D1442046

# Endocrinology

# Endocrinology

Volume 3

## FIFTH EDITION

### Senior Editors

**Leslie J. DeGroot, MD**
Professor of Medicine (Research)
Brown University
Providence, Rhode Island
Professor of Medicine, Emeritus
University of Chicago
Chicago, Illinois

**J. Larry Jameson, MD, PhD**
Irving S. Cutter Professor and Chairman
Department of Medicine
Northwestern University Feinberg School of
    Medicine
Chicago, Illinois

### Section Editors

**David de Kretser, AO, FAA, FTSE, MD, FRACP**
Director, Monash Insitute of Medical
    Research
Monash University
Monash Medical Centre
Clayton, Victoria
Australia

**Ashley B. Grossman, BA, BSc, MD, FRCP, F Med Sci**
Professor of Neuroendocrinology
Barts and the London School of Medicine
    and Dentistry
Queen Mary, University of London
Honorary Consultant Physician
St. Bartholomew's Hospital
London, United Kingdom

**John C. Marshall, MD, PhD**
Andrew D. Hart Professor of Medicine
Director, Center for Research in Reproduction
University of Virginia School of Medicine
Charlottesville, Virginia

**Shlomo Melmed, MD**
Senior Vice President, Academic Affairs
Director, Burns and Allen Research Institute
Associate Dean, UCLA School of Medicine
Cedars-Sinai Medical Center
Los Angeles, California

**John T. Potts, Jr, MD**
Jackson Distinguished Professor of Clinical
    Medicine
Department of Medicine
Harvard Medical School
Physician-in Chief Emeritus,
Department of Medicine
Massachusetts General Hospital
Boston, Massachusetts

**Gordon C. Weir, MD**
Head, Section on Islet Transplantation
    and Cell Biology
Diabetes Research and Wellness
    Foundation Chair
Joslin Diabetes Center
Professor of Medicine
Harvard Medical School
Boston, Massachusetts

ELSEVIER
SAUNDERS

ELSEVIER
SAUNDERS

Elsevier
1600 John F. Kennedy Blvd.
Ste 1800
Philadelphia, PA 19103-2899

ENDOCRINOLOGY

Part number 9-9976-3674-0 (vol 1)
Part number 9-9976-3675-9 (vol 2)
Part number 9-9976-3676-7 (vol 3)
ISBN 0-7216-0376-9 (set)

Previous editions copyrighted 2001, 1995, 1989, 1979 by Elsevier Inc.

**Library of Congress Cataloging-in-Publication Data**

Endocrinology / senior editors, Leslie J. DeGroot, J. Larry Jameson; section editors,
    David de Krester . . . [et al.].— 5th ed.
        p. ; cm.
Includes bibliographical references and index.
    ISBN 0-7216-0376-9 (set)
        1. Endocrine glands—Diseases. 2. Endocrinology. I. DeGroot, Leslie J. II. Jameson, J. Larry.
        [DNLM: 1. Endocrine Diseases. 2. Endocrine Glands. 3. Hormones. WK 140 E5585 2005]
    RC648.E458 2005 2006
    616.4—dc22

                                                                    2004051091

*Acquisitions Editor:* Rebecca Schmidt Gaertner
*Developmental Editor:* Jennifer Shreiner
*Project Manager:* Mary Stermel

Working together to grow
libraries in developing countries

www.elsevier.com | www.bookaid.org | www.sabre.org

ELSEVIER    BOOK AID International    Sabre Foundation

Printed in the United States of America

Last digit is the print number: 9 8 7 6 5 4 3 2 1

# Contributors

**Lloyd Paul Aiello, MD, PhD**
Associate Director, Beetham Eye Institute
Joslin Diabetes Center;

Director, Section Eye Research
Joslin Diabetes Center;

Associate Professor of Ophthalmology
Harvard Medical Center
Boston, Massachusetts
*Diabetic Eye Disease*

**Carolyn A. Allan, MBBS(Hons), DRCOG, FRACP**
Clinical Research Fellow
Male Reproduction Group
Prince Henry's Institute of Medical Research
Clayton, Victoria, Australia
*Androgen Deficiency Disorders*

**Nobuyuki Amino, MD**
Kuma Hospital
Center for Excellence in Thyroid Care
Chuo-ku
Kobe, Japan
*Chronic (Hashimoto's) Thyroiditis*

**Marianne S. Anderson, MD**
Assistant Professor
Pediatrics
University of Colorado Health Sciences Center
Aurora, Colorado
*Fuel Homeostasis in the Fetus and Neonate*

**Josephine Arendt, PhD, FRCPath**
Professor of Endocrinology, Emeritus
School of Biomedical and Molecular Sciences
University of Surrey
Guildford, Surrey, United Kingdom
*The Pineal Gland: Basic Physiology and Clinical
Implications*

**Richard J. Auchus, MD, PhD**
Assistant Professor
Internal Medicine/Endocrinology and Metabolism
University of Texas Southwestern Medical School;

Staff Endocrinologist
Internal Medicine
Zale Lipshy University Hospital/St. Paul University Hospital;

Staff Endocrinologist
Internal Medicine
Veterans' Administration Hospitals of North Texas
Dallas, Texas
*The Principles, Pathways, and Enzymes of Human
Steroidogenesis*

**Joseph Avruch, MD**
Professor, Medicine
Harvard Medical School;
Physician and Chief, Diabetes Unit
Medical Services
Massachusetts General Hospital;

Member
Department of Molecular Biology
Massachusetts General Hospital
Boston, Massachusetts
*Hormone Signaling via Tyrosine Kinase Receptors*

**Lloyd Axelrod, MD**
Associate Professor of Medicine
Department of Medicine
Harvard Medical School;

Physician and Chief of the James Howard Means Firm
Medical Services
Massachusetts General Hospital
Boston, Massachusetts
*Glucocorticoid Therapy*

**Eric S. Bachman, MD, PhD**
Senior Research Fellow
Pharmacology Division
Merck Research Laboratories
Boston, Massachusetts
*Appetite Regulation and Thermogenesis*

**Rebecca S. Bahn, MD**
Professor of Medicine
Mayo Clinic College of Medicine,
Consultant in Endocrinology, Mayo Clinic
Department of Internal Medicine, Mayo Clinic
Rochester, Minnesota
*Graves' Ophthalmopathy*

**H. W. Gordon Baker, MD, PhD, FRACP**
Professor, Department of Obstetrics and Gynaecology
(Royal Women's Hospital)
University of Melbourne
Melbourne IVF
Melbourne, Victoria, Australia
*Clinical Management of Male Infertility*

**Stephen G. Ball, MD**
BHF Heart Research Centre (Clinical)
Leeds General Infirmary
Leeds, United Kingdom
*Vasopressin, Diabetes Insipidus, and Syndrome of Inappropriate
Antidiuresis*

**Randall B. Barnes, MD**
Associate Professor
Department of Obstetrics and Gynecology
University of Chicago Pritzker School of Medicine;

Attending Physician
Chicago Lying-in Hospital
Chicago, Illinois
*Hyperandrogenism, Hirsutism, and the Polycystic Ovary Syndrome*

**Peter H. Baylis, BSc, MD, FRCP, FMedSci**
Pro-Vice-Chancellor, Faculty of Medical Sciences
University of Newcastle upon Tyne;

Consultant Endocrinologist, Endocrinology Unit
Newcastle Hospital NHS Trust
Newcastle upon Tyne, United Kingdom
*Vasopressin, Diabetes Insipidus, and Syndrome of Inappropriate
Antidiuresis*

**Paolo Beck-Peccoz, MD**
Professor of Endocrinology
Institute of Endocrine Sciences
University of Milan
Ospedale Maggiore IRCCS
Milan, Italy
*TSH-Producing Adenomas
Resistance to Thyroid Hormone*

**Graeme I. Bell, PhD**
Professor of Biochemistry and Molecular Biology
Medicine and Human Genetics
University of Chicago
Chicago, Illinois
  *Chemistry and Biosynthesis of the Islet Hormones: Insulin, Islet*
    *Amyloid Polypeptide (Amylin), Glucagon, Somatostatin,*
    *and Pancreatic Polypeptide*

**Norman H. Bell, MD**
Distinguished University Professor of Medicine
Medical University of South Carolina;

Attending Physician
Medical University Hospital
Charleston, South Carolina
  *Disorders of Calcification: Osteomalacia and Rickets*

**Laura Berman, LCSW, PhD**
Clinical Assistant Professor
Northwestern University;

Director
Berman Center
Chicago, Illinois
  *Female Sexual Dysfunction*

**Vikas Bhalla, MD**
Division of Cardiology
Department of Medicine
Veterans Affairs Medical Center and University of California, San
  Diego
San Diego, California
  *Neurohormonal Alterations in Heart Failure*

**Meenakshi A. Bhalla, MD**
Division of Cardiology
Department of Medicine
Veterans Affairs Medical Center
  and University of California, San Diego
San Diego, California
  *Neurohormonal Alterations in Heart Failure*

**Shalender Bhasin, MD**
Professor of Medicine,
Chief, Section of Endocrinology
Boston University School of Medicine;

Chief, Section of Endocrinology
Evans Department of Medicine
Boston Medical Center
Boston, Massachusetts
  *Sexual Dysfunction in Men*

**Neil A. Bhowmick, PhD**
Assistant Professor
Urologic Surgery and Cancer Biology
Vanderbilt University
Nashville, Tennesse
  *Endocrinology of the Prostate and Benign Prostatic Hyperplasia*

**John P. Bilezikian, MD**
Professor of Medicine and Pharmacology
Department of Medicine
College of Physicians and Surgeons, Columbia University;

Chief, Division of Endocrinology,
Director, Metabolic Bone Diseases Unit
Department of Medicine
New York Presbyterian Hospital
New York, New York
  *Primary Hyperparathyroidism*

**Stephen R. Bloom, MA, MD, DSc, FRCP, FRCPath, FMedSci**
Head of Division of Investigative Science
Metabolic Medicine
Imperial College London;

Professor of Medicine
Pathology and Therapy Services
Hammersmith Hospitals NHS Trust
London, United Kingdom
  *Gastrointestinal Hormones and Tumor Syndromes*

**Jeffrey A. Bluestone, MD**
A.W. and Mary Margaret Distinguished Professor
UCSF Diabetes Center
University of California San Francisco
San Francisco, California
  *Immunologic Mechanisms Causing Autoimmune Endocrine Disease*

**Manfred Blum, MD, FACP**
Professor of Medicine and Radiology,
Director of the Nuclear Endocrine Laboratory
Medicine and Radiology
NYU School of Medicine;

Attending Physician
Tisch Hospital of NYU Medical Center;

Attending Physician
Bellevue Hospital
New York, New York
  *Thyroid Imaging*

**Steen J. Bonnema, MD, PhD**
Associate Professor
Endocrinological Research Unit, Institute of Clinical Research
University of Southern Denmark;

Associate Professor, Staff Specialist
Department of Endocrinology and Metabolism
Odense University Hospital
Odense, Denmark
  *Multinodular Goiter*

**Roger Bouillon, MD, PhD, FRCP**
Laboratory of Experimental Medicine and Endocrinology
Katholieke Univeriteit Leuven
Leuven, Belgium
  *Vitamin D: From Photosynthesis, Metabolism, and Action to Clinical*
    *Applications*

**Andrew J. M. Boulton, MD, DSc(Hon), FRCP**
Professor of Medicine
Academic Division of Medicine
University of Manchester;

Consultant Physician
Manchester Royal Infirmary
Manchester, United Kingdom;

Professor of Medicine
Division of Endocrinology
University of Miami
Miami, Florida
  *Diabetes Mellitus: Neuropathy*

**Glenn D. Braunstein, MD**
Professor of Medicine
The David Geffen School of Medicine at UCLA;

Chairman, Department of Medicine
The James R. Klinenberg, MD Chair in Medicine
Department of Medicine
Cedars-Sinai Medical Center
Los Angeles, California
  *Hypothalamic Syndromes*

**F. Richard Bringhurst, MD**
Associate Professor
Medicine
Harvard Medical School;

Physician
Massachusetts General Hospital
Boston, Massachusetts
*Regulation of Calcium and Phosphate Homeostasis*

**Arthur E. Broadus, MD, PhD**
Professor
Internal Medicine, Section of Endocrinology
Yale University School of Medicine
New Haven, Connecticut
*Malignancy-Associated Hypercalcemia*

**Marcello D. Bronstein, MD**
Associate Professor of Medicine
Department of Internal Medicine
University of Sao Paulo Medical School;

Chief, Neuroendocrine Unit
Division of Endocrinology and Metabolism
Department of Internal Medicine
Hospital das Clinicas, University of Sao Paulo Medical School
Sao Paulo, Brazil
*Disorders of Prolactin Secretion and Prolactinomas*

**Edward M. Brown, MD**
Professor of Medicine
Department of Medicine
Harvard Medical School;

Senior Physician
Endocrine-Hypertension Division, Department of Medicine
Brigham and Women's Hospital
Boston, Massachusetts
*Parathyroid Hormone and Parathyroid Hormone–Related Peptide in the Regulation of Calcium Homeostasis and Bone Development*
*Familial Hypocalciuric Hypercalcemia and Other Disorders Due to Calcium-Sensing Receptor Mutations*

**Chuong Bui, MD**
Resident, Department of Radiology
University of Michigan Medical Center
Ann Arbor, Michigan
*Adrenal Gland Imaging*

**Henry B. Burch, MD, FACP, FACE**
Chair, Endocrinology Division
Department of Medicine
Uniformed Services University of the Health Sciences
Bethesda, Maryland;

Chief
Endocrinology, Diabetes, and Metabolism Service
Walter Reed Army Medical Center
Washington, DC
*Graves' Ophthalmopathy*

**Henry G. Burger, AO, FAA, MD, BS, FRCP, FRACP, FCP (SA), FRCOG, FRANZCOG**
Professor
Faculty of Medicine
Monash University;

Professor
Prince Henry's Institute of Medical Research at Monash Medical Centre
Melbourne, Victoria, Australia
*Gonadal Peptides: Inhibins, Activins, Follistatin, Müllerian-Inhibiting Substance (Antimüllerian Hormone)*

**John B. Buse, MD, PhD**
Chief, Division of General Medicine and Clinical Epidemiology
Director, Diabetes Care Center
University of North Carolina School of Medicine;

Director, Diabetes Care Center
UNC Health Care
Chapel Hill, North Carolina
*Management of Type 2 Diabetes Mellitus*

**Peter C. Butler, MD**
Professor of Medicine
Larry L. Hillblom Islet Research Center
David Geffen School of Medicine at UCLA;

Director
Larry L. Hillblom Islet Research Center
David Geffen School of Medicine at UCLA
Los Angeles, California
*Insulin Secretion*

**Paolo Cappabianca, MD**
Professor and Chairman of Neurological Surgery
Department of Neurological Sciences, Division of Neurosurgery
Università degli Studi di Napoli Federico II
Naples, Italy
*Pituitary Surgery*

**Esther Carlton, CLS**
Project Manager, Clinical Correlations Department
Quest Diagnostics Nichols Institute
San Juan Capistrano, California
*Endocrine Testing*

**Jose F. Caro, MD**
Professor of Medicine
Indiana University School of Medicine;

Vice President, Endocrine Research and Clinical Investigation
Lilly Research Laboratories
Eli Lilly and Company
Indianapolis, Indiana
*Obesity: The Problem and Its Management*

**Don H. Catlin, MD**
Professor, Molecular and Medical Pharmacology
University of California, Los Angeles;

Professor, Molecular and Medical Pharmacology
David Geffen School of Medicine at UCLA;

Director
UCLA Olympic Analytical Laboratory
University of California, Los Angeles
Los Angeles, California
*Anabolic Steroids*

**Francesco Cavagnini, MD**
Head
Chair of Endocrinology
University of Milan;

Chief
Department of Endocrinology
Istituto Auxologico Italiano, Ospedale San Luca, IRCCS
Milan, Italy
*Adrenal Causes of Hypercortisolism*

**Jerry Cavallerano, PhD**
Assistant to the Director
Beetham Eye Institute
Joslin Diabetes Center
Boston, Massachusetts
*Diabetic Eye Disease*

**Luigi Maria Cavallo, MD, PhD**
Staff Neurosurgeon
Department of Neurological Sciences, Division of Neurosurgery
Università degli Studi di Napoli Federico II
Naples, Italy
   *Pituitary Surgery*

**John R. G. Challis, PhD, DSc, FIBiol, FRCOG, FRSC**
Vice-President
Research and Associate Provost;

Professor
Physiology, Ob/Gyn, Medicine
University of Toronto
Toronto, Ontario, Canada
   *Endocrinology of Parturition*

**Shu J. Chan, PhD**
Associate Professor of Biochemistry and Molecular Biology
University of Chicago Pritzker School of Medicine;

Senior Research Associate
Howard Hughes Medical Institute
Chicago, Illinois
   *Chemistry and Biosynthesis of the Islet Hormones: Insulin,*
   *Islet Amyloid Polypeptide (Amylin), Glucagon, Somatostatin, and*
   *Pancreatic Polypeptide*

**Roland D. Chapurlat, MD, PhD**
Assistant Professor
Rheumatology
Université Claude Bernard;

Assistant Professor
Rheumatology and Bone Diseases
Hôpital E Herriot;

Assistant Professor
Unit 403
INSERM
Lyon, France
   *Osteoporosis*

**V. Krishna Chatterjee, BMBCh, FRCP**
Professor of Endocrinology
Department of Medicine
University of Cambridge;

Honorary Consultant Physician
Department of Diabetes and Endocrinology
Addenbrooke's Hospital
Cambridge, United Kingdom
   *Resistance to Thyroid Hormone*
   *Adrenarche and Adrenopause*

**Luca Chiovato, MD, PhD**
Professor of Endocrinology
Internal Medicine and Medical Therapy
University of Pavia;

Head, Unit of Internal Medicine and Endocrinology
Fondazione Salvatore Maugeri I.R.C.C.S
Pavia, Italy
   *Graves' Disease*

**Kyung J. Cho, MD, FACR**
William Martell Professor of Radiology
University of Michigan Medical Center
Ann Arbor, Michigan
   *Adrenal Gland Imaging*

**Daniel Christophe, PhD**
Research Director FNRS
IRIBHM-IBMM
Université Libre de Bruxelles
Charleroi (Gosselies), Belgium
   *Thyroid Regulatory Factors*

**George P. Chrousos, MD**
Pediatrics
Athens University
Athens, Greece
   *Interactions of the Endocrine and Immune Systems*

**John A. Cidlowski, PhD**
Chief
Laboratory of Signal Transduction
National Institute of Environmental Health Science
National Institutes of Health
Research Triangle Park, North Carolina
   *Glucocorticoid Receptors and Their Mechanisms of Action*

**Adrian J. L. Clark, DSc FRCP**
Professor
Department of Endocrinology
Barts and the London, Queen Mary, University of London
London, United Kingdom
   *Adrenal Insufficiency*

**David R. Clemmons, MD**
Kenan Professor of Medicine
Internal Medicine
University of North Carolina School of Medicine;

Attending Physician
Internal Medicine
University of North Carolina Hospitals
Chapel Hill, North Carolina
   *Insulin-like Growth Factor 1 and Its Binding Proteins*

**Jack W. Coburn, MD[†]**
Formerly, Adjunct Professor of Medicine
UCLA School of Medicine
University of California, Los Angeles;

Formerly, Staff Physician
VA West Los Angeles Medical Center
Los Angeles, California
   *The Renal Osteodystrophies*

**P. Conton, MD**
Department of Medical and Surgical Sciences
OU of Endocrinology
University of Padova
Azienda Ospedaliera di Padova
Padova, Italy
   *Adrenal Cancer*

**Georges Copinschi, MD, PhD**
Professor Emeritus of Endocrinology
Laboratory of Physiology
Faculty of Medicine, Université Libre de Bruxelles;

Formerly Chief
Division of Endocrinology
Hôpital Universitaire Saint-Pierre;

Formerly Chairman
Department of Medicine
Hôpital Universitaire Saint-Pierre
Brussels, Belgium
   *Endocrine and Other Biologic Rhythms*

**C. Hamish Courtney, MD, MRCP**
Consultant Physician
Regional Centre for Diabetes and Endocrinology
Royal Victoria Hospital
Belfast, Ireland
   *Type 2 Diabetes Mellitus: Etiology, Pathogenesis, and Natural History*

---

[†]Deceased

**Vincent L. Cryns, MD**
Associate Professor
Departments of Medicine and Cell and Molecular Biology
Feinberg School of Medicine, Northwestern University;

Attending Physician
Department of Medicine
Northwestern Memorial Hospital
Chicago, Illinois
  *Cell Division, Differentiation, Senescence, and Death*

**Gerald R. Cunha, PhD**
Professor
Anatomy, Urology and Obstetrics and Gynecology
University of California
San Francisco, California
  *Endocrinology of the Prostate and Benign Prostatic Hyperplasia*

**Gary C. Curhan, MD, ScD**
Associate Professor of Medicine
Department of Medicine
Harvard Medical School;

Renal Division, Department of Medicine
Brigham and Women's Hospital;

Associate Professor of Epidemiology
Harvard School of Public Health
Boston, Massachusetts
  *Nephrolithiasis*

**Leona Cuttler, MD**
Professor, Pediatrics
Case Western Reserve University;

Chief, Endocrinology, Diabetes, and Metabolism
Pediatrics
Rainbow Babies and Children's Hospital
Cleveland, Ohio
  *Somatic Growth and Maturation*

**Jamie Dananberg, MD**
Executive Director
Exploratory and Program Medical
Lilly Research Laboratories, Eli Lilly and Co.
Indianapolis, Indiana
  *Obesity: The Problem and Its Management*

**Mehul T. Dattani, FRCP, MD**
Reader in Paediatric Endocrinology
Biochemistry, Endocrinology, and Metabolism
Institute of Child Health London;

Consultant in Paediatric Endocrinology
Endocrinology
Great Ormond Street Children's Hospital;

Consultant in Paediatric Endocrinology
Adolescent Endocrinology
Middlesex Hospital
London, United Kingdom
  *Growth Hormone Deficiency in Children*

**Marlyse A. Debrincat**
Division of Cancer and Haematology
The Walter and Eliza Hall Institute of Medical Research
Parkville, Victoria, Australia
  *Hormone Signaling via Cytokine Receptors*

**Oreste de Divitiis, MD**
Associate Professor of Neurosurgery
Department of Neurological Sciences, Division of Neurosurgery
Università degli Studi di Napoli Federico II
Naples, Italy
  *Pituitary Surgery*

**Mario De Felice, MD**
Senior Scientist
Laboratory of Animal Genetics
Stazione Zoologica Anton Dohrn
Naples, Italy
  *Anatomy and Development of the Thyroid*

**Ralph A. DeFronzo, MD**
Professor of Medicine; Chief, Diabetes Division
University of Texas Health Science Center
San Antonio, Texas
  *Regulation of Intermediatory Metabolism during Fasting and Feeding*

**Leslie J. DeGroot, MD**
Professor of Medicine (Research)
Brown University
Providence, Rhode Island;

Professor of Medicine, Emeritus
University of Chicago
Chicago, Illinois
  *Endocrinology: Impact on Science and Medicine*
  *Nonthyroidal Illness Syndrome*
  *Thyroid Neoplasia*

**David de Kretser, AO, FAA, FTSE, MD, FRACP**
Director, Monash Institute of Medical Research
Monash University
Monash Medical Centre
Clayton, Victoria, Australia
  *Gonadal Peptides: Inhibins, Activins, Follistatin, Müllerian-Inhibiting*
    *Substance (Antimüllerian Hormone)*
  *Functional Morphology of the Testis*

**Pierre D. Delmas, MD, PhD**
Professor of Medicine
Claude Bernard University of Lyon;

Chief of Department, Rheumatology
Hôpital E. Herriot;

Director, Research Unit 403 (Pathophysiology of Osteoporosis)
INSERM
Lyon, France;

President, International Osteoporosis Foundation
Nyon, Switzerland
  *Osteoporosis*

**Paul Devroey, PhD**
AZ-Vrije Universiteit Brussel
Centre for Reproductive Medicine
Brussels, Belgium
  *Ovulation Induction and Assisted Reproduction*

**Roberto Di Lauro, MD**
Full Professor of Human Genetics
University of Naples Frederico II Medical School;

Head, Laboratory of Biochemistry and Molecular Biology
Stazione Zoologica Anton Dohrn
Naples, Italy
  *Anatomy and Development of the Thyroid*

**Ruben Diaz, MD, PhD**
Instructor in Pediatrics
Harvard Medical School;

Assistant in Medicine
Endocrinology
Children's Hospital Boston
Boston, Massachusetts
  *Familial Hypocalciuric Hypercalcemia and Other Disorders Due to*
    *Calcium-Sensing Receptor Mutations*

**Sean F. Dinneen, MD, FACP, FRCPI**
Consultant Diabetologist
Addenbrooke's Hospital
Cambridge, United Kingdom
  *Classification and Diagnosis of Diabetes Mellitus*

**Annemarie A. Donjacour**
Assistant Research Anatomist
University of California at San Francisco
San Francisco, California
  *Endocrinology of the Prostate and Benign Prostatic Hyperplasia*

**Daniel J. Drucker, MD**
Director, Banting and Best Diabetes
Professor of Medicine
University of Toronto;

Staff Physician
Toronto General Hospital
Toronto, Ontario, Canada
  *Glucagon and the Glucagon-like Peptides*

**Jacques E. Dumont, MD, PhD**
Founding Director
Institute of Interdisciplinary Research (IRIBHM)
University of Brussels
Brussels, Belgium
  *Thyroid Regulatory Factors*

**Christopher R. W. Edwards, MD, FRCP, FRCPEd, FRSE, FMedSci**
Professor, Vice-Chancellor
University of Newcastle upon Tyne
Newcastle upon Tyne, United Kingdom
  *Primary Mineralocorticoid Excess Syndromes*

**David A. Ehrmann, MD**
Professor of Medicine and Associate Director
The University of Chicago General Clinical Research Center
The University of Chicago
Chicago, Illinois
  *Hyperandrogenism, Hirsutism, and the Polycystic Ovary Syndrome*

**Graeme Eisenhofer, PhD**
Staff Scientist
Clinical Neurocardiology Section, National Institutes of
  Neurological Disorders and Stroke
National Institutes of Health
Bethesda, Maryland
  *Pheochromocytoma*

**Ilia J. Elenkov, MD**
Division of Rheumatology
Immunology, and Allergy
Georgetown University Medical Center
Washington, DC
  *Interactions of the Endocrine and Immune Systems*

**Gregory F. Erickson, PhD**
Professor
Reproductive Medicine
University of California, San Diego
La Jolla, California
  *Folliculogenesis, Ovulation, and Luteogenesis*

**Barbro Eriksson, MD, PhD**
Professor, Department of Medical Sciences
Senior Consultant, Department of Endocrine Oncology
University Hospital Uppsala
Uppsala, Sweden
  *Carcinoid Syndrome*

**Eric A. Espiner, MBChB, MD, FRACP, FRS (NC)**
Emeritus Professor, Medicine
Christ Church School of Medicine and Health Sciences
Christ Church, New Zealand
  *Hormones of the Cardiovascular System*

**Victoria Esser, PhD**
Associate Professor, Internal Medicine
University of Texas Southwestern Medical Center at Dallas
Dallas, Texas
  *Ketoacidosis and Hyperosmolar Coma*

**Erica A. Eugster, MD**
Associate Professor of Clinical Pediatrics, School of Medicine
Indiana University;

Director, Section of Pediatric Endocrinology/Diabetology
Riley Hospital for Children
Indianapolis, Indiana
  *Precocious Puberty*
  *Delayed Puberty*

**I. Sadaf Farooqi, MD**
Department of Medicine and Clinical Biochemistry
University of Cambridge
Adderbrooke's Hospital
Cambridge, United Kingdom
  *Genetic Syndromes Associated with Obesity*

**Bart C. J. M. Fauser, MD, PhD**
Department of Reproductive Medicine
University of Medical Center Utrecht
Utrecht, The Netherlands
  *Female Subfertility: Evaluation and Management*

**Eleuterio Ferrannini, MD**
Professor, Department of Internal Medicine
University of Pisa
Pisa, Italy
  *Regulation of Intermediatory Metabolism during Fasting and Feeding*

**David M. Findlay, PhD**
Associate Professor, Orthopaedics and Trauma
The University of Adelaide;

Member, Hanson Institute
Adelaide, South Australia, Australia
  *Calcitonin*

**Joel S. Finkelstein, MD**
Associate Professor of Medicine
Harvard Medical School;

Associate Physician, Department of Medicine
Massachusetts General Hospital
Boston, Massachusetts
  *Medical Management of Hypercalcemia*

**Delbert A. Fisher, MD**
Professor of Pediatrics and Medicine Emeritus
UCLA School of Medicine;

VP Science and Innovation
Quest Diagnostics Incorporated
San Juan Capistrano, California
  *Fetal and Neonatal Endocrinology*
  *Endocrine Testing*

**Susan J. Fisher, PhD**
Professor, Cell and Tissue Biology
University of California, San Francisco
San Francisco, California
  *Implantation and Placental Physiology in Early Human Pregnancy:*
  *The Role of the Maternal Decidua and the Trophoblast*

**Jeffrey S. Flier, MD**
George C. Reisman Professor of Medicine
Harvard Medical Center;

Chief Academic Officer, Research
Beth Israel Deaconess Medical School;

Harvard Faculty Dean for Academic Programs
Beth Israel Deaconess Medical Center
Boston, Massachusetts
  *Syndromes of Insulin Resistance and Mutant Insulin*

**Maguelone G. Forest, MD, PhD**
Directeur de Recherche à Titre Exceptional, Professor Emeritus
Hôpital Debrousse
INSERM
Lyon, Rhône, France
  *Diagnosis and Treatment of Disorders of Sexual Development*

**Daniel W. Foster, MD**
John Denis McGarry, PhD Distinguished Chair in Diabetes and
    Metabolic Research
Department of Internal Medicine
The University of Texas Southwestern Medical School
Dallas, Texas
*Ketoacidosis and Hyperosmolar Coma*

**Aaron L. Friedman, MD**
Professor and Chair, Department of Pediatrics
University of Wisconsin School of Medicine
Madison, Wisconsin
*Hormonal Regulation of Electrolyte and Water Metabolism*

**Eli A. Friedman, MD, FACP, FRCP (London)**
Distinguished Teaching Professor of Medicine
Chief, Renal Disease Division
Department of Medicine
Downstate Medical Center;

Director, Nephrology, Department of Medicine
Kings County Hospital Center
Brooklyn, New York
*Diabetic Nephropathy*

**Mark Frydenberg, MBBS, FRACS (Urol)**
Chairman of the Department of Urology
Monash Medical Centre;

Clinical Associate Professor, Department of Surgery
Clinical Director of the Centre of Urological Research
Monash Institute of Reproduction and Development
Monash University
Clayton, Victoria, Australia
*Endocrinology of Prostate Cancer*

**Peter J. Fuller, MBBS, BMedSc(Hons), PhD, FRACP**
Professorial Fellow, Medicine and Biochemistry
    and Molecular Biology
Monash University
Melbourne, Victoria, Australia;

Director, Endocrinology
Southern Health;

NHMRC Senior Principal Research Fellow
Prince Henry's Institute of Medical Research
Clayton, Victoria, Australia
*Aldosterone: Secretion and Action*

**John W. Funder, MD, PhD, FRACP**
Professor, Medicine
Monash University;

Prince Henry's Institute of Medical
Monash Medical Center
Clayton, Victoria, Australia
*Essential Hypertension and Endocrine Hypertension*

**Dana Gaddy, PhD**
Associate Professor, Physiology and Biophysics
University of Arkansas for Medical Sciences
Little Rock, Arkansas
*Hormone Signaling via Serine Kinase Receptors*

**Robert F. Gagel, MD**
Professor of Medicine and Division Head
Division of Internal Medicine
University of Texas Health Science Center;

Professor of Medicine and Division Head
Division of Internal Medicine
MD Anderson Cancer Center
Houston, Texas
*Multiple Endocrine Neoplasia Type 2*

**Jason L. Gaglia, MD**
Clinical Fellow, Department of Medicine
Harvard Medical School;

Clinical Fellow, Endocrinology, Diabetes, and Metabolism
Beth Israel Deaconess Medical Center;

Clinical Fellow, Adult Diabetes
Joslin Diabetes Center
Boston, Massachusetts
*Pancreatic and Islet Transplantation*

**David Galton, MD, FRCP**
Professor, Human Metabolism and Genetics
Wolfson Institute of Preventive Medicine;

Hon. Consultant, Metabolism and Genetics
St. Bartholomew's Hospital;

Consultant Physician, Diabetes and Metabolism
London Medical Center
London, United Kingdom
*Diabetes, Lipids, and Atherosclerosis*

**Thomas J. Gardella, PhD**
Associate Professor, Medicine
Harvard Medical School;

Associate Professor, Medicine, Endocrine Unit
Massachusetts General Hospital
Boston, Massachusetts
*Parathyroid Hormone and Parathyroid Hormone–Related Peptide in the
    Regulation of Calcium Homeostasis and Bone Development*

**Bruce D. Gaylinn, PhD**
Research Assistant Professor
Internal Medicine Division of Endocrinology
University of Virginia Health System
Charlottesville, Virginia
*Growth Hormone–Releasing Hormone, Ghrelin, and Growth Hormone
    Secretagogues*

**Harry K. Genant, MD**
Professor, Emeritus
Radiology, Medicine and Orthopaedic Surgery;
Executive Director, Osteoporosis and Arthritis Research Group
Department of Radiology
University of California, San Francisco;

Chairman, Emeritus and Member, Board of Directors, Synarc, Inc.
San Francisco, California
*Bone Density and Imaging of Osteoporosis*

**Hans Gerber, MD**
Privatdozent, University of Bern School of Medicine;

Head of Division, Department of Clinical Chemistry
University Hospital
Inselspital
Bern, Switzerland
*Multinodular Goiter*

**John E. Gerich, MD**
Professor of Medicine
University of Rochester;

Endocrine Attending
Strong Memorial Hospital
Rochester, New York
*Hypoglycemia*

**Michael S. German, PhD**
Professor, Medicine and Diabetes Center
University of California, San Francisco
San Francisco, California
*Development of the Endocrine Pancreas*

**Marvin C. Gershengorn, MD**
Director, Division of Intramural Research
National Institute of Diabetes and Digestive and Kidney
    Diseases, NIH
Bethesda, Maryland
    *Second Messenger Signaling Pathways: Phospholipids and Calcium*

**Mohammad A. Ghatei, MD**
Department of Metabolic Medicine
Imperial College School of Medicine
London, United Kingdom
    *Gastrointestinal Hormones and Tumor Syndromes*

**William Gibb, PhD**
Professor, Obstetrics and Gynecology, and Cellular and Molecular
    Medicine
University of Ottawa
Ottawa, Ontario, Canada
    *Endocrinology of Parturition*

**Lisa K. Gilliam, MD, PhD**
Senior Fellow, Medicine
University of Washington Medical Center
Seattle, Washington
    *Type 1 (Insulin-dependent) Diabetes Mellitus:*
    *Etiology, Pathogenesis, and Natural History*

**Monica Girotra, MD**
Clinical Fellow in Endocrinology
College of Physicians and Surgeons, Columbia University;

Clinical Fellow in Endocrinology
New York-Presbyterian Hospital
New York, New York
    *Immunologic Mechanisms Causing Autoimmune Endocrine Disease*

**Linda C. Giudice, MD, PhD**
Stanley McCormick Memorial Professor
Obstetrics and Gynecology
Stanford University School of Medicine;

Physician, Obstetrics and Gynecology
Stanford University Hospital;

Chief, Division of Reproductive Endocrinology and Infertility
Stanford University Hospital and Clinics;

Associate Chair of Research
Department of Obstetrics and Gynecology
Stanford University
Stanford, California
    *Endometriosis*
    *Implantation and Placental Physiology in Early Human Pregnancy:*
        *The Role of the Maternal Decidua and the Trophoblast*

**Anna Glasier, BSc, MD, FRCOG, MFFP**
Director, Family Planning and Well Woman Services
Lothian Primary Care NHS Trust;

Senior Lecturer, Department of Obstetrics and Gynaecology
University of Edinburgh
Edinburgh, Scotland
    *Contraception*

**Francis H. Glorieux, MD, PhD**
Professor, Surgery, Pediatrics and Human Genetics
McGill University;

Director of Research, Shriners Hospital for Children
Montreal, Canada
    *Genetic Defects in Vitamin D Metabolism and Action*

**Steven R. Goldring, MD**
Professor of Medicine, Harvard Medical School;

Chief of Rheumatology
Beth Israel Deaconess Medical Center;

Chief of Rheumatology
New England Baptist Hospital
Boston, Massachusetts
    *Disorders of Calcification: Osteomalacia and Rickets*

**Javier González-Maeso, PhD**
Research Associate, Department of Neurology
Mount Sinai School of Medicine
New York, New York
    *Hormone Signaling via G Protein-Coupled Receptors*

**Theodore L. Goodfriend, MD**
Professor Emeritus, Medicine and Pharmacology
University of Wisconsin Medical School;

Associate Chief of Staff for Research
Wm. S. Middleton Memorial Veterans Hospital
Madison, Wisconsin
    *Hormonal Regulation of Electrolyte and Water Metabolism*

**Louis J. G. Gooren, MD**
Professor of Endocrinology
Vrije Universiteit Medical Center
Amsterdam, The Netherlands
    *Gender Identity and Sexual Behavior*

**William J. Gradishar, MD**
Associate Professor of Medicine
Division of Hematology and Oncology
Northwestern University; Northwestern Memorial Hospital;

Director Breast Medical Oncology
Robert H. Lurie Comprehensive Cancer Center
Chicago, Illinois
    *Endocrine Management of Breast Cancer*

**Karen A. Gregerson, PhD**
Associate Professor of Physiology
College of Pharmacy, Division of Pharmaceutical Sciences
University of Cincinnati
Cincinnati, Ohio
    *Prolactin*

**Milton D. Gross, MD**
Professor, Radiology and Internal Medicine
University of Michigan Medical School
Ann Arbor, Michigan;

Director/Chief
Nuclear Medicine and Radiation Safety Service
Department of Veterans Affairs Health System
Ann Arbor, Michigan and Washington, DC (field-based)
    *Adrenal Gland Imaging*

**Ashley B. Grossman, BA, BSc, MD, FRCP, F Med Sci**
Professer of Neuroendocrinology
Barts and the London School of Medicine and Dentistry
Queen Mary, University of London
Honorary Consultant Physician
St. Bartholomew's Hospital
London, United Kingdom
    *Cushing's Syndrome*
    *Adrenal Insufficiency*

**Valeria C. Guimarães, MD**
Institute of Biological Sciences
Federal University of Minas Geiras (ICB-UFMG)
Belo Horizonte-MG, Brazil;

Unité de Recherches Laitières et de Génétique Appliquée,
Institut National de la Recherche Agronomique, Domaine
    de Vilvert
Cedex, France
    *Subacute and Riedel's Thyroiditis*

**Mark Gurnell, BSc(Hons), MBBS, MRCP(UK), PhD**
University Lecturer, Medicine, University of Cambridge;

Honorary Consultant Physician
Endocrinology and Diabetes Mellitus
Addenbrooke's Hospital
Cambridge, United Kingdom
    *Resistance to Thyroid Hormone*

**Joel F. Habener, MD**
Professor, Medicine
Harvard Medical School;

Chief
Laboratory of Molecular Endocrinology
Massachusetts General Hospital;

Investigator
Howard Hughes Medical Institute
Boston, Massachusetts
*The Cyclic AMP Second Messenger Signaling Pathway*

**Charles B. Hammond, MD**
E.C. Hamblen Professor
Department of Obstetrics and Gynecology
Duke University Medical Center
Durham, North Carolina
*Gestational Trophoblastic Neoplasms*

**David J. Handelsman, MB, BS, PhD, FRACP**
Professor of Reproductive Endocrinology and Andrology
Director, ANZAC Research Institute
Head, Andrology Department, Concord Hospital
ANZAC Research Institute
University of Sydney
Sydney, NSW, Australia
*Androgen Action and Pharmacologic Uses*
*Male Contraception*

**John B. Hanks, MD**
C. Bruce Morton Professor and Chief
Division of General Surgery
University of Virginia Health System
Charlottesville, Virginia
*Adrenal Surgery*

**Shun-ichi Harada, MD**
Senior Research Fellow
Molecular Endocrinology/Bone Biology
Merck Research Laboratories
West Point, Pennsylvania
*Bone Development and Remodeling*

**William W. Hay, Jr, MD**
Professor, Pediatrics
Scientific Director, Perinatal Research Center
University of Colorado Health Sciences Center
Aurora, Colorado;

Director, Neonatal Clinical Research Center (NIH – Pediatric GCRC)
University of Colorado School of Medicine and The Children's
   Hospital
Denver, Colorado
*Fuel Homeostasis in the Fetus and Neonate*

**Simon W. Hayward, PhD**
Assistant Professor
Urologic Surgery and Cancer Biology
Vanderbilt University Medical Center
Nashville, Tennessee
*Endocrinology of the Prostate and Benign Prostatic Hyperplasia*

**David Heber, MD, PhD**
Professor of Medicine, Department of Medicine
David Geffen School of Medicine at UCLA;

Director, Department of Medicine
UCLA Center for Human Nutrition
Los Angeles, California
*Starvation and Parenteral Nutrition*

**Matthias Hebrok, PhD**
Assistant Professor in Residence
Diabetes Center and Department of Medicine
University of California, San Francisco (UCSF)
San Francisco, California
*Development of the Endocrine Pancreas*

**Laszlo Hegedüs, MD, DMSc**
Professor, Department of Endocrinology and Metabolism
Odense University;

Head of Department
Department of Endocrinology and Metabolism
Odense University Hospital
Odense, Denmark
*Multinodular Goiter*

**Wayne J. G. Hellstrom, MD, FACS**
Chief, Section of Andrology and Male Infertility
Department of Urology
Tulane University School of Medicine
New Orleans, Louisiana
*Sexual Dysfunction in Men*

**Georg Hennemann, MD, PhD, FRCP, FRCP(E)**
Professor of Medicine and Endocrinology
Medical Faculty
Erasmus University
Rotterdam, The Netherlands
*Autonomously Functioning Thyroid Nodules and Other Causes*
*of Thyrotoxicosis*

**Kevan C. Herold, MD**
Associate Professor of Medicine
College of Physicians and Surgeons
Columbia University
New York, New York
*Immunologic Mechanisms Causing Autoimmune Endocrine Disease*

**Yoh Hidaka, MD**
Associate Professor, Laboratory Medicine
Osaka University Graduate School of Medicine
Suita, Osaka, Japan
*Chronic (Hashimoto's) Thyroiditis*

**Douglas J. Hilton, PhD**
Division of Cancer and Haematology
The Walter and Eliza Hall Institute of Medical Research
Parkville, Victoria, Australia
*Hormone Signaling via Cytokine Receptors*

**Peter C. Hindmarsh, BSc, MD, FRCP, FRCPCH**
Professor of Paediatric Endocrinology
Institute of Child Health
University College London;

Hon Consultant in Paediatric Endocrinology
London Centre for Paediatric Endocrinology and Metabolism
Great Ormond Street Hospital for Children
London, United Kingdom
*Growth Hormone Deficiency in Children*

**Patricia M. Hinkle, PhD**
Professor, Pharmacology and Physiology
University of Rochester Medical Center
Rochester, New York
*Second Messenger Signaling Pathways: Phospholipids and Calcium*

**Clement K. M. Ho, MBBS, DRCOG, PhD**
Clinical Biochemistry
Royal Infirmary of Edinburgh
Edinburgh, Scotland
*Ovarian Hormone Synthesis*

**Ken K. Y. Ho, FRACP, MD**
Professor, Medicine
University of New South Wales;

Head, Endocrinology
St. Vincent's Hospital;

Head, Pituitary Research Unit
Garvan Institute of Medical Research
Sydney, NSW, Australia
*Growth Hormone Deficiency in Adults*

**Ana O. Hoff, MD**
Assistant Professor of Medicine
Endocrine Neoplasia and Hormonal Disorders
University of Texas
MD Anderson Cancer Center
Houston, Texas
*Multiple Endocrine Neoplasia Type 2*

**Anthony N. Hollenberg, MD**
Associate Professor, Medicine
Harvard Medical School;

Chief, Thyroid Unit
Division of Endocrinology
Beth Israel Deaconess Medical Center
Boston, Massachusetts
*Mechanisms of Thyroid Hormone Action*

**Nelson D. Horseman, PhD**
Professor of Molecular and Cellular Physiology
Department of Molecular and Cellular Physiology
University of Cincinnati
Cincinnati, Ohio
*Prolactin*

**Ieuan A. Hughes, MD**
Department of Paediatrics
University of Cambridge
Addenbrooke's Hospital
Cambridge, United Kingdom
*Adrenarche and Adrenopause*

**Hero K. Hussain, MD**
Siemens Medical Systems/RSNA Fellow
Department of Radiology
University of Michigan Health System
Ann Arbor, Michigan
*Adrenal Gland Imaging*

**John M. Hutson, MD, FRACS, FAAP(Hon)**
Professor of Paediatric Surgery, Paediatrics
University of Melbourne;

Director, General Surgery
Royal Children's Hospital;

Associate Director, Clinical Research
Murdoch Childrens Research Institute
Melbourne, Victoria, Australia
*Cryptorchidism and Hypospadias*

**Peter Illingworth MB, MD(Hon), FRANZCOG**
Associate Professor, Obstetrics and Gynaecology
University of Sydney;

Director of Reproductive Medicine
Westmead Hospital
Sydney, NSW, Australia
*Amenorrhea, Anovulation, and Dysfunctional Uterine Bleeding*

**J. Larry Jameson, MD, PhD**
Irving S. Cutter Professor and Chairman
Department of Medicine
Northwestern University Feinberg School of Medicine
Chicago, Illinois
*Endocrinology: Impact on Science and Medicine*
*Applications of Genetics in Endocrinology*
*Mechanisms of Thyroid Hormone Action*
*Endocrinology of Sexual Maturation*

**Michael Jergas, MD**
Assistant Professor of Radiology
Teaching Hospital at the University of Cologne;

Director, Department of Radiology
St. Katharinen-Hospital
Frechen, Germany
*Bone Density and Imaging of Osteoporosis*

**V. Craig Jordan, OBE, PhD, DSc**
Vice President and Research Director for Medical Sciences
Alfred G. Knutson Chair of Cancer Research
Fox Chase Cancer Center
Philadelphia, Pennsylvania
*Endocrine Management of Breast Cancer*

**Nathalie Josso**
Institut Paris-Sud sur les Cytokines
Université Paris-Sud;

Attaché, Service d' Endocrinologie Pédiatrique
Hôpital Saint Vincent-de-Paul;

Directeur de Recherches, Unité 493
Institut National de la Santé et de la Recherche Médicale
Paris, France
*Embryology and Control of Fetal Sex Differentiation*

**Andreas Jöstel, MD**
Clinical Research Fellow
Department of Endocrinology
Christie Hospital
Manchester, United Kingdom
*Hypopituitarism*

**Harald Jüppner, MD**
Associate Professor of Pediatrics
Harvard Medical School;

Associate Pediatrician
Endocrine Unit and Pediatric Nephrology Unit
Massachusetts General Hospital
Boston, Massachusetts
*Parathyroid Hormone and Parathyroid Hormone–Related Peptide in the Regulation of Calcium Homeostasis and Bone Development*
*Genetic Disorders of Calcium Homeostasis Caused by Abnormal Regulation of Parathyroid Hormone Secretion or Responsiveness*

**Ursula B. Kaiser, MD**
Associate Professor of Medicine
Harvard Medical School;

Associate Physician and Director
Neuroendocrine Program
Department of Medicine
Brigham and Women's Hospital
Boston, Massachusetts
*Gonadotropin-Releasing Hormone and Gonadotropins*

**Edwin L. Kaplan, MD**
Professor, Surgery
The University of Chicago, Pritzker School of Medicine;

Professor, Surgery
The University of Chicago Hospitals
Chicago, Illinois
*Surgery of the Thyroid*

**Jeffrey A. Kalish, MD**
General Surgery Resident
Boston Medical Center
Boston, Massachusetts
*Diabetic Foot and Vascular Complications*

**Gerard Karsenty, MD, PhD**
Professor, Molecular and Human Genetics
Baylor College of Medicine
Houston, Texas
*Genetic Analysis of Skeleton Physiology*

**Rasa Kazlauskaite, MD**
Assistant Professor
Department of Medicine
Division of Endocrinology
Rush University
John H. Stroger, Jr. Hospital of Cook County
Chicago, Illinois
*Thyroid-Stimulating Hormone and Regulation of the Thyroid Axis*

**Gary L. Keeney, MD**
Assistant Professor, Mayo Medical School;

Consultant
Department of Laboratory Medicine and Pathology
Division of Anatomic Pathology
Mayo Clinic
Rochester, Minnesota
*Ovarian Tumors with Endocrine Manifestations*

**Harry Keiser, MD**
Scientist Emeritus, Attending Physician
The Clinical Center
National Institutes of Health
Bethesda, Maryland
*Pheochromocytoma*

**Ruth A. Keri, PhD**
Assistant Professor
Department of Pharmacology;

Assistant Professor
Division of General Medical Sciences, Oncology
Case Western Reserve University School of Medicine
Cleveland, Ohio
*Transgenic and Genetic Animal Models*

**Jeffrey B. Kerr, PhD**
Department of Anatomy and Cell Biology
Faculty of Medicine
Monash University
Melbourne, Victoria, Australia
*Functional Morphology of the Testis*

**Paul Kim, MD**
System Director
Department of Endocrinology
Geisinger Health System
Danville, Pennsylvania
*Thyroid Hormone Formation*

**Ronald Klein, MD, MPH**
Professor, University of Wisconsin
Ophthalmology and Visual Sciences
Medical School
Madison, Wisconsin
*Diabetic Eye Disease*

**David L. Kleinberg, MD**
Professor, Medicine
Director, Neuroendocrine Unit
New York University School of Medicine;

Attending, Medicine
New York University Medical Center
New York, New York
*Endocrinology of Lactation*

**Meyer Knobel, MD**
Thyroid Unit, Division of Endocrinology
University of Sao Paulo Medical School
Sao Paulo, Brazil
*Iodine Deficiency Disorders*

**Isaac S. Kohane, MD, PhD**
Associate Professor, Pediatrics
Harvard Medical School;

Director, Informatics Program
Children's Hospital;

Director, Harvard Partners Center for Genetics and Genomics
Brigham and Women's Hospital;

Henderson Professor
Health Sciences and Technology
Harvard University-Massachusetts Institute of Technology
Boston, Massachusetts
*Genomics and Proteomics*

**Efstratios M. Kolibianakis, MD, PhD**
Consultant, Centre for Reproductive Medicine
Dutch Speaking Brussels Free University
Brussels, Belgium
*Ovulation Induction and Assisted Reproduction*

**John J. Kopchick, PhD**
Goll-Ohio Professor of Molecular Biology
Edison Biotechnology Institute;

Professor of Molecular Biology
Department of Biomedical Sciences
College of Osteopathic Medicine, Ohio University
Athens, Ohio
*Growth Hormone*

**Peter Kopp, MD**
Associate Professor, Associate Division Chief for Education
Division of Endocrinology, Metabolism and Molecular Medicine
Feinberg School of Medicine, Northwestern University
Chicago, Illinois
*Applications of Genetics in Endocrinology*

**Kenneth S. Korach, MD**
Chief, Laboratory of Reproductive and Developmental Toxicology
Director, Environmental Disease & Medicine Program
Division of Intramural Research
National Institute of Environmental Health Sciences, NIH
Research Triangle Park, North Carolina
*Environmental Agents and the Reproductive System*

**Márta Korbonits, MD, PhD**
MRC Clinician Scientist
Senior Lecturer in Endocrinology
Department of Endocrinology
St. Bartholomew's Hospital
London, United Kingdom
*Growth Hormone–Releasing Hormone, Ghrelin, and Growth Hormone Secretagogues*

**Melvyn Korobkin, MD**
Professor, Department of Radiology
University of Michigan
Ann Arbor, Michigan
*Adrenal Gland Imaging*

**Stephen M. Krane, MD**
Persis, Cyrus and Marlow B. Harrison Distinguished Professor of Medicine
Harvard Medical School;

Physician
Massachusetts General Hospital
Boston, Massachusetts
*Disorders of Calcification: Osteomalacia and Rickets*

**Henry M. Kronenberg, MD**
Professor of Medicine, Harvard Medical School;

Chief, Endocrine Unit
Massachusetts General Hospital
Boston, Massachusetts
*Parathyroid Hormone and Parathyroid Hormone–Related Peptide in the Regulation of Calcium Homeostasis and Bone Development*

**Wendy Kuohung, MD**
Assistant Professor, Department of Obstetrics and Gynecology
Boston University School of Medicine;

Associate Physician of the Research Staff
Department of Medicine, Division of Endocrinology, Diabetes, and Hypertension
Brigham and Women's Hospital;

Visiting Assistant Professor
Harvard Medical School
Boston, Massachusetts
*Gonadotropin-Releasing Hormone and Gonadotropins*

**John M. Kyriakis, PhD**
Professor, Medicine
Tufts University School of Medicine;

Investigator, Molecular Cardiology Research Institute
Tufts-New England Medical Center
Boston, Massachusetts
  *Map Kinase and Growth Factor Signaling Pathways*

**Ruth B. Lathi, MD**
Clinical Assistant Professor
Division of Reproductive Endocrinology and Infertility
Department of Obstetrics & Gynecology
Stanford University School of Medicine
Stanford, California
  *Implantation and Placental Physiology in Early Human Pregnancy:
  The Role of the Maternal Decidua and the Trophoblast*

**Joop S. E. Laven, MD, PhD**
Senior Lecturer
Obstetrics and Gynecology, Division of Reproductive Medicine;

Senior Consultant OBGYN, Subspecialist Reproductive Medicine
Obstetrics and Gynecology, Division of Reproductive Medicine
Erasmus Medical Center
Rotterdam, The Netherlands
  *Female Subfertility: Evaluation and Management*

**Diana L. Learoyd, MD**
Molecular Genetics Unit
Kolling Institute of Medical Research (DLL, MM, BGR);

Departments of Endocrinology (DLL, BGR) and Surgery (AIG, LWD)
Royal North Shore Hospital and University of Sydney
Sydney, NSW, Australia;

Department of Surgery
Karolinska Hospital (JZ)
Stockholm, Sweden
  *Medullary Thyroid Carcinoma*

**Harold E. Lebovitz, MD, FACE**
Professor of Medicine
State University of New York Health Science Center at Brooklyn
Brooklyn, New York
  *Hyperglycemia Secondary to Nondiabetic Conditions and Therapies*

**Benjamin Z. Leder, MD**
Assistant Professor of Medicine
Harvard Medical School;

Endocrine Unit
Massachusetts General Hospital
Boston, Massachusetts
  *Regulation of Calcium and Phosphate Homeostasis*

**Colin A. Leech, PhD**
Laboratory of Molecular Endocrinology
Massachusetts General Hospital
Boston, Massachusetts
  *The Cyclic AMP Second Messenger Signaling Pathway*

**Åke Lernmark, Med. Dr.**
Robert H. Williams Professor of Medicine
University of Washington
Seattle, Washington;

Adjunct Professor of Experimental Diabetes
Clinical Medicine
University Hospital MAS
Malmö, Sweden
  *Type 1 (Insulin-dependent) Diabetes Mellitus:
  Etiology, Pathogenesis, and Natural History*

**Michael A. Levine, MD**
Chairman, Department of Pediatrics
Cleveland Clinic Lerner College of Medicine of Case Western
    Reserve University;

Physician-in-Chief
The Children's Hospital
The Cleveland Clinic Foundation
Cleveland, Ohio;

Visiting Professor, Department of Pediatric
The Johns Hopkins University School of Medicine
Baltimore, Maryland
  *Hypoparathyroidism and Pseudohypoparathyroidism*

**David M. Levy, MD, FRCP**
Consultant Physician, Diabetes & Endocrinology
Gillian Hanson Centre for Diabetes & Endocrinology
Whipps Cross University Hospital;

London Diabetes & Lipid Centre
London, United Kingdom
  *Diabetes, Lipids, and Atherosclerosis*

**Laura J. Lewis-Tuffin, PhD**
Laboratory of Signal Transduction
National Institute of Environmental Health Sciences, NIH, HHS
Research Triangle Park, North Carolina
  *Glucocorticoid Receptors and Their Mechanisms of Action*

**Jonathan Lindzey, PhD**
Assistant Professor, Department of Biology
University of South Florida
Tampa, Florida
  *Environmental Agents and the Reproductive System*

**Ling Choo LIM, MBBS, MMed, MRCP(UK)**
Associate Consultant, Division of Endocrinology
Alexandra Hospital
Singapore
  *Medullary Thyroid Carcinoma*

**Catherine Ann Lissett, MBChB, MRCP**
Department of Endocrinology
Christie Hospital
Manchester, United Kingdom
  *Hypopituitarism*

**Frank W. LoGerfo, MD**
William V. McDermott Professor of Surgery
Harvard Medical School;

Chief, Division of Vascular and Endovascular Surgery
Beth Israel Deaconess Medical Center
Boston, Massachusetts
  *Diabetic Foot and Vascular Complications*

**B. Macino, MD**
Molecular Targeting Unit
Department of Experimental Oncology
Istituto Nazionale Tumori
Milan, Italy
  *Adrenal Cancer*

**Noel K. Maclaren, M.D.**
Director, Research Institute for Children
Harahan, Louisiana
  *Autoimmune Polyglandular Syndromes*

**Carine Maenhaut, PhD**
Assistant Professor, IRIBHM
Free University of Brussels
Brussels, Belgium
  *Thyroid Regulatory Factors*

**Alan Maisel, MD**
Professor of Medicine
University of California, San Diego;

Director, Coronary Care Unit and Heart Failure Program
San Diego, California
*Neurohormonal Alterations in Heart Failure*

**Carl D. Malchoff, MD, PhD**
Associate Professor, Medicine
University of Connecticut Health Center
Farmington, Connecticut
*Generalized Glucocorticoid Resistance*

**Diana M. Malchoff, PhD**
Assistant Professor, Medicine
University of Connecticut Health Center
Farmington, Connecticut
*Generalized Glucocorticoid Resistance*

**Rayaz A. Malik, BSc, MSc, MB.ChB, MRCP, PhD**
Senior Lecturer, Medicine
University of Manchester;

Consultant Physician
Manchester Royal Infirmary
Manchester, United Kingdom
*Diabetes Mellitus: Neuropathy*

**Susan J. Mandel, MD, MPH**
Associate Professor of Medicine and Radiology
Division of Endocrinology, Diabetes, and Metabolism
University of Pennsylvania School of Medicine;

Associate Chief for Clinical Affairs
Division of Endocrinology, Diabetes, and Metabolism
Hospital of the University of Pennsylvania
Philadelphia, Pennsylvania
*Diagnosis and Treatment of Thyroid Disease during Pregnancy*

**F. Mantero, MD, PhD**
Professor of Endocrinology
Department of Medical and Surgical Sciences
University of Padua;

Director, Division of Endocrinology
University Hospital
Padua, Italy
*Adrenal Cancer*

**Christos Mantzoros, MD, DSc**
Associate Professor in Internal Medicine
Division of Endocrinology, Diabetes, and Metabolism
Harvard Medical School
Boston, Massachusetts
*Syndromes of Insulin Resistance and Mutant Insulin*

**Eleftheria Maratos-Flier, MD**
Associate Professor of Medicine
Harvard Medical School;

Division of Endocrinology
Beth Israel Deaconess Medical Center
Boston, Massachusetts
*Appetite Regulation and Thermogenesis*

**Michele Marinò, MD**
Assistant Professor, Endocrinology
University of Pisa
Pisa, Italy
*Graves' Disease*

**John C. Marshall, MD, PhD**
Andrew D. Hart Professor of Medicine
Director, Center for Research in Reproduction
University of Virginia School of Medicine
Charlottesville, Virginia
*Regulation of Gonadotropin Synthesis and Secretion*
*Hormonal Regulation of the Menstrual Cycle and Mechanisms*
*of Ovulation*

**T. John Martin, MD, DSc, FRS**
Emeritus Professor, Medicine
University of Melbourne;

John Holt Fellow
St. Vincent's Institute of Medical Research
Melbourne, Australia
*Calcitonin*

**Thomas F. J. Martin, PhD**
Professor of Biochemistry
University of Wisconsin
Madison, Wisconsin
*Control of Hormone Secretion*

**Christopher J. Mathias, PhD, FMedSci**
Clinical Professor
Division of Neurosciences and Mental Health, Medicine
Imperial College
London, United Kingdom
*Orthostatic Hypotension and Orthostatic Intolerance*

**Neil J. McKenna, MD**
Department of Molecular and Cellular Biology
Baylor College of Medicine
Houston, Texas
*Nuclear Receptors: Structure, Function, and Cofactors*

**Robert I. McLachlan, MD, PhD**
Professor, Obstetrics and Gynecology
Monash University;

Deputy Director, Endocrinology
Monash Medical Centre;

Director of Clinical Research
Prince Henry's Institute of Medical Research
Clayton, Victoria, Australia
*Androgen Deficiency Disorders*

**Michael J. McPhaul, MD**
Professor
Department of Internal Medicine/Endocrinology and Metabolism
University of Texas Southwestern Medical Center
Dallas, Texas
*Mutations That Alter Androgen Receptor Function: Androgen*
*Insensitivity and Related Disorders*

**Geraldo Medeiros-Neto, MD, FACP**
Professor of Endocrinology
Department of Clinical Medicine
University of Sao Paulo Medical School;

Chief of Thyroid Unit
Division of Endocrinology
Department of Clinical Medicine
Hospital Das Clinicas
Sao Paulo Medical School
Sao Paulo, Brazil
*Iodine Deficiency Disorders*

**Juris J. Meier, MD**
Research Fellow
Larry L. Hillblom Islet Research Center
University of California, Los Angeles
Los Angeles, California
*Insulin Secretion*

**Shlomo Melmed, MD**
Senior Vice President, Academic Affairs
Director, Burns and Allen Research Institute
Associate Dean, UCLA School of Medicine
Cedars-Sinai Medical Center
Los Angeles, California
*Evaluation of Pituitary Masses*
*Acromegaly*

**Boyd E. Metzger, MD**
Tom D. Spies Professor
Northwestern University Feinberg School of Medicine;

Attending Physician
Northwestern Memorial Hospital
Chicago, Illinois
*Diabetes Mellitus and Pregnancy*

**Walter L. Miller, MD**
Professor, Pediatrics
University of California, San Francisco;

Chief of Endocrinology
University of California, San Francisco Children's Hospital
San Francisco, California
*The Principles, Pathways, and Enzymes of Human Steroidogenesis*

**Mark E. Molitch, MD**
Professor of Medicine
Division of Endocrinology, Metabolism & Molecular Medicine
Department of Medicine
Northwestern University Feinberg School of Medicine;

Attending Physician
Northwestern Memorial Hospital
Chicago, Illinois
*Hormonal Changes and Endocrine Testing in Pregnancy*

**David D. Moore, PhD**
Professor, Molecular and Cellular Biology
Baylor College of Medicine
Houston, Texas
*Nuclear Receptors: Structure, Function, and Cofactors*

**Damian G. Morris, MBBS, BSc, MRCP**
Department of Endocrinology
St. Bartholomew's and the Royal London School of Medicine and
   Dentistry
London, United Kingdom
*Cushing's Syndrome*

**Allan Munck, PhD**
Third Century Professor of Physiology, Emeritus
Physiology
Dartmouth Medical School
Lebanon, New Hampshire
*Glucocorticoid Physiology*

**Monzur Murshed, PhD**
Postdoctoral Associate
Molecular and Human Genetics
Baylor College of Medicine
Houston, Texas
*Genetic Analysis of Skeleton Physiology*

**Anikó Náray-Fejes-Tóth, MD**
Professor of Physiology
Dartmouth Medical School
Lebanon, New Hampshire
*Glucocorticoid Physiology*

**Ralf Nass, MD**
Research Associate
University of Virginia School of Medicine
Charlottesville, Virginia
*Growth Hormone–Releasing Hormone, Ghrelin,
   and Growth Hormone Secretagogues*

**David M. Nathan, MD**
Professor, Medicine
Harvard Medical School;

Director, Diabetes Center and General Clinical Research Center
Massachusetts General Hospital
Boston, Massachusetts
*Diabetes Control and Long-term Complications*

**Maria I. New, MD**
Professor of Pediatrics
Director, Adrenal Steroid Disorders Program
Attending Pediatrician, Department of Pediatrics
Mount Sinai School of Medicine
New York, New York
*Defects of Adrenal Steroidogenesis*

**Lynnette K. Nieman, MD**
Senior Investigator
Pediatric and Reproductive Endocrinology Branch, NICHD
National Institutes of Health
Bethesda, Maryland
*Cushing's Syndrome*

**John H. Nilson, PhD**
Edward R. Meyer Distinguished Professor Director
School of Molecular Biosciences
Washington State University
Pullman, Washington
*Hormones and Gene Expression: Basic Principles*

**Christopher F. Njeh, MSc, PhD, CPhys**
Assistant Adjunct Professor, Physics
California State University;

Senior Medical Physicist
Radiation Oncology
Saint Agnes Medical Center
Fresno, California
*Bone Density and Imaging of Osteoporosis*

**Jeffrey A. Norton, MD**
Professor of Surgery, Chief of Surgical Oncology
Stanford University;

Surgery
Stanford University Hospital
Stanford, California
*Surgical Management of Hyperparathyroidism*

**Kjell Öberg, MD, PhD**
Medical Faculty
Department of Medical Sciences
Uppsala University;

Department of Endocrine Oncology
University Hospital
Uppsala, Sweden
*Carcinoid Syndrome*

**William D. Odell, MD, PhD, MACP**
Emeritus Professor of Medicine and Physiology
University of Utah School of Medicine
Salt Lake City, Utah
*Endocrinology of Sexual Maturation*

**Jerrold M. Olefsky, MD**
Professor of Medicine
Department of Medicine
University of California, San Diego;

Associate Dean for Scientific Affairs
School of Medicine
University of California, San Diego
La Jolla, California
*Type 2 Diabetes Mellitus: Etiology, Pathogenesis, and Natural History*

**Stephen O'Rahilly, MD, FRS**
Professor of Clinical Biochemistry and Medicine
Clinical Biochemistry
University of Cambridge;

Honorary Consultant
Diabetes and Endocrinology
Addenbrooke's Hospital
Cambridge, United Kingdom
*Genetic Syndromes Associated with Obesity*

**Karel Pacak, MD, PhD, DSc**
Chief, Unit on Clinical Neuroendocrinology
Pediatric and Reproductive Endocrinology Branch
National Institute of Child Health and Human Development
National Institutes of Health
Bethesda, Maryland
*Pheochromocytoma*

**Furio Pacini, MD**
Professor of Endocrinology
Internal Medicine, Endocrinology and Metabolism
Sienna, Italy
*Thyroid Neoplasia*

**Samuel Parry, MD**
Assistant Professor
Obstetrics and Gynecology
University of Pennsylvania
Philadelphia, Pennsylvania
*Placental Hormones*

**Francesca Pecori Giraldi, MD**
Researcher
Chair of Endocrinology
University of Milan;

Staff Physician
Department of Endocrinology
Istituto Auxologico Italiano, Ospedale San Luca, IRCCS
Milan, Italy
*Adrenal Causes of Hypercortisolism*

**Luca Persani, MD, PhD**
Associate Professor
Institute of Endocrine Science
University of Milan;

Head, Laboratory of Experimental Endocrinology
IRCCS Instituto Auxologico Italiano
Milan, Italy
*TSH-Producing Adenomas*

**Ora Hirsch Pescovitz, MD**
Executive Associate Dean for Research Affairs
Edwin Letzer Professor of Pediatrics
Professor of Cellular and Integrative Physiology
School of Medicine
Indiana University;

President and CEO
Riley Hospital for Children
Indianapolis, Indiana
*Precocious Puberty*
*Delayed Puberty*

**Richard L. Phelps, MD**
Assistant Clinical Professor of Medicine
Northwestern University Medical School;

Attending Physician
Northwestern Memorial Hospital
Chicago, Illinois
*Diabetes Mellitus and Pregnancy*

**Aldo Pinchera, PhD**
Department of Endocrinology
University of Pisa
Cisanello Hospital
Pisa, Italy
*Graves' Disease*

**John T. Potts, Jr., MD**
Jackson Distinguished Professor of Clinical Medicine
Department of Medicine
Harvard Medical School;

Physician-in-Chief Emeritus
Department of Medicine
Massachusetts General Hospital
Boston, Massachusetts
*Parathyroid Hormone and Parathyroid Hormone–Related Peptide in*
*the Regulation of Calcium Homeostasis and Bone Development*
*Medical Management of Hypercalcemia*

**Lisa P. Purdy, MD, CM, MPH**
Assistant Professor of Medicine
University of Rochester School of Medicine and Dentistry;

Attending Physician
Genesee Hospital
Rochester General Hospital
Strong Memorial Hospital
Rochester, New York
*Diabetes Mellitus and Pregnancy*

**Charmian A. Quigley, MBBS**
Assistant Professor
Indiana University School of Medicine
Indiana University;

Senior Clinical Research Physician
Endocrinology
Lilly Research Laboratories
Indianapolis, Indiana
*Genetic Basis of Gonadal and Genital Development*

**Marcus O. Quinkler, MD**
Clinical Endocrinology, Department of Medicine
Charité Campus Mitte
Berlin, Germany
*Mineralocorticoid Deficiency*

**Christine Campion Quirk, PhD**
Assistant Professor
Medical Sciences Program
Indiana University School of Medicine
Bloomington, Indiana
*Hormones and Gene Expression: Basic Principles*

**Miriam T. Rademaker, MD**
Christchurch School of Medicine
Christchurch, New Zealand
*Hormones of the Cardiovascular System*

**Ewa Rajpert-De Meyts, MD, PhD**
Senior Scientist
Deparment of Growth and Reproduction
Copenhagen University Hospital (Rigshopitalet)
Copenhagen, Denmark
*Testicular Tumors with Endocrine Manifestations*

**Valerie Anne Randall, PhD**
Professor of Biomedical Sciences
The University of Bradford
Bradford, United Kingdom
*Physiology and Pathophysiology of Androgenetic Alopecia*

**Eric Ravussin, PhD**
Professor, Human Physiology
Pennington Biomedical Research Center
Louisiana State University
Baton Rouge, Louisiana
*Role of the Adipocyte in Metabolism and Endocrine Function*

**David W. Ray**
Senior Lecturer in Medicine
Centre for Molecular Medicine and Endocrine Sciences Research
  Group
University of Manchester;

Consultant in Endocrinology
Manchester Royal Infirmary
Manchester, United Kingdom
  *Ectopic Hormone Syndromes*

**Nancy E. Reame, MSN, PhD, FAAN**
The Rhetaugh Graves Dumas Professor of Nursing
School of Nursing;

Research Scientist
Reproductive Sciences Program
Department of Obstetrics-Gynecology
The University of Michigan
Franklin, Michigan
  *Premenstrual Syndrome*

**Samuel Refetoff, PhD**
Professor of Medicine, Pediatrics, Genetics
University of Chicago
Chicago, Illinois
  *Diagnostic Tests of the Thyroid*

**Ravi Retnakaran, MD, MSc, FRCPC**
Endocrinology Fellow
Division of Endocrinology and Metabolism
University of Toronto;

Endocrinology Fellow
Leadership Sinai Centre for Diabetes
Mount Sinai Hospital
Toronto, Ontario, Canada
  *Treatment of Type 1 Diabetes Mellitus in Adults*

**Rodolfo Rey, MD, PhD**
Centro de Investigaciones en Reproducción
Department of Histology, Cell Biology, Embryology and Genetics
School of Medicine, University of Buenos Aires;

Centro do Investigaciones Endocrinológicas (CONICET)
Hospital de Niños R. Gutiérrez
Buenos Aires, Argentina
  *Embryology and Control of Fetal Sex Differentiation*

**Gail P. Risbridger, PhD**
Professor and Associate Director
Monash Institute of Reproduction and Development
Monash University
Clayton, Victoria, Australia
  *Endocrinology of Prostate Cancer*

**Robert A. Rizza, MD**
Earl and Arlene McDonough Professor of Medicine
Division of Endocrinology, Diabetes, Metabolism and Nutrition
Mayo School of Medicine
Rochester, Minnesota
  *Classification and Diagnosis of Diabetes Mellitus*

**Bruce G. Robinson, MD**
Professor
Royal North Shore Hospital
University of Sydney
Syndey, NSW, Australia
  *Medullary Thyroid Carcinoma*

**Gideon A. Rodan, MD, PhD**
Adjunct Professor
Biochemistry and Biophysics
University of Pennsylvania
Philadelphia, Pennsylvania
  *Bone Development and Remodeling*

**Pierre P. Roger, MD**
Department of Endocrinology and Reproductive Diseases
Assistance Publique-Hopitaux de Paris
Centre Hospitalier d'Universite Bicetre
Le Kremlin-Bicetre, France.
  *Thyroid Regulatory Factors*

**Michael G. Rosenfeld, PhD**
Professor of Medicine
Endocrinology and Metabolism
University of California, San Diego
La Jolla, California
  *Development of the Pituitary*

**Robert L. Rosenfield, MD**
Professor, Pediatrics and Medicine
The University of Chicago Pritzker School of Medicine;

Pediatric Endocrinologist
The University of Chicago Comer Children's Hospital
Chicago, Illinois
  *Somatic Growth and Maturation*
  *Hyperandrogenism, Hirsutism, and the Polycystic Ovary Syndrome*

**Peter Rotwein, MD**
Professor and Chair
Department of Biochemistry and Molecular Biology;

Director, Molecular Medicine Division
Department of Medicine
Oregon Health and Science University
Portland, Oregon
  *Peptide Growth Factors Other than Insulin-like Growth Factors*
  *or Cytokines*

**Arthur H. Rubenstein, MD**
Dean
Mount Sinai School of Medicine
New York, New York
  *Chemistry and Biosynthesis of the Islet Hormones: Insulin,*
  *Islet Amyloid Polypeptide (Amylin), Glucagon, Somatostatin, and*
  *Pancreatic Polypeptide*

**Robert T. Rubin, MD, PhD**
Professor, Psychiatry and Biobehavioral Sciences
David Geffen School of Medicine at UCLA;

Chair, Department of Psychiatry
Veterans Affairs Greater Los Angeles Healthcare System
Los Angeles, California
  *Anorexia Nervosa, Bulimia Nervosa, and Other Eating Disorders*

**Neil Ruderman, MD, DPhil**
Professor of Medicine, Physiology, and Biophysics
Boston University School of Medicine;

Director, Diabetes Unit
Boston Medical Center
Boston, Massachusetts
  *The Metabolic Syndrome*

**Irma H. Russo, MD, FCAP, FASCP**
Adjunct Professor of Pathology and Cell Biology
Jefferson Medical College
Thomas Jefferson University;

Chief, Molecular Endocrinology Section
Breast Cancer Research Laboratory
Department of Pathology;
Active Staff
Department of Surgical Oncology
American Oncologic Hospital;
Member, Medical Science Division
Fox Chase Cancer Center
Philadelphia, Pennsylvania
  *Hormonal Control of Breast Development*

**Jose Russo, MD**
Professor of Pathology and Laboratory Medicine
Jefferson School of Medicine;

American Oncology Hospital, Pathology
Director, Breast Cancer and the Environment Research Center
Fox Chase Cancer Center;
Philadelphia, Pennsylvania
*Hormonal Control of Breast Development*

**Isidro B. Salusky, MD**
Professor of Pediatrics
Director, Pediatric Dialysis Program
Director, General Clinical Research
David Geffen School of Medicine at UCLA
Los Angeles, California;

Treasurer, International Pediatric Nephrology Association (IPNA)
Freibrug, Germany
*The Renal Osteodystrophies*

**Richard J. Santen, MD**
Professor of Internal Medicine
Department of Internal Medicine
Division of Endocrinology and Metabolism
University of Virginia Health System
Charlottesville, Virginia
*Hormonal Control of Breast Development*
*Benign Breast Disorders*
*Gynecomastia*

**Nanette Santoro, MD**
Professor and Director
Division of Reproductive Endocrinology and Infertility
Albert Einstein College of Medicine
Bronx, New York
*Mechanisms of Menopause and the Menopausal Transition*

**Stuart C. Sealfon, MD**
Saunders Professor of Neurology
Mount Sinai School of Medicine
New York, New York
*Hormone Signaling via G Protein-Coupled Receptors*

**Patrick M. Sexton, PhD**
Senior Research Fellow, Molecular Pharmacology
Howard Florey Institute
The University of Melbourne
South Carlton, Victoria, Australia
*Calcitonin*

**Stephen Michael Shalet, BSc, MBBS, MD, FRCP**
Professor of Medicine (Endocrinology)
University of Manchester;

Head of Department, Endocrinology
Christie Hospital
Manchester, England
*Hypopituitarism*

**Yoram Shenker, MD**
Associate Professor, Medicine
University of Wisconsin;

Staff Physician
University of Wisconsin;

Chief, Section of Endocrinology
William S. Middleton Memorial VA Hospital
Madison, Wisconsin
*Hormonal Regulation of Electrolyte and Water Metabolism*

**Gerald I. Shulman, MD, PhD**
Professor of Medicine and Cellular and Molecular Physiology
Internal Medicine
Yale School of Medicine;

Doctor
Endocrinology
Yale New Haven Hospital
New Haven, Connecticut
*The Metabolic Syndrome*

**Alison Silverberg, MD**
Albert Einstein College of Medicine
Division of Reproductive Endocrinology
Bronx, New York
*Mechanisms of Menopause and the Menopausal Transition*

**Shonni J. Silverberg, MD**
Professor of Clinical Medicine
Columbia University, College of Physicians and Surgeons;

Attending, Division of Endocrinology
New York Presbyterian Hospital
New York, New York
*Primary Hyperparathyroidism*

**Frederick R. Singer, MD**
Clinical Professor of Medicine
David Geffen School of Medicine
Los Angeles, California;

Director, Endocrine/Bone Disease Program
John Wayne Cancer Institute
Santa Monica, California
*Paget's Disease of Bone*

**Niels E. Skakkebœk, MD, DSc**
Professor
University of Copenhagen;

Head, Department of Growth and Reproduction
Copenhagen University Hospital (Rigshospitalet)
Copenhagen, Denmark
*Testicular Tumors with Endocrine Manifestations*

**Carolyn L. Smith, PhD**
Associate Professor
Molecular and Cellular Biology
Baylor College of Medicine
Houston, Texas
*Estrogen and Progesterone Action*

**Steven R. Smith, MD**
Associate Professor
Chief, Inpatient Unit
Experimental Endocrinology
Pennington Biomedical Research Center
Baton Rouge, Louisianna
*Role of the Adipocyte in Metabolism and Endocrine Function*

**Peter J. Snyder, MD**
Professor of Medicine
University of Pennsylvania
Philadelphia, Pennsylvania
*Gonadotroph and Other Clinically Nonfunctioning Pituitary Adenomas*

**John T. Soper, MD**
Professor, Department of Obstetrics and Gynecology
Duke University Medical Center
Durham, North Carolina
*Gestational Trophoblastic Neoplasms*

**Richard Stanhope, MD, FRCP**
Honorary Senior Lecturer
Department of Biochemistry, Endocrinology and Metabolism
Institute of Child Health;

Consultant Paediatric Endocrinologist
Department of Endocrinology
Great Ormond Street Hospital for Children;

Consultant Paediatric Endocrinologist
Department of Adolescent Endocrinology
University College Hospital;

Consultant Paediatric Endocrinologist
Department of Paediatrics
The Portland Hospital for Women and Children
London, United Kingdom
*Evaluation and Management of Childhood Hypothalamic and
Pituitary Tumors*

**René St-Arnaud, PhD**
Associate Professor
Medicine, Surgery, and Human Genetics
McGill University;

Scientist, Genetics Unit
Shriners Hospital for Children
Montreal, Quebec, Canada
*Genetic Defects in Vitamin D Metabolism and Action*

**Donald L. St. Germain, MD**
Professor, Medicine and Physiology
Dartmouth Medical School
Lebanon, New Hampshire
*Thyroid Hormone Metabolism*

**Donald F. Steiner, MD**
Professor, Biochemistry and Molecular Biology
The University of Chicago;

Senior Investigator
Howard Hughes Medical Institute
Chicago, Illinois
*Chemistry and Biosynthesis of the Islet Hormones: Insulin, Islet
Amyloid Polypeptide (Amylin), Glucagon, Somatostatin, and
Pancreatic Polypeptide*

**Andrew F. Stewart, MD**
Professor and Chief
Division of Endocrinology and Metabolism
University of Pittsburgh School of Medicine
Pittsburgh, Pennsylvania
*Malignancy-Associated Hypercalcemia*

**Paul M. Stewart, MD**
Professor of Medicine
University of Birmingham
Queen Elizabeth Hospital
Birmingham, United Kingdom
*Mineralocorticoid Deficiency*

**Jim Stockigt, MD, FRACP, FRCPA**
Professor of Medicine
Monash University;

Senior Endocrinologist
Ewen Downie Metabolic Unit
Alfred Hospital;

Consultant Endocrinologist
Epworth Hospital
Melbourne, Australia
*Thyroid Hormone Binding and Variants of Transport Proteins*

**Michael Stowasser, MBBS, FRACP, PhD**
Associate Professor
Hypertension Unit, Department of Medicine
University of Queensland;

Director, Hypertension Unit
Princess Alexandra Hospital;

Director, Hypertension Unit
Greenslopes Hospital
Brisbane, Queensland, Australia
*Primary Mineralocorticoid Excess Syndromes*

**Jerome F. Strauss, III, MD, PhD**
The Luigi Mastroianni Jr. Professor and Director
Center for Research on Reproduction and Women's Health
University of Pennsylvania;

Associate Chairman
Department of Obstetrics and Gynecology
University of Pennsylvania Health System
Philadelphia, Pennsylvania
*Ovarian Hormone Synthesis*
*Placental Hormones*

**Lillian M. Swiersz, MD**
Departments of Gynecology and Obstetrics and Radiation Biology
Stanford University
Stanford, California
*Endometriosis*

**Mariusz W. Szkudlinski, MD, PhD**
Vice President for Research and Development
Trophogen, Inc
Rockville, Maryland
*Thyroid-Stimulating Hormone and Regulation of the Thyroid Axis*

**Shahrad Taheri BSc, MSc, PhD, MB, BS, MRCP**
Lecturer in Medicine and Endocrinology
Henry Wellcome Laboratories for Integrative Neuroscience and
Endocrinology
University of Bristol;

Lecturer in Medicine and Endocrinology
Diabetes and Endocrinology
Bristol Royal Infirmary;

Lecturer in Medicine and Endocrinology
Diabetes and Endocrinology
Southmead Hospital
Bristol, United Kingdom
*Gastrointestinal Hormones and Tumor Syndromes*

**Rajesh V. Thakker, MD, FRCP, FRCPath, FMedSci**
May Professor of Medicine
Nuffield Department of Medicine
University of Oxford
Oxford, Oxon, United Kingdom
*Genetic Disorders of Calcium Homeostasis Caused by Abnormal
Regulation of Parathyroid Hormone Secretion or Responsiveness*
*Multiple Endocrine Neoplasia Type 1*

**Axel A. Thomson, PhD**
Programme Leader, MRC Human Reproductive Sciences Unit
Edinburgh, Scotland
*Endocrinology of the Prostate and Benign Prostatic Hyperplasia*

**Michael O. Thorner, MB, BS, DSc**
Henry B. Mulholland Professor and Chair
Internal Medicine
University of Virginia School of Medicine
Charlottesville, Virginia
*Growth Hormone–Releasing Hormone, Ghrelin, and Growth Hormone
Secretagogues*

**Jorma Toppari, MD, PhD**
Professor, Departments of Physiology and Pediatrics
University of Turku
Turku, Finland
*Testicular Tumors with Endocrine Manifestations*

**Cristina Traggiai, MD**
Department of Paediatrics
Institute G. Gaslini
Genoa, Italy
*Evaluation and Management of Childhood Hypothalamic and Pituitary Tumors*

**Greet Van den Berghe, MD, PhD**
Professor of Medicine
Faculty of Medicine
Catholic University of Leuven;

Director, Department of Intensive Care
University Hospital Gasthuisberg-Catholic University of Leuven
Leuven, Belgium
*Endocrine Aspects of Critical Care Medicine*

**Eve Van Cauter, PhD**
Department of Medicine
The University of Chicago
Chicago, Illinois
*Endocrine and Other Biologic Rhythms*

**André C. Van Steirteghem, MD, PhD**
Professor, Embryology and Genetics
Vrije Universiteit Brussel (VUB);

Co-Director, Centre for Reproductive Medicine
Academisch Ziekenhuis VUB
Brussels, Belgium
*Ovulation Induction and Assisted Reproduction*

**Gilbert Vassart, MD, PhD**
Institut de Recherche Interdisciplinaire en Biologie Humaine et
    Moléculaire
Université Libre de Bruxelles
Campus Erasme;

Department of Medical Genetics
Université Libre de Bruxelles
Hôpital Erasme
Brussels, Belgium
*Thyroid Regulatory Factors*
*Thyroid-Stimulating Hormone Receptor Mutations*

**Jan J. M. de Vijlder, MSc, PhD**
Professor of Biochemistry
University of Amsterdam;

Emma Children's Hospital
Academic Medical Center
Amsterdam, The Netherlands
*Genetic Defects in Thyroid Hormone Synthesis and Action: Defects in Thyroid Hormone Synthesis*

**Thomas Vulsma, MD, PhD, MSc**
Associate Professor of Pediatric Endocrinology
University of Amsterdam;

Pediatric Endocrinologist
Emma Children's Hospital
Academic Medical Center
Amsterdam, The Netherlands
*Genetic Defects in Thyroid Hormone Synthesis and Action: Defects in Thyroid Hormone Synthesis*

**Michael P. Wajnrajch, MD**
Assistant Professor of Pediatrics
Department of Pediatrics
Division of Pediatric Endocrinology
Weill Medical College of Cornell University;

Visiting Associate Research Scientist
Department of Pediatrics
Division of Molecular Genetics
Columbia University College of Physicians and Surgeons
New York, New York
*Defects of Adrenal Steroidogenesis*

**Kathleen E. Walsh, DO, MS**
Assistant Clinical Professor, School of Medicine
University of Wisconsin-Madison
Madison, Wisconsin;

Emergency Medicine Physician, The Monroe Clinic
Monroe, Wisconsin
*Female Sexual Dysfunction*

**Anthony P. Weetman, MD, DSc**
Professor of Medicine and Dean
School of Medicine and Biomedical Sciences
University of Sheffield;

Honorary Consultant Endocrinologist
Sheffield Teaching Hospitals
Sheffield, United Kingdom
*Autoimmune Thyroid Disease*

**Nancy L. Weigel, PhD**
Professor, Molecular and Cellular Biology
Baylor College of Medicine
Houston, Texas
*Estrogen and Progesterone Action*

**David A. Weinstein, MD, MMSc**
Instructor in Pediatrics, Harvard Medical School;

Director, Glycogen Storage Disease Program
Division of Endocrinology
Children's Hospital Boston
Boston, Massachusetts
*Management of Diabetes in Children*

**Bruce D. Weintraub, MD**
Chief Operating Officer, Chief Scientific Officer
Trophogen Inc.
Rockville, Maryland
*Thyroid-Stimulating Hormone and Regulation of the Thyroid Axis*

**Gordon C. Weir, MD**
Head, Section on Islet Transplantation and Cell Biology
Diabetes Research and Wellness Foundation Chair
Joslin Diabetes Center;

Professor of Medicine
Harvard Medical School
Boston, Massachusetts
*Pancreatic and Islet Transplantation*

**Roy E. Weiss, MD, PhD, FACP**
Professor of Medicine, Program Director
General Clinical Research Center
University of Chicago, Pritzker School of Medicine
Chicago, Illinois
*Diagnostic Tests of the Thyroid*

**Katherine Wesseling, MD**
Fellow, Pediatrics, Division of Nephrology
University of California at Los Angeles;

Doctor, Pediatric Nephrology
Mattel Children's Hospital, UCLA
Los Angeles, California
*The Renal Osteodystrophies*

**Anne White, PhD**
Professor, Endocrine Sciences
University of Manchester
Manchester, United Kingdom
*Adrenocorticotropic Hormone*

**Morris F. White, PhD**
Principal Investigator
Harvard Medical School
Joslin Diabetes Center
Boston, Massachusetts
*The Molecular Basis of Insulin Action*

**Wilmar M. Wiersinga, MD**
Professor of Endocrinology
Endocrinology Metabolism
Academic Medical Center, University of Amsterdam;

Professor and Doctor
Department of Endocrinology and Metabolism
Academic Medical Center
Amsterdam, The Netherlands
*Hypothyroidism and Myxedema Coma*

**Joseph I. Wolfsdorf, MB, BCh**
Associate Professor, Pediatrics
Harvard Medical School
Boston, Massachusetts;

Director, Diabetes Program
Associate Chief, Division of Endocrinology
Department of Medicine
Children's Hospital Boston
Boston, Massachusetts
*Management of Diabetes in Children*

**Yalemzewd Woredekal, MD**
Assistant Professor of Medicine
Medicine Renal Division
SUNY-Downstate Medical Center;

Medical Director of Dialysis Service
Medicine Renal Division
Kings County Hospital Center
Brooklyn, New York
*Diabetic Nephropathy*

**Sharon Y. Wu, MD**
Fellow, Section of Endocrinology
Department of Medicine
University of Chicago
Chicago, Illinois
*Diagnostic Tests of the Thyroid*

**Wei Wu, PhD**
Assistant Project Scientist
University of California at San Diego
La Jolla, California
*Development of the Pituitary*

**Run Yu**
Fellow, Cedars-Sinai Research Institute
University of California Los Angeles School of Medicine;

Fellow, Division of Endocrinology, Diabetes, and Metabolism
Cedars-Sinai Medical Center
Los Angeles, California
*Cell Division, Differentiation, Senescence, and Death*

**Bernard Zinman, MDCM, FRCPC, FACP**
Professor of Medicine
University of Toronto;

Director
Leadership Sinai Centre for Diabetes
Mount Sinai Hospital;

Senior Scientist
Samuel Lunenfeld Research Institute
Mount Sinai Hospital
Toronto, Ontario, Canada
*Treatment of Type 1 Diabetes Mellitus in Adults*

# Preface

The origins of the fifth edition of *Endocrinology* go back nearly 40 years, which is a long time in the history of contemporary textbooks, although obviously a mere step in the march of medical history. In 1966, John B. Stanbury, MD, who had just successfully published a new and important text called "The Metabolic Basis of Inherited Disease," suggested that a similar approach to endocrinology would be useful. The idea was to develop a book that combined basic mechanisms with diagnosis and management of endocrine diseases, in sharp contrast to the quite clinically oriented texts then available. The idea took root, but a very long gestation followed.

George Cahill and David Kipnis were instrumental in nurturing the concept, but it finally took nine editors and years of work to bring the first edition to press in 1979. The second edition followed in 1989, third edition in 1995, and fourth edition in 2001. Of the original editors, Leslie J. DeGroot, John C. Marshall, and John T. Potts have persisted through each edition. Gordon M. Besser, Don H. Nelson, William D. Odell, Arthur Rubenstein, Emil Steinberger, Henry G. Burger, and D. Lynn Loriaux made immense contributions to these earlier editions. We proudly add Gordon C. Weir, Ashley B. Grossman, and David de Kretser to the masthead of the fifth edition. The authors include more than 300 experts from all over the globe, reflecting the international contributions to the science of endocrinology.

Our goals, as stated in the first edition, remain unchanged. We want our text to provide a complete, contemporary source of basic and clinical aspects of endocrinology. Our book is directed to serious students of endocrinology—a group that includes undergraduates, residents, fellows, and practicing physicians, as well as researchers.

The goals we sought to achieve in 1966 are as crucial today as they were then: to review basic knowledge of endocrine physiology and biochemistry in a complete and up-to-date manner; to provide a thorough clinical discussion of each topic; to integrate the basic and clinical material around human endocrinology; to make clear the integration of the endocrine system in a gland-by-gland manner, as well as the important multi-hormonal integration in endocrine function; and to have our presentation made by the most accomplished endocrinologists in the world.

We recognize the enormous transformation in the use of medical information. Readers, especially those in training, desire instant access to information on the internet. Powerful search engines can track down even the most obscure facts within seconds. While this strategy is valuable for locating snippets of information, it often lacks context and depth. Thus, while great effort and cost are necessary to prepare a multi-authored book, such texts remain important because an expert synthesizes the daunting body of available information. A growing number of students are rediscovering the value of well-written chapters as a means to gain a deep understanding of a topic.

The best of both worlds is a living text that is continuously updated and designed to complement other forms of electronically available information. That is why the fifth edition is available as a hardcover text and on the internet. The online e-dition will be updated regularly with a particular focus on ground-breaking studies. The e-dition also provides a means to keep diagnostic and treatment guidelines updated between editions.

In closing, the editors express their deep gratitude to the authors who once again have provided very readable chapters filled with carefully organized medical information. It is their dedication to teaching that makes our book valuable to readers.

**Leslie J. DeGroot, MD**

**Larry Jameson, MD**

# Contents

*A complete index appears at the end of each volume.*

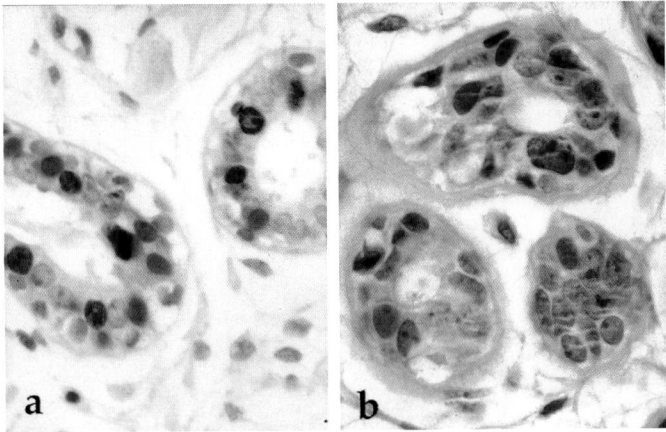

*Figure 164-9*  Lob I ductules of the human breast. **A,** The single-layered epithelium lining the ductule contains Ki67-positive cells (brown nuclei), and ER-positive cells (red-purple nuclei) (×40). **B,** the single-layered epithelium lining the ductule contains brown Ki67-positive cells, and red-purple PR-positive cells. Sections were stained with DAB/alkaline phosphatase-vector red, with light hematoxylin counterstain and photographed at ×40.

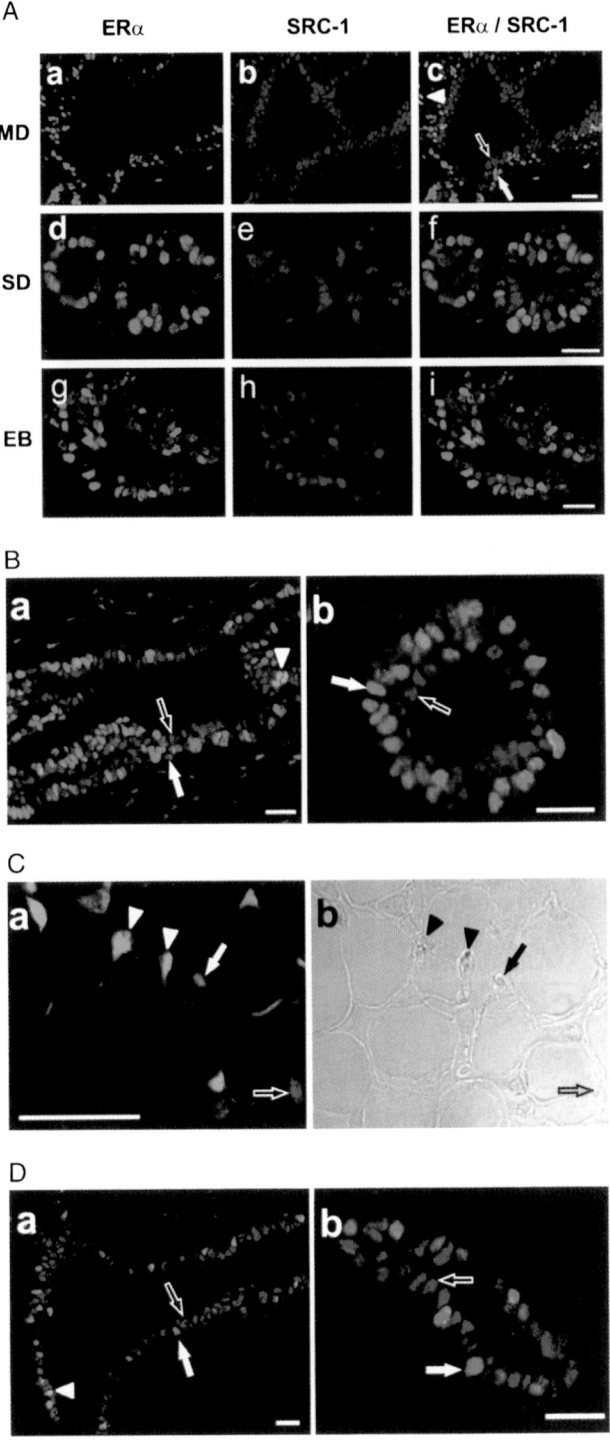

*Figure 164-11*  Segregation of steroid receptor coactivator 1 (SRC-1) expression from ER-α-positive cells as illustrated by dual fluorescence labeling of SRC-1 and ER-α. **A,** mammary glands from 3-week-old virgin female rats were stained simultaneously for SRC-1 (b, e, and h; red) and ER-α (a, d, and g; green). Green and red images were superimposed (c, f, and i). Main duct (MD), small duct (SD), and end bud (EB) are shown. **B,** The discrete distribution pattern of ER-α (green) and SRC-1 (red) was confirmed with the combination of two different antibodies (α and b). **C,** Stroma expressing ER-α alone (green), SRC-1 alone (red), or both (yellow). The phase contrast image from α is shown in b. **D,** Staining from 10-week-old virgin female rat mammary gland also demonstrated the segregation of SRC-1 from ER-α in epithelial cells. *Solid arrow,* Cells expressing only ER-α; *open arrow,* cells expressing only SRC-1; *solid arrowhead,* cells expressing both ER-α and SRC-1. (Bar = 100 μm.)

# CARDIOVASCULAR ENDOCRINOLOGY

# Hormones of the Cardiovascular System

## Miriam T. Rademaker and Eric A. Espiner

## INTRODUCTION

Body fluid volume and blood pressure regulation, which are crucial to sustaining organ perfusion and function, are maintained in health by the integrated actions of the autonomic nervous system (maintaining cardiac output and peripheral vascular resistance), by renal modulation of sodium excretion, and by a complex series of interlocking neurohumoral (endocrine) responses. Traditionally, endocrine regulation of body fluid volume has focused on the renal-adrenal axis (renin-angiotensin-aldosterone system), the nonosmotic release of vasopressin from the neurohypophysis, and changes in local (and possibly circulatory) levels of norepinephrine under the influence of the sympathetic nervous system. However, discoveries over the past 2 decades have made it clear that both cardiac and vascular tissues have the ability to synthesize hormones and local peptides and autacoids that have important local and humoral actions affecting blood pressure and body fluid volume and distribution. Although a large number of peptides with potent hemodynamic effects have been identified within vascular tissue, this chapter is concerned with the natriuretic peptide family (i.e., atrial natriuretic peptide [ANP], brain natriuretic peptide [BNP], and C-type natriuretic peptide [CNP]), the endothelins (ETs), and adrenomedullin (AM). However, in contrast to ANP and BNP, which have clearly defined physiologic roles as circulating hormones, the systemic contributions of CNP, the ETs, and AM are controversial and remain to be clarified.

## NATRIURETIC PEPTIDES

### INTRODUCTION

The discovery by de Bold and colleagues in 1981 of a natriuretic factor in atrial extracts[1] was instrumental in establishing the heart as a true endocrine organ; it also spawned an enormous research effort culminating 3 years later in the isolation and sequencing of a 28-amino acid peptide[2] that was designated ANP. Soon to follow was the identification of other structurally and functionally related peptides, first BNP[3] and then CNP.[4] These three peptides, all present in a wide range of species, constitute a family of natriuretic peptides characterized by strong homology in amino acid sequence within a 17-member ring structure (Fig. 132-1). The actions of this structure are largely directed toward the regulation of blood pressure/volume homeostasis and cardiovascular remodeling. Of the three hormones, the CNP sequence is the most conserved across mammalian species. Whereas both ANP and BNP are true *circulating* hormones (secreted predominantly by the atria and ventricles of the heart, respectively), CNP, in contrast, is not primarily a product of cardiac secretion but appears to act locally (as an autocrine/paracrine factor) within various tissues and organ systems.

### BIOCHEMISTRY

#### Synthesis and Structure

In humans, the two genes encoding ANP and BNP are arranged in tandem (approximately 8 kb apart) on the short arm of chromosome 1. Transcription of the ANP gene yields a 151-amino acid precursor, prepro-ANP, which is cleaved to produce the 126-amino acid prohormone (pro-ANP), the main storage form and the chief constituent of atrial granules.[5] Final processing of the stored pro-ANP by proteolytic cleavage takes place during the hormone's release into the circulation and culminates in the 28-amino acid peptide $ANP_{99-126}$ (or ANP-28, the major bioactive and circulating form) (see Fig. 132-1) and the amino-terminal (NT) fragment $ANP_{1-98}$.[6] Constitutive secretion of ANP-28 and pro-ANP may also occur from the ventricle in pathologic states (e.g., left ventricular hypertrophy and heart failure). BNP gene transcription and processing in humans yields a 134-amino acid precursor, followed by a 108-amino acid propeptide, and finally the mature 32-amino acid $BNP_{77-108}$ (or BNP-32) (see Fig. 132-1) and the NT fragment $BNP_{1-76}$. In humans, both forms circulate in plasma, together with a higher-molecular-weight component, probably the prohormone itself (pro-$BNP_{1-108}$).[7] The main storage form of BNP within the human atria is the mature peptide (BNP-32),[6] which indicates that posttranslational processing of the BNP precursor occurs within the heart and not during secretion, as in the case of ANP. In the ventricle, BNP appears to be predominantly secreted directly from myocytes as the mature peptide via a constitutive pathway.[8] It follows that regulation of BNP secretion primarily occurs during gene expression, in contrast to ANP, which is largely regulated at the level of release from storage granules.

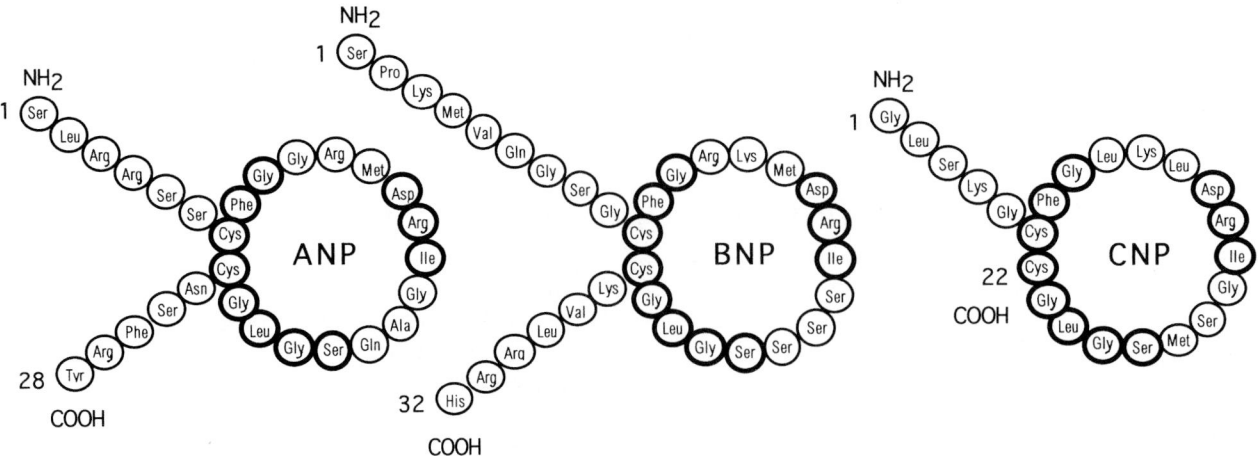

*Figure 132-1*   Mature forms of human atrial natriuretic peptide (ANP), brain natriuretic peptide (BNP), and C-type natriuretic peptide (CNP). *Bold circles* represent amino acids common to the three human hormones. The biologically active forms shown are ANP, BNP-32, and CNP-22.

Distinct from ANP and BNP, the gene encoding CNP is located on chromosome 2 in humans and is transcribed to produce a 126-amino acid precursor molecule that yields a 103-amino acid pro-CNP peptide. Processing of pro-CNP appears to be specifically mediated intracellularly by the enzyme furin[9] to yield an NT fragment (NT-pro-CNP$_{1-50}$); and CNP-53 (pro-CNP$_{51-103}$) (see Fig. 132-1), which is the predominant biologically active form of the peptide in vascular endothelium.[6] CNP-53 is further processed at unknown sites to yield CNP-22 (pro-CNP$_{82-103}$), which retains full biologic activity. In contrast to NT-pro-CNP,[10] plasma levels of CNP-53 and CNP-22 are extremely low and are not readily measurable in human plasma.

### Tissue Distribution

The major site of ANP gene expression is the cardiac atria, which in health produce approximately 95% of the total ANP secreted. The normal ventricle also expresses the gene but at a level 100-fold lower than the atrium. However, expression in the ventricle may increase markedly in pathologic states such as congestive heart failure and ventricular hypertrophy, and thus it may become an important source of circulating forms of ANP.[5] Extracardiac ANP gene expression occurs (although at much lower levels) in the lung, aortic arch, adrenal medulla, gastrointestinal tract, immune system, eye, and central nervous system.[11] In the kidney, processing at amino acid 94/95 yields urodilatin (pro-ANP$_{95-126}$), which may have unique intrarenal paracrine functions.[12] As with ANP, the highest levels of BNP are found in atrial tissue (albeit at 5% of ANP levels), where it is co-stored with ANP within a subset of atrial granules. Whereas immunoreactive levels of BNP in the ventricle are low in comparison (consistent with its constitutive secretion from ventricular myocytes[8]), concentrations of ventricular BNP mRNA are similar to those of atrial tissue. When chamber weights are taken into account, some 60% to 80% of the cardiac secretion of BNP arises from the ventricle.[8] As with ANP, BNP transcripts and secretion are markedly increased in states of chronic left ventricular strain or overload.[8] Other sites of BNP synthesis include the brain (humans excepted), kidney, lung, thyroid, spleen, and amnionic tissue.[11] CNP was first described in the central nervous system,[4] where the concentration of the peptide exceeds that of either ANP or BNP, suggesting a functional role for CNP as a neuropeptide. CNP and transcripts have also been identified outside the central nervous system, most notably within vascular endothelial tissue, where the peptide may serve as a vasodilator and inhibitor of vascular cell proliferation. Low levels of CNP have also been found in human atrial and ventricular myocardium, possibly reflecting its production within the coronary arterial endothelium; and in other tissues including pituitary, kidney, cornea, reproductive organs, and skeletal tissue.[11]

### Receptors and Metabolism

The diverse biologic actions of the natriuretic peptides (see below) are mediated via binding to specific membrane-associated receptors that have been identified in all known target tissues. To date, three different subtypes of natriuretic peptide receptor (NPR) have been identified.[13] Two of these subtypes, NPR-A and NPR-B, are coupled to particulate guanylate cyclase (GC)[14] and appear to mediate most of the well-known actions of the natriuretic peptides through production of the intracellular second messenger, cyclic guanosine monophosphate (cGMP). A splice variant of the NPR-B (NPR-Bi) lacking a functional GC domain has recently been identified in humans.[15] NPR-A selectively binds both ANP and BNP (with preference for ANP) and is present in high concentration in the kidney (particularly within the glomerulus and inner medullary collecting duct), adrenals, heart, vascular smooth muscle, lung, and brain. NPR-B is highly specific for CNP,[16] and its distribution overlaps to some extent with that of NPR-A. The third (and most prevalent) receptor subtype, NPR-C, has no GC domain and is thought to function largely as a "clearance" receptor by internalizing the peptide for lysosomal degradation.[14] However, receptor stimulation has been shown to inhibit adenyl cyclase in several tissues (including vascular smooth muscle cells [VSMCs]), to stimulate phosphoinositide hydrolysis, and to mediate some of the antimitogenic effects of the natriuretic peptides.[17] NPR-C is widely distributed and appears to represent most of the natriuretic peptide receptors in vascular endothelial and smooth muscle cells; it is also prominent in the heart, adrenal gland, kidney, and skeleton.[11,14] In humans, NPR-C affinity for BNP is appreciably less than for ANP and CNP.[16]

In addition to receptor-mediated endocytosis via NPR-C, the other major pathway involved in metabolism of the natriuretic peptides is enzymatic cleavage by neutral endopeptidase (NEP) 24.11. This enzyme, a membrane-bound zinc metalloproteinase that exhibits broad substrate specificity, is present in many epithelial tissues including the vasculature, lung, and kidney (particularly concentrated in the proximal tubular membrane).[18] A soluble form of the enzyme is also detectable in human plasma. In humans, BNP is much more resistant to enzyme hydrolysis than is either ANP or CNP,[19] which together with its lower affinity for NPR-C may in part explain the prolonged plasma half-life of BNP (approximately 22 minutes) compared with ANP and CNP (2 to 4 minutes). Nevertheless, the metabolic clearance rates of all three hormones are similar in adult humans (approximately 2 to 4 L/min),[11,20] thus indicating a markedly greater volume of distribution of BNP than of the other two peptides.

## CONTROL MECHANISMS

The most important stimulus to the secretion of ANP is an increase in atrial wall tension: ANP secretion is increased in acute as well as in chronic states of volume expansion such as congestive heart failure.[21] In humans it has been calculated that each 1-mm Hg rise in atrial pressure is associated with a rise of approximately 10 to 14 pmol/L in venous plasma ANP concentration.[21] As expected, acute reduction of atrial pressure reduces ANP secretion. Despite the generally strong relationship between atrial pressure (wall tension) and ANP secretion, discrepancies can occur, as has been observed during cardiac tamponade and after acute intravenous volume loading.[11] In addition to atrial stretch, many other factors may affect secretion of the peptide, including mechanical factors such as the heart rate (particularly the frequency of atrial contraction) and numerous physiologic and pathophysiologic factors (e.g., increased sodium intake, supine posture, water immersion, exercise, hypoxia, and myocardial ischemia and hypertrophy). In addition, multiple chemical stimuli (particularly ET and angiotensin II[22] but also adrenergic agonists, acetylcholine, glucocorticoids, calcium ionophores, prostaglandin F2α, vasopressin, calcitonin gene-related peptide [CGRP], growth factors, thrombin, platelet-activating factor, relaxin, corticotropin-releasing factor, estradiol, as well as ANP itself) may directly stimulate ANP release or enhance its response to acute volume load.[5,23] Conversely, nitric oxide, testosterone, and perhaps AM inhibit ANP secretion.[23]

Although less attention has focused on the mechanisms of BNP release from the heart, several studies suggest that both peptides respond similarly in many circumstances.[11] Like ANP, plasma BNP is increased by chronic (dietary) sodium loading and in other hypervolemic states (e.g., chronic renal failure and some forms of hypertension).[24] In most of these situations, the increases in plasma ANP and BNP are comparable; however, BNP appears to be less responsive than ANP to abrupt changes in intracardiac pressure (e.g., acute changes in posture, exercise, rapid ventricular pacing, and acute saline loading).[11] These findings presumably reflect the relative content of the two hormones within the atrial granules. Proportionately greater increases in plasma BNP concentrations (vs. ANP) occur after acute myocardial infarction,[25] in patients with heart failure,[8] and in hypertrophic cardiomyopathy.[26] These latter differences are consistent with the markedly augmented gene expression of BNP in comparison to ANP in overloaded ventricles and contrast with the relatively unchanged levels of atrial BNP mRNA and secretion observed in these states, thus suggesting differential regulation of BNP secretion from atrial and ventricular tissues.

Although little is currently known about the regulation of CNP in vivo, studies directed toward identifying a vascular CNP system provide evidence that a variety of factors affecting vascular tone and cell growth have the capacity to stimulate CNP production in vitro. Transforming growth factor-β, interleukin-1, tumor necrosis factor-β, thrombin, lipopolysaccharide, and endotoxin, most of which are derived from VSMCs, macrophages, and platelets, have been shown to enhance CNP secretion from cultured endothelial cells. On the other hand, CNP secretion is inhibited by oxidized low-density lipoprotein, insulin, and vascular endothelial cell growth factor.[11,27] CNP is not considered to be primarily a product of cardiac secretion, and plasma levels of the peptide (as well as NT-pro-CNP) are only minimally raised in chronic cardiac failure[28] (in strong contrast to ANP and BNP). However, CNP concentrations in ventricular myocardium are reported to increase some threefold in severe heart failure,[29] suggesting a local (paracrine) action within the heart. A small arteriovenous CNP gradient across the heart[30] is in keeping with these findings.

## FUNCTION

The natriuretic peptides exhibit a broad range of effects in a variety of tissues, affecting sodium and blood pressure homeostasis (Fig. 132-2). Some of these actions, particularly in the kidney, are influenced by a variety of other physiologic variables, including resting arterial blood pressure, sodium status, the degree of neurohormonal activation, and age. Intriguingly (with only a few exceptions), the physiologic

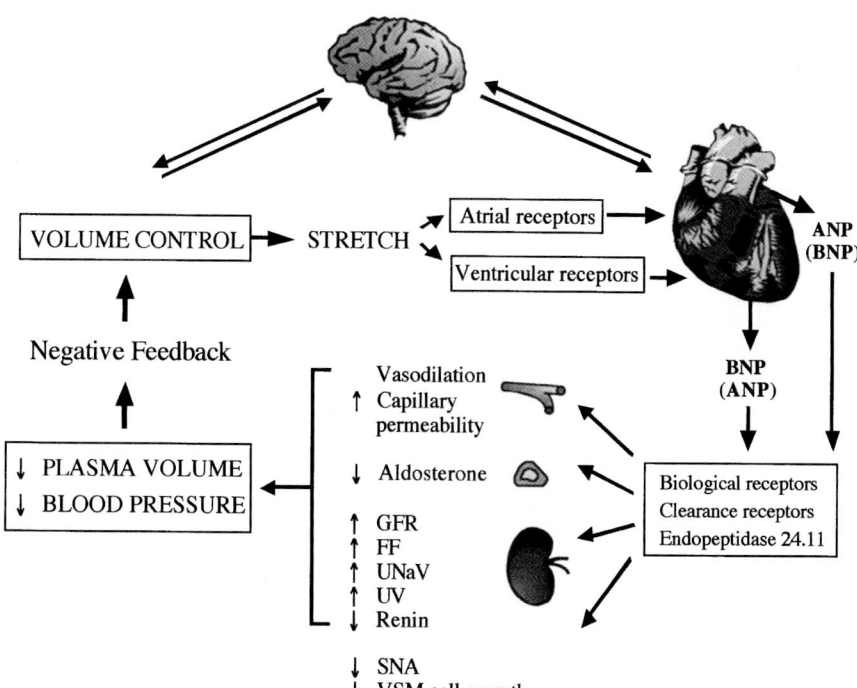

Figure 132-2  Schematic diagram showing the regulation and integrated actions of atrial natriuretic peptide (ANP) and brain natriuretic peptide (BNP). Possible regulation of cardiac synthesis and secretion of ANP/BNP by the brain and the actions of circulating natriuretic peptides on circumventricular brain tissues are discussed in the text. Paracrine actions of the natriuretic peptides (also C-type) on the vessel wall, kidney, and other tissues are omitted for reasons of clarity. FF, filtration fraction; GFR, glomerular filtration rate; SNA, sympathetic nervous activity; UNaV, urine sodium excretion; UV, urine volume; VSM, vascular smooth muscle. (From Rademaker MT, Espiner EA: The endocrine heart. In Becker KL [ed]: Principles and Practice of Endocrinology and Metabolism, 3d ed. Philadelphia, Lippincott Williams & Wilkins, 2001, pp 1622–1634.)

effects of the natriuretic peptides appear to oppose those of the renin-angiotensin system. Apparently standing outside these actions is the recently recognized role of the natriuretic peptides (especially CNP) in endochondral bone formation.[31]

## Renal Effects

Administration of ANP in normovolemic states induces prompt natriuresis, diuresis, and smaller increases in divalent ions without significantly elevating potassium excretion.[11] Larger doses of ANP have been shown to elevate the glomerular filtration rate (GFR). The most striking renal effect of ANP is to increase the fractional excretion of sodium (the fraction of total sodium filtered at the glomerulus that is excreted in the urine), acting largely at tubular sites. In most studies, the filtration fraction (the fraction of total renal blood flow filtered at the glomerulus) is also increased, indicating that renal hemodynamic actions contribute to the natriuresis (see Fig. 132-2). Although a direct effect of ANP on proximal tubular epithelial cation transport has been difficult to demonstrate, direct (receptor-mediated) actions in the glomerulus and the collecting duct are generally agreed upon. ANP has also been shown to redistribute blood flow to the deeper nephrons with less sodium reabsorptive capacity. A number of the proposed actions of ANP appear to be mediated by inhibition of the action of angiotensin II and, to a lesser extent, arginine vasopressin and aldosterone.[32]

Although not studied in as much detail, it seems likely that natriuretic potency and the mode of action of BNP are analogous to those of ANP.[33,34] In contrast to ANP and BNP, CNP appears to lack natriuretic activity,[20] even when administered in high doses directly into the renal artery.

## Hemodynamic Effects

One of the best-documented hemodynamic effects of ANP and BNP is a fall in arterial (chiefly systolic) blood pressure (see Fig. 132-2), which in normal health is mediated largely by a fall in cardiac output caused by a reduction in cardiac filling pressure. Some of this effect is because of a reduction in plasma volume (as evidenced by an increase in venous hematocrit) associated with a shift of plasma from the vascular to the extravascular space.[11] This latter action is mediated by enhanced capillary hydraulic conductivity (see Fig. 132-2) and by an increase in permeability of the vascular endothelium. Additional factors contributing to the reduction in cardiac preload include dilation of capacitance veins and increased resistance to venous return. A direct effect of ANP on atrial (and ventricular) myocytes in reducing their tension or excitability has also been proposed. However, cardiac muscle contractility is largely unaffected by either ANP or BNP, whereas coronary blood flow is increased and myocardial oxygen consumption is decreased.[35] A further important hemodynamic action of ANP is its effect to reduce sympathetic tone in the peripheral vasculature by a direct inhibitory action on sympathetic nerve outflow, in addition to sensitizing vagal afferents (leading to reflex bradycardia) and dampening arterial baroreflex responses.[36] Other actions contributing to the hypotensive effect include early natriuresis/diuresis, inhibition of renin and aldosterone secretion, and inhibition of the vasopressor response to angiotensin II and ET.

A range of studies have shown that CNP has vasodilator activity that is enhanced by removal of the endothelium. Proportionately greater venodilator effects have been observed in dogs in contrast to the possible arterial bias of ANP and BNP. In normotensive humans, high-dose infusions of CNP reduced systemic blood pressure without altering heart rate or cardiac output (suggesting a reduction in peripheral vascular resistance),[27] whereas lower, more physiologic doses had no hemodynamic effect.[20] CNP has also been shown to induce vasorelaxation of coronary arteries[37] and the pulmonary vasculature.[27]

## Endocrine Effects

One of the remarkable aspects of ANP (and BNP) action is the nearly universal inhibition of the effects of angiotensin II. Although some of these interactions have already been discussed in the context of the renal and hemodynamic actions of ANP and BNP, the antagonism extends to many endocrine actions (e.g., inhibition of angiotensin II–induced aldosterone and vasopressin secretion) and other central effects mediated by the brain renin-angiotensin system. In humans, inhibition of renin secretion appears to be a consistent and prompt effect of ANP (and BNP) administration,[33] and a direct inhibitory effect by ANP on renin release is supported by in vitro studies. It is also likely that inhibition is mediated by increased delivery of sodium and chloride to the macula densa. ANP and BNP have a selective inhibitory effect on the zona glomerulosa whereby aldosterone production is reduced (mainly via inhibition of cholesterol uptake into mitochondria).[38] In humans, ANP inhibits the aldosterone-stimulating effects of potassium; adrenocorticotrophic hormone (ACTH); metoclopramide; and, in particular, angiotensin II. Other endocrine actions of ANP (and BNP) include inhibition of ET, ACTH, arginine vasopressin, prolactin, and luteinizing hormone secretion. On the other hand, the peptides (usually at higher dosage) appear to *stimulate* testosterone and progesterone secretion. In contrast to the cardiac natriuretic peptides, antagonism of the renin-angiotensin-aldosterone system by CNP appears negligible.[20] However, like ANP and BNP, CNP has been shown to attenuate stimulated ET-1 production in vitro[27] and to inhibit arginine vasopressin and luteinizing hormone secretion. The significance of many of the above findings (all of which are drawn from in vitro systems, or have employed pharmacological doses) is unclear.

## Antiproliferative Effects

All three natriuretic peptides (ANP, BNP, and CNP) have antiproliferative (antimitogenic) effects in a variety of tissues, including vascular smooth muscle, adrenal gland, kidney, brain, myocardiocytes, and endothelial cells.[39] ANP itself, acting via NPR-A, induces apoptosis in neonatal rat cardiac myocytes.[40] ANP and BNP also inhibit both ET-1 and angiotensin II–stimulated $^3$H-thymidine incorporation into cardiac fibroblasts,[41] whereas reciprocal antagonism between CNP and mitogens has been reported in these cells.[42] These findings raise the possibility that natriuretic peptides regulate cell growth within the cardiac and vascular systems, thereby influencing remodeling and, possibly, vessel wall changes accompanying atheroma or other trauma. In this context it is interesting to note that striking ventricular overgrowth together with perivascular fibrosis occurs in transgenic mice lacking functional NPR-A,[43] findings that support the view that ANP and BNP have important roles in regulating ventricular cell growth in vivo. Furthermore, it has been speculated that CNP, as an endothelium-derived factor, might also play an important antimitogenic role in the prevention of vascular and cardiac remodeling.[44] Indeed, adenoviral gene transfer of CNP in rabbits not only suppresses vascular neointimal formation after injury but also accelerates reendothelialization and angiogenesis, indicating the peptide has both vasculoprotective and regenerative actions.[45]

## Neuroendocrine and Other Effects

The expression of all three natriuretic peptides (particularly CNP) and their receptors in discrete and diverse regions of the brain and spinal cord suggests a central (brain) natriuretic peptide system that is analogous to the brain renin-angiotensin system. The actions and role of the natriuretic peptides within the brain have been difficult to unravel. However, consistent with complementary actions with systemic hormones are the effects of centrally administered ANP and BNP to reduce systemic blood pressure and heart rate; to suppress basal, dehydration-induced, and angiotensin II–induced drinking; and to attenuate the pressor action of central angiotensin II.[46] In some circumstances, centrally administered ANP has been shown to induce natriuresis and diuresis and to reduce salt appetite. Even though ANP and BNP do not cross the blood-brain barrier, the presence of NPR-A in subfornical and circumventricular tissues suggests that these circulating hormones may affect the central neural tissues that regulate blood pressure and fluid homeostasis[46] (see Fig. 132-2). Although not studied in as much detail, central injection of CNP also appears to reduce blood pressure and adrenocortical activity and to inhibit angiotensin II–stimulated vasopressin secretion and luteinizing hormone secretion. However, in contrast to central ANP, CNP may actually stimulate thirst and prolactin secretion.[27]

Contrary to their antiproliferative activities, all three natriuretic peptides (particularly CNP) have been shown to stimulate the growth of osteoblasts in vitro.[47] Marked skeletal overgrowth develops in transgenic mice that overexpress the BNP gene,[48] whereas mice lacking the NPR-C gene exhibit skeletal deformities associated with significantly increased bone turnover.[49] These novel findings suggest that natriuretic peptides, particularly CNP, may act as paracrine factors regulating endochondral ossification and/or bone formation.

## ROLE IN PHYSIOLOGY AND PATHOPHYSIOLOGY

The striking range of actions of the natriuretic peptides (e.g., reductions in cardiac filling pressure, arterial vasodilation, promotion of sodium and water excretion, inhibition of the renin-angiotensin-aldosterone system, and reduced baroreflex sensitivity) provides strong circumstantial evidence that they play a fundamental role in maintaining blood pressure and volume. More concrete evidence is supplied by studies showing that blockade of the natriuretic peptide system increases plasma renin-aldosterone, ET, and norepinephrine levels; reduces sodium excretion and GFR[50]; and accelerates the development of hypertension and heart failure.[51] Further studies using transgenic models show that mice overexpressing the ANP or BNP gene exhibit elevated plasma natriuretic peptide concentrations in conjunction with marked and life-long hypotension, in comparison to normal mice,[52] whereas mice entirely lacking a functional gene encoding NPR-A (and thus largely unable to respond to either ANP or BNP) have not only elevated blood pressure but also marked cardiac hypertrophy (and fibrosis) with dilatation.[43] In males, there is an increased incidence of sudden death. Taken together, these findings provide strong support for the view that cardiac natriuretic peptides play a critical role in circulatory homeostasis. Although information on the physiology and pathophysiology of CNP is relatively limited, it appears that this peptide is likely to play a lesser role than ANP and BNP in sodium homeostasis. In support of this view, the phenotype of transgenic mice lacking a functional CNP gene, although exhibiting profound dwarfism, appears to show normal cardiovascular function (including blood pressure).[31] These findings do not exclude the possibility that CNP participates as a paracrine factor, possibly interdigitating with the other (circulating) natriuretic peptides in a "vascular CNP system" concerned with the regulation of local vasomotor tone and vascular cell growth.[53]

Plasma venous levels of immunoreactive ANP in young healthy adults range from 5 to 25 pmol/L and show little evidence of pulsatile secretion or diurnal rhythmicity. Concentrations increase with age and are elevated by supine posture, high dietary sodium intake, and volume expansion. Circulating BNP levels in normal humans are consistently lower (0.3 to 10 pmol/L) than those of ANP. Similar to ANP, BNP levels are higher in the elderly, increase in sodium-loaded states, but show less fluctuation than ANP with acute maneuvers such as changes in posture and exercise. As previously mentioned, plasma ANP and BNP levels are elevated in a number of hypervolemic states, in keeping with increased intracardiac pressure. The most striking increases occur in congestive heart failure, where both ANP and BNP concentrations correlate with severity[8] (Fig. 132-3). These marked increases in plasma levels are largely caused by augmented ventricular secretion of both peptides. Other disorders of cardiac muscle (e.g., dilated cardiomyopathy) or valvular function are also associated with elevated circulating levels of cardiac natriuretic peptides. Plasma BNP is reported to be uniquely elevated in hypertrophic obstructive cardiomyopathy. Plasma ANP and BNP are also increased soon after myocardial infarction (see Fig. 132-3), even in the absence of clinical cardiac decompensation, with concentrations reflecting infarct size and the increase in cardiac filling pressure.[54] Both ANP and BNP are increased after subarachnoid hemorrhage (BNP more than ANP), possibly as a consequence of transient subendocardial ischemia associated with intense cardiac sympathetic nervous activation.[55] Increased concentrations of ANP and BNP in chronic renal failure may also reflect "volume overload" inasmuch as levels fall after dialysis (ANP more than BNP) (see Fig. 132-3). Raised levels of both hormones are observed in pulmonary hypertension (reflecting right ventricular dysfunction)[56]; in patients with acute lung injury[57]; and in a variety of other noncardiac edematous states including the nephrotic syndrome and cirrhosis, where central blood volume may be increased. Significant, but smaller, increases in both ANP and BNP levels occur in hypertension and correlate with left ventricular hypertrophy.[24] A variety of tachyarrhythmias may markedly increase plasma hormone levels (ANP more than BNP in humans). A number of other noncardiac disorders (e.g., the "syndrome of inappropriate antidiuretic hormone secretion," Cushing's

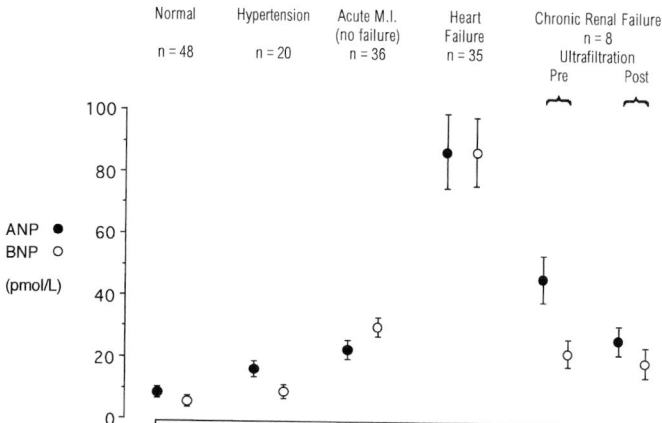

*Figure 132-3*  Venous plasma atrial natriuretic peptide (ANP, *filled circles*) and concurrent brain natriuretic peptide (BNP, *open circles*) levels in normal subjects and patients with circulatory disorders. Values are means + SEM. n, number of subjects in each group. All samples were assayed in the same laboratory (Endocrine Department, Christchurch Hospital, New Zealand) by previously published techniques. Hypertensive patients showed no evidence of significant end-organ disease (data from Richards et al: Hypertension 22:231–236, 1993; and Pidgeon et al: Hypertension 27:906–913, 1996). Patients with acute (uncomplicated) myocardial infarction (MI) had blood drawn within 24 hours of admission (data from Foy et al: Eur Heart J 16:770–779, 1995). Heart failure was of recent onset, New York Heart Association functional class II to IV (normal and heart failure data from Yandle et al: J Clin Endocrinol Metab 76:832–838, 1993). In patients with chronic renal failure, blood was drawn before and after acute volume depletion by ultrafiltration (data from Corboy et al: Clin Sci 87:679–684, 1994.) (From Rademaker MT, Espiner EA: The endocrine heart. In Becker KL (ed): Principles and Practice of Endocrinology and Metabolism, 3d ed. Philadelphia, Lippincott Williams & Wilkins, 2001, pp. 1622–1634.)

syndrome, Bartter's syndrome, and orthostatic hypotension) are also reported to be associated with raised plasma ANP.

To date, the only validated report of a primary disorder of cardiac natriuretic peptide secretion or action resulting in disease is that of familial open-angle glaucoma.[58] However, analogous with transgenic animal studies,[43,52] there are several reports that polymorphism in the genes of the natriuretic peptides and their receptors may contribute or predispose to some types of cardiovascular disease. In humans, not only have mutations in the ANP,[59] NPR-A,[60] and NPR-C[61] genes been found to be associated with the development of hypertension, but genetic mutations in the natriuretic peptide system may also be associated with left ventricular hypertrophy[60]; coronary artery disease; and nonfatal myocardial infarction,[62] stroke,[63] and proteinuria.[64]

CNP is present at very low plasma concentrations in health, whereas the amino-terminal fragment (NT-pro-CNP) is clearly detectable,[10] and circulating levels of the peptide do not appear to change greatly in patients with hypertension or severe heart failure[27,28] (in strong contrast to ANP and BNP). Recent studies have reported that polymorphism in the human CNP gene[65] and in its receptor, NPR-B,[66] is associated with the development of hypertension. In view of the lack of obvious cardiovascular complications in CNP-disrupted transgenic mice models and other spontaneous mutations of the genes affecting CNP formation or actions, further studies in humans are awaited with interest. Elevated plasma CNP levels have been reported in patients with severe sepsis,[67] chronic renal failure (with levels decreasing significantly after hemodialysis), cor pulmonale, hypoxia, and aneurysmal subarachnoid hemorrhage.[27] In patients with chronic renal failure, CNP was the only natriuretic peptide to significantly correlate with systolic blood pressure.[68] Whether these increases constitute a response to specific stimuli or reflect widespread endothelial damage or impaired clearance is unknown.

## CLINICAL APPLICATIONS

### Diagnosis/Prognosis/Guiding Therapy

The close relationship between natriuretic peptide plasma levels and cardiac load has led to their use in clinical diagnosis and as markers of cardiac dysfunction. Raised plasma concentrations of ANP and, in particular, BNP and its N-terminal fragment (NT-proBNP) (by virtue of predominant ventricular origin, more rapid gene induction, and slower clearance rate from plasma) are not only markers of left ventricular dysfunction but also predict subsequent hemodynamic deterioration in asymptomatic subjects and the development of overt heart failure.[69] Raised BNP (or NT-pro-BNP) levels distinguish cardiac dyspnea from other causes such that a low concentration of the hormone accurately rules out the presence of decompensated heart failure in patients presenting with acute breathlessness.[70] A large and increasing body of evidence indicates that measurement of BNP/NT-pro-BNP can assist in the evaluation of a variety of disorders affecting the cardiovascular system, some of which are summarized in Table 132-1. Taken together, these findings indicate that measurement of BNP hormones are likely to become a routine part of care of any subject with a known or suspected cardiac disorder.[69]

Measurement of natriuretic peptide levels in the assessment of "volume" status in noncardiac disorders is also a possibility. Already it has been shown that assay of plasma ANP is useful in determining the adequacy of mineralocorticoid replacement in patients with Addison's disease.[71] Similarly, it is possible that along with aldosterone and renin, measurement of plasma cardiac natriuretic peptides may prove to be a useful marker of the hyperexpanded state associated with primary hyperaldosteronism. Thus, a relatively cheap and rapid blood test may ultimately be a guide to the identification of subjects

| Table 132-1 | Clinical Uses of BNP/NT-pro-BNP Measurement |
|---|---|

Screening for left ventricular dysfunction
Diagnosis of newly symptomatic heart failure
Diagnosis of diastolic dysfunction
Diagnosis of cor pulmonale in chronic respiratory disease
Predicting cardiovascular events in hypertension
Predicting mortality in unstable angina
Predicting mortality and future myocardial infarction in acute coronary syndrome
Risk stratification following acute myocardial infarction
Risk stratification in known heart failure
Predicting successful cardioversion in atrial fibrillation
Predicting outcome after coronary/cardiac surgery
Predicting poor outcome in pulmonary embolism
Predicting future cardiac events in chronic hemodialysis
Predicting LV dysfunction in recipients of hemopoietic stem cell transplantation
Predicting mortality in the elderly
Titration of antifailure treatment

requiring more detailed (and costly) investigations, or to the introduction or intensification of treatment.[69]

### Treatment

Because of their protean effects (i.e., vasodilatory, natriuretic/diuretic, renin-angiotensin-aldosterone system–inhibitory, and antimitogenic actions), any maneuver that increases the circulating and tissue levels of the natriuretic peptides is likely to be favorable in the treatment of a variety of cardiovascular and hypervolemic disorders. Indeed, BNP (nesiritide) has recently become the first new parenteral agent to be approved for treating heart failure in over a decade. In (acutely) decompensated heart failure, nesiritide infusion is associated with rapid hemodynamic and symptomatic improvement[72] and a significant reduction in length of stay in hospital. In a comparative study with dobutamine, nesiritide was equally as effective, was safer, and significantly lowered the 21-day all-cause hospital readmission rate as well as the 6-month mortality.[71,73] In another study, nesiritide was found to be more effective and better tolerated than the vasodilator nitroglycerin.[74] In view of these findings, nesiritide represents an attractive choice for first-line therapy for patients with acutely decompensated heart failure. BNP may also prove useful in the treatment of noncardiogenic acute pulmonary edema[75] and management of postoperative cardiac patients,[76] whereas ANP is reported to attenuate reperfusion phenomena and preserve left ventricular function in patients undergoing direct coronary angioplasty for acute myocardial infarction.[77] In patients with acute renal failure, long-term infusion of ANP markedly improved renal blood flow and glomerular function,[78] whereas in patients with cor pulmonale, both cardiac peptides produced pulmonary vasodilation without worsening oxygen saturation.[79] The use of NEP 24.11 inhibitors (which enhance endogenous levels of the peptides through inhibition of their enzymatic breakdown) has been shown to have beneficial effects that mimic those of exogenous ANP and BNP.[80] Other advantages of these drugs include oral availability, a relatively prolonged duration of action, and enhanced renal activity.[80] In chronic renal failure, NEP inhibition is reported to induce marked diuresis at a stage when loop diuretics have little effect. Chronic use of NEP inhibitors has also been shown to reduce intraocular pressure, and it may have a place in the management of glaucoma. The development of drug combinations with NEP- and angiotensin-converting enzyme (ACE)–inhibitory actions,[81] or combinations with endothelin-converting enzyme (ECE) inhibitors,[82] shows particular promise. The long-term use of such compounds also has important actions in promoting the antiproliferative effects of the natriuretic peptides, thereby reducing endothelial proliferation and vascular smooth muscle and cardiac hypertrophy. For example, in rats, CNP gene transfer to balloon-injured carotid arteries reduced neointimal formation by 90%,[83] whereas ANP gene therapy is reported to reduce blood pressure for up to 12 weeks.[84]

## ENDOTHELIN

### INTRODUCTION

The vascular endothelium, once considered to be an inert barrier between the blood and vascular wall, is now recognized as an independent functional system. By 1989, the three members of the ET family of 21-amino acid peptides (ET-1, ET-2, and ET-3) had been identified,[85] with ET-1 being the major isoform generated in the human vasculature and considered the most important functionally in regulating local vascular tone. In combination with other diverse effects in various tissues (see below), these actions serve to maintain circulatory pressure and tissue blood flow.[86] To date, the physiologic functions of ET-2 and ET-3 are much less clear; some evidence, however, suggests that ET-2 may mediate actions within the kidney, whereas ET-3 may mediate effects within the gut and nervous system. As already shown for angiotensin II, ET and the natriuretic peptides appear to be mutually opposing forces in many tissues and cellular pathways.

### BIOCHEMISTRY

#### Synthesis, Structure, and Distribution

In humans, the genes encoding ET-1, ET-2, and ET-3 are located on chromosomes 6, 1, and 20, respectively.[85,87] Transcription and processing of the ET genes yields a precursor peptide (prepro-ET), followed by the inactive pro-ET ("big" ET) isoforms (38, 37, and 41 amino acids for big ET-1, ET-2, and ET-3, respectively). Subsequent cleavage, yielding the mature 21-amino acid bioactive peptides (Fig. 132-4) and inactive C-terminal fragments, occurs through the action of a unique ECE (relatively selective for big ET-1), which is the rate-limiting step in ET synthesis.[88] The major site of ET-1

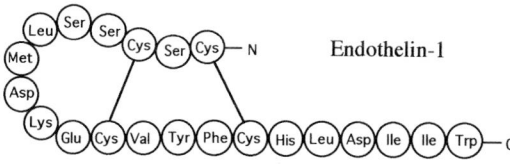

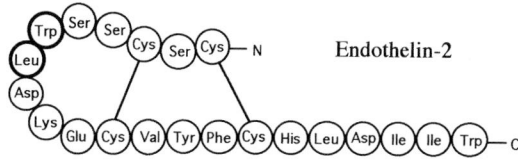

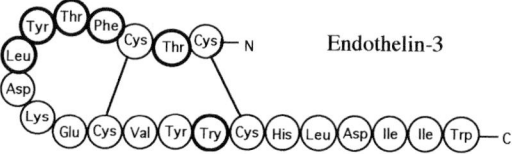

*Figure 132-4* The three mature isoforms of human endothelin: endothelin-1, endothelin-2, and endothelin-3. *Bold circles* represent amino acids different from those of endothelin-1.

generation is the vascular endothelium, but a variety of other cells secrete the peptide (e.g., epithelial cells, VSMCs, cardiac myocytes, macrophages, and mast cells). ET-1 gene expression has been demonstrated in many tissues, including the vasculature, heart, lung, kidney, pancreas, spleen, liver, placenta, endometrium, and central nervous system.[86,88,89] ET-2 has been found in the kidneys and intestines, as well as the heart, placenta, and uterus, whereas ET-3 is expressed predominantly in the central nervous system but is also found throughout the gastrointestinal tract, lung, and kidney. ET-3 is not detected in endothelial cells.

#### Receptors and Metabolism

Two ET receptors have been identified: ETA and ETB, both of which are G protein coupled.[89,90] The ETA receptor is highly selective for ET-1 (ET-1 more than ET-2 more than ET-3), and can be detected in a variety of tissues, the highest expression being evident in VSMCs, cardiac myocytes, and the renal glomeruli and vasculature. The ETA receptor largely mediates the vasoconstrictor action of ET-1 (through activation of phospholipase C), as well as mitogenesis (via protein kinase C activation) and the stimulation of aldosterone secretion.[86,89] The ETB receptor binds all three ETs equally but is the preferred receptor for ET-3; it is expressed predominantly in endothelial cells and, to a lesser extent, in VSMCs, brain, lung, and kidney.[90] Activation of vascular endothelial ETB receptors evoke transient vasodilatation (through stimulation of nitric oxide and prostacyclin), although vasoconstriction has been reported in some tissues, including the coronary arteries[91] and renal vasculature.[87] The ETB receptor also appears to mediate the growth-inhibitory effects associated with apoptosis, as well as inhibition of platelet aggregation.[89] In addition, the ETB receptor plays a major role in the clearance of ET-1 through binding and internalization of the peptide[92] in a variety of vascular beds, but primarily in the lungs and kidneys.[93] Enzymatic degradation of the ETs by endopeptidases, particularly by NEP 24.11, also occurs.

### CONTROL MECHANISMS

The process of peptide release is not well understood but appears to be largely constitutive (at least in endothelial cells) and is regulated predominantly at the level of mRNA transcription. However, both ET-1 and big ET-1 have been identified in secretory vesicles isolated from bovine aortic endothelial cells. Induction of ET-1 mRNA (and/or increased peptide release) occurs in response to various mechanical and chemical stimuli (e.g., pulsatile stretch, low shear stress, hypoxia, thrombin, transforming growth factor-β, and other cytokines) as well as vasoactive agents (e.g., catecholamines, arginine vasopressin, angiotensin II, bradykinin, and insulin)[86–89] (Fig. 132-5). Conversely, factors that inhibit ET-1 gene expression include high shear stress, ET-3, the natriuretic peptides, AM, nitric oxide, prostacyclin, prostaglandin $E_2$, estrogen, dilator prostanoids, and heparin[88,89] (see Fig. 132-5).

### FUNCTION

#### Hemodynamic Effects

One of the best-defined actions of ET (mediated largely by the ETA receptor) is smooth muscle contraction, particularly vascular smooth muscle of arteries, veins, and resistance vessels (see Fig. 132-5). Characteristically, this action is slow both to develop and reverse. ET-1 is generally the most potent vasoconstrictor of the three isoforms, with coronary, renal, and cerebral vascular beds being especially sensitive.[94] Of note, the vasoconstricting actions of ET-1 are greatly increased in atherosclerotic vessels (in which the opposing biologic effect of nitric oxide is largely lost), and ET-1 constriction of coronary vessels has been associated with the development of fatal ventricular arrhythmias. As well as having direct effects on

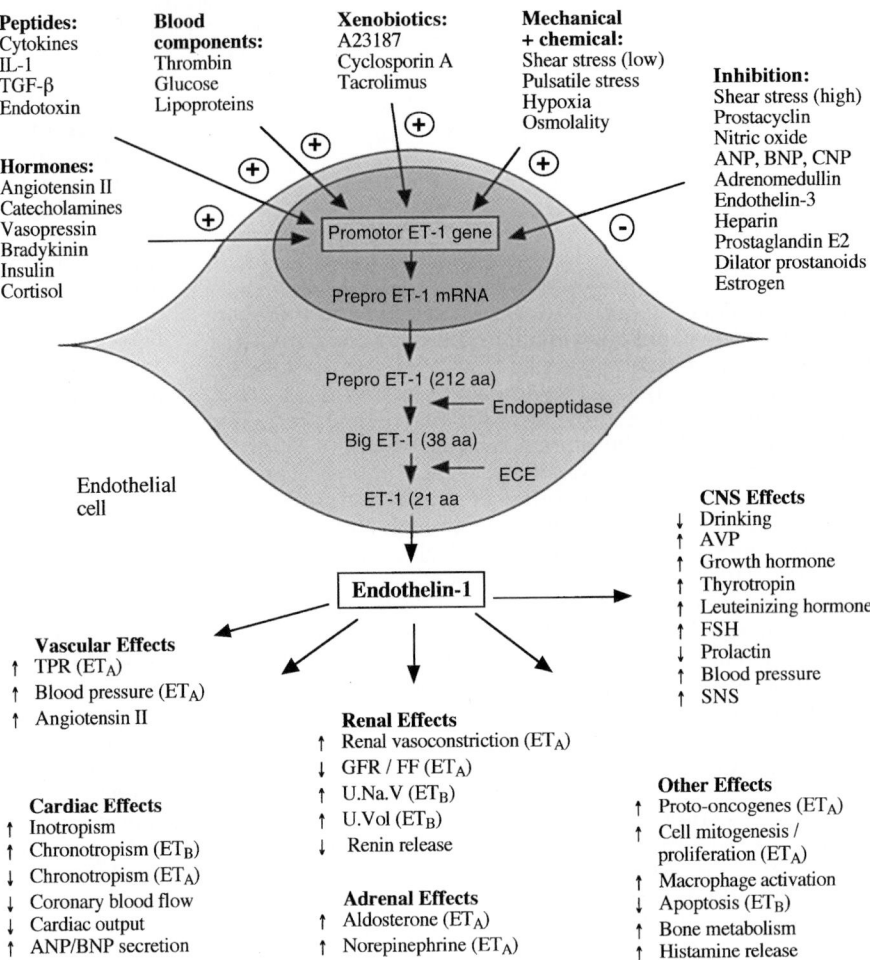

**Peptides:**
Cytokines
IL-1
TGF-β
Endotoxin

**Hormones:**
Angiotensin II
Catecholamines
Vasopressin
Bradykinin
Insulin
Cortisol

**Blood components:**
Thrombin
Glucose
Lipoproteins

**Xenobiotics:**
A23187
Cyclosporin A
Tacrolimus

**Mechanical + chemical:**
Shear stress (low)
Pulsatile stress
Hypoxia
Osmolality

**Inhibition:**
Shear stress (high)
Prostacyclin
Nitric oxide
ANP, BNP, CNP
Adrenomedullin
Endothelin-3
Heparin
Prostaglandin E2
Dilator prostanoids
Estrogen

Promotor ET-1 gene
Prepro ET-1 mRNA
Prepro ET-1 (212 aa)
← Endopeptidase
Big ET-1 (38 aa)
← ECE
ET-1 (21 aa)

Endothelial cell

**Endothelin-1**

**Vascular Effects**
↑ TPR (ET$_A$)
↑ Blood pressure (ET$_A$)
↑ Angiotensin II

**Cardiac Effects**
↑ Inotropism
↑ Chronotropism (ET$_B$)
↓ Chronotropism (ET$_A$)
↓ Coronary blood flow
↓ Cardiac output
↑ ANP/BNP secretion

**Renal Effects**
↑ Renal vasoconstriction (ET$_A$)
↓ GFR / FF (ET$_A$)
↑ U.Na.V (ET$_B$)
↑ U.Vol (ET$_B$)
↓ Renin release

**Adrenal Effects**
↑ Aldosterone (ET$_A$)
↑ Norepinephrine (ET$_A$)

**CNS Effects**
↓ Drinking
↑ AVP
↑ Growth hormone
↑ Thyrotropin
↑ Leuteinizing hormone
↑ FSH
↓ Prolactin
↑ Blood pressure
↑ SNS

**Other Effects**
↑ Proto-oncogenes (ET$_A$)
↑ Cell mitogenesis / proliferation (ET$_A$)
↑ Macrophage activation
↓ Apoptosis (ET$_B$)
↑ Bone metabolism
↑ Histamine release

**Figure 132-5** Synthesis regulation, generation, and biologic actions of endothelin-1 (ET-1). Receptors (ETA/ETB) mediating actions if known are shown in parentheses. See the text for details. AVP, arginine vasopressin; CNS, central nervous system; ECE, endothelin-converting enzyme; FF, filtration fraction; FSH, follicle-stimulating hormone; GFR, glomerular filtration rate; IL-1 interleukin-1; SNS, sympathetic nervous system; TGF-β, transforming growth factor-β; TPR, total peripheral resistance; U.Na.V, urine sodium excretion; U.Vol, urine volume. (Modified from Haynes WG, Webb DJ: Endothelin as a regulator of cardiovascular function in health and disease. J Hypertens 16:1081–1098, 1998.)

vascular tone, ET-1 acts indirectly by augmenting vasoconstriction caused by other agents (e.g., angiotensin II, serotonin, and catecholamines) and by enhancing central and peripheral sympathetic function.[89,95] Other cardiovascular effects of ET-1 include potent positive inotropic effects,[96] and both positive (via ETB receptor) and negative (via ETA receptor) chronotropic actions[86] (see Fig. 132-5). Low-dose intravenous infusion of ET-1, sufficient to increase plasma levels twofold, is reported to reduce heart rate and cardiac output and to increase renal and systemic vascular resistance without affecting mean arterial pressure and coronary vascular resistance.[97] ET-1 is also a constrictor of nonvascular smooth muscle, including those of respiratory, intestine, bladder, myometrium, mesangium, prostate, and vas deferens tissues,[86] and has been implicated in stimulation of uterine contractions during spontaneous labor and closure of umbilical vessels and the ductus arteriosus at birth.

### Renal Effects

ET within the kidney has direct effects on renal hemodynamics and tubular function. As mentioned above, the renal circulation is particularly sensitive to the vasoconstrictor actions of ET (via the ETA receptor), where it acts to reduce renal plasma flow, GFR, and the glomerular capillary ultrafiltration coefficient (see Fig. 132-5), resulting in marked sodium retention.[98] However, the tubular effects of ET, which are mediated via the ETB receptor, actually inhibit sodium reabsorption in the proximal tubule and collecting duct by inhibiting tubular sodium/potassium-ATPase activity, and block water reabsorption in the collecting duct by inhibiting the effects of vasopressin on tubular osmotic permeability

(see Fig. 132-5).[88] An important physiologic role for the renal ETB receptor is supported by the finding that mice and rats lacking the gene for this receptor exhibit salt-sensitive hypertension that is not reversed by blocking the ETA receptor.[99]

### Endocrine Effects

ET-1 has multiple and contrasting effects on the renin-angiotensin-aldosterone system. Whereas the peptide has been shown to inhibit the release of renin from isolated rat glomeruli, ET-1 stimulates endothelial ACE activity and secretion of aldosterone from adrenal zona glomerulosa cells.[88] Furthermore, blockade of ETA receptors is reported to prevent the hemodynamic effects and vascular hypertrophy induced by angiotensin II.[100] ET-1 also interacts with the natriuretic peptide system, stimulating the cardiac secretion of ANP and BNP, whereas they in turn inhibit both ET-1 production and its vasoconstricting actions. Other endocrine effects of ET-1 include the stimulation of epinephrine, vasopressin, histamine, estrogen, prostaglandin, growth hormone, thyrotropin, and follicle-stimulating hormone secretion and the inhibition of prolactin.[86–89]

### Proliferative Effects

ET-1, acting via the ETA receptor, is a potent mitogen for VSMCs, cardiac myocytes, fibroblasts, glomerular mesangial cells, and bronchial smooth muscle cells (mediated via the ETA receptor).[86,88] Indeed, transgenic mice overexpressing ET-1 develop renal cysts, interstitial fibrosis, and glomerulosclerosis,[101] whereas ETA receptor antagonism attenuates cardiac hypertrophy provoked by myocardial infarction in rats.[102] ET-1 is also a strong chemoattractant for circulating monocytes and activates macrophages,[87] thereby contributing to the pathogenesis of atherosclerosis; and it is implicated in the restenotic process.[103] In addition, ET is expressed in several tumors, and has been shown to induce the expression of a number of proto-oncogenes (e.g., c-*fos*, c-*jun*, c-*myc*) and promote the growth of some cancers.[104]

### Neuroendocrine and Other Effects

ET-3 and smaller amounts of ET-1, along with specific receptors, are found throughout the brain.[86] ETB receptors predominate, at least in astrocytes, and mediate the stimulation of DNA synthesis and inhibition of second messenger generation by other neurotransmitters.[89] Both ET-1 and ET-3 activate the sodium-potassium-chloride transporter function of brain capillary endothelial cells, thereby assisting in the maintenance of a low potassium environment in the central nervous system. Evidence also suggests that ET-1 contributes to the vasospasm associated with subarachnoid hemorrhage and to ischemia after cerebral thrombosis and infarction.[86] Central administration of ET-1 increases blood pressure (through the stimulation of central sympathetic outflow and the central production and action of arginine vasopressin)[105]; inhibits baroreceptor responses and stimulates chemoreceptor responses at the carotid bifurcation; blocks the water-seeking behavior induced by central angiotensin II[86]; and may potentiate the peripheral actions of the sympathetic nervous system.[88]

The ET system also appears to play an important role in developmental biology. Mice lacking genes encoding for ET-1 or the ETA receptor have craniofacial and cardiac abnormalities, and die of respiratory failure soon after birth,[106] whereas mice deficient in ET-3 or the ETB receptor exhibit aganglionic megacolon (associated with coat color spotting),[107] which resembles Hirschsprung's disease in humans. As noted for the natriuretic peptides, evidence also suggests a role for ET in the regulation of bone metabolism.[108]

### ROLE IN PHYSIOLOGY AND PATHOPHYSIOLOGY

ET immunoreactivity is present in normal human plasma at levels usually less than 5 pmol/L. At least three components contribute to immunoreactivity: (1) big ET-1 (60%); (2) ET-1 (30%); and (3) ET-3 (10%). ET-2 has not been detected.[88] ET-1 concentrations at the interface between endothelial cells and VSMCs, however, are likely to be much higher because as much as 75% of ET-1 secreted by endothelial cells is abluminal (toward the adjacent vascular smooth muscle), again suggesting a largely paracrine role for this peptide.

Plasma ET-1 is decreased by volume expansion and increased by orthostasis in normal subjects,[109] yet it appears to be unaffected by cold stress or exercise. A variety of disease states are associated with increased plasma concentrations of ET-1, including myocardial infarction, heart failure, atherosclerosis, pulmonary hypertension, renal failure, septic shock, diabetes, and systemic sclerosis.[110,111] Subjects with Raynaud's syndrome show elevated values and augmented responses to local cooling when compared with normal subjects.[112] Some, but not all, studies report increased levels of circulating ET-1 in essential hypertension.[113] Higher than normal levels have also been found in patients with pre-eclampsia, hyperlipoproteinemia, cirrhosis with ascites, Crohn's disease and ulcerative colitis, biliary atresia, sickle-cell disease (particularly those in acute vaso-occlusive crisis), subarachnoid hemorrhage, ischemic stroke, obstructive sleep apnea, Paget's bone disease, and pseudoxanthoma elasticum. In many of these disorders the source and significance of the abnormal ET-1 levels are unclear. However, the actions of ET-1 in increasing vascular tone, activating the angiotensin-aldosterone and sympathetic nervous systems, and augmenting mitogenesis make it a likely candidate in the pathogenesis of

a range of cardiovascular disorders. Obvious examples include states of sustained vasoconstriction, intermittent vasospasm, and other vasospastic states such as may occur in stroke and brain injury. ET-1 is a potent bronchoconstrictor and is implicated in the development of acute asthma, primary pulmonary hypertension, and pulmonary fibrosis. ET-1 also has extensive renovascular and parenchymal effects within the kidney.

In at least one disorder (malignant hemangioendothelioma), a causal connection between hypertension and increased circulating levels of ET-1 appears to have been established.[114] In addition, increased (threefold) plasma ET concentrations in hypertensive blacks, as compared with whites, suggest possible racial differences in the formation of ET-1.[115] There are also several reports indicating that polymorphism in the genes of the endothelin peptides, their receptors, and ECE are associated with the development of essential hypertension,[116–119] as well as with the degree of vascular stiffness, thickness,[120] and reactivity.[121] Mutations of the ETA receptor gene may be a risk factor for idiopathic dilated cardiomyopathy[122] and predict survival in patients with this disease.[123] Conversely, polymorphisms in the ET-1 gene are reported to be associated with reduced risk for chronic heart failure with higher levels of big endothelin.[124] Other associations have been found in patients at risk for malignant ventricular arrhythmia,[125] migraine,[126] asthma and rhinitis,[127] and Hirschsprung's disease.[128]

### CLINICAL APPLICATIONS

#### Diagnosis/Prognosis

In patients with congestive heart failure, ET plasma levels correlate with the degree of left ventricular impairment[129] and myocardial mass,[130] are inversely associated with prognosis, and predict mortality or the need for cardiac transplantation.[131] Circulating ET also appears to be a marker (as well as instigator) of ventricular ectopy in decompensated congestive heart failure.[132] In patients with myocardial infarction, plasma concentrations 3 days after infarction have been shown to predict 1-year mortality.[133] These findings suggest both a diagnostic and prognostic role for this peptide in heart failure. Plasma ET levels may also serve as prognostic markers for patients with primary pulmonary hypertension,[134] as well as indicators of poor outcome in severe acute respiratory distress[135] and of myocardial depression and mortality in septic shock.[136] In addition, ET-1 levels in exhaled breath condensate may be useful for early diagnosis and clinical monitoring of pulmonary fibrosis.[137]

#### Treatment

Increasing interest is being expressed in the potential therapeutic use of ET receptor blockers or ECE inhibitors in a number of disorders associated with increased expression of ET-1, vasoconstriction, and vascular dysfunction. Indeed, bosentan, an orally available mixed ETA/ETB receptor antagonist, was recently approved as a therapeutic drug for pulmonary hypertension: Its administration is associated with improved exercise tolerance, improved cardiopulmonary hemodynamics, and increased time to clinical worsening.[138] Although initial short-term dual ET receptor blockade in patients with hypertension,[139] coronary artery disease,[140] and chronic heart failure[141] were promising, longer-term clinical trials have been less convincing. In chronic heart failure, whereas some trials suggest ET antagonism may improve hemodynamic performance and symptoms and may reduce morbidity,[142] the two longer-term trials found an increased early risk of worsening heart failure in a significant percentage of patients (as a consequence of fluid retention)[143,144] with no overall mortality benefits.[143] In patients with acute decompensated heart failure associated with acute coronary syndrome, the mixed antagonist, tezosentan, did not significantly improve any of the primary clinical end points (i.e., death, recurrent or new ischemia, or myocardial infarction) and demonstrated a non-significant trend toward a higher incidence of worsening heart failure.[145] There has been much debate over whether selective ETA rather than nonselective ETA/ETB receptor blockade would be more beneficial, given the actions mediated via the ETB receptor (i.e., natriuresis, diuresis, positive chronotropism, and vasodilation) and its significant role in ET clearance. Recent studies have shown that although treatment with the ETA antagonist, darusentan, in patients with hypertension[146] and heart failure[147] produced some hemodynamic improvement, there were again trends toward more adverse events. The possible therapeutic applicability of ETA receptor blockade in these diseases requires longer-term studies as well as comparative trials with dual receptor antagonists.

In addition to its blood pressure–lowering effects, inhibition of the growth-promoting effects of ET-1 is under investigation in a range of disorders. Recent results from clinical trials (e.g., those with the ETA-receptor antagonist atrasentan in prostate cancer) are encouraging.[148] Blockade of ET-1's growth-promoting effects may also have therapeutic potential for vascular and cardiac remodeling,[149] atherosclerosis,[150] restenosis,[103] and renal fibrosis.[88] Other areas potentially benefiting from ET antagonism include subarachnoid hemorrhage,[151] renal failure,[152] ischemic cardiac arrhythmia,[153] and acute myocardial infarction.[154]

## ADRENOMEDULLIN

### INTRODUCTION

Kitamura and colleagues' discovery in 1993 of AM,[155] a potent and long-acting vasodepressor peptide, has generated intense interest in its function and role in cardiovascular homeostasis. At present, substantial evidence indicates that AM has potentially important actions on tissues concerned with pressure-volume regulation, but its precise role and any

unique contribution to disorders in humans still remain to be clarified. AM is widely distributed in tissues and organs, where it may function as an autocrine/paracrine rather than endocrine factor. However, because AM circulates in plasma and is increased in a variety of cardiovascular disorders (including heart failure), important endocrine effects cannot be excluded.

### BIOCHEMISTRY

#### Synthesis, Structure, and Distribution

Transcription and processing of the AM gene, situated in a single locus on chromosome 11 in humans, yields a 185-amino acid precursor (prepro-AM), followed by a 164-amino acid prohormone, and ultimately two biologically active hormones: (1) the C-terminal 52-amino acid AM peptide, containing a 6-residue ring structure and a C-terminal amide group (Fig. 132-6); and (2) the N-terminal 20-amino acid peptide PAMP. AM shows structural and pharmacologic similarities to calcitonin, CGRP, and amylin, and may thus belong to the CGRP superfamily of peptides.

AM immunoreactivity is widely distributed: The highest concentrations are found in the adrenal medulla and anterior pituitary glands, with lower levels found in such tissues as the heart, lung, kidney, brain, and vasculature.[156,157] Both endothelial cells and VSMCs have been shown to actively synthesize and secrete AM.[158] Indeed, current evidence in humans points to vascular tissue as the likely major source of circulating AM in health because no major step-up in plasma levels occurs across any particular organ (including the adrenal gland).[159] However, a small gradient (increase) across the heart in patients with heart failure suggests that some cardiac contribution to the raised plasma levels may occur in this disorder.[160]

#### Receptors and Metabolism

To date, at least three types of AM receptors (all G protein–linked) have been reported. Whereas one appears to be specific for AM,[161] the other two receptors (i.e., the orphan

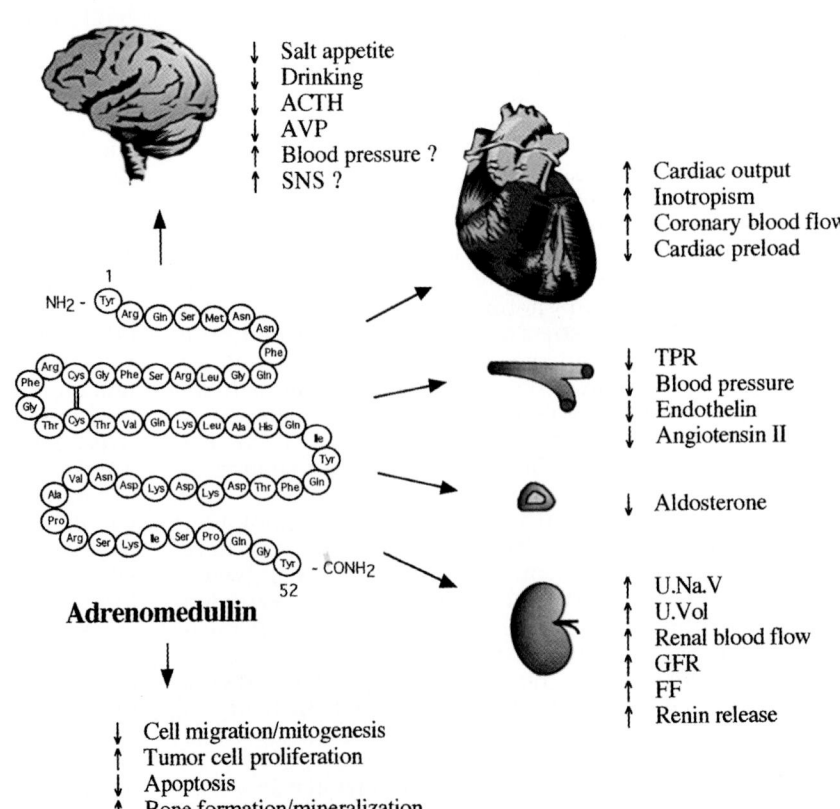

*Figure 132-6* The mature form and integrated actions of human adrenomedullin₁₋₅₂. See the text for details. ACTH, adrenocorticotropic hormone; AVP, arginine vasopressin; FF, filtration fraction; GFR, glomerular filtration rate; SNS, sympathetic nervous system; TPR, total peripheral resistance; U.Na.V, urine sodium excretion; U.Vol, urine volume.

receptor RDC-1 and the CGRP1 receptor[157]) appear to bind to both AM and CGRP. Interactions between AM and CGRP and the latter two receptors remain unclear and may vary according to species, tissue type, and experimental setting. Specific binding sites for AM are present in both endothelial cells and VSMCs and in multiple tissue beds, and colocalization of the AM receptor and ligand in most organs supports the hypothesis that AM acts locally in a short-range autocrine or paracrine mode. Although cyclic adenosine monophosphate (cAMP) is considered the major intracellular second messenger for AM, alternative signal transduction pathways have also been reported, including nitric oxide, prostaglandins, intracellular calcium mobilization, and activation of the inositol phosphate pathway. In addition, AM's antiproliferative activity may be mediated, at least partly, by inhibiting the MAP kinase pathway.[156]

Little is yet understood about the mechanisms of clearance of AM from plasma. Estimates in humans indicate a half-life approximating 22 minutes, a metabolic clearance rate of 27 mL/kg/min, and a volume of distribution of 900 mL/kg.[162] Sites of clearance include the lungs and, possibly, the kidney.[163] Degradation in vitro has been shown to be prevented by metalloproteinase inhibitors.

## CONTROL MECHANISMS

Stimuli for the secretion of AM have been studied primarily in cultured endothelial cells and VSMCs, where a variety of factors (e.g., interleukin-1, tumor necrosis factor, lipopolysaccharide, adrenal corticosteroids, and retinoic acid) all promote message expression or production of the peptide. Other less powerful stimuli for enhanced AM production include fibroblast growth factor, endothelial growth factor, platelet-derived growth factor, angiotensin II, ET-1, bradykinin, substance P, and thyroxine. In addition, AM mRNA expression is augmented by shear stress in endothelial cells, and by hypoxia in ventricular myocytes. Physical factors, including volume overload and rapid ventricular pacing in dogs, are reported to increase AM gene expression in the heart.[156,157] On the other hand, interferon-γ, vasoactive intestinal peptide, forskolin, 8-bromo-cAMP, and thrombin all suppress AM production. These findings suggest that AM secretion from vascular tissues is subject to complex regulation by multiple local and circulating factors, many of which are elevated in a variety of pathophysiologic conditions (e.g., endotoxic shock, atherosclerosis, inflammation, and volume overload).[164]

## FUNCTION

### Hemodynamic Effects

The most pronounced effect of administered AM is a prolonged dose-dependent fall in vascular resistance and blood pressure,[156,165] resulting largely from the generation of nitric oxide within the vessel wall. The hypotensive effect of AM may also be mediated in part by its inhibitory actions on procontractile factors (e.g., ET-1 and angiotensin II), as well as reversal of norepinephrine-induced venoconstriction. In addition, AM may dampen baroreceptor reflexes.[156] Larger doses of AM are also associated with falls in cardiac preload and a rise in heart rate and cardiac output. These latter effects may be caused in part by direct cardiostimulatory actions, because AM is reported to increase coronary blood flow and conductance, and cardiac contractility[166] (see Fig. 132-6). AM induces dilatation of several major vascular beds, including those in the lungs, heart, spleen, kidneys, adrenal glands, small intestine, and brain,[157] suggesting a role for AM in the regulation of regional vascular resistance and blood flow.

### Renal Effects

AM exerts potent natriuretic and diuretic effects as a result of both renal hemodynamic and tubular actions. AM increases renal blood flow through preglomerular and postglomerular arteriolar vasodilatation (nitric oxide dependent), and by lowering renal vascular resistance (prostaglandin-dependent)[156,158]; at higher doses, it increases GFR and filtration fraction[158] (see Fig. 132-6). AM also decreases tubular sodium reabsorption and osmotic permeability of the inner medullary collecting duct. These effects of AM in the kidney are complemented by hypothalamic actions to inhibit vasopressin release, and adrenal effects to inhibit aldosterone secretion (see below).[156]

### Endocrine Effects

A number of neuroendocrine actions of AM have been described, many of which have the potential to contribute to its hemodynamic and renal effects. Whereas AM directly stimulates renin production,[167] it inhibits angiotensin II and aldosterone secretion.[168] AM also inhibits ET-1 and gastric acid release, reduces plasma ACTH and cortisol levels, and regulates insulin secretion.[157,163] The effect of AM on the natriuretic peptide system is unclear. Whereas AM appears to inhibit ANP mRNA expression and secretion in vitro, AM may actually stimulate ANP in vivo.[165]

### Proliferative/Antiproliferative Effects

AM appears to influence both cell migration and proliferation. AM inhibits VSMC migration[169] as well as the secretion of cytokine-induced neutrophil chemoattractant, a key mediator of neutrophil migration in inflammatory sites.[170] In addition, AM suppresses mitogenesis of mesangial cells, VSMCs,[157] and cardiomyocytes,[171] which suggests autocrine/paracrine actions with the potential to affect vascular and cardiac remodeling. Conversely, AM is reported to increase proliferation in a variety of tumor cells,[172] although the suppression of prostate cancer cells by AM has also been demonstrated.[173] Of interest, AM has been shown to both increase apoptosis (cAMP-dependent event) in rat mesangial cells[174] and to suppress apoptosis (cAMP-independent event) in endothelial cells.[175]

### Neuroendocrine and Other Effects

AM immunoreactivity and evidence of receptor binding are widespread throughout the central nervous system, particularly within the thalamus, hypothalamus, and pituitary.[156,157] Central actions of AM include the inhibition of salt appetite, angiotensin II–induced drinking, ACTH release, and hyperosmolar and hypovolemia-induced vasopressin release. Central AM administration increases plasma oxytocin levels, and usually leads to a rise in blood pressure and heart rate (see Fig. 132-6).

AM also appears to play a role in bone physiology[176] and embryogenesis,[177] and may be involved in the body's defense against microorganisms.[178]

## ROLE IN PHYSIOLOGY AND PATHOPHYSIOLOGY

Plasma levels of immunoreactive AM in normal healthy humans are typically low (2 to 8 pmol/L) and do not appear to be significantly increased by either acute or chronic salt loading[179]; however, they do rise with increasing age[180] and, possibly, with severe exercise.[181] Elevated concentrations have been reported in normal pregnancy.[182] Significant increases in plasma AM levels in human pathology are numerous, with the most striking increase (12-fold) occurring in acute sepsis.[183] Smaller rises are reported in patients with hemorrhagic and cardiogenic shock,[183] untreated Addison's disease,[184] chronic renal failure (Fig. 132-7),[185] asthma,[186] chronic obstructive pulmonary disease,[185] hepatic insufficiency with ascites, hyperthyroidism, subarachnoid hemorrhage, and gastrointestinal and pulmonary neoplasms.[183,185] In several of these disorders, hormone elevation has correlated with increases in C-reactive protein, a marker of acute inflammation. Significant, but lesser

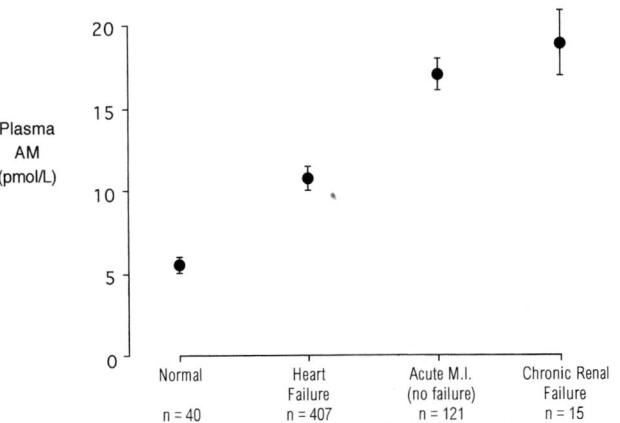

*Figure 132-7* Venous plasma adrenomedullin (AM) levels in normal subjects and patients with circulatory disorders. Values are means + SEM. n, number of subjects in each group. All samples were assayed in the same laboratory (Endocrine Department, Christchurch Hospital, New Zealand) by previously published techniques. Heart failure was due to coronary artery disease, New York Heart Association functional class I to III (ejection fraction less than 45%). Patients with acute (uncomplicated) myocardial infarction (MI) had blood drawn within 24 hours of admission. Patients with chronic renal failure were all receiving maintenance hemodialysis. (MI data from Richards AM, Nicholls MG, Yandle TG, et al: Plasma N-terminal pro-brain natriuretic peptide and adrenomedullin: New neurohormonal predictors of left ventricular function and prognosis after myocardial infarction. Circulation 97:1921–1929, 1998.)

increases in AM, occur in a number of cardiovascular disorders including congestive heart failure,[185] myocardial infarction[25] (see Fig. 132-7), and hypertension.[185] The source of the increase in plasma AM in many of these disorders is uncertain; increased cardiac secretion may occur in heart failure, but multiple tissues appear to contribute in sepsis. Decreased renal clearance may also be an underlying factor in some disorders, particularly in chronic renal failure. It remains to be seen whether these pathologic elevations reflect tissue/organ damage or, alternatively, represent increased production as part of compensatory homeostasis.

Although infusion studies provide strong circumstantial evidence supporting a central role for AM in pressure/volume homeostasis,[165] a clearer definition of its importance in normal physiologic and pathophysiologic states are supplied by work with AM antagonists and transgenic models which affect hormone production and action. Transgenic mice overexpressing AM in the vasculature exhibit reduced blood pressure in comparison to wild-type littermates,[150] whereas heterozygous AM knockout mice (embryonic lethal in the homozygous state) show increased blood pressure and susceptibility to vascular and cardiac injury.[187] Administration of AM antagonists results in elevated vascular tone.[188] These data suggest that endogenous AM plays a role in the regulation of blood pressure and is cardioprotective. As yet, no instance of a primary disorder of AM production or action resulting in disease has been reported, although a number of recent studies have suggested that a polymorphism of the human AM gene is associated with genetic predispositions to develop essential hypertension and diabetic nephropathy.[189]

## CLINICAL APPLICATIONS

### Diagnosis/Prognosis

Increased circulating levels of AM have been reported to be useful markers of blood volume in hemodialysis patients,[190] of atherosclerosis in patients with ischemic stroke (independent of blood pressure or the presence of risk factors),[191] and of recurrent pregnancy loss caused by impaired uterine perfusion.[192] Plasma AM might also be a promising tool for

identifying preterm infants at risk of intraventricular hemorrhage immediately after birth, when imaging assessment and clinical symptoms of hemorrhage are still silent.[193]

Because the increase in plasma AM is related to disease severity in many instances, a prognostic role for this peptide is also indicated. In subjects with left ventricular dysfunction after myocardial infarction, AM levels correlate inversely with ejection fraction, correlate positively with other markers of cardiac decompensation (e.g., plasma levels of BNP and ET-1[25]), and are independent predictors of mortality and heart failure[194]; however, in chronic heart failure, plasma levels of the peptide are inversely associated with prognosis.[195] In patients with systemic inflammatory response syndrome, circulating AM concentrations might serve not only as a marker for evaluating severity of disease but also as an early predictor of subsequent organ failure and outcome in septic shock.[196] Plasma AM levels may also serve as a marker of clinical symptomatology and prognosis in bipolar affective disorder[197] and in schizophrenia,[198] whereas AM gene expression in epithelial ovarian cancer is associated with histological grade and poor prognosis.[199]

### Treatment

AM holds promise as a therapeutic strategy in a variety of pathologic conditions. As with the natriuretic peptides, the vasodilatory, natriuretic, counter-neurohormonal, and antimitogenic actions of AM are likely to be favorable in the treatment of a variety of cardiovascular disorders associated with volume overload. The positive inotropic action of AM is likely to be an important additional benefit. Indeed, short-term administration of AM has been shown to improve hemodynamic performance, renal function, and hormonal parameters in patients with heart failure[200] and chronic renal impairment.[201] In addition, recent studies have reported that long-term infusion or AM gene therapy significantly reduces blood pressure, myocardial infarction, cardiovascular remodeling, and renal injury; and it prolongs survival in experimental models of hypertension, myocardial injury, and heart failure.[202] AM (and CNP) have also been shown to reduce vascular calcification.[203]

Another action of AM is to increase regional blood flow. Not only is the hormone protective in ischemic brain injury[204] and vascular reperfusion injury,[205] but AM also induces coronary vasodilatation[166] and improves microcirculation in hepatic cirrhosis.[206] Other potential benefits include stimulation of bone growth[176] and bronchodilation. Indeed, a recent study in experimental pulmonary hypertension reported that aerosolized AM significantly reduced pulmonary artery pressure and profoundly improved the arterial oxygen tension.[207]

## OVERVIEW

By direct natriuretic effects, vascular relaxation, and inhibition of the production and actions of vasoconstrictor peptides, the natriuretic peptide system (both hormonal and paracrine) appears to be the chief defense against the threat of volume expansion (hypervolemia). In the longer term (and equally important), these hormones reset the sympathetic nervous system (reducing sympathetic nervous activity) and restrain vascular and cardiac cell growth (Table 132-2). Although the biologic roles of ANP and BNP appear to be very similar, differences in source, secretion, regulation, and metabolism (at least in humans) suggest that the two hormones function as independent regulators of intra-atrial and intraventricular pressure, respectively. CNP appears to be uniquely placed within the vascular system to interact with numerous other peptides and autacoids, to reduce vascular tone, and to contribute to vascular remodeling. As noted with the natriuretic peptides, AM also exerts multiple effects on a

**Table 132-2** Comparative Overview of Secretion and Cardiovascular Actions*

| Feature | ANP/BNP | CNP | Endothelin-1 | | Adrenomedullin |
|---|---|---|---|---|---|
| Major site of synthesis | Cardiac atrium/ cardiac ventricle | Vascular endothelium/brain | Vascular endothelium | | Vascular endothelium? |
| Major stimulus to secretion | Atrial/ventricular transmural pressure | Multiple local factors | Multiple local factors | | Multiple local factors |
| Normal plasma levels (pmol/L) | 5–25/0.3–10 | ? Very low | <5 | | 2–8 |
| Plasma half-life (min) | 3/22 | 2–3 | 1–1.5 | | 22 |
| Main biologic receptor | NPR-A | NPR-B | ETA | ETB | AM-R, CGRP-R, RDC-1 |
| Major intracellular mediator | cGMP | cGMP | [Ca] | NO | cAMP/NO |
| Major effects | | | | | |
|   Vasculature | Dilation | Dilation | Constriction | Dilation (and constriction) | Dilation |
| | ↓ ET-1 ↓ Ang II ↑ Vascular permeability | | ↑ Ang II | | ↓ ET-1 / ↓ Ang II |
|   Heart | Negative inotropism | ↑ Coronary BF | Negative chronotropism | Positive chronotropism | Positive chronotropism |
| | ↑ Coronary BF | | Positive inotropism ↓ Coronary BF ↑ ANP/BNP | | Positive inotropism ↑ Coronary BF |
|   Kidney | Natriuresis ↓ Renin | — — | Antinatriuresis ↓ Renin | Natriuresis | Natriuresis ↑ Renin |
|   Adrenal gland | ↓ Aldosterone | — | ↑ Aldosterone | | ↓ Aldosterone |
|   Other: | Antimitogenesis ↓ SNA | Antimitogenesis Mitogenic in skeleton | Mitogenesis ↑ SNA | | Antimitogenesis ↓ SNA |

*Comparative overview of the natriuretic peptides (atrial, brain, and C-type natriuretic peptide: ANP, BNP, and CNP, respectively), endothelin-1 (ET-1), and adrenomedullin (AM). Data relating to BNP, if different from ANP, are in parentheses.
AM-R, adrenomedullin receptor; Ang II, angiotensin II; BF, blood flow; cAMP, cyclic adenosine monophosphate; cGMP, cyclic guanosine monophosphate; CGRP-R, calcitonin gene–related peptide receptor; NO, nitric oxide; NPR, natriuretic peptide receptor; RDC-1, orphan receptor; SNA, sympathetic nervous activity.

variety of tissues, the combined actions of which promote a reduction in blood volume and pressure (see Table 132-2). Superficially, this function might suggest redundancy; however, differences in their production and effects on tissues suggest otherwise. For example, in contrast to the natriuretic peptides, AM is clearly inotropic and appears to *stimulate* renin release (see Table 132-2). Much more work is needed to define the respective roles of the natriuretic peptides and AM in vasodilatation or any commonality in intracellular action (e.g., via nitric oxide synthesis and action). Counterbalancing these dilator hormonal systems are the highly potent vasoconstrictor peptides ET-1 and angiotensin II. ET-1, acting as a local autocrine/paracrine mediator, exerts uniquely sustained vasoconstrictor actions, augments angiotensin II activity, stimulates aldosterone, and at the same time increases sympathetic nervous activity and promotes mitogenesis (see Table 132-2). Although likely to be important in controlling peripheral resistance, the major role of tissue ET may be to counterbalance other endothelial factors (e.g., nitric oxide, prostacyclin, AM, and CNP), thereby contributing to the maintenance of blood fluidity and tissue perfusion. The remarkable interplay among the natriuretic peptides, AM, ETs, and angiotensin II (along with prostaglandins) appears to dictate the local actions of these hormones in many tissues.

## REFERENCES

1. de Bold AJ, Borenstein HB, Veress AT, et al: A rapid and potent natriuretic response to intravenous injection of atrial myocardial extract in rats. Life Sci 28:89–94, 1981.
2. Kangawa K, Matsuo H: Purification and complete amino acid sequence of alpha-human atrial natriuretic polypeptide (alpha-hANP). Biochem Biophys Res Commun 118:131–139, 1984.
3. Sudoh T, Kangawa K, Minamino N, et al: A new natriuretic peptide in porcine brain. Nature 322:78–81, 1988.
4. Sudoh T, Minamino N, Kangawa K, et al: C-type natriuretic peptide (CNP): A new member of natriuretic peptide family identified in porcine brain. Biochem Biophys Res Commun 168:863–870, 1990.
5. Ruskoaho H: Atrial natriuretic peptide: Synthesis, release, and metabolism. Pharmacol Rev 44:479–602, 1992.
6. Yandle TG: Biochemistry of natriuretic peptides. J Intern Med 235:561–576, 1994.
7. Hunt PJ, Yandle TG, Nicholls MG, et al: The amino-terminal portion of pro-brain natriuretic peptide (Pro-BNP) circulates in human plasma. Biochem Biophys Res Commun 214:1175–1183, 1995.
8. Mukoyama Y, Nakao K, Hosoda K, et al: Brain natriuretic peptide as a novel cardiac hormone in humans: Evidence for an exquisite dual natriuretic peptide system, ANP and BNP. J Clin Invest 87:1402–1412, 1991.
9. Wu C, Wu F, Pan J, et al: Furin-mediated processing of Pro-C-type natriuretic peptide. J Biological Chem 278:25847–25852, 2003.
10. Prickett TC, Yandle TG, Nicholls MG, et al: Identification of amino-terminal pro-C-type natriuretic peptide in human plasma. Biochem Biophys Res Comm 286:513–517, 2001.
11. Espiner EA, Richards AM, Yandle TG, et al: Natriuretic hormones. Endocrinol Metab Clin North Am 24:481–509, 1995.
12. Forssmann W, Meyer M, Forssmann K: The renal urodilatin system: Clinical implications. Cardiovasc Res 51:450–462, 2001.
13. Koller KJG, Goeddel DV: Molecular biology of the natriuretic peptides and their receptors. Circulation 86:1081–1088, 1992.
14. Maack T, Nikonova LN, Friedman O, et al: Functional properties and dynamics of natriuretic peptide receptors. Exp Biol Med 213:109–116, 1996.
15. Hirsch JR, Skutta N, Schlatter E: Signaling and distribution of NPR-Bi, the human splice form of the natriuretic peptide receptor type B. Am J Physiol 285:F370–F374, 2003.

16. Suga S, Nakao K, Hosoda K, et al: Receptor selectivity of natriuretic peptide family, atrial natriuretic peptide, brain natriuretic peptide, and C-type natriuretic peptide. Endocrinology 130:229–239, 1992.

17. Levin ER: Natriuretic peptide C-receptor: More than a clearance receptor. Am J Physiol 264:E483–E489, 1993.

18. Olins GM, Spear KL, Siegel NR, et al: Atrial peptide inactivation by rabbit-kidney brush-border membranes. Eur J Biochem 170:431–434, 1987.

19. Smith MW, Espiner EA, Yandle TG, et al: Delayed metabolism of human brain natriuretic peptide reflects resistance to neutral endopeptidase. J Endocrinol 167:239–246, 2000.

20. Hunt PJ, Richards AM, Espiner EA, et al: Bioactivity and metabolism of C-type natriuretic peptide in normal man. J Clin Endocrinol Metab 78:1428–1435, 1994.

21. Raine AE, Erne P, Burgisser E, et al: Atrial natriuretic peptide and atrial pressure in patients with congestive heart failure. N Engl J Med 315:533–537, 1986.

22. Leskinen H, Vuolteenaho O, Ruskoaho H: Combined inhibition of endothelin and angiotensin II receptors blocks volume load-induced cardiac hormone release. Circ Res 80:114–123, 1997.

23. Thibault G, Amiri F, Garcia R: Regulation of natriuretic peptide secretion by the heart. Annu Rev Physiol 61:193–217, 1999.

24. Richards AM: The natriuretic peptides and hypertension. J Intern Med 235:543–560, 1994.

25. Richards AM, Nicholls MG, Yandle TG, et al: Plasma N-terminal pro-brain natriuretic peptide and adrenomedullin: New neurohormonal predictors of left ventricular function and prognosis after myocardial infarction. Circulation 97:1921–1929, 1998.

26. Yoshibayashi M, Kamiya T, Saito Y, et al: Increased plasma levels of brain natriuretic peptide in hypertrophic cardiomyopathy. N Engl J Med 329:433–434, 1993.

27. Barr CS, Rhodes P, Struthers AD: C-type natriuretic peptide. Peptides 17:1243–1251, 1996.

28. Wright SP, Prickett TC, Doughty RN, et al: Amino-terminal pro-C-Type natriuretic peptide in heart failure. Hypertens 43:94–100, 2004.

29. Wei CM, Heublein DM, Perrella MA, et al: Natriuretic peptide system in human heart failure. Circulation 88:1004–1009, 1993.

30. Kalra PR, Clague JR, Bolger AP, et al: Myocardial production of C-type natriuretic peptide in chronic heart failure. Circ 107:571–573, 2003.

31. Chusho H, Tamura N, Ogawa Y, et al: Dwarfism and early death in mice lacking C-type natriuretic peptide. Proc Natl Acad Sci U S A 98:4016–4021, 2001.

32. Brenner BM, Ballermann BJ, Gunning ME, et al: Diverse biological actions of atrial natriuretic peptide. Physiol Rev 70:665–699, 1990.

33. Cody RJ, Atlas SA, Laragh JH, et al: Atrial natriuretic factor in normal subjects and heart failure patients. Plasma levels and renal, hormonal, and hemodynamic responses to peptide infusion. J Clin Invest 78:1362–1374, 1986.

34. Jensen KT, Eiskjaer H, Carstens J, et al: Renal effects of brain natriuretic peptide in patients with congestive heart failure. Clin Sci 96:5–15, 1999.

35. Michaels AD, Klein A, Madden JA, et al: Effects of intravenous nesiritide on human coronary vasomotor regulation and myocardial oxygen uptake. Circulation 107:2697–2701, 2003.

36. Levin ER, Gardner DG, Samson WK: Natriuretic peptides. N Engl J Med 339:321–328, 1998.

37. Wei CM, Hu S, Kim CH, et al: The in-vitro actions of C-type natriuretic peptide in coronary arteries. Circulation 88:I-181, 1993.

38. Cherradi N, Brandenburger Y, Rossier MF, et al: Atrial natriuretic peptide inhibits calcium-induced steroidogenic acute regulatory protein gene transcription in adrenal glomerulosa cells. Mol Endocrinol 12:962–972, 1998.

39. Appel RG: Growth-regulatory properties of atrial natriuretic factor. Am J Physiol 262:F911–F918, 1992.

40. Wu CF, Bishopric NH, Pratt RE: Atrial natriuretic peptide induces apoptosis in neonatal rat cardiac myocytes. J Biol Chem 272:14860–14866, 1997.

41. Fujisaki H, Ito H, Hirata Y, et al: Natriuretic peptides inhibit angiotensin II-induced proliferation of rat cardiac fibroblasts by blocking endothelin-1 gene expression. J Clin Invest 96:1059–1065, 1995.

42. Chrisman TD, Garbers DL: Reciprocal antagonism coordinates C-type natriuretic peptide and mitogen-signaling pathways in fibroblasts. J Biol Chem 274:4293–4299, 1999.

43. Oliver PM, Fox JE, Kim R, et al: Hypertension, cardiac hypertrophy, and sudden death in mice lacking natriuretic peptide receptor A. Proc Natl Acad Sci U S A 94:14730–14735, 1997.

44. Itoh H, Suga S, Ogawa Y, et al: Significance of vascular natriuretic peptide system in vascular remodeling in humans and its application to gene therapy. Ann N Y Acad Sci 811:533–541, 1997.

45. Yamahara K, Itoh H, Chun TH, et al: Significance and therapeutic potential of the natriuretic peptides/cGMP/cGMP-dependent protein kinase pathway in vascular regeneration. Proc Natl Acad Sci U S A 100:3404–3409, 2003.

46. Imura H, Nakao K, Itoh H: The natriuretic peptide system in the brain: Implications in the central control of cardiovascular and neuroendocrine functions. Front Neuroendocrinol 13:217–249, 1992.

47. Hagiwara H, Inoue A, Yamaguchi A, et al: cGMP produced in response to ANP and CNP regulates proliferation and differentiation of osteoblastic cells. Am J Physiol 270:C1311–C1318, 1996.

48. Suda M, Ogawa Y, Tanaka K, et al: Skeletal overgrowth in transgenic mice that overexpress brain natriuretic peptide. Proc Natl Acad Sci U S A 95:2337–2342, 1998.

49. Matsukawa N, Grzesik WJ, Takahashi N, et al: The natriuretic peptide clearance receptor locally modulates the physiological effects of the natriuretic peptide system. Proc Natl Acad Sci U S A 96:7403–7408, 1999.

50. Wada A, Tsutamoto T, Matsuda Y, et al: Cardiorenal and neurohumoral effects of endogenous atrial natriuretic peptide in dogs with severe congestive heart failure using a specific antagonist for guanylate cyclase-coupled receptors. Circulation 89:2232–2240, 1994.

51. Lee ME, Miller WL, Edwards BS, et al: Role of endogenous atrial natriuretic factor in acute congestive heart failure. J Clin Invest 84:1962–1966, 1989.

52. Barbee RW, Perry BD, Re RN, et al: Hemodynamics in transgenic mice with overexpression of atrial natriuretic factor. Circ Res 74:747–751, 1994.

53. Chen HH, Burnett JC Jr: C-type natriuretic peptide: The endothelial component of the natriuretic peptide system. J Cardiovasc Pharmacol 32:S22–S28, 1998.

54. Nicholls MG: The natriuretic peptides in heart failure. J Intern Med 235:515–526, 1994.

55. Espiner EA, Leikis R, Ferch RD, et al: The neuro-cardio-endocrine response to acute subarachnoid haemorrhage. Clin Endocrinol 56:629–635, 2002.

56. Nagaya N, Nishikimi T, Okano Y, et al: Plasma brain natriuretic peptide levels increase in proportion to the extent of right ventricular dysfunction in pulmonary hypertension. J Am Coll Cardiol 31:202–208, 1998.

57. Mitaka C, Hirata Y, Nagura T, et al: Increased plasma concentrations of brain natriuretic peptide in patients with acute lung injury. J Crit Care 12:66–71, 1997.

58. Sheffield VC, Stone EM, Alward WL, et al: Genetic linkage of familial open angle glaucoma to chromosome 1q21–q31. Nat Genet 4:47–50, 1993.

59. Rutledge DR, Sun Y, Ross EA: Polymorphisms within the atrial natriuretic peptide gene in essential hypertension. J Hypertens 13:953–955, 1995.

60. Nakayama T, Soma M, Takahashi Y, et al: Functional deletion mutation of the 5′-flanking region of type A human natriuretic peptide receptor gene and its association with essential hypertension and left ventricular hypertrophy in the Japanese. Cir Res 86:841–845, 2000.

61. Sarzani R, Dessi-Fulgheri P, Salvi F, et al: A novel promoter variant of the natriuretic peptide clearance receptor gene is associated with lower atrial natriuretic peptide and higher blood

pressure in obese hypertensives. J Hypertens 17:1301–1305, 1999.

62. Gruchala M, Ciecwierz D, Wasag B, et al: Association of the ScaI atrial natriuretic peptide gene polymorphism with nonfatal myocardial infarction and extent of coronary artery disease. Am Heart J 145:125–131, 2003.

63. Rubattu S, Ridker P, Stampfer MJ, et al: The gene encoding atrial natriuretic peptide and the risk of human stroke. Circulation 100:1722–1726, 1999.

64. Nannipieri M, Posadas R, Williams K, et al: Association between polymorphisms of the atrial natriuretic peptide gene and proteinuria: a population-based study. Diabetologia 46:429–432, 2003.

65. Ono K, Mannami T, Baba S, et al: A single-nucleotide polymorphism in C-type natriuretic peptide gene may be associated with hypertension. Hypertens Res -Clin and Exp 25:727–730, 2002.

66. Rehemudula D, Nakayama T, Soma M, et al: Structure of the type B human natriuretic peptide receptor gene and association of a novel microsatellite polymorphism with essential hypertension. Circ Res 84:605–610, 1999.

67. Hama N, Itoh H, Shirakami G, et al: Detection of C-type natriuretic peptide in human circulation and marked increase of plasma CNP level in septic shock patients. Biochem Biophys Res Commun 198:1177–1182, 1994.

68. Takahashi M, Nagake Y, Ichikawa H, et al: Plasma concentrations of natriuretic peptides in patients on hemodialysis. Res Commun Mol Pathol Pharmacol 92:19–30, 1996.

69. de Lemos JA, McGuire DK, Drazner MH: B-type natriuretic peptide in cardiovascular disease. Lancet 362:316–322, 2003.

70. Lainchbury JG, Campbell E, Frampton CM, et al: Brain natriuretic peptide and N-terminal brain natriuretic peptide in the diagnosis of heart failure in patients with acute shortness of breath. JACC 42(4):728–735, 2003.

71. Cohen N, Gilbert R, Wirth A, et al: Atrial natriuretic peptide and plasma renin levels in assessment of mineralocorticoid replacement in Addison's disease. J Clin Endocrinol Metab 81:1411–1415, 1996.

72. Keating GM, Goa KL: Nesiritide: A review of its use in acute decompensated heart failure. Drugs 63:47–70, 2003.

73. Burger AJ, Horton DP, LeJemtel T, et al: Prospective randomized evaluation of cardiac ectopy with dobutamine or natrecor therapy: Effect of nesiritide (B-type natriuretic peptide) and dobutamine on ventricular arrhythmias in the treatment of patients with acutely decompensated congestive heart failure: The PRECEDENT study. Am Heart J 144:1102–1108, 2002.

74. Publication Committee for the VMAC Investigators: Intravenous nesiritide vs. nitroglycerin for treatment of decompensated congestive heart failure: A randomized controlled trial. JAMA 287:1531–1440, 2002.

75. Bobadilla RV, Oppelt TF, Hirshy TC: Nesiritide treatment of noncardiogenic pulmonary edema. Ann Pharmacotherapy 37:530–533, 2003.

76. Moazami N, Damiano RJ, Bailey MS, et al: Nesiritide (BNP) in the management of postoperative cardiac patients. Ann Thoracic Surgery 75:1974–1976, 2003.

77. Kuga H, Ogawa K, Oida A, et al: Administration of atrial natriuretic peptide attenuates reperfusion phenomena and preserves left ventricular regional wall motion after direct coronary angioplasty for acute myocardial infarction. Circ J 67:443–448, 2003.

78. Sward K, Valson F, Ricksten SE: Long-term infusion of atrial natriuretic peptide (ANP) improves renal blood flow and glomerular filtration rate in clinical acute renal failure. Acta Anaesthesiologica Scandinavica 45:536–542, 2001.

79. Cargill RI, Lipworth BJ: Atrial natriuretic peptide and brain natriuretic peptide in cor pulmonale. Hemodynamic and endocrine effects. Chest 110:1220–1225, 1996.

80. Rademaker MT, Charles CJ, Kosoglou T, et al: Clearance receptors and endopeptidase: Equal role in natriuretic peptide metabolism in heart failure. Am J Physiol 273:H2372–H2379, 1997.

81. Packer M, Califf RM, Konstam MA, et al: Comparison of omapatrilat and enalapril in patients with chronic heart failure: The Omapatrilat Versus Enalapril Randomized Trial of Utility in Reducing Events (OVERTURE). Circ 106:920–926, 2002.

82. Dickstein K, de Voogd H, Miric M, et al: Inhibition of both neutral endopeptidase and endothelin converting enzyme lowers pulmonary pressure in congestive heart failure. JACC 41(6–Suppl A):266, 2003.

83. Ueno H, Haruno A, Morisaki N, et al: Local expression of C-type natriuretic peptide markedly suppresses neointimal formation in rat injured arteries through an autocrine/paracrine loop. Circulation 96:2272–2279, 1997.

84. Phillips MI: Gene therapy for hypertension: Sense and antisense strategies. Expert Opin Biol Ther 1:655–662, 2001.

85. Inoue A, Yanagisawa M, Kimura S, et al: The human endothelin family: Three structurally and pharmacologically distinct isopeptides predicted by three separate genes. Proc Natl Acad Sci U S A 86:2863–2867, 1989.

86. Miyauchi T, Masaki T: Pathophysiology of endothelin in the cardiovascular system. Annu Rev Physiol 61:391–415, 1999.

87. Hocher B, Thone-Reineke C, Bauer C, et al: The paracrine endothelin system: Pathophysiology and implications in clinical medicine. Eur J Clin Chem Clin Biochem 35:175–189, 1997.

88. Haynes WG, Webb DJ: Endothelin as a regulator of cardiovascular function in health and disease. J Hypertens 16:1081–1098, 1998.

89. Levin ER: Endothelins. N Engl J Med 333:356–363, 1995.

90. Sakurai T, Yanagisawa M, Masaki T: Molecular characterization of endothelin receptors. Trends Pharmacol Sci 13:103–108, 1992.

91. Wang QD, Hemsen A, Li XS, et al: Local overflow and enhanced tissue content of endothelin following myocardial ischaemia and reperfusion in the pig: Modulation by L-arginine. Cardiovasc Res 29:44–49, 1995.

92. Fukuroda T, Fujikawa T, Ozaki S, et al: Clearance of circulating endothelin-1 by ETB receptors in rats. Biochem Biophys Res Commun 199:1461–1465, 1994.

93. Weitzberg E, Ahlborg G, Lundberg JM: Long-lasting vasoconstriction and efficient regional extraction of endothelin-1 in human splanchnic and renal tissues. Biochem Biophys Res Commun 180:1298–1303, 1991.

94. Clozel M, Clozel JP: Effects of endothelin on regional blood flows in squirrel monkeys. J Pharmacol Exp Ther 250:1125–1131, 1989.

95. Webb DJ, Strachan FE: Clinical experience with endothelin antagonists. Am J Hypertens 11(Suppl):71–79, 1998.

96. Ishikawa T, Yanagisawa M, Kimura S, et al: Positive inotropic action of novel vasoconstrictor peptide endothelin on guinea pig atria. Am J Physiol 255:H970–H973, 1988.

97. Lerman A, Hildebrand FL, Aarhus LL, et al: Endothelin has biological actions at pathophysiological concentrations. Circulation 83:1808–1814, 1991.

98. Rabelink TJ, Kaasjager KA, Boer P, et al: Effects of endothelin-1 on renal function in humans: Implications for physiology and pathophysiology. Kidney Int 46:376–381, 1994.

99. Webb DJ, Monge JC, Rabelink TJ, et al: Endothelin: New discoveries and rapid progress in the clinic. Trends Pharmacol Sci 19:5–8, 1998.

100. Moreau P, d'Uscio LV, Shaw S, et al: Angiotensin II increases tissue endothelin and induces vascular hypertrophy: Reversal by ET(A)-receptor antagonist. Circulation 96:1593–1597, 1997.

101. Hocher B, Thone-Reineke C, Rohmeiss P, et al: Endothelin-1 transgenic mice develop glomerulosclerosis, interstitial fibrosis, and renal cysts but not hypertension. J Clin Invest 99:1380–1389, 1997.

102. Sakai S, Miyauchi T, Kobayashi M, et al: Inhibition of myocardial endothelin pathway improves long-term survival in heart failure. Nature 384:353–355, 1996.

103. McKenna CJ, Burke SE, Opgenorth TJ, et al: Selective ET(A) receptor antagonism reduces neointimal hyperplasia in a porcine coronary stent model. Circulation 97:2551–2556, 1998.

104. Shichiri M, Hirata Y, Nakajima T, et al: Endothelin-1 is an autocrine/paracrine growth factor for human cancer cell lines. J Clin Invest 87:1867–1871, 1991.

105. Nishimura M, Takahashi H, Matsusawa M, et al: Chronic intracerebroventricular infusions of endothelin elevate arterial pressure in rats. J Hypertens 9:71–76, 1991.

106. Kurihara Y, Kurihara H, Suzuki H, et al: Elevated blood pressure and craniofacial abnormalities in mice deficient in endothelin-1. Nature 368:703–710, 1994.

107. Hosoda K, Hammer RE, Richardson JA, et al: Targeted and natural (piebald-lethal) mutations of endothelin-B receptor gene produce megacolon associated with spotted coat color in mice. Cell 79:1267–1276, 1994.

108. Tsukahara H, Hori C, Hiraoka M, et al: Endothelin subtype A receptor antagonist induces osteopenia in growing rats. Metab Clin Exp 47:1403–1407, 1998.

109. Schichiri M, Hirata Y, Ando K, et al: Postural change and volume expansion affect plasma endothelin levels. JAMA 263:661, 1990.

110. Monge JC: Neurohormonal markers of clinical outcome in cardiovascular disease: Is endothelin the best one? J Cardiovasc Pharmacol 329(Suppl):36–42, 1998.

111. Groeneveld AB, Hartemink KJ, de Groot MC, et al: Circulating endothelin and nitrate-nitrite relate to hemodynamic and metabolic variables in human septic shock. Shock 11:160–166, 1999.

112. Zamora MR, O'Brien RF, Rutherford RB, et al: Serum endothelin-1 concentrations and cold provocation in primary Raynaud's phenomenon. Lancet 336:1144–1147, 1990.

113. Saito Y, Nakao K, Mukoyama M, et al: Increased plasma endothelin level in patients with essential hypertension. N Engl J Med 322:205, 1990.

114. Yokokawa K, Tahara H, Kohno M, et al: Hypertension associated with endothelin-secreting malignant hemangioendothelioma. Ann Intern Med 114:213–215, 1991.

115. Ergul S, Parish DC, Puett D, et al: Racial differences in plasma endothelin-1 concentrations in individuals with essential hypertension. Hypertension 28:625–655, 1996.

116. Stevens PA, Brown MJ: Genetic variability of the ET-1 and the ETA receptor genes in essential hypertension. J Cardiovasc Pharmacol 26(Suppl):9–12, 1995.

117. Jin JJ, Nakura J, Wu Z, et al: Association of endothelin-1 gene variant with hypertension. Hypertension 41:163–167, 2003.

118. Sharma P, Hingorani A, Jia H, et al: Quantitative association between a newly identified molecular variant in the endothelin-2 gene and human essential hypertension. J Hypertens 17:1281–1287, 1999.

119. Funke-Kaiser H, Reichenberger F, Kopke K, et al: Differential binding of transcription factor E2F-2 to the endothelin-converting enzyme-1b promoter affects blood pressure regulation. Human Mol Genetics 12:423–433, 2003.

120. Lajemi M, Gautier S, Poirier O, et al: Endothelin gene variants and aortic and cardiac structure in never-treated hypertensives. Am J Hypertens 14:755–760, 2001.

121. Iglarz M, Benessiano J, Philip I, et al: Preproendothelin-1 gene polymorphism is related to a change in vascular reactivity in the human mammary artery in vitro. Hypertension 39:209–213, 2002.

122. Charron P, Tesson F, Poirier O, et al: Identification of a genetic risk factor for idiopathic dilated cardiomyopathy. Involvement of a polymorphism in the endothelin receptor type A gene. CARDIGENE group. Eur Heart J 20:1587–1591, 1999.

123. Herrmann S, Schmidt-Petersen K, Pfeifer J, et al: A polymorphism in the endothelin-A receptor gene predicts survival in patients with idiopathic dilated cardiomyopathy. Eur Heart J 22:1948–1953, 2001.

124. Vasku A, Spinarova L, Goldbergova M, et al: The double heterozygote of two endothelin-1 gene polymorphisms (G8002A and -3A/-4A) is related to big endothelin levels in chronic heart failure. Exp Mol Path 73:230–233, 2002.

125. Kozak M, Holla LI, Krivan L, et al: Endothelin-1 gene polymorphism in the identification of patients at risk for malignant ventricular arrhythmia. Med Sci Monitor 8:BR164–167, 2002.

126. Tzourio C, El Amrani M, Poirier O, et al: Association between migraine and endothelin type A receptor (ETA -231 A/G) gene polymorphism. Neurology 56:1273–1277, 2001.

127. Holla L, Vasku A, Znojil V, et al: Association of 3 gene polymorphisms with atopic diseases. J Allergy Clin Immunol 103:702–708, 1999.

128. Inoue M, Kusafuka T, Okada A: Endothelin B receptor system and Hirschsprung disease. Nippon Rinsho 56:1876–1880, 1998.

129. Wei CM, Lerman A, Rodeheffer RJ, et al: Endothelin in human congestive heart failure. Circulation 89:1580–1586, 1994.

130. Groenning BA, Nilsson JC, Sondergaard L, et al: Evaluation of impaired left ventricular ejection fraction and increased dimensions by multiple neurohumoral plasma concentrations. Eur J Heart Fail 3:699–708, 2001.

131. Selvais PL, Robert A, Ahn S, et al: Direct comparison between endothelin-1, N-terminal proatrial natriuretic factor, and brain natriuretic peptide as prognostic markers of survival in congestive heart failure. J Cardiac Failure 6:201–207, 2000.

132. Aronson D, Burger AJ: Neurohumoral activation and ventricular arrhythmias in patients with decompensated congestive heart failure: Role of endothelin. Pacing Clin Electrophys 26:703–710, 2003.

133. Omland T, Lie RT, Aakvaag A, et al: Plasma endothelin determination as a prognostic indicator of 1-year mortality after acute myocardial infarction. Circulation 89:1573–1579, 1994.

134. Rubens C, Ewert R, Halank M, et al: Big endothelin-1 and endothelin-1 plasma levels are correlated with the severity of primary pulmonary hypertension. Chest 120:1562–1569, 2001.

135. Dobyns EL, Eells PL, Griebel JL, et al: Elevated plasma endothelin-1 and cytokine levels in children with severe acute respiratory distress syndrome. J Pediatr 135:246–249, 1999.

136. Hartemink KJ, Groeneveld AB, de Groot MC, et al: alpha-atrial natriuretic peptide, cyclic guanosine monophosphate, and endothelin in plasma as markers of myocardial depression in human septic shock. Crit Care Med 29:80–82, 2001.

137. Carpagnano GE, Kharitonov SA, Wells AU, et al: Increased vitronectin and endothelin-1 in the breath condensate of patients with fibrosing lung disease. Respiration 70:154–160, 2003.

138. Kenyon KW, Nappi JM: Bosentan for the treatment of pulmonary arterial hypertension. Ann Pharmacother 37:1055–1062, 2003.

139. Krum H, Viskoper RJ, Lacourciere Y, et al: The effect of an endothelin-receptor antagonist, bosentan, on blood pressure in patients with essential hypertension. N Engl J Med 338:784–790, 1998.

140. Wenzel RR, Fleisch M, Shaw S, et al: Hemodynamic and coronary effects of the endothelin antagonist bosentan in patients with coronary artery disease. Circulation 98:2235–2240, 1998.

141. Suetsch G, Christen S, Yan XY, et al: Clinical and hemodynamic effects of an orally active endothelin-1 receptor antagonist in patients with refractory chronic heart failure. Circulation 96:193–194, 1997.

142. Louis A, Cleland JG, Crabbe S, et al: Clinical trials update: CAPRICORN, COPERNICUS, MIRACLE, STAF, RITZ-2, RECOVER and RENAISSANCE and cachexia and cholesterol in heart failure. Highlights of the Scientific Sessions of the Am Coll Cardiol, 2001. Eur J Heart Failure 3:381–387, 2001.

143. Kalra PR, Moon JC, Coats AJ: Do results of the ENABLE (Endothelin Antagonist Bosentan for Lowering Cardiac Events in Heart Failure) study spell the end for non-selective endothelin antagonism in heart failure? Int J Cardiol 85:195–197, 2002.

144. Mylona P, Cleland JG: Update of REACH-1 and MERIT-HF clinical trials in heart failure. Eur J Heart Fail 1:197–200, 1999.

145. O'Connor CM, Gattis WA, Adams KF Jr, et al: Tezosentan in patients with acute heart failure and acute coronary syndromes: Results of the Randomized Intravenous TeZosentan Study (RITZ-4). JAAC 41:1452–1457, 2003.

146. Nakov R, Pfarr E, Eberle S, et al: Darusentan: An effective endothelin-A receptor antagonist for treatment of hypertension. Am J Hypertens 15:583–589, 2002.

147. Luscher TF, Enseleit F, Pacher R, et al: Heart Failure ET(A) Receptor Blockade Trial. Hemodynamic and neurohumoral effects of selective endothelin A (ET(A)) receptor blockade in chronic heart failure: The Heart Failure ET(A) Receptor Blockade Trial (HEAT). Circulation 106:2666–2672, 2002.

148. Carducci MA, Padley RJ, Breul J, et al: Effect of endothelin-A receptor blockade with atrasentan on tumor progression in men with hormone-refractory prostate cancer: A randomized, phase II, placebo-controlled trial. J Clin Oncol 21:679–689, 2003.

149. Teerlink JR: Reversal of left ventricular remodeling: Role of the endothelin pathway. J Cardiac Fail 8:S494–S499, 2002.

150. Kowala MC, Rose PM, Stein PD, et al: Selective blockade of the endothelin subtype A receptor decreases early atherosclerosis in hamsters fed cholesterol. Am J Pathol 146:819–826, 1995.

151. Shaw MD, Vermeulen M, Murray GD, et al: Efficacy and safety of the endothelin, receptor antagonist TAK-044 in treating subarachnoid hemorrhage: A report by the Steering Committee on behalf of the UK/Netherlands/Eire TAK-044 Subarachnoid Haemorrhage Study Group. J Neurosurgery 93:992–997, 2000.

152. Takaoka M, Kuro T, Matsumura Y: Role of endothelin in the pathogenesis of acute renal failure. Drug News Perspect 13:141–146, 2000.

153. Xu H, Lin L, Yuan WJ: Antiarrhythmic effect of endothelin-A receptor antagonist on acute ischemic arrhythmia in isolated rat heart. Acta Pharmacologica Sinica 24:37–44, 2003.

154. Cernacek P, Stewart DJ, Monge JC, et al: The endothelin system and its role in acute myocardial infarction. Can J Physiol Pharmacol 81:598–606, 2003.

155. Kitamura K, Kangawa K, Kawamoto M, et al: Adrenomedullin: A novel hypotensive peptide isolated from human pheochromocytoma. Biochem Biophys Res Commun 192:553–560, 1993.

156. Samson WK: Adrenomedullin and the control of fluid and electrolyte homeostasis. Annu Rev Physiol 61:363–389, 1999.

157. Kitamura K, Eto T: Adrenomedullin-physiological regulator of the cardiovascular system or biochemical curiosity? Curr Opin Nephrol Hypertens 6:80–87, 1997.

158. Edwards RM, Trizna W, Aiyar N: Adrenomedullin: A new peptide involved in cardiorenal homeostasis? Exp Nephrol 5:18–22, 1997.

159. Nishikimi T, Kitamura K, Saito Y, et al: Clinical studies on the sites of production and clearance of circulating adrenomedullin in human subjects. Hypertension 24:600–604, 1994.

160. Nishikimi T, Horio T, Sasaki T, et al: Cardiac production and secretion of adrenomedullin are increased in heart failure. Hypertension 30:1369–1375, 1997.

161. Kapas S, Catt KJ, Clark JL: Cloning and expression of cDNA encoding a rat adrenomedullin receptor. J Biol Chem 270:25344–25347, 1995.

162. Meeran K, O'Shea D, Upton PD, et al: Circulating adrenomedullin does not regulate systemic blood pressure but increases plasma prolactin after intravenous infusion in humans: A pharmacokinetic study. J Clin Endocrinol Metab 82:95–100, 1997.

163. Massart PE, Hodeige D, Donckier J: Adrenomedullin: View on a novel vasodilatory peptide with natriuretic properties. Acta Cardiol 51:259–269, 1996.

164. Minamino N, Kikumoto K, Isumi Y: Regulation of adrenomedullin expression and release. Microsc Res Tech 57:28–39, 2002.

165. Rademaker MT, Charles CJ, Espiner EA, et al: Long-term adrenomedullin administration in experimental heart failure. Hypertension 40:667–672, 2002.

166. Parkes DG: Cardiovascular actions of adrenomedullin in conscious sheep. Am J Physiol 268:H2574–H2578, 1995.

167. Jensen BL, Kramer BK, Kurtz A: Adrenomedullin stimulates renin release and renin mRNA in mouse juxtaglomerular granular cells. Hypertension 29:1148–1155, 1997.

168. Yamaguchi T, Baba K, Doi Y, et al: Effect of adrenomedullin on aldosterone secretion by dispersed rat adrenal zona glomerulosa cells. Life Sci 56:379–387, 1995.

169. Horio T, Kohno M, Kano H, et al: Adrenomedullin as a novel antimigration factor of vascular smooth muscle cells. Circ Res 77:660–664, 1995.

170. Kamoi H, Kanazawa H, Hirata K, et al: Adrenomedullin inhibits the secretion of cytokine-induced neutrophil chemoattractant, a member of the interleukin-8 family, from rat alveolar macrophages. Biochem Biophys Res Commun 211:1031–1035, 1995.

171. Tsuruda T, Kato J, Kitamura K, et al: Adrenomedullin: A possible autocrine or paracrine inhibitor of hypertrophy of cardiomyocytes. Hypertension 31:505–510, 1998.

172. Zudaire E, MartA-nez A, Cuttitta F: Adrenomedullin and cancer. Reg Pep 112:175–183, 2003.

173. Abasolo I, Yang L, Haleem R, et al: Overexpression of adrenomedullin gene markedly inhibits proliferation of PC3 prostate cancer cells in vitro and in vivo. Mol Cell Endocrinol 199:179–187, 2003.

174. Parameswaran N, Nambi P, Brooks DP, et al: Regulation of glomerular mesangial cell proliferation in culture by adrenomedullin. Eur J Pharmacol 372:85–95, 1999.

175. Kato H, Shichiri M, Marumo F, et al: Adrenomedullin as an autocrine/paracrine apoptosis survival factor for rat endothelial cells. Endocrinology 138:2615–2620, 1997.

176. Cornish J, Naot D, Reid IR: Adrenomedullin: A regulator of bone formation. Reg Pept 112:79–86, 2003.

177. Montuenga LM, Martinez A, Miller MJ, et al: Expression of adrenomedullin and its receptor during embryogenesis suggests autocrine or paracrine modes of action. Endocrinology 138:440–451, 1997.

178. Allaker RP, Kapas S: Adrenomedullin and mucosal defence: Interaction between host and microorganism. Reg Pept 112:147–152, 2003.

179. Ishimitsu T, Nishikimi T, Matsuoka H, et al: Behaviour of adrenomedullin during acute and chronic salt loading in normotensive and hypertensive subjects. Clin Sci 91:293–298, 1996.

180. Kato J, Kitamura K, Uemura T, et al: Plasma levels of adrenomedullin and atrial and brain natriuretic peptides in the general population: Their relations to age and pulse pressure. Hypertens Res Clin Exp 25:887–892, 2002.

181. Morimoto A, Nishikimi T, Takaki H, et al: Effect of exercise on plasma adrenomedullin and natriuretic peptide levels in myocardial infarction. Clin Exp Pharmacol Physiol 24:315–320, 1997.

182. Hoshimoto K, Hayashi M, Ohkura T: Mature adrenomedullin concentrations in plasma during pregnancy. J Matern Fetal Neonatal Med 11:126–129, 2002.

183. Ehlenz K, Koch B, Preuss P, et al: High levels of circulating adrenomedullin in severe illness: Correlation with C-reactive protein and evidence against the adrenal medulla as site of origin. Exp Clin Endocrinol Diabetes 105:156–162, 1997.

184. Letizia C, Cerci S, Centanni M, et al: Circulating levels of adrenomedullin in patients with Addison's disease before and after corticosteroid treatment. Clin Endocrinol 48:145–148, 1998.

185. Cheung B, Leung R: Elevated plasma levels of human adrenomedullin in cardiovascular, respiratory, hepatic and renal disorders. Clin Sci 92:59–62, 1997.

186. Ceyhan BB, Karakurt S, Hekim N: Plasma adrenomedullin levels in asthmatic patients. J Asthma 38:221–227, 2001.

187. Ando K, Fujita T: Lessons from the adrenomedullin knockout mouse. Reg Pept 112:185–188, 2003.

188. Nishimatsu H, Hirata Y, Shindo T, et al: Endothelial responses of the aorta from adrenomedullin transgenic mice and knockout mice. Hypertens Res Clin Exp 26:S79–S84, 2003.

189. Ishimitsu T, Tsukada K, Minami J, et al: Variations of human adrenomedullin gene and its relation to cardiovascular diseases. Hypertens Res Clin Exp 26:S129–S34, 2003.

190. Kanozawa K, Shimosawa T, Nagasawa R, et al: Mature form of adrenomedullin is a useful marker to evaluate blood volume in hemodialysis patients. Am J Kid Dis 40:794–801, 2002.

191. Shinomiya K, Ohmori K, Ohyama H, et al: Association of plasma adrenomedullin with carotid atherosclerosis in chronic ischemic stroke. Peptides 22:1873–1880, 2001.

192. Nakatsuka M, Habara T, Noguchi S, et al: Increased plasma adrenomedullin in women with recurrent pregnancy loss. Obstet Gynecol 102:319–324, 2003.

193. Gazzolo D, Marinoni E, Giovannini L, et al: Circulating adrenomedullin is increased in preterm newborns developing intraventricular hemorrhage. Pediatr Res 50:544–547, 2001.

194. Richards AM, Doughty R, Nicholls MG, et al: Australia-New Zealand Heart Failure Group. Plasma N-terminal pro-brain natriuretic peptide and adrenomedullin: Prognostic utility and prediction of benefit from carvedilol in chronic ischemic left ventricular dysfunction. JACC 37:1781–1787, 2001.

195. Pousset F, Masson F, Chavirovskaia O, et al: Plasma adrenomedullin, a new independent predictor of prognosis in patients with chronic heart failure. Eur Heart J 21:1009–1014, 2000.

196. Ueda S, Nishio K, Minamino N, et al: Increased plasma levels of adrenomedullin in patients with systemic inflammatory response syndrome. Am J Respir Crit Care Med 160:132–136, 1999.

197. Savas HA, Herken H, Yurekli M, et al: Possible role of nitric oxide and adrenomedullin in bipolar affective disorder. Neuropsychobiology 45:57–61, 2002.

198. Zoroglu SS, Herken H, Yurekli M, et al: The possible pathophysiological role of plasma nitric oxide and adrenomedullin in schizophrenia. J Psych Res 36:309–315, 2002.

199. Hata K, Takebayashi Y, Akiba S, et al: Expression of the adrenomedullin gene in epithelial ovarian cancer. Mol Hum Reprod 6:867–872, 2000.

200. Lainchbury JG, Nicholls MG, Espiner EA, et al: Bioactivity and interactions of adrenomedullin and brain natriuretic peptide in patients with heart failure. Hypertension 34:70–75, 1999.

201. McGregor DO, Troughton RW, Frampton C, et al: Hypotensive and natriuretic actions of adrenomedullin in subjects with chronic renal impairment. Hypertension 37:1279–1284, 2001.

202. Nishikimi T, Yoshihara F, Mori Y, et al: Cardioprotective effect of adrenomedullin in heart failure. Hypertens Res Clin Exp 26:S121–S127, 2003.

203. Huang Z, Li J, Jiang Z, et al: Effects of adrenomedullin, C-type natriuretic peptide, and parathyroid hormone-related peptide on calcification in cultured rat vascular smooth muscle cells. J Cardiovasc Pharmacol 42:89–97, 2003.

204. Dogan A, Suzuki Y, Koketsu N, et al: Intravenous infusion of adrenomedullin and increase in regional cerebral blood flow and prevention of ischemic brain injury after middle cerebral artery occlusion in rats. J Cereb Blood Flow Metab 17:19–25, 1997.

205. Kato T, Bishop AT, Tu YK, et al: Function of the vascular endothelium after hypothermic storage at four degrees Celsius in a canine tibial perfusion model. The role of adrenomedullin in reperfusion injury. J Bone Joint Surg Am 80:1341–1348, 1998.

206. Ueno T, Tanikawa K: Intralobular innervation and lipocyte contractility in the liver. Nutrition 13:141–148, 1997.

207. Kandler MA, Von Der Hardt K, Mahfoud S, et al: Pilot intervention: Aerosolized adrenomedullin reduces pulmonary hypertension. J Pharmacol Exp Therapeut 306:1021–1026, 2003.

# Hormonal Regulation of Electrolyte and Water Metabolism

## *Theodore L. Goodfriend, Aaron L. Friedman, and Yoram Shenker*

In normal humans, the volume, distribution, and composition of body fluids are held within relatively narrow limits despite wide variations in the quantity and relative proportions of water and electrolytes ingested. Such stability of the internal environment requires coordination among the many factors that can affect water and electrolyte metabolism. This chapter addresses the diverse efferent humoral and neural signals, each of which responds to its own afferent stimuli, that are integrated to enable the kidney to make appropriate adjustments in renal excretion of water and electrolytes. The chapter begins with a brief review of renal mechanisms that govern water and electrolyte excretion. The major focus throughout this discussion is on sodium and potassium; acid-base balance, magnesium, and calcium-phosphate metabolism are not covered.

It should be noted that regulation of electrolyte and water metabolism differs from many other endocrine systems in the degree to which physical parameters play an important part. Blood volume and blood pressure are as relevant as blood sodium or aldosterone in overall regulation. This chapter does not, however, discuss in great detail the regulation of the physical parameters themselves.

## NORMAL PHYSIOLOGY

### *EXTRACELLULAR FLUID HOMEOSTASIS*

Osmolality of body fluids depends on the regulation of water metabolism, primarily by the hypothalamic centers, which regulate release of antidiuretic hormone (ADH) and modulate thirst. Because most cell membranes are freely permeable to water, the osmolality of the intracellular and extracellular compartments is identical. As a corollary, the distribution of body water depends on the amounts of solute in the intracellular and extracellular compartments. Sodium is the principal extracellular cation, so sodium and its associated anions are the major determinants of osmolality and volume of the extracellular space. Potassium plays an analogous role inside the cell.[1]

An abrupt increase in total body sodium transiently increases extracellular osmolality, leading to the movement of water from the intracellular to the extracellular space down an osmotic gradient. The movement of water expands the extracellular fluid volume; volume expansion leads to increased salt and water excretion by mechanisms that are discussed in the following. Conversely, a loss of body sodium, which usually results in decreased osmolality and extracellular volume contraction, decreases salt and water excretion. The renal mechanisms that control sodium excretion are responsive to changes in extracellular fluid volume; however, extracellular fluid volume is not restored by corrections in sodium excretion alone. Further adjustments involve alterations in water handling by the kidney, which are mediated by ADH. Therefore, extracellular fluid volume is regulated by renal mechanisms that govern both sodium and water.[2,3]

When a normal person increases sodium intake for a prolonged period, there is a delay before the added sodium is excreted quantitatively; the rate of sodium excretion rises progressively, and sodium balance is restored after 3 to 5 days (Fig. 133-1). Because of the initial delay in excreting the sodium load, there is net retention of sodium and water with associated weight gain, which does not abate as sodium balance resumes but persists as long as the augmented sodium intake is continued. In that way, increased sodium intake results in a new steady state marked by a sustained increment in body sodium content and expanded extracellular fluid volume.[4] Conversely, a reduction in sodium intake initially results in a loss of body sodium and weight before sodium excretion decreases enough to restore sodium balance, usually within 3 or 4 days. These initial losses also persist as long as sodium intake is restricted, and a new steady state is established with a sustained reduction in body sodium content and extracellular fluid volume.

### *RENAL HANDLING OF SALT AND WATER*

The amount of sodium excreted in urine represents the net difference between glomerular filtration and tubular reabsorption. In an adult with a normal glomerular filtration rate (GFR) who is ingesting a typical Western diet, approximately 20,000 mEq of sodium are filtered per day, but only the equivalent of the ingested sodium is excreted. Even if dietary sodium intake is markedly increased, the total sodium excretion is still a small percentage of the total filtered sodium. The sodium transporting capacity of the renal tubule is substantial, reabsorbing more than 99% of the total filtered sodium. If uncompensated, small percentage changes in filtration and tubular reabsorption could result in very large changes in sodium excretion.

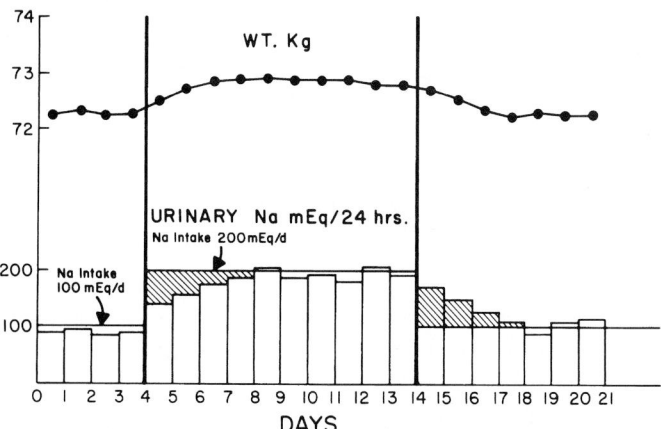

*Figure 133-1*   Renal response to a prolonged increase in dietary sodium intake.

Glomerular filtration depends on glomerular hydrostatic pressure, the opposing filtrate pressure, and specific properties of the ultrafiltration barrier.[5] Changes in GFR can be induced by changes in arterial pressure, and a number of humoral factors (e.g., angiotensin II, bradykinin, prostaglandins, natriuretic peptides, nitric oxide, and ADH). These hormones alter afferent or efferent glomerular arteriolar tone, changing the impact of renal arterial pressure on filtration. The ultrafiltration coefficient, a reflection of the filtration properties of the glomerulus, can also be altered by humoral factors. Nevertheless, with ordinary variations in dietary sodium intake, GFR changes very little. Even with marked changes in systolic blood pressure, renal blood flow and GFR remain constant. Constancy of blood flow is achieved by vascular adaptations referred to as *autoregulation.*

Increases and decreases in GFR under normal conditions are associated with compensatory changes in sodium reabsorption by the tubules and collecting ducts. This adaptation,

called *glomerulotubular balance,* is the result of several mechanisms.[6,7] The first of these affects the proximal tubule (Fig. 133-2). Peritubular Starling's forces promote increased sodium reabsorption by the proximal tubule when GFR is increased. The rise in filtration increases the concentration of protein in the plasma in postglomerular capillaries, promoting reabsorption of sodium and water from the urine into the blood. The reverse of this process occurs when GFR falls. A second intrarenal mechanism by which a rise in GFR stimulates sodium reabsorption is the increased sodium reabsorbed through cotransport with other solutes such as glucose or phosphate. With increased filtration, more sodium is cotransported; and with decreased filtration, less sodium cotransport occurs. Angiotensin II directly stimulates sodium reabsorption in the proximal tubule. Because the concentration of angiotensin II usually varies inversely with intravascular volume and pressure, and because volume and pressure are affected by sodium balance, the renin-angiotensin system is part of the mechanism affecting glomerulotubular balance. Other aspects of the renin-angiotensin system are discussed in the following.

The loop of Henle is the next important segment of the nephron that plays a role in urinary dilution or concentration and in sodium excretion[8] (see Fig. 133-2). Tubular fluid reaching the loop is isotonic. The thin descending limb is impermeable to solute but permeable to water. The interstitium of the kidney is progressively more hypertonic the deeper into the medulla one examines. Because it is permeable to water, the thin descending limb permits movement of water out of the tubule into the hypertonic interstitium, concentrating the fluid in the tubule lumen. The thick ascending limb is impermeable to water but has the machinery to move sodium and chloride into the interstitium, which helps maintain the hypertonicity of the medullary interstitium. Sodium and chloride make up a part of the osmotically active solute in the interstitium, but a substantial portion of the hypertonicity is produced by urea that moves into the interstitium from the collecting duct. When sodium and chloride are reabsorbed from the ascending limb without water, the tubule

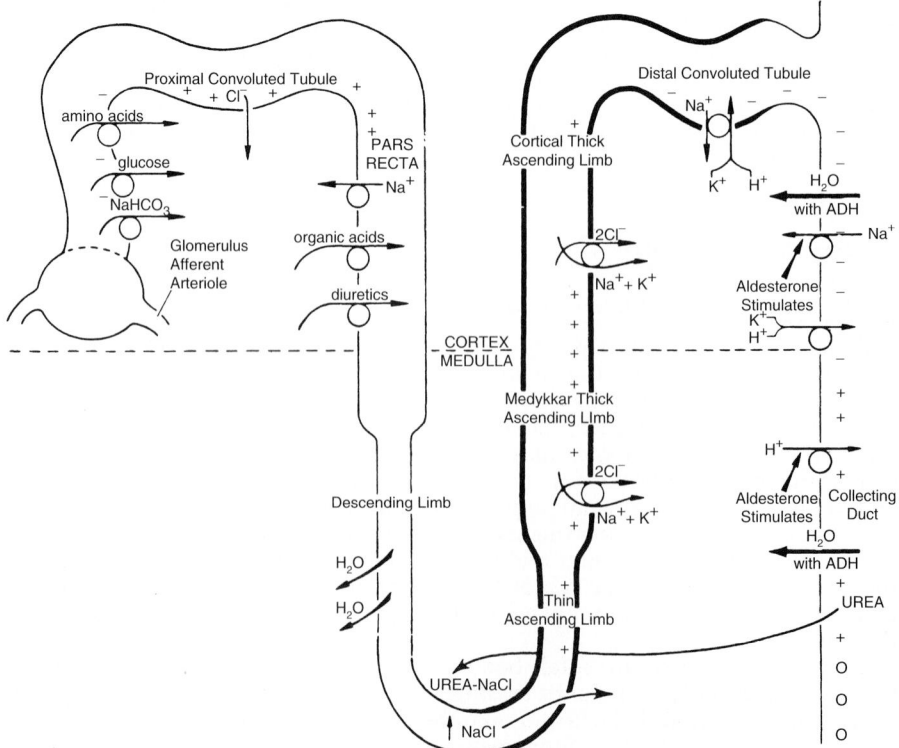

*Figure 133-2*   Summary of reabsorption and excretion of ions and water in the nephron. ADH, antidiuretic hormone. (From Kokko JP: Site and mechanism of action of diuretics. Am J Med 77[A]:11–17, 1984.)

fluid becomes increasingly more dilute as it progresses up the ascending limb of Henle's loop toward the distal tubule.

The "distal nephron" (i.e., the distal tubule and collecting duct) reabsorbs only a small fraction of filtrate, less than 20% of the total.[9] By contrast with the proximal tubule, where filtrate is reabsorbed iso-osmotically, the distal nephron can adjust sodium and water reabsorption separately to compensate for changes in fluid and electrolyte intake and losses. The distal convoluted tubule and connecting tubule actively reabsorb sodium, resulting in a negative intraluminal electrical potential; chloride passively follows the sodium down the electrochemical gradient. Aldosterone is not important in this segment of the nephron. In the absence of ADH, the entire distal tubule is impermeable to water, so the reabsorption of sodium chloride further dilutes tubule fluid. However, in the presence of ADH, the last portion of the distal tubule becomes permeable to water, and the osmolality of tubule fluid increases nearly to that of plasma.

Active sodium reabsorption also occurs against a steep electrochemical gradient in both the cortical and the medullary collecting ducts. Sodium reabsorption in the cortical collecting duct is influenced by aldosterone and atrial natriuretic factor[10,11] (see the following). Permeability to water is low in the collecting ducts when ADH is absent, so that further dilution can be accomplished in these segments as more salt is extracted. Although only a small fraction of overall sodium reabsorption takes place in the collecting ducts, extremely low sodium concentrations (e.g., as low as 1 to 2 mEq/L) are achieved in this segment during salt deprivation.

Water reabsorption in the distal nephron is passive, being governed by permeability changes induced by ADH.[12] In nearly all situations, the osmolality of filtrate entering the distal nephron is approximately 100 mOsm/kg. During water diuresis, further dilution of tubule fluid occurs because the distal nephron is relatively impermeable to water, preventing little water reabsorption while active transport of ions continues. On the other hand, when ADH is released during water deprivation, permeability to water increases, and urine osmolality can exceed 1200 mOsm/kg as water in the collecting ducts diffuses from the lumen into the hypertonic medullary interstitium.

## FACTORS AFFECTING RENAL SODIUM EXCRETION

As described above, the amount of sodium excreted in the urine represents the small difference between the large quantities of sodium that are filtered and those that are reabsorbed by the kidney. Because changes in glomerular filtration ordinarily have a minimal influence on sodium excretion, factors that control reabsorption must be the major determinant. Physical factors, such as hydrostatic and oncotic pressures that influence proximal tubule reabsorption, also affect the distal tubule, but the mechanism of their distal effect is incompletely understood. The humoral factors affecting distal tubular sodium reabsorption and consequent net sodium balance are described in the following.

## ALDOSTERONE

Steroids from the adrenal cortex with mineralocorticoid activity, primarily aldosterone and deoxycorticosterone (DOC), conserve sodium by stimulating its reabsorption from luminal fluids in the renal tubule, colon, and salivary and sweat glands.[11] Mineralocorticoids have their greatest sodium-conserving effects on the distal nephron; mineralocorticoid receptors are in highest concentration in the cortical collecting duct.[10,13,14] The cortical collecting duct is composed of at least two types of epithelial cells. The most abundant cell type, the "principal cell," is primarily responsible for sodium and potassium transport. "Intercalated cells" are involved in excretion of hydrogen and bicarbonate ions.

Mineralocorticoid receptors can also bind the predominant glucocorticoid, cortisol, but not its oxidation product, cortisone. Therefore, selectivity of steroid binding to mineralocorticoid receptors is not conferred by binding specificity but by the enzyme 11β-hydroxysteroid dehydrogenase, which converts cortisol to cortisone.[15] This is true only where the enzyme exists in proximity to the receptor, as in the kidney. By contrast, glucocorticoids and aldosterone compete equally for mineralocorticoid receptors in tissues such as brain, hippocampus, and heart, where 11β-hydroxysteroid dehydrogenase activity is lacking (see Chapter 129).

The response of cortical collecting duct cells to a mineralocorticoid is characterized by an early phase, within 1 or 2 hours, in which sodium transport is increased by the insertion of existing sodium channels into the apical cell membrane. This promotes sodium influx into the cells. Mineralocorticoid action also has a late phase in which new $Na^+/K^+$-ATPase molecules are synthesized and incorporated into the basolateral cell membrane.[16] The influx of sodium into the tubule cell through apical channels directly stimulates basolateral $Na^+/K^+$-ATPase activity, which pumps sodium out of the cell toward the blood in exchange for potassium. The rise in intracellular potassium, and the negative charge in the lumen resulting from sodium flux into the cell, drive potassium into the urine. The net result of these linked processes is reabsorption of sodium from urine to blood, and excretion of potassium from blood to urine. Because potassium ultimately derives from intracellular stores, the tubule conserves the principal extracellular cation at the expense of the principal intracellular one. During the late phase of mineralocorticoid activity, potassium excretion is augmented further by upregulation of potassium channels in both the apical and basolateral cell membranes. Aldosterone action is discussed further in Chapter 122.

## OTHER MINERALOCORTICOIDS SECRETED BY THE ADRENAL CORTEX

DOC is produced by zona fasciculata cells, as a byproduct of cortisol biosynthesis; and by glomerulosa cells, where it is a precursor of aldosterone biosynthesis[17] (see Chapter 119). Other mineralocorticoids include 18-hydroxydeoxycorticosterone and 18-hydroxycorticosterone[18,19]; both of these are biologically weak. The demethylated steroid 19-nordeoxycorticosterone is of intermediate potency but unknown significance in humans.[20] The 19-norsteroids are derived by two reactions: (1) 19-hydroxylation or oxidation in the adrenal; and (2) 19-demethylation outside of the gland. Aldosterone can be metabolized in a similar way to 19-noraldosterone, which is a potent mineralocorticoid of unknown significance.[17] Aldosterone is extensively metabolized by the liver, where it is first reduced. Reduced metabolites of the mineralocorticoids, including 3,5-tetrahydroaldosterone, are relatively weak mineralocorticoids as measured by standard bioassays, but they may have other important properties, such as modulating the effects of the primary adrenal products.[21] Reduced metabolites make up the bulk of the urinary excretory products derived from corticosteroids.

Classic glucocorticoids (e.g., cortisol and corticosterone) have finite mineralocorticoid activity, especially when they have unimpeded access to the mineralocorticoid receptor. If they are produced in large quantities (as in Cushing's disease), or if their access is unimpeded because of inadequate activity of the enzyme that usually oxidizes the 11-hydroxyl group (as in the syndrome of apparent mineralocorticoid excess or the ingestion of licorice), their mineralocorticoid effects can be significant.[22,23] Hydroxylation or oxidation of the 18-methyl group of cortisol increases its mineralocorticoid activity 10-fold, to 2% of that of aldosterone. The physiologic relevance of this steroid is also unknown.[24]

## REGULATION OF MINERALOCORTICOID SECRETION

Aldosterone is produced by the zona glomerulosa cells that lie just under the adrenal capsule. This zone produces 50 to 150 μg of aldosterone per day.[11] Secretion of this steroid can be affected by over 20 hormones, autacoids, and ions (Table 133-1). Among these, the predominant stimulant is angiotensin II, synthesized by the sequential action of renin and angiotensin converting enzyme (ACE) on a plasma protein made in the liver (angiotensinogen). The renin-angiotensin axis provides the best understood link between aldosterone secretion and the volume and circulatory status of mammals. Renin is released from the kidney in response to a drop in perfusion of the juxtaglomerular apparatus, or in response to adrenergic discharge from nerves supplying the kidney. Adrenergic nerve traffic to the kidneys is increased, in turn, by a drop in intravascular volume as sensed by the low-pressure baroreceptors of the central circulation. Among other stimuli of renin release is decreased tubular chloride concentration, which can result from a drop in glomerular filtration. Most, but not all, stimuli to renin release are triggered by decreases or threatened decreases in renal perfusion.[25,26]

Angiotensin III is a heptapeptide produced by removal of the N-terminal aspartic acid residue from angiotensin II. It, too, is a potent stimulus of aldosterone secretion, but it is more susceptible to proteolytic degradation than is the octapeptide, so it probably plays a smaller role in the regulation of aldosterone secretion by the blood-borne renin-angiotensin axis.[27]

Stimulation of aldosterone secretion by either angiotensin II or III is mediated by the $AT_1$ subtype of angiotensin receptor, a classic G protein–linked receptor that increases protein phosphorylation in adrenal cells by elevating intracellular calcium, diacylglycerol, and inositol phosphates.[28]

Angiotensin is also synthesized by renin or other proteolytic enzymes within cells outside the kidney, including the adrenal, heart, and brain.[29,30] At these sites, synthesis of angiotensin is regulated by unknown factors that are distinct from volume status.

The second most prominent regulator of aldosterone secretion is potassium in the extracellular fluid. Aldosterone secretion increases sharply in response to small increments in extracellular (plasma) potassium concentration, and falls when plasma potassium drops.[31,32] Potassium stimulates the zona glomerulosa cell by depolarizing its membrane and increasing the inward flux of calcium.[33] The actions of

potassium and angiotensin are complementary and interrelated.[34,35] High concentrations of either potassium or angiotensin accentuate the adrenal response to the other agonist, and low concentrations of either potassium or angiotensin blunt the response to the other.

In addition to the acute effects of potassium, chronic exposure to elevated concentrations of the ion increases responsiveness of the adrenal to various stimuli by increasing synthesis of steroidogenic enzymes.[36] Dietary potassium is a trophic factor for the adrenal glomerulosa. Chronic exposure to endogenous angiotensin has a similar positive effect, which includes upregulation of angiotensin receptors.[37]

Adrenocorticotropic hormone (ACTH) has a biphasic effect on aldosterone secretion, stimulating it for a day or two, then inhibiting it.[38] The mechanism of the stimulatory action involves activation of adenylate cyclase and protein kinase A. The mechanism of the inhibitory effect is unclear, and may involve the ability of ACTH to convert zona glomerulosa cells into zona fasciculata cells, depleting the potential of the gland to make aldosterone.[39] The inhibitory effect of ACTH is not seen if the hormone is administered in bursts.[38] Because that pattern approximates the secretory rhythm of normal humans, ACTH may not be an aldosterone inhibitor under normal conditions.

Aldosterone secretion can be stimulated by administration of other hormones, ions, and autacoids, but the physiologic relevance of these stimuli is uncertain.[40,41] Among the more potent stimuli are serotonin, prostaglandin $E_2$, and ammonium ion. Other molecules that can be shown to stimulate isolated adrenal glomerulosa cells include endothelin, melanocyte-stimulating hormone, vasopressin, and epinephrine.

Secretion of aldosterone can be inhibited by a large number of endogenous substances (see Table 133-1). Inhibitors most likely to be relevant to volume status are ACTH (given chronically), natriuretic peptides, and dopamine. The inhibitory influence of dopamine is most evident when it is blocked by dopamine antagonists such as metaclopramide.[42] Other substances that inhibit aldosterone secretion under experimental conditions include oleic and other unsaturated fatty acids, somatostatin, and adrenomedullin.[43] The relevance of these effects to control of aldosterone secretion in humans is uncertain. The zona glomerulosa is innervated by autonomic fibers, and there is evidence that aldosterone secretion can be regulated by catecholamines or acetylcholine released by these nerves.[41] It is not clear that these signals are integrated into a volume-sensitive reflex loop, although autonomic nerve traffic is affected by intravascular volume.

Secretion of mineralocorticoids like DOC that arise in the zona fasciculata is regulated by ACTH.[44] Integration of the various stimuli and inhibitors of mineralocorticoid secretion is discussed in the following.

### HUMORAL NATRIURETIC FACTORS

Endogenous natriuretic factors that participate in the regulation of renal sodium excretion include a family of natriuretic peptides first identified in the heart; other peptides such as bradykinin; some eicosanoids; and, possibly, an endogenous sodium pump inhibitor similar or identical to ouabain.[45,46]

#### Atrial Natriuretic Peptide

The principal natriuretic peptide in human blood is atrial natriuretic peptide (ANP), isolated from mammalian atria.[47] ANP is a 28-amino acid peptide derived from an inactive 126-amino acid precursor (pro-ANP). The precursor is stored in perinuclear granules in atrial cardiomyocytes. These granules are not found in normal mammalian ventricular myocardial cells. Pro-ANP is derived from its precursor, prepro-ANP, by cleavage of a signal peptide.

**Table 133-1** Stimuli and Inhibitors of Aldosterone Secretion

| Stimuli | Inhibitors |
| --- | --- |
| **VOLUME-SENSITIVE** | |
| Angiotensin II and III | Atrial natriuretic peptides |
| Autonomic innervation | Autonomic innervation |
| Catecholamines | |
| Vasopressin | |
| **POSSIBLY VOLUME-SENSITIVE** | |
| ACTH (acute) | ACTH (chronic) |
| Potassium | Hyperosmolality |
| | Dopamine |
| | Hypoxia |
| **NOT VOLUME-SENSITIVE** | |
| Serotonin | Somatostain |
| Endothelin | Adrenomedullin |
| Interleukin-6 | Interleukin-1β |
| Insulin | Fatty acids |
| Vasoactive intestinal peptide | Tumor necrosis factor |
| Bradykinin | |
| Enkephalins | |
| Melanocortin | |

ANP's effects are summarized in Table 133-2. In the kidney, ANP dilates afferent glomerular arterioles, constricts efferent arterioles, and relaxes mesangial cells. These changes increase glomerular filtration. ANP also inhibits angiotensin-stimulated sodium reabsorption, inhibits ADH-induced water transport, and directly blocks tubular reabsorption of sodium. The net effect is to increase excretion of sodium and water.

ANP has three known receptor subtypes. The principal receptor mediating ANP actions, the A receptor, is coupled to guanylate cyclase. Another receptor, the B receptor, is also coupled to guanylate cyclase but is activated more prominently by brain natriuretic peptide (BNP) than by ANP. The third receptor, C receptor, does not mediate a known biologic response but may serve to clear ANP from some sites; it is sometimes called the "clearance receptor."

Release of ANP from the atria is directly related to atrial stretch, possibly mediated through release of endothelin-1, NO, or angiotensin II.[48] In congestive heart failure (CHF) and chronic renal failure, plasma ANP levels are elevated.[45,49,50] In CHF, ANP levels increase with the severity of the disease[49] (see Chapter 134). In most forms of hypertension, high ANP plasma levels have been found,[51] with a positive correlation between the severity of hypertension and degree of ANP elevation.

The physiologic role of ANP is not completely understood because there is no practical way to remove it from living humans. Low-dose infusions that result in plasma levels within the high-normal range cause natriuresis and suppression of the renin-angiotensin-aldosterone system.[50] Deletion of the ANP gene in mice leads to hypertension. These mice are able to cope with a gradual, sustained increase in dietary sodium but show an attenuated renal response to an acute volume load administered to animals on a low-salt diet.[45] Receptor gene knockout mice also show little increase in sodium excretion after acute volume expansion.[45] ANP clearly

plays a role in mineralocorticoid escape, as shown by significant inhibition of this escape by administration of a blocker of the A and B receptors.[49] These findings suggest a role for ANP in defending against mineralocorticoid- and salt-induced hypertension, but ANP is probably not essential to normal chronic sodium and water homeostasis.[45] Multiple observations support the involvement of ANP in the pathophysiology of congestive heart failure, hypertension, and cardiovascular remodeling.[45,51]

### Brain Natriuretic Peptide

Another member of the family of natriuretic peptides was first isolated from porcine brain, so it was called "brain natriuretic peptide." The circulating form in humans is a 32-amino acid peptide with a remarkable homology to ANP.[45,47,49] Prepro-BNP contains 134 amino acids; the first 26 comprise a signal peptide whose removal creates pro-BNP. This peptide is found in atrial myocytes in normal hearts and in ventricular myocytes in failing hearts.

Plasma concentrations of BNP in normal subjects are only about 20% of the corresponding ANP levels, but in severe cases of CHF, BNP levels are higher than those of ANP.[49] This suggests that BNP is synthesized primarily in the heart, probably in the ventricle in the failing heart. Plasma BNP levels are a better reflection of the severity of CHF or postmyocardial infarction status than are ANP levels. For this reason, BNP measurements are now widely used in the diagnosis and the follow-up of CHF.[49] Infusion of BNP (nesiritide) can be used to treat acutely decompensated heart failure in the hospital setting[52] (see Chapter 134).

### C Natriuretic Peptide

In 1990, another peptide was isolated from porcine brain and called C natriuretic peptide (CNP). This peptide has the same 17-residue ring sequence as other natriuretic peptides but lacks C-terminal extensions from the ring structure. Two forms, 22 and 53 amino acids in length, have been identified in vivo.[45] The diuretic, natriuretic, and hypotensive effects of CNP are minimal, and plasma concentrations are very low.[45,47,50,51] CNP acts through the B receptor and is primarily produced in vascular endothelial cells, where it has a paracrine vasodilating effect on smooth muscle cells.[45,47] CNP is also present in the hypothalamus and may play a role in neuroendocrine control of reproduction.[53]

### Sodium Pump Inhibitor

Experiments by Lee and de Wardener[54] and others suggested the existence of an endogenous natriuretic factor with the ability to inhibit $Na^+/K^+$-ATPase. This enzyme is responsible for establishing the gradient of sodium and potassium across cell membranes, including renal tubular cells. The putative endogenous ATPase inhibitor was postulated to be secreted in response to plasma volume expansion. An ATPase inhibitor could also elevate vascular smooth muscle cytosolic $Ca^{2+}$ and cause vasoconstriction, contributing to hypertension.[46] Such an inhibitor would, therefore, increase sodium excretion in two ways: (1) inhibition of renal tubular reabsorption; and (2) stimulation of pressure natriuresis.

A strong body of evidence suggests that there is an ATPase inhibitor in human plasma that is identical to the plant glycoside ouabain.[46,55] The highest concentration of ouabain is found in the adrenals, particularly in the zona glomerulosa. Circulating levels of ouabain depend on the presence of an intact adrenal cortex, and experiments suggest that the compound is synthesized in the adrenal under the influence of catecholamines and angiotensin.[46] Inhibition of ouabain action by antibodies lowers blood pressure in animal models of DOC-saline hypertension. In many patients with low-renin essential hypertension, ouabain levels are elevated.[46] Whether ouabain is simply a marker of volume expansion in such patients or actually plays a role in the development of their

---

### Table 133-2    Effects of Atrial Natriuretic Peptide

**SYSTEMIC EFFECTS**
Decrease in blood pressure
Hemoconcentration

**HORMONAL EFFECTS**
Fall in plasma renin
Fall in aldosterone
Inhibition of vasopressin secretion

**RENAL EFFECTS**
Rise in glomerular filtration rate (by dilation of afferent renal arterioles and constriction of efferent arterioles)
Rise in filtration (relaxation of mesangial cells)
Tubular actions (inhibition of angiotensin II–stimulated sodium and water transport, inhibition of vasopressin-induced water transport, direct blocking of sodium absorption)
Rise in urinary volume and electrolytes

**CENTRAL NERVOUS SYSTEM EFFECTS**
Decrease in sympathetic tone
Inhibition of salt appetite and water drinking
Inhibitory effects on blood pressure–volume–regulatory regions in the brain

**CARDIOVASCULAR EFFECTS**
Reduction in peripheral vascular resistance
Decrease in cardiac preload (by shifting of intravascular fluid to extravascular compartment and increase in venous capacitance)

**PULMONARY EFFECTS**
Relaxation of vascular smooth muscle cells

**CELLULAR EFFECTS**
Antiproliferative action in endothelial cells, cardiac fibroblasts, and vascular smooth muscle

hypertension is unknown. Ouabain also can be found in the hypothalamus. Elevated levels may affect the central nervous system and activate pathways that mediate sympathetic nerve activity.[55] Related compounds that can inhibit sodium pumps (e.g., marinobufagenin) have been identified in mammals, but their physiologic or pathologic roles are uncertain.[46]

## OTHER FACTORS AFFECTING THE KIDNEY

Other important determinants of salt and water reabsorption are neural influences; hormones aside from those previously described; and physical factors, especially arterial pressure. The kidney is richly supplied by sympathetic neurons.[56] α-Adrenergic receptors are found in abundance along the proximal tubule, the thick ascending loop of Henle, and the distal tubule. Stimulation of renal nerves causes antidiuresis, increased sodium reabsorption by activation of $\alpha_1$-receptors, and renin release by activation of $\beta_1$-receptors. The larger vessels and glomeruli also have α-adrenergic receptors that mediate vasoconstriction, reduce renal blood flow, and lower GFR. Dopamine receptors of the $D_1$ class are found along the renal tubule and on renal vessels.[57] Stimulation of these receptors causes natriuresis, diuresis, and renal vasodilation, the opposite of α-adrenergic receptors. However, dopamine in high concentrations and nonspecific synthetic dopamine agonists can also activate other dopamine and adrenergic receptors, with unpredictable net effects on sodium balance and blood pressure.

Hormonal effects on the kidney can be categorized as primarily glomerular or tubular. In the glomerulus, angiotensin II, norepinephrine, and endothelin lead to contraction of arterioles, whereas prostaglandins I and E, bradykinin, ANP, and dopamine relax them.[58] In the tubules, angiotensin II, norepinephrine, and insulin stimulate sodium reabsorption, whereas dopamine and parathormone inhibit reabsorption.[59,60] At the loop of Henle, catecholamines stimulate sodium reabsorption, whereas prostaglandin E inhibits it.[60]

In addition to all of the factors previously mentioned, and perhaps superseding them, the kidney responds to variations in arterial pressure. As described by Guyton[61] (Fig. 133-3), increased arterial pressure causes increased sodium and water excretion, a phenomenon called "pressure natriuresis."[61] By Guyton's analysis, the relationship between arterial pressure

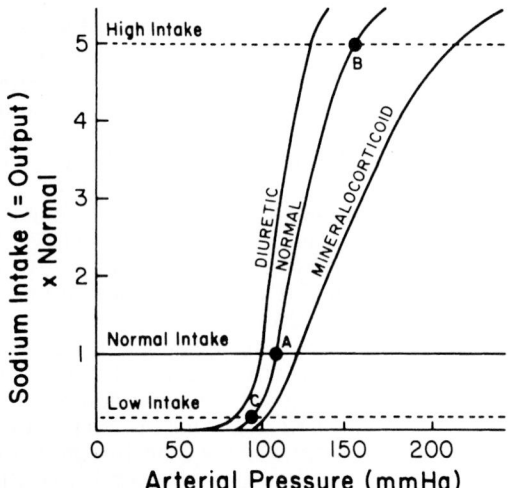

**Figure 133-3** Relationship between arterial pressure and renal sodium excretion. The intersections of lines indicate the arterial pressure required to excrete the sodium ingested. Three curves describe the pressure-natriuresis relationship under three conditions. (Modified from Guyton AC, Coleman TG, Cowley AW Jr, et al: Arterial pressure regulation: Overriding dominance of the kidney in long-term regulation and in hypertension. Am J Med 52:584–594, 1972.)

and sodium excretion (i.e., the "pressure-natriuresis curve") closely links renal and cardiovascular function through the mediation of extracellular fluid volume.[61] The mechanism by which the kidney responds to renal arterial pressure is not known; it probably involves the renal medulla rather than GFR.[62] The previously described hormones and nerves that influence renal function clearly affect the pressure-natriuresis relationship, shifting the curve to the left (facilitating sodium excretion at a given pressure) or to the right (blunting sodium excretion at a given pressure), but they do not abrogate the relationship. Although the existence of a pressure-natriuresis relationship is well accepted, there is continuing debate over its relative rank among other factors affecting sodium balance, volume status, and blood pressure.

## OTHER ISSUES IN VOLUME AND SODIUM REGULATION

The importance of volume and sodium regulation to the survival of land-based animals is attested by the number and interrelationships of the systems that can affect these parameters. This complexity makes it difficult to understand and describe how all the humoral, neural, and physical factors are integrated. As pointed out by Guyton, the individual factors have different power and time constants.[61] For example, aldosterone cannot be responsible for moment-to-moment adjustments in sodium excretion, because changes in aldosterone secretion and action take a while to occur, and the steroid has a long duration of action. More rapid adjustments are made by nerve traffic to the kidneys and by short-lived hormones such as ANP.

We know a huge number of facts like these, but many puzzles remain. Many of the factors that regulate sodium have other effects as well. It is unclear how those other effects can be isolated and regulated, apart from volume, when a change in volume is the perturbation that initiates the correction. For example, it is unclear if the effects of aldosterone and angiotensin on the growth of cells in the cardiovascular system are a constant accompaniment to effects on sodium reabsorption by the kidney; and, if not, how the growth effects are independently regulated.

One situation that presents an apparent conflict to the regulatory system is volume contraction caused by pure water deprivation. Renin is released in response to the shrunken intravascular volume, and that would be expected to stimulate aldosterone release. In pure dehydration, however, plasma sodium concentrations are usually increased. Schneider and Kramer[63] showed that high concentrations of sodium or other osmolytes inhibit aldosterone secretion, even when angiotensin is present. Therefore, when water alone is lost, aldosterone secretion is not stimulated as much as it would be if the volume loss were isosmotic. By contrast, ADH release is stimulated appropriately in pure dehydration by the combined effects of afferent nerves from the atrium, increased serum osmolality, and increased levels of angiotensin in the blood.

Another situation with apparently conflicting requirements is volume contraction in the presence of inadequate potassium. Aldosterone would help restore volume but might waste more potassium. Here, the secretion of aldosterone is restrained by low serum potassium concentrations. Even in the presence of high concentrations of angiotensin, the adrenal is relatively unresponsive because the synergism of potassium with other agonists is missing. Furthermore, when intravascular volume is contracted, the amount of sodium reaching the distal nephron is reduced, so renal potassium loss linked to sodium reabsorption in the distal tubule is minimized (see the following). It is less clear how sodium and volume status are adjusted when aldosterone is secreted in response to a pure potassium load, or when secretion is inhibited by isolated potassium depletion. Variations in ANP may contribute to the fine-tuning of sodium balance.

Another question raised by the interaction of so many factors in volume regulation concerns stimuli and inhibitors that are not known to be integrated into volume-homeostatic loops. Although it is relatively easy to describe the feedback loops that include volume, renin, aldosterone, and sodium reabsorption, it is difficult to understand how serotonin or prostaglandins fit in, for example. These and other autacoids are potentially powerful regulators of aldosterone secretion, and some of them have direct effects on renal function, but it is not known how their own formation is linked to intravascular volume. ACTH is a powerful acute stimulus to aldosterone release, but its own formation is largely independent of intravascular volume. However, the volume and stress reflex arcs are segregated by the influence of time. By mechanisms not fully understood, ACTH changes from a stimulus to an inhibitor of aldosterone secretion after a day or two. Therefore, prolonged stimulation of the hypothalamo-pituitary axis causes sustained cortisol secretion but only transitory aldosterone secretion.

Among all renal regulators, physical forces affecting the kidney are least well understood. Interstitial pressure and arterial pressure are clearly important in salt and water balance. Interstitial pressure is difficult to measure, especially in humans. Compared to the wealth of data on humoral influences, we have almost none on interstitial pressure, and although arterial pressure is easy to measure, we do not yet understand how its influence is transduced to affect sodium excretion.

## POTASSIUM METABOLISM

Potassium homeostasis depends on mechanisms that govern total body potassium and that maintain the critical ratio between the high intracellular and low extracellular potassium concentrations essential to the normal excitability of cell membranes.[64,65] When dietary potassium intake is augmented, there is a gradual increase in urinary potassium associated with an increased rate of aldosterone excretion, and balance is restored in 4 or 5 days.[66] The delayed excretion of the potassium load is associated with an appreciable rise in the plasma potassium concentration. If high intake is prolonged, a state of "potassium tolerance" develops in which an increment in potassium intake is excreted promptly without the usual rise in plasma potassium level. These renal adaptations are facilitated by, but not dependent on, the kaliuretic effect of aldosterone. Several renal mechanisms operate independently of aldosterone to promote the excretion of a potassium load or to contribute to potassium tolerance. Other renal mechanisms are involved in potassium conservation. In the face of severe extrarenal losses, urinary potassium excretion can fall to negligible quantities.

The kidney is incapable of responding sufficiently promptly to defend against the threat of hyperkalemia imposed by the sudden influx of large amounts of potassium that may be ingested with some foods (e.g., meat). A single meal may provide more potassium than the total amount in the extracellular fluid. Moment-to-moment adjustments are accomplished by increasing the cellular uptake of potassium under the influence of insulin and epinephrine. Thus, external potassium balance is controlled by relatively ponderous renal mechanisms that are largely aldosterone-dependent, whereas internal balance is regulated by insulin and adrenergic agents that have rapid, direct effects on the cellular uptake of potassium.

Potassium excretion by the kidneys is the result of glomerular filtration, tubular reabsorption, and tubular secretion. Most of the potassium filtered at the glomerulus (approximately 65%) is reabsorbed by the proximal tubule.[67] Reabsorption at the proximal tubule is passive, closely following water and sodium reabsorption. A significant amount of further reabsorption of potassium occurs in the thick ascending limb of the loop of Henle, mediated by a $Na^+/K^+$-2Cl cotransporter.[68] This transporter is the target of loop diuretics such as furosemide and bumetanide.

Potassium secretion, starting in the thick ascending limb of the loop of Henle and continuing in the cortical collecting duct, is mediated by potassium channels termed *ROM K*. These channels allow for the preferential movement of potassium, powered by a favorable electrochemical gradient.[69] Under normal conditions, potassium secretion by the distal tubule, and especially the cortical collecting duct, contributes significantly to net urinary potassium excretion. The excreted amount can be equivalent to 20% of the filtered load, although it is not derived from the potassium filtered at the glomerulus.[70] Another important potassium transporter, a hydrogen/potassium ATPase, results in the movement of hydrogen ions out of the intercalated cells of the cortical collecting duct and the movement of potassium into these cells. Potassium secretion also is directly related to urine flow rate and to blood pH. In summary, tubular secretion of potassium in the distal nephron is influenced by mineralocorticoid activity, distal sodium delivery, urine flow rate, and acid-base status.

## PATHOPHYSIOLOGY

### EFFECTS OF EXCESS MINERALOCORTICOID ACTIVITY

Mineralocorticoids increase renal sodium reabsorption and potassium secretion, but the syndrome of mineralocorticoid excess does not always include all of the logical sequelae of these classical effects of the steroid. For example, there is no edema; instead, the syndrome is usually marked by hypokalemia and hypertension, and even these manifestations are not found in all cases. Other possible components of the full-blown syndrome include metabolic alkalosis and mild impairment of renal concentrating ability. In syndromes of mineralocorticoid excess, sodium balance is normal despite continued exposure to high concentrations of the steroid. The apparent refractoriness to the sodium-retaining action of mineralocorticoids has been termed *mineralocorticoid escape.*

During mineralocorticoid escape, proximal tubular reabsorption of sodium is suppressed by volume hyperexpansion, which releases ANP, and by increased arterial pressure. ANP increases renal sodium excretion directly, and increased arterial pressure drives sodium and water excretion by pressure natriuresis.[62] The renal response during mineralocorticoid escape does not differ fundamentally from that during prolonged high salt intake, but excessive mineralocorticoid causes a greater increase in blood volume and blood pressure than excessive sodium ingestion. In other words, mineralocorticoids shift the pressure-natriuresis relationship to higher pressures.

The escape phenomenon is not caused by refractoriness of target sites in the nephron to mineralocorticoid action. The sodium-retaining effect on the distal tubule is mitigated by the high flux of sodium to that site. This flux results from decreased proximal sodium reabsorption. Enhanced excretion of potassium and hydrogen ions (caused by the mineralocorticoid) is not diminished and may even be increased by the increased sodium delivered to the distal nephron. Overt edema does not occur because cumulative sodium retention usually is limited to 200 to 300 mEq, and aldosterone has no direct effect to increase capillary permeability.

The small accumulation of body sodium and the large loss of potassium characteristic of primary aldosteronism can be reproduced by administering mineralocorticoids to normal subjects. Exogenous mineralocorticoids, however, have a variable effect on blood pressure when administered to humans.[71] The increase in pressure is related to volume hyperexpansion and can be prevented by restricting salt intake. Some portion of mineralocorticoid-induced hypertension may be caused by direct effects of the steroid on vascular smooth muscle.

Mineralocorticoids also increase secretion of hydrogen ions in the distal nephron by an exchange process that depends on the rate of active sodium transport. The medullary collecting duct is the major acidification site. Hydrogen ion secretion in this segment is increased by aldosterone but does not depend on sodium transport.[72] Mineralocorticoids preferentially enhance tubular secretion of potassium ions, but hydrogen ion secretion progressively increases as potassium depletion develops. Accordingly, generation of metabolic alkalosis in the syndrome of mineralocorticoid excess can be moderated or prevented if potassium depletion is avoided by providing supplemental potassium chloride.[73] Volume expansion depresses proximal bicarbonate reabsorption, lessening alkalosis; this is opposite to the alkalosis-promoting effect of volume contraction. Therefore, the metabolic alkalosis in the volume-expanded syndrome of mineralocorticoid excess tends to be less severe than the metabolic alkalosis induced by diuretics or by protracted vomiting.[74]

The syndrome of mineralocorticoid excess includes impaired ability to concentrate the urine, which is caused by the deleterious effect of potassium depletion on distal tubular cells, and inhibition of ADH production by volume expansion.[75]

Aldosterone excess is also described in Chapter 128.

## EFFECTS OF ALDOSTERONE DEFICIENCY

Impaired ability to conserve sodium is a characteristic feature of uncomplicated selective aldosterone deficiency. The severity of symptoms depends on the extent of sodium depletion; substantial depletion ultimately leads to hyponatremia with mild to moderate hyperkalemia. Severe hyperkalemia does not occur unless renal function is diminished by intrinsic renal disease.[76]

Patients with selective aldosterone deficiency who have normal renal function do not invariably develop acidosis, and they may be able to lower urinary pH normally in response to an acid load.[77] Urinary ammonium excretion is distinctly reduced in patients with aldosterone deficiency, and this abnormality has been ascribed to an inhibitory effect of hyperkalemia on urinary ammonium production. Acidosis in patients with aldosterone deficiency can be ameliorated by reducing potassium levels to normal with an exchange resin, which enables increased ammonium production.

The ability to tolerate mineralocorticoid deficiency is directly related to sodium intake. In normal subjects on a high sodium intake, aldosterone is not needed and is, in fact, suppressed to negligible levels. Providing salt supplements to patients with adrenal insufficiency produces a similar state. Moreover, sodium deprivation does not result in unremitting sodium loss in the absence of a mineralocorticoid. Nonaldosterone-dependent factors come into play, and renal sodium excretion decreases as volume depletion progresses.[78] Although sodium balance can be maintained, the plasma volume and blood pressure are extremely susceptible to changes in sodium intake or loss in the absence of a mineralocorticoid. Beyond a certain point, additional sodium losses or reduced dietary sodium intake results in rapid development of symptomatic hypovolemia; hypotension; and, eventually, hyponatremia and hyperkalemia.

Aldosterone deficiency is also described in Chapter 129.

## SECONDARY ALDOSTERONISM VS. COMPENSATORY RESPONSES TO VOLUME DEPLETION

The term *aldosteronism* should be restricted to the clinical syndrome that results from the effects of excessive amounts of aldosterone. An elevated secretion rate or plasma level of aldosterone does not, in itself, justify the conclusion that there is a clinically significant abnormality. Aldosterone secretion normally varies considerably in response to changes in dietary sodium intake or effective blood volume. With extreme sodium deprivation, vasodilatation, or vascular volume contraction, aldosterone secretion rates are markedly elevated, reaching levels as high as, or higher than, some cases of primary aldosteronism. Because of our inability to measure effective blood volume, it can be very difficult to determine in a given patient whether increased activity of the renin-angiotensin-aldosterone system reflects hyperfunction or a normal compensatory response.

*Secondary aldosteronism* is a pathologic state that results from overproduction of aldosterone caused by hyperactivity of the renin-angiotensin system. Typically, secondary aldosteronism is characterized by hypertension and metabolic features of mineralocorticoid excess such as hypokalemia and alkalosis. Secondary aldosteronism may be caused by disorders that compromise renal perfusion (e.g., renovascular hypertension or diffuse arteriolar sclerosis associated with severe hypertension). Reduced mean pressure in afferent glomerular arterioles activates the renin-angiotensin system which, in turn, stimulates aldosterone production. Although the renin-angiotensin system is activated by renal ischemia, cases of renovascular hypertension or of accelerated essential hypertension presenting with hypokalemic alkalosis are uncommon; hypokalemia is present in only 10% to 20% of patients.[79] Renin-secreting tumors are an extremely rare cause of secondary aldosteronism, and are associated with very high renin levels and severe hypokalemia.[80] Most of these tumors arise from elements of the juxtaglomerular apparatus, but they also may be ectopic in origin.

By contrast with secondary aldosteronism, the elevated level of aldosterone that occurs with sodium depletion does not lead to the development of hypertension or hypokalemia. The lack of kaliuresis is related to decreased distal tubular sodium delivery; proximal reabsorption is enhanced by hypovolemia. Thus, when aldosterone increases in response to sodium deprivation, it results in renal sodium retention unaccompanied by potassium wasting; the threat of volume depletion is successfully countered by an appropriate reduction in sodium excretion. Some clinical conditions in which renin activity and aldosterone secretion are perturbed in tandem are discussed in the following.

### Diuretic Therapy

Diuretics induce a net loss of body salt and water by interfering with transport processes at various nephron sites. The urinary potassium wasting and hypokalemia that result from chronic treatment with loop or thiazide diuretics exemplify a situation in which a compensatory response has undesirable consequences. Treatment with a diuretic activates the renin-angiotensin-aldosterone axis, which limits the saliuretic effect of the drug but also increases urinary potassium excretion. Potassium wasting occurs because inhibition of tubular sodium reabsorption by the diuretic increases sodium delivery to the distal nephron, where sodium-potassium exchange is greatly augmented by high levels of aldosterone. Salt balance is restored with a shrunken intravascular volume (at least initially), but potassium loss, hypokalemia, and alkalosis persist.

### Bartter's and Other Genetic Syndromes

Bartter's, Gitelman's, and Liddle's syndromes arise from defects in ion transporters or channels, primarily located in the distal tubule or the ascending limb of the loop of Henle. *Bartter's syndrome* is characterized by hypokalemic alkalosis, elevated plasma renin activity and aldosterone levels, and hyperplasia of the juxtaglomerular cells; however, blood pressures are normal. Typically, Bartter's syndrome patients also have hypercalciuria and normal magnesium levels. Prostaglandin production by the kidney is increased.

Antenatal Bartter's syndrome is a more severe variant, with polyhydramnios, prematurity, significant neonatal salt wasting and nephrocalcinosis, and renal insufficiency or failure. Classic Bartter's syndrome, with its presentation well after the neonatal period, typically does not result in renal failure. The majority of patients with Bartter's syndrome manifest an autosomal-recessive inheritance pattern.[81] At least four defects have been found. The most common is a defect in the $Na^+/K^+$-2Cl transporter of the thick ascending limb of the loop of Henle; this explains the solute wasting. A defect in the ROM K potassium channel causes another variant of Bartter's syndrome; this is less common than the $Na^+/K^+$-2Cl transport defect. Two other rare forms of Bartter's syndrome have defects in the basal lateral chloride channel and in the protein barttin, a chloride channel subunit. The barttin defect was described in a small set of families with antenatal Bartter's syndrome and sensorineural deafness.[82–85]

*Gitelman's syndrome* occurs in children and adults and is also inherited in an autosomal-recessive pattern. It is similar to Bartter's syndrome with two important differences: (1) very low calcium excretion (hypocalciuria); and (2) increased magnesium excretion with hypomagnesemia. The defect is in the thiazide-sensitive sodium chloride cotransporter in the distal tubule. Most patients with Gitelman's syndrome do not develop renal insufficiency or renal failure; and, of course, they do not develop nephrocalcinosis, because there is little calcium loss.[86] Both Bartter's and Gitelman's syndromes are marked by low or normal blood pressure. There is speculation that some patients with extreme sensitivity to diuretics may be heterozygous for a tubular defect found in these two syndromes (especially Gitelman's).

*Liddle's syndrome* is marked by severe hypertension. It generally appears in childhood, together with hypokalemic metabolic alkalosis. The defect is a constitutive activation of the epithelial sodium channel (ENaC) on the apical surface of the collecting duct. The syndrome is caused by a dominant mutation on chromosome 16.[87] This constitutive activation results in increased tubular sodium reabsorption and loss of potassium, independent of aldosterone. Renin and aldosterone are suppressed by the volume expansion caused by uncontrolled sodium reabsorption. Liddle's syndrome is ameliorated by amiloride, which inhibits the epithelial sodium channel that is overactive as a result of the mutation.

### Pregnancy

Normal pregnancy is characterized by markedly increased levels of aldosterone and DOC.[88] Nonetheless, pregnant women do not exhibit serum electrolyte changes typical of mineralocorticoid excess. Aldosterone secretion is regulated by angiotensin, as expected. Although extracellular and intravascular fluid volumes are greatly expanded in pregnancy, blood pressure actually falls during the first trimester, and responsiveness of the renin-angiotensin-aldosterone axis to postural change is exaggerated.[89,90] The prevailing view is that increased levels of renin activity and aldosterone in pregnancy represent a normal compensatory response to vascular underfilling.[91] The effective blood volume is reduced, despite the high absolute intravascular fluid volume, because of peripheral vasodilatation that is mediated largely by nitric oxide (NO) from the endothelium. NO synthase is activated by estrogen. Prostaglandins may also play a role in the expanded vascular capacity.[92] A decrease in plasma osmolality is a consistent finding in pregnancy; this may be related to high levels of ADH, which upregulates aquaporin-2 water channels in the collecting ducts.[93] Salt loss in pregnancy is promoted by progesterone, which inhibits the renal action of mineralocorticoids at the level of the mineralocorticoid receptor.[94]

The cause of hypertension and excessive sodium retention in pre-eclampsia is obscure. Aldosterone secretion and activity of the renin-angiotensin-aldosterone system are decreased. This congruent suppression is probably the result of the disease itself, which increases sodium retention and promotes vasoconstriction. Generalized dysfunction of the endothelium has been well demonstrated in pre-eclampsia. This leads to decreased production of vasodilators (e.g., NO and prostaglandin) and increased production of vasoconstrictors (e.g., thromboxane $A_2$ and endothelin). One result of these changes is increased vascular sensitivity to angiotensin II, norepinephrine, and ADH, as well as a decrease in GFR.[92,95] The clinical picture includes proteinuria, hypertension, and edema.

A mutation in the mineralocorticoid receptor has been described that increases intrinsic receptor activity and expands its specificity to include progesterone as an agonist.[96] Patients with this mutation experience hypertension aggravated by pregnancy, because the elevated progesterone levels increase sodium reabsorption instead of reducing it.

### EDEMATOUS DISORDERS

Congestive heart failure, hepatic cirrhosis, and nephrotic syndromes are characterized by retention of sodium and water and by peripheral edema and effusions. Activity of the renin-angiotensin-aldosterone system is often, but not always, increased. Sodium retention in these disorders can occur in the absence of elevated aldosterone levels, and even in those cases where aldosterone is increased, it may not account for all of the sodium retention. The pathophysiology of these disorders is complex. As mentioned previously, even when aldosterone levels are extremely high as a result of adrenal adenomas, edema does not occur. Factors other than the renin-angiotensin-aldosterone system that regulate volume and vascular permeability may participate in edema formation. These may include the sympathetic nervous system, ADH, vasoactive autacoids, and natriuretic factors.[95,97,98]

Heart failure, aside from high-output failure, lowers cardiac output and peripheral vascular perfusion. Peripheral edema is common. The absolute blood volume is usually increased; but the effective blood volume is diminished, which activates neurohumoral effectors. These effectors, which include angiotensin, aldosterone, ADH, endothelin, and catecholamines, promote retention of salt and water, pulmonary congestion, and vasoconstriction.[98] Vasoconstriction is aggravated by impaired endothelial release of vasodilators. Sodium retention and vasoconstriction add to cardiac afterload and preload, which may further burden the compromised heart.

Hyponatremia is a common occurrence in severe congestive failure, and its development is closely correlated with increased activity of the renin-angiotensin-aldosterone system.[98] Circulating levels of ANP are markedly elevated in patients with CHF and contribute to the hyponatremia.[99] Angiotensin activates receptors in the brain that stimulate thirst and the release of ADH, promoting free water retention. Treatment with ACE inhibitors often relieves the hyponatremia and decreases vascular congestion. The sodium retention and edema that occur in CHF are not caused by impaired ability of the damaged heart to secrete ANP; secretion of ANP is usually increased. On the other hand, the natriuretic and diuretic responses to infused ANP are attenuated in animals with low-output heart failure.[45,49] The endocrine aspects of heart failure are discussed in Chapter 134.

Cirrhosis causes splanchnic vasodilatation; increased production of NO probably plays a role. Splanchnic pooling activates counter-regulatory mechanisms including the renin-angiotensin-aldosterone axis, sympathetic nervous system, and ADH. With decompensation, vasodilatation worsens and the counter-regulatory hormones increase.[97] Low albumin contributes to peripheral edema and ascites. In the final stage of cirrhosis, marked renal vasoconstriction occurs, adding renal failure to hepatic failure (i.e., the hepatorenal syndrome).

The nephrotic syndrome reduces blood volume by the loss of plasma osmotic pressure. This alone would stimulate sodium-retaining counter-regulatory mechanisms. However, some cases of nephrotic syndrome are accompanied by sodium and water retention as a result of the intrinsic renal abnormality.[99] In such cases of hypervolemic nephrotic syndrome, plasma renin activity and aldosterone secretion are suppressed, in sharp contrast to the more common "classic" cases of the nephrotic syndrome.[95]

## Acknowledgment
We wish to thank Dr. Edward Ehrlich for his contributions to previous editions.

## REFERENCES

1. Pitts RF: Volume and composition of the body fluids. In Pitts RF (ed): Physiology of the Kidney and Body Fluids. St Louis, Mosby-Year Book, 1974, pp 11–35.
2. Senkfer SI, Anger MS, Berl T: Control of water metabolism. In Massry SG, Glasscok RJ (eds): Textbook of Nephrology. Baltimore, Williams & Wilkins, 1995, pp 258–265.
3. Rodriguez RA, Humphreys RA: Control of sodium excretion. In Massry SG, Glasscock RJ (eds): Textbook of Nephrology. Baltimore, Williams & Wilkins, 1995, pp 266–275.
4. Seely JF, Levy M: Control of extracellular fluid volume. In Brenner BM, Rector FC Jr (eds): The Kidney: Regulation of Renal Sodium Secretion, 2d ed. Philadelphia, WB Saunders, 1981, pp 371–407.
5. Dworkin LD, Brenner BM: The biophysical basis of glomerular function in the kidney. In Seldin DW, Geibisch G (eds): Physiology and Pathophysiology. New York, Raven Press, 1992.
6. Berry CA, Rector FC Jr: Mechanisms of proximal NaCl reabsorption in the proximal tubule of the mammalian kidney. Semin Nephrol 11:86–100, 1991.
7. Briggs JP, Schnermann J: The glomerulotubular feedback mechanism: Functional and biochemical aspects. Annu Rev Physiol 49:251–268, 1986.
8. Greger R: Ion transport mechanisms in the thick ascending limb of Henle's loop of the mammalian nephron. Physiol Rev 65:760–797, 1985.
9. Reeves WB, Andreoli TE: Tubular sodium transport. In Schrier RW, Gottschalk CW (eds): Diseases of the Kidney. Boston, Little, Brown, 1993, pp 139–179.
10. O'Neil RG: Aldosterone regulation of sodium and potassium transport in the cortical collecting duct. Semin Nephrol 10:365–374, 1990.
11. Mulrow PJ, Forman BH: The tissue effects of mineralocorticoids. Am J Med 53:561–572, 1972.
12. Lassiter WE, Gottschalk CW: Regulation of water balance: Urine concentration and dilution. In Schrier RW, Gottschalk CW (eds): Diseases of the Kidney. Boston, Little, Brown, 1993, pp 139–179.
13. Marver D, Kokko JP: Renal target sites and the mechanism of action of aldosterone. Miner Electrolyte Metab 9:1–18, 1983.
14. Fanestil DD, Park CS: Steroid hormones and the kidney. Annu Rev Physiol 46:637–649, 1981.
15. Funder JW, Pearce PT, Smith R, et al: Mineralocorticoid action: Target tissue specificity is enzyme, not receptor, mediated. Science 242:583–585, 1988.
16. Rossier BC: Mechanism of action of mineralocorticoid hormones. Endocr Res 15:203–226, 1989.
17. Gomez-Sanchez CE: Mineralocorticoid biosynthetic pathways and hypertension. In Levin ER, Nadler JL (eds): Endocrinology of Cardiovascular Function. Boston, Kluwer Academic, 1998, pp 311–325.
18. Melby JC, Dale SL, Wilson TE: 18-Hydroxy-11-deoxycorticosterone in human hypertension. Circ Res 28(Suppl 2):143–152, 1971.
19. Fraser R, Lantos CP: 18-Hydroxycorticosterone: A review. J Steroid Biochem 9:273–286, 1978.
20. Gomez-Sanchez CE, Holland OB, Murray BA, et al: 19-Nordeoxycorticosterone: A potent mineralocorticoid isolated from the urine of rats with regenerating adrenals. Endocrinology 105:708–711, 1979.
21. Morris DJ, Kenyon CJ, Latif SA, et al: The possible biological role of aldosterone metabolities. Hypertension 5(Suppl 1):I35–I40, 1983.
22. Stewart PM, Carrie JET, Shackleton CHL, et al: Syndrome of apparent mineralocorticoid excess: A defect in the cortisol-cortisone shuttle. J Clin Invest 82:340–349, 1988.
23. Monder C, Stewart PM, Lakhmi I, et al: Licorice inhibits corticosteroid 11-beta dehydrogenase of rat kidney and liver. In vivo and in vitro studies. Endocrinology 125:1046–1053, 1989.
24. Gomez-Sanchez CE, Gomez-Sanchez EP, Smith JS, et al: Receptor binding and biologic activity of 18-oxocortisol. Endocrinology 116:6–10, 1985.
25. Davis JO: The control of renin release. Am J Med 55:333–350, 1973.
26. Gibbons GH, Dzau VJ, Farhi ER, et al: Interaction of signals influencing renin release. Annu Rev Physiol 46:291–308, 1984.
27. Goodfriend TL, Peach MJ: Angiotensin III: (des-aspartic acid¹)-angiotensin II: Evidence and speculation for its role as an important agonist in the renin-angiotensin system. Circ Res 36–37(Suppl 1):I38–I48, 1975.
28. Goodfriend TL, Elliott ME, Catt KJ: Angiotensin receptors and their antagonists. N Engl J Med 334:1649–1654, 1996.
29. Ganong WF: The brain renin-angiotensin system. Annu Rev Physiol 46:17–31, 1984.
30. Mulrow PJ: Adrenal renin: A possible local regulator of aldosterone production. Yale J Biol Med 62:503–510, 1989.
31. Brunner HR, Baer L, Sealey J, et al: The influence of potassium administration and potassium deprivation on plasma renin in normal and hypertensive subjects. J Clin Invest 49:2123–2138, 1970.
32. Himathongkam T, Dluhy RG, Williams GH: Potassium-aldosterone-renin interrelationships. J Clin Endocrinol Metab 41:153–159, 1975.
33. Quinn SJ, Williams GH: Regulation of aldosterone secretion. Annu Rev Physiol 50:409–426, 1988.
34. Pratt JH: Role of angiotensin II in potassium-mediated stimulation of aldosterone secretion in the dog. J Clin Invest 70:667–672, 1982.
35. Young DB, Smith MJ Jr, Jackson TE, et al: Multiplicative interaction between angiotensin II and K concentration in stimulation of aldosterone. Am J Physiol 247:E328–E335, 1984.
36. Müller J, Lauber M: Regulation of aldosterone biosynthesis: A continual challenge. Am J Hypertens 4:280–282, 1991.
37. Aguilera G, Hauger RL, Catt KJ: Control of aldosterone secretion during sodium restriction: Adrenal receptor regulation and increased adrenal sensitivity to angiotensin II. Proc Natl Acad Sci U S A 75:975–979, 1978.
38. Seeley EW, Conlin PR, Brent GA, et al: Adrenocorticotropin stimulation of aldosterone: Prolonged continuous versus pulsatile infusion. J Clin Endocrinol Metab 69:1028–1032, 1989.
39. Abayasekara DRE, Vazir H, Whitehouse BJ, et al: Studies on the mechanisms of ACTH-induced inhibition of aldosterone biosynthesis in the rat adrenal cortex. J Endocrinol 122:625–632, 1989.
40. Ehrhart-Bornstein M, Hinson J, Bornstein S, et al: Intraadrenal interactions in the regulation of adrenocortical steroidogenesis. Endocr Rev 19:101–143, 1998.
41. Nussdorfer GG: Paracrine control of adrenal cortical function by medullary chromaffin cells. Pharmacol Rev 48:495–530, 1996.
42. Campbell DJ, Mendelsohn FAO, Adam WR, et al: Is aldosterone secretion under dopaminergic control? Circ Res 49:1217–1227, 1981.
43. Goodfriend TF, Ball DL, Elliott ME, et al: Fatty acids are endogenous regulators of

aldosterone secretion. Endocrinology 128:2511–2519, 1991.

44. Kater CE, Biglieri EG, Brust N, et al: Stimulation and suppression of the mineralocorticoid hormones in normal subjects and adrenocortical disorders. Endocr Rev 10:149–164, 1989.

45. Rubattu S, Volpe M: The atrial natriuretic peptide: A changing view. J Hypertens 19:1923–1931, 2001.

46. Schoner W: Endogenous cardiac glycosides, a new class of steroid hormones. Eur J Biochem 269:2440–2448, 2002.

47. Silberbach M, Roberts CT Jr: Natriuretic peptide signaling. Molecular and cellular pathways to growth regulation. Cell Signal 13:221–231, 2001.

48. Ruskoaho H, Leskinen H, Magga J, et al: Mechanisms of mechanical load-induced atrial natriuretic peptide secretion: Role of endothelin, nitric oxide, and angiotensin II. J Mol Med 75:876–885, 1997.

49. Boomsma F, van den Meiracker AH: Plasma A- and B-type natriuretic peptides: Physiology, methodology and clinical use. Cardiovasc Res 51:442–449, 2001.

50. Richards AM: The renin-angiotensin-aldosterone system and the cardiac natriuretic peptides. Heart 76(Suppl 3):36–44, 1996.

51. Prins BA, Biesiada E, Levin ER: Natriuretic peptides and hypertension. Curr Opin Nephrol Hypertens 5:170–173, 1996.

52. Mills RM, Hobbs RE, Young JB: "BNP" for heart failure: Role of nesiritide in cardiovascular therapeutics. CHF 8:270–273, 2002.

53. Fowkes RC, McArdle CA: C-type natriuretic peptide: An important neuroendocrine regulator? Trends Endocrinol Metab 11:333–338, 2000.

54. Lee J, de Wardener HE: Neurosecretion and sodium excretion. Kidney Int 6:323–330, 1974.

55. Hamlyn JM, Lu Z-R, Manunta P, et al: Observations on the nature, biosynthesis, secretion and significance of endogenous ouabain. Clin Exp Hypertens 20:523–533, 1998.

56. DiBona GF: Neural control of renal function: Cardiovascular implications. Hypertension 13:539–551, 1989.

57. DiBona GF: Renal dopamine containing nerves: What is their functional significance? Am J Hypertens 3:645–695, 1990.

58. Carmines PK, Fleming JT: Control of the renal microvasculature by vasoactive peptides. FASEB J 4:3300–3307, 1990.

59. Rabkin R: Hormones and the kidney. In Schrier RW, Gottschalk CW (eds): Diseases of the Kidney. Boston, Little, Brown, 1993, pp 283–331.

60. Morel F: Regulation of kidney function by hormones: A new approach. Recent Prog Horm Res 39:271–291, 1983.

61. Guyton AC: Blood pressure control: Special role of the kidneys and body fluids. Science 252:1813–1816, 1991.

62. Cowley AW Jr: Long-term control of arterial blood pressure. Physiol Rev 72:231–300, 1992.

63. Schneider ED, Kramer RE: Effect of osmolality on angiotensin-stimulated aldosterone production by primary cultures of bovine adrenal glomerulosa cells. Biochem Biophys Res Commun 139:46–51, 1986.

64. Rabinowitz L: Homeostatic regulation of potassium excretion. J Hypertens 7:433–442, 1989.

65. Giebisch C, Malnic G, Berliner RW: Control of renal potassium excretion. In Brenner BM, Rector FC Jr (eds): The Kidney, 5th ed. Philadelphia, WB Saunders, 1996, pp 371–407.

66. Silva P, Brown RS, Epstein FH: Adaptation to potassium. Kidney Int 11:466–475, 1977.

67. Solomon S: Absolute rates of sodium and potassium reabsorption by proximal tubule of immature rat. Biol Neonate 25:340, 1974.

68. Malnic G, Klose RM, Giebisch G: Micropuncture studies of distal tubular potassium and sodium transport in rat nephron. Am J Physiol 211:529, 1966.

69. Giebisch G: Physiological roles of renal potassium channels. Semin Nephrol 19:458, 1999.

70. Giebisch G: Renal potassium transport: Mechanisms and regulation. Am J Physiol 274:F817, 1998.

71. Schalekamp MA, Wenting GJ, Man In'T, Veld AJ: Pathogenesis of mineralocorticoid hypertension. J Clin Endocrinol Metab 10:397–418, 1981.

72. Stone DK, Cider BP, Xiao Song X: Aldosterone and urinary acidification. Semin Nephrol 10:375–379, 1990.

73. Seldin DW, Rector FC Jr: Symposium on acid-base homeostasis: The generation and maintenance of metabolic alkalosis. Kidney Int 1:306–321, 1972.

74. Kurtzman NA: Regulation of renal bicarbonate reabsorption by extracellular volume. J Clin Invest 49:586–595, 1970.

75. Hollander W Jr, Blyth WB: Nephropathy of potassium depletion. In Strauss MB, Welt LG (eds): Diseases of the Kidney. Boston, Little, Brown, 1971, p 592.

76. Hills AG: Pathogenesis of hyperkalemia in hypoaldosteronism. J Clin Endocrinol Metab 29:988–989, 1969.

77. Williams GH: Aldosterone, potassium and acidosis. N Engl J Med 294:392–393, 1976.

78. Lipsett MB, Pearson OH: Sodium depletion in adrenalectomized humans. J Clin Invest 37:1394–1402, 1958.

79. Dustan H: Renal arterial disease and hypertension. Med Clin North Am 81:1199–1212, 1997.

80. Corry DB, Tuck ML: Secondary aldosteronism. Endocrinol Metab Clin North Am 24:511–529, 1995.

81. Rodriguez-Soriano J: Bartter's and related syndromes: The puzzle is almost solved. Pediatr Nephrol 12:315, 1998.

82. Simon DB, Caret FE, Hamdan JM, et al: Bartter's syndrome, hypokalemic alkalosis with hypercalciuria is caused by mutations in the Na-K-2Cl transporter NKCC2. Nat Genet 13:183–188, 1996.

83. Lorenz JN, Baird NR, Judd LN, et al: Impaired renal Na-Cl absorption in mice lacking the ROM K potassium channel, a model for type II Bartter's syndrome. J Biol Chem 277:37871–37880, 2002.

84. Konrad M, Vollmer M, Lemmink HH, et al: Mutations in the chloride channel gene CLCNKB as a cause of classic Bartter's syndrome. J Am Soc Nephrol 11:1449–1459, 2000.

85. Vollmer M, Jeck N, Lemmink HH, et al: Antenatal Bartter's syndrome with sensorineural deafness: Refinement of the locus on chromosome 1p31. Nephrol Dial Transplant 15:970–974, 2000.

86. Simon DB, Nelson-Williams C, Bia MJ, et al: Gitelman's as a variant of Bartter's syndrome, inherited hyperkalemic alkalosis is caused by mutations in the thiazide sensitive Na-Cl co-transporter. Nat Genet 12:24–30, 1996.

87. Abriel H, Loffing J, Rebhum JF, et al: Defective regulation of the epithelial Na channel by Nedd4 in Liddle's syndrome. J Clin Invest 103:667–673, 1999.

88. Ehrlich EN, Oparil S, Lindheimer MD: Role of the augmented aldosterone secretion in regulation of volume homeostasis in pregnancy. In Fregly MJ, Fregly MS (eds): Oral Contraceptives and High Blood Pressure. Gainesville, FL, Dolphin, 1974, pp 274–293.

89. Lindheimer MD, del Greco F, Ehrlich EN: Postural effects on Na and steroid excretion, and serum renin activity during pregnancy. J Appl Physiol 35:343–348, 1973.

90. Wilson M, Morganti AA, Zervoudakis J, et al: Blood pressure, the renin-aldosterone system and sex steroids throughout normal pregnancy. Am J Med 68:97–104, 1980.

91. Schrier RW, Dürr JA: Pregnancy: An overfill or underfill state. Am J Kidney Dis 9:284–289, 1987.

92. Davison JM: Edema in pregnancy. Kidney Int Suppl 51(suppl 59):S90–S96, 1997.

93. Schrier RW, Ohara M, Rogachev B, et al: Aquaporin-2 water channels and vasopressin antagonists in edematous disorders. Mol Genetics Metab 65:255–263, 1998.

94. Landau RL, Lugibihl K: Inhibition of the sodium retaining influence of aldosterone by progesterone. J Clin Endocrinol Metab 18:1237–1245, 1958.

95. Martin P-Y, Schrier RW: Renal sodium excretion and edematous disorders. Endocrinol Metab Clin North Am 24:459–479, 1995.

96. Geller DS, Farhi A, Pinkerton N, et al: Activating mineralocorticoid receptor mutation in hypertension exacerbated by pregnancy. Science 289:119–123, 2000.

97. Suzuki H, Stanley AJ: Current management and novel therapeutic strategies for refractory ascites and hepatorenal syndrome. Q J Med 94:293–300, 2001.

98. Lilly LS, Dzau VJ, Williams GH, et al: Hyponatremia in congestive heart failure: Implications for neurohumoral activation and responses to orthostasis. J Clin Endocrinol Metab 59:924–930, 1984.

99. Schrier RW: Pathogenesis of sodium and water retention in high-output and low-output cardiac failure, nephrotic syndrome, cirrhosis, and pregnancy: Part one. N Engl J Med 319:1065–1071, 1988.

# Neurohormonal Alterations in Heart Failure

## *Alan Maisel, Meenakshi A. Bhalla, and Vikas Bhalla*

RENIN-ANGIOTENSIN-ALDOSTERONE SYSTEM

SYMPATHETIC NERVOUS SYSTEM

ANTIDIURETIC HORMONE

ENDOTHELIN

INSULIN AND OTHER METABOLIC
NEUROHORMONAL CHANGES IN CHF

THE NATRIURETIC PEPTIDE FAMILY
Physiologic Effects of BNP

NEUROHORMONES AS CARDIAC MARKERS

CONCLUSION

Congestive heart failure (CHF) is a complex clinical syndrome characterized by dysfunction of the left, right, or both ventricles; it results in the impairment of the heart's ability to circulate blood at a rate sufficient to maintain the metabolic needs of peripheral tissues and various organs. The causes for the loss of a critical amount of functioning myocardium could be acute myocardial infarction (MI); prolonged cardiovascular stress (e.g., hypertension or valvular disease); toxins (e.g., alcohol abuse); or infection. In some cases, there is no apparent cause (idiopathic cardiomyopathy).

This syndrome is accompanied by exercise intolerance; shortness of breath (i.e., dyspnea at rest and during exertion, orthopnea, or paroxysmal nocturnal dyspnea); and fluid retention. The compensatory hemodynamic and neurohumoral mechanisms triggered by poor cardiac output and decreased renal perfusion result in jugular vein distension, peripheral pitting edema, sinus tachycardia, basal rales, cardiomegaly, S3 gallop sound, and liver enlargement; these lead to tremendous morbidity and shortened survival. Late stage heart failure often indicates that all reserve capacity and compensatory mechanisms of the myocardium and peripheral circulation have been exhausted.

Several complex interactions between myocardial hemodynamic and neurohumoral compensatory events follow the initial cardiac damage, together giving rise to a clinical syndrome characterized by elevated intracardiac pressures, cardiac hypertrophy, reduced cardiac output, and diminished functional reserve. These mechanisms include activation of the renin-angiotensin-aldosterone system (RAS), natriuretic peptide system, sympathetic nervous system (SNS), endothelins, and other neurohormonal factors. Thus, cardiorenal, hemodynamic, and neurohormonal factors all play a role in the pathogenesis of heart failure.[1] Activation of these compensatory mechanisms leads to progressive worsening of left ventricular function, in part by increasing remodeling and the overall work of the heart. The development of heart failure is complicated by a complex balance between vasodilatory and vasoconstrictive influences (Fig. 134-1). Natriuresis, diuresis, and vasodilatory mechanisms work to relieve stress on the heart, but are essentially overwhelmed by the SNS, RAS, and endothelins; this leads to peripheral vasoconstriction and hemodynamic alterations. The end result is progressive deterioration of heart function with worsened symptoms of heart failure (i.e., dyspnea, peripheral edema, tachycardia, and volume overload). This chapter discusses some of the important neurohormonal factors involved in heart failure.

Because heart failure results from the impairment of the heart's ability to circulate blood at a rate sufficient to maintain the metabolic needs of the body, the initial neurohormonal changes are geared toward:

1. Restoration of cardiac output by increasing myocardial contractility, heart rate, and blood volume.
2. Increasing the systemic blood pressure by vasoconstriction to maintain perfusion to vital organs.

Mentioned in the following are some of the prominent neurohormonal systems that play a part in pathogenesis of heart failure (HF).

### RENIN-ANGIOTENSIN-ALDOSTERONE SYSTEM

The renin-angiotensin-aldosterone system is a classic endocrine system, and angiotensin II is the primary effector hormone. Angiotensin II is an oligopeptide of eight amino acids, formed from its original precursor, angiotensinogen, by a series of two enzymatic cleavages. Angiotensinogen is released into the circulation by the liver. Renin, produced by the kidney in response to glomerular hypoperfusion, catalyzes cleavage of angiotensinogen to angiotensin I, a decapeptide. Angiotensin I is in turn cleaved by angiotensin-converting enzyme (ACE) to produce the octapeptide angiotensin II. There are two well-described subtypes of angiotensin II receptors, designated AT1 and AT2, both of which are present in the heart and have a high affinity for angiotensin II.[2] The AT1 subtype mediates the vasoconstrictor effect of angiotensin II, and is generally thought to mediate angiotensin II–induced growth in the left ventricle and the arterial wall.[3] The AT1 subtype is further subdivided into AT1A and AT1B.

The actions of the AT2 receptor are less well understood. The circulating angiotensin II:

- Promotes sodium and water reabsorption, thereby increasing intravascular fluid volume, which in turn increases cardiac preload and, therefore, stroke volume.
- Causes systemic arteriolar vasoconstriction, increasing vascular resistance and cardiac afterload.
- Affects the autonomic nervous system, stimulating the sympathetic nervous system and reducing vagal activity.[4]

### SYMPATHETIC NERVOUS SYSTEM

Activation of the sympathetic nervous system is one of the first responses to a decrease in cardiac output; it results in both increased release and decreased uptake of norepinephrine (NE) at adrenergic nerve endings.

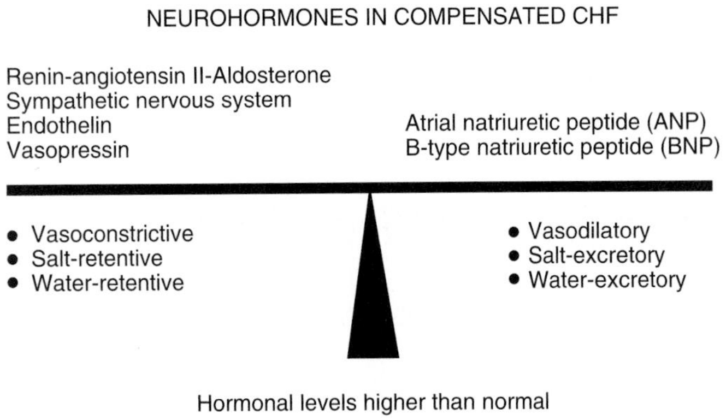

## NEUROHORMONES IN COMPENSATED CHF

Renin-angiotensin II-Aldosterone
Sympathetic nervous system
Endothelin                        Atrial natriuretic peptide (ANP)
Vasopressin                       B-type natriuretic peptide (BNP)

- Vasoconstrictive                 • Vasodilatory
- Salt-retentive                   • Salt-excretory
- Water-retentive                  • Water-excretory

Hormonal levels higher than normal

*Figure 134-1*   The complex balance between vasodilatory and vasoconstrictive influences in CHF.

Increased sympathetic activity leads to systemic and pulmonary vasoconstriction and enhanced venous tone, thereby increasing ventricular preload, which initially helps in maintaining systemic blood pressure. Renal vasoconstriction (mediated by both NE and angiotensin II), primarily at the efferent arteriole, produces an increase in filtration fraction that allows glomerular filtration to be relatively well maintained despite a fall in renal blood flow. Both NE and angiotensin II also stimulate proximal tubular sodium reabsorption, which further contributes to the sodium retention. Initially, the catecholamine-induced augmentation of ventricular contractility and heart rate helps maintain cardiac output, particularly during exercise. However, with progressive worsening of ventricular function, these mechanisms are no longer sufficient.

Sympathetic activation results in an increase in the plasma NE concentration, which correlates directly with the severity of the cardiac dysfunction and correlates inversely with survival.[1] The Val-HeFT trial, involving more than 4000 patients, found that those with an initial plasma NE concentration in the highest quartile (572 pg/mL) had a significantly higher mortality rate at 2 years than did those with an initial plasma NE concentration in the lowest quartile (< 274 pg/mL) (24.2% vs. 13.8%).[5]

## ANTIDIURETIC HORMONE

Low cardiac output in heart failure activates the carotid sinus baroreceptors, which leads to enhanced release of antidiuretic hormone (ADH) and stimulation of thirst. Elevated levels of ADH via stimulation of the V1A receptor, found on vascular smooth muscle cells, may contribute to the increase in systemic vascular resistance in HF, and also promote water retention via the V2 receptor by enhancing water reabsorption in the collecting tubules. The combination of decreased water excretion and increased water intake via thirst often leads to a fall in the plasma sodium concentration. The severity of these defects tends to parallel the severity of the heart failure. As a result, the degree of hyponatremia is an important prognostic factor in these patients.

A study of 142 patients with class III/IV heart failure who were treated with intravenous conivaptan, a dual V1A/V2 vasopressin receptor antagonist, supports the role of ADH in HF.[6] In patients with advanced heart failure, vasopressin receptor antagonism with conivaptan, as compared with placebo, resulted in favorable changes in hemodynamics and urine output without affecting cardiac index, systemic or pulmonary vascular resistance, blood pressure, or heart rate.

## ENDOTHELIN

Endothelin, produced by the vascular endothelium, may contribute to the regulation of myocardial function, vascular tone, and peripheral resistance in HF. ET-1, the predominant isoform synthesized in the human vasculature, is the most potent vasoconstrictor. Plasma endothelin concentrations are increased in patients with HF, and angiotensin II may contribute to the high circulating levels in HF.[7-9] This has led to the evaluation of endothelin inhibition as a therapy for heart failure.

## INSULIN AND OTHER METABOLIC NEUROHORMONAL CHANGES IN CHF

Swan and colleagues[10] demonstrated that CHF is associated with marked insulin resistance, and that it is also characterized by both fasting and stimulated hyperinsulinemia. They found a 58% reduction in insulin sensitivity in patients with CHF and a 131% increase in fasting insulin concentration compared with values in a healthy control group. Increased severity of CHF in terms of peak VO2 (i.e., functional exercise capacity) was significantly related to increased insulin resistance. Resistance to the action of insulin at the myocardial level may reduce the availability of glucose as an energy source for the heart muscle cells; and, along with its marked antinatriuretic effect, insulin[11] could in the long term be detrimental to the clinical condition of patients with CHF. Similarly, Anker and colleagues[12] showed that compared with control subjects and noncachectic patients, cachectic CHF patients had increased norepinephrine, epinephrine, cortisol, tumor necrosis factor (TNF)-α, and human growth hormone; and that insulin, cortisol, TNF-α, and norepinephrine correlated independently with wasting in CHF. This led to evaluation of the usefulness of insulin sensitization as a therapy for heart failure, and there are new drugs currently under evaluation in the phase 3 trials.

## THE NATRIURETIC PEPTIDE FAMILY

The recognition of role of B-type natriuretic peptide as an objective marker for the diagnosis, severity, and prognosis of CHF has generated great interest in the natriuretic peptide family (see also Chapter 132). There are three major natriuretic peptides: atrial (A-type) natriuretic peptide (ANP) and B-type natriuretic peptide (BNP) are of myocardial cell origin, whereas C-type natriuretic peptide (CNP) is of endothelial origin (Fig. 134-2). All three major natriuretic peptides share a common 17-amino acid ring structure, and are secreted in an attempt to correct the vasoconstrictive, sodium retaining, antidiuretic, and antifibrotic effects caused by the neurohormonal imbalance (Fig. 134-3).

The natriuretic peptides exert their action through binding to high-affinity receptors, mainly on endothelial cells and vascular smooth muscle cells, but also other target cells. Three distinct natriuretic peptide receptors (NPRs) known as NPR A, NPR B, and NPR C have been identified in mammalian tissues.[13] NPR A and NPR B are structurally similar, with a 44% homology in the ligand-binding domain.[14,15] Both types of receptors utilize a cyclic guanosine monophosphate-signaling cascade.[16] NPR B is mostly found in the brain, whereas NPR A is more commonly located in large blood vessels. Both receptor types are also found in the adrenal glands and kidneys. NPR A binds preferentially to ANP, but it also binds to BNP. On the other hand, CNP is the natural ligand for B receptors.

BNP is cleared from the circulation through two distinct mechanisms: (1) endocytosis; and (2) enzymatic degradation

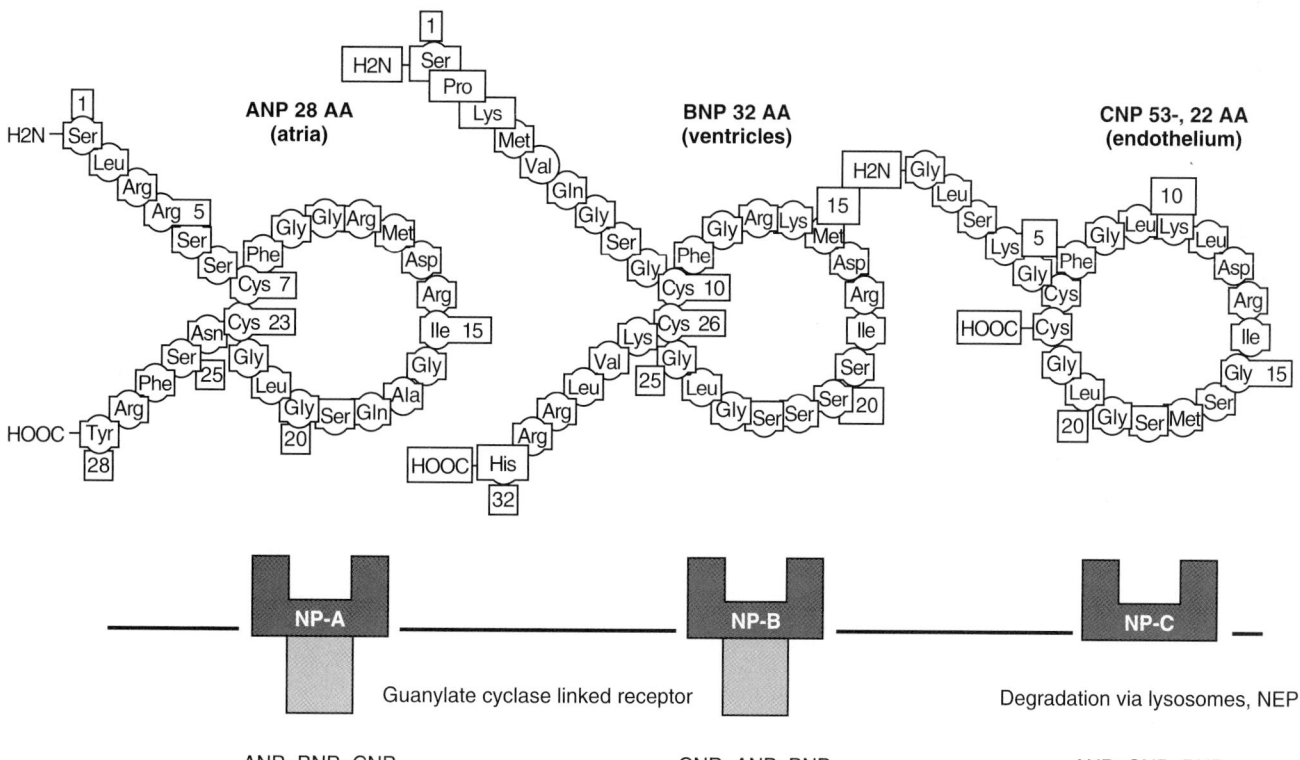

*Figure 134-2* The amino acid ring structure of three major natriuretic peptides: atrial (A-type) natriuretic peptide (ANP), B-type natriuretic peptide (BNP), and C-type natriuretic peptide (CNP).

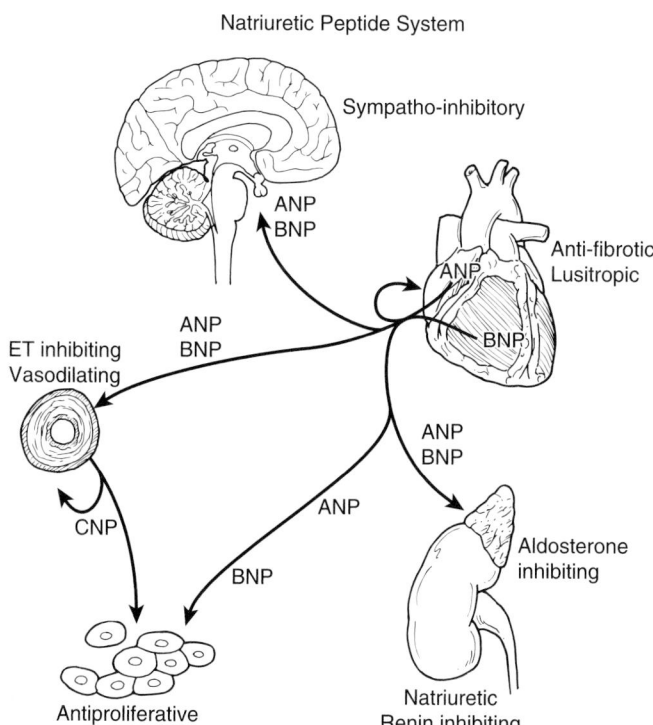

*Figure 134-3* The physiologic effects of natriuretic peptides as they attempt to correct the vasoconstrictive, sodium retaining, antidiuretic, and antifibrotic effects caused by the neurohormonal imbalance. (Copyright Mayo Clinic.)

by endopeptidases. NPR C binds to all members of natriuretic peptide family with equal affinity. When a ligand-receptor complex forms, the complex undergoes receptor-mediated endocytosis. The C-type receptors are recycled to the cellular membrane, and the various natriuretic peptides are degraded to building blocks. The second mechanism to remove natriuretic peptides from plasma involves zinc-containing endopeptidases. These enzymes are present in renal tubules and in vascular endothelial cells. They chew and degrade natriuretic peptides (among other proteins).

## PHYSIOLOGIC EFFECTS OF BNP

BNP is a potent natriuretic, diuretic, and vasorelaxant peptide; it coordinates fluid and electrolyte homeostasis through its activity in the central nervous system and peripheral tissue. BNP promotes vascular relaxation and lowers blood pressure, particularly in states of hypervolemia. It inhibits sympathetic tone; the renin-angiotensin axis; and synthesis of vasoconstrictor molecules such as catecholamines, angiotensin II, aldosterone, and endothelin-1.[14] An improvement in central hemodynamics (including the cardiac index) in patients with CHF is achieved through suppression of myocyte proliferation, cardiac growth, and compensatory hypertrophy of the heart. Its renal effects include increasing glomerular filtration rate (GFR) and enhancing sodium excretion. BNP reinforces the diuretic effects through suppressing centers for salt appetite, and it counteracts sympathetic tone via its action in the brainstem.

The major source of plasma BNP is the cardiac ventricles. This is unlike ANP, whose major storage sites include both the atria and ventricles.[17] Figure 134-4 shows the structure of proBNP, BNP, and N-terminal natriuretic peptide (NT-BNP). Unlike ANP, which is mainly released from its storage granules in response to atrial wall tension, BNP (as the nucleic acid

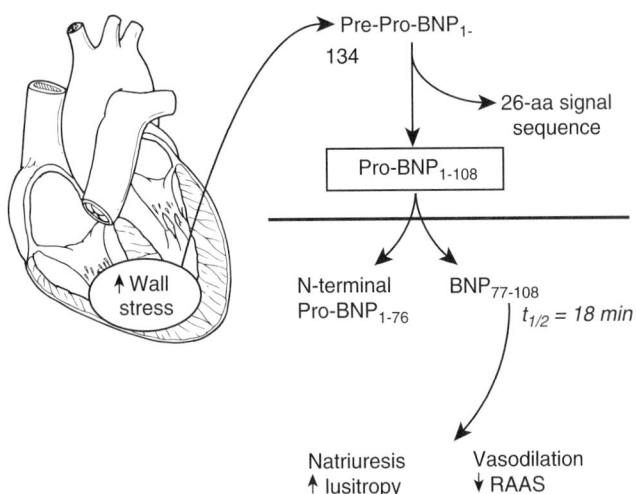

*Figure 134-4* The secretion of prepro BNP (132 amino acids) in response to wall stress, and its sequential breakdown to a 76–amino acid N-terminal fragment (NT-BNP) and a 32–amino acid active hormone (BNP).

sequence of the preproBNP gene with high turnover of mRNA suggests) is synthesized in bursts by increased gene expression, owing to stretch stimulus to the ventricular wall as prepro-BNP (132 amino acids),[18] and is then released in direct proportion to ventricular volume expansion and pressure overload from ventricular myocytes as a 76-amino acid N-terminal fragment (NT-BNP) and a 32-amino acid active hormone (BNP) (see Fig. 134-4).[19–21]

Because ANP is stored in granules and released episodically, a minor stimulus (e.g., exercise) can trigger the release of significant amounts of ANP into the bloodstream.[22] In contrast, BNP levels show only minor changes with vigorous exercise, making it unlikely that a normal patient would be classified as having CHF based on a BNP level obtained after activity.[23] This suggests that BNP may be a more sensitive and specific indicator of ventricular disorders than other natriuretic peptides.[24] BNP levels accurately reflect the decompensated state of circulatory congestion.[25] BNP has been found to be an independent predictor of high left ventricular (LV) end-diastolic pressure, and it is more useful than ANP or other neurohormones for assessing mortality in patients with chronic CHF. The half-life of BNP is 22 minutes, and studies have established that BNP can accurately reflect pulmonary capillary wedge pressure changes every 2 hours.[26,27]

Recognition of the potent natriuretic, diuretic, and vasorelaxant effect of BNP led to the development and approval of the first intravenous drug for acute decompensated congestive heart failure (CHF) in 15 years, nesiritide (Natrecor® Scios Inc.; Sunnyvale, CA). Manufactured via recombinant technology, nesiritide is structurally identical to endogenous human BNP; because of its rapid impact on salt and volume overload, along with favorable effects on hemodynamics and neurohormones, it has become a rational choice of initial intravenous therapy for decompensated heart failure.[28–31]

## NEUROHORMONES AS CARDIAC MARKERS

Owing to the drastic increase in CVD risk factors (e.g., obesity and diabetes), and improved survival rate after acute myocardial infarction (and subsequent development of CHF), there has been an increase in incidence and prevalence of heart failure in the United States.[32]

Because most of the CHF patients present to the emergency department, and determining the cause of dyspnea has been difficult because traditional subjective methods of distinguishing heart failure from pulmonary conditions may be unreliable, physicians are increasingly reluctant to rely on these subjective data alone.

Rapid, inexpensive, point-of-care biomarker tests that are simple to administer in a variety of clinical settings, and that promise to simplify clinical decision making and enable care providers to facilitate and optimize care of patients, are often adopted enthusiastically by practitioners.

As mentioned, heart failure is characterized by complicated neurohormonal alterations.[33,34] Increased levels of vasoconstrictor neurohumoral factors (e.g., NE, renin, endothelin-1, interleukin-6, and tumor necrosis factor-α) have been found to have significant prognostic value in CHF, suggesting an important role of vasoconstrictors in the pathogenesis of the disorder.[35–37]

Even though pharmacologic modulation of these factors has led to improvements in cardiac function in some cases,[38,39] relying on these factors to monitor therapy has proved impractical. Levels of neurohormones and cytokines (e.g., tumor necrosis factor and interleukin-6) have wide ranges, have assay stability issues, and may vary considerably over time; hence, they have not been shown to be useful as biomarkers in CHF.[40]

On the other hand, in studies involving patients presenting with acute dyspnea to the emergency department,[41,42] BNP has been found to be an accurate, independent predictor of heart failure. BNP measurement substantially increased the explanatory power of the diagnostic model and decreased the indecision (Fig. 134-5). BNP also distinguishes heart failure from pulmonary disease and other clinical presentations with a high specificity, sensitivity, and accuracy.[43] High BNP levels (> 480 pg/mL) are also highly predictive of cardiac events and death within 6 months.[44] In another study, patients with BNP level above 130 pg/mL were also found to be at high risk for sudden cardiac death.[45] Recently, Wang and colleagues (investigators from the Framingham Offspring Study), after adjusting for traditional risk factors, found that the level of B-type natriuretic peptide was independently predictive of the risk of death, heart failure, atrial fibrillation, and stroke over a mean follow-up period of about 5 years in asymptomatic, middle-aged persons.[46]

In long-term care, the BNP assay can be used to guide therapy.[47] The assay provides simplicity, high predictive value of a negative screen, and a potential early indication of heart-failure decompensation. In a small population, patients whose therapy was guided by BNP levels had fewer hospitalizations and lower mortality than did those treated by physicians blinded to BNP levels.[48] Several large-scale, ongoing studies (e.g., RABBIT and BATTLE-SCARRED) are testing the hypothesis that monitoring BNP levels leads to better long-term management.

In the landmark Valsartan Heart Failure Trial (Val-HeFT),[5] changes in BNP over time induced by pharmacologic therapy were shown for the first time to correlate with morbidity and mortality. Patients with the greatest percentage decrease in BNP and NE from baseline had the lowest morbidity and mortality, whereas patients with greatest percentage increase in BNP and NE were at greatest risk. The authors found BNP to be more predictive of morbidity and mortality than NE or, in a separate analysis, than aldosterone.[49]

## CONCLUSION

Several complex interactions between myocardial hemodynamic and neurohumoral compensatory events follow the initial cardiac damage; these together give rise to a clinical

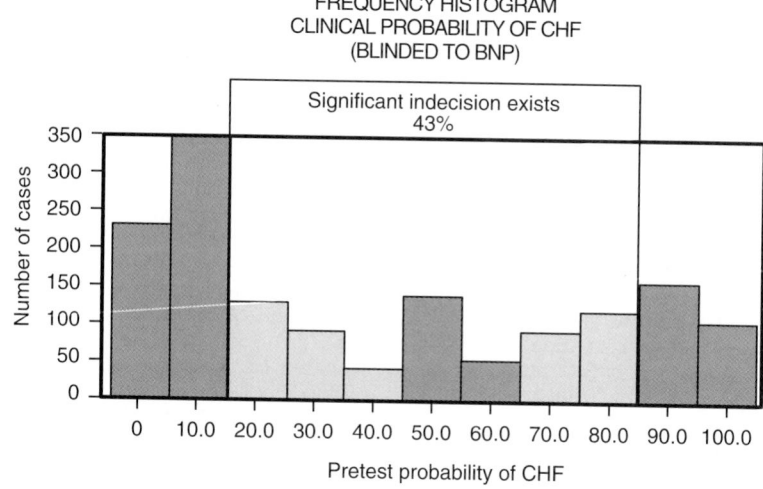

FREQUENCY HISTOGRAM
CLINICAL PROBABILITY OF CHF
(BLINDED TO BNP)

A

PRIMARY ENDPOINT

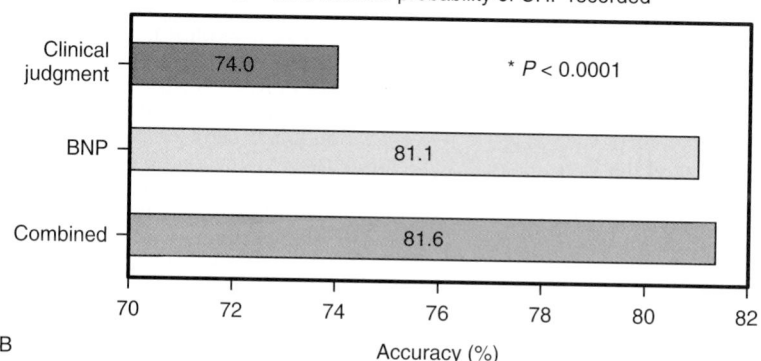

B

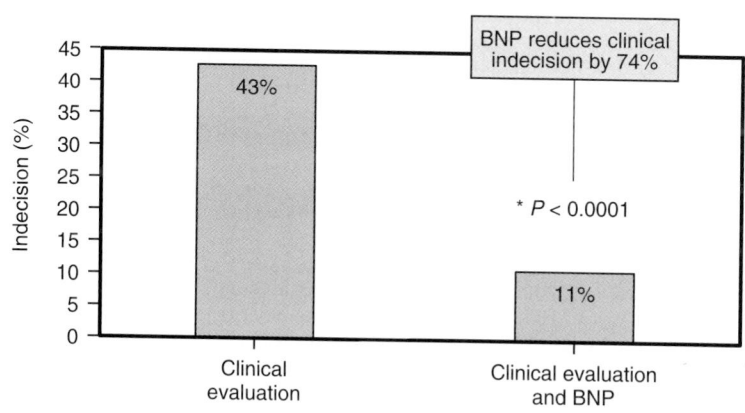

CLARIFICATION OF DIAGNOSIS & BNP

C

*Figure 134-5* **A,** the significant indecision that exists in the ED regarding diagnosis of heart failure. **B,** BNP measurement substantially increases the explanatory power of the diagnostic model. **C,** BNP measurement decreases this indecision.

syndrome of heart failure. Recognition of this neurohormonal imbalance has led to interest in evaluation of:

- Biomarker potential of these factors in accurately diagnosing, screening, and monitoring patients with heart failure.
- Therapeutic approaches utilizing pharmacologic modulation of these factors in improving cardiac function in CHF patients.

BNP has been found to be the first biomarker to prove its prognostic value in monitoring patients, in tailoring management and titrating therapy, in providing objectivity in assessing discharge and admission criteria, and in predicting and decreasing adverse cardiac events and readmissions in patients with heart failure.

Emerging clinical data will help refine biomarker-guided therapeutic and monitoring strategies involving BNP and other neurohormones in HF.

## REFERENCES

1. Cohn JN, Levine TB, Olivari MT, et al: Plasma norepinephrine as a guide to prognosis in patients with chronic congestive heart failure. N Engl J Med 311:819–823, 1984.

2. Timmermans PBMWM, Wong PC, Chiu AT, et al: Angiotensin II receptors and angiotensin II receptor antagonists. Pharmacol Rev 45:205, 1993.

3. Goodfriend TL, Elliott ME, Catt KJ: Angiotensin receptors and their antagonists. N Engl J Med 334:1649, 1996.

4. Clemson B, Gaul L, Gubin SS, et al: Prejunctional angiotensin II receptors: Facilitation of norepinephrine release in the human forearm. Clin Invest 93(2):684–691, 1994.

5. Anand IS, Fisher LD, Chiang YT, et al: Changes in brain natriuretic peptide and norepinephrine over time and mortality and morbidity in the Valsartan Heart Failure Trial (Val-HeFT). Circulation 107(9):1278–1283, 2003.

6. Udelson JE, Smith WB, Hendrix GH, et al: Acute hemodynamic effects of conivaptan, a dual V(1A) and V(2) vasopressin receptor antagonist, in patients with advanced heart failure. Circulation 104(20):2417–2423, 2001.

7. Good JM, Nihoyannopoulos P, Ghatei MA, et al: Elevated plasma endothelin concentrations in heart failure: An effect of angiotensin II? Eur Heart J 15(12):1634–1640, 1994.

8. Kiowski W, Sutsch G, Hunziker P, et al: Evidence for endothelin-1-mediated vasoconstriction in severe chronic heart failure. Lancet 346(8977):732–736, 1995.

9. McMurray JJ, Ray SG, Abdullah I, et al: Plasma endothelin in chronic heart failure. Circulation 85(4):1374–1379, 1992.

10. Swan JW, Anker SD, Walton C, et al: Insulin resistance in chronic heart failure: Relation to severity and etiology of heart failure. J Am Coll Cardiol 30:527–532, 1997.

11. DeFronzo RA: The effect of insulin on renal sodium metabolism: A review with clinical implications. Diabetologia 21:165–171, 1981.

12. Anker SD, Chua TP, Ponikowski P, et al: Hormonal changes and catabolic/anabolic imbalance in chronic heart failure and their importance for cardiac cachexia. Circulation 96:526–534, 1997.

13. Yasue H, Yoshimura M, Sumida H, et al: Localization and mechanism of secretion of B-type natriuretic peptide in comparison with those of A-type natriuretic peptide in normal subjects and patients with heart failure. Circulation 90:195–203, 1994.

14. Koller KJ, Goeddel DV: Molecular biology of the natriuretic peptides and their receptors. Circulation 86:1081–1088, 1992.

15. Davidson NC, Naas AA, Hanson JK, et al: Comparison of atrial natriuretic peptide, B-type natriuretic peptide, and N-terminal proatrial natriuretic peptide as indicators of left ventricular systolic dysfunction. Am J Cardiol 77:828–831, 1996.

16. Levin ER, Gardner DG, Samson WK: Natriuretic Peptides. N Engl J Med 339(5):321–328, 1998.

17. Luchner A, Stevens TL, Borgeson DD, et al: Differential atrial and ventricular expression of myocardial BNP during evolution of heart failure. Am J Physiol 274:H1684–H1689, 1998.

18. Nagagawa O, Ogawa Y, Itoh H, et al: Rapid transcriptional activation and early mRNA turnover of BNP in cardiocyte hypertrophy: Evidence for BNP as an "emergency" cardiac hormone against ventricular overload. J Clin Invest 96:1280–1287, 1995.

19. Tsutamoto T, Wada A, Maeda K, et al: Attenuation of compensation of endogenous cardiac natriuretic peptide system in chronic heart failure: Prognostic role of plasma brain natriuretic peptide concentration in patients with chronic symptomatic left ventricular dysfunction. Circulation 96:509–516, 1997.

20. Maeda K, Takayoshi T, Wada A, et al: Plasma brain natriuretic peptide as a biochemical marker of high left ventricular end-diastolic pressure in patients with symptomatic left ventricular dysfunction. Am Heart J 135:825–832, 1998.

21. Klinge R, Hystad M, Kjekshus J, et al: An experimental study of cardiac natriuretic peptides as markers of development of CHF. Scand J Clin Lab Invest 58:683–691, 1998.

22. Yasue H, Yoshimura M, Sumida H, et al: Localization and mechanism of secretion of B-type natriuretic peptide in comparison with those of A-type natriuretic peptide in normal subjects and patients with heart failure. Circulation 90:195–203, 1994.

23. McNairy M, Gardetto N, Clopton P, et al: Stability of B-type natriuretic peptide levels during exercise in patients with congestive heart failure: implications for outpatient monitoring with B-type natriuretic peptide. Am Heart J 143(3):406–411, 2002.

24. Nagagawa O, Ogawa Y, Itoh H, et al: Rapid transcriptional activation and early mRNA turnover of BNP in cardiocyte hypertrophy. Evidence for BNP as an "emergency" cardiac hormone against ventricular overload. J Clin Invest 96:1280–1287, 1995.

25. Muders F, Kromer EP, Griese DP, et al: Evaluation of plasma natriuretic peptide as markers for left ventricular dysfunction. Am Heart J 134:442–449, 1997.

26. Triage BNP (package insert). San Diego, CA: Biosite Inc, 2002.

27. Kazanagra R, Cheng V, Garcia A, et al: A rapid test for B-type natriuretic peptide correlates with falling wedge pressures in patients treated for decompensated heart failure: A pilot study. J Card Fail 7(1):21–29, 2001.

28. Abraham WT, Lows BD, Ferguson DA, et al: Systemic hemodynamic, neurohormonal, and renal effects of a steady-state infusion of human brain natriuretic peptide in patients with hemodynamically decompensated heart failure. J Card Fail 4:37–44, 1998.

29. Publication Committee for the VMAC Investigators: Intravenous nesiritide versus nitroglycerin for the treatment of decompensated congestive heart failure: A randomized controlled trial. JAMA 287:1531–1540, 2002.

30. Fonarow GC: Pharmacologic therapies for acutely decompensated heart failure. Rev Cardiovasc Med 3:S18–S27, 2002.

31. Emerman CL: Safety and efficacy of nesiritide for the treatment of decompensated heart failure. Rev Cardiovasc Med 3:S28–S34, 2002.

32. Rich M: Epidemiology, pathophysiology, and etiology of congestive heart failure in older adults. J Am Geriatr Soc 45:968–974, 1997.

33. Swedberg K, Eneroth P, Kjekshus J, et al: Hormones regulating cardiovascular function in patients with severe congestive heart failure and their relation to mortality. CONSENSUS Trial Study Group. Circulation 82:1730–1736, 1990.

34. Mann DL: Mechanisms and models of heart failure: A combinatorial approach. Circulation 100:999–1008, 1999.

35. Cohn JN, Levine TB, Olivari MT, et al: Plasma norepinephrine as a guide to prognosis in patients with chronic congestive heart failure. N Engl J Med 311:819–823, 1984.

36. Francis GS, Benedict C, Johnstone DE, et al: Comparison of neuroendocrine activation in patients with left ventricular dysfunction with and without congestive heart failure: A substudy of the studies of left ventricular dysfunction (SOLVD). Circulation 82:1724–1729, 1990.

37. Remes J, Tikkanen I, Fyhrquist F, et al: Neuroendocrine activity in untreated heart failure. Br Heart J 65:249–255, 1991.

38. Bristow MR, Gilbert EM, Abraham WT, et al: Carvedilol produces dose-related improvements in left ventricular function and survival in subjects with chronic heart failure. Circulation 94:2807–2816, 1996.

39. The SOLVD Investigators: Effect of enalapril on mortality and the development of heart failure in asymptomatic patients with reduced ventricular ejection fractions and congestive heart failure. N Engl J Med 325:293–302, 1991.

40. Dibbs Z, Thornby J, White BG, et al: Natural variability of circulating levels of cytokines and cytokine receptors in patients with heart failure: Implications for clinical trials. J Am Coll Cardiol 33:1935–1941, 1999.

41. Dao Q, Krishnaswamy P, Kazanegra R, et al: Utility of B-type natriuretic peptide (BNP) in the diagnosis of heart

failure in an urgent care setting. J Am Coll Cardiol 37:379–385, 2001.

42. Maisel AS, Krishnaswamy P, Nowak RM, et al: Rapid measurement of B-type natriuretic peptide in the emergency diagnosis of heart failure. N Engl J Med 347:161–167, 2002.

43. Morrison L, Harrison A, Krishnaswamy P, et al: Utility of rapid B-type natriuretic peptide in differentiating congestive heart failure from lung disease in patients presenting with dyspnea. J Am Coll Cardiol 39:202–209, 2002.

44. Harrison A, Morrison LK, Krishnaswamy P, et al: B-type natriuretic peptide predicts future cardiac events in patients presenting to the emergency department with dyspnea. Ann Emerg Med 39:131–138, 2002.

45. Berger R, Huelsman M, Strecker K, et al: B-type natriuretic peptide predicts sudden death in patients with chronic heart failure. Circulation 105:2392–2397, 2002.

46. Wang TJ, Larson MG, Levy D, et al: Plasma natriuretic peptide levels and the risk of cardiovascular events and death. N Engl J Med 350:655–663, 2004.

47. Cheng V, Kazanagra R, Garcia A, et al: A rapid bedside test for B-type peptide predicts treatment outcomes in patients admitted for decompensated heart failure: A pilot study. J Am Coll Cardiol 37:386–391, 2001.

48. Troughton RW, Frampton CM, Yandle TG, et al: Treatment of heart failure guided by plasma amino terminal brain natriuretic peptide (N-BNP) concentrations. Lancet 355:1126–1130, 2000.

49. Cohn JN, Anand IS, Latini R, et al: Sustained reduction of aldosterone in response to the angiotensin receptor blocker valsartan in patients with chronic heart failure: Results from the Valsartan Heart Failure Trial. Circulation 108:1306–1309, 2003.

# Diabetes, Lipids, and Atherosclerosis

## David M. Levy and David Galton

## INTRODUCTION

It is well known that atherosclerotic cardiovascular disease (myocardial infarction [MI], stroke, and peripheral vascular disease) is the most common cause of death in type 2 diabetes, accounting for approximately 75% to 80% of deaths in adult patients.[1] Type 1 diabetes also carries a high cardiovascular risk, but in the past this has been overshadowed by the premature mortality associated with diabetic microvascular complications, especially nephropathy (though the high mortality associated with established diabetic nephropathy is overwhelmingly cardiovascular rather than renal). A significant contributor to the cardiovascular morbidity in both forms of diabetes is dyslipidemia, and the long-term use of safe and effective drugs, especially the statins, in the past 15 years, is now established as a major risk-reducing strategy in people with diabetes. In addition, in the past decade, there has been an explosion of interest in the mechanisms by which both traditional and nontraditional lipid factors contribute to the accelerated atherosclerosis of diabetes. This chapter, therefore, reviews recent clinical and physiologic studies of lipoproteins and their metabolism, especially in type 2 diabetes, but also in type 1 diabetes and the insulin resistance syndrome.

## EPIDEMIOLOGY OF CARDIOVASCULAR DISEASE IN DIABETES

### TYPE 1 DIABETES

Type 1 patients who have not yet developed microvascular complications, especially nephropathy, have a lipid profile indistinguishable from that of nondiabetic people, but they still have accelerated atherosclerosis.[2,3] The excess risk varies from study to study, up to 10-fold in comparison with nondiabetic people in one older report from the Pittsburgh type 1 epidemiology study.[4] A recent study of more than 23,000 British patients found that cardiovascular disease was the most important cause of death in those older than 30 years of age. Standardized mortality ratios for cardiovascular disease were 4 to 11 times higher at all ages and consistently higher in women than men.[5] Whereas usual cardiovascular risk factors (hypertension, smoking) operate in type 1 diabetes, as shown in a recent 10-year follow-up report from the Pittsburgh study, glycemic control did not predict future coronary events in this cohort.[6] The presence of type 2 diabetes eliminates gender differences in atherosclerosis, but it appears also to be the case in type 1 diabetes; the British Diabetic Association report suggests this, and there is supporting evidence from studies using surrogate measures of atherosclerosis. Two studies measuring coronary artery calcification (CAC) have demonstrated this phenomenon.[7,8] The more recent CACTI study concluded that gender differences in insulin resistance–associated fat distribution might explain the fact that after adjustment for anthropometric measures of central obesity, there were no significant differences in CAC between males and females in this large group of subjects (n = 656). Different results were obtained for another surrogate measure of atherosclerosis, carotid intima-media thickness (IMT), in the Epidemiology of Diabetes Interventions and Complications (EDIC) follow-up cohort of the Diabetes Control and Complications Trial (DCCT). Mean common and internal carotid artery IMT were consistently greater in males than females, in both the previously intensively and conventionally treated groups. In contrast with the Pittsburgh study, IMT was associated with mean $HbA_{1c}$ during the trial; in addition, age, the EDIC-baseline systolic but not diastolic blood pressure, smoking, high-density lipoprotein (HDL)/low-density lipoprotein (LDL) cholesterol ratio, and albumin excretion rate were associated with progression of IMT.[9]

## TYPE 2 DIABETES

A large body of epidemiologic evidence confirms the considerable excess risk of cardiovascular disease in people with established type 2 diabetes, of which coronary heart disease (CHD) is the most important. The degree of excess risk is widely debated, however, and appears to vary with gender and ethnicity; the general consensus is that there is a twofold to fourfold increased risk. The huge Multiple Risk Factor Intervention Trial (MRFIT) found a threefold higher absolute risk of cardiovascular disease death in men with diabetes at every age (screenees were between 35 and 57 years at recruitment), in every ethnic group, and at every conventional risk factor level.[10] CHD mortality rates were lower in black men as compared with white men after adjustment for income, but still accounted for 31% and 44% of deaths, respectively, after a 16-year follow-up period.[11]

Two other classical studies reached broadly the same conclusions, both also conducted on men. Diabetic men (types 1 and 2 combined) in the Framingham Study had a 1.7-fold greater age-adjusted incidence in CHD mortality compared with nondiabetic subjects.[12] The United Kingdom Whitehall Study included only type 2 patients (but also glucose-intolerant subjects) and found a 15-year relative risk of 1.2 to 2.6, increasing with worsening glucose tolerance status.[13] A 5-year follow-up of the relatively small number of type 2 patients (135) enrolled in the Helsinki Heart Study found a significantly increased risk of MI and cardiac death compared with nondiabetic subjects (7.4% vs. 3.3%).[14]

While these studies included only men, there is abundant evidence that women with diabetes carry a higher relative risk of CHD than do men. A large prospective study in Iceland found a hazard ratio (HR) of 2.65 for MI, significantly greater than the risk for men (HR 2.08); this study excluded the possible bias of undiagnosed diabetes by combining self-reported diabetes with those who had a fasting capillary glucose greater than 120 mg/dL.[15] The absolute risk of CHD, however, has generally been found to be greater in men than in women[16]—the exception being the Framingham Study.[17]

### TYPE 2 DIABETES AS A CORONARY DISEASE EQUIVALENT

In the past 5 years, there has been increasing acceptance of the concept of type 2 diabetes as a "coronary disease equivalent"; that is, that people with type 2 diabetes, but with no overt evidence of atherosclerotic disease, nevertheless have a similar cardiovascular disease risk as nondiabetic people who have already suffered a vascular event, with the corollary that they should be treated for cardiovascular risk factors with the same vigor as nondiabetic secondary prevention patients. The concept arose from a 7-year observational study of 890 Finnish patients with diabetes who had no history of MI, and 69 patients without diabetes who had previously suffered an MI.[18] At follow-up, there was no significant difference in death rate between the two groups. A similar study, but of an American population, within the Insulin Resistance Atherosclerosis Study (IRAS), found that carotid IMT was the same in these two groups.[19] The National Cholesterol Education Panel Adult Treatment Panel III (NCEP ATP III) guidelines (2001) cite type 2 diabetes as one of a group of CHD equivalents[20] (Table 135-1). Several larger population-based studies have challenged this conclusion, however. While confirming the higher overall mortality in diabetic, compared with nondiabetic subjects, especially in women, an Australian study with an 8-year follow-up period found a hazard ratio of 0.67 using an extended definition of CHD (as opposed to MI alone, which was considered in the Haffner study).[21] Recent cross-sectional and cohort studies from Scotland in more than 250,000 subjects found that a nondiabetic MI group had a consistently higher mortality than a group with diabetes over 8 years,[22] and an 18-year follow-up

**Table 135-1 NCEP-Defined Coronary Heart Disease Risk Equivalents**

Other manifestations of atherosclerotic disease:
- Peripheral arterial disease
- Abdominal aortic aneurysm
- Symptomatic carotid artery disease

Diabetes

Multiple risk factors that confer a 10-year risk of CHD >20% (Framingham Risk Score)

NCEP, National Cholesterol Education Panel.

of the MRFIT quoted a hazard ratio of 1.88 for CHD mortality in patients with incident cardiovascular disease compared with those with diabetes.[23] The ARIC (Atherosclerosis Risk in Communities) study recently indicated a very similar result: Nondiabetic MI patients had a 1.9-fold increased risk of cardiovascular death compared with diabetic patients after 9 years' follow-up.[24] On the weight of this contrary evidence, the ARIC investigators rightly conclude that there is still an important role for risk stratification in people with diabetes, and that the therapeutic consequences of the coronary disease equivalent concept, for example, the recommendation that all or nearly all type 2 patients should be treated with a statin, may not be the best clinical or cost-effective approach.

While the overall mortality from ischemic heart disease has consistently fallen in the United States and Europe in the past 25 years, the mortality seems to be falling more slowly in the diabetic population. Results from the National Health and Nutrition Examination Survey (NHANES) study in the United States show that whereas age-adjusted mortality from heart disease fell substantially (36%) in nondiabetic men between the 1971 to 1975 and the 1982 to 1984 cohort, it fell much less in diabetic men (13%); nondiabetic women experienced a 27% fall, whereas there was an increase of 23% in women with diabetes.[25] The number of diabetic subjects was still rather small in this study, and the differences in women were not statistically significant, but whereas the trends in other epidemiological studies are not consistent for men with diabetes, the paradoxical increase in mortality in women has been noted in at least two other studies.[26,27]

Once myocardial infarction has occurred, outcomes are invariably worse in diabetic compared with nondiabetic subjects. Death rates from cardiogenic shock,[28] early (1-month) mortality,[29] and late (5-year)[30] mortality are all higher in diabetic people, with mortality rates that are consistently 50% to 60% higher than in people without diabetes.

### STROKE

Many studies, some as far back as the 1970s, have identified diabetes as an important risk factor for stroke, with relative risk estimates between 3 and 6. It is not clear whether short-term mortality rates after stroke are higher in diabetic than nondiabetic people, or whether diabetic men or women fare worse than their nondiabetic counterparts. A long-term prospective study of a middle-aged Finnish population confirmed earlier work, including the MRFIT study: Diabetes was the strongest factor for the development of stroke, though smoking and systolic blood pressure were significant risk factors in both sexes, and serum cholesterol in men.[31] Cholesterol levels in women, however, and body mass index (BMI) and the use of antihypertensive treatment in both men and women, were not found to be associated with stroke in a multivariate analysis. This and other studies also confirm that duration of diabetes is an important risk factor,[32] though the long preclinical period of up to 12 years before the onset of clinical diabetes may be important in the risk of cerebrovascular disease, as shown in the Honolulu Heart Program.[33]

## PERIPHERAL VASCULAR DISEASE

Type 2 patients have a 10- to 15-fold increased risk of lower extremity amputation.[34] Hypercholesterolemia is a risk factor for intermittent claudication in diabetes, but it may not be applicable to lower extremity amputation in all groups of people with diabetes. Smoking is a significant risk factor in both diabetic and nondiabetic people.[35] End points in peripheral vascular disease are difficult to define, and studies are complicated by the highly variable symptomatology and the diffuse nature of lower extremity atherosclerosis characteristic of people with diabetes.

## LIPOPROTEIN METABOLISM (FIG.135-1)

Cholesterol and triglycerides are hydrophobic molecules, and their transport through the body is facilitated by their incorporation into complex particles, lipoproteins, which solubilize them (Table 135-2). Two pathways have been identified: the exogenous pathway, for the uptake and catabolism of dietary fats; and the endogenous pathway, which describes the metabolism of lipoproteins synthesised in the liver.[36] Drugs affecting both pathways play an important part in the modification of diabetic dyslipidemia, and the distinctions between the two pathways are not as clear as previously thought.

## EXOGENOUS PATHWAY

The end products of small intestinal lipid digestion (2-monoglycerides, free [nonesterified] fatty acids [NEFA], and cholesterol) diffuse across the brush-border membrane of the intestinal mucosal cells. Triglycerides and cholesterol are reformed within the cells, and packaged into large triglyceride-rich lipoproteins, the chylomicrons, together with their characteristic apolipoprotein, B-48. The chylomicrons are released into the lymphatics, then into the general circulation, where they acquire apo C and apo E from circulating HDL. The extracellular endothelial enzyme lipoprotein lipase (LPL), predominantly attached to the luminal surfaces of capillary membranes in adipose tissue, muscle, and the heart, releases NEFAs, which are either stored as triglycerides in adipose tissue or oxidized for energy in the heart and skeletal muscle. Through the action of LPL, the chylomicrons are progressively depleted of triglyceride. Apo C returns to circulating HDL, while the chylomicron remnants are taken up into the liver by receptor-mediated endocytosis involving binding of apo E to the remnant receptor.

## ENDOGENOUS PATHWAY

The endogenous pathway originates in the liver, which secretes large, triglyceride-rich very low-density lipoproteins

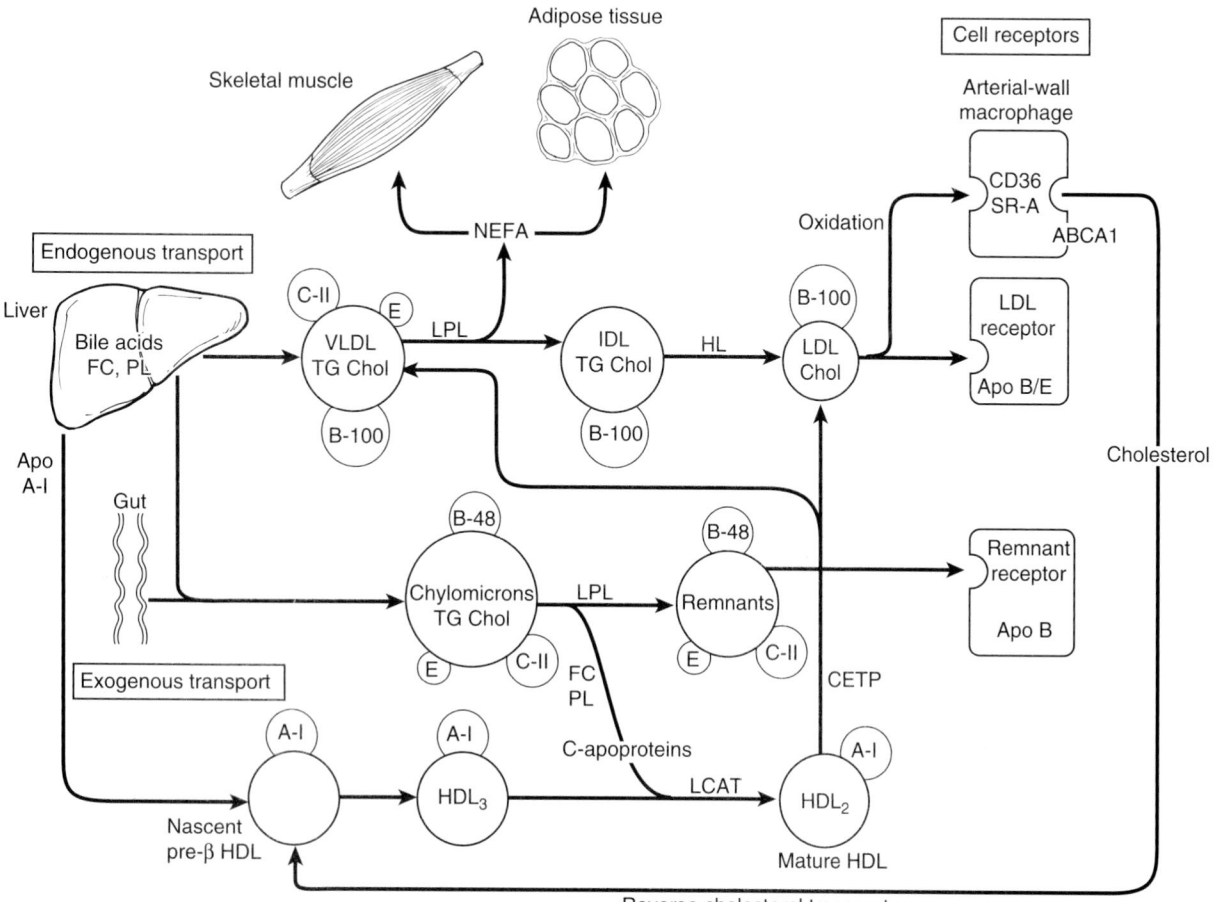

*Figure 135-1* Outline of lipoprotein metabolism. Major apolipoproteins are indicated. ABCA, adenosine triphosphate (ATP)-binding cassette transporter; CETP, cholesteryl ester transfer protein; FC, free cholesterol; HDL, high-density lipoprotein; HL, hepatic lipase; IDL, intermediate-density lipoprotein; LCAT, lecithin: cholesterol acyltransferase; LDL, low-density lipoprotein; LPL, lipoprotein lipase; NEFA, nonesterified fatty acids; PL, phospholipid; TG, triglyceride; VLDL, very low-density lipoprotein.

**Table 135-2** Plasma Lipoprotein Function and Apolipoprotein Composition

| Lipoprotein | Source | Function | Apoproteins |
|---|---|---|---|
| Chylomicron | Intestine | Transport dietary triglyceride to peripheral tissues | Apo B-48, apo C-II, apo E |
| Very low-density lipoprotein (VLDL) | Liver | Transport endogenous triglyceride to peripheral tissues | Apo B-100, apo C-II, apo E |
| Intermediate-density lipoprotein (IDL) | Plasma VLDLs | Triglyceride transport and precursor of LDL | Apo B-100, apo C-II, apo E |
| Low-density lipoprotein (LDL) | Plasma IDLs | Transport cholesterol to peripheral tissues | Apo B-100 |
| High-density lipoprotein (HDL) | Liver and intestine | Reverse cholesterol transport and source of lipoproteins | Apo A, apo C, apo E |

(VLDLs), derived partly from de novo synthesis of triglycerides and cholesterol, and also from degradation of chylomicron remnants. The major apolipoprotein associated with VLDL is apo B-100. LPL continues to hydrolyze the triglycerides of VLDLs into fatty acids, resulting in the smaller, heterogeneous population of intermediate-density lipoproteins (IDLs) and eventually LDLs. IDLs lose their apo C-II to HDL as they become smaller; since LPL activity depends on apo C-II, the conversion of IDLs to LDLs is mediated not by LPL but by hepatic lipase (HL), an extracellular enzyme located on the sinusoidal surfaces of the liver. The remaining, approximately 75%, of the IDLs are internalized by the liver via receptor-mediated processes. Conversion of IDL to LDL is accompanied by the return of apo E to circulating HDL; LDL contains only apo B.

All nucleated cells contain LDL receptors that recognize the single apo B-100 molecule of the LDL particle. The liver normally clears LDL from the circulation, though a substantial proportion of LDL is removed by low-affinity receptors, known as scavenger receptors. Modification of LDL, particularly by oxidation, enhances uptake via this mechanism, particularly in macrophages, and is a key process in atherogenesis (see later).

HDLs, synthesized in the liver, are circulating repositories of apolipoproteins apo A, apo C, and apo E. Apo C and E are exchanged with other lipoproteins, though apo A is uniquely associated with HDL. HDL is critical in reverse cholesterol transport, the process by which free cholesterol is transferred from peripheral tissues to the liver. Free cholesterol transferred to HDL is converted to cholesteryl ester by the enzyme lecithin: cholesterol acyltransferase (LCAT), a process stimulated by apo A-I. The cholesteryl esters, transferred to VLDL and chylomicron remnants, replace triglycerides removed from the particles by LPL; there is, therefore, a close link between reverse cholesterol transport and LPL-catalyzed triglyceride hydrolysis, so that high LPL activity results in higher concentrations of HDL cholesterol, especially the larger, more buoyant and more cholesterol-rich $HDL_2$ subfraction, compared with $HDL_3$. When functioning optimally, this pattern of lipoprotein metabolism—rapid removal of chylomicrons from the circulation, low hepatic production rate of VLDL, high activity of the hepatic apo B/E receptor that results in rapid clearance of LDL particles, and high LPL activity—results in low fasting and postprandial triglyceride concentrations, absent fasting chylomicrons, low VLDL and LDL levels, and high HDL concentrations.[36] Many of these features are absent in uncontrolled type 1 diabetes, in treated type 2 diabetes, and in the metabolic syndrome.

### INSULIN AND LIPOPROTEIN METABOLISM

Resistance to the antilipolytic effects of insulin on adipose tissue is characteristic of patients with both type 2 diabetes and the metabolic syndrome.[37] Normal function of LPL requires insulin; it is also needed for normal clearance of LDL via the LDL receptor[38] and it suppresses free fatty acid release by hormone-sensitive lipase in the adipocyte. Insulin may

also play a role in the processing of remnant and HDL particles by hepatic lipase in obesity and in type 2 diabetes.[39] Untreated type 1 and 2 diabetes, which are both insulin-deficient states, result in impaired LPL activity. This causes increased chylomicrons and VLDL, with consequent increased levels of triglycerides and total cholesterol, and reduced HDL cholesterol levels. LPL activity returns slowly to normal after institution of treatment with insulin or oral hypoglycemic agents. Lipid profiles in untreated diabetes are therefore unreliable.

### LIPOPROTEIN(a)

There is continuing interest in this unique lipoprotein, which was discovered more than 40 years ago. It consists of an LDL-like particle, with an associated glycosylated protein, apolipoprotein(a), which is, in turn, linked to the apo B-100 of the LDL particle. Unlike apo B-100, however, apolipoprotein(a) is highly variable in size due to the varying numbers of kringles that make up its plasminogen-like molecule. Because of its dual LDL-like and plasminogen-like properties, many studies have focused on its role in both atherosclerosis and thrombosis. A meta-analysis of prospective studies up to 2000 concluded that there was a clear association between lipoprotein(a) and CHD in the general population, but that its relevance in the causation of CHD was less well established. Few individual studies have given clearcut results; a recent study suggested that elevated lipoprotein(a) level was an independent risk factor for stroke, and vascular and all-cause death in elderly men but not women.[40] It may be, however, that such a functionally and structurally variable molecule may have multiple effects in different situations. There are several reports that lipoprotein(a) may be an independent risk factor for atherosclerosis in certain groups of diabetic subjects, for example, in silent coronary artery disease detected using various methods[41] and asymptomatic carotid artery disease (IMT) in South Indians.[42] Intensive blood glucose control does not appear to have significant lipoprotein(a)-lowering effects. Until more definitive studies are published, the measurement of lipoprotein(as) remains a component of the more intensive screening tests for coronary risk in type 2 diabetes.

### OXIDATION, GLYCATION, AND GLYCOXIDATION OF LIPOPROTEINS

The concept of atherosclerosis and of type 2 diabetes as inflammatory conditions is gaining wide acceptance. Key mediators of the inflammatory process are lipoproteins, which are not simply passive transporters of lipids, but carry various enzymes and bioactive phospholipids that are involved in the process of atherogenesis.[43] The phospholipids, lecithin in particular, are highly susceptible to oxidation, and it is this process, rather than the simple accumulation of lipids, that is implicated in atherogenesis. The general view is that oxidation of the major proatherogenic LDL particles occurs in the subendothelial region of the arterial wall, though there is some evidence that the process may start in the general circulation, perhaps through interaction with red cells or diet-derived oxidized and oxidizable lipids, to be continued in the artery.[44] The LDL receptor does not recognize the oxidized LDL as efficiently as it does native LDL, leading to accumulation of oxidized LDL in the serum and increased uptake by scavenger receptors on macrophages and smooth muscle cells. Oxidized LDL modulates transcription factors such as activator protein-1 and nuclear factor-κB, which, in turn, promote vascular inflammatory genes such as monocyte chemotactic protein-1 and various adhesion molecules, respectively.[45] Among the many proatherogenic properties of angiotensin II, it enhances oxidation and uptake of LDL by macrophages and endothelial cells; oxidized LDL upregulates expression of the angiotensin type-1 (AT$_1$) receptor.[46] Several non-lipid-lowering drugs in widespread clinical use in diabetes reduce LDL oxidation. The angiotensin receptor blocker candesartan reduces LDL oxidation in an experimental rabbit model, and losartan (and also the dihydropyridine calcium-channel blocker lercanidipine, but not nifedipine) have the same effect in humans.[47] This interesting property is also shared by the angiotensin-converting enzyme (ACE) inhibitor enalapril.[48] There is an intriguing link between C-reactive protein (CRP), an acute-phase marker currently of great interest as a sensitive indicator of atherothrombotic risk, and oxidized LDL; CRP, which localizes in both atheromatous plaques and in myocardial infarcts, has been shown to bind oxidized, though not native, LDL. This is another possible mechanism by which modified LDL might accelerate the atheromatous process in diabetes, which is characteristically associated with elevated CRP levels.[49]

Increased oxidative susceptibility of the small dense LDL particles characteristic of type 2 diabetes and the metabolic syndrome is assumed to be a significant factor in accelerated atherogenesis, and the inverse relationship between LDL size, and in vivo but not in vitro oxidation has been confirmed in well-controlled type 2 patients.[50] Two studies have failed to confirm a relationship between glycemic control and LDL oxidizability, however, one in the DCCT/EDIC cohort[51] and another in type 2 patients in the IRAS study, which paradoxically suggested lower oxidizability with increasing degrees and duration of glucose intolerance.[52] Lack of standardization of methodology for measuring oxidized LDL probably accounts for much of the divergence in results in these studies.

## Glycation

Major advances have also recently occurred in the understanding of the chemistry and biology of advanced glycation end products (AGEs). All proteins, both long- and short-lived, are glycated in the hyperglycemic environment of diabetes, and the glycated products have both structural and functional effects. Glycation of amino groups of certain phospholipids on apo B and LDL is well documented and, as with oxidation, results in reduced clearance by the LDL receptor.[53] AGE-LDL is then further susceptible to oxidation, and both processes occur at a rate that is proportional to glucose concentration.[54] There is good experimental evidence that glycated LDL is more readily oxidizable than native LDL.[55] A significant correlation has been described between serum AGE-apo B and AGE levels in endarterectomy specimens of nondiabetic patients with occlusive carotid artery disease[56]; a similar or even stronger association would be expected in people with diabetes, but has not been described. There is a complex AGE receptor system, of which receptor for advanced glycation end products (RAGE) is the best-known and which mediates the intracellular signal-transducing and pro-inflammatory effects of AGEs. This is a fast-moving field, and multiple deleterious effects of AGEs continue to be described; for example, an experimental study suggests that AGE proteins may inhibit reverse cholesterol transport by acting as ligands for the scavenger receptor class B type 1, the first HDL receptor to be identified.[57]

## LIPIDS IN TYPE 1 DIABETES

Type 1 patients who have not developed microvascular complications, especially microalbuminuria, have a traditional lipid profile indistinguishable from that of nondiabetic subjects, yet macrovascular complications, particularly myocardial infarction, are common in type 1 diabetes of long duration; clearly, there are many mechanisms by which nonlipid factors could be contributory, especially the multiple effects of hyperglycemia,[58] but several subtle alterations in lipoproteins have been identified that may be of importance.

The epidemiologic follow-up study of the DCCT cohort (EDIC) showed overall lipid profiles that were no different at follow-up, whether the patients were initially in the intensively or conventionally treated cohort. Men had significantly lower HDL levels but similar total and LDL cholesterol and triglyceride levels compared with the women. The nuclear magnetic resonance (NMR)-determined lipid profiles, however, showed considerable differences in men, who had smaller VLDL particles, lower IDL (VLDL remnant) levels, lower levels of large (good) HDL, higher levels of small (bad) HDL, and, overall, smaller HDL particles. The study also found higher LDL particle concentrations in men. There were many weak but statistically significant associations between these measurements and simultaneous HbA$_{1c}$ levels.[51] These results, however, are at variance with those of the EURODIAB study of type 1 patients, which found the more atherogenic HDL pattern in both males and females, whereas the adverse LDL pattern was found in women but not in men. Interestingly, while increasing adverse NMR profiles were associated with increased CAC scores in nondiabetic subjects, these relationships did not hold for type 1 patients.[59]

The inconsistency of these epidemiologic studies suggests that other lipid-related factors may be of importance. Glycated and oxidized lipoproteins may be significant (see previous discussion), while a common promoter polymorphism in the hepatic lipase gene has been reported to be associated with CAC in type 1 diabetes.[60] Other enzymes that have an effect on triglycerides, for example, cholesteryl ester transfer protein (CETP) and LCAT, have been implicated, as has paraoxonase, which is associated with HDL and can retard lipoprotein oxidation and metabolize oxidized lipids.[61] There is recent evidence for increased absorption and decreased cholesterol synthesis in type 1, compared with type 2 diabetes, possibly due to downregulation of the enterocyte and hepatic adenosine triphosphate–binding cassette (ABC) transport system, caused by ineffective insulin action.[62]

### EFFECTS OF INTENSIFIED CONTROL

Improvement in glycemic control in type 1 diabetes from HbA$_{1c}$ levels of 9% to 13% to 7% or less results in continuing falls in triglycerides and total and LDL cholesterol, following from decreased synthesis of apo B–containing particles, rather than increased removal,[63] while HDL levels remain unchanged, possibly due to the HDL-lowering effect of weight gain resulting from intensive insulin therapy. This effect was noted in the DCCT.[64] Overall, triglycerides (TG), total cholesterol, LDL, apo B, and lipoprotein(a) were lower in the intensively treated, compared with the conventionally treated, group in the DCCT. Total and LDL cholesterol levels were lower in intensively treated women, but not in the men,[65] despite higher baseline LDL levels in conventionally treated women compared with men in the same study.[66] Intensive treatment in the DCCT was associated with lower cholesterol levels in the VLDL and dense LDL fractions, but with more cholesterol in the buoyant HDL fractions. There was a tendency toward lower levels in the IDL fractions, but this did not reach statistical significance. There were minor differences in the cholesterol content of various fractions between women and men, but these were, in both cases, associated with a generally beneficial change in profiles.

## INSULIN RESISTANCE IN TYPE 1 DIABETES

Most patients in the DCCT gained weight over the course of the study, weight gain being more marked in the intensively treated group compared with the conventionally treated group.[67] These results confirm earlier findings from the same study.[68] The highest quartile of weight gain in the intensively treated group resulted in clinical obesity (mean BMI 31 kg/m[2]); this was associated with significantly increased levels of total cholesterol, LDL, and apo B, as well as systolic blood pressure, compared with the first quartile of weight gain. In contrast, there were no significant differences in triglycerides, LDL relative flotation (Rf, a measure of buoyancy of the LDL particles), HDL, apo A-I, or diastolic blood pressure. The first quartile of the intensively treated group did not gain weight over the course of the study, and lipid and other changes can be attributed solely to the effects of reducing $HbA_{1c}$ by about 2%; for example, mean triglycerides fell from 85 to 71 mg/dL, mean total cholesterol from 177 to 174 mg/dL, and LDL from 111 to 106 mg/dL. HDL increased from 49 to 54 mg/dL, but there were no significant changes in apo B, LDL, Rf, apo A-I, or lipoprotein(a). This elegant analysis confirms earlier reports of the small but beneficial effects on lipoprotein levels that accompany intensification of glycemic control.[69] The conclusion is that type 1 patients who develop excessive weight gain with intensive glycemic control show changes in lipid profile, blood pressure, and measures of central obesity that are typical of the insulin resistance syndrome (including computed tomography [CT]-determined intra-abdominal fat [IAF] measured 4 years after DCCT closeout in subjects studied at one center),[70] and, although there are no sufficiently long-term follow-up studies of these relatively young people to demonstrate any increases in macrovascular events, they are likely to be at increased risk. Type 1 patients with a family history of type 2 diabetes have also been confirmed to have several insulin-resistant characteristics, for example, higher blood pressure and insulin doses, larger waist circumference, and slightly increased triglycerides (though similar LDL and HDL levels) compared with type 1 patients with no such family history.[71] A follow-up study of a subgroup of the DCCT cohort examined the relationships between IAF, dyslipidemia, and HL; previous studies had indicated a close association between IAF and HL activity that could lead to the observed insulin-resistant dyslipidemia in nondiabetic subjects.[72] The authors conclude that the same associations occur in type 1 diabetes.[70]

## LIPIDS AND NEPHROPATHY IN TYPE 1 DIABETES

There are more experimental than clinical studies showing that abnormal lipid levels have a pathogenic role in initiating and continuing glomerular and tubulointerstitial damage.[73,74] Several studies have investigated the predictive role of lipoproteins in the development of diabetic nephropathy and the association with lipid abnormalities once nephropathy has developed, though there are more studies relating to type 2 diabetes than to type 1 (see discussion to follow). The Pittsburgh Epidemiology of Diabetes Complications Study confirmed that dyslipidemia predicted early-onset nephropathy (within 5 years) but not later nephropathy, which was predicted by $HbA_{1c}$. Glucose disposal was found to be a significant predictor throughout, suggesting that insulin resistance characteristics are associated with the development of nephropathy.[75] In the same study, polymorphisms of two lipoprotein-related genes, apolipoprotein E and lipoprotein lipase, were strongly predictive of nephropathy (odds ratio

[OR] 7.1 for non-apo E3/3 vs. apo E3/3, and 3.6 for the common HindIII lipoprotein lipase +/–, –/– vs. +/+). There is increasing experimental evidence that reduced levels of lipoprotein lipase and reduced lipoprotein binding to it are responsible for the high levels of VLDL in the nephrotic syndrome.[76] A cross-sectional study found that the concentrations of oxidized LDL–antioxidized LDL complexes were increased in patients with type 1 diabetes and macroalbuminuria (albumin excretion rate >300 mg/24 hr), compared with normoalbuminuric patients, especially when these complexes were formed with high avidity antibodies.[77] These abnormalities and others besides have been found in patients with nephropathy and type 2 diabetes (see discussion to follow).

A high proportion of type 1 patients with microalbuminuria regress to normoalbuminuria (around 60% within 6 years)[78]; interestingly, this recent study found that while the use of ACE inhibitor treatment was not associated with regression, low levels of both cholesterol (<198 mg/dL) and triglycerides (<145 mg/dL) were independently associated with regression, though simultaneous control of other risk factors (glycemia and hypertension) markedly enhanced the rate of regression. Considering other microvascular complications in type 1 diabetes, there are various reports of independent associations between lipids, and neuropathy and retinopathy. A publication from the DCCT/EDIC cohort has shown an independent association between the degree of diabetic retinopathy and triglycerides, and in men, small LDL and HDL, but no significant associations with apo A-I, lipoprotein(a), or susceptibility of LDL to oxidation.[79]

## LIPIDS IN TYPE 2 DIABETES

The dyslipidemia of type 2 diabetes is characterized, as in the metabolic syndrome, by mildly or moderately elevated total and LDL cholesterol levels, increased VLDL levels, and depressed HDL cholesterol. Garg and Grundy have made a good case for using non-HDL cholesterol (total –HDL cholesterol) in place of LDL cholesterol as the major therapeutic target, arguing that non-HDL cholesterol represents the total atherogenic potential of all the apo B–containing lipoproteins (LDL, VLDL, and IDL).[80] Non-HDL cholesterol was found to be a powerful predictor of CHD in men and women with type 2 diabetes.[81] They also argue that in many diabetic subjects there is an increased proportion of non-HDL cholesterol contained in the VLDL fraction, thereby underestimating cardiovascular risk if just the LDL fraction is used alone. They conclude that therapeutic targets should therefore be aimed at two distinct, though slightly overlapping components, and in the following order of priority: (1) LDL cholesterol + VLDL remnants (which are cholesterol enriched), clinically equivalent to non-HDL cholesterol; and (2) the atherogenic lipoprotein phenotype (raised triglycerides, small dense LDL particles, and low HDL cholesterol). Further refinements of the atherogenic phenotype continue to be described, for example, the hypertriglyceridemic hyperapoB phenotype, comprising hypertriglyceridemia, elevation of LDL particle number, small dense LDL, and low HDL.[82] It is not yet known which of these overlapping profiles best predicts clinical atherosclerosis in type 2 diabetes. As discussed later, although the atherogenic lipoprotein phenotype is probably an independent risk factor for atherosclerosis and there are effective means (lifestyle and drugs) to manage it, clinical trial evidence for it is less strong than for LDL reduction; firm secondary prevention data has only recently emerged, and there is evidence that the statins, drugs that have a predominant LDL-lowering effect, may also have significant beneficial effects on the atherogenic phenotype as well.

The United Kingdom Prospective Diabetes Study (UKPDS) provides a good example of a conventional lipid profile in a large cohort of newly diagnosed type 2 patients.[83] Mean total cholesterol was 212 mg/dL in males, 224 in females; LDL cholesterol was 139 mg/dL in males, 151 in females; HDL was 39 mg/dL in males, 42 mg/dL in females; triglycerides 159 mg/dL in males, 162 in females. Therefore, apart from the higher HDL cholesterol, the profile was more adverse in females than in males, possibly reflecting the much higher prevalence of obesity (>120% ideal body weight) in the females (81%) compared with the males (58%). The recent Heart Protection Study (HPS) provides a broad picture of British patients in their early 60s, nondiabetic subjects all with evidence of cardiovascular disease and diabetic patients, 50% of whom had cardiovascular disease: Total and LDL cholesterol were slightly lower in the diabetic patients compared to the nondiabetic (220 mg/dL vs. 228 and 123 vs. 131, respectively). HDL cholesterol was identical in the two groups (41 mg/dL), but triglycerides slightly higher (205 vs. 179 mg/dL).[84]

Secondary causes of hyperlipidemia, especially hypercholesterolemia, should be excluded in all patients by urinalysis, screening for renal function, or testing for microalbuminuria, liver function, and thyroid function. Hypothyroidism elevates cholesterol levels through a deficit in expression of the hepatic LDL receptor gene mediated by thyroid hormone–regulated sterol regulatory element binding transcription factor 2 (SREBP2), resulting in reduced clearance of LDL cholesterol.[85]

## EFFECTS OF INTENSIFIED CONTROL

Three months of intensive diet therapy in the initial UKPDS cohort, resulting in mean weight reduction of 4.5 kg, and a fall in $HbA_{1c}$ from 9% to 7%, had predictable effects on the lipid profile: Mean triglycerides fell by 37 mg/dL in men, 21 mg/dL in women; total cholesterol fell in men by 11 mg/dL, and 4 mg/dL in women; and there were small but significant increases in HDL cholesterol, up to 0.77 mg/dL. Larger changes were noted in those subjects with initial measurements in the highest tertiles (males: 37% fall in triglyceride, 12% fall in cholesterol), but it should be noted that the final measurements were still outside current lipid targets, and the continued weight gain and deterioration in glycemic control noted in the UKPDS after the first year of treatment are likely to have undermined these initially encouraging results.

## INSULIN

Few studies have specifically investigated the effects of intensive insulin therapy alone on lipids in type 2 diabetes. The Veterans Affairs Cooperative Study in Type II Diabetes Mellitus (VA CSDM) reported lipid changes in the 2-year stepped therapy study, which included glipizide together with insulin as the first step, then proceeded to increasingly intensive insulin-alone regimens.[86] Metformin was not available in the United States at the time. A 2% $HbA_{1c}$ differential was maintained between the intensive and standard groups throughout the study. There were no significant changes in lipid levels in the standard-treatment group, but in the intensive-treatment group triglycerides fell by 63 mg/dL and total cholesterol by 14 mg/dL (1 year data), and LDL cholesterol fell from 133 to 122 mg/dL. Apo B decreased in both groups, while apo A-I fell in the standard treatment arm; lipoprotein(a) levels showed no changes in either group. Again, these final results are not at current target levels, and both the VA CSDM and UKPDS confirm that the major beneficial effect of intensive glycemic control falls on triglyceride levels, and not on total or LDL cholesterol. In practice, therefore, in patients with elevated LDL, intensification of glycemic treatment should be accompanied by specific LDL-lowering therapy.

## METFORMIN

There is much literature suggesting that metformin has overall beneficial effects on lipid profiles, and these may account, in part, for the finding in the UKPDS that, despite similar glycemic control compared with insulin and sulfonylurea-treated patients, there was a definite advantage in terms of reduction in myocardial infarction in obese patients.[87] These advantages appear to have been maintained in the 5 years since completion of the UKPDS. Metformin also has several nonlipid and nonglycemic effects, however, that might contribute to improvement in the cardiovascular risk profile, for example, reductions in insulin, plasminogen activator inhibitor-1 (PAI-1), and methylglyoxal levels, and, in a few studies, a minor reduction in blood pressure.[88,89] Earlier clinical studies found general improvements in lipid profile, including fasting triglycerides, total, LDL, and HDL cholesterol, together with a decrease in insulin and free fatty acid levels; these results were consistent in diabetic patients in poor control, those with mild hypertriglyceridemia and type 2 diabetes diagnosed on glucose tolerance test, and also in patients with relatively poor control on sulfonylurea treatment. In addition, the benefit of metformin appeared to be greater in the postprandial than in the fasting state, and there were particularly marked effects on postprandial triglyceride-rich lipoproteins (summarized by Reaven[90]). Free fatty acids were also reduced throughout the day. Recent clinical trials and studies have yielded less clear-cut results, and this may be because the effects of metformin on lipid metabolism are greater in patients with a more severe metabolic disturbance.[91] A large, recently reported study from Holland found small reductions in total cholesterol and LDL cholesterol in patients treated with metformin who had been stabilized on intensive insulin therapy (10 mg/dL and 8 mg/dL, respectively), but no changes in HDL cholesterol and triglycerides, the changes being independent of improvement in glycemic control.[92] A study from the United Kingdom gave similar results.[93] A recent comprehensive study of free fatty acid kinetics in patients poorly controlled on a sulfonylurea found excessive free fatty acid release both during the night and after meals, compared with control subjects; in contrast to the earlier studies, however, metformin had no effect on free fatty acid metabolism.[94]

## THIAZOLIDINEDIONES AND OTHER ORAL HYPOGLYCEMIC DRUGS

These important drugs reduce insulin resistance, mostly at the level of the muscle, but also in the liver. They have well-documented effects on glycemic control, and have generally beneficial effects on lipid profiles, free fatty acids, and many of the other nonlipid factors associated with the metabolic syndrome and type 2 diabetes, including PAI-1, CRP, interleukin-6, and matrix metalloproteinase-9.[95,96] There are many studies using the prototype drug troglitazone, but it is chemically quite different from the currently available agents, rosiglitazone and pioglitazone, and was withdrawn in the United States in early 2000. All three glitazones have slightly different lipid effects. A recent summary analysis of all published double-blind, placebo-controlled studies of rosiglitazone and pioglitazone concluded that pioglitazone had a broadly more beneficial effect on lipids than rosiglitazone: Considering monotherapy trials, mean total cholesterol increased by 26 mg/dL with rosiglitazone, 2 mg/dL with pioglitazone; LDL cholesterol by 17 mg/dL with rosiglitazone, 3 mg/dL with pioglitazone; HDL cholesterol increased by 1 mg/dL with rosiglitazone, 4 mg/dL with pioglitazone; and triglycerides increased by 19 mg/dL with rosiglitazone, but fell by 46 mg/dL with pioglitazone.[97] Interestingly, these adverse effects of rosiglitazone appeared to be attenuated in combination therapy trials. The long-term significance of any adverse effects on lipid profiles is not yet known. Rosiglitazone increases large buoyant $HDL_2$, while decreasing small dense LDL, and this may moderate the apparent proatherogenic effects seen in the traditional lipid profile.[98,99] Rosiglitazone also increases insulin sensitivity in adipocytes, resulting in lower fasting, post glucose load, and basal plasma fatty acid turnover.[100] A recent comparative 3-month study of metformin, pioglitazone, and gliclazide monotherapy showed beneficial effects of metformin and pioglitazone on the lipid profile, but no changes with gliclazide, confirming that sufonylureas do not appear to have significant vascular protective effects beyond their glucose-lowering capacity.[101] Glyburide and the short-acting meglitinide nateglinide have also been shown to have no effect on fasting and postprandial lipemia,[102] but both glimepiride and repaglinide appear to reduce lipoprotein(a), PAI-1, and homocysteine.[103] In addition to reducing the progression to type 2 diabetes, the α-glucosidase inhibitor acarbose has been shown to reduce cardiovascular events and hypertension over 3 years in patients with impaired glucose tolerance in the STOP-NIDDM study, though the only significant lipid effect of this drug was to reduce triglycerides; other mechanisms, for example, reduction in postprandial glucose levels, with possible associated reduction in oxidative stress, may have been more important,[104] and concerns have been expressed about the validity of the cardiovascular outcomes.[105] Thus, among the oral hypoglycemic agents, only metformin and acarbose have so far been shown in clinical trials to have a beneficial effect on cardiovascular outcomes.

## DYSLIPIDEMIA IN THE METABOLIC SYNDROME

The multiple proatherogenic components of the metabolic syndrome are underpinned by the phenomenon of insulin resistance, the impairment of insulin-mediated glucose uptake in skeletal muscle, adipose tissue, and the liver.[106,107] Insulin resistance precedes the development of diabetes by many years and accounts for the high rate of atherosclerosis in newly diagnosed type 2 patients, but, even in the absence of baseline diabetes and cardiovascular disease, it is associated with a twofold to threefold increase in cardiovascular and all-cause mortality.[108] This important fact, that hyperglycemia itself is a weak predictor of CHD in the absence of the metabolic syndrome, has been reinforced in a report from the NHANES III study (using NCEP-defined metabolic syndrome), in which diabetic subjects without the metabolic syndrome had no greater risk of CHD than nondiabetic subjects without the metabolic syndrome.[109] It is not possible to measure insulin resistance in routine clinical practice, and three pragmatic definitions have recently been formulated (NCEP ATP III,[20] World Health Organization [WHO],[110] and American Association of Clinical Endocrinologists [AACE][111]) (Table 135-3). However, four components are invariably present—central (upper body) obesity, hypertriglyceridemia, hypertension, and depressed HDL cholesterol[112]—though multiple abnormalities of lipoprotein metabolism have been described. Additional components of the syndrome include hypertension, abnormalities of coagulation, inflammation, fibrinolysis, hyperuricemia, microalbuminuria, the spectrum of nonalcoholic fatty liver disease (NAFLD) including nonalcoholic steatohepatitis (NASH), and polycystic ovary syndrome (PCOS) (Table 135-4).

The prevalence of the metabolic syndrome is high and, with the relentlessly increasing trends in worldwide obesity, it is bound to be increasing. Depending on the definition used, 8.8% to 14.3% of Finnish males in a recent population study had the syndrome.[107] The Botnia study uncovered it in 10% and 15% of men and women, respectively, with normal glucose tolerance, 42% and 64% of subjects with impaired

| *Table 135-3* Definitions of the Metabolic Syndrome | | | |
|---|---|---|---|
| | **NCEP ATP III** | **WHO** | **AACE** |
| **NCEP Criteria for Definition of Metabolic Syndrome** | | | |
| Obesity | Waist circumference: >102 cm (men) (94–102 if other risk factors) >88 cm (women) | BMI >30 kg/m² and/or W:H ratio >0.9 (men), >0.85 (women) | BMI ≥25 kg/m² |
| Blood pressure (mm Hg) | ≥130/≥85 | ≥140/≥90 and/or antihypertensive medication | ≥135/85 |
| Triglycerides (mg/dL) | ≥150 | ≥150 | ≥150 |
| HDL cholesterol (mg/dL) | <40 (men) <50 (women) | <35 (men) <39 (women) | <40 (men) <50 (women) |
| Glycemia/insulin resistance | FPG ≥110 mg/dL (recent suggestion ≥100) | Insulin resistance<br>• Type 2 diabetes<br>• Impaired fasting glucose<br>• Impaired glucose tolerance<br>• Low glucose uptake (below lowest quartile using hyperinsulinemic, euglycemic conditions) | FPG 110–126 2-hr post glucose challenge >140 |
| Others | - | Urinary albumin excretion ≥20 μg/min or alb:cr ratio ≥30 mg/g | • Family history of type 2 diabetes mellitus, high blood pressure, or cardiovascular disease<br>• Polycystic ovarian syndrome<br>• Sedentary lifestyle<br>• Advancing age<br>• Ethnic group with high risk for type 2 diabetes mellitus or cardiovascular disease |
| **Definition** | | | |
| | ≥3 factors | Insulin resistance + 2 other risk factors | Clinical judgement |

AACE, American Association of Clinical Endocrinologists; BMI, body mass index; FPG, fasting plasma glucose; HDL, high-density lipoprotein; NCEP ATP III, National Cholesterol Education panel Adult Treatment Panel III; WHO, World Health Organization.

**Table 135-4** Traditional and Nontraditional Cardiovascular Risk Factors in Diabetes

| Traditional | Commonly Used Lipid Measurements | Extended Lipid Measurements | Nonlipid Factors |
|---|---|---|---|
| Systolic hypertension<br>Smoking<br>Family history of<br>　premature CVD<br>Dyslipidemia<br>Age | Total cholesterol<br>LDL cholesterol<br>HDL cholesterol<br>Triglycerides<br>(Non-HDL cholesterol) | Non-HDL cholesterol<br>Apo B<br><br>Lipoprotein(a)<br>small dense LDL<br>Peak LDL diameter<br>$HDL_2$, $HDL_3$<br>Oxidized LDL | Insulin resistance<br>High-sensitivity C-reactive protein, white<br>　blood count<br>Plasminogen activator inhibitor-1<br>Fibrinogen<br>Homocysteine<br>Microalbuminuria<br>Intima media thickness, coronary artery<br>　calcification<br>Postprandial glucose and lipid abnormalities<br>　(endothelial dysfunction)<br>Urate<br>Liver functions (transaminases, gamma GT) |

CVD, cardiovascular disease; HDL, high-density lipoprotein; LDL, low-density lipoprotein.

fasting glycemia or impaired glucose tolerance, and, not surprisingly, a large majority of patients with type 2 diabetes (78% males, 84% females).[113] High prevalence rates of 20% to 30% have also recently been reported from the United States, the rates being higher in African-American and Mexican-American subjects.[114] Even in people with strictly normal glucose tolerance studied in the Framingham Offspring cohort, the levels of all metabolic risk factors for cardiovascular disease and type 2 diabetes (obesity, high waist-hip ratio, hypertension, hyperinsulinemia, and dyslipidemia) increased continuously across quintiles of fasting glucose.[115]

The dyslipidemia of the metabolic syndrome results from abnormal metabolism of lipoproteins containing apo B-100 (contained in VLDL, IDL, and LDL) and apo A-I (contained in HDL). Hyperapolipoprotein B (hyperapo B) is increasingly recognized as an important component of an unconventional metabolic triad (the others being hyperinsulinemia and small dense LDL) that may more accurately predict CHD than the conventional definitions of the metabolic syndrome.[116] Increased hepatic secretion of apo B results from several features of the insulin resistance syndrome: increased free fatty acid flux to the liver, increased de novo lipogenesis, increased triglyceride availability, and resistance to a direct inhibitory effect of insulin on apo B secretion.[117] There is also increasing evidence that free fatty acids affect insulin action at many peripheral target tissues (lipotoxicity); accumulation of excess lipids in skeletal muscle is associated with insulin resistance, while it can induce apoptosis in pancreatic β cells (leading to dysregulation of insulin secretion) and possibly also in cardiac muscle.[118]

In terms of prognosis for CHD, there is increasing evidence that low HDL cholesterol is an important factor, and may be more significant than a moderately elevated LDL cholesterol. An analysis of a very large cohort of Israeli men, followed for 21 years, found that one sixth had an isolated low HDL cholesterol less than 35 mg/dL. This group had a 36% higher age-adjusted CHD mortality than those subjects who had a total cholesterol less than 200 mg/dL but HDL cholesterol greater than 35 mg/dL. The combination of diabetes and low HDL carried an even worse outcome, with a 65% increased death rate compared with those who had diabetes and HDL cholesterol greater than 35 mg/dL.[119]

## LDL PARTICLE SIZE

It has been known for several years that small LDL particles are associated with an increased risk of coronary heart disease[120] and risk of progression.[121] Quantitatively, a peak LDL particle diameter greater than 26.3 nm has been recom-

mended as the upper normal cut-off level, cardiovascular events being less common above this level. Insulin resistance induces increased CETP activity, which increases exchange between cholesterol esters in LDL and triglycerides in VLDL; the resulting triglyceride-enriched LDL particles are rapidly lipolyzed by hepatic lipase, the activity of which also appears to be increased in insulin resistance.[122] Increased hepatic lipase is also associated with decreased large buoyant $HDL_2$. There are close interrelations between the components of the insulin resistance syndrome, so it is difficult to establish the strength of this particular measurement as a risk factor, but higher PAI-1 concentrations are strongly associated with small LDL.[123] The mechanisms by which small dense LDL increase atherogenesis are discussed later. Three categorical patterns of LDL size are recognized; A is large and buoyant, B is small and dense. There is also an intermediate pattern (I). These are difficult measurements to make, and there is no agreement on the best method; currently, density (ultracentrifugation) and size (electrophoresis) are both used.[124]

## FAMILIAL COMBINED HYPERLIPIDEMIA

This complex disorder shares many of the features of the insulin resistance syndrome and is present in about 17% of families with at least one case of premature CHD; 65% of all patients with familial combined hyperlipidemia (FCHL) met the NCEP criteria for the metabolic syndrome, 20% had diabetes, and common carotid IMT was significantly greater than in unaffected controls.[125] FCHL is characterized by two separate genetic defects, one determining increased apo B, resulting from increased VLDL secretion, and a second for insulin resistance together with small dense LDL and hypertriglyceridemia.[126] Although there are variable lipoprotein phenotypes, the common lipid characteristics remain hyperapo B and increased small dense LDL. Treatment is with appropriate combination lipid-lowering therapy; a recent study showed that several of the abnormalities were corrected by a high dose of Omacor, a fish-oil preparation.[127]

## MANAGEMENT OF THE METABOLIC SYNDROME

In routine clinical practice, measurements of LDL particle distribution, apo B, and insulin are not available. As in type 2 diabetes, measurement of waist circumference and a simple fasting lipid profile, consisting of total cholesterol, triglycerides, HDL cholesterol, and calculated LDL cholesterol, will identify most patients with the syndrome. Fasting plasma glucose will identify those with impaired fasting glycemia and diabetes, but formal oral glucose tolerance testing is still of relevance in those with persistent impaired fasting glycemia to characterize fully the degree of glucose intolerance. The place of more sophisticated measures, for example, apo B (which will reflect the increased total concentration of VLDL, IDL, and small dense LDL), high sensitivity CRP, fibrinogen, lipoprotein(a), and homocysteine, is not clear, and the threshold of number of abnormalities that would warrant noninvasive cardiac testing has not been established either. For the time being, further investigations should be determined by the severity of the syndrome, together with local availability of these tests. The management of patients with the metabolic syndrome must be comprehensive, addressing weight loss ($\approx$7% to 10% of body weight, with a 500–1000 calorie/day reduction), increasing activity (regular bouts of 15–60 minutes' exercise), treating hypertension with lipid-neutral drugs, and correction of the dyslipidemia, using a fibrate or a statin, or, in patients with combined hyperlipidemia, both. Low-dose aspirin should be given in those with a 10-year CHD risk of 10% or greater.[128] There is good recent evidence for the benefits of exercise, diet, metformin, and acarbose in reducing the risk of progression to diabetes in those with impaired glucose tolerance, of whom approximately 50% or more will have the full-blown syndrome. The importance of the syndrome as a major public health issue cannot be overstated; the recent study of Ford suggests that, based on the 2000 U.S. census, about 47 million people have the metabolic syndrome, many of whom will have overt or subclinical ischemic heart disease[114]; approximately 44% of adults more than 50 years old in the United States have the NCEP-defined syndrome.[108]

## DYSLIPIDEMIA IN DIABETIC RENAL DISEASE

Accelerated atherosclerosis in advanced renal disease has been recognized for many years, hypertension and diabetes being commonly associated factors. Abnormalities of the conventional lipid profile are well described, and include increased triglycerides, VLDL, and IDL and decreased HDL; surprisingly, however, total and LDL cholesterol levels are lower than in people without renal failure.[129] Apo B and lipoprotein(a) are also elevated, as are nonlipid atherogenic factors, including homocysteine and fibrinogen.[130] Lipid abnormalities increase with progressing proteinuria and are particularly marked in nephrotic patients.[131] Multiple mechanisms have been described that might account for the deleterious effects of dyslipidemia on renal function. Mesangial cells bind LDL cholesterol via specific receptors, and cause cellular hypertrophy.[132] LDL can be oxidized in mesangial cells, leading to cytokine formation[133] and, thereby, cell injury, and oxidized LDL can also reduce glomerular nitric oxide, leading to vasoconstriction. LDL also stimulates collagen formation and activates vasoactive substances, for example, endothelin, thromboxane, and angiotensin II.[134]

Clinical evidence for the effect of dyslipidemia on the progression of renal disease is suggestive, but not conclusive, because of the absence of studies specifically designed to test this hypothesis. In the whole population of the Helsinki Heart Study, low HDL and LDL/HDL ratio were found to be risk factors for decline of renal function, but only in hypertensives. Diabetes was not considered. The drug used in this trial, gemfibrozil, did not appear to have any effect on the rate of progression of renal dysfunction.[135] After adjusting for known risk factors for decrease in renal function (age, diabetes, use of antihypertensive agents, elevated baseline serum creatinine and blood pressure, and African-American ethnic origin), low HDL and triglycerides were identified as risk factors for progression of renal impairment in the ARIC Study.[136] A post hoc analysis of the Reduction of Endpoints in NIDDM with the Angiotensin II Agonist Losartan (RENAAL) study that investigated the effect of the angiotensin receptor blocker losartan on progression of diabetic nephropathy

found that total cholesterol, LDL cholesterol, and triglycerides, but not low HDL cholesterol, were associated with increased risk of developing a composite end point of doubling of serum creatinine, end-stage renal disease, or all-cause deaths.[137] The most persuasive evidence in diabetes comes from a recent report from Casale Monferrato in Italy, in which both apo B and HDL cholesterol levels, together with the expected nonlipid risk factors (and fibrinogen) were found to be independent risk factors for progression from micro- to macroalbuminuria.[138]

Despite these results, there is no convincing evidence from clinical trials that lipid-lowering agents have an impact on renal function in diabetes, again because the particular question has not been addressed. There was a hint from the Medical Research Council/British Heart Foundation (MRC/BHF) Heart Protection Study, however, that treatment with simvastatin (40 mg daily) for about 5 years resulted in a smaller fall in estimated glomerular filtration rate compared with placebo-treated patients, and that this effect was greater in people with diabetes.[84] A specific study of lipid lowering in nondiabetic proteinuric (>1 g/24 hr) patients has recently been reported.[139] Subjects had been stabilized on ACE inhibitor or angiotensin receptor blockade treatment (or both) for a year, and were then randomized to atorvastatin up to 40 mg daily, targeting LDL less than 120 mg/dL, or no treatment. After 1 year, mean protein excretion had fallen from 2.2 to 1.2 g/24 hr in the atorvastatin group, with no change in the control group. There was a significant fall in creatinine clearance in the untreated group, and a smaller but not significant fall in the treated group.

There is much evidence that statin treatment reduces cardiovascular events in people with varying degrees of renal impairment of diabetic or nondiabetic origin. Pravastatin reduced major coronary events and coronary vascularization and marginally reduced stroke, but not total mortality, in patients in the secondary prevention Cholesterol and Recurrent Events (CARE) study who had a creatinine clearance of 75 mL/min or less (mean serum creatinine 1.2 mg/dL).[140] A large registry-based study of patients starting dialysis in 1996 concluded that any statin use reduced relative risk of all-cause and cardiovascular death by 32% and 37%, respectively, though fibric acid drugs (used in very few subjects) did not confer any benefit.[141] Nonlipid effects of statins are probably important; atorvastatin and simvastatin both reduce in vivo LDL oxidation,[142] and reductions in high-sensitivity CRP have also been described in hemodialysis patients.[143] There are no specific analyses of diabetic patients with renal impairment, but since diabetic patients on dialysis have a higher cardiovascular event rate than nondiabetic patients, the absolute benefit is likely to be greater. In practical terms, diabetes associated with any degree of renal impairment is an indication for long-term treatment with a statin.

## TREATMENT (TABLES 135-5 AND 135-6)

### DIET

Although current lipid-lowering agents are effective, potent, and safe, attempts should always be made to maximally modify lipid levels, as well as weight, through a prudent diet. Both have been shown to have significant beneficial effects on the lipid profile. The dietary approach toward the primary target of the NCEP ATP III guidelines for people with diabetes, that is, serum LDL less than 100 mg/dL, is contained in the American Diabetes Association (ADA) recommendation that saturated fat and polyunsaturated fat should each comprise less than 10% of the total energy intake, and that total daily cholesterol intake should be less than 300 mg; the more recent NCEP guideline is that saturated fat should comprise

**Table 135-5** Effect of Different Classes of Lipid-Modifying Agents on Major Lipoproteins (Percentage Change, Range)

| Drug/Nutrient Class | LDL | HDL | TG |
|---|---|---|---|
| Statins | ↓18–60 | ↑5–15 | ↓7–30 |
| Fibric acids | ↓0–20 | ↑10–20 | ↓20–50 |
| Nicotinic acid | ↓5–25 | ↑15–35 | ↓20–50 |
| Ezetimibe | ↓15–20 | ↑5 | ↓10 |
| n-3 fatty acids | ↔, ↑mild | ↔ | ↓15–35 |
| Phytosterols/stanols | ↓11–13 | ↔ | ↔ |

HDL, high-density lipoprotein; LDL, low-density lipoprotein; TG, triglycerides.

**Table 135-7** NCEP ATP III (2001)—Features of Relevance for People with Diabetes

Primary target: LDL <100 mg/dL (non-HDL-C goal <130 mg/dL)
- Therapeutic lifestyle changes should be initiated at LDL ≥100 mg/dL:
  - Reduced intakes of saturated fat (<7% total calories) and cholesterol (<200 mg/day)
  - Increased physical activity
  - Weight control
  - Plant stanols/sterols (2 g/day) and increased viscous (soluble) fiber (10–25 g/day)
- Consider drug therapy at LDL ≥130 mg/dL (optional: 100–129 mg/dL)—statin, bile acid sequestrant, or nicotinic acid

Secondary target: Metabolic syndrome
- Control LDL
- Triglycerides: target <150 mg/dL
  - Weight reduction, increased physical activity
  - Intensify LDL-lowering therapy (to reach non-HDL cholesterol goal)
  - Add fibrate or nicotinic acid
- Low HDL (<40 mg/dL)
  - No specific goal stated for HDL-raising (limited evidence base)
  - Weight reduction, increased physical activity
  - HDL-raising drugs—fibrates or nicotinic acid

HDL, high-density lipoprotein; LDL, low-density lipoprotein; NCEP ATP III, National Cholesterol Education Panel Adult Treatment Panel III.

less than 7% of total energy intake, and dietary cholesterol intake should be less than 200 mg/day (Table 135-7). The mechanism by which dietary saturated fat and cholesterol increase serum LDL is thought to be through upregulation of hepatocyte LDL receptors.[144] An alternative approach, particularly for people with hypertriglyceridemia, those of Mediterranean origin, or those aspiring to the additional cardiovascular benefits of the Mediterranean diet, can be to increase cis monounsaturated fats (contained in canola, olive, and peanut oils and in avocados) up to 20% of total energy, so long as carbohydrate is restricted.[145] Trans unsaturated fatty acids, contained in partially hydrogenated vegetable oils, as well as other high saturated-fat foods, also raise serum LDL, though less potently than do saturated fatty acids.

Two additional dietary recommendations are included in NCEP ATP III: the recognition of the importance of the exogenous lipid pathway through the inclusion of dietary soluble fiber up to 10 to 25 g/day, and addition of 2 g/day of plant stanols/sterols (see discussion to follow). A well-controlled study, comparing a lower fiber diet (16 g insoluble and 8 g soluble fiber/day), with a high-fiber diet (25 g/day each of soluble and insoluble fiber) in type 2 patients, found that the higher fiber diet reduced mean plasma glucose and insulin by 9% and 12%, respectively, more than the lower fiber diet did. Total cholesterol fell by 7% more, LDL by 6%, triglycerides by 10%, and decreased intestinal absorption of cholesterol by an additional 10%.[146] While these are encouraging results in a short-term (6-week) study, the average daily fiber intake in people with diabetes in the NHANES study was only 16 g. There is, therefore, a long way to go in dietary education before we achieve these valuable goals.

## STATINS

Statins inhibit hepatic 3-hydroxy-3-methylglutaryl coenzyme A (HMG-CoA) reductase, which is rate limiting in cholesterol synthesis. Lower intrahepatocyte cholesterol levels upregulate LDL receptors and enhance plasma clearance of LDL. They are the most widely used lipid-modifying agents and have been available for clinical use for more than 15 years. Although the

**Table 135-6** Qualitative Effects of Different Classes of Lipid-Modifying Agents on Some Nontraditional Cardiovascular Risk Factors*

| Drug/Nutrient Class | Lp(a) | sdLDL | Homocysteine | hsCRP |
|---|---|---|---|---|
| Statins | ↓ | ↓ | ↔ | ↓ |
| Fibric acids | ↔ | ↓ | ↑ (mild, variable) | ↓ |
| Nicotinic acid | ↓ | ↓ | ↑ | ↓ |
| Ezetimibe | ↓ | ? | ? | ↓ |
| n-3 fatty acids | ↔ | ↔ | ↔ | ↔ |
| Phytosterols/stanols | ↔ | ↔ | ↔, ↓ | ↔ |

*In some cases, the data are very limited.
hsCRP, high-sensitivity C-reactive protein; Lp(a), lipoprotein (a); sdLDL, small, dense LDL.

major effect of the statins is to lower LDL cholesterol, the more powerful agents (atorvastatin and rosuvastatin) have clinically significant effects on triglyceride and HDL levels. The triglyceride-lowering effect is thought to be due to reduction in secretion of apo B–containing lipoproteins.[147]

There is now much evidence relating to the benefits of statins in reducing risk of recurrent events in people with diabetes. The major secondary prevention studies using statins (4S, CARE, LIPID, HPS, ALLHAT-LLT, ASCOT-LLA) have now all reported subgroup analyses of diabetic subjects, some of them extending the analyses to nondiabetic levels of dysglycemia. The early studies (4S, CARE, LIPID), however, all strictly secondary prevention studies in patients who had suffered a definite macrovascular event, recruited few people with diabetes and, although their results are highly suggestive, none reached statistical significance. The second phase of studies, represented by HPS, ALLHAT, PROSPER, and ASCOT, have been characterized by inclusion of substantial proportions (11% to 35%) of diabetic subjects, but, in all cases, mixtures of patients with either a definite vascular history or those with a well-defined high risk of a first event (coronary risk equivalents). In addition, mean recruitment LDL levels have been progressively falling. While these studies much more realistically represent patients in routine clinical practice, for various reasons the results have not always been clear-cut, including the heterogeneity of the subjects, the relatively low LDL levels, and the relatively poor responses of people with the metabolic syndrome to statin treatment. Two diabetes-only studies have been carried out; the Lipids in Diabetes Study, part of the UKPDS, was discontinued after the withdrawal of cerivastatin, and CARDS, a study using atorvastatin in more than 2800 diabetic patients with no history of previous coronary events, terminated early because of a significant reduction in cardiovascular end points (see later discussion).[148]

### Early Statin Studies
The Scandinavian Simvastatin Survival Study (4S) recruited only 202 out of 4444 with clinical diabetes (mean initial LDL, 189 mg/dL), but a later analysis included a further 281

subjects who had diagnostic fasting glucose levels of 125 mg/dL or greater.[149,150] Treatment with simvastatin (20–40 mg daily) reduced CHD events in this combined group by 42%, not significantly different from the 32% in nondiabetic subjects.

In the CARE study, using pravastatin at 40 mg daily, there was a similar proportion of diabetic subjects as in the 4S (14% vs. 11%, respectively); mean initial LDL was lower (139 mg/dL). There was no significant reduction in cardiac end points or stroke, but the risk of any coronary event was marginally significantly reduced by 25%; using an expanded events end point, diabetic patients were confirmed as having a greater absolute reduction in event rates than nondiabetic patients (8.1% vs. 5.2%).[151] An interesting analysis identified a group of subjects without known diabetes who had fasting glucose levels between 110 and 125 mg/dL. These levels conferred a similar risk compared with known diabetic subjects who had the same fasting levels.

The last of these studies to report, Long-term Intervention with Pravastatin in Ischemic Disease (LIPID) study, used pravastatin (40 mg daily). The reduction in death from coronary heart disease and nonfatal myocardial infarction (19%) was not significant in diabetic subjects, and has not changed in a long-term follow-up study.[152,153]

The Prospective Pravastatin Pooling Project combined the results of the CARE and LIPID studies (and the primary prevention WOSCOPS study, which excluded people with known diabetes), and not surprisingly found no significant reduction overall in coronary death and nonfatal myocardial infarction, though all coronary end points were significantly reduced by 25%.[154] The 2607 patients in the Pooling Project with pretreatment LDL less than 125 mg/dL did not show significant risk reduction. They were more likely to have the characteristics of the metabolic syndrome (higher rate of diabetes, hypertension, male gender, and triglycerides, and lower HDL cholesterol). Nondiabetic individuals in this group did not benefit from pravastatin treatment, though diabetic subjects did. HDL cholesterol and triglycerides were stronger predictors of events in low LDL patients than they were in the higher LDL group.[155]

## More Recent Statin Studies

The Heart Protection Study (HPS) reported in 2003 on 5963 diabetic patients, treated with simvastatin (40 mg daily) for nearly 5 years; 50% of the subjects had no history of vascular disease.[84] Major coronary events were reduced by 27% and stroke, revascularization, and combined vascular events by about 25%. Analysis by all baseline characteristics gave similar results; although not statistically significant, it appeared that the small number of patients with type 1 diabetes (615) benefited to the same extent as type 2 patients. Reducing LDL from less than 116 to less than 77 mg/dL conferred the same relative benefit as at higher LDL levels. The study authors suggest that all diabetic patients at risk of any vascular event or intervention should be treated with a statin.

Two huge studies, both investigating the effects of combined antihypertensive and lipid-lowering treatment, have also recently reported. The Anglo-Scandinavian Cardiac Outcomes Trial–Lipid Lowering Arm (ASCOT-LLA) studied a very high risk group of hypertensive diabetic subjects with at least two additional risk factors, treated with atorvastatin (10 mg daily).[156] Despite the large number of diabetic subjects (2532), there were very few primary events (CAD death or nonfatal myocardial infarction): 38 in the atorvastatin group and 46 in the placebo, not significantly different. Of the ASCOT population, 38% had the metabolic syndrome (NCEP definition), but atorvastatin did not significantly reduce CHD events in this group, compared with a significant reduction in those without the syndrome.[157] The hypertension treatment arm has not yet reported, and it is likely that patients derived much of the benefit from the antihypertensive treatment. The lipid-lowering arm of the Antihypertensive and Lipid-Lowering Treatment to Prevent Heart Attack Trial (ALLHAT-LLT) also recruited a large number of diabetic subjects (3638, 35%) in this mixed group of patients with and without CAD at baseline, and treated either with usual care or pravastatin (40 mg daily).[158] The results for people with diabetes were not reported separately, but, in the whole group, there was no significant difference in all-cause or CHD mortality. Insufficient recruitment, the open-label nature of the study, resulting in reduced adherence to treatment and significant crossover (26% of the usual-care group were taking a statin by the end of the study), and a consequent small difference in LDL between usual-care and pravastatin-treated groups (14% difference at 6 years; compare 31% in ASCOT-LLA) were thought to be the major reasons for the result; however, the small reduction in end points was consistent with the other major statin trials, and suggested that robust and persistent LDL reduction is a prerequisite for useful outcomes in clinical practice.[159] This long-held view has been confirmed in two novel and important studies that have directly compared moderate LDL lowering (pravastatin, 40 mg) with more intensive LDL lowering (atorvastatin, 80 mg). In the angiographic REVERSAL study, atheroma progression was prevented by atorvastatin but not pravastatin. This effect was not seen, however, in the approximately 20% of patients with diabetes or in the much larger group (≈40%) with the metabolic syndrome.[160] The secondary prevention PROVE-IT-TIMI 22 study randomized immediately post acute coronary syndrome patients to the same regimens. High-dose atorvastatin reduced events over a mean of 2 years by 16% compared with pravastatin. Of the subjects in the study, 18% had diabetes; 2-year event rates were reduced by about 6%, though this was not statistically significant. Metabolic syndrome patients were not analyzed separately.[161] These two studies resulted in on-treatment LDL levels of 60 to 80 mg/dL with high-dose atorvastatin, and it is certain that intensive LDL lowering to these levels, rather than the current level of less than 100 mg/dL, will be recommended for all secondary prevention and high-risk patients.[161a]

CARDS (Collaborative AtoRvastatin Diabetes Study) reported in mid-2004 after early termination.[162] It was a large primary prevention study in 2838 diabetic subjects, mean age 62, with no clinical history of cardiovascular disease, but one significant cardiovascular risk factor (hypertension or current smoking) or microvascular complication (retinopathy, micro- or macroalbuminuria). The population was overwhelmingly white (94%) and, although baseline mean LDL was reasonably low (118 mg/dL), triglycerides were also relatively low (150 mg/dL), and, importantly, HDL was remarkably high (55 mg/dL). The profile was substantially less insulin resistant than those in the HPS and UKPDS (see previous discussion). Subjects were randomized to atorvastatin (10 mg daily) or placebo; median follow-up was 4 years. Mean LDL difference between the two groups was maintained at 46 mg/dL, resulting in a mean LDL on medication of approximately 70 mg/dL. The difference in triglycerides between the two groups was 35 mg/dL, but there was no difference in HDL levels, presumably because of the high baseline levels. Relative risk reduction for major coronary events was 37%, and 48% for stroke; revascularizations were reduced nonsignificantly by 31%. This study confirms the findings of the REVERSAL and PROVE-IT studies in a non–secondary care setting; target LDL should be 60 to 80 mg/dL in type 2 diabetic patients, but the preliminary report does not include an analysis of the effects of of atorvastatin in type 2 patients with the characteristic insulin-resistant dyslipidemia.

## FIBRATES

The fibrates (gemfibrozil, ciprofibrate, bezafibrate, and fenofibrate) are peroxisome-proliferator-activated receptor α (PPAR-α) agonist drugs with a broad spectrum of lipid actions, though their major clinical effects are to increase HDL cholesterol and to decrease triglyceride levels. Their role is less in reducing LDL than in tackling the subtle dyslipidemia of the insulin resistance syndrome, and, like the statins, they have several nonlipid actions, including improved vasomotor function and reductions in inflammatory and oxidative markers.[163] Actions beyond lipid modification cannot, in themselves, be the basis for clinical use; fortunately, there is now a sound evidence base for the use of fibrates in people with diabetes, and those with the insulin resistance syndrome.

Fibrates have multiple actions on lipoprotein metabolism (Table 135-8), and one single effect does not seem to be dominant.[155] In relation to their primary effect, normalizing HDL levels, they enhance reverse cholesterol transport at several stages; increase hepatic synthesis of major HDL apoproteins, for example, apo A-I and apo A-II; and increase cholesterol efflux into HDL, by increasing expression of peripheral cholesterol transporters that are PPAR-α responsive. In addition, they increase hepatic cholesterol uptake from plasma HDL by increasing expression of the hepatic sinusoidal membrane receptor, scavenger receptor class B type 1, and increase biliary cholesterol secretion. Their second major effect is to reduce both fasting and postprandial levels of triglyceride-rich lipoproteins; for example, fenofibrate decreases postprandial chylomicrons and VLDL mass concentration.[164] Reduced postprandial triglyceride enrichment of all lipoproteins is associated with improved flow-mediated endothelium-dependent vasodilatation and reduced postprandial oxidative stress after treatment with ciprofibrate.[165] Fibrates inhibit hepatic triglyceride synthesis and secretion and increase triglyceride clearance[166] through stimulation of lipoprotein lipase, and decrease expression and concentration of apo C-III, which inhibits LPL activity. Finally, fibrates shift LDL from the small dense pattern to a larger, more buoyant fraction that is less prone to oxidation.

Gemfibrozil, the prototypic earlier fibric acid drug, has no effects on LDL level, an important finding in the VA-HIT (see later). Fenofibrate has been shown to reduce LDL by 15% in a group of type 2 diabetic patients with combined hyperlipidemia.[167] Fenofibrate, but not simvastatin or atorvastatin, has been reported to increase homocysteine in a group of nondiabetic subjects, but it is not known what, if any effect, this has on long-term cardiovascular outcomes, probably rather small if compared with the multiple beneficial effects of fibrates.[168]

## Clinical Trials with Fibrates
If the early statin studies enrolled few people with diabetes, there have been even fewer fibrate trials with substantial numbers of diabetic subjects. The paradox here is evident:

The Helsinki Heart Study, discussed earlier, suggested that gemfibrozil had a disproportionately beneficial effect on the few patients with diabetes. The secondary prevention Bezafibrate Infarction Prevention (BIP) Study included only 10% of subjects with diabetes.[169] Only one study, the angiographic Diabetes Atherosclerosis Intervention Study (DAIS), has been performed specifically on diabetic subjects[170]; 418 diabetic subjects were treated with 200 mg micronized fenofibrate daily or placebo for 3 years. There was significantly less progression of focal atherosclerosis than in the placebo-treated subjects. Major CHD events were reduced from 50 in the placebo group, compared with 38 in the fenofibrate group This reduction was not statistically significant; the study was not powered to show a clinical effect. Fenofibrate had the expected effects on the lipid profile: Triglycerides fell by 28% from a relatively low baseline (≈215 mg/dL), cholesterol fell by 9.0%, LDL fell by 3.5%, and HDL rose by 7.5%. LDL peak particle diameter increased in relation to the fall in triglycerides and statistically contributed to the beneficial effect of fenofibrate.[171] A primary prevention study, FIELD (Fenofibrate Intervention and Event Lowering in Diabetes), has enrolled more than 9000 patients, and will report in 2005 to 2007.

The VA-HIT (Veterans Affairs High-Density Lipoprotein Cholesterol Intervention Trial) is an important secondary prevention study that showed that a fibrate (gemfibrozil) could have similar effects on event reduction as a statin, and that people with diabetes and the metabolic syndrome derived even greater benefit than those without.[172] The 5-year trial, of 2531 subjects, 25% with diabetes, had several important features: (1) baseline lipids were characteristic of a population with coronary artery disease (low-normal LDL [mean 111 mg/dL] and total cholesterol [175 mg/dL], low HDL cholesterol [32 mg/dL], but only slightly elevated triglycerides [162 mg/dL]); (2) the fortuitous choice of gemfibrozil, which had no effect on LDL, but a typical fibrate effect on HDL (6% increase) and triglycerides (31% decrease); and (3) the inclusion of a significant number of people with diabetes and a large number of people with the metabolic syndrome.

The overall reduction in primary end points (nonfatal MI, CHD death, or confirmed stroke) was 24%, very similar to the reduction found in the major statin trials; there was an identical and significant reduction (24%) in these events in diabetic subjects. Reduction in CHD death in people with diabetes was markedly greater than in nondiabetic subjects (39% vs. 3%). Robins contrasted this with CARE, where most of the benefit of pravastatin occurred in nondiabetic subjects compared with diabetic subjects (23% vs. 3%).[163] Reduction in these events was correlated with treatment HDL concentrations, but not with either baseline or treatment triglyceride levels. There was a significant reduction in events (28%)

| Table 135-8 | Potentially Beneficial Effects of Fibrates |
|---|---|

Lipid effects
1. Increased HDL-mediated reverse cholesterol transport
   a. Increased hepatic synthesis of HDL apolipoproteins*
   b. Increased LPL synthesis and TG-rich lipoprotein catabolism; transfer of lipoprotein surface components to form new HDL*
   c. Increasing macrophage cholesterol efflux into HDL*
   d. Increased hepatic cholesterol uptake by increasing hepatic receptors and scavenger receptors
2. Reduced TG-rich lipoproteins (increased LPL, reduced synthesis of apo C-III)*
3. Decreased small, dense LDL
4. Decreased hepatic cholesterol 7-α-hydroxylase activity, bile acid synthesis, and micellar solubilization and absorption of intestinal cholesterol*
Nonlipid effects
1. Increased endothelium-mediated vasodilatation through decrease in triglycerides (especially postprandial)
2. Decreased procoagulant activity, e.g., reduction in plasminogen activator inhibitor 1, tissue plasminogen activator, fibrinogen
3. Decreased inflammatory mediators, e.g., tissue factor, tissue necrosis factor-α, interleukin-6, C-reactive proteins, and cellular adhesion molecules

*Peroxisome-proliferator-activated receptor α–mediated effects
HDL, high-density lipoprotein; LDL, low-density lipoprotein; LPL, lipoprotein lipase; TG, triglycerides.

in those with the highest tertile baseline triglyceride levels (>180 mg/dL), but lipid levels explained only 23% of the favorable effects of gemfibrozil, so it is possible that its non-lipid effects are important.[173] In fact, insulin resistance predicted new CHD events much more strongly than either HDL cholesterol or triglycerides. The benefit of gemfibrozil was greater in insulin-resistant people than non-insulin-resistant people at most levels of HDL or triglycerides; in the absence of diabetes, insulin resistance (highest tertile of homeostasis model assessment–Insulin Resistance [HOMA-IR]) carried a significantly higher risk of cardiovascular events (27.7%) compared with the non-insulin-resistant group (19.8%). Importantly, however, the increases in HDL and decreases in triglycerides were least in the presence of insulin resistance, where, nevertheless, clinical benefit was greater. The preferential effects in insulin-resistant and diabetic subjects in VA-HIT may account for the lack of significant benefit seen in the BIP Study, which, in addition to the very small proportion of people with diabetes, excluded those treated with insulin and those with even modest hyperglycemia (fasting glucose > 160 mg/dL). No diabetic subgroup analyses from BIP have been presented. As in VA-HIT, hypertriglyceridemic subjects (triglycerides ≥ 200 mg/dL) derived a significant benefit, but only in those with baseline HDL cholesterol less than 35 mg/dL.

## Clinical Use

Apart from a disputed increase in mortality associated with the obsolete clofibrate, fibric acid drugs have a long safety history. They are more effective in the treatment of severe hypertriglyceridemia than even the potent new statins; the ADA suggests that people with triglycerides consistently more than 400 mg/dL should be treated with a fibrate in order to reduce the risk of acute pancreatitis, though, in clinical practice, pancreatitis does not usually occur until triglyceride levels are more than 1000 to 2000 mg/dL. VA-HIT supports the use of a fibrate in MI subjects with low-normal LDL levels and low HDL, but, in practice, the majority of these patients, regardless of LDL or HDL levels, will have been started on a statin. In addition, in the majority of patients who do not have marked hypertriglyceridemia, the measurable benefits of fibrate treatment are small; for example, a 6% increase in HDL level, found in VA-HIT, is not reliably detectable with usual current laboratory methods, and the paradox found in VA-HIT, that clinical benefits were greatest in the insulin-resistant patients in whom there were the smallest changes in HDL and triglycerides,[174] means that treatment with a fibrate is more reliant on clinical outcome data than laboratory findings. The clinical dilemma, then, is using a fibrate without reliable simple laboratory means to detect response or clinical outcome. The problem becomes more severe in combination therapy, where there is an increased risk of side effects, though the risk of myositis is low, as long as fenofibrate (or bezafibrate or ciprofibrate where available), rather than gemfibrozil, is used. Combination statin-fibrate treatment, according to the epidemiology, should be employed in about 20% of all MI patients. There are no end-point clinical trials demonstrating that a statin-fibrate combination is preferable to statin treatment alone. Several studies, however, have reported safety and efficacy in nondiabetic subjects with mixed hyerlipidemia and coronary heart disease. In 120 diabetic subjects with mixed hyperlipidemia studied for 6 months, the combination of atorvastatin (20 mg daily) and micronized fenofibrate (200 mg daily) had a greater effect on all lipid measurements (other than lipoprotein(a), which was unchanged) than either drug alone. With combination therapy, mean LDL fell by 46%, triglycerides by 50%, apo B-100 by 41%, and fibrinogen by 19% (fenofibrate effect); mean HDL increased by 22%.[175] No patient withdrew because of side effects and there was no reported myalgia. This is, therefore, a potentially valuable combination.

## EZETIMIBE

Originally discovered during a search for potential acyl coenzyme A: cholesterol transferase (ACAT) inhibitors, ezetimibe, the first of a class of agents known as the 2-azetidinones, has no such activity; although its precise mode of action is not known, its characteristics are those of a cholesterol absorption inhibitor, probably acting through inhibition of a putative cholesterol transporter. It would therefore be expected to reduce blood chylomicron cholesterol levels, decrease hepatic cholesterol uptake, and thereby upregulate hepatic LDL receptors. Patients who respond poorly to statins, and who may therefore have high cholesterol absorption rates but low synthesis rates, might be expected to respond well to ezetimibe monotherapy.[176] It is important to recognize that ezetimibe acts in quite a different way from other lipid-lowering agents that act on the intestine, for example, resins and polymers.

In monotherapy, ezetimibe reduces LDL levels by about 17%, raises HDL cholesterol by 2% to 3%, and has a variable and slight effect on triglycerides (falls of 4% to 11%). When added to any statin, it further reduces LDL by 21% to 22% and triglycerides by 11%, and increases HDL cholesterol by about 2%.[177] The effects of ezetimibe on nontraditional markers of atherosclerosis, for example, homocysteine, lipoprotein(a), and LDL particle size, are not known, but it reduces hsCRP more than statins alone. A single reported retrospective study of ezetimibe in a small group of type 2 diabetic patients, of whom nearly 90% were taking additional lipid-lowering treatment (75% a statin), found a 21% reduction in total cholesterol and a 34% fall in LDL, but no significant changes in triglycerides or HDL cholesterol.[178] These results are likely to be replicated in larger studies of diabetic subjects.

This novel agent has, therefore, an important potential role as add-on treatment to maximum-dose statin treatment where target LDL is not being achieved in those patients who have a suboptimal response to statins, and as the principal LDL-lowering agent where there is intolerance of statins. It carries no additional risk of myositis, though there have been occasional reports of elevations of transaminases, especially in patients with preexisting elevated transaminase levels and in combination therapy with statins. Although there are no reported studies, it is likely to be safe and effective in combination with a fibrate. Fixed-dose combinations of simvastatin and ezetimibe have been introduced, and their judicious use will increase attainment of the more rigorous LDL targets discussed earlier.

## PHYTOSTEROLS/PHYTOSTANOLS

Hydrogenation converts plant sterols, which have a structure very similar to that of cholesterol, to their corresponding stanols; subsequent esterification renders them fat soluble, and they can then be incorporated into easily consumable fat-containing products, where they are much more effective in reducing LDL than the native crystalline sterols or stanols.[173] Unesterified sterols/stanols reduce cholesterol absorption[179] by displacing cholesterol from micelles, but there is recent evidence that they may also have effects in the enterocyte and hepatocyte, especially through adenosine triphosphate–binding cassette (ABC) proteins that cause efflux of cholesterol and phytosterols from cells.[180] The NCEP recommended intake of about 2 g/day, a dose that has the maximum cholesterol-lowering effect, can be achieved by taking 1 to 1½ tablespoonsful of sterol/stanol-enriched margarine daily. This dose reduces total cholesterol by 12% to 13%, and LDL cholesterol by 13% to 16%, but has no effect on triglycerides or HDL cholesterol. LDL reductions in a large group of type 2 diabetic subjects with initial LDL of 140 mg/dL or greater were less marked after taking 1.6 g of phytosterol-enriched spread daily; at 4 weeks, LDL fell by 6.8%, but this effect diminished at 8 and 12 weeks, suggesting that compliance is difficult to maintain.[181] Combinations of sterols and other functional foods can have more dramatic effects on LDL levels; in nondiabetic hyperlipidemic subjects, a further 23% reduction beyond that achieved by a low saturated fat was described in a study combining sterols with soy protein, viscous fiber, and almonds, but adherence to such regimens is likely to be poor.[182] Ezetimibe inhibits absorption of phytosterols, but there is no functional interaction. Plant sterols are entirely safe when taken in recommended doses, and, used consistently, together with other lifestyle measures, nutraceuticals, and medication where required, should enable a higher proportion of the diabetic population to achieve recommended LDL levels.

## n-3 POLYUNSATURATED FATTY ACIDS

The n-3 (also known as omega-3) polyunsaturated fatty acids (PUFAs) are "essential" in that they cannot be endogenously synthesized and must be obtained from food, largely from marine vertebrates. Progressive elongation and desaturation of the parent fatty acid, $\alpha$-linolenic (C18:3n-3) results in the two major long-chain forms, eicosapentaenoic acid (EPA, C20:5n-3), and, the longest of them all, docosahexaenoic acid (DHA, C22:6n-3), found in greatest concentrations in the oil of fatty fish.[183] There is sound epidemiologic evidence that increased intake of fish oils reduces the risk of sudden death,[184] and the GISSI-Prevenzione study provided clinical trial evidence for the benefit of daily supplementation with approximately 1 g of DHA+EPA in reducing sudden, presumed arrhythmic, death in post myocardial infarction patients.[185] These antiarrhythmic effects are mediated without changes in the lipid profile, however. In higher doses, long-chain fish oils have a long history of use in the treatment of hypertriglyceridemia, acting through lowering VLDL synthesis. There has been some concern, however, that they may be associated with worsening glycemic control in diabetic people. A systematic review of diabetic studies published in 2000 concluded that approximately 2 to 3 g/day fish oil supplementation resulted in a mean fall in triglyceride level of 50 mg/dL, but 65 mg/dL in hypertriglyceridemic subjects and 76 mg/dL when higher doses of fish oil were used. Total cholesterol showed little change, but there was a tendency to higher LDL levels (8 mg/dL), possibly accounted for by an increase in larger, more buoyant LDL particles. Both fasting glucose and $HbA_{1c}$ showed very small increases (0.26 mg/dL and 0.15%, respectively).[186] Larger increases in mean fasting glucose levels were seen in a 6-week Australian study of supplementation with 4 g of DHA or EPA (25 mg/dL and 18 mg/dL, respectively), with corresponding falls of 19% and 15% in triglyceride levels. This study found no significant changes in total, LDL, or HDL cholesterol, but there was a small decrease in $HDL_2$ and a small increase in $HDL_3$. There were no changes in $HbA_{1c}$ or in insulin sensitivity or secretion in this very short-term study.[187] Another review of studies in nondiabetic populations estimated the fall in triglycerides to be approximately 10% to 35%, corresponding to a dose range of 2 to 9 g/day n-3 PUFAs.[188] Fish oils appear to have no effect either on C-reactive protein[189] or homocysteine levels.[190] There are no reported studies of combination therapy with fish oils, though they should act synergistically with other agents, for example, statins, fibrates, or niacin.

## NIACIN (NICOTINIC ACID)

Niacin (nicotinic acid), a B-complex vitamin, has a long history of use in lipid disorders. High doses are required to exert a therapeutic effect, however, and these have been associated with significant side effects, especially flushing and hepatotoxicity; there have also been concerns that niacin adversely affects glycemic control in people with diabetes. Recently, the introduction of an extended-release niacin preparation (Niaspan) has reduced the incidence of side effects, and the effects on blood glucose levels in short-term use appear to be small.

The mechanisms of action of niacin are not clear. Its most dramatic effect is elevation of HDL cholesterol levels, which it does to a greater extent than any other lipid-modifying agent. This is due to a decrease in the rate of removal of apo A-I, and not an increase in its synthesis, or through any effect on the hepatic scavenger receptor SR-BI.[191] It also reduces activity of hepatic lipase, thereby making HDL and LDL particles more buoyant and probably less atherogenic. Finally, it reduces lipolysis, and fewer free fatty acids are available for hepatic synthesis into VLDL, thereby also reducing LDL levels.[192] This last action cannot account for all the effect of niacin on VLDL-TG production, since VLDL-TG production rates continue to be low for several hours after the antilipolytic action of niacin has abated.[193] The spectrum of antidyslipidemic effects is similar to that of the fibrates. Treatment with the maximum recommended dose of Niaspan (2000 mg daily) reduces LDL cholesterol by about 16%, total cholesterol 12%, triglycerides 30%, and lipoprotein(a) 25%, and increases HDL cholesterol by about 24%. HDL levels continue to climb slowly over the course of many weeks. A study comparing gemfibrozil (1200 mg/day) and Niaspan (up to 2000 mg/day) in patients with low HDL cholesterol ($\leq$40 mg/dL) gave broadly similar results, but indicated the comparative differences between the fibric acid drugs and niacin; niacin had a greater effect on HDL cholesterol and apo A-I than gemfibrozil (increases of 26.0% vs. 13.0% and 11.2% vs. 31%, respectively), but a smaller effect on triglycerides (decreases of 30% vs. 40%). Niacin had a neutral effect on LDL cholesterol (9% increase with gemfibrozil), a marked effect on lipoprotein(a) (reduction of 20% compared with neutral effect of gemfibrozil), and a slight reduction in fibrinogen (compared with a slight increase on gemfibrozil).[194]

There have been several end-point studies in nondiabetic patients, but, so far, none specifically in people with diabetes. The results of the secondary prevention Coronary Drug Project, published nearly 30 years ago, showed that coronary death, nonfatal MI, and stroke were significantly reduced by 6 years of treatment with 3 g of niacin daily, the effect persisting for at least a further 9 years.[195,196] Two later angiographic studies (the Cholesterol-Lowering Atherosclerosis Study [CLAS] and the Familial Atherosclerosis Treatment Study [FATS]) used combination niacin and the bile acid resin colestipol in post–coronary artery bypass grafts and high-risk people with established CHD, respectively. Both studies found that progression of coronary lesions was reduced and lesion regression increased. Active treatment in FATS reduced clinical events, though not significantly.[197,198]

Niacin therapy has been reported in combination with a variety of statins, with the expected added beneficial effects on LDL, triglycerides, and HDL. A 3-year angiographic study (HDL-Atherosclerosis Treatment Study, HATS) in people with low HDL (baseline mean 31 mg/dL), but relatively low LDL (baseline mean 125 mg/dL) used a combination of simvastatin (mean daily dose 13 mg) and niacin (mean daily dose 2.4 g), resulting in 42% and 36% reductions in LDL and triglycerides, respectively, and a 26% increase in HDL cholesterol. Treatment was associated with a slight (0.4%) regression in coronary stenosis, compared with an increase of 3.9% in the placebo group. There was a significant reduction in composite cardiovascular end points in the simvastatin-niacin group.[199] Interestingly, the effect of antioxidant vitamins in the same trial was to blunt both the lipid-modifying and antiatherogenic effects of the niacin-simvastatin combination; in particular, they suppressed $HDL_2$ subfraction levels and blunted its rise. The niacin-statin combination appears to have no excess adverse hepatic effects.

Concerns about deteriorating glycemic control with niacin have been addressed in a recent study in type 2 patients, nearly half of whom were treated with a statin. Patients were required to have more than one of the following: LDL cholesterol of 130 mg/dL or greater, HDL cholesterol of 40 mg/dL or less, or triglyceride of 200 mg/dL or greater, but baseline glycemic control was good (mean $HbA_{1c}$ 7.1% to 7.2%).[200] $HbA_{1c}$ increased nonsignificantly by 0.29% after 16 weeks of treatment with 1500 mg of extended-release niacin. There were small increases in fasting glucose at 4 and 8 weeks, which settled after 16 weeks, suggesting that the oral hypoglycemic regimen was being appropriately adjusted; glycemic control was thought to have worsened in about 30% of the patients on the higher dose, but in only 12% of the placebo-treated group. In the comparative study previously mentioned, 2000 mg of Niaspan daily increased mean fasting glucose by 4.5% in a group of predominantly nondiabetic subjects.[190] The effects of low-dose extended-release niacin on glycemic control are therefore small and manageable, but caution should be exercised in patients who are borderline for a change in diabetes treatment regimen such as a change from oral hypoglycemic agents to insulin. There would be little justification for withholding niacin treatment in a patient with persistent poor glycemic control despite maximum efforts.

### Clinical Use

The long-standing, but largely unjustified, anxieties about the effects of niacin on glycemic control have resulted in its role not being well defined in the treatment of diabetic dyslipidemia; in addition, it has only recently been introduced in its extended-release form in Europe. While it has excellent effects on triglycerides, most authorities would still recommend a fibric acid drug for predominant or isolated hypertriglyceridemia. Niacin's dramatic effects on HDL cholesterol, however, make it an important drug for the treatment of isolated low HDL with or without moderate hypertriglyceridemia. The increasing recognition of the importance of low HDL levels in atherosclerosis has prompted a search for HDL-raising agents even more powerful than niacin. Early clinical studies of two inhibitors of cholesteryl ester transfer protein (CETP) have been reported. The more powerful, torcetrapib, almost doubled HDL levels when given at a dose of 120 mg twice daily to a small group of nondiabetic subjects with HDL levels less than 40 mg/dL. LDL cholesterol fell by 17% and triglycerides by 26%, and there were very marked increases in the large $HDL_2$ and LDL subfractions.[201] Results of larger trials including people with diabetes are eagerly awaited.

## CONCLUSIONS

The mechanisms by which diabetes and its nearly universal precursor and accompaniment, the metabolic syndrome, affect lipid metabolism and its interaction with other potent risk factors for atherosclerosis are complex. Dyslipidemia increases cardiovascular risk in diabetes to approximately the same extent as other risk factors, but the drugs now available have a predictable effect that persist unchanged as long as the drug is taken; this means that lipid abnormalities are among the most readily treatable of the risk factors in diabetes. The evidence base for monotherapy is well established, though the importance of the fibric acid drugs compared with the statins has probably been underestimated in diabetes. The challenge is now to use clinical trial data to extend medication to all diabetic patients who are likely to benefit and to tailor medication, especially combination therapy, to suit different clinical and metabolic profiles in individual subjects. Despite the potency of drugs, therapeutic lifestyle changes and functional foods still have a major role in the management of dyslipidemia in the diabetic patient.

### Acknowledgments
I am grateful to the librarians at the Medical Education Centre, Whipps Cross University Hospital, for their help in the preparation of this chapter.

## REFERENCES

1. Pyörälä K, Laakso M, Uusitupa M: Diabetes and atherosclerosis: An epidemiologic view. Diabetes Metab Rev 3:463–524, 1987.
2. Dorman JS, Laport RE, Kuller LH, et al: The Pittsburgh insulin-dependent diabetes mellitus (IDDM) morbidity and mortality study: Mortality results. Diabetes 33:271–276, 1984.
3. Krolewski AS, Kosinski EJ, Warram JH, et al: Magnitude and determinants of coronary artery disease in juvenile-onset, insulin-dependent diabetes mellitus. Am J Cardiol 59:750–755, 1987.
4. Dorman JS, Laporte RE, Kuller LH, et al: The Pittsburgh insulin-dependent diabetes mellitus (IDDM) morbidity and mortality study: Mortality results. Diabetes 33:271–276, 1984.
5. Laing SP, Swerdlow AJ, Slater SD, et al: The British Diabetic Association Cohort Study, II: Cause-specific mortality in patients with insulin-treated diabetes mellitus. Diabet Med 16:466–471, 1999.
6. Orchard TJ, Olson JC, Erbey JR, et al: Insulin resistance-related factors, but not glycemia, predict coronary artery disease in type 1 diabetes: 10-year follow-up data from the Pittsburgh Epidemiology of Diabetes Complications study. Diabetes Care 26:1374–1379, 2003.
7. Colhoun HM, Rubens MB, Underwood SR, et al: The effect of type 1 diabetes mellitus on the gender difference in coronary artery calcification. J Am Coll Cardiol 36:2160–2167, 2000.
8. Dabelea D, Kinney G, Snell-Bergeon JK, et al: Effect of type 1 diabetes on the gender difference in coronary artery calcification: A role for insulin resistance? The Coronary Artery Calcification in Type 1 Diabetes (CACTI) Study. Diabetes 52:2833–2839, 2003.
9. The Diabetes Control and Complications Trial/Epidemiology of Diabetes Interventions and Complications Research Group: Intensive diabetes therapy and carotid intima-media thickness in type 1 diabetes mellitus. N Engl J Med 348:2294–2303, 2003.
10. Stamler J, Vaccaro O, Neaton JD, et al: Diabetes, other risk factors, and 12-yr cardiovascular mortality for men screened in the Multiple Risk Factor Intervention Trial. Diabetes Care 16:434–444, 1993.
11. Vaccaro O, Stamler J, Neaton JD, for the Multiple Risk Factor Intervention Trial Research group: Sixteen-year coronary mortality in black and white men with diabetes screened for the Multiple Risk Factor Intervention Trial (MRFIT). Int J Epidemiol 27:636–641, 1998.
12. Kannel WB, McGee DL: Diabetes and cardiovascular disease: The Framingham Study. JAMA 241:2035–2038, 1979.
13. Jarrett RJ, Shipley MJ: Type 2 (non-insulin-dependent) diabetes mellitus and cardiovascular disease—putative association via common antecedents: Further evidence from the Whitehall study. Diabetologia 31:737–740, 1988.
14. Koskinen P, Manttari M, Manninen V, et al: Coronary heart disease incidence in NIDDM patients in the Helsinki Heart Study. Diabetes Care 15:820–825, 1992.
15. Jonsdottir LS, Sigfusson N, Gunason V, et al: Do lipids, blood pressure, diabetes, and smoking confer equal risk of myocardial infarction in women as in men? The Reykjavik Study. J Cardiovasc Risk 9:67–76, 2002.
16. West KM, Ahuja MM, Bennett PH, et al: The role of circulating glucose and triglyceride concentrations and their interactions with other "risk factors" as determinants of arterial disease in nine diabetic population samples from the WHO multinational study. Diabetes Care 6:361–369, 1983.
17. Kannel WB, McGee DL: Diabetes and glucose tolerance as risk factors for

cardiovascular disease: The Framingham Study. Diabetes Care 2:120–126, 1979.

18. Haffner SM, Lehto S, Ronnemaa T, et al: Mortality from coronary heart disease in subjects with type 2 diabetes and in nondiabetic subjects with and without prior myocardial infarction. N Engl J Med 339:229–234, 1998.

19. Haffner SM, D'Agostino R, Saad MF, et al: Carotid artery atherosclerosis in type-2 diabetic and nondiabetic subjects with and without symptomatic coronary artery disease. The Insulin Resistance Atherosclerosis Study. Am J Cardiol 85:1395–1400, 2000.

20. Expert Panel on detection, evaluation, and treatment of high blood cholesterol in adults: Executive summary of the Third Report of the National Cholesterol Education Panel (NCEP) Expert Panel on detection, evaluation, and treatment of high blood cholesterol in adults (Adult Treatment Panel III): JAMA 285:2486–2497, 2001.

21. Simons LA, Simons J: Diabetes and coronary heart disease. N Engl J Med 339:1714–1716, 1998.

22. Evans JMM, Wang J, Morris AD: Comparison of cardiovascular risk between patients with type 2 diabetes and those who had had a myocardial infarction: Cross sectional and cohort studies. Br Med J 324:939–942, 2002.

23. Eberly LE, Cohen JD, Prineas R, Yang L, for the Multiple Risk Factor Intervention Trial Research Group: Impact of incident diabetes and incident nonfatal cardiovascular disease on 18-year mortality. The Multiple Risk Factor Intervention Trial experience. Diabetes Care 26:848–854, 2003.

24. Lee CD, Folsom AR, Pankow JS, et al, for the Atherosclerosis Risk in Communities (ARIC) Study investigators: Cardiovascular events in diabetic and non diabetic adults with or without history of myocardial infarction. Circulation 109:855–860, 2004.

25. Gu K, Cowie CC, Harris MI: Diabetes and decline in heart disease mortality in US adults. JAMA 281:1291–1297, 1999.

26. Leibson CL, O'Brien PC, Atkinson E, et al: Relative contribution of incidence and survival to increasing prevalence of adult-onset diabetes mellitus: A population based study. Am J Epidemiol 146:12–22, 1997.

27. Sievers ML, Nelson RG, Bennett PH: Sequential trends in overall and cause-specific mortality in diabetic and nondiabetic Pima Indians. Diabetes Care 19:107–111, 1996.

28. Shindler DM, Palmeri ST, Antonelli TA, et al: Diabetes mellitus in cardiogenic shock complicating acute myocardial infarction: A report from the SHOCK Trial Registry. Should we emergently revascularize occluded coronaries for cardiogenic shock? J Am Coll Cardiol 36:1097–1103, 2000.

29. Miettinen H, Lehto S, Salomaa V, et al: Impact of diabetes on mortality after the first myocardial infarction. The FINMONICA Myocardial Infarction Register Study Group. Diabetes Care 21:69–75, 1998.

30. Herlitz J, Karlson BW, Lindqvist J, et al: Rate and mode of death during five years of follow-up among patients with acute chect pain with and without a history of diabetes mellitus. Diabet Med 15:308–314, 1998.

31. Tuomilehto J, Rastenyte D, Jousilahti P, et al: Diabetes mellitus as a risk factor for death from stroke. Stroke 27:210–215, 1996.

32. Kuusisto J, Mykkanen L, Pyörälä K, Laakso M: Non-insulin dependent diabetes and its metabolic control are important predictors of stroke in elderly subjects. Stroke 25:1157–1164, 1994.

33. Burchfiel CM, Curb D, Rodriguez BL, et al: Glucose intolerance and 22-year stroke incidence: The Honolulu Heart Program. Stroke 25:951–957, 1994.

34. Siitonen OI, Niskanen LK, Laakso M, et al: Lower-extremity amputations in diabetic and nondiabetic patients: A population-based study in eastern Finland. Diabetes Care 16:16–20, 1993.

35. Palumbo PJ, O'Fallon WM, Osmundson PJ, et al: Progression of peripheral occlusive arterial disease in diabetes mellitus: What factors are predictive. Arch Intern Med 151:717–721, 1991.

36. Poirier P, Desprès J-P: Lipid disorders in diabetes. In Pickup JC, Williams G (eds): Textbook of Diabetes. London, Blackwell, 2003, pp 54.1–54.21.

37. Basu A, Basu R, Shah P, et al: Systemic and regional free fatty acid metabolism in type 2 diabetes. Am J Physiol 280:E1000–E1006, 2001.

38. Hiramatsu K, Bierman ET, Chait A: Metabolism of low density lipoprotein from patients with diabetic hypertriglyceridemia by cultured human skin fibroblasts. Diabetes 34:8–14, 1985.

39. Purnell JQ, Brunzell JD: Effect of intensive diabetes therapy on diabetic dyslipidemia. Diabet Rev 5:434–444, 1997.

40. Ariya AA, Thach C, Tracy R, for the Cardiovascular Health Study investigators: Lp(a) lipoprotein, vascular disease, and mortality in the elderly. N Engl J Med 349:2108–2115, 2003.

41. Gazzaruso C, Garzaniti A, Giordanetti S, et al: Silent coronary artery disease in type 2 diabetes mellitus: The role of Lipoprotein(a), homocysteine and apo(a) polymorphism. Cardiovasc Diabetol 1:5, 2002.

42. Velmurugan K, Deepa R, Ravikumar R, et al: Relationship of lipoprotein(a) with intimal medial thickness in the carotid artery in type 2 diabetic patients in south India. Diabet Med 20:455–461, 2003.

43. Navab M, Hama SY, Ready ST, et al: Oxidized lipids as mediators of coronary heart disease. Curr Opin Lipidol 13:363–372, 2002.

44. Kovanen PT, Pentikäinen MO: Circulating lipoproteins as proinflammatory and anti-inflammatory particles in atherogenesis. Curr Opin Lipidol 14:411–419, 2003.

45. Norata GD, Pirillo A, Catapano AL: Statins and oxidative stress during atherogenesis. J Cardiovasc Risk 10:181–189, 2003.

46. Papademetriou V: The potential role of AT1-receptor blockade in the prevention and reversal of atherosclerosis. J Hum Hypertens 16(Suppl 3):S34–S41, 2002.

47. Rachmani R, Levi Z, Bat-Sheva Z, Ravid M: Losartan and lercanidipine attenuate low-density lipoprotein oxidation in patients with hypertension and type 2 diabetes mellitus: A randomized, prospective crossover study. Clin Pharmacol Ther 72:302–307, 2002.

48. Brosh D, Lvi Z, Ravid M: Oxidation of low-density lipoprotein in normotensive type 2 diabetic patients. Comparative effects of enalapril versus nifedipine: A randomized cross-over study. Diabetes Res Clin Pract 48:139–145, 2000.

49. Hirschfield GM, Pepys MB: C-reactive protein and cardiovascular disease: New insights from an old molecule. Q J Med 96:793–807, 2003.

50. Scheffer PG, Bos G, Volwater HG, et al: Associations of LDL size with in vitro oxidizability and plasma levels of in vivo oxidized LDL in type 2 diabetic patients. Diabet Med 20:563–567, 2003.

51. Jenkins AJ, Lyons TJ, Zheng D, et al: Serum lipoproteins in the Diabetes Control and Complications Trial/Epidemiology of Diabetes Intervention and Complications cohort: Associations with gender and glycemia. Diabetes Care 26:810–818, 2003.

52. Schwenke DC, D'Agostino RB Jr, Goff DC Jr, et al: Differences in LDL oxidizability by glycemic status. The Insulin Resistance Atherosclerosis Study. Diabetes Care 26:1449–1455, 2003.

53. Bucala R, Mitchell R, Arnold K, et al: Identification of the major site of apolipoprotein B modification by advanced glycosylation and end products blocking uptake by the low density lipoprotein receptor. J Biol Chem 270:10828–10832, 1995.

54. Vlassara H, Palace MR: Diabetes and advanced glycation endproducts. J Intern Med 251:87–101, 2002.

55. Sobal G, Menzel J, Sinzinger H: Why is glycated LDL more sensitive to oxidation than native LDL? A comparative study. Prostaglandins Leukot Essent Fatty Acids 63:177–186, 2000.

56. Stitt AW, He C, Friedman S, et al: Elevated AGE-modified ApoB in the sera of euglycemic, normolipidemic patients with atherosclerosis: Relationship to tissue AGEs. Mol Med 3:617–627, 1997.

57. Ohgami N, Miyazaki A, Sakai M, et al: Advanced glycation end products (AGE) inhibit scavenger receptor class B type 1-mediated reverse cholesterol transport: A new crossroad of AGE to cholesterol metabolism. J Atheroscler Thromb 10:1–6, 2003.

58. Tilton RG:s Diabetic vascular dysfunction: Links to glucose-induced reductive stress and VEGF. Microsc Res Tech 57:390–407, 2002.

59. Colhoun HM, Otvos JD, Robens MB, et al: Lipoprotein subclasses and particle sizes and their relationship with coronary artery calcification in men and women with and without type 1 diabetes. Diabetes 51:1949–1956, 2002.

60. Hokanson JE, Cheng S, Snell-Bergeon JK, et al: A common promoter polymorphism in the hepatic lipase genet (LIPC-480C>T) is associated with an increase in coronary artery calcification in type 1 diabetes. Diabetes 51:1208–1213, 2002.

61. Jenkins AJ, Garvey TW, Kelin RL: Lipoprotein abnormalities in type 1 diabetes. Curr Opin Endocrinol Diabetes 10:245–250, 2003.

62. Miettinen TA, Gylling H, Tuominen J, et al: Low synthesis and high absorption of cholesterol characterize type 1 diabetes. Diabetes Care 27:53–58, 2004.

63. Pietri AO, Dunn FL, Grundy SM, Raskin P: The effect of continuous subcutaneous insulin infusion on very-low-density lipoprotein triglyceride metabolism in type I diabetes mellitus. Diabetes 32:75–81, 1983.

64. Haffner SM, Mykkanen L, Stern MP, et al: Greater effect of diabetes on LDL size in women than in men. Diabetes Care 17:1164–1171, 1994.

65. Purnell JQ, Marcovina SM, Hokanson JE, et al: Levels of Lp(a), apolipoprotein B, and lipoprotein cholesterol distribution in IDDM: Results from follow-up in the Diabetes Control and Complications Trial. Diabetes 44:1218–1226, 1995.

66. The DCCT Research Group: Lipid and lipoprotein levels in patients with IDDM. Diabetes Care 15:886–894, 1992.

67. Purnell JQ, Hokanson JE, Marcovina SM, et al: Effect of excessive weight gain with intensive therapy of type 1 diabetes and blood pressure: Results from the DCCT. JAMA 280:140–146, 1998.

68. The Diabetes Control and Complications Trial Research Group: Adverse events and their association with treatment regimens in the Diabetes Control and Complications Trial. Diabetes Care 18:1415–1427, 1995.

69. Pietri AO, Dunn FL, Raskin P: The effect of improved diabetic control on plasma lipid and lipoprotein levels: A comparison of conventional therapy and continuous subcutaneous insulin infusion. Diabetes 29:1001–1005, 1980.

70. Sibley SD, Palmer JP, Hirsch IB, Brunzell JD: Visceral obesity, hepatic lipase activity, and dyslipidemia in type 1 diabetes. J Clin Endocrinol Metab 88:3379–3384, 2003.

71. Damci T, Osar Z, Ilkova H: Higher blood pressure in mornoalbuminuric type 1 diabetic patients with a familial history of type 2 diabetes. Diabetes Metab 28:417–420, 2002.

72. Carr MC, Hokanson JE, Zaambon A, et al: The contribution of intraabdominal fat to gender differences in hepatic lipase activity and low/high density lipoprotein heterogeneity. J Clin Endocrinol Metab 86:2831–2837, 2001.

73. Remuzzi G, Ruggenenti P, Benigni A: Understanding the nature of renal disease progression. Kidney Int 51:2–15, 1997.

74. Humes HD, Nguyen VD, Cieslinski DA, et al: The role of free fatty acids in hypoxia-induced injury to renal proximal tubule cells. Am J Physiol 256:F688–F696, 1989.

75. Orchard TJ, Chang YF, Ferrell RE, et al: Nephropathy in type 1 diabetes: A manifestation of insulin resistance and multiple genetic susceptibilities? Further evidence from the Pittsburgh Epidemiology of Diabetes Complications Study. Kidney Int 62:963–970, 2002.

76. Sahadevan M, Kasiske BL: Hyperlipidemia in kidney disease: Causes and consequences. Curr Opin Nephrol Hypertens 11:323–329, 2002.

77. Atchley DH, Lopes-Virella MF, Zheng D, et al: Oxidised LDL-anti-oxidised LDL immune complexes and diabetic nephropathy. Diabetologia 45:1562–1571, 2002.

78. Berkins BA, Dicociello LH, Silva KH, et al: Regression of microalbuminuria in type 1 diabetes. New Engl J Med 348:2285–2293, 2003.

79. Lyons TJ, Jenkins AJ, Zheng D, et al: Diabetic retinopathy and serum lipoprotein subclasses in the DCCT/EDIC cohort. Invest Ophthalmol Vis Sci 45:910–918, 2004.

80. Garg A, Grundy SM: Diabetic dyslipidemia and its therapy. Diabetes Rev 5:425–433, 1997.

81. Lu W, Resnick HE, Jablonski KA, et al: Non-HDL cholesterol as a predictor of cardiovascular disease in type 2 diabetes. The Strong Heart Study. Diabetes Care 26:16–23, 2003.

82. Sniderman AD, Scantlebury T, Cianfole K: Hypertriglyceridemic hyperapoB: The unappreciated atherogenic dysliproteinemia in type 2 diabetes mellitus. Ann Int Med 135:447–459, 2001.

83. Manley SE, Stratton IM, Cull CA, et al: Effects of three months' diet after diagnosis of type 2 diabetes on plasma lipids and lipoproteins (UKPDS 45). UK Prospective Diabetes Study Group. Diabet Med 17:518–523, 2000.

84. Heart Protection Study Collaborative Group: MRC/BHF Heart Protection Study of cholesterol-lowering with simvastatin in 5963 people with diabetes: A randomized placebo-controlled trial. Lancet 361:2005–2016, 2003.

85. Roberts CGP, Ladenson PW: Hypothyroidism. Lancet 363:793–803, 2004.

86. Emmanuele N, Azad N, Abraira C, et al: Effect of intensive glycemic control on fibrinogen, lipids, and lipoproteints. Veterans Affairs Cooperative Study in Type II diabetes mellitus. Arch Intern Med 158:2485–2490, 1998.

87. UK Prospective Study (UKPDS) Group. Effect of intensive blood-glucose control with metformin on complications in overweight patients with type 2 diabetes (UKPDS 34). Lancet 352:854–865, 1998.

88. Nagi DK, Yudkin JS: Effects of metformin on insulin resistance, risk factors for cardiovasculoar disease, and plasminogen activator inhibitor in NIDDM subjects: A study of two ethnic groups. Diabetes Care 16:621–629, 1993.

89. Beisswenger PJ, Howell SK, Touchette AD, et al: Metformin reduces systemic methylglyoxal levels in type 2 diabetes. Diabetes 48:198–202, 1999.

90. Reaven GM: Effect of metformin on various aspects of glucose, insulin and lipid metabolism in patients with non-insulin-dependent diabetes mellitus with varying degrees of hyperglycemia. Diabet Metab Rev 11:S97–S108, 1995.

91. Grosskopf I, Ringel Y, Charach G, et al: Metformin enhances clearance of chylomicrons and chylomicron remnants in nondiabetic mildly overweight glucose-intolerant subjects. Diabetes Care 20:1598–1602, 1997.

92. Wulffelé MG, Kooy A, Lehert P, et al: Combination of insulin and metformin in the treatment of type 2 diabetes. Diabetes Care 25:2133–2140, 2002.

93. Robinson AC, Burke J, Robinson S, et al: The effects of metformin on glycemic control and serum lipids in insulin-treated NIDDM patients with suboptimal metabolic control. Diabetes Care 21:701–705, 1998.

94. Miles JM, Wooldridge D, Grellner WJ, et al: Nocturnal and postprandial free fatty acid kinetics in normal and type 2 diabetic subjects: Effects of insulin sensitization therapy. Diabetes 52:675–681, 2003.

95. Haffner SM, Greenberg AS, Weston WM, et al: Effect of rosiglitazone treatment on nontraditional markers of cardiovascular disease in patients with type 2 diabetes mellitus. Circulation 106:679–684, 2002.

96. Parulkar AA, Pendergrass ML, Granda-Ayala R, et al: Nonhypoglycemic effects of thiazolidinediones. Ann Intern Med 135:61–71, 2001.

97. Van Wijk JPH, de Koning EJP, Martens EP, Rabelink TJ: Thiazolidinediones and blood lipids in type 2 diabetes. Arterioscler Thromb Vasc Biol 23:1744–1749, 2003.

98. Freed MI, Ratner R, Marcovina SM, et al, on behalf of the Rosiglitazone Study 108 investigators: Effects of rosiglitazone alone and in combination with atorvastatin on the metabolic abnormalities in type 2 diabetes mellitus. Am J Cardiol 90:947–952, 2002.

99. Ovalle F, Bell DS: Lipoprotein effects of different thiazolidinediones in clinical practice. Endocr Pract 8:406–410, 2002.

100. Miyazaki Y, Glass L, Triplitt C, et al: Effect of rosiglitazone on glucose and non-esterified fatty acid metabolism in type II diabetic patients. Diabetologia 44:2210–2219, 2001.

101. Lawrence JM, Reid J, Taylor GJ, et al: Favorable effects of pioglitazone and metformin compared with gliclazide on lipoprotein subfractions in overweight patients with early type 2 diabetes. Diabetes Care 27:41–46, 2004.

102. Vakkilainen J, Mero N, Schweizer A, et al: Effects of nateglinide and glibenclamide on postprandial lipid and glucose metabolism in type 2 diabetes. Diabetes Metab Res Rev 18:484–490, 2002.

103. Derosa G, Mugellini A, Ciccarelli L, et al: Comparison between repaglinide and glimepiride in patients with type 2 diabetes mellitus: A one-year, randomized, double-blind assessment of metabolic parameters and cardiovascular risk factors. Clin Ther 25:472–484, 2003.

104. Chiasson J-L, Josse RG, Gomis R, et al, for the STOP-NIDDM Trial Research Group: Acarbose treatment and the risk of cardiovascular disease and hypertension in patients with impaired glucose tolerance. The STOP-NIDDM Trial. JAMA 290:486–494, 2003.

105. Kaiser T, Sawicki PT: Acarbose for prevention of diabetes, hypertension and cardiovascular events? A critical analysis of the STOP-NIDDM data. Diabetologia 47:575–580, 2004.

106. Reaven GM: Banting lecture 1988: Role of insulin resistance in human disease. Diabetes 37:1595–1607, 1988.

107. Ginsberg HN: Insulin resistance and cardiovascular disease. J Clin Invest 106:453–458, 2000.

108. Lakka H-M, Laaksonen DE, Lakka TA, et al: The metabolic syndrome and total and cardiovascular disease mortality in middle-aged men. JAMA 288:2709–2716, 2002.

109. Alexander CM, Landsman PB, Teutsch SM, Haffner SM: NCEP-defined metabolic syndrome, diabetes, and prevalence of coronary geart disease among NHANES III participants age 50 years and older. Diabetes 52:1210–1214, 2003.

110. Alberti KG, Zimmet PZ: Definition, diagnosis and classification of diabetes mellitus and its complications, 1: Diagnosis and classification of diabetes mellitus provisional reports of a WHO consultation. Diabet Med 15:539–553, 1998.

111. Einhorn D, Reaven GM, Cobin RH, et al: American College of Endocrinology position statement on the insulin resistance syndrome. Endocr Pract 9:237–252, 2003.

112. Lemieux I, Pascot A, Couillard C, et al: Hypertriglyceridemic waist: A marker of the atherogenic metabolic triad (hyperinsulinaemia; hyperapoplipoprotein B; small, dense LDL) in men? Circulation 102:179–184, 2000.

113. Isomaa B, Almgren P, Tuomi T, et al: Cardiovascular morbidity and mortality associated with the metabolic syndrome. Diabetes Care 24:683–689, 2001.

114. Ford ES, Giles WH, Dietz WH: Prevalence of the metabolic syndrome among US adults: findings from the third National Health and Nutrition Examination Survey. JAMA 287:356–359, 2002.

115. Meigs JB, Nathan DM, Wilson PWF, et al: Metabolic risk factors worsen continuously across the spectrum of nondiabetic glucose tolerance: The Framingham Offspring Study. Ann Intern Med 128:524–533, 1998.

116. Lamarche B, Tchernof A, Mauriège P, et al: Fasting insulin and apolipoprotein B levels and low-density lipoprotein particle size as risk factors for ischemic heart disease. JAMA 279:1955–1961, 1998.

117. Watts GF, Barrett HR, Ji J, et al: Differential regulation of lipoprotein kinetics by atorvastatin and fenofibrate in subjects with the metabolic syndrome. Diabetes 52:803–811, 2003.

118. Listenberger LL, Han X, Lewis SE, et al: Triglyceride accumulation protects against fatty acid-induced lipotoxicity. Proc Natl Acad Sci U S A 100:3077–3082, 2003.

119. Goldbourt U, Yaari S, Medalie JH: Isolated low HDL cholesterol as a risk factor for coronary heart disease mortality: A 21-year follow-up of 8000 men. Arterioscler Thromb Vasc Biol 17:107–113, 1997.

120. Austin M, Breslow JL, Hennekens CH, et al: Low density lipoprotein subclass patterns and risk of myocardial infarction. JAMA 260:1917–1921, 1988.

121. Williams PT, Superko HR, Haskell WL, et al: Smallest LDL particles are most strongly related to coronary disease progression in men. Arterioscler Throm Vasc Biol 23:314–321, 2003.

122. Ruotolo G, Howard BV: Dyslipidemia of the metabolic syndrome. Curr Cardiol Rep 4:494–500, 2002.

123. Festa A, D'Agostino R Jr, Mykkanen L, et al: Low-density lipoprotein particle size is inversely related to plasminogen activator inhibitor-1 levels. The Insulin Resistance Atherosclerosis Study. Arterioscler Thromb Vasc Biol 19:605–610, 1999.

124. Marais AD: Therapeutic modulation of low-density lipoprotein size. Curr Opin Lipidol 11:597–602, 2000.

125. Hopkins PN, Heiss G, Ellison C, et al: Coronary artery disease risk in familial combined hyperlipidemia and familial hypertriglyceridemia: A case-control comparison from the National Heart, Lung, and Blood Institute Family Heart Study. Circulation 108:519–523, 2003.

126. Purnell JQ, Kahn SE, Schwartz RS, Brunzell JD: Relationship of insulin sensitivity and ApoB levels to intra-abdominal fat in subjects with familial combined hyperlipidemia. Arterioscler Thromb Vasc Biol 21:567–572, 2001.

127. Calabresi L, Villa B, Canavesi M, et al: An omega-3 polyunsaturated fatty acid concentrate increases plasma high-density lipoprotein 2 cholesterol and paraoxonase levels in patients with familial combined hyperlipidemia. Metabolism 53:153–158, 2004.

128. Grundy SM, Hansen B, Smith SC, et al, for conference participants: Clinical management of metabolic syndrome: Report of the American Heart Association/National Heart, Lung, and Blood Institute/American Diabetes Association conference on scientific issues related to management. Circulation 109:551–556, 2004.

129. Shoji T, Nishizawa Y, Kawagishi T, et al: Atherogenic lipoprotein changes in the absence of hyperlipidemia in patients with chronic renal failure treated by hemodialysis. Atherosclerosis 131:229–236, 1997.

130. Elisaf M, Mikhailidis DP: Statins and renal function. Angiology 53:493–502, 2002.

131. Radhakrishnan J, Appel AS, Valeri A, Appel GB: The nephritic syndrome, lipids and risk factors for cardiovascular diseases. Am J Kidney Dis 22:135–142, 1993.

132. Takemura T, Yoshioka K, Aya N, et al: Apolipoproteins and lipoprotein-receptors in glomeruli in human kidney diseases. Kidney Int 43:918–927, 1993.

133. Oda H, Keane WF: Recent advances in statins and the kidney. Kidney Int 71(Suppl):S2–S5, 1999.

134. Galle J, Heermeier K: Angiotensin II and oxidized LDL: An unholy alliance creating oxidative stress. Nephrol Dial Transplant 14:2585–2589, 1999.

135. Manttari M, Tiula E, Alikosko T, et al: Effects of hypertension and dyslipidemia on the decline in renal function. Hypertension 26:670–675, 1995.

136. Muntner P, Coresh J, Smith C, et al: Plasma lipids and risk of developing renal dysfunction: The Atherosclerosis Risk in Communities Study. Kidney Int 58:293–301, 2000.

137. Appel GB, Radhakrishnan J, Avram MM, et al, for the RENAAL study investigators: Analysis of metabolic parameters as predictors of risk in the RENAAL study. Diabetes Care 26:1402–1407, 2003.

138. Bruno G, Merletti F, Biggeri A, et al: Progression to overt nephropathy in type 2 diabetes: The Casale Monferrato Study. Diabetes Care 26:2150–2155, 2003.

139. Bianchi S, Bigazzi R, Caiazza A, Campese VM: A controlled, prospective study of the effects of atorvastatin on proteinuria and progression of kidney disease. Am J Kidney Dis 41:565–570, 2003.

140. Tonelli M, Moyé L, Sacks FM, et al: Pravastatin for secondary prevention of cardiovascular events in persons with mild chronic renal insufficiency. Ann Intern Med 138:98–104, 2003.

141. Seliger SL, Weiss NS, Gillen DL, et al: HMG-CoA reductase inhibitors are associated with reduced mortality in ESRD patients. Kidney Int 61:297–304, 2002.

142. Van der Akker JM, Bredie SJH, Diepenveen SHA, et al: Atorvastatin and simvastatin in patients on hemodialysis: Effects on lipoproteins, C-reactive protein and in vivo oxidized LDL. J Nephrol 16:238–244, 2003.

143. Chang JW, Yang WS, Min WK, et al: Effects of simvastatin on high sensitivity C-reactive protein and serum albumin in hemodialysis patients. Am J Kidney Dis 39:1213–1217, 2002.

144. Denke MA, Grundy SM: Dietary influences on serum lipids and lipoproteins. J Lipid Res 31:1149–1172, 1997.

145. Cater NB, Garg A: The effect of dietary intervention on serum lipid levels in type 2 diabetes mellitus. Curr Diab Rep 2:289–294, 2002.

146. Chandalia M, Garg A, Lutjohann D, et al: Beneficial effects of high dietary fiber intake in patients with type 2 diabetes mellitus. N Engl J Med 342:1392–1398, 2000.

147. Burnett JR, Wilcox LJ, Telford DE, et al: Inhibition of HMG-CoA reductase by atorvastatin decreases both VLDL and LDL apolipoprotein B production in miniature pigs. Arterioscler Thromb Vasc Biol 17:2589–2600, 1997.

148. Colhoun HM, Thomason MJ, Mackness, et al, for the Collaborative AtoRvastatin Diabetes Study (CARDS) investigators: Design of the Collaborative AtoRvastatin Diabetes Study (CARDS) in patients with type 2 diabetes. Diabet Med 19:201–211, 2002.

149. Pyörälä K, Pedersen TR, Kjekshus J, et al: Cholesterol lowering with simvastatin improves prognosis of diabetic patients with coronary heart disease. A subgroup analysis of the Scandinavian Simvastatin Survival Study (4S). Diabetes Care 20:614–620, 1997.

150. Haffner SM, Alexander CM, Cook TJ, et al: Reduced coronary events in simvastatin-treated patients with coronary heart disease and diabetes or impaired fasting glucose levels. Subgroup analyses in the Scandinavian Simvastatin Survival Study. Arch Intern Med 159:2661–2667, 1999.

151. Goldberg RB, Mellies MJ, Sacks FM, et al, for the CARE investigators: Cardiovascular events and their reduction with pravastatin in diabetic and glucose-intolerant myocardial infarction survivors with average cholesterol levels. Subgroup analyses in the Cholesterol and Recurrent Events (CARE) Trial. Circulation 98:2513–2519, 1998.

152. LIPID Study Group: Long-term intervention with pravastatin in ischemic disease: Prevention of cardiovascular events and death with pravastatin in patients with coronary heart disease and a broad range of initial cholesterol levels. N Engl J Med 339:1349–1357, 1998.

153. The LIPID Study Group: Long-term effectiveness and safety of pravastatin in 9014 patients with coronary heart disease and average cholesterol concentrations: The LIPID trial follow-up. Lancet 359:1379–1387, 2002.

154. Sacks FM, Tonkin AM, Shepherd J, et al: Effect of pravastatin on coronary disease events in subgroups defined by coronary risk factors. The Prospective Pravastatin Pooling Project. Circulation 102:1893–1900, 2000.

155. Sacks FM, Tonkin AM, Craven T, et al: Coronary heart disease in patients with low LDL-cholesterol: Benefit of pravastatin in diabetics and enhanced role for HDL-cholesterol and triglycerides as risk factors. Circulation 105:1424–1428, 2002.

156. Sever PS, Dahlof B, Poulter NR, et al; ASCOT investigators: Prevention of coronary and stroke events with atorvastatin in hypertensive patients who have average or lower-than-average cholesterol concentration in the Anglo-Scandinavian Cardiac Outcomes Trial–Lipid Lowering Arm (ASCOT-LLA): A multicentre randomised controlled trial. Lancet 361:1149–1158, 2003.

157. Robins SJ: Cardiovascular disease with diabetes or the metabolic syndrome: Should statins or fibrates be first line lipid therapy? Curr Opin Lipidol 14:575–583, 2003.

158. The ALLHAT Officers and Coordinators for the ALLHAT Collaborative Research Group: Major outcomes in moderately hypercholesterolemic, hypertensive patients randomized to pravastatin vs usual care. The Antihypertensive and Lipid-Lowering Treatment to Prevent Heart Attack Trial (ALLHAT-LLT). JAMA 288:2998–3007, 2002.

159. Pasternak RC: The ALLHAT Lipid Lowering Trial: Less is less. JAMA 288:3042–3044, 2002.

160. Nissen SE, Tuzcu EM, Schoenhagen P, et al, for the REVERSAL Investigators: Effect of intensive compared with moderate lipid-lowering therapy on progression of coronary atherosclerosis: A randomized controlled trial. JAMA 291:1071–1080, 2004.

161. Cannon CP, Braunwald E, McCabe CH, et al, for the Pravastatin or Atorvastatin Evaluation and Infection Therapy–Thrombolysis in Myocardial Infarction 22 Investigators: Comparison of intensive and moderate lipid lowering with statins after acute coronary syndromes. N Engl J Med 350:1495–1504, 2004.

161a. Grundy SM, Cleeman JI, Merz NB, et al for the Coordinating Committee of the National Cholesterol Education Program: Implication of recent clinical trials for the National Cholesterol Education Program Adult Treatment Panel II guidelines. Circulation 110:227–239, 2004.

162. Available at www.cardstrial.org. Website accessed on June 16, 2004.

163. Robins SJ: Fibrates and coronary heart disease reduction in diabetes. Curr Opin Endocrinol Diabetes 94:312–322, 2002.

164. Cavallero E, Dachet C, Assadolahi F, et al: Micronised fenofibrate normalises the enhanced lipidemic response to a fat load in patients with type 2 diabetes and optimal glucose control. Atherosclerosis 166:151–161, 2003.

165. Evans M, Anderson RA, Graham J, et al: Ciprofibrate therapy improves endothelial function and reduces postprandial lipemia and oxidative stress in type 2 diabetes mellitus. Circulation 101:1773–1779, 2000.

166. Forcheron F, Cachefo A, Thevenon S, et al: Mechanisms of the triglyceride- and cholesterol-lowering effect of fenofibrate in hyperlipidemic type 2 diabetic patients. Diabetes 51:3486–3491, 2002.

167. Athyros VG, Papageorgiou AA, Athyrou VV, et al: Atorvastatin and micronized fenofibrate alone and in combination in type 2 diabetes with combined hyperlipidemia. Diabetes Care 25:1198–1202, 2002.

168. Milionis HJ, Papakostas J, Kakafika A, et al: Comparative effects of atorvastatin, simvastatin, and fenofibrate on serum homocysteine levels in patients with primary hyperlipidemia. J Clin Pharmacol 43:825–830, 2003.

169. The BIP Study Group: Secondary prevention by raising HDL-cholesterol and reducing triglycerides in patients with coronary artery disease. The Bezafibrate Infarction Prevention (BIP) Study. Circulation 102:21–27, 2000.

170. Diabetes Atherosclerosis Intervention Study Investigators: Effect of fenofibrate on progression of coronary-artery disease in type 2 diabetes: The Diabetes Atherosclerosis Intervention Study, a randomized study. Lancet 357:905–910, 2001.

171. Vakkilainen J, Steiner G, Ansquer J-C, et al, on behalf of the DAIS Group: Relationships between low-density lipoprotein particle size, plasma lipoproteins, and progression of coronary artery disease. The Diabetes Atherosclerosis Intervention Study (DAIS). Circulation 107:1733–1737, 2003.

172. Rubins HB, Robins SJ, Collins D, et al, for the Veterans Affairs High-Density Lipoprotein Cholsterol Intervention Trial Study Group: Gemfibrozil for the secondary prevention of coronary heart disease in men with low levels of high-density lipoprotein cholesterol. N Engl J Med 341:410–418, 1999.

173. Robins SJ, Collins D, Wittes JT, et al, for the VA-HIT Study Group: Relation of gemfibrozil treatment and lipid levels with major coronary events: VA-HIT, a randomized controlled trial. JAMA 285:1585–1591, 2001.

174. Robins SJ, Rubins HB, Faas FH, et al: Insulin resistance and cardiovascular events with low HDL cholesterol. The Veterans Affairs HDL Intervention Trial (VA-HIT). Diabetes Care 26:1513–1517, 2003.

175. Athyros VG, Papageorgiou AA, Athyrou VV, et al: Atorvastatin and micronized fenofibrate alone and in combination in type 2 diabetes with combined hyperlipidemia. Diabetes Care 25:1198–1202, 2002.

176. Bays H: Ezetimibe. Expert Opin Investig Drugs 11:1587–1604, 2002.

177. Gagne C, Bays HE, Weiss SR, et al: the Ezetimibe Study Group: Efficacy and safety of ezetimibe added to ongoing statin therapy for treatment of patients with primary hypercholesterolemia. Am J Cardiol 90:1084–1091, 2002.

178. Stroup JS, Kane MP, Busch R: The antilipidemic effects of ezetimibe in patients with diabetes. Diabetes Care 26:2958–2959, 2003.

179. Vanstone CA, Raeini-Sarjaz M, Parsons WE, Jones PJ: Unesterified plant sterols and stanols lower LDL-cholesterol concentrations equivalently in hypercholesterolemic persons. Am J Clin Nutr 76:1272–1278, 2002.

180. Ostlund RE Jr: Phytosterols and cholesterol metabolism. Curr Opin Lipidol 15:37–41, 2004.

181. Lee YM, Haastert B, Scherbaum W, Hauner H: A phytosterol-enriched spread improves the lipid profile of subjects with type 2 diabetes mellitus: A randomized controlled trial under free-living conditions. Eur J Nutr 42:111–117, 2003.

182. Jenkins DJ, Kendall CW, Marchie A, et al: The effect of combining plant sterols, soy protein, viscous fibers, and almonds in treating hypercholesterolemia. Metabolism 52:1478–1483, 2003.

183. Leaf A, Kang JX, Xiao Y-F, Billman GE: Clinical prevention of sudden cardiac death by n-3 polyunsaurated fatty acids and mechanism of prevention of arrhythmias by n-3 fish oils. Circulation 107:2646–2652, 2003.

184. Albert CM, Campos H, Stampfer MJ, et al: Blood levels of long-chain n-3 fatty acids and the risk of sudden death. N Engl J Med 346:1113–1118, 2002.

185. Marchioli R, Barzi F, Bomba E, et al: Early protection against sudden death by n-3 polyunsaturated fatty acids after myocardial infarction: Time-course analysis of the results of the Gruppo Italiano per lo Studio della Sopravvivenza nell'Infarto Miocardico (GISSI)–Prevenzione. Circulation 105:1897–1903, 2002.

186. Montori VM, Farmer A, Wollan PC, Dinneen SF: Fish oil supplementation in type 2 diabetes: A quantitative systematic review. Diabetes Care 23:1407–1415, 2000.

187. Woodman RJ, Mori TA, Burke V, et al: Effects of purified eicosapentaenoic and docosahexaenoic acids on glycemic control, blood pressure, and serum lipids in type 2 diabetic patients with treated hypertension. Am J Clin Nutr 76:1007–1015, 2002.

188. Roche HM, Gibney MJ: Effect of long-chain n-3 polyunsaturated fatty acids on fasting and postprandial triacylglycerol metabolism. Am J Clin Nutr 71(Suppl):232S–237S, 2000.

189. Madsen T: The effect on dietary n-3 fatty acids on serum concentrations of C-reactive protein: A dose-response study. Br J Nutr 89:517–522, 2003.

190. Piolot A: Effect of fish oil on LDL oxidation and plasma homocysteine concentrations in health. J Lab Clin Med 141:41–49, 2003.

191. Kashyap ML: Mechanistic studies of high-density lipoproteins. Am J Cardiol 82:42U–48U, 1998.

192. Pan J, Van JT, Chan E, et al: Extended-release niacin treatment of the atherogenic lipid profile and lipoprotein(a) in diabetes. Metabolism 51:1120–1127, 2002.

193. Wang W, Basinger A, Neese RA, et al: Effect of nicotinic acid administration on hepatic very low density lipoprotein-triglyceride production. Am J Physiol Endocrinol Metab 43:E540–E547, 2001.

194. Guyton JR, Blazing MA, Hagar J, et al, for the Niaspan-Gemfibrozil Study Group: Extended-release niacin vs gemfibrozil for the treatment of low levels of high-density lipoprotein cholesterol. Arch Intern Med 160:1177–1184, 2000.

195. The Coronary Drug Project Research Group: Clofibrate and niacin in coronary heart disease. JAMA 231:360–379, 1975.

196. Canner PL, Burgle KG, Wenker NK, et al: Fifteen year mortality in Coronary Drug Project patients: Long-term benefit with niacin. J Am Coll Cardiol 8:1245–1255, 1986.

197. Blankenhorn DH, et al: Beneficial effects of combined colestipol-niacin therapy on coronary atherosclerosis and coronary venous bypass grafts. JAMA 257:3232–3240, 1987.

198. Brown G, et al: Regression of coronary artery disease as a result of intensive lipid-lowering therapy in men with high levels of apolipoprotein B. N Engl J Med 323:1289–1298, 1990.

199. Brown BG, Zhao X-Q, Chait A, et al: Simvastatin and niacin, antioxidant vitamins, or the combination for the prevention of coronary disease. N Engl J Med 345:1583–1592, 2001.

200. Grundy SM, Vega GL, McGovern ME, et al, for the Diabetes Multicenter Research Group: Efficacy, safety, and tolerability of once-daily niacin for the treatment of dyslipidemia associated with type 2 diabetes: Results of the Assessment of Diabetes Control and Evaluation of the Efficacy of Niaspan Trial. Arch Intern Med 162:1568–1576, 2002.

201. Brousseau ME, Schaefer EJ, Wolfe ML, et al: Effects of an inhibitor of cholesteryl ester transfer protein on HDL cholesterol. N Engl J Med 350:1505–1515, 2004.

# Essential Hypertension and Endocrine Hypertension

## *John W. Funder*

## INTRODUCTION

Blood pressure is relatively easily measured, from casual sphygmomanometry to 24-hour monitoring. Such measurements yield maximal (systolic) and minimal (diastolic) values for pressure within the brachial artery, as representative of the major vessels. Because it is easy to measure, blood pressure has assumed a central place in pathophysiology, as one determinant of and a first approximation to blood flow. Blood flow can be differentially regulated on a tissue-by-tissue or even vascular bed–by–vascular bed basis, and is much closer in terms of physiologic centrality than brachial artery pressure. We are used to thinking about physiology in terms of things that we can measure—blood volume, electrolytes, hemoglobin, viscosity—all of which affect blood pressure, and to draw inferences on aortic distensibility and total peripheral resistance from systolic and diastolic pressure values. All these factors are, in turn, important at the tissue level in terms of blood flow, but they are not the only determinants. One example might suffice to illustrate such between-tissue differences. The kidneys normally receive between 20% and 25% of the cardiac output; the only tissue with a higher perfusion rate on a weight basis is the carotid body. The liver, in contrast, with both portal venous and hepatic arterial circulations, has a much longer capillary transit time, so that, for instance, it sees albumin-bound steroids as "free," in contrast to high transit tissues such as the kidney.

Normal blood pressure is commonly assumed to be 120 (systolic)/80 (diastolic) mm Hg, although increasingly epidemiologic evidence suggests that lower blood pressures in otherwise healthy individuals are associated with reduced levels of cardiovascular morbidity and mortality. Blood pressure is normally subject to a moderate (~20 mm Hg) diurnal variation and is modulated over different time frames to changes in posture, exercise, or volume, for example, by a series of what have perhaps unhelpfully been dubbed neurohumoral mechanisms. Changes in posture are rapidly compensated, by volume shifts and changes in sympathetic nervous system activity, to produce appropriate vasoconstriction; although the latter is well recognized, the 10% or more of blood volume shift from pulmonary to the systemic circulation from lying down to standing up is often less appreciated. In exercise, the sympathetic drive leading to increased cardiac output and vasoconstriction is to some extent balanced at the muscular level by local vasodilatory mechanisms, again relatively rapidly, with a time course of minutes. When blood volume is threatened, either because of dehydration or sodium deficiency on the one hand or uncompensated (commonly via the gut) fluid and electrolyte loss on the other, a range of homeostatic mechanisms is activated, particularly involving the renin-angiotensin-aldosterone system. These range from renin release in response to sympathetic drive (which is also directly vasoconstrictor) to angiotensin (and aldosterone)-induced vasoconstriction to vasopressin release in dehydration to aldosterone-driven increases in salt appetite and epithelial sodium retention in sodium deficiency.

## PATHOGENESIS OF ESSENTIAL HYPERTENSION AND SECONDARY HYPERTENSION

Although there are many inputs to the maintenance of tissue perfusion (and by extension normal blood pressure), they are commonly interdependent, and rarely redundant across the range of environmental challenges to homeostasis. This is reflected in the causes of both clinical hypotensive and hypertensive states. Autonomic insufficiency, for example, is associated with low blood pressure and postural hypotension; autonomic overactivity, on the other hand, is commonly considered to be the proximate efferent mechanism, if not the cause, of essential hypertension. Of the clearly inherited forms of disturbed blood pressure control, all to date involve abnormalities in electrolyte and, by extension, fluid handling, with consequent effects to up or downregulate circulatory volume. In unilateral renal artery stenosis, renin release in response to reduced blood flow to the affected kidney serves to raise systemic pressure toward normalizing flow in the affected kidney, at the expense of vessels elsewhere vasoconstricted to sustain the elevated blood pressure. In few, if any, instances can deficiency or overactivity in one of the major components of blood pressure regulation be accommodated except by a change in blood pressure and, by extension, in tissue perfusion at a local or the systemic level.

## CLINICAL FEATURES OF ESSENTIAL HYPERTENSION

Essential hypertension is a term of convenience to define the clear majority of clinical situations of blood pressure elevation above 140/90 mm Hg, as opposed to hypertension secondary to a particular pathologic cause, for example, renal artery stenosis, pheochromocytoma, primary aldosteronism, congenital syndromes of inappropriate sodium handling. Systolic hypertension reflects, *inter alia*, the relative elasticity of the walls of the major arteries, the aorta in particular, which commonly decreases with age. Diastolic hypertension reflects, again *inter alia*, the extent of constriction of the arteriolar resistance vessels. Whereas it was previously thought, and taught, that elevation of diastolic pressure was more dangerous than that of systolic, the opposite is now known to be the case, perhaps linked at least in part to coronary flow occurring during diastole.

The interdependence of the various systems involved in blood pressure control is mirrored by the therapeutic options currently available for and used in essential hypertension. Diuretics promote sodium excretion and thus water with the sodium (and sometimes other electrolytes such as potassium and magnesium); β-adrenoceptor blockers lower sympathetic tone, with their effects being thus on vasoconstriction and renin release. Calcium-channel antagonists similarly lower vascular smooth muscle contractility and thus tone and have cardiac effects. Angiotensin-converting enzyme inhibitors block the production of angiotensin II, with consequent effects on vascular tone and (at least temporarily) aldosterone production; angiotensin II receptor blockers antagonize the effect of angiotensin at $AT_1R$ receptors; mineralocorticoid receptor antagonists block the effect of aldosterone on epithelial sodium retention, and amiloride blocks epithelial sodium retention via an effect on epithelial sodium channels. Although there is some variation in responsiveness (e.g., African-Americans characteristically respond much better to diuretics than to angiotensin-converting enzyme inhibitors), by and large, all the various therapeutic interventions show a remarkable ability to lower blood pressure to more or less the same extent.[1-3] In moderate hypertension (e.g., systolic 155/diastolic 100 mm Hg) blood pressure is commonly lowered by 12 to 20 mm Hg systolic, and 8 to 15 mm Hg diastolic. Angiotensin levels do not have to be elevated for angiotensin-converting enzyme inhibitors or angiotensin II receptor blockers to be effective in terms of blood pressure control; aldosterone levels similarly can be well within the normal range and mineralocorticoid receptor blockade will lower an elevated blood pressure.

## ENDOCRINE HYPERTENSION

In these terms, then, basically all essential hypertension is endocrine hypertension, although clearly not in terms of relative or absolute overproduction of catecholamines or angiotensin/aldosterone being the ultimate cause. Endocrine hypertension, *senso strictu*, would then be represented by pheochromocytoma, by renal vascular disease leading to increased renin levels or estrogen administration to increased angiotensinogen levels, or to autonomous secretion of aldosterone. The blood pressure effects of inappropriate catecholamine secretion and overproduction of angiotensin are dealt with elsewhere (see Chapters 129 and 130),[4] as are the very uncommon but equally very illustrative genetic causes of salt and water imbalance with blood pressure effects.[5-7] The section on endocrine hypertension, therefore, focuses on what in the past decade has emerged as an area of increasing reevaluation, that of autonomous overproduction of aldosterone as a cause of hypertension, as an example of new ways of considering the interaction of the endocrine sytem and blood pressure control. More details on hyperaldosteronism are given in Chapter 129.

## PRIMARY ALDOSTERONISM

### HISTORY

Aldosterone was first discovered and characterized in 1953, and in the following year, Jerome Conn reported the diagnosis and successful surgical treatment of a patient with hypertension due to an aldosterone-producing adenoma. Although Conn predicted that as many as 20% of patients with essential hypertension would be found to have primary aldosteronism, conventional wisdom (and medical school teaching) over the following 40 years put the incidence of primary aldosterone (or Conn syndrome) at 1% or less of those with essential hypertension. Over the past decade, however, this figure has been steadily reevaluated, so that today primary aldosteronism is commonly reckoned to represent 8% to 13% of essential hypertension, with as many as 40% of the hypertensive population showing abnormal aldosterone-to-renin ratios, evidence of autonomous (i.e., not angiotensin supported) aldosterone production (Table 136-1). This evolution in classification has profound therapeutic implications for patients with Conn syndrome, for patients with abnormal aldosterone-to-renin ratios but plasma aldosterone levels within the normal range, and possibly for essential hypertension as a whole.

In parallel with the emergence of aldosterone as having a key role in patients previously characterized as having essential hypertension has been the development of the second-generation mineralocorticoid receptor antagonist eplerenone. This development was prompted by the demonstration in the Randomized Aldactone Evaluation Study of the 30% improvement in survival and 35% fewer hospitalizations in patients with progressive cardiac failure given low-dose spironolactone in addition to standard of care.[8] The studies over the past

| *Table 136-1* Literature Data on High Aldosterone-to-Renin Ratio in Different Countries | | | |
|---|---|---|---|
| **Ref, year, country** | **Subjects** | **Clinical setting** | **Prevalence** |
| Hiramatsu et al.,[9] 1981, Japan | 348 patients with hypertension | Hypertension unit | 2.5% (aldosterone-producing adenoma) |
| Gordon et al.,[20] 1993, Australia | 52 pharmacologic trial volunteers | Hypertension unit | 12% |
| Gordon et al.,[21] 1994, Australia | 199 patients with hypertension | Hypertension unit | 8.5% |
| Brown et al.,[22] 1996, Australia | 74 patients with hypertension | Hospital | 8% |
| Lim et al.,[10] 1999, United Kingdom | 125 patients with hypertension of one GP | Primary care | 14% |
| Kreze et al.,[23] 1999, Slovakia | 115 patients with hypertension | Outpatient department | 13% |
| Mosso et al.,[24] 1999, Chile | 100 patients with hypertension | Outpatient department | 10% |
| Fardella et al.,[25] 2000, Chile | 305 patients with hypertension | Outpatient department | 9.5% |
| Loh et al.,[26] 2000, Singapore | 350 patients with hypertension | Hospital | 18% |
| Rayner et al.,[27] 2000, South Africa | 216 patients with hypertension | Hypertension unit | 32% |
| Gallay et al.,[28] 2001, United States | 90 patients with hypertension | Hypertension unit | 17% |
| Schwarz et al.,[13] 2002, United States | 505 patients (volunteers) with hypertension | Outpatient department | 40% |
| Calhoun et al.,[29] 2002, United States | 88 patients with resistant hypertension | Hypertension unit | 20% |
| Olivieri et al.,[11] 2004, Italy | 287 patients with hypertension of multiple GPs | Primary care | 32% |

GP, general practitioner.
Adapted from Olivieri et al.[11]

decade on patients with hypertension with an elevated plasma aldosterone-to-renin ratio, and the concurrent studies on eplerenone in essential hypertension,[1–3] thus form the basis for a reevaluation of both the pathogenesis and treatment of a substantial subpopulation of those with essential hypertension.

## DIAGNOSIS

The first demonstration that Conn syndrome may account for more than 1% of essential hypertension came from Japan, with an incidence of 2.5% based on using the aldosterone-to-renin ratio as a pointer to diagnosis.[9] Over the past decade, studies from around the world have addressed both specialist clinic populations and in two instances patients with commonly milder hypertension in general practice. Although numerical values of the aldosterone-to-renin ratio are often different between laboratories (reflecting assay variation and degree of conservatism), and sometimes very different (reflecting different units) there is now consensus, at least within the cardiovascular endocrine community, that Conn syndrome may represent as many as 15% of patients with essential hypertension referred to specialist hypertension clinics. From the two studies on general practice populations, in Scotland[10] and in Italy,[11] on patients with milder blood pressure elevation, the values may be 15% to 30% for autonomous aldosterone production, as demonstrated by abnormal aldosterone-to-renin ratios.

Part of the emerging consensus from studies around the world is that of a possible continuum in terms of the clinical picture, from autonomous overproduction of aldosterone through bilateral and possibly micronodular adrenal hyperplasia to adrenal adenoma. The erstwhile characteristic diagnostic criterion of hypokalemia similarly shows a progressive increase, from very uncommon in autonomous overproduction to present in a clear minority of cases in bilateral hyperplasia to being found in approximately one half of the adenoma population. With the increasing use of the aldosterone-to-renin ratio for screening, and the subsequent use (especially in patients with elevated plasma aldosterone levels) of bilateral adrenal venous catheterization to distinguish between adenoma and hyperplasia, it has also become apparent that the majority of cases of Conn syndrome are due to bilateral hyperplasia rather than a discrete adenoma. Although bilateral aldosterone-to-cortisol ratios commonly give a clearcut diagnosis of adenoma or hyperplasia, there are sufficient borderline differences to be consistent with a progression from autonomous aldosterone secretion through hyperplasia to adenoma. The distinction between autonomous aldosterone secretion and bilateral hyperplasia is even more blurred; whether aldosterone levels are within normal limits for renin levels clearly does not factor in other determinants of aldosterone secretion. The example of the angiotensinogen knockout mouse,[12] which responds to sodium restriction in terms of plasma aldosterone levels indistinguishably from the wild type, is a pointed reminder that the renin-angiotensin system does not appear vital for the regulation of aldosterone secretion unless potassium intake is severely limited.

## TREATMENT

The therapeutic implications of the finding of abnormal aldosterone-to-renin ratios as high as 40% in clinic patients,[13] and of more than 30% in general practice populations,[11] are profound. Although, as previously noted, there is a range of interventions that appears to be equipotent in terms of blood pressure lowering, and treatment with more than one class of antihypertensive is now accepted as standard of care for moderate to severe elevation of blood pressure, it is also clear that subgroups of patients are resistant even to multiple-drug reg-

imens. Among these patients with resistant hypertension, it is common clinical experience to find a dramatic response to the further addition of low doses (e.g., 25 mg) of spironolactone; this constitutes indirect evidence that this group of patients with hypertension resistant to combination therapy not including mineralocorticoid receptor antagonists may represent the proportion of the hypertensive population, as many as 40% in studies to date, with inappropriate aldosterone secretion for their renin status. If this is the case, there would appear to be considerable merit in treating at least this subgroup of hypertensives with a mineralocorticoid receptor antagonist as a first-line component of a multiple-drug regimen. Given the current low cost of spironolactone, cost-benefit ratio considerations might even indicate inclusion of 25 mg as a routine part of starting antihypertensive therapy, with replacement by a more selective mineralocorticoid antagonist such as eplerenone if adverse effects (e.g., gynecomastia, erectile dysfunction, mastodynia, menstrual disturbances) of spironolactone therapy are seen.

## IMPLICATIONS

What has, however, only recently been highlighted is that approximately 20% of patients with moderately severe essential hypertension do not show a significant blood pressure response to high-dose (200 mg eplerenone) antihypertensive therapy.[14] That this group, however, may still benefit from mineralocorticoid receptor blockade has been shown in principle in various animal models. In stroke-prone spontaneously hypertensive rats, for example, mineralocorticoid receptor blockade with spironolactone dramatically reduces the incidence of stroke and proteinuria, subsequent to substantial vascular protection, without a substantial change in blood pressure.[15] Similarly, in uninephrectomized rats on 0.9% NaCl solution to drink and infused with angiotensin II, there are no differences in blood pressure between angiotensin II–infused, adrenalectomized angiotensin II–infused, and angiotensin II–infused with eplerenone added to their chow. The two latter groups, however, show almost complete vascular protection, which is abolished in adrenalectomized rats by aldosterone replacement.[16] These blood pressure–independent vasculoprotective effects in animal models are reminiscent of the dramatic reduction seen with perindopril plus indapamide in the secondary prevention Progress trial,[17] in which a 28% overall lower incidence of stroke was seen, with no difference between hypertensive and normotensive patients. Similarly, in the context of heart failure, no change in blood pressure was seen on the average dose of 26 mg spironolactone in the Randomized Aldactone Evaluation Study,[8] or 43 mg eplerenone in Eplerenone Post-Acute Myocardial Infarction Heart Failure Efficacy and Survival Study (EPHESUS),[18] despite which very positive outcomes were seen.

## SUMMARY

Essential hypertension is a clinical classification based on blood pressure and in which there is no obvious precipitating cause for the elevation in measured blood pressure. Blood pressure itself is a sometimes distracting surrogate for a complex series of cardiovascular mechanisms ensuring tissue perfusion. Whereas, for most essential hypertension, overactivity of the sympathetic nervous system appears to be the proximal efferent cause of the elevated blood pressure, no single component of the neurohumoral factors involved in blood pressure elevation appears redundant, in that a wide variety of therapeutic interventions are all able to modestly reduce blood pressure, and a combination of different therapeutic agents often produces almost additive blood pressure decreases. To this extent, nearly all essential hypertension has an endocrine component, with largely independent contributions from the renin-angiotensin system and activation of mineralocorticoid receptors, as shown in the 4E trial.[3] The salient area of change in terms of endocrine hypertension is that of autonomous aldosterone secretion, inappropriate for renin status as determined by the aldosterone-to-renin ratio, which has been reported to be elevated in as many as 40% of patients with otherwise essential hypertension. It is possible that such a group represents a progression of clinical course from hypertension with an elevated aldosterone-to-renin ratio to bilateral adrenal hyperplasia to Conn syndrome. Similarly, given the growing appreciation of the vascular protection produced experimentally by mineralocorticoid receptor blockade, consideration must be given to including mineralocorticoid receptor antagonists as first-line agents in treatment regimens at least for those with elevated aldosterone-to-renin ratios and potentially for all patients with hypertension.[11,19]

## REFERENCES

1. White WB, Duprez D, St. Hillaire R: Effects of selective aldosterone blocker eplerenone versus the calcium antagonist amlodipine in systolic hypertension. Hypertension, 41:1021–1026, 2003.
2. Weinberger M, Roniker B, Krause SL, et al: Eplerenone, a selective aldosterone blocker, in mild-to-moderate hypertension. Am J Hypertens 15:709–716, 2002.
3. Pitt B, Reichek N, Willenbrock R: Effects of eplerenone, enalapril, and eplerenone/enalapril in patients with essential hypertension and left ventricular hypertrophy: The 4E-left ventricular hypertrophy study. Circulation 108:1831–1838, 2003.
4. DeGroot LJ, Jameson JL (eds): Endocrinology, 5th ed. Philadelphia, Elsevier, 2005.
5. Rogerson FM, Fuller PJ: Mineralocorticoid action. Steroids 65:61–73, 2000.
6. Funder JW: Aldosterone and mineralocorticoids. In Oparil S, Weber M (eds): Hypertension: A Companion to Brenner and Rector's The Kidney. Philadelphia, Elsevier, 2004.
7. Geller D, Farhi A, Pinkerton N: Activating mineralocorticoid receptor mutation in hypertension exacerbated by pregnancy. Science 289:119–123, 2000.
8. Pitt B, Zannad F, Remme WJ: The effect of spironolactone on morbidity and mortality in patients with severe heart failure. N Engl J Med 341:709–717, 1999.
9. Hiramatsu K, Yamada T, Yukimura Y: A screening test to identify aldosterone-producing adenoma by measuring plasma renin activity. Arch Intern Med 141:1589–1593, 1981.
10. Lim PO, Rodgers P, Cardale K: Potentially high prevalence of primary aldosteronism in a primary-care population. Lancet 353:40, 1999.
11. Olivieri O, Ciacciarelli A, Signorelli D: Aldosterone to renin ratio in a primary care setting: The Bussolengo study. J Clin Endocrinol Metab 2004 (in press).
12. Okubo S, Niimura F, Nishimura H: Angiotensin-independent mechanism for aldosterone synthesis during chronic extracellular fluid volume depletion. J Clin Invest 99:855–860, 1997.
13. Schwarz GL, Chapman AB, Boerwinkle E: Screening for primary aldosteronism: Implications of an increased plasma aldosterone/renin ratio. Clin Chem 48:1919–1923, 2002.
14. Levy D, Rocha R, Funder JW: Distinguishing the antihypertensive and electrolyte effects of eplerenone. J Clin Endocrinol Metab 89:2736–2740, 2004.
15. Rocha R, Chander PN, Khanna K: Mineralocorticoid blockade reduces vascular injury in stroke-prone hypertensive rats. Hypertension 31:451–458, 1998.
16. Rocha R, Martin-Berger C, Yang P: Selective aldosterone blockade prevents angiotensin II/salt-induced vascular inflammation in the rat heart. Endocrinology 143:4828–4836, 2002.
17. Progress Collaborative Group: Randomised trial of a perindopril-based blood-pressuring-lowering regimen among 6105 individuals with previous stroke or transient ischaemic attack. Lancet 358:1033–1041, 2001.
18. Pitt B, Remme W, Zannad F: Eplerenone, a selective aldosterone blocker, in patients with left ventricular dysfunction after myocardial infarction. N Engl J Med 348:1309–1321, 2003.
19. Funder JW: Aldosterone-renin ratios in the context of primary care. J Clin Endocrinol Metab 2004 (in press).
20. Gordon RD, Ziezak MD, Tunny TJ: Evidence that primary aldosteronism may not be uncommon—twelve percent incidence among antihypertensive drug trial volunteers. Clin Exp Pharmacol Physiol 20:296–298, 1993.
21. Gordon RD, Stowasser M, Tunny TJ: High incidence of primary aldosteronism in 199 patients referred with hypertension. Clin Exp Pharmacol Physiol 21:315–318, 1994.
22. Brown MA, Cramp HA, Zammit VC: Primary aldosteronism: A missed diagnosis in "essential hypertensives"? Aust N Z J Med 26:533–538, 1996.
23. Kreze AJ, Okalova D, Vanuga P: Occurrence of primary aldosteronism in a group of ambulatory hypertensive patients. Vnitr Lek 45:17–21, 1999.
24. Mosso L, Fardella C, Montero J: High prevalence of undiagnosed primary hyperaldosteronism among patients with essential hypertension. Rev Med Child 127:800–806, 1999.
25. Fardella CE, Mosso L, Gomez-Sanchez CE: Primary aldosteronism in essential hypertensives: Prevalence, biochemical profile and molecular biology. J Clin Endocrinol Metab 85:1863–1867, 2000.
26. Loh K-C, Koay ES, Khaw M-C: Prevalence of primary aldosteronism among Asian hypertensive patients in Singapore. J Clin Endocrinol Metab 85:2854–2859, 2000.
27. Rayner BL, Opie LH, Davidson JS: The aldosterone/renin ratio as a screening test for primary aldosteronism. S Afr Med J 90:394–400, 2000.
28. Gallay BJ, Ahmad S, Xu L: Screening for primary aldosteronism without discontinuing hypertensive medications: Plasma aldosterone-renin ratio. Am J Kidney 37:699–705, 2001.
29. Calhoun DA, Nishizaka MK, Zaman MA: Hyperaldosteronism among black and white subjects with resistant hypertension. Hypertension 40:892–896, 2002.

# Orthostatic Hypotension and Orthostatic Intolerance

## Christopher J. Mathias

INTRODUCTION

CLASSIFICATION

CLINICAL FEATURES

INVESTIGATION OF ORTHOSTATIC HYPOTENSION
AND ORTHOSTATIC INTOLERANCE

DESCRIPTION OF KEY DISORDERS
   Nonneurogenic Causes of Orthostatic Hypotension

Neurogenic Orthostatic Hypotension
Drugs, Chemicals, Toxins
Intermittent Autonomic Dysfunction

MANAGEMENT
   Orthostatic Hypotension
   Intermittent Autonomic Dysfunction

## INTRODUCTION

Various features, some resulting from evolutionary processes, distinguish humans from animals. One of these is our transformation from quadrupeds into bipeds, which has resulted in certain advantages but has exposed us to the effects of gravitational (Newtonian) forces. These forces are of particular influence in the functioning of the cardiovascular system, of which a prime aim is to ensure adequate perfusion of organs. Standing upright results in translocation of between 500 and 700 mL of blood from central compartments to the lower limbs that cause marked pressure differentials, with a substantial increase in pressure below and a decrease in pressure above heart level (Fig. 137-1).[1] Adaptive mechanisms therefore are essential in ensuring the maintenance of arterial blood pressure and provision of an adequate perfusion pressure to organs to avoid malfunction, especially while standing upright.

Comparative biology has provided information on how our forebears developed the means to circumvent the effects of gravitational stress. This is necessary even in quadrupeds, who can rapidly become hypotensive when suspended with their legs dependent.[2] Adaptive mechanisms, even in the same species, provide the ability to cope with differences in morphology, activities, and terrain, as observed in the snake.[3] Aquatic (sea) snakes can cope with vertical pressure gradients because they are unaffected by gravity despite their low level of blood pressure (15–39 mm Hg), as the density of their blood is similar to that of seawater. Terrestrial (land) snakes have a higher level of blood pressure and by the use of body coiling and tail movements maintain cerebral perfusion pressure, for instance, when poised to attack when the head is raised. Arboreal (tree) snakes have a higher level of pressure (50–90 mm Hg) due to increased vascular tone; they are slimmer with a thinner tail to prevent vascular pooling and have their heart closer to the head, thus aiding cerebral perfusion. The morphology of some mammals, such as the giraffe whose head is 20 ft above the heart, poses specific challenges. The giraffe has a markedly elevated systemic blood pressure (almost twice that of humans), which is helped by a large and muscular heart, a series of one-way valves in the jugular vein to prevent blood backflow, and thick-walled arteries in the lower limbs beneath an extremely tight skin that prevents pooling.

In humans, the ability to overcome the effects of gravitational stress is dependent on a variety of factors that include cardiac output, tone in resistance vessels, the state of capacitance vessels, vasoactive hormones that are circulating (the

renin-angiotensin-aldosterone system) and locally produced (nitric oxide and endothelin), intravascular volume and overall fluid status, and the baroreceptor reflex, which is part of a highly developed autonomic nervous system. Afferent pathways in the carotid sinus, heart, and major cardiopulmonary vessels relay information to the brain through the vagus and glossopharyngeal nerves. Within the brain are numerous cerebral connections. The efferent pathways consist of the sympathetic outflow to blood vessels and heart and the parasympathetic (vagus) nerves to the heart. The baroreflex enables beat-by-beat control of blood pressure through vasoconstriction induced by sympathetic activation, as has been demonstrated in humans using the technique of sympathetic microneurography (Fig. 137-2).[4] These factors maintain blood pressure and heart rate when upright. Impairment of one or more of vascular, endocrine, volume, or neurogenic factors can result in orthostatic intolerance when standing upright, although this may occur even while sitting. *Orthostatic* or *postural hypotension* is the term used to describe the decrease in blood pressure that may occur when upright. It is defined as a decrease in systolic blood pressure of 20 mm Hg or diastolic blood pressure of 10 mm Hg or greater while either standing or tilted head-up for 3 minutes. Orthostatic intolerance may occur independently of orthostatic hypotension, for instance, in the postural tachycardia syndrome (PoTS).

## CLASSIFICATION

There are many causes of orthostatic hypotension. Nonneurogenic causes are more frequently encountered (Table 137-1). They include disorders that reduce intravascular fluid volume, impair the function of the heart, or dilate blood vessels.[5] Neurogenic causes result from disease affecting the autonomic nervous system: This may occur within the brain, spinal cord, or periphery or at multiple sites.[6] In primary disorders, there is no clear etiology or association, as in pure autonomic failure (PAF) and multiple-system atrophy (MSA) (Table 137-2). Secondary causes include genetic disorders (familial dysautonomia) and enzyme deficiencies (dopamine β-hydroxylase deficiency) and when there is an association with a clearly defined disease (diabetes mellitus and spinal cord injuries). A variety of drugs can cause orthostatic hypotension by direct pharmacologic effects on the autonomic nervous system or by causing an autonomic neuropathy (Table 137-3).

Orthostatic hypotension results usually in orthostatic intolerance, with difficulties when standing and occasionally even

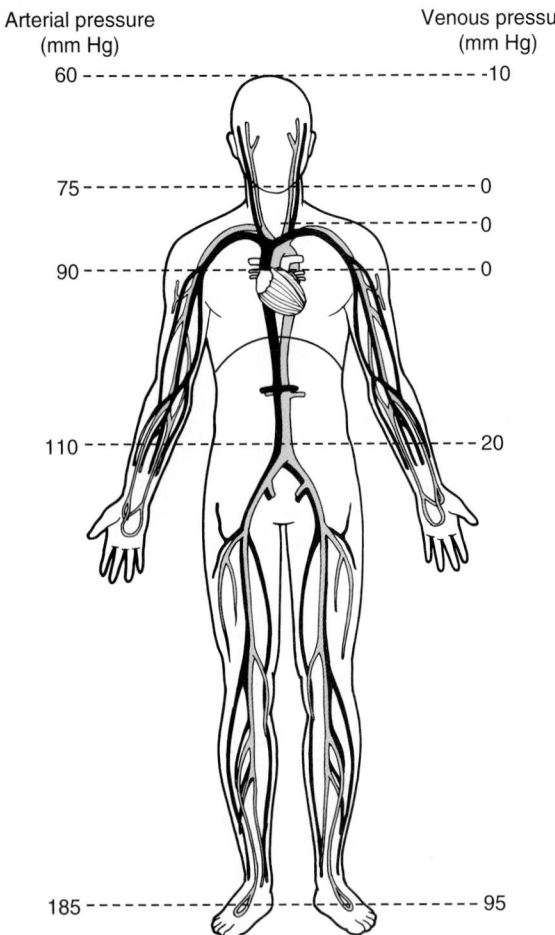

**Figure 137-1** Effects of gravity on arterial and venous blood pressures in an erect, motionless man. Arterial and venous pressures in the lower part of the body are increased and are decreased in the upper part of the body. Note that cerebral arterial pressure is approximately 15 mm Hg lower than aortic root pressure. Because the brain is enclosed by the rigid skull, the venous pressures may be less than atmospheric pressure. This results in a relatively constant arteriovenous pressure difference in different parts of the brain. (From Hainsworth R: Arterial blood pressure. In Henderby GEH [ed]: Hypotensive Anaesthesia. Edinburgh, Churchill Livingstone, 1985, pp 3–29.)

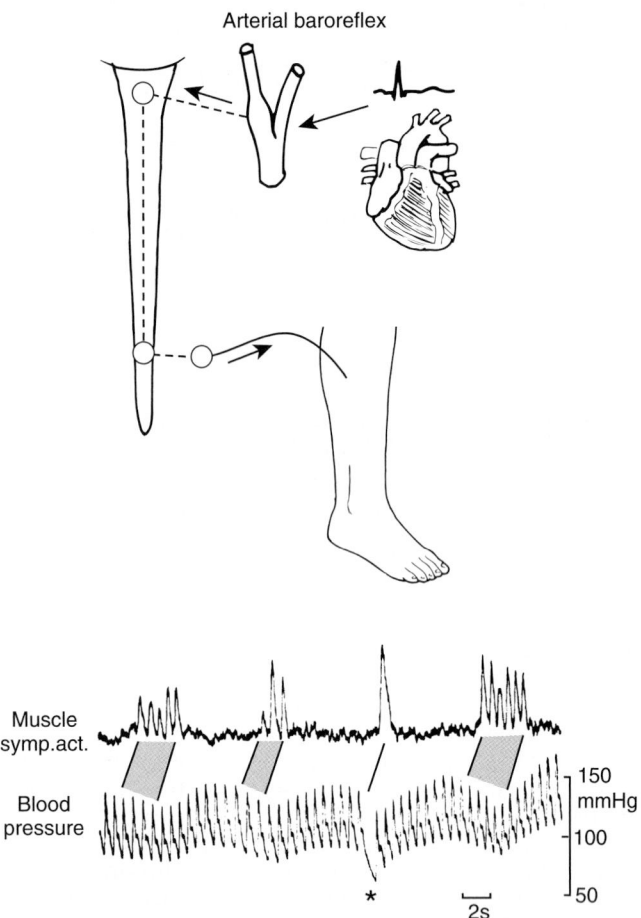

**Figure 137-2** Relationship between spontaneous fluctuations of blood pressure and muscle nerve sympathetic activity (symp. act.) (*left*) recorded in the right peroneal nerve. The baroreceptor reflex accounts for the pulse synchrony of nerve activity and the inverse relationship to blood pressure fluctuations. The *star* indicates a diastolic blood pressure decrease due to sudden atrioventricular block. *Stippling* indicates corresponding sequences of bursts and heart beats. bpm, beats per minute. (From Wallin BG, Linblad L-E: Baroreflex mechanisms controlling sympathetic outflow to the muscles. In Sleight P [ed]: Arterial Baroreceptors and Hypertension. Oxford, Oxford University Press, 1988, p 101.)

sitting. This may be a consistent feature, as often is seen in disorders with fixed damage to autonomic nerves. However, there are intermittent autonomic disorders, such as neurally mediated syncope, in which transient autonomic dysfunction results in a decrease in blood pressure, heart rate, or both, with effects that are more substantial while upright (Table 137-4). In PoTS, symptoms occur predominantly while standing upright or during exertion but often without a decrease in blood pressure. Orthostatic intolerance may occur even in healthy subjects, as in astronauts exposed to negative gravity for a prolonged period.[7]

## CLINICAL FEATURES

Orthostatic hypotension causes a variety of symptoms that mainly arise from underperfusion of organs, especially those above the level of the heart, such as the brain (Table 137-5).[8] There may be similar features in both nonneurogenic and neurogenic orthostatic hypotension, although there are certain aspects that differentiate the two when blood pressure decreases. Neurogenic causes of orthostatic hypotension often also involve the cardiac parasympathetic nerves, and, in such cases, the decrease in blood pressure is not accompanied by an appropriate increase in heart rate, as may otherwise

occur in an attempt to correct hypotension. Thus, in nonneurogenic orthostatic hypotension, tachycardia and palpitations are more likely to accompany the decrease in blood pressure. In such subjects, additional compensatory mechanisms to increase blood pressure usually are triggered, causing peripheral vasoconstriction with symptoms of clamminess and sweating. This is less likely to occur in widespread autonomic failure. In orthostatic intolerance due to PoTS, there is a marked increase in heart rate of more than 30 beats per minute, without a decrease in blood pressure (Fig. 137-3).[9]

The symptoms arising from orthostatic hypotension can be considered under those arising from hypoperfusion of specific organs (see Table 137-5). The brain is at particular risk, and transient loss of consciousness (syncope, fainting, blackouts) may occur. Symptoms that precede syncope include dizziness, visual disturbances, and, in some, transient cognitive deficits. A number of disorders can result in similar symptoms, but the hallmark in orthostatic hypotension is the onset of symptoms on assuming the upright posture and regression of symptoms, usually fairly rapidly, on returning to a horizontal position. In orthostatic hypotension associated or caused by chronic disorders, many recognize the association with head-up postural change, either before or during the initial onset of symptoms, and introduce corrective means, such as sitting down, lying flat, or assuming curious postures such as squatting or stoop-

**Table 137-1** Examples of Nonneurogenic Causes of Orthostatic Hypotension

**LOW INTRAVASCULAR VOLUME**
Blood/plasma loss
  Hemorrhage, burns, hemodialysis
Fluid/electrolyte deficiency
  Diminished intake—Anorexia nervosa
  Loss from gut—Vomiting, ileostomy losses, diarrhea
  Loss from kidney—Salt losing nephropathy, diuretics
  Endocrine deficiency—Adrenal insufficiency (Addison's disease)

**CARDIAC INSUFFICIENCY**
Myocardial
  Myocarditis
Impaired ventricular filling
  Atrial myxoma, constrictive pericarditis
Impaired output
  Aortic stenosis

**VASODILATATION**
Endogenous
  Hyperpyrexia
  Hyperbradykininism
  Systemic mastocytosis
  Varicose veins
Exogenous
  Drugs such as glyceryl trinitrate (GTN)
  Alcohol
  Excessive heat

**Table 137-2** Neurogenic Causes of Orthostatic Hypotension

Primary
  Acute/subacute dysautonomias
    Pure pandysautonomia
    Pandysautonomia with neurologic features
  Chronic autonomic failure syndromes
    Pure autonomic failure
    Multiple system atrophy (Shy-Drager syndrome)
    Autonomic failure with Parkinson's disease
Secondary
  Congenital
    Nerve growth factor deficiency
  Hereditary
    Autosomal-dominant trait
      Familial amyloid neuropathy
    Autosomal-recessive trait
      Familial dysautonomia, Riley-Day syndrome
      Dopamine $\beta$-hydroxylase deficiency
  Metabolic
    Diabetes mellitus
    Chronic renal failure
    Chronic liver disease
    Alcohol induced
  Inflammatory
    Guillain-Barré syndrome
    Transverse myelitis
  Infections
    Bacterial: tetanus
    Viral: human immunodeficiency virus infection
  Neoplasia
    Brain tumors, especially of the third ventricle or posterior fossa
    Paraneoplastic, including adenocarcinomas of the lung and pancreas
  Surgery
    Vagotomy and drainage procedures; "dumping syndrome"
  Trauma
    Cervical and high thoracic spinal cord transection
Drugs, chemicals, poisons, toxins
  By their direct effects
  By causing a neuropathy

Adapted from Mathias CJ: Autonomic diseases: Clinical features and laboratory evaluation. Neurol Neurosurg Psychiatry 74:iii31–iii41, 2003.

ing. The adaptive mechanisms depend in part on the rapidity with which blood pressure may decrease. In some, there may be no time because the blood pressure decreases precipitously and syncope may occur rapidly, similar to a drop attack, but often with syncope. Loss of consciousness may result in injury. In some, seizures may result due to cerebral hypoxia. The decrease in blood pressure and symptoms may vary considerably even within the same patient because there is dependence on a number of factors, including tolerance to a low cerebral perfusion pressure. Symptomatic tolerance may develop with time, probably as a result of improved cerebrovascular autoregulation and may explain why some are at their worst in the early stages of their disorder, but later tolerate a head-up postural change despite a similar decrease in blood pressure. Some hyperventilate when the blood pressure decreases; this should be discouraged because it has the potential to further reduce cerebral perfusion through cerebral vasoconstriction. In some disorders, such as high spinal cord injuries, subjects learn techniques to increase blood pressure, such as initiating autonomic dysreflexia (due to activation of skeletal muscle spasms or urinary bladder contraction), that can trigger spinal reflexes, increase blood pressure, and thus prevent or reduce the postural decrease in blood pressure.[10] In subjects in whom adaptive mechanisms have not or cannot be induced, the reduction in blood pressure may result in falling to the ground with the potential for trauma that in some may result in fractures and even death. Patients with cerebrovascular insufficiency due to atheroma and stenosis are at risk because a relatively small decrease in blood pressure can induce cerebral ischemia more readily.

There are a number of symptoms due to organ hypoperfusion, some of which are more common in chronic orthostatic hypotension. Hypoperfusion of tonically active suboccipital and paracervical muscles may result in neck and shoulder ache in a "coat-hanger" distribution, where the pain is related to the head-up position when blood pressure is low.[11] Unlike other causes of neck pain, such as cervical spondylitis, it tends to rapidly resolve when the blood pressure recovers, while sitting or lying flat. Chest pain may occur even in the young with apparently normal coronary arteries; mechanisms include chest wall ischemia. Symptoms of low back pain and

occasionally even calf claudication may occur; whether this is due to impaired perfusion of muscles or to spinal cord ischemia during standing is difficult to ascertain. Some give a clear history of worsening symptoms and loss of consciousness while activating arm muscles, such as while putting out

**Table 137-3** Drugs, Chemicals, Poisons, and Toxins Causing Neurogenic Orthostatic Hypotension

Decreasing sympathetic activity
  Centrally acting
    Clonidine
    Methyldopa
    Moxonidine
    Reserpine
    Barbiturates
    Anesthetics
  Peripherally acting
    Sympathetic nerve endings (guanethidine, bethanidine)
    $\alpha$-Adrenoceptor blockade (phenoxybenzamine)
    $\beta$-Adrenoceptor blockade (propranolol)
Miscellaneous
  Alcohol
  Vincristine, perhexiline maleate
  Ciguatera toxicity
  Jellyfish and marine animal venoms
  First dose of some drugs (prazosin, captopril)

Adapted from Mathias CJ: Autonomic diseases: Clinical features and laboratory evaluation. J Neurol Neurosurg Psychiatry 74:iii31–iii41, 2003.

**Table 137-4** Intermittent Autonomic Disorders That Cause Orthostatic Intolerance

Neurally mediated syncope
   Vasovagal syncope
   Carotid sinus hypersensitivity
   Miscellaneous (or situational) syncope
Postural tachycardia syndrome

---

**Table 137-5** Some of the Symptoms Resulting from Orthostatic Hypotension and Impaired Perfusion of Various Organs

Cerebral hypoperfusion
   Dizziness
   Visual disturbances
      Blurred; tunnel
      Scotoma
      Graying out; blacking out
      Color defects
   Loss of consciousness
   Cognitive deficits
Muscle hypoperfusion
   Paracervical and suboccipital ("coat-hanger") ache
   Lower back/buttock ache
Subclavian steal-like syndrome
Renal hypoperfusion
   Oliguria
Spinal cord hypoperfusion
Nonspecific
   Weakness, lethargy, fatigue
   Falls

Adapted from Mathias CJ: Autonomic diseases: Clinical features and laboratory evaluation. J Neurol Neurosurg Psychiatry 74:iii31–iii41, 2003.

the washing, reaching upward, or using a lawn mower. This may result in increased blood supply to the pectoral girdle musculature, and a subclavian steal, further impairing low vertebrobasilar blood flow.

Orthostatic hypotension can reduce renal hyperperfusion and result in oliguria while upright. The reverse, polyuria, may occur, especially at night, when the subject is supine.[12]

In some, there may be few of the symptoms listed, but nonspecific symptoms such as weakness, lethargy, and fatigue.[8] In the elderly, the key symptom may be falls of otherwise unknown etiology.

There are many factors that influence the postural decrease in blood pressure, especially in patients with autonomic failure (Table 137-6). Some are worse in the morning, probably because of nocturia reducing intravascular fluid volume; this also has been observed after prolonged recumbency. The speed of postural change is of importance because rapid movement into the head-up position may lower blood pressure further. Cutaneous vasodilatation, in hot weather or after a warm bath, increases the tendency to orthostatic symptoms. Patients with widespread autonomic failure often have impairment of micturition and defecation, and straining can induce a Valsalva-like maneuver with a further decrease in blood pressure. Similar changes may occur during coughing and even laughing. Ingestion of water alone, for reasons that remain unclear, can increase blood pressure.[13] This differs from the ingestion of food and alcohol that can lower blood pressure substantially, presumably because of splanchnic vasodilatation that in autonomic failure is not opposed by vasoconstriction in other vascular regions, as occurs normally[14–16] (Fig. 137-4). Physical exertion, even of a modest nature, also can lower blood pressure substantially because of vasodilatation in exercising skeletal muscle[17–19] (Fig. 137-5). Of importance are the vasodilatatory actions of drugs, to

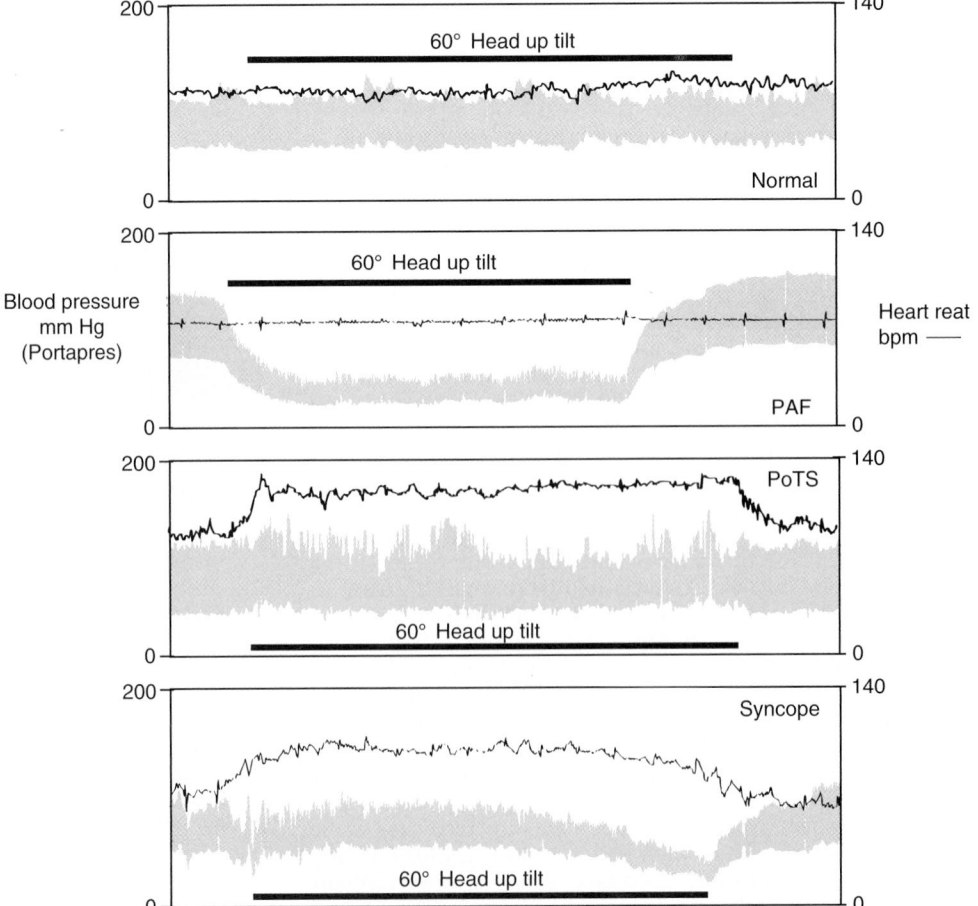

**Figure 137-3** Blood pressure and heart rate measured continuously before, during, and after a 60-degree head-up tilt by the Portapres II in a normal subject and in subjects with three different autonomic disorders: pure autonomic failure (PAF), postural tachycardia syndrome (PoTS), and vasovagal syncope. (From Mathias CJ: To stand on ones' own legs. Clin Med 2:237–245, 2002.)

**Table 137-6** Factors That May Influence Orthostatic Hypotension

Speed of positional change
Time of day (worse in the morning)
Prolonged recumbency
Warm environment (hot weather, hot bath)
Raising intrathoracic pressure: micturition, defecation, or coughing
Water ingestion*
Food and alcohol ingestion
Physical exertion
Physical maneuvers and positions (bending forward, abdominal compression, leg crossing, squatting, activating calf muscle pump)†
Drugs with vasoactive properties

*This increases blood pressure in autonomic failure.
†These maneuvers usually reduce the postural decrease in blood pressure in neurogenic causes of orthostatic hypotension, unlike the others.
Adapted from Mathias CJ: Autonomic diseases: Clinical features and laboratory evaluation. J Neurol Neurosurg Psychiatry 74:iii31–iii41, 2003.

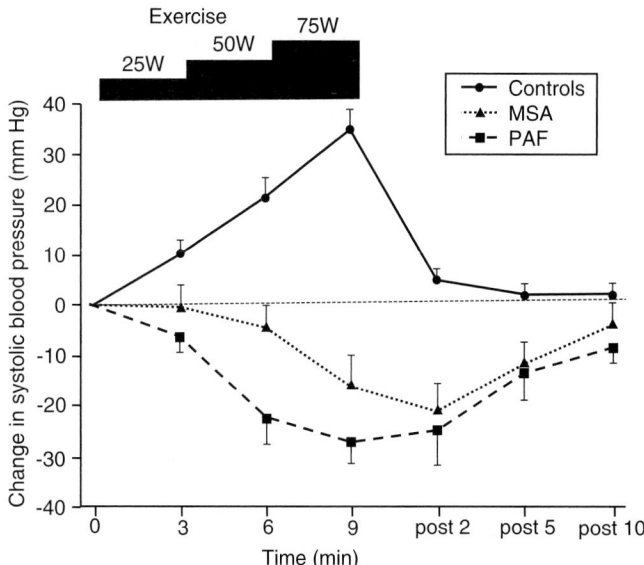

**Figure 137-5** Changes in systolic blood pressure during supine bicycle exercise at three incremental levels (25, 50, and 75 W) in normal subjects (controls) and patients with multiple-system atrophy (MSA) and pure autonomic failure (PAF). The bars indicate standard error of the mean. Unlike controls, in whom there is an increase, there is a decrease in blood pressure in both MSA and PAF. Blood pressure returns rapidly to the baseline in controls, unlike in the two patient groups in whom it takes almost 10 minutes. All remained horizontal during and for 10 minutes postexercise. (From Smith GDP, Watson LP, Pavitt DV, Mathias CJ: Abnormal cardiovascular and catecholamine responses to supine exercise in human subjects with sympathetic dysfunction. J Physiol [Lond] 485:255–265, 1995.)

which patients with autonomic failure are supersensitive because of their inability to compensate adequately.[20] Examples are patients with Parkinson's disease in whom the drug L-dopa, in part through the formation of dopamine, can unmask or aggravate orthostatic hypotension. In diabetics with an autonomic neuropathy, administration of insulin, either by reducing blood volume through increasing transcapillary albumin escape or by vasodilatatory effects, occasionally may exacerbate orthostatic hypotension.

In the intermittent autonomic disorders, such as neurally mediated syncope, the decrease in blood pressure and heart rate is transient and often related to specific events, although it may occur without a recognized provoking cause. This may cause symptoms of dizziness, palpitations, and clamminess (presyncope) that may be followed by syncope. The warning signs vary between individuals and even between episodes in the same subject. In the cardioinhibitory form, heart rate decreases because of increased vagal activity; in the vasodepressor form, blood pressure falls due to withdrawal of sym-

pathetic nerve activity to blood vessels; in the mixed form, there is a varying combination of the two. There are three major causes of neurally mediated syncope: vasovagal, carotid sinus hypersensitivity, and a miscellaneous group (see Table 137-4). The majority of subjects with neurally mediated syncope are otherwise healthy individuals in whom autonomic screening shows no abnormalities.[21] A variety of factors that include fear and pain may induce a vasovagal episode, hence the term *emotional syncope*. In carotid sinus hypersensitivity, there may be a history of syncope while turning the head, tightening the collar, or shaving. In the elderly, such associations often are not provided. There is a variety of miscellaneous causes that include micturition-induced syncope, as observed mainly in the male. Choking on food may also induce syncope. Neurally mediated syncope is more likely to occur in the upright position.

In another intermittent autonomic disorder, the PoTS orthostatic intolerance often is accompanied by palpitations with a heart rate rise of over 30 beats per minute, during head-up tilt or standing, without a decrease in blood pressure. Many find that the tachycardia is worse during exercise; decompensation due to lack of physical activity may complicate the disorder. In some, there may be features of hyperventilation and panic attacks may occur, although whether this is primary or secondary to the problem remains difficult to determine.

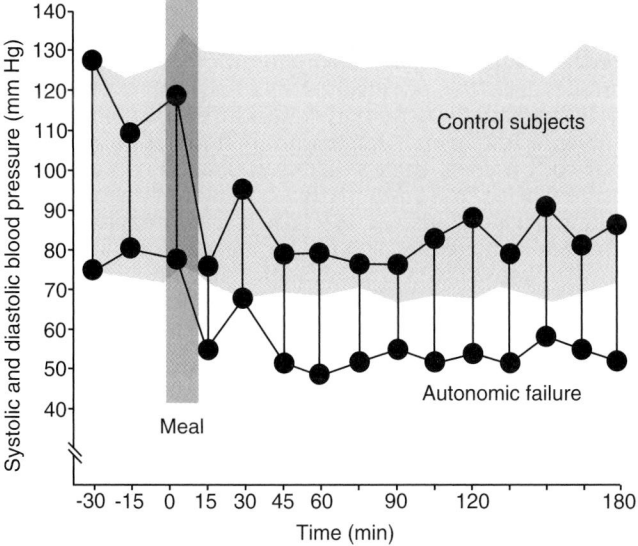

**Figure 137-4** Supine systolic and diastolic blood pressures before and after a standard meal in a group of normal subjects *(stippled area)* and in a patient with autonomic failure. Blood pressure does not change in the normal subjects after a meal taken while lying flat. In the patient, there is a rapid decrease in blood pressure to levels of approximately 80/50 mm Hg, which remains low while in the supine position over the 3-hour observation period. (From Mathias CJ, Bannister R: Postprandial hypotension in autonomic disorders. In Mathias CJ, Bannister R [eds]: Autonomic Failure: A Textbook of Clinical Disorders of the Autonomic Nervous System, 4th ed. Oxford, Oxford University Press, 2002, pp 283–295.)

## INVESTIGATION OF ORTHOSTATIC HYPOTENSION AND ORTHOSTATIC INTOLERANCE

In nonneurogenic orthostatic hypotension, investigation will depend on the suspected cause, underlying deficit, and associated disorder. The key reasons for investigation are to confirm diagnosis, aid prognosis, and enable investigation-based management.

In neurogenic causes of orthostatic hypotension, a multi-pronged approach is often needed for evaluation, ideally in an autonomic laboratory. Outlined are screening tests to evaluate cardiovascular autonomic function (Table 137-7); additional tests may be needed. Laboratory investigation is needed for at least three purposes: (1) to determine whether autonomic function is normal or abnormal; (2) to determine if an abnormality has been observed, to evaluate the degree of autonomic dysfunction, with an emphasis on the site of lesion and the functional deficits; (3) to ascertain the cause of autonomic dysfunction, as this determines the extent of further investigations and the prognosis and may modify management strategies.

In neurally mediated syncope, testing may need to be designed around the individual patient and circumstances. In generalized autonomic diseases, extensive investigation of the nervous system may be required.

In the clinic, orthostatic hypotension can be measured while lying down and then sitting or standing. In the laboratory, head-up tilt to 60 degrees often is used as the postural stimulus, especially when the neurologic deficit or severe hypotension makes it difficult for the patient to stand. Blood pressure and heart rate can be accurately measured using non-invasive techniques, many of which are automated and provide a printout at preset intervals. In autonomic failure, there may be considerable variability in the basal supine levels and the postural decrease in blood pressure; the greatest changes often occur in the morning, after a meal, and after physical exertion. In such patients, nonneurogenic causes also must be considered, especially as they worsen neurogenic orthostatic hypotension.

Autonomic screening tests, in addition to head-up tilt testing, help determine the site and extent of the cardiovascular autonomic abnormality. The responses to Valsalva's maneuver, during which intrathoracic pressure is increased to a maximum of 40 mm Hg, depend on the integrity of the entire baroreflex pathway. Changes in heart rate alone may provide a useful guide. Some patients, however, may increase mouth pressure without necessarily increasing intrathoracic pressure, resulting in a falsely abnormal heart rate response. Stimuli that increase blood pressure, such as isometric exercise (e.g., by sustained hand grip for 3 minutes), the cold pressor test (e.g., immersing the hand in ice slush for 90 seconds), and mental arithmetic (e.g., using serial-7 or -17 subtraction), activate different afferent or central pathways, which then stimulate the sympathetic outflow. The heart rate responses to postural change, deep breathing (sinus arrhythmia), and hyperventilation assess the cardiac parasympathetic (vagus) nerves.

Additional investigations may be needed to determine factors causing or contributing to orthostatic hypotension and syncope. These include the responses to food ingestion, exercise, and carotid sinus massage. To assess postprandial hypotension, the cardiovascular responses to a balanced liquid meal containing carbohydrate, protein, and fat are measured while supine, with comparisons of the blood pressure res-

ponse to head-up tilt before the meal and 45 minutes later. To evaluate exercise-induced hypotension, responses are obtained during graded incremental supine exercise using a bicycle ergometer with measurement of postural responses before and after exercise. In suspected carotid sinus hypersensitivity, resuscitation facilities should be available because carotid massage may cause profound bradycardia or cardiac arrest. Carotid massage also should be performed during head-up tilt because hypotension may occur only in this position because of the greater dependence on sympathetic tone. Intermittent ambulatory blood pressure and heart rate recordings over a 24-hour period using small computerized lightweight devices are of particular value, especially at home, in determining the effects of various stimuli in daily life. However, it is essential in autonomic disease, in contrast to hypertensive patients, that appropriate protocols are followed and an accurate diary of events maintained to determine the effects of postural change, food, and exercise (Fig. 137-6). The information from such recordings also is of value in determining the beneficial effects of therapy.

Plasma catecholamine measurements are available in specialized laboratories and may be of value (Fig. 137-7). Plasma norepinephrine provides a measure of sympathetic neural activity and plasma epinephrine of adrenomedullary activity. In PAF, the supine basal levels of plasma norepinephrine are low and suggest a distal lesion compared with MSA, in which supine levels are often within the normal range. In both groups, there is an attenuation or lack of increase in plasma norepinephrine during head-up tilt, indicating impairment of sympathetic neural activity. In high spinal cord lesions, basal plasma norepinephrine and epinephrine levels are low and do not increase with postural change. There is, however, an increase (but only moderately above the basal levels of normal subjects) during severe hypertension accompanying autonomic dysreflexia, which differs from paroxysmal hypertension due to a pheochromocytoma, when plasma norepinephrine or epinephrine levels usually are greatly elevated. Extremely low or undetectable levels of plasma norepinephrine and epinephrine with elevated plasma dopamine levels occur in sympathetic failure caused by deficiency of the enzyme dopamine β-hydroxylase, which converts dopamine into norepinephrine.

Muscle and skin sympathetic nervous activity can be recorded directly by percutaneous insertion of tungsten microelectrodes into the peroneal or median nerves (Fig. 137-8). Muscle sympathetic activity is closely linked to the baroreceptor reflex, with a clear relationship to blood pressure. In high spinal cord lesions, there is reduced baseline neural activity consistent with low basal plasma norepinephrine and blood pressure levels because of the lack of transmission of tonic brain stem sympathetic activity. Increased nerve firing occurs in the Guillain-Barré syndrome, with hypertension and tachycardia. These microneurographic approaches have aided our understanding of the pathophysiologic processes but are of limited clinical application, especially in the investigation of autonomic failure.

Pharmacologic approaches determine the degree of sensitivity of different receptors and the functional integrity of sympathetic nerves and cardiac vagi. Some have value in the clinical situation. Repeat head-up tilt after stepwise intravenous atropine (to a maximum of 1.8 mg), when the rate increases to 120 beats per minute, helps determine the role of maintaining the heart rate, such as by cardiac pacing, in the cardioinhibitory forms of vasovagal syncope. A vasodepressor response while the heart rate is maintained indicates that pacing is unlikely to be effective.

Some pharmacologic challenges, often combined with hormonal measurement, provide information in different disorders. Basal plasma norepinephrine levels may be elevated due to stress and other factors; in these situations, the central sympatholytic actions of clonidine suppress plasma norepinephrine levels, which does not occur with autonomous

| **Table 137-7** Investigation of Neurogenic Orthostatic Hypotension |
|---|
| Head-up tilt (60 degrees),* standing,* Valsalva's maneuver* |
| Pressor stimuli* (isometric exercise, cold pressor, mental arithmetic) |
| Heart rate responses to deep breathing,* hyperventilation,* standing,* head-up tilt* |
| Liquid meal challenge |
| Modified exercise testing |
| Carotid sinus massage |

*Indicates screening autonomic tests used in our London Units.
Adapted from Mathias CJ: Autonomic diseases: Clinical features and laboratory evaluation. J Neurol Neurosurg Psychiatry 74:iii31–iii41, 2003.

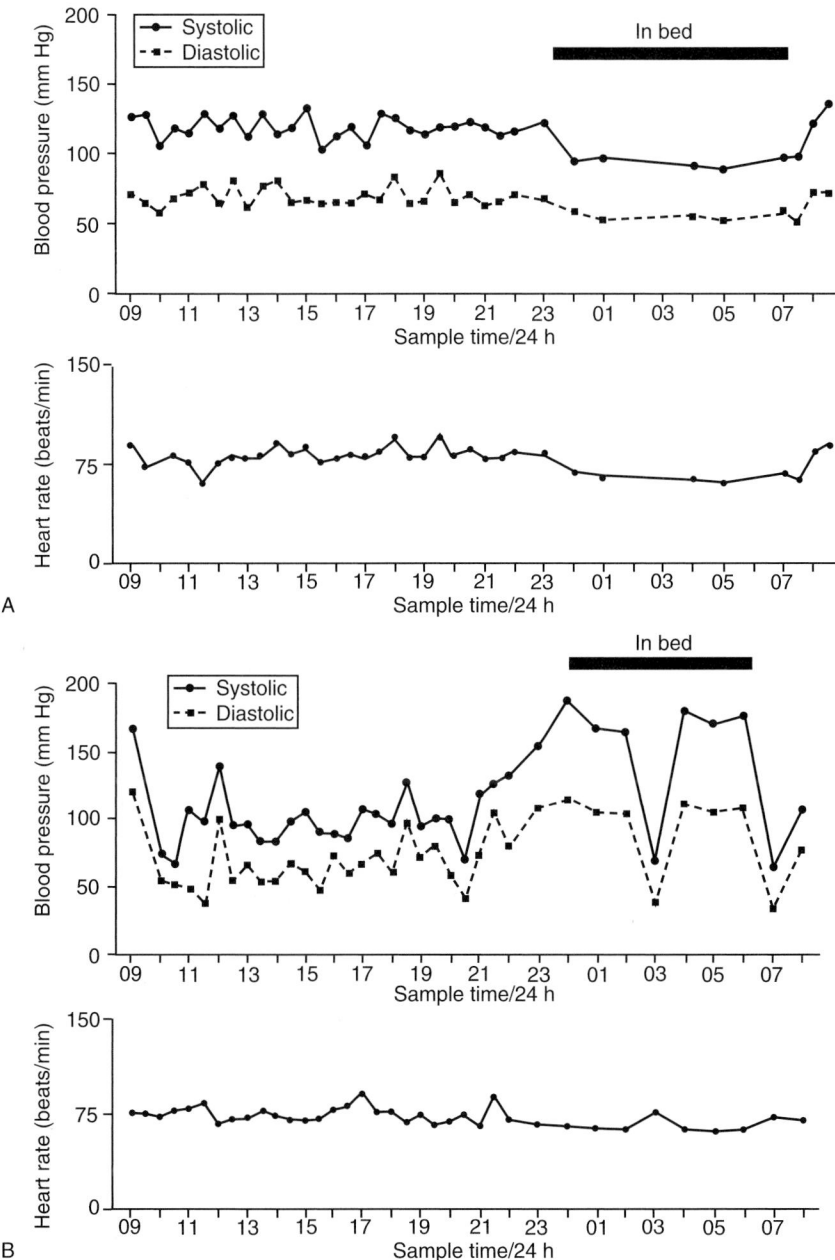

*Figure 137-6* Twenty-four-hour noninvasive ambulatory blood pressure profile showing systolic and diastolic blood pressures and heart rate at intervals throughout the day and night. **A,** The changes in a normal subject with no postural decrease in blood pressure: There was a decrease in blood pressure at night while asleep, with an increase in blood pressure on waking. **B,** Changes in a subject with autonomic failure. The marked decreases in blood pressure are usually the result of postural changes, either sitting or standing. Supine blood pressure, particularly at night, is elevated. Getting up to micturate causes a marked decrease in blood pressure (at 3:00 A.M.). There is a reversal of the diurnal changes in blood pressure. There are relatively small changes in heart rate, considering the marked changes in blood pressure. (From Mathias CJ, Bannister R [eds]: Investigation of autonomic disorders. In Autonomic Failure: A Textbook of Clinical Disorders of the Autonomic Nervous System, 4th ed. Oxford, Oxford University Press, 2002.)

secretion in pheochromocytoma. Another central action of clonidine, through the hypothalamus and anterior pituitary, is stimulation of growth hormone (GH) release. Serum GH levels rise in normal subjects and in PAF who have distal autonomic lesions; there is no response in MSA, in whom the lesions are central.

Advances in modern technology enable noninvasive measurement of autonomic cardiac function and blood flow in various regions. A variety of spectral analytic techniques assess cardiovascular function. Invasive techniques measure total body and regional norepinephrine spillover in the heart, splanchnic and renal circulations, and the brain. Radionuclide [123]I-metaiodobenzylguanidine imaging assesses cardiac sympathetic innervation. These techniques have a role in the clinical research setting, and in due course, some may be applied to the clinical investigation of cardiovascular autonomic function.

Details of investigations in neurogenic orthostatic hypotension are described in specialized textbooks.[22,23]

## DESCRIPTION OF KEY DISORDERS

### NONNEUROGENIC CAUSES OF ORTHOSTATIC HYPOTENSION

Many of the causes of orthostatic hypotension outlined in Table 137-1 do not warrant further description, other than some endocrine deficiencies. Further details of these disorders are provided in other chapters.

#### Adrenal Failure

A reduction in either cortisol or aldosterone levels or a combination of the two that occurs in Addison's disease can cause orthostatic hypotension.

*Hypocortisolism*

Low cortisol levels may result from a primary adrenocortical defect, a deficiency of adrenocorticotropic hormone, or a reduction in corticotrophic releasing hormone, as may occur in intracranial disorders and pituitary tumors. Prolonged

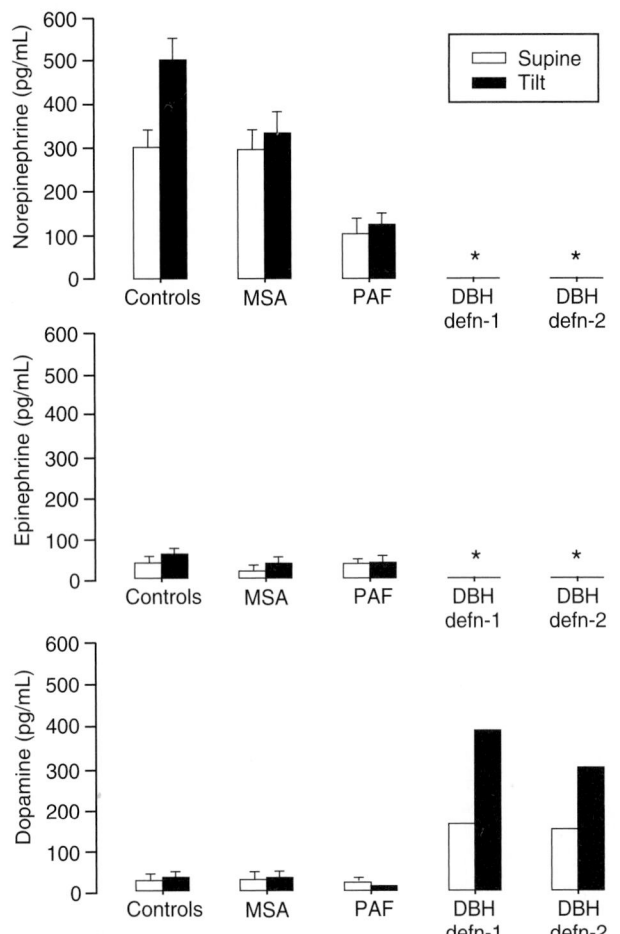

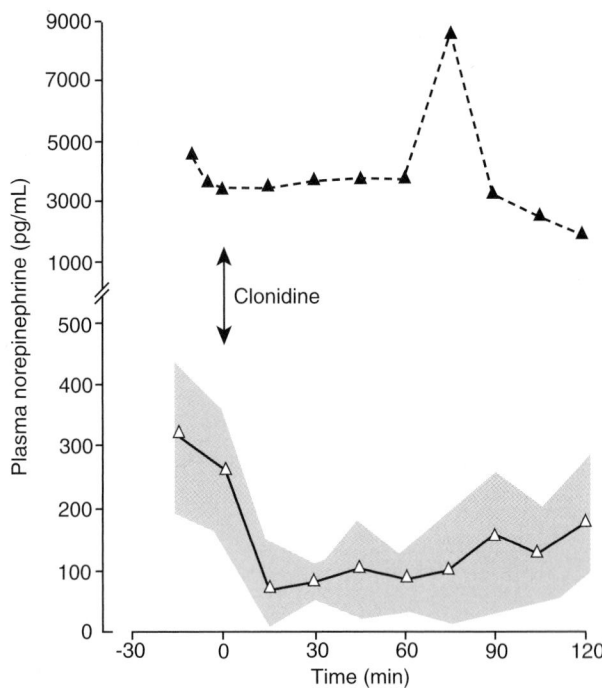

**Figure 137-8** Plasma norepinephrine levels in a patient with a pheochromocytoma (*solid triangles*) and in a group of patients with essential hypertension (*open triangles*) before and after intravenous clonidine, indicated by an *arrow* (2 µg/kg over 10 minutes). Plasma norepinephrine levels fall rapidly in the essential hypertensives after clonidine and remain low over the period of observation. The *stippled area* indicates the mean ± SEM. Plasma norepinephrine levels are considerably higher in the patient with pheochromocytoma and are not affected by clonidine. (From Mathias CJ, Bannister R: Investigation of autonomic disorders. In Mathias CJ, Bannister R (eds): Autonomic Failure. A Textbook of Clinical Disorders of the Autonomic Nervous System, 4th ed. Oxford, Oxford University Press, 2002, pp 169–195.)

**Figure 137-7** Plasma norepinephrine, epinephrine, and dopamine levels (measured by high-pressure liquid chromatography) in normal subjects (controls), patients with multiple-system atrophy (MSA), pure autonomic failure (PAF), and two individual patients with dopamine β-hydroxylase (DBH defn) while supine and after 45-degree head-up tilt to for 10 minutes. The *asterisks* indicate levels below the detection limits for the assay, which are less than 5 pg/mL for norepinephrine and less than 20 pg/mL for dopamine. *Bars* indicate ± SEM. (From Bannister R, Mathias CJ: Investigation of autonomic disorders. In Bannister R, Mathias CJ (eds): Autonomic Failure. A Textbook of Clinical Disorders of the Autonomic Nervous System, 4th ed. Oxford, Oxford University Press, 2002, pp 169–195.)

glucocorticoid therapy may suppress adrenocorticotropic hormone, with effects when the steroids are rapidly withdrawn or when associated with severe stress. Normal recumbent levels of blood pressure may be seen even when there is a marked reduction in cortisol levels. Supine hypotension often is an indication of severe adrenocortical failure. Tachycardia often is present, as autonomic responses are not impaired. Current concepts of the pathophysiology of orthostatic hypotension in hypocortisolism depend largely on previous observations, which suggested that adrenal insufficiency impaired the contractility of the vasculature. These included the visually obvious blanching of the surgically exposed mesoappendix of the rat in response to local application of norepinephrine that was absent in adrenalectomized animals but was rapidly restored by adrenal extract.[24] An important additional role of fluid maldistribution in bilaterally adrenalectomized dogs has been demonstrated.[25] Swingle and colleagues[25] observed profound hypotension, hemoconcentration, hyponatremia, oliguria, and azotemia of adrenalectomized dogs when steroid replacement was withdrawn that could be dramatically corrected by glucocorticoid administration alone in the absence of access of the dogs to oral or intravenous fluids. This sug-

gested that glucocorticoid therapy mobilized a presumably intracellular accumulation of water to restore blood pressure, to reverse hemoconcentration, and to result in diuresis and the correction of azotemia. One of the first clinical tests for the diagnosis of Addison's disease was the demonstration of the strikingly subnormal ability of these patients to dilute their urine and to excrete an administered water load.[26] Patients subjected to this test were often sickened by the procedure, sometimes became stuporous and had excessive swelling of erythrocytes (indicated by an excessive decrease in mean corpuscular hemoglobin concentration) compared with healthy subjects.[27] These changes could all be restored to the normal ranges with cortisone given a few hours before the water load.[28] The observations suggested that low cortisol levels were severely reducing water excretion, partly by impairment of sodium reabsorption in the ascending limb of the loop of Henle[29,30] and partly because of excessive water sequestration in the erythrocytes and probably other cells of the body.

Whether cortisol affects cellular water channels is unclear. With low cortisol levels, plasma volume is reduced[25] and probably plays an important role in the orthostatic hypotension of adrenal insufficiency.

### Hypoaldosteronism

Low levels of plasma aldosterone may be the result of low plasma renin levels as may occur in some forms of autonomic failure[31] or from a secretory defect primarily in the adrenal zona glomerulosa. When it results from hyporeninism, the consequent decrease in angiotensin II formation may reduce sympathetic function by loss of its normal actions on the area postrema as well as in the potentiation of sympathetic ganglionic transmission.[32] Hypoaldosteronism may contribute to, or be the sole cause of, orthostatic hypotension that is correctable with fludrocortisone replacement therapy. This effect of hypoaldosteronism presumably results from diminished reabsorption of sodium in the distal nephron and consequent reduction in plasma volume. In addition, patients may develop orthostatic hypotension through loss of the mineralocorticoid action enhancing the normal vasoconstrictive effect of norepinephrine on human arterioles[33] and veins.[34] Whether the effect of aldosterone on intracellular concentrations of sodium[35] contributes is not known.

## Pheochromocytoma

In 11 patients with pheochromocytoma, orthostatic hypotension in 46% and tachycardia in 55% were reported when the adrenal glands were explored during lumbodorsal sympathectomy for severe hypertension.[36] Of 18 patients with subsequently proven pheochromocytoma,[37] 16 (89%) had orthostatic systolic hypotension, 12 (67%) had orthostatic tachycardia, and 10 (56%) had both orthostatic abnormalities (Fig. 137-9). In striking contrast, of 350 consecutively studied patients with essential hypertension whose plasma norepinephrine concentrations were all less than 400 pg/mL, 6% had orthostatic systolic hypotension, 7% had orthostatic tachycardia, and only two patients (0.6%) had both abnormalities. Because the prevalence of pheochromocytomas has been estimated to be between 0.32% and 0.64% of hypertensives, it is likely that when patients with pheochromocytoma are questioned about their experience of any of the symptoms of orthostatic hypotension, several of them reply in the affirmative. These unexpected accompaniments of excessive circulating catecholamines occur only in patients whose tumors are persistently secreting norepinephrine.[37] When such patients were given intravenous infusions of norepinephrine at increasing rates, they were found to require significantly greater increments in plasma norepinephrine concentrations than normal subjects to increase their systolic blood pressure by 15 mm Hg and their diastolic blood pressure by 7 mm Hg, confirming previous findings.[38] Measurements also revealed subnormal sensitivity of the veins to the contractile action of increasing rates of norepinephrine infusion in patients with pheochromocytoma.[37] These findings probably result from downregulation of arteriolar and venous α-adrenergic receptors, as has been found in the platelets of patients with pheochromocytoma, which is the

usual response to persistently (but not intermittently) elevated concentration of the circulating agonist norepinephrine.[38–41] Because of this phenomenon, most patients with pheochromocytoma fail to experience normal orthostatic contraction of their veins and arterioles, causing orthostatic hypotension, despite the huge orthostatic increments in circulating norepinephrine that have been shown to occur in these patients.[37]

## NEUROGENIC ORTHOSTATIC HYPOTENSION

The causes are outlined in Tables 137-2 and 137-3.

### Primary Causes
The primary causes of autonomic failure include acute/subacute dysautonomias and chronic autonomic failure.

#### Acute/Subacute Dysautonomia
These are rare disorders. In pure pandysautonomia, there are features of both sympathetic and parasympathetic failure, with orthostatic hypotension usually a major problem. In pandysautonomia, the peripheral somatic nerves may also be affected. The prognosis in the pandysautonomias is variable, with complete recovery in some.[42]

#### Chronic Autonomic Failure
These mainly include PAF, MSA, and diseases with overlapping features.

**Pure Autonomic Failure** The diagnosis usually is considered when orthostatic hypotension is detected.[6] The onset may be insidious because compensatory mechanisms, often unwittingly used, help reduce symptoms of orthostatic hypotension. Erroneous diagnoses, from epilepsy to a psychiatric disorder, may previously have been considered. Nocturia is frequent, along with constipation. Impairment of sweating may not be recognized in temperate climates. Heat intolerance and collapse may occur in tropical areas. In males, impotence is common. The clinical and laboratory features include widespread sympathetic failure, usually with parasympathetic deficits. The neuropathologic data available,[43] along with the physiologic and biochemical tests, indicate a peripheral autonomic lesion.

In PAF, management of orthostatic hypotension is of importance because it contributes to morbidity and may result in injury. Control of bowel and bladder function, and, in males,

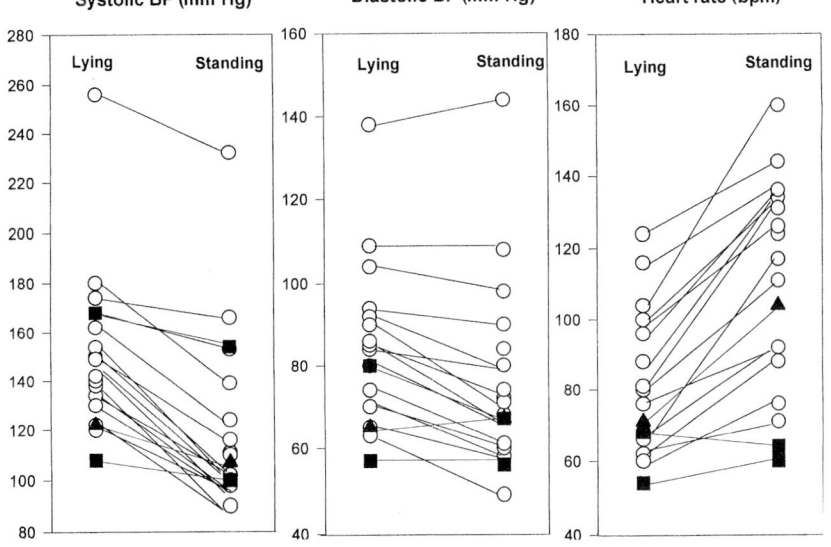

*Figure 137-9* Orthostatic changes in blood pressure (BP) and heart rate induced by standing for 5 minutes in 18 patients with pheochromocytoma. Orthostatic systolic hypotension was present in 13 patients whose plasma norepinephrine levels were consistently elevated (*open circles*) but not in the patient with exclusive elevation of plasma epinephrine (*solid triangles*) or in the two patients with only intermittently increased plasma norepinephrine levels (*solid squares*). Excessive orthostatic tachycardia occurred in 10 patients with persistently increased plasma norepinephrine levels and the patient with exclusively increased plasma epinephrine levels but not in the two patients with intermittently elevated plasma catecholamine concentrations. (Data from Streeten DHP, Anderson GH Jr: Mechanisms of orthostatic hypotension and tachycardia in patients with pheochromocytoma. Am J Hypertens 9:760–769, 1996.)

sexual function, may need to be addressed. These patients often are older than the age of 50 at presentation. The overall prognosis in PAF is good, with a life expectancy similar to that of healthy individuals of an equivalent age.

**Multiple System Atrophy** This disorder is synonymous with the Shy-Drager syndrome. It is a sporadic, nonfamilial disorder with autonomic, parkinsonian, cerebellar, and pyramidal features that occur in any combination over a varying time scale[44-46] (see Table 137-1). In humans, it probably is the most common neurodegenerative condition affecting the autonomic nervous system. It is a relentlessly progressive disorder but with an unpredictable rate of progression; this adds to difficulties in diagnosis. Most patients have parkinsonian features at some stage of the disease. There often is difficulty in distinguishing MSA from idiopathic Parkinson's disease (IPD), and this may account for why as many as 25% of patients diagnosed *in vivo* as having IPD are found at postmortem to have the characteristic neuropathologic features of MSA. In the early stages, depending on the presenting features, patients may consult a range of specialists, from internists, neurologists, and cardiologists to urologists and psychiatrists.

There are three major subgroups of MSA based on their neurologic features: parkinsonian (MSA-P), cerebellar (MSA-C), and mixed (MSA-M), with a combination of these features. A characteristic neuropathologic feature is the presence of intracytoplasmic argyrophilic inclusions in oligodendrocytes within defined areas of the brain and spinal cord.[47] Cell loss in various brain stem nuclei (including the vagus), the intermediolateral cell mass in the thoracic and lumbar spinal cord, and Onuf's nucleus in the sacral spinal cord accounts for various abnormalities. The paravertebral ganglia and visceral (enteric) plexuses are not affected.

In the parkinsonian forms of MSA, the onset of bradykinesia and rigidity often is bilateral, with minimal or no tremor, unlike IPD. Lack of a motor response to dopaminergic drugs alone is not helpful because two thirds of patients with MSA respond initially, although side effects and refractoriness to the motor benefits with time lowers this to a third or less. The presence of autonomic failure (especially cardiovascular and genitourinary) in a patient with parkinsonism should alert one to the possibility of MSA. Respiratory abnormalities and oropharyngeal dysphagia favor MSA, although these often only occur as the disease advances.

Neuroimaging (especially positron emission tomography and magnetic resonance scanning of the brain) and proton magnetic resonance spectroscopy of the basal ganglia may help distinguish MSA from other parkinsonian syndromes.[6] The presence of orthostatic hypotension alone does not necessarily indicate autonomic failure because there are many contributing causes (Table 137-8). A combined neuropharmacologic-neuroendocrine approach, using intravenous clonidine-GH testing separates central from peripheral autonomic failure.[48] The centrally acting $\alpha_2$-adrenoceptor agonist clonidine stimulates hypothalamic GH-releasing hormone that acts on the anterior pituitary to release GH[49,50] (Fig. 137-10). In PAF, in which there is no central autonomic abnormality, levels of GH rise after clonidine administration. In MSA, there is no GH response to clonidine. In MSA, the GH secretagogue L-dopa increases GH-releasing hormone and GH levels,[51] whereas apomorphine increases GH, although there is a greater response in Parkinson's disease.[52] This indicates that the abnormal GH response to clonidine is not the result of widespread neuronal fallout and probably indicates a specific $\alpha_2$-adrenoceptor-hypothalamic deficit. In nondrug-treated IPD, there is preservation of the clonidine-GH response[50] that may not apply to drug-treated IPD (see Fig. 137-10).

The prognosis in MSA is poor compared with that of IPD and PAF because there is progressive worsening of the motor and autonomic deficits; refractoriness to antiparkinsonian

| *Table 137-8* Possible Causes of Orthostatic Hypotension in a Patient with Parkinsonism |
|---|
| Side effects of antiparkinsonian drugs |
|   L-dopa, bromocritine, pergolide |
|   L-dopa and catecholamine-*O*-methyl transferase inhibitors (tolcapone) |
|   Monoamine oxidase B inhibitor (selegeline) |
| Coincidental disease causing autonomic dysfunction |
|   Diabetes mellitus |
| Coincidental drugs for allied conditions |
|   Hypertension: antihypertensives |
|   Prostatic hypertrophy: $\alpha$-adrenoceptor blockers |
|   Ischemic heart disease: vasodilators |
|   Cardiac failure: diuretics |
|   Erectile failure: sildenafil |
| Autonomic failure |
|   Multiple-system atrophy |
|   Parkinson's disease with autonomic failure |
|   Diffuse Lewy body disease |

Adapted from Mathias CJ: Autonomic diseases: Clinical features and laboratory evaluation. J Neurol Neurosurg Psychiatry 74:iii31–iii41, 2003.

agents and orthostatic hypotension further impair mobility.[6,44,45] Communication becomes increasingly difficult. In the cerebellar forms, truncal ataxia may cause falls and an inability to stand upright; incoordination in the upper limbs, speech deficits, and nystagmus add to the disability. Oropharyngeal dysphagia enhances the risk of aspiration, especially because many have vocal cord abnormalities; a percutaneous feeding gastrostomy may be needed. Respiratory abnormalities that include obstructive apnea (due to laryngeal abductor cord paresis) and central apnea may necessitate a tracheostomy.

In MSA, there currently is no means of reversing the neurologic decline. Supportive therapy is an essential component in the management and should incorporate the family, therapists, and community. Many autonomic features can be helped, and this includes orthostatic hypotension and bowel, bladder, and sexual dysfunction.

**Idiopathic Parkinson's Disease and Other Parkinsonian Disorders** In IPD, especially in the early stages, autonomic features usually are not prominent. The prevalence of orthostatic hypotension varies from rare to high (58%, with 38.5% symptomatic)[53] and may vary depending on the duration of the disease, age, and multiple drug therapy.[54] [123]I-metaidobenzylguanidine with $\gamma$-scintiscanning and fluorodopamine with positron emission tomography scanning of the heart indicate cardiac sympathetic denervation that may occur early in the disorder, often without other detectable autonomic features.[55-57] In MSA, there is cardiac uptake, excluding sympathetic denervation; this is consistent with a preganglionic sympathetic lesion and intact postganglionic sympathetic nerves. The implications of cardiac sympathetic denervation in Parkinson's disease is unclear; whether this is of relevance to cardiac arrhythmias induced by drug therapy in IPD is unknown.

A smaller group, often older and with apparent classic IPD, who have been successfully treated with L-dopa for many years, develop features of autonomic failure, often with severe postural hypotension. They differ from the majority of patients with IPD in whom autonomic deficits, if present, are relatively mild. Cardiac scanning techniques indicate sympathetic denervation, favoring a peripheral lesion similar to PAF.[58] They also have low basal plasma norepinephrine levels, with orthostatic hypotension that does not respond to yohimbine (whose actions are dependent on intact sympathetic nerves). The etiology of IPD with autonomic failure is unknown; it may be a coincidental association of a common condition with an uncommon disorder (PAF), an indication of

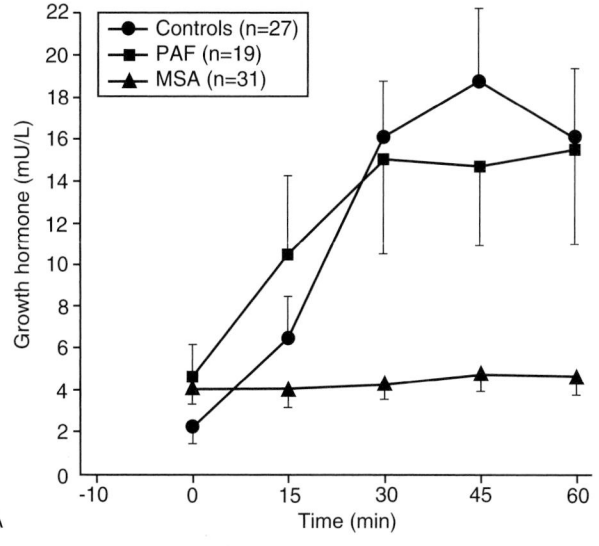

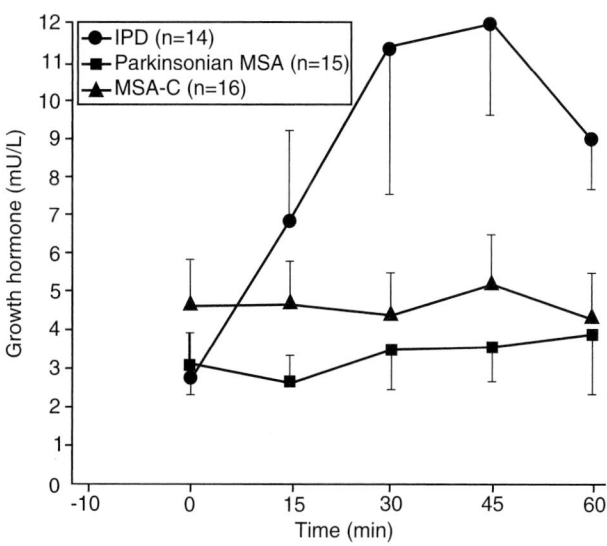

*Figure 137-10* **A,** Serum growth hormone (GH) concentrations before (0) and at 15-minute intervals for 60 minutes after clonidine (2 μg/kg/min) in normal subjects (controls) and in patients with pure autonomic failure (PAF) and multiple-system atrophy (MSA). GH concentrations increase in controls and in patients with PAF with a peripheral lesion; there is no increase in patients with MSA with a central lesion.[50] **B,** Lack of serum GH response to clonidine in MSA (the cerebellar form [MSA-C] and the parkinsonian forms) in contrast to patients with idiopathic Parkinson's disease (IPD) with no autonomic deficit, in whom there is a significant rise in GH levels. (From Kimber JR, Watson L, Mathias CJ: Distinction of idiopathic Parkinson's disease from multiple system atrophy by stimulation of growth hormone release with clonidine. Lancet 349:1877–1881, 1997.)

vulnerability to autonomic degeneration in a subgroup of IPD that may be linked to increasing age, long-term drug therapy, an inherent metabolic susceptibility, or a combination of these factors. These patients do not appear to have the many complications of MSA and clinically appear to differ from them.

Dizziness and orthostatic hypotension are more common in diffuse Lewy body disease than previously recognized.[59,60] These patients with orthostatic hypotension may be mistakenly diagnosed as PAF or MSA. In PAF, Lewy bodies also are present in the peripheral autonomic nervous system, raising the possibility that it may be a forme fruste, or early stage, of diffuse Lewy body disease. In PSP, orthostatic hypotension and cardiovascular autonomic features are exclusionary features in diagnosis.[61]

## Secondary Causes

Autonomic failure may be caused by or associated with a wide range of disorders (see Table 137-3), some of which are described here.

### Hereditary

These include both autosomal-dominant and autosomal-recessive disorders. In some disorders, such as congenital nerve growth factor deficiency,[62] the neurogenetics is unclear.

**Riley-Day Syndrome: Familial Dysautonomia**　The diagnosis may be made soon after birth in children of Ashkenazi-Jewish extraction.[63] Characteristic features are absent fungiform papillae, lack of corneal reflexes, decreased deep tendon reflexes, and a diminished response to pain. An abnormal intradermal histamine skin test (with an absent flare response) and pupillary hypersensitivity to cholinomimetics confirm the diagnosis. The defective gene has been mapped to the long arm of chromosome 9 (q31).

A variety of symptoms resulting from both autonomic underactivity and overactivity may occur. These include a labile blood pressure (with orthostatic hypotension and hypertension) and gastrointestinal and urinary bladder disturbances. With neurologic abnormalities, scoliosis, and renal failure, these features previously contributed to a poor prognosis. The ability to anticipate, prevent, and treat complications has resulted in a number of children now reaching adulthood.

**Amyloid Polyneuropathy**　Autonomic dysfunction occurs in familial amyloid polyneuropathy and light chain amyloidosis.[64] In familial amyloid polyneuropathy, symptoms usually occur in adulthood. Sensory, motor, and autonomic abnormalities result from deposition of mutated amyloid protein, mainly produced in the liver in peripheral nerves. Motor and sensory neuropathy often begins in the lower limbs. There are various forms based on the chemical and molecular nature of the constituent proteins: transthyretin familial amyloid polyneuropathy, familial amyloid polyneuropathy Ala 60 (Irish/Appalachian), and familial amyloid polyneuropathy Ser 84 and His 58. The cardiovascular system, gut, and urinary bladder can be affected at any stage. The disease relentlessly progresses at a variable speed. There may be dissociation of autonomic symptoms from functional deficits; this is of importance because evaluation of cardiovascular autonomic abnormalities is essential to prevent morbidity and mortality, especially during major procedures such as liver transplantation. This is the only currently effective means to reduce levels of variant transthyretin and its deposition in nerves; it prevents progression and may even reverse some of the neuropathic features. It may be of greater value if performed before substantial nerve damage occurs. In the light chain amyloidosis form, amyloid is derived from monoclonal light chains, secondary to multiple myeloma, malignant lymphoma, or Waldenström's macroglobulinemia. The prognosis is often poor.

**Dopamine β-Hydroxylase Deficiency**　This disorder, initially recognized in the mid-1980s, has been described in seven patients, two of whom are siblings.[65] Although symptoms are present in childhood, diagnosis had not been made until the teenage years, when orthostatic hypotension was first recognized. Whether the symptoms became more prominent or easier to detect at this time is unclear. The clinical features indicate sympathetic adrenergic failure with sparing of sympathetic cholinergic and parasympathetic function. Sweating is preserved, and urinary bladder and bowel function is normal; in one of the males, erection was possible but ejaculation was difficult to achieve. The diagnosis may be made from basal levels of plasma catecholamines because norepinephrine and epinephrine levels are undetectable, whereas

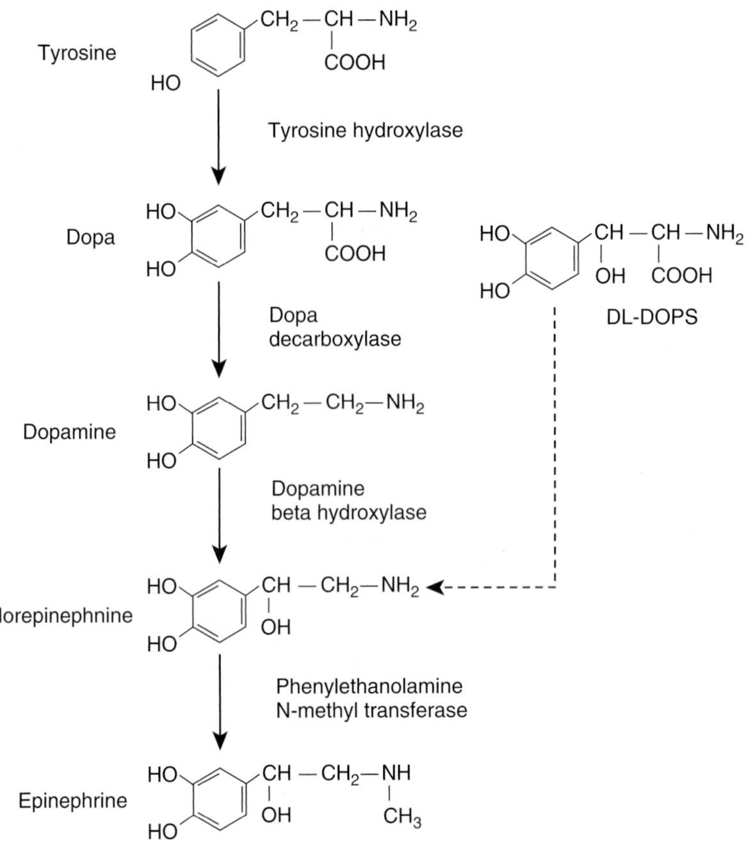

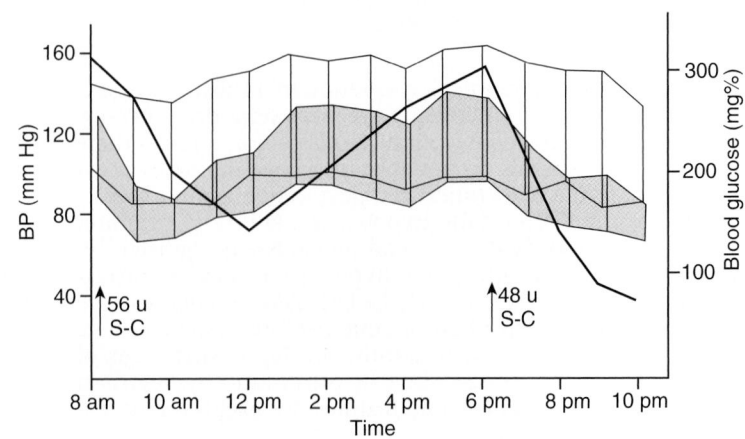

**Figure 137-11** Biosynthetic pathway in the formation of epinephrine and norepinephrine. The structure of DL-DOPS is indicated on the right. It is converted directly to norepinephrine by dopa decarboxylase, thus bypassing dopamine β-hydroxylase. (From Mathias CJ, Bannister R, Cortelli P, et al: Clinical autonomic and therapeutic observations in two siblings with postural hypotension and sympathetic failure due to an inability to synthesize noradrenaline from dopamine because of a deficiency of dopamine beta-hydroxylase. Q J Med 278:617–633, 1990.)

dopamine levels are elevated (Fig. 137-11).[66] This is a highly specific enzymatic defect, with sympathetic nerve pathways and terminals otherwise intact, as demonstrated by electron microscopy, and preservation of muscle sympathetic nerve activity using microneurography. Treatment is with the pro-drug L-dihydroxyphenylserine, which has a structure similar to that of norepinephrine except for a carboxyl group that is acted on by the enzyme dopa-decarboxylase (abundantly present in extraneuronal tissues such as the liver and kidneys), thus transforming it into norepinephrine. This reduces orthostatic hypotension and has resulted in remarkable improvements in the patients' ability to lead active lives.

### Metabolic

**Diabetes Mellitus**  There is a high incidence of both peripheral and autonomic neuropathy, especially in poorly controlled, older, and long-standing diabetics on insulin therapy.[67] Their

morbidity and mortality are considerably higher than without a neuropathy. A number of factors may be involved, which include activation of the polyol pathway, with an excessive amount of sorbitol accumulating in nerves when glucose is reduced by aldose reductase.[68] It initially may involve the vagus (Fig. 137-12), with characteristic features of cardiac vagal denervation.[69] This may occur in conjunction with partial preservation of the cardiac sympathetic and may predispose patients with diabetes, many of whom have ischemic heart disease, to sudden death from cardiac dysrhythmias. In some, sympathetic failure may cause orthostatic hypotension, but often there are additional nonneurogenic factors, which include dehydration (as may occur with hypoglycemia-induced osmotic diuresis and watery diarrhea), anemia, and at times even the effects of therapy with insulin, that lower blood pressure further.[70] Although vagal denervation (synonymous with cardiac autonomic neuropathy) is often an initial feature, there is evidence that sympathetic impairment may occur even

**Figure 137-12** Diurnal variation of lying and standing blood pressures in a 48-year-old man with severe autonomic neuropathy. Insulin was given subcutaneously (S-C) at the times shown by the *vertical arrows*. The *unhatched area* shows supine blood pressure, the *hatched area* shows the standing blood pressure, and the *solid line* shows the blood glucose. (From Watkins PJ, Edmonds ME: Diabetic autonomic failure. In Mathias CJ, Bannister R [eds]: Autonomic Failure: A Textbook of Clinical Disorders of the Autonomic Nervous System, 4th ed. Oxford, Oxford University Press, 2002, pp 378–386.)

at an early stage in patients with type 2 diabetes in whom there are subnormal vasoconstrictor responses to cold.[71] It may be that sympathetic denervation predisposes to excessive gravitational blood pooling, either in the legs or splanchnic circulation, that accounts for the description of hyperadrenergic orthostatic hypotension,[72] in which there is tachycardia and even an increase in plasma norepinephrine levels. Factors such as anemia may contribute.[73] Compensatory tachycardia, often attributed to impaired vagal function in diabetes, may therefore have an alternative cause and may be associated with intermittent episodes of orthostatic symptoms.

In the later stages of diabetes, impairment of baroreceptors, sympathetic denervation of the heart and blood vessels, and various other factors can result in severe orthostatic hypotension. In some, the capacity to maintain blood pressure is further compromised by damage to innervation of the renal juxtaglomerular apparatus, leading to hyporeninemic hyperaldosteronism.[74] When given intravenously, insulin may cause dilatation and hypotension, as it does in patients with primary autonomic failure, even when blood glucose is maintained by a euglycemia clamp.

Awareness of hypoglycemia may be diminished with autonomic nerve damage. There may be involvement of the gastrointestinal tract (gastroparesis diabeticorum and diabetic diarrhea) and urinary bladder (diabetic cystopathy), whereas in the male, impotence may result. Sudomotor abnormalities include gustatory sweating. Damage to other organs may occur through nonneuropathic factors and compound the problems caused by the neuropathy. Other than maintaining normoglycemia, there is no known means to prevent and reverse the neuropathy except by strict glycemic control and possibly pancreatic transplantation.

*Trauma*

**Spinal Cord Injuries** The entire sympathetic outflow is from the spinal cord. The level of completeness of the lesion determines the degree of autonomic dysfunction.[10] Cardiovascular autonomic dysfunction is common, especially in cervical and high thoracic spinal cord lesions. Orthostatic hypotension results from the inability of the brain to activate efferent sympathetic pathways, despite preservation of baroreceptor afferent and central connections because of the interruption of sympathetic outflow to blood vessels and the heart[75] (Fig. 137-13). In these subjects, the reverse, paroxysmal hypertension, may occur after large bowel and urinary bladder contraction as part of the mass reflex in the syndrome of autonomic dysreflexia.[76] This is due to isolated spinal cord reflex activity (without the restraint of cerebral control) and can be induced by a variety of stimuli, from cutaneous, skeletal muscle, or visceral sources, below the level of the lesion. In the acute phase after injury, such patients may be in spinal shock when isolated spinal sympathetic activity cannot be provoked.[77]

A combination of autonomic underactivity and overactivity may occur in other neurologic disorders. In the Guillain-Barré syndrome, hypotension and tachycardia may alternate with hypertension and bradycardia. The precise mechanisms are unclear. Cardiovascular disturbances of a similar nature may occur in tetanus, especially in those on assisted respiration.

### DRUGS, CHEMICALS, TOXINS

Drugs may cause autonomic dysfunction through their recognized pharmacologic effects on the sympathetic nervous system, such as the sympatholytic agents (see Table 137-3). A side effect of a drug may cause clinical problems when used in a high dose over a prolonged period or when deficits are unmasked or induced in susceptible individuals. Examples of the latter include L-dopa worsening orthostatic hypotension in MSA. Drugs such as perhexiline maleate, vincristine, and alcohol may induce orthostatic hypotension independently of their pharmacologic properties by causing an autonomic neuropathy.

### INTERMITTENT AUTONOMIC DYSFUNCTION

#### Neurally Mediated Syncope
These disorders are characterized by an intermittent cardiovascular autonomic abnormality resulting in syncope (loss of consciousness synonymous with fainting, blackouts) (see

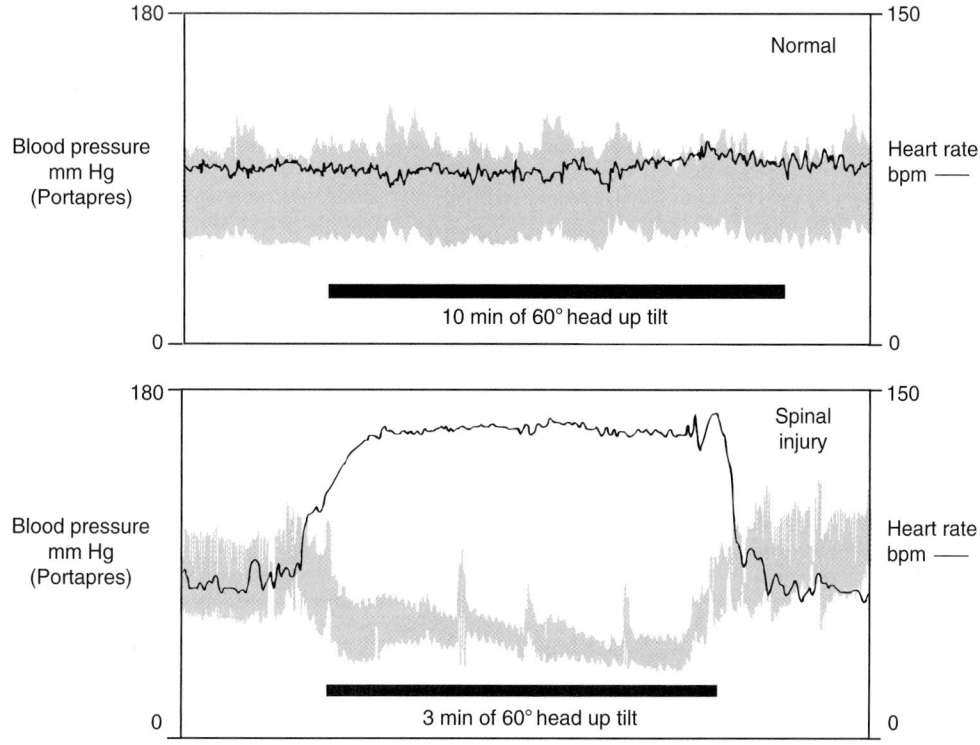

*Figure 137-13* Blood pressure (in mmHg) and heart rate (in beats per minute, bpm) measured continuously with the Portapres II in a patient with a high cervical spinal cord lesion. There is a decrease in blood pressure because of impairment of the sympathetic outflow disrupted in the cervical spine. Heart rate increases because of the withdrawal of vagal activity in response to the increase in pressure.

Table 137-4). Withdrawal of sympathetic nerve activity results in hypotension (vasodepressor form), and an increase in cardiac parasympathetic activity causes severe bradycardia or cardiac arrest (cardioinhibitory form). The two may occur separately or together as the mixed form (Fig. 137-14). Between episodes, there often are no abnormalities detected on autonomic screening.

### Vasovagal syncope

In the young, vasovagal syncope is a common cause of neurally mediated syncope. There is often a family history when presentation is in teenagers.[78] It appears to be more common in women. It may be induced by various stimuli, from fear and the sight of blood to venepuncture and at times even discussion of venepuncture. Standing still, a warm environmental temperature and other factors that promote vasodilation, including gravitational pooling, can induce syncope. Cardiac conduction disorders and other causes of syncope, including pseudosyncope[79] need to be excluded. Tilt table testing, and, in some, application of a provocative stimulus (including venepuncture or pseudovenepuncture) may induce an episode (Fig. 137-14).[21] Some advocate supraphysiologic (head-up tilt and lower body negative pressure) and pharmacologic (head-up tilt and isoprenaline infusion) testing if physiologic measures alone do not induce an episode; these stimuli, however, may provoke a vasovagal episode in subjects who have never fainted.[80]

### Carotid sinus hypersensitivity

In the elderly, carotid sinus hypersensitivity may be more common than previously thought; in this age group it may be a major cause of unexplained falls.[81] There may be a classic history of syncope induced by head movements, collar tightening, or shaving. The occurrence of falls without a clear cause should prompt one to consider a diagnosis of carotid sinus hypersensitivity in older patients. Investigation should include carotid sinus massage performed with requisite precautions in a laboratory with adequate resuscitation facilities, ideally using beat-by-beat blood pressure and heart rate recording (Fig. 137-15).[82] Carotid massage also should be performed with the subject tilted head-up because hypotension is more likely to occur in situations in which sympathetic nerve activity is needed.[83]

### Miscellaneous causes

A variety of stimuli may induce neurally mediated syncope. Syncope induced by swallowing (and, in some, associated glossopharyngeal neuralgia) and during pelvic and rectal examina-tions or instrumentation, are examples. Malignancies in the pharynx and thorax may increase the tendency to reflexly induced syncope. In micturition and defecation syncope, changes in intrathoracic pressure may contribute, as in syncope induced by paroxysms of coughing, laughter, trumpet blowing, weightlifting, and volition ("fainting lark"). In extremely fit subjects, especially those performing isometric and dynamic exercise such as rowers and cyclists, increased vagal tone may result in syncope. The first-dose hypotensive effect of some drugs may be neurally mediated via the Bezold-Jarisch reflex.

### Postural Tachycardia Syndrome

PoTS is a disorder mainly affecting women between the ages of 20 and 50 years, with symptoms of orthostatic intolerance (light headedness and other manifestations of cerebral hypoperfusion), often with palpitations.[84] The symptoms disappear on sitting or lying down. Investigations exclude orthostatic hypotension and autonomic failure; during postural challenge, heart rate increases by 30 beats per minute or more (see Fig. 137-3).[9] There are similarities with the syndromes initially described by Da Costa and Lewis (also known as soldier's heart or neurocirculatory esthenia), mitral valve prolapse syndrome, chronic fatigue syndrome and deconditioning after prolonged bed rest, and microgravity during space flight. Hypovolemia may contribute. In some, the disorder appears to follow a viral infection. There may be features of a partial autonomic neuropathy, with lower limb denervation.[85] Antibodies to autonomic ganglia have been related to the autonomic deficits.[86] In a family with affected twins, a genetic basis has been proposed, and there was a mutation of the gene encoding the norepinephrine transporter system; this defect may have accounted for the increased basal norepinephrine levels and hyperadrenergic state.[87] There is an association with joint hypermobility syndrome (Ehlers-Danlos 3).[88]

## MANAGEMENT

### ORTHOSTATIC HYPOTENSION

Orthostatic hypotension may cause considerable disability, with the potential risk of serious injury. In nonneurogenic orthostatic hypotension, the underlying problem needs to be resolved. It may be an indicator of substantial blood or fluid loss or of a serious underlying disorder, such as adrenal insufficiency. This may include reducing fluid loss, replacing blood and fluids, correcting the endocrine deficiency, improving car-

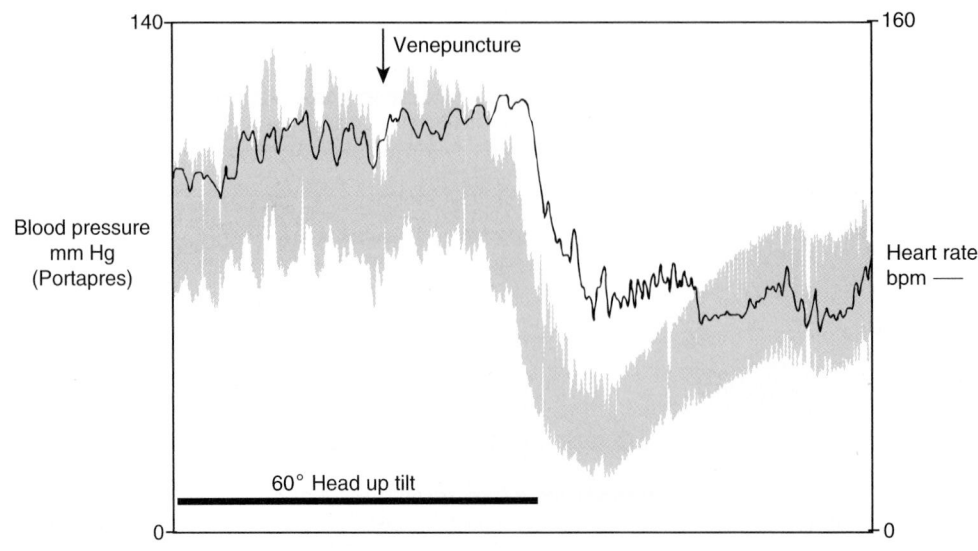

**Figure 137-14** Blood pressure and heart rate with continuous recordings from the Portapres II in a patient with the mixed (cardioinhibitory and vasodepressor) form of vasovagal syncope.

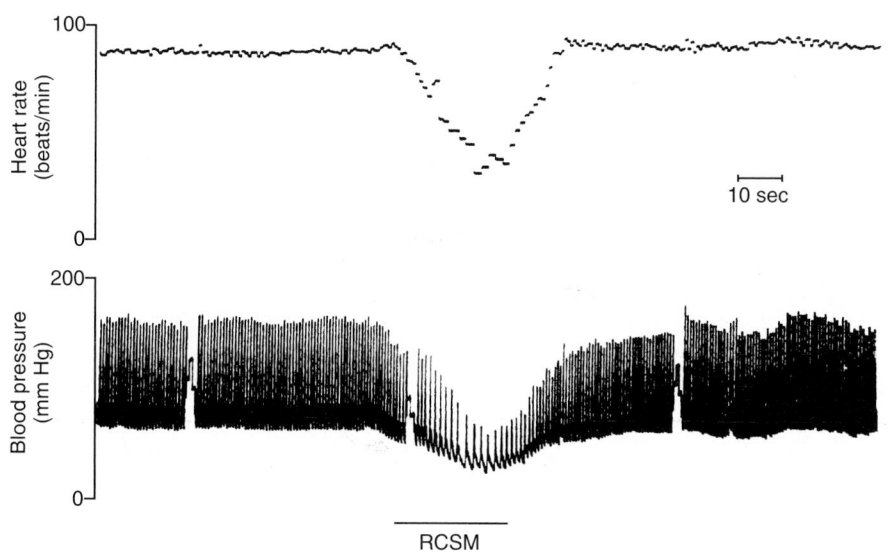

*Figure 137-15* Blood pressure and heart rate with continuous recordings from the Portapres II in a patient with the mixed (cardioinhibitory and vasodepressor) form of carotid sinus hypersensitivity. (From Mathias CJ: Autonomic dysfunction. In Grimley-Evans J, Franklin Williams T, Lynn Beattie B, et al [eds]: Oxford Textbook of Geriatric Medicine, 2nd ed. Oxford, Oxford University Press, 2000, pp 833–852.)

diac function, and preventing vasodilatation. In neurogenic orthostatic hypotension, cure is less likely and long-term management often needs to be considered. This is in part dependent on the pathophysiologic processes and primary disease responsible. It should be emphasized that the management of associated nonneurogenic factors (such as those resulting from fluid and blood loss) is essential because they can considerably exacerbate neurogenic orthostatic hypotension. Nonpharmacologic measures are an essential component of management, even when drugs are used.[89] Because no single drug can effectively mimic the actions of the sympathetic nervous system, a multipronged approach is needed (Table 137-9). They include factors to avoid, to institute, and to consider.

Increasing patient awareness of the many factors, other than postural change, that lower blood pressure is important. These include simple measures such as avoiding rapid postural change, especially in the morning when getting out of bed because the supine blood pressure often is lowest at this time, probably because nocturnal polyuria reduces extracellular fluid volume. Prolonged bed rest and recumbency, especially postoperatively, should be avoided. Head-up tilt at night is beneficial and probably reduces salt and water loss by stimulating the renin-angiotensin-aldosterone system or by activating other hormonal, neural, or local renal hemodynamic mechanisms, which reduce recumbency-induced diuresis. When head-up tilt is impractical or the degree of tilt achieved is inadequate, nocturnal polyuria and nocturia can be reduced with the antidiuretic agent desmopressin.[90] Straining during micturition and bowel movement should be avoided. In hot weather, the elevation of body temperature because of impairment of thermoregulatory mechanisms, such as sweating, may further increase vasodilatation and worsen orthostatic hypotension. Ingestion of alcohol or large meals, especially those containing a high carbohydrate content, may cause postprandial hypotension and aggravate postural hypotension. Various physical maneuvers,[91] such as leg crossing, squatting, sitting in the knee-chest position, and abdominal compression, are of value in reducing orthostatic hypotension (Fig. 137-16).[92]

Consideration should be given to introducing devices aimed at preventing venous pooling during standing. These include lower limb elastic stockings, abdominal binders, and, in extreme cases, positive-gravity suits. Each has its limitations and may increase susceptibility to orthostatic postural hypotension when not in use. In patients with amyloidosis and accompanying hypoalbuminemia, positive-gravity suits may be the last resort because it is often impossible to maintain intravascular volume without causing tissue edema.

Tachypacing with an implanted cardiac pacemaker is of no benefit in the management of orthostatic hypotension due to sympathetic failure except in the rare situation when bradycardia also occurs. This is because increasing the heart rate without increasing venous return does not elevate cardiac output and therefore does not increase blood pressure. Recent observations indicate that ingestion of 500 mL of water increases blood pressure substantially in primary autonomic failure (Fig. 137-17); this may be of value, although the ensuing diuresis may be troublesome, especially in patients with MSA who have associated bladder disturbances.[93,94]

The nonpharmacologic measures described earlier may need to be supplemented by drugs to sustain blood pressure when upright. The major mechanisms by which they act are outlined in Table 137-10. In autonomic failure, enhanced responses usually occur to pressor and vasodepressor agents; the former may result in severe hypertension, especially when supine, whereas vasodepressor substances may cause marked

| **Table 137-9** | **Some Approaches Used in the Management of Orthostatic Hypotension, Especially in Patients with Chronic Autonomic Failure** |
|---|---|

Nonpharmacologic measures
To be avoided
 Sudden head-up postural change (especially on waking)
 Prolonged recumbency
 Straining during micturition and defecation
 High environmental temperature (including hot baths)
 Severe exertion
 Large meals (especially with refined carbohydrate)
 Alcohol
 Drugs with vasodepressor properties
To be introduced
 Head-up tilt during sleep
 Small, frequent meals
 High-salt intake
 Judicious exercise (including swimming)
 Body positions and maneuvers
To be considered
 Elastic stockings
 Abdominal binders
 Water ingestion
Pharmacologic measures
 Starter drug: fludrocortisone
 Sympathomimetics: ephedrine, midodrine
 Specific targeting: octreotide, desmopressin, erythropoietin

Adapted from Mathias CJ, Kimber JR: Treatment of postural hypotension. J Neurol Neurosurg Psychiatry 65:285–289, 1998.

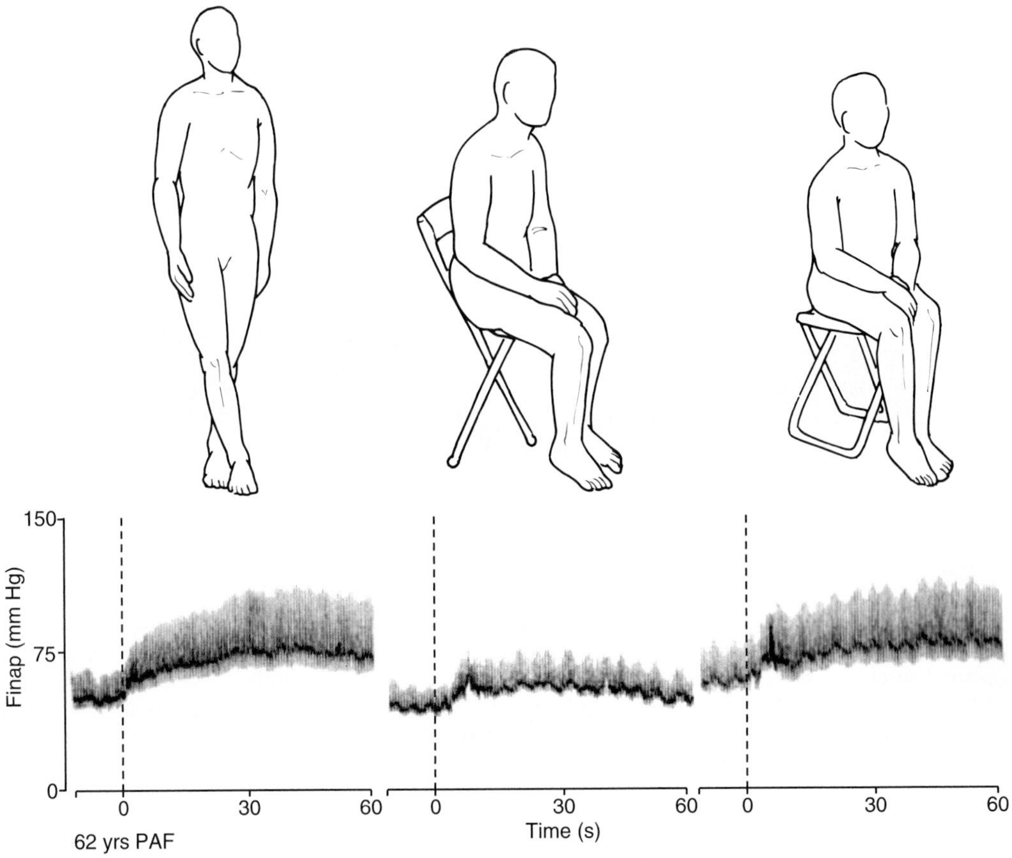

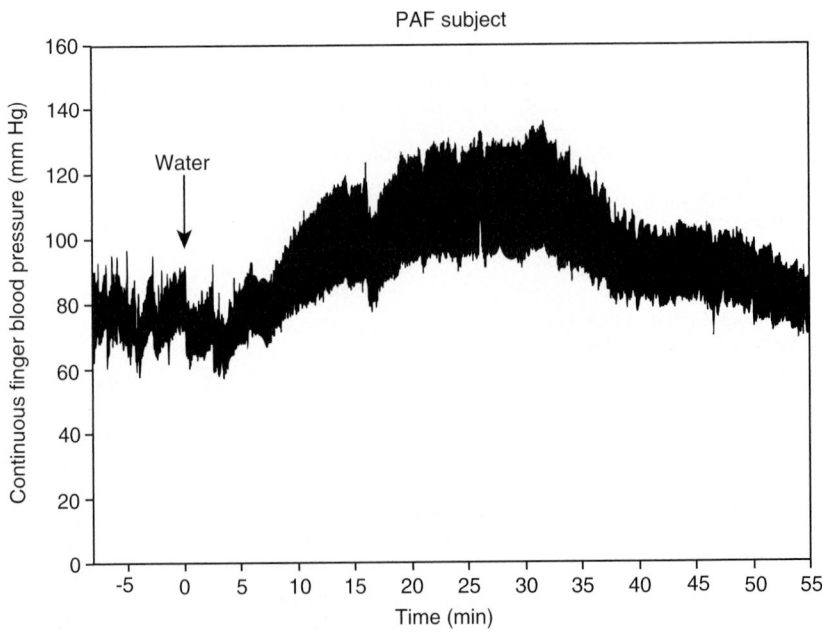

**Figure 137-16** Finger arterial blood pressure (Finapres) while standing in the crossed-leg position with leg muscle contraction (*left*) and sitting on a derby chair (*middle*) and fishing chair (*right*) in a patient with autonomic failure. Orthostatic symptoms were present initially when standing and disappeared on crossing the legs and sitting on the fishing chair. Sitting on the derby chair caused the least increase in blood pressure and did not relieve completely the patient's symptoms.[92] (Redrawn from Smit AAJ, Hardjowijono MA, Wieling W: Are portable folding chairs useful to combat orthostatic hypotension. Ann Neurol 42:975–978, 1997.)

62 yrs PAF

hypotension. There are exceptions, as patients with infiltration of blood vessels due to amyloidosis may not exhibit supersensitivity, despite a peripheral autonomic neuropathy.

In those with a precise biochemical deficit, such as in dopamine β-hydroxylase deficiency, agents can be given that bypass deficient enzyme systems and result in appropriate neurotransmitter replacement (see Fig. 137-11). The amino acid l-threo-3,4-dihydroxyphenylserine is directly converted by dopa-decarboxylase into norepinephrine. Whether this occurs intra- or extraneuronally or both is unclear. Its potential value in the management of orthostatic hypotension due to other neurogenic causes remains to be determined.[95]

Although there is no evidence of a mineralocorticoid deficiency in primary autonomic failure, a valuable starter drug is fludrocortisone, in a low dose of 0.1 or 0.2 mg at night. Low-dose fludrocortisone probably acts by reducing the inability to retain salt and water, especially when recumbent, and by increasing the sensitivity of blood vessels to pressor

PAF subject

Water

**Figure 137-17** Changes in blood pressure before and after 500 mL of distilled water ingested at time 0 in a patient with pure autonomic failure (PAF). Blood pressure is measured continuously using the Portapres II. (From Cariga P, Mathias CJ: The hemodynamics of the pressor effect of oral water in human sympathetic denervation due to autonomic failure. Clin Sci 101:313–319, 2001.)

**Table 137-10** Outline of the Major Actions by Which a Variety of Drugs May Reduce Orthostatic Hypotension

Reducing salt loss/plasma volume expansion
  Mineralocorticoids (fludrocortisone)
Reducing nocturnal polyuria
  $V_2$-receptor agonists (desmopressin)
Sympathetic vasoconstriction
  On resistance vessels (ephedrine, midodrine, phenylephrine, norepinephrine, clonidine, tyramine with monoamine oxidase inhibitors, yohimbine, L-dihydroxyphenylserine)
  On capacitance vessels (dihydroergotamine)
Nonsympathomimetic vasoconstriction
  $V_1$-receptor agents: terlipressin
Ganglionic nicotinic-receptor stimulation
  Anticholinesterase inhibitors
Preventing vasodilatation
  Prostaglandin synthetase inhibitors (indomethacin, flurbiprofen)
  Dopamine receptor blockade (metoclopramide, domperidone)
  $\beta_2$-adrenoceptor blockade (propranolol)
Preventing postprandial hypotension
  Adenosine receptor blockade (caffeine)
  Peptide release inhibitors (somatostatin analogue: octreotide)
Increasing cardiac output
  β-blockers with intrinsic sympathomimetic activity (pindolol, xamoterol)
  Dopamine agonists (ibopamine)
Increasing red cell mass
  Erythropoietin

Adapted from Mathias CJ: Autonomic diseases: Clinical features and laboratory evaluation. J Neurol Neurosurg Psychiatry 74:iii31–iii41, 2003.

substances. In the doses used, it is less likely to induce side effects such as ankle edema and hypokalemia. If nocturnal polyuria is not reduced by head-up tilt, fludrocortisone can be effectively combined with desmopressin, a vasopressin-2 receptor agonist with potent antidiuretic but minimal direct pressor activity. Five to 40 mg intranasally or 100 to 400 mg orally at night reduces the diuresis but when used without fludrocortisone does not prevent nocturnal natriuresis. These trials have been performed mainly in chronic autonomic failure.[96] Smaller doses (usually 5–10 mg only) are used in PAF because they appear to be more sensitive to the drug than patients with MSA. Plasma sodium must be monitored to exclude hyponatremia and water intoxication. These can be reversed by stopping the drug and withholding water, but diuresis then ensues, which may enhance orthostatic hypotension.

Drugs that mimic the activity of norepinephrine, either directly or indirectly, include ephedrine and midodrine. Ephedrine acts both directly and indirectly and is of value in central and incomplete autonomic lesions, including MSA. In severe peripheral sympathetic lesions (as in PAF), it may have minimal or no effects. A dose of 15 mg three times daily initially can be increased to 30 or 45 mg three times daily, although central side effects limit use of the higher doses. Drugs that act directly on α-adrenoceptors are often needed, especially in peripheral lesions. These drugs often act mainly on resistance vessels; they have the potential risk of deleterious arterial constriction, especially in the elderly and those with peripheral vascular disease. They include midodrine, which is converted to the active metabolite desglymidodrine.[97] The ergot alkaloid dihydroergotamine acts predominantly on venous capacitance vessels, but its effects are limited by its poor absorption; high oral doses (5–10 mg three times daily) may be needed.

Other therapeutic attempts to increase blood pressure have concentrated on pre- and postsynaptic $\alpha_2$-adrenoceptor mechanisms. They have limited application in practice. Clonidine is mainly an $\alpha_2$-adrenoceptor agonist, which predominantly lowers blood pressure through its central effects by reducing sym-

pathetic outflow. It also has peripheral actions on postsynaptic α-adrenoceptors, which may increase blood pressure in the presence of pressor supersensitivity. These peripheral vasoconstrictor effects probably account for its modest success in severe, distal sympathetic lesions. Yohimbine blocks presynaptic $\alpha_2$-adrenoceptors, which normally suppress release of norepinephrine and should theoretically be of benefit in incomplete sympathetic lesions, as observed in single-dose studies. Acetylcholinesterase inhibitors have been reported to increase blood pressure when given in single doses.[98] Their value in long-term management is not known.

Supine hypertension may occur in chronic autonomic failure and may be worsened by treatment (see Fig. 137-6). It may occasionally result in cerebral hemorrhage, aortic dissection, myocardial ischemia, or cardiac failure. This may be a greater problem with some drug combinations, such as tyramine (which releases norepinephrine) and monoamine oxidase inhibitors (such as tranylcypromine and moclobemide), which prolong its actions. Supine hypertension may increase symptoms of cerebral ischemia during subsequent postural change, probably through an unfavorable resetting of cerebral autoregulatory mechanisms. To prevent these problems, head-up tilt, omission of the evening dose of vasopressor agents, a prebedtime snack to induce postprandial hypotension, and even the nocturnal use of short-acting vasodilators have been suggested.

To overcome the problems with lability of blood pressure, a subcutaneous infusion pump, as in the control of hyperglycemia with insulin in diabetes mellitus, has been used to administer the short-acting vasoconstrictor norepinephrine. Previous studies with a pilot device had been successful but with a number of practical problems, including accurate monitoring of blood pressure without an intra-arterial catheter. Some of these problems have been overcome.[99] This may benefit the severely hypotensive patient who is refractory to the combination of nonpharmacologic and conventionally administered drug therapy.

To prevent vasodilatation, prostaglandin synthetase inhibitors, such as indomethacin and flurbiprofen, have been used with some success. They may act by blocking vasodilatatory prostaglandins, by causing salt and water retention through their renal effects, or both. They have potentially serious side effects, however, such as gastrointestinal ulceration and hemorrhage. The dopamine antagonists metoclopramide and domperidone are occasionally of value when an excess of dopamine is contributory. Whether preventing the vasodilator effects of nitric oxide will be of value remains speculative.[100]

β-Adrenoceptor blockers, such as propranolol, may be successful when orthostatic hypotension is accompanied by tachycardia; the combination of blocking $\beta_2$-adrenoceptor vasodilatation and $\beta_1$-adrenoceptor-induced tachycardia may account for the benefit. Some β-adrenoceptor blockers, such as pindolol, with a high degree of intrinsic sympathomimetic activity, may increase cardiac output and through this, or other less well-understood mechanisms, increase blood pressure. Cardiac failure may complicate treatment. Xamoterol, another agent with similar properties, had limited success and was withdrawn because of deleterious effects. The dopamine agonist ibopamine has been used in a few patients with varying success.

Various therapeutic approaches have been used to reduce severe postprandial hypotension. Caffeine may act by blocking vasodilatatory adenosine receptors. A dose of 250 mg, the equivalent of two cups of coffee, may be of benefit. The prodrug L-dihydroxyphenylserine, presumably through adrenoceptor-induced vasoconstriction, reduces postprandial hypotension in primary autonomic failure.[101] The somatostatin analogue octreotide, which inhibits release of a variety of gastrointestinal tract peptides, including those with vasodilatatory properties, has been successfully used to prevent postprandial hypotension; it also may partly reduce postural and exercise-induced hypotension.[102] The need for subcutaneous administration is a drawback. It does not enhance nocturnal (supine) hypertension.[103] The development of an oral preparation would be a substantial advance in therapy.

## INTERMITTENT AUTONOMIC DYSFUNCTION

### Neurally Mediated Syncope

Management includes reducing or preventing exposure to precipitating causes, although these may be unclear; in some, behavioral therapy, especially in patients with phobias, is needed. A high-salt diet, fluid repletion,[104] and various drugs such as fludrocortisone, vasopressor agents, and antidepressants (including the serotonin uptake release inhibitors) have been used with varying success. In some with the cardioinhibitory form, a cardiac demand pacemaker may be of value.[105] Lower limb exercises, sympathetic activation techniques, and antipooling measures are useful maneuvers, especially in the presyncopal phase.[106,107] The long-term prognosis is favorable, and in many, the frequency of attacks are reduced, especially after the third decade.

In carotid sinus hypersensitivity, a cardiac demand pacemaker may be of benefit in the cardioinhibitory form; in the mixed and vasodepressor forms, the use of vasopressor drugs may be necessary. Denervation of the carotid sinus has been used, especially in unilateral hypersensitivity. Bradycardia in patients with high spinal cord injuries who are on respirators may require a combination of atropine, oxygen, and, if necessary, a temporary demand pacemaker.[10]

### Postural Tachycardia Syndrome

In PoTS, the underlying disorder may warrant either the use of a β-blocker or approaches similar to those used for orthostatic hypotension, including fludrocortisone and ephedrine and/or midodrine. β-Blockers may help. Correcting hypovolemia and other factors is also of particular importance. Some recover with time.

## REFERENCES

1. Hainsworth R: Arterial blood pressure. In Henderby GEH (ed): Hypotensive Anaesthesia. Edinburgh, Churchill Livingstone, 1985, pp 3–29.
2. Hill L: The influence of the force of gravity on the circulation of the blood. J Physiol (Lond) 18:15–53, 1895.
3. Lillywhite HB: Snakes, blood circulation and gravity. Sci Am 66–72, 1988.
4. Wallin BG, Linblad L-E: Baroreflex mechanisms controlling sympathetic outflow to the muscles. In Sleight P (ed): Arterial Baroreceptors and Hypertension. Oxford, Oxford University Press, 1988, p 101.
5. Mathias CJ: Autonomic diseases—clinical features and laboratory evaluation. J Neurol Neurosurg Psychiatry 74:31–41, 2003.
6. Mathias CJ: Disorders of the autonomic nervous system. In Bradley WG, Daroff RB, Fenichel GM, Jancovich J (eds): Neurology in Clinical Practice, 3d ed. Boston, Butterworth-Heinemann, 2004, pp 2403–2240.
7. Bungo MW, Goldwater DJ, Popp RL, Sandler H: Cardiovascular deconditioning during space flight and the use of saline as a countermeasure to orthostatic intolerance. Aviat Space Environ Med 56:985–990, 1985.
8. Mathias CJ, Mallipeddi R, Bleasdale-Barr K: Symptoms associated with orthostatic hypotension in pure autonomic failure and multiple system atrophy. J Neurol 246:893–898, 1999.
9. Mathias CJ: To stand on ones' own legs. Clin Med 2:237–245, 2002.
10. Mathias CJ, Frankel H: Autonomic disturbances in spinal cord lesions. In Mathias CJ, Bannister R (eds): Autonomic Failure: A Textbook of Clinical Disorders of the Autonomic Nervous System, 4th ed. Oxford, Oxford University Press, 2002, pp 494–513.
11. Bleasdale-Barr K, Mathias CJ: Neck and other muscle pains in autonomic failure: Their association with orthostatic hypotension. J R Soc Med 91:355–359, 1998.
12. Mathias CJ, Fosbraey P, da Costa DF, et al: The effect of desmopressin on nocturnal polyuria, overnight weight loss and morning postural hypotension in patients with autonomic failure. Br Med J 293:353–354, 1986.
13. Mathias CJ: A 21(st) century water cure. Lancet 356:1046–1048, 2000.
14. Mathias CJ, Bannister R: Postprandial hypotension in autonomic disorders. In Mathias CJ, Bannister R (eds): Autonomic Failure: A Textbook of Clinical Disorders of the Autonomic Nervous System, 4th ed. Oxford, Oxford University Press, 2002, pp 283–295.
15. Mathias CJ, da Costa DF, Fosbraey P, et al: Cardiovascular, biochemical and hormonal changes during food induced hypotension in chronic autonomic failure. J Neurol Sci 94:255–269, 1989.
16. Mathias CJ, Holly E, Armstrong E, et al: The influence of food on postural hypotension in three groups with chronic autonomic failure: Clinical and therapeutic implications. J Neurol Neurosurg Psychiatry 54:726–730, 1991.
17. Smith GDP, Watson LP, Pavitt DV, Mathias CJ: Abnormal cardiovascular and catecholamine responses to supine exercise in human subjects with sympathetic dysfunction. J Physiol (Lond) 485:255–265, 1995.
18. Smith GDP, Mathias CJ: Postural hypotension enhanced by exercise in patients with chronic autonomic failure. Q J Med 88:251–256, 1995.
19. Puvi-Rajasingham S, Smith GDP, Akinola A, Mathias CJ: Abnormal regional blood flow responses during and after exercise in human sympathetic denervation. J Physiol 505:481–489, 1997.
20. Mathias CJ, Matthews WB, Spalding JMK: Postural changes in plasma renin activity and response to vasoactive drugs in a case of Shy-Drager syndrome. J Neurol Neurosurg Psychiatry 2:147–156, 1977.
21. Mathias CJ, Deguchi K, Schatz I: Observations on recurrent syncope and presyncope in 641 patients. Lancet 357:348–353, 2001.
22. Mathias CJ, Bannister R (eds): Investigation of autonomic disorders. In Autonomic Failure: A Textbook of Clinical Disorders of the Autonomic Nervous System, 4th ed. Oxford, Oxford University Press, 2002.
23. Low PA: Clinical Autonomic Disorders, 2nd ed. Philadelphia, Lippincott–Raven, 1997.
24. Fritz I, Levine R: Action of adrenal cortical steroids and norepinephrine on vascular responses of stress in adrenalectomized rats. Am J Physiol 165:456–465, 1951.
25. Swingle WW, DaVanzo JP, Crossfield HC, et al: Glucocorticoids and maintenance of blood pressure and plasma volume of adrenalectomized dogs subjected to stress. Proc Soc Exp Biol Med 100:617–622, 1959.
26. Robinson FJ, Power MH, Kepler EJ: Two new procedures to assist in the recognition and exclusion of Addison's disease. Proc Staff Meet Mayo Clin 16:577–583, 1941.
27. Streeten DHP, Thorn GW: Use of changes in the mean corpuscular hemoglobin concentration as an index of erythrocyte hydration. J Lab Clin Med 49:661–671, 1957.
28. Dingman JF, Streeten DHP, Thorn GW: Effect of cortisone on the abnormal distribution of intravascular water in adrenal cortical insufficiency in man. J Lab Clin Med 49:7–18, 1957.
29. Yunio SL, Bercovitch DD, Stein RM, et al: Renal tubular effects of hydrocortisone and aldosterone in normal hydropenic man: Comment on sites of action. J Clin Invest 43:1668–1676, 1964.
30. Jick H, Snyder JG, Finkelstein EM, et al: On the renal site and mode of action of glucocorticoid in cirrhosis. J Clin Invest 42:1561–1568, 1963.
31. Gordon RD, Kuchel O, Liddle GW, et al: Role of the sympathetic nervous system in regulating renin and aldosterone production in man. J Clin Invest 46:599–605, 1967.
32. Mathias CJ, May CN, Taylor GM: The renin-angiotensin system and hypertension—basic and clinical aspects. In Malcolm ADB (ed): Molecular Medicine, vol 1. Oxford and Washington, DC, IRL Press, 1984, pp 177–208.

33. Schmid PG, Eckstein JW, Abboud FM: Effect of 9-α-fluorohydrocortisone on forearm vascular responses to norepinephrine. Circulation 34:620–626, 1966.

34. Schmid PG, Eckstein JW, Abboud FM: Effect of 9-α-fluorohydrocortisone on forearm venous responses to norepinephrine and tyramine. J Appl Physiol 23:571–574, 1967.

35. Spach C, Streeten DHP: Retardation of sodium exchange in dog erythrocytes by physiological concentrations of aldosterone in vitro. J Clin Invest 43:217–227, 1964.

36. Smithwick RH, Greer WER, Robertson CW, et al: Pheochromocytoma. A discussion of symptoms, signs and procedures of diagnostic value. N Engl J Med 242:252–257, 1950.

37. Streeten DHP, Anderson GH Jr: Mechanisms of orthostatic hypotension and tachycardia in patients with pheochromocytoma. Am J Hypertens 9:760–769, 1996.

38. Leonetti G, Terzoli L, Bianchini G, et al: Noradrenaline reactivity in patients with phaeochromocytoma before and after surgical correction. Clin Sci (Colch) 6(Suppl 7):211s–213s, 1981.

39. Davies IB, Mathias CJ, Sudera D, Sever PS: Agonist regulation of alpha-adrenergic receptor responses in man. J Cardiovasc Pharmacol 4:s139–s144, 1982.

40. Brodde O-E, Bock KD: Changes in platelet alpha$_2$-adrenergic receptors in human phaeochromocytoma. Eur J Clin Pharmacol 26:265–267, 1984.

41. McLeod JG: Autonomic dysfunction in peripheral nerve disease. In Autonomic Failure: A Textbook of Clinical Disorders of the Autonomic Nervous System, 4th ed. Oxford, Oxford University Press, 2002, pp 367–377.

42. Mathias CJ: Neurodegeneration, parkinsonian syndromes and autonomic failure. Autonomic Neuroscience: Basic and Clinical 96:50–58, 2002.

43. Matthews M: Autonomic ganglia and preganglionic neurones in autonomic failure. In Mathias CJ, Bannister R (eds): Autonomic Failure: A Textbook of Clinical Disorders of the Autonomic Nervous System, 4th ed. Oxford, Oxford University Press, 2002, pp 329–339.

44. Mathias CJ, Williams AC: The Shy Drager syndrome (and multiple system atrophy). In Calne DB (ed): Neurodegenerative Diseases. Philadelphia, WB Saunders, 1994, pp 743–768.

45. Wenning GK, Ben Shlomo Y, Magalhaes M, et al: Clinical features and a natural history of multiple system atrophy. An analysis of 100 cases. Brain 117:835–845, 1994.

46. Gilman S, Low P, Quinn N, et al: Consensus statement on the diagnosis of multiple system atrophy. Clin Auton Res 8:359–362, 1998.

47. Daniel S: The neuropathology and neurochemistry of multiple system atrophy. In Mathias CJ, Bannister R (eds): A Textbook of Clinical Disorders of the Autonomic Nervous System, 4th ed. Oxford, Oxford University Press, 2002, pp 321–328.

48. Kimber J, Sivenandan M, Watson L, Mathias CJ: Age and gender related growth hormone responses to intravenous clonidine in healthy adults. Growth Horm IGF Res 11:128–135, 2001.

49. Thomaides T, Chaudhuri KR, Maule S, et al: The growth hormone response to clonidine in central and peripheral primary autonomic failure. Lancet 340:263–266, 1992.

50. Kimber JR, Watson L, Mathias CJ: Distinction of idiopathic Parkinson's disease from multiple system atrophy by stimulation of growth hormone release with clonidine. Lancet 349:1877–1881, 1997.

51. Kimber JR, Mathias CJ: Neuroendocrine responses to Levodopa in multiple system atrophy (MSA). Mov Disord 14:981–987, 1999.

52. Friess E, Kuempfel T, Winkelmann J, et al: Increased growth hormone response to apomorphine in Parkinson Disease compared with multiple system atrophy. Arch Neurol 5:241–246, 2001.

53. Senard J-M, Rai S, Lapeyre-Mestre M, et al: Prevalence of orthostatic hypotension in Parkinson's disease. J Neurol Neurosurg Psychiatry 63:578–589, 1997.

54. Mathias CJ: Cardiovascular autonomic dysfunction in parkinsonian patients. Clin Neurosci 5:153–166, 1998.

55. Hakusui S, Yasuda T, Yanagi T, et al: A radiological analysis of heart sympathetic functions with meta-[$^{123}$I] iodobenzylguanidine in neurological patients with autonomic failure. J Auton Nerv Syst 49:81–84, 1994.

56. Orimo S, Ozawa E, Nakade S, et al: $^{123}$I-metaiodobenzylguanidine myocardial scintigraphy in Parkinson's disease. J Neurol Neurosurg Psychiatry 67:189–194, 1999.

57. Courbon F, Brefel-Courbon C, Thalamas C, et al: Cardiac MIBG scintigraphy is a sensitive tool for detecting cardiac sympathetic denervation in Parkinson's disease. Mov Disord 18:890–897, 2003.

58. Goldstein DS, Holmes C, Cannon RO III, et al: Sympathetic cardioneuropathy in dysautonomias. N Engl J Med 336:696–702, 1997.

59. Larner AJ, Mathias CJ, Rossor MN: Autonomic failure preceding dementia with Lewy bodies. J Neurol 247:229–231, 2000.

60. Horimoto Y, Matsumoto M, Akatsu H, et al: Autonomic dysfunction in dementia with Lewy bodies. J Neurol 250:530–533, 2003.

61. Kimber J, Mathias CJ, Lees AJ, et al: Physiological, pharmacological and neurohormonal assessment of autonomic function in progressive supranuclear palsy. Brain 123:1422–1430, 2000.

62. Anand P, Rudge P, Mathias CJ, et al: New autonomic and sensory neuropathy with loss of adrenergic sympathetic function and sensory neuropeptides. Lancet 337:1253–1254, 1991.

63. Axelrod FB: Familial dysautonomia. In Mathias CJ, Bannister R (eds): Autonomic Failure: A Textbook of Clinical Disorders of the Autonomic Nervous System, 4th ed. Oxford, Oxford University Press, 1999, pp 402–409.

64. Reilly MM, Thomas PK: Amyloid polyneuropathy. In Mathias CJ, Bannister R (eds): Autonomic Failure: A Textbook of Clinical Disorders of the Autonomic Nervous System, 4th ed. Oxford, Oxford University Press, 1999, pp 410–420.

65. Mathias CJ, Bannister R: Dopamine beta-hydroxylase deficiency and other genetically determined autonomic disorders. In Mathias CJ, Bannister R (eds): Autonomic Failure. A Textbook of Clinical Disorders of the Autonomic Nervous System, 3rd ed. Oxford, Oxford University Press, 2002, pp 387–401.

66. Mathias CJ, Bannister R, Cortelli P, et al: Clinical autonomic and therapeutic observations in two siblings with postural hypotension and sympathetic failure due to an inability to synthesize noradrenaline from dopamine because of a deficiency of dopamine beta-hydroxylase. Q J Med 278:617–633, 1990.

67. Watkins PJ: The enigma of autonomic failure in diabetes. J R Coll Phys Lond 32:360–365, 1998.

68. Greene DA, Lattimer SA, Sima AAF: Are disturbances of sorbitol, phosphoinositide, and Na$^+$K$^+$ ATPase regulation involved in pathogenesis of diabetic neuropathy? Diabetes 37:688–693, 1988.

69. Ewing DJ, Campbell IW, Burt AA, Clarke BF: Vascular reflexes in diabetic autonomic neuropathy. Lancet 2:1354–1356, 1973.

70. Watkins PJ, Edmonds ME: Diabetic autonomic failure. In Mathias CJ, Bannister R (eds): Autonomic Failure: A Textbook of Clinical Disorders of the Autonomic Nervous System, 4th ed. Oxford, Oxford University Press, 2002, pp 378–386.

71. Sundkvist G, Bornmyr S, Svensson H, et al: Sympathetic neuropathy is more frequent than parasympathetic neuropathy in patients with a short duration of type 2 diabetes. Clin Auton Res 8:281, 1998.

72. Cryer PE, Silverberg AB, Santiago JV, et al: Plasma catecholamines in diabetes. Am J Med 64:407–416, 1978.

73. Hoeldtke RD, Streeten DHP: Treatment of orthostatic hypotension with erythropoietin. N Engl J Med 329:611–615, 1993.

74. Christlieb AR, Bratten JJ: Decreased response of plasma renin activity to orthostasis in diabetic patients with orthostatic hypotension. Diabetes 23:835–840, 1974.

75. Mathias CJ, Christensen NJ, Corbett JL, et al: Plasma catecholamines, plasma renin activity and plasma aldosterone in tetraplegic man, horizontal and tilted. Clin Sci Mol Med 49:291–299, 1975.

76. Mathias CJ, Christensen NJ, Corbett JL, et al: Plasma catecholamines during paroxysmal neurogenic hypertension in quadriplegic man. Circ Res 39:204–208, 1976.

77. Mathias CJ, Christensen NJ, Frankel HL, Spalding JMK: Cardiovascular control in recently injured tetraplegics in spinal shock. Q J Med 48:273–287, 1979.

78. Mathias CJ, Deguchi K, Bleasdale-Barr K, Kimber JR: Frequency of family history in vasovagal syncope. Lancet 352:33–34, 1998.

79. Mathias CJ, Deguchi K, Bleasdale-Barr K, Smith S: Familial vasovagal syncope and pseudosyncope: Observations in a case with both natural and adopted siblings. Clin Auton Res 10:43–45, 2000.

80. El Badawi KM, Hainsworth R: Combined head-up tilt and lower body suction: A test of orthostatic intolerance. Clin Auton Res 4:41–47, 1994.

81. McIntosh SJ, Lawson J, Kenny RA: Clinical characteristics of vasodepressor, cardioinhibitory and mixed carotid sinus syndrome in the elderly. Am J Med 95:203–208, 1993.

82. Mathias CJ: Autonomic dysfunction. In Grimley-Evans J, Franklin Williams T, Lynn Beattie B, et al (eds): Oxford Textbook of Geriatric Medicine, 2nd ed. Oxford, Oxford University Press, 2000, pp 833–852.

83. Mathias CJ, Armstrong E, Browse N, et al: Value of non-invasive continuous blood pressure monitoring in the detection of carotid sinus hypersensitivity. Clin Auton Res 2:157–159, 1991.

84. Low PA, Schondorf R, Rummans TA: Why do patients have orthostatic symptoms in PoTS? Clin Auton Res 11:223–224, 2001.

85. Jacob G, Costa F, Shannon JR, et al: The neuropathic postural tachycardia syndrome. N Engl J Med 343:1008–1014, 2000.

86. Vernino S, Low PA, Fealey RD, et al: Autoantibodies to ganglionic acetylcholine receptors in autoimmune autonomic neuropathies. N Engl J Med 343:847–855, 2000.

87. Shannon JR, Flatten NL, Jordan J, et al: Orthostatic intolerance and tachycardia associated with norepinephrine-transporter deficiency. N Engl J Med 342:541–549, 2000.

88. Gazit Y, Nahir AM, Grahame R, Jacob G: Dysautonomia in the joint hypermobility syndrome. Am J Med 115:33–40, 2003.

89. Mathias CJ: Autonomic diseases: Management. J Neurol Neurosurg Psychiatry 74:iii42–iii47, 2003.

90. Mathias CJ, Young TM: Plugging the leak—the benefits of the vasopressin-2 agonist, desmopressin in autonomic failure. Clin Auton Res 13:85–87, 2003.

91. Wieling W, van Lieshout JJ, van Leeuwen AM: Physical manoeuvres that reduce postural hypotension. Clin Auton Res 3:57–65, 1993.

92. Smit AAJ, Hardjowijono MA, Wieling W: Are portable folding chairs useful to combat orthostatic hypotension? Ann Neurol 42:975–978, 1997.

93. Cariga P, Mathias CJ: The haemodynamics of the pressor effect of oral water in human sympathetic denervation due to autonomic failure. Clin Sci 101:313–319, 2001.

94. Young TM, Mathias CJ: The effects of water ingestion on orthostatic hypotension in two groups with chronic autonomic failure: Multiple system atrophy and pure autonomic failure. J Neurol Neurosurg Psychiatry 75(12):1737–1741, 2004.

95. Mathias CJ, Senard J, Braune S, et al: L-Theo-dihydroxphenylserine (L-threo-DOPS; droxidopa) in the management of neurogenic orthostatic hypotension: A multi-national, multi-centre, dose-ranging study in multiple system atrophy and pure autonomic failure. Clin Auton Res 11:235–242, 2001.

96. Sakakibara R, Matsuda S, Uchiyama T, et al: The effect of intranasal desmopressin on nocturnal waking in urination in multiple system atrophy patients with nocturnal polyuria. Clin Auton Res 13:106–108, 1993.

97. Low PA, Gilden JL, Freeman R, et al: Efficacy of midodrine vs. placebo in neurogenic orthostatic hypotension. A randomized, double-blind multicenter study. JAMA 277:1046–1051, 1997.

98. Singer W, Opfer-Gehrking TL, McPhee BR, et al: Acetylcholinesterase inhibition: A novel approach in the treatment of neurogenic orthostatic hypotension. J Neurol Neurosurg Psychiatry 74:1294–1298, 2003.

99. Oldenburg O, Mitchell AN, Nurnberger J, et al: Ambulatory norepinephrine treatment of severe autonomic orthostatic hypotension. J Am Coll Cardiol 37:219–223, 2001.

100. Kimber J, Watson L, Mathias CJ: Cardiovascular and neurohormonal responses to i.v. l-arginine in two groups with primary autonomic failure. J Neurol 248:1036–1041, 2001.

101. Freeman R, Young J, Landsbert L, Lipsitz L: The treatment of postprandial hypotension in autonomic failure with 3,4-DL-threo-dihydroxphenylserine. Neurology 47:1414–1420, 1996.

102. Smith GDP, Alam M, Watson LP, Mathias CJ: Effects of the somatostatin analogue, octreotide, on exercise induced hypotension in human subjects with chronic sympathetic failure. Clin Sci 89:367–373, 1995.

103. Alam M, Smith GDP, Bleasdale-Barr K, et al: Effects of the peptide release inhibitor, octreotide, on daytime hypotension and on nocturnal hypertension in primary autonomic failure. J Hypertens 13:1664–1669, 1995.

104. Cooper VL, Hainsworth R: Effects of dietary salt on orthostatic tolerance, blood pressure and baroreceptor sensitivity in patients with syncope. Clin Auton Res 12:234–241, 2002.

105. Benditt DG: Cardiac pacing for prevention of vasovagal syncope. J Am Coll Cardiol 33:21–23, 1999.

106. Brignole M, Croci F, Menozzi C, et al: Isometric arm contraction at the onset of prodromal symptoms: A new first-line treatment for vasovagal syncope. In Raviele A (ed): Cardiac Arrhythmias. Springer, 2004, pp 641–650.

107. van Dijk N, Harms MP, Linzer M, Wieling W: Treatment of vasovagal syncope: Pacemaker or crossing legs? Clin Auton Res 10:347–349, 2000.

# ENDOCRINE CHANGES IN CRITICALLY ILL PATIENTS

# Endocrine Aspects of Critical Care Medicine

## Greet Van den Berghe

INTRODUCTION

PATHOGENESIS, CLINICAL FEATURES,
AND TREATMENT OPTIONS
    Somatotropic Axis
    Thyrotropic Axis

Lactotropic Axis
Luteinizing Hormone–Testosterone Axis
Pituitary-Adrenal Axis
Insulin
What Are the Implications for Clinical Practice?

## INTRODUCTION

Critical illness is any condition requiring support of failing vital organ systems without which survival would not be possible. This life-threatening condition, which may be evoked by trauma, extensive surgery, or severe medical illnesses, is an ultimate example of acute, severe physical stress. If onset of recovery does not follow within a few days of intensive care, critical illness often becomes prolonged and vital organ support is frequently needed for weeks or even months. Feeding alone is unable to reverse ongoing wasting of protein from skeletal muscle and solid organs, which causes impairment of vital functions, weakness, and delayed or hampered recovery.[1,2] This is a frustrating clinical problem because, despite adequate and successful treatment of the underlying disease, dependence on intensive care persists and susceptibility to potentially lethal complications, often of septic origin, increases. Indeed, mortality from prolonged critical illness is high: Almost 3 of 10 adult patients with an intensive care stay of more than 3 weeks do not survive the intensive care phase.[3] Male patients seem to have a higher risk of adverse outcome of prolonged critical illness than female patients do, an observation that remains unexplained.[3] In line with the foregoing is the inability of the classic scoring systems for severity of illness, such as the Acute Physiology and Chronic Health Evaluation (APACHE) II score,[4] to predict mortality in an individual chronically critically ill patient. This enigma reflects our lack of understanding of the pathophysiologic mechanisms underlying onset of recovery or, conversely, the failure to recover from prolonged critical illness.

Until recently, the endocrine changes occurring during critical illness were considered to be part of a uniform stress response that is sustained throughout intensive care and that reflects a beneficial adaptation of the human body contributing to survival. Recent new data, however, have become available that indicate that this is not correct because the acute and chronic phases of critical illness are associated with distinct endocrine alterations.[5,6] It still remains a matter of debate whether or to what extent these biphasic changes are adaptive or contributing to the metabolic disturbances present in the critically ill. The endocrine stress responses are partially central and partially peripheral in origin. In addition, patients admitted to intensive care units may have preexisting central and/or peripheral endocrine diseases, either previously diagnosed or unknown. Hence, the puzzle is complex and endocrine function testing in a critically ill patient represents a major challenge. Furthermore, the inability to label the endocrine changes either as adaptation or as pathology renders the issue of treatment even more controversial.

This chapter reviews the novel insights into the dynamic neuroendocrine alterations as they occur during the course of critical illness. It also highlights the complexity of the differential diagnosis with preexisting endocrine diseases as well as the available evidence of benefit and/or harm of some endocrine interventions.

## PATHOGENESIS, CLINICAL FEATURES, AND TREATMENT OPTIONS

### SOMATOTROPIC AXIS

In normal physiology, growth hormone (GH) is released from the pituitary somatotropes in a pulsatile fashion under the interactive control of the hypothalamic GH-releasing hormone (GHRH), which is stimulatory, and somatostatin, which exerts an inhibitory effect.[7] Since the 1980s, a series of synthetic GH-releasing peptides (GHRPs) and nonpeptide analogues has been developed with potent GH-releasing capacities acting through a specific G protein–coupled receptor located in the hypothalamus and the pituitary.[8,9] The highly conserved endogenous ligand for this receptor has recently been discovered and named ghrelin.[10] Ghrelin originates in peripheral tissues such as the stomach as well as in the hypothalamic arcuate nucleus and appears to be a third key factor in the complex physiologic regulation of pulsatile GH secretion. As originally shown in rodents,[11] there is now evidence that, also in the human,[12] the pulsatile nature of GH secretion is important for its metabolic effects.[3,13]

#### Alterations within the Somatotropic Axis in the Acute Phase of Critical Illness

During the first hours and days after an acute insult, such as surgery, trauma, or infection, circulating GH levels become elevated and the normal GH profile, consisting of peaks alternating with virtually undetectable troughs, is altered: Peak GH levels as well as interpulse concentrations are high and the GH pulse frequency is elevated[5,14,15] (Fig. 138-1). It is still unclear which factor ultimately controls the stimulation of GH release in response to stress. As in starvation,[16] more frequent withdrawal of the inhibitory somatostatin and/or an increased availability of stimulatory (hypothalamic and/or peripheral) GH-releasing factors could hypothetically be involved. Second, serum concentrations of insulin-like growth factor 1 (IGF-1) and the GH-dependent-binding protein IGF-binding protein 3 (IGFBP-3) and its acid-labile subunit (ALS) decrease, which is preceded by a decrease in serum levels of GH-binding protein (GHBP).[17] The latter was found to reflect reduced GH receptor expression in peripheral tissues.[17] Circulating levels of the small IGF-binding proteins, such as

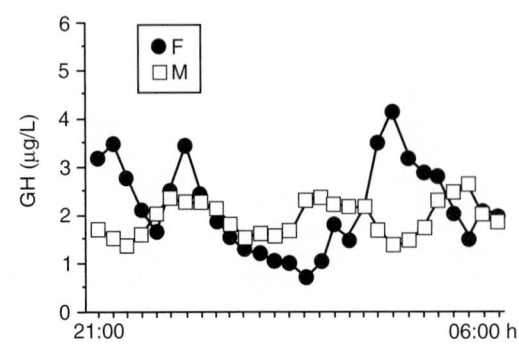

**Figure 138-1** Nocturnal serum concentration profiles of growth hormone (GH) illustrate the differences between the acute phase and the chronic phase of critical illness in an intensive care setting. (From Van den Berghe G: Novel insights into the neuroendocrinology of critical illness. Eur J Endocrinol 143:1–13, 2000.)

IGFBP-1, IGFBP-2, and IGFBP-6, are elevated.[18,19] This constellation, which has been confirmed in experimental human and animal models of acute stress and in acutely ill patients, has been interpreted as acquired peripheral resistance to GH.[14,18] It has been suggested that these changes are brought about by the effects of cytokines such as tumor necrosis factor-alpha, interleukin-1, and interleukin-6, the hypothesis being that reduced GH receptor expression and thus low IGF-1 levels are the primary events (cytokine induced) that in turn, through reduced negative feedback inhibition, induce the abundant release of GH during acute stress, exerting direct lipolytic, insulin-antagonizing, and immune-stimulating actions, whereas the indirect IGF-1 mediated effects of GH are attenuated.[20,21] This explanation is plausible in that such changes would prioritize essential substrates such as glucose, free fatty acids, and amino acids (glutamine) toward survival rather than anabolism. Increased IGFBP-3 protease activity in plasma has also been reported, however, and is thought to result in increased dissociation of IGF-1 from the ternary complex, thereby shortening the IGF-1 half-life in the circulation. The latter could theoretically be an adaptive escape mechanism to secure availability of free IGF-1 at the tissue level.[22]

## Distinct Alterations within the Somatotropic Axis during Chronic Critical Illness

In chronic critical illness, the changes observed within the somatotropic axis are different. First, the pattern of GH secretion is very chaotic and the amount of GH, which is released in pulses, is now much reduced compared with the acute phase[6,23–25] (see Fig. 138-1). Moreover, although the nonpulsatile fraction is still somewhat elevated and the number of pulses is still high, the mean nocturnal GH serum concentrations are scarcely elevated, if at all,[23] compared with the healthy, nonstressed condition, and substantially lower than

in the acute phase of stress.[5] We observed that, when intensive care patients are studied from 7 to 10 days of illness onward, in the absence of drugs known to exert profound effects on GH secretion such as dopamine,[26,27] calcium entry blockers, and glucocorticoids, mean nocturnal GH levels are uniformly approximately 1 µg/L,[23] trough levels are easily detectable (and thus still elevated), and peak GH levels hardly ever exceed 2 µg/L.[6,23–25] These results are surprisingly independent of the patient's age, gender, body composition, and type of underlying disease.[3,5] Second, only the pulsatile fraction of GH secretion, which is substantially reduced, correlates positively with circulating levels of IGF-1, IGFBP-3, and ALS, all of which are low.[6,24,25] Thus, the smaller that the GH pulses become, the lower the circulating levels of GH-dependent IGF-1 and ternary complex binding proteins. This clearly no longer represents a pure state of GH resistance. Serum levels of GHBP,[3] assumed to reflect GH receptor expression in peripheral tissues, which are increased in patients who are critically ill for several weeks compared with those measured in a matched control group, are in line with recovery of GH responsiveness with time during severe illness.[3,6] Moreover, low serum levels of GH-dependent IGF-1 and IGF-binding proteins (IGFBP-3, ALS, and IGFBP-5) are closely related to biochemical markers of impaired anabolism, such as low serum osteocalcin and leptin concentrations during prolonged critical illness.[6] These findings suggest that relative GH deficiency, epitomized by reduced pulsatile GH secretion, participates in the pathogenesis of the wasting syndrome, especially in the chronic phase of critical illness. Furthermore, there is a gender dissociation in that men show a greater loss of pulsatility and regularity within the GH secretory pattern than women (despite indistinguishable total GH output) and concomitantly have lower circulating IGF-1 and ALS levels[3] (Fig. 138-2). It remains unknown whether the (paradoxic) sexual dimorphism within the GH/IGF-1 axis and the fact

**Figure 138-2** The more feminized pattern of growth hormone (GH) secretion (more irregular and less pulsatile GH secretory pattern for an identical mean nocturnal GH level) in prolonged critically ill men compared with women is illustrated by the representative nocturnal (21:00–06:00 hr) GH serum concentration series (sampling every 20 minutes) obtained in a male and a matched female patient. Concomitantly, prolonged critically ill men have lower circulating levels of insulin-like growth factor 1 (IGF-1) than female patients do. IGF-1 results are presented as mean ± standard deviation. **$P < 0.01$. (From Van den Berghe G: Novel insights into the neuroendocrinology of critical illness. Eur J Endocrinol 143:1–13, 2000.)

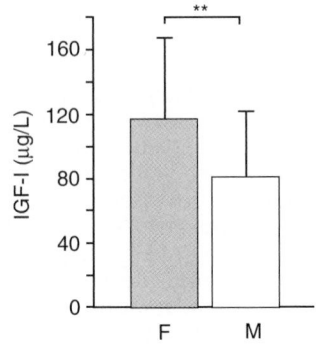

that males seem to be at higher risk of an adverse outcome from chronic critical illness than females[3] is a casual or causal association.

## Pathophysiology of Chronic Changes within the Somatotropic Axis

The pathogenesis of the secretory pattern of GH in prolonged critical illness is probably complex. One of the possibilities is that the pituitary is taking part in the multiple organ failure syndrome, becoming unable to synthesize and secrete GH. An alternative explanation could be that the lack of pulsatile GH secretion is due to increased somatostatin tone and/or reduced stimulation by endogenous releasing factors such as GHRH and/or ghrelin. Studying GH responses to administration of GH secretagogues (GHRH and GHRP), in a saturating dose, enables the differentiation between a primarily pituitary origin and a hypothalamic origin of the relatively impaired GH release in prolonged critically ill patients. Indeed, the combined administration of GHRH and GHRP appears to be a most powerful stimulus for pituitary GH release in humans.[28] A low GH response in critical illness would thus corroborate a pituitary dysfunction and/or a high somatostatin tone, whereas a high GH response would be compatible with reduced (hypothalamic) stimulation of the somatotropes.

GH responses to a bolus injection of GHRP have been found to be high in prolonged critically ill patients and severalfold higher than the response to GHRH, the latter being normal or often subnormal.[29] GHRH + GHRP evokes a clear synergistic response in this condition, revealing the highest GH responses ever reported in a human study.[29] The high GH responses to secretagogues exclude the possibility that the blunted GH secretion during protracted critical illness is due to either the lack of pituitary capacity to synthesize GH or accentuated somatostatin-induced suppression of GH release. Inferentially, one of the mechanisms that could be involved is reduced availability of ghrelin. Ultimately, the combination of low availability of somatostatin and an endogenous GHRP-like ligand such as ghrelin emerges as a plausible mechanism that clarifies (1) the reduced GH burst amplitude, (2) the increased frequency of spontaneous GH secretory bursts, (3) the elevated interpulse levels, and (4) the striking responsiveness to GHRP alone or in combination with GHRH, and this without markedly increased responsiveness to GHRH alone. Female patients with prolonged critical illness have a markedly higher response to a bolus of GHRP compared with male patients, a difference that is nullified when GHRH is injected together with GHRP[3] (Fig. 138-3). Less endogenous GHRH action in prolonged critically ill men, possibly due to the concomitant profound hypoandrogenism,[3] accompanying loss of action of an endogenous GHRP-like ligand with prolonged stress in both genders, may explain this finding.

## Effects of GH-Releasing Factors in the Chronic Phase of Critical Illness

The hypothesis of reduced endogenous stimulation of GH secretion in prolonged critical illness was further explored by examining the effects of continuous infusion of GHRP ± GHRH. Continuously infusing GHRP (1 µg/kg/hr) and, even more so, GHRH + GHRP (1 + 1 µg/kg/hr), for as long as 2 days was found to substantially amplify pulsatile GH secretion (more than sixfold and more than 10-fold, respectively) in this condition, without altering the relatively high burst frequency[24,25] (Fig. 138-4). Reactivating pulsatile GH secretion evoked a proportionate increase in serum IGF-1 (66% and 106%), IGFBP-3 (50% and 56%), and ALS (65% and 97%), indicating peripheral GH responsiveness[24,25] (see Fig. 138-4). The presence of considerable responsiveness to reactivated pulsatile GH secretion in these patients and the high serum levels of GHBP clearly delineate the distinct pathophysiologic paradigm present in the chronic phase of critical illness as opposed to the acute phase, which is thought to be primarily a condition of GH resistance. After 2 days, treatment with GHRP, (near) normal levels of IGF-1, IGFBP-3, IGFBP-5, and ALS are reached, and, as shown in a subsequent study, this normalization is maintained for at least 5 days[6] (Fig. 138-5). Concomitantly, GH secretion after 5 days of treatment with GH secretagogues was found to be lower than after 2 days of treatment, suggesting active feedback inhibition loops, which most likely prevented overtreatment.[6,25] In this study, in which GHRP was infused together with thyrotropin-releasing hormone (TRH) for 5 days, the self-limiting endocrine responses induced anabolism at the level of several peripheral tissues, as indicated by an increase in the serum levels of osteocalcin, insulin, and leptin and a decrease in urea production.[6] Usually, infusion of GHRP without GHRH suffices to reactivate pulsatile GH secretion and to elicit the IGF-1 and IGFBP responses in prolonged critical illness. However, in critically ill men, in particular those with a very long intensive care stay, it may be necessary to add a low dose of GHRH (0.1 µg/kg/hr suffices) (Van den Berghe, unpublished

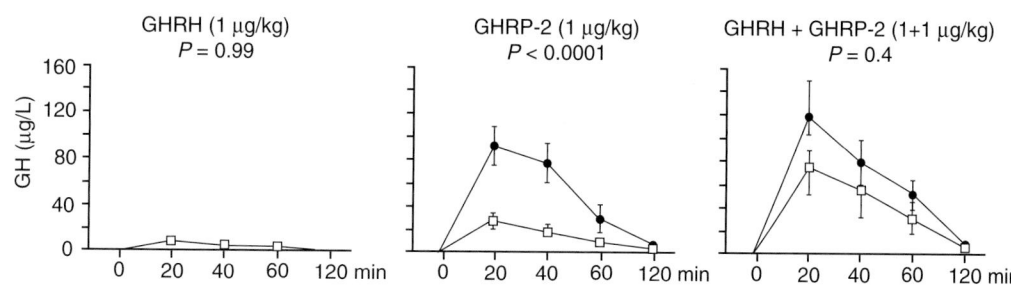

**Figure 138-3** Responses (increments above baseline) of growth hormone (GH) obtained 20, 40, 60, and 120 minutes after intravenous bolus administration of GH-releasing hormone (GHRH) (1 µg/kg), GH-releasing peptide 2 (GHRP-2) (1 µg/kg), and GHRH + GHRP-2 (1 + 1 µg/kg) in matched male and female prolonged critically ill patients. Five men and five women were randomly allocated to each secretagogue group. Results are presented as mean ± standard error of the mean. *Filled circles* depict results from female patients and *open squares* depict results from male patients. *P* values were obtained using repeated measures analysis of variance. (From Van den Berghe G: Novel insights into the neuroendocrinology of critical illness. Eur J Endocrinol 143:1–13, 2000.)

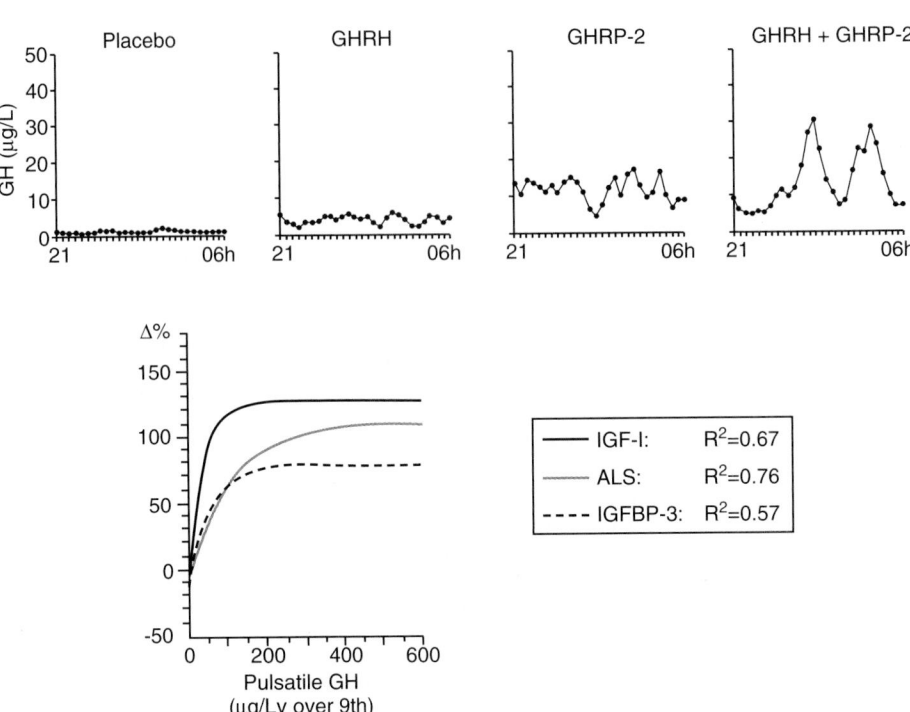

*Figure 138-4* Nocturnal serum growth hormone (GH) profiles in the prolonged phase of illness illustrate the effects of continuous infusion of placebo, GH-releasing hormone (GHRH) (1 μg/kg/hr), GH-releasing peptide-2 (GHRP-2) (1 μg/kg/hr), or GHRH + GHRP-2 (1 + 1 μg/kg/hr). Exponential regression lines have been reported between pulsatile GH secretion and the changes in circulating insulin-like growth factor 1 (IGF-1), acid-labile subunit (ALS), and IGF-binding protein 3 (IGFBP-3) obtained with 45-hour infusion of placebo, GHRP-2, or GHRH + GHRP-2. They indicate that the parameters of GH responsiveness increase in proportion to GH secretion up to a certain point, beyond which further increase of GH secretion has apparently little or no additional effect. It is noteworthy that the latter point corresponds to a pulsatile GH secretion of approximately 200 μg/L over 9 hours or less, a value that can usually be evoked by the infusion of GHRP-2 alone. In chronic critical illness, GH sensitivity is clearly present, in contrast to the acute phase of illness, which is thought to be primarily a condition of GH resistance. (From Van den Berghe G: Novel insights into the neuroendocrinology of critical illness. Eur J Endocrinol 143:1–13, 2000.)

observations) because of the simultaneous lack of endogenous GHRH activity accompanying the reduced availability of the GHRP-like ligand.[3]

## Treatment with Growth Hormone during Critical Illness

In view of the anabolic properties of GH and IGF-1, a large multicenter study investigated the effects of high-dose GH treatment in long-stay intensive care patients.[30] Instead of improving outcome, this intervention doubled mortality and worsened morbidity. Although the authors of this study did not provide an explanation for the unexpected outcome, the difference between the acute and chronic stress responses may be important. The rationale for the use of high GH doses

in that trial has presumably been the extrapolation, now invalidated, that all conditions of stress-associated hypercatabolism, and thus also the catabolic state of prolonged critical illness, are brought about primarily by resistance to GH in the presence of normal or adaptively altered pituitary function and that the induction of anabolism in these conditions would thus require very high GH doses. The knowledge that is now available on the different states of the somatotropic axis in acute and prolonged critical illness clarifies, at least partially, why the administration of high GH doses to sick, but often GH-responsive, patients may have evoked side effects. Indeed, high doses of GH administered in the chronic phase of critical illness can induce IGF-1 levels into the

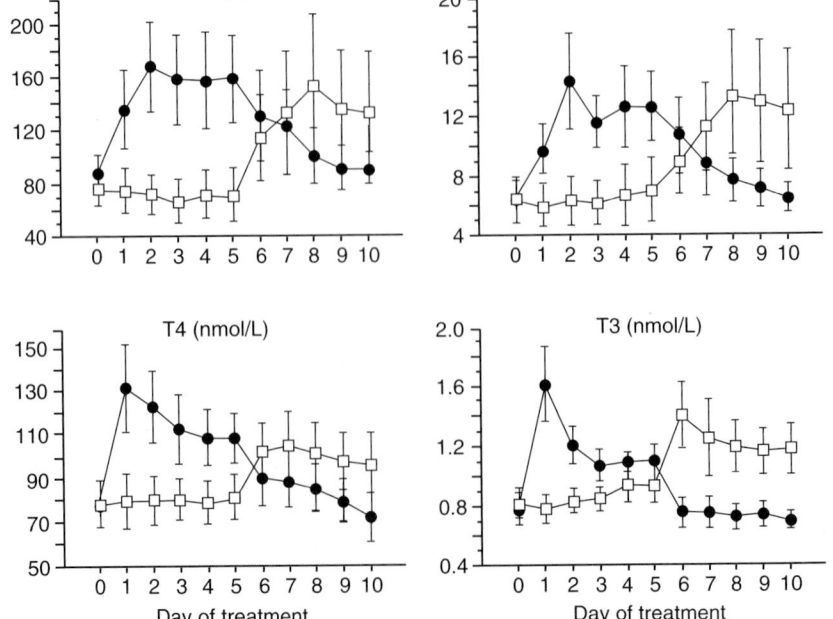

*Figure 138-5* Serum concentrations (mean ± standard error of the mean) of insulin-like growth factor 1 (IGF-1), acid-labile subunit (ALS), thyroxine ($T_4$), and triiodothyronine ($T_3$) in response to a randomized treatment with either 5 days GHRP-2 + thyrotropin-releasing hormone (TRH) infusion (1 + 1 μg/kg/hr) followed by 5 days of placebo (*filled circles*) or 5 days of placebo followed by 5 days GHRP-2 + TRH infusion (1 + 1 μg/kg/hr) (*open squares*) in a group of 10 male and 4 female critically ill patients on ventilation in the intensive care unit. All $P < 0.0001$ with analysis of variance. The mean age of the patients was 68 years. The mean intensive care unit stay at the time of study start was 40 days. (From Van den Berghe G: Novel insights into the neuroendocrinology of critical illness. Eur J Endocrinol 143:1–13, 2000.)

acromegalic range, excessive fluid retention (as much as 20% of body weight), hypercalcemia, and pronounced insulin resistance with hyperglycemia.[31] In view of the broad spectrum of target tissues for GH and taking into account the pre-existing impairment of vital organ functions in the critically ill, the excessive doses of GH may have further deteriorated the function of multiple organs.

A question that arises from the results of this trial is what intensive care physicians should do when patients who are GH deficient and on GH treatment become critically ill and admitted to the intensive care unit. Should GH substitution therapy be discontinued in that situation? A consensus statement from the Growth Hormone Research Society[32] advises not to discontinue GH in view of the lack of evidence that the low GH doses used for substitution therapy are harmful.

## THYROTROPIC AXIS

### Changes in the Acute Phase of Critical Illness

Within 2 hours after surgery or trauma, serum levels of triiodothyronine ($T_3$) decrease, whereas thyroxine ($T_4$) and thyroid-stimulating hormone (TSH) briefly increase (Fig. 138-6).[33] Apparently, low $T_3$ levels at that stage are mainly caused by a decreased peripheral conversion of $T_4$ to $T_3$.[34] Subsequently, circulating TSH and $T_4$ levels often return to "normal," whereas $T_3$ levels remain low. Although mean serum TSH concentrations are indistinguishable from normal at that time point, the normal nocturnal TSH surge is absent.[35,36] The magnitude of the $T_3$ decrease within 24 hours has been found to reflect the severity of illness.[37,38] The cytokines tumor necrosis factor-alpha, interleukin-1, and interleukin-6 have been investigated as putative mediators of acute low $T_3$ syndrome. Although these cytokines are capable of mimicking the acute stress–induced alterations in thyroid status, cytokine antagonism in a human model failed to restore normal thyroid function.[39] Low concentrations of binding proteins and inhibition of hormone binding, transport, and metabolism by elevated levels of free fatty acids and bilirubin have been proposed as factors contributing to the low $T_3$ syndrome at the tissue level.[40] Teleologically, the acute changes in the thyroid axis may reflect an attempt to reduce energy expenditure, as happens during starvation,[41] and thus as an appropriate response that does not warrant intervention. This, however, remains a controversial issue because valid data to support or refute this statement are lacking.[42] Indeed, although short-term intravenous administration of $T_3$

to patients after cross-clamp removal during elective coronary bypass grafting has been shown to improve postoperative cardiac function,[43,44] the doses of $T_3$ resulted in supranormal serum $T_3$ levels and support but do not prove an adaptive nature of the "acute" low $T_3$ syndrome.

### Changes in Prolonged Critical Illness

Patients treated in intensive care units for several weeks present with a somewhat different set of changes within the thyroid axis (see Fig. 138-6). A single sample usually reveals low or low-normal TSH values and low $T_4$ and $T_3$ serum concentrations.[45] However, overnight repeated sampling revealed that, essentially, the pulsatility in the TSH secretory pattern is dramatically diminished and that, as for the GH axis, it is the loss of TSH pulse amplitude that is related to low serum levels of thyroid hormone.[45] Moreover, Fliers and colleagues[46] elegantly demonstrated by postmortem examination of human brain specimens that when death follows chronic severe illness, the expression of the TRH gene in hypothalamic paraventricular nuclei is reduced, whereas this is not the case after death from acute insults such as lethal trauma due to a motor vehicle accident. These researchers observed a positive correlation between TRH mRNA in the paraventricular nuclei and blood levels of TSH and $T_3$. Together, these findings indicate that production and/or release of thyroid hormones is reduced in the chronic phase of critical illness due to reduced hypothalamic stimulation of the thyrotropes, in turn leading to reduced stimulation of the thyroid gland. In line with this concept is the increase of TSH marking onset of recovery from severe illness.[47] The exact mechanisms underlying the neuroendocrine pathogenesis of the low thyroid hormone levels in prolonged critical illness are unknown. As circulating cytokine levels are usually much lower at that stage,[48] other mechanisms operational within the central nervous system are presumably involved. Endogenous dopamine and prolonged hypercortisolism may each play a role because exogenous dopamine and glucocorticoids are known to provoke or severely aggravate hypothyroidism in critical illness.[49,50]

Recent data indicate that in addition to the resetting of hypothalamic control, the activity in the liver of type 1 deiodinase (D1) is suppressed and of type 3 deiodinase (D3) is increased in prolonged critically ill patients. These alterations in enzyme activity were found to determine the ratio of active to inactive thyroid hormone ($T_3$/reverse $T_3$), indicating that changes in thyroid hormone metabolism are contributing to the picture of low $T_3$ syndrome in the chronic phase of critical illness.[51] Interestingly, in a rabbit model of critical illness, the downregulation of D1 and upregulation of D3 was reversed by the simultaneous infusion of TRH and GHRP-2.[52]

It has been shown that alternative splicing gives rise to two receptor isoforms for thyroid hormone, TR-1 and TR-2. The TR-1 isoform is a bona fide $T_3$ receptor, whereas the TR-2 acts as a dominant negative isoform. The ratio of these splice variants could therefore have a marked influence on $T_3$-regulated gene expression, especially in view of the changing metabolism of thyroid hormone during illness. An inverse correlation between $T_3$/reverse $T_3$ ratio and the TR-1/TR-2 ratio in liver biopsies of prolonged critically ill patients was recently observed.[53] Furthermore, higher TR-1/TR-2 ratios were present in sicker and older patients compared with the less sick and younger ones. Hence, critically ill patients appear to adapt to the decreasing thyroid hormone levels by increasing the expression of the active form of the thyroid hormone receptor gene and thereby possibly increasing the cellular sensitivity to the hormone. This constellation does not corroborate an adaptive nature of the low $T_3$ syndrome in prolonged critically ill patients.

Low thyroid hormone levels in protracted critical illness correlate inversely with urea production and bone degradation, which could again reflect either an adaptive, protective mechanism against hypercatabolism or a causal relationship.[6]

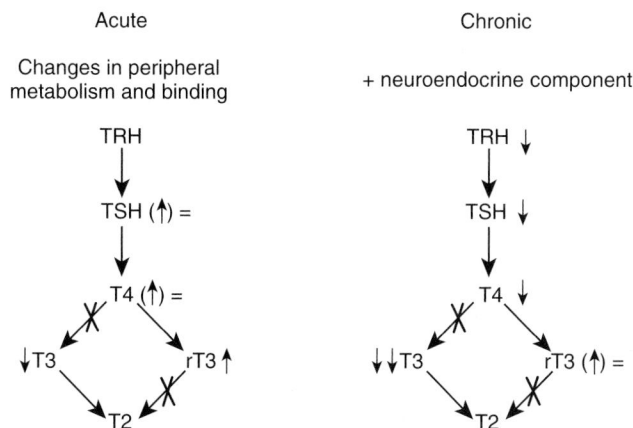

**Figure 138-6** Simplified overview of the major changes occurring within the thyroid axis during the acute and chronic phases of critical illness. r$T_3$, reverse triiodothyronine; $T_3$, triiodothyronine; $T_4$, thyroxine; TRH, thyrotropin-releasing hormone; TSH, thyroid-stimulating hormone. (From Van den Berghe G: Novel insights into the neuroendocrinology of critical illness. Eur J Endocrinol 143:1–13, 2000.)

Restoring physiologic levels of thyroid hormones by continuously infusing TRH together with GHRP-2 (see Fig. 138-5), however, was found to reduce rather than increase hypercatabolism,[6] an effect that was related only to thyroid hormone changes. During TRH infusion in prolonged critical illness, the negative feedback exerted by thyroid hormones on the thyrotropes was found to be maintained, thus precluding overstimulation of the thyroid axis.[23,25] This self-limitation may be extremely important during critical illness to avoid hyperthyroidism, which would inadvertently aggravate catabolism. The coinfusion of TRH and GH-releasing factors appears to be a better strategy than the infusion of TRH alone because the combination, but not TRH alone, avoids an increase in circulating reverse $T_3$.[6,23] The latter is in line with the effects that TRH and GHRP-2 exert on the activity of type 1 and 3 deiodinases and eventually with other important interactions among different anterior pituitary axes for optimal peripheral responses.[54]

### Treatment with Thyroid Hormone or Releasing Factors during Prolonged Critical Illness

It remains controversial whether correction of the illness-associated low serum and tissue concentrations of $T_3$ by either $T_4$ or $T_3$ administration is required to improve clinical problems distinctively associated with prolonged critical illness.[55,56] Pioneering studies with $T_4$ administration so far have failed to demonstrate clinical benefit within an intensive care setting, but in view of the impaired conversion of $T_4$ to $T_3$, this is not really surprising.[57,58] A recent report on thyroid hormone treatment using substitution doses of $T_3$ in dopamine-treated pediatric patients after correction of a congenital cardiac anomaly revealed improvement in postoperative cardiac function.[59] In contrast to treatment with thyroid hormones, infusing TRH allows peripheral shifts in thyroid hormone metabolism during intercurrent events and, accordingly, permits the body to elaborate appropriate concentrations of thyroid hormones in the circulation and at the tissue level, thus setting the scene for a safer treatment than the administration of $T_3$.[25] Also, the peripheral tissue responses to the normalization of serum concentrations of IGF-1 and binding proteins as evoked by GHRP infusion seem to depend on the coinfusion of TRH and the concomitant normalization of the thyroid axis. Indeed, GHRP-2 infused alone evokes identical increments in serum concentrations of IGF-1, IGFBP-3, and ALS but is devoid of the anabolic tissue responses that are present with the combined infusion of GHRP and TRH.[23] Outcome benefit of TRH infusion alone or in combination with GH secretagogues in prolonged critical illness is yet to be studied.

The diagnosis of *preexisting* thyroid disease and its management during critical illness also can be extremely difficult and recommendation for clinical practice is often not evidence based. In view of the hypothalamic-pituitary suppression occurring in the chronic phase of critical illness, in patients with and without previous endocrine disease, it is virtually impossible to diagnose preexisting central hypothyroidism during intensive care. Patients with preexisting primary hypothyroidism, myxedema coma being the extreme presentation, are expected to reveal low serum levels of $T_4$ and $T_3$ in combination with very high TSH concentrations. However, when primary hypothyroidism and severe nonthyroidal critical illness coincide, the TSH increase may be absent. Indeed, the nonthyroidal critical illness evokes the sum of changes within the hypothalamus-pituitary-thyroid axis as described previously. A decrease in serum $T_3$ and an increase in serum reverse $T_3$ are the most common changes in acute nonthyroidal critical illness, but serum $T_3$ may be undetectable and serum $T_4$ may also be dramatically reduced in patients with protracted nonthyroidal critical illness. Therefore, in patients with myxedema coma and severe comorbidity (e.g., pneumonia, sepsis), serum $T_3$ and $T_4$ levels are very low but could be indistinguishable from those values observed in prolonged nonthyroidal critical illness. Whereas serum TSH is markedly increased in uncomplicated primary hypothyroidism, it is paradoxically normal or even decreased in severely ill patients. Therefore, serum TSH may be lower than anticipated, from the severe hypothyroid condition of the patient with myxedema coma and concomitant illness, or even frankly low. Thus, a high serum TSH concentration, when observed, is in agreement with primary hypothyroidism but a normal or a low TSH does not exclude it during intercurrent critical illness. Indeed, serum TSH may be paradoxically low in this setting because of concomitant nonthyroidal critical illness, especially in patients given high-dose corticosteroids and/or dopamine. Other iatrogenic factors causing hypothyroidism, particularly in a surgical intensive care unit, are iodine wound dressings, iodine-containing contrast agents used for radiologic imaging, and drugs such as somatostatin and amiodarone. The finding of a high ratio of $T_3$ to $T_4$ in serum, a low thyroid hormone–binding ratio, and a low serum reverse $T_3$ may favor the presence of primary hypothyroidism, whereas opposite changes occur in nonthyroidal critical illness. However, the diagnostic accuracy of any of these measurements is limited, and, in many patients, no definite laboratory diagnosis can be established. In these patients, history, physical examination, and the possible presence of thyroid autoantibodies may give further clues to the presence or absence of thyroid disease. Repeated thyroid function tests after improvement of the nonthyroidal illness are required to confirm the diagnosis.

When and how to treat primary hypothyroidism during the course of an intercurrent nonthyroidal critical illness also remain controversial. One exception, however, is a presumed diagnosis of myxedema coma, for which there is general agreement that patients should be treated with a parenteral form of thyroid hormone. The proper initiation of thyroid hormone replacement therapy, however, is controversial because controlled studies on the optimal treatment regimen are lacking. The first uncertainty relates to the type of thyroid hormone to be given: Should it be $T_4$ alone, $T_3$ alone, or a combination of both? The second uncertainty is the optimal initial dose of any thyroid hormone replacement regimen. Many clinicians prefer a loading dose of as high as 300 to 500 μg of intravenous $T_4$ to quickly restore circulating levels of $T_4$ to approximately 50% of the euthyroid value,[60,61] followed by 50 to 100 μg of intravenous $T_4$ daily until oral medication can be given. Higher doses do not seem to be beneficial, although Kaptein and associates[62] found no increased cardiovascular risk in severely ill hypothyroid patients treated with larger doses of $T_4$.

Some authors have advocated the use of $T_3$ in addition to $T_4$ because $T_3$ does not require conversion by 5'-deiodinase enzymes to a biologically active form. In an animal experimental study by Morreale de Escobar and colleagues,[63] replacement therapy for hypothyroidism with $T_4$ alone did not ensure euthyroidism in all tissues, and a subsequent study showed that only the combined treatment with both $T_4$ and $T_3$ induces euthyroidism in all tissues. Tissue-specific deiodinase activity acting as local regulatory mechanisms may explain these findings. In a more recent study in patients with hypothyroidism, it appeared that partial substitution of $T_3$ for $T_4$ may improve mood and neuropsychological function, possibly by the increased bioavailability of $T_3$ in the central nervous system.[64] While these fascinating results await confirmation by others, replacement therapy with a combination of $T_4$ and $T_3$ in compensated hypothyroidism remains an experimental modality.[65]

The author's experimental protocol for thyroid hormone therapy during intensive care of presumed hypothyroidism, either preexisting or iatrogenically induced when reversal of the iatrogenic cause appears impossible, advises administering a 100- to 200-μg bolus of $T_4$ intravenously per 24 hours combined with T$_3$ at 0.6 µg/kg ideal body weight per 24 hours in a continuous intravenous infusion, targeting serum thyroid hormone levels in the low normal range.

## LACTOTROPIC AXIS

### Prolactin Responses to Acute and Prolonged Critical Illness

It has been suggested that the changes in prolactin secretion in response to stress may contribute to altered immune function during the course of critical illness. The evidence of this includes the presence of prolactin receptors on human T and B lymphocytes[66] and the prolactin dependence on T lymphocytes for maintaining immune competence.[67] In mice, inhibition of prolactin release results in impaired lymphocyte function, in depressed lymphokine-dependent macrophage activation and in death from a normally nonlethal exposure to bacteria.[68] The immune suppressive drug cyclosporine is known to compete with prolactin for a common binding site on T cells, which may explain part of its effects.[69,70] The prolactin-suppressing drug bromocriptine has been shown to be an adjuvant immunosuppressant in humans after heart transplantation.[70] Prolactin was among the first hormones known to have increased serum concentrations in response to acute physical or psychological stress,[71] an increase that may be mediated by vasoactive intestinal peptide, oxytocin, dopaminergic pathways, and/or other still uncharacterized factors. Cytokines may again play a signaling role. Whether hyperprolactinemia during the initial phase of critical illness contributes to the vital initial activation of the immune cascade remains speculative.

In chronic critical illness, serum prolactin levels are no longer as high as in the acute phase and the secretory pattern is characterized by a reduced pulsatile fraction.[25,41] A role for endogenous dopamine has been suggested.[72] It is unknown whether the blunted prolactin secretion in the chronic phase plays a role in the anergic immune dysfunction or in the increased susceptibility to infections characterizing the chronically ill.[73] However, exogenous dopamine, often infused as an inotropic drug in intensive care–dependent patients, has been shown to further suppress prolactin secretion and was found to aggravate concomitantly both T-lymphocyte dysfunction and impaired neutrophil chemotaxis.[72,74]

### Prolactin as a Therapeutic Target?

Prolactin is currently not available for therapy. Future studies are needed to evaluate the therapeutic potential of TRH-induced prolactin release for optimizing immune function during critical illness.[50] Also, it remains unknown whether patients on treatment for prolactinoma should interrupt or continue this treatment during an intercurrent critical illness.

## LUTEINIZING HORMONE–TESTOSTERONE AXIS

### Changes in the Luteinizing Hormone–Testosterone Axis in Acute and Prolonged Critical Illness

Also for luteinizing hormone (LH), the pulsatility in the secretory pattern is important for its bioactivity.[75,76] Because testosterone is the most important endogenous anabolic steroid, changes within the LH-testosterone axis in the male could be relevant to the catabolic state of critical illness. A variety of catabolic states are accompanied by low serum testosterone levels in men. These conditions include starvation,[77,78] the postoperative phase,[79] myocardial infarction,[80] burn injury,[81,82] psychological and physical stress,[83,84] and chronic critical illness.[85]

Low serum testosterone concentrations and elevated LH levels observed during the acute stress of surgery or myocardial infarction[79,80,86] suggest an immediate Leydig cell suppression, the exact cause of which remains obscure. Inflammatory cytokines (interleukin-1 and -2) may play a role, as suggested

by experimental studies.[87,88] It may be considered appropriate that the secretion of anabolic androgens be switched off in circumstances of acute stress to conserve energy and metabolic substrates for, at that time at least, less vital functions.

When critical illness becomes prolonged, hypogonadotropism develops.[81,89] Concomitantly, circulating levels of testosterone become extremely low (often undetectable) in men, whereas estimated free estradiol concentrations remain normal, suggesting increased aromatization of adrenal androgens.[3] The progressive decrease of serum gonadotropin levels, however, appears to lag behind the rapid decline in serum testosterone.[80,86,90] In prolonged critically ill men, a high LH pulse frequency with an abnormally low LH pulse amplitude has been observed,[85] which was interpreted as impaired compensatory LH hypersecretion in response to the very low serum testosterone levels. Thus, again, it seems to be mainly impairment of the pulsatile component of LH secretion that occurs in response to the sustained stress of prolonged critical illness.[85] Endogenous dopamine, opiates, and the preserved levels of circulating estradiol[3] may be involved in the pathogenesis of hypogonadotropism because exogenous dopamine, opioids, and estrogens may further decrease blunted LH secretion.[85,91] Animal data suggest that prolonged exposure of the brain to interleukin-1 may also play a role through the suppression of LH-releasing hormone synthesis.[87] The pioneering studies evaluating androgen treatment in prolonged critical illness failed to demonstrate conclusive clinical benefit.[92] In view of the secretory characteristics of the other anterior pituitary hormones, we recently investigated the therapeutic potential of LH-releasing hormone pulses in prolonged critically ill men, alone and together with GHRP-2 and TRH. LH-releasing hormone alone appears only partially and transiently effective.[93] However, when LHRH pulses were given together with GHRP-2 and TRH infusion, target organ responses and anabolic effects followed.[23] These data underline the importance of correcting all the hypothalamic/pituitary defects instead of applying a single hormone treatment.

### Sex Steroid Substitution Therapy during Critical Illness?

Because critical illness in itself induces profound hypoandrogenism in male patients (it remains unknown whether this reflects adaptation or pathology), it is not clear whether androgen substitution therapy for preexisting hypogonadism should be interrupted or continued during the course of an intercurrent critical illness. Sex steroids in women are usually not continued during critical illness.

## PITUITARY-ADRENAL AXIS

### Pituitary-Adrenal Responses to Acute and Prolonged Critical Illness

The pituitary-adrenal axis also responds differently to acute and prolonged critical illness. It has been long known that the vital stress-induced hypercortisolism induced by surgery, trauma, or sepsis, is associated with augmented adrenocorticotropic hormone release, which, in turn, is presumably driven by corticotropin-releasing hormone, cytokines, and the noradrenergic system. Concomitantly, circulating aldosterone increases markedly, most likely under the control of an activated renin-angiotensin system.[94] Hypercortisolism acutely shifts carbohydrate, fat, and protein metabolism so that energy is instantly and selectively available to vital organs, such as the brain, and anabolism is delayed. Intravascular fluid retention and the enhanced inotropic and vasopressor response to respectively catecholamines and angiotensin II offer hemodynamic advantages in the fight-and-flight reflex. In addition, hypercortisolism elicited by acute disease or trauma can be interpreted as an attempt of the organism to mute its own inflammatory cascade, thus protecting itself against overresponses.[95–97]

In chronic critical illness, serum adrenocorticotropic hormone was found to be low, whereas cortisol concentrations remained elevated, indicating that cortisol release may in this phase be driven through an alternative pathway, possibly involving endothelin.[98] Why adrenocorticotropic hormone levels are low in chronic critical illness is unclear; a role for atrial natriuretic peptide or substance P has been suggested.[98] In contrast to serum cortisol, circulating levels of adrenal androgens such as dehydroepiandrosterone sulfate, which has immunostimulatory properties on Th1-helper cells, are low during chronic critical illness.[99–101] Moreover, despite increased plasma renin activity, paradoxically decreased concentrations of aldosterone are found in protracted critical illness.[102] This constellation suggests a shift of pregnenolone metabolism away from both mineralocorticoid and adrenal androgen pathways toward the glucocorticoid pathway, orchestrated by an unknown peripheral drive. Ultimately, the latter mechanism may also fail, as indicated by a 20-fold higher incidence of adrenal insufficiency present in critically ill patients older than the age of 50 years and being treated in the intensive care unit for more than 14 days.[103] The fact that this type of relative adrenal failure coincides with adverse outcome suggests that high levels of glucocorticoids remain essential for hemodynamic stability. Whether hypercortisolism in the chronic phase of critical illness is exclusively beneficial remains uncertain. Sustained hypercortisolism in the presence of low levels of dehydroepiandrosterone sulfate and prolactin could theoretically evoke imbalance between immunosuppressive and immunostimulatory pathways and thus could be seen as participating in the increased susceptibility to infectious complications. Other conceivable, although unproven, drawbacks of prolonged hypercortisolism include impaired wound healing and myopathy, complications that are often observed during protracted critical illness.

### Treatment of Adrenal Failure during Critical Illness

In a patient with previously diagnosed primary or central adrenal insufficiency and in patients previously treated with systemic glucocorticoids, treatment should be continued and additional coverage for the stress of critical illness should be provided. Also, it goes without saying that a true addisonian crisis needs treatment in severe stress conditions: hydrocortisone 100 mg followed by 50 to 100 mg every 6 hours on the first day, 50 mg every 6 hours on the second day, and 25 mg every 6 hours on the third day, tapering to a maintenance dose by the fourth to fifth day. In prolonged critical conditions, the maintenance dose should be kept two to three times the basal need. Special attention should be given to patients with concomitant diabetes insipidus because the lack of cortisol may prevent polyuria because cortisol is needed for free-water clearance. Inversely, in these patients, glucocorticoid therapy may induce or aggravate diabetes insipidus. Another specific condition is the posthypophysectomy phase for Cushing's syndrome, characterized by a high vulnerability to an addisonian-like crisis. Drugs such as phenytoin, barbiturates, rifampicin, and thyroid hormone can accelerate glucocorticoid metabolism by induction of microsomal enzyme activity and can increase the glucocorticoid replacement dose requirements. If this increased requirement is not met, adrenal crisis may occur.

Recently, however, the concept of relative hyopthalamic-pituitary-adrenal insufficiency in patients with sepsis or septic shock was launched.[104–106] This concept advocates short-term treatment with stress doses of glucocorticoids as beneficial in patients with sepsis without a full blown adrenal failure.[107,108] The controversy about this concept of relative adrenal axis failure in acute stress conditions is in part explained by a problematic methodology for diagnosis. Indeed, accurate "normal" values for baseline cortisol levels in this type of stress as well as normal reference values for cortisol responses to a short adrenocorticotropic hormone test, not to mention the option to use a low- or high-dose adrenocorticotropic hormone test,[106,109] are still unavailable. Another controversial issue regarding the concept of relative adrenal failure in acute sepsis is the dose and the duration of treatment once it has been initiated. Indeed, treating patients with sepsis with glucocorticoids in too high a dose and for too long a time will conceivably aggravate the loss of lean tissue, increase the risk of polyneuropathy and myopathy, prolong the intensive care unit dependence, and increase the susceptibility to potentially lethal complications.

## INSULIN

### A High Serum Concentration of Insulin-like Growth Factor–Binding Protein 1 Predicts Adverse Outcome: A Link to Insulin?

In the acute phase of critical illness, a high serum cortisol and/or low $T_3$ level[37] appear to indicate poor prognosis. In the prolonged critically ill patient, however, these markers lack sensitivity. Recently, another endocrine parameter, a high serum concentration of IGFBP-1, was found to better predict outcome of chronic critical illness[3,6,110] (Fig. 138-7). IGFBP-1 is a small IGFBP produced almost exclusively by the liver (except in pregnancy). It is distinct among the members of the IGFBP family in that it is acutely regulated by metabolic stimuli.[111] Studies with cultured human liver explants suggest that the major regulatory influences on IGFBP-1 production are insulin, which is inhibitory, and hepatic substrate deprivation, which is stimulatory, acting through a cyclic adenosine monophosphate–dependent mechanism.[112,113] Moreover, an inverse correlation of IGFBP-1 with IGF-1 and the GH-dependent proteins ALS and IGFBP-3 during critical illness is consistent with its inverse regulation by GH, as previously suggested.[114–116] The higher IGFBP-1 levels observed in prolonged critically ill patients who did not survive coincided with lower insulin concentrations compared with survivors, for the same range of blood glucose level, a surprising finding considering that these patients are thought to be insulin resistant (see Fig. 138-7). Whether this indicates that insulin

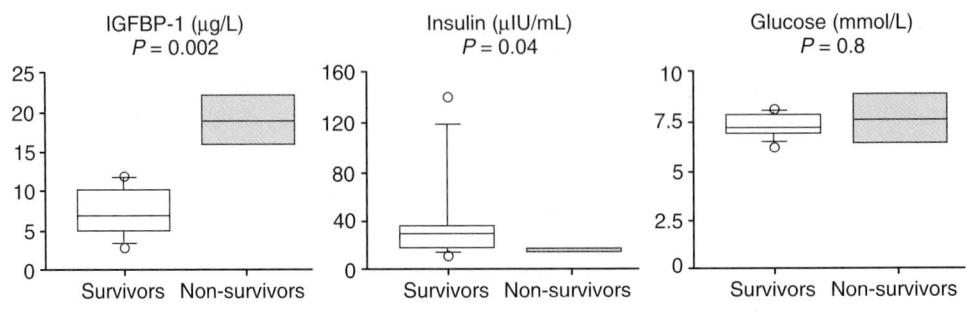

**Figure 138-7** Serum insulinlike growth factor binding protein 1 (IGFBP-1) concentration is higher in nonsurvivors compared with survivors in prolonged critical illness. Concomitantly, nonsurvivors revealed lower serum insulin levels for the same blood glucose level. *Box plots* represent medians, P25-P75 and P10-P90 and *circles* represent the absolute values for outliers. (From Van den Berghe G: Novel insights into the neuroendocrinology of critical illness. Eur J Endocrinol 143:1–13, 2000.)

secretion is also becoming impaired in prolonged critically ill patients remains unclear. It is clear, however, that in unfavorable metabolic conditions, the hepatocyte alters its production of IGF regulatory proteins, for which the trigger might be reduced hepatocyte substrate availability (theoretically caused by either hepatic hypoperfusion or hypoxia, hypoglycemia, relative insulin deficiency, or hepatic insulin resistance) leading to increased cyclic adenosine monophosphate production, which would both suppress IGF-1 and ALS[117] and stimulate IGFBP-1.[113] It is unclear to what extent loss of GH pulsatility may contribute to this switch, but recent data[6] suggest that activation of hepatic IGF-1 and ALS expression may require pulsatile GH, and animal studies similarly suggest that suppression of hepatic IGFBP-1 expression by insulin requires acute, rather than prolonged or nonpulsatile, GH action.[118]

Why prolonged critically ill patients fail to recover and eventually die despite optimal intensive care remains incompletely understood. An exploration of the link between high serum IGFBP-1 levels, relatively low circulating insulin levels, and adverse outcome of prolonged critical illness suggested that particular effects of insulin, specifically in the liver, may be crucial for recovery and survival. This novel concept generated the hypothesis that treatment with insulin may offer therapeutic potential to improve the outcome of critical illness.

### Intensive Insulin Therapy Reduces Morbidity and Mortality of Critical Illness

Hyperglycemia is a well-known accompaniment of trauma, burns, and critical illness resulting from the combined action of counterregulatory hormones, cytokines, and nervous signals on glucose metabolic pathways. Insulin resistance develops during critical illness, manifested by increased serum insulin levels, impaired peripheral glucose uptake, and elevated hepatic glucose production. Recently, we demonstrated that strict maintenance of normoglycemia (less than 110 mg/dL) with intensive insulin therapy markedly reduces mortality of intensive care patients, particularly of those with prolonged critical illness (mortality reduced by half)[119] (Fig. 138-8). Furthermore, intensive insulin therapy was protective against acute renal failure, with a 42% reduction in dialytic therapy for loss of renal function, and prevented the occurrence of critical illness polyneuropathy. Controlling hyperglycemia with insulin has also been shown to restore the impaired immunity during critical illness by preventing the disturbed phagocytosis capacity of monocytes.[120]

Furthermore, hyperglycemia in the critically ill is also associated with a deranged serum lipid profile, which can be partially normalized by intensive insulin therapy, totally eliminating hypertriglyceridemia and substantially increasing the low serum levels of high- and low-density lipoproteins.[121] In addition, intensive insulin therapy exerted an anti-inflammatory effect[122] in critically ill patients. From these findings, it is now clear that blood glucose levels should be tightly controlled at less than 110 mg/dL by continuous insulin infusion, in critically ill patients with and without diabetes.

### WHAT ARE THE IMPLICATIONS FOR CLINICAL PRACTICE?

The difference between the acute and chronic endocrine stress response may not be trivial in relation to the outcome of critical illness. It was the (inappropriate) assumption that acute stress responses, such as GH resistance, persist throughout the course of critical illness, which (inappropriately) justified administration of high doses of GH to long-stay intensive care patients to induce anabolism.[30] The concomitant endocrine changes in chronic critical illness may have predisposed to severe side effects of high doses of GH. In view of the significant benefits of strict glycemic,[119] GH-induced insulin resistance and hyperglycemia may have played a role.

Although it has been shown that anabolism can be reinitiated when GH secretagogues, TRH, and gonadotropin-releasing hormone are coinfused in critically ill patients, the effect on survival remains unknown. Hence, because of the lack of appropriately designed and powered clinical trials, these and other endocrine interventions in the critically ill should at this time still be considered experimental. One notable exception is maintenance of normoglycemia with intensive insulin therapy, a strategy that has shown to substantially improve outcome of intensive care patients.

### Acknowledgments

The work summarized in this chapter has been supported by research grants from the Belgian Fund for Scientific Research (G.0144.00 and G.0278.03), the Research Council of the University of Leuven (OT/99/33 and OT/03/56), and the Belgian Foundation for Research in Congenital Heart Diseases. Dr. Van den Berghe is a Fundamental Clinical Researcher for the Fund for Scientific Research Flanders, Belgium (G.3C05.95N) and recipient of the K.U. Leuven/Novo Nordisk Chair for Research on Insulin in Critical Illness.

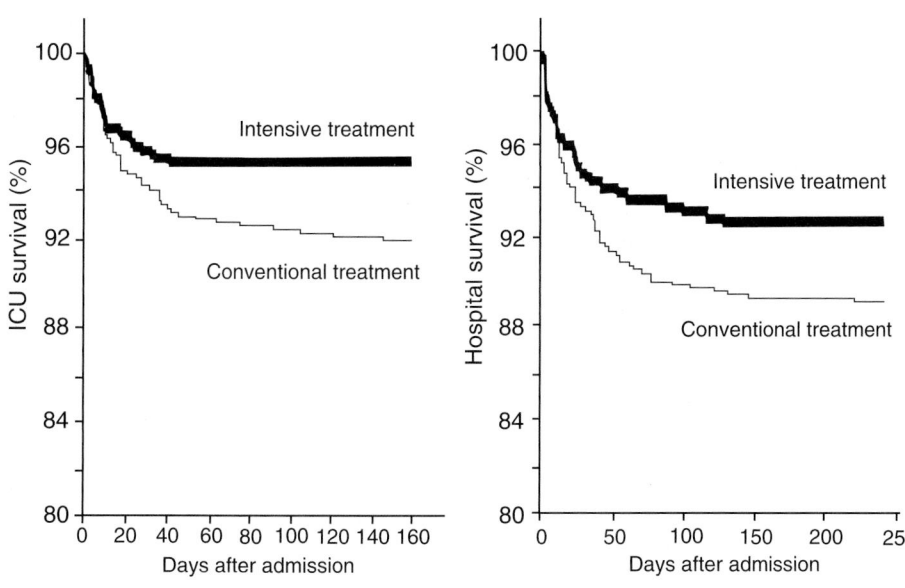

**Figure 138-8**  Kaplan-Meier cumulative survival plots for intensive care and in-hospital survival shows the effect of intensive insulin treatment in a study of 1548 critically ill patients. Patients discharged alive from intensive care (**left**) and hospital (**right**), respectively, were considered survivors. $P$ values were obtained by log-rank (Mantel-Cox) significance testing. The difference between the intensive care insulin group and the conventional group was significant for intensive care survival (unadjusted $P = 0.005$; adjusted $P < 0.04$) and for hospital survival (unadjusted $P = 0.01$). (From Van den Berghe G, Wouters P, Weekers F, et al: Intensive insulin therapy in critically ill patients. N Engl J Med 345:1357–1367, 2001.)

## REFERENCES

1. Streat SJ, Beddoe AH, Hill GL: Aggressive nutritional support does not prevent protein loss despite fat gain in septic intensive care patients. J Trauma 27:262–266, 1987.
2. Carroll P: Protein metabolism and the use of growth hormone and insulin-like growth factor-I in the critically ill patient. Growth Horm IGF Res 9:400–413, 1999.
3. Van den Berghe G, Baxter RC, Weekers F, et al: A paradoxical gender dissociation within the growth hormone/insulin-like growth factor I axis during protracted critical illness. J Clin Endocrinol Metab 85:183–192, 2000.
4. Knaus WA, Draper EA, Wagner DP, et al: APACHE II: A severity of disease classification system. Crit Care Med 13:818–829, 1985.
5. Van den Berghe G, de Zegher F, Bouillon R: Acute and prolonged critical illness as different neuroendocrine paradigms. J Clin Endocrinol Metab 83:1827–1834, 1998.
6. Van den Berghe G, Wouters P, Weekers F, et al: Reactivation of pituitary hormone release and metabolic improvement by infusion of growth hormone releasing peptide and thyrotropin-releasing hormone in patients with protracted critical illness. J Clin Endocrinol Metab 84:1311–1323, 1999.
7. Thorner MO, Vance ML, Laws ER, et al: The anterior pituitary. In Wilson JD, Foster DW, Kronenberg HM, Larsen PR (eds): Williams Textbook of Endocrinology, 9th ed. Philadelphia, WB Saunders, 1998, pp 249–340.
8. Bowers CY, Momany FA, Reynolds GA, et al: On the in vitro and in vivo activity of a new synthetic hexapeptide that acts on the pituitary to specifically release growth hormone. Endocrinology 114:1537–1545, 1984.
9. Howard AD, Feighner SD, Cully DF, et al: A receptor in pituitary and hypothalamus that functions in growth hormone release. Science 273:974–977, 1996.
10. Kojima M, Hosoda H, Date Y, et al: Ghrelin is a growth-hormone-releasing acylated peptide from stomach. Nature 402:656–660, 1999.
11. Gevers EF, Wit JM, Robinson IC: Growth, growth hormone (GH) binding protein, and GH receptors are differentially regulated by peak and trough components of GH secretory pattern in the rat. Endocrinology 137:1013–1018, 1996.
12. Giustina A, Veldhuis JD: Pathophysiology of the neuroregulation of growth hormone secretion in experimental animals and the human. Endocr Rev 19:717–797, 1998.
13. Hindmarsh PC, Dennison E, Pincus SM, et al: A sexually dimorphic pattern of growth hormone secretion in the elderly illness. J Clin Endocrinol Metab 84:2679–2685, 1999.

14. Ross R, Miell J, Freeman E, et al: Critically ill patients have high basal growth hormone levels with attenuated oscillatory activity associated with low levels of insulin-like growth factor-1. Clin Endocrinol 35:47–54, 1991.
15. Voerman HJ, Strack van Schijndel RJM, de Boer H, et al: Growth hormone: Secretion and administration in catabolic adult patients, with emphasis on the critically ill patient. Neth J Med 41:229–244, 1992.
16. Hartman ML, Veldhuis JD, Johnson ML, et al: Augmented growth hormone secretory burst frequency and amplitude mediate enhanced GH secretion during a two day fast in normal men. J Clin Endocrinol Metab 74:757–765, 1992.
17. Hermansson M, Wickelgren RB, Hammerqvist F, et al: Measurement of human growth hormone receptor messenger ribonucleic acid by a quantitative polymerase chain reaction-based assay: Demonstration of reduced expression after elective surgery. J Clin Endocrinol Metab 82:421–428, 1997.
18. Baxter RC, Hawker FH, To C, et al: Thirty day monitoring of insulin-like growth factors and their binding proteins in intensive care unit patients. Growth Horm IGF Res 8:455–463, 1998.
19. Rodriguez-Arnao J, Yarwood Y, Ferguson C, et al: Reduction in circulating IGF-I and hepatic IGF-I mRNA levels after cecal ligation and puncture are associated with differential regulation of hepatic IGF-binding protein-1, -2 and -3 mRNA levels. J Endocrinol 151:287–292, 1996.
20. Bentham J, Rodriguez-Arnao-J, Ross RJ: Acquired growth hormone resistance in patients with hypercatabolism. Horm Res 40:87–91, 1993.
21. Timmins AC, Cotterill AM, Cwyfan Hughes SC, et al: Critical illness is associated with low circulating concentrations of insulin-like growth factors-I and -II, alterations in insulin-like growth factor binding proteins, and induction of an insulin-like growth factor binding protein-3 protease. Crit Care Med 24:1460–1466, 1996.
22. Gibson FA, Hinds CJ: Growth Hormone and insulin-like growth factors in critical illness. Intensive Care Med 23:369–378, 1997.
23. Van den Berghe G, Baxter RC, Weekers F, et al: The combined administration of GH-releasing peptide-2 (GHRP-2), TRH and GnRH to men with prolonged critical illness evokes superior endocrine and metabolic effects than treatment with GHRP-2 alone. Clin Endocrinol 56:655–669, 2002.
24. Van den Berghe G, de Zegher F, Veldhuis JD, et al: The somatotropic axis in critical illness: Effect of continuous GHRH and GHRP-2 infusion. J Clin Endocrinol Metab 82:590–599, 1997.

25. Van den Berghe G, de Zegher F, Baxter RC, et al: Neuroendocrinology of prolonged critical illness: Effect of continuous thyrotropin-releasing hormone infusion and its combination with growth hormone-secretagogues. J Clin Endocrinol Metab 83:309–319, 1998.
26. Van den Berghe G, de Zegher F, Lauwers P, et al: Growth hormone secretion in critical illness: Effect of dopamine. J Clin Endocrinol Metab 79:1141–1146, 1994.
27. Van den Berghe G, de Zegher F: Anterior pituitary function during critical illness and dopamine treatment. Crit Care Med 24:1580–1590, 1996.
28. Micic D, Popovic V, Doknic M, et al: Preserved growth hormone (GH) secretion in aged and very old subjects after testing with the combined stimulus GH-releasing hormone plus GH-releasing hexapeptide-6. J Clin Endocrinol Metab 83:2569–2572, 1998.
29. Van den Berghe G, de Zegher F, Bowers CY, et al: Pituitary responsiveness to growth hormone (GH) releasing hormone, GH-releasing peptide-2 and thyrotropin releasing hormone in critical illness. Clin Endocrinol 45:341–351, 1996.
30. Takala J, Ruokonen E, Webster NR, et al: Increased mortality associated with growth hormone treatment in critically ill adults. N Engl J Med 341:785–792, 1999.
31. Van den Berghe G: Whither growth hormone in the catabolic state of critical illness? Growth Horm IGF Res 9:397–399, 1999.
32. Christiansen JS, Bengtsson BA, Thorner MO, et al: Critical Evaluation of the safety of recombinant human growth hormone administration: Statement from the growth hormone research society. J Clin Endocrinol Metab 86:1868–1870, 2001.
33. Michalaki M, Vagenakis A, Makri M, et al: Dissociation of the early decline in serum T3 concentration and serum IL-6 rise and TNF alfa in non-thyroidal illness syndrome induced by abdominal surgery. J Clin Endocrinol Metab 86:4198–4205, 2001.
34. Chopra IJ, Huang TS, Beredo A, et al: Evidence for an inhibitor of extrathyroidal conversion of thyroxine to 3,5,3'-triiodothyronine in sera of patients with non-thyroidal illness. J Clin Endocrinol Metab 60:666–672, 1985.
35. Romijn JA, Wiersinga WM: Decreased nocturnal surge of thyrotropin in nonthyroidal illness. J Clin Endocrinol Metab 70:35–42, 1990.
36. Bartalena L, Martino E, Brandi LS, et al: Lack of nocturnal serum thyrotropin surge after surgery. J Clin Endocrinol Metab 70:293–296, 1990.
37. Schlienger JL, Sapin R, Capgras T, et al: Evaluation of thyroid function after myocardial infarction. Ann Endocrinol (Paris) 52:283–288, 1991.

38. Rothwell PM, Lawler PG: Prediction of outcome in intensive care patients using endocrine parameters. Crit Care Med 23:78–83, 1995.

39. van der Poll T, van Zee K, Endert E, et al: Interleukin-1 receptor blockade does not affect endotoxin-induced changes in plasma thyroid hormone and thyrotropin concentration in man. J Clin Endocrinol Metab 80:1341–1346, 1995.

40. Lim CF, Doctor R, Visser TJ, et al: Inhibition of thyroxine transport into cultured rat hepatocytes by serum of non-uremic critically ill patients: Effects of bilirubin and non-esterified fatty acids. J Clin Endocrinol Metab 76:1165–1172, 1993.

41. Gardner DF, Kaplan MM, Stanley CA, et al: Effect of triiodothyronine replacement on the metabolic and pituitary responses to starvation. N Engl J Med 300:579–584, 1979.

42. De Groot LJ: Dangerous dogmas in medicine: the non-thyroidal illness syndrome. J Clin Endocrinol Metab 84:151–164, 1999.

43. Kemperer JD, Klein I, Gomez M, et al: Thyroid hormone treatment after coronary bypass surgery. N Engl J Med 333:1522–1527, 1995.

44. Mullis-Jansson SL, Argenziano M, Corwin S, et al: A randomized double blind study on the effect of triiodothyronine on cardiac function and morbidity after coronary bypass surgery. J Thorac Cardiovasc Surg 117:1128–1134, 1999.

45. Van den Berghe G, de Zegher F, Veldhuis JD, et al: Thyrotropin and prolactin release in prolonged critical illness: Dynamics of spontaneous secretion and effects of growth hormone secretagogues. Clin Endocrinol 47:599–612, 1997.

46. Fliers E, Guldenaar SEF, Wiersinga WM, et al: Decreased hypothalamic thyrotropin-releasing hormone gene expression in patients with non-thyroidal illness. J Clin Endocrinol Metab 82:4032–4036, 1997.

47. Bacci V, Schussler GC, Kaplan TC: The relationship between serum triiodothyronine and thyrotropin during systemic illness. J Clin Endocrinol Metab 54:1229–1235, 1982.

48. Damas P, Reuter A, Gysen P, et al: Tumor necrosis factor and interleukin-1 serum levels during severe sepsis in humans. Crit Care Med 17:975–978, 1989.

49. Faglia G, Ferrari C, Beck-Peccoz P, et al: Reduced plasma thyrotropin response to thyrotropin releasing hormone after dexamethasone administration in normal humans. Horm Metab Res 5:289–291, 1973.

50. Van den Berghe G, de Zegher F, Vlasselaers D, et al: Thyrotropin Releasing Hormone in critical illness: From a dopamine-dependent test to a strategy for increasing low serum triiodothyronine, prolactin and growth hormone concentrations. Crit Care Med 24:590–595, 1996.

51. Peeters R, Wouters P, Kaptein E, et al: Reduced activation and increased inactivation of thyroid hormone in tissues of critically ill patients. J Clin Endocrinol Metab 88:3202–3211, 2003.

52. Weekers F, Michalaki M, Coopmans W, et al: Endocrine and metabolic effects of growth hormone (GH) compared with GH-releasing peptide, thyrotropin releasing hormone and insulin infusion in a rabbit model of prolonged critical illness. Endocrinology 145:205–213, 2004.

53. Timmer DC, Peeters RP, Wouters PJ, et al: Thyroid hormone receptor alpha splice variants in livers of critically ill patients (submitted).

54. Van den Berghe G, Wouters P, Bowers CY, et al: Growth hormone releasing peptide-2 infusion synchronizes growth hormone, thyrotropin and prolactin secretion in prolonged critical illness. Eur J Endocrinol 140:17–22, 1999.

55. Arem R, Wiener GJ, Kaplan SG, et al: Reduced tissue thyroid hormone levels in fatal illness. Metabolism 42:1102–1108, 1993.

56. Vaughan GM, Mason AD, McManus WF, et al: Alterations of mental status and thyroid hormones after thermal injury. J Clin Endocrinol Metab 60:1221–1225, 1985.

57. Brent GA, Hershman JM: Thyroxine therapy in patients with severe non-thyroidal illnesses and low serum thyroxine concentrations. J Clin Endocrinol Metab 63:1–7, 1986.

58. Becker RA, Vaughan GM, Ziegler MG, et al: Hypermetabolic low triiodothyronine syndrome in burn injury. Crit Care Med 10:870–875, 1982.

59. Bettendorf M, Schmidt KG, Grulich-Henn J, et al: Triiodothyronine treatment in children after cardiac surgery: A double-blind, randomized, placebo-controlled study. Lancet 356:529–534, 2000.

60. Nicoloff JT: Thyroid storm and myxedema coma. Med Clin North Am 69:1005–1017, 1985.

61. Ringel MD: Management of hypothyroidism and hyperthyroidism in the intensive care unit. Crit Care Clin 17:59–74, 2001.

62. Kaptein EM, Quion-Verde H, Swinney RS, et al: Acute hemodynamic effects of levothyroxine loading in critically ill hypothyroid patients. Arch Intern Med 146:662–666, 1986.

63. Escobar-Morreale HF, Obregon MJ, Escobar del Rey F, et al: Replacement therapy for hypothyroidism with thyroxine alone does not ensure euthyroidism in all tissues, as studied in thyroidectomized rats. J Clin Invest 96:2828–2838, 1995.

64. Bunevicius R, Kazanavicius G, Zalinkevicius R, et al: Effects of thyroxine plus triiodothyronine in patients with hypothyroidism. N Engl J Med 340:424–429, 1999.

65. Wiersinga WM: Thyroid hormone replacement therapy. Horm Res 56:74–81, 2001.

66. Russell DH: New aspects of prolactin and immunity: A lymphocyte-derived prolactin-like product and nuclear protein kinase C activation. Trends Pharmacol Sci 10:40–44, 1989.

67. Bernton EW, Meltzer MS, Holaday JW: Suppression of macrophage activation and T-lymphocyte function in hypoprolactinemic mice. Science 239:401–404, 1988.

68. Russell DH, Larson DF, Cardon SB, et al: Cyclosporin inhibits prolactin induction of ornithine decarboxilase in rat tissue. Mol Cell Endocrinol 35:159–166, 1984.

69. Russell DH, Kibler R, Matrisian L, et al: Prolactin receptors on human T- and B-lymphocytes: Antagonism of prolactin-binding by cyclosporin. J Immunol 134:3027–3031, 1985.

70. Carrier M, Wild J, Pelletier C, et al: Bromocriptine as an adjuvant to cyclosporine immunosuppression after heart transplantation. Ann Thorac Surg 49:129–132, 1990.

71. Noel GL, Suh HK, Stone SJG, et al: Human prolactin and growth hormone release during surgery and other conditions of stress. J Clin Endocrinol Metab 35:840–851, 1972.

72. Van den Berghe G, de Zegher F, Lauwers P: Dopamine and the euthyroid sick syndrome in critical illness. Clin Endocrinol 41:731–737, 1994.

73. Meakins JL, Pietsch JB, Bubenick O, et al: Delayed hypersensitivity: Indicator of acquired failure of host defenses in sepsis and trauma. Ann Surg 188:241–250, 1977.

74. Devins SS, Miller A, Herndon BL, et al: Effects of dopamine on T-lymphocyte proliferative responses and serum prolactin concentrations in critically ill patients. Crit Care Med 263:9682–9685, 1992.

75. Belchetz PE, Plant TM, Nakai Y, et al: Hypophyseal responses to continuous and intermittent delivery of hypothalamic gonadotropin-releasing hormone. Science 202:631–633, 1978.

76. Santoro N, Filicori M, Crowley WF Jr: Hypogonadotropic disorders in men and women: Diagnosis and therapy with pulsatile gonadotropin releasing hormone. Endocr Rev 7:11–23, 1986.

77. Klibanski A, Beitens IZ, Badger TM, et al: Reproductive function during fasting in man. J Clin Endocrinol Metab 53:258–266, 1981.

78. Veldhuis JD, Iranmanesh A, Evans WS, et al: Amplitude suppression of the pulsatile mode of immunoradiometric LH release in fasting-induced hypoandrogenemia in normal men. J Clin Endocrinol Metab 76:587–593, 1993.

79. Wang C, Chan V, Yeung RTT: Effect of surgical stress on pituitary-testicular function. Clin Endocrinol 9:255–266, 1978.

80. Wang C, Chan V, Tse TF, et al: Effect of acute myocardial infarction on pituitary testicular function. Clin Endocrinol 9:249–253, 1978.

81. Vogel AV, Peake GT, Rada RT: Pituitary-testicular axis dysfunction in

burned men. J Clin Endocrinol Metab 60:658–665, 1985.

82. Lephart ED, Baxter CR, Parker CR Jr: Effect of burn trauma on adrenal and testicular steroid hormone production. J Clin Endocrinol Metab 64:842–848, 1987.

83. Kreutz LD, Rose RM, Jennings JR: Suppression of plasma testosterone levels and psychological stress: A longitudinal study of young men in officer candidate school. Arch Gen Psychiatry 26:479–482, 1972.

84. Aakvaag A, Bentdal O, Quigstad K, et al: Testosterone and testosterone binding globulin in young men during prolonged stress. Int J Androl 1:22–31, 1978.

85. Van den Berghe G, de Zegher F, Lauwers P, et al: Luteinizing hormone secretion and hypoandrogenemia in critically ill men: Effect of dopamine. Clin Endocrinol 41:563–569, 1994.

86. Dong Q, Hawker F, McWilliam D, et al: Circulating immunoreactive inhibin and testosterone levels in patients with critical illness. Clin Endocrinol 36:399–404, 1992.

87. Rivier C, Vale W: In the rat, interleukin 1-a acts at the level of the brain and the gonads to interfere with gonadotropin and sex steroid secretion. Endocrinology 124:2105–2109, 1989.

88. Guo H, Calkins JH, Sigel MM, et al: Interleukin-2 is a potent inhibitor of Leydig cell steroidogenesis. Endocrinology 127:1234–1239, 1990.

89. Woolf PD, Hamill RW, McDonald JV, et al: Transient hypogonadotropic hypogonadism caused by critical illness. J Clin Endocrinol Metab 60:444–450, 1985.

90. Spratt DI, Cox P, Orav J, et al: Reproductive axis suppression in acute illness is related to disease severity. J Clin Endocrinol Metab 76:1548–1554, 1993.

91. Cicero TJ, Bell RD, Wiest WG, et al: Function of the male sex organs in heroin and methadone users. N Engl J Med 292:882–887, 1975.

92. Tweedle D, Walton C, Johnston IDA: The effect of an anabolic steroid on postoperative nitrogen balance. Br J Clin Pract 27:130–132, 1972.

93. Van den Berghe G, Weekers F, Baxter RC, et al: Five days pulsatile GnRH administration unveils combined hypothalamic-pituitary-gonadal defects underlying profound hypoandrogenism in men with prolonged critical illness. J Clin Endocrinol Metab 86:3217–3226, 2001.

94. O'Leary E, Hubbard K, Tormey W, et al: Laparoscopic cholecystectomy: Hemodynamic and neuroendocrine responses after pneumoperitoneum and changes in position. Br J Anaesth 76:640–644, 1996.

95. Munck A, Guyre P, Holbrook N: Physiological functions of glucocorticoids during stress and their relation to pharmacological actions. Endocr Rev 5:25–44, 1984.

96. Starling EH: The Wisdom of the Body. The Harveian Oration Delivered to the Royal College of Physicians, London, 1923. London, H. K. Lewis, 1923.

97. Cannon WB: The Wisdom of the Body. New York, Norton, 1932.

98. Vermes I, Bieshuizen A, Hampsink RM, et al: Dissociation of plasma adrenocorticotropin and cortisol levels in critically ill patients: Possible role of endothelin and atrial natriuretic hormone. J Clin Endocrinol Metab 80:1238–1242, 1995.

99. Suzuki T, Suzuki N, Daynes RA, et al: Dehydroepiandrosterone enhances IL2 production and cytotoxic effector function of human T-cells. Clin Immunol Immunopathol 61:202–211, 1991.

100. Parker LN, Levin ER, Lifrak E: Evidence for adrenocortical adaptation to severe illness. J Clin Endocrinol Metab 60:947–952, 1985.

101. Van den Berghe G, de Zegher F, Schetz M, et al: Dehydroepiandrosterone sulphate in critical illness: Effect of dopamine. Clin Endocrinol 43:457–463, 1995.

102. Zipser RD, Davenport MW, Martin KL, et al: Hyperreninemic hypoaldosteronism in the critically ill: A new entity. J Clin Endocrinol Metab 53:867–873, 1981.

103. Barquist E, Kirton O: Adrenal insufficiency in the surgical intensive care unit patient. J Trauma 42:27–31, 1997.

104. Beishuizen A, Vermes I, Hylkema BS, et al: Relative eosinophilia and functional adrenal insufficiency in critically ill patients [letter]. Lancet 353:1675–1676, 1999.

105. Annane D, Sebille V, Troche G, et al: A 3-level prognostic classification in septic shock based on cortisol levels and cortisol response to corticotropin. JAMA 283:1038–1045, 2000.

106. Richards ML, Caplan RH, Wickus GG, et al: The rapid low-dose (1 microgram) cosyntropin test in the immediate postoperative period: Results in elderly subjects after major abdominal surgery. Surgery 125:431–440, 1999.

107. Bollaert PE, Charpentier C, Levy B, et al: Reversal of late septic shock with supraphysiological doses of hydrocortisone. Crit Care Med 26:645–650, 1998

108. Briegel J, Forst H, Haller M, et al: Stress doses of hydrocortisone reverse hyperdynamic septic shock: A prospective, randomized, double-blind, single-center study. Crit Care Med 27:723–733, 1999.

109. Streeten DHP: What test for hypothalamic-pituitary adrenocortical insufficiency? Lancet 354:179–180, 1999.

110. Van den Berghe G: Novel insights into the neuroendocrinology of critical illness. Eur J Endocrinol 143:1–13, 2000.

111. Yeoh SI, Baxter RC: Metabolic regulation of the growth hormone independent insulin-like growth factor binding protein in human plasma. Acta Endocrinol 119:465–473, 1988.

112. Lewitt MS, Baxter RC: Regulation of growth hormone-independent insulin-like growth factor-binding protein (BP-28) in cultured human fetal liver explants. J Clin Endocrinol Metab 69:246–252, 1989.

113. Lewitt MS, Baxter RC: Inhibitors of glucose uptake stimulate the production of insulin-like growth factor binding protein (IGFBP-1) by human fetal liver. Endocrinology 126:1527–1533, 1990.

114. Baxter RC: Circulating binding proteins for the insulin-like growth factors. Trends Endocrinol Metab 4:91–96, 1993.

115. Norrelund H, Fisker S, Vahl N, et al: Evidence supporting a direct suppressive effect of growth hormone on serum IGFBP-1 levels, experimental studies in normal, obese and GH-deficient adults. Growth Horm IGF Res 9:52–60, 1999.

116. Olivecrona H, Hilding A, Ekström C, et al: Acute and short-term effects of growth hormone on insulin-like growth factors and their binding proteins: Serum levels and hepatic messenger ribonucleic acid responses in humans. J Clin Endocrinol Metab 84:553–560, 1999.

117. Delhanty PJD, Baxter RC: The regulation of acid-labile subunit gene expression and secretion by cyclic adenosine 3′,5′-monophosphate. Endocrinology 139:260–265, 1998.

118. Hu M, Robertson DG, Murphy LJ: Growth hormone modulates insulin regulation of hepatic insulin-like growth factor binding protein-1 transcription. Endocrinology 137:3702–3709, 1996.

119. Van den Berghe G, Wouters P, Weekers F, et al: Intensive insulin therapy in critically ill patients. N Engl J Med 345:1357–1367, 2001.

120. Weekers F, Giuletti A-P, Michalaki M, et al: Metabolic, endocrine and immune effects of stress hyperglycemia in a rabbit model of prolonged critical illness. Endocrinology 144:5329–5338, 2003.

121. Mesotten D, Swinnen J, Vanderhoydonc F, et al: Contribution of circulating lipids to the improved outcome of critical illness by glycemic control with intensive insulin therapy. J Clin Endocrinol Metab 89:219–226, 2004.

122. Hansen TK, Thiel S, Wouters PJ, et al: Intensive insulin therapy exerts anti-inflammatory effects in critically ill patients, as indicated by circulating mannan-binding lectin and C-reactive protein levels. J Clin Endocrinol Metab 88:1082–1088, 2003.

# PART 14

# REPRODUCTIVE ENDOCRINOLOGY AND SEXUAL FUNCTION

# Gonadotropin-Releasing Hormone and Gonadotropins

## *Wendy Kuohung and Ursula B. Kaiser*

## INTRODUCTION

Gonadotropin-releasing hormone (GnRH) is a decapeptide central to the initiation of the reproductive hormone cascade. Formed in hypothalamic neurons from a precursor polypeptide by enzyme processing, GnRH is released in a pulsatile manner into the hypothalamic-hypophyseal portal circulation for delivery to the anterior pituitary, where it stimulates gonadotropin biosynthesis and secretion.[1,2] This physiologic pulsatile pattern has been employed in clinical therapies. Low-dose GnRH administered in a pulsatile fashion restores fertility in hypogonadal patients and effectively treats delayed puberty.[3-5] In contrast, large doses of GnRH or GnRH agonists desensitize the gonadotroph and inhibit gonadal function, facilitating their application in a wide range of gonadotropin-dependent disorders.[5,6]

The gonadotropins human luteinizing hormone (LH) or lutropin, human chorionic gonadotropin (hCG), and human follicle-stimulating hormone (FSH) or follitropin play a well-established role in reproduction. The gonadotropins regulate sex steroid synthesis and the final steps in gametogenesis. FSH is required for follicular development and for the selection of dominant follicles fated to ovulate. In males, FSH has an important role in spermatogenesis. The major functions of LH are the induction of ovulation, luteinization of fully developed follicles, and stimulation of steroidogenesis in the theca cells of the follicle and the Leydig cells of the testis.

This chapter describes the structure, synthesis, and secretion of GnRH and gonadotropins; their tissue distribution and putative functions; their interaction with their cognate receptors; and the intracellular (IC) mechanisms mediating GnRH actions on the gonadotrope. The physiologic changes in GnRH release occurring in different clinical states are also reviewed. Regulation of gonadotropin synthesis and secretion is discussed elsewhere in this textbook (see Chapter 142).

## PHYSIOLOGY OF GONADOTROPIN-RELEASING HORMONE

### DEVELOPMENT OF THE GONADOTROPIN-RELEASING HORMONE NEURONAL SYSTEM

GnRH-producing neurons are located primarily in the arcuate nucleus of the medial basal hypothalamus and the preoptic area of the anterior hypothalamus in humans. Unlike other hypothalamic neurons, GnRH neurons are spread throughout these areas and do not form a discrete nucleus. Early in development, neurons displaying GnRH immunoreactivity are found in the epithelia of the olfactory pit. In mice, GnRH progenitor cells are found in the septopreoptic-hypothalamic area with a concomitant decrease in the number of GnRH cells in the olfactory pit and nasal septum as gestation advances.[7] Using immunocytochemistry and in situ hybridization, a similar migratory pattern of GnRH neurons from the nasal region to the basal hypothalamus was discovered in fetal rhesus monkeys.[8] This migratory route of GnRH neurons supports the notion of an olfactory pit origin. However, more recent dye-labeling studies in the zebrafish have suggested that the hypothalamic GnRH cell population arises from the adenohypophyseal region of the anterior neural plate while neuromodulatory GnRH cells of the terminal nerve arise from the cranial neural crest.[9] These findings may signify the earliest origins of GnRH neurons before their development of GnRH immunoreactivity.

An olfactory developmental pathway for GnRH neurons explains the anosmia associated with hypogonadotropic hypogonadism in patients with Kallmann's syndrome. This hypothesis was confirmed in a 19-week-old fetus with a complete deletion of the X-linked Kallmann locus; autopsy studies revealed that GnRH neurons had failed to migrate into the brain.[10] In the most common X-linked form of Kallmann's syndrome, GnRH neuronal migration is impaired due to a mutation in an extracellular (EC) matrix protein encoded by the KAL1 gene, anosmin-1, which mediates neural cell adhesion.[11-14] Recently, loss-of-function mutations in the *FGFR1* gene have been found to cause autosomal-dominant Kallmann's syndrome.[15] Evidence suggests that anosmin-1 is involved in fibroblast growth factor signaling through fibroblast growth factor receptor 1 as anosmin-1 binds to heparan sulfate proteoglycan,[16] and heparan sulfate proteoglycans are important in the formation of the fibroblast growth factor–fibroblast growth factor receptor complex.[17]

## STRUCTURE OF GONADOTROPIN-RELEASING HORMONE AND ANALOGUES

Comparison of the amino acid sequences of GnRH from protochordate and vertebrate species reveals a remarkable conservation in peptide length (10 amino acids) and in the N terminus (pGlu-His-Trp-Ser) and C terminus (Pro-Gly NH2) (Fig. 139-1). The preservation of these features over 500 million years of evolution supports their crucial role in receptor binding and activation. Structure and activity data from thousands of analogues developed empirically support the functional importance of these characteristics. Position 8 is the most variable amino acid (Arg, Gln, Ser, Asn, Leu, Tyr, Lys, Ala, Trp). Although the mammalian pituitary GnRH receptor requires arginine in position 8 for binding,[18,19] studies of cloned nonmammalian receptors reveal different specificities for the amino acid in position 8.[20-23] These findings suggest an important role for this residue in the selectivity of the nonmammalian receptors for the ligand. The mammalian pituitary GnRH receptor has more rigorous ligand conformation requirements than the nonmammalian receptor.[18,21,22,24] Studies have shown that the conserved N- and C-terminal domains of GnRH are closely apposed when mammalian GnRH binds its receptor. This folded conformation results from a βII-type turn involving residues 5 to 8 (Fig. 139-2).[18,19] Substitution of Arg8 (e.g., Gln8) results in a more extended structure and loss of binding affinity.[20,25,26]

Native GnRH is cleaved by peptidases in the hypothalamus and pituitary gland at the Gly6-Leu7 bond and at position 10.[19] This degradation accounts for the short half-life of GnRH of 2 to 4 minutes.[27] Substitution of a D-amino acid for Gly6 enhances the βII-type folded configuration, increasing the activity of GnRH approximately 10-fold and overcoming the deleterious effects of Arg8 substitution.[22,28] This substitution at position 6 accounts for increased metabolic stability, while replacement of the C-terminal glycinamide residue by an ethylamide group increases receptor-binding affinity 10-fold.[19] Agonists such as leuprolide, buserelin, and nafarelin are 200 times more effective in stimulating gonadotropin release than is native GnRH (Table 139-1).

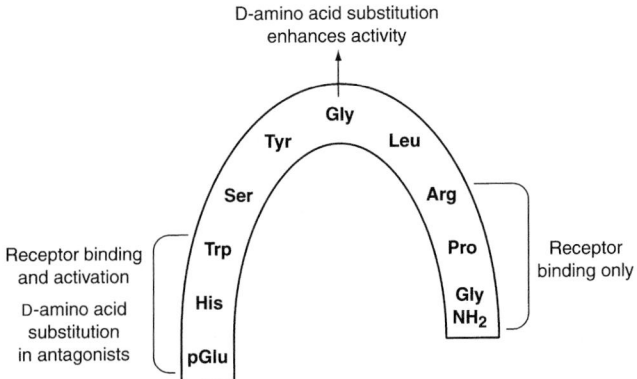

**Figure 139-2** Schematic representation of gonadotropin-releasing hormone (GnRH) in the folded conformation in which it is bound to the GnRH receptor. The molecule is bent at glycine at position 6, where substitution with D-amino acids (as in GnRH agonist and antagonist analogues) stabilizes the folded configuration, increases binding affinity, and decreases metabolic clearance. The N and C termini are involved in receptor binding. The N terminus is involved in receptor activation, and substitutions in this region produce antagonists.

Alteration of the conserved N-terminal residues in GnRH yields analogues with antagonistic properties.[18,19] This modification together with the substitution of Gly6 with a D-amino acid forms the basis of all antagonists (see Table 139-1). Unlike agonists, GnRH antagonists have the advantage of triggering an immediate decrease in circulating gonadotropin levels with rapid reversal.[29] GnRH agonist and antagonist action will be covered in more detail later in this chapter.

## STRUCTURAL VARIANTS OF GONADOTROPIN-RELEASING HORMONE

After the original discovery of diverse forms of GnRH in vertebrates,[30,31] more than a dozen different structures sharing 10% to 50% amino acid identity have been identified.[21,24,32-35] Variant GnRH molecules are widely distributed in vertebrate tissues, including the placenta, the preimplantation embryo, the endometrium, the gonads, GnRH neurons, immune system cells, breast and prostate cancer cells, and the central and peripheral nervous system including the sympathetic ganglion and the midbrain.[18,21,24,32,33,36-42] In these tissues, GnRH functions in autocrine, paracrine, and neuromodulatory roles in addition to its neuroendocrine action. Moreover, it is evident that at least two and usually three forms of GnRH are present in most of the more than 80 species examined.[18,21,24,32-34]

**Figure 139-1** Comparison of amino acid sequences of gonadotropin-releasing hormone (GnRH) through evolution of protochordates to mammals. *Boxed regions* indicate conserved N- and C-terminal residues that serve important functional roles. Nonconserved residues may confer ligand selectivity for a particular GnRH receptor. Each GnRH is named according to the species in which it was first discovered and may be present in more than one species. For example, mammalian GnRH is found in amphibians and chicken GnRH II is present in most vertebrates, including humans.

| | 1 | 2 | 3 | 4 | 5 | 6 | 7 | 8 | 9 | 10 | |
|---|---|---|---|---|---|---|---|---|---|---|---|
| Mammal | pGlu | His | Trp | Ser | Tyr | Gly | Leu | Arg | Pro | Gly | NH2 |
| Guinea Pig | pGlu | His | Tyr | Ser | Tyr | Gly | Val | Arg | Pro | Gly | NH2 |
| Chicken I | pGlu | His | Trp | Ser | Tyr | Gly | Leu | Gln | Pro | Gly | NH2 |
| Rana | pGlu | His | Trp | Ser | Tyr | Gly | Leu | Trp | Pro | Gly | NH2 |
| Salmon | pGlu | His | Trp | Ser | Tyr | Gly | Trp | Leu | Pro | Gly | NH2 |
| Catfish | pGlu | His | Trp | Ser | His | Gly | Leu | Asn | Pro | Gly | NH2 |
| Chicken II | pGlu | His | Trp | Ser | His | Gly | Trp | Tyr | Pro | Gly | NH2 |
| Lamprey III | pGlu | His | Trp | Ser | His | Asp | Trp | Lys | Pro | Gly | NH2 |
| Lamprey I | pGlu | His | Tyr | Ser | Leu | Glu | Trp | Lys | Pro | Gly | NH2 |
| Tunicate I | pGlu | His | Trp | Ser | Asp | Tyr | Phe | Lys | Pro | Gly | NH2 |
| Tunicate II | pGlu | His | Trp | Ser | Leu | Cys | His | Ala | Pro | Gly | NH2 |

**Table 139-1** Gonadotropin-Releasing Hormone Analogues Available as Approved Drugs in the United States

| Name | Structure | Route of Administration |
|---|---|---|
| GnRH decapeptide | pGlu-His-Trp-Ser-Tyr-Gly-Leu-Arg-Pro-Gly-NH$_2$ | Intravenous pulsatile pump |
| **GnRH AGONISTS** | | |
| Leuprolide (Lupron) | pGlu-His-Trp-Ser-Tyr-DLeu-Leu-Arg-Pro-NHEt | Subcutaneous or intramuscular (daily or depot), depot implant |
| Nafarelin (Synarel) | pGlu-His-Trp-Ser-Tyr-D2Nal-Leu-Arg-Pro-GlyNH$_2$ | Nasal (daily) |
| Goserelin (Zoladex) | pGlu-His-Trp-Ser-Tyr-DSer(O$^t$Bu)-Leu-Arg-Pro-AzaglyNH$_2$ | Intramuscular (depot), depot implant |
| **GnRH ANTAGONISTS** | | |
| Cetrorelix (Cetrotide) | [Ac-DNal$^1$,DCpa$^2$,DPal$^3$, DCit$^6$,DAla$^{10}$]GnRH | Subcutaneous (daily) |
| Ganirelix (Antagon) | [Ac-DNal$^1$,DCpa$^2$,DPal$^3$, DhArg(Et)$_2$$^6$, hArg(Et)$_2$$^8$,DAla$^{10}$]GnRH | Subcutaneous (daily) |
| Abarelix (Plenaxis) | [Ac-DNal$^1$,DCpa$^2$,DPal$^3$, NMeTyr$^5$, DAsn$^6$,Lys(iPr)$^8$]GnRH | Intramuscular (depot) |

GnRH, gonadotropin-releasing hormone.

The most common GnRH structural variant is called chicken GnRH type II (cGnRH II) because it was first isolated from chicken brain; it differs from mammalian GnRH (GnRH I) by three amino acid residues at positions 5, 7, and 8. cGnRH II and its messenger RNA (mRNA) has been demonstrated in humans.[43,44] The complete conservation of cGnRH II sequence in vertebrates from primitive fish to mammals[43,45] implies an essential function. The location of cGnRH II in the extrahypothalamic brain suggests a neurotransmitter or neuromodulatory role. Indeed, one of the established functions specific to cGnRH II is the potent inhibition of potassium channels in amphibian sympathetic ganglia, facilitating fast excitatory transmission by conventional neurotransmitters and possibly providing a general neuromodulatory mechanism for cGnRH II in the nervous system.[45] Moreover, cGnRH II (but not GnRH I) has been shown to activate mating in energy-challenged musk shrews, suggesting a role in coordinating energy and reproductive behavior.[46] A growing number of extrapituitary functions of cGnRH II have been identified in the human such as the suppression of tumor proliferation,[42,47–49] although full-length cGnRH II receptor transcript has not yet been detected.

Stopa and colleagues[50] detected a third nonmammalian GnRH isoform, a lamprey-like GnRH III in human hypothalami using a combination of immunocytochemistry, high-performance liquid chromatography, and radioimmunoassay. Unlike cGnRH II, the hypothalamic distribution of immunopositive lamprey GnRH III neurons was similar to that observed for those containing GnRH type I, suggesting a role for lamprey GnRH III in the regulation of pituitary function. Studies in the rat brain also showed colocalization of GnRH I and lamprey GnRH III in neurons in the ventromedial preoptic area, a region known to control the preovulatory release of gonadotropins.[51,52]

## SYNTHESIS AND PROCESSING

The human GnRH I gene consists of four exons separated by three introns and resides on chromosome 8p11.2-p21.[53,54] The first exon of the gene is untranslated and is composed of 61 base pairs in mRNA expressed in the hypothalamus. The second exon encodes the signal sequence, the GnRH decapeptide, a GKR processing signal, and the initial 11 residues of the GnRH-associated peptide (GAP). The third exon contains the next 32 GAP residues, and the fourth exon encodes the remaining 13 GAP residues, the translation termination codon, and the entire 160-base pair (bp) 3'-untranslated region (UTR).[53,55] (Fig. 139-3). The cloning of GnRH I cDNAs from human hypothalamus and placenta revealed identical coding and 3'-UTRs.[55,56] However, the placental cDNA has a much longer 5'-UTR because the first intron is included in the transcript.[53,55]

The GnRH I cDNA contains an open reading frame of 276 bp encoding a precursor protein of 92 amino acids. The initial 23 amino acids form a signal sequence followed by the GnRH decapeptide. Cleavage of the signal peptide generates an N-terminal glutamic acid residue, which undergoes cyclization to pyroglutamic acid. The decapeptide is followed by a GKR sequence and a 56-amino acid peptide, GAP. The GKR sequence signals amidation of the carboxyl terminus and enzymatic cleavage of the decapeptide from the precursor protein. The precise function of the GAP is not known, but it has been suggested to have prolactin release inhibitory activity.[57,58]

The human cGnRH II gene has been cloned and mapped to chromosome 20p13 by fluorescence in situ hybridization.[43] It is also composed of four exons separated by three introns, and the predicted preprohormone is organized in a manner identical to that of the GnRH I precursor. However, the human GnRH I gene (5 kilobase) is longer than cGnRH II gene (2.1 kilobase) because introns 2 and 3 of the former are larger.[43] In addition, the GAP is 50% longer in the cGnRH II precursor (84 vs. 56 amino acids).

## GONADOTROPIN-RELEASING HORMONE SECRETION

In elegant experiments performed in the rhesus monkey, Knobil[59] established that gonadotropin secretion depends on pulsatile GnRH discharge within a defined frequency and amplitude. The pulsatile rhythm of GnRH and gonadotropin secretion is critical to the regulation of the gonadotropin-gonadal axis. These pulses occur at approximately hourly intervals and

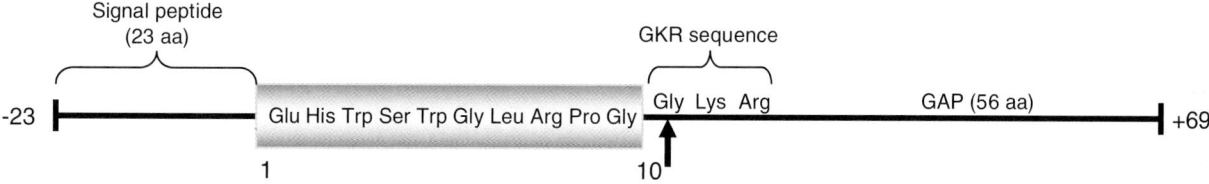

**Figure 139-3** The processing of preprogonadotropin-releasing hormone (prepro-GnRH). In the 92-amino acid prepro-GnRH polypeptide, the GnRH decapeptide is located between the 23-amino acid signal peptide and the GKR processing sequence. The *arrow* indicates the site of enzymatic cleavage from the precursor protein and C-terminal amidation. The GnRH decapeptide and GnRH-associated peptide (GAP) are secreted in tandem into the hypophyseal portal circulation.

originate in the area of the arcuate nucleus in the medial basal hypothalamus. This manner of GnRH secretion occurs in all mammalian species.

Pulses of GnRH in the hypophyseal portal blood and LH pulses in the peripheral blood display remarkable synchrony.[59–62] Thus, the medial basal hypothalamus sets the rhythm of GnRH pulsatile discharges from the nerve terminals at the median eminence, which in turn controls pituitary gonadotropin secretion, and hence governs the entire reproductive process. In humans, patterns of hypothalamic pulsatile GnRH secretion are deduced by the characteristics of LH pulses determined by frequent blood sampling. In studies of isolated medial basal hypothalamus from the human fetus (at 20 to 23 weeks of gestation) and adult in an in vitro perfusion system, the periodicity of GnRH pulses was found to be approximately 60 minutes for the fetal medial basal hypothalamus and 60 to 100 minutes for the adult medial basal hypothalamus.[63] Studies of the immortalized GT1 neuronal cell line in culture suggest that GnRH pulsatile release is an intrinsic property of GnRH neurons.[64]

Although it has long been established that episodic secretion of GnRH from the hypothalamus is required for normal gonadotropin release, the molecular and cellular mechanisms underlying the synchronous release of GnRH are not well understood. Findings from hamster studies suggest that circadian regulation of LH release may be mediated through direct input of the suprachiasmatic nucleus, the central hypothalamic pacemaker, to GnRH neurons.[65] Studies of circadian clock genes in GT1-7 cells demonstrated that perturbation of circadian clock function by transient expression of a dominant-negative Clock gene disrupts normal ultradian patterns of GnRH secretion, significantly decreasing mean pulse frequency.[66] This finding indicates that an endogenous clock in GnRH neurons assists in the control of normal patterns of pulsatile GnRH secretion.

## MECHANISM OF ACTION

GnRH is transported from the hypothalamus to the pituitary through the hypothalamic-hypophyseal portal circulation and binds to the G protein–coupled cell surface GnRH receptor on the gonadotroph with high affinity.[67,68] The GnRH receptor number varies in response to GnRH pulse frequency and according to physiologic conditions, such as during sexual maturation and the estrous cycle.[69] Changes in GnRH receptor concentration on the surface of the gonadotrope are highly correlated with alterations in the gonadotrope response to GnRH. The concentration of GnRH receptors in the pituitary gland is highest with a GnRH pulse frequency of 30 minutes in rodents, and lower concentrations are observed with a GnRH pulse frequency of 2 hours. These changes in the levels of GnRH receptors are correlated with cyclic synthesis and release of LH and FSH during an ovulatory cycle. The variations in levels of GnRH receptors during pituitary development, the menstrual cycle, pregnancy, lactation, and oophorectomy in the presence or absence of estrogen replacement further suggest that such changes are physiologically important.[70–72]

Initially, GnRH receptors are distributed evenly on the cell surface, but coupling with GnRH causes clustering and probably dimerization of GnRH receptors.[73] These clusters are then internalized and incorporated into lysosomes, where some of the hormone-receptor complexes undergo degradation. A large fraction of GnRH receptors is rapidly shuttled back to the cell surface. GnRH receptors are also upregulated by GnRH, contributing to the recycling process.[74] In fact, GnRH itself has been shown to be the major determinant of receptor concentration, and the number of receptors increases when endogenous GnRH secretion is elevated, such as after castration.[71] A GnRH antagonist, in contrast, binds to the GnRH receptor but cannot induce clustering of receptors.[73] In this manner, antagonists decrease gonadotropin secretion by occupying the receptor without triggering hormone action.[74]

As discussed earlier, a number of GnRH agonists were generated by substitution of amino acids at the 6 or 10 position (see Table 139-1). The increased biologic activity of agonist peptides has been attributed to their high binding affinity to GnRH receptors and resistance to enzymatic degradation. GnRH agonists are administered subcutaneously, intranasally, or intramuscularly. An initial agonist response (i.e., the flare effect) is associated with an increase in the circulating levels of LH and FSH. The most potent agonist response is seen when GnRH agonist is administered during the early follicular phase, when the combined effects of GnRH agonist and elevated estradiol create a large reserve pool of gonadotropins.[75] The administration of a long-acting depot formulation of a GnRH agonist gives rise eventually to downregulation of the gonadotropin-gonadal axis within 1 to 3 weeks. The downregulation effect is due to a combination of factors that are discussed later in this chapter.

The U.S. Food and Drug Administration has approved the use of GnRH agonists for the treatment of GnRH-dependent precocious puberty, endometriosis, and prostate cancer. Another indication is the preoperative improvement of anemia in patients with uterine leiomyomas. GnRH agonists have also been used for downregulation of the pituitary during ovulation induction, induction of endometrial atrophy before endometrial ablation surgery, and prevention of menstrual bleeding in patients with coagulation disorders. GnRH agonists have also been used to suppress ovarian steroidogenesis in hirsute patients.[76] Additionally, native GnRH may be employed in the treatment of delayed puberty and infertility in hypogonadal patients when administered in a pulsatile fashion by a portable infusion pump.[3,77,78]

Multiple amino acid substitutions also permit the synthesis of GnRH antagonists (see Table 139-1). These include modifications of the pyroglutamic and glycine termini at positions 1 and 10 or deletion and substitution of hydrophobic amino acids at positions 2 and 3.[19] GnRH antagonists bind to the GnRH receptor and provide competitive inhibition for endogenous GnRH. As stated earlier, GnRH antagonists have the advantage of inducing an immediate decrease in circulating gonadotropin levels with rapid reversal.[29] The early antagonists either lacked potency or were associated with undesirable side effects related to histamine release. Newer GnRH antagonists are at various stages of development.[79–85] These newer antagonists are more potent in the downregulation of the gonadotropin-gonadal axis and do not cause histamine release (see Table 139-1).

## CONTROL OF GONADOTROPE FUNCTION

Gonadotropes are specialized cell types of the anterior pituitary that synthesize and secrete LH and FSH. These cells constitute 7% to 15% of the total number of anterior pituitary cells and are detected in this location early in fetal life.[86] The majority of the gonadotropes are capable of synthesizing both LH and FSH.[86,87]

As discussed earlier, the activation of gene expression for gonadotropin subunits is governed by the periodicity of GnRH signals to pituitary gonadotropes.[88] During the menstrual cycle, the LH pulse frequency is approximately 90 minutes in the early follicular phase, 60 to 70 minutes during the late follicular phase, 100 minutes during the early luteal phase, and 200 minutes during the late luteal phase.[89] This variation alters FSH and LH secretion and resultant ovarian steroid release during the phases of the menstrual cycle. GnRH pulse frequency dictates both the absolute levels and the ratio of LH and FSH release, in which more rapid pulse frequencies promote LH secretion, and slower frequencies favor FSH.[90]

The effect of GnRH pulse rhythms on gonadotropin secretion has been studied in hypophysectomized animals receiving exogenous GnRH as well as in in vitro systems. The relative stimulation of gonadotropin subunits in the rat pituitary is influenced by GnRH pulse frequency. High pulse frequencies stimulate LH-β mRNA levels more than FSH-β, whereas the converse is true at low pulse frequencies.[91,92] Thus, the combination of alterations in pulse frequency together with differential phasing and duration of the various signaling pathways provides the potential for fine regulation of gonadotropin secretion. Feedback by gonadal steroid and peptide hormones[93] at the gonadotrope provides additional modulation (see also Chapters 142 and 154).

## REGULATORS OF GONADOTROPIN-RELEASING HORMONE SECRETION

Studies of immortalized GnRH-secreting GT1 neurons,[64] primary GnRH neurons,[94,95] and GnRH neurons in vivo in animal models[96-99] have permitted the study of mechanisms underlying the pulsatile secretion of GnRH and its regulation. GT1 cells secrete GnRH, and there is processing of pro-GnRH to GnRH and GAP.[100,101] The most noteworthy biologic effect of these cells is their ability to reverse the hypogonadism of mutant *hpg* mice (GnRH deficient due to a mutation of GnRH gene) after injection into the hypothalamus.[102] GT1 neurons have been found to express GnRH receptor, the activation of which is associated with a rapid, prominent, and dose-dependent elevation of cytoplasmic calcium concentrations and GnRH release, indicating autocrine regulation of GnRH release by GnRH itself,[103] a finding also suggested by in vivo studies.[104] Recent data from perifused fetal rat GnRH neurons showed that GnRH pulse amplitude was increased by GnRH agonist treatment and diminished during GnRH antagonist treatment, additional evidence that an autocrine interaction between GnRH and its receptor influences GnRH pulsatile release.[105]

### NEUROTRANSMITTERS

GnRH pulsatility is modulated by locally released neurotransmitters, including norepinephrine and dopamine. Norepinephrine and dopamine stimulate GnRH release.[106] The identification of β$_1$-adrenergic and D$_1$-dopaminergic receptors on GT1 GnRH neurons suggests that the effects of norepinephrine and dopamine on gonadotropin release are mediated by direct synapses on GnRH neurons. β$_1$-Adrenergic and D$_1$-dopaminergic receptors are positively coupled to adenylate cyclase on GT1 cells.[107,108] Another study of GT1-7 cells demonstrated that calcium mobilization was blocked by the β-adrenergic antagonist propranolol but not by the α-adrenergic antagonist phentolamine.[109]

Experiments in primates and humans have shown that GnRH pulse generator activities and associated LH pulses are subject to adrenergic modulation. In contrast to the GT1 cell model, blockade of the α$_1$-adrenergic receptor by phentolamine or prazosin and the dopamine antagonist metoclopramide inhibits the frequency of pulse generation or arrests it altogether in ovariectomized rhesus monkeys.[110,111] These data provide evidence that central catecholaminergic systems modulate inputs to GnRH neurons. Unlike the findings in the rhesus monkey, α-adrenergic blocking agents do not alter LH pulsatile frequency in humans. The acute administration of dopamine and dopamine agonists has been shown to decrease mean LH levels.[112-114]

Glutamate, one of the major excitatory transmitters in the hypothalamus, serves as a critical central mediator in the neuroendocrine regulation of diverse processes such as cognition, memory, puberty, menstrual cyclicity, and reproductive behavior.[115] Once released into the synaptic cleft, glutamate may bind to N-methyl-D-aspartate (NMDA) receptors on presynaptic or postsynaptic neurons, or it may be cleared

from the synaptic cleft by either glial or neuronal transporter protein. Agents that can inhibit glutamate exocytosis by acting at presynaptic receptors include γ-aminobutyric acid (GABA) agonists and opioids.[116,117] In GT1 cells, receptors for glutamate (NMDA), GABA$_A$, and GABA$_B$ have been identified.[118] The nitric oxide–cyclic guanosine monophosphate pathway is also operative in these cells, modulating GnRH release in vitro.[119] A proposed interaction of glutamate neurons, nitric oxide, and opioid neurons may occur in the control of GnRH secretion.[115]

In immature female rats, the GnRH neuronal system was precociously activated by the episodic administration of an NMDA receptor analogue.[120] Conversely, NMDA receptor antagonist given to prepubertal female rats significantly delayed but did not prevent puberty, as determined by the age at vaginal opening and first ovulation.[120] These results demonstrate that blockade of NMDA receptors can prevent the development of enhanced LH secretion in female rats undergoing sexual maturation.

GABA, an inhibitory neurotransmitter, appears to suppress GnRH release. In green fluorescent protein(GFf)–identified adult mouse GnRH neurons in brain slices, rapid GABA application and activation of GABA$_A$ receptors excited GnRH neurons, whereas prolonged activation reduced excitability.[121] Moreover, in GnRH-LacZ and GnRH-GFP transgenic mouse models, approximately 80% of GnRH neurons responded to the selective GABA$_A$ receptor antagonist bicuculline with a rapid and reversible membrane depolarization and/or increase in firing rate.[122] These observations show that endogenous GABA signaling through the GABA$_A$ receptor exerts a powerful net inhibitory effect on the excitability of mature GnRH neurons.

### NEUROPEPTIDES

Opioids are known inhibitors of GnRH neuronal activity as demonstrated both in vitro and in vivo.[123,124] Using GT1 cells, it was found that opioids have a direct effect on GnRH neurons to attenuate the stimulatory action of α-adrenergic and dopaminergic inputs. β-Endorphin and other opioids may also serve to suppress the hypothalamic release of GnRH.[125] Thus, the inhibitory effect of opioids on GnRH release in vivo is by way of reducing the responsiveness to GnRH stimulators and may not require an interneuron.[126] This inhibitory effect can be reversed by the administration of the opiate antagonist naloxone.[127-129]

Corticotropin-releasing factor (CRF) administered peripherally immediately suppresses GnRH pulse generator activity in the rhesus monkey, an effect that appears to be mediated through the activation of endogenous opiates.[59,60,128] Similar experiments in humans failed to identify an inhibitory effect of CRF on LH pulsatile secretion.[130] The presence of a high-affinity CRF-binding protein unique to humans may account for disparate results by a rapid binding of CRF to CRF-binding protein, thereby reducing free CRF at the receptor site.

Tyrosine kinase receptors including receptors for insulin-like growth factor 1 (IGF-1) and IGF-2, insulin, epidermal growth factor, basic fibroblast growth factor, and prolactin are expressed in GT1 cells. The presence of the insulin receptor family in GT1-7 cells has permitted the demonstration of mitogenic effects of insulin, IGF-1, and IGF-2 (at a 100-fold higher dose than IGF-1 or insulin).[131] GnRH secretion by GT1-7 cells treated with IGF-1 or IGF-2 but not insulin showed an increase (80%–100%) at 2 hours of treatment followed by a decrease (46%) at 6 hours that continued as long as 24 hours.[132] This initial stimulation and then suppression by IGFs suggests an uncoupling of biosynthesis and secretion.[133] In GT1-1 cells, basic fibroblast growth factor priming counteracted an epidermal growth factor–induced decrease in GnRH release and significantly stimulated GnRH secretion after IGF-1 or insulin, suggesting that basic fibroblast growth factor may sensitize GnRH neurons to the differentiating effects of specific growth factors during development.[134] It is unknown whether these receptor mRNAs are expressed in native hypothalamic GnRH neurons as well as GT1 cells; however, the potent neurotropic effects of basic fibroblast growth factor[135] together with the ability of IGFs to stimulate mitogenesis and GnRH secretion indicate that these growth factor receptors may be important regulators of GnRH neuronal expansion, survival, migration, and connectivity. Derangements in the physiology of insulin and IGFs have been implicated in the pathogenesis of polycystic ovary syndrome, a disorder of insulin resistance, hyperpulsatile LH secretion, and overactive ovarian and adrenal androgen synthesis in adolescent and adult women.[136-138]

Neuropeptide Y, galanin, and aspartate are also putative excitatory neuromodulators of GnRH release in primates and rodents. Although aspartate appears to exert a direct effect by increasing the activity of the GnRH pulse generator, neuropeptide Y and galanin require gonadal steroids for their action.[139,140]

Leptin, an adipocyte-derived peptide hormone, increases GnRH hypothalamic secretion in prepubertal and peripubertal rats.[141] In peripubertal rats, leptin exerts a stimulatory effect on GnRH by inducing release of excitatory amino acids (aspartate) and reducing release of inhibitory amino acids (GABA) involved in GnRH control. In contrast, the stimulatory effect of leptin on GnRH in prepubertal rats appears to be mediated by the stimulation of GABA, which at this age increases GnRH release.[141] In humans, leptin has been administered to a 9-year-old leptin-deficient girl, resulting in a gonadotropin secretory pattern consistent with early puberty.[142]

### STEROID HORMONES

Changes in GnRH pulse frequency are modulated by gonadal steroid feedback. Depending on the level and duration of exposure, estradiol may either stimulate or inhibit GnRH pulsatility, whereas elevated progesterone levels decrease GnRH pulse frequency.[88,90,143] Thus, the increased progesterone levels of the late luteal phase in the menstrual cycle may lead to a decrease in GnRH pulse frequency, accounting for the predominant biosynthesis and secretion of FSH.[88]

The gonadal steroids modify endogenous opioid activity, and the negative feedback of steroids on gonadotropins appears to be mediated at least in part by endogenous opioids.[144] Thus, it was proposed that sex steroids enhance the activity of endogenous opioids that in turn inhibit GnRH secretion.[145] The negative effect of opioids on GnRH secretion is also biologically plausible because the reduced GnRH secretion in hypothalamic amenorrhea may be mediated by an increase in endogenous opioid inhibitory tone.[146]

Because estrogen receptors (ER-α and ER-β), progesterone receptors, glucocorticoid receptors, and thyroid hormone receptor have all been identified in GT1 cells as well as in the GnRH neurons,[147-151] steroid feedback sites and thyroid hormone targets in the brain now include GnRH neurons. Potential interactions of estrogen and thyroid hormone receptors on a progesterone receptor–estrogen response element sequence may occur and suggest a neuroendocrine-metabolic integration that is important for reproductive function.[152] GnRH release may also be modified by direct steroid action on receptors expressed in the neurons. In the GT1 cell model, both 5α-dihydrotestosterone and 17β-estradiol were found to repress GnRH gene expression.[153,154]

Estrogen exerts an important regulatory influence on the functioning of GnRH neurons in vivo. Using female mice with targeted disruptions of ER-α and ER-β (ERαKO and ERβKO, respectively), Dorling and colleagues[155] investigated the role of the two ERs in the negative feedback influence of estrogen on GnRH mRNA expression. Compared with intact wild-type mice, plasma LH levels were substantially higher in intact ERαKO females and increased modestly in intact

ERβKO mice. Three weeks after ovariectomy, LH concentrations were elevated significantly in wild-type and ERβKO mice but unchanged in ERαKO females. GnRH mRNA content was greater in intact ERαKO mice compared with intact wild-type and ERβKO mice, and after ovariectomy, GnRH mRNA expression was elevated in wild-type and ERβKO females but not ERαKO mice. These data demonstrate that both ER-α and ER-β are involved in inhibiting LH levels at times of estrogen-negative feedback in vivo. However, only ER-α appears to be critical for the estrogen-negative feedback suppression of GnRH mRNA expression in the female mouse.[155]

## PHYSIOLOGIC CHANGES IN GONADOTROPIN-RELEASING HORMONE RELEASE

### GONADOTROPIN-RELEASING HORMONE RHYTHMS FROM FETAL LIFE TO PUBERTY

LH-containing cells develop in the human fetal anterior pituitary as early as 10 weeks of gestation, and GnRH has been identified in the human hypothalamus at 14 to 16 weeks.[156] By 20 to 23 weeks, isolated medial basal hypothalamus from the mid-gestational human fetus releases GnRH in a pulsatile manner in vitro,[63] and the fetal gonadotrope has the capacity to respond in vivo and in vitro to GnRH stimulation with the release of LH.[157] Thus, by mid-gestation in the human fetus, the hypothalamic GnRH pulse generator and the pituitary gonadotrope form a functional unit for maintaining LH and FSH secretion.

Concentrations of immunoreactive LH in serum and in the pituitary are significantly greater in the female than in the male human fetus at mid-gestation.[158,159] Because GnRH secretion at this time is quantitatively similar in the male and female medial basal hypothalamus,[160,161] this sex-associated difference in LH secretion may result from negative feedback by factors from the fetal testis that attenuate pituitary sensitivity to GnRH stimulation. Indeed, during repetitive GnRH pulse dosing, LH responses are six times greater in pituitary tissue from female than that from male fetuses.[157]

The progression of pulsatile GnRH/gonadotropin secretion conforms to a U-shaped curve (Fig. 139-4). During the first several months of life, gonadotropin levels are elevated, followed by a progressive decline until a quiescent hypogonadotropic state is reached at the age of 2 to 3 years. A parallel decrease in pituitary responsiveness to exogenous GnRH is also achieved. As the gonadotropin nadir occurs in the

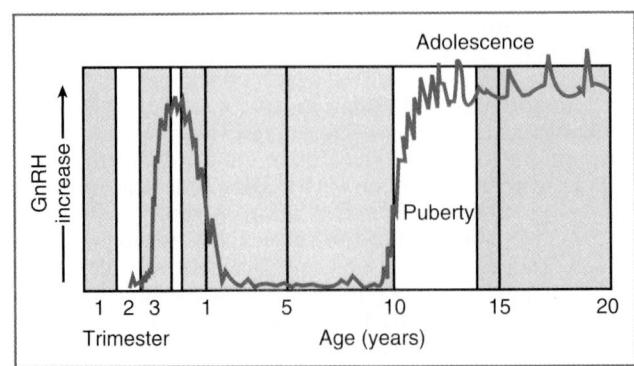

*Figure 139-4* Gonadotropin-releasing hormone (GnRH) secretion from fetal life to adolescence. GnRH secretion is high during late fetal and neonatal periods, decreases during the first year of life, and remains low until the increase in activity at the onset of puberty. (Redrawn from Yen SSC: Reproductive strategy in women: Neuroendocrine basis of endogenous contraception. In Roland R [ed]: Neuroendocrinology of Reproduction. Amsterdam, Excerpta Medica, 1988, pp 231–239.)

absence of ovarian function,[162] this prepubertal restriction on gonadotropin secretion may be attributed to central inhibition of hypothalamic GnRH secretion. Attempts to implicate endogenous opioids as the central inhibitor of GnRH neuronal activities have been unsuccessful.[163,164] The role of the neurotransmitters aspartate and glutamate in the activation of GnRH neuronal secretion during puberty are being investigated. Glutamate enhances GnRH release from arcuate nucleus-median eminence fragments in vitro,[165] and prolonged intermittent intravenous injection of an analogue of aspartate, NMDA, triggers the onset of precocious puberty in immature monkeys and rats.[120,166]

The onset of puberty is determined by the brain through an increase in pulsatile GnRH release from the hypothalamus. This increase is initiated even when the gonads are absent, as in patients with gonadal dysgenesis.[162] In the prepubertal monkey, puberty may be activated prematurely by exogenous pulsatile GnRH administration.[167] Recently, loss-of-function mutations of the gene encoding GPR54, the putative receptor for the KiSS-1-derived peptide metastin, have been associated with lack of puberty onset and hypogonadotropic hypogonadism.[168-170] In rodents, metastin administered subcutaneously or directly into the cerebral ventricles induced a dramatic increase in LH secretion in prepubertal animals.[171-173] This activation was abolished by pretreatment with GnRH antagonists. These findings along with the detection of maximal levels of KiSS-1 and GPR54 mRNA at puberty suggest that metastin-GPR54 signaling may play a pivotal role in governing hypothalamic GnRH secretion.[171]

After puberty, cyclic menses require pulsatile GnRH release within a defined range of frequencies as discussed earlier. Slower GnRH pulse frequency causes anovulation and amenorrhea due to inadequate stimulation. Higher GnRH pulse frequency or constant exposure to GnRH also gives rise to anovulation by downregulating GnRH receptor expression, thereby abolishing gonadotropin responses. Thus, a changing frequency of GnRH stimulation of the gonadotrope is critical for differential gonadotropin secretion during ovulatory cycles. In cases of hypothalamic amenorrhea, patients exhibit a persistent slow frequency of LH (and hence GnRH) pulses, which reflects excess hypothalamic opioid tone and can be reversed temporarily by opioid antagonists. In contrast, LH (GnRH) pulses are persistently rapid and favor LH synthesis, hyperandrogenism, and impaired follicular maturation in polycystic ovarian syndrome.[174] The hormonal regulation of the menstrual cycle is covered in greater detail in Chapter 154.

## EFFECTS OF STRESS ON GONADOTROPIN-RELEASING HORMONE PULSATILITY

Various stressors, including metabolic, infectious, physical, and chronic illness, have been shown to interfere with GnRH pulsatility. Studies in young healthy humans and in experimental animals suggest that reduced release of hypothalamic GnRH plays a key role in the acute fasting-associated suppression of reproductive function in both the male and female.[175] It also appears that age-related differences in hypothalamic-pituitary axis regulation occur because short-term fasting in young but not older men reduces 24-hour LH secretory burst frequency and mass, enhances the orderliness of LH release patterns, and alters 24-hour LH rhythmicity.[176]

Administration of lipopolysaccharide, representing infectious stress, to gonadectomized rats and goats inhibits existing pulsatile LH release.[177-179] In experiments on ovariectomized estrogen-primed rats, acute immobilization stress and intravenous lipopolysaccharide were shown to suppress LH release induced by NMDA or naloxone but not to inhibit basal LH secretion or LH release induced by GnRH.[180-182] These findings suggest that different stressors may facilitate a common mechanism in inhibiting GnRH neurons and that

these two stressors in particular have a suprapituitary site of action to suppress GnRH neurons in female rats. In prolonged critically ill men, decreased LH secretion associated with blunted pulsatility is a common feature along with reduced serum concentrations of androgens, consistent with acquired hypogonadotropic hypogonadism.[183,184]

## GONADOTROPIN-RELEASING HORMONE RECEPTOR

### STRUCTURE OF THE GONADOTROPIN-RELEASING HORMONE RECEPTOR

In 1992, the amino acid sequence of the GnRH receptor was first elucidated for the mouse in the $\alpha$T3-1 gonadotrope-derived cell line.[185,186] Since then, the sequence formed the basis for cloning pituitary GnRH receptors from the rat,[187-189] human,[190,191] sheep,[192,193] cow,[194] pig,[195] catfish,[196] Xenopus, and chicken.[21] These receptors have been designated type I. Cloning of type II GnRH receptor from marmoset cDNA has been reported; the type II receptor is more widely distributed than the type I receptor and is expressed throughout the marmoset brain, including areas associated with sexual arousal, and in the testis, prostate, mammary glands, seminal vesicles, and epididymis.[197] Substantial expression was also detected in adrenal, thyroid, heart, and skeletal muscle, suggesting a variety of functions.[197] A third form with closer homology to type II than type I has also been found in Rana.[198] These findings suggest an early evolution of the three GnRH receptor subtypes in vertebrates in parallel with that of the GnRH ligands. The human gene homologue of the type II GnRH receptor, however, has a frame shift and stop codon, and it appears that GnRH II signaling occurs through the type I GnRH receptor.[199]

A 60-kilodalton glycoprotein, the GnRH receptor is a G protein–coupled receptor (GPCR) with an N-terminal EC domain, followed by seven $\alpha$-helical transmembrane (TM) domains connected by three EC domains and three IC loop domains (Fig. 139-5). Peptide hormones such as GnRH are bound by the EC domains and superficial TM regions. A negatively charged domain interacts primarily with Arg8 of the GnRH molecule. The TMs are presumed to be involved in conformational change related to signal propagation and receptor activation, whereas the IC domains interact with G proteins to facilitate signal transduction. The absence of a C-terminal tail distinguishes the mammalian GnRH receptor from all other GPCRs and all nonmammalian GnRH receptors.

Downregulation of the GnRH receptor involves several mechanisms, including agonist-stimulated internalization of GnRH receptors via clathrin-coated vesicles, reduction in the number of cell-surface receptors, and the uncoupling of associated second messenger systems including inositol triphosphate production and calcium mobilization.[200] Mammalian GnRH receptors are unique in that they lack C-terminal tails and do not rapidly desensitize,[201,202] whereas nonmammalian GnRH receptors have C-terminal tails and have been found to rapidly desensitize and internalize.[203] The evolution of the nondesensitizing GnRH receptor may confer a reproductive advantage in mammals, which is discussed later.

The structures of the genes encoding the mouse[204] and human[205-207] GnRH receptors have been deduced. In the human, the GnRH receptor gene is localized on chromosome 4. In both the mouse and human genes, three exons are separated by introns in the coding regions of TM4 and IC3, and numerous splice variants exist.[185,193,204] The function of these splice variants may be regulatory because some truncated receptor variants affect the expression of the functional receptor.[208] Moreover, expression of the mouse and human receptors is highly regulated by GnRH and by gonadal steroid and peptide hormones.[209,210]

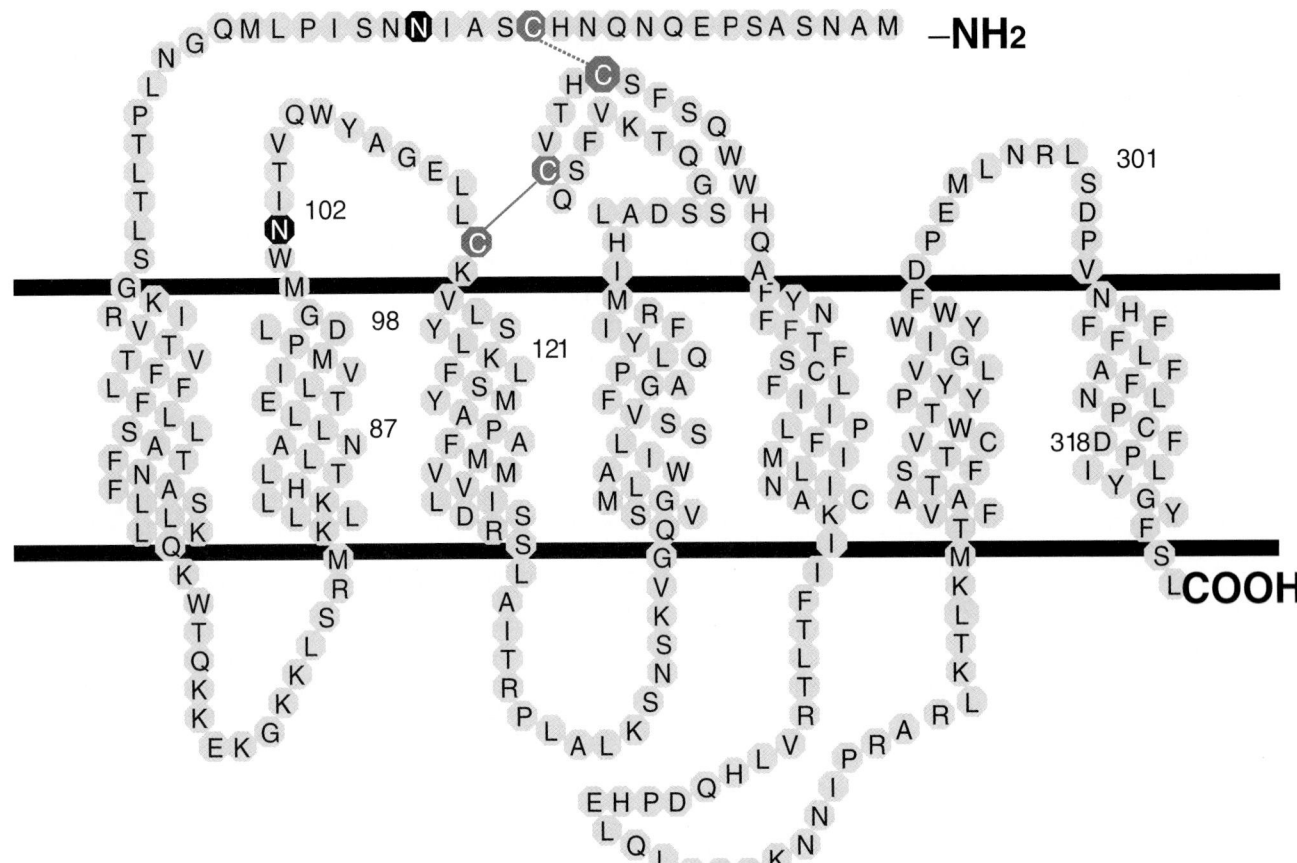

**Figure 139-5** Schematic representation of the human gonadotropin-releasing hormone (GnRH) receptor. The receptor is composed of an extracellular N-terminal domain, seven transmembrane domains, and three extracellular and three intracellular loops. The mammalian GnRH receptor is notable for the absence of an intracellular C-terminal tail. Two N-linked glycosylation sites (*dark*) and two putative disulfide bridges (*shaded*) are depicted.

Three-dimensional structural information on the GnRH receptor has been derived from computer-based molecular models[18]; it has not yet been possible to crystallize any GPCR to obtain x-ray structural information with the exception of bovine rhodopsin.[211] Consequently, a molecular model of the GnRH receptor has been generated and refined by several experimental studies.[18] For example, the observation that two residues are highly conserved in GPCRs, aspartate in TM2 and asparagine in TM7, suggests that the two residues interact with each other. Indeed, these two residues appear to have undergone reciprocal mutation to Asn87 and Asp318 in the mouse GnRH receptor (Asp319 in the human). Mutation of Asn87 to aspartate in the mouse receptor abolished receptor function, which was restored by mutation of Asp318 to Asn318 (recreating the arrangement in other GPCRs). Thus, the restoration of binding by reciprocal mutation indicates that the side chains of the two residues in TM2 and TM7 play complementary roles in maintaining receptor structure.

Further studies on receptor structure have defined glycosylation sites at Asn4 and Asn18 in the mouse and Asn18 in the human receptor.[212,213] Glycosylation does not affect the receptor-binding affinity of GnRH but increases the expression of the receptor on the cell membrane; introducing the additional mouse receptor glycosylation site in the human receptor increased expression.[213]

## LIGAND-RECEPTOR INTERACTIONS

Considerable advances in identifying putative ligand contact sites have been made by the systematic targeted mutation of amino acid residues in the GnRH receptor.[21] One approach is to mutate a highly conserved amino acid (presumably essential to receptor function), followed by an assessment of agonist binding. This technique was employed in replacing Lys121 with aspartate, alanine, or leucine, leading to a total loss in agonist binding. Mutation to glutamine resulted in a 1000-fold reduction in agonist-binding affinity without influencing antagonist binding.[214] It is postulated that the lysine interacts with His2 or pGlu1 of GnRH. Similarly, mutation of Asn102 to alanine results in a 100- to 1000-fold loss of potency in Gly10-NH2-GnRH in stimulating phosphoinositol hydrolysis but has a reduced effect on the potency of NH-CH2-CH2 GnRH analogues.[6,215]

Another method to elucidate which amino acids in the receptor interact with ligand was to mutate all EC amino acids that might interact with a side chain of GnRH. Flanagan and colleagues[28] created mutations of all EC acidic amino acids in the mouse receptor that might interact with the positive arginine side chain of GnRH; only mutation of Glu301 in EC3 resulted in a 100-fold decrease in ligand affinity and loss of selectivity between Arg8- and Gln8-GnRH. The Glu301 mutant retained selectivity for GnRH analogues with amino acid changes other than Arg8. The same properties were later demonstrated for the equivalent residue in the human, Asp302.[216] In the study mutating all EC amino acids in the mouse receptor, it was also noted that mutation of Asp98 to asparagine resulted in a large drop in inositol phosphate production.[28] Further investigation has revealed that this mutation has little effect on potency of Trp2-GnRH while decreasing that of the native ligand containing His2.[217] Thus, the amino group of tryptophan can substitute for the histidine amino group in the wild-type receptor and can also interact with the Asn98 mutant, whereas the histidine NH is unable to interact with the mutant receptor, possibly due to the longer side chain.

Thus, putative ligand contact sites may be identified using these experimental approaches. All these sites (Asp302, Lys121, Asn102, and Asp98) are conserved in vertebrate GnRH receptors cloned from bony fish, amphibians, and bird species.

## RECEPTOR ACTIVATION AND G PROTEIN COUPLING

Molecular mechanisms of ligand-mediated receptor activation have only been partially elucidated for GPCRs other than rhodopsin. Hormone messages are conveyed by the receptor to signal transduction pathways within the cell via changes in receptor conformation.[218] In GPCRs, the active conformation is formed by a ternary complex consisting of hormone, receptor, and G protein. An initial binding step common to both agonists and antagonists is followed by a transition step exclusive to agonists, leading to formation of the ternary complex. This model also allows spontaneous formation of a receptor–G protein complex, which has higher affinity for and is stabilized by binding of agonist ligands. The receptor returns to the low-affinity conformation when guanosine triphosphate binds to the G protein and the complex dissociates.[219] A revised model hypothesizes that receptors change from an inactive R confirmation to an active R* conformation.[220] Agonist binding shifts the equilibrium toward the R* conformation, which has high affinity for agonists and is the only form that can bind G proteins.

Studies of the GnRH receptor have provided some insight into the mechanism of receptor activation. Mutation of Asn87 and Asp318 in the mouse GnRH receptor (Asp319 in the human) revealed that the Asp318 is involved in receptor activation (signal propagation) as the mutants Asn87Asn318 and Asp87Asn318 both retained ligand binding but had reduced inositol phosphate production.[221] These findings suggest that the aspartate in TM7 in the GnRH receptor is an essential component of ligand-mediated receptor activation, as is the aspartate in TM2 of other nonmammalian GPCR,[222] which have aspartate in both TM2 and TM7.[21,196] Other elements of the GnRH receptor that have been implicated in receptor activation include the highly conserved DRXXXI/V motif at the IC end of TM3 involving Arg138: Mutation of the arginine to glutamine leads to very poor coupling efficiency.[223,224]

The IC loops and C-terminal tail participate in coupling GPCRs to their cognate G proteins, but their involvement varies among different receptors. The conservation of the C-terminal sequence of IC3 in vertebrate GnRH receptors suggests that this region may be essential for coupling to the primary mediator, $G_{q/11}$.[21] Within this region, Ala261 was identified as an important residue: Mutation of Ala261 to bulky amino acids resulted in uncoupling of the receptor and failure to produce inositol phosphate.[225] Mutation of the conserved adjacent basic amino acid Arg262 to alanine and natural mutations of Arg262 in families with hypogonadotropic hypogonadism have similarly been shown to cause uncoupling.[217,226]

GnRH has been shown to rapidly stimulate cyclic adenosine monophosphate production in COS-7 cells transfected with the rat GnRH receptor.[227] These studies also identified a G protein recognition motif BBXXB (where B is a basic amino acid) in IC2 and determined that mutation of some of these residues leads to uncoupling of cyclic adenosine monophosphate production but not of inositol phosphate production.[227]

## RECEPTOR UNCOUPLING AND INTERNALIZATION

Continuous exposure of the gonadotrope to high doses of GnRH agonists results in the phenomenon of desensitization. Several mechanisms contribute to gonadotrope desensitization, including GnRH receptor downregulation, receptor uncoupling from cognate G proteins, additional downstream uncoupling (e.g., inositol phosphate production, $Ca^{2+}$ mobilization), inhibition of gonadotropin synthesis, and alterations in the glycosylation of gonadotropins, rendering them biologically inactive or even antagonistic.[228,229] For many GPCRs, agonist stimulation leads to the activation of protein kinases, which phosphorylate IC domains, resulting in uncoupling from G proteins and internalization of the receptor.[230–232] However, the mammalian GnRH receptors lack the C-terminal IC tail, which is a prime target for phosphorylation by receptor and protein kinases followed by docking of arrestins, resulting in uncoupling and receptor internalization. The absence of the C-terminal tail in the mammalian GnRH receptor may prevent rapid desensitization[202,233,234] and slow receptor internalization; the internalization rate is sevenfold less than that of the cGnRH II receptor, which has a C-terminal tail.[235] Removal of the C-terminal tail from the chicken receptor reduced the rate of internalization to that found in the human receptor. Addition of the C-terminal tail of the thyrotropin-releasing hormone receptor to the rat GnRH receptor conveys both rapid desensitization of ligand-stimulated inositol phosphate production and more rapid internalization.[203]

These findings suggest that during evolution, selection favored the removal of the C-terminal tail in the mammalian GnRH receptor, precluding rapid desensitization. This adaptation may have been driven by the physiologic need for a prolonged LH surge for ovulation in mammals.[235] Although many clinical applications use the ability of pharmacologic doses of GnRH to desensitize the gonadotrope, the GnRH receptor is less susceptible to ligand-mediated desensitization than other GPCRs.

## INTRACELLULAR SIGNAL TRANSDUCTION

The coupling of the GnRH receptor to IC signaling pathways has been an area of intense study.[209,210,236–238] A wide spectrum of IC signaling pathways has been implicated in GnRH action, but the consensus is that the primary pathway is the activation of phospholipase Cβ through the $G_{q/11}$ family of G proteins (Fig. 139-6).[239–247] Stimulation of LH release after injection of GnRH agonist persists in both $G\alpha_q$ and $G\alpha_{11}$ knockout mice, suggesting that the two G proteins may be able to substitute for each other in GnRH receptor signaling.[248]

In addition to its interaction with the $G_{q/11}$ subclass of G proteins, the GnRH receptor has also been proposed to activate $G_i$[88,243,249,250] and $G_s$ subtype G proteins.[210,243,249,251–254] Coupling of the GnRH receptor to the $G_{i/o}$ subtype of G proteins is not reproducibly observed in the gonadotrope. GnRH receptor coupling to $G_s$ and/or increased production of cyclic adenosine monophosphate has been reported with heterologous expression of the receptor, transiently in COS-7 cells and stably in somatolactotroph GH3 cells (GGH3 cells).[210,254,255] Although studies with either the heterologous human receptor expressed in CHO-K1 cells or with the endogenous mouse receptor in αT3-1 cells showed activation solely of the $G_{q/11}$ family of G proteins,[240] a subsequent study of the mouse LβT2 gonadotrope cell line using cell permeable G protein inhibitory peptides and guanosine triphosphate loading assays indicated that the endogenous mouse receptor in these cells can also activate both $G_{q/11}$ and $G_s$ subtypes of G proteins.[251]

After activation by GnRH complexing with its receptor and recruitment of $G\alpha_{q/11}$, PLCβ in the plasma membrane hydrolyzes phosphatidylinositol 4,5-bisphosphate to inositol 1,4,5-trisphosphate and diacylglycerol.[256] Inositol 1,4,5-trisphosphate binds to receptors in the endoplasmic reticulum to induce the transient release of $Ca^{2+}$ from IC stores, eliciting a rapid spike of LH release and activating conventional protein kinase C (PKC) isoforms.[257–260] Diacylglycerol activates calcium-independent novel PKC isoforms, the expression of which is also induced by GnRH receptor

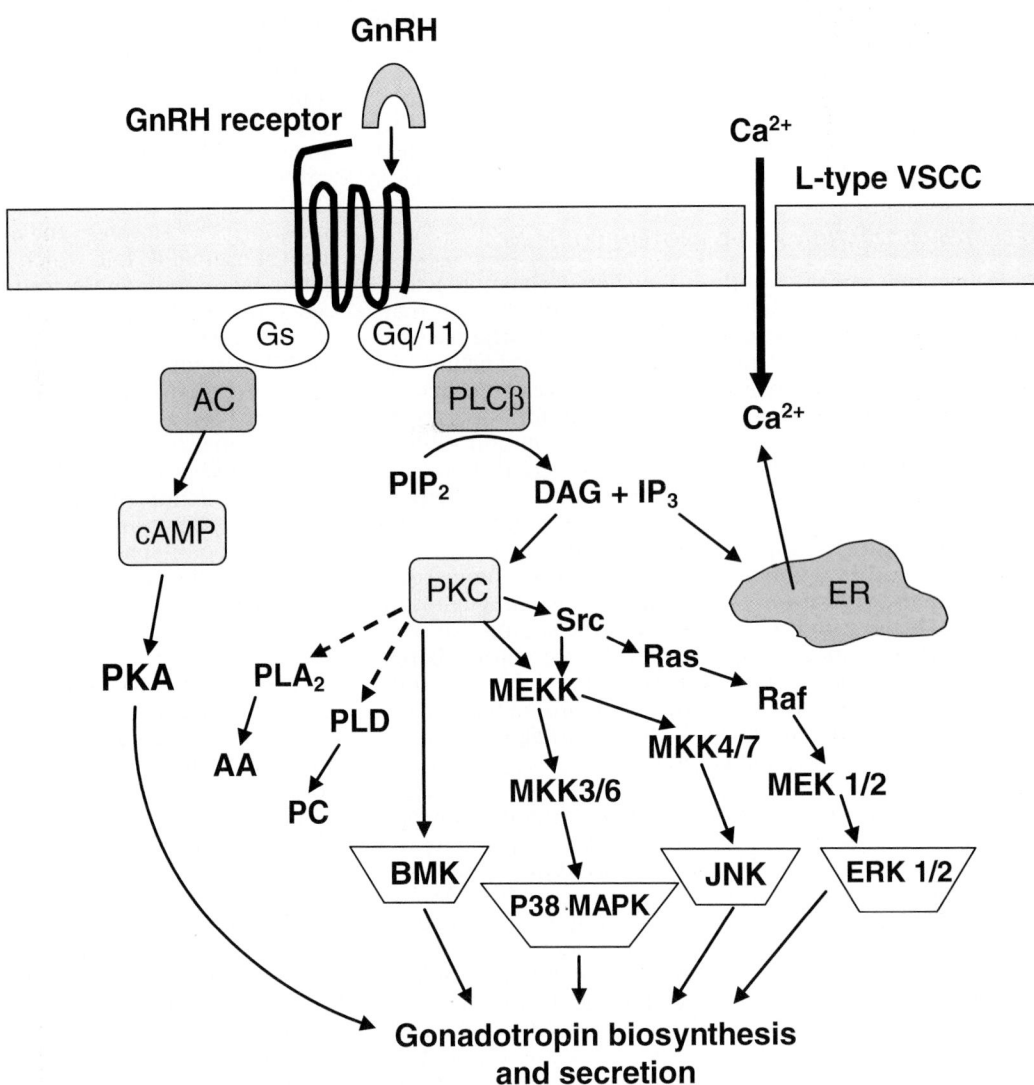

**Figure 139-6** Gonadotropin-releasing hormone (GnRH) receptor–activated signaling pathways. The primary pathway involves the activation of phospholipase Cβ (PLCβ) via $G_{q/11}$, resulting in the hydrolysis of phosphatidylinositol 1,4-bisphosphate ($PIP_2$) to diacylglycerol (DAG), which activates protein kinase C (PKC), and to inositol 1,4,5-trisphosphate ($IP_3$), which triggers $Ca^{2+}$ release from the endoplasmic reticulum (ER). GnRH binding also activates L-type voltage-sensitive $Ca^{2+}$ channels (VSCC). Coupling to $G_s$ stimulates adenylate cyclase (AC), which increases cAMP (cyclic adenosine monophosphate) production. *Broken lines* indicate pathways that are less certain, including the activation of phospholipase $A_2$ ($PLA_2$), which generates arachidonic acid (AA), and of phospholipase D (PLD), which may hydrolyze phosphatidylcholine (PC). Four kinase cascades are activated by GnRH receptor signaling, leading to activation of extracellular signal-regulated kinase (ERK), c-Jun N-terminal kinase (JNK), p38 mitogen-activated protein kinase (MAPK), and big MAPK (BMK). MEK, MAPK extracellular signal-regulated kinase kinase; MEKK, MEK kinase; MKK, MAP kinase kinase; PKA, protein kinase A.

activity.[237,261–264] Phospholipase D and phospholipase A2 are sequentially activated by GnRH receptor signaling,[265–268] probably via PKC.[265,269] Another major effect of GnRH binding to its receptor is the activation of L-type voltage-operated $Ca^{2+}$ channels, causing the influx of EC $Ca^{2+}$ required to recharge IC stores and for sustained LH release.[270–273]

GnRH receptor activation triggers several mitogen-activated protein kinase (MAPK) cascades that mediate gene induction (see Fig. 140-6).[264,274–276] Activation of the MAPK cascade by GnRH involves PKC-dependent and PKC-independent pathways.[276] Four kinase cascades are activated by GnRH receptor signaling, leading to activation of EC signal-regulated kinase (ERK),[241,244,274,277–280] c-Jun N-terminal kinase,[281–284] p38 MAPK,[279] and big MAPK.[276]

Activation of ERK occurs primarily via PKC in αT3-1 cells, with some contribution through dynamin.[282,283] In LβT2 cells, blocking conventional PKC does not inhibit completely the phosphorylation of ERK by GnRH treatment.[258] The mode of signaling from the GnRH receptor to ERK remains controversial. It has been reported that the GnRH receptor transactivates the epidermal growth factor receptor, which then activates ERK signaling pathways in αT3-1 cells.[240] However, another group found that ERK activation by GnRH occurs independently of the epidermal growth factor receptor in αT3-1 cells.[282] Calcium influx through L-type calcium channels depends on PKC activation and appears to facilitate

ERK activation in αT3-1 cells and in primary pituitary cultures.[283,285]

Although the activation of ERK by GnRH in αT3-1 cells requires influx of calcium through L-type calcium channels, c-Jun N-terminal kinase activation is dependent only on mobilization of calcium from IC stores.[283] One study of αT3-1 cells reported that c-Jun N-terminal kinase activation is PKC dependent,[284] whereas other groups studying αT3-1 cells[283] and LβT2 cells[281] have found that c-Jun N-terminal kinase activation occurs independently of PKC. Induction of p38 MAPK has also been reported to be PKC dependent.[279] The activated MAPKs translocate to the nucleus where they regulate transcription factors, such as the Ets family proteins, thereby modulating the promoter activity of various genes.[275,286–292]

## NATURALLY OCCURRING MUTATIONS OF THE GONADOTROPIN-RELEASING HORMONE RECEPTOR

A functioning GnRH receptor is crucial for both normal pubertal development and reproductive function. Loss-of-function mutations of the GnRH receptor gene have been described as a cause of hypogonadotropic hypogonadism. Patients carrying GnRH receptor mutations have normal olfaction and exhibit a wide spectrum of phenotypes, ranging from normal testicular volumes and spermatogenesis[226,293] to complete lack of pubertal development.[104,294,295] The majority of described patients are compound heterozygotes for two different GnRH receptor mutations. Homozygous mutations identified thus far have been associated with complete hypogonadotropic hypogonadism[294–296] except for Gln106Arg, which was reported as a homozygous mutation in a woman with partial hypogonadotropic hypogonadism who subsequently conceived spontaneously.[297]

Functional characterization of these mutations in vitro distinguishes between substitutions with complete or partial loss of function. However, the same mutations of the GnRH receptor may cause variable degrees of hypogonadism in affected kindred.[217] Moreover, patients with GnRH receptor mutations who are treated with pulsatile GnRH may display a rightward shift of the dose-response curves of their gonadotropin responses to pulsatile GnRH and differential sensitivities of LH and FSH to GnRH.[298] Also, the varied phenotypes observed among patients harboring these mutations may be due to differential stimulation of gonadotropin subunit gene expression by the mutant receptor and effects on signal transduction pathways.[299]

## PHYSIOLOGY OF GONADOTROPINS

The gonadotropins LH, FSH, and hCG are essential for human reproduction. The gonadotropins regulate the synthesis of sex steroids and the final steps in gametogenesis. FSH is required for development of ovarian follicles and recruitment of dominant follicles. In males, FSH is important in spermatogenesis, as demonstrated by the small testes and lower numbers of sperm in FSH-β knockout mice compared with wild-type littermate controls.[300] Although FSH is not necessary for resumption of meiosis, lack of FSH results in infertility.[300] Insufficient FSH stimulation causes follicles to undergo atresia.[301] FSH also promotes formation of the antrum and induces granulosa cell LH receptors[302] in preparation for the mid-cycle LH surge.

Major functions of LH include the induction of ovulation, luteinization of graafian follicles, and stimulation of steroidogenesis in the theca cells of the follicle and the Leydig cells of the testis. LH acts on Leydig cells to stimulate androgen synthesis required for spermatogenesis[303] and for development of male secondary sexual characteristics. As FSH promotes the aromatization of androgens to estradiol, LH and FSH have synergistic effects on ovarian estradiol synthesis.[302] hCG is essential during early pregnancy as it supports luteal progesterone synthesis. Assays of hCG have been used to detect early fetal loss,[304] ectopic pregnancy,[305] Down syndrome,[306] and gonadotropin-secreting tumors.[307]

### HORMONE STRUCTURE

FSH, LH, and hCG are structurally related. Each gonadotropin is a heterodimer, and both LH and FSH are composed of two noncovalently bound peptide subunits termed α and β. The α subunits of LH, FSH, and hCG, as well as thyroid-stimulating hormone, are identical in polypeptide structure. The β subunit of each hormone has a unique amino acid sequence and confers its specific biologic activity. Each subunit is cysteine-rich with multiple disulfide linkages and contains multiple carbohydrate residues that influence hormone biologic activity and metabolism. The common α subunit contains 92 amino acids. The β subunits of FSH, LH, and hCG contain 117, 121, and 145 amino acids, respectively.[308–311]

### GONADOTROPIN SYNTHESIS AND SECRETION

The human α subunit gene is located on the short arm of chromosome 6. The human FSH-β subunit gene is located on the short arm of chromosome 11 and encodes a 117-amino acid peptide.[312] The human LH and hCG β subunit genes are located on chromosome 19q13.3, which contains a cluster of seven β subunit–like genes,[311] of which only the LH and hCG β subunit genes give rise to two distinct and functional mRNA species. The LH-β subunit mRNA encodes a 145-amino acid precursor protein that is then cleaved to produce a 24-amino acid leader sequence and a 121-amino acid biologically active peptide. The βhCG subunit mRNA also encodes a 145-amino acid protein, which does not undergo posttranslational processing and functions as the biologically active βhCG subunit. The βhCG subunit contains an additional 24-amino acid extension at the C terminus and four serine O-linked oligosaccharide units in this carboxyterminal peptide. The carboxyterminal peptide influences the IC processing of the subunit and is important for maintaining the biologic half-life of hCG.[308–311,313,314] The amino acid sequences of the human LH and hCG β subunits share 82% homology. When associated with the α subunit, these two β subunits activate the same receptor.[308,309,311,314]

The mechanisms governing the formation and combination of the α and β subunits of FSH and LH are not well understood. Because the pituitary contains excess α subunit mRNA and levels of free α subunit are readily detected in serum, it appears that the free β subunit, present at relatively low levels in the pituitary and rarely found in serum or urine,[315] may be the rate-limiting factor in the synthesis of these glycoprotein hormones.

LH and FSH are produced by the anterior pituitary, whereas hCG is synthesized by the placenta. Upon binding of GnRH to its receptor, the biosynthesis of the gonadotropins proceeds by transcription of the subunit genes, translation of the subunit mRNAs, posttranslational modifications of the precursor polypeptides, subunit folding and combination, mature hormone packaging, and hormone secretion. Serum levels of gonadotropins are proportional to their secretion rates and serum half-lives, which are regulated by the number of oligosaccharide moieties. The higher the content of carbohydrate residues, especially sialic acid residues, the lower the rate of metabolism and the higher the serum half-life and biologic activity.[316–319] Hormones with oligosaccharides terminating in galactose or galactosamine or that are sulfated have shorter half-lives[320] and are excreted through liver parenchymal cell receptors.[317] The higher content of sialic acid in FSH compared with LH is responsible for the slower clearance of FSH from the circulation; the half-life of FSH ranges from 1 to 4 hours.[321–323] LH has the shortest half-life, generally considered to be less than 20 minutes,[321] but a range of 2 to 50 minutes has been reported.[320,324] Due to differences in the carboxyterminal peptide and high sialylation, hCG has the longest half-life (24 hours).[313]

## CONCLUSION

The creation of immortalized hypothalamic and gonadotrope cell lines, the cloning of hormone receptors, and in vivo disease models have advanced significantly our understanding of the regulation of GnRH and gonadotropins and of hormone-receptor interactions. Further improvements in our knowledge of this field may lead to the development of novel methods of contraception and treatments for infertility, cancers, and disorders of puberty.

### Acknowledgments
The authors acknowledge Dr. Robert P. Millar and Dr. William R. Moyle for the use of some of the materials in this chapter. Dr. Millar and Dr. Moyle were the authors of the corresponding chapters in the fourth edition of this textbook.

## REFERENCES

1. Fink G: Gonadotropin secretion and its control. In Knobil E, Neill J (eds): The Physiology of Reproduction. New York, Raven Press, 1988, pp 1349–1377.
2. Seeburg PH, Mason AJ, Stewart TA, et al: The mammalian GnRH gene and its pivotal role in reproduction. Recent Prog Horm Res 43:69–98, 1987.
3. Crowley WF Jr, McArthur JW: Simulation of the normal menstrual cycle in Kallmann's syndrome by pulsatile administration of luteinizing hormone-releasing hormone (LHRH). J Clin Endocrinol Metab 51:173–175, 1980.
4. Conn PM, Crowley WF Jr: Gonadotropin-releasing hormone and its analogs. Annu Rev Med 45:391–405, 1994.
5. Barbieri RL: Clinical applications of GnRH and its analogues. Trends Endocrinol Metab 3:30–34, 1992.
6. Moghissi KS: Clinical applications of gonadotropin-releasing hormones in reproductive disorders. Endocrinol Metab Clin North Am 21:125–140, 1992.
7. Schwanzel-Fukuda M, Pfaff DW: Origin of luteinizing hormone-releasing hormone neurons. Nature 338:161–164, 1989.
8. Ronnekleiv OK, Resko JA: Ontogeny of gonadotropin-releasing hormone-containing neurons in early fetal development of rhesus macaques. Endocrinology 126:498–511, 1990.
9. Whitlock KE, Wolf CD, Boyce ML: Gonadotropin-releasing hormone (GnRH) cells arise from cranial neural crest and adenohypophyseal regions of the neural plate in the zebrafish, Danio rerio. Dev Biol 257:140–152, 2003.
10. Schwanzel-Fukuda M, Bick D, Pfaff DW: Luteinizing hormone-releasing hormone (LHRH) expressing cells do not migrate normally in an inherited hypogonadal (Kallmann syndrome). Mol Brain Res 6:311–326, 1989.
11. Legouis R, Hardelin JP, Levilliers J, et al: The candidate gene for the X-linked Kallmann syndrome encodes a protein related to adhesion molecules. Cell 67:423–435, 1991.
12. Franco B, Guioli S, Pragliola A, et al: A gene deleted in Kallmann's syndrome shares homology with neural cell adhesion and axonal path-finding molecules. Nature 353:529–536, 1991.
13. Seminara SB, Hayes FJ, Crowley WF Jr: Gonadotropin-releasing hormone deficiency in the human (idiopathic hypogonadotropic hypogonadism and Kallmann's syndrome): Pathophysiological and genetic considerations. Endocr Rev 19:521–539, 1998.
14. Schwanzel-Fukuda M, Jorgenson KL, Bergen HT, et al: Biology of normal luteinizing hormone-releasing hormone neurons during and after their migration from olfactory placode. Endocr Rev 13:623–634, 1992.

15. Dode C, Levilliers J, Dupont JM, et al: Loss-of-function mutations in FGFR1 cause autosomal dominant Kallmann syndrome. Nat Genet 33:463–465, 2003.
16. Soussi-Yanicostas N, Hardelin JP, Arroyo-Jimenez MM, et al: Initial characterization of anosmin-1, a putative extracellular matrix protein synthesized by definite neuronal cell populations in the central nervous system. J Cell Sci 109:1749–1757, 1996.
17. Pellegrini L: Role of heparan sulfate in fibroblast growth factor signalling: A structural view. Curr Opin Struct Biol 11:629–634, 2001.
18. Sealfon SC, Weinstein H, Millar RP: Molecular mechanisms of ligand interaction with the gonadotropin-releasing hormone receptor. Endocr Rev 18:180–205, 1997.
19. Karten MJ, Rivier JE: Gonadotropin-releasing hormone analog design. Structure-function studies toward the development of agonists and antagonists: Rationale and perspective. Endocr Rev 7:44–66, 1986.
20. Maliekal J, Jackson GE, Flanagan CA, et al: Solution conformations of gonadotropin-releasing hormone (GnRH) and [Gln8] GnRH. S Afr Med J Chem 50:217–219, 1997.
21. Millar RP, Troskie B, Sun YM, et al: Plasticity in the structural and functional evolution of GnRH: A peptide for all seasons. Presented at the 13th International Congress of Comparative Endocrinology, Yokohama, Japan, 1997, pp 15–27.
22. Millar RP, Flanagan CA, Milton RC, et al: Chimeric analogues of vertebrate gonadotropin-releasing hormones comprising substitutions of the variant amino acids in positions 5, 7, and 8. Characterization of requirements for receptor binding and gonadotropin release in mammalian and avian pituitary gonadotropes. J Biol Chem 264:21007–21013, 1989.
23. Illing N, Troskie BE, Nahorniak CS, et al: Two gonadotropin-releasing hormone receptor subtypes with distinct ligand selectivity and differential distribution in brain and pituitary in the goldfish (Carassius auratus). Proc Natl Acad Sci U S A 96:2256–2531, 1999.
24. King JA, Millar RP: Evolutionary aspects of gonadotropin-releasing hormone and its receptor. Cell Mol Neurobiol 15:5–23, 1995.
25. Milton RC, King JA, Badminton MN, et al: Comparative structure activity studies of mammalian [Arg8]LHRH and chicken [Gln8]LHRH by fluorimetric titration. Biochem Biophys Res Commun 111:1082–1088, 1983.
26. Guarnieri F, Weinstein H: Conformational memories and the exploration of biologically relevant peptide conformations: An illustration for the gonadotropin-releasing hormone. J Am Chem Soc 118:5580–5589, 1996.

27. Handelsman DJ, Swerdloff RS: Pharmacokinetics of gonadotropin-releasing hormone and its analogs. Endocr Rev 7:95–105, 1986.
28. Flanagan CA, Becker II, Davidson JS, et al: Glutamate 301 of the mouse gonadotropin-releasing hormone receptor confers specificity for arginine8 of mammalian gonadotropin-releasing hormone. J Biol Chem 269:22636–22641, 1994.
29. Cetel NS, Rivier JE, Vale WW, et al: The dynamics of gonadotropin inhibition in women induced by an antagonistic analog of gonadotropin-releasing hormone. J Clin Endocrinol Metab 57:62–65, 1983.
30. King JA, Millar RP: Heterogeneity of vertebrate luteinizing hormone-releasing hormone. Science 206:67–69, 1979.
31. King JA, Millar RP: Comparative aspects of luteinizing hormone-releasing hormone structure and function in vertebrate phylogeny. Endocrinology 106:707–717, 1980.
32. King JA, Millar RP: Evolution of gonadotropin-releasing hormone. Trends Endocrinol Metab 3:339–346, 1992.
33. Sherwood N: The GnRH family of peptides. Trends Neurosci 10:129–132, 1987.
34. Sherwood NM, Lovejoy DA, Coe IR: Origin of mammalian gonadotropin-releasing hormones. Endocr Rev 14:241–254, 1993.
35. Dubois EA, Zandbergen MA, Peute J, et al: Evolutionary development of three gonadotropin-releasing hormone (GnRH) systems in vertebrates. Brain Res Bull 57:413–418, 2002.
36. Casan EM, Raga F, Polan ML: GnRH mRNA and protein expression in human preimplantation embryos. Mol Hum Reprod 5:234–239, 1999.
37. Chegini N, Rong H, Dou Q, et al: Gonadotropin-releasing hormone (GnRH) and GnRH receptor gene expression in human myometrium and leiomyomata and the direct action of GnRH analogs on myometrial smooth muscle cells and interaction with ovarian steroids in vitro. J Clin Endocrinol Metab 81:3215–3221, 1996.
38. Chatzaki E, Bax CM, Eidne KA, et al: The expression of gonadotropin-releasing hormone and its receptor in endometrial cancer, and its relevance as an autocrine growth factor. Cancer Res 56:2059–2065, 1996.
39. Bahk JY, Hyun JS, Chung SH, et al: Stage specific identification of the expression of GnRH mRNA and localization of the GnRH receptor in mature rat and adult human testis. J Urol 154:1958–1961, 1995.
40. Hsueh AJ, Schaeffer JM: Gonadotropin-releasing hormone as a paracrine hormone and neurotransmitter in extra-pituitary sites. J Steroid Biochem 23:757–764, 1985.

41. Jennes L, Conn PM: Gonadotropin-releasing hormone and its receptors in rat brain. Front Neuroendocrinol 15:51–77, 1994.

42. Choi KC, Auersperg N, Leung PC: Expression and antiproliferative effect of a second form of gonadotropin-releasing hormone in normal and neoplastic ovarian surface epithelial cells. J Clin Endocrinol Metab 86:5075–5078, 2001.

43. White RB, Eisen JA, Kasten JL, et al: Second gene for gonadotropin-releasing hormone in humans. Proc Natl Acad Sci U S A 95:305–309, 1998.

44. Miyamoto K, Hasegawa Y, Nomura M, et al: Identification of the second gonadotropin-releasing hormone in chicken hypothalamus: evidence that gonadotropin secretion is probably controlled by two distinct gonadotropin-releasing hormone in avian species. Proc Natl Acad Sci U S A 81:3874–3878, 1984.

45. Millar RP: GnRH II and type II GnRH receptors. Trends Endocrinol Metab 14:35–43, 2003.

46. Temple JL, Millar RP, Rissman EF: An evolutionarily conserved form of gonadotropin-releasing hormone coordinates energy and reproductive behavior. Endocrinology 144:13–19, 2003.

47. Grundker C, Gunthert AR, Millar RP, et al: Expression of gonadotropin-releasing hormone II (GnRH-II) receptor in human endometrial and ovarian cancer cells and effects of GnRH-II on tumor cell proliferation. J Clin Endocrinol Metab 87:1427–1430, 2002.

48. Chou CS, Zhu H, MacCalman CD, et al: Regulatory effects of gonadotropin-releasing hormone (GnRH) I and GnRH II on the levels of matrix metalloproteinase (MMP)-2, MMP-9, and tissue inhibitor of metalloproteinases-1 in primary cultures of human extravillous cytotrophoblasts. J Clin Endocrinol Metab 88:4781–4790, 2003.

49. Chen A, Ganor Y, Rahimipour S, et al: The neuropeptides GnRH-II and GnRH-I are produced by human T cells and trigger laminin receptor gene expression, adhesion, chemotaxis and homing to specific organs. Nat Med 8:1421–1426, 2002.

50. Stopa EG, Sower SA, Svendsen CN, et al: Polygenic expression of gonadotropin-releasing hormone (GnRH) in human? Peptides 9:419–423, 1988.

51. Dees WL, Hiney JK, Sower SA, et al: Localization of immunoreactive lamprey gonadotropin-releasing hormone in the rat brain. Peptides 20:1503–1511, 1999.

52. Hiney JK, Sower SA, Yu WH, et al: Gonadotropin-releasing hormone neurons in the preoptic-hypothalamic region of the rat contain lamprey gonadotropin-releasing hormone III, mammalian luteinizing hormone-releasing hormone, or both peptides. Proc Natl Acad Sci U S A 99:2386–2391, 2002.

53. Radovick S, Wondisford FE, Nakayama Y, et al: Isolation and characterization of the human gonadotropin-releasing hormone gene in the hypothalamus and placenta. Mol Endocrinol 4:476–480, 1990.

54. Yang-Feng TL, Seeburg PH, Francke U: Human luteinizing hormone-releasing hormone gene (LHRH) is located on short arm of chromosome 8 (region 8p11.2—p21). Somat Cell Mol Genet 12:95–100, 1986.

55. Adelman JP, Mason AJ, Hayflick JS, et al: Isolation of the gene and hypothalamic cDNA for the common precursor of gonadotropin-releasing hormone and prolactin release-inhibiting factor in human and rat. Proc Natl Acad Sci U S A 83:179–183, 1986.

56. Seeburg PH, Adelman JP: Characterization of cDNA for precursor of human luteinizing hormone releasing hormone. Nature 311:666–668, 1984.

57. Chavali GB, Nagpal S, Majumdar SS, et al: Helix-loop-helix motif in GnRH associated peptide is critical for negative regulation of prolactin secretion. J Mol Biol 272:731–740, 1997.

58. Nikolics K, Mason AJ, Szonyi E, et al: A prolactin-inhibitory factor within the precursor for human gonadotropin-releasing hormone. Nature 316:511–517, 1985.

59. Knobil E: The neuroendocrine control of the menstrual cycle. Recent Prog Horm Res 36:53–88, 1980.

60. Knobil E: The electrophysiology of the GnRH pulse generator. J Steroid Biochem 33:669–671, 1989.

61. Clarke IJ, Cummins JT: The temporal relationship between gonadotropin releasing hormone (GnRH) and luteinizing hormone (LH) secretion in ovariectomized ewes. Endocrinology 111:1737–1739, 1982.

62. Minami S, Frautschy SA, Plotsky PM, et al: Facilitatory role of neuropeptide Y on the onset of puberty: effect of immunoneutralization of neuropeptide Y on the release of luteinizing hormone and luteinizing-hormone-releasing hormone. Neuroendocrinology 52:112–115, 1990.

63. Rasmussen DD, Gambacciani M, Swartz W, et al: Pulsatile gonadotropin-releasing hormone release from the human mediobasal hypothalamus in vitro: Opiate receptor-mediated suppression. Neuroendocrinology 49:150–156, 1989.

64. Mellon PL, Windle JJ, Goldsmith PC, et al: Immortalization of hypothalamic GnRH neurons by genetically targeted tumorigenesis. Neuron 5:1–10, 1990.

65. de la Iglesia HO, Blaustein JD, Bittman EL: The suprachiasmatic area in the female hamster projects to neurons containing estrogen receptors and GnRH. Neuroreport 6:1715–1722, 1995.

66. Chappell PE, White RS, Mellon PL: Circadian gene expression regulates pulsatile gonadotropin-releasing hormone (GnRH) secretory patterns in the hypothalamic GnRH-secreting GT1-7 cell line. J Neurosci 23:11202–11213, 2003.

67. Clayton R: Gonadotropin-releasing hormone: Its actions and receptors. Endocr Rev 120:11–19, 1989.

68. Conn P: The molecular basis of gonadotropin-releasing hormone action. Endocr Rev 7:3–10, 1986.

69. Savoy-Moore RT, Schwartz NB, Duncan JA, et al: Pituitary gonadotropin releasing hormone receptors during the estrous cycle. Science 209:942–945, 1980.

70. Bauer-Dantoin A, Weiss J, Jameson J: Roles of estrogen, progesterone, and gonadotropin-releasing hormone (GnRH) in the control of pituitary GnRH receptor gene expression at the time of the preovulatory gonadotropin surges. Endocrinology 136:1014–1019, 1995.

71. Clayton RN, Catt KJ: Gonadotropin-releasing hormone receptors—Characterization, physiological regulation, and relationship to reproductive function. Endocr Rev 2:186–209, 1981.

72. Kaiser U, Jakubowiak A, Steinberger A: Regulation of rat pituitary gonadotropin-releasing hormone receptor mRNA levels in vivo and in vitro. Endocrinology 133:931–934, 1993.

73. Cornea A, Conn PM: Measurement of changes in fluorescence resonance energy transfer between gonadotropin-releasing hormone receptors in response to agonists. Methods 27:333–339, 2002.

74. Hazum E, Conn PM: Molecular mechanism of gonadotropin releasing hormone (GnRH) action. I. The GnRH receptor. Endocr Rev 9:379–386, 1988.

75. Lemay A, Maheux R, Faure N, et al: Reversible hypogonadism induced by a luteinizing hormone-releasing hormone (LHRH) agonist (buserelin) as a new therapeutic approach for endometriosis. Fertil Steril 41:863–871, 1984.

76. Carr BR, Breslau NA, Givens C, et al: Oral contraceptive pills, gonadotropin-releasing hormone agonists, or use in combination for treatment of hirsutism: A clinical research center study. J Clin Endocrinol Metab 80:1169–1178, 1995.

77. Hoffman AR, Crowley WF Jr: Induction of puberty in men by long-term pulsatile administration of low-dose gonadotropin-releasing hormone. N Engl J Med 307:1237–1241, 1982.

78. Homburg R, Eshel A, Armar NA, et al: One hundred pregnancies after treatment with pulsatile luteinising hormone releasing hormone to induce ovulation. Br Med J 298:809–812, 1989.

79. Wong SL, Lau DT, Baughman SA, et al: Pharmacokinetics and pharmacodynamics of a novel depot formulation of abarelix, a gonadotropin-releasing hormone (GnRH) antagonist, in healthy men ages 50 to 75. J Clin Pharmacol 44:495–502, 2004.

80. Andreyko JL, Monroe SE, Marshall LA, et al: Concordant suppression of serum immunoreactive luteinizing hormone (LH), follicle-stimulating hormone, alpha subunit, bioactive LH, and testosterone in postmenopausal women by a potent gonadotropin releasing hormone antagonist (detirelix). J Clin Endocrinol Metab 74:399–405, 1992.

81. Pavlou SN, Wakefield G, Schlechter NL, et al: Mode of suppression of pituitary and gonadal function after acute or prolonged administration of a luteinizing hormone-releasing hormone antagonist in normal men. J Clin Endocrinol Metab 68:446–454, 1989.

82. Pavlou SN, Wakefield GB, Island DP, et al: Suppression of pituitary-gonadal function by a potent new luteinizing hormone-releasing hormone antagonist in normal men. J Clin Endocrinol Metab 64:931–936, 1987.

83. Pavlou SN, Debold CR, Island DP, et al: Single subcutaneous doses of a luteinizing hormone-releasing hormone antagonist suppress serum gonadotropin and testosterone levels in normal men. J Clin Endocrinol Metab 63:303–308. Erratum in J Clin Endocrinol Metab 63:940, 1986.

84. Fujimoto VY, Monroe SE, Nelson LR, et al: Dose-related suppression of serum luteinizing hormone in women by a potent new gonadotropin-releasing hormone antagonist (Ganirelix) administered by intranasal spray. Fertil Steril 67:469–473, 1997.

85. Behre HM, Kliesch S, Puhse G, et al: High loading and low maintenance doses of a gonadotropin-releasing hormone antagonist effectively suppress serum luteinizing hormone, follicle-stimulating hormone, and testosterone in normal men. J Clin Endocrinol Metab 82:1403–1408, 1997.

86. Childs GV, Hyde C, Naor Z, et al: Heterogeneous luteinizing hormone and follicle-stimulating hormone storage patterns in subtypes of gonadotropes separated by centrifugal elutriation. Endocrinology 113:2120–2128, 1983.

87. Childs GV: Division of labor among gonadotropes. Vitam Horm 50:215–286, 1995.

88. Haisenleder DJ, Dalkin AC, Ortolano GA, et al: A pulsatile gonadotropin-releasing hormone stimulus is required to increase transcription of the gonadotropin subunit genes: Evidence for differential regulation of transcription by pulse frequency in vivo. Endocrinology 128:509–517, 1991.

89. Filicori M, Santoro N, Merriam GR, et al: Characterization of the physiological pattern of episodic gonadotropin secretion throughout the human menstrual cycle. J Clin Endocrinol Metab 62:1136–1144, 1986.

90. Wildt L, Hausler A, Marshall G, et al: Frequency and amplitude of gonadotropin-releasing hormone stimulation and gonadotropin secretion in the rhesus monkey. Endocrinology 109:376–385, 1981.

91. Kaiser UB, Jakubowiak A, Steinberger A, et al: Differential effects of gonadotropin-releasing hormone (GnRH) pulse frequency on gonadotropin subunit and GnRH receptor messenger ribonucleic acid levels in vitro. Endocrinology 138:1224–1231, 1997.

92. Dalkin AC, Haisenleder DJ, Ortolano GA, et al: The frequency of gonadotropin-releasing-hormone stimulation differentially regulates gonadotropin subunit messenger ribonucleic acid expression. Endocrinology 125:917–924, 1989.

93. Brown P, McNeilly AS: Transcriptional regulation of pituitary gonadotrophin subunit genes. Rev Reprod 4:117–124, 1999.

94. Maurer JA, Wray S: Luteinizing hormone-releasing hormone (LHRH) neurons maintained in hypothalamic slice explant cultures exhibit a rapid LHRH mRNA turnover rate. J Neurosci 17:9481–9491, 1997.

95. Tobet SA, Hanna IK, Schwarting GA: Migration of neurons containing gonadotropin releasing hormone (GnRH) in slices from embryonic nasal compartment and forebrain. Brain Res Dev Brain Res 97:287–292, 1996.

96. Levine JE, Chappell P, Besecke LM, et al: Amplitude and frequency modulation of pulsatile luteinizing hormone-releasing hormone release. Cell Mol Neurobiol 15:117–139, 1995.

97. Barrell GK, Moenter SM, Caraty A, et al: Seasonal changes of gonadotropin-releasing hormone secretion in the ewe. Biol Reprod 46:1130–1135, 1992.

98. Gore AC, Terasawa E: A study of the hypothalamic pulse-generating mechanism responsible for LH release: Electrical stimulation of the medial basal hypothalamus in the ovariectomized guinea pig. Brain Res Bull 560:268–275, 1991.

99. Negro-Vilar A, Advis JP, Ojeda SR, et al: Pulsatile luteinizing hormone (LH) patterns in ovariectomized rats: Involvement of norepinephrine and dopamine in the release of LH-releasing hormone and LH. Endocrinology 111:932–938, 1982.

100. Wetsel WC, Valenca MM, Merchenthaler I, et al: Intrinsic pulsatile secretory activity of immortalized luteinizing hormone-releasing hormone-secreting neurons. Proc Natl Acad Sci U S A 89:4149–4153, 1992.

101. Wetsel WC, Liposits Z, Seidah NG, et al: Expression of candidate pro-GnRH processing enzymes in rat hypothalamus and an immortalized hypothalamic neuronal cell line. Neuroendocrinology 62:166–177, 1995.

102. Silverman AJ, Roberts JL, Dong KW, et al: Intrahypothalamic injection of a cell line secreting gonadotropin-releasing hormone results in cellular differentiation and reversal of hypogonadism in mutant mice. Proc

Natl Acad Sci U S A 89:10668–10672, 1992.

103. Cesnjaj M, Krsmanovic LZ, Catt KJ, et al: Autocrine induction of c-fos expression in GT1 neuronal cells by gonadotropin-releasing hormone. Endocrinology 133:3042–3045, 1993.

104. Padmanabhan V, Evans NP, Dahl GE, et al: Evidence for short or ultrashort loop negative feedback of gonadotropin-releasing hormone secretion. Neuroendocrinology 62:248–258, 1995.

105. Martinez-Fuentes AJ, Hu L, Krsmanovic LZ, et al: Gonadotropin-releasing hormone (GnRH) receptor expression and membrane signaling in early embryonic GnRH neurons: Role in pulsatile neurosecretion. Mol Endocrinol 18:1808–1817, 2004.

106. Herbison AE: Noradrenergic regulation of cyclic GnRH secretion. Rev Reprod 2:1–6, 1997.

107. Findell PR, Wong KH, Jackman JK, et al: Beta 1-adrenergic and dopamine (D1)-receptors coupled to adenylyl cyclase activation in GT1 gonadotropin-releasing hormone neurosecretory cells. Endocrinology 132:682–688, 1993.

108. Martinez de la Escalera G, Gallo F, Choi AL, et al: Dopaminergic regulation of the GT1 gonadotropin-releasing hormone (GnRH) neuronal cell lines: Stimulation of GnRH release via D1-receptors positively coupled to adenylate cyclase. Endocrinology 131:2965–2971, 1992.

109. Uemura T, Nishimura J, Yamaguchi H, et al: Effects of noradrenaline on GnRH-secreting immortalized hypothalamic (GT1-7) neurons. Endocr J 44:73–78, 1997.

110. Kaufman JM, Kesner JS, Wilson RC, et al: Electrophysiological manifestation of luteinizing hormone-releasing hormone pulse generator activity in the rhesus monkey: Influence of alpha-adrenergic and dopaminergic blocking agents. Endocrinology 116:1327–1333, 1985.

111. Gearing M, Terasawa E: The alpha-1-adrenergic neuronal system is involved in the pulsatile release of luteinizing hormone-releasing hormone in the ovariectomized female rhesus monkey. Neuroendocrinology 53:373–381, 1991.

112. Pehrson JJ, Jaffee WL, Vaitukaitis JL: Effect of dopamine on gonadotropin-releasing hormone-induced gonadotropin secretion in postmenopausal women. J Clin Endocrinol Metab 56:889–892, 1983.

113. Lachelin GC, Leblanc H, Yen SS: The inhibitory effect of dopamine agonists on LH release in women. J Clin Endocrinol Metab 44:728–732, 1977.

114. Leblanc H, Lachelin GC, Abu-Fadil S, et al: Effects of dopamine infusion on pituitary hormone secretion in humans. J Clin Endocrinol Metab 43:668–674, 1976.

115. Brann DW, Mahesh VB: Excitatory amino acids: evidence for a role in the control of reproduction and anterior pituitary hormone secretion. Endocr Rev 18:678–700, 1997.

116. Weisskopf MG, Zalutsky RA, Nicoll RA: The opioid peptide dynorphin mediates heterosynaptic depression of hippocampal mossy fibre synapses and modulates long-term potentiation. Nature 365:188, 1993.

117. Potashner SJ: Baclofen: Effects on amino acid release and metabolism in slices of guinea pig cerebral cortex. J Neurochem 32:103–109, 1979.

118. Stojilkovic SS, Krsmanovic LZ, Spergel D, et al: Gonadotropin-releasing hormone neurons. Intrinsic pulsatility and receptor-mediated regulation. Trends Endocrinol Metab 5:201–209, 1994.

119. Moretto M, Lopez FJ, Negro-Vilar A: Nitric oxide regulates luteinizing hormone-releasing hormone secretion. Endocrinology 133:2399–2402, 1993.

120. Urbanski HF, Ojeda SR: Activation of luteinizing hormone-releasing hormone release advances the onset of female puberty. Neuroendocrinology 46:273–276, 1987.

121. DeFazio RA, Heger S, Ojeda SR, et al: Activation of A-type gamma-aminobutyric acid receptors excites gonadotropin-releasing hormone neurons. Mol Endocrinol 16:2872–2891, 2002.

122. Han SK, Todman MG, Herbison AE: Endogenous GABA release inhibits the firing of adult gonadotropin-releasing hormone neurons. Endocrinology 145:495–499, 2004.

123. Grosser PM, O'Byrne KT, Williams CL, et al: Effects of naloxone on estrogen-induced changes in hypothalamic gonadotropin-releasing hormone pulse generator activity in the rhesus monkey. Neuroendocrinology 57:115–119, 1993.

124. Kalra SP, Kalra PS: Opioid-adrenergic-steroid connection in regulation of luteinizing hormone secretion in the rat. Neuroendocrinology 38:418–426, 1984.

125. Gindoff P, Ferin M: Brain opioid peptides and menstrual cyclicity. Semin Reprod Endocrinol 5:125–133, 1987.

126. Nazian SJ, Landon CS, Muffly KE, et al: Opioid inhibition of adrenergic and dopaminergic but not serotonergic stimulation of luteinizing hormone releasing hormone release from immortalized hypothalamic neurons. Mol Cell Neurosci 5:642–648, 1994.

127. Van Vugt DA, Webb MY, Reid RL: Comparison of the duration of action of nalmefene and naloxone on the hypothalamic-pituitary axis of the rhesus monkey. Neuroendocrinology 49:275–280, 1989.

128. Williams CL, Nishihara M, Thalabard JC, et al: Duration and frequency of multiunit electrical activity associated with the hypothalamic gonadotropin releasing hormone pulse generator in the rhesus monkey: Differential effects of morphine. Neuroendocrinology 52:225–228, 1990.

129. Ferin M, Wehrenberg WB, Lam NY, et al: Effects and site of action of morphine on gonadotropin secretion in the female rhesus monkey. Endocrinology 111:1652–1656, 1982.

130. Fischer UG, Wood SH, Bruhn J, et al: Effect of human corticotropin-releasing hormone on gonadotropin secretion in cycling and postmenopausal women. Fertil Steril 58:1108–1112, 1992.

131. Olson BR, Scott DC, Wetsel WC, et al: Effects of insulin-like growth factors I and II and insulin on the immortalized hypothalamic GTI-7 cell line. Neuroendocrinology 62:155–165, 1995.

132. Anderson RA, Zwain IH, Arroyo A, et al: The insulin-like growth factor system in the GT1-7 GnRH neuronal cell line. Neuroendocrinology 70:353–359, 1999.

133. Longo KM, Sun Y, Gore AC: Insulin-like growth factor-I effects on gonadotropin-releasing hormone biosynthesis in GT1-7 cells. Endocrinology 139:1125–1132, 1998.

134. Gallo F, Morale MC, Tirolo C, et al: Basic fibroblast growth factor priming increases the responsiveness of immortalized hypothalamic luteinizing hormone releasing hormone neurones to neurotrophic factors. J Neuroendocrinol 12:941–959, 2000.

135. Tsai PS, Werner S, Weiner RI: Basic fibroblast growth factor is a neurotropic factor in GT1 gonadotropin-releasing hormone neuronal cell lines. Endocrinology 136:3831–3838, 1995.

136. Nobels F, Dewailly D: Puberty and polycystic ovarian syndrome: The insulin/insulin-like growth factor I hypothesis. Fertil Steril 58:655–666, 1992.

137. Barreca A, Del Monte P, Ponzani P, et al: Intrafollicular insulin-like growth factor-II levels in normally ovulating women and in patients with polycystic ovary syndrome. Fertil Steril 65:739–745, 1996.

138. Thierry van Dessel HJ, Lee PD, Faessen G, et al: Elevated serum levels of free insulin-like growth factor I in polycystic ovary syndrome. J Clin Endocrinol Metab 84:3030–3035, 1999.

139. Woller MJ, Terasawa E: Estradiol enhances the action of neuropeptide Y on in vivo luteinizing hormone-releasing hormone release in the ovariectomized rhesus monkey. Neuroendocrinology 56:921–925, 1992.

140. Brann DW, Chorich LP, Mahesh VB: Effect of progesterone on galanin mRNA levels in the hypothalamus and the pituitary: Correlation with the gonadotropin surge. Neuroendocrinology 58:531–538, 1993.

141. Reynoso R, Ponzo OJ, Szwarcfarb B, et al: Effect of leptin on hypothalamic release of GnRH and neurotransmitter amino acids during sexual maturation in female rats. Exp Clin Endocrinol Diabetes 111:274–277, 2003.

142. Farooqi IS, Jebb SA, Langmack G, et al: Effects of recombinant leptin therapy in a child with congenital leptin deficiency. N Engl J Med 341:879–884, 1999.

143. Wildt L, Hutchison JS, Marshall G, et al: On the site of action of progesterone in the blockade of the estradiol-induced gonadotropin discharge in the rhesus monkey. Endocrinology 109:1293–1294, 1981.

144. Shoupe D, Montz FJ, Lobo RA: The effects of estrogen and progestin on endogenous opioid activity in oophorectomized women. J Clin Endocrinol Metab 60:178–183, 1985.

145. Goodman RL, Parfitt DB, Evans NP, et al: Endogenous opioid peptides control the amplitude and shape of gonadotropin-releasing hormone pulses in the ewe. Endocrinology 136:2412–2420, 1995.

146. Wildt L, Leyendecker G, Sir-Petermann T, et al: Treatment with naltrexone in hypothalamic ovarian failure: Induction of ovulation and pregnancy. Hum Reprod 8:350–358, 1993.

147. Jansen HT, Lubbers LS, Macchia E, et al: Thyroid hormone receptor (alpha) distribution in hamster and sheep brain: Colocalization in gonadotropin-releasing hormone and other identified neurons. Endocrinology 138:5039–5047, 1997.

148. Morte B, Iniguez MA, Lorenzo PI, et al: Thyroid hormone-regulated expression of RC3/neurogranin in the immortalized hypothalamic cell line GT1-7. J Neurochem 69:902–909, 1997.

149. Chandran UR, Attardi B, Friedman R, et al: Glucocorticoid repression of the mouse gonadotropin-releasing hormone gene is mediated by promoter elements that are recognized by heteromeric complexes containing glucocorticoid receptor. J Biol Chem 271:20412–20420, 1996.

150. Attardi B, Tsujii T, Friedman R, et al: Glucocorticoid repression of gonadotropin-releasing hormone gene expression and secretion in morphologically distinct subpopulations of GT1-7 cells. Mol Cell Endocrinol 131:241–255, 1997.

151. Ahima RS, Harlan RE: Glucocorticoid receptors in LHRH neurons. Neuroendocrinology 56:845–850, 1992.

152. Scott RE, Wu-Peng XS, Yen PM, et al: Interactions of estrogen- and thyroid hormone receptors on a progesterone receptor estrogen response element (ERE) sequence: A comparison with the vitellogenin A2 consensus ERE. Mol Endocrinol 11:1581–1592, 1997.

153. Belsham DD, Evangelou A, Deboleena R, et al: Regulation of gonadotropin-releasing hormone (GnRH) gene expression by 5a-dihydrotestosterone

in GnRH-secreting GT1-7 hypothalamic neurons. Endocrinology 139:1108–1114, 1998.

154. Roy D, Angelini NL, Belsham DD: Estrogen directly represses gonadotropin-releasing hormone (GnRH) gene expression in estrogen receptor-α (ERα)-and ERβ-expressing GT1-7 GnRH neurons. Endocrinology 140:5045–5053, 1999.

155. Dorling AA, Todman MG, Korach KS, et al: Critical role for estrogen receptor alpha in negative feedback regulation of gonadotropin-releasing hormone mRNA expression in the female mouse. Neuroendocrinology 78:204–209, 2003.

156. Kaplan SL, Grumbach MM, Aubert ML: The ontogenesis of pituitary hormones and hypothalamic factors in the human fetus: Maturation of central nervous system regulation of anterior pituitary function. Recent Prog Horm Res 32:161–243, 1976.

157. Rossmanith WG, Swartz WH, Tueros VS, et al: Pulsatile GnRH-stimulated LH release from the human fetal pituitary in vitro: Sex-associated differences. Clin Endocrinol (Oxf) 33:719–727, 1990.

158. Reyes FI, Boroditsky RS, Winter JS, et al: Studies on human sexual development. II. Fetal and maternal serum gonadotropin and sex steroid concentrations. J Clin Endocrinol Metab 38:612–617, 1974.

159. Kaplan SL, Grumbach MM: Pituitary and placental gonadotrophins and sex steroids in the human and sub-human primate fetus. Clin Endocrinol Metab 7:487–511, 1978.

160. Rasmussen DD, Liu JH, Swartz WH, et al: Human fetal hypothalamic GnRH neurosecretion: Dopaminergic regulation in vitro. Clin Endocrinol (Oxf) 25:127–132, 1986.

161. Rasmussen DD, Liu JH, Wolf PL, et al: Endogenous opioid regulation of gonadotropin-releasing hormone release from the human fetal hypothalamus in vitro. J Clin Endocrinol Metab 57:881–884, 1983.

162. Ross JL, Loriaux DL, Cutler GB Jr: Developmental changes in neuroendocrine regulation of gonadotropin secretion in gonadal dysgenesis. J Clin Endocrinol Metab 57:288–293, 1983.

163. Petraglia F, Bernasconi S, Iughetti L, et al: Naloxone-induced luteinizing hormone secretion in normal, precocious, and delayed puberty. J Clin Endocrinol Metab 63:1112–1116, 1986.

164. Medhamurthy R, Gay VL, Plant TM: The prepubertal hiatus in gonadotropin secretion in the male rhesus monkey (Macaca mulatta) does not appear to involve endogenous opioid peptide restraint of hypothalamic gonadotropin-releasing hormone release. Endocrinology 126:1036–1042, 1990.

165. Donoso AO, Lopez FJ, Negro-Vilar A: Glutamate receptors of the non-N-methyl-D-aspartic acid type mediate the increase in luteinizing hormone-releasing hormone release by excitatory amino acids in vitro. Endocrinology 126:414–420, 1990.

166. Plant TM, Gay VL, Marshall GR, et al: Puberty in monkeys is triggered by chemical stimulation of the hypothalamus. Proc Natl Acad Sci U S A 86:2506–2510, 1989.

167. Wildt L, Marshall G, Knobil E: Experimental induction of puberty in the infantile female rhesus monkey. Science 207:1373–1375, 1980.

168. de Roux N, Genin E, Carel JC, et al: Hypogonadotropic hypogonadism due to loss of function of the KiSS1-derived peptide receptor GPR54. Proc Natl Acad Sci U S A 100:10972–10976, 2003.

169. Seminara SB, Messager S, Chatzidaki EE, et al: The GPR54 gene as a regulator of puberty. N Engl J Med 349:1614–1627, 2003.

170. Funes S, Hedrick JA, Vassileva G, et al: The KiSS-1 receptor GPR54 is essential for the development of the murine reproductive system. Biochem Biophys Res Commun 312:1357–1363, 2003.

171. Navarro VM, Castellano JM, Fernandez-Fernandez R, et al: Developmental and hormonally regulated messenger ribonucleic acid expression of KiSS-1 and its putative receptor, GPR54, in rat hypothalamus and potent luteinizing hormone releasing activity of KiSS-1 peptide. Endocrinology 145:4565–4574, 2004.

172. Matsui H, Takatsu Y, Kumano S, et al: Peripheral administration of metastin induces marked gonadotropin release and ovulation in the rat. Biochem Biophys Res Commun 320:383–388, 2004.

173. Gottsch ML, Cunningham MJ, Smith JT, et al: A role for Kisspeptins in the regulation of gonadotropin secretion in the mouse. Endocrinology 145:4073–4077, 2004.

174. Marshall JC, Eagleson CA, McCartney CR: Hypothalamic dysfunction. Mol Cell Endocrinol 183:29–32, 2001.

175. Bergendahl M, Veldhuis JD: Altered pulsatile gonadotropin signaling in nutritional deficiency in the male. Trends Endocrinol Metab 6:145–159, 1995.

176. Bergendahl M, Aloi JA, Iranmanesh A, et al: Fasting suppresses pulsatile luteinizing hormone (LH) secretion and enhances orderliness of LH release in young but not older men. J Clin Endocrinol Metab 83:1967–1975, 1998.

177. Takeuchi Y, Nagabukuro H, Kizumi O, et al: Lipopolysaccharide-induced suppression of the hypothalamic gonadotropin-releasing hormone pulse generator in ovariectomized goats. J Vet Med Sci 59:93–96, 1997.

178. Refojo D, Arias P, Moguilevsky JA, et al: Effect of bacterial endotoxin on in vivo pulsatile gonadotropin secretion in adult male rats. Neuroendocrinology 67:275–281, 1998.

179. Yoo MJ, Nishihara M, Takahashi M: Tumor necrosis factor-alpha mediates endotoxin induced suppression of gonadotropin-releasing hormone pulse generator activity in the rat. Endocr J 44:141–148, 1997.

180. He D, Sato I, Kimura F, et al: Lipopolysaccharide inhibits luteinizing hormone release through interaction with opioid and excitatory amino acid inputs to gonadotropin-releasing hormone neurones in female rats: Possible evidence for a common mechanism involved in infection and immobilization stress. J Neuroendocrinol 15:559–563, 2003.

181. Akema T, Chiba A, Shinozaki R, et al: Acute stress suppresses the N-methyl-D-aspartate-induced luteinizing hormone release in the ovariectomized estrogen-primed rat. Neuroendocrinology 62:270–276, 1995.

182. Akema T, Chiba A, Shinozaki R, et al: Acute immobilization stress and intraventricular injection of CRF suppress naloxone-induced LH release in ovariectomized estrogen-primed rats. J Neuroendocrinol 8:647–652, 1996.

183. Spratt DI, Cox P, Orav J, et al: Reproductive axis suppression in acute illness is related to disease severity. J Clin Endocrinol Metab 76:1548–1554, 1993.

184. Van den Berghe G, de Zegher F, Lauwers P, et al: Luteinizing hormone secretion and hypoandrogenemia in critically ill men: Effect of dopamine. Clin Endocrinol (Oxf) 41:563–569, 1994.

185. Tsutsumi M, Zhou W, Millar RP, et al: Cloning and functional expression of a mouse gonadotropin-releasing hormone receptor. Mol Endocrinol 6:1163–1169, 1992.

186. Reinhart J, Mertz LM, Catt KJ: Molecular cloning and expression of cDNA encoding the murine gonadotropin-releasing hormone receptor. J Biol Chem 267:21281–21284, 1992.

187. Kaiser UB, Zhao D, Cardona GR, et al: Isolation and characterization of cDNAs encoding the rat pituitary gonadotropin-releasing hormone receptor. Biochem Biophys Res Commun 189:1645–1652, 1992.

188. Eidne KA, Sellar RE, Couper G, et al: Molecular cloning and characterisation of the rat pituitary gonadotropin-releasing hormone (GnRH) receptor. Mol Cell Endocrinol 90:R5–R9, 1992.

189. Perrin MH, Bilezikjian LM, Hoeger C, et al: Molecular and functional characterization of GnRH receptors cloned from rat pituitary and a mouse pituitary tumor cell line. Biochem Biophys Res Commun 191:1139–1144, 1993.

190. Kakar SS, Musgrove LC, Devor DC, et al: Cloning, sequencing, and expression of human gonadotropin releasing hormone (GnRH) receptor.

Biochem Biophys Res Commun 189:289–295, 1992.

191. Chi L, Zhou W, Prikhozhan A, et al: Cloning and characterization of the human GnRH receptor. Mol Cell Endocrinol 91:R1–R6, 1993.

192. Brooks J, Taylor PL, Saunders PT, et al: Cloning and sequencing of the sheep pituitary gonadotropin-releasing hormone receptor and changes in expression of its mRNA during the estrous cycle. Mol Cell Endocrinol 94:R23–R27, 1993.

193. Illing N, Jacobs GF, Becker II, et al: Comparative sequence analysis and functional characterization of the cloned sheep gonadotropin-releasing hormone receptor reveal differences in primary structure and ligand specificity among mammalian receptors. Biochem Biophys Res Commun 196:745–751, 1993.

194. Kakar SS, Rahe CH, Neill JD: Molecular cloning, sequencing, and characterizing the bovine receptor for gonadotropin releasing hormone (GnRH). Domest Anim Endocrinol 10:335–342, 1993.

195. Weesner GD, Matteri RL: Rapid communication: Nucleotide sequence of luteinizing hormone-releasing hormone (LHRH) receptor cDNA in the pig pituitary. J Anim Sci 72:1911, 1994.

196. Tensen C, Okuzawa K, Blomenrohr M, et al: Distinct efficacies for two endogenous ligands on a single cognate gonadoliberin receptor. Eur J Biochem 243:134–140, 1997.

197. Millar R, Lowe S, Conklin D, et al: A novel mammalian receptor for the evolutionarily conserved type II GnRH. Proc Natl Acad Sci U S A 98:9636–9641, 2001.

198. Wang L, Bogerd J, Choi HS, et al: Three distinct types of GnRH receptor characterized in the bullfrog. Proc Natl Acad Sci U S A 98:361–366, 2001.

199. Millar RP, Lu ZL, Pawson AJ, et al: Gonadotropin-releasing hormone receptors. Endocr Rev 25:235–275, 2004.

200. McArdle CA, Willars GB, Fowkes RC, et al: Desensitization of gonadotropin-releasing hormone action in alphaT3-1 cells due to uncoupling of inositol 1,4,5-trisphosphate generation and Ca2+ mobilization. J Biol Chem 271:23711–23717, 1996.

201. Willars GB, Heding A, Vrecl M, et al: Lack of a C-terminal tail in the mammalian gonadotropin-releasing hormone receptor confers resistance to agonist-dependent phosphorylation and rapid desensitization. J Biol Chem 274:30146–30153, 1999.

202. Davidson JS, Wakefield IK, Millar RP: Absence of rapid desensitization of the mouse gonadotropin-releasing hormone receptor. Biochem J 300:299–302, 1994.

203. Heding A, Vrecl M, Bogerd J, et al: Gonadotropin-releasing hormone receptors with intracellular carboxyl-terminal tails undergo acute desensitization of total inositol phosphate production and exhibit accelerated internalization kinetics. J Biol Chem 273:11472–11477, 1998.

204. Zhou W, Sealfon SC: Structure of the mouse gonadotropin-releasing hormone receptor gene: Variant transcripts generated by alternative processing. DNA Cell Biol 13:605–614, 1994.

205. Fan NC, Jeung EB, Peng C, et al: The human gonadotropin-releasing hormone (GnRH) receptor gene: Cloning, genomic organization and chromosomal assignment. Mol Cell Endocrinol 103:R1–R6, 1994.

206. Fan NC, Peng C, Krisinger J, et al: The human gonadotropin-releasing hormone receptor gene: Complete structure including multiple promoters, transcription initiation sites, and polyadenylation signals. Mol Cell Endocrinol 107:R1–R8, 1995.

207. Kakar SS: Molecular structure of the human gonadotropin-releasing hormone receptor gene. Eur J Endocrinol 137:183–192, 1997.

208. Grosse R, Schoneberg T, Schultz G, et al: Inhibition of gonadotropin-releasing hormone receptor signaling by expression of a splice variant of the human receptor. Mol Endocrinol 11:1305–1318, 1997.

209. Stojilkovic SS, Catt KJ: Expression and signal transduction pathways of gonadotropin-releasing hormone receptors. Recent Prog Horm Res 50:161–205, 1995.

210. Kaiser UB, Conn PM, Chin WW: Studies of gonadotropin-releasing hormone (GnRH) action using GnRH receptor-expressing pituitary cell lines. Endocr Rev 18:46–70, 1997.

211. Palczewski K, Kumasaka T, Hori T, et al: Crystal structure of rhodopsin: A G protein-coupled receptor. Science 289:733–734, 2000.

212. Davidson JS, Flanagan CA, Zhou W, et al: Identification of N-glycosylation sites in the gonadotropin-releasing hormone receptor: Role in receptor expression but not ligand binding. Mol Cell Endocrinol 107:241–245, 1995.

213. Davidson JS, Flanagan CA, Davies PD, et al: Incorporation of an additional glycosylation site enhances expression of functional human gonadotropin-releasing hormone receptor. Endocrine 4:207–212, 1996.

214. Zhou W, Rodic V, Kitanovic S, et al: A locus of the gonadotropin-releasing hormone receptor that differentiates agonist and antagonist binding sites. J Biol Chem 270:18853–18857, 1995.

215. Davidson JS, McArdle CA, Davies P, et al: Asn102 of the gonadotropin-releasing hormone receptor is a critical determinant of potency for agonists containing C-terminal glycinamide. J Biol Chem 271:15510–15514, 1996.

216. Fromme BJ, Katz AA, Roeske RW, et al: Role of aspartate7.32[302] of the human gonadotropin-releasing hormone receptor in stabilizing a high-affinity ligand conformation. Mol Pharmacol 60:1280–1287, 2001.

217. de Roux N, Young J, Brailly-Tabard S, et al: The same molecular defects of the gonadotropin-releasing hormone receptor determine a variable degree of hypogonadism in affected kindred. J Clin Endocrinol Metab 84:567–572, 1999.

218. Kenakin T: Pharmacologic Analysis of Drug-Receptor Interaction. New York, Raven Press, 1993.

219. De Lean A, Stadel JM, Lefkowitz RJ: A ternary complex model explains the agonist-specific binding properties of the adenylate cyclase-coupled beta-adrenergic receptor. J Biol Chem 255:7108–7117, 1980.

220. Samama P, Cotecchia S, Costa T, et al: A mutation-induced activated state of the beta 2-adrenergic receptor. Extending the ternary complex model. J Biol Chem 268:4625–4636, 1993.

221. Zhou W, Flanagan C, Ballesteros JA, et al: A reciprocal mutation supports helix 2 and helix 7 proximity in the gonadotropin-releasing hormone receptor. Mol Pharmacol 45:165–170, 1994.

222. Blomenrohr M, Bogerd J, Leurs R, et al: Differences in structure-function relations between nonmammalian and mammalian gonadotropin-releasing hormone receptors. Biochem Biophys Res Commun 238:517–522, 1997.

223. Arora KK, Cheng Z, Catt KJ: Mutations of the conserved DRS motif in the second intracellular loop of the gonadotropin-releasing hormone receptor affect expression, activation, and internalization. Mol Endocrinol 11:1203–1212, 1997.

224. Ballesteros J, Kitanovic S, Guarnieri F, et al: Functional microdomains in G-protein-coupled receptors. The conserved arginine-cage motif in the gonadotropin-releasing hormone receptor. J Biol Chem 273:10445–10453, 1998.

225. Myburgh DB, Millar RP, Hapgood JP: Alanine-261 in intracellular loop III of the human gonadotropin-releasing hormone receptor is crucial for G-protein coupling and receptor internalization. Biochem J 331:893–896, 1998.

226. de Roux N, Young J, Misrahi M, et al: A family with hypogonadotropic hypogonadism and mutations in the gonadotropin-releasing hormone receptor. N Engl J Med 337:1597–1602, 1997.

227. Arora KK, Krsmanovic LZ, Mores N, et al: Mediation of cyclic AMP signaling by the first intracellular loop of the gonadotropin-releasing hormone receptor. J Biol Chem 273:25581–25586, 1998.

228. Timossi CM, Barrios de Tomasi J, Zambrano E, et al: A naturally occurring basically charged human follicle-stimulating hormone (FSH) variant inhibits FSH-induced androgen aromatization and tissue-type plasminogen activator enzyme activity in vitro. Neuroendocrinology 67:153–163, 1998.

229. Sairam MR, Linggen J, Sairam J, et al: Influence of carbohydrates on the antigenic structure of gonadotropins: Distinction of agonists and antagonists. Biochem Cell Biol 68:889–893, 1990.

230. Sibley DR, Benovic JL, Caron MG, et al: Regulation of transmembrane signaling by receptor phosphorylation. Cell 48:913–922, 1987.

231. Leeb-Lundberg LM, Cotecchia S, DeBlasi A, et al: Regulation of adrenergic receptor function by phosphorylation. I. Agonist-promoted desensitization and phosphorylation of alpha 1-adrenergic receptors coupled to inositol phospholipid metabolism in DDT1 MF-2 smooth muscle cells. J Biol Chem 262:3098–3105, 1987.

232. Nussenzveig DR, Heinflink M, Gershengorn MC: Agonist-stimulated internalization of the thyrotropin-releasing hormone receptor is dependent on two domains in the receptor carboxyl terminus. J Biol Chem 268:2389–2392, 1993.

233. McArdle CA, Forrest-Owen W, Willars G, et al: Desensitization of gonadotropin-releasing hormone action in the gonadotrope-derived alpha T3-1 cell line. Endocrinology 136:4864–4871, 1995.

234. Anderson L, McGregor A, Cook JV, et al: Rapid desensitization of GnRH-stimulated intracellular signalling events in alpha T3-1 and HEK-293 cells expressing the GnRH receptor. Endocrinology 136:5228–5231, 1995.

235. Pawson AJ, Katz A, Sun Y-M, et al: Contrasting internalization kinetics of human and chicken gonadotropin-releasing hormone receptors mediated by C-terminal tail. J Endocrinol 156:R009–R012, 1997.

236. Hille B, Tse A, Tse FW, et al: Signaling mechanisms during the response of pituitary gonadotropes to GnRH. Recent Prog Horm Res 50:75–95, 1995.

237. Naor Z, Harris D, Shacham S: Mechanism of GnRH receptor signaling: combinatorial cross-talk of Ca2+ and protein kinase C. Front Neuroendocrinol 19:1–19, 1998.

238. Conn PM, Janovick JA, Stanislaus D, et al: Molecular and cellular bases of gonadotropin-releasing hormone action in the pituitary and central nervous system. Vitam Horm 50:151–214, 1995.

239. Cornea A, Janovick JA, Stanislaus D, et al: Redistribution of G(q/11)alpha in the pituitary gonadotrope in response to a gonadotropin-releasing hormone agonist. Endocrinology 139:397–402, 1998.

240. Grosse R, Schmid A, Schoneberg T, et al: Gonadotropin-releasing hormone receptor initiates multiple signaling pathways by exclusively coupling to G(q/11) proteins. J Biol Chem 275:9193–9200, 2000.

241. Han XB, Conn PM: The role of protein kinases A and C pathways in the regulation of mitogen-activated protein kinase activation in response to gonadotropin-releasing hormone receptor activation. Endocrinology 140:2241–2251, 1999.

242. Hsieh KP, Martin TF: Thyrotropin-releasing hormone and gonadotropin-releasing hormone receptors activate phospholipase C by coupling to the guanosine triphosphate-binding proteins Gq and G11. Mol Endocrinol 6:1673–1681, 1992.

243. Krsmanovic LZ, Mores N, Navarro CE, et al: An agonist-induced switch in G protein coupling of the gonadotropin-releasing hormone receptor regulates pulsatile neuropeptide secretion. Proc Natl Acad Sci U S A 100:2969–2974, 2003.

244. Reiss N, Llevi LN, Shacham S, et al: Mechanism of mitogen-activated protein kinase activation by gonadotropin-releasing hormone in the pituitary of alphaT3-1 cell line: Differential roles of calcium and protein kinase C. Endocrinology 138:1673–1682, 1997.

245. Shah BH, MacEwan DJ, Milligan G: Gonadotrophin-releasing hormone receptor agonist-mediated down-regulation of Gq alpha/G11 alpha (pertussis toxin-insensitive) G proteins in alpha T3-1 gonadotroph cells reflects increased G protein turnover but not alterations in mRNA levels. Proc Natl Acad Sci U S A 92:1886–1890, 1995.

246. Shah BH, Milligan G: The gonadotrophin-releasing hormone receptor of alpha T3-1 pituitary cells regulates cellular levels of both of the phosphoinositidase C-linked G proteins, Gq alpha and G11 alpha, equally. Mol Pharmacol 46:1–7, 1994.

247. Stanislaus D, Janovick JA, Brothers S, et al: Regulation of G(q/11)alpha by the gonadotropin-releasing hormone receptor. Mol Endocrinol 11:738–746, 1997.

248. Stanislaus D, Janovick JA, Ji T, et al: Gonadotropin and gonadal steroid release in response to a gonadotropin-releasing agonist in Gqalpha and G11alpha knockout mice. Endocrinology 139:2710–2717, 1998.

249. Hawes BE, Barnes S, Conn PM: Cholera toxin and pertussis toxin provoke differential effects on luteinizing hormone release, inositol phosphate production, and gonadotropin-releasing hormone (GnRH) receptor binding in the gonadotrope: Evidence for multiple guanyl nucleotide binding proteins in GnRH action. Endocrinology 132:2124–2130, 1993.

250. Imai A, Takagi H, Horibe S, et al: Coupling of gonadotropin-releasing hormone receptor to Gi protein in human reproductive tract tumors. J Clin Endocrinol Metab 81:3249–3253, 1996.

251. Liu F, Usui I, Evans LG, et al: Involvement of both G(q/11) and G(s) proteins in gonadotropin-releasing hormone receptor-mediated signaling in L beta T2 cells. J Biol Chem 277:32099–32108, 2002.

252. Ulloa-Aguirre A, Stanislaus D, Arora V, et al: The third intracellular loop of the rat gonadotropin-releasing hormone receptor couples the receptor to Gs- and G(q/11)-mediated signal transduction pathways: Evidence from loop fragment transfection in GGH3 cells. Endocrinology 139:2472–2478, 1998.

253. Lin X, Conn PM: Transcriptional activation of gonadotropin-releasing hormone (GnRH) receptor gene by GnRH: involvement of multiple signal transduction pathways. Endocrinology 140:358–364, 1999.

254. Kuphal D, Janovick JA, Kaiser UB, et al: Stable transfection of GH3 cells with rat gonadotropin-releasing hormone receptor complementary deoxyribonucleic acid results in expression of a receptor coupled to cyclic adenosine 3′,5′-monophosphate-dependent prolactin release via a G-protein. Endocrinology 135:315–320, 1994.

255. Faure M, Voyno-Yasenetskaya TA, Bourne HR: cAMP and beta gamma subunits of heterotrimeric G proteins stimulate the mitogen-activated protein kinase pathway in COS-7 cells. J Biol Chem 269:7851–7854, 1994.

256. Andrews WV, Conn PM: Gonadotropin-releasing hormone stimulates mass changes in phosphoinositides and diacylglycerol accumulation in purified gonadotrope cell cultures. Endocrinology 118:1148–1158, 1986.

257. Liu JP: Protein kinase C and its substrates. Mol Cell Endocrinol 116:1–29, 1996.

258. Liu F, Austin DA, Mellon PL, et al: GnRH activates ERK1/2 leading to the induction of c-fos and LHbeta protein expression in LbetaT2 cells. Mol Endocrinol 16:419–434, 2002.

259. Junoy B, Maccario H, Mas JL, et al: Proteasome implication in phorbol ester- and GnRH-induced selective down-regulation of PKC (alpha, epsilon, zeta) in alpha (T31) and L beta T2 gonadotrope cell lines. Endocrinology 143:1386–1403, 2002.

260. Johnson MS, MacEwan DJ, Simpson J, et al: Characterisation of protein kinase C isoforms and enzymic activity from the alpha T3-1 gonadotroph-derived cell line. FEBS Lett 333:67–72, 1993.

261. Asaoka Y, Yoshida K, Sasaki Y, et al: Potential role of phospholipase A2 in HL-60 cell differentiation to macrophages induced by protein kinase C activation. Proc Natl Acad Sci U S A 90:4917–4921, 1993.

262. Bell RM, Burns DJ: Lipid activation of protein kinase C. J Biol Chem 266:4661–4664, 1991.

263. Harris D, Reiss N, Naor Z: Differential activation of protein kinase C delta and epsilon gene expression by gonadotropin-releasing hormone in alphaT3-1 cells. Autoregulation by protein kinase C. J Biol Chem 272:13534–13540, 1997.

264. Shacham S, Cheifetz MN, Lewy H, et al: Mechanism of GnRH receptor signaling: from the membrane to the nucleus. Ann Endocrinol (Paris) 60:79–88, 1999.

265. Zheng L, Stojilkovic SS, Hunyady L, et al: Sequential activation of phospholipase-C and -D in agonist-stimulated gonadotrophs. Endocrinology 134:1446–1454, 1994.

266. Shraga-Levine Z, Ben-Menahem D, Naor Z: Arachidonic acid and lipoxygenase products stimulate protein kinase C beta mRNA levels in pituitary alpha T3-1 cell line: Role in gonadotropin-releasing hormone action. Biochem J 316:667–670, 1996.

267. Ben-Menahem D, Shraga-Levine Z, Limor R, et al: Arachidonic acid and lipoxygenase products stimulate gonadotropin alpha-subunit mRNA levels in pituitary alpha T3-1 cell line: Role in gonadotropin releasing hormone action. Biochemistry 33:12795–12799, 1994.

268. Cesnjaj M, Zheng L, Catt KJ, et al: Dependence of stimulus-transcription coupling on phospholipase D in agonist-stimulated pituitary cells. Mol Biol Cell 6:1037–1047, 1995.

269. Mitchell R, Wolbers WB, Sim P, et al: The regulation of phospholipase C (PLC) and phospholipase D (PLD) by G protein receptor-activated tyrosine kinases in alpha T3-1 cells. Biochem Soc Trans 23:208S, 1995.

270. Stojilkovic SS, Torsello A, Iida T, et al: Calcium signaling and secretory responses in agonist-stimulated pituitary gonadotrophs. J Steroid Biochem Mol Biol 41:453–467, 1992.

271. Smith CE, Wakefield I, King JA, et al: The initial phase of GnRH-stimulated LH release from pituitary cells is independent of calcium entry through voltage-gated channels. FEBS Lett 225:247–250, 1987.

272. Merelli F, Stojilkovic SS, Iida T, et al: Gonadotropin-releasing hormone-induced calcium signaling in clonal pituitary gonadotrophs. Endocrinology 131:925–932, 1992.

273. Davidson JS, Wakefield IK, King JA, et al: Dual pathways of calcium entry in spike and plateau phases of luteinizing hormone release from chicken pituitary cells: Sequential activation of receptor-operated and voltage-sensitive calcium channels by gonadotropin-releasing hormone. Mol Endocrinol 2:382–390, 1988.

274. Sundaresan S, Colin IM, Pestell RG, et al: Stimulation of mitogen-activated protein kinase by gonadotropin-releasing hormone: Evidence for the involvement of protein kinase C. Endocrinology 137:304–311, 1996.

275. Roberson MS, Misra-Press A, Laurance ME, et al: A role for mitogen-activated protein kinase in mediating activation of the glycoprotein hormone alpha-subunit promoter by gonadotropin-releasing hormone. Mol Cell Biol 15:3531–3539, 1995.

276. Naor Z, Benard O, Seger R: Activation of MAPK cascades by G-protein-coupled receptors: The case of gonadotropin-releasing hormone receptor. Trends Endocrinol Metab 11:91–99, 2000.

277. Wolbers B, Simpson J, Mitchell R: LHRH-induced tyrosine phosphorylation and MAP kinase activation in alpha T3-1 cells. Biochem Soc Trans 23:145S, 1995.

278. Sim PJ, Wolbers WB, Mitchell R: Activation of MAP kinase by the LHRH receptor through a dual mechanism involving protein kinase C and a pertussis toxin-sensitive G protein. Mol Cell Endocrinol 112:257–263, 1995.

279. Roberson MS, Zhang T, Li HL, et al: Activation of the p38 mitogen-activated protein kinase pathway by gonadotropin-releasing hormone. Endocrinology 140:1310–1318, 1999.

280. Haisenleder DJ, Cox ME, Parsons SJ, et al: Gonadotropin-releasing hormone pulses are required to maintain activation of mitogen-activated protein kinase: Role in stimulation of gonadotrope gene expression. Endocrinology 139:3104–3111, 1998.

281. Yokoi T, Ohmichi M, Tasaka K, et al: Activation of the luteinizing hormone beta promoter by gonadotropin-releasing hormone requires c-Jun NH2-terminal protein kinase. J Biol Chem 275:21639–21647, 2000.

282. Benard O, Naor Z, Seger R: Role of dynamin, Src, and Ras in the protein kinase C-mediated activation of ERK by gonadotropin-releasing hormone. J Biol Chem 276:4554–4563, 2001.

283. Mulvaney JM, Roberson MS: Divergent signaling pathways requiring discrete calcium signals mediate concurrent activation of two mitogen-activated protein kinases by gonadotropin-releasing hormone. J Biol Chem 275:14182–14189, 2000.

284. Levi NL, Hanoch T, Benard O, et al: Stimulation of Jun N-terminal kinase (JNK) by gonadotropin-releasing hormone in pituitary alpha T3-1 cell line is mediated by protein kinase C, c-Src, and CDC42. Mol Endocrinol 12:815–824, 1998.

285. Mulvaney JM, Zhang T, Fewtrell C, et al: Calcium influx through L-type channels is required for selective activation of extracellular signal-regulated kinase by gonadotropin-releasing hormone. J Biol Chem 274:29796–29804, 1999.

286. Yordy JS, Muise-Helmericks RC: Signal transduction and the Ets family of transcription factors. Oncogene 19:6503–6513, 2000.

287. Wolfe MW, Call GB: Early growth response protein 1 binds to the luteinizing hormone-beta promoter and mediates gonadotropin-releasing hormone-stimulated gene expression. Mol Endocrinol 13:752–763, 1999.

288. Weck J, Anderson AC, Jenkins S, et al: Divergent and composite gonadotropin-releasing hormone-responsive elements in the rat luteinizing hormone subunit genes. Mol Endocrinol 14:472–485, 2000.

289. Padmanabhan V, Dalkin A, Yasin M, et al: Are immediate early genes involved in gonadotropin-releasing hormone receptor gene regulation? Characterization of changes in GnRH receptor (GnRH-R), c-fos, and c-jun messenger ribonucleic acids during the ovine estrous cycle. Biol Reprod 53:263–269, 1995.

290. Maurer RA, Kim KE, Schoderbek WE, et al: Regulation of glycoprotein hormone alpha-subunit gene expression. Recent Prog Horm Res 54:455–484, 1999.

291. Gur G, Bonfil D, Safarian H, et al: GnRH receptor signaling in tilapia pituitary cells: Role of mitogen-activated protein kinase (MAPK). Comp Biochem Physiol B Biochem Mol Biol 129:517–524, 2001.

292. Call GB, Wolfe MW: Gonadotropin-releasing hormone activates the equine luteinizing hormone beta promoter through a protein kinase C/mitogen-activated protein kinase pathway. Biol Reprod 61:715–723, 1999.

293. Pitteloud N, Boepple PA, DeCruz S, et al: The fertile eunuch variant of idiopathic hypogonadotropic hypogonadism: Spontaneous reversal associated with a homozygous mutation in the gonadotropin-releasing hormone receptor. J Clin Endocrinol Metab 86:2470–2475, 2001.

294. Pralong FP, Gomez F, Castillo E, et al: Complete hypogonadotropic hypogonadism associated with a novel inactivating mutation of the gonadotropin-releasing hormone receptor. J Clin Endocrinol Metab 84:3811–3816, 1999.

295. Costa EM, Bedecarrats GY, Mendonca BB, et al: Two novel mutations in the gonadotropin-releasing hormone receptor gene in Brazilian patients with hypogonadotropic hypogonadism and normal olfaction. J Clin Endocrinol Metab 86:2680–2686, 2001.

296. Soderlund D, Canto P, de la Chesnaye E, et al: A novel homozygous mutation in the second transmembrane domain of the gonadotrophin releasing hormone receptor gene. Clin Endocrinol (Oxf) 54:493–498, 2001.

297. Dewailly D, Boucher A, Decanter C, et al: Spontaneous pregnancy in a patient who was homozygous for the Q106R mutation in the gonadotropin-releasing hormone receptor gene. Fertil Steril 77:1288–1291, 2002.

298. Meysing AU, Kanasaki H, Bedecarrats GY, et al: GnRHR mutations in a woman with idiopathic hypogonadotropic hypogonadism highlight the differential sensitivity of luteinizing hormone and follicle-stimulating hormone to gonadotropin-releasing hormone. J Clin Endocrinol Metab 89:3189–3198, 2004.

299. Bedecarrats GY, Linher KD, Kaiser UB: Two common naturally occurring mutations in the human gonadotropin-releasing hormone (GnRH) receptor have differential effects on gonadotropin gene expression and on GnRH-mediated signal transduction. J Clin Endocrinol Metab 88:834–843, 2003.

300. Kumar TR, Wang Y, Lu N, et al: Follicle stimulating hormone is required for ovarian follicle maturation but not male fertility. Nat Genet 15:201–204, 1997.

301. Amsterdam A, Dantes A, Hosokawa K, et al: Steroid regulation during apoptosis of ovarian follicular cells. Steroids 63:314–318, 1998.

302. Hsueh AJ, Adashi EY, Jones PB, et al: Hormonal regulation of the differentiation of cultured ovarian granulosa cells. Endocr Rev 5:76–127, 1984.

303. Steinberger E: Hormonal control of mammalian spermatogenesis. Physiol Rev 51:1–22, 1971.

304. Wilcox AJ, Weinberg CR, O'Connor JF, et al: Incidence of early loss of pregnancy. N Engl J Med 319:189–194, 1988.

305. Emancipator K, Bock JL, Burke MD: Diagnosis of ectopic pregnancy by the rate of increase of choriogonadotropin in serum: Diagnostic criteria compared. Clin Chem 36:2097–2101, 1990.

306. Bahado-Singh RO, Oz U, Kovanci E, et al: New triple screen test for Down syndrome: Combined urine analytes and serum AFP. J Matern Fetal Med 7:111–114, 1998.

307. Hussa RO: The Clinical Marker hCG. New York, Praeger, 1987.

308. Jameson JL, Chin WW, Hollenberg AN, et al: The gene encoding the beta-subunit of rat luteinizing hormone. Analysis of gene structure and evolution of nucleotide sequence. J Biol Chem 259:15474–15480, 1984.

309. Jameson JL, Becker CB, Lindell CM, et al: Human follicle-stimulating hormone beta-subunit gene encodes multiple messenger ribonucleic acids. Mol Endocrinol 2:806–815, 1988.

310. Gharib SD, Wierman ME, Shupnik MA, et al: Molecular biology of the pituitary gonadotropins. Endocr Rev 11:177–199, 1990.

311. Talmadge K, Vamvakopoulos NC, Fiddes JC: Evolution of the genes for the beta subunits of human chorionic gonadotropin and luteinizing hormone. Nature 307:37–40, 1984.

312. Themmen APN, Huhtaniemi IT: Mutations of gonadotropins and gonadotropin receptors: Elucidating the physiology and pathophysiology of pituitary-gonadal function. Endocr Rev 21:551–583, 2000.

313. Garcia-Campayo V, Sugahara T, Boime I: Unmasking a new recognition signal for O-linked glycosylation in the chorionic gonadotropin beta subunit. Mol Cell Endocrinol 194:63–70, 2002.

314. Chin W: Glycoprotein hormone genes. In Habener JF (ed): Genes Encoding Hormones and Regulatory Peptides. Clifton, NJ, Humana Press, 1986, pp 137–172.

315. Beitins IZ, Derfel RL, O'Loughlin K, et al: Immunoreactive luteinizing hormone, follicle stimulating hormone and their subunits in human urine following gel filtration. J Clin Endocrinol Metab 44:149–159, 1977.

316. de Leeuw R, Mulders J, Voortman G, et al: Structure-function relationship of recombinant follicle stimulating hormone (Puregon). Mol Hum Reprod 2:361–369, 1996.

317. Baenziger JU, Green ED: Pituitary glycoprotein hormone oligosaccharides: Structure, synthesis and function of the asparagine-linked oligosaccharides on lutropin, follitropin and thyrotropin. Biochim Biophys Acta 947:287–306, 1988.

318. Matzuk MM, Keene JL, Boime I: Site specificity of the chorionic gonadotropin N-linked oligosaccharides in signal transduction. J Biol Chem 264:2409–2414, 1989.

319. Sairam MR, Jiang LG: Comparison of the biological and immunological properties of glycosylation deficient human chorionic gonadotropin variants produced by site directed mutagenesis and chemical deglycosylation. Mol Cell Endocrinol 85:227–235, 1992.

320. Baenziger JU, Kumar S, Brodbeck RM, et al: Circulatory half-life but not interaction with the lutropin/chorionic gonadotropin receptor is modulated by sulfation of bovine lutropin oligosaccharides. Proc Natl Acad Sci U S A 89:334–338, 1992.

321. Yen SC, Llerena LA, Pearson OH, et al: Disappearance rates of endogenous follicle-stimulating hormone in serum following surgical hypophysectomy in man. J Clin Endocrinol Metab 30:325–329, 1970.

322. Urban RJ, Padmanabhan V, Beitins I, et al: Metabolic clearance of human follicle-stimulating hormone assessed by radioimmunoassay, immunoradiometric assay, and in vitro Sertoli cell bioassay. J Clin Endocrinol Metab 73:818–823, 1991.

323. Peckham WD, Yamaji T, Dierschke DJ, et al: Gonadal function and the biological and physicochemical properties of follicle stimulating hormone. Endocrinology 92:1660–1666, 1973.

324. Veldhuis JD, Johnson ML: In vivo dynamics of luteinizing hormone secretion and clearance in man: Assessment by deconvolution mechanics. J Clin Endocrinol Metab 66:1291–1300, 1988.

# Gonadal Peptides: Inhibins, Activins, Follistatin, Müllerian-Inhibiting Substance (Antimüllerian Hormone)

## Henry G. Burger and David de Kretser

## INTRODUCTION

In addition to steroid hormones, the gonads produce regulatory peptides that act in endocrine, paracrine, and autocrine modes to control sexual differentiation and reproductive function. The term *inhibin* was given to the active ingredient in aqueous testicular extracts that was shown to prevent the appearance of castration cells in the rat pituitary.[1] Inhibin activity, present in both testicular extracts and ovarian follicular fluid, was first isolated from the latter in 1985 and shown to be a dimeric protein.[2] Isolation had involved bioassay of chromatographic column fractions of follicular fluid extracts, with inhibition of follicle-stimulating hormone (FSH) synthesis or release from rat pituitary cell cultures used as an end point. It was noted that some fractions stimulated rather than inhibited FSH, and this observation led to the isolation of both the activins[3,4] and another peptide, originally designated FSH-suppressing protein and subsequently follistatin, that had inhibin-like activity.[5,6] In initially totally unrelated studies, the hormone responsible for regression of developing female müllerian structures was isolated, characterized, and shown to be structurally related to the inhibins.[7-9] In this chapter, the structural properties and relationships of these gonadal peptides are described, as are their receptors. The inhibins, activins, and follistatins are then considered individually in terms of their sites of production, knowledge gained from the creation of mice transgenic for deletion of the hormones or their subunits, the relevant assays, physiology, and, where relevant, clinical applications of the assays. The major emphasis of this chapter is on the inhibins, activins, and follistatin, whereas müllerian-inhibiting substance (MIS) is largely covered in Chapter 143.

## STRUCTURAL PROPERTIES AND RELATIONSHIPS OF GONADAL PEPTIDES

The structural characteristics of the inhibins, activins, and follistatins are shown diagrammatically in Figures 140-1 and 140-2. The inhibins are dimers made up of a common $\alpha$ subunit and one of two $\beta$ subunits designated $\beta_A$ and $\beta_B$, the respective dimers being called inhibins A($\alpha\beta_A$) and B($\alpha\beta_B$).[10] The three subunits are products of separate genes located on chromosomes 2 ($\alpha$ and $\beta$B) and 7 ($\beta$A). The $\alpha$ subunit is synthesized in a preproform of approximately 51 kilodalton. This form incorporates a proregion of 6 kilodalton and an $\alpha$ subunit of 43 kilodalton that can be cleaved proteolytically to give an N-terminal segment ($\alpha$N) of approximately 20 kilodalton and a C-terminal segment ($\alpha$C) of approximately 20 kilodalton. Combination of the 43-kilodalton $\alpha$ subunit with a 15-kilodalton $\beta$ subunit gives rise to the 55-kilodalton species of inhibin. Proteolytic cleavage gives rise to a 33- to 36-kilodalton form, the lowest molecular weight dimer that is biologically active. The $\beta$ subunits are synthesized as precursors that are 55 kilodalton in molecular weight and then proteolytically cleaved to give the mature 15-kilodalton subunits. Higher molecular weight forms of inhibin dimers occur in biologic fluids, the main species in addition to 33 and 55 kilodalton being 66 and 95 kilodalton in molecular weight.[11] The highest molecular weight forms are not biologically active.[12] The $\beta_A$ and $\beta_B$ subunits can be isolated from follicular fluid.[13]

Activins are dimers of the $\beta$ subunits and occur in three major forms, activin A ($\beta_A\beta_A$), activin AB ($\beta_A\beta_B$), and activin B ($\beta_B\beta_B$),[10] although the additional forms $\beta_C$, $\beta_D$, and $\beta_E$ have now been identified (see later).

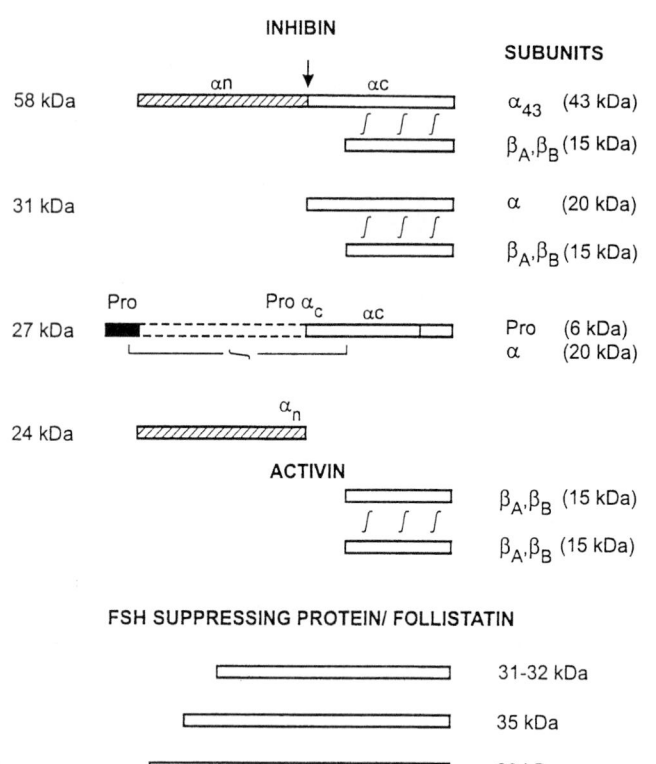

**Figure 140-1** Schema of the structures of inhibin, the α subunit containing peptide Pro-αaC, αN, activin, and follistatin. Note that 31-kilodalton inhibin is derived from the 58-kilodalton form by proteolytic cleavage of αN from the $\alpha_{43}$ subunit. FSH, follicle-stimulating hormone.

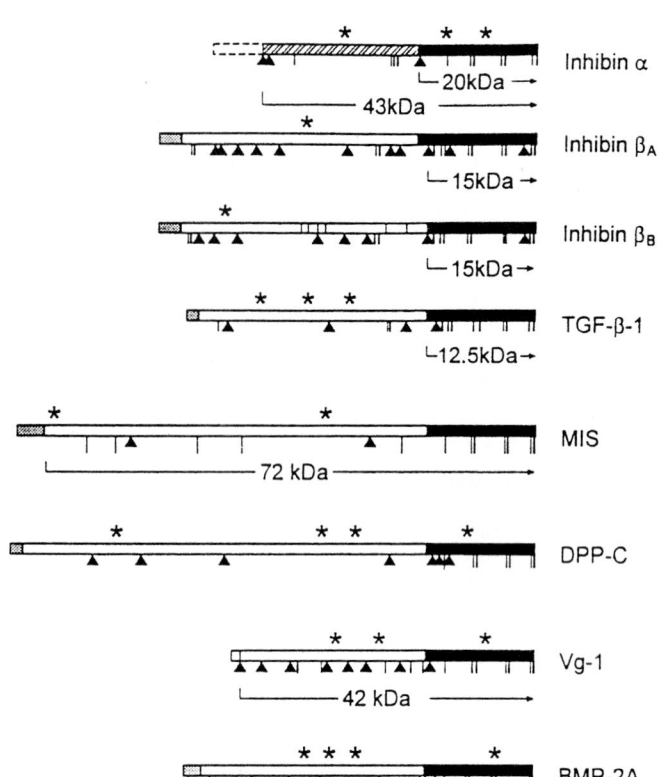

**Figure 140-2** Schematic diagram of subunit precursor sequences of the transforming growth factor-β/inhibin family members as deduced from their cDNA structure. The *darkened region* corresponds to the region of highest homology between sequences and the region associated with biologic activity.*, potential glycosylation site; ▲, potential proteolytic site. Vg-1 mRNA and its protein are localized in the vegetal region of oocytes and embryos. Cysteine residues are denoted by *vertical bars*. BMP, bone morphogenetic protein; DPP-C, decapentaplegic complex; MIS, müllerian-inhibiting substance; TGF-$\beta_1$, transforming growth factor beta 1.

Substantial interspecies homology among the inhibins and activins is demonstrable.[10] Eighty-five percent homology is seen in the sequence of the α chain among human, bovine, porcine, murine, and ovine inhibins and 100% homology in the $\beta_A$ subunit sequences among human, bovine, porcine, and murine species, with a single amino acid substitution in the ovine $a_A$ subunit. The $\beta_B$ subunits are 95% homologous among species, and 70% homology is found between the $\beta_A$ and $\beta_B$ subunits.

Follistatin is quite different in structure from the inhibins and activins and occurs in a range of molecular weight forms between 31 and 44 kilodalton.[14] The follistatin gene, with its five exons, may undergo differential splicing to give two major forms, FS-288 and FS-315, which can in turn be cleaved to an FS-300 form.[15] The amino acid sequences of rat, mouse, human, bovine, ovine, and porcine follistatin are highly homologous (97%). No follistatin receptor has been identified, although the molecule, in particular FS-288, has a high affinity for many cell-surface heparan sulfate proteoglycans, which suggests that it may have a facilitatory action, particularly in regulating the action of activin.[16]

MIS is a dimer made up of two 72-kilodalton subunits, the C-terminal domain of which shows homologies with inhibin A, both of the inhibin B subunits, and a variety of other peptides, including transforming growth factor beta (TGF-β); decapentaplegic and related molecules; nodal, Vg-1, and related molecules; osteogenic proteins; bone morphogenesis factors; cartilage-derived morphogenetic proteins; and various growth and differentiation factors.[17] Thus, the inhibins, activins, and MIS are related proteins, whereas follistatin is structurally unrelated but functionally influences the activity of the activins in particular. Recent crystallographic studies suggest that all members of the TGF-β superfamily may share a similar three-dimensional structure characterized by a central cysteine knot generated by disulfide bridges between six of the seven conserved cysteine residues in the C-terminal portion of the proteins.[18]

## GONADAL PEPTIDE RECEPTORS

The major family of receptors that has been extensively characterized is that for the activins[19] (see also Chapter 10). They are single, membrane-spanning serine-threonine kinases. Two distinct receptors occur, ActRI and ActRII, as well as a number of subtypes (two for ActRI and five for ActRII). Similar receptor types and subtypes occur for TGF-β and MIS. This family of receptors is thought to function by initial binding of the ligand to ActRII, which dictates ligand specificity. This binding in turn allows dimerization with ActRI, which promotes phosphorylation at a serine or threonine type 1 receptor. This activates a second messenger system involving Smads (sons of mothers against decapentaplegia), of which there are eight subtypes.[20] Details of the signal transduction pathway have been reviewed recently.[21] Inhibin A binds to ActRII with 10- to 20-fold lower affinity than activin A does, and inhibin B binds with even lower affinity. The signaling pathway for the inhibins is less well understood. No specific receptor has been isolated. Inhibin may antagonize the binding or signaling of activin to the activin receptor. Inhibin binds to betaglycan, the type III TGF-β receptor, which in turn facilitates its binding to ActRII.[22] Further, a factor termed *p120* facilitates the antagonism of activin signaling by inhibin.[23] Mechanisms of inhibin action may however vary depending on the ligand and receptor types involved.[24] The MIS receptor system functions similarly to the activin system.[16]

## THE INHIBINS

### SITES OF PRODUCTION

The facts that circulating concentrations of inhibin, whether measured by bioassay or radioimmunoassay (RIA), decrease to undetectable levels after gonadectomy in animals and that inhibin is also undetectable in most normal postmenopausal women as well as in castrate men indicate that the gonads are the major source of the circulating molecule.[25–28] The main source of inhibin during the follicular phase of the reproductive cycle is the granulosa cell.[29] The biologic and immunologic activities of inhibin were detected in media in which rat, bovine, porcine, or human granulosa cells had been cultured.[29–32] With the use of antibodies generated against either 32-kilodalton inhibin or the inhibin α-subunit, immunoreactivity was localized in the ovarian granulosa cells in various species, including humans.[33] mRNAs for the α, $\beta_A$, and $\beta_B$ subunits were detectable in rat granulosa cells by in situ hybridization[34,35] but have also been demonstrated in bovine and primate ovaries. Weak $\beta_B$ subunit immunoreactivity was detectable in the granulosa cells of some primary follicles in mid-gestation human fetal ovaries, but all three subunits were demonstrable in the granulosa cells of primary and secondary follicles late in gestation in the rhesus monkey ovary.[36] In the adult human ovary, preantral and early antral follicular granulosa cells showed positive immunostaining, particularly for the α and $\beta_B$ subunits, whereas medium-sized healthy antral follicles and preovulatory follicles were positive for α and $\beta_A$.[37]

In primates, the corpus luteum is also a site of inhibin production. Tsonis and colleagues[38] demonstrated the production of inhibin in vitro by luteinized human granulosa cells, and cells from isolated human corpora lutea were shown to be capable of producing inhibin in vitro under basal conditions; these cells responded to human chorionic gonadotropin (hCG) with an increase in inhibin production when isolated from the corpus luteum in the early luteal to mid-luteal phase.[39] The subunit genes for inhibin subunit α and inhibin subunit $\beta_A$ were demonstrable in human and monkey corpora lutea.[40,41] Immunocytochemical studies with α subunit antiserum have shown localization in human luteal cells.[42]

Inhibin subunit mRNAs have also been demonstrated in the placenta[43] and the decidua[44] as well as in both fetal and adult adrenal glands.[45] Inhibin subunit α mRNA is present in extracts of early pregnancy placenta and is much more abundant than inhibin $\beta_A$ mRNA, with $\beta_B$ mRNA being detected at low levels only in term placenta.[46] Inhibin α subunit was demonstrable in the cytotrophoblast and $\beta_B$ in the syncytial layer of the villi; $\beta_A$ was widely distributed. Partial characterization of human placental inhibin, activin, and follistatin has been described.[47] Regulation of placental inhibin secretion has been reviewed.[48,49]

The major source of inhibin production by the testis is the Sertoli cell. Early studies showed that cultured rat Sertoli cells produce an FSH-inhibiting factor.[50] Secretion of both immunoreactive and biologically active inhibin from Sertoli cell cultures has subsequently been confirmed, and both α and β subunits are located in those cells as determined by immunohistochemistry.[51] In addition, Leydig cells have been shown to secrete immunoreactive inhibin, and both α and β subunit expression has been demonstrated in those cells and cell cultures.[51,52] The function of secreted Leydig cell inhibin remains uncertain. Sertoli cells can secrete inhibin both from their apical surfaces into the seminiferous tubule lumen and from their basal cells into interstitial fluid. The relative importance of each route of secretion is controversial.[53] As demonstrated by studies in the rhesus monkey, inhibin B secretion is governed by the inhibitory and stimulatory actions of luteinizing hormone (LH) and FSH, respectively.[54] The actions of LH may be mediated by testosterone inhibition of βB gene expression.

The pituitary is another potential site of inhibin production. In the rat, gonadotrophs have been shown to contain immunoreactive inhibin α and inhibin $\beta_B$ subunits and their mRNAs.[54] In male monkeys, inhibin-like immunoreactivity was noted in clusters of chromophobe cells, frequently lying close to gonadotrophs,[55] which suggests a possible paracrine role for inhibin in the regulation of gonadotropin production. Inhibin β subunits (but not α subunits) were reported in monkey pituitary,[56] and the entire range of inhibin/activin subunit genes and the ActRII gene have been demonstrated in normal and adenomatous human pituitary tissue.[57–59] A candidate receptor for inhibin has been identified. It corresponds to the type III TGF-β receptor betaglycan. Specificity for inhibin occurs when this receptor functions together with the ActRII.[22] It has, however, not been possible to detect inhibin bioactivity or immunoreactivity in medium from cultured rat anterior pituitary cells, and incubation of such cells in medium that contains anti-inhibin antiserum does not alter basal FSH secretion. Thus, the possible role of any inhibin that might be secreted by pituitary cells remains unclear.

Finally, current studies in prostatic diseases, particularly prostate cancer, suggest that progression to malignancy is accompanied by loss of the α subunit in prostatic epithelium, a topic not considered further here.[60,61]

### CONSEQUENCES OF INHIBIN GENE DELETION

Targeted disruption of the inhibin α subunit gene led to elevated levels of activin A concentrations, and the results of α subunit deletion have been reviewed in detail.[62,63] The most striking consequence is the development of gonadal sex cord–stromal tumors in mice of both sexes, leading to the hypothesis that the α subunit gene is a tumor suppressor. Tumors develop in essentially 100% of mice in the absence of inhibin. Tumor development is followed by a wasting syndrome resembling the human cancer cachexia syndromes.[63] The cachexia was prevented when inhibin α subunit gene knockout mice were crossed with mice with targeted disruption of the gene for ActRII.[64] However, the tumors developed, indicating that this pathology was related to the absence of the inhibin α subunit, whereas the cachexia was related to activin action. From the point of view of reproductive function, male mice were shown to be capable of normal copulation and to have normal spermatogenesis, relatively normal seminal vesicles, and fertility. These data were obtained from young mice before tumor development. The fact that inhibin is not essential for spermatogenesis in males contrasts with the situation in inhibin-deficient female mice, in which normal folliculogenesis was interfered with and corpora lutea did not develop. Mice in which granulosa cell tumors developed showed evidence of elevated estradiol levels.[62]

### ASSAYS

#### Bioassays

The isolation and characterization of inhibin were based on in vitro bioassays that used dispersed cultured rat anterior pituitary cells and measured basal FSH release, cell content, or gonadotropin-releasing hormone–stimulated release.[65] However, the release of activin and follistatin from these cells, which respectively stimulate or suppress FSH secretion, compromises the specificity of these bioassays. Bioassays using dispersed ovine pituitary cells have been of sufficient sensitivity for application to physiologic studies of inhibin regulation.[66] These bioassays have a place in the validation of newly developed RIA systems and in the characterization of inhibin and related molecules synthesized by recombinant techniques and were crucial in the identification of substances such as activin and follistatin.[67,68]

## Radioimmunoassays

A number of early RIAs for human inhibin used antibodies directed to the NH$_2$-terminal region of the α subunit; the best known is the Monash assay.[26,69,70] However, subsequent studies demonstrated very significant cross-reactivity with the α subunit precursor pro-αC, which is present in follicular fluid,[71,72] and in peripheral blood.[11,73] Nevertheless, the Monash assay measures both dimeric inhibin A and B as well as α subunit products and in the absence of the latter provide accurate measures. Thus, in the follicular phase of the human menstrual cycle,[74] the Monash assay provided an accurate measure, but in the luteal phase, the corpus luteum secreted predominantly α subunit products, providing a poor index of inhibin biologic activity The major findings with respect to inhibin physiology in humans, when such RIAs were used, were in accord with a physiologic role for inhibin as a component of the closed-loop feedback regulating system involved in the control of FSH secretion.[74,75] The inhibin assay field was revolutionized by the development of enzyme-linked immunosorbent assays (ELISAs) specific for each of the inhibin dimers. The first of these assays to be developed was the assay for inhibin A,[76] the results of which, when applied to human serum samples, in general paralleled those previously obtained with the inhibin RIAs. The development of an assay specific for inhibin B[77] clarified many previously puzzling findings, particularly with regard to inhibin physiology in the male. Inhibin A is undetectable by ELISA in the male, and the major species of inhibin secreted in the male is inhibin B.[77,78] Both males and females secrete significant quantities of α subunit–related peptides.[11] Whereas use of the specific assays is now regarded as mandatory in the definition of inhibin physiology, nonspecific RIAs or more recently developed assays of similar specificity still appear to be the method of choice in the application of inhibin assays to the field of ovarian malignancies (see later).

## PHYSIOLOGY

### Male

Initial studies of inhibin physiology in the male using the relatively nonspecific inhibin RIA led to paradoxic findings, for example, that α subunit-containing inhibin levels (immunoreactive inhibin) were normal or even elevated in patients with severe seminiferous tubule damage, including men with Klinefelter syndrome.[79] No evidence could be demonstrated for the postulated inverse relationship between immunoreactive inhibin and serum FSH in men with testicular disorders despite the initial observation that bioassayable inhibin in seminal plasma was inversely related to serum FSH.[79,80] The specific inhibin B ELISA showed that in fractionation studies of male serum, the predominant biologically active inhibin species in the male is inhibin B, with activity concentrated in two molecular weight species of 66 and 32 kDA.[11] However, in addition to inhibin B, large amounts of α subunit–related peptides circulate in the male and are measured in the inhibin RIA, although not in the specific inhibin B assay.[11]

#### Early Postnatal Period and Prepuberty

In the pituitary-gonadal axis of boys in the first few months of life, FSH levels are around the lower limit of adult values and inhibin B concentrations are above the adult male level at 3 months of age and remain elevated until about 15 months.[81,82] A nadir in levels occurs at 6 to 10 years of age. In prepubertal boys, inhibin B correlates with age but not with FSH.[83]

#### Puberty

Inhibin B levels are low from the age of 2 or 3 years to 10 or 11 years, possibly due to constitutive secretion, but rising total immunoreactive and inhibin B levels occur during pubertal development.[84–86] In early puberty, inhibin B correlates with testosterone, whereas from mid-puberty, the correlation with FSH is inverse, consistent with the establishment of negative feedback.[85] The two peaks of inhibin B in infancy and early puberty may reflect periods of Sertoli cell proliferation.

#### Adulthood

In men, an inverse correlation is found between the levels of FSH and inhibin B as a function of increasing age, and it appears to be primarily falling inhibin B levels associated with the rise in FSH that is a feature of aging in the male.[86] Other studies[87] have shown a weak correlation of inhibin B with age and a significant negative correlation of FSH and inhibin B in all age groups from 16 to 89 years. Several authors have demonstrated positive correlations between spermatogenesis and inhibin B concentrations.[88–90] The most striking demonstration that inhibin B is the specific gonadal peptide regulator of FSH was a study of 12 men with a variety of lymphomas and other hematologic malignancies evaluated before and during chemotherapy containing agents toxic to the seminiferous epithelium.[91] Serum inhibin B levels fell rapidly after administration of these agents, with an inverse rise in serum FSH levels and no significant change in the levels of testosterone. However, Pro-αC–containing peptides rose in response to the induction of testicular damage. Other studies in which the pituitary testicular axis was manipulated are also consistent with the fundamental role of inhibin B in FSH regulation.[88,89] Thus, administration of exogenous FSH leads to a delayed, but clearcut, increase in circulating serum inhibin B, whereas suppression of the pituitary by using a combination of testosterone and a synthetic progestin resulted in suppression of inhibin B levels. In pathologic states characterized by either gonadotropin deficiency or seminiferous tubule damage, serum inhibin B levels reflected the expected alteration in Sertoli cell function.[88–92] The relative roles of inhibin B and testosterone in FSH regulation are discussed in Chapter 171.

### Female
#### Fetus

Although it has been demonstrated that the fetal gonad in sheep secretes immunoreactive inhibin when FSH is administered in a pulsatile manner[93] and that administration of porcine follicular fluid treated with charcoal leads to decreased circulating FSH but not LH levels in ovine fetuses,[94] no data are available regarding the secretion of inhibin or activin by the human or primate fetal gonad. Rabinovici and coworkers[95] showed weak immunostaining for the β$_A$ subunit in some of the follicles that had formed at mid-gestation (16–23 weeks) but were unable to demonstrate α or β$_B$ subunit staining. In late-gestation fetal rhesus monkey ovaries, granulosa cells surrounding oocytes showed positive immunostaining for all three inhibin subunits. Inhibin levels were undetectable in media from cultures of mid-gestation human ovaries, and no studies were reported on rhesus monkey fetal ovary cultures. In the fetal bovine ovary, both inhibin bioactivity and immunoactivity have been detected, as has follistatin.[96]

#### Early Postnatal Period

Just as in the male, immunoreactive inhibin and the specific dimeric inhibins appear to participate in activation of the pituitary-gonadal axis in the first few months of life. In a study of girls aged 2 months to 2 years, immunoreactive inhibin levels were found to be in the low follicular phase range of adults in the youngest girls, with FSH levels elevated at times into the postmenopausal range and LH in the early follicular phase range. Estradiol was in the mid-follicular range in the youngest girls studied, but beyond the age of 1 year, all four hormones were at extremely low concentrations.[81] More extensive documentation of the levels of the inhibins, FSH, LH, estradiol, and sex hormone binding–globulin in 473 unselected, healthy, 3-month-old girls has shown marked intraindividual variation, with concentrations corresponding to those observed in puberty.[97] The authors supported the concept that a "mini-puberty" occurs in infant girls similar to that in boys.

### Prepuberty

In a large study of 345 girls aged 0 to 18 years, median inhibin B levels were low until age 6, subsequently rose slightly, and increased further after age 10. The finding of increased levels of both inhibins in some individual samples, together with their positive relationship with FSH, provided evidence to support the occurrence of sporadic follicular development throughout infancy and childhood under the influence of FSH.[98]

### Puberty

Serum immunoreactive inhibin concentrations in girls were low before the onset of puberty and rose in parallel with levels of FSH, LH, and estradiol.[84] The values were lower than those seen in boys at equivalent stages. A wide range of values was seen at different stages of puberty, but the increase in mean concentration with increasing maturation was highly significant. Levels of inhibin A and B behaved similarly to those of immunoreactive inhibin.[85,98] Inhibin levels have been reported in children treated with cytotoxic therapy for childhood leukemia who have shown disturbances in pubertal development.[99] Such children may undergo puberty at a significantly earlier age than normal, and many of these patients had undetectable inhibin concentrations, presumably reflecting the ovarian damage caused by chemotherapy. A further study reported inhibin B concentrations before and during chemotherapy in 25 prepubertal children (9 females) who had other solid tumors or acute lymphoblastic leukemia. In the girls, inhibin B decreased to undetectable levels in the majority during treatment without any change in FSH or LH. Posttreatment recovery of inhibin B was variable. In boys, inhibin B was normal for age and sex and no significant change occurred during or after treatment. Thus, in girls, cancer chemotherapy may be associated with arrest of follicle development and sustained suppression of inhibin B may be indicative of permanent ovarian damage. In prepubertal boys, chemotherapy appears to have little immediate effect on Sertoli cell production of inhibin B.[100]

### Menstrual Cycle

The endocrinology of the menstrual cycle is described comprehensively in Chapter 153. Only a brief summary of inhibin physiology is given here.

The initial report of immunoreactive serum inhibin levels throughout the menstrual cycle[101] showed that levels remained relatively constant throughout most of the follicular phase, rose immediately before the mid-cycle gonadotropin surge, fell transiently, and rose again to reach their highest levels during the mid-luteal phase. With development of the specific inhibin A ELISA, immunoreactive inhibin concentrations were shown to reflect the secretory pattern of inhibin A.[76]

The patterns of inhibin B secretion differ from those of inhibin A[76] because they rise during the luteal follicular transition, in close correlation with levels of FSH. They follow the early follicular phase rise and fall in serum FSH and show a small mid-cycle peak with a progressive decline thereafter throughout the luteal phase, at a time when inhibin A levels rise and fall. The behavior of inhibin B strongly suggests that it is a product of the pool of small FSH-responsive antral follicles from which the dominant follicle is selected and that it is not a product of the corpus luteum. Recent evidence suggests that the intercycle rise in inhibin B is dependent on rising levels of FSH.[102]

Different regulatory mechanisms appear to be involved in the control of inhibin secretion during the follicular and luteal phases. During the follicular phase, the inhibins are predominantly under FSH control. Urinary gonadotropin preparations that contain both FSH and LH given for the purpose of ovarian hyperstimulation[103] or biologically purified FSH given to women with polycystic ovarian disease undergoing ovulation induction[104] leads to increases in circulating immunoreactive inhibin and estradiol, and dose-response relationships were demonstrated between immunoreactive inhibin levels and FSH given as single injections in the early follicular phase of the menstrual cycle.[105] Both inhibin A and inhibin B participate in this response, the dose-response curve for inhibin B being steeper than that for inhibin A.[106] In studies of ovarian hyperstimulation using recombinant FSH, serum inhibin B levels determined during the early stages of fixed-dose FSH treatment provided an early indicator of the number of recruited follicles destined to form mature oocytes.[107]

During the luteal phase, LH appears to be the major regulatory gonadotropin. Human granulosa lutein cells in long-term culture responded to LH and testosterone with increased inhibin production,[38] and a gonadotropin-releasing hormone antagonist given to normal women in the mid-luteal phase caused a fall in circulating inhibin levels that could be prevented or reversed by hCG but not FSH administration.[108] Similar data have been obtained in the macaque monkey treated with a gonadotropin-releasing hormone antagonist, with hCG but not FSH reversing the inhibitory effects on inhibin levels.[109] However, FSH can also stimulate inhibin A secretion during the luteal phase of the cycle.[110] The possible role of inhibin in the phenomenon of twinning was examined in one study[111]; elevated early follicular phase levels of FSH and LH were accompanied by increased inhibin concentrations, thus suggesting a hypothalamic-pituitary cause for the increased gonadotropin concentrations. It should be noted that immunoreactive inhibin $\alpha$ and $\beta_A$ subunits have been demonstrated in human endometrium.[112]

### Pregnancy and Lactation

The circulating levels of both bioactive and immunoreactive inhibin rise throughout normal pregnancy,[113,114] an early rise being originally noted in the studies of McLachlan and colleagues,[115] who observed parallel increasing concentrations of inhibin and hCG in women pregnant after embryo transfer following in vitro fertilization. Levels rose from the mid-luteal phase to peak at approximately week 11 of gestation, with a subsequent decline to a plateau from 14 to 25 weeks and a further slow rise to peak concentrations at 41 weeks, the levels then being as high as four times those of the mid-luteal phase. The levels subsequently fell in a biexponential manner after delivery.[116] An increase in inhibin was noted relatively early in pregnancy in women without endogenous ovarian function,[117] indicating that the ovary was not essential for the early inhibin increase in pregnancy. It is clear that the major form of bioactive, dimeric inhibin circulating in pregnant women is inhibin A.[118,119] Inhibin A levels in early pregnancy peak at approximately 8 weeks, declining subsequently at approximately 16 weeks. The concentrations remain low throughout the second trimester but increase approximately fivefold during the third trimester to reach a maximum at 36 weeks. Inhibin B concentrations do not increase in early pregnancy and are near the detection limit of the assay, and unpublished observations indicate that such is also the case at delivery. A fetoplacental source of inhibin A in early pregnancy is consistent with the detection of both bioactive and immunoactive inhibin in the placenta, with hCG having been shown capable of stimulating inhibin secretion from cultured placental cells.[120] Physiologic doses of hCG given to normal women during the mid-luteal phase stimulate increases in both progesterone and inhibin, compatible with the corpus luteum as a significant source of inhibin early in pregnancy.[121] Another possible source of inhibin during pregnancy is the decidua because α, βA, and βB inhibin subunits have been demonstrated in decidual tissue.[44] Higher inhibin A levels are found in multiple pregnancies than in singleton pregnancies, and levels in missed abortions are very low. These observations suggest a prognostic role for inhibin A measurements, particularly in the management of early pregnancy in patients who conceive as a result of in vitro fertilization.[122,123]

Inhibin A (and activin A) concentrations are increased in preeclampsia, and it has been proposed that women who have increased inhibin A concentrations at 16 weeks' gestation are at higher risk of preeclampsia.[124] Studies using both inhibin α–directed assays and dimeric inhibin A assays have shown that measurement of maternal serum inhibin A in the second trimester can make a contribution to current screening tests for Down syndrome; the physiology of the inhibins and activins in normal and abnormal pregnancy has been reviewed recently.[125,126]

### Reproductive Aging and the Menopausal Transition

Serum FSH levels increase in women older than 40 years who continue to have regular menstrual cycles.[127,128] Lenton and associates[129] found a significant increase in serum FSH in a group of women aged 40 to 41 with a further gradual rise throughout their 40s. LH became significantly elevated in the 48- to 49-year-old age group. When related to the time of menopause, the increase in FSH was seen 5 to 6 years earlier, whereas the LH increase occurred 3 to 4 years earlier. This group further reported that follicular phase immunoreactive inhibin concentrations in cycles from older women (mean age, 44.2 years) were lower than those of younger women (mean age, 27.4 years) in cycles in which pregnancy did not occur but were similar to those of a group with a mean age of 29.7 years when sampled during a conception cycle.[130] When estradiol and progesterone levels were measured as a function of increasing age, no change was seen.[131] The major regulator of early follicular phase serum FSH levels is inhibin B. Thus, serum inhibin B levels (but not inhibin A or estradiol levels) were significantly lower in a group of older, regularly cycling women selected to have elevated follicular phase serum FSH levels when compared with a younger control group[132] and inhibin B was inversely correlated with early follicular phase serum FSH in women aged 20 to 50 years, particularly those in the 40- to 50-year age group.[133] A decrease in serum inhibin B appears to be the earliest endocrine marker of the onset of the menopausal transition, that is, that time when menstrual cycle irregularity becomes manifest. Early perimenopausal subjects were shown to have significantly lower levels of inhibin B in the presence of a small, statistically nonsignificant increase in FSH and no change in estradiol and inhibin A.[134]

Circulating estradiol and inhibin concentrations fluctuate widely in individual women during the menopausal transition. In a prospective study,[135] it was noted that mean FSH levels begin to increase and E2 levels decrease approximately 2 years before final menses, with the levels of inhibin A and inhibin B showing a similar pattern and being undetectable in the majority of women by the time of their final menstrual period.

Some evidence suggests differential secretion of inhibin and estradiol by the aging granulosa cell. Although parallel changes in estradiol and inhibin were observed during ovarian hyperstimulation for the purposes of in vitro fertilization,[103] an age-related reduction in inhibin but not in estradiol responses in women older than 35 years of age was noted.[136] Serum inhibin may thus provide a sensitive and early index of declining ovarian function with advancing age, a view supported by the finding of elevated early follicular phase FSH levels in women with "incipient" ovarian failure, whose serum inhibin levels were lower than normal, with

estradiol being in the normal range.[137] After menopause, inhibin levels are usually undetectable by the currently available immunoassays. Comprehensive reviews of the human endocrinology of inhibins[138] and the endocrinology of the menopausal transition[139] are available.

## CLINICAL APPLICATIONS OF INHIBIN ASSAYS

The growing use of the specific dimeric assays as well as the less specific assays for immunoreactive inhibin is pointing to a number of diagnostic possibilities. In the male, the demonstration that inhibin B is the major gonadal peptide regulator of FSH and that it reflects Sertoli cell function has suggested that inhibin B measurements may provide evidence regarding seminiferous tubule function, in addition to that provided by serum FSH measurement. Thus, inhibin B may be a sensitive marker of spermatogenesis[140] and may help resolve some of the uncertainties regarding the diagnostic classification in men with severe oligospermia or azoospermia and normal serum FSH levels.[89]

In women, inhibin B measurements may be of prognostic value in the management of those undergoing ovarian hyperstimulation for the purposes of in vitro fertilization.[107,141] Current studies suggest that low levels of serum inhibin B in the early follicular phase before ovarian hyperstimulation may indicate a poor prognosis for the outcome of in vitro fertilization cycles. Whether inhibin B measurements will provide evidence of impending ovarian failure has yet to be established.[126] The clinical applications of inhibin A assays have been mentioned previously with reference to the monitoring of early pregnancy, prediction of preeclampsia, and screening for Down syndrome.[126]

Because inhibin is a product of the corpus luteum, it might be predicted that it could provide a useful marker of luteal insufficiency. Published reports to date are conflicting in this regard, with one group reporting that women with an inadequate luteal phase had lowered serum inhibin concentrations during that time[142] and another group reporting that women with luteal phases of normal length but markedly decreased progesterone concentrations had normal concentrations of inhibin and estradiol.[130]

The major area of diagnostic promise is in the monitoring of patients with stromal and epithelial tumors of the ovary.[143] An initial report indicated that circulating immunoreactive inhibin concentrations were markedly elevated in patients with granulosa cell tumors of the ovary[144] (Fig. 140-3) and that at least in some patients rising inhibin levels were observed up to 20 months before clinical evidence of tumor recurrence was obtained. Inhibin assays are clearly of greatest value in patients who have previously undergone bilateral oophorectomy or in those who are postmenopausal, both situations in which endogenous inhibin levels are expected to be undetectable. Serum inhibin concentrations are elevated in most postmenopausal women with mucinous cystadenocarcinoma of the ovary and in approximately 15% of patients with nonmucinous epithelial cancers. Successful surgical removal of such tumors leads to a rapid fall in serum inhibin to nonsignificant levels by 1 week postoperatively.[145] In postmenopausal women with proven ovarian cancer, serum inhibin is inversely correlated with FSH and positively correlated with estradiol and progesterone, particularly in those with granulosa cell tumors. In women with mucinous tumors, the inverse correlation with FSH is lost; one possible explanation for this is that mucinous tumors may secrete α subunit–related peptides. Recent studies indicate that in addition to their production of α subunit–related peptides, granulosa cell tumors produce both inhibins A and B.[146] Mucinous epithelial tumors also have the capacity to secrete the dimeric inhibins, more frequently inhibin B than inhibin A, but the levels are less consistently elevated than in granulosa cell tumors. Some patients with serous cystadenocarcinomas

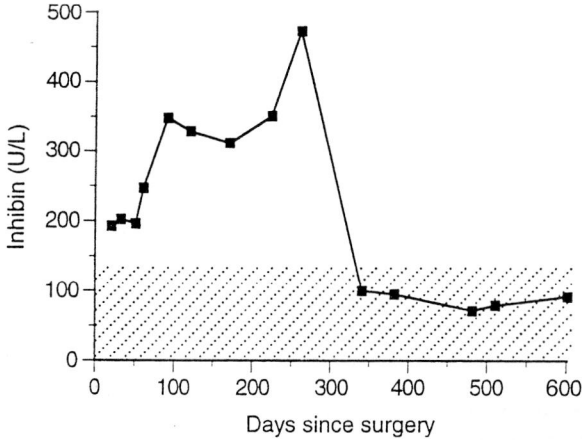

*Figure 140-3* Serum inhibin concentrations in an 80-year-old patient with a stage 2 granulosa cell tumor of the right ovary. Despite apparent clinical remission, serum inhibin levels rose steadily for 9 months after cytoreductive surgery. Second-look laparotomy 272 days after primary surgery confirmed residual granulosa cell tumor that was successfully removed, after which the patient remained clinically disease free. The serum inhibin range seen in functionally agonadal postmenopausal women is shown as a *hatched band.*

produce the dimeric inhibins. Current studies are directed at establishing whether a combination of a nonspecific inhibin measurement with a standard marker such as CA125 may have value for screening in addition to diagnostic value for ovarian tumors.[147]

One report indicates that inhibin levels may be of diagnostic value in patients with hydatidiform mole.[148] Levels were elevated in patients with this tumor and fell much more rapidly after evacuation than did levels of the traditional marker hCG. Failure to remove all diseased tissue led to a decrease in inhibin but not into the normal range, whereas complete evacuation restored inhibin levels to normal.

## THE ACTIVINS

### SITES OF PRODUCTION

Activins are homodimers or heterodimers of the inhibin $\beta$ subunits $\beta_A$ and $\beta_B$, with three isoforms being recognized: activin A ($\beta_A \beta_A$), activin B ($\beta_B \beta_B$), and activin AB ($\beta_A \beta_B$).[3,4] Three further $\beta$ subunits have been cloned, including mammalian $\beta_C$ and $\beta_E$ subunits and a *Xenopus* $\beta_D$ subunit.[149-151] There is evidence to suggest that $a_C$ can dimerize with $a_A$ and $a_B$ to form inactive proteins.[152] Activins are synthesized as precursor proteins and are characterized in particular by having a bioneutralizing binding protein, follistatin,[5,6] that modulates activin activity.[153] Activins also bind to the broad-spectrum protease inhibitor $\alpha_2$-macroglobulin.[154] Although the activins signal through serine threonine kinase receptors, there are numerous other mechanisms that can regulate their biologic activity.[19-21] Given the widespread actions of these proteins, these mechanisms serve to limit their actions to specific tissues and cell types (reviewed in Ref. 155). Activin $\beta$ subunits can be identified by immunohistochemistry and in situ hybridization in a wide variety of tissues, thus reflecting the evidence that they are local regulators of growth and differentiation in a number of organs.

All three species of activin have been isolated from porcine follicular fluid.[3,4,156] The $\beta_A$ subunit monomer is calculated to be present at 25% to 60% of the level of activin A dimer in bovine follicular fluid and resembles it in both biologic and immunologic activity.[13] The erythroid differentiation factor isolated from the culture medium of a human leukemia cell line has been shown to be activin A and shares its biologic activity.[157] Activins may play fundamental roles in embryonic differentiation, specifically in mesoderm induction.[158,159] Exposure of animal pole cells of the *Xenopus* embryo to activin A or activin B leads to the formation of a miniature embryo complete with head and rudimentary trunk. Activin B is transcribed very early in embryonic development, at the blastula stage, several hours before activin A.[158] Related studies in the chick embryo showed that activins can induce the formation of organized axial structures from epiblasts and that activin B is expressed in the hypoblast, which normally induces axial differentiation in the epiblast.[159] Other diverse effects of activin include the stimulation of insulin secretion by rat pancreatic islets and glucose production in isolated rat adipocytes. The effects on pituitary cells other than gonadotrophs have included a reduction in growth hormone–releasing factor–mediated growth hormone release and thyrotropin-releasing hormone–mediated prolactin release, together with inhibition of somatotroph growth and growth hormone biosynthesis and secretion.[160] There are widespread actions on many tissues including the induction of apoptosis in the liver and B lymphocytes as well as other roles in bone biology, wound healing, inflammation, and neuronal survival.[161-167] These multifunctional actions of the activins indicate that these proteins function as growth factors or cytokines rather than hormones because, in many states, the circulating levels are bound with high affinity to follistatin thereby neutralizing its actions.[168,169] Given the capacity of follistatin to bind activin A[153] and in turn also bind to heparin sulfate proteoglycans,[170,171] there are significant quantities of both activin A and follistatin that can be released by heparin from cell surfaces and basement membranes.[172]

### CONSEQUENCES OF ACTIVIN AND ACTIVIN RECEPTOR GENE DELETIONS

Extensive studies have been reported on the consequences of deletion of the genes coding for the $\beta_A$ and $\beta_B$ subunits as well as deletion of the genes coding for the activin receptors.[62] Activin $\beta_B$–deficient mice have developmental defects in eyelid closure,[173] and males have normal reproductive capacity. The gestation time of activin $\beta_B$–deficient females is prolonged and live-born litters fail to survive postnatally due to the failure of mothers to nurse their young, consistent with the role of activin B in control of hypothalamic oxytocin secretion.[174]

Activin $\beta_A$–deficient mice die within 24 hours of birth because of multiple craniofacial abnormalities that prevent suckling.[175] The defects include cleft palate and other palatal abnormalities, absence of whiskers, and lack of lower incisors. It is thus clear that activin $\beta_A$ is essential for normal craniofacial development.[175] Insertion of the $a_B$ subunit gene at the $a_A$ locus prevented the major palatal defects, but the mice had smaller testes and exhibited a delay in the onset of spermatogenesis.[176] Whether activin $\beta_C$ or a putative mammalian activin $\beta_D$ may compensate for the absence of activin $\beta_A$ or activin $\beta_B$ during embryogenesis or in adult physiology is not clear.

Mice deficient in ActRII mostly develop normally to adulthood but have suppressed FSH levels and show a decrease in testis size and some delay in the acquisition of fertility.[177] Quantitative studies of spermatogenesis show a decrease in Sertoli cell number and diminished germ cell counts.[178] ActRII receptor–deficient female mice are infertile. It is not clear whether this infertility results from reduced serum FSH levels, absent activin signaling in the ovaries, or both.

The fact that mice that lack both activin $\beta_A$ and activin $\beta_B$, ActRII, or follistatin[179] show normal mesoderm formation and neurulation suggests that activins are not required for mesoderm induction or neural development in mammals.

## ASSAYS

The development of suitable ligand-binding assays for the activins has proved to be difficult. Activin binds with relatively high affinity to follistatin, which itself circulates. Although several assays are available for activin A, the most commonly used assay is an ELISA.[180,181] Levels have been measured by assays in which detergents are used to separate activin from follistatin and other binding proteins to give a measure of total activin A rather than the free or biologically available form.[182] It is noteworthy that the $\beta_A$ subunit monomer is present at 25% to 60% of the levels of the dimer, for example, in bovine follicular fluid, and it may therefore be a potential source of cross-reactivity in binding assays.[183]

## PHYSIOLOGY

There have been significant developments in our understanding of the physiology of the activins in recent years.[155,184] Detailed consideration is not possible within this chapter, and the reader should consult some of the references provided for more information. The use of the activin ELISAs has greatly added to our understanding, and, as in the past, the demonstration of inhibin $\beta$ subunits by RNA analysis or by immunocytochemistry, in the absence of a demonstrable $\alpha$ subunit, has been taken as implicit evidence of the production of activin rather than inhibin. Although in the past there was debate as to whether activin has primarily paracrine or endocrine functions,[185] recent data clearly indicate that the major actions are paracrine.

There is no doubt that infusion of exogenous activin A into monkeys results in a moderate increase in circulating FSH, consistent with a possible endocrine role.[186] Consistent with this finding is the demonstration that activin A levels are higher in the mid-follicular phase in older than in younger women of reproductive age, suggesting that activin is promoting the increase in FSH levels seen with increasing age.[187] Activin levels appear to be relatively independent of gonadal status, and total activin A concentrations are similar in premenopausal, postmenopausal, and castrated women.[188] Serum activin A levels were reported to be similar in men and women and showed an age-related progressive increase between the ages of 20 and 50.[188] However, the concentrations did not change after the age of 50 years in women but increased further in men to reach peak concentrations between 70 and 90 years. Circulating concentrations do not in general change significantly throughout the menstrual cycle nor are they influenced by castration. Finally, castration of male rats did not alter circulating levels of activin A, indicating that many other tissues are contributing to the circulating pool.[182] These data all support the conclusion that circulating activin A is not a hormone of the reproductive axis, in contrast to inhibin physiology as outlined previously. The widespread expression of activin subunits in tissues as diverse as the placenta, bone marrow, brain, and endothelium is not characteristic of a classic endocrine hormone. The coexpression of follistatin in activin-producing tissues is also consistent with a local modulatory role.

### Ovarian Function

The activins play an important role in early folliculogenesis by promoting granulosa cell growth and differentiation.[189] As follicular development proceeds, activin stimulates FSH receptor expression and enhances FSH-induced aromatase activity and the expression of LH receptors and progesterone production.[190-192] In general, activin promotes folliculogenesis, prevents atresia, and inhibits luteinization, all actions that can be inhibited by follistatin. The theca cell also responds to activin, which inhibits androgen substrate production for granulosa cell estrogen synthesis.[193] Activin may therefore play a pivotal role in folliculogenesis by both controlling granulosa cell differentiation and affecting the availability of substrate for estrogen synthesis.

### Testicular Function

There are time-dependent changes in the expression of the $\beta$ subunits in the rat testis.[194] Before birth, gonocytes express the $\beta_A$ subunit and activin stimulates the numbers of these cells.[195] However, after birth, expression declines and is replaced by follistatin as the gonocytes progress to spermatogonia. Activin has been shown to stimulate spermatogonial proliferation of germ cells cocultured with Sertoli cells from 21-day-old rats.[196] The testicular and circulating levels of activin A are highest until approximately 15 days postnatal, a period during which activin A stimulates Sertoli cell proliferation synergistically with FSH.[194,197] Sertoli cell production of activin in vitro has been demonstrated,[198] consistent with an autocrine action in stimulating proliferation, although the peritubular cells are known to secrete activin A.[199] Earlier studies have shown that the Leydig cells also are capable of producing activin.[200]

### Neural Actions

Activin A is produced at neural sites, and further physiologic studies have shown that it can protect neural tissues from the toxic actions of several agents.[201,202] $\beta_A$ subunit protein is expressed in the nucleus of the tractus solitarius with projections to the paraventricular nucleus and is involved in the milk let-down reflex via oxytocin secretion,[174] in keeping with the failure of female mice with targeted disruption of the $\beta_B$ gene to suckle their young.[173]

### Actions in the Pituitary

Inhibin $\beta$ subunits, particularly $\beta_B$, are also demonstrable in rat gonadotrophs, and culture of pituitary cells in the presence of an anti–activin B monoclonal antibody results in suppression of spontaneous FSH release consistent with a local role of activin B in maintaining FSH secretion.[16,203,204] This action is consistent with the low FSH levels in mice with targeted disruption of the activin type IIA receptor gene.[177] It emphasizes the local role of activin B consistent with a paracrine action and with the capacity for its action on FSH to be modulated by the local production of follistatin by the folliculostellate cells.[205]

Castration has been reported to lead to increased expression of the $\beta$ subunits of inhibin/activin, follistatin, and the ActRI, ActRII, and ActRIIB genes in rat pituitary tissues.[16] Steroid replacement prevents these increases other than the increase in ActRII. The potential roles of intrapituitary inhibin/activin/follistatin have been reviewed in detail.[16]

### Actions in Pregnancy

Activin A levels rise during pregnancy, particularly after 24 weeks' gestation, with a substantial increase from approximately 34 weeks to term.[206-208] The levels fall rapidly post partum.[209] Activin A has been isolated from the placenta and amniotic fluid in the human,[210] and in the early placenta, activin stimulates hCG secretion. The late increase in activin A levels has been implicated in the onset of labor in some studies but not others.[211,212] Other studies showed that the induction of fetal hypoxemia resulted in elevation of fetal activin A levels, perhaps in an effort to combat the hypoxia by stimulating erythropoiesis.[213] Elevated levels of activin A have been reported in women with gestational diseases, including preterm labor, gestational diabetes,[214] and in women with preeclampsia.[215,216] Further studies have since been published suggesting that the elevation of activin A levels in early pregnancy may be predictive of the later development of preeclampsia,[217] but more data are necessary to determine the accuracy of such predictions.

## Role in Inflammation

The link between activin A and inflammation arose from studies that showed elevated levels of activin A in synovial fluid from patients with rheumatoid arthritis but not in those with osteoarthritis.[218] There are also data to indicate that activin A expression was elevated in patients with chronic inflammatory bowel disease.[219] In vitro studies on macrophages in culture indicated that activin A is a proinflammatory cytokine stimulating tumor necrosis factor-alpha, interleukin-6, and interleukin-1.[220] The ability to measure activin A in serum has shown that the injection of lipopolysaccharide into sheep was followed by a rapid rise in serum activin A levels that peaked within 30 minutes of the injection.[221] This peak spanned approximately 2 hours and preceded that of tumor necrosis factor-alpha by 5 to 10 minutes (Fig. 140-4). Interleukin-1 and interleukin-6 increased after 3 to 5 hours, accompanied by a follistatin secretory response. These data suggest the possibility that activin A may be involved in the initiation of the cytokine cascade. Further studies indicated that the activin A response was not dependent on tumor necrosis factor-alpha because a soluble tumor necrosis factor-alpha inhibitor did not alter the magnitude of the initial activin response but did attenuate the later stages. In addition, blocking the actions of prostaglandins by the use of fluroprofen attenuated the fever response but did not alter the initial activin A peak.[222]

In the human, serum activin and follistatin levels are markedly elevated in patients in intensive care for septicemia, indicating that the link was not limited to one species.[223]

In murine models of allergic pulmonary inflammation, activin A, produced locally by mast cells, has been linked to remodeling of the bronchial tree.[224] These studies require further extension to determine their applicability to asthma in humans.

A recent study has shown that elevated levels of activin A are found in patients with heart failure compared with healthy controls with the magnitude of the rise correlating positively with indicators of disease severity.[225] They also showed that in a rat model of heart failure induced by ischemia, activin A and its receptors were induced in cardiomyocytes. In these cells, activin A–induced mediators associated with tissue repair and remodeling such as atrial

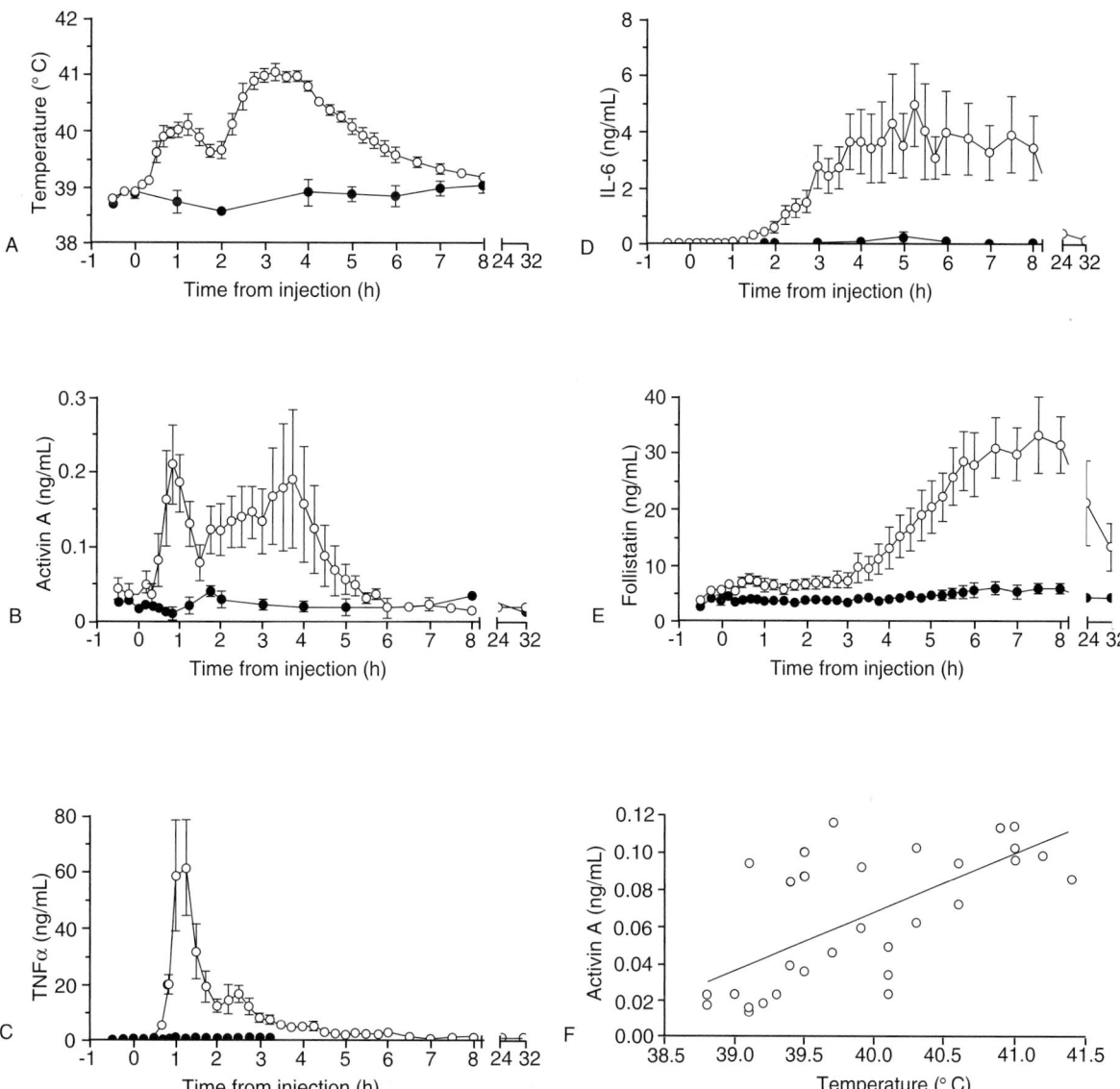

*Figure 140-4*  The changes in key measures of the inflammatory response in adult ewes after the injection of lipopolysaccharide (50 μg) (o) or nonpyrogenic saline (●) are shown. Changes in body temperature (**A**), activin A (**B**), tumor necrosis factor-alpha (**C**), interleukin-6 (**D**), follistatin (**E**), and the correlation between activin A concentrations and temperature (**F**) in individual ewes. Values are mean ± standard error of the mean. (From Jones KL, de Kretser DM, Phillips DJ: Effect of heparin administration to sheep on the release profiles of circulating activin A and follistatin. J Endocrinol 181:307–314, 2004. © 2004, The Endocrine Society.)

natriuretic peptide, brain natruretic peptide, matrix metalloproteinase-9, and tissue inhibitor of metalloproteinase-1. These studies open new directions in the field of activin biology and further reinforce the role of this protein in the inflammatory response and tissue repair.

Further, several studies have shown that activin A and follistatin are expressed at the sites of wound healing in mice. Overexpression of the follistatin gene under a keratinocyte promoter resulted in slower wound healing but limited fibrosis at the site.[164,226] This observation could represent a local inflammatory response at the site of the wound, and, provided healing occurred rapidly, the degree of fibrosis and scar formation is limited. Further studies are required to determine the scope and magnitude of the response of this cytokine to these crucial pathophysiologic responses.

## CLINICAL APPLICATIONS OF ACTIVIN ASSAYS

No clearcut diagnostic role for activin assays has thus far been described. Increased activin A concentrations have been found in patients with renal failure, liver disease, and some solid tumors.[214,227] Whether such increased levels make any contribution to cancer cachexia is uncertain. As mentioned previously, mice transgenic for deletion of the inhibin α subunit show markedly elevated activin levels and a cachexia syndrome mediated via the activin type II receptor.[63,64]

## FOLLISTATINS

### SITES OF PRODUCTION

The follistatins are molecules originally isolated on the basis of their ability to suppress FSH secretion by pituitary cells in vitro, but they showed no structural similarity to the inhibins.[5,6] There are differing forms based on alternative splicing mechanisms and the degree of glycosylation.[15] However, two major forms are recognized because of their physiologic implications. Follistatin 288, a 288-amino acid form has the capacity to bind avidly to heparin sulfate proteoglycans, whereas follistatin 315 does not demonstrate this property and represents the circulating form[170,171] (reviewed in ref. 169). Subsequent studies have shown that the capacity of follistatin to suppress FSH relates to its capability to bind and neutralize the biologic activity of the activins, which, in the context of the pituitary, is their ability to stimulate FSH.[153] Because of the binding of follistatin to heparin sulfate proteoglycans, administration of heparin can release significant quantities of follistatin and bound activin into the circulation in both humans and sheep[172] (Fig. 140-5). These studies indicate the presence of significant quantities of tissue stores linked to basement membranes, some of the activins being targeted through this pathway to intracellular degradation via lysosomal pathways.[170] Various tissues express the follistatin gene including the kidney, muscle, uterus, brain, pancreas, testis, pituitary, and adrenal,[228] with high levels in the ovary.[229] In the ovary, follistatin mRNA and protein are present in granulosa and luteal cells but not in other ovarian cell types,[228] and expression in granulosa cells is regulated by FSH, with the response to FSH stimulation being inhibited by epidermal growth factor.[228–231] In addition, it is produced by endothelial cells.[232] In principle, follistatin is induced by the actions of activin A either within the same cell or in an adjacent cell type within the same tissue. The locally produced follistatin can modulate the biologic action of activin at the site, or, when local production leads to an overflow into the circulation, the follistatin contributes to the binding capacity of serum for activin, providing a circulating pool from which activin can be released by heparin.

It is not possible in this chapter to consider the detailed physiology of follistatin, but, in general, it can neutralize all the biologic actions of the activins. Further, there are emerging data to suggest that follistatin can inhibit the actions of other growth factors such as bone morphogenetic protein 4, 6, 7, and 15, thereby influencing physiologic processes beyond those of the actions of the activins.[183] This is in keeping with

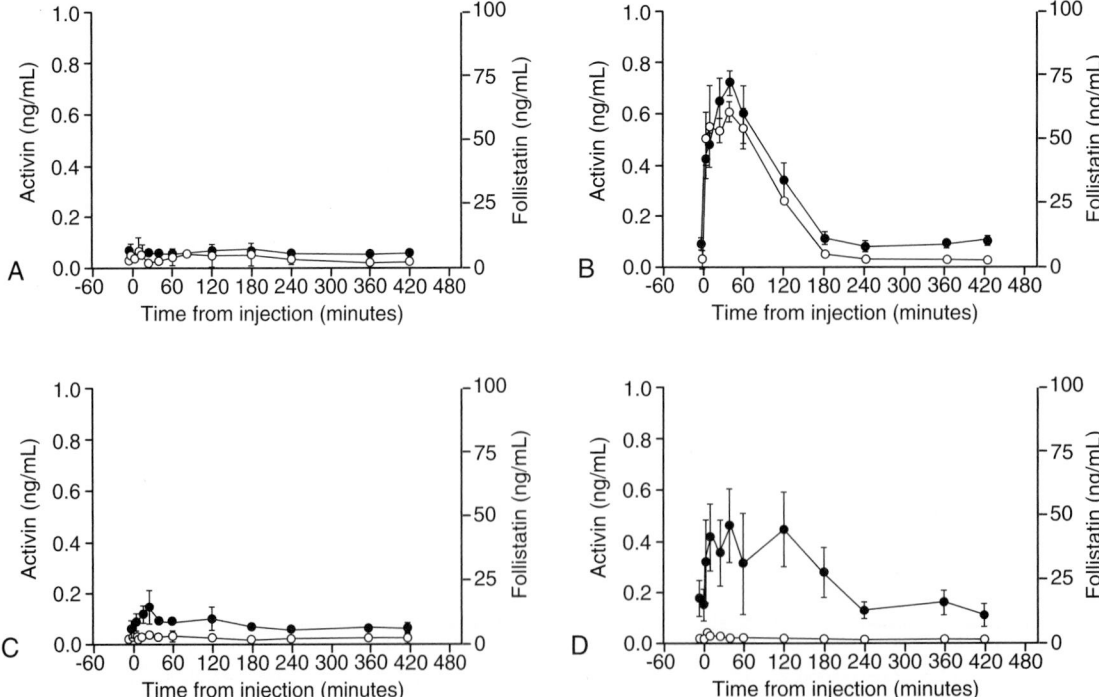

**Figure 140-5** Changes in the plasma concentrations of follistatin (l) and activin A (o) in the serum of adult ewes given a variety of treatments: **A,** saline only; **B,** heparin (100 U/kg); **C,** premixed heparin and protamine; **D,** protamine (2 mg/kg). Note the release of both activin and follistatin by heparin, the attenuation of the release when heparin and protamine are premixed and the release of follistatin only by protamine given alone. (From Jones KL, de Kretser DM, Phillips DJ: Effect of heparin administration to sheep on the release profiles of circulating activin A and follistatin. J Endocrinol 181:307–314, 2004. © 2004, The Endocrine Society.)

the observations that the phenotype of mice with targeted disruption of the follistatin gene does not replicate that seen in mice with disruption of the activin subunit genes.[179]

## CONSEQUENCES OF FOLLISTATIN GENE DELETION

Mice transgenic for follistatin gene deletion died within hours of delivery and showed shiny, taut skin, similar to that observed in mice with overexpression of TGF-$\beta_1$ to the epidermis.[179] The transgenic mice also had abnormal whiskers, a cleft hard palate, and abnormal lower incisors, suggestive of the modulatory role of follistatin in the activity of activin A.

Defects in axial skeletal components were noted in the ribs and vertebrae. The authors concluded that the phenotype of follistatin-deficient mice was consistent with the possibility that follistatin modulates the activities of multiple members of the TGF family in addition to the activins as discussed previously.[183]

## ASSAYS

Follistatin was recognized and isolated based on its biologic activity in dispersed cultured rat anterior pituitary cells. Its inhibition of FSH production in such cells appears to result primarily from its ability to bind activin. Additionally, follistatin can be measured in bioassays for activin A, such as the apoptotic action on MPC-11 (mouse plasmacytoma) cells,[233] wherein follistatin inhibits the readout. A variety of follistatin immunoassays has been described, variously specific for FS-288 or FS-315. Interpretation of such assays is rendered complex by the ability of activin to bind follistatin.[234–237] An assay primarily for FS-288 measured total follistatin.[174] Because levels were similar throughout the menstrual cycle and in postmenopausal women, it appears that circulating FS-288 is not an ovarian product. This is in keeping with results of castration experiments in sheep in which the levels did not decrease.[238] The binding of activin to follistatin clearly defines two potential pools, namely, free and bound, but to date, there are insufficient data to provide clear guidance as to the general applicability of these methods. The majority of the data to date are based on assays that measure total follistatin, with questions still about whether these assays measure both the FS-288 and FS-315 isoforms equally. Further developments in this field are needed to assist in clarifying the physiology of this protein.

## PHYSIOLOGY

It has now become abundantly clear that follistatins act primarily as activin-binding molecules.[14,153] The resulting activin-follistatin complexes are likely to be biologically inactive. As discussed earlier, the physiology of follistatin mirrors that of the activins. There remains the strong possibility that other actions of follistatin will reflect its capacity to bind other members of the TGF-$\beta$ family.

A further property of follistatin that complicates interpretation of its biologic activities is its ability to bind sulfated proteoglycans on the granulosa cell surface.[170] Such binding can be inhibited by the addition of heparin or heparin sulfate, and granulosa cells remain responsive to activin even after removal of follistatin with heparin. FS-288 in particular binds to cell-surface proteoglycans and sulfated matrices, whereas FS-315 shows essentially no binding. The heparin sulfate–binding site of follistatin is in a basic amino acid–rich region.[239] The precise role of cell surface–bound follistatin in

either enhancing or inhibiting the actions of activin remains controversial.[16] Whether it promotes activin clearance from the circulation or restricts the range of tissues in which activin acts has not been clearly established.[240]

The tissue localization provides an indication of the widespread actions of follistatin, but additional data are emerging from studies in which the measurement of this protein and the activins in disease states provides evidence of pathophysiologic roles. A clear example is the elevated levels of these proteins in patients with severe sepsis, indicating that these proteins are involved in the inflammatory response. Further, levels were elevated in patients with chronic liver disease, chronic renal failure, and advanced solid cancer.[187]

Follistatin is secreted by cultured rat[240] and bovine[236] granulosa cells, whereas cultured theca interna tissue does not produce the hormone. One report of follistatin measurements in women has indicated a twofold increase in its levels after ovarian hyperstimulation with gonadotropins.[237] A direct positive relationship was seen between follistatin and estradiol levels. Corresponding data have been obtained in vitro in cattle, in which FSH stimulates granulosa cell follistatin secretion.[236]

Like activin A, serum follistatin levels were elevated in pregnant women and increased similarly to activin throughout gestation.[208] Levels decreased after delivery. Free follistatin levels were also higher in pregnant than in nonpregnant women. The data were interpreted as indicating a placental origin for follistatin in pregnancy and is supported by the presence of follistatin in the placenta.[210] The role of these proteins in pregnancy disorders is the subject of ongoing studies.

## MÜLLERIAN-INHIBITING SUBSTANCE

### CLINICAL APPLICATIONS OF ASSAYS

The major characteristics of MIS (also known as antimüllerian hormone) are described in Chapter 143. It is relevant to mention MIS briefly in this chapter because of its structural relationships with other gonadal peptides. In terms of clinical application, descriptions of normal circulating levels from infancy to adulthood have been published. Mean MIS levels for males rise rapidly during the first year of life, are highest during late infancy, and gradually decline until puberty.[241] MIS levels in females are lowest at birth and show a minimal increase throughout the prepubertal years, with most subjects having undetectable levels. Values above the upper limits for females are discriminatory for the presence of testicular tissue or an ovarian tumor, and those below the lower limits for males are consistent with dysgenetic or absent testes or the presence of ovarian tissue. Substantial overlap was noted in MIS levels in adult males and females, with levels generally being similar to those of pubertal females. The same authors demonstrated that measurements of serum MIS can be used to determine testicular status in prepubertal children with nonpalpable gonads, thus allowing differentiation of anorchism from undescended testes in boys with bilateral cryptorchidism and giving a measure of testicular integrity in children with intersexual anomalies.[242] Recent publications[243,244] suggest that serum MIS is more strongly related to ovarian follicular status than inhibin B, estradiol, or FSH on day 3 of the menstrual cycle. However, during controlled ovarian hyperstimulation, levels actually decline, probably reflecting a decline in the numbers of small antral follicles.[244]

## REFERENCES

1. McCullagh DR: Dual endocrine activity of the testis. Science 76:19–20, 1932.
2. Robertson DM, Foulds LM, Leversha L, et al: Isolation of inhibin from bovine follicular fluid. Biochem Biophys Res Commun 126:220–226, 1985.
3. Ling N, Ying SY, Ueno N, et al: Pituitary FSH is released by a heterodimer of the subunits of the two forms of inhibin. Nature 321:779–782, 1986.
4. Vale W, Rivier J, Vaughan J, et al: Purification and characterization of an

FSH releasing protein from porcine follicular fluid. Nature 321:776–779, 1986.

5. Robertson DM, Klein R, de Vos FL, et al: The isolation of polypeptides with FSH suppressing activity from bovine follicular fluid which are structurally different from inhibin. Biochem Biophys Res Commun 149:744–749, 1987.

6. Ueno N, Ling N, Ying SY, et al: Isolation and partial characterization of follistatin: A single chain $M_r$ 35000 monomeric protein that inhibits the release of follicle stimulatory hormone. Proc Natl Acad Sci U S A 84:8282–8286, 1987.

7. Picard J-Y, Josso N: Purification of testicular anti-müllerian hormone allowing direct visualization of the pure glycoprotein and determination of yield and purification factor. Mol Endocrinol 34:23–29, 1984.

8. Budzik GP, Powell SM, Kamagata S, Donahoe PK: Müllerian inhibiting substance fractionation by dye affinity chromatography. Cell 34:307–314, 1983.

9. Cate RL, Mattaliano RJ, Hession C, et al: Isolation of the bovine and human genes for müllerian inhibiting substance and expression of the human gene in animal cells. Cell 45:685–698, 1986.

10. Vale W, Rivier C, Hsueh A, et al: Chemical and biological characterization of the inhibin family of protein hormones. Recent Prog Horm Res 44:1–34, 1988.

11. Robertson DM, Cahir N, Findlay JK, et al: The biological and immunological characterization of inhibin A and B forms in human follicular fluid and plasma. J Clin Endocrinol Metab 82:889–896, 1997.

12. Mason AJ, Farnworth PG, Sulligan J: Characterization and determination of the biological activities of non cleavable high molecular weight forms of inhibin A and activin A. Mol Endocrinol 10:1055–1065, 1996.

13. Robertson DM, Foulds LM, Prisk M, Hedger MP: Inhibin/activin subunit monomer: Isolation and characterization. Endocrinology 130:1680–1687, 1992.

14. Michel U, Farnworth P, Findlay JK: Follistatins: More than follicle-stimulating hormone suppressing proteins. Mol Cell Endocrinol 91:1–11, 1993.

15. Shimasaki S, Koga M, Esch F, et al: Primary structure of the human follistatin precursor and its genomic organization. Proc Natl Acad Sci U S A 85:4218–4222, 1988.

16. DePaolo LV: Inhibins, activins, and follistatins: The saga continues. Proc Soc Exp Med Biol 214:328–339, 1997.

17. Haqq CM, Donahoe PK: Regulation of sexual dimorphism in mammals. Physiol Rev 78:1–33, 1998.

18. Sun PD, Davies DR: The cystine-knot growth-factor superfamily. Annu Rev Biophys Biomol Struct 24:269–291, 1995.

19. Woodruff TK: Regulation of cellular and system function by activin. Biochem Pharmacol 55:953–963, 1998.

20. Wrana JL, Attisano L: The Smad pathway. Cytokine Growth Factor Rev 11:5–13, 2000.

21. Massague J, Chen YG: Controlling TGF-beta signaling. Genes Dev 15:627–644, 2000.

22. Lewis KA, Gray PC, Blount AL, et al: Beta-glycan binds inhibin and can mediate functional antagonism of activin signalling. Nature 404:411–414, 2000.

23. Bernard DJ, Chapman SC, Woodruff TK: Inhibin binding protein (INH-BP/P120), betaglycan and its continuing search for the inhibin receptor. Mol Endocrinol 16:207–212, 2002.

24. Chapman SC, Bernard DJ, Jelan J, Woodruff TK: Properties of inhibin binding to beta-glycan, INH-BP/P120 and the activin type II receptors. Mol Cell Endocrinol 196:79–93, 2002.

25. Lee VWK, McMaster J, Quigg H, Leversha L: Ovarian and circulating inhibin levels in immature female rats treated with gonadotropin and after castration. Endocrinology 111:1849–1854, 1982.

26. Robertson DM, Hayward S, Irby D, et al: Radioimmunoassay of rat serum inhibin: Changes after PMSG stimulation and gonadectomy. Mol Cell Endocrinol 58:1–8, 1988.

27. McLachlan RI, Robertson DM, Burger HG, de Kretser DM: The radioimmunoassay of bovine and human follicular fluid and serum inhibin. Mol Cell Endocrinol 46:175–185, 1986.

28. Ishida H, Tashiro H, Watanabe M, et al: Measurement of inhibin concentrations in men: Study of changes after castration and comparison with androgen levels in testicular tissue, spermatic vein blood and peripheral venous blood. J Clin Endocrinol Metab 70:1019–1022, 1990.

29. Erickson GF, Hsueh AJW: Secretion of "inhibin" by rat granulosa cells in vitro. Endocrinology 103:1960–1961, 1978.

30. Henderson KM, Franchimont P: Inhibin production by bovine ovarian tissues in vitro and its regulation by androgens. J Reprod Fertil 67:291–298, 1983.

31. Channing CP, Hoover DJ, Anderson LD, Tanabe K: Control of follicular secretion of inhibin in vitro and in vivo. Adv Biosci 34:41–55, 1982.

32. Channing CP, Tanabe K, Chacon M, Tildon JT: Stimulatory effects of follicle-stimulating hormone and luteinizing hormone upon secretion of progesterone and inhibin activity by cultured infant human ovarian granulosa cells. Fertil Steril 42:598–605, 1984.

33. Merchenthaler I, Culler MD, Petrusz P, Negro-Vilar A: Immunocytochemical localization of inhibin in rat and human reproductive tissues. Mol Cell Endocrinol 54:239–243, 1987.

34. Meunier H, Rivier C, Evans RM, Vale W: Gonadal and extragonadal expression of inhibin $\alpha$, $\beta_A$ and $\beta_B$ subunits in various tissues predicts diverse functions. Proc Natl Acad Sci U S A 85:247–251, 1988.

35. Woodruff TK, D'Agostino J, Schwartz NB, Mayo KE: Dynamic changes in inhibin messenger RNAs in rat ovarian follicles during the reproductive cycle. Science 239:1296–1299, 1988.

36. Rabinovici J, Goldsmith PC, Roberts VJ, et al: Localization and secretion of inhibin/activin subunits in the human and subhuman primate fetal gonads. J Clin Endocrinol Metab 73:1141–1149, 1991.

37. Roberts VJ, Barth S, El-Roeiy A, Yen SSC: Expression of inhibin/activin subunits and follistatin messenger ribonucleic acids and proteins in ovarian follicles and the corpus luteum during the human menstrual cycle. J Clin Endocrinol Metab 77:1402–1410, 1993.

38. Tsonis CG, Hillier SG, Baird DT: Production of inhibin bioactivity by human granulosa-lutein cells; stimulation by LH and testosterone in vitro. J Endocrinol 112:R11–R14, 1987.

39. Wang H-Z, Lu S-H, Han X-J, et al: Control of inhibin production by dispersed human luteal cells in vitro. Reprod Fertil Dev 4:67–75, 1992.

40. Davis SR, Krozowski Z, McLachlan RI, Burger HG: Inhibin gene expression in the human corpus luteum. J Endocrinol 115:R21–R23, 1987.

41. Schwall RH, Mason AJ, Wilcox JN, et al: Localization of inhibin/activin subunit mRNAs within the primate ovary. Mol Endocrinol 4:75–79, 1990.

42. Smith KB, Millar MR, McNeilly AS, et al: Immunocytochemical localization of inhibin $\alpha$-subunit in the human corpus luteum. J Endocrinol 129:155–160, 1991.

43. Mayo KE, Cerelli GM, Spiess J, et al: Inhibin-A subunit cDNAs from porcine ovary and human placenta. Proc Natl Acad Sci U S A 83:5849–5853, 1986.

44. Petraglia F, Calza L, Garuti GC, et al: Presence and synthesis of inhibin subunits in human decidua. J Clin Endocrinol Metab 71:487–492, 1990.

45. Voutilainen R, Eramaa M, Ritvos O: Hormonally regulated inhibin gene expression in human fetal and adult adrenals. J Clin Endocrinol Metab 73:1026–1030, 1991.

46. Petraglia F, Garuti GC, Calza L, et al: Inhibin subunits in human placenta: Localization and messenger ribonucleic acid levels during pregnancy. Am J Obstet Gynecol 165:750–758, 1991.

47. deKretser DM, Foulds LM, Hancock M, Robertson DM: Partial characterization of inhibin, activin and follistatin in the term human placenta. J Clin Endocrinol Metab 79:502–507, 1994.

48. Petraglia F, Florio P, Nappi C, Genazzani AR: Peptide signaling in human placenta and membranes: Autocrine, paracrine, and endocrine mechanisms. Endocr Rev 17:156–186, 1996.

49. Qu J, Thomas K: Inhibin and activin production in human placenta. Endocr Rev 16:485–507, 1995.

50. Steinberger A, Steinberger E: Secretion of an FSH-inhibiting factor by cultured Sertoli cells. Endocrinology 99:918–921, 1976.

51. Roberts V, Meunier H, Sawchenko PE, Vale W: Differential production and regulation of inhibin subunits in rat testicular cell types. Endocrinology 125:2350–2359, 1989.

52. Risbridger G, Clements J, Robertson DM, et al: Immuno- and bioactive inhibin and inhibin α subunit expression in rat Leydig cell cultures. Mol Cell Endocrinol 66:119–122, 1989.

53. Janecki A, Jakubowiak A, Steinberger A: Vectorial secretion of inhibin by immature rat Sertoli cells in vitro: Reexamination of previous results. Endocrinology 127:1896–1903, 1990.

54. Ramaswamy S, Marshall GR, Pohl CR, et al: Inhibitory and stimulatory regulation of testicular inhibin B secretion by luteinising hormone and follicle stimulating hormone, respectively, in the rhesus monkey (*Macaca mulatta*). Endocrinology 144:1175–1185, 2003.

55. Roberts V, Meunier H, Vaughan J, et al: Production and regulation of inhibin subunits in pituitary gonadotropes. Endocrinology 124:552–554, 1989.

56. Schlatt S, Weinbauer GF, Nieschlag E: Inhibin-like and gonadotropin-like immunoreactivity in pituitary cells of male monkeys (*Macaca fascicularis*, *Macaca mulatta*). Cell Tissue Res 265:203–209, 1991.

57. Attardi B, Marshall GR, Zorub DS, et al: Effects of orchidectomy on gonadotropin and inhibin sub-unit messenger ribonucleic acids in the pituitary of the rhesus monkey (*Macaca mulatta*). Endocrinology 130:1238–1244, 1992.

58. Alexander JM, Swearinger B, Tindall GT, Klibanski A: Human pituitary adenomas express endogenous inhibin subunit and follistatin messenger ribonucleic acids. J Clin Endocrinol Metab 80:147–152, 1995.

59. Demura R, Tajima S, Suzuki T, et al: Expression of inhibin-α and inhibin-βA subunit and activin type II receptor mRNAs in various human pituitary adenomas. Endocr J 42:95–100, 1995.

60. Thomas TZ, Wang H, Niclasen P, et al: Expression and localization of activin subunits and follistatins in tissues from men with high grade prostate cancer. J Clin Endocrinol Metab 82:3851–3858, 1997.

61. Mellor SL, Richards MG, Pedersen JS, et al: Loss of the expression and localization of inhibin alpha-subunit in high grade prostate cancer. J Clin Endocrinol Metab 83:969–975, 1998.

62. Matzuk MM, Kumar TR, Shou W, et al: Transgenic models to study the roles of inhibins and activins in reproduction, oncogenesis and development. Recent Prog Horm Res 51:123–157, 1996.

63. Matzuk MM, Finegold MJ, Mather JP, et al: Development of cancer cachexia-like syndrome and adrenal tumors in inhibin-deficient mice. Proc Natl Acad Sci U S A 91:8817–8821, 1994.

64. Coerver KA, Woodruff TK, Finegold MJ, et al: Activin signaling through activin receptor type II causes the cachexia-like symptoms in inhibin-deficient mice. Mol Endocrinol 10:534–543, 1996.

65. McLachlan RI, Robertson DM, de Kretser DM, Burger HG: Advances in the physiology of inhibin and inhibin-related peptides. Clin Endocrinol 29:77–114, 1988.

66. Tsonis CG, McNeilly AS, Baird DT: Measurement of exogenous and endogenous inhibin in sheep serum using a new and extremely sensitive bioassay for inhibin based on inhibition of ovine pituitary FSH secretion in vitro. J Endocrinol 110:341–352, 1986.

67. Tierney ML, Goss NH, Tomkins SM, et al: Physicochemical and biological characterization of recombinant human inhibin A. Endocrinology 126:3268–3270, 1990.

68. Rivier C, Schwall R, Mason A, et al: Effect of recombinant inhibin on luteinizing hormone and follicle-stimulating hormone secretion in the rat. Endocrinology 128:1548–1554, 1991.

69. McLachlan RI, Robertson DM, Healy DL, et al: Circulating immunoreactive inhibin levels during the normal human menstrual cycle. J Clin Endocrinol Metab 65:954–961, 1987.

70. Burger HG: Clinical review—clinical utility of inhibin measurements. J Clin Endocrinol Metab 76:1391–1396, 1993.

71. Robertson DM, Giacometti M, Foulds LM, et al: Isolation of inhibin α-subunit precursor proteins from bovine follicular fluid. Endocrinology 125:2141–2149, 1989.

72. Sugino K, Nakamura T, Takio N, et al: Inhibin α-subunit monomer is present in follicular fluid. Biochem Biophys Res Commun 159:1323–1329, 1989.

73. Schneyer AL, Mason AJ, Burton LE, et al: Immunoreactive inhibin α-subunit in human serum: Implications for radioimmunoassay. J Clin Endocrinol Metab 70:1208–1212, 1990.

74. Robertson DM, Tsonis CG, McLachlan RI: Comparison of inhibin immunological and in vitro biological activities in human serum. J Clin Endocrinol Metab 67:438–443, 1988.

75. Burger HG: Inhibin. Reprod Med Rev 1:1–20, 1992.

76. Groome NP, Illingworth PJ, O'Brien M, et al: Detection of dimeric inhibin throughout the human menstrual cycle by two-site enzyme immunoassay. Clin Endocrinol (Oxf) 40:717–723, 1994.

77. Groome NP, Illingworth PJ, O'Brien M, et al: Measurement of dimeric inhibin B throughout the human menstrual cycle. J Clin Endocrinol Metab 81:1401–1405, 1996.

78. Illingworth PJ, Groome NP, Byrd W, et al: Inhibin B: A likely candidate for the physiologically important form of inhibin in men. J Clin Endocrinol Metab 81:1321–1325, 1996.

79. de Kretser DM, McLachlan RI, Robertson DM, Burger HG: Serum inhibin levels in normal men and men with testicular disorders. J Endocrinol 120:517–523, 1989.

80. Scott RS, Burger HG: An inverse relationship exists between seminal plasma inhibin and serum FSH in man. J Clin Endocrinol Metab 52:796–803, 1981.

81. Burger HG, Yamada Y, Bangah ML, et al: Serum gonadotropin, sex steroid and immunoreactive inhibin levels in the first two years of life. J Clin Endocrinol Metab 72:682–686, 1991.

82. Andersson AM, Toppari J, Haavisto AM, et al: Longitudinal reproductive hormone profiles in infants: Peak of inhibin B levels in infant boys exceeds levels in adult men. J Clin Endocrinol Metab 83:675–681, 1998.

83. Crofton PM, Evans AEM, Groome NP et al: Inhibin B in boys from birth to adulthood: Relationship with age, pubertal stage FSH and testosterone. Clin Endocrinol 56:215–221, 2002.

84. Burger HG, McLachlan RI, Bangah ML, et al: Serum inhibin concentrations rise throughout normal male and female puberty. J Clin Endocrinol Metab 67:689–694, 1988.

85. Crofton PM, Illingworth PJ, Groome NP, et al: Changes in dimeric inhibin A and B during normal early puberty in boys and girls. Clin Endocrinol 46:109–114, 1997.

86. Byrd W, Bennett MJ, Carr BR, et al: Regulation of biologically active dimeric inhibin A and B from infancy to adulthood in the male. J Clin Endocrinol Metab 83:2849–2854, 1998.

87. Bohring C, Krause W: Serum levels of inhibin B in men of different age groups. Aging Male 6:73–78, 2003.

88. Anawalt BD, Bebb RA, Matsumoto AM, et al: Serum inhibin B levels reflect Sertoli cell function in normal men and men with testicular dysfunction. J Clin Endocrinol Metab 81:3341–3345, 1996.

89. Anderson RA, Wallace EM, Groome NP, et al: Physiological relationship between inhibin B, follicle stimulating hormone secretion and spermatogenesis in normal men and response to gonadotrophin suppression by exogenous testosterone. Hum Reprod 12:746–751, 1997.

90. Klingmuller D, Haidl G: Inhibin B in men with normal and disturbed spermatogenesis. Hum Reprod 12:2376–2378, 1997.

91. Wallace EM, Groome NP, Riley SC, et al: Effects of chemotherapy-induced testicular damage on inhibin, gonadotropin, and testosterone secretion: A prospective, longitudinal study. J Clin Endocrinol Metab 82:3111–3115, 1997.

92. Seminara SB, Boepple PA, Nachtigall LB, et al: Inhibin B in males with gonadotropin-releasing hormone (GnRH) deficiency: Changes in serum concentrations after short term physiologic GnRH replacement—a clinical research center study. J Clin Endocrinol Metab 81:3692–3696, 1996.

93. Albers N, Bettendorf M, Hart CS, et al: Hormone ontogeny in the ovine fetus. XXIII. Pulsatile administration of follicle-stimulating hormone stimulates inhibin production and decreases testosterone synthesis in the ovine fetal gonad. Endocrinology 124:3089–3094, 1989.

94. Albers N, Hart CS, Kaplan SL, Grumbach MM: Hormone ontogeny in the ovine fetus. XXIV. Porcine follicular fluid "inhibins" selectively suppress plasma follicle-stimulating hormone in the ovine fetus. Endocrinology 125:675–678, 1989.

95. Rabinovici J, Goldsmith PC, Roberts VJ, et al: Localization and secretion of inhibin/activin subunits in the human and subhuman primate fetal gonads. J Clin Endocrinol Metab 73:1141–1149, 1991.

96. Torney AH, Robertson DM, de Kretser DM: Characterization of inhibin and related proteins in bovine fetal testicular and ovarian extracts: Evidence for the presence of inhibin subunit products and FSH-suppressing protein. J Endocrinol 133:111–120, 1992.

97. Chellakooty M, Schmidt IM, Haavisto AM, et al: Inhibin A, inhibin B, follicle stimulating hormone, luteinising hormone, estradiol, and sex hormone binding globulin levels in 473 healthy infant girls. J Clin Endocrinol Metab 88:3515–3520, 2003.

98. Crofton PM, Evans AEM, Groome NP, et al: Dimeric inhibins in girls from birth to adulthood: Relationship with age, pubertal stage, FSH and estradiol. Clin Endocrinol 56:223–230, 2002.

99. Quigley C, Cowell C, Jimenez M, et al: Normal or early development of puberty despite gonadal damage in children treated for acute lymphoblastic leukemia. N Engl J Med 321:143–151, 1989.

100. Crofton PM, Thomson AB, Evans AEM, et al: Is inhibin B a potential marker of gonadotoxicity in pre-pubertal children treated for cancer? Clin Endocrinol 58:296–301, 2003.

101. McLachlan RI, Robertson DM, Healy DL, et al: Circulating immunoreactive inhibin levels during the normal human menstrual cycle. J Clin Endocrinol Metab 65:954–961, 1987.

102. Welt CK, Martin KM, Taylor AE, et al: Frequency modulation of follicle-stimulating hormone (FSH) during the luteal-follicular transition: Evidence for FSH control of inhibin B in normal women. J Clin Endocrinol Metab 82:2645–2652, 1997.

103. McLachlan RI, Robertson DM, Healy DL, et al: Plasma inhibin levels during gonadotrophin-induced ovarian hyperstimulation for IVF: A new index of follicular function? Lancet 1:1233–1234, 1986.

104. Buckler HM, Healy DL, Burger HG: Purified FSH stimulates inhibin production from the human ovary. J Endocrinol 122:279–285, 1989.

105. Hee J, MacNaughton J, Bangah M, et al: FSH induces dose-dependent stimulation of immunoreactive inhibin secretion during the follicular phase of the human menstrual cycle. J Clin Endocrinol Metab 76:1340–1343, 1993.

106. Burger HG, Groome NP, Robertson DM: Both inhibin A and B respond to exogenous follicle-stimulating hormone in the follicular phase of the human menstrual cycle. J Clin Endocrinol Metab 83:4167–4169, 1998.

107. Eldar-Geva AT, Robertson DM, Cahir N, et al: Relationship between serum inhibin A and B and ovarian follicle development after a daily fixed dose of administration of recombinant follicle-stimulating hormone. J Clin Endocrinol Metab 85:607–613, 2000.

108. McLachlan RI, Cohen NL, Vale WW, et al: The importance of LH in the control of inhibin and progesterone secretion by the human corpus luteum. J Clin Endocrinol Metab 68:1078–1085, 1989.

109. Smith KB, Fraser HM: Control of progesterone and inhibin secretion during the luteal phase in the macaque. J Endocrinol 128:107–113, 1991.

110. Burger HG, Hee J, Bangah M, et al: Effects of FSH on serum immunoreactive inhibin levels in the luteal phase of the menstrual cycle. Clin Endocrinol 45:431–434, 1996.

111. Martin NG, Robertson DM, Chenevix-Trench G, et al: Elevation of follicular phase inhibin and luteinizing hormone levels in mothers of dizygotic twins suggests nonovarian control of human multiple ovulation. Fertil Steril 56:469–474, 1991.

112. Leung PHY, Salamonsen LA, Findlay JK: Immunolocalization of inhibin and activin subunits in human endometrium across the menstrual cycle. Hum Reprod 13:3469–3477, 1998.

113. Qu J, Vankrieken L, Brulet C, Thomas K: Circulating bioactive inhibin levels during human pregnancy. J Clin Endocrinol Metab 72:862–866, 1991.

114. Abe Y, Hasegawa Y, Miyamoto K, et al: High concentrations of plasma immunoreactive inhibin during normal pregnancy in women. J Clin Endocrinol Metab 71:133–137, 1990.

115. McLachlan RI, Healy DL, Robertson DM, et al: Circulating immunoreactive inhibin in the luteal phase and early gestation of women undergoing ovulation induction. Fertil Steril 48:1001–1005, 1987.

116. Kettel LM, Roseff SJ, Bangah ML, et al: Circulating levels of inhibin in pregnant women at term: Simultaneous disappearance with estradiol and progesterone after delivery. Clin Endocrinol 34:19–23, 1991.

117. McLachlan RI, Healy DL, Lutjen PJ, et al: The maternal ovary is not the source of circulating inhibin levels during human pregnancy. Clin Endocrinol 27:663–668, 1987.

118. Illingworth PJ, Groome NP, Duncan WC, et al: Measurement of circulating inhibin forms during the establishment of pregnancy. J Clin Endocrinol Metab 81:1471–1475, 1996.

119. Muttukrishna S, George L, Fowler PA, et al: Measurement of serum concentrations of inhibin-A (alpha-beta A dimer) during human pregnancy. Clin Endocrinol (Oxf) 42:391–397, 1995.

120. Petraglia F, Sawchenko P, Lim ATW, et al: Localization, secretion, and action of inhibin in human placenta. Science 237:187–189, 1987.

121. Illingworth PJ, Reddi K, Smith K, Baird DT: Pharmacological "rescue" of the corpus luteum results in increased inhibin production. Clin Endocrinol 33:323–332, 1990.

122. Yohkaichiya T, Polson DW, Hughes EG, et al: Serum immunoactive inhibin levels in early pregnancy after in vitro fertilisation and embryo transfer. Fertil Steril 59:1081–1089, 1993.

123. Clifford K, Rai R, Regan L: Future pregnancy outcome in unexplained recurrent first trimester miscarriage. Hum Reprod 12:387–389, 1997.

124. Muttukrishna S, Knight PG, Groome NP, et al: Activin A and inhibin A as possible endocrine markers for pre-eclampsia. Lancet 349:1285–1288, 1997.

125. Lockwood GM, Muttukrishna S, Ledger WL: Inhibins and activins in human ovulation, conception and pregnancy. Hum Reprod 4:284–295, 1998.

126. Tong S, Wallace EM, Burger HG: Inhibins and activins: Clinical advances in reproductive medicine. Clin Endocrinol 58:115–127, 2003.

127. Sherman BM, West JH, Korenman SG: The menopausal transition: Analysis of LH, FSH, estradiol, and progesterone concentrations during menstrual cycles of older women. J Clin Endocrinol Metab 42:629–636, 1976.

128. Reyes FI, Winter JSD, Faiman C: Pituitary-ovarian relationships preceding the menopause. Am J Obstet Gynecol 129:557–564, 1977.

129. Lenton EA, Sexton L, Lee S, Cooke ID: Progressive changes in LH and FSH and LH:FSH ratio in women throughout reproductive life. Maturitas 10:35–43, 1988.

130. Lenton LA, de Kretser DM, Woodward AJ, Robertson DM: Inhibin concentrations throughout the menstrual cycles of normal, infertile, and older women compared with those during spontaneous conception cycles. J Clin Endocrinol 73:1180–1190, 1991.

131. Lee SJ, Lenton EA, Sexton L, Cooke ID: The effect of age on the cyclical patterns of plasma LH, FSH, oestradiol and progesterone in women with regular menstrual cycles. Hum Reprod 3:851–855, 1988.

132. Klein NA, Illingworth PJ, Groome NP, et al: Decreased inhibin secretion is associated with the monotropic FSH rise in older, ovulatory women: A study of serum and follicular fluid levels of dimeric inhibin A and B in spontaneous menstrual cycles. J Clin Endocrinol Metab 81:2742–2745, 1996.

133. Burger HG, Dudley EC, Cui J, et al: Early follicular phase serum FSH as a function of age: The roles of inhibin B, inhibin A and oestradiol. Climacteric 3:17–24, 2000.

134. Burger HG, Cahir N, Robertson DM, et al: Serum inhibins A and B fall differentially as FSH rises in perimenopausal women. Clin Endocrinol 48:809–813, 1998.

135. Burger HG, Dudley EC, Hopper JL, et al: Prospectively measured levels of serum FSH, oestradiol and the dimeric inhibins during the menopausal transition in a population-based cohort of women. J Clin Endocrinol Metab 84:4025–4030, 1999.

136. Hughes EG, Robertson DM, Handelsman DJ, et al: Inhibin and estradiol responses to ovarian hyperstimulation: Effects of age and predictive value for in vitro fertilization outcome. J Clin Endocrinol Metab 70:358–364, 1990.

137. Buckler HM, Evans CA, Mamtora H, et al: Gonadotropin, steroid and inhibin levels in women with incipient ovarian failure during anovulatory and ovulatory rebound cycles. J Clin Endocrinol Metab 72:116–124, 1991.

138. Hayes FJ, Hall JE, Boepple PA, Crowley WJ Jr: Clinical review 96: Differential control of gonadotropin secretion in the human: Endocrine role of inhibin. J Clin Endocrinol Metab 83:1835–1841, 1998.

139. Burger HG, Dudley EC, Robertson DM, et al: Hormonal changes in the menopausal transition. Rec Prog Horm Res 57:257–275, 2002.

140. Jensen TK, Andersson A-M, Hjollund NHI, et al: Inhibin B as a serum marker of spermatogenesis: Correlation to differences in sperm concentration and follicle-stimulating hormone levels. A study of 349 Danish men. J Clin Endocrinol Metab 82:4059–4063, 1997.

141. Seifer DB, Lambert-Messerlian G, Hogan JW, et al: Day 3 serum inhibin-B is predictive of assisted reproductive technologies outcome. Fertil Steril 67:110–114, 1997.

142. Soules MR, McLachlan RI, Marit EK, et al: Luteal phase deficiency: Characterization of reproductive hormones over the menstrual cycle. J Clin Endocrinol Metab 69:804–812, 1989.

143. Robertson DM, Burger HG, Fuller PJ: Inhibin/activin and ovarian cancer. Endocr Relat Cancer 11:35–49, 2004.

144. Lappohn R, Burger H, Bouma J, et al: Inhibin as a marker for granulosa-cell tumors. N Engl J Med 321:790–793, 1989.

145. Healy DL, Burger HG, Mamers P, et al: Inhibin: A serum marker for mucinous ovarian cancers. N Engl J Med 329:1539–1541, 1993.

146. Robertson DM, Cahir N, Burger HG: Inhibin forms in serum from postmenopausal women with ovarian cancers. Clin Endocrinol (Oxf) 50:381–386, 1999.

147. Robertson DM, Cahir N, Burger HG: Combined inhibin and CA125 assays in the detection of ovarian cancer. Clin Chem 45:651–658, 1999.

148. Yohkaichiya T, Fukaya T, Hoshiai H, et al: Inhibin: A new circulating marker of hydatidiform mole? Br Med J 298:1684–1686, 1989.

149. Schmitt J, Hotten G, Jenkins NA, et al: Structure, chromosomal localization, and expression analysis of the mouse inhibin/activin $\beta_C$ (Inhbc) gene. Genomics 32:358–366, 1996.

150. Oda S, Nishimatsu S, Murakami K, Ueno N: Molecular cloning and functional analysis of a new activin $\beta$ subunit: A dorsal mesoderm-inducing activity in *Xenopus*. Biochem Biophys Res Commun 210:581–588, 1995.

151. Fang J, Yin W, Smiley E, et al: Molecular cloning of the mouse activin $\beta_E$ subunit gene. Biochem Biophys Res Commun 228:669–784, 1996.

152. Mellor SL, Cranfield M, Ries R, et al: Localization of activin, $\beta_A$-, $\beta_B$-, and $\beta_C$-subunits in human prostate and evidence for formation of new activin heterodimers of $\beta_C$-subunit. J Clin Endocrinol Metab 85:4851–4858, 2000.

153. Nakamura T, Takio K, Eto Y, et al: Activin-binding protein from rat ovary is follistatin. Science 247:836–838, 1989.

154. Vaughan JM, Vale WW: $\alpha_2$-Macroglobulin is a binding protein of inhibin and activin. Endocrinology 132:2038–2050, 1993.

155. Phillips DJ: Regulation of activin's access to the cell: Why is Mother Nature such a control freak? Bioessays 22:689–696, 2000.

156. Nakamura T, Asashima M, Eto Y, et al: Isolation and characterization of native activin B. J Biol Chem 267:16385–16389, 1992.

157. Eto Y, Takazawa M, Takano S, et al: Purification and characterization of erythroid differentiation factor (EDF) isolated from human leukemia cell line THP-1. Biochem Biophys Res Commun 142:1095–1103, 1987.

158. Thomsen G, Woolf T, Whitman M, et al: Activins are expressed early in *Xenopus* embryogenesis and can induce axial mesoderm and anterior structures. Cell 63:485–493, 1990.

159. Mitrani E, Ziv T, Thomsen G, et al: Activin can induce the formation of axial structures and is expressed in the hypoblast of the chick. Cell 63:495–501, 1990.

160. Ying SY: Inhibins, activins and follistatins: Gonadal proteins modulating the secretion of follicle-stimulating hormone. Endocr Rev 9:267–293, 1988.

161. Kogure K, Zhang Y-Q, Kanzaki M, et al: Intravenous administration of follistatin: Delivery to the liver and effect on liver regeneration after partial hepatectomy. Hepatology 24:361–366, 1996.

162. Brosh N, Sternberg D, Honigwachs-Sha'anani J: The plasmacytoma growth inhibitor restricting-P is an antagonist of interleukin 6 and interleukin 11—Identification as a stroma-derived activin A. J Biol Chem 270:29594–29600, 1995.

163. Sakai R, Miwa K, Eto Y: Local administration of activin promotes fracture healing in the rat fibula fracture model. Bone 25:191–196, 1999.

164. Hübner C, Smola H, Werner S: Strong indication of activin expression after injury suggests an important role of activin in wound repair. Dev Biol 173:490–498, 1996.

165. de Kretser DM, Hedger MP, Phillips DJ: Activin A and follistatin: Their role in the acute phase reaction and inflammation. J Endocrinol 161:195–198, 1999.

166. Andreasson K, Worley PF: Induction of beta-A activin expression by synaptic activity and during neocortical development. Neuroscience 69:781–796, 1995.

167. Wu DD, Lai M, Hughes Paul E, et al: Expression of the activin axis and neuronal rescue effects of recombinant activin A following hypoxic-ischemic brain injury in the infant rat. Brain Res 835:369–378, 1999.

168. Mather JP, Woodruff TK, Krummen LA: Paracrine regulation of reproductive function by inhibin and activin. Proc Soc Exp Biol Med 201:1–15, 1992.

169. Phillips DJ, de Kretser DM: Follistatin: A multifunctional regulatory protein. Front Neuroendocrinol 19:287–322, 1998.

170. Nakamura T, Sugino S, Titani K, Sugino H: Follistatin, an activin binding protein associates with heparin sulphate proteoglycans on follicular granulosa cells. J Biol Chem 266:19432–19437, 1991.

171. Sugino K, Kurosawa N, Nakamura T, et al: Molecular heterogeneity of follistatin, an activin binding protein. Higher affinity of the carboxyl-terminal truncated forms for heparan sulfate proteoglycans on the ovarian granulose cell. J Biol Chem 268:15579–15587, 1993.

172. Phillips DJ, Jones KL, McGaw DJ, et al: Release of activin and follistatin during cardiovascular procedures is largely due to heparin administration. J Clin Endocrinol Metab 85:2411–2415, 2000.

173. Vassilli A, Matzuk MM, Gardner HAR, et al: Activin/inhibin $\alpha_B$ subunit gene disruption leads to defects in eyelid development and female reproduction. Genes Dev 8:414–427, 1994.

174. Sawchenko PE, Plotsky PM, Pfeiffer SW, et al: Inhibin in central neural pathways involved in the control of oxytocin secretion. Nature 334:615–617, 1988.

175. Matzuk MM, Kumar TR, Vassalli A, et al: Functional analysis of activins during mammalian development. Nature 374:354–356, 1995.

176. Brown CW, Houston-Hawkins DE, Woodruff TK, Matzuk MM: Insertion of Inhbb into the Inhba locus rescues the Inhba-null phenotype and reveals new activin functions. Nat Genet 25:453–457, 2000.

177. Matzuk MM, Kumar TR, Bradley A: Different phenotypes for mice deficient in either activins or activin receptor type II. Nature 374:356–360, 1995.

178. Wreford NG, Kumar TR, Matzuk MM, de Kretser DM: Analysis of the testicular phenotype of the follicle stimulating hormone (FSH) β subunit knock-out and the activin type II receptor knock-out mice by stereological analysis. Endocrinology 142:2916–2920, 2001.

179. Matzuk MM, Lu N, Vogel H, et al: Multiple defects and perinatal death in mice deficient in follistatin. Nature 374:360–363, 1995.

180. Knight PG, Muttukrishna S, Groome NP: Development and application of a two-site enzyme immunoassay for the determination of "total" activin A concentrations in serum and follicular fluid. J Endocrinol 148:267–279, 1996.

181. Groome NP, Tsigou A, Cranfield M, et al: Enzyme immunoassays for inhibins, activins and follistatins. Mol Cell Endocrinol 180:73–77, 2001.

182. McFarlane JR, Foulds LM, Pisciotta A, et al: Measurement of activin in biological fluids by radioimmunoassay, utilizing dissociating agents to remove the interference of follistatin. Eur J Endocrinol 134:481–489, 1996.

183. Robertson DM, Foulds LM, Prisk M, Hedger MP: Inhibin/activin beta-subunit monomer: Isolation and characterization. Endocrinology 130:1680–1687, 1992.

184. Lin SY, Morrison JR, Phillips DJ, de Kretser DM: Regulation of ovarian function by the TGF-a superfamily and follistatin. Reproduction 126:133–148, 2003.

185. Welt CK, Crowley WF Jr: Activin: An endocrine or paracrine agent? Eur J Endocrinol 139:469–471, 1998.

186. McLachlan RI, Dahl KD, Bremner WJ, et al: Recombinant human activin A stimulates basal and GNRH-stimulated FSH and LH release in the adult male macaque, Macaca fascicularis. Endocrinology 125:2787–2789, 1989.

187. Loria P, Petraglia F, Concari M, et al: Influence of age and sex on serum concentrations of total dimeric activin A. Eur J Endocrinol 139:487–492, 1998.

188. Shintani Y, Wakatsuki M, Harada K, et al: Immunoassays for activin and follistatin: Results in normal and diseased subjects. In Aono T, Sugino H, Vale W (eds): Inhibin, Activin and Follistatin. Norwell, MA, Serono Symposia, 1997, pp 130–140.

189. Findlay JK: An update on the roles of inhibin, activin and follistatin as local regulators of folliculogenesis. Biol Reprod 48:15–23, 1993.

190. Xiao S, Robertson DM, Findlay JK: Effects of activin and follicle stimulating hormone (FSH) suppressing protein/follistatin on FSH receptors and differentiation of cultured rat granulosa cells. Endocrinology 131:1009–1016, 1992.

191. Xiao S, Findlay JK, Robertson DM: The effect of bovine activin and follicle stimulating hormone (FSH) suppressing protein/follistatin on FSH-induced differentiation of rat granulosa cells in vitro. Mol Cell Endocrinol 69:1–8, 1990.

192. Miro F, Smyth CD, Hillier SG: Development-related effects of recombinant activin on steroid synthesis in rat granulosa cells. Endocrinology 129:3388–3394, 1991.

193. Hillier SG, Yong EL, Illingworth PJ, et al: Effect of recombinant activin on androgen synthesis in cultured human thecal cells. J Clin Endocrinol Metab 72:1206–1211, 1991.

194. Buzzard JJ, Loveland KL, O'Bryan MK, et al: Changes in circulating and testicular levels of inhibin A and B and activin A during post-natal development in the rat. Endocrinology 145:3532–3541, 2004.

195. Meehan T, Schlatt S, O'Bryan MK, et al: Regulation of germ cell and Sertoli cell development by activin, follistatin and FSH. Dev Biol 220:225–237, 2000.

196. Mather JP, Attie K, Woodruff T, et al: Activin stimulates spermatogonial proliferation in germ-Sertoli cell cocultures from immature rat testis. Endocrinology 127:3206–3214, 1990.

197. Buzzard JJ, Farnworth PG, de Kretser DM, et al: Proliferative phase Sertoli cells display a developmentally regulated response to activin in vitro. Endocrinology 144:474–483, 2003.

198. de Winter JP, Vanderstichele HMJ, Timmerman MA, et al: Activin is produced by rat Sertoli cells in vitro and can act as an autocrine regulator of Sertoli cell function. Endocrinology 132:975–982, 1993.

199. de Winter JP, Vanderstichele HM, Verhoeven G, et al: Peritubular myoid cells from immature rat testes secrete activin A and express activin receptor type II in vitro. Endocrinology 135:759–767, 1994.

200. Lee W, Mason AJ, Schwall R, et al: Secretion of activin by interstitial cells in the testis. Science 243:396–398, 1989.

201. Schubert D, Kimura H, LaCorbiere M: Activin is a nerve survival molecule. Nature 344:868–870, 1990.

202. Lai M, Sirimanne H, Williams C, Gluckman P: Sequential patterns of inhibin/activin gene expression following hypoxic-ischemic injury to the rat brain. Neuroscience 70:1013–1024, 1996.

203. Corrigan AZ, Bilezikjian LM, Carroll RS, et al: Evidence for an autocrine role of activin B within rat anterior pituitary cultures. Endocrinology 128:1682–1684, 1991.

204. Bilezikjian LM, Corrigan AZ, Blount AL, Vale WW: Pituitary follistatin and inhibin subunit messenger ribonucleic acid levels and differentially regulated by local and hormonal factors. Endocrinology 137:4277–4284, 1996.

205. Gospodarowicz D, Lau K: Pituitary follicular cells secrete both vascular endothelial growth factor and follistatin. Biochem Biophys Res Commun 165:292–298, 1989.

206. Petraglia F, Garg S, Horio P, et al: Activin A and activin B measured in maternal serum, cord blood serum, and amniotic fluid during human pregnancy. Endocr J 1:323–327, 1993.

207. Muttukrishna S, Fowler PA, George L, et al: Changes in peripheral serum levels of total activin A during the human menstrual cycle and pregnancy. J Clin Endocrinol Metab 81:3328–3334, 1996.

208. O'Connor AE, McFarlane JR, Hayward S, et al: Serum activin A and follistatin levels during human pregnancy: A cross-sectional and longitudinal study. Hum Reprod 14:827–832, 1999.

209. Florio P, Cobellis S, Luisi P, et al: Changes in inhibins and activin secretion in healthy and pathological pregnancies. Mol Cell Endocrinol 180:123–130, 2001.

210. de Kretser DM, Foulds LM, Hancock M, Robertson DM: Partial characterization of inhibin, activin and follistatin in the term human placenta. J Clin Endocrinol Metab 79:502–507, 1994.

211. Petraglia F, Garg S, Florio P, et al: Activin A and Activin B measured in maternal serum, cord blood serum and amniotic fluid during human pregnancy. Endocr J 1:323–327, 1993.

212. Schneider-Kolsky M, D'Antona D, Evans LW, et al: Maternal serum total activin A and follistatin in pregnancy and parturition. Br J Obstet Gynaecol 107:995–1000, 2000.

213. Jenkin G, Ward J, Hooper S, O'Connor A, et al: Feto-placental hypoxemia regulates the release of fetal activin A as prostaglandin E$_2$. Endocrinology 142:963–966, 2001.

214. Harada K, Shintani Y, Sakamoto Y, et al: Serum immunoreactive activin A levels in normal subjects and patients with various diseases. J Clin Endocrinol Metab 81:2125–2130, 1996.

215. Petraglia F, De Vita D, Gallinelli A, et al: Abnormal concentration of maternal serum activin A in gestational diseases. J Clin Endocrinol Metab 80:558–561, 1995.

216. Petraglia F, Aguzzoli L, Gallinelli A, et al: Hypertension in pregnancy: Changes in activin A maternal serum

concentration. Placenta 16:447–454, 1995.

217. Muttukrishna S, Knight PG, Groome NP, et al: Activin A and inhibin A as possible markers for pre-eclampsia. Lancet 349:1285–1288, 1997.

218. Yu EW, Dolter KL, Shao L-E, Yu J: Suppression of IL-6 biological activities by activin A and implications for inflammatory arthropathies. Clin Exp Immunol 112:126–132, 1998.

219. Hubner G, Brauchle M, Gregor M, Werner S: Activin A: A novel player and inflammatory marker in inflammatory bowel disease. Lab Invest 77:311–317, 1997.

220. Nüsing RM, Barsig J: Induction of prostanoid, nitric oxide and cytokine formation in rat bone marrow derived macrophages by activin A. Br J Pharmacol 127:919–926, 1999.

221. Jones KL, Brauman JN, Groome NP, et al: Activin A release into the circulation is an early event in systemic inflammation and precedes the release of follistatin. Endocrinology 141:1905–1908, 2000.

222. Jones KL, de Kretser DM, Clarke IJ, et al: Characterisation of the rapid release of activin A following acute lipopolysaccharide challenge in the ewe. J Endocrinol 182:69–80, 2004.

223. Michel U, Ebert S, Phillips D, Nau R: Serum concentrations of activin and follistatin are elevated and run in parallel in patients with septicemia. Eur J Endocrinol 148:1–6, 2003.

224. Funaba M, Ikeda T, Ogawa K, et al: Role of activin A in murine mast cells: Modulation of cell growth, differentiation and migration. J Leukoc Biol 73:793–801, 2003.

225. Yndestad A, Ueland T, Oie E, et al: Elevated levels of activin A in heart failure: Potential role in myocardial remodeling. Circulation 109:1379–1385, 2004.

226. Wankell M, Munz B, Hübner G, et al: Impaired wound healing in transgenic mice overexpressing the activin antagonist follistatin in the epidermis. EMBO J 20:5361–5273, 2001.

227. Welt CK, Lambert-Messerlian G, Zheng W, et al: Presence of activin, inhibin, and follistatin in epithelial ovarian carcinoma. J Clin Endocrinol Metab 82:3720–3727, 1997.

228. Michel U, Albiston A, Findlay JK: Rat follistatin: Gonadal and extragonadal expression and evidence for alternative splicing. Biochem Biophys Res Commun 173:401–407, 1990.

229. Nakatani A, Shimasaki S, DePaolo LV, et al: Cyclic changes in follistatin messenger ribonucleic acid and its protein in the rat ovary during the estrous cycle. Endocrinology 129:603–611, 1991.

230. Shimasaki S, Koga M, Buscaglia ML, et al: Follistatin gene expression in the ovary and extragonadal tissues. Mol Endocrinol 3:651–659, 1989.

231. Michel U, McMaster JW, Findlay JK: Regulation of steady-state follistatin mRNA levels in rat granulosa cells in vitro. J Mol Endocrinol 9:147–156, 1992.

232. Michel U, Schneider O, Kirchhof C, et al: Production of follistatin in porcine endothelial cells: Differential regulation by bacterial compounds and the synthetic glucocorticoid RU28362. Endocrinology 137:4925–4934, 1996.

233. Phillips DJ, Brauman JN, de Kretser DM, et al: A sensitive and specific in vitro bioassay for activin using a mouse plasmacytoma cell line, MPC-11. J Endocrinol 162:111–116, 1999.

234. Wakatsuki M, Shintani Y, Abe M, et al: Immunoradiometric assay for follistatin: Serum immunoreactive follistatin levels in normal adults and pregnant women. J Clin Endocrinol Metab 81:630–634, 1996.

235. Sakamoto Y, Shintani Y, Harada K, et al: Determination of free follistatin levels in sera of normal subjects and patients with various diseases. Eur J Endocrinol 135:345–351, 1996.

236. Klein R, Robertson DM, Shukovski L, et al: The radioimmunoassay of follicle stimulating hormone (FSH)-suppressing protein (FSP); stimulation of bovine granulosa cell FSP secretion by FSH. Endocrinology 128:1048–1056, 1991.

237. Sugawara S, DePaolo L, Nakatani A, et al: Radioimmunoassay of follistatin: Application for in vitro fertilization procedures. J Clin Endocrinol Metab 71:1672–1674, 1990.

238. Phillips DJ, Hedger MP, McFarlane JR, et al: Follistatin concentrations in male sheep increase following sham castration or injection of interleukin-1-a. J Endocrinol 151:119–124, 1996.

239. Inouye S, Ling N, Shimasaki S: Localization of the heparin binding site of follistatin. Mol Cell Endocrinol 90:1–6, 1992.

240. Saito S, Nakamura T, Titani K, Sugino H: Production of activin-binding protein by rat granulosa cells in vitro. Biochem Biophys Res Commun 176:413–422, 1991.

241. Lee MM, Donahoe PK, Hasegawa T, et al: Müllerian inhibiting substance in humans: Normal levels from infancy to adulthood. J Clin Endocrinol Metab 81:571–576, 1996.

242. Lee MM, Donahoe PK, Silverman BL, et al: Measurements of serum müllerian inhibiting substance in the evaluation of children with nonpalpable gonads. N Engl J Med 336:1480–1486, 1997.

243. Fanchin R, Schonauer LM, Righini C, et al: Serum anti-Mullerian hormone is more strongly related to ovarian follicular status than serum inhibin B, oestradiol, FSH and LH on day 3. Hum Reprod 18:323–327, 2003.

244. Fanchin R, Schonauer LM, Righini C, et al. Serum anti-mullerian hormone dynamics during controlled ovarian hyperstimulation. Hum Reprod 18:328–332, 2003.

# Regulation of Gonadotropin Synthesis and Secretion

## John C. Marshall

HYPOTHALAMIC-PITUITARY-OVARIAN AXIS

GnRH SECRETION AND MECHANISMS
OF GnRH ACTION
    Patterns of GnRH Secretion
    Mechanisms of GnRH Action
    Self-Priming Action of GnRH

FACTORS THAT MODULATE GONADOTROPE
RESPONSES TO GnRH
    Hypothalamic Peptides
    Prolactin

    Estradiol
    Progesterone
    Testosterone
    Inhibins, Activins, and Follistatin

EXPRESSION OF THE GONADOTROPIN
SUBUNIT GENES
    Gonadal Steroids and Peptides
    Estrous Cycle
    Role of GnRH Pulse Amplitude and Frequency
    Regulation of FSH-β mRNA Expression

## HYPOTHALAMIC-PITUITARY-OVARIAN AXIS

The major hormones involved in the regulation of reproductive function in women are shown in Figure 141-1.

Gonadotropin-releasing hormone (GnRH) is a decapeptide secreted by hypothalamic neurons that stimulates the synthesis and secretion of both luteinizing hormone (LH) and follicle-stimulating hormone (FSH) by pituitary gonadotrope cells. Secretion of GnRH is regulated by neurotransmitters and, in general, the catecholamines norepinephrine and epinephrine increase GnRH release, whereas endogenous opioid peptides such as β-endorphin inhibit GnRH secretion. LH and FSH are glycoprotein hormones composed of two subunits, a common α subunit and structurally dissimilar β subunits that convey specificity to the hormones. Both LH and FSH are secreted by the same gonadotrope cells, which constitute 7% to 10% of cells in the anterior pituitary gland. Metabolic clearance rates of the two hormones are different, with the plasma half-life of LH (about 60–90 minutes) being shorter than that of FSH (about 180–200 minutes). FSH and LH act sequentially in concert to produce ovarian follicular maturation, ovulation, and secretion of estradiol and progesterone. Prolactin regulates ovarian function in rodents but does not appear to be important in humans. The inhibins are proteins with a common α subunit linked to either a $\beta_A$ subunit (inhibin A) or a $\beta_B$ subunit (inhibin B). The activins are homodimers or heterodimers of the β subunits, activin A ($\beta_A$, $\beta_A$) and activin B ($\beta_B$, $\beta_B$). Follistatin is an unrelated single-chain protein that binds to and inactivates activin. Inhibins, activins, and follistatin were originally obtained from gonadal extracts, but are widely distributed and exert multiple actions in different tissues (inhibins and activins are related to transforming growth factor-β compounds). In relation to gonadotropins, inhibin and follistatin reduce and activin increases FSH synthesis and secretion (see Chapter 139). They are active in both sexes, with effects being more marked in females and immature males. Plasma inhibin and FSH are inversely related, which indicates an endocrine role for inhibin of ovarian origin. The exact roles of circulating activin and follistatin are less clear, and because both compounds are also present in the pituitary, they exert paracrine or autocrine actions.

Evidence from animal studies has shown that the suprahypothalamic portion of the central nervous system (CNS) can exert a major influence on reproductive function. In rodents, odors from a male mouse can coordinate the timing of estrous cycles in female mice housed together (Whitten effect). These effects are mediated by pherohormones,[1] and similar mechanisms may be active in primates. If vaginal secretions from a female rhesus monkey at midcycle are placed on the perineum of a castrate female, males are attracted to the castrate animal.[2] Exposure to light and, in particular, the duration of light exposure are also important factors in some species, the effects varying with the species. Regulation of light exposure (constant day-night length) can regularize the estrous cycle of rats, and constant light can advance puberty in female rats. The duration of light exposure is a major factor in the regulation of reproductive function in seasonal breeding species. In female sheep, LH secretion is inhibited during summer (long days), and during fall, gonadotropin secretion increases and cyclic estrous function continues during the winter breeding season (short days).[3] The transition from anestrus (summer) to the breeding season is associated with an increase in the frequency of pulsatile LH secretion, which suggests that the duration of light exposure regulates secretion of GnRH. The exact CNS mechanisms mediating these effects remain uncertain, and little evidence is available that similar factors play any role in reproductive function in women. Higher CNS regulation of reproductive function exists, however, as evidenced by the anovulation and amenorrhea seen in some women under conditions of stress or after weight loss or intensive exercise (see Chapter 152).

GnRH is the major regulator of both LH and FSH synthesis and secretion. Thus, in this summary of regulation of gonadotropin secretion, we review the secretion and actions of GnRH and also examine the factors that modulate GnRH actions on the pituitary gonadotrope.

## GnRH SECRETION AND MECHANISMS OF GnRH ACTION

### PATTERNS OF GnRH SECRETION

Early studies of LH secretion in humans revealed that LH was released into the circulation in a series of pulses[4,5] and that similar secretory patterns are present in all species. These data suggested that each LH pulse resulted from the episodic release of GnRH by the hypothalamus. Direct evidence is lacking in humans, but data from sheep, rodents, and primates support this view. Simultaneous measurement of GnRH in

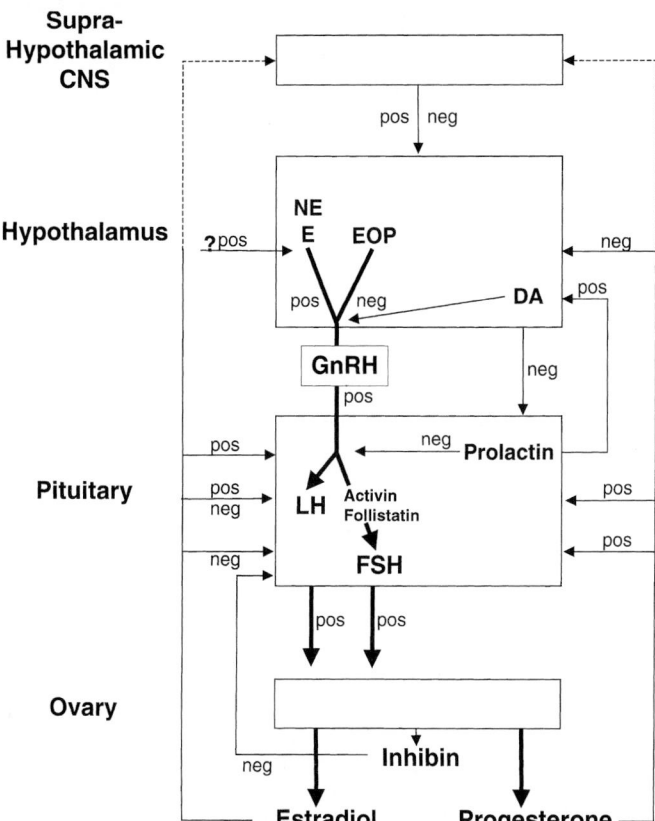

**Figure 141-1** Schematic representation of the hormones and feedback control mechanisms in the hypothalamic-pituitary-ovarian axis. *Solid lines* indicate established and *dotted lines* indicate putative regulatory pathways. Pos shows stimulatory and neg shows inhibitory regulation. DA, dopamine; E, epinephrine; EOP, endogenous opioid peptides; FSH, follicle-stimulating hormone; GnRH, gonadotropin-releasing hormone; LH, luteinizing hormone; NE, norepinephrine.

interval between pulses. Regulation of GnRH secretion is complex and consists of stimulatory and inhibitory actions of steroids and neurotransmitters acting to modify the intrinsic pulsatile secretion of GnRH neurons (see Chapter 138). In sum, GnRH secretion is increased by the catecholamines epinephrine and norepinephrine and by neuropeptide Y (NPY), galanin, and *N*-methyl-D-aspartic acid. Estradiol exerts complex actions with initial inhibition and subsequent stimulation of GnRH release. Endogenous opioid peptides (β-endorphin), progesterone, testosterone, and prolactin exert inhibitory actions on GnRH secretion.

Pulsatile secretion of GnRH is essential for maintenance of normal gonadotropin synthesis and secretion. The crucial importance of a pulsatile GnRH stimulus was initially observed in a GnRH-deficient castrate monkey model.[7] If GnRH is given in a pulsatile manner, LH and FSH secretion is maintained for prolonged periods, whereas subsequent continuous GnRH infusion resulted in a decline in serum LH and FSH (Fig. 141-2).

These observations have been confirmed in humans, and pulsatile administration of GnRH to patients with isolated GnRH deficiency can stimulate gonadotropin secretion and induce pubertal maturation,[8,9] reproduce the hormonal changes seen during the menstrual cycle, and induce ovulation.[10,11]

The frequency of the pulsatile GnRH stimulus is also important in determining gonadotropin secretion. Increasing the frequency of GnRH pulses from one per hour to two or three per hour reduces plasma gonadotropins in monkeys with hypothalamic lesions, and slower frequencies of GnRH stimulation (one pulse every 3–4 hours) do not maintain serum LH concentrations.[12] These data indicate that a narrow range of GnRH pulse frequency is required to maintain normal gonadotropin secretion. Additional evidence suggests that the frequency of GnRH stimulation may regulate differential release of LH or FSH by the gonadotroph. GnRH pulse frequencies of one per hour induce the release of both LH and FSH in monkeys, sheep, and humans. Slower frequencies, one pulse every 3 to 4 hours, increase serum FSH, but LH declines. The fall in LH may reflect the short half-life of LH, but the rise in FSH suggests that a slow frequency of GnRH stimulation favors FSH release by the pituitary.[12,13] In rats, a GnRH pulse frequency of one every 30 minutes was required to maintain LH responses, whereas FSH release continued after pulses given every 60 to 120 minutes.[14] GnRH pulse frequency may also determine the amount of LH released in response to a GnRH pulse. The amplitude of LH release is small when the GnRH pulse frequency is high and increases after a slower

portal blood and LH in jugular venous blood[6] has shown good concordance between GnRH and LH pulses, which suggests that the patterns of GnRH secretion can be inferred from measurement of LH pulses in peripheral plasma. FSH is also secreted in a pulsatile manner, but FSH peaks are often obscured because the long half-life of FSH often exceeds the

**Figure 141-2** The effects of pulsatile or continuous administration of gonadotropin-releasing hormone (GnRH) to ovariectomized monkeys rendered GnRH deficient by placement of a lesion in the hypothalamus. Gonadotropin secretion was restored by hourly GnRH pulses, reduced during a continuous GnRH infusion, and again increased after reinstitution of pulsatile GnRH administration. FSH, follicle-stimulating hormone; LH, luteinizing hormone. (From Belchetz PE, Plant TM, Nakai Y, et al: Hypophysial responses to continuous and intermittent delivery of hypothalamic gonadotropin-releasing hormone. Science 202:631–633; © 1978 by the American Association for the Advancement of Science.)

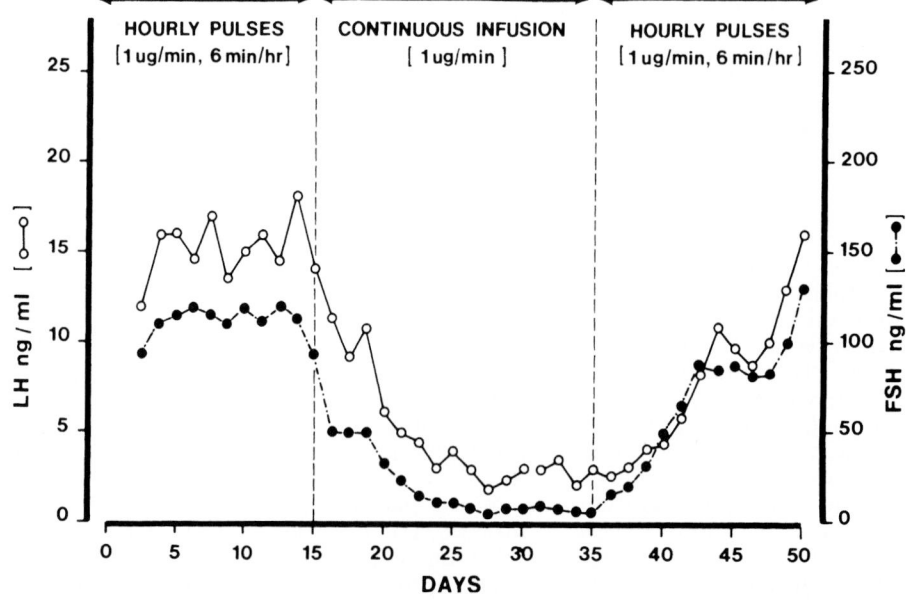

frequency of GnRH stimulation.[13] This finding may in part explain the differences in LH release seen during the follicular (faster frequency) and the luteal phases of the menstrual cycle (slower frequency).[15,16]

These data demonstrate the critical importance of a pulsatile GnRH stimulus in the maintenance of normal gonadotropin secretion and indicate a role of GnRH pulse frequency in the differential secretion of LH and FSH. The exact frequencies and amount of GnRH required to produce optimal gonadotrope stimulation vary in different species, but all share a requirement for an intermittent stimulus.

## MECHANISMS OF GnRH ACTION

GnRH acts on pituitary gonadotropes to stimulate the acute release and synthesis of both LH and FSH. The mechanisms involved in GnRH action are shown in Figure 141-3 and have been reviewed.[17–20]

GnRH action is initiated by binding to its receptor on the gonadotrope plasma membrane. The number of GnRH receptors varies in different physiologic situations, such as during sexual maturation and during the estrous cycle.[21] GnRH receptors are highest when responsiveness to GnRH is maximal, thus suggesting that the number of receptors plays a role in modulating GnRH action. GnRH itself has been shown to be the main factor regulating receptor concentration, and the number of receptors is elevated when endogenous GnRH secretion is increased, such as after castration.[22] Thus, the number of GnRH receptors reflects endogenous GnRH secretion, but the pattern of GnRH stimulation also determines receptor response. In rats, GnRH pulses given every 30 minutes produce a maximum increase in receptor concentration,[14] and faster or slower GnRH frequencies result in smaller responses. The number of GnRH receptors may play a role in differential activation of intracellular signaling pathways and subunit gene expression. Luteinizing hormone-β (LH-β) expression is favored in the presence of elevated GnRH-R, suggesting preferential activation of signaling cascades, which activate LH-β transcription.[23,24]

After GnRH binding to the membrane receptor, multiple steps appear to be involved in GnRH-stimulated LH and FSH secretion and subunit gene expression. GnRH stimulates a phospholipase C enzyme in the plasma membrane, a step that involves guanosine triphosphate–binding proteins. Phosphatidylinositol 4,5-diphosphate is hydrolyzed to inositol triphosphate and diacylglycerol.[25] The increase in inositol triphosphate releases calcium from intracellular stores, and this transient calcium increase effects the initial burst of LH release lasting from 1 to 1½ minutes. Both the elevated intracellular calcium and diacylglycerol probably induce the translocation of protein kinase C (PKC) subspecies from the cytosol to the membrane. Activated PKC phosphorylates proteins involved in initiating LH and FSH secretion, as well as proteins in the mitogen-activated protein kinase (MAPK) pathway, which are involved in stimulating gonadotropin subunit transcription.[26,27] GnRH receptor binding also initiates the influx of extracellular calcium by way of calcium channels, which leads to a further increase in intracellular calcium; the increased intracellular calcium appears to be necessary, together with the effects of PKC, to maintain the sustained phase (over several minutes) of gonadotropin secretion. GnRH also induces the production of arachidonic acid and lipoxygenase and/or epoxygenase products of the fatty acid, which appear to be involved in exocytosis.

GnRH stimulates transcription of the α, LH-β, and follicle-stimulating hormone-β (FSH-β) genes, and several intracellular pathways appear to be involved in transmitting the GnRH signal. After receptor activation, prominent calcium oscillations occur in gonadotrope cells, and experimentally, episodic increases in intracellular calcium at different frequencies differentially increase α, LH-β, and FSH-β mRNA in a manner similar to GnRH pulses[26] (see later discussion). PKC activation also increases α and LH-β messenger RNA (mRNA) expression,[27] and GnRH is relatively ineffective in stimulating LH mRNA in PKC-depleted cells.[28] The exact role of PKC activation is unclear but appears to involve the MAPK pathway.[29] GnRH stimulates MAPK, and blockade of MAPK activation abolishes α and FSH-β but not LH-β mRNA responses to GnRH.[30] Studies of the α subunit promoter have suggested that PKC and MAPK act via an Ets (E twenty-six specific) domain protein that binds to the GnRH response element. Other mechanisms may be involved inasmuch as GnRH stimulates steroidogenic factor 1 (SF-1) expression and in some reports increases intracellular cyclic adenosine monophosphate (cAMP). The α subunit promoter contains cAMP and SF-1 sites involved in basal expression and a GnRH response

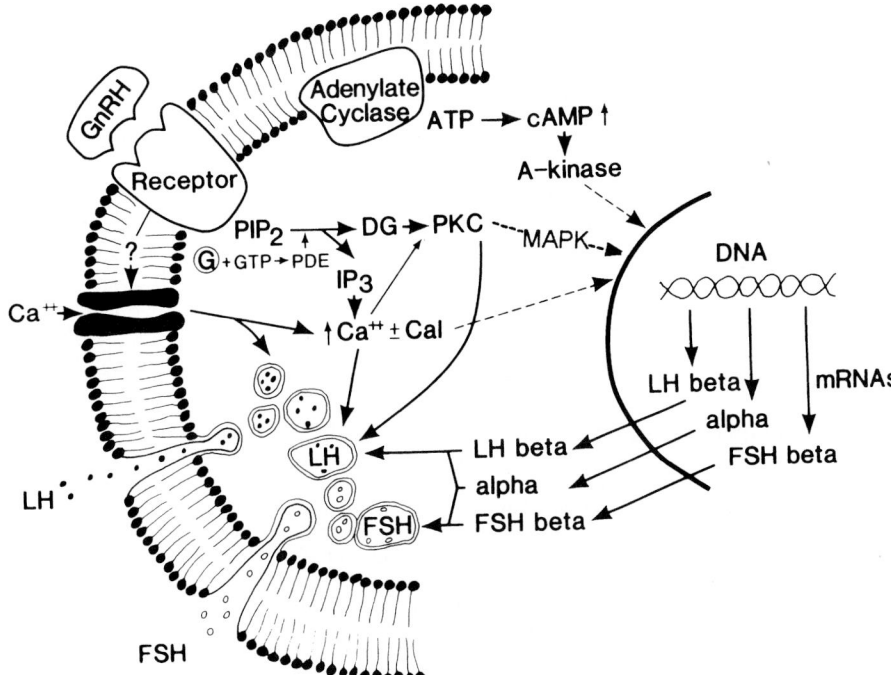

Figure 141-3 Mechanisms involved in gonadotropin-releasing hormone (GnRH) action on the gonadotroph. *Dashed lines* indicate pathways where the mechanisms are uncertain. ATP, adenosine triphosphate; cal, calmodulin; cAMP, cyclic adenosine monophosphate; DG, diacylglycerol; FSH, follicle-stimulating hormone; G, G protein; GTP, guanosine triphosphate; IP₃, inositol triphosphate; LH, luteinizing hormone; MAPK, mitogen-activated protein kinase; PDE, phosphodiesterase (phospholipase C); PIP₂, phosphatidylinositol 4,5-phosphate; PKC, protein kinase C.

element responsive to MAPK activation. The LH-β promoter is responsive to steroid feedback and to GnRH and contains SF-1 and NFY sites (basal) and SP1, CaRG, Egr, and AP1 sites involved in GnRH action. The FSH-β promoter also contains SF-1 and NFY, AP1, and Ptx (pituitary homeobox 1) sites in addition to Smad response elements (activin stimulated) and androgen response elements (AREs).[31] In sum, GnRH receptor binding activates several intracellular pathways, including calcium, PKC, and MAPK, which are involved in regulating subunit gene expression. At present, it remains unclear which pathways specifically mediate stimulation of α versus LH-β versus FSH-β.

### SELF-PRIMING ACTION OF GnRH

In addition to stimulating LH and FSH release, GnRH enhances pituitary responsiveness to subsequent stimulation by GnRH.[32] When a second GnRH injection is given within 1 to 2 hours, enhanced secretion of LH occurs in response to the second stimulus. This phenomenon is termed a *self-priming effect* and depends on protein synthesis. The self-priming effect of GnRH is enhanced in the presence of estradiol, such as during the late follicular and mid-luteal phases of the menstrual cycle.[33] The self-priming action of GnRH is one component of the positive-feedback effect of estradiol in enhancing pituitary responses to GnRH (see discussion to follow).

cAMP and progesterone also augment responses to subsequent GnRH stimulation. These effects are blocked by the progesterone receptor antagonist RU486 (mifepristone), which suggests that GnRH activation of protein kinase A may interact with the progesterone receptor (PR) and mediate GnRH self-priming. In pituitary cells transfected with a progesterone response element linked to a reporter gene, GnRH increases reporter gene activity and GnRH self-priming is blunted in progesterone receptor knockout (PRKO) mice. These data suggest that GnRH self-priming may result from GnRH-stimulated intracellular mechanisms (? cAMP) acting by way of the progesterone receptor to enhance responsiveness to subsequent GnRH stimuli.[34,35]

### FACTORS THAT MODULATE GONADOTROPE RESPONSES TO GnRH

GnRH stimulation of LH and FSH release can be modified by other hormones, which may enhance or inhibit gonadotrope responses. Evidence points to estradiol, progesterone, and inhibin as the most important hormones regulating gonadotrope responsiveness in females. The hypothalamic peptides NPY and galanin, prolactin, and adrenal steroids may also play roles in modulating responses to GnRH.

### HYPOTHALAMIC PEPTIDES

NPY is a 36-amino acid member of the pancreatic polypeptide family that is present in high concentrations in the hypothalamus. NPY enhances GnRH binding to gonadotropes and augments LH responses to GnRH.[36,37] Immunoneutralization of NPY attenuates the proestrous LH surge, and NPY is elevated in portal blood during the surge, thus suggesting a role in augmenting GnRH action on proestrus.

Galanin is a 29-amino acid peptide that is present in GnRH neurons and cosecreted with GnRH. Galanin augments LH responses to GnRH in the presence of estradiol and, together with NPY, is involved in mediating the marked increase in LH secretion during the preovulatory LH surge.[38,39]

### PROLACTIN

The major action of prolactin on LH and FSH secretion is exerted by inhibiting secretion of GnRH, but prolactin also

inhibits gonadotrope responses. In vitro, GnRH-stimulated LH release is impaired in the presence of elevated prolactin, and this action is reversed by bromocriptine.[40] Similar results are observed in vivo,[41] and prolactin inhibition of responses to GnRH contributes to the low gonadotropin levels seen in hyperprolactinemic states.

### ESTRADIOL

The administration of estradiol to women or female animals is followed by an initial suppression of plasma LH and FSH, but both gonadotropins, particularly LH, are subsequently increased.[42] These observations have been confirmed in numerous studies, and the time course of the biphasic action depends on the species and the dose of estradiol used. In women, the inhibitory effects persist for 2 to 3 days and are followed by augmentation of LH secretion—"positive feedback." With the use of exogenous GnRH, both the inhibitory and the stimulatory effects of estradiol have been shown to be exerted on the gonadotrope cell. In women, LH responses to GnRH are suppressed during the first 36 hours but are augmented after 48 hours, and the enhanced responses persist for several days.[43,44] The temporal relationships in sheep, together with the pituitary site of estradiol action,[45] are shown in Figure 141-4. Estradiol initially inhibits LH release at each GnRH pulse, but responses are then augmented and mean plasma LH increases. This positive action of estradiol accounts in part for variations in LH responsiveness to GnRH during the menstrual cycle. LH responses are augmented during the late follicular and mid-luteal phases of the cycle, when plasma estradiol is elevated. In vitro studies have confirmed that the positive action of estradiol is exerted directly on the gonadotrope cell. In rat pituitary cells, LH responses to GnRH are augmented after 12 hours of exposure to estradiol. The mechanisms of estradiol action include enhancing GnRH receptor upregulation by GnRH and increasing both the amount of LH released by each cell and the number of cells releasing LH.[46]

In contrast to its action on LH, estradiol inhibits FSH release. The differential effects of estradiol on pituitary LH and FSH secretion are seen in studies in which GnRH pulses

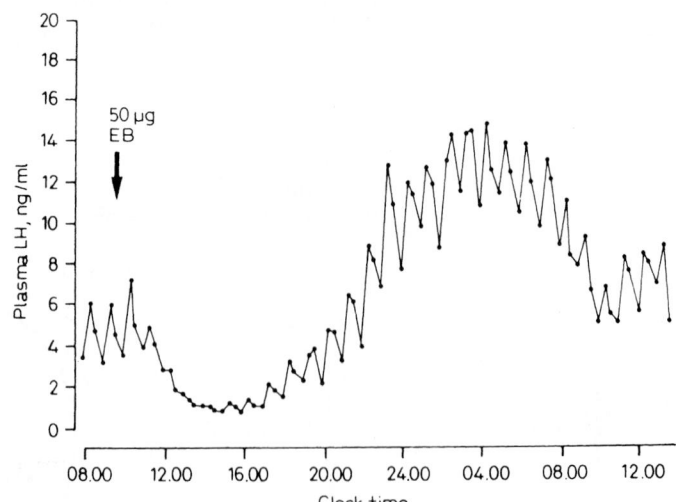

**Figure 141-4** Inhibitory and stimulatory effects of estradiol on luteinizing hormone (LH) responsiveness to gonadotropin-releasing hormone (GnRH). Ovariectomized ewes, with surgical disconnection of the hypothalamus from the pituitary, were given GnRH pulse injections (500 ng every hour). LH responses to each GnRH pulse were measured after the injection of 50 μg of estradiol benzoate (EB). LH responses were diminished between 12 noon and 4:00 P.M. and subsequently augmented between 8:00 P.M. and 9:00 A.M. (From Clarke IJ, Cummins JT: Direct pituitary effects of estrogen and progesterone on gonadotropin secretion in the ovariectomized ewe. Neuroendocrinology 39:267–274, 1984.)

are given to women with isolated GnRH deficiency (Kallmann's syndrome). Pretreatment with estradiol abolishes FSH responses to GnRH, but LH responsiveness is maintained.[47] As shown in Figure 141-5, the inhibitory effect of estradiol on FSH release is evident when endogenous plasma estradiol exceeds 50 to 75 pg/mL, and FSH release is abolished by the addition of exogenous estradiol. In vitro studies using pituitary cells have shown that estradiol inhibition of FSH secretion involves inhibition of FSH synthesis after 6 to 8 hours' exposure to steroid.[48]

## PROGESTERONE

Progesterone can also augment gonadotropin responses to GnRH, but only after previous exposure to estradiol, which induces PRs.[49] LH responses to GnRH are inhibited when progesterone alone is added to rat pituitary cells in culture. In

contrast, after prior incubation with estradiol, progesterone produces a transient (12- to 16-hour) augmentation of LH release and a more prolonged enhancement of FSH responsiveness to GnRH.[50] Transient augmentation of responsiveness to GnRH also occurs in vivo, data for which are shown in Figure 141-5.

Thus, progesterone acts synergistically with estrogen to augment gonadotrope responsiveness to GnRH. The combined effects of these steroids are crucial for production of the midcycle LH and FSH surge (see Chapter 152), and progesterone augments and prolongs the positive-feedback effects of estradiol.[51]

## TESTOSTERONE

Testosterone exerts complex actions on gonadotropin secretion by actions at both the hypothalamic and pituitary levels. Evidence in several species indicates that an elevated plasma testosterone is associated with impaired progesterone action on gonadotropin secretion. Moderate elevations of testosterone are associated with increased plasma LH while higher levels lower both LH and FSH. In female pituitary cells cultured with estradiol ($E_2$), androgen pretreatment (testosterone or dihydrotestosterone [DHT]) inhibited LH responses to GnRH and also suppressed progesterone augmentation of responses to GnRH.[52] Data in humans, primates, and rodents indicate that testosterone can modify normal gonadotropin physiology in females. In women, markedly elevated testosterone from ovarian tumors suppresses plasma LH and FSH,[53] whereas moderate hyperandrogenemia (two- to threefold elevation) is associated with disrupted cyclicity, infertility, and increased LH.[54,55] In moderately hyperandrogenemic women and adolescents, plasma LH is elevated and LH pulse frequency increased,[56] which in part reflects an impaired suppressive action of progesterone.[57,58]

Other data suggest that androgens in early life can modify responses to progesterone on a long-term basis. In monkeys and sheep, androgen exposure in utero is associated with enhanced LH secretion during subsequent puberty and impaired positive feedback actions of progesterone and $E_2$.[59-61] Thus, considerable evidence indicates that testosterone impairs the actions of progesterone on GnRH/LH secretion, but the mechanisms of testosterone action at the hypothalamic and/or pituitary remain uncertain.

## INHIBINS, ACTIVINS, AND FOLLISTATIN

The concept that ovarian follicular fluid contains proteins that selectively inhibit FSH secretion has existed for more than half a century, and recent studies have clarified this area. The inhibins A and B, activins, and follistatin are compounds that regulate FSH synthesis and secretion.[62] All three compounds were originally isolated from gonadal tissue, but either the protein or mRNA for all three compounds is widely distributed. Of importance, inhibin-$\alpha$, activin-$\beta_B$, and follistatin are present in pituitary cells and specifically in gonadotropes.

Inhibin B in plasma is secreted by ovarian granulosa cells during the follicular phase (under the control of FSH) and inhibin A by the corpus luteum in the luteal phase under the control of LH.[63] In vitro, inhibin reduces FSH release from the gonadotrope. Together, these data suggest that inhibins act synergistically with estradiol to reduce plasma FSH in the late follicular phase and to inhibit FSH secretion in the luteal phase of the menstrual cycle. In female rats, injection of recombinant inhibin produced dose-related decreases in plasma FSH with little or no effect on LH. Similarly, inhibin decreased the evening proestrous FSH surge and abolished the secondary FSH surge the subsequent morning.[64] These actions are exerted directly on the gonadotrope and appear to reflect interference with the positive actions of activin on FSH

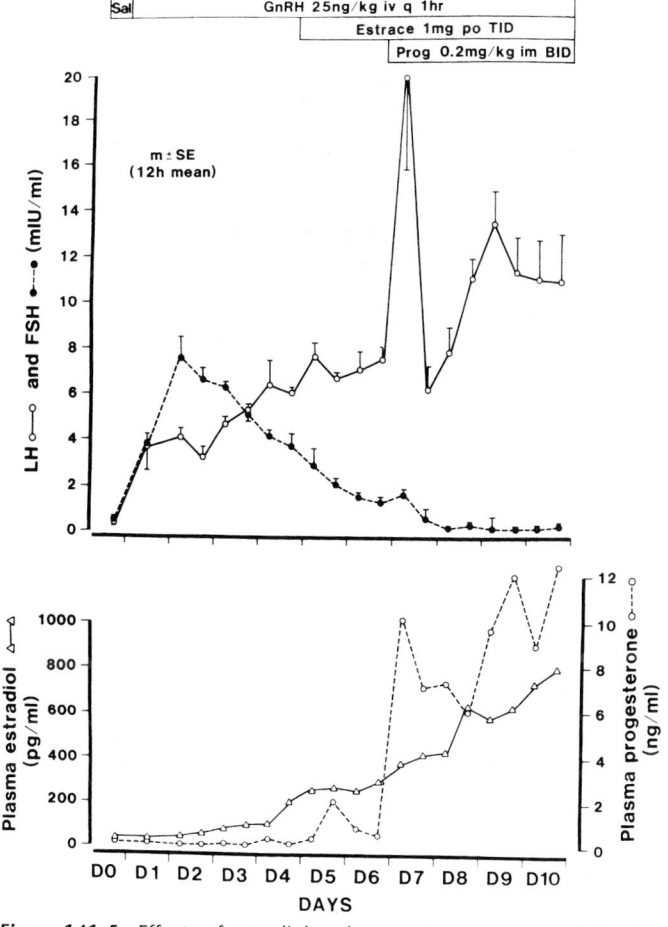

**Figure 141-5** Effects of estradiol and progesterone on gonadotropin responses to gonadotropin-releasing hormone (GnRH). GnRH pulses (25 ng/kg per pulse) were given hourly for 10 days to a woman with isolated GnRH deficiency. The effects of addition of estrogen alone (Estrace [estradiol] on days 4–6) and estrogen together with progesterone (days 6–10) on plasma luteinizing hormone (LH) and follicle-stimulating hormone (FSH) are shown. Plasma LH and FSH (mean values over 4 hours from samples obtained before GnRH pulses) are shown in the **upper panel** and ovarian steroids in the **lower panel**. Serum FSH declines as endogenous estradiol increases (days 2–4). The rapid transient augmentation of LH and, to a lesser extent, FSH responses to GnRH is evident soon after the addition of progesterone on day 6. (Redrawn from Nippoldt TB, Khoury S, Barkan A, et al: Gonadotropin responses to GnRH pulses in hypogonadotropic hypogonadism: LH responsiveness is maintained in the presence of luteal phase concentrations of estrogen and progesterone. Clin Endocrinol 26:293–301, 1987.)

synthesis and secretion. The exact mechanisms are unclear and inhibin binds to but does not activate the activin receptor complex.[65] Two potential inhibin receptors have been identified.[66,67] The betaglycan receptor binds inhibin at high affinity with formation of an inhibin/betaglycan/type II activin receptor complex[68] and is localized to gonadotropes.[69] In vitro, inhibin rapidly reduces FSH-β mRNA[70] and, in vivo, anti-inhibin sera increase FSH-β mRNA during the proestrous surge in rats.[71]

Activin plays a critical role in FSH production, increasing secretion of FSH by pituitary cells in vitro, and elevating plasma FSH and FSH-β mRNA in female rats.[72,73] Ovarian activin does not appear to act in an endocrine manner, and as activin subunits are present in gonadotropes, activin exerts its effects by autocrine mechanisms to increase FSH synthesis and secretion selectively.

Follistatin exerts potent and specific inhibition of pituitary FSH secretion with actions similar to those of inhibin but of longer duration in vivo.[74] As with activin, follistatin does not appear to act in an endocrine manner, and its presence in the pituitary indicates a predominantly autocrine or paracrine action.

Activin, inhibin, and follistatin play important roles in FSH synthesis and secretion. Present evidence suggests that ovarian inhibin acts in an endocrine manner to reduce FSH secretion by inhibiting the effects of gonadotrope-derived activin. Circulating activin and follistatin have less clear roles, and data indicate that autocrine/paracrine actions of intrapituitary activin and follistatin regulate FSH synthesis and secretion (see discussion to follow).

## EXPRESSION OF THE GONADOTROPIN SUBUNIT GENES

The cDNAs and genes for the common α and the specific LH-β and FSH-β subunits have been isolated and characterized in several species.[75] For α, a single gene is composed of four exons and three introns, and a pituitary glycoprotein hormone basal element, SF-1, GnRH, and cAMP response elements are present in the 5' flanking region.[76] The LH gene is smaller, with three exons and two introns. The promoter is responsive to steroid feedback and contains an SF-1 site, an estrogen response element,[77] and SP1, CaRG, Egr, and AP1 sites involved in GnRH action. The FSH-β subunit is also coded by a single gene with three exons, but it differs in having a long 3' untranslated region containing sequences that have been shown to be important in determining RNA stability.[78] The promoter contains SF-1, NPY (basal), and Ptx 1 (pituitary homebox 1), AP1 (GnRH responsive), Smad (activin responsive), and ARE (androgen responsive) sites.[79]

### GONADAL STEROIDS AND PEPTIDES

Gonadectomy in male and female rats has revealed evidence of differential expression of the gonadotropin subunit genes,[75,80] which reflect changes in GnRH secretion, gonadal steroids and peptides, and intrapituitary activin $\beta_B$ and follistatin. In females, serum LH and α and LH-β subunit mRNA do not increase until several days after ovariectomy, whereas serum FSH and FSH-β mRNA increase within hours.[81] In males, all three subunit mRNAs increase within 24 hours, although the rise in FSH-β is less marked than in females.

Replacement of estradiol and progesterone at the time of ovariectomy prevents the increase in α and LH-β transcription and mRNA expression, but the rise in FSH-β expression is only partially suppressed. Similar changes occur in the presence of a GnRH antagonist, which suggests that the increase in α and LH-β mRNA depends on GnRH, but other factors in addition to GnRH regulate FSH-β mRNA.[82,83] The early increase in

FSH-β expression follows loss of ovarian inhibin in female animals, and inhibin rapidly reduces FSH-β transcription and mRNA in pituitary cells.[70,83]

In male rats, testosterone replacement or administration of a GnRH antagonist at castration prevents the increase in all three subunit mRNAs. In previously castrate animals, testosterone suppresses α and LH-β, but FSH-β mRNA remains elevated. Testosterone selectively increases FSH-β mRNA in the absence of GnRH by increasing transcription[84] and by prolonging the half-life of FSH mRNA.[85]

The gonadal peptides activin and follistatin also modify FSH-β transcription and mRNA stability.[86] Both compounds are active in vitro, and their presence in the pituitary suggests that activin may normally enhance transcription and also stabilize newly synthesized FSH-β mRNA, an action that can be modified by inhibin and follistatin (see discussion to follow).

## ESTROUS CYCLE

During the 4-day estrous cycle in female rats, the concentrations of serum LH and FSH and subunit mRNA in the pituitary change in both a coordinated and a differential manner[87] (Fig. 141-6). During metestrus, FSH-β mRNA alone is increased, whereas during diestrus, α and LH-β mRNA expression increases and FSH remains unchanged. During the proestrous gonadotropin surge, α mRNA is unchanged, LH-β mRNA is increased, and FSH-β mRNA increases several hours later. The increase in β subunit mRNA at the time of elevated

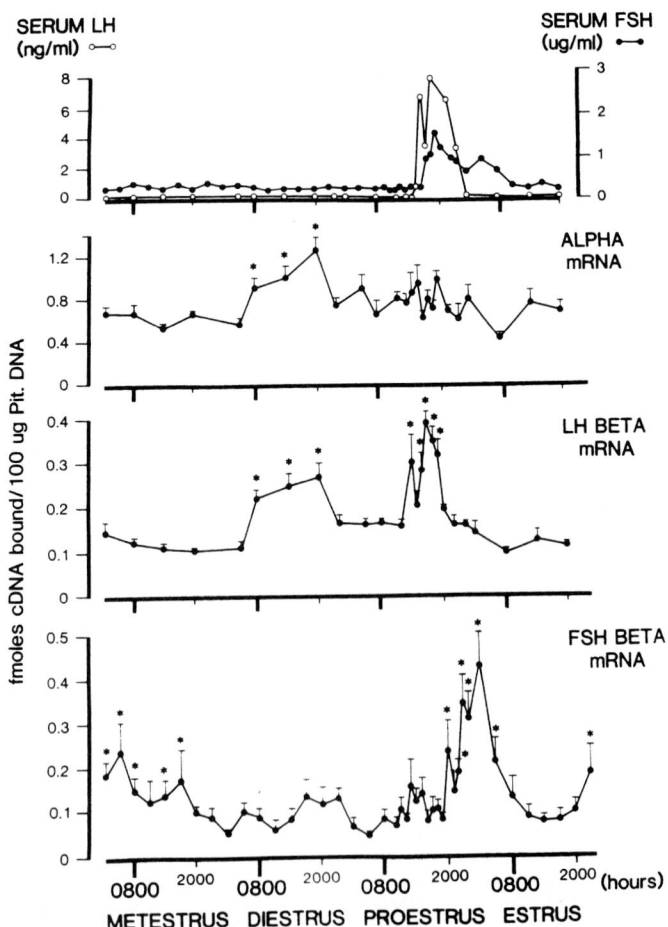

**Figure 141-6**  Serum luteinizing hormone (LH) and follicle-stimulating hormone (FSH) and gonadotropin subunit mRNAs during the 4-day estrous cycle in rats. *$P < 0.05$ vs. basal values. (From Marshall JC, Dalkin AC, Haisenleder DJ, et al: Gonadotropin releasing hormone pulses: Regulators of gonadotropin synthesis and ovulatory cycles. Recent Prog Horm Res 47:155–189, 1991.)

gonadotropin secretion suggests dependence on GnRH during the surge. The increase in FSH-β mRNA during metestrus occurs when GnRH secretion is low, which suggests that it may reflect a reduction in the actions of ovarian inhibin.[88]

These physiologic data during ovulatory cycles in rats indicate that complex mechanisms are involved in the differential expression of gonadotropin subunit genes. Present data indicate that these mechanisms include altered patterns of GnRH secretion and the actions of intrapituitary activin and follistatin on FSH-β mRNA expression.

## ROLE OF GnRH PULSE AMPLITUDE AND FREQUENCY

GnRH is the major stimulus of subunit gene expression, and GnRH antagonists reduce the elevated transcription and mRNA expression seen in castrate animals. A pulsatile GnRH stimulus is as important in increasing subunit gene expression as it is in maintaining hormone release. Thus, when long-acting GnRH agonists or a continuous GnRH infusion is used to stimulate the gonadotrope, β subunit mRNA expression is not increased although α subunit mRNA concentrations rise, indicating that α subunit mRNA expression is not as dependent on intermittent GnRH stimuli. Studies in GnRH-deficient sheep and rodent models have shown that GnRH pulses can increase subunit transcription rates and mRNA concentrations, and that both the amplitude and the frequency of GnRH stimuli are important determinants of differential gene expression.[20,89]

In general, similar responses to GnRH pulse amplitude occur in both sexes. α Subunit mRNA expression is increased by a wide range of pulse doses, but only lower-amplitude pulses increase LH-β. In males, FSH-β is also increased over the range of pulse doses used, but in females, higher-amplitude pulses are ineffective. Figure 141-7 shows that the variation in the frequency of GnRH pulses also affects differential expression of the subunit genes and the patterns of subunit mRNA responses to different GnRH pulse frequencies. Rapid frequencies (one pulse every 8 minutes) increased α, LH-β, and also FSH-β in females.[90] Fast physiologic pulses (every 30 minutes is the frequency of GnRH pulses in castrate rats) increased all three subunit genes, whereas slower-frequency pulses (as in intact rats) did not stimulate α and LH-β but maintained elevated FSH-β mRNA expression. Thus, LH and FSH synthesis and secretion are highly dependent on the GnRH stimulus pattern, with rapid frequencies favoring LH and slower pulses favoring FSH synthesis. These effects of GnRH pulse frequency are exerted predominantly at the level of subunit gene transcription.[91] GnRH pulses increased the α subunit transcription rate, only 30-minute pulses increased LH-β, and FSH-β was increased only by slower (every 2 hours) pulses.[92,93] The time course of changes in subunit transcription, follistatin, and activin β_B expression after different GnRH frequencies is shown in Figure 141-8. GnRH pulses given every 30 or 240 minutes increased α subunit transcription, but only 30-minute pulses stimulated LH-β transcription over 24 hours. FSH-β transcription rates were dependent on the duration of GnRH stimuli. GnRH pulses every 30 minutes initially (1–6 hours) increased FSH-β primary transcripts, but by 24 hours values had returned to basal and were inversely correlated to increased follistatin expression. In contrast, GnRH pulses every 240 minutes maintained FSH-β transcription through 24 hours, while follistatin was unchanged. These data imply that activin mediates FSH-β transcription, with the increase in follistatin neutralizing activin action after 30-minute GnRH pulses. GnRH also exerts direct actions, however, as in the presence of exogenous follistatin, slow (240 minutes) GnRH pulses increase FSH-β, albeit to a lesser degree.[94]

Overall, these data suggest that alterations in the frequency and amplitude of pulsatile GnRH secretion are a critical part of mechanisms that allow a single GnRH molecule to

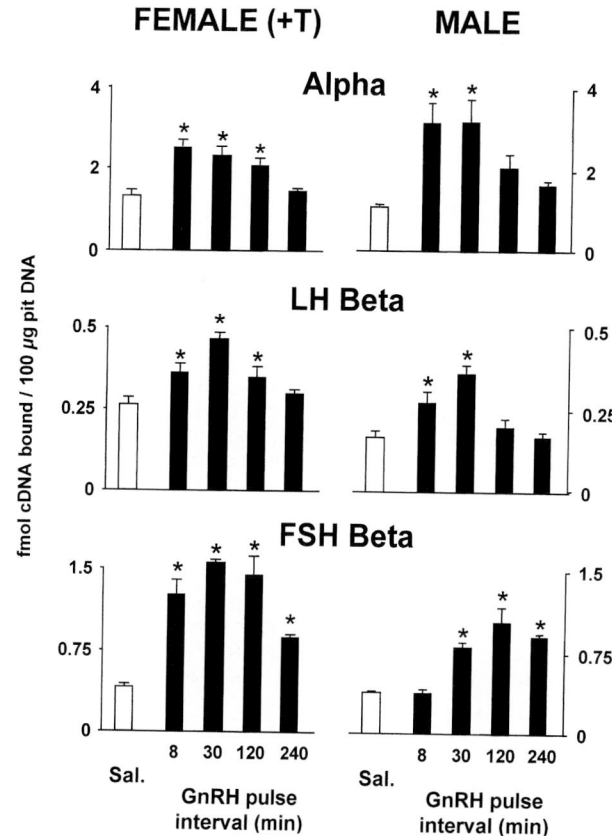

**Figure 141-7** Effect of gonadotropin-releasing hormone (GnRH) pulse frequency on gonadotropin subunit mRNA concentrations in GnRH-deficient male and female rats also given replacement testosterone (+T) to allow LH-β expression (see Ref. 91). Animals received saline (*open bars*) or GnRH (*solid bars*) pulses for 24 hours (males, 25 ng per pulse; females, 5 ng per pulse). *$P < 0.05$ vs. saline. FSH, follicle-stimulating hormone; LH, luteinizing hormone.

differentially stimulate expression of the three gonadotropin subunit genes. This property, in turn, imparts physiologic import to the changes in GnRH pulse frequency observed during ovulatory cycles in several species.

## REGULATION OF FSH-β mRNA EXPRESSION

In the data reviewed above, expression of α and LH-β mRNA is similar in both sexes, but FSH-β exhibited different responses to frequency and amplitude of GnRH pulses between the sexes. These data suggest that factors in addition to GnRH are active in regulating FSH-β expression. Both the mRNA and protein for inhibin-α, inhibin-β_B, and follistatin are present in pituitary gonadotrope cells.[95–97] Activin B and follistatin (but not inhibin) are secreted by pituitary cells, and activin receptors[98] are present on gonadotropes. Thus, activin acts in an autocrine manner, and its action in increasing FSH mRNA can be antagonized by antibodies to activin B[99] and by follistatin, which binds to the β_B subunit and reduces activin activity.[100] Activin stimulates FSH-β transcription[101] and appears to act synergistically with GnRH. Activin also stabilizes FSH-β mRNA by actions that probably involve the long 3′ untranslated region of the mRNA. These findings indicate that an intrapituitary regulatory system is present in the gonadotrope and plays a significant role in regulating FSH-β mRNA expression.

A series of in vitro studies have shown complex interactions between activin, follistatin, and inhibin. Activin stimulates follistatin expression and reduces production of the β_B subunit. Inhibin and follistatin both exert similar actions in

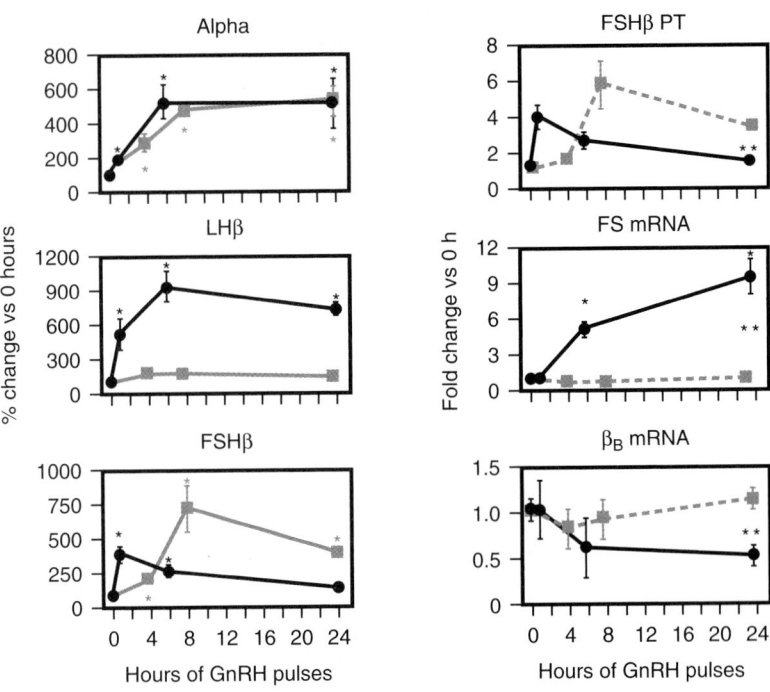

**Figure 141-8** The time course of gonadotropin subunit primary transcript (**L panel**) and follistatin and activin $\beta_B$ expression (**R panel**) to GnRH pulses (25 ng/pulse) given every 30 min (●) or 240 min (■) to GnRH-deficient male rats. Data are shown as increases over zero hour values. *$P < 0.05$ vs. 0 hr; ** 30 vs. 240 min. FSH-β, follicle-stimulating hormone-β; GnRH, gonadotropin-releasing hormone; LH-β, luteinizing hormone-β. (Redrawn with permission from Burger LL, Dalkin AC, Aylor KW, et al: GnRH pulse frequency modulation of gonadotropin subunit gene transcription in normal gonadotropes: Assessment by primary transcript assay provides evidence for roles of GnRH and follistatin. Endocrinology 143:3243–3249, 2002.)

reducing follistatin and increasing $\beta_B$ subunit mRNA and protein.[102-104] These studies suggest mechanisms whereby activin secretion by the gonadotrope acts to increase FSH-β mRNA but also increases follistatin production, which, in turn, reduces the effectiveness of activin—a self-limiting intragonadotrope mechanism to determine FSH-β mRNA concentrations. These mechanisms are active during normal physiology. Although only minor changes (twofold) in $\beta_B$ mRNA expression occur during the estrous cycle, marked elevation of follistatin mRNA and protein is seen just before the proestrous LH surge and is dependent on secretion of GnRH.[105,106] This proestrous increase in follistatin modulates FSH-β mRNA expression on proestrus and estrus.[107]

In vivo studies have also clarified the nature of factors regulating gonadotrope follistatin and $\beta_B$ mRNA; data after gonadectomy are shown in Figure 141-9. In males, castration results in an increase in FSH-β and follistatin, whereas inhibin-α and inhibin-$\beta_B$ mRNA is unchanged. The increase in follistatin could be abolished by administration of a GnRH antagonist, thus suggesting that the rise in follistatin depends on increased GnRH secretion.[108] Subsequent work in GnRH-deficient rats showed that the pattern of GnRH stimulus modulates follistatin mRNA expression, with an inverse relationship between follistatin and FSH-β mRNA occurring as a function of GnRH pulse frequency.[94,109] Thus, in males, GnRH regulation of FSH-β appears to be affected by changes in follistatin, with no evidence of changes in $\beta_B$ mRNA and hence activin production.

Testosterone also selectively stimulates FSH-β transcription and mRNA expression in male rats. In GnRH antagonist–treated animals, testosterone increased FSH-β transcription while suppressing that of LH-β.[84] In vivo, the increase in FSH-β transcription may in part reflect suppression of follistatin expression (Fig. 141-10). However, testosterone also exerts direct actions, as FSH-β transcription is increased in vitro in the presence of excess follistatin.

The intrapituitary regulatory systems in females appear more complex. After ovariectomy, FSH-β, $\beta_B$, and follistatin mRNAs increase and are only partly inhibited by GnRH antagonists, suggesting actions of factors in addition to GnRH. The increase in $\beta_B$ subunit can be prevented by administration of estradiol in ovariectomized animals, whereas blockade of inhibin feedback by anti-inhibin sera in intact rats results in a

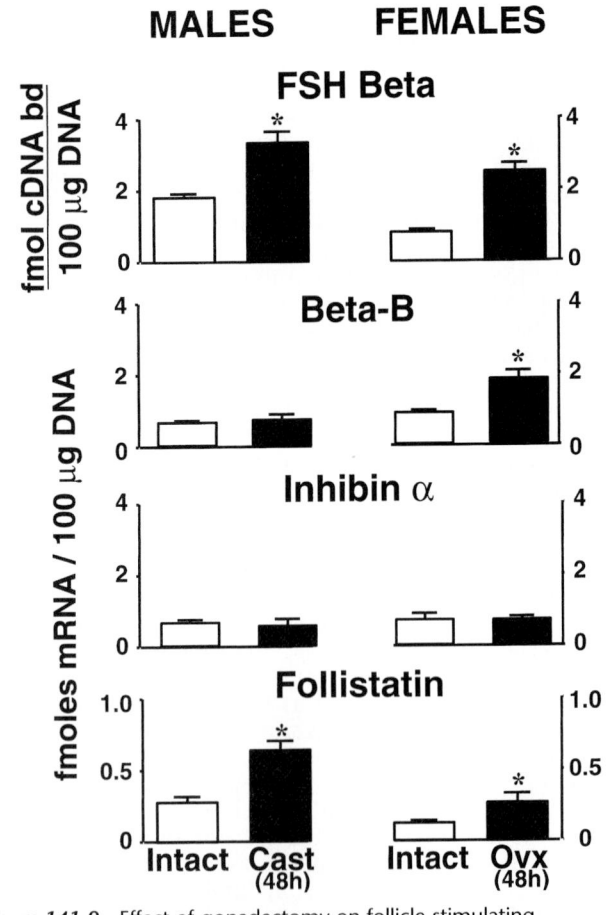

**Figure 141-9** Effect of gonadectomy on follicle-stimulating hormone-β (FSH-β), follistatin, and inhibin/activin subunit mRNA concentrations in male and female rats. Pituitary RNA was examined 48 hours after gonadectomy; FSH-β mRNA was measured by hybridization; and $\beta_B$, inhibin-α, and follistatin mRNAs were measured by quantitative reverse transcriptase polymerase chain reaction. *$P < 0.05$ vs. intact animals. (From Dalkin AC, Haisenleder DJ, Gilrain JT, et al: Regulation of pituitary follistatin and inhibin/activin subunit mRNAs in male and female rats: Evidence for inhibin regulation of follistatin mRNA in females. Endocrinology 139:2818–2823, 1998; © 1998, The Williams & Wilkins Company, Baltimore.)

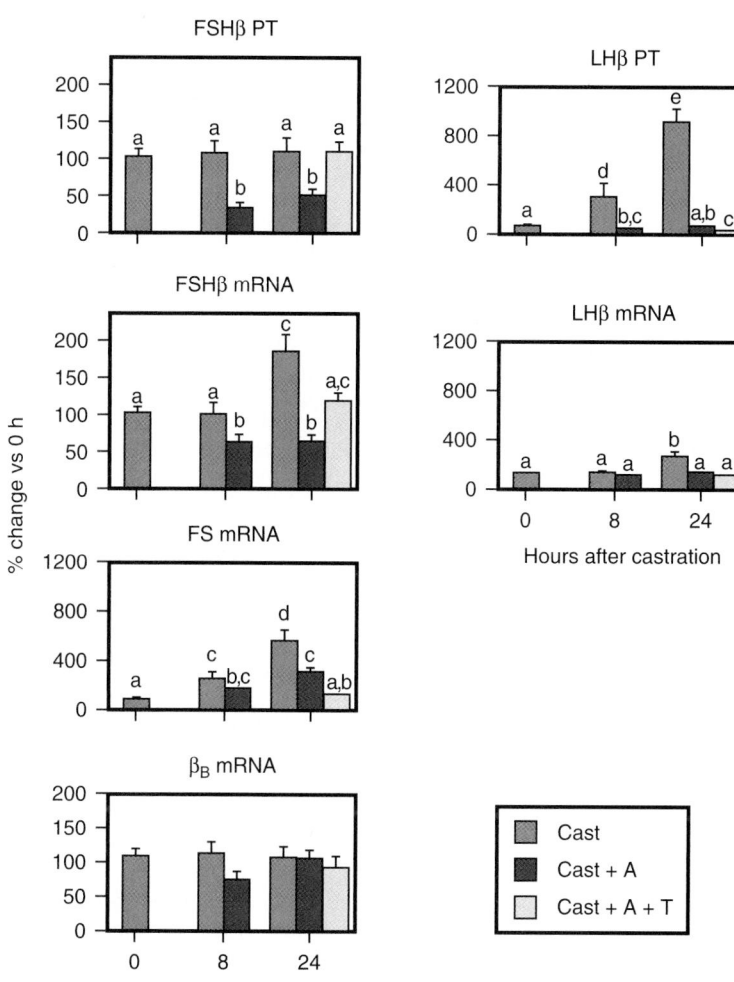

**Figure 141-10** The effects of testosterone on follicle-stimulating hormone-β (FSH-β) and luteinizing hormone-β (LH-β) transcription in male rats. Rats were castrated (*dark gray bars*) and some treated with a gonadotropin-releasing hormone (GnRH) antagonist (*black bars*) and testosterone (*light gray bars*). Data are percent change over zero hours. Different letters indicate differences (*P* < 0.05). (With permission from Burger LL, Haisenleder DJ, Aylor KW, et al: Regulation of LH beta and FSH beta gene transcription by androgens: Testosterone directly stimulates FSH beta transcription independent of its role on follistatin gene expression. Endocrinology 145:71–78, 2004.)

marked increase in follistatin mRNA. Thus, GnRH appears to stimulate the expression of FSH-β, β$_B$, and follistatin mRNA, whereas estradiol exerts an inhibitory effect on β$_B$ and inhibin suppresses follistatin expression.[108] The pattern of the GnRH pulse stimulus also differentially regulates follistatin and β$_B$ mRNA in the pituitary. In a GnRH-deficient female model, low-amplitude GnRH pulses increased FSH-β and β$_B$ mRNA, whereas follistatin mRNA was unchanged. In contrast, high-amplitude pulses produced an inverse pattern, with follistatin increasing and β$_B$ and FSH-β mRNA remaining unchanged. Differential expression of follistatin and β$_B$ mRNA also occurs as a function of GnRH pulse frequency, although the results in relation to FSH-β expression are not as clear-cut.[110] In females, rapid GnRH pulses increase FSH-β and follistatin, intermediate (every 30 minutes) pulses increase FSH-β and β$_B$, and slower-frequency pulses only increase FSH-β expression.

These observations indicate the presence of a complex intra-pituitary autocrine/paracrine regulatory system that governs the expression of FSH-β mRNA and FSH secretion. A model of the proposed intragonadotrope regulatory system is shown in Figure 141-11. GnRH increases FSH-β, activin (β$_B$), and follistatin mRNA as a function of the pattern of the pulsatile stimulus. Activin is secreted by the gonadotrope and increases both FSH-β mRNA and follistatin, with inhibitory effects on β$_B$ production. Because the net effect of activin action is to increase FSH-β mRNA, its action in increasing FSH-β transcription and stabilizing FSH mRNA appears to exceed its effects on follistatin. Follistatin is also secreted by the gonadotrope and binds to activin at an extracellular site, which reduces its action at the activin receptor. It is proposed that in females inhibin reduces the effectiveness of activin at the activin receptor, and as a consequence, FSH-β mRNA levels decline.

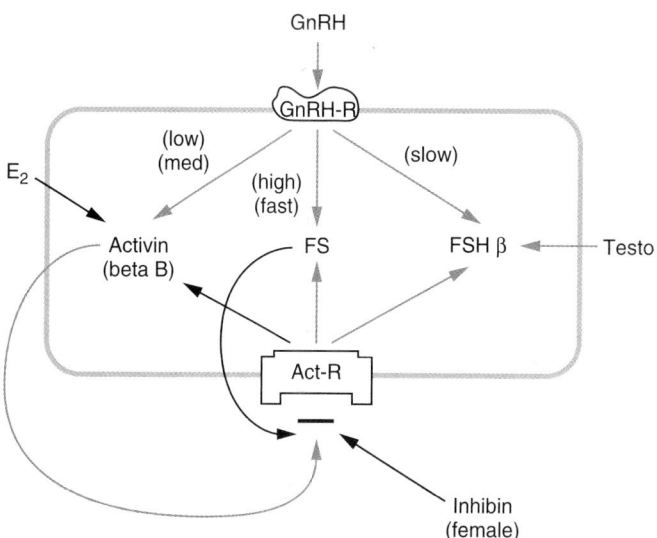

**Figure 141-11** Proposed model of intragonadotrope regulation of follicle-stimulating hormone-β (FSH-β) mRNA expression. *Gray arrows* indicate stimulatory and *black arrows* indicate inhibitory pathways. High and low refer to gonadotropin-releasing hormone (GnRH) pulse amplitude, and fast, med (medium), and slow refer to GnRH pulse frequency. Act-R, activin receptor complex; E$_2$, estradiol; FS, follistatin; GnRH-R, GnRH receptor.

## REFERENCES

1. Bronson FH: Pherohormonal influences on mammalian reproduction. In Diamond N (ed): Perspectives in Reproduction and Sexual Behavior. Bloomington, Indiana University Press, 1968.
2. Michael RP: Hormone steroids and sexual communication in primates. J Steroid Biochem 6:161–168, 1975.
3. Karsch FJ: Seasonal reproduction: A saga of reversible fertility. Physiologist 23:29–38, 1981.
4. Midgley AR, Jaffe RB: Regulation of human gonadotropins: Episodic fluctuation of LH sduring the menstrual cycle. J Clin Endocrinol Metab 33:962–969, 1971.
5. Santen RJ, Bardin CW: Episodic luteinizing hormone secretion in man. J Clin Invest 52:2617–2628, 1973.
6. Clarke IJ, Cummins JT: The temporal relationship between gonadotropin releasing hormone (GnRH) and luteinizing hormone (LH) secretion in ovariectomized ewes. Endocrinology 111:1737–1739, 1982.
7. Belchetz PE, Plant TM, Nakai Y, et al: Hypophysial responses to continuous and intermittent delivery of hypothalamic gonadotropin-releasing hormone. Science 202:631–633, 1978.
8. Marshall JC, Kelch RP: Low dose pulsatile gonadotropin-releasing hormone in anorexia nervosa: A model of human pubertal development. J Clin Endocrinol Metab 49:712–718, 1979.
9. Hoffman AR, Crowley WF: Induction of puberty in men by long term pulsatile administration of low dose gonadotropin-releasing hormone. N Engl J Med 307:1237–1241, 1982.
10. Valk TW, Marshall JC, Kelch RP: Simulation of the follicular phase of the menstrual cycle by intravenous administration of low dose pulsatile gonadotropin-releasing hormone. Am J Obstet Gynecol 141:842–843, 1981.
11. Crowley WF, McArthur JW: Simulation of the normal menstrual cycle in Kallmann's syndrome by pulsatile administration of LHRH. J Clin Endocrinol Metab 51:173–175, 1980.
12. Wildt L, Hausler A, Marshall G, et al: Frequency and amplitude of gonadotropin-releasing hormone stimulation and gonadotropin secretion in the rhesus monkey. Endocrinology 109:376–385, 1981.
13. Clarke IJ, Cummins JT, Findlay JK, et al: Effects on plasma LH and FSH of varying frequency and amplitude of gonadotropin-releasing hormone pulses in ovariectomized ewes with hypothalamic-pituitary disconnection. Neuroendocrinology 39:214–221, 1984.
14. Katt JA, Duncan JA, Herbon L, et al: The frequency of gonadotropin-releasing hormone stimulation determines the number of pituitary gonadotropin-releasing hormone receptors. Endocrinology 116:2113–2116, 1985.
15. Backstrom CT, McNeilly AS, Leask RM, et al: Pulsatile secretion of LH, FSH prolactin, oestradiol and progesterone during the human menstrual cycle. Clin Endocrinol (Oxf) 17:29–42, 1982.
16. Reame N, Sauder SE, Kelch RP, et al: Pulsatile gonadotropin secretion during the human menstrual cycle: Evidence for altered frequency of gonadotropin-releasing hormone secretion. J Clin Endocrinol Metab 59:328–337, 1984.
17. Conn PM, Janovick JA, Stanislaus D, et al: Molecular and cellular bases of gonadotropin releasing hormone (GnRH) action in the pituitary and central nervous system. Vitam Horm 50:151–214, 1995.
18. Stojilkovic SS, Catt KJ: Expression and signal transduction pathways of gonadotropin releasing hormone receptors. Recent Prog Horm Res 50:161–205, 1995.
19. Naor Z: Signal transductor mechanisms of Ca$^{2+}$ mobilizing hormones: The case of gonadotropin releasing hormone. Endocr Rev 11:326–353, 1990.
20. Burger LL, Haisenleder DJ, Dalkin AC, Marshall JC: Regulation of gonadotropin subunit gene transcription. J Mol Endocrinol 2004 (in press).
21. Savoy-Moore RT, Schwartz NB, Duncan JA, et al: Pituitary gonadotropin releasing hormone receptors during the estrous cycle. Science 209:942–945, 1980.
22. Clayton RN, Katt KJ: Gonadotropin-releasing hormone receptors: Characterization, physiological regulation, and relationship to reproductive function. Endocr Rev 2:186–209, 1981.
23. Kaiser UB, Conn PM, Chin WW: Studies of GnRH action using GnRH receptor-expressing pituitary cell lines. Endocr Rev 18:46–70, 1997.
24. Bedecarrats GY, Kaiser UB: Differential regulation of gonadotropin subunit gene promoter activity by pulsatile GnRH in perifused LβT$_2$ cells: Role of GnRH receptor concentration. Endocrinology 144:1802–1811, 2003.
25. Andrews WV, Conn PM: Gonadotropin-releasing hormone stimulates mass changes in phosphoinositides and diacylglycerol accumulation in purified gonadotrope cell cultures. Endocrinology 118:1148–1158, 1986.
26. Haisenleder DJ, Yasin M, Marshall JC: Gonadotropin subunit and GnRH receptor gene expression are regulated by alterations in the frequency of calcium pulsatile signals. Endocrinology 138:5227–5230, 1997.
27. Haisenleder DJ, Yasin M, Marshall JC: Regulation of gonadotropin, thyrotropin subunit and prolactin mRNA expression by pulsatile or continuous protein kinase C (PKC) stimulation. Endocrinology 136:13–19, 1995.
28. Andrews WV, Conn PM: Stimulation of rat luteinizing hormone beta mRNA levels by gonadotropin releasing hormone. J Biol Chem 263:13755–13758, 1988.
29. Sundaresan S, Colin IM, Restell RG, et al: Stimulation of MAPK by GnRH: Evidence for the involvement of PKC. Endocrinology 137:304–311, 1996.
30. Haisenleder DJ, Cox ME, Parsons SJ, et al: GnRH pulses are required to maintain activation of mitogen-activated protein kinase (MAPK): Role in stimulation of gonadotrope gene expression. Endocrinology 139:3104–3111, 1998.
31. Spady TJ, Shayya R, Thackray UG, et al: Androgen regulates FSHβ gene expression in an activin dependent manner in immortalized gonadotropes. Mol Endocrinol 18:925–940, 2004.
32. Aiyer MS, Chiappa SA, Fink G: A priming effect of luteinizing hormone–releasing factor on the anterior pituitary gland in the female rat. J Endocrinol 62:573–588, 1974.
33. Wang CF, Lasley BL, Lein A, et al: The functional changes of the pituitary gonadotrophs during the menstrual cycle. J Clin Endocrinol Metab 42:718–728, 1976.
34. Chappel P, Schneider J, Kim P, et al: Absence of gonadotropin surges and GnRH self priming in ovariectomized estrogen-treated progesterone receptor knock-out mice. Endocrinology 140:3653–3658, 1999.
35. Turgeon J, Waring D: LH secretion from wild type and progesterone receptor knock-out mouse anterior pituitary cells. Endocrinology 142:3108–3115, 2002.
36. Sutton SW, Toyama TT, Otto S, et al: Evidence that neuropeptide Y (NPY) released into the hypophysial-portal circulation participates in priming gonadotropes to the effects of GnRH. Endocrinology 123:1208–1210, 1988.
37. Bauer-Dantoin A, McDonald JK, Levine JE: Neuropeptide Y potentiates LH-RH stimulated LH surges in pentobarbital-blocked proestrus rats. Endocrinology 129:402–408, 1991.
38. Lopez FJ, Merchenthaler I, Ching M, et al: Galanin: A hypothalamic-hypophysiotropic hormone modulating reproductive functions. Proc Natl Acad Sci U S A 88:4508–4512, 1991.
39. Merchenthaler I, Lopez FJ, Lennard DE, et al: Sexual differences in the distribution of neurons coexpressing galanin and LH-RH in the rat brain. Endocrinology 129:1977–1986, 1991.
40. Cheung CY: Prolactin suppresses luteinizing hormone secretion and pituitary responses to LHRH by a direct action at the anterior pituitary. Endocrinology 113:632–638, 1983.
41. Duncan JA, Barkan A, Herbon L, et al: Regulation of pituitary GnRH receptors by pulsatile GnRH in female rats: Effects of estradiol and prolactin. Endocrinology 118:320–327, 1986.
42. Tsai CC, Yen SSC: The effect of ethinyl estradiol administration during the early follicular phase of the cycle on gonadotropin levels and ovarian function. J Clin Endocrinol Metab 33:917–923, 1971.

43. Shaw RW, Butt WR, London DR: The effect of estrogen pretreatment on subsequent response to luteinizing hormone–releasing hormone in normal women. Clin Endocrinol (Oxf) 4:297–304, 1975.

44. Jaffe RB, Keyes WR: Estradiol augmentation of pituitary responsiveness to gonadotropin-releasing hormone in women. J Clin Endocrinol Metab 39:850–856, 1974.

45. Clarke IJ, Cummins JT: Direct pituitary effects of estrogen and progesterone on gonadotropin secretion in the ovariectomized ewe. Neuroendocrinology 39:267–274, 1984.

46. Smith PF, Frawley LS, Neill JD: Detection of LH release from individual pituitary cells by the reverse hemolytic plaque assay: Estrogen increases the fraction of gonadotropes responding to GnRH. Endocrinology 115:2484–2486, 1984.

47. Marshall JC, Case GD, Valk TW, et al: Selective inhibition of follicle-stimulating hormone secretion by estradiol: A mechanism for modulation of gonadotropin responses to low dose pulses of gonadotropin-releasing hormone. J Clin Invest 71:248–257, 1983.

48. Miller WL, Knight MM, Grimek HJ, et al: Estrogen regulation of follicle-stimulating hormone in cell cultures of sheep pituitaries. Endocrinology 100:1306–1316, 1977.

49. Szabo M, Kileon S, Nho S, Schwartz N: Progesterone receptor A and B mRNAs in the anterior pituitary of rats are regulated by estrogen. Biol Reprod 62:95–102, 2000.

50. Lagace L, Massicotte J, Labrie F: Acute stimulatory effects of progesterone on luteinizing hormone and follicle-stimulating hormone release in rat anterior pituitary cells in culture. Endocrinology 106:684–692, 1980.

51. Nippoldt TB, Khoury S, Barkan A, et al: Gonadotropin responses to GnRH pulses in hypogonadotropic hypogonadism: LH responsiveness is maintained in the presence of luteal phase concentrations of estrogen and progesterone. Clin Endocrinol 26:293–301, 1987.

52. Turgeon J, Waring D: Androgen modulation of LH secretion by female rat gonadotropes. Endocrinology 140:1767–1774, 1999.

53. Barkan A, Cassorla F, Loriaux D, et al: Steroid and gonadotropin secretion in a patient with virilization due to a lipoid cell ovarian tumor. Obstet Gynecol 63:287–295, 1984.

54. Venturoli S, Porcu E, Fabri R, et al: Longitudinal evaluation of different gonadotropin pulsatile patterns in anovulatory cycles of young girls. J Clin Endocrinol Metab 74:836–841, 1992.

55. Apter D, Vihko R: Endocrine determinants of fertility: Serum androgen concentrations during followup of adolescents into the third decade of life. J Clin Endocrinol Metab 71:970–974, 1990.

56. Apter D, Butzow T, Laughlin G, Yen S: Accelerated 24 hour LH pulsatile activity in adolescent girls with ovarian hyperandrogenism: Relevance to the developmental phase of PCOS. J Clin Endocrinol Metab 79:119, 1994.

57. Daniels T, Berga S: Resistance of GnRH drive to sex steroid induced suppression in hyperandrogenemic anovulation. J Clin Endocrinol Metab 82:4179–4183, 1997.

58. Pastor C, Griffin-Korf M, Aloi J, et al: Polycystic ovarian syndrome: Evidence for reduced sensitivity of the GnRH pulse generator to inhibition by estradiol and progesterone. J Clin Endocrinol Metab 83:582–590, 1998.

59. Dumesic D, Abbott D, Eisner J, Goy R: Prenatal exposure of female rhesus monkeys to testosterone propionate increases serum LH levels in adulthood. Fertil Steril 67:155–163, 1997.

60. Robinson J, Forsdike R, Taylor J: In-utero exposure of female lambs to testosterone reduces the sensitivity of the GnRH neuronal network to inhibition by progesterone. Endocrinology 140:5797–5805, 1999.

61. Sharma T, Herkimer C, West C, et al: Fetal programming: Prenatal androgen disrupts positive feedback actions of estradiol but does not effect timing of puberty in female sheep. Biol Reprod 66:924–933, 2002.

62. Ying SY: Inhibins, activins, and follistatins: Gonadal proteins modulating the secretion of follicle-stimulating hormone. Endocr Rev 9:267–293, 1988.

63. McLachlan RI, Robertson DM, Healy DL, et al: Circulating immunoreactive inhibin levels during the normal human menstrual cycle. J Clin Endocrinol Metab 65:954–961, 1987.

64. Rivier C, Schwall R, Mason A, et al: Effect of recombinant inhibin on gonadotropin secretion during proestrus and estrus in the rat. Endocrinology 128:2223–2228, 1991.

65. DePaolo LV: Inhibins, activins and follistatins: The saga continues. Proc Soc Exp Biol Med 214:328–339, 1997.

66. Chang G, Pangas SA, Bernard DJ, et al: Structure and expression of a membrane component of the inhibin receptor system. Endocrinology 141:2600–2607, 2000.

67. Lewis KA, Gray PC, Blount AL, et al: Betaglycan binds inhibin and can mediate functional antagonism of activin signaling. Nature 404:411–414, 2000.

68. Chapman SC, Bernard DJ, Jelen J, Woodruff TK: Properties of inhibin binding to betaglycan, Inh BP/p120 and the activin type II receptors. Mol Cell Endocrinol 196:79–93, 2002.

69. Chapman SC, Woodruff TK: Betaglycan localization in the female rat pituitary: Implications for the regulation of FSH by inhibin. Endocrinology 144:5640–5649, 2003.

70. Carroll RS, Corrigan AZ, Gharib SD, et al: Inhibin, activin and follistatin: Regulation of follicle-stimulating hormone messenger ribonucleic acid levels. Mol Endocrinol 3:1969–1976, 1989.

71. Attardi B, Vaughan J, Vale W: Regulation of FSH beta mRNA levels in the rat by endogenous inhibin. Endocrinology 129:2802–2804, 1991.

72. Rivier C, Vale W: Effect of recombinant activin-A on gonadotropin secretion in the female rat. Endocrinology 129:2463–2465, 1991.

73. Carroll RS, Kowash PM, Lofgren JA, et al: In vivo regulation of FSH synthesis by inhibin and activin. Endocrinology 129:3299–3304, 1991.

74. Inouye S, Guo Y, DePaolo L, et al: Recombinant expression of human follistatin with 315 and 288 amino acids: Chemical and biological comparison with native porcine follistatin. Endocrinology 129:815–822, 1991.

75. Gharib SD, Wierman ME, Shupnik MA, et al: Molecular biology of the pituitary gonadotropins. Endocr Rev 11:177–199, 1990.

76. Albanese C, Colin IM, Crowley WF, et al: The gonadotropin genes: Evolution of distinct mechanisms for hormonal control. Recent Prog Horm Res 51:23–61, 1996.

77. Fallest PC, Trader TM, Darrow JM, Shupnik MA: Regulation of the rat luteinizing hormone beta gene expression in transgenic mice by steroids and a GnRH antagonist. Biol Reprod 53:103–109, 1995.

78. Shaw G, Kamen R: A conceived AU sequence from the 3′ untranslated region of GM-CSF mRNA mediates selective mRNA degradation. Cell 46:659–663, 1980.

79. Spady TJ, Shayya R, Thackray UG, et al: Androgen regulates FSH beta gene expression in an activin dependent manner in immortalized gonadotropes. Mol Endocrinol 18:925–940, 2004.

80. Papavasiliou SS, Zmeili S, Herbon L, et al: α and LHβ mRNA of male and female rats after castration: Quantitation using an optimized RNA dot blot hybridization assay. Endocrinology 119:691–698, 1986.

81. Dalkin AC, Haisenleder DJ, Ortolano GA, et al: Gonadal regulation of gonadotropin subunit gene expression: Evidence for regulation of FSH beta mRNA by non-steroidal hormones in female rats. Endocrinology 127:798–806, 1990.

82. Dalkin AC, Haisenleder DJ, Gilrain JT, et al: GnRH regulation of gonadotropin subunit gene expression in female rats: Actions on FSH beta mRNA involve differential expression of pituitary activin (beta B) and follistatin mRNAs. Endocrinology 140:903–908, 1999.

83. Burger LL, Dalkin AC, Aylor KW, et al: Regulation of gonadotropin subunit transcription after ovariectomy in the rat: Measurement of subunit primary transcripts reveals differential roles of GnRH and inhibin. Endocrinology 142:3435–3442, 2001.

84. Burger LL, Haisenleder DJ, Aylor KW, et al: Regulation of LH beta and FSH beta gene transcription by androgens: Testosterone directly stimulates FSH beta transcription independent of its role on follistatin gene expression. Endocrinology 145:71–78, 2004.

85. Paul SJ, Ortolano GA, Haisenleder DJ, et al: Gonadotropin subunit mRNA concentrations after blockade of GnRH action: Testosterone selectively increases FSH beta subunit mRNA by posttranscriptional mechanisms. Mol Endocrinol 4:1943–1955, 1990.

86. Carroll RS, Corrigan AZ, Vale W, et al: Activin stabilizes FSH-beta mRNA levels. Endocrinology 129:1721–1726, 1991.

87. Marshall JC, Dalkin AC, Haisenleder DJ, et al: Gonadotropin releasing hormone pulses: Regulators of gonadotropin synthesis and ovulatory cycles. Recent Prog Horm Res 47:155–189, 1991.

88. Haisenleder DJ, Ortolano GA, Jolly D, et al: Inhibin secretion during the rat estrous cycle: Relationships to FSH secretion and FSH beta subunit mRNA concentrations. Life Sci 47:1769–1773, 1990.

89. Haisenleder DJ, Dalkin AC, Marshall JC: Regulation of gonadotropin gene expression. In Knobil E, Neill JD (eds): The Physiology of Reproduction, 2d ed. New York, Raven, 1994, pp 1793–1832.

90. Yasin M, Dalkin AC, Haisenleder DJ, et al: Testosterone is required for GnRH stimulation of LHβ mRNA expression in female rats. Endocrinology 137:1265–1271, 1996.

91. Dalkin AC, Burger LL, Aylor KW, et al: Regulation of gonadotropin subunit gene transcription by GnRH: Measurement of primary transcript RNAs by quantitative RT-PCR assays. Endocrinology 142:139–146, 2001.

92. Haisenleder DJ, Dalkin AC, Ortolano GA, et al: A pulsatile GnRH stimulus is required to increase transcription of the gonadotropin subunit genes: Evidence for differential regulation of transcription by pulse frequency in vivo. Endocrinology 128:509–517, 1991.

93. Shupnik MA: GnRH effects on rat gonadotropin subunit gene transcription in vitro: Requirement for pulsatile administration for LH beta gene stimulation. Mol Endocrinol 4:1444–1450, 1990.

94. Burger LL, Dalkin AC, Aylor KW, et al: GnRH pulse frequency modulation of gonadotropin subunit gene transcription in normal gonadotropes: Assessment by primary transcript assay provides evidence for roles of GnRH and follistatin. Endocrinology 143:3243–3249, 2002.

95. Roberts V, Meunier H, Vaughan J, et al: Production and regulation of inhibin subunits in pituitary gonadotropes. Endocrinology 124:552–554, 1989.

96. Kogawa K, Nakamura T, Sugino K, et al: Activin-binding protein is present in pituitary. Endocrinology 128:1434–1440, 1991.

97. Kaiser UB, Lee BL, Carroll RS, et al: Follistatin gene expression in the pituitary: Localization in gonadotropes and folliculo-stellate cells in diestrus rats. Endocrinology 130:3048–3056, 1992.

98. Tsuchida K, Mathews LS, Vale WW: Cloning and characterization of a transmembrane serine kinase that acts as an activin type 1 receptor. Proc Natl Acad Sci U S A 90:11242–11246, 1993.

99. Corrigan AZ, Bilezikjian LM, Carroll RS, et al: Evidence for an autocrine role of activin B within anterior pituitary cultures. Endocrinology 128:1682–1684, 1991.

100. Shimonaka M, Inouye S, Shimasaki S, et al: Follistatin binds to both activin and inhibin through the common beta subunit. Endocrinology 128:3313–3315, 1991.

101. Weiss J, Guendner MJ, Halvorson LH, et al: Transcriptional activation of the FSHβ subunit gene by activin. Endocrinology 136:1885–1891, 1995.

102. Bilezikjian LM, Vaughan JM, Vale WW: Characterization and the regulation of inhibin/activin subunit proteins of cultured rat anterior pituitary cells. Endocrinology 133:2545–2553, 1993.

103. Bilezikjian LM, Corrigan AZ, Vaughan JM, et al: Activin-A regulates follistatin secretion from cultured rat anterior pituitary cells. Endocrinology 133:2554–2560, 1993.

104. Bilezikjian LM, Corrigan AZ, Blount AL, et al: Pituitary follistatin and inhibin subunit mRNAs are differentially regulated by local and hormonal factors. Endocrinology 137:4277–4284, 1996.

105. Halvorson LM, Weiss J, Bauer-Dantoin AC, et al: Dynamic regulation of pituitary follistatin, but not inhibin subunit, messenger ribonucleic acids during the rat estrus cycle. Endocrinology 134:1247–1253, 1994.

106. Bauer-Dantoin AC, Weiss J, Jameson JL: GnRH regulation of pituitary follistatin gene expression during the primary FSH surge. Endocrinology 137:1634–1639, 1996.

107. Besecke LM, Guendner MJ, Sluss PA, et al: Pituitary follistatin regulates activin-mediated production of follicle-stimulating hormone during the rat estrus cycle. Endocrinology 138:2841–2848, 1997.

108. Dalkin AC, Haisenleder DJ, Gilrain JT, et al: Regulation of pituitary follistatin and inhibin/activin subunit messenger ribonucleic acids (mRNAs) in male and female rats: Evidence for inhibin regulation of follistatin mRNA in females. Endocrinology 139:2818–2823, 1998.

109. Kirk SE, Dalkin AC, Yasin M, et al: GnRH pulse frequency regulates expression of pituitary follistatin mRNA: A mechanism for differential gonadotrope function. Endocrinology 135:876–880, 1994.

110. Dalkin AC, Haisenleder DJ, Gilrain JT, et al: Gonadotropin-releasing hormone regulation of gonadotropin subunit gene expression in female rats: Actions on follicle-stimulating hormone beta messenger ribonucleic acid (mRNA) involve differential expression of pituitary activin (beta-B) and follistatin mRNAs. Endocrinology 140:903–908, 1999.

# Genetic Basis of Gonadal and Genital Development

## *Charmian A. Quigley*

## INTRODUCTION

Sex determination and differentiation are distinct, consecutive processes that follow the establishment of chromosomal sex at the time of gamete fertilization, subsequently requiring the coordinated spatiotemporal expression of a specific set (or sets) of genes. The term *sex determination* (alternatively called *primary sex differentiation*) refers to the development of gonadal sex, a process that occurs at approximately 6 to 7 weeks' gestation in the human male fetus and significantly later, around 10 to 11 weeks' gestation in the female fetus. As generally used, the term *sex differentiation* refers to the processes downstream of gonadal development, the processes that are regulated by gonadal secretions (also called *secondary sex differentiation*). In essence, the sex chromosome complement endowed at fertilization determines gonad type and the latter determines the pattern of differentiation in the genital ducts and external genitalia.

Normal development of the gonads and genitalia has three major phases. First, in the earliest stages of gestation, the fetus develops a bipotential gonad, two sets of embryonic internal genitalia, and undifferentiated ambisexual external genitalia. The next step is the differentiation of the bipotential gonads into either ovaries or testes, and the final phase is the differentiation and development of the internal and external genital primordia along male or female lines, depending on the nature of the hormonal products of the gonads (or lack thereof). Each phase is described separately in the sections that follow.

The initial event in sex determination—the development of the primordial, bipotential gonad—is a process dependent on a network of interacting factors encoded by at least a dozen, and possibly hundreds, of genes, most of which are probably yet to be discovered. After development of the primordial gonad, the development of either the testis or the ovary is exquisitely regulated by a team of cooperative transcriptional activators and repressors that selectively upregulate or downregulate the genes required for sex-specific gonadal differentiation. The genes involved in the regulation of sex determination and sex differentiation reside on both the sex chromosomes and the autosomes. Based on studies of sex determination in other species, it has been hypothe-sized that the mammalian sex chromosomes evolved from a homologous autosome pair.

Numerous disorders of sex determination have been reported in association with defects of the many genes involved in these processes. Sex reversal is present when an individual with a 46,XX karyotype develops testes and varying degrees of masculinization or an individual with 46,XY karyotype develops ovaries and is feminized. Male-to-female (i.e., 46,XY) sex reversal has been reported in association with mutations of *WT1*, *SF1*, *ATRX*, *SRY*, and *SOX9* and also occurs in association with deletions of the region of chromosome 9 in which *DMRT1/2* reside, and with duplication of the chromosomal regions in which *DAX1* and *Wnt4* reside. Details of each of these genes are provided in the following sections. Female-to-male sex reversal is found in association with translocation of *SRY* onto the X chromosome and with duplication of the chromosomal region containing *SOX9*. Notably, many 46,XX males have no currently definable genetic lesion. The finding that approximately 10% of 46,XX males with testes are completely negative for all Y-encoded sequences (XX$^{Y-}$) indicates that non-Y sequences must be responsible for testis determination in these cases. The absence of spermatogenesis in 46,XX males has been attributed to two factors: the presence of the extra X chromosome, and the absence of Y-chromosomal genes involved in spermatogenesis.

True hermaphroditism is present when there is coexistence of ovarian and testicular tissue in the same individual (either an ovary on one side and a testis on the other [≈20% of patients], bilateral ovotestes [≈30%], or one ovotestis and one testis or ovary [≈50%]), regardless of karyotype. The majority of patients with 46,XX true hermaphroditism are negative for any detectable Y-chromosomal sequences. While the molecular basis of this condition is as yet unknown, genetic causes are implicated by the finding of familial cases of the disorder. The term *pseudohermaphroditism* describes conditions in which the gonads are congruent with the karyotype (46,XX with ovaries; 46,XY with testes), but the internal and/or external genitalia are partially or completely those of the opposite sex. Examples include individuals with 46,XY karyotype and testes whose phenotype is female or ambiguous (e.g., androgen insensitivity syndromes, disorders of testosterone biosynthesis) and those with 46,XX karyotype and ovaries whose phenotype is male or masculinized (e.g., congenital adrenal hyperplasia).

## DEVELOPMENT OF THE BIPOTENTIAL GONADS AND PRIMORDIAL GENITALIA

### EMBRYOLOGY OF DEVELOPMENT OF THE BIPOTENTIAL GONADS AND PRIMORDIAL GENITALIA

In the first few weeks of gestation, the primordial gonads develop from the condensation of a ridge of mesenchymal tissue located medial to the mesonephros (the forebear of the embryonic kidney) accompanied by thickening and proliferation of the coelomic epithelium, which penetrates the underlying mesenchyme.[1] Blood vessels grow into the developing gonad from the mesonephros, subsequently developing in a sexually dimorphic manner. At approximately 5 weeks of gestation in the human fetus, the intermediate mesoderm in the area that will become the kidney, adrenal, and gonad condenses into its distinct regions. As development progresses, the nephrogenic tissue forms urogenital ridges on the dorsal wall of the body cavity. The urogenital ridge consists of the mesonephros (primitive kidney) and the primitive gonad. The genital ridge (the subregion of the urogenital ridge from which the gonad arises) is located medial to the mesonephric ridge. The primitive gonadal or genital ridges initially contain no germ cells. Between the fifth and sixth weeks of gestation (embryonic day [E]10.5–12 in the mouse), primordial germ cells migrate by ameboid movement from the endoderm of the yolk sac along the dorsal mesentery of the hindgut and into the indifferent gonad, where they invade the developing primary sex cords (Fig. 142-1A). At this stage, the gonad comprises an outer cortex and inner medulla, and there is still no morphologic difference between the gonads of male and female fetuses. Following the arrival of the germ cells, the gonad begins to differentiate: In the 46,XX fetus, the cortex develops under the influence of the germ cell lineage and the medulla regresses; in the 46,XY fetus, the reverse occurs, with development of the medullary sex cords under the influence of the supporting cell lineage. Timing is critical as there is only a limited window during which these events can occur.[2]

Both the urinary and genital components of the urogenital system are derived, to a large extent, from the intermediate mesoderm. The intermediate mesoderm becomes segmented into units termed *nephrotomes*. The lateral portions of the nephrotomes unite, forming a longitudinal duct on each side of the embryo, the mesonephric duct (later to become the Wolffian duct), by about week 4 of human gestation (Fig. 142-1B). Later, at around 6 weeks, the paramesonephric duct (forebear of the Müllerian duct) forms by invagination of a tube from the epithelium on the surface of the urogenital ridge, such that, by 6 weeks' gestation, male and female fetuses are endowed with two sets of internal duct structures[1,3] (Fig. 142-2).

Just as the gonads and internal genitalia are indistinguishable between the sexes for the first few weeks of life, so it is for the external genital primordia. In the fourth week of gestation, the external genitalia of both karyotypic sexes are represented simply by a midline protuberance, the genital tubercle. By week 6 (still indifferent), two medial folds—the urethral folds—flank the urogenital groove and two larger folds—the labioscrotal folds—are present laterally[3,4] (Fig. 142-3A).

### GENETICS OF DEVELOPMENT OF THE BIPOTENTIAL GONADS AND PRIMORDIAL GENITALIA

There is a relationship between renal, adrenal, and gonadal cellular precursors that underlies both normal and abnormal development, since these tissues all arise from the same regions of the primitive mesoderm and coelomic epithelium known as the *adrenogenital primordium*.[5] The adrenal cortex derives from mesenchymal cells attached to the coelomic cavity lining adjacent to the urogenital ridge within the intermediate mesoderm; similarly, the steroid-producing cells of the gonads (Leydig and theca cells) differentiate from

mesenchymal stem cells. The specific ontogeny of steroidogenic tissues has particular relevance for the understanding of the genetic regulation of gonadal development. Since these tissues have common cellular ancestors, it is not surprising that they share aspects of their genetic makeup. Thus, the roles and responsibilities of a number of transcription factors involved in the early stages of renal, adrenal, and gonadal development overlap, when tissues are undifferentiated and the major developmental need of the organism is to increase cell mass. As development progresses and populations of cells begin to differentiate along specific, irreversible paths, there is a requirement for a much more focused program of transcription factor action. This concept may help in the understanding of the diverse roles served by transcription factors such as SF1, WT1, and LIM1 compared with the much more limited roles, expression, timing, and cellular specificity of factors such as SRY and AMH.

Transcription factors and other molecules implicated in the early development of the bipotential gonadal and reproductive tract primordia include LIM1, EMX2, LHX9, SF1, WT1, and Wnt4 (internal reproductive tract). In addition, the ligand/receptor pair, Steel/c-kit, is known, at least in mice, to be vital to the process of primordial germ cell migration from the yolk sac to the gonadal primordium in both sexes. Exact relationships between these factors and the precise timing and order of their expression remain to be determined; a hypothetical scheme for their potential roles in regulating the processes of early development of the reproductive tract is shown in Figure 142-4B. Following are descriptions of the molecular biology of individual factors.

### Lim Homeobox Gene 1 (LIM1 or LHX1)

LIM transcription factors constitute a large family (at least 40 members) of proteins that carry two tandem copies of the LIM domain (the acronym stands for Lin-11, Islet-1, and Mec-3—the 3 original members of the family), a unique cysteine-rich, zinc-binding domain (two zinc fingers per LIM domain, for a total of four zinc fingers) involved in protein-protein interactions, followed downstream by a homeodomain that mediates DNA binding.[6] LIM domains can physically interact with other proteins to form protein complexes that regulate transcription. LIM homeodomain proteins are critical regulators of embryonic development.[7] Some studies have suggested that LIM domains negatively regulate the transcriptional activity of their associated homeodomains, by interfering with DNA binding. LIM homeobox* gene 1 (*LIM1* or *LHX1*), an early member of the family that appears to be a transcriptional activator, plays a major role in organizing the development of the head in mice and is implicated in gonadal and renal development.[8] Mice homozygous for a null mutation (knockout) of *Lim1* or for mutations that alter conserved amino acids required for zinc-finger structure in the LIM domains were severely defective. Most mutant mice died in utero, but the few that survived to delivery had no heads, kidneys, or gonads. It can be assumed that these findings were true for both XX and XY embryos, although this was not specifically reported. The complete urogenital phenotype of these mice has not been reported, but it would seem likely that other derivatives of the mesonephros, such as internal genital ducts, would also be deficient.

Human LIM1 shares more than 99% identity at the amino acid level with mouse Lim1 and the gene has been localized to 11p12-13, making it quite a close neighbor to *WT1* (see discussion to follow), also at 11p13.[9,10] The *Lim1* gene comprises 5 exons and encodes a 384–amino acid polypeptide. The two LIM domains are encoded by the first and second exons, while the homeodomain is encoded by exons 3 and 4.

---

*The homeo*box* is the ~180 base pair sequence in the gene that encodes the ~60 amino acid homeo*domain* of its respective protein.

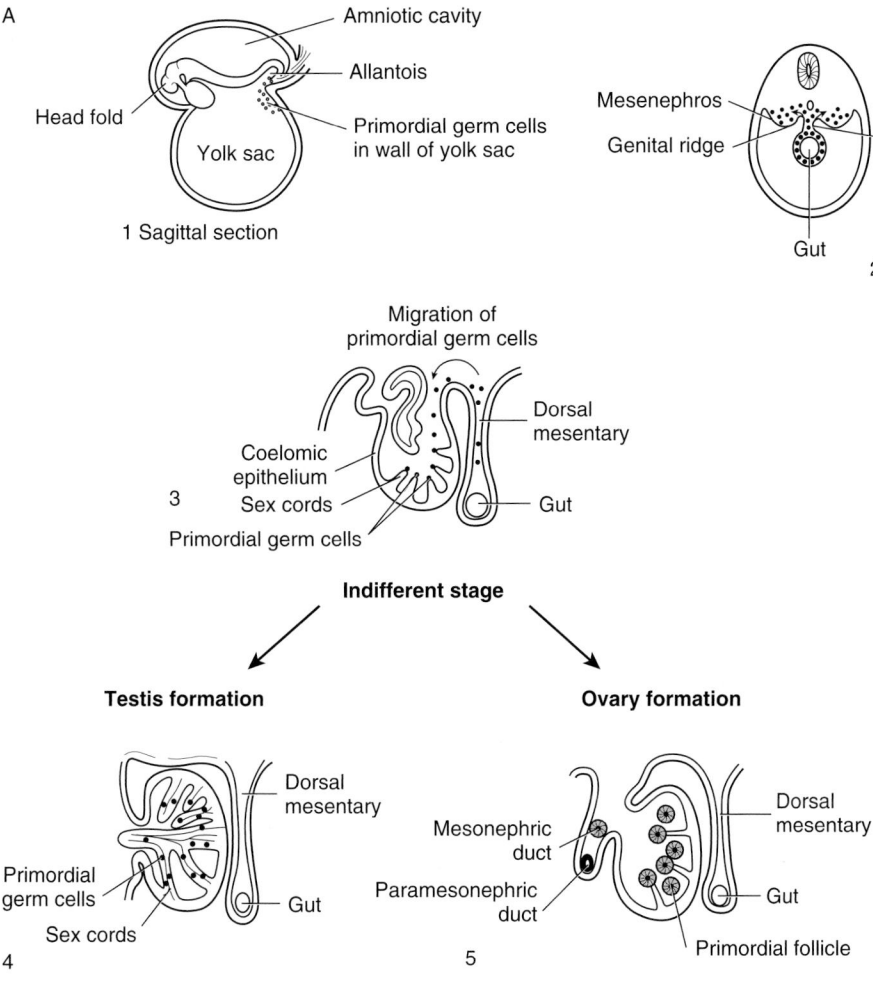

**Figure 142-1A** Embryology of the gonads. **1** and **2,** The primordial germ cells are located in the wall of the yolk sac in early embryogenesis. **3,** At about the fifth to sixth week of human gestation, germ cells migrate by ameboid movement from the coelomic epithelium, along the dorsal mesentery of the hindgut, to the genital ridge, the site of the future gonad. During formation of the indifferent (bipotential) gonad, the primordial germ cells infiltrate the primary sex cords, which subsequently become the seminiferous tubules of the testis, or the primordial follicles of the ovary. **4** and **5,** Formation of the testis continues after arrival of the germs cells, although these are not required for the process to occur. Probably under the direction of the newly differentiated Sertoli cells, the primitive sex cords differentiate as the seminiferous tubules, in which germ cells are embedded. Morphologic development of the testis is complete by 8 weeks' gestation. Formation of the ovary occurs later than that of the testis, at around week 10 of gestation, and does require the presence of germ cells. The primary sex cords develop into primordial follicles at about week 16 of gestation.

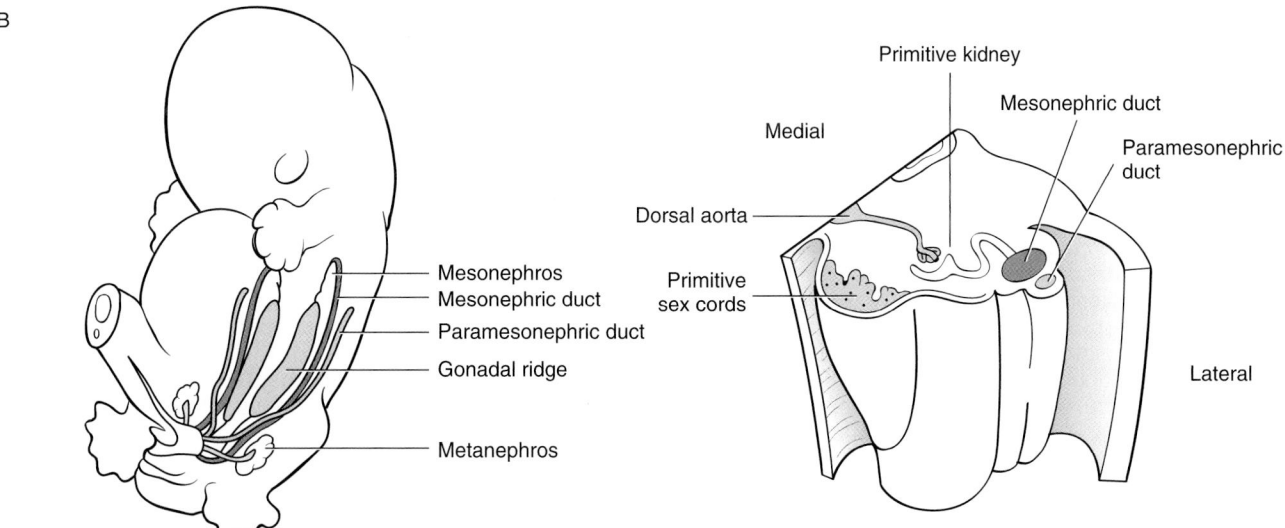

**Figure 142-1B** Anatomic relationships between renal and gonadal primordia during embryogenesis. **Left,** Diagram of human fetus at 5 to 6 weeks of gestation. The primordial genital ridges are located just medial to the mesonephros, the primitive fetal kidney. The mesonephros is functional only during early fetal life and is replaced later in gestation by the metanephros (located more caudally in this diagram), which becomes the definitive kidney. The mesonephric duct, which later becomes the Wolffian duct, runs in a craniocaudal direction just lateral to the mesonephros; the paramesonephric duct, which later becomes the Müllerian duct, runs almost parallel to the mesonephric duct, a little farther laterally on the posterior abdominal wall. **Right,** Partial horizontal section of the 5 to 6 weeks' gestation fetus, showing (from medial to lateral) the primitive sex cords (containing primordial germ cells), primitive kidney, mesonephric duct, and paramesonephric duct.

*Figure 142-2* Embryologic development of the internal genitalia. **Top,** Indifferent stage. The primitive internal genitalia at 7 weeks' gestation have both paramesonephric or Müllerian (female) and mesonephric or Wolffian (male) duct systems. **Lower left,** Female development. In the 9- to 13-week female fetus, the Wolffian ducts regress (*dotted lines*) while Müllerian ducts (*shaded*) differentiate and develop. The upper portions of the Müllerian ducts form the fallopian tubes; the lower portions fuse to form the uterus, cervix, and upper part of the vagina. The urogenital sinus remains patent in the absence of androgen action, forming the lower part of the vagina. **Lower right,** Male development. Differentiation of the Wolffian ducts in the male fetus occurs under the influence of testosterone between 8 and 13 weeks of gestation. These develop as the epididymides, vas deferentia, and seminal vesicles (*shaded*). By week 11, the Müllerian ducts are obliterated by a process of apoptosis that occurs under the direction of antimüllerian hormone (AMH) secreted by Sertoli cells (*dotted lines*).

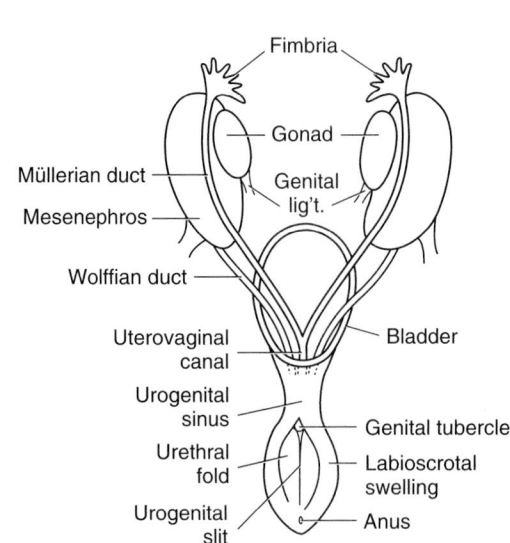

Indifferent stage

Female development

Male development

*Lim1* expression in the mouse occurs extremely early, at the stage of the primitive streak, then in the intermediate mesoderm and nephrogenic cord.[11] Consequently, the action of Lim1 in gonad formation is likely at the level of the primordial gonad. *Lim1* is also expressed later in development in several urogenital tissues such as mesonephros, Wolffian ducts, ureteric buds, and definitive kidney. Subsequently, mouse *Lim1* expression can be detected in the central nervous system from the telencephalon through the spinal cord and in the developing excretory system including the pronephric region, mesonephros, nephric duct, and metanephros.[12] Target genes for transcriptional regulation by Lim1 are currently unknown.

Human *LIM1* expression has been detected in the brain, tonsil, and thymus, and also in a number of leukemia cell lines, but not in the adult testis or ovary. While this latter finding may appear incongruous with a role in gonadal development, it should be noted that human fetal expression has not yet been reported. If this gene plays a role in human gonadogenesis, it would be expected that expression is limited to a specific time window during development of the primordial human gonad. Human mutations have not been described.

## Empty Spiracles 2

Another homeodomain transcription factor, empty spiracles 2 (EMX2), appears in mice to have somewhat similar functions to LIM1, being essential for the development of the dorsal telencephalon and components of the developing urogenital system.[13] In addition to developmental defects of the brain, *Emx2* null mutant mice lack kidneys, ureters, gonads, and genital tracts, implying a role for this transcription factor in very early development of the renal, gonadal, and internal genital primordia, probably at the stage of development of the mesonephros. Degeneration of the Wolffian duct and mesonephric tubules was abnormally accelerated, and Müllerian ducts did not form.

The 3-exon human *EMX2* gene maps to 10q26.1, which is, incidentally, the site of a putative endometrial tumor suppressor.[14,15] The 3.0-kb transcript encodes a deduced 252–amino acid protein containing a 61–amino acid homeodomain, encoded by exons 2 and 3. A second gene of unknown significance is transcribed from the opposite DNA strand.[16]

*Emx2* is intensely expressed in the bipotential gonads and ovaries and is also expressed in epithelial components of the

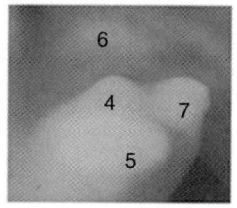
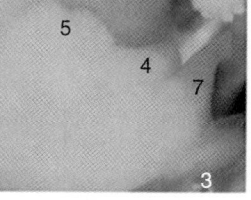

**A    Indifferent stage male or female - 5 weeks**

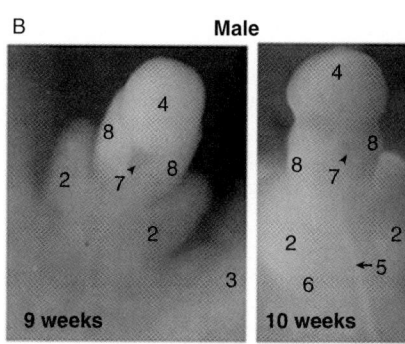
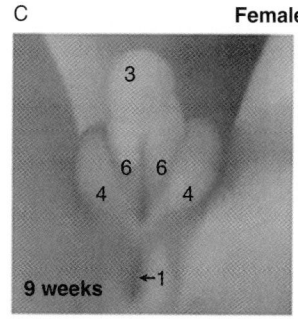
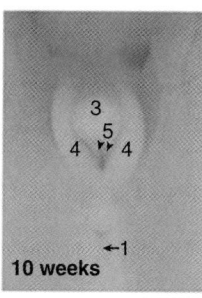

**B    Male**

9 weeks    10 weeks

**C    Female**

9 weeks    10 weeks

*Figure 142-3*  Embryology of external genital development. **A,** Indifferent stage: *4,* Genital tubercle; *5,* Leg bud; *6,* Umbilical cord; *7,* Tail. **B,** Male development: *2,* Labioscrotal swelling; *4,* Phallus; *5,* Median raphe; *7,* Urethral groove; *8,* Urogenital folds. **C,** Female development: *1,* Anus; *3,* Clitoris; *4,* Labioscrotal swelling; *5,* Labia minora; *6,* Urogenital folds. (Reproduced with permission from England M: Color Atlas of Life Before Birth. Chicago, Year Book Medical Publishers, 1983.)

developing urogenital system, specifically the pronephros and mesonephros, Wolffian and Müllerian ducts, ureteric buds, and early epithelial structures derived from metanephrogenic mesenchyme.[17] *Emx2* is also detected in brain, kidney, and uterus. *Emx2* is expressed in the adult urogenital tract in an inverse temporal pattern from *Hoxa10,* another homeobox gene, suggesting a negative regulatory relationship.[18] Notably, *Emx2* null mice had reduced expression of *Lim1* and that of *Wnt4* (described later) was absent, suggesting that Emx2 may modulate expression of these factors.[13]

Heterozygous mutations in EMX2 have been detected in a number of patients with the rare, severe cerebral malformation syndrome schizencephaly.[19] A urogenital phenotype has not been reported in these patients; however, since a pair of brothers has been reported with the mutation, it appears that male urogenital development was normal, so the role of this gene in human, as distinct from murine, gonadal development remains in question. It will be important to review further patients with *EMX2* mutations carefully for evidence of urogenital maldevelopment, especially in light of the finding of sex reversal in association with deletions of distal chromosome 10q, the site of the *EMX2* gene in humans.

## LIM Homeobox Gene 9

An early-acting factor in gonadal development (and other developmental processes) appears to be LIM homeobox gene 9 (*Lhx9*), encoding another member of the LIM family of transcription factors. A role for Lhx9 in development of the primordial gonad was established by the finding of complete gonadal agenesis in *Lhx9* null mice of both sexes,[20] without apparent extragonadal defects (in contrast with the headless *Lim1* null mutants). As would be expected in the situation of gonadal agenesis, the mice had high follicle-stimulating hormone (FSH) concentrations and no detectable testosterone or estradiol. All null mice were phenotypically female. They had atrophic uteri, vaginas, and oviducts, indicating that Lhx9 is not required for development of the internal genital primordia and also suggesting that gonadal secretions are required for optimal development of these structures. Gonadal agenesis appeared to be due to failure of gonadal cell proliferation at around day 12 of gestation rather than exaggeration of apoptosis, suggesting a role for Lhx9 in stimulating proliferation of cells of the primordial gonad.

The human gene encoding LHX9 is located at 1q31-32 and encodes a protein with over 98% amino acid identity with mouse LHX9.[21,22] The gene contains 6 exons spanning 10 kb

of genomic sequence, resulting in a predominant 4.7-kb transcript. A number of alternate splice products are detectable in a variety of human tissues. Like other LIM family members the protein contains 2 amino-terminal cysteine-rich LIM protein domains, each comprised of 2 zinc fingers, followed by a DNA-binding homeodomain.

Lhx9 appears to be necessary for proliferation and invasion of the epithelial (somatic) cells of the genital ridge into the underlying mesenchyme and subsequent formation of sex cords—an essential step in formation of the gonads.[23] Its primary role may be in regulation of expression of steroidogenic factor-1 (SF1), a key regulator of adrenal and gonadal development (discussed later); LHX9 can bind directly to the SF1 promoter and may act synergistically with an isoform of Wt1 (the form lacking the lysine, threonine, serine amino acid triplet, known as the –KTS isoform, described later) in activating Sf1.[24] Lhx9 may regulate Sf1 specifically in the gonad, as evidenced by the findings in *Lhx9* null mice of normal adrenal SF1 expression in the face of minimal SF1 expression in genital ridges.[20] *Wt1* was expressed quite normally in *Lhx9* null mice indicating that Lhx9 does not appear to have a role in regulation of *Wt1* expression.

*Lhx9* is expressed in epithelial and subjacent mesenchymal cells of the early gonadal ridge, detectable at mouse E9.5. *Lhx9* expression localizes to the interstitial region of the developing gonad as morphologic differentiation occurs, then disappears as epithelial cells differentiate into Sertoli cells and begin to express antimüllerian hormone (AMH). In the fetal rat ovary, *Lhx9* is highly expressed in epithelial cords. Similar to the downregulation that occurs once testicular Sertoli cells differentiate, expression is downregulated as ovarian epithelial cells differentiate into granulosa cells during the process of folliculogenesis. Thus, it appears that *Lhx9* expression is inversely correlated with the degree of differentiation of mesenchymal cells of the gonad.

Studies in human embryos demonstrate *LHX9* expression in the abdominal region of both sexes at the time of gonad formation. It is widely expressed in adult tissues, including testis, ovary, prostate, bowel, lung, heart, liver, and leukocytes. The finding of a number of different transcripts in different human tissues suggests complex, partly sex-specific, regulatory events involving transcription initiation and alternative splicing. Human *LHX9* mutations have not been reported, despite a careful search in at least one study of 27 patients with 46,XY gonadal agenesis or dysgenesis.[22]

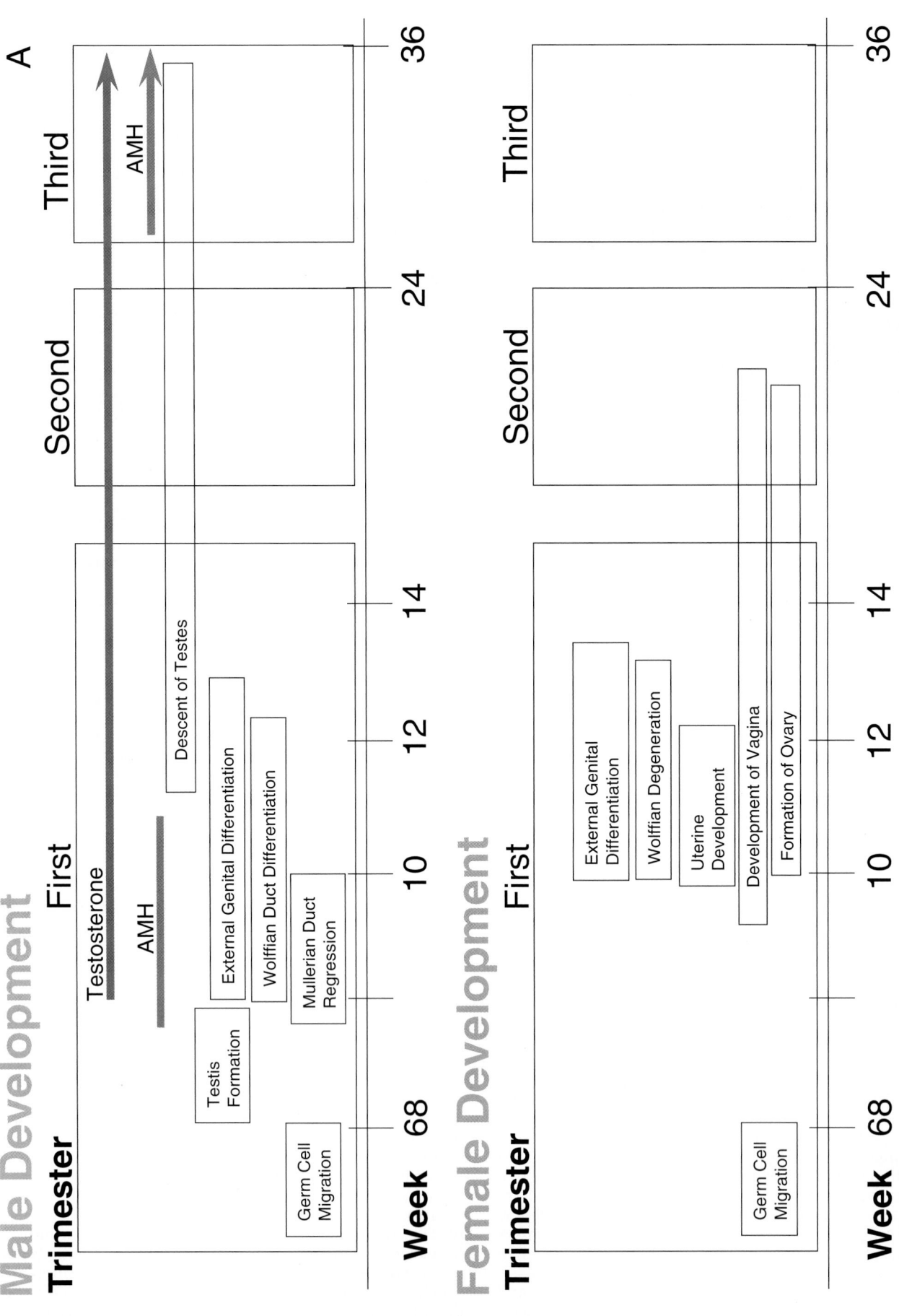

**Figure 142-4A** Timetable of gonadal and genital differentiation. In both male and female development, the first event of sex differentiation is the migration of germ cells, at around 5 to 6 weeks' gestation. This is followed by testicular development in the male. After onset of antimüllerian hormone (AMH) and testosterone secretion at approximately 7 to 8 weeks' gestation, the Müllerian ducts regress and Wolffian ducts differentiate. Male development is complete by the end of the first trimester of gestation, although penile enlargement and testicular descent continue into the third trimester. The pattern of development is parallel, but essentially opposite and somewhat delayed for female fetuses. In particular, there is a marked lag between testicular and ovarian development; ovarian differentiation and vaginal development continue into the middle of the second trimester.

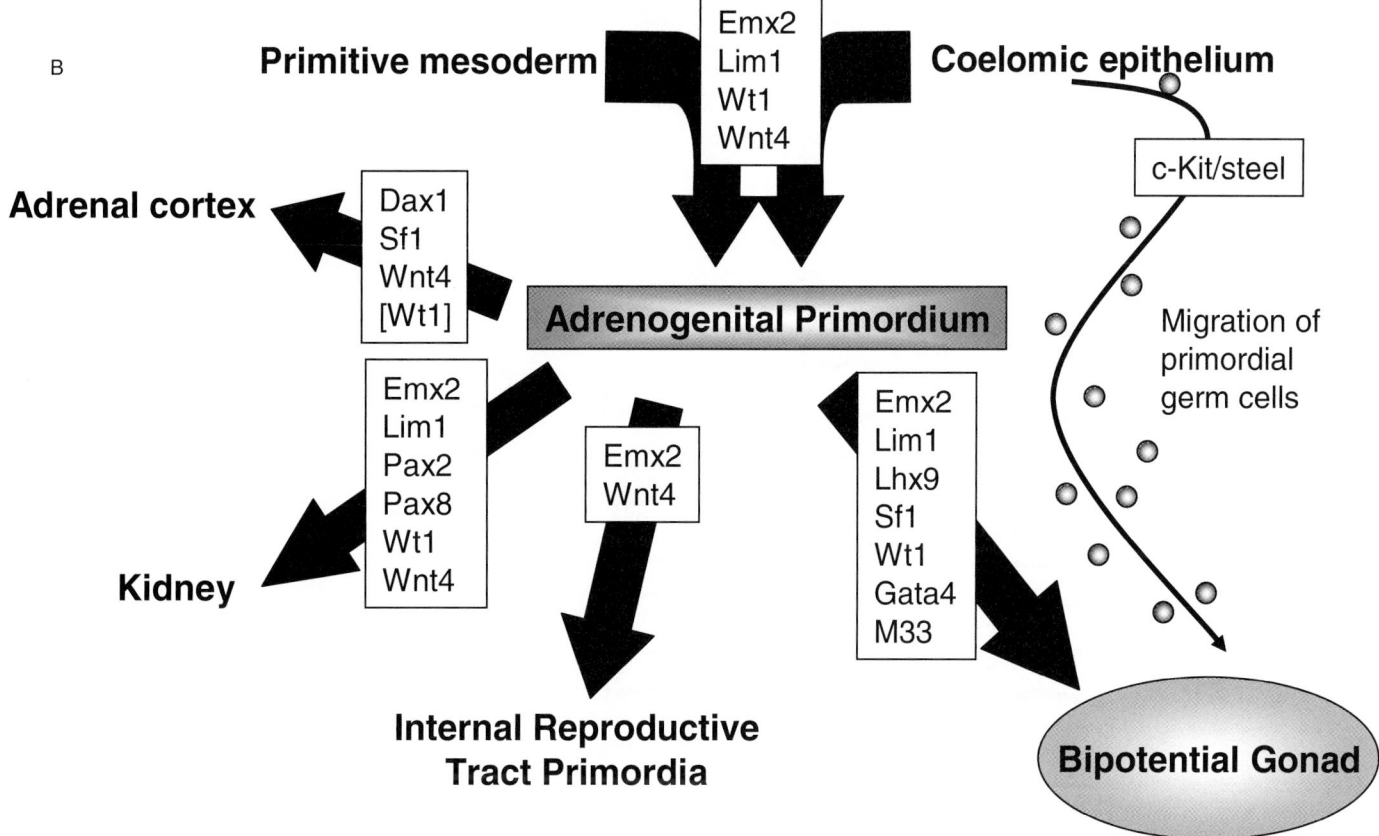

**Figure 142-4B**  Genetic determinants of development of the primordial gonad. Transcription factors Emx2, Lim1, Wt1, and Wnt4 are required for development of the adrenogenital primordium, which forms following condensation of primitive mesoderm and coelomic epithelium. Thereafter, various combinations of transcription factors direct the fate of the various undifferentiated primordial cells down one of a number of pathways to form the adrenal cortex, kidney, bipotential gonad, and various internal reproductive tract primordia.

### Steroidogenic Factor-1

The orphan nuclear receptor transcription factor, steroidogenic factor-1 (SF1, also referred to as adrenal 4–binding protein [Ad4BP] and officially termed nuclear receptor subfamily 5, group A, member 1 [NR5A1]) appears to be one of the earliest-acting and most critical factors in the primitive development of the reproductive tract, impacting reproductive function at all three levels of the hypothalamic-pituitary-gonadal axis, and subsequently regulating factors acting further down the pathway of gonadal/genital development in a male-specific fashion.[25–27] This transcription factor is also critical for normal development of the adrenal gland. Importantly, SF1 appears to act in a dose-dependent manner in both mice and humans.[28]

The human gene encoding SF1 is located at chromosome 9q33, spans 30 kb of genomic DNA and contains 7 exons including an initial noncoding exon.[29] Two distinct proteins—SF1 and ELP (embryonal long terminal repeat)—are produced by alternative promoter usage and splicing; however, the critical protein with respect to reproductive tract development is SF1 itself, a 461–amino acid protein with a molecular weight of 53 kilodaltons.[30] SF1 contains two central DNA-binding zinc fingers typical of nuclear receptors, an activation domain and a carboxyterminal ligand-binding domain (for which no ligand has yet been identified). SF1 differs structurally from most nuclear receptors by lacking an amino-terminal domain and differs functionally by binding as a monomer, rather than as the more usual dimer, to a nonpalindromic DNA steroid response element half-site, 5'-AGGTCA-3'. Based on studies of human mutations, two regions of the protein appear particularly critical for function: The so-called P-box, located in the

proximal portion of the first zinc finger, is responsible for interaction with the major groove of DNA; the A-box region located downstream of the DNA-binding domain modulates monomeric binding to DNA.[31]

SF1 is implicated in the regulation of numerous genes, as SF1 binding sites have been located within the promoter regions of at least 20 target genes, including those encoding a number of other transcription factors (DAX1, WT1, SRY), hormones (luteinizing hormone [LH]–β, AMH, oxytocin, Isnl3, inhibin, gonadotropin subunits), receptors (AMH-R, ACTH-R, PRL-R), proteins and enzymes of steroidogenesis (StAR, P450scc, steroid 21-hydroxylase, the aldosterone synthase isozyme of steroid 11α-hydroxylase, aromatase), and the signaling molecule Wnt4.[31–37] SF1 has been clearly demonstrated to upregulate AMH expression in a sexually dimorphic manner and, in so doing, associates with WT1 (the –KTS isoform, discussed later).[38–41] Notably, although SF1 binds to the promoter of the *AMH* gene, it is unable to regulate *AMH* expression in cotransfection assays using a heterologous cell line unless its ligand-binding domain is deleted. This finding suggests a role for a possible ligand for SF1 in its regulation of *AMH* expression in vivo, perhaps a Sertoli cell-specific factor[32] (Fig. 142-5).

The gene that encodes Sf1 in the mouse is termed *FtzF1*, on the basis of its similarity to the drosophila gene, fushi tarazu factor 1. *Sf1* is expressed in the urogenital ridge of male and female mice at embryonic day 9 to day 9.5, the earliest stage of organogenesis of the indifferent gonads.[42] Consistent with its role in regulation of steroidogenesis, *Sf1* is expressed before expression of the first enzyme of steroidogenesis, p450scc. Since both *Sf1* and *Wt1* (discussed later) are expressed in the gonadal primordium at a similar time, before

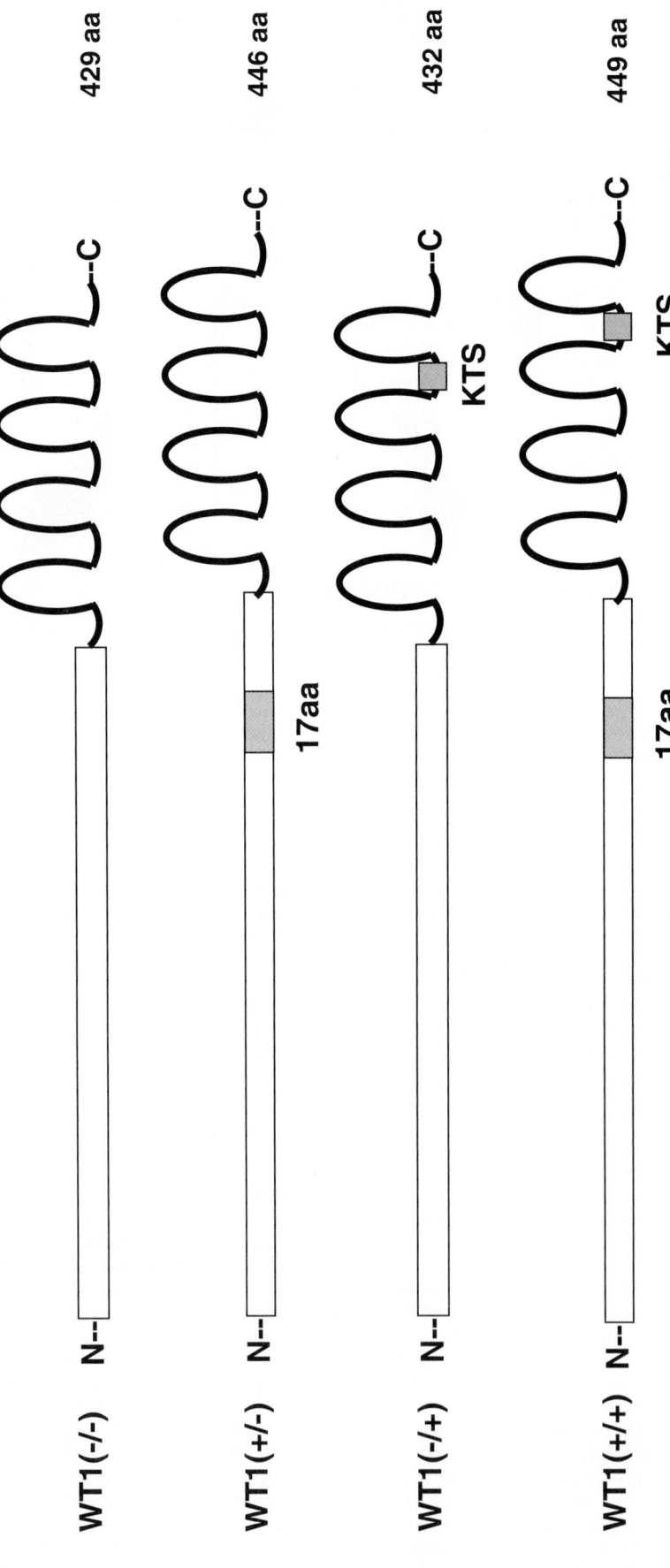

*Figure 142-5A* Structure and function of transcription factor WT1. **A,** Major isoforms of WT1. WT1 is a potent transcriptional activator or repressor, depending on the specific cellular and genetic context. There are four major isoforms of WT1, formed by differential splicing of exons 5 and 9 that either include or exclude a 17–amino acid sequence in the central region of the protein (encoded by exon 5) and a lysine-serine-threonine triad (KTS) between the third and fourth zinc fingers (encoded by exon 9) that alters the DNA-binding specificity of the protein. The −/− isoform, lacking both inserts, has greater transcriptional activation potential than the main isoform (+/+) that contains both inserts.

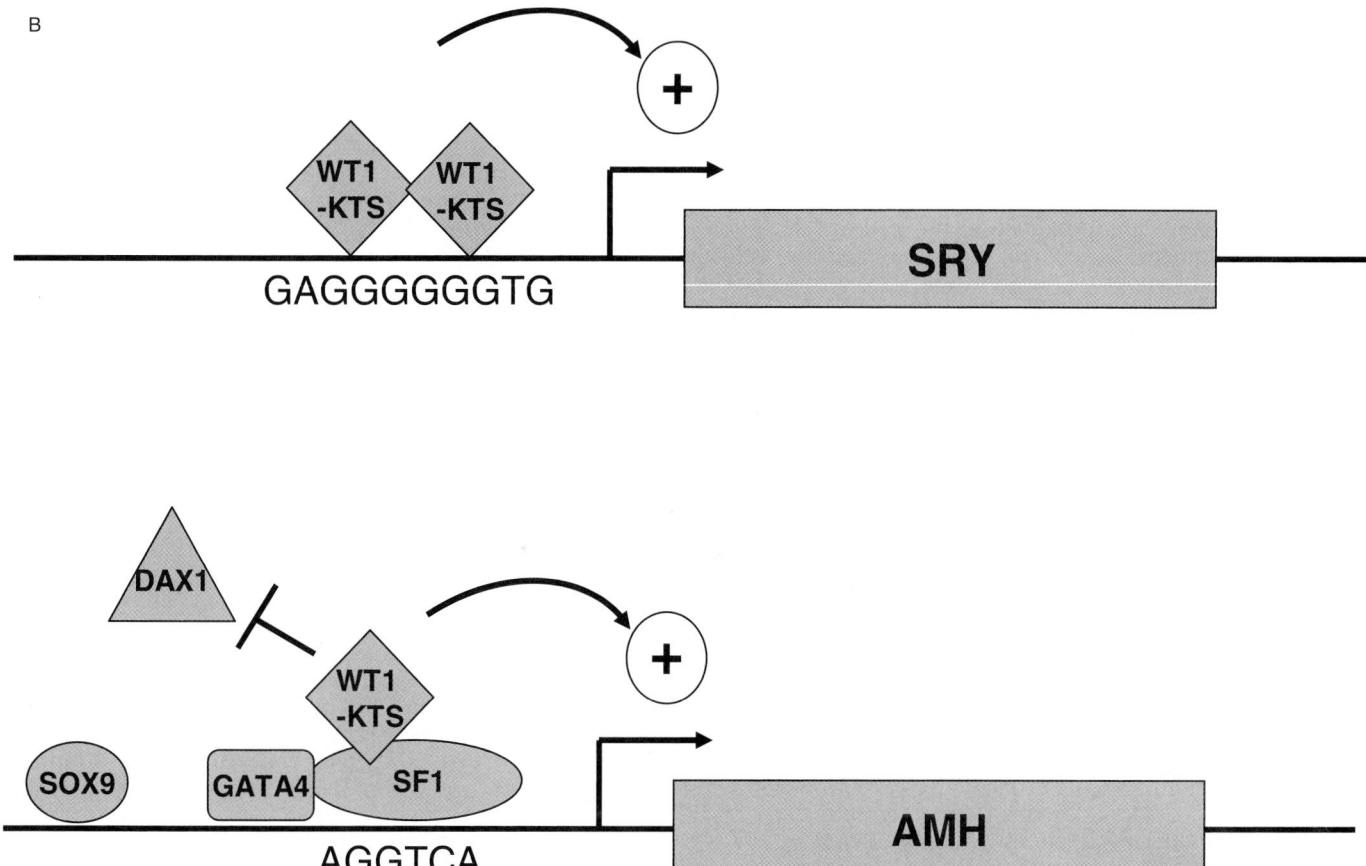

*Figure 142-5B* **B,** WT1 binding at target genes. WT1 regulates transcription of numerous target genes involved in various aspects of sex determination and differentiation, including SRY, DAX1, and AMH. WT1 (–KTS) binds as a homodimer to the promoter of the SRY gene to upregulate its transcription. In contrast, at the AMH gene, WT1-KTS binds as a heterodimer with SF1, antagonizing binding of DAX1 to the promoter.

gonadal differentiation occurs, Sf1 interaction with Wt1 may play a role in proper development of the gonadal precursor.[24] After a sex-specific gonad can be discerned, *Sf1* expression becomes sexually dimorphic, presumably under the regulation of other sex-specific factors; *Sf1* expression in the fetal testis, specifically Sertoli and Leydig cells, continues at a high level. In contrast to the continued high *Sf1* expression in males, expression in fetal ovaries is quite low.[42,43] In XX mouse gonads, *Sf1* is expressed in somatic cells until embryonic day 13 and disappears altogether between embryonic days 13.5 and 16.5, in keeping with the lack of ovarian steroidogenic activity at that time. In adult mice, *Sf1* is expressed in all primary steroidogenic tissues, including all zones of the adrenal cortex, testicular Leydig and Sertoli cells, ovarian theca and granulosa cells, and corpus luteum.

The expression of SF1 and DAX1, another orphan nuclear receptor described in further detail later, overlap in their tissue distribution. DAX1 appears, in fact, to repress or antagonize SF1 activity, particularly the synergy between SF1 and WT1, probably via a protein-protein interaction with SF1.[44,45] On the basis of this finding, it has been proposed that DAX1 and SF1 functionally oppose each other. These interactions may be key for the differential expression of genes involved in female versus male development.

Not only does SF1 regulate gonadal and adrenal development, it also appears to control development of an important hypothalamic nucleus and of pituitary gonadotropes.[46] *Sf1* mRNA is detectable in the developing mouse pituitary at embryonic days 13.5 to 14.5 and can be specifically detected in gonadotropes. *Sf1* is also expressed in nonmammalian

vertebrates including chicken and alligator, but expression patterns (and, therefore, likely functional roles) vary among species.

Expression of *Sf1* appears to be regulated by other transcription factors, including a helix-loop-helix protein (upstream stimulatory factor[47]) that binds to a region in the promoter of the gene designated the E box and by the homeodomain transcription factor Lhx9, which has an additive effect with Wt1 at the *Sf1* promoter.[47,48] Furthermore, pituitary expression of *Sf1* appears to be regulated by gonadotropin-releasing hormone (GnRH), at least in the rat pituitary, and this may be relevant for the Sf1 regulation of gonadotrope development.[49] *Sf1* expression beyond the pituitary gland, however, is not controlled by the hypothalamic-pituitary-adrenal axis, since hypophysectomized rats display normal *Sf1* expression in the adrenals and gonads.[50]

*SF1* mRNA is expressed widely in human tissues, both steroidogenic and nonsteroidogenic, including the adrenal cortex, gonads, spleen (primarily the reticuloendothelial cells), adult liver, heart, and brain (including several components of the limbic system).[51] *SF1* is expressed at high levels in the human pituitary gonadotrope and is also expressed in the human placenta from the first trimester to term.[52] The diverse expression of *SF1* in tissues such as spleen and brain suggests that SF1 may play a role in reticuloendothelial/immune cell maturation and/or function, as well as nervous system development and/or neurosteroid biosynthesis.

Key information regarding the developmental roles of SF1 came initially from studies in transgenic null mice, which demonstrated the requirement for Sf1 in both sexes for development of the organs that derive from the adrenogenital primordium—primordial gonads and adrenal cortex—as well as the hypothalamus and pituitary.[25,26,53] Male and female mice homozygous for deletion of *FtzF1* failed to develop steroidogenic tissues, having neither gonads nor adrenal glands. The mice had phenotypically female internal and external genitalia and died in the neonatal period of adrenal insufficiency. These mice did display mesenchymal thickening in the gonadal ridge area at the earliest stages of gonadal development (E10.5), but, thereafter, the cells of this region underwent apoptosis, suggesting that the role of Sf1 may be in maintaining rather than initiating gonadal development. The mice also had abnormal development of the ventromedial hypothalamic nucleus, a region important in control of pituitary gonadotropin secretion. Expression of proteins specific to gonadotrope cells, LH, FSH, and GnRH receptor was absent, implicating Sf1 in gonadotrope development and LH/FSH expression.

The presence of female internal genitalia in the null animals of both sexes indicates that the Müllerian ducts did not regress as would normally occur in the males, reflecting lack of Amh action. Since Sf1 regulates expression of *Amh*, deficiency of Sf1 in males would result in lack of *Amh* expression and, therefore, retention of Müllerian structures. These findings imply that Sf1 is active earlier than Amh in the ontogeny of sexual differentiation. In females, expression of *Sf1* during the critical period of genital development would be detrimental to normal sex differentiation since this would lead to Müllerian regression and failure of oviduct and uterine development. The fact that *Sf1* expression in normal developing ovaries is low supports this contention.

In contrast to the complete absence of adrenal development in the *Sf1* null mice, haploinsufficiency for *Sf1* produces a different phenotype. Mice heterozygous for *Sf1* deletion had significant defects in adrenal development and organization, but, by compensation via cellular hypertrophy and increased expression of steroidogenic acute regulatory protein (StAR), were able to maintain adequate basal adrenal function.[54] Furthermore, the heterozygous mice developed testes and ovaries, albeit somewhat smaller than those of wild-type animals, indicating that a single active gene is adequate for this function.

The rare mutations identified in the human *SF1* gene suggest dosage effects for the function of this transcription factor in human development. 46,XY sex reversal (streak gonads and female genitalia) and adrenal hypoplasia were reported in a patient with homozygous *SF1* mutation, but no effect was evident in the heterozygous state.[55] There was no obvious effect on ovarian development in a 46,XX patient with partial adrenal hypoplasia due to heterozygous *SF1* mutation, similar to the *Sf1* haploinsufficiency phenotype in mice.[56]

## Wilms Tumor 1

Like SF1, the transcription factor Wilms tumor 1 (WT1), plays a pivotal role in early development of the primordial gonad and the bipotential internal genital duct systems before sex determination, and, in addition, a specific isoform appears to be required for subsequent development of the testis. In renal tissue, WT1 acts as a tumor suppressor.[41,57] WT1 is a member of the early growth response (EGR) family of transcription factors (proteins expressed early in the cell cycle, at G0 to G1 transition) and acts as a transcriptional activator or repressor, depending on the cellular or chromosomal context.[58-61] There appears to be a general requirement for WT1 in the formation of organs derived from the intermediate mesoderm, particularly the differentiation of glomerular epithelial cells and gonadal primordium.[62] WT1 is implicated in gonadal and genital development by analysis of human mutations and transgenic mice with *WT1* deletions or mutations.[41,63]

The human *WT1* gene is a complex locus at 11p13 that in fact consists of two genes, *WT1* and *WIT-1*, expressed from opposite DNA strands.[64,65] The function of the *WIT-1* transcript is unknown, but a role as an antisense regulator of *WT1* has been postulated. The highly conserved *WT1* gene itself spans 50 kb and contains 10 exons that can be alternatively spliced to yield four distinct mRNA species of approximately 3 to 3.5 kb each. The primary WT1 protein is a 429–amino acid ($\approx$50 kilodaltons) transcription factor with four contiguous Cys2-His2 zinc-finger domains (encoded by exons 7–10) and an amino terminus rich in proline and glutamine, typical of certain transcription factors. Zinc fingers 2, 3, and 4 of WT1 have greater than 60% amino acid identity with the zinc fingers of the EGR1 transcription factor. Separate domains subserve transcriptional repression and activation: residues 85 to 124 encompass the repressor domain, and 181 to 250 the activator domain. These regions are distinct from the DNA-binding domain and their activities are probably mediated by protein-protein interaction. The four mRNA species encode four major proteins, designated WT1 (A–D), differing mainly on the basis of the presence or absence of an additional 17 amino acids in the central region of the protein (present only in placental mammals) and a lysine/threonine/serine triad (KTS) between the third and fourth zinc fingers (see Fig. 142-5*A*); perhaps as many as 32 different isoforms of WT1 result from additional variations in translational start site, either 5' or 3' of the main translation initiator.[41,57,66] Two of the four major WT1 isoforms contain the KTS sequence (+KTS) and two do not (–KTS). The presence of the KTS amino acid triad alters the spacing between the third and fourth zinc fingers, thereby changing the DNA-binding specificity, likely preventing its binding to the typical EGR1-like DNA-binding sequence. The –KTS and +KTS isoforms also have differential expression patterns within cell nuclei and appear to have distinct but somewhat overlapping roles. Of note, the smaller –/– isoform, lacking both inserts, has greater transcriptional activation potential than the main isoform (+/+) that contains both inserts. The fact that all transcripts are expressed at similar levels suggests that each encoded protein makes a significant contribution to WT1 function, and interactions between the proteins, each of which may have distinct targets and functions, may be important in the control of cellular proliferation and differentiation exerted by WT1.

Various forms of WT1 regulate *SRY*, *DAX1*, *SF1*, and *AMH* expression[45,67-69] (Fig.142-5*B*). WT1-KTS isoforms associate and synergize with SF1 to promote *AMH* expression. DAX1 antagonizes the synergy between SF1 and WT1, most likely through a direct protein-protein interaction with SF1, suggesting that WT1 and DAX1 functionally oppose each other in testis development by modulating SF1-mediated transactivation. WT1-KTS can also activate the *DAX1* promoter. The fact that WT1 can upregulate expression of *DAX1*, which, in turn, antagonizes WT1/SF1-mediated stimulation of *AMH* expression suggests that the relative dosages of WT1-KTS and DAX1 and the timing of their expression during embryogenesis are critical in the delicate balance of transcription factor activity required for gonadal development. The –KTS isoforms of WT1 also upregulate *SRY* gene expression through the EGR1-like sequence in the core promoter.

Expression patterns for *Wt1* in normal mouse embryogenesis also support a role for Wt1 in development of urogenital tissues: *Wt1* expression occurs very early in the fetal life of the mouse, at about the same time as *Sf1* and before *Dax1*.[70-72] *Wt1* is faintly detectable as early as embryonic day 9 and readily detectable in pronephric and mesonephric tissues on day 10.5, at which time *Sry* expression (discussed later) is detectable in pre–Sertoli cells. By embryonic day 11.5, the nephrogenic cord, condensing metanephric tissue, and urogenital ridge display high levels of *Wt1* message. In the developing gonad, *Wt1* expression is localized to the developing sex cords, and, in mature gonads, it is confined to the Sertoli cells and tunica albuginea of the testis and the granulosa and epithelial cells of the ovary. Whereas the role for Wt1 in development of the primordial gonad is fairly clear, its roles in specific testis or ovary development are less well understood and it seems likely that the various forms of Wt1 may function differentially in the different genetic contexts of testicular versus ovarian development. Consistent with this concept, Wt1 expression is differentially regulated during development, depending on the sexual differentiation of the gonad.

The expression pattern of WT1 in human fetal development is similar to that seen in the mouse during the period between days 28 and 70 of gestation, equivalent to mouse embryonic days 10 to 15.[57,71] During this time, WT1 is expressed mainly in mesodermally derived tissues—kidneys, gonads, and mesothelium—but is also expressed in spinal cord and brain (tissues of ectodermal origin). In mid-trimester human embryos, there is strong expression in kidneys and gonads. WT1 expression is limited to Sertoli cells in adult testes.

Transgenic mice homozygous for a knockout mutation of the entire Wt1 gene had failure of renal and gonadal development in the initial study, with additional failure of adrenal gland development in a later study (the reason for the difference in phenotype between these studies is not clear).[62,63,73] Specifically, at day 11 of gestation, the cells of the metanephric blastema underwent apoptosis, the ureteric bud failed to grow out from the Wolffian duct, and the formation of the metanephric kidney did not occur. The mice were nonviable, probably due to abnormal development of the mesothelium, heart, and lungs. A later study also demonstrated a requirement for Wt1 in the development of epicardium and adrenal gland and throughout nephrogenesis.

Different phenotypes are seen when the knockout targets a specific isoform of Wt1.[69] Heterozygous (as distinct from homozygous) mice with a reduction of either Wt1 isoform have normal fetal urogenital development. Thus, the level of Wt1 expressed from a single wild-type Wt1 allele is adequate for normal development. Mice with reduced Wt1 +KTS levels develop glomerulosclerosis after 2 to 3 months, representing a model for the human disease Frasier syndrome, indicating that Wt1 +KTS dosage is important for normal postnatal renal function. Male mice homozygous for deletion of the +KTS isoforms (which, therefore, completely lack the +KTS isoforms but retain normal levels of the –KTS isoforms) showed complete XY sex reversal, their embryonic gonads having the morphologic appearance of ovaries, associated with a dramatic reduction of gonadal Sry and Sox9 expression and female-type Dax1 expression. These findings imply a key role for the +KTS isoforms in regulation of the critical testis-determining Sox genes in male gonadal development. Female mice lacking the +KTS isoforms had normal ovaries, indicating lack of absolute requirement for the +KTS isoforms for ovarian development. Kidney development was severely impaired in both sexes. Mice completely lacking the –KTS Wt1 isoforms had tiny streak gonads in both males and females, associated with reduced Dax1 expression. The mice also had abnormal development of the internal genital ducts and severely impaired renal development. These data demonstrate distinct functions for the WT1 +/–KTS isoforms and place the WT1 +KTS variants as likely regulators of SRY in the sex determination pathway.

It appears from these different transgenic experiments that some form of WT1 is absolutely required for primordial gonad development, but that the subsequent more specific development of the testis requires the +KTS isoform. The absence of both sets of internal genital duct anlagen in one patient with a WT1 mutation is also compatible with a primary role of WT1 in early development of the bipotential internal duct systems, although this has yet to be confirmed.[73]

Human mutations confirm the developmental importance of WT1. The Denys-Drash syndrome is associated with heterozygous germline mutations in WT1 (mainly in the zinc-finger encoding regions) in more than 90% of cases. The disorder is genetically dominant, since no patients have been described with mutations in both alleles of the gene. Complete deletion of the WT1 gene produces milder genital abnormalities (cryptorchidism and/or hypospadias in 46,XY individuals) than does a mutation that encodes expression of an abnormal WT1 protein (46,XY sex reversal with streak gonads), suggesting a dominant negative mechanism of the action of mutant WT1 proteins, perhaps due to abnormal DNA binding.[74] Defective gonadal development has also been reported in 46,XX individuals, underscoring the role of WT1 in both male and female gonadal development.

## GATA4

GATA4 is a member of a group of structurally related DNA-binding zinc-finger transcription factors that control gene expression and differentiation in a variety of cell types.[75-78] Members of this family contain one or two zinc fingers that recognize a consensus GATA DNA sequence known as the GATA motif ([TA]GATA[A/G], hence the name of this class), which is an important element in the promoters of many genes. GATA-family transcription factors are critical to the development of diverse tissues. In particular, GATA4 has been implicated in formation of the vertebrate heart. With respect to sex determination and differentiation, GATA4 may, like WT1, have dual roles, being involved both in early development of the primordial gonad and later in male-specific development.

The human gene for GATA4 is located at 8p23.1-p22 and encodes a 48-kilodalton protein that has a highly conserved zinc-finger domain consisting of two zinc-finger motifs and two adjacent stretches of basic amino acids.[80,81] The carboxyterminal zinc finger confers the DNA-binding ability. The protein also contains a nuclear localization domain and two amino-terminal transcription activation domains.[75]

The genes encoding many steroidogenic enzymes may be targets of GATA proteins as they contain the consensus GATA sequence within their 5′ regulatory regions, suggesting a role for GATA4 in regulation of steroidogenesis.[78] GATA4 has been demonstrated to regulate the StAR promoter in the ovary. GATA4 and SF1 may act synergistically in regulation of AMH expression; binding sites for both factors are adjacent to each other on the AMH promoter, resulting in protein-protein interaction via the zinc-finger region of GATA4.[82] The affinities of various GATA factors for specific promoters probably depend on interactions with cofactors and other, more restricted transcription factors. For example, Leydig cells express factors known as "Friends of GATA" or "FOG" (FOG1 and FOG2), which may play a role in tissue-specific effects and also appear to be necessary for normal gonadal development in both sexes.[77,83]

Most tissues of mesodermal origin express either GATA4, -5, or -6 at some stage.[75] GATA4 is expressed from early stages of gonadal development (E 11.5 in mouse) in both sexes in the somatic cell population (later to become the testicular Sertoli and ovarian granulosa cells) of the indifferent gonad, but not in the primordial germ cells.[84,85] Abundant GATA4 expression continues in Sertoli cells throughout embryonic testis development. During early ovarian development, GATA4 mRNA and protein localize to the granulosa cells; GATA4 is markedly downregulated shortly after the histologic differentiation of the ovary on embryonic day 13.5, resulting in a sexually dimorphic pattern of greater expression in developing testes than ovaries. Because GATA4 is involved in regulating AMH activity, reduced GATA4 expression in the latter stages of ovary development is consistent with the requirement for absence of AMH to allow normal Müllerian duct development in the female. GATA4 is expressed from early human fetal testicular development to adulthood.[85] Like AMH, GATA4 represents an early marker of Sertoli cells; expression in Sertoli cells peaks at 19 to 22 weeks' gestation, at the time of high circulating fetal FSH and testosterone. *GATA4* is also expressed in a number of steroidogenic tissues, and this finding, coupled with the presence of GATA consensus sequences in the promoter regions of the genes encoding many steroidogenic enzymes, is consistent with a role in regulation of steroidogenesis. In Leydig cells, *GATA4* is expressed during the fetal period and after puberty, coinciding with the periods of most active androgen synthesis in the testis. Other steroidogenic tissues in which *GATA4* is expressed include fetal and postnatal granulosa cells, adult theca cells, and fetal adrenal cortex (human and mouse). Fetal germ cells and prepubertal spermatogonia also express *GATA4*; it is downregulated in these cells after puberty.

As the mouse *GATA4* knockout is an early embryonic lethal (days 7–9, before the normal onset of gonadal *GATA4* expression), a gonadal phenotypye of the null mutation has not been described.[75] Targeted mutations that disrupt *Fog2* or its interaction with GATA4 result, however, in significant reduction in expression of *Sry*, *Sox9*, *Amh*, and *Dhh*, as well as the genes encoding steroidogenic enzymes p450scc, 3β-hydroxysteroid dehydrogenase (3β-HSD), and p450c17. There was also failure of upregulation of *Sf1* and *Wt1* in XY gonads, as normally occurs in the developing testis, whereas *Wnt4*, which is normally downregulated in testicular development, was overexpressed. These abnormalities resulted in abnormal gonadal development in both XX and XY fetuses.[77] Human mutations are associated with cardiac defects but no gonadal phenotype has been described.

## Chromobox Homologue 2

Chromobox homologue 2 (CBX2), which maps to 17q25, is the human homologue of a mouse gene called *M33*, which in turn is homologue of a *Drosophila* gene called *polycomb*.[86] The *Drosophila* polycomb genes encode factors that repress homeotic and other developmentally regulated genes by mediating changes in higher order chromatin structure. Both XX and XY mice homozygous for deletion of M33 had retarded formation of genital ridges and those that survived the immediate postnatal period showed male-to-female sex reversal.[87] Formation of genital ridges was disturbed in both XX and XY embryos, suggesting a role for M33 in primordial gonad formation.

## Wingless-Type MMTV Integration Site Family

The *Wnt* genes belong to a family of protooncogenes with at least 16 known mammalian members that are expressed in species ranging from *Drosophila* to man.[88] (The acronym "Wnt" is an amalgamation of "w" from "wingless" and "int-1," a mouse protooncogene so named because it is a target for insertional activation by the mouse mammary tumor virus [MMTV].) These genes encode 38- to 43-kilodalton cysteine-rich glycoproteins with features typical of secreted growth factors (extracellular signaling molecules): a hydrophobic signal sequence and 21 conserved cysteine residues whose relative spacing is maintained. Transcription of *Wnt* family genes appears to be developmentally regulated in a precise temporal and spatial manner. Interaction of Wnt factors with Frizzled receptors (at least eight mammalian members that are part of the seven-transmembrane family of receptors) results in an intracellular signal cascade that in turn leads to transcriptional activation of target genes. By these interactions, the Wnts regulate cell proliferation, morphology, and fate in a wide variety of developmental processes[89]; with regard to urogenital development, the Wnts have particular relevance for development of the kidney and female reproductive tract.[90]

### Wnt4

Wnt4 is required for kidney development and for the initial stages of Müllerian duct formation from the coelomic epithelium in both sexes in mice.[91,92] Homozygous *Wnt4* null mice of both sexes had failure of differentiation of kidney mesenchyme, and Müllerian ducts were absent prior to the time at which *Amh* expression causes Müllerian degeneration in males, indicating that the ducts had failed to form, rather than having formed and then regressed.

*Wnt4* expression is first detected in the mesonephric mesenchyme, which later forms the bipotential gonad; it is subsequently expressed in the indifferent gonads of both sexes, then is downregulated in male gonads. *Wnt4* is also expressed in the adrenal cortex of both sexes, consistent with a role in regulation of steroidogenesis. The approximately 25-kb five-exon human *WNT4* gene located at chromosome 1p35 encodes a protein with 99% sequence conservation with mouse Wnt4.[93,94] *Wnt4* is discussed in greater detail in the section on ovary development. A heterozygous human *WNT4* mutation recapitulates many features seen in a mouse *Wnt4* knockout model, as it appears to function in a dominant negative manner.[95] The mutation occurred in a 46,XX female who had clinical features of Mayer-Rokitansky-Kuster-Hauser syndrome, in addition to mild virilization and excess androgen levels. Combining information from mice and humans, WNT4: (1) suppresses Leydig cell development and expression of the steroidogenic enzymes required for androgen synthesis; (2) is required for normal development of Müllerian structures (upper vagina, uterus, fallopian tubes); (3) suppresses migration of vascular endothelial cells that form the blood vessels characteristic of the testis; and (4) supports normal kidney development.

### Wnt5a

This member of the Wnt family is expressed in the genital tubercle and the genital tract mesenchyme during embryogenesis and in the genital tract mesenchyme postnatally.[90] Mutant mice have stunted growth of the genital tubercle, resulting in lack of external genitalia.[96]

## SEX DETERMINATION (DEVELOPMENT OF TESTIS OR OVARY)

Once development of the primordial gonadal and genital structures has occurred, the next steps diverge between the sexes. The primary event governing the path down which morphologic sex differentiation proceeds is the development of the gonad. In the mid twentieth century the elegant experiments of Jost determined that "maleness" was a state imposed upon the fetus that would otherwise develop as a "female" (at least, phenotypically).[97] These findings led to the theory that development of the ovary and female phenotype occur when the fetus is not exposed to the influences of specific "maleness-determining" genes. Newer information indicates that rather than being a passive, "default" process, ovarian/female development likely also requires activation of specific, perhaps opposing, gene pathways. From these findings, the concept has developed that sex determination represents the primordial "Battle of the Sexes"—the dominance of one set of gonad-specific genes over another.[1] The key event determining the winner of the battle appears to be whether or not the primordial germ cells that colonize the indifferent gonad enter meiosis or are prevented from doing so. Testis cord development under the influence of the *SOX* genes during a narrow developmental window arrests the primordial germ cells in mitosis; in the absence of testis cord development, germ cells enter meiosis and ovarian development ensues.[2,98]

Sex-specific development of the gonads depends on carefully coordinated enhancement of expression of certain genes, with parallel repression of others. This coordinated expression allows for the specificity of timing and level of gene expression required to facilitate differentiation, as opposed to the more general expression and action of factors involved in early phase organogenesis. Thus, in this phase of development, the undifferentiated cell lineages—supporting cells and steroidogenic cells—that colonize the primordial gonad are directed down one of two irreversible paths, toward either testis or ovary. It makes sense that genes required for sex-specific differentiation would either be encoded on the sex-specific chromosomes or vary in dosage between the sexes. Thus, testis development requires that *SRY* (a Y-encoded gene) and *SOX9* (an autosomal gene that appears to be dosage sensitive) are active. Conversely, ovary development requires that *SOX9* is repressed and *WNT4* is active. The long-held concept of the "dominant" and "default" gonad is derived in part from the differential timing of development of testis versus ovary, testicular development occurring in a narrow window at least 3 to 4 weeks before ovarian development. Thus, it is believed that action of male-specific genes must occur at a critical time, to inhibit or repress the function of the ovary-defining genes that are otherwise destined to become active. Not only does testis development begin before ovarian development, the whole process is completed more rapidly. This phenomenon of the relative timing of development of the dominant and default pathways is seen in many mammalian species, indicating that it is a primary feature of sex determination.[99]

## EMBRYOLOGY OF TESTIS DEVELOPMENT

The first discernible event in testis development is the appearance of primordial Sertoli cells, which differentiate from somatic cells of the coelomic epithelium at around 7 weeks of human gestation. Soon after their appearance in the gonadal ridge, Sertoli cells proliferate, aggregate around the primitive germ cells, and align into cordlike structures that subsequently become the seminiferous tubules.[1,100,101] The seclusion of germ cells within the tubules prevents meiosis and commits the germ cells to spermatogenic development. The prevention of meiosis may be the key event that directs gonadal development away from the ovarian pathway, and it is believed that testis cord formation and germ cell entry into meiosis are competing pathways in gonad development. This organizational process appears to be regulated by the Sertoli cells themselves; germ cells are not required for the processes of testis development to occur, since morphologic testis development occurs in their absence. About 1 week later (around 8 weeks), steroidogenic Leydig cells differentiate from primitive interstitial cells of mesonephric origin. This process may be controlled by paracrine influences from Sertoli cells, possibly antimüllerian hormone (AMH). Another key event in testis development is the differentiation of peritubular myoid cells, thought to derive from the same interstitial cell lineage as Leydig cells. These myoepithelial cells are required for the development of the testis cords—the defining event in testicular organogenesis.[102] Finally, establishment of testis-specific vasculature (a coelomic blood vessel) enables testicular secretions to be exported to the developing fetal internal and external genitalia to direct masculinization.

## GENETICS OF TESTIS DEVELOPMENT

Male sex determination is synonymous with testis determination. The process of testis development in the karyotypic male appears to be controlled by a switchlike mechanism that involves the Y-chromosomal *SRY* gene and its encoded protein, a related homeobox gene *SOX9*, and no doubt other genes and proteins that either regulate or are regulated by these factors.[103,104] One of the earliest effects of *SRY* expression is the induction of somatic cell migration from the mesonephros into the XY gonad, a critical first step in preparation for development of testis cords.[100,101] Subsequently, SOX9 directs the process of seminiferous tubule organization by Sertoli cells and regulates transcription of the Sertoli cell glycoprotein AMH; AMH, in turn, may play a role in directing undifferentiated interstitial cells to develop as Leydig cells.[105,106] Once testicular differentiation is established, other Y-encoded genes are required to maintain spermatogenesis. A number of other molecules have been identified as having involvement in testis

development, but their exact positions in this pathway, their functions, and the factors that they regulate or by which they are regulated remain to be elucidated. These include the +KTS isoform of WT1 (as described previously, WT1 is also critical for development of the primordial gonad); the helicase enzyme ATRX, which is involved in DNA recombination, repair, and regulation of transcription; perhaps the intracellular signaling molecule desert hedgehog (Dhh); and a gene or genes located on the distal long arm of chromosome 10. Additional X-chromosomal sequences are also likely to affect testis development, perhaps negatively, since the presence of one or more extra X chromosomes (as found in Klinefelter syndrome and its variants) is associated with reduced testicular size. There are many hypothetical schemes for the interactions of the ever-expanding coterie of transcription factors involved in sex determination, but no definitive model for this process currently exists. What is clear is that the system is extremely complex, involving a network of interacting transcription factors in a nonlinear web of upregulation or activation and downregulation or repression steps. One hypothetical model is as follows: (1) Establishment of the gonadal primordium (multiple factors, as already described), (2) WT1 activation of *SRY*, (3) SRY repression of *WNT4* and perhaps *FOXl2*, thus (5) allowing SF1 to (6) stimulate expression of *SOX9*, leading to (7) development of Sertoli cells followed by (8) DAX1-mediated differentiation of peritubular myoid cells and formation of testis cords, (9) WT1/SF1/SOX9-mediated induction of AMH secretion, (10) action of AMH via the AMH receptor(s) causing Müllerian duct regression, (11) concurrent activity of ATRX to modulate chromatin structure allowing access of transcription factors to target genes, and (12) SF1-mediated stimulation of steroidogenic activity by fetal Leydig cells. A simplified diagram of a possible mechanism for testis development is depicted in Figure 142-6A. While analyses of humans with gonadal dysgenesis, mouse models, and in vitro cell culture assays have provided important insights, it is important to note that there may be quite marked species differences. Although the mouse is generally a convenient model, differences between mice and men must not be overlooked, and the details of sex determination and differentiation elucidated in rodents cannot necessarily be extrapolated to human development. Moreover, the phenotypic effects of many mutations differ among mouse strains, emphasizing the importance of genetic modifiers. Each of these genes and factors is described individually in further detail in the following sections.

### SRY-Related Homeobox Genes

There is an ever-expanding family of DNA-binding, atypical transcription-regulating proteins related to each other by the presence of a central high-mobility-group (HMG) domain* homologous to the HMG domain of the founding member of the family: sex-determining region of the Y (SRY).[107-109] Following the discovery of the *SRY* gene, many related genes were soon identified. Those that encode proteins with more than 60% similarity to the SRY HMG domain are termed *SOX* genes (*SOX* derives from *SRY box*). At least 20 *SOX* genes have been described, and a number of these appear to be involved in sex determination or have testis-specific expression, including *SRY* itself, *SOX9*, *SOX3*, and perhaps *SOX8*. In the interest of space, only the most well-characterized genes—*SRY* and *SOX9*—are discussed here.

### Sex-Determining Region of the Y (SRY)

The existence of a Y-chromosomal "maleness-determining" gene was postulated in the 1930s, and in the 1960s this was designated the *testis-determining factor (TDF)*. Many candidates were proposed and rejected over the years, until 1990, when

---

*The HMG domain is a 70–80 AA DNA-binding motif, comprised mainly of hydrophobic and charged residues, shared by a group of architectural proteins involved in DNA transcription, replication, recombination, and repair.

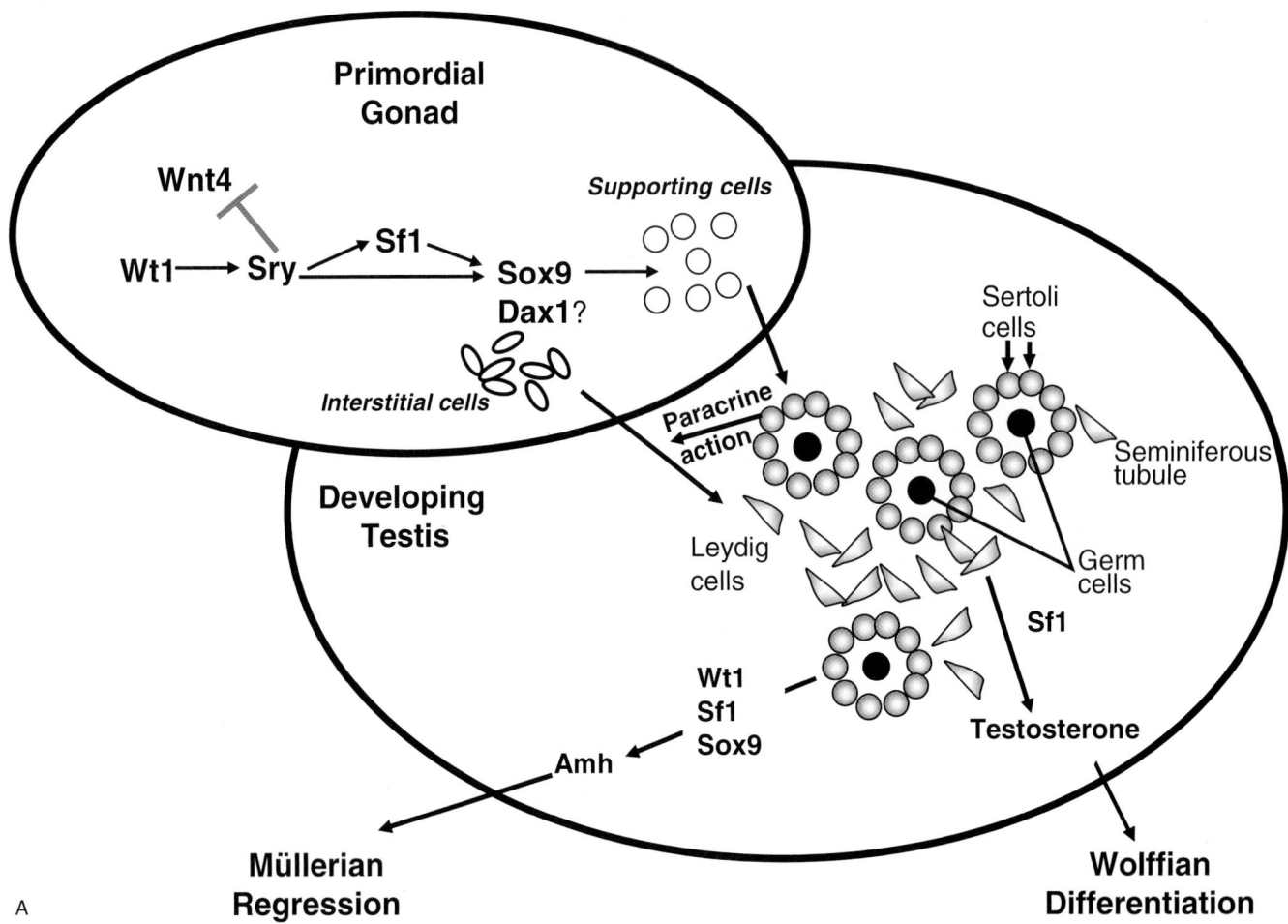

*Figure 142-6A* Hypothetical model of testis determination. The bipotential gonad of an XY fetus expresses the key testis-determining gene *Sry*, which is upregulated by Wt1. Sry, in turn, upregulates expression of a related gene *Sox9* and represses the "antitestis" gene *Wnt4*. A critical role of *Sox9* is to stimulate differentiation of primitive supporting cells into Sertoli cells, which are the primary organizers of the seminiferous tubule. Dax1 acts in parallel to Sox9 and plays a role in the formation of testis cords. The seclusion of germ cells within the tubules prevents germ cell meiosis and commits them to spermatogenic development. Under the influence of Sertoli cells, interstitial cells differentiate as Leydig cells, subsequently secreting testosterone under the drive of Sf1. Meanwhile, Sertoli cell secretion of antimüllerian hormone (Amh) is upregulated by the combined influences of Wt1, Sf1, and Sox9. Testis secretion of tesosterone and Amh cause Wolffian duct differentiation and Müllerian duct regression, respectively.

the existence of such a gene was confirmed, with the discovery the *SRY* gene (*Sry* in the mouse).[110] Insertion of the mouse *Sry* gene into XX-fertilized mouse eggs resulted in development of testes and male genitalia (female-to-male sex reversal).[111] These seminal studies demonstrated that *Sry* was the key Y-chomosomal gene sufficient to induce maleness. Replacement of the HMG box of *Sry* with that of *Sox3* or *Sox9* also results in sex reversal in XX mice, indicating that Sox3 or Sox9 can functionally replace Sry and elicit development of testis cords, male patterns of gene expression, and male genital development.[112]

The human *SRY* gene is a 3.8-kb single-exon gene located just centromeric to the pseudoautosomal region of Yp (Yp11.3) that encodes a 204–amino acid (24 kilodalton) protein.[110] Approximately the middle third of the protein (79 amino acids) represents the HMG domain, which endows SRY with its sequence-specific DNA binding to a target nucleotide sequence: 5′-AACAAAG-3′.[113] This region is the most critical to protein function and almost all human *SRY* mutations are located here. Outside the HMG domain, the remainder of the protein is poorly conserved among mammals.

The target genes of SRY are largely unknown, but may include those encoding AMH, SOX9, and the steroidogenic enzyme CYP11; a fundamental role of SRY appears to be the regulation of *SOX9* expression.[109,114] Similarly, the exact

mechanisms of action, whether or not SRY has any direct transcriptional regulating capacity, and whether it functions as a transcriptional activator or repressor, or both, remain to be determined.[109] Since human SRY lacks a transcription activation domain (present in mice), it has been suggested that SRY function depends solely on the HMG domain (as noted, the HMG domain of SOX3 or SOX9 can functionally replace that of SRY) and that it acts as an "architectural" transcription factor by creating the spatial arrangement needed for the transcription "machinery" to work.[104] It has been proposed that SRY controls the splicing of pre-mRNA substrates whose products act in the gonadal ridge of XY embryos to trigger the male differentiation program. Possible functional roles include bringing together distant DNA sequences, promoting contacts between factors bound at distant sites on DNA or recruiting proteins that by themselves do not bind to DNA, facilitating access of other important transcription-regulating proteins to regulator sequences within specific testis-inducing target genes. Nuclear magnetic resonance spectroscopy analysis of the interaction between the SRY protein and the *AMH* gene promoter reveals that SRY binds in a sequence-specific manner in the minor groove of the DNA helix, causing some unwinding of the strands and 70- to 80-degree bending of the DNA.[115,116] In addition, SRY displays sequence-independent binding at four-way DNA junctions,

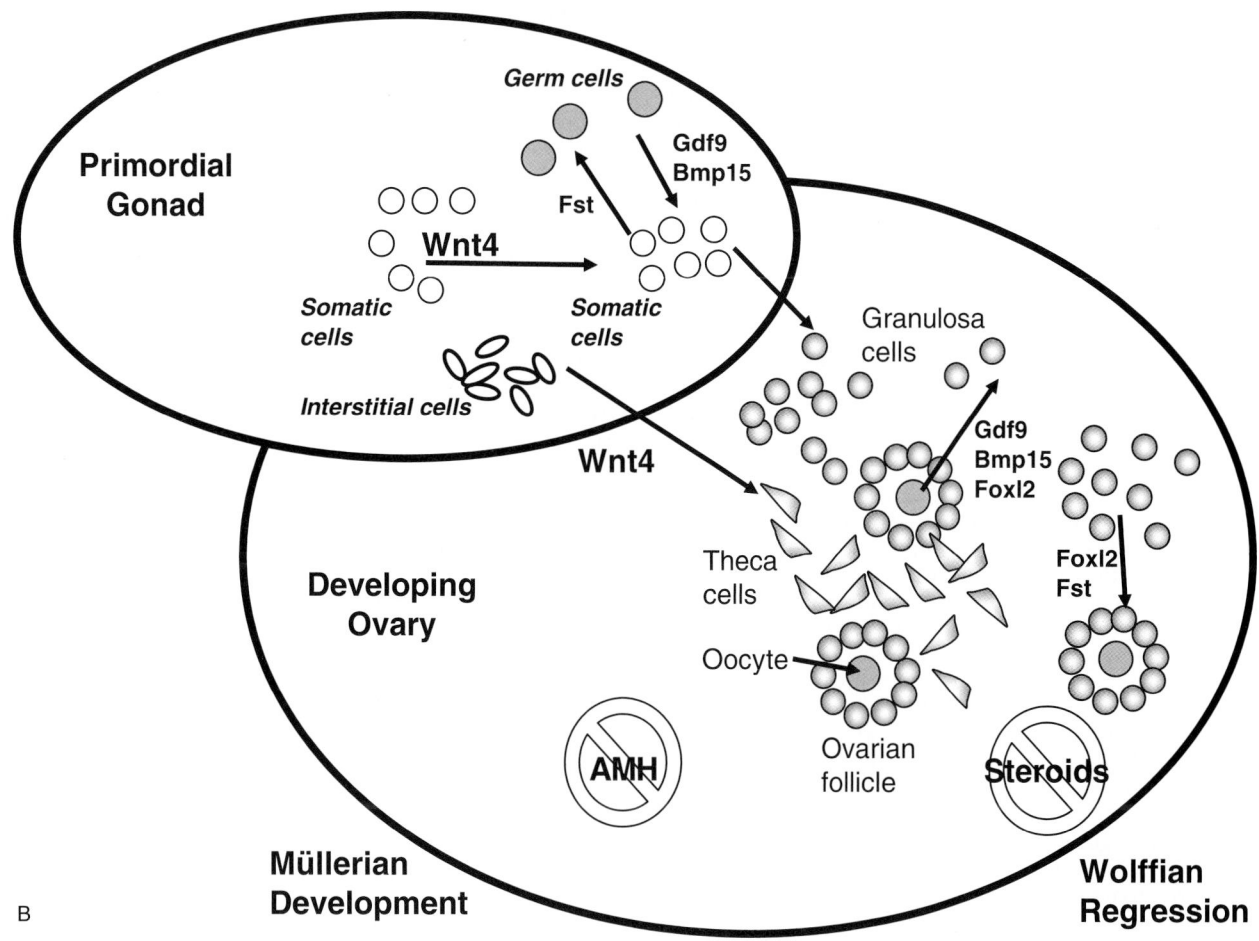

**Figure 142-6B**  Hypothetical model of ovary determination. In the normal XX ovary, Sry and Sox9 are not expressed. Consequently, Sertoli cells do not differentiate and testis cords do not form. Instead, follistatin is differentially expressed and may bind members of the TGF-β family, such as activins or Bmp2. Granulosa cells surround germ cells to form ovarian follicles, perhaps under the influence of Foxl2. Meanwhile, interstitial cells are prevented from developing as Leydig cells by the action of Wnt4 secreted by supporting cells; instead, they develop as theca cells. In the absence of Leydig cells and Sertoli cells, neither testosterone nor AMH is secreted. Consequently, Wolffian ducts regress and Müllerian ducts differentiate.

which are intrinsically bent. Since mouse Sry does appear to contain an activation domain, it may act via a fundamentally different biochemical mechanism in mice compared with other mammals.

Expression of *Sry* occurs in the gonadal tissue of fetal mice in the earliest period of specific testis formation, being first detected at embryonic day 10.5 in pre-Sertoli cells in the developing gonadal ridge, about a day before testicular morphology can be discerned.[98,100,117,118] This finding suggests that these cells are integral to the process of testis development; indeed, one of the primary events in testis development is the induction of Sertoli cell differentiation. *Sry* expression peaks at day 11.5 and declines once testicular development is established, at day 12.5; expression is quite restricted to the urogenital ridge at this critical time, with no evidence for expression in any other tissue. One of the earliest changes that occurs following *Sry* expression in XY mouse gonads is dramatic proliferation of somatic cells leading to a notable increase in the size of the developing XY gonad compared with the XX gonad within 24 hours of the onset of *Sry* expression.[119] *Sry* expression and Sertoli cell differentiation are followed by testis differentiation, most notably, Sertoli cell-regulated organization of seminiferous tubules and Leydig cell differentiation.

Despite its preeminent role in testis determination, other transcription factors appear to regulate *SRY* expression, including WT1.[67,109] There is also evidence of a cooperative interaction between WT1 and SRY in regulation of other

genes involved in testis development.[120] In the adult testis, SRY may continue to act as a splicing factor in Sertoli cells and germ cells. In addition to the testis, *Sry* is also expressed in the hypothalamus and midbrain of adult male but not adult female mice.[121] *SRY* mRNA expression in human male testes begins at around 6 weeks' gestation, just before specific testis development. SRY protein is localized to nuclei of somatic and germ cells in the genital ridge during testis development and is detectable in both Sertoli cells and germ cells until adulthood.[122]

Although SRY is probably the key positive regulator of testis determination, there are clearly other upstream and downstream factors that must be activated or repressed to allow testis development to occur. This is implied by the following: (1) the majority of 46,XY females with gonadal dysgenesis have an intact *SRY* gene; and (2) some 46,XX males with testes are completely Y negative, indicating that non-Y sequences must be responsible for testis determination in these cases. Furthermore, the tight ontogeny of *Sry* expression during embryogenesis in the mouse suggests the presence of a "controller," that is, at least one upstream regulator of expression.

Human *SRY* mutations are fairly common and are found more frequently in 46,XY sex-reversed females with complete rather than partial gonadal dysgenesis. The majority of *SRY* mutations reported to date produce nonconservative amino acid substitutions at highly conserved sites within the SRY HMG domain.[123]

*SRY Homeobox-like Gene (SOX 9)*

Another member of the *SOX* gene family, *SRY* homeobox-like gene 9 (*SOX9*), is significantly involved in the process of testis formation and, like *Sry*, can induce testis formation when inserted into XX mouse embryos.[124] In fact, *Sox9* appears to be equally as important as the related gene *Sry* in the process of testis development.[105,109] Human *SOX9* was identified by cloning of a chromosomal translocation breakpoint from a sex-reversed patient with campomelic dysplasia, a severe form of autosomal dominant skeletal dysplasia that typically is fatal in infancy. The gene is located at 17q24-25, in a region termed *sex reversal autosomal 1 (SRA1)*.[125] The 3.9-kb cDNA encodes a 509–amino acid protein with features of a transcription regulator—a DNA-binding HMG domain and two transcriptional activation domains, including a proline- and glutamine-rich domain in its carboxyterminal region, similar to activation domains of other transcription factors.[126] In vitro deletion of this latter region destroys the transactivating function of the protein.[127] Unlike *SRY*, the *SOX9* gene displays strong sequence conservation throughout mammalian evolution. Furthermore, the sequence similarity between *SOX9* and *SRY* suggests a relationship between the two that may represent evolution from a dosage-dependent autosomal sex-determination system (dosage sensitivity is a feature of many regulatory genes) to a dominant Y-chromosomal system.

*Sox9* expression can be detected in mRNA isolated from whole mouse embryos as early as embryonic day 8.5, and it is highly expressed in fetal skeletal, neural, and cardiac tissues.[128] *Sox9* is initially expressed in the genital ridges of both sexes at low levels. Subsequently, consistent with a role in testis determination, *Sox9* is upregulated in male genital ridges and downregulated in female genital ridges, and its expression parallels Sertoli cell differentiation; indeed, the main action of Sox9 appears to be the induction of Sertoli cell differentiation from interstitial precursors.[129] Sox9 appears to be acting just downstream of Sry and, based on timing of expression and the presence of a potential binding site for Sry within the *Sox9* promoter, may represent a target gene for Sry.[128,129] However, there is probably not an absolute requirement for Sry regulation of *Sox9*, since Sox9 can induce testis development in the absence of Sry as evidenced by transgenic insertion of *Sox9* into XX mice.[124] Sex- and tissue-specific regulation of *Sox9* expression is controlled by a proximal region in the *Sox9* promoter; *Sox9* is also under the control of distant upstream sequences including a locus about 1 mB upstream.[130–132] This locus, called *Odsex*, appears to play a role in suppressing Sox9 activity in XX gonads, since deletion of the gene resulted in a dominant form of XX sex reversal.[132] In male gonads, *Sox9* expression precedes that of *Amh*, and Sox9 appears to play the pivotal role in activating *Amh* expression, a role befitting a key maleness-determining factor.[133] In this function, Sox9 interacts with Sf1, Wt1, and Gata4. Sox9 activates transcription via a nucleotide motif recognized by other HMG domain transcription factors—AACAAT; binding specificity is conferred by nucleotide pairs on either side of the central sequence.[134,135] Sox9 may represent another switchlike mechanism, as it appears to act in a dominant fashion, similar to Sry. Indeed, Sox9 may, in fact, be the pivotal maleness-determining factor, potentially displacing Sry in this role—a battle whose outcome is yet to be decided.

In the human fetus, *SOX9* mRNA is detectable by Northern analysis in brain, liver, and kidney. By in situ hybridization, *SOX9* expression is detectable by week 6 of gestation in the undifferentiated presumptive testis, later localizing clearly to the sex cords where it is maintained until 18 weeks with an expression pattern similar to that of *SRY*.[136] No *SOX9* expression is detectable in 46,XX gonads prior to week 6, consistent with a sex-specific role of SOX9 in testis determination, but low-level expression is apparent later in the embryonic ovary. In the adult human, *SOX9* message is expressed most strongly in the testis. It is also highly expressed in the pancreas, prostate, kidney, brain, and skeleton and at a low level in most other adult tissues.[126,137,138]

Mice heterozygous for deletion of *Sox9* had skeletal malformations equivalent to those seen in the human disease campomelic dysplasia and died soon after birth.[139] The testes were normal in the male mutant mice, in contrast to many human *SOX9* mutations, well known for causing male-to-female sex reversal, suggesting differences in Sox9/*SOX9* function between mice and humans. Release of repression (de-repression) of *Sox9* expression in XX gonads is associated with testis development in *Odsex* mice (which have a deletion of a presumed regulatory region upstream of the *Sox9* gene), providing additional evidence for the importance of Sox9 in testis determination. The importance of SOX9 for human sex determination is evidenced by the rare disorder of campomelic dysplasia, in which heterozygous mutations of *SOX9* are associated with 46,XY male-to-female sex reversal (with or without skeletal dysplasia), while duplication of the chromosomal region containing human *SOX9* has resulted in 46,XX female-to-male sex reversal, suggesting that the action of SOX9 is dosage sensitive.[126,137,138,140–142]

## Alpha-Thalassemian/Mental Retardation, X-Linked

Alpha-thalassemian/mental retardation, X-linked (ATRX, also known as X-linked helicase-2 [XH2]) is a helicase—an enzyme that catalyzes the unwinding of double-stranded nucleic acids—and is a member of a family of proteins involved in DNA recombination and repair, chromatin remodeling, chromosome segregation, and regulation of transcription. It is implicated in testicular development by the finding of mutations in the encoding gene in patients with the ATRX syndrome accompanied by male-to-female sex reversal.[143] The large (>200 kb) human *ATRX* gene is located at Xq13.3 (and is also on the mouse X chromosome) and comprises 35 exons, which are subject to alternate splicing in different tissues.[144–146] The *ATRX* gene has a homologue on the Y chromosome of marsupial mammals (not present in mouse or human) that is expressed specifically in the testis, giving additional weight to its role in male sex determination, at least in this mammalian family.[147] The putative approximately 275 kilodalton (2453– or 2492– amino acid) protein contains a nuclear localization signal and three zinc fingers in the amino-terminal region; the carboxyterminal region contains six helicase domains and a glutamine-rich sequence common in transcription factors.[146,148] The ATRX protein is believed to function by binding to DNA via the zinc-finger region, then opening the DNA double helix with the helicase region in an adenosine triphosphatase (ATPase)-dependent manner. Immunofluoresence and confocal microscopy have demonstrated that the protein is associated with pericentromeric chromatin during interphase and mitosis, suggesting that ATRX may act as part of a protein complex that modulates chromatin structure.[149] Apart from the fact that human mutations are associated with sex reversal, little is known about the function of this protein in sex determination and differentiation, as comprehensive studies in mice are lacking.

*ATRX* is expressed in a wide range of embryonic and adult human tissues, including developing brain and testis.[143,145–147] Because of its X-chromosomal location, the gene undergoes X-inactivation in females; *ATRX* is transcribed only from the active X chromosome, presumably maintaining equivalence of expression between males and females. Since a single active copy of the gene in normal females is not associated with testis development, while a single copy is adequate for testis development in males, ATRX likely functions downstream of a male-specific transcription factor such as SRY or SOX9, requiring activation or upregulation by such a factor.

In sex-reversed patients with *ATRX* mutations, the gonads are streaks; however, Müllerian ducts are absent, suggesting that *AMH* expression and, therefore, Sertoli cell development were retained during the critical period. This implies that the critical period for *ATRX* expression occurs after Sertoli cell development. Diverse mutations in the *ATRX* gene have been reported in individuals with the ATRX syndrome,[147] an X-linked condition characterized by variable expression of alpha thalassemia, mental retardation, and undermasculinization or sex reversal.

## Desert Hedgehog

Desert hedgehog (Dhh) is a signaling molecule involved in interactions between Sertoli cells and germ cells and differentiation of Leydig cells from their precursors.[150] The three-exon human *DHH* gene located at chromosome 12q13.1 encodes a 396–amino acid polypeptide.[151]

*Dhh* is expressed only in the testis and not in the ovary. Expression is initiated in Sertoli cell precursors shortly after activation of *Sry* expression, and persists to adulthood. In the embryonic testis, Dhh has roles in regulation of germ cell proliferation and Leydig cell development. This system appears to regulate mitosis and meiosis in male germ cells, its role varying at different stages of development; in the postnatal testis, Dhh directs maturation of germ cells. The receptor for Dhh, Patched2, is expressed on Leydig cells and peritubular cells, and one of the key roles of Dhh appears to be in the proper development of peritubular tissue.[152] Consequently, the mechanism by which Dhh regulates germ cell development may be indirect, via other cell types, and may be secondary to the more general effects on organization of testicular structure. In the initial murine studies, male mice homozygous for a null mutation of *Dhh* had small testes and were infertile due to lack of mature sperm.[153] Apart from the deficiency of germ cells, however, the testes were structurally and microscopically normal, including the Dhh-producing Sertoli cells themselves. In a subsequent study in mice from a different genetic background, over 90% of null male mice were feminized, with female external genitalia and a blind vagina, accompanied by very small undescended ectopically located testes and poor Leydig cell development with low serum testosterone.[154] The latter study demonstrated requirement for Dhh for normal development of peritubular myoid cells and the basal lamina, and subsequent well-organized development of seminiferous tubules. Thus, Dhh may or may not be required for testicular organogenesis, depending on genetic background, and there is phenotypic heterogeneity of the null mutation even within a single genetic background. *Dhh* mutant females show no gonadal abnormality. Human *DHH* mutations are associated with 46,XY partial gonadal dysgenesis accompanied by an unusual form of peripheral neuropathy.[155,156]

## EMBRYOLOGY OF OVARY DEVELOPMENT

In contrast with the testes, normal ovarian differentiation requires the presence of germ cells.[98,101] Without the germ cell seeding of the gonadal primordium, the tissue degenerates into a nonfunctional, mainly fibrous "streak." Before week 10 of human gestation, the only feature that distinguishes an ovary is the absence of testicular features. Thereafter, ovarian structure becomes distinguishable, with the development of the primary medullary sex cords. Secondary cortical sex cords provide the supporting structure for the arriving germ cells. Within the sex cords, the primary germ cells undergo vigorous mitotic replication to become oogonia, then the sex cords break up into clusters, becoming the primordial follicles at about week 16. The primordial follicles contain the diploid (i.e., 46 chromosomes) primary oocytes, which, after entering into the first stage of meiosis (reduction division), remain quiescent until puberty. Follicular (granulosa) cells arise from the same somatic cell lineage as Sertoli cells. Theca cells represent the ovarian counterpart of Leydig cells.

There is a notable difference in the chronology of testicular versus ovarian development, the process of testis formation being completed by 8 weeks' gestation, at which time the process of ovarian development has not yet begun.[157] In fact, germ cells migrate much earlier to the developing testis than to the ovarian primordium under the influence of extracellular matrix proteins and adhesion molecules, such as catenins and cadherins, and the process seems to be influenced by the sex of the germ cells. Morphologic ovarian development is not completed until after most of the processes of phenotypic sex differentiation have occurred. This, and the fact that phenotypic development is normal even in complete absence of the ovary, highlights the lack of involvement of the ovary in the processes of normal female phenotypic development. The embryologic development of the testis and ovary are summarized in Figure 142-1A.

## GENETICS OF OVARY DEVELOPMENT

At present, the factors directing ovarian development are less well characterized than those governing testis development. There is presumably an equally complex network of controls guiding this process, which likely requires action on two fronts: repression of autosomal testis-inducing genes such as *SOX9* (but not *SRY*, since this is absent from the normal XX embryo), and either de-repression (removal of an inhibitory influence) or activation (direct stimulation) of ovary-inducing genes. Importantly, any factor that functions as a "testis inhibitor" must be expressed and active prior to the time that expression of non-Y-specific testis-determining factors would be expected to occur. One such gene likely resides on the X chromosome and is probably a dosage-sensitive locus. A former candidate for this role was *DAX1*, since 46,XY individuals with duplication of the region of the X chromosome containing this gene have streak ovaries rather than testes. *DAX1* became less convincing as the "anti-testis" gene, however, with the discovery of a normally developed 46,XX human female with homozygous deletion of the gene who might have been expected to develop testes under the influence of autosomal testis-determining genes such as *SOX9*. Other candidates for the role of a "testis inhibitor" are Wnt4, described later, and *Odsex*, a locus on chromosome 17 upstream of *Sox9*. No candidate for the role of a positive "ovary-determining factor" has yet been proposed; however, such a gene is probably also a dosage-sensitive locus (therefore, likely X-chromosomal) required for germ cell survival in the ovarian milieu. This is suggested by the findings in girls and women with Turner syndrome, who, in the absence of two functional copies of the X chromosome, have regression of the ovaries due to early fetal demise of germ cells. It is, therefore, reasonable to speculate that initial ovarian differentiation occurs under the influence of a factor (or factors) expressed from a single copy of the X chromosome in the absence of the Y chromosome (since ovarian development initiates normally in 45,X girls with Turner syndrome), and that, subsequently, dosage-sensitive X-chromosomal genes (required in double copy) are responsible for ovarian maintenance.

As was discussed regarding male/testis determination, there is not yet a clear understanding of the sequence of steps in the pathway of ovarian development and, in fact, it is likely that this is not a linear process, but rather a complex series of interconnected upregulatory and downregulatory events. A speculative model, based on some of the known and hypothetical genetic events is as follows: (1) An unknown factor induces expression of *WNT4*; (2) *WNT4* increases expression of *DAX1*; (3) DAX1 antagonizes SF1 and represses *SOX9*, thus, bipotential supporting cells do not differentiate as Sertoli cells but instead as granulosa cells; (4) secretion of Bmp15 and Fox12 by oocytes and Fst and Fox12 by granulosa cells; (5) WNT4, produced by somatic (interstitial) cells of the ovary is upregulated, inhibiting development of bipotential interstitial cells to Leydig cells; (6) since Sertoli cells do not develop, AMH is not produced during fetal life; thus, (7) Müllerian structures are maintained and subsequently differentiate under the influence of Wnt7a and other factors; (8) in the absence of Leydig cells, the fetal gonad does not produce sex steroids; therefore, the Wolffian ducts regress and external genitalia develop as female (see Fig. 142-3C; Fig. 142-6B).

## Wnt4

As noted in the section on the development of the primordial reproductive system, the signaling molecule/growth factor Wnt4 is required for the initial stages of Müllerian duct formation in both sexes in mice.[91,92] In addition, Wnt4 appears to be required for normal ovarian development in females and is a prime candidate for a role as an "anti-testis" gene, perhaps mediating its action via increased expression of Dax1.[158] Evidence for the role of Wnt4 in ovarian development comes from studies in which the gene was homozygously deleted in XX female mice or overexpressed in male mice, from the phenotype of 46,XY male-to-female sex reversal in human individuals with duplication of the chromosomal region encompassing the WNT4 gene, and from the findings in a 46,XX individual with a WNT4 mutation.[92,93,95,158,159] The identification of WNT4 as a key driver of normal ovarian differentiation has finally refuted the long-held misconception of female development as a passive "default" process.

Wnt4 is initially expressed in the gonad in both sexes in the mouse. However, at the onset of sex-specific gonadal differentiation, Wnt4 expression is maintained in the female, but is downregulated in the male.[92] Ovarian expression of Wnt4 occurs within somatic cell lineages (i.e., non–germ cell) and is maintained throughout fetal life in the female. Wnt4 is strongly expressed in the mesenchyme underlying the Müllerian ducts but is absent from the Wolffian ducts. Another member of the Wnt family, Wnt7a, appears to regulate the more female-specific development of the Müllerian ducts (discussed later in further detail).[160-162] Indirect evidence for the role of Wnt4 in supporting ovarian development through suppression of testicular development comes from in vitro studies in Sertoli and Leydig cell lines, where Wnt4 upregulates Dax1, which, as described previously, is an antagonist of Sf1. This hypothetical mechanism of action is consistent with the timing of expression of these transcription factors in male mice: Sry is highly expressed at E11.5, at which time Wnt4 is downregulated; Dax1 is subsequently downregulated in males at E12.5. There is also in vitro evidence for downregulation of Wnt4 by Wt1, consistent with the known role of Wt1 in testis development.[94] Thus, in a hypothetical multistep process in the male, Sry and Wt1 downregulate Wnt4, and lack of Wnt4 stimulation results in reduced expression of Dax1 and full expression of Sf1 and Sox9, allowing the subsequent steps of testis development to occur.

In the female, the opposite set of developmental events would be proposed. Absence of Sry allows Wnt4 to be fully expressed. In ovarian development, Wnt4 is proposed to act via a number of mechanisms to suppress gonadal vascular development, migration of steroidogenic cells from the adrenogenital primordium to the gonad, and differentiation of primordial interstitial cells into Leydig cells.[92,163] These actions would thereby inhibit testosterone synthesis and secretion, allowing female development to occur. Female mice homozygous for a null mutation of Wnt4 had masculinization of the gonad and proximal sex ducts (regression of Müllerian ducts and development of Wolffian ducts) due to lack of repression of gonadal steroidogenesis by Leydig cell precursors.[92] Of note, these mice had no masculinization of the external genitalia, probably because testosterone was produced in insufficient quantities from the mutant gonads. The Wnt4 knockout mice had reduced Dax1 expression in gonads reflecting the role of Wnt4 as a regulator of Dax1. Furthermore, the XX null mice had accelerated loss of oocytes in the ovaries to less than 10% of the number present in wild-type littermates, suggesting a role for Wnt4 in maintenance of the female germ cell line and oocyte development. Wnt4-deficient males were normal,

consistent with lack of a functional role for Wnt4 in testicular development. Wnt4 has also been shown to regulate both the pattern of vascular development and the recruitment of steroidogenic cells in the gonad in a sex-specific manner.[163] Thus, in female gonads, Wnt4 suppresses development of the coelomic blood vessel that appears to be important in male development for transport of testicular secretions to the general circulation and suppresses steroidogenic cell migration from the adrenogenital primordium into the developing gonad. In contrast, overexpression of WNT4 in XY mice caused repression of Sf1 action and reduced expression of StAR, leading to reduction of testicular steroidogenesis; testicular vasculature was also disturbed. The mice had only mild evidence of undermasculinization—underdevelopment of the seminal vesicles and reduction of spermatids—but were nevertheless fertile. These findings are consistent with the interpretation of Wnt4 as a mild "anti-male" factor.[158]

Mirroring the findings in mice, the phenotype of a 46,XX woman with a WNT4 mutation (WNT4 is located at human chromosomal locus 1p35) included absence of the right kidney, Müllerian duct regression (absent uterus and vagina) and signs of mild androgen excess, including a small vaginal introitus (but no clitoromegaly) and acne.[95] The extent of phenotypic similarity between the transgenic mouse model and the naturally occurring human mutation is unknown, however, as no information was available regarding ovarian morphology.

## Odsex

The Odsex locus is a region approximately 1 mb upstream of the SOX9 gene on human chromosome 17. Deletion of the equivalent region in XX mice resulted in male-pattern Sox9 expression and development of testes—female-to-male sex reversal.[132] No specific gene has yet been identified within the region and, instead, the region may contain a gonad-specific regulatory sequence. It is proposed that when bound by a repressor factor, this sequence turns off SOX9 expression in the normal XX gonad. Absence of the sequence therefore results in aberrant SOX9 expression and testis development. It is further hypothesized that one function of SRY in male development is to inhibit the repressor of SOX9 expression—a "double-repressor" mechanism of action.

## Winged Helix/Forkhead Transcription Factor 2

Winged helix/forkhead transcription factor 2 (FOXL2) is implicated as a player in the process of ovarian development by the finding of gonadal dysgenesis in some individuals with heterozygous mutations of the gene encoding FOXL2 and by the XX sex-reversed goat, which has a deletion in the chromosomal region containing the gene.[164-167] The single-exon gene is located at human chromosome 3q23 and encodes a member of the winged helix/forkhead transcription factor family (there are at least 20 known human forkhead genes encoding transcription factors involved in cell cycle regulation).[164] These proteins contain a characteristic 100–amino acid DNA-binding domain (the forkhead domain) and are involved in the development of tissues from all three germ layers. Foxl2 appears to be required for maintenance of ovarian follicles, which, in turn, is required for completion of ovarian development.[168] In the absence of ovarian follicles, the gonad develops as a fibrous streak (similar to that found in Turner syndrome); when follicles develop but undergo early atresia, premature ovarian failure ensues. A suggested mechanism of action of this transcription factor is inhibition of proapoptotic genes that would otherwise induce ovarian follicular atresia.[164] Foxl2 is highly conserved and abundantly expressed in the early developing ovary of several species with different mechanisms of sex determination (mouse, chicken, and turtle); expression occurs around the time of sex determination and is sexually dimorphic, consistent with a conserved role of this factor in ovarian differentiation.[167] In fact, Foxl2 appears to be the earliest marker of ovarian differentiation in mammals. *Foxl2* expression in the developing mouse ovary begins at around E12.5 and continues throughout gestation and into postnatal life; some expression is also detectable in the developing oviducts. Foxl2 is detectable in both somatic and germ cell populations in the developing ovary, and in granulosa cells and some oocytes in the adult ovary. There is a high degree of structural conservation of this transcription factor during evolution, another finding consistent with an important developmental role. How this factor fits into the scheme of ovarian differentiation, how and by what it is regulated, and its transcriptional targets are unknown, but a role in regulation of transforming growth factor β–related signaling pathways has been proposed. Inhibition of *Foxl2* expression by Sry has been suggested as one of the switch mechanisms that promotes testis development. Further understanding of the role of Foxl2 in ovarian determination awaits analysis of transgenic mice deleted for the gene and in vitro studies of the activities of the transcription factor.

### OTHER GENES WITH PUTATIVE OR UNCLEAR ROLES IN GONADAL DEVELOPMENT OR FUNCTION

#### Dosage-Sensitive Sex Reversal Adrenal Hypoplasia Congenita Locus on the X Chromosome, Gene 1

DAX1, dosage-sensitive sex-reversal adrenal hypoplasia congenita locus on the X chromosome, gene 1 (also known as nuclear receptor subfamily 0, group B, member1 [NR0B1]), is an orphan member of the nuclear hormone receptor superfamily of transcription factors that appears to function primarily as a transcriptional repressor. For some time, DAX1 bore the title of main contender for the role of "anti-testis" factor, until targeted mutagenesis revealed an unanticipated role in testis development.[169] The role of this transcription factor in the physiology of sex determination (as opposed to its roles in experimentally induced mutations) is unclear and at present there is conflicting evidence for roles in development of both testis and ovary. Humans with *DAX1* mutations form testes, but also have evidence of postnatal testicular dysfunction manifesting as primary hypogonadism and impaired spermatogenesis. Thus, DAX1 may be involved in normal testis development, but its function may be modified or compensated by other genes in the sex-determination pathway. The *DAX1* gene was initially discovered by cloning the region in Xp21 duplicated in a number of patients with 46,XY sex reversal, and deleted in patients with adrenal hypoplasia congenita.[170,171] The 5.0-kb two-exon *DAX1* gene is located at Xp21.3-21.2 and encodes a 470 amino acid protein.[172] The amino terminal region of the DAX1 protein, encoded by the first exon of the gene, contains an unusual DNA-binding domain comprising three repeats of a novel amino acid sequence (LxxLL) that has little homology with that of other nuclear receptors; the protein does not contain the central two-zinc-finger DNA-binding domain typical of the nuclear receptor family. The ligand-binding domain, however, encoded in part by the first and in part by the second exon of the gene, has homology with another orphan nuclear receptor, small heterodimer partner (SHP), and with the retinoic acid and retinoid X receptors (RAR and RXR).[173,174] The gene demonstrates a degree of evolutionary conservation, homologous sequences being detected in an X-linked pattern of distribution in many mammalian species, including mice. *Dax1* is autosomal rather than X-chromosomal, however, in the tammar wallaby and the chicken, and appears not to have a sex-determining function in these species, suggesting that any sex-determining role in placental mammals arose fairly recently in evolution. Furthermore, comparison of the predicted protein products between mouse and human DAX1 show that specific domains of this transcription factor are evolving rapidly, a finding that may explain different functions of the protein in mice versus humans and differing effects of DAX1 excess or deficiency in the different species.

Evidence for the role of Dax1 in sex determination and differentiation comes from strong expression of the homologous gene in the mouse *(Ahch)* seen in the first stages of gonadal and adrenal differentiation and in the developing hypothalamus and pituitary gonadotropes.[175–177] *Dax1* expression is downregulated at the time of overt differentiation of the testis, but persists in the developing ovary, consistent with a role in ovarian development (although such a role remains hypothetical). Expression at lower levels has also been detected by reverse transcriptase polymerase chain reaction (RT-PCR) in numerous other tissues in the mouse.[175] *Dax1* expression in cultured postnatal rat Sertoli cells suggests a role in spermatogenesis in that species.[178] There is significant overlap in the distribution of expression of *Dax1* and *Sf1* in numerous tissues, supporting the concept of linkage between these two transcription factors in regulation of development of steroidogenic tissues.[176,179,180] The promoter region of the *Dax1* gene contains binding sites for Sf1, and there is substantial evidence that Sf1 is required for regulation of *Dax1* expression in vitro and some evidence that it is required in vivo, since *Sf1*-disrupted mice lacked *Dax1* expression in the developing genital ridge in one study, although not in another.[176,179,181–184] The Sf1-mediated upregulation of *Dax1* appears to occur synergistically with another factor, the signaling molecule β-catenin.[184] In addition, Wnt4 may also regulate *Dax1* expression, potentially explaining increased expression in ovary.[184] The physiology of Dax1 is complicated, because while Sf1 regulates expression of *Dax1*, Dax1 inhibits Sf1-mediated transcription of other genes, suggesting a complex regulatory loop. Indeed, the fact that Dax1 blocks Sf1-mediated steroidogenesis suggests a possible negative feedback mechanism. Obviously, many aspects of Dax1 remain to be unraveled.

In human studies, *DAX1* is expressed in Sertoli cells of the fetal testis by 16 weeks' gestation (perhaps earlier), adult testis and adrenal cortex, in the hypothalamus and pituitary gland, and at low levels in adult ovary and liver.[136,171,185,186] The expression of *DAX1* at all levels of the hypothalamic-pituitary-adrenal/gonadal axis supports its role in the coordinated development of the adrenal and reproductive systems and suggests that the DAX1 protein may be directly or indirectly involved in gonadal regulation of hypothalamic-pituitary function. Since human *DAX1* is located in a region of Xp that normally undergoes X inactivation, single-copy expression would be predicted for both males and females. Differential regulation by sexually dimorphic factors such as Wnt4, however, could help explain differences in role and function of Dax1 in male and female development.

Dax1 has been demonstrated to repress *StAR* and *Cyp17* expression, to inhibit Sf1-mediated transactivation, thereby blocking steroidogenesis, and to antagonize the synergy between Sf1 and Wt1 in their upregulation of *Amh* expression; however, this latter action appears to be via a protein-protein interaction with Sf1, rather than an effect at the target gene.[44,45,187–190] Sequences responsible for the suppressive function reside in the ligand-binding domain and in the amino-terminal leucine repeat region of the protein.[184,187,191] Although not yet described, a transcription activating function for Dax1 at other target sites is conceivable, much as has been described for Wt1, which has target-specific activating and repressive functions.

Analysis of targeted disruption or transgenic overexpression of *Dax1* in mice highlights the importance of gene dosage and the genetic background on which such experimental changes are expressed (Table 142-1). XY mice with deletion of *Dax1* have normal testis development and masculinization (but have small testes and are sterile due to spermatogenetic defects) when the deletion is introduced into a normal mouse strain; in contrast, complete sex reversal (ovarian and phenotypic female development) occurs when the deletion is introduced into a strain of mice that carries a "weak" Sry gene

**Table 142-1** Factors Involved in Sex Determination and Differentiation

| Gene Name or Pseudonyms | Human Gene Locus | Protein Name | Protein Type | Genetic or Cellular Targets | Action/Expression | Effects of Over- or Underexpression |
|---|---|---|---|---|---|---|
| **FACTORS INVOLVED IN PRIMORDIAL GONAD/REPRODUCTIVE TRACT FORMATION** | | | | | | |
| LIM1 LHX1 | 11p12-13 | LIM1 | Homeodomain transcription factor with 2 LIM domains (4 zinc fingers) | Not reported | Expressed at stage of primitive streak. Organizes development of anterior neural tissues. | KO mice lack heads, kidneys, and genital ridges. |
| EMX2* | 10q26.1 | EMX2 | Homeodomain transcription factor | Wnt4, possibly Lim1 | Similar to Lim1. Probably functions downstream of WT1. | KO mice (XX or XY) lack kidneys, ureters, gonads, and genital tracts and have brain defects. Human mutation causes schizencephaly; no urogenital phenotype reported. |
| LHX9 | 1q31-32 | LHX9 | LIM homeodomain transcription factor, similar to LIM1 | Binds Sf1 promoter. May have additive effect with –KTS isoform of WT1 in activating Sf1 | Drives formation of sex cords. | XX and XY KO mice have gonadal agenesis. |
| SF1* Ftzf1 AD4BP NR5A1 | 9q33 | SF1 | Orphan nuclear receptor/zinc-finger transcription factor | WT1, SRY, SOX9, DAX1, GnRH-R, LHβ, ACTH-R, AMH, AMH-R, StAR, P450scc, 21-OH'lase, 11β-OH'lase, oxytocin, SF1, others | Activates transcription of many genes in development of gonads, adrenals; regulates steroidogenesis. Synergizes with WT1; antagonizes DAX1. Dose-dependent activity. | KO mice: no gonads or adrenals; retained müllerian structures; abnormal hypothalamus. Haploinsufficient mice: reduced but not absent adrenal function. Homozygous human mutation: 46,XY sex reversal and adrenal hypoplasia. Heterozygous human mutation: 46,XX normal ovary, partial adrenal insufficiency. |
| WT1* | 11p13 | WT1 | Zinc-finger transcription factor; tumor repressor | DAX1, IGF-2, type 1 IGF receptor, PDGF-A, Pax2, WT1, SRY | Represses transcription; activates transcription of Sry. Dose-dependent effects. | XY homozygous deletion of WT1+KTS isoform: male-to-female sex reversal; XY homozygous deletion of WT1-KTS isoform: streak gonads in XX and XY. Human Denys-Drash syndrome: gonadal dysgenesis, congenital nephropathy, Wilms' tumor; |
| GATA4 | 8p23.1-p22 | GATA4 | Zinc-finger transcription factor | "GATA" DNA binding motif; AMH; steroidogenic enzymes | Expressed early in both ovary and testis. | KO mice embryonic lethal, no gonadal phenotype reported. Human mutation—cardiac defects; no gonadal phenotype reported. |
| M33 CBX2 | 17q25, near Sox9 | M33 | Transcription repressor | Possibly SRY | Mediates changes in chromatin structure. | KO mice (XX or XY) have retarded development of gonadal ridges; XY mice have male-to-female sex reversal. |
| WNT4 | 1p35 | WNT4 | Cysteine-rich signaling molecule/secreted growth factor | Mesonephric mesenchyme | Directs müllerian duct formation. | XX and XY KO mice have müllerian agenesis. |
| c-KIT | 4q12 | Kit | Transmembrane tyrosine kinase receptor; proto-oncogene | Germ cell, hematopoietic and melanocyte precursors | Suppresses apoptosis, directs migration proliferation of stem cell populations. | Mouse mutations: white coat color, sterility, anemia. Human mutation: piebaldism, mast cell leukemia. |
| STEEL | 12q22 | Slf/KL | Ligand for c-kit | Unknown | As for c-kit | Mouse mutations: white coat color, sterility, anemia. |

**Table 142-1** Factors Involved in Sex Determination and Differentiation—cont'd

| Gene Name or Pseudonyms | Human Gene Locus | Protein Name | Protein Type | Genetic or Cellular Targets | Action/Expression | Effects of Over- or Underexpression |
|---|---|---|---|---|---|---|
| **FACTORS INVOLVED IN TESTIS/MALE SEX DETERMINATION/DIFFERENTIATION** | | | | | | |
| SRY* | Yp11.3 | SRY | HMG domain–containing transcription factor | SF1, SOX9, CYP19, AMH | Bends DNA. | XX mice expressing transgenic Sry have female-to-male sex reversal. Human SRY mutations: 46,XY sex reversal. Translocation of SRY to X chromosome: 46,XX female-to-male sex reversal or true hermaphroditism. |
| SOX9* | 17q24-25 | SOX9 | HMG domain–containing transcription factor of SRY family | Supporting cells of gonadal primordium | Simulates differentiation of Sertoli cells. | Odsex mice: de-repression of Sox9 expression in XX gonads → testis development. |
| ATRX* XH2 XNP | Xq13.3 | ATRX | Helicase; transcription factor | Widespread expression early in mouse embryogenesis, more restricted expression later | Gene regulation at interphase and chromosomal segregation at mitosis | Human mutations cause α thalassemia, mental retardation, and genital anomalies → male-to-female sex reversal |
| DHH | 12q13.1 | DHH | Signaling molecule | Expressed only in testis | Involved in interactions between Sertoli cells and germ cells. May regulate mitosis and meiosis in male germ cells. | Strain-specific effects: XY null mice have defective Leydig cell development and are feminized. |
| LH/CG-R* | 2p21 | LH/CG receptor | G-protein-coupled, 7-transmembrane domain peptide hormone receptor | Not applicable | Transduces LH signal to activate Gsα → cAMP. Required for Leydig cell testosterone production. | Mouse mutation: normal sex differentiation. Males and females infertile. Human mutation: Leydig cell hypoplasia → male pseudohermaphroditism. |
| STAR* | 8p11.2 | StAR | Mitochondrial transport protein | Not applicable | Transports cholesterol to inner mitochondrial membrane. | Human mutation: congenital lipoid adrenal hyperplasia and male pseudohermaphroditism. |
| SRD5A1* | 5p15 | 5α-reductase 2 | Mitochondrial enzyme | Not applicable | Converts testosterone → DHT. | Male pseudohemaphroditism due to 5α-reductase deiciency. |
| AR* | Xq11-12 | AR | Ligand-dependent nuclear receptor | AMH-R, ?CYP19 | Regulates transcription. | Androgen insensitivity syndromes: male pseudohermaphrodatism. |
| AMH* | 19p13.2-13.3 | AMH | Glycoprotein homodimer of TGF-β family | Not reported | Ligand for AMH-R. | Persistent müllerian duct syndrome. |
| AMH-R2* | 12q13 | Type II AMH receptor | Transmembrane serine/threonine kinase receptor | Mesenchymal and epithelial cells of müllerian ducts | Stimulates apoptosis of müllerian duct. | Persistent müllerian duct syndrome. |
| **FACTORS INVOLVED IN OVARY/FEMALE SEX DETERMINATION** | | | | | | |
| WNT4 | 1p35 | WNT4 | Cysteine-rich signaling molecule/secreted growth factor | Mesonephric mesenchyme | Directs initial müllerian duct formation in both sexes; possible "anti-testis" factor in ovarian development. | XX and XY null mice: müllerian duct agenesis. Overexpression in XY: male-to-female sex reversal. Human: duplication of WNT4 associated with male-to-female sex reversal. |
| FOXL2* | 3q23 | FOXL2 | Transcription factor | Not reported | Expressed predominantly in ovary; earliest known marker of ovarian differentiation in mammals. | Goat: deletion associated with XX sex reversal. Human mutation: 46,XX gonadal dysgenesis. |
| HOXA13 | 7p15-p14.2 | HOXA13 | Homeodomain transcription factor | Fgf8, Bmp7 | Involved in epithelial-mesenchymal interactions required for morphogenesis of terminal gut and urogenital tract, including müllerian structures. | Mouse: XX null have hypoplasia of cervix and vagina. Human mutation: hand-foot-genital syndrome with uterine malformation in 46,XX. |

Continued

**Table 142-1**    Factors Involved in Sex Determination and Differentiation—cont'd

| Gene Name or Pseudonyms | Human Gene Locus | Protein Name | Protein Type | Genetic or Cellular Targets | Action/Expression | Effects of Over- or Underexpression |
|---|---|---|---|---|---|---|
| **FACTORS WITH POSSIBLE ROLES IN EITHER SEX** | | | | | | |
| DAX1* Ahch NR0B1 | Xp21 | DAX1 | Orphan nuclear receptor transcription factor | RAR, RXR, StAR, P450scc, 3β-HSD | Represses SF-1 transcription; antagonizes SF-1; regulates testis cord organization. Dose dependent. | Strain-specific defects in XY mice: over-expression → testis maldevelopment and sex reversal; homozygous deletion → adrenal hypoplasia, normal testes. Human mutations: adrenal hypoplasia congenita, hypothalamic hypogonadism. |
| WNT7a | 3p25 | WNT7a | Signaling molecule | Mesenchymal and epithelial cells of müllerian ducts | XY: involved in müllerian duct regression; XX: stimulates development of müllerian duct. | XY KO mice have retained müllerian ducts; female Wnt7a-deficient mice have defective, though not absent, development of oviducts and uterus. |
| DMRT1/2 | 9p24.3 | DMRT1 DMRT2 | DM domain transcription factors | | Expressed only in genital ridge. Dose-dependent effect on postnatal testis development. | XY KO mice have normal prenatal testis development, but abnormal postnatal testis differentiation. Human monosomy 9p: 46,XY testis maldevelopment; 46,XX primary hypogonadism. |

A number of the genes listed have been implicated in gonadal/genital development only by studies in mice, and defects have not been reported in humans.
*Genes in which human mutations have been reported.
See Table 142-2 for enzymes of steroidogenesis.

(*M. domesticus poschiavinus*).[37,169] Thus, depending on the genetic background in which it is acting, Dax1 could be interpreted as unnecessary for testis formation but required for postnatal spermatogenesis on the one hand, or required for normal testis determination on the other. Findings are equally enigmatic in mice expressing excess *Dax1*. When these experiments are performed in the *M. domesticus poschiavinus* (weak Sry) strain, overexpression of *Dax1* results in XY sex reversal (just as deletion of the gene does), postulated to be due to Dax1 antagonism of Sry resulting in a "toxic" effect on testicular development.[174] When the excess *Dax1* was expressed on the background of a normal *Sry* gene (*M. musculus*), however, only a transient delay in testis development was observed.[174] Effects of mutation or even homozygous deletion of *Dax1* in XX mice appear to be negligible, as such mice have been reported to be fertile, challenging earlier speculation regarding the role of this transcription factor as a critical ovary-determining factor.[37,192] Females with overexpression of *Dax1* are also fertile, giving no indication of a dosage effect on ovarian differentiation.[174]

Studies of naturally occurring mutations in humans also fail to clarify exactly how DAX1 fits into the sex-determination pathway. Duplication of the region of Xp containing DAX1 results in 46,XY sex reversal (the basis for the name of this chromosomal region).[170] The 160-kb region, however, contains at least another four or five genes at this locus and beyond the conflicting murine studies already described, there is no direct evidence that DAX1 itself is the mediator of this sex-reversal effect in humans. Deletion or disruptive mutations of the gene in 46,XY individuals have no impact on testis determination or male sex differentiation in humans, but affected males have the syndrome of adrenal

hypoplasia congenita and typically have hypogonadotropic hypogonadism with evidence of postnatal testicular dysfunction and reduced fertility.[31,171,193,194] Of note, the reported missense mutations in the gene all reside within the region encoding the ligand-binding domain, suggesting that a ligand may in fact exist for this orphan. Just as the role for DAX1 in human testis determination is unclear, there is equally little evidence from human studies of a role for DAX1 in ovarian determination; apart from varying degrees of pubertal delay/hypogonadotropic hypogonadism, ovarian development and function are normal in XX individuals with *DAX1* deletion or mutation, including a rare homozygous mutation due to gene conversion.[56]

Thus, the genetic background (between or even within species) on which excess or deficiency of *DAX1* is expressed appears to be a primary determinant of the effects of alteration in this gene. This may reflect species differences in levels or timing of expression of *DAX1* versus *SRY* or other relevant genes relative to critical thresholds and prompts caution in interpreting the relevance of murine models with respect to human development and disease.

### Dsx and MAB-3–Related Transcription Factor 1 and Related DM Family Genes

Transcription factors related to the sexual regulatory factors dsx (for *doublesex*, in *Drosophila*) and mab3 (for *male abnormal gene*, in earthworm) contain a conserved DNA-binding motif referred to as the *DM* (doublesex/mab) domain.[197] These are the only transcription factors that share sex-determining functions across different phyla.[198] Seven genes encoding such transcription factors, referred to as *DM genes*, have been discovered to date in humans and mice.[199,200] DM-related ranscription factor

**Table 142-2** Proteins Involved in Steroidogenesis: Nomenclature, Function, and Dysfunction

| Gene Name | Gene Locus | Protein Names | Enzyme Common Names | Protein Function | Effects of Deficiency |
|---|---|---|---|---|---|
| StAR | 8p11.2 | STAR STARD1 | Steroidogenic acute regulatory protein | Transport of cholesterol to inner mitochondrial membrane | Congenital lipoid adrenal hyperplasia Adrenal insufficiency with— 46,XY: defective masculinization 46,XX: post-pubertal ovarian failure |
| CYP11A | 15q23-q24 | P450scc P450C11A1 | Cholesterol side chain cleavage enzyme 20,22-desmolase | Converts cholesterol to pregnenolone by 20- and 22-hydroxylation and removal of carbon side chain at C20-22 bond | Lipoid adrenal hyperplasia with later onset than STAR defects, and— 46,XY: defective masculinization 46,XX: normal female with sexual infantilism |
| HSD3B2 | 1p13.1 | 3βHSD2 | 3β-hydroxysteroid dehydrogenase | Converts pregnenolone, 17-OH-pregnenolone, DHEA, and androstenediol to progesterone, 17-OH-progesterone, androstenedione, and testosterone by sequential dehydrogenation and isomerization ($\delta^5 \to \delta^4$ steroids) | Adrenal insufficiency with— 46,XY: defective masculinization 46,XX: mild to moderate virilization |
| POR | 7q12 | POR CYPOR CPR | P450 oxidoreductase | Electron donor for all cytochrome p450 enzymes | Virilization of pregnant woman during pregnancy and— 46,XY: normal or undervirilized male 46,XX: virilization of external genitalia Both sexes: Antley-Bixler syndrome |
| CYP17 CYP17A1 | 10q24.3 | P450$_{17\alpha}$ P450c17 | 17α-hydroxylase 17,20-lyase 17,20-desmolase | 17α-hydroxylation of pregnenolone and progesterone to 17-OH-pregnenolone and 17-OH-progesterone; conversion of 17-OH-pregnenolone and 17-OH-progesterone to DHEA and androstenedione | Adrenal insufficiency with hypertension and— 46,XX: defective masculinization 46,XX: normal female with sexual infantilism due to primary gonadal failure |
| CYP21 CYP21A2 | 6p21.3 | P450c21 | 21-hydroxylase | 21-hydroxylation of progesterone and 17-OH-progesterone to 11-deoxycorticosterone and 11-deoxycortisol | Adrenal insufficiency with— 46,XY: normal masculinization; precocious pseudopuberty 46,XX: virilization of external genitalia |
| CYP11B1 | 8q21 | P450c11 P450c11B1 | 11β-hydroxylase | 11-hydroxylation of deoxycortisol to cortisol | Adrenal insufficiency with hypertension 46,XY: normal masculinization; precocious pseudopuberty 46,XX: virilization of external genitalia |
| CYP11B2 | 8q21 | P450XIB2 P450cmo P450AS CMOI CMOII | 18 hydroxylase 18 hydroxysteroid dehydrogenase Aldosterone synthase | 18-hydroxylation of corticosterone; 18-oxidation of 18-OH-corticosterone to aldosterone | Isolated aldosterone deficiency → hyponatremia, hyperkalemia, failure to thrive No effect on sex differentiation |
| HSD17B3 EDH17B2 | 9q22 | 17βHSDIII | 17β-hydroxysteroid dehydrogenase 3; 17-ketosteroid reductase; 17β-hydroxysteroid oxidoreductase | Reversible conversion of DHEA, androstenedione, and estrone to androstenediol, testosterone, and estradiol | No effect on adrenal steroidogenesis 46,XY: defective masculinization 46,XX: normal female |
| CYP19A1 | 15q21.1 | P450arom | Aromatase Estrogen synthetase | Converts androstenedione to estrone and testosterone to estradiol by addition of 2 double bonds to steroid A ring | Virilization of pregnant woman in latter part of pregnancy and— 46,XX: normal male 46,XX: virilization of external genitalia |
| SRD5A2 | 2p23 | 5α-reductase 2 | 5α-reductase | 5α-reduction of testosterone to dihydrotestosterone | 46,XY: defective masculinization with normal Wolffian duct development 46,XX: normal female |

1 (DMRT1, also known as DMT1[201]) may have roles similar to WT1, functioning as an early regulator of primordial gonad formation, and later as a testis-specific factor. Human chromosomal band 9p24.3 harbors the *DMRT1, -3,* and *-2* genes, in this order from telomeric to centromeric.[200,202] These genes are located at less than 30 kb from the critical region for sex reversal on chromosome 9, determined by analysis of sex-reversed 46,XY patients with monosomy of distal 9p, thus placing them in the lineup for roles in testis determination.[200,203–207] The genes encode 226–amino acid peptides that share approximately 80% identity in the 29–amino acid core region of the DM domain.[204]

Studies in a number of species (mice, humans, chickens, amphibians, alligators, lizards, turtles, fish) demonstrate gonad-specific expression of various DM domain factors. Given the different sex-determining switches in these verte-

brate groups, the DMRTs, which may overlap to some extent in their functional roles, are thought to represent an ancient, conserved component of the vertebrate sex-determining pathway, upstream of SRY.[199,202,208,209] Early in development, murine *Dmrt1* mRNA is expressed exclusively in the genital ridge of both XX and XY embryos, before gonadal sex determination.[205,210] *Dmrt1* expression becomes sexually dimorphic, being upregulated in testes compared to ovaries during early gonadal development. Testicular expression is restricted to the Sertoli cells and germ cells of the seminiferous tubules as development proceeds. *Dmrt1* expression in Sertoli cells may be FSH-driven, as studies in postnatal rat testes have demonstrated significant increases in expression with FSH treatment.[211] Expression is also upregulated by the transcription factors Sp1 and Sp3 and the cell cycle regulator early growth response 1 (Egr1).[212] Three other *DM* genes—*Dmrt3,*

*Dmrt4*, and *Dmrt7*—are also significantly expressed in the embryonic mouse gonad.[200] *Dmrt4* is expressed at similar levels in the gonads of both sexes, while *Dmrt3* is more highly expressed in male gonads and *Dmrt7* in female gonads, suggesting yet to be determined sex-specific roles for these other members of the DM family.

Male mice with homozygous deletion of *Dmrt1* had normal fetal testis development, but had severe defects in postnatal testis differentiation, resembling those associated with human deletions.[213] Prior to postnatal day 7, the testes of the null mice appeared grossly normal. Thereafter, the testes were hypoplastic with disorganized seminiferous tubules, absent germ cells, and evidence of fatty degeneration of Leydig cells. Notably, the gonadal tissue was not ovarian and there were no Müllerian duct–derived structures. Thus, the murine *Dmrt1* null phenotype represents a postnatal failure of testis development, accompanied by germ cell death, rather than a prenatal failure of male sex determination and subsequent ovarian development. In contrast to the postnatal testis maldevelopment seen in the mutant mouse, deletion of the human chromosomal region 9p24, containing *DMRT1*, *-2*, and *-3*, in a 46,XY individual was associated with full-blown male-to-female sex reversal. The effects of *DMRT1* appear to be similarly discordant between mouse and human in ovarian development. No effect of *Dmrt1* deletion on gonadal development was seen in female mice; however, deletion of 9p (including *DMRT1* and nearby loci) in humans apparently does impair ovarian development.[214] These contrasting findings suggest differing roles for *DMRT1* in human and murine gonadal development.

## SEX DIFFERENTIATION (DEVELOPMENT OF MALE OR FEMALE INTERNAL AND EXTERNAL GENITALIA)

Differentiation of the internal and external genitalia along male or female lines is dependent on the presence or absence of functional testicular tissue, the resultant production of AMH and testosterone, and their action at target tissues (see Chapter 143).

### EMBRYOLOGY OF MALE SEX DIFFERENTIATION

The primitive internal genital tracts are indistinguishable between the sexes until 7 weeks' gestation. Once function of the testis is established at around 8 weeks of human gestation, development of the male sexual phenotype (internal and external genitalia) is under control of testicular secretions and the receptors that mediate their action.[3,215] These include fetal luteinizing hormone (LH), the LH/chorionic gonadotropin receptor (LH/CG-R), at least five steroidogenic enzymes involved in testosterone biosynthesis, steroid 5α-reductase 2 required for conversion of testosterone to dihydrotestosterone, the androgen receptor (AR), antimüllerian hormone (AMH) and the AMH receptor. Initially, the Wolffian ducts are stabilized (prevented from undergoing resorption) by the action (mainly local) of testosterone and thereafter undergo differentiation into the epididymides, vasa deferentia and seminal vesicles; these processes occur between 9 and 13 weeks' gestation. Development of Wolffian structures requires testosterone, which is produced by testicular Leydig cells following activation of the cell surface LH/CG-R. During the first trimester of gestation, the ligand for this receptor is probably CG, produced in large quantity by the placenta. Subsequently, endogenous fetal LH is the primary ligand. The lack of dependence upon fetal LH during genital morphogenesis is evidenced by the normal penile development of male infants with hypopituitarism; however, the subnormal penile size of these infants highlights the role of LH/testosterone action in the penile growth that occurs in the third trimester. Action of CG or LH at the Leydig cell LH/CG-R stimulates testicular steroidogenesis. Sertoli cells may also help regulate Leydig cell secretion in a paracrine fash-

ion. The biochemistry and molecular biology of the steroidogenic enzymes is described in further detail below. The outcome of this multistep process is a high local, and to a lesser extent systemic, concentration of testosterone. Testosterone action is mediated by the AR, a nuclear receptor/transcription factor found in high concentration in the tissues of the Wolffian ducts (where testosterone itself is the ligand) and external genitalia (where the ligand is dihydrotestosterone). Dihydrotestosterone does not appear to mediate the processes of Wolffian development, since the enzyme required for its production (5α-reductase 2) is not expressed in Wolffian tissues at the time of their differentiation. In the absence of high androgen concentration, as in the female or androgen deficient fetus, there is insufficient activated AR to induce transcription of target genes required for stabilization and development of the Wolffian system and for masculinization of the external genitalia.

In parallel to the masculinization of the internal genitalia represented by Wolffian development, a process of "defeminization" of the genital ducts occurs as the Müllerian ducts regress under the influence of locally acting AMH, a glycoprotein hormone secreted by testicular Sertoli cells that acts via a complex of serine/threonine kinase receptors. Action of AMH at its receptor(s) results in involution of Müllerian structures by apoptosis. By this process the Müllerian ducts are obliterated by the eleventh week of human gestation, the only remnant of their existence in the 46,XY fetus being the prostatic utricle. Absence of one testis results in retention of the ipsilateral Müllerian structures and only limited Wolffian development on that side, indicating that the effects of AMH and testosterone are mediated to some extent in a paracrine fashion (see Fig. 142-2).[157]

Meanwhile, under the influence of androgen action (primarily dihydrotestosterone), the genital tubercle elongates to form the body of the penis, and the urethral folds fuse ventrally from behind forward, to form the penile urethra.[3,157,216] The labioscrotal swellings/folds grow toward each other, fusing in the midline to form the scrotum. Dihydrotestosterone (DHT) also induces the urogenital sinus to differentiate as the prostate, and inhibits the formation of the vesico-vaginal septum (described below). These processes are completed by week 12 of gestation (see Fig. 142-3B).

Between 12 and 24 weeks' gestation the testes migrate from their original lumbar location to the level of the internal inguinal ring above the scrotum. Descent of the testes through the inguinal ring and into the scrotum begins around week 28, and in most infants is completed by term. This process, which can perhaps be considered the final phase of masculinization, is controlled in part by a Leydig cell secreted protein, insulin-like protein 3, which belongs to the insulin-like hormone superfamily (including insulin, relaxin, and insulin-like growth factors 1 and 2).

### GENETICS OF MALE SEX DIFFERENTIATION

The following sections describe the genetic regulation of proteins, enzymes, hormones, and receptors involved in secretion and action of the two primary male sex hormones: testosterone and AMH. Deficiencies of these processes in human males result in various forms of male (46,XY) pseudohermaphroditism. This term describes the condition in which an individual with male karyotype and normally formed testes has abnormal masculinization of the internal and/or external genitalia. In essence, there are two major classes: defects of production or response to testosterone, and defects of production or response to AMH.

#### Luteinizing Hormone/Chorionic Gonadotropin Receptor
Testosterone production by fetal Leydig cells is essential for masculinization of the Wolffian system and external genitalia. It appears, however, that this may occur independent of gonadotropin stimulation in the earliest stages of human sex

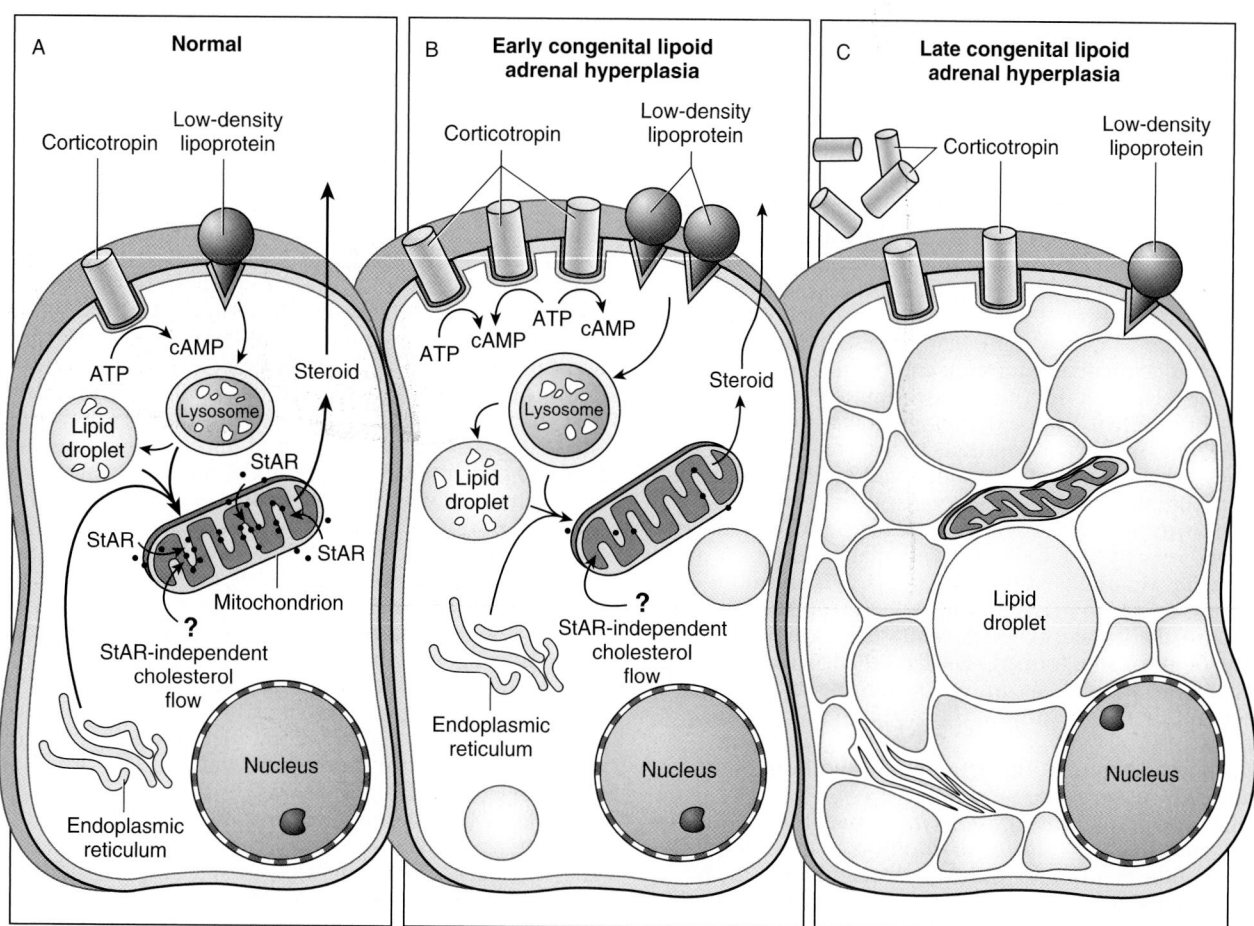

**Figure 142-7** Steroidogenic acute regulatory protein (StAR) and mechanism of adrenal damage in congenital lipoid adrenal hyperplasia. **A,** In the healthy adrenal cortical cell, binding of adrenocorticotropic hormone (ACTH) stimulates transport of low-density lipoprotein (LDL) cholesterol into the cell by endocytosis. LDL is processed by lysososmes and either stored in lipid droplets or transferred to the mitochondria. Meanwhile, cholesterol is also synthesized independently by the endoplasmic reticulum and transferred to the mitochondria, where it is transported from the outer to the inner mitochondrial membrane for processing—the rate-limiting step in steroidogenesis—by mechanisms that may be StAR dependent or independent. **B,** In the absence of StAR, as in early congenital lipoid adrenal hyperplasia (or the placenta), StAR-independent mechanisms can move some cholesterol into the mitochondria, resulting in a low level of steroidogenesis. The limited production of steroids results in increased ACTH secretion, stimulating further production of cholesterol and its accumulation as cholesterol esters in lipid droplets. **C,** As lipid droplets accumulate, they engorge the cell, damaging its cytoarchitecture through both physical displacement and the chemical action of cholesterol auto-oxidation products. Steroidogenic capacity is destroyed, and ACTH stimulation increases. ATP, adenosine triphosphate; cAMP, cyclic adenosine monophosphate. (From Bose HS, et al: The pathophysiology and genetics of congenital lipoid adrenal hyperplasia. N Engl J Med 335:1870–1878, 1996.)

differentiation. The lack of dependence on fetal LH secretion during the early stages of genital morphogenesis (weeks 6 through 8 of gestation) is evidenced by the normal penile development of male infants with hypopituitarism and normal masculinization in a reported case of LH-β gene mutation.[217] The severe defects in masculinization seen in individuals with mutations of the LH/CG-R underscore, however, the importance of this system in male sex differentiation.[218] Fetal Leydig cell development and function in the mouse do not require gonadotropins, as evidenced by normal Leydig cell development and expression of steroidogenic enzymes in mice lacking GnRH,[219] and there is evidence that the initial phases of Leydig cell development and function occur independent of the receptor.[220,221] The subnormal penile size of infants with hypopituitarism reflects the role of LH-testosterone action in normal penile growth in the third trimester of gestation.

The LH/CG-R is a seven-transmembrane domain G-protein coupled receptor responsible for modulating the hormonal effects of LH and CG.[221] The 60-kb gene encoding the LH/CG-R is located at 2p21 and is comprised of 11 exons transcribed into a number of mRNA splice variants whose differential function is unclear.[220,222] Exons 1 through 10 encode the major portion of the amino-terminal extracellular domain, containing a leucine-rich repeat, while exon 11 codes for a small part of the extracellular domain, as well as all seven transmembrane loops and the carboxyterminal intracellular region. The LH/CG-R is a protein of 85 to 95 kilodaltons and has significant homology with the FSH and thyroid-stimulating hormone (TSH) receptors. Ligand binding induces increased intracellular production of cyclic adenosine monophosphate (cAMP), the principal mediator of hormone action in this system. Stimulation of the receptor by binding of its ligand results in increased steroidogenesis via a number of different stimulatory events. The receptor-mediated increase in cAMP causes stimulation of intracellular cholesterol transport, via activation of StAR (described later), activation of cholesterol side-chain cleavage enzyme, and activation of steroidogenic enzymes including 3β-hydroxysteroid dehydrogenase, 17α-hydroxylase, and 17,20-lyase. LH/CG-R is expressed predominantly in gonads, including testicular Leydig cells and ovarian granulosa, theca, interstitial, and luteal cells. In mice, testicular Leydig cells constitutively express LH/CG-R in the absence of hormone, and early steroidogenesis is also GnRH independent in the fetal rat testis.[219,223] In contrast, in mouse ovary, LH/CG-R mRNA can be detected only on day 5 postnatally, after the onset of LH stimulation of gonadal function, implying that LH/CG-R is not required for normal ovarian development.[222,224] The receptor appears to be regulated by its ligand (LH or CG) via two processes: uncoupling (a fairly immediate process, which results in reduced cAMP production in response to ligand, without reducing receptor number) and downregulation (a slower, biphasic process, resulting in reduced receptor number due to internalization and degradation of already formed receptors, followed by reduced receptor mRNA transcription, via a cAMP-mediated process). These regulatory events are believed to contribute to the phenomenon of desensitization that occurs in the presence of continuous hormonal stimulation. For reasons that are as yet unclear, expression of LH/CG-R has also been found in a number of extragonadal tissues including prostate, fallopian tubes, uterus, placenta, adrenal gland (human and mouse), and brain. Targeted disruption of the LH/CG-R in the mouse resulted in underdevelopment of internal and external genitalia in both sexes, including, in males, abdominal testes, marked prostatic hypoplasia, and micropenis, accompanied by dramatic reduction in serum testosterone and increase in serum LH.[225,226] Overall growth and development of gonads and reproductive tracts were severely reduced, and both male and female mice were infertile. Mutations of the human LH/CG-R result in even more severe defects in masculinization than seen in the mouse, with essentially female external genital development in the presence of normally formed, Leydig cell–deficient testes in affected 46,XY individuals in the syndrome of Leydig cell hypoplasia.[218,220,227,228]

### Proteins and Enzymes of Testosterone Biosynthesis
#### Steroidogenic Acute Regulatory Protein
The first and rate-limiting step in gonadal and adrenal steroidogenesis is the transfer of cholesterol from the mitochondrial outer membrane to the inner membrane, mediated by steroidogenic acute regulatory protein (StAR) (Fig. 142-7). The cholesterol transport protein StAR is encoded by an 8-kb seven-exon gene located at 8p11.2 that contains an 855-bp open reading frame. The StAR protein comprises 285 amino acids and is produced as a 37-kilodalton cytosolic precursor that is imported to the mitochondria, where it is processed to four mature 30-kilodalton forms.[229–231]

StAR is not required for basal (chronic) steroidogenesis, but is essential for the increased rate of steroid production required under trophic stimulation.[232,233] The acute response of steroidogenic cells to trophic hormone (e.g., LH, adrenocorticotropic hormone [ACTH]) stimulation is the transport of cholesterol to the inner mitochondrial membrane, where the first enzyme of steroidogenesis—the cholesterol side-chain cleavage enzyme—is located, resulting in a rapid increase in pregnenolone synthesis.[234] The mechanism of action of StAR in this process is thought to involve formation of contact sites between the inner and outer mitochondrial membranes.[229,233] StAR comprises two major functional domains: the amino-terminal domain contains the hydrophobic mitochondrial targeting sequence and the carboxyl terminus comprises the StAR-related lipid transfer (START) domain, responsible for the translocation of cholesterol between the two mitochondrial membranes. The central region of the protein, between residues 63 and 193, is believed to slow the protein's transit into the mitochondria, permitting the biologically active carboxyl terminus to have more interactions with the outer mitochondrial membrane.

Star mRNA expression in the mouse is localized to the adrenals and gonads, first appearing in the urogenital ridge at day 10.5 (just after Sf1 and at the same time as Sry).[232,233] Subsequently, expression is restricted to the adrenal cortical cells and the interstitial regions of the testis (where Leydig cells reside) and is not seen in the embryonic ovary. Human StAR mRNA expression is seen in the ovary, testis, adrenal cortex, and kidney—tissues that carry out mitochondrial sterol oxidations subject to acute regulation by cAMP.[230,235] Star is also expressed in the brain, consistent with a role in production of neurosteroids. Although the placenta is an abundantly

steroidogenic tissue, StAR is not expressed there since placenta does not exhibit acute regulation of steroidogenesis and is not expressed in any nonsteroidogenic tissues. Star mRNA expression is stimulated by LH and ACTH via their receptors that induce cAMP-mediated events.[234] In addition, the promoters of the StAR genes of a number of species contain binding sites for SF1 and the estrogen receptor, and SF1 has been demonstrated to have a major role in regulation of Star expression.[36,234,236,237] Exposure of adrenocortical cells to either low-density lipoproteins (LDLs) or high-density lipoproteins (HDLs) increases Star expression, perhaps reflecting a positive feedback circuit linking cholesterol availability with steroid output. Negative regulation of Star expression has been demonstrated for two hypothetical "anti-male" factors, Dax1 and Wnt4, in keeping with the demonstrated lack of steroidogenesis during ovarian development.[158,188]

Homozygous deletion of Star in mice resulted in adrenal cortical abnormalities highly reminiscent of the human disease congenital lipoid adrenal hyperplasia.[237] Adrenal defects included florid lipid deposition in steroidogenic cells, very low levels of adrenal cortical hormones, high ACTH and corticotropin-releasing hormone (CRH), and early postnatal death. The testes of the male mice, although grossly normal, showed similar cytologic changes with lipid deposits in steroidogenic cells. Although postnatal testosterone levels were not frankly abnormal, prenatal testosterone levels must have been low, as the male mice had phenotypically female external genitalia. The internal genitalia, however, were normally masculinized, indicating that the testes had retained at least enough steroidogenic capability during fetal development for adequate local testosterone concentrations in the vicinity of the Wolffian ducts. The ovaries of the female mice were normal. The sex-specific differences in gonadal involvement reflect a "two-hit" mode of pathogenesis of StAR deficiency: Trophic hormone stimulation induces progressive accumulation of lipids within the steroidogenic cells; the lipid accumulation eventually causes cell death and adrenal failure.

Homozygous and compound heterozygous mutations have been detected in the gene encoding StAR in patients with the clinical syndrome of congenital lipoid adrenal hyperplasia (CLAH), which is the rarest and most severe form of congenital adrenal hyperplasia.[238–243] A defect in the transport of cholesterol to the inner mitochondrial membrane to serve as substrate for steroidogenesis causes the disorder by a two-hit process. The gene defect results in absent or dysfunctional transport protein, which, in turn, leads to accumulation of intracellular lipid (hence, "lipoid hyperplasia"). Affected males, deficient in testosterone, have phenotypically female external genitalia and fail to masculinize the Wolffian ducts. These mutations have tended to cluster in families of Eastern or Middle Eastern origin (Japanese, Korean, Vietnamese, and Palestinian), perhaps suggesting a founder effect.

#### P450 Side-Chain Cleavage Enzyme
P450 side-chain cleavage enzyme (P450scc; previously known as 20,22-desmolase) is a mixed function oxidase located on the inner mitochondrial membrane where it is in complex with two other proteins, adrenodoxin and adrenodoxin reductase. It is the first enzyme of steroidogenesis, catalyzing the conversion of cholesterol to pregnenolone in three distinct biochemical reactions: 20α-hydroxylation, 22-hydroxylation, and side-chain cleavage of the C20–C22 bond (Fig. 142-8). Electrons are transferred from nicotinamide adenine dinucleotide phosphate hydrogen (NADPH) to adrenodoxin reductase, a membrane-bound flavoprotein, then to adrenodoxin, a soluble iron/sulfur protein, and finally to the enzyme P450scc itself.

P450scc is encoded by the 20-kb 9-exon CYP11A gene localized to the q23-q24 region of human chromosome 15.[244] The gene is expressed in steroidogenic tissues such as adrenal cortex, ovarian granulosa cells, testicular Leydig cells, and placenta and is also expressed in skin, heart, and brain. Expression in brain colocalizes with that of StAR, consistent with a role in production of neurosteroids. Expression of *CYP11A* in classic steroidogenic sites is enhanced by ACTH, gonadotropins, cAMP, and SF1 (for which binding sites are located in the *CYP11A* promoter, and which may act in conjunction with the ubiquitous transcription factor Sp1, at least in bovine adrenocortical cells). There is also evidence for insulinlike growth factor 1 (IGF-1)–mediated stimulation of *Cyp11a* expression in mouse Leydig cells and for downregulation of adrenal expression by glucocorticoids such as dexamethasone. Expression patterns are tissue specific and involve the use of alternate promoter sequences. Expression is likely also species specific, since Amh causes downregulation of testicular *Cyp11a* in rats but not in mice.

Mice with targeted disruption of the *Cyp11a1* gene were unable to make steroids, had markedly elevated ACTH, and died shortly after birth.[245] Male mice had small testes, epididymides, and vasa deferentia; no prostate or seminal vesicles; and feminized external genitalia. Similar to the findings reported in mice with *Star* gene deletions, the *Cyp11a1*-deleted mice had abnormal lipid deposits in the adrenals and testes, whereas the ovaries of the females were normal. Findings in individuals with mutations of the human *CYP11A* gene are similar to those in the transgenic mice, with the phenotype of male-to-female sex reversal in 46,XY individuals, and normal ovary development and sex differentiation with postnatal adrenal failure in 46,XX individuals.[246,247]

### 3β-Hydroxysteroid Dehydrogenase

The 3β-hydroxysteroid dehydrogenase/$\delta^5$-$\delta^4$ isomerases (3β-HSD1 and 3β-HSD2) are two highly homologous noncytochrome, nicotine adenine dinucleotide (NAD)+-dependent, membrane-bound short-chain alcohol dehydrogenases located in the endoplasmic reticulum and mitochondria. Both have two separate, sequential enzymatic activities: dehydrogenase activity and isomerase activity (conversion of $\delta^5$-steroids to $\delta^4$-steroids), the net result of which is the conversion of 3β-hydroxy-$\delta^5$-steroids (pregnenolone, 17-hydroxypregnenolone, dehydroepiandrosterone, and androstenediol) to the 3-keto-$\delta^4$-steroids (progesterone, 17α-hydroxyprogesterone, $\delta^4$-androstenedione, and testosterone, respectively) (Fig. 142-8).[248,249] Reduced nicotinamide adenine dinucleotide (NADH), the product of the rate-limiting dehydrogenase reaction, induces a conformational change around the bound 3-oxo-$\delta^5$-steroid (the substrate for the second enzymatic step) to activate the isomerase reaction. This bifunctional dimeric enzyme is therefore required for the biosynthesis of all classes of steroid hormones. Deficiency of 3β-HSD activity in steroidogenic tissues impairs both adrenal and gonadal (testicular and ovarian) steroidogenesis and is reported to be the second most common cause of congenital adrenal hyperplasia. There are two highly homologous human genes encoding isoenzymes responsible for 3β-HSD activity, *HSD3B1* and *HSD3B2*, encoding 3β-HSD1 and 3β-HSD2, respectively.[250,251] The genes are approximately 7 to 8 kb in size and contain four exons. There is evidence for tight linkage between these genes, which are both located at 1p13.1. Three pseudogenes containing stop codons and/or deletions have also been identified. The *HSD3B1* gene is the predominant form expressed in placenta, liver, kidney, skin, mammary gland, and prostate and encodes a 372–amino acid (42-kilodalton) protein. The *HSD3B2* gene encodes the 371–amino acid 3β-HSD2 isoform, which shares 93.5% identity with the type 1 isozyme and has the same enzymatic activities, but has a somewhat lower affinity for its substrates and is expressed almost exclusively in the steroidogenic cells of the adrenals and gonads. In bovine adrenocortical cells, the enzyme colocalizes with P450scc at the inner mitochodrial membrane, suggesting a possible functional association between the two enzymes in regulation of steroidogenesis. Specific amino acid residues have been shown to be required for the separate enzymatic activities: His261 for the dehydrogenase activity, and Tyr263 or -264 for the isomerase activity.

3β-HSD is detectable in human testicular interstitial cells from 8 weeks' gestation, consistent with the requirement for the Leydig cell testosterone production essential for embryonic masculinization. In contrast, as might be expected from the fact that fetal ovarian steroid production is not required for female sex differentiation, 3β-HSD expression in the ovary is not observed until 28 weeks of human gestation, at which time it is detected in theca and interstitial cells. Expression in the adrenal gland can be detected from around 11 weeks' gestation, but then seems to decline at mid-gestation, rising again in the third trimester.[252] In cultured human adrenal cells, 3β-HSD mRNA and protein levels are regulated by ACTH and angiotensin II. A putative SF1 binding site is present in the promoter of the *HSD3B2* gene, and activity of the *HSD3B2* promoter is enhanced by SF1, and even more so by a related factor called liver receptor homologue 1 (LRH1; designated NR5A2), which is expressed at high levels in the testis and ovary. In mouse Leydig cells, expression is regulated by LH/CG.

Deficiency of human 3β-HSD impairs steroidogenesis in the adrenals and gonads, resulting in reduced synthesis of all classes of steroids—cortisol, aldosterone, and gonadal steroids—associated with congenital adrenal hyperplasia (which may or may not be of the salt-losing variety) and disturbances of external genital development in both males (undermasculinization) and females (virilization).

### 17α-Hydroxylase and 17,20-Lyase

A single microsomal enzyme, cytochrome $P450_{17\alpha}$ (p450c17), catalyzes two consecutive oxidation reactions, the 17α-hydroxylase and 17,20-lyase (17,20-desmolase) reactions of adrenal and gonadal steroidogenesis.[253,254] $P450_{17\alpha}$ is encoded by *CYP17*, a 6.6-kb 8-exon gene located on chromosome 10q24.3. The *CYP17* gene is similar to *CYP21* (encoding the 21-hydroxylase enzyme, described later), and the two may have originated from a common ancestral gene. The two genes share an average homology of almost 30%, with some regions of high homology and others of low homology. The main difference is that *CYP17* has lost two exons present in *CYP21*.

Cytochrome $P450_{17\alpha}$ is a 508–amino acid, 57-kilodalton protein that is part of the $P450_{17\alpha}$ complex anchored to the smooth endoplasmic reticulum of steroidogenic cells, which also includes a 78-kilodalton flavoprotein reductase, termed P450 oxidoreductase. $P450_{17\alpha}$ comprises an amino-terminal membrane-attachment domain, a steroid-binding domain, a redox-interaction domain, and a heme-binding domain. The enzyme accepts electrons from NADPH via P450 reductase to catalyze the overall oxidation reaction; P450 oxidoreductase contains binding domains for NADPH, flavin mononucleotide (FMN), and flavin-adenine dinucleotide (FAD). The 17α-hydroxylase reaction converts pregnenolone to 17-hydroxypregnenolone and progesterone to 17-hydroxyprogesterone, respectively (see Fig. 142-8). This reaction is the rate-limiting step in androgen biosynthesis. The 17,20-lyase reaction cleaves the C17,20 bond to convert the C21 steroid 17-hydroxypregnenolone to the C19 steroid dehydroepiandrosterone (DHEA) and catalyzes the equivalent conversion of 17-hydroxyprogesterone to $\delta^4$-androstenedione, although this latter reaction occurs much more slowly. DHEA and androstenedione are the major precursors of testosterone and estradiol, respectively, although, because of the enzyme's preference for $\delta^5$-steroids, most human sex steroids derive from DHEA. Specific amino acid residues are critical for either the 17α-hydroxylase or the 17,20-lyase activity.[254–257] Serine phosphorylation of the enzyme increases lyase activity, while dephosphorylation eliminates this activity. Other regulatory features may include variation in the ratio of the NADPH P450 oxidoreductase to the $P450_{17\alpha}$ enzyme itself, resulting in alteration of electron transfer to the enzyme.

$P450_{17\alpha}$ is expressed in human adrenal, testis, and ovarian theca cells, but not in ovarian granulosa cells or placenta.

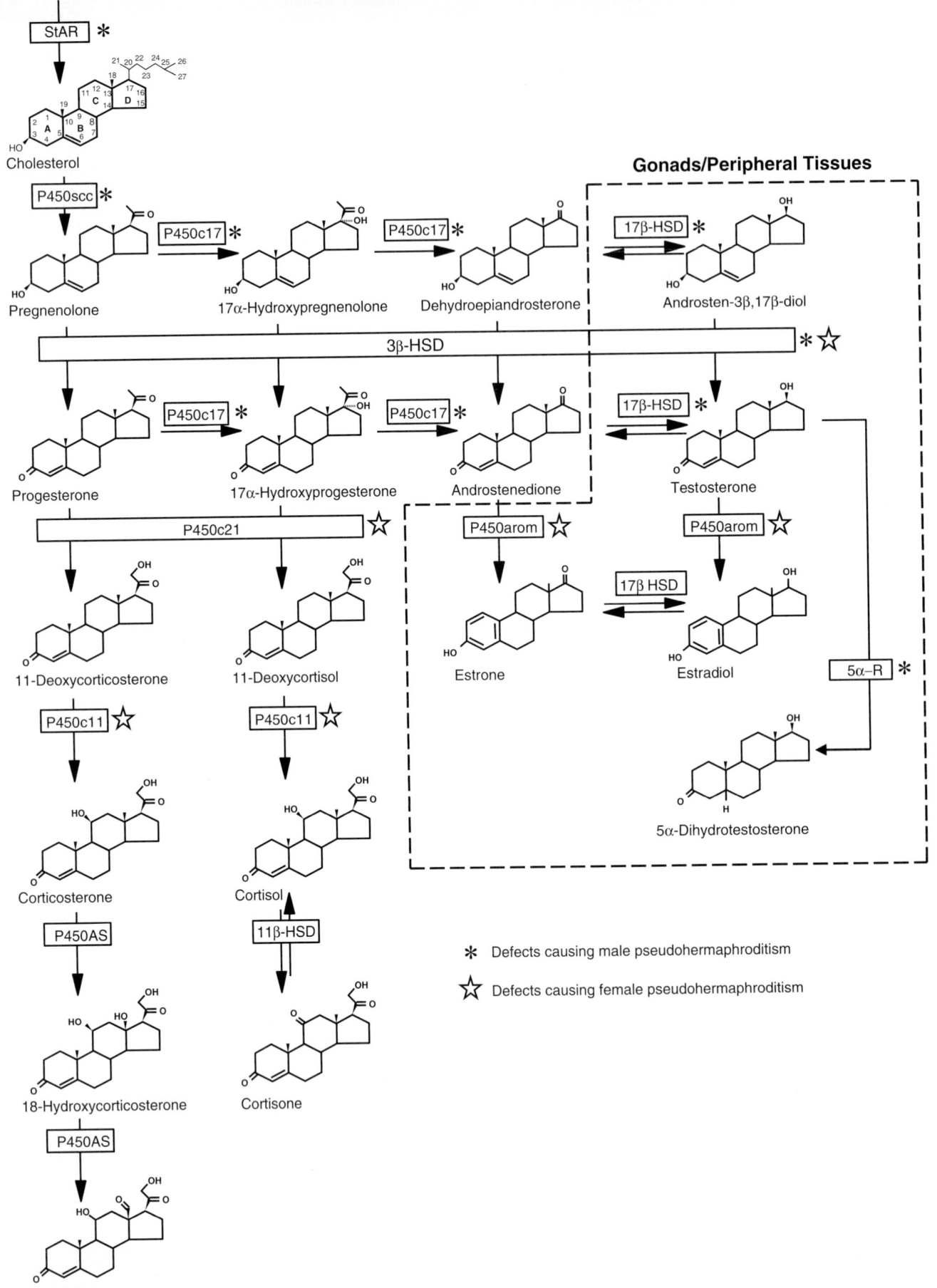

**Figure 142-8** Pathway of steroid biosynthesis and defects in steroidogenesis. The first step in steroidogenesis is the transport of cholesterol across the mitochondrial membrane, mediated by steroidogenic acute regulatory protein (StAR). The remaining steps in adrenal and gonadal steroidogenesis are accomplished by a number of enzymes. Most are of the P450 cytochrome family; however, 3β-hydroxysteroid dehydrogenase (3β-HSD) and 17β-hydroxysteroid dehydrogenase (17β-HSD)are of the short-chain alcohol dehydrogenase family. Molecular defects that cause male pseudohermaphroditism are designated by *triangles*. Defects that cause female pseudohermaphroditism are designated by *stars*. 3β-HSD deficiency can cause either male or female pseudohermaphroditism.

*CYP17* expression begins between 41 and 44 days post-conception in the human fetus, limited to the adrenal fetal zone. *CYP17* mRNA is upregulated by ACTH via cAMP; cAMP regulatory regions have been identified in the 5'-flanking region of the bovine *CYP17* gene. Expression is also regulated by the inhibin/activin system in the ovary. A key regulator of *CYP17* in adernocortical and Leydig cells is SF1.[258] The 5'-flanking region of the human *CYP17* gene contains three functional SF1 elements that collectively mediate at least 25-fold induction of promoter activity by SF1. SF1 regulation of *CYP17* may be inhibited by DAX1.

The ratio of 17α-hydroxylase to 17,20-lyase activity differs between adrenal and testis and is developmentally regulated at adrenarche, an increase in the ratio of lyase to hydroxylase activity occurring at this time. The basis for the time- and tissue-specific differential regulation of the enzyme's two main activities is not yet fully understood.

Deficiency of this enzyme is another fairly uncommon cause of male pseudohemaphroditism. A variety of molecular defects have been described in the *CYP17* genes of individuals with 17α-hydroxylase deficiency, either in a homozygous or compound heterozygous state.

### 17β-Hydroxysteroid Dehydrogenase 3

The 17β-hydroxysteroid dehydrogenases (17β-HSDs, also known as 17β-ketosteroid reductases and as estradiol 17β-dehydrogenases) are NAD+/NADPH-dependent, membrane-bound enzymes involved in the final steps of gonadal steroid synthesis. There are at least 11 17β-HSD enzymes encoded by separate genes; only those related to gonadal steroidogenesis are discussed here.[259-262] The nomenclature of this group of genes and enzymes is quite daunting: The type 1 enzyme, 17β-HSD I, also known as estradiol-17β hydroxysteroid dehydrogenase II, is encoded by a gene located at 17q11-12, referred to as *HSD17B1* or *EDH17B2*.[263] This locus, in fact, contains two genes: *h17β-HSDI* and *-II*. The active gene is *h17β-HSDII*; *h17β-HSDI* is a pseudogene, also referred to as *EDH17BP1*, which is 89% homologous to the active gene.[264] 17β-HSD I appears to be the isozyme responsible for ovarian 17β-HSD activity. The type 2 isoform, 17β-HSDII, encoded by *HSD17B2*, is responsible for 17β-HSD activity in placenta and endometrium. The testicular isoform, relevant for the process of sex differentiation, is 17β-HSD3 (III). This enzyme, responsible for the final step in testosterone synthesis—reduction of androstenedione to testosterone—is encoded by *HSD17B3* (*EDH17B3*), which shares only 23% sequence homology with the *HSD17B1* and 2 genes. The 60-kb gene located at 9q22 contains 11 exons and encodes a 310–amino acid protein.[265,266] The finding of small amounts of testosterone in patients with deficiency of the type III isozyme suggests that one of the other isozymes can also convert androstenedione to testosterone.

These steroidogenic enzymes (which are not of the cytochrome P450 type) catalyze the only reversible steps in the steroid biosynthetic pathway: interconversion of δ⁴-androstenedione↔testosterone, DHEA↔δ⁵-androstenediol and estrone↔estradiol by oxidation or reduction of C-18 and C-19 steroids (see Fig. 142-8).

The 17β-HSD enzymes are expressed in a tissue-specific fashion, some being expressed predominantly in estrogenic or androgenic tissues and others more widely.[265-268] In addition to being found in the ovary, testis, and placenta, significant levels of *HSD17B* mRNAs are found in peripheral sites such as uterus, breast, prostate, and adipose tissue. In these peripheral locations, 17β-HSD may play a role in regulating the levels of active androgens and estrogens, by utilizing either their oxidative or reductive functions. The 17β-HSDs are not expressed in the adrenals. The tissue-specific isozymes have differing specificity for either the oxidative or the reductive reaction, based on their affinity for specific cofactors and substrates.[269] The testicular isozyme preferentially utilizes NADPH as its cofactor in the reduction of androstendione to testosterone.[270]

Deficiency of this enzyme is the most common defect of androgen production, due to impaired testicular conversion of androstenedione to testosterone; adrenal function is unaffected. 17β-HSD deficiency is inherited in an autosomal-recessive fashion and a number of extensive inbred Arab kindreds with numerous affected individuals have been reported. Although 46,XY individuals with deficiency of testicular 17β-HSD3 activity have female (or, less often, mildly to moderately masculinized) external genitalia, their internal genitalia are well masculinized, with development of epididymides, vasa deferentia, and seminal vesicles. This finding may be due to activity of 17β-HSD isozymes other than 17β-HSD3 converting testis-derived androstenedione to testosterone in the proximity of the Wolffian ducts. In contrast, there is insufficient testosterone at the level of the external genital primordia to act as substrate for 5α-reductase conversion to dihydrotestosterone. A striking feature of this disorder is the marked virilization that occurs at puberty. Affected 46,XY individuals develop a male body habitus with abundant body and facial hair, enlargement of the penis and testes to normal adult size, and pigmentation and rugation of the labioscrotal folds. Gynecomastia is variably present. Many affected individuals spontaneously adopt the male gender role, with apparently adequate sexual function, but with infertility. These clinical observations correlate with normalization of peripheral and spermatic vein testosterone levels. Part of this effect appears likely to be related to increased LH secretion and Leydig cell hyperplasia.

### 5α-Reductase

The 5α-reductases are microsomal enzymes that catalyze the 5α-reduction of many C19 and C21 steroids, utilizing NADPH as a cofactor.[271-273] There are two isozymes of 5α-reductase encoded by separate genes, 5-reductase 1 by the *SRD5A1* gene at 5p15, and 5α-reductase 2, encoded by the *SRD5A2* gene located at 2p23.[274] In the context of sexual differentiation, the most important of these enzymes is 5α-reductase 2 (II), which mediates the conversion of testosterone to dihydrotestosterone (DHT) in androgenic target tissues. This is an essential step in normal male fetal sex differentiation, since external genital masculinization is dependent on adequate local concentrations of the most potent androgen, DHT. The genes encoding the enzymes are structurally similar, with 5 coding exons each. The two enzymes share approximately 50% amino acid identity; the 5α-reductase 2 isozyme is a 254–amino acid protein.[275]

The 5α-reductase isozymes have differential expression patterns.[271,274,276] The type 1 isozyme is not detectable in the fetus, but is transiently expressed in newborn scalp and skin and postpubertal skin and is permanently expressed in the liver. The type 2 isozyme is expressed in the liver and in androgen target tissues, including the external genitalia, accessory sex organs, and prostate. It is expressed in the primordia of the prostate and external genitalia before their differentiation, but is not expressed in the embryonic Wolffian ducts until after their differentiation, supporting the contention that testosterone rather than DHT is the relevant androgen in this process.[271,276] The expression of the enzyme is upregulated by androgens, as demonstrated by the marked increase in *Srd5a2* mRNA level in the prostate of castrate animals after testosterone administration. Expression appears to be regulated in the opposite fashion in the liver.

Deficiency of the enzyme 5α-reductase 2 results in a form of male pseudohermaphroditism previously referred to as *pseudovaginal perineoscrotal hypospadias*, now called *5α-reductase deficiency*. The condition is inherited in an autosomal-recessive fashion, and there is a high frequency of consanguinity within affected kindreds that cluster in inbred populations in the Dominican Republic, Pakistan, Lebanon, and New Guinea. The genital phenotype varies widely between and even within affected kindreds, the most consistent findings being underdevelopment of the penis and prostate. As seen with

17α-hydroxylase deficiency, one of the most intriguing and well-documented features of this disorder is the striking virilization, including increased muscularity and deepening of the voice, that occurs at puberty in many affected individuals. In addition, the testes often enlarge and descend and Leydig cell hyperplasia is noted.

### Androgen Receptor

The androgen receptor (AR) is a ligand-activated nuclear transcription factor that mediates the effects of androgens in induction of target gene transcription in androgen-dependent tissues.[277,278] The eight-exon 75 to 90-kb AR gene is localized to the q11-12 region of the human X chromosome.[279] The encoded 110-kilodalton AR protein is comprised of three major functional domains: amino-terminal (transcription-regulating), DNA-binding (zinc finger), and steroid-binding. This protein plays a key role in mediating androgenic effects on external genital development during normal male sex differentiation, as evidenced by mutations in the AR gene in humans and rodents, which result in varying degrees of defective masculinization.[277,278,280]

Binding of androgen to AR activates the receptor to assume a state in which it is capable of binding DNA. In this state, the receptor/ligand complex binds as a homodimer to induce transcription of target genes by interaction with androgen response element (ARE) DNA sequences in their promoter regions. The polyglutamine repeat in the AR amino terminus is important for transactivation function of the receptor and, consequently, for many androgen-dependent processes. Numerous cofactors have been identified that either enhance or repress transcriptional regulation by AR.[281,282] Although the exact targets of the AR in genital development are largely unknown, one gene identified as being AR regulated is that encoding the AMH receptor (AMH-R). Thus, in addition to their pivotal role in inducing masculinization of the male fetus, androgens/AR appear to be indirectly involved in the process of "defeminization" by enhancing transcription of the AMH-R, the factor primarily responsible for Müllerian duct regression.

The AR is expressed in a wide array of genital and nongenital tissues, reflecting its role as a ubiquitous transcription factor. In external genital tissues, testosterone is converted by steroid 5α-reductase 2 to DHT, which has greater affinity for the AR. Nevertheless, the same molecular events occur following interaction of either testosterone or DHT with AR. The female fetus bears the same AR as the male, thus, it is primarily the available concentration of androgens that is the major determinant of genital morphogenesis, since in the absence of bound androgen the AR is, functionally quiescent.

Absence or defective function of the AR results in resistance or insensitivity to the effects of androgens (the heterogeneous androgen insensitivity syndromes [AIS], previously referred to as testicular feminization), which is believed to comprise the single most common identifiable cause of male pseudohermaphroditism. Affected individuals display variable degrees of reduced masculinization: In the complete form of AIS, not only is the phenotype unequivocally female, the labia minora and majora and clitoris may also, in fact, be underdeveloped, suggesting a role for a mild degree of androgen effect in normal female external genital development. Depending on the severity of the androgen resistance, varying degrees of virilization and/or feminization occur at puberty. The complete form of AIS has a prevalence of approximately 1:20,000 46,XY births. The prevalence of the partial forms of AIS is unknown. Numerous mutations of the AR gene causing complete or partial androgen insensitivity have been reported, affecting the various functional regions of the protein.[277,278,283]

### Antimüllerian Hormone

Antimüllerian hormone (AMH) or Müllerian-inhibiting substance (MIS) is a member of the transforming growth factor beta (TGF-β) family of growth factors that also includes activin and inhibin and an ancestral group called the decapentaplegic/bone morphogenetic proteins. This product of testicular Sertoli cells mediates regression of the Müllerian duct structures during normal male embryogenesis. The five-exon 2.75-kb AMH gene is located on human chromosome 19p13.3-13.2 and encodes a 560–amino acid glycoprotein that forms a 140-kilodalton homodimer.[39,40,284,285]

After SRY, AMH is the first molecular marker specific for testis (Sertoli cell) differentiation. Amh expression in developing mouse testis begins about 2 days later than that of Sry, at about E13.5. Initially believed to be regulated by SRY, it was subsequently determined that the key SOX factor in AMH regulation is actually another Sertoli cell product, SOX9.[133] It has been suggested that AMH transcription is initiated by SOX9 and subsequently upregulated by SF1 binding to the promoter and interacting with SOX9, WT1, and GATA4 (Fig. 142-9).[39,40,133] DMRT1 may also play a role in regulation of AMH transcription. In postnatal life, androgens, acting via the AR, cause marked repression of AMH secretion. There is also evidence for regulation of AMH by gonadotropins and by germ cells.[39,40,286]

The primary effect of AMH is the induction of regression of Müllerian ducts during a short window of male sex differentiation (weeks 9–11 of human gestation). AMH functions in a paracrine fashion, with hormone secretion from one testis mediating only the regression of the ipsilateral Müllerian duct. The events of Müllerian regression are remarkably well coordinated in a spatiotemporal manner by the interaction of AMH with two membrane-bound serine/threonine kinase receptors, the type 2 and type 1 AMH receptors, that act via a signaling pathway involving Smad proteins (named for their homology with "Sma" in C. elegans and "mothers against decapentaplegic" [mad] in drosophila). Details of events downstream of AMH binding to AMH-R2 are provided in the following section.

AMH is produced by Sertoli cells, not only during the period of sex differentiation, but also in late gestation, after birth, and even, albeit at a much reduced rate, in adulthood, suggesting that AMH may have physiologic roles in the male other than its control of Müllerian duct regression. After puberty, AMH production is downregulated by androgens (this feature is absent in individuals with androgen insensitivity). AMH is not expressed prenatally in the ovary, but low amounts are released into the follicular fluid by mature granulosa cells.

As expected from the known function of this protein, male mice with homozygous deletion of Amh had normal male reproductive tracts, but also had uteri and oviducts that obstructed their male sex ducts, rendering them infertile despite production of normal sperm[287] and Leydig cell hyperplasia. In contrast, mice with mutations in the Amh promoter that affect the regulation of Amh transcription had variable phenotypes. Mutation at the Sf1 binding site was associated with reduced Amh expression, but expression that was nevertheless adequate to induce Müllerian regression. Strinkingly, male mice homozygous for a mutant Sox9 binding site did not initiate Amh transcription, resulting in complete retention of Müllerian ducts.

Female mice overexpressing human AMH had no uteri or fallopian tubes and blind-ending vaginas.[288] The ovaries were devoid of germ cells and underwent reorganization into seminiferous tubule-like structures after birth. Males were also abnormal, with undervirilized external genitalia and impaired Wolffian duct development associated with undescended testes notable for Leydig cell hypoplasia. These changes were due to effects of excess Amh on Leydig cell development and inhibition of steroidogenesis and, in conjuction with the finding of Leydig cell hyperplasia in Amh-null mice, implicate Amh as a paracrine regulator of Leydig cell development.

Naturally occurring human AMH mutations mirror those induced in mice, resulting in retention and development of Müllerian structures in otherwise normally masculinized

## Müllerian Duct

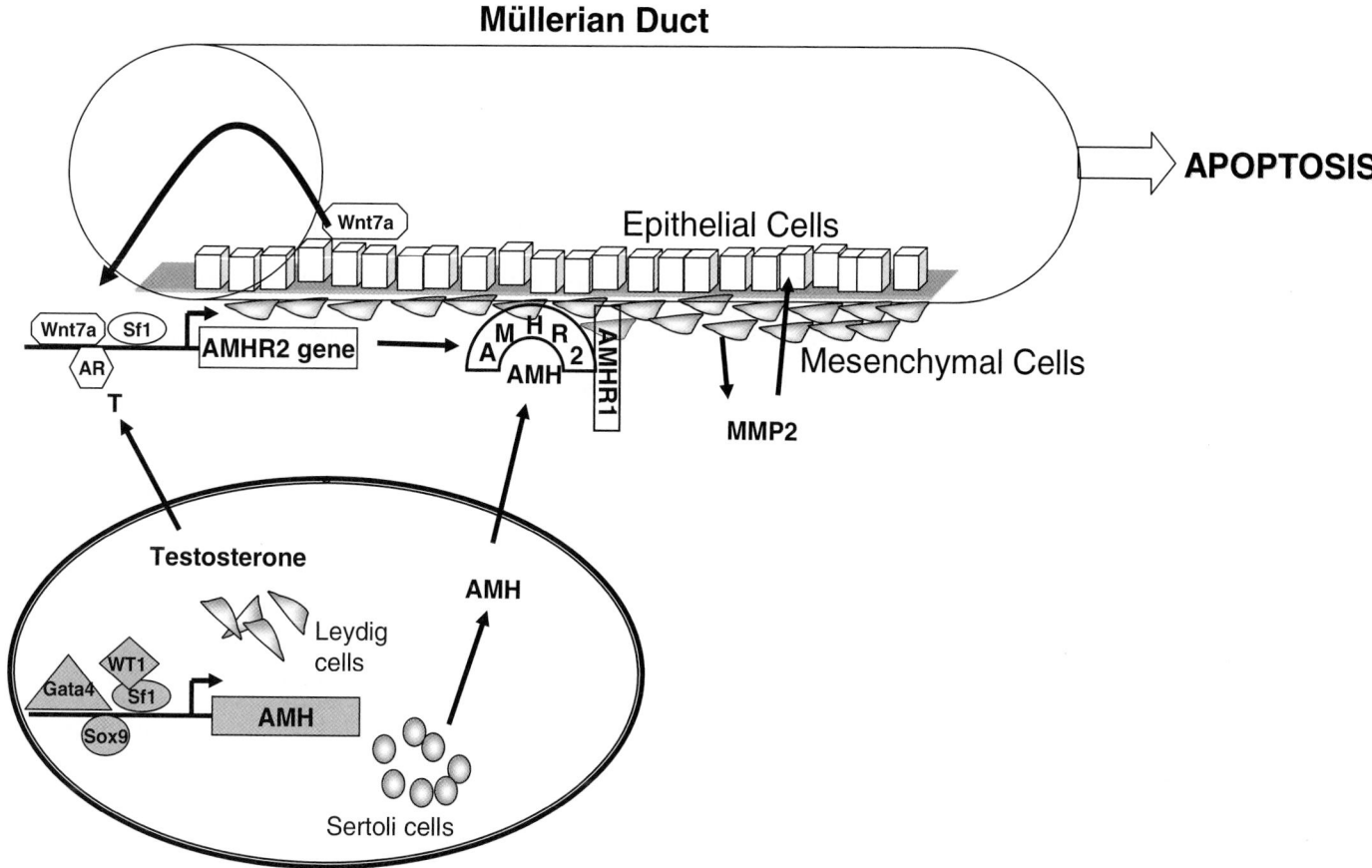

## Fetal Testis

**Figure 142-9** Interactions between antimüllerian hormone (AMH), its receptor (AMH-R 1 and 2), and other transcription factors in induction of Müllerian regression during male embryogenesis. Within the fetal testis, a synergistic combination of transcription factors including Wt1, Sf1, Sox9, and Gata4 stimulates Sertoli cell production of Amh. Meanwhile, Leydig cells produce testosterone, under the stimulatory influence of Sf1 and other factors. The primitive Müllerian ducts comprise epithelial and mesenchymal elements that contribute to their structure and function. Epithelial cells secrete Wnt7a, an extracellular signaling molecule. Wnt7a interacts with SF1 and the androgen receptor (AR), activated by testosterone secreted by Leydig cells, to stimulate transcription of the AMH-R gene and receptor expression by the mesenchymal cells surrounding the duct. Binding of Sertoli cell–derived AMH to the AMH-R stimulates apoptosis of the Müllerian epithelium, leading to obliteration of the duct lumen progressing in a craniocaudal direction down the duct and mediated by a paracrine "death factor" that may be a product of the activated AMH-R. This process occurs during weeks 9 through 11 of male gestation. MMP2, matrix metalloproteinase 2.

46,XY individuals—*the persistent Müllerian duct syndrome type 1.*[39,40,289]

### Antimüllerian Hormone Receptors, Type I and II

In the Müllerian mesenchyme, AMH acts by binding to the type II AMH receptor (AMH-R2), a transmembrane serine/threonine kinase, which in turn phosphorylates a type I receptor. The active complex comprises a tetraheteromer of two molecules each of the type II and type I receptor. The type II receptor is a member of the TGF-β family, but, unlike other family members, its expression is restricted to the gonads and reproductive tracts.[285] The 11-exon 8-kb gene encoding human AMH-R2 is located at 12q13. The 573–amino acids protein comprises an extracellular domain, encoded by exons 1–3, a short transmembrane domain encoded by exon 4, and an intracellular domain responsible for the serine/threonine kinase enzymatic activity, encoded by exons 5–11. AMH-R2 is expressed in mesenchymal cells adjacent to the Müllerian duct epithelium during embryogenesis, in keeping with the fact that the effects of AMH occur via changes in the mesenchyme surrounding the Müllerian ducts, which, in turn, induces apoptosis of the Müllerian epithelium and duct regression.

Binding of AMH to the type II receptor and subsequent phosphorylation of the type I receptor initiates an intracellular signal cascade that leads to target gene activation.[285] On the basis of studies in transgenic mice, candidates for the role of the specific type I receptor with which the type II receptor interacts include activin receptor-like kinase 2 (ALK2) and bone morphogenetic protein receptor 1a (Bmpr1a), also known as ALK3.[290] Strong evidence for Bmpr1a as the type I receptor through which AMH-R2 signals was provided by conditional knockout of *Bmpr1a* in mice, which had retention and development of Müllerian ducts. Unlike the type II receptors, type I receptors are widely expressed in many tissues and likely used by other members of the TGF-β family.[285] It is the interaction between the type II and type I receptors that mediates the specific action of AMH in reproductive tissues. The activated complex of type II and type I receptors initiates a signaling pathway that utilizes a number of Smad molecules, which, after phosphorylation by the type 1 enzyme enter the nucleus to activate target genes.

The action of AMH via its receptors causes regression of the cranial part of the Müllerian duct while the duct continues to grow caudally. This pattern of regression is associated with a cranial-to-caudal gradient of expression of AMH-R2 protein, followed by a wave of apoptosis spreading along the Müllerian duct as it progresses caudally.[291] Induction of this signaling pathway in the Müllerian mesenchymal cells results in apoptosis in the adjacent epithelial cells. Expression of the type 2 receptor within perimüllerian mesenchymal cells is followed by accumulation of β-catenin, an adherens junction protein (a factor that mediates cell-cell adhesion). Müllerian epithelial apoptosis seems to be mediated, at least in part, by an extracellular proteinase, matrix metalloproteinase 2 (MMP2), a downstream target of AMH/AMH-R2 signaling that functions as a paracrine "death factor."[292] Inhibition of MMP2 activity in vitro can prevent AMH-induced duct regression, so this enzyme does appear to be a key player in the process of eliminating the primitive female reproductive tract in males by inducing degradation of the extracellular matrix.

*AMH-R2* expression can be detected in fetal Sertoli cells, in fetal and adult granulosa cells, and in Müllerian duct tissue at the time the duct is undergoing regression.[293] *AMH-R2* expression has also been observed in Leydig cells, and there is evidence that AMH action on Leydig cells causes downregulation of testosterone production. Like AMH itself, the receptor is also expressed postpubertally. Expression of both ligand and receptor in the same cells suggests an autocrine action. *AMH-R2* expression is stimulated by SF1 (which also regulates expression of *AMH* itself) and by the signaling molecule Wnt7a.[133,162] The receptor may also be regulated by its ligand, which might explain the fact that expression of the receptor in female Müllerian mesenchyme does not result in duct regression, since ligand is absent in females; expression may also be regulated in part by the androgen receptor.

Male mice with homozygous deletion of *Amh-r2* were a phenocopy of those with *Amh* deletion: their internal reproductive tracts comprised a complete set of male and female duct structures.[294] The phenotype of *Amh/Amh-r2* double-knockout mutant males was indistinguishable from that of either single mutant. Similarly, the phenotype of 46,XY individuals with mutations in the human *AMH-R2* gene is identical to those with mutations in the gene encoding the hormone itself,[289] so the condition is termed *persistent Müllerian duct syndrome type 2*.

### Wnt7a

Studies in mice have demonstrated a role for Wnt7a, another member of the WNT glycoprotein growth factor/signaling molecule family whose members are involved in regulation of cell fate and patterning, in the process of Müllerian duct regression.[162] These secreted proteins bind to the extracellular domain of Frizzled receptors, members of the seven-transmembrane family, to mediate signal transduction.[88] *Wnt7a* is expressed in mice of both sexes, but appears to have differing roles in male versus female development. *Wnt7a* is expressed along the length of the Müllerian epithelium from embryonic day 12.5 to 14.5, while *Amhr2* is expressed in the mesenchymal cells surrounding the Müllerian ducts at day 14.5. *Wnt7a* expression declines following Müllerian duct regression in the male. It is hypothesized that the Wnt7a signal from the epithelial cells is involved in regulation of *Amhr2* gene expression in the adjacent mesenchyme (see Fig. 142-9).

Male mice with homozygous deficiency of *Wnt7a* have retained Müllerian ducts and do not express *Amhr2* in the mesenchyme of the ducts.[162] Thus, Wnt7a deficiency results in failure of *Amhr2* expression and, therefore, failure of Müllerian duct regression. In contrast, female *Wnt7a* deficient mice have defective, though not absent, development of the oviducts and uterus (described later).

The human gene homologous to mouse *Wnt7a* is localized to 3p35 and encodes a 349–amino acid protein.[160] Human *WNT7a* is expressed in placenta, kidney, testis, uterus, fetal lung, and fetal and adult brain. The role of WNT7a in human development is unknown and no human mutations have been reported.

### EMBRYOLOGY OF FEMALE SEX DIFFERENTIATION

In the absence of testicular secretions, as in the normal 46,XX fetus, the inverse set of genital tract developmental processes occurs.[215,216] Without local androgen action, the Wolffian ducts regress. Similarly, in the absence of AMH, the Müllerian ducts are permitted to develop. Their upper portions form the fallopian tubes; the lower sections fuse and differentiate as the uterus and upper part of the vagina. The lower portion of the vagina derives from the urogenital sinus (the ventral part of the embryonic mammalian cloaca formed by the growth of a fold dividing the cloaca where the gut and allantois meet), which remains patent when not exposed to androgen (see Fig. 142-2).

External genital development in the normal female fetus (or androgen-deficient or -resistant male) is a much less dramatic process than male development, since the changes that must occur to complete development from the starting point of the genital primordia are more limited and subtle. The genital tubercle elongates only slightly to form the clitoris (see Fig. 142-3) and the urogenital sinus remains open. The vesico-vaginal septum (a fold of tissue that develops in the female to separate the posterior wall of the bladder from the anterior wall of the vagina) forms, so that the urethra opens anteriorly and the vagina posteriorly.[3,157,216] The vestibule of the urogenital sinus is bordered laterally by the urethral folds, which do not fuse and instead develop as the labia minora. Further laterally, the labioscrotal swellings enlarge somewhat but also remain unfused, forming the labia majora. There is minor fusion posteriorly, forming the posterior commissure, and anteriorly, producing the mons pubis. These events occur from about week 7 to week 12 of human gestation. The timetable of gonadal and genital differentiation in both sexes is shown in Figure 142-4A.

There are far fewer known causes of virilization of a female fetus than there are of undermasculinization of a male fetus. Individuals with female (46,XX) pseudohermaphroditism have normally developed ovaries, but varying degrees of defeminization and masculinization of internal and external genitalia. Essentially, disorders of female sex differentiation represent the converse of male pseudohermaphroditism, resulting, in general, from prenatal exposure to excessive androgen concentrations. Maternal androgen excess caused by androgen-secreting tumors or drugs with androgenic activity, such as progestational agents that were previously used to sustain threatened pregnancies or anabolic steroids taken for medical or other purposes, can also result in masculinization of the female fetus.

### GENETICS OF FEMALE SEX DIFFERENTIATION

Little is known about factors involved in female development downstream of the ovary. Normal internal genital (reproductive duct) development requires persistence and differentiation of the Müllerian ducts into the fallopian tubes, uterus, and upper vagina, and regression of the Wolffian ducts. Thus, AMH and testosterone action must be absent. Sertoli cells do not develop and AMH is not produced during fetal life, thus Müllerian structures are maintained and subsequently differentiate under the influence of Wnt7a and other factors; meanwhile, in the absence of Leydig cells (which do not develop due to the repressive action of Wnt4), the fetal gonad does not produce sex steroids, therefore, the Wolffian ducts regress and external genitalia develop as female. The finding of familial disorders of reproductive tract development (discussion follows) implies that genetic factors must, indeed, play a role in either stimulating Müllerian development or inhibiting its repression. Although there is much less known about the genetic basis of female sex differentiation than of male, some information from murine and human studies of *Wnt* and *Hox* genes has emerged.

### Wnt Family

The finding that *Wnt4*-deficient mice of both sexes completely lack Müllerian ducts establishes *Wnt4* expression as a crucial factor for development of the primordial Müllerian ducts.[92] Subsequently, other members of the Wnt family such as Wnt5a and Wnt7a were found to be involved in female reproductive development and function.[90] Whereas Wnt4 is required for initiation of Müllerian duct formation, Wnt7a appears to regulate its subsequent fate in both sexes. During normal embryogenesis, Wnt4 is expressed in the mesenchyme of the future uterine horn, while Wnt7a is expressed throughout the epithelium of the Müllerian duct. Wnt4-deficient females have masculinization of the gonads and lack Müllerian ducts, due to the failure of their early development rather than abnormal regression; Wnt7a-deficient female mice are sterile due to abnormal development of the oviduct and uterus, possibly reflecting loss of Wnt7a control of normal epithelial-mesenchymal signaling via members of the Hox family.[161,162] Wnt5a is expressed in the external genital primordia of both sexes and Wnt5a mutant mice lack external genitalia.

The effects of human WNT4 mutation are similar to those seen in female null mice. A 46,XX individual with a loss-of-function WNT4 mutation had absent vagina and uterus and ectopically located ovaries.[95] She also had slightly increased ovarian androgen secretion, but this was presumably not present prenatally, as she had no evidence of genital virilization, and had a normal female phenotype apart from a small vaginal introitus.

### Hoxa13 and Related Genes

Hoxa13 is a member of the homeobox family of genes that encode the developmentally important homeodomain proteins. Hoxa13 and related genes play important roles in the morphogenesis of the terminal part of the gut and urogenital tract and seem to be involved in Müllerian development. Hoxa13 is specifically discussed because, in addition to abnormalities in Hoxa13-deficient mice, mutations affecting uterine development have been reported in humans.[295]

The human gene encoding HOXA13 is located within a cluster of at least eight homeobox genes on chromosome 7, at 7p15-p14.2. Within the protein, certain residues and amino acid motifs are strongly conserved in fish, amphibian, reptile, chicken, and marsupial and placental mammals.

Hoxa13 is expressed early in the tissues of the developing hindgut in a manner that suggests a fundamental role for epithelial-specific expression of the factor in the epithelial-mesenchymal interaction necessary for tail growth and posterior gut/genitourinary patterning. In the development of the embryonic mouse Müllerian tract, Hoxa9, Hoxa10, Hoxa11, and Hoxa13 are all expressed along the length of the paramesonephric duct.[296] Later in development, expression of Hoxa13, as detected by whole-mount in situ hybridization, is localized to the cervical and vaginal tissues.[297] After birth, a spatial Hox axis is established, corresponding to the postnatal differentiation of this organ system in the mouse: Hoxa9 is expressed in the fallopian tubes, Hoxa10 in the uterus, Hoxa11 in the uterus and uterine cervix, and Hoxa13 in the upper vagina. In the developing mouse genital tubercle, Hoxa13 is essential for normal expression of fibroblast growth factor 8 (Fgf8) and Bmp7 in the urethral plate epithelium. Administration of diethylstilbestrol to mice in utero produces changes in the expression pattern of several Hox genes involved in patterning of the reproductive tract.

Mice with the semidominant mutation hypodactyly have a 50-bp deletion in the first exon of the Hoxa13 gene. Hoxa13-deficient adult female mice have profound hypoplasia of the cervix and vaginal cavity.[297] Hoxa13 null fetuses show agenesis of the caudal portion of the Müllerian ducts, lack of development of the presumptive urinary bladder, and have premature stenosis of the umbilical arteries, which could account for the lethality of this mutation at mid-gestational stages. Female mice with compound mutations of Hoxa13 and

a related gene, Hoxd13, have malpositioning of the vaginal, urethral, and anal openings and incorrect separation of the vagina from the urogenital sinus; double null (Hoxa13[−/−]/Hoxd13[−/−]) fetuses display even more severe defects, with no separation of the terminal (cloacal) hindgut cavity into a urogenital sinus and presumptive rectum, and no development of the genital bud.[298] The findings in these compound mutants demonstrate that both genes act, in a partly redundant manner, during early gut and urogenital morphogenesis.

Mutations in human HOXA13 produce the hand-foot-genital syndrome (also known as hand-foot-uterine syndrome) or the related Guttmacher syndrome, dominantly inherited conditions characterized by Müllerian duct fusion defects of varying degree in females (and hypospadias in males).[295,299]

### CONCLUSIONS

Since sexual dimorphism is imperative for the survival of all mammalian species, sex determination and differentiation involve great complexity and exquisite coordination of genes and transcription factors. The foundation of gonadal development requires that cells of the adrenogenital primordium differentiate to become the primordial gonad. Factors now known to play a role in this very early stage include SF1 and WT1, mutations of which are associated with complete absence of gonadal tissue. Additional factors, such as the homeodomain proteins LIM1 and EMX2, appear to contribute to this phase of gonadal development, and others will undoubtedly be described. The Steel/c-Kit system mediates germ cell colonization of the primordial gonad, and WNT4 is required for early development of the Müllerian duct system in both sexes. Once the basic ingredients of the reproductive systems have developed—bipotential gonads, two sets of internal ducts, and sexually indifferent external genitalia—the developmental processes become more specific. In this second phase of development, the sexually dimorphic phase, alternate, perhaps antagonistic, sets of genes must be either activated or repressed to mediate the correct pattern of cellular development. Thus, the factors involved in sex-specific gonadal development seem to fall into one of two camps. In the "pro-male" corner are SRY, SF1, SOX9, and perhaps DAX1. In the "pro-female" corner are WNT4, follistatin, and FOXL2. The following hypotheticals may serve as summary models for understanding the divergent pathways that operate after development of the primordial gonad. Under normal circumstances in a 46,XY embryo, SRY and SF1 stimulate expression of SOX9, which results in differentiation of the Sertoli cell, the cell that controls, directs, and organizes other cellular elements of the gonad (presumably via paracrine interactions) to form the seminiferous tubules. In the 46,XX embryo, WNT4 impedes SF1 from stimulating SOX9, blocking differentiation of supporting cells to Sertoli cells and interstitial cells as Leydig cells. Thus, in the absence of Sertoli or Leydig cells, an ovary develops. Differentiation events thereafter depend on fetal gonadal activity. The testis actively secretes two hormones that mediate the defeminization and masculinization of the internal and external genitalia. In the female, ovarian steroidogenesis is repressed, and adrenal androgens are "detoxified" by the placenta, protecting the fetus from potential virilization. Notably, the long-held concept of female development as a passive process, resulting simply from the absence of maleness, seems to have been replaced by a new paradigm that involves transcription factors and signaling molecules in a process parallel to male development. In both male and female sex determination and differentiation, much remains to be learned regarding the exact sequence of events and interactions that drive these fundamental processes.

## REFERENCES

1. Capel B: The battle of the sexes. Mech Dev 92:89–103, 2000.
2. Yao HH, Tilmann C, Zhao GQ, Capel B: The battle of the sexes: Opposing pathways in sex determination. Novartis Found Symp 244:187–198, discussion 198–206, 253–187, 2002.
3. Larsen W: Development of the urogenital system. In Sherman LS, Potter SS, Scott WJ (eds): Human Embryology, 3d ed. New York, Churchill Livingstone, 2001.
4. Sadler T: Urogenital system. In Langman's Medical Embryology, 7th ed. Baltimore, Williams and Wilkins, 1995.
5. Morohashi K: The ontogenesis of the steroidogenic tissues. Genes Cells 2:95–106, 1997.
6. Hobert O, Westphal H: Functions of LIM-homeobox genes. Trends Genet 16:75–83, 2000.
7. Cheah SS, Kwan KM, Behringer RR: Requirement of LIM domains for LIM1 function in mouse head development. Genesis 27:12–21, 2000.
8. Shawlot W, Behringer RR: Requirement for Lim1 in head-organizer function. Nature 374:425–430, 1995.
9. Dong WF, Heng HH, Lowsky R, et al: Cloning, expression, and chromosomal localization to 11p12-13 of a human LIM/HOMEOBOX gene, hLim-1. DNA Cell Biol 16:671–678, 1997.
10. National Center for Biotechnology Information: Online Mendelian Inheritance in Man.
11. Barnes JD, Crosby JL, Jones CM, et al: Embryonic expression of Lim-1, the mouse homolog of Xenopus Xlim-1, suggests a role in lateral mesoderm differentiation and neurogenesis. Dev Biol 161:168–178, 1994.
12. Karavanov AA, Saint-Jeannet JP, Karavanova I, et al: The LIM homeodomain protein Lim-1 is widely expressed in neural, neural crest and mesoderm derivatives in vertebrate development. Int J Dev Biol 40:453–461, 1996.
13. Miyamoto N, Yoshida M, Kuratani S, et al: Defects of urogenital development in mice lacking Emx2. Development 124:1653–1664, 1997.
14. Kastury K, Druck T, Huebner K, et al: Chromosome locations of human EMX and OTX genes. Genomics 22:41–45, 1994.
15. Noonan FC, Mutch DG, Ann Mallon M, Goodfellow PJ: Characterization of the homeodomain gene EMX2: Sequence conservation, expression analysis, and a search for mutations in endometrial cancers. Genomics 76:37–44, 2001.
16. Noonan FC, Goodfellow PJ, Staloch LJ, et al: Antisense transcripts at the EMX2 locus in human and mouse. Genomics 81:58–66, 2003.
17. Pellegrini M, Pantano S, Lucchini F, et al: Emx2 developmental expression in the primordia of the reproductive and excretory systems. Anat Embryol (Berl) 196:427–433, 1997.
18. Troy PJ, Daftary GS, Bagot CN, Taylor HS: Transcriptional repression of peri-implantation EMX2 expression in mammalian reproduction by HOXA10. Mol Cell Biol 23:1–13, 2003.
19. Faiella A, Brunelli S, Granata T, et al: A number of schizencephaly patients including 2 brothers are heterozygous for germline mutations in the homeobox gene EMX2. Eur J Hum Genet 5:186–190, 1997.
20. Birk OS, Casiano DE, Wassif CA, et al: The LIM homeobox gene Lhx9 is essential for mouse gonad formation. Nature 403:909–913, 2000.
21. Failli V, Rogard M, Mattei MG, et al: Lhx9 and Lhx9alpha LIM-homeodomain factors: Genomic structure, expression patterns, chromosomal localization, and phylogenetic analysis. Genomics 64:307–317, 2000.
22. Ottolenghi C, Moreira-Filho C, Mendonca BB, et al: Absence of mutations involving the LIM homeobox domain gene LHX9 in 46,XY gonadal agenesis and dysgenesis. J Clin Endocrinol Metab 86:2465–2469, 2001.
23. Mazaud S, Oreal E, Guigon CJ, et al: Lhx9 expression during gonadal morphogenesis as related to the state of cell differentiation. Gene Expr Patterns 2:373–377, 2002.
24. Wilhelm D, Englert C: The Wilms' tumor suppressor WT1 regulates early gonad development by activation of SF1. Genes Dev 16:1839–1851, 2002.
25. Ingraham HA, Lala DS, Ikeda Y, et al: The nuclear receptor steroidogenic factor 1 acts at multiple levels of the reproductive axis. Genes Dev 8:2302–2312, 1994.
26. Luo X, Ikeda Y, Parker KL: A cell-specific nuclear receptor is essential for adrenal and gonadal development and sexual differentiation. Cell 77:481–490, 1994.
27. Parker KL, Schimmer BP: Steroidogenic factor 1: A key determinant of endocrine development and function. Endocr Rev 18:361–377, 1997.
28. Achermann JC, Ozisik G, Ito M, et al: Gonadal determination and adrenal development are regulated by the orphan nuclear receptor steroidogenic factor-1, in a dose-dependent manner. J Clin Endocrinol Metab 87:1829–1833, 2002.
29. Oba K, Yanase T, Nomura M, et al: Structural characterization of human Ad4bp (SF1) gene. Biochem Biophys Res Commun 226:261–267, 1996.
30. Lala DS, Rice DA, Parker KL: Steroidogenic factor I, a key regulator of steroidogenic enzyme expression, is the mouse homolog of fushi tarazu-factor I. Mol Endocrinol 6:1249–1258, 1992.
31. Achermann JC, Meeks JJ, Jameson JL: Phenotypic spectrum of mutations in DAX-1 and SF1. Mol Cell Endocrinol 185:17–25, 2001.
32. Shen WH, Moore CC, Ikeda Y, et al: Nuclear receptor steroidogenic factor 1 regulates the mullerian inhibiting substance gene: A link to the sex determination cascade. Cell 77:651–661, 1994.
33. Cammas FM, Pullinger GD, Barker S, Clark AJ: The mouse adrenocorticotropin receptor gene: Cloning and characterization of its promoter and evidence for a role for the orphan nuclear receptor steroidogenic factor 1. Mol Endocrinol 11:867–876, 1997.
34. Barbara PS, Moniot B, Poulat F, et al: Steroidogenic factor-1 regulates transcription of the human anti-mullerian hormone receptor. J Biol Chem 273:29654–29660, 1998.
35. Naville D, Penhoat A, Marchal R, et al: SF1 and the transcriptional regulation of the human ACTH receptor gene. Endocr Res 24:391–395, 1998.
36. Sandhoff TW, Hales DB, Hales KH, McLean MP: Transcriptional regulation of the rat steroidogenic acute regulatory protein gene by steroidogenic factor 1. Endocrinology 139:4820–4831, 1998.
37. Yu RN, Ito M, Jameson JL: The murine Dax-1 promoter is stimulated by SF1 (steroidogenic factor-1) and inhibited by COUP-TF (chicken ovalbumin upstream promoter-transcription factor) via a composite nuclear receptor-regulatory element. Mol Endocrinol 12:1010–1022, 1998.
38. Giuili G, Shen WH, Ingraham HA: The nuclear receptor SF1 mediates sexually dimorphic expression of Mullerian inhibiting substance, in vivo. Development 124:1799–1807, 1997.
39. Josso N, di Clemente N, Gouedard L: Anti-Mullerian hormone and its receptors. Mol Cell Endocrinol 179:25–32, 2001.
40. Teixeira J, Maheswaran S, Donahoe PK: Mullerian inhibiting substance: An instructive developmental hormone with diagnostic and possible therapeutic applications. Endocr Rev 22:657–674, 2001.
41. Scharnhorst V, van der Eb AJ, Jochemsen AG: WT1 proteins: Functions in growth and differentiation. Gene 273:141–161, 2001.
42. Ikeda Y, Shen WH, Ingraham HA, Parker KL: Developmental expression of mouse steroidogenic factor-1, an essential regulator of the steroid hydroxylases. Mol Endocrinol 8:654–662, 1994.
43. Luo X, Ikeda Y, Parker KL: The cell-specific nuclear receptor steroidogenic factor 1 plays multiple roles in reproductive function. Philos Trans R Soc Lond B Biol Sci 350:279–283, 1995.
44. Crawford PA, Dorn C, Sadovsky Y, Milbrandt J: Nuclear receptor DAX-1 recruits nuclear receptor corepressor N-CoR to steroidogenic factor 1. Mol Cell Biol 18:2949–2956, 1998.
45. Nachtigal MW, Hirokawa Y, Enyeart-VanHouten DL, et al: Wilms' tumor 1 and Dax-1 modulate the orphan nuclear receptor SF1 in sex-specific gene expression. Cell 93:445–454, 1998.

46. Asa SL, Bamberger AM, Cao B, et al: The transcription activator steroidogenic factor-1 is preferentially expressed in the human pituitary gonadotroph. J Clin Endocrinol Metab 81:2165–2170, 1996.

47. Harris AN, Mellon PL: The basic helix-loop-helix, leucine zipper transcription factor, USF (upstream stimulatory factor), is a key regulator of SF1 (steroidogenic factor-1) gene expression in pituitary gonadotrope and steroidogenic cells. Mol Endocrinol 12:714–726, 1998.

48. Nomura Y, Yagi H, Onigata K, et al: A sex reversal infant with XX karyotype and complete male external genitalia. Acta Paediatr Jpn 37:706–709, 1995.

49. Haisenleder DJ, Yasin M, Dalkin AC, et al: GnRH regulates steroidogenic factor-1 (SF1) gene expression in the rat pituitary. Endocrinology 137:5719–5722, 1996.

50. Nomura M, Kawabe K, Matsushita S, et al: Adrenocortical and gonadal expression of the mammalian Ftz-F1 gene encoding Ad4BP/SF1 is independent of pituitary control. J Biochem (Tokyo) 124:217–224, 1998.

51. Ramayya MS, Zhou J, Kino T, et al: Steroidogenic factor 1 messenger ribonucleic acid expression in steroidogenic and nonsteroidogenic human tissues: Northern blot and in situ hybridization studies. J Clin Endocrinol Metab 82:1799–1806, 1997.

52. Bamberger AM, Ezzat S, Cao B, et al: Expression of steroidogenic factor-1 (SF1) mRNA and protein in the human placenta. Mol Hum Reprod 2:457–461, 1996.

53. Parker KL, Schimmer BP: The role of nuclear receptors in steroid hormone production. Semin Cancer Biol 5:317–325, 1994.

54. Bland ML, Jamieson CA, Akana SF, et al: Haploinsufficiency of steroidogenic factor-1 in mice disrupts adrenal development leading to an impaired stress response. Proc Natl Acad Sci U S A 97:14488–14493, 2000.

55. Achermann JC, Ito M, Hindmarsh PC, Jameson JL: A mutation in the gene encoding steroidogenic factor-1 causes XY sex reversal and adrenal failure in humans. Nat Genet 22:125–126, 1999.

56. Merke DP, Tajima T, Baron J, Cutler GB Jr: Hypogonadotropic hypogonadism in a female caused by an X-linked recessive mutation in the DAX1 gene. N Engl J Med 340:1248–1252, 1999.

57. Reddy JC, Licht JD: The WT1 Wilms' tumor suppressor gene: How much do we really know? Biochim Biophys Acta 1287:1–28, 1996.

58. Madden SL, Cook DM, Rauscher FJ III: A structure-function analysis of transcriptional repression mediated by the WT1, Wilms' tumor suppressor protein. Oncogene 8:1713–1720, 1993.

59. Rauscher FJ III: Tumor suppressor genes which encode transcriptional repressors: Studies on the EGR and Wilms' tumor

60. Wang ZY, Qiu QQ, Deuel TF: The Wilms' tumor gene product WT1 activates or suppresses transcription through separate functional domains. J Biol Chem 268:9172–9175, 1993.

61. Reddy JC, Morris JC, Wang J, et al: WT1-mediated transcriptional activation is inhibited by dominant negative mutant proteins. J Biol Chem 270:10878–10884, 1995.

62. Moore AW, McInnes L, Kreidberg J, et al: YAC complementation shows a requirement for WT1 in the development of epicardium, adrenal gland and throughout nephrogenesis. Development 126:1845–1857, 1999.

63. Kreidberg JA, Sariola H, Loring JM, et al: WT-1 is required for early kidney development. Cell 74:679–691, 1993.

64. Call KM, Glaser T, Ito CY, et al: Isolation and characterization of a zinc finger polypeptide gene at the human chromosome 11 Wilms' tumor locus. Cell 60:509–520, 1990.

65. Hewitt JA, Kessler PM, Campbell CE, Williams BR: Tissue-specific regulation of the WT1 locus. Med Pediatr Oncol 27:456–461, 1996.

66. Scharnhorst V, Dekker P, van der Eb AJ, Jochemsen AG: Internal translation initiation generates novel WT1 protein isoforms with distinct biological properties. J Biol Chem 274:23456–23462, 1999.

67. Hossain A, Saunders GF: The human sex-determining gene SRY is a direct target of WT1. J Biol Chem 276:16817–16823, 2001.

68. Kim J, Prawitt D, Bardeesy N, et al: The Wilms' tumor suppressor gene (wt1) product regulates Dax-1 gene expression during gonadal differentiation. Mol Cell Biol 19:2289–2299, 1999.

69. Hammes A, Guo JK, Lutsch G, et al: Two splice variants of the Wilms' tumor 1 gene have distinct functions during sex determination and nephron formation. Cell 106:319–329, 2001.

70. Pelletier J, Schalling M, Buckler AJ, et al: Expression of the Wilms' tumor gene WT1 in the murine urogenital system. Genes Dev 5:1345–1356, 1991.

71. Armstrong JF, Pritchard-Jones K, Bickmore WA, et al: The expression of the Wilms' tumour gene, WT1, in the developing mammalian embryo. Mech Dev 40:85–97, 1993.

72. Rackley RR, Flenniken AM, Kuriyan NP, et al: Expression of the Wilms' tumor suppressor gene WT1 during mouse embryogenesis. Cell Growth Differ 4:1023–1031, 1993.

73. Pelletier J, Bruening W, Kashtan CE, et al: Germline mutations in the Wilms' tumor suppressor gene are associated with abnormal urogenital development in Denys-Drash syndrome. Cell 67:437–447, 1991.

74. Lee SB, Haber DA: Wilms' tumor and the WT1 gene. Exp Cell Res 264:74–99, 2001.

75. Molkentin JD: The zinc finger–containing transcription factors

(WT1) gene products. Adv Exp Med Biol 348:23–29, 1993.

GATA-4, -5, and -6: Ubiquitously expressed regulators of tissue-specific gene expression. J Biol Chem 275:38949–38952, 2000.

76. Patient RK, McGhee JD: The GATA family (vertebrates and invertebrates). Curr Opin Genet Dev 12:416–422, 2002.

77. Tevosian SG, Albrecht KH, Crispino JD, et al: Gonadal differentiation, sex determination and normal Sry expression in mice require direct interaction between transcription partners GATA4 and FOG2. Development 129:4627–4634, 2002.

78. Tremblay JJ, Viger RS: A mutated form of steroidogenic factor 1 (SF1 G35E) that causes sex reversal in humans fails to synergize with transcription factor GATA-4. J Biol Chem 278:42637–42642, 2003.

79. Ko LJ, Engel JD: DNA-binding specifics of the GATA transcription factor family. Mol Cell Biol 13:4011–4022, 1993.

80. Huang WY, Cukerman E, Liew CC: Identification of a GATA motif in the cardiac alpha-myosin heavy-chain-encoding gene and isolation of a human GATA-4 cDNA. Gene 155:219–223, 1995.

81. Huang WY, Heng HH, Liew CC: Assignment of the human GATA4 gene to 8p23.1—>p22 using fluorescence in situ hybridization analysis. Cytogenet Cell Genet 72:217–218, 1996.

82. Tremblay JJ, Viger RS: Transcription factor GATA-4 enhances mullerian inhibiting substance gene transcription through a direct interaction with the nuclear receptor SF1. Mol Endocrinol 13:1388–1401, 1999.

83. Robert NM, Tremblay JJ, Viger RS: Friend of GATA (FOG)-1 and FOG-2 differentially repress the GATA-dependent activity of multiple gonadal promoters. Endocrinology 143:3963–3973, 2002.

84. Viger RS, Mertineit C, Trasler JM, Nemer M: Transcription factor GATA-4 is expressed in a sexually dimorphic pattern during mouse gonadal development and is a potent activator of the mullerian inhibiting substance promoter. Development 125:2665–2675, 1998.

85. Ketola I, Pentikainen V, Vaskivuo T, et al: Expression of transcription factor GATA-4 during human testicular development and disease. J Clin Endocrinol Metab 85:3925–3931, 2000.

86. Gecz J, Gaunt SJ, Passage E, et al: Assignment of a polycomb-like chromobox gene (CBX2) to human chromosome 17q25. Genomics 26:130–133, 1995.

87. Katoh-Fukui Y, Tsuchiya R, Shiroishi T, et al: Male-to-female sex reversal in M33 mutant mice. Nature 393:688–692, 1998.

88. Dale TC: Signal transduction by the Wnt family of ligands. Biochem J 329( Pt 2):209–223, 1998.

89. Moon RT, Brown JD, Torres M: WNTs modulate cell fate and behavior during vertebrate development. Trends Genet 13:157–162, 1997.

90. Heikkila M, Peltoketo H, Vainio S: Wnts and the female reproductive system. J Exp Zool 290:616–623, 2001.

91. Stark K, Vainio S, Vassileva G, McMahon AP: Epithelial transformation of metanephric mesenchyme in the developing kidney regulated by Wnt-4. Nature 372:679–683, 1994.

92. Vainio S, Heikkila M, Kispert A, et al: Female development in mammals is regulated by Wnt-4 signalling. Nature 397:405–409, 1999.

93. Jordan BK, Mohammed M, Ching ST, et al: Up-regulation of WNT-4 signaling and dosage-sensitive sex reversal in humans. Am J Hum Genet 68:1102–1109, 2001.

94. Sim EU, Smith A, Szilagi E, et al: Wnt-4 regulation by the Wilms' tumour suppressor gene, WT1. Oncogene 21:2948–2960, 2002.

95. Biason-Lauber A, Konrad D, Navratil F, Schoenle EJ: A WNT4 mutation associated with Mullerian-duct regression and virilization in a 46,XX woman. N Engl J Med 351:792–798, 2004.

96. Suzuki K, Bachiller D, Chen YP, et al: Regulation of outgrowth and apoptosis for the terminal appendage: External genitalia development by concerted actions of BMP signaling [corrected]. Development 130:6209–6220, 2003.

97. Jost A: Problems of fetal endocrinology: The gonadal and hypophyseal hormones. Recent Prog Horm Res 8:379–418, 1953.

98. Cotinot C, Pailhoux E, Jaubert F, Fellous M: Molecular genetics of sex determination. Semin Reprod Med 20:157–168, 2002.

99. Mittwoch U: Phenotypic manifestations during the development of the dominant and default gonads in mammals and birds. J Exp Zool 281:466–471, 1998.

100. Merchant-Larios H, Moreno-Mendoza N: Onset of sex differentiation: Dialog between genes and cells. Arch Med Res 32:553–558, 2001.

101. Tilmann C, Capel B: Cellular and molecular pathways regulating mammalian sex determination. Recent Prog Horm Res 57:1–18, 2002.

102. Meeks JJ, Crawford SE, Russell TA, et al: Dax1 regulates testis cord organization during gonadal differentiation. Development 130:1029–1036, 2003.

103. Parker KL, Schedl A, Schimmer BP: Gene interactions in gonadal development. Annu Rev Physiol 61:417–433, 1999.

104. Lovell-Badge R, Canning C, Sekido R: Sex-determining genes in mice: Building pathways. Novartis Found Symp 244:4–18; discussion 18–22, 35–42, 253–257, 2002.

105. Marshall OJ, Harley VR: Molecular mechanisms of SOX9 action. Mol Genet Metab 71:455–462, 2000.

106. Koopman P, Bullejos M, Bowles J: Regulation of male sexual

development by Sry and Sox9. J Exp Zool 290:463–474, 2001.

107. Clarkson MJ, Harley VR: Sex with two SOX on: SRY and SOX9 in testis development. Trends Endocrinol Metab 13:106–111, 2002.

108. Harley VR: The molecular action of testis-determining factors SRY and SOX9. Novartis Found Symp 244:57–66; discussion 66–57, 79–85, 253–257, 2002.

109. Harley VR, Clarkson MJ, Argentaro A: The molecular action and regulation of the testis-determining factors, SRY (sex-determining region on the Y chromosome) and SOX9 (SRY-related high-mobility group [HMG] box 9). Endocr Rev 24:466–487, 2003.

110. Sinclair AH, Berta P, Palmer MS, et al: A gene from the human sex-determining region encodes a protein with homology to a conserved DNA-binding motif. Nature 346:240–244, 1990.

111. Koopman P, Gubbay J, Vivian N, et al: Male development of chromosomally female mice transgenic for Sry. Nature 351:117–121, 1991.

112. Bergstrom DE, Young M, Albrecht KH, Eicher EM: Related function of mouse SOX3, SOX9, and SRY HMG domains assayed by male sex determination. Genesis 28:111–124, 2000.

113. Harley VR, Jackson DI, Hextall PJ, et al: DNA binding activity of recombinant SRY from normal males and XY females. Science 255:453–456, 1992.

114. Canning CA, Lovell-Badge R: Sry and sex determination: How lazy can it be? Trends Genet 18:111-113, 2002.

115. van de Wetering M, Clevers H: Sequence-specific interaction of the HMG box proteins TCF-1 and SRY occurs within the minor groove of a Watson-Crick double helix. EMBO J 11:3039–3044, 1992.

116. King CY, Weiss MA: The SRY high-mobility-group box recognizes DNA by partial intercalation in the minor groove: A topological mechanism of sequence specificity. Proc Natl Acad Sci U S A 90:11990–11994, 1993.

117. Koopman P, Munsterberg A, Capel B, et al: Expression of a candidate sex-determining gene during mouse testis differentiation. Nature 348:450–452, 1990.

118. Capel B: Sex in the 90s: SRY and the switch to the male pathway. Annu Rev Physiol 60:497–523, 1998.

119. Schmahl J, Eicher EM, Washburn LL, Capel B: Sry induces cell proliferation in the mouse gonad. Development 127:65–73, 2000.

120. Matsuzawa-Watanabe Y, Inoue J, Semba K: Transcriptional activity of testis-determining factor SRY is modulated by the Wilms' tumor 1 gene product, WT1. Oncogene 22:7900–7904, 2003.

121. Lahr G, Maxson SC, Mayer A, et al: Transcription of the Y chromosomal

gene, Sry, in adult mouse brain. Brain Res Mol Brain Res 33:179–182, 1995.

122. Salas-Cortes L, Jaubert F, Bono MR, et al: Expression of the human SRY protein during development in normal male gonadal and sex-reversed tissues. J Exp Zool 290:607–615, 2001.

123. Hawkins JR: Mutational analysis of SRY in XY females. Hum Mutat 2:347–350, 1993.

124. Vidal VP, Chaboissier MC, de Rooij DG, Schedl A: Sox9 induces testis development in XX transgenic mice. Nat Genet 28:216–217, 2001.

125. Tommerup N, Schempp W, Meinecke P, et al: Assignment of an autosomal sex reversal locus (SRA1) and campomelic dysplasia (CMPD1) to 17q24.3-q25.1. Nat Genet 4:170–174, 1993.

126. Foster JW, Dominguez-Steglich MA, Guioli S, et al: Campomelic dysplasia and autosomal sex reversal caused by mutations in an SRY-related gene. Nature 372:525–530, 1994.

127. Sudbeck P, Schmitz ML, Baeuerle PA, Scherer G: Sex reversal by loss of the C-terminal transactivation domain of human SOX9. Nat Genet 13:230–232, 1996.

128. Morais da Silva S, Hacker A, Harley V, et al: Sox9 expression during gonadal development implies a conserved role for the gene in testis differentiation in mammals and birds. Nat Genet 14:62–68, 1996.

129. Kent J, Wheatley SC, Andrews JE, et al: A male-specific role for SOX9 in vertebrate sex determination. Development 122:2813–2822, 1996.

130. Wunderle VM, Critcher R, Hastie N, et al: Deletion of long-range regulatory elements upstream of SOX9 causes campomelic dysplasia. Proc Natl Acad Sci U S A 95:10649–10654, 1998.

131. Kanai Y, Koopman P: Structural and functional characterization of the mouse Sox9 promoter: Implications for campomelic dysplasia. Hum Mol Genet 8:691–696, 1999.

132. Bishop CE, Whitworth DJ, Qin Y, et al: A transgenic insertion upstream of sox9 is associated with dominant XX sex reversal in the mouse. Nat Genet 26:490–494, 2000.

133. De Santa Barbara P, Bonneaud N, Boizet B, et al: Direct interaction of SRY-related protein SOX9 and steroidogenic factor 1 regulates transcription of the human anti-mullerian hormone gene. Mol Cell Biol 18:6653–6665, 1998.

134. Denny P, Swift S, Connor F, Ashworth A: An SRY-related gene expressed during spermatogenesis in the mouse encodes a sequence-specific DNA-binding protein. EMBO J 11:3705–3712, 1992.

135. Mertin S, McDowall SG, Harley VR: The DNA-binding specificity of SOX9 and other SOX proteins. Nucleic Acids Res 27:1359–1364, 1999.

136. Hanley NA, Ball SG: Genes, mice and the internet: Is WT1 the shape of

things to come? Clin Endocrinol (Oxf) 52:399–400, 2000.

137. Wagner T, Wirth J, Meyer J, et al: Autosomal sex reversal and campomelic dysplasia are caused by mutations in and around the SRY-related gene SOX9. Cell 79:1111–1120, 1994.

138. Schafer AJ, Dominguez-Steglich MA, Guioli S, et al: The role of SOX9 in autosomal sex reversal and campomelic dysplasia. Philos Trans R Soc Lond B Biol Sci 350:271–277, discussion 277–278, 1995.

139. Bi W, Huang W, Whitworth DJ, et al: Haploinsufficiency of Sox9 results in defective cartilage primordia and premature skeletal mineralization. Proc Natl Acad Sci U S A 98:6698–6703, 2001.

140. Kwok C, Weller PA, Guioli S, et al: Mutations in SOX9, the gene responsible for campomelic dysplasia and autosomal sex reversal. Am J Hum Genet 57:1028–1036, 1995.

141. Meyer J, Sudbeck P, Held M, et al: Mutational analysis of the SOX9 gene in campomelic dysplasia and autosomal sex reversal: lack of genotype/phenotype correlations. Hum Mol Genet 6:91–98, 1997.

142. Huang B, Wang S, Ning Y, et al: Autosomal XX sex reversal caused by duplication of SOX9. Am J Med Genet 87:349–353, 1999.

143. Gibbons RJ, Higgs DR: Molecular-clinical spectrum of the ATR-X syndrome. Am J Med Genet 97:204–212, 2000.

144. Gecz J, Pollard H, Consalez G, et al: Cloning and expression of the murine homologue of a putative human X-linked nuclear protein gene closely linked to PGK1 in Xq13.3. Hum Mol Genet 3:39–44, 1994.

145. Stayton CL, Dabovic B, Gulisano M, et al: Cloning and characterization of a new human Xq13 gene, encoding a putative helicase. Hum Mol Genet 3:1957–1964, 1994.

146. Villard L, Lossi AM, Cardoso C, et al: Determination of the genomic structure of the XNP/ATRX gene encoding a potential zinc finger helicase. Genomics 43:149–155, 1997.

147. Pask A, Renfree MB, Marshall Graves JA: The human sex-reversing ATRX gene has a homologue on the marsupial Y chromosome, ATRY: Implications for the evolution of mammalian sex determination. Proc Natl Acad Sci U S A 97:13198–13202, 2000.

148. Picketts DJ, Tastan AO, Higgs DR, Gibbons RJ: Comparison of the human and murine ATRX gene identifies highly conserved, functionally important domains. Mamm Genome 9:400–403, 1998.

149. McDowell TL, Gibbons RJ, Sutherland H, et al: Localization of a putative transcriptional regulator (ATRX) at pericentromeric heterochromatin and the short arms of acrocentric chromosomes. Proc Natl

Acad Sci U S A 96:13983–13988, 1999.

150. Yao HH, Capel B: Disruption of testis cords by cyclopamine or forskolin reveals independent cellular pathways in testis organogenesis. Dev Biol 246:356–365, 2002.

151. Tate G, Satoh H, Endo Y, Mitsuya T: Assignment of desert hedgehog (Dhh) to human chromosome bands 12q12—>q13.1 by in situ hybridization. Cytogenet Cell Genet 88:93–94, 2000.

152. Carpenter D, Stone DM, Brush J, et al: Characterization of two patched receptors for the vertebrate hedgehog protein family. Proc Natl Acad Sci U S A 95:13630–13634, 1998.

153. Bitgood MJ, Shen L, McMahon AP: Sertoli cell signaling by Desert hedgehog regulates the male germline. Curr Biol 6:298–304, 1996.

154. Clark AM, Garland KK, Russell LD: Desert hedgehog (Dhh) gene is required in the mouse testis for formation of adult-type Leydig cells and normal development of peritubular cells and seminiferous tubules. Biol Reprod 63:1825–1838, 2000.

155. Umehara F, Yamaguchi N, Kodama D, et al: Polyneuropathy with minifascicle formation in a patient with 46XY mixed gonadal dysgenesis. Acta Neuropathol (Berl) 98:309–312, 1999.

156. Umehara F, Tate G, Itoh K, et al: A novel mutation of desert hedgehog in a patient with 46,XY partial gonadal dysgenesis accompanied by minifascicular neuropathy. Am J Hum Genet 67:1302–1305, 2000.

157. Warne GL, Kanumakala S: Molecular endocrinology of sex differentiation. Semin Reprod Med 20:169–180, 2002.

158. Jordan BK, Shen JH, Olaso R, et al: Wnt4 overexpression disrupts normal testicular vasculature and inhibits testosterone synthesis by repressing steroidogenic factor 1/beta-catenin synergy. Proc Natl Acad Sci U S A 100:10866–10871, 2003.

159. Vilain E: Anomalies of human sexual development: clinical aspects and genetic analysis. Novartis Found Symp 244:43–53, discussion 53–46, 79–85, 253–257, 2002.

160. Ikegawa S, Kumano Y, Okui K, et al: Isolation, characterization and chromosomal assignment of the human WNT7A gene. Cytogenet Cell Genet 74:149–152, 1996.

161. Miller C, Sassoon DA: Wnt-7a maintains appropriate uterine patterning during the development of the mouse female reproductive tract. Development 125:3201–3211, 1998.

162. Parr BA, McMahon AP: Sexually dimorphic development of the mammalian reproductive tract requires Wnt-7a. Nature 395:707–710, 1998.

163. Jeays-Ward K, Hoyle C, Brennan J, et al: Endothelial and steroidogenic cell migration are regulated by WNT4

in the developing mammalian gonad. Development 130:3663–3670, 2003.

164. Crisponi L, Deiana M, Loi A, et al: The putative forkhead transcription factor FOXL2 is mutated in blepharophimosis/ptosis/epicanthus inversus syndrome. Nat Genet 27:159–166, 2001.

165. Pailhoux E, Vigier B, Chaffaux S, et al: A 11.7-kb deletion triggers intersexuality and polledness in goats. Nat Genet 29:453–458, 2001.

166. De Baere E, Beysen D, Oley C, et al: FOXL2 and BPES: Mutational hotspots, phenotypic variability, and revision of the genotype-phenotype correlation. Am J Hum Genet 72:478–487, 2003.

167. Loffler KA, Zarkower D, Koopman P: Etiology of ovarian failure in blepharophimosis ptosis epicanthus inversus syndrome: FOXL2 is a conserved, early-acting gene in vertebrate ovarian development. Endocrinology 144:3237–3243, 2003.

168. Schlessinger D, Herrera L, Crisponi L, et al: Genes and translocations involved in POF. Am J Med Genet 111:328–333, 2002.

169. Meeks JJ, Weiss J, Jameson JL: Dax1 is required for testis determination. Nat Genet 34:32–33, 2003.

170. Bardoni B, Zanaria E, Guioli S, et al: A dosage sensitive locus at chromosome Xp21 is involved in male to female sex reversal. Nat Genet 7:497–501, 1994.

171. Zanaria E, Muscatelli F, Bardoni B, et al: An unusual member of the nuclear hormone receptor superfamily responsible for X-linked adrenal hypoplasia congenita. Nature 372:635–641, 1994.

172. Guo W, Burris TP, Zhang YH, et al: Genomic sequence of the DAX1 gene: An orphan nuclear receptor responsible for X-linked adrenal hypoplasia congenita and hypogonadotropic hypogonadism. J Clin Endocrinol Metab 81:2481–2486, 1996.

173. Seol W, Choi HS, Moore DD: An orphan nuclear hormone receptor that lacks a DNA binding domain and heterodimerizes with other receptors. Science 272:1336–1339, 1996.

174. Swain A, Narvaez V, Burgoyne P, et al: Dax1 antagonizes Sry action in mammalian sex determination. Nature 391:761–767, 1998.

175. Bae DS, Schaefer ML, Partan BW, Muglia L: Characterization of the mouse DAX-1 gene reveals evolutionary conservation of a unique amino-terminal motif and widespread expression in mouse tissue. Endocrinology 137:3921–3927, 1996.

176. Ikeda Y, Swain A, Weber TJ, et al: Steroidogenic factor 1 and Dax-1 colocalize in multiple cell lineages: Potential links in endocrine development. Mol Endocrinol 10:1261–1272, 1996.

177. Swain A, Zanaria E, Hacker A, et al: Mouse Dax1 expression is consistent with a role in sex determination as well as in adrenal and hypothalamus

function. Nat Genet 12:404–409, 1996.

178. Tamai KT, Monaco L, Alastalo TP, et al: Hormonal and developmental regulation of DAX-1 expression in Sertoli cells. Mol Endocrinol 10:1561–1569, 1996.

179. Kawabe K, Shikayama T, Tsuboi H, et al: Dax-1 as one of the target genes of Ad4BP/SF1. Mol Endocrinol 13:1267–1284, 1999.

180. Ikeda Y, Takeda Y, Shikayama T, et al: Comparative localization of Dax-1 and Ad4BP/SF1 during development of the hypothalamic-pituitary-gonadal axis suggests their closely related and distinct functions. Dev Dyn 220:363–376, 2001.

181. Burris TP, Guo W, Le T, McCabe ER: Identification of a putative steroidogenic factor-1 response element in the DAX-1 promoter. Biochem Biophys Res Commun 214:576–581, 1995.

182. Yu RN, Ito M, Saunders TL, et al: Role of Ahch in gonadal development and gametogenesis. Nat Genet 20:353–357, 1998.

183. Hoyle C, Narvaez V, Alldus G, et al: Dax1 expression is dependent on steroidogenic factor 1 in the developing gonad. Mol Endocrinol 16:747–756, 2002.

184. Suzuki T, Mizusaki H, Kawabe K, et al: Concerted regulation of gonad differentiation by transcription factors and growth factors. Novartis Found Symp 244:68–77; discussion 77–85, 253–257, 2002.

185. Guo W, Burris TP, McCabe ER: Expression of DAX-1, the gene responsible for X-linked adrenal hypoplasia congenita and hypogonadotropic hypogonadism, in the hypothalamic-pituitary-adrenal/gonadal axis. Biochem Mol Med 56:8–13, 1995.

186. Majdic G, Saunders PT: Differential patterns of expression of DAX-1 and steroidogenic factor-1 (SF1) in the fetal rat testis. Endocrinology 137:3586–3589, 1996.

187. Ito M, Yu R, Jameson JL: DAX-1 inhibits SF1-mediated transactivation via a carboxy-terminal domain that is deleted in adrenal hypoplasia congenita. Mol Cell Biol 17:1476–1483, 1997.

188. Zazopoulos E, Lalli E, Stocco DM, Sassone-Corsi P: DNA binding and transcriptional repression by DAX-1 blocks steroidogenesis. Nature 390:311–315, 1997.

189. Hanley NA, Hagan DM, Clement-Jones M, et al: SRY, SOX9, and DAX1 expression patterns during human sex determination and gonadal development. Mech Dev 91:403–407, 2000.

190. Hanley NA, Rainey WE, Wilson DI, et al: Expression profiles of SF1, DAX1, and CYP17 in the human fetal adrenal gland: potential interactions in gene regulation. Mol Endocrinol 15:57–68, 2001.

191. Lalli E, Bardoni B, Zazopoulos E, et al: A transcriptional silencing domain in DAX-1 whose mutation causes adrenal hypoplasia congenita. Mol Endocrinol 11:1950–1960, 1997.

192. Goodfellow PN, Camerino G: DAX-1, an "antitestis" gene. EXS 91:57–69, 2001.

193. Habiby RL, Boepple P, Nachtigall L, et al: Adrenal hypoplasia congenita with hypogonadotropic hypogonadism: Evidence that DAX-1 mutations lead to combined hypothalmic and pituitary defects in gonadotropin production. J Clin Invest 98:1055–1062, 1996.

194. Zhang YH, Guo W, Wagner RL, et al: DAX1 mutations map to putative structural domains in a deduced three-dimensional model. Am J Hum Genet 62:855–864, 1998.

195. Seminara SB, Achermann JC, Genel M, et al: X-linked adrenal hypoplasia congenita: A mutation in DAX1 expands the phenotypic spectrum in males and females. J Clin Endocrinol Metab 84:4501–4509, 1999.

196. Quigley CA: Unpublished observations.

197. Shen MM, Hodgkin J: mab-3, A gene required for sex-specific yolk protein expression and a male-specific lineage in C. elegans. Cell 54:1019–1031, 1988.

198. Hodgkin J: The remarkable ubiquity of DM domain factors as regulators of sexual phenotype: Ancestry or aptitude? Genes Dev 16:2322–2326, 2002.

199. Ottolenghi C, Fellous M, Barbieri M, McElreavey K: Novel paralogy relations among human chromosomes support a link between the phylogeny of doublesex-related genes and the evolution of sex determination. Genomics 79:333–343, 2002.

200. Kim S, Kettlewell JR, Anderson RC, et al: Sexually dimorphic expression of multiple doublesex-related genes in the embryonic mouse gonad. Gene Expr Patterns 3:77–82, 2003.

201. Aoyama S, Shibata K, Tokunaga S, et al: Expression of Dmrt1 protein in developing and in sex-reversed gonads of amphibians. Cytogenet Genome Res 101:295–301, 2003.

202. Brunner B, Hornung U, Shan Z, et al: Genomic organization and expression of the doublesex-related gene cluster in vertebrates and detection of putative regulatory regions for DMRT1. Genomics 77:8–17, 2001.

203. McDonald MT, Flejter W, Sheldon S, et al: XY sex reversal and gonadal dysgenesis due to 9p24 monosomy. Am J Med Genet 73:321–326, 1997.

204. Raymond CS, Parker ED, Kettlewell JR, et al: A region of human chromosome 9p required for testis development contains two genes related to known sexual regulators. Hum Mol Genet 8:989–996, 1999.

205. De Grandi A, Calvari V, Bertini V, et al: The expression pattern of a mouse doublesex-related gene is consistent with a role in gonadal differentiation. Mech Dev 90:323–326, 2000.

206. Muroya K, Okuyama T, Goishi K, et al: Sex-determining gene(s) on distal 9p: Clinical and molecular studies in six cases. J Clin Endocrinol Metab 85:3094–3100, 2000.

207. Shan Z, Zabel B, Trautmann U, et al: FISH mapping of the sex-reversal region on human chromosome 9p in two XY females and in primates. Eur J Hum Genet 8:167–173, 2000.

208. Raymond CS, Shamu CE, Shen MM, et al: Evidence for evolutionary conservation of sex-determining genes. Nature 391:691–695, 1998.

209. Smith CA, McClive PJ, Western PS, et al: Conservation of a sex-determining gene. Nature 402:601–602, 1999.

210. Raymond CS, Kettlewell JR, Hirsch B, et al: Expression of Dmrt1 in the genital ridge of mouse and chicken embryos suggests a role in vertebrate sexual development. Dev Biol 215:208–220, 1999.

211. Chee GH, Mathias DB, James RA, Kendall-Taylor P: Transsphenoidal pituitary surgery in Cushing's disease: Can we predict outcome? Clin Endocrinol (Oxf) 54:617–626, 2001.

212. Lei N, Heckert LL: Sp1 and Egr1 regulate transcription of the Dmrt1 gene in Sertoli cells. Biol Reprod 66:675–684, 2002.

213. Raymond CS, Murphy MW, O'Sullivan MG, et al: Dmrt1, a gene related to worm and fly sexual regulators, is required for mammalian testis differentiation. Genes Dev 14:2587–2595, 2000.

214. Ogata T, Muroya K, Ohashi H, et al: Female gonadal development in XX patients with distal 9p monosomy. Eur J Endocrinol 145:613–617, 2001.

215. Rey R, Picard JY: Embryology and endocrinology of genital development. Baillieres Clin Endocrinol Metab 12:17–33, 1998.

216. Sadler TW: Urogenital system. In Sadler TW (ed): Langman's Medical Embryology, 7th ed. Baltimore, Williams and Wilkins, 1995.

217. Jameson JL: Inherited disorders of the gonadotropin hormones. Mol Cell Endocrinol 125:143–149, 1996.

218. Themmen AP, Verhoef-Post M: LH receptor defects. Semin Reprod Med 20:199–204, 2002.

219. O'Shaughnessy PJ, Baker P, Sohnius U, et al: Fetal development of Leydig cell activity in the mouse is independent of pituitary gonadotroph function. Endocrinology 139:1141–1146, 1998.

220. Themmen APN, Huhtaniemi IT: Mutations of gonadotropins and gonadotropin receptors: Elucidating the physiology and pathophysiology of pituitary-gonadal function. Endocr Rev 21:551–583, 2000.

221. Habert R, Lejeune H, Saez JM: Origin, differentiation and regulation of fetal and adult Leydig cells. Mol Cell Endocrinol 179:47–74, 2001.

222. Segaloff DL, Ascoli M: The lutropin/choriogonadotropin

receptor . . . 4 years later. Endocr Rev 14:324–347, 1993.

223. El-Gehani F, Zhang FP, Pakarinen P, et al: Gonadotropin-independent regulation of steroidogenesis in the fetal rat testis. Biol Reprod 58:116–123, 1998.

224. Huhtaniemi I: The Parkes lecture. Mutations of gonadotrophin and gonadotrophin receptor genes: What do they teach us about reproductive physiology? J Reprod Fertil 119:173–186, 2000.

225. Lei ZM, Mishra S, Zou W, et al: Targeted disruption of luteinizing hormone/human chorionic gonadotropin receptor gene. Mol Endocrinol 15:184–200, 2001.

226. Rao CV, Lei ZM: Consequences of targeted inactivation of LH receptors. Mol Cell Endocrinol 187:57–67, 2002.

227. Latronico AC, Anasti J, Arnhold IJ, et al: Brief report: Testicular and ovarian resistance to luteinizing hormone caused by inactivating mutations of the luteinizing hormone-receptor gene. N Engl J Med 334:507–512, 1996.

228. Richter-Unruh A, Martens JW, Verhoef-Post M, et al: Leydig cell hypoplasia: Cases with new mutations, new polymorphisms and cases without mutations in the luteinizing hormone receptor gene. Clin Endocrinol (Oxf) 56:103–112, 2002.

229. King SR, Ronen-Fuhrmann T, Timberg R, et al: Steroid production after in vitro transcription, translation, and mitochondrial processing of protein products of complementary deoxyribonucleic acid for steroidogenic acute regulatory protein. Endocrinology 136:5165–5176, 1995.

230. Sugawara T, Lin D, Holt JA, et al: Structure of the human steroidogenic acute regulatory protein (StAR) gene: StAR stimulates mitochondrial cholesterol 27-hydroxylase activity. Biochemistry 34:12506–12512, 1995.

231. Christenson LK, Strauss JF III: Steroidogenic acute regulatory protein: An update on its regulation and mechanism of action. Arch Med Res 32:576–586, 2001.

232. Clark JT: Sexual function in altered physiological states: Comparison of effects of hypertension, diabetes, hyperprolactinemia, and others to "normal" aging in male rats. Neurosci Biobehav Rev 19:279–302, 1995.

233. Stocco DM, Clark BJ: Regulation of the acute production of steroids in steroidogenic cells. Endocr Rev 17:221–244, 1996.

234. Sugawara T, Kiriakidou M, McAllister JM, et al: Multiple steroidogenic factor 1 binding elements in the human steroidogenic acute regulatory protein gene 5′-flanking region are required for maximal promoter activity and cyclic AMP responsiveness. Biochemistry 36:7249–7255, 1997.

235. Pollack SE, Furth EE, Kallen CB, et al: Localization of the steroidogenic acute regulatory protein in human tissues. J Clin Endocrinol Metab 82:4243–4251, 1997.

236. Sugawara T, Holt JA, Kiriakidou M, Strauss JF III: Steroidogenic factor 1-dependent promoter activity of the human steroidogenic acute regulatory protein (StAR) gene. Biochemistry 35:9052–9059, 1996.

237. Caron KM, Ikeda Y, Soo SC, et al: Characterization of the promoter region of the mouse gene encoding the steroidogenic acute regulatory protein. Mol Endocrinol 11:138–147, 1997.

238. Bose HS, Sugawara T, Strauss JF III, Miller WL: The pathophysiology and genetics of congenital lipoid adrenal hyperplasia. International Congenital Lipoid Adrenal Hyperplasia Consortium. N Engl J Med 335:1870–1878, 1996.

239. Bose HS, Pescovitz OH, Miller WL: Spontaneous feminization in a 46,XX female patient with congenital lipoid adrenal hyperplasia due to a homozygous frameshift mutation in the steroidogenic acute regulatory protein. J Clin Endocrinol Metab 82:1511–1515, 1997.

240. Nakae J, Tajima T, Sugawara T, et al: Analysis of the steroidogenic acute regulatory protein (StAR) gene in Japanese patients with congenital lipoid adrenal hyperplasia. Hum Mol Genet 6:571–576, 1997.

241. Bose HS, Sato S, Aisenberg J, et al: Mutations in the steroidogenic acute regulatory protein (StAR) in six patients with congenital lipoid adrenal hyperplasia. J Clin Endocrinol Metab 85:3636–3639, 2000.

242. Stocco DM: Clinical disorders associated with abnormal cholesterol transport: Mutations in the steroidogenic acute regulatory protein. Mol Cell Endocrinol 191:19–25, 2002.

243. Fujieda K, Okuhara K, Abe S, et al: Molecular pathogenesis of lipoid adrenal hyperplasia and adrenal hypoplasia congenita. J Steroid Biochem Mol Biol 85:483–489, 2003.

244. Chung BC, Matteson KJ, Voutilainen R, et al: Human cholesterol side-chain cleavage enzyme, P450scc: cDNA cloning, assignment of the gene to chromosome 15, and expression in the placenta. Proc Natl Acad Sci U S A 83:8962–8966, 1986.

245. Hu MC, Hsu NC, El Hadj NB, et al: Steroid deficiency syndromes in mice with targeted disruption of Cyp11a1. Mol Endocrinol 16:1943–1950, 2002.

246. Tajima T, Fujieda K, Kouda N, et al: Heterozygous mutation in the cholesterol side chain cleavage enzyme (p450scc) gene in a patient with 46,XY sex reversal and adrenal insufficiency. J Clin Endocrinol Metab 86:3820–3825, 2001.

247. Katsumata N, Ohtake M, Hojo T, et al: Compound heterozygous mutations in the cholesterol side-chain cleavage enzyme gene (CYP11A) cause congenital adrenal insufficiency in humans. J Clin Endocrinol Metab 87:3808–3813, 2002.

248. Lachance Y, Luu-The V, Labrie C, et al: Characterization of human 3 beta-hydroxysteroid dehydrogenase/delta 5-delta 4-isomerase gene and its expression in mammalian cells. J Biol Chem 265:20469–20475, 1990.

249. Lachance Y, Luu-The V, Verreault H, et al: Structure of the human type II 3 beta-hydroxysteroid dehydrogenase/delta 5-delta 4 isomerase (3 beta-HSD) gene: Adrenal and gonadal specificity. DNA Cell Biol 10:701–711, 1991.

250. Lorence MC, Corbin CJ, Kamimura N, et al: Structural analysis of the gene encoding human 3 beta-hydroxysteroid dehydrogenase/delta 5–4-isomerase. Mol Endocrinol 4:1850–1855, 1990.

251. Penning TM: Molecular endocrinology of hydroxysteroid dehydrogenases. Endocr Rev 18:281–305, 1997.

252. Parker CR Jr, Faye-Petersen O, Stankovic AK, et al: Immunohistochemical evaluation of the cellular localization and ontogeny of 3 beta-hydroxysteroid dehydrogenase/delta 5–4 isomerase in the human fetal adrenal gland. Endocr Res 21:69–80, 1995.

253. Yanase T, Simpson ER, Waterman MR: 17 alpha-hydroxylase/17,20-lyase deficiency: from clinical investigation to molecular definition. Endocr Rev 12:91–108, 1991.

254. Auchus RJ: The genetics, pathophysiology, and management of human deficiencies of P450c17. Endocrinol Metab Clin North Am 30:101–119, vii, 2001.

255. Kitamura M, Buczko E, Dufau ML: Dissociation of hydroxylase and lyase activities by site-directed mutagenesis of the rat P45017 alpha. Mol Endocrinol 5:1373–1380, 1991.

256. Lin D, Black SM, Nagahama Y, Miller WL: Steroid 17 alpha-hydroxylase and 17,20-lyase activities of P450c17: Contributions of serine106 and P450 reductase. Endocrinology 132:2498–2506, 1993.

257. Auchus RJ, Miller WL: Molecular modeling of human P450c17 (17alpha-hydroxylase/17,20-lyase): Insights into reaction mechanisms and effects of mutations. Mol Endocrinol 13:1169–1182, 1999.

258. Zhang P, Mellon SH: Multiple orphan nuclear receptors converge to regulate rat P450c17 gene transcription: Novel mechanisms for orphan nuclear receptor action. Mol Endocrinol 11:891–904, 1997.

259. Andersson S, Moghrabi N: Physiology and molecular genetics of 17 beta-hydroxysteroid dehydrogenases. Steroids 62:143–147, 1997.

260. Labrie F, Luu-The V, Lin SX, et al: Role of 17 beta-hydroxysteroid dehydrogenases in sex steroid formation in peripheral intracrine tissues. Trends Endocrinol Metab 11:421–427, 2000.

261. Adamski J, Jakob FJ: A guide to 17beta-hydroxysteroid dehydrogenases. Mol Cell Endocrinol 171:1–4, 2001.

262. Luu-The V: Analysis and characteristics of multiple types of human 17beta-hydroxysteroid dehydrogenase. J Steroid Biochem Mol Biol 76:143–151, 2001.

263. Winqvist R, Peltoketo H, Isomaa V, et al: The gene for 17 beta-hydroxysteroid dehydrogenase maps to human chromosome 17, bands q12-q21, and shows an RFLP with ScaI. Hum Genet 85:473–476, 1990.

264. Luu-The V, Labrie C, Simard J, et al: Structure of two in tandem human 17 beta-hydroxysteroid dehydrogenase genes. Mol Endocrinol 4:268–275, 1990.

265. Isomaa VV, Ghersevich SA, Maentausta OK, et al: Steroid biosynthetic enzymes: 17 Beta-hydroxysteroid dehydrogenase. Ann Med 25:91–97, 1993.

266. Rosler A, Silverstein S, Abeliovich D: A (R80Q) mutation in 17 beta-hydroxysteroid dehydrogenase type 3 gene among Arabs of Israel is associated with pseudohermaphroditism in males and normal asymptomatic females. J Clin Endocrinol Metab 81:1827–1831, 1996.

267. Blomquist CH: Kinetic analysis of enzymic activities: Prediction of multiple forms of 17 beta-hydroxysteroid dehydrogenase. J Steroid Biochem Mol Biol 55:515–524, 1995.

268. Poutanen M, Isomaa V, Peltoketo H, Vihko R: Role of 17 beta-hydroxysteroid dehydrogenase type 1 in endocrine and intracrine estradiol biosynthesis. J Steroid Biochem Mol Biol 55:525–532, 1995.

269. Huang YW, Pineau I, Chang HJ, et al: Critical residues for the specificity of cofactors and substrates in human estrogenic 17beta-hydroxysteroid dehydrogenase 1: Variants designed from the three-dimensional structure of the enzyme. Mol Endocrinol 15:2010–2020, 2001.

270. Rosler A, Belanger A, Labrie F: Mechanisms of androgen production in male pseudohermaphroditism due to 17 beta-hydroxysteroid dehydrogenase deficiency. J Clin Endocrinol Metab 75:773–778, 1992.

271. Thigpen AE, Silver RI, Guileyardo JM, et al: Tissue distribution and ontogeny of steroid 5 alpha-reductase isozyme expression. J Clin Invest 92:903–910, 1993.

272. Wilson CA, di Clemente N, Ehrenfels C, et al: Mullerian inhibiting substance requires its N-terminal domain for maintenance of biological activity: A novel finding within the transforming growth factor-beta superfamily. Mol Endocrinol 7:247–257, 1993.

273. Jin Y, Penning T4M: Steroid 5alpha-reductases and 3alpha-hydroxysteroid dehydrogenases: Key enzymes in androgen metabolism. Best Pract Res Clin Endocrinol Metab 15:79–94, 2001.

274. Russell DW, Wilson JD: Steroid 5 alpha-reductase: Two genes/two enzymes. Annu Rev Biochem 63:25–61, 1994.

275. Andersson S, Berman DM, Jenkins EP, Russell DW: Deletion of steroid 5 alpha-reductase 2 gene in male pseudohermaphroditism. Nature 354:159–161, 1991.

276. Siiteri PK, Wilson JD: Testosterone formation and metabolism during male sexual differentiation in the human embryo. J Clin Endocrinol Metab 38:113–125, 1974.

277. Quigley CA, De Bellis A, Marschke KB, et al: Androgen receptor defects: Historical, clinical, and molecular perspectives. Endocr Rev 16:271–321, 1995.

278. Brinkmann AO, Trapman J: Genetic analysis of androgen receptors in development and disease. Adv Pharmacol 47:317–341, 2000.

279. Lubahn DB, Joseph DR, Sar M, et al: The human androgen receptor: Complementary deoxyribonucleic acid cloning, sequence analysis and gene expression in prostate. Mol Endocrinol 2:1265–1275, 1988.

280. Yarbrough WG, Quarmby VE, Simental JA, et al: A single base mutation in the androgen receptor gene causes androgen insensitivity in the testicular feminized rat. J Biol Chem 265:8893–8900, 1990.

281. Gobinet J, Poujol N, Sultan C: Molecular action of androgens. Mol Cell Endocrinol 198:15–24, 2002.

282. Heinlein CA, Chang C: Androgen receptor (AR) coregulators: An overview. Endocr Rev 23:175–200, 2002.

283. McPhaul MJ: Androgen receptor mutations and androgen insensitivity. Mol Cell Endocrinol 198:61–67, 2002.

284. Lee KS, Na YG, Dean-McKinney T, et al: Alterations in voiding frequency and cystometry in the clomipramine induced model of endogenous depression and reversal with fluoxetine. J Urol 170:2067–2071, 2003.

285. Josso N, Clemente N: Transduction pathway of anti-Mullerian hormone, a sex-specific member of the TGF-beta family. Trends Endocrinol Metab 14:91–97, 2003.

286. Al-Attar L, Noel K, Dutertre M, et al: Hormonal and cellular regulation of Sertoli cell anti-Mullerian hormone production in the postnatal mouse. J Clin Invest 100:1335–1343, 1997.

287. Behringer RR, Finegold MJ, Cate RL: Mullerian-inhibiting substance function during mammalian sexual development. Cell 79:415–425, 1994.

288. Behringer RR, Cate RL, Froelick GJ, et al: Abnormal sexual development in transgenic mice chronically expressing mullerian inhibiting substance. Nature 345:167–170, 1990.

289. Belville C, Josso N, Picard JY: Persistence of mullerian derivatives in males. Am J Med Genet 89:218–223, 1999.

290. Jamin SP, Arango NA, Mishina Y, et al: Requirement of Bmpr1a for Mullerian duct regression during male sexual development. Nat Genet 32:408–410, 2002.

291. Allard S, Adin P, Gouedard L, et al: Molecular mechanisms of hormone-mediated mullerian duct regression: Involvement of beta-catenin. Development 127:3349–3360, 2000.

292. Roberts LM, Visser JA, Ingraham HA: Involvement of a matrix metalloproteinase in MIS-induced cell death during urogenital development. Development 129:1487–1496, 2002.

293. di Clemente N, Wilson C, Faure E, et al: Cloning, expression, and alternative splicing of the receptor for anti-mullerian hormone. Mol Endocrinol 8:1006–1020, 1994.

294. Mishina Y, Rey R, Finegold MJ, et al: Genetic analysis of the Mullerian-inhibiting substance signal transduction pathway in mammalian sexual differentiation. Genes Dev 10:2577–2587, 1996.

295. Goodman FR, Bacchelli C, Brady AF, et al: Novel HOXA13 mutations and the phenotypic spectrum of hand-foot-genital syndrome. Am J Hum Genet 67:197–202, 2000.

296. Taylor HS, Vanden Heuvel GB, Igarashi P: A conserved Hox axis in the mouse and human female reproductive system: Late establishment and persistent adult expression of the Hoxa cluster genes. Biol Reprod 57:1338–1345, 1997.

297. Post LC, Innis JW: Infertility in adult hypodactyly mice is associated with hypoplasia of distal reproductive structures. Biol Reprod 61:1402–1408, 1999.

298. Warot X, Fromental-Ramain C, Fraulob V, et al: Gene dosage-dependent effects of the Hoxa-13 and Hoxd-13 mutations on morphogenesis of the terminal parts of the digestive and urogenital tracts. Development 124:4781–4791, 1997.

299. Mortlock DP, Innis JW: Mutation of HOXA13 in hand-foot-genital syndrome. Nat Genet 15:179–180, 1997.

# Embryology and Control of Fetal Sex Differentiation

## Nathalie Josso and Rodolfo Rey

## INTRODUCTION

Fetal sex differentiation can be defined as the acquisition of male or female characteristics in anlage that are initially similar regardless of the genetic sex. Normally, genetic sex, gonadal sex, and somatic sex are concordant with one another and with the sex that is assigned to the neonate based on external appearance; if not, there is sexual ambiguity. A clear understanding of the mechanisms of normal sex differentiation is crucial to the analysis of intersex disorders and provides guidelines for adequate diagnosis and treatment.

## HISTORY

Modern history of fetal sex differentiation begins in 1903, when two pathologists from Nancy (France), Bouin and Ancel,[1] studying the testes of fetal pigs, noticed the presence of cells closely resembling the Leydig cells of pubertal animals and suggested that their secretion product was responsible for the modeling of the male reproductive tract. In 1917, the observations of Frank Lillie,[2] a professor of zoology in Chicago, supported the "endocrine theory" of sex differentiation, but, at first, experimental confirmation could not be obtained. In 1947, frustrated with his negative results in the opossum, Carl Moore,[3] a pupil of Lillie, wrote that hormones have nothing to do with fetal sex differentiation.

The same year, the PhD thesis of a young Frenchman contradicted this hasty conclusion. Using microsurgery to remove the gonads from fetal rabbits at the ambisexual stage of fetal sex differentiation, Alfred Jost[4] showed that all developed female somatic characteristics, regardless of the histologic nature of the fetal gonads. This demonstrated the key role of testicular secretion, which overcomes the default pathway toward female genital differentiation. Jost then went on to show that distinct testicular hormones promote male characteristics and inhibit female ones. Jost's hypothesis still serves as the basis for understanding clinical defects of sex differentiation (Fig. 143-1). However, recent findings have stressed the importance of control mechanisms involving tissue interactions and growth factors.

## ANATOMY AND DEVELOPMENT OF SEX DIFFERENTIATION

### GONADAL DIFFERENTIATION

#### The Primitive Gonad

The primitive gonad, or genital ridge, develops at about day 32 (Table 143-1) as a thickening of the coelomic epithelium covering the ventral side of the cranial mesonephros, close to the dorsal mesentery. Soon these gonadal ridges shorten and project into the coelomic cavity. Genital ridges of both sexes express SOX 9, an SRY-related gene also needed for cartilage development[5]; steroidogenic factor-1, an orphan nuclear receptor involved in the control of gonadal, adrenal, and hypothalamic function and development[6]; Wnt4, a signaling molecule required for renal development[7]; the Wilms' tumor–associated gene (WT-1), a transcription factor important for urogenital development[8]; and DAX-1, an atypical member of the nuclear hormone receptor superfamily.[9] DAX-1 and steroidogenic factor-1 have striking similarities in their tissue sites of expression, suggesting that these orphan nuclear receptors might converge on common developmental pathways.

Germ cells, which derive from pluripotent cells of the embryonic epiblast, are first identified outside the embryo proper near the stalk of the allantois. From there, they become incorporated in the hindgut and migrate through the dorsal mesentery and into the genital ridges. Their morphology and their expression of alkaline phosphatase, Oct4, and the tyrosine kinase receptor c-kit identify them throughout their journey (Fig. 143-2).

#### Testicular Differentiation

Testicular differentiation can be detected in human fetuses between 42 and 50 days (see Table 143-1). It is heralded by the differentiation of a new cell type, the primitive Sertoli cell, characterized by a large, clear cytoplasm with abundant rough endoplasmic reticulum and complex membrane interdigitations. The interaction between differentiating peritubular myoid and primitive Sertoli cells results in the formation of testicular cords that enclose germ cells.[10] Soon after the

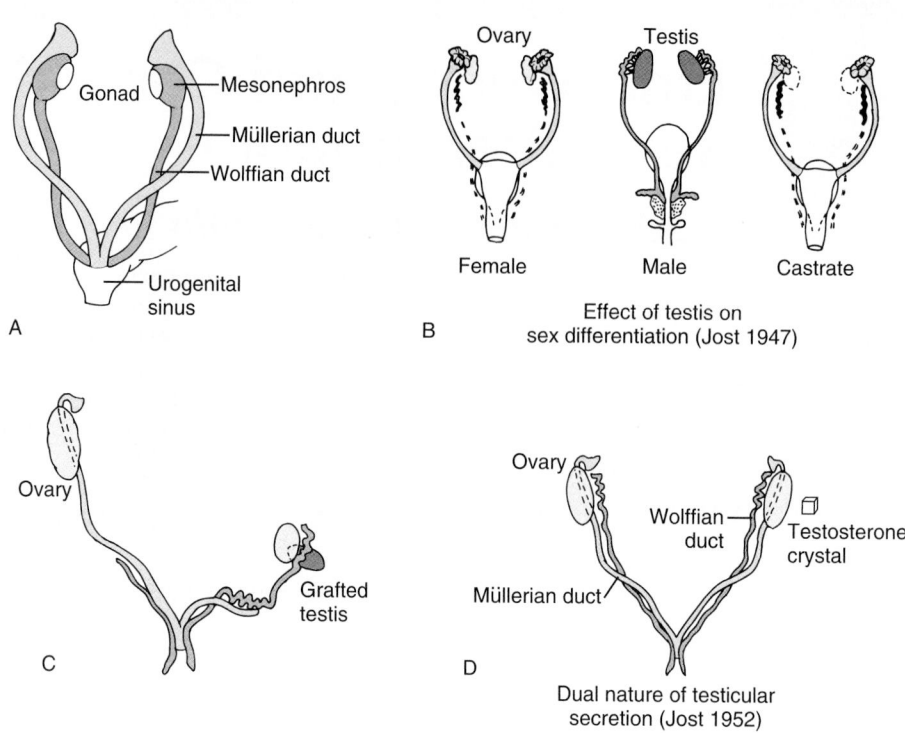

*Figure 143-1* Jost's pioneering experiments showing the dual nature of testicular hormone secretion and its effect on fetal sexual differentiation. **A,** The urogenital tract in the ambisexual stage consists of undifferentiated gonads and müllerian and wolffian ducts in fetuses of both sexes. **B,** Differentiation of the internal genital tract. In normal females, müllerian ducts are maintained and wolffian ducts regress, whereas in males, the opposite occurs. In castrated fetuses, irrespective of genetic or gonadal sex, the reproductive tract differentiates according to the female pattern. **C,** A testis, unilaterally grafted at the ambisexual stage in an XX embryo, induces homolateral male differentiation of the genital tract. **D,** A testosterone crystal, unilaterally grafted at the ambisexual stage in an XX embryo, induces male differentiation of the wolffian duct but not the regression of the müllerian duct. (Modified from Josso N, Rey R, Gonzalès J: Sexual differentiation. In New M [ed]: Pediatric Endocrinology. Available at *http://www.endotext.org/pediatrics/pediatrics7/ pediatricsframe7.htm*. Accessed March 20, 2003. © 2003, MDTEXT.COM, INC.)

differentiation of seminiferous tubules, the testis becomes rounded and blood vessels appear at the surface, allowing easy macroscopic recognition, and mesenchymal cells and blood vessels fill the interstitial space. The basement membrane beneath the coelomic epithelium thickens to form the tunica albuginea.

At the same time, approximately 8 weeks in the human fetus, Leydig cells differentiate in the intertubular compartment. From the 14th to the 18th week, the interstitium is crowded with them[11]; their number remains stable until the 24th week at which time they begin to involute, to finally disappear within 3 weeks post partum.

Functional testicular differentiation begins in genital ridges before morphologic differentiation. Sertoli cell precursors begin to express SRY, inducing a testis-specific pattern of cell migration,[12] coincident with upregulation of SOX9, and steroidogenic factor-1[13] and downregulation of Wnt4 and DAX-1. Primitive Sertoli cells also express proteases vanin and nexin,[14] desert hedgehog, a molecule that plays an essential role in spermatogenesis,[15] its receptor Patched2 and antimüllerian hormone (AMH), also called müllerian-inhibiting substance or factor (Fig. 143-3). Fetal Leydig cells produce testosterone, which triggers the virilization of the reproductive tract, and INSL3, which promotes migration of the testes to the scrotum.[16]

### Ovarian Differentiation

Morphologically, the first sign of ovarian differentiation is a negative one, as put by Gilman (cited in Ref. 17): "actually the gonad is an ovary, not because it has that structure, but rather because it is not a testis." Mingled germ and somatic cells are arranged in stacks, often called ovigerous cords, separated by mesenchyme and blood vessels; they extend to the periphery of the gonad and are confluent with the surface epithelium, whereas in the male, epithelial cells are excluded from the gonadal surface by the tunica albuginea. The hallmark of ovarian differentiation is the entry of germ cells in meiotic prophase. In the human fetus at 10 to 11 weeks, while vigorous mitotic activity is continuing in the superficial layers of the ovarian cortex, a few cells in the deepest layer enter the leptotene stage of meiotic prophase (Fig. 143-4).[18]

Progressively, meiotic prophase proceeds to the dictyotene stage, at which it remains until ovulation, 12 to 40 years later. In parallel, the number of germ cells decreases; mitotic activity ceases at 7 months while successive waves of degeneration hit the germ cell population. From 6.8 million at 5 months, the germ cell population declines to approximately 2 million at birth.[18]

## DIFFERENTIATION OF SOMATIC SEX

### Ambisexual Stage

Until the eighth week of gestation, human reproductive organs consist of unipotential wolffian and müllerian ducts and bipotential sinusal and external genital primordia. Wolffian ducts, the primordia for the male sex accessory organs, are originally the excretory canals of the primitive kidney, the mesonephros, and become incorporated in the genital system when renal function is taken over by the metanephros or definitive kidney. Müllerian or paramesonephric ducts, the primordia for the female internal reproductive organs, arise from a cleft lined by coelomic epithelium that originates between the gonadal ridge and the mesonephros and express Wnt4, which is required for the initial development of müllerian ducts in both sexes.[7] The newly formed müllerian duct grows caudally along the mesonephros, parallel to the preexisting wolffian duct with which it fuses, entering its basal membrane below the caudal tip of the mesonephros. Failure to do so arrests the downward growth of the müllerian duct and is a possible cause of Mayer-Küster-Rokitansky syndrome, characterized by the aplasia of the corpus uteri and the upper part of the vagina.[19] Normally, at 8 weeks, the müllerian ducts have crossed to the midline, fused with one another, and reached the dorsal wall of the urogenital sinus where they cause an elevation, the müllerian tubercle. The müllerian tubercle separates the cranial vesicourethral canal from the caudal urogenital sinus (Fig. 143-5).

The undifferentiated external genitalia are represented by the genital membrane, which closes the ventral part of the cloaca and is surrounded ventrally by the genital tubercle and laterally by the genital folds or labioscrotal swellings

| Table 143-1 | Chronology of Sex Differentiation | |
| --- | --- | --- |
| **Age from Conception** | **CR Length (mm)** | **Event** |
| 32 days | 5 | Gonadal primordia develop |
| | | Growth of wolffian ducts |
| | | Primordial germ cell differentiation |
| 37 days | 10 | Primordial germ cells reach gonadal ridge |
| | | Differentiation of müllerian ducts |
| 42–50 days | 15–20 | Seminiferous cord differentiation |
| 55–60 days | 30 | Beginning of secretion of AMH |
| | | Leydig cell differentiation |
| | | Cranial part of müllerian ducts begins to regress |
| 9 weeks | 40 | Leydig cells produce testosterone |
| | | Beginning of masculinization of urogenital sinus and external genitalia |
| 10 weeks | 45–50 | Meiotic entry of oocytes in the medulla |
| | | Beginning of degeneration of female wolffian ducts |
| | | Male müllerian ducts have disappeared |
| | | Prostatic buds appear |
| 12 weeks | 55–60 | The vaginal cord is formed |
| | | Primordial follicles appear |
| | | Seminal vesicles develop |
| | | Testis at internal inguinal ring |
| 14 weeks | 70 | Completion of male urethral organogenesis |
| 16 weeks | 100 | Primary follicles appear |
| 20 weeks | 150 | Testosterone serum level is low |
| | | Formation of prostatic utricle |
| 22 weeks | 180 | Vagina reaches perineum |
| 24 weeks | 200 | Graafian follicles appear |
| | | Beginning of penile growth |
| 25–32 weeks | 230–265 | Inguinoscrotal descent of the testis |
| 36 weeks | 300 | Secondary and tertiary follicles produce AMH |

(Fig. 143-6). After the corpora cavernosa and glans have differentiated, the genital tubercle elongates to form the phallus, whose ventral surface is depressed by a deep furrow, the urethral groove or urogenital slit. No external sex difference is detectable in human fetuses before 9 to 10 weeks.

## Male Differentiation

The first step of somatic male differentiation is müllerian duct regression through apoptosis and epithelial-mesenchymal cell remodeling.[20] Testis-mediated müllerian regression begins at 8 weeks; however, müllerian ducts will undergo regression only if exposed to testicular tissue before that time. In the human, müllerian ducts have nearly completely disappeared at 10 weeks.

The second aspect of internal male differentiation is the integration of wolffian ducts in the genital system and their subsequent development into epididymis, vasa deferentia, and seminal vesicles. Prostatic buds appear at approximately 10 weeks at the site of the müllerian tubercle and grow into solid branching cords. Maturation of the prostatic gland is accompanied by development of the prostatic utricle, the male equivalent of the vagina (see Fig. 143-6).

Masculinization of the external genital organs (see Fig. 143-6) begins at 9 weeks by lengthening of the anogenital distance, followed by fusion of the labioscrotal folds and closure of the rims of the urethral groove, leading to the formation of a perineal and penile urethra. Fusion of the labioscrotal folds, in a proximal to distal fashion, forms the epithelial seam, which closes the primary urethral groove. The urethral plate, an extension of the urogenital sinus that is present within the genital tubercle from the earliest stages of development,[21] lies in the roof of the primary urethral groove and extends to the tip of the phallus. Urethral organogenesis is complete at 16 weeks; however, at that time, no difference exists between penile or clitoral size.[22]

Descent of the testis from its initial pararenal position to its terminal location in the scrotum is a complex process that has been subdivided into several phases. Transabdominal movement brings the testis to the internal inguinal ring at 12 weeks. The actual passage of the testis through the inguinal canal into the scrotum occurs between 25 and 32 weeks[23] but may be delayed until the immediate postnatal period. The gubernaculum testis, a jelly-like structure that extends from the caudal pole of the testis to the inguinal ring

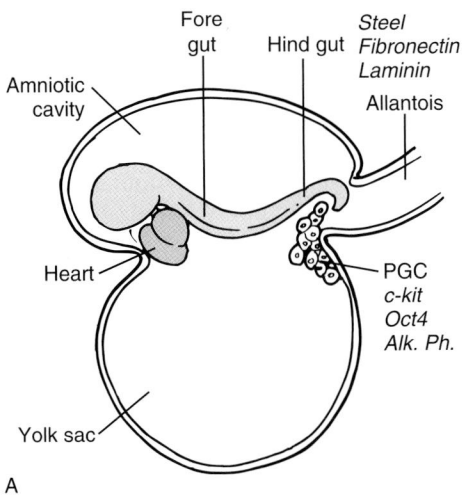
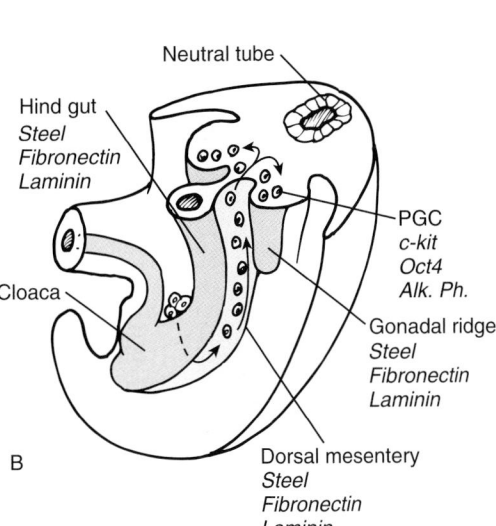

**Figure 143-2** Regulation of germ cell migration. Factors expressed by the different tissular components are indicated in italics. **A,** Four-week human embryo. Differentiation of primordial germ cells (PGC) occurs from epiblast-derived cells present in the yolk sac near the base of the allantois. PGC express alkaline phosphatase (Alk.Ph.), Oct4, and c-kit. Steel factor (also called stem cell factor), which binds to the receptor c-kit, and extracellular matrix proteins, such as fibronectin and laminin, are expressed along the PGC pathway. **B,** Five-week embryo. PGC migrate along the dorsal mesentery of the hindgut to the gonadal ridges. (Modified from Josso N, Rey R, Gonzalès J: Sexual differentiation. In New M [ed]. Pediatric Endocrinology. Available at http://www.endotext.org/pediatrics/pediatrics7/pediatrics frame7.htm. Accessed March 20, 2003. © 2003, MDTEXT.COM, INC.)

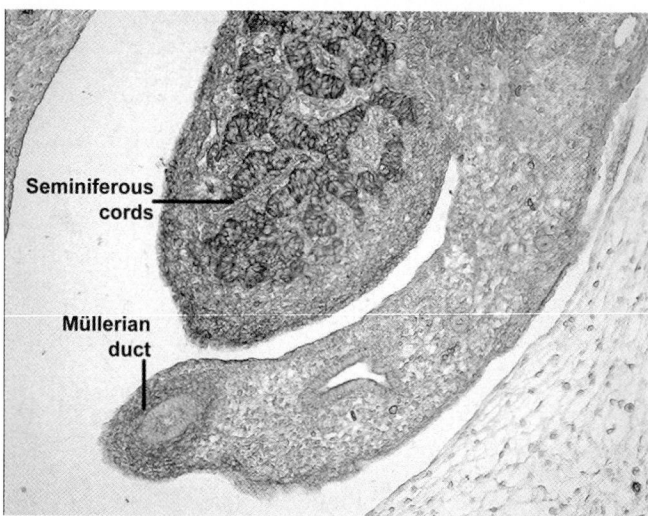

*Figure 143-3*   Immunocytochemical detection of antimüllerian hormone expression in differentiating testicular cords forming in an 8-week-old human fetus.

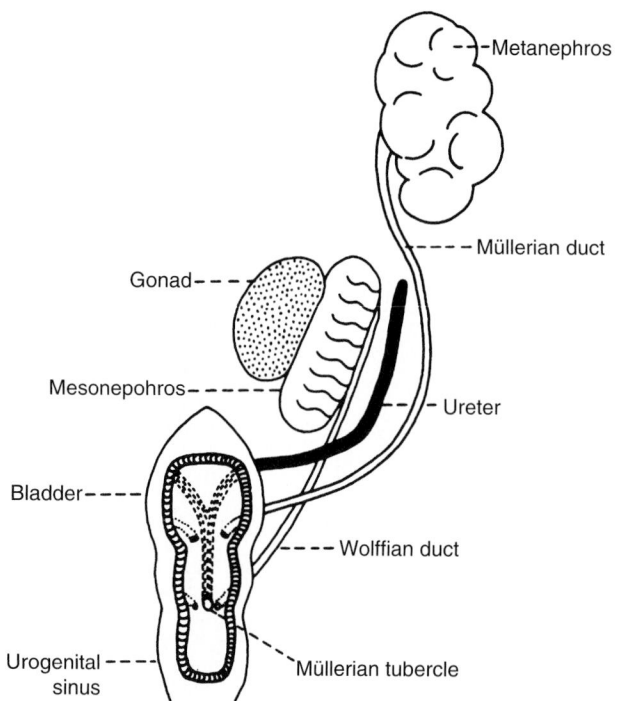

*Figure 143-5*   Undifferentiated reproductive tract. Both wolffian and müllerian ducts are present. Müllerian ducts open in the urogenital sinus at the level of the müllerian tubercle between the orifices of the wolffian duct. (From Josso N: Physiology of sex differentiation: A guide to the understanding and management of the intersex child. In Josso N [ed]. The Intersex Child. Basel, Karger, 1981, pp 1–13. © 1981 S. Karger AG, Basel.)

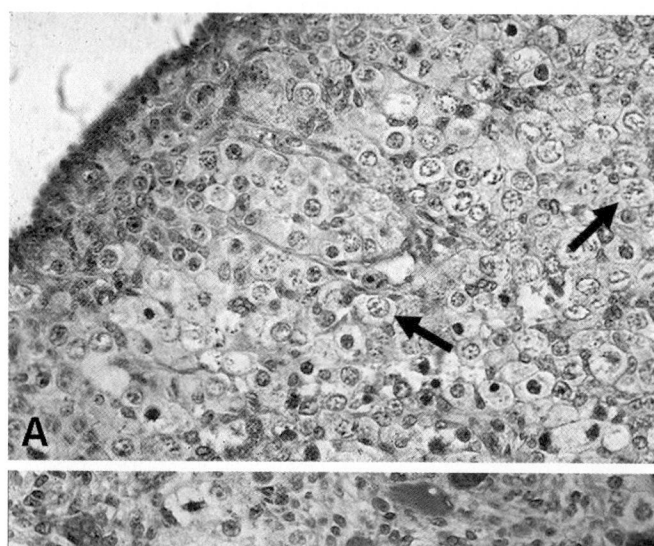
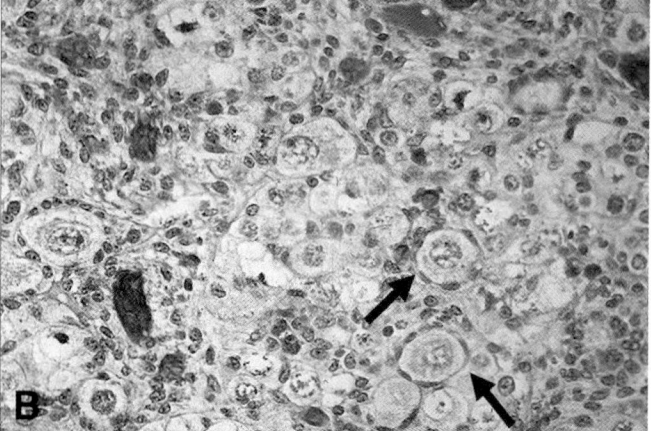

*Figure 143-4*   Developing human fetal ovaries. **A,** In the cortex of the 14-week-old gonad, germ cells are aligned in rows; some of them have entered the meiotic prophase *(arrows)*. **B,** In the medulla, primordial follicles *(arrows)* are visible.

and precedes the testis into the inguinal canal, is believed to play a critical role, but the factors that control its growth and differentiation are not totally elucidated.[24]

### Female Differentiation

Female orientation of the genital tract is characterized essentially by the stabilization of müllerian ducts and their differentiation into tubes and the uterus. Wolffian ducts begin to degenerate at 10 weeks, and their obliterated remnants are incorporated into müllerian derivatives.

At 11 weeks, the vaginal primordium is formed by the caudal tip of the müllerian ducts and by outgrowths of the posterior sinusal wall, the sinovaginal bulbs laterally and the müllerian tubercle medially. At 15 weeks, these structures fuse to form the vaginal plate or cord, which acquires a lumen about halfway through prenatal life. The major difference between male and female organogenesis lies in the downgrowth of the vaginal cord. Whereas in males, the prostatic utricle, the male equivalent of the vagina, opens just beneath the bladder neck, in females, the vaginal cord proliferates and its caudal end "slides" down the urethra to acquire a separate opening on the perineum (see Fig. 143-6). The hymen delineates the vagina and the dwindling urogenital sinus, whose pars pelvina gives rise to the vestibule.

## CONTROL BY TESTICULAR HORMONES

Male differentiation of the reproductive tract involves two discrete steps: müllerian regression and wolffian stabilization. Is the same testicular hormone responsible for both? By grafting a testosterone crystal near the ovary of a developing rabbit at the ambisexual stage, Jost[25] showed that the müllerian ducts were impervious to androgen but regressed when

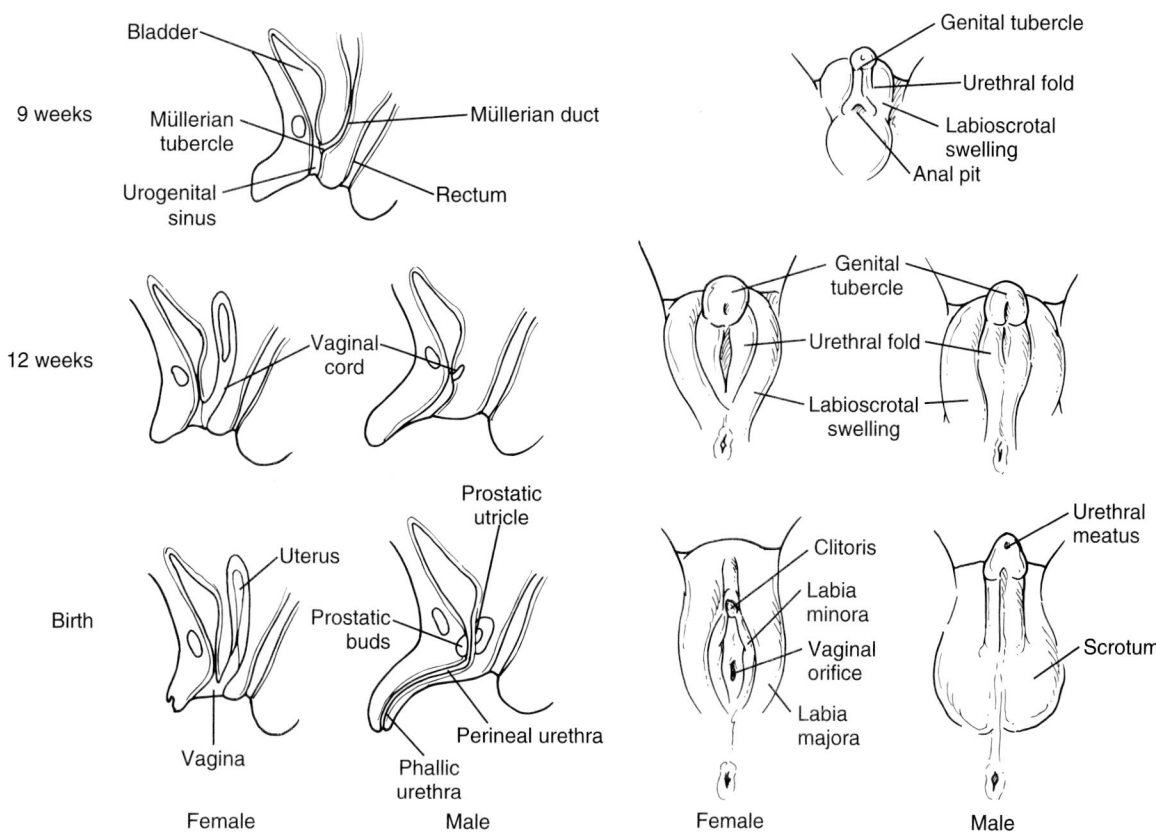

***Figure 143-6*** Sex differentiation of urogenital sinus *(left)* and external genitalia *(right)*. (Modified from Josso N, Rey R, Gonzalès J: Sexual differentiation. In New M [ed]: Pediatric Endocrinology. Available at *http://www.endotext.org/pediatrics/pediatrics7/pediatricsframe7.htm.* Accessed March 20, 2003. © 2003 MDTEXT.COM, INC.)

exposed to a graft of testicular tissue (see Fig. 143-1). Jost named the putative testicular factor responsible for müllerian regression the müllerian inhibitor, now known as either AMH or müllerian-inhibiting substance or factor. Figure 143-7 shows the hormones and receptors involved in control of male sex differentiation.

## ANTIMÜLLERIAN HORMONE

### Biosynthesis, Biochemistry, and Molecular Biology
A glycoprotein dimer linked by disulfide bonds,[26] AMH is a member of the transforming growth factor-beta (TGF-β) family. The 2.8-kb human gene has been cloned[27] and mapped to human chromosome 19. Its expression is under tight transcriptional control. It is produced by Sertoli cells, from testicular differentiation to puberty and by granulosa cells from birth to menopause. SOX9, steroidogenic factor-1,[28] WT-1,[29] and GATA-4[30] binding sites play a role in the initiation, whereas more distant promoter sequences are necessary for the maintenance[31,32] or the hormonal regulation[32] of AMH expression by Sertoli cells (Fig. 143-8).

AMH is detectable by enzyme-linked immunoassay in serum but not amniotic fluid of human male fetuses[33] and, for this reason, is not widely used in prenatal diagnosis. After birth, however, AMH assay is very useful for the investigation of cryptorchidism, micropenis,[34] intersex states,[35] and sterility in both sexes.[36,37]

### AMH Receptors and Target Organs
Members of the TGF-β family usually signal through two distantly related serine/threonine receptors, a primary receptor named type II, which binds the ligand, and a smaller one, type I, involved in signal transduction. The AMH receptor

type II has been cloned[38,39] and mapped to chromosome 12.[40] Three type I receptors used for bone morphogenetic protein signaling are involved in AMH transduction (reviewed in Ref. 41).

The type II receptor for AMH is expressed in Sertoli and granulosa cells, in the mesenchyme surrounding the müllerian duct[38,39] (Fig. 143-9), and in the gravid uterus.[42] Fetal müllerian ducts are the main target organs of AMH, as demonstrated by mutation analysis and gene targeting. Patients with mutations of either the AMH or the AMH receptor type II gene have persistent müllerian duct syndrome, characterized by the persistence of uterus and tubes in otherwise normally masculinized genetic males.[43] In mice, inactivation of either the AMH or the AMH receptor[44,45] genes also results in retention of müllerian derivatives in males.

Type II AMH receptors are also expressed in Leydig cells where they mediate the inhibitory effect of the hormone on Leydig cell differentiation and function.[46,47] AMH is normally not expressed by the ovary before the end of gestation and thus has no physiologic target organ in the female fetus. One exception is the freemartin condition in cattle. In bovine heterosexual pregnancies, the twins are joined by chorionic vascular anastomoses. The female product of such gestations, the freemartin, lacks müllerian derivatives and her ovaries are stunted and masculinized by AMH produced by the testes of her male twin.

## TESTOSTERONE

### Testosterone Biosynthesis and Regulation
Testosterone is produced from cholesterol by fetal Leydig cells through the coordinated action of steroidogenic proteins (reviewed in Ref. 48). Testosterone is detectable at approximately

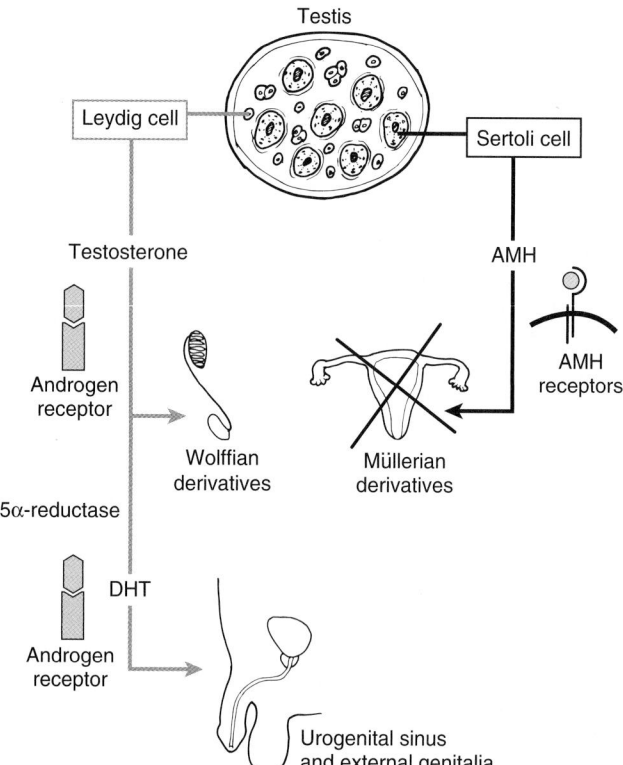

**Figure 143-7** Hormonal control of fetal male sex differentiation. Wolffian ducts are maintained by testosterone produced by Leydig cells and acting through the androgen receptor. Müllerian ducts regress under the influence of antimüllerian hormone (AMH) produced by Sertoli cells, acting through the membrane-bound AMH receptors. The urogenital sinus and external genitalia are virilized by dihydrotestosterone (DHT), resulting from the reduction of testosterone by the enzyme 5α-reductase. Testosterone and DHT act through the same androgen receptor. (Modified from Rey R, Picard JY: Embryology and endocrinology of genital development. Baillière Clin Endocrinol Metab 12:17–33, 1998. © 1998, Baillière Tindall.)

9 weeks, shortly after the time that Leydig cells form in the interstitium. There is a brisk increase in serum and testicular testosterone concentrations to a peak at mid-pregnancy and then a decline, in close correlation with the histologic pattern of fetal Leydig cell development.[11] Testosterone concentration in amniotic fluid at mid-pregnancy is also significantly higher in males than in females.[49] In the human fetus, placental human chorionic gonadotropin is not required for initiation of Leydig cell function but is regarded as the stimulus that maintains testicular steroidogenesis until the hypothalamic-pituitary axis gains control.[50] Fetal Leydig cells apparently escape human chorionic gonadotropin desensitization, allowing them to maintain a high testosterone output during the several weeks necessary to complete male differentiation of the genital tract.

### Androgen Metabolism in the Reproductive Tract: Dihydrotestosterone and 5α-Reductase
The mechanisms whereby androgens virilize the male embryo have been elucidated mainly by the work of Wilson and his associates.[51] Testosterone is the major steroid released by fetal testes in the bloodstream and enters cells by passive diffusion. Organs such as the wolffian duct that are adjacent to the fetal testis also take up testosterone by pinocytosis.[52] This local source of androgen is important for wolffian duct development, which does not occur if testosterone is supplied only via the peripheral circulation,

as in female pseudohermaphroditism caused by adrenal hyperplasia.

Inside the cell, testosterone is converted to dihydrotestosterone (DHT) by the enzyme 5α-reductase. DHT cannot be aromatized to estrogen, and thus its effects are purely androgenic. Also, DHT binds to the androgen receptor with greater affinity and stability than does testosterone. Therefore, in tissues wih 5α-reductase activity such as the prostate, urogenital sinus, and external genitalia, DHT is the active androgen. Patients with 5α-reductase deficiency show poor virilization of these tissues.[53] The androgen receptor gene, a member of the steroid receptor family, is located on the X chromosome (reviewed in Refs. 54 and 55). The human androgen receptor gene, which spans a minimum of 54 kb, is divided into eight exons. Most mutations occur in exons 4 through 8, which code for the steroid hormone–binding domain (see Chapter 150 for details).

### ENDOCRINE CONTROL OF TESTICULAR DESCENT

Control of testicular descent is still a hotly disputed issue, which we will not attempt to resolve here. A role for AMH has been suspected, but in mice, inactivation of either the AMH or the AMH receptor[56] genes does not lead to cryptorchidism. More importantly, mutations of insulin-like hormone 3 (INSL3), a member of the insulin/relaxin hormone superfamily secreted by fetal Leydig cells and shown to affect gubernaculum development in mutant mice,[16] have been detected in cryptorchid patients.[57] Prenatal DES treatment, which is associated with cryptorchidism, interferes with Insl3 expression in the mouse testis.[58] Androgens mediate the disappearance of the cranial suspensory ligament[59] and are required for the inguinoscrotal phase of testicular descent, perhaps acting through the genitofemoral nerve and the neuropeptide calcitonin gene-related peptide.[24]

### XENOESTROGENS, ENDOCRINE DISRUPTERS

In the human male, the increasing incidence of testicular cancer, cryptorchidism, and hypospadias has been attributed to intrauterine exposure to inappropriate levels of compounds with weak estrogenic activity, called xenoestrogens or endocrine disrupters, for example, plastics and insecticides.[60] Their role is analyzed in Chapter 149.

## CONTROL BY PARACRINE, GROWTH, AND TRANSCRIPTION FACTORS

### GONADAL DEVELOPMENT

Two members of the bone morphogenetic protein family, Bmp8b[61] and Bmp4,[62] are required for generation of primordial germ cells from the epiblast in the mouse embryo. Furthermore, mice homozygous for a mutation at the *Steel* locus, which controls the ligand for the tyrosine kinase receptor *c-kit*, are sterile because primordial germ cells fail to proliferate and do not reach the gonadal primordia (see Fig. 143-2). Testicular development is not hindered by the lack of germ cells[63] but is heavily dependent on cell migration from the mesonephros.[64] The characteristic vasculature of the testis is disrupted by overexpression of Wnt4.[65]

Although ovarian development does not apparently require specific genes,[66] ovaries cannot survive in the absence of germ cells. Thus, factors involved in the proliferation and migration of primordial germ cells and in stabilization and meiosis of oocytes are needed (reviewed in Ref. 67). Furthermore, FIGα is crucial to the formation of primordial follicles[68] whose recruitment is regulated by AMH,[69] whereas GDF9 is important for follicle growth beyond the primary stage.[70]

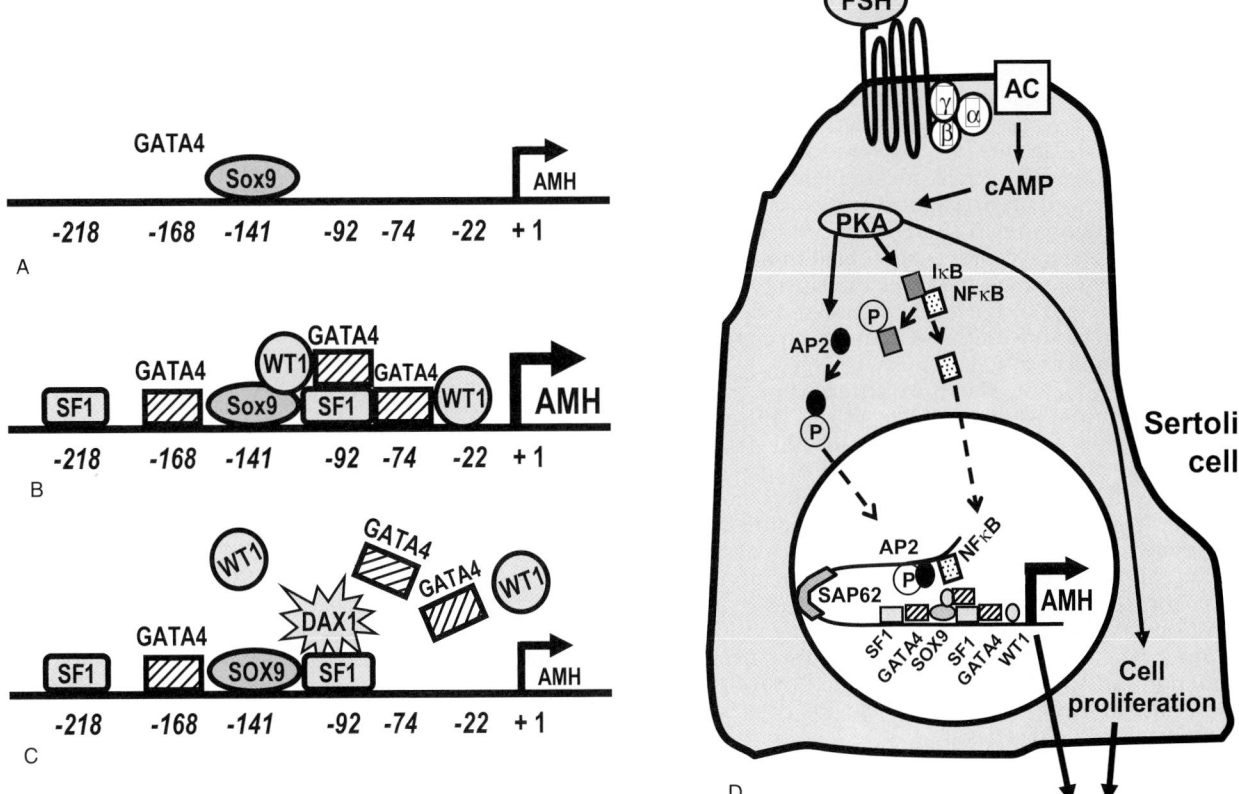

**Basal AMH expression**　　　　**FSH-dependent increase in AMH secretion**

*Figure 143-8* Regulation of antimüllerian hormone (AMH) expression in Sertoli cells. **A,** SOX9 initiates AMH expression through binding to a specific response element. **B,** Steroidogenic factor-1 (SF1), GATA4, and WT1 also bind to the proximal AMH promoter and enhance transcriptional activation. GATA4 and WT1 may also act by interacting with SF1, without binding to DNA. **C,** DAX1 is capable of interacting with SF1 and disrupts GATA4/SF1 and WT1/SF1 synergisms, resulting in a decrease in AMH expression. **D,** Upon binding to its specific receptor in the cell membrane, follicle-stimulating hormone (FSH) activates adenylate cyclase (AC) which increases intracellular concentration of adenosine cyclic 3′,5′-monophosphate (cAMP), resulting in an activation of protein kinase A (PKA). PKA phosphorylates AP2 and IκB, which releases nuclear factor-κB (NF-κB). Both transcription factors are translocated to the nucleus where they bind to specific response elements present more than 1.9 kb upstream of the AMH transcription start site, beyond the SAP62 gene. (**C,** Modified from Lasala C, Carré-Eusèbe D, Picard JY, Rey R: Subcellular and molecular mechanisms regulating anti-Müllerian hormone gene expression in mammalian and non-mammalian species. DNA Cell Biol 23:572–585, 2004. © 2004, Mary Ann Liebert Inc. **D,** Modified from Lukas-Croisier C, Lasala C, Nicaud J, et al: Follicle stimulating hormone increases testicular anti-Müllerian hormone (AMH) production through Sertoli cell proliferation and a non-classical cyclic AMP-mediated activation of the AMH gene. Mol Endocrinol 17:550–561, 2003. © 2003, The Endocrine Society.)

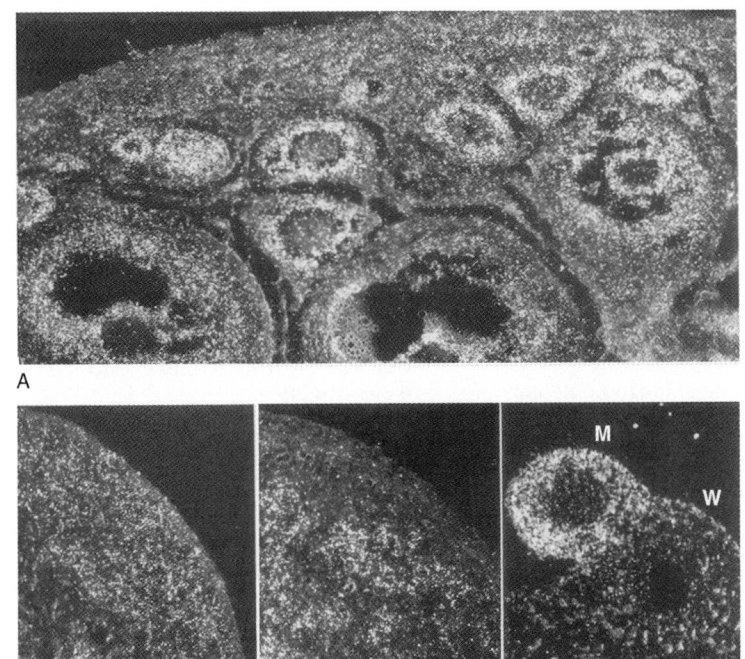

*Figure 143-9* In situ hybridization analysis of antimüllerian hormone receptor type 2 (AMHR2) expression in various rabbit tissues. **A,** In a 16-week-old adult ovary, AMHR2 is expressed by granulosa cells of preantral and small antral follicles. **B,** In the fetal testis, it is detected in Sertoli cells. **C,** In the reproductive tract of an 18-day-old female fetus, at the time of müllerian duct regression in males, AMHR2 is expressed by mesenchymal cells surrounding the müllerian epithelium (M) but not around the wolffian duct (W). (Modified from di Clemente N, Wilson C, Faure E, et al: Cloning, expression, and alternative splicing of the receptor for anti-Müllerian hormone. Mol Endocrinol 8:1006–1020, 1994. © 2003, The Endocrine Society. )

## MALE SEX DIFFERENTIATION

Testicular hormones are not the only factors shaping the sexual phenotype. Epithelial-mesenchymal interactions, probably mediated through growth factors, are also crucial regulators of male sex differentiation.[71] Mesenchyme and epithelium of reproductive organs interact, playing an instructive role in dictating the fate of the neighboring tissue. Both the AMH type II receptor[39] and the androgen receptor[72] are located in the mesenchyme, whereas Wnt7a, which mediates the emergence of AMH receptors, is expressed in the epithelium. Normal seminal vesicle growth and cytodifferentiation require the presence of the BMP family member *Gdf7*.[73]

Growth factors are also involved in the differentiation of the prostate and male external genitalia (Table 143-2). Although experiments have mainly been conducted in rodents, in whom organogenesis of genital accessory organs occurs after birth, they probably apply to humans at the end of fetal development. *Sonic hedgehog (Shh)* signaling from the epithelium controls development of the prostate[74] and male external genitalia.[75,76] In mice, *Hoxa13* function is essential for the normal expression of the downstream regulating genes *Fgf8* and *BMP7*[77]; mutations of *HOXa13* in humans lead to hand-foot-genital syndrome.[78] The prostate ductal system is also affected by loss of function of *BMP4* in the mesenchyme.[79] *Hoxd-13*[80] and *Hox-10*[81] mutations are also associated with defects in male accessory organ morphogenesis.[82]

## FEMALE SEX DIFFERENTIATION

Patterning of the female reproductive tract is also controlled by mesenchymal-epithelium interaction and growth factors. *Wnt4*, expressed in the mesonephric mesenchyme and coelomic epithelium, is essential in both sexes for initial müllerian duct formation[7] and *Wnt7a*, expressed in the epithelium, is required for appropriate uterine patterning.[83] The abnormal cytoarchitecture of the female reproductive tract of *Wnt7a* mutant mice closely resembles the situation reported in women exposed to the synthetic estrogen diethylstilbestrol during fetal development and indeed, mice with diethylstilbestrol-induced uterine malformation express only low levels of *Wnt7a* transcripts in the uterus at birth.[84]

*Hox* genes are also important in the development of the female reproductive tract. *Hox10* is required for defining

**Table 143-2** Growth Factors in Sex Differentiation of the Reproductive Tract

| Growth Factors | Function in Urogenital Development |
| --- | --- |
| HOXA13 | Deletion in mice leads to limb defects, vaginal hypoplasia, and deficiency of the os penis (hypodactyly syndrome)[86] |
| | Human mutation produces limb and uterine abnormalities and urinary tract malformations (hand-foot-genital syndrome)[87] |
| HOXD13 | Male accessory organ morphogenesis[80] |
| HOX10 | Male accessory organ morphogenesis[81] |
| TGF-β | Opposes action of androgen on prostatic cells[88] |
| BMP4 | Prostate differentiation[79] |
| FGF8 and 10 | Growth of genital tubercle[82] |
| SHH | Development of external genitalia[75] |
| | Prostate development[74] |
| | Penile morphogenesis[76] |
| WNT4 | Growth of müllerian ducts[7] |
| WNT7a | Uterine patterning[89] |
| | Sex-specific development of müllerian ducts[90] |
| | Repression of Leydig cells in the ovary[90] |

tissue boundaries; *Hoxa* and *Hoxd13* lack the caudal portion of the müllerian duct (reviewed in Ref. 85)

## PATHOPHYSIOLOGY

Understanding fundamental physiologic processes is a great asset in the diagnosis and treatment of human diseases, and intersexuality is no exception. For example, the development of a female phenotype in agonadal XY patients can be explained by the experiments of Jost[4] in fetal rabbits. Similarly, the association of external sexual ambiguity and persistence of müllerian derivatives should be expected in patients with gonadal dysgenesis who lack both androgens and AMH. In contrast, mutations of steroidogenic genes or of the androgen receptor cannot affect the synthesis or action of AMH, explaining why patients with these defects may have a completely female external phenotype and yet do not have a uterus or fallopian tubes. Paradoxically, at the same time that our knowledge progresses, other black boxes appear, which can best be solved by interaction between the clinic and the laboratory.

## REFERENCES

1. Bouin P, Ancel P: Sur la signification de la glande interstitielle du testicule embryonnaire. C R Soc Biol 55:1632–1634, 1903.
2. Lillie FR: The freemartin, a study of the action of sex hormones in foetal life of cattle. J Exp Zool 23:371–452, 1917.
3. Moore CR: Embryonic Sex Hormones and Sexual Differentiation. Springfield, Charles C Thomas, 1947.
4. Jost A: Recherches sur la différenciation sexuelle de l'embryon de lapin. III. Rôle des gonades foetales dans la différenciation sexuelle somatique. Arch Anat Microsc Morphol Exp 36:271–315, 1947.
5. Kent J, Wheatley SC, Andrews JE, et al: A male specific role for SOX9 in vertebrate sex determination. Development 122:2813–2822, 1996.
6. Parker KL, Schimmer BP: Steroidogenic factor 1: A key determinant of endocrine development and function. Endocr Rev 18:361–377, 1997.
7. Vainio S, Heikkil M, Kispert A, et al: Female development in mammals is regulated by Wnt-4 signaling. Nature 397:405–409, 1999.
8. Hastie ND: Life, sex, and WT1 isoforms—Three amino acids can make all the difference. Cell 106:391–394, 2001.
9. Hoyle C, Narvaez V, Alldus G, et al: Dax1 expression is dependent on steroidogenic factor 1 in the developing gonad. Mol Endocrinol 16:747–756, 2002.
10. Tilmann C, Capel B: Cellular and molecular pathways regulating mammalian sex determination. Recent Prog Horm Res 57:1–18, 2002.
11. Murray TJ, Fowler PA, Abramovich DR, et al: Human fetal testis: Second trimester proliferative and steroidogenic capacities. J Clin Endocrinol Metab 85:4812–4817, 2000.
12. Capel B: The role of SRY in cellular events underlying mammalian sex determination. Curr Top Dev Biol 32:1–37, 1996.
13. Parker KL, Schedl A, Schimmer BP: Gene interactions in gonadal development. Annu Rev Physiol 61:417–433, 1999.
14. Grimmond S, van Hateren N, Siggers P, et al: Sexually dimorphic expression of protease nexin-1 and vanin-1 in the developing mouse gonad prior to overt differentiation suggests a role in mammalian sexual development. Hum Mol Genet 9:1553–1560, 2000.
15. Bitgood MJ, Shen LY, McMahon AP: Sertoli cell signaling by desert hedgehog regulates the male germline. Curr Biol 6:298–304, 1996.
16. Nef S, Parada LF: Cryptorchidism in mice mutant for Insl3. Nat Genet 22:295–299, 1999.
17. Jost A: A new look at the mechanisms controlling sex differentiation in mammals. Johns Hopkins Med J 130:38–53, 1972.
18. Baker TG: A quantitative and cytological study of germ cells in human ovaries. Proc R Soc Lond B Biol Sci 158:417–433, 1963.

19. Ludwig KS: The Mayer-Rokitansky-Küster syndrome. An analysis of its morphology and embryology. Part II: Embryology. Arch Gynecol Obstet 262:27–42, 1998.

20. Allard S, Adin P, Gouédard L, et al: Molecular mechanisms of hormone-mediated müllerian duct regression: Involvement of α-catenin. Development 127:3349–3360, 2000.

21. Penington EC, Hutson JM: The urethral plate: Does it grow into the genital tubercle or within it ? Br J Urol 89:733–739, 2002.

22. Zalel Y, Pinhas-Hamiel O, Lipitz S, et al: The development of the fetal penis—An in utero sonographic evaluation. Ultrasound Obstet Gynecol 17:129–131, 2001.

23. Achiron R, Pinhas-Hamiel O, Zalel Y, et al: Development of fetal male gender: Prenatal sonographic measurement of the scrotum and evaluation of testicular descent. Ultrasound Obstet Gynecol 11:242–245, 1998.

24. Hutson JM, Hasthorpe S, Heyns CF: Anatomical and functional aspects of testicular descent and cryptorchidism. Endocr Rev 18:259–280, 1997.

25. Jost A: Problems of fetal endocrinology: The gonadal and hypophyseal hormones. Recent Prog Horm Res 8:379–418, 1953.

26. Picard JY, Josso N: Purification of testicular anti-müllerian hormone allowing direct visualization of the pure glycoprotein and determination of yield and purification factor. Mol Cell Endocrinol 34:23–29, 1984.

27. Cate RL, Mattaliano RJ, Hession C, et al: Isolation of the bovine and human genes for müllerian inhibiting substance and expression of the human gene in animal cells. Cell 45:685–698, 1986.

28. Arango NA, Lovell-Badge R, Behringer RR: Targeted mutagenesis of the endogenous mouse Mis gene promoter: In vivo definition of genetic pathways of vertebrate sexual development. Cell 99:409–419, 1999.

29. Hossain A, Saunders GF: Role of Wilms tumor 1 (WT1) in the transcriptional regulation of the mullerian-inhibiting substance promoter. Biol Reprod 69:1808–1814, 2003.

30. Watanabe K, Clarke TR, Lane AH, et al: Endogenous expression of müllerian inhibiting substance in early postnatal rat Sertoli cells requires multiple steroidogenic factor-1 and GATA-4-binding sites. Proc Natl Acad Sci U S A 97:1624–1629, 2000.

31. Beau C, Vivian N, Münsterberg A, et al: In vivo analysis of the regulation of the anti-müllerian hormone, as a marker of Sertoli cell differentiation during testicular development, reveals a multi-step process. Mol Reprod Dev 59:256–264, 2001.

32. Lukas-Croisier C, Lasala C, Nicaud J, et al: Follicle stimulating hormone increases testicular anti-müllerian hormone (AMH) production through Sertoli cell proliferation and a non-classical AMP-mediated activation of the AMH gene. Mol Endocrinol 17:550–561, 2003.

33. Josso N, Lamarre I, Picard JY, et al: Anti-müllerian hormone in early human development. Early Hum Dev 33:91–99, 1993.

34. Misra M, MacLaughlin DT, Donahoe PK, et al: Measurement of müllerian inhibiting substance facilitates management of boys with microphallus and cryptorchidism. J Clin Endocrinol Metab 87:3598–3602, 2002.

35. Rey RA, Belville C, Nihoul-Fékété C, et al: Evaluation of gonadal function in 107 intersex patients by means of serum anti-Müllerian hormone measurement. J Clin Endocrinol Metab 84:627–631, 1999.

36. van Rooij IAJ, Broekmans FJM, te Velde ER, et al: Serum anti-Müllerian hormone levels: A novel measure of ovarian reserve. Hum Reprod 17:3065–3071, 2002.

37. Fénichel P, Rey R, Poggioli S, et al: Anti-müllerian hormone as a seminal marker for spermatogenesis in non-obstructive azoospermia. Hum Reprod 14:2020–2024, 1999.

38. di Clemente N, Wilson CA, Faure E, et al: Cloning, expression and alternative splicing of the receptor for anti-müllerian hormone. Mol Endocrinol 8:1006–1020, 1994.

39. Baarends WM, van Helmond MJL, Post M, et al: A novel member of the transmembrane serine/threonine kinase receptor family is specifically expressed in the gonads and in mesenchymal cells adjacent to the müllerian duct. Development 120:189–197, 1994.

40. Imbeaud S, Faure E, Lamarre I, et al: Insensitivity to anti-müllerian hormone due to a spontaneous mutation in the human anti-müllerian hormone receptor. Nat Genet 11:382–388, 1995.

41. Josso N, di Clemente N: The AMH/MIS transduction pathway. Trends Endocrinol Metab 14:91–97, 2003.

42. Teixeira J, He WW, Shah PC, et al: Developmental expression of a candidate mullerian inhibiting substance type II receptor. Endocrinology 137:160–165, 1996.

43. Josso N, Belville C, Picard JY: Persistence of müllerian derivatives in males. In Fauser BCJM (ed): Molecular Biology in Reproductive Medicine. New York, Parthenon Press, 2003, p 575.

44. Mishina Y, Rey R, Finegold MJ, et al: Genetic analysis of the müllerian-inhibiting substance signal transduction pathway. Genes Dev 10:2577–2587, 1996.

45. Jamin SP, Arango NA, Mishina Y, et al: Requirement of Bmpr1a for müllerian duct regression during male sexual development. Nat Genet 32:408–410, 2002.

46. Racine C, Rey R, Forest MG, et al: Receptors for anti-müllerian hormone on Leydig cells are responsible for its effects on steroidogenesis and cell differentiation. Proc Natl Acad Sci U S A 95:594–599, 1998.

47. Lee MM, Seah CC, Masiakos PT, et al: Müllerian-inhibiting substance type II receptor expression and function in purified rat Leydig cells. Endocrinology 140:2819–2827, 1999.

48. Rey R: Intersex disorders: Biochemical and molecular diagnosis. In Robaire B, Chemes H, Morales C (eds): Andrology in the 21(st). Century. Englewood, NJ, Medimond Publishing, 2001, p 383.

49. Wudy SA, Dorr HG, Solleder C, et al: Profiling steroid hormones in amniotic fluid of midpregnancy by routine stable isotope dilution/gas chromatography-mass spectrometry: Reference values and concentrations in fetuses at risk for 21-hydroxylase deficiency. J Clin Endocrinol Metab 84:2724–2728, 1999.

50. Rabinovici J, Jaffe RB: Development and regulation of growth and differentiated function in human and subhuman primate fetal gonads. Endocr Rev 11:532–557, 1990.

51. Wilson JD, George FW, Renfree MB: The endocrine role in mammalian sexual differentiation. Recent Prog Horm Res 50:349–364, 1995.

52. Tong SYC, Hutson JM, Watts LM: Does testosterone diffuse down the wolffian duct during sexual differentiation? J Urol 155:2057–2059, 1996.

53. Imperato-McGinley J, Zhu YS: Androgens and male physiology the syndrome of 5 alpha-reductase-2 deficiency. Mol Cell Endocrinol 198:51–59, 2002.

54. Cato ACB, Peterziel HL: The androgen receptor as mediator of gene expression and signal transduction pathways. Trends Endocrinol Metab 9:150–154, 1998.

55. Quigley CA, De Bellis A, Marschke KB, et al: Androgen receptor defects: Historical, clinical, and molecular perspectives. Endocr Rev 16:271–321, 1995.

56. Mishina Y, Behringer RR: The in vivo function of Müllerian inhibiting substance during mammalian sexual development. Adv Dev Biol 4:1–25, 1996.

57. Tomboc M, Lee PA, Mitwally MF, et al: Insulin-like 3/relaxin-like factor gene mutations are associated with cryptorchidism. J Clin Endocrinol Metab 85:4013–4018, 2000.

58. Emmen JMA, McLuskey A, Adham IM, et al: Involvement of insulin-like factor 3 (Insl3) in diethylstilbestrol-induced cryptorchidism. Endocrinology 141:846–849, 2000.

59. van der Schoot PCJM, Elger WH: Perinatal development of gubernacular cones in rats and rabbits: Effect of exposure to anti-androgens. Anat Rec 236:399–407, 1993.

60. Sharpe RM: The 'oestrogen hypothesis'—Where do we stand now? Int J Androl 26:2–15, 2003.

61. Ying Y, Liu XM, Marble A, et al: Requirement of BMP8b for the generation of primordial germ cells in

the mouse. Mol Endocrinol 14:1053–1063, 2000.

62. Lawson KA, Dunn NR, Roelen BAJ, et al: Bmp4 is required for the generation of primordial germ cells in the mouse embryo. Genes Dev 13:424–436, 1999.

63. McLaren A: Germ and somatic cell lineages in the developing gonad. Mol Cell Endocrinol 163:3–9, 2000.

64. Ross AJ, Tilman C, Yao H, et al: AMH induces mesonephric cell migration in XX gonads. Mol Cell Endocrinol 211:1–7, 2003.

65. Jordan BK, Shen JHC, Olaso R, et al: Wnt4 overexpression disrupts normal testicular vasculature and inhibits testosterone synthesis by repressing steroidogenic factor 1/beta-catenin synergy. Proc Natl Acad Sci U S A 100:10866–10871, 2003.

66. Yu RN, Ito M, Saunders TL, et al: Role of Ahch in gonadal development and gametogenesis. Nat Genet 20:353–357, 1999.

67. Josso N, Rey R, Gonzalès J: Sexual differentiation. In New M (ed): Pediatric Endocrinology. Available at *http://www. endotext.org/pediatrics/pediatrics7/pediatric sframe7.htm.* Accessed March 20, 2003.

68. Soyal SM, Amleh A, Dean J: FIGα, a germ cell-specific transcription factor required for ovarian follicle formation. Development 127:4645–4654, 2000.

69. Durlinger ALL, Gruijters MJG, Kramer P, et al: Anti-Müllerian hormone attenuates the effects of FSH on follicle development in the mouse ovary. Endocrinology 142:4891–4899, 2001.

70. Dong J, Albertini DF, Nishimori K, et al: Growth differentiation factor-9 is required during early ovarian folliculogenesis. Nature 383:531–535, 1996.

71. Baskin LS, Erol A, Jegatheesan P, et al: Urethral seam formation and hypospadias. Cell Tissue Res 305:379–387, 2001.

72. Cooke PS, Young P, Cunha GR: Androgen receptor expression in developing male reproductive organs. Endocrinology 128:2867–2873, 1991.

73. Settle S, Marker P, Gurley K, et al: The BMP family member Gdf7 is required for seminal vesicle growth, branching morphogenesis, and cytodifferentiation. Dev Biol 234:138–150, 2001.

74. Podlasek CA, Barnett DH, Clemens JQ, et al: Prostate development requires sonic hedgehog expressed by the urogenital sinus. Dev Biol 209:28–39, 1999.

75. Perriton CL, Powles N, Chiang C, et al: Sonic hedgehog signaling from the urethral epithelium controls external genital development. Dev Biol 247:26, 2002.

76. Podlasek CA, Zelner DJ, Jiang HB, et al: Sonic hedgehog cascade is required for penile postnatal morphogenesis differentiation and adult homeostasis. Biol Reprod 63:423–438, 2003.

77. Morgan EA, Nguyen SB, Scott V, et al: Loss of Bmp7 and Fgf8 signaling in Hoxa13-mutant mice causes hypospadia. Development 130:3095–3109, 2003.

78. Goodman FR, Baccheli C, Brady AF, et al: Novel HOXA13 mutations and the phenotypic spectrum of hand-foot-genital syndrome. Am J Hum Genet 67:197–202, 2000.

79. Lamm MLG, Podlasek CA, Barnett DH, et al: Mesenchymal factor bone morphogenetic protein 4 restricts ductal budding and branching morphogenesis in the developing prostate. Dev Biol 232:301–314, 2001.

80. Podlasek CA, Duboule D, Bushman W: Male accessory organ morphogenesis is altered by loss of function of Hoxd-13. Dev Dyn 208:454–465, 1997.

81. Podlasek CA, Seo RM, Clemens JQ, et al: Hoxa-10 deficient male mice exhibit abnormal development of the accessory sex organs. Dev Dyn 214:1–12, 1999.

82. Haraguchi R, Suzuki K, Murakami R, et al: Molecular analysis of external genitalia formation: The role of fibroblast growth factor (Fgf) genes during genital tubercle formation. Development 127:2471–2479, 2000.

83. Sassoon D: Wnt genes and endocrine disruption of the female reproductive tract: a genetic approach. Mol Cell Endocrinol 158:1–5, 1999.

84. Miller C, Degenhardt K, Sassoon DA: Fetal exposure to DES results in de-regulation of Wnt7a during uterine morphogenesis. Nat Genet 20:228–230, 1998.

85. Kobayashi A, Behringer RR: Developmental genetics of the female reproductive tract in mammals. Nat Rev Genet 4:969–980, 2003.

86. Post LC, Innis JW: Infertility in adult hypodactyly mice is associated with hypoplasia of distal reproductive structures. Biol Reprod 61:1402–1408, 1999.

87. Mortlock DP, Innis JW: Mutation of HOXA13 in hand-foot-genital syndrome. Nat Genet 15:179–180, 1997.

88. Gerdes MJ, Dang TD, Larsen M, et al: Transforming growth factor-beta 1 induces nuclear to cytoplasmic distribution of androgen receptor and inhibits androgen response in prostate smooth muscle cells. Endocrinology 139:3569–3577, 1998.

89. Miller C, Sassoon DA: Wnt-7 maintains appropriate uterine patterning during the development of the mouse female reproductive tract. Development 125:3201–3211, 1998.

90. Parr BA, McMahon AP: Sexually dimorphic development of the mammalian reproductive tract requires Wnt-7a. Nature 395:707–710, 1998.

# Endocrinology of Sexual Maturation

## William D. Odell and J. Larry Jameson

**ENDOCRINE PHYSIOLOGY OF SEXUAL MATURATION**
　Hypothalamic-Pituitary-Gonadal Systems
　Triggers for the Onset of Puberty
　Adrenarche
　Changes in Bone Mineral Density during Sexual
　Maturation

Changes in Growth Hormone and Insulin-like Growth
Factor 1 during Sexual Maturation

**TIMING AND TEMPO OF PUBERTY**

**PHYSICAL CHANGES OF PUBERTY IN BOYS**

**PHYSICAL CHANGES OF PUBERTY IN GIRLS**

Sexual maturation, the process of puberty, consists of a complex series of interrelated endocrine and physiologic changes that transform a sexually immature individual to a sexually mature one capable of reproduction. The direct cause of sexual maturation is increasing production of steroids during puberty, predominantly testosterone and its metabolic products dihydrotestosterone (DHT) and estradiol in boys and ovarian estradiol, progesterone, and adrenal androgen precursors in girls. However, these changes in sex steroids are, in turn, regulated by neuroendocrine changes that integrate growth and reproduction. The pathways regulating the onset of puberty remain one of the great mysteries in endocrinology but recent discoveries of new hormones and receptors are providing new insight into this important physiologic process. In this chapter, we review the endocrine physiology of adrenarche, puberty, and the accompanying changes in growth, bone mineral density (BMD), and physical changes that accompany these dynamic hormonal events. This chapter serves as the background to understanding diseases resulting in delayed or precocious sexual maturation described in Chapters 147 and 148.

## ENDOCRINE PHYSIOLOGY OF SEXUAL MATURATION

### HYPOTHALAMIC-PITUITARY-GONADAL SYSTEMS

The pulsatile secretion of the gonadotropins, luteinizing hormone (LH), and follicle-stimulating hormone (FSH) is regulated by hypothalamic gonadotropin-releasing hormone (GnRH). Frequent blood sampling studies in adult males and females demonstrate that gonadotropin pulses occur about every 60 to 120 minutes and vary with sleep, and in response to sex steroid feedback, as occurs during the menstrual cycle[1] (see Chapter 141). Ultrasensitive gonadotropin assays demonstrate that while LH and FSH levels are low before puberty, they are secreted in a pulsatile fashion, indicating that there is ongoing pulsatile GnRH secretion.[2,3] This prepubertal hypothalamic-pituitary-gonadal system is held under a partial or modified negative-feedback control. Mean LH concentrations are 0.026 IU/L in prepubertal girls and 0.025 IU/L in prepubertal boys, whereas mean FSH concentrations were 1.9 in prepubertal girls and 0.73 in prepubertal boys.[4] In prepubertal agonadal girls, these values increase about 20- to 40-fold to 1.1 IU/L for LH and 34 IU/L for FSH. In agonadal boys, there is a 5- to 10-fold increase with LH values of 0.13 IU/L and FSH values of 6.5 IU/L. Although prepubertal gonadotropins rise in the absence of gonadal feedback, it is notable that these concentrations of LH and FSH are not increased to the degree seen in sexually mature men and women, suggesting that

gonadal steroids and peptides do not account fully for the low prepubertal gonadotropins; intrinsic hypothalamic regulatory systems must also exist.[5] In fact, gonadotropins are increased during fetal development and during the first few months after birth.[6] In boys, the high fetal level of LH is accompanied by increased testosterone and DHT, which are important for inducing virilization of the external genitalia (see Chapter 143). This transient increase in gonadotropins is sometimes referred to as *mini-puberty of infancy*.[7] The fact that gonadotropins rise and are subsequently suppressed during early childhood provides additional evidence for active neural control of puberty. These hormonal events and some of the putative regulatory steps are summarized in Figure 144-1.

As puberty progresses, there is little change in the frequency of LH pulsations. However, the mass of hormone secreted during each pulse, and the amplitude of each pulse, increase strikingly,[8] suggesting that the sexual maturation change in LH consists of a specific mass/amplitude-dependent mechanism. Because the metabolic clearance rate of FSH is much slower than that of LH, it is more difficult to characterize the pulsation characteristics of FSH. However, GnRH induces the release of both LH and FSH and cross-correlation studies confirm that LH and FSH secretory bursts occur simultaneously at all ages. In boys studied longitudinally, the percentage of peaks with high pulse amplitude increases steadily with each stage of puberty[9] (Figure 144-2). In early puberty, there is a nocturnal increase in LH, suggesting a sleep-associated regulatory mechanism that either activates or de-represses pathways controlling GnRH release. At the completion of puberty, there is no day/night difference in LH/FSH pulsations.[8,9] Thus, the nocturnal activity of the GnRH pulse generator appears to represent a discrete developmental stage. In patients with anorexia nervosa who develop hypogonadotropic hypogonadism, but then gain weight, recovery of the reproductive axis is heralded by nocturnal increases in gonadotropins,[10] suggesting that this feature is characteristic of reactivation of the GnRH pulse generator rather than an age-specific event. The pubertal rise in mean LH and FSH stimulates the ovaries to secrete increasing amounts of estradiol and the testes to secrete increasing amounts of testosterone. These steroids then stimulate the development of secondary sex characteristics.

In addition to these changes in LH, FSH, and gonadal steroids, gonadal production of inhibin A and B changes during puberty. The chemistry and function of the inhibins and activins are described separately in Chapter 140. Girls have higher mean FSH, particularly during puberty stages II to IV, than boys.[11] This difference likely reflects the relatively low activity of inhibin, which is produced by the Sertoli cells of the testis, and the granulosa/theca cells of the ovary (see below). Inhibin B is the physiologically important form in

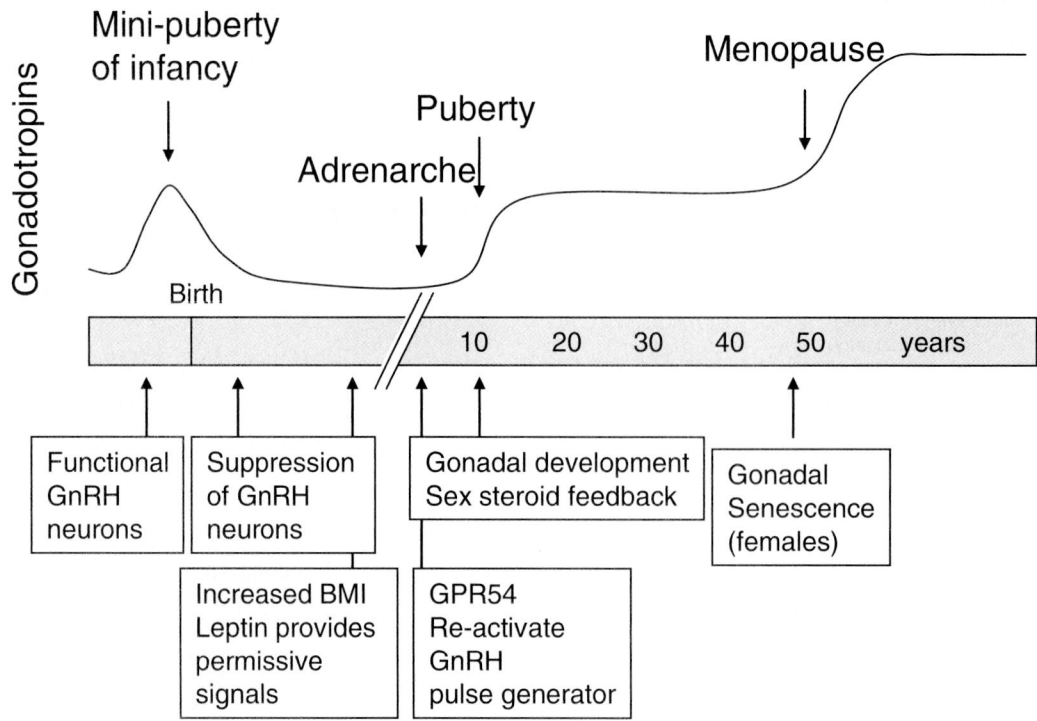

**Figure 144-1** Timeline of changes in the reproductive axis.

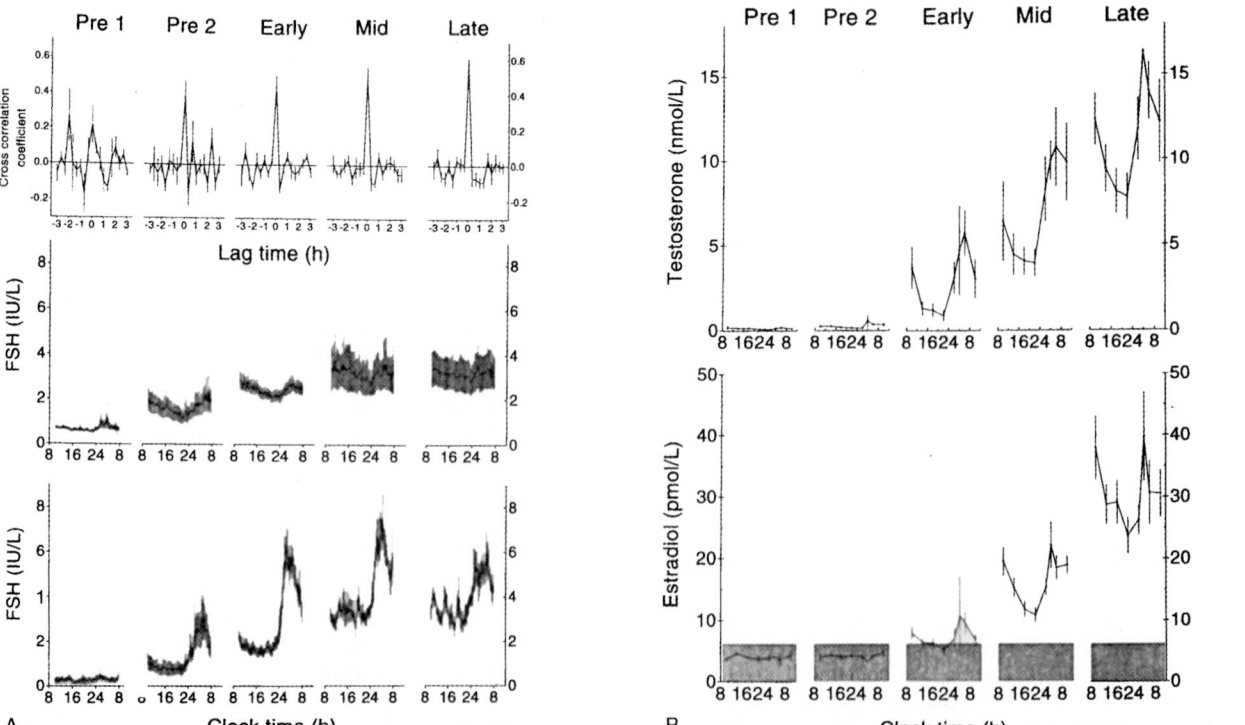

**Figure 144-2** **A,** Mean luteinizing hormone (LH) and follicle-stimulating hormone (FSH) measured each 20 minutes for 24 hours in 12 boys monitored throughout puberty. Pre 1 and Pre 2 designate two prepubertal times. Pre 1 had testicular volumes of 1 to 2 mL; Pre 2 had testicular volumes of 2 mL. Early, mid, and late designates early puberty, midpuberty, and late puberty. **B,** Mean 24-hour blood testosterone and estradiol in the same 12 subjects. (From Albertsson-Wikland K, Rosberg S, Lawering B, et al: Twenty-four-hour profiles of luteinizing hormone, follicle-stimulating hormone, testosterone and estradiol levels: A semi-longitudinal study throughout puberty in healthy boys. J Clin Endocrinol Metab 82:541, © 1997, The Endocrine Society.)

men.[12] Serum levels of inhibin B increase between stages I and II of puberty and remain constant from stage II to stage V. This finding is in contrast to FSH concentrations, which increase to stage III and remain constant thereafter. In late puberty (stage II and on), inhibin B is negatively correlated with FSH, a phenomenon that is also present in adult men. Inhibin production by the ovary varies during the menstrual cycle.[13] Inhibin B increases during the follicular phase, whereas inhibin A increases during the luteal phase. Inhibin B has been used as an index of ovarian reserve, perhaps reflecting the pool of primordial follicles.[14]

### TRIGGERS FOR THE ONSET OF PUBERTY

The physiologic mechanisms controlling the onset of puberty remain an important unsolved problem in endocrinology. As noted above, the onset of puberty is perhaps more accurately described as reactivation of the reproductive axis. Although the regulatory mechanisms that control puberty are not completely understood, genetic disorders provide important clues to the critical steps.[15] Mutations have been identified in: (1) the pathway that controls the development of GnRH-producing neurons (KAL1 or fibroblast growth factor receptor 1 [FGFR-1]; (2) transcription factors that regulate normal development of the ventromedial hypothalamus and pituitary (steroidogenic factor-1 [SF-1] or DAX1); (3) GnRH receptor (GnRHR); and (4) the gonadotropin genes (luteinizing hormone-beta [LH-β] or follicle-stimulating hormone-beta [FSH-β]. Genes that affect hypothalamic regulation of GnRH secretion (LEP, LEPR) can also cause inherited hypogonadotropic hypogonadism. Thus, each of these steps is necessary for GnRH stimulation of gonadotropin secretion. However, there is no evidence that changes in the expression or regulation of these genes is the key regulatory step for activation of puberty.

In 2003, a candidate regulator of puberty was discovered based on studies of subjects with idiopathic hypogonadotropic hypogonadism without anosmia or other features associated Kallmann's syndrome. Linkage studies localized a candidate gene, GPR54, which encodes a G protein–coupled receptor.[16] Mutations were identified in the original pedigree as well as in unrelated patients.[16,17] Targeted mutagenesis of this receptor in mice causes a similar syndrome with gonadotropin deficiency and failure to undergo secondary sexual maturation.[16] The GPR54 knockout mice have apparently normal GnRH-producing neurons and respond to exogenous GnRH by producing pituitary gonadotropins. The affected patients respond to exogenous GnRH and are actually hypersensitive with a left-shifted dose-response curve. Thus, pituitary function is normal and the defect appears to involve an upstream pathway that regulates GnRH release. The GPR54 receptor binds a ligand referred to as kisspeptin. Administration of kisspeptin stimulates GnRH secretion in mice[18] and preliminary data suggests that it may be sufficient to induce gonadotropin secretion in prepubertal primates. While further studies of this pathway are needed, these findings suggest that kisspeptin or related ligands, acting via GPR54, may be the proximate pathway for reactivating the GnRH pulse generator and regulating the onset of puberty. If correct, this idea begs the question, what regulates production of kisspeptin and GPR54? Moreover, it is important to integrate other physiologic events that occur at the time of puberty. For example, leptin signals that adequate fat mass is available before entering the reproductive phase.[19] In leptin-deficient patients, there is initiation or resumption of gonadotropin secretion after leptin replacement.[19] Recombinant leptin restores gonadotropin secretion in women with hypothalamic amenorrhea associated with anorexia nervosa.[20] Leptin levels rise by 50% just before the onset of puberty and then fall to baseline after stage II.[21,22] Thus, leptin is necessary for activation of the GnRH pulse generator but there is no compelling evidence that it is the

primary trigger for the onset of puberty. The initial nocturnal GnRH surges suggest a link to circadian pathways, or possibly disinhibition during rapid eye movement (REM) sleep. Thus, multiple pathways may converge to signal the onset of puberty; key steps involve activation of GPR54, the leptin receptor, and activation of the GnRH pulse generator.

### ADRENARCHE

The adrenal cortex in humans secretes three classes of steroid hormones: glucocorticoids, mineralocorticoids, and androgen precursors. The androgen precursors are mainly dehydroepiandrosterone (DHEA), dehydroepiandrosterone sulfate (DHEA-S), and androstenedione. These steroids do not bind to androgen receptors or act as androgens per se. Androgenic potency is derived from conversion, in peripheral tissues (e.g., skin, hair follicle, and liver), to the potent androgens testosterone and DHT.

During development, the human adrenal consists of fetal and adult zones.[23] Patients with X-linked adrenal hypoplasia congenita (AHC), which is caused by mutations in the orphan nuclear receptor DAX1, develop adrenal insufficiency because the adult zone does not form.[24] The fetal zone secretes large amounts of DHEA-S because of relatively low expression of 3β-hydroxysteroid dehydrogenase (3β-HSD). The fetal zone normally regresses in early infancy and the adult zone persists and forms the characteristic zona reticularis, zona fasciculate, and zona glomerulosa. In adolescents and adults, DHEA-S is synthesized mainly by the zona reticularis.[25]

Adrenarche is defined as the time when adrenal androgens, principally DHEA, DHEA-S, and androstenedione, increase in a process that is largely independent of sexual maturation.[26] Adrenarche is associated with increased growth of pubic and axillary hair, and occurs before increases in gonadal sex steroid secretion.[27] Premature adrenarche, which occurs more commonly in girls than boys, is associated with precocious development of axillary and pubic hair and is caused by premature increases in adrenal DHEA-S production. The usual age of adrenarche onset is about 6 years. Studies of 17-ketosteroid excretion published in the early 1940s showed that at about 6 years of age, 17-ketosteroid excretion begins to increase and rises steadily thereafter reaching adult values by about ages 20 to 21.[28,29] These observations have been confirmed with serum steroid measurements (Fig. 144-3).

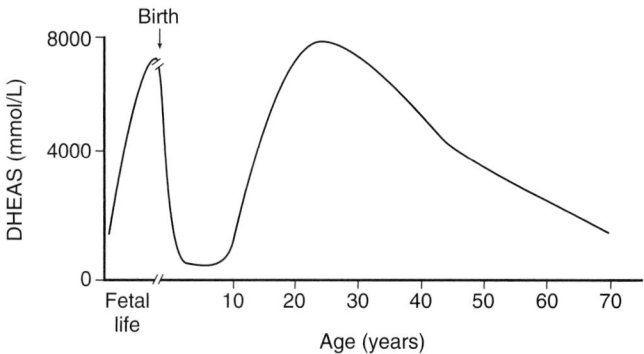

*Figure 144-3* Variation in circulating dehydroepiandrosterone sulphate (DHEA-S) concentration throughout human life. DHEA-S concentrations reach a peak at term; following birth, there is a rapid decline. At about 6 years of age, DHEA-S concentrations rise again (adrenarche) and reach a peak during early adulthood, declining thereafter in a process often called adrenopause (Permission from Auchus RJ, Rainey WE: Adrenarche—Physiology, biochemistry and human disease. Clin Endocrinol [Oxf] 60:288–296, 2004.)

The factors that regulate adrenarche remain enigmatic. Adrenocorticotropic hormone (ACTH) is necessary and is an important modulator of adrenal androgen, as well as glucocorticoid, secretion. However, its potency relative to control of cortisol secretion is much less, by a factor of about 1000.[30] In addition to ACTH, several other hormones have been postulated or demonstrated to modify adrenal androgen secretion. These hormones include estrogens, prolactin, growth hormone (GH), gonadotropins, lipotropin, and a postulated pituitary hormone called cortical androgen-stimulating hormone.[30] Under selected circumstances, each of these hormones may affect adrenal androgen secretion, but none appears to be a major modulator. Of note, estrogen treatment of prepubertal and preadrenarchal girls with gonadal dysgenesis commonly leads to the development of axillary and pubic hair, as well as inducing estrogenic effects. However, serum DHEA and DHEA-S do not change significantly in such children.[31,32] Both estrone and estradiol are inhibitors of 3β-HSD. Several investigators have postulated that estrogens, directly or indirectly, modify adrenal steroidogenesis, which could, in turn, explain the onset of adrenarche.

Although the factors regulating adrenarche remain unknown, it appears that changes in the constitution of adrenal cells, and their specific enzymatic pathways, account primarily for variations in adrenal androgen production. The activities of CYP11A, CYP17, and SULT2A1, all of which are abundant in the zona reticularis, direct steroidogenesis towards production of DHEA-S.[27] In addition, DHEA-S production is increased by expression of cofactor proteins, such as cytochrome b5, which enhance the 17,20-lyase activity of CYP17.

Abnormalities in the timing and intensity of adrenarche may be linked to insulin resistance and polycystic ovary syndrome (PCOS).[33,34] Thus, this topic remains an important area of research.

### CHANGES IN BONE MINERAL DENSITY DURING SEXUAL MATURATION

In a study of 403 white Dutch children, dual-energy x-ray absorptiometry was used to estimate BMD and was correlated data with pubertal stage, fat mass, and lean tissue mass.[35] The percentage of body fat was higher in girls than boys at all ages and was increased in girls in consecutive pubertal stages. In contrast, body fat was lower in stage IV than in stage III in boys. Tanner stage was positively correlated with BMD in both boys and girls and also with body fat percentage in girls. In a separate study of 295 girls and 205 boys, spinal BMD was shown to positively correlate in both sexes with calcium intake, pubertal stage, and physical activity.[36] The major determinant of BMD was Tanner stage in girls and body weight in boys. In a longitudinal study of 68 males and 72 females, it was found that over 35% of total body bone mineral and 27% of bone mineral at the femoral neck is laid down in a 4-year adolescent period during peak linear growth velocity.[37] This corresponds to as much bone mineral as most adults lose during their remaining life. In a prospective study of peak height velocity and peak bone mineral content (BMC) velocity, peak BMC velocity peaked 1.2 years after peak height velocity in boys and 1.6 years after peak height velocity in girls.[38] Within 3 years before or after peak BMC velocity, boys consistently had higher BMC than girls, and this difference increased steadily throughout puberty. Calcium accretion into bone was estimated to be about 500 mg/day at time of peak BMC velocity.

In summary, BMD increases in parallel with pubertal stage in both sexes. The bone mineral accretion rate is very high during these years, and attainment of optimal peak bone density demands a high calcium intake of over 1 g daily during adolescence. Studies in humans and in animal models have suggested that estrogen, formed from aromatization of testosterone in boys and directly secreted from the ovary in girls, is a key mediator of this increasing bone density.

### CHANGES IN GROWTH HORMONE AND INSULIN-LIKE GROWTH FACTOR 1 DURING SEXUAL MATURATION

The dynamics and disorders of growth are discussed in other chapters (Chapters 36 and 37) and will not be discussed in detail here. However, the changes in gonadal steroids occurring during puberty are associated with and appear to cause the striking increase in height velocity and the increases in insulin-like growth factor 1 (IGF-1) and GH secretion seen during sexual maturation.[39–42] Growth velocity is approximately 6 cm/year during prepubertal childhood. This velocity increases in girls of approximately 11 years of age, peaks on average at age 12, and falls thereafter. In boys, growth velocity increases later, beginning at approximately 13 years old and peaking at about 14 years old[40] (Fig. 144-4). Changes in IGF-1 parallel these changes in growth velocity as depicted in Figure 144-5.[40] The mean 24-hour concentration of GH is approximately 5 to 7 µg/L in prepubertal children and in early puberty and increases strikingly during mid to late puberty to about 13 to 15 µg/L.[41] These changes in GH are responsible for the striking pubertal changes in IGF-1 and growth velocity. As is true for changes in LH and FSH during puberty, the rise in the mean GH concentration is caused primarily by increases in pulse amplitude and an increase in mass of the GH pulse secretory burst rather than by changes in pulse frequency.[41,42]

### TIMING AND TEMPO OF PUBERTY

Sexual maturation in girls and probably in boys has occurred at younger and younger ages over the past 100 years.[43] Between 1850 and 1950, the mean age of menarche decreased by 3 to 4 months each decade in developed nations. Most

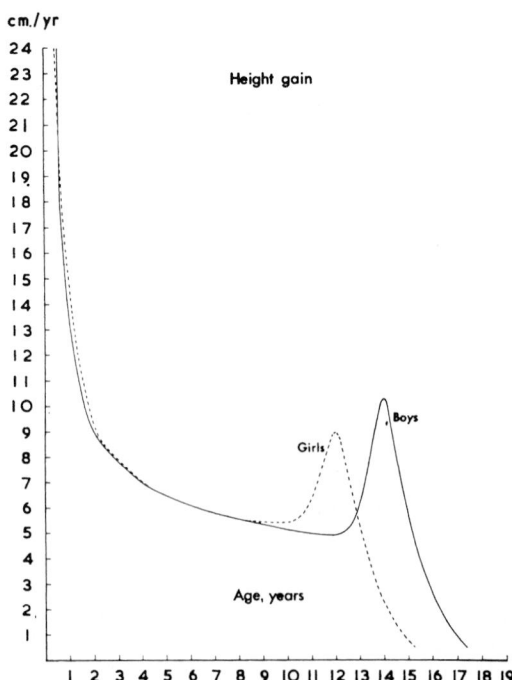

**Figure 144-4** Typical individual curves for supine length or height in boys and girls. These curves represent the velocity of the typical boy and girl at any given instant. (From Tanner JM, Whitehouse RH, Takaishi M: Standards from birth to maturity for height, weight, height velocity, and weight velocity: British children, 1995. Arch Dis Child 41:454, 1966.)

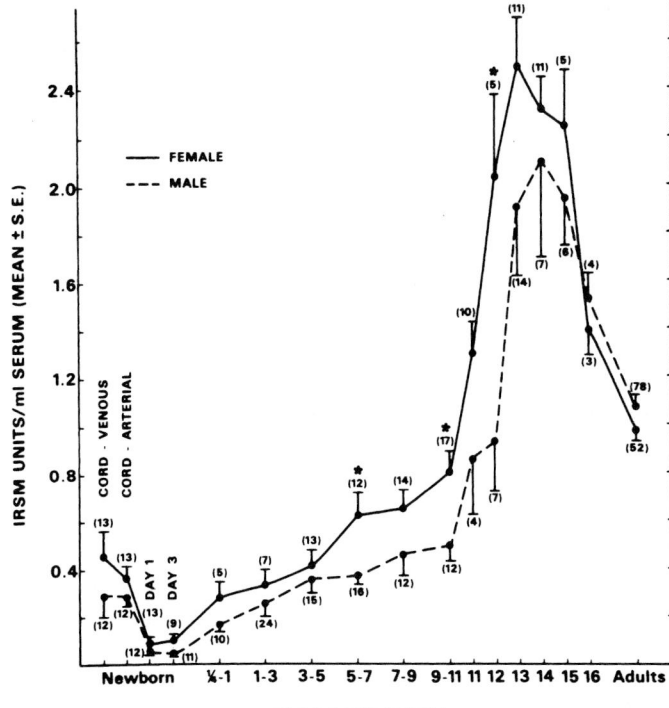

*Figure 144-5* Comparison of somatomedin (Insulin-like growth factor 1, IGF-1) levels in normal male and female newborns, children at various ages, and adults. Sera were obtained from the same newborns at delivery (CAS and CVS) and again 1 and 3 days after birth. The number of subjects in each group is indicated in parentheses. *Asterisk,* significant difference between mean levels of immunoreactive somatomedin in the sera of males and females in each age group, as determined by one-way analysis of variance ($P < 0.001$), followed by Duncan's multiple range test ($P < 0.05$). (From Bala RM, Lapatka J, Leung A, et al: Serum immunoreactive somatomedin levels in normal adults, pregnant women at term, children at various ages, and children with constitutionally delayed growth. J Clin Endocrinol Metab 52:508–512, © 1981, The Endocrine Society.)

investigators believe that improved nutritional status accounts for these changes.[44] However, as depicted in Figure 144-6, there is considerable variability in the age of menarche among ethnic groups, and even within a defined population. In the United States population, the age of menarche of African-American girls occurs significantly earlier than that of non-Hispanic white and Mexican-American girls.[45] Given this variability, some of which is likely to be genetically determined, it is difficult to discern whether the trend toward earlier puberty has continued over the last 50 years.[43]

With the onset of adrenarche, the adrenal gland secretes androgen precursors that stimulate axillary and pubic hair growth independent of gonadal steroids. Whereas in girls these precursor androgens are the major source of androgens, in boys the adrenal androgen precursors produce only a small fraction (less than 5% in adults) of the circulating androgens. Therefore, in boys, changes in axillary and pubic hair proceed in parallel with an increase in testicular size. The most widely used descriptive system of pubertal events in boys and girls is that of Marshall and Tanner[46,47] who examined groups of English boys and girls as they went through the process of sexual maturation. The relative timing of growth and puberty in boys and girls is summarized in Figure 144-7. These events are interrelated in that gonadotropin-induced sex steroids enhance GH secretion and ultimately induce epiphyseal closure.

## PHYSICAL CHANGES OF PUBERTY IN BOYS

The physical changes that occur in the genitalia and pubic hair in boys are summarized in Table 144-1 and Figure 144-8. Increasing testosterone concentrations also produce changes in many other organs. In some of these tissues, testosterone produces the effects; in other tissues, metabolic products of testosterone may produce the changes. Estradiol, for example, is produced by peripheral aromatization of testosterone in fat, muscle, and liver.[48] Estradiol is a much more potent inhibitor of LH and FSH secretion than testosterone, even though it is present in blood in much smaller concentrations than testosterone. Estradiol is probably the major feedback regulator of LH and FSH secretion in men,[49] acting both at the

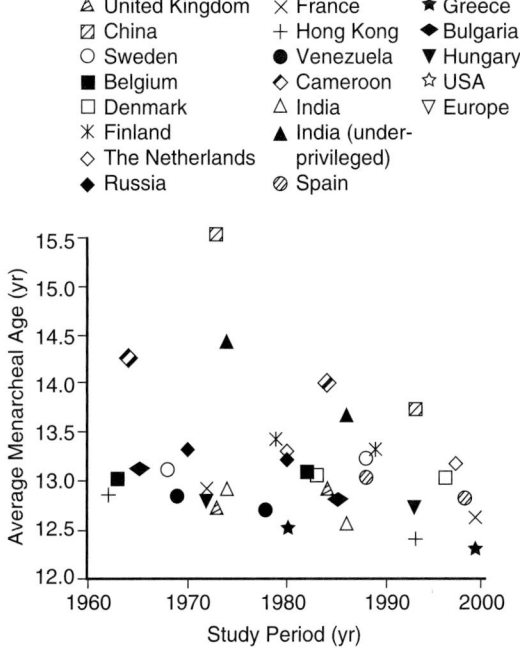

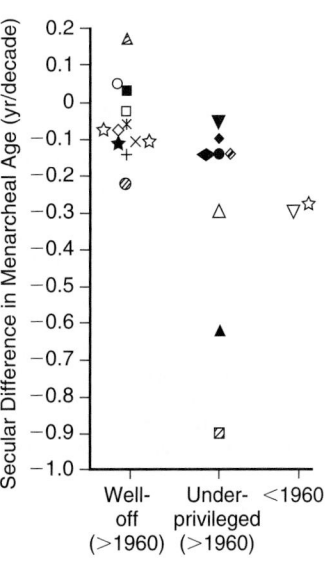

*Figure 144-6* Recent trends in the average age of menarche in different countries. **Left,** Data obtained after 1960 in different countries at several 10-year intervals. **Right,** Secular differences in menarcheal age calculated from those data. (With permission from Parent AS, Teilmann G, Juul A, et al: The timing of normal puberty and the age limits of sexual precocity: Variations around the world, secular trends, and changes after migration. Endocr Rev 24:668–693, 2003.)

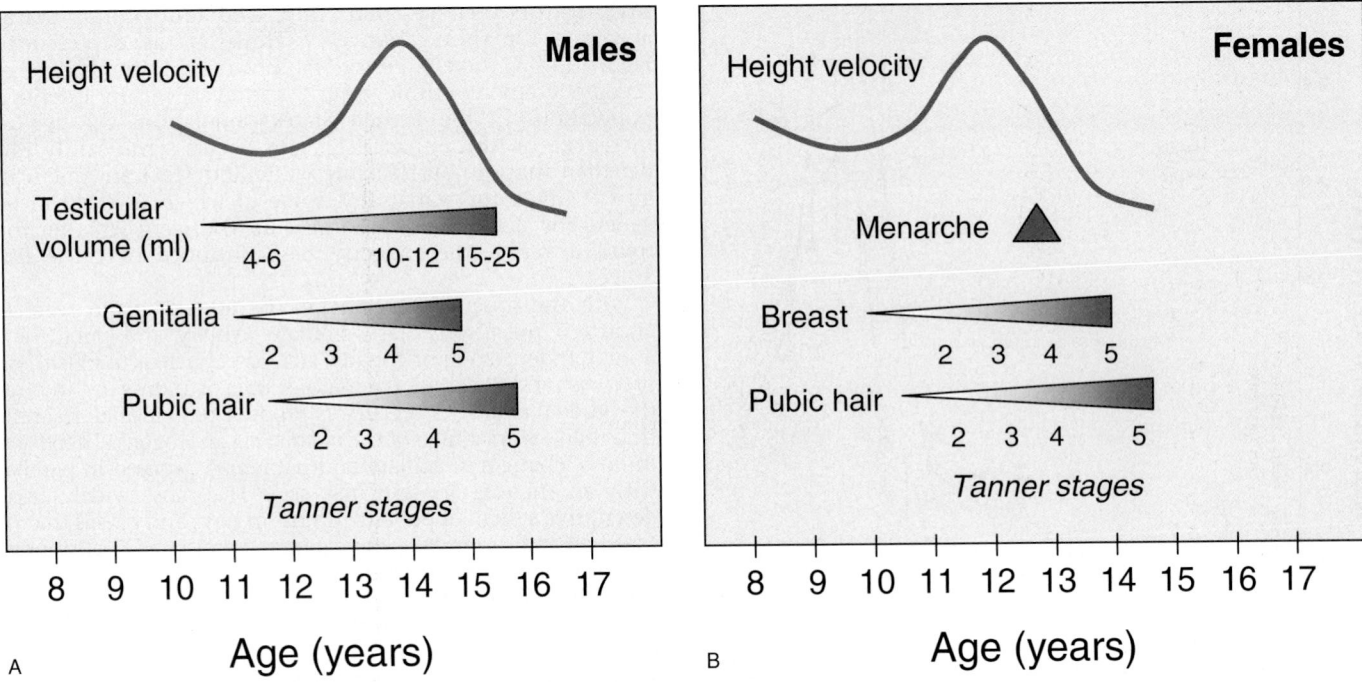

*Figure 144-7* Tempo of growth and puberty in males and females. (With permission from Dattani MT, Brook CGD: Adolescent Medicine [Chapter 8]. In Braunwald E, Fauci AS, Kasper DL, et al [eds]: Harrison's Principles of Internal Medicine, 15th ed. New York, McGraw-Hill, 2001.)

hypothalamic and pituitary levels. The antiestrogen clomiphene increases LH and FSH secretion in men. Aromatization of testosterone occurs in hypothalamic and pituitary tissues, and such conversion may modulate LH and FSH secretion at these sites. As discussed previously, several observations suggest that changes in BMD are produced by estradiol actions on bone in both boys and girls, including the observation that mutations in the estrogen receptor reduce bone density.[50] Another metabolic product of testosterone is DHT, which is produced in peripheral and target tissues. During embryogenesis, DHT is required for the normal devel-opment of tissues derived from the genital tubercle and the urogenital sinus. Thus, in response to testosterone or its meta-bolic products, a host of changes develop in most tissues of the body in boys. The larynx increases in size and the voice deepens, the bones increase in mass, muscle strength increases, a growth spurt results, the red blood cell mass increases, the skin thickens, and hair increases on the trunk in the pubic and axillary areas and on the face. Over the years, hair recedes on the head. Behavior is altered as testosterone or estradiol produced from testosterone in the nervous system stimulates sexual libido and aggressiveness. Many of these

| | | Age at Onset (yr) | |
|---|---|---|---|
| Stage | Description | Mean | Range (95% CI) |
| 1 | Preadolescent: The vellus over the pubes is no further developed than that over the abdominal wall, i.e., no pubic hair. | | |
| 2 | Sparse growth of long, slightly pigmented downy hair, straight or only slightly curled, appears chiefly at the base of the penis. This stage is difficult to see on photographs, particularly of fair-haired subjects. Although the rating of stage 2 was used in this study, it cannot be regarded as reliable, and ages at which subjects are said to have reached stage 2 are almost certainly too late. | 13.4* | 11.2–15.6 |
| 3 | Hair is considerably darker, coarser, and mostly curled. Hair spreads sparsely over the pubic junction. This and subsequent stages were clearly recognizable on photographs. | 13.9* | 11.9–16.0 |
| 4 | Hair is now adult in type, but the area covered is still considerably smaller than in most adults. Hair has not spread to the medial surface of the thighs. | 14.4* | 12.2–16.5 |
| 5 | Hair is adult in quantity and type and distributed as an inverse triangle of the classically feminine pattern. Spread has occurred to the medial surface of the thighs but not up to the linea alba or elsewhere above the base of the inverse triangle. In about 80% of men, pubic hair spreads farther beyond the triangular pattern, but this pattern takes some time to occur after stage 5 has been reached. This more widespread pubic hair may be rated as "stage 6"; this stage is not usually reached before the mid-20s. | 15.2* | 13.0–17.3 |

**Table 144-1** Stages of Pubic Hair in Boys

*Values may be too high because of error in experimental observations.
CI, confidence interval.
Data from Marshall WA, Tanner JM: Variations in the pattern of pubertal changes in boys. Arch Dis Child 45:13–23, 1970; and Root AW, Reiter EO: Evaluation and management of the child with delayed pubertal development. Fertil Steril 27:745–755, 1976.

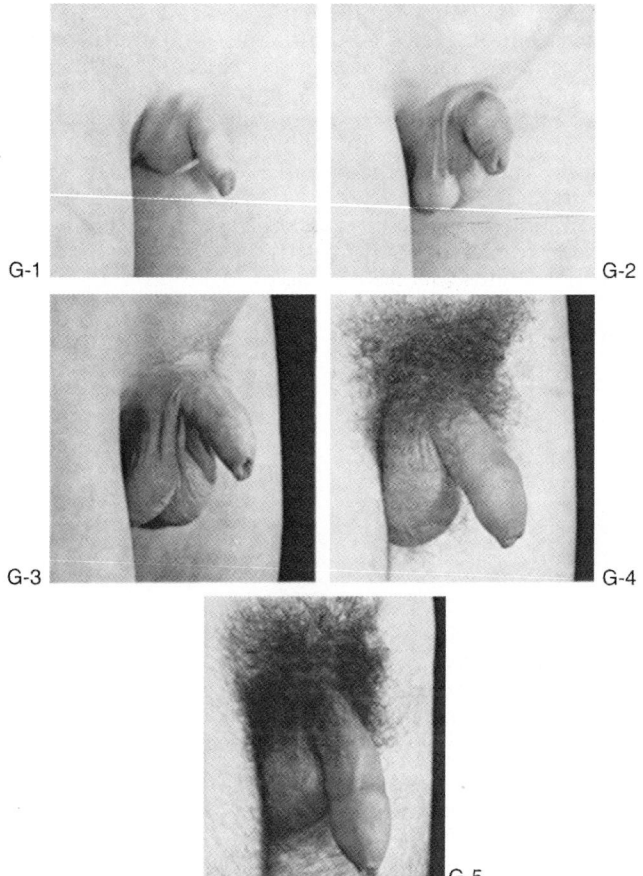

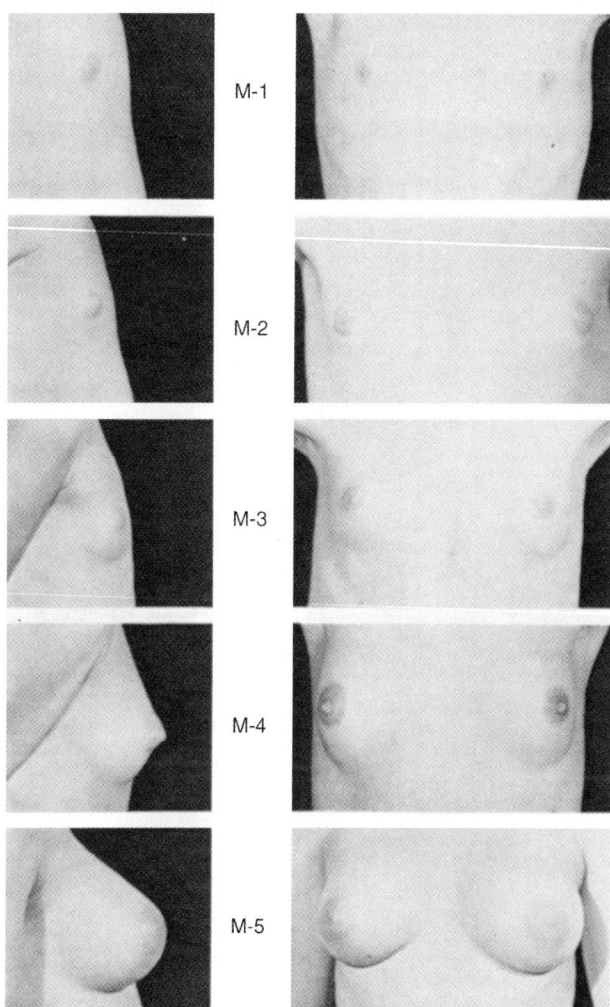

**Figure 144-8** Stages of male genital development and pubic hair development. *Genital development,* Stage 1 **(G-1)**: Preadolescent. Testes, scrotum, and penis are about the same size and proportion as in early childhood. Stage 2 **(G-2)**: The scrotum and testes have enlarged; the scrotal skin shows a change in texture and also some reddening. Stage 3 **(G-3)**: Growth of the penis has occurred, at first mainly in length but with some increase in breadth; there is further growth of the testes and scrotum. Stage 4 **(G-4)**: The penis is further enlarged in length and breadth with development of the glans. The testes and scrotum are further enlarged. The scrotal skin has further darkened. Stage 5 **(G-5)**: Genitalia are adult in size and shape. No further enlargement takes place after staeg 5 is reached. *Pubic hair development,* Stage 1 **(G-1)**: Preadolescent. The vellus over the pubic region is not further developed than that over the abdominal wall; that is, there is no pubic hair. Stage 2 **(G-2)**: Sparse growth of long, slightly pigmented, downy hair, straight or slightly curled, appearing chiefly at the base of the penis. Stage 3 **(G-3)**: Hair is considerably darker, coarser, and curlier and spreads sparsely over the junction of the pubes. Stage 4 **(G-4)**: Hair is now adult in type, but the area it covers is still considerable smaller than in most adults. There is no spread to the medial surface of the highes. Stage 5 **(G-5)**: Hair is adult in quantity and type, distributed as an inverse triangle. The spread is to the medial surface of the thighs but not up the linea alba or elsewhere above the base of the inverse triangle. Most men will have further spread of the pubic hair. (Stages according to Marshall WA, Tanner JM: Variations in the pattern of pubertal changes in boys. Arch Dis Child 45:13–23, 1970; Reynolds EL, Wines JV: Individualized differences in physical changes associated with adolescence in girls. Am J Dis Child 75:329–350, 1948; and Dupertuis CW, Atkinson WB, Elftman H: Sex differences in pubic hair distribution. Hum Biol 16:137–142, 2002. Photographs from Van Wieringen JD, Wafelbakker F, Verbrugge HP, et al: Growth Diagrams 1965 Netherlands: Second National Survey on 0–24 Year Olds. Netherlands Insitute for Preventative Medicine TNO, Groningen, Wolters-Noordhoff, 1971. © Wolters-Noordhoff, Groningen.)

**Figure 144-9** Stages of breat development. Stage 1 **(M-1)**: Preadolescent; elevation of papilla only. Stage 2 **(M-2)**: Breast bud stage; elevation of breast and papilla as a small mound, enlargement of areolar diameter. Stage 3 **(M-3)**: Further enlargement of breast and areola with no separation of their contours. Stage 4 **(M-4)**: Projection of areola and pailla to form a secondary mound above the level of the breast. Stage 5 **(M-5)**: Mature stage; projection of pailla only, resulting from recession of the areola to the general contour of the breast. (Stages according to Marshall WA, Tanner JM: Variations in the pattern of pubertal changes in girls. Arch Dis Child 44:291, 1969; and Reynolds EL, Wines JV: Individualized differences in physical changes associated with adolescence in girls. Am J Dis Child 75:329–350, 1948. Photographs from Van Wieringen JD, Wafelbakker F, Verbrugge HP, et al: Growth Diagrams 1965 Netherlands: Second National Survey on 0–24 Year Olds. Netherlands Insitute for Preventative Medicine TNO, Groningen, Wolters-Noordhoff, 1971. © Wolters-Noordhoff, Groningen.)

testosterone-induced changes take years to fully develop. For example, even though adult testosterone concentrations in blood are reached by age 15 or so, growth of the adult male beard is not usually complete until 20 to 25 years of age.

## PHYSICAL CHANGES OF PUBERTY IN GIRLS

The development of axillary and pubic hair growth in females is mediated primarily by adrenal androgens. Ovarian secretion of estradiol and progesterone produces the changes in breast development, body fat deposition, and vaginal and uterine tissues and their secretions, as well as the growth and psychologic development that occur during puberty in girls. Marshall and Tanner have also developed standards for breast development (estrogen and progesterone effects) and pubic hair development (an androgen effect).[46] The ovaries secrete small amounts of androgens and androgen precursors, and, additionally, estrogens probably stimulate some axillary and pubic hair growth. Therefore, in normal females, pubic hair results from the total effect of androgens secreted by the adrenals and ovaries with possibly some effects of estradiol. The term *thelarche* is used to define the onset of breast development at puberty. The staging of breast and pubic hair development in girls is depicted in Figures 144-9 and 144-10, respectively. Tables 144-2 and 144-3 describe these changes and their usual age of occurrence.

The proximate causes of these physical changes in girls are the increasing estradiol concentrations and the increasing adrenal and ovarian androgen concentrations. The major source of estradiol in the ovary is the granulosa cells surrounding the ova. Groups of these follicles undergo development and then atresia as the pubertal stages proceed before menarche. The cause of these ovarian changes is activation of the GnRH pulse generator leading to increased LH and FSH concentrations. The duration of puberty (time from the start of puberty to menarche) is related to the age of onset.[51] In a study of 163 girls at follow-up of 10 to 17 years, the overall average duration of puberty was $1.96 \pm 0.06$ years. For subgroups starting puberty at 9, 10, 11, 12, and 13 years, the duration was $2.77 \pm 0.16$, $2.27 \pm 0.16$, $1.78 \pm 0.08$, $1.44 \pm 0.1$, and $0.65 \pm 0.09$ years, respectively.

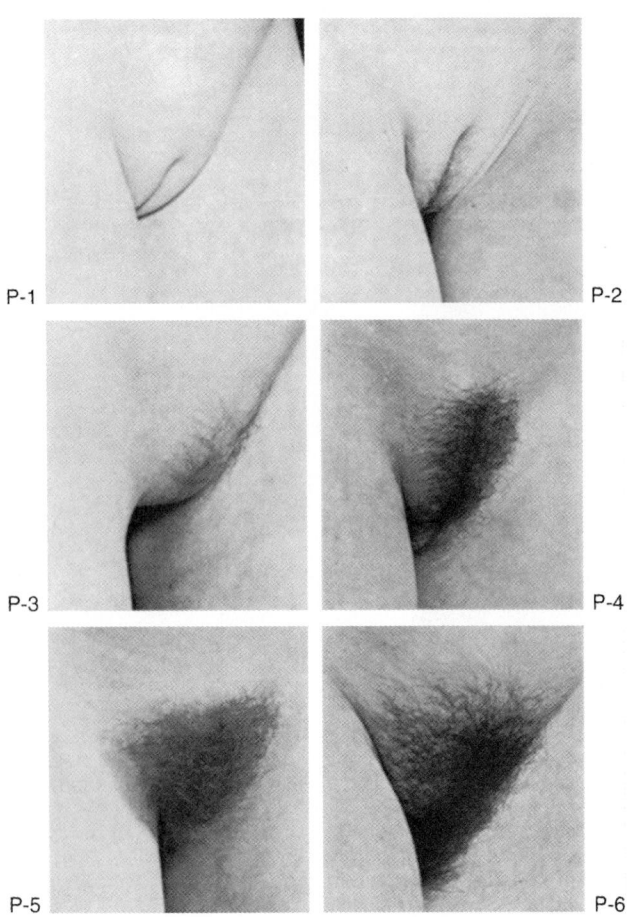

**Figure 144-10** Stages of female pubic hair development. Stage 1 **(P-1)**: Preadolescent. The vellus over the pubes is not further developed than that over the anterior abdominal wall; that is, there is no pubic hair. Stage 2 **(P-2)**: Sparse growth of long, slightly pigmented, downy hair, straight or only slightly curled, appearing chiefly along the labia. This stage is difficult to see on photographs. Stage 3 **(P-3)**: Hair is considerably darker, coarser, and curlier. The hair spreads sparsely over the junction of the pubic region. Stage 4 **(P-4)**: Hair is now adult in type, but the area covered by it is still considerable smaller than in most adults. There is no spread to the medial surface of the thighs. Stage 5 **(P-5)**: Hair is adult in quantity and type, distributed as an inverse triangle of the classical feminine pattern. Stage 6 **(P-6)**: The spread is to the medial surface of the thighs but not up the linea alba or elsewhere above the base of the inverse triangle. (Stages according to Marshall WA, Tanner JM: Variations in the pattern of pubertal changes in girls. Arch Dis Child 44:291, 1969; and Reynolds EL, Wines JV: Individualized differences in physical changes associated with adolescence in girls. Am J Dis Child 75:329–350, 1948; and Dupertuis CW, Atkinson WB, Elftman H: Sex differences in pubic hair distribution. Hum Biol 16:137–142, 2002. Photographs from Van Wieringen JD, Wafelbakker F, Verbrugge HP, et al: Growth Diagrams 1965 Netherlands: Second National Survey on 0–24 Year Olds. Netherlands Insitute for Preventative Medicine TNO, Groningen, Wolters-Noordhoff, 1971. © Wolters-Noordhoff, Groningen.)

| Table 144-2 | Stages of Breast Development in Girls | | |
|---|---|---|---|
| | | **Age at Onset (yr)** | |
| **Stage** | **Description** | **Mean** | **Range (95% CI)** |
| 1 | Preadolescent: Only the papilla is elevated. | | |
| 2 | Breast bud stage: The breast and papilla are elevated as a small mound; areola diameter is enlarged. | 11.2 | 9.0–13.3 |
| 3 | Further enlargement of breast and areola has occurred, with no separation of their contours. | 12.2 | 10.0–14.3 |
| 4 | The areola and papilla project to form a secondary mound above the level of the breast. | 13.1 | 10.8–15.3 |
| 5 | Mature stage: Only the papilla projects because of recession of the areola to the general contour of the breast. | 15.3 | 11.9–18.8 |

CI, confidence interval.
Data from Marshall WA, Tanner JM: Variations in pattern of pubertal changes in girls. Arch Dis Child 44:291–303, 1969; and Root AW, Reiter EO: Evaluation and management of the child with delayed pubertal development. Fertil Steril 27:745–755, 1976.

**Table 144-3** Stages of Pubic Hair in Girls

| Stage | Description | Age at Onset (yr) | |
|---|---|---|---|
| | | Mean | Range (95% CI) |
| 1 | Preadolescent: The vellus over the pubes is no further developed than that over the anterior abdominal wall, i.e., no pubic hair. | | |
| 2 | Sparse growth of long, slightly pigmented, downy hair, straight or only slightly curled, appears chiefly along labia. This stage is difficult to see on photographs, particularly of fair-haired subjects. Although a stage 2 rating was used in this study, it cannot be regarded as reliable, and ages at which subjects are said to have reached stage 2 are almost certainly too late. | 11.7* | 4*9.3–14.1* |
| 3 | Hair is considerably darker, coarser, and more curled. Hair spreads sparsely over the pubic junction. This and subsequent stages were clearly recognizable on photographs. | 12.4* | 10.2–14.6 |
| 4 | Hair is now adult in type, but the area covered by it is still considerably smaller than in most adults. Hair has not spread to the medial surface of the thighs. | 13.0* | 10.8–15.1 |
| 5 | Adult in quantity and type and distributed as an inverse triangle in the classically feminine pattern. Spread occurs to the medial surface of the thighs but not up the linea alba or elsewhere above the base of inverse triangle. | 14.4* | 12.2–16.7 |

*Values may be too high because of error in experimental observations.
CI, confidence interval.
Data from Marshall WA, Tanner JM: Variations in pattern of pubertal changes in girls. Arch Dis Child 44:291–303, 1969; and Root AW, Reiter EO: Evaluation and management of the child with delayed pubertal development. Fertil Steril 27:745–755, 1976.

## REFERENCES

1. Santoro N, Filicori M, Crowley WF Jr: Hypogonadotropic disorders in men and women: Diagnosis and therapy with pulsatile gonadotropin-releasing hormone. Endocr Rev 7:11–23, 1986.
2. Dunkel L, Alfthan H, Stenman UH, et al: Pulsatile secretion of LH and FSH in prepubertal and early pubertal boys revealed by ultrasensitive time-resolved immunofluorometric assays. Pediatr Res 27:215–219, 1990.
3. Wu FC, Butler GE, Kelnar CJ, et al: Ontogeny of pulsatile gonadotropin releasing hormone secretion from midchildhood, through puberty, to adulthood in the human male: A study using deconvolution analysis and an ultrasensitive immunofluorometric assay. J Clin Endocrinol Metab 81:1798–1805, 1996.
4. Ropelato MG, Escobar ME, Gottlieb S, Bergada C: Gonadotropin secretion in prepubertal normal and agonadal children evaluated by ultrasensitive time-resolved immunofluorometric assays. Horm Res 48:164–172, 1997.
5. Odell WD, Swerdloff RS: Etiologies of sexual maturation: A model system based on the sexually maturing rat. Recent Prog Horm Res 32:245–288, 1976.
6. Kaplan SL, Grumbach MM, Aubert ML: The ontogenesis of pituitary hormones and hypothalamic factors in the human fetus: maturation of central nervous system regulation of anterior pituitary function. Recent Prog Horm Res 32:161–243, 1976.
7. Kaiserman KB, Nakamoto JM, Geffner ME, McCabe ER: Minipuberty of infancy and adolescent pubertal function in adrenal hypoplasia congenita. J Pediatr 133:300–302, 1998.
8. Clark PA, Iranmanesh A, Veldhuis JD, Rogol AD: Comparison of pulsatile luteinizing hormone secretion between prepubertal children and young adults: Evidence for a mass/amplitude-dependent difference without gender or day/night contrasts. J Clin Endocrinol Metab 82:2950–2955, 1997.
9. Albertsson-Wikland K, Rosberg S, Lannering B, et al: Twenty-four-hour profiles of luteinizing hormone, follicle-stimulating hormone, testosterone, and estradiol levels: A semilongitudinal study throughout puberty in healthy boys. J Clin Endocrinol Metab 82:541–549, 1997.
10. Dunkel L, Alfthan H, Stenman UH, et al: Developmental changes in 24-hour profiles of luteinizing hormone and follicle-stimulating hormone from prepuberty to midstages of puberty in boys. J Clin Endocrinol Metab 74:890–897, 1992.
11. Manasco PK, Umbach DM, Muly SM, et al: Ontogeny of gonadotrophin and inhibin secretion in normal girls through puberty based on overnight serial sampling and a comparison with normal boys. Hum Reprod 12:2108–2114, 1997.
12. Andersson AM, Juul A, Petersen JH, et al: Serum inhibin B in healthy pubertal and adolescent boys: Relation to age, stage of puberty, and follicle-stimulating hormone, luteinizing hormone, testosterone, and estradiol levels. J Clin Endocrinol Metab 82:3976–3981, 1997.
13. Hayes FJ, Hall JE, Boepple PA, Crowley WF Jr: Clinical review 96: Differential control of gonadotropin secretion in the human: Endocrine role of inhibin. J Clin Endocrinol Metab 83:1835–1841, 1998.
14. Welt CK, McNicholl DJ, Taylor AE, Hall JE: Female reproductive aging is marked by decreased secretion of dimeric inhibin. J Clin Endocrinol Metab 84:105–111, 1999.
15. Achermann JC, Ozisik G, Meeks JJ, Jameson JL: Genetic causes of human reproductive disease. J Clin Endocrinol Metab 87:2447–2454, 2002.
16. Seminara SB, Messager S, Chatzidaki EE, et al: The GPR54 gene as a regulator of puberty. N Engl J Med 349:1614–1627, 2003.
17. de Roux N, Genin E, Carel JC, et al: Hypogonadotropic hypogonadism due to loss of function of the KiSS1-derived peptide receptor GPR54. Proc Natl Acad Sci U S A 100:10972–10976, 2003.
18. Gottsch ML, Cunningham MJ, Smith JT, et al: A role for kisspeptins in the regulation of gonadotropin secretion in the mouse. Endocrinology 145:4073–4077, 2004.
19. O'Rahilly S: Leptin: Defining its role in humans by the clinical study of genetic disorders. Nutr Rev 60:S30–S34; discussions S68–S84 and 85–37, 2002.
20. Welt CK, Chan JL, Bullen J, et al: Recombinant human leptin in women with hypothalamic amenorrhea. N Engl J Med 351:987–997, 2004.
21. Mantzoros CS, Flier JS, Rogol AD: A longitudinal assessment of hormonal and physical alterations during normal puberty in boys. V. Rising leptin levels may signal the onset of puberty. J Clin Endocrinol Metab 82:1066–1070, 1997.
22. Garcia-Mayor RV, Andrade MA, Rios M, et al: Serum leptin levels in normal children: Relationship to age, gender, body mass index, pituitary-gonadal hormones, and pubertal stage. J Clin Endocrinol Metab 82:2849–2855, 1997.

23. Ratcliffe J, Nakanishi M, Jaffe RB: Identification of definitive and fetal zone markers in the human fetal adrenal gland reveals putative developmental genes. J Clin Endocrinol Metab 88:3272–3277, 2003.

24. Achermann JC, Meeks JJ, Jameson JL: Phenotypic spectrum of mutations in DAX1 and SF-1. Mol Cell Endocrinol 185:17–25, 2001.

25. Endoh A, Kristiansen SB, Casson PR, et al: The zona reticularis is the site of biosynthesis of dehydroepiandrosterone and dehydroepiandrosterone sulfate in the adult human adrenal cortex resulting from its low expression of 3 beta-hydroxysteroid dehydrogenase. J Clin Endocrinol Metab 81:3558–3565, 1996.

26. Wierman ME, Beardsworth DE, Crawford JD, et al: Adrenarche and skeletal maturation during luteinizing hormone releasing hormone analogue suppression of gonadarche. J Clin Invest 77:121–126, 1986.

27. Auchus RJ, Rainey WE: Adrenarche—Physiology, biochemistry and human disease. Clin Endocrinol (Oxf) 60:288–296, 2004.

28. Nathanson IT, Towne LE, Aub JC: Normal excretion of sex hormones in childhood. Endocrinology 28:851, 1941.

29. Talbot N, Butler A, Berman R, et al: Excretion of 17-ketosteroids by normal and abnormal children. Am J Dis Child 65:364, 1943.

30. Parker LN, Odell WD: Control of adrenal androgen secretion. Endocr Rev 1:392–410, 1980.

31. Lee PA, Kowarski A, Migeon CJ, Blizzard RM: Lack of correlation between gonadotropin and adrenal androgen levels in agonadal children. J Clin Endocrinol Metab 40:664–669, 1975.

32. Sklar CA, Kaplan SL, Grumbach MM: Lack of effect of oestrogens on adrenal androgen secretion in children and adolescents with a comment on oestrogens and pubic hair growth. Clin Endocrinol (Oxf) 14:311–320, 1981.

33. Ibanez L, Dimartino-Nardi J, Potau N, Saenger P: Premature adrenarche—Normal variant or forerunner of adult disease? Endocr Rev 21:671–696, 2000.

34. Legro RS: Detection of insulin resistance and its treatment in adolescents with polycystic ovary syndrome. J Pediatr Endocrinol Metab 15(Suppl 5):1367–1378, 2002.

35. Boot AM, Bouquet J, de Ridder MA, et al: Determinants of body composition measured by dual-energy X-ray absorptiometry in Dutch children and adolescents. Am J Clin Nutr 66:232–238, 1997.

36. Boot AM, de Ridder MA, Pols HA, et al: Bone mineral density in children and adolescents: Relation to puberty, calcium intake, and physical activity. J Clin Endocrinol Metab 82:57–62, 1997.

37. Bailey DA: The Saskatchewan Pediatric Bone Mineral Accrual Study: Bone mineral acquisition during the growing years. Int J Sports Med 18(Suppl 3):S191–S194, 1997.

38. Martin AD, Bailey DA, McKay HA, Whiting S: Bone mineral and calcium accretion during puberty. Am J Clin Nutr 66:611–615, 1997.

39. Reiter EO, Rosenfield RG: Nomal and aberrant growth. In Wilson JD, Foster DW, Kronenberg HM, Larson RR (eds): Williams Textbook of Endocrinology, 9th ed. Philadelphia, WB Saunders, 1998, pp 1427–1507.

40. Bala RM, Lopatka J, Leung A, et al: Serum immunoreactive somatomedin levels in normal adults, pregnant women at term, children at various ages, and children with constitutionally delayed growth. J Clin Endocrinol Metab 52:508–512, 1981.

41. Link K, Blizzard RM, Evans WS, et al: The effect of androgens on the pulsatile release and the twenty-four-hour mean concentration of growth hormone in peripubertal males. J Clin Endocrinol Metab 62:159–164, 1986.

42. Martha PM Jr, Gorman KM, Blizzard RM, et al: Endogenous growth hormone secretion and clearance rates in normal boys, as determined by deconvolution analysis: Relationship to age, pubertal status, and body mass. J Clin Endocrinol Metab 74:336–344, 1992.

43. Parent AS, Teilmann G, Juul A, et al: The timing of normal puberty and the age limits of sexual precocity: Variations around the world, secular trends, and changes after migration. Endocr Rev 24:668–693, 2003.

44. Winter JS: Nutrition and the neuroendocrinology of puberty. Curr Concepts Nutr 11:3–12, 1982.

45. Chumlea WC, Schubert CM, Roche AF, et al: Age at menarche and racial comparisons in US girls. Pediatrics 111:110–113, 2003.

46. Marshall WA, Tanner JM: Variations in pattern of pubertal changes in girls. Arch Dis Child 44:291–303, 1969.

47. Marshall WA, Tanner JM: Variations in the pattern of pubertal changes in boys. Arch Dis Child 45:13–23, 1970.

48. Longcope C, Pratt JH, Schneider SH, Fineberg SE: Aromatization of androgens by muscle and adipose tissue in vivo. J Clin Endocrinol Metab 46:146–152, 1978.

49. Odell WD, Swerdloff RS, Wollesen F: Selected aspects of control of LH and FSH secretion in women. In James VHT, Serio M, Giusti G (eds): The Endocrine Function of the Human Ovary. New York, Academic Press, 1976, pp 89–108.

50. Smith EP, Boyd J, Frank GR, et al: Estrogen resistance caused by a mutation in the estrogen-receptor gene in a man. N Engl J Med 331:1056–1061, 1994.

51. Marti-Henneberg C, Vizmanos B: The duration of puberty in girls is related to the timing of its onset. J Pediatr 131:618–621, 1997.

# Environmental Agents and the Reproductive System

## Jonathan Lindzey and Kenneth S. Korach

**POTENTIAL SITES OF ENDOCRINE DISRUPTER ACTION**

**ENDOCRINE DISRUPTERS WITHOUT INTRINSIC HORMONAL ACTIVITY**
Metals
Dioxins
Atrazines

**ENVIRONMENTAL AGENTS WITH INTRINSIC HORMONAL ACTIVITY**
Polychlorinated Biphenyls
Synthetic "Estrogens"

Alkylphenols
Phytoestrogens
Mycotoxins
Pesticides
DDT and DDT Metabolites
Methoxychlor
Vinclozolin
Lindane

**CONCLUSIONS**

The explosion of technology and industrialization that began during the twentieth century has greatly increased both the amounts and the diversity of compounds that are released into the environment. In recent decades, it has become clear that exposures to some of these compounds not only pose significant health risks but may also have significant effects on the reproductive health of humans and wildlife. Environmental agents with known or potential reproductive effects include heavy metals, dioxins, polychlorinated biphenyls, pesticides, synthetic hormones or antihormones, alkylated phenols, and naturally occurring plant and fungal products. Collectively, exogenous compounds that alter normal reproductive development and adult reproduction have been referred to as *endocrine disrupters*. Many of these compounds or their metabolites have been shown to exhibit some degree of intrinsic hormonal activity in receptor binding studies, cell culture, or in vivo bioassays. Many of these compounds, however, may also have overt toxic effects. Therefore, even in well-documented cases of reproductive effects, a recurring question is whether these compounds exert their reproductive effects by acting as environmental hormones (i.e., through direct interaction with endocrine receptor signaling pathways) or via nonhormonal actions (i.e., non–endocrine receptor mediated actions and/or generalized cellular toxicity). It is important to keep in mind, however, that these two pathways are not mutually exclusive and that compounds with intrinsic hormonal activity may also be overtly toxic. In addition, compounds with no intrinsic hormonal activity can alter normal functions of endocrine systems and, hence, affect peripheral endocrine targets.

## POTENTIAL SITES OF ENDOCRINE DISRUPTER ACTION

Regulation of normal reproductive development and physiology is a complex process involving the coordinated interaction of neurotransmitter systems, hypothalamic releasing factors, pituitary hormones, steroid hormones, and growth factors. Therefore, delineating the exact mechanisms by which endocrine disrupters exert an effect is problematic. For instance, neurotoxic compounds that alter neurotransmitters systems may cause changes in secretion of gonadotropin-releasing hormone (GnRH), gonadotropins, and steroids that ultimately cause downstream changes in steroid-sensitive peripheral tissues such as the uterus or

prostate. Similarly, a compound that exerts toxic effects on a peripheral steroid target might be assumed to act as an antisteroid via direct interactions with steroid receptors. In addition, inhibition of steroidogenic enzymes may decrease circulating hormone levels and mimic a peripheral response consistent with receptor antagonism. Therefore, without careful analysis of the effects of this agent in steroid receptor binding assays and in vivo effects on hormone profiles, hormone metabolism, and peripheral targets, such a compound might be assumed to act directly through steroid receptors.

Both estrogens and androgens are clearly involved in numerous aspects of normal sexual differentiation and regulation of the hypothalamus, pituitary, gonads, and accessory reproductive structures in adults. Classically, most steroid effects are thought to be mediated through interactions with specific nuclear steroid receptors, although other cellular mechanisms have been described including non-genomic actions of steroid hormones (Fig. 145-1). 17-$\beta$ Estradiol ($E_2$), the most active estrogen of vertebrates, exerts most of its effects on reproduction through the nuclear estrogen receptors (ER)-$\alpha$ and ER-$\beta$,[1,2] whereas androgens exert most of their effects through a nuclear androgen receptor (AR)[3] or via aromatization to estrogens and activation of ER signaling pathways. It is important, however, to keep in mind that unknown receptor pathways may mediate observed effects of some compounds. For instance, recent reports suggest the presence of a novel but uncharacterized estrogen signaling pathway in uterine tissues.[4,5]

In addition to "ligand-dependent" activation of steroid receptors by their specific ligand(s), it is important to remember that "ligand-independent" activation of steroid receptors can occur through activation of growth factor–signaling cascades and mitogen-activated protein kinase (MAPK).[6,7] Furthermore, nuclear receptors recruit various coactivators or corepressors in the course of altering gene expression. Thus, cellular mechanisms of endocrine disruption may also involve alterations in growth factor pathways or coactivators that ultimately impact the ability of steroid hormones and steroid receptors to modulate transcription and receptor-mediated responsiveness. Indeed, a recent report suggests that short-chain fatty acids such as methoxyacetic acid, a component in many paints and solvents, can augment ligand-dependent activation of ER-$\beta$ or progesterone receptor (PR), possibly through activation of MAPK and, perhaps, phosphorylation of coactivators.[8]

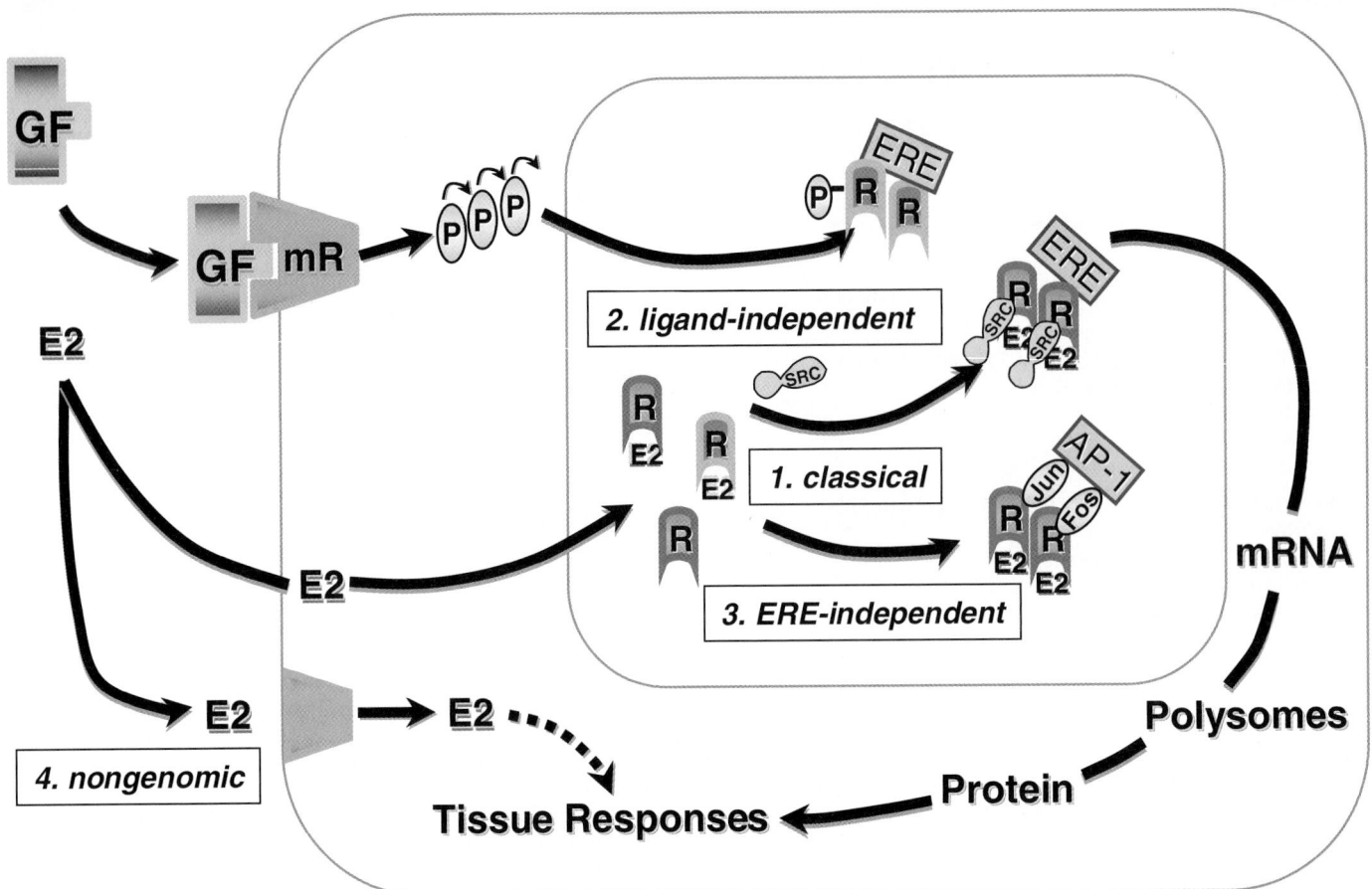

*Figure 145-1* Cellular mechanisms of estrogen action. Four modes of estrogen hormone action are depicted in this cellular model. (1) classical ligand-dependent receptor activity involving DNA binding; (2) ligand-independent receptor activation; (3) ligand-dependent ERE-independent receptor activity not involving direct DNA binding; and (4) non-genomic membrane receptor pathways. AP-1, DNA-binding site for *fos jun* transcription factors; E2, estradiol estrogen; ERE, DNA estrogen response element; GF, growth factor; mR, membrane or growth factor receptor; P, phosphorylation kinase activity; R, nuclear estrogen receptor; SRC, coregulator proteins, coactivator. (Modified from Hall JM, Couse JF, Korach KS: The multifaceted mechanisms of estradiol and estrogen receptor signaling. J Biol Chem 276:36869–36872, 2001.)

While normal reproductive physiology hinges on the coordinated actions of estrogens and androgens, inappropriate exposure to these endogenous steroids or exposure to exogenous compounds with steroidal activity during critical periods can result in gross alterations in adult phenotypes such as masculinization, feminization, teratogenesis, or carcinogenesis. A recurring theme in reproductive toxicology is that perinatal periods of development are more sensitive to endocrine disruption and that perinatal exposure can result in profound and permanent effects that are manifested during adulthood.

In this review, we discuss the reproductive effects of selected endocrine disrupters on reproductive development and adult reproductive physiology and the possible cellular mechanisms underlying these effects. For convenience, we have divided our discussion into two mechanistically defined groups: endocrine disrupters without intrinsic hormonal activity and those with demonstrated hormonal activity.

## ENDOCRINE DISRUPTERS WITHOUT INTRINSIC HORMONAL ACTIVITY

### METALS

Although many metals are reported to have deleterious effects on early embryogenesis,[9] the following discussion focuses mainly on the effects of lead, a common environmental contaminant that has been shown to exert reproductive effects in animal models. Lead exposure occurs primarily through intake of water and food. It poses a significant health problem due to environmental persistence and bioaccumulation in the food chain. In humans, childhood exposure to lead has been linked to slower growth and severely reduced brain development and cognitive abilities.[9] Many of these same effects have been reported in rodent models.

To our knowledge, lead has never been demonstrated to exhibit any significant binding activity with any of the steroid receptors. Therefore, it seems likely that reproductive effects of lead are due to cellular toxicity. Indeed, the well-characterized neurotoxicity of lead may cause reproductive deficits via alterations in neuroendocrine development and function.

Relatively few studies have examined the link between lead exposure in humans and effects on reproduction. A study of workers in high-lead versus low-lead environments showed, however, a correlation between higher lead content and compromised spermatogenesis, but it was unclear whether this was due to testicular toxicity or alterations in serum testosterone.[10] A subsequent study supported this relationship between higher lead levels and reduced sperm counts. In females, increased maternal exposures to lead have been correlated with reduced fertility, shortened gestation, and increased incidence of premature delivery and stillbirths.[11,12] A recent in vitro study using cultured human granulosa cells found that lead can reduce levels of aromatase enzyme and ER-β protein and mRNA.[13] Although this study used high doses of lead (10 μM), these findings propose potential mechanisms to explain some of the observed correlations between lead exposure and reduced fertility in women.

A number of animal studies lend credence to the idea that lead exposure may exert harmful effects on human reproduction. Chronic lead exposure in adult male rats leads to a reduced capacity for fertilization and decreased implantation of embryos.[14] Other studies have demonstrated a correlation between reduced spermatogenesis and reduced serum and intratesticular testosterone levels.[15,16] In light of reduced serum testosterone, gonadotropins would normally be elevated. Gonadotropin levels were normal, however, suggesting a hypothalamic or pituitary site of lead toxicity. A subsequent study revealed that lead may interfere with naloxone-induced GnRH secretion.[17] While this study supports a hypothalamic site of action, other studies suggest that both the testis and the hypothalamus/pituitary are sites of lead toxicity.

In utero, neonatal and/or prepubertal lead exposure has led to variable effects on the reproductive health of the offspring. In rats exposed to lead in utero from gestational day (GD) 5 to sacrifice, vaginal opening was delayed and prostate weights were diminished. Coincident with these delays in sexual maturation were decreased serum levels of testosterone and $E_2$ during puberty in male and female rats.[18] Levels of luteinizing hormone (LH) were suppressed in serum and elevated in the pituitary of pubertal males. Only pituitary LH was elevated in females. In this same report, however, serum levels of steroids and LH in adults were not affected despite continuous lead exposure into adulthood. Although this suggests the possibility of compensatory mechanisms or adaptation to chronic lead exposure, other studies suggest more permanent organizational changes. In utero treatments from GD 14 to birth have been reported to decrease sperm counts in adult male rats,[19] whereas another study reports no effect on epididymal sperm counts in mice exposed from gestational day 1 through postnatal day (PND) 60.[20] In addition to potential effects on spermatogenesis, perinatal lead treatments of females can lead to disrupted estrous cycles and an absence of corpora lutea.[16,19,21] Perinatal and lactational exposure to lead can also decrease uterine expression of ER,[22] levels of ovarian gonadotropin receptors, and alter adult steroid profiles.[23] Thus, there is evidence of permanent ovarian cycling deficits in perinatally lead-exposed females.

In recent years, the reproductive consequences of cadmium exposure have gained increasing attention. It is apparent from in vivo and in vitro studies that cadmium can interfere with normal gonadal steroidogenesis. For instance, in vivo exposures have been reported to suppress serum LH, serum testosterone, and mRNA levels for the LH receptor in the testes of rats.[24,25] An intriguing finding, however, is that cadmium exhibits estrogenic actions on peripheral target tissues. In vivo treatments increased uterine wet weights, stimulated endometrial hypertrophy, and induced progesterone receptor expression.[26] In addition, mammary gland development was stimulated along with increased expression of milk proteins and progesterone receptor.[26] Female pups exposed in utero also exhibited classic signs of estrogen exposure such as accelerated puberty and altered mammary gland development.[26] In terms of mammary gland effects, qualitatively similar results were reported in studies using cultured breast cancer cells. Significantly, these in vitro studies found that the estrogen antagonist ICI 164,384 blocked the estrogenic actions of cadmium,[27] suggesting that cadmium acts through ER-α. Indeed, cadmium has been demonstrated to bind to ER-α (Kd = 4 − 5 ×10⁻¹⁰) and activate estrogen-dependent gene activity.[28] This latter study suggests that cadmium binds to the ligand-binding domain of the ER-α. It is also interesting to note that other metals (nickel, cobalt) are able to bind ER and activate estrogen-dependent gene activity in MCF-7 cells.[29] Thus, unlike the mechanisms of action of lead, it appears that some metals may exert reproductive effects through direct interactions with nuclear steroid receptors.

A recent study has also revealed another potential mode of action for "estrogenic" endocrine disrupters. In utero arsenic exposure increased the incidence of hepatocellular carcinoma in male mice coupled with a feminized pattern of cytochrome P-450 enzyme expression.[30] The former is consistent with exposure to estrogen during adulthood, whereas the latter is consistent with estrogen exposure during a critical developmental window. Interestingly, this study found that hepatic ER-α mRNA levels were significantly elevated and were correlated with hypomethylation of the ER-α promoter. These findings suggest that some compounds may have persistent "estrogenic" effects by permanently altering the signaling mechanisms that mediate the effects of endogenous steroids.

## DIOXINS

Dioxins are polychlorinated hydrocarbons produced as a byproduct of herbicide production and other types of combustive and industrial processes. The best studied of the dioxins is 2,3,7,8-tetrachlorodibenzo-p-dioxin (TCDD). Although the degree of toxicity varies with species, it is, in general, highly toxic to adult animals and can cause a classic wasting syndrome prior to death. In addition, it has numerous fetotoxic effects in mammals. Although no firm reproductive effects have been documented in the few epidemiologic studies evaluating humans, extrapolation from animal studies suggests that exposure during fetal life may have an impact on human reproductive health.

After relatively large postnatal TCDD exposure in rats, there are reports of decreased testicular weight[31] and reduced serum testosterone associated with diminished cholesterol conversion to steroids.[32] Additional reports indicate reduced fertility associated with decreased testis, seminal vesicle, and ventral prostate weights.[31,33,34] However, most of these effects require high doses that are overtly toxic to the rats and result in diminished body weights.

In immature female rats, TCDD exerts antiestrogenic effects. Some of these effects include decreased $E_2$-induced uterine weight, decreased uterine ER expression,[35,36] and decreased basal and $E_2$-induced levels of uterine peroxidase, c-fos, and epidermal growth factor (EGF) receptor.[37–39] Thus, it appears that TCDD has seemingly antiestrogenic effects on morphology, gene expression, and enzyme activity. These data, coupled with evidence of outright fetotoxicity and reduced litter sizes, indicate that large doses of TCDD during adulthood or peripubertal stages interfere with adult reproductive physiology.

Perinatal treatments with TCDD doses that more closely approximate environmental TCDD exposures may also have long-lasting effects on surviving offspring. In rats exposed to TCDD on GD 15, there are reports of reduced anogenital distance (AGD) in male pups at birth,[40] decreased accessory sex organ weights,[40] and decreased testicular and epididymal sperm counts later in life.[41] The deficits in sperm counts are variable, with some studies reporting deficits in testicular and epididymal sperm counts,[40,41] whereas other studies report no significant deficits.[42] These discrepancies may stem from different strains of rats. The deficits in AGD and organ weights were largely confirmed by subsequent studies, although the decreased AGD may be due an overall decrease in body weight.[41–43]

The observed deficits in AGD, organ weights, and sperm counts could all be explained by either reduced serum testosterone levels or reduced levels of AR. Indeed, the original report suggested that these effects might be secondary to decreased levels of testosterone during perinatal and pubertal stages.[40] Subsequent reports have not supported this hypothesis, however, and it appears that both reduced prostate and seminal vesicle weights can occur despite normal serum testosterone.[41–45] The sexually dimorphic nucleus of the hypothalamus, which is developmentally sensitive to changes in serum testosterone, appears to be normal in adult males that were treated in utero.[46] These data suggest that the deficits may arise from end-organ insensitivity to testosterone or non-hormonal sources. The issue of end-organ responsiveness has been addressed by examining expression patterns of AR and 5α-reductase. One study reports normal levels of AR in accessory glands of TCDD-treated males,[41] whereas others report a decrease in prostatic AR protein or mRNA.[42,45] Although there are variable reports of AR expression, 5α-reductase levels do not appear to be reduced, and, therefore, this mechanism does not appear to be a viable explanation for observed effects on the prostate.[42,45] These data suggest that abnormalities in male sex accessory sex structures may stem from direct actions on the target tissues that are largely androgen independent.

Prenatal exposure to TCDD at either GD 8 or GD 15 also results in reproductive tract abnormalities in female offspring. The most consistent finding is a delay in vaginal opening, presence of a persistent thread of tissue across the vaginal opening, and clefting of the external genitalia.[39] These effects are most pronounced in offspring prenatally treated on GD 15, and do not seem to be accompanied by alterations in estrous cycles. This suggests that hormonal profiles are largely normal and that these abnormalities stem from aryl-hydrocarbon receptor (AhR)-mediated effects of TCDD on the developing urogenital system.

Given the lack of TCDD binding to either ER-α or ER-β,[47] it is assumed that the reported antiestrogenic effects are mediated through the AhR and/or the AhR nuclear translocator protein (ARNT). Potential mechanisms may involve AhR-mediated suppression of ER protein levels, direct downregulation of ER-regulated genes, or altered CYP-450 enzyme profiles that might alter endogenous steroid hormone levels. Indeed, recent studies provide support for all of these possible levels of TCDD action. For instance, it appears that TCDD may decrease ER levels due to AhR interactions with both ER-α and a proteasome complex, resulting in degradation of ER-α.[48] Further studies indicate that ER-induced gene expression may be suppressed via (1) AhR-ARNT heterodimers binding to xenobiotic response elements (XREs) that overlap naturally occurring estrogen response elements,[47] and (2) AhR competition for transcriptional coactivators (e.g., RIP 140) that interact with steroid receptors.[49] This would also provide a potential mechanism for TCDD to interfere with other steroid hormone receptors. Further evidence also supports the possibility that TCDD may reduce $E_2$ levels via suppression of P-450c17 enzyme levels and the androgen precursors for $E_2$ synthesis.[50,51]

TCDD may also alter development through growth factor signaling pathways such as epidermal growth factor (EGF), insulin-like growth factor (IGF), or transforming growth factor (TGF). For instance, TCDD treatments have been demonstrated to affect expression of EGF receptors in the ureteric epithelial layers.[52] Another study has demonstrated that dioxin inhibits estrogenic stimulation of the mouse uterus through disruption of normal cyclin and TGF-β expression.[53] Given the interactions between estrogen and growth factor signaling pathways in the female reproductive tract,[6,7] it is tempting to postulate that some of dioxins affects on estrogen-dependent events in the female may be through alterations in such signaling pathways.

Whereas TCDD can clearly exert antiestrogenic effects, it appears to have dual actions in that it has also been reported to exert estrogenic effects such as induction of endometriosis in animal models.[54] A recent study found that the AhR-ARNT heterodimer can interact with either ER-α or ER-β.[55] Functionally, this resulted in estrogen-independent recruitment of ER-α and p300, a coactivator, and stimulation of estrogen-dependent genes. When estrogen was present, however, estrogen-dependent gene induction was inhibited, suggesting that the effect of TCDD may vary with the endocrine status of the female. Significantly, the estrogenic actions of AhR agonists were not observed in ER-α knockout mice.[55] Thus, it appears that TCDD may exert estrogenic effects through complex protein-protein interactions involving ER-α, and, possibly, ER-β.

## ATRAZINES

Atrazines are the most widely used herbicides in the United States and have recently received a great deal of attention because of a potential link to mammary gland cancer. Although the risk to human mammary gland cancer has been minimized,[56] studies have revealed that atrazine may pose significant risks to reproductive health. Atrazine is clearly not estrogenic in the classical sense, as it does not bind ER and fails to stimulate estrogen-dependent processes.[57] It does, however, interfere with ovarian cycling[58] and hypothalamic control of LH and prolactin (PRL) secretion in Long-Evans rats,[59] and has been demonstrated to increase levels of aromatase in different cell types.[60,61] Perhaps the most alarming findings are that exposure of some frog species to low levels of atrazines is reported to result in hermaphroditism[62,63] and/or varying degrees of ovarian or testicular dysfunction.[64,65] Associated with these defects is a pronounced decrease in circulating testosterone that might be explained by elevated levels of aromatase and, hence, an altered testosterone-to-estrogen ratio that could drive some of the gonadal changes observed in vivo.[63] These effects are not uniform in all amphibians, however, and low-dose atrazine effects were not detected in *Xenopus laevis* larvae[66] or cricket frogs.[67] Nonetheless, the findings of altered development in some studies are sufficiently alarmingly that this area warrants further investigation.

## ENVIRONMENTAL AGENTS WITH INTRINSIC HORMONAL ACTIVITY

A number of compounds have been demonstrated to exert estrogenic activity through in vitro binding assays or in vivo bioassays (i.e., uterotropic bioassays). These compounds include polychlorinated biphenyls (PCBs), pesticides, pharmaceutical products (diethylstilbestrol [DES] and ethinyl estradiol), and naturally occurring phytoestrogens and fungal products. The structures of some of the estrogenic compounds are shown in Figure 145-2. Although all of these compounds are hormonally active in uterine bioassays and receptor binding assays, there are no consistent structural features that predict the estrogenicity of a compound. With the exception of the synthetic estrogens, the ER-binding affinities of these "environmental estrogens" are generally much lower than that of $E_2$.[1,2] (Table 145-1). However, due to (1) bioaccumulation of multiple compounds, (2) the potential for persistent exposure and additivity of weak estrogen effects, and (3) exposure during sensitive critical periods, there is still good reason to be concerned about potential reproductive consequences. It is also interesting to note that some environmental estrogens such as phytoestrogens exhibit higher affinities for ER-β than for ER-α. This raises the possibility that phytoestrogens may exert more profound effects on ER-β expressing cells.

## POLYCHLORINATED BIPHENYLS

PCBs are a diverse class of compounds that are produced in the manufacturing of dielectrics and hydraulic fluids. Their production has been banned in the United States, but due to their chemical structures, PCBs are highly persistent and are still found in the environment in low levels. Because of their lipophilic nature, PCBs also exhibit significant bioaccumulation in fatty tissues and significant levels have been reported

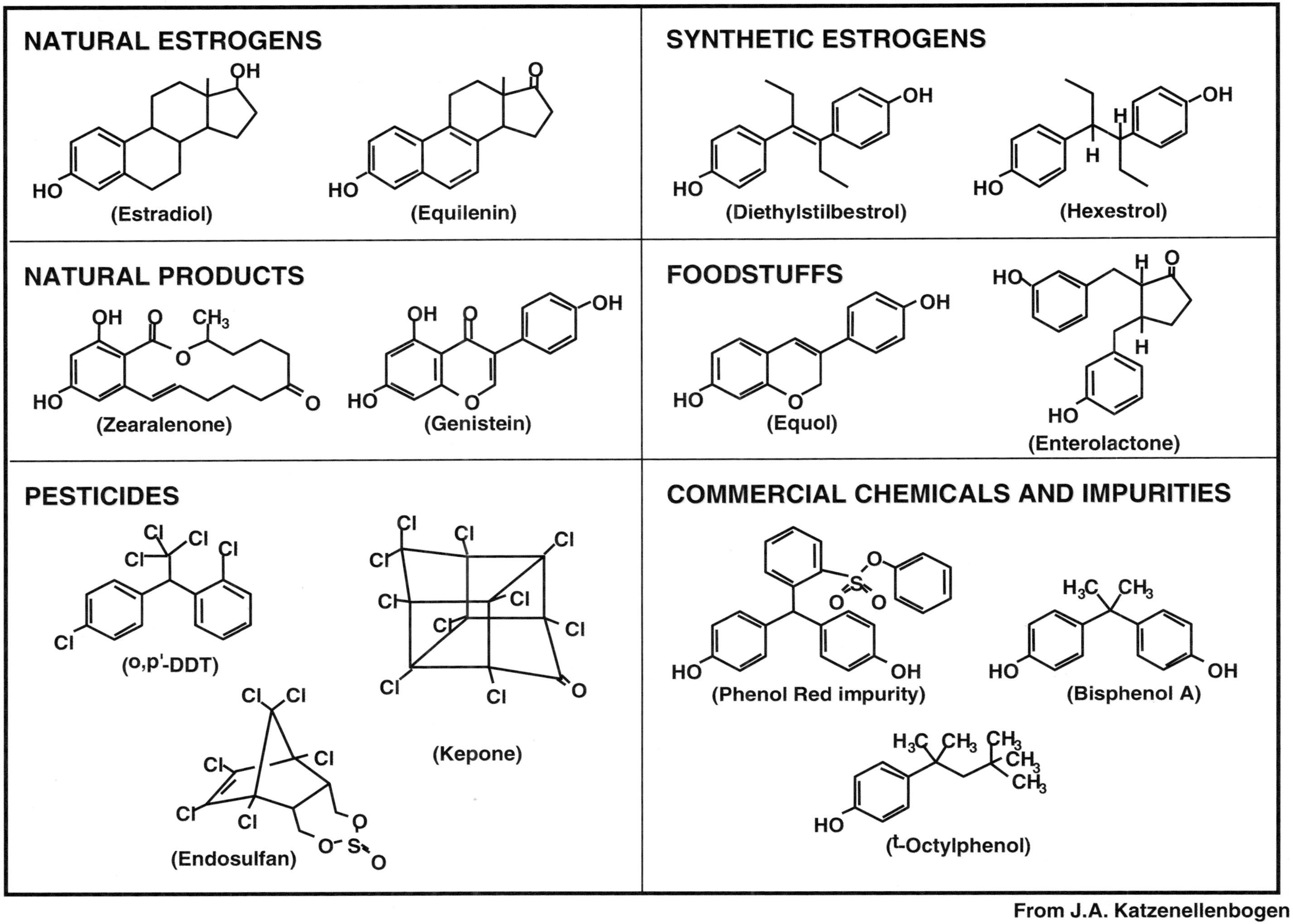

*Figure 145-2* Examples of the diversity of the chemical structures of some estrogenic compounds. Sources and examples are given in respective boxes. Figure modified from Katzenellenbogen JA: The structural pervasiveness of estrogenic activity. Environ Health Perspect 103(Suppl 7):99–101, 1995.

From J.A. Katzenellenbogen

**Table 145-1** Relative Binding Affinities (RBA) of Endocrine Disrupters for ER-α and ER-β

| Compound | RBA | |
|---|---|---|
| | ER-α | ER-β |
| 17β-estradiol | 100 | 100 |
| DES | 236 | 221 |
| 2',4',6'-trichloro-4-biphenylol | 2.4 | 4.7 |
| 2',3',4',5'-tetrachloro-4-biphenylol | 3.4 | 7.2 |
| 4-octylphenol | 0.02 | 0.07 |
| Nonylphenol | 0.05 | 0.09 |
| Bisphenol A | 0.01 | 0.01 |
| o,p'-DDT | 0.01 | 0.02 |
| p,p'-DDT | <0.01 | <0.01 |
| o,p-DDE | <0.01 | <0.01 |
| Methoxychlor | <0.01 | <0.01 |
| Endosulfan | <0.01 | <0.01 |
| Chlordecone | 0.06 | 0.1 |
| Coumestrol | 20 | 140 |
| Genistein | 4 | 87 |
| Zearalenone | 7 | 5 |

RBA of competitors were calculated as the ratio of 17β-estradiol to competitor required to suppress binding to ER-α or ER-β by 50% (ratio of IC50 values).
RBA data extracted from Kuiper G, Lemmen J, Carlsson B, et al: Interaction of estrogenic chemicals and phytoestrogens with estrogen receptor beta. Endocrinology 139:4252–4263, 1998.

in different fish species as well as human populations. Indeed, data suggests a potential link between PCB exposure and earlier onset of puberty in young women,[68] an effect that can be interpreted as "estrogenic" in nature.

One of the problems with examining the effects of PCBs is the number and diversity of different compounds and the fact that commercial mixtures of PCBs contain multiple PCB congeners. Coupled with this is the diversity of biologic effects of different PCBs. For instance, PCBs with coplanar structures that resemble TCDD often exert dioxin-like toxicity and exhibit antiestrogenic activity like dioxin, but have very low affinity for the estrogen receptor. In general, the toxicity of a PCB can be correlated with its ability to interact with the AhR that mediates the effects of TCDD. Conversely, noncoplanar PCBs can be less overtly toxic and some possess low affinity for the ER and are estrogenic in vivo. Several studies have suggested that mixtures of PCBs with low Cl⁻ content may have estrogenic activity. It also appears that the hydroxylated metabolites of these compounds are more potent estrogens.[69,70] A further requirement for the estrogenic actions of hydroxylated PCBs is that the 4-hydroxyl group is unhindered by Cl⁻ substitutions.[69–71] Our discussion is largely limited to those PCBs exhibiting estrogenic action.

Exposure of adult rats to Aroclor 1221, a mixture of PCBs, results in uterotropic responses.[72] Aroclor 1221 was also able to upregulate leves of GnRH mRNA and peptide in the GT1-7 cell line.[73] Only the effect on mRNA could be blocked by antiestrogen treatments, however, suggesting that some of the effects might be ER independent. Similar to in vivo studies with Aroclor 1221, treatments of immature rats with 2,5,2',5'-tetrachlorobiphenyl and 4'OH-2,4,6-trichlorobiphenyl or Aroclor 1242 significantly stimulated uterine weights and DNA synthesis.[74] Aroclor 1242 was also able to mimic the effects of estradiol on gonadotropin synthesis and secretion in primary pituitary cultures.[74] Two PCB congeners (4-OH-2',4',6' trichlorobiphenyl and 4-OH-2,3,4,5 tetrachlorbiphenyl) were also demonstrated to induce vitellogenin synthesis in trout, a highly sensitive bioassay for estrogenicity.[75] (Vitellogenin is a phospholipoprotein that is normally produced by the liver of female fish when circulating levels of E$_2$ are elevated.) Aroclor 1242 treatment of adult male rhesus suppressed testis weight, serum testosterone, and sperm

counts.[76] In contrast to the estrogenic actions of these PCB mixtures or congeners, however, 3,4,3',4'-tetrachlorobiphenyl failed to exhibit estrogenic effects. Indeed, 3,4,3',4'-tetrachlorobiphenyl acted as an antiestrogen and was able to suppress the effects of E$_2$ or Aroclor 1242 on the uterus.[74] Thus, some mixtures of PCBs or PCB congeners are able to elicit estrogenic effects in adult mammals whereas others exert antiestrogenic actions.

One of the more dramatic examples of PCB effects on reproduction is the ability of in ovo PCB exposures to reverse sex in turtles exposed in laboratory settings.[77,78] In addition, a correlation between environmental exposure to elevated levels of PCBs and skewed sex ratios (more males) in wild populations of cricket frogs has been observed.[67] Although less dramatic than sex reversal, perinatal PCB treatments of mammals indicate that early life exposures to these compounds can also result in significant effects on adult mammalian reproductive physiology. Despite an inability of perinatal Aroclor treatments to alter androgen status in males,[79] Aroclor 1254 has been demonstrated to reduce ventral prostate weight,[79,80] increase testis weight, and increase spermatogenesis.[81] The testicular effects of Aroclor 1254 are likely due to a hypothyroid state that results in increased testis size and spermatogenesis.[81] While lactational exposure to Aroclor 1254 suppressed ventral prostate weights, neonatal treatments with Aroclor 1221, 1242, and 1260 have no effect on prostate weights.[82] These differences in prostate effects may be due to the timing of treatments and/or different compounds in the mixtures.

In terms of fertility, perinatal treatments of male Sprague-Dawley rats with Aroclor 1221, 1242, and 1260 had no effect when males were mated with untreated females.[82] In contrast to these data, another study using in vitro fertilization assays found that a combination of perinatal and lactational exposure to Aroclor 1242 severely compromised sperm function, but did not affect AGD or testis weight of mice.[83] This suggests a pronounced germ cell effect at dosages that fail to alter androgenic status and accessory sex glands. Similarly, lactational exposure of male Holtzman rats to Aroclor 1254 resulted in decreased numbers of pregnancies and increased levels of postimplantation loss.[80] These data suggest that these compounds have different effects or that strain and species differences may play a role. In addition, the mode of exposure and developmental window may also play critical roles in susceptibility.

Translactational exposure of female rats to Aroclor 1254 resulted in delayed vaginal opening and a delay in first estrus. In addition to delayed puberty, these treatments resulted in diminished uterine weights, decreased uterotropic responses to exogenous E$_2$, and decreases in successful implantation.[84]

## SYNTHETIC "ESTROGENS"

### Diethylstilbestrol

The best-studied example of an agent exhibiting "endocrine disrupter" activity is diethylstilbestrol (DES). Although based on chemical structure, DES is not a steroid, but it is perhaps the most potent estrogenic compound synthesized by man. Beginning in the 1940s, it was used to treat women thought to be in danger of miscarriages. Data now indicate that it had no effect on the rate of miscarriage and, more significantly, resulted in numerous reproductive abnormalities in offspring that were exposed in utero. In female offspring, these included an increased incidence of a rare form of vaginal adenocarcinoma and increased incidence of structural abnormalities of the uterus and cervix, vaginal adenosis, and vaginal polyps.[85] Reduced fertility and elevated serum testosterone levels have also been reported. In the male, there are reports of reduced fertility, decreased sperm counts, hypoplastic and cryptorchid testes, and testicular tumors. There are also reports of microphallus and hypospadia, and prostatic abnormalities.[86] Fortunately, DES is no longer used to treat pregnant women, but it remains the prototypical model compound for comparing effects of different endocrine disrupters.

In an attempt to delineate the mechanisms by which DES affected human offspring, in utero and neonatal DES treatment models have been developed in rodents. Although there are some differences in the spectrum of abnormalities induced by in utero versus neonatal DES treatments, most of the human affects are replicated by either in utero or neonatal treatments of rodents.[87] Due to the wealth of literature on DES effects, the following section provides only an overview of the major reproductive effects and the reader is referred to several excellent reviews for a more in-depth discussion.

In the female mouse, in utero/neonatal treatments result in compromised fertility, uterine tumors, ovarian cysts and tumors, structural abnormalities of the uterus and cervix, cervical and vaginal polyps, vaginal adenosis, and persistent vaginal cornification. In male mice, in utero/neonatal treatments result in reduced fertility, decreased sperm counts, epididymal cysts, hypoplastic and cryptorchid testes, testicular tumors, hypospadia, retention of müllerian derivatives, tumors of the seminal vesicle and prostate, and feminization of musculoskeletal components.

The proposed mechanisms of action of DES fall into two general categories: receptor dependent and receptor independent. Various researchers have postulated that the carcinogenic actions of DES stem from oxidative metabolism into more reactive intermediates such as DES-4',4''-quinone which can result in formation of DNA adducts and mutations.[88] They hypothesize that these original mutational events are required for the carcinogenic effects and, therefore, the initial insult to the tissue should be considered receptor independent. Indeed, DES has been demonstrated to result in mutational events in mammary and uterine cells. It has been shown, however, that DES-4',4''-quinone can also bind irreversibly to the ER-$\alpha$, suggesting that a receptor-dependent path may also be involved in the effects of the highly reactive DES-quinone.[89] Perinatal DES treatments can also permanently increase basal expression of uterine c-fos[90,91] by hypomethylation of the CG region of the promoter.[90] The receptor-dependent theories postulate that action through the ER is required for many of the carcinogenic and teratogenic effects of DES. In this scenario, exposure to DES during an inappropriate window or critical period for differentiation results in the abnormal and persistent activation of gene expression and cellular proliferation. Support for the receptor-dependent mechanisms is found in several recent studies utilizing transgenic lines of mice. In one line of mouse that overexpressed ER-$\alpha$, the onset of DES-induced uterine tumors was accelerated.[92] Additionally, it was recently reported that many DES-induced developmental anomalies are absent in neonatally treated female ER-$\alpha$ knockout mice while female wild-type littermates exhibit many of the expected developmental abnormalities.[93] Interestingly, DES-induced suppression of Hoxa10, Hoxa11, and Wnt7a genes proved to be ER-$\alpha$ dependent, whereas DES effects on Wnt4 and Wnt5a were observed in both genotypes.[93] The latter finding suggests that ER-$\beta$ or another ER signaling pathway may play some developmental role in mediating the uterine effects of DES. Further studies with male ER-$\alpha$ knockout ($\alpha$-ERKO) and ER-$\beta$ knockout ($\beta$-ERKO) mice demonstrate that ER-$\alpha$ but not ER-$\beta$ mediates the teratogenic effects of neonatal DES treatments on the prostate.[94,95] These data provide very strong evidence that many of the adverse developmental effects of DES require the ER-$\alpha$ signaling pathways. It in important to note, however, that receptor-dependent and -independent mechanisms are not mutually exclusive. It may be that both an initial mutational insult coupled with subsequent hormonally induced proliferation is required for the full carcinogenic effects of DES to be elaborated.

## Ethinyl Estradiol

Another pharmaceutical estrogen of concern is ethinyl estradiol (EE), an estrogen commonly used in birth control pills. Not only is this compound released into the environment in large quantities, but due to some cases of inappropriate usage and failure to prevent conception, there is concern that some fetuses may be exposed to ethinyl estradiol in utero. Although EE is a potent estrogen in adults, relatively few studies have examined the developmental effects of in utero or perinatal EE exposure. EE treatment of pregnant mice resulted, however, in a significant increase in cryptorchid testes with no significant effect on incidence of testicular teratocarcinoma.[96] In utero treatments of rats resulted in persistent estrus, follicular cysts, and delayed anovulation in female offspring,[97] whereas EE treatments of pups at postnatal days 1 to 5 decreased uterine weights by day 26.[98] Thus, these few studies that have examined in utero or neonatal exposures find effects that are similar to those for DES exposure. This raises the possibility that in utero exposures of human fetuses might lead to similar effects as those observed in DES daughters and sons. Interestingly, another study examined the effects of postnatal EE treatment on the incidence of vaginal epithelial tumors in female rats exposed in utero to DES.[99] This study reported no significant effect of postnatal EE treatment on DES-induced tumors, despite the ability of in utero or neonatal EE exposures to mimic many DES effects.

While the potential for deleterious EE-induced developmental effects in humans is still speculative, developmental defects in wildlife populations appear to stem from the large amounts of EE released into the environment. It was found that male fish living downstream of sewage effluent were producing large amounts of vitellogenin.[100] As noted previously, vitellogenin is a phospholipoprotein normally produced by the liver of female fish when circulating levels of $E_2$ are elevated. In male fish, this protein is not normally produced in significant amounts but can be induced with exogenous $E_2$ treatments. Apparently, the overproduction of vitellogenin in these fish was due to the high levels of ethinyl estradiol in the sewage effluent.[100] It should be kept in mind, however, that sewage effluent contains other potential endocrine disrupters such as alkyl phenols and, therefore, conclusions concerning the causative agent(s) may prove problematic. Nonetheless, this line of work has led to additional studies demonstrating that exposure to EE can indeed result in feminization of male vertebrates and invertebrates.[101–103] A question that remains to be addressed is whether such point sources of contamination have a significant effect on anything more than the immediate local population of animals.

## ALKYLPHENOLS

Alkylphenols are produced in large amounts through the synthesis of plastics and are also used as nonionic surfactants. These compounds are released in great amounts into the environment and, due to their chemical structure, may exhibit significant bioaccumulation. Based on in vitro binding assays, yeast reporter assays, and mammalian cotransfection assays, both octylphenols and nonylphenols exhibit some weak estrogenicity.[1,2]

In adult rats, the administration of octylphenol has produced estrogenic effects in both males and females. In males, large doses of octylphenol (80 mg) administered three times a week for 1 or 2 months suppressed serum levels of testosterone, LH, and FSH and pituitary contents of LH and FSH. In addition, serum and pituitary levels of PRL were elevated and pituitary weights increased.[104] In another study, the antiestrogen tamoxifen was effective in blocking PRL induction by octylphenols, suggesting that octylphenols acted through ER.[105] In female rats, octyphenol stimulated uterine growth in prepubertal rats[106] and, in large doses, also resulted in persistent estrus and disruption of ovarian cycling.[107] Normal ovarian cycling returned, however, after octylphenol treatments were discontinued. These data indicate that large doses of octylphenol can indeed exert classical estrogenic effects and disrupt normal reproductive processes in adult rats, but that the effects may be transient in nature.

Nonylphenol has also been demonstrated to exert estrogenic effects by stimulating proliferation of MCF7 cells, an estrogen-sensitive mammary cell line, and proliferation of rat endometrium.[108] Potential environmental relevance was shown by studies indicating that nonylphenol also stimulates aberrant production of vitellogenin in adult males of a variety of fish species.[109–113] It has also been reported to decrease the gonado-somatic-index in male teleosts.[112]

Although large doses of alkylphenols are clearly estrogenic in adult vertebrates, the more pressing question is whether alkylphenols exert long-lasting developmental effects. Prenatal nonylphenol treatment of rats (gestational days 11–18) were found to have no effect on numbers of Sertoli cells[114] or on the seminal vesicle/body weight ratio.[115] Neonatal treatments (days 1–15) of male rats with nonylphenol, however, is reported to reduce fertility with accompanying decreases in testis, epididymis, seminal vesicle, and ventral prostate weights. This study also reported an increase in cryptorchidism,[116] but relatively high doses (>20.8 mg/kg) were required before these effects were observed.

Interestingly, very low maternal doses of octylphenol (2 ng/kg) during gestational days 11 to 17 of mice also resulted in testicular abnormalities with decreased sperm production.[117] These findings are particularly intriguing because of the effects observed at relatively low doses. Another study utilizing low-dose in utero exposures demonstrated that serum FSH, testis weight, and Sertoli cell number were all decreased in male sheep at birth.[118] Similarly, postnatal octylphenol treatments reduced testis size and pituitary FSH-β mRNA levels. Such studies suggest that testicular effects of octylphenol may stem from changes in FSH levels. Additional studies suggest that octylphenol may also have direct effects on steroidogenic enzymes. For instance, in utero treatments with high doses of DES or octylphenol results in diminished levels of expression of $17\alpha$-hydroxylase activity and steroidogenic factor-1 (SF-1) in fetal rat testes (GD 17.5).[119–121] Similar results were found in a study in which low-dose octylphenol exposures of bullfrog embryos altered sex-specific profiles of SF-1.[122] In vitro cell culture experiments also demonstrated that high concentrations of octylphenol can suppress human chorionic gonadotropin (hCG) stimulated steroidogenesis by mouse Leydig tumor cells.[123] In contrast to the studies reporting effects on steroidogenesis, however, a recent study failed to detect any significant effect of prenatal octylphenol treatments on testicular content of testosterone at gestational day 19.5.[124] Thus, despite some inconsistencies in the literature, the bulk of the studies suggest that alkylphenols may have the capacity to alter pituitary function and steroidogenic capacity of testes and, subsequently, masculine phenotypes. On the whole, all of the perinatal effects of octylphenol are consistent with the reported effects of perinatal treatments with other estrogenic compounds.

One of the most convincing series of studies dealing with alkylphenol-based endocrine disruption has been conducted in the United Kingdom where different populations of wild roach, a teleost fish, were examined for endocrine disruption. Populations exposed to high levels of sewage effluent were found to have a high level of intersex, both testes and ovaries, and the amount of ovarian tissue correlated with serum vitellogenin levels.[125,126] More important, fish exhibiting a significant degree of intersex gonads were found to have reduced spermatogenesis,[126] low rates of milt release, and reduced motility and in vitro fertilization success.[125] Again, with complex mixtures such as sewage effluent, it is difficult to pinpoint the causative agent(s). Nonetheless, this provides documentation of a functional deficit in reproduction that is correlated with exposure to sewage effluent. Furthermore, an additional study supports the hypothesis that alkylphenols may be a feminizing factor in sewage effluent. This study examined changes in estrogenicity of sewage effluent as regulatory changes resulted in lower nonylphenol discharges in the course of 4 years.[127] It was found that male trout exposed to the waters exhibited less dramatic changes in levels of vitellogenesis and abnormal gonadosomatic index (GSI) as nonylphenol levels dropped. Such findings strongly implicate alkylphenols as a causative agent in the roach studies.

The effects of bisphenol A (BPA) have also been addressed in a number of studies that have led to some degree of controversy regarding "low-dose effects." High doses of BPA clearly suppress serum testosterone and elevate serum LH levels in adult rats, suggesting that testosterone synthesis is compromised.[128] Peripubertal exposures (postnatal days 21–35) to low doses of BPA resulted in lower serum levels of both testosterone and LH, with concomitant increases in LH-β and ER-β mRNA levels.[129] In this same study, BPA was able to suppress testosterone synthesis in cultured Leydig cells,[129] suggesting that BPA might act centrally as an estrogen to suppress LH synthesis as well as peripherally to suppress testosterone synthesis.

A number of studies employing in utero exposures of rat fetuses have been conducted but have produced variable results. In exposed male offspring, increased stromal proliferation in the prostate[130] and decreased numbers of AR-positive stromal cells have been observed in the ventral prostate.[131] Although these effects appear to be transient, it was also found that levels of ER MRNA were increased in the medial preoptic area of males.[130] Another study found significant effects of in utero treatments on vaginal morphology and aberrant downregulation of vaginal ER-α.[132] In stark contrast to these studies, a recent study reported minimal effects of in utero BPA treatments, with the only effects being a decrease in daily sperm production and increased latency for vaginal opening in a single strain of rat exposed to the highest dosage.[133]

Mouse studies employing low, environmentally relevant BPA treatments in utero have reported increased prostate size, reduced epididymal size, and reduced sperm production in adults.[117,134,135] Still further studies have demonstrated significant in utero effects, which include accelerated puberty[136,137]; altered mammary gland morphology including increased numbers of ducts, terminal end buds, and alveolar buds[138]; and decreased maternal behaviors.[139] A single study, however, sought to replicate the vom Saal findings[117,134] and reported no significant reproductive effects in male or female offspring.[140] In light of this contradictory report, it is important to consider nonmammalian studies that support the likelihood that BPA may well disrupt normal reproduction. For instance, low doses of BPA have been found to suppress sperm counts in guppies,[141] alter gonadal differentiation of Japanese medaka,[109] and alter spermatogenesis and induce vitellogenin synthesis in male fathead minnows.[142] Thus, the bulk of the data suggest that BPA may indeed exert disruptive effects on reproduction. The critical issue is whether this is occurring in human and wildlife populations at current levels of environmental exposure.

## PHYTOESTROGENS

Many plants produce nonsteroidal compounds that exhibit estrogenic activity in both in vitro and in vivo bioassays. Two of the most intensively studied classes of phytoestrogens are the coumestans and isoflavones. Compounds from both of these classes have been demonstrated to bind to both ER-α and ER-β.[2] The fact that coumestrol and genistein have approximately fivefold higher affinities for ER-β raises the possibility, however, that phytoestrogens may have more pronounced effects on ER-β rich targets such as the prostate and ovary.

Although vertebrates have coevolved with plants producing phytoestrogens, it is still possible for these compounds to have potentially adverse or beneficial effects on reproduction. For instance, sheep feeding on subterranean clover were found to have suppressed reproductive cycles, which has since been attributed to the effects of high levels of coumestrol present in the forage.[143] In addition, some cultures consume vast quantities of soy products, which can contain relatively high concentrations of genistein. It has been suggested that a high soy diet may be partly responsible for the lower incidence of some cancers reported in these societies (see discussion to follow). Indeed, genistein poses a particularly interesting case because it binds to ER-α and ER-β and is also a potent tyrosine kinase inhibitor. Given the ubiquitous role of tyrosine kinase in cellular signaling pathways, it is interesting to speculate that some of the reproductive effects may be through an ER-independent pathway. Furthermore, given the intimate cross-talk between ER signaling and EGF signaling pathways,[6] it is entirely possible that genistein may alter reproduction through a combination of ER and tyrosine-kinase signaling pathways.

The aforementioned "clover disease" is one of the most dramatic examples of endocrine disruption resulting from environmental exposure to an estrogenic agent. The infertility of these sheep was accompanied by a number of estrogen-like morphologic effects including mammary gland enlargement and altered cervical and uterine morphology. Similarly, acute (3-day) dietary exposure to coumestrol in peripubertal rats results in progesterone receptor induction in the uterus, pituitary, and hypothalamic preoptic area.[144] Chronic dietary exposure in this study also resulted in accelerated vaginal opening and irregular cycles. Another dietary study in ovariectomized adult rats indicates that genistein stimulated uterine weight, increased uterine c-fos expression, reduced mammary gland regression, and stimulated serum PRL levels.[145] Acute treatments of ovariectomized mice with genistein also stimulate uterine hypertrophy and induction of lactoferrin and progesterone receptor gene expression that can be antagonized by administration of the estrogen antagonist ICI 182,780 (J. Lindzey and K.S. Korach, unpublished data). This effect of genistein is also absent in female α-ERKO mice, further indicating that these uterotropic effects of genistein are mediated through ER-α. Treatment of adult female rats and dietary exposures of women have also been demonstrated to suppress serum LH.[146,147] Similarly, adult male mice treated with genistein exhibit estrogenic effects such as reduced pituitary LH levels, serum and testicular testosterone levels, and prostate weight.[148] Thus, in adult and peripubertal animals, phytoestrogens can clearly exert estrogenic effects in peripheral target tissues and the pituitary that appear to be mediated through ER.

Neonatal treatments with phytoestrogens tend to elicit many of the same peripheral effects as neonatal administration of $E_2$ or DES. For instance, neonatal coumestrol treatment of mice results in advanced vaginal opening, persistent vaginal cornification, cervical adenosis, cystic uterine glands, and squamous metaplasia of the uterus.[149,150] Neonatal genistein treatments also resulted in an increased incidence of uterine adenocarcinomas in mice[151] and the presence of multioocyte follicles.[152] The reported effects of perinatal genistein treatments on mammary gland development are more variable, with one study reporting that daily gavage from GD 12 through PND 20 did not result in any abnormal mammary gland development of pubertal mice,[153] whereas a second study reported that genistein or $E_2$ treatments from GD 15 to 20 resulted in increased density of terminal end buds.[154] A third study utilized dietary genistein treatments of rats from GD 7 through PND 50 and reported ductal and alveolar hyperplasia in both female and male offspring.[155] Discrepancies between some of these studies may be due to methodologic and species differences.

In contrast to effects of perinatal genistein treatments on ovaries, several studies report relatively minor or no effects on testis function of rats and mice exposed to genistein either perinatally or prepubertally.[156–159] One study utilizing prolonged dietary exposure (GD 7–PND 50) in rats[155] reported an effect on spermatogenesis, however, as well as reduced ventral prostate weight. Additional studies have reported some decrease in dorsolateral prostate (DLP),[160] decreased DLP ER-β expression,[161] decreased AR expression,[160] and altered methylation patterns[162] after genistein treatments.

In addition to peripheral effects, perinatal phytoestrogen exposures are clearly able to alter hypothalamic-pituitary function in a manner that is consistent with estrogenic actions. For instance, neonatal coumestrol treatments were also observed to increase basal levels of LH secretion in both male and female rats.[163,164] Neonatal exposure to high doses of coumestrol also suppressed GnRH-induced surges in the females, but did not result in an increase in volume of the sexually dimorphic nucleus (SDN) of the preoptic area (POA), an estrogen-sensitive hypothalamic nucleus.[163] Similarly, neonatal exposure to high doses of genistein also suppressed LH responses to GnRH challenge,[165–167] but, in contrast to the effects of coumestrol, increased the volumes of the SDN-POA. Thus, phytoestrogens are clearly able to elicit a number of permanent estrogenizing effects in both the peripheral reproductive structures and central neuroendocrine regulation, although it does appear that genistein may be more effective than coumestrol in terms of neural differentiation. All evidence points to the fact that most of these estrogenic effects are likely mediated by interactions with one of the two known forms of ER.

While much of the research on environmental estrogens has focused on potentially harmful effects, it has recently been postulated that phytoestrogens may play a role in cancer prevention or suppression. Epidemiologic data suggest that cultures that consume high levels of dietary phytoestrogens may have a lower incidence of breast and prostate cancer.[168,169] Indeed, a number of laboratory studies seem to support these epidemiologic studies. For instance, genistein or soy isoflavones suppress development of chemically induced prostate cancer[170,171] or LnCaP tumors in vivo,[172] transplanted Dunning prostate tumors in rats,[173] human benign prostatic hyperplasia (BPH) tissue and prostate cancer in culture,[174] and several prostate cancer cell lines.[175,176] Possible mechanisms for effects on the prostate include reduced expression of epidermal growth factor and ErbB2/ Neu receptors,[177] inhibition of 5α-reductase,[178] increased apoptosis,[179] and suppression of insulin-like growth factor signaling pathways.[176] Genistein has also been demonstrated to be antiangiogenic,[180] an effect that would be expected to slow the growth of many tumor types.

The effects of genistein on mammary gland carcinogenesis seem more variable. In mice, dietary genistein stimulates 7,12-dimethylbenz (a) anthracene (DMBA)-induced development of tumors[181] as well as estrogen-dependent MCF-7 tumors.[182] In mice implanted with mouse mammary adenocarcinoma cells (F3II), however, genistein inhibited growth of adenocarcinomas.[183] In utero treatments of rats have been alternately reported to have no effect when exposure is dietary,[184] to increase the incidence when dams are injected daily,[185] or to significantly delay and reduce DMBA-induced tumor onset through in utero dietary treatments.[186] Prepubertal injections[187,188] or peripubertal dietary exposures[189] seem to inhibit the growth of DMBA-induced tumors, however. It is possible that this inhibitory effect is due to reduced DMBA-adduct formation, as reported by Giri and Lu.[190] Part of the inconsistency in observed effects of genistein exposures may stem from differences in mode of treatment, timing of treatments, estrogen dependency of the tumors, and levels of endogenous estrogens. As suggested by Hilakivi-Clarke and colleagues,[191] however, it appears that maternal exposures may prove to increase offspring risks due to increased terminal end buds (TEB) and ER-α levels whereas prepubertal or peripubertal exposures may be protective by promoting early differentiation of epithelial cells.

## MYCOTOXINS

Estrogenic mycotoxins include zearalenone and zearanol. Identification of the hormonal activity of this class of compounds was first observed by the induction of infertility and persistent vaginal cornification in swine that were fed moldy corn found to contain mycotoxins. Recent studies using purified zearalenone have confirmed that a zearalenone-supplemented diet induces infertility, constant estrus, diminished fertility, and reduced litter size in sows.[192] Zearalenone binds to both ER-α and ER-β[2] and, indeed, neonatal treatments seem to mimic the effects of neonatal DES treatments with reports of delayed vaginal opening, persistent estrus, and sterility.[193] Another neonatal exposure study has reported diminished corpora lutea and increased squamous metaplasia in adult mice that were treated neonatally with zearalenone.[194] In rats, neonatal zearalenone has also resulted in increased volume of the SDN-POA and diminished pituitary responses to GnRH challenges.[166] Recent studies also indicate that zearalenone treatments of adult males can reduce testis size and sperm concentrations in deer[195] and induce germ cell apoptosis in rats.[196] In utero treatments also resulted in increased regression of germinal epithelium in mice.[197] Thus, it appears that this class of compounds can exert significant estrogenic activity that is mechanistically very similar to the effects of $E_2$.

## PESTICIDES

A number of organochlorine pesticides have been synthesized in the past 50 years including DDT, chlordecone (Kepone), lindane, and methoxychlor. There are numerous accounts of pesticides exerting effects on reproduction. As with highly toxic compounds such as lead, TCDD, and PCBs, however, one of the major issues is whether these compounds or their metabolites can exert reproductive effects directly via intrinsic hormonal activity or indirectly via their well-characterized neurotoxic effects. Indeed, all of the aforementioned pesticides have been suggested to exert some degree of hormonelike activity either in vitro or in vivo.

One of the more interesting aspects of this group of endocrine disrupters is that some seem to act as weak estrogens while others seem to act as weak antiandrogens. Indeed, there is often overlap with some compounds exhibiting both estrogenic and antiandrogenic effects. For instance, o,p′-DDD, o,p′-DDE, p,p′-DDT, and o,p′-DDT have all been demonstrated to bind to human estrogen receptor although their affinities are orders of magnitude less than $E_2$.[198] In transient transfections, these compounds and p,p-DDE also act as androgen antagonists.[199,200] The same dual actions can be attributed to methoxychlor and its active metabolite 2, 2-bis(p-hydroxyphenyl)1,1,1-trichloroethane (HPTE), which exert both estrogenic and antiandrogenic effects (see methoxychlor section). This duality of action makes mechanistic interpretations of in vivo data somewhat problematic, as perinatal treatments with estrogens and antiandrogens can result in similar phenotypes in the offspring. In this section, we provide examples of some pesticides that have the potential to alter reproduction through their intrinsic hormonal activity. Given recent reports that dichlorodiphenyltrichloroethane (DDT) and its metabolites can alter AP1 gene activity through ER-independent activation of the p38 MAPK pathway in cell culture, however, it is important to keep in mind that these chemicals may also have "nonhormonal" mechanisms of action.[201,202]

## DDT AND DDT METABOLITES

Although DDT has been banned from use in the United States and many parts of Europe, it is still used in some countries and therefore continues to be a significant health concern for humans and wildlife populations. This risk is compounded by the fact that DDT and its metabolites are environmentally persistent organochlorine compounds that are highly lipophilic and readily bioaccumulate. Thus, although environmental levels of DDT and its many metabolites have diminished in this country, these compounds still persist in low levels in the environment and can be detected in tissues of humans and wildlife. Despite this persistence, there are few reports of reproductive effects of DDT in humans, although epidemiologic data indicate that higher DDT or DDE levels may be correlated with an increased incidence of breast cancer[203] and with shorter periods of lactation in women.[204]

Historically, the most infamous effects of DDT involved one of its metabolites, dichlorodiphenyldichloroethylene (DDE). This compound reduced fecundity in birds, due to bioaccumulation in the female birds and compromised activity of shell glands that led to thinning of the shells and consequent mortality. In laboratory studies, oral dosing of DDT for 2 to 3 weeks resulted in lower serum and intratesticular testosterone levels despite normal serum FSH and LH levels in adult rats.[205] Several studies support the classification of DDT as a weak estrogen. For instance, treatments of immature rats with o,p-DDT cause increased DNA synthesis in epithelial, stromal, and myometrial layers of the uterus.[206] These uterotropic effects were also observed in mice in whom o,p-DDT increased uterine weight and induced estrogen-responsive genes.[207] Additionally, o,p-DDT has been demonstrated to stimulate growth of estrogen-responsive tumor cells.[208]

Neonatal studies indicate that either DES or o,p′-DDT treatment of rats on postnatal days 1 to 10 suppressed basal LH levels or GnRH induction of LH in castrated adult males.[165] An additional study reports that low-dose prenatal treatments increase aggression in both sexes and, at some doses, result in lower testis size.[209] These actions of o,p′-DDT are consistent with the effects of known estrogens. As mentioned earlier, however, the DDT metabolite p,p′-DDE exerts antiandrogenic effects. For instance, perinatal p,p′-DDE treatments of rats resulted in decreased anogenital distance and retention of thoracic nipples in male offspring.[200,210] A recent finding that p,p-DDE can induce hepatic aromatase levels also raises the possibility that some observed "antiandrogenic" actions may stem partly from elevated levels of estrogens.[211]

Examples of developmental effects of pesticides are also emerging from studies of lower vertebrates. Studies of neonate red-bellied turtles from Lake Apopka in Florida indicate that high levels of contaminants (particularly p,p-DDE) are associated with reduced numbers of individuals with normal testes and an increased incidence of ovotestes.[212] Juvenile alligators from this lake have reduced serum testosterone levels and reduced penis size and, in laboratory experiments, treatment of alligator eggs with $E_2$ or DDE results in effects similar to those observed in the Lake Apopka population.[212] In addition to effects in reptiles, injection of o,p-DDT into seagull eggs results in feminization of males.[213] Similarly, exposure of fish eggs through microinjection has shown that o,p-DDT induces sex reversal (male to female) of Japanese medaka,[214] whereas o,p-DDE simply reduces gonadal size and compromises ovarian function.[215] In flounder, o,p-DDT also reduces testis size, decreases serum testosterone, and induces synthesis of vitellogenin.[216]

## METHOXYCHLOR

Methoxychlor (MTX) is a pesticide that is structurally related to DDT. Methoxychlor and its metabolite HPTE are reported to have both estrogenic and antiandrogenic effects when tested in vitro and in vivo. Recent studies reported, however, that HPTE is an ER-α agonist but an antagonist for ER-β and AR.[217,218] In addition, methoxychlor was reported to stimulate estrogen-responsive genes, lactoferrin, and glucose-6-phosphate dehydrogenase through a mechanism that does not involve ER-α or ER-β.[5] These multiple modes of action greatly complicate interpretation of in vivo effects of methoxychlor and HPTE.

Chronic treatments of mice with MTX have resulted in increased incidence of interstitial cell carcinomas[219] and decreased spermatogenesis.[220] In an earlier study, MTX also caused decreased prostate, seminal vesicle, and testis size in adult male rats.[221] The effects on testicular carcinoma and reduced spermatogenesis are consistent with reports of estrogenic activity, and binding data indicate that MTX can indeed interact weakly with ER.[222] Either antiandrogenic action at the peripheral targets or estrogenic suppression of the hypothalamic-pituitary-gonadal (HPG) axis could explain reduced weights of accessory sex glands, however. The testicular atrophy might suggest that secretion of LH and FSH was reduced due to estrogenic action at the level of the hypothalamus or pituitary. Studies in intact male mice using high doses of MTX revealed reduced seminal vesicle weight (30%) but no significant effects on either serum LH or testosterone levels (unpublished data). In contrast, flutamide very effectively reduced seminal vesicle weight and resulted in significantly elevated serum LH and testosterone (unpublished data). Similar selectivity in target organ effects was reported for a chronic MTX study in which spermatogenesis and accessory sex structures were inhibited while serum LH and testosterone were unaffected.[223] These selective effects occur despite an apparent ability of HPTE to inhibit GnRH expression in cultured GT1-7 cells[224] and testosterone synthesis by cultured Leydig cells.[225] It is possible that a lack of overt effect on serum LH and serum testosterone in vivo stems from the mutally antagonistic effects of estrogenic negative feedback versus antiandrogenic blockade of androgenic negative feedback. Nonetheless, these data suggest that, in adult rodents, MTX is a relatively weak antiandrogen at high doses.

In adult female mice, HPTE is clearly uterotropic, based on stimulation of uterine hypertrophy and estrogen-dependent genes.[207] A single MTX treatment of pseudopregnant rats has been demonstrated to reduce fertility and decrease uterine decidualization response, a progesterone-regulated event, without affecting ovarian weight, numbers of corpora lutea, or serum progesterone levels. Since MTX mimicked the effects of the estrone control but had no apparent effect on serum progesterone, this suggested that methoxychlor may have estrogen-like effects on decidualization, independent of any alterations in serum progesterone.[226] A subsequent study, however, demonstrated that MTX administered on gestational days 1 to 8 resulted in decreased implantation associated with a decrease in serum progesterone.[227] Further studies suggest that MTX on gestational days 2 to 3 results in accelerated movement of embryos into the uterus. Thus, MTX treatments of pregnant rats has effects on embryo movement, implantation, and decidualization that may involve direct effects of MTX and indirect effects through changes in serum progesterone. MTX treatment of immature female rats results in vaginal estrus, induction of uterine EGFR, and peroxidase activity.[228,229] Another study demonstrated that MTX stimulated uterine weights, induced persistent vaginal estrus, and, in conjunction with progesterone treatments, stimulated sexual behaviors.[230] On the whole, most of these effects are similar to those of naturally occurring estrogens and support the hypothesis that MTX or its metabolite HPTE may have reproductive effects in vivo by interacting with estrogen receptors.

In mice, neonatal MTX treatment (PND 1–10 or 1–14) has been reported to stimulate precocial vaginal opening and persistent vaginal estrus, increase uterine weight, stimulate epithelial hypertrophy of the uterus and vagina, and produce some degree of uterine dysplasia.[231,232] MTX treatments on PND 1 to 4 have also been reported to accelerate expression of ER in the uterine epithelium.[233] Ovarian atrophy and decreased superovulation responses have also been observed in adult mice that were treated neonatally with MTX.[234] Male pups treated with $E_2$ or MTX on PND 1 to 9 exhibited decreased serum testosterone and reduced DNA content in the seminal vesicle and ventral prostate.[235]

Perinatal MTX treatments of rats have also been reported to accelerate the onset of puberty in females and disrupt estrous cycling during adulthood,[236] whereas male offspring exhibited delayed puberty[236] and reduced testis size, epididymal sperm counts, and Seroli cell numbers.[237] An additional study demonstrated that perinatal MTX treatment resulted in increased size of the ventral prostate associated with inflammation.[238] Many of the reported effects in females are consistent with an estrogenic mode of action mediated by ER, whereas the effects in males may be attributed to either an estrogenic or antiandrogenic mode of action mediated by activation of either ER or AR.

Although they are not pesticides, recent studies of di(n-butyl) phthalate and methoxyacetic acid warrant comment here as they reveal other potential mechanisms by which seemingly antiandrogenic effects can be exerted. Di(n-butyl) phthalate can exert antiandrogenic effects including decreased AGD, retention of nipples, and degeneration of seminiferous tubules. It appears that some of these effects stem from reduced cholesterol transport and testosterone synthesis by Leydig cells rather than by antagonism of AR.[239] Methoxyacetic acid (MAA) disrupts spermatogenesis, an effect consistent with reduced serum testosterone or antiandrogens. It appears, however, that MAA-induced apoptosis of primary spermatocytes is correlated with increased cytoplasmic expression of ER-β-in spermatocytes[239] and, perhaps, augmented ER-β-mediated gene transcription.[8] These studies suggest that different compounds may be able to alter androgen-dependent structures and spermatogenesis by altering steroid hormone profiles and inappropriate activation of steroid receptors expressed within germ cells.

## VINCLOZOLIN

Vinclozolin, a dicarboxamide fungicide, and it metabolites have been demonstrated to antagonize androgen effects by binding to and blocking androgen receptor–mediated events such as androgen-induced transactivation in transient transfections. One of these metabolites is remarkably effective and exhibits only a twofold lower antiandrogenic activity than hydroxyflutamide, a very potent antiandrogen.[240] In adult rats, vinclozolin treatments resulted in reduced sperm counts, increased LH-β and FSH-β mRNA levels, increased serum levels of LH and testosterone, and higher levels of testicular 17α-hydroxylase.[241] Similarly, treatments of adult guppies reduced sperm counts, sexually dimorphic coloration, and sex behaviors in male guppies.[242,243] Perinatal treatments of rats with vinclozolin have also been demonstrated to reduce AGD, induce cryptorchidism, inhibit development on spinal nuclei, reduce sizes of levator ani/bulbocavernosum muscles, and reduce ventral prostate weight.[241,244–246] As adults, perinatally treated males exhibited diminished levels of intromission and an inability to ejaculate, despite normal mounting behaviors. It appears that, rather than an effect on motivational aspects of sex behavior, the failure to intromit was due to cleft phallus and hypospadias. Many of these effects are similar to those of perinatal flutamide treatment and suggest that vinclozolin acts in vivo as an antiandrogen[247] and does so over a wide range of vertebrate classes.

Other reports have documented the existence of antidrogenic activity in other pesticides such as linuron, an herbicide, and fenitrothion, an insecticide. In utero linuron treatments of rats are reported to alter normal development of the epididymis and vas deferens. It appears these "antiandrogenic" effects may be related to altered growth factor signaling between mesynchemal and epithelial cells.[248] In utero exposures to fenitrothion resulted in transient effects such as reduced AGD and retention of nipples at postnatal days 1 and 13, respectively.[249] These effects disappeared by postnatal day 100, indicating that fenitrothion is a relatively weak antiandrogen when compared to vinclozolin, linuron, or flutamide.

## LINDANE

It appears that lindane can alter reproduction and that the effects can be classified as either estrogenic or antiestrogenic. For instance, when ovexed mice are treated chronically with low levels of lindane, uterine epithelial height and vaginal thickness are increased.[250] Similarly, lindane can stimulate growth of estrogen-dependent cell lines and stimulate ERE-regulated gene activity.[251,252] Lindane also stimulated vitellogenin synthesis by cultured trout hepatocytes.[253] Interestingly, although ICI 164,384 or other ER antagonists blocked these estrogenic effects, lindane was unable to bind ER in any of the studies that tested binding activities.[251-253] Thus, in the absence of endogenous or exogenous estrogen, it appears that lindane can activate ER-dependent events without binding to the ligand-binding domain of the ER.

In contrast to these "estrogenic" effects of lindane, several studies report effects in female rodents that are primarily "antiestrogenic" in nature. For instance, chronic lindane treatments caused delayed vaginal opening, disrupted estrous cycling, and reduced pituitary and uterine weights.[254,255] Chronic lindane treatments of female rats were also demonstrated to decrease serum and pituitary levels of LH and PRL while effects on serum $E_2$ were variable.[255] Later studies indicate that these antiestrogenic effects occur without alterations in $E_2$ levels or numbers of ER and $E_2$-induced PR in either the hypothalamus, pituitary, or uterus.[256] Thus, in contrast to its estrogenic effects in the absence of estrogens, it appears that lindane may sometimes act in an antiestrogenic fashion when endogenous estrogens are present.

## CONCLUSIONS

Based on laboratory experiments, there is little question that a number of nonsteroidal environmental contaminants have the potential to affect vertebrate reproduction adversely. These effects can occur through steroid receptor–mediated actions or through steroid receptor independent changes in production of endogenous hormones, activation or inhibition of steroid receptors, nonhormonal effects on transcription of steroid sensitive genes, or cellular toxicity. Laboratory experiments continue to prove that exposures during perinatal or immature stages have the most persistent and dramatic effects on reproduction.

Unfortunately, the laboratory experiments do not address the issue of whether normal environmental exposures to endocrine disrupters pose a significant health risk to wildlife and humans. These are difficult questions to answer and, presently, there are limited epidemiologic data to support human effects for most of the compounds discussed in this chapter. Recent studies of wild populations and "low-dose" studies are sufficiently alarming, however, that this area continues to warrant significant research efforts. We suggest that, in addition to survey studies of humans and wildlife populations, future studies should continue to address mechanistic questions, dose response relationships, low-dose effects of "environmentally relevant" exposures, and effects of commonly found mixtures or "environmental cocktails" of endocrine disrupters. It is through the continued application of laboratory screening, mechanistic studies, and characterization of wildlife and human exposure that we will be able to determine the underlying mechanisms of reproductive disruption and the extent to which endocrine disrupters threaten the reproductive capacities of vertebrates. Ultimately, by understanding the mechanisms of endocrine disruption, we will be able to devise better preventive measures to minimize exposure and the effects of endocrine disrupters.

## REFERENCES

1. Gaido K, Leonard L, Lovell S, et al: Evaluation of chemicals with endocrine modulating activity in a yeast-based steroid hormone receptor gene transcription assay. Toxicol Appl Pharmacol 143:205–212, 1997.
2. Kuiper G, Lemmen J, Carlsson B, et al: Interaction of estrogenic chemicals and phytoestrogens with estrogen receptor beta. Endocrinology 139:4252–4263, 1998.
3. Lindzey J, Kumar MV, Grossman M, et al: Molecular mechanisms of androgen action. In Litwak G (ed): Steroids. San Diego, CA, Academic, 1994, 383–432.
4. Das SK, Taylor JA, Korach KS, et al: Estrogenic responses in estrogen receptor (ER)–deficient mice reveal a novel non-ER mediated signaling pathway. Proc Natl Acad Sci U S A 94:12786–12791, 1997.
5. Ghosh D, Taylor JA, Green JA, et al: Methoxychlor stimulates estrogen-responsive messenger ribonucleic acids in mouse uterus through a non-estrogen receptor (non-ER) alpha and non-ER beta mechanism. Endocrinology 140:3526–3533, 1999.
6. Curtis SW, Washburn T, Sewall C, et al: Physiological coupling of growth factor and steroid receptor signaling pathways: Estrogen receptor knockout mice lack estrogen-like response to epidermal growth factor. Proc Natl Acad Sci U S A 93:12626–12630, 1996.
7. Klotz DM, Hewitt SC, Ciana P, et al: Requirement of estrogen receptor-alpha in insulin-like growth factor-1 (IGF-1)–induced uterine responses and in vivo evidence for IGF-1/estrogen receptor cross-talk. J Biol Chem 277:8531–8537, 2002.
8. Jansen MS, Nagel SC, Miranda PJ, et al: Short-chain fatty acids enhance nuclear receptor activity through mitogen-activated protein kinase activation and histone deacetylation. Proc Natl Acad Sci U S A 101:7199–7204.
9. Dwivedi R, Iannaccone P: Effects of environmental chemicals on early development. In Korach KS (ed): Reproductive and Developmental Toxicology. New York, Marcel Dekker, 1998, pp 11–46.
10. Lancranjan I, Popescu H, Gavanescu O, et al: Reproductive ability of workmen occupationally exposed to lead. Arch Environ Health 30:396–401, 1975.
11. Nordstrom S, Beckman L, Nordenson I, et al: Occupational and environmental risks in and around a smelter in northern Sweden. III. Frequencies of spontaneous abortions. Hereditas 88:51–54, 1978.
12. McMichael A, Vimpani G, Robertson E, et al: The Port Pirie cohort study: Maternal blood lead and pregnancy outcome. J Epidemiol Community Health 40:18–25, 1986.
13. Taupeau C, Poupon J, Treton D, et al: Lead reduces messenger RNA and protein levels of cytochrome p450 aromatase and estrogen receptor beta in human ovarian granulosa cells. Biol Reprod 68(6):1982–1988, 2003.
14. Johansson L, Sjoblol P, Wide M: Effects of lead on the male mouse as investigated by in vitro fertilization and blastocyst culture. Environ Res 42:140–148, 1987.
15. Sokol RZ, Madding CE, Swerdloff RS: Lead toxicity and the hypothalamic-pituitary-testicular axis. Biol Reprod 33:722–728, 1985.
16. Ronis MJ, Badger TM, Shema SJ, et al: Reproductive toxicity and growth effects in rats exposed to lead at different periods of development. Toxicol Appl Pharmacol 136:361–371, 1996.
17. Sokol RZ: Hormonal effects of lead acetate in the male rat: Mechanism of action. Biol Reprod 37:1135–1138, 1987.
18. Ronis MJ, Gandy J, Gadger T: Endocrine mechanisms underlying reproductive toxicity in the developing rat exposed

chronically to dietary lead. J Toxicol Environ Health 54:77–99, 1998.

19. McGivern RF, Sokol RZ, Berman NG: Prenatal lead exposure in the rat during the third week of gestation: Long-term behavioral, physiological, and anatomical effects associated with reproduction. Toxicol Appl Pharmacol 110:206–215, 1991.

20. Pinon-Lataillade G, Thoreaux-Manlay A, Coffigny H, et al: Reproductive toxicity of chronic lead exposure in male and female mice. Hum Exp Toxicol 14:872–878, 1995.

21. Ronis MJ, Badger TM, Shema SJ, et al: Effects on pubertal growth and reproduction in rats exposed to lead prenatally or continuously throughout development. J Toxicol Environ Health 53:327–341, 1998.

22. Wiebe J, Barr K: Effect of prenatal and neonatal exposure to lead on the affinity and number of estradiol receptors in the uterus. J Toxicol Environ Health 24:451–460, 1988.

23. Wiebe J, Barr K, Buckingham K: Effect of prenatal and neonatal exposure to lead on gonadotropin receptors and steroidogenesis in rat ovaries. J Toxicol Environ Health 24:461–476, 1988.

24. Gunnarsson D, Nordberg G, Lundgren P, et al: Cadmium-induced decrement of the Lh receptor expression and cAMP levels in the testis of rats. Toxicology 183:57–63, 2003.

25. Lafuente A, Marquez N, Perez-Lorenzo M, et al: Cadmium effects on hypothalamic-pituitary-testicular axis in male rats. Exp Biol Med (Maywood) 226:605–611, 2001.

26. Johnson MD, Kenney N, Stoica A, et al: Cadmium mimics the in vivo effects of estrogen in the uterus and mammary gland. Nat Med 9:1081–1084, 2003.

27. Garcia-Morales P, Saceda M, Kenney N, et al: Effect of cadmium on estrogen receptor levels and estrogen-induced responses in human breast cancer cells. J Biol Chem 269:16896–16901, 1994.

28. Stoica A, Katzenellenbogen BS, Martin MB: Activation of estrogen receptor-alpha by the heavy metal cadmium. Mol Endocrinol 14:545–553, 2000.

29. Martin MB, Reiter R, Pham T, et al: Estrogen-like activity of metals in MCF-7 breast cancer cells. Endocrinology 144:2425–2436, 2003.

30. Waalkes MP, Liu J, Chen H, et al: Estrogen signaling in livers of male mice with hepatocellular carcinoma induced by exposure to arsenic in utero. J Natl Cancer Inst 96:466–474, 2004.

31. Moore RW, Potter CL, Theobald HM, et al: Androgenic deficiency in male rats treated with 2,3,7,8-tetrachlorodibenzo-p-dioxin. Toxicol Appl Pharmacol 79:99–111, 1985.

32. Moore RW, Jeffcoate CR, Peterson RE, et al: 2,3,7,8-Tetrachlorodibenzo-p-dioxin inhibits steroidogenesis in the rat testis by inhibiting mobilization of cholesterol to cytochrome P450. Toxicol Appl Pharmacol 109:85–97, 1991.

33. Rune GM, de Souza P, Krowke R, et al: Morphological and histochemical pattern of response in rat testes after administration of 2,3,7,8-tetrachlorodibenzo-p-dioxin (TCDD). Histol Histopathol 6:459–467, 1991.

34. Johnson L, DSickerson R, Safe SH, et al: Reduced Leydig cell volume and function in adult rats exposed to 2,3,7,8-tetrachlorodibenzo-p-dioxin without a significant effect on spermatogenesis. Toxicology 76:103–118, 1992.

35. Romkes M, Piskorska-Pliszczynska J, Safe S: Effects of 2,3,7,8-tetrachlorodibenzo-p-dioxin on hepatic and uterine estrogen receptor levels in rats. Toxicol Appl Pharmacol 87:306–314, 1987.

36. Romkes M, Safe S: Comparative activities of 2,3,7,8-tetrachlorodibenzo-p-dioxin and progesterone as antiestrogens in the female rat uterus. Toxicol Appl Pharmacol 92:368–380, 1988.

37. Astroff B, Rowlands C, Dickerson R, et al: 2,3,7,8-Tetrachlorodibenzo-p-dioxin inhibition of 17 beta-estradiol-induced increases in rat uterine epidermal growth factor receptor binding activity and gene expression. Mol Cell Endocrinol 72:247–252, 1990.

38. Astroff B, Safe S: 2,3,7,8-Tetrachlorodibenzo-p-dioxin as an antiestrogen: Effect on rat uterine peroxidase activity. Biochem Pharmacol 39:485–488, 1990.

39. Astroff B, Eldridge B, Safe S: Inhibition of the 17 beta-estradiol-induced and constitutive expression of the cellular protooncogene c-fos by 2,3,7,8-tetrachlorodibenzo-p-dioxin (TCDD) in the female rat uterus. Toxicol Lett 56:305–315, 1991.

40. Mably TA, Moore RW, Peterson RE: In utero and lactational exposure of male rats to 2,3,7,8-tetrachlorodibenzo-p-dioxin. 1. Effects on androgenic status. Toxicol Appl Pharmacol 114:97–107, 1992.

41. Gray LE Jr, Kelce WR, Monosson E, et al: Exposure to TCDD during development permanently alters reproductive function in male Long Evans rats and hamsters: Reduced ejaculated and epididymal sperm numbers and sex accessory gland weights in offspring with normal androgenic status. Toxicol Appl Pharmacol 131:108–118, 1995.

42. Ohsako S, Miyabara Y, Nishimura N, et al: Maternal exposure to a low dose of 2,3,7,8-tetrachlorodibenzo-p-dioxin (TCDD) suppressed the development of reproductive organs of male rats: Dose-dependent increase of mRNA levels of 5alpha-reductase type 2 in contrast to decrease of androgen receptor in the pubertal ventral prostate. Toxicol Sci 60:132–143, 2001.

43. Gray LE, Ostby JS, Kelce WR: A dose-response analysis of the reproductive effects of a single gestational dose of 2,3,7,8-tetrachlorodibenzo-p-dioxin in male Long Evans hooded rat offspring. Toxicol Appl Pharmacol 146:11–20, 1997.

44. Roman BL, Sommer RJ, Shinomiya K, et al: In utero and lactational exposure of the male rat to 2,3,7,8-tetrachlorodibenzo-p-dioxin: Impaired prostate growth and development without inhibited androgen production. Toxicol Appl Pharmacol 134:241–250, 1995.

45. Theobald HM, Roman BL, Lin TM, et al: 2,3,7,8-Tetrachlorodibenzo-p-dioxin inhibits luminal cell differentiation and androgen responsiveness of the ventral prostate without inhibiting prostatic 5alpha-dihydrotestosterone formation or testicular androgen production in rat offspring. Toxicol Sci 58:324–338, 2000.

46. Bjerke DL, Brown TJ, MacLusky NJ, et al: Partial demasculinization and feminization of sex behavior in male rats by in utero and lactational exposure to 2,3,7,8-tetrachlorodibenzo-p-dioxin is not associated with alterations in estrogen receptor binding or volumes of sexually differentiated brain nuclei. Toxicol Appl Pharmacol 127:258–267, 1994.

47. Klinge CM, Bowers JL, Kulakosky PC, et al: The aryl hydrocarbon receptor (AHR)/AHR nuclear translocator (ARNT) heterodimer interacts with naturally occurring estrogen response elements. Mol Cell Endocrinol 157:105–119, 1999.

48. Wormke M, Castro-Rivera E, Chen I, et al: Estrogen and aryl hydrocarbon receptor expression and crosstalk in human Ishikawa endometrial cancer cells. J Steroid Biochem Mol Biol 72:197–207, 2000.

49. Kumar MB, Tarpey RW, Perdew GH: Differential recruitment of coactivator RIP140 by Ah and estrogen receptors: Absence of a role for LXXLL motifs. J Biol Chem 274:22155–22164, 1999.

50. Moran FM, VandeVoort CA, Overstreet JW, et al: Molecular target of endocrine disruption in human luteinizing granulosa cells by 2,3,7,8-tetrachlorodibenzo-p-dioxin: Inhibition of estradiol secretion due to decreased 17alpha-hydroxylase/17,20-lyase cytochrome P450 expression. Endocrinology 144:467–473, 2003.

51. Moran FM, Conley AJ, Corbin CJ, et al: 2,3,7,8-Tetrachlorodibenzo-p-dioxin decreases estradiol production without altering the enzyme activity of cytochrome P450 aromatase of human luteinized granulosa cells in vitro. Biol Reprod 62:1102–1108, 2000.

52. Abbott BD, Birnbaum LS: Effects of TCDD on embryonic ureteric epithelial EGF receptor expression and cell proliferation. Teratology 41:71–84, 1990.

53. Buchanan DL, Ohsako S, Tohyama C, et al: Dioxin inhibition of estrogen-induced mouse uterine epithelial mitogenesis involves changes in cyclin and transforming growth factor-beta expression. Toxicol Sci 66:62–68, 2002.

54. Rier S, Foster WG: Environmental dioxins and endometriosis. Reprod Toxicol 16:299–307, 2002.

55. Ohtake F, Takeyama K, Matsumoto T, et al: Modulation of oestrogen receptor signalling by association with the activated dioxin receptor. Nature 423:545–550, 2003.

56. Eldridge JC, Wetzel LT, Tyrey L: Estrous cycle patterns of Sprague-Dawley rats during acute and chronic atrazine administration. Reprod Toxicol 13:491–499, 1999.

57. Fujimoto N, Honda H: Effects of environmental estrogenic compounds on growth of a transplanted estrogen responsive pituitary tumor cell line in rats. Food Chem Toxicol 41:1711–1717, 2003.

58. Cooper RL, Stoker TE, Goldman JM, et al: Effect of atrazine on ovarian function in the rat. Reprod Toxicol 10:257–264, 1996.

59. Cooper RL, Stoker TE, Tyrey L, et al: Atrazine disrupts the hypothalamic control of pituitary-ovarian function. Toxicol Sci 53:297–307, 2000.

60. Sanderson JT, Letcher RJ, Heneweer M, et al: Effects of chloro-s-triazine herbicides and metabolites on aromatase activity in various human cell lines and on vitellogenin production in male carp hepatocytes. Environ Health Perspect 109:1027–1031, 2001.

61. Sanderson JT, Seinen W, Giesy JP, et al: 2-Chloro-s-triazine herbicides induce aromatase (CYP19) activity in H295R human adrenocortical carcinoma cells: A novel mechanism for estrogenicity? Toxicol Sci 54:121–127, 2000.

62. Hayes T, Haston K, Tsui M, et al: Atrazine-induced hermaphroditism at 0.1 ppb in American leopard frogs (Rana pipiens): Laboratory and field evidence. Environ Health Perspect 111:568–575, 2003.

63. Hayes TB, Collins A, Lee M, et al: Hermaphroditic, demasculinized frogs after exposure to the herbicide atrazine at low ecologically relevant doses. Proc Natl Acad Sci U S A 99:5476–5480, 2002.

64. Tavera-Mendoza L, Ruby S, Brousseau P, et al: Response of the amphibian tadpole Xenopus laevis to atrazine during sexual differentiation of the ovary. Environ Toxicol Chem 21:1264–1267, 2002.

65. Tavera-Mendoza L, Ruby S, Brousseau P, et al: Response of the amphibian tadpole (Xenopus laevis) to atrazine during sexual differentiation of the testis. Environ Toxicol Chem 21:527–531, 2002.

66. Carr JA, Gentles A, Smith EE, et al: Response of larval Xenopus laevis to atrazine: Assessment of growth, metamorphosis, and gonadal and laryngeal morphology. Environ Toxicol Chem 22:396–405, 2003.

67. Reeder AL, Foley GL, Nichols DK, et al: Forms and prevalence of intersexuality and effects of environmental contaminants on sexuality in cricket frogs (Acris crepitans). Environ Health Perspect 106:261–266, 1998.

68. Rogan WJ, Ragan NB: Evidence of effects of environmental chemicals on the endocrine system in children. Pediatrics 112:247–252, 2003.

69. Korach KS, Sarver P, Chae K, et al: Estrogen receptor-binding activity of polychlorinated hydroxybiphenyls: Conformationally restricted structural probes. Mol Pharmacol 33:120–126, 1988.

70. Fielden MR, Chen I, Chittim B, et al: Examination of the estrogenicity of 2,4,6,2′,6′-pentachlorobiphenyl (PCB 104), its hydroxylated metabolite 2,4,6,2′,6′-pentachloro-4-biphenylol (HO-PCB 104), and a further chlorinated derivative, 2,4,6,2′,4′,6′-hexachlorobiphenyl (PCB 155). Environ Health Perspect 105:1238–1248, 1997.

71. Connor K, Ramamoorthy K, Moore M, et al: Hydroxylated polychlorinated biphenyls (PCBs) as estrogens and antiestrogens: Structure-activity relationships. Toxicol Appl Pharmacol 145:111–123, 1997.

72. Gellert RJ: Uterotrophic activity of polychlorinated biphenyls (PCB) and induction of precocious reproductive aging in neonatally treated female rats. Environ Res 16:123–130, 1978.

73. Gore AC, Wu TJ, Oung T, et al: A novel mechanism for endocrine-disrupting effects of polychlorinated biphenyls: Direct effects on gonadotropin-releasing hormone neurones. J Neuroendocrinol 14:814–823, 2002.

74. Jansen HT, Cooke PS, Porcelli J, et al: Estrogenic and antiestrogenic actions of PCBs in the female rat: In vitro and in vivo studies. Reprod Toxicol 7:237–248, 1993.

75. Carlson DB, Williams DE: 4-Hydroxy-2′,4′,6′-trichlorobiphenyl and 4-hydroxy-2′,3′,4′,5′-tetrachlorobiphenyl are estrogenic in rainbow trout. Environ Toxicol Chem 20:351–358, 2001.

76. Ahmad SU, Tariq S, Jalali S, et al: Environmental pollutant Aroclor 1242 (PCB) disrupts reproduction in adult male rhesus monkeys (Macaca mulatta). Environ Res 93:272–278, 2003.

77. Bergeron RM, Crews D, McLachlan JA: PCBs as environmental estrogens: Turtle sex determination as a biomarker of environmental contamination. Environ Health Perspect 102:780–781, 1994.

78. Willingham E, Crews D: Sex reversal effects of environmentally relevant xenobiotic concentrations on the red-eared slider turtle, a species with temperature dependent sex determination. Gen Comp Endocrinol 113:429–435, 1999.

79. Sager DB, Girard DM, Nelson D: Early postnatal exposure to PCBs: Sperm function in rats. Environ Toxicol Chem 10:737–746, 1991.

80. Sager DB: Effect of postnatal exposure to polychlorinated biphenyls on adult male reproductive function. Environ Res 31:76–94, 1983.

81. Cooke PS, Zhao YD, Hansen LG: Neonatal polychlorinated biphenyl treatment increases adult testis size and sperm production in the rat. Toxicol Appl Pharmacol 136:112–117, 1996.

82. Gellert RJ, Wilson C: Reproductive function in rats exposed prenatally to pesticides and polychlorinated biphenyls (PCB). Environ Res 18:437–443, 1979.

83. Fielden MR, Halgren RG, Tashiro CH, et al: Effects of gestational and lactational exposure to Aroclor 1242 on sperm quality and in vitro fertility in early adult and middle-aged mice. Reprod Toxicol 15:281–292, 2001.

84. Sager DB, Girard DM: Long-term effects on reproductive parameters in female rats after translactational exposure to PCBs. Environ Res 66:52–76, 1994.

85. Robboy SJ, Scully RE, Welch WR, et al: Intrauterine diethylstilbestrol exposure and its consequences: Pathologic characteristics of vaginal adenosis, clear cell adenocarcinoma, and related lesions. Arch Pathol Lab Med 101:1–5, 1977.

86. Newbold R: Influence of estrogenic agents on mammalian male reproductive tract development. In Korach KS (ed): Reproductive and Developmental Toxicology. New York, Marcel Dekker, 1998, pp 531–552.

87. Newbold R: Cellular and molecular effects of developmental exposure to diethylstilbestrol: Implications for other environmental estrogens. Environ Health Perspect 103(Suppl 7):83–87, 1995.

88. Liehr JG: Genotoxic effects of estrogens. Mutat Res 238:269–276, 1990.

89. Chae K, Lindzey J, Korach K: Estrogen-dependent gene regulation by an oxidative metabolite of diethylstilbestrol, diethylstilbestrol-4′,4″-quinone. Steroids 63:149–157, 1998.

90. Li S, Hansman R, Newbold R, et al: Neonatal diethylstilbestrol exposure induces persistent elevation of c-fos expression and hypomethylation in its exon-4 in mouse uterus. Mol Carcinog 38:78–84, 2003.

91. Yamashita S, Takayanagi A, Shimizu N: Effects of neonatal diethylstilbestrol exposure on c-fos and c-jun protooncogene expression in the mouse uterus. Histol Histopathol 16:131–140, 2001.

92. Couse JF, Davis VL, Hanson RB, et al: Accelerated onset of uterine tumors in transgenic mice with aberrant expression of the estrogen receptor after neonatal exposure to diethylstilbestrol. Mol Carcinog 19:236–242, 1997.

93. Couse JF, Dixon D, Yates M, et al: Estrogen receptor-alpha knockout mice exhibit resistance to the developmental effects of neonatal diethylstilbestrol exposure on the female reproductive tract. Dev Biol 238:224–238, 2001.

94. Prins GS, Birch L, Couse JF, et al: Estrogen imprinting of the developing prostate gland is mediated through stromal estrogen receptor alpha: Studies with alphaERKO and betaERKO mice. Cancer Res 61:6089–6097, 2001.

95. Risbridger G, Wang H, Young P, et al: Evidence that epithelial and mesenchymal estrogen receptor-alpha mediates effects of estrogen on prostatic epithelium. Dev Biol 229:432–442, 2001.

96. Walker AH, Bernstein L, Warren DW, et al: The effect of in utero ethinyl oestradiol exposure on the risk of cryptorchid testis and testicular teratoma in mice. Br J Cancer 62:599–602, 1990.

97. Sawaki M, Noda S, Muroi T, et al: In utero through lactational exposure to ethinyl estradiol induces cleft phallus and delayed ovarian dysfunction in the offspring. Toxicol Sci 75:402–411, 2003.

98. Branham WS, Zehr DR, Chen JJ, et al: Uterine abnormalities in rats exposed neonatally to diethylstilbestrol, ethynylestradiol, or clomiphene citrate. Toxicology 51:201–212, 1988.

99. Baggs RB, Miller RK, Odoroff CL: Carcinogenicity of diethylstilbestrol in the Wistar rat: Effect of postnatal oral contraceptive steroids. Cancer Res 51:3311–3315, 1991.

100. Sumpter JP: Xenoendorine disrupters: Environmental impacts. Toxicol Lett 102:337–342, 1998.

101. Jobling S, Casey D, Rodgers-Gray T, et al: Comparative responses of molluscs and fish to environmental estrogens and an estrogenic effluent. Aquat Toxicol 65:205–220, 2003.

102. Andersen L, Holbech H, Gessbo A, et al: Effects of exposure to 17alpha-ethinylestradiol during early development on sexual differentiation and induction of vitellogenin in zebrafish (Danio rerio). Comp Biochem Physiol C Toxicol Pharmacol 134:365–374, 2003.

103. van Aerle R, Pounds N, Hutchinson TH, et al: Window of sensitivity for the estrogenic effects of ethinylestradiol in early life-stages of fathead minnow, Pimephales promelas. Ecotoxicology 11:423–434, 2002.

104. Blake CA, Boockfor FR: Chronic administration of the environmental pollutant 4-tert-octylphenol to adult male rats interferes with the secretion of luteinizing hormone, follicle-stimulating hormone, prolactin, and testosterone. Biol Reprod 57:255–266, 1997.

105. Abraham EJ, Frawley LS: Octylphenol (OP), an environmental estrogen, stimulates prolactin (PRL) gene expression. Life Sci 60:1457–1465, 1997.

106. Bicknell RJ, Herbison AE, Sumpter JP: Oestrogenic activity of an environmentally persistent alkylphenol in the reproductive tract but not the brain of rodents. J Steroid Biochem Mol Biol 54:7–9, 1995.

107. Blake C, Ashiru O: Disruption of rat estrous cyclicity by the environmental estrogen 4-tert-octophenol. Proc Soc Exp Biol Med 216:446–451, 1997.

108. Soto AM, Justicia H, Wray JW, et al: p-Nonyl-phenol: An estrogenic xenobiotic released from "modified" polystyrene. Environ Health Perspect 92:167–173, 1991.

109. Kang IJ, Yokota H, Oshima Y, et al: Effects of bisphenol A on the reproduction of Japanese medaka (Oryzias latipes). Environ Toxicol Chem 21:2394–2400, 2002.

110. Kang IJ, Yokota H, Oshima Y, et al: Effects of 4-nonylphenol on reproduction of Japanese Medaka, Oryzias latipes. Environ Toxicol Chem 22:2438–2445, 2003.

111. Pait AS, Nelson JO: Vitellogenesis in male Fundulus heteroclitus (killifish) induced by selective estrogenic compounds. Aquat Toxicol 64:331–342, 2003.

112. Christiansen T, Korsgaard B, Jespersen A: Effects of nonylphenol and 17 beta-oestradiol on vitellogenin synthesis, testicular structure and cytology in male eelpout Zoarces viviparus. J Exp Biol 201(Pt 2):179–192, 1998.

113. van Aerle R, Nolan TM, Jobling S, et al: Sexual disruption of wild cyprinid fish (the gudgeon, Gobio gobio) in United Kingdom freshwaters. Environ Toxicol Chem 20:2841–2847, 2001.

114. Dalgaard M, Pilegaard K, Ladefoged O: In utero exposure to diethylstilboestrol or 4-n-nonylphenol in rats: Number of sertoli cells, diameter and length of seminiferous tubules estimated by stereological methods. Pharmacol Toxicol 90:59–65, 2002.

115. Hossaini A, Dalgaard M, Vinggaard AM, et al: In utero reproductive study in rats exposed to nonylphenol. Reprod Toxicol 15:537–543, 2001.

116. Lee PC: Disruption of male reproductive tract development by administration of the xenoestrogen, nonylphenol, to male newborn rats. Endocrine 9:105–111, 1998.

117. vom Saal FS, Cooke PS, Buchanan DL, et al: A physiologically based approach to the study of bisphenol A and other estrogenic chemicals on the size of reproductive organs, daily sperm production, and behavior. Toxicol Ind Health 14:239–260, 1998.

118. Sweeney T, Nicol L, Roche JF, et al: Maternal exposure to octylphenol suppresses ovine fetal follicle-stimulating hormone secretion, testis size, and sertoli cell number. Endocrinology 141:2667–2673, 2000.

119. Majdic G, Sharpe R, O'Shaughnessy P, et al: Expression of cytochrome P450 17alpha-hydroxylase/C17-20lyase in the fetal rat testis is reduced by maternal exposure to exogenous estrogens. Endocrinology 137:1063–1070, 1996.

120. Majdic G, Sharpe R, Saunders P: Maternal oestrogen/xenoestrogen exposure alters expression of steroidogenic factor-1 (Sf-1/Ad4Bp) in fetal rat testis. Mol Cell Endocrinol 127:91–98, 1997.

121. Saunders PT, Majdic G, Parte P, et al: Fetal and perinatal influence of xenoestrogens on testis gene expression. Adv Exp Med Biol 424:99–110, 1997.

122. Mayer LP, Dyer CA, Propper CR: Exposure to 4-tert-octylphenol accelerates sexual differentiation and disrupts expression of steroidogenic factor 1 in developing bullfrogs. Environ Health Perspect 111:557–561, 2003.

123. Nikula H, Talonpoika T, Kaleva M, et al: Inhibition of hCG-stimulated steroidogenesis in cultured mouse Leydig tumor cells by bisphenol A and octylphenols. Toxicol Appl Pharmacol 157:166–173, 1999.

124. Haavisto TE, Adamsson NA, Myllymaki SA, et al: Effects of 4-tert-octylphenol, 4-tert-butylphenol, and diethylstilbestrol on prenatal testosterone surge in the rat. Reprod Toxicol 17:593–605, 2003.

125. Jobling S, Coey S, Whitmore JG, et al: Wild intersex roach (Rutilus rutilus) have reduced fertility. Biol Reprod 67:515–524, 2002.

126. Jobling S, Beresford N, Nolan M, et al: Altered sexual maturation and gamete production in wild roach (Rutilus rutilus) living in rivers that receive treated sewage effluents. Biol Reprod 66:272–281, 2002.

127. Sheahan DA, Brighty GC, Daniel M, et al: Reduction in the estrogenic activity of a treated sewage effluent discharge to an English river as a result of a decrease in the concentration of industrially derived surfactants. Environ Toxicol Chem 21:515–519, 2002.

128. Tohei A, Suda S, Taya K, et al: Bisphenol A inhibits testicular functions and increases luteinizing hormone secretion in adult male rats. Exp Biol Med (Maywood) 226:216–221, 2001.

129. Akingbemi BT, Sottas CM, Koulova AI, et al: Inhibition of testicular steroidogenesis by the xenoestrogen bisphenol A is associated with reduced pituitary luteinizing hormone secretion and decreased steroidogenic enzyme gene expression in rat Leydig cells. Endocrinology 145:592–603, 2004.

130. Ramos JG, Varayoud J, Kass L, et al: Bisphenol A induces both transient and permanent histofunctional alterations of the hypothalamic-pituitary-gonadal axis in prenatally exposed male rats. Endocrinology 144:3206–3215, 2003.

131. Ramos JG, Varayoud J, Sonnenschein C, et al: Prenatal exposure to low doses of bisphenol A alters the periductal stroma and glandular cell function in the rat ventral prostate. Biol Reprod 65:1271–1277, 2001.

132. Schonfelder G, Flick B, Mayr E, et al: In utero exposure to low doses of bisphenol A leads to long-term deleterious effects in the vagina. Neoplasia 4:98–102, 2002.

133. Tinwell H, Haseman J, Lefevre PA, et al: Normal sexual development of two strains of rat exposed in utero to low doses of bisphenol A. Toxicol Sci 68:339–348, 2002.

134. vom Saal FS, Timms BG, Montano MM, et al: Prostate enlargement in mice due to fetal exposure to low doses of estradiol or diethylstilbestrol and opposite effects at high doses. Proc Natl Acad Sci U S A 94:2056–2061, 1997.

135. Welshons WV, Nagel SC, Thayer KA, et al: Low-dose bioactivity of xenoestrogens in animals: Fetal exposure to low doses of methoxychlor and other xenoestrogens increases adult prostate size in mice. Toxicol Ind Health 15:12–25, 1999.

136. Howdeshell KL, Hotchkiss AK, Thayer KA, et al: Exposure to bisphenol A advances puberty. Nature 401:763–764, 1999.

137. Honma S, Suzuki A, Buchanan DL, et al: Low dose effect of in utero exposure to bisphenol A and diethylstilbestrol on female mouse reproduction. Reprod Toxicol 16:117–122, 2002.

138. Markey CM, Luque EH, Munoz De Toro M, et al: In utero exposure to bisphenol A alters the development and tissue organization of the mouse mammary gland. Biol Reprod 65:1215–1223, 2001.

139. Palanza PL, Howdeshell KL, Parmigiani S, et al: Exposure to a low dose of bisphenol A during fetal life or in adulthood alters maternal behavior in mice. Environ Health Perspect 110(Suppl 3):415–422, 2002.

140. Ashby J, Tinwell H, Haseman J: Lack of effects for low dose levels of bisphenol A and diethylstilbestrol on the prostate gland of CF1 mice exposed in utero. Regul Toxicol Pharmacol 30:156–166, 1999.

141. Haubruge E, Petit F, Gage MJ: Reduced sperm counts in guppies (*Poecilia reticulata*) following exposure to low levels of tributyltin and bisphenol A. Proc R Soc Lond B Biol Sci 267:2333–2337, 2000.

142. Sohoni P, Tyler CR, Hurd K, et al: Reproductive effects of long-term exposure to bisphenol A in the fathead minnow (*Pimephales promelas*). Environ Sci Technol 35:2917–2925, 2001.

143. Hughes C, Tansey G: Phytoestrogens and reproductive medicine. In Korach KS (ed): Reproductive and Developmental Toxicology. New York, Marcel Dekker, 1998, pp 277–298.

144. Whitten P, Naftolin F: Effects of a phytoestrogen diet on estrogen-dependent reproductive processes in immature female rats. Steroids 57:56–61, 1992.

145. Santell R, Chang Y, Nair M, et al: Dietary genistein exerts estrogenic effects upon the uterus, mammary gland and the hypothalamic/pituitary axis in rats. J Nutr 127:263–269, 1997.

146. Hughes C: Effects of phytoestrogens on GnRH-induced luteinizing hormone secretion in ovariectomized rats. Reprod Toxicol 1:179–181, 1988.

147. Cassidy A, Bingham S, Setchell K: Biological effects of isoflavones in young women: Importance of the chemical composition of soyabean products. Br J Nutr 74:587–601, 1995.

148. Strauss L, Makela S, Joshi S, et al: Genistein exerts estrogen-like effects in male mouse reproductive tract. Mol Cell Endocrinol 144:83–93, 1998.

149. Burroughs C, Mills K, Bern H: Long-term genital tract changes in female mice treated neonatally with coumestrol. Reprod Toxicol 4:127–135, 1990.

150. Burroughs C, Mills K, Bern H: Reproductive abnormalities in female mice exposed neonatally to various doses of coumestrol. J Toxicol Environ Health 30:105–122, 1990.

151. Newbold RR, Banks EP, Bullock B, et al: Uterine adenocarcinoma in mice treated neonatally with genistein. Cancer Res 61:4325–4328, 2001.

152. Jefferson WN, Couse JF, Padilla-Banks E, et al: Neonatal exposure to genistein induces estrogen receptor (ER)alpha expression and multioocyte follicles in the maturing mouse ovary: Evidence for ERbeta-mediated and nonestrogenic actions. Biol Reprod 67:1285–1296, 2002.

153. Fielden MR, Fong CJ, Haslam SZ, et al: Normal mammary gland morphology in pubertal female mice following in utero and lactational exposure to genistein at levels comparable to human dietary exposure. Toxicol Lett 133:181–191, 2002.

154. Hilakivi-Clarke L, Cho E, Clarke R: Maternal genistein exposure mimics the effects of estrogen on mammary gland development in female mouse offspring. Oncol Rep 5:609–616, 1998.

155. Delclos KB, Bucci TJ, Lomax LG, et al: Effects of dietary genistein exposure during development on male and female CD (Sprague-Dawley) rats. Reprod Toxicol 15:647–663, 2001.

156. Fritz WA, Cotroneo MS, Wang J, et al: Dietary diethylstilbestrol but not genistein adversely affects rat testicular development. J Nutr 133:2287–2293, 2003.

157. Wisniewski AB, Klein SL, Lakshmanan Y, et al: Exposure to genistein during gestation and lactation demasculinizes the reproductive system in rats. J Urol 169:1582–1586, 2003.

158. Fielden MR, Samy SM, Chou KC, et al: Effect of human dietary exposure levels of genistein during gestation and lactation on long-term reproductive development and sperm quality in mice. Food Chem Toxicol 41:447–454, 2003.

159. Roberts D, Veeramachaneni DN, Schlaff WD, et al: Effects of chronic dietary exposure to genistein, a phytoestrogen, during various stages of development on reproductive hormones and spermatogenesis in rats. Endocrine 13:281–286, 2000.

160. Fritz WA, Eltoum IE, Cotroneo MS, et al: Genistein alters growth but is not toxic to the rat prostate. J Nutr 132:3007–3011, 2002.

161. Dalu A, Blaydes BS, Bryant CW, et al: Estrogen receptor expression in the prostate of rats treated with dietary genistein. J Chromatogr B Analyt Technol Biomed Life Sci 777:249–260, 2002.

162. Day JK, Bauer AM, DesBordes C, et al: Genistein alters methylation patterns in mice. J Nutr 132:2419S–2423S, 2002.

163. Register B, Bethel M, Thompson N, et al: The effect of neonatal exposure to diethylstilbestrol, coumestrol, and beta-sitosterol on pituitary responsiveness and sexually dimorphic nucleus volume in the castrated adult rat. Proc Soc Exp Biol Med 208:72–77, 1995.

164. Hughes CL Jr, Chakinala M, Reece S, et al: Acute and subacute effects of naturally occurring estrogens on luteinizing hormone secretion in the ovariectomized rat: Part 2. Reprod Toxicol 5:133–137, 1991.

165. Faber K, Basham K, Hughes CL Jr: The effect of neonatal exposure to DES and o,p′-DDT on pituitary responsiveness to GnRH in adult castrated rats. Reprod Toxicol 5:363–369, 1991.

166. Faber KA, Hughes CL Jr: The effect of neonatal exposure to diethylstilbestrol, genistein, and zearalenone on pituitary responsiveness and sexually dimorphic nucleus volume in the castrated adult rat. Biol Reprod 45:649–653, 1991.

167. Faber K, Hughes CL Jr: Dose-response characteristics of neonatal exposure to genistein on pituitary responsiveness to gonadotropin releasing hormone and volume of the sexually dimorphic nucleus of the preoptic area (SDN-POA) in postpubertal castrated female rats. Reprod Toxicol 7:35–39, 1993.

168. Adlercreutz H: Phytoestrogens and human health. In Korach KS (ed): Reproductive and Developmental Toxicology. New York, Marcel Dekker, 1998, pp 299–372.

169. Castle EP, Thrasher JB: The role of soy phytoestrogens in prostate cancer. Urol Clin North Am 29:viii–ix, 71–81, 2002.

170. Wang J, Eltoum IE, Lamartiniere CA: Dietary genistein suppresses chemically induced prostate cancer in Lobund-Wistar rats. Cancer Lett 186:11–18, 2002.

171. Onozawa M, Kawamori T, Baba M, et al: Effects of a soybean isoflavone mixture on carcinogenesis in prostate and seminal vesicles of F344 rats. Jpn J Cancer Res 90:393–398, 1999.

172. Aronson WJ, Tymchuk CN, Elashoff RM, et al: Decreased growth of human prostate LNCaP tumors in SCID mice fed a low-fat, soy protein diet with isoflavones. Nutr Cancer 35:130–136, 1999.

173. Landstrom M, Zhang JX, Hallmans G, et al: Inhibitory effects of soy and rye

diets on the development of Dunning R3327 prostate adenocarcinoma in rats. Prostate 36:151–161, 1998.

174. Geller J, Sionit L, Partido C, et al: Genistein inhibits the growth of human-patient BPH and prostate cancer in histoculture. Prostate 34:75–79, 1998.

175. Hempstock J, Kavanagh J, George N: Growth inhibition of prostate cell lines in vitro by phyto-oestrogens. Br J Urol 82:560–563, 1998.

176. Wang S, DeGroff VL, Clinton SK: Tomato and soy polyphenols reduce insulin-like growth factor-I–stimulated rat prostate cancer cell proliferation and apoptotic resistance in vitro via inhibition of intracellular signaling pathways involving tyrosine kinase. J Nutr 133:2367–2376, 2003.

177. Dalu A, Haskell J, Coward L, et al: Genistein, a component of soy, inhibits the expression of the EGF and ErbB2/Neu receptors in the rat dorsolateral prostate. Prostate 37:36–43, 1998.

178. Evans B, Griffiths K, Morton M: Inhibition of 5 alpha-redutase in genital skin fibroblasts and prostate tissue by dietary lignans and isoflavonoids. J Endocrinol 147:295–302, 1995.

179. Kyle E, Neckers L, Takimoto C, et al: Genistein-induced apoptosis of prostate cancer cells is preceded by a specific decrease in focal adhesion kinase activity. Mol Pharmacol 51:193–200, 1997.

180. Buchler P, Reber HA, Buchler MW, et al: Antiangiogenic activity of genistein in pancreatic carcinoma cells is mediated by the inhibition of hypoxia-inducible factor-1 and the down-regulation of VEGF gene expression. Cancer 100:201–210, 2004.

181. Day JK, Besch-Williford C, McMann TR, et al: Dietary genistein increased DMBA-induced mammary adenocarcinoma in wild-type, but not ER alpha KO, mice. Nutr Cancer 39:226–232, 2001.

182. Ju YH, Allred CD, Allred KF, et al: Physiological concentrations of dietary genistein dose-dependently stimulate growth of estrogen-dependent human breast cancer (MCF-7) tumors implanted in athymic nude mice. J Nutr 131:2957–2962, 2001.

183. Hewitt AL, Singletary KW: Soy extract inhibits mammary adenocarcinoma growth in a syngeneic mouse model. Cancer Lett 192:133–143, 2003.

184. Hilakivi-Clarke L, Cho E, Cabanes A, et al: Dietary modulation of pregnancy estrogen levels and breast cancer risk among female rat offspring. Clin Cancer Res 8:3601–3610, 2002.

185. Hilakivi-Clarke L, Cho E, Onojafe I, et al: Maternal exposure to genistein during pregnancy increases carcinogen-induced mammary tumorigenesis in female rat offspring. Oncol Rep 6:1089–1095, 1999.

186. Fritz W, Coward L, Wang J, et al: Dietary genistein: Perinatal mammary cancer prevention, bioavailability and toxicity testing in the rat. Carcinogenesis 19:2151–2158, 1998.

187. Hilakivi-Clarke L, Onojafe I, Raygada M, et al: Prepubertal exposure to zearalenone or genistein reduces mammary tumorigenesis. Br J Cancer 80:1682–1688, 1999.

188. Lamartiniere C, Zhang J, Controneo M: Genistein studies in rats: Potential for breast cancer prevention and reproductive and developmental toxicity. Am J Clin Nutr 68(Suppl):1400S–1405S, 1998.

189. Gallo D, Giacomelli S, Cantelmo F, et al: Chemoprevention of DMBA-induced mammary cancer in rats by dietary soy. Breast Cancer Res Treat 69:153–164, 2001.

190. Giri A, Lu L: Genetic damage and the inhibition of 7,12-dimethylbenz[a]anthracene-induced genetic damage by the phytoestrogens, genistein and daidzein, in female ICR mice. Cancer Lett 95:125–133, 1995.

191. Hilakivi-Clarke L, Cho E, deAssis S, et al: Maternal and prepubertal diet, mammary development and breast cancer risk. J Nutr 131(Suppl):154S–157S, 2001.

192. Chang K, Kurtz HJ, Mirocha CJ: Effects of the mycotoxin zearalenone on swine reproduction. Am J Vet Res 40:1260–1267, 1979.

193. Ito Y, Ohtsubo K: Effects of neonatal administration of zearaleone on the reproductive physiology of female mice. J Vet Med Sci 56:1155–1159, 1994.

194. Williams B, Mills K, Burroughs C, et al: Reproductive alterations in female C57Bl/Crgl mice exposed neonatally to zearalenone, an estrogenic mycotoxin. Cancer Lett 46:225–230, 1989.

195. Wilson TW, Neuendorff DA, Lewis AW, et al: Effect of zeranol or melengestrol acetate (MGA) on testicular and antler development and aggression in farmed fallow bucks. J Anim Sci 80:1433–1441, 2002.

196. Kim IH, Son HY, Cho SW, et al: Zearalenone induces male germ cell apoptosis in rats. Toxicol Lett 138:185–192, 2003.

197. Perez-Martinez C, Ferreras-Estrada MC, Garcia-Iglesias MJ, et al: Effects of in utero exposure to nonsteroidal estrogens on mouse testis. Can J Vet Res 61:94–98, 1997.

198. Chen C, Hurd C, Vorojeikina D, et al: Transcriptional activation of the human estrogen receptor by DDT isomers and metabolites in yeast and MCF-7 cells. Biochem Pharmacol 53:1161–1172, 1997.

199. Maness S, McDonnell D, Gaido K: Inhibition of androgen receptor-dependent transcriptional activity by DDT isomers and methoxychlor in HepG2 human hepatoma cells. Toxicol Appl Pharmacol 151:135–142, 1998.

200. Kelce W, Stone C, Laws S, et al: Persistent DDT metabolite p,p'-DDE is a potent androgen receptor antagonist. Nature 375:581–585, 1995.

201. Frigo DE, Burow ME, Mitchell KA, et al: DDT and its metabolites alter gene expression in human uterine cell lines through estrogen receptor-independent mechanisms. Environ Health Perspect 110:1239–1245, 2002.

202. Frigo DE, Tang Y, Beckman BS, et al: Mechanism of AP-1-mediated gene expression by select organochlorines through the p38 MAPK pathway. Carcinogenesis 25:249–261, 2004.

203. Wolff MS, Toniolo PG, Lee EW, et al: Blood levels of organochlorine residues and risk of breast cancer. J Natl Cancer Inst 85:648–652, 1993.

204. Rogan WJ, Gladen BC, McKinney JD, et al: Polychlorinated biphenyls (PCBs) and dichlorodiphenyl dichloroethene (DDE) in human milk: Effects on growth, morbidity, and duration of lactation. Am J Public Health 77:1294–1297, 1987.

205. Krause W: Influence of DDT, DDVP and malathion of FSH, LH, and testosterone serum levels and testosterone concentration in testis. Bull Environ Contam Toxicol 18:231–242, 1997.

206. Robison A, Schmidt W, Stancel G: Estrogenic activity of DDT: Estrogen-receptor profiles and the responses of individual uterine cell types following o,p'-DDT administration. J Toxicol Environ Health 16:493–508, 1985.

207. Newbold RR, Jefferson WN, Padilla-Banks E, et al: Cell response endpoints enhance sensitivity of the immature mouse uterotropic assay. Reprod Toxicol 15:245–252, 2001.

208. Robison AK, Sirbasku DA, Stancel GM: DDT supports the growth of an estrogen-responsive tumor. Toxicol Lett 27:109–113, 1985.

209. Palanza P, Parmigiani S, vom Saal FS: Effects of prenatal exposure to low doses of diethylstilbestrol, o,p'DDT, and methoxychlor on postnatal growth and neurobehavioral development in male and female mice. Horm Behav 40:252–265, 2001.

210. You L, Casanova M, Archibeqye-Engle S, et al: Impaired male sexual development in perinatal Sprauge-Dawley and Long-Evans hooded rats exposed in utero and lactationally to p,p'-DDE. Toxicol Sci 45:162–173, 1998.

211. You L, Sar M, Bartolucci E, et al: Induction of hepatic aromatase by p,p'-DDE in adult male rats. Mol Cell Endocrinol 178:207–214, 2001.

212. Guillette LJ Jr, Crain DA, Rooney AA, et al: Organization versus activation: The role of endocrine-disrupting contaminants (EDCs) during embryonic development in wildlife. Environ Health Perspect 103(Suppl 7):157–164, 1995.

213. Fry DM: Reproductive effects in birds exposed to pesticides and industrial chemicals. Environ Health Perspect 103(Suppl 7):165–171, 1995.

214. Edmunds JS, McCarthy RA, Ramsdell JS: Permanent and functional

male-to-female sex reversal in d-rR strain medaka (*Oryzias latipes*) following egg microinjection of o,p'-DDT. Environ Health Perspect 108:219–224, 2000.

215. Papoulias DM, Villalobos SA, Meadows J, et al: In ovo exposure to o,p'-DDE affects sexual development but not sexual differentiation in Japanese medaka (*Oryzias latipes*). Environ Health Perspect 111:29–32, 2003.

216. Mills LJ, Gutjahr-Gobell RE, Haebler RA, et al: Effects of estrogenic (o,p'-DDT; octylphenol) and anti-androgenic (p,p'-DDE) chemicals on indicators of endocrine status in juvenile male summer flounder (*Paralichthys dentatus*). Aquat Toxicol 52:157–176, 2001.

217. Gaido KW, Leonard LS, Maness SC, et al: Differential interaction of the methoxychlor metabolite 2,2-bis-(p-hydroxyphenyl)-1,1,1-trichloroethane with estrogen receptors alpha and beta. Endocrinology 140:5746–5753, 1999.

218. Gaido KW, Maness SC, McDonnell DP, et al: Interaction of methoxychlor and related compounds with estrogen receptor alpha and beta, and androgen receptor: structure-activity studies. Mol Pharmacol 58:852–858, 2000.

219. Reuber M: Interstitial cell carcinomas of the testis in Balb/C male mice ingesting methoxychlor. J Cancer Res Clin Oncol 93:173–179, 1979.

220. Bal H: Effect of methoxychlor on reproductive systems of the rat. Proc Soc Exp Biol Med 176:187–196, 1984.

221. Tullner WW, Edgcomb JH: Cystic tubular nephropathy and decrease in testicular weight in rats following oral methoxychlor treatment. J Pharmacol Exp Ther 138:126–130, 1962.

222. Matthews J, Celius T, Halgren R, et al: Differential estrogen receptor binding of estrogenic substances: A species comparison. J Steroid Biochem Mol Biol 74:223–234, 2000.

223. Gray LE Jr, Ostby J, Cooper RL, et al: The estrogenic and antiandrogenic pesticide methoxychlor alters the reproductive tract and behavior without affecting pituitary size or LH and prolactin secretion in male rats. Toxicol Ind Health 15:37–47, 1999.

224. Roy D, Angelini NL, Belsham DD: Estrogen directly represses gonadotropin-releasing hormone (GnRH) gene expression in estrogen receptor-alpha (ERalpha)- and ERbeta-expressing GT1-7 GnRH neurons. Endocrinology 140:5045–5053, 1999.

225. Akingbemi BT, Ge RS, Klinefelter GR, et al: A metabolite of methoxychlor, 2,2-bis(p-hydroxyphenyl)-1,1,1-trichloroethane, reduces testosterone biosynthesis in rat leydig cells through suppression of steady-state messenger ribonucleic acid levels of the cholesterol side-chain cleavage enzyme. Biol Reprod 62:571–578, 2000.

226. Cummings A, Gray LJ: Methoxychlor affects the decidual cell response of the uterus but not other progestational parameters in female rats. Toxicol Appl Pharmacol 90:330–336, 1987.

227. Cummings A, Gray LJ: Antifertility effect of methoxychlor in female rats: Dose- and time-dependent blockade of pregnancy. Toxicol Appl Pharmacol 97:454–462, 1989.

228. Metcalf J, Laws S, Cummings A: Methoxychlor mimics the action of 17 beta-estradiol on induction of uterine epidermal growth factor receptors in immature female rats. Reprod Toxicol 10:393–399, 1996.

229. Cummings A, Metcalf J: Mechanisms of the stimulatin of rat uterine peroxidase activity by methoxychlor. Reprod Toxicol 8:477–486, 1994.

230. Gray LJ, Ostby J, Ferrell J, et al: Methoxychlor induces estrogen-like alterations of behavior and the reproductive tract in the female rat and hamster: Effects on sex behavior, running wheel activity, and uterine morphology. Toxicol Appl Pharmacol 96:525–540, 1988.

231. Eroschenko V: Ultrastructure of vagina and uterus in young mice after methoxychlor exposure. Reprod Toxicol 5:427–435, 1991.

232. Walters L, Rourke A, Eroschenko V: Purified methoxychlor stimulates the reproductive tract in immature female mice. Reprod Toxicol 7:599–606, 1993.

233. Eroschenko V, Rourke A, Sims W: Estradiol or methoxychlor stimulates estrogen receptor (ER) expression in uteri. Reprod Toxicol 10:265–271, 1996.

234. Eroschenko VP, Swartz WJ, Ford LC: Decreased superovulation in adult mice following neonatal exposures to technical methoxychlor. Reprod Toxicol 11:807–814, 1997.

235. Cooke P, Eroschenko V: Inhibitory effects of technical grade methoxychlor on development of neonatal male mouse reproductive organs. Biol Reprod 42:585–596, 1990.

236. Masutomi N, Shibutani M, Takagi H, et al: Impact of dietary exposure to methoxychlor, genistein, or diisononyl phthalate during the perinatal period on the development of the rat endocrine/reproductive systems in later life. Toxicology 192:149–170, 2003.

237. Johnson L, Staub C, Silge RL, et al: The pesticide methoxychlor given orally during the perinatal/juvenile period, reduced the spermatogenic potential of males as adults by reducing their Sertoli cell number. Reprod Nutr Dev 42:573–580, 2002.

238. Stoker TE, Robinette CL, Cooper RL: Perinatal exposure to estrogenic compounds and the subsequent effects on the prostate of the adult rat: Evaluation of inflammation in the ventral and lateral lobes. Reprod Toxicol 13:463–472, 1999.

239. Thompson CJ, Ross SM, Gaido KW: Di(n-butyl) phthalate impairs cholesterol transport and steroidogenesis in the fetal rat testis through a rapid and reversible mechanism. Endocrinology 145:1227–1237, 2004.

240. Wong C, Kelce W, Sar M, et al: Androgen receptor antagonist versus agonist activities of the fungicide vinclozolin relative to hydroxyflutamide. Biol Chem 270:19998–20003, 1995.

241. Kubota K, Ohsako S, Kurosawa S, et al: Effects of vinclozolin administration on sperm production and testosterone biosynthetic pathway in adult male rat. J Reprod Dev 49:403–412, 2003.

242. Bayley M, Larsen PF, Baekgaard H, et al: The effects of vinclozolin, an anti-androgenic fungicide, on male guppy secondary sex characters and reproductive success. Biol Reprod 69:1951–1956, 2003.

243. Baatrup E, Junge M: Antiandrogenic pesticides disrupt sexual characteristics in the adult male guppy *Poecilia reticulata*. Environ Health Perspect 109:1063–1070, 2001.

244. Shono T, Suita S, Kai H, et al: Short-time exposure to vinclozolin in utero induces testicular maldescent associated with a spinal nucleus alteration of the genitofemoral nerve in rats. J Pediatr Surg 39:217–219, 2004.

245. Shono T, Suita S, Kai H, et al: The effect of a prenatal androgen disruptor, vinclozolin, on gubernacular migration and testicular descent in rats. J Pediatr Surg 39:213–216, 2004.

246. Wolf CJ, LeBlanc GA, Ostby JS, et al: Characterization of the period of sensitivity of fetal male sexual development to vinclozolin. Toxicol Sci 55:152–161, 2000.

247. Gray LJ, Ostby J, Klece W: Developmental effects of an environmental antiandrogen: The fungicide vincloxolin alters sex differentiation of the male rat. Toxicol Appl Pharmocol 129:46–52, 1994.

248. Turner KJ, McIntyre BS, Phillips SL, et al: Altered gene expression during rat wolffian duct development in response to in utero exposure to the antiandrogen linuron. Toxicol Sci 74:114–128, 2003.

249. Turner KJ, Barlow NJ, Struve MF, et al: Effects of in utero exposure to the organophosphate insecticide fenitrothion on androgen-dependent reproductive development in the Crl:CD(SD)BR rat. Toxicol Sci 68:174–183, 2002.

250. Ulrich EM, Caperall-Grant A, Jung SH, et al: Environmentally relevant xenoestrogen tissue concentrations correlated to biological responses in mice. Environ Health Perspect 108:973–977, 2000.

251. Maruyama S, Fujimoto N, Yin H, et al: Growth stimulation of a rat pituitary line MtT/E-2 by environmental estrogens in vitro and in vivo. Endocr J 46:513–520, 1999.

252. Steinmentz R, Young PC, Caperell-Grant A, et al: Novel estrogenic action of the pesticide residue beta-hexachlorochyclohexane in human breast cancer cells. Cancer Res 56:5403–5409, 1996.

253. Flouriot G, Pakdel F, Ducouret B, et al: Influence of xenobiotics on rainbow trout liver estrogen receptor and vitellogenin gene expression. J Mol Endocrinol 15:143–151, 1995.

254. Chadwick RW, Cooper RL, Chang J, et al: Possible antiestrogenic activity of lindane in female rats. J Biochem Toxicol 3:147–158, 1988.

255. Cooper RL, Chadwick RW, Rehnberg GL, et al: Effect of lindane on hormonal control of reproductive function in the female rat. Toxicol Appl Pharmacol 99:384–394, 1989.

256. Laws SC, Carey SA, Hart DW, et al: Lindane does not alter the estrogen receptor or the estrogen-dependent induction of progesterone receptors in sexually immature or ovariectomized adult rats. Toxicology 92:127–142, 1994.

# Diagnosis and Treatment of Disorders of Sexual Development

## *Maguelone G. Forest*

## PATHOGENESIS AND CLASSIFICATION

In the past decade, advances in experimental endocrinology, biochemistry, genetics, and molecular biology have all contributed to our understanding of the process of human sex differentiation (see Chapters 142 and 143). In brief, normal sex development consists of three sequential processes (Fig. 146-1). The first is the *genetic sex* determined at the time of fertilization by the constitution of the sex chromosome. In the second phase, the genetic information determines that an undifferentiated gonad differentiates into either a testis or an ovary (*gonadal sex*). Finally, *sex phenotype* is the result of male differentiation, which is an active process resulting in testicular secretions: antimüllerian hormone (AMH), which is produced by the Sertoli cells, inhibits the müllerian ducts; testosterone is produced by the Leydig cells and is responsible for stabilization of the wolffian ducts and, via its transformation into dihydrotestosterone (DHT), is responsible for virilization of the external genitalia. In the absence of testis, the genital primordia are irreversibly committed to femaleness.

Classification of intersex disorders is complex. Based on the recognition of the underlying anomaly in the process of sex differentiation,[1] intersex disorders may be divided into abnormal gonadal determination and abnormal genital differentiation (including male pseudohermaphroditism [MPH] and female pseudohermaphroditism [FPH]). Abnormal gonadal determination is mainly dependent on sex chromosomal defects that can be detected by cytogenetic analysis or by the DNA probes for genes located on the Y chromosome. Male

pseudohermaphrodites are individuals with ambiguous genitalia but two differentiated testes. MPH results mainly from abnormal testosterone biosynthesis or metabolism, androgen receptor defects (lack or insufficient tissue sensitivity to androgens), or intrauterine structural insults. Some authors prefer the term *undervirilized males*. Female pseudohermaphrodites are genetic females with ambiguous external genitalia but normal ovaries and normal internal genitalia. FPH results mainly from exposure to abnormal levels of androgens in utero at the critical time of sex differentiation (because the genital tubercle has androgen receptors and 5α-reductase activity irrespective of the gonadal sex) or intrauterine structural insults. Intersex problems may also be classified according to the presenting gonadal status. On the other hand, in most disorders there is a wide range of presenting phenotypes. Therefore, any classification is somewhat arbitrary. The classification used here (Table 146-1) is based on the recent knowledge of the genetic basis of sex determination (gonadal differentiation and development) and sex differentiation (for differentiation and development of internal and external genitalia, see Chapters 142 and 143). Indeed, several conditions previously classified as pseudohermaphroditism associated with malformations or unclassified forms of abnormal sexual development are now recognized as resulting from defects in genes implicated in gonadal determination.

It is very important to recognize all intersex problems as early as possible in life and not to delay the etiologic diagnosis. The diagnosis should be as precise as possible for instituting substitutive treatment in case of an enzymatic defect in

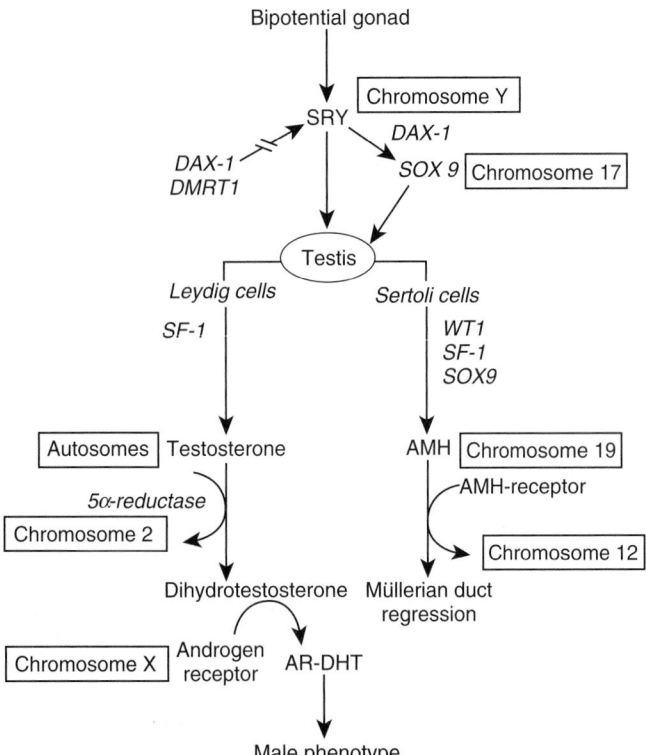

***Figure 146-1*** Schematic representation of the genetic and hormonal factors involved in testicular determination and sex differentiation. AMH, antimüllerian hormone; AR, androgen receptor; DHT, dihydrotestosterone; SRY, sex-determining region Y.

steroid biosynthesis but also primarily for helping the choice of the most appropriate gender for rearing. Also, investigations should anticipate the chances of the best somatic and psychological development in the sex assigned. As intersex states may be caused by genetic abnormalities as well as by environmental factors, genetic counseling is possible only when the etiology and the mode of transmission are known.

## ABNORMAL GONADAL DIFFERENTIATION

### *DEFECTIVE DEVELOPMENT OF THE PRIMORDIAL GONAD AND THE BIPOTENTIAL REPRODUCTIVE SYSTEM*

Several situations of XY sex reversal that, in the past, were described as part of various malformative syndromes have being recognized as resulting from mutations in some, but not all, genes controlling the gonadal primordium and bipotential reproductive ducts (see Chapter 142).

#### Mutation in the Gene Encoding Steroidogenic Factor-1
**Genetics** Steroidogenic factor-1 (SF-1) is a nuclear receptor that regulates the transcription of an array of genes involved in reproduction, steroidogenesis, and male sex differentiation, among which the genes encoding AMH, DAX1 gene (NROB1), CYP11A, steroidogenic acute regulatory protein (StAR), and the genes encoding steroid hydroxylases, gonadotropins, and aromatase. The gene NR5A1, cloned in 1995,[2] contains seven exons, including the noncoding first exon, and has been mapped to chromosome 9q33.[3]

**Clinical Findings** Disruption of the SF-1 gene causes failure of adrenal function, XY sex reversal, and persistence of müllerian structures in males. The first case was reported in 1999[4] in a patient presenting with adrenal insufficiency, XY complete sex reversal, and persistent müllerian structures. The phenotypi-

***Table 146-1*** **Classification of Intersex Disorders**

I. Defective development of the primordial gonad and the bipotential reproductive system
  A. Mutation in the gene-encoding steroidogenic factor-1 (SF-1)
  B. Ambiguous genitalia associated with degenerative renal disease
    1. Denys-Drash syndrome (DDS)
    2. Frasier syndrome (FS)
    3. WAGR syndrome
II. Abnormal gonadal determination
  A. Defective testis formation or maintenance
    1. Pure gonadal dysgenesis, 46,XY (Swyer's syndrome)
    2. Mixed gonadal dysgenesis
    3. Dysgenetic male pseudohermaphroditism
    4. Testicular regression syndrome
    5. Seminiferous tubule dysgenesis (Klinefelter syndrome and variants, XX males)
    6. 46,XX males
    7. Campomelic dysplasia: an autosomal sex reversal
    8. Dosage-sensitive sex reversal (DSS)
  B. Defective ovary formation or maintenance
    1. Gonadal dysgenesis, 46,XX
    2. Turner's syndrome, 45,X and variants
  C. Bisexual gonads: true hermaphroditism
II. Male pseudohermaphroditism (MPH): incomplete masculinization of XY male
  A. Impaired gonadotropic action or function
    1. Leydig cell aplasia or hypoplasia
    2. Fetal luteinizing hormone (LH) deficiency
  B. Inborn error of cholesterol biosynthesis
    1. 7-Dehydrocholesterol reductase deficiency
  C. Impaired androgen biosynthesis, metabolism, or action
    1. Inborn errors of testosterone biosynthesis
      a. Deficient formation of pregnenolone (side-chain cleavage deficiency)
      b. 3β-Hydroxysteroid dehydrogenase (3β-HSD) deficiency
      c. 17α-Hydroxylase (17-OH) deficiency
      d. 17,20-Desmolase (17,20-D) deficiency
      e. 17β-Hydroxysteroid dehydrogenase (17β-HSD) deficiency
    2. Impaired metabolism of testosterone: 5α-reductase deficiency
    3. Androgen receptor defects: androgen insensitivity syndrome (AIS), complete and incomplete forms
  D. Impaired antimüllerian hormone (AMH) production or action: persistent müllerian duct syndrome types 1 and 2
  E. MPH associated with various malformations
  F. MPH unclassified, iatrogenic, and idiopathic
III. Female pseudohermaphroditism (FPH): virilization of an XX female
  A. Fetal source
    1. Congenital adrenal hyperplasia due to inborn errors in cortisol biosynthesis
      a. 21-Hydroxylase deficiency
      b. 11β-Hydroxylase deficiency
      c. 3β-Hydroxysteroid dehydrogenase deficiency
    2. Aromatase deficiency
  B. Excessive androgen production of maternal origin
    1. Adrenal or ovarian tumors, luteoma of pregnancy
    2. Iatrogenic: maternal ingestion of androgens, progestagens, or drugs
  C. FPH associated with various malformations
  D. FPH unclassified and idiopathic

WAGR, Wilms' tumor, aniridia, genitourinary abnormalities, and mental retardation.

cally female subject presented primary adrenal failure in the first weeks of life, and was first misdiagnosed as having lipoid congenital adrenal hypoplasia (see later). At 10 years, her hormonal status was examined further before the induction of puberty. Pituitary gonadotropins responded to gonadotropin-releasing hormone (GnRH) stimulation, but no testosterone response was present after human chorionic gonadotropin (hCG) stimulation. Streak gonads and normal müllerian structures were found at laparotomy. Normal uterine growth and regular menstruation were induced by cyclical progestogen. Mutation analysis revealed a de novo mutation heterozygous (G35E in exon 3) within the proximal box (P-box) of the

DNA-binding domain of SF-1, which apparently prevents SF-1 stimulation of its target genes. This finding indicates that haploinsufficiency of this factor is sufficient to cause severe clinical phenotype. This case also demonstrates that SF-1 is essential for normal adrenal and gonadal development, as predicted from targeted disruption of the SF-1 gene (FTZ-F1) in mice (see Chapter 142). Moreover, it also regulates the regression of the müllerian structures either through direct action of AMH promoter or secondary to an abnormality of Sertoli cell function, and fails to synergize with transcription factor GATA-4, given that both activate the promotor of AMH.[5]

Only three other cases have been reported to date. The sole SF-1 mutation described in an XX female is also a de novo mutation (R255L) affecting a conserved residue in the hinge region of SF-1.[6] Although the mutation renders the molecule transcriptionally inactive, it does not appear to impair ovarian function. As in the previous case, the mode of inheritance appears to be autosomal dominant. Thus, SF-1 is probably not necessary for female gonadal development, although it has a crucial role in adrenal gland formation in both sexes.

An additional SF-1 mutation was identified in a 46,XY subject who presented with the same clinical phenotype as the first patient described,[4] but with a different mode of inheritance that interestingly appeared to be autosomal recessive.[7] Indeed, in this family the index case was homozygous for the mutation R92Q, affecting a codon within the A-box of SF-1, a region that functions as a secondary DNA-binding domain. Heterozygous family members were phenotypically normal despite having one mutant allele. This mutation partially impaired SF-1 function, underscoring the dose-dependent action of this gene, as inheritance of two copies of the mutant protein were required for phenotypic expression of the adrenal and gonadal defects.

Finally, a heterozygous frameshift resulting from the deletion of eight nucleotides at position 2783, leading to a carboxy-terminal truncated protein, was described in a subject with 46,XY sex reversal and clitoromegaly, but no uterus and no adrenal insufficiency.[8]

Thus, it appears that mutations in different regions of the gene would produce variant phenotypes. Although the number of reported cases is still small, it appears that patients with SF-1 mutations may have variable degrees of adrenal insufficiency and gonadal dysgenesis. It can be expected that most cases will be sporadic new mutations, though recessive transmission may occur for milder mutations.

### Ambiguous Genitalia Associated with Degenerative Renal Disease

These situations, characterized by the association of dysgenetic gonads and degenerative renal diseases, were classically classified as subtypes of dysgenetic MPH. Today, three distinct entities are recognized: (1) Denys-Drash syndrome (DDS), (2) Frasier syndrome (FS), and (3) WAGR syndrome (Wilms' tumor, aniridia, genitourinary abnormalities, and mental retardation).

#### Denys-Drash Syndrome

**Definition and Clinical Findings**   DDS is characterized by the clinical triad of genital abnormalities, nephropathy, and Wilms' tumor.[9–11] Most individuals with DDS have a female phenotype or ambiguous genitalia and dysgenetic gonads. Although the XY karyotype is the most frequent, patients with 46,XXY or with 46,XX and hypoplastic gonads or streaks have been reported.[11,12] The nephropathy is characterized by proteinuria at an early age, evolving into nephrotic syndrome and eventually into renal failure owing to focal or diffuse mesangial sclerosis.[13,14] Wilms' tumor is an embryonal malignancy of the kidney resulting from the continuous proliferation of embryonic kidney blastemal cells. These cells account for 85% of all childhood kidney cancer and affect probably 1 in 10,000 children.[15] The tumor develops before 2 years of age and is frequently bilateral.

**Genetics**   The disease is autosomal dominant. DDS is the result of a mutation in the Wilms' tumor suppressor gene (WT1), which is located at chromosome 11p13. WT1 consists of 10 exons and encodes a protein with four zinc-finger motifs and transcriptional and tumor-suppressor activities. Mueller[16] reviewed DDS in detail on the basis of 150 reported cases. Furthermore, a tabulation was provided of 25 reported mutations in the WT1 gene, including 6 arg394-to-trp mutations, 1 arg394-to-pro mutation, and 2 different mutations at codon 396 (namely, asp396-to-asn in 2 cases and asp396-to-gly in 1 case). Also, to date, five different mutations that alter amino acids predicted to interact specifically with nucleotides in the target DNA sequence have been described. Two of these mutations are located in zinc finger 2 (R366H, R366C) and three are located in finger 3 (R374W, D396G, D396N). According to Borel and associates,[15] in these situations the clinical phenotype of DDS would be associated with a modest reduction in the DNA-binding affinity of WT1. In DDS, the risk of a tumor is high. The dominant-negative mutant allele is defective, and loss of the second allele (according to the two-hit model) may be an important step in tumor formation. Nevertheless, the mechanism whereby mutations of WT1 affect the embryonic kidney adversely has not been elucidated.

On the other hand, Devriendt and colleagues[17] described a newborn infant with MPH and glomerular lesions but without Wilms' tumor. In addition, the child had a large diaphragmatic hernia, a previously undescribed feature of DDS. A constitutional heterozygous arg366-to-his mutation was identified. The expression of the WT1 gene in pleural and abdominal mesothelium and the occurrence of diaphragmatic hernia in transgenic mice with a homozygous WT1 deletion strongly suggested that the diaphragmatic hernia in this patient was part of the malformation pattern caused by the WT1 mutation (see Chapter 142). Finally, by systematic screening with polymerase chain reaction–single-strand conformation polymorphism (PCR-SSCP) analysis and sequencing, of 15 boys with severe hypospadias, but no endocrine abnormality or Wilms' tumor, 3 were found to have mutations in the WT1 gene (V13X, R326X, R390X).[18] This finding should prompt the initiation of systematic mutational screening of the WT1 gene in idiopathic hypospadias. Because of the increased risk of malignancy of the Wilms' tumors and their fatal prognosis, nephrectomy is performed as soon as the tumor is diagnosed. Prophylactic bilateral nephrectomies and early renal transplantation have been proposed, because nephrectomy specimens demonstrate nephrogenic rests (nephroblastomatosis), which have a potential for malignant transformation.[19]

#### Frasier Syndrome

**Definition**   Moorthy and associates[20] suggested that some of the patients reported as cases of DDS, in fact, had a different disorder, for which they suggested the designation to be FS.[21] This rare disease is defined by the association of an XY female with gonadal dysgenesis, progressive glomerulopathy, and a significant risk of gonadoblastoma. Glomerular symptoms consist of childhood proteinuria and nephrotic syndrome, characterized by unspecified focal and segmental glomerular sclerosis, progressing to end-stage renal failure in adolescence or early adulthood. In several of the patients, the diagnosis was established only after successful kidney transplantation during an evaluation for primary amenorrhea. With the exception of one report,[22] no case of Wilms' tumor has been reported in patients with FS, even with extended follow-up.

**Genetics**   In contrast to patients with DDS, there are no mutations in the coding sequence of WT1 gene in patients with FS,[23] or in the SRY (sex-determining region Y) gene.[24] It was demonstrated that FS is caused by mutations in the donor splice site in intron 9 of WT1.[25] Klamt and colleagues[26] showed that no mutant protein is produced by the mutations in WT1 causing FS. Rather, the mutation results in an altered ratio of the two spliced isoforms of the protein, those with and those without the extra three amino acids (KTS). In contrast to DDS, patients with FS have one normal copy of WT1 and one that can only produce a shorter isoform. Allele loss would thus lead to cells that cannot produce the +KTS isoform of WT1, but still have large amounts of the −KTS isoform. In this respect, it is interesting to note that tumorigenicity of the G401 Wilms' tumor cell line in nude mice can be suppressed to the same extent by +KTS and −KTS isoforms (see Chapter 142).

An unusual case of FS phenotype—male ambiguous genitalia and absence of gonadal dysgenesis—due to IVS9 + 4V>T mutation in the WT1 gene, which predicts a change in splice site utilization has been reported.[27] This case suggests that DDS and FS may represnt two ends of a spectrum of disorders caused by alterion in the WT1 gene.

### WAGR Syndrome

**Definition** Wilms' tumor can be associated with *a*niridia, *g*enitourinary anomalies, and mental *r*etardation.[28] The syndrome subsequently became known as WAGR syndrome,[29] in which bilateral gonadoblastoma are less frequent. In addition to genitourinary abnormalities, the G in WAGR refers to ambiguous genitalia[30] or gonadoblastoma.[31] A systematic evaluation of the clinical and pathologic features of the WAGR syndrome has only recently been realized in a large cohort of 8533 children with Wilms tumor-aniridia syndrome.[32] WAGR is rare, representing only 0.75% of this cohort. In the WAGR syndrome, the average birth weight was 2.94 kg and the median age at diagnosis was 22 months. The percentage with bilateral disease was 17%; metastatic disease, 2%; favorable histology tumors, 100%; and intralobar nephrogenic rests, 77%. Survival estimates were 95% plus or minus 3% at 4 years, but 48% plus or minus 17% at 27 years from diagnosis. These all differed from the non-WAGR patients.[32] The excess of bilateral disease, intralobar nephrogenic rests–associated favorable histology tumors of mixed cell type, and early age at diagnosis in WAGR patients all fit the known phenotypic spectrum of constitutional deletion of chromosome 11p13. Despite a favorable response of their Wilms' tumor to treatment, WAGR patients have a high risk of end-stage renal disease as they approach adulthood.

**Genetics** WAGR syndrome is one of the best studied *contiguous gene syndromes* (as defined by Schmickel[33]). The evidence from studies of balanced translocations and other observations suggested that the genitourinary dysplasia, like aniridia, is caused by a separate gene in close proximity to the WT1 gene on chromosome 11p13. Aniridia (AN2) is distal to WT1, and genitourinary dysplasia is proximal.[34,35] From a review of many reported cases,[36] it was concluded that single breaks are associated with isolated aniridia, the genetic cause of which is mutations in the PAX6 gene,[37] whereas deletion on chromosomal region 11p13 results in WAGR syndrome. The explanation for low birth weights in patients with del11p13 has not yet been determined.

Aniridia was part of WAGR syndrome in a female whose brother presented with hypospadias.[38] Thus, the identification and definition of the deletions in the WAGR region, which include the WT1 locus, are important in order to identify a high tumor risk in infant patients with aniridia, including those without other WAGR anomalies. A comprehensive mutational analysis of aniridia cases showed the detection of mutations in 68% of sporadic cases and 89% in familial cases.[37] Moreover, it showed a smaller risk for Wilms' tumor than in previous estimates, and that tumor development requires deletion of WT1.[37]

**Diagnosis** The diagnosis is made on the finding of a microdeletion of the 11p13 chromosome by using highly sophisticated cytogenetic techniques or suspected by blood enzymatic markers of chromosome 11 (mainly catalase).

**Management** As for patients with DDS, kidney sonographic follow-up is highly recommended because of the high risk of developing Wilms' tumor, which, however, may not be clinically detectable until several months or years after birth.[32,39]

### DEFECTIVE TESTIS DETERMINATION OR MAINTENANCE

#### Pure Gonadal Dysgenesis 46,XY

**Pathogenesis** Gonadal dysgenesis is characterized by abnormal testicular determination. The syndrome, described by Swyer[40] as the association of female phenotype, female internal genitalia, normal or tall stature, and sexual infantilism with primary amenorrhea, represents by definition the complete form of the so-called pure gonadal dysgenesis. These patients have streak gonads that do not secrete testosterone or AMH and, therefore, müllerian duct derivatives develop. The 46,XY gonadal dysgenesis syndrome is, however, both clinically and genetically heterogeneous. It can be sporadic or familial. Familial reported cases are compatible with either X-linked recessive transmission or sex-limited dominant autosomal transmission.[41,42] The phenotypic differences observed in complete or partial gonadal dysgenesis depend on the extent of testicular differentiation. Patients with partial gonadal dysgenesis have a mixture of wolffian and müllerian duct derivatives and some functional capacity to produce testosterone or AMH.

**Clinical Findings** Patients with the complete form have a female phenotype. Primary amenorrhea with hypergonadotropic sexual infantilism is the most frequent presenting symptom in a child reared as a female who has a normal or tall stature and no stigmata of Turner's syndrome despite a negative chromatin. Such a child has a 46,XY karyotype and no evidence of mosaicism. A uterus is demonstrated by ultrasonography and gynecologic examination. Moderate hypertrophy of the clitoris may be observed without any other evidence of virilization and, in fact, a continuum of phenotypes ranging from the complete syndrome to ambiguous external genitalia has been described. At laparotomy, two streak gonads are found, which may contain androgen-secreting hilus cells, and sometimes corpora albicans–like formations.[43] A more frequent occurrence of streak gonad tumors is found together with the possibility of tracing the merged gonadoblastoma into a dysgerminoma. In 95% of the streak gonads checked, an ovary-like stroma is found. In approximately half of the patients, one of the aforementioned tumors is found.[43] A frequent finding is the presence of Leydig-type cells, calcifications, and the remains of wolffian canals. In cases of partial gonadal dysgenesis, gonadal tissue may contain areas of poorly differentiated seminiferous tubules in combination with areas of ovary-like stroma.[43] Spontaneous breast development may be the first evidence of an estrogen-secreting gonadal tumor.

Within families, variable expression has been reported; in one family, two siblings were typical XY females, whereas another had genital ambiguity with bilateral dysgenetic testes and müllerian derivatives.[44]

**Molecular Genetics** Studies have shown that the genetics of XY sex reversal is heterogeneous. Attention was first focused on the gene SRY, a Y chromosomal gene that acts as a switch to direct the determination of the testis. Mutations that may account for this phenotype have been described in the sex-determining sequence SRY of the Y chromosome of sporadic cases,[45,46] owing to de novo mutation,[47] and familial cases,[48] more often in complete forms,[49] but they appear uncommon in general.[50] Indeed, deletions or mutations in the SRY gene account for only an estimated 15% of 46,XY females.[51] SRY could play a role, however, in the formation of gonadal tumors, especially dysgerminoma.[52]

Another cause of XY sex reversal may be a rearranged Y chromosome secondary to a paternal X-Y interchange, deletion in the short arm of the Y (Yp),[53] or a 46,YXp resulting from a translocation of an extra fragment of Xp on an otherwise normal Y chromosome.[54] A novel gene on the Y chromosome has been characterized,[55] highly homologous to a previously isolated gene from Xp22.3, PRKX; both are members of the cyclic adenosine monophosphate (cAMP)-dependent serine-threonine protein kinase gene family. An abnormal interchange occurred particularly frequently (27% to 35%) between PRKX and PRKY at different sites within the gene, explaining the high frequency of abnormal pairing and subsequent ectopic recombination leading to XY females as well as XX males[55] (see later).

Studies of familial cases have shown that the genetic defect in this disorder might involve other sex-determining genes involved in testis formation or maintenance, which need not map to the Y but rather on the X chromosome,[54,56] or even on autosomes. XY sex reversal was found to be associated with autosomal structural abnormalities, including terminal deletion of 10p,[57] 9p monosomy,[58] 9p deletion,[51] and duplication of 1p.[59] Finally, sporadic cases may represent teratologic defects in gonadal morphology.

**Endocrinology and Management**  Sex steroid levels remain extremely low, and there is a progressive and marked elevation in the gonadotropins with age. As a result, pubertal development should be initiated by estrogen replacement therapy in patients brought up in the female gender. In the incomplete form, assignment of a male gender role may be possible, depending on the degree of virilization of the genitalia. Nevertheless, all these patients are at high risk of dysgerminoma, seminoma, and especially of gonadoblastoma. Therefore, when a laparotomy is performed for diagnostic purposes, prophylactic removal of the streak gonads is advised with histologic examination. Although gonadoblastoma may be found before puberty, the risk of neoplastic change usually appears after puberty. Gonadoblastoma may also affect XY male siblings.[60] Exceptionally, in a 46,XY female infant, a few primordial follicles and numerous germ cells were found in a dysgenetic streak gonad in which a gonadoblastoma developed several years later.[61] Ovarian development would occur if the lack of testis induction allowed the constitutive ovarian pathway of gonadal development to be expressed.[62,63]

## Mixed Gonadal Dysgenesis
**Pathogenesis**  Mixed gonadal dysgenesis (MGD), also called atypical or asymmetric gonadal dysgenesis, is a syndrome of abnormal sexual development defined on the basis of gonadal morphologic features (i.e., an abnormal testis on one side and a rudimentary gonad, streak, or no gonad at all on the opposite side).[63a,63b] Typically, the patients have ambiguous asymmetric, external genitalia, persistent müllerian duct structures, and a cell line with a Y chromosome, often part of a mosaic karyotype. The most common karyotype is 45,XO/46,XY.

**Clinical Features**  At birth, the ambiguous external genitalia are often asymmetric, with labioscrotal folds and a testis palpable unilaterally (Fig. 146-2). This testis is capable of some endocrine function, but is histologically dysgenetic.[64] The karyotype is diagnostic of gonadal dysgenesis by generally showing a mosaic containing an XY cell line. The elevation of basal or hCG-stimulated plasma testosterone, although below normal male values, indicates the presence of testicular tissue. Genitography demonstrates the persistence of müllerian structures. Usually, these patients have a uterus, normal or partly developed, with a fallopian tube on the side of the streak. The development of the genital tract correlates with the gonadal differentiation. Müllerian ducts—fallopian tube and uterus—are always associated with the streak gonad and frequently with the dysgenetic testis. Depending on the activity of the dysgenetic testis on the opposite side, the suppression of the müllerian ducts is complete or partial, and a vas deferens may develop. The testis is dysgenetic with widely separated seminiferous tubules and poorly differentiated tubules in the hilar region, absence of germ cells, and tubular fibrosis. The streak gonads may show some evidence of tubule formation.

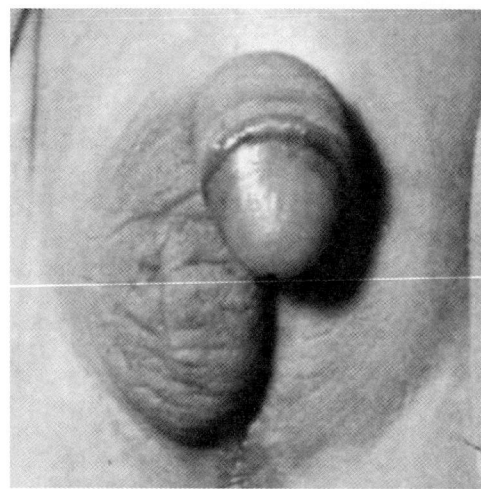

*Figure 146-2*  Patient with mixed gonadal dysgenesis. Note the typical asymmetrical development of external genitalia.

Reported cases with 45,X/46,XY mosaicism, however, show a wide spectrum of phenotypes as Turner's syndrome, MGD, MPH, and an apparently normal male.[65] Besides this classic and most frequent clinical phenotype, various degrees of sex reversal can be seen from females with clitoral hypertrophy and males with hypospadias or abnormal internal genitalia or unilateral cryptorchidism.[64,66-69] The testicular capacity for testosterone secretion may allow normal plasma levels after hCG stimulation and pubertal virilization of patients raised as males.[70]

Turner stigmata and short stature are found in about half of the reported cases, in keeping with the chromosomal mosaicism containing an XO cell line. The presence of a Y chromosome indicates the likely presence of testicular tissue and hence predicts the occurrence of virilization at puberty as well as a high risk of gonadal tumors.[71,72] The latter are often discovered at histologic examination of the gonadal streak or of the dysgenetic testis.

One report documents the fact that substantial differences exist between prenatally and postnatally diagnosed cases of 45,X/46,XY mosaicism.[69] Ninety percent of prenatally diagnosed cases show a normal male phenotype, whereas the postnatally diagnosed cases show a wide spectrum of phenotypes. Thus, the 10% risk of an abnormal outcome in prenatally diagnosed cases requires further attention. In this cohort of 27 cases, no correlation was found between the proportion of the 45,X/46,XY cell lines in the blood or the fibroblasts and the phenotype. Mild mental retardation was present in four patients, and two patients showed signs of autism.[69]

**Genetics**  Although a 45,X/46,XY karyotype is most frequently found in patients with MGD, other mosaics have been reported that contain a structurally normal or abnormal Y chromosome.[73] MGD may also occur with a 46,XY karyotype in sporadic and familial cases with ambiguous genitalia. In these cases, a low proportion of 45,XO cells may be missed or undetectable by conventional techniques. Pure gonadal dysgenesis and MGD, both with 46,XY karyotype, have been reported in the same family.[74] It is thought that the 45,X/46,XY mosaicism is caused by the loss of a structurally abnormal Y.[75] Because of such a clinical heterogeneity, MGD appears more likely to be one of the various clinical and anatomic conditions associated with defective Y function. An X-linked molecule-like DAX1 may have a role in MGD, since overexpression of DAX1 suppresses testicular differentiation and loss of DAX1 also impairs testis development.[1]

**Differential Diagnosis**  Based on anatomic and karyotypic findings, the main differential diagnosis is with true hermaphroditism. If primordial follicles are found in the streak gonad, the diagnosis of true hermaphroditism should be considered.

Some cases may be difficult to classify unless a thorough pathologic examination of the removed streak gonad is performed. On the other hand, MGD shares many features with the syndromes of either gonadal dysgenesis or dysgenetic MPH,[76] in which patients have bilateral dysgenetic testes and failure to secrete AMH normally. This is why the frontiers between the three entities are somewhat arbitrary and, for some authors, all three represent variants of gonadal dysgenesis.

**Management** Most patients with MGD have been reared as females.[66] This is the best choice for patients seen during infancy or at birth, because surgical repair of the vagina is usually easy; a uterus or hemiuterus is present; and the dysgenetic gonad, which is at high risk of tumor development, should be removed early. In patients raised as males and diagnosed late, sex reassignment is not possible. Surgical correction of the hypospadias and the unilateral cryptorchidism is performed, and the testis, if conserved, should be observed regularly to detect the possible development of gonadoblastoma. These individuals virilize at puberty but remain sterile. One study considered the significance of prenatally diagnosed 45,X/46,XY mosaicism at amniocentesis.[77] Of 76 patients, only 1 had a female phenotype with clitoromegaly, 3 had ambiguous genitalia, and the remaining were apparently normal males. Histology of the gonads available in 11 cases of the latter group showed bilateral ovotestes in 2 cases. It was concluded that dysgenetic gonads may occur even in children with a normal phenotype and 45,X/46,XY mosaicism. The outcome of gonadal function in these phenotypic males prenatally diagnosed remains to be established, however. In any case, these findings are in contrast with the classical presentation of MGD with ambiguous genitalia.

### Dysgenetic Male Pseudohermaphroditism

**Pathogenesis** The term *dysgenetic MPH* does not designate a distinct clinical identity. Federman[76] used it as a convenient clinical classification of 46,XY patients presenting with bilateral dysgenetic testes and evidence of embryonic gonadal regression having occurred at various stages of early or late development.[72] The combined failure of Leydig and Sertoli cell functions is characteristic of fetal testicular dysgenesis. Here again, there is a clinical heterogeneity and possibly various causes of the syndrome. For instance, familial 46,XY cases have been reported in which both pure gonadal dysgenesis and rudimentary testes have occurred.[44] Bilateral testicular dysgenesis, as described earlier, is also found in patients with an additional XO cell line or with structural anomaly of the Y chromosome such as 46,X(Yp–).

**Clinical Features** In any case, all these patients present with ambiguous genitalia, bilateral cryptorchidism, or rarely palpable gonads, urogenital sinus, and a uterus. Some patients have associated abnormalities of the kidney and thus are also classified in a subgroup of MPH (see earlier). Although the XY karyotype is the most frequent, patients with 46,XXY or with 46,XX and hypoplastic gonads or streaks have been reported.[11,12]

**Diagnosis and Management** In order to differentiate dysgenetic MPH and MGD, the histology of the testes is very important, showing in the former case bilateral dysgenetic testes and no streak.[72] Although female gender assignment is usually preferred, male assignment is a justifiable alternative in cases of extreme virilization and a descended testis. In these male-assigned patients, however, consideration must be given to the role of periodic testicular biopsies. In light of tumor potential, all intra-abdominal gonads should be removed. Patients would undergo hypospadias repair or feminizing genitoplasty, depending on the gender assigned.[78]

### XYY Males

The XYY karyotype, which is said to occur in about 1 of every 1000 males,[79] does not usually produce a disorder of testicular differentiation. Hypotonia, delayed speech, and poor neuromuscular coordination are common in these individuals. Tall stature is often reported, but is not constant. Testicular function is usually normal, and many individuals affected are fertile. Variable, but severe, abnormalities of spermatogenesis are found at systematic testicular biopsies of institutionalized patients, however. In addition, the association of ambiguous genitalia and even of complete female phenotype with the 47,XYY karyotype has been reported in approximately 10 cases,[80] suggesting the possibility of widespread Y chromosomal damage during paternal spermatogenesis.

In the past decade, there has been a significant increase in the proportion of XYY males detected prenatally, mostly as a fortuitous finding. From birth on, weight, height, and head circumference are above average values. A recent follow-up study[81] has concluded the following: (1) These patients are at considerably increased risk for delayed language and/or motor development; (2) The majority attends kindergarten in the normal education circuit, although, in 50% of the cases, psychosocial problems are documented; (3) From primary school age on, there is an increased risk for child psychiatric disorders such as autism; and (4) Although normally intelligent, many of these boys are referred to special education programs.[81] Despite the classic belief that these patients commit criminal acts more frequently than expected, a study of 17 XYY men and 60 controls[82] provided evidence for a slightly increased liability to antisocial behavior and, if they show somewhat higher criminal convictions, this is through lowered intelligence. Property offences were the majority of offences in all groups.

At least two mechanisms cause nondisjunction of the Y chromosome, most often a nondisjunction at meiosis II after a nullichiasmate meiosis I or a postzygotic mitotic error.[83]

The condition may be viewed as a variant of gonadal dysgenesis. Management of such cases is the same as earlier, keeping in mind that XYY, like trisomy 21, predisposes to leukemia.[84]

### Testicular Regression Syndromes

**Pathogenesis** *Testicular regression* refers to a group of conditions defined by the presence of a 46,XY karyotype and evidence of testicular formation followed by gonadal regression. The pathogenesis of testicular regression remains unknown, and its eventual precise timing does not depend on its genetic determinant. The patients have perfectly normal male differentiation of their internal and external genitalia but no longer have any gonadal tissue.

**Clinical Features** The range of virilizing effects owing to early testicular tissue extends from none in phenotypic females with only slightly hypoplastic normal external genitalia, well-formed but hypoplastic uterus, and well-formed tubes[85] to the anorchid phenotypic male.[86] According to the clinical picture, variable timing for the regression may be assigned (Table 146-2). The spectrum of testicular regression includes three clinical conditions: true agonadism, rudimentary testes, and congenital anorchia.

*True agonadism* presents with various degrees of ambiguity of external genitalia. Müllerian derivatives are absent or rudimentary. This situation can be explained by complete or partial AMH activity, an event that precedes the secretion of testosterone by Leydig cells that fail to develop normally.[87] Craniofacial, vertebral, and cardiac abnormalities have been observed in some of these patients.[88] True agonadism and anorchia have been associated in the same kindred. On the basis of familial occurrences of bilateral congenital anorchia, a possible genetic etiology has been hypothesized, namely mutations of the SRY gene, which initiates the genetic cascade leading to testis development in mammals. In several studies, SRY gene is present in these patients as well as in normal boys.[89,90] Thus, the condition does not seem to be related to

**Table 146-2** Testicular Dysgenesis and Testicular Regression Syndromes: Varying Phenotypes and Timing of Testicular Development

| | Gonadal Dysgenesis | True Agonadism | Rudimentary Testes | Congenital Anorchia |
|---|---|---|---|---|
| Genetic sex | 46,XY | 46,XY | 46,XY | 46,XY |
| Familial occurrence | Yes | Rare | Rare | Rare |
| Onset of testicular dysfunction* | <8 wk | 8–12 wk | 14–20 wk | >20 wk |
| External genitalia | Female | Ambiguous | Micropenis | Male |
| Vagina | Present | Present | No | No |
| Müllerian duct derivatives | Present | No | No | No |
| Wolffian duct derivatives | No | No | Present | Present |
| Gonads | Streak† | No | No | No |

*Weeks of gestation.
†Risk of gonadoblastoma.
Adapted from David M, Forest M, Chatelain P, et al: Pseudohermaphrodismes féminins. Pediatrie 45:65S–71S, 1990.

an anomaly of the opening reading frame sequence of the SRY gene. Nevertheless, familial occurrences suggest a genetic etiology. Further studies must, therefore, evaluate the possibility of punctiform mutations of the SRY gene.

*Rudimentary testes* occur with a male phenotype and micropenis.[91,92] Small atrophic testes may be palpable. They contain scanty small testicular tubules, pre-Sertoli and pre-Leydig cells, and some spermatogonia. In some cases, the genital ridge contains fibrous tissue and clumps of fetal Leydig cells. Some patients may have penile or perineal hypospadias with persistent müllerian elements. Familial cases have been reported. Rudimentary testes may be a manifestation of XY primary gonadal dysplasia, as it has been found to be associated with pure gonadal dysgenesis in a family.[44]

*Congenital anorchia* is characterized by the complete absence of testicular tissue at birth, but a normal male sex differentiation, without müllerian derivatives. It is considered to result from vanishing testes,[93] and should rather be called *embryonic testicular regression syndrome.*[91] These two denominations encompass the same entity that is referred to in the urologist literature as the *vanishing testis syndrome,* or in the pathologic literature as the *testicular regression syndrome,* since the presence of spermatic cord structure is evidence of the presence of the testis in early intrauterine life. Pathologic assessment included identification of vas deferens, epididymis, dystrophic calcification, hemosiderin, dominant vein, pampiniform plexus–like vessels, and vascularized fibrous nodule formation. At minimum, the presence of a vascularized fibrous nodule (VFN) with calcification or hemosiderin or VFN with cord element(s) was required for diagnosis.[94] In the typical situation in which a blind ending spermatic cord is submitted for tissue analysis, characterization of such cases as consistent with regressed testis is desirable and achievable in a high percentage of cases. Pathologists may play a pivotal role in management of these patients since histologic confirmation of the testis as regressed[94] reassures the surgeon and the family of the correctness of diagnosis and can eliminate the necessity for further intervention.

The coexistence of anorchia and true agonadism in one sibship suggests that they are fundamentally the same and due to regression of the embryonic testis.[91] Finally, besides some unknown genetic factor, congenital anorchia is thought to result also from the late suppression of the vascular supply to the testes (in utero testicular torsion). The most likely is that fetal testes developed normally and are destroyed in utero, in the perinatal period, or even soon after birth. The most frequent mechanism with a genetic predisposition seems to be bilateral pedicle twisting.

**Diagnosis and Management** All these patients have a normal 46,XY karyotype and signs of testicular regression. The diagnosis should be considered in all males with bilateral cryptorchidism. In the absence of palpable gonads, a critical diagnostic finding is the evidence of basal or hCG-stimulated

testosterone secretion above the female range. If some testosterone is produced, it is taken as evidence of some persistent testicular tissue. In agonadic patients, basal gonadotropins are greatly elevated during early infancy or at pubertal age. In childhood, GnRH elicits a rise in luteinizing hormone (LH) and follicle-stimulating hormone (FSH) levels greater than in normal prepubertal children. But further evaluation, eventually including laparotomy or celioscopy and histology of the gonads, is necessary to make a precise diagnosis. The internal and external genitalia phenotype provides information as to the timing of the testicular failure. If, as usual, there is no uterus, these conditions should be distinguished from MPH with failure of testosterone synthesis or action. These individuals are usually brought up as males, and with testosterone replacement therapy they have a normal pubertal and sexual life. Implantation of prosthetic testes is recommended for cosmetic and, above all, for psychological benefit.

### Seminiferous Tubular Dysgenesis: Klinefelter Syndrome and Variants

**Definition** Klinefelter syndrome, the most common cause of male hypogonadism, was first described in 1942[95] as the association of eunuchoidism, gynecomastia, small testes, azoospermia, and elevated FSH excretion. Several groups subsequently reported that a high proportion of patients with this syndrome were chromatin positive, a finding explained in 1959 when the XXY constitution was reported.[96] An extra X chromosome is seen in 0.23 out of 1000 live-born males.[79,97] The presence of an extra X chromosome is significantly higher (0.45% to 2.5%), however, in surveys of mentally retarded males. An association with the fragile X syndrome has been reported.[98] Patients with the XXY genotype have classic Klinefelter syndrome. In the past 3 decades, the clinical spectrum of the syndrome expanded to include patients with various 46,XY/47,XXY mosaicisms, those with three or more X chromosomes and a Y chromosome, and males with a 46,XX sex chromosome complement. All are considered to have variant forms of Klinefelter syndrome.[99]

**Pathogenesis** The basic genetic defect, a 47,XXY karyotype, arises from a nondisjunction during the first (34%) or second (9%) meiotic division of maternal gametogenesis, which results in an egg with two X chromosomes. The origin of the extra X has been documented by using X-linked markers such as color vision in pedigree studies, which showed that meiotic nondisjunction during spermatogenesis occurs in 53% of the cases. Although both parents tend to be older than average at the time of conception, a significant association has been found only between maternal age and the frequency of first meiotic division abnormalities.[100,101] There is no phenotypic difference between maternally and paternally derived patients.

The characteristic feature is seminiferous tubule dysgenesis, expressed at the age of puberty. As the gonadotropins increase, the seminiferous tubules do not enlarge, but rather undergo fibrosis and hyalinization, which results in small firm testes. Sertoli cells and spermatogonia may be present in some sections. Absence of elastic fibers in the tunica propria is indicative of the dysgenetic nature of the tubules. Obliteration of the seminiferous tubules results in azoospermia. Onset of puberty is associated with accelerated germ cell depletion.[102] By contrast, inhibin B and AMH secretions are normal in infancy,[103] and display pathologic changes later, in midpuberty.[102]

The marked reduction of tubular volume accounts for the apparent hyperplasia of the interstitial tissue. Leydig cells are present in clumps and, although their total mass is normal, they are functionally abnormal from birth on. Indeed, the postnatal rise in testosterone is lower than in controls, while the gonadotropins do not differ from controls.[103] In adulthood, testosterone production rate is reduced, with compensatory LH hypersecretion, and the response to hCG stimulation is subnormal. Because of the high LH levels, estradiol secretion is stimulated, with an increased estradiol-testosterone ratio, which is believed to account for the development of gynecomastia. The pathogenesis of eunuchoidism, personality disturbances, intellectual deficits, and associated medical disorders is still unexplained.

**Clinical Features**    At birth, there are generally no particular stigmata in Klinefelter syndrome. Although five cases of phenotypic females with a 47,XXY karyotype are described in the literature,[104] external genitalia usually exhibit a normal male phenotype and the patients are reared as males. During childhood there are no specific signs or symptoms, except for bilateral cryptorchidism, micropenis, learning disabilities, behavior disorders, or mental retardation in some patients.[105,106] As a rule, no symptoms occur until the age of puberty. The clinical expression of the androgen deficiency varies considerably in timing and among patients. Some have virtually no pubertal development, whereas others virilize normally. Puberty may be delayed, but usually by no more than 1 to 2 years. A spontaneous pubertal development is most often observed. In all cases, the predominant features are the small size of the testes (100%), which do not increase normally at puberty, and pubertal gynecomastia (60%). The testes are less than 2 to 3 cm in their longest axis and firm as a result of fibrosis and hyalinization. Other complaints are decreased pubic hair (88%), infertility, poor libido, or impotency. Osteopenia may be severe in patients with long-standing androgen deficiency,[105] but can be prevented with early diagnosis and treatment The growth of the lower extremities is relatively greater than that of the trunk and upper extremities.[107] The patients are classically described as being eunuchoid, but in fact they have abnormal skeletal proportions (pubis-to-floor height greater than crown-to-pubis height, and span less than total height) that are not the result of androgen deficiency (which leads to span greater than height).

Intellectual impairment is noted in many, but not all, patients. The true proportion of affected individuals with subnormal intelligence is, however, not known. Antisocial behavior is common. Association with the following disorders is greater than chance: chronic pulmonary disease, emphysema or chronic bronchitis, varicose veins, glucose intolerance or mild diabetes mellitus, and primary hypothyroidism. There is also a 20-fold increased risk for breast carcinoma,[108] and a significant association with other malignancies such as leukemia, lymphoma, bladder cancer, or primary mediastinal germ cell tumor.[109]

**Laboratory Findings**    The plasma levels of total testosterone are low to normal; however, owing to increased sex hormone–binding globulin, free testosterone levels are decreased. The testosterone response to hCG is lower than normal. During puberty, plasma FSH increases greatly, usually after pubertal stage IV. After puberty, plasma LH and FSH levels are both elevated, with a hyperresponse to GnRH.[110] Gonadotropin can be suppressed, but only with high doses of sex steroids. Serum

inhibin levels are relatively low and do not correlate with FSH levels.[111] Basal and thyroid-stimulating hormone (TSH)-stimulated prolactin levels are normal. Abnormal thyroid function with blunted response to thyrotropin-releasing hormone (TRH) is found in some cases.[110]

**Diagnosis**    Klinefelter syndrome should be distinguished from other causes of hypogonadism. Small, firm testes are orientating, especially if normal puberty has occurred. Elevated gonadotropins place the site of the lesion at the testicular level. A positive buccal smear is not sufficient to confirm the diagnosis. Chromosomal analysis is required to recognize the variant forms of the syndrome.[112]

**Treatment and Prognosis**    Testosterone replacement is necessary at some point. Indeed, although pubertal development is often normal, testicular involution is inevitable, occurring as a rule after age 30. Therapy consists of the injections of long-acting testosterone esters every 3 to 4 weeks or use of transdermal testosterone preparations. The dose of injected esters should be increased gradually (100 to 250 mg) to decrease the risk of aggressive behavior or to induce pubertal development if needed. Long-term psychiatric counseling is often required. Moreover, it has been suggested that testosterone administration in early puberty would improve the psychological behavior at adolescence.[106,113] Mastectomy may be indicated if gynecomastia presents a cosmetic problem. Most patients are sterile, although some cases of fertility have been reported.[114] The report of the birth of a healthy neonate following the intracytoplasmic injection of testicular spermatozoa from a patient with Klinefelter syndrome[115] provides further evidence that normal spermatozoa with fertilization potential are produced in the testes of these patients.

Long-term follow-up indicates a high incidence of breast cancer,[116] and mortality due to neoplastic disease is higher than in the general population.[113]

**Variant Forms of Seminiferous Tubule Dysgenesis**
In this group, there is at least an XXY cell line in at least some tissues. Numerous variants of Klinefelter syndrome are reported, with mosaicisms such as 46,XY/47,XXY karyotype or 48,XXXY, or 49,XXXXY cell lines.[117] Patients with both an extra X and Y and karyotypes such as 48,XXYY or 49,XXXYY are also considered as variants of seminiferous tubule dysgenesis. These patients tend to be tall. Mosaicism with any Y cell line may modify the clinical syndrome and result in less severe gynecomastia or degree of testicular pathology. Indeed, subjects with XY/XXY mosaics have less obvious manifestations of Klinefelter syndrome, and fertility has been reported in some patients. On the other hand, the severity of the clinical and gonadal aberration is linked to the number of X chromosomes. Thus, any of the other variants tend to have more severe mental retardation than is found in XXY patients. In addition, individuals with three or more extra X chromosomes have associated anomalies such as radioulnar synostosis, epiphyseal dysplasia, patent ductus arteriosus, small genitalia, and cryptorchidism.[118] In some of these individuals, an unusual facies with prognathism, hypertelorism, strabismus, and myopia is observed.

**Management**    As in the classical form of Klinefelter syndrome, detection of its variant forms is important to providing early help for both the androgen deficiency and the emotional and social dysfunctions. Therapy depends on the severity of the clinical and gonadal aberrations.

**46,XX Males**
This condition, also called *sex reversal syndrome*, is characterized by testicular development in subjects who have two X chromosomes but lack a normal Y chromosome. About 200 cases have been reported in the past 30 years, but it would appear that 1 in 20,000 to 30,000 males have a 46,XX

karyotype.[100] Most are sporadic cases. The subjects usually have a normal male phenotype, although hypospadias or more severe genital ambiguity with cryptorchidism is seen in about 10% of them.[119] At puberty, the patients develop gynecomastia (75%) and some degree of testosterone deficiency with elevated plasma FSH and LH, whereas spermatogenesis is impaired. The testes present the same features as those observed in Klinefelter syndrome. The patients differ from the latter in that they are not tall and show no impairment of intelligence.

A low degree of mosaicism for an XXY cell line in tissue culture has been considered as a possible explanation for the sex reversal.[120] The XX males may be divided into three subgroups: 46,XX males with the SRY gene; 46,XX males without the SRY gene; and XX/XY mosaics. Most of these patients have part of the short arm of the Y chromosome transferred to one of the two X chromosomes, suggesting a form of X-Y paternal interchange.[121] Two hot spots of ectopic Xp-Yp recombination have been shown to be at the origin of XX maleness in about half of the affected subjects[122] in whom the presence of a Y-specific material is found. Male sex differentiation in these patients results from the transfer of the sex-determining chromosomal region by accidental crossover during paternal meiosis.[55,119]

Some XX males have no demonstrable Y sequences, however, and differ from the previous group by the occurrence of hypospadias or micropenis, and the association of multiple anomalies.[123]

Thus, there is genetic as well as phenotypic heterogeneity in 46,XX maleness in which some subjects have SRY, whereas other lack it,[123] thus indicating that non-Y genes may also be necessary to achieve testicular differentiation. In this respect, some 46,XX males with abnormal external genitalia more closely resemble XX true hermaphrodites.[124] Unless careful gonadal examination is performed by a trained pathologist, true hermaphroditism may be missed.

### Campomelic Dysplasia: An Autosomal Sex Reversal
**Definition** Campomelic dysplasia (CD) is a rare, often lethal, dominantly inherited, congenital osteochondrodysplasia associated with male-to-female autosomal sex reversal in affected karyotypic males.

**Clinical Features** This is a disorder of the newborn characterized by congenital bowing and angulation of long bones, together with other skeletal and extraskeletal defects. The designation *campomelic* (or *camptomelic*) *dwarfism*, proposed by Maroteaux and colleagues,[125] comes from the bowing of the legs, especially the tibiae. The scapulae are very small, and the pelvis and spine show changes. Eleven pairs of ribs are usually present. The inferior part of the scapula is hypoplastic. Cleft palate, micrognathia, flat face, and hypertelorism are also features. Most patients die in the neonatal period of respiratory distress. Disarray of the hair ("unruly" hair) is present in some patients. Severe anomalies of the lower cervical spine may lead to an appearance of pterygium colli. The syndrome includes severe respiratory distress. Approximately three quarters of cases of 46,XY affected individuals show complete or partial sex reversal.[126]

**Pathogenesis and Genetics** CD syndrome is caused by mutations within the SOX9 gene (a member of the SOX family of transcription factors) or chromosomal rearrangement breakpoints outside SOX9. Chromosomal translocations in individuals with both syndromes had localized an autosomal sex-reversal locus (SRA1) and a campomelic dysplasia locus (CMPD1) to the long arm of human chromosome 17. The molecular cloning of a translocation breakpoint in a sex-reversed campomelic dysplasia patient revealed its proximity to SOX9, a gene that is related to SRY. Analysis of SOX9 in patients without chromosomal rearrangements demonstrated

single allele mutations in sex-reversed campomelic individuals, linking this gene with both bone formation and control of testis development. The fact that all mutations found affect a single allele is consistent with a dominant mode of inheritance and with the hypothesis that CD results from haploinsufficiency of SOX9. No mutations were found in the SOX9 open reading frame of two patients with chromosome 17q rearrangements, suggesting that the translocations affect SOX9 expression. SOX9 should not, however, be considered a candidate gene for XY sex reversal without skeletal malformation.[127] There is no correlation between genotype and phenotype.[128] This may be explained by several possible mechanisms, such as variable penetrance of the mutation, increased activity of the nonmutant SOX9 allele, or stochastic environmental factors. These results also demonstrate that paternal germ cell mosaicism of a mutant SOX9 sequence can result in a CD phenotype among his offspring. Finally, it has been shown that SOX9 duplication can cause XX sex reversal and that SOX9 is sufficient to initiate testis differentiation in the absence of SRY.[129]

### Dosage-Sensitive Sex Reversal
Male-to-female sex reversal has been observed in individuals with duplications of the short arm of the X chromosome. The first demonstration that sex reversal could result from the presence of two active copies of an Xp locus rather than from its rearrangement and that alterations at this locus constitute one of the causes of sex reversal in individuals with a normal 46,XY karyotype was made by Bardoni and colleagues.[130] They named this locus *dosage-sensitive sex reversal* (DSS) and localized it to a 160-kb region of chromosome Xp21, adjacent to the adrenal hypoplasia congenita locus. The identification of male individuals deleted for DSS suggests that this locus is not required for testis differentiation. The same authors proposed that DSS plays a role in ovarian development or functions as a link between ovary and testis formation. It is now well recognized that the DSS phenotype, a male-to-female sex reversal syndrome, is caused by the duplication of a small region of human chromosome Xp21, which contains the DAX1 gene and perhaps others.[131] The phenotype is heterogeneous, however. Among 22 patients with duplication in Xp, 9 had unambiguous female genitalia and a well-documented duplication of the DSS region. Two patients with duplication of DSS showed ambiguous external genitalia. Thus, induction of testicular tissue may start in these patients, but the type of genitalia depends on the degree of subsequent degeneration by a gene in DSS.[132]

## DEFECTIVE OVARY FORMATION OR MAINTENANCE

Both X chromosomes are necessary for the maintenance of an ovary with normal follicular maturation. It is not clear whether there is also a specific defect in ovary formation. Several parts of the X chromosome, mainly the Xq2-q28 segment[133] and possibly an autosomal-recessive gene, may play an important role in this control. In females who have only one X, or deletions of the short or long arm of the X, the ovaries undergo regression to the structure called a streak gonad, devoid of follicles. Most of the sex differentiation abnormalities involved combine a normal female phenotype with absent or hypoplastic ovaries.

### Pure Gonadal Dysgenesis 46,XX
Patients with pure gonadal dysgenesis and 46,XX karyotype have a normal stature, sexual infantilism, and bilateral streak gonads.[134] There is a marked heterogeneity, both genetically and clinically, in the expression of the disease, even in the same kindred. The molecular basis of the condition is still not well understood. The frequency of consanguinity in affected families points to an autosomal gene necessary for normal ovarian development and function. Alternatively, the condition may

result from an X-linked gene mutation or deletion in sporadic cases. Recent studies showing that adult height is lower in 46,XX than in 46,XY gonadal dysgenesis supports the existence of a Y-specific growth gene that promotes statural growth independent of gonadal steroids.[135]

The main clinical features are the lack of stigmata of Turner's syndrome and female internal and external genitalia. Presenting symptoms at the age of puberty are primary amenorrhea, lack of breast development, and elevated gonadotropins. Occasionally, patients may develop mild virilization such as clitoral enlargement, hirsutism, and elevated serum testosterone, which is assumed to be produced by highly stimulated hilar cells.[136] This is a sensible hypothesis because gonadal neoplasia, an alternative cause of virilization, does not seem to occur in XX gonadal dysgenesis. Familial cases are frequent, and affected siblings may show distinct features such as extreme ovarian hypoplasia or precocious menopause.[134] Various associations have been reported such as sensorineural deafness in Perrault syndrome, cerebellar ataxia, or other neurologic defects that may be caused by coincident genetic defects. The diagnosis is made on the association of normal karyotype in a sexually infantile female with hypergonadotropic hypogonadism. In sporadic cases, it is important to confirm the absence of normal ovaries by ultrasonography or pelvic magnetic resonance imaging (MRI) or even by laparotomy and rule out other causes of hypergonadotropic ovarian failure. Replacement therapy with estrogen is as for patients with Turner's syndrome.

### Turner's Syndrome

It was described by Turner in 1938 as a distinct entity associating sexual infantilism, webbed neck, and cubitus valgus.[137] As early as 1930, Ullrich had in fact described the same physical characteristics in female patients,[138] but neither one correctly suggested a cause. It was not until 1944 that Wilkins and Fleishmann established that underdeveloped ovaries were present. In subsequent years, gonadal dysgenesis was recognized as part of Ullrich-Turner syndrome (called exclusively Turner's syndrome in the Anglo-Saxon literature). Definitive evidence for X-chromosomal abnormality was provided in 1959.[139] Turner's syndrome occurs in approximately 1 in 2500 live female births. There is a much larger number of unborn affected fetuses, however, because approximately 98% of pregnancies with Turner's syndrome abort spontaneously for reasons that are not yet understood. Also, approximately 10% of fetuses from miscarried pregnancies have Turner's syndrome. Familial cases are reported rarely.[139]

**Pathogenesis** The cause of Turner's syndrome is the total or partial absence of one of the two X chromosomes in some or all of the body cells. The loss of an entire chromosome is observed in about 60% of patients with Turner's syndrome. It results from a nondisjunction that occurs either before zygotic formation or in the first or second postzygotic division. If an X chromosome is lost by faulty distribution during later cell division, this results in a 45,X/46,XX mosaicism. Partial X-chromosome losses may also occur from either transverse division leading to isochromosomes made of two parts of the long i(X)q or two parts of the short chromosome segment i(Xp) or from major deletions (denoted "del" or "−"). Minor deletions, or the loss of small X fragments, can only be visualized through banding techniques or by DNA probes. Finally, an X chromosome may fail to develop in the usual rod form, but instead close to form a ring; the karyotype is then 46,X,r(X). The normal X chromosome comes from the mother in most patients with a 45,X karyotype, but only in about half of those with a different karyotype.[140] The percentage of 45,X chromosomes versus mosaics or isochromosomes varies somewhat among populations. For example, the proportions of mosaics and isochromosome, 46,X,i(Xq), was found to be higher in a large Korean population than those reported in other countries.

**Genetics** Structural abnormalities involving the terminal short arms of the X and Y chromosomes have been shown to lead to short stature. A putative locus affecting height has been localized to a 170-kb critical region within the pseudoautosomal region (PAR). It contains a homeodomain and functions as a transcription factor. Most of the PAR, including PHOG/SHOX, is lost as a result of a translocation.[142]

A gene has been isolated from this critical deleted region that encodes a novel homeodomain-containing transcription factor and is expressed at highest levels in osteogenic cells. It has been called a pseudoautosomal homeobox-containing osteogenic gene (PHOG). Its deletion in patients with short stature, the predicted altered dosage in 45,X individuals, along with the nature of the encoded protein and its expression pattern, has made PHOG an attractive candidate for involvement in the short stature of Turner's syndrome.[143] Rao and colleagues[144] have isolated a short-stature homeobox-containing gene (SHOX) on the PAR of the sex chromosomes (Xp22 and Yp11.3), which has at least two alternatively spliced forms, encoding proteins with different patterns of expression. The involvement of SHOX in idiopathic growth retardation and in the short stature phenotype of Turner's syndrome patients is now well recognized. There are 29 unique intragenic mutations of the SHOX gene recorded.[145] Point mutations or complete deletions of SHOX have been found not only in Turner's patients, but also in several families with Leri-Weill dyschondrosteosis (LWD) syndrome.[146]

Haploinsufficiency of SHOX causes not only short stature, but also Turner's skeletal anomalies (e.g., short fourth metacarpals, cubitus valgus, and LWD), and growth pattern is primarily dependent on the presence or absence of LWD. Short stature owing to SHOX deletions is not a rare entity.[142] SHOX is most strongly expressed in bone-marrow fibroblasts, implying that it plays a positive role in bone growth and development.[143,147] In addition, SHOX is expressed in both the inactive X chromosome as well as in the active X and Y chromosome, suggesting that SHOX escapes inactivation and exerts a dosage effect in patients with sex chromosome aberrations.[144] Aneuploidy, rather than specific gene loss, may also explain growth failure.[148] Several matters remain to be determined for the skeletal features in Turner's syndrome other than short stature.[142]

**Clinical Features** The syndrome represents a wide spectrum of clinical presentations.[149–151] The main characteristics are, however, abnormal physical features, gonadal dysgenesis, and short stature (Fig. 146-3). Children with Turner's syndrome may have the following physical findings: short, thick, and webbed neck; dysmorphic face (fishlike mouth, hypertelorism, epicanthus, ptosis of the eyelids, prominent ears, high-arched palate, micrognathia) and low posterior hairline; congenital lymphedema (puffy hands and feet at birth); broad childlike chest; hypoplastic or inverted nipples; cubitus valgus; short fourth metacarpals; multiple pigmented nevi; abnormal fingernails (turned out at the end); intestinal telangiectasia; recurrent otitis media; and a tendency to keloid formation. Turner's patients also show a prevalence of celiac disease in childhood or adolescence. Immunoglobulin gamma (IgA)-antiendomysium antibodies (EMA) are a good immunologic marker for use in screening for celiac disease, and such screening seems to be justified in patients with Turner's syndrome.[152] Cardiovascular anomalies are common, and the most clinically frequent is coarctation of the aorta. Echographic studies, however, showed that nonstenotic bicuspid aorta might be the most common cardiovascular lesion in Turner's syndrome. A routine echocardiogram is thus indicated in all 45,X patients. Kidney anomalies occur in one third to one half of girls with Turner's syndrome, with monosomic patients at greater risk. The most common anomaly is a horseshoe kidney. The prevalence of mental retardation appears no greater than in the general population. Many patients have a specific deficit in special ability,

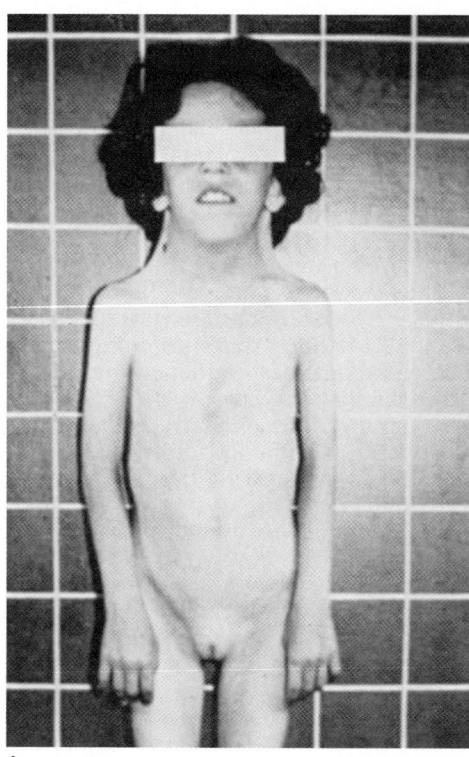 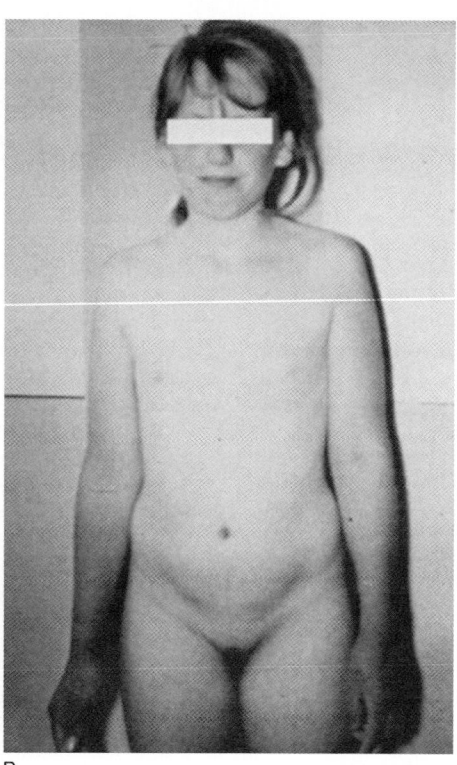

A                                    B

*Figure 146-3*  Phenotypic spectrum in patients with 45,X Turner's syndrome. **A,** This girl has typical morphologic anomalies, in particular, a pronounced webbed neck, whereas the girl in **B** has very few. Both girls were very short.

however, and frequently exhibit gross and fine motor dysfunction. The bone age is delayed. Osteoporosis may also be seen.

In a cohort of 115 women with Turner's syndrome, a dose-response relationship was found between the karyotype and hearing function. Hearing deteriorates more rapidly with increasing age in those lacking the whole p-arm of chromosome X (i.e., monosomy 45,X, or isochromosome cases 46,X,i(Xq)) compared with women having a partial deletion of the p-arm (structural deletions or mosaicism cases), who, in turn, had poorer hearing than a female random population sample (46,XX) ($P < 0.001$). This supports the hypothesis that lack of growth-regulating genes such as SHOX, which is located within the PAR on the p-arm of the X chromosome, may increase the occurrence of auricular malformations and otitis media and also induce an earlier loss of hearing function.[153]

Normal pubertal development and spontaneous menstrual periods do not occur in most children with Turner's syndrome. Mosaic forms of Turner's syndrome are usually seen in female adolescents with primary amenorrhea and in young women with premature ovarian failure. It is estimated, however, that 3% to 8% of 45,X karyotype patients and 12% to 21% of females with sex chromosome mosaicism may have normal pubertal development and spontaneous menstrual periods, but their final height is not significantly greater.[154] Spontaneous pregnancy is an exceptional event, but occurs in approximately 2% of cases and more often in patients with structural anomalies of the X chromosomes in which the Xq13-q26 region, containing the genes that are thought to control ovarian function, is spared or in patients with a mosaic karyotype containing a 46,XX cell line (45,X and 45,X/46,XX), which preserves ovarian development. Excellent results have been obtained with embryo transfers; 46% resulted in pregnancy.[155]

Short stature is almost a constant finding in Turner's syndrome. This does not mean that all patients are short at every period of their lives, particularly if their parents are tall. As a group, the newborn are smaller than average both in length and weight.[156] Usually, the postnatal growth lies in the normal range for the first 2 to 3 years but then decreases. Body length further deviates from the norm with age. The deficit in height results, however, mainly because of a lack of pubertal growth spurt. The ultimate mean height is below the third percentile (ranging from 139 to 147 cm). Family height plays a role in determining the ultimate height in girls with Turner's syndrome,[157,158] and there are significant differences in final height in Turner's patients from different ethnic groups. Growth charts adapted to Turner's spontaneous growth have been established in various populations.[156] Body proportions are altered (increased upper-to-lower segment ratio) in most cases, which is not improved by growth hormone (GH) therapy.[159] Furthermore, treatment seems to aggravate the disproportionate growth of feet.[159] There is an increase in subcutaneous adipose tissue with age and frequent obesity.[160]

**Laboratory Findings**  Longitudinal studies of both basal and GnRH-stimulated gonadotropin secretion indicate a lack of feedback inhibition of the hypothalamic-pituitary axis in affected infants and children. However, the restraint in gonadotropin secretions, which is characteristic of the human childhood, also occurs in patients with gonadal dysgenesis (Fig. 146-4). Thus, plasma and urinary gonadotropin, particularly FSH, are unambiguously elevated during infancy and after 10 years of age.[161] With the use of more sensitive assays using monoclonal antibodies, however, gonadotropin levels are found above the normal range throughout childhood in girls with Turner's syndrome. Studies concerning GH and somatomedins are controversial. Early studies demonstrated GH deficiency in only a few patients. More recent investigations have shown that GH levels measured over 24 hours or during sleep are below normal from 8 years of life onward. Adrenal steroids are normal. Thyroid hormones are usually normal, although subclinical thyroid dysfunction may be present.

There is an increased frequency for chronic lymphocytic thyroiditis, diabetes mellitus, rheumatoid arthritis, and inflammatory bowel disease. An increased prevalence of thyroid autoantibodies in Turner's syndrome has been reported repeatedly, but has been shown to be not significantly higher than in age-matched control children, suggesting that such a prevalence does not exist from birth.[162] It is possible that

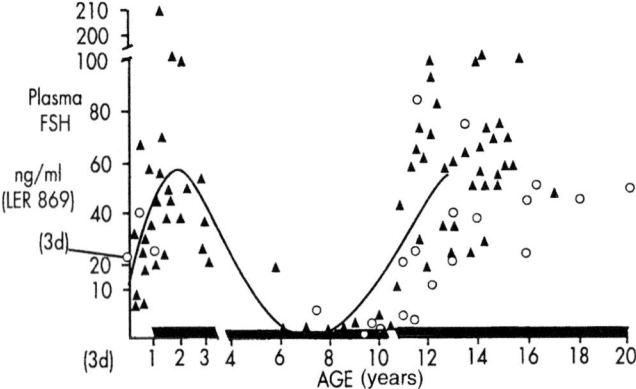

**Figure 146-4** Pattern of plasma follicle-stimulating hormone (FSH) concentrations in relation to age in subjects with gonadal dysgenesis. *Closed triangle,* 45,X karyotype; *open circles,* patients with structural abnormalities of the X chromosome and mosaics. The *hatched* area represents the mean range in normal females. (From Conte FA, Kaplan SL, Grumbach MM: A diphasic pattern of gonadotropin secretion in patients with the syndrome of gonadal dysgenesis. J Clin Endocrinol Metab 40:670–674; © 1975, The Endocrine Society.)

Turner's syndrome is associated with factors that render these patients more susceptible to endocrine autoimmunity later in life.

**Diagnosis** Typically, the syndrome is suspected because of the combination of short stature, gonadal dysgenesis, and lymphedema. There are, however, no pathognomonic clinical features of Turner's syndrome. Many girls have distinctive characteristics, whereas some girls may show a few characteristics (see Fig. 146-3). Gonadal dysgenesis should be entertained in all short girls, girls with unexpected primary or secondary amenorrhea, and girls with lymphedema. Chromosome studies are indicated in the workup of suspected patients. Heart and kidney evaluation is indicated if the diagnosis of Turner's syndrome is confirmed. These findings point to the diagnosis. The only disorder that has an overall similar picture is Noonan's syndrome, the distinguished features of which are listed in Table 146-3. Noonan's syndrome, however, is an autosomal-dominant congenital malformation syndrome.[163] Heterozygous point mutation in the gene PTPN11 has been identified in families showing linkage to the NS1 locus in 12q24 and in some sporadic cases, but only in 33% to 50% of 255 patients diagnosed.[164]

**Treatment**

*General Management* Much attention should be paid to the psychological aspects in managing these patients. All aspects of the disorder should be taken into consideration, and the various problems discussed with the patient and her family in order to improve the emotional impact. Pterygium colli is amenable to plastic reconstruction. Other malformations, such as heart or vascular anomalies, require specific surgery. Pigmented nevi do not usually require a specific treatment except for moderate sun exposure. They should be kept under close surveillance if the child is given GH therapy, however, because of the risk for rapid growth with pathologic signs of activation.[165]

*Growth* Although current data suggest that the short stature is not due to overt GH deficiency, recombinant human GH (r-hGH) has been used since 1984, with increased predicted final height. The response to GH therapy varies from one patient to another, and different modalities of therapy have been used: GH alone or in combination with either oxandrolone (0.05 to 0.1 mg/kg/day) or low doses of ethinyl estradiol (0.1 μg/kg/day) or even both. It is certainly too early to draw definitive conclusions, but from many multicentric trials the following emerges.[150] Increased growth rate is seen with doses of r-hGH (0.60 to 1.82 IU/kg/wk) twice as high as that used in GH-deficient children, and r-hGH is given in six or seven subcutaneous injections per week. Growth velocity is usually faster when oxandrolone is involved, but androgenic side effects are noticed and bone age accelerates. Long-term studies show that GH therapy augments the final height of girls with Turner's syndrome by a mean of about 5 cm, depending on the method of evaluation, and that shorter girls may be preferred candidates for such therapy. GH therapy can be initiated after 10 years of age, but results are apparently better when GH treatment is started earlier.[166] Indirect evidence suggests that high-dose GH therapy may surmount a pathophysiologic resistance in the GH–insulin-like growth factor 1 axis, thus long-term results are not necessarily better. A mathematic model for predicting the growth response has been developed in order to provide realistic expectations of therapy outcomes and to adjust treatment on the basis of detected differences between observed and predicted height velocities.[167] Growth-promoting therapy with r-hGH is effective with regard to height gain, but a tendency to disproportionate growth is apparent.[168] In cases of unexplained growth failure, especially if associated with any mild skeletal disproportion, genetic analysis of SHOX should be considered.[145,168]

There is no reason to delay estrogen therapy beyond 12 years of age.[169,170] There is no correlation between the clinical phenotype and the deletion size. Low-dose estrogen therapy does not have any potentializing effect on growth velocity,[171] as predicted by a study showing that physiologic estrogen secretion would not increase ultimate stature in girls with Turner's syndrome.[154] Also, long-term estrogen therapy does not prevent the decrease in bone mass.[172] Several groups (Germany, Netherlands, Scotland, and Belgium) have reported final height after GH therapy. They all found an improved final height (FH). The optimal GH dosage depends on height and age at the start of treatment and first-year height velocity (HV). GH treatment leads to a normalization of final height in most girls, even when puberty is induced at a normal pubertal age. GH treatment leads to a normalization of final height in most girls, even when puberty is induced at a normal pubertal age. The optimal GH dosage depends on height and age at the start of treatment and first-year height velocity. Continued surveillance into adult life is crucial, however, particularly in children receiving supra physiologic doses of GH or whose underlying condition increases their risk of adverse effects.[173] Finally, late induced, or spontaneous puberty does not affect final height.

*Pubertal Development and Fertility* Most patients with Turner's syndrome require substitution of female hormone therapy for development of secondary sexual characteristics and menstruation. The time of initiation of therapy varies with each patient. Until recently, it was recommended that therapy

| Table 146-3 | Distinguishing Features of Turner's Syndrome and Noonan's Syndrome | |
| --- | --- | --- |
| | **Turner's Syndrome** | **Noonan's Syndrome** |
| General appearance | Typical | Very similar to Turner's syndrome |
| Sex of patient | Female | Male or female |
| Karyotype | 45,X (or mosaics) | Normal 46,XY or 46,XX |
| Inheritance | No | ? Dominant |
| Size at birth | Reduced | Normal |
| Final height | Reduced | In only half |
| Typical heart defect | Coarctation of the aorta | Pulmonary stenosis (62%) |
| Gonads | Streaks | Usually normal |
| Mental ability | Usually normal | Often impaired |

begin when the patient expresses concern about the onset of puberty. Instituting growth-promoting therapy at an early age (when growth decelerates below 2 SD), however, may allow the introduction of replacement estrogen at a more age-appropriate time (i.e., 12 to 13 years).

Spontaneous pregnancy is exceptional. A review of the literature shows that of 160 pregnancies that occurred in 74 women with Turner's syndrome, 29% ended in spontaneous abortion; 7% led to the perinatal death of the fetus; 20% gave birth to malformed babies (e.g., Turner's or Down syndrome); and only in 38% of cases were healthy children born. This study suggests that the rare patients with Turner's syndrome who are able to procreate should undergo prenatal diagnosis techniques. In sterile patients with Turner's syndrome, the use of artificial fertilization techniques is a possible solution,[174] although it raises important ethical issues concerning the required oocyte or egg donation.

### Variants of Turner's Syndrome

These are patients with various mosaicisms with a 45,X, a Y-bearing cell line, or a structurally abnormal Y chromosome. Clinical phenotypes range from females with typical turnerian features to ambiguous genitalia. The full syndrome results from monosomy for the X chromosome (chromatin-negative buccal smear) and is also seen in patients with major deletions of the short arm of the X chromosome (46,XXp–). In some patients, in addition to highly variable features of Turner's syndrome, there is evidence of masculinization at birth, ranging from isolated clitoromegaly to ambiguous genitalia without palpable gonads. Such masculinization is due to the presence of a Y chromosome, which allowed some functional testicular tissue to develop. The most frequent karyotype is a 45,X/46,XY mosaicism, also referred as to MGD (described earlier). These cases are mentioned because of the somatic abnormalities related to the presence of a 45,X cell line (Table 146-4).

### BISEXUAL GONADS

### True Hermaphroditism

**Definition** True hermaphrodites are individuals who have both ovarian and testicular tissues in either the same gonad or opposite gonads. True hermaphroditism is the rarest of the intersex disorders (10%), except in blacks of Southern Africa in whom it is the most common intersex condition.[175] The first case was described in 1899[175a] and about 400 cases have been reported since then. The disorder's rarity may be explained by the finding of an approximately 1% incidence of true hermaphrodites in spontaneously aborted fetuses of less than 2 months of gestation, suggesting that most of these fetuses do not survive the rigors of intrauterine life.[176]

Familial forms have been reported in Africa and elsewhere. The bisexual gonad contains testicular tissue with distinct tubules, and the ovarian tissue has follicles. The ovarian tissue must contain oocytes for the diagnosis; however, the presence of only ovarian stroma is not an adequate criterion.

**Clinical Features** According to an extensive review of the literature,[177] the most frequent presenting symptom before puberty is the abnormal appearance of the external genitalia with labioscrotal folds and variable degrees of genital ambiguity. A normal female phenotype, as well as almost normal male appearance with penile hypospadias or small penis, has been reported, however, especially in late-diagnosed cases.[178] In some patients who are reared as females, virilization may cause hirsutism and clitoromegaly. In others, normal ovarian function and fertility may even happen. In phenotypic males, gynecomastia and urethral bleeding have been reported as well as testosterone deficiency and infertility. Association with microphthalmia has been reported.[179] Undescended gonads and inguinal hernia are frequent. The inguinal hernia may contain a gonad or a uterus. In some cases, the palpable gonad is irregular and only partly firm, suggesting an ovotestis. The ovotestis is the most frequent gonad found (59%), the two components being arranged end to end. The ovarian tissue is usually normal, contrasting with dysgenetic testicular tissue lacking spermatogonia. A vas deferens may be palpable. The gonadal descent occurs more frequently on the right side. The internal genital differentiation is variable and reflects the gonadal endocrine capabilities. It is often asymmetric. Most, but not all, hermaphrodites have a uterus, which may be fully developed. According to the nature and the location of the gonadal tissue a classification has been proposed: (1) bilateral with two ovotestes; (2) lateral with testis on one side, ovary on the other; and (3) unilateral with a normal gonad on one side and an ovotestis on the other side, the most frequent condition. The descended gonad usually contains some testicular tissue.

**Genetics** The karyotype in approximately 60% of such patients reveals a 46,XX karyotype; 10% show a 46,XY karyotype and the remainder is characterized by various forms of mosaicism, XX/XY.[177] In some cases there is cytogenetic evidence of Y material when karyotypes are 46,XY or 46,XX/46,XY chimeras,[180] or various mosaics containing a Y chromosome. In these conditions, the suggested mechanisms are sex chromosome mosaicism due to mitotic or meiotic errors or chimeras from double fertilization or fusion of two normally fertilized ova. The most frequent karyotype, however, is 46,XX structurally normal. In a few of these patients, translocations of the testis-determining region from the paternal Y to the X chromosome has been demonstrated.[181–183] It is interesting that the study of XX males and XX hermaphrodites has permitted the redefinition of the region in which the

---

**Table 146-4  Variants of the Syndrome of Gonadal Dysgenesis: Relationships between Chromosomal Abnormalities and Clinical Manifestations**

| Chromosomal Abnormality | Karyotype | Sexual Infantilism* | Short Stature | Somatic Anomalies[†] |
|---|---|---|---|---|
| Monosomy haplo X | 45,X | Yes | Yes | Yes |
| Mosaicism | 45,X/46,XX | Yes | Yes | Variable |
|  | 45,X/46,XX/47,XX | Yes | Yes | Variable |
|  | 45,X/47,XXX | Yes | Yes | Variable |
| Structurally abnormal X | Short-arm deletion (Xp–) | Variable | Variable | Not always |
|  | Long-arm deletion (Xq–) | Yes | Often not | Rather rare |
| Isochromosome | 46,XXqi | Often | Yes | Yes |
| X ring chromosome | 46,XXr | Not in all | Yes | Not always |
| Miscellaneous | 45,X/46,XY | Yes | Variable | In about half |
|  | 47,XXX | Usually not | No | No |

*Female phenotype, except in miscellaneous patients in whom ambiguous genitalia may be seen.
[†]Those found in typical Turner's syndrome.

testis-determining factor (TDF) would be located.[184,185] The zinc-finger Y (ZFY) coded gene initially described by Page and colleagues[184] is absent. The presence of SRY, however, has been reported in some cases.[45,181,186]

At present, most of these 46,XX patients have yielded negative results for both ZFY and SRY.[187] For this reason, it is believed that other unknown mutations on the X or an autosome may have impaired normal testicular differentiation in these patients.[188] Genetic counseling is still based on the predominance of sporadic cases, as very few familial cases have been reported.[189] Those may result from autosomal-recessive or autosomal-dominant mutant genes. It is, therefore, likely that true hermaphroditism is caused by various dysgenetic defects.

**Diagnosis**    Internal as well as external genitalia show various ambiguous forms, ranging from male to almost female phenotypes. Most of the case reports are based on clinical, cytogenetic, and endocrine investigations, and only a few include histologic examinations of the gonadal tissue. With increasing age, ovarian tissue is often normally developed and even pregnancies have been reported.[190,191] The testicular portion is often immature,[192] and spermatogenesis is rare.[177] The diagnosis of true hermaphroditism should be considered in any patient typically combining ambiguous genitalia, one or no palpable gonad, and 46,XX karyotype. Basal or hCG-stimulated plasma testosterone level above the female range is indicative of the presence of Leydig cells. Another important point is the presence of a uterus. Genitography and ultrasonography of the pelvis may be difficult to perform in neonates and infants, however, and may fail to demonstrate müllerian structures. The cervix may eventually be identified by pelvic examination. Finally, the diagnosis of true hermaphroditism depends on the careful search for ovarian tissue during surgery in an apparently male gonad. Unless appropriate biopsies are performed and the whole gland, if removed, is examined by the pathologist, there is a risk of ignoring true hermaphroditism and of misdiagnosing the child as having dysgenetic MPH or XX male dysgenesis. A further difficulty is the lack of a reliable functional test to demonstrate the presence of ovarian tissue before surgery.

**Management**    The treatment and sex assignment are dependent on the age at diagnosis. Many patients are referred in the neonatal period. Neonates with true hermaphroditism are often rather masculinized and present with one palpable gonad. The male sex assignment has, therefore, been preferably considered if there was good phallic size, correctable hypospadias, and sufficient testicular tissue that could descend into the scrotum. Preservation of testicular tissue should allow normal virilization at puberty, but infertility is constant. The descended gonads should be controlled for the later development of tumors, which may eventually be malignant. Because of the latter risk, some authors prefer to choose female sex rearing if a uterus is present with a vagina, and especially if sufficient ovarian tissue can be preserved.[193] When the ovarian portion of the gonad has been preserved, some patients exhibited spontaneous puberty.[188] In these female-reared patients, partial gonadectomy limited to the testicular component must be performed during infancy at the time of reconstructive surgery.[194] Its complete removal is confirmed by the lack of postoperative testosterone secretion. It is important to consider that pregnancy is possible and that normal infants have been delivered.[191,195] Therefore, it is felt at present that most patients with true hermaphroditism should be raised as females. This was confirmed by patients as well, which underlines the significance of early diagnosis.[196]

At adolescence, whatever the sex of rearing, the requirement of replacement sex steroid therapy depends on the functional activity of the residual tissue. Interestingly, at variance with the testicular tissue, the ovary is not at a greater risk of malignancy than the testis is.[197]

## DYSGENETIC GONAD AND NEOPLASTIC DEGENERATION

Most gonadal tumors that occur in intersex patients are of germ cell origin[198] (see also Chapter 175). Their spectrum ranges from benign microscopic lesions to highly malignant, invasive tumors.[199] Most frequently, they are associated with dysgenetic gonads. Reported cases have frequently been detected only histologically in a gonad or streak gonad that has been removed or biopsied. An early stage of malignancy would be intratubular germ cell with in situ signs of seminoma-like modifications.[200] Gonadoblastoma is the most frequent type of benign tumor and is often bilateral. It consists of germ cells and sex cord–derived cells that resemble Sertoli cells or granulosa cells. In patients older than 15 years of age, Leydig cells are also present in the adjacent stroma.[198] Round collections of basement membrane–like material develop and may obliterate the tumor cells. They contain calcifications. This tumor may be seen during childhood, but it is more frequent during early adulthood. It may provoke virilization at puberty with the presence of Leydig-like cells. Its prognosis is excellent if both gonads are excised. A gonadoblastoma in itself poses little threat to the patients, but half of them have associated dysgerminoma and another 10% of them are associated with malignant tumors. Seminoma is the most frequent invasive malignant tumor, which consists of neoplastic germ cells. Metastasis occurs late, and this tumor is radiosensitive. More rarely, an embryonal carcinoma or yolk sac tumor may be diagnosed on the basis of elevated β-hCG or α-fetoprotein plasma levels. In patients with gonadal dysgenesis carrying a Y chromosome and reared as female, the prophylactic management of these gonadal tumors is bilateral gonadectomy or removal of gonadal streaks. In a patient reared as a boy with palpable intrascrotal gonads, regular clinical examination should be performed during adulthood. The conditions associated with gonadal tumors are listed in Table 146-5.

## ABNORMAL GENITAL DIFFERENTIATION

### IMPAIRED GONADOTROPIC ACTION OR FUNCTION

#### Leydig Cell Agenesis or Hypoplasia
This is a rare form of MPH resulting from inadequate fetal testicular Leydig cell differentiation, and, thus, impaired testosterone production. This is a rare cause of incomplete testicular differentiation. Berthezène and colleagues[201] first described the disorder in its complete form, in which the patient is 46,XY but has female external genitalia and cryptorchidism. Owing to normal secretion of AMH by apparently normally differentiated Sertoli cells, there are no müllerian derivatives. The testes are usually intra-abdominal. The patient does not secrete testosterone during hCG stimulation; plasma LH is elevated, but FSH is normal. This was believed to result from normal inhibin secretion by the testis, because FSH levels rise after castration. On histologic examination, the gonads are found to be testes with normal Sertoli cells but no mature Leydig cells. Incomplete forms, also named *Leydig cell hypoplasia*, have been reported.[202] Affected individuals presented a wide phenotypic spectrum, ranging from complete female external genitalia to males with a micropenis. In such cases,

| Table 146-5 | Disorders of Sexual Differentiation Associated with Increased Risk of Gonadal Neoplasm |
|---|---|

Pure gonadal dysgenesis
Mixed gonadal dysgenesis
Dysgenetic male pseudohermaphroditism
Variants of Turner's syndrome with Y cell line
True hermaphroditism
Androgen insensitivity syndrome

partial posterior fusion of the labia and the presence of the vas deferens with epididymis is attributed to partial and transient fetal Leydig cell function.[203–205]

As postulated earlier,[206,207] the failure of Leydig cells to differentiate normally is due to receptor loss-of-function mutations in the LH receptor gene. The human lutropin-choriogonadotropin receptor (hLHCGR) is a member of the G protein–coupled receptors characterized by the presence of seven transmembrane (TM) helixes. Gene dosing reveals four copies of the human hLHCGR in contrast to a single copy in the rat genome.[208] Chromosomal mapping localizes all copies of the human LHCGR to the chromosome 2p16–21 loci. Recessive mutations in the LH receptor gene have been identified as responsible for the condition. Laue and coworkers[209] described the first case of a nonsense cys545-to-ter mutation in exon 11 of the LHCGR gene in two sisters with this disorder. The mutation was an A-to-C transversion at nucleotide 1635, which caused loss of function of the receptor by introducing a stop codon at residue 545 in TM helix 5 of the LH receptor. Surface expression of the truncated gene product in human embryonic kidney cells stably transfected with cDNA encoding the mutant protein was diminished compared with the wild-type gene, and hCG-induced cAMP accumulation was impaired.[210] Most of the hLHCGR mutations are point mutations located in exon 11 of the gene. Deletion and missense mutations in exon 8 have been described, however, in different alleles of the hLHCGR.[211] Latronico and colleagues[212] reported a 46,XY pseudohermaphrodite who presented with female external genitalia and his 46,XX sister who had oligomenorrhea and infertility. Both affected siblings were homozygous for a deletion of nucleotides 1822 to 1827 (CTGGTT), resulting in the deletion of leu608 (CTG) and val609 (GTT) in the seventh TM helix of the LHCGR gene. These findings support the concept that a functional LH receptor is necessary for the early development and multiplication of Leydig cells, if not for their differentiation. Familial cases have an autosomal-recessive inheritance.[203,210]

### Fetal Luteinizing Hormone Deficiency

Alterations in sexual differentiation due to gonadotropin abnormalities are questionable, because there is considerable evidence that chorionic gonadotropin may be sufficient to stimulate early fetal Leydig cell activity. The absence of fetal Leydig cell activity, resulting in micropenis and hypospadias, has been reported, however.[213] Delayed development of hCG/LH receptors has also been suggested as a cause of defective masculinization.[214,215]

## INBORN ERROR OF CHOLESTEROL BIOSYNTHESIS

### 7-Dehydrocholesterol Reductase Deficiency

**Definition** Smith-Lemli-Opitz syndrome (SLOS) is an autosomal-recessive syndrome of multiple malformations and mental retardation[216] that was relegated to the atlases of genetic esoterica for years. A decade ago, the relative inactivity of 7-dehydrocholesterol reductase, the final enzyme of the cholesterol biosynthetic pathway, was identified as a causative factor of SLOS.[217] Therefore, cholesterol biosynthesis is impaired, leading to reduced plasma and tissue cholesterol concentrations, and the accumulation of 7-dehydrocholesterol (7-DHC) in all tissues. The 8-dehydrocholesterol (8-DHC) is also produced in elevated amounts because of the presence in mammalian tissues of an active $\Delta^8$-$\Delta$ isomerase.[218] This finding made SLOS the first true metabolic syndrome of multiple congenital malformations.[219] This is a relatively common inborn error of metabolism, thought to be most common among European Caucasians, with an incidence of 1 in 20,000 to 1 in 30,000 births.[220] The incidence of SLOS in the United States is fewer than 1 in 60,000, and it is even lower in Japan; the number of cases among persons

with African, Asian, or South American ancestry is quite low.[219]

The recent recognition of the important role of cholesterol in vertebrate embryogenesis, especially with regard to the hedgehog embryonic signaling pathway and its effects on the expression of homeobox genes, has provided an explanation for the abnormal morphogenesis in the syndrome. The well-known role of cholesterol in the formation of steroid hormones has also provided a possible explanation for the abnormal behavioral characteristics of SLOS.[219] It is clear that a deficiency of cholesterol, the adrenal hormones' precursor, leads to insufficient synthesis of adrenal and gonadal steroid hormones. The pathogenesis, that is, the developmental pathways involved in the multisystem structural abnormalities and different phenotypes occurring in this syndrome, is not yet fully elucidated, however.

**Clinical Features** SLOS is defined by a constellation of severe birth defects that affect most organ systems. It is characterized by striking craniofacial features, characteristic facial appearance, microcephaly, hypotonia, profound mental retardation, severe failure to thrive, growth retardation, practically constant two to three toe syndactyly, and hypogenitalism or genital malformations.[221] About 20 anomalies are recorded, with a variable frequency and association.[219] A high infant mortality rate is observed. Photosensitivity has been evidenced as a common and prominent feature of SLOS and appears to be ultraviolet activity-mediated.[222] The kinetics of phototransduction are slow in children with SLOS, likely a consequence of altered sterol composition in the cell membranes of the rod photoreceptors.[223] Adrenal insufficiency may also be a previously undetected and treatable manifestation in SLOS.[224] Until recently, the syndrome has been diagnosed only from its clinical presentation. There is a wide range of clinical expression,[219,225] however, and sexual ambiguity is not always present in genetic males.

**Genetics** SLOS is caused by mutations within the human DHCR7 gene. In 1998, the gene encoding DHCR7 was identified and mapped to chromosome 11q13.[226] To date, 91 different mutations have been described.[221] Among these, mutations impairing the activity of the C terminus appear to be the most severe. One mutation affecting the splice acceptor site 5' of exon 9 was frequently found in affected individuals,[227] whereas T93M was a common mutation in Italy, as well as all patients in the world whose ancestors originate in the region of the Mediterranean Sea basin, whether their genotypes were compound heterozygous or homozygous for T93M.[220] These findings are suggestive of either a founder effect or a mutational hot spot. Polymerase chain reaction–based assay has been developed to detect this common mutation.[227] This simple assay allows the diagnosis of atypical cases, carrier testing, prediction of prognosis based on genotype, and prenatal diagnosis. There is one report of the IVS8-1G→C mutation in a person of African ancestry.[220]

**Diagnosis** The discovery of the biochemical defect causing SLOS has resulted in the development of diagnostic tests. Low cholesterol and high concentrations of its direct precursor DHC in plasma and tissues are the diagnostic biochemical hallmarks of the syndrome. Indeed, because about 10% of patients with SLOS have normal serum cholesterol at any age, a blood cholesterol level in itself is not a reliable screening test for SLOS. The plasma sterol concentrations correlate with severity and disease outcome, but there are exceptions.[219] The accumulation of 7- and 8-DHC is very high in the brain, and the 7- and 8-DHC/cholesterol ratios in nonsurviving SLOS newborns were five and eight times the mean values for other organs and tissues, respectively.[228] Prenatal diagnosis has successively been made on high levels of 7-DHC or its metabolites in amniotic fluid,[229] or maternal serum or urine.[230,231] As reported by several authors, one of the early signs of SLOS in a fetus is an abnormally low maternal level of unconjugated estriol. Fetal sonographies can identify multiple suggestive anomalies. The diagnosis is now possible by molecular studies.[232] The simplicity and accuracy of biochemical testing, in particular the level of 7-DHC in the amniotic fluid, however, obviate the need for molecular analysis, except, perhaps, in a rare case with equivocal biochemical results.[219]

**Management** The phenotype is often female in 46,XY-affected infants. The sex of rearing is dictated by the phenotype, and surgical repair is made accordingly. It has also been suggested that prenatal supplementation of cholesterol could potentially arrest some of the adverse consequences of cholesterol deficiency at an earlier stage of development.[233] The first trials of postnatal treatment with cholesterol supplementation have shown improvement of plasma sterol levels, and, apparently, infants and young children with SLOS have shown improvement in growth, behavior, and general health; older children and adults have shown some improvement in development and intellectual functioning.[234] The striking behavioral changes do not correlate with any specific change in the sterol plasma profile, but return when cholesterol supplementation is stopped. This treatment is difficult to administer, and has severe complications (esophageal reflux, nutritional problems, idiopathic hypermetabolism). Despite the overall significant improvements reported at several ages, a recent long-term study (6-year period) suggests that cholesterol supplementation in its current form (50 to 300 mg/kg/day, either in natural form, i.e., eggs, cream, liver, meats, and meat-based formula, or as purified food grade cholesterol with or without supplement in bile acids) does not improve the developmental progress in the area of cognitive, motor, and adaptive skills of children and adolescents with SLOS.[235] This might be due to the fact that the blood-brain barrier is impervious to circulating cholesterol.[236] The use of MRI and ¹H magnetic resonance spectroscopy (MRS)

is an effective way to demonstrate brain structural abnormalities in patients with SLOS, and may prove to be an effective method for the assessment of the effects of cholesterol replacement therapy in the brain.[237] Despite the excitement these developments have elicited among geneticists and biochemists, this syndrome remains relatively unknown to many primary care physicians. Increased awareness of SLOS is needed to identify affected patients so that these patients and their families can benefit from appropriate care and genetic counseling.

## INBORN ERRORS OF TESTOSTERONE BIOSYNTHESIS

Five enzymes are necessary for the synthesis of testosterone from cholesterol (Fig. 146-5).[238] If there is a deficit in any one of these enzymes, testosterone production is impaired and, as a consequence, there is incomplete male sexual differentiation.[239] The first three enzymes are common to both cortisol and testosterone biosynthetic pathways: 20,22-desmolase or cholesterol side-chain cleavage (P-450scc), 3β-hydroxysteroid dehydrogenase (3β-HSD), and 17α-hydroxylase (P-450c17). A deficiency in one of the three will result in both congenital adrenal hyperplasia (CAH) and MPH. The last two, 17,20-lyase or -desmolase (17,20-D) and 17β-hydroxysteroid dehydrogenase/17-ketosteroid reductase (17β-HSD), are obligatory enzymes in the biosynthesis of C19 steroids only, and a defect in either one results only in MPH.

### Features Common to All Inborn Errors in Testosterone Biosynthesis

These disorders are inherited as an autosomal-recessive trait, and both genetic males and females can be affected. Male individuals with an enzymatic defect in testosterone biosynthesis have MPH and also, by definition, a normal 46,XY karyotype and bilateral testes. Because the secretion of AMH

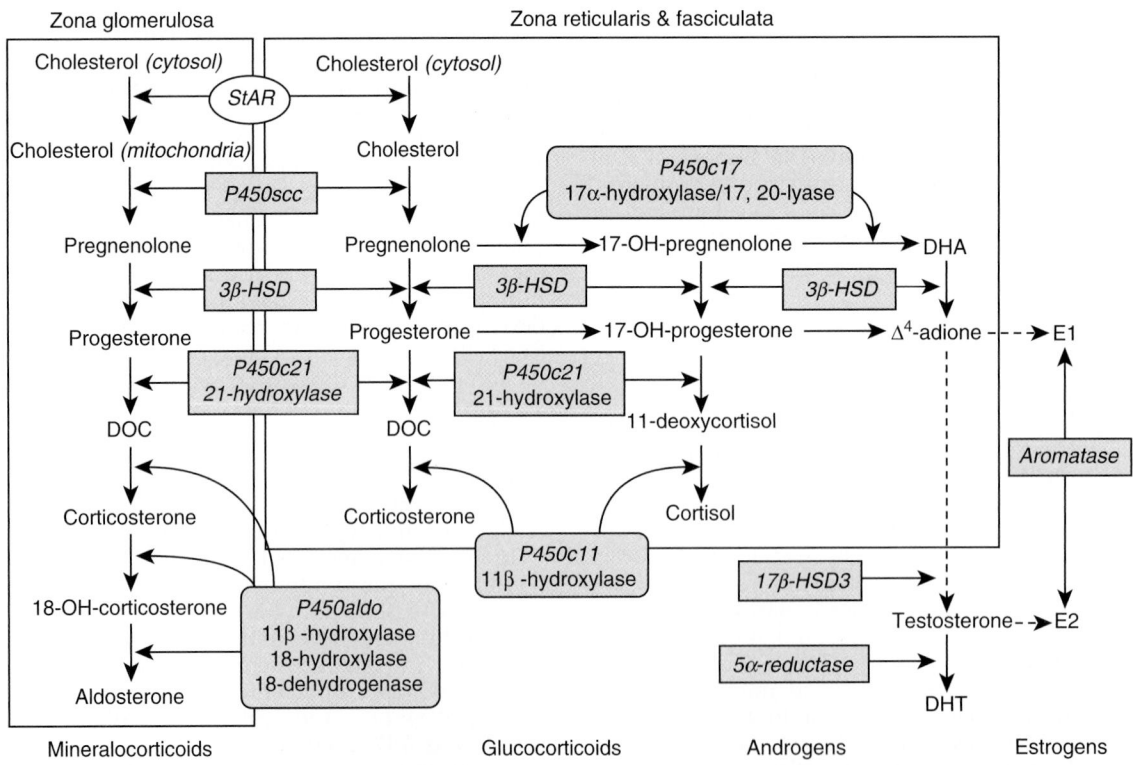

*Figure 146-5*   Steroid biosynthetic pathways in the adrenal glands (with its three functional zones in the *rectangles*) and in gonads (outside the *rectangle*). Five enzymatic steps are necessary for the biosynthesis of testosterone (T): (1) P450scc, cholesterol side-chain cleavage; (2) 3β-HSD, 3β-hydroxysteroid dehydrogenase isomerase; P450c17 for both (3) 17α-hydroxylase and (4) 17,20-desmolase; and (5) 17β-HSD 3, 17β-hydroxysteroid dehydrogenase type 3, located only in the testis. 5α-reductase type 2 reduces T into DHT (dihydrotestosterone) in target organs. Aromatase, P450_AROM, converts androgens to estrogens mainly in the ovary, but also in various tissues. DOC, deoxycorticosterone; DHEA, dehydroepiandrosterone; E1, estrone; E2,17β-estradiol; StAR, steroidogenic acute regulatory protein.

by the Sertoli cells is normal, the internal müllerian ducts (as expected) regress. Commonly, a blind vaginal pouch may be seen, being an embryologic derivative of the urogenital sinus that normally forms the lower third of the vagina. Because the fetal secretion of testosterone is impaired, there may be incomplete wolffian duct development and there is incomplete virilization of the external genitalia.

Ambiguity of the external genitalia ranges from complete female phenotype to pseudovaginal perineoscrotal hypospadias. The aspect of the external genitalia is not pathognomonic, and the phenotypic heterogeneity relates rather to the severity of the enzyme defect.

The activity of 5α-reductase is normal, and hence the metabolism of testosterone in tissues is normal. Androgen receptors are normal, thus the target cells are responsive to the action of androgens (replacement therapy). Finally, fertility is not possible because spermatogenesis is usually absent or defective.

Therefore, identification of the different enzymatic defects in testosterone biosynthesis must be based on biochemical findings and not on phenotype. Familial history, timing and expression of the disorder, and association or not with adrenal dysfunction confer on each defect, however, its own particular profile (Table 146-6).

### Impaired Formation of Pregnenolone
**Pathogenesis**   The first and rate-limiting step in the synthesis of all steroid hormones is the conversion of cholesterol to pregnenolone by the mitochondrial enzyme P-450scc (see Fig. 146-5). This conversion occurs in the inner mitochondrial membrane and requires three distinct chemical reactions: 20α-hydroxylation, 22R-hydroxylation, and scission of the cholesterol side chain at the C20-22 carbon bond.[240,241] It has been thought that three separate enzymes were involved until it was shown that a single cytochrome P-450 is the only protein responsible for all three reactions.[242] This P-450, named P-450scc (for cholesterol side-chain cleavage), is encoded in both the testis and the adrenal[243] by a single gene,[244] designated CYP11A, according to the recent nomenclature.[245] This gene is at least 20 kb long, has nine exons, and is located at chromosome 15q23–q24.[246] P-450scc is a hemoprotein functioning as the terminal oxidase in a mitochondrial electron-transport chain wherein electrons are transferred from nicotinamide adenosine dinucleotide phosphate (NADPH) to a flavoprotein (adrenodoxin reductase), then to an iron-sulfur protein (adrenodoxin), and, finally, to P-450scc.[238] Two pseudogenes for adrenodoxin have been identified on chromosome 20, but they are not transcribed.[247] The functional human genes for adrenodoxin and adrenodoxin reductase have been isolated, cloned, and localized on chromosome 11[247,248] and on chromosome 17,[249] respectively. A total defect in P-450scc activity would result in the failure of both the gonad and the adrenal cortex to produce any steroid compound.

Brutschy[250] first described the disorder and named it the *massive lipoid hyperplasia of the adrenals*. Prader and colleagues[251,252] suggested, however, that the disorder was a defect in the early steps in steroid biosynthesis and later correctly defined the site of the defect.[253] The disorder was first referred to as Prader's syndrome. However, because pathologic examination revealed a considerable lipid accumulation in both the adrenals and the testes,[254,255] it is also called *congenital lipoid adrenal hyperplasia*. A similar disorder has been observed in a strain of rabbit[256] and can be reproduced by the administration to pregnant rats of aminoglutethimide, a compound blocking 20α-hydroxylation.[257]

**Epidemiology and Clinical Features**   This is a rare disease, but it may well be more frequent because it may not be recognized. The real incidence is unknown. Lipoid CAH is common among the Japanese, Korean, and Palestinian Arab populations, but is rare elsewhere.[258] In Japan, a large spectrum of presentation is found with less severe forms in male patients presenting with ambiguous genitalia.[254] This suggests a substantially broader spectrum of clinical findings in this disease than has been appreciated previously.[258] Lipoid CAH is an autosomal-recessive disorder in which the clinical history differs between sexes. Most patients are born after an uneventful pregnancy, and the disease becomes manifest in both sexes in the first 2 weeks of life. The symptoms are those of a complete adrenal insufficiency: vomiting, diarrhea, weight loss, skin pigmentation, and urinary salt loss. Sudden deaths without any clinical symptom of adrenal insufficiency have been reported, as have frequent infections.[254] Some cases can eventually present in midinfancy, causing unexplained infant death that resembles sudden infant death syndrome (SIDS).[259]

In affected 46,XY genetic males, the additional cardinal features are MPH (female phenotype) and sexual infantilism, whereas affected 46,XX females do have normal feminization at the time of puberty, cyclic vaginal bleeding,[260] but subsequently develop polycystic ovaries.[261–264]

**Biologic Findings**   These include very low to unmeasurable levels of all steroid hormones in blood or urine and high levels of plasma adrenocorticotropic hormone (ACTH) and plasma renin activity (PRA),[254,265] which do not rise after stimulation with ACTH or hCG. It is not possible to detect the heterozygous carriers by hormonal evaluation since they exhibit normal responses of adrenal steroid hormones to exogenous ACTH administration.[266]

In vitro studies performed on either testicular tissue or adrenal or testicular mitochondria have shown the incapacity to transform cholesterol into pregnenolone[254,265] due to a single gene,[244] and, in one autopsied patient, the P-450scc protein appeared to be absent.[267]

**Table 146-6**  Main Characteristics of the Five Inborn Errors in Testosterone Biosynthesis

| Enzyme Defect | Salt Loss | Hypertension | PRA* | Selective Marker* | 17KS† | 17-OHCS† |
|---|---|---|---|---|---|---|
| SCC | Yes | No | ↑↑ | No steroid measurable | ~0 | ~0 |
| 17α-OH | No | Yes | ↓↓ | P, DOC, corticosterone | ↓↓ | ↓↓ |
| 3β-HSD | Yes | No | ↑↑ | Δ5-17-OHP, DHEA, DHEA-S | ↑ | ±↓ |
| 17,20-D | No | No | Normal | 17-OHP | ±↑ | Normal |
| 17β-HSD | No | No | Normal | Δ4-Androstenedione | ±↑ | Normal |

*In plasma.
†Urinary excretion. These measurements are rarely performed nowadays, replaced by gas chromatography of steroid excretion patterns.
3b-HSD, 3β-hydroxysteroid dehydrogenase isomerase; 17α-OH, 17α-hydroxylase; 17β-HSD, 17β-hydroxysteroid dehydrogenase type 3; 17,20-D, 17,20-desmolase; DHEA, dehydroepiandrosterone; DHEA-S, DHEA sulfate; DOC, deoxycorticosterone; 17KS, 17-cetosteroids; 17-OHCS, 17-hydroxycorticosteroids; 17-OHP, 17α-hydroxyprogesteron; P, progesterone; PRA, plasma renin activity; SCC, side-chain cleavage enzymatic complex.

**Molecular Genetics**    The concept that the disease represents a genetic defect in the human CYP11A gene has been challenged by the successive molecular studies performed. Although the possibility of adrenodoxin or adrenodoxin reductase lesions in this disorder seemed unlikely because these proteins also serve as electron transports for nonsteroidogenic mitochondrial P-450 that are unaffected in this disease, studies of the cloned human cDNAs for adrenodoxin reductase and adrenodoxin were performed. They showed that these electron transport cofactors were normal, as were all three known factors involved in cholesterol transport to the mitochondria (sterol carrier protein 2, endozepine, and steroidogenesis activator peptide).[268] Thus, attention focused on P-450scc, but no deletion and no mutation could be demonstrated in the coding sequence of the CYP11A gene.[244,268,269] Therefore, the gene lesion in lipoid CAH was not considered at that time to be in the P-450scc system or in any known step upstream from it.

The disease is associated with mutations in the steroidogenic acute regulatory protein (StAR). Sugawara and colleagues[270] mapped the StAR gene to 8p, and a pseudogene to chromosome 13. The StAR gene spans 8 kb in the human, and is organized into seven exons and six introns.[270] It is expressed only in the adrenal, testis, and ovary,[271] not in other tissues, including the brain, that express P-450scc. Furthermore, StAR is absent from the human placenta,[270] where progesterone production is essential during pregnancy. This demonstrates that StAR is an absolute requirement in the rate-limiting step in steroidogenesis, the transfer of cholesterol into the mitochondria.

To date, 34 different mutations in the StAR gene have been recorded in the world literature, overlapping in a few reviews, not including the latest reported.[272] There are 31 exonic missense, nonsense, and frameshift mutations, and four intronic mutations.[272] Mutations can be found in any exon, but mostly in exon 5 to exon 7, and affect the critical StAR-related lipid transfer.[258] Mutations altering the reading frame or causing premature translational termination are common, and result in no StAR activity (i.e., not greater than the StAR-independent background conversion of cholesterol to pregnenolone; see later). All missense mutations are found in the carboxy-terminal region of the 285-amino acid StAR protein, and most are null mutations. The mutation Q258X was found in 80% of affected alleles from Japanese and Korean patients, whereas the mutation R182L was found in 78% of affected alleles from Palestinian patients.[273] Further studies showed that the Q258X mutation can be used as a genetic marker for the screening of Japanese for lipoid CAH and confirmed that the C terminus of StAR plays an important role in the protein's activity.[263] A few mutations, however, are associated with some residual StAR activity (10% to 30%). Thus, it appears to be a good correlation between the severity of the StAR mutations as assessed in vitro and the age of onset of the disease.[274]

Tropic hormones such as ACTH and gonadotropins induce steroidogenesis via cAMP by elaborating intracellular cAMP, which stimulates P-450scc activity in two distinct ways. Chronic stimulation and consequent increased steroidogenic capacity occur. StAR appears to mediate the rapid increase in pregnenolone synthesis stimulated by tropic hormones. StAR increases the flow of cholesterol into mitochondria, thus regulating substrate availability to whatever amount of P-450scc is available. StAR acts on the outer mitochondrial membrane to promote sterol translocation to P-450scc, and the importation of StAR into the mitochondria terminates its action. StAR works solely on or in the outer mitochondrial membrane and undergoes a partially open molten globule conformation while picking up and discharging cholesterol.[275] This is an unusual example of a protein that exerts its biologic activity in a cellular location it occupies only transiently.[275] The mutated StAR gene results in tropic hormone-induced intracellular accumulation of cholesterol in the adrenals and gonads. In the absence of StAR, up to 14% of maximal StAR-induced level of steroidogenesis persists as StAR-independent steroidogenesis.[274,276]

The sex-specific differences in gonadal involvement provide evidence for a two-stage model of the pathogenesis of StAR deficiency, with tropic hormone stimulation causing progressive accumulation of lipids within the steroidogenic cells which ultimately kills them. Bose and colleagues[277] proposed a two-hit model in order to explain the differences in the extent of functional impairment of the testes and ovaries in lipoid CAH. This model considers the persistence of StAR-independent steroidogenesis and the differences in the fetal and postnatal ages at which the testis, adrenal zona glomerulosa, adrenal zona fasciculata, and ovary are stimulated. The model also predicts and explains all of the various clinical manifestations of lipoid CAH, which is spared ovarian steroidogenesis through puberty when the StAR gene product is inactive. This is in marked contrast to the early onset of severe defects in testicular and adrenocortical steroidogenesis, which are characteristics of the disease.[262] The StAR knockout mice mimic all the features of the human disease.[278]

At the time of the first reports, all patients studied had mutations in StAR, suggesting that such mutations were the sole cause of lipoid CAH. StAR mutations were not found, however, in some patients undoubtedly presenting lipoid CAH on clinical and hormonal grounds. Recently, a de novo heterozygous mutation (inframe insertion of gly and asp between asp[271] and val[272]) in the CYP11A gene has been reported in a 46,XY patient presenting adrenal failure and MPH.[279] The patient was somewhat atypical in that he survived for 4 years without replacement therapy. Thus, haploinsufficiency of CYP11A is able to cause the disease, and can also lead to a late onset form of lipoid CAH. A year later, compound heterozygous mutations in the CYP11A gene were reported in a girl with congenital adrenal insufficiency: a maternally inherited R353W mutation and a de novo A189V in the paternal allele.[280] The single amino acid substitution mutation R353W resulted in markedly reduced P-450scc activity while the other A189V was a splicing mutation creating a novel alternative splice-donor site, resulting in a 61 nucleotide deletion that only partially inactivated CYP11A. The mother heterozygote for the inactivating mutation was normal.[280]

**Differential Diagnosis**    The differential diagnosis is made essentially with the presence of congenital adrenal hypoplasia. The diagnosis of lipoid CAH is inherently indirect, because there is no characteristic accumulation of a precursor steroid. Rather easy in genetic males, the diagnosis is made on the association of MPH (normal 46,XY karyotype, cryptorchid testes) and severe adrenal insufficiency. The lack of response to both ACTH and hCG confirms the diagnosis. In females, the differential diagnosis with congenital adrenal hypoplasia is very difficult. In both sexes, LH/FSH levels are greatly elevated at puberty, as in agonadic patients. The findings of markedly enlarged lipid-laden adrenals and downward displacement of the kidney on ultrasound, computed tomography (CT), or MRI scans are most helpful.[281]

**Treatment**    Lipoid CAH is a very severe disease. Of the first 35 patients reported, only 11 have survived infancy. With appropriate glucocorticoid and mineralocorticoid substitutive therapy, however, long survival is possible. The possibility of an overproduction of abnormal sterols and their deleterious effects remains to be clarified.[282] Affected males raised as females require a gonadectomy because of the risk of carcinoma in situ, and additional estrogen replacement therapy at puberty. In genetic female patients, it has been recommended to treat them with oral contraceptives to suppress the high level of LH/FSH to prevent the development of cysts or polycystic ovaries.[261]

## 3β-Hydroxysteroid Dehydrogenase Deficiency

**Pathogenesis**    An enzyme complex is required for the conversion of 3β-5 steroids to the 3-keto-4 configuration seen in all physiologically active C21 and C19 steroids (see Fig. 146-5).

This requires the oxidation of the 3β-hydroxyl group and the shifting of the double bond from the 5–6 to the 4–5 position (5–4 isomerization). Both activities are found in the endoplasmic reticulum and involve a single non-P-450 enzyme, requiring nicotinamide adenine dinucleotide (NAD) as cofactor. Both activities have been found in a single protein of molecular weight (MW) 46,000 isolated from rat adrenals and testes.[283,284] In the testis, 3β-HSD functions primarily to convert Δ[5]-androstenediol to testosterone. Studies in several strains of mice have shown that the 3β-HSD enzyme is encoded by the same structural gene in the adrenal as in the testes but is under separate regulatory control in the two glands.[285] Reduced 3β-HSD activity impairs the production of all classes of steroids: glucocorticoids and mineralocorticoids as well as sex steroid hormones (see Fig. 146-5).

**Epidemiology and Clinical Findings**    Since the first report by Bongiovanni,[286] many patients of both sexes have been described, and the heterogeneity of the clinical presentation is in evidence. When the enzymatic blockade is severe, affected individuals of both sexes present with life-threatening salt loss in infancy. The male infants also have MPH; if they are cryptorchidic,[287] they resemble females with classic 21-hydroxylase deficiency. One may find in the literature the report of a boy with 3β-HSD deficiency that was originally described as having a paradoxical association with 21-hydroxylase deficiency and third-degree hypospadias.[288] It has been claimed that female infants with 3β-HSD deficiency may be paradoxically virilized (clitoral enlargement and variable degree of posterior labial fusion).[289,290] This has been attributed to the peripheral conversion of the increased Δ[5]-precursors through extragonadal, mainly hepatic, fetal 3β-HSD.[286] In the experience of the author and others (Morel, personal communication), however, female patients have little or no ambiguity of the external genitalia. Indeed, the 3β-HSD activity develops only during the second or third trimester,[291] that is, too late to provide enough testosterone for virilization. In both sexes, mild signs of androgen excess (premature pubarche) develop during childhood, due to their high [dehydroepiandrosterone (DHEA)/dehydroepiandrosterone sulfate (DHEA-S)] levels for age.

There is no correlation between the impairment in male sex differentiation and salt wasting. No salt wasting could be detected in some genetic males with mild hypospadias at birth,[289,292,293] nor even in patients with severe hypospadias[294] or complete female phenotype.[295] In contrast, severe salt loss can be observed in both male and female patients with normal genitalia.[296,297] In recent years, it has been said that there is a late-onset or "nonclassical" form of 3β-HSD deficiency,[298] just as there is with 21-hydroxylase deficiency, and that there is a great heterogeneity in both forms.[289] In some patients, the enzyme defect is only expressed as premature pubarche.[292,299]

At puberty, boys with 3β-HSD deficiency may develop gynecomastia.[286,300–302] It was also thought that the testicular defect improves because testosterone production could be sufficient for pubertal virilization.[303] These observations have suggested that the severity of the enzymatic block may be less in gonads than in the adrenals, or vice versa. In fact, sufficient testosterone was produced through the peripheral conversion of the Δ[5]-steroids produced in very high amounts.[303] There are very few reports of the evaluation of gonadal function after puberty.[304] The only patients for whom the long-term evolution after puberty has been reported were a male who fathered two children[305] and a female who was hypogonadal.[297] There is a single report of an affected female presenting with severe salt-wasting 3β-HSD deficiency who had progressive breast development, regular menses, and evidence of progesterone secretion.[306] The same authors describe a genetic male with defective prenatal masculinization and neonatal salt loss who later experienced normal male puberty, as previously seen in males with severe 3β-HSD deficiency.[303] Unhappily, the patient was azoospermic at 18.5 years of age. The discovery of

bilateral accessory adrenal tissue in the ovaries and in the para-aortic region in a female whose definitive diagnosis of 3β-HSD deficiency was made late, at 41 years of age,[307] points out the difficulties of the diagnosis in hyperandrogenic women and the importance of compliance to treatment. The occurrence of hyperplasia of adrenal rests among women with classical congenital adrenal hyperplasia may not be rare, especially among patients with a late diagnosis.

**Biologic Findings**    The pathognomonic biologic finding is the accumulation of all five precursors. In early studies, diagnosis of 3β-HSD deficiency was made on urinary metabolites. Urinary DHEA is not a good discriminator.[286] In infancy, the most preponderant urinary steroids include Δ[5]-pregnenetriol, 16-hydroxypregnenolone, and 16-hydroxy-DHEA.[286] Pregnanediol is variably elevated, but is constantly less than Δ[5]-pregnenetriol. Plasma levels are now more often used. There is an increase in plasma pregnenolone, 17α-pregnenolone, DHEA, its sulfate (DHEA-S), and Δ[5]-androstenediol. Plasma cortisol levels are slightly reduced or normal, but they do not rise sufficiently after ACTH stimulation. Plasma ACTH levels are usually high. Plasma aldosterone may be decreased or normal. In the latter case, PRA is also normal. Paradoxically, the plasma levels of Δ[4]-androstenedione, 17α-hydroxyprogesterone, and even progesterone might be well above normal.[287,294,297,308] As mentioned earlier for the fetus, this has been attributed to (normal) extragonadal conversion of the high levels of DHEA, 17α-hydroxypregnenolone, and pregnenolone.[292,294] Plasma testosterone is decreased but might be in the low-normal range in pubertal subjects. Testicular production of testosterone has been shown by measuring spermatic testosterone levels.[296] The testosterone response to hCG is usually poor in infancy,[294] but may be substantial in pubertal boys.[309] An abnormal rise in either DHEA-S[294] or Δ[5]-androstenediol[296,309] is still observed, however. Finally, obligate heterozygotes for the disease exhibit normal ACTH-stimulated hormonal profiles.[310]

In vitro incubations of testicular tissue have shown the low conversion of labeled pregnenolone or DHEA to Δ[4]-androstenedione and testosterone and the accumulation of Δ[5]-androstenediol.[288,295]

**Diagnosis**    The findings of elevated levels of DHEA-S for age are not sufficient for the positive diagnosis of 3β-HSD deficiency. Elevation of 17α-hydroxypregnenolone is the best marker of the enzymatic defect. It must be emphasized that variable patterns in steroid levels can be observed, depending on the severity of the enzymatic block. In any case, the diagnosis relies more on the abnormally high ratio of Δ[5]/Δ[4] steroids than on absolute levels, both in basal conditions and after ACTH or hCG stimulation. With time, the hormonal criteria for bona fide mild variants of 3β-HSD deficiency proposed by Pang and colleagues[298]—that is, ACTH-stimulated 17α-hydroxypregnenolone and DHEA levels and ratios of 17α-hydroxypregnenolone/17α-hydroxyprogesterone, 17α-hydroxypregnenolone/cortisol, or DHA/Δ[4]-androstenedione greater than 2 SD above pubertal stage–matched normal mean values—have been revised upward or must even be reappraised.[310] Although an elevated ratio of Δ[5]/Δ[4] steroids was for long considered to be the best biologic parameter for the diagnosis of the disorder, in the author and coworkers' experience,[311,312] the most accurate criteria now appears to be plasma levels of 17α-hydroxypregnenolone greater than 100 nmol/L after ACTH stimulation.[313] Others have a much higher mean cut-off.[314] This may be due to assay variations. Genotypically proven heterozygotes can't be identified by hormonal testing.[315]

**Molecular Genetics**    The existence of two human 3β-HSD isoenzymes has long been suspected,[296] then characterized. They differ only by 23 amino acids, and were chronologically designated type 1 and type 2.[316–318] The corresponding genes are named *HSD3B1* and *HSD3B2*, respectively. The complete nucleotide sequence of the two genes shows that both consist of four exons and three introns included within a DNA fragment of approximately 7.8 kb and assigned to chromosome 1p13.1.[319-321] The two genes are highly homologous (93.5% nucleotide identity), but present a specific tissue distribution. The HSD3B1 gene encodes the 3β-HSD type 1 isoenzyme, widely distributed in the placental nonsteroidogenic peripheral tissues.[322] In contrast, the HSD3B2 gene encodes the predominant 3β-HSD type 2 isoenzyme expressed in the adrenal gland, ovary, and testis and its deficiency is responsible for this rare form of CAH.[318]

The first report of the molecular basis of the disease evidenced nonsense and frameshift mutations in the gene of patients with the severe salt-losing form of the disease.[305] These mutations account for an almost complete enzymatic block in steroidogenic tissues. Deficiencies in activity of this enzyme have been attributed to other specific amino acid changes resulting from single base changes within the coding region of the HSD3B2 type 2 gene, whereas type 1 was normal in all cases.[323-325] These observations help to understand why subnormal testosterone levels can be observed in affected boys at the time of puberty; the intact peripheral type 1 3β-HSD isoenzyme converts the five precursors produced in increasing amounts by the testis.

To date, a total of 37 mutations (5 frameshift, 4 nonsense, 1 in-frame deletion, 1 splicing, and 26 missense) have been identified in the HSD3B2 gene in 60 individuals from 47 families suffering from classical 3β-HSD deficiency (personal communication,[312,313]). All nonsense and frameshift mutations introducing a premature termination codon were associated with the classical salt-losing form. The locations of these nonsense mutations suggest that at least the first 318 amino acids out of 371 are required for 3β-HSD activity.[311] Moreover, it could be shown that no functional 3β-HSD type 2 isoenzyme is expressed in the adrenals and gonads of the patients suffering from a severe salt-wasting form of CAH owing to classical 3β-HSD deficiency. A rare presentation in two girls with undiagnosed salt-wasting 3β-HSD in early childhood, and thus delayed diagnosis until a checkup for premature pubarche, has recently been described.[326]

In almost all cases, the functional characterization of HSD3B2 mutations has provided a molecular explanation for the heterogeneous clinical presentation of this disorder. Indeed, these experiments confirm that no functional 3β-HSD type 2 isoenzyme is expressed in the adrenals and gonads of the patients suffering from a severe salt-wasting form, whereas the non-salt-losing form results from specific missense mutation(s) in the HSD3B2 gene, which causes an incomplete loss of enzymatic activity, thus leaving sufficient enzymatic activity to prevent salt wasting.[327] Moreover, various mutations appear to have a drastic effect upon stability of the protein, therefore providing molecular evidence of a new mechanism involved in classical 3β-HSD deficiency.[312] Thus, the elucidation of the molecular basis of 3β-HSD deficiency has highlighted the fact that mutations in the HSD3B2 gene can result in a wide spectrum of molecular repercussions, which are associated with the different phenotypic manifestations of classical 3β-HSD deficiency and also provide valuable information concerning the structure-function relationships of the 3β-HSD superfamily.[311-313]

A "nonclassical form of 3β-HSD deficiency" has been described in children with premature pubarche[299] and in women with hyperandrogenism.[298] Mutations of the HSD3B1 gene have been found in only a few children with premature pubarche.[328-330] In hirsute women, the diagnosis of "nonclassic" 3β-HSD deficiency was made on empirical $\Delta^5/\Delta^4$ steroid ratios after ACTH stimulation.[298] Several molecular studies have not, however, been able to demonstrate mutations in either HSD3B1 or HSD3B2 genes in these women with mild to moderate eleva-

tions in ACTH-stimulated 17α-hydroxypregnenolone levels and particularly in $\Delta^5/\Delta^4$ steroid ratios.[311,331-335]

The functional data described by Moisan and colleagues[312] concerning the sequence variants A167V, S213G, K216E, and L236S, which were detected in children with premature pubarche or in hyperandrogenic adolescent girls suspected of being affected by nonclassic 3β-HSD deficiency, combined with the studies cited, strongly support the conclusion that the so-called nonclassic forms of 3β-HSD deficiency do not result from a mutant 3β-HSD isoenzyme. The question whether this disorder, clinically defined, results from a dysregulation of the enzyme activity itself is still debatable.

**Treatment** Treatment for 3β-HSD deficiency is much the same as for 21-hydroxylase deficiency (see Chapter 124). It includes glucocorticoids and mineralocorticoids at substitutive doses in the severe forms. Glucocorticoids alone are indicated in the late-onset or mild forms with normal and plasma renin activity. At puberty, sex steroid replacement therapy might be needed.

### 17α-Hydroxylase/17,20-Desmolase Deficiency

**Pathogenesis** One of the essential steps in the formation of both cortisol and sex hormones is 17α-hydroxylation of either pregnenolone or progesterone into 17α-hydroxypregnenolone or 17α-hydroxyprogesterone, respectively (see Fig. 146-5). These 17-hydroxylated derivatives are further converted to C19 steroid precursors by cleavage of the C17–C20 carbon bond by a 17,20-desmolase (or lyase) to yield DHEA in the $\Delta^5$-pathway. These two enzymes' activities can readily be distinguished by examination of the pattern of circulating steroid levels in patients apparently lacking either 17α-hydroxylase or 17,20-desmolase.[336] Both enzymes' activities are catalyzed, however, by a single species of cytochrome P-450, named *P-450c17*, which is the key enzyme in leading the choice of pathways from progesterone to glucocorticoids or mineralocorticoids (17α-hydroxylase activity) and from 17α-hydroxyprogesterone to glucocorticoids or androgens (17,20-desmolase activity) (see Fig. 146-5). In contrast to rodent, pig, or chicken,[337] the human enzyme does not have significant capacity to convert the C21 progestin 17α-hydoxyprogesterone to the 19 androgen $\Delta^4$-androstenedione.[338] Thus, in the human testis, the $\Delta^5$-pathway, in which DHEA is the immediate precursor for $\Delta^5$-androstenediol, predominates. Like P-450c21 (21-hydroxylase), P-450c17 is bound to the endoplasmic reticulum and accepts electrons from a flavoprotein distinct from adrenodoxin and does not employ an iron-sulfur protein such as adrenodoxin.[238] P-450c17 has been purified[339] and is encoded by a single gene called *CYP17α*. The gene is 6.6 kb long and has eight exons. It is cloned, sequenced,[340] and localized at chromosome 10q24–q25.[341]

The two activities of P-450c17 can, however, be distinguished genetically (since a deficiency of human 17,20-desmolase exists in which 17α-hydroxylase activity remains normal[336]) as well as physiologically. Indeed, the expression of P-450c17 is regulated hormonally,[342] developmentally,[343] and in a tissue-specific manner. The human adrenal has abundant P-450c17 with considerable 17α-hydroxylase activity but little 17,20-desmolase activity.[344] The latter increases during a prepubertal event called *adrenarche*,[345] an increase that is controlled by yet unknown factors. Both activities are expressed at high levels in the testis,[346] whereas in the ovary they are confined to the granulosa cells.[347] Because the same P-450c17 mRNA is found in the human adrenal gland and testis,[348] the differences in the ontogenic timing and tissue specificity of P-450c17 might "lie in enhancer-like elements regulated by tissue-specific *transacting* factors."[340]

On the basis of clinical presentation and hormonal studies, patients have been identified as having only 17α-hydroxylase deficiency,[349] only 17,20-desmolase deficiency,[336] or both.[350,351]

## 17α-Hydroxylase Deficiency

**Clinical Features**   The disease was first reported in a female by Biglieri and colleagues.[352] The first genotypically male patient was identified 4 years later.[353] Two decades later, 65 cases have been reported in genetic males,[239,349] including 1 case associated with complete gonadal agenesis[354] and about 55 genetic females or presumably 46,XX.[355] In this rare form of CAH, diminished 17α-hydroxylase activity leads to deficient production of both cortisol and sex hormones, resulting in MPH in genetic males and sexual infantilism in genetic females. In both sexes, the other cardinal symptoms are hypertension, hypokalemic alkalosis, and carbohydrate intolerance. Most 46,XY patients have been raised as females because they present with a complete female phenotype and are usually diagnosed at puberty with a presentation similar to that of genetic females (infantilism). In rare cases, the diagnosis was made in infancy,[356] or in childhood on either hypertension or ambiguous external genitalia. The onset and natural course of hypertension vary. Hypertension might be undiagnosed until late in life or progress to malignant hypertension with renal failure.[355] Other complications result from reduced sex steroid secretions, bone age retardation, osteoporosis, and eunuchoidism.

**Biologic Findings**   The relative deficiency in cortisol biosynthesis is reflected by a rise in ACTH, which, in turn, stimulates steroidogenesis up to 17α-hydroxylation. Plasma levels of pregnenolone and progesterone are elevated to a variable extent. The overproduction of deoxycorticosterone (DOC) and corticosterone (>50 times normal) produces sufficient glucocorticoid for survival. DOC produces hypertension. In contrast, aldosterone production is usually suppressed after the DOC-induced sodium retention, expansion of circulating volume, and suppression of plasma renin activity.[357] A block in 18-hydroxylase has been evoked to explain the inhibition of aldosterone secretion,[358–360] but is unlikely because it eventually recovers with dexamethasone treatment.[349,357,361,362] Surprisingly, normal or elevated aldosterone levels (despite suppressed renin activity) have been reported in some patients.[355,363] The reason for this is unclear. Plasma testosterone levels are extremely low with a blunted response to hCG,[359,360] and virtually no androgen is present in testicular tissue.[360] Plasma FSH and LH concentrations are elevated, as they are in agonadal subjects.[359,364]

This is only one defect in testosterone biosynthesis in which obligate carriers and sibling heterozygotes may be identified in biochemical abnormalities (exaggerated responses of DOC and corticosterone[349,364,365] or progesterone[366] to ACTH stimulation).

Early in vitro studies[365,367,368] demonstrated the existence of 17α-hydroxylase testicular defect in 17α-hydroxylase deficiency, but did not investigate the 17,20-desmolase activity. When examined in two patients, it was found that both 17α-hydroxylase and 17,20-desmolase activities were impaired in this disorder.[369] Although the same observation was subsequently made in six other cases,[364] gonadal tissue was, nevertheless, shown to possess 17,20-desmolase activity in another.[370] It is likely that a spectrum of combined or relative deficiency in one of the two enzyme activities may exist.

**Differential Diagnosis**   A typical defect in 17α-hydroxylase is easy to distinguish from other causes of MPH or sexual infantilism on the typical hormonal profile in basal and stimulated states. In hypertensive patients with high aldosterone levels, however, differential diagnosis should be made from glucocorticoid responsive aldosteronism, but in the latter there are no sexual abnormalities. In the exceptional case of testicular adrenal-like tissue associated with 17α-hydroxylase deficiency, the major differential diagnosis is one of the Leydig cell tumors.[363]

**Molecular Genetics**   The first hybridization studies of DNA samples from three patients with classic 17α-hydroxylase deficiency have not demonstrated gross deletions or rearrangements of the P-450c17 gene.[338] Subsequently, a 4 basepair duplication in exon 8, which caused a loss of both 17α-hydroxylase and 17,20-desmolase activities as a result of a reading frameshift and altered C-terminal amino acid sequence has been found in nine cases.[371–373] Molecular genetic studies showed a marked heterogeneity in genetic lesions: mutations, missense, nonsense, deletions, insertions, and a bizarre deletion/insertion.[374–377] These lesions were first classified in two groups[378]: class I mutations that change the primary sequence by a single base change, deletion, or insertion and lead to a P-450 with reduced or absent activities; and class II mutations that lead to stop codons before heme-binding cysteine, which is absolutely required for a functional P-450. A correlation was found between the genetic lesions and the clinical symptoms of 17α-hydroxylase deficiency. To date, about 20 different mutations in 30 individuals have been identified, and all of them are located in the coding region of CYP17. Only one splice site mutation in the CYP17 gene has been described.[379] Several mutations have been reconstructed in human P-450c17 cDNA and expressed in COS cells to characterize the kinetic properties of 17α-hydroxylase and 17,20-lyase activities. The molecular bases of cases clinically reported as 17α-hydroxylase deficiency have turned out to result from complete or partial combined deficiencies of 17α-hydroxylase/17,20-lyase.[377,380–382] These studies also suggest that the essential role of Ser106 is in the active site, rather than in interacting with P-450 reductase, and that electron transfer may play an important role in regulating the 17,20-lyase activity of P-450c17.[375] In partial combined 17α-hydroxylase/17,20-lyase deficiency, there seems to be a threshold of 17,20-lyase enzyme activity for the phenotypic expression of the defect. Greater than 20% of the total normal 17,20-lyase activity should be required for complete virilization in the male.

**Management**   In newborns, sex assignment in affected males is very important. In most cases of 17α-hydroxylase, the individuals have been brought up as females, with adequate psychosocial orientation.[384] Substitutive treatment is only to replace the deficient glucocorticoid production. It suppresses ACTH overproduction (hence, the overproduction of mineralocorticoids) and improves hypertension. Control of treatment is best performed on clinical parameters.[384] The prognosis is better than it is for other forms of CAH because there is no risk of adrenal crisis. Sex steroid replacement therapy is needed after the normal age of puberty.

## 17,20-Desmolase Deficiency

**Clinical Features**   The disorder was first described by Zachmann and Prader.[336] Twelve reported cases of MPH are due to isolated 17,20-desmolase deficiency with normal 17α-hydroxylase activity as evidenced by high levels of 17α-hydroxylated precursors (17α-hydroxypregnenolone and 17α-hydroxyprogesterone) with low androgen production and near-normal cortisol levels.[336] Variable phenotypes are seen, from complete female external genitalia,[385] severe hypospadias,[336,385] to normal male phenotype.[351,385] The disorder has also been described in genetic females.[386,387]

**Biologic Findings**   Cortisol secretion and cortisol metabolites are normal. In plasma, there is an accumulation of C21 precursors (progesterone, 17α-hydroxyprogesterone, and, to a variable degree, 17α-hydroxypregnenolone, pregnenolone, and pregnenolone sulfate),[385] whereas DHEA and Δ4-androstenedione levels are more or less low. Testosterone, Δ4-androstenedione, and DHEA secretions and excretions do not rise normally after adrenal or gonadal stimulation. Zachmann and colleagues[388] have delineated two biochemical forms. In type 1, urinary pregnanetriolone (a unique metabolite of 17α-hydroxyprogesterone) is increased and further rises after ACTH or hCG stimulation, and plasma DHEA and DHEA-S are low and increase little or not at all after ACTH. In type 2, there is no excretion of pregnanetriolone in basal conditions, and plasma DHEA is normal and responds more to ACTH. Accordingly, type 1 would represent an incomplete defect in both the $\Delta^5$- and $\Delta^4$-pathways, and type 2 is a more complete defect but limited to the $\Delta^4$-pathway.

In vitro studies with testicular tissues have demonstrated a defect in the conversion of C21 to C19 steroids,[336] and that the $\Delta^4$-pathway is more affected than the $\Delta^5$-pathway in type 1.[389]

**Diagnosis** In both types, the patients do not present any clinical symptom evocative of the disorder other than incomplete virilization in affected males. The diagnosis is established on systematic hormonal studies. Both ACTH and hCG tests should be performed to bring out the abnormal ratio between C21 and C19 steroids more clearly.

**Molecular Genetics** The association of 17,20-desmolase deficiency with the 18q deletion syndrome had led to the hypothesis that a "structural or regulatory gene for 17,20-desmolase may be located on chromosome 17."[390] Not all patients with 18q deletion have sexual ambiguity, however. Human male sexual differentiation requires production of fetal testicular testosterone, the biosynthesis of which requires steroid 17,20-lyase activity. The existence of true isolated 17,20-lyase deficiency has been questioned because 17α-hydroxylase and 17,20-lyase activities are catalyzed by a single enzyme, microsomal cytochrome P-450c17, and because combined deficiencies of both activities were found in a patient thought to have had isolated 17,20-lyase deficiency. Molecular genetic studies performed on one patient originally reported as having normal 17α-hydroxylase activity found that the patient carried two different mutations in the CYP17 gene, one on each allele.[391] Subsequent reevaluation of this patient, however, showed an age-dependent loss of 17α-hydroxylase activity.[392] Geller and colleagues[393] studied two patients with clinical and hormonal findings suggestive of isolated 17,20-lyase deficiency. They found that the patients were homozygous for substitution mutations (F417C) in the CYP17 gene. When expressed in COS-1 cells, the mutants retained 17α-hydroxylase activity and had minimal 17,20-lyase activity.

Miller and coworkers[394,395] have shown that P-450c17 must be phosphorylated on serine and threonine residues by a cAMP-dependent protein kinase to acquire 17,20-lyase activity. They also found two cases of isolated 17,20-lyase deficiency in whom there were mutations of residues in the proposed redox partner-binding site. These authors proposed a unified view of the regulation of 17,20-lyase activity. The ratio of 17,20-lyase to 17α-hydroxylase activity of P-450c17 would be regulated by the availability of reducing equivalents flowing to the enzyme; this can be increased by increasing the molar concentration of electron-donating redox partners, such as P-450 oxidoreductase or possibly cytochrome $b_5$, as appears to be the case in the gonads.

This hypothesis is in agreement with molecular in vitro studies in a 17,20-lyase deficient patient carrying a nonsense mutation, which gave no functional product, and a missense mutation causing the synthesis of a protein that retains 17α-hydroxylase activity but almost no 17,20-lyase activity. Experiments based on the use of an electron donor independent from enzyme binding (iodosobenzene) demonstrated that the addition of electrons restores, at least in part, in vitro 17,20-lyase activity, with no significant influence on the 17α-hydroxylase activity. This study supports the concept that the electron transfer system plays a major role in the differential regulation of the two P-450c17 activities.[396]

The previously described CYP17 mutation, F417C, was found in another case of isolated 17,20-desmolase deficiency.[397] A second CYP17 mutation (E305G) caused isolated 17,20-desmolase deficiency by selectively altering steroid binding.[398] In the other cases of isolated 17,20-desmolase deficiency, mutations found in the CYP17 gene affected the activities of both enzymes. In several other cases, no mutation was found (see later).

It is possible that additional (unknown) factors regulating androgen biosynthesis are involved or that previously apparently isolated 17,20-desmolase deficiency can with time be complicated by additional 17α-hydroxylase deficiency, as reported in two patients.[351,392]

**Management**
Except for surgical repair of the external genitalia and sex steroid substitution therapy at the normal age of puberty, there is no need for other treatment. Since an age-dependent loss of 17α-hydroxylase activity may occur, however, the patients diagnosed as having pure 17,20-desmolase deficiency should be reevaluated at time intervals, because of the risk of developing hypertension.

**Multiple P-450 Deficiencies: The P-450 Oxidoreductase Deficiency**
The association of 21-hydroxylase deficiency with a deficiency in 17α-hydroxylase and 17,20-desmolase[399,400] or 17,20-desmolase alone has been reported as a new variant of CAH. No mutations have been found, however, in the CYP17 and CYP21 genes, which encode these P-450 enzymes. Because these are combined defects of microsomal mixed-function oxidases, the possibility of a defect in the flavoprotein NADPH-cytochrome P-450 reductase has been tested in one case and excluded.[400] In fact, this form of CAH is, indeed, due to mutations in P-450 oxidoreductase (POR),[401] with and without Antley-Bixler syndrome,[402] a skeletal abnormality primarily affecting head and limbs. POR is a flavoprotein that donates electrons to all microsomal P-450 enzymes, including the steroidogenic enzymes P-450c17 (CYP17A1), P-450c21 (CYP21 A2), and CYP51A1. POR is encoded by a single gene (POR), long ago isolated and mapped to chromosome 7q11.2.[403]

Affected girls are born with ambiguous genitalia, but their circulating androgens are low and virilization does not progress. Affected boys have normal genitalia at birth,[404] but present micropenis later on (personal data). Diagnosis can be made on steroid analysis.[405] The distinctive steroid metabolite "metabolone" has been proposed by the author as the primary parameter for diagnosis, at least in the forms not associated with fibroblast growth factor receptor 2 (FGFR2) mutations (found in Antley-Bixler syndrome). Excessive maternal excretion of epiallopregnanediol with low estriol may be prenatally diagnostic for oxidoreductase.[404]

Management, in both sexes, includes glucocorticoids if needed, and inevitable induction of puberty by sex steroids. In boys, micropenis should be treated as soon as possible.

**17β-Hydroxysteroid Dehydrogenase-3 Deficiency**
**Pathogenesis** The last step in testosterone biosynthesis is the conversion of $\Delta^4$-androstenedione to testosterone, which is performed by an enzyme previously named 17-ketosteroid reductase (17-KSR). This is the only reversible step in testosterone biosynthesis. This is the reason why this enzyme is also called 17-oxidoreductase, or 17β-hydroxysteroid dehydrogenase (17β-HSD), which describes the conversion of testosterone back to $\Delta^4$-androstenedione. The enzyme also catalyzes the interconversion of DHEA and $\Delta^5$-androstenediol in the $\Delta^5$-pathway and that of estrone and estradiol (see Fig. 146-5). This enzymatic complex of MW 35,000[406] is an NADPH-dependent non-P-450 enzyme located in the endoplasmic reticulum. The gene encoding the human placental 17β-HSD has been cloned.[407] This single gene, which encodes two mRNAs,[408] lies on the long arm of chromosome 17.[409] The product of this gene, however, is the estradiol 17β-hydroxysteroid dehydrogenase. In fact, the 17β-HSD reaction is catalyzed by several isoenzymes in the gonads and also in multiple extragonadal tissues (see later). Our knowledge in this field expands very fast and at least 11 types of 17-HSDs can be distinguished to date.[410] A nomenclature for 17β-HSD was proposed, based on genetic identity of

the enzymes and their functionality.[411] The canonical name for 17β-HSD, approved by the Human Genome Organization (HUGO) Gene Nomenclature Committee, became HSD17Bn where "n" stays for the enzyme number. HSD17B6 and HSD17B9 have not as yet been identified in humans.[410]

In 17β-HSD3 deficiency, only sex steroid synthesis is altered, and the adrenal function is normal. Neher and Kahnt[412] have observed the enzymatic defect in their in vitro studies of testicular tissue from patients believed to have partial androgen insensitivity syndrome (AIS), but the defect was first identified as such by Peretti and colleagues.[413] The disorder was first reported in a pubertal patient.[414] Since then, 77 other individuals have been described,[239,415] with 23 other cases in the Dutch population,[416] 25 patients in the French,[417] a large Arab kindred of 25 cases or more,[418,419] and likely more to date.

In vitro studies have confirmed a major impairment in the reduction of $\Delta^4$-androstenedione to testosterone. The oxidation of $\Delta^4$-androstenedione in testosterone is affected in diverse ways; it either proceeds normally or is also deficient but is always less than the reductive step. The defect is also expressed on the $\Delta^5$-pathway; however, owing to increased 3β-HSD activity, the testicular testosterone biosynthesis is shifted toward the $\Delta^4$-pathway.[415] In contrast, peripheral 17β-HSD activities are normal, as evidenced by studies of the fate of injected labeled testosterone[414] or in vitro studies on skin.[420] The suggestion that the enzymes in the testis and liver or peripheral tissues were under a different regulatory control was confirmed by molecular studies.

**Molecular Genetics** The first enzymatic complex identified (a soluble NADH-dependent non-P-450 enzyme isolated from the placenta) is encoded by a duplicated gene (17β-HSD type 1) lying on the long arm of chromosome 17. The product of this gene, however, is only estradiol 17β-HSD. The long search for the gene responsible for the enzymatic defect has led to the identification of four other 17β-HSD genes bound to the endoplasmic reticulum. The 17β-HSD2 gene (on chromosome 16q24), coding an enzyme expressed also in the liver, small intestine, endometrium, and placenta, promotes mainly the oxidative pathway of both testosterone and estradiol. The 17β-HSD3 gene (located on chromosome 9q–22) encodes an NADPH-dependent enzyme that is capable of catalyzing the reduction of both androgens and estrogens in the testis.[421] Furthermore, 17β-HSD4 (expressed in the liver, heart, prostate, and testis) and 17β-HSD5, which possesses higher homology with the aldo-ketose reductase family, have been described.[416,422]

The enzyme involved in the testicular biosynthesis is the 17β-HSD3, which is expressed almost exclusively in the testis and not in the ovary. Mutations on the HSD17B3 gene are associated with the human disease.[422] The gene spans at lesat 60 kb, has 11 exons, and is located on chromosme 9q22. The inherited disease causes a form of MPH that is rare in the general population but frequent among a highly inbred Arab population in the Gaza Strip. To date, 19 different mutations, spread from exons 3 to 11 of the gene, have been defined in affected individuals from different families from Western Europe,[416] the United States, Brazil,[423] and the Middle East.[419,424] This recurrence of some mutations (325+4:A(→T, 655-1;G(→C, R80G, N74T, N130S, A188V) as well as de novo recurrent mutations (326-1;G→C, P282L) supports the conclusion that the genetic basis of the disease is determined by multiple founders and recurrent de novo mutations.[416] An interesting founder effect is represented by the point mutation R80Q in exon 3 common among Arabs in various parts of Israel (from Gaza, Jerusalem, and Lod-Ramle) and some with Druze ancestors from Syria and Lebanon.[419]

**Clinical Features** The natural history is remarkable (Fig. 146-6). Deficiency in the 17β-HSD3 gene gives rise to genetic males with female external genitalia who, however, do virilize extensively at puberty. The phenotype is almost always female in character;

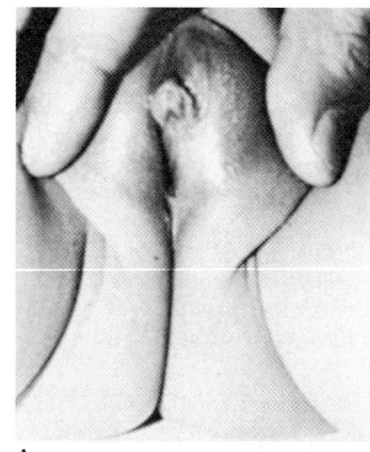

A

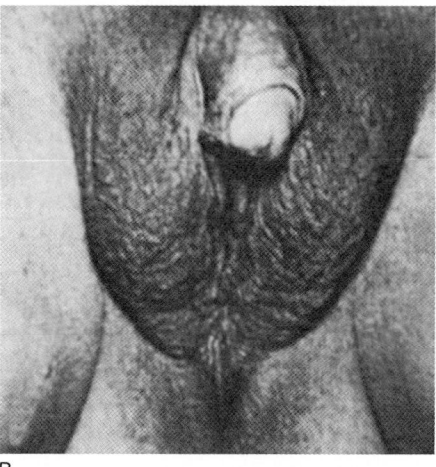

B

***Figure 146-6*** **A** and **B,** Patients with 17β-hydroxysteroid dehydrogenase (17β-HSD) deficiency. Note the almost complete female phenotype seen at birth and the marked virilization that occurs spontaneously in adulthood. Note the gonadal bulges in the labioscrotum (testes).

the affected males are born with female genitalia or a slightly enlarged clitoris.[415,418,420] Male wolffian duct–derived internal genitalia are found, however. At the normal age of puberty, the patients present rapid and intense virilization, with[414] or without[415] gynecomastia. This is believed to be caused mainly by extragonadal peripheral conversion of the high circulating levels of both $\Delta^4$-androstenedione and estrone into testosterone and estradiol, because testicular testosterone formation (as estimated by spermatic testosterone levels) remains low.[415] On the other hand, despite intrafamilial variation,[420] it appears there is a progressive restoration of the 17β-HSD activity in adulthood in the highly inbred population of the Gaza Strip.[425] In addition, there is a remarkable heterogeneity in the clinical presentation of genotypically identical siblings or cases, phenotypic variations in external genitalia appearance, from female phenotype to MPH, and even only idiopathic gynecomastia and hypogonadism, the latter reported as a late-onset form of the disorder.[426]

Although 17β-HSD3 deficiency is a rather rare genetic disorder, it is an underestimated cause of MPH because it is often mistaken for complete AIS at birth (about 20 cases in three large series[416,417]), for gonadal dysgenesis (on low testosterone levels, but $\Delta^4$-androstenedione and AMH/müllerian-inhibiting substance [MIS] not measured), or abnormalities of LH receptor.[417]

In contrast to what was hypothesized in the literature earlier, affected females, whether homozygotes or compound heterozygotes, are asymptomatic.[416,417,419] Indeed, 17HSDB3 is expressed in the testis but not in the ovary.

**Biologic Findings** Most patients with 17β-HSD deficiency are diagnosed at puberty or as adults.[239,415] In those patients, the marker of the enzymatic block is the accumulation of $\Delta^4$-androstenedione in blood, whereas plasma testosterone is low or near normal. The testicular origin of the $\Delta^4$-androstenedione overproduction is shown by the fact that the high $\Delta^4$-androstenedione levels are not suppressed by dexamethasone,[415,418] but are reduced by exogenous administration of either testosterone or estrogens. Plasma levels of LH are constantly elevated; those of FSH are normal or subnormal.[415] Owing to this hypergonadotropic stimulation, plasma levels of 17α-hydroxyprogesterone are also increased; those of DHEA are slightly increased[415]; and plasma $\Delta^5$-androstenediol is decreased.[420] Plasma levels of ACTH, glucocorticoid hormones, and mineralocorticoid hormones are normal. In spermatic blood, there is a marked increase in $\Delta^4$-androstenedione and estrone, and a moderate increase in testosterone precursors such as pregnenolone, 17α-hydroxyprogesterone, and DHEA, whereas testosterone levels are considerably low.[415]

**Differential Diagnosis** In pubertal or adult patients, the diagnosis of 17β-HSD deficiency is easy, because the hyperplastic Leydig cells secrete predominantly $\Delta^4$-androstenedione. The abnormal $\Delta^4$-androstenedione/testosterone ratio is diagnostic, even in the basal state. In infants or children, a differential diagnosis should be made with AIS.[416] Indeed, in infants, the clinical presentation is much the same as it is in the AIS female, that is, near-normal female phenotype, no clinical symptoms other than gonads palpable in the inguinal canal (which are classically mistaken for ovarian hernia), 46,XY karyotype, and normal basal levels of all measured steroid hormones, except for low testosterone levels for age in early infancy.[415] In the absence of sufficient gonadotropic stimulation, the prepubertal testis does not produce excessive amounts of $\Delta^4$-androstenedione. Thus, in contrast to pubertal subjects, baseline levels of $\Delta^4$-androstenedione are normal in prepubertal patients, and a diagnosis can only be made by finding a high ratio of $\Delta^4$-androstenedione to testosterone (>1) after hCG stimulation. Because the defect is expressed only in the testis, at no age can it be diagnosed on hormonal findings after castration.

**Management** Due to the practically complete lack of virilization, infants with 17β-HSD deficiency are usually given a female sex assignment at birth. Most often, the diagnosis is made at or after puberty, with the frightful consequence of severe virilization in a female. Thus, it seems advisable to recommend prepubertal castration and estrogen replacement therapy with this disorder. Management of the disorder has become a matter of controversy, however.[427] Rösler and Kohn have observed a spontaneous change at puberty to the male gender in several individuals of a large Arab kindred.[418] On this basis, and owing to the good response to exogenous testosterone therapy in infancy,[418] these authors propose raising all affected genetic males in the male gender. The context and advantage of being a male in this particular Arabic society in Israel probably promote the aforementioned situation. In addition, because most of the patients with 17β-HSD deficiency are naturally brought up as females and remain cryptorchid until their teens, particular attention should be given to the possible development of a malignancy in those who change their gender role to male at puberty and retain their testes.[428] The question of whether exposure to high $\Delta^4$-androstenedione levels in utero leads postnatally to disturbed female gender identity in later life is not settled, for the most part. The best management is dictated by the age at diagnosis and also by the familial and cultural context.

## IMPAIRED METABOLISM OF TESTOSTERONE

### Steroid 5α-Reductase Deficiency

**Pathogenesis and Clinical Findings** Steroid 5α-reductase deficiency is a rare disorder, except in some areas of the world. This recessive-autosomal disorder refers to 46,XY genetic males who have incomplete virilization of their external genitalia and two testes. This condition was first described as *perineoscrotal hypospadias*, because the infant usually presents with a severely hypoplastic penis with the urethra opening on the perineum.[429] It was later established that the disorder resulted from a deficiency in steroid 5α-reductase, the key enzyme for the conversion of testosterone to dihydrotestosterone (DHT), the metabolite responsible for normal external masculinization.[430,431] The receptors of the external structures respond most efficiently to DHT, and genitalia are predominantly female when only testosterone is present (Fig. 146-7). The wolffian duct derivatives are normal, but the prostate is rudimentary.[432] The müllerian ducts normally regress, which is a feature critical for the diagnosis. The disease is inherited as autosomal recessive and is best described in several Dominican kindreds[431] and in small clusters in some parts of the world.[424] Different phenotypes (hypospadias, isolated micropenis) can be seen in the same kindred.[433] The typical patient, however, presents at birth with a female external phenotype and male internal genital structures. Clitoral enlargement may be present. There is a urogenital sinus with a perineal opening. Since wolffian differentiation occurs normally, there is vas deferens with seminal vesicles, and epididymis terminates in a vaginal pouch of variable size. As in AIS, regression of the müllerian ducts occurs because Sertoli cells produce normal or elevated levels of AMH/MIS. At birth, these individuals are believed to be girls and are often raised as such. Virilization occurs at puberty, frequently with a gender role change. Indeed, they present phallic enlargement, descent of the testes, and deepening of the voice without gynecomastia. This paradox is explained by a normal increase in the activity of the 5α-reductase isoform-1, which, together with normal pubertal testosterone increase, results in sufficient DHT to complete the virilization of these genetic males. Facial and body hair often remains scanty, however, but balding has not been reported. There is no prostatic tissue. Spermatogenesis is incomplete, but can be normal if the testes are descended.[434] The activity of the enzyme may decrease rapidly with age, but residual activity could account for the fact that even in older patients low but detectable concentrations of DHT are present. At all ages, the affected enzyme causes a decrease in hepatic 5α-reductase, which leads to low

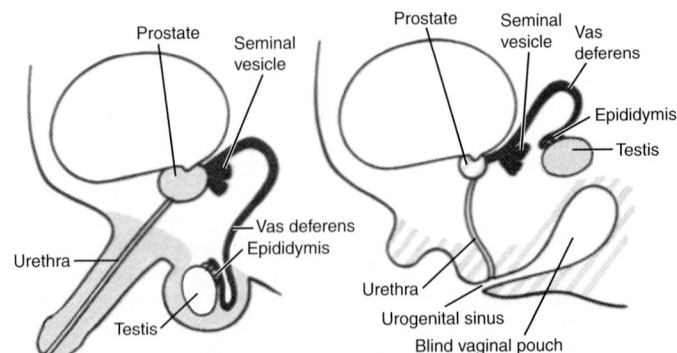

**Figure 146-7** Schematic representation of the genitalia of a normal male on the left and that of a subject with 5α-reductase deficiency on the right, illustrating the relative roles of testosterone and dihydrotestosterone (DHT) in male sexual development (organs dependent on testosterone in *black* and that dependent on DHT in light *stippled* areas). (Adapted from Imperato-McGinley J, Peterson RE: Male pseudohermaphroditism: The complexities of male phenotypic development. Am J Med 61:251–272, 1976.)

excretion of 5α-allotetrahydrocortisol and androsterone, allowing biochemical detection of the abnormality.

**Diagnosis** The biochemical abnormalities characteristic of 5α-reductase deficiency are clearly described in adults in whom the endocrine characteristics demonstrate the lack of formation of DHT or its metabolites. This is easily shown at puberty with a plasma basal testosterone/DHT ratio above 35, a diminished urinary ratio of 5α-reductase/5β-reductase steroid metabolites, and decreased urinary androstanediol excretion. Only recently has the diagnosis been made in infants or children born with ambiguous genitalia.[435] The typical pattern is that of normal or raised concentration of plasma testosterone with an increased testosterone/DHT ratio only after hCG stimulation[436] or testosterone administration.[437] This parameter might, however, be normal at birth and become abnormal with age.[438] The ratio of tetrahydrocortisol/5α-tetrahydrocortisol appears to be more discriminatory in infancy, but 5α-tetrahydrocortisol requires sensitive and specific detection methods.[438] Decreased production of DHT from testosterone in cultured genital skin fibroblasts may also aid the diagnosis.[431]

**Molecular Genetics** The enzyme 5α-reductase is a key enzyme in the process of masculinization of external genitalia in the male. Studies have confirmed the presence of two functional 5α-reductase isoenzymes with distinct biochemical, genetic, and pharmacologic properties. The disorder is caused by mutations in a 5α-reductase enzyme with an acidic pH optimum. Genetic analysis has excluded the 5α-reductase type 1 gene (SRD5A1) as being responsible for the disorder.[439] The 5α-reductase type 2 gene (SRD5A2), which contains five exons and four introns, has been cloned and mapped to chromosome 2 band p23.[440] A deletion in SRD5A gene has been found[441] in affected subjects from the small tribe in New Guinea previously diagnosed by Imperato-McGinley and colleagues.[442] Analysis of the molecular genetics and biochemistry of the enzyme from 25 families from various parts of the world has shown 18 mutations in 11 homozygotes and a high proportion of compound heterozygotes, which suggests that the carrier frequency of mutations in this gene may be higher than was previously thought.[440] Later on, systematic screening of a skin specimen from boys with isolated hypospadias showed that 7 of 81 (8.6%) boys carried a mutation in at least one SRD5A2 gene, whereas 2 patients had mutations in both alleles. The mutations identified were A49T, L113V, and H231R. The A49T mutation in 5 patients was the most common (71%), and it was generally present in less severe forms of hypospadias. Apparently, neither the A49T nor the L113V mutation has been previously reported in association with 5α-reductase-2 deficiency and, to date, they have only been identified in cases of isolated hypospadias. This finding suggests that a partial deficiency of 5α-reductase activity and inadequate levels of DHT in the fetal urethra may be sufficient to cause the phenotype of hypospadias without other clinical features of 5α-reductase deficiency.[443] Mutations have been described in all five exons, and range from a single point defect to deletion of the entire gene. Correlation between the severity of the syndrome and a particular gene has not been observed.[434] Mutations in the SRD5A2 gene has been found in 3 out of 81 patients with micropenis.[444] The R227Q mutation was present in all three (one homozygote, two compound heterozygotes with Y26X or G34R). One study found differences in the mode of transmission for the disease, a patient being found to be homozygous, but only for the paternal mutation. Because this finding could not be explained on the basis of nonpaternity or a chromosomal abnormality, uniparental disomy was suggested, and confirmed.[445] This appears as an alternate mechanism whereby this enzymatic disorder can derive from a single parent.[445]

**Management** Classically, even in subjects born with a clitoris-like penis, bifid scrotum, and severe hypospadias, the penis enlarges at puberty with significant muscular development. It is believed that because brain receptors probably respond to testosterone, children often choose to be male at that time.[442,446] If recognized early, infants can now be treated specifically with DHT and respond well.[438] Thus, if the diagnosis is made during the neonatal period, a male sex for rearing is recommended, and androgen therapy can be used to enhance penile growth and facilitate surgical repair of the genitalia. In such patients, further virilization can be expected at puberty, and fertility is theoretically possible. Those diagnosed later in life, who have an unambiguous female gender identity, should undergo an orchiectomy and receive estrogen therapy at the time of puberty. There are reports, however, of patients who were raised as females and who underwent a reversal of gender role behavior (and married) at adolescence.[447-449] Finally, paternity by intrauterine insemination with sperm from a man with 5α-reductase-2 deficiency demonstrates that spermatogenesis can occur in this disorder.[450]

## ANDROGEN RECEPTOR DEFECTS: SYNDROMES OF ANDROGEN RESISTANCE

These disorders are caused by end-organ resistance to the action of androgens. Male sexual differentiation and development proceed under the direct control of testicular androgens, testosterone, and DHT. The latter is formed at its site of action in embryonic tissues of the prostate and the external genitalia and causes the male development, whereas the development of the wolffian ducts into epididymis, vas deferens, and seminal vesicles requires testosterone. The actions of both testosterone and DHT are mediated by a specific intracellular receptor, the androgen receptor (AR). The AR belongs to a superfamily of ligand-responsive DNA-binding transcription factors that includes the other steroid receptors, the receptors for thyroid hormones, vitamin D, and retinoid acid, and also several so-called orphan receptors, for which the ligand remains to be found.[451] Once androgen binds to the AR, the receptor is activated and is then found predominantly in the nucleus, where it binds to chromosomal DNA target sites (androgen-response elements) and initiates transcription. Messenger RNA is synthesized and exported to the cytoplasm, where ribosomes translate it into new proteins, which ultimately leads to the androgenic effect. Mutations in the AR cause abnormalities in transformation of the steroid-receptor complex, its binding to DNA, or its transcription exportation or translation. Receptor or postreceptor defects cause various androgen resistance syndromes (also named AIS) that have a wide range of clinical presentations ranging from subjects with a complete female phenotype to undervirilized infertile men with normal male genitalia.[452] In all cases, the müllerian ducts have normally regressed (a feature that is essential for the diagnosis).

### Complete Androgen Resistance or Complete Form of Androgen Insensitivity Syndrome
**Clinical Features** Complete androgen resistance or complete form of androgen insensitivity syndrome (CAIS), formerly named *syndrome of Morris* or *testicular feminization* (a term which should be abandoned) is a distinct entity. All the patients are 46,XY (chromatin negative). Their testes are capable of normal testosterone secretion, and they also have induced a normal fetal regression of the müllerian derivatives. Patients come to medical attention at pubertal age as phenotypic girls with primary amenorrhea and during infancy because of an inguinal hernia containing a palpable gonad that turns out to be a testis. At puberty, these patients have a normal female habitus, well-developed breasts, and a small clitoris (Fig. 146-8). Pubic and axillary hair is sparse or absent. The vagina is short and blind ending, but in many CAIS patients, surgical elongation of the vagina is not indicated.[453] No cervix is seen at gynecologic examination; the uterus and

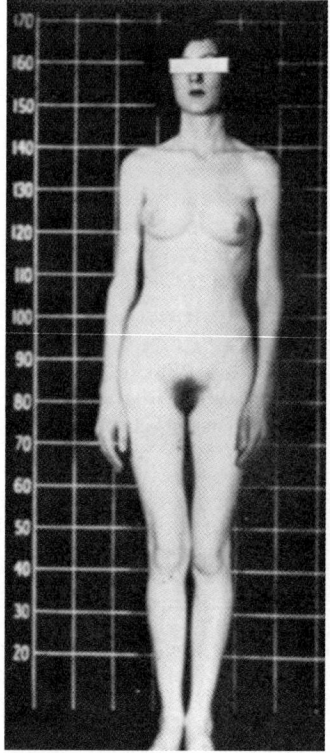 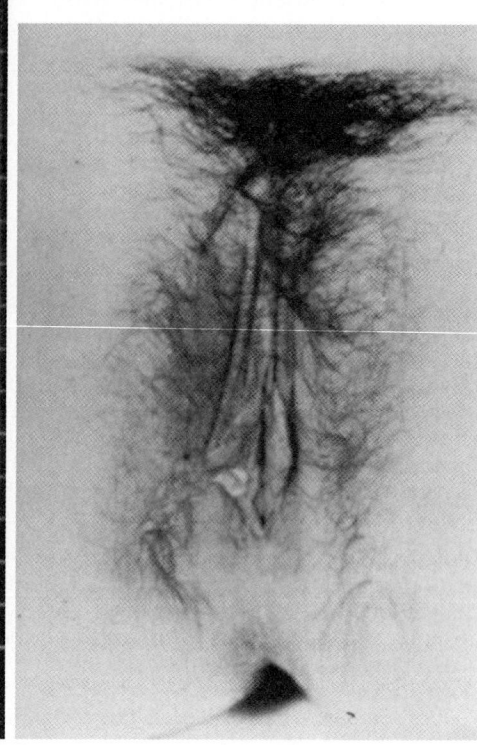

*Figure 146-8* Patient with the syndrome of complete androgen resistance. Note the paucity of pubic hair, the normal female breast development, and the relatively tall stature.

A                    B

fallopian tubes are absent. The testes are variably located: intra-abdominal, inguinal, or in the labia majora. There are no spermatogenesis or wolffian duct structures. Because of their apparently normal female phenotype, these patients are always reared as girls. They are sterile, but, in most cases, capable of satisfactory sexual intercourse without vaginal corrective surgery.[454]

**Laboratory Findings** The typical hormonal profile with normal or elevated testosterone levels and high LH levels is found at puberty.[455,456] During the neonatal transient phase of activation of the hypothalamic-pituitary-testicular axis, plasma testosterone values are below the normal range in most CAIS infants at 30 and 60 days of age, and plasma LH values are low.[457] These findings suggest that the postnatal testosterone rise requires the receptivity of the hypothalamic-pituitary axis to testosterone. In contrast, the testosterone response to hCG is in the range or greater than that of normal infants.[458] Plasma AMH levels are high in infants, children, and even pubertal boys.[459]

Determination of AR binding in cultured genital skin fibroblasts has shown biochemical heterogeneity. Three situations can be seen. Some patients have a complete absence of androgen binding and are called receptor negative, whereas others with quantitatively low or normal binding are called receptor positive.[460] Among the latter cases, the AR may be defective, because the complex with the steroid is not stable and cannot be normally translocated to the nucleus.[461] These are named *qualitatively abnormal receptors.*

**Molecular Genetics** Although family studies have pointed to the existence of the AR on the X chromosome for many years, the AR was only first cloned in 1988 by several groups.[462–465] The AR gene (>90 kb) has eight exons and encodes a protein with three functional domains: a central domain encoded by exons B and C (or 2 and 3), involved in the binding of the receptor to chromosomal DNA; a C-terminal domain encoded by exons D–H (or 4–8), responsible for the binding of androgen to the receptor; and an N-terminal domain encoded

by the large exon A (or 1), involved in transcriptional regulation to androgen. The AR gene has been localized to the q11–12 region of the long arm of the X chromosome.

Molecular analysis of the AR has been studied extensively. Various strategies have been used: Southern blotting with various probes, amplification of the coding regions of the AR gene by polymerase chain reaction (PCR), and screening of amplified fragments by single-strand conformation polymorphism (SSCP) or sequencing putative mutants fragments of the entire gene.[466,467] Results show a great heterogeneity in molecular lesions. Androgen insensitivity can exceptionally result from a deletion of the AR structural gene.[468] Various point mutations have been demonstrated in critical domains of the gene. As expected, mutations have been found in the steroid-binding domain of receptor-negative patients and in the DNA-binding domain in receptor-positive patients.

The molecular basis of the androgen insensitivity has been reviewed.[452,466,469,470] Complete or gross deletions of the androgen receptor gene have not been frequently found in persons with complete AIS, whereas point mutations at several different sites in exons 2 to 8 encoding the DNA- and androgen-binding domains have been reported in both partial and complete forms of AIS, with a relatively high number of mutations in two clusters in exons 5 and 7. The number of mutations in exon 1 is extremely low, and no mutations have been reported in the hinge region, which is located between the DNA-binding domain and the ligand-binding domain. It is still difficult to make close correlations between the clinical forms and the molecular lesions. In addition, in some patients with AIS, no lesions have been identified in the AR gene.

In addition, two polymorphisms in the AR gene have been described: an intronic Hind III,[471] and the other concerning a repeated CAG sequence in exon 1.[472] After adequate studies of an index case and the nuclear family, these polymorphisms can be used prenatally or postnatally to recognize affected individuals and heterozygous females carrying mutant AR genes.[473]

Arg607-Gln and Arg608-Lys point mutations in the DNA-binding domain of the AR gene have been associated with male breast cancer in partial AIS or with early development of the germ cell tumor in complete AIS.[474]

Another disorder is associated with modifications of the AR. The identification of a mutation of the AR gene in Kennedy's disease or X-linked amyotrophic lateral sclerosis (ALS), a rare form of progressive lower motor neuron degeneration that is also associated with clinical signs of androgen insensitivity and infertility,[475] raises the possibility that androgen function may be disturbed in other motor neuron disorders (including ALS). The molecular cause of spinal and bulbar muscle atrophy is the increased size (>40 residues) of a highly polymorphic CAG repeat sequence in the first exon of the AR gene, coding for a polyglutamine tract.[476,477] A relationship between CAG repeat length in the AR gene and the risk of defective spermatogenesis has also been suggested.[476,477]

Finally, the finding of a submicroscopic deletion of the AR gene in patients presenting with complete AIS and mental retardation has led to the postulate that the deletion involves, in addition to the AR gene, one or more neighboring genes that are implicated in nonspecific mental retardation.[478]

**Management** Even in complete AIS, it is necessary to confirm the initial female assignment and to remove the testes because of predisposition to gonadal tumors.[474] There is some controversy among pediatricians with regard to the best time for castration in patients diagnosed in infancy. Because it is inevitable, the author believes that early orchiectomy has more positive psychological advantages than a delayed decision for surgery. Estrogen replacement therapy is required at the time of puberty.

### Incomplete Form of Androgen Insensitivity Syndrome

**Clinical Features** A certain percentage of patients present with partial androgen resistance (partial androgen insensitivity syndrome, or PAIS) and show incomplete fetal masculinization. Among them, there is a clinical heterogeneity, occasionally within the same pedigree.[479–481] The most frequently encountered variant in neonates is a phenotypic male with perineoscrotal or penile hypospadias, a small vaginal pouch seen at genitography, a hooded phallus and preputial folds unfused ventrally, and a bifid scrotum that occasionally contains gonads. The testes are small with arrested spermatogenesis and normal Leydig cells. Other presentations have been reported, such as male phenotype with microphallus, perineoscrotal hypospadias, idiopathic gynecomastia with infertility, or isolated azoospermia. The term *Reifenstein syndrome* was formerly used to describe this less severe variant of AIS, but it comprises a heterogeneous group of disorders, including patients with 5α-reductase deficiency and partial androgen insensitivity. Other variants described as the syndromes of Lubs, Rosewater, or Gilbert-Dreyfus[481] likely fit in the group of incomplete AIS, but recognition of these various presentations as distinct syndromes should no longer be made. All these patients may also have scanty pubic and axillary hair and, at puberty, show some, but not complete, virilization and develop gynecomastia.

It is remarkable that phenotypic variations are absent in families with CAIS,[453] but distinct phenotypic variations are relatively frequent in families with PAIS.[482–484]

**Molecular Genetics** Variable defects in androgen binding have been reported in PAIS. Qualitative androgen binding abnormalities appear to be a good guide to the presence of AR abnormalities in PAIS. On the other hand, it appears likely that PAIS may result from anomalies in other as yet unidentified genes or postreceptor defects when androgen binding is normal. The molecular basis of PAIS has been studied in many patients. Single amino acid mutations have been found in both the steroid-binding domain[485] and the DNA-binding domain.[454,486,487] The number of mutations described is so large that a database of AR gene mutations has been established and regularly updated.[488] This database is a compre-

hensive listing of mutations published in journals and meetings' proceedings. Most mutations are point mutations identified in individual patients with AIS. The database includes information regarding the phenotype, the nature and location of the mutations, and also the effects of the mutations on the androgen-binding activity of the receptor. The total number of reported mutations has risen from 309 to 374 in the past year,[489] and from 374 to 605 in the past 5 years.[488]

Complete or gross deletions of the AR gene have not been frequently found in persons with CAIS, whereas point mutations at several different sites in exons 2 to 8 encoding the DNA- and androgen-binding domains have been reported in both partial and complete forms of AIS, with a relatively high number of mutations in two clusters in exons 5 and 7.[469] Interestingly, the number of mutations in the large exon 1 is extremely low, because only 11 mutations in exon 1 have been identified in 15 individuals with AIS.[490] No mutations have been reported in the hinge region. Postzygotic de novo mutations do occur at the expected high rate of an X-linked-recessive mutation in AIS,[491] and somatic mosaicism is of particular clinical relevance for genetic counseling in this disorder.[492] Finally, there is no apparent correlation between phenotypes and genotypes, because the same M780I mutation in exon 6 in the same family can result in clinical phenotypes characteristic of complete or partial AIS.[482] Therefore, the molecular defect of the AR gene may not alone predict the phenotype in families with AIS.

**Diagnosis and Management** The diagnosis is easier if there is a family history. In sporadic cases, the diagnosis of partial androgen insensitivity remains difficult to assess, and other causes of MPH with normal AMH activity must first be ruled out.[473,481] Diagnosis is likely when both plasma testosterone and LH concentrations are elevated, as can be seen in the first trimester of life and at puberty. Additional evidence comes from the poor responsiveness to the intramuscular (IM) injection of long-acting testosterone (e.g., 100 mg/m$^2$ four times at 15-day intervals), which should bring the penile length into the normal range. This test is difficult to interpret in most cases, however, except when there is a total lack of response. Unfortunately, it also remains to be proved that a positive response in infancy correctly predicts normal penile development at the time of puberty, because an underdeveloped penis is a frequent and severe complication in patients reared as males. Therefore, a male sex assignment may only be chosen if the phallus is developed enough to allow corrective surgery. For some authors, male sex rearing is acceptable only if the penis is significantly responsive to stimulation by intramuscular testosterone and if the vaginal cavity is too small that it precludes easy immediate corrective female-oriented surgery. Therefore, when androgen insensitivity is suspected, the best choice remains to rear the child as a female, with immediate reconstructive surgery. The testes are removed at the same time or at puberty. Estrogen and progesterone replacement therapy is necessary at puberty. Progesterone is needed to avoid the risk of estrogen-induced breast tumors. At present, unless there is an obvious family history with X-linked transmission, the diagnosis of partial androgen insensitivity is problematic. Procedures looking for gene defects directly or by the restriction length polymorphism technique in affected families[473] will, it is to be hoped, allow rapid early diagnosis if appropriate laboratory facilities are immediately available.

### Androgen Resistance in Phenotypic Males

Androgen receptor mutations are rare in patients with micropenis.[493] Moreover, some androgen resistance might be manifest in men with normal male genitalia but azoospermia. Some present with gynecomastia. Plasma levels of testosterone and LH are often elevated, but are normal in some of those men whose only symptom is infertility. Androgen receptors are decreased,[494] but no molecular defect has been described to date. These cases likely represent the extreme end of the PAIS spectrum. Because infertility is not necessarily associated with androgen resistance,[484] however, the frontier between mild androgen resistance and normality will remain difficult to establish until reliable diagnostic tools are developed.

## IMPAIRED ANTIMÜLLERIAN HORMONE PRODUCTION OR ACTION

### Persistent Müllerian Duct Syndrome
**Clinical and Anatomic Features**   The persistent müllerian duct syndrome (PMDS) is a rare form of MPH characterized by the persistence of müllerian derivatives in otherwise normal males. The situation is usually discovered in patients undergoing surgical repair of cryptorchidism or inguinal hernia (at various ages in the past, but now more often in children because of earlier treatment of undescended testes). This situation is also referred to as *hernia uteri inguinalis*.[495] The testis and hernia (containing the uterus and tubes) are always palpable together because of the tight attachment of the testis to the fallopian tube. Sometimes the two testes are in the same inguinal canal (a situation known as *transverse testicular ectopia*, which is almost never encountered except in cases of PMDS).[70] More rarely, the persistence of a uterus and fallopian tubes is discovered in apparently normal males during laparotomy or herniorrhaphy. In such cases, both testes are in an ovarian position and no inguinal hernia can be palpated. The testes of these patients are usually normal, except for cryptorchidism. The failure of testicular descent would result from mechanical restraint by the abdominal müllerian organs.[70] Vasa deferentia are present, as well as an epididymis, so that fertility is possible if normal spermatogenesis occurs. Paternity has been recorded.[496] This disease is often familial and presents as an autosomal-recessive trait, an inheritance pattern that correlates with the etiology of the disorder.

**Pathogenesis and Molecular Genetics**   Normal regression of müllerian ducts normally occurs at 8 to 10 weeks in utero under the action of the AMH, also called müllerian-inhibiting factor (MIF) or substance (MIS). This glycoprotein dimer is secreted by the Sertoli cells of the immature testis. AMH can be detected in male serum until puberty.[497] AMH is a member of the transforming growth factor (TGF)-β superfamily. Its gene has been cloned,[498] and located at 19p13.3–p13.2.[499]

The AMH receptor (AMHR or AMHR2) is a serine/threonine kinase with a single transmembrane domain that belongs to the family of type 2 receptors for TGF-β-related proteins. Type 2 receptors bind the ligand on their own but require the presence of a type 1 receptor for signal transduction. Imbeaud and colleagues have cloned the AMH receptor gene and determined that the AMHR2 gene is located on 12q13.[500]

PMDS, characterized by lack of regression of müllerian derivatives, uterus, and tubes in otherwise normally masculinized males, is a genetically transmitted disorder. The phenotype can be produced by a mutation in the gene encoding AMH[501–504] or by a mutation in the AMH receptor.[500] These two forms of PMDS are now referred to as types 1 and 2, respectively. The type of genetic defect could be predicted from the level of serum AMH, which is very low or undetectable in PMDS type 1 patients and at the upper limit of normal in type 2.[505] Both types are consistent with an autosomal-recessive mode of transmission. Whereas mutations in the AMH gene are extremely diverse, about two thirds of the patients with AMH receptor mutations had a bp deletion in exon 10 on either one or two alleles (i.e., homozygous or heterozygous for this mutation).[506] As a result, this mutation is implicated in approximately 25% of patients with PMDS.

**Management**   Therapy involves orchiopexy and hysterectomy. The free segment of the spermatic cord is too short,

however, and a partial hysterectomy leaving the cervix intact is recommended to avoid injury to the vas deferens embedded in the uterine wall. This procedure allows the descent of the testes after an extensive dissection of the cord to preserve fertility.[507] More recently, it has been suggested that optimal surgical management is orchiopexy, leaving the uterus and fallopian tubes in situ.[508] Meticulous proximal salpingectomy and hysterectomy are indicated only in patients whose müllerian structures limit intrascrotal placement of the testes. In the past, the testes of these patients have not been considered to be predisposed to form tumors. The occurrence of testicular cancer has been reported, however, in nine patients with PMDS.[509] Whether the risk for testicular cancer is increased in this disorder or is the same as for cryptorchid patients is still an open question. Thus, orchiectomy has been advised for testes that cannot be mobilized to a palpable location.[508] On the other hand, it is not necessary to perform testicular biopsy to detect a tumor if the testis is in the scrotal position, because an impalpable tumor can be localized by ultrasound.[510]

## MALE PSEUDOHERMAPHRODITISM ASSOCIATED WITH MALFORMATIONS

### Ambiguous Genitalia Associated with Multiple Congenital Anomalies
The wolffian ducts may atrophy at the mesonephros stage, so that the epididymis, ductus deferens, seminal vesicle, ureter, and kidney are lacking. After it has reached the cloaca, resorption of the wolffian duct can lead to absence of the epididymis, ductus epididymis, and proximal ductus deferens. Failure of development of the wolffian duct structures and rete testes is reported in as many as 1% of patients with cryptorchid testes, but is probably rarer in patients with descended testes.[511]

In the syndrome of *lethal acrodysgenital dwarfism*, failure to thrive, facial dysmorphism (anteverted nostrils and micrognathia), syndactyly, postaxial polydactyly, Hirschsprung's disease, cardiac and renal anomalies, and ambiguous genitalia may be found. Many of the features are similar to those of the Smith-Lemli-Opitz syndrome, but it has been proposed that they are separate entities.[512]

The Opitz G/BBB syndrome, also known as the hypospadias-dysphagia syndrome or telecanthus with associated abnormalities, is associated with midline abnormalities such as cleft lip, laryngeal cleft, heart defects, hypospadias, and agenesis of the corpus callosum.

In Crigler-Najjar syndrome, ambiguous genitalia are found in association with cardiomyopathy and mental retardation.

Numerous other syndromes combine dysmorphology and abnormalities of sexual differentiation, including hypospadias with or without cryptorchidism and without persistence of the müllerian duct[118] (Table 146-7). The mechanism is unknown. It may involve so-called contiguous gene syndromes because of the gene location on the sex chromosomes or some unknown autosomal control of embryonic development.

## IATROGENIC CAUSES

### Maternal Ingestion of Progestins and Estrogens
Animal evidence suggests that ingestion of progesterone by a mother can feminize a male fetus, but proof of this tendency in the human is incomplete. Some studies, however, have suggested a link between hypospadias and maternal intake of progestins.[513] Diethylstilbestrol (DES) may have effects on a male fetus, such as meatal stenosis, epididymal cysts, and hypoplasia of the testes.[514] One case of MPH has been reported, but there is little evidence to link DES with feminization of an otherwise normal male fetus.

### Endocrine Disrupters
Considerable attention has been given in the past few years to the possibility that man-made chemicals (xenobiotics) in the

**Table 146-7** Male or Female Pseudohermaphroditism Frequently Associated with Birth Defects

**Hypospadias or ambiguous external genitalia, frequent in:**
Aniridia-Wilms' tumor association
Exstrophy of bladder sequence (epispadias)
Exstrophy of cloaca sequence
Fetal trimethadione or hydantoin effects
Frasier's syndrome
Opitz syndrome
Rapp-Hodgkin ectodermal dysplasia syndrome
Rieger's syndrome
Robinow's syndrome
Schinzel-Giedion syndrome
Short rib polydactyly, Majewski type
Triploidy syndrome
4p– syndrome
13q– syndrome

**Bicornuate uterus or double vagina frequent in:**
Exstrophy of cloaca sequence
Frasier's syndrome
Johanson-Blizzard syndrome
Mayer-Rokitansky-Küster-Hauser syndrome
Trisomy 13 syndrome

environment may pose a hazard to human reproductive health (see Chapter 145).[515] The endocrine-disrupting effects of many xenobiotics can be interpreted as interference with the normal regulation of reproductive processes by steroid hormones. One review[516] concluded that there is evidence that xenobiotics bind to androgen and estrogen receptors in target tissues, to androgen-binding protein, and to sex hormone–binding globulin. Although environmental chemicals have weak hormonal activity, their ability to interact with more than one steroid-sensitive pathway provides a mechanism by which their hazardous nature can be augmented. A given toxicant may be present in low concentration in the environment and, therefore, be harmless. However, we are not exposed to one toxicant at a time, but, rather, to all of the xenobiotics present in the environment. Therefore, numerous potential agonists and antagonists, working together through several steroid-dependent signaling pathways, could prove to be hazardous to normal sex differentiation.[516]

## UNCLASSIFIED FORMS OF ABNORMAL SEXUAL DEVELOPMENT IN MALES

### Hypospadias
Tertiary or perineoscrotal hypospadias is a feature of many of the syndromes discussed in this chapter, and such a finding should cause concern that there is an abnormality of sex differentiation. In most cases, however, first-degree or coronal or glandular hypospadias in an individual with an otherwise normal male phenotype appears to have no endocrine basis; the condition is sometimes referred to as *idiopathic MPH* or *simple hypospadias*. Hypospadias is generally explained in terms of malformation of the urethra. For Mouriquand,[517] hypospadias can be defined as a hypoplasia of the tissues forming the ventral aspect (ventral radius) of the penis beyond the division of the corpus spongiosum. The incidence of this anomaly is between 1 and 8 in 1000 births,[518] and incidence rates have been widely reported to be increasing in the past 2 decades.[515] It is significantly associated with increasing maternal age (older than 35), and this is more evident in severe cases.[519] There are reports of cases of minimal hypospadias associated with an abnormality of the AR, but the prevalence and importance of such a finding in a wider range of patients is unknown. Steroid 5α-reductase activity is normal.[520] Although some mutations in the WT1, AR, or 5α-reductase genes have been found in systematic mutational

screenings for these candidate genes (see earlier), they seem to be uncommon causes of isolated hypospadias.[521]

There seems to be a controversial issue in the definition itself of hypospadias, since in one study an etiology was found in one third of 63 cases of "severe" hypospadias: complex genetic syndromes (17%), chromosomal anomalies (9.5%), and 1% involving AIS, vanishing testes syndrome, or 5α-reductase-2 deficiency, respectively.[522] In some authors' opinions, including this author, these "severe" hypospadias with a proven etiology would have been included in disorders of sexual development (see later). Interestingly, in the 16 families with familial hypospadias, no etiology was found, except one case due to AIS

### Cryptorchidism
Some degree of cryptorchidism is common in many of the syndromes noted in this chapter. There is a more than 25% chance of presence of an intersex problem in patients with undescended testes and hypospadias, and the frequency increases if the disorder is bilateral and hypospadias is severe. AR gene alterations are not associated with isolated cryptorchidism.[523] Although there is a marked increased incidence of cryptorchidism in hypogonadotropic hypogonadism, cryptorchidism can occur as an isolated finding. The pathophysiology of isolated undescended testes is still a matter of debate.

### Micropenis
Microphallus without hypospadias results from a heterogeneous group of disorders. Strictly speaking, the condition is not categorized as a defect in male sexual differentiation, but it often results from fetal testosterone deficiency. In any case, it frequently generates debate with regard to the appropriate sex assignment. A course of androgen therapy (see later) is mandatory to enlarge the penis to the normal range for age and, hence, to evaluate the responsiveness of the penis to testosterone, which will help to predict the pubertal growth potential of the phallus.

## FEMALE PSEUDOHERMAPHRODITISM: MASCULINIZATION OF AN XX FEMALE

### FETAL SOURCE OF THE CAUSE OF FETAL MASCULINIZATION

#### Excessive Production of Androgens by the Fetal Adrenal: Congenital Adrenal Hyperplasias
Virilizing congenital adrenal hyperplasias (CAHs) are the most frequent causes of FPH. The enzymatic defects that cause female masculinization involve only three enzymatic steps on the biosynthetic pathway of cortisol and aldosterone (see Fig. 146-5). The specifics of these conditions are presented in Chapter 124 and are only briefly discussed here for the sake of completeness.

##### Steroid 21-Hydroxylase Deficiency
This is the most common type of CAH. Salt loss occurs in approximately 80% of cases, whereas virilization of the female fetus is by definition a constant feature in the classic forms. The degree of virilization varies, however, and is usually described in five stages according to Prader.[524] Virilization might be quite important (Fig. 146-9); even a female fetus with a severe form may present with an apparently normal male phenotype, except for bilateral cryptorchidism. Some children have moderate virilization at birth with clitoral enlargement and a partial posterior fusion of the labioscrotal folds; they may be misdiagnosed unless a careful genital examination is performed. In the nonclassic forms (e.g., late-onset, acquired, cryptic), the affected females are, by definition, not virilized at birth. The disorder may then cause virilization later in childhood or adolescence and is a cause of pseudoprecocious puberty rather than sexual ambiguity.

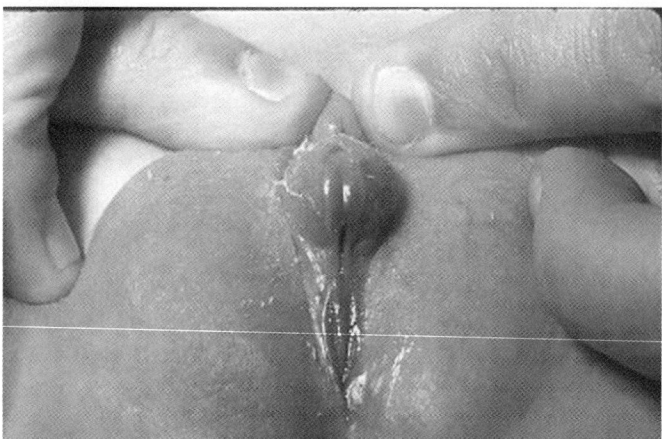

*Figure 146-9* Genitalia of a female infant with 21-hydroxylase deficiency. Note the enlarged phallus, the common urogenital sinus below, and the pigmented fused labioscrotal folds.

Diagnosis is made on the marked accumulation of the steroid proximal to the enzymatic block, that is, 17α-hydroxyprogesterone. In most congenital forms, the elevation is so large that it is diagnostic. Management is straightforward, and the decision about the sex of rearing is easy to make. The child should be brought up in her female gender, because she will develop normally and have a normal reproductive female life with glucocorticoid and mineralocorticoid replacement therapy and appropriate plastic surgery. This disease is the only one in which there is a possibility to prevent the occurrence of sex ambiguity. Prenatal treatment can be offered to the mother of a CAH girl following pregnancy. Suppression of the overproduction of androgen by the fetal adrenals can be achieved by giving the mother an appropriate dose of glucocorticoid (a daily dose of 20 μg of dexamethasone per kilogram of maternal weight, split in two or three doses, is currently advised).[525] Such treatment should be initiated after careful genetic counseling, however, and monitored by highly specialized teams of pediatric endocrinologists, biologists, and gynecologists.

### 11β-Hydroxylase Deficiency

11β-hydroxylase deficiency usually causes a severe virilization of an affected female fetus, associated with salt retention, potassium loss, and hypertension from the overproduction of 11-deoxycorticosterone (DOC). The hormonal marker of the disorder is the selective elevation of 11-deoxycortisol (compound S), although there is a variable elevation in several other precursors in relation to the intensity of ACTH overproduction. Adrenal crisis is rare, because salt loss is not a feature. Glucocorticoid deficiency might, however, cause hypoglycemia and shock under stress or at the time of initiation of the replacement therapy.

### 3β-Hydroxysteroid Dehydrogenase Deficiency

This enzyme defect is associated with salt loss and potassium retention. Virilization of female fetuses may occur in severe forms but is always minimal (hypertrophy of clitoris, small labial fusion). As discussed earlier, this is caused by the conversion of the five steroids produced in excess by the adrenals into more active Δ⁴ androgens by intact 3β-HSD type 1 enzyme in peripheral tissues.

In all three CAHs, the association of ambiguous genitalia and the occurrence of a salt-losing syndrome are orientating. Karyotyping should be performed in all cases. Visualization of a uterus and ovaries remains the safest and more rapid way to identify genetic females, but might be difficult to interpret in newborns. Together with the appropriate hormonal evaluation, this allows rapid diagnosis, correct female assignment, and appropriate treatment to avoid further virilization.

Eventually, a differential diagnosis must be made in preterm infants, with the exceptional situation in which isolated hypertrophy of the clitoris is associated with persistent high concentrations of adrenal fetal zone androgens.[526]

### P-450 Aromatase Deficiency (Placental Aromatase Deficiency)

Aromatase, also called estrogen synthetase, catalyzes formation of aromatic C18 estrogens from C19 androgens (see Fig. 146-5) and constitutes a unique gene family (CYP19 gene) in the cytochrome P-450 superfamily.[245] This enzyme is localized in the placenta and ovary or testes as well as in various extragonadal tissues. It plays a key role in the control of reproductive function by regulating the production of estrogens. The entire gene spans more than 123 kb of DNA. Only the 30-kb 3' region encodes aromatase, whereas a large 93-kb 5' flanking region serves as the regulatory unit of the gene. CYP19 gene comprises 10 exons. The translational initiation site and the termination site are located in exon 2 and exon 10, respectively. The aromatase gene is mapped to 15q21.

The first case of FPH related to placental aromatase deficiency was described in 1991.[527] Maternal and fetal virilization and then infant FPH were observed. Estrogen production was greatly diminished. In vitro studies during gestation and in vitro studies post partum indicated a marked decrease in the ability of the fetoplacental unit to aromatize androgens to estrogens; the aromatase deficiency was apparently confined to the placenta. Further studies showed that the placental aromatase deficiency depended on a genetic defect in the fetus, resulting in the expression of an abnormal larger protein molecule with 29 extra amino acids[528] that was caused by a point mutation at the splicing site of intron 6 in the aromatase gene.[529] The parents were heterozygotes for the mutation, suggesting that the disorder is an autosomal hereditary disease. Conte and colleagues[530] reported a phenotypically similar infant with ambiguous genitalia in whom aromatase deficiency was persistent in childhood. At puberty, androgen levels increased, but plasma estrone and estradiol levels remained extremely low, despite elevated plasma levels of gonadotropins, and there was development of large follicular cysts. Direct analysis of genomic DNA from ovarian fibroblasts and blood lysates indicated that the patient had two different single base mutations in the coding region of the P-450_{AROM} gene in exon 10.[530,531] The hypothesis was made that aromatase deficiency may also be responsible for polycystic ovary syndrome (PCOS), which presented in this patient.[531] Since then, four other cases presenting with a similar phenotype—the association of marked virilization in both the mother and the newborn—and hormonal features have been reported.[532-535] A seventh case has recently been reported, with a follow-up of 7 years, and two novel mutations.[536] The authors' finding was mainly that, in girls, aromatase deficiency results in a decrease of the negative feedback of both serum LH and FSH, which can be detected as early as the second week after birth and persists up to the sixth month of life, and of FSH during the rest of prepuberty.[536]

Mutations were different in each of the seven reported cases of aromatase deficiency in genetic females. There was missense, nonsense, or stop codon mutations in exons 9 (two) and 10 (three), and two splicing mutations, one between exon and intron 3, and the other between exon 6 and intron 6.

The cardinal features of this syndrome are a consequence of P-450 aromatase deficiency: (1) The fetal masculinization in this syndrome can be ascribed to defective placental conversion of C19 steroids to estrogens, leading to exposure of the female fetus to excessive amounts of testosterone; (2) the pubertal failure, mild virilization, multicystic ovaries, and hyperstimulation of the ovaries by FSH and LH are the result of the inability of the ovary to aromatize testosterone and androstenedione to estrogens; and (3) the striking delay in bone age at 14 2/12 years of age supports the notion that estrogens, in contrast to androgens, are the major sex steroid driving skeletal maturation during puberty.

## MATERNAL SOURCE OF THE CAUSE OF FETAL MASCULINIZATION

### Excessive Androgen Production by the Mother

Masculinization of external genitalia of a female fetus can occur if it is exposed to maternal-produced androgens crossing the placental barrier. Internal genitalia are normal. This concerns female offspring of mothers with CAH,[537] adrenal tumors,[538] ovarian tumors,[539] or hCG-dependent luteoma of pregnancy. It has been suggested that some cases of virilization of newborns may be attributed to maternal cysts that regress after delivery. Because more responsive to the action of androgens than the mother, the fetus may virilize while the mother escapes these effects. Investigation of the mother for abnormal steroid secretion must be performed immediately after delivery.

Familial glucocorticoid resistance (FGR) is characterized by increased cortisol secretion without clinical signs of hypercortisolism, but with manifestations of androgen and mineralocorticoid excess. The condition is mainly cause by mutation in glucocorticoid receptor (GR). FGR due to a novel mutation in the GR gene is a newly recognized cause of FPH, through maternal androgen excess.[540]

### Iatrogenic: Maternal Exposure to Androgen and Progestins

Girls whose mothers were treated with androgenic substances are vulnerable to virilization. In the past, the medication consisted of progestational agents given to attempt to prolong a pregnancy threatened with abortion. Such medications could cause posterior fusion of the vagina, scrotalization of the labia, and even some degree of fusion of the urethral folds if given before 13 weeks of gestation, but the medications would only cause clitoral enlargement when administered later.[541] Compounds that caused virilization included 19-nortestosterone (norethindrone, ethisterone, norethynodrel), testosterone,[542] and danazol.[543] Several cases of diethylstilbestrol have also been reported to cause virilization for unknown reasons. In addition, the risk of development of clear cell adenocarcinoma of the vagina and cervix should preclude the use of diethylstilbestrol in pregnancy. The actual incidence of such virilization is low (<3%), and the effects depend on the medication, dose, and duration. Iatrogenic fetal virilization has become less frequent since hormonal treatment is no longer advised during pregnancy.

## FEMALE PSEUDOHERMAPHRODITISM ASSOCIATED WITH VARIOUS MALFORMATIONS

A number of birth defects may also include features that mimic mild virilization, such as an enlargement of the clitoris in genetic females. However, this represents nonandrogen-dependent causes of FPH (also called nonspecific FPH). The pathogenesis of the anomalies should be considered in the context of teratologic conditions owing to embryonic defects. Indeed, the common embryonic derivation of the internal sexual ducts and the excretory system predisposes to concurrence with anomalies of the kidney and intestines. Genital abnormalities are frequently associated with imperforate anus, renal agenesis, and other congenital malformations of the intestine and urinary tract (some of them being incompatible with life). It should be remembered that renal failure, which is often associated with pyelonephritis, is a frequent feature and that the child presents then with salt loss, which may confuse the picture with CAH. Hormonal and anatomic studies are rapidly orientating the diagnostic. In contrast with the androgen-induced forms of FPH, the internal genitalia may also be malformed, and persistence of a cloaca is not exceptional. When studied, Y-specific DNA sequences were found to be normal.[544] Masculinization in these cases might result from abnormal expression of genes, which would normally be regulated by testosterone. Familial occurrence has been reported.[118] In all these cases, the only treatment is gen-

ital surgical repair of the external genitalia. Such surgery may be more difficult when there is an associated imperforate anus or malformations of the urinary and intestinal tracts.

## UNCLASSIFIED FORMS OF ABNORMAL SEXUAL DEVELOPMENT IN FEMALES

### Sexual Abnormalities of Unknown Cause

Developmental defects of the female reproductive tract may mimic intersexuality and should not be misinterpreted at the time of sex assignment or even at adolescence.[545,546] Some are easily recognizable, such as fusion of the labia minora or imperforate hymen. In other situations, congenital absence or abnormal development of the vagina is associated with variable anomalies of the müllerian duct structures. Several presentations may be individualized.

**Mayer-Rokitansky-Küster-Hauser Syndrome**   This syndrome is characterized by the association of the congenital absence of the upper four fifths of the vagina with a rudimentary uterus.[547] It occurs in 1 per 4000 to 5000 female live births, may be familial, and is the second most frequent cause of primary amenorrhea. The fallopian tubes might be well developed. Absence of the uterus is always associated with the absence of the vagina, but a small uterus might be found in females without a vagina. Because the ovaries are normal, the patients have normal development of secondary sex characteristics, but they do have amenorrhea. At least one fourth of women with primary amenorrhea have this syndrome. The anatomic anomaly is discovered at the time of evaluation of primary amenorrhea, but also of infertility or a pelvic mass. These abnormalities may be associated with renal, skeletal, or other anomalies such as developmental defects of the urinary tract (see Table 146-6). Cases of the Mayer-Rokitansky-Küster-Hauser (MRKH) syndrome with vertebral anomalies are considered part of the VATER (vertebral anomalies, anal atresia, tracheoesophageal fistula, radial limb dysplasia, and renal or cardiac anomalies, single umbilical artery, bicornuate uterus, and vaginal atresia) syndrome.

Bilateral ovarian agenesis and the presence of the testis-specific protein-1 Y-linked gene are two new features of MRKH syndrome.[548] The Y chromosome genes such as testis specific protein 1-Y-linked (TSPY) seem to be involved in the pathogenesis of MRKH.

**Vaginal Atresia**   This entity differs from the congenital absence of the vagina in that there is a failure of formation of the urogenital sinus and failure to canalize the solid vaginal plug. The müllerian duct structures and the ovaries are normal. Normal pubertal development occurs. Problems arise at puberty when there is an obstruction to the menstrual flux and abdominal pain caused by increased pressure.

**Atresia of the Uterine Cervix**   Atresia occurs rarely. The patients are apparently normal females with normal pubertal development; they have a normal vaginal opening, but they have cramping, which occurs during menses or with the absence of vaginal bleeding.

**Other Anomalies**   A transverse vaginal septum represents the most common vaginal abnormality, whereas a longitudinal vaginal septum is seen exceptionally in the absence of incomplete fusion of the müllerian duct structures. The latter condition is rather common and occurs in 0.1% to 3% of females. The lack of fusion may lead to uterus unicornis, uterus arcuatus, or uterus septus. Duplication of müllerian ducts may also occur, leading to uterus bicornis bicollis, uterus didelphys, or separate hemiuteri with one fallopian tube, each with separate vaginas and possibly a duplicated colon and anus. True duplication of the müllerian ducts with two separate uteri, each with two fallopian tubes, is exceptional.

**Differential Diagnosis**   In all situations, any hormonal cause of MPH should be eliminated. This is relatively easy to accomplish. Normal adrenal steroid values and the fact that clitoromegaly is not a feature of the MRKH syndrome demarcate it from the androgen-induced forms of FPH. The differential diagnosis is mainly with AIS. A normal 46,XX karyotype, normal gonadal and gonadotropic values, and anatomic findings help to differentiate the disorder from AIS. Indeed, at ultrasound, a uterus can be seen, and its structure can be determined eventually by CT scan or MRI. Management is purely surgical and limited to vaginal reconstruction, if necessary, at an appropriate age.

*Idiopathic*

On rare occasions, female hermaphroditism remains unexplained despite extensive infant and maternal studies. The condition is then idiopathic. Other local changes should be recognized, however, and should not be mistaken for sexual ambiguity, apparent enlargement of the clitoris in the premature infant, or clitoral abnormalities owing to lipoma, hemangioma, or plexiform neuroma.

## INVESTIGATIONS

### FULL CHROMOSOME ANALYSIS

Karyotype is usually performed on blood leukocytes. This is the analysis of chromosome number and morphology, completed by the examination of Y fluorescence and banding, and, eventually, fluorescent in situ hybridization (FISH)

Determination of mosaics may necessitate karyotyping of other tissues, including skin and gonadal tissue. This analysis is one basis for orientating the classification of an intersex in the category of MPH or FPH or some classes of gonadal dysgenesis. Normal 46,XY karyotype is found in pure gonadal dysgenesis,[42] agonadism,[91] bilateral gonadal dysgenesis,[549] and MPH. A 46,XX karyotype is found most frequently in true hermaphrodites,[177,550] and in all forms of female MPH.

### MOLECULAR GENETICS

#### Sex Chromosomes

Chromosome analysis has some limitations, for instance, in determining the presence of testicular tissue in XX males in the absence of recognizable Y chromosome or the impaired testicular differentiation in 46,XY males. Determination of the sex-determining region Y (SRY) gives complementary information. SRY is an intronless gene that spans 3.8 kb and has one exon.

It is located on chromosome Yp11.3. The SRY gene encodes a transcription factor that is a member of the high mobility group (HMG)-box family of DNA-binding proteins. SRY might be translocated on a chromosome X in XX males,[551] true hermaphroditism,[552] or an autosome[553] or might be structurally abnormal.[554] Mutations in this gene give rise to XY females with gonadal dysgenesis (one type of Swyer's syndrome) or some XX males.[54] This can only be known by molecular genetic studies. The presence of a normal SRY sequence can now be easily determined by PCR. If an abnormal pattern is found, further mutational analysis can be made by gene sequencing.[49,54] Determination of SRY might also be useful to detect a Y cell line in patients with Turner's syndrome in whom a mosaic has been missed.[555]

Alternatively to regular karyotyping, which remains a costly and time-consuming technique, the use of polymorphic DNA markers for the X chromosome has been proposed.[556] It appears quite valuable and accurate and is capable of detecting heterozygosity with multiallelic polymorphism in 83% of the cases.

Genetic lesions on various autosomes or chromosome X are responsible for steroid enzyme defects or androgen resistance, respectively. Adequate probes are used to detect genetic defects when diagnosis has been made for the first time in a family by conventional testing (see earlier). Molecular genetic studies in the relatives of the index case will thereafter be used for identification of other cases in the kindred, genetic counseling, and prenatal diagnosis, as discussed later. Such studies are still not applicable for immediate diagnosis or for population screening.

### ANTIMÜLLERIAN HORMONE AND INTERSEX STATES

Specific assays for human serum antimüllerian hormone (AMH or MIS) are available, and have permitted the establishment of control values from birth to adulthood in normal subjects (Fig. 146-10). Although testicular function has traditionally been assessed only by examining the steroidogenic capacity of Leydig cells and spermatogenesis, the measurement of AMH as a marker of Sertoli cell function has opened new perspectives in the investigation of intersex states, providing information regarding testicular function in infancy.[497] In particular, without the need for hCG stimulation, elevated AMH levels are indicative of the presence of testicular tissue.[459]

The combined measurement of androgens, AMH, and gonadotropins helps to establish the diagnosis in intersex patients, as follows, for example:

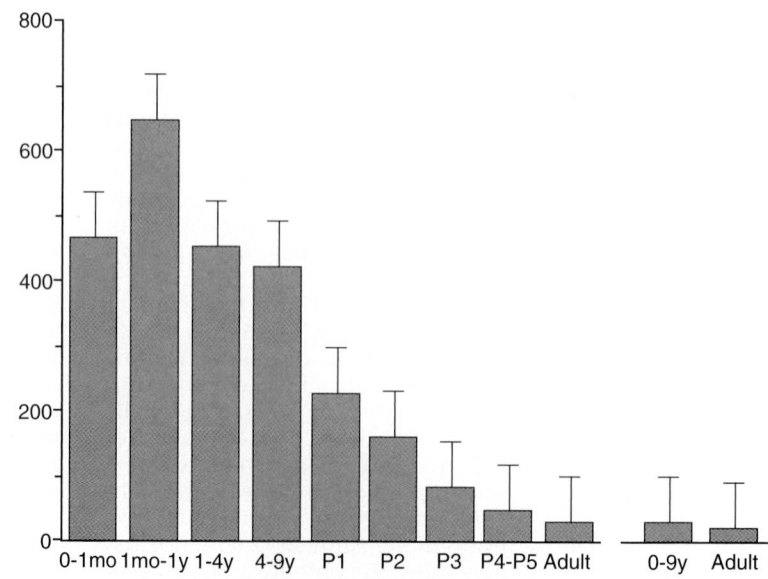

**Figure 146-10** Postnatal serum levels of AMH (antimüllerian hormone). Note the fall during puberty. (From Rey RA, Belville C, Nihoul-Fékété C, et al: Evaluation of gonadal function in 107 intersex patients by means of serum antimüllerian hormone measurement. J Clin Endocrinol Metab 84:627–631, 1999.)

- Whereas testosterone is low and gonadotropins elevated in patients with either gonadal dysgenesis (GD) or 3β-HSD deficiency, AMH is low in the former and high in the latter.
- Serum AMH and gonadotropins are normal or high in patients with 3β-HSD deficiency or AIS, but these could be distinguished by testosterone levels.
- Serum testosterone and gonadotropins are normal or high in AIS and SRD5A2 deficiency patients. Whereas AMH is elevated in AIS, it is not the case in SRD5A2 deficiency patients, indicating that testosterone is sufficient to inhibit AMH within the testis.
- In childhood, when testosterone is normally low, levels of AMH can distinguish GD and anorchidy from AIS or steroid enzyme defects before an hCG test.
- In idiopathic cases, gonadotropins and testosterone are normal, and AMH is normal or low.

## HORMONAL STUDIES OF THE HYPOTHALAMIC-PITUITARY-GONADAL AND ADRENAL AXES

These hormonal studies are very important to show evidence of any enzymatic defect in adrenal or testicular biosynthesis. Although some of these disorders are rare, it is important to identify the causal defect for the further choice of molecular genetics studies and for appropriate treatment. In the mild form of any enzyme defect, dynamic tests may be necessary. In genetic males, testing the response to hCG stimulation is a necessity. It is necessary in infants or children not only for the correct identification of the enzyme defect in the two last steps of testosterone biosynthesis, but also to diagnose agonadism and assess the Leydig cell secretory capacity, thus to anticipate the possibilities of spontaneous male puberty. Finally, testing pituitary function is also recommended, not so much for identifying a defect in LH during fetal life as a possible and exceptional cause of MPH,[557] but to document pituitary function in complex syndromes with multiple malformations.

### Adrenal Function

**Short ACTH Stimulation Test**  This test consists of a bolus intravenous (IV) injection of 0.25 mg of ACTH1-24 (synacthen). A catheter is placed in a peripheral vein. Blood is sampled at 10 to 30 minutes before and just before the injection (to exclude an interfering stress) and at 15, 30, 60, 90, and 120 minutes later. In young infants, blood sampling can be restricted to 15 minutes before, just before the injection, and 60 minutes after.

**Long ACTH Test**  This test consists of six IM injections of 0.5 mg per $m^2$ of body surface area of depot synacthen every 12 hours. Blood is obtained before the first injection and 12 hours after the last injection.

For both the short and long ACTH tests, reference values should be established because the responses change with age and whether the stimulation is long[558,559] or short.[560,561]

**Dexamethasone Suppression Test**  This is a two-step test: Dexamethasone is given orally, first at a small dose (20 μg/kg/day) for 3 days, then at a high dose (8 mg/day) for the next 3 days. Both doses are split in four daily intakes (every 6 hours). Blood is obtained before the test, on the morning of the fourth day (just before switch to the high dose), and on the seventh day (i.e., 6 hours after the last dose).

### Testicular Function

**Long hCG Stimulation Test**  This test consists of seven IM injections of 1500 IU of hCG every other day. Blood is obtained before the first injection and the day after the last injection. The advantages of the test are simplicity, the requirement of only two blood samples, and control values established not only for testosterone, but also for its precursors in infants and prepubertal boys.[562]

**Short hCG Stimulation Test**  This test consists of a single IM injection of 100 IU/$m^2$ of hCG. Blood samples are obtained in the early morning before the injection and daily thereafter for 1 week. The advantages are that the test is shorter and allows a better investigation of the dynamics of response of testosterone and its precursors, but it requires repeated blood samplings. Normal values have been established in children.[562]

### Pituitary Gonadotropin Function

**Luteinizing Hormone–Releasing Hormone (LHRH) Test**  It consists of a bolus injection of 100 mg/$m^2$ of LHRH. Blood samples are obtained 10 to 20 minutes before and just before the injection and 30, 45, 60, 90, and 120 minutes later for the measurement of LH and FSH. Plasma testosterone is also measured at 0 and 120 minutes. This test is best performed before any dynamic test of adrenal or gonadal function. If not, the test should be performed at least 2 weeks after an ACTH test and 1 month after an hCG test.

## EVALUATION OF ANDROGEN SENSITIVITY

Tissue androgen sensitivity is appreciated on the *clinical response* (growth of the genitalia) after the long hCG test and after exogenous administration of testosterone. Local treatment with testosterone cream has been abandoned, because it is difficult to standardize and because of the negative psychological effect (drawing attention to the problem two or three times a day). The author's clinic presently uses the following protocol described by Forest and David[562a]: four IM injections of 100 mg/$m^2$ of Depo-Testosterone (testosterone ester) at 2-week intervals. Careful examination of the scrotum (pigmentation, rugosity, size) and measurement of the penis are made before the injections and a few days after the last injection. If necessary, two more injections are prescribed. The fall in sex steroid–binding protein (SBP) (also called SHBG) is a useful marker of normal androgen sensitivity.[563,564] The test is more informative with the use of anabolic steroids, but is sometimes not sufficiently informative in PAIS.

## ANATOMIC STATUS OF THE GENITOURINARY TRACT

Ultrasonic imaging of the pelvis and abdomen is helpful in visualizing a uterus or some müllerian remnants and in appreciating the kidney morphology. This can be completed by an abdominal CT scan or by MRI. Genital anatomy is well demonstrated with MRI, a very useful tool that offers unsurpassed soft-tissue contrast, multiplanar capability, and no exposure to radiation.[565,566]

Genitography and cystoscopy are commonly used to determine the status of the urogenital sinus and the internal ducts' structure. Genitography may involve the use of retrograde urethrography or voiding cystourethrography, and is readily used in the preoperative state. Cystoscopy is useful to determine the presence of a vaginal pouch, a posterior utricle, or a cervix. Urethroscopy appreciates the anatomy of the urethra (one or two segments, the presence or not of veru montanum, and opening of the vagina). Pyelography is also recommended.

## HISTOLOGIC EXAMINATION OF THE GONADS

Gonadal biopsy is indicated in all patients who are suspected of presenting gonadal dysgenesis,[66,76] true hermaphroditism,[567] or Leydig cell aplasia/hypoplasia.[201] It is useless in all forms of FPH, as well as in most male pseudohermaphrodite patients with an inborn error in testosterone biosynthesis, AIS, or iatrogenic MPH. It may be interesting in patients with PMDS,[496] as well as in idiopathic MPH, to eventually exclude any form of bilateral gonadal dysgenesis (formerly named dysgenetic MPH).[549] Diagnosis of bilateral gonadal dysgenesis is made on the histologic identification of both gonads as being true dysgenetic testes.[568] Differentiation between dysgenetic MPH and normal cryptorchid testes may be very difficult,[76] however, and most male pseudohermaphrodite patients have undescended testes. This is why some pediatricians or pediatric urologists are reluctant to perform testicular biopsy when Leydig cell function is normal.

## ETIOLOGIC DIAGNOSIS

The aims of the etiologic diagnosis are: (1) to establish the genetic sex; (2) to evaluate the anatomic status of the urogenital sinus, internal genitalia, and gonads; (3) to recognize an enzymatic defect; (4) to assess Leydig cell and gonadotropic functions; (5) to estimate tissue sensitivity to androgens; and (6) to exclude an exceptional iatrogenic cause.

The appearance of the genitalia (stage of hypospadias) may orientate, but does not help, the etiologic diagnosis. The battery of tests described earlier should be made systematically in all patients presenting ambiguous genitalia or an intersex state, before making a decision regarding the sex of rearing, or treatment. In particular, the investigations are clearly suggested in cases of familial occurrence, all chances being that an affected child presents the same disorder as a previously affected sibling or relative. Etiologic diagnosis must be made in progressive steps.

## THE FIRST STEP

### Delay Birth Registration
The clinician should tell the parents that recognition of the sex of the child is difficult on simple external examination and can be made only after complete investigation, rather than saying that the child is neither a boy nor a girl.

### Thorough Clinical Examination
Examination should be performed on the external genitalia; a search should be made for gonads (in the labia or inguinal canal), pigmentation of the genitalia, nipples, symptoms of salt loss (failure to thrive, diarrhea, vomiting), and other somatic anomalies.

### Family Investigation
The clinician should directly question the parents regarding familial pedigree. The discovery of other cases can aid in directing the diagnosis and may help to elucidate the genetic mode of transmission. A maximum of medical information should be obtained about possibly affected family members.

If the child also presents somatic malformations, whenever possible, family members should be carefully examined for evidence of these malformations, even in the absence of sexual ambiguity. Questioning includes a search for maternal treatment during pregnancy (androgens, synthetic progestins such as medroxyprogesterone, norethynodrel, or drugs such as aminoglutethimide and danazol).

## THE NEXT STEPS: THE PRESENCE OF PALPABLE GONADS DETERMINES THE CHOICE AND THE ORDER OF THE INVESTIGATION

### If No Gonad Is Palpable (Figure 146-11)
The first priority is to exclude FPH due to CAH. The most common cause (90% to 95%) of CAH[569] is 21-hydroxylase deficiency. The findings of high levels of ACTH and PRA are suggestive of adrenal insufficiency, and adrenal insufficiency associated with ambiguous genitalia is indicative of CAH. The findings of extremely high levels (to 10,000 ng/dL or 300 nmol/L) of 17α-hydroxyprogesterone are diagnostic of 21-hydroxylase deficiency. In other forms of CAH, namely deficiencies in either 3β-HSD or 11β-hydroxylase, 17α-hydroxyprogesterone may also be elevated, but to a lesser extent. Therefore, when repeating blood sampling (or on the first if some is left), the measurement of testosterone, $\Delta^4$-androstenedione, DHEA or its sulfate (DHEA-S), and 11-deoxycortisol are sufficient to document the diagnosis of the given enzymatic block (Fig. 146-12). ACTH testing is not indicated when the biologic marker of a given enzymatic block is unambiguously elevated and is even dangerous, precipitating adrenal crisis in the infant.

However, 17α-hydroxyprogesterone may not be unequivocally elevated the first day of life in 21-hydroxylase deficiency, and hormonal investigations must be repeated daily.[570] Concentration of 17α-hydroxyprogesterone can easily be measured on dried blood spots on filter paper. In the mild form of any CAH, an ACTH test is required. Unless there is documented proof that the child does not present any salt loss, the test should be performed in the hospital under IV salt infusion. The choice of short or long ACTH testing is indicated by the local conditions. In most cases, the short ACTH test will provide the answer, by evidencing a rise in the precursor proximal to the enzymatic block. When all hormone levels are very low to undetectable and do not rise after long ACTH testing, the child is likely to present cholesterol side-chain cleavage deficiency.

Meanwhile, studies of salt balance ($Na^+$, $K^+$ in blood and urine) are performed, and a karyotype is demanded, except if the diagnosis of 21-hydroxylase or 11β-hydroxylase deficiency

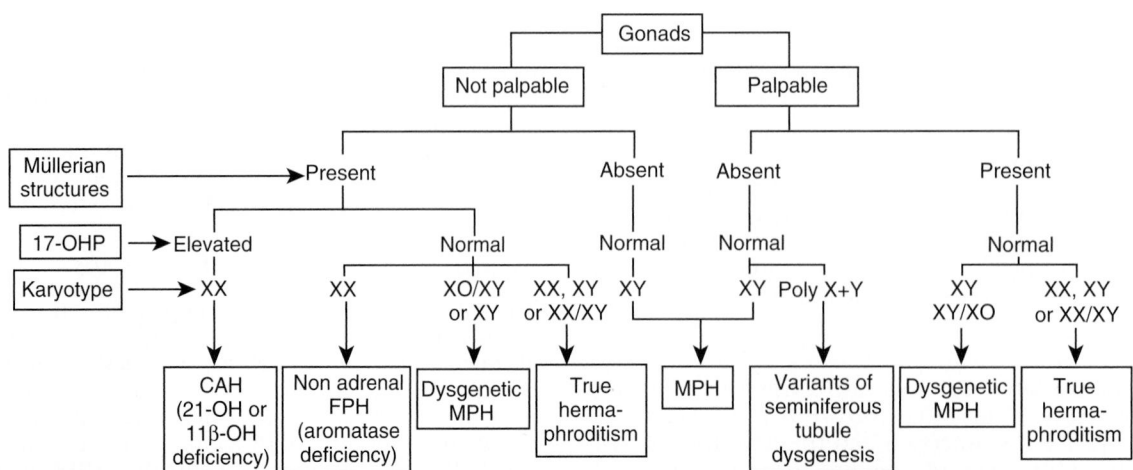

***Figure 146-11***  Flow chart of the initial steps and analysis of intersexuality in infancy and eventually in childhood. 11β-OH, 11β-hydroxylase; 17-OHP, 17α-hydroxyprogesterone; 21-OH, 21-hydroxylase; CAH, congenital adrenal hyperplasia; FPH, female pseudohermaphroditism; MPH, male pseudohermaphroditism.

is unambiguous and the blood karyotype 46,XX (no sex ambiguity in a genetic male with these disorders). Also, the determination of SRY can be performed. It is easy and fast. It is important to make certain of the genetic sex because the clinical presentation may be quite similar in a genetic female with 21-hydroxylase deficiency and a cryptorchid genetic male with 3β-HSD deficiency.

## If Gonads Are Palpated in the Inguinal Canal or the Scrotum
The gonads are most likely testes, and diagnosis should be made between gonadal dysgenesis and MPH (Fig. 146-13).

### Karyotyping Is a Necessity
This test is in order to establish whether the patient has a normal 46,XY constitution or a mosaicism or some chromosomal abnormalities on either gonosomes or autosomes. As mentioned earlier, determination of SRY may be complementary.

### Hormonal Studies Are Performed in the Following Order
**Measurement of Steroid Hormones in Basal Conditions** Since the availability of radioimmunoassays (RIAs), plasma determinations are preferred because they are more accurate and easier to perform than the measurement of urinary metabolites. Also, complete 24-hour urinary collection is difficult to obtain in an ambiguous child. Adapted techniques, utilizing a chromatographic step in order to have specific RIAs and to separate various hormones from the same plasma extract, enable the measurement of progesterone, 17α-hydroxypregnenolone, 17α-hydroxyprogesterone, Δ4-androstenedione, testosterone, and DHT from a single 5-mL blood sample. Plasma DHEA-S is rapidly measured using a commercial kit, which the author has adapted for infants and children (Forest, unpublished). DHEA-S can also be measured on dried blood spots on filter paper, after elution in distilled water or phosphate, by a direct RIA.

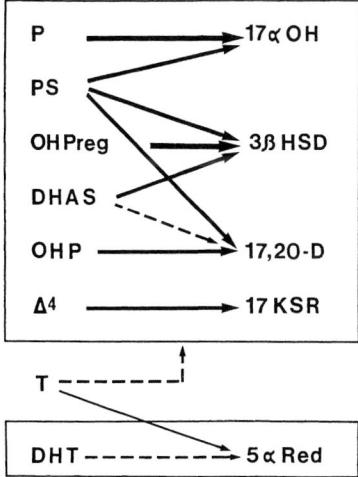

*Figure 146-12* Steroid hormone levels (on the left) orienting toward specific enzyme defects (on the right). Steroid levels can be markedly elevated (*thickened line*), decreased (*dashed line*), or normal (*continued line*). High progesterone (P) levels in an ambiguous child are evocative of 17-hydroxylase (17α-OH) deficiency. Elevation of both 17α-hydroxypregnenolone (OH Preg) and dehydroepiandrosterone sulfate (DHEA-S) is evocative of 3β-hydroxysteroid dehydrogenase (3β-HSD) deficiency, whereas low DHEA-S and high 17α-hydroxyprogesterone (OHP) levels are seen in 17,20 desmolase (17,20-D) deficiency. Marked elevation of Δ4-androstenedione (Δ4) is characteristic of a defect in 17-ketosteroid reductase (17-KSR). Testosterone (T) is reduced in all four enzyme defects, but it is normal and dihydrotestosterone (DHT) is diminished in 5α-reductase deficiency (5α Red). Elevation of pregnenolone sulfate (PS) is indicative of disrupted negative feedback.

The selective increase of one testosterone precursor may already orientate the diagnosis (see Fig. 146-12).

**LHRH Test** The test may be combined with the steroid hormone determinations and are performed on the blood sample taken at the time of the test.

**hCG Stimulation Test** This test, as mentioned earlier, is a necessity, except if the patient is seen at puberty. At that time, endogenous gonadotropic stimulation is sufficient to evidence any abnormality in the testicular secretion of testosterone or its precursors.

**Anatomic Studies (Genitography, Urethrography)** Ultrasonic imaging of the kidney should be repeated regularly in patients suspected of presenting with Denys-Drash syndrome in order to recognize Wilms' tumor as early as possible.[571]

**Test of Androgen Sensitivity** This is important to perform if AIS is suspected (very poor virilization, normal 46,XY, normal secretion of testosterone and its precursors, family history), not only for the diagnosis, but also to dictate the choice of gender in the incomplete forms. The test is also useful before reconstructive surgery for the treatment of a microphallus, which is so often associated with hypospadias. It is not performed when the decision to rear the child as a female has been taken.

**Search for Associated Malformations (Using Pyelography, Cardiac Examination, Bone Radiographs)** It should be kept in mind that in malformative syndromes associated with intersexuality, malformations can involve every organ or system from the central nervous system to the skin, viscera, kidney, bones, and orofacial structures.[572]

## LAST STEPS ARE DICTATED BY THE RESULTS OF PREVIOUS INVESTIGATIONS

A dexamethasone suppression test may be indicated to evidence the adrenal or testicular origin of high steroid hormone levels in various enzyme defects and exceptionally to exclude a virilizing adrenal tumor developed in utero (high levels of DHEA, DHEA-S) in girls with apparent non-salt-losing 3β-HSD deficiency.

Laparotomy is essential in the diagnosis of true hermaphroditism[197] or sex reversal.[91] There is no particular indication for laparoscopy or celioscopy because the risk for the child is not less and visualization of internal genitalia is not as complete as with laparotomy.

Determination of ARs on cultured skin fibroblasts helps to confirm the diagnosis of AIS,[573] although some of these patients are receptor positive.[460] More sophisticated studies of the instability or various biochemical abnormalities of the AR have been possible in specialized laboratories. Because these techniques are not easily available and are time consuming, they cannot help the clinician to make a rapid decision of sex assignment. Moreover, they are now supplanted by molecular genetic studies.[574]

There are situations in which the differential diagnosis may be difficult because of a similar clinical presentation and comparable hormonal anomalies. For instance:

- Cryptorchid male with deficient cholesterol side-chain cleavage (e.g., 20,22-desmolase) and female with complete adrenal insufficiency (importance of karyotype)
- Deficiency in 17,20-desmolase and so-called simple hypospadias[385]
- Deficiency in 17α-hydroxylase and AIS or idiopathic MPH
- Mild 3β-HSD deficiency without clinical salt loss and incomplete AIS[293]
- 17-ketosteroid reductase deficiency and complete AIS[416]

The importance of systematic studies of testosterone precursors before and after the hCG test is evident in the last four examples.

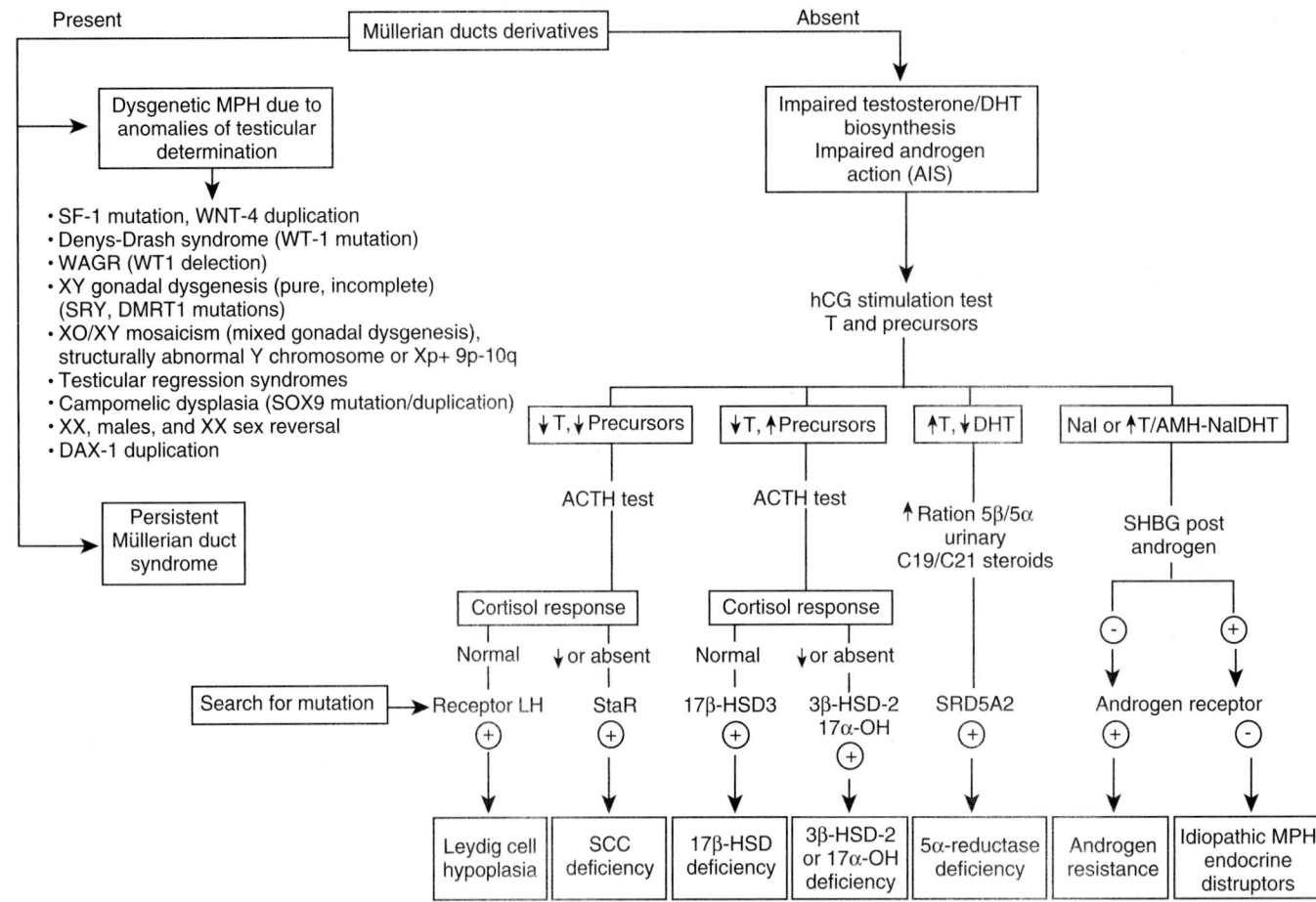

**Figure 146-13** Flow chart of the investigations to make for the etiologic diagnosis of MPH (male pseudohermaphroditism), that is, an infant with 46,XY karyotype and ambiguous genitalia. DHT, dihydrotestosterone; 3β-HSD, 3β-hydroxysteroid dehydrogenase; T, testosterone. See text for other abbreviations.

### WHEN ALL RESULTS ARE NORMAL

This situation is classified as *idiopathic MPH*. The decision to make this diagnosis is not very satisfactory, because the cause of abnormal sex differentiation has not been explained. It is possible that those cases with normal Leydig cell function in postnatal life may result from a delayed timing of Leydig cell maturation, which thus could explain the defective fetal masculinization.[215] This hypothesis is quite impossible to prove after birth. Also, some idiopathic MPH may well be incomplete forms of AIS. The condition may have been ignored if the investigations performed early in life showed normal or near-normal AR levels. Such patients may be recognized only at puberty on the findings of high endogenous levels of both testosterone and LH and florid gynecomastia.[481,575] The possible impact of endocrine disrupters is controversial.[515,576,577]

### GENETIC COUNSELING AND PRENATAL DIAGNOSIS

When the etiologic diagnosis has been made in a patient presenting with a disorder of sex differentiation, genetic counseling is indicated in all conditions recognized to be familial or inherited. Genetic counseling should be initiated immediately by giving the family all current information about the disease, the possibilities of treatment, complications, fertility,[578] and, finally, prenatal diagnosis.[579,580] Cultural differences not only influence the patient's psychosexual development, but also medical decisions regarding sex assignment and consecutive management.[581] Parental decisions should be taken into consideration.[582]

The prenatal diagnosis in families with an index case requires previous familial investigations. Possibilities for prenatal diagnosis are summarized in Table 146-8. The antenatal diagnosis of sex differentiation may involve different approaches. Karyotype analysis on chorion villus cells or amniocytes provides information on sex chromosomes. Currently, the determination of SRY is a more rapid screening for the presence of an Y chromosome. Amniotic fluid steroids have been widely studied and provide a basis for the study of enzymatic defects, independent of an index case.[583] Maternal estriol in plasma or urine reflects the functional capacity of the fetal adrenal if an X-linked steroid sulfatase is ruled out. Ultrasound performed at 11 weeks and repeated after 20 weeks can give information on the aspect of fetal genitalia. Direct fetoscopy has been used for earlier morphologic evaluation. Some patients may be fortuitously diagnosed when fetal karyotype is examined for another purpose (most often because of maternal age) or as a finding during routine ultrasound. This is true especially for Klinefelter syndrome or for Turner's syndrome and variants of the 45,X/46,XY constitution.

### RELATIVE FREQUENCY OF THE CAUSE OF INTERSEX

In the literature, the relative frequency of the causes of intersex is highly variable, likely due to small numbers in some series, the definition of etiologic categories, and even exclusion of the so-called idiopathic cases.

In a 25-year experience in the Lyon's Pediatric Clinics, 325 infants or children seen for intersexuality have been recorded, excluding Klinefelter or Turner's syndromes and variants.

**Table 146-8** Prenatal Diagnosis of Intersexuality in A Fetus at Risk of A Known Disorder

| Condition | Determination on Amniotic Fluid,* Amniocytes,[†] and CVS[‡], Ultrasound[587] |
|---|---|
| Fetal sexing | Karyotype[†,589] SRY,[†] and fetal SRY in maternal blood[591] at 6–11 weeks |
| Sex chromosome disorders (i.e., XX-male,[593] Klinefelter syndrome[594]) | Karyotype[†,592] SRY,[†] ultrasound |
| Inpaired cholesterol synthesis (SLOS) | Steroid marker[219] and molecular genetics[232] |
| | 7-/8-Dehydrocholesterol (7/8DHCR) or its metabolites in amniotic fluid[229] or maternal serum or urine[231] |
| | Molecular studies on CVS[232] |
| Steroid enzyme defects | Steroid marker,* fetal sexing,[†] and molecular genetic studies[†] for all |
| StAR | Low maternal estriol,[595] MRI[281] |
| 3β-HSD | 17-OH-pregnenolone (17-OHP),* DHEA-S* and C21 $\Delta^{5}/\Delta^{4}$ ratios*[583] |
| 17α-Hydroxylase | Low maternal estriol[596] |
| 17,20-Desmolase | High 17-OHP and low androgens (C21/C19 ratios)*[385] |
| 21-Hydroxylase | High 17-OHP and high androgens (T and $\Delta^{4}$*)[525] |
| 11-Hydroxylase | High 11-deoxycortisol*[597,598] |
| 17β-HSD | Low T,* high $\Delta^{4}$,* high $\Delta^{4}/T$ ratio*[599] |
| Aromatase | In mother, low estriol and very high T and $\Delta^{4}$ |
| P-450 oxidoreductase | Excessive excretion of epiallopregnanediol and low estriol[404] |
| 5α-Reductase deficiency | Fetal sexing[†] to identify a male at risk, molecular genetics studies[†] |
| Androgen insensitivity | Fetal sexing[†] to identify a male at risk, normal T polymorphism of X,[†473] molecular genetic studies[†] |

3β-HSD, 3β-hydroxysteroid dehydrogenase; 17-OHP, 17α-hydroxyprogesterone; CVS, chorionic villus sampling; $\Delta^{4}$, $\Delta^{4}$-androstenedione; DHEA, dehydroepiandrosterone; DHEA-S, DHEA sulfate; OH, hydroxylase; SLOS, Smith-Lemli-Opitz syndrome; SRY, sex-determining region Y; StAR, Steroidogenic acute regulatory protein; T, testosterone.

There was a similar number of MPH (49%) and FPH (51%), as observed elsewhere.[584] In contrast, very few FPH were found in another study of 429 patient with sexual ambiguity.[585] In the Lyon's experience, among the 167 cases of FPH, 134 girls had CAH (80%), mainly owing to 21-hydroxylase deficiency (125 cases). Maternal hyperandrogeny was found in 3% and malformations in 6%; the remaining 10% were idiopathic. The 150 other patients had abnormal male sex differentiation, owing to gonadal dysgenesis or hermaphroditism (27%), testicular deficiency in AMH or testosterone (13%), AIS (16%) MPH associated with malformations (14%), or idiopathic MPH (30%). The etiologies were similar to that in the author's own experience, with a somewhat higher rate of idiopathic cases (35%). In contrast, in a recent collaborative study,[586] no diagnosis could be reached in 52% of cases, despite an exhaustive clinical and laboratory workup, including routine sequencing of exons 2 to 8 of the androgen receptor. The latter, after study of testosterone precursors following hCG stimulation, is recommended when gonadal dysgenesis and true hermaphroditism can be excluded.

In the studies found in the literature, the percentage of the various etiologies is strikingly variable. This is likely due to bias in recruitment, but overall to the definition of MPH versus that of hypospadias.

## REFERENCES

1. MacLaughlin DT, Donahoe PK: Sex determination and differentiation. N Engl J Med 350:367–378, 2004.
2. Oba K, Yanase T, Nomura M, et al: Structural characterization of human Ad4bp (SF-1) gene. Biochem Biophys Res Commun 226:261–267, 1996.
3. Wong M, Ramayya M, Chrousos G, et al: Cloning and sequence analysis of the human gene encoding steroidogenic factor 1. J Mol Endocrinol 17:139–147, 1996.
4. Achermann JC, Ito M, Ito M, et al: A mutation in the gene encoding steroidogenic factor-1 causes XY sex reversal and adrenal failure in humans. Nat Genet 22:125–126, 1999.
5. Tremblay JJ, Viger RS: A mutated form of steroidogenic factor 1 (SF-1 G35E) that causes sex reversal in humans fails to synergize with transcription factor GATA-4. J Biol Chem 278:42637–42642, 2003.
6. Biason-Lauber A, Schoenle EJ: Apparently normal ovarian differentiation in a prepubertal girl with transcriptionally inactive steroidogenic factor 1 (NR5A1/SF-1) and adrenocortical insufficiency. Am J Hum Genet 67:1563–1568, 2000.
7. Achermann JC, Ozisik G, Ito M, et al: Gonadal determination and adrenal development are regulated by the orphan nuclear receptor steroidogenic factor-1, in a dose-dependent manner. J Clin Endocrinol Metab 87:1829–1833, 2002.
8. Correa RV, Domenice S, Bingham NC, et al: A microdeletion in the ligand binding domain of human steroidogenic factor 1 causes XY sex reversal without adrenal insufficiency. J Clin Endocrinol Metab 89:1767–1772, 2004.
9. Denys P, Malvaux P, van den Berghe H, et al: Association d'un syndrome anatomo-pathologique de pseudohermaphroditisme masculin, d'une tumeur de Wilms, d'une néphropathie parenchymateuse et d'un mosaicisme XX/XY. Arch Fr Pediatr 24:729–739, 1967.
10. Drash A, Sherman F, Hartmann WH, et al: A syndrome of pseudohermaphroditism, Wilms' tumor, hypertension, and degenerative renal disease. J Pediatr 76:565–593, 1970.
11. Jadresic L, Leake J, Gordon I, et al: Clinicopathologic review of 12 children with nephropathy, Wilms tumor, and genital abnormalities (Drash sydrome). J Pediatr 117:717–725, 1990.
12. Fisher JE, Andres GA, Cooney DR, et al: A syndrome of pure gonadal dysgenesis gonadoblastoma, Wilms' tumour and nephron disease. Lab Invest 48:4P–5P, 1983.
13. Habib R, Loirat C, Gubler MC, et al: The nephropathy associated with male pseudohermaphroditism and Wilms' tumor (Drash sydrome): A distinctive glomerular lesion—report of 10 cases. Clin Nephrol 24:269–278, 1985.
14. Jensen JC, Ehrlish RM, Hanna MK, et al: A report of four patients with the Drash syndrome and a review of the literature. J Urol 141:1174–1176, 1989.
15. Borel F, Barilla KC, Hamilton TB, et al: Effects of Denys-Drash syndrome point mutations on the DNA binding activity of the Wilms' tumor suppressor protein WT1. Biochemistry 35:12070–12076, 1996.
16. Mueller RF: The Denys-Drash syndrome. J Med Genet 31:471–477, 1994.
17. Devriendt K, Deloof E, Moerman P, et al: Diaphragmatic hernia in Denys-Drash syndrome. Am J Med Genet 57:97–101, 1995.
18. Köhler A, Schumacher V, Royer-Pokora B, et al: Mutational screening of the WT1 gene in boys with severe hypospadias. Horm Res 51 (Suppl 2):P257, 1999.
19. Hu M, Zhang GY, Arbuckle S, et al: Prophylactic bilateral nephrectomies in

two paediatric patients with missense mutations in the WT1 gene. Nephrol Dial Transplant 19:223–226, 2004.

20. Moorthy AV, Chesney RW, Lubinsky M: Chronic renal failure and XY gonadal dysgenesis: "Frasier" syndrome—a commentary on reported cases. Am J Med Genet 3:297–302, 1987.

21. Frasier SD, Bashore RA, Mosier HD: Gonadoblastoma associated with pure gonadal dysgenesis in monozygotic twins. J Pediatr 64:7740–7745, 1964.

22. Barbosa AS, Hadjiathanasiou CG, Theodoridis C, et al: The same mutation affecting the splicing of WT1 gene is present on Frasier syndrome patients with or without Wilms' tumor. Hum Mutat 13:146–153, 1999.

23. Poulat F, Morin D, Konig A, et al: Distinct molecular origins for Denys-Drash and Frasier syndromes. Hum Genet 91:285–286, 1993.

24. Berta P, Morin D, Poulat F, et al: Molecular analysis of the sex-determining region from the Y chromosome in two patients with Frasier syndrome. Horm Res 37:103–106, 1992.

25. Barbaux S, Niaudet P, Gubler MC, et al: Donor splice-site mutations in WT1 are responsible for Frasier syndrome. Nat Genet 17:467–470, 1997.

26. Klamt B, Koziell A, Poulat F, et al: Frasier syndrome is caused by defective alternative splicing of WT1 leading to an altered ratio of WT1 +/–KTS splice isoforms. Hum Mol Genet 7:709–714, 1998.

27. Melo KF, Martin RM, Costa EM, et al: An unusual phenotype of Frasier syndrome due to IVS9 +4C→T mutation in the WT1 gene: Predominantly male ambiguous genitalia and absence of gonadal dysgenesis. J Clin Endocrinol Metab 87:2500–2505, 2002.

28. Miller RW, Fraumeni JF, Larsen H-W, et al: Association of Wilms' tumor with aniridia, hemihypertrophy and other congenital malformations. New Engl J Med 270:922–927, 1964.

29. Turleau C, de Grouchy J, Dufier JL, et al: Aniridia, male pseudohermaphroditism, gonadoblastoma, mental retardation and del 11p13. Hum Genet 57:300–306, 1981.

30. Riccardi VM, Sujansky E, Smith AC, et al: Chromosomal imbalance in the aniridia-Wilms tumor association: 11p Interstitial deletion. Pediatrics 61:604–610, 1978.

31. Anderson SR, Geertinger P, Larsen H-W, et al: Aniridia, cataract and gonadoblastoma in a mentally retarded girl with deletion of chromosome 11: A clinicopathological case report. Ophthalmologica 176:171–177, 1978.

32. Breslow NE, Norris R, Norkool PA, et al: Characteristics and outcomes of children with the Wilms tumor-Aniridia syndrome: A report from the National Wilms Tumor Study Group. J Clin Oncol 21:4579–4585, 2003.

33. Schmickel RD: Chromosomal deletions and enzyme deficiencies. J Pediatr 108:244–246, 1986.

34. Bickmore WA, Hastie ND: Aniridia, Wilms' tumor and human chromosome 11. Ophthalmic Paediatr Genet 10:229–248, 1989.

35. Glaser T, Driscoll DJ, Antonarakis S, et al: A highly polymorphic locus cloned from the breakpoint of a chromosome 11p13 deletion associated with the WAGR syndrome. Genomics 5:880–893, 1989.

36. Moore JW, Hyman S, Antonarakis SE, et al: Familial isolated aniridia associated with a translocation involving chromosomes 11 and 22 (t[11;22][p13;q12.2]). Hum Genet 72:297–302, 1986.

37. Gronskov K, Olsen J, Sand A, et al: Population-based risk estimates of Wilms tumor in sporadic aniridia: A comprehensive mutation screening procedure of PAX6 identifies 80% of mutations in aniridia. Hum Genet 109:11–18, 2001.

38. Lorda-Sanchez I, Sanz R, Diaz-Guillen MA, et al: Aniridia as part of a WAGR syndrome in a girl whose brother presented hypospadias. Genet Couns 13:171–177, 2002.

39. Compton DA, Weil MM, Jones C, et al: Long range physical map of Wilms tumor–aniridia region on human chromosome 11. Cell 55:827–836, 1988.

40. Swyer GIM: Male pseudohermaphroditism: A hitherto undescribed form. Br Med J 2:709–712, 1955.

41. German J, Simpson JL, Chaganti RSK, et al: Genetically determined sex reversal in 46,XY humans. Science 202:53–56, 1978.

42. Simpson JL, Blogowidow N, Martin AO: XY gonadal dysgenesis: Genetic heterogeneity based upon observations, H-Y antigen status and segregation analysis. Hum Genet 58:91–97, 1981.

43. Radakovic B, Jukic S, Bukovic D, et al: Morphology of gonads in pure XY gonadal dysgenesis. Coll Antropol 23:203–211, 1999.

44. Chemke J, Carmichael R, Stewart JM, et al: Familial XY gonadal dysgenesis. J Med Genet 7:105–111, 1970.

45. Berta P, Hawkins JR, Sinclair AH, et al: Genetic evidence equating SRY and the testis-determining factor. Nature 348:448–450, 1990.

46. Jäger RJ, Anvret M, Hall K, et al: A human XY female with a frame shift mutation in the candidate testis-determining gene SRY. Nature 348:452–454, 1990.

47. Battiloro E, Angeletti B, Tozzi MC, et al: A novel double nucleotide substitution in the HMG box of the SRY gene associated with Swyer syndrome. Hum Genet 100:585–587, 1997.

48. Hines RS, Tho SP, Zhang YY, et al: Paternal somatic and germ-line mosaicism for a sex-determining region on Y (SRY) missense mutation leading to recurrent 46,XY sex reversal. Fertil Steril 67:675–679, 1997.

49. Hawkins JR, Taylor A, Goodfellow PN, et al: Evidence for increased prevalence of SRY mutations in XY females with complete rather than partial gonadal dysgenesis. Am J Hum Genet 51:979–984, 1992.

50. Pivnick EK, Watchel S, Woods D, et al: Mutations in the conserved domain of SRY are uncommon in XY gonadal dysgenesis. Hum Genet 90:308–310, 1992.

51. Raymond CS, Parker ED, Kettlewell JR, et al: A region of human chromosome 9p required for testis development contains two genes related to known sexual regulators. Hum Mol Genet 8:989–996, 1999.

52. Uehara S, Funato T, Yaegashi N, et al: SRY mutation and tumor formation on the gonads of XY pure gonadal dysgenesis patients. Cancer Genet Cytogenet 113:78–84, 1999.

53. Levilliers J, Quack B, Weissenbach J, et al: Exchange of terminal portions of X- and Y-chromosomal short arms in human XY females. Proc Natl Acad Sci U S A 86:2296–2300, 1989.

54. Ogata T, Hawkins JR, Taylor A, et al: Sex reversal in a child with a 46,X,Xp+ karyotype: Support for the existence of a gene(s), located in distal Xp, involved in testes formation. J Med Genet 29:226–230, 1992.

55. Schiebel K, Winkelmann M, Mertz A, et al: Abnormal XY interchange between a novel isolated protein kinase gene, PRKY, and its homologue, PRKX, accounts for one third of all (Y+)XX males and (Y–)XY females. Hum Mol Genet 6:1985–1989, 1997.

56. Fechner PY, Marcantonio SM, Ogata T, et al: Report of a kindred with X-linked (or autosomal dominant sex-limited) 46,XY partial gonadal dysgenesis. J Clin Endocrinol Metab 76:1248–1253, 1993.

57. Wilkie AO, Campbell FM, Daubeney P, et al: Complete and partial XY sex reversal associated with terminal deletion of 10p: Report of two cases and literature review. Am J Med Genet 46:597–600, 1993.

58. McDonald MT, Flejter W, Sheldon S, et al: XY sex reversal and gonadal dysgeneis due to 9p monosomy. Am J Med Genet 73:321–326, 1997.

59. Wieacker P, Missbach D, Jakubiczka S, et al: Sex reversal in a child with the karyotype 46,XY, dup(1)(p22.3p32.3). Clin Genet 49:271–273, 1996.

60. Kingsbury AC, Frost F, Cookson WO, et al: Dysgerminoma, gonadoblastoma, and testicular germ cell neoplasia in phenotypically female and male siblings with 46,XY genotype. Cancer 59:288–291, 1987.

61. Cussen LJ, McMahon RA: Germ cells and ova in dysgenetic gonads of a 46,XY female dizygotic twin. Am J Dis Child 133:373–375, 1979.

62. Bernstein R, Koo CG, Watchel SS: Abnormalities of the X chromososme in human 46,XY female siblings with dysgenetic ovaries. Science 207:768–769, 1980.

63. Russell MH, Watchel SS, Davis BW, et al: Ovarian development in 46,XY gonadal dysgenesis. Hum Genet 60:196–199, 1982.

63a. Bergada C, Cleveland WW, Jones HW, et al: Variants of embryonic testicular dysgenesis, bilateral anorchia and the syndrome of rudimentary testes. Acta Endocrinol (Copenh) 40:521–535, 1962.

63b. Sohval AR: Hermaphroditism with atypical or "mixed" gonadal dysgenesis. Relationship to gonadal neoplams. Am J Med 36:281–292, 1964.

64. Morishima A, Grumbach MM: The interrelationship of sex chromosome constitution and phenotype in the syndrome of gonadal dysgenesis and its variants. Ann N Y Acad Sci 155:695–715, 1968.

65. Kelly TE, Franko B, Rogol A, et al: Discordant phenotypes and 45,X/46,X,idic(Y). J Med Genet 35:862–864, 1998.

66. Zäh H, Kalderon HE, Tucci JR: Mixed gonadal dysgenesis. Acta Endocrinol (Copenh) 79(Suppl):3–39, 1975.

67. Donahoe PK, Crawford JD, Hendren WH: Mixed gonadal dysgenesis, pathogenesis and management. J Pediatr Surg 14:287–300, 1979.

68. Yamakita N, Yasuda K, Mori H, et al: A case of mixed gonadal dysgenesis (MGD) with a review of MGD patients reported in Japan. Jpn J Med 28:744–750, 1989.

69. Telvi L, Lebbar A, Del Pino O, et al: 45,X/46,XY mosaicism: Report of 27 cases. Pediatrics 104:304–308, 1999.

70. Josso N, Fékété C, Cachin O, et al: Persistance of müllerian ducts in male pseudohermaphrodism, and its relationship to cryptorchidism. Clin Endocrinol 19:247–258, 1983.

71. Josso N, Nezelof C, Picon R, et al: Gonadoblastoma in gonadal dysgenesis: A report of two cases with 46,XY/45,XO mosaicism. J Pediatr 74:425–437, 1969.

72. Rajfer J, Walsh PC: Mixed gonadal dysgenesis-dysgenetic male pseudohermaphrodism. In Josso N (ed): The Intersex Child. Basel, Karger, 1981, pp 105–115.

73. Yanagisawa S: Structural abnormalities of the Y chromosome and abnormal external genitalia. Hum Genet 53:183–188, 1980.

74. Cohen MM, Shaw MW: Two siblings with gonadal dysgenesis and a female phenotype. N Engl J Med 272:1083–1088, 1965.

75. Kaluzewski B, Jokinen A, Hortling H, et al: A theory explaining the abnormality in 45/46XY mosaicism with non-fluorescent Y chromosome: Presentation of three cases. Ann Genet (Paris) 21:5–11, 1978.

76. Federman DD: Abnormal Sexual Development: A Genetic and Endocrine Approach. Philadelphia, WB Saunders, 1967.

77. Chang HJ, Clark RD, Bachman H: The phenotype of 45,X/46,XY mosaicism: An analysis of 92 prenatally diagnosed cases. Am J Hum Genet 46:156–167, 1990.

78. Borer JG, Nitti VW, Glassberg KI: Mixed gonadal dysgenesis and dysgenetic male pseudohermaphrodism. J Urol 153:1267–1273, 1995.

79. Nielsen J, Wohlert M: Sex chromosomes abnormalities found among 34,910 newborn children: Results from a 13-year incidence study in Arhuus, Denmark. In Birth Defects: Original Article Series 26. New York, Alan R. Liss, Inc., 1990, pp 209–223.

80. Bosch-Banyeras JM, Audi L, Bau A, et al: A case of male pseudohermaphrodism with normal androgen receptor binding and 47,XYY karyotype. Ann Genet 28:125–129, 1985.

81. Geerts M, Steyaert J, Fryns JP: The XYY syndrome: A follow-up study on 38 boys. Genet Couns 14:267–279, 2003.

82. Gotz MJ, Johnstone EC, Ratcliffe SG: Criminality and antisocial behaviour in unselected men with sex chromosome abnormalities. Psychol Med 29:953–962, 1999.

83. Robinson DO, Jacobs PA: The origin of the extra Y chromosome in males with a 47,XYY karyotype. Hum Mol Genet 8:2205–2209, 1999.

84. Hecht F: Risks of hematologic malignancy with constitutional chromosome abnormalities. Cancer Genet Cytogent 24:375–377, 1987.

85. De Marchi M, Campagnoli C, Guiringhello B, et al: Gonadal agenesis in a phenotypically normal female with positive H-Y antigen. Hum Genet 56:417–419, 1981.

86. Edman CD, Winter AJ, Porter JC, et al: Embryonic testicular regression: A clinical spectrum of XY agonadal individuals. Obstet Gynecol 49:208–212, 1977.

87. Overzier C, Linden H: Echter Agonadismus (anorchismus) bei Geschwistern. Gynaecologia 142:215–233, 1956.

88. Schoen EJ, King AL, Baritell AL, et al: Pseudohermaphrodism with multiple congenital anomalies. Pediatrics 16:363–371, 1955.

89. Sorgo W, Gortner L, Bartmann P, et al: Gonadal agenesis in a 46,XY female with multiple malformations and positive testing for the sex-determining region of the Y-chromosome. Horm Res 35:124–131, 1991.

90. Parigi G, Bardoni B, Avoltini V, et al: Is bilateral congenital anorchia genetically determined? Eur J Pediatr Surg 9:312–315, 1999.

91. Josso N, Briard ML: Embryonic testicular regression syndrome: Variable phenotypic expression in siblings. J Pediatr 97:200–204, 1980.

92. Bergada C, Cleveland WW, Jones HWJ, et al: Variants of embryonic testicular dysgenesis: Bilateral anorchia and the syndrome of rudimentary testes. Acta Endocrinol (Copenh) 40:521–536, 1962.

93. Aynsley-Green A, Zachmann M, Illig R, et al: Congenital bilateral anorchia in childhood: A clinical, endocrine and therapeutic evaluation of 21 cases. Clin Endocrinol 5:381–391, 1976.

94. Spires SE, Woolums CS, Pulito AR, et al: Testicular regression syndrome: A clinical and pathologic study of 11 cases. Arch Pathol Lab Med 124:694–698, 2000.

95. Klinefelter HFJ, Reifenstein ECJ, Albright F: Syndrome characterized by gynecomastia, aspermatogenis with A-Leydigism, and increased excretion of follicle-stimulating hormone. J Clin Endocrinol Metab 2:615–627, 1942.

96. Jacobs PA, Strong JA: A case of human intersexuality having a possible XXY sex-determining mechanism. Nature 83:302–303, 1959.

97. Perwein E: Incidence of Klinefelter's syndrome. In Badmann HJ, Breit R, Perwein E (eds): Klinefelter's Syndrome. Berlin, Springer-Verlag, 1984.

98. Filippi G, Pecile V, Rinaldi A, et al: Fragile X mutation and Klinefelter's syndrome: A reappraisal. Am J Med Genet 30:99–107, 1988.

99. Klinefelter HF: Klinefelter syndrome: Historical background and development. South Med J 79:1089–1093, 1986.

100. de la Chapelle A: Nature and origin of males with XX sex chromosomes. Am J Hum Genet 24:71–105, 1972.

101. Jacobs PA, Hassold TJ, Whittington E, et al: Klinefelter's syndrome: An analysis of the origin of the additional sex chromosome using molecular probes. Ann Hum Genet 52:93–109, 1988.

102. Wikstrom AM, Raivio T, Hadziselimovic F, et al: Klinefelter syndrome in adolescence: Onset of puberty is associated with accelerated germ cell depletion. J Clin Endocrinol Metab 89:2263–2270, 2004.

103. Lahlou N, Fennoy I, Carel JC, et al: Inhibin B and anti-Mullerian hormone, but not testosterone levels, are normal in infants with nonmosaic Klinefelter syndrome. J Clin Endocrinol Metab 89:1864–1868, 2004.

104. Schmid M, Guttenbach M, Endres H, et al: A 47,XXY female with unusual genitalia. Hum Genet 90:346–349, 1992.

105. Schwartz ID, Root AW: The Klinefelter's syndrome of testicular dysgenesis. Endocrinol Metab Clin North Am 20:615–627, 1991.

106. Mandoki MW, Gavla SS, Hoffman RP, et al: A review of Klinefelter's syndrome in children and adolescents. J Am Acad Child Adolesc Psychiatry 30:167–172, 1991.

107. Schilber D, Brook CG, Kind HP, et al: Growth and body proportions in 54 boys and men with Klinefelter's syndrome. Helv Pædiatr Acta 29:325–333, 1974.

108. Scheike O, Visfeldt J, Petersen B: Male breast carcinoma in association with the Klinefelter's syndrome. Acta Pathol Microbiol Scand 81:352–358, 1973.

109. Hasle H, Jacobsen BB, Asschenfeldt P, et al: Mediastinal germ cell tumor associated with Klinefelter's syndrome: A report of case and review of the literature. Eur J Pediatr 151:735–739, 1992.

110. Cheikh IE, Hamilton BPM, Hsu TH, et al: Studies using releasing factors in Klinefelter's syndrome: The responses

of LH and FSH to luteinizing hormone-releasing hormone and prolactin and TSH to thyrotropin-releasing hormone before and after testosterone. Psychoneuroendocrinology 6:37–44, 1981.

111. De Kretzer DM, McLachlan RI, Robertson DM, et al: Serum inhibin levels in normal men and in men with testicular disorders. J Endocrinol 120:517–523, 1989.

112. Mark HF, Feldman D, Sigman M: Conventional and molecular cytogenetic identification of a variant Klinefelter syndrome patient with a deleted X chromosome. Pathobiology 67:107, 1999.

113. Nielsen J, Pelsen B, Sorensen K: Follow-up of 30 Klinefelter males treated with testosterone. Clin Genet 33:262–269, 1988.

114. Warburg E: A fertile patient with Klinefelter's syndrome. Acta Endocrinol (Copenh) 43:829–838, 1963.

115. Ron-el R, Friedler S, Strassburger D, et al: Birth of a healthy neonate following the intracytoplasmic injection of testicular spermatozoa from a patient with Klinefelter's syndrome. Hum Reprod 14:368–370, 1999.

116. Hultborn R, Hanson C, Kopf I, et al: Prevalence of Klinefelter's syndrome in male breast cancer patients. Anticancer Res 17:4293–4297, 1997.

117. Sepulveda W, Ivankovic M, Be C, et al: Sex chromosome pentasomy (49,XXXXY) presenting as cystic hygroma at 16 weeks' gestation. Prenat Diagn 19:257–259, 1999.

118. Jones KL: Smith's Recognizable Patterns of Human Malformations. Philadelphia, WB Saunders, 1988.

119. Ferguson-Smith MA, Cooke A, Affara NA, et al: Genotype-phenotype correlations in XX males and their bearing on current theories of sex determination. Hum Genet 84:198–202, 1990.

120. Miro R, Cabellin MR, Marsini S, et al: Mosaicism in XX males. Hum Genet 45:103–106, 1978.

121. de la Chapelle A, Tipett PA, Wetterstrand G, et al: Genetic evidence of X-Y interchange in a human XX male. Nature 307:170–171, 1984.

122. Wang I, Weil D, Levilliers J, et al: Prevalence and molecular analysis of two hot spots for ectopic recombination leading to XX maleness. Genomics 28:52–58, 1995.

123. Fechner PY, Marcantonio SM, Jaswaney V, et al: The role of the sex-determining region Y gene in the etiology of 46,XX maleness. J Clin Endocrinol Metab 3:690–695, 1993.

124. Abbas NE, Toublanc JE, Boucekkine C, et al: A possible common origin of "Y-negative" human XX males and XX true hermaphroditism. Hum Genet 84:356–360, 1990.

125. Maroteaux P, Spranger JW, Opitz JM, et al: Le syndrome campomélique. Presse Med 22:1157–1162, 1971.

126. Schafer AJ, Dominguez-Steglich MA, Guioli S, et al: The role of SOX9 in autosomal sex reversal and campomelic dysplasia. Philos Trans R Soc Lond B Biol Sci 350:271–277, discussion 277–278, 1995.

127. Kwok C, Goodfellow PN, Hawkins JR: Evidence to exclude SOX9 as a candidate gene for XY sex reversal without skeletal malformation. J Med Genet 33:800–801, 1996.

128. Meyer J, Sudbeck P, Held M, et al: Mutational analysis of the SOX9 gene in campomelic dysplasia and autosomal sex reversal: Lack of genotype/phenotype correlations. Hum Mol Genet 6:91–98, 1997.

129. Huang B, Wang S, Ning Y, et al: Autosomal XX sex reversal caused by duplication of SOX9. Am J Med Genet 87:349–353, 1999.

130. Bardoni B, Zanaria E, Guioli S, et al: A dosage sensitive locus at chromosome Xp21 is involved in male to female sex reversal. Nat Genet 7:497–501, 1994.

131. Goodfellow PN, Camerino G: DAX-1, an "antitestis" gene. Cell Mol Life Sci 55:857–863, 1999.

132. Baumstark A, Barbi G, Djalali M, et al: Xp-duplications with and without sex reversal. Hum Genet 97:79–86, 1996.

133. Krauss CM, Turksoy RN, Atkins L, et al: Familial premature ovarian failure due to interstitial deletion of the long arm of the X chromosome. N Engl J Med 317:125–131, 1987.

134. Simpson JL: Disorders of sexual differentiation, etiology and clinical delineation. New York, Academic Press, 1976.

135. Ogata T, Matsuo N: Comparison of adult height between patients with XX and XY gonadal dysgenesis: Support for a Y specific growth gene(s). J Med Genet 29:539–541, 1992.

136. Judd HL, Scully RE, Atkins L, et al: Pure gonadal dysgenesis with progressive hirsutism. N Engl J Med 282:881–885, 1970.

137. Turner HH: A syndrome of infantilism, congenital webbed neck and cubitus valgus. Endocrinology 23:566–578, 1938.

138. Ullrich O: Uber typische Kombinationsbilder multipler Abartung. Z Kinderheilkd 49:271–276, 1930.

139. Ford CE, Jones KW, Polani PE, et al: A sex chromosome anomaly in a case of gonadal dysgenesis (Turner's syndrome). Lancet 82:711–713, 1959.

140. Connor JM, Loughlin SAR: Molecular genetic of Turner's syndrome. Acta Paediatr Scand 356(Suppl):77–80, 1990.

141. Kim SS, Jung SC, Kim HJ, et al: Chromosome abnormalities in a referred population for suspected chromosomal aberrations: A report of 4117 cases. J Korean Med Sci 14:373–376, 1999.

142. Kosho T, Muroya K, Nagai T, et al: Skeletal features and growth patterns in 14 patients with haploinsufficiency of SHOX: Implications for the development of Turner syndrome. J

Clin Endocrinol Metab 84:4613–4621, 1999.

143. Ellison JW, Wardak Z, Young MF, et al: PHOG, a candidate gene for involvement in the short stature of Turner syndrome. Hum Mol Genet 6:1341–1347, 1997.

144. Rao E, Weiss B, Fukami M, et al: Pseudoautosomal deletions encompassing a novel homeobox gene cause growth failure in idiopathic short stature and Turner syndrome [see comments]. Nat Genet 16:54–63, 1997.

145. Niesler B, Fisher CR, Rappold GA: The human SHOX mutation database. Hum Mutat 20:338–341, 2002.

146. Cormier-Daire V, Belin V, Cusin V, et al: SHOX gene mutations and deletions in dyschondrosteosis or Leri-Weill syndrome. Acta Paediatr Suppl 88:55–59, 1999.

147. Belin V, Cusin V, Viot G: SHOX mutations in dyschondrosteosis (Leri-Weill syndrome). Nat Genet 19:67–69, 1999.

148. Haverkamp F, Wolfle J, Zerres K, et al: Growth retardation in Turner syndrome: Aneuploidy, rather than specific gene loss, may explain growth failure. J Clin Endocrinol Metab 84:4578–4582, 1999.

149. Hall JG, Gilchrist DM: Turner syndrome and its variants. Pediatr Clin North Am 37:1421–1440, 1990.

150. Rosenfeld R, Grumbach MM: Turner Syndrome. New York, Marcel Dekker, 1990.

151. Lippe B: Turner syndrome. Endocrinol Metab Clin North Am 20:121–152, 1991.

152. Ivarsson SA, Carlsson A, Bredberg A, et al: Prevalence of coeliac disease in Turner syndrome. Acta Paediatr 88:933–936, 1999.

153. Barrenas ML, Nylen O, Hanson C: The influence of karyotype on the auricle, otitis media and hearing in Turner syndrome. Hear Res 138:163–170, 1999.

154. Page LY: Final heights in 45,X Turner's syndrome with spontaneous sexual development: Review of European and American reports. J Pediatr Endocrinol 6:153–158, 1993.

155. Hovatta O: Pregnancies in women with Turner's syndrome. Ann Med 31:106–110, 1999.

156. Ranke MB, Pfugler H, Rosendahl W, et al: Turner's syndrome: Spontaneous growth in 150 cases and review of the literature. Eur J Pediatr 141:81–88, 1983.

157. Brook CG, Gasser T, Werder EA, et al: Height correlations between parents and mature offspring in normal subjects with Turner's and Klinefeleter's and other syndromes. Ann Hum Biol 4:17–22, 1977.

158. Massa G, Vanderschueren-Lodeweyckx M, Malvaux P: Linear growth in patients with Turner's syndrome: Influence of spontaneous puberty and parental height. Eur J Pediatr 149:246–250, 1990.

159. Sas TC, Gerver WJ, de Bruin R, et al: Body proportions during long-term

growth hormone treatment in girls with Turner syndrome participating in a randomized dose-response trial. J Clin Endocrinol Metab 84:4622–4628, 1999.

160. Hughes PCR, Ribeiro J, Hughes IA: Body proportions in Turner's syndrome. Arch Dis Child 61:506–517, 1986.

161. Conte FA, Kaplan SL, Grumbach MM: A diphasic pattern of gonadotropin secretion in patients with the syndrome of gonadal dysgenesis. J Clin Endocrinol Metab 40:670–674, 1975.

162. Glück M, Attanasio A, Speer U, et al: Prevalence of autoantibodies to endocrine organs in girls with Ullrich-Turner syndrome. Horm Res 38:114–119, 1992.

163. Sharland M, Burch M, McKenna WM, et al: A clinical study of Noonan syndrome. Arch Dis Child 67:178–183, 1992.

164. Zenker M, Buheitel G, Rauch R, et al: Genotype-phenotype correlations in Noonan syndrome. J Pediatr 144:368–374, 2004.

165. Ernould C, Bourguignon JP, Pierard GE: Activation of pigmented skin naevi (PSN) during growth hormone (GH) therapy. Horm Res 35:27, 1991.

166. Sas TC, de Muinck Keizer-Schrama SM, Stijnen T, et al: Normalization of height in girls with Turner syndrome after long-term growth hormone treatment: Results of a randomized dose-response trial. J Clin Endocrinol Metab 84:4607–4612, 1999.

167. Ranke MB, Lindberg A, Chatelain P, et al: Predicting the response to recombinant human growth hormone in Turner syndrome: KIGS models. KIGS International Board. Kabi International Growth Study. Acta Paediatr Suppl 88:122–125, 1999.

168. Binder G, Schwarze CP, Ranke MB: Identification of short stature caused by SHOX defects and therapeutic effect of recombinant human growth hormone. J Clin Endocrinol Metab 85:245–249, 2000.

169. Hochberg Z, Zadik Z: Final height in young women with Turner syndrome after GH therapy: An open controlled study [see comments]. Eur J Endocrinol 141:218–224, 1999.

170. Cacciari E, Mazzanti L: Final height of patients with Turner's syndrome treated with growth hormone (GH): Indications for GH therapy alone at high doses and late estrogen therapy. Italian Study Group for Turner Syndrome. J Clin Endocrinol Metab 84:4510–4515, 1999.

171. Vanderschueren-Lodeweyckx M, Massa G, Maes MM, et al: Growth promoting effect of GH and low doses of ethinylestradiol in girls with Turner's syndrome. J Clin Endocrinol Metab 70:122–128, 1990.

172. Lanes R, Gunczler P, Esaa S, et al: Decreased bone mass despite long-term estrogen replacement therapy in young women with Turner's syndrome and previously normal bone density. Fertil Steril 72:896–899, 1999.

173. Harris M, Hofman PL, Cutfield WS: Growth hormone treatment in children: Review of safety and efficacy. Paediatr Drugs 6:93–103, 2004.

174. Chan CLK, Cameron IT, Findlay JK, et al: Ovocyte donation and in vitro fertilization for hypergonadotropic hypogonadism: Clinical state of the art. Obstet Gynecol Surv 42:350–362, 1987.

175. Ramsay M, Bernstein R, Zwane W, et al: XX true hermaphroditism in Southern African blacks: An enigma of primary sexual differentiation. Am J Hum Genet 43:4–13, 1988.

175a. Salèn E: Ein Fall von Hermaphroditismus verus beim Menschen. Verh dt Ges Path 2:241–243, 1899.

176. Lee S: High incidence of true hermaphroditism in the early human embryos. Biol Neonate 18:418–425, 1971.

177. van Niekerk WA: True hermaphroditism: An analytic review with a report of three new cases. Am J Obstet Gynecol 126:890–907, 1976.

178. Montero M, Mendez R, Valverde D, et al: True hermaphroditism and normal male external genitalia: A rare presentation. Acta Paediatr 88:909–911, 1999.

179. Hayashi T, Kageyama Y, Ishizaka K, et al: True hermaphroditism associated with microphthalmia. Eur J Endocrinol 140:62–65, 1999.

180. Josso N, de Grouchy J, Auvert J, et al: True hermaphroditism with XX/XY mosaicism, probably due to double fertilization of the ovum. J Clin Endocrinol Metab 25:114–126, 1965.

181. Fellous M, Abbas N, Souleyreau M: 46,XX true hermaphroditism positive for Y DNA sequence is due to an X/Y terminal exchange. Horm Res 35 (Suppl 2):A26, 1991.

182. Braun A, Kammerer S, Cleve H, et al: True hermaphroditism in a 46,XY individual, caused by a postzygotic somatic point mutation in the male gonadal sex-determining locus (SRY): Molecular genetics and histological findings in a sporadic case. Am J Hum Genet 52:578–585, 1993.

183. Kojima Y, Hayashi Y, Asai N, et al: Detection of the sex-determining region of the Y chromosome in 46,XX true hermaphroditism. Urol Int 60:235–238, 1998.

184. Page DC, Mosher R, Simpson EM, et al: The sex-determining region of the human Y chromosome encodes a finger protein. Cell 51:1091–1104, 1987.

185. Palmer MS, Sinclair AH, Berta P, et al: Genetic evidence that ZFY is not the testes determining factor. Nature 342:937–939, 1989.

186. Tanoue A, Nakamura T, Endo F, et al: Sex-determining region Y (SRY) in a patient with 46,XX true hermaphroditism. Jpn J Human Genet 37:311–320, 1992.

187. McElreavey K, Rappaport R, Vilain E, et al: A minority of 46,XX true hermaphrodites are positive for the

Y-DNA sequence including SRY. Hum Genet 90:121–125, 1992.

188. Damiani D, Fellous M, McElreavey K, et al: True hermaphroditism: Clinical aspects and molecular studies in 16 cases. Eur J Endocrinol 136:201–204, 1997.

189. Abbas N, McElreavey K, Leconiat M, et al: Familial case of 46,XX male and 46,XX true hermaphrodite associated with a paternal-derived SRY-bearing X chromosome. C R Acad Sci III 316:375–383, 1993.

190. Kim MH, Gumpel JA, Graff P: Pregnancy in a true hermaphrodite. Obstet Gynecol 535:40–42, 1979.

191. Tiltman AJ, Sweerts M: Multiparity in a covert true hermaphrodite. Obstet Gynecol 60:752–754, 1982.

192. Bergmann M, Schleicher G, Böcker R, et al: True hermaphroditism with bilateral ovotestes: A case report. Int J Androl 12:139–147, 1989.

193. Nihoul-Fékété C, Lortat-Jacob S, Cachin O, et al: Preservation of gonadal function in true hermaphroditism. J Pediatr Surg 19:49–55, 1984.

194. Tillem SM, Stock JA, Hanna MK: Vaginal construction in children. J Urol 160:186–190, 1998.

195. Starceski PJ, Sieber WK, Lee PA: Fertility in true hermaphroditism. Adolesc Pediatr Gynecol 1:55–56, 1988.

196. Krstic ZD, Smoljanic Z, Vukanic D, et al: True hermaphroditism: 10 years' experience. Pediatr Surg Int 16:580–583, 2000.

197. Aaronson IA: True hermaphroditism: A review of 41 cases with observations on testicular histology and function. Br J Urol 57:775–779, 1985.

198. Scully RE: Neoplasia associated with anomalous sexual development and abnormal sex chromosomes. Pediatr Adolesc Endocrinol 8:203–217, 1981.

199. Savage MO, Lowe DG: Gonadal neoplasia and abnormal sexual differentiation. Clin Endocrinol (Oxf) 32:519–533, 1990.

200. Müller J, Skakkebaek NE: Testicular carcinoma in situ in children with the androgen insensitivity (testicular feminization) syndrome. Br Med J 288:1419–1420, 1984.

201. Berthezène F, Forest MG, Grimaud JA, et al: Leydig cell agenesis: A new cause of male pseudohermaproditism. N Engl J Med 292:969–972, 1976.

202. Forest MG: Disorders of Leydig cell differentiation: Leydig cell agenesis or hypoplasia, gonadotropin resistance. In Martinez-Mora J (ed): Textbook: Intersexual States. Barcelona, Doyma SA, 1994, pp 200–215.

203. Pérez-Palacios G, Scaglia HE, Kofman-Alfaro S, et al: Inherited male pseudohermaphroditism due to gonadotropin unresponsiveness. Acta Endocrinol 98:148–155, 1981.

204. Lee PA, Rock JA, Brown TR: Leydig cell hypofunction resulting in male pseudohermaphroditism. Fertil Steril 37:675–679, 1982.

205. Saldanha PH, Arnhold IJP, Mendoça BB, et al: A clinico-genetic investigation of Leydig cell hypoplasia. Am J Med Gen 26:337–344, 1987.
206. Schwartz M, Imperato-McGinley J, Peterson RE, et al: Male pseudohermaphroditism secondary to an abnormality in Leydig cell differentaition. J Clin Endocrinol Metab 52:123–127, 1981.
207. Martinez-Mora J, Sáez JM, Torán N, et al: Male pseudohermaphroditism due to Leydig cell agenesia and absence of testicular LH receptors. Clin Endocrinol 34:485–491, 1991.
208. Tsai-Morris CH, Geng Y, Buczko E, et al: A novel human luteinizing hormone receptor gene. J Clin Endocrinol Metab 83:288–291, 1998.
209. Laue L, Wu SM, Kudo M, et al: A nonsense mutation of the human luteinizing hormone receptor gene in Leydig cell hypoplasia. Hum Mol Genet 4:1429–1433, 1995.
210. Kremer H, Kraaij R, Toledo SP, et al: Male pseudohermaphroditism due to a homozygous missense mutation of the luteinizing hormone receptor gene. Nat Genet 9:160–164, 1995.
211. Laue LL, Wu SM, Kudo M, et al: Compound heterozygous mutations of the luteinizing hormone receptor gene in Leydig cell hypoplasia. Mol Endocrinol 10:987–997, 1996.
212. Latronico AC, Anasti J, Arnhold IJ, et al: Brief report: Testicular and ovarian resistance to luteinizing hormone caused by inactivating mutations of the luteinizing hormone-receptor gene. N Engl J Med 334:507–512, 1996.
213. Park IJ, Burnett LS, Jones HWJ, et al: A case of male pseudohermaphroditism associated with elevated LH, normal FSH and low testosterone possibly due to the secretion of an abnormal LH molecule. Acta Endocrinol (Copenh) 83:173–181, 1976.
214. Axelrod L, Neer R, Kliman B: Hypogonadism in a male with immunologically active biologically inactive luteinizing hormone: An exception to a venerable rule. J Clin Endocrinol Metab 48:593–603, 1978.
215. Meyer WJ 3rd, Keenan BS, Lacerda LD, et al: Familial male pseudohermaprodistism with normal Leydig cell function at puberty. J Clin Endocrinol Metab 46:593–603, 1978.
216. Smith DW, Lemli L, Opitz JM: A newly recognized syndrome of multiple congenital anomalies. J Pediatr 64:210–217, 1964.
217. Tint GS, Irons M, Elias ER, et al: Defective cholesterol biosynthesis associated with the Smith-Lemli-Opitz syndrome [see comments]. N Engl J Med 330:107–113, 1994.
218. Batta AK, Tint GS, Shefer S, et al: Identification of 8-dehydrocholesterol (cholesta-5,8-dien-3β-ol) in patients with Smith-Lemli-Opitz syndrome. J Lipid Res 36:705–713, 1995.

219. Kelley RI, Hennekam RC: The Smith-Lemli-Opitz syndrome. J Med Genet 37:321–335, 2000.
220. Nowaczyk MJ, Nakamura LM, Eng B, et al: Frequency and ethnic distribution of the common DHCR7 mutation in Smith-Lemli-Opitz syndrome. Am J Med Genet 102:383–386, 2001.
221. Jira PE, Waterham HR, Wanders RJ, et al: Smith-Lemli-Opitz syndrome and the DHCR7 gene. Ann Hum Genet 67:269–280, 2003.
222. Anstey AV: Photosensitivity in the Smith-Lemli-Opitz syndrome. Photodermatol Photoimmunol Photomed 15:217–218, 1999.
223. Elias ER, Hansen RM, Irons M, et al: Rod photoreceptor responses in children with Smith-Lemli-Opitz syndrome. Arch Ophthalmol 121:1738–1743, 2003.
224. Andersson HC, Frentz J, Martinez JE, et al: Adrenal insufficiency in Smith-Lemli-Opitz syndrome. Am J Med Genet 82:382–384, 1999.
225. Cunniff C, Kratz LE, Moser A, et al: Clinical and biochemical spectrum of patients with RSH/Smith-Lemli-Opitz syndrome and abnormal cholesterol metabolism. Am J Med Genet 68:263–269, 1997.
226. Waterham HR, Wijburg FA, Hennekam RC, et al: Smith-Lemli-Opitz syndrome is caused by mutations in the 7-dehydrocholesterol reductase gene [see comments]. Am J Hum Genet 63:329–338, 1998.
227. Battaile KP, Maslen CL, Wassif CA, et al: A simple PCR-based assay allows detection of a common mutation, IVS8-1G→C, in DHCR7 in Smith-Lemli-Opitz syndrome. Genet Test 3:361–363, 1999.
228. Tint GS, Seller M, Hughes-Benzie R, et al: Markedly increased tissue concentrations of 7-dehydrocholesterol combined with low levels of cholesterol are characteristic of the Smith-Lemli-Opitz syndrome. J Lipid Res 36:89–95, 1995.
229. Abuelo DN, Tint GS, Kelley R, et al: Prenatal detection of the cholesterol biosynthetic defect in the Smith-Lemli-Opitz syndrome by the analysis of amniotic fluid sterols. Am J Med Genet 56:281–285, 1995.
230. Bradley LA, Palomaki GE, Knight GJ, et al: Levels of unconjugated estriol and other maternal serum markers in pregnancies with Smith-Lemli-Opitz (RSH) syndrome fetuses [letter]. Am J Med Genet 82:355–358, 1999.
231. Shackleton CH, Roitman E, Kratz LE, et al: Midgestational maternal urine steroid markers of fetal Smith-Lemli-Opitz (SLO) syndrome (7-dehydrocholesterol 7-reductase deficiency). Steroids 64:446–452, 1999.
232. Loeffler J, Utermann G, Witsch-Baumgartner M: Molecular prenatal diagnosis of Smith-Lemli-Opitz syndrome is reliable and efficient. Prenat Diagn 22:827–830, 2002.
233. Irons MB, Nores J, Stewart TL, et al: Antenatal therapy of Smith-Lemli-

Opitz syndrome. Fetal Diagn Ther 14:133–137, 1999.
234. Irons M, Elias ER, Abuelo D, et al: Treatment of Smith-Lemli-Opitz syndrome: Results of a multicenter trial. Am J Med Genet 68:311–314, 1997.
235. Sikora DM, Ruggiero M, Petit-Kekel K, et al: Cholesterol supplementation does not improve developmental progress in Smith-Lemli-Opitz syndrome. J Pediatr 144:783–791, 2004.
236. Dietschy JM, Turley SD: Cholesterol metabolism in the brain. Curr Opin Lipidol 12:105–112, 2001.
237. Caruso PA, Poussaint TY, Tzika AA, et al: MRI and (1)H MRS findings in Smith-Lemli-Opitz syndrome. Neuroradiology 46:3–14, 2004.
238. Miller WL: Molecular biology of steroid hormone synthesis. Endocr Rev 9:292–318, 1988.
239. Forest MG: Inborn error of testosterone biosynthesis. In Josso N (ed): The Intersex Child. Basel, Karger, 1981, pp 133–155.
240. Duque C, Morisaki M, Ikekawa N, et al: The enzyme activity of bovine adrenocortical cytochrome P-450 producing pregnenolone from cholesterol: Kinetic and electrophoretic studies of the reactivity of activity hydrocholesterol intermediates. Biochem Biophys Res Commun 82:174–178, 1978.
241. Takikawa O, Gomi T, Suhara K, et al: Properties of an adrenal cytochrome P-450 (P-450scc) for the side chain cleavage of cholesterol. Arch Biochem Biophys 190:300–306, 1978.
242. Shikita M, Hall PF: Cytochrome P-450 from bovine adrenocortical mitochondria: An enzyme for the side chain cleavage of cholesterol. I. Purification and properties. J Biol Chem 248:5596–5604, 1973.
243. Chung B, Matteson KJ, Voutilainen R, et al: Human cholesterol side-chain cleavage enzyme, P450scc: cDNA cloning, assignment of the gene to chromosome 15, and expression in the placenta. Proc Natl Acad Sci U S A 83:8962–8966, 1986.
244. Matteson KJ, Chung B, Urdea M, et al: Study of cholesterol side-chain cleavage (20,22-desmolase) deficiency causing congenital lipoid adrenal hyperplasia using bovine sequence P450scc oligodeoxyribonucleotide probes. Endocrinology 118:1296–1305, 1986.
245. Nebert DW, Nelson DR, Coon MJ, et al: The P450 gene superfamily: Update on new sequences, gene mapping and recommended nomenclature. DNA Cell Biol 10:1–14, 1991.
246. Sparkes RS, Llisak I, Miller WL: Regional mapping of genes encoding human steroidogenic enzymes: P450scc to 15q23-q24; adrenodoxin to 11q22; adrenodoxin reductase to 17q24-q25; and P450c17 to 10q24-q25. DNA Cell Biol 10:359–366, 1991.

247. Morel Y, Picado-Leonard J, Wu DA, et al: Assignment of the functional gene for human adrenodoxin to chromosome 11q13→qter and of adrenodoxin pseudogenes to chromosome 20cen→q13.1. Am J Hum Genet 43:52–59, 1988.

248. Chang CY, Wu DA, Lai CC, et al: Cloning and structure of the human adrenodoxin gene. DNA 7:609–616, 1988.

249. Solish SB, Picardo-Leonard J, Morel Y, et al: Human adrenodoxin reductase: Two mRNAs encoded by a single gene on chromosome 17cen→q25 are expressed in steroidogenic tissues. Proc Natl Acad Sci U S A 85:7104–7108, 1988.

250. Brutschy P: Hochgradige Lipoidhyperplasie beider Niebennieren mit herdförmigen Kalkablagerungen bei einem Fall von Hypospadias penisscrotalis und droppelseitigem Kryptorchismus mit unechter akzessorisher Nebenniere am rechten Hoden (Pseudohermaphroditismus masculinus externus). Frankf Z Pathol 24:203–240, 1920.

251. Prader A, Gurtner HP: Das Syndrom des Pseudohermaphroditismus masculinus bei kongenitaler Nebennierenindenhyperplasie ohne androgenüberproduktion (adrenaler Pseudohermaphroditismus masculinus). Helv Pædiatr Acta 10:397–411, 1955.

252. Prader A, Siebenmann RE: Nebenniereninsuffieiznz bei kongenitaler Lipodhyperplasie der Nebennieren. Helv Pædiatr Acta 12:569–595, 1957.

253. Prader A, Anders CJPA: Zur Genetik der kongenitalen Lipoidhyperplasie der Niebennieren. Helv Pædiatr Acta 17:285–289, 1962.

254. Degenhart HJ: Prader's syndrome (congenital adrenal hyperplasia). In New MI, Levine LS (eds): Adrenal Diseases in Childhood. Basel, Karger, 1984, pp 125–144.

255. Aya M, Ogata T, Sakaguchi A, et al: Testicular histopathology in congenital lipoid adrenal hyperplasia: A light and electron microscopic study. Horm Res 47:121–125, 1997.

256. Fox RR, Crary DD: Genetics and pathology of hereditary μcongenital adrenal hyperplasia in the rabbit. J Hered 69:251–254, 1978.

257. Goldman AS: Production of congenital lipoid adrenal hyperplasia in rats and inhibition of cholesterol side chain cleavage. Endocrinology 86:1245–1251, 1970.

258. Bose HS, Sato S, Aisenberg J, et al: Mutations in the steroidogenic acute regulatory protein (StAR) in six patients with congenital lipoid adrenal hyperplasia. J Clin Endocrinol Metab 85:3636–3639, 2000.

259. Gassner HL, Toppari J, Quinteiro Gonzalez S, et al: Near-miss apparent SIDS from adrenal crisis. J Pediatr 145:178–183, 2004.

260. Tanae A, Katsumata N, Sato N, et al: Genetic and endocrinological

261. Bose HS, Pescovitz OH, Miller WL: Spontaneous feminization in a 46,XX female patient with congenital lipoid adrenal hyperplasia due to a homozygous frame-shift mutation in the steroidogenic acute regulatory protein. J Clin Endocrinol Metab 82:1511–1515, 1997.

262. Fujieda K, Tajima T, Nakae J, et al: Spontaneous puberty in 46,XX subjects with congenital lipoid adrenal hyperplasia: Ovarian steroidogenesis is spared to some extent despite inactivating mutations in the steroidogenic acute regulatory protein (StAR) gene. J Clin Invest 99:1265–1271, 1997.

263. Nakae J, Tajima T, Sugawara T, et al: Analysis of the steroidogenic acute regulatory protein (StAR) gene in Japanese patients with congenital lipoid adrenal hyperplasia. Hum Mol Genet 6:571–576, 1997.

264. Shima M, Tanae A, Miki K, et al: Mechanism for the development of ovarian cysts in patients with congenital lipoid adrenal hyperplasia. Eur J Endocrinol 142:274–279, 2000.

265. Hauffa BP, Miller WL, Grumbach MM, et al: Congenital adrenal hyperplasia due to deficient cholesterol side chain cleavage activity (20,22 desmolase) in a patient treated for 18 years. Clin Endocrinol (Oxf) 23:481–493, 1985.

266. Katsumata N, Tanae A, Shinagawa T, et al: Homozygous Q258X mutation in the steroidogenic acute regulatory gene in a Japanese patient with congenital lipoid adrenal hyperplasia. Endocr J 44:441–446, 1997.

267. Koizumi S, Kyoya S, Miyawaki T, et al: Cholesterol side-chain cleavage enzyme activity and cytochrome P-450 content an adrenal mitochondria of a patient with congenital lipoid adrenal hyperplasia (Prader disease). Clin Chim Acta 77:301–306, 1977.

268. Saenger P, lin D, Gitelman SE, et al: Congenital lipoid adrenal hyperplasia-genes for P450scc, side chain cleavage enzyme, are normal. J Steroid Biochem Mol Biol 45:87–97, 1993.

269. Lin D, Gitelman SE, Saenger P, et al: Normal genes for the cholesterol side chain cleavage enzyme, P450scc, in congenital lipoid adrenal hyperplasia. J Clin Invest 88:1955–1962, 1991.

270. Sugawara T, Holt JA, Driscoll D, et al: Human steroidogenic acute regulatory protein: Functional activity in COS-1 cells, tissue-specific expression, and mapping of the structural gene to 8p11.2 and a pseudogene to chromosome 13. Proc Natl Acad Sci U S A 92:4778–4482, 1995.

271. Clark BJ, Soo SC, Caron KM, et al: Hormonal and developmental regulation of the steroidogenic acute regulatory protein. Mol Endocrinol 9:1346–1355, 1995.

272. Gonzalez AA, Reyes ML, Carvajal CA, et al: Congenital lipoid adrenal hyperplasia caused by a novel splicing mutation in the gene for the steroidogenic acute regulatory protein. J Clin Endocrinol Metab 89:946–951, 2004.

273. Bose HS, Sugawara T, Strauss III JF, et al: The pathophysiology and genetics of congenital lipoid adrenal hyperplasia. N Engl J Med 335:1870–1878, 1996.

274. Miller WL: Congenital lipoid adrenal hyperplasia: The human gene knockout for the steroidogenic acute regulatory protein. J Mol Endocrinol 19:227–240, 1997.

275. Bose HS, Lingappa VR, Miller WL: The steroidogenic acute regulatory protein, StAR, works only at the outer mitochondrial membrane. Endocr Res 28:295–308, 2002.

276. Stocco DM: An update on the mechanism of action of the steroidogenic acute regulatory (StAR) protein. Exp Clin Endocrinol Diabetes 107:229–235, 1999.

277. Bose HS, Sugawara T, Strauss JF III, et al: The pathophysiology and genetics of congenital lipoid adrenal hyperplasia. International Congenital Lipoid Adrenal Hyperplasia Consortium. N Engl J Med 335:1870–1878, 1996.

278. Caron KM, Soo SC, Parker KL: Targeted disruption of StAR provides novel insights into congenital adrenal hyperplasia. Endocr Res 24:827–834, 1998.

279. Tajima T, Fujieda K, Kouda N, et al: Heterozygous mutation in the cholesterol side chain cleavage enzyme (p450scc) gene in a patient with 46,XY sex reversal and adrenal insufficiency. J Clin Endocrinol Metab 86:3820–3825, 2001.

280. Katsumata N, Ohtake M, Hojo T, et al: Compound heterozygous mutations in the cholesterol side-chain cleavage enzyme gene (CYP11A) cause congenital adrenal insufficiency in humans. J Clin Endocrinol Metab 87:3808–3813, 2002.

281. Ogata T, Ishikawa K, Kodha E, et al: Computed tomography in the early detection of congenital lipoid adrenal hyperplasia. Pediatr Radiol 18:360–361, 1988.

282. Korsch E, Peter M, Hiort O, et al: Gonadal histology with testicular carcinoma in situ in a 15-year-old 46,XY female patient with a premature termination in the steroidogenic acute regulatory protein causing congenital lipoid adrenal hyperplasia. J Clin Endocrinol Metab 84:1628–1632, 1999.

283. Ishi-Ohba H, Saiki N, Inano H, et al: Purification and characterization of rat adrenal 3β-hydroxysteroid dehydrogenase with steroid 5-ene 4-ene isomerase. J Steroid Biochem 24:753–760, 1986.

284. Ishi-Ohba H, Juano H, Tamaoki BI: Purification and properties of testicular

3β-hydroxy-5-ene steroid dehydrogenase and 5-ene-4-ene isomerase. J Steroid Biochem 25:555–560, 1986.

285. Stalvey JRD, Meisler MH, Payne AH: Evidence that the same structural gene encodes testicular and adrenal 3β-hydroxysteroid dehydrogenase-isomerase. Biochem Genet 25:181–190, 1987.

286. Bongiovanni AM: Adreno-genital syndrome with deficiency of 3β-hydroxysteroid dehydrogenase. J Clin Invest 41:2086–2092, 1962.

287. Perrone L, Criscuolo T, Sinisi AA, et al: Male pseudohermaphroditism due to 3β-hydroxysteroid dehydrogenase deficiency associated with atrial septal defect. Acta Endocrinol (Copenh) 110:532–539, 1985.

288. Schneider G, Genel M, Bongiovanni AM, et al: Persistent testicular Δ⁵-isomerase-3β-hydroxysteroid dehydrogenase (Δ⁵-3β-HSD) deficiency in the Δ⁵-3β-HSD form of congenital adrenal hyperplasia. J Clin Invest 55:681–690, 1975.

289. Bongiovanni AM: Acquired adrenal hyperplasia with special reference to 3β-hydroxysteroid dehydrogenase. Fertil Steril 35:599–608, 1981.

290. Gendrel D, Chaussain JL, Roger M, et al: L'hyperplasie surrénale congénitale par bloc de la 3β-hydroxystéroïde déshydogénase. Arch Fr Pediatr 36:647–655, 1979.

291. Goldman AS, Yakovac WC, Bongiovanni AM: Development of activity of 3β-hydroxysteroid dehydrogenase in human fetal tissues and in two anencephalic newborns. J Clin Endocrinol Metab 26:14–22, 1966.

292. Pang S, Levine LS, Stoner E, et al: Non salt-losing congenital adrenal hyperplasia due to 3β-hydroxysteroid dehydrogenase deficiency with normal glomerulosa function. J Clin Endocrinol Metab 56:808–818, 1983.

293. Mébarki F, Sanchez R, Rhéaume E, et al: Non salt-losing male pseudohermaphroditism due to the novel homozygous N100S mutation in the type II 3β-hydroxysteroid dehydrogenase (HSD3B2) gene. J Clin Endocrinol Metab 80:2127–2134, 1995.

294. Peretti Ed, Forest MG, Feit JP, et al: Endocrine studies in two children with male pseudohermaphroditism due to to 3β-hydroxysteroid dehydrogenase defect. In Genazzani AR, Thijssen JHH, Siiteri PK (eds): Adrenal Androgens. New York, Raven Press, 1980, pp 141–145.

295. Mendonça B, Bloise W, Arnhold I, et al: Male pseudohermaphroditism due to 3β-hydroxysteroid dehydrogenase deficiency without clinical salt losing in two adult cousins. J Steroid Biochem 25 (Suppl):20S, 1986.

296. Cravioto MACd, Ulloa-Aguirre A, Bermudez JA, et al: A new inherited variant of 3β-hydroxysteroid dehydrogenase-isomerase deficiency syndrome: Evidence for the existence of two isoenzymes. J Clin Endocrinol Metab 62:360–367, 1986.

297. Zachmann M, Forest MG, de Peretti E: 3β-hydroxysteroid dehydrogenase deficiency: Follow-up studies in a girl with pubertal bone age. Horm Res 11:292–302, 1979.

298. Pang S, Lerner AJ, Stoner E: Late onset adrenal 3β-hydroxysteroid dehydrogenase deficiency: A cause of hirsutism in pubertal and post pubertal women. J Clin Endocrinol Metab 60:428–439, 1985.

299. Temek JW, Pang S, Nelson C, et al: Genetic defects of steroidogenesis in premature pubarche. J Clin Endocrinol Metab 64:609–617, 1987.

300. Parks GA, Bermudez JA, Anast CS, et al: A pubertal boy with a 3β-hydroxysteroid dehydrogenase defect. J Clin Endocrinol Metab 38:269–278, 1971.

301. Jänne O, Perheentupa J, Viinikka L, et al: Testicular endocrine function in a pubertal boy with a 3β-hydroxysteroid dehydrogenase deficiency. J Clin Endocrinol Metab 39:206–209, 1974.

302. Martin F, Perheentupa J, Adlerkreutz H: Plasma and urinary androgens and œstrogens in a pubertal boy with 3β-hydroxysteroid dehydrogenase deficiency. J Steroid Biochem 13:197–201, 1980.

303. Kenny FM, Reynolds JW, Green OC: Partial 3β-hydroxysteroid dehydrogenase (3β-HSD) deficiency in a family with congenital adrenal hyperplasia: Evidence for increasing 3β-HSD activity with age. Pediatrics 56:756–765, 1971.

304. Forest MG: Pubertal expression in enzymatic and receptor steroid defects. In Bergadà C, Moguilevsky JA (eds): Puberty: Basic and Clinical Aspects. Rome, Ares-Serono Symposia Publications, 1995, pp 305–318.

305. Rhéaume E, Simard J, Morel Y, et al: Congenital adrenal hyperplasia due to a homozygous nonsense mutation in the type II 3β-hydroxysteroid dehydrogenase gene. Nat Genet 1:239–245, 1992.

306. Alos N, Moisan AM, Ward L, et al: A novel A10E homozygous mutation in the HSD3B2 gene causing severe salt-wasting 3β-hydroxysteroid dehydrogenase deficiency in 46,XX and 46,XY French-Canadians: Evaluation of gonadal function after puberty. J Clin Endocrinol Metab 85:1968–1974, 2000.

307. Paula FJ, Dick-de-Paula I, Pontes A, et al: Hyperandrogenism due to 3β-hydroxysteroid dehydrogenase deficiency with accessory adrenocortical tissue: A hormonal and metabolic evaluation. Braz J Med Biol Res 27:1149–1158, 1994.

308. Cara JF, Moshang TJ, Bongiovanni AM, et al: Elevated 17-hydroxyprogesterone and testosterone in a newborn with 3β-hydroxysteroid dehydrogenase deficiency. N Engl J Med 313:618–621, 1985.

309. Rosenfield RL, Barmach de Niepmniszshe A, Kenny FM, et al: The response to human chorionic gonadotropin (hCG) administration in boys with and without Δ⁵-3β-hydroxysteroid dehydrogenase deficiency. J Clin Endocrinol Metab 39:370–374, 1974.

310. Pang S: The molecular and clinical spectrum of 3β-hydroxy steroid dehydrogenase deficiency disorder. Trends Endocrinol Metab 9:82–86, 1998.

311. Morel Y, Mebarki F, Rheaume E, et al: Structure-function relationships of 3β-hydroxysteroid dehydrogenase: Contribution made by the molecular genetics of 3β hydroxysteroid dehydrogenase deficiency. Steroids 62:176–184, 1997.

312. Moisan AM, Ricketts ML, Tardy V, et al: New insight into the molecular basis of 3β-hydroxysteroid dehydrogenase deficiency: Identification of 8 mutations in the HSD3B2 gene in 11 patients from 7 new families and comparison of the functional properties of 25 mutant enzymes. J Clin Endocrinol Metab 84:4410–4425, 1999.

313. Simard J, Moisan AM, Morel Y: Congenital adrenal hyperplasia due to 3β-hydroxysteroid dehydrogenase/Δ⁵-Δ⁴ isomerase deficiency. Semin Reprod Med 20:255–276, 2002.

314. Lutfallah C, Wang W, Mason JI, et al: Newly proposed hormonal criteria via genotypic proof for type II 3β-hydroxysteroid dehydrogenase deficiency. J Clin Endocrinol Metab 87:2611–2622, 2002.

315. Pang S, Carbunaru G, Haider A, et al: Carriers for type II 3β-hydroxysteroid dehydrogenase (HSD3B2) deficiency can only be identified by HSD3B2 genotype study and not by hormone test. Clin Endocrinol (Oxf) 58:323–331, 2003.

316. Luu-The V, Lachance Y, Labrie C, et al: Full lenght cDNA structure and deduced amino acid sequence of human 3β-hydroxy-5-ene steroid dehydrogenase. Mol Endocrinol 3:1310–1312, 1989.

317. Lorence MC, Corbin CJ, Kamimura N, et al: Structural analysis of the gene encoding human 3β-hydroxysteroid dehydrogenase Δ⁵-Δ4-isomerase. Mol Endocrinol 4:1850–1855, 1990.

318. Rhéaume E, Lachance Y, Zhao HF, et al: Structure and expression of a new complementary DNA encoding the almost exclusive 3β-hydroxysteroid dehydrogenase/Δ⁵-Δ⁴-isomerase in human adrenals and gonads. Mol Endocrinol 5:1147–1157, 1991.

319. Lachance Y, Luu-The V, Labrie C, et al: Characterization of human 3β-hydroxysteroid dehydrogenase/Δ⁵-Δ⁴ isomerase gene and its expression in mammalian cells. J Biol Chem 265:20469–20475, 1990.

320. Lachance Y, Luu-The V, Verreault H, et al: Structure of the human type-II 3β-hydroxysteroid dehydrogenase/Δ⁴-Δ⁵ isomerase (3β-HSD) gene: Adrenal

and gonadal specificity. DNA Cell Biol 10:701–711, 1991.

321. Morrison N, Nickson DA, McBride MW, et al: Regional chromosomal assignment of human 3-β-hydroxy-5-ene steroid dehydrogenase to 1p13.1 by non-isotopic in situ hybridization. Hum Genet 87:223–225, 1991.

322. Labrie F, Simard J, Luu-The V, et al: Structure, and tissue-specific expression of 3β-hydroxysteroid dehydrogenase/5-ene-4-ene isomerase genes in human and rat classical and peripheral steroidogenic tissues. J Steroid Biochem Mol Biol 41:421–435, 1992.

323. Simard J, Rhéaume E, Sanchez R, et al: Molecular basis of congenital adrenal hyperplasia due to 3β-hydroxysteroid dehydrogenase deficiency. Mol Endocrinol 7:716–728, 1993.

324. Simard J, Rheaume E, Leblanc JF, et al: Congenital adrenal hyperplasia caused by a novel homozygous frameshift mutation 273 delta AA in type II 3 beta-hydroxysteroid dehydrogenase gene (HSD3B2) in three male patients of Afghan/Pakistani origin. Hum Mol Genet 3:327–330, 1994.

325. Zhang L, Sakkal-Alkaddour H, Chang YT, et al: A new compound heterozygous frameshift mutation in the type II 3β-hydroxysteroid dehydrogenase (3β-HSD) gene causes salt-wasting 3β-HSD deficiency congenital adrenal hyperplasia. J Clin Endocrinol Metab 81:291–295, 1996.

326. Johannsen TH, Mallet D, Dige-Petersen N, et al: Delayed diagnosis of congenital adrenal hyperplasia with salt wasting due to type II 3β-Hydroxysteroid dehydrogenase deficiency. J Clin Endocr Metab 2004 (in press).

327. Rhéaume E, Sanchez R, Simard J, et al: Molecular basis of congenital adrenal hyperplasia in two siblings with classical nonsalt-losing 3β-hydroxysteroid dehydrogenase deficiency. J Clin Endocrinol Metab 79:1012–1018, 1994.

328. McCartin S, Russell AJ, Fisher RA, et al: Phenotypic variability and origins of mutations in the gene encoding 3β-hydroxysteroid dehydrogenase type II. J Mol Endocrinol 24:75–82, 2000.

329. Marui S, Castro M, Latronico AC, et al: Mutations in the type II 3β-hydroxysteroid dehydrogenase (HSD3B2) gene can cause premature pubarche in girls. Clin Endocrinol (Oxf) 52:67–75, 2000.

330. Pang S, Wang W, Rich B, et al: A novel nonstop mutation in the stop codon and a novel missense mutation in the type II 3β-hydroxysteroid dehydrogenase (3β-HSD) gene causing, respectively, nonclassic and classic 3β-HSD deficiency congenital adrenal hyperplasia. J Clin Endocrinol Metab 87:2556–2563, 2002.

331. Zerah M, Rheaume E, Mani P, et al: No evidence of mutations in the genes for type I and type II 3β-hydroxysteroid dehydrogenase (3β-HSD) in nonclassical 3β-HSD deficiency. J Clin Endocrinol Metab 79:1811–1817, 1994.

332. Chang YT, Zhang L, Alkaddour HS, et al: Absence of molecular defect in the type II 3β-hydroxysteroid dehydrogenase (3β-HSD) gene in premature pubarche children and hirsute female patients with moderately decreased adrenal 3β-HSD activity. Pediatr Res 37:820–824, 1995.

333. Sakkal-Alkaddour H, Zhang L, Yang X, et al: Studies of 3β-hydroxysteroid dehydrogenase genes in infants and children manifesting premature pubarche and increased adrenocorticotropin-stimulated $\Delta^5$-steroid levels. J Clin Endocrinol Metab 81:3961–3965, 1996.

334. Marui S, Russell AJ, Paula FJ, et al: Genotyping of the type II 3β-hydroxysteroid dehydrogenase gene (HSD3B2) in women with hirsutism and elevated ACTH-stimulated $\Delta^5$-steroids. Fertil Steril 74:553–557, 2000.

335. Carbunaru G, Prasad P, Scoccia B, et al: The hormonal phenotype of nonclassic 3β-hydroxysteroid dehydrogenase (HSD3B) deficiency in hyperandrogenic females is associated with insulin-resistant polycystic ovary syndrome and is not a variant of inherited HSD3B2 deficiency. J Clin Endocrinol Metab 89:783–794, 2004.

336. Zachmann M, Prader A: 17,20-Desmolase deficiency. In New MI, Levine LS (eds): Adrenal Diseases in Childhood. Basel, Karger, 1984, pp 95–109.

337. Fevold RH, Lorence MC, McCarthy JL, et al: Rat P450c17 from testes: Characterization of a full-length cDNA encoding a unique steroid hydroxylase capable of catalyzing both $\Delta^4$- and $\Delta^5$-steroid-17,20-lyase reactions. Mol Endocrinol 3:968–975, 1989.

338. Bradshaw KD, Wareman MR, Couch RT, et al: Characterization of complementary deoxyribonucleic acid for human adrenocortical 17α-hydroxylase: A probe for analysis of 17α-hydroxylase deficiency. Mol Endocrinol 1:348–354, 1987.

339. Nakajin S, Shinoda M, Haniu M, et al: C21 steroid side chain cleavage enzyme from porcine adrenal microsomes: Purification and characterization of the 17α-hydroxylase/C17-20 lyase cytochrome P-450. J Biol Chem 259:3971–3976, 1984.

340. Picado-Leonard J, Miller WL: Cloning and sequence of the human gene for P450c17 (steroid 17α-hydroxylase/17,20-lyase): Similarity with the gene for P450c21. DNA 6:439–448, 1987.

341. Matteson KJ, Picado-Leonard J, Chung BC, et al: Assignment of the gene for adrenal P450c17 (steroid 17α-hydroxylase/17,20-lyase) to human chromosome 10. J Clin Endocrinol Metab 63:789–791, 1986.

342. Voutilainen R, Tapanainen J, Chung BC, et al: Hormonal regulation of P450scc (20,22-desmolase) and P450c17 (17α-hydroxylase/17,20-lyase) in cultured human granulosa cells. J Clin Endocrinol Metab 63:202–207, 1986.

343. Voutilainen R, Miller WL: Developmental and hormonal regulation of mRNA's for insulin-like growth factor II and steroidogenic enzymes in human fetal adrenals and gonads. DNA 7:9–15, 1988.

344. Diblasio AM, Voutilainen R, Jaffe RB, et al: Hormonal regulation of mRNAs for P450scc (cholesterol side chain cleavage enzyme) and P450c17 (17α-hydroxylase/17,20-lyase) in cultured human fetal adrenal cells. J Clin Endocrinol Metab 65:170–175, 1987.

345. Schiebinger RJ, Albertson BD, Cassorla FG, et al: The developmental changes in plasma adrenal androgens during infancy and adrenarche are associated with changing activities of adrenal microsomal 17-hydroxylase and 17-20 desmolase. J Clin Endocrinol Metab 67:1177–1182, 1981.

346. Voutilainen R, Miller WL: Developmental expression of genes for the steroidogenic enzymes P450cc (20,22 desmolase), P450c17 (17α-hydroxylase/17,20 lyase) and P450c21 (21-hydroxylase) in the human fetus. J Clin Endocrinol Metab 63:1145–1150, 1986.

347. Erikson GF, Magoffin DA, Dyer CA, et al: The ovarian androgen producing cells: A review of structure/function relationship. Endocr Rev 6:371–379, 1985.

348. Chung B, Picado-Leonard J, Haniu M, et al: Cytochrome P450c17 (steroid 17α-hydroxylase/ 17-20 lyase): Cloning of human adrenal and testes cDNAs indicate the same gene is expressed in both tissues. Proc Natl Acad Sci U S A 84:407–411, 1987.

349. Mantero F, Scaroni C: Enzymatic defects of steroidogenesis: 17α-Hydroxylase. In New MI, Levine LS (eds): Adrenal Diseases in Childhood. Basel, Karger, 1984, pp 83–94.

350. Bosson D, Wolter R, Toppet M, et al: Partial 17,20-desmolase and 17α-hydroxylase deficiencies in a 16 year old boy. J Endocrinol Invest 11:527–534, 1988.

351. Forest M, Jacard V, Morel Y, et al: Combined 17-hydroxylase and 17,20-desmolase deficiencies: Natural history in a female and diagnosis by systematic studies in her brother. Horm Res 33(Suppl 3):14, 1990.

352. Biglieri EG, Herron MA, Brust N: 17α-hydroxylation deficiency in man. J Clin Invest 45:1946–1954, 1966.

353. New MI: Male pseudohermaphroditism due to 17α-hydroxylase deficiency. J Clin Invest 49:1930–1941, 1970.

354. Tvedegaard E, Frederiksen V, Ølgaard K, et al: Two cases of 17α-hydroxylase deficiency—one combined with complete gonadal agenesis. Acta Endocrinol (Copenh) 98:267–273, 1981.

355. Yanase T, Simpson ER, Waterman MR: 17α-hydroxylase/17,20-lyase deficiency: From clinical investigation to molecular definition. Endocr Rev 12:91–108, 1991.

356. Dean RJ, Shackleton CHL, Winter JSD: Diagnosis and natural history of 17-hydroxylase deficiency in a newborn male. J Clin Endocrinol Metab 59:513–520, 1984.

357. Biglieri EG: Mechanisms establishing the mineralocorticoid hormone patterns in the 17α-hydroxylase deficiency syndrome. J Steroid Biochem 11:653–657, 1979.

358. Bricaire H, Luton JP, Laudat P, et al: A new male pseudohermaphroditism associated with hypertension due to a block of 17α-hydroxylation. J Clin Endocrinol Metab 35:67–71, 1972.

359. Tourniaire J, Audi-Parera L, Loras B, et al: Male pseudohermaphroditism with hypertension due to 17α-hydroxylation deficiency. Clin Endocrinol 5:53–61, 1976.

360. Waldhäusl W, Herkner K, Notwotny P, et al: Combined 17α- and 18-hydroxylase deficiency associated with complete male pseudohermaphroditism and hypoaldosteronism. J Clin Endocrinol Metab 46:236–246, 1978.

361. Saruta T, Kondo K, Saito I, et al: Control of aldosterone in 17α-hydroxylase deficiency. Horm Res 13:98–108, 1980.

362. Kater CE, Biglieri EG, Brust N, et al: The unique pattern of plasma aldosterone and 18-hydroxycorticosterone concentrations in the 17α-hydroxylase deficiency syndrome. J Clin Endocrinol Metab 55:295–302, 1982.

363. Garcia-Mayor RVG, Sopeña B, Fluiters E, et al: Testicular adrenal-like tissue in a patient with 17α-hydroxylase deficiency. Horm Res 38:241–244, 1992.

364. Winter JSD, Couch RM, Muller J, et al: Combined 17-hydroxylase and 17,20-desmolase deficiencies: Evidence for synthesis of a defective cytochrome P450c17. J Clin Endocrinol Metab 68:309–316, 1989.

365. D'Armiento M, reda G, Kater C, et al: 17α-hydroxylase deficiency: Mineralocorticoid hormone profiles in an affected family. J Clin Endocrinol Metab 56:697–701, 1983.

366. Rohmer V, Barbot N, Bertrand P, et al: A Case of male pseudohermaphroditism due to 17α-hydroxylase deficiency and hormonal profiles in the nuclear family. J Clin Endocrinol Metab 71:523–529, 1990.

367. Hammerstein J, Zielske F, Distler A, et al: 17α-hydroxylase deficiency of the gonads and adrenals in a male pseudohermaphrodite. Acta Endocrinol (Copenh) 173(Suppl):76A, 1973.

368. Salti IS, Hajj H, Dhib-Jalbut S: Testicular in vitro conversion of progesterone to testosterone and androstenedione in 17α-hydroxylase deficiency. J Steroid Biochem 17:155–157, 1982.

369. Peretti de E, Cadillon E: In vitro testicular biosynthesis in two cases of 17α-hydroxylase deficiency. Proceedings of the 65th Meeting of the Endocrine Society 1983, p 944 (abstract).

370. Vargas A, Reiter EO, Kula R, et al: Direct determination of 17α-hydroxylase (17OHase) deficiency in a male pseudohermaphrodite by in vitro studies of testicular steroid biosynthesis. Pediatr Res 15:515, 1981.

371. Kagimoto M, Winter JSD, Simpson ER, et al: Structural characterization of normal and mutant human steroid 17α-hydroxylase genes: Molecular basis of one example of combined 17α-hydroxylase/17,20-lyase deficiency. Mol Endocrinol 2:564–570, 1988.

372. Yanase T, Sanders D, Shibata A, et al: Combined 17α-hydroxylase/17,20-lyase deficiency due to a 7 basepair duplication in the N-terminal region of the cytochrome P-45017alpha (CYP17) gene. J Clin Endocrinol Metab 70:1325–1329, 1990.

373. Imai T, Yanase T, Waterman MR, et al: Canadian Mennonites and individuals residing in the Friesland region of the Netherlands share the same molecular basis of 17α-hydroxylase deficiency. Hum Genet 89:95–96, 1992.

374. Biason A, Mantero F, Scaroni C, et al: Deletion within the CYP17-gene together with insertion of foreign DNA is the cause of combined complete 17α-hydroxylase/17,20-lyase deficiency in an Italian patient. Mol Endocrinol 5:2037–2045, 1991.

375. Lin D, Black SM, Nagahama Y, et al: Steroid 17α-hydroxylase and 17,20-lyase activities of P450c17: Contributions of serine106 and P450 reductase. Endocrinology 132:2498–2506, 1993.

376. Oshiro C, Takasu N, Wakugami T, et al: Seventeen α-hydroxylase deficiency with one base pair deletion of the cytochrome P450c17 (CYP17) gene. J Clin Endocr Metab 80:2526–2529, 1995.

377. Yanase T: 17α-Hydroxylase/17,20-lyase defects. J Steroid Biochem Mol Biol 53:153–157, 1995.

378. Waterman MR, Keeney DS: Genes involved in androgen biosynthesis and the male phenotype. Horm Res 38:217–211, 1992.

379. Yamaguchi H, Nakazato M, Miyazato M, et al: A 5'-splice site mutation in the cytochrome P450 steroid 17α-hydroxylase gene in 17α-hydroxylase deficiency. J Clin Endocrinol Metab 82:1934–1938, 1997.

380. Laflamme N, Leblanc JF, Mailloux J, et al: Mutation R96W in cytochrome P450c17 gene causes combined 17α-hydroxylase/17-20-lyase deficiency in two French Canadian patients. J Clin Endocrinol Metab 81:264–268, 1996.

381. Suzuki Y, Nagashima T, Nomura Y, et al: A new compound heterozygous mutation (W17X, 436 + 5G→T) in the cytochrome P450c17 gene causes 17α-hydroxylase/17,20-lyase

deficiency. J Clin Endocrinol Metab 83:199–202, 1998.

382. Yamaguchi H, Nakazato M, Miyazato M, et al: Identification of a novel splicing mutation and 1-bp deletion in the 17α-hydroxylase gene of Japanese patients with 17α-hydroxylase deficiency. Hum Genet 102:635–639, 1998.

383. Ahlgren R, Yanase T, Simpson ER, et al: Compound heterozygous mutations (Arg 239→Stop, Pro 342→Thr) in the CYP17(P450$_{17\alpha}$) gene lead to ambiguous external genitalia in a male patient with partial combined 17 alpha-hydroxylase/17, 20-lyase deficiency. J Clin Endocrinol Metab 70:1325–1329, 1992.

384. Peter M, Sippell WG, Wernze H: Diagnosis and treatment of 17-hydroxylase deficiency. J Steroid Biochem Mol Biol 45:107–116, 1993.

385. Forest MG, Lecornu M, de Peretti E: Familial male pseudohermaphroditism due to 17,20 desmolase deficiency. I. In vivo endocrine studies. J Clin Endocrinol Metab 50:826–833, 1980.

386. Larrea F, Lisker R, Baarnuelos R, et al: Hypergonadotrophic hypogonadism in an XX female subject due to 17,20-desmolase deficiency. Acta Endocrinol (Copenh) 103:400–405, 1983.

387. Peretti Ed, Pradon M, Forest MG: 17,20-desmolase deficiency in a female newborn paradoxically virilized in utero. J Steroid Biochem 20:455–458, 1984.

388. Zachmann M, Werder EA, Prader A: Two types of male pseudohermaphroditism due to 17, 20-desmolase deficiency. J Clin Endocrinol Metab 55:487–490, 1982.

389. Peretti Ed, Cadillon E, Forest MG: In vitro studies in testicular 17,20-desmolase deficiency. Proceedings of the 63rd Meeting of the Endocrine Society 97(Abstr 58), 1981.

390. Chasalow F, Bletsen SL, Knight SM, et al: 18q Deletion syndrome in a child with steroid 17,20-lyase deficiency. Steroids 47:421–429, 1986.

391. Yanase T, Waterman MR, Zachmann M, et al: Molecular basis of apparent isolated 17,20-lyase deficiency: Compound heterozygous mutations in the C-terminal region (Arg(496)→Cys, Gln(461)→Stop) actually cause combined 17α-hydroxylase/17,20-lyase deficiency. Biochim Biophys Acta 1139:275–279, 1992.

392. Zachmann M, Kempken B, Manella B, et al: Conversion from 17,20-desmolase to 17α-hydroxylase with age. Acta Endocrinol (Copenh) 127:97–99, 1992.

393. Geller DH, Auchus RJ, Mendonca BB, et al: The genetic and funtional basis of isolated 17,20 lyase deficiency. Nat Genet 17:201–205, 1997.

394. Miller WL, Geller DH, Auchus RJ: The molecular basis of isolated 17,20 lyase deficiency. Endocr Res 24:817–825, 1998.

395. Miller WL, Auchus RJ, Geller DH: The regulation of 17,20 lyase activity. Steroids 62:133–142, 1997.

396. Biason-Lauber A, Leiberman E, Zachmann M: A single amino acid substitution in the putative redox partner-binding site of P450c17 as cause of isolated 17,20-lyase deficiency. J Clin Endocrinol Metab 82:3807–3812, 1997.

397. Biason-Lauber A, Kempken B, Werder E, et al: 17α-hydroxylase/17,20-lyase deficiency as a model to study enzymatic activity regulation: Role of phosphorylation. J Clin Endocrinol Metab 85:1226–1231, 2000.

398. Sherbet DP, Tiosano D, Kwist KM, et al: CYP17 mutation E305G causes isolated 17,20-lyase deficiency by selectively altering substrate binding. J Biol Chem 278:48563–48569, 2003.

399. Peterson RE, Imperato-McGinley J, Gauthier T, et al: Male pseudohermaphroditism due to multiple defects in steroid-biosynthetic microsomal mixed-function oxidases: A new variant of congenital adrenal hyperplasia. N Engl J Med 313:1182–1191, 1985.

400. Kagawa J, Tanae A, Hashimoto N, et al: A new variant of congenital adrenal hyperplasia (CAH) with combined deficiencies of 17α-hydroxylase, 17,20-desmolase and 21-hydroxylase. Acta Paediatr Jpn 30(Suppl):239, 1988.

401. Arlt W, Walker EA, Draper N, et al: Congenital adrenal hyperplasia caused by mutant P450 oxidoreductase and human androgen synthesis: Analytical study. Lancet 363(9427):2128–2135, 2004.

402. Fluck CE, Tajima T, Pandey AV, et al: Mutant P450 oxidoreductase causes disordered steroidogenesis with and without Antley-Bixler syndrome. Nat Genet 36:228–230, 2004.

403. Shephard EA, Phillips IR, Santisteban I, et al: Isolation of a human cytochrome P-450 reductase cDNA clone and localization of the corresponding gene to chromosome 7q11.2. Ann Hum Genet 53:291–301, 1989.

404. Shackleton C, Marcos J, Arlt W, et al: Prenatal diagnosis of P450 oxidoreductase deficiency (ORD): A disorder causing low pregnancy estriol, maternal and fetal virilization, and the Antley-Bixler syndrome phenotype. Am J Med Genet 129A:105–112, 2004.

405. Shackleton C, Marcos J, Malunowicz EM, et al: Biochemical diagnosis of Antley-Bixler syndrome by steroid analysis. Am J Med Genet 128A:223–231, 2004.

406. Inano H, Ohba H, Tamaoki B: Porcine testicular 17β-hydroxysteroid dehydrogenase: Affinity chromatography with dye-ligand agarose and demonstration of multiple forms of the enzyme. J Steroid Biochem 6:291–296, 1981.

407. Luu-The V, Labrie C, Zhao HF, et al: Characterization of cDNAs for human estradiol 17β-dehydrogenase and assignment of the gene to chromosome 17: Evidence of two mRNA species with distinct 5′-termini in human placenta. Mol Endocrinol 3:1301–1309, 1989.

408. Luu-The V, Labrie C, Simard J, et al: Structure of two in tandem human 17β-hydroxysteroid dehydrogenase genes. Mol Endocrinol 4:268–275, 1990.

409. Tremblay Y, Ringler GE, Morel Y, et al: Regulation of the gene for estrogenic 17-ketosteroid reductase lying on chromosome 17cen→q25. J Biol Chem 264:20458–20462, 1989.

410. Adamski J, Jakob FJ: A guide to 17β-hydroxysteroid dehydrogenases. Mol Cell Endocrinol 171:1–4, 2001.

411. Peltoketo H, Luu-The V, Simard J, et al: 17β-hydroxysteroid dehydrogenase (HSD)/17-ketosteroid reductase (KSR) family: Nomenclature and main characteristics of the 17HSD/KSR enzymes. J Mol Endocrinol 23:1–11, 1999.

412. Neher R, Kahnt FW: Gonadal steroid biosynthesis in vitro in four cases of testicular feminization. In Vermeulen A, Exley D (eds): Androgens in Normal and Pathological Conditions. Amsterdam, EMF, International Congress Series, 1966, pp 132.

413. Peretti de E, Saez J, Bertrand J: Familial male pseudohermaphroditism (MHP) due to 17-ketosteroid reductase defect: In vitro study and testicular incubation. Amsterdam, Excerpta Medica Intern Congress Series, 1970, p 205.

414. Saez J, de Perreti E, Morera A, et al: Familial male hermaphroditism with gynaecomastia due to a testicular 17-ketosteroid reductase defect: Studies in vivo. J Clin Endocrinol Metab 32:604–610, 1971.

415. Forest MG: Les pseudo-hermaphrodismes masculins par déficit en 17 céto-réductase. In Chaussain JL, Roger M (eds): Les ambiguités sexuelles. Paris, Sepe, 1988, pp 97–131.

416. Boehmer AL, Brinkmann AO, Sandkuijl LA, et al: 17β-hydroxysteroid dehydrogenase-3 deficiency: Diagnosis, phenotypic variability, population genetics, and worldwide distribution of ancient and de novo mutations. J Clin Endocrinol Metab 84:4713–4721, 1999.

417. Michel-Calemard L, Bertrand AM, Forest MG, et al: Le déficit en 17-céto-réductase est une étiologie très sous-estimée de pseudo-hermaphrosimsme masculin, mais est asymptomatique chez la femme. Ann Endocrinol (Paris) 60:278–279, 1999.

418. Rösler A, Kohn G: Male pseudohermaphroditism due to 17β-hydroxysteroid dehydrogenase deficiency: Studies on the natural history of the defect and effect of androgens on gender role. J Steroid Biochem 19:663–674, 1983.

419. Rösler A, Silverstein S, Abeliovich D: A (R80Q) mutation in 17β-hydroxysteroid dehydrogenase type 3 gene among Arabs of Israel is associated with pseudohermaphroditism in males and normal asymptomatic females. J Clin Endocrinol Metab 81:1827–1831, 1996.

420. Wilson SC, Hodgins MB, Scott JS: Incomplete masculinization due to a deficiency of 17β-hydroxysteroid dehydrogenase: Comparison of pubertal and peripubertal siblings. Clin Endocrinol (Oxf) 26:459–469, 1987.

421. Geissler WM, Davis DL, Wu L, et al: Male pseudohermaphroditism caused by mutations of testicular 17β-hydroxysteroid dehydrogenase 3. Nat Genet 7:34–39, 1994.

422. Andersson S, Moghrabi N: Physiology and molecular genetics of 17β-hydroxysteroid dehydrogenases. Steroids 62:143–147, 1997.

423. Andersson S, Russell DW, Wilson JD: 17β-hydroxysteroid dehydrogenase 3 deficiency. Trends Endocrinol Metab 7:121–126, 1996.

424. Can S, Zhu YS, Cai LQ, et al: The identification of 5α-reductase-2 and 17β-hydroxysteroid dehydrogenase-3 gene defects in male pseudohermaphrodites from a Turkish kindred. J Clin Endocrinol Metab 83:560–569, 1998.

425. Eckstein B, Cohen S, Farkas A, et al: The nature of the defect in familial male pseudohermaphroditism in Arabs of Gaza. J Clin Endocrinol Metab 68:477–485, 1989.

426. Castro-Magana M, Angulo M, Uy J: Male hypogonadism with gynecomastia caused by late-onset deficiency of testicular 17-ketosteroid reductase. N Engl J Med 328:1297–1301, 1993.

427. Gross DJ, Landau H, Kohn G, et al: Male pseudohermaphroditism due to 17β-hydroxysteroid dehydrogenase deficiency: Gender reassignment in early infancy. Acta Endocrinol (Copenh) 112:238–246, 1986.

428. Imperato-McGinley J, Peterson RE, Stoller R, et al: Male pseudohermaphroditism secondary to 17-hydroxysteroid dehydrogenase deficiency: Gender role change with puberty. J Clin Endocrinol Metab 49:391–395, 1979.

429. Nowakowski H, Lentz W: Genetic aspects in male hypogonadism. Recent Prog Horm Res 17:53–95, 1961.

430. Peterson RE, Imperato-McGinley J, Gautier T, et al: Male pseudohermaphroditism due to steroid 5α-reductase deficiency. Am J Med 62:170–191, 1977.

431. Imperato-McGinley J, Guerrero L, Gautier T, et al: Steroid 5α-reductase deficiency in man: An inherited form of male pseudohermaphroditism. Science 186:1213–1215, 1974.

432. Imperato-McGinley J, Peterson RE: Male pseudohermaphroditism: The complexities of male phenotypic development. Am J Med 61:251–272, 1976.

433. Ng WK, Taylor NF, Hughes IA, et al: 5α-reductase deficiency without hypospadias. Arch Dis Child 65:1166–1167, 1990.

434. Imperato-McGinley J, Zhu YS: Androgens and male physiology the

syndrome of 5α-reductase-2 deficiency. Mol Cell Endocrinol 198:51–59, 2002.

435. Imperato-McGinley J, Gautier T, Pichardo M, et al: The diagnosis of 5α-reductase deficiency in infancy. J Clin Endocrinol Metab 63:1313–1318, 1986.

436. Saenger P, Goldman AS, Levine LS, et al: Prepubertal diagnosis of steroid 5α-reductase deficiency in infancy. J Clin Endocrinol Metab 46:627–634, 1978.

437. Greene S, Zachmann M, Manella B, et al: Comparison of two tests to recognize or exclude 5α-reductase deficiency in prepubertal children. Acta Endocrinol (Copenh) 114:113–117, 1987.

438. Odame I, Donaldson MDC, Wallace AM, et al: Early diagnosis and management of 5α-reductase deficiency. Arch Dis Child 67:720–723, 1992.

439. Jenkins EP, Andersson S, Imperato-McGinley J, et al: Genetic and pharmacological evidence for more than one human steroid 5α-reductase. J Clin Invest 89:293–300, 1991.

440. Thigpen AE, Davis DL, Milatovitch A, et al: Molecular genetics of steroid 5α-reductase 2 deficiency. J Clin Invest 90:799–809, 1992.

441. Andersson S, Berman DM, Jenkins EP, et al: Deletion of steroid 5α-reductase 2-gene in male pseudohermaphroditism. Nature 354:159–161, 1991.

442. Imperato-McGinley J, Miller M, Wilson JD, et al: A cluster of male pseudohermaphrodites with 5α-reductase deficiency in Papua New Guinea. Clin Endocrinol (Oxf) 34:293–298, 1991.

443. Silver RI, Russell DW: 5α-Reductase type 2 mutations are present in some boys with isolated hypospadias. J Urol 162:1142–1145, 1999.

444. Sasaki G, Ogata T, Ishii T, et al: Micropenis and the 5α-reductase-2 (SRD5A2) gene: Mutation and V89L polymorphism analysis in 81 Japanese patients. J Clin Endocrinol Metab 88:3431–3436, 2003.

445. Chavez B, Valdez E, Vilchis F: Uniparental disomy in steroid 5α-reductase 2 deficiency. J Clin Endocrinol Metab 85:3147–3150, 2000.

446. Imperato-McGinley J, Peterson RE, Gautier T, et al: Androgens and the evolution of male gender identity among male pseudohermaphrodites with 5α-reductase deficiency. N Engl J Med 300:1233–1237, 1979.

447. Nordenskjold A, Magnus O, Aagenaes O, et al: Homozygous mutation (A228T) in the 5α-reductase type 2 gene in a boy with 5alpha-reductase deficiency: genotype-phenotype correlations. Am J Med Genet 80:269–272, 1998.

448. Mendonca BB, Inacio M, Costa EM, et al: Male pseudohermaphroditism due to steroid 5α-reductase 2 deficiency: Diagnosis, psychological evaluation, and management. Medicine (Baltimore) 75:64–76, 1996.

449. Ferraz LF, Mathias Baptista MT, Maciel-Guerra AT, et al: New frameshift mutation in the 5α-reductase type 2 gene in a Brazilian patient with 5α-reductase deficiency. Am J Med Genet 87:221–225, 1999.

450. Katz MD, Kligman I, Cai LQ, et al: Paternity by intrauterine insemination with sperm from a man with 5α-reductase-2 deficiency. N Engl J Med 336:994–997, 1997.

451. Carson-Jurica M, Schrader W, O'Malley B: Steroid receptor family: Structure and functions. Endocr Rev 11:201–220, 1990.

452. Wilson JD: Syndromes of androgen resistance. Biol Reprod 46:168–173, 1992.

453. Boehmer AL, Brinkmann O, Bruggenwirth H, et al: Genotype versus phenotype in families with androgen insensitivity syndrome. J Clin Endocrinol Metab 86:4151–4160, 2001.

454. Quigley CA, De Bellis A, Marschke KB, et al: Androgen receptor defects: Historical, clinical, and molecular perspectives. Endocr Rev 16:271–321, 1995 [published erratum appears in Endocr Rev 16:546, 1995].

455. Lee PA, Brown TR, La Torre H: Diagnosis of the partial androgen insensitivity syndrome during infancy. JAMA 16:2207–2209, 1986.

456. Nagel RA, Lippe BM, Griffin JE: Androgen resistance in the neonate: Use of hormones of hypothalamic-pituitary-gonadal axis for diagnosis. J Pediatr 109:486–488, 1984.

457. Bouvattier C, Carel JC, Lecointre C, et al: Postnatal changes of T, LH, and FSH in 46,XY infants with mutations in the AR gene. J Clin Endocrinol Metab 87:29–32, 2002.

458. Forest MG: La réponse stéroïdogénique testiculaire à la gondotrophine chorionique est augmentée pendant le premier trimestre de la vie dans le syndrome de féminisation testiculaire. In Saez JM, Forest MG, Dazord A, et al (eds): Recent Progress in Cellular Endocrinology of the Testis. Paris, Editions INSERM, 1985, pp 341–346.

459. Rey RA, Belville C, Nihoul-Fékété C, et al: Evaluation of gonadal function in 107 intersex patients by means of serum antimullerian hormone measurement. J Clin Endocrinol Metab 84:627–631, 1999.

460. Griffin JE, Wilson JD: The androgen resistance syndromes: 5α-reductase deficiency, testicular feminization, and related syndromes. In Scriver CR, Beaudet AI, Sly WS, et al (eds): The Metabolic Basis of Inherited Disease, 6th ed. New York, McGraw-Hill, 1989, pp 1919–1944.

461. Jukier L, Kaufman M, Pinsky L, et al: Partial androgen resistance associated with secondary 5α-reductase deficiency: Identification of a novel qualitative androgen receptor defect and clinical implications. J Clin Endocrinol Metab 49:678–688, 1984.

462. Chang C, Kokontis J, Liao S: Molecular cloning of human and rat complementary DNA encoding androgen receptors. Science 240:324–326, 1988.

463. Lubahn DB, Joseph DR, Sullivan PM: Cloning of human androgen receptor complementary DNA and localization to the X chromosome. Science 240:327–330, 1988.

464. Tilley WD, Marcelli M, Wilson JD, et al: Characterization and expression of a cDNA encoding the human androgen receptor. Proc Natl Acad Sci U S A 86:327–331, 1989.

465. Trapman J, Klassen P, Kuiper GG, et al: Cloning, structure and expression of a cDNA encoding the human androgen receptor. Biochem Biophys Res Commun 153:241–248, 1988.

466. French FS, Lubahn DB, Brown TR, et al: Molecular basis of androgen insensitivity. Recent Prog Horm Res 46:1–42, 1990.

467. Marcelli M, Tilly WD, Zoppi S, et al: Androgen resistance associated with a mutation of the androgen receptor at amino acid 772 (Arg→Cys): Results from a combination of decreased messenger ribonucleic acid levels and impairment of receptor function. J Clin Endocrinol Metab 73:318–325, 1991.

468. Brown TR, Lubahn DB, Wilson EM, et al: Deletion of the steroid-binding domain of the human androgen receptor gene in one family with complete androgen insensitivity syndrome: Evidence for further genetic heterogeneity in this syndrome. Proc Natl Acad Sci U S A 85:8151–8155, 1988.

469. Brinkmann A, Jenster G, Ris-Stalpers C, et al: Molecular basis of androgen insensitivity. Steroids 61:172–175, 1996.

470. McPhaul MJ, Griffin JE: Male pseudohermaphroditism caused by mutations of the human androgen receptor. J Clin Endocrinol Metab 84:3435–3441, 1999.

471. Brown CJ, Goss SJ, Lubahn DB, et al: Androgen receptor locus on the human X chromosome regional localization to xq11-12 and description of a DNA polymorphism. Am J Hum Genet 44:264–269, 1989.

472. Marcelli M, Zoppi S, Grino PB, et al: A mutation in the DNA-binding domain of the androgen receptor gene causes complete testicular feminization in a patient with receptor-positive androgen resistance. J Clin Invest 87:1123–1126, 1991.

473. Mebarki F, Forest MG, Chatelain P, et al: Analysis of exon 1 polymorphism and mutations of the androgen receptor gene makes possible the detection of heterozygote carriers and the prenatal diagnosis of the androgen insensitivity syndrome. Horm Res 35(Abstr):7, 1991.

474. Chen CP, Chern SR, Wang TY, et al: Androgen receptor gene mutations in 46,XY females with germ cell tumours. Hum Reprod 14:664–670, 1999.

475. Kennedy WR, Alter M, Sung JH: Progressive proximal spinal and bulbar

muscular atrophy of late onset: A sex-linked recessive trait. Neurology 18:671–680, 1968.

476. La Spada AR, Wilson EM, Lubahn DB, et al: Androgen receptor gene mutations in X-linked spinal and bulbar muscular atrophy. Nature 352:77–79, 1991.

477. La Spada AR, Roling DB, Harding AE, et al: Meiotic stability and genotype-phenotype correlation of the trinucleotide repeat in X-linked spinal and bulbar muscular atrophy. Nat Genet 2:301–304, 1992.

478. Davies HR, Hughes IA, Savage MO, et al: Androgen insensitivity with mental retardation: a contiguous gene syndrome? J Med Genet 34:158–160, 1997.

479. Maes M, Lee PA, Jejjs RD, et al: Phenotypic variation in a family with partial androgen insensitivity syndrome. Am J Dis Child 134:470–473, 1980.

480. Sultan C, Terraza A, Chalab A, et al: Pseudo-hermaphroditisme masculin par insensibilité partielle aux androgènes: Hétérogénéité clinique et biochimique. Arch Fr Pediatr 42:569–574, 1985.

481. Forest MG, Mollard P, David M, et al: Syndrome d'insensibilité incomplète aux androgènes: Difficultés du diagnostic et de la conduite à tenir. Arch Fr Pediatr 47:107–113, 1990.

482. Rodien P, Mebarki F, Mowszowicz I, et al: Different phenotypes in a family with androgen insensitivity caused by the same M780I point mutation in the androgen receptor gene. J Clin Endocrinol Metab 81:2994–2998, 1996.

483. Boehmer AL, Brinkmann AO, Nijman RM, et al: Phenotypic variation in a family with partial androgen insensitivity syndrome explained by differences in 5α-dihydrotestosterone availability. J Clin Endocrinol Metab 86:1240–1246, 2001.

484. Quigley CA, Tan J, He B, et al: Partial androgen Insensitivity with phenotypic variation caused by androgen receptor mutations that disrupt activation function 2 and the NH2- and carboxyl-terminal interaction. Mech Ageing Dev 2004 (in press).

485. McPhaul MJ, Marcelli M, Tilley WD, et al: Molecular basis of androgen resistance in a family with a qualitative abnormality of the androgen receptor and responsive to high-dose androgen therapy. J Clin Invest 87:1413–1421, 1991.

486. Batch J, Williams D, Davies H, et al: Androgen receptor mutations identified by SSCP in 14 subjects with androgen insensitivity syndrome. Hum Mol Genet 1:197–503, 1992.

487. Nakao R, Yanase T, Sakai Y, et al: A single amino-acid substitution (gly743→val) in the steroid-binding domain of the human androgen receptor leads to Reifenstein syndrome. J Clin Endocrinol Metab 77:103–107, 1993.

488. Gottlieb B, Beitel LK, Wu JH, et al: The androgen receptor gene mutations database (ARDB): 2004 update. Hum Mutat 23:527–533, 2004.

489. Gottlieb B, Beitel LK, Lumbroso R, et al: Update of the androgen receptor gene mutations database. Hum Mutat 14:103–114, 1999.

490. Gottlieb B, Vasiliou DM, Lumbroso R, et al: Analysis of exon 1 mutations in the androgen receptor gene. Hum Mutat 14:527–539, 1999.

491. Holterhus PM, Wiebel J, Sinnecker GH, et al: Clinical and molecular spectrum of somatic mosaicism in androgen insensitivity syndrome. Pediatr Res 46:684–690, 1999.

492. Boehmer AL, Brinkmann AO, Niermeijer MF, et al: Germ-line and somatic mosaicism in the androgen insensitivity syndrome: Implications for genetic counseling [letter]. Am J Hum Genet 60:1003–1006, 1997.

493. Ishii T, Sato S, Kosaki K, et al: Micropenis and the AR Gene: Mutation and CAG repeat-length analysis. J Clin Endocrinol Metab 86:5372–5378, 2001.

494. Aiman J, Griffin J: The frequency of androgen receptor deficiency in infertile men. J Clin Endocrinol Metab 54:725–732, 1982.

495. Nilson O: Hernia uteri inguinalis. Acta Chir Scand 83:231–249, 1939.

496. Brook CGD, Wagner H, Zachmann M, et al: Familial occurrence of persistent müllerian structures in otherwise normal males. Br Med J 1(5856): 771–773, 1973.

497. Josso N, Boussin L, Knebelmann B, et al: Anti-müllerian hormone and intersex states. Trends Endocrinol Metab 2:227–233, 1991.

498. Cate RL, Mattaliano Rj, Hession C, et al: Isolation of the bovine and human genes for müllerian inhibiting substance and expression of the human gene in animal cells. Cell 45:685–698, 1986.

499. Cohen-Haguenauer O, Picard JY, Mattei MG, et al: Mapping of the gene for anti-müllerian hormone to the short arm of human chromosome 19. Cytogenet Cell Genet 44:2–6, 1987.

500. Imbeaud S, Faure E, Lamarre I, et al: Insensitivity to anti-mullerian hormone due to a mutation in the human anti-mullerian hormone receptor. Nat Genet 11:382–388, 1995.

501. Knebelmann B, Boussin L, Guerrier D, et al: Anti-müllerian hormone Bruxelles: A nonsense mutation associated with the persistant müllerian duct syndrome. Proc Natl Acad Sci U S A 88:3767–3771, 1991.

502. Imbeaud S, Carré-Eusèbe D, Boussin L, et al: Biologie moléculaire de l'hormone anti-Müllérienne normale et pathologique. Ann Endocrinol 52:415–419, 1991.

503. Carré-Eusèbe D, Imbeaud S, Harbison M, et al: Variants of the anti-müllerian hormone gene in a compound heterozygote with the persistent müllerian duct syndrome and his family. Hum Genet 90:389–394, 1992.

504. Imbeaud S, Carre-Eusebe D, Rey R, et al: Molecular genetics of the persistent mullerian duct syndrome: A study of 19 families. Hum Mol Genet 3:125–131, 1994.

505. Guerrier D, Tran D, Van der Winden JM, et al: The persistent Müllerian duct syndrome: A molecular approach. J Clin Endocrinol Metab 68:46–52, 1989.

506. Imbeaud S, Belville C, Messika-Zeitoun L, et al: A 27 base-pair deletion of the anti-mullerian type II receptor gene is the most common cause of the persistent mullerian duct syndrome. Hum Mol Genet 5:1269–1277, 1996.

507. Sloan WR, Walsh PC: Familial persistent müllerian duct syndrome. J Urol 115:459–461, 1976.

508. Vandersteen DR, Chaumeton AK, Ireland K, et al: Surgical management of persistent mullerian duct syndrome. Urology 49:941–945, 1997.

509. Melman A, Leiter E, Perez JM, et al: The influence of neonatal orchidopexy upon the testes in persistent müllerian duct syndrome. J Urol 125:856–858, 1981.

510. Berkmen F: Persistent mullerian duct syndrome with or without transverse ectopia and testis tumours. Br J Urol 79:122–126, 1997.

511. Nelson RE: Congenital absence of the vas deferens: A review of the literature and report of three cases. J Urol 63:176–178, 1950.

512. Le Merrer M, Briard ML, Girard S, et al: Lethal acrodysgenital dwarfism: A severe lethal condition resembling Smith-Lemli-Opitz syndrome. J Med Genet 25:88–95, 1988.

513. Aarskog D: Maternal progestins as a possible cause of hypospadias. N Engl J Med 300:75–78, 1979.

514. Driscoll SG, Taylor SH: Effects of prenatal maternal estrogen on the male urogenital system. Obstet Gynecol 56:537–542, 1980.

515. Skakkebaek NE: Testicular dysgenesis syndrome. Horm Res 60(Suppl 3):49, 2003.

516. Danzo BJ: The effects of environmental hormones on reproduction. Cell Mol Life Sci 54:1249–1264, 1998.

517. Mouriquand P, Mure PY: Hypospadias. In Gearhart JP, Rink R, Moutiquand P (eds): Pediatric Urology. Philadelphia, WB Sauders, 2001, pp 713–728.

518. Sweet RA, Schrott HG, Kurland R, et al: Study of the incidence of hypospadias in Rochester, Minnesota, 1940–1970, and a case control comparison of possible etiologic factors. Mayo Clin Proc 49:52–58, 1974.

519. Fisch H, Golden RJ, Libersen GL, et al: Maternal age as a risk factor for hypospadias. J Urol 165:934–936, 2001.

520. Svensson J, Snochowski M: Androgen receptor levels in preputial skin from boys with hypospadias. J Clin Endocrinol Metab 49:340–345, 1979.

521. Nordenskjold A, Friedman E, Tapper-Persson M, et al: Screening for mutations in candidate genes for hypospadias. Urol Res 27:49–55, 1999.

522. Boehmer AL, Nijman RJ, Lammers BA, et al: Etiological studies of severe or familial hypospadias. J Urol 165:1246–1254, 2001.

523. Wiener JS, Marcelli M, Gonzales ET Jr, et al: Androgen receptor gene alterations are not associated with isolated cryptorchidism. J Urol 160:863–865, 1998.

524. Prader A: Der genitalbefund beim pseudohermaphroditismus femininus des kongenitalen adrenogenitalen syndroms: Morphologie, häufigkeit, entwicklung und vererbung der verschiedenen genital formen. Helv Paediatr Acta 9:231–248, 1954.

525. Forest MG: Prenatal diagnosis, treatment, and outcome in infants with congenital adrenal hyperplasia. Curr Opin Endocrinol Diabet 4:209–217, 1997.

526. Midgley PC, Azzopardi D, Oates N, et al: Virilization of female preterm infants. Arch Dis Child 65:701–703, 1990.

527. Shozu M, Akasofu K, Harada T, et al: A new cause of female pseudohermaphroditism: Placental aromatase deficiency. J Clin Endocrinol Metab 72:560–566, 1991.

528. Harada N, Ogawa H, Shozu M, et al: Biochemical and molecular genetic analyses on placental aromatase (P-450$_{AROM}$) deficiency. J Biol Chem 267:4781–4785, 1992.

529. Harada N, H, Shozu M, Yamada K: Genetic studies to characterize the origin of the mutation in placental aromatase deficiency. Am J Hum Genet 51:666–672, 1992.

530. Conte FA GM, Ito Y, Fisher CR, Simpson ER: A syndrome of female pseudohermaphrodism, hypergonadotropic hypogonadism, and multicystic ovaries associated with missense mutations in the gene encoding aromatase (P450arom). J Clin Endocrinol Metab 78:1287–1292, 1994.

531. Ito Y, Fischer CR, Conte FA, et al: Identification of two novel mutations (R435C and C437Y) in the aromatase cytochrome P4500 (CYP19) gene of a patient with polycystic ovaries. 75th Annual Meeting of the Endocrine Society, Las Vegas, 1993.

532. Forest MG, Nicolino M, Portrat S, et al: Une cause exeptionelle de pseudohermaphrodisme féminin (PHF): Déficit en aromatase fœto-placentaire. Ann Endocrinol (Paris) 56:282, 1995.

533. Morishima A, Grumbach MM, Simpson ER, et al: Aromatase deficiency in male and female siblings caused by a novel mutation and the physiological role of estrogens. J Clin Endocrinol Metab 80:3689–3698, 1995.

534. Ludwig M, Beck A, Wickert L, et al: Female pseudohermaphroditism associated with a novel homozygous G-to-A (V370-to-M) substitution in the P-450 aromatase gene. J Pediatr Endocrinol Metab 11:657–664, 1998.

535. Mullis PE, Yoshimura N, Kuhlmann B, et al: Aromatase deficiency in a female who is compound heterozygote for two new point mutations in the P450arom gene: Impact of estrogens on hypergonadotropic hypogonadism, multicystic ovaries, and bone densitometry in childhood. J Clin Endocrinol Metab 82:1739–1745, 1997.

536. Belgorosky A, Pepe C, Marino R, et al: Hypothalamic-pituitary-ovarian axis during infancy, early and late prepuberty in an aromatase-deficient girl who is a compound heterocygote for two new point mutations of the CYP19 gene. J Clin Endocrinol Metab 88:5127–5131, 2003.

537. Kai H, Nose O, Iida Y, et al: Female pseudohermaphroditism caused by maternal congenital adrenal hyperplasia. J Pediatr 95:418–420, 1979.

538. Kirk JMW, Perry LA, Shand WS, et al: Female pseudohermaphroditism due to a maternal adrenocortical tumor. J Clin Endocrinol Metab 70:1280–1284, 1990.

539. Forest MG, Orgiazzi J, Tranchant D, et al: Approach to the mechanism of the androgen overproduction in a new case of Krukenberg tumor responsible for virilization during pregnacy. J Clin Endocrinol Metab 47:428–434, 1978.

540. Mendonca BB, Leite MV, de Castro M, et al: Female pseudohermaphroditism caused by a novel homozygous missense mutation of the GR gene. J Clin Endocrinol Metab 87:1805–1809, 2002.

541. Grumbach MM, Ducharme JR: The Effects of androgens on fetal sexual development, androgen induced female pseudo-hermaphroditism. Fertil Steril 11:157–180, 1960.

542. Carson SA, Simpson JL: Virilization of female fetuses following maternal ingestion of progestational and androgenic steroids. In Mahesh CVB, Greenblatt RB (eds): Hirsutism and virilism. London, Butterworths, 1983, pp 177–188.

543. Castro-Magana M, Cheruvanky T, Collip PJ, et al: Transient adrenogenital syndrome due to exposure to danazol in utero. Am J Dis Child 135:1032–1034, 1981.

544. Seaver LH, Grimes J, Erickson RP: Female pseudohermaphroditism with multiple caudal anomalies: Absence of Y-specific DNA sequences as pathogenetic factors. Am J Med Genet 51:16–21, 1994.

545. Shulman LP, Elias S: Developmental abnormalities of the female reproductive tract: Pathogenesis and nosology. Adolesc Pediatr Gynecol 1:203–238, 1988.

546. Gearhart JP, Rock JD: Female pseudohermaphroditism: Unusual variants and their management. Adolesc Pediatr Gynecol 2:3–9, 1989.

547. Bergh PA, Breen JL, Gregori CA: Minireview: Congenital absence of the vagina: The Mayer-Rokitansky-Kuster-Hauser syndrome. Adolesc Pediatr Gynecol 2:73–85, 1989.

548. Plevraki E, Kita M, Goulis DG, et al: Bilateral ovarian agenesis and the presence of the testis-specific protein 1-Y-linked gene: Two new features of Mayer-Rokitansky-Kuster-Hauser syndrome. Fertil Steril 81:689–692, 2004.

549. Rafjer L, Mendelson G, Arnheim J, et al: Dysgenetic male pseudo hermaphroditism. J Urol 119:525–527, 1978.

550. Skordis NA, Stetka DG, MacGillivray MH, et al: Familial 46,XX males coexisting with familial 46,XX true hermaphrodites in same pedigree. J Pediatr 110:244–248, 1987.

551. Margarit E, Soler A, Carrio A, et al: Molecular, cytogenetic, and clinical characterisation of six XX males including one prenatal diagnosis. J Med Genet 35:727–730, 1998.

552. Margarit E, Coll MD, Oliva R, et al: SRY gene transferred to the long arm of the X chromosome in a Y-positive XX true hermaphrodite. Am J Med Genet 90:25–28, 2000.

553. de la Chapelle A: Genetic and molecular studies on 46,XX and 45,X males. Symposia on Quantitative Biology, vol XI, Cold Spring Harbor, NY, 1986.

554. Uehara S, Hashiyada M, Sato K, et al: Complete XY gonadal dysgenesis and aspects of the SRY genotype and gonadal tumor formation. J Hum Genet 47:279–284, 2002.

555. Medlej R, Lobaccaro JM, Berta P, et al: Screening for Y-derived sex determining gene SRY in 40 patients with Turner syndrome. J Clin Endocrinol Metab 75:1289–1292, 1992.

556. Gicquel C, Cabrol S, Schneid H, et al: Molecular diagnosis of Turner's Syndrome. J Med Genet 29:547–551, 1992.

557. Prader A, Illig R, Zachmann M: Prenatal LH-deficiency as a posssible cause of male pseudohermaphroditism, hypospadias, hypogenitalism and cryptorchidism. Pediatr Res 10:883, 1976.

558. Forest MG: Age-related response of plasma testosterone, $\Delta^4$-androstenedione and cortisol to ACTH in infants, children and adults. J Clin Endocrinol Metab 47:931–937, 1978.

559. Forest MG, Peretti de E, Bertrand J: Age-related shift in the response of plasma $\Delta^4$- and $\Delta^5$-androgens, their precursors and cortisol to ACTH from infancy to puberty. In Cacciari E, Prader A (eds): Pathophysiology of Puberty. London, Academic Press, 1980, pp 137–155.

560. Lashansky G, Saenger P, Fishman K, et al: Normative data for adrenal steroidogenesis in a healthy pediatric population: Age- and sex-related changes after adrenocorticotropin stimulation. J Clin Endocrinol Metab 73:674–686, 1991.

561. Lashansky G, Saenger P, Dimartino-Nardi J, et al: Normative data for the steroidogenic response of mineralocorticoids and their precursors to adrenocorticotropin in a healthy pediatric population. J Clin Endocrinol Metab 75:1491–1496, 1992.

562. Forest MG, Bertrand J: Cinétique de la réponse stéroïdogénique testiculaire à la stimulation par la gonadotrophine chorionique placentaire. IV. Chez le garçon impubère. Arch Fr Pediatr 41:103–106, 1984.

562a. Forest MG, David M: Le micropénis: Données étiologiques et traitement dans une série de 88 cas. Rev Fr Endocr Clin 27:31–35, 1986.

563. Forest MG, Lecoq A, David M, et al: Effects of human chorionic gonadotropin, androgens, adrenocorticotropin hormone, dexamethasone and hyperprolactinemia on plasma sex binding protein. Ann N Y Acad Sci 538:214–234, 1988.

564. Krause A, Sinnecker GH, Hiort O, et al: Applicability of the SHBG androgen sensitivity test in the differential diagnosis of 46,XY gonadal dysgenesis, true hermaphroditism, and androgen insensitivity syndrome. Exp Clin Endocrinol Diabetes 112:236–240, 2004.

565. Tanaka YO, Mesaki N, Kurosaki Y, et al: Testicular feminization: Role of MRI in diagnosing this rare male pseudohermaphroditism. J Comput Assist Tomogr 22:884–888, 1998.

566. Choi HK, Cho KS, Lee HW, et al: MR imaging of intersexuality. Radiographics 18:83–96, 1998.

567. Yordam N, Alikasifoglu A, Kandemir N, et al: True hermaphroditism: Clinical features, genetic variants and gonadal histology. J Pediatr Endocrinol Metab 14:421–427, 2001.

568. Robboy SJ, Miller T, Donahoe PK, et al: Dysgenesis of testicular and streak gonads in the syndrome of mixed gonadal dysgenesis. Hum Pathol 13:700–716, 1982.

569. Morel Y, Miller WL: Clinical and molecular genetics of congenital adrenal hyperplasia due to 21-hydroxylase deficiency. Adv Hum Genet 20:1–68, 1991.

570. Peretti Ed, Forest MG: Pitfalls in the etiological diagnosis of congenital adrenal hyperplasia in early infancy. Horm Res 16:10–22, 1982.

571. Goldman SM, Garfinkel DJ, Sang OK, et al: The Drash syndrome: Male pseudohermaphroditism, nephritis and Wilms tumor. Radiology 141:87–91, 1981.

572. Svensson J: Male hypospadias, 625 cases, associated malformations and possible etiological factors. Acta Pediatr Scand 68:587–592, 1979.

573. Morris JM: The syndrome of testicular feminization in male pseudohermaphroditism. Am J Obstet Gynecol 65:1192–1211, 1953.

574. Brinkmann AO, Jenster G, Ris-Stalpers C, et al: Androgen receptor mutations. J Steroid Biochem Mol Biol 53:443–448, 1995.

575. Wilson JD, Harrod MJ, Goldstein JL: Familial incomplete male pseudohermaphroditism, type 1: Evidence for androgen resistance and variable clinical manifestations in a family with the Reifenstein syndrome. N Engl J Med 290:1097–1103, 1974.

576. Norgil Damgaard I, Main KM, Toppari J, et al: Impact of exposure to endocrine disrupters in utero and in childhood on adult reproduction. Best Pract Res Clin Endocrinol Metab 16:289–309, 2002.

577. Sharpe RM, Irvine DS: How strong is the evidence of a link between environmental chemicals and adverse effects on human reproductive health? Br Med J 328:447–451, 2004.

578. Sobel V, Imperato-McGinley J: Gender identity in XY intersexuality. Child Adolesc Psychiatr Clin North Am 13:609–622, 2004.

579. Hines M: Psychosexual development in individuals who have female pseudohermaphroditism. Child Adolesc Psychiatr Clin North Am 13:641–656, 2004.

580. Zucker KJ: Intersexuality and gender idenity differentiation. J Pediatr Adolesc Gynecol 15:3–13, 2002.

581. Kuhnle U, Krahl W: The impact of culture on sex assignment and gender development in intersex patients. Perspect Biol Med 45:85–403, 2002.

582. Hamamy HA, Dahoun S: Parental decisions following the prenatal diagnosis of sex chromosome abnormalities. Eur J Obstet Gynecol Reprod Biol 116:59–62, 2004.

583. Forest MG: Prenatal diagnosis of inborn errors in steroid metabolism causing sexual ambiguity. In Slob AK, Baum MJ (eds): Psychoneuroendocrinology of Growth and Development. Bussum, Netherlands, Medicon Europe, 1990, pp 151–164.

584. Nimkarn S, Likitmaskul S, Sangacharoenkit P, et al: Ambiguous genitalia: An overview of 22 years experience and the diagnostic approach in the Pediatric Department, Siriraj Hospital. J Med Assoc Thai 85:S496–S505, 2002.

585. Alvarez-Nava F, Gonzalez-Ferrer S, Soto M: Diagnosis and management of patients with sex differentiation disorders: Experience at the Unit of Medical Genetics of the University of Zulia, Maracaibo, Venezuela. Invest Clin 39:273–292, 1998.

586. Morel Y, Rey R, Teinturier C, et al: Aetiological diagnosis of male sex ambiguity: A collaborative study. Eur J Pediatr 161:49–59, 2002.

587. Pinhas-Hamiel O, Zalel Y, Smith E, et al: Prenatal diagnosis of sex differentiation disorders: The role of fetal ultrasound. J Clin Endocrinol Metab 87:4547–4553, 2002.

588. Amor D, Delatycki MB, Susman M, et al: 46,XX/46,XY at amniocentesis in a fetus with true hermaphroditism. J Med Genet 36:866–869, 1999.

589. Kilpatrick MW, Tafas T, Evans MI, et al: Automated detection of rare fetal cells in maternal blood: Eliminating the false-positive XY signals in XX pregnancies. Am J Obstet Gynecol 190:1571–1578, discussion 1578–1581, 2004.

590. Vialard F, Ottolenghi C, Gonzales M, et al: Deletion of 9p associated with gonadal dysfunction in 46,XY but not in 46,XX human fetuses. J Med Genet 39:514–518, 2002.

591. Costa JM, Benachi A, Gautier E, et al: First-trimester fetal sex determination in maternal serum using real-time PCR. Prenat Diagn 21:1070–1074, 2001.

592. Kolon TF, Gray CL, Borboroglu PG: Prenatal karyotype and ultrasound discordance in intersex conditions. Urology 54:1097, 1999.

593. Ginsberg NA, Cadkin A, Strom C, et al: Prenatal diagnosis of 46,XX male fetuses. Am J Obstet Gynecol 180:1006–1007, 1999.

594. Bojesen A, Juul S, Gravholt CH: Prenatal and postnatal prevalence of Klinefelter syndrome: A national registry study. J Clin Endocrinol Metab 88:622–666, 2003.

595. Saenger P, Klonari Z, Black SM, et al: Prenatal diagnosis of congenital lipoid adrenal hyperplasia. J Clin Endocrinol Metab 80:200–205, 1995.

596. Reschini E, Catania A, D'Alberton A: On the antenatal diagnosis of 17-hydroxylase deficiency. J Endocrinol Invest 14:981–982, 1991.

597. Rösler A, Weshler N, Leiberman E, et al: 11β-hydroxylase deficiency congenital adrenal hyperplasia: Update of prenatal diagnosis. J Clin Endocrinol Metab 68:309–321, 1989.

598. Cerame BI, Newfield RS, Pascoe L, et al: Prenatal diagnosis and treatment of 11β-hydroxylase deficiency congenital adrenal hyperplasia resulting in normal female genitalia. J Clin Endocrinol Metab 84:3129–3134, 1999.

599. Forest MG, Nivelon-Chevallier A, Tenebaum D, et al: Familial 17-ketosteroid reductase (17-KSR) deficiency: Post-natal and prenatal diagnosis. Proceedings of the 67th Meeting of the Endocrine Society 89 (Abstr 354), 1985.

# Precocious Puberty

## Erica A. Eugster and Ora Hirsch Pescovitz

Precocious puberty is among the most fascinating and complex areas of pediatric endocrinology. The combination of an extensive differential diagnosis, dramatic clinical manifestation, and intricate pathophysiology provides continual challenges for clinicians and scientists alike. Although many questions remain unanswered, recent years have witnessed phenomenal breakthroughs in elucidation of the molecular genetics, lifelong implications, and therapeutic outcomes of different forms of precocious puberty. Undoubtedly, future advances will continue to enhance our understanding of the biologic basis of normal and abnormal secondary sexual development.

## INTRODUCTION

*Precocious puberty* has historically been defined as the onset of any sign of puberty in girls younger than 8 years and in boys younger than 9 years.[1,2] However, there has been considerable debate in the past several years about whether these guidelines are appropriate for girls.[3] This was precipitated by a large, office-based, cross-sectional study in which pubertal development was documented in a substantial proportion of normal girls who were younger than age 8.[4] Subsequent analysis of the original data has demonstrated a correlation between body mass index and the onset of puberty, suggesting that heavier girls may be entering puberty at slightly younger ages than lean peers.[5] Despite this observation, studies in the United States and internationally indicate that the average age of menarche has been quite stable over several decades, which argues against a meaningful shift in the secular trend of pubertal onset.[6] In contrast, racial differences in the onset of pubertal development are well documented, with African-American children typically starting puberty 6 to 12 months earlier than white children and Hispanic children having an onset of puberty intermediate between the other racial groups.[7,8] Regardless of the ultimate consensus in terms of what should be considered "normal," individual factors such as growth parameters, body mass index, skeletal maturation, height prediction, family history, and psychosocial status need to be taken into consideration when evaluating a child who presents with early puberty. It is also important to recognize that the tempo of puberty varies among children, with duration of normal puberty often being inversely proportional to age of pubertal onset.[9] A general approach to the evaluation and diagnosis of precocious puberty in girls and in boys is outlined in Figures 147-1 and 147-2, respectively.

## VARIANTS OF PRECOCIOUS PUBERTY

Evidence of pubertal development at a younger than normal age does not necessarily imply a pathologic condition that requires intervention. There are two distinct conditions that commonly occur in children when there is isolated development of a secondary sexual characteristic. *Premature thelarche* refers to isolated breast enlargement in girls, whereas *premature pubarche* describes early onset of pubic hair in boys or girls. Although different in terms of etiology, pathogenesis, and implications for future health, both conditions may be considered variations of normal development.

### PREMATURE THELARCHE

#### Clinical Features
Premature thelarche occurs most commonly in girls between infancy and age 3, although it can occur anytime before the normal onset of puberty.[10] The typical history is that breast tissue has been noted since birth or that there is gradual enlargement of the breasts over several months without any other evidence of puberty.[11] Growth velocity and skeletal maturation are within the normal range for age.[12,13] On physical examination, breast tissue is usually easily discernible, with a texture characterized by firm elasticity and a palpable margin at the periphery. The breast enlargement may be unilateral or bilateral and usually does not exceed a Tanner stage III level of development (Fig. 147-3). The nipples may remain immature, and the vaginal mucosa typically appears unestrogenized, although estrogenization does not exclude a diagnosis of premature thelarche. Using an ultrasensitive assay, estradiol levels have been found to be higher in girls with premature thelarche compared with controls.[14] Despite this, ovarian and uterine volumes remain in a prepubertal range, in contrast to the enlargement of these structures, which is characteristic of central precocious puberty.[15,16]

#### Pathophysiology
The precise cause of premature thelarche remains unknown, although several theories about its pathogenesis have been proposed. These include individual differences in peripheral

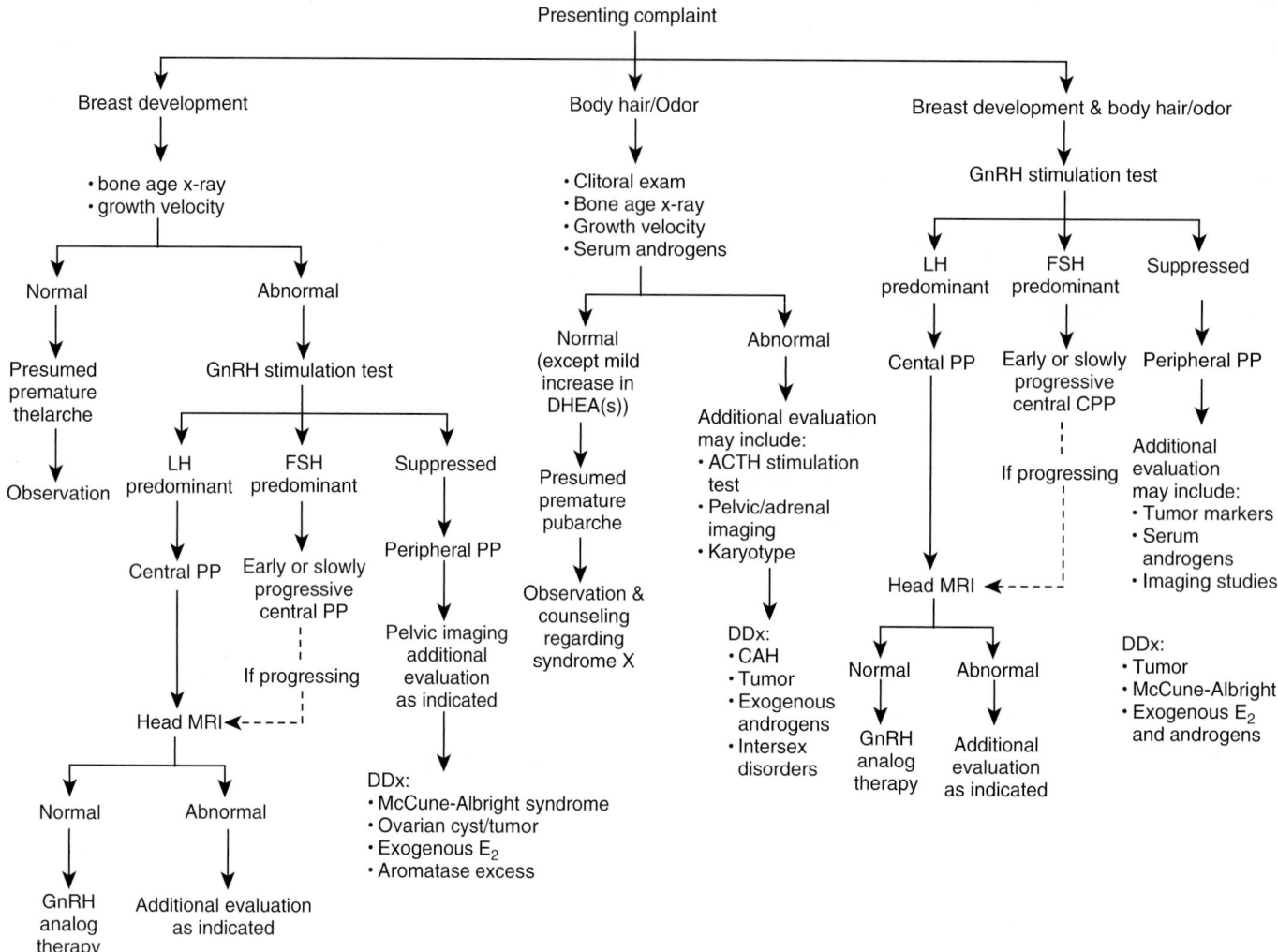

**Figure 147-1** Diagnostic approach to evaluation of precocious puberty in girls. ACTH, adrenocorticotropic hormone; CAH, congenital adrenal hyperplasia; CPP, central precocious puberty; DDx, differential diagnosis; DHEA(S), dehydroepiandrosterone (sulfate); $E_2$, estradiol; FSH, follicle-stimulating hormone; GnRH, gonadotropin-releasing hormone; LH, luteinizing hormone; MRI, magnetic resonance imaging; PP, precocious puberty.

sensitivity to estradiol as well as an alteration in the ratio of estrogen to androgens from increased sex hormone–binding globulin levels.[17] Gain-of-function mutations in the follicle-stimulating hormone (FSH) receptor or $G_s\alpha$ have also been hypothesized to be a cause of premature thelarche, although a search for molecular genetic abnormalities in these patients has been negative thus far.[18] Most cases of premature thelarche are characterized by an FSH-predominant response to gonadotropin-releasing hormone (GnRH) stimulation testing.[19] However, it is still unclear whether this indicates involvement of the hypothalamic-pituitary-gonadal (HPG) axis in causing this condition because this response is also characteristic of the prepubertal state.[20–23] One likely hypothesis is that premature thelarche exists along a continuum of hypothalamic-pituitary-ovarian activity, representing one end of a clinical spectrum that, in some patients, manifests as full-blown central precocious puberty characterized by a luteinizing hormone (LH)-predominant response to GnRH stimulation.[23] What governs whether activation of this axis is mild, partial, transient, or complete remains a mystery. Interestingly, premature thelarche is relatively common in girls, whereas prepubertal gynecomastia is uncommon in boys, and both FSH and estradiol levels are higher in girls compared with boys at all ages.[24]

## Natural History

Follow-up studies of patients with premature thelarche have indicated several possible scenarios in terms of clinical course. Complete regression of breast tissue occurs in a substantial percentage of girls with premature thelarche, particularly in girls with onset before age 2.[25] In other patients, breast tissue may persist, or even enlarge, although initial studies failed to identify an increased risk of pubertal progression or additional medical problems.[12,26] In some series, as many as 14% of girls with classic premature thelarche progress to central precocious puberty, although baseline clinical and biochemical characteristics of these patients are indistinguishable from those whose condition remains stable.[20,27] Reassuringly, adult stature and the timing of central puberty appear to be normal in girls with nonprogressive premature thelarche.[28]

## Management

In girls with typical premature thelarche, reassurance, and follow-up are all that are indicated. Careful clinical assessment, including determination of growth velocity, should be performed at 3- to 6-month intervals. A bone age radiograph is helpful at the time of diagnosis and is reassuring if it is consistent with the chronologic age. Additional radiographs are indicated if there is evidence of secondary sexual progression or

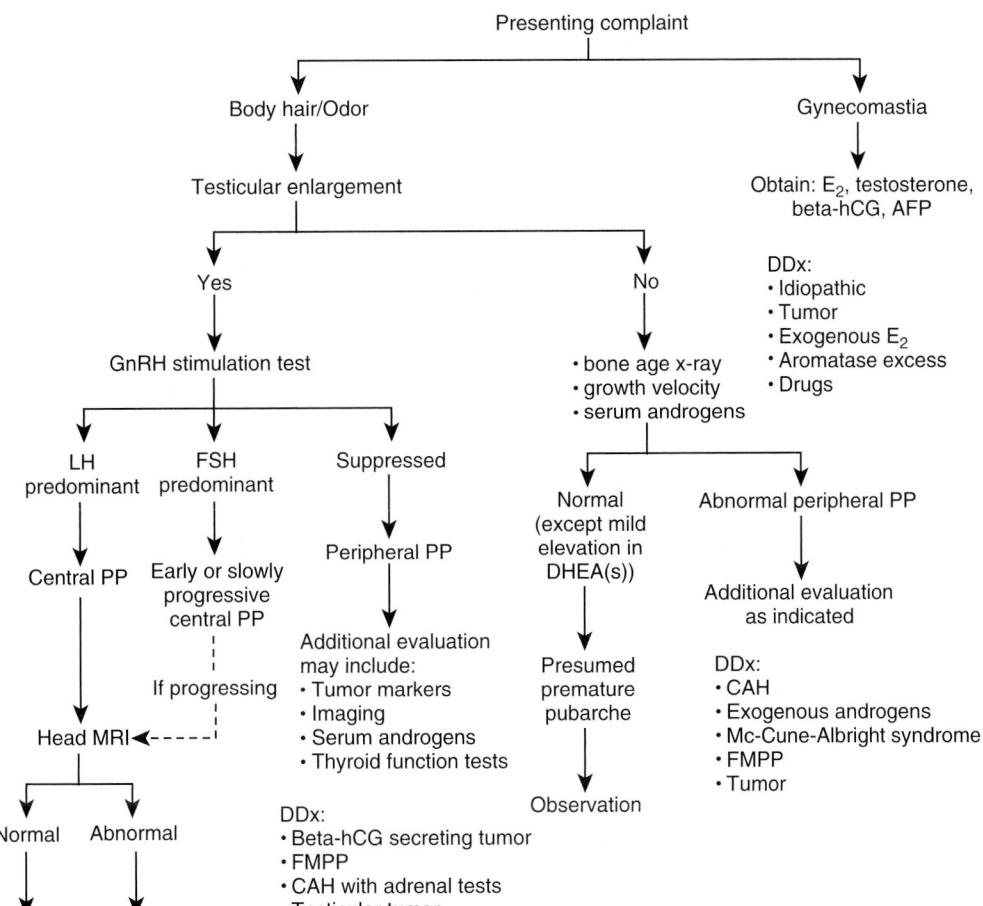

Presenting complaint

Body hair/Odor → Testicular enlargement

Gynecomastia → Obtain: E₂, testosterone, beta-hCG, AFP

Testicular enlargement:

**Yes** → GnRH stimulation test

- LH predominant → Central PP
- FSH predominant → Early or slowly progressive central PP — If progressing → Head MRI
- Suppressed → Peripheral PP → Additional evaluation may include:
  - Tumor markers
  - Imaging
  - Serum androgens
  - Thyroid function tests

  DDx:
  - Beta-hCG secreting tumor
  - FMPP
  - CAH with adrenal tests
  - Testicular tumor
  - Hypothyroidism

Central PP → Head MRI:
- Normal → GnRH analog therapy
- Abnormal → Additional evaluation as indicated

**No** →
- bone age x-ray
- growth velocity
- serum androgens

- Normal (except mild elevation in DHEA(s)) → Presumed premature pubarche → Observation
- Abnormal peripheral PP → Additional evaluation as indicated

  DDx:
  - CAH
  - Exogenous androgens
  - Mc-Cune-Albright syndrome
  - FMPP
  - Tumor

Gynecomastia DDx:
- Idiopathic
- Tumor
- Exogenous E₂
- Aromatase excess
- Drugs

*Figure 147-2* Diagnostic approach to evaluation of precocious puberty in boys. FMPP, familial male precocious puberty; hCG, human chorionic gonadotropin; for other abbreviations, see legend for Figure 147-1.

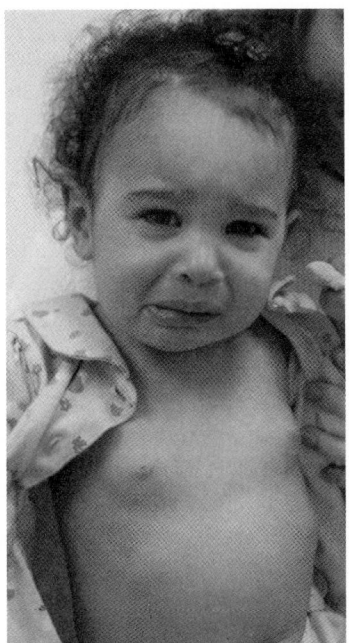

*Figure 147-3* Typical appearance of premature thelarche in a 2½-year-old girl.

acceleration of linear growth. Because of the possibility of progression to central precocious puberty, it is recommended to continue follow-up by the primary care physician. Other causes of breast masses in children include fibroadenomas, abscesses, hemorrhagic cysts, or, rarely, metastatic disease.[29]

### PREMATURE PUBARCHE

#### Clinical Features

Premature pubarche is characterized by the development of pubic hair in prepubertal children. Additional findings often include axillary hair, body odor, and mild acne.[13,30] Most cases of premature pubarche are secondary to premature adrenarche, which is characterized by mildly elevated serum adrenal androgen levels, especially dehydroepiandrosterone sulfate, for age, with values corresponding to the degree of Tanner stage development.[31,32] Premature adrenarche usually occurs in children between the ages of 6 and 8 but may occur earlier. Additional diagnostic criteria include the absence of other signs of puberty, such as breast development. Although growth velocity and skeletal maturation may be slightly advanced, significant virilization such as clitoromegaly, voice change, or increased muscle mass is absent.[33] Because premature pubarche can be the presenting sign in congenital adrenal hyperplasia (CAH) or virilizing adrenal or gonadal tumors, these conditions should be considered and excluded.

#### Pathophysiology

Attempts to define the precise clinical and biochemical profile of premature adrenarche have yielded significant heterogeneity in terms of underlying pathophysiology and concurrent metabolic features. Physiologic adrenarche, which occurs normally during mid-childhood, refers to the development of the zona reticularis and an associated increase in adrenal androgen secretion.[34,35] This is accompanied by alterations in adrenal enzyme activity, characterized by increases in 17,20-desmolase and 17-hydroxylase enzymes and a decrease in 3β-hydroxysteroid dehydrogenase activity.[36,37] While much progress has been made in understanding the physiology of adrenarche, the driving force behind this process, in both premature and physiologic adrenarche, remains unknown. Differences in peripheral metabolism of adrenal androgens have been implicated as a contributing factor in some patients, supported by the finding of elevated 3α-androstanediol glucuronide, a marker of peripheral adrenal androgen activity, in children with premature adrenarche compared with controls.[32,38] Partial adrenal enzyme deficiencies, including 21-hydroxylase, 3β-hydroxysteroid dehydrogenase, and 11-hydroxylase deficiencies, have been reported at variable frequencies among patients presenting with premature adrenarche,[39–43] whereas the prevalence of heterozygosity for 21-hydroxylase deficiency has also been found to be increased in this population.[44,45] A search for genetic markers associated with premature adrenarche has revealed sequence variants in a number of genes encoding for steroidogenic enzymes and related receptors, although the functional consequence of these variants is unclear.[46,47] Last, a subset of patients has been identified with steroid hormone profiles intermediate between those with "typical" premature adrenarche and those with CAH, a condition described as "exaggerated adrenarche."[48] An increased incidence of premature adrenarche has been noted in children with a history of central nervous system insult such as head trauma or hypoxic-ischemic injury, suggesting that a central cause may play a role in its development.

### Natural History

Despite the fact that children with premature adrenarche experience a normal onset of central puberty and achieve normal adult heights,[49,50] the previous assumption that this developmental variation was always "benign" has proved to be incorrect. For many children, premature adrenarche may now be thought of as one stage in a continuum of metabolic abnormalities that ultimately manifests as syndrome X, which is typified by insulin resistance, hyperandrogenism, and dyslipidemia.[51] Indeed, as many as 45% of girls with premature adrenarche may develop polycystic ovarian syndrome later in life.[52] Even lean girls with premature adrenarche have demonstrable alterations in body composition and insulin and androgen levels when compared with controls.[53] Insulin resistance has also been reported in boys with premature adrenarche, suggesting that a propensity for future development of cardiovascular disease and type 2 diabetes pertains to both genders with this condition.[54,55] Prenatal growth restriction resulting in low birth weight has been established as a common risk factor for premature adrenarche, functional ovarian hyperandrogenism, and hyperinsulinemia, implying that these metabolic derangements may be related via a shared primary abnormality.[56] However, identifying predictive factors in patients who will develop hyperandrogenism in later life have thus far eluded detection.[57] Further biochemical and molecular genetic characterization of patients with premature adrenarche and its postmenarchal corollaries should yield greater understanding of pathogenesis and allow improved diagnostic discrimination and prognostic accuracy.

### Management

In patients with isolated pubic hair and normal linear growth, a bone age radiograph may be the only diagnostic study indicated,[30] although the finding of normal or only mildly elevated adrenal androgens provides additional reassurance. Further investigation, including baseline or stimulated serum adrenal androgen and steroid precursor levels, is warranted if there is marked growth acceleration, advanced skeletal maturation, clitoromegaly, or other significant virilization on physical examination. Patients with typical premature adrenarche should be monitored at 3- to 6-month intervals to allow determination of growth velocity and clinical status. Because the condition is progressive, most patients experience a gradual increase in body hair over time, accompanied by a normal rate of skeletal advancement. It is recommended that girls are monitored until menarche and a pattern of regular menses has been established because of the increased incidence of functional ovarian hyperandrogenism in this population. Accumulating evidence suggests an important role for metformin in the treatment of hyperandrogenism and hyperinsulinism during adolescence.[58] However, to date there is no evidence that pharmacologic intervention in premature adrenarche is indicated, especially because we are not yet able to predict which children will develop more serious adverse associations.[59]

## PATHOLOGIC PRECOCIOUS PUBERTY

### CENTRAL PRECOCIOUS PUBERTY

Also termed *gonadotropin dependent*, central precocious puberty refers to early activation of the HPG, and thus "central," axis. The underlying physiology of this form of precocious puberty is therefore identical to that of normal puberty, with the distinction being that it occurs at an abnormal time and may be the result of a pathologic condition.

#### Clinical Features

Girls with central precocious puberty typically present with breast enlargement and other estrogenic changes accompanied by growth acceleration and skeletal maturation. Unlike puberty beginning at a normal age, in central precocious puberty, there is often dissociation between gonadarche and adrenarche, which may be a result of lower adrenal androgen levels during early childhood. Testicular enlargement, which is the first sign of central precocious puberty in boys, often goes unrecognized, with the subsequent genital and body hair development prompting medical evaluation.

#### Pathophysiology

Causes of central precocious puberty can be divided into two general categories. *Idiopathic* central precocious puberty is used to designate cases in which no anatomic abnormality is identified, whereas in the remaining cases, a central nervous system insult, either congenital or acquired, is believed to be the trigger. Central precocious puberty is far more common in girls than in boys, with as many as 90% of cases being designated as idiopathic.[60] This is in contrast to the frequency of idiopathic central precocious puberty in boys, reported to account for 10% to 50% of cases.[61] Several forms of intracranial lesions have been implicated in the etiology of central precocious puberty, the most common being a hypothalamic hamartoma, a heterotopic mass located typically in the region of the tuber cinereum[62] (Figs. 147-4 and 147-5). This congenital malformation consists of GnRH-secreting neurons or transforming growth factor alpha–producing astroglial cells, both of which are believed to function as ectopic triggers on the hypothalamic pulse generator, resulting in an escape from the normal central nervous system inhibitory constraint on pubertal onset.[63,64] Rarely, hypothalamic hamartomas are associated with an increased incidence of seizures, particularly gelastic, or laughing, seizures.[65] Other central nervous system abnormalities that are associated with central precocious puberty include hypothalamic-pituitary or optic chiasm tumors, pineal or suprasellar cysts, septo-optic dysplasia, neurofibromatosis, head trauma, and hydrocephalus.[66,67] The

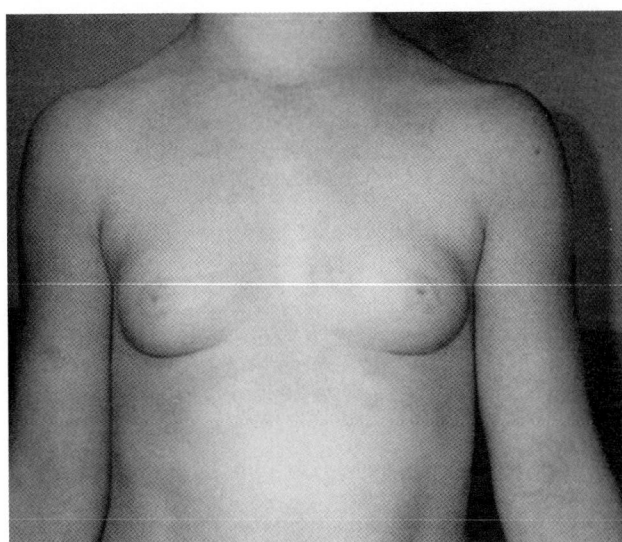

**Figure 147-4** Tanner stage III breast development in a 6-year-old girl with a hypothalamic hamartoma. Bone age was 8¹⁰/₁₂ years, pubic hair was Tanner stage I, and the vaginal mucosa was estrogenized.

mechanism of intracranial abnormalities leading to precocious puberty is believed to be caused by a disruption of the neural pathways that normally exert tonic inhibition on the brain in terms of activation of puberty. This process results in a seemingly paradoxic situation in which many disorders associated with deficiencies of anterior pituitary hormones may also be associated with excessive gonadotropin secretion.

### Diagnosis

The diagnosis of central precocious puberty is based on the ability to detect activation of the HPG axis, during which there is increased sensitivity to stimulation at each level of the axis. The GnRH stimulation test takes advantage of the fact that a "primed" pituitary gland responds to GnRH with a brisk elevation of gonadotropins, which in turn stimulates gonadal sex steroid secretion.[68] Although several different protocols have been developed, the most widely used is a 1-hour test employing intravenous synthetic GnRH (Factrel) and multiple blood sampling. Alternative methods include random or first warning (AM) gonadotropins using ultrasensitive assays, other GnRH agonists, such as nafarelin or leuprolide, and the use of a single-sample rapid subcutaneous stimulation test.[69–73] A pubertal response to GnRH stimulation is classically character-ized by a pattern of LH predominance indicating an elevation of LH above that of FSH, whereas a prepubertal response is marked by a minimal increase in LH, if any, but may elicit an FSH response above baseline. An intermediate response, typified by an FSH-predominant response, is seen in early central puberty and in premature thelarche. Additional evaluation of patients with central precocious puberty includes a magnetic resonance imaging scan of the brain to rule out an intracranial lesion.[74] A bone age radiograph provides important information about the degree of skeletal maturation and remaining growth potential. Pelvic ultrasonography is useful in documenting uterine and ovarian enlargement, ovarian symmetry, or the presence of cysts or other ovarian abnormalities.[75] In patients with a prepubertal or suppressed response to GnRH stimulation, further investigation for causes of gonadotropin-independent precocious puberty is indicated (see Figs. 147-1 and 147-2).

### Treatment

Potential negative consequences of precocious puberty include compromise of adult stature due to premature fusion of epiphysial growth plates, and psychosocial issues related to a discrepancy between physical and emotional maturity. Therefore, the primary goal of therapy is to temporarily suppress the HPG axis to allow improved adult height and to simultaneously restore the child to a physiologic state comparable with that of his or her peers. The discovery of safe and effective treatment in the form of GnRH agonists revolutionized the therapy of central precocious puberty in the mid-1980s and is the treatment of choice for this condition.[76,77] Although the mechanism of action of GnRH analogue therapy is not completely understood, it is believed that down-regulation of pituitary gonadotroph receptors occurs as a result of sustained high levels of GnRH.[78] Six long-acting GnRH analogues have been used in the treatment of precocious puberty, with subcutaneous, intranasal, and intramuscular routes of administration.[79] The depot preparation of leuprolide acetate, given in the form of monthly intramuscular injections, is the most commonly used agent in the United States and has been shown to provide safe and effective long-term therapy in children with central precocious puberty.[80,81] There are initial reports of longer acting formulations of GnRH analogues administered at 3-month intervals that also appear promising.[82] Although untested, it is possible that GnRH antagonists may eventually have a role in the treatment of central precocious puberty as well.[83] Therapy is characterized by a suppression of gonadotropins below the pubertal range and a return of gonadal steroids to prepubertal levels, along with a deceleration of growth velocity and skeletal maturation. Therapeutic efficacy may be biochemically

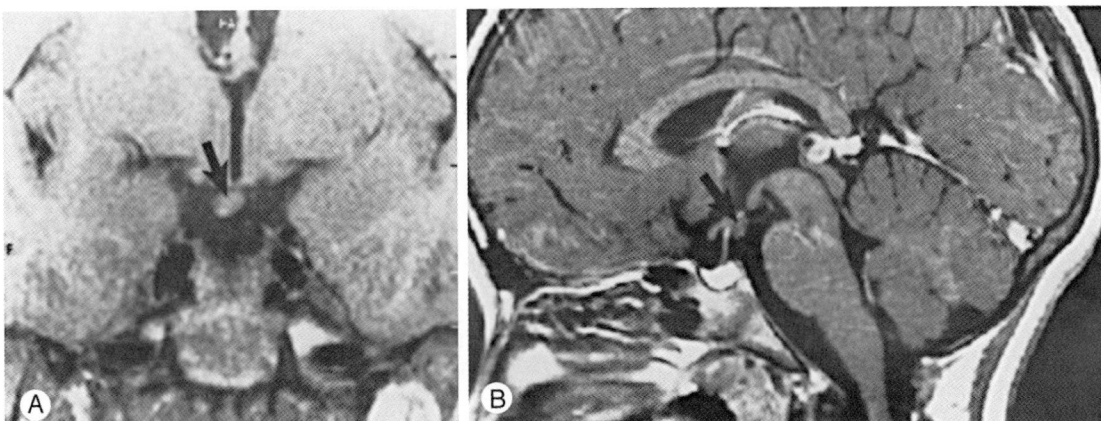

**Figure 147-5** Head magnetic resonance imaging scan revealed a pedunculated hypothalamic hamartoma in the region of the tuberous cinereum, as indicated by the *arrows* in frontal (**A**) and sagittal (**B**) sections.

documented by gonadotropin suppression in response to GnRH testing, whereas pelvic ultrasonography represents a potentially useful tool for monitoring the effects of treatment in girls, which is characterized by a regression of the internal genitalia from a pubertal to a prepubertal size.[84] In boys, a decrease in testicular volume provides similar information. Although therapy has a profound impact on the outcome of many patients, a subset of patients with precocious puberty has been identified in whom height prognosis is quite favorable, even without treatment. These patients are characterized by having an indolent form of precocious puberty, in which pubertal progression occurs gradually and bone age advancement is minimal.[85,86] Distinguishing features at presentation among this subset of patients include an increased height age–bone age ratio and predicted adult height similar to target height when compared with patients who have rapidly progressive precocious puberty.[87]

## Therapeutic Outcomes

A number of different outcome measures have been examined in regards to the safety and efficacy of GnRH analogue therapy for central precocious puberty, including adult height, bone mineralization, and resumption of puberty after treatment. Each of these is discussed individually.

### Adult Height

Numerous studies have demonstrated a significant improvement in adult height with gains ranging from 2.9 to 12.5 cm in patients with central precocious puberty treated with GnRH analogues.[86,88–91] Combination therapy in the form of a GnRH analogue plus growth hormone also improves final height in patients who experience a marked slowing of growth velocity on analogue therapy alone.[92–94] Additional proposed applications of GnRH analogue therapy for the purposes of preservation of height include its use in the delay of normal puberty in children with or without growth hormone deficiency[95,96] and in patients with deterioration of height potential occurring as a result of an underlying condition, such as CAH.[97–99]

### Bone Mineralization

The effects of sex steroids on bone density are well described, with peak acquisition of bone mass occurring during puberty.[100] Reports of a rapid decrease in bone mineralization after GnRH analogue therapy in adults initially led to concerns about potential similar negative consequences of GnRH analogue therapy in children with precocious puberty. However, several follow-up studies have now demonstrated normal bone mineral density in adult patients previously treated with a GnRH analogue.[90,101,102]

### Resumption of Puberty

Once pubertal suppression is removed via discontinuation of GnRH analogue therapy, there must be reactivation of the HPG axis for resumption of puberty to occur. Although the vast majority of patients experience spontaneous resumption of puberty, rare exceptions exist in cases in which there is a history of central nervous system insult such as cranial irradiation. A number of studies have examined the onset of progression of secondary sexual development as well as the age of menarche in girls treated for precocious puberty with GnRH analogues. Results have indicated a resumption of pubertal LH pulsatile secretion in most patients by 4 months after therapy,[103] as well as normal menarche, which most girls experience within 18 months after stopping treatment.[91,103] It has been found that normal ovulatory cycles are established in this population within a time frame identical to that of the untreated adolescent.[104] Similarly, gonadal function in adults previously treated with

GnRH analogues for central precocious puberty appears to be normal.[90,101]

## PERIPHERAL PRECOCIOUS PUBERTY

Also termed *gonadotropin independent*, peripheral precocious puberty refers to cases in which sex steroid exposure leads to pubertal development through a source other than activation of the HPG axis. This broad category encompasses an extremely heterogeneous group of abnormalities. Evaluation and differential diagnosis depend on whether the child is a girl or a boy and on whether the clinical presentation reveals changes associated with estrogens, androgens, or both. Individual causes of peripheral precocious puberty are discussed here, and the genotype-phenotype relationships seen in these disorders are outlined in Table 147-1.

### Abnormalities of Enzymes Involved in Steroid Biosynthesis
#### Congenital Adrenal Hyperplasia
CAH represents a group of diseases stemming from an autosomal-recessive inherited deficiency of an enzyme required for adrenal steroidogenesis. The resulting disorders represent a wide spectrum of molecular genetic abnormalities and phenotypic characteristics. Excess adrenal androgen secretion as a consequence of CAH is the most common cause of abnormal postnatal virilization in children. The hallmark of these disorders is an enzymatic block in the cortisol biosynthetic pathway leading to a lack of negative feedback stimulation at the level of the pituitary gland. The resulting increase in pituitary adrenocorticotropic hormone and a buildup of steroid precursors proximal to the enzyme block, results in an "overflow" of these precursors to the androgen synthetic pathway and subsequent overproduction of adrenal androgens. Once the diagnosis has been made, glucocorticoid replacement is intended to result in a cessation of adrenal hyperstimulation and a return of adrenal androgens to near-normal levels. The three types of CAH that may result in abnormal adrenal androgen production and subsequent virilization in prepubertal children are 21-hydroxylase,[105,106] 3β-hydroxysteroid dehydrogenase,[107] and 11-hydroxylase deficiencies.[108] Typical physical findings in girls may include pubic and axillary hair, body odor, growth acceleration, advanced bone age, and clitoromegaly. However, not all these features may be present at diagnosis. Boys present with similar changes, including increased phallic size and increased muscle mass. Testicular volume, however, is in the prepubertal range, in contrast to that observed in central precocious puberty. Rare cases of CAH with adrenal rest tissue represent an exception, in which unilateral or even bilateral enlargement of the testes may be found.[109]

#### Aromatase Excess Syndrome
Aromatase is the enzyme responsible for the conversion of androgens to estrogen in many tissues, including the gonads and adipocytes. Increased aromatization has been reported to be a cause of familial and prepubertal gynecomastia.[110] Kindreds have been described in whom the aromatase excess syndrome appears to be inherited in an autosomal-dominant fashion, resulting in gynecomastia in boys and precocious puberty in girls, accompanied by elevations of estradiol and estrone.[111] Aberrant expression of the P-450 aromatase gene is thought to form the basis of the condition in at least one case,[112] whereas an activating mutation in the aromatase gene has also been reported as a cause of familial aromatase excess.[113]

### Gain-of-Function Mutations
#### Abnormalities of G Proteins
**McCune-Albright Syndrome** McCune-Albright syndrome (MAS), first described in 1937 by Albright and colleagues,[114] is a rare disorder characterized by the clinical triad of precocious puberty, polyostotic fibrous dysplasia of bone, and

**Table 147-1** Genotype/Phenotype Relationships in Peripheral Precocious Puberty

| Disorder | Affected Product | Molecular Genetic Abnormality | Functional Consequence | Clinical presentation | | Inheritance |
|---|---|---|---|---|---|---|
| | | | | **Classic** | **Late-onset** | |
| Congenital adrenal hyperplasia | 21-hydroxylase, 11-hydroxylase, 3β-hydroxysteroid dehydrogenase enzymes | CYP21, CYP11B1, HSD3B2 mutations | Enzymatic block in cortisol biosynthesis | F: ambiguous genitalia ± salt wasting; M: ± salt wasting precocious puberty | F,M: premature pubarche | Autosomal recessive |
| Aromatase excess syndrome | Aromatase enzyme | Polymorphism of P-450 aromatase gene; inversions of chromosome 15q21.2-3 | Aberrant transcription of aromatase gene; gain-of-function mutation of aromatase gene | F: precocious puberty | M: gynecomastia | Autosomal dominant, X linked |
| McCune-Albright syndrome | G$_s$α | Missense mutation in G$_s$α gene resulting in ARG$^{201}$ → CYS or HIS | Mosaic distribution of constitutive G$_s$α activation | F,M: precocious puberty, café-au-lait spots, fibrous dysplasia of bone, other hyperfunctioning endocrinopathies | | Sporadic |
| Tissue-specific G$_s$α mutation | G$_s$α | Point mutation in G$_s$α gene resulting in ALA$^{366}$ → SER | Constitutive activation in testes, inactivation in other tissues | M: testotoxicosis and pseudohypoparathyroidism | Sporadic | |
| Familial male precocious puberty | Luteinizing hormone receptor | Single amino acid substitution in LH receptor | Constitutive activation of LH receptor in Leydig cells | M: precocious puberty | | Autosomal dominant, sporadic |
| FSH activating mutation | FSH receptor | Single amino acid substitutions: THR$^{449}$ → I in 3rd transmembrane domain of FSH receptor, ASP$^{567}$ → ASN in 6th transmembrane domain; ASP$^{567}$ → GLY in 3rd cytoplasmic loop of FSH receptor | Increased affinity of FSH receptor for human chorionic gonadotropin, constitutive activation of FSH receptor | F: familial gestational ovarian hyperstimulation syndrome, ? ovarian cysts, ? premature thelarche | M: preservation of spermatogenesis after hypophysectomy | ? |

F, female; FSH, follicle-stimulating hormone; LH, Luteinizing hormone; M, male.

café-au-lait spots. Molecular genetic investigation led to the discovery that MAS is caused by an activating mutation in $G_s\alpha$, the stimulatory subunit of the G protein involved in intracellular signaling.[115,116] This somatic mutation, which usually involves substitution of arginine for histidine or cysteine at the 201 position, is believed to occur in early embryogenesis, leading to a mosaic distribution of affected tissues. The result is a phenomenon of unregulated intracellular accumulation of cyclic adenosine monophosphate known as constitutive activation (see Chapters 11 and 12), which in turn stimulates downstream gene transcription.[117] Hyperfunction of endocrine glands is a cardinal feature of MAS, with numerous organs affected, including the adrenals, parathyroid glands, pituitary gland, thyroid, and gonads.[118] Rare involvement of nonendocrine tissues has also been reported in MAS and has included hepatobiliary disease, cardiac disease, and sudden death.[119,120] Unregulated sex steroid secretion from the gonads in prepubertal children forms the basis of the precocious puberty in MAS, which, although occurring in both sexes, is more commonly reported in females. In prepubertal girls, the precocious puberty is characterized by sporadic ovarian cysts with subsequent elevations in serum estradiol levels.[121] Spontaneous regression of the cysts can lead to withdrawal bleeding, whereas chronic unopposed estrogen can also result in uterine breakthrough bleeding.

The clinical presentation of MAS is extremely variable, ranging from patients with extensive skin (Fig. 147-6) and bone involvement (Fig. 147-7) and progressive precocious puberty to patients with only mild manifestations. Increasingly, patients exhibiting a forme fruste of MAS are being recognized, in whom isolated involvement of bone,[122] adrenals,[123] or gonads may occur.[124] The variable clinical presentation reflects, in part, the fact that the $G_s\alpha$ mutations that cause MAS are postzygotic and mosaic.[117] Thus, different individuals, and different organs within the same individual, may contain variable proportions of cells that harbor the $G_s\alpha$ mutation. Tissue-specific imprinting of the *GNAS-1* gene may also contribute to the observed phenotypic heterogeneity.[125] In patients with rapidly progressive precocious puberty, treatment has traditionally been with an aromatase inhibitor, such as testolactone. Unfortunately, this therapy has been largely disappointing, due to problems with both efficacy and compliance.[126] Thus far, limited experience with the newer generation aromatase inhibitors fadrozole, anastrozole, and

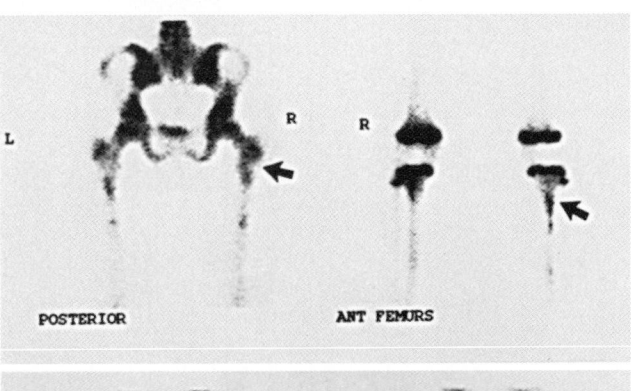

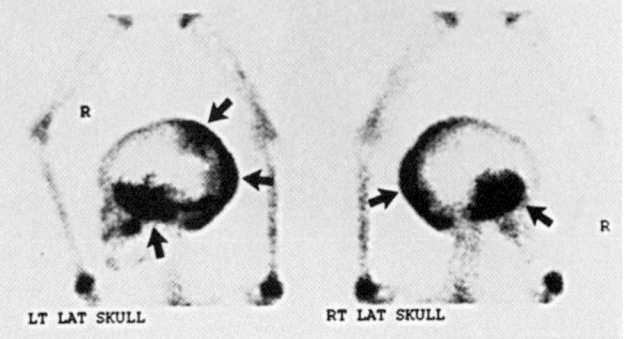

*Figure 147-7*  Bone scan of a patient with polyostotic fibrous dysplasia. The *arrows* indicate areas of increased uptake.

letrozole has yielded mixed results.[127,128] In contrast, tamoxifen, a selective estrogen receptor modulator, was shown to be safe and efficacious in 25 girls with McCune-Albright MAS and precocious puberty.[129] It remains to be seen whether pure estrogen receptor antagonists, such as Faslodex,[130] will prove to be superior to existing treatments for the precocious puberty of MAS. Regardless of the pharmacologic agent used, the underlying disease process is unchanged, as manifested by periodic elevations in serum estradiol even while clinical evidence of pubertal progression is completely suppressed (Fig. 147-8). Once the onset of central puberty commences, the HPG axis usually overrides the independent gonadal

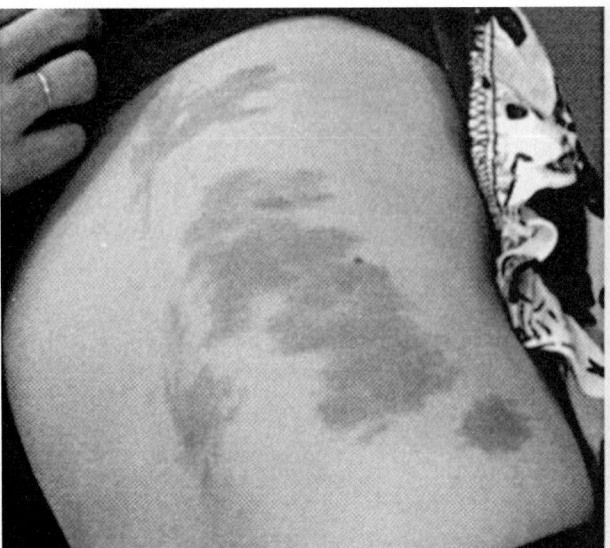

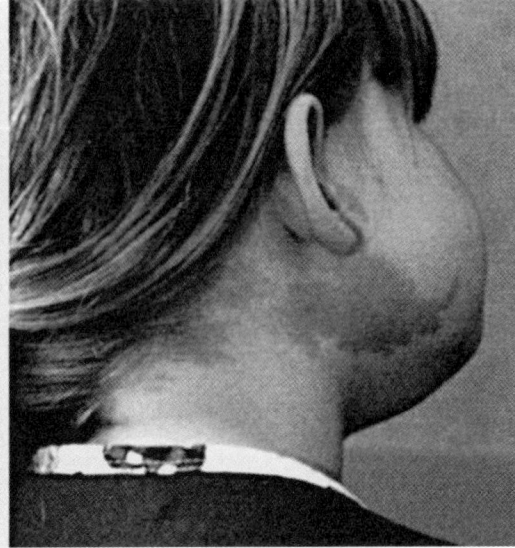

*Figure 147-6*  Café-au-lait skin pigmentation in a 4-year-old girl with McCune-Albright syndrome who presented with precocious puberty. The irregular borders of these lesions designate them as "coast of Maine" café-au-lait spots, as opposed to the smooth-bordered "coast of California" variety characteristic of neurofibromatosis. The propensity of these lesions to stop abruptly at the midline is demonstrated.

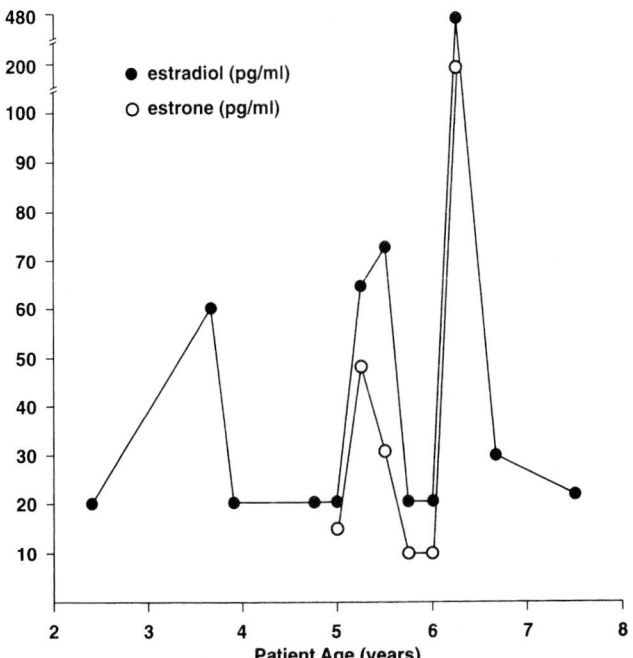

*Figure 147-8* The autonomous gonadal function of McCune-Albright syndrome is characterized by sporadic and periodic elevations in serum estrogens. This continues despite clinical suppression of puberty, which in this patient was achieved with the use of tamoxifen.

function, although persistent autonomous ovarian activity has been documented in some postmenarchal girls and women with MAS.[131,132]

**$G_s\alpha$ Mutations with Tissue Specificity** A rare and fascinating mutation of $G_s\alpha$ has been described in two unrelated males in which a mutant G protein subunit exhibits temperature dependence, resulting in both activating and inactivating properties, depending on the tissue involved. In the testes, which are cooler than the core body temperature, the abnormal $G_s\alpha$ is activated, leading to autonomous sex steroid production and testotoxicosis. In contrast, in skin fibroblasts, which are at 37°C, thermal instability of the abnormal protein is observed, leading to rapid degradation of $G_s\alpha$ with a subsequent decrease in $G_s\alpha$ activity and pseudohypoparathyroidism.[133,134]

### Abnormalities of Gonadotropin Receptors
**Familial Male Precocious Puberty** Familial male precocious puberty, also termed *testotoxicosis,* is a form of gonadotropin-independent precocious puberty that occurs in males. In this disorder, the LH receptor exhibits constitutive activation, leading to autonomous sex steroid secretion and early pubertal development. The underlying abnormality is a heterozygous mutation in the gene encoding the LH receptor, which results in transcription of an abnormal receptor product with aberrant function. The first described mutation, found in eight affected individuals in different families, involved the substitution of glycine for aspartate at position 578 in the sixth transmembrane helix of the LH receptor.[135] Since then, at least 13 additional mutations involving the first, second, and third transmembrane domains and third intracellular loop of the LH receptor have been described.[136,137] Although the typical inheritance pattern for familial male precocious puberty is autosomal dominant, patients with sporadic mutations have also been identified.[138,139] Females with activating mutations of the LH receptor have no phenotypic

abnormalities, likely because both LH and FSH are required for ovarian steroidogenesis.[140]

Patients with familial male precocious puberty present in early childhood (typically by age 4) with growth acceleration and progressive virilization, including growth of pubic hair and phallic enlargement. The testes are usually small in comparison with the degree of virilization and may be nodular,[141] with histology demonstrating Leydig cell hyperplasia.[142] Serum testosterone levels are in the adult male range, whereas serum gonadotropins are prepubertal, as is the response to GnRH testing. Untreated, males with familial male precocious puberty experience continued skeletal maturation with early epiphyseal closure and final short stature. Fertility is generally normal, although oligospermia and morphologic testicular abnormalities have been described in some affected individuals.[143] Pharmacologic regimens shown to be effective in the treatment of familial male precocious puberty have included the antisteroidogenic agent ketoconazole,[144] although there are concerns regarding potential liver toxicity.[145] To date, the greatest efficacy and safety have been achieved using combination therapy with the androgen receptor blocker spironolactone and the aromatase inhibitor testolactone.[146] The addition of a long-acting GnRH analogue once central puberty begins has provided useful adjunctive therapy.[147] It is likely that improved efficacy will eventually be achieved through the use of third-generation aromatase inhibitors in combination with pure antiandrogens in boys with this disorder.[148]

**Follicle-Stimulating Hormone Receptor–Activating Mutations** Heterozygous mutations in the FSH receptor have been discovered as the etiology for familial and sporadic spontaneous gestational ovarian hyperstimulation syndrome.[149,150] In this instance, the specificity of the mutated receptor is altered such that human chorionic gonadotropin and FSH result in stimulation of the receptor. One case of an FSH receptor mutation exhibiting constitutive activation has also been reported in a hypophysectomized male who was able to autonomously maintain spermatogenesis.[151] Although a search for FSH-activating receptor mutations in prepubertal girls has been negative thus far,[18,152] such mutations could theoretically cause autonomous ovarian sex steroid production, resulting in granulosa cell tumors, premature thelarche, or precocious puberty.

**Ovarian Cysts** Use of high-resolution ultrasonography has revealed that ovarian cysts are quite common in prepubertal girls of all ages.[153,154] Although these cysts are typically asymptomatic, they may also become transiently functional, causing acute onset of breast development because of elevated ovarian estradiol secretion.[155] Spontaneous resolution of these cysts is followed by a decrease in breast tissue, leading to a history of waxing and waning breast development. The underlying pathophysiology of this cause of precocious puberty is poorly understood and may represent transient activity of the HPG axis, a $G_s\alpha$ mutation (forme fruste of MAS),[124,156] or an unidentified FSH receptor mutation.

### TUMORS
Sex steroid production by neoplastic tissue in prepubertal children is a rare but important cause of peripheral precocious puberty. Presenting symptoms depend on the location and type of tumor and whether androgens, estrogens, or both are being produced.

### Gonadal Tumors
**Ovarian Tumors** Primary ovarian neoplasms in children may originate from sex cord or stromal tissue, epithelium, or the germ cell line,[157] with granulosa cell tumors being the most frequent ovarian tumor inducing precocious puberty.[158] Although the average age of prepubertal children presenting with ovarian tumors is 10 years, precocious puberty caused by

ovarian neoplasms has been reported in infants.[159,160] The majority of ovarian tumors produce estrogen, resulting in feminization, although androgen production may also occur, leading to hirsutism and other signs of virilization.[157,161] Additional clinical findings often include abdominal symptoms such as pain, distension, ascites, or a palpable mass. The frequency of precocious puberty as a feature of ovarian tumors varies, depending on the type of tissue involved, but may be as high as 71%.[162] Primary treatment is surgical with or without adjuvant chemotherapy,[163] and the prognosis is generally good, particularly in patients with the juvenile granulosa cell tumor variety.[159]

**Testicular Tumors**    Leydig cell tumors, which make up approximately 3% of all testicular neoplasms,[164] are the most common gonadal stromal tumors associated with precocious puberty in boys.[165] Although 10% of such tumors are malignant in adults, they are usually benign in children. Precocious puberty caused by testicular tumors is typically characterized by elevated serum testosterone levels and evidence of virilization. However, sex cord (Sertoli cell) tumors have rarely been described in which gynecomastia, as well as virilization, is a feature of the clinical presentation.[166] In several cases, somatic activating mutations of the LH receptor have been shown to form the basis for Leydig cell tumors associated with precocious puberty.[167,168]

*Adrenal Tumors*
Adrenocortical adenomas and carcinomas are extremely rare causes of precocious puberty in childhood but have been reported to occur even during infancy.[169] The vast majority of such tumors are virilizing (Fig. 147-9), due to elevations in serum adrenal androgen levels, which may or may not be accompanied by hypercortisolism.[170] However, in rare instances, variations in biosynthetic enzyme activity within the tumor may also result in increased plasma concentrations of estrogens, with subsequent feminization.[171] The majority of functioning childhood adrenocortical neoplasms are benign, and surgical resection is the treatment method of choice.[172] Secondary activation of the hypothalamic-pituitary-adrenal axis has been reported after removal of a virilizing adrenal tumor.[173]

*Germ Cell Tumors*
Nongonadal germ cell tumors as a cause of precocious puberty have been reported to arise in numerous locations, including

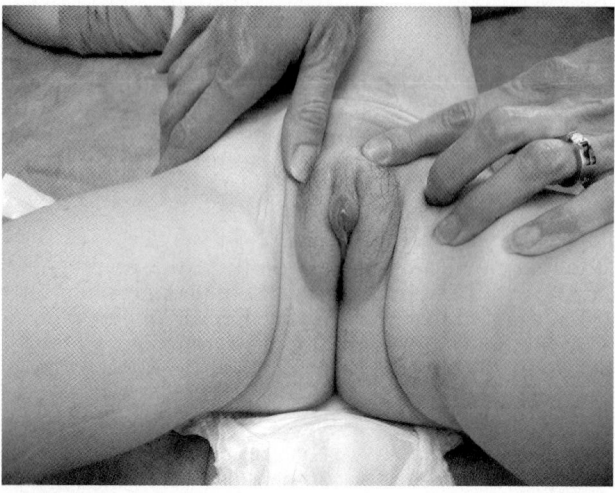

*Figure 147-9*    Virilization of the genitalia in a 2-year-old girl with an androgen-secreting adrenocortical adenoma. (Photo courtesy of Dr. Emily Walvoord.)

the liver,[174] lungs,[175] mediastinum,[176] pineal gland,[177] basal ganglia, thalamus, and hypothalamus.[178] Tumor markers useful in the diagnosis and follow-up of germ cell tumors include α-fetoprotein, β–human chorionic gonadotropin, and pregnancy-specific $β_1$-glycoprotein.[179] Because precocious puberty in this setting occurs as a result of ectopic β–human chorionic gonadotropin secretion, which mimics the action of LH on testicular Leydig cells, the overwhelming majority of cases are reported in boys. Increased tumor aromatase activity in the setting of simultaneous β–human chorionic gonadotropin production has been postulated to account for rare cases of precocious feminization in girls presenting with germ cell tumors.[180,181]

### Exogenous Sex Steroids
Exogenous sex steroids, either estrogens or androgens, can lead to the development of secondary sexual characteristics in prepubertal children. Examples of widely available exogenous steroids include oral contraceptive pills and estrogen- or androgen-containing topical preparations. Systemic absorption of estrogens found in various cosmetics and hair products have also been linked to precocious puberty.[182] Increasingly, attention has focused on the potential deleterious developmental effects of environmental exposures to endocrine disruptors. Phthalates represent one class of pollutants widely used in manufacturing that was present in higher concentrations in the serum of Puerto Rican girls with premature thelarche when compared with controls.[183] Naturally occurring dietary substances such as phytoestrogens are also known to affect the reproductive system; however, it remains unclear whether they have any role in abnormal pubertal development.[184]

### Hypothyroidism
More appropriately thought of as a form of *pseudoprecocious puberty*, the rare association between severe long-standing hypothyroidism and early sexual development (Van Wyk-Grumbach syndrome) was described in the 1960s.[185] In this condition, apparent precocious puberty is accompanied by the seemingly paradoxic finding of significantly delayed skeletal maturation and growth arrest. In girls, the clinical presentation consists of estrogenic manifestations, including breast development and changes of the vaginal mucosa. Galactorrhea and vaginal bleeding may be present, which in some patients are severe.[186,187] Pelvic ultrasonography reveals enlarged ovaries with multiple cysts. Boys present with macro-orchidism, often without evidence of virilization (Figs. 147-10 and 147-11), which is consistent with the finding of low serum testosterone levels.

Investigation of the HPG axis of boys with severe primary hypothyroidism and macro-orchidism reveals a prepubertal pattern of gonadotropin response to GnRH stimulation, although baseline levels of thyroid-stimulating hormone, prolactin, and pituitary gonadotropins are elevated.[188,189] The original hypothesis for pituitary overproduction of gonadotropins in addition to thyroid-stimulating hormone has been supported by the finding of an elevated FSH response to thyroid-stimulating hormone stimulation in a patient with hypothyroidism-induced macro-orchidism,[190] whereas evidence also exists of a component of cross-reactivity of thyroid-stimulating hormone at the level of the FSH receptor.[191] Both of these mechanisms would theoretically result in FSH-mediated gonadal stimulation, causing Sertoli cell proliferation with subsequent testicular enlargement in boys and ovarian hyperstimulation in girls. The lack of LH-induced testosterone secretion in hypothyroid boys with elevated gonadotropins has been attributed to an inhibitory influence of prolactin on LH action at the Leydig cell.[188] The majority of the clinical and biochemical abnormalities in these patients gradually resolve with restoration of a

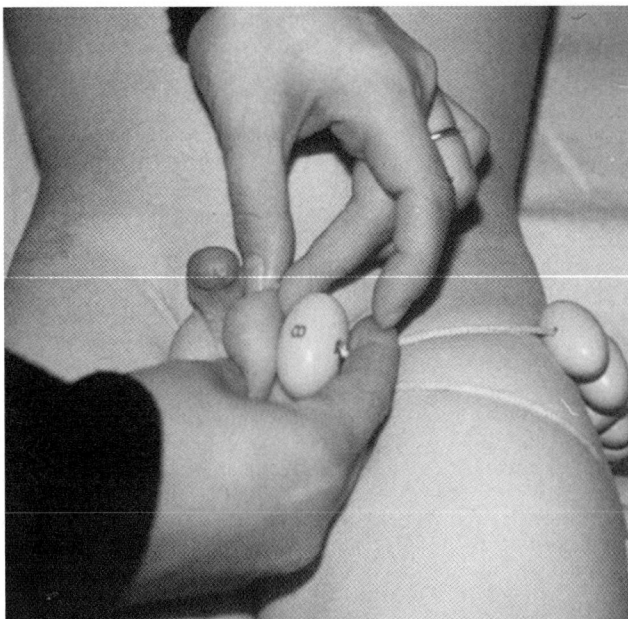

**Figure 147-10** Macro-orchidism in an 8-year-old boy with severe long-standing hypothyroidism secondary to autoimmune thyroiditis. Testicular volume was 8 mL, in contrast to a normal prepubertal testicular volume of 1 to 3 mL.

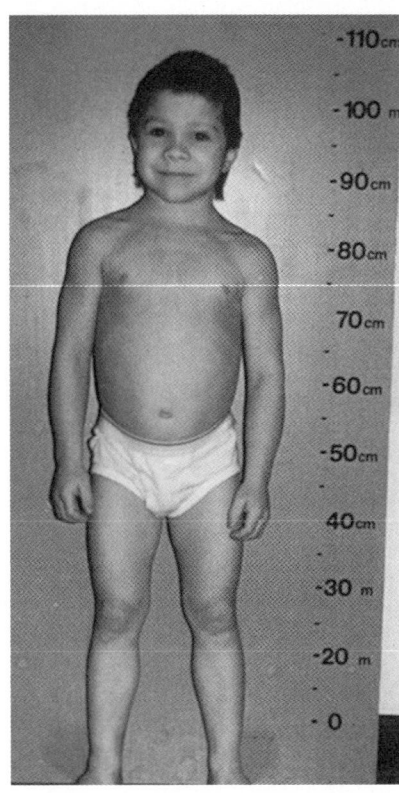

**Figure 147-11** Additional manifestations of hypothyroidism in this child included severe growth arrest, coarse facial features, dry skin, and sallow complexion. Bone age radiograph was significantly delayed at 5 years.

euthyroid status, although macro-orchidism may persist.[190] Treatment with a GnRH agonist, often in combination with growth hormone, should be considered in patients with hypothyroidism who rapidly progress through puberty once thyroid replacement therapy is initiated.[192]

### Gynecomastia

Although some degree of breast development in boys during puberty is nearly universal,[193] prepubertal gynecomastia is uncommon and always abnormal. A review of published cases reveals that onset of prepubertal gynecomastia is usually between the ages of 2 and 7 and may be bilateral or unilateral.[194] Causes of prepubertal gynecomastia include gonadal, adrenal, or human chorionic gonadotropin–secreting tumors,[166,171,195,196] exogenous estrogen exposure,[197] and idiopathic reasons.[198] Prepubertal gynecomastia has also been associated with exogenous growth hormone therapy and is usually mild and self-limited in this setting.[199] Familial cases of gynecomastia typically represent forms of the aromatase excess syndrome.[112,113,200] Evaluation of prepubertal gynecomastia includes a careful investigation for underlying abnormalities. Treatment commonly consists of surgical excision, which, in idiopathic cases, is curative.[201] Medical therapy in the form of antiestrogens or aromatase inhibitors, both of which have been used in pubertal gynecomastia, may prove to be effective in patients with prepubertal gynecomastia as well.

### REFERENCES

1. Marshall WA, Tanner JM: Variations in the pattern of pubertal changes in girls. Arch Dis Child 44:291–303, 1969.
2. Lee PA: Normal ages of pubertal events among American males and females. J Adolesc Health Care 1:26–29, 1980.
3. Kaplowitz PB, Oberfield SE: Reexamination of the age limit for defining when puberty is precocious in girls in the United States: Implications for evaluation and treatment. Drug and Therapeutics and Executive Committees of the Lawson Wilkins Pediatric Endocrine Society. Pediatrics 104:936–941, 1999.
4. Herman-Giddens ME, Slorla EJ, Wasserman RC, et al: Secondary sexual characteristics and menses in young girls seen in office practice: A study from the pediatric research in office settings network. Pediatrics 99:505–512, 1997.
5. Kaplowitz PB, Slora EJ, Wasserman RC, et al: Earlier onset of puberty in girls: Relation to increased body mass index and race. Pediatrics 108:347–343, 2001.
6. Bourguignon JP: Control of the onset of puberty. In Pescovitz OH, Eugster EA (eds): Pediatric Endocrinology: Mechanisms, Manifestations and Management. Philadelphia, Lippincott Williams & Wilkins, 2004, pp 285–298.
7. Chumlea WC, Schubert CM, Roche AF, et al: Age at menarche and racial comparisons in us girls. Pediatrics 111:110–113, 2003.
8. Sun SS, Schubert CM, Chumlea WC, et al: National estimates of the timing of sexual maturation and racial differences among US children. Pediatrics 110:911–919, 2002.
9. Marti-Henneberg C, Vizmanos B: The duration of puberty in girls is related to the timing of its onset. J Pediatr 131:618–621, 1997.
10. Volta C, Bernasconi S, Cisternino M, et al: Isolated premature thelarche and thelarche variant: Clinical and auxological follow-up of 119 girls. J Endocrinol Invest 21:180–183, 1998.
11. Ilicki A, Prager Lewin R, et al: Premature thelarche-natural history and sex hormone secretion in 68 girls. Acta Paediatr Scand 73:756–762, 1984.

12. Mills JL, Stolley PD, Davies J, et al: Premature thelarche: Natural history and etiologic investigation. Am J Dis Child 135:743–745, 1981.

13. Pang S: Precocious thelarche and premature adrenarche. Pediatr Ann 10:340–345, 1981.

14. Klein KO, Meriq V, Brown-Dawson JM, et al: Estrogen levels in girls with premature thelarche compared with normal prepubertal girls as determined by an ultrasensitive recombinant cell bioassay. J Pediatr 134:19–22, 1999.

15. Haber HP, Wollmann HA, Ranke MB: Pelvic ultrasonography: Early differentiation between isolated premature thelarche and central precocious puberty. Eur J Pediatr 154:182–186, 1995.

16. Buzi F, Pilotta A, Dordini D, et al: Pelvic ultrasonography in normal girls and in girls with pubertal precocity. Acta Paediatr 88:246–247, 1999.

17. Belgorosky A, Chaler E, Rivarola MA: High serum sex hormone-binding globulin (SHBG) in premature thelarche. Clin Endocrinol 37:203–206, 1992.

18. Hannon TS, King DW, Brinkman AD, et al: Premature thelarche and granulosa cell tumors: A search for FSH receptor and Gsα activating mutations. J Pediatr Endocrinol Metab 15:891–895, 2002.

19. Choubtum L, Mahachoklertwattana P, Sriphrapradang A, et al: Gonadotropin-releasing hormone testing in premature thelarche. J Med Assoc Thai 82(Suppl 1):S33–S38, 1999.

20. Verrotti A, Ferrari M, Morgese G: Premature thelarche: A long-term follow-up. Gynecol Endocrinol 10:241–247, 1996.

21. Aritaki S, Takagi A, Someya H, et al: A comparison of patients with premature thelarche and idiopathic true precocious puberty in the initial stage of illness. Acta Paediatr Jpn 39:21–27, 1997.

22. Wang C, Zhong CQ, Leung A, et al: Serum bioactive follicle-stimulating hormone levels in girls with precocious sexual development. J Clin Endocrinol Metab 70:615–619, 1990.

23. Pescovitz OH, Hench KD, Barnes KM, et al: Premature thelarche and central precocious puberty: The relationship between clinical presentation and the gonadotropin response to luteinizing hormone-releasing hormone. J Clin Endocrinol Metab 67:474–479, 1988.

24. Klein KO, Baron J, Colli MJ, et al: Estrogen levels in childhood determined by an ultrasensitive recombinant cell bioassay. J Endocrinol Invest 94:2475–2480, 1994.

25. Pasquino AM, Tebaldi L, Cioschi L, et al: Premature thelarche: A follow-up study of 40 girls. Natural history and endocrine findings. Arch Dis Child 60:1180–1182, 1985.

26. Van Winter JT, Noller KL, Zimmerman D, et al: Natural history of premature thelarche in Olmsted County, Minnesota, 1940 to 1984. J Pediatr 116:278–280, 1990.

27. Pasquino AM, Pucarelli I, Passeri F, et al: Progression of premature thelarche to central precocious puberty. J Pediatr 126:11–14, 1995.

28. Salardi S, Cacciari E, Mainetti B, et al: Outcome of premature thelarche: Relation to puberty and final height. Arch Dis Child 79:173–174, 1998.

29. West KW, Rescorla FJ, Scherer LR III, et al: Diagnosis and treatment of symptomatic breast masses in the pediatric population. J Pediatr Surg 30:182–186, 1995.

30. Reiter EO, Saenger P: Premature adrenarche. Endocrinologist 7:85–88, 1997.

31. Voutilainen R, Perheentupa J, Apter D: Benign premature adrenarche: Clinical features and serum steroid levels. Acta Paediatr Scand 72:707–711, 1983.

32. Riddick LM, Garibaldi LR, Wang ME, et al: 3α-Androstanediol glucuronide in premature and normal pubarche. J Clin Endocrinol Metab 72:46–50, 1991.

33. Saenger P, Reiter E: Premature adrenarche: A normal variant of puberty. J Clin Endocrinol Metab 74:236–238, 1992.

34. Kelner CJ, Brook CG: A mixed longitudinal study of adrenal steroid excretion in childhood and the mechanism of adrenarche. Clin Endocrinol 19:117, 1983.

35. Kecskes L, Juricskay Z, Tatai Z, et al: Dynamics of adrenal steroidogenesis in childhood: Steroid excretion in prepubertal and pubertal girls. Acta Paediatr Acad Sci Hung 23:151–165, 1982.

36. Schiebinger RJ, Albertson BD, Cassorla FG, et al: The developmental changes in plasma adrenal androgens during infancy and adrenarche are associated with changing activities of adrenal microsomal 17-hydroxylase and 17,20-desmolase. J Clin Invest 67:1177–1182, 1981.

37. Gell JS, Carr BR, Sasano H, et al: Adrenarche results from development of a 3β-hydroxysteroid dehydrogenase-deficient adrenal reticularis. J Clin Endocrinol Metab 83:3695–3701, 1998.

38. Horton R, Lobo R: Peripheral androgens and the role of androstanediol glucuronide. Clin Endocrinol 15:293–306, 1986.

39. Cathro DM, Golombek SG: Non-classical 3β-hydroxysteroid dehydrogenase deficiency in children in central Iowa. Difficulties in differentiating this entity from cases of precocious adrenarche without an adrenal enzyme defect. J Pediatr Endocrinol 7:19–32, 1994.

40. Morris AH, Reiter EO, Geffner ME, et al: Absence of nonclassical congenital adrenal hyperplasia in patients with precocious adrenarche. J Clin Endocrinol Metab 69:709–715, 1989.

41. Temeck JW, Pang S, Nelson C, et al: Genetic defects of steroidogenesis in premature pubarche. J Clin Endocrinol Metab 64:609–617, 1987.

42. Siegel SF, Finegold DN, Urban MD, et al: Premature pubarche: Etiological heterogeneity? J Clin Endocrinol Metab 74:239–247, 1992.

43. Balducci R, Boscherini B, Mangiantini A, et al: Isolated precocious pubarche: An approach. J Clin Endocrinol Metab 79:582–589, 1993.

44. Witchel SF, Lee PA, Suda-Hartman M, et al: Hyperandrogenism and manifesting heterozygotes for 21-hydroxylase deficiency. Biochem Mol Med 62:151–158, 1997.

45. Dacou-Voutetakis C, Dracopoulou M: High incidence of molecular defects of the CYP21 gene in patients with premature adrenarche. J Clin Endocrinol Metab 84:1570–1574, 1999.

46. Witchel SF, Smith R, Tomboc M, Aston CE: Candidate gene analysis in premature pubarche and adolescent hyperandrogenism. Fertil Steril 75:724–730, 2001.

47. Ibanez L, Marcos MV, Potau N, et al: Increased frequency of the G972R variant of the insulin receptor substrate-1 (irs-1) gene among girls with a history of precocious pubarche. Fertil Steril 78:1288–1293, 2002.

48. Likitmaskul S, Cowell CT, Donaghue K, et al: "Exaggerated adrenarche" in children presenting with premature adrenarche. Clin Endocrinol 42:265–272, 1995.

49. Ibanez L, Virdis R, Potau N, et al: Natural history of premature pubarche: An auxological study. J Clin Endocrinol Metab 74:254–257, 1992.

50. Ghizzoni L, Milani S: The natural history of premature adrenarche. J Pediatr Endocrinol Metab 13(Suppl 5):1247–1251, 2000.

51. Silverstein JH, Rosenbloom AL: Type 2 diabetes in children. Curr Diabetes Rep 1:19–27, 2001.

52. Ibanez L, Potau N, Virdis R, et al: Postpubertal outcome in girls diagnosed of premature pubarche during childhood: Increased frequency of functional ovarian hyperandrogenism. J Clin Endocrinol Metab 76:1599–1603, 1993.

53. Ibanez L, Ong K, de Zegher F, et al: Fat distribution in non-obese girls with and without precocious pubarche: Central adiposity related to insulinaemia and androgenaemia from prepuberty to postmenarche. Clin Endocrinol 58:372–379, 2003.

54. Denburg MR, Silfen ME, Manibo AM, et al: Insulin sensitivity and the inulin-like growth factor system in prepubertal boys with premature adrenarche. J Clin Endocrinol Metab 87:5604–5609, 2002.

55. Ibanez L, Potau N, Zampolli M, et al: Hyperinsulinemia and decreased insulin-like growth factor-binding protein-1 are common features in prepubertal and pubertal girls with a history of premature pubarche. J Clin Endocrinol Metab 82:2283–2288, 1997.

56. Ibanez L, Potau N, François I, et al: Precocious pubarche, hyperinsulinism, and ovarian hyperandrogenism in girls: Relation to reduced fetal growth. J Clin Endocrinol Metab 83:3558–3562, 1998.

57. Ibanez L, Valls C, Potau N, et al: Polycystic ovary syndrome after precocious pubarche: Ontogeny of the low-birthweight effect. Clin Endocrinol 55:667–672, 2001.

58. Ibanez L, Ferrer A, Ong K, et al: Insulin sensitization early after menarche prevents progression from precocious pubarche to polycystic ovary syndrome. J Pediatr 144:23–29, 2004.

59. Ibanez L, Ong K, Ferrer A, et al: Low-dose flutamide-metformin therapy reverses insulin resistance and reduces fat mass in nonobese adolescents with ovarian hyperandrogenism. J Clin Endocrinol Metab 88:2600–2606, 2003.

60. Dacou-Voutakis C: Female sexual precocity. Ann N Y Acad Sci 816:209–218, 1997.

61. De Sanctis V, Corrias A, Rizzo V, et al: Etiology of central precocious puberty in males: Results of the Italian study group for physiopathology of puberty. J Pediatr Endocrinol Metab 13(Suppl 1):687–693, 2000.

62. Robben SG, Oostdijk W, Drop SL: Idiopathic isosexual central precocious puberty: Magnetic resonance findings in 30 patients. Br J Radiol 68:34–38, 1995.

63. Mahachaklertwattana P, Kaplan SL, Grumbach MM: The luteinizing hormone-releasing hormone-secreting hypothalamic hamartoma is a congenital malformation: Natural history. J Clin Endocrinol Metab 77:118–124, 1993.

64. Jung H, Carmel P, Schwartz MS, et al: Some hypothalamic hamartomas contain transforming growth factor alpha, a puberty-inducing growth factor, but not luteinizing hormone-releasing hormone neurons. J Clin Endocrinol Metab 84:4695–4701, 1999.

65. Jung H, Neumaier Probst E, Hauffa BP, et al: Association of morphological characteristics with precocious puberty and/or gelastic seizures in hypothalamic hamartoma. J Clin Endocrinol Metab 88:4590–4595, 2003.

66. Pescovitz OH: Precocious puberty. Pediatr Rev 11:229–237, 1990.

67. Sockalosky JJ, Kriel RL, Krach LE, et al: Precocious puberty after traumatic brain injury. J Pediatr 110:373–377, 1987.

68. Pescovitz OH, Comite F, Hench K, et al: The NIH experience with precocious puberty: Diagnostic subgroups and response to short-term luteinizing hormone releasing hormone analogue therapy. J Pediatr 108:47–54, 1986.

69. Neely EK, Wilson DM, Lee PA: Spontaneous serum gonadotropin concentrations in the evaluation of precocious puberty. J Pediatr 127:47–52, 1995.

70. Rosenfield RL, Garibaldi LR, Moll GW Jr, et al: The rapid ovarian secretory response to pituitary stimulation by the gonadotropin-releasing hormone agonist nafarelin in sexual precocity. J Clin Endocrinol Metab 63:1386–1389, 1986.

71. Ibanez L, Potau N, Zampolli M, et al: Use of leuprolide acetate response

patterns in the early diagnosis of pubertal disorders: Comparison with the gonadotropin-releasing hormone test. J Clin Endocrinol Metab 78:30–35, 1994.

72. Rosenfield RL, Perovic N, Ehrmann DA: Acute hormonal responses to the gonadotropin releasing hormone agonist leuprolide: Dose response studies and comparison to nafarelin—A clinical research center study. J Clin Endocrinol Metab 81:3408–3411, 1996.

73. Eckert KL, Wilson DM, Bachrach LK, et al: A single-sample, subcutaneous gonadotropin-releasing hormone test for central precocious puberty. Pediatrics 97:517–519, 1996.

74. Ng SM, Kumar Y, Cody D, et al: Cranial MRI scans are indicated in all girls with central precocious puberty. Arch Dis Child 88:414–418, 2003.

75. Herter LD, Golendziner E, Flores JA, et al: Ovarian and uterine findings in pelvic sonography: Comparisons between prepubertal girls, girls with isolated thelarche, and girls with central precocious puberty. J U S Med 21:1237–1246, 2002.

76. Crowley WF Jr, Comite F, Vale W, et al: Therapeutic use of pituitary desensitization with a long-acting LHRH agonist: A potential new treatment for idiopathic precocious puberty. J Clin Endocrinol Metab 52:370–372, 1981.

77. Breyer P, Haider A, Pescovitz OH: Gonadotropin-releasing hormone agonists in the treatment of girls with central precocious puberty. Clin Obstet Gynecol 36:764–772, 1993.

78. Conn PM, Jankovick JA, Stanislaus K, et al: Molecular and cellular bases of gonadotropin-releasing hormone action in the pituitary and central nervous system. Vitam Horm 50:151–214, 1995.

79. Hardin DS, Pescovitz OH: Central precocious puberty and its treatment with long-acting GnRH analogs. Endocrinologist 1:163, 1991.

80. Clemons RD, Kappy MS, Stuart TE, et al: Long-term effectiveness of depot gonadotropin-releasing hormone analogue in the treatment of children with central precocious puberty. Am J Dis Child 147:653–657, 1993.

81. Neely EK, Hintz RL, Parker B, et al: Two-year results of treatment with depot leuprolide acetate for central precocious puberty. J Pediatr 121:634–640, 1993.

82. Carel JC, Lahlou N, Jaramillo O, et al: Treatment of central precocious puberty by subcutaneous injections of leuprorelin 3-month depot. J Clin Endocrinol Metab 87:4111–4116, 2002.

83. Roth C: Therapeutic potential of GnRH antagonists in the treatment of precocious puberty. Exp Opin Invest Drug 1:253–259, 2002.

84. Beck-Jensen AM, Brocks V, Holm K, et al: Central precocious puberty in girls: Internal genitalia before, during, and after treatment with long-acting gonadotropin-releasing hormone analogues. J Pediatr 132:105–108, 1998.

85. Ghirri P, Bottone U, Gasperi M, et al: Final height in girls with slowly progressive untreated central precocious puberty. Gynecol Endocrinol 11:301–305, 1997.

86. Kauli R, Galatzer A, Kornreich L, et al: Final height of girls with central precocious puberty, untreated versus treated with cyproterone acetate or GnRH analogue. A comparative study with re-evaluation of predictions by the Bayley-Pinneau method. Horm Res 47:54–61, 1997.

87. Kreiter M, Burstein S, Rosenfield RL, et al: Preserving adult height potential in girls with idiopathic true precocious puberty. J Pediatr 117:364–370, 1990.

88. Mul D, Bertelloni S, Carel JC, et al: Effect of gonadotropin releasing hormone agonist treatment in boys with central precocious puberty: Final height results. Horm Res 58:1–7, 2002.

89. Klein KO, Barnes KM, Jones JV, et al: Increased final height in precocious puberty after long-term treatment with lhrh agonists: The National Institutes of Health experience. J Clin Endocrinol Metab 86:4711–4726, 2001.

90. Bertelloni S, Baroncelli GI, Ferdeghini M, et al: Final Height, gonadal function and bone mineral density of adolescent males with central precocious puberty after therapy with gonadotropin-releasing hormone analogues. Eur J Pediatr 159:369–374, 2000.

91. Oostdijk W, Rikken B, Schreuder S, et al: Final height in central precocious puberty after treatment with a slow release GnRH agonist. Arch Dis Child 75:292–297, 1996.

92. Pasquino AM, Municchi G, Pucarelli I, et al: Combined treatment with gonadotropin-releasing hormone analog and growth hormone in central precocious puberty. J Clin Endocrinol Metab 81:948–951, 1996.

93. Saggese G, Pasquino AM, Bertelloni S: Effect of combined treatment with gonadotropin releasing hormone analogue and growth hormone in patients with central precocious puberty who had subnormal growth velocity and impaired height prognosis. Acta Paediatr 84:299–304, 1995.

94. Walvoord EC, Pescovitz OH: Precocious puberty: Combined use of GH and GnRH analogues: Theoretical and practical considerations. Pediatrics 104:1010–1014, 1999.

95. Adan L, Souberbielle JC, Zucker JM, et al: Adult height in 24 patients treated for growth hormone deficiency and early puberty. J Clin Endocrinol Metab 82:229–233, 1997.

96. Yanovski JA, Rose SR, Municchi G, et al: Treatment with a luteinizing hormone-releasing hormone agonist in adolescents with short stature. N Engl J Med 348:908–917, 2003.

97. Pescovitz OH, Comite F, Cassorla F, et al: True precocious puberty

complicating congenital adrenal hyperplasia: Treatment with a luteinizing hormone releasing hormone analogue. J Clin Endocrinol Metab 58:857–861, 1984.

98. Soliman AT, Al Lamki M, Al Salmi I, et al: Congenital adrenal hyperplasia complicated by central precocious puberty: Linear growth during infancy and treatment with gonadotropin-releasing hormone analog. Metabolism 46:513–517, 1997.

99. Quintos JB, Vogiatzi MG, Harbison MD, et al: Growth hormone therapy alone or in combination with gonadotropin-releasing hormone analog therapy to improve the height deficit in children with congenital adrenal hyperplasia. J Clin Endocrinol Metab 86:1511–1517, 2002.

100. Saggese G, Bertelloni S, Baroncelli GI: Sex steroids and the acquisition of bone mass. Horm Res 48(Suppl 5):65–71, 1997.

101. Heger S, Partsch CJ, Sippell WG: Long-term outcome after depot gonadotropin releasing hormone agonist treatment of central precocious puberty: Final height, body proportions, body composition, bone mineral density, and reproductive function. J Clin Endocrinol Metab 84:4583–4590, 1999.

102. Antoniazzi F, Zamboni G, Bertoldo F, et al: Bone mass at final height in precocious puberty after gonadotropin releasing hormone agonist with and without calcium supplementation. J Clin Endocrinol Metab 88:1096–1101, 2003.

103. Schroor EJ, Van Weissenbruch MM, Delemarre-van de Waal HA: Long-term GnRH-agonist treatment does not postpone central development of the GnRH pulse generator in girls with idiopathic precocious puberty. J Clin Endocrinol Metab 80:1696–1701, 1995.

104. Jay N, Mansfield MJ, Blizzard RM, et al: Ovulation and menstrual function of adolescent girls with central precocious puberty after therapy with gonadotropin-releasing hormone agonists. J Clin Endocrinol Metab 75:890–894, 1992.

105. Miller WL: Genetics, diagnosis and management of 21-hydroxylase deficiency. J Clin Endocrinol Metab 78:241–246, 1994.

106. Cutler GB Jr, Laue L: Congenital adrenal hyperplasia due to 21-hydroxylase deficiency. N Engl J Med 323:1806–1813, 1990.

107. Sakkal-Alkaddour H, Zhang L, Yang X, et al: Studies of 3β-hydroxysteroid dehydrogenase genes in infants and children manifesting premature pubarche and increased adrenocorticotropin-stimulated Δ5-steroid levels. J Clin Endocrinol Metab 81:3961–3965, 1996.

108. White PC, Pascoe L: Disorders of steroid 11β-hydroxylase isoenzymes. Trends Endocrinol Metab 3:229, 992.

109. Speiser PW, White PC: Congenital adrenal hyperplasia. N Engl J Med 349:776–788, 2003.

110. Berkovitz GD, Guerami A, Brown TR, et al: Familial gynecomastia with increased extraglandular aromatization of plasma carbon-19 steroids. J Clin Invest 75:1763–1769, 1985.

111. Brodie A, Inkstar S, Yue W: Aromatase expression in the human male. Mol Cell Endocrinol 178:23–28, 2001.

112. Stratakis CA, Vottero A, Brodie A, et al: The aromatase excess syndrome is associated with feminization of both sexes and autosomal dominant transmission of aberrant P450 aromatase gene transcription. J Clin Endocrinol Metab 83:1348–1357, 1998.

113. Shozu M, Sebastian S, Takayama K, et al: Estrogen excess associated with novel gain-of-function mutations affecting the aromatase gene. N Engl J Med 348:1855–1865, 2003.

114. Albright F, Butler AM, Hampton AO, et al: Syndrome characterized by osteitis fibrosa disseminata, areas of pigmentation and endocrine dysfunction, with precocious puberty in females. N Engl J Med 216:727–746, 1937.

115. Weinstein LS, Shenker A, Gejman PV, et al: Activating mutations of the stimulatory G protein in the McCune-Albright syndrome. N Engl J Med 325:1688–1695, 1991.

116. Shenker A, Weinstein LS, Sweet DE, et al: An activating mutation is present in fibrous dysplasia of bone in the McCune-Albright syndrome. J Clin Endocrinol Metab 79:750–755, 1994.

117. Spiegel AM: The molecular basis of disorders caused by defects in G proteins. Horm Res 47:89–96, 1997.

118. Foster CM: Endocrine manifestations of McCune-Albright syndrome. Endocrinologist 3:359–364, 1993.

119. Shenker A, Weinstein L, Moran A, et al: Severe endocrine and nonendocrine manifestations of the McCune-Albright syndrome associated with activating mutations of stimulatory G protein Gs. J Pediatr 123:509–518, 1993.

120. Silva ES, Lumbroso S, Medina M, et al: Demonstration of McCune-Albright mutations in the liver of children with high gamma GT progressive cholestasis. J Hepatol 32:154–158, 2000.

121. Foster CM, Feuillan P, Padmanabhan V, et al: Ovarian function in girls with McCune-Albright syndrome. Pediatr Res 20:859–863, 1986.

122. Hannon TS, Noonan K, Steinmetz R, et al: Is McCune-Albright syndrome overlooked in subjects with fibrous dysplasia of bone? J Pediatr 142:532–538, 2003.

123. Fragoso MC, Domenice S, Latronico AC, et al: Cushing's syndrome secondary to adrenocorticotropin-independent macronodular adrenocortical hyperplasia due to activating

mutations of GNAS1 gene. J Clin Endocrinol Metab 88:2147–2151, 2003.

124. Pienkowski C, Lumbroso S, Bieth E, et al: Recurrent ovarian cyst and mutation of the Gs alpha gene in ovarian cyst fluid cells: What is the link with McCune-Albright syndrome? Acta Paediatr 86:1019–1021, 1997.

125. Weinstein LS, Chen M, Lui J: Gs (alpha) mutations and imprinting in human disease. Ann N Y Acad Sci 968:173–197, 2002.

126. Feuillan PB, Jones J, Cutler GB: Long term testolactone therapy for precocious puberty in girls with the McCune-Albright syndrome. J Clin Endocrinol Metab 77:647–651, 1993.

127. Roth C, Freiberg C, Zappel H, Albers N: Effective aromatase inhibition by anastrozole in a patient with gonadotropin-independent precocious puberty in McCune-Albright syndrome. J Pediatr Endocrinol Metab 15(Suppl 3):945–948, 2002.

128. Nunez SB, Calis K, Cutler GB, et al: Lack of efficacy of Fadrozole in treating precocious puberty in girls with the McCune-Albright syndrome. J Clin Endocrinol Metab 88: 5730–5733, 2003.

129. Eugster EA, Rubin SD, Reiter EO, et al, and the McCune-Albright Study Group: Tamoxifen treatment for precocious puberty in McCune-Albright syndrome: A multicenter trial. J Pediatr 143:60–66, 2003.

130. Jones SE: A new estrogen receptor antagonist-an overview of available data. Br Cancer Res Treat 75(Suppl 1):S19–S21, 2002.

131. Escobar ME, Gryngarten M, Domene H, et al: Persistence of autonomous ovarian activity after discontinuation of therapy for precocious puberty in McCune-Albright syndrome. J Pediatr Adolesc Gynecol 10:147–151, 1997.

132. Maesaka H, Abe Y, Tachibana K, et al: Ovarian function in three female patients with McCune-Albright syndrome with persistent autonomous ovarian activity. J Pediatr Endocrinol Metab 15(Suppl 3):903–911, 2002.

133. Iiri T, Herzmark P, Nakamoto JM, et al: Rapid GDP release from Gsα in patients with gain and loss of endocrine function. Nature 371:164–168, 1994.

134. Nakamoto JM, Zimmerman D, Jones EA, et al: Concurrent hormone resistance (pseudohypoparathyroidism type Ia) and hormone independence (testotoxicosis) caused by a unique mutation in the G alpha s gene. Biochem Mol Med 58:18–24, 1996.

135. Shenker A, Laue L, Kosugi S, et al: A constitutively activating mutation of the luteinizing hormone receptor in familial male precocious puberty. Nature 365:652–654, 1993.

136. Shenker A: Activating mutations of the lutropin choriogonadotropin receptor in precocious puberty. Receptor Channel 8:3–18, 2002.

137. Latronico AC, Shinozaki H, Guerra G Jr, et al: Gonadotropin-independent precocious puberty due to luteinizing hormone receptor mutations in Brazilian boys: A novel constitutively activating mutation in the first transmembrane helix. J Clin Endocrinol Metab 85:4799–4805, 2000.

138. Latronico AC, Abell AN, Arnhold JP, et al: A unique constitutively activating mutation in third transmembrane helix of luteinizing hormone receptor causes sporadic male gonadotropin-independent precocious puberty. J Clin Endocrinol Metab 83:2435–2440, 1998.

139. Kremmer H, Martens JWM, van Reel M, et al: A limited repertoire of mutations of the luteinizing hormone (LH) receptor gene in familial and sporadic patients with male LH-independent precocious puberty. J Clin Endocrinol Metab 84:1136–1140, 1999.

140. DiMeglio LA, Pescovitz OH: Disorders of puberty: Inactivating and activating molecular mutations. J Pediatr 131:S8–S12, 1997.

141. Leschek EW, Chan WY, Diamond DA, et al: Nodular Leydig cell hyperplasia in a boy with familial male-limited precocious puberty. J Pediatr 138:949–951, 2001.

142. Schedewie HK, Reiter EO, Beitins IZ, et al: Testicular Leydig cell hyperplasia as a cause of familial sexual precocity. J Clin Endocrinol Metab 52:271–278, 1981.

143. Egli CA, Rosenthal SM, Grumbach MM, et al: Pituitary gonadotropin-independent male-limited autosomal dominant sexual precocity in nine generations: Familial testotoxicosis. J Pediatr 106:33–40, 1985.

144. Holland FJ, Fishman L, Bailey JD, et al: Ketoconazole in the management of precocious puberty not responsive to LHRH-analogue therapy. N Engl J Med 312:1023–1028, 1985.

145. Babovic-Vuksanovic D, Donaldson MD, Gibson NA, Wallace AM: Hazards of ketoconazole therapy in testotoxicosis. Acta Paediatr 83:994–997, 1994.

146. Laue L, Kenigsberg D, Pescovitz OH, et al: The treatment of familial male precocious puberty with spironolactone and testolactone. N Engl J Med 320:496–502, 1989.

147. Leschek EW, Jones J, Barnes KM, et al: Six-year results of spironolactone and testolactone treatment of familial male-limited precocious puberty with addition of deslorelin after central puberty onset. J Clin Endocrinol Metab 84:175–178, 1999.

148. Eugster EA, Pescovitz OH: Advances in the treatment of precocious puberty. Exp Opin Invest Drug 10:1623–1630, 2001.

149. Vasseur C, Rodien P, Beau I, et al: A chorionic gonadotropin-sensitive mutation in the follicle-stimulating hormone receptor as a cause of familial gestational spontaneous ovarian hyperstimulation syndrome. N Engl J Med 349:753–759, 2003.

150. Smits G, Olatunbosun O, Delbaere A, et al: Ovarian hyperstimulation syndrome due to a mutation in the follicle-stimulating hormone receptor. N Engl J Med 349:760–766, 2003.

151. Gromoll J, Simoni M, Nieschlag E: An activating mutation of the follicle-stimulating hormone receptor autonomously sustains spermatogenesis in a hypophysectomized man. J Clin Endocrinol Metab 81:1367–1370, 1996.

152. Batista MC, Kohek MB, Frazzatto ES: Mutation analysis of the follicle-stimulating hormone receptor gene in girls with gonadotropin-independent precocious puberty resulting from autonomous cystic ovaries. Fertil Steril 73:280–283, 2000.

153. Cohen HL, Eisenberg P, Mandel F, et al: Ovarian cysts are common in premenarchal girls: A sonographic study of 101 children 2–12 years old. Am J Roentgenol 159:89–91, 1992.

154. Strickland JL: Ovarian cysts in neonates, children and adolescents. Curr Opin Obstet Gynecol 14:459–465, 2002.

155. Pienkowski C, Tauber MT, Beladj N, et al: How to manage a symptomatic ovarian follicular cyst in a female child? Arch Pediatr 1:903–907, 1994.

156. Rodriguez-Macias KA, Thibaud E, Houang M, et al: Follow up of precocious pseudopuberty associated with isolated ovarian follicular cysts. Arch Dis Child 81:53–56, 1999.

157. Skinner MA, Schlatter MG, Heifetz SA, et al: Ovarian neoplasms in children. Arch Surg 128:849–853, 1993.

158. Merras-Salmio L, Vettenranta K, Mottonen M, et al: Ovarian granulosa cell tumors of childhood. Pediatr Hematol Oncol 19:145–156, 2002.

159. Bouffet E, Basset T, Chetail N, et al: Juvenile granulosa cell tumor of the ovary in infants: A clinicopathologic study of three cases and review of the literature. J Pediatr Surg 32:762–765, 1997.

160. Choong CS, Fuller PJ, Chu S, et al: Sertoli-Leydig cell tumor of the ovary, a rare cause of precocious puberty in a 12-month old infant. J Clin Endocrinol Metab 87:49–56, 2002.

161. Nakashima N, Young RH, Scully RE: Androgenic granulosa cell tumors of the ovary. A clinicopathologic analysis of 17 cases and review of the literature. Arch Pathol Lab Med 108:786–791, 1984.

162. Cronje HS, Niemand I, Bam RH, et al: Granulosa and theca cell tumors in children: A report of 17 cases and literature review. Obstet Gynecol Surv 53:240–247, 1998.

163. Schneider DT, Calaminus G, Wessalowski R, et al: Ovarian sex cord-stromal tumors in children and adolescents. J Clin Oncol 21:357–363, 2003.

164. Masur Y, Steffens J, Ziegler M, et al: Leydig cell tumors of the testes-clinical and morphologic aspects. Urologe A 35:468–471, 1996.

165. Perilongo G, Rigon F, Murgia A: Oncologic causes of precocious puberty. Pediatr Hematol Oncol 6:331–340, 1989.

166. Diamond FB, Root AW, Hoover DL, et al: Hetero- and isosexual pseudoprecocity associated with testicular sex-cord tumors in an 8 year-old male. J Pediatr Endocrinol Metab 9:407–414, 1996.

167. Richter-Unruh A, Wessels HT, Menken U, et al: Male LH-independent sexual precocity in a 3.5 year old boy caused by a somatic activating mutation of the LH receptor in a Leydig cell tumor. J Clin Endocrinol Metab 87:1052–1056, 2002.

168. Liu G, Duranteau L, Carel JC, et al: Leydig-cell tumors caused by an activating mutation of the gene encoding the luteinizing hormone receptor. N Engl J Med 341:1731–1736, 1999.

169. Wolthers OD, Cameron FJ, Scheimberg I, et al: Androgen secreting adrenocortical tumors. Arch Dis Child 80:46–50, 1999

170. Lee PD, Winter RJ, Green OC: Virilizing adrenocortical tumors in childhood: Eight cases and a review of the literature. Pediatrics 76:437–444, 1985.

171. Phornphutkul C, Okubo T, Wu K, et al: Aromatase p450 expression in a feminizing adrenal adenoma presenting as isosexual precocious puberty. J Clin Endocrinol Metab 86:649–652, 2001.

172. Patil KK, Ransley PG, McCullagh M, et al: Functioning adrenocortical neoplasms in children. BJU Int 89:562–565, 2002.

173. Pescovitz OH, Comite F, Hench K, et al: Central precocious puberty complicating a virilizing adrenal tumor: Treatment with a long-acting LHRH analog. J Pediatr 106:612–614, 1985.

174. Heimann A, White PF, Riely CA, et al: Hepatoblastoma presenting as isosexual precocity. The clinical importance of histologic and serologic parameters. J Clin Gastroenterol 9:105–110, 1987.

175. Otsuka T, Ohshima Y, Sunaga Y, et al: Primary pulmonary choriocarcinoma in a four month old boy complicated with precocious puberty. Acta Paediatr Jpn 36:404–407, 1994.

176. Billmire D, Vinocur C, Rescorla F, et al: Malignant mediastinal germ cell tumors: an intergroup study. J Pediatr Surg 36:18–24, 2001.

177. Cohen AR, Wilson JA, Sadeghi-Nejad A: Gonadotropin-secreting pineal teratoma causing precocious puberty. Neurosurgery 28:597–602, 1991.

178. Rivarola, Belgorosky A, Mendilaharzu H, et al. Precocious puberty in children with tumours of the suprasellar and pineal areas: Organic central precocious puberty. Acta Paediatr 90:751–756, 2001.

179. Englund AT, Geffner ME, Nagal RA, et al: Pediatric germ cell and human chorionic gonadotropin-producing tumors. Clinical and laboratory features. Am J Dis Child 145:1294–1297, 1991.

180. Kukuvitis A, Matte C, Polychronakos C: Central precocious puberty following feminizing right ovarian granulosa cell tumor. Horm Res 44:268–270, 1995.

181. Starzyk J, Starzyk B, Bartnik-Mikuta A, et al: Gonadotropin releasing hormone-independent precocious puberty in a 5 year old girl with suprasellar germ cell tumor secreting beta-hCG and alpha-fetoprotein. J Pediatr Endocrinol Metab 14:789–796, 2001.

182. Zimmerman PA, Francis GL, Poth M: Hormone-containing cosmetics may cause signs of early sexual development. Mil Med 160:628–630, 1995.

183. Colon I, Caro D, Bourdony CJ, et al: Identification of phthalate esters in the serum of young Puerto Rican girls with premature thelarche. Environ Health Perspect 108:895–900, 2000.

184. Haddad NG, Fuqua JS: Phytoestrogens: Effects on the reproductive system. Endocrinologist 11:498–505, 2001.

185. Van Wyk JJ, Grumbach MM: Syndrome of precocious menstruation and galactorrhea in juvenile hypothyroidism: An example of hormonal overlap in pituitary feedback. J Pediatr 57:416–435, 1960.

186. Gordon CM, Austin DJ, Radovick S: Primary hypothyroidism presenting as severe vaginal bleeding in a prepubertal girl. J Pediatr Adolesc Gynecol 10:35–38, 1997.

187. Chemaitilly W, Thalassinos C, Emond S, et al: Metrorrhagia and precocious puberty revealing primary hypothyroidism in a child with Down's syndrome. Arch Dis Child 88:330–331, 2003.

188. Castro-Magana M, Angulo M, Canas A, et al: Hypothalamic-pituitary gonadal axis in boys with primary hypothyroidism and macroorchidism. J Pediatr 112:397–402, 1987.

189. Niedziela M, Korman E: Severe hypothyroidism, due to autoimmune atrophic thyroiditis-predicted target height and a plausible mechanism for sexual precocity. J Pediatr Endocrinol Metab 14:901–907, 2001.

190. Bruder JM, Samuels MH, Bremner WJ, et al: Hypothyroidism-induced macroorchidism: Use of a gonadotropin-releasing hormone agonist to understand its mechanism and augment adult stature. J Clin Endocrinol Metab 80:11–16, 1995.

191. Anasti JN, Flack MR, Froehlich J, et al: A potential novel mechanism for precocious puberty in juvenile hypothyroidism. J Clin Endocrinol Metab 80:276–279, 1995.

192. Watanabe T, Minamatani K, Minagawa M, et al: Severe juvenile hypothyroidism: Treatment with GH and GnRH agonist in addition to thyroxine. Endo J 45(Suppl):S159–S162, 1998.

193. Braunstein GD: Gynecomastia. N Engl J Med 328:490–495, 1993.

194. Haibach H, Rosenholtz MJ: Prepubertal gynecomastia with lobules and acini: A case report and review of the literature. Am J Clin Pathol 80:252–255, 1983.

195. Coen P, Kulin H, Ballantine T, et al: An aromatase-producing sex-cord tumor resulting in prepubertal gynecomastia. N Engl J Med 324:317–322, 1991.

196. Hertl MC, Wiebel J, Schafer H, et al: Feminizing Sertoli cell tumors associated with Peutz-Jeghers syndrome: an increasingly recognized causes of prepubertal gynecomastia. Plast Reconstr Surg 102:1151–1157, 1998.

197. Felner EI, White PC: Prepubertal gynecomastia: Indirect exposure to estrogen cream. Pediatrics 105:E55, 2000.

198. Latorre H, Kenny FM: Idiopathic gynecomastia in seven preadolescent boys. Am J Dis Child 126:771–773, 1973.

199. Malazowski S, Stadel BV: Prepubertal gynecomastia during growth hormone therapy. J Pediatr 126:659–661, 1995.

200. Martin RM, Lin CJ, Nishi MY, et al: Familial hyperestrogenism in both sexes: Clinical, hormonal, and molecular studies of two siblings. J Clin Endocrinol Metab 88:3027–3034, 2003.

201. Reiter EO, Braunstein GD: Gynecomastia. In Pescovitz OH, Eugster EA (eds): Pediatric Endocrinology: Mechanisms, Manifestations and Management. Philadelphia, Lippincott Williams & Wilkins, 2004, pp 349–359.

# Delayed Puberty

## Erica A. Eugster and Ora Hirsch Pescovitz

| DEFINITION | TREATMENT OF DELAYED PUBERTY |
|---|---|
| **BENIGN VARIANT** | Girls |
| Constitutional Delay of Growth and Puberty | Boys |
| **PATHOLOGIC DELAYED PUBERTY** | |
| Hypothalamic-Pituitary Hypogonadism | |
| Primary Hypogonadism | |

Delayed puberty refers to the absence of pubertal onset by the expected age or, once puberty has commenced, failure of appropriate progression. While its outward manifestations are subtle, delayed puberty is, nonetheless, profoundly distressing to the adolescents affected by it, who continually compare themselves to their peers, and find themselves lacking. A fascinating array of disorders may manifest as delayed puberty, necessitating a diagnostic process that incorporates patience, astute observation, and an open mind. Discovery of the molecular genetic basis for both benign and pathologic forms of delayed puberty will continue to offer tremendous insight into the biology of human reproduction.

## DEFINITION

Girls are considered to have delayed puberty if they reach the age of 13 without evidence of pubertal changes, whereas in boys the analogous age is 14. Progression of puberty denotes the development of secondary sexual characteristics according to a predictable and sequential series of stages, first described by Dr. James Tanner.[1,2] Whereas a postponement of pubertal onset often represents a benign variation of normal development (discussed in the following section), arrest of puberty once it has begun is almost always abnormal and indicative of an underlying pathologic condition. The general approach to the evaluation of delayed puberty in girls and in boys is outlined in Figures 148-1 and 148-2, respectively.

## BENIGN VARIANT

### CONSTITUTIONAL DELAY OF GROWTH AND PUBERTY

Constitutional delay of growth and puberty (CDGP) refers to a well-described variation of normal growth that is the most common cause of delayed puberty in both boys and girls.[3] Children with this condition are short for their genetic background, often below the third percentile, and have delayed skeletal maturation, as well as delayed puberty. In many cases, there is a family history of "late bloomers," manifested by an older age at menarche in women or significant linear growth occurring in the late teenage years in men. The precise cause of the altered growth pattern observed in CDGP is unknown. Observations of the strong familial nature of the condition have led to investigations of potential inheritance patterns.[4] Evidence thus far suggests the possible presence of single genes whose effects are modified by environmental and genetic factors.[5] However, precisely which genes and/or modifiers are responsible for CDGP remains unknown.

### Diagnosis

The diagnosis of CDGP rests on the typical clinical findings of short stature, delayed bone age, and low-normal growth velocity, combined with the absence of any other identifiable cause of short stature and pubertal delay. Baseline gonadotropin levels are low. These clinical and biochemical features are virtually indistinguishable from those observed in patients with gonadotropin deficiency, resulting in an historic "wait and see" policy in terms of determining which patients would ultimately experience spontaneous puberty.[6] However, the ability to differentiate CDGP from pathologic causes is desirable because of anxiety regarding whether or not puberty will ensue. Although no single test is considered foolproof, strategies that appear useful for this purpose include stimulation tests using gonadotropin-releasing hormone (GnRH) analogues such as nafarelin, leuprolide, and triptorelin. Peak luteinizing hormone (LH) levels following administration of GnRH analogue are reported to be significantly higher in patients with constitutional delay as compared with patients with hypogonadotropic hypogonadism.[7-9] High sensitivity and specificity for discrimination of CDGP from other etiologies of delayed puberty in boys has also been reported using human chorionic gonadotropin (hCG) stimulation tests,[10] while another approach relies on measurements of the free α glycoprotein subunit after GnRH stimulation.[11] Alternatively, failure of spontaneous pubertal onset by a bone age of 12 for girls, and 13 for boys, would clearly be inconsistent with a diagnosis of CDGP, and causes of pathologic hypogonadism should be sought.

### Treatment

The practice of using anabolic agents in adolescents with CDGP originated from recognizing the potential adverse psychological consequences of sexual immaturity,[12,13] and from concerns about possible decreased bone mineral density in these patients. Short-term low-dose anabolic therapy has shown to be both safe and effective in promoting growth and sexual maturity without advancing bone age. Specific agents that have been used include fluoxymesterone,[14] oxandrolone,[15] and oral or transdermal testosterone.[16] However, the mainstay of therapy employs low-dose intramuscular (IM) testosterone, given monthly on a continuous or intermittent basis for several months and up to a year.[17] Another proposed advantage of such therapy is based on the concept that exogenous androgens may advance maturation of the hypothalamic-pituitary-gonadal (HPG) axis, to "jump-start" puberty. Despite this hypothesis, there is little evidence that treatment with exogenous testosterone affects the timing and tempo of endogenous pubertal development in boys with constitutional delay[18] in whom considerable heterogeneity in baseline HPG activation has been well documented.[19,20] Similar

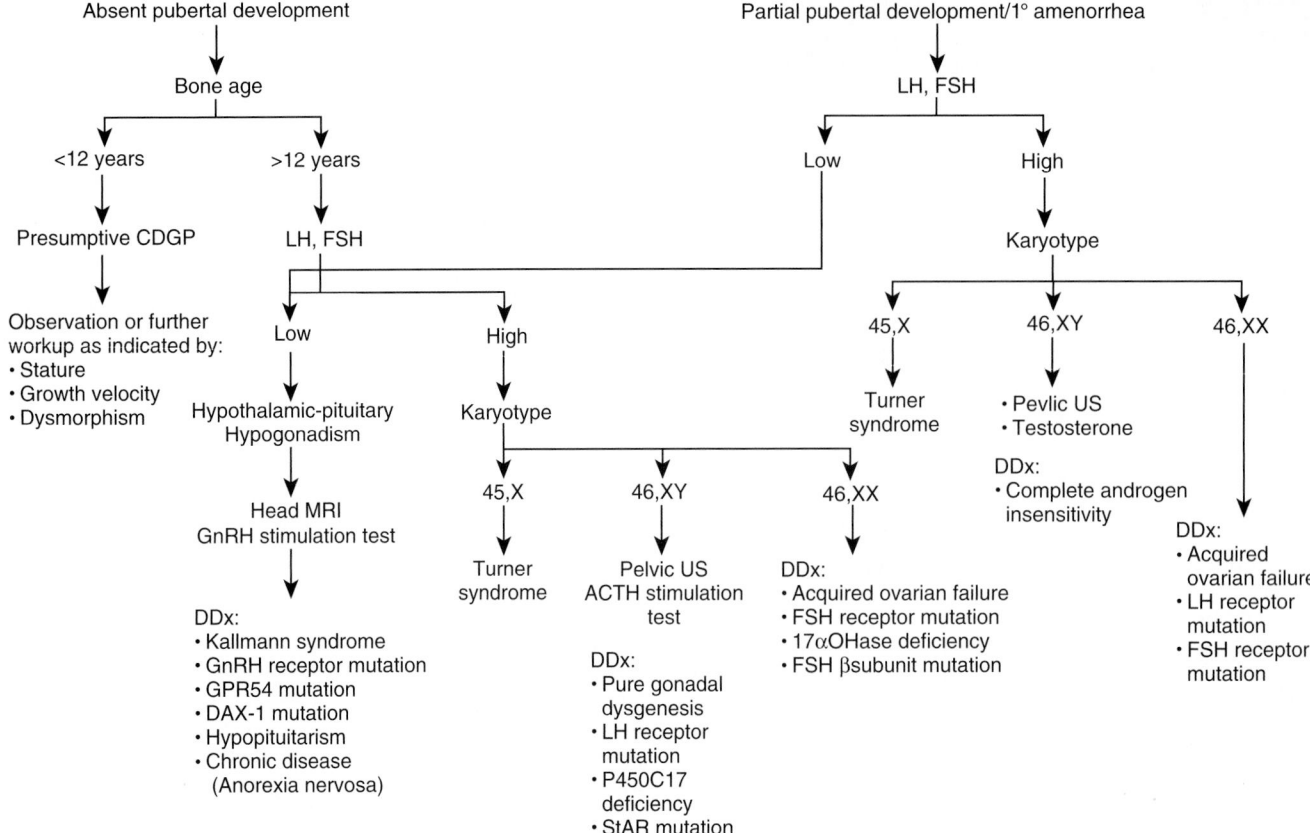

**Figure 148-1**  Diagnostic approach to delayed puberty in girls. CDGP, constitutional delay of growth and puberty; LH, luteinizing hormone; FSH, follicle-stimulating hormone; MRI, magnetic resonance imaging; GnRH, gonadotropin-releasing hormone; DDx, differential diagnosis; US, ultrasound; ACTH, adrenocorticotropic hormone; StAR, steroidogenic acute regulatory protein.

therapeutic regimens have been administered in girls with CDGP, using conjugated or unconjugated oral estrogens or transdermal 17β-estradiol, with comparable results.[21] An emerging therapeutic option for boys with constitutional delay aims to improve adult stature by blocking the effects of estrogen on skeletal maturation and epiphyseal fusion.

Promising results have been reported thus far, when using the third generation aromatase inhibitor letrozole in combination with testosterone, in significantly increasing predicted adult heights in boys with CDGP after 18 months, compared to controls.[22] Reassuringly, no differences in growth velocity or pubertal progression were noted in patients treated with

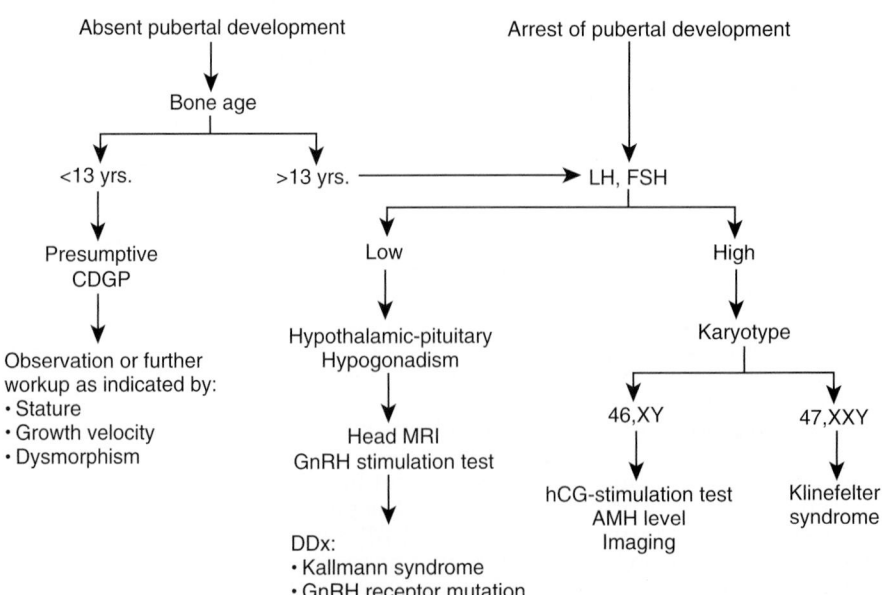

**Figure 148-2**  Diagnostic approach to evaluation of delayed puberty in boys. CNS, central nervous system; hCG, human chorionic gonadotropin; AMH, anti-müllerian hormone. For other abbreviations, see legend for Figure 145-1.

letrozole, and bone mineral density in the experimental group also appeared to be unaffected.[23] It is unknown whether similar findings could be achieved with estrogen receptor blockers or other aromatase inhibitors, and this remains an area of active investigation.

## Outcome
### Adult Stature
Adult height in patients with CDGP has been examined in relation to predicted height and target height. The majority of studies indicate that individuals with CDGP attain an adult height that is below the target height but within the mid-parental range,[24–27] whether or not treatment with short-term anabolic agents is undertaken. Accuracy of predicted heights varies in these patients, as determined by the Bayley-Pinneau method. While most investigators have found that height predictions are fairly reliable,[24,25,28,29] overestimating and underestimating adult heights have also been reported using this method.[30] Disproportionality, when the spine is short in relation to the limbs (eunuchoid body habitus), has also been described in CDGP, and has been attributed to decreased spinal growth during the characteristically attenuated pubertal growth spurt observed in these patients, as well as a longer period for limb growth.[31] It remains to be seen whether the projected height gains suggested by short-term treatment with antiestrogenic agents will translate into actual increases in adult stature.

### Bone Mineralization
The effects of sex steroids on the acquisition of bone mineral density are well known, and hypogonadal states are a cause of osteoporosis in adulthood.[32] Although normal bone mineral density has been reported in affected boys and men with a history of CDGP,[33,34] a significant decrease in bone mineral density has also been identified in this population,[35,36] suggesting a possible negative impact of delayed sex steroid exposure on bone accretion. Treatment with exogenous testosterone during adolescence has shown to improve bone density and bone turnover,[37] providing additional support for the use of short-term anabolic agents in these patients. The effects of androgens on bone mineralization and skeletal maturation are mediated via aromatization to estrogen. This has been demonstrated by rare clinical examples of estrogen receptor mutations and aromatase deficiency in males, conditions which are characterized by profoundly decreased bone mineral density and skeletal maturation, despite normal serum testosterone levels.[38,39]

## PATHOLOGIC DELAYED PUBERTY

Pathologic causes of delayed puberty have conventionally been grouped into two distinct categories, depending on which portion of the HPG axis is affected. *Hypogonadotropic hypogonadism* refers to conditions in which gonadotropins are low, implying an abnormality at the level of the hypothalamus or pituitary, or both, whereas *hypergonadotropic hypogonadism* refers to conditions in which LH and follicle-stimulating hormone (FSH) are elevated, indicating a lack of negative feedback at the level of the pituitary gland, and localizing the problem to the gonads. This delineation has become less useful with the recognition of genetic mutations involving hypothalamic-pituitary hormones and their receptors, some of which result in *hyper*gonadotropism rather than *hypo*gonadotropism. Therefore, causes of hypogonadism are grouped according to the location within the HPG axis of the affected hormone. The term *hypothalamic-pituitary hypogonadism* is used to designate disorders of hormones (and their receptors) originating from this portion of the axis, whereas *primary hypogonadism* encompasses disorders of the gonads themselves. In both forms of hypogonadism, the end result is a failure of normal ovarian or testicular sex steroid production. Discussed later in this chapter, exogenous sex steroid replacement is therefore the cornerstone of therapy for all types of pathologic delayed puberty, regardless of the cause.

## HYPOTHALAMIC-PITUITARY HYPOGONADISM

Hypothalamic-pituitary hypogonadism refers to conditions in which hypothalamic GnRH or pituitary gonadotropins, or both, are either deficient or inactive. This includes a diverse group of disorders with varied pathophysiology. While some causes stem from an isolated abnormality in hypothalamic GnRH, and others from an isolated abnormality in pituitary gonadotropins (LH and/or FSH), conditions also exist in which both hypothalamic and pituitary dysfunction are present. Similarly, hypothalamic-pituitary hypogonadism may be the sole manifestation of the disorder, or there may be wide-ranging effects on additional body systems. Partial progression through puberty in a subset of affected individuals is a common feature of many conditions, leading to clinical heterogeneity even within the same kindred. Another shared trait among patients with hypothalamic-pituitary hypogonadism is a characteristic body habitus. An arm span of at least 5 cm more than height, and an upper-to-lower segment ratio of less than 0.9 confirm the presence of "eunuchoid" proportionality.[40] When left untreated, hypothalamic-pituitary hypogonadism is also associated with an increase in adult height, due to the lack of sex steroid–induced skeletal maturation and epiphyseal fusion.[41] While the exact cause of many cases of hypothalamic-pituitary hypogonadism remains unknown, there has been significant progress in identifying the precise molecular genetic abnormalities responsible for several specific disorders.[42] The list of single gene defects associated with hypothalamic-pituitary hypogonadism continues to grow, and is summarized in Table 148-1 along with descriptions of the associated phenotypes. Once a diagnosis of hypothalamic-pituitary hypogonadism has been made, magnetic resonance imaging is recommended to rule out an intracranial lesion. Ultrasensitive gonadotropin assays, a GnRH stimulation test, or a GnRH analogue stimulation test, may be useful in confirming and determining the degree of hypogonadotropism. Hypothalamic GnRH deficiency may be differentiated from pituitary gonadotropin deficiency by administration of pulsatile GnRH, which usually results in subsequent elevations of LH and FSH in individuals with isolated hypothalamic defects.[43] Fertility is, therefore, potentially possible with the use of exogenous GnRH or gonadotropin therapy, although sex steroid replacement is generally the therapy of choice for induction of puberty and maintenance of secondary sexual characteristics. Specific causes of hypothalamic-pituitary hypogonadism are discussed in the following sections.

### Kallmann Syndrome
The prototype of GnRH deficiency exists in the form of Kallmann syndrome, which refers to the association between hypogonadotropic hypogonadism and anosmia, first described in 1944.[44] Sporadic cases and multiple heritable forms have been described, including X-linked, autosomal recessive and autosomal dominant. The X-linked form of the disease is caused by mutations in the KAL gene on Xp22.3.[45] This gene encodes for the extracellular matrix glycoprotein anosmin-1, which is a cell adhesion molecule essential for normal neuronal migration during embryogenesis.[46,47] Highly conserved across species, anosmin-1 appears to have direct as well as permissive roles in olfactory bulb development, GnRH-neuronal migration, and axonal growth.[48,49] Numerous mutations within the KAL gene have been described in patients with Kallmann syndrome.[50–52] Interestingly, significant clinical heterogeneity in the degree

**Table 148-1** Genotype/Phenotype Relationships in Hypothalamic-Pituitary Hypogonadism

| Affected Hormone/Product | Abnormality | Functional Consequence | LH | FSH | Inheritance | Clinical Characteristics | |
|---|---|---|---|---|---|---|---|
| GnRH | KAL mutation (Kallmann syndrome) | Abnormal neuronal migration resulting in GnRH deficiency | ↓ | ↓ | X-linked | • Hypogonadotropic hypogonadism<br>• Anosmia/hyposmia<br>• Associated congenital anomalies | |
| | FGFR1 mutation | Abnormal neuronal migration resulting in GnRH deficiency | ↓ | ↓ | Autosomal dominant | | |
| | GnRH receptor mutation | Loss of function of GnRH receptor | ↓ | ↓ | Autosomal recessive | • Partial hypogonadotropic hypogonadism | |
| | GPR54 mutation | Abnormal GnRH release | ↓ | ↓ | Autosomal recessive | • Hypogonadotropic hypogonadism | |
| Pituitary gonadotropes | PROP-1 mutation | Abnormal pituitary ontogenesis | ↓ | ↓ | Autosomal recessive | • Combined pituitary deficiency | |
| | LHX3 mutation | Abnormal pituitary ontogenesis | ↓ | ↓ | Autosomal dominant | • Combined pituitary deficiency | |
| | HESX1 | Abnormal pituitary ontogenesis | ↓ | ↓ | Autosomal recessive | • Septo-optic dysplasia<br>• Variable pituitary function | |
| DAX-1 | DAX-1 mutation | Abnormal development of adrenals and pituitary | ↓ | ↓ | X-linked | M<br>• Adrenal hypoplasia congenita, hypogonadotropic hypogonadism | F<br>• Unaffected carrier, delayed puberty, hypogonadotropic hypogonadism |
| SF-1 | SF-1 mutation | Abnormal development of adrenals and pituitary | ↑ | ↑ | Autosomal dominant, autosomal recessive | M<br>• XY sex reversal, adrenal failure | F<br>• Adrenal failure |
| FSH | FSH β subunit mutation | Truncated FSH with abnormal function | ↑ | ↓ | Autosomal recessive | M<br>• Delayed puberty, azoospermia, normal testosterone | F<br>• Primary amenorrhea absent breast development |
| | FSH receptor mutation | Loss of function of FSH receptor | ↑ | ↑ | Autosomal recessive | M<br>• Low-normal testicular volume and sperm count | F<br>• Ovarian dysgensis or premature ovarian failure |
| LH | LH β subunit mutation<br>LH receptor mutation | Loss of LH bioactivity | ↑ | ↓ | Autosomal recessive | M<br>• Delayed puberty | F<br>• Unaffected |
| | | Loss of function of LH receptor | ↑ | nl | Autosomal recessive | M<br>• Leydig cell hypoplasia<br>• External genitalia female, or micropenis ± hypospadius | F<br>• Primary amenorrhea |
| Leptin | Leptin gene or leptin receptor mutation | Abnormal leptin function | ↓ | ↓ | Autosomal recessive | Obesity | |
| Prohormone convertase 1 | PC1 mutation | Abnormal neuropeptide processing | ↓ | ↓ | Autosomal recessive | Obesity | |

of hyposmia/anosmia and hypogonadism exists among patients bearing identical mutations, implying the presence of important modifier genes and/or environmental factors in the expression of the syndrome.[53,54] The specific genes underlying the other forms of Kallmann syndrome are unknown, although loss-of-function mutations in FGFR1 have been reported in association with the autosomal-dominant form.[55] A wide range of associated congenital anomalies have been reported in patients with Kallmann syndrome, including cleft palate, hearing loss, color blindness, abnormal eye movements, unilateral renal agenesis, and synkinesia, although the relationship between these features and specific abnormalities of the KAL gene are unclear.[56]

### GnRH Receptor Mutations

While the search for GnRH gene mutations has been negative thus far,[57] mutations in the GnRH receptor have increasingly been identified as a cause of familial isolated hypothalamic-pituitary hypogonadism (see Chapter 139).[58] This disorder is transmitted in an autosomal-recessive fashion, affecting both males and females, and olfaction is normal. Several different loss-of-function mutations in the GnRH receptor gene have been described, resulting in a phenotypic spectrum of hypogonadotropic hypogonadism.[59–61] Both homozygous and compound heterozygous cases occur, and carriers for the mutations are unaffected.[62] As in Kallmann syndrome, pulsatile GnRH administration may restore normal gonadal function and fertility in patients with a GnRH receptor mutation.[63]

### GPR54 Gene Mutations

A novel etiology for autosomal-recessive isolated hypothalamic-pituitary hypogonadism has been discovered in the form of mutations in the GPR54 gene, which encodes an orphan G protein–coupled receptor that is a member of the rhodopsin family of receptors.[64] Several consanguineous families have been identified, as well as one unrelated individual found to be a compound heterozygote for GPR54 mutations. The putative ligand of GPR54 is derived from kisspeptin-1, a tumor suppressor gene.[65] Although the frequency of GPR54 mutations appears to be low among kindreds with autosomal recessive hypothalamic-pituitary hypogonadism, studies from a transgenic mouse model suggest that GPR54 may be a key regulator of hypothalamic GnRH release and pubertal onset.[66] This exciting discovery paves the way for a new direction in the investigation of mammalian reproductive physiology.

## Mutations in Pituitary Transcription Factors and Orphan Nuclear Receptors

Normal embryologic hypothalamic-pituitary development relies on a tightly regulated, complex cascade of tissue-, cell-, and stage-specific transcription factors. Mutations within the genes encoding for these transcription factors, therefore, may result in a spectrum of combined anterior pituitary hormone deficiencies and abnormal function of the hypothalamic-pituitary axis. While the etiology of many forms of hypopituitarism remains unknown (Fig. 148-3), molecular genetic abnormalities in several pituitary transcription factors have now been elucidated. The first identified transcription factor, pituitary-specific transcription factor (Pit-1), is essential for normal activation of the genes encoding for growth hormone, prolactin, and thyrotropin-stimulating hormone, as well as for normal differentiation and proliferation of the pituitary cell types responsible for the expression of these hormones.[67,68] Following its discovery in 1988, numerous additional transcription factors have been identified, some of which are also involved in normal function of hypothalamic GnRH and pituitary gonadotrophs.[69,70] Orphan nuclear receptors that regulate development within multiple levels of the HPG axis are also associated with hypothalamic-pituitary hypogonadism. Human genetic mutations that have been identified in these factors are discussed in the following sections.

### Prop-1

Prop-1 (Prophet of Pit-1) is a paired-like homeodomain transcription factor that is required for normal expression of Pit-1.[71] Since its discovery as the defective gene responsible for the Ames mouse phenotype,[72] in which there is profound growth hormone, prolactin and TSH deficiency, mutations of Prop-1, have been identified in several human kindreds with a similar phenotype.[73] In contrast with the mouse, Prop-1 in humans also appears to be involved in the differentiation of pituitary gonadotrophs, resulting in LH and FSH deficiencies in patients with Prop-1 mutations. Pubertal progression has been quite variable in reported cases, with several individuals completing pubertal maturation prior to the development of permanent hypogonadism by their early 20s.[74,75]

### LHX3

Another etiology of combined pituitary hormone deficiency has been traced to mutations within LHX3, a pituitary transcription factor gene located on chromosome 9.[76] Although a limited number of cases have been identified, all affected individuals have had gonadotropin deficiency and unresponsiveness to exogenous GnRH.[77]

### HESX1

Several different mutations within the transcription factor HESX1 gene have been implicated in septo-optic dysplasia associated with variable pituitary function. While some patients exhibit apparently normal pituitary hormone secretion, a continuum ranging from isolated growth hormone deficiency to panhypopituitarism has been described.[78] Studies from the mouse model have indicated that HESX1 has an important role in embryologic development of the optic nerves and the hypothalamic-pituitary axis.

### DAX-1

Hypogonadotropic hypogonadism is a feature of X-linked adrenal hypoplasia congenita. The gene responsible for this condition, DAX-1, encodes for an orphan nuclear receptor that is expressed in adrenal, pituitary, hypothalamic, and gonadal tissue.[79] More than 100 different mutations within

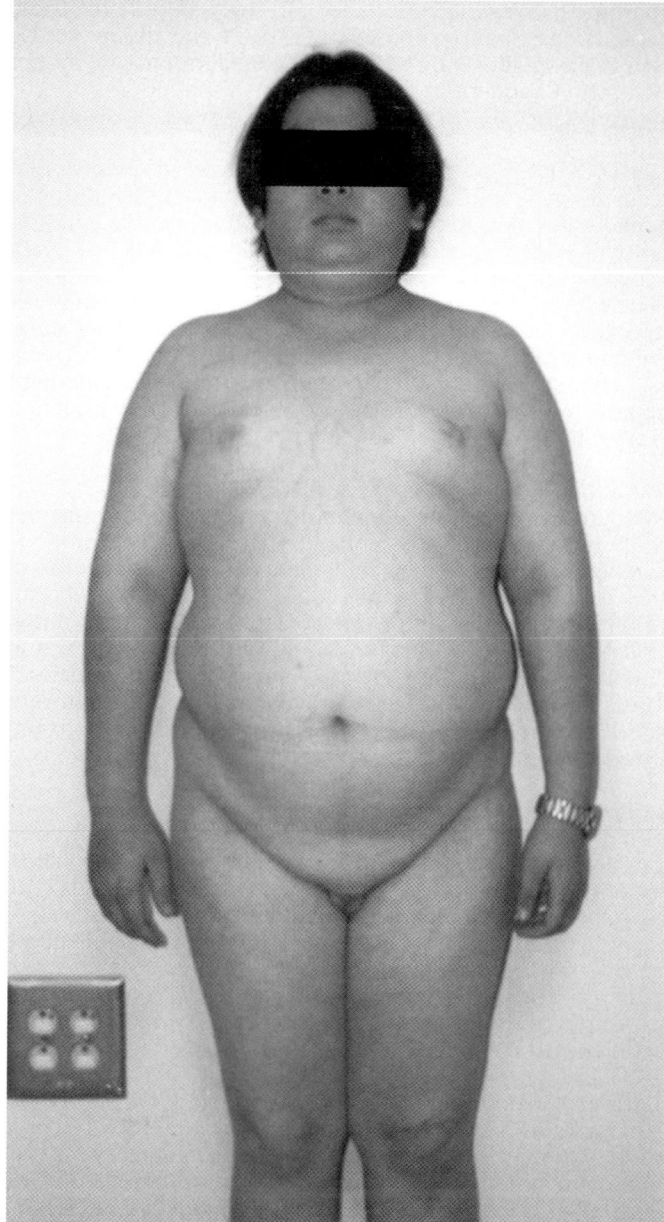

***Figure 148-3*** Delayed puberty in a 19-year-old boy with hypopituitarism of unknown etiology. Bone age was 14 years and height was 148 cm. (Reproduced with permission from Becker KL [ed]: Principles and Practice of Endocrinology and Metabolism, 3d ed. Philadelphia, LWW.)

DAX-1 have been identified.[80] Males with the disorder typically present with adrenal crisis during infancy, whereas the hypothalamic-pituitary hypogonadism emerges in adolescence.[81] However, there appears to be significant clinical variability among individuals with adrenal hypoplasia congenita. Congenital gonadotropin deficiency has been suggested by cryptorchidism in some newborns with DAX-1 mutations, while a normal mini-puberty of infancy has also been reported in affected boys.[82,83] Atypical presentations have included hypothalamic-pituitary hypogonadism in a female with a homozygous DAX-1 mutation,[84] delayed puberty in heterozygous females,[85] and the delayed onset of adrenal insufficiency and partial hypogonadism in adulthood in a few affected individuals.[86] Studies from the *Ahch* (*Dax1*) knockout mouse suggest that DAX-1 has a critical role in testis development and spermatogenesis, as well as in the function of the HPG axis.[87] This finding, as well as recognition of the combined hypothalamic and pituitary defect in these patients, has been proposed to explain the disappointing results using exogenous GnRH or gonadotropins to induce virilization and fertility.[88]

### SF-1

Like DAX-1, SF-1 encodes for an orphan nuclear receptor that regulates gene transcription in multiple tissues including the gonads, adrenals, hypothalamus, and pituitary.[89] The importance of SF-1 for normal gonadotrope function was first established by the knockout mouse, which exhibits gonadotropin deficiency and hypoplastic gonads.[90] Human SF-1 mutations have been identified as a cause of 46,XY sex reversal and adrenal failure.[91,92] Some SF-1 mutations cause testicular dysgenesis, without affecting adrenal function. Ovarian development appears to be normal thus far in a prepubertal girl with a heterozygous SF-1 mutation and adrenal insufficiency.[93]

## Mutations in Gonadotropins and Their Receptors

FSH and LH comprise a common α subunit and a distinct β subunit and exert their biologic effects through G protein–coupled receptors (see Chapter 11). While no mutations of the α subunits have been described to date, FSH-β subunit, LH-β subunit, and inactivating gonadotropin receptor mutations have been identified as causes of delayed puberty and abnormal reproductive function in males and females.[94] These mutations continue to provide important insight into the relative roles of FSH and LH in gonadal function and human physiology.

### FSH-β Subunit Mutations

Mutations in the FSH-β subunit gene have been reported to cause hypogonadism in both females and males.[95] The majority of cases have occurred in females with complete absence of pubertal development, although partial breast development in an affected girl has been reported.[96,97] The phenotype of males with FSH-β gene mutations ranges from delayed puberty and azoospermia to azoospermia alone.[98] As expected, serum LH levels are high in these patients, and FSH is undetectable.

### FSH Receptor Mutations

Homozygous inactivating mutations in the FSH receptor were first identified as the cause of autosomal-recessive premature ovarian failure in several Finnish families.[99] The females in these kindreds demonstrated uneven degrees of pubertal development followed by complete ovarian failure, in association with elevated serum gonadotropins and hypoplastic ovaries. Subsequently, a number of novel FSH receptor mutations have been described in association with primary or secondary amenorrhea.[100,101] In contrast, men with homozygous mutations have normal LH and testosterone levels and low-normal testicular volumes, with elevated FSH levels and unpredictable degrees of impaired spermatogenesis and infertility.[102]

### LH-β Subunit Mutation

One case of delayed puberty due to an LH gene mutation has been described. The 17-year-old male proband was homozygous for a single base substitution in the LH-β subunit gene.[103] Serum LH was elevated, while FSH and testosterone levels were low. The finding of LH immunoreactivity with complete loss of LH bioactivity in this patient was consistent with the clinical phenotype. Three maternal uncles, all heterozygous for the same mutation, were infertile, while female carriers appeared unaffected.

### LH Receptor Mutations

Homozygous loss-of-function mutations of the LH receptor, inherited via autosomal-recessive transmission, have been recognized as a rare cause of hypogonadism in males and females. The first such mutation was reported in two 46,XY individuals with female external genitalia, but complete absence of breast development and primary amenorrhea.[104] Serum levels of LH were markedly elevated, while testosterone levels were low, and FSH levels were normal. Histologic examination of the testes revealed Leydig cell hypoplasia. Since then, multiple additional mutations of the LH receptor have been identified.[105-107] Males with inactivating LH receptor mutations exhibit a clinical spectrum ranging from female external genitalia to hypospadias or micropenis.[108] The testes are usually cryptorchid and müllerian structures are absent. In females, LH receptor mutations result in amenorrhea with normal secondary sexual development, and elevations of LH and FSH.[109] The finding of ovarian follicular development at all stages suggests that LH may be necessary for ovulation but that follicular development may occur under the influence of FSH and ovarian paracrine factors alone.[110] Conversely, activating mutations of the LH receptor cause a form of male-limited familial precocious puberty, and are discussed in Chapter 147.

## Metabolism-Related Genetic Defects

Naturally occurring genetic mutations associated with obesity have indicated important interactions between metabolism and human reproduction. Hypothalamic-pituitary hypogonadism has been a feature of rare human mutations within the leptin gene and leptin receptor.[111,112] A similar phenotype was observed in a girl with primary amenorrhea and hypothalamic-pituitary hypogonadism in association with compound heterozygous mutations in prohormone convertase 1, an endopeptidase involved in neuropeptide processing.[113] The precise role of these genes in GnRH release and/or function is unknown.

## Chronic Disease

Any significant chronic disease or inflammation can result in delayed puberty, which is usually seen in association with poor growth and retarded skeletal maturation. Malnutrition also has a profound impact on gonadal function through loss of normal hypothalamic-pituitary pulsatile secretion. This is exemplified by the hypothalamic amenorrhea often observed in young women with anorexia nervosa, in whom chronic caloric restriction leads to aberrations in neuroendocrine function.[114] The same phenomenon is observed in individuals engaging in frequent, high-intensity exercise such as runners or ballet dancers, in whom osteopenia is a common correlate.[115,116] Hypothalamic-pituitary hypogonadism has also been documented in women of normal weight who practice severe restriction of dietary fat intake.[117] These forms of hypogonadism are transient, and are characterized by a restoration of normal HPG function once the underlying abnormality is resolved. In contrast, permanent hypothalamic-pituitary hypogonadism may result from acquired central nervous system insults such as infection, cranial irradiation, tumor, or trauma. Paradoxically, children with intracranial abnormalities are at increased risk for the development of precocious puberty (see Chapter 147).

## Syndromes

Hypothalamic-pituitary hypogonadism is a common feature of a number of different genetic syndromes with otherwise heterogeneous manifestations. For example, individuals with Prader-Willi syndrome often have hypogonadism secondary to hypothalamic-pituitary dysfunction.[118] Other syndromes that share this characteristic include Boucher-Neuhauser,[119] Bardet-Biedl,[120] and Noonan syndromes.[121] Associated abnormalities often include cryptorchidism, micropenis, or both. Hypothalamic-pituitary hypogonadism also occurs in patients with pseudohypoparathyroidism type IA, in association with multiple hormone resistance from a loss-of-function mutation in the GNAS1 gene.[122]

## PRIMARY HYPOGONADISM

Primary hypogonadism refers to conditions in which there is failure of normal sex steroid production due to an intrinsic abnormality of the gonads. Using traditional assays, individual gonadotropin levels in prepubertal children with primary hypogonadism may be indistinguishable from normal controls, with the development of elevated gonadotropins by the time pubertal age is reached. Using ultrasensitive methods, supranormal LH and FSH concentrations are detectable in prepubertal agonadal children of all ages compared to controls.[123] In contrast, serum inhibin B levels tend to be inversely proportional to gonadotropins in boys with primary gonadal failure.[124,125] The causes of primary hypogonadism include congenital and acquired gonadal abnormalities, as discussed in the next section and summarized in Table 148-2.

### Congenital Primary Hypogonadism

#### Chromosomal Abnormalities

It has been recognized for many years that normal ovarian activity depends on the presence and function of specific X chromosomal genetic loci. Therefore, abnormalities involving any significant portion of the X chromosome in females are associated with aberrant ovarian function. Varying degrees of gonadal dysregulation are also observed in males with an abnormal complement of X chromosomes. The most common karyotypic abnormalities leading to primary hypogonadism are discussed in the next sections.

**Turner Syndrome** With an incidence of 1 in 2000 to 5000 live-born females, Turner syndrome is the most common cause of primary ovarian failure. First described in 1938 by Dr. Henry Turner,[126] the syndrome consists of a missing or structurally abnormal X chromosome combined with characteristic phenotypic features. Although a wide range of physical characteristics may manifest, nearly 100% of affected individuals have short stature. Gonadal dysgenesis, as evidenced by "streak ovaries," is present in approximately 94% of patients, and appears to occur as a consequence of accelerated oocyte atresia with subsequent fibrosis of ovarian stroma.[127] The multisystem involvement is demonstrated by the frequent occurrence of cardiac, renal, lymphatic, and musculoskeletal anomalies,[128] while common phenotypic features include low-set, posteriorly rotated ears, high-arched palate, low posterior hairline, webbed neck, the appearance of widely spaced nipples, cubitus valgus, and hypoplastic hyperconvex fingernails and toenails (Figs. 148-4 to 148-6). While many of these somatic characteristics are believed to be the consequence of intrauterine lymphedema, the Turner syndrome phenotype in general is thought to result from a haploid dosage of genes on the X chromosome that normally escape X inactivation.[129] One such gene, SHOX (short stature homeobox-containing gene), located in the pseudoautosomal region of the X chromosome, has been implicated in the genesis of multiple skeletal abnormalities in Turner syndrome, including short stature.[130,131] Girls may come to medical attention in several ways. Lymphedema noted at birth may precipitate an early diagnosis. Alternatively, girls may present in mid-childhood or adolescence with progressive short stature or delayed puberty. Cytogenetic analysis reveals a heterogeneous group of X chromosomal abnormalities, with approximately 50% of patients exhibiting some form of mosaicism.[132] The diagnosis of ovarian failure is based on the finding of elevated gonadotropins. These follow a diphasic pattern, with plasma LH and FSH levels rising during early and late childhood and exhibiting a nadir during middle years, although increased for age.[133] Although the vast majority of patients will require exogenous sex steroid replacement, approximately 30% of girls will experience spontaneous pubertal onset and up to 16% percent will achieve menarche unassisted.[134] Rarely, women with Turner syndrome are able to conceive, although pregnancies in this population are complicated by a high incidence of fetal loss and congenital anomalies.[135,136] Significant improvement in adult height is achieved with the use of growth hormone (GH) therapy, with optimal outcomes when treatment is initiated early.[137]

**Xq and Other Chromosomal Abnormalities** Patients with deletions or rearrangements of the long arm of the X chromosome typically have premature ovarian failure without

| Table 148-2 | Etiologies of Primary Hypogonadism | | |
|---|---|---|---|
| **Type of Abnormality** | **Defect** | **Inheritance** | **Clinical Characteristics** |
| Chromosomal abnormality | Turner syndrome 45,X | Sporadic | • Short stature<br>• Characteristic phenotype<br>• Renal, cardiac, lymphatic, musculoskeletal anomalies |
| | Klinefelter syndrome 47,XXY | | • Seminiferous tubule dysgenesis<br>• Variable hypogonadism, infertility |
| | Xq Deletion, X translocations, triple X, penta X | | • Premature ovarian failure |
| Biosynthetic enzyme deficiency | StAR mutation | Autosomal recessive | • Lipoid adrenal hyperplasia<br>• Adrenal crisis<br>• External genitalia undervirilized or female (M's) |
| | P-450C17 mutation | | • Delayed puberty (F's)<br>• External genitalia female, intra-abdominal testes (M's) |
| Disorder of sexual differentiation | Complete androgen insensitivity (TF) | X-linked recessive | • Female phenotype, blind pouch vagina, primary amenorrhea, normal breast development<br>• Intra-abdominal testes, absent internal reproductive organs<br>• Paucity of body hair |
| | Pure 46,XY gonadal dysgenesis | X-linked recessive autosomal dominant sporadic | • Female phenotype without Turner stigmata<br>• "Streak" gonads at risk for neoplasia |
| | Testicular regression (vanishing testes) | Sporadic, rare familial cases | • External genitalia normal or undervirilized<br>• Complete absence of identifiable testes |
| Acquired primary hypogonadism | Chemotherapy (rare) radiation<br>Autoimmune disease<br>Trauma/torsion galactosemia (F's) | Not heritable except autoimmune polyglandular failure and galactosemia (autosomal recessive) | • Variable onset and degree of primary hypogonadism |

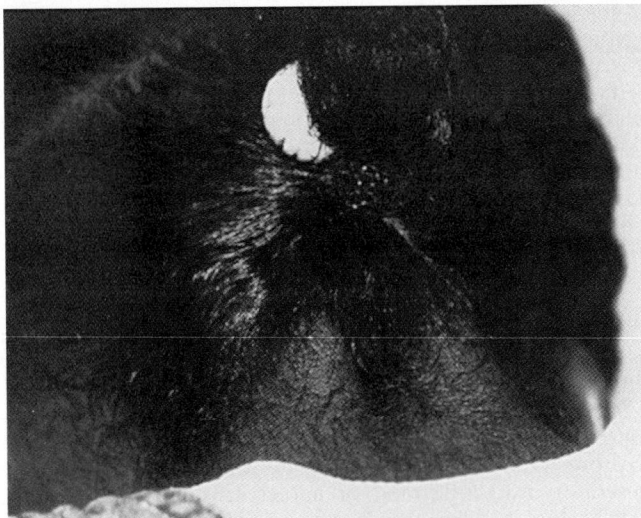

*Figure 148-4*  Girls with Turner syndrome often have a low posterior hairline, which typically has a "tripartite" (double arch) configuration.

phenotypic features of Turner syndrome.[138] Molecular genetic analysis of inherited cases has led to the localization within the distal region of Xq of one or more genes essential for ovarian maintenance.[139] Many cases of sporadic X chromosome:autosomal translocations are also associated with premature ovarian failure, as are mutations within a forkhead transcription gene (FOXL2) located on chromosome 3.[140] Triple and penta-X syndromes represent other examples of X chromosome aneuploidy in which premature ovarian failure is a frequent correlate.[141]

**Klinefelter Syndrome**  First described in 1942,[142] Klinefelter syndrome results from X chromosome polysomy in males, with the majority of patients demonstrating a 47,XXY karyotype. It is the most common disorder of the sex chromosomes, with an estimated incidence ranging from 1 in 400[143] to 1 in 1000[144] live-born males. Typical features include tall stature with eunuchoid body proportions, hypogonadism, a variety of learning and behavioral problems, and borderline-to-normal intelligence.[144] The testes, which are usually small and firm, and may be cryptorchid, are characterized by seminiferous tubule dysgenesis[145] and a spectrum of Leydig cell dysfunction. While pubertal onset may occur normally, serum testosterone levels are generally at the low end of the normal

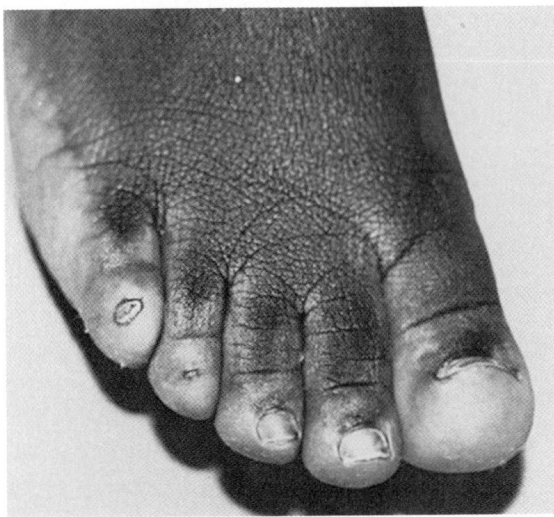

*Figure 148-5*  Hypoplasia of the fourth and fifth toenails in a patient with Turner syndrome.

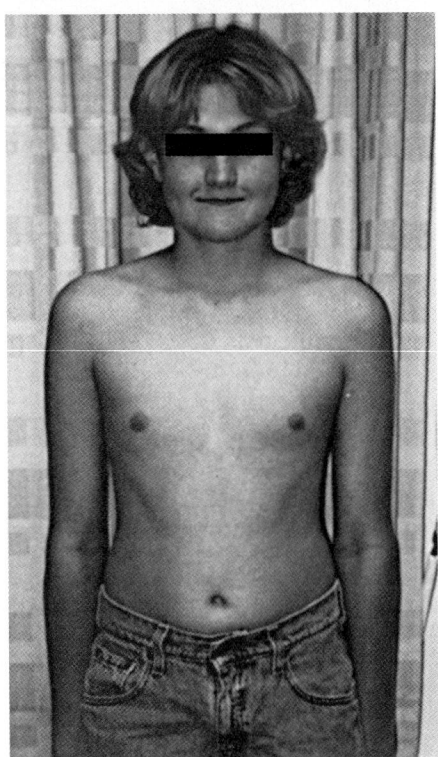

*Figure 148-6*  Complete absence of breast development in a 15-year-old girl presenting with delayed puberty. Arm span was 8.3 cm greater than height and upper-to-lower body segment ratio was 0.7, confirming a "eunuchoid habitus." Karyotype was 46,XY.

range, and inhibin B levels gradually decrease in conjunction with progressive testicular failure.[146] Gynecomastia, due to an abnormal estrogen-androgen ratio, and elevated serum gonadotropins are important clues to the presence of Klinefelter syndrome in a boy at pubertal age. However, many patients remain undiagnosed through adolescence[147] and may present in adulthood with infertility, azoospermia, or hypogonadism.[148] A propensity for the development of certain malignancies has long been recognized in individuals with Klinefelter syndrome. Breast cancer, historically believed to occur at increased frequency,[149] has not been observed in other large series,[148,150] whereas germ cell tumors have been found to be 50 times more common in this population, and have been implicated in rare cases of precocious puberty in boys with Klinefelter syndrome.[151]

*Enzymatic Defects in Steroid Biosynthesis*
Congenital adrenal hyperplasia represents a group of disorders originating from an inherited deficiency of one or more enzymes necessary for normal adrenal steroid production (see Chapter 124). Although the most common forms of congenital adrenal hyperplasia are associated with an excess of adrenal androgen secretion, rare defects exist in which there may be a complete inability to synthesize both androgens and estrogens. These include deficiencies of 17α-hydroxylase and 17,20-lyase enzymes, as well as a deficiency of the steroidogenic acute regulatory protein, which plays a key role in cholesterol transport, the rate-limiting step of steroid hormone biosynthesis.[152] Lipoid adrenal hyperplasia results from mutations within the steroidogenic acute regulatory gene, with more than 34 different mutations identified to date.[80,153] Clinical manifestations consist of severe electrolyte imbalance usually beginning in infancy, as well as complete deficiency of adrenal and testicular steroidogenesis, resulting in phenotypically female genitalia in both sexes. A fascinating aspect of lipoid adrenal hyperplasia is that some affected 46,XX

individuals experience spontaneous puberty and normal menstrual cycles, presumably due to steroidogenic acute regulatory-independent steroidogenesis within the ovary.[154] Mutations in the *CYP17* gene (responsible for both 17α-hydroxylase and 17,20-lyase activity) is another rare cause of delayed puberty in males and females.[155] Both sexes appear phenotypically female, with affected males demonstrating absence of müllerian structures, and intra-abdominal testes. Diagnosis is based on extreme elevations of adrenal steroid precursors, and treatment consists of glucocorticoid and sex steroid replacement as indicated by the phenotypic sex. Genetic males with severe 17α-hydroxylase deficiencies are, therefore, typically raised as females, using estrogen therapy to induce breast development at puberty once the diagnosis is made.

### Disorders of Sexual Differentiation

Abnormalities of sexual determination and differentiation result in a number of conditions typified by either overvirilization of genetic females or undervirilization of genetic males, and are usually associated with genital ambiguity (see Chapters 142 and 143). However, rare disorders exist where a phenotypically normal appearance is present, which may result in a delay of diagnosis until abnormal pubertal development prompts medical evaluation. Discussion of these disorders will be limited to genetic males, who may appear phenotypically female, as discussed in the next sections.

### Complete Androgen Insensitivity (Testicular Feminization Syndrome)

A variety of mutations within the androgen receptor gene may result in qualitative or quantitative abnormalities in androgen receptor function (see Chapter 169).[156,157] While partial androgen insensitivity is a cause of undervirilization of a male infant, complete androgen insensitivity results in an apparently normal female phenotype in a 46,XY individual. These patients are typically tall, and present in adolescence with normal breast development, primary amenorrhea, and a paucity of pubic and axillary hair. The external genitalia are those of a normal female, although the vagina ends blindly. The testes are intra-abdominal, and no female internal reproductive organs are found. As in XY gonadal dysgenesis, women with complete androgen insensitivity are at risk for gonadal neoplasms, although the incidence appears to be low in this setting.[158] Therefore, most clinicians advocate leaving the gonads in place until pubertal development is complete, after which time gonadectomy is recommended and estrogen replacement is necessary to maintain secondary sexual characteristics.

### Pure 46,XY Gonadal Dysgenesis (Swyer Syndrome)

First described in 1955,[159] pure 46,XY gonadal dysgenesis manifests as a normal female phenotype with complete absence of secondary sexual development (see Fig 148-6; Table 148-3). Stature is normal to tall, and there are no stigmata of Turner syndrome. A uterus and fallopian tubes are present, while the gonads are characterized by fibrotic "streaks." Heritable forms of pure 46,XY gonadal dysgenesis exist, with postulated modes of transmission including X-linked and autosomal inheritance patterns.[160,161] Although the causes of gonadal dysgenesis are largely unknown, approximately 15% of patients harbor mutations within SRY.[162,163] Additional etiologies implicated in pure XY sex reversal include deletions or mutations in genes involved in male sex determination including SOX-9, SF-1, WT-1, and DAX-1.[164] Regardless of the precise genetic cause, patients with pure 46,XY gonadal dysgenesis require prophylactic gonadectomy due to an estimated 20% to 30% incidence of gonadoblastoma or dysgerminoma in this population.[165]

### Testicular Regression (Vanishing Testes) Syndrome

Testicular regression syndrome refers to a rare condition in which the testes become nonfunctional and involute (thus the term *vanishing*) at some point during intrauterine life or the early postnatal period. Depending on the timing of testicular regression, ambiguous or normally formed male genitalia may result. The cause of testicular regression is poorly understood but is hypothesized to be the result of a vascular insult to the testes during intrauterine life. Familial cases have rarely been reported.[166] Males may go undiagnosed until adolescence or even adulthood.[167] A human chorionic gonadotropin stimulation test is useful in the evaluation of Leydig cell function,[168] while müllerian-inhibiting substance (MIS, antimüllerian hormone) levels, secreted by Sertoli cells, provide additional information regarding the presence and integrity of testicular tissue.[169] There is controversy whether inguinal exploration of these patients is always mandatory, as the incidence of residual gonadal tissue is extremely low.[170]

### Acquired Primary Hypogonadism

There are several causes of acquired primary hypogonadism, all stemming from significant insult or injury to the gonads. While trauma and torsion represent rare causes of acquired primary hypogonadism,[171] improved survival rates of childhood cancer have resulted in a rise in cases of primary hypogonadism occurring as sequelae of irradiation, chemotherapy, and bone marrow transplantation.[172] Autoimmune-related gonadal failure is a feature of type I and type II polyglandular autoimmune syndromes, and may have an insidious onset many years after the development of adrenal insufficiency.[173] Conversely, ovarian failure may be the first presenting sign of these disorders, and as such, girls with unexplained premature ovarian failure should be screened for other autoimmune disorders.[174] Metabolic diseases associated with acquired gonadal failure include galactosemia,[175] where premature ovarian failure may occur in up to 60% of affected females, resulting in complete or partial lack of pubertal development.[176]

---

**Table 148-3** Clinical, Laboratory, and Radiographic Data in a Patient with Pure 46,XY Gonadal Dysgenesis

| Clinical Characteristics | Laboratory Data | Radiographic Studies |
|---|---|---|
| • Presenting complaint: primary amenorrhea | • LH:15.8 mIU/mL (1.0–18) | • Bone age x-ray: 11 6/12 years |
| • Chronologic age: 15 yr | • FSH:64.7 mIU/mL (4–13) | • Pelvic ultrasound: small uterus, no visible gonads |
| • Height:162.7 cm (50 percentile on female growth chart, 25 percentile on male growth chart) | • Estradiol:13 pg/mL (10–178) | • Genitogram: normal vagina with cervical impression |
| • Arm span:171 cm | | |
| • Upper/lower body ratio: percentile 0.7 | • Thyroxine: 7.6 µg/dL (4.5–12) | |
| • Breasts: Tanner I | | |
| • Pubic hair: Tanner II | | |
| • External genitalia: normal female | • TSH: 3.9 (.45–6.0) uIU/mL | |
| | • Prolactin: 10.7 ng/mL (5.3–22) | |
| | • Karyotype: 46,XY | |
| | • MIH: 0 ng/mL | |

## TREATMENT OF DELAYED PUBERTY

The goal of therapy in children with hypogonadism is to initiate secondary sexual development in a way that simulates normal puberty. This is achieved by using low doses of sex steroids at initiation of therapy, gradually increasing the dosage over time. Once pubertal development is complete, adult replacement doses of gonadal steroids are required for the maintenance of secondary sexual characteristics and normal sexual function.

### GIRLS

Multiple protocols exist for estrogen replacement therapy. The most commonly used in the United States involve oral conjugated or unconjugated estrogen preparations, such as premarin or ethinyl estradiol, at typical daily starting doses of 0.15 to 0.30 mg or 5 µg, respectively. Concurrently monitoring growth, skeletal maturation, and pubertal progression, the dose of estrogen is then gradually increased by 6- to 12-month increments to an adult daily dose of 0.625 to 1.25 mg of conjugated estrogen, or 20 µg of unconjugated estrogen, depending on end-organ response. Although optimal breast maturation in some girls requires estrogen at the high end of the dose range, this can typically be reduced once pubertal development is complete. Once Tanner stage IV breast development has been achieved, progesterone is added in the form of medroxyprogesterone acetate 5 to 10 mg/day for 10 days or micronized progesterone at a dose of 200 mg, which allows for the commencement of monthly bleeding. Once puberty is complete, oral contraceptive pills offer a convenient method of combined estrogen-progesterone therapy. Oral 17β-estradiol (starting dose 0.25 mg) and transdermal 17β-estradiol patches (1/2 of a 0.025 mg patch) represent alternative means of estrogen replacement, and may be more physiologic.[21,128] As has been observed in hypogonadal boys, sex steroid replacement in girls with hypogonadism significantly improves calcium absorption and retention, with important implications in terms of the acquisition of bone mineral density.[177,178]

### BOYS

The most commonly employed method of sex steroid replacement therapy in adolescent hypogonadal boys consists of intramuscular depot preparations of testosterone such as testosterone enanthate or cypionate. The typical starting dose is 50 to 100 mg intramuscularly every 4 weeks, which is followed by gradual increases of 25 to 50 mg every 6 to 12 months as indicated by rates of growth, skeletal maturation, and pubertal progression. An adult replacement dose of testosterone consists of 200 to 300 mg intramuscularly every 2 to 4 weeks, resulting in elevation of serum testosterone levels to within the normal range. Alternate forms of maintenance testosterone replacement include transdermal testosterone patches and testosterone gels.[179] Although experience with these preparations during adolescence is limited,[180] ongoing investigation may reveal that they are safe and effective for pubertal induction.

## REFERENCES

1. Marshall WA, Tanner JM: Variations in pattern of pubertal changes in girls. Arch Dis Child 44:291–303, 1969.
2. Marshall WA, Tanner JM: Variations in pattern of pubertal changes in boys. Arch Dis Child 45:13–23, 1970.
3. Sedlmeyer IL, Palmert MR: Delayed puberty: Analysis of a large case series from an academic center. J Clin Endocrinol Metab 87:1613–1620, 2002.
4. Palmert MR, Boepple PA: Variation in the timing of puberty: Clinical spectrum and genetic investigation. J Clin Endocrinol Metab 86:2364–2368, 2001.
5. Sedlmeyer IL, Hirschhorn JN, Palmert MR: Pedigree analysis of constitutional delay of growth and maturation: Determination of familial aggregation and inheritance patterns. J Clin Endocrinol Metab 87:5581–5586, 2002.
6. Rosen DS, Kletter GB, Kelch RP: Puberty: What to do when the clock doesn't ring. J Pediatr Endocrinol 5:129, 1992.
7. Ehrmann DA, Rosenfield RL, Cuttler L, et al: A new test of combined pituitary-testicular function using the gonadotropin-releasing hormone agonist nafarelin in the differentiation of gonadotropin deficiency from delayed puberty: Pilot studies. J Clin Endocrinol Metab 69:963–967, 1989.
8. Street ME, Bandello MA, Terzi C, et al: Luteinizing hormone responses to leuprolide acetate discriminate between hypogonadotropic hypogonadism and constitutional delay of puberty. Fertil Steril 77(3):555–560, 2002.
9. Ozkan B, Topaloglu AK, Bilginturan N: A practical GnRH analogue (triptorelin) stimulation test to distinguish constitutional delay of puberty from hypogonadotropic hypogonadism in prepubertal boys. Turk J Pediatr 43(2):114–117, 2001.
10. Degros V, Cortet-Rudelli C, Soudan B, et al: The human chorionic gonadotropin test is more powerful than the gonadotropin-releasing hormone agonist test to discriminate male isolated hypogonadotropic hypogonadism. Eur J Endocrinol 149(1):23–29, 2003.
11. Mainieri AS, Elnecave RH: Usefulness of the free alpha-subunit to diagnose hypogonadotropic hypogonadism. Clin Endocrinol 59(3):307–313, 2003.
12. Lee PK, Rosenfeld RG: Psychosocial correlates of short stature and delayed puberty. Pediatr Adolesc Endocrinol 34:851–863, 1987.
13. Brack CJ, Orr DP, Ingersoll G: Pubertal maturation and adolescent self-esteem. J Adolesc Health Care 9:280–285, 1988.
14. Strickland AL: Long-term results of treatment with low-dose fluoxymesterone in constitutional delay of growth and puberty and in genetic short stature. Pediatrics 91:716–720, 1993.
15. Wilson DM, McCauley E, Brown DR, et al: Oxandrolone therapy in constitutionally delayed growth and puberty. Pediatrics 96:1095–1100, 1995.
16. Reiter EO, Lee PA: Delayed puberty. Adol Med St Ar Rev 13(1):101–118, 2002.
17. De Luca F, Argente J, Cavallo L, et al: Management of puberty in constitutional delay of growth and puberty. J Pediatr Endocrinol Metab 14 (Suppl 2):953–957, 2001.
18. Gupta MK, Brown DC, Faiman C, et al: Effect of low-dose testosterone treatment of androgen regulated proteins prostate specific antigen and sex hormone binding globulin in short prepubertal boys: Lack of initiation of puberty. J Pediatr Endocrinol Metab 16(1):55–62, 2003.
19. Kulin HE, Finkelstein JW, D'Arcangelo MR: Diversity of pubertal testosterone changes in boys with constitutional delay in growth and/or adolescence. J Pediatr Endocrinol Metab 10:395–400, 1997.
20. Crowne EC, Wallace WH, Moore C, et al: Degree of activation of the pituitary-testicular axis in early pubertal boys with constitutional delay of growth and puberty determines the growth response to treatment with testosterone or oxandrolone. J Clin Endocrinol Metab 80:1869–1870, 1995.
21. Kiess W, Conway G, Ritzen M, et al: Induction of puberty in the hypogonadal girl—Practices and attitudes of pediatric endocrinologists in Europe. Horm Res 57:66–71, 2002.
22. Wickman S, Sipila I, Ankarberg-Lindgren C, et al: A specific aromatase inhibitor and potential increase in adult height in boys with delayed puberty: A randomised controlled trial. Lancet 357(9270):1743–1748, 2001.

23. Wickman S, Kajantie E, Dunket L: Effects of suppression of estrogen action by the p450 aromatase inhibitor letrozole on bone mineral density and bone turnover in pubertal boys. J Clin Endocrinol Metab 88(8):3785–3793, 2003.

24. Arrigo T, Cisternino M, Luca De F, et al: Final height outcome in both untreated and testosterone-treated boys with constitutional delay of growth and puberty. J Pediatr Endocrinol Metab 9:511–517, 1996.

25. Salerno M, De Filippo G, Di Maio S: Definitive body height in constitutional retardation of growth and puberty. Arch Pediatr 3:866–869, 1996.

26. Crowne EC, Shalet SM, Wallace W, et al: Final height in girls with untreated constitutional delay in growth and puberty. Eur J Pediatr 150:708–712, 1991.

27. LaFranchi S, Hanna CE, Mandel SH: Constitutional delay of growth: Expected versus final adult height. Pediatrics 87:82–87, 1991.

28. Crowne EC, Shalet SM, Wallace WH, et al: Final height in boys with untreated constitutional delay in growth and puberty. Arch Dis Child 65:1109–1112, 1990.

29. Kelly BP, Paterson WF, Donaldson MD: Final height outcome and value of height prediction in boys with constitutional delay in growth and adolescence treated with intramuscular testosterone 125 mg per month for 3 months. Clin Endocrinol 58(3):267–272, 2003.

30. Blethen SL, Gaines S, Weldon V: Comparison of predicted and adult heights in short boys: Effect of androgen therapy. Pediatr Res 18:467–469, 1984.

31. Albanese A, Stanhope R: Does constitutional delayed puberty cause segmental disproportion and short stature? Eur J Pediatr 152(4):293–296, 1993.

32. Saggese G, Bertelloni S, Baroncelli GI: Sex steroids and the acquisition of bone mass. Horm Res 48 (Suppl 5):65–71, 1997.

33. Bertelloni S, Baroncelli GI, Ferdeghini M, et al: Normal bone mineral density and bone turnover in young men with histories of constitutional delay of puberty. J Clin Endocrinol Metab 83:4280–4283, 1998.

34. Krupa B: Evaluation of bone mineral density and selected metabolic markers of bone in boys with constitutional delay of growth and puberty. Ann Acad Med Stetin 46:165–176, 2000.

35. Lubushitzky R, Front D, Iosilevsky G, et al: Quantitative bone SPECT in young males with delayed puberty and hypogonadism: Implications for treatment of low bone mineral density. J Nucl Med 39:104–107, 1998.

36. Moreira-Andres MN, Canizo FJ, de la Cruz FJ: Bone mineral status in prepubertal children with constitutional delay of growth and puberty. Eur J Endocrinol 139(3):271–275, 1998.

37. Bergada I, Bergada C: Long term treatment with low dose testosterone in constitutional delay of growth and puberty: Effect on bone age maturation and pubertal progression. J Pediatr Endocrinol Metab 8(2):117–122, 1995.

38. Smith EP, Boyd J, Frank GR, et al: Estrogen resistance caused by a mutation in the estrogen-receptor gene in a man. N Engl J Med 331:1056–1061, 1994.

39. Morishima A, Grumbach MM, Simpson ER, et al: Aromatase deficiency in male and female siblings caused by a novel mutation and the physiological role of estrogens. J Clin Endocrinol Metab 80:3689–3698, 1995.

40. Styne DM: The testes: Disorders of sexual differentiation and puberty. In Kaplan SA (ed): Clinical Pediatric Endocrinology. Philadelphia, WB Saunders, 1990, p 367.

41. Uriarte MM, Baron J, Garcia HB, et al: The effect of pubertal delay on adult height in men with isolated hypogonadotropic hypogonadism. J Clin Endocrinol Metab 74:436–440, 1992.

42. Silviera LF, MacColl GS, Bouloux PM: Hypogonadotropic hypogonadism. Semin Reprod Med 20(4):327–338, 2002.

43. Santoro N, Filicori M, Crowley WF Jr: Hypogonadotropic disorders in men and women: Diagnosis and therapy with pulsatile gonadotropin-releasing hormone. Endocr Rev 7:11–23, 1986.

44. Kallmann FJ, Schoenfeld WA, Barrera SE: The genetic aspects of primary eunuchoidism. Am J Ment Retard 48:203, 1944.

45. Meitinger T, Heye B, Petit C, et al: Definitive localization of X-linked Kallmann syndrome (hypogonadotropic hypogonadism and anosmia) to Xp22.3: Close linkage to the hypervariable repeat sequence CRI-S232. Am J Hum Genet 47:664–669, 1990.

46. Franco B, Guioli S, Pragliola A, et al: A gene deleted in Kallmann's syndrome shares homology with neural cell adhesion and axonal path-finding molecules. Nature 353:529–536, 1991.

47. Hu T, Tanriverdi F, MacColl GS, et al: Kallmann's syndrome: Molecular pathogenesis. Int J Biochem Cell Biol 35(8):1157–1162, 2003.

48. Soussi-Yanicostas N, de Castro F, Julliard AK, et al: Anosmin-1, defective in the X-linked form of 48. Kallmann syndrome, promotes axonal branch formation from olfactory bulb output neurons. Cell 109(2):217–228, 2002.

49. MacColl G, Bouloux P, Quinton R: Kallmann syndrome: Adhesion, afferents and anosmia. Neuron 34(5):675–678, 2002.

50. Maya-Nunez G, Zenteno JC, Ulloa-Aguirre A, et al: A recurrent missense mutation in the KAL gene in patients with X-linked Kallmann's syndrome. J Clin Endocrinol Metab 83(5):1650–1653, 1998.

51. Soderlund D, Canto P, Mendez JP: Identification of three novel mutations in the KAL1 gene in patients with Kallmann syndrome. J Clin Endocrinol Metab 87(6):2589–2592, 2002.

52. Hardelin JP, Levilliers J, Blanchard S, et al: Heterogeneity in the mutations responsible for X chromosome-linked Kallmann syndrome. Hum Mol Genet 2(4):373–377, 1993.

53. Massin N, Pecheux C, Eloit C, et al: X chromosome-linked Kallmann syndrome: Clinical heterogeneity in three siblings carrying an intragenic deletion of the KAL-1 gene. J Clin Endocrinol Metab 88(5):2003–2008, 2003.

54. Matsuo T, Okamoto S, Izumi Y, et al: A novel mutation of the KAL1 gene in monozygotic twins with Kallmann syndrome. Eur J Endocrinol 143(6):783–787, 2000.

55. Dode C, Levelliers J, Dupont JM, et al: Loss of function mutations in FGFR1 cause autosomal dominant Kallmann syndrome. Nat Genet 33(4):463–465, 2003.

56. Izumi Y, Tatsumi K, Okamoto S, et al: Analysis of the KAL1 gene in 19 Japanese patients with Kallmann syndrome. Endocrinol J 48(2):143–149, 2001.

57. Bo-Abbas Y, Acierno JS Jr, Shagoury JK, et al: Autosomal recessive idiopathic hypogonadotropic hypogonadism: Genetic analysis excludes mutations in the gonadotropin-releasing hormone (GnRH) and GnRH receptor genes. J Clin Endocrinol Metab 88(6):2730–2737, 2003.

58. De Roux N, Young J, Misrahi M, et al: A family with hypogonadotropic hypogonadism and mutations in the gonadotropin-releasing hormone receptor. N Engl J Med 337:1597–1602, 1997.

59. Costa EM, Bedecarrats GY, Mendoca BB, et al: Two novel mutations in the gonadotropin-releasing hormone receptor gene in Brazilian patients with hypogonadotropic hypogonadism and normal olfaction. J Clin Endocrinol Metab 86(6):2680–2686, 2001.

60. Karges B, Karges W, Mine M, et al: Mutation Ala(171)Thr stabilizes the gonadotropin-releasing hormone receptor in its inactive conformation, causing familial hypogonadotropic hypogonadism. J Clin Endocrinol Metab 88(4):1873–1879, 2003.

61. Wolczynski S, Laudanski P, Jarzabek K, et al: A case of complete hypogonadotropic hypogonadism with a mutation in the gonadotropin-releasing hormone receptor gene. Fertil Steril 79(2):442–444, 2003.

62. Kottler ML, Chauvin S, Lahlou N, et al: A new compound heterozygous mutation of the gonadotropin-releasing hormone receptor (L314X, Q106R) in a woman with complete hypogonadotropic hypogonadism: Chronic estrogen administration amplifies the gonadotropin defect.

J Clin Endocrinol Metab 85(9):3002–3008, 2000.

63. Seminara SB, Beranova M, Oliveira LM, et al: Successful use of pulsatile gonadotropin-releasing hormone (GnRH) for ovulation induction and pregnancy in a patient with GnRH receptor mutations. J Clin Endocrinol Metab 85(2):556–562, 2000.

64. De Roux N, Genin E, Carel JC, et al: Hypogonadotropic hypogonadism due to loss of function of the KiSS1-derived peptide receptor GPR54. Proc Natl Acad Sci U S A 100(19):10972–10976, 2003

65. Lee JH, Miele ME, Hicks DJ, et al: Kiss-1, a novel human malignant melanoma metastasis-suppressor gene. J Natl Cancer Inst 88(1):731–737, 1996.

66. Seminara SB, Messager S, Emmanouella E, et al: The GPR54 gene as a regulator of puberty. N Engl J Med 349(17):1614–1627, 2003.

67. Radovick S, Nations M, Du Y, et al: A mutation in the POU-homeodomain of Pit-1 responsible for combined pituitary hormone deficiency. Science 257:1115–1118, 1992.

68. Ward J, Chavez M, Huot C, et al: Severe combined hypopituitarism with low prolactin levels and age-dependent anterior pituitary hypoplasia: A clue to a PIT-1 mutation. J Pediatr 132:1036, 1998.

69. Sheng HZ, Zhadanov AB, Mosinger B Jr, et al: Specification of pituitary cell lineages by the LIM homeobox gene Lhx. Science 272:1004–1007, 1996.

70. Parks JS, Adess ME, Brown MR: Genes regulating hypothalamic and pituitary development. Acta Paediatr Suppl 423:28–32, 1997.

71. Dutour A: A new step understood in the cascade of tissue-specific regulators orchestrating pituitary lineage determination: The Prophet of Pit-1 (PROP-1). Eur J Endocrinol 137:616–617, 1997.

72. Sornson MW, Wu W, Dasen JS, et al: Pituitary lineage determination by the Prophet of Pit-1 homeodomain factor defective in Ames dwarfism. Nature 384:327–333, 1996.

73. Wu W, Cogan JD, Pfaffle RW, et al: Mutations in PROP-1 cause familial combined pituitary hormone deficiency. Nat Genet 18:147, 1998.

74. Fluck C, Deladoey J, Rutishauser K, et al: Phenotypic variability in familial combined pituitary hormone deficiency caused by a PROP1 gene mutation resulting in the substitution of arg→cys at codon 120 (R120C). J Clin Endocrinol Metab 83:3727–3734, 1998.

75. Rosenbloom AL, Almonte AS, Brown MR, et al: Clinical and biochemical phenotype of familial anterior hypopituitarism from mutation of the PROP1 gene. J Clin Endocrinol Metab 84:50–57, 1999.

76. Sloop K, Meier BC, Bridwell JL, et al: Differential activation of pituitary hormone genes by human Lhx3 isoforms with distinct DNA binding properties. Mol Endocrinol 13:2212–2225, 1999.

77. Netchine I, Sobrier M-L, Krude H, et al: Mutations in LHX3 result in a new syndrome revealed by combined pituitary hormone deficiency. Nat Genet 25:182–186, 2000.

78. Thomas PQ, Dattani MT, Brickman JM, et al: Heterozygous HESX1 mutations associated with isolated pituitary hypoplasia and septo-optic dysplasia. Hum Mol Genet 10:39–45, 2001.

79. Zenaria E, Muscatelli F, Bardoni B, et al: An unusual member of the nuclear hormone receptor superfamily responsible for X-linked adrenal hypoplasia congenita. Nature 372:635–641, 1994.

80. Fujieda K, Okuhara K, Abe S, et al: Molecular pathogenesis of lipoid adrenal hypoplasia congenital. J Steroid Biochem Mol Biol 85(2-5):483–489, 2003.

81. Reutens AT, Achermann JC, Ito M, et al: Clinical and functional effects of mutations in the DAX-1 gene in patients with adrenal hypoplasia congenita. J Clin Endocrinol Metab 84:504–511, 1999.

82. Kaiserman KB, Nakamoto JM, Geffner ME, et al: Minipuberty of infancy and adolescent pubertal function in adrenal hypoplasia congenita. J Pediatr 133:300–302, 1998.

83. Takahashi T, Shoji Y, Shoji Y, at el: Active hypothalamic-pituitary-gonadal axis in an infant with X linked adrenal hypoplasia congenital. J Pediatr 130:485–488, 1997.

84. Merke DP, Tajima T, Baron J, et al: Hypogonadotropic hypogonadism in a female caused by an X-linked recessive mutation in the DAX-1 gene. N Engl J Med 340:1248–1252, 1999.

85. Seminara SB, Achermann JC, Genel M, et al: X-linked adrenal hypoplasia congenital: A mutation in DAX1 expands the phenotypic spectrum in males and females. J Clin Endocrinol Metab 84:4501–4509, 1999.

86. Ozisik G, Mantovani G Achermann JC, et al: An alternate translation initiation site circumvents an amino-terminal DAX1 nonsense mutation leading to a mild form of X-linked adrenal hypoplasia congenital. J Clin Endocrinol Metab 88:417–423, 2003.

87. Achermann JC, Meeks JJ, Jameson JL: X-linked adrenal hypoplasia congenital and DAX-1. Endocrinologist 10:289–290, 2000.

88. Tabarin A, Achermann JC, Recan D, et al: A novel mutation in DAX1 causes delayed onset adrenal insufficiency and incomplete hypogonadotropic hypogonadism. J Clin Invest 105:321–328, 2000.

89. Ingraham HA, Lala DS, Ikeda Y, et al: The nuclear receptor steroidogenic factor 1 acts at multiple levels of the reproductive axis. Genes Dev 8:2302–2312, 1994.

90. Zhao L, Bakke M, Krimkevich Y, et al: Steroidogenic factor 1 (SF1) is essential for pituitary gonadotrope function. Development 128:147–154, 2001.

91. Achermann JC, Ito M, Ito M, et al: A mutation in the gene encoding steroidogenic factor-1 causes XY sex-reversal and adrenal failure in humans. Nat Genet 22:125–126, 1999.

92. Achermann JC, Ozisik G, Ito M, et al: Gonadal determination and adrenal development are regulated by the orphan nuclear receptor steroidogenic factor-1, in a dose-dependent manner. J Clin Endocrinol Metab 87:1829–1833, 2002.

93. Biason-Lauber A, Schoenle EJ: Apparently normal ovarian differentiation in a prepubertal girl with transcriptionally inactive steroidogenic factor 1 (NR5A1/SF-1) and adrenocortical insufficiency. Am J Hum Genet 67(6):1563–1568, 2000.

94. Themman APN, Huhtaniemi IT: Mutations of gonadotropins and gonadotropin receptors: Elucidating the physiology and pathophysiology of pituitary-gonadal function. Endocr Rev 21(5):551–583, 2000.

95. Matthews CH, Borgato S, Beck-Peccoz P, et al: Primary amenorrhoea and infertility due to a mutation in the β-subunit of follicle stimulating hormone. Nat Genet 5:83–86, 1993.

96. Layman LC, Lee EJ, Peak DB, et al: Delayed puberty and hypogonadism caused by a mutation in the follicle-stimulating hormone β-subunit gene. N Engl J Med 337:607–611, 1997.

97. Layman LC, Porto ALA, Xie J, et al: FSHβ gene mutations in a female with partial breast development and a male sibling with normal puberty and azoospermia. J Clin Endocrinol Metab 87:3702–3707, 2002.

98. Phillip M, Arbelle JE, Segev Y, et al: Male hypogonadism due to a mutation in the gene for the β-subunit of follicle stimulating hormone. N Engl J Med 338:1729–1732, 1998.

99. Aittomaki K, Dieguez Lucena JL, et al: Mutation in the follicle-stimulating hormone receptor gene causes hereditary hypergonadotropic ovarian failure. Cell 82:959–968, 1995.

100. Meduri G, Touraine P, Beau I, et al: Delayed puberty and primary amenorrhea associated with a novel mutation of the human follicle-stimulating hormone receptor: Clinical, histological and molecular studies. J Clin Endocrinol Metab 88:3491–3498, 2003.

101. Allen LA, Achermann JC, Pakarinen P, et al: A novel loss of function mutation in exon 10 of the FSH receptor gene casuing hypogonadotropic hypogonadism: Clinical and molecular characteristics. Hum Reprod 18(2):251–256, 2003.

102. Tapanainen JS, Aittomaki K, Min J, et al: Men homozygous for an inactivating mutation of the follicle-stimulating hormone (FSH) receptor gene present variable suppression of spermatogenesis and fertility. Nat Genet 15:205–206, 1997.

103. Weiss J, Axelrod L, Whitcomb RW, et al: Hypogonadism caused by a

single amino acid substitution in the β-subunit of luteinizing hormone. N Engl J Med 326:179–183, 1992.

104. Kremer H, Kraaij R, Sergio PA, et al: Male pseudohermaphroditism due to a homozygous missense mutation of the luteinizing hormone receptor gene. Nat Genet 9:160–164, 1995.

105. Chan WY: Molecular genetic, biochemical and clinical implications of gonadotropin receptor mutations. Mol Genet Metab 63:75–84, 1998.

106. Stavrou SS, Zhu YS, Cai LQ: A novel mutation of the human luteinizing hormone receptor in 46XY and 46XX sisters. J Clin Endocrinol Metab 83:2091–2098, 1998.

107. Gromoll J, Schulz A, Borta H, et al: Homozygous mutation within the conserved Ala-Phe-Asn-Glu-Thr motif of exon 7 of the LH receptor causes male pseudohermaphroditism. Eur J Endocrinol 147(5):597–608, 2002.

108. Tsigos C, Latronico C, Chrousos GP: Luteinizing hormone resistance syndromes. Ann N Y Acad Sci 816:263–273, 1997.

109. Latronico AC, Anasti J, Arnhold IJP, et al: Brief report: Testicular and ovarian resistance to luteinizing hormone caused by inactivating mutations of the luteinizing hormone-receptor gene. N Engl J Med 334:507–601, 1996.

110. Toledo SPA, Brunner HG, Kraaij R, et al: An inactivating mutation of the luteinizing hormone receptor causes amenorrhea in a 46,XX female. J Clin Endocrinol Metab 81:3850–3854, 1996.

111. Strobel A, Issad T, Camoin L, et al: A leptin missense mutation associated with hypogonadism and morbid obesity. Nat Genet 18:213–215, 1998.

112. Clement K, Vaisse C, Lahlou N, et al: A mutation in the human leptin receptor gene causes obesity and pituitary dysfunction. Nature 392:398–401, 1998.

113. Jackson RS, Creemers JW, Ohagi S, et al: Obesity and impaired prohormone processing associated with mutations in the human prohormone convertase 1 gene. Nat Genet 16:303–306, 1997.

114. Yen SSC: Female hypogonadotropic hypogonadism: Hypothalamic amenorrhea syndrome. Endocrinol Metab Clin North Am 22:29–58, 1993.

115. Kazis K, Iglesias A: The female athlete triad. Adol Med State Art Rev 14(1):87–95, 2003.

116. Warren MP, Brooks-Gunn J, Fox RP: Osteopenia in exercise-associated amenorrhea using ballet dancers as a model: A longitudinal study. J Clin Endocrinol Metab 87(7):3162–3168, 2002.

117. Laughlin GA, Dominguez CE, Yen SSC: Nutritional and endocrine-metabolic aberrations in women with functional hypothalamic amenorrhea. J Clin Endocrinol Metab 83:25–32, 1998.

118. Muller J: Hypogonadism and endocrine metabolic disorders in Prader-Willi syndrome. Acta Paediatr 423:58–59, 1997.

119. Tojo K, Ichinose M, Nakayama M, et al: A new family of Boucher-Neuhauser syndrome: Coexistence of Holmes type cerebellar atrophy, hypogonadotropic hypogonadism and retinochoroidal degeneration: Case reports and review of literature. Endocr J 42:367–376, 1995.

120. Green JS, Parfrey PS, Harnett JD, et al: The cardinal manifestations of Bardet-Biedl syndrome, a form of Laurence-Moon-Biedl syndrome. N Engl J Med 321:1002–1009, 1989.

121. Mendez HMM, Opitz JM: Noonan syndrome: A review. Am J Med Genet 21:493–506, 1985.

122. Germain-Lee L, Groman J, Crane JL, et al: Growth hormone deficiency in pseudohypoparathyroidism type 1a-another manifestation of multihormone resistance. J Clin Endocrinol Metab 88(9):4059–4068, 2003.

123. Ropelato MG, Escobar ME, Gottlieb S, et al: Gonadotropin secretion in prepubertal normal and agonadal children evaluated by ultrasensitive time-resolved immunofluorometric assays. Horm Res 48:164–192, 1997.

124. Dunkel L, Siimes MA, Bremner WJ: Reduced inhibin and elevated gonadotropin levels in early pubertal boys with testicular defects. Pediatr Res 33:514–518, 1993.

125. Meachem SJ, Nieschlag E, Simoni M: Inhibin B in male reproduction: Pathophysiology and clinical relevance. Eur J Endocrinol 145(5):561–571, 2001.

126. Turner HH: A syndrome of infantilism, congenital webbed neck and cubitus valgus. Endocrinology 23:566, 1938.

127. Weiss L: Additional evidence of gradual loss of germ cells in the pathogenesis of streak ovaries in Turner's syndrome. J Med Genet 8:540–544, 1971.

128. Davenport M, Calikoglu AS: Turner syndrome. In Pescovitz OH, Eugster EA (eds): Pediatric Endocrinology: Mechanisms, manifestations and management. Philadelphia, Lippincott, Williams & Wilkins, 2004.

129. Zinn AR, Page DC, Fisher EMC: Turner syndrome: The case of the missing sex chromosome. Trends Genet 9:90–93, 1993.

130. Rao E, Weiss B, Fukami M, et al: Pseudoautosomal deletions encompassing a novel homeobox gene cause growth failure in idiopathic short stature and Turner syndrome. Nat Genet 16:54–63, 1997.

131. Clement-Jones M, Schiller S, Rao E, et al: The short stature homeobox gene SHOX is involved in skeletal abnormalities in Turner syndrome. Hum Mol Genet 9(5):695–702, 2000.

132. Hall JG, Gilchrist DM: Turner syndrome and its variants. Pediatr Clin North Am 37:1421–1440, 1990.

133. Conte FA, Grumbach MM, Kaplan SL: A diphasic pattern of gonadotropin secretion in patients with the syndrome of gonadal dysgenesis. J Clin Endocrinol Metab 40:670–674, 1974.

134. Pasquino AM, Passeri F, Pucarelli I, et al: Spontaneous pubertal development in Turner's syndrome. J Clin Endocrinol Metab 82(6):1810–1813, 1997.

135. Kaneko N, Kawagoe S, Hiroi M: Turner's syndrome-review of the literature with reference to a successful pregnancy outcome. Gynecol Obstet Invest 29:81–87, 1990.

136. Tarani L, Lampariello S, Raguso G, et al: Pregnancy in patients with turner syndrome: Six new cases and review of the literature. Gynecol Endocrinol 12:83–87, 1998.

137. Rosenfeld RG, Attie KM, Frane J, et al: Growth hormone therapy of Turner's syndrome: Beneficial effect on adult height. J Pediatr 132:319–324, 1998.

138. Ponzio G, Chiodo F, Messina M, et al: Non-mosaic isodicentric X-chromosome in a patient with secondary amenorrhea. Clin Genet 32:20–23, 1987.

139. Tharapel AT, Anderson KP, Simpson JL, et al: Deletion (X)(q26.1→q28) in a proband and her mother: Molecular characterization and phenotypic-karyotypic deductions. Am J Hum Genet 52:463–471, 1993.

140. Schlessinger D, Herrera L, Crisponi L, et al: Genes and translocations involved in POF. Am J Med Genet 111(3):328–333, 2002.

141. Rooman RP, Van Driessche K, Du Caju MV: Growth and ovarian function in girls with 48,XXXX karyotype-patient report and review of the literature. J Pediatr Endcrinol Metab 15(7):1051–1055, 2002

142. Klinefelter HF Jr, Reifenstein EC Jr, Albright F: Syndrome characterized by gynecomastia, aspermatogenesis without aleydigism and increased excretion of follicle-stimulating hormone. J Clin Endocrinol Metab 2:615, 1942.

143. Smyth CM, Bremner WJ: Klinefelter syndrome. Arch Intern Med 158:1309, 1998.

144. Sotos JF: Overgrowth section IV, Genetic disorders associated with overgrowth. Clin Pediatr 36:39–49, 1997.

145. Ahmad KN, Dykes JR, Ferguson-Smith MA, et al: Leydig cell volume in chromatin-positive Klinefelter's syndrome. J Clin Endocrinol Metab 33:517–520, 1971.

146. Christiansen P, Andersson AM, Skakkebaek NE: Longitudinal studies of inhibin B levels in boys and young adults with Klinefelter syndrome. J Clin Endocrinol Metab 88(2):888–891, 2003.

147. Bojesen A, Juul S, Gravholt CH: Prenatal and postnatal prevalence of Klinefelter syndrome: A national registry study. J Clin Endocrinol Metab 88(2):622–626, 2003.

148. Kleczhowska A, Fryns JP, Van den Berghe: X-chromosome polysomy in the male. The Leuven

experience 1966–1987. Hum Genet 80:16, 1988.

149. Dodge OG, Path MC, Jackson AW, et al: Breast cancer and interstitial cell tumors in a patient with Klinefelter's syndrome. Cancer 24:1027–1032, 1969.

150. Hasle H, Mellemgaard A, Nielsen J, et al: Cancer incidence in men with Klinefelter syndrome. Br J Cancer 71:416–420, 1995.

151. Kurzock EA, Tunuguntla HS, Busby JE, at al: Klinefelter's syndrome and precocious puberty: A harbinger for tumor. Urol 60(3):514, 2002.

152. Stocco DM: Clinical disorders associated with abnormal cholesterol transport: Mutations in the steroidogenic acute regulatory protein. Mol Cel Endocrinol 191(1):19–25, 2002.

153. Bose HS, Sugawara T, Strauss JF III, et al: The pathophysiology and genetics of congenital lipoid adrenal hyperplasia. N Engl J Med 335:1870–1878, 1996.

154. Bose HS, Pescovitz OH, Miller W: Spontaneous feminization in a 46,XX female patient with congenital lipoid adrenal hyperplasia due to a homozygous frameshift mutation in the steroidogenic acute regulatory protein. J Clin Endocrinol Metab 82:1511–1515, 1997.

155. Kater CE, Biglieri EG: Disorders of steroid 17 alpha-hydroxylase deficiency. Endocrinol Metab Clin North Am 23:341–357, 1994.

156. Quigley CA, De Bellis A, Marschke KB, et al: Androgen receptor defects: Historical, clinical and molecular perspectives. Endocr Rev 16:271–321, 1995.

157. Brinkman AO: Molecular basis of androgen insensitivity. Mol Cell Endocrinol 179(1-2):105–109, 2001.

158. Verp MS, Simpson JL: Abnormal sexual differentiation and neoplasia. Cancer Genet Cytogenet 25:191–218, 1987.

159. Swyer GIM, Phil D: Male pseudohermaphroditism: A hitherto undescribed form. Br Med J 2:709–712, 1955.

160. Simpson JL, Blagowidow N, Martin AO: XY gonadal dysgenesis: Genetic heterogeneity based upon clinical observations, H-Y antigen status and segregation analysis. Hum Genet 58:91–97, 1981.

161. Le Caignec C, Baron S, McElreavey K, et al: 46,XY gonadal dysgenesis: Evidence for autosomal dominant transmission in a large kindred. Am J Med Genet 116A(1):37–43, 2003.

162. Hawkins JR, Taylor A, Goodfellow PN, et al: Evidence for increased prevalence of SRY mutations in XY females with complete rather than partial gonadal dysgenesis. Am J Hum Genet 51:979–984, 1992.

163. Mitchell CL, Harley VR: Biochemical defects in eight SRY missense mutations causing XY gonadal dysgenesis. Mol Genet Metab 77(3):217–225, 2002.

164. Gallagher MP, Oberfield SE: Disorders of sexual differentiation. In Pescovitz OH, Eugster EA (eds): Pediatric Endocrinology: Mechanisms, manifestations and management. Philadelphia, Lippincott, Williams & Wilkins, 2004, pp 243–254.

165. Kempe A, Engels H, Schubert R, et al: Familial ovarian dysgerminomas (Swyer syndrome) in females associated with 46, XY karyotype. Gyencol Endocrinol 16(2):107–111, 2002.

166. De Grouchy J, Gompel A, Salmon-Bernard Y: Embryonic testicular regression syndrome and severe mental retardation in sibs. Ann Genet 28:154–160, 1985.

167. Sahin C, Yigit T, Ozbey I, et al: Adult nonpalpable testis: Is laparoscopy always required? J Laparendosc Adv Surg Tech A 12(6):431–434, 2002.

168. Davenport M, Brian C, Vanderberg C, et al: The use of the hCG stimulation test in the endocrine evaluation of cryptochidism. Br J Urol 76:790–794, 1995.

169. Lee MM, Donahoe K, Silverman BL, et al: Measurements of serum mullerian inhibiting substance in the evaluation of children with nonpalpable gonads. N Engl J Med 336:1480–1486, 1997.

170. Grady RW, Mitchell ME, Carr MC: Laparoscopic and histologic evaluation of the inguinal vanishing testis. Urol 52(5):866–869, 1998.

171. Ozcan C, Celik A, Ozok G, et al: Adnexal torsion in children may have a catastrophic sequel: Asynchronous bilateral torsion. J Pediatr Surg 37(11):1617–1620, 2002.

172. Cicognani A, Pasini A, Pession A, et al: Gonadal function and pubertal development after treatment of a childhood malignancy. J Pediatr Endocrinol Metab 16 (Suppl 2):321–326, 2003.

173. Maclaren N, Chen QY, Kukreja A, et al: Autoimmune hypogonadism as part of an autoimmune polyglandular syndrome. J Soc Gynecol Invest 8(1 Suppl):S52–S54, 2001.

174. Betterle C, Volpato M: Adrenal and ovarian autoimmunity. Eur J Endocrinol 138:16–25, 1998.

175. Twigg S, Wallman L, McElduff A: The resistant ovary syndrome in a patient with galactosemia: A clue to the natural history of ovarian failure. J Clin Endocrinol Metab 81:1329–1331, 1996.

176. Gitzelmann R, Steinman B: Galactosemia: How does long-term treatment change the outcome? Enzyme 32:37–46, 1984.

177. Mauras N, Vieira NE, Yergey AL: Estrogen therapy enhances calcium absorption and retention and diminishes bone turnover in young girls with Turner's syndrome: A calcium kinetic study. Metabolism 46:908–913, 1997.

178. Kanaoka Y, Honda K, Ishiko O, et al: Long-term effects of hormone replacement therapy on bone mineral density in girls oophorectomized in adolescence. Gynecol Obstet Invest 55(3):168–172, 2003.

179. McNichols TA, Dean JD, Mulder H, et al: A novel testosterone gel formulation normalizes androgen levels in hypogonadal men, with improvements in body composition and sexual function. BJU Int 91(1):69–74, 2003.

180. Meikle AW, Mazer NA, Moellmer JF, et al: Enhanced transdermal delivery of testosterone across nonscrotal skin produces physiological concentrations of testosterone and its metabolites in hypogonadal men. J Clin Endocrinol Metab 74:623–628, 1992.

# Gender Identity and Sexual Behavior

## Louis J. G. Gooren

## PRENATAL, POSTNATAL, AND CHILDHOOD YEARS

### PRENATAL HORMONAL EFFECTS

This chapter deals with the effect of hormones on differentiation and maintenance of the dimorphism of sexual behavior during the life span. Sex steroids are the primary hormonal regulators of sexual behavior. Sexual behavior is governed chiefly by sex hormones in lower mammals, less so in the lower primates, and, least of all, but still recognizably, in humans.[1-4]

Programming of sexual behavior is in part prenatal in origin, with long-term effects of sex steroids on the central nervous system (CNS). However, whatever the prenatal hormonal programming of the CNS, in humans it is enormously influenced by social environmental programming in the postnatal years.[1,3-5] In fact, a large component of gender identity and sexual behavior is not exclusively hormonally determined but is also a product of an individual's postnatal experience.[1,3-5]

### SEXUAL DIFFERENTIATION

Sexual differentiation begins with the sex difference of the chromosomes established at conception (see Chapter 142). In humans, no evidence can be found that the combination of chromosomes present in all cells of the body has a direct effect on erotosexual status. Rather, the influence is indirect and derivative through determination of the nature of the embryonic gonadal anlagen and their hormonal products.[1,3-5]

### BRAIN SEXUAL DIFFERENTIATION

In the early 1900s, it became clear from animal experimentation that the process of sexual differentiation is not completed with formation of the external genitalia, but that the brain, as the substrate of sexual and nonsexual behavior, also undergoes sexual differentiation to match the other characteristics of sex. In lower animals, evidence has accumulated that the same hormonal organizing principles of sexual dimorphic differentiation account for both the genitalia and the brain.[4-8] This hormonal action of testosterone has been termed *organizational*, and it is exerted during a rather circumscribed, so-called critical period of prenatal or early postnatal development. In lower mammals, part of this action is mediated by estrogens through aromatization of testosterone,[9] but this is not the case in primates and the human.[10] The main regions of the mammalian brain involved in sexual differentiation are the hypothalamus, the septum, the bed nucleus of the stria terminalis, the preoptic area, and the amygdala.[7-9]

The sexual dimorphic differentiation of the human brain is less well documented, but a number of sexual dimorphic nuclei have been found (sexual dimorphic nucleus [SDN] and the bed nucleus of the stria terminalis).[7,8] The morphologic sex difference in the SDN is not established until the first postnatal years, and that of the bed nucleus of the stria terminalis may extend into adulthood.[8] During childhood, there are no significant sex differences in circulating sex steroids. While the mechanism of sexual differentiation in laboratory animals is clearly induced by gonadal steroids[7,8] as well as other genetic factors,[11] in humans the mechanism and the clinical relevance of brain sexual dimorphism are not yet certain. In humans this information has been deduced from "experiments of nature": genetic and endocrine disorders that spontaneously occur in the fetus or result from exposure to exogenous hormones, such as estrogenic drugs during pregnancy.[1,3-5] Clinical observations support the hypothesis that in human prenatal development, sexual brain differentiation is subject to effects of androgens, but these are not of the hormonal-robot type found in subprimate mammals, in which sex steroids typically exert a simple on-off effect on sexual behavior.[1,3-5]

### DISORDERS OF SEXUAL DIFFERENTIATION

Human sexual differentiation is a multistep, sequentially interrelated process in which genetic information is translated into the phenotype of a person who subsequently establishes a male or female identity and an awareness of sexual orientation.[1,3] The human embryo is initially bipotential with respect to gonadal and genital development and, consequently, disorders in any of these steps can result in ambiguity of the gonads/genitalia.[5,6] A child born with ambiguous genitalia constitutes a psychosocial emergency in which sex assignment must take place without delay, in days rather than weeks (see Chapter 143).[12] Western society demands two clearly defined sexes, with an absolute distinction between male and female. Modern techniques such as karyotyping, molecular biology, and imaging techniques allow a rather precise diagnosis of the condition, but decisions regarding sex assignment are still based on very limited empiric data.[12]

Most experts would agree that biologic characteristics (such as chromosomal pattern, nature of the gonad, and so on) are not sufficient to provide reliable indicators for determining a person's "true" sex status as a man or woman.[1,3-5] Though relevant, they do not fully govern the decision to assign a particular sex to a newborn with ambiguous genitalia. A widely adopted policy is to arrive at a prognosis on the "optimal sex" for the newborn, the elements of which are an overall sex-appropriate appearance with stable gender identity, good sexual function (preferably combined with reproductive function if attainable), minimal medical procedures, and a reasonably fulfilling life hampered as little as possible by the condition.[4,5,12]

This policy has recently been called into question. While it is reasonable to assume that a neural substrate corresponding to traits and self-concepts of being male or female will eventually be present in a person's life, the factors that determine these self-concepts remain a matter of debate. Assignment of a newborn with ambiguous genitalia to one sex or the other on the basis of a prognosticated best future functioning as male or female presupposes psychosexual neutrality of children at that stage of their lives. In other words, the clinical and scientific question is whether at the time of birth a (biologically determined) "neural bias" is already present with regard to future gender identity/role and sexual orientation. Are the latter shaped (exclusively) by postnatal factors in the course of rearing a child as boy or girl or is this development wholly or partially determined by prenatal factors such as the hormonal milieu?[3-5,12]

Brain research, mostly performed on lower mammals, demonstrates a significant role of prenatal and perinatal sex hormones in the sexual differentiation of brain and behavior.[7-9] Several reports provide evidence that such hormonal effects are present in humans, but the association is not absolute, and the information too preliminary to constitute solid guidelines for sex assignment of children with ambiguous genitalia.[1,3,12,13]

The clinical syndromes that allow assessment of prenatal androgen effects on future gender identity/role, sexual orientation, and other behaviors are 46,XX subjects with congenital adrenal hyperplasia (CAH),[14-17] 46,XY subjects with hypoandrogenism,[18-23] such as partial androgen insensitivity (PAIS), and children with nonhormonally induced severe genital malformations such as cloacal exstrophy and penile agenesis/ablation who have been assigned to the female sex but whose prenatal androgen production/exposure has been similar to other males.[24,25] Available data allow the preliminary conclusion that effective prenatal exposure to androgens is indeed associated with masculinization of gender role behavior. Girls with CAH, particularly the more severe salt-wasting form, exhibit a spectrum of masculinized gender role behavior, though this is often compatible with a core female gender identity. The likelihood of a gender change later in life in such females correlates with the presumed degree of prenatal androgen exposure, though the association is not very strong.

Naturally, the degree of prenatal and postnatal androgen exposure also determines the extent of genital ambiguity, which, together with the postnatal experience and considerations of quality of life, may also be a factor in a change of gender. Predictors of gender change are stigmatization, gonadectomy, and/or feminizing surgery after the age of 3 years. A relative absence of gender dysphoria in childhood does not preclude a gender change later in life.

The majority of 46,XY intersex patients (such as in PAIS) seem to develop an identity commensurate with the assigned gender and do not change their gender later.[18,21-23] Childhood gender identity will in most cases continue into adolescence and adulthood, but patient-initiated gender change in intersex patients does seem to happen more often in adolescence and adulthood than in childhood. More female-assigned 46,XY patients initiate a gender change to male than male-assigned 46,XY patients to female, possibly indicating the prenatal effects of androgens.[18,21,22]

Boys born with a cloacal exstrophy have normal testes and have had a presumed normal prenatal exposure to androgens. About 50% of those assigned to the female sex report dissatisfaction with this assignment and change to male, but these data are still rather preliminary.[25] In a series of 18 children born with a micropenis, all subjects were satisfied with their sex of rearing in adulthood, though both men and women expressed dissatisfaction with their genital status.[24] In summary, the evidence available to date permits only tentative policy-relevant conclusions: (1) the organizational effects of prenatal androgens are more noticeable in gender role behavior than in gender identity; (2) gender identity can develop as female or male over wide variations of gender role behavior; and (3) there is suggestive, but not conclusive, evidence that a male gender identity/role is more frequent in patients with a history of fully male-typical prenatal androgenization. There is, at this stage of research, no unambiguous evidence for or against female gender assignment of 46,XY patients, even in the prenatally most androgenized conditions.

Obviously, the policy of sex assignment of intersexed newborns is based on a number of insufficiently substantiated presuppositions, but this must also be weighed against the consequences of allowing infants to grow up intersexed until they are old enough to make their own choices. Not intervening can be a complicated decision as well, with the risk of not taking adequate account of the two-sexed world in which the children have to live, and the depth of feeling of parents who might find it difficult to cope with their child's sexual ambiguity.[12]

A rigorous policy of early sex assignment has been criticized by interest groups of intersexed people, who advocate a safe space for the development of identities as intersexuals, as occurs in some societies.[26] Some of these individuals, having undergone hormonal and surgical sex assignment treatment, are unable to identify themselves as belonging to either sex. This group believes that surgical therapy should be limited to instances necessary for physical health and comfort. In particular, it opposes clitorectomy or substantial reduction of the clitoris and poor surgical repair of penile abnormalities, both of which reduce the prospects for later pleasurable sexual activity.[26] These views deserve serious attention.

## COMPLETE ANDROGEN INSENSITIVITY

Children afflicted with the androgen insensitivity syndrome (AIS) have a 46,XY karyotype and testes as gonads (see Chapter 169).[27-29] An abbreviated blind vaginal pouch is present, but no uterus or fallopian tubes. Because the external genitalia have a normal female appearance, the disorder of these patients is often unnoticed at birth. Surgical repair of an inguinal hernia containing a testis may reveal the condition. Hormonal puberty is, without intervention, feminizing, due to the aromatization of endogenous androgens to estrogens. In cases of complete AIS, sex assignment and rearing are almost invariably female. The differentiation of gender identity/role is feminine.[18,21-23,27-29] This fact is theoretically important in showing that the nature of the chromosomes and gonads per se do not dictate gender identity and role.

In adulthood, gender identity/role and sexuality conform to typical heterosexual feminine expectations. Patients with complete AIS are phenotypically normal women whose first complaint may be primary amenorrhea.[27] Up to that point, they have usually lived unambiguously as girls. Their female gender identity/role should therefore be bolstered. Sexual functioning may be problematic due to vaginal hypoplasia, requiring interventions.[30]

Because of the risk of malignant degeneration of the testes, orchidectomy is indicated in all patients with complete AIS. Counseling is a sensitive issue for a patient with complete AIS and for the parents. Patients most often complain of amenorrhea, with no awareness of an underlying endocrine disorder. Undue and severe psychologic trauma may be produced by a physician who informs the patient that she is, in fact, a male or has sexual characteristics of both sexes. Both the patient and her parents need to be reassured that the patient is a female who will become a woman. In all likelihood, her sexual orientation will be to men. Many such families have children by adoption.[27–29]

## PARTIAL ANDROGEN RESISTANCE SYNDROMES

The spectrum of phenotypes in 46,XY may include individuals with almost normal female external genitalia, children with ambiguous genitalia (perineoscrotal hypospadias, a microphallus, and cryptorchidism), and a normal male phenotype.[18–23]

There may be some[19,20] relation between the nature of the androgen receptor defect and the phenotype at puberty, but, because of the androgen insensitivity, the development of male secondary sex characteristics is not very pronounced. Gynecomastia develops as a result of an imbalance in androgen-estrogen action. Less severe cases may have either hypospadias or a normal male phenotype and normal male development at puberty with azoospermia.

Because of the variability in expression of partial AIS, no standard therapy is available.[18–23] Minor deviations may go unnoticed or may be repaired by surgery (e.g., hypospadias). In more severe cases, the child has ambiguous genitalia. In these children the problem of sex assignment arises.

Consideration should be given first to the morphologic appearance of the external genitalia. If the anatomy is thoroughly ambiguous and the possibilities for surgical correction are equally promising in either direction, the potential for fertility may be a determining factor.[18–23] The growth potential of the penis must be estimated, however.[31]

In practice, the chances for relatively normal development are better in a female direction.[18–23] For older infants, children, and adults, first consideration should be given to the degree that a gender role has been established in the sex already assigned.

If a female sex of rearing is decided upon, plastic surgical repair of the genitalia should be performed at an appropriate age. Guidelines similar to those specified for patients with complete AIS could be followed. At least 50% of subjects are neither informed about their medical condition and surgical history nor satisfied with their level of knowledge in adulthood.[22]

If a male sex of rearing is chosen, reconstructive surgery of the genitalia should be performed in childhood. Pubertal gynecomastia is to be expected and may require early surgical correction.

## 5α-REDUCTASE DEFICIENCY

5α-dihydrotestosterone (DHT), the most potent natural androgen, is formed exclusively through 5α-reduction of testosterone by the enzyme 5α-reductase.[32,33] Affected people are born with labioscrotal folds and a clitoridean penis. At puberty they become moderately virilized or remain eunuchoid with enlargement of the clitoridean penis. No breast development is seen.

In the first reports, it was claimed that these people were reared as girls during childhood, but, after pubertal physical changes, took up life as men.[33] The interpretation offered was that testosterone apparently induces a reversal of gender identity and role and generates a "male sex drive."[32] Subsequent studies cast doubt on this interpretation.[33] Local people are usually aware of the genital disorder of these neonates and of their potential future male pubertal development. In the recent study from Brazil,[33] 25 of 26 affected with 5α-reductase type 2 deficiency were assigned at birth to the female sex and raised as girls. Thirteen changed to the male sex after puberty. This was associated with some virilization of the external genitalia. There was no straightforward relationship between the severity of the condition and change of gender.[33]

## 17β-HYDROXYSTEROID DEHYDROGENASE DEFIENCY

17β-hydroxysteroid dehydrogenase 3 is involved in the terminal step in the synthesis of testosterone in the Leydig cell and of estradiol in the ovarian granulosa cell.[34] Subjects with an XY chromosomal pattern and testes affected with 17β-hydroxysteroid dehydrogenase 3 deficiency are born with more or less female external genitalia due to lack of an effective androgenic stimulus at the time of the differentiation of the external genitalia.[34–36] Such children are usually assigned to the female sex at birth and raised as girls.[35] A particular feature of this disorder is that the testosterone production increases with age (due to a higher luteinizing hormone [LH] drive and alternative pathways of testosterone production), and subjects may have near-normal testosterone levels at the time of puberty, inducing substantial virilization. There are several reports of affected individuals raised as females who have changed their gender role behavior from female to male at the time of expected puberty.[35] This is not universally the case, but appears to happen in approximately 50% of the reported cases in the literature.[34,36]

## CONGENITAL ADRENAL (VIRILIZING) HYPERPLASIA

Congenital adrenal hyperplasia (CAH) is a disorder occurring in both sexes involving excessive/untimely exposure to androgens (see Chapter 124). Early reports indicated an overriding influence of the sex of assignment and rearing on the gender identity of CAH girls.[3,16] If CAH subjects were assigned as girls, they turned out to have a female gender identity, but with tomboyish behavior in play and activity and high energy expenditure—a marked masculine shift on the scale of sex dimorphic behavior likely due to prenatal and possibly postnatal androgen exposure.[13,14,16]

These observations also extend to childhood and later indices of maternal interest. This is more true for the salt-wasting form of CAH than for the simple virilizing form.[14] Some are less contented with life as women, without having an explicit gender identity disorder.[13,14] In a report of older CAH subjects reared as girls, 37% rated themselves as homosexual or bisexual or they had fewer heterosexual experiences than the comparison group.[13] This finding has been further corroborated.[14] Another study was less affirmative in this regard.[16] Nevertheless, retrospective studies indicate that that there may be a decreased sexual interest and below-average engagement in heterosexual relationships. This may also be due to androgenic effects on the genitalia.[13,14,16] Further, hirsutism may be a disruptive factor. By contrast, it has been reported that those subjects assigned as boys due to the degree of masculinization of their external genitalia successfully developed a male gender identity and role though patient-initiated reassignments to the female gender have been reported.[16]

In both sexes, an aim of treatment must be to maximize adult height potential, while fertility may also be an issue. Both height and fertility are related to the quality of endocrine care.[17]

Prenatal dexamethasone treatment of pregnant mothers possibly bearing a child affected with CAH has become an option, though it is still experimental.[37] Treatment must start "blindly" by or before the sixth or seventh postmenstrual week until the diagnosis can be made by chorionic villous biopsy at week 10 or 11 or by amniocentesis at week 14 to 16.[37,38] The treatment requires intensive guidance of the patient, but is efficacious.[38]

### PRENATAL EXPOSURE TO EXOGENOUS HORMONES

Estrogens or estrogenic drugs (predominantly diethylstilbestrol [DES]) and progestins were administered to pregnant women, notably between 1940 and 1970. Synthetic progestins have, depending on their chemical formulas, antiandrogenic or weak androgenic biologic activity. In male fetuses, prenatal exposure to progestins and/or estrogens may have suppressed their endogenous testosterone production by the powerful negative feedback action on the hypothalamic-pituitary-testicular axis.[1] Prenatal exposure of female fetuses to DES or progestins has not impaired their subsequent self-identification as female,[39] but a higher incidence of homosexuality or bisexuality (25%) in adulthood has been reported in a sample of such women.[40] Several follow-up studies of prenatal exposure to DES and/or progestin in men have indeed found them to display a degree of nonconformity in stereotyped gender behavior, but a clear-cut effect on sexual orientation or gender identity has not been established.[3]

### PRECOCIOUS AND DELAYED HORMONAL PUBERTY

Precocious puberty occurs more often in girls than boys. Affected children typically mature sexually between the ages of 6 and 8 years and sometimes earlier. Their erotosexual behavior matches their chronologic age more closely than their physical maturation.[41,42] Erections in boys are usually associated with erotic ideation and imagery corresponding to their calendar age. Signs of erotic interest may be in evidence from time to time, but they usually do not lead to sexual encounters, possibly through lack of potential partners,[42] though these children are usually somewhat ahead of their peers in erotosexual activity at the normal time of puberty.[41,42] With this advanced physical maturation, children may seek friends close to their stage of sexual development even though they lack the age-appropriate development of these children. Outsiders may have unrealistic expectations arising from the stage of physical maturation, with the potential for sexual abuse and the risk of pregnancy in girls. Studies indicate that many of the behavioral problems of precocious puberty are mediated by the perception, of self and by others, of the discrepancy of physical sexual maturation and behavior appropriate for calendar age.[41,42] Both parents and the child need guidance to cope with this premature sexual development. Parents' anxieties and concerns should be carefully addressed. They often fear premature sexual activity.[41,42] The gap between chronologic age and physical age may be minimized by planned acceleration in school and social life.

Delayed puberty is the converse of precocious puberty. Similar to precocious puberty, behavioral problems may arise from the perception, of self and by others, of the discrepancy between calendar age and physical sexual maturation.[42]

In most cases, the delay of puberty is constitutional, but it may also be based on disturbances in gonadotropin and sex steroid production. The problems of being out of step in sexual maturation with peers are underrated by many parents and medical professionals. Pubertal delay may lead to shyness and withdrawal from group activities (sports, heterosexual social activities, flirtation, and erotic overtures) because of shame about physique.

## PUBERTY YEARS

### TURNER'S SYNDROME

In Turner's syndrome, with a 45,X0 or related mosaic chromosomal disorder, the gonads fail to produce hormones. The genitalia are normally female and gender identity/role is typically feminine.[43-45] Awareness of infertility and the lifelong short stature typical of this syndrome do not interfere with a desire for marriage and motherhood. Secondary sexual characteristics must be induced by estrogen administration.[43-45] This is often delayed until the late teenage years, sexual development being temporarily sacrificed for statural growth, for which synthetic growth hormone is often added. Psychologic problems may arise when estrogen therapy is initiated later than at approximately the age of 13 years. As a result of delay in sexual maturation, there may be relative romantic and erotic inertia.[43-45] The absence of ovarian androgen production may also be relevant. Girls with Turner's syndrome have a specific cognitive deficit that does not affect verbal intelligence though speech may be delayed, but does affect nonverbal intelligence and is manifested as a handicap in visuospatial capacity (direction sense, map reading), mathematics, and a motor deficit.[43-45]

### KLINEFELTER SYNDROME

Klinefelter syndrome (47,XXY and its mosaics) is not infrequent. A recent study found an incidence ratio of 1:667 male births.[46] The condition is often not diagnosed until the age of puberty because, until teenage years, affected boys are only moderately different from control subjects: Patients may be taller or have undescended testes or relatively small external genitalia, but these features are not always present. Puberty may progress slowly with permanently weak virilization and, often, gynecomastia. Patients usually receive treatment with testosterone to increase virilization and to promote synchrony with the development of chronologic age peers.

The intelligence quotient (IQ) of most 47,XXY males is usually average or somewhat lower. Verbal IQ is usually more affected than nonverbal or performance IQ and is manifested in infancy as a developmental delay in speech.[47]

Executive skills (such as concept formation, problem solving, switching tasks, and initiating rapid and fluent response) may be also be impaired.[47,48] If Klinefelter syndrome is diagnosed early, remedial teaching may help improve educational performance. In sexologic counseling, attention is given, as needed, to surgical correction of gynecomastia, cosmetic prosthetic testes, and coping with infertility. With regard to erotosexuality, no systematic epidemiologic statistics are available to permit a statement about the prevalence of paraphilias or gender transpositions in the 47,XXY population versus the 46,XY population. The dominant trend is for 47,XXY men to be timid and hyposexual. The sexuality of Klinefelter patients in infertility clinics is indistinguishable from a comparison group.[49]

### ABNORMAL BODY SHAPE AND IMAGE

Hormones have a profound impact on body shape and consequently on body self-image. Patients with conditions that affect appearance, such as gynecomastia, precocious/delayed puberty, small/tall stature, hirsutism, Klinefelter syndrome, Turner's syndrome, obesity, and the like, may suffer from a negative body image.[42]

In particular, adolescents often view themselves through the eyes of their peers and constantly compare themselves with them. Any deviation in appearance may evoke peer ridicule and can result in low self-esteem and feelings of inadequacy, shame, and stress; this combination may lead to withdrawal from social activities and poor academic performance and may impair healthy erotic and sexual interaction and development.[42,50]

Therefore, body image dissatisfaction must be addressed when treating the aforementioned conditions even though the complaints may lack technical medical significance. Reassurance based on medical examination that pathology has been ruled out and that no relevant medical problems are present may not be sufficient. Alternatively, it may even be counterproductive if the patient believes that the absence of disease leaves no room for discussing body image problems. It may be up to the physician to initiate discussion of these issues. Inquiries such as "Other people with the same condition often experience discomfort with their bodies. How is this condition affecting your life?" may pave the way for an assessment of how patients experience their deviation from the norm. The physician may offer the information that joining a patient self-help group is sometimes helpful.

## ADULT YEARS

### ADULT MALE SEXUAL FUNCTIONING

The evidence for testosterone-induced masculinization of certain aspects of sexual behavior in men is persuasive. Most of the information has been collected from androgen withdrawal/replacement studies of hypogonadal men. It is now clear that androgens are fundamental to normal sexual behavior in men, although they do not have a simple on-off effect on sexual functions, and are not the only factor involved in male sexual behavior.[2,51,52] When androgen production is deficient from the fetal stage, as in hypogonadotropic hypogonadism and Klinefelter syndrome, the response to androgen replacement during puberty or later may be manifestly impaired, expressing itself as relative sexual inertia. However, emotional, cognitive, and social learning are also elements of testosterone manifestation in adolescent and adult sexuality.[2]

The distinction between sexual interest and erectile function and its subdivision has helped considerably in clarifying the role of androgens in male function.[2,51,52] Spontaneous erections, particularly those that occur during sleep, and probably fantasy-induced erections are androgen dependent, whereas erections in response to erotic (e.g., visual or tactile) stimuli are less so.[2,52] But androgens do affect penile responses to erotic stimuli with regard to the duration of response, degree of rigidity, and speed of detumescence.[53] In men, the principal target of androgen appears to be sexual interest or appetite.[2,52] Androgen might enhance the persistence of attention to eroticism, which, in turn, might affect sexual behavior. It has been argued that androgen influences pleasurable awareness during sexual activity, possibly by enhancing sensory (genital) function. It is not certain how androgens exert their action on the brain; they may also influence cellular activity in a nongenomic fashion by acting directly on cell membranes or by modulating other membrane receptors or secondary messenger systems.[51]

Although it has been convincingly established that the main effect of androgens on male sexual functioning is on the central nervous system, additional evidence now suggests that they also affect nitric oxide synthase in the corpus cavernosum (nitric oxide induces smooth muscle relaxation of the penile vasculature, essential for penile erection) and that androgen administration may be helpful in men who respond poorly to treatment of erectile dysfunction with phosphodiesterase inhibitors.[54]

The blood level of testosterone critical for normal male sexual function varies among individuals.[52,55,56] In most males, 60% to 70% of the reference values was sufficient.[55,56] In men with sexual dysfunction and normal androgen levels, additional testosterone is likely to be of no help, although a short-lived beneficial effect from additional testosterone in eugonadal men who complained of lack of sexual interest has been found.

Pubertal development is associated with a gradual though variable increase in sexual interest and activity, but it has been difficult to relate levels of androgens to the development of adolescent sexuality, probably because there is a fair but individually different amount of socially influenced learning that impacts on this hormone-behavior relationship. Physical pubertal development may be a better predictor of sexual interest and behavior than free testosterone,[57,58] but one study was able to demonstrate a more direct relationship between salivary/plasma testosterone and sexual activity.[57] Sexual functions decline with aging. Aging is also associated with a variable decline in bioavailable testosterone levels, but levels remain well above minimum testosterone levels for normal sexual functioning established in younger men. The hypothesis has been advanced that aging men are less sensitive to the actions of testosterone.[59]

Information on the timing of onset of behavioral effects after withdrawal of androgens is limited. With both naturally occurring and pharmacologically induced hypotestosteronemia, behavioral effects and a reduction in seminal emission become clear after 2 weeks and reach a maximum after 4 weeks or longer. A sexually active partner may be a factor in prolongation of sexual activity.[2] In the majority of men, the ejaculatory capacity is profoundly decreased after androgen withdrawal, affecting sexual behavior in its own right.[2]

Restoration of testosterone effects is probably somewhat quicker, approximately over 1 to 2 weeks, and there may be a relationship with the duration of foregoing androgen deficiency.[52]

### ADULT FEMALE SEXUAL FUNCTIONING

In contrast to males, it has been difficult to ascertain the effect of sex steroids on female sexual functioning. Yet most women find that their erotosexual functioning increases with the advent of puberty. The menopausal transition is usually associated with a decline in sexual activity. Women experience profoundly different hormonal patterns in the course of their reproductive and postmenopausal years. Notwithstanding, it has been difficult to relate elements of sexual functioning closely to their serum estrogen/progesterone levels.[2,60] Also, the effects of oral contraceptives have been difficult to assess with certainty.[2] Almost all studies show that the sexuality of women is powerfully influenced by mood, energy, and well-being,[2] obscuring an unambiguous definition of endocrine factors. Estrogen administration to estrogen-deficient women improves vaginal lubrication and this effect, rather than or in addition to effects on the neural substrate, may be a factor in improved sexual functioning.[2]

Some evidence suggests that testosterone is a factor in prompting sexual interest in women. The matter has been extensively reviewed.[61] There are a number of methodological difficulties in assessing the significance of androgens in women. With the low plasma testosterone in women, the levels of adrenal androgens may be biologically significant. Plasma androgen levels vary over the menstrual cycle, and there may be a relationship between midcycle testosterone peaks and sexual motivation and arousability.[61] In women who undergo oophorectomy, there is a decline in circulating androgens. Some but not all experience a deterioration of their sexual function and some benefit from testosterone treatment.[61] The natural menopause is associated with a decrease in estrogens and a decrease in plasma sex hormone–binding globulin (SHBG), while plasma testosterone does not decline for the next 7 years after menopause. Usually, sexual functioning declines with the menopausal transition. In the studies measuring the effects of exogenous testosterone as part of hormonal replacement therapy in women with low androgen levels,[61] sexual desire, arousability, frequency of sexual activity, and orgasm and sexual satisfaction were enhanced. It has been found that testosterone may improve mood in women and, theoretically, the beneficial effects of androgens on female sexuality could be secondary to mood effects. It is not quite certain whether the effects of androgen administration must be viewed as physiologic or pharmacologic actions of testosterone. From an endocrine viewpoint, it is interesting that females respond to androgen levels to which males are not behaviorally sensitive.[61]

## HYPERPROLACTINEMIA

In contrast to that in women, the role of prolactin in males is less well understood. No convincing evidence has emerged that a lower than normal prolactin level impairs sexual functioning in humans.[53] In women, the initial symptom of hyperprolactinemia is mostly a disturbance in reproductive physiology (amenorrhea, infertility), leading to a relatively early discovery of the condition. Interference with female sexual functioning has been reported but is less clear-cut than in men. It may be manifested as a depressive disorder affecting orgasmic capacity, which improves upon treatment with dopamine agonists.

In men, sexual dysfunction, but more often symptoms of a pituitary tumor, may lead to the discovery of hyperprolactinemia. This condition accounts for less than 2% of cases of sexual dysfunction in men.[53] About 80% to 90% of men with chronic hyperprolactinemia have complaints such as loss of libido, erectile weakness, and, frequently, difficulty ejaculating.[53] The mechanism by which hyperprolactinemia impairs sexual function is not completely understood. In cases of associated testosterone deficiency, testosterone substitution did not reverse the symptoms.[53] Dopaminergic drugs restored sexual function even before testosterone levels had risen to normal.[53]

Most experts now believe that hyperprolactinemia impairs sexual function through a CNS mechanism by interference with neurotransmitter activity, in particular, dopamine and endogenous opioids.[62] In some men with sexual complaints, serum prolactin levels may be found to be elevated in the presence of normal gonadotropin and testosterone levels. They may have macroprolactinemia, and their sexual problems cannot be ascribed to their spurious hyperprolactinemia.[63] Administration of antipsychotic drugs can be associated with marked hyperprolactinemia. And it is increasingly clear that this drug-induced hyperprolactinemia may produce menstrual irregularities, galactorrhea, gynecomastia, sexual dysfunction, and mood disturbances.[64] The condition is often not diagnosed since the psychological effects are viewed as part of the disease requiring antipsychotic medication. In cases of clinically relevant hyperprolactinemia, the dose of the antipsychotic drug may be lowered or an alternative drug may be chosen.[64]

## PARAPHILIAS AND THEIR PHARMACOLOGIC TREATMENT

Persons with a paraphilia are compulsively responsive to and dependent on an unusual and often personally or socially unacceptable sexual stimulus for sexual arousal and orgasm.[65] No known correlation between paraphilic behavior and an endocrine condition, past or present, has been detected.[65] Paraphilias occur predominantly in men, but may also occur in women. There is no convincing evidence that circulating testosterone levels are higher in (violent) sex offenders than controls.[65] The socially intolerable paraphilias (such as rape, exhibitionism, and pedophilia) may bring persons in conflict with the law, and (forensic) medicine may play a part in pharmacologic interventions aimed at helping paraphiliacs. When dealing with this category, it is mandatory to observe professional neutrality. As in normal persons, testosterone lowers

the threshold of occurrence of erotosexual imagery and sexual activity in paraphiliacs. It has no effect on the contents of the imagery, however.[65] Antiandrogens may be of benefit, particularly for those paraphilias characterized by intense and frequent sexual desire and arousal. To be effective, hormonal treatment must be accompanied by sexologic counseling. The most widely used drug in the United States is medroxyprogesterone acetate, and in Canada and Europe, cyproterone acetate. Of late, LH-releasing hormone (LHRH) agonists and antagonists have also been used successfully.[66] Both are available in injectable form, thus facilitating greater compliance with the treatment program. Long-term androgen deprivation may lead to osteopenia. Some forms of paraphilia are not so much characterized by sexual desire but are obsessive-compulsive or impulse control disorders or are acted out in depressive mood states, and do not respond well to antiandrogenic intervention. These can be successfully treated with psychotropic drugs such as modern antidepressants in view of the role of the dopaminergic system in motivational processes.[65]

## GENDER IDENTITY/ROLE AND SEXUAL ORIENTATION

The very existence of such phenomena as transsexualism and homosexuality indicates that a gender identity in agreement with other sex characteristics and a heterosexual orientation are not foreordained but are apparently the outcome of a developmental process, the mechanisms of which are virtually unknown. Transsexuals, in spite of having the normal biologic characteristics of one sex, experience and present themselves as members of the opposite sex. Homosexuality is distinct from transsexualism in that homosexuals experience no discomfort with their physical state of being male or female, but are able to interact erotosexually only with others of the same morphologic sex. By and large, the determinants of gender identity and sexual orientation are not known. Prenatal androgen exposure appears to predispose to the development of male gender identity, a sexual orientation toward women, and male gender behavior,[1,14–17] but other factors may override this.[1] There is almost never evidence of an abnormal prenatal endocrine condition in transsexuals and homosexuals.[1]

Some researchers view both transsexualism and homosexuality[1] as incidents in the perinatal sexual differentiation process of the brain.

## HOMOSEXUALITY

Family and twin studies in men and DNA linkage analysis in men[67] suggest that familial and genetic factors are relevant in (some) men with a homosexual orientation, but not in women. The route by which genotype could influence sexual orientation/behavior remains to be specified. Some epidemiologic findings suggest that a late birth order and a higher brother-to-sister ratio in the family correlate with a homosexual orientation in men—again, a finding that is not easy to interpret in terms of biologic mechanisms.[68]

In addition, vast numbers of homosexual men can be found in whom the aforementioned features cannot be identified. Some women have a prenatal endocrine history atypical for their sex, such as exposure to DES,[40] or a higher than normal androgen exposure due to CAH.[13,14,16] In these women, the incidence of partial or complete lesbian erotosexuality is elevated, although homoerotic sexuality does not develop in the majority of subjects with an identical history. Critical analysis shows that no simple cause-and-effect relationship between the prenatal endocrine milieu and postnatal sexual orientation can be established, and these studies show, at best, rather weak correlations between a biologic variable and sexual orientation.[1]

A non–sex dimorphic nucleus, the suprachiasmatic nucleus (SCN), has been found to be larger in homosexuals.[8] But some researchers are critical of neuroanatomic findings.[69] The SCN has not been implicated in known sexual functions in humans.

## TRANSSEXUALISM

### Definition
Transsexualism is a condition in which a person with apparently normal somatic sexual differentiation is convinced that he or she is actually a member of the opposite sex. It is associated with an irresistible urge to be hormonally and surgically adapted to that sex. Transsexualism cannot be explained by variations in chromosomal pattern or by gonadal, genital, or hormonal anomalies.[1] Nor is there an indication that genetic factors play a role. Though occasionally identical twins have both manifested as transsexuals, this is not common, and no familial clustering has been observed. Traditionally, transsexualism has been conceptualized as a psychological phenomenon, but research on the brains of male-to-female transsexuals has found that the sexual differentiation of one brain area (the bed nucleus of the stria terminalis) follows a female pattern.[70]

The latter finding may lead to a concept of transsexualism as a form of intersex, where the sexual differentiation of the brain is not consistent with the other variables of sex: chromosomal pattern and nature of the gonad and the internal/external gonads. So it could be argued that transsexualism is a sexual differentiation disorder.

Adult transsexuals often recall that their gender dysphoria started early in life, well before puberty. Children with gender identity problems increasingly come to the attention of the psychomedical care system. A reliable estimation indicates that only about 20% will become transsexuals in adolescence.[71] Homosexuality will more often be the outcome.

If, in expert opinion, a child's cross-sex gender identity will not change during long-term follow-up, the individual may be spared the torment of (full) pubescent development of the "wrong" secondary sex characteristics.[72,73] Depot forms of LHRH antagonists/agonists, following the regimen used in children with precocious puberty, can be used when clear signs of sexual maturation are evident in order to delay pubertal development until an age that a balanced and responsible decision can be made.[74]

### Diagnostic Procedures
In the final analysis, the etiology of transsexualism and related expressions of gender dysphoria is unknown and initial assessment will be based on psychodiagnostic instruments and will generally be done by a mental health professional. Guidelines are spelled out in the "Standards of Care" of the Harry Benjamin International Gender Dysphoria Association.[75]

The criterion for reassignment treatment is the reasonable expectation that hormonal/surgical treatment will alleviate the sufferings of gender dysphoria. Serious psychiatric comorbidity and adverse personal social conditions may constitute a serious impediment to successful transition to the desired sex.

When hormone treatment starts, or perhaps even before that, the "real-life test" should begin. It is an extended period of full-time living as a member of the desired sex. The real-life test allows the subject to monitor experiences in the new sex.[75]

### Hormonal Reassignment
Secondary sex characteristics are contingent on sex steroids. No fundamental difference in sensitivity to the biologic action of sex steroids on the basis of genetic configurations or gonadal status is known. Adult transsexuals have the disadvantage that at that age a normal average degree of hormonal masculinization or feminization has already taken place. Hormonal reassignment has two aims: (1) to eliminate as much as possible the hormonally induced secondary sex characteristics of the original sex, and (2) to induce those of the new sex.[76,77] Adult male beard growth is very resistant to the hormonal interventions and, in Caucasian subjects, extra measures to eliminate facial hair are almost always necessary. Breast formation starts almost immediately after estrogen administration. After 2 years of hormone administration, no further development can be expected. It is quantitatively satisfactory in 40% to 50% of subjects.

### Regrets
It has been estimated that 1% to 2% of transsexuals who opt for transition to the desired sex will have regrets; almost all of these are male-to-female transsexuals.[78] Some of these subjects will only have experienced gender dysphoria relatively late in adult life; others have difficulty in making the transition to the new sex because of their appearance or limited social skills. Also of significance (for all transsexuals) is the quality of surgical construction of the genitalia.[78]

## REFERENCES

1. Gooren LJ: The endocrinology of transsexualism: A review and commentary. Psychoneuroendocrinology 15:3–14, 1990.
2. Bancroft J: Biological factors in human sexuality. J Sex Res 39:15–21, 2002.
3. Money J: The development of sexuality and eroticism in humankind. Q Rev Biol 56:379–404, 1981.
4. MacLaughlin DT, Donahoe PK: Mechanism of disease: Sex determination and differentiation. N Engl J Med 350:367–378, 2004.
5. Migeon CJ, Wisniewski AB: Human sex differentiation and its abnormalities. Best Pract Res Clin Obstet Gynaecol 17:1–18, 2003.
6. Hughes IA: Minireview: Sex differentiation. Endocrinology 142:3281–3287, 2001.
7. Gorski RA: Hypothalamic imprinting by gonadal steroid hormones. Adv Exp Med Biol 511:57–70, 2002.
8. Swaab DF, Chun WC, Kruijver FP, et al: Sexual differentiation of the human hypothalamus. Adv Exp Med Biol 511:75–100, 2002.
9. McEwen BS: Invited review: Estrogens effects on the brain: Multiple sites and molecular mechanisms. J Appl Physiol 91:2785–2801, 2001.
10. Rochira V, Balestrieri A, Madeo B, et al: Congenital estrogen deficiency in men: A new syndrome with different phenotypes—clinical and therapeutic implications in men. Mol Cell Endocrinol 193:19–28, 2002.
11. Tobet SA: Genes controlling hypothalamic development and sexual differentiation. Eur J Neurosci 16:373–376, 2002.
12. Meyer-Bahlburg HF: Gender assignment and reassignment in intersexuality: Controversies, data, and guidelines for research. Adv Exp Med Biol 511:199–223, 2002.
13. Meyer-Bahlburg HF: Gender and sexuality in classic congenital adrenal hyperplasia. Endocrinol Metab Clin North Am 30:155–171, viii, 2001.
14. Meyer-Bahlburg HF, Bakker SW, Dolezal C, et al: Long-term outcome in congenital adrenal hyperplasia: Gender and sexuality. Endocrinologist 13:227–232, 2003.
15. Hrabovszky Z, Hutson JM: Androgen imprinting of the brain in animal models and humans with intersex disorders: Review and recommendations. J Urol 168:2142–2148, 2002.
16. Money J: Biographies of Gender and Hermaphroditism in Paired Comparisons. Amsterdam, Elsevier Science, 1991.
17. Warne G: Congenital adrenal hyperplasia: Long-term outcome studies. Endocrinologist 13:179–181, 2003.
18. Meyer-Bahlburg HF: Gender assignment and reassignment in 46,XY pseudohermaphroditism and related conditions. J Clin Endocrinol Metab 84:3455–3458, 1999.

19. Ahmed SF, Cheng A, Dovey L, et al: Phenotypic features, androgen receptor binding, and mutational analysis in 278 clinical cases reported as androgen insensitivity syndrome. J Clin Endocrinol Metab 85:658–665, 2000.

20. Boehmer AL, Brinkmann O, Bruggenwirth H, et al: Genotype versus phenotype in families with androgen insensitivity syndrome. J Clin Endocrinol Metab 86:4151–4160, 2001.

21. Migeon CJ, Wisniewski AB, Gearhart JP, et al: Ambiguous genitalia with perineoscrotal hypospadias in 46,XY individuals: Long-term medical, surgical, and psychosexual outcome. Pediatrics 110:e31– 2002.

22. Migeon CJ, Wisniewski AB, Brown TR, et al: 46,XY intersex individuals: Phenotypic and etiologic classification, knowledge of condition, and satisfaction with knowledge in adulthood. Pediatrics 110:e32–***, 2002.

23. Melo KF, Mendonca BB, Billerbeck AE, et al: Clinical, hormonal, behavioral, and genetic characteristics of androgen insensitivity syndrome in a Brazilian cohort: Five novel mutations in the androgen receptor gene. J Clin Endocrinol Metab 88:3241–3250, 2003.

24. Wisniewski AB, Migeon CJ, Gearhart JP, et al: Congenital micropenis: Long-term medical, surgical and psychosexual follow-up of individuals raised male or female. Horm Res 56:3–11, 2001.

25. Reiner WG, Gearhart JP: Discordant sexual identity in some genetic males with cloacal exstrophy assigned to female sex at birth. N Engl J Med 350:333–341, 2004.

26. Intersex Society of North America: Recommendations for treatment. Available at *http://www.isna.org.*

27. Wisniewski AB, Migeon CJ, Meyer-Bahlburg HFL, et al: Complete androgen insensitivity syndrome: Long-term medical, surgical, and psychosexual outcome. J Clin Endocrinol Metab 85:2664–2669, 2000.

28. Hines M, Ahmed SF, Hughes IA: Psychological outcomes and gender-related development in complete androgen insensitivity syndrome. Arch Sex Behav 32:93–101, 2003.

29. Wisniewski AB, Migeon CJ: Long-term perspectives for 46,XY patients affected by complete androgen insensitivity syndrome or congenital micropenis. Semin Reprod Med 20:297–304, 2002.

30. Minto CL, Liao KL, Conway GS, et al: Sexual function in women with complete androgen insensitivity syndrome. Fertil Steril 80:157–164, 2003.

31. Ghali SA, Gottlieb B, Lumbroso R, et al: The use of androgen receptor amino/carboxyl-terminal interaction assays to investigate androgen receptor gene mutations in subjects with varying degrees of androgen insensitivity. J Clin Endocrinol Metab 88:2185–2193, 2003.

32. Russell DW, Wilson JD: Steroid 5 alpha-reductase: Two genes/two enzymes. Annu Rev Biochem 63:25–61, 1994.

33. Mendonca BB: Male pseudohermaphroditism due to 5a-reductase 2 deficiency: Outcome of a brazilian cohort. Endocrinologist 13:201–204, 2003.

34. Andersson S, Geissler WM, Wu L, et al: Molecular genetics and pathophysiology of 17 beta-hydroxysteroid dehydrogenase 3 deficiency. J Clin Endocrinol Metab 81:130–136, 1996.

35. Wilson JD: The role of androgens in male gender role behavior. Endocr Rev 20:726–737, 1999.

36. Boehmer AL, Brinkmann AO, Sandkuijl LA, et al: 17Beta-hydroxysteroid dehydrogenase-3 deficiency: Diagnosis, phenotypic variability, population genetics, and worldwide distribution of ancient and de novo mutations. J Clin Endocrinol Metab 84:4713–4721, 1999.

37. New MI, Carlson AD, Obeid JS, et al: Update: prenatal diagnosis for congenital adrenal hyperplasia in 595 pregnancies. Endocrinologist 13:233–239, 2003.

38. Forest MG, Dörr HG: Prenatal therapy in congenital adrenal hyperplasia due to 21-hydroxylase deficiency: Retrospective follow-up study of 253 treated pregnancies in 215 families. Endocrinologist 13:252–259, 2003.

39. Money J, Mathews D: Prenatal exposure to virilizing progestins: An adult follow-up study of 12 women. Arch Sex Behav 11:73–83, 1982.

40. Ehrhardt AA, Meyer-Bahlburg HF, Rosen LR, et al: Sexual orientation after prenatal exposure to exogenous estrogen. Arch Sex Behav 14:57–77, 1985.

41. Ehrhardt AA, Meyer-Bahlburg HF: Psychosocial aspects of precocious puberty. Horm Res 41(Suppl 2):30–35, 1994.

42. Mazur T, Clopper RR: Pubertal disorders: Psychology and clinical management. Endocrinol Metab Clin North Am 20:211–230, 1991.

43. Frias JL, Davenport ML: Health supervision for children with Turner syndrome. Pediatrics 111:692–702, 2003.

44. Karnis MF, Reindollar RH: Turner syndrome in adolescence. Obstet Gynecol Clin North Am 30:303–320, 2003.

45. Conway GS: The impact and management of Turner's syndrome in adult life. Best Pract Res Clin Endocrinol Metab 16:243–261, 2002.

46. Bojesen A, Juul S, Gravholt CH: Prenatal and postnatal prevalence of Klinefelter syndrome: A national registry study. J Clin Endocrinol Metab 88:622–626, 2003.

47. Simpson JL, de la Cruz F, Swerdloff RS, et al: Klinefelter syndrome: Expanding the phenotype and identifying new research directions. Genet Med 5:460–468, 2003.

48. Temple CM, Sanfilippo PM: Executive skills in Klinefelter's syndrome. Neuropsychologia 41:1547–1559, 2003.

49. Yoshida A, Miura K, Nagao K, et al: Sexual function and clinical features of patients with Klinefelter's syndrome with the chief complaint of male infertility. Int J Androl 20:80–85, 1997.

50. Sandberg DE, Voss LD: The psychosocial consequences of short stature: A review of the evidence. Best Pract Res Clin Endocrinol Metab 16:449–463, 2002.

51. Mills TM, Reilly CM, Lewis RW: Androgens and penile erection: A review. J Androl 17:633–638, 1996.

52. Gooren LJ, Kruijver FP: Androgens and male behavior. Mol Cell Endocrinol 198:31–40, 2002.

53. Carani C, Granata AR, Fustini MF, et al: Prolactin and testosterone: Their role in male sexual function. Int J Androl 19:48–54, 1996.

54. Aversa A, Isidori AM, Spera G, et al: Androgens improve cavernous vasodilation and response to sildenafil in patients with erectile dysfunction. Clin Endocrinol (Oxf) 58:632–638, 2003.

55. Gooren LJ: Androgen levels and sex functions in testosterone-treated hypogonadal men. Arch Sex Behav 16:463–473, 1987.

56. Alexander GM, Swerdloff RS, Wang C, et al: Androgen-behavior correlations in hypogonadal men and eugonadal men. I. Mood and response to auditory sexual stimuli. Horm Behav 31:110–119, 1997.

57. Halpern CT, Udry JR, Suchindran C: Monthly measures of salivary testosterone predict sexual activity in adolescent males. Arch Sex Behav 27:445–465, 1998.

58. Finkelstein JW, Susman EJ, Chinchilli VM, et al: Effects of estrogen or testosterone on self-reported sexual responses and behaviors in hypogonadal adolescents. J Clin Endocrinol Metab 83:2281–2285, 1998.

59. Schiavi RC, Rehman J: Sexuality and aging. Urol Clin North Am 22:711–726, 1995.

60. Van Goozen SH, Wiegant VM, Endert E, et al: Psychoendocrinological assessment of the menstrual cycle: The relationship between hormones, sexuality, and mood. Arch Sex Behav 26:359–382, 1997.

61. Bachmann G, Bancroft J, Braunstein G, et al: Female androgen insufficiency: The Princeton consensus statement on definition, classification, and assessment. Fertil Steril 77:660–665, 2002.

62. Meston CM, Frohlich PF: The neurobiology of sexual function. Arch Gen Psychiatry 57:1012–1030, 2000.

63. Schlechte JA: The macroprolactin problem. J Clin Endocrinol Metab 87:5408–5409, 2002.

64. Halbreich U, Kinon BJ, Gilmore JA, et al: Elevated prolactin levels in patients with schizophrenia: mechanisms and related adverse effects. Psychoneuroendocrinology 28(Suppl 1):53–67, 2003.

65. Gijs L, Gooren LJ: Hormonal and psychopharmacological interventions in

the treatment of paraphilias: An update. J Sex Res 33:273–290, 1996.

66. Reilly DR, Delva NJ, Hudson RW: Protocols for the use of cyproterone, medroxyprogesterone, and leuprolide in the treatment of paraphilia. Can J Psychiatry 45:559–563, 2000.

67. Mustanski BS, Chivers ML, Bailey JM: A critical review of recent biological research on human sexual orientation. Annu Rev Sex Res 13:89–140, 2002.

68. Zucker KJ, Blanchard R, Siegelman M: Birth order among homosexual men. Psychol Rep 92:117–118, 2003.

69. Lasco MS, Jordan TJ, Edgar MA, et al: A lack of dimorphism of sex or sexual orientation in the human anterior commissure. Brain Res 936:95–98, 2002.

70. Kruijver FP, Zhou JN, Pool CW, et al: Male-to-female transsexuals have female neuron numbers in a limbic nucleus. J Clin Endocrinol Metab 85:2034–2041, 2000.

71. Cohen-Kettenis PT: Gender identity disorder in DSM? J Am Acad Child Adolesc Psychiatry 40:391, 2001.

72. Cohen-Kettenis PT, Van Goozen SH: Pubertal delay as an aid in diagnosis and treatment of a transsexual adolescent. Eur Child Adolesc Psychiatry 7:246–248, 1998.

73. Cohen-Kettenis PT, Pfäfflin F: Transgenderism and Intersexuality in Childhood and Adolescence: Making Choices. Thousand Oaks, CA, Sage, 2003.

74. Gooren LJ, Delemarre–van de Waal HA: Memo on the feasibility of endocrine interventions in juvenile transsexuals. J Psychol Hum Sex 8:69–74, 1996.

75. The Harry Benjamin International Gender Dysphoria Association: Standards of care for the treatment of gender dysphoria. Available at *http://www.hbigda.org/socv6.html*.

76. Moore E, Wisniewski A, Dobs A: Endocrine treatment of transsexual people: A review of treatment regimens, outcomes, and adverse effects. J Clin Endocrinol Metab 88:3467–3473, 2003.

77. Levy A, Crown A, Reid R: Endocrine intervention for transsexuals. Clin Endocrinol (Oxf) 59:409–418, 2003.

78. Lawrence AA: Factors associated with satisfaction or regret following male-to-female sex reassignment surgery. Arch Sex Behav 32:299–315, 2003.

# Folliculogenesis, Ovulation, and Luteogenesis

## Gregory F. Erickson

OVARY ANATOMY AND HISTOLOGY

**FOLLICULOGENESIS**
Preantral Follicles
Antral or Graafian Follicles
Atresia

**OVULATION**

LUTEOGENESIS
Luteinization
Luteolysis

**THE GROWTH FACTOR CONCEPT**

**CONCLUSION**

During the reproductive years, there are two primary functions of the human ovary: (1) to produce regularly a single graafian follicle that secretes estradiol ($E_2$) and ovulates a mature oocyte at about midpoint in the menstrual cycle; and (2) to produce an endocrine structure, the corpus luteum, which secretes large amounts of $E_2$ and progesterone ($P_4$), which acts on the uterus to prepare it for implantation of the embryo. A major feature of this ovarian activity is its cyclic nature, a feature strikingly reflected in the growth and development of the dominant follicle and corpus luteum, respectively. These cyclic changes are regulated predominantly by changing concentrations of the anterior pituitary hormones follicle-stimulating hormone (FSH) and luteinizing hormone (LH). Here, we focus our attention on the structure/function changes that occur in the human ovary to evoke a menstrual cycle, namely folliculogenesis, ovulation, and luteogenesis.

## OVARY ANATOMY AND HISTOLOGY

In normal adult women, the ovaries are oval-shaped bodies, each measuring 2.5 to 5.0 cm in length, 1.5 to 3.0 cm in width, and 0.6 to 1.5 cm in thickness. The ovaries are covered by a sheet of squamous or cuboidal epithelium, the *germinal* or *serous epithelium*, which rests on a basement membrane. Beneath the serous epithelium is a layer of dense connective tissue termed the *tunica albuginea*. One edge of the ovary, the *hilum*, is attached to the broad ligament by the mesovarium.

The ovary is organized into two principal parts, a central part called the *medulla* and a peripheral part called the *cortex* (Fig. 150-1). Embedded in the stroma of the medulla is a mass of blood vessels and associated nerves, which pass toward the cortex. In the hilum are nests of typical Leydig cells, called *hilus cells*, which are capable of secreting testosterone in response to LH stimulation.[1]

The cortex is a dynamic structure with follicles and corpora lutea (see Fig. 150-1). These histologic units exhibit a specialized architecture that reflects their stage in growth and development. The pool of follicles can be divided into two major classes: growing and nongrowing. Most (90% to 95%) of the follicles are the nongrowing or *primordial follicles*. Once a primordial follicle has been recruited to grow, its size, structure, and position in the cortex begin to change dramatically. During this process, the follicle passes through three developmental stages: the *primary*, *secondary*, and *tertiary* or *graafian* stages (see Fig. 150-1). Selection of a dominant follicle occurs during the graafian stage, and those follicles that are not selected degenerate by a process called *atresia*. After ovulation of the large dominant follicle, the follicle wall transforms into a corpus luteum by a process called *luteinization*. The corpus

luteum of the cycle ultimately degenerates by a process called *luteolysis*.

## FOLLICULOGENESIS

The ability of a primordial follicle to undergo folliculogenesis is at the very foundation of the expression of a menstrual cycle. As a follicle grows and develops, important changes occur within the three major cell populations, the oocytes, granulosa, and theca cells. These cellular changes include proliferation, differentiation, growth, and apoptosis. Two major classes of regulatory molecules control these cellular activities, namely, hormones and growth factors. Folliculogenesis can be divided into two phases, the preantral and antral periods. That period from recruitment of a primordial follicle to the end of the secondary stage is referred to as the *preantral* or *gonadotropin-independent phase*. In the *antral* or *gonadotropin-dependent phase*, a fluid-filled cavity or antrum develops within the follicle. The tertiary or graafian follicle becomes larger, predominantly through the accumulation of increasing amounts of follicular fluid in the antrum. The fully developed graafian follicle is termed a *preovulatory follicle*.

### PREANTRAL FOLLICLES

The development of a preantral follicle is characterized by three major developmental events: (1) the recruitment (entry) of a primordial follicle into the pool of growing follicles; (2) the growth and differentiation of the oocyte; and (3) the acquisition of FSH and LH receptors in the granulosa and theca cells, respectively.

#### Primordial Follicle

The *primordial follicles* constitute a pool of nongrowing follicles from which all preovulatory follicles are ultimately derived. A primordial follicle consists of a small (~15 µm in diameter) oocyte arrested in the dictyotene stage of meiosis, a single layer of squamous granulosa cells, and a thin basal lamina that encloses both cell types (Fig. 150-2). There is no blood vascular system directly associated with the primordial follicles[2]; however, there is evidence in the rhesus monkey that they may be innervated, most notably by *vasoactive intestinal peptide (VIP) nerves*.[3]

In humans, the primordial follicles are formed in the fetal ovaries between the sixth and ninth months of gestation.[4] Since all the female germ cells have committed to meiosis, there are no unspecialized stem cells that are capable of producing new oocytes by the end of gestation. Consequently, all the oocytes in a woman's ovaries are present at birth. Once

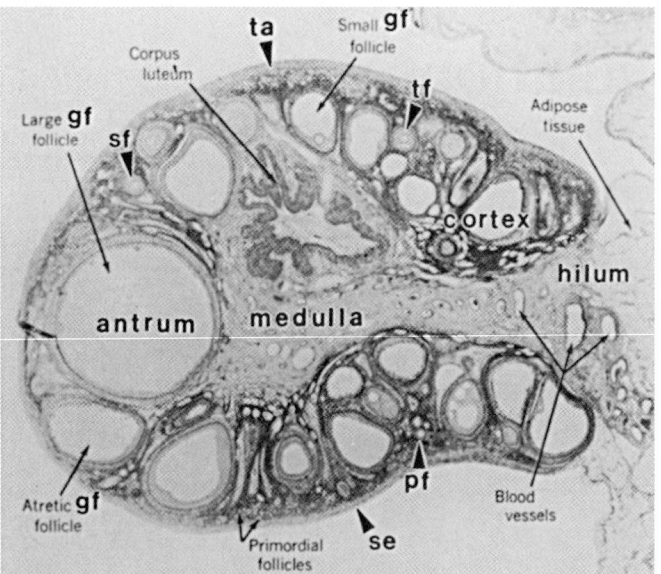

**Figure 150-1** Photomicrograph of an adult primate ovary showing the follicular and luteal units in the cortex and large blood vessels and nerves in the medulla. Gf, graafian follicle; pf, primary follicle; se, serous or surface epithelium; sf, secondary follicle; ta, tunica albuginea; tf, tertiary follicle. (Modified from Bloom W, Fawcett DW [eds]: A Textbook of Histology. Philadelphia, WB Saunders, 1975, p 860.)

the primordial follicles are formed, some become recruited to grow. As a woman ages, the process of recruitment continues on a regular basis until the total primordial follicle compartment is exhausted: This event, the *menopause*, occurs in most women at about 51 years of age.[5] An important concept is that the loss of primordial follicles or *ovary reserve* (OR) is not constant during aging. For example, a significant accelerated

decrease in OR occurs at about 37 years in most women (Fig. 150-3). Clinically, the age-related acceleration of primordial follicle depletion is of great importance because it is associated with a significant decrease in fecundity.[5]

Certainly, one of the foremost questions in reproductive biology concerns the basis of recruitment. Structurally, recruitment or the primordial-to-primary follicle transition begins with a change in shape in the granulosa cells from the squamous to a cuboidal shape, which, in turn, is accompanied by or associated with a commitment of the granulosa to divide, albeit very slowly.[6,7] During or immediately following this sequence of events, the oocyte genome becomes activated and the oocyte begins to grow.[8,9] That the first visible signs of recruitment occur in the granulosa cells fits the prediction that granulosa cells may play a key role in the process. There has been recent progress in our understanding of how recruitment might be regulated. The general principle to emerge is that recruitment may be controlled by positive and negative growth factors.[10,11] For example, there is evidence in laboratory animals that recruitment is inhibited by epidermal growth factor[12] and Müllerian inhibiting substance[13] and stimulated by a variety of factors including kit ligand,[14] insulin,[15] testosterone,[16] bone morphogenetic protein-7,[17] and restricted food intake.[18] It will be of great interest to find out how some of these signaling pathways regulate OR in women.

### Primary Follicle

A primary follicle consists of a growing oocyte, a single layer of one or more cuboidal granulosa cells, and a basal lamina (see Figs. 150-2 and 150-4). In the primary follicle, several fundamental and important activities are expressed, including *FSH receptors* in the granulosa cells, *gap junctions* between the oocyte and granulosa cells, dramatic *oocyte growth* and *zona pellucida* deposition.

During the evolution of the primary follicle, the gene encoding the FSH receptor is turned on in the granulosa cells,[19] which, in turn, is followed by the acquisition of cell

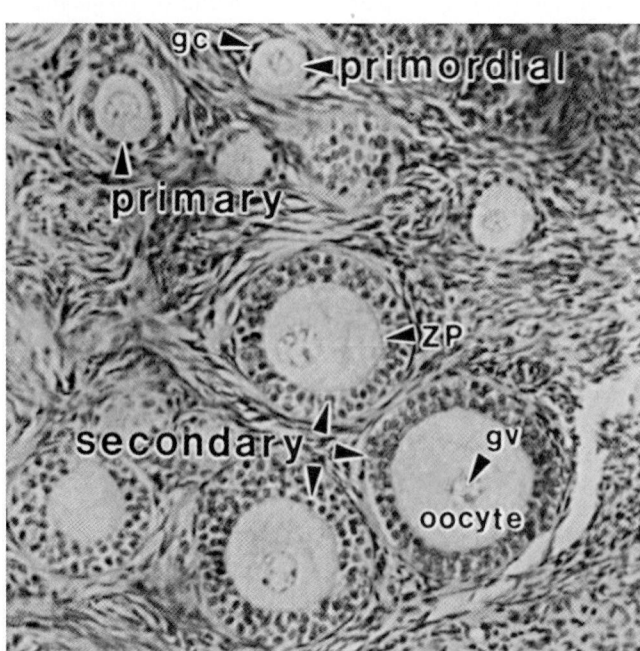

**Figure 150-2** Photomicrograph of a portion of the cortex of the ovary. Primordial (nongrowing) follicles consisting of a small oocyte arrested in diplotene of meiosis I surrounded by a single layer of squamous granulosa cells (gc). Primary follicle containing a growing oocyte and a single layer of cuboidal granulosa cells. Secondary follicles containing a near–full-grown diplotene oocyte with an intact germinal vesicle (gv) or nucleus, a thin zona pellucida (ZP), and two or more layers of cuboidal granulosa cells.

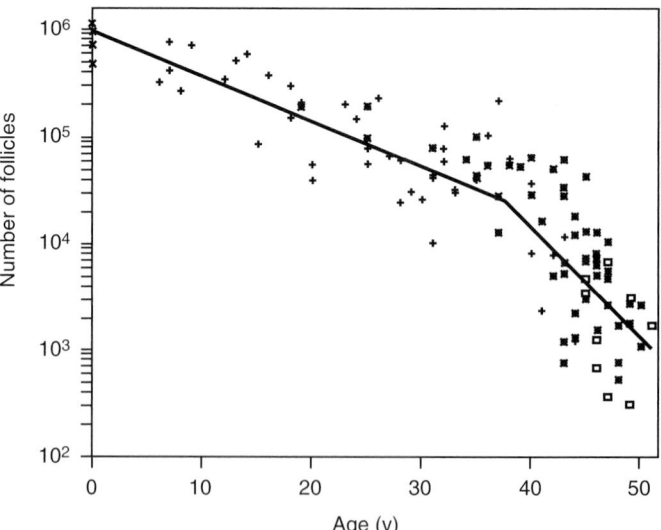

**Figure 150-3** Morphometric analysis of normal human ovaries showing the age-related decrease in the total number of primordial follicles (PF) within both ovaries from birth to the menopause. As a consequence of recruitment, the number of PFs decreases progressively from approximately 1 million at birth to about 25,000 at age 37. Note that the rate of loss of PF accelerates approximately twofold at 37.5 ± 1.2 years, with the number being reduced to about 1000 at approximately 51 years of age. (From Faddy MJ, Gosden RG, Gougeon A, et al: Accelerated disappearance of ovarian follicles in midlife: Implications for forecasting menopause. Hum Reprod 7:1342–1346, 1992.)

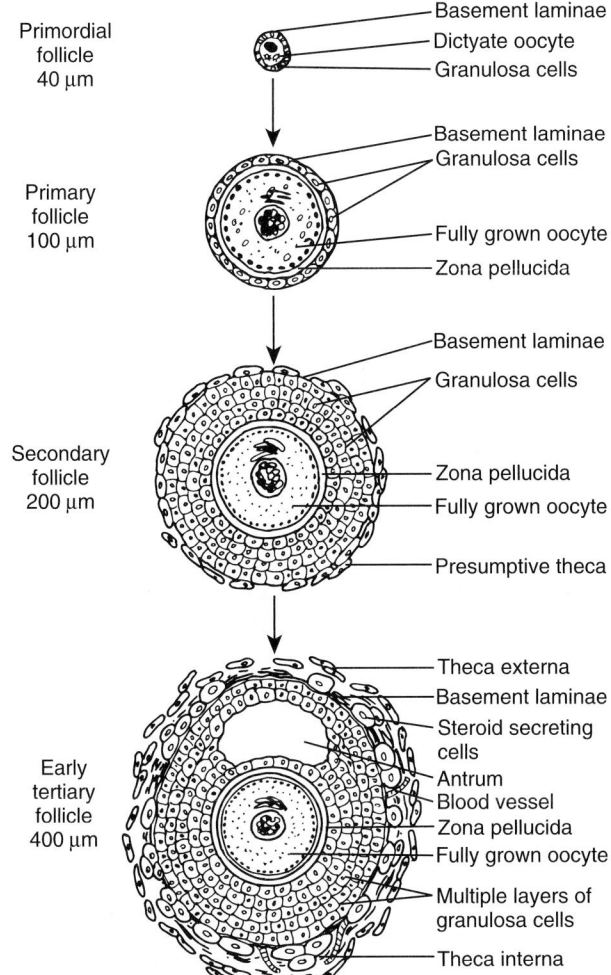

Figure 150-4 components labels:

Primordial follicle 40 µm
- Basement laminae
- Dictyate oocyte
- Granulosa cells

Primary follicle 100 µm
- Basement laminae
- Granulosa cells
- Fully grown oocyte
- Zona pellucida

Secondary follicle 200 µm
- Basement laminae
- Granulosa cells
- Zona pellucida
- Fully grown oocyte
- Presumptive theca

Early tertiary follicle 400 µm
- Theca externa
- Basement laminae
- Steroid secreting cells
- Antrum
- Blood vessel
- Zona pellucida
- Fully grown oocyte
- Multiple layers of granulosa cells
- Theca interna

*Figure 150-4*   Diagram of developing preantral follicles showing steps in the gonadotropin-independent stages of folliculogenesis from recruitment of a primordial follicle into the growing pool through its development to the early antrum or tertiary (cavitation) stage. (From Erickson GF: The ovary: Basic principles and concepts. In Felig P, Baxter JD, Frohman LA [eds]: Endocrinology and Metabolism, 3d ed. New York, McGraw-Hill, 1995, pp 973–1015.)

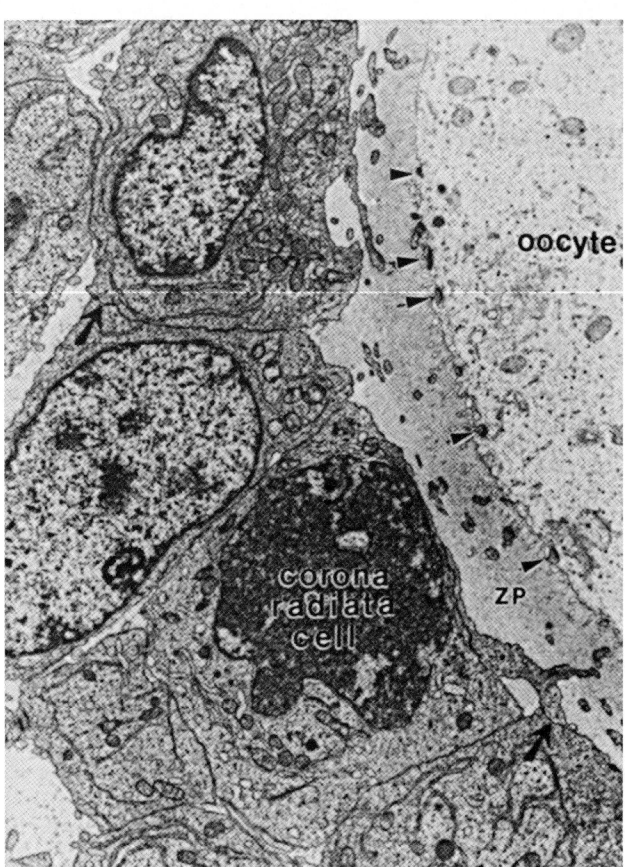

*Figure 150-5*   Electron micrograph of a portion of an oocyte-cumulus complex. Gap junctions (comprised of connexin 37) between the processes of corona radiata cells traversing the zona pellucida (ZP) and the oolemma are illustrated by *arrowheads*. Gap junctions between the corona granulosa cells are illustrated by *black arrows*. (From Gilula NB, Epstein ML, Beers WH: Cell-to-cell communication and ovulation: A study of the cumulus-oocyte complex. J Cell Biol 78:58–75, 1978.)

surface FSH receptors that can be identified using [125]I FSH autoradiography.[20] This is an important event because it allows the potential of the follicle to be stimulated by FSH signaling pathways. Although the process of FSH receptor expression is poorly understood in women, there is evidence in rodents that activin produced by the granulosa cells can increase FSH receptor expression by autocrine mechanisms.[5,21]

A second key event that occurs in the primary follicle (Fig. 150-5) is the development of gap junctions between the granulosa cells and the oocyte.[22] Gap junctions are formed by a family of proteins termed *connexins* (Cx).[23] Functionally, they allow for nonspecific transfer between cells of low-molecular-weight molecules, including the second messengers cyclic adenosine monophosphate (cAMP) and calcium.[22–24] Gap junctions between the granulosa cells consist of Cx43 and are expressed at the earliest stages of primary follicle development.[22] The gap junctions between the oocyte and surrounding granulosa cells are comprised of Cx37.[25] Importantly, Cx37-deficient female mice (Cx37 knockouts) lack mature (graafian) follicles, fail to ovulate, and develop numerous inappropriate corpora lutea.[25] Thus, the physiologically important interactions between the oocytes and granulosa cells via Cx37 channels are obligatory for normal folliculogenesis and fertility in mice.

A third event is the growth and differentiation of the oocyte in the primary follicle (see Figs. 150-2 and 150-4). Studies in rodents have demonstrated that the granulosa cells are essential to oocyte growth and development.[26,27] It seems likely that the Cx37 connections between the granulosa and oocyte allow for the exchange of nutrient and regulatory molecules that are required for proper oocyte function. Specifically, they evoke changes in oocyte metabolism that influence gene expression. One example is a marked increase in zona pellucida gene expression. As the oocyte grows, it synthesizes and secretes an extracellular matrix, the *zona pellucida* (ZP), which in time encapsulates the egg (see Figs. 150-2, 150-4, and 150-5). The importance of the ZP is demonstrated by the fact that it contains the species-specific receptor for capacitated sperm and provides a block to polyspermy.[28] The ZP consists of three glycoproteins designated ZP-1, ZP-2, and ZP-3.[29] ZP-3 is particularly important in sperm binding through its carbohydrate moiety.[30] Clinically, there is considerable interest in the development of immunocontraceptive vaccines based on the ZP-3 antigen.[31,32]

### Secondary Follicle

The secondary follicle consists of a fully grown oocyte surrounded by a complete zona pellucida, two to eight layers of cuboidal or columnar granulosa cells, and a presumptive theca layer immediately peripheral to the basal lamina (see Fig. 150-4). The acquisition of a theca layer is a major new feature of developing secondary follicles. The presumptive theca consists of several layers of elongated fibroblast-like cells that run radially around the entire follicle (see Fig. 150-2). Theca development is accompanied by *angiogenesis*. Consequently, the secondary follicle is exposed to important blood hormones such as FSH, LH, and insulin. The mechanisms of theca formation and angiogenesis during secondary follicle development are not clear[1]; however, it involves growth factors, including oocyte-derived *growth differentiation factor-9* (GDF-9).[33,34]

## ANTRAL OR GRAAFIAN FOLLICLES

During the late stages of growth in the secondary follicle, a clear fluid begins to accumulate between some granulosa cells. When the follicle reaches approximately 400 μm in diameter, the fluid coalesces into a crescentic space called the *antrum*.[35] By definition, the follicle is now a *tertiary* or *graafian follicle* (see Figs. 150-4 and 150-6). This process, termed *cavitation* or *beginning antrum formation*, results in the remodeling of the granulosa cells to form a miniature graafian follicle (see Fig. 150-6). Cavitation is gonadotropin-independent.[35] Precisely how the antrum forms is unknown, but direct evidence for a role of activin has been provided.[36]

Theca differentiation is an important step that occurs at cavitation. It is characterized by a change in which a subpopulation of theca cells becomes epithelial-like and acquires the ultrastructural and functional characteristics typical of active steroid-secreting cells.[1] This tissue is called the *theca interna*. As these changes occur, the cells, now called *theca interstitial* cells, express LH receptors.[1] At the periphery of the theca interna is a layer of concentrically arranged fusiform cells that have the ultrastructural and functional characteristics of smooth muscle cells.[35] They constitute the *theca externa* of the tertiary follicle (see Fig. 150-6).

By the time of cavitation, the oocyte has attained its full size (~120 μm in diameter) and appears fully developed structurally (see Fig. 150-6). Therefore, the oocyte does not grow further, despite the fact that the graafian follicle as a whole might continue to enlarge to a diameter of 2 cm or more.[37]

### Classification of Graafian Follicles

*Graafian follicles* can be defined structurally as a heterogeneous family of relatively large follicles (400 μm to >2 cm at ovulation) that display an antrum containing *follicular fluid*, or *liquor folliculi*. The antrum is a characteristic structural feature of all graafian follicles. As such, the term *antral follicle* is a synonym for graafian follicle.

In a broad sense, graafian follicles can be divided into two major groups: healthy and atretic (Fig. 150-7). The main difference between these two groups is whether or not *apoptosis*, or *programmed cell death*, is occurring in the granulosa cells. All graafian follicles (healthy or atretic) follow a progressive course during their development over time. The healthy graafian follicle becomes progressively larger and more differentiated with increasing time until it reaches the preovulatory stage (see Fig. 150-7). The mechanism by which a healthy graafian follicle is formed depends on pituitary gonadotropins and involves the differential and temporal pattern of expression of specific genes that lead to cytodifferentiation and proliferation of the follicle cells.[38] In a similar manner, the atretic or nondominant graafian follicles undergo a temporal pattern of expression of specific genes, which, in turn, results in the cessation of growth and the activation of apoptosis (see Fig. 150-7).

### Structure of the Graafian Follicle

A healthy graafian follicle is a complex tissue comprised of multiple layers of precisely positioned cells (Fig. 150-8). The *theca externa* is innervated by autonomic nerves that seem to play an active role in their contraction.[35,39] The full significance of the theca externa is not known, but the regulated contraction of these cells has been implicated in the processes of both ovulation and atresia.[35] In the *theca interna*, the number of differentiated theca interstitial cells increases progressively and their endocrine function is reflected in the large capillary plexus. It is not uncommon to have five to eight layers of theca interstitial cells in a graafian follicle.[1]

Internal to the theca is a basal lamina that functions as a barrier to vascular tissue, and multiple layers of granulosa cells that appear heterogeneous by virtue of their position within the follicle wall (Fig. 150-9). The position of the granulosa cells creates at least four different domains: (1) an outer or *membrana domain* comprised of a pseudostratified epithelium, which makes contact with the basal lamina; (2) an inner or *periantral domain*, which makes contact with the membrana cells; (3) the *cumulus domain*, which makes contact with the periantral cells; and (4) a *corona radiata domain*, which makes contact with the cumulus cells as well as the ZP and oocyte (see Fig. 150-9). By virtue of their position, the granulosa cells are directed to express different cellular functions in

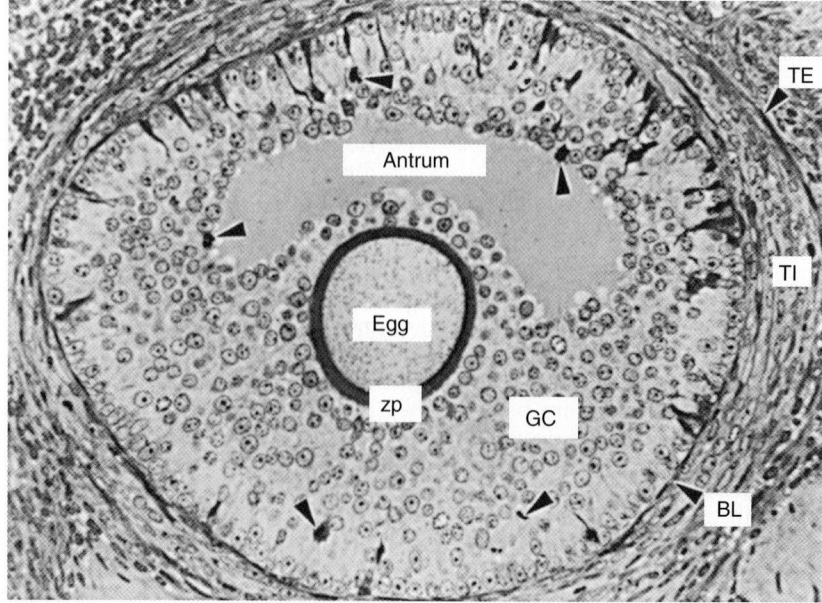

**Figure 150-6** Photomicrograph of a tertiary follicle approximately 400 μm in diameter at the time of cavitation or early antrum formation. It comprises a fully growing dictyate oocyte (egg) surrounded by a thick zona pellucida (zp); an antrum containing follicular fluid; multiple layers of granulosa cells (GC) organized morphologically into recognizable zones; a basal lamina (BL); a theca interna (TI); and a theca externa (TE). Note the presence of dividing GCs (*arrowheads*) and the presence of light and dark GCs, the physiologic significance of which is unknown. (From Bloom W, Fawcett DW [eds]: A Textbook of Histology. Philadelphia, WB Saunders, 1975, p 869.)

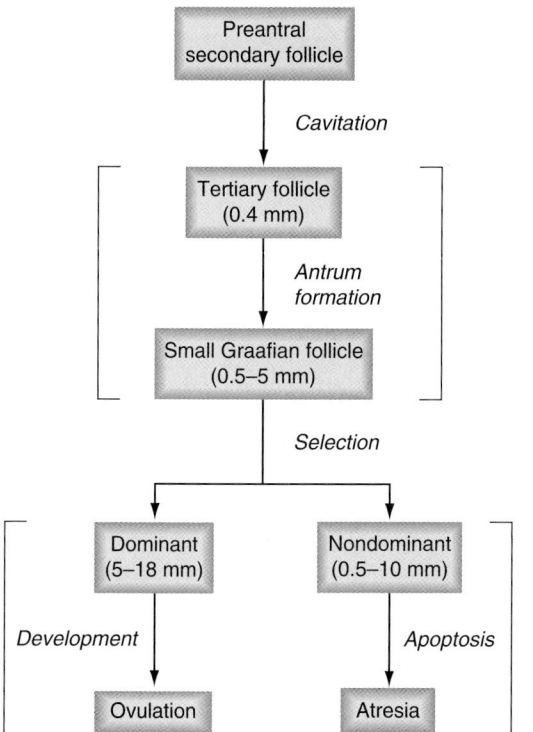

**Figure 150-7** Diagram of the major steps involved in the life cycle of a graafian follicle. (From Erickson GF: The graafian follicle: A functional definition. In Adashi EY (ed): Ovulation: Evolving Scientific and Clinical Concepts. New York, Springer-Verlag, 2000.)

preovulatory stages (18 to 23 mm). The size of a graafian follicle is determined largely by the size of the antrum, which, in turn, is determined by the volume of follicular fluid. The atretic follicle passes from the small to the medium stage, but, under physiologic conditions, an atretic follicle rarely reaches a size greater than 10 mm.[35]

### Chronology of Development

Folliculogenesis in women is a very long process.[7,40,41] In normal cycling women, the dominant follicle that will ovulate originates from a primordial follicle that was recruited to grow about 1 year earlier (Fig. 150-10). The preantral or gonadotropin-independent stage of folliculogenesis proceeds very slowly—a period taking 300 or more days to complete (see Fig. 150-10). The slow nature of the development of preantral follicles results from the long doubling time (~250 hours) of the granulosa cells.[40] The rate of follicle growth increases dramatically when follicular fluid begins to accumulate, and the healthy graafian follicle passes through the gonadotropin-dependent or antral phases (small, medium, and large) relatively rapidly, for example, in about 40 to 50 days (see Fig. 150-10).

### Selection of the Dominant Follicle

In normal women, it appears that the *dominant follicle* is selected from a cohort of small graafian follicles (see Fig. 150-10, the class 5 follicles). Once selected, it requires about 20 days to complete its growth and development to the preovulatory stage. It is important to note that the vast majority of graafian follicles die by atresia. Atresia can occur at any stage in the process, but generally is most frequent in the small and medium graafian follicles (see Fig. 150-10).

**The Process.**   Selection of the dominant follicle is a critical event in the ovarian cycle. In the human, the dominant follicle that will ovulate is believed to be selected from a cohort of healthy small graafian follicles (4.7 ± 0.7 mm) at the end of the luteal phase of the menstrual cycle.[7,40,41] The selected follicle is characterized by a high, sustained rate of mitosis during its maturation. Initially, there occurs a simulation of mitosis in all cohort small graafian follicles during the luteolytic period of the cycle, with the granulosa cells in all follicles showing a sharp increase (~twofold) in the rate of mitosis.[7,40,41] The first visible sign that one cohort follicle has been selected is that granulosa cell division continues at a rapid rate in the chosen follicle while the mitotic rate becomes low in nondominant follicles.[7,40] Since this distinction becomes apparent in the late luteal phase, it is argued that selection takes place at this stage in the cycle. The dominant follicle continues to show a high rate of mitosis and follicular fluid production throughout the follicular phase of the cycle (Fig. 150-11). Accordingly, the dominant follicle grows rapidly, reaching 6.9 ± 0.5 mm at days 1 to 5, 13.7 ± 1.2 mm

response to FSH stimulation.[33,34] For example, in the central domains (corona radiata, cumulus, periantral), the granulosa cells continue dividing throughout graafian follicle development, suggesting the cells might be stem cells. By contrast, the cells in the membrana domain become postmitotic and respond to FSH with the expression of their fully differentiated state (see Fig. 150-9). How such a heterogeneity of granulosa cells is generated and precisely what is accomplished by it are important questions, the answers to which remain largely unknown. Interestingly, however, the concept is emerging that morphogens produced by the oocyte function as novel determinants of granulosa proliferation and differentiation are responses to FSH stimulation.[33,34]

During the course of its development, the graafian follicle can be arbitrarily divided into four stages based on size.[35] The healthy human graafian follicle passes through small (1 to 6 mm), medium (7 to 11 mm), large (12 to 17 mm), and

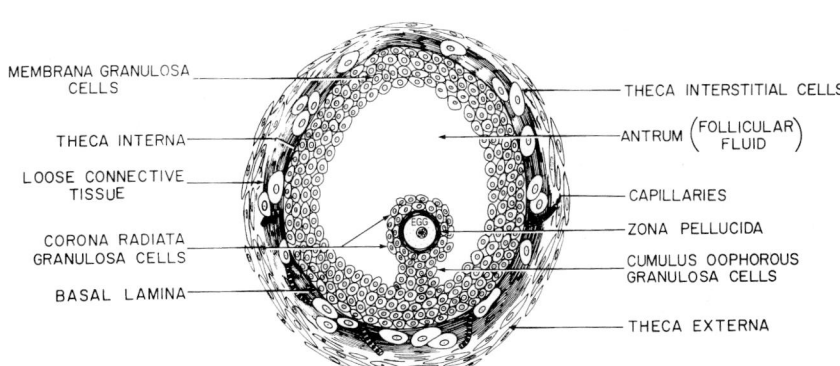

**Figure 150-8** Diagram of the cross-sectional appearance of a typical healthy graafian follicle showing the organization of its various cell types. (From Erickson GF: Primary cultures of ovarian cells in serum-free medium as models of hormone-dependent differentiation. Mol Cell Endocrinol 29:21–49, 1983.)

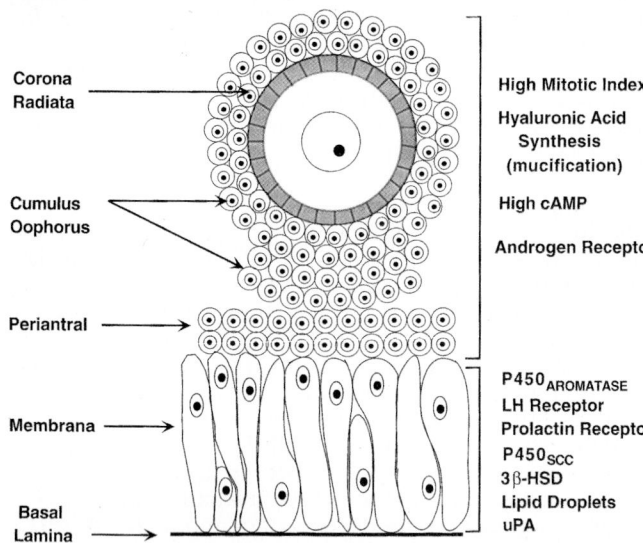

Corona Radiata

Cumulus Oophorus

Periantral

Membrana

Basal Lamina

High Mitotic Index

Hyaluronic Acid Synthesis (mucification)

High cAMP

Androgen Receptor

P450$_{AROMATASE}$
LH Receptor
Prolactin Receptor
P450$_{SCC}$
3β-HSD
Lipid Droplets
uPA

**Figure 150-9** Diagram of the structure-function heterogeneity of the granulosa cells in a healthy graafian follicle. By virtue of their position in the follicle wall, the granulosa cells become different from one another and this is reflected in different patterns of proliferation and differentiation. (From Erickson GF: The graafian follicle: A functional definition. In Adashi EY (ed). Ovulation: Evolving Scientific and Clinical Concepts. New York, Springer-Verlag, 2000.)

at days 6 to 10, and 18.8 ± 0.5 mm at days 11 to 14 of the cycle.

A fundamental question is how selection occurs. The secondary rise in plasma FSH is obligatory for, and the basis of, *dominant follicle selection*.[42] In women, plasma FSH begins to rise about the same time that plasma $P_4$ and $E_2$ levels fall to baseline levels at the end of the luteal phase (Fig. 150-12). The *secondary FSH rise* (the primary FSH rise being at midcycle) also occurs concomitantly with decreases in inhibin A emanating from the corpus luteum (see Fig. 150-12). The inverse relationship between plasma FSH and *inhibin A* (a known inhibitor of pituitary FSH secretion) could suggest an endocrine role for inhibin A in the regulation of the secondary FSH rise. By contrast, *inhibin B* increases before menses

coincident with the FSH rise. It is possible that elevated inhibin B levels emanating from the cohort follicles might play a role in suppressing the secondary FSH rise during the follicular phase (see Fig. 150-12).

One effect of the secondary FSH rise is a progressive increase in the concentration of FSH in the follicular fluid of the dominant follicle. Intriguingly, FSH levels become low or nondetectable in the follicular fluid of nondominant follicles.[43,44] How a dominant follicle sequesters FSH is not known. Nonetheless, when the concentration of FSH in the microenvironment reaches threshold levels, dominance is established and the chosen follicle becomes committed to develop along the ovulatory pathway. In the absence of threshold levels of FSH, the mitotic rate falls to low levels and the nondominant cohort follicles proceed along the atretic pathway. It should be mentioned that treating women with exogenous FSH can stimulate granulosa mitosis in nondominant follicles during the early follicular phase.[40] Thus, if the amount of FSH is elevated to threshold levels in nondominant follicles, they might be rescued from atresia. This could have implications for understanding how exogenous FSH provokes multiple ovulatory follicles in women undergoing ovulation induction.

**The Consequence.** The relatively high concentrations of FSH in the follicular fluid of the dominant follicle act on the granulosa cells to stimulate the expression of specific genes required for further development to the preovulatory stage. Three of the most intensively studied and best understood FSH-stimulated functions include: (1) the increasing synthesis of $E_2$; (2) the induction of receptors for $P_4$ and LH or human chorionic gonadotropin (hCG); and (3) the acquisition of the potential for synthesizing progesterone. The precise spatial and temporal pattern of expression of the genes that control these processes are critical for ovulation and luteinization.

*Cell Proliferation.* As development of the dominant follicle proceeds, the granulosa and theca cells show a high continual proliferative capacity (see Fig. 150-11). Although the physiologic mechanisms controlling granulosa cell proliferation remain poorly understood, it has been shown in vivo[7,40] and in vitro[44,45] that FSH can directly stimulate mitosis in human granulosa cells. Such observations support a model in which FSH signaling plays a fundamental role in stimulating mitosis in granulosa cells of human dominant follicles. There is also evidence from in vitro studies that fibroblast growth factor

**Figure 150-10** The chronology of folliculogenesis in normal human ovaries. The steps from primordial follicle recruitment, dominant follicle selection, and ovulation can be seen flanked by a time line. The follicles are labeled to indicate developmental stage, size, and the percentage in atresia. (From Gougeon A: Dynamics of follicular growth in the human: A model from preliminary results. Hum Reprod 2:81, 1986.)

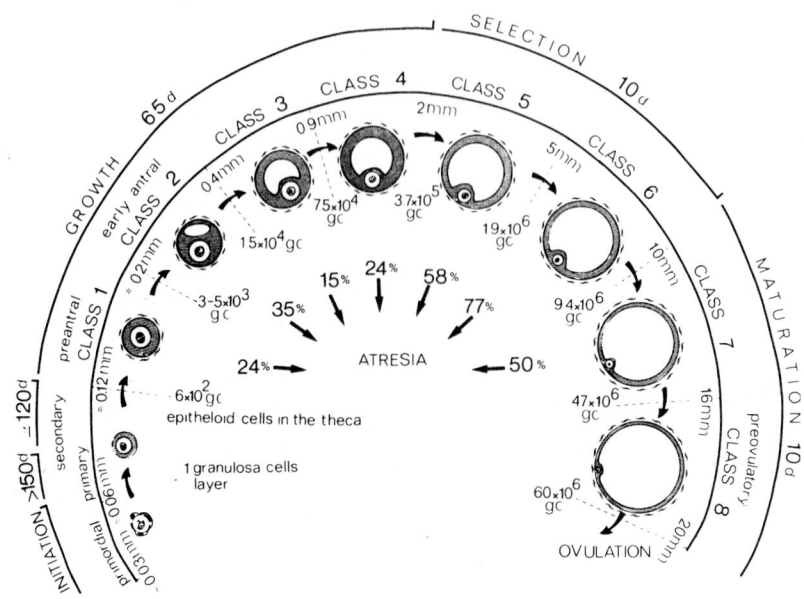

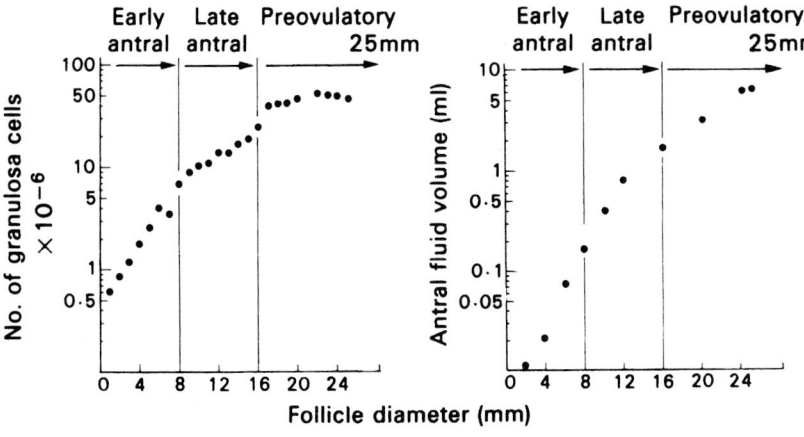

**Figure 150-11** Changes in the number of granulosa cells (*left panel*) and volume of follicular fluid (*right panel*) during the growth (diameter) of a healthy (dominant) human graafian follicle. (From McNatty KP: Hormonal correlates of follicular development in the human ovary. Aust J Biol Sci 34:249–268, 1981.)

and epidermal growth factor are potent stimulators of mitosis by mechanisms independent of FSH.[46] The physiologic relevance of these growth factors in human granulosa proliferation remains to be established. During the histogenesis of the dominant follicle, the number of theca interstitial and theca externa cells increases concurrently with the granulosa cells,[47,48] but the mechanisms and controls of theca mitosis are virtually unknown.

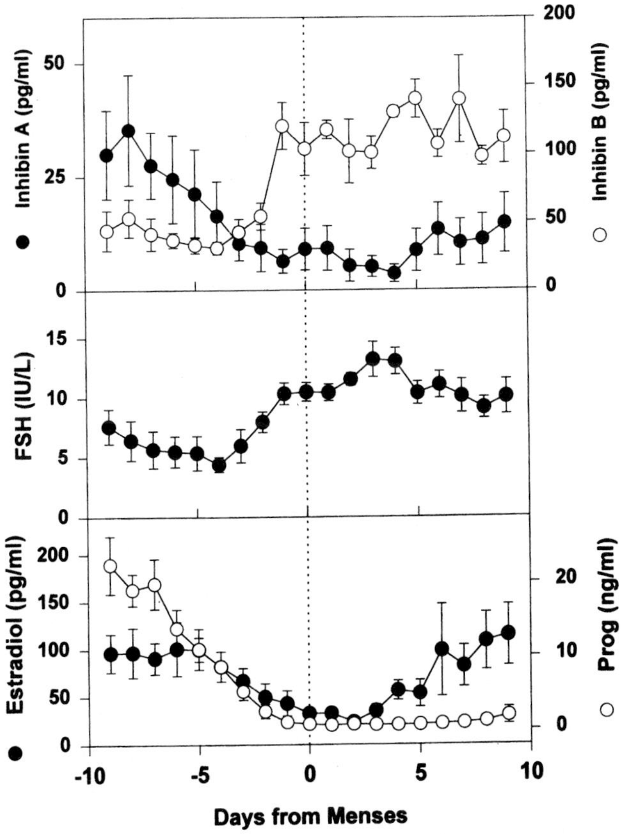

*Estradiol Synthesis.* An important event in dominant follicle development is the ability of FSH to elicit profound increases in P450arom gene expression in the granulosa cells. This is reflected in progressive increases of estradiol ($E_2$) production, which, in turn, is directly involved in the regulation of endometrial growth and the generation of the preovulatory surge of LH at midcycle. The cellular mechanism by which follicular $E_2$ is produced is called the *two-cell, two-gonadotropin concept for follicular estrogen biosynthesis* (Fig. 150-13). The synthesis of follicular $E_2$ requires two cell types (the theca

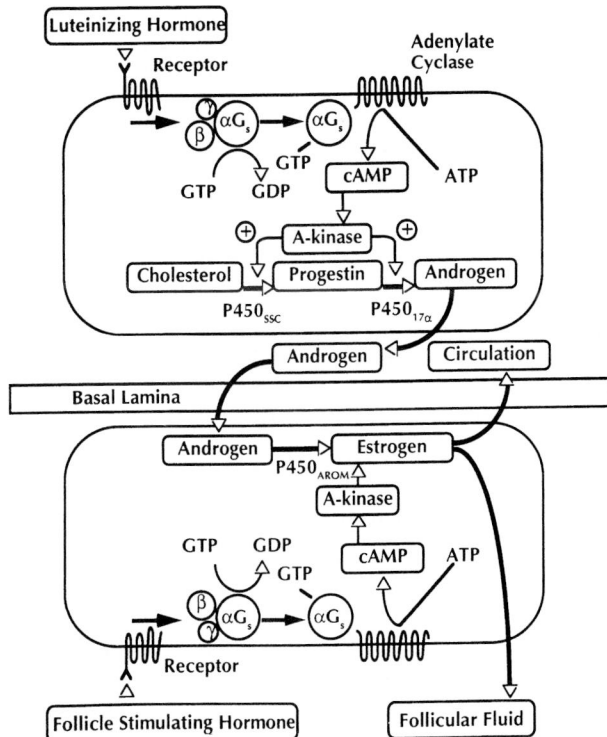

**Figure 150-13** Diagram of the two-cell, two-gonadotropin concept for follicular estradiol biosynthesis. G proteins include $G_s\alpha$, β, γ; A kinase or cyclic adenosine monophosphate (cAMP)-dependent protein kinase A. ATP, adenosine triphosphate; GDP, guanosine diphosphate; GTP, guanosine triphosphate. (From Kettel LM, Erickson GF: Basic and clinical concepts of ovulation induction. In Rock J, Alverez-Murphy A [eds]: Advances in Obstetrics and Gynecology. St Louis, Mosby–Year Book, 1994.)

**Figure 150-12** The secondary rise of plasma follicle-stimulating hormone (FSH) as it occurs in normal cycling women during the luteal-follicular transition. Data are mean ± SEM of daily FSH, estradiol, progesterone, inhibin A, and inhibin B levels in plasma of five normal cycling women. Data are centered to the day of menses. (From Welt CK, Martin KA, Taylor AE, et al: Frequency modulation of follicle-stimulating hormone [FSH] during the luteal-follicular transition: Evidence for FSH control of inhibin B in normal women. J Clin Endocrinol Metab 82:2645–2652, 1997; © 1997, The Endocrine Society.)

interstitial and granulosa cells) and two gonadotropins (FSH and LH).

The theca interstitial cells produce *androstenedione* (aromatase substrate) in response to LH stimulation.[49] When LH interacts with its transmembrane receptor, the binding event is transduced into an intracellular signal by means of the heterotrimeric G proteins. The LH-activated receptor is coupled to the Gα stimulatory ($G_s$α), adenylate cyclase, cAMP, protein kinase A (PKA) signal transduction pathway, which, in turn, is coupled to the differential activation of those genes encoding the steroidogenic enzymes in the androstenedione biosynthetic pathway. These regulatory proteins include steroidogenic acute regulatory protein (StAR), cytochrome P450 side-chain cleavage (P450c22), 3β-hydroxysteroid dehydrogenase (3β-HSD), and the P450 17α-hydroxylase and 17,20-lyase (P450c17). The end result is the production of high levels of androstenedione, which accumulates at very high concentrations in the follicular fluid. It is noteworthy that the androstenedione synthetic activity of the theca interstitial cells can be markedly stimulated by other regulatory proteins, including insulin, insulin-like growth factor 1 (IGF-1), activins, low-density lipoprotein (LDL), and high-density lipoprotein (HDL).[35,49] Although the functional significance of these regulatory molecules is poorly understood, it is notable that *hyperinsulinemia* in women with *polycystic ovary syndrome* (PCOS) is marked by *hyperandrogenism* and infertility.[50] Thus, although LH is clearly the most important stimulator of follicular androstenedione production, there are other proteins that can effect changes in theca androgen production, for better or for worse.

The granulosa cells are the only cell types known to express FSH receptors. It follows, therefore, that the FSH-mediated responses in the dominant follicle occur in the granulosa cells. Like LH, the FSH ligand interacts with a cell surface transmembrane receptor, which, when bound, activates the $G_s$α, adenylate cyclase, cAMP, PKA signaling pathway.[51] The activation of this FSH-dependent signaling mechanism (see Fig. 150-13) leads to the expression of specific genes that control the potential for estradiol production, namely, the expression of the P450 aromatase (P450arom)[52] and perhaps the type 1 17β-hydroxysteroid dehydrogenase (17β-HSD) genes.[53,54] By virtue of the presence of these key steroidogenic enzymes, the granulosa cells have the capacity to convert androstenedione to testosterone, which then is aromatized to estradiol by P450arom. The temporal pattern and level of expression of P450arom enzymes determine the time course and the level of $E_2$ produced by the dominant follicle during the follicular phase of the menstrual cycle.

*Induction of LH and Progesterone Receptors.* FSH receptor signals also elicit increases in LH receptor gene expression in the granulosa cells. As with P450arom, only the granulosa cells in the dominant follicle express the LH receptor gene; however, in contrast to the relatively early expression of P450arom, granulosa LH receptors are not expressed until late in the follicular phase of the cycle.[20,55] The LH receptors provide the granulosa cells in the dominant follicle with the capacity to respond to the midcycle surge of LH and undergo ovulation. An important event of this LH signaling in the granulosa cells is to induce the expression of $P_4$ receptors.[56,57] The induction of $P_4$ receptors by LH plays an obligatory role in the physiologic process of ovulation.[57] The general principle to emerge is that FSH induction of granulosa LH receptors plays an obligatory role in directing ovulation by formulating LH-dependent induction of progesterone receptors.

## ATRESIA

Of the 2 million or so primary oocytes present in the ovaries at birth (see Fig. 150-3), only about 400 will survive to be ovulated from a preovulatory follicle. Thus, 99.9% of the oocytes in the ovaries are destroyed by *apoptosis*, or *programmed cell death*.[58] The process of apoptosis is governed by the activation of a genetically controlled cell suicide program.[58] Studies over the past decade have highlighted pathways for directing the expression of proteins that are involved in both promoting and suppressing apoptosis in the ovary.[58–61] The current challenges are to identify how specific *atretogenic ligands* promote apoptosis and how these interactions are integrated into the overall pattern of folliculogenesis during the cycle. Notably, the ability of high concentrations of FSH to inhibit apoptosis in rodent granulosa cells[62] supports the concept that apoptosis in nondominant follicles may be causally connected to subthreshold levels of FSH in the microenvironment. Implicit in this idea is the concept that FSH not only exerts an inductive effect on granulosa cytodifferentiation, but also acts as a survival factor through its ability to inhibit the activation of apoptosis. Understanding the nature of FSH signaling pathways that control granulosa apoptosis and follicle atresia is a major goal of reproductive research.

## OVULATION

On or about the fifteenth day of an ideal 28-day cycle, the preovulatory follicle secretes the egg-cumulus complex by a process termed *ovulation* (Fig. 150-14). Normal ovulation requires the coordinate action of LH, FSH, and progesterone. How do these events occur?

During ovulation, the oocytes undergo *meiotic maturation*, or *resumption of meiosis*. This critically important change is evoked by the preovulatory surge of LH. Up to this point in folliculogenesis, the process of meiosis has been arrested. How meiosis is suppressed during folliculogenesis is poorly understood, but evidence suggests that the maintenance of high levels of intraoocyte cAMP is important. The cAMP appears to be provided by the granulosa cells through Cx37 gap junctions.[9,63] The preovulatory LH/FSH surge in some way causes

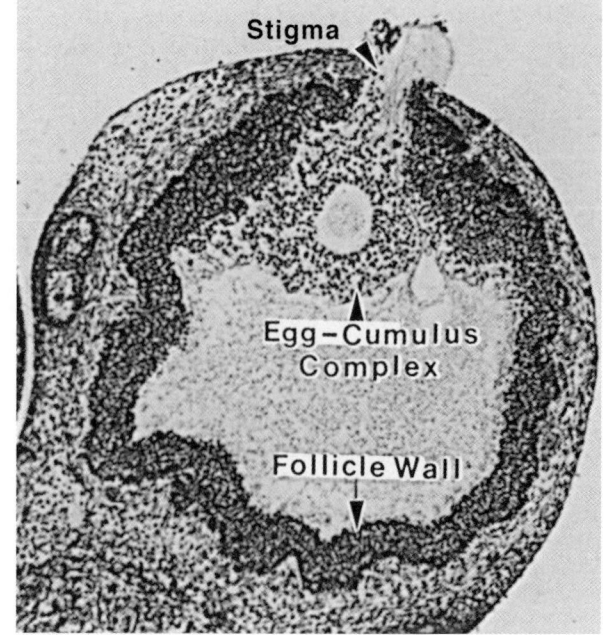

*Figure 150-14* Photomicrograph of ovulation in situ. (From Hartman CG, Leathem JH: Oogenesis and ovulation. In Conference on Physiological Mechanisms Concerned with Conception. New York, Pergamon, 1959.)

the level of cAMP in the oocyte to fall, perhaps by mechanisms involving *desensitization* and *downregulation* of the granulosa LH (and perhaps FSH) receptors. When this occurs, the oocyte resumes meiosis.[9] In the resulting division, the oocyte reaches the second meiotic metaphase, or *first polar body stage* (Fig. 150-15); the meiotic process proceeds no further unless the ovulated egg is fertilized. Concomitantly, the cumulus granulosa cells undergo a series of structure-function changes called *mucification* (see Fig. 150-14). In response to the preovulatory surge of FSH, the cumulus cells secrete large quantities of a glycoprotein mucous substance into the extracellular spaces; this change results in the dispersal of the cumulus cells and causes the egg-cumulus complex to expand tremendously.[9,63,64] The process of mucification is physiologically important because it is critical for transport and fertilization of the egg in the fallopian tube.

The actual secretion of the egg-cumulus complex is intimately coupled to the production of proteases[65] that degrade the ovarian tissues in a small highly localized area called the *macula pellucida*, or *stigma*. Animal studies have demonstrated that LH-stimulated $P_4$ and prostaglandin production by the follicle wall play an obligatory role in the expression of the proteolytic activities that occur during ovulation. The most compelling data come from gene knockout experiments showing that female mice lacking either the $P_4$ receptor[66] or the prostaglandin synthase gene (cyclooxygenase [COX-2],[67] the first rate-limiting enzyme in the biosynthesis of prostaglandins from arachidonic acid)[68] fail to ovulate and are infertile. Histologic studies of rodent preovulatory follicles treated with indomethacin (an inhibitor of prostaglandin production) indicate that the LH-induced prostaglandins are critical for stigma formation.

Based on these results, the following model has been constructed: The mid-cycle surge of LH stimulates the production of $P_4$; the $P_4$ ligand interacts with its receptor in the follicle cells, which, in turn, is responsible for the induction of prostaglandin synthase and prostaglandin production; the prostaglandins interact with specific receptors in the surface epithelial cells of the presumptive stigma; the prostaglandin receptor signaling causes the release of lysosomal (proteolytic) enzymes that degrade the underlying tissue; this ultimately results in stigma formation and follicle rupture (Fig. 150-16).

## LUTEOGENESIS

After ovulation, the follicle transforms into an endocrine organ, the *corpus luteum* (see Figs. 150-14 and 150-17). The theca interstitial and granulosa cells become the *theca lutein* and *granulosa lutein cells*, respectively. The corpus becomes richly vascularized, and serves as the site of $P_4$ and $E_2$ production during the luteal phase of the cycle. The major changes that occur during the life and death of the corpus luteum constitute the process called *luteogenesis*. Typically, this process is divided into two stages: luteinization and luteolysis. *Luteinization* begins shortly after the preovulatory LH surge, and full expression of the differentiated state of the lutein cells by the end of 1 week (day 21 or 22 of the cycle). If the egg is not fertilized, the corpus luteum of menstruation undergoes apoptosis,[69] a process termed *luteolysis*. The features of luteogenesis are reflected in the biphasic production of $P_4$, $E_2$, and inhibin A during the luteal phase of the cycle.

### LUTEINIZATION

LH is a central regulator of luteinization. In response to the preovulatory surge of LH, the genes encoding StAR, P450c22, 3β-HSD, and P450arom are expressed at high levels in the granulosa lutein cells. As such, the biochemical pathways that lead to the production of large amounts of $P_4$ and $E_2$ are induced in the corpus luteum by LH. Although mean plasma LH levels are low over the luteal phase, small amounts of LH are critical for proper corpus luteum function during luteinization.[70] It should be mentioned that luteinization is almost certainly more complex, and most certainly involves other regulatory molecules including LDL,[71] blood cells, and cytokines.[72] If fertilization and embryo implantation occur, the corpus luteum enlarges further to become a *corpus luteum of pregnancy*; it can persist for about 6 weeks, after which it declines in size and function. The hCG produced by the blastocyst is responsible for the development of the corpus luteum of pregnancy.

### LUTEOLYSIS

*Luteolysis*, or corpus luteum demise, is accompanied by the progressive expression of apoptosis in the lutein and vascular cells. During this process, there occurs a striking decrease in $P_4$ and $E_2$ production by the corpus luteum. Despite its great significance to female fertility, the physiologic mechanism governing luteolysis remain unknown. It is possible that prostaglandin $F_2\alpha$ is somehow involved, but its importance in women has yet to be proven.

## THE GROWTH FACTOR CONCEPT

It is clear that the ovarian cycle is governed by the combinational and sequential action of key hormones including FSH, LH, progesterone, androgen, estradiol, and insulin. Large scale cellular and mutational analyses have led to the identification of local signaling pathways in distinct groups of ovarian cells that can modulate, either amplifying or attenuating,

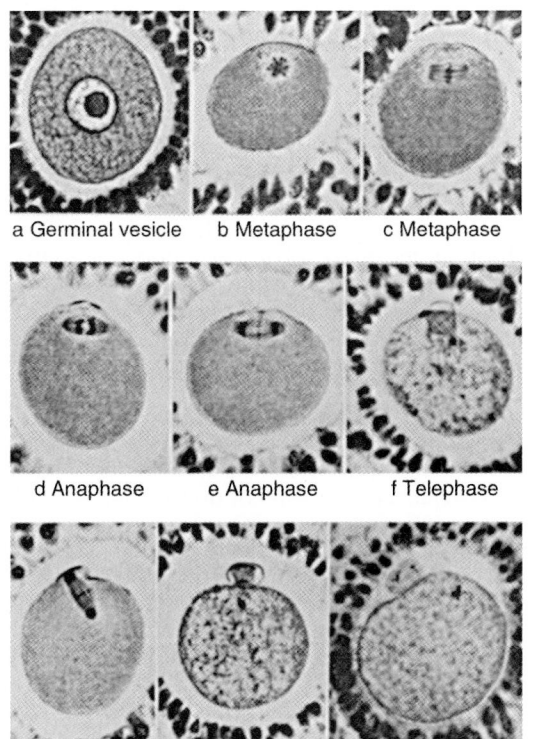

a Germinal vesicle    b Metaphase    c Metaphase

d Anaphase    e Anaphase    f Telephase

g Telephase    h Polar body    i Polar body

*Figure 150-15* Photomicrograph showing the stages of meiotic maturation of the oocyte following the resumption of meiosis in the dominant follicle. (From Witschi E: Development of Vertebrates. Philadelphia, WB Saunders, 1956.)

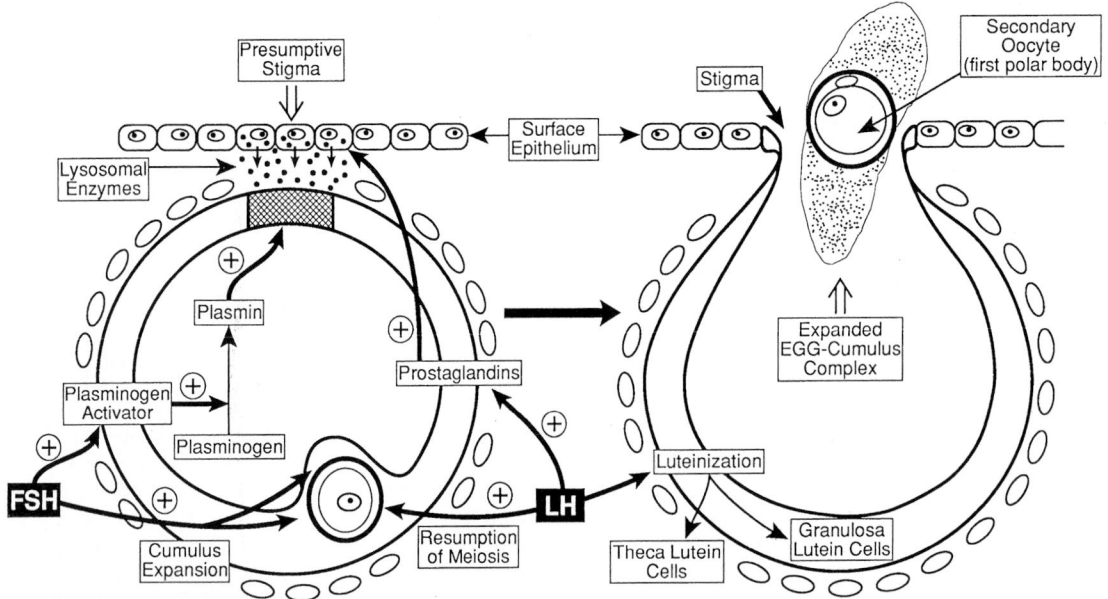

**Figure 150-16** A model illustrating the cellular activities involved in gonadotropin (follicle-stimulating hormone [FSH] and luteinizing hormone [LH])-induced ovulation. (From Erickson GF: The ovary: Basic principles and concepts. In Felig P, Baxter JD, Frohman LA [eds]: Endocrinology and Metabolism, 3d ed. New York, McGraw Hill, 1995, pp 973–1015.)

the hormone effects.[73] These local ligands, termed *growth factors*, are capable of interacting with receptors to activate signal transduction pathways that affect multifunctional responses, including cell proliferation, differentiation, and apoptosis. The most intensely and best studied ovarian growth factors include IGF,[74,75] transforming growth factor-β (TGF-β),[73,76] transforming growth factor-α (TGF-α) or epidermal growth factor (EGF),[7] fibroblast growth factor (FGF), and cytokines. Collectively, this work has led to the concept that the developmental programs of folliculogenesis, ovulation, and luteogenesis involve a precise spatial and temporal pattern of expression of members in these growth factor families. The current concept is that the expression patterns of these growth factors form a controlling network that ensures the proper sequences and timing of the developmental events evoked by key hormones such as FSH and LH. Indeed, genetic studies in animals have demonstrated that growth factor

signaling pathways play an obligatory role in folliculogenesis, ovulations, luteogenesis, and female fertility.

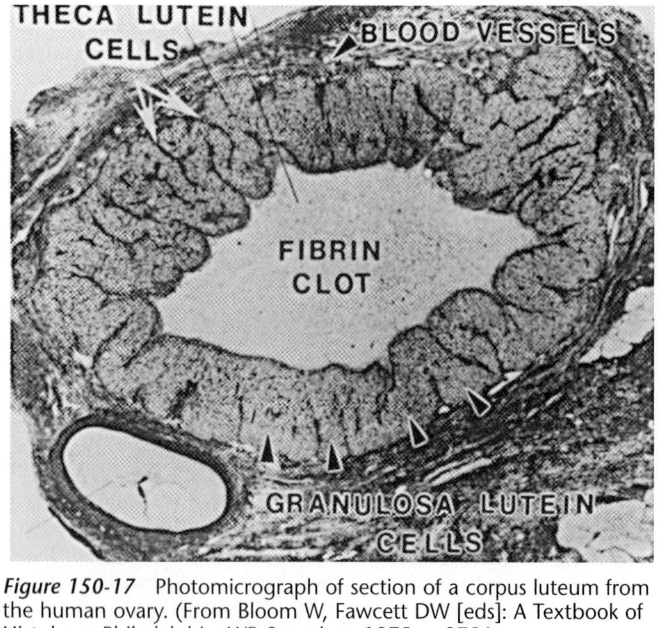

It is certainly important to note that growth factor research on the bone morphogenetic proteins (BMPs) has attracted the attention of reproductive biologists.[34] For example, BMP-15 and GDF-9 are oocyte-derived growth factors that act to control ovulation quota[77] by regulating mitosis and the supporting activities of FSH and LH. Therefore, there is a great excitement in the BMP field because animal studies have suggested that they are obligatory factors that control the hormone-dependent ovarian cycle. It is almost certain that growth factors play critical roles in directing the proliferation, differentiation, and death of cells in the human ovary; indeed, there is evidence suggesting aberrant GDF-9 expression in oocytes of women with PCOS.[78] It will be of great interest to find out how specific growth factor signaling pathways lead to activation of particular effector genes and ultimately to specific biological responses in the process of folliculogenesis, ovulation, and luteogenesis. Such investigations could have far reaching implications for understanding ovarian physiology, infertility, and pathophysiology including cancer.

## CONCLUSION

The developmental programs of folliculogenesis, ovulation, and luteogenesis form the basis of the ovarian cycle, which in turn forms the basis of the menstrual cycle and female fertility. These programs are dependent on the careful regulation of many cellular functions including mitosis, meiosis, differentiation, growth, and apoptosis. That reproductive and metabolic hormones play critical roles in directing the cellular functions is clear. However, recent studies have established the exciting new concept that the regulated expression of growth factor signaling pathways also plays an obligatory role in specifying ovarian cell fates through local autocrine/paracrine mechanisms. The emerging model is that ovarian growth factors are the controlling modulators that ensure the proper level, timing, and spatial pattern of the developmental programs evoked by hormones. The clinical significance and excitement of the growth factor concept is that it may prove to be a major new way of understanding and treating fertility and infertility in women.

**Figure 150-17** Photomicrograph of section of a corpus luteum from the human ovary. (From Bloom W, Fawcett DW [eds]: A Textbook of Histology. Philadelphia, WB Saunders, 1975, p 875.)

# REFERENCES

1. Erickson GF, Magoffin DA, Dyer CA, et al: The ovarian androgen producing cells: A review of structure/function relationships. Endocr Rev 6:371–399, 1985.

2. Reynolds SRM: The vasculature of the ovary and ovarian function. Recent Prog Horm Res 5:65, 1950.

3. Schultea TD, Dees WL, Ojeda SR: Postnatal development of sympathetic and sensory innervation of the rhesus monkey ovary. Biol Reprod 47:760–767, 1992.

4. Ohno S, Klinger HP, Atkin NB: Human oogenesis. Cytogenetics 1:42–51, 1962.

5. Erickson GF: Basic biology: Ovarian anatomy and physiology. In Lobo R, Marcus R, Kelsey J (eds): Menopause. San Diego, Academic, 2000, pp 13–32.

6. Gougeon A, Chainy GBN: Morphometric studies of small follicles in ovaries of women at different ages. J Reprod Fertil 81:433–442, 1987.

7. Gougeon A: Regulation of ovarian follicular development in primates: Facts and hypotheses. Endocr Rev 17:121–155, 1996.

8. Bachvarova R, De Leon V, Johnson A, et al: Changes in total RNA, polyadenylated RNA, and actin mRNA during meiotic maturation of mouse oocytes. Dev Biol 108:325–331, 1985.

9. Erickson GF: Analysis of follicle development and ovum maturation. Semin Reprod Endocrinol 4:233–254, 1986.

10. Fortune JE, Cushman RA, Wahl CM, et al: The primordial to primary follicle transition. Mol Cell Endocrinol 163:53–60, 2000.

11. McGee EA, Hsueh AJW: Initial and cyclic recruitment of ovarian follicles. Endocr Rev 21:200–214, 2000.

12. Lintern-Moore S, Moore GPM, Panaretto BA, et al: Follicular development in the neonatal mouse ovary: Effect of epidermal growth factor. Acta Endocrinol 96:123–126, 1981.

13. Durlinger ALL, Gruijters MJG, Kramer P, et al: Anti-Müllerian hormone inhibits initiation of primordial follicle growth in the mouse ovary. Endocrinology 143:1076–1084, 2002.

14. Parrott JA, Skinner MK: Kit-ligand/stem cell factor induces primordial follicle development and initiates folliculogenesis. Endocrinology 140:4262–4271, 1999.

15. Kezele PR, Nilsson EE, Skinner MK: Insulin but not insulin-like growth factor-1 promotes the primordial to primary follicle transition. Mol Cell Endocrinol 192:37–43, 2002.

16. Vendola K, Zhou J, Wang J, et al: Androgens promote oocyte insulin-like growth factor 1 expression and initiation of follicle development in the primate ovary. Biol Reprod 61:353–357, 1999.

17. Lee W, Otsuka F, Moore RK, et al: The effect of bone morphogenetic protein-7 on folliculogenesis and ovulation in the rat. Biol Reprod 65:994–999, 2001.

18. Lintern-Moore S, Everitt AV: The effect of restricted food intake on the size and composition of the ovarian follicle population in the Wistar rat. Biol Reprod 19:688–691, 1978.

19. Oktay K, Briggs D, Gosden RG: Ontogeny of follicle-stimulating hormone receptor gene expression in isolated human ovarian follicles. J Clin Endocrinol Metab 82:3748–3751, 1997.

20. Yamoto M, Shima K, Nakano R: Gonadotropin receptors in human ovarian follicles and corpora lutea throughout the menstrual cycle. Horm Res 37(Suppl 1):5–11, 1992.

21. Nakamura M, Minegishi T, Hasegawa Y, et al: Effect of an activin A on follicle-stimulating hormone (FSH) receptor messenger ribonucleic acid levels and FSH receptor expressions in cultured rat granulosa cells. Endocrinology 133:538–544, 1993.

22. Grazul-Bilska AT, Reynolds LP, Redmer DA: Gap junctions in the ovaries. Biol Reprod 57:947–957, 1997.

23. Bruzzone R, White TW, Paul DL: Connections with connexins: The molecular basis of direct intercellular signaling. Eur J Biochem 238:1–27, 1996.

24. Kumar NM, Gilula NB: The gap junction communication channel. Cell 84:381–388, 1996.

25. Simon AM, Goodenough DA, Li E, et al: Female infertility in mice lacking connexin 37. Nature 385:525–529, 1997.

26. Heller DT, Cahill DM, Schultz RM: Biochemical studies of mammalian oogenesis: Metabolic cooperativity between granulosa cells and growing mouse oocytes. Dev Biol 84:455–464, 1981.

27. Brower PT, Schultz RM: Intercellular communication between granulosa cells and mouse oocytes: existence and possible nutritional role during oocyte growth. Dev Biol 90:144–153, 1982.

28. Wassarman PM: The biology and chemistry of fertilization. Science 235:553–560, 1987.

29. Moos J, Faundes D, Kopf GS, et al: Composition of the human zona pellucida and modifications following fertilization. Hum Reprod 10:2467–2471, 1995.

30. Gong X, Dubois DH, Miller DJ, et al: Activation of a G protein complex by aggregation of a-1,4-galactosyltransferase on the surface of sperm. Science 269:1718–1721, 1995.

31. Tesarik J: Targeting the zona pellucida for immunocontraception: A minireview. Hum Reprod 10(Suppl 2):132–139, 1995.

32. Skinner SM, Prasad SV, Ndolo TM, et al: Zona pellucida antigens: Targets for contraceptive vaccines. Am J Reprod Immunol 35:163–174, 1996.

33. Erickson GF, Shimasaki S: The role of the oocyte in folliculogenesis. Trends Endocrinol Metab 11:193–198, 2000.

34. Shimasaki S, Moore RK, Otsuka F, et al: The bone morphogenetic protein system in mammalian reproduction. Endocr Rev, 2004 (in press).

35. Erickson GF: The graafian follicle: A functional definition. In Adashi EY (ed): Ovulation: Evolving Scientific and Clinical Concepts. New York, Springer-Verlag, 2000, pp 31–48.

36. Li R, Phillips DM, Mather JP: Activin promotes ovarian follicle development in vitro. Endocrinology 136:849–856, 1995.

37. Green SH, Zuckerman S: Quantitative aspects of the growth of the human ovum and follicle. J Anat 85:373, 1951.

38. Richards JS: Hormonal control of gene expression in the ovary. Endocr Rev 15:725–751, 1994.

39. Erickson GF: The ovary: Basic principles and concepts. In Felig P, Baxter JD, Frohman LA (eds): Endocrinology and Metabolism, 3d ed. New York, McGraw-Hill, 1995, pp 973–1015.

40. Gougeon A: Dynamics of follicular growth in the human: A model from preliminary results. Hum Reprod 1:81–87, 1986.

41. Gougeon A, Lefèvre B: Evolution of the diameters of the largest healthy and atretic follicles during the human menstrual cycle. J Reprod Fertil 69:497–502, 1983.

42. Zeleznik AJ: Dynamics of primate follicular growth: A physiologic perspective. In Adashi EY, Leung PCK (eds): The Ovary. New York, Raven, 1993, pp 41.

43. McNatty KP, Hunter WM, McNeilly AS, et al: Changes in the concentration of pituitary and steroid hormones in the follicular fluid of human graafian follicles throughout the menstrual cycle. J Endocrinol 64:555–571, 1975.

44. McNatty KP, Sawers RS: Relationship between the endocrine environment within the graafian follicle and the subsequent rate of progesterone secretion by human granulosa cells in vitro. J Endocrinol 66:391–400, 1975.

45. Yong EL, Baird DT, Hillier SG: Mediation of gonadotrophin-stimulated growth and differentiation of human granulosa cells by adenosine-3′,5′-monophosphate: One molecule, two messages. Clin Endocrinol 37:51–58, 1992.

46. Gospodarowicz D, Bialecki H: Fibroblast and epidermal growth factors are mitogenic agents for cultured granulosa cells of rodent, porcine, and human origin. Endocrinology 104:757–764, 1979.

47. McNatty KP, Moore-Smith D, Osathanondh R, et al: The human antral follicle: Functional correlates of growth and atresia. Ann Biol Anim Biochem Biophys 19:1547–1558, 1979.

48. McNatty KP: Hormonal correlates of follicular development in the human ovary. Aust J Biol Sci 34:249–268, 1981.

49. Erickson GF: Ovarian androgen biosynthesis: Endocrine regulation. In Azziz R, Nestler JE, Dewailly D (eds): Androgen Excess Disorders in Women, Lippincott-Raven, 1997, pp 3–11.

50. Franks S: Polycystic ovary syndrome. N Engl J Med 333:853–861, 1995.

51. Simoni M, Gromoll J, Nieschlag E: The follicle-stimulating hormone receptor: Biochemistry, molecular biology, physiology, and pathophysiology. Endocr Rev 18:739–773, 1997.

52. Suzuki T, Sasano H, Tamura M, et al: Temporal and spatial localization of steroidogenic enzymes in premenopausal human ovaries: In situ hybridization and immunohistochemical study. Mol Cell Endocrinol 97:135–143, 1993.

53. Sawetawan C, Milewich L, Word RA, et al: Compartmentalization of type I 17 a-hydroxysteroid oxidoreductase in the human ovary. Mol Cell Endocrinol 99:161–168, 1994.

54. Ghersevich SA, Poutanen MH, Martikainen HK, et al: Expression of 17 a-hydroxysteroid dehydrogenase in human granulosa cells: Correlation with follicular size, cytochrome P450 aromatase activity and oestradiol production. J Endocrinol 143:139–150, 1994.

55. Minegishi T, Tano M, Abe Y, et al: Expression of luteinizing hormone/human chorionic gonadotrophin (LH/HCG) receptor mRNA in the human ovary. Mol Hum Reprod 3:101–107, 1997.

56. Suzuki T, Sasano H, Kimura N, et al: Immunohistochemical distribution of progesterone, androgen and oestrogen receptors in the human ovary during the menstrual cycle: Relationship to expression of steroidogenic enzymes. Hum Reprod 9:1589–1595, 1994.

57. Graham JD, Clarke CL: Physiological action of progesterone in target tissues. Endocr Rev 18:502–519, 1997.

58. Erickson GF: Defining apoptosis: Players and systems. J Soc Gynecol Investig 4:219–228, 1997.

59. Hsueh AJ, Billig H, Tsafriri A: Ovarian follicle atresia: A hormonally controlled apoptotic process. Endocr Rev 15:707–724, 1994.

60. Tilly JL: Apoptosis and ovarian function. Rev Reprod 1:162–172, 1996.

61. Tilly JL: Apoptosis and the ovary: A fashionable trend or food for thought? Fertil Steril 67:226–228, 1997.

62. Chun SY, Billig H, Tilly JL, et al: Gonadotropin suppression of apoptosis in cultured preovulatory follicles: Mediatory role of endogenous insulin-like growth factor-I. Endocrinology 135:1845–1853, 1994.

63. Eppig JJ: Regulation of mammalian oocyte maturation. In Adashi EY, Leung PCK (eds): The Ovary. New York, Raven, 1993, pp 185.

64. Eppig JJ: Oocyte-somatic cell communication in the ovarian follicles of mammals. Semin Dev Biol 5:51–59, 1994.

65. Tsafriri A, Chun SY, Reich R: Follicular rupture and ovulation. In Adashi EY, Leung PCK (eds): The Ovary. New York, Raven, 1993, pp 227.

66. Lydon JP, DeMayo FJ, Funk CR, et al: Mice lacking progesterone receptor exhibit pleiotropic reproductive abnormalities. Genes Dev 9:2266–2278, 1995.

67. Lim H, Paria BC, Das SK, et al: Multiple female reproductive failures in cyclooxygenase 2-deficient mice. Cell 91:197–208, 1997.

68. Herschman HR: Prostaglandin synthase 2. Biochim Biophys Acta 1299:125–140, 1996.

69. Shikone T, Yamoto M, Kokawa K, et al: Apoptosis of human corpora lutea during cyclic luteal regression and early pregnancy. J Clin Endocrinol Metab 81:2376–2380, 1996.

70. Vande Wiele RL, Bogumil J, Dyrenfurth I, et al: Mechanisms regulating the menstrual cycle in women. Recent Prog Horm Res 26:63–103, 1970.

71. Carr BR, MacDonald PC, Simpson ER: The role of lipoproteins in the regulation of progesterone secretion by the human corpus luteum. Fertil Steril 38:303–311, 1982.

72. Brännström M, Norman RJ: Involvement of leukocytes and cytokines in the ovulatory process and corpus luteum function. Hum Reprod 8:1762–1775, 1993.

73. Chang H, Brown CW, Matzuk MM: Genetic analysis of the mammalian transforming growth factor-a superfamily. Endocr Rev 23:787–823, 2002.

74. Poretsky L, Cataldo NA, Rosenwaks Z, et al: The insulin-related ovarian regulatory system in health and disease. Endocr Rev 20:535–582, 1999.

75. Monget P, Fabre S, Mulsant P, et al: Regulation of ovarian folliculogenesis by IGF and BMP system in domestic animals. Domest Anim Endocrinol 23:139–154, 2002.

76. Matzuk MM, Kumar TR, Shou W, et al: Transgenic models to study the roles of inhibins and activins in reproduction, oncogenesis, and development. Recent Prog Horm Res 51:123–157, 1996.

77. Juengel JL, Hudson NL, Heath DA, et al: Growth differentiation factor-9 and bone morphogenetic protein 15 are essential for ovarian follicular development in sheep. Biol Reprod 67:1777–1789, 2002.

78. Teixeira Filho FL, Baracat EC, Lee TH, et al: Aberrant expression of growth differentiation factor-9 in oocytes of women with polycystic ovary syndrome. J Clin Endocrinol Metab 87:1337–1344, 2002.

# Ovarian Hormone Synthesis

## Clement K. M. Ho and Jerome F. Strauss III

## INTRODUCTION

Ovarian hormones can be divided into two groups according to their chemical nature: (1) lipids, including steroids and prostaglandins; and (2) peptide hormones. In the ovary, germ cell production and hormone synthesis take place in the same functional unit, the follicle, which consists of an outer layer of theca cells encircling inner layers of granulosa cells, which, in turn, surround the oocyte. The androgen-producing theca cells and the estrogen-secreting granulosa cells respond to the pituitary gonadotropins luteinizing hormone (LH) and follicle-stimulating hormone (FSH), respectively. During the final stage of follicle maturation, LH receptors are also expressed on granulosa cells, and the preovulatory LH surge acts on both granulosa and theca cells of the graafian follicle to induce ovulation. Locally produced growth factors and cytokines, as well as the sex steroids produced by the ovarian cells, amplify or attenuate the actions of gonadotropins. Together, these factors participate in the intricate dialogue among the oocyte, granulosa cells, theca cells, and the adjacent stroma to coordinate growth and maturation of the follicle and oocyte.

Before puberty, the human ovary is relatively quiescent in terms of steroidogenesis despite the presence of significant levels of gonadotropins during fetal life and early infancy. The factors that restrain ovarian sex steroid secretion during these times include the relative absence of expression of LH receptors. Gonadarche, the first evidence of substantial ovarian function in response to rising pituitary gonadotropin secretion at puberty, heralds the transition into the reproductive years. During this reproductive stage of life, some 400 to 500 follicles complete the full developmental cycle. Under the influence of cyclical gonadotropin stimulation, the selected follicle elaborates substantial amounts of estradiol, which ultimately triggers the preovulatory LH surge and subsequently the transformation of the follicle into a corpus luteum. The majority (>99%) of ovarian follicles never reach the preovulatory stage due in part to a lack of appropriate FSH stimulation. When follicular units are depleted as a consequence of this unrelenting process of atresia, the ovarian capacity to synthesize estradiol is lost and the residual hilar and corticostromal cells are the only sources of ovarian steroids.

## OVERVIEW OF OVARIAN STEROID HORMONE SYNTHESIS

The human ovary produces three main classes of steroid hormones, namely, C-18 estrogens, C-19 androgens, and C-21 progestins. Enzymes involved in steroid biosynthesis and metabolism can be classified into two broad groups: the cytochrome P-450s and the oxidoreductases. Cytochrome P-450s are heme-containing proteins with a characteristic light absorption maximum at 450 nm in the presence of carbon monoxide. The second main group of steroid-metabolizing enzymes, oxidoreductases, can be further divided into two families based on their structures and functions, namely, short-chain dehydrogenase/reductase (SDR) and aldo-keto reductase (AKR) families.[1,2] SDRs belong to a highly divergent group of proteins including 3β-hydroxysteroid dehydrogenase (3β-HSD) types 1 and 2, and most of the known 17β-HSDs. Of the AKR family, 17β-HSD type 5 is expressed in the ovary and considered essential for androgen production.

The rate of production of steroid hormones is determined largely by the delivery of cholesterol to the first enzyme in the steroidogenic pathway, cytochrome P-450 side-chain cleavage enzyme (P-450scc, encoded by *CYP11A*), and also by the levels and activities of this and other enzymes that catalyze subsequent biosynthetic steps.[3,4] Gonadotropins acutely increase ovarian steroid synthesis by stimulating cholesterol transport to P-450scc and, in the longer term, control the content of the steroidogenic machinery, mainly by stimulating transcription of the genes encoding steroidogenic enzymes. These acute and long-term changes are primarily initiated by a cAMP (cyclic adenosine monophosphate)-mediated signaling system.[4,5] Emerging evidence suggests, however, that FSH regulates expression of steroidogenic enzymes such as aromatase in granulosa cells via an alternative intracellular signaling system controlled by Akt/protein kinase B.[6]

## ACQUISITION OF CHOLESTEROL

Ovarian cells, like other steroidogenic cells, acquire cholesterol either by de novo synthesis or by the uptake of lipoprotein-carried cholesterol. The trophic hormones that stimulate steroidogenesis generally increase both cellular cholesterol synthesis and lipoprotein uptake. Lipoprotein-associated cholesterol and cholesterol esters enter steroidogenic cells by two receptor-mediated pathways, the low-density lipoprotein (LDL) and the high-density lipoprotein (HDL) pathways (Fig. 151-1). Human steroidogenic cells are enriched with LDL receptors. These receptors mediate lipoprotein and cholesterol uptake by an endocytic mechanism that delivers the endocytosed contents to the lysosomal compartment, where the apolipoproteins are degraded and the lipoprotein-associated cholesterol esters are hydrolyzed by lysosomal acid lipase. Stimulation of steroidogenic cells by trophic hormones increases the number of LDL receptors and also accelerates the rate of LDL internalization and degradation. HDLs mediate cholesterol uptake by a process different from the "LDL pathway."[7,8] HDL particles bind to scavenger receptors (e.g., SR-BI and its human counterparts CD36 and CLA-1), which have broad ligand specificity, recognizing HDL apolipoproteins as well as lipids.[9] HDL-binding scavenger receptors are highly expressed in steroidogenic organs including the ovary. HDL cholesterol esters are selectively internalized, leaving the apolipoproteins on the cell surface.[7,9] Existing evidence indicates that the internalized HDL cholesterol esters are not cleaved by lysosomal acid lipase and that other sterol esterases release free cholesterol from esters; these include the cytosolic neutral cholesterol ester hydrolase (NCEH) and carboxyl ester lipase.[10,11] The itineraries of this HDL-derived

cholesterol, as well as free cholesterol generated in lysosomes from the hydrolysis of LDL-delivered cholesterol esters, remain obscure.

Active steroidogenic glands accumulate the majority of their cholesterol from lipoproteins. The quantitative importance of circulating cholesterol as a hormone precursor is demonstrated by the fact that radiolabeled plasma cholesterol in humans is almost fully equilibrated with the steroidogenic pool of cholesterol.[12] The access of lipoproteins to certain ovarian cells may affect their ability to synthesize hormones. A partial blood-follicle barrier excludes high molecular weight substances including LDL from the follicular antrum.[7] Thus, LDL cannot reach the granulosa cells until after the preovulatory surge of LH initiates breakdown of the follicular wall and vascularization of the developing corpus luteum.

A characteristic feature of steroidogenic cells is the presence of numerous cytoplasmic lipid droplets containing cholesterol esters.[13] Sterol esters in these droplets are synthesized by acyl coenzyme A: cholesterol acyltransferase type 1 (ACAT-1), an endoplasmic reticulum enzyme.[14] The esters generated by ACAT-1 accumulate within the endoplasmic reticulum membranes and subsequently bud off as lipid droplets. The sterol esters in lipid droplets are hydrolyzed by the soluble NCEH (see Fig. 151-1). Gonadotropin stimulation of cAMP-dependent protein kinase activates NCEH by phosphorylation of its serine residues, thus promoting the association of the enzyme to perilipins, proteins, coating lipid droplets, and the hydrolysis of the lipid droplet sterol esters.[15] The size and the number of lipid droplets change as the ester pool expands or contracts. Cellular cholesterol ester storage is dependent on the acquisition of cholesterol by de novo synthesis or accumulation of lipoprotein-carried cholesterol, on the one hand, and cholesterol depletion through steroidogenic activity of the cell, on the other.[16] Trophic stimulation promotes cholesterol ester hydrolysis and diverts cholesterol into the steroidogenic pool away from ACAT-1, preventing reesterification and resulting in a net depletion of cholesterol from the lipid droplets.

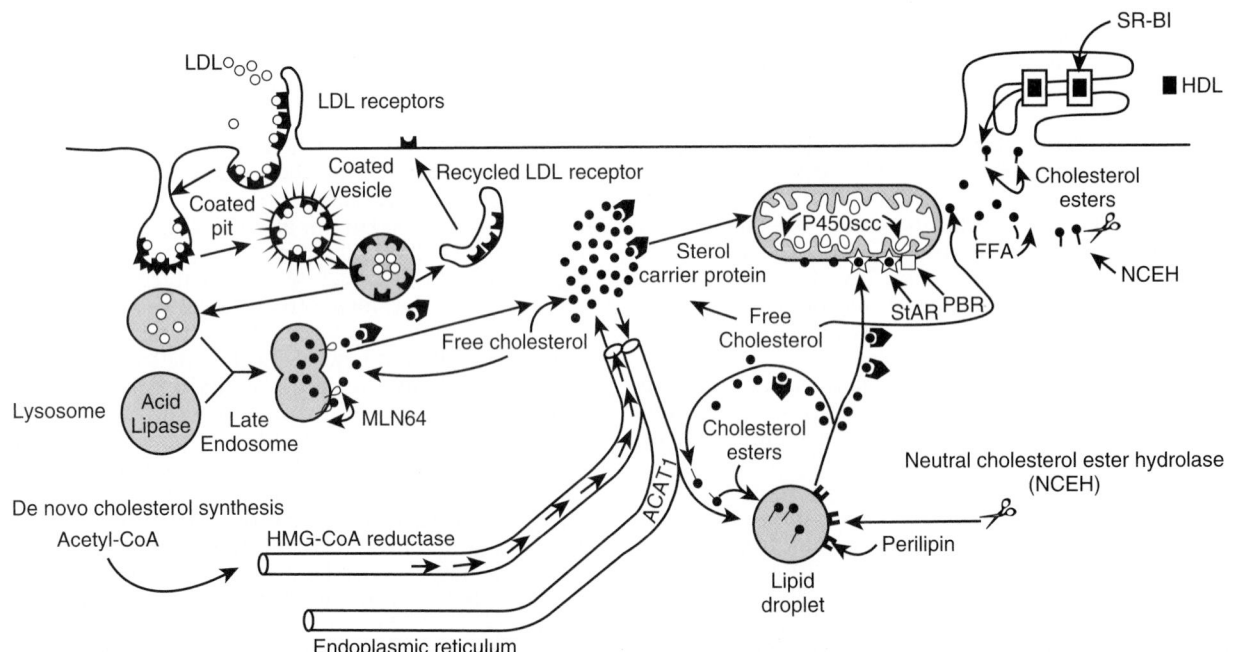

*Figure 151-1* The acquisition, storage, and trafficking of cholesterol in steroidogenic cells. ACAT-1, acyl coenzyme cholesterol acyltransferase type 1; FFA, free fatty acid; HDL, high-density lipoprotein; HMG-CoA, 3-hydroxy-3-methylglutaryl-coenzyme A; LDL, low-density lipoprotein; NCEH, neutral cholesterol ester hydrolase; P-450scc, cholesterol side-chain cleavage enzyme; MLN64, a StAR-related lipid transfer protein; PBR, peripheral benzodiazepine receptor; SR-BI, HDL receptor; StAR, steroidogenic acute regulatory protein.

## THE CHOLESTEROL SIDE-CHAIN CLEAVAGE REACTION

The cholesterol side-chain cleavage reaction is the first committed step as well as the rate-limiting process in steroid hormone synthesis.[17] This reaction takes place on the inner mitochondrial membranes, catalyzed by P-450scc (Fig. 151-2) and its associated electron transport system consisting of a flavoprotein reductase (ferredoxin or adrenodoxin reductase) and an iron sulfoprotein (ferredoxin or adrenodoxin). The dissociation constant ($K_d$) for binding of cholesterol is about 5000 nM, whereas P-450scc's affinities for the intermediate substrates (22R) 22-hydroxycholesterol and (20R, 22R) 20,22-dihydroxycholesterol are more than 60-fold higher ($K_d$ = 4.9 and 81 nM, respectively). Thus, once cholesterol is bound to the enzyme, it is committed to completing the reaction sequence. The estimated $K_d$ for pregnenolone is 2900 nM, which permits the dissociation of the final reaction product from the enzyme.

The rate of formation of pregnenolone is determined by multiple factors: (1) the delivery of cholesterol to the mitochondria; (2) the access of cholesterol to the inner mitochondrial membranes; (3) the amount of cholesterol side-chain cleavage enzyme, and secondarily its flavoprotein and iron-sul-

fur protein electron transport chain; and (4) the catalytic activity of P-450scc. Acute alterations in steroidogenesis generally result from changes in the delivery of cholesterol to P-450scc, whereas long-term alterations involve changes in the quantities of enzyme proteins as well as cholesterol delivery.

The mechanisms involved in the transport of cholesterol from various substrate pools including lipid droplets and the plasma membrane to the mitochondria remain unclear. However, it is the translocation of cholesterol deposited in the outer mitochondrial membranes to the relatively sterol-poor inner mitochondrial membranes that is the critical step in the cholesterol side-chain cleavage process. The steroidogenic acute regulatory protein (StAR), a protein with a short biological half-life, appears to play a pivotal role in this translocation process.[18,19] Human StAR is synthesized in the cytoplasm as a preprotein containing an amino-terminal leader sequence that directs StAR to mitochondria. After entering into the mitochondria, the leader sequence is cleaved to yield the 30 kiloDaltons (kDa) mature form of the protein. Phosphorylation is believed to be the mechanism by which preexisting or newly synthesized StAR can be rapidly activated. StAR contains several consensus sequences for cAMP-dependent protein kinase phosphorylation and experi-

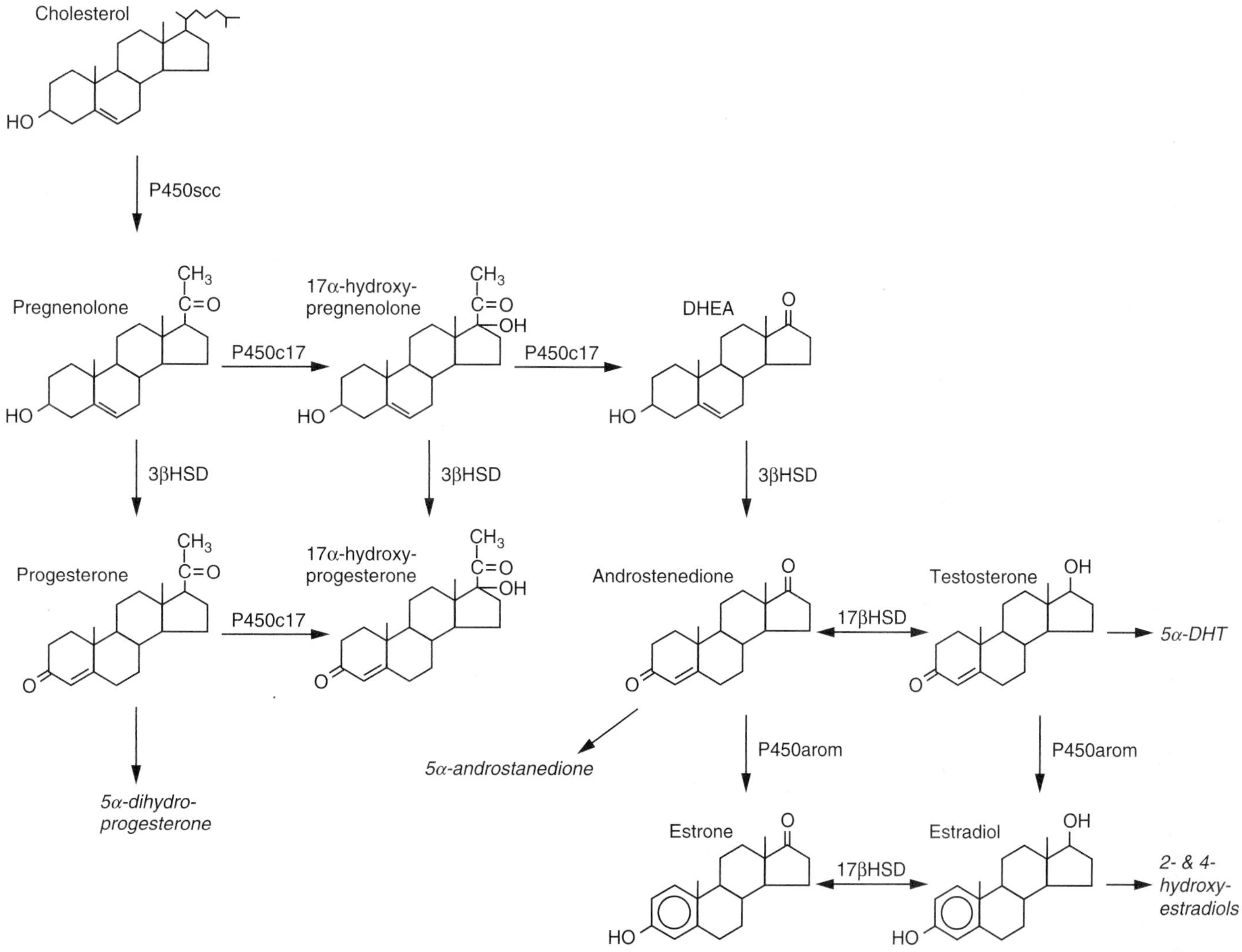

**Figure 151-2**  Major pathways of steroid biosynthesis and metabolism in the human ovary. Steroid metabolites in italics have unclear roles in the ovary and their speculative functions are described in the text. 3β-HSD, 3β-hydroxysteroid dehydrogenase; 5α-DHT, 5α-dihydrotestosterone; 17β-HSD, 17β-hydroxysteroid dehydrogenase; DHEA, dehydroepiandrosterone; P-450arom, aromatase; P-450c17, 17α hydroxylase/17,20 desmolase; P-450scc, cholesterol side-chain cleavage enzyme.

mental evidence indicates that serine 195 must be phosphorylated to achieve StAR's maximal steroidogenic activity.

Multiple lines of evidence demonstrate that StAR plays a critical role in steroid hormone synthesis. Expression of StAR mRNA and protein is correlated with steroidogenesis, and transfection of cells with a StAR expression plasmid enhances pregnenolone synthesis. The etiologic identification of lipoid congenital adrenal hyperplasia (lipoid CAH), caused by inactivating mutations of the StAR gene, conclusively established an essential role for StAR in adrenal and gonadal steroidogenesis[20]; patients suffering from this relatively rare autosomal-recessive disorder are characterized by impaired biosynthesis of all classes of adrenal and gonadal steroid hormones due to a defect at the cholesterol side-chain cleavage step. However, 46,XX females with lipoid CAH develop female sexual characteristics at puberty and menstrual bleeding despite nonfunctional StAR proteins and adrenal insufficiency.[21] The latter findings suggest that, although biosynthesis of large amounts of steroids in organs such as the adrenal gland requires StAR protein function, secretion of small amounts of estrogens by the ovary sufficient to produce secondary sexual development and endometrial growth can take place independent of StAR.

The exact mechanism by which StAR increases mitochondrial cholesterol metabolism is not known. It has been speculated that StAR interacts with the outer mitochondrial membranes, causing cholesterol to flow down a chemical gradient to the inner membranes and cytochrome P-450scc.[20] The import of StAR into the mitochondria is thought to represent the mechanism by which StAR's actions are terminated. This model holds that StAR has two key domains: the N-terminal mitochondrial targeting sequence, which ensures that the protein is directed to the site of action; and the C terminus, which promotes cholesterol movement. Although this model has several attractive features, there are key unknowns, such as the identity and nature of the outer mitochondrial membrane molecule that StAR recognizes. One possibility is that StAR can bind to and activate the peripheral benzodiazepine receptor (PBR), a protein integrated into the outer mitochondrial membrane. The five transmembrane domains of PBR are thought to be capable of forming a cholesterol pore, which enables a cholesterol molecule to pass through the membrane.[22,23] The N terminus and a central region of StAR have also been shown to interact with the cytosolic hormone sensitive lipase (HSL, shown as NCEH in Fig. 151-1); HSL and StAR together may facilitate cholesterol movement from lipid droplets to mitochondria for steroidogenesis.[24]

### 3β-HYDROXYSTEROID/Δ⁴-Δ⁵ ISOMERASE (3β-HSD)

The 3β-hydroxysteroid/$\Delta^4$-$\Delta^5$ isomerases convert pregnenolone to progesterone, 17α-hydroxypregnenolone to 17α-hydroxyprogesterone, and dehydroepiandrosterone (DHEA) to androstenedione (see Fig. 151-2). Using NAD⁺ as cofactor, these microsomal enzymes catalyze the dehydrogenation of the 3β-hydroxyl group and the subsequent isomerization of the $\Delta^5$ olefinic bond to yield the $\Delta^4$,3-ketone structure.[25] The importance of 3β-HSD to steroidogenesis is highlighted by the observation that inhibitors of 3β-HSD such as epostane effectively block progesterone synthesis and interrupt early human pregnancy. Two different but highly homologous human 3β-HSD genes have been identified and localized to chromosome 1p13.1.[26] The type 1 gene (HSD3B1) is expressed primarily in the human placenta, skin, and adipose tissue. The type 2 gene (HSD3B2) encodes the primary 3β-HSD enzyme expressed in the gonads and adrenal cortex. DNA sequences of the exons of HSD3B1 and HSD3B2 are so similar that the two encoded proteins, 372 and 371 amino acids, respectively, differ in only 23 amino acid residues.

Before the midcycle LH surge, 3β-HSD is localized to the theca but not granulosa cells; this differential distribution of the enzyme is concordant with the androgen-synthesizing function of theca cells. The type 2 3β-HSD in human corpus luteum has been localized to the perimitochondrial endoplasmic reticulum by electron microscope cytochemistry.[27] The enzyme is, therefore, positioned to convert pregnenolone produced by the mitochondrial cholesterol side-chain cleavage system to progesterone. Because steroidogenic cells have a large capacity to generate progesterone when presented with exogenous pregnenolone, 3β-HSD is not thought to be a rate-determining enzyme. The level of 3β-HSD increases, however, after trophic hormone stimulation.[28]

### 17α-HYDROXYLASE/17,20 DESMOLASE (P-450c17 ENCODED BY CYP17)

Theca cells of the follicle and theca-lutein cells of the corpus luteum as well as the ovarian hilus cells express P-450c17. This single microsomal enzyme catalyzes two reactions in the ovary: (1) hydroxylation of pregnenolone and progesterone at $C_{17}$, and (2) conversion of 17α-hydroxypregnenolone into DHEA (lyase reaction).[29] The 17α-hydroxylation reaction requires a pair of electrons and one molecule of $O_2$; a second electron pair and $O_2$ molecule are needed for the lyase reaction. The electrons are transferred from NADPH to the P-450c17 heme iron by reduced nicotinamide adedine dinucleotide phosphate (NADPH)-cytochrome P-450 reductase, the importance of which is demonstrated by disordered steroidogenesis in patients harboring mutations of the POR gene encoding NADPH-cytochrome P-450 reductase.[30] Several factors determine whether substrates undergo only 17α-hydroxylation or the subsequent scission of the 17,20 bond. These include the nature of the substrate, the flux of reducing equivalents, post-translational modification of P-450c17, and allosteric effectors.[28] The human P-450c17 only utilizes $\Delta^5$ substrates for 17,20 bond cleavage (see Fig. 151-2). Phosphorylation of P-450c17 appears to be necessary for maximal 17,20-lyase activity[31] and cytochrome $b_5$ increases 17,20 lyase activity by acting as an allosteric effector rather than an electron donor.[32]

### AROMATASE (P-450arom ENCODED BY CYP19) AND THE SYNTHESIS OF ESTRADIOL

Estrogens are synthesized in granulosa cells and lutein cells by the action of P-450arom (aromatase).[33] In most cases, P-450arom-expressing cells utilize androgen precursors derived from another cell type, placing ovarian estrogen synthesis under complex regulation epitomized by the "two cell–two gonadotropin" model of follicular steroid biosynthesis. According to this model, LH drives thecal synthesis of androgens, which are subsequently aromatized to estrogens in adjacent granulosa cells (Fig. 151-3). FSH is the primary stimulator of P-450arom gene expression in granulosa cells, which contain greater than 99% of the aromatization capacity of the follicle.[34] All granulosa cells are not equal in their capacity to form estrogens, however. There is a gradient of activity with highest aromatase expression located in the mural granulosa cells and lowest levels in the proliferating cells near the antrum.

Aromatase is a microsomal member of the family of cytochrome P-450 enzymes. It catalyzes three sequential hydroxylations of a C-19 substrate using three molecules of NADPH and three molecules of oxygen to produce a C-18 estrogen characterized by a phenolic A ring, with the elimination of the C-19 methyl group as formic acid.[35] The first hydroxylation yields a C-19 hydroxyl derivative; this is followed by a second hydroxylation step to produce an unstable gem-diol, which collapses to yield a C-19 aldehyde. The final hydroxylation event involves the formation of a 19-hydroxy-19-hydroperoxide intermediate, resulting in the subsequent

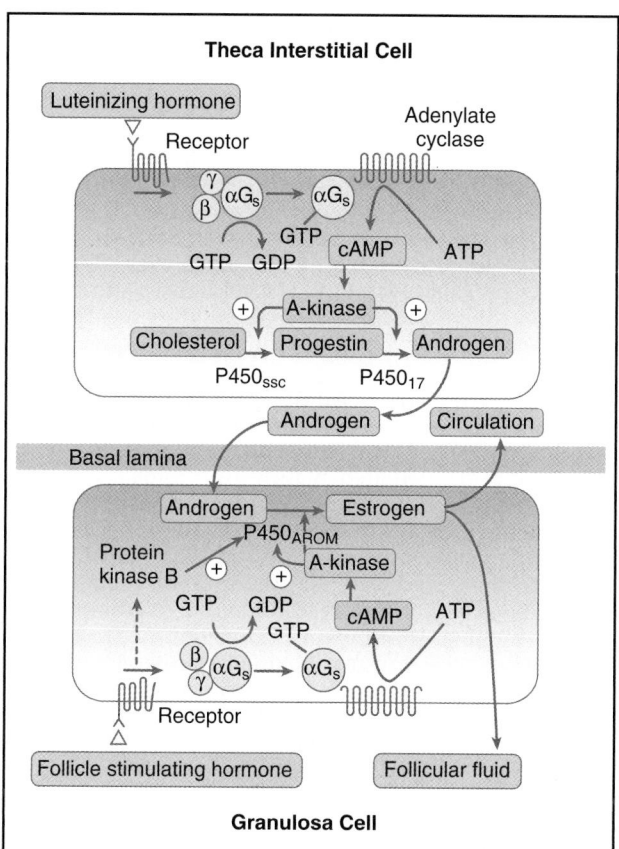

*Figure 151-3*  Gonadotropin regulation of follicular androgen and estrogen biosynthesis and the two cell–two gonadotropin model. αGS, G protein; ATP, adenosine triphosphate; cAMP, cyclic adenosine monophosphate; GDP, guanosine diphosphate; GTP, guanosine triphosphate; P-450arom, aromatase; P-450c17α, 17α-hydroxylase; P-450scc, cholesterol side-chain cleavage enzyme.

elimination of a formic acid molecule and aromatization of the steroid A ring. This sequence of reactions takes place at a single active site on the enzyme with reducing equivalents transferred to P-450arom by NADPH-cytochrome P-450 reductase.[36] The aromatase protein is encoded by a single gene (CYP19) on chromosome 15q21.1, which gives rise to mRNAs of various sizes as a result of the use of alternative promoters within the large gene spanning more than 123 kilobases (kb).[33,37,38] The promoter (promoter II) that drives ovarian aromatase expression lies adjacent to the exon encoding the translation start site. In granulosa cells, FSH stimulates transcription of both CYP19 and the gene encoding NADPH-cytochrome P-450 reductase.[36]

Gonadal tissues reduce 17-ketosteroids into 17β-hydroxysteroids, which have greater biological potency.[39] More than 10 different 17β-HSDs, designated types 1 through 10, according to the chronological order in which their respective cDNAs were cloned, have been identified. The type 1 enzyme is also referred to as the "estrogenic" 17β-HSD since it catalyzes the final step in estrogen biosynthesis by preferentially reducing the weak estrogen, estrone, to yield 17β-estradiol, a potent estrogen, using either NADH or NADPH as cofactor. Having 100-fold higher affinity for C-18 steroids over C-19 steroids, the type 1 enzyme is located in the cytosol and is expressed in granulosa cells under the influence of FSH.[40,41] The type 3 enzyme is referred to as the "androgenic" 17β-HSD because it catalyzes the final step in androgen biosynthesis by reducing androstenedione, a weak androgen, to testosterone, a potent androgen, using NADPH as cofactor. The type 3 enzyme does not appear to be expressed

in the human ovary, and the primary androgen produced by the theca is androstenedione.[42] The absence of the type 3 enzyme mRNA from the human ovary indicates that another 17β-HSD is responsible for ovarian testosterone production. The most likely 17β-HSD participating in ovarian testosterone synthesis is the type 5 enzyme, which is expressed in theca cells and the corpus luteum. Type 7 17β-HSD is also expressed in the ovary[43]; its murine homologue prefers estrone as a substrate and is most abundantly expressed in the ovaries of pregnant mice.[44]

### ROLES FOR CHOLESTEROL PRECURSORS AND STEROID METABOLITES IN OVARIAN FUNCTION?

Intermediates in the cholesterol biosynthetic pathway from lanosterol have been found to induce oocytes to resume meiosis.[45] 4,4-Dimethyl-5α-cholesta-8,14,24-triene-3β-ol was extracted from human follicular fluid and named follicular fluid (FF) meiosis activating substance (MAS) or FF-MAS. A related compound, 4,4-dimethyl-5α-cholest-8,24-diene-3β-ol, was isolated from bull testis and called T-MAS.[46] Present in micromolar concentrations in preovulatory follicle follicular fluid, both compounds are synthesized from lanosterol by P-450 14α-demethylase encoded by the CYP51 gene. The accumulation of FF-MAS and T-MAS in mature follicles may be the result of increased synthesis or inhibition of cholesterol synthesis at steps beyond the formation of FF-MAS and T-MAS. Gonadotropins have been reported to cause a several-fold increase in CYP51 gene expression in rodent ovaries, which could contribute to enhanced MAS formation.rogesterone during the luteal phase. Since pregnancy can be established and maintained in the absence of these molecules, they do not appear to have essential roles in reproductive physiology.

Two distinct isozymes of 5α-reductase, namely type I (5αRI) and type II (5αRII), have been identified. Both isozymes reduce the double bond between $C_4$ and $C_5$, and can convert progesterone to 5α-dihydroprogesterone, testosterone to dihydrotestosterone (DHT), and androstenedione to 5αs-androstanedione. Whereas 5αRI mRNA expression has been clearly shown in the ovary, mRNA expression of 5αRII is contentious.[50,51] Although DHT is present in follicular fluid, its precise role in normal human ovarian physiology is unclear. In rhesus monkeys that received a gonadotropin-releasing hormone (GnRH) antagonist to interrupt spontaneous gonadotropin secretion and were infused with human FSH and LH, systemic administration of DHT significantly reduced estrogen secretion,[52] whereas elevated DHT may also inhibit aromatase activity (discussed later). Together, these observations suggest that high concentrations of DHT are antagonistic to gonadotropin-stimulated estradiol secretion in primates.

The primary estrogens, estradiol and estrone, can undergo hydroxylation at $C_2$ and $C_4$ positions in the ovary, resulting in the formation of catecholestrogens, which are estrogens containing a dihydroxybenzene A ring. Conversion of estradiol is catalyzed by the enzymes estrogen 2-hydroxylase (CYP1A1) and estrogen 4-hydroxylase (CYP1B1) to the catecholestrogens 2-hydroxyestradiol and 4-hydroxyestradiol, respectively. Both of these metabolites bind to the two known estrogen receptors, ERα and ERβ, with 7% to 13% relative binding affinity compared with estradiol.[53] Catecholestrogens can be further O-methylated by catechol-O-methyl transferase (COMT) to form methoxyestrogens. The precise physiologic functions of these steroid metabolites in the ovary are unclear. Some studies suggest their roles as paracrine/autocrine regulators of steroidogenesis and follicular development.[54] Catecholestrogens can also be oxidized to potent genotoxic molecules implicated in carcinogenesis,[55] whereas antiangiogenic and antitumor activities have been associated with 2-methoxyestradiol.[56]

## GONADOTROPIN CONTROL OF OVARIAN STEROID PRODUCTION

### FSH AND LH

Gonadotropins control the growth and differentiation of the steroid hormone–secreting cells of the ovary, intrinsically linking form and function. A defined sequence of gonadotropin action propels the growth of follicles and the production of steroid hormones. Positive feedback on the pituitary by high concentrations of estrogens leads to the ovulatory surge of LH, which, in turn, triggers a dramatic differentiation event, resulting in structural reorganization of the preovulatory follicle, release of the ovum, and striking changes in the steroidogenic capacity of the luteinizing cells.

Follicular growth that culminates in ovulation and corpus luteum formation requires both FSH and LH. Steroidogenic competence of the ovarian follicle is not achieved in the absence of FSH, even though LH is present in abundance. FSH promotes proliferation of the granulosa cells and induces the expression of genes involved in estradiol biosynthesis.[33,36,37] Thus, mutations that lead to the synthesis of an inactive FSH β subunit[57] or inactivate both alleles of the FSH receptor gene[58,59] produce symptoms of primary hypogonadism with deficient ovarian estrogen production in the face of elevated plasma LH levels. Likewise, FSH cannot achieve complete regulation of follicular development by itself. In gonadotropin-deficient women or LH-deprived monkeys treated with FSH alone, follicles grow to a preovulatory size, but there is no parallel increase in estradiol production due to a relative deficiency in androgen precursors[60–62] (Fig. 151-4). The small amount of estradiol that is made in this situation may be derived from androgens secreted by the adrenal cortex or thecal androgens produced in response to paracrine factors released by the granulosa cells. During the last phase of follicular maturation, when granulosa cells acquire LH receptors, LH is then able to sustain follicular growth and estradiol synthesis.[63] This LH drive may compensate for the diminished levels of FSH resulting from the negative feedback action of follicular estradiol and inhibin.

LH stimulation is indispensable for normal ovarian hormone production, not only before but also after ovulation. Suppression of LH release leads to a prompt decline in progesterone levels that precede changes in the abundance of mRNAs encoding steroidogenic enzymes or structural changes in the corpus luteum.[64] This acute regulation of ovarian progesterone secretion is controlled by LH via the expression of StAR. StAR mRNA and protein, present in both theca-lutein and granulosa-lutein cells throughout the luteal phase, are highly expressed in the early and midluteal phases, whereas declining StAR mRNA and protein levels are characteristic of the late luteal phase. Moreover, StAR protein levels in the corpus luteum are highly correlated with plasma progesterone levels; suppression of LH levels during the mid-luteal phase markedly decreases plasma progesterone levels and abundance of StAR mRNA transcripts in the corpus luteum.[65]

### MECHANISMS OF GONADOTROPIN ACTION

LH stimulates an almost immediate increase in gonadal steroid secretion, mediated mainly by proteins phosphorylated by the cAMP-dependent protein kinase.[3] The rapid enhancement of cholesterol delivery to the inner mitochondrial membranes is driven by posttranslational changes in existing proteins, resulting in increases in their activities. These include the phosphorylation and activation of cholesterol ester hydrolase,[66] the phosphorylation of StAR,[67] which appears to be necessary for maximal steroidogenic activity, and possibly the phosphorylation of components of the cholesterol side-chain cleavage system.[68]

Longer term regulation of steroid hormone production over hours or days is exerted at the level of gene transcription. In general, increases in cAMP concentrations stimulate transcription of all of the genes involved in steroid hormone synthesis.[5] However, many of these genes do not contain consensus cAMP response elements in their promoters, so that transcriptional activation is mediated by other sequence motifs. Steroidogenic factor 1 (SF-1), encoded by the NR5A1 gene, is involved in the control of most of these genes.[69,70] SF-1-binding elements are present in the promoters of the StAR, P-450scc, 3β-HSD type 2, P-450c17, and P-450arom genes. The interaction of SF-1 with coactivators, including cAMP response element binding (CREB) binding protein (CBP) and steroid receptor coactivator-1 (SRC-1), may coordinate the cAMP response.[71,72] Whereas SF-1 expression decreases after ovulation, mRNA levels of the orphan nuclear

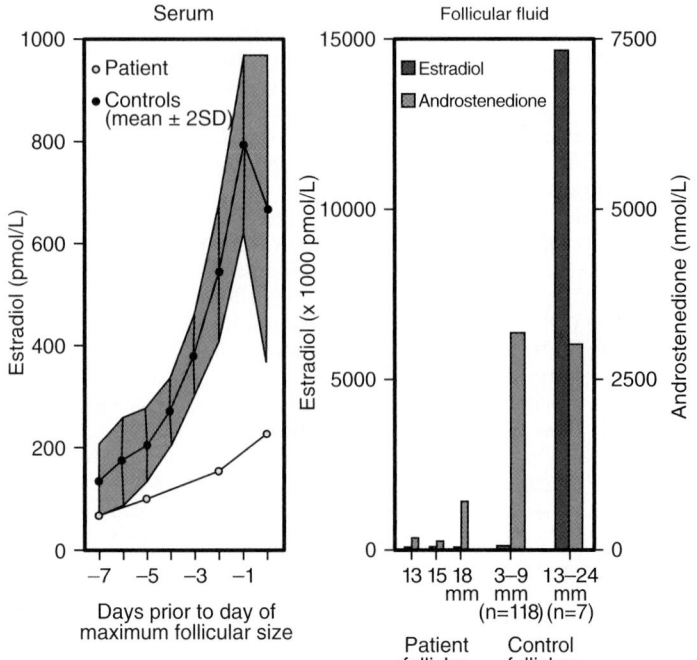

**Figure 151-4** *Left panel,* Serum estradiol concentrations of a patient with isolated gonadotropin deficiency after administration of recombinant FSH before the day when ovarian follicles reach their maximum size (day 17). As a reference, daily serum estradiol levels (mean ± 2 SD) are shown in seven normally cycling women up to the day of LH peak. *Right panel,* Follicular fluid concentrations of estradiol and androstenedione in three separate follicles (13-, 15-, 18-mm diameter) from a patient with isolated gonadotropin deficiency after administration of recombinant FSH. Median estradiol (E₂) and androstenedione (AD) concentrations in small (3–9 mm) follicles (n = 118), and large (13–24 mm) follicles (n = 7) are shown. (Reprinted from Schoot DC, Coelingh Bennink H, Mannaerts BM, et al: Human recombinant follicle-stimulating hormone induces growth of preovulatory follicles without concomitant increase in androgen and estrogen biosynthesis in a woman with isolated gonadotropin deficiency. J Clin Endocrinol Metab 74:1471–1473, 1992.)

receptor LRH-1 (encoded by *NR5A2*) are higher in corpus luteum than in mature follicles. Unlike SF-1, the expression of which is reduced in the ovary during gestation, the expression of LRH-1 is induced significantly in the corpus luteum during pregnancy.[73] The stage-specific expression of LRH-1 in the ovary, which differs from that of SF-1, implies its specific role in regulating follicular and luteal functions. Cotransfection of granulosa cells demonstrated a dose-dependant effect of LRH-1 on 3β-HSD type 2 promoter activity, suggesting that LRH-1 can contribute to progesterone synthesis in the corpus luteum.[74] The GATA family of transcription factors has recently emerged as an important group of transcription factors regulating expression of multiple steroidogenic enzymes. This b-helix-loop-helix family includes GATA-4 and GATA-6, which have roles in regulating the expression of StAR, P-450scc, and P-450c17, among other steroidogenic enzymes. The GATA family of transcription factors also interacts with other transcription factors including SF-1 and specificity protein 1 (Sp1) as part of a combinatorial code that regulates steroidogenic enzyme gene expression.

FSH-mediated granulosa cell differentiation has been shown to be protein kinase B (PKB) dependent. Expression of constitutively active LH receptors in rat granulosa cells resulted in increased cAMP production without increasing aromatase activity or LH receptor mRNA levels, whereas stimulation of granulosa cells by FSH in the presence of PKB led to an amplification of FSH-induced aromatase and LH receptor mRNA levels.[6] FSH via cAMP stimulates the activation of the PI 3-kinase/PKB pathway in granulosa cells, leading to the activation of multiple intracellular signaling molecules.[75]

The transcription of genes encoding steroidogenic enzymes is also suppressed at specific stages of follicular and luteal function. For example, the expression of thecal P-450c17 declines transiently after the LH surge as does the expression of aromatase and 17β-HSD type 1 in the luteinizing granulosa cells.[39,72,76] A decline in expression of the StAR gene is associated with functional luteolysis.[77] Factors that block expression of steroidogenic proteins include the orphan nuclear receptor DAX-1, which interacts directly with SF-1 to prevent activation of the transcriptional machinery.[78,79] Stimulation of P-450arom promoter activity by SF-1 in ovarian granulosa cells is inhibited by the transcription factors DAX-1 and WT1[80]; all of the three transcription factors are expressed in granulosa cells of the human ovarian follicle, indicating the presence of a finely coordinated regulation of P-450arom expression.[81,82] Posttranscriptional control (e.g., changes in mRNA stability) is also important in certain circumstances and may account, in part, for the actions of insulin-like growth factors on the expression of components of the steroidogenic machinery.[83,84]

### OTHER GONADOTROPIC HORMONES WITH POSSIBLE ACTIONS IN THE OVARY

Besides FSH and LH, other hormones also exhibit gonadotropic activity; these include prolactin, growth hormone, insulin, and insulin-like growth factors. Although prolactin plays an important role in regulating luteal function in rodents, the physiological role of prolactin in human ovarian function is less certain. The human ovary expresses prolactin and prolactin receptors, and high levels of prolactin suppress steroidogenesis by granulosa cells.[85,86] However, the menstrual disturbances observed in hyperprolactinemic women are primarily due to the consequences of reduced gonadotropin secretion, and the impact of elevated prolactin levels on the ovary appears to be secondary.

Growth hormone (GH) has been reported to have direct effects on animal and human granulosa cells; its cognate receptor is expressed on granulosa cells of human antral follicles and luteal cells.[87] In addition, GH administration increases the ovarian response to gonadotropins in hypopituitary subjects. Yet, supplemental GH does not appear to have dramatic effects on gonadotropin action in individuals with normal pituitary function.[88]

Ovarian theca and granulosa cells express the insulin receptor, through which insulin augments steroid production.[89] Mechanisms of this insulin effect on steroidogenesis remain to be clarified. Insulin can increase steady state levels of steroidogenic enzyme mRNAs, but it is not yet known whether this is a transcriptional or posttranscriptional response. To date, insulin-response elements have not been identified in steroidogenic enzyme genes or their promoters. There is, however, evidence for insulin effects on mRNA stability. Additionally, insulin is known to activate translation rapidly, and it is yet to be determined if such a translational action of insulin takes place in ovarian cells.

## INTRAOVARIAN CONTROL MECHANISMS

The growth of follicles and the function of the corpus luteum, while under the primary direction of the pituitary, are highly influenced by intraovarian factors that modulate the action of gonadotropins. These intraovarian factors most likely account for gonadotropin-independent follicular growth, observed differences in the rate and extent of development of ovarian follicles, arrest and initiation of meiosis, dominant follicle selection, and luteolysis. The list of potential paracrine factors that can influence steroid production by theca and granulosa cells is long and diverse. It includes various growth factors, cytokines, peptide hormones, and steroids such as epidermal growth factor, transforming growth factor-α and -β, platelet-derived growth factor, fibroblast growth factors, activins, inhibins, antimüllerian hormone, insulin-like growth factors, estradiol, progesterone, and GnRH (Table 151-1).[90–93]

**Table 151-1 Intraovarian Regulators**

| Growth Factor/Cytokine | Ovarian Actions |
| --- | --- |
| Activin | Stimulates follicular maturation and FSH receptor expression |
| | Inhibits thecal steroidogenesis |
| EGF | Stimulates mitosis of granulosa cells |
| | Inhibits expression of aromatase |
| FGF | Stimulates mitosis of granulosa cells |
| | Inhibits steroidogenesis |
| GDF-9 | Increases follicular growth |
| | Regulates granulosa cell steroidogenesis |
| GnRH | Modulates steroidogenesis |
| | Activates oocyte maturation |
| IGF-1, IGF-2 | Stimulates granulosa and theca cell mitosis and steroidogenesis, and augments gonadotropin-stimulated steroidogenesis |
| IL-1 | Inhibits gonadotropin-stimulated steroidogenesis |
| | Participates in the process of ovulation |
| Inhibins A & B | Increases thecal androgen synthesis |
| PDGF | Augments FSH-induced LH receptor expression and steroidogenesis |
| TGF-α | Same as EGF |
| TGF-β | Augments FSH-mediated steroidogenesis |
| TNF-α | Inhibits gonadotropin-stimulated steroidogenesis |

EGF, epidermal growth factor; FGF, fibroblast growth factor; GDF-9, growth and differentiation factor-9; GnRH, gonadotropin-releasing hormone; IGF, insulin-like growth factor; IL-1, interleukin 1; TGF, transforming growth factor; TNF, tissue necrosis factor.

## INSULIN-LIKE GROWTH FACTORS AND THEIR BINDING PROTEINS

In response to FSH, granulosa cells produce insulin-like growth factors (IGFs) as well as IGF-binding proteins (IGFBPs), which have higher affinities for the IGFs than the receptor that mediates IGF action.[91–93] In animal follicles, IGF-1 is the primary IGF produced, whereas, in the human ovary, IGF-2 is the major IGF. In general, IGFs amplify the actions of FSH on granulosa cells, including effects on cell proliferation, cAMP accumulation, and transcriptional stimulation of some genes, including the StAR gene.[83,84] Similarly, IGFs increase theca-cell androgen production and amplify the stimulatory effects of LH.[94] There are also reports that IGF-1 and IGF-2 have differential effects on human ovarian cell function. Whereas they both stimulate progesterone secretion by granulosa-lutein cells, IGF-1, but not IGF-2, increases basal aromatase activity and synergizes with FSH to increase aromatase expression.

The pattern of expression of IGFBPs is determined by the stage of follicular maturation and the status of the follicle.[91–93,95] IGFBP-2 is expressed by theca and the granulosa cells of small antral atretic follicles, whereas IGFBP-3 is expressed by theca and granulosa cells of the dominant follicle. IGFBP-4, expressed by ovarian stroma, theca, and the granulosa cells of small antral follicles and the dominant follicle, is a potent inhibitor of IGF action in vitro. Therefore, its cleavage by IGFBP-4 protease, also known as pregnancy-associated plasma protein-A (PAPP-A), acts as a positive regulatory mechanism of IGF bioavailability.[96] Consistent with the notion that PAPP-A is a marker of ovarian follicle selection, the metalloproteinase is secreted by cultured luteinizing granulosa cells and granulosa cells from large antral follicles, but not small antral follicles.[97] IGFBP-5 is expressed in stroma as well as theca and granulosa cells in follicles of all sizes. IGFBP-6 is not detectable in the human ovary.

Healthy follicles are characterized by a microenvironment in which IGFs are present in the unbound form. The high levels of free IGF are achieved in part through reduced levels of IGFBP-2 and the production of an FSH-stimulated IGFBP protease by granulosa cells. In contrast, IGFBP-2 and IGFBP-4 are abundant in atretic follicles, restricting availability of free IGF. The IGF system represents a prototype for amplifying the effects of FSH during the follicular phase, permitting the dominant follicle to survive in the face of declining FSH levels. Inhibins, activins, and follistatin inhibins, which are heterodimeric glycoproteins produced mainly by granulosa cells during the follicular phase, augment thecal androgen synthesis under the influence of LH and IGFs, but have no direct effect on granulosa cell steroidogenesis.[98,99] FSH stimulates inhibin production by granulosa cells and, in this way, a feed-forward system for estrogen synthesis is developed by, on the one hand, the combined effects of FSH on the expression of P-450arom and NADPH cytochrome P-450 reductase and, on the other hand, the amplifying effects of inhibins on theca cell androgen formation.[100] Activins, primarily produced by granulosa cells, have more complex actions in the follicle. They potentially play a role early in follicular growth by stimulating the expression of FSH receptor and aromatase, and inhibin production by granulosa cells. Activins suppress thecal androgen production and block the stimulatory effects of inhibin on thecal steroidogenesis. Consequently, activins can keep thecal androgen synthesis in check during early follicular development. Activins also increase the production of IGFBP-2 and IGFBP-4 by granulosa cells, which, in turn, promote follicular atresia. As follicles progress through the maturation process, they evidently transit through an early activin-dominated state to a later inhibin-dominated state.

Follistatin is a monomeric protein first identified in and isolated from ovarian follicular fluid. An activin-binding protein, it is produced by granulosa cells under FSH stimulation and blocks the actions of activin.[101] Serum levels of follistatin do not fluctuate across normal menstrual cycles.[102] Likewise, intrafollicular concentrations of free follistatin do not vary with size or maturity of the follicle.[103] However, female transgenic mice overexpressing follistatin exhibit small ovaries due to a block in folliculogenesis at various stages, confirming its role of follistatin in follicular development.[104]

## ANTIMÜLLERIAN HORMONE (MÜLLERIAN-INHIBITING SUBSTANCE)

Antimüllerian hormone (AMH), also known as müllerian-inhibiting substance/factor, is another member of the TGF-β family of growth and differentiation factors. In females, AMH is expressed in granulosa cells of large preantral and small antral follicles of the ovary. Expression of AMH receptor has been localized to granulosa and theca cells of the rat ovary. Compared with wild-type controls, ovaries of prepubertal AMH null mice contained more growing follicles, whereas ovaries of adult AMH null mice had significantly less primordial follicles.[105] By 13 months of age, AMH null ovaries were almost depleted of primordial follicles. Collectively, these observations suggest a role for AMH in inhibiting the recruitment of primordial follicles to the growing pool. In women, serum AMH levels are positively correlated with the number of antral follicles detectable by ultrasonography, but negatively correlated with age, indicating that AMH is a potential serum marker of ovarian reserve.[106,107]

## OOCYTE-DERIVED FACTORS

The oocyte also participates in the paracrine dialogue involving the somatic cells in the follicle. Growth and differentiation factor-9 (GDF-9) is highly expressed by growing oocytes and to a lesser extent by primate granulosa cells. It presumably activates putative receptors in granulosa and theca cells.[108] Disruption of the GDF-9 gene in mice prevents follicle development beyond the primary/early secondary stage.[109] The follicles of GDF-9-deficient mice arrest in growth at the primary stage, yet their oocytes continue to grow, indeed, at a faster rate than wild-type oocytes, and progress to advanced stages of differentiation seen in the antral follicles of normal mice.[109,110] However, there are ultrastructural abnormalities in the interconnections between granulosa cells and oocytes. The theca also fails to form around the follicles, implicating GDF-9 in the organization and/or proliferation of this follicular component.

In vitro, GDF-9 has a variety of species-specific effects on granulosa and theca cells.[111] In rodents, GDF-9 stimulates granulosa cell differentiation including induction of LH receptors and steroidogenesis. In cumulus cells, GDF-9 promotes expression of proteins that are incorporated into the proteoglycan extracellular matrix of the cumulus-oophorus complex and follicular fluid. It also stimulates cyclooxygenase-2 (COX-2) and prostaglandin synthesis, and progesterone formation.[112,113] LH receptor expression is suppressed, which would discourage luteinization of the cumulus cells. These actions of GDF-9 give the granulosa cells immediately surrounding the oocyte, which would be exposed to the highest GDF-9 concentrations, a unique phenotype. GDF-9 inhibits human granulosalutein and theca cell steroidogenesis in vitro, with the inhibitory effect on theca cells being more pronounced.[114] It also stimulates theca cell proliferation, a finding consonant with the apparent role of GDF-9 in controlling thecal development in the murine ovary. Bone morphogenic protein-15 (BMP-15) is another member of the TGF-β superfamily produced by oocytes.[115] It is structurally related to and shares a similar pattern of expression with

GDF-9. BMP-15 stimulates the proliferation of rat granulosa cells in primary culture, a mitogenic effect independent of FSH stimulation. Although BMP-15 has no effect on FSH-stimulated estradiol production, it decreases FSH-induced progesterone production, indicating that BMP-15 is a selective modulator of FSH action.[116] In vitro, BMP-15 stimulates granulosa cell mitosis, but suppresses FSH receptor expression. Mutations in the human GDF-9 and BMP-15 genes have yet to be identified and linked to alterations in ovarian function.

## ROLE OF ESTROGENS

In addition to their systemic effects on the reproductive tract, hypothalamus, and pituitary, estrogens act on granulosa, theca, and luteal cells in the ovaries of laboratory animals and domestic species. Not only are estrogen receptors (ERs) expressed in the ovary, but high levels of estrogens are also characteristically found in the antral fluid of healthy mature follicles.[117] There are conflicting reports in the literature regarding the expression of the two estrogen receptor subtypes, ERα and ERβ, in the primate ovary.[118] The most convincing of these studies indicates that both ER subtypes are expressed by the germinal epithelium, granulosa cells with ERβ predominating over ERα in medium-sized and preovulatory follicles, theca cells, and luteinized granulosa cells. Some researchers have detected ERα transcripts by polymerase chain reaction (PCR) in human oocytes, but these findings have not been confirmed by others. The discrepancies among various reports probably reflect sensitivities of the detection methods used. Existing data support the notion that the ovary is a site of estrogen action via the classical receptor-mediated signaling pathways. Given the high intraovarian estrogen concentrations achieved during follicular maturation and corpus luteum function, the physiologic roles of estrogen within the primate ovary and the mechanisms by which they might influence cellular function (i.e., genomic versus nongenomic actions) are matters of current debate.[118] Indeed, the extremely high levels of estradiol reached in the antrum of the preovulatory follicle (~1 μg/mL) raise serious questions as to the roles of the classical estrogen receptors, which would be fully saturated by ligand during the later stages of follicular maturation. Estrogens have pleiotropic effects on animal granulosa cells. They promote proliferation and exert antiatretic effects. Estrogens also augment intercellular gap junction and antrum formation, and increase the estrogen receptor content of granulosa cells. Estrogens synergize with gonadotropins at several levels, including the promotion of ovarian growth, LH and FSH receptor expression, and augment aromatase activity. However, high levels of estrogens are not essential for growth of follicles to the size equivalent to the preovulatory stage.[119,120] There are pharmacologic data suggesting that estrogens are important for oocyte function.[121] In vitro studies on primate granulosa cells have yielded inconsistent findings with respect to the actions of estrogens. Estradiol inhibits progesterone secretion by rhesus monkey granulosa cells, whereas in marmoset granulosa cells, it has no effect on progesterone production, but stimulates aromatase in the presence of IGF-1. Exogenous estrogen exerts a luteolytic effect on the primate corpus luteum, probably through actions on the central nervous system.

In summary, while the primate ovary expresses the receptors that allow a variety of cells to respond to estradiol, the physiologic significance of estrogens in follicular maturation and luteal function in the primate ovary is still unknown. It is evident that follicle growth per se does not require high levels of estradiol, but the orchestration of events that result in a mature oocyte capable of developing into a viable embryo after fertilization may require estrogen action on granulosa cells, oocyte, or both.

## ROLE OF ANDROGENS

In the human, primate, and rat ovary, androgen receptor (AR) is expressed mainly in granulosa cells of the follicle and, to a lesser extent, also in theca cells and stroma,[122-125] suggesting that, in addition to serving as substrates for estrogen production, thecal androgens may have paracrine and autocrine functions. Androgens have a number of effects on the primate ovary.[124,126,127] It has been proposed that androgens have complex actions on granulosa cells, amplifying the effects of FSH during intermediate stages of follicular development, but potentially inducing atresia during the late preovulatory period. Administration of testosterone or DHT to rhesus monkeys promotes accumulation of primary follicles as well as follicle survival, suggesting a folliculotropic action. Moreover, androgen receptors were positively correlated with a marker of cell proliferation (Ki-67) and negatively correlated with apoptosis. These observations are in sharp contrast with the notion that androgens are atretogenic, a concept that emerged primarily from studies on the rodent ovary in which androgens block granulosa cell proliferation in vitro and promote follicular atresia. Taken together, these discrepancies suggest species-specific androgen actions in the ovary.

Stage-dependent effects of androgens on granulosa cell function in vitro have been reported in the marmoset.[128] Androgens enhanced FSH-stimulated aromatase expression and progesterone production, while inhibiting human chorionic gonadotropin (hCG)-stimulated aromatase activity and progestin synthesis in cells from large preovulatory follicles. Evidence that androgens have a detrimental effect on human follicular function includes the observation that follicular fluid enriched in DHT and poor in estradiol is characteristic of atresia. This steroid profile may be a consequence rather than a cause of atresia, however. Favoring a causal relationship are reports that high follicular concentrations of 5α-reduced androgens such as DHT act as competitive inhibitors of granulosa cell aromatase activity.[129] Both DHT and 5α-androstanedione are potent inhibitors of the rat aromatase in granulosa cells in vitro.[130] Thus, androgens may exert both positive and negative effects on follicular growth and function in a stage-dependent manner through androgen receptors as well as nonreceptor mediated mechanisms.

## ROLE OF PROGESTERONE

Although a role for progesterone in maintaining the secretory endometrium is well documented, its functions within the ovary are not entirely clear. In women, granulosa cells from preovulatory follicles do not contain significant amounts of progesterone receptors (PRs), whereas granulosa cells of the dominant follicle highly express PR at the time of LH surge.[131] After follicle rupture, PR expression persists in the luteinized granulosa cells of the corpus luteum,[131] with mRNA concentrations of both PR isoforms (PR-A and PR-B) at the early and mid-luteal phases higher than those at the late luteal phase.[132] These data are concordant with the hypothesis that progesterone is a "local luteotropin" that promotes luteal development and sustains luteal structure and function.[133] Progesterone plays a key role in the periovulatory period and may be essential for the normal luteinization process and maintenance of luteal function.[133-135] For instance, ovulation does not occur in mutant mice with disruption of the PR gene, or in animals treated with the PR antagonist RU-486. Pharmacologic blockade of ovarian progesterone production with a 3β-HSD inhibitor indicated that progesterone exerts antiapoptotic and prodifferentiation effects on luteinizing cells and maintains luteal function. Progesterone also appears to play a role in oocyte maturation. In rhesus monkeys treated with the progestin R5020, a significant percentage of oocytes resumed meiosis to enter metaphase 2,despite the absence of a gonadotropin surge or follicle rupture.[136] Collectively, the cited studies indicate that progesterone produced in response to the mid-cycle LH surge is important for luteinization of the dominant follicle, oocyte maturation, ovulation, and subsequent maintenance of luteal function.

## OTHER INTRAOVARIAN REGULATORS

Prostaglandins (PGs) are members of the eicosanoid family of biologically active molecules derived from arachidonic acid, which is, in turn, mobilized from cell membrane phospholipids mainly via the action of phospholipase $A_2$ ($PLA_2$). Arachidonic acid is converted to $PGH_2$ by the two isozymes of cyclooxygenase, COX-1 and COX-2. COX-1 is constitutively expressed at low levels, but induction of COX-2 in granulosa cells before ovulation is highly conserved across many mammalian species.[137] Indeed, COX-2 knockout mice are infertile due to ovulation failure.[138,139] The preovulatory gonadotropin surge markedly increases COX-2 expression and concentrations of both $PGE_2$ and $PGF_{2\alpha}$ in follicular fluid.[140] Transgenic mice lacking the $PGE_2$ receptor subtype EP2 show decreased ovulation and exhibit abnormal cumulus expansion.[139,141] Although a role for $PGF_{2\alpha}$ in ovulation is unclear, its negative effects on progesterone biosynthesis and its function as a luteolytic agent have been reported. Administration of $PGF_{2\alpha}$ to ewes decreases serum progesterone levels and mRNA concentrations of both StAR and 3β-HSD type 2 in their corpora lutea.[142,143]

Oxytocin is another intraluteal regulator implicated in the regulation of gap junction formation between luteal cells, stimulation of estradiol synthesis, and, in animals, the process of luteolysis.[144] Primate corpora lutea have the highest contents of oxytocin during the mid-luteal phase and oxytocin receptor transcripts are detectable in the corpus luteum at this time. The observation that oxytocin knockout mice do not show abnormalities in corpus luteum function suggests, however, that oxytocin is not a major factor in controlling the rodent corpus luteum.

The proinflammatory cytokines interleukin-1α (IL-1α) and interleukin-1β (IL-1β) inhibit steroid production and suppress the steady state levels of StAR and steroidogenic enzymes in ovarian cells.[145] These cytokines, together with their cognate receptor, IL-1R1, are produced by resident ovarian macrophages and both granulosa and theca cells. Studies have shown multiple functions of the IL-1 system in the developing follicle. In vitro, IL-1 inhibited FSH-induced estradiol and progesterone production by granulosa cells, and also gonadotropin-induced androstenedione production by theca cells.[146-148] IL-1 treatment can increase prostaglandin accumulation in the rat ovary by stimulating the expression of two of the key enzymes in prostaglandin formation, that is, $PLA_2$ and COX-2. The exact physiologic role of these cytokines in the ovary remains to be elucidated, but evidence suggests that the IL-1 system participates in the control of folliculogenesis, ovulation, and luteal function.

In addition to playing a pivotal role in the hypothalamus-pituitary-gonad axis, GnRH modulates steroidogenesis in the ovary as a local autocrine/paracrine factor. Two isoforms of this decapeptide hormone have been identified, namely, GnRH-1 and GnRH-2; mRNA transcripts of both GnRH isoforms and GnRH-1 receptor are expressed in granulosalutein and ovarian surface epithelial cells.[149-151] Progesterone secretion from granulosa cells in culture was decreased by the addition of a GnRH agonist, an effect reversed by the coadministration of a GnRH antagonist.[152] At low concentrations, the GnRH agonist buserelin stimulates estrogen production in granulosa-lutein cells, but suppresses steroidogenesis at higher concentrations.[153,154] GnRH-1, GnRH-2, and GnRH-1 receptor mRNA expression levels in the ovary are regulated by multiple factors including FSH, hCG, estradiol, and GnRH-1 and GnRH-2 themselves.

## HORMONE PRODUCTION DURING THE OVARIAN LIFE CYCLE

### THE FETAL AND PREPUBERTAL OVARY

The human fetal ovary displays very limited steroidogenic activity. It contains no detectable StAR in theca or granulosa cells and expresses very low levels of P-450scc.[155,156] Homogenates of fetal ovaries convert pregnenolone into progesterone, 17α-hydroxyprogesterone and 5α-reduced compounds. Androgens are not formed in any significant quantity, however, indicating the lack of 17,20 lyase activity.[156] Consistent with these observations, P-450c17 mRNA in the fetal ovary is less than 2% of the levels found in fetal testis. Homogenates of fetal ovaries can, however, aromatize androstenedione and testosterone at low rates. The paucity of 17,20 lyase activity as well as low aromatase gene expression would restrict fetal estradiol synthesis.[157]

### THE OVARY DURING REPRODUCTIVE LIFE

The plasma levels of the two major female sex steroid hormones, estradiol and progesterone, change dramatically during the menstrual cycle, primarily reflecting their rate of secretion from the ovary. During the follicular phase, the theca of maturing follicles contributes 30% of the circulating androstenedione, increasing to 60% immediately before ovulation. The rising estradiol levels in the follicular phase are derived almost exclusively from the follicle selected for ovulation. After ovulation, the luteinization of the theca and granulosa cells gives rise to the corpus luteum. The granulosa-lutein cells (large luteal cells) and theca-lutein cells (small luteal cells) display a different repertoire of steroidogenic enzymes.[158] Capable of progesterone production, both cell types express P-450scc and 3β-HSD type 2. Theca-lutein cells express P-450c17 and appear to be the primary site of 17α-hydroxyprogesterone production as well as the source of androgen substrates to be converted to estrogens by the aromatase-expressing granulosa-lutein cells,[159] a compartmentalization of steroidogenic enzymes reminiscent of the theca-granulosa cooperation in estrogen synthesis during the follicular phase. The granulosa-lutein and theca-lutein have an intimate relationship in the formed corpus luteum, and their interactions may be promoted by the action of locally produced hormones, including oxytocin, which stimulates the formation of gap junctions between these cells, facilitating intercellular communication.[160]

The steroidogenic activity of the corpus luteum is dependent on LH stimulation.[161,162] Administration of a GnRH antagonist to nonhuman primates results in an immediate and profound decline in plasma progesterone levels and sharp reduction in ovarian StAR mRNA expression,[65] but without significant changes in P-450scc and 3β-HSD mRNA levels.[64] In monkeys with hypothalamic lesions that destroy GnRH-producing neurons, luteal function can be maintained by pulsatile administration of GnRH. Cessation of GnRH infusion results in a rapid fall in progesterone levels, which can be restored by reinitiation of infusion. Interestingly, the functional life span of the corpus luteum in this experimental paradigm cannot be extended beyond the usual life of 14 to 16 days, despite continued administration of GnRH. Only treatment with progressively increasing amounts of LH or hCG can "rescue" the corpus luteum from luteolysis.[163,164] These observations suggest that luteolysis in primates is the result of a loss of sensitivity to LH, presumably as a consequence of intraluteal events, and that decreased luteal sensitivity to LH can be overcome with higher levels of gonadotropin stimulation.

During the first 8 weeks of pregnancy, the corpus luteum produces large amounts of progesterone. Secretory function then declines as assessed by the measurement of the levels of 17α-hydroxyprogesterone, a steroid that is not secreted by the placenta and is, therefore, assumed to provide an index of luteal function[48] (Fig. 151-5). In the absence of an hCG rescue signal, the corpus luteum undergoes a process of functional and structural regression that has been likened to an immune-mediated event characterized by apoptotic death of luteal cells.[165,166]

## ENDOCRINE ACTIVITY OF THE POSTMENOPAUSAL OVARY

The postmenopausal ovary contains two different populations of cells with steroidogenic capacity: hilar cells, and corticostromal cells that may represent residual thecal elements.[167] In vitro studies suggest that the postmenopausal ovary has some steroidogenic potential. Incubation of postmenopausal ovarian stromal slices with pregnenolone yielded progesterone, DHEA, and testosterone. Incubation of strips of ovarian hilar tissue from postmenopausal women revealed a steroidogenic pattern similar to that of the postmenopausal ovarian stroma. However, the overall amount of steroids produced was substantially greater compared with stroma. Measurable in vitro formation of estradiol by postmenopausal cortical stroma and hilar cells has also been reported.[168,169] Immunohistochemical studies found that less than 1% of stromal cells showed evidence of expression of P-450scc, 3β-hydroxysteroid dehydrogenase, and P-450c17.

The postmenopausal ovary is thought to be a source of circulating testosterone, although there may be considerable variation among individuals with respect to androgen output. The circulating levels of testosterone in postmenopausal women are only slightly lower than those observed in premenopausal women. The postmenopausal ovary probably can contribute no more than 20% of the daily production of androstenedione and multiple lines of evidence indicate that the adrenal glands are the major source of androstenedione in women. Although some authors have concluded that the postmenopausal ovary is a significant site of androgen

biosynthesis, others have questioned this idea. Cauley and colleagues[170] examined hormone levels in postmenopausal women with and without ovaries and observed no statistically significant differences in circulating levels of testosterone or androstenedione between the two groups. Couzinet and coworkers[171] reported that plasma androgen levels were very low in all postmenopausal women with adrenal insufficiency, and were similar between oophorectomized and nonoophorectomized postmenopausal women with normal adrenal function. A recent study reported that P-450scc mRNA levels were increased threefold in the ovarian stroma of postmenopausal women with endometrial cancer or hyperplasia compared with postmenopausal women without an endocrine or endometrial pathology.[172] Although P-450arom mRNA was not detectable in any of the ovaries examined, the same study found P-450c17 mRNA expression by northern analysis in the ovarian stroma of all women with endometrial cancer or hyperplasia, but only in two of the five control postmenopausal women, suggesting a potential to produce androgens in some postmenopausal ovaries. Collectively, these data indicate that the ovarian contribution to circulating androgens is highly variable among postmenopausal women.

Estrogens in the postmenopausal women appear to arise almost exclusively from extraglandular aromatization of androstenedione.[173] Oophorectomy results in no significant reduction in urinary estrogen excretion by postmenopausal women. Adrenalectomy after oophorectomy virtually eliminates measurable estrogens from the urine, however. In vitro studies concluded that the postmenopausal ovarian stroma is unable to aromatize androgens.[174] Others have suggested, however, that the postmenopausal ovary may synthesize limited amounts of estrogens because the concentrations of estradiol and estrone are two times higher in ovarian venous blood than in peripheral blood of postmenopausal women.[175]

There is some evidence that ovarian androgen production in postmenopausal women can be gonadotropin dependent. Administration of hCG to postmenopausal women results in a small increase in the circulating levels of testosterone.[176] Daily injection of hCG causes hyperplasia of the ovarian hilar cells and histochemical evidence suggestive of active steroidogenesis.[177] Administration of hCG, but not adrenocorticotropic hormone (ACTH), resulted in increased androgen but not estrogen production by the ovaries.[178] Binding sites for both LH and FSH were identified in the cortical stroma and in hilar cells.[179] Addition of hCG to hilar cells results in increased cAMP formation and steroid biosynthesis, indicating preserved responsiveness to gonadotropins. Taken together, these observations suggest that ovarian androgen biosynthesis is at least partially gonadotropin dependent.

The postmenopausal ovary is occasionally involved in pathologic endocrine activity. Stromal hyperplasia can occur with the ovary enlarging with hyperplastic stromal nodules consisting of lipid-rich luteinized cells that resemble theca interna. The ovaries with stromal hyperplasia produce large amounts of androstenedione, resulting in hirsutism and virilization.[180] Hilar cells can give rise to functional hilar cell tumors, which produce excess amounts of androgens, leading to virilization.[181-183] Signs and symptoms of estrogen excess may also be evident in circumstances of significant peripheral aromatization. For instance, the finding of threefold higher P-450scc mRNA levels in the ovarian stroma of postmenopausal women with endometrial cancer and endometrial hyperplasia suggests that aberrant steroid biosynthetic activity in the postmenopausal ovary might lead to these two disorders known to be associated with excessive estrogen stimulation.[172]

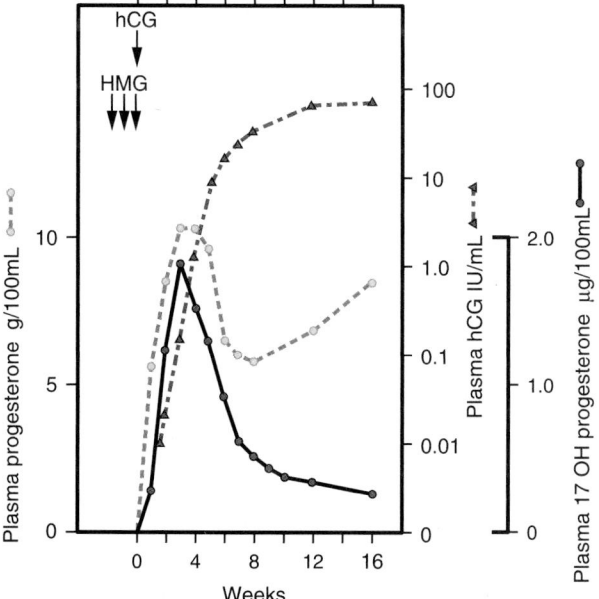

*Figure 151-5* Mean plasma levels of progesterone, 17-hydroxyprogesterone, and human chorionic gonadotropin (hCG) after induction of ovulation with human menopausal gonadotropins (HMG) and hCG. (Reprinted with permission from Yoshimi T, Strott CA, Marshall JR, et al: Corpus luteum function in early pregnancy. J Clin Endocrinol Metab 29[2]:225–230, 1969.)

## PROTEIN SECRETORY PRODUCTS OF THE OVARY

The endocrine products of the adult ovary include the protein hormones inhibin, activin, and relaxin. Both activins and inhibins are disulfide-linked dimers of subunits derived from larger preproteins. Activins are dimers consisting of two β subunits, βA and βB, assembled into three different combinations, namely, activin A (βA-βA), activin B (βB-βB), and activin AB (βA-βB). One unique α subunit is complexed to either of the two β subunits to give two isoforms of inhibin, inhibin A (α-βA) and inhibin B (α-βB). In addition to their role as intraovarian regulators, described previously, inhibins appear to have important functions in the control of FSH secretion. Inhibins and estrogens inhibit, whereas GnRH stimulates, FSH secretion by the anterior pituitary. Although infusions of activin A have been shown to stimulate FSH secretion in monkeys, it is believed that circulating activins are rendered inactive by binding to follistatin, a single-chain glycoprotein hormone that does not share significant homology with the actin/inhibin α or β subunits.

The two different forms of inhibin display a divergent secretory pattern. Circulating inhibin B levels closely parallel serum FSH levels, rising in the early follicular phase, then declining, followed by a mid-cycle peak and a subsequent decline during the luteal phase. In contrast, serum inhibin A levels are low during the early follicular phase and rise with the growth of the dominant follicle.[184] In the luteal phase, the granulosa and theca-lutein cells of the corpus luteum are a source of inhibin α subunits with the corpus luteum primarily secreting inhibin A.[185] Because inhibin B is produced by growing small follicles, circulating levels of this hormone have been postulated to be a marker for depletion of the follicle pool, preceding the onset of menopause.[186]

Relaxin, a member of the insulin family of hormones, is produced by the corpus luteum of the cycling ovary and during pregnancy.[187,188] In humans, relaxin is a two-chain peptide hormone encoded by two nonallelic genes H1 and H2, also known as RLN1 and RLN2. The H2 gene is expressed in the ovary, term placenta, decidua, and prostate gland, whereas H1 gene expression is detectable only in the prostate.[189] Immunohistochemical studies have localized relaxin to large luteal cells but not small luteal cells. Luteal immunostaining was low in early luteal phase; it increased progressively, reaching the highest level in late luteal phase, and then decreased greatly in corpora albicantia.[190] Circulating relaxin is essentially of luteal origin. The pattern of relaxin secretion by the corpus luteum of pregnancy mirrors its steroidogenic function, with levels reaching peak concentrations of 1.2 ng/mL between 8 and 12 weeks of gestation, declining to a level of 1 ng/mL, which is maintained until term. As an early pregnancy hormone, relaxin participates in the decidual response of the endometrium and the maintenance of myometrial quiescence. hCG appears to be the primary stimulus for luteal relaxin secretion. This action of hCG is independent of the stimulation of progesterone production since relaxin levels are unaffected in monkeys treated with hCG and the 3β-HSD inhibitor trilostane, which markedly reduces circulating progesterone concentrations.[191] The precise role played by relaxin in human pregnancy, cervical ripening, and parturition is currently unclear. Recent developments in the relaxin field include the discovery of a third gene encoding relaxin-3 (RLN3) and two G protein–coupled receptors, LGR7 and LGR8, which can respond to relaxin stimulation.[192]

## REFERENCES

1. Penning TM: Molecular endocrinology of hydroxysteroid dehydrogenases. Endocr Rev 18:281–305, 1997.
2. Bird IM, Conley AJ: Steroid biosynthesis: Enzymology, integration and control. In Mason JI (ed): Genetics of Steroid Biosynthesis and Function. London, Taylor and Francis, 2002, pp 1–35.
3. Strauss JF III, Penning TM: Synthesis of the sex steroid hormones: Molecular and structural biology with applications to clinical practice. In Fauser B, Rutherford A, Strauss JF III, et al (eds): Molecular Biology in Reproductive Medicine. New York, Parthenon, 1999, pp 201–232.
4. Hanukoglu I: Steroidogenic enzymes: Structure, function, and role in regulation of steroid hormone biosynthesis. J Steroid Biochem Mol Biol 43:779–804, 1992.
5. Waterman MR, Keeney DS: Signal transduction pathways combining peptide hormones and steroidogenesis. Vitam Horm 52:129–148, 1996.
6. Zeleznik AJ, Saxena D, Little-Ihrig L: Protein kinase B is obligatory for follicle-stimulating hormone-induced granulosa cell differentiation. Endocrinology 144:3985–3994, 2003.
7. Gwynne JT, Strauss J III: The role of lipoproteins in steroidogenesis and cholesterol metabolism in steroidogenic glands. Endocr Rev 3:295–329, 1982.
8. Cao G, Garcia CK, Wyne KL, et al: Structure and localization of the human gene encoding SR-BI/CLA-1: Evidence for transcriptional control by steroidogenic factor 1. J Biol Chem 272:33068–33076, 1997.

9. Azhar S, Tsai L, Medicherla S, et al: Human granulosa cells use high density lipoprotein cholesterol for steroidogenesis. J Clin Endocrinol Metab 83:983–991, 1998.
10. Connelly MA, Kellner-Weibel G, Rothblat GH, et al: SR-BI-directed HDL-cholesteryl ester hydrolysis. J Lipid Res 44:331–341, 2003.
11. Camarota LM, Chapman JM, Hui DY, et al: Carboxyl ester lipase cofractionates with scavenger receptor-BI in hepatocyte lipid rafts and enhances selective uptake and hydrolysis of cholesteryl esters from HDL. J Biol Chem 279:27599–27606, 2004.
12. Bolte E, Coudert S, Lefebvre Y: Steroid production from plasma cholesterol. II. In vivo conversion of plasma cholesterol to ovarian progesterone and adrenal C19 and C21 steroids in humans. J Clin Endocrinol Metab 38:394–400, 1974.
13. Claesson L: The intracellular localization of the esterified cholesterol in the living interstitial gland cell of the rabbit ovary. Acta Physiol Scand Suppl 31:53–78, 1954.
14. Chang TY, Chang CCY, Chen D: Acyl-coenzyme A: cholesterol acyltransferase. Annu Rev Biochem 66:613–638, 1997.
15. Yeaman SJ: Hormone-sensitive lipase: New roles for an old enzyme. Biochem J 379:11–22, 2004.
16. Strauss JF III, Schuler LA, Rosenblum MF, et al: Cholesterol metabolism by ovarian tissue. Adv Lipid Res 18:99–157, 1981.

17. Hall P: Cytochrome P-450 and the regulation of steroid synthesis. Steroids 48:131–196, 1986.
18. Stocco DM, Clark BJ: Regulation of the acute production of steroids in steroidogenic cells. Endocr Rev 17:221–244, 1996.
19. Strauss JF III, Kallen CB, Christenson LK, et al: The steroidogenic acute regulatory protein (StAR): A window into the complexities of intracellular cholesterol trafficking. Recent Prog Horm Res 54:369–394, discussion 394–365, 1999.
20. Lin D, Sugawara T, Strauss JF III, et al: Role of steroidogenic acute regulatory protein in adrenal and gonadal steroidogenesis. Science 267:1828–1831, 1995.
21. Fujieda K, Tajima T, Nakae J, et al: Spontaneous puberty in 46,XX subjects with congenital lipoid adrenal hyperplasia: Ovarian steroidogenesis is spared to some extent despite inactivating mutations in the steroidogenic acute regulatory protein (StAR) gene. J Clin Invest 99:1265–1271, 1997.
22. Papadopoulos V: Structure and function of the peripheral-type benzodiazepine receptor in steroidogenic cells. Proc Soc Exp Biol Med 217:130–142, 1998.
23. Li H, Yao Z, Degenhardt B, et al: Cholesterol binding at the cholesterol recognition/ interaction amino acid consensus (CRAC) of the peripheral-type benzodiazepine receptor and inhibition of steroidogenesis by an HIV

TAT-CRAC peptide. Proc Natl Acad Sci U S A 98:1267–1272, 2001.

24. Shen W-J, Patel S, Natu V, et al: Interaction of hormone-sensitive lipase with steroidogeneic acute regulatory protein: Facilitation of cholesterol transfer in adrenal. J Biol Chem 278:43870–43876, 2003.

25. Simard J, Durocher F, Mebarki F, et al: Molecular biology and genetics of the 3 beta-hydroxysteroid dehydrogenase/delta5-delta4 isomerase gene family. J Endocrinol 150(Suppl):S189–S207, 1996.

26. Morel Y, Mebarki F, Rheaume E, et al: Structure-function relationships of 3 beta-hydroxysteroid dehydrogenase: Contribution made by the molecular genetics of 3 beta-hydroxysteroid dehydrogenase deficiency. Steroids 62:176–184, 1997.

27. Laffargue P, Chamlian A, Adechy-Senkoel L: Localization probable en microscopie electronique de la 3b-hydrosteeroide dehydrogenase de la glucose-6-phosphate dehydrogenase et de la NADH diaphorase dans le corps jaune ovarien de la femme. J Microsc 13:325–327, 1972.

28. Mason JI, Keeney DS, Bird IM, et al: The regulation of 3 beta-hydroxysteroid dehydrogenase expression. Steroids 62:164–168, 1997.

29. Miller WL, Auchus RJ, Geller DH: The regulation of 17,20 lyase activity. Steroids 62:133–142, 1997.

30. Fluck CE, Tajima T, Pandey AV, et al: Mutant P450 oxidoreductase causes disordered steroidogenesis with and without Antley-Bixler syndrome. Nat Genet 36:228–230, 2004.

31. Zhang L, Rodriguez H, Ohno S, et al: Serine phosphorylation of human P450c17 increases 17,20 lyase activity: Implications for adrenarche and for polycystic ovary syndrome. Proc Natl Acad Sci U S A 92:10619–10623, 1995.

32. Auchus RJ, Lee TC, Miller WL: Cytochrome B5 augments the 17,20-lyase activity of human P450c17 without direct electron transfer. J Biol Chem 273:3158–3165, 1998.

33. Simpson ER, Zhao Y, Argawal VR, et al: Aromatase expression in health and disease. Recent Prog Horm Res 7:185–213, 1997.

34. Hillier SG, Reichert LE Jr, Van Hall EV: Control of preovulatory follicular estrogen biosynthesis in the human ovary. J Clin Endocrinol Metab 52:847–856, 1981.

35. Cole PA, Robinson CH: Mechanism and inhibition of cytochrome P-450 aromatase. J Am Chem Soc 33:2933–2942, 1990.

36. Durham CR, Zhu H, Masters BS, et al: Regulation of aromatase activity of rat granulosa cells: Induction of synthesis of NADPH-cytochrome P-450 reductase by FSH and dibutyryl cyclic AMP. Mol Cell Endocrinol 40:211–219, 1985.

37. Hinshelwood MM, Dodson Michael M, Sun T, et al: Regulation of aromatase expression in the ovary and placenta: A comparison between two species.

J Steroid Biochem Mol Biol 61:399–405, 1997.

38. Sebastian S, Bulun SE: A highly complex organization of the regulatory region of the human CYP19 (aromatase) gene revealed by the Human Genome Project. J Clin Endocrinol Metab 86:4600–4602, 2001.

39. Peltoketo H, Vihko P, Vihko R: Regulation of estrogen action: Role of 17 beta-hydroxysteroid dehydrogenases. Vitam Horm 55:353–398, 1999.

40. Sawetawan C, Milewich L, Word RA, et al: Compartmentalization of type I 17 beta-hydroxysteroid oxidoreductase in the human ovary. Mol Cell Endocrinol 99:161–168, 1994.

41. Zachow RJ, Ramski BE, Lee H: Modulation of estrogen production and 17β-hydroxysteroid dehydrogenase type 1, cytochrome p450 aromatase, c-met, and protein kinase b α messenger ribonucleic acid content in rat ovarian granulosa cells by hepatocyte growth factor and follicle-stimulating hormone. Biol Reprod 62:1851–1857, 2000.

42. Zhang Y, Word RA, Fesmire S, et al: Human ovarian expression of 17 beta-hydroxysteroid dehydrogenase types 1, 2, and 3. J Clin Endocrinol Metab 81:3594–3598, 1996.

43. Krazeisen A, Breitling R, Imai K, et al: Determination of cDNA, gene structure and chromosomal localization of the novel human 17beta-hydroxysteroid dehydrogenase type 7. FEBS Lett 460:373–379, 1999.

44. Nokelainen P, Peltoketo H, Vihko R, et al: Expression cloning of a novel estrogenic mouse 17 beta-hydroxysteroid dehydrogenase/17-ketosteroid reductase (m17HSD7), previously described as a prolactin receptor–associated protein (PRAP) in rat. Mol Endocrinol 12:1048–1059, 1998.

45. Hegele-Hartung C, Grutzner M, Lessl M, et al: Activation of meiotic maturation in rat oocytes after treatment with follicular fluid meiosis-activating sterol in vitro and ex vivo. Biol Reprod 64:418–424, 2001.

46. Filicori M, Butler JP, Crowley WF Jr: Neuroendocrine regulation of the corpus luteum in the human: Evidence for pulsatile progesterone secretion. J Clin Invest 73:1638–1647, 1984.

47. Vaknin KM, Lazar S, Popliker M, et al: Role of meiosis-activating sterols in rat oocyte maturation: Effects of specific inhibitors and changes in the expression of lanosterol 14alpha-demethylase during the preovulatory period. Biol Reprod 64:299–309, 2001.

48. Yoshimi T, Strott CA, Marshall JR, et al: Corpus luteum function in early pregnancy. J Clin Endocrinol Metab 29:225–230, 1969.

49. Backstrom T, Andersson A, Baird DT, et al: The human corpus luteum secretes 5 alpha-pregnane-3,20-dione. Acta Endocrinol (Copenh) 111:116–121, 1986.

50. Haning RV Jr, Tantravahi U, Zhao Q, et al: 5alpha-reductase 1 and 2 expression and activity in human ovarian follicles, stroma and corpus

luteum as compared to neonatal foreskin. J Steroid Biochem Mol Biol 59:199–204, 1996.

51. Jakimiuk AJ, Weitsman SR, Magoffin DA: 5α-Reductase activity in women with polycystic ovary syndrome. J Clin Endocrinol Metab 84:2414–2418, 1999.

52. Zeleznik AJ, Little-Ihrig L, Ramasawamy S: Administration of dihydrotestosterone to rhesus monkeys inhibits gonadotropin-stimulated ovarian steroidogenesis. J Clin Endocrinol Metab 89:860–866, 2004.

53. Kuiper GGJM, Carlsson B, Grandien K, et al: Comparison of the ligand binding specificity and transcript tissue distribution of estrogen receptors α and β. Endocrinology 138:863–870, 1997.

54. Spicer LJ, Hammond JM: Regulation of ovarian function by catecholestrogens: Current concepts. J Steroid Biochem 33:489–501, 1989.

55. Cavalieri E, Frenkel K, Liehr JG, et al: Estrogens as endogenous genotoxic agents: DNA adducts and mutations. J Natl Cancer Inst Monogr 75–93, 2000.

56. Mabjeesh NJ, Escuin D, LaVallee TM, et al: 2ME2 inhibits tumor growth and angiogenesis by disrupting microtubules and dysregulating HIF. Cancer Cell 3:363–375, 2003.

57. Matthews CH, Borgato S, Beck-Peccoz P, et al: Primary amenorrhoea and infertility due to a mutation in the beta-subunit of follicle-stimulating hormone. Nat Genet 5:83–86, 1993.

58. Aittomaki K, Herva R, Stenman UH, et al: Clinical features of primary ovarian failure caused by a point mutation in the follicle-stimulating hormone receptor gene. J Clin Endocrinol Metab 81:3722–3726, 1996.

59. Tapanainen JS, Vaskivuo T, Aittomaki K, et al: Inactivating FSH receptor mutations and gonadal dysfunction. Mol Cell Endocrinol 145:129–135, 1998.

60. Couzinet B, Lestrat N, Brailly S, et al: Stimulation of ovarian follicular maturation with pure follicle-stimulating hormone in women with gonadotropin deficiency. J Clin Endocrinol Metab 66:552–556, 1988.

61. Schoot DC, Coelingh Bennink HJ, Mannaerts BM, et al: Human recombinant follicle-stimulating hormone induces growth of preovulatory follicles without concomitant increase in androgen and estrogen biosynthesis in a woman with isolated gonadotropin deficiency. J Clin Endocrinol Metab 74:1471–1473, 1992.

62. Zelinski-Wooten MB, Hutchison JS, Hess DL, et al: Follicle stimulating hormone alone supports follicle growth and oocyte development in gonadotrophin-releasing hormone antagonist–treated monkeys. Hum Reprod 10:1658–1666, 1995.

63. Sullivan MW, Stewart-Akers A, Krasnow JS, et al: Ovarian responses in women to recombinant follicle-stimulating hormone and luteinizing hormone (LH): A role for LH in the final stages of follicular maturation. J Clin Endocrinol Metab 84:228–232, 1999.

64. Ravindranath N, Little-Ihrig L, Benyo DF, et al: Role of luteinizing hormone in the expression of cholesterol side-chain cleavage cytochrome P450 and 3 beta-hydroxysteroid dehydrogenase, delta 5-4 isomerase messenger ribonucleic acids in the primate corpus luteum. Endocrinology 131:2065–2070, 1992.

65. Devoto L, Kohen P, Gonzalez RR, et al: Expression of steroidogenic acute regulatory protein in the human corpus luteum throughout the luteal phase. J Clin Endocrinol Metab 86:5633–5639, 2001.

66. Wiltbank MC, Belfiore CJ, Niswender GD: Steroidogenic enzyme activity after acute activation of protein kinase (PK) A and PKC in ovine small and large luteal cells. Mol Cell Endocrinol 97:1–7, 1993.

67. Arakane F, King SR, Du Y, et al: Phosphorylation of steroidogenic acute regulatory protein (StAR) modulates its steroidogenic activity. J Biol Chem 272:32656–32662, 1997.

68. Monnier N, Defaye G, Chambaz EM: Phosphorylation of bovine adrenodoxin: Structural study and enzymatic activity. Eur J Biochem 169:147–153, 1987.

69. Wong M, Ikeda Y, Luo X, et al: Steroidogenic factor 1 plays multiple roles in endocrine development and function. Recent Prog Horm Res 52:167–184, 1997.

70. Omura T, Morohashi K-I: Gene regulation of steroidogenesis. J Steroid Biochem Mole Biol 53:19–25, 1995.

71. Ito M, Yu RN, Jameson JL: Steroidogenic factor-1 contains a carboxy-terminal transcriptional activation domain that interacts with steroid receptor coactivator-1. Mol Endocrinol 12:290–301, 1998.

72. Hedin L, Rodgers RJ, Simpson ER, et al: Changes in content of cytochrome P450(17)alpha, cytochrome P450scc, and 3-hydroxy-3-methylglutaryl CoA reductase in developing rat ovarian follicles and corpora lutea: Correlation with theca cell steroidogenesis. Biol Reprod 37:211–223, 1987.

73. Hinshelwood MM, Repa JJ, Shelton JM, et al: Expression of LRH-1 and SF-1 in the mouse ovary: Localization in different cell types correlates with differing function. Mol Cell Endocrinol 207:39–45, 2003.

74. Peng N, Kim JW, Rainey WE, et al: The role of the orphan nuclear receptor, liver receptor homologue-1, in the regulation of human corpus luteum 3beta-hydroxysteroid dehydrogenase type II. J Clin Endocrinol Metab 88:6020–6028, 2003.

75. Alam H, Maizels ET, Park Y, et al: Follicle-stimulating hormone activation of hypoxia-inducible factor-1 by the phosphatidylinositol 3-kinase/AKT/ras homolog enriched in brain (Rheb)/mammalian target of rapamycin (mTOR) pathway is necessary for induction of select protein markers of follicular differentiation. J Biol Chem 279:19431–19440, 2004.

76. Fitzpatrick SL, Richards JS: Regulation of cytochrome P450 aromatase messenger ribonucleic acid and activity by steroids and gonadotropins in rat granulosa cells. Endocrinology 129:1452–1462, 1991.

77. Chung PH, Sandhoff TW, McLean MP: Hormone and prostaglandin F2 alpha regulation of messenger ribonucleic acid encoding steroidogenic acute regulatory protein in human corpora lutea. Endocrine 8:153–160, 1998.

78. Zazopoulos E, Lalli E, Stocco DM, et al: DNA binding and transcriptional repression by DAX-1 blocks steroidogenesis. Nature 390:311–315, 1997.

79. Lalli E, Melner MH, Stocco DM, et al: DAX-1 blocks steroid production at multiple levels. Endocrinology 139:4237–4243, 1998.

80. Gurates B, Amsterdam A, Tamura M, et al: WT1 and DAX-1 regulate SF-1-mediated human P450arom gene expression in gonadal cells. Mol Cell Endocrinol 208:61–75, 2003.

81. Sato Y, Suzuki T, Hidaka K, et al: Immunolocalization of nuclear transcription factors, DAX-1 and COUP-TF II, in the normal human ovary: Correlation with adrenal 4 binding protein/steroidogenic factor-1 immunolocalization during the menstrual cycle. J Clin Endocrinol Metab 88:3415–3420, 2003.

82. Makrigiannakis A, Amin K, Coukos G, et al: Regulated expression and potential roles of p53 and Wilms' tumor suppressor gene (WT1) during follicular development in the human ovary. J Clin Endocrinol Metab 85:449–459, 2000.

83. LaVoie HA, Garmey JC, Veldhuis JD: Mechanisms of insulin-like growth factor I augmentation of follicle-stimulating hormone-induced porcine steroidogenic acute regulatory protein gene promoter activity in granulosa cells. Endocrinology 140:146–153, 1999.

84. LaVoie HA, Garmey JC, Day RN, et al: Concerted regulation of low density lipoprotein receptor gene expression by follicle-stimulating hormone and insulin-like growth factor I in porcine granulosa cells: Promoter activation, messenger ribonucleic acid stability, and sterol feedback. Endocrinology 140:178–186, 1999.

85. Schwarzler P, Untergasser G, Hermann M, et al: Prolactin gene expression and prolactin protein in premenopausal and postmenopausal human ovaries. Fertil Steril 68:696–701, 1997.

86. Soto EA, Tureck RW, Strauss JF III: Effects of prolactin on progestin secretion by human granulosa cells in culture. Biol Reprod 32:541–545, 1985.

87. Sharara FI, Nieman LK: Identification and cellular localization of growth hormone receptor gene expression in the human ovary. J Clin Endocrinol Metab 79:670–672, 1994.

88. Franks S: Growth hormone and ovarian function. Baillieres Clin Endocrinol Metab 12:331–340, 1998.

89. Willis D, Franks S: Insulin action in human granulosa cells from normal and polycystic ovaries is mediated by the insulin receptor and not the type-I insulin-like growth factor receptor. J Clin Endocrinol Metab 80:3788–3790, 1995.

90. Giudice LC, Cataldo NA, van Dessel HJ, et al: Growth factors in normal ovarian follicle development. Semin Reprod Endocrinol 14:179–196, 1996.

91. Adashi EY: Insulin-like growth factors as determinants of follicular fate. J Soc Gynecol Investig 2:721–726, 1995.

92. Norman RJ, Brannstrom M: Cytokines in the ovary: Pathophysiology and potential for pharmacological intervention. Pharmacol Ther 69:219–236, 1996.

93. Zhou J, Bondy C: Anatomy of the human ovarian insulin-like growth factor system. Biol Reprod 48:467–482, 1993.

94. Barbieri RL, Makris A, Randall RW, et al: Insulin stimulates androgen accumulation in incubations of ovarian stroma obtained from women with hyperandrogenism. J Clin Endocrinol Metab 62:904–910, 1986.

95. Cataldo NA: Insulin-like growth factor binding proteins: Do they play a role in polycystic ovary syndrome? Semin Reprod Endocrinol 15:123–136, 1997.

96. Lawrence JB, Oxvig C, Overgaard MT, et al: The insulin-like growth factor (IGF)–dependent IGF binding protein-4 protease secreted by human fibroblasts is pregnancy-associated plasma protein-A. Proc Natl Acad Sci U S A 96:3149–3153, 1999.

97. Conover CA, Faessen GF, Ilg KE, et al: Pregnancy-associated plasma protein-A is the insulin-like growth factor binding protein-4 protease secreted by human ovarian granulosa cells and is a marker of dominant follicle selection and the corpus luteum. Endocrinology 142:2155, 2001.

98. Knight PG: Roles of inhibins, activins, and follistatin in the female reproductive system. Front Neuroendocrinol 17:476–509, 1996.

99. DePaolo LV: Inhibins, activins, and follistatins: The saga continues. Proc Soc Exp Biol Med 214:328–339, 1997.

100. Peng C, Ohno T, Khorasheh S, et al: Activin and follistatin as local regulators in the human ovary. Biol Signals 5:81–89, 1996.

101. Patel K: Follistatin. Int J Biochem Cell Biol 30:1087–1093, 1998.

102. Khoury RH, Wang QF, Crowley WF Jr, et al: Serum follistatin levels in women: Evidence against an endocrine function of ovarian follistatin. J Clin Endocrinol Metab 80:1361–1368, 1995.

103. Schneyer AL, Fujiwara T, Fox J, et al: Dynamic changes in the intrafollicular inhibin/activin/follistatin axis during human follicular development: Relationship to circulating hormone

concentrations. J Clin Endocrinol Metab 85:3319–3330, 2000.

104. Guo Q, Kumar TR, Woodruff T, et al: Overexpression of mouse follistatin causes reproductive defects in transgenic mice. Mol Endocrinol 12:96–106, 1998.

105. Durlinger AL, Kramer P, Karels B, et al: Control of primordial follicle recruitment by anti-Müllerian hormone in the mouse ovary. Endocrinology 140:5789–5796, 1999.

106. de Vet A, Laven JS, de Jong FH, et al: Antimullerian hormone serum levels: A putative marker for ovarian aging. Fertil Steril 77:357–362, 2002.

107. Gruijters MJ, Visser JA, Durlinger AL, et al: Anti-Müllerian hormone and its role in ovarian function. Mol Cell Endocrinol 211:85–90, 2003.

108. McGrath SA, Esquela AF, Lee SJ: Oocyte-specific expression of growth/differentiation factor-9. Mol Endocrinol 9:131–136, 1995.

109. Dong JW, Albertini DF, Nishimori K, et al: Growth differentiation factor-9 is required during early ovarian folliculogenesis. Nature 383:531–535, 1996.

110. Carabatsos MJ, Elvin J, Matzuk MM, et al: Characterization of oocyte and follicle development in growth differentiation factor-9-deficient mice. Dev Biol 204:373–384, 1998.

111. Vitt UA, Mazerbourg S, Klein C, et al: Bone morphogenetic protein receptor type II is a receptor for growth differentiation factor-9. Biol Reprod 67:473–480, 2002.

112. Elvin JA, Clark AT, Wang P, et al: Paracrine actions of growth differentiation factor-9 in the mammalian ovary. Mol Endocrinol 13:1035–1048, 1999.

113. Elvin JA, Yan C, Wang P, et al: Molecular characterization of the follicle defects in the growth differentiation factor 9–deficient ovary. Mol Endocrinol 13:1018–1034, 1999.

114. Yamamoto N, Christenson LK, McAllister JM, et al: Growth differentiation factor-9 inhibits 3′5′-adenosine monophosphate–stimulated steroidogenesis in human granulosa and theca cells. J Clin Endocrinol Metab 87:2849–2856, 2002.

115. Shimasaki S, Moore RK, Otsuka F, et al: The bone morphogenetic protein system in mammalian reproduction. Endocr Rev 25:72–101, 2004.

116. Otsuka F, Yao Z, Lee T, et al: Bone morphogenetic protein-15. Identification of target cells and biological functions. J Biol Chem 275:39523–39528, 2000.

117. Tonetta SA, diZerega GS: Intragonadal regulation of follicular maturation. Endocr Rev 10:205–229, 1989.

118. Palter SF, Tavares AB, Hourvitz A, et al: Are estrogens of import to primate/human ovarian folliculogenesis? Endocr Rev 22:389–424, 2001.

119. Rabinovici J, Blankstein J, Goldman B, et al: In vitro fertilization and primary embryonic cleavage are possible in 17 alpha-hydroxylase deficiency despite extremely low intrafollicular 17 beta-estradiol. J Clin Endocrinol Metab 68:693–697, 1989.

120. Fisher CR, Graves KH, Parlow AF, et al: Characterization of mice deficient in aromatase (ArKO) because of targeted disruption of the cyp19 gene. Proc Natl Acad Sci U S A 95:6965–6970, 1998.

121. Zelinski-Wooten MB, Hess DL, Baughman WL, et al: Administration of an aromatase inhibitor during the late follicular phase of gonadotropin-treated cycles in rhesus monkeys: Effects on follicle development, oocyte maturation, and subsequent luteal function. J Clin Endocrinol Metab 76:988–995, 1993.

122. Saunders PT, Millar MR, Williams K, et al: Differential expression of estrogen receptor-alpha and -beta and androgen receptor in the ovaries of marmosets and humans. Biol Reprod 63:1098–1105, 2000.

123. Horie K, Takakura K, Fujiwara H, et al: Immunohistochemical localization of androgen receptor in the human ovary throughout the menstrual cycle in relation to oestrogen and progesterone receptor expression. Hum Reprod 7:184–190, 1992.

124. Weil SJ, Vendola K, Zhou J, et al: Androgen receptor gene expression in the primate ovary: Cellular localization, regulation, and functional correlations. J Clin Endocrinol Metab 83:2479–2485, 1998.

125. Szoltys M, Slomczynska M: Changes in distribution of androgen receptor during maturation of rat ovarian follicles. Exp Clin Endocrinol Diabetes 108:228–234, 2000.

126. Vendola KA, Zhou J, Adesanya OO, et al: Androgens stimulate early stages of follicular growth in the primate ovary. J Clin Invest 101:2622–2629, 1998.

127. Weil S, Vendola K, Zhou J, et al: Androgen and follicle-stimulating hormone interactions in primate ovarian follicle development. J Clin Endocrinol Metab 84:2951–2956, 1999.

128. Hillier SG, Tetsuka M: Role of androgens in follicle maturation and atresia. Baillieres Clin Obstet Gynaecol 11:249–260, 1997.

129. Agarwal SK, Judd HL, Magoffin DA: A mechanism for the suppression of estrogen production in polycystic ovary syndrome. J Clin Endocrinol Metab 81:3686–3691, 1996.

130. Hillier SG, van den Boogaard AM, Reichert LE Jr, et al: Alterations in granulosa cell aromatase activity accompanying preovulatory follicular development in the rat ovary with evidence that 5alpha-reduced C19 steroids inhibit the aromatase reaction in vitro. J Endocrinol 84:409–419, 1980.

131. Iwai T, Nanbu Y, Iwai M, et al: Immunohistochemical localization of oestrogen receptors and progesterone receptors in the human ovary throughout the menstrual cycle. Virchows Arch A Pathol Anat Histopathol 417:369–375, 1990.

132. Misao R, Nakanishi Y, Iwagaki S, et al: Expression of progesterone receptor isoforms in corpora lutea of human subjects: Correlation with serum oestrogen and progesterone concentrations. Mol Hum Reprod 4:1045–1052, 1998.

133. Stouffer RL: Progesterone as a mediator of gonadotrophin action in the corpus luteum: Beyond steroidogenesis. Hum Reprod Update 9:99–117, 2003.

134. Duffy DM, Stouffer RL: Gonadotropin versus steroid regulation of the corpus luteum of the rhesus monkey during simulated early pregnancy. Biol Reprod 57:1451–1460, 1997.

135. Duffy DM, Hess DL, Stouffer RL: Acute administration of a 3 beta-hydroxysteroid dehydrogenase inhibitor to rhesus monkeys at the midluteal phase of the menstrual cycle: Evidence for possible autocrine regulation of the primate corpus luteum by progesterone. J Clin Endocrinol Metab 79:1587–1594, 1994.

136. Borman SM, Chaffin CL, Schwinof KM, et al: Progesterone promotes oocyte maturation, but not ovulation, in nonhuman primate follicles without a gonadotropin surge. Biol Reprod 71:366–373, 2004.

137. Sirois J, Boreboom D, Sayasith K: Prostaglandin biosynthesis and action in the ovary. In Leung PCK, Adashi EY (eds): The Ovary, 2d ed. San Diego, CA, Elsevier, 2004, pp 233–247.

138. Lim H, Paria BC, Das SK, et al: Multiple female reproductive failures in cyclooxygenase 2–deficient mice. Cell 91:197–208, 1997.

139. Ochsner SA, Russell DL, Day AJ, et al: Decreased expression of tumor necrosis factor-alpha–stimulated gene 6 in cumulus cells of the cyclooxygenase-2 and EP2 null mice. Endocrinology 144:1008–1019, 2003.

140. Duffy DM, Stouffer RL: The ovulatory gonadotrophin surge stimulates cyclooxygenase expression and prostaglandin production by the monkey follicle. Mol Hum Reprod 7:731–739, 2001.

141. Hizaki H, Segi E, Sugimoto Y, et al: Abortive expansion of the cumulus and impaired fertility in mice lacking the prostaglandin E receptor subtype EP2. Proc Natl Acad Sci U S A 96:10501–10506, 1999.

142. McGuire WJ, Juengel JL, Niswender GD: Protein kinase C second messenger system mediates the antisteroidogenic effects of prostaglandin F2 alpha in the ovine corpus luteum in vivo. Biol Reprod 51:800–806, 1994.

143. Juengel JL, Meberg BM, Turzillo AM, et al: Hormonal regulation of messenger ribonucleic acid encoding steroidogenic acute regulatory protein in ovine corpora lutea. Endocrinology 136:5423–5429, 1995.

144. Khan-Dawood FS: Oxytocin in intercellular communication in the corpus luteum. Semin Reprod Endocrinol 15:395–407, 1997.
145. Terranova PF, Rice VM: Review: cytokine involvement in ovarian processes. Am J Reprod Immunol 37:50–63, 1997.
146. Hurwitz A, Payne DW, Packman JN, et al: Cytokine-mediated regulation of ovarian function: Interleukin-1 inhibits gonadotropin-induced androgen biosynthesis. Endocrinology 129:1250–1256, 1991.
147. Gottschall PE, Uehara A, Hoffmann ST, et al: Interleukin-1 inhibits follicle stimulating hormone–induced differentiation in rat granulosa cells in vitro. Biochem Biophys Res Commun 149:502–509, 1987.
148. Gottschall PE, Katsuura G, Arimura A: Interleukin-1 suppresses follicle-stimulating hormone–induced estradiol secretion from cultured ovarian granulosa cells. J Reprod Immunol 15:281–290, 1989.
149. Peng C, Fan NC, Ligier M, et al: Expression and regulation of gonadotropin-releasing hormone (GnRH) and GnRH receptor messenger ribonucleic acids in human granulosa-luteal cells. Endocrinology 135:1740–1746, 1994.
150. Kang SK, Choi KC, Cheng KW, et al: Role of gonadotropin-releasing hormone as an autocrine growth factor in human ovarian surface epithelium. Endocrinology 141:72–80, 2000.
151. Choi KC, Auersperg N, Leung PC: Expression and antiproliferative effect of a second form of gonadotropin-releasing hormone in normal and neoplastic ovarian surface epithelial cells. J Clin Endocrinol Metab 86:5075–5078, 2001.
152. Tureck RW, Mastroianni L Jr, Blasco L, et al: Inhibition of human granulosa cell progesterone secretion by a gonadotropin-releasing hormone agonist. J Clin Endocrinol Metab 54:1078–1080, 1982.
153. Parinaud J, Beaur A, Bourreau E, et al: Effect of a luteinizing hormone–releasing hormone agonist (Buserelin) on steroidogenesis of cultured human preovulatory granulosa cells. Fertil Steril 50:597–602, 1988.
154. Maeda K, Kitawaki J, Yokota K, et al: [Effects of gonadotropin–releasing hormone and its analogue (buserelin) on aromatase in cultured human granulosa cells]. Nippon Sanka Fujinka Gakkai Zasshi 48:89–95, 1996.
155. Pollack SE, Furth EE, Kallen CB, et al: Localization of the steroidogenic acute regulatory protein in human tissues. J Clin Endocrinol Metab 82:4243–4251, 1997.
156. Voutilainen R, Miller WL: Developmental expression of genes for the stereoidogenic enzymes P450scc (20,22-desmolase), P450c17 (17 alpha-hydroxylase/17,20-lyase), and P450c21 (21-hydroxylase) in the human fetus.

J Clin Endocrinol Metab 63:1145–1150, 1986.
157. Tapanainen J, Voutilainen R, Jaffe RB: Low aromatase activity and gene expression in human fetal testes. J Steroid Biochem 33:7–11, 1989.
158. Sanders SL, Stouffer RL: Localization of steroidogenic enzymes in macaque luteal tissue during the menstrual cycle and simulated early pregnancy: Immunohistochemical evidence supporting the two-cell model for estrogen production in the primate corpus luteum. Biol Reprod 56:1077–1087, 1997.
159. Sasano H, Suzuki T: Localization of steroidogenesis and steroid receptors in human corpus luteum: Classification of human corpus luteum (CL) into estrogen-producing degenerating CL, and nonsteroid-producing degenerating CL. Semin Reprod Endocrinol 15:345–351, 1997.
160. Grazul-Bilska AT, Redmer DA, Reynolds LP: Cellular interactions in the corpus luteum. Semin Reprod Endocrinol 15:383–393, 1997.
161. Hutchison JS, Zeleznik AJ: The rhesus monkey corpus luteum is dependent on pituitary gonadotropin secretion throughout the luteal phase of the menstrual cycle. Endocrinology 115:1780–1786, 1984.
162. Hutchison JS, Zeleznik AJ: The corpus luteum of the primate menstrual cycle is capable of recovering from a transient withdrawal of pituitary gonadotropin support. Endocrinology 117:1043–1049, 1985.
163. Zeleznik AJ: In vivo responses of the primate corpus luteum to luteinizing hormone and chorionic gonadotropin. Proc Natl Acad Sci U S A 95:11002–11007, 1998.
164. Benyo DF, Little-Ihrig L, Zeleznik AJ: Noncoordinated expression of luteal cell messenger ribonucleic acids during human chorionic gonadotropin stimulation of the primate corpus luteum. Endocrinology 133:699–704, 1993.
165. Bukovsky A, Caudle MR, Keenan JA, et al: Is corpus luteum regression an immune-mediated event? Localization of immune system components and luteinizing hormone receptor in human corpora lutea. Biol Reprod 53:1373–1384, 1995.
166. Shikone T, Yamoto M, Kokawa K, et al: Apoptosis of human corpora lutea during cyclic luteal regression and early pregnancy. J Clin Endocrinol Metab 81:2376–2380, 1996.
167. Plouffe L Jr: Ovaries, androgens and the menopause: Practical applications. Semin Reprod Endocrinol 16:117–120, 1998.
168. Dennefors BL, Janson PO, Knutson F, et al: Steroid production and responsiveness to gonadotropin in isolated stromal tissue of human postmenopausal ovaries. Am J Obstet Gynecol 136:997–1002, 1980.
169. Dennefors BL, Janson PO, Hamberger L, et al: Hilus cells from

human postmenopausal ovaries: Gonadotrophin sensitivity, steroid and cyclic AMP production. Acta Obstet Gynecol Scand 61:413–416, 1982.
170. Cauley JA, Gutai JP, Kuller LH, et al: The epidemiology of serum sex hormones in postmenopausal women. Am J Epidemiol 129:1120–1131, 1989.
171. Couzinet B, Meduri G, Lecce MG, et al: The postmenopausal ovary is not a major androgen-producing gland. J Clin Endocrinol Metab 86:5060–5066, 2001.
172. Nagamani M, Urban RJ: Expression of messenger ribonucleic acid encoding steroidogenic enzymes in postmenopausal ovaries. J Soc Gynecol Investig 10:37–40, 2003.
173. Grodin JM, Siiteri PK, MacDonald PC: Source of estrogen production in postmenopausal women. J Clin Endocrinol Metab 36:207–214, 1973.
174. Mattingly RF, Huang WY: Steroidogenesis of the menopausal and postmenopausal ovary. Am J Obstet Gynecol 103:679–693, 1969.
175. Judd HL, Judd GE, Lucas WE, et al: Endocrine function of the postmenopausal ovary: Concentration of androgens and estrogens in ovarian and peripheral vein blood. J Clin Endocrinol Metab 39:1020–1024, 1974.
176. Vermeulen A: The hormonal activity of the postmenopausal ovary. J Clin Endocrinol Metab 42:247–253, 1976.
177. Poliak A, Jones G, Goldberg B: Effect of human chorionic gonadotropin on postmenopausal women. Am J Obstet Gynecol 101:731, 1968.
178. Greenblatt RB, Colle ML, Mahesh VB: Ovarian and adrenal steroid production in the postmenopausal woman. Obstet Gynecol 47:383–387, 1976.
179. Nakano R, Shima K, Yamoto M, et al: Binding sites for gonadotropins in human postmenopausal ovaries. Obstet Gynecol 73:196–200, 1989.
180. Braithwaite SS, Erkman-Balis B, Avila TD: Postmenopausal virilization due to ovarian stromal hyperthecosis. J Clin Endocrinol Metab 46:295–300, 1978.
181. Sternberg WH: The morphology, androgenic function, hyperplasia, and tumors of the human ovarian hilus cells. Am J Pathol 25:493, 1947.
182. Mandel FP, Voet RL, Weiland AJ, et al: Steroid secretion by masculinizing and "feminizing" hilus cell tumors. J Clin Endocrinol Metab 52:779–784, 1981.
183. Merkow LP, Slifkin M, Acevedo HF, et al: Ultrastructure of an interstitial (hilar) cell tumor of the ovary. Obstet Gynecol 37:845–859, 1971.
184. Groome NP, Illingworth PJ, O'Brien M, et al: Measurement of dimeric inhibin B throughout the human menstrual cycle. J Clin Endocrinol Metab 81:1401–1405, 1996.
185. Illingworth PJ, Groome NP, Duncan WC, et al: Measurement of circulating inhibin forms during the

establishment of pregnancy. J Clin Endocrinol Metab 81:1471–1475, 1996.

186. Welt CK, McNicholl DJ, Taylor AE, et al: Female reproductive aging is marked by decreased secretion of dimeric inhibin. J Clin Endocrinol Metab 84:105–111, 1999.

187. Goldsmith LT, Weiss G, Steinetz BG: Relaxin and its role in pregnancy. Endocrinol Metab Clin North Am 24:171–186, 1995.

188. Bani D: Relaxin: A pleiotropic hormone. Gen Pharmacol 28:13–22, 1997.

189. Gunnersen JM, Fu P, Roche PJ, et al: Expression of human relaxin genes: Characterization of a novel alternatively spliced human relaxin mRNA species. Mol Cell Endocrinol 118:85–94, 1996.

190. Stoelk E, Chegini N, Lei ZM, et al: Immunocytochemical localization of relaxin in human corpora lutea: Cellular and subcellular distribution and dependence on reproductive state. Biol Reprod 44:1140–1147, 1991.

191. Duffy DM, Stouffer RL, Stewart DR: Dissociation of relaxin and progesterone secretion from the primate corpus luteum by acute administration of a 3 beta-hydroxysteroid dehydrogenase inhibitor during the menstrual cycle. Biol Reprod 53:447–453, 1995.

192. Bathgate RA, Samuel CS, Burazin TC, et al: Relaxin: New peptides, receptors and novel actions. Trends Endocrinol Metab 14:207–213, 2003.

# Estrogen and Progesterone Action

## Nancy L. Weigel and Carolyn L. Smith

## INTRODUCTION

Estrogen and progesterone are required for female reproductive function, playing key roles in growth and differentiation of the uterus and mammary glands. The actions of these steroids are, for the most part, mediated by their cognate nuclear receptors. Estrogen and progesterone receptors (ER and PR, respectively) are members of a very large family of lig-and-activated transcription factors that encompasses receptors for other steroids, thyroid hormone, the active forms of vitamins A and D, as well as a variety of other small hydrophobic compounds.[1-3] Members of the nuclear receptor family share several common structural features. Family members were first identified by their highly conserved 66 amino acid DNA-binding domains and two smaller, less conserved regions in the carboxyl-terminal hormone-binding domain of the proteins.[4] The regions of the receptors have, by convention, been named A–F with the DNA-binding domain (C) and the hormone-binding domain (E) being the most highly conserved regions.[5,6] Some receptors, such as the PR, lack an F domain, and others contain extremely short A/B regions.

The mechanisms of action of steroid hormone receptors share many common features. Figure 152-1 shows a simplified model of steroid receptor activation. In the absence of hormone, receptor monomers are each bound by protein complexes that contain heat shock protein 90 (hsp90), hsp70, and a number of other proteins that are required for formation of the mature ligand-binding conformation of the receptors.[7,8] Most of the estrogen receptors and progesterone receptors are localized to the nucleus in the absence of hormone; nevertheless, hormone binding promotes DNA binding. Because estradiol and progesterone are lipophilic hormones (Fig. 152-2), they can diffuse passively across the plasma membrane and bind to their cognate receptors. Hormone binding induces conformational changes in the receptor,[9,10] releasing it from the heat shock protein complex[8] and allowing the receptors to form homodimers that bind to specific hormone response elements in the DNA. Receptors recruit coactivators and interact directly with components of the basal transcription complex to induce transcription of target genes.

## STRUCTURE OF ESTROGEN AND PROGESTERONE RECEPTORS

### ESTROGEN RECEPTOR-α

The structure of the human estrogen receptor-α (ER-α) is shown in Figure 152-3. The amino terminal region (A/B) contains one of the transcriptional activation functions of ER-α. This activity, originally termed TAF1,[11] has been renamed activation function 1 (AF1). The A/B region in ER-α is substantially shorter than that of other steroid receptors such as the PR shown in Figure 152-4. Adjacent to the A/B region is the DNA-binding domain (C), the most highly conserved domain in steroid receptors. This region contains two zinc-finger motifs, each containing four cysteines that coordinately bind $Zn^{2+}$. The consensus DNA response element for the estrogen receptor is an inverted palindrome separated by three nucleotides (AGGTCAnnnTGACCT), although natural response elements may differ substantially from this consensus. The D or hinge region is poorly conserved among steroid receptors, but contains a nuclear localization signal.[12] The E region is required for hormone binding and contains dimerization domains,[13] a second activation function, AF2, and sites for interaction with other proteins including hsp90[14] and a variety of coactivators. The estrogen receptor contains an additional region, F, at the carboxyl terminus.

### ESTROGEN RECEPTOR-β

For many years, it was thought that there was only one estrogen receptor. However, a second estrogen receptor was cloned from a prostate library in 1996.[15] The classical estrogen receptor described in the previous section was therefore renamed ER-α, and the more recently discovered estrogen receptor is referred to as ER-β. This second estrogen receptor is encoded by a separate gene. It shares roughly 84% homology with ER-α in the DNA-binding domain, but only 58% in the E region and less in the other domains. There have been discrepancies in the reported length of the A/B region of ER-β, as predicted by DNA sequencing, but in all cases, ER-β is shorter than ER-α. Western blot analysis generally reveals ER-β to be approximately 6 kilodalton smaller than ER-α. In addition to forming homodimers, ER-β can heterodimerize with ER-α

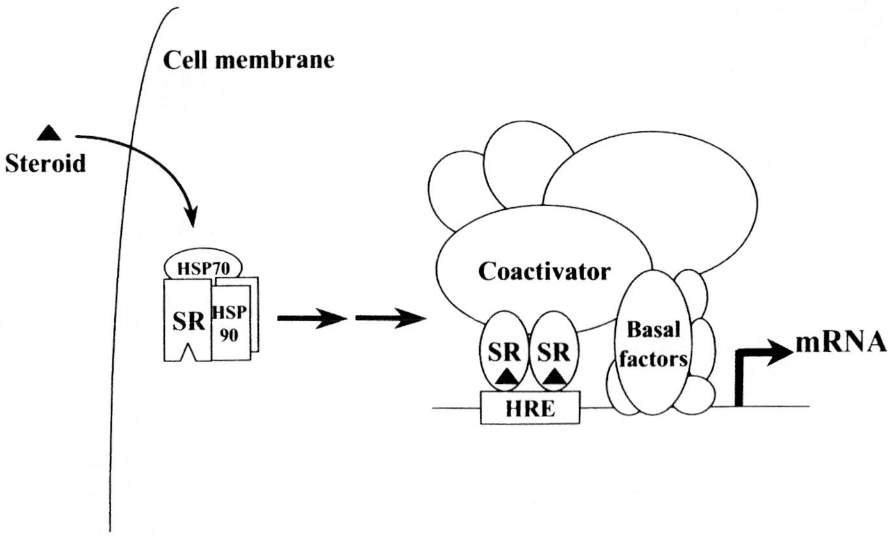

**Cell membrane**

**Steroid**

*Figure 152-1* Activation of steroid receptors. In the absence of ligand, steroid receptors (SRs) reside in an inactive complex containing heat shock proteins (HSPs) and other proteins. Upon steroid binding, the receptor undergoes a conformational change and dissociates from the HSP complex. The receptor-ligand complex dimerizes and interacts with hormone responsive elements (HREs) in the promoter region of steroid-responsive genes. The steroid receptor dimer at the HRE is thought to recruit coactivator proteins that in turn recruit other factors that together induce gene transcription.

with the resulting activity intermediate between that of ER-α and ER-β homodimers.[16] Cellular responses to estrogens are therefore dependent on the relative abundance of the two forms.

### PROGESTERONE RECEPTORS A AND B

Shown in Figure 152-4 are the structures of the PR-A and PR-B forms of the human PR. Although there is only one gene for the PR, most species (with the exception of rabbit) express two forms of the receptor.[17–19] Multiple mRNAs are produced from the progesterone receptor gene and some of these lack the 5′ region that encodes the portion unique to the B receptor.[20] The shorter form is produced by initiation of translation at an internal AUG.[21] Thus, the two forms have identical hormone-binding and DNA-binding domains, but the shorter A form lacks the first 164 amino acids of the B form. The structure of the DNA-binding domain is similar to that of the ER. The consensus DNA-binding site (AGAACAnnnTGTTCT) for the PR is an inverted palindrome separated by three nucleotides.[22] As is true for estrogen response elements, progesterone response elements can differ substantially from the consensus sequence, and promoters of target genes may have multiple response elements and/or half-sites that contribute to the activity. Androgen receptors, glucocorticoid receptors, and mineralocorticoid receptors also bind to the PR consensus sequence.[22]

The hinge region (D) of PR contains a nuclear localization sequence that is responsible for constitutive nuclear localization of the receptor.[12] The E region contains the hormone-binding region, an AF2 function, and sites for dimerization and interaction with other proteins. Unlike the ER, PR lacks an F region; deletion of even a few of the carboxyl-terminal amino acids of PR results in loss of hormone binding.

The amino terminal domains of PR-A and PR-B also contain an activation function, AF1. The relative importance of AF1 and AF2 in transcriptional activation depends on the cell type and promoter sequence. In many cases, the two act synergistically. There is an additional activation region, termed *AF3*, in the region unique to PR-B.[23]

### COACTIVATORS AND COREPRESSORS

#### COACTIVATORS

Until recently, the molecular basis for hormones binding to receptors and acting either as agonists or antagonists was unknown. Similarly, the means by which the activation

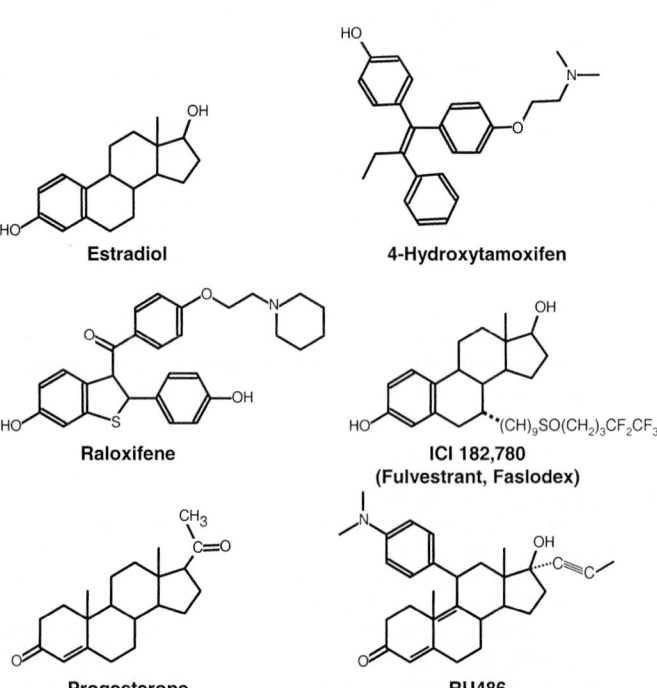

**Estradiol**

**4-Hydroxytamoxifen**

**Raloxifene**

**ICI 182,780
(Fulvestrant, Faslodex)**

**Progesterone**

**RU486
(Mifepristone)**

*Figure 152-2* Structure of ER and PR agonists and antagonists. 17β-estradiol is the natural ER agonist. 4-Hydroxytamoxifen, raloxifene, and ICI 182,780 (fulvestrant, Faslodex) are estrogen receptor antagonists. Progesterone is the natural PR agonist and RU486 (mifepristone) is an antagonist of PR action.

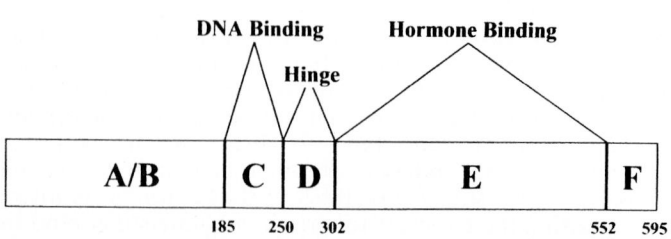

*Figure 152-3* Structure of estrogen receptor-α. A to F represent the previously defined regions of the receptor described in the text.[5] The numbers denote the amino acids at the boundaries of the regions.

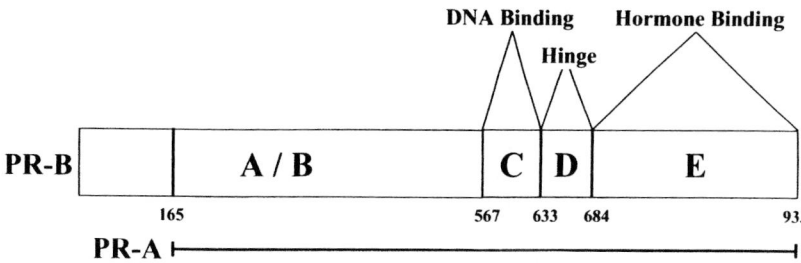

**Figure 152-4** Structure of progesterone receptor A (PR-A) and B (PR-B) forms. PR, like the estrogen receptor, contains modular domains A to E with corresponding functions. The numbers denote the amino acids at the boundaries of the regions with 1 corresponding to the first amino acid of the PR-B sequence.

functions enhanced transcription was, for the most part, unknown. The discovery of coactivators and corepressors that regulate the activities of transcription factors has provided insight into these issues. Coactivators typically are recruited to active forms of transcription factors and enhance target gene transcription, whereas corepressors bind to inactive forms of transcription factors, repressing transcription.

In the case of steroid receptors, the activating signal is typically binding of agonist. Coactivators for steroid receptors were originally sought as proteins that bind to the hormone-binding domain only in the presence of agonist. The first nuclear receptor coactivator to be identified, steroid receptor coactivator-1 (SRC-1), is one of three related coactivators termed *p160 coactivators*.[24] Its structure is shown in Figure 152-5. It is a very complex protein with both enzymatic activity and the capacity to interact with multiple proteins simultaneously. The protein contains four LXXLL (L = leucine, X = any amino acid) sequences, a motif that has been implicated in the binding of coactivators to steroid receptors[25] as well as in other protein-protein interactions. The region labeled "HAT" contains the intrinsic histone acetyltransferase activity of the protein.[26] HATs acetylate histones, opening up the structure for more efficient transcription. Although histones are substrates for HATs, some HATs also acetylate transcription factors, including p53 and some of the steroid receptors.[27]

Coactivators form complexes with other proteins, and recent data on isolation of coactivator complexes and on the kinetics of association of coactivator proteins with receptors on promoters suggest that groups of proteins are recruited as complexes through one or more proteins in the complex that interact directly with the receptor.[28] In the case of SRC-1, the region containing the intrinsic HAT activity also binds another histone acetyltransferase, pCAF (p300/CBP-associated factor). Two activation domains (AD) have been identified in SRC-1 as well as another region that interacts with the cyclic adenosine monophosphate (cAMP) response element binding protein (CREB)-binding protein (CBP) coactivator. In addition, PAS (Per-Arnt-Sim) and basic helix-loop-helix domains have been identified that are likely involved in interactions with other proteins containing similar motifs. Additional p160 interacting proteins include the histone methyltransferases CARM1 and PRMT1.[29]

In addition to the complexes containing p160 proteins, several other complexes are recruited to the promoters that modify chromatin and/or interact with and modify basal transcription factors. These include SWI/SNF complexes that induce adenosine triphosphate (ATP)-dependent chromatin remodeling and the TRAP/mediator complex that enhances phosphorylation of RNA polymerase II.[30]

## COREPRESSORS

The steroid receptor family corepressors were initially identified as proteins that interact with two steroid receptor family members (thyroid hormone receptor and retinoic acid receptor) that repress basal transcription of their target genes. The corepressors bind to these proteins in the absence of ligand, but are released when the receptors bind to their cognate agonist ligands. Two corepressors have been well characterized. NCoR (nuclear receptor corepressor[31]) and SMRT (silencing mediator of retinoic acid and thyroid hormone receptors[32]) bind to unliganded retinoic acid receptors and thyroid hormone receptors and recruit protein complexes that contain histone deacetylases.[33] Deacetylation of the histones results in a more compact and therefore less accessible chromatin structure. Their role in the hormone-dependent activation of estrogen and progesterone receptors is less well defined, although some evidence indicates that histone deacetylases, independent of SMRT and NCoR, may play a role in attenuating estrogen-stimulated expression of the pS2 gene.[28] However, NCoR and SMRT are important in the actions of steroid receptor antagonists. Several studies have shown that SMRT and NCoR can bind to antagonist- but not agonist-bound ER and PR in vivo.[34–36] Overexpression of these proteins reduces the partial agonist activity of 4-hydroxytamoxifen bound to ER and the partial agonist activity of RU486 (mifepristone) bound to PR. Hence, the activity of this class of proteins is extremely important clinically in situations where receptor antagonists are administered.

## ESTROGEN RECEPTOR ACTION

The group of hormones referred to as estrogens are steroids that play important roles during development and various aspects of reproduction, but which also exert significant biological effects in the brain and the cardiovascular and skeletal systems. The ability of estrogens to increase uterine size due to epithelial cell proliferation and accumulation of water has long been used to monitor estrogen action in animal studies.[37] Likewise, the effects of estrogen in the mammary gland, where they induce ductal growth and branching as well as formation of terminal end buds,[38,39] and in the skeleton,

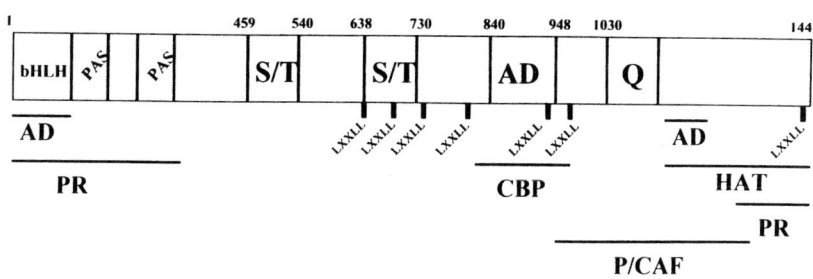

**Figure 152-5** Structure of steroid receptor coactivator-1 (SRC-1). Regions of SRC-1 shown to interact with PR, CREB-binding protein (CBP), and p300/CBP-associated factor (P/CAF) are as indicated. HAT (histone acetyltransferase) refers to the regions containing the intrinsic HAT activity. The locations of the LXXLL motifs, activation domains (ADs), bHLH (basic helix-loop-helix) motif, PAS (Per-Arnt-Sim) domain, S/T (serine/threonine-rich) region, and Q (glutamine-rich) region are also indicated.

where they promote skeletal maturation and maintenance of bone mineral density, are well recognized.[40] Differences in the incidence of cardiovascular disease in premenopausal women in comparison to men suggest that estrogens may be cardio-protective, and there is evidence that estrogens reduce the levels of serum cholesterol and have positive effects on serum lipoprotein profiles.[41] This view, however, is at least partially contradicted by the results of the Women's Health Initiative Study, which reveals a small, but significant increase in cardiovascular events in postmenopausal women receiving hormone replacement therapy.[42,43] Evidence also indicates that estrogen action in the central nervous system is associated with protection against cognitive aging and a reduction in the risk of Alzheimer's disease.[44]

With the finding that there are at least two estrogen receptors and that these receptors can be activated in the absence of hormone, simple elimination of estrogens is insufficient to assess the role of a specific receptor in vivo. Mice lacking ER-α (known as ERKO), generated by disruption of the ER-α gene by homologous recombination in embryonic stem cells, have been used to evaluate the role of this receptor in vivo.[39,45] Both male and female mice lacking ER-α are viable; the females are infertile, whereas the males exhibit reduced fertility. Although prenatal reproductive tract development proceeds normally, several reproductive tract abnormalities, including hypoplastic uteri and hyperemic ovaries lacking corpora lutea, have been identified in the adult animals. Moreover, these animals fail to display characteristic responses to estrogen, including increases in uterine wet weight and vaginal cornification. The animals also exhibit reduced bone mineral density as well as elevated levels of gonadal steroids, indicating that feedback control at the level of the hypothalamus and pituitary is absent.[40] Thus, it appears that these actions of estrogen are mediated by ER-α and that ER-β cannot act as a substitute.

Mice lacking ER-β due to homologous recombination technology are viable and develop normally; and as might be expected from differences in the expression patterns of ER-α and ER-β, the phenotype of ER-β knockout (BERKO) mice is distinct from ERKO mice.[39,46] Female BERKO mice have reduced fertility due to compromised follicular maturation, as evidenced by sparse corpora lutea. This appears to be due to a defect intrinsic to the ovary, as opposed to hyperstimulation of the ovary by pituitary luteinizing hormone as is the case for ERKO animals. Male BERKO mice are fertile, but exhibit signs of prostatic hyperplasia.[47] Only female BERKO mice exhibit a bone phenotype consisting of increased bone length and cortical bone mineral content.[40] Taken together, analyses of ER-α and ER-β knockout mice indicate that the two receptors play different biological roles, and that the receptors are unable to act as a substitute for one another. Thus, the overall effects of estrogens result from a range of activities mediated by two distinct receptors as well as by the non-genomic effects of these ligands.

## ER AGONISTS AND ANTAGONISTS

In the absence of stimuli that activate ERs, the receptor monomers associate with heat shock protein complexes and are inactive. Agonist binding induces conformational changes that favor dissociation from the heat shock proteins, receptor dimerization, and binding to DNA. Synthetic compounds that compete with estradiol for binding to the ER and antagonize its activity have been developed. These have been useful both in understanding ER function and clinically in the treatment of breast cancer.

Antiestrogens for ER-α have been separated into two classes based on their activities (reviewed in MacGregor and Jordan[48]). Whereas the type I antiestrogens have mixed estrogen/antiestrogen activity, the type II compounds are pure antagonists. Tamoxifen and related derivatives containing the

core triphenylethylene structure and the benzothiophene raloxifene are examples of type I antiestrogens (see Fig. 152-2). These compounds induce receptor dimerization and DNA binding. In some cases, they produce transcriptionally inactive complexes, whereas in others they function as weak agonists; the nature of the response is cell/tissue and target gene specific. For example, tamoxifen exerts estrogen-like activity in the uterus but antiestrogen effects in the normal breast.[49] Although the type I antagonists are incapable of inducing AF2 function, they do not block AF1 activity. For this reason, under conditions in which AF1 is an important activation function, type I antagonists can function as partial agonists. Conversely, in contexts where AF2 function is required, they are effective antagonists. The differences in responses between the agonists and type I antagonists correlate with the ability of the agonist-bound receptor to efficiently recruit p160 coactivators while antagonist-bound receptors recruit corepressors. A comparison between the x-ray crystallographic structure of the ER ligand-binding domains containing either estradiol or type I antagonists reveals that raloxifene binding[50] or 4-hydroxytamoxifen binding[51] displaces a critical α-helix, helix 12, into a position that occludes the interaction of p160 coactivators with the receptor's coactivator binding surface. That corepressors play an active role in repressing transcription by antagonist-bound receptors is supported by the finding that under conditions where corepressor levels are low, the type 1 antagonists can function as agonists.[35,36,52]

The type II antagonists typified by ICI 164,384 and ICI 182,780 are 7α-substituted derivatives of estradiol with no agonist activity.[48] These antagonists have been shown to promote DNA binding. However, cystallographic analyses of ER-β liganded by ICI 164,384 reveals a structure in which the coactivator binding groove of the receptor is not formed. Moreover, these antagonists promote the rapid degradation of estrogen receptors, and this is likely important for the pure antagonist effects of these compounds.[53]

Most of the work characterizing ER antagonists has centered on the responses of ER-α. Studies of ER-β reveal that there are differences in the responses of the two forms of the receptor to antiestrogens. Whereas agonists typically function to stimulate the transcriptional activity of both receptors, although with somewhat different efficacies, and the type II antagonists act as pure antagonists for both, the type 1 antagonists for ER-α appear to act as pure antagonists of ER-β as measured on estrogen response element (ERE)-containing reporter genes.[54]

## ER ACTION INDEPENDENT OF CONSENSUS RESPONSE ELEMENTS

Although the most completely characterized actions of the estrogen receptors are those induced through ER-α binding to classical estrogen response elements, there is an increasing body of evidence demonstrating that steroid receptors also act through interaction with other transcription factors. For example, estrogen receptors may regulate gene expression indirectly through interactions with the Sp1 transcription factor.[55] Interactions that induce transcription as well as those that inhibit transcription also have been described. Webb and colleagues have shown that ER-α can induce transcription through AP-1 sites by binding to the fos/jun complex.[56] Under these conditions, both estradiol and type 1 antagonists such as tamoxifen function as agonists of ER-α. The actions of ER-β at AP-1 elements appear to differ. Paech and colleagues[57] reported that estradiol-bound ER-β inhibits AP-1-dependent gene expression, whereas the type I antagonists tamoxifen and raloxifene, as well as the type II antagonist ICI 164,384, act as agonists at this element. In addition to this example of antagonists functioning as agonists, there have been reports of induced ER-α-dependent gene expression by the antagonist-bound receptor.[58]

It should be noted that the genomic actions of estrogens and antiestrogens described here are not the only effects mediated by these compounds. An increasing body of literature details the abilities of agonists and antagonists to alter rapidly (≤5 minutes) the activity of a variety of intracellular signaling molecules, such as src kinase and mitogen-activated protein kinases (MAPKs), or the levels of second messengers such as calcium or cAMP (cyclic adenosine monophosphate).[59] These events are independent of the ability of estrogen receptors to alter gene expression, and are therefore referred to as non-genomic actions. Collectively, it is clear that the actions of compounds defined as agonists and antagonists and the estrogen receptors are not as simple as previously envisioned.

## PROGESTERONE RECEPTOR ACTION

Progesterone is required for female fertility and plays numerous roles in female reproduction. Because PR is induced by activated ER, it has historically been difficult to distinguish between the contributions of ER and PR to biological responses. Based on the distribution of PR, likely targets of progesterone action include the ovary, uterus, mammary gland, and brain. Consistent with this, biological changes in response to progesterone are observed in these organs and PR-null mice exhibit altered phenotypes in these sites. In the uterus, PR is expressed in both the epithelial and stromal cells of the endometrium as well as in the myometrium.[60,61] In the normal menstrual cycle, progesterone antagonizes the proliferative action of estrogen in the epithelial cells, but appears to stimulate stromal cell growth late in the luteal phase.[61] Consistent with this, the uteri of PR-null mice treated with both estrogen and progesterone appear morphologically similar to uteri of normal mice treated with estrogen alone. The uteri were larger than normal, filled with fluid, and contained hyperplastic epithelium and enlarged endometrial glands.[62,63] Interestingly, there was evidence of inflammation, supporting an additional role for progesterone in suppressing inflammation. Progesterone is also required for normal ovarian function. Treatment with the PR antagonist RU486 prevents ovulation.[61] Studies of PR-null (knockout) mice reveal that PR action is required for release of follicles from the ovary and production of corpora lutea.[62,63] Thus, female PR-null mice are infertile.

Progesterone is required both for the initial development and differentiation of mammary glands as well as during pregnancy. Whereas the glands of normal mice undergo extensive growth, branching, and lobuloalveolar development, the PR-null mice have greatly reduced ductal development and branching. Moreover, there is no lobuloalveolar development.[62,63] In women, there is a higher rate of epithelial cell proliferation in the late luteal phase as well as in pregnancy when levels of progesterone are high (reviewed in Ref. 61). Progesterone also acts to prevent the premature synthesis of the milk proteins α-lactalbumin and casein during pregnancy (reviewed in Ref. 61).

Progesterone plays multiple roles in implantation and maintenance of pregnancy. Early actions of progesterone include the stimulation of the synthesis of degradative enzymes responsible for lysis of the zona pellucida and the stimulation of growth factor production facilitating implantation and growth.[61] Consistent with these findings, uterine stromal cells in PR-null mice fail to decidualize, the mice are infertile, and wild-type embryos will not implant in pseudopregnant PR-null mice.[62,63] Thus, there are defects both in the ovary and the uterus.

Progesterone also reduces myometrial contractility (reviewed in Ref. 61), which is important to prevent expulsion of the fetus. This is accomplished both by regulating free intracellular calcium levels and reducing the expression of factors that promote contractility. Studies in various animal models indicate that progesterone prevents increases of intracellular calcium levels through induction of calcitonin and reduction in the calcium transporter calbindin-D9K. In addition, progesterone decreases expression of prostaglandins, resulting in decreased expression of oxytocin receptors. The ability of the progesterone receptor antagonist RU486 to stimulate prostaglandin synthesis contributes to the abortifacient activity of RU486. Progesterone also induces expression of relaxin, further contributing to the reduction in myometrial contractility.

As previously noted, two major forms of PR have been identified: PR-A and PR-B. Cells that express PR generally express both forms, although the ratios may differ. For instance, the levels and ratios of PR-A to PR-B have been reported to vary throughout the menstrual cycle and in some tumors. Although these forms share common sequences, with the exception of the 164 amino acids at the N terminus of B that are unique to this form,[20] their activities are quite different. In most instances, PR-B is a better transcriptional activator than PR-A. However, this response is, in part, cell-type specific.[64,65] The most striking difference is the capacity of PR-A, but not PR-B, to function as an inhibitor of the activity of other steroid receptors including the estrogen receptor.[66] The most convincing evidence that the two forms have unique functions comes from genetically engineered mice that express only PR-B (PRAKO) or PR-A (PRBKO). Whereas the mammary gland development in PRAKO mice appears normal, the uterus has a phenotype similar to that of an animal lacking PR.[67] In contrast, PRBKO exhibit aberrant mammary gland differentiation but normal uterine development.[67]

### PR ANTAGONIST AND AGONIST FUNCTION

The natural ligand for the progesterone receptor is progesterone. Although there are no known natural antagonists, synthetic compounds such as RU486 (see Fig. 152-2), which function as antagonists, have been useful in elucidating receptor function and in clinical applications. In the absence of hormone, the heat shock protein complexes containing progesterone receptor are in a dynamic equilibrium with free receptor with cycles of dissociation and reassociation.[8] Binding of hormone induces a conformational change that prevents the reassociation of the receptors with the heat shock proteins. Comparison of the structures of the ligand-binding domains of various steroid receptor family members in the presence and absence of ligand reveals that there are substantial conformational changes. The most significant change is the movement of the most carboxyl-terminal α helix (helix 12) from a relatively open position to a position that covers the hormone-binding pocket.[51]

Antagonists compete with agonists for binding to the receptor, thereby blocking the hormone-induced activity. In the case of the PR, two types of antagonists have been identified[68]; pure antagonists block the activity of agonists and lack any activity when used alone, whereas partial antagonists reduce the activity in the presence of agonist, but have low levels of intrinsic activity. The activity of the partial antagonist is frequently dependent on the cell type and target gene. RU486, which is used for inducing abortions, is an example of a partial antagonist. Identification of antagonists has been empirical; since antagonists induce DNA binding, the molecular basis for the failure to induce transcription was unknown prior to the discovery of coactivators and corepressors. As described previously, the ability to induce a conformation that recruits a coactivator plays an important role in the ability of a hormone to induce transcriptional activity. Conversely, ligands that induce conformations that bind corepressors act as antagonists. RU486 and other antagonists substantially alter the orientation of helix 12, inhibiting PR interaction with coactivators and promoting interaction with corepressors.

## MODULATION OF RECEPTOR ACTIVITY BY CELL SIGNALING PATHWAYS

Although the steroid receptors are ligand-activated transcription factors, they are also phosphoproteins. Phosphorylation of steroid receptors and their associated proteins modulates their activity. Both ER and PR are phosphorylated on multiple sites, and phosphorylation of the sites is typically increased by agonist treatment.[69] In addition, coactivators such as the p160 proteins and CBP are phosphoproteins. Many of the phosphorylation sites in the receptors as well as in the coactivators contain the sequence motif Ser-Pro suggesting that the kinases involved in their regulation are proline directed kinases such as the cyclin-dependent kinases or the MAPKs. Consistent with this, modulation of the activities of these kinases alters receptor activity.

Until the last decade, it was believed that the signal to activate steroid receptors was the binding of hormone and that, in the absence of hormone, these receptors are inactive. Denner and colleagues first showed that chicken PR, transiently transfected into CV1 cells, can be activated by treatment of cells with 8-Br-cAMP (8-bromoadenosine cyclic adenosine monophosphate) in the absence of progesterone.[70] Although some steroid receptors do not appear to be activated in the absence of hormone, there are numerous studies showing that alterations in cell signaling pathways can activate the ER. These responses depend on cell type and target gene. ER-α can be activated by treatment with EGF (epidermal growth factor) both in vivo and in cell culture models.[71,72] Other compounds that induce activation of ER include cAMP, dopamine, and IGF-1 (insulin-like growth factor-1).[73–75] The mechanism(s) by which ligand-independent activation is achieved has not been elucidated. There is evidence that altered receptor and/or coregulator phosphorylation is required and that the targets are cell signaling pathway, receptor, and cell-type specific.[76,77] Although the significance of the contribution of the ligand-independent pathways to overall ER action in vivo has not been determined, it is evident that cell signaling pathways can potentiate the response of ER to ligands. Stimulators of kinase activity can both enhance the activity of agonists as well as

cause antagonists such as tamoxifen to function as agonists. A clinically relevant example of this phenomenon is the finding that overexpression of Her2/neu (which activates MAPK) can cause tamoxifen resistance. Treatment of cells with cAMP or activators of tyrosine kinase signaling pathways reduces the interaction of corepressors with antagonist-occupied steroid receptors, causing the antagonists to function as agonists.[36]

In contrast to ER, human PR does not appear to respond to cell signaling pathways in the absence of hormone. However, activators of protein kinases A and C stimulate hormone-dependent activity. Moreover, treatment with 8-Br-cAMP causes RU486 to act as an agonist in T47D breast cancer cells.[78] Although the mechanism by which this occurs has not been completely elucidated, Wagner and colleagues[34] have shown that 8-Br-cAMP treatment reduces interactions of RU486-bound receptor with corepressors.

## SUMMARY

Although the ER and PR are hormone-activated transcription factors, recent studies indicate that there are many factors that will determine the response to hormone. These include levels and types of receptors (ER-α and ER-β, PR-A and PR-B), the activation states of cell signaling pathways, the complement of coactivators and corepressors, and the target gene. Figure 152-6 contains a current model of receptor action depicting roles for hormone, cell signaling pathways, and coactivators in the activity of receptors. These findings have led to a quest for antagonists that will be unaffected by cell signaling pathways. In addition, selective agonists that have agonist activity in tissues where it is desirable to have estrogen or progesterone action, but lack activity or act as antagonists in tissues where agonist activity is deleterious are being sought. In the case of the ER, these compounds have been termed *SERMs* (selective estrogen receptor modulators)[79] and much effort has been devoted to development of compounds that are agonists in bone and in the cardiovascular system, but not in breast or uterus where they might promote tumor development. With the availability of three-dimensional structures for the hormone-binding domains, the discovery of the ER-β, coactivators, and corepressors, and the substantial roles of cell signaling pathways, it is likely that compounds with the desired specificity will be developed in the near future.

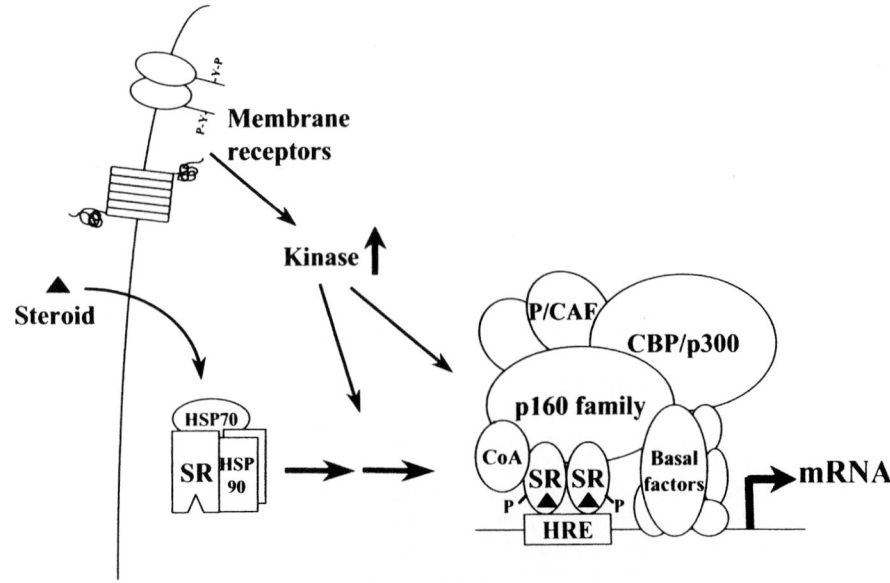

*Figure 152-6* The role of signaling pathways in steroid receptor activation. Growth factors and other hormones that interact with their membrane receptors (serpentine or tyrosine kinase) induce signal transduction pathways that result in an increase in intracellular kinase activity. Active kinases can phosphorylate steroid receptors, p160 family members, and possibly other coactivator-like proteins that interact with both steroid receptors and p160 family members. Changes in steroid receptor and coactivator phosphorylation can alter protein-protein interactions and affect the overall level of gene transcription. CBP, CREB-binding protein; CoA, coactivator; HRE, hormone responsive element; HSP, heat shock protein; P/CAF, p300-CBP-associated factor; SR, steroid receptor.

## REFERENCES

1. Evans RM: The steroid and thyroid hormone receptor superfamily. Science 240:889–895, 1988.
2. O'Malley BW, Conneely OM: Minireview: Orphan receptors: in search of a unifying hypothesis for activation. Mol Endocrinol 6:1359–1361, 1992.
3. Nuclear Receptors Nomenclature Committee: A unified nomenclature system for the nuclear receptor superfamily. Cell 97:161–163, 1999.
4. Wang LH, Tsai SY, Cook RG, et al: COUP transcription factor is a member of the steroid receptor superfamily. Nature 340:163–166, 1989.
5. Krust A, Green S, Argos P, et al: The chicken oestrogen receptor sequence: Homology with v-erbA and the human oestrogen and glucocorticid receptors. EMBO J 5:891–897, 1986.
6. Green S, Chambon P: The oestrogen receptor: From perception to mechanism. In Parker MG (ed): Nuclear Hormone Receptors. San Diego, CA, Academic Press, 1991, pp 15–38.
7. Smith DF, Toft DO: Steroid receptors and their associated proteins. Mol Endocrinol 7:4–11, 1993.
8. Smith DF: Dynamics of heat shock protein 90-progesterone receptor binding and the disactivation loop model for steroid receptor complexes. Mol Endocrinol 7:1418–1429, 1993.
9. Beekman JM, Allan GF, Tsai SY, et al: Transcriptional activation by the estrogen receptor requires a conformational change in the ligand binding domain. Mol Endocrinol 7:1266–1274, 1993.
10. Allan GF, Leng XH, Tsai SY, et al: Hormone and antihormone induce distinct conformational changes which are central to steroid receptor activation. J Biol Chem 267:19513–19520, 1992.
11. Tora L, White JH, Brou C, et al: The human estrogen receptor has two independent nonacidic transcriptional activation functions. Cell 59:477–487, 1989.
12. Guiochon-Mantel A, Loosfelt H, Lescop P, et al: Mechanisms of nuclear localization of the progesterone receptor: Evidence for interaction between monomers. Cell 57:1147–1154, 1989.
13. Fawell SE, Lees JA, White R, et al: Characterization and colocalization of steroid binding and dimerization activities in the mouse estrogen receptor. Cell 60:953–962, 1990.
14. Carson-Jurica MA, Schrader WT, O'Malley BW: Steroid receptor family: Structure and functions. Endocr Rev 11:201–220, 1990.
15. Kuiper GG, Enmark E, Pelto-Huikko M, et al: Cloning of a novel estrogen receptor expressed in rat prostate and ovary. Proc Natl Acad Sci U S A 93:5925–5930, 1996.
16. Pettersson K, Grandien K, Kuiper GG, et al: Mouse estrogen receptor β forms estrogen response element-binding heterodimers with estrogen receptor α. Mol Endocrinol 11:1486–1496, 1997.
17. Schrader WT, O'Malley BW: Progesterone-binding components of chick oviduct IV: Characterization of purified subunits. J Biol Chem 247:51–59, 1972.
18. Horwitz KB, Alexander PS: In situ photolinked nuclear progesterone receptors of human breast cancer cells: Subunit molecular weights after transformation and translocation. Endocrinology 113:2195–2201, 1983.
19. Loosfelt H, Logeat F, Hai MTV, et al: The rabbit progesterone receptor: Evidence for a single steroid-binding subunit and characterization of receptor mRNA. J Biol Chem 259:14196–14202, 1984.
20. Kastner P, Krust A, Turcotte B, et al: Two distinct estrogen-regulated promoters generate transcripts encoding the two functionally different human progesterone receptor forms A and B. EMBO J 9:1603–1614, 1990.
21. Conneely OM, Kettelberger DM, Tsai M-J, et al: The chicken progesterone receptor A and B isoforms are products of an alternate translation initiation event. J Biol Chem 264:14062–14064, 1989.
22. Cooney AJ, Tsai SY: Nuclear receptor–DNA Interactions. In Tsai M-J, O'Malley BW (eds): Mechanism of Steroid Hormone Regulation of Gene Transcription. Austin, TX, RG Landes, 1994, ch 2.
23. Sartorius CA, Melville MY, Hovland AR, et al: A third transactivation function (AF3) of human progesterone receptors located in the unique N-terminal segment of the B-isoform. Mol Endocrinol 8:1347–1360, 1994.
24. Onate SA, Tsai SY, Tsai M-J, et al: Sequence and characterization of a coactivator for the steroid hormone receptor superfamily. Science 270:1354–1357, 1995.
25. Heery DM, Kalkhoven E, Hoare S, et al: A signature motif in transcriptional co-activators mediates binding to nuclear receptors. Nature 387:733–736, 1997.
26. Spencer TE, Jenster G, Burcin MM, et al: Steroid receptor coactivator-1 is a histone acetyltransferase. Nature 389:194–198, 1997.
27. Wang C, Fu M, Angeletti RH, et al: Direct acetylation of the estrogen receptor-α hinge region by p300 regulates transactivation and hormone sensitivity. J Biol Chem 6:18375–18383, 2001.
28. Métivier R, Penot G, Hübner MR, et al: Estrogen receptor-a directs ordered, cyclical, and combinatorial recruitment of cofactors on a natural target promoter. Cell 115:751–763, 2003.
29. Chen D, Ma H, Hong H, et al: Regulation of transcription by a protein methyltransferase. Science 284:2174–2177, 1999.
30. Glass CK, Rosenfeld MG: The coregulator exchange in transcriptional functions of nuclear receptors. Genes Dev 14:121–141, 2000.
31. Horlein AJ, Naar AM, Heinzel T, et al: Ligand-independent repression by the thyroid hormone receptor mediated by a nuclear receptor co-repressor. Nature 377:397–404, 1995.
32. Chen JD, Evans RM: A transcriptional co-repressor that interacts with nuclear hormone receptors. Nature 377:454–457, 1995.
33. Nagy L, Kao HY, Chakravarti D, et al: Nuclear receptor repression mediated by a complex containing SMRT, mSin3A, and histone deacetylase. Cell 89:373–380, 1997.
34. Wagner BL, Norris JD, Knotts TA, et al: The nuclear corepressors NCoR and SMRT are key regulators of both ligand- and 8-bromo-cyclic AMP-dependent transcriptional activity of the human progesterone receptor. Mol Cell Biol 18:1369–1378, 1998.
35. Smith CL, Nawaz Z, O'Malley BW: Coactivator and corepressor regulation of the agonist/antagonist activity of the mixed antiestrogen, 4-hydroxytamoxifen. Mol Endocrinol 11:657–666, 1997.
36. Lavinsky RM, Jepsen K, Heinzel T, et al: Diverse signaling pathways modulate nuclear receptor recruitment of N-CoR and SMRT complexes. Proc Natl Acad Sci U S A 95:2920–2925, 1998.
37. Walters MR: Steroid hormone receptors and the nucleus. Endocr Rev 6:512–543, 1985.
38. Daniel CW, Silberstein GB, Strickland P: Direct action of 17 b-estradiol on mouse mammary ducts analyzed by sustained release implants and steroid autoradiography. Cancer Res 47:6052–6057, 1987.
39. Couse JF, Korach KS: Estrogen receptor null mice: What have we learned and where will they lead us? Endocr Rev 2003:358–417, 1999.
40. Windahl SH, Andersson G, Gustafsson J-Å: Elucidation of estrogen receptor function in bone with the use of mouse models. Trends Endocrinol Metab 13:195–200, 2002.
41. Mendelsohn ME, Karas RH: The protective effects of estrogen on the cardiovascular system. New Engl J Med 340:1801–1811, 2004.
42. Writing Group for the Women's Health Initiative Investigators: Risks and benefits of estrogen plus progestin in healthy postmenopausal women. JAMA 288:321–333, 2002.
43. Fitzpatrick LA: Hormones and the heart: controversies and conundrums. J Clin Endocrinol Metab 88:5609–5610, 2003.
44. Sherwin BB: Estrogen and cognitive functioning in women. Endocr Rev 24:133–151, 2003.
45. Lubahn DB, Moyer JS, Golding TS, et al: Alteration of reproductive function but not prenatal sexual development after insertional disruption of the mouse estrogen receptor gene. Proc Natl Acad Sci U S A 90:11162–11166, 1993.

46. Pettersson K, Gustafsson J-Å: Role of estrogen receptor beta in estrogen action. Annu Rev Physiol 63:165–192, 2001.

47. Weihua Z, Warner M, Gustafsson J-Å: Estrogen receptor beta in the prostate. Mol Cell Endocrinol 193:1–5, 2002.

48. MacGregor J, Jordan VC: Basic guide to the mechanisms of antiestrogen action. Pharmacol Rev 50:151–196, 1998.

49. Cosman F, Lindsay R: Selective estrogen receptor modulators: Clinical spectrum. Endocr Rev 20:418–434, 1999.

50. Brzozowski AM, Pike AC, Dauter Z, et al: Molecular basis of agonism and antagonism in the oestrogen receptor. Nature 389:753–758, 1997.

51. Shiau AK, Barstad D, Loria PM, et al: The structural basis of estrogen receptor/coactivator recognition and the antagonism of this interaction by tamoxifen. Cell 95:927–937, 1998.

52. Jepsen K, Hermanson O, Onami TM, et al: Combinatorial roles of the nuclear receptor corepressor in transcription and development. Cell 102:753–763, 2000.

53. Dauvois S, Danielian S, White R, et al: Antiestrogen ICI 164,384 reduces cellular estrogen receptor content by increasing its turnover. Proc Natl Acad Sci U S A 89:4037–4041, 1992.

54. Barkhem T, Carlsson B, Nilsson Y, et al: Differential response of estrogen receptor α and estrogen receptor β to partial estrogen agonists/antagonists. Mol Pharmacol 54:105–112, 1998.

55. Safe S: Transcriptional activation of genes by 17β-estradiol through estrogen receptor-Sp1 interactions. Vitam Horm 62:231–252, 2001.

56. Webb P, Lopez GN, Uht RM, et al: Tamoxifen activation of the estrogen receptor/AP-1 pathway: Potential origin for the cell-specific estrogen-like effects of antiestrogens. Mol Endocrinol 9:443–456, 1995.

57. Paech K, Webb P, Kuiper GG, et al: Differential ligand activation of estrogen receptors ERα and ERβ at AP-1 sites. Science 277:1508–1510, 1997.

58. Montano MM, Katzenellenbogen BS: The quinone reductase gene: A unique estrogen receptor-regulated gene that is activated by antiestrogens. Proc Natl Acad Sci U S A 94:2581–2586, 1997.

59. Coleman KM, Smith CL: Intracellular signaling pathways: Nongenomic actions of estrogens and ligand-independent activation of estrogen receptors. Front Biosci 6:D1379–D1391, 2001.

60. Punyadeera C, Verbost P, Groothuis P: Oestrogen and progestin responses in human endometrium. J Steroid Biochem Mol Biol 84:393–410, 2003.

61. Graham JD, Clarke CL: Physiological action of progesterone in target tissues. Endocr Rev 18:502–519, 1997.

62. Lydon JP, DeMayo FJ, Funk CR, et al: Mice lacking progesterone receptor exhibit pleiotropic reproductive abnormalities. Genes Dev 9:2266–2278, 1995.

63. Lydon JP, DeMayo FJ, Conneely OM, et al: Reproductive phenotypes of the progesterone receptor null mutant mouse. J Steroid Biochem Mol Biol 56:67–77, 1996.

64. Meyer ME, Pornon A, Ji JW, et al: Agonistic and antagonistic activities of RU486 on the functions of the human progesterone receptor. EMBO J 9:3923–3932, 1990.

65. Vegeto E, Shahbaz MM, Wen DX, et al: Human progesterone receptor A form is a cell- and promoter-specific repressor of human progesterone receptor B function. Mol Endocrinol 7(10):1244–1255, 1993.

66. McDonnell DP, Goldman ME: RU486 exerts antiestrogenic activities through a novel progesterone receptor A form-mediated mechanism. J Biol Chem 269:11945–11949, 1994.

67. Conneely OM, Mulac-Jericevic B, DeMayo F, et al: Reproductive functions of progesterone receptors. Recent Prog Horm Res 57:339–355, 2002.

68. Edwards DP, Altmann M, DeMarzo A, et al. Progesterone receptors and the mechanism of action of progesterone antagonists. J Steroid Biochem Mol Biol 53:449–458, 1995.

69. Weigel NL: Steroid hormone receptors and their regulation by phosphorylation. Biochem J 319:657–667, 1996.

70. Denner LA, Weigel NL, Maxwell BL, et al: Regulation of progesterone receptor-mediated transcription by phosphorylation. Science 250:1740–1743, 1990.

71. Ignar-Trowbridge DM, Nelson KG, Bidwell MC, et al: Coupling of dual signaling pathways: Epidermal growth factor action involves the estrogen receptor. Proc Natl Acad Sci U S A 89:4658–4662, 1992.

72. Curtis SW, Washburn T, Sewall C, et al: Physiological coupling of growth factor and steroid receptor signaling pathways: Estrogen receptor knockout mice lack estrogen-like response to epidermal growth factor. Proc Natl Acad Sci U S A 93:12626–12630, 1996.

73. Smith CL, Conneely OM, O'Malley BW: Modulation of the ligand-independent activation of the human estrogen receptor by hormone and antihormone. Proc Natl Acad Sci U S A 90:6120–6124, 1993.

74. Fujimoto N, Katzenellenbogen BS: Alteration in the agonist/antagonist balance of antiestrogens by activation of protein kinase A signaling pathways in breast cancer cells: Antiestrogen selectively and promoter dependence. Mol Endocrinol 8:296–304, 1994.

75. Newton CJ, Buric R, Trapp T, et al: The unliganded estrogen receptor (ER) transduces growth factor signals. J Steroid Biochem Mol Biol 48:481–486, 1994.

76. Bunone G, Briand P-A, Miksicek RJ, et al: Activation of the unliganded estrogen receptor by EGF involves the MAP kinase pathway and direct phosphorylation. EMBO J 15:2174–2183, 1996.

77. Weigel NL, Zhang Y: Ligand-independent activation of steroid hormone receptors. J Mol Med 76:469–479, 1997.

78. Beck CA, Weigel NL, Moyer ML, et al: The progesterone antagonist RU486 acquires agonist activity upon stimulation of cAMP signaling pathways. Proc Natl Acad Sci U S A 90:4441–4445, 1993.

79. Bryant HU, Dere WH: Selective estrogen receptor modulators: An alternative to hormone replacement therapy. Proc Soc Exp Biol Med 217:45–52, 1998.

# Hormonal Regulation of the Menstrual Cycle and Mechanisms of Ovulation

## John C. Marshall

**HORMONAL CHANGES DURING THE MENSTRUAL CYCLE—OVERVIEW**

**MECHANISMS THAT REGULATE HORMONE SECRETION**
Follicular Phase and the Midcycle Gonadotropin Surge
Luteal Phase and Initiation of the Next Wave
of Follicular Recruitment
Role of GnRH Secretory Patterns in Cycle Regulation

**MECHANISMS OF ANOVULATION**
Hypothalamic Amenorrhea
Hyperprolactinemia
Polycystic Ovary Syndrome

In women and female primates, reproductive function follows a cyclic pattern between menarche and menopause that is termed the *menstrual cycle*. Cyclic function is recognized clinically by menstrual bleeding, and the first day of bleeding is designated day 1 of the cycle. During the 12 to 18 months after menarche, cycles are often anovulatory and cycle length is irregular. Regular menses occur for the next 20 to 25 years, and cycle length is usually between 25 and 30 days. Before menopause, irregular cycles of longer duration are again seen. Early studies of vaginal and endometrial histology together with measurement of urinary steroids indicated different hormonal activity during the cycle that was divided into two parts: the follicular phase and the luteal phase, separated by ovulation. The follicular phase persists for 12 to 16 days and is the stage of growth and maturation of ovarian follicles, one of which is destined to become the ovulatory follicle. Conventionally, the follicular phase begins on the first day of menstrual bleeding, but follicular maturation begins during the latter part of the preceding luteal phase. After ovulation, the luteal phase persists for 10 to 16 days and is associated with the presence of a corpus luteum in the ovary. Estradiol and progesterone secreted by the corpus luteum induce proliferation and secretory changes in the endometrial glands. In the absence of a fertilized ovum, the corpus luteum regresses 9 to 11 days after ovulation, and the decline in estradiol and progesterone results in shedding of the endometrium as the menstrual flow.

## HORMONAL CHANGES DURING THE MENSTRUAL CYCLE—OVERVIEW

The dynamic relationship between pituitary gonadotropin and ovarian steroid secretion has been recognized for several decades, but detailed understanding of the nature of these interactions has occurred only in recent years. Sensitive assays have allowed delineation of the temporal and causal relationships between luteinizing hormone (LH), follicle-stimulating hormone (FSH), estradiol, progesterone, and inhibins, on a day-to-day and on a minute-to-minute basis. These studies have resulted in our current understanding of the control mechanisms that regulate the menstrual cycle. A schematic diagram of the day-to-day changes of hormones in plasma during an ovulatory menstrual cycle are shown in Figure 153-1 and are based on studies using radioimmunoassays.[1–6]

The first few days of the follicular phase are characterized by plasma levels of FSH that are relatively high and by low levels of LH, estradiol, progesterone, and inhibins A and B.

The initial predominance of FSH stimulation of the ovary is critical for the recruitment and maturation of a cohort of ovarian follicles, one of which is destined to ovulate.[7–10] FSH stimulates follicular growth and inhibin secretion, induces the appearance of LH receptors on granulosa cells, and stimulates the activity of the aromatase enzymes that are required to convert androstenedione (from theca cells) to estradiol (see Chapter 151). The combined effects of FSH and LH stimulate secretion of estradiol, which by the middle to the late follicular phase is secreted predominantly by the follicle destined to ovulate, the dominant follicle. The exact mechanisms whereby one follicle achieves dominance while many others become atretic are not fully understood, but FSH appears to be important in primates. Suppression of plasma FSH by exogenous estradiol during the early follicular phase delays development of the dominant follicle[11] and prolongs the follicular phase in both monkeys and humans. Large doses or continued administration of lower doses of FSH to prolong the elevation in plasma FSH for 5 to 6 days result in more than one follicle being stimulated to develop—often several in women and primates.[12] If an antiestrogen is given to hypophysectomized rats along with FSH, this FSH-stimulated folliculogenesis is prevented. Thus, estrogens acting locally within the ovary are involved in follicular maturation initiated by FSH. In addition, regulatory proteins are secreted by granulosa cells, which can inhibit follicle growth and have been termed *follicle regulatory proteins* or *oocyte maturation inhibitors*.[13] It is postulated that these materials assist the dominant follicle to be selected by producing atresia and failure to survive in smaller follicles (see Chapter 150). Just as an adequate FSH stimulus is important in initiating follicle development, it is also important for determining subsequent function of the corpus luteum inasmuch as women with short luteal phases have lower levels of serum FSH during the follicular phase of the cycle.

The magnitude and duration of plasma FSH elevation appear to be critical determinants of monofollicular development, and insight into the regulation of FSH secretion has followed the recent development of specific two-site enzyme-linked immunosorbent assays (ELISAs) for the inhibins A and B.[6,7] The patterns of inhibin A and B in plasma during an ovulatory cycle are shown in Figure 153-2. These data show that inhibin B is the predominant form secreted during the follicular phase and inhibin A is secreted by the corpus luteum. Inhibin B levels rise rapidly during the early to mid follicular phase and limit FSH secretion, which is also selectively inhibited by the late follicular rise in estradiol[14] and inhibin A. This reduction in FSH may be causally related to

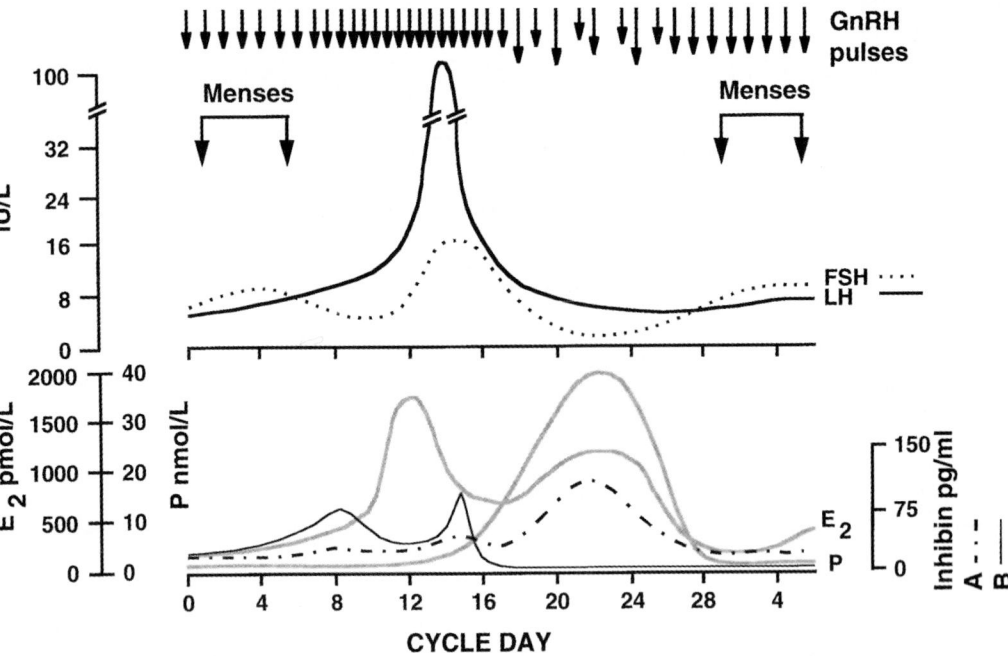

*Figure 153-1* Diagram of plasma concentrations of pituitary gonadotropins (luteinizing hormone [LH], follicle-stimulating hormone [FSH]; **top**) and ovarian steroids (estradiol [E₂], progesterone [P], and inhibins A and B; **bottom**) during an ovulatory menstrual cycle. The *arrows* above the figure represent pulses of gonadotropin-releasing hormone (GnRH) secretion from the hypothalamus. For estradiol, divide by 3.7 pg/mL to convert to picograms per milliliter; for progesterone, divide by 3.2 ng/mL to convert to nanograms per milliliter.

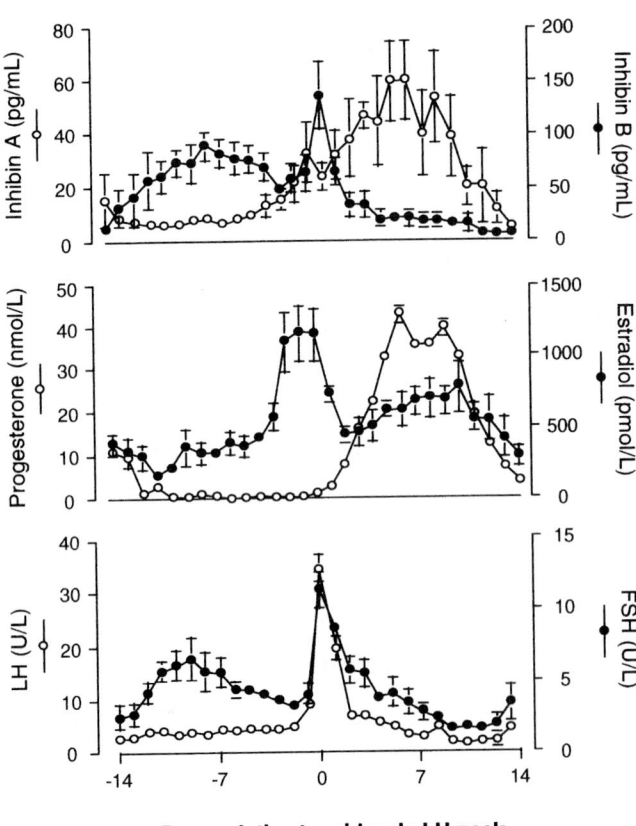

*Figure 153-2* Plasma concentrations of inhibins A and B **(top)**, progesterone and estradiol **(middle)**, and luteinizing hormone (LH) and follicle-stimulating hormone (FSH) **(bottom)** during ovulatory cycles in women. Data are aligned to the day of the midcycle LH peak (day 0). Mean ± SE is shown. (From Groome NP, Illingworth PJ, O'Brien M, et al: Measurement of dimeric inhibin B throughout the human menstrual cycle. J Clin Endocrinol Metab 81:1401–1405; © 1969, The Endocrine Society.)

atresia of the nondominant follicles. The increase in estradiol in the late follicular phase is important in development of the midcycle LH surge. Estradiol exerts a positive feedback effect and enhances LH responsiveness to gonadotropin-releasing hormone (GnRH). Plasma progesterone is also rising and augments LH responses to GnRH,[15] with the combined effects resulting in markedly enhanced LH release and the midcycle LH surge. GnRH secretion is also increased in sheep and monkeys, and estradiol can increase secretion of GnRH.[16] Thus, this ovarian estradiol-progesterone signal system produced by the mature follicle induces the GnRH-LH-FSH ovulatory surge. The LH surge persists for 40 to 48 hours and induces rupture of the mature follicle and release of the ovum, which occurs 16 to 24 hours after initiation of the LH surge. Concomitant with the abrupt rise in LH, serum estradiol falls precipitously and progesterone secretion increases, which is a reflection of the altered function of the luteinized follicle. After ovulation, the luteinized follicle secretes progesterone, 17-hydroxyprogesterone, estradiol, estrone, and inhibin A, and plasma concentrations of these hormones increase during the 7 to 8 days after ovulation. The elevated plasma inhibin A and estradiol suppress FSH secretion, and plasma FSH remains low during the luteal phase. LH appears to be essential for normal function of the corpus luteum. The nature of other factors that dictate the duration of corpus luteum function is uncertain, but in many species, prostaglandins of ovarian or uterine origin appear to be involved.[17] If the ovum is fertilized, corpus luteum function is maintained by human chorionic gonadotropin (hCG), but in the absence of conception, plasma levels of inhibin A, estradiol, and progesterone decline during the final days of the cycle. The fall in ovarian hormones allows an increase in plasma gonadotropins, particularly FSH, which initiates the recruitment and maturation of ovarian follicles for the next cycle.

## MECHANISMS THAT REGULATE HORMONE SECRETION

The mechanisms involved in interactions of the hypothalamic-pituitary-ovarian axis to produce the orderly sequential hormonal changes seen during the normal cycle are complex and incompletely understood. Detailed examination of blood samples obtained every 10 to 20 minutes during the cycle have revealed different patterns of LH and FSH secretion that suggest that alterations in pulsatile hypothalamic GnRH secretion are important for the maintenance of normal cyclicity. In humans, estimation of GnRH secretion has to be indirect, and changes in GnRH secretion are inferred from the patterns of LH or free α subunit in plasma. Studies in animals have shown that GnRH is secreted in an intermittent manner and each episode of GnRH release from the hypothalamus is followed by an acute increase in plasma LH. Thus, the frequency and/or amplitude of LH pulses in peripheral blood can be used as an indirect measurement of GnRH secretion. FSH is less helpful in this regard because the long half-life (about 3 hours) of FSH obscures pulsatile patterns. The frequency of LH pulses varies during different stages of the cycle.[18–21] In the early follicular phase, LH pulses are of constant amplitude and occur at a frequency of every 1 to 2 hours. Slower frequencies (every 2 to 6 hours) of LH pulses are present during the luteal phase, and the amplitude of LH pulses is much more variable. The patterns of plasma LH and FSH during cycles in two normal women are shown in Figure 153-3.

## FOLLICULAR PHASE AND THE MIDCYCLE GONADOTROPIN SURGE

During the early follicular phase (days 1–5), plasma concentrations of FSH exceed those of LH, and LH pulses occur every 90 to 100 minutes. FSH stimulates the increase in inhibin B during the midfollicular phase inasmuch as exogenous FSH stimulates ovarian secretion of both inhibin A and B.[22] The source of inhibin B is probably the small antral follicles, which are rich in inhibin-α and inhibin-$\beta_B$ subunit mRNA,[23] and the elevated plasma inhibin B suppresses FSH secretion by direct actions on the gonadotrope. In the late follicular phase, inhibin B levels decline and $\beta_B$ mRNA expression is markedly reduced in the preovulatory follicle.[24] LH pulse frequency increases to about one pulse per hour during the late luteal phase and stimulates estradiol secretion by the maturing follicle.[25,26] The increase in estradiol probably maintains suppression of FSH secretion together with an increase in inhibin A during the days before the LH surge. Granulosa cells of the dominant follicle contain both α and $\beta_A$ mRNA and are the probable source of secreted inhibin A.[23] The mechanisms involved in increasing the frequency of LH pulses in humans

## PULSATILE LH AND FSH SECRETION DURING A NORMAL MENSTRUAL CYCLE

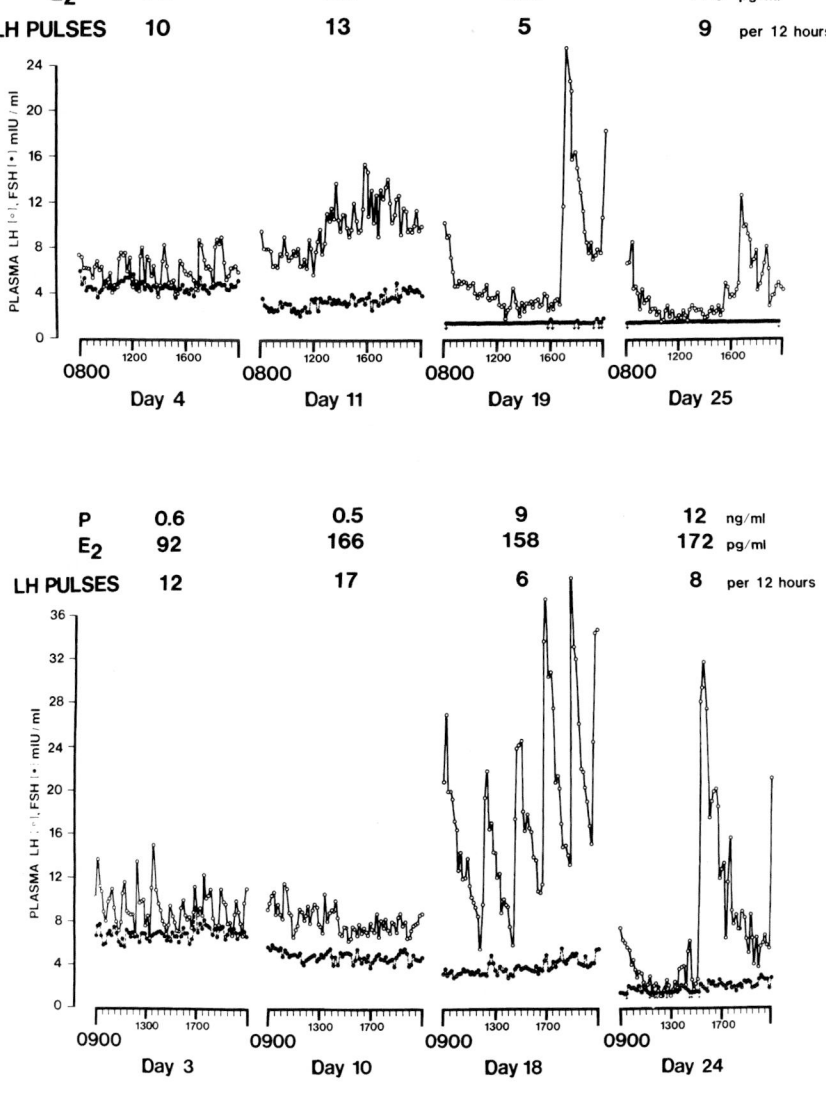

*Figure 153-3* Pulsatile luteinizing hormone (LH) and follicle-stimulating hormone (FSH) secretion in two women during ovulatory menstrual cycles. Blood samples were obtained at 10-minute intervals during the early and late stages of both the follicular and the luteal phases of the cycle. Mean values for ovarian steroids are shown. The number of LH pulses per 12 hours is shown for each day. $E_2$, estradiol; P, progesterone. (From Reame N, Sauder SE, Kelch RP, Marshall JC: Pulsatile gonadotropin secretion during the human menstrual cycle: Evidence for altered frequency of gonadotropin-releasing hormone secretion. J Clin Endocrinol Metab 59:328–337; © 1984, The Endocrine Society.)

are unclear and may reflect the gradual loss of progesterone inhibition in the previous luteal phase[27] and/or the rise in estradiol. Similar changes occur in sheep and appear to depend on the rise in estradiol.[28,29] Direct measurement of portal blood GnRH in sheep after estradiol administration has shown that GnRH pulse frequency and amplitude increase and estradiol induces a massive increase in GnRH secretion.[16,28] The pulsatile release of GnRH is obscured, and GnRH levels remain elevated throughout and beyond the termination of the LH surge. Estradiol only appears to be required to initiate increased GnRH secretion and, once begun, GnRH secretion continues despite falling estradiol levels.[30] In primates and humans, the requirement for a marked increase in GnRH secretion to induce the LH surge is less clear. Although GnRH is increased in rhesus monkeys,[31] ovulatory LH surges can be induced by the administration of constant-amplitude GnRH pulses to GnRH-deficient monkeys and humans,[32,33] though the magnitude of LH secretion is less than occurs spontaneously. These data suggest that an increase in GnRH secretion is not an absolute requirement to produce an LH surge. However, supraphysiologic doses of GnRH were given and the amount of GnRH delivered to the pituitary may have approached concentrations of endogenous GnRH that are present only during a spontaneous midcycle surge.

In addition to the increase in GnRH secretion, both estradiol and progesterone enhance LH responsiveness to GnRH. Plasma estradiol is maximal, and progesterone and 17α-hydroxyprogesterone concentrations rise immediately before the LH surge[34] (Fig. 153-4). Thus, the increase in estradiol is probably the primary signal that triggers increased GnRH secretion and enhanced LH responsiveness to GnRH. The latter is augmented by the rise in progesterone, which results in the ovulatory LH surge.[35]

FSH also increases transiently during the midcycle surge, although levels are much lower than those of LH. This difference probably reflects increased GnRH secretion, although activin A has been reported to be increased in some studies.[36] Inhibin B is also increased after the rise in FSH, but because β_B mRNA is not detectable in corpora lutea, this increase may reflect release of inhibin B from the ruptured follicle.[37] During the LH surge, progesterone concentrations continue to rise, but estradiol falls rapidly. These changes reflect the LH-induced luteinization of granulosa cells and an acute change in steroidogenesis to favor progesterone secretion.[38] The duration of the LH surge is probably limited by a combination of factors. The fall in estradiol results in loss of enhanced LH responses to GnRH, and progesterone is not effective in maintaining LH responsiveness in the absence of estradiol. GnRH secretion continues to be elevated during the declining part of the surge.[29] Thus, the reduced amplitude of LH pulsatile secretion may also reflect a degree of gonadotrope desensitization after the prolonged rapid frequency or even continuous stimulation by GnRH.

### LUTEAL PHASE AND INITIATION OF THE NEXT WAVE OF FOLLICULAR RECRUITMENT

During the 3 to 4 days after ovulation, LH pulse frequency falls, and by the midluteal stage, LH pulses occur every 3 to 5 hours. In addition, the pattern of LH pulses varies through the luteal phase. In the early luteal phase, LH pulses occur regularly and are of large amplitude, whereas irregularity in both amplitude and frequency is seen in the midluteal to late luteal phase (see Fig. 153-3). The variable LH secretory patterns reflect altered hypothalamic GnRH secretion inasmuch as LH responsiveness to GnRH is not impaired during the luteal phase.[39] The elevation in progesterone is the main factor that reduces GnRH secretion in the luteal phase. Administration of progesterone during the follicular phase results in LH secretory patterns that resemble those of the normal luteal phase[40]

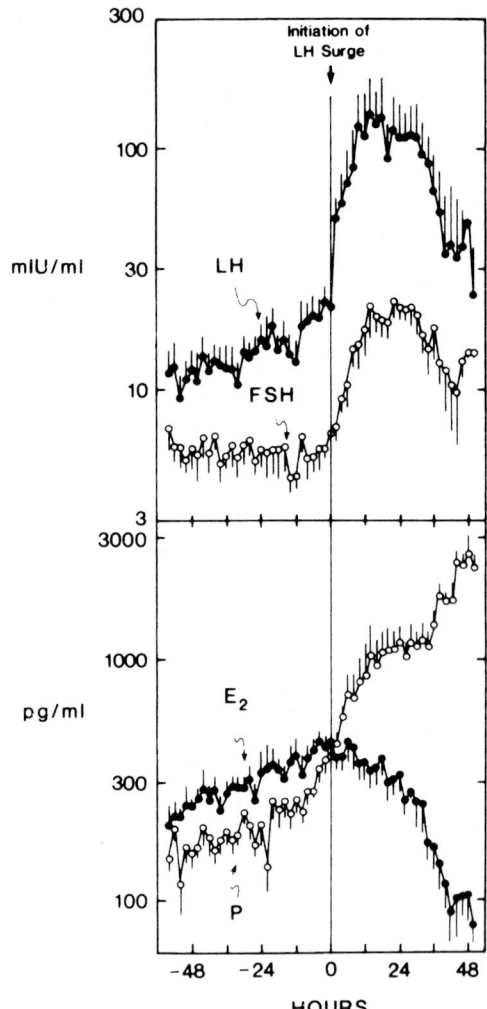

**Figure 153-4**  Plasma luteinizing hormone (LH), follicle-stimulating hormone (FSH), estradiol (E_2), and progesterone (P) concentrations in samples obtained at 2-hour intervals for 5 days at midcycle during seven cycles. Zero time represents initiation of the gonadotropin surge. Data are plotted on a logarithmic scale. (From Hoff JD, Quigley ME, Yen SCC: Hormonal dynamics at mid cycle: A reevaluation. J Clin Endocrinol Metab 57:792–796; © 1983, The Endocrine Society.)

(Fig. 153-5). Similar effects of progesterone in slowing LH pulse frequency have been observed in castrate estrogen-replaced ewes.[41]

The mechanism of progesterone slowing of GnRH secretion involves increased hypothalamic opioid activity. β-Endorphin is increased hypothalamic portal blood in the luteal phase, and administration of naloxone, an opiate receptor blocker, increases LH pulse frequency during the luteal phase in both women and monkeys.[42,43] Naloxone is ineffective during the follicular phase. The slowing of GnRH pulsatile secretion during the luteal phase may have important consequences for the life span of the corpus luteum. The factors that regulate the life span of the corpus luteum are uncertain, but LH is required for normal luteal function in primates. In the absence of LH secretion, the corpus luteum life span is shortened; in the presence of large doses of exogenous LH or the secretion of hCG (an LH-like hormone) in normal pregnancy, the corpus luteum life span is lengthened.[44] In the early luteal phase, before LH pulse frequency has decreased, serum progesterone is stable and only minor fluctuations occur. During the midluteal to late luteal phase, progesterone secretion only occurs coincident with LH pulses.[20,45] Thus, alteration in the pattern of the LH stimulus may be important for corpus luteum function, and the reduced LH pulse frequency may

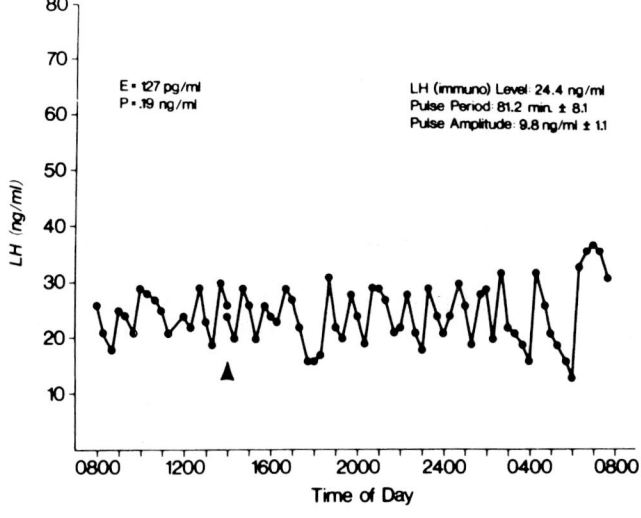

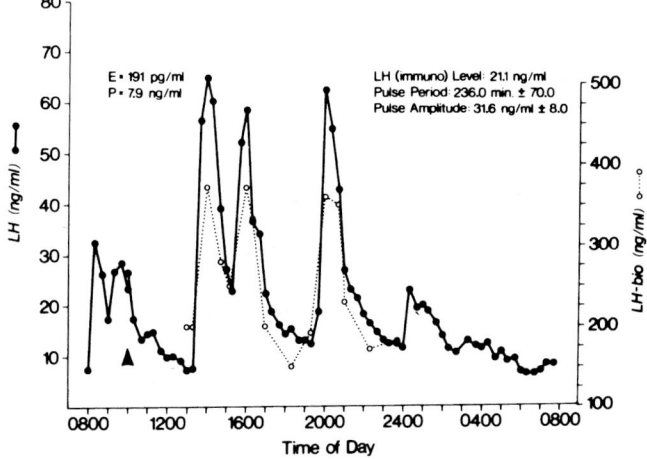

*Figure 153-5*  Patterns of plasma luteinizing hormone (LH) in samples obtained at 20-minute intervals during the late follicular phase **(top)** and during the late follicular phase after the administration of progesterone (P) for 8 days **(bottom)** in a normally cycling woman. The *dotted lines* in the lower panel represent serum LH measured by bioassay. E$_2$, estradiol. (From Soules MR, Steiner RA, Clifton DK, et al: Progesterone modulation of pulsatile luteinizing hormone secretion in normal women. J Clin Endocrinol Metab 58:378–383; © 1984, The Endocrine Society.)

play a role in demise of the corpus luteum. The slower frequency of GnRH pulses may also affect gonadotropin synthesis in the luteal phase. GnRH is essential for gonadotropin synthesis, and in rodents, faster-frequency GnRH pulses favor LH synthesis and slower pulses favor FSH synthesis.[46] The slow irregular luteal GnRH stimulus would thus be expected to maintain FSH synthesis, but may not be optimal for LH synthesis. Reduced LH synthesis, together with ongoing LH release, would result in depletion of pituitary LH stores during the luteal phase.

Plasma FSH remains low during the luteal phase (see Fig. 153-3), which reflects inhibition of release by estradiol and inhibin A secreted by the corpus luteum.[5,46,47] With the demise of the corpus luteum, serum progesterone, estradiol, and inhibin A levels fall and LH pulse frequency and plasma FSH levels increase during the last 2 to 3 days of the cycle. Detailed studies of the late luteal–early follicular phase transition in individual patients suggest that the fall in progesterone allows an increase in GnRH pulse frequency (Fig. 153-6), which continues to rise over the next 1 to 2 weeks.[27] The increase in GnRH stimulation of the pituitary results in predominantly FSH release because the selective inhibition by estradiol and inhibin A is no longer present and LH stores have been depleted. Activin A also rises during the late luteal phase[36] and may contribute to FSH release, which together with the long half-life of FSH, effects a selective increase in plasma FSH. Studies in GnRH-deficient women have emphasized the role of increased GnRH secretion in the selective intercycle rise in FSH and subsequent follicular secretion of inhibin B. When a slow frequency (every 240 minutes) of GnRH pulses was continued during menses, a smaller increase in FSH and inhibin B occurred than when GnRH pulses were given at a physiologic, early follicular frequency of every 90 minutes.[48] Thus, although FSH bioassay has suggested that bioactive FSH may be present during the entire luteal phase,[49] the critically important increase in plasma FSH that initiates recruitment of ovarian follicles for the next cycle occurs during the late luteal phase and results from increased GnRH stimulation of a pituitary that is primed to release FSH.

### ROLE OF GnRH SECRETORY PATTERNS IN CYCLE REGULATION

Regulation of the normal menstrual cycle involves a complex series of timely interactions among the hypothalamus, pituitary, and ovaries. Changes in the pattern of GnRH secretion appear to play an important role, and the presumed patterns of GnRH secretion are shown in Figures 153-1, 153-3, and 153-6.

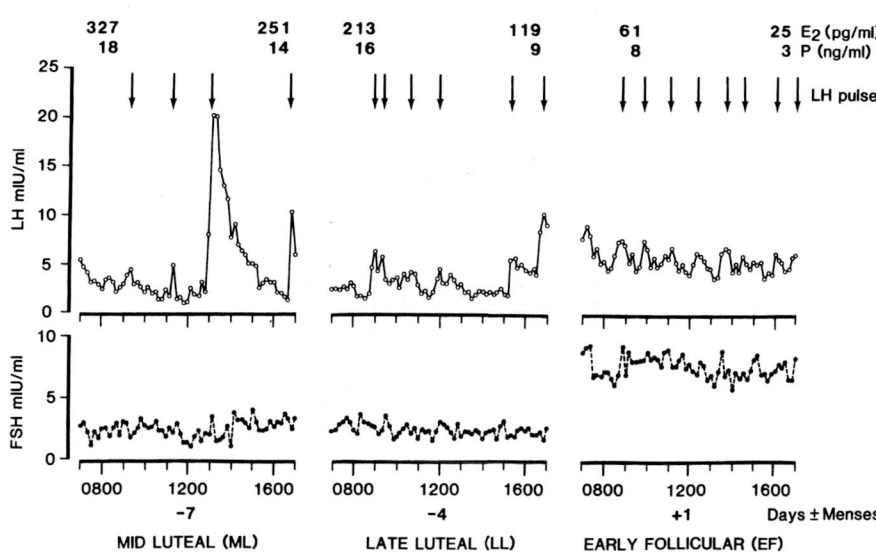

*Figure 153-6*  Gonadotropin secretion and gonadal steroids during the intercycle period of an ovulatory cycle. The transition of hormone secretion from the midluteal to the early follicular phase is shown. *Arrows* indicate luteinizing hormone (LH; gonadotropin-releasing hormone) pulses. E$_2$, estradiol; FSH, follicle-stimulating hormone; P, progesterone. (From Marshall JC, Dalkin AC, Haisenleder DJ, et al: Gonadotropin-releasing hormone pulses: Regulators of gonadotropin synthesis and ovulatory cycles. Recent Prog Horm Res 47:155–189, 1991.)

Follicular recruitment and maturation are initiated by FSH, secretion of which is enhanced by the late luteal increase in GnRH pulse frequency in the presence of low levels of estradiol and inhibin A and B. Estradiol from the maturing follicle selectively inhibits FSH secretion and, in some species, stimulates the late follicular increase in GnRH pulse frequency. This, in turn, increases plasma LH, and subsequent estradiol secretion by the dominant follicle triggers markedly enhanced GnRH secretion at midcycle. The LH surge results from both an increased frequency and amplitude of GnRH secretion and augmentation of LH responses to GnRH. After ovulation, progesterone increases hypothalamic opioid activity, which slows the frequency of GnRH secretion, thereby favoring FSH synthesis. The slow, irregular GnRH pulses do not release FSH (inhibited by elevated estradiol and inhibin A levels), and gonadotrope FSH stores are maintained. The fall in progesterone allows an increase in GnRH pulse frequency, which now effects FSH secretion because estradiol and inhibin A levels are low.

This synopsis of the role of GnRH secretion is based on patterns of hormone secretion consistently observed in women and several animal species. The importance of changes in GnRH secretion remains uncertain, however, because the administration of a fixed dose of GnRH at a fixed frequency can induce ovulation, both in women with GnRH deficiency and in GnRH-deficient monkeys (induced by hypothalamic lesions).[32,33,50–52] This apparent contradiction may reflect the manner of GnRH administration. In most cycles in which ovulation has been induced with exogenous GnRH, the dose of GnRH used was supraphysiologic, which may override the need to change the frequency of the GnRH stimulus. Additionally, few studies have examined the efficacy of uninterrupted exogenous GnRH pulse regimens in the stimulation of ovulatory cycles over prolonged periods, and the ability to alter GnRH frequency may be important in the continued maintenance of normal cyclicity. Slowing of pulse frequency in the luteal phase appears to be important in this regard. The administration of GnRH at rapid frequencies in the luteal phase has led to deficient follicular development and corpus luteum function in subsequent cycles, perhaps a consequence of inadequate late luteal/early follicular FSH secretion.[53–55] The fact that GnRH pulse frequency varies during the cycle appears well established and has led to the use of varied GnRH dose/frequency regimens for induction of ovulation with excellent (>90%) ovulation rates in GnRH-deficient women.[56] However, the exact role and the requirement for altered frequency to maintain ongoing cyclicity await the results of future studies.[57]

The changes in the pattern of GnRH secretion during the cycle, particularly the increase in frequency from the luteal to the follicular phase, are similar to the changes in GnRH secretion that occur during pubertal maturation. In prepubertal girls, LH (by inference, GnRH) pulse amplitude is low and pulses occur infrequently, every 3 to 4 hours, with a minor augmentation during sleep.[58–60] Pubertal maturation is initiated by increased GnRH secretion initially during sleep, subsequently throughout 24 hours, and responses to GnRH change from a predominant FSH response in prepubertal girls to the adult pattern of LH release. Thus, the increase in frequency of GnRH secretion during pubertal maturation in girls is similar to that seen during the luteal/follicular transition, when FSH responses to GnRH also change to the LH-dominated responses of the late follicular phase. The ability to secrete GnRH at a rapid frequency (one pulse per hour) is reacquired at puberty (data suggest that fast-frequency secretion is present in infancy), and is necessary for the development of ovulatory cycles. A rapid frequency of GnRH secretion is needed to allow estradiol augmentation of GnRH secretion and LH responses to GnRH, important events in the genesis of the LH surge. The luteal phase could then be viewed as a time when ovarian steroids restrict GnRH release to a pattern that is not optimal for LH secretion, but allows ongoing FSH synthesis to stimulate the next wave of follicular development.[46,57]

## MECHANISMS OF ANOVULATION

In view of the complex nature of the interrelations between the hypothalamus-pituitary and the ovary that are required for normal cyclic function, it is not surprising that disorders of any part of this axis can result in anovulation and amenorrhea. In many instances, however, anovulation occurs in the absence of recognized pathologic abnormalities. Anovulatory cycles frequently occur during the year after menarche, and because regular cycles subsequently ensue, this pattern suggests that hormonal interrelationships are established over time. Specifically, the ability of estradiol to induce positive feedback and increase LH release is absent in immature girls,[61] which may, in part, account for the anovulatory cycles that occur soon after menarche.

In several instances, anovulation has been shown to be associated with abnormal patterns of LH (GnRH) pulsatile secretion, and these patterns are discussed in the sections that follow.

### HYPOTHALAMIC AMENORRHEA

Hypothalamic amenorrhea, the most common form of amenorrhea, is a diagnosis made only after exclusion of pituitary and ovarian abnormalities. Conditions that often precede anovulation include marked weight loss, strenuous exercise such as gymnastics or competitive running, psychologic stress, and, occasionally, the prior use of combination oral contraceptive preparations.[62] In most women (about 70%), removal of these antecedent conditions results in the return of ovulatory menses within 12 months, but, in the remainder, anovulation and amenorrhea persist. Basal hormone measurements show that plasma LH, FSH, and estradiol levels are often normal or low, prolactin is not elevated, and LH and FSH responsiveness to GnRH is usually preserved. Daily hormone measurements have shown that cyclic changes do not occur, and abnormalities of estrogen and progesterone feedback, with failure of positive feedback, have been described.[63–66] Studies from several groups have shown that the frequency of GnRH pulsatile secretion is markedly reduced in most women with hypothalamic amenorrhea[67–69] (Fig. 153-7). GnRH pulse frequency (one pulse every 3 to 4 hours) and the irregular amplitude of LH pulses resemble the patterns seen during the luteal phase of ovulatory cycles. This similarity suggested that the disorder may reflect abnormal suppression of GnRH pulse frequency by increased hypothalamic opioid activity. Administration of the opiate receptor blocker naloxone results in rapid (within 1 to 2 hours) restoration of normal-frequency GnRH secretion in some 60% to 70% of women with hypothalamic amenorrhea[70–72] (Fig. 153-8). This opiate antagonist–induced restoration of GnRH secretion suggests that most women with this disorder are anovulatory on the basis of a persistent slow frequency of pulsatile GnRH secretion that is inadequate to maintain the level of LH synthesis and secretion required for the production of an ovulatory LH surge. Support for this view is found in studies in which GnRH pulses given at a slow frequency (every 3 hours) to GnRH-deficient primates did not maintain plasma LH concentrations.[73]

The observation that patterns of GnRH secretion are variable but slower than normal pulse frequency would also explain observations that some women with hypothalamic amenorrhea ovulate after the administration of clomiphene citrate (Clomid). If pulse frequency were markedly impaired, clomiphene would not enhance GnRH and gonadotropin secretion to the levels required for an LH surge. On the other hand, lesser degrees of GnRH slowing may be overcome by clomiphene and permit follicular maturation and ovulation.

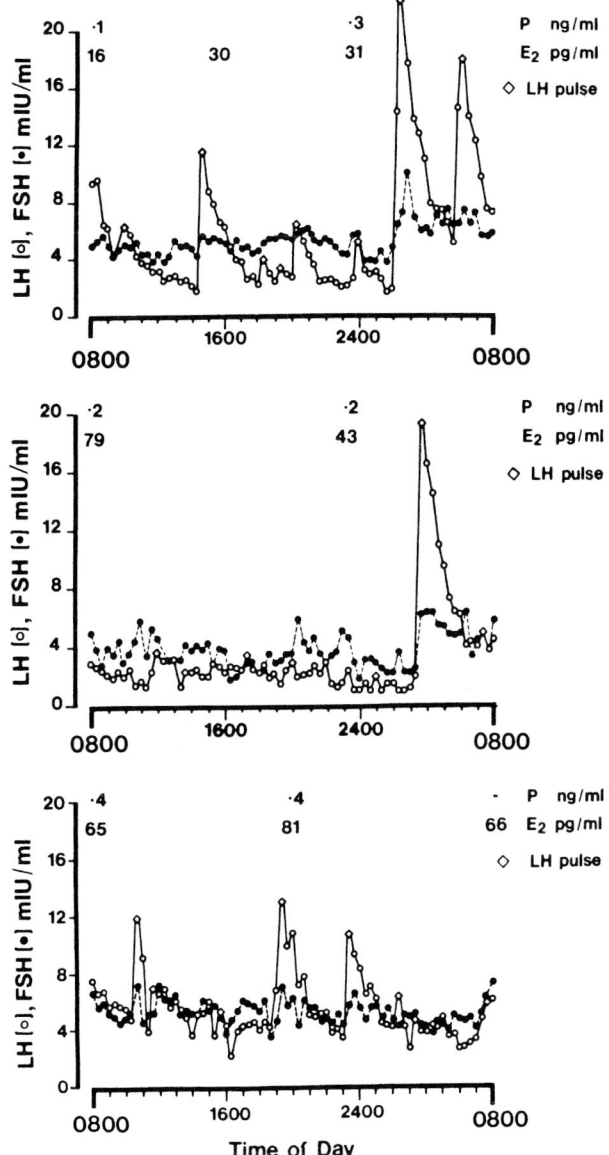

*Figure 153-7* Patterns of pulsatile luteinizing hormone (LH) secretion over a 24-hour period in women with hypothalamic amenorrhea. Plasma estradiol ($E_2$) and progesterone (P) levels are also shown. From top to bottom panels, patients showed 4, 3.5, and 5 pulses per 12 hours, respectively. FSH, follicle-stimulating hormone. (From Reame NE, Sauder SE, Kelch RP, et al: Pulsatile gonadotropin secretion in women with hypothalamic amenorrhea: Evidence for reduced frequency of GnRH secretion. J Clin Endocrinol Metab 61:851–858; © 1985, The Endocrine Society.)

As noted previously, not all women with hypothalamic amenorrhea have slow-frequency GnRH pulses at the time of study, and not all those who do have slow-frequency pulses respond to opiate blockade. The mechanisms of amenorrhea in these women are uncertain, but some data have suggested that abnormalities of the hypothalamic-pituitary-adrenal axis may be involved.[74,75] Stress can elevate corticotropin-releasing hormone (CRH), and CRH has been shown to directly inhibit GnRH secretion and reproductive function in animal studies. Some women with hypothalamic amenorrhea have elevated plasma cortisol levels and blunted responses to CRH, which suggests stress-induced abnormalities in CRH secretion.[76] In women where amenorrhea is associated with strenuous exercise, data suggest a negative energy balance is a precipitating factor and plasma leptin levels are reduced.[77–79] Studies in a primate monkey model have supported this concept[80] and

provision of additional calories while maintaining the same level of exercise restored reproductive cyclicity.[81] The mechanisms involved remain unclear; however, evidence suggests that most women with hypothalamic amenorrhea are anovulatory on the basis of slow-frequency GnRH secretion, reflecting enhanced hypothalamic opioid activity. Naltrexone (an orally active opiate receptor blocker) has been given to these patients for 2 to 3 weeks and in a few studies has induced ovulation,[82] although this action appears to be short lived and repetitive ovulatory cycles rarely ensue.

### HYPERPROLACTINEMIA

Amenorrhea and anovulation commonly occur when serum prolactin is elevated. Increased prolactin may result from medications that reduce hypothalamic dopamine secretion or block dopamine action, or it may reflect the presence of a prolactinoma in the pituitary gland. Initial studies revealed slow, irregular patterns of GnRH secretion, which were restored to normal follicular-phase patterns after suppression of serum prolactin by the dopamine agonist bromocriptine[83,84] (Fig. 153-9).

Of interest, the mechanisms of reduced GnRH pulsatile secretion in hyperprolactinemic patients also appear to involve a final common pathway of increased hypothalamic opioid activity. Administration of naloxone to hyperprolactinemic women (serum prolactin remains elevated) results in a rapid increase in pulsatile GnRH secretion in a manner similar to that seen in women with hypothalamic amenorrhea.[85,86] This response suggests that an elevated prolactin level enhances hypothalamic opioid activity, which, in turn, reduces GnRH secretion by reducing pulse frequency.

These data suggest that in both hypothalamic amenorrhea and hyperprolactinemia, anovulation depends on a continuing slow frequency of endogenous GnRH secretion. The inability to increase pulsatile GnRH secretion results in failure of follicular maturation and failure of estradiol/progesterone augmentation of LH release (the latter would not occur in the absence of an adequate GnRH stimulus). In addition, data show that the abnormalities in GnRH secretion may be variable[72] and not consistently present on a week-to-week basis. This variability may account for why some women with apparent hypothalamic amenorrhea have "normal" LH pulse frequencies during some studies. If an underlying abnormality such as stress increases hypothalamic opioid activity, this response may be variable in both degree and duration. When such abnormalities are present for long enough to affect the hypothalamic mechanisms involved in normal follicular maturation and ovulation, anovulation would be expected to ensue.

### POLYCYSTIC OVARY SYNDROME

Polycystic ovary syndrome (PCOS) is a heterogeneous disorder of unknown cause associated with anovulation, hirsutism, obesity, insulin resistance, and multiple cysts in the ovaries (see Chapter 157). The excess androgen secretion in PCOS has been shown to be predominantly of ovarian origin, but insulin resistance and adrenal abnormalities exist, and it is likely that the clinical syndrome encompasses several different etiologies.[87,88] Ovarian abnormalities, including abnormal steroidogenesis and follicular maturation, may be the primary cause of excess androgen secretion in some patients.[89] In most, however, the syndrome is associated with increased LH secretion, and some 75% of patients with PCOS have elevated mean serum LH levels, increasing to 90% when recent spontaneous ovulation is excluded.[90] In obese subjects, plasma LH tends to be lower and mean LH is inversely related to body mass index (BMI). LH and GnRH pulse frequency are elevated, however, in both lean and obese women with PCOS.[91] Desensitization of LH secretion by using a long-acting GnRH

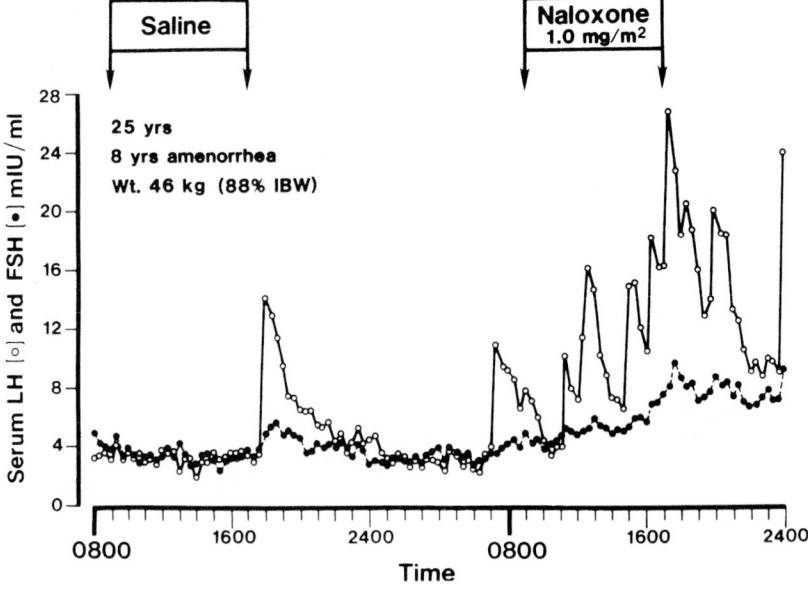

**Figure 153-8** Effects of naloxone on pulsatile luteinizing hormone (LH, *open circles*) and follicle-stimulating hormone (FSH, *closed circles*) secretion in a woman with hypothalamic amenorrhea. The 25-year-old woman had a history of weight loss and amenorrhea for 8 years and, despite regaining weight to 90% of ideal 1 year ago, had remained amenorrheic. IBW, ideal body weight. (Data from Khoury SA, Reame NE, Kelch RP, Marshall JC: Diurnal patterns of pulsatile luteinizing hormone secretion in hypothalamic amenorrhea: Reproducibility and responses to opiate blockade and in α₂-adrenergic agonist. J Clin Endocrinol Metab 64:755–762; © 1987, The Endocrine Society.)

agonist is followed by reduced androgen secretion, thus confirming the importance of LH stimulation of the ovary.[92] Studies have demonstrated that the frequency and amplitude of LH pulses are usually increased in patients with PCOS.[93,94] This finding suggests the possibility that a persistent rapid frequency of GnRH secretion causes the excess LH synthesis and secretion, which, in turn, produces enhanced androgen production by the ovary and failure of follicular maturation. The abnormal GnRH secretion could be viewed as being secondary to anovulation and consequent reduced ovarian progesterone secretion and is a factor in anovulatory women. An alternative view is that the abnormal pulsatile GnRH secretion reflects an underlying abnormality in PCOS.[95–97] In normal cycles, estradiol and progesterone inhibit pulse frequency in the luteal phase, and if a relative hypothalamic insensitivity to these steroids were present, persistently increased GnRH and LH secretion would result. Many patients with PCOS had an onset of symptoms soon after pubertal maturation, a time when the ability to secrete GnRH at a rapid frequency is reacquired. Thus, if women in whom PCOS is destined to develop were relatively resistant to estradiol and progesterone slowing

of GnRH secretion, the normal luteal phase slowing may not occur. This lack of normal slowing would be expected to result in a relative deficiency in FSH secretion, with consequent impaired follicular maturation and infrequent ovulation. Over time, increased GnRH pulse frequency and LH secretion would increase ovarian androgen production and lead to cyst formation.

Evidence to support this concept is found in adolescents with hyperandrogenemia. In half of the adolescent girls with anovulation studied, LH pulse amplitude and frequency were increased, and this increase was associated with elevated plasma androgens, estradiol, and progesterone.[98–100] A detailed study over 24 hours confirmed these findings. When compared with age-matched controls, hyperandrogenemic adolescent girls had higher LH pulse frequency (one pulse every 80 minutes) and mean LH during both waking and sleeping hours.[101] It is uncertain whether changes consistent with PCOS will later develop in these adolescents, but only 40% subsequently established ovulatory cycles.[100]

Further evidence suggests that elevated androgens may interfere with normal regulation of GnRH secretion. In pre- and

## LH PULSES IN A WOMAN WITH HYPERPROLACTINEMIA

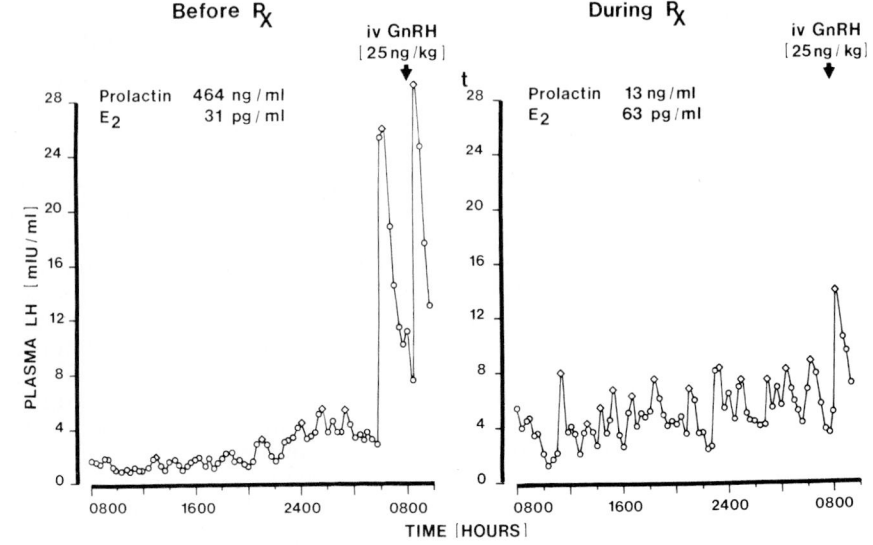

**Figure 153-9** Patterns of pulsatile luteinizing hormone (LH) secretion before and after administration of bromocriptine in a woman with hyperprolactinemia. Note the initial irregular amplitude and infrequent LH pulses (6 per 24 hours) **(left)**, which return to a more regular pulsatile pattern similar to that of the follicular phase (12 pulses per 24 hours) after the administration of bromocriptine and reduction in serum prolactin **(right)**. *Open diamond*, LH pulses. E₂, plasma estradiol; GnRH, gonadotropin-releasing hormone. (From Sauder SE, Frager M, Case GD, et al: Abnormal patterns of pulsatile luteinizing hormone secretion in women with hyperprolactinemia and amenorrhea: Responses to bromocriptine. J Clin Endocrinol Metab 59:941–948; © 1984, The Endocrine Society.)

early pubertal girls, testosterone exceeds estradiol concentrations in plasma by 10-fold.[102,103] This exposure of the hypothalamus to androgens may reduce GnRH sensitivity to steroid inhibition and, as puberty progresses, lead to higher circulating levels of both LH and ovarian steroids. Studies in monkeys and sheep have shown that prenatal exposure to elevated androgens results in reduced GnRH inhibition by progesterone and elevated plasma LH during subsequent adolescence and adulthood.[104,105]

To explore these possibilities, the ability of physiologic luteal concentrations of estradiol and progesterone to suppress the rapid frequency of GnRH secretion has been assessed in women with PCOS.[106] Administration of estrogen and progesterone for 3 weeks initially slowed the frequency of GnRH secretion (by day 10), with later persistent slowing and marked reduction in LH pulse amplitude. Withdrawal of ovarian steroids was associated with increased GnRH pulse frequency and a selective increase in FSH, which increased more rapidly than LH. This relative increase in FSH after steroids and normalization of the LH/FSH ratio to unity is shown in Figure 153-10. The enhanced FSH secretion resulted in follicular maturation in all patients studied and ovulation in some. These data show that luteal steroids can suppress the frequency of GnRH secretion in women with PCOS, but recent studies have indicated that the hypothalamic GnRH pulse generator is relatively resistant to the inhibitory effects of sex steroids. After administration of a combined oral contraceptive, GnRH pulse frequency was higher in women with PCOS than in controls, both during treatment and after steroid use was discontinued.[107] Similarly, administration of estradiol and progesterone for 7 days to normal controls and patients with PCOS showed that GnRH pulse frequency was suppressed to a greater degree in controls after exposure to similar levels of steroids.[108] Lower plasma levels of progesterone (<10 ng/mL) were more effective in suppressing GnRH pulse frequency in normal controls than in women with PCOS, while higher concentrations of progesterone suppressed GnRH pulse frequency to a similar degree in both groups. These findings suggest that the GnRH pulse generator is relatively resistant to suppression by progesterone in women with PCOS.

Subsequent studies have indicated that the hypothalamic insensitivity to progesterone reflects the effects of hyperandrogenemia.[109] When women with PCOS were pretreated with the androgen receptor blocker flutamide, the ability of lower concentrations of progesterone to suppress GnRH pulse frequency was restored to normal (Fig. 154-11). Plasma testosterone was not reduced and basal LH pulsatility was not altered, suggesting that excess androgens selectively impair progesterone inhibition of the GnRH pulse generator. These data strongly support a role for hyperandrogenemia in the etiology of the elevated LH in PCOS, but it remains uncertain when the abnormality developed. Some results suggest that similar insensitivity to progesterone is present in hyperandrogenic adolescents,[110] which, if confirmed, indicates a role for hyperandrogenemia in the genesis of abnormal LH secretion in PCOS.

Overall, these observations in anovulatory patients indicate that some disorders resulting in anovulation are associated with abnormalities in GnRH secretory patterns. Both slow frequency with an inability to increase GnRH pulse frequency and persistence of rapid GnRH frequencies have been recognized. This variability suggests that the ability to change the pattern of GnRH secretion in normal cycles is an important part of the process of repeated cyclic ovulation. Moreover, these data suggest new approaches to therapy whereby administration of exogenous hormones to slow GnRH frequency in PCOS may be efficacious in restoring normal pulsatile GnRH secretion and ovulatory cycles.

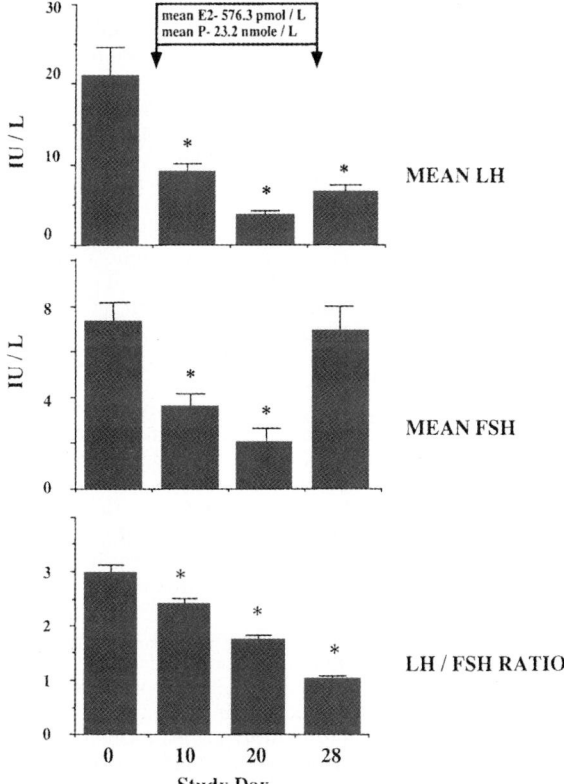

*Figure 153-10*  Mean plasma concentrations of luteinizing hormone (LH) and follicle-stimulating hormone (FSH) and LH/FSH ratios in six women with polycystic ovary syndrome given estradiol (E2) and progesterone (P) on days 1 through 20. *$P < 0.001$ vs. day 0. (From Christman GM, Randolph J, Kelch RP, et al: Reduction of GnRH pulse frequency is associated with subsequent selective FSH secretion in women with polycystic ovarian disease. J Clin Endocrinol Metab 72:1278–1285; © 1991, The Endocrine Society.)

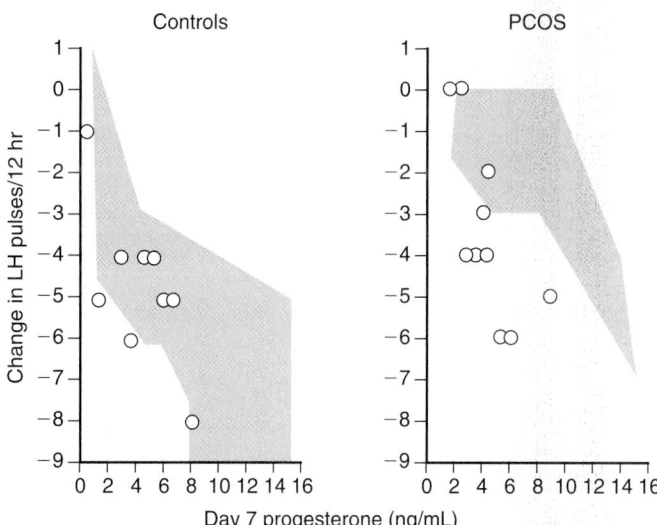

*Figure 153-11*  Effect of the androgen receptor blockade by flutamide on progesterone suppression of luteinizing hormone (LH) pulse frequency. Both normal control and women with polycystic ovary syndrome (PCOS) received 250 mg of flutamide twice daily for 5 weeks. During the last 7 days, estradiol (E2, plasma conc$^n$ approx 120 pg/nl) and variable doses of progesterone (P) were also given. Blood was drawn every 10 minutes for 12 hours before and on day 7 of E2 + P treatment and pulsatile LH secretion analyzed. The data (*circles*) show the decrement in LH pulse frequency after 7 days of E2 + P as a function of plasma progesterone on day 7. The *shaded areas* indicate the range of response in the absence of flutamide pretreatment. Flutamide had little effect in controls, but enhanced the ability of low doses of progesterone to inhibit LH (gonadotropin-releasing hormone [GnRH]) pulse frequency in women with PCOS.

## REFERENCES

1. Cargille CM, Ross GT, Yoshimi TJ: Daily variations in plasma follicle-stimulating hormone, luteinizing hormone and progesterone in a normal menstrual cycle. J Clin Endocrinol Metab 29:12–16, 1969.
2. Abraham GE, Odell WD, Swerdloff RS, et al: Simultaneous radioimmunoassay of plasma FSH, LH, progesterone, 17-hydroxyprogesterone and estradiol-17 during the menstrual cycle. J Clin Endocrinol Metab 34:312–318, 1972.
3. Speroff L, Vande Weile L: Regulation of the human menstrual cycle. Am J Obstet Gynecol 109:234–237, 1971.
4. Baird DT, Fraser HM, Hillier SG, et al: Production and secretion of ovarian inhibin in women. In Yen SSC, Vale WW (eds): Neuroendocrine Regulation of Reproduction. Norwell, MA, Serono Symposia USA, 1990, pp 195–206.
5. Groome NP, Illingworth PJ, O'Brien M, et al: Detection of dimeric inhibin throughout the human menstrual cycle by two-site enzyme immunoassay. Clin Endocrinol (Oxf) 40:717–723, 1994.
6. Groome NP, Illingworth PJ, O'Brien M, et al: Measurement of dimeric inhibin B throughout the human menstrual cycle. J Clin Endocrinol Metab 81:1401–1405, 1996.
7. DiZerega GS, Hodgen GD: Folliculogenesis in the primate ovarian cycle. Endocr Rev 2:27–49, 1981.
8. Baird DT: Factors regulating the growth of the pre-ovulatory follicle in the sheep and human. J Reprod Fertil 69:343–352, 1983.
9. Tonetta SA, DiZerega GS: Intragonadal regulation of follicular maturation. Endocr Rev 10:205–229, 1989.
10. Adashi EY: The potential relevance of cytokines to ovarian physiology: The emerging role of ovarian cells of the white blood cell series. Endocr Rev 11:454–464, 1990.
11. Zeleznik AJ: Premature elevation of systemic estradiol reduces serum FSH and lengthens the follicular phase of the menstrual cycle in rhesus monkeys. Endocrinology 109:352–355, 1981.
12. Schipper I, Hop WCJ, Fauser BCJM: The FSH threshold/window concept examined by different interventions with exogenous FSH during the follicular phase of the normal menstrual cycle: Duration rather than magnitude of FSH increase affects follicle development. J Clin Endocrinol Metab 83:1292–1298, 1998.
13. Hsueh AJW, Adashi EY, Jones PBC, Welsh TH Jr: Hormonal regulation of the differentiation of cultured ovarian granulosa cells. Endocr Rev 5:76–127, 1984.
14. Marshall JC, Case GD, Valk TW, et al: Selective inhibition of follicle-stimulating hormone secretion by estradiol: Mechanism for modulation of gonadotropin responses to low dose pulses of gonadotropin-releasing hormone. J Clin Invest 71:248–258, 1983.
15. Odell WD, Swerdloff RS: Progesterone induced luteinizing and follicle-stimulating hormone surge in postmenopausal women: A stimulated ovulatory peak. Proc Natl Acad Sci U S A 61:629–631, 1968.
16. Moenter SM, Caraty A, Karsch FJ: The estradiol induced surge of GnRH in the ewe. Endocrinology 127:1375–1384, 1990.
17. Auletta FJ, Flint ADF: Mechanisms controlling corpus luteum function in sheep, cows, nonhuman primates and women especially in relation to the time of luteolysis. Endocr Rev 9:88–105, 1988.
18. Yen SSC, Tsai CC, Naftolin F, et al: Pulsatile patterns of gonadotropin release in subjects with and without ovarian function. J Clin Endocrinol Metab 34:671–676, 1972.
19. Santen RJ, Bardin CW: Episodic luteinizing hormone secretion in man. J Clin Invest 52:2617–2628, 1973.
20. Backstrom CT, McNeilly AS, Leask RM, Baird DT: Pulsatile secretion of LH, FSH, prolactin, estradiol and progesterone during the human menstrual cycle. Clin Endocrinol (Oxf) 17:29–40, 1982.
21. Reame N, Sauder SE, Kelch RP, Marshall JC: Pulsatile gonadotropin secretion during the human menstrual cycle: Evidence for altered frequency of gonadotropin-releasing hormone secretion. J Clin Endocrinol Metab 59:328–337, 1984.
22. Burger HG, Groome NP, Robertson DM: Both inhibin A and B respond to exogenous FSH in the follicular phase of the human menstrual cycle. J Clin Endocrinol Metab 83:4167–4169, 1998.
23. Roberts VJ, Barth S, el-Roeiy A, Yen SS: Expression of inhibin/activin subunits and follistatin mRNAs and proteins in ovarian follicles and the corpus luteum during the human menstrual cycle. J Clin Endocrinol Metab 77:1402–1410, 1993.
24. Schwall RH, Mason AJ, Willcox JN, et al: Localization of inhibin/activin subunit mRNAs within the primate ovary. Mol Endocrinol 4:75–79, 1990.
25. Baird DT: Pulsatile secretion of LH and ovarian estradiol in the follicular phase of the sheep estrous cycle. Biol Reprod 18:359–364, 1978.
26. Djahanbakhch O, Warner P, McNeilly AS, Baird DT: Pulsatile release of LH and oestradiol during the periovulatory period in women. Clin Endocrinol (Oxf) 20:579–589, 1984.
27. McCartney CR, Gingrich MB, Hu Y, et al: Hypothalamic regulation of cyclic ovulation: Evidence that the increase in GnRH pulse frequency during the follicular phase reflects the gradual loss of the restraining effects of progesterone. J Clin Endocrinol Metab 87:2194–2200, 2002.
28. Karsch FJ, Foster DL, Bittman EL, Goodman RL: A role for estradiol in enhancing LH pulse frequency during the follicular phase of the estrous cycle of sheep. Endocrinology 113:1333–1339, 1983.
29. Moenter SM, Caraty A, Locatelli A, Karsch FJ: Pattern of GnRH secretion leading up to ovulation in the ewe: Existence of a preovulatory GnRH surge. Endocrinology 129:1175–1182, 1991.
30. Evans NP, Dahl GE, Padmanabhan V, et al: Estradiol requirements for induction and maintenance of the GnRH surge: Implications for neuroendocrine processing of the estradiol signal. Endocrinology 138:5408–5414, 1997.
31. Pau K-YF, Berria M, Hess DL, et al: Preovulatory GnRH surge in ovarian intact rhesus macaques. Endocrinology 133:1650–1656, 1993.
32. Knobil E, Plant TM, Wildt L, et al: Control of the rhesus monkey menstrual cycle: Permissive role of hypothalamic gonadotropin-releasing hormone. Science 207:1371–1374, 1980.
33. Leyendecker G, Wildt L, Hansmann M: Pregnancies following chronic intermittent (pulsatile) administration of GnRH by means of a pulsatile pump (zyklomat): A new approach to the treatment of infertility in hypothalamic amenorrhea. J Clin Endocrinol Metab 51:1214–1216, 1980.
34. Hoff JD, Quigley ME, Yen SSC: Hormonal dynamics at mid cycle: A reevaluation. J Clin Endocrinol Metab 57:792–796, 1983.
35. Liu JH, Yen SSC: Induction of the mid cycle gonadotropin surge by ovarian steroids in women: A critical evaluation. J Clin Endocrinol Metab 57:797–802, 1983.
36. Muttukrishna S, Fowler PA, George L, et al: Changes in peripheral serum levels of total activin A during the human menstrual cycle and pregnancy. J Clin Endocrinol Metab 81:3328–3334, 1996.
37. Hayes FJ, Hall JE, Boepple PA, et al: Differential control of gonadotropin secretion in the human: Endocrine role of inhibin. J Clin Endocrinol Metab 83:1835–1841, 1998.
38. McNatty KP, Makras A, DeGrazia C, et al: The production of progesterone, androgens and estrogens by human granulosa cells, thecal tissue and stromal tissue from human ovaries in vitro. J Clin Endocrinol Metab 49:687–694, 1979.
39. Nippoldt TB, Khoury S, Barkan A, et al: Gonadotropin responses to GnRH pulses in hypogonadotropic hypogonadism: LH responsiveness is maintained in the presence of luteal phase concentrations of estrogen and progesterone. Clin Endocrinol 26:293–301, 1987.
40. Soules MR, Steiner RA, Clifton DK, et al: Progesterone modulation of pulsatile luteinizing hormone secretion in normal women. J Clin Endocrinol Metab 58:378–383, 1984.

41. Goodman RL, Bittman EL, Foster DL, Karsch FJ: The endocrine basis of the synergistic suppression of luteinizing hormone by estradiol and progesterone. Endocrinology 109:1414–1417, 1981.

42. Ropert JF, Quigley ME, Yen SSC: Endogenous opiates modulate pulsatile luteinizing hormone release in humans. J Clin Endocrinol Metab 52:583–588, 1981.

43. Van Vugt DA, Lam NY, Ferin M: Reduced frequency of pulsatile luteinizing hormone secretion in the luteal phase of the rhesus monkey: Involvement of endogenous opiates. Endocrinology 115:1095–1101, 1984.

44. Vande Wiele RL, Bogumil J, Dyrenfurth I, et al: Mechanisms regulating the menstrual cycle in women. Recent Prog Horm Res 26:63–103, 1970.

45. Filicori M, Butler JP, Crowley WF: Neuroendocrine regulation of the corpus luteum in the human: Evidence for pulsatile progesterone secretion. J Clin Invest 73:1638–1647, 1984.

46. Marshall JC, Dalkin AC, Haisenleder DJ, et al: Gonadotropin-releasing hormone pulses: Regulators of gonadotropin synthesis and ovulatory cycles. Recent Prog Horm Res 47:155–189, 1991.

47. Le Nestour E, Marraoui J, Lahlau N, et al: Role of estradiol in the rise of FSH levels during the luteal-follicular transition. J Clin Endocrinol Metab 77:439–442, 1993.

48. Welt CK, Martin KA, Taylor AE, et al: Frequency modulation of FSH during the luteal-follicular transition: Evidence for FSH control of inhibin B in normal women. J Clin Endocrinol Metab 82:2645–2652, 1997.

49. Christin-Maitre S, Taylor AE, Khoury RH, et al: Homologous in vitro bioassay for FSH reveals increased FSH biological signal during the mid-late luteal phase of the human menstrual cycle. J Clin Endocrinol Metab 81:2080–2088, 1996.

50. Crowley WF, MacArthur JW: Simulation of the normal menstrual cycle in Kallmann's syndrome by pulsatile administration of luteinizing hormone–releasing hormone (LHRH). J Clin Endocrinol Metab 51:173–175, 1980.

51. Valk TW, Marshall JC, Kelch RP: Simulation of the follicular phase of the menstrual cycle by intravenous administration of low dose pulsatile gonadotropin-releasing hormone. Am J Obstet Gynecol 141:842–844, 1981.

52. Filicori M, Flamigni C, Merriggiola MC, et al: Ovulation induction with pulsatile gonadotropin-releasing hormone: Technical modalities and clinical perspectives. Fertil Steril 56:1–13, 1991.

53. Lam NY, Ferin M: Is the decrease in the hypophysiotropic signal frequency normally observed during the luteal phase important for menstrual cyclicity in the primate? Endocrinology 120:2044–2050, 1987.

54. Soules MR, Clifton DK, Bremner WJ, Steiner RA: Corpus luteum insufficiency induced by a rapid gonadotropin-releasing hormone–induced gonadotropin secretion pattern in the follicular phase. J Clin Endocrinol Metab 65:457–464, 1987.

55. Schweiger U, Laessle RG, Tuschl RJ, et al: Decreased follicular phase gonadotropin secretion is associated with both impaired $E_2$ and P secretion during the follicular and luteal phases in normally menstruating women. J Clin Endocrinol Metab 68:888–893, 1989.

56. Santoro N, Wierman M, Filicori M, et al: Intravenous administration of pulsatile GnRH in hypothalamic amenorrhea: Effects of dosage. J Clin Endocrinol Metab 62:109–114, 1986.

57. Marshall JC, Kelch RP: Gonadotropin-releasing hormone: Role of pulsatile secretion in the regulation of reproduction. N Engl J Med 315:1459–1468, 1986.

58. Hale PM, Khoury S, Foster CM, et al: Increased luteinizing hormone pulse frequency during sleep in early to midpubertal boys: Effects of testosterone infusion. J Clin Endocrinol Metab 66:785–791, 1988.

59. Wu FC, Butler GE, Kelner CJ, et al: Patterns of pulsatile luteinizing hormone and follicle-stimulating hormone secretion in prepubertal (midchildhood) boys and girls and patients with idiopathic hypogonadotropin hypogonadism (Kallmann's syndrome): A study using an ultrasensitive time-resolved immunofluorometric assay. J Clin Endocrinol Metab 72:1229–1237, 1991.

60. Apter D, Butzow TL, Laughlin GA, et al: GnRH pulse generator activity during pubertal transition in girls: Pulsatile and diurnal patterns of circulating gonadotropins. J Clin Endocrinol Metab 76:940–946, 1993.

61. Reiter EO, Kulin HE, Hamwood SM: The absence of positive feedback between estrogen and luteinizing hormone in sexually immature girls. Pediatr Res 8:740–745, 1974.

62. Schwartz B, Cumming DC, Riordan E, et al: Exercise-associated amenorrhea: A distinct entity? Am J Obstet Gynecol 141:662–668, 1981.

63. Santen RJ, Friend JN, Trojanowski D, et al: Prolonged negative feedback suppression after estradiol administration: Proposed mechanism of eugonadal secondary amenorrhea. J Clin Endocrinol Metab 47:1220–1229, 1978.

64. Shaw RW, Butt WR, London DR, Marshall JC: The estrogen provocation test: A method for assessing the hypothalamic-pituitary axis in patients with amenorrhea. Clin Endocrinol (Oxf) 4:267–276, 1975.

65. Shaw RW, Butt WR, London DR: Pathological mechanisms to explain some cases of amenorrhea without organic disease. Br J Obstet Gynaecol 82:337–340, 1975.

66. Rakoff JS, Rigg LA, Yen SSC: The impairment of progesterone induced pituitary release of prolactin and gonadotropin in patients with hypothalamic chronic anovulation. Am J Obstet Gynecol 130:807–812, 1978.

67. Reame NE, Sauder SE, Kelch RP, et al: Pulsatile gonadotropin secretion in women with hypothalamic amenorrhea: Evidence for reduced frequency of GnRH secretion. J Clin Endocrinol Metab 61:851–858, 1985.

68. Veldhuis JD, Evans WS, Demers LM, et al: Altered neuroendocrine regulation of gonadotropin secretion in women distance runners. J Clin Endocrinol Metab 61:557–563, 1985.

69. Crowley WF, Filicori M, Spratt DI, Santoro NF: The physiology of GnRH secretion in men and women. Recent Prog Horm Res 41:473–531, 1985.

70. Quigley ME, Sheehan KL, Casper RF, Yen SSC: Evidence for increased dopaminergic and opiate activity in patients with hypothalamic hypogonadotropic amenorrhea. J Clin Endocrinol Metab 50:949–954, 1980.

71. Sauder SE, Case GD, Hopwood NJ, et al: The effects of opiate antagonism on gonadotropin secretion in children and in women with hypothalamic amenorrhea. Pediatr Res 18:322–328, 1984.

72. Khoury SA, Reame NE, Kelch RP, Marshall JC: Diurnal patterns of pulsatile luteinizing hormone secretion in hypothalamic amenorrhea: Reproducibility and responses to opiate blockade and in $\alpha_2$-adrenergic agonist. J Clin Endocrinol Metab 64:755–762, 1987.

73. Pohl CR, Richardson DW, Hutchison JS, et al: Hypophysiotropic signal frequency and the functioning of the pituitary-ovarian axis in the rhesus monkey. Endocrinology 112:2076–2080, 1983.

74. Berga SL, Mortola JF, Girton L, et al: Neuroendocrine abnormalities in women with functional amenorrhea. J Clin Endocrinol Metab 68:301–308, 1989.

75. Loucks AB, Mortola JF, Girton L, et al: Alteration in hypothalamic-pituitary ovarian and adrenal axes in athletic women. J Clin Endocrinol Metab 68:402–407, 1989.

76. Biller BMK, Federoff HJ, Koenig JI, Klibanski A: Abnormal cortisol secretion and responses to corticotropin-releasing hormone in women with hypothalamic amenorrhea. J Clin Endocrinol Metab 70:311–317, 1990.

77. Bullen BA, Skrinar GS, Beitins IZ, et al: Induction of menstrual disorders by strenuous exercise in untrained women. N Engl J Med 312:1349–1353, 1985.

78. Kopp-Woodroffe SA, Manore MM, Dueck CA, et al: Energy and nutrient status of amenorrheic athletes participating in a diet and exercise training intervention program. Int J Sport Nutr 9:70–88, 1999.

79. Laughlin GA, Yen SSC: Hypoleptinemia in women athletes: Absence of a diurnal rhythm with amenorrhea. J Clin Endocrinol Metab 82:318–322, 1997.

80. Williams NI, Caston-Balderrama AL, Helmreich DL, et al: Longitudinal changes in reproductive hormones and menstrual cyclicity in cynomolgus monkeys during strenuous exercise training: Abrupt transition to exercise induced amenorrhea. Endocrinology 142:2381–2389, 2001.

81. Williams NI, Helmreich DL, Parfitt D, et al: Evidence for a causal role of low energy availability in the induction of menstrual cycle disturbances during strenuous exercise training. J Clin Endocrinol Metab 86:5184–5193, 2001.

82. Wildt L, Leyendecker G: Induction of ovulation by the chronic administration of naltrexone in hypothalamic amenorrhea. J Clin Endocrinol Metab 64:1334–1335, 1987.

83. Klibanski A, Beitins IZ, Merriam GR, et al: Gonadotropin and prolactin pulsations in hyperprolactinemic women before and during bromocriptine therapy. J Clin Endocrinol Metab 58:1141–1147, 1984.

84. Sauder SE, Frager M, Case GD, et al: Abnormal patterns of pulsatile luteinizing hormone secretion in women with hyperprolactinemia and amenorrhea: Responses to bromocriptine. J Clin Endocrinol Metab 59:941–948, 1984.

85. Grossman A, Moult PJA, McIntyre H, et al: Opiate mediation of amenorrhea in hyperprolactinemia and in weight loss related amenorrhea. Clin Endocrinol (Oxf) 17:379–388, 1982.

86. Cook CB, Nippoldt TB, Kletter GB, et al: Naloxone increases the frequency of pulsatile LH secretion in women with hyperprolactinemia. J Clin Endocrinol Metab 73:1099–1105, 1991.

87. Franks S: The polycystic ovary syndrome. N Engl J Med 333:853–861, 1995.

88. Dunaif A: Insulin resistance and the polycystic ovary syndrome: Mechanisms and implications for pathogenesis. Endocr Rev 18:774–800, 1997.

89. Ehrmann DA, Barnes RB, Rosenfield RL: Polycystic ovary syndrome as a form of functional ovarian hyperandrogenism due to dysregulation of androgen secretion. Endocr Rev 16:322–353, 1995.

90. Taylor AE, McCourt B, Martin KA, et al: Determinants of abnormal gonadotropin secretion in clinically defined women with polycystic ovary syndrome. J Clin Endocrinol Metab 82:2248–2254, 1997.

91. Morales AJ, Laughlin GA, Butzow T, et al: Insulin, somatotrophic and luteinizing hormone axes in non-obese and obese women with polycystic ovary syndrome: common and distinct features. J Clin Endocrinol Metab 81:2854–2864, 1996.

92. Chang RJ, Laufer LR, Meldrum DR, Judd HL: Steroid secretion in polycystic ovarian disease after ovarian suppression by a long acting GnRH agonist. J Clin Endocrinol Metab 56:897–903, 1983.

93. Kazer RR, Kessel B, Yen SSC: LH pulse frequency in women with PCOS. J Clin Endocrinol Metab 65:223–226, 1987.

94. Waldstreicher J, Santoro NF, Hall JE, et al: Hyperfunction of the hypothalamic pituitary axis in women with PCOS. J Clin Endocrinol Metab 66:165–172, 1988.

95. Marshall JC, Eagleson CA: Neuroendocrine aspects of polycystic ovary syndrome. Endocrinol Metab Clin North Am 28:295–324, 1999.

96. McCartney CR, Eagleson CA, Marshall, JC: Regulation of gonadotropin secretion: implications for polycystic ovarian syndrome. Semin Reprod Med 20(4):317–325, 2002.

97. Marshall JC, Eagleson CA, McCartney CR: Neuroendocrine dysfunction in polycystic ovarian syndrome. In Chang J, Heindel F, Dunaif A (eds): Polycystic Ovary Syndrome. New York, Marcel Dekker, 2002, pp 89–104.

98. Porcu E, Venturoli S, Magini O, et al: Circadian variations of luteinizing hormones can have two different profiles in adolescent anovulation. J Clin Endocrinol Metab 65:488–494, 1987.

99. Zumoff B, Freeman R, Coupey S, et al: A chronobiologic abnormality in luteinizing hormone secretion in teenage girls with polycystic ovary syndrome. N Engl J Med 309:1206–1209, 1983.

100. Venturoli S, Porcu E, Fabri R, et al: Longitudinal evaluation of different gonadotropin pulsatile patterns in anovulatory cycles of young girls. J Clin Endocrinol Metab 74:836–842, 1992.

101. Apter D, Butzow T, Laughlin GA, et al: Accelerated 24 h pulsatile activity in adolescent girls with ovarian hyperandrogenism: Relevance to the developmental phase of polycystic ovary syndrome. J Clin Endocrinol Metab 79:119–125, 1994.

102. Ankarberg C, Norjavaara E: Diurnal rhythm of testosterone secretion before and through puberty in healthy girls: Correlation with 17 beta estradiol and DHEA-S. J Clin Endocrinol Metab 84:975–984, 1999.

103. Mitamura R, Yana K, Suzuki N, et al: Diurnal rhythms of LH, FSH, testosterone and estradiol secretion before the onset of female puberty in short children. J Clin Endocrinol Metab 85:1074–1080, 2000.

104. Robinson JE, Forsdike RA, Taylor JA: In utero exposure of female lambs to testosterone reduces the sensitivity of the GnRH neuronal network to inhibition by progesterone. Endocrinology 140:5797–5805, 1999.

105. Dumesic DA, Abbott DH, Eisner JC, Goy RW: Prenatal exposure of female rhesus monkeys to testosterone proprionate increases serum luteinizing hormone in adulthood. Fertil Steril 67:155–163, 1997.

106. Christman GM, Randolph J, Kelch RP, Marshall JC: Reduction of GnRH pulse frequency is associated with subsequent selective FSH secretion in women with polycystic ovarian disease. J Clin Endocrinol Metab 72:1278–1285, 1991.

107. Daniels TL, Berga SL: Resistance of GnRH drive to sex steroid induced suppression in hyperandrogenemic anovulation. J Clin Endocrinol Metab 82:4179–4183, 1997.

108. Pastor CL, Griffin-Korf ML, Aloi JA, et al: Polycystic ovary syndrome: Evidence for reduced sensitivity of the GnRH pulse generator to inhibin by estradiol and progesterone. J Clin Endocrinol Metab 83:582–590, 1998.

109. Eagleson CA, Gingrich MB, Pastor CL, et al: Polycystic ovarian syndrome: Evidence that flutamide restores sensitivity of the GnRH pulse generator to inhibition by estradiol and progesterone. J Clin Endocrinol Metab 85:4047–4052, 2000.

110. Chhabra S, Bellows AB, Prendergast KA, et al: The hypothalamic GnRH pulse generator in normal and hyperandrogenemic girls: Evidence for reduced sensitivity to progesterone inhibition in hyperandrogenemic adolescents. Proceedings 85th Meeting of the Endocrine Society, Abs P2-203, pp 355, New Orleans, LA, June 2003.

# Amenorrhea, Anovulation, and Dysfunctional Uterine Bleeding

*Peter Illingworth*

## INTRODUCTION

Interruption of the normal pattern of menstruation resulting in amenorrhea or irregular menses is the most common manifestation of disordered function of the hypothalamic-pituitary-ovarian axis in women. The current pattern of regular menstrual cyclicity, however, appears to be a product of the evolution to a Westernized society from primitive hunter-gatherer arrangements.[1] As human social development has proceeded, changes including earlier menarche and, particularly, loss of the extended lactational amenorrhea have resulted in a significant increase in the number of menstrual cycles in an average lifetime.[2]

Nowadays, disorders of menstruation are a common cause of morbidity.[3] They are the second most common gynecologic condition leading to hospital referral and affect up to one third of women of child-bearing age. As a result, menstrual disorders have a high economic impact in developed countries and the resulting iron-deficiency anemia can be a common cause for ill health in developing countries.

One notable scientific difficulty in studying disorders of menstruation has been that, in contrast to most other processes in endocrinology, periodic menstruation is restricted to women and Old World primates and is completely distinct from the phenomenon of estrus seen in lower orders. Thus, whereas ovarian function and its control have many common processes across different mammalian species, study of the human uterus and its disorders has been heavily dependent on research that can be carried out in women and other primates such as rhesus monkeys.

## THE NORMAL MENSTRUAL CYCLE

The normal menstrual cycle is one in which regular menstrual bleeding occurs at intervals of 25 to 35 days. Variations in menstrual cycle length are more common at the start and the end of the reproductive years (Fig. 154-1). After menarche, the early adolescent cycles may be quite variable, but tend to regulate over the first 2 to 3 years and, by the third year after menarche, 60% to 80% of cycles should be of normal length.[4] In the first year after menarche, most cycles range from 21 to 45 days but, despite the variable cycle length, many cycles are still ovulatory. From a clinical perspective, it is quite reasonable to reassure a young girl, and her parents, that these variations in menstrual function are not a sign of serious disease and that, in the absence of other clinical features, full endocrine evaluation is not necessary until the age of 16. Anovulation is also common at the other end of the reproductive spectrum and considerable variations in menstrual pattern can be observed.[5] The decline in estradiol secretion that characterizes menopause, in fact, occurs at a relatively late stage of the endocrine transition. Before this, anovulatory cycles may occur with often very high estradiol concentrations. In any case, if a woman experiences menstrual disruption after the age of 45 years with associated symptoms of hypoestrogenism, it is likely that she has entered her menopausal transition and detailed endocrine evaluation is unnecessary.

## PHYSIOLOGY OF THE MENSTRUAL CYCLE

Clinical problems of menstruation occur as a result of abnormalities in the physiologic function of either the hypothalamic-pituitary-ovarian axis or the uterus. Full details of the functions of these endocrine systems are contained elsewhere in this textbook. For an understanding of the pathophysiology discussed here, however, a brief summary of the normal menstrual cycle follows, highlighting the areas in which clinical disorders can arise.

The ovary is formed in utero when the primordial germ cells migrate from the yolk sac to the gonadal ridge before proliferating and differentiating into approximately 6 million primordial oogonia by 16 to 20 weeks' gestation,[6] followed by progression of meiosis as far as arrest at the diplotene stage. From this point onward, there is a rapid loss of oocytes through a process of follicle recruitment and, by the time of birth, the number has dropped to approximately 2 million. After recruitment, the majority of follicles become atretic and only a minority go on to further development.[7] The control of follicle recruitment is unclear.[7] A number of genes, including antimüllerian hormone, c-kit, and kit ligand, have been implicated and the step of initial follicle recruitment appears to be largely hormone independent. By contrast, follicle-stimulating hormone (FSH) is an essential requirement for the later stages of antrum formation.[8]

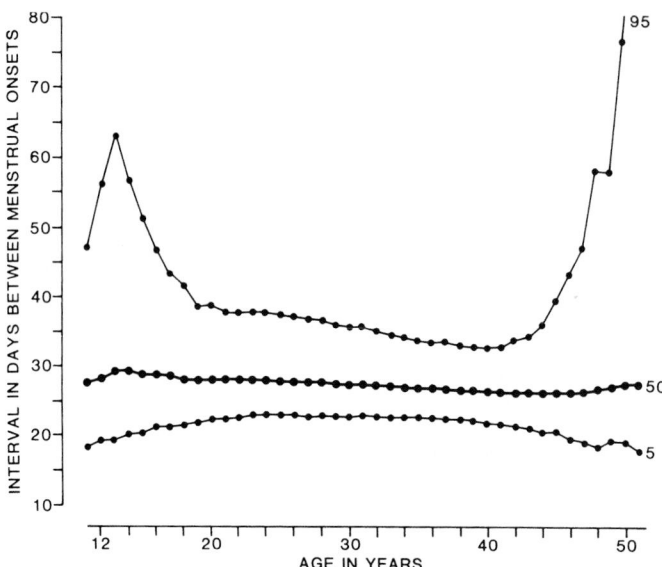

**Figure 154-1**   Menstrual cycle length in relation to age. The median and 5th and 95th percentiles are indicated. Note the marked variation in length of the menstrual cycle at the extremes of reproductive life. (Redrawn from Treloar AE, Boynton RE, Behn BG, Brown BW: Variation of the human menstrual cycle through reproductive life. Int J Fertil 12:77–126, 1967.)

Abnormalities in early follicle development result in the clinical picture of primary ovarian failure. This may occur as a result of abnormal germ cell development (as seen in 46,XY gonadal dysgenesis), accelerated oocyte loss (as seen in Turner's syndrome), a failure of follicle recruitment (as seen in autoimmune disorders), or insensitivity to FSH (as seen in "resistant ovary syndrome").

From a clinical perspective, the critical point of the ovarian cycle is the process of follicle selection, whereby a rise in FSH stimulates a single antral follicle (in a normal unstimulated menstrual cycle) to be selected as the dominant follicle and acquire a number of distinctive features.[9] The granulosa cells proliferate rapidly with increased synthesis of aromatase and inhibin α subunit. There is downregulation of granulosa cell androgen receptors, thus removing the atretic effect of thecal cell androgens on the follicle.[10] Finally, luteinizing hormone (LH) receptors are expressed in granulosa cells, giving these cells the capacity to respond to both LH and FSH by a common cyclic adenosine monophosphate (cAMP)-dependent pathway. Abnormalities in follicle selection account for most cases of chronic anovulation, including the more extreme form, polycystic ovary syndrome (PCOS). Follicle selection is also the step suppressed by hormonal inhibitors of ovulation such as the oral contraceptive pill and is the point at which different doses of gonadotropins can be administered to achieve either monofollicular development for ovulation induction or multifollicular development for in vitro fertilization treatment.

After growth of the dominant follicle, the rising concentrations of estradiol and progesterone evoke a surge of LH from the pituitary gland. LH acts on the ovary to stimulate a group of processes comprising ovulation, including rupture of the follicle, nuclear and cytoplasmic maturation of the oocyte, cumulus expansion, and luteinization of the follicle.[11] The corpus luteum that forms at the time of ovulation functions for 14 days before luteolysis sets in by a mechanism that remains unclear in women.[12] In women, unlike in some other species, the corpus luteum secretes both estradiol and inhibin A, resulting in a suppression of FSH until the time of the luteal-follicular shift at luteolysis.[12] Although the LH surge can readily be manipulated for the purposes of either

contraception or fertility treatment, pathologic disorders of this step are not commonly seen. The actions of LH on the ovary may be affected, however, by medical treatments such as nonsteroidal anti-inflammatory drugs.

During the first half of the menstrual cycle, the endometrium proliferates under the influence of estrogen. Thereafter, under the influence of progesterone, the stroma and epithelium undergo a precisely timed transition to a highly differentiated glandular structure with the capacity to support implantation through glycogen secretion.[13] When pregnancy occurs, progesterone continues to maintain synthesis of the prostaglandin-metabolizing enzyme prostaglandin dehydrogenase and to suppress inflammatory actions in the endometrium.[14] In contrast, during the nonpregnant menstrual cycle, the declining progesterone secretion results in a fall in prostaglandin dehydrogenase synthesis and an activation of the cytokine network, leading to an increase in local prostaglandin concentrations and an influx of leucocytes to the endometrium. This initiates the irreversible stage of menstruation, with an increase in tissue edema, local vasospasm, and hypoxia in a process that involves tissue metalloproteinase activation and finally results in sloughing of the tissues and menstruation.

Clinical abnormalities of endometrial function are common and include a failure of the endometrium to proliferate due to the actions of androgenic forms of the oral contraceptive, excessive bleeding during menstruation due to excessive prostaglandin concentrations and breakthrough bleeding, due to abnormalities of angiogenesis.

## AMENORRHEA

### HISTORY AND EXAMINATION

*Amenorrhea* is defined as either the absence of periods for more than 6 months (secondary amenorrhea) or the absence of periods at age 16 (primary amenorrhea), while *oligomenorrhea* is bleeding that occurs at intervals between 35 days and 6 months.

History should include coverage of the following points:

- Full menstrual history including details of the events and timing of puberty.
- Full past medical history including details of any past significant disease, details of all drug ingestion (particularly steroidal contraception and major tranquilizers), and comprehensive details of any past surgical procedures. Psychological stress resulting from such factors as bereavement and separation may coincide with cessation of menstruation. Various psychotropic drugs may interfere with normal hypothalamic function either by depleting the amounts of catecholamines (e.g., reserpine) or by blocking dopamine receptors (e.g., phenothiazines).
- As much information as available about recent weight changes, dietary history, and exercise patterns.
- Specific enquiry about the symptoms of headache, galactorrhea, hirsutism, and hot flashes.

One of the most important parts of assessment of the amenorrheic woman, particularly the young amenorrheic woman, is to have a sensitive and empathetic discussion with the young woman. It may often be appropriate to include her mother in this discussion. This discussion should include consideration of the future consequences of the diagnoses under consideration. What outcome does she anticipate from her investigation? Is she frightened of "abnormality" by comparison with her peers? Is she looking to achieve a pregnancy at this stage or simply to reach a diagnosis? In any case, the patient will need the sympathetic support of her physician throughout the process of diagnosis to explain fully and accurately the nature of the problem and the possible outcomes. In some instances, particularly with emotionally traumatic diagnoses such as the intersex variations, formal supportive counseling will also be required.

The extent of the examination to be performed should reflect the circumstances of the patient. Measurement of height and weight and calculation of body mass index are an essential part of the assessment. The general examination should include breast examination with careful check of the nipples for galactorrhea as well as abdominal examination. The external genitalia should be examined carefully to check for genital development and the clitoris assessed for possible clitoromegaly. This examination enables the pubertal stage to be identified and also allows early identification of major degrees of hirsutism and pelvic masses secondary to hematocolpos from low outflow obstruction (see later discussion). Internal pelvic examination can often be traumatic, particularly for a young adolescent, and its role is less clear in this era of high-resolution pelvic imaging. If in doubt, this aspect of the examination can be safely deferred until after the initial investigation has identified the general nature of the problem.

### INITIAL INVESTIGATION OF AMENORRHEA AND IDENTIFICATION OF THE GENERAL CAUSE

The investigations shown in Figure 154-2 should normally be performed during the initial assessment of amenorrhea.

The gonadotropin concentrations, particularly FSH, are pivotal to allocation of the case to the diagnostic categories shown in Figure 154-2, and human chorionic gonadotropin (hCG) is important to exclude pregnancy. The measurement of estradiol and testosterone are similarly important as, despite the undoubted value of the progestogen challenge test (see discussion to follow), it is still useful to measure the circulating concentrations of these two steroids. The measurement of thyroid-stimulating hormone (TSH), prolactin, and

dehydroepiandrosterone sulfate (DHEA-S) are important in making an early identification of thyroid, pituitary, and adrenal disease, respectively. Although a range of complex dynamic tests of function of the hypothalamic-pituitary-ovarian axis were previously used, their use is now largely restricted to research with little application in everyday clinical practice.[15]

Measurement of the estradiol concentration is helpful in distinguishing conditions characterized by low to absent estrogen production from those characterized by ongoing estrogen production such as chronic anovulation and uterine outflow abnormalities. The estradiol concentration can fluctuate significantly, however, and overlap between these conditions is not uncommon. It is for this reason that the progestogen challenge test is a particularly valuable investigation. This is normally performed by administering either intramuscular progesterone (100 mg) or a pure progestogenic preparation such as medroxyprogesterone acetate (10 mg daily for 10 days). Within a few days of cessation of the progestogen, there will either be a significant vaginal bleed (a positive progestogen challenge test) or an absent or very scanty bleed (a negative progestogen challenge test). This test allows conditions with either low estrogen production or a genital tract disorder to be distinguished from other conditions, such as chronic anovulation or polycystic ovary syndrome, in which there is both estrogen production and a normal genital tract.

Ultrasound examination of the pelvis is another important part of the initial investigation. This can be performed as an abdominal ultrasound where the woman is young or has never had sexual intercourse. A transvaginal ultrasound provides more information and is preferable when the woman is older and has previously had sexual intercourse. Ultrasound examination of the pelvis will establish the presence and general structure of the uterus and enables assessment of the ovaries for a polycystic appearance (discussion to follow). The thickness or lack of thickness of the endometrium is a useful

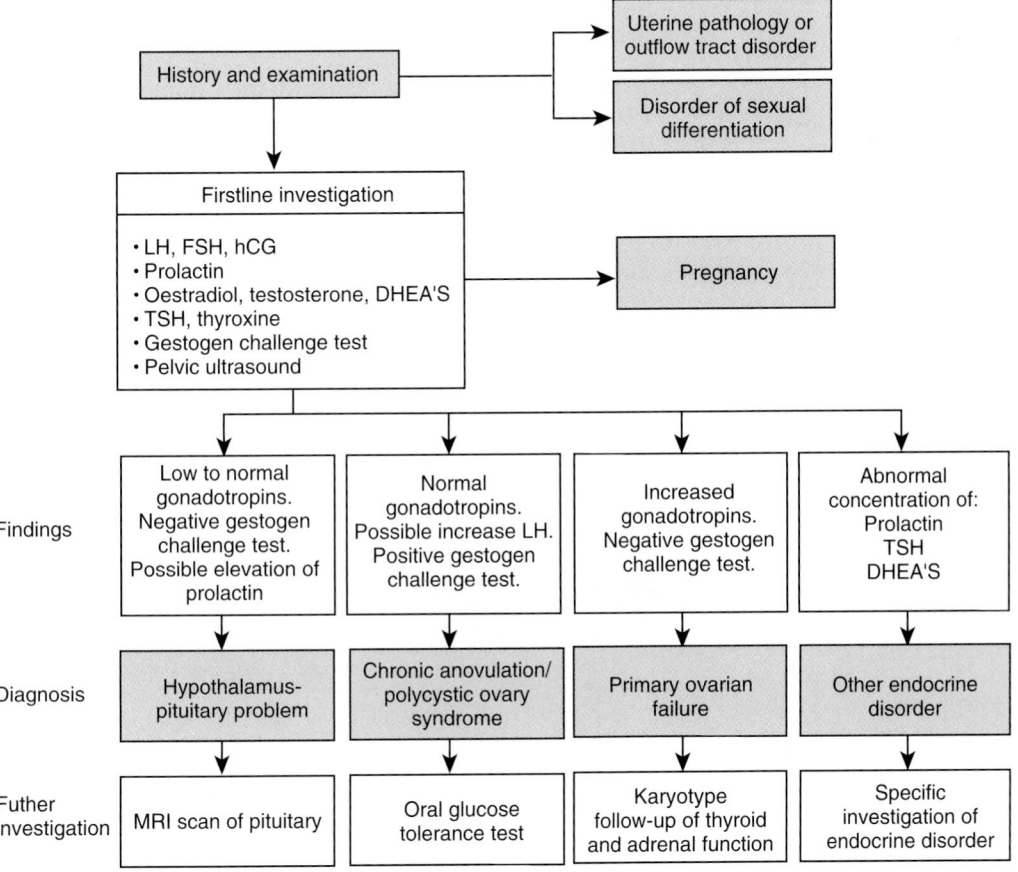

Figure 154-2 Algorithm for investigation of women with amenorrhea. DHEA-S, dehydroepiandrosterone sulfate; FSH, follicle-stimulating hormone; hCG, human chorionic gonadotropin; LH, luteinizing hormone; MRI, magnetic resonance imaging; TSH, thyroid-stimulating hormone.

guide to the degree of estrogenization that is present. When the initial assessment suggests a genital outflow disorder, magnetic resonance imaging (MRI) is likely to be a more appropriate method of establishing the final diagnosis.[4]

On the basis of history, examination, and initial investigation, it is usually possible to identify the general cause of the amenorrhea, as shown in Figure 154-2. The initial classification also gives a high level of prediction of future fertility as, in most forms of amenorrhea, pregnancy is a likely outcome of treatment (Fig. 154-3). By contrast, in hypergonadotropic amenorrhea, the prospects for pregnancy are very limited. In the past, great emphasis was placed on the distinction between primary and secondary amenorrhea. Although some conditions may be specifically associated with either primary or secondary amenorrhea, it is nowadays recognized that there is a significant overlap and that the distinction between primary and secondary amenorrhea is not particularly helpful in reaching the final diagnosis. Thus, the remainder of this chapter is presented according to the primary pathology involved.

## PHYSIOLOGIC CAUSE

Pregnancy and lactation are two common physiologic causes of amenorrhea. The early signs of pregnancy are easy to overlook, and all women in the reproductive age group who have missed a period should be assumed to be pregnant until proven otherwise. Ovulation and pregnancy can occur without resumption of menstruation after lactation or after recovery from hypothalamic suppression associated with weight loss. Measurement of hCG in blood or urine can exclude pregnancy.

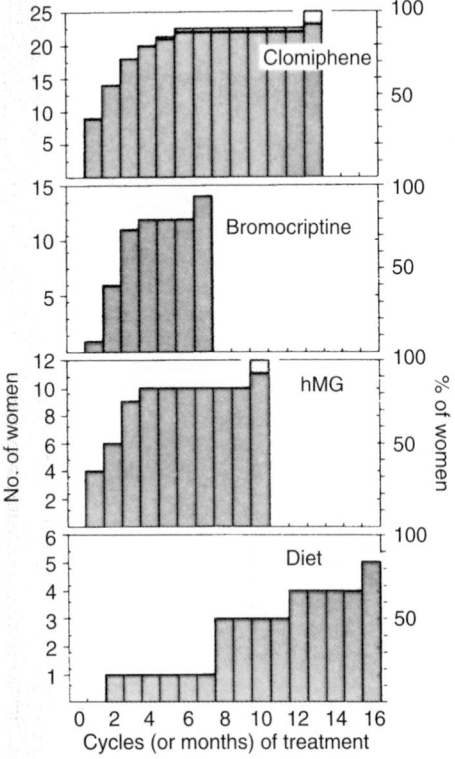

*Figure 154-3* Time to conception: Conceptions after treatment of amenorrheic women with clomiphene, human menopausal gonadotropin (hMG), bromocriptine, or diet. Selection of therapy was based on the cause of the amenorrhea. (From Hull MGR, Savage PE, Jacobs HS: Investigation and treatment of amenorrhea resulting in normal fertility. Br Med J 1:1257–1261, 1979.)

## DISORDERS OF THE HYPOTHALAMUS-PITUITARY

Failure of the hypothalamus and/or anterior pituitary is a much more common cause of amenorrhea than ovarian failure. A disturbance in ovarian function also occurs if the feedback loops are interrupted by steroids or gonadotropins extrinsic to the hypothalamic-pituitary-ovarian (HPO) axis. In the absence of clearly localized destruction, injury, or disease (e.g., pituitary infarction, as in Sheehan's syndrome), it is often difficult to distinguish between disorders of the hypothalamus and the anterior pituitary. It is, therefore, convenient to regard the hypothalamus and pituitary as a single unit and to classify the conditions accordingly. Disorders of the hypothalamus-pituitary that result in amenorrhea are shown in Table 154-1.

The characteristic feature of amenorrhea resulting from hypothalamic-pituitary disorder is a reduction in the pulsatile secretion of LH.[16,17] Although basal levels of LH and FSH may be within the range of the normal follicular phase of the cycle, careful analysis of the pattern of pulsatile secretion of gonadotropins demonstrates a reduction in the frequency of pulses of LH and FSH (Fig. 154-4). Hypothalamic-pituitary disorders are also characterized by loss of the normal responses to physiologic stimuli such as estrogen provocation (Fig. 154-5). These effects occur in most disorders of the hypothalamus-pituitary, including disorders of prolactin secretion, and result in a continuum ranging from a hypogonadotropic state resembling infancy to minor abnormalities of cycle control, as represented by the formation of an inadequate corpus luteum. Although the degree of inactivity of the hypothalamic-pituitary unit can be tested directly by measuring the pattern of gonadotropin secretion, in practice, it is much more convenient to assess estrogenic status. In the absence of adequate gonadotropic stimulation, the ovaries secrete minimal quantities of estradiol, levels of which are very low (<50 pg/mL).

### Hyperprolactinemia Including Prolactin-Secreting Tumors

Hyperprolactinemia normally presents with reasonably short onset secondary amenorrhea and prolactin measurements above the normal range (>20 ng/mL, Friesen Standard; 360 mU/L, International Standard) are common. Mild elevations are of little clinical significance and, due to the sensitivity of prolactin to even trivial stress effects such as venepuncture, it is important to ensure that any elevations observed are consistent. A mild elevation in prolactin concentration may also be seen in amenorrhea due to polycystic ovary syndrome, presumably due to the unopposed estrogens stimulating growth of the lactotrophs. The other clinical features, particularly hypoestrogenism, should enable the clinician to distinguish amenorrhea due to primary hyperprolactinemia from polycystic ovary syndrome.

Prolactin has a physiologic role in lactogenesis, and thus, galactorrhea is an unsurprising symptom of pathologic hyperprolactinemia. The association of amenorrhea and galactorrhea has previously been described under a number of

| *Table 154-1* | Causes of Amenorrhea Due to Disorders of the Hypothalamus-Pituitary |
|---|---|

Hyperprolactinemia
  Prolactin-secreting tumor
  Centrally acting medications, including dopamine antagonists
Pituitary Disease
  Non–prolactin secreting pituitary tumor
  Generalized pituitary insufficiency including previous pituitary surgery
Hypothalamic amenorrhea
  Nutrition/exercise disorders
  Idiopathic hypogonadotropic hypogonadism

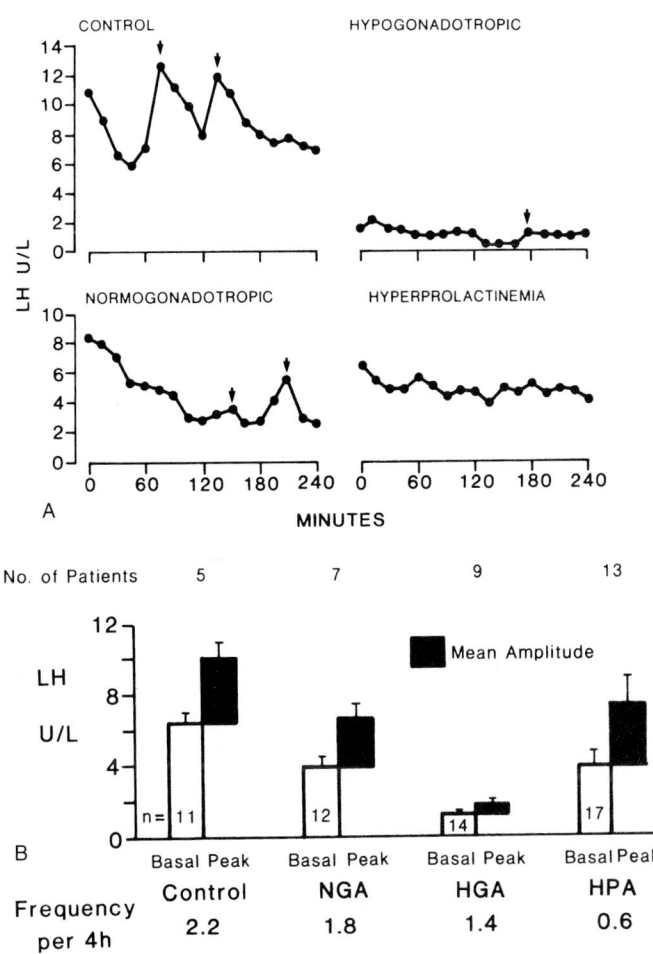

**Figure 154-4** Luteinizing hormone (LH) secretion in relation to diagnosis. **A,** Patterns of concentration of LH in the serum of patients with secondary amenorrhea. Note the absence of pulsatile release of LH in hyperprolactinemic patients, although the basal level is within the normal range. **B,** Mean basal level and pulse amplitude and frequency in women with amorrhea. HGA, hypogonadotropic; HPA, hyperprolactinemic; NGA, normogonadotropic. (Courtesy of C.W. Vaughan Williams and D.T. Baird.)

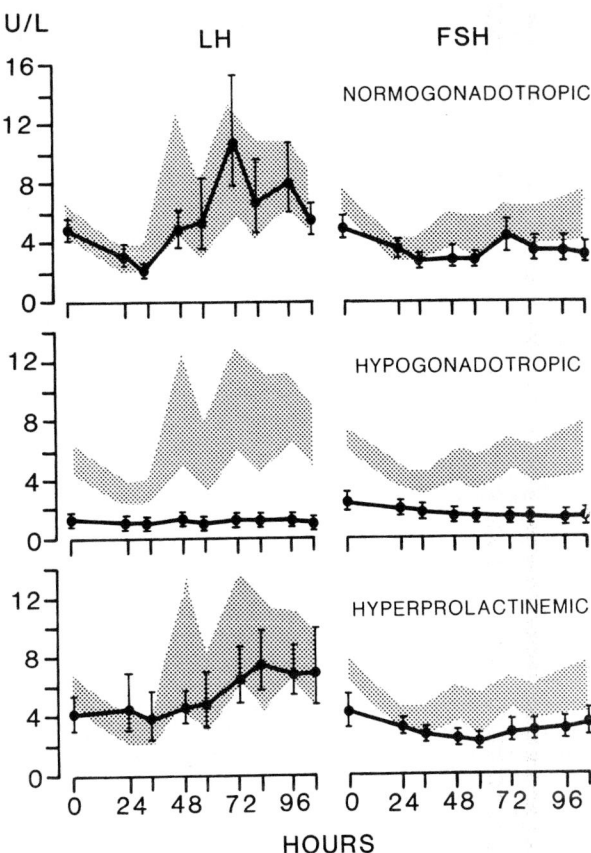

**Figure 154-5** Loss of luteinizing hormone (LH) response. Estrogen provocation test in women with secondary amenorrhea. The range of normal control women in the early follicular phase of the cycle is indicated by the shaded area. Note the absence of a secondary rise in LH concentration in the hypogonadotropic women. FSH, follicle-stimulating hormone. (From Vaughan Williams CW, McNeilly AS, Baird DT: The effects of chronic treatment with LHRH on gonadotrophin secretion and pituitary responsiveness to LHRH in women with secondary hypogonadism. Clin Endocrinol 19:9–19, 1983.)

eponyms,[18] such as Chiari-Frommel syndrome (postpartum), Argonz–Del Castillo syndrome (without a relationship to pregnancy), and Forbes-Albright syndrome (galactorrhea with a pituitary tumor). The relationship with galactorrhea is complex, however. Only about half of amenorrheic women with hyperprolactinemia have demonstrable galactorrhea. Conversely, only about half the women with galactorrhea have raised levels of prolactin, and when galactorrhea is present in the absence of amenorrhea, the prolactin concentration is usually normal.[19] Galactorrhea may also be present in hypothyroid women who have normal levels of prolactin, and it is thus likely that other factors, such as thyroxine, may affect the sensitivity of the breast to prolactin.

The amenorrhea of hyperprolactinemia is likely to result from a direct central effect of prolactin, as characteristic disturbances of LH pulsatility can be demonstrated in women with hyperprolactinemia[20] (Fig. 154-6) and selective enucleation of a prolactin-secreting tumor results in restoration of normal secretion of gonadotropins and cyclic ovarian activity. It has been reported that naloxone administration increases the frequency of LH pulses, thus suggesting the involvement of endogenous opioids in the amenorrhea of hyperprolactinemia.[21] This finding is not consistent, however, even in women without a prolactin-secreting adenoma. A direct effect on the gonad is also possible and has been suggested on the

basis of the evident actions of prolactin in a range of transgenic and knockout mice.[22] Prolactin actions vary between species, however, and normal ovulation can be induced in untreated hyperprolactinemic women after treatment with pulsatile gonadotropin-releasing hormone (GnRH) alone.[23] Although this does not preclude a direct gonadal effect of prolactin, the significance is likely to be limited.

A number of conditions including hypothyroidism, stress, and use of major tranquilizers can result in hyperprolactinemia. The first step in investigation is to exclude a prolactin-secreting tumor of the pituitary. MRI of the sella turcica is now the investigation of choice and tumors can be identified in about 50% of women with hyperprolactinemia (see Chapter 27). Most of these tumors are microadenomas (<10 mm diameter) and do not need specific treatment other than for symptomatic relief or treatment of infertility. In the remainder, it is assumed there is either a tumor too small to be identified or a defect in the hypothalamic production of dopamine leading to hypertrophy of the lactotrophs. The latter occurs physiologically during pregnancy and is important in maintaining the increased secretion of prolactin during lactation. In hypothyroidism, excessive secretion of thyrotropin-releasing hormone has been suggested as being responsible for the increased secretion of prolactin from lactotrophs, but this theory has not been proved.

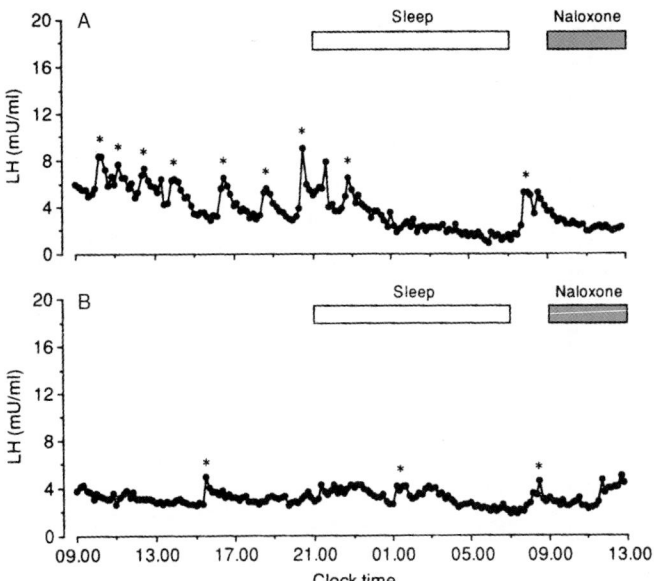

*Figure 154-6* Twenty-four-hour secretory pattern of luteinizing hormone (LH) in two women with amenorrhea caused by hyperprolactinemia and during 4-hour infusions with naloxone (1.6 mg/hr). Statistically significant LH pulses are indicated by an *asterisk*. Note the reduced number of LH pulses in both women. (From Tay CCK, Glasier AF, Illingworth PJ, Baird DT: Abnormal 24 pattern of pulsatile luteinising hormone secretion and response to naloxone in women with hyperprolactinaemic amenorrhea. Clin Endocrinol 39:599–606, 1993.)

The clinical features and detailed investigation of patients with pituitary tumors are dealt with elsewhere in this textbook. The degree of hypogonadism in hyperprolactinemic women can vary from gross evidence of estrogenic deficiency to a minor disturbance in the regulation of ovarian function. Many women with amenorrhea associated with hyperprolactinemia complain of dyspareunia associated with vaginal dryness and estrogen deficiency. Although single measurements of the basal concentration of gonadotropins can be within the normal range, the concentration of estradiol may be less than 50 pg/mL, and no bleeding is induced in response to progestogen challenge. Others may have spontaneous episodes of vaginal bleeding that reflect estrogen concentrations in the range of 50 to 200 pg/mL in association with follicular activity. In these women, LH pulses are present, although at a reduced frequency.[20]

Management of a hyperprolactinemic woman with amenorrhea depends on whether she wants to become pregnant, the presence and size of a pituitary tumor, and the presence of associated symptoms such as galactorrhea. If the tumor diameter exceeds 1 cm, it should normally be treated before the patient becomes pregnant.[24] If untreated, these women have a small but definite risk of further enlargement of the tumor during pregnancy, with subsequent pressure on the optic chiasma. Many of these tumors may be safely enucleated by the transsphenoidal route with minimal morbidity and preservation of function of the anterior pituitary.[25] The operation is not totally without risk, however, and is curative in only about 60% to 80% of patients.

Even in the presence of significant tumors, medical treatment with a dopamine agonist is the first line of treatment.[25] Cabergoline is now the treatment of first choice, with a higher remission rate and a significantly lower level of side effects than bromocriptine.[22] Dopamine agonists interact with the dopamine receptors of the lactotrophs and inhibit the secretion of prolactin. Using a twice-weekly dosage with a total weekly dosage of up to 3 mg, cabergoline reduces the concentration of prolactin[26] and produces a coincidental rise

in the frequency of LH pulses. Although menses usually return within 3 months, the first few cycles may be anovulatory or have a short and/or inadequate luteal phase. Normal ovarian cyclicity is restored within 6 months, in most cases, and the fertility rates are satisfactory.

It is usually recommended that a dopamine agonist should be stopped as soon as pregnancy is diagnosed, although there is no conclusive evidence of teratogenicity. Some authorities recommend use of bromocriptine for women trying to conceive, on the basis that cabergoline is a newer preparation, but it is not clear that bromocriptine is less likely to be teratogenic than cabergoline. In the rare instance of tumor enlargement in pregnancy, a dopamine agonist can safely be restarted during pregnancy and usually results in prompt shrinkage of the tumor. There is increasing evidence that permanent remission can sometimes be achieved with cabergoline[22] and, in the absence of a significant tumor, it is reasonable to have a trial cessation of therapy after 1 to 2 years.

It is not necessary to use a dopamine agonist to treat hyperprolactinemic women with no symptoms, no tumor, and no desire to conceive. Moreover, not all hyperprolactinemic women are deficient in estrogen, and restoration of cyclic ovarian function may provoke menstrual symptoms that require treatment. If a dopamine agonist is not given, however, some form of therapy is required to treat the osteoporosis in estrogen-deficient women. If a dopamine agonist is given to those who are sexually active, it is necessary to provide some form of contraception (avoiding the combined pill) to prevent unwanted pregnancy. The long-term consequences of repeated ovarian cycles (breast and endometrial cancer) may well outweigh the risks of osteoporosis. The relative health risks and benefits of treatment versus no treatment must be carefully weighed in each case. Whatever the choice, the woman should be informed of the possible long-term risks and monitored at intervals of 6 to 12 months.

### Pituitary Disease
Rare pituitary tumors may cause amenorrhea without significant prolactin secretion through compression of the portal tract. An MRI scan is thus important in all otherwise-undiagnosed women with amenorrhea of hypothalamic-pituitary origin. Hypogonadotropic amenorrhea is also likely in all cases of clinical hypopituitarism, whether the latter is due to previous surgery, Sheehan's syndrome, or other pituitary disease. Measurement of other pituitary hormones will clarify this.

### Hypothalamic Amenorrhea
Women with hypothalamic amenorrhea are characterized by progestogen-negative amenorrhea in the presence of either low or normal gonadotropins and the absence of any demonstrable pathology such as hyperprolactinemia, tumors, or pituitary disease.

Eugonadotropic hypothalamic amenorrhea is commonly related to metabolic disorders subsequent to stress, weight loss, and extremes of exercise. In particular, hypothalamic amenorrhea is an important feature of serious psychological diseases such as anorexia nervosa and bulimia. It is thus very important to ensure that the underlying psychological disease is adequately treated before managing the amenorrhea and that body weight has returned to normal before starting any endocrine therapy. Ovulation induction in women significantly below ideal body weight may result in a pregnancy complicated by intrauterine growth retardation, with significant health consequences for the child.

As discussed, amenorrhea in the presence of apparently normal gonadotropin concentrations results from changes in the normal pattern of GnRH pulsatility. There are a number of metabolic changes and endocrine changes in women who are either underweight or strenuously exercising that can contribute to this. The principle of a critical body weight above which menstruation returns is generally accepted and appears to be approximately 15% below ideal body weight.[27] There is considerable interindividual variation on this model, however, for reasons that have not been apparent until recently. A greater understanding has emerged since the identification of leptin, a small protein hormone secreted by adipocytes that plays a critical role in regulation of appetite and metabolism.[28,29] It is now clear that a reduced body weight is associated with reduced secretion of leptin and that a consequently reduced leptin stimulus to the GnRH pulse generator may play a role in the amenorrhea associated with significant weight loss.[30] Exercise is also associated with metabolic changes, in particular, increases in corticotropin-releasing hormone (CRH) and β-endorphin concentrations in the hypothalamus that may inhibit GnRH pulsatility.[31] In some trials, a restoration of normal LH pulsatility and ovulation has been observed in response to treatment with opioid inhibitors such as naltrexone,[32] although the effects of opioid inhibitors have not been consistent.

## Idiopathic Hypogonadotropic Hypogonadism

Idiopathic hypogonadotropic hypogonadism (IHH) has been defined as GnRH deficiency in the absence of a hypothalamic or pituitary lesion.[33] GnRH deficiency (with a correspondingly low gonadotropin concentration) accounts for only a small proportion of women whose amenorrhea is due to hypothalamic-pituitary dysfunction. Patients with anosmia were previously considered to form the separate group defined as Kallmann's syndrome,[34] a condition that occurs five to seven times more commonly in men than in women, in whom it is seen only rarely. However, it is now clear that there is considerable overlap between Kallmann's syndrome and IHH, and both entities have been described in the same family.[33] GnRH deficiency has also been associated with a number of other genetic defects in addition to mutations in the classic KAL gene of Kallmann's syndrome, the adhesion molecule anosmin-1.[35] Other genes involved in IHH include the DAX-1 gene and the GnRH receptor gene, although no defects have been identified in the GnRH gene itself.[33] The

classic X-linked inheritance of Kallmann's syndrome appears to represent only a small number of cases, and autosomal-dominant or autosomal-recessive modes of inheritance are also possible.[36] Even among the carefully defined group of women with IHH, however, the incidence of identifiable genetic abnormalities is low and routine search for them in clinical practice is not appropriate.[36]

## Treatment

If there is no apparent primary pathology or if the primary pathology has been appropriately treated without restoring normal endocrinology, then the treatment options lie between estrogen replacement (or the oral contraceptive in a younger woman) to prevent osteoporosis and ovulation induction to restore fertility.

Ovulation induction is described in detail in Chapter 158. There are, however, some differences in the approach for ovulation induction in women with hypothalamic disorders. Estrogen antagonists are usually ineffective in inducing ovulation in progestogen-negative women and treatment with either pulsatile GnRH or gonadotropin treatment is normally required. Treatment with pulsatile GnRH involves the woman carrying a small portable pump, but has the important advantage of a lower multiple pregnancy rate than with gonadotropin treatment (Fig. 154-7). Women with a low LH concentration (<4 IU/L) require treatment with combined gonadotropin regimens that include both FSH and LH bioactivity. The older urinary gonadotropin preparations have sufficient LH bioactivity, but when a recombinant FSH is used, it needs to be supplemented with either recombinant LH or a low dosage of urinary hCG.

## PRIMARY OVARIAN FAILURE

Primary ovarian failure is the absence of any detectable ovarian activity despite stimulation by gonadotropins. Possible causes for primary ovarian failure are shown in Table 154-2. Unlike the testis, an ovary without gametes (oocytes) cannot function as an endocrine gland and, in the absence of

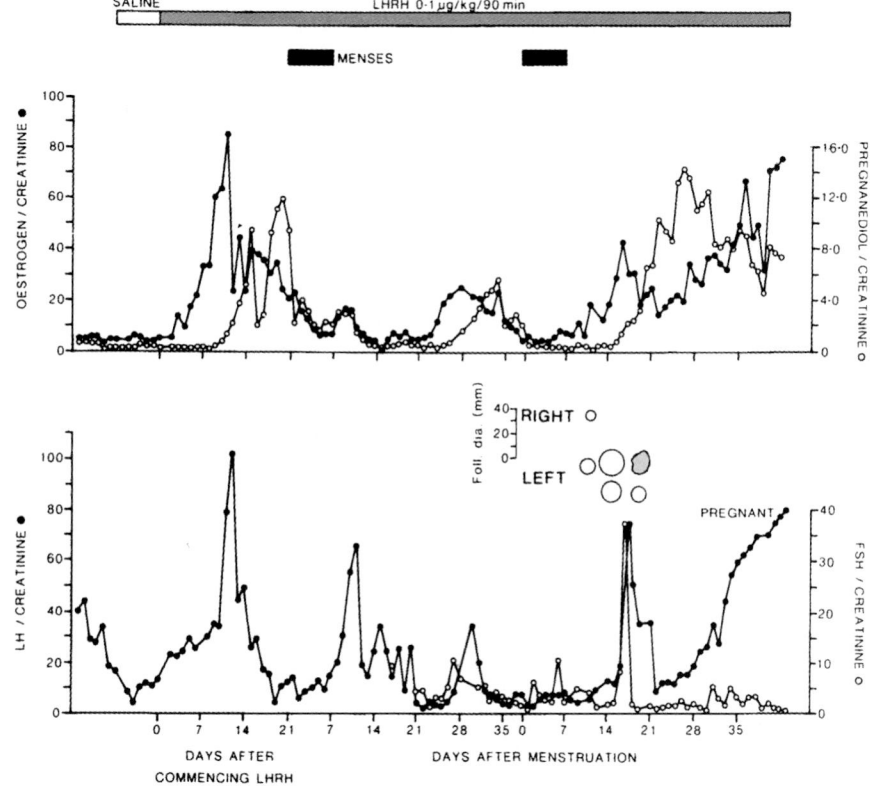

*Figure 154-7* Induction of ovulation with pulsatile gonadotropin-releasing hormone (GnRH) therapy in women with hypogonadotropic hypogonadism. GnRH was administered subcutaneously by way of a portable pump as a 40-mL bolus at a dosage of 0.1 mg/kg every 90 minutes. Note the occurrence of a luteinizing hormone (LH) surge without a change in the frequency of LH pulses. Pregnancy occurred during the third cycle. (Courtesy of A.F. Glasier, A.S. McNeilly, and D.T. Baird.)

**Table 154-2** Causes of Primary Ovarian Failure

Iatrogenic
  Surgery
  Chemotherapy
  Radiotherapy
Environmental
  Smoking
  Viral infections
Autoimmune
  Association with other autoimmune disease
Abnormal karyotypes
  46,XY
  45,XO
Genetic disorders with a normal karyotype
  Fragile X premutations
  Galactosemia
  Carbohydrate-deficient glycoprotein syndrome type1 (CDG1)
  Inhibin α gene mutations
  Follicle-stimulating hormone (FSH) receptor gene
    mutations

gametes, will not develop normally and will be present in adulthood merely as a streak. The diagnosis of primary ovarian failure is made on the basis of a negative progestogen challenge test accompanied by elevated gonadotropin concentrations with FSH concentration greater than that of LH. Once this diagnosis is made, the prognosis for future fertility is poor. In women younger than 40, the karyotype should be checked to diagnose Turner's syndrome (45,XO) and 46,XY gonadal dysgenesis. The value of checking the karyotype in women aged 30 to 40 with premature menopause has been discussed.[37] Although no cases of 46,XY gonadal dysgenesis have ever been described in women older than 30, a number of karyotypic abnormalities with a potentially etiologic role have been identified. Beyond this, in the presence of a normal karyotype, current diagnostic methods are able to reach a pathologic diagnosis in only a small proportion of cases.

Nowadays, one of the most common causes for premature menopause is chemotherapy and radiotherapy used in treatment regimens for childhood cancer. Treatment with most forms of chemotherapy, particularly the alkylating agents, will significantly reduce the number of primordial follicles in the ovary by a mechanism involving induction of apoptosis in the follicles.[38] The long-term consequences for reproductive function, however, depend on the dosage, duration, and type of chemotherapy involved, as well as, critically, the age of the patient.[39] Many of the modern chemotherapy regimens for first-line treatment of hematologic malignancy in young women are relatively ovarian sparing and a good long-term prognosis for fertility can be given. In contrast, the more intense regimens required for either bone-marrow transplant or cancer recurrence will almost inevitably induce a premature menopause with amenorrhea.[39]

Environmental factors such as smoking and viral infections may also affect the number of oocytes in the ovary. Although smoking clearly affects the age of menopause, as well as making osteoporosis more likely, the overall effect is unlikely to be greater than a year and is not likely to contribute to a diagnosis of amenorrhea in young women.[40] A history of past infections such as mumps should always be sought, although oophoritis leading to premature ovarian failure is a very rare complication of such an infection.[41]

### Turner's Syndrome
Turner's syndrome was first described in the 1930s and has a characteristic phenotype including short stature, a shield chest and web-shaped neck, short fourth metacarpal, and congenital heart disease.[42] This syndrome is common and is observed in 1 in 2500 neonates,[43] although the incidence in spontaneous abortions is much higher and suggests that less than 1% of affected fetuses will reach viability.[44]

The karyotype is commonly 45,XO, but a number of variations are now recognized. Approximately 50% of cases are either XO/XX mosaics or 46,XX with an abnormal X chromosome. Long-arm deletions are associated with primary amenorrhea, whereas short-arm deletions are associated with the physical features of Turner's syndrome, particularly short stature. One particular variant, the ring chromosome, is associated with an increased incidence of mental retardation and fetal abnormalities.[45] The cytogenetic abnormalities appear to result from abnormalities in epigenetic development.[45] Oogonia are formed in fetal life in the ovaries of women with Turner's syndrome, but do not develop to primordial oocytes[46] and, by the time puberty is expected, the ovary is usually devoid of oocytes. Although the majority of women with Turner's syndrome are completely sterile, a range of phenotypes can occur, from impaired fertility with recurrent miscarriage to permanent amenorrhea. On the rare occasions of spontaneous pregnancy, the rate of fetal abnormality is almost 30%. Pregnancy can often be successfully achieved in amenorrheic women with Turner's syndrome using donated oocytes. Care is required during pregnancy, however, as cases have been reported of serious complications of congenital cardiovascular disease in pregnant women with Turner's syndrome.[47]

### 46,XY Gonadal Dysgenesis
In this condition, Swyer's syndrome, there are streak gonads with an intact uterus and fallopian tubes.[48] Once this condition is diagnosed, the gonads are required to be removed as the presence of any part of the Y chromosome means that there is a very high risk of development of a gonadoblastoma with the subsequent risk of transformation to an immature teratoma.

Approximately 20% of these cases have a deletion of SRY (locus Yp11.3), a gene that codes for a DNA-binding protein.[49] In the presence of this gene, the undifferentiated cells in the gonad differentiate into Sertoli cells; in the gene's absence, they differentiate into granulosa cells.[50] The genetic cause for the remaining 80% of cases is unknown, although it is presumed that downstream genes in testicular development are likely to be involved. One other candidate gene is SOX-9, in which a deletion has been demonstrated to be responsible for the sex reversal seen in XY camptomelic dwarfism.[51]

### Genetic Abnormalities in the Presence of a Normal Karyotype
In addition to karyotypic abnormalities, a number of other genetic abnormalities have been identified in association with premature ovarian failure.

The most common genetic association is with a premutation for fragile X syndrome (FRAXA). This is an X-linked-dominant condition resulting from CGG trinucleotide expansion in the untranslated region of the fragile X mental retardation (FMR1) gene located at Xq27.3.[52] Premutations (i.e., 60–200 triplet repeat insertions) of this gene are found in 2% to 6% of women with premature ovarian failure, whereas carriers of full mutations (>200 triplet repeats) and their sisters appear to have no increase in risk of premature ovarian failure.[53]

A number of rare genetic metabolic syndromes, including galactosemia, carbohydrate-deficient glycoprotein syndrome type 1 (CDG1), blepharophimosis-ptosis-epicanthus inversus syndrome (BPES), and autoimmune polyendocrinopathy-candidiasis-ectodermal dystrophy (APECED) include premature ovarian failure as part of their phenotype.[37] In each of these syndromes, however, the other clinical features are normally apparent and amenorrhea is rarely the presenting feature. Galactosemia is associated with mutations of the galactose 1–phosphate uridyltransferase gene (GALT, chromosome 9,p13).[54] The phenotype is variable, but usually includes hepatomegaly and mental retardation with cataract. Most females experience premature ovarian failure due to the buildup of galactose interfering with migration of the germ cells from the urogenital ridge to the gonad in fetal life.

Rare mutations in some of the critical genes of reproduction have been described in association with amenorrhea. A number of cases of premature ovarian failure due to FSH receptor defects were reported in Finland.[55] Subsequent studies have not found this to be a common mutation.[56] In rare cases of LH receptor defects, women have normal secondary sexual characteristics, but have anovulation.[57] Mutations in the inhibin α gene, which result in premature ovarian failure, have also been described. Abnormalities in estrogen synthesis (aromatase deficiency) result in sexual infantilism. At birth, the babies show a degree of virilization (clitoromegaly) because of an inability of the placenta to aromatize dehydroepiandrosterone and its consequent conversion to more potent androgens.[58] At the time of puberty, they have amenorrhea and failure of breast development in association with hypergonadotropic hypogonadism and cystic ovaries.

Most women with primary ovarian failure, have no identifiable cause or genetic abnormality. The role of genetic investigation beyond a karyotype in routine clinical practice is unclear at present. Although screening for a FRAXA premutation may be of value in the sister donating oocytes to a woman with premature ovarian failure, investigating for these rare genetic defects is not otherwise part of routine clinical practice. It is likely that, in the next few years, increased understanding of the molecular basis of ovarian function and thus of the clinical syndromes of premature ovarian failure will require a revision of the genetic investigation of the woman with premature ovarian failure.

### Autoimmune Ovarian Failure

Ovarian failure can occur in association with autoantibodies to ovarian tissue.[59,60] There is a clear association between premature ovarian failure and other endocrinopathies that have a clear autoendocrine basis such as thyroid disease, type 1 diabetes, and Addison's disease.[59] Approximately 2% of cases of idiopathic premature failure are associated with subsequent development of Addison's disease. Some methodologies for the detection of autoantibodies to ovarian tissue have found antibodies to ovarian tissue in patients with premature ovarian failure (Fig. 154-8) and there are clinical reports of women with elevated FSH concentrations conceiving after steroid treatment.[61] In addition, it has been demonstrated that active immunization of primates with antigens to ovary-specific proteins such as ZP3 leads to premature ovarian failure.[62] An autoendocrine basis for some cases of premature ovarian failure thus seems likely.

The reproducibility of clinical measurement of auto-ovarian antibodies in women with premature ovarian failure is poor,[63] however, probably because the antibodies involved have a heterogeneous range of antigens. A more practical approach for routine clinical practice may be to follow up all women with otherwise-undiagnosed premature ovarian failure with regular measurement of thyroid function, oral glucose tolerance, and adrenal assessment in order to facilitate early detection of an endocrinopathy in other organs.

### Resistant Ovary Syndrome and the Role of Ovarian Biopsy

Resistant ovary syndrome has been described as premature ovarian failure with oocytes present within the ovary and some authorities have advised ovarian biopsy. Laparoscopic ovarian biopsy is accompanied by a risk of morbidity, however, and the contribution to the clinical management is not clear. Amenorrhea with an elevated FSH concentration has a poor prognosis for fertility, regardless of the etiology. In addition, a biopsy may fail to show oocytes even when they are

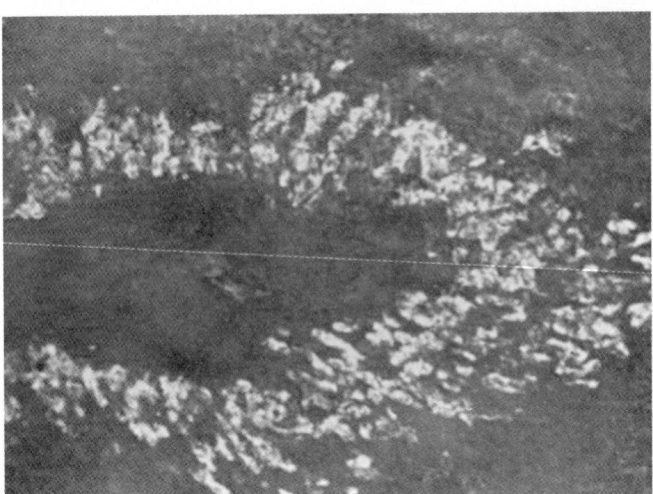

*Figure 154-8*  Immunofluorescent photomicrograph of antibodies to granulosa cells in the serum of patient with premature ovarian failure. Note that the immunofluorescence is localized in the granulosa cells of the follicle (x144). (From Irvine WJ: Autoimmune ovarian failure. In Irvine WJ, Loraine JA [eds]: Reproductive Endocrinology. Edinburgh, Churchill Livingstone, 1970, pp 106–114.)

present elsewhere in the ovary. In view of this, an ovarian biopsy is not normally recommended as part of the routine investigation of a woman with primary ovarian failure.

### Treatment

Young women with primary ovarian failure are at increased risk of osteoporosis and, therefore, long-term estrogen, in some form, is indicated, as is serial monitoring of bone density. Prospects for fertility are very poor and are essentially dependent on oocyte donation with hormone replacement. Despite sometimes very high levels of FSH, spontaneous ovulation can occur in rare instances. It is important, while giving an otherwise poor prognosis for fertility, to warn young women of this. It is also my clinical practice to use low-dose estrogen replacement therapy that will not prevent the rare chance of a spontaneous ovulation in women who would be delighted to be pregnant.

### GENITAL TRACT DISORDERS

Abnormalities of the lower genital tract are relatively common and are usually associated with normal ovarian development and function and, consequently, normal endocrinology. The initial clinical symptoms depend on the degree of abnormality.

A transverse membrane or incompletely canalized vagina results in primary amenorrhea with normal secondary sex characteristics and cyclic abdominal pain during puberty. The diagnosis can be easily made from the history and presence of pelvic swelling and a bulging septum at the introitus. It is important to make the diagnosis promptly because, unless surgically corrected, the distention of the uterus and tubes with retrograde menstruation may produce permanent damage and sterility. The surgery required for an outflow disorder may be a simple stellate incision of the membrane or, where the defect is greater, may involve more complex surgery to lift the vagina into the abdominal cavity to repair the deficit.[4]

Complete müllerian agenesis or Mayer-Rokitansky-Kuster-Hauser syndrome (MRKH or Rokitansky syndrome) consists of the absence of a uterus in association with vaginal agenesis, and occurs in approximately 1 in 5000 female births.[64] The external genitalia have a normal appearance and the karyotype is normal. Müllerian agenesis may be suspected on the basis of either the initial ultrasound scan or the finding of a short blind-ending vagina on clinical examination. The presence of normal axillary and pubic hair excludes androgen insensitivity syndrome. Laparoscopy may rarely be required to confirm the diagnosis. Full evaluation, with an MRI scan, is recommended before laparoscopy to distinguish complete müllerian agnesis from a transverse occlusion of the vagina so effective intervention is possible and can be planned for the time of surgery. In the case of complete vaginal agenesis, surgery is not usually indicated. The vaginal dimple is normally small but can be up to several centimeters long, and vaginal dilators can be used to create an elongated vagina. Due to the embryologic association between genital and urinary tract development, renal abnormalities may be detected in 15% to 20% of cases of müllerian tract abnormality. Renal imaging with either intravenous pyelogram (IVP) or ultrasound should thus be performed.

Secondary amenorrhea of uterine origin may also arise from endometrial abnormalities. These can be due either to medical suppression of the endometrium through the use of androgenic progestogens in the combined oral contraceptive pill or to synechiae resulting from uterine surgery or infection (Asherman's syndrome). Where the cause has been androgenic progestogens, short-term treatment with estrogens should be sufficient to restore endometrial function. Potential causes of synechiae include repeated curettage of the uterus, abortion, myomectomy, cesarean section, pyogenic endometritis, or tuberculous infection. With increasing awareness of the potential hazards of repeated uterine surgery, however, such cases are becoming less frequent. Treatment is normally by hysteroscopic division of the adhesions followed by short-term insertion of an intrauterine device to maintain the endometrial cavity. The subsequent prognosis is highly dependent on the level of adhesions present before treatment.[65]

### DISORDERS OF SEXUAL DIFFERENTIATION

Complete failure of either androgen synthesis or androgen action in a genetic male may rarely present as a pubertal girl with primary amenorrhea.

Congenital disorders of androgen synthesis caused by an absence or reduction in five key enzymes (20,22-cholesterol desmolase, 3β-hydroxy-$\Delta^5$-steroiddehydrogenase, 17-ketoreductase, 17α-hydroxylase, and 17,20-desmolase) required in the synthesis of testosterone are dealt with in Chapters 143 and 146. In these genetic males, incomplete masculinization of the urogenital sinus and external genitalia may result in male pseudohermaphroditism. If unrecognized at birth, these people may be raised as girls and have primary amenorrhea at the time that puberty is expected. The diagnosis can be made by the presence of a normal XY karyotype and by detection of raised levels of precursor steroids, reflective of the defects in steroid enzymes.

Complete androgen insensitivity syndrome should be suspected at birth in the presence of inguinal hernia in a girl without genital ambiguity.[66] In the complete syndrome, previously described as testicular feminization,[67] the phenotype is fully female, although the uterus and upper part of the vagina are absent because of the production of antimüllerian hormone by the fetal testes. The testes fail to descend into the scrotum and are retained within the abdominal cavity or inguinal canal. Because of the secretion of estradiol, breast development is good and the normal female contours are present. Axillary and pubic hair is scanty or absent. The diagnosis is easily made from the family history, absence of body hair, XY karyotype, and the male levels of testosterone in plasma and can be confirmed by identification of the androgen receptor gene mutation. Complete androgen insensitivity resulting from disruptions of the androgen receptor open reading frame or from single amino acid mutations in the gene has been described.[68]

In complete androgen insensitivity, the intra-abdominal testes are more likely to become tumorous and should be surgically removed as soon as growth and breast development are complete. Gender allocation in androgen insensitivity syndromes is complex, although complete androgen insensitivity patients are normally raised as girls. Professional psychological support and follow-up are necessary, however.

Partial androgen insensitivity syndromes can result from abnormalities in 5α-reductase-2 deficiency or from the relatively common partial defects in the receptor protein, although these abnormalities are beyond the scope of this chapter and are discussed in detail in Chapter 169.

### EXTRAOVARIAN ENDOCRINE DISEASES

Disturbances of ovarian cyclicity can also occur as part of other endocrine disorders such as thyroid and adrenal disease.

In thyroid disease, the disturbance in menstrual pattern may range from amenorrhea to dysfunctional uterine bleeding.[69] In hyperthyroidism, the most common manifestation is simple oligomenorrhea (with decreased menstrual flow), and anovulatory cycles are very common, with over 20% of patients with thyrotoxicosis experiencing menstrual cycle disturbances.[69] Increased bleeding may occur, although this is not common. These effects may be related to the altered concentration of sex hormone–binding globulin (SHBG) increasing the concentrations of both estradiol and testosterone. The metabolic clearance rate of both steroids is reduced, and the extraglandular production of estrogens from androgens increases, as in polycystic ovary syndrome.[70]

In hypothyroidism, polymenorrhea is more common. This may be due to a variety of factors. The elevated TSH concentrations may have weak gonadotropin-like actions.[69] Estradiol is preferentially metabolized in favor of estriol, which has weak intrinsic biologic activity[71] and, because the concentration of SHBG is reduced, the amount of unbound estradiol is increased, although the total concentration is reduced due to the increased metabolic clearance rate. Finally, the concentration of prolactin may be elevated because of stimulation with thyrotropin-releasing hormone, and galactorrhea may be a feature. Treatment with thyroxine causes a reduction in TSH and prolactin, with the disappearance of galactorrhea and resumption of normal menstrual cyclicity.

The normal adrenal secretes large quantities of androgens (androstenedione, testosterone, and dehydroepiandrosterone and its sulfate) but little estrogen. Androstenedione, an important precursor for estrogen, is produced in the liver, skin, and fatty tissue. Although adrenal androgens may modulate the sensitivity of the HPO axis, they are not essential for ovarian cyclicity, which apparently occurs normally in their absence in Addison's disease or after bilateral adrenalectomy. In contrast, excessive adrenal secretion due to Cushing's syndrome, adrenal carcinoma, or congenital adrenal hyperplasia normally leads to amenorrhea.[72] There are a number of potential mechanisms for this. Secretion of gonadotropins may be suppressed by androgens directly or after aromatization to estrogens either in peripheral adipose tissue or centrally in the pituitary itself. In addition, glucocorticoids can inhibit pituitary LH and ovarian estrogen and progesterone secretion and can render estrogen-target tissues, such as the endometrium, resistant to gonadal steroids.[72] In addition to this, the involvement of the hypothalamic-pituitary-adrenal axis in physiologic stress responses may be a contributor to stress-related central amenorrhea through the suppressive actions of both CRH and the CRH-induced propiomelanocortin peptides inhibiting hypothalamic GnRH secretion.[72]

## ANOVULATION

### *CHRONIC ANOVULATION/POLYCYSTIC OVARY SYNDROME*

#### Definition

Chronic anovulation is the failure of follicle selection in the presence of a normal hypothalamic-pituitary-ovarian axis. Chronic anovulation may present with amenorrhea, in which case there is a clear bleed in response to progestogens, or oligomenorrhea, in which there is sometimes heavy bleeding at irregular intervals. Many anovulatory patients with normal levels of gonadotropins display some or all of the features of polycystic ovary syndrome (PCOS), such as obesity, hirsutism, and anovulation associated with enlarged microcystic ovaries.[73] A consensus meeting of the American Society for Reproductive Medicine and the European Society for Human Reproduction and Embryology defined polycystic ovary syndrome as the presence of two out of the three clinical features of oligomenorrhea and/or anovulation, clinical and/or biochemical signs of hyperandrogenism, and polycystic ovaries on ultrasound after the exclusion of other etiologies (congenital adrenal hyperplasia, androgen-secreting tumors, Cushing's syndrome).[74] The ultrasound appearances necessary to make the diagnosis have been defined as the presence of either 12 or more follicles measuring 2 to 9 mm in diameter or increased ovarian volume (>10 cm$^3$).[75] The essential abnormality is thus the presence of multiple follicles that do not easily mature from the antral stage to the dominant preovulatory stage, but can be stimulated to do so by exogenous gonadotropin. Polycystic ovary syndrome is described in detail in Chapter 157.

#### Etiology

The etiology of polycystic ovary syndrome appears to be closely related to abnormalities of insulin metabolism.[76] PCOS in both lean and obese women is associated with increased insulin resistance and compensatory hyperinsulinemia in comparison to weight-matched controls.[77] The severity of the hyperinsulinemia is correlated with the severity of many of the characteristic features of PCOS, particularly the degree of anovulation and the level of hyperandrogenism present. Both the adrenal gland and the ovary contribute to the increased circulating androgen concentration. The thecal cells of the ovary are particularly responsive to stimulation by the increased circulating concentrations of both insulin and LH.[78] At present, it appears to be the increased insulin action stimulating increased thecal androgen secretion, with possibly a genetic predisposition, that leads to the block in follicle development that characterizes this condition.[79]

#### Investigation

On investigation, the gonadotropin concentrations in chronic anovulation are typically normal although women with polycystic ovary syndrome may have a moderate elevation in LH to 10 to 20 IU/L. The LH concentration is elevated as a result of increased frequency and amplitude of LH pulses, possibly due to unopposed (by progesterone) estradiol stimulation of the hypothalamic GnRH pulse generator and estrogen provocation produces an LH surge (positive feedback) (see Fig. 154-5). The concentration of estradiol is usually between 50 and 100 pg/mL and bleeding occurs in response to progestogen challenge. Due to the association with increased insulin resistance, an oral glucose tolerance test should be performed to exclude frank glucose intolerance. With all the components of the HPO axis intact and responding appropriately to dynamic stimuli, it not clear why these women remain anovulatory. It may be that they have reverted to a state that is equivalent to early puberty, when the hypothalamus remains so sensitive to the inhibitory effects of ovarian steroids that follicular development is inhibited shortly after its initiation.

#### Treatment

Management of chronic anovulation depends on the presenting clinical feature. Where amenorrhea or anovulatory dysfunctional uterine bleeding is the principal presenting feature and pregnancy is not desired, treatment with cyclical progestogens, possibly in the form of the combined oral contraceptive pill, is indicated to reduce menstrual loss and prevent endometrial hyperplasia. Where fertility is sought, ovulation induction, as described later, and in detail in Chapter 158, is appropriate. Treatment of polycystic ovary syndrome, as described in detail in Chapter 157, includes the use of antiandrogens or 5α-reductase inhibitors to treat symptoms of hyperandrogenism.[80]

Induction of ovulation and restoration of fertility in chronic anovulation can be achieved relatively easily by the administration of an antiestrogen such as clomiphene citrate or tamoxifen.[81] Clomiphene has a long half-life and is a mixture of two isomers, of which the *trans (zu)* isomer is the active component.[82] Clomiphene is normally started in the early follicular phase at an initial dosage of 50 mg/day, although overweight women can be started on 100 mg/day. Treatment should be monitored with regular estradiol measurements and transvaginal ultrasound and, if ovulation is not observed, the dose may be increased up to 150 mg/day. Treatment causes a rise in both FSH and LH, which stimulate follicular development, leading to increased secretion of estradiol, which, in turn, induces a surge of LH by a positive feedback mechanism. Clomiphene is thus only effective in inducing ovulation in progestogen-positive amenorrhea when both negative and positive feedback mechanisms are intact. Ovulation may be triggered by the administration of hCG (5,000–10,000 U), but the injection must be timed to coincide with maximum follicular development as assessed by ultrasonography and/or estradiol levels. Although an ovulation rate of more than 70% may be achieved if patients are properly selected for antiestrogen therapy, the pregnancy rate is only 30% to 40%.[83] The low pregnancy rate is a result of the long-acting antiestrogenic effects of clomiphene on cervical mucus and endometrial development. There has consequently been great interest in the potential of aromatase inhibitors as ovulation induction agents,[84] but comparison with antiestrogens in a large-scale clinical trial is still awaited. A number of case-control studies have suggested that the risk of ovarian cancer may be increased in women who have previously been treated with clomiphene, particularly after repeated courses.[85,86] Although it is not clear that the association is causal, it is wise to limit the number of months of treatment to 12.

About 25% of women with PCOS fail to ovulate in response to clomiphene and in this circumstance there are a number of potential approaches. The standard treatment for women with clomiphene-resistant PCOS is exogenous FSH. Women with PCOS are extremely sensitive to FSH, however, and it can be difficult to restrict the number of ovulatory follicles, with the result that multiple pregnancy is a serious complication of treatment (see Chapter 158). Using clomiphene continuously until ovulation may be effective, but thorough monitoring with serial estradiol and ultrasound measurements is required. If evidence of excessive secretion of adrenal androgens is present, treatment with corticosteroids (e.g., 0.5 mg of dexamethasone per day) may restore cyclic ovarian activity or make them responsive to clomiphene. Use of the insulin-lowering agent metformin has been shown to be an effective treatment for anovulation in PCOS, both alone and as an adjunct to clomiphene.[87] This effect is particularly marked when the PCOS is associated with increased body mass index; it may not be as significant in lean women with

PCOS. The previously used treatment of wedge resection restored ovulation in about 70% of women, but, due to the risk of postoperative adhesions, has since been replaced by laparoscopic ovarian drilling. Meta-analysis of the available randomized trials shows that ovarian drilling is as effective as exogenous FSH in achieving a pregnancy, but with a significantly lower multiple pregnancy rate (odds ratio 0.16, 95% confidence intervals [CI] 0.03, 0.98).[88]

There are growing concerns about the long-term health of women diagnosed with polycystic ovary syndrome; these concerns are predominantly related to the associated insulin resistance state. Women with PCOS have a greater susceptibility to subsequent development of type 2 diabetes, and this risk appears to be higher in anovulatory women and women with a family history of type 2 diabetes.[74] Women with insulin-resistance states generally have a higher risk of subsequent cardiovascular disease. There is, so far, however, little direct evidence to link PCOS itself with increased cardiovascular disease risk.[89]

### LUTEAL PHASE DEFECT

The concept of the luteal phase defect is controversial. It has historically been defined in one of two ways: (1) as a defect of progesterone secretion by the corpus luteum, or (2) as a lag of more than 2 days (on more than one occasion) in histologic development of the endometrium relative to the day of the cycle.[90] The defect is estimated to affect 3% to 20% of the infertile population and 23% to 60% of women with recurrent miscarriage.[91] It is thus suggested that the defect in endometrial function affects embryo implantation, leading to subsequent problems in early pregnancy. Although some researchers have demonstrated that the incidence of histologic abnormalities in the endometrium is higher in women with unexplained infertility or recurrent miscarriage, more recent work suggests this variation to be a chance finding.[92,93]

The etiology of the endometrial abnormality has been related to the circulating progesterone concentration. In most ovarian cycles, the luteal phase lasts for at least 10 days, during which time the concentration of progesterone exceeds 5 ng/mL on at least 1 day. A luteal phase that falls below these limits is deemed to be inadequate, although the precise values incompatible with the maintenance of pregnancy are not clear.[94] The diagnosis of an inadequate luteal phase depends on accurate timing of the cycle and frequent measurements of plasma progesterone in the luteal phase. The fact that the concentration of progesterone varies considerably from minute to minute may add to the difficulties of confirming a diagnosis.

It is clear that short luteal phases do occur in specific circumstances such as lactation and after treatment of hyperprolactinemic amenorrhea with bromocriptine.[95] These physiologic states of infertility are associated with an abnormality in the preovulatory pattern of LH pulses, and it therefore seems likely that follicular development is abnormal. Treatment during the early follicular phase with clomiphene or human menopausal gonadotropin (hMG) restores the pattern of ovarian steroids to normal, whereas luteal phase treatment with hCG to stimulate increased secretion of endogenous progesterone and administration of exogenous progesterone both produce a lengthening of the luteal phase. None of these treatments has conclusively improved fertility,[96] however, and, consequently, the clinical significance of the luteal phase defect remains uncertain.

### LUTEINIZED UNRUPTURED FOLLICLE SYNDROME

Luteinization of the follicle is the process whereby the basement membrane breaks down, resulting in vascularization of the granulosa cells in association with a rapid increase in steroidogenic enzyme capacity leading to a rapid rise in prog-esterone secretion. The condition whereby this process takes place in the absence of follicle rupture is called *luteinized unruptured follicle syndrome (LUFS)*. A number of studies have suggested an association between this condition and endometriosis and have postulated that the reduction in peritoneal steroid levels due to the absence of follicle rupture may be an etiologic factor in endometriosis.[97] These observations remain to be tested by properly controlled studies, however, and it is entirely possible that, in most cases, luteinized unruptured follicle syndrome arises as an occasional feature of an otherwise normal menstrual cycle. Due to the important role of cyclooxygenase (COX)-2 in follicle rupture,[98] luteinized unruptured follicle syndrome can specifically arise after treatment with high doses of nonsteroidal anti-inflammatory drugs.[99]

## DYSFUNCTIONAL UTERINE BLEEDING

### DEFINITION

Dysfunctional uterine bleeding may be anovulatory or ovulatory. Anovulatory dysfunctional uterine bleeding has already been discussed. In most women with excessively heavy menses, no abnormality in ovarian activity can be identified.[100] Ovulatory dysfunctional uterine bleeding is defined as the presence of excessively heavy, prolonged, or frequent bleeding of uterine origin that is not due to pregnancy or to recognizable pelvic or systemic disease.[3] Heavy bleeding is defined as a total menstrual blood loss of more than 80 mL.[3] Approximately half of women presenting with heavy periods have a measured blood loss below this level, however.[101] The diagnosis of dysfunctional uterine bleeding is, thus, one of exclusion.

### ETIOLOGY

A number of local pathophysiologic mechanisms have been proposed for the excessive blood loss. First, abnormalities in prostaglandin metabolism appear to contribute to many cases. When incubated in vitro, the endometrial tissue of women with excessive menstrual blood loss synthesizes more prostaglandins than seen in women with normal blood loss.[102,103] These prostaglandins influence a range of processes in the endometrium, including angiogenesis, apoptosis and proliferation, tissue invasion and metastases, and immunosuppression.[104] Moreover, more $PGE_2$ and $PGI_2$, prostaglandins that induce vasodilation and inhibition of platelet aggregation, are produced relative to $PGF_{2\alpha}$, a vasoconstrictor.[105] Second, abnormalities in fibrinolysis have been demonstrated, with increased levels of plasminogen activator being found in the endometrium of women with heavy menstrual bleeding compared to those with normal menstrual loss.[106] Finally, angiogenesis has recently been identified as a critical process in the growth of both eutopic and ectopic endometria, raising the possibility of new therapeutic possibilities for antiangiogenic agents.[107]

### INVESTIGATION

Investigation is based on the exclusion of contributing pathology and should include pelvic ultrasound and endometrial biopsy. Hysteroscopy should also be performed when there is either an abnormally thickened endometrium or irregular bleeding despite evidence of ovulation.

### TREATMENT

A number of medical therapies have proven efficacy in the management of dysfunctional uterine bleeding. A meta-analysis of the effects of antifibrinolytics for heavy menstrual bleeding[108] demonstrated that treatment during menses with tranexamic acid resulted in a significant reduction in mean blood loss (approximately 50%) compared with placebo, luteal phase norethisterone, mefenamic acid, or ethamsylate as well as significant improvements in quality of life measures and few significant side effects. Nonsteroidal anti-inflammatory agents such as mefenamic acid (1.5 g/day in three divided doses) started on day 1 for the duration of bleeding also result in a reduction in menstrual blood loss, but are not as effective as tranexamic acid.[109] Progestogens administered from day 15 or 19 to day 26 of the cycle offer no advantage over other medical therapies such as danazol, tranexamic acid, nonsteroidal anti-inflammatories, and the intrauterine system (IUS) in the treatment of menorrhagia in women with ovulatory cycles.[110] Progestogen therapy for 21 days of the cycle results in a significant reduction in menstrual blood loss, although women find the treatment less acceptable than intrauterine levonorgestrel.[110] Progestogen delivered locally to the endometrium via the levonorgestrel-releasing intrauterine system (LNG-IUS) is a highly effective way of reducing blood loss (Fig. 154-9), although irregular spotting may occur in the few months after insertion. A systematic review[111] of nine randomized controlled trials found a significant reduction in average menstrual blood loss using LNG-IUS (range, 74% to 97%). The LNG-IUS was found to be more effective than tranexamic acid, but slightly less effective than endometrial resection at reducing menstrual blood loss. Danazol, in amounts insufficient to suppress ovarian function (200 mg/day), has been demonstrated to result in a significant reduction in blood loss compared to luteal phase progestogen and nonsteroidal anti-inflammatory agents.[112] The mechanism is unknown, although the androgenic action is likely to reduce proliferation of the endometrium. The androgenicity of danazol, particularly at high doses also limits its clinical utility due to the resultant adverse effects of weight gain and hirsutism. Excessive menstrual loss can be controlled medically by inducing suppression of the pituitary-ovarian axis with analogues of GnRH.[113] The side effects of estrogen withdrawal, however, preclude long-term use of GnRH analogues.

The surgical alternatives to medical treatment include endometrial ablation, either by hysteroscopy or by the

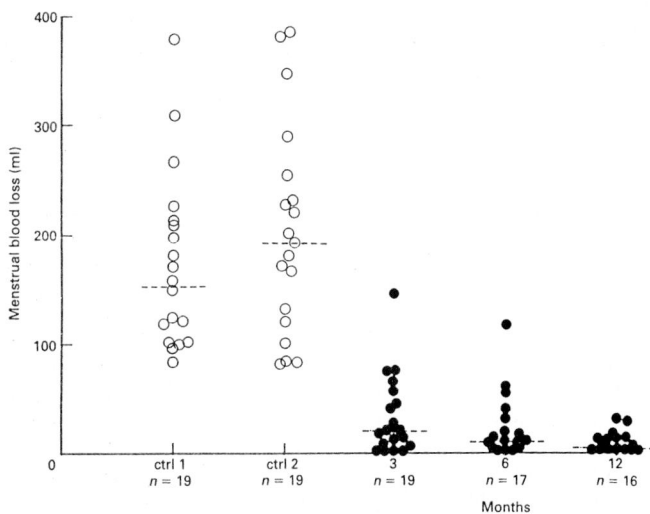

**Figure 154-9**  Menstrual blood loss in menorrhagic women at two control periods (ctrl) before levonorgestrel-releasing intrauterine system (LNG-IUS) insertion and after 3, 6, and 12 months of use. All individual values are indicated and median values are marked. (From Andersson R, Rybo G: Levonorgestrel-releasing intrauterine device in the treatment of menorrhagia. Br J Obstet Gynaecol 97:690–694, 1990).

second-generation, nonhysteroscopy techniques. Hysteroscopy techniques have a high level of patient satisfaction, but a portion of patients require further surgery. Hysterectomy is the definitive treatment for heavy menstrual bleeding, with satisfaction rates consistently greater than 90%. Hysterectomy is a major operation, however, with a potential for serious morbidity and, rarely, mortality,[101] and should thus be regarded as a treatment of last resort.

### Acknowledgment
I acknowledge, with immense gratitude, the author of the previous edition of this chapter, Professor David Baird, on whose work and inspirational teaching this revision is based.

## REFERENCES

1. Short R: Oestrus and menstrual cycles. In Austin C, Short R (eds): Hormonal Control of Reproduction. Cambridge, Mass, Cambridge University Press, 1984, pp 115–152.
2. Howie PW, McNeilly AS: Effect of breast-feeding patterns on human birth intervals. J Reprod Fertil 65:545–557, 1982.
3. Fraser I, Hickey M: Dysfunctional uterine bleeding. In Fraser I, Jansen R, Lobo R, et al (eds): Estrogens and Progestogens in Clinical Practice. London, Churchill Livingstone, 1998, pp 419–436.
4. Hickey M, Balen A: Menstrual disorders in adolescence: Investigation and management. Hum Reprod Update 9:493–504, 2003.
5. Santoro N: The menopause transition: An update. Hum Reprod Update 8:155–160, 2002.
6. Motta PM, Makabe S, Nottola SA: The ultrastructure of human reproduction. I. The natural history of the female germ cell: Origin, migration and differentiation inside the developing ovary. Hum Reprod Update 3:281–295, 1997.
7. McNatty KP, Heath DA, Lundy T, et al: Control of early ovarian follicular development. J Reprod Fertil Suppl 54:3–16, 1999.
8. Elvin JA, Matzuk MM: Mouse models of ovarian failure. Rev Reprod 3:183–195, 1998.
9. Baird DT: The primate ovary: Critique and perspectives. In Stouffer RL (ed): The Primate Ovary. New York, Plenum, 1988, pp 249–259.
10. Hillier SG, Tetsuka M: Role of androgens in follicle maturation and atresia. Baillieres Clin Obstet Gynaecol 11:249–260, 1997.
11. Richards JS, Russell DL, Ochsner S, et al: Ovulation: New dimensions and new regulators of the inflammatory-like response. Annu Rev Physiol 64:69–92, 2002.
12. Duncan WC: The human corpus luteum: Remodelling during luteolysis and maternal recognition of pregnancy. Rev Reprod 5:12–17, 2000.
13. Noyes RW, Hertig AT, Rock J: Dating the endometrial biopsy. Fertil Steril 1:33–25, 1950.
14. Kelly RW, King AE, Critchley HO: Cytokine control in human endometrium. Reproduction 121:3–19, 2001.
15. Baird DT: Amenorrhoea. Lancet 350:275–279, 1997.
16. Leyendecker G, Wildt L: Induction of ovulation with chronic intermittent (pulsatile) administration of Gn-RH in women with hypothalamic amenorrhoea. J Reprod Fertil 69:397–409, 1983.
17. Crowley WF Jr, Filicori M, Spratt DI, et al: The physiology of gonadotropin-releasing hormone (GnRH) secretion in men and women. Recent Prog Horm Res 41:473–531, 1985.
18. Blackwell RE: Diagnosis and treatment of hyperprolactinemic syndromes. Obstet Gynecol Annu 14:310–327, 1985.
19. Kleinberg DL, Noel GL, Frantz AG: Galactorrhea: A study of 235 cases, including 48 with pituitary tumors. N Engl J Med 296:589–600, 1977.

20. Tay CC, Glasier AF, Illingworth PJ, et al: Abnormal 24 hour pattern of pulsatile luteinizing hormone secretion and the response to naloxone in women with hyperprolactinaemic amenorrhoea. Clin Endocrinol (Oxf) 39:599–606, 1993.

21. Grossman A, Moult PJ, McIntyre H, et al: Opiate mediation of amenorrhoea in hyperprolactinaemia and in weight-loss related amenorrhoea. Clin Endocrinol (Oxf) 17:379–388, 1982.

22. Davis JR: Prolactin and reproductive medicine. Curr Opin Obstet Gynecol 16:331–337, 2004.

23. Matsuzaki T, Azuma K, Irahara M, et al: Mechanism of anovulation in hyperprolactinemic amenorrhea determined by pulsatile gonadotropin-releasing hormone injection combined with human chorionic gonadotropin. Fertil Steril 62:1143–1149, 1994.

24. Mah PM, Webster J: Hyperprolactinemia: Etiology, diagnosis, and management. Semin Reprod Med 20:365–374, 2002.

25. Molitch ME: Medical management of prolactin-secreting pituitary adenomas. Pituitary 5:55–65, 2002.

26. Di Sarno A, Landi ML, Cappabianca P, et al: Resistance to cabergoline as compared with bromocriptine in hyperprolactinemia: Prevalence, clinical definition, and therapeutic strategy. J Clin Endocrinol Metab 86:5256–5261, 2001.

27. Frisch RE: Fatness, menarche, and female fertility. Perspect Biol Med 28:611–633, 1985.

28. Bray GA, York DA: Clinical review 90: Leptin and clinical medicine: A new piece in the puzzle of obesity. J Clin Endocrinol Metab 82:2771–2776, 1997.

29. Zhang Y, Proenca R, Maffei M, et al: Positional cloning of the mouse obese gene and its human homologue. Nature 372:425–432, 1994.

30. Moschos S, Chan JL, Mantzoros CS: Leptin and reproduction: A review. Fertil Steril 77:433–444, 2002.

31. Laatikainen TJ: Corticotropin-releasing hormone and opioid peptides in reproduction and stress. Ann Med 23:489–496, 1991.

32. Wildt L, Leyendecker G, Sir-Petermann T, et al: Treatment with naltrexone in hypothalamic ovarian failure: Induction of ovulation and pregnancy. Hum Reprod 8:350–358, 1993.

33. Hall JE: Physiologic and genetic insights into the pathophysiology and management of hypogonadotropic hypogonadism. Ann Endocrinol (Paris) 60:93–101, 1999.

34. Kallman F, Schoefield W, Barrera S: The genetic aspects of primary eunuchoidism. Am J Ment Defic 48:203–236, 1944.

35. Franco B, Gbuioli S, Pragiola A: A gene deleted in Kallmann's syndrome shares homology with neural cell adhesion and axonal path-finding molecules. Nature 353:529–536, 1991.

36. Waldstreicher J, Seminara SB, Jameson JL, et al: The genetic and clinical heterogeneity of gonadotropin-releasing hormone deficiency in the human. J Clin Endocrinol Metab 81:4388–4395, 1996.

37. Laml T, Preyer O, Umek W, et al: Genetic disorders in premature ovarian failure. Hum Reprod Update 8:483–491, 2002.

38. Perez G, Knudson CM, Leykin L, et al: Apoptosis-associated signaling pathways are required for chemotherapy-mediated female germ cell destruction. Nat Med 3:1228–1232, 1998.

39. Muller J: Impact of cancer therapy on the reproductive axis. Horm Res 59(Suppl 1):12–20, 2003.

40. Harlow BL, Signorello LB: Factors associated with early menopause. Maturitas 35:3–9, 2000.

41. Morrison JC, Givens JR, Wiser WL, et al: Mumps oophoritis: A cause of premature menopause. Fertil Steril 26:655–659, 1975.

42. Turner H: A syndrome of infantilism, congenital webbed neck and cubitus valgus. Endocrinology 23:566–568, 1938.

43. Maclean N, Harnden DG, Brown WM, et al: Sex-chromosome abnormalities in newborn babies. Lancet 13:286–290, 1964.

44. Gravholt CH, Juul S, Naeraa RW, et al: Prenatal and postnatal prevalence of Turner's syndrome: A registry study. Br Med J 312:16–21, 1996.

45. Leppig KA, Disteche CM: Ring X and other structural X chromosome abnormalities: X inactivation and phenotype. Semin Reprod Med 19:147–157, 2001.

46. Reynaud K, Cortvrindt R, Verlinde F, et al: Number of ovarian follicles in human fetuses with the 45,X karyotype. Fertil Steril 81:1112–1119, 2004.

47. Karnis MF, Zimon AE, Lalwani SI, et al: Risk of death in pregnancy achieved through oocyte donation in patients with Turner syndrome: A national survey. Fertil Steril 80:498–501, 2003.

48. Swyer G: Male pseudohermaphroditism: A hitherto undescribed form. Br Med J ii:709–712, 1955.

49. Hines RS, Tho SP, Zhang YY, et al: Paternal somatic and germ-line mosaicism for a sex-determining region on Y (SRY) missense mutation leading to recurrent 46,XY sex reversal. Fertil Steril 67:675–679, 1997.

50. Goodfellow PN, Lovell-Badge R: SRY and sex determination in mammals. Annu Rev Genet 27:71–92, 1993.

51. Foster JW, Dominguez-Steglich MA, Guioli S, et al: Campomelic dysplasia and autosomal sex reversal caused by mutations in an SRY-related gene. Nature 372:525–530, 1994.

52. Warren ST, Ashley CT Jr: Triplet repeat expansion mutations: The example of fragile X syndrome. Annu Rev Neurosci 18:77–99, 1995.

53. Sherman SL: Premature ovarian failure in the fragile X syndrome. Am J Med Genet 97:189–194, 2000.

54. Kaufman FR, Kogut MD, Donnell GN, et al: Hypergonadotropic hypogonadism in female patients with galactosemia. N Engl J Med 304:994–998, 1981.

55. Aittomaki K, Lucena JL, Pakarinen P, et al: Mutation in the follicle-stimulating hormone receptor gene causes hereditary hypergonadotropic ovarian failure. Cell 82:959–968, 1995.

56. Layman LC, Amde S, Cohen DP, et al: The Finnish follicle-stimulating hormone receptor gene mutation is rare in North American women with 46,XX ovarian failure. Fertil Steril 69:300–302, 1998.

57. Latronico AC, Anasti J, Arnhold IJ, et al: Brief report: Testicular and ovarian resistance to luteinizing hormone caused by inactivating mutations of the luteinizing hormone-receptor gene. N Engl J Med 334:507–512, 1996.

58. Morishima A, Grumbach MM, Simpson ER, et al: Aromatase deficiency in male and female siblings caused by a novel mutation and the physiological role of estrogens. J Clin Endocrinol Metab 80:3689–3698, 1995.

59. Irvine WJ, Chan MM, Scarth L, et al: Immunological aspects of premature ovarian failure associated with idiopathic Addison's disease. Lancet 2:883–887, 1968.

60. Hoek A, Schoemaker J, Drexhage HA: Premature ovarian failure and ovarian autoimmunity. Endocr Rev 18:107–134, 1997.

61. Blumenfeld Z, Halachmi S, Peretz BA, et al: Premature ovarian failure: The prognostic application of autoimmunity on conception after ovulation induction. Fertil Steril 59:750–755, 1993.

62. Aitken RJ, Paterson M, van Duin M: The potential of the zona pellucida as a target for immunocontraception. Am J Reprod Immunol 35:175–180, 1996.

63. Wheatcroft NJ, Salt C, Milford-Ward A, et al: Identification of ovarian antibodies by immunofluorescence, enzyme-linked immunosorbent assay or immunoblotting in premature ovarian failure. Hum Reprod 12:2617–2622, 1997.

64. Gell JS: Mullerian anomalies. Semin Reprod Med 21:375–388, 2003.

65. Magos A: Hysteroscopic treatment of Asherman's syndrome. Reprod Biomed Online 4(Suppl 3):46–51, 2002.

66. Sultan C, Lumbroso S, Paris F, et al: Disorders of androgen action. Semin Reprod Med 20:217–228, 2002.

67. Morris J: The syndrome of testicular feminization in male pseudohermaphrodites. Am J Obstet Gynecol 65:1192–1211, 1953.

68. McPhaul MJ: Androgen receptor mutations and androgen insensitivity. Mol Cell Endocrinol 198:61–67, 2002.

69. Koutras DA: Disturbances of menstruation in thyroid disease. Ann N Y Acad Sci 816:280–284, 1997.

70. Ridgway EC, Longcope C, Maloof F: Metabolic clearance and blood production rates of estradiol in hyperthyroidism. J Clin Endocrinol Metab 41:491–497, 1975.

71. Fishman J, Hellman L, Zumoff B, et al: Influence of thyroid hormone on estrogen metabolism in man. J Clin Endocrinol Metab 22:389–392, 1962.

72. Magiakou MA, Mastorakos G, Webster E, et al: The hypothalamic-pituitary-adrenal axis and the female reproductive system. Ann N Y Acad Sci 816:42–56, 1997.

73. Stein I, Leventhal M: Amenorrhoea associated with bilateral polycystic ovaries. Am J Obstet Gynecol 29:181–191, 1935.

74. The Rotterdam FSHRE/ASRM-Sponsored Consensus Workshop Group: Revised 2003 consensus on diagnostic criteria and long-term health risks related to polycystic ovary syndrome. Fertil Steril 81:19–25, 2004.

75. Balen AH, Laven JS, Tan SL, et al: Ultrasound assessment of the polycystic ovary: International consensus definitions. Hum Reprod Update 9:505–514, 2003.

76. Sam S, Dunaif A: Polycystic ovary syndrome: Syndrome XX? Trends Endocrinol Metab 14:365–370, 2003.

77. Norman RJ, Noakes M, Wu R, et al: Improving reproductive performance in overweight/obese women with effective weight management. Hum Reprod Update 10:267–280, 2004.

78. Nelson VL, Legro RS, Strauss JF III, et al: Augmented androgen production is a stable steroidogenic phenotype of propagated theca cells from polycystic ovaries. Mol Endocrinol 13:946–957, 1999.

79. Strauss JF III: Some new thoughts on the pathophysiology and genetics of polycystic ovary syndrome. Ann N Y Acad Sci 997:42–48, 2003.

80. Azziz R: The evaluation and management of hirsutism. Obstet Gynecol 101:995–1007, 2003.

81. Adashi E: Ovulation induction: Clomiphene citrate. In Adashi E, Rock J, Rosenwaks Z (eds): Reproductive Endocrinology, Surgery and Technology. Philadelphia, Lippincott-Raven, 1996, pp 1181–1206.

82. Glasier AF, Irvine DS, Wickings EJ, et al: A comparison of the effects on follicular development between clomiphene citrate, its two separate isomers and spontaneous cycles. Hum Reprod 4:252–256, 1989.

83. Homburg R: The management of infertility associated with polycystic ovary syndrome. Reprod Biol Endocrinol 1:109, 2003.

84. Mitwally MF, Casper RF: Use of an aromatase inhibitor for induction of ovulation in patients with an inadequate response to clomiphene citrate. Fertil Steril 75:305–309, 2001.

85. Rossing MA, Daling JR, Weiss NS, et al: Ovarian tumors in a cohort of infertile women. N Engl J Med 331:771–776, 1994.

86. Tarlatzis BC, Grimbizis G, Bontis J, et al: Ovarian stimulation and ovarian tumours: A critical reappraisal. Hum Reprod Update 1:284–301, 1995.

87. Lord JM, Flight IH, Norman RJ: Metformin in polycystic ovary syndrome: Systematic review and meta-analysis. Br Med J 327:951–953, 2003.

88. Farquhar C, Vandekerckhove P, Lilford R: Laparoscopic "drilling" by diathermy or laser for ovulation induction in anovulatory polycystic ovary syndrome. Cochrane Database Syst Rev CD001122, 2001.

89. Legro RS: Polycystic ovary syndrome and cardiovascular disease: A premature association? Endocr Rev 24:302–312, 2003.

90. Li TC, Cooke ID: Evaluation of the luteal phase. Hum Reprod 6:484–499, 1991.

91. Balasch J, Vanrell JA: Luteal phase deficiency: An inadequate endometrial response to normal hormone stimulation. Int J Fertil 31:368–371, 1986.

92. Wentz AC, Kossoy LR, Parker RA: The impact of luteal phase inadequacy in an infertile population. Am J Obstet Gynecol 162:937–943, discussion 943–935, 1990.

93. Balasch J, Fabregues F, Creus M, et al: The usefulness of endometrial biopsy for luteal phase evaluation in infertility. Hum Reprod 7:973–977, 1992.

94. Hamilton MP, Fleming R, Coutts JR, et al: Luteal phase deficiency: Ultrasonic and biochemical insights into pathogenesis. Br J Obstet Gynaecol 97:569–575, 1990.

95. McNeilly AS: Neuroendocrine changes and fertility in breast-feeding women. Prog Brain Res 133:207–214, 2001.

96. Karamardian LM, Grimes DA: Luteal phase deficiency: Effect of treatment on pregnancy rates. Am J Obstet Gynecol 167:1391–1398, 1992.

97. Koninckx PR, Kennedy SH, Barlow DH: Endometriotic disease: The role of peritoneal fluid. Hum Reprod Update 4:741–751, 1998.

98. Sirois J, Sayasith K, Brown KA, et al: Cyclooxygenase-2 and its role in ovulation: A 2004 account. Hum Reprod Update 10:373–385, 2004.

99. Smith G, Roberts R, Hall C, et al: Reversible ovulatory failure associated with the development of luteinized unruptured follicles in women with inflammatory arthritis taking non-steroidal anti-inflammatory drugs. Br J Rheumatol 35:458–462, 1996.

100. Drife J: Dysfunctional uterine bleeding and menorrhagia. Baillieres Clin Obstet Gynaecol 3:271–291, 1989.

101. Lethaby A, Farquhar C: Treatments for heavy menstrual bleeding. Br Med J 327:1243–1244, 2003.

102. Rees MC, Anderson AB, Demers LM, et al: Prostaglandins in menstrual fluid in menorrhagia and dysmenorrhoea. Br J Obstet Gynaecol 91:673–680, 1984.

103. Smith SK, Abel MH, Kelly RW, et al: Prostaglandin synthesis in the endometrium of women with ovular dysfunctional uterine bleeding. Br J Obstet Gynaecol 88:434–442, 1981.

104. Sales KJ, Jabbour HN: Cyclooxygenase enzymes and prostaglandins in pathology of the endometrium. Reproduction 126:559–567, 2003.

105. Smith SK, Abel MH, Kelly RW, et al: A role for prostacyclin (PGI2) in excessive menstrual bleeding. Lancet 1:522–524, 1981.

106. Gleeson NC: Cyclic changes in endometrial tissue plasminogen activator and plasminogen activator inhibitor type 1 in women with normal menstruation and essential menorrhagia. Am J Obstet Gynecol 171:178–183, 1994.

107. Reynolds LP, Grazul-Bilska AT, Redmer DA: Angiogenesis in the female reproductive organs: Pathological implications. Int J Exp Pathol 83:151–163, 2002.

108. Lethaby A, Farquhar C, Cooke I: Antifibrinolytics for heavy menstrual bleeding. Cochrane Database Syst Rev CD000249, 2000.

109. Lethaby A, Augood C, Duckitt K: Nonsteroidal anti-inflammatory drugs for heavy menstrual bleeding. Cochrane Database Syst Rev CD000400, 2002.

110. Lethaby A, Irvine G, Cameron I: Cyclical progestogens for heavy menstrual bleeding. Cochrane Database Syst Rev CD001016, 2000.

111. Stewart A, Cummins C, Gold L, et al: The effectiveness of the levonorgestrel-releasing intrauterine system in menorrhagia: A systematic review. Brit J Obstet Gynaecol 108:74–86, 2001.

112. Beaumont H, Augood C, Duckitt K, et al: Danazol for heavy menstrual bleeding. Cochrane Database Syst Rev CD001017, 2002.

113. Fraser HM, Baird DT: Clinical applications of LHRH analogues. Baillieres Clin Endocrinol Metab 1:43–70, 1987.

# Endometriosis

## Lillian M. Swiersz and Linda C. Giudice

Endometriosis, present in 10% of women of reproductive age and up to 50% of women with infertility, is an enigmatic gynecologic disorder characterized by the growth of endometrial tissue (glands *and* stroma) at extrauterine sites (Fig. 155-1) Its clinical manifestations include dysmenorrhea, dyspareunia, pelvic pain, and infertility.[1,2] Endometriosis is most commonly found on the ovaries, the pelvic peritoneum, and the bowel and less commonly on the pleura of the lungs, on the pericardium, and in previous abdominal and/or vaginal incisions. No correlation has been established between the amount of disease present and symptomatology, although pain does correlate well with the site of disease.[2,3] The steroid hormone dependence of this disorder is striking[4]: prolonged periods of unopposed estrogen predispose women, female primates, and men to the disorder, and natural or surgical menopause results in inactivity of the disorder.[5-7] Endometriosis occurs during the reproductive years and is more prevalent in women with few pregnancies (relatively more menstrual cycles) and higher endogenous estrogen levels, and it is lower in women with decreased estrogen levels and fewer menstrual cycles, such as women with hypothalamic amenorrhea. This chapter reviews the current literature on the pathogenesis and mechanisms underlying the establishment of endometriosis and its clinical diagnosis and management.

## PATHOGENESIS

Despite its description by von Rokitansky over 100 years ago,[8] the precise pathogenesis of endometriosis continues to elude physicians and scientists. For nearly 80 years, three theories have dominated thinking about this disorder: the retrograde menstruation theory of Sampson,[9] the coelomic metaplasia theory,[10] and the müllerian embryonic rest theory.[11] Although the past decade has witnessed the potential roles of the immune system, genetic influences, and environmental chemicals in the pathogenesis of endometriosis, evolving genomic and proteomic research is poised to aid in the development of diagnostic tests and rational development of molecular therapeutics for endometriosis.

### RETROGRADE MENSTRUATION/METAPLASIA

In menstruating women, approximately 90% of menstrual blood emerges through the cervix, and about 10% is refluxed through the fallopian tubes into the peritoneal cavity.[12] Sampson's theory of retrograde menstruation postulates that sloughed endometrial tissue, fluxed through the fallopian tubes, contains viable, steroid-sensitive cells that are capable of implanting outside the uterus.[9] Although this hypothesis is attractive, it does not explain why retrograde menstruation, a physiologic event,[12] does not result in endometriosis in all women. The volume of regurgitated menstrual debris has been considered to be relevant to establishment of the disorder inasmuch as women with endometriosis have a higher volume of refluxed menstrual blood than those without the disorder.[12] The findings of hypotonia of the uterotubal junction in women with endometriosis, but not in controls,[13] supports this theory and, in part, may explain why only some women are affected. In addition, during the menstrual phase, the occurrence of subendometrial myometrial contractile waves exhibiting a retrograde pattern in women with endometriosis, versus controls with a normal antegrade pattern,[14] further supports the Sampson theory and suggests that endometriosis, long considered to be an endometrial disorder, may, in part, be a disorder of normal *myometrial* function. The greatest support for Sampson's theory derives from the nonhuman primate. Spontaneous endometriosis is found in approximately 25% of baboons, and its prevalence increases with the duration of captivity, lack of conception, and incidence of retrograde menstruation.[15,16] In addition, endometriosis can be induced in baboons by cervical occlusion,[15] much as endometriosis is uniformly observed in young girls with primary amenorrhea caused by cervical hypoplasia or aplasia, vaginal agenesis, or other müllerian anomalies associated with obstruction to the outflow of menstrual blood.[16]

The theory of coelomic metaplasia proposes that undefined stimuli activate totipotent cells of the mesothelium (peritoneal epithelium) to differentiate into ectopic endometrium.[10] This theory is based on the common embryologic origin of endometrial and mesothelial cells; however, little experimental evidence supports this theory.[17] Alternatively, müllerian cells or embryonic rests, after prolonged periods of hormonal

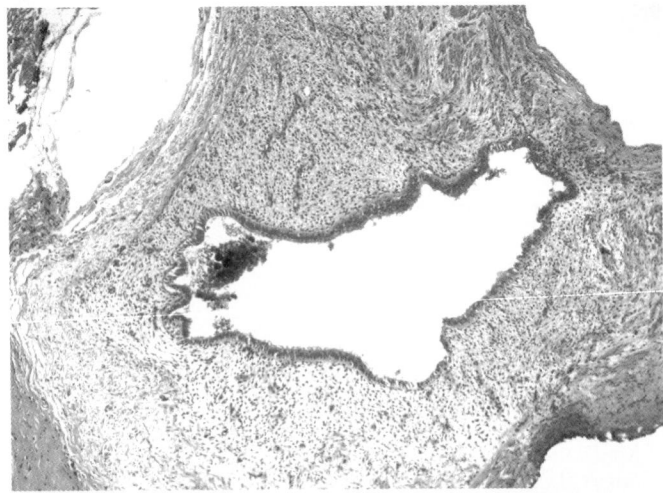

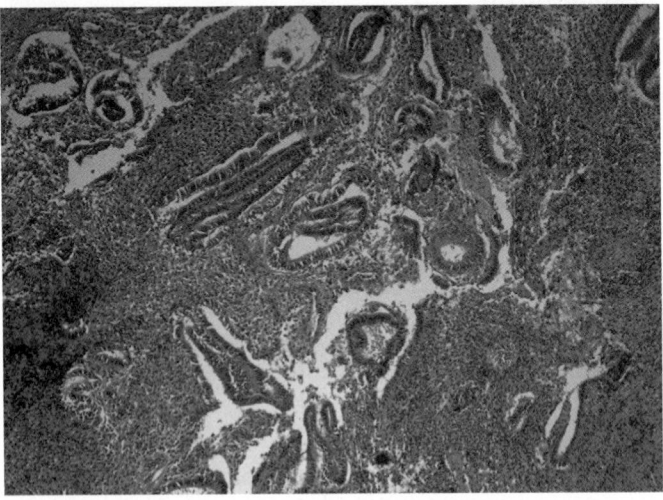

*Figure 155-1* **A**, 10× hematoxylin and eosin stain of a peritoneal lesion of endometriosis. Note the presence of glands and stroma surrounded by fibrosis. **B**, 10× hematoxylin and eosin stain of late proliferative endometrium taken from the same patient at the time of surgery.

stimulation, could give rise to endometriosis,[11] and this may contribute to the pathogenesis of rectovaginal disease.[18]

Of all these possibilities, the one that has the greatest support is the theory of retrograde menstruation resulting in endometrial tissue that may implant on peritoneal or abdominal/pelvic visceral surfaces. In addition, the tissue may be transported to distant sites by vascular or lymphatic channels.[19] Implicit in this theory is that endometrial tissue so desquamated must have viable cells that are capable of implanting in heterologous tissue.

## IMMUNE SYSTEM

There is abundant evidence demonstrating that endometriosis is accompanied by an inflammatory reaction in the peritoneum, resulting in abnormal levels of cytokines and chemokines in the peritoneal fluid. There have been observations of higher levels of activated macrophages and cytokines in peritoneal fluid from women with endometriosis than in those without the disorder.[20,21] In addition, there is some evidence to suggest a role for abnormal macrophage activity in endometriosis, which is supported by numerous studies showing altered macrophage-dependent cytokine levels and activity that can affect the survival and growth of ectopic endometrial cells.[22,23] In addition to inflammation, a growing

body of evidence supports relative immune dysfunction in women with endometriosis.[22,24] It has been suggested that endometriosis is part of an autoimmune disorder,[25] on the basis of observations that women with endometriosis have increased generalized B-cell activity[26] and an association with abnormal autoantibodies, such as autoantibodies to phospholipids[27] and to endometrium.[28,29] In addition, an increased association with other autoimmune phenomena such as premature ovarian failure and atopic disease supports the hypothesis.[30] The actual significance of the increased multiple antibodies remains unknown, however, and the mechanisms by which such an increase in antibodies leads to the development of endometriosis remains uncertain. The possibility exists that the increased antibody production is the consequence of a general inflammatory response initiated by activated macrophages and other antigen-presenting cells in response to the ectopic endometrial tissue rather than the cause of the development of endometriosis. Before an immune basis for endometriosis can be determined with certainty, however, well-controlled prospective studies need to be conducted. The role of the humoral and cellular immune systems in the pathophysiology of endometriosis is presented later in the section on pathophysiology.

## GENETICS

A genetic predisposition to the development of endometriosis has been recognized.[31] An increased risk (5% to 8%) of endometriosis is seen among first-degree relatives of affected women in comparison to the general population.[32–34] Recurrence risks of this magnitude are most consistent with polygenic/multifactorial etiology. Additional support for a polygenic inheritance is the earlier age of onset for familial versus nonfamilial cases and similar age of onset among affected relatives.[35] In addition, a strong familial tendency is found in nonhuman primates.[36]

## ENVIRONMENT

Monkeys exposed to total body proton irradiation had an increased prevalence of endometriosis when compared with controls (53% vs. 26%).[37] Irradiation may contribute to the establishment and/or growth of endometriosis.[38,39] In addition, severe endometriosis developed in rhesus monkeys exposed to tetrahydrochlorodibenzo-*p*-dioxin (TCDD or dioxin) at 5 to 25 parts per trillion (ppt) daily for 4 years.[40] The severity of the disease was dose dependent. Studies in rodents exposed to TCDD have shown both an increase[41] and decrease in endometriotic lesions.[42] Epidemiologic studies demonstrate that Belgium, a country with one of the highest levels of dioxin pollution in the world, has the highest incidence of endometriosis and prevalence of severe disease.[43] In 1976 in Seveso, Italy, a cohort of women were acutely exposed to dioxin and were evaluated for endometriosis 20 years later. The study demonstrated a doubled, nonsignificant risk for endometriosis among women with serum TCDD levels of 100 ppt or higher; however, no clear dose response was found. A more recent case-control study carried out on Italian and Belgian women of reproductive age, with and without endometriosis, showed no significant differences in dioxin-like compound body burdens between women with and without endometriosis.[44] Overall, TCDD is unlikely to be a significant factor in the etiology of most endometriosis cases.

## ABERRANT GENE EXPRESSION

The use of rapidly emerging technologies that include high-throughput expression analysis by microarrays,[45] protenomics, and accompanying strategies for data analysis (bioinformatics) have recently been applied to the study of endometriosis. Kao and colleagues performed global gene profiling of 12,686 genes during the window of implantation from eight subjects with and seven subjects without endometriosis.[46] Dysregulation of a number of genes including aromatase, progesterone receptor, and angiogenic factors was determined as likely contributing to the pathogenesis of endometriosis. Interestingly, kallikrein was 100-fold upregulated in the endometrium of women with endometriosis. Tissue kallikrein belongs to a family of serine proteases involved in the generation of bioactive peptide kinins in many organs. These enzymes may participate in proteolysis of extracellular matrix, which may be important in the establishment of the disease in the peritoneal cavity. Genes such as B61 and semaphorin E may participate in the neovascularization and survival of endometrium, leading to the establishment of endometriosis. cDNA microarrays were used to compare expression patterns between endometriotic tissues and corresponding eutopic endometria. Fifteen genes were identified that were upregulated in the endometrial cysts. The upregulated elements included genes encoding some human leukocyte antigens (HLAs), complement factors, ribosomal proteins, and transforming growth factor beta 1 (TGF-β1).[47] With development and use of these new technologies, the stage is set for the development of diagnostic tools and targeted drug therapies for endometriosis.

## GENOMIC ALTERATIONS

Alterations in DNA copy numbers in human endometriosis lesions have been detected by comparative genomic hybridization.[48] In addition, a recent study, using a similar approach, revealed several regions of genomic alteration in eutopic endometrium from women with endometriosis compared to normal controls. Some of the regions were the same as previously found in the endometriotic lesions, suggesting that genomic alterations may be a proximate cause for endometriosis.[49] Two-color fluorescence in situ hybridization was used for analysis of endometriotic and normal archival tissue, and increased heterogeneity of chromosome 17 aneuploidy in endometriosis was found. These findings support a multistep pathway involving somatic genetic alterations in the development and progression of endometriosis.[50]

## PATHOPHYSIOLOGY

### CELL SURVIVAL/CELL ADHESION

For tissue to implant and thrive in an ectopic location, it must survive after detachment from its original location, attach itself and invade into a new environment, proliferate, and establish a new blood supply. These processes involve inhibition of apoptosis; cell-cell and cell-substratum interactions; matrix degradation, inhibition, and repair; controlled cellular proliferation; and angiogenesis. As with normal endometrium, endometriosis tissue responds to cyclic changes in steroid hormones by proliferation and glandular secretion, as well as by production of autocrine and paracrine factors that affect these processes.[51]

Endometrial cells undergo apoptosis as part of their natural cell death at the time of menstruation.[52,53] In women with endometriosis, however, the percentage of sloughed endometrial cells undergoing apoptosis is greatly reduced, thereby resulting in increased numbers of cells that may survive in ectopic sites.[54] After survival, endometrial cells must adhere to the mesothelium or other surfaces and then begin the process of invasion. An in vitro model of endometriosis using confocal microscopy has demonstrated the adherence and invasion of endometrial cells through peritoneal mesothelium.[55] The expression of cellular adhesion molecules by endometriotic lesions has been investigated to help understand mechanisms involved in the maintenance of endometrial tissue in ectopic locations.[56] Of interest is the finding that refluxed endome-

trial cells, but not tissue fragments, downregulate expression of the E-cadherin cell adhesion molecule.[57] It is possible that proteases, cytokines, or growth factors in the peritoneal fluid of women with endometriosis alter some endometrial structures and may result in their selective adhesion to the peritoneum.

### MATRIX DEGRADATION/INVASION

Endometriosis, a benign disorder, can invade tissues and surfaces with as much aggression as a malignancy. Matrix metalloproteinases (MMPs) and their inhibitors (tissue inhibitors of metalloproteinases [TIMPs]) are involved in extracellular matrix remodeling[58,59] and have been implicated in the endometrial remodeling that occurs during the proliferative phase of the menstrual cycle and as participants in tissue desquamation at the time of menses.[60,61] The balance between MMPs and TIMPs is critical in maintaining the appropriate level of MMP activity, and failure to maintain this balance may contribute to matrix breakdown and cellular invasion, as observed in endometriosis.

In eutopic endometrium, mRNA for all the MMPs has been detected during the menstrual phase.[60,62,63] Matrilysin (MMP-7) mRNA is localized to the epithelium, whereas all others are expressed in the stroma. Only MMP-2 and TIMP-1 mRNA is constitutively expressed throughout the cycle. MMP-10 and MMP-9 are expressed only in late secretory and menstrual endometrium, whereas MMP-7, MMP-2, and MMP-11 mRNA is consistently detected in proliferative endometrium, which suggests steroid regulation of MMPs in this tissue. This theory is supported by experimental studies in vitro.[61,64,65]

Recent studies have focused on the role of MMP production in endometriosis.[61] Epithelial-specific MMP-7 is expressed in endometriotic lesions during the secretory phase, whereas it is absent in eutopic endometrium,[66] which suggests that progesterone suppression of MMP-7 may be dysregulated in endometriosis and that this MMP may play a role in growth or progression of the disorder. MMP-3 has also been identified in lesions of endometriosis, and such expression is diminished after danazol treatment.[67] MMP-1 is expressed focally in red peritoneal and ovarian endometriosis lesions regardless of the menstrual phase, but not in black peritoneal and rectovaginal lesions.[68] Foci of MMP-1 expression closely correlate with matrix breakdown and with the absence of progesterone receptors in adjacent epithelial cells, thus suggesting that MMP-1 expression may be involved in tissue remodeling and bleeding and possibly reimplantation of endometriotic lesions. An endometriosis-specific protein, ENDO-II, has homology with TIMP-1.[69] Recent studies indicate that both eutopic and ectopic tissue from women with endometriosis exhibit patterns of altered MMP regulation in vivo. A lack of responsiveness to progesterone was demonstrated in vitro, associated with a failure to suppress MMP expression and an enhanced ability of the tissue to establish experimental endometriosis. In vitro treatments with retinoic acid and TGF-β, however, restored the ability of progesterone to suppress MMPs in vitro and prevented the establishment of experimental disease.[70] In vitro studies using endometrial cell cultures suggest that interleukin-8 (IL-8) increases MMP activity and the invasive capability of endometrial stromal cells in culture.[71] Studies have also shown that MMP expression in human peritoneal endometriotic lesions were much greater than that in eutopic endometrium.[72] Specifically, endometriotic tissue possesses higher level of gelatinase activity than eutopic endometrium from patients with endometriosis does, and MMP-9 might be of importance for the implantation and invasive growth of endometriotic tissue that may lead to endometriosis.[73] Uterine endometrium from women with endometriosis expressed higher levels of MMP-2 and membrane type (MT)1-MMP and lower levels of TIMP-2 than did endometrium from normal women.[74] MMP-2, MMP-9, and

MT1-MMP mRNA expression levels in clinically aggressive pigmented lesions were significantly higher than those in normal eutopic endometrium.[75]

The hypogonadal, athymic nude mouse is a useful model to investigate steroid dependence of MMPs in the pathogenesis of endometriosis.[76] Endometrial explant cultures treated with estradiol secrete MMPs and establish ectopic peritoneal lesions when injected into recipient animals. Suppressing MMP secretion with progesterone or blocking MMP activity with TIMP-1, however, inhibits the formation of ectopic lesions.[76] This model provides insight into a mechanistic link between steroidal regulation of MMP secretion in the establishment of an endometriosis-like disease and may prove useful in designing therapeutic agents to inhibit or minimize endometriosis lesions in the peritoneal cavity. It is still not understood, however, how misexpression of MMPs and TIMPs are due to an innate anomaly of the endometrium, immune system, or peritoneum of women with endometriosis.

### GROWTH FACTORS, ANGIOGENIC FACTORS, CHEMOATTRACTANTS, MORPHOGENS

Peritoneal fluid from women with endometriosis has mitogenic, angiogenic, morphogenic, and chemoattractant activities (Table 155-1). It contains growth factors and cytokines secreted by monocytes/macrophages, as well as endometrial, ovarian, and mesothelial cells in the peritoneal cavity.[51,77–79]

These cytokines and growth factors can induce or suppress cell survival, proliferation, differentiation, angiogenesis, and the inflammatory response. In women with endometriosis, levels of proinflammatory cytokines are elevated, such as macrophage colony-stimulating factor,[80] IL-1,[81,82] IL-6,[83–88] and tumor necrosis factor-α (TNF-α),[81,86,88–90] all of which are secreted by macrophages/monocytes. IL-1 and TNF-α, in turn, can stimulate the secretion of other cytokines such as IL-8,[91,92] monocyte chemotactic protein-1,[93–95] and RANTES (regulated upon activation, normal, T-cell expressed and secreted),[96,97] which are chemoattractants for neutrophils, T lymphocytes, monocytes, and macrophages, as well as a potent angiogenic factor (IL-8). These factors may contribute to pelvic pain[86] or infertiity.[79]

Growth factors may also play a fundamental role in the pathogenesis of endometriosis by independently stimulating cell survival, growth, or differentiation. Macrophage-conditioned media contain mitogenic activity, some of which is attributable to TGF-β,[98] platelet-derived growth factor (PDGF),[86,99] and basic fibroblast growth factor (bFGF).[100] Epidermal growth factor (EGF),[100,101] insulin-like growth factors (IGFs),[102–104] PDGF,[86,99] and bFGF are potent mitogens for endometrial stromal cells in vitro. Hepatocyte growth factor is a mitogen and morphogen for endometrial epithelial cells when cocultured with stromal cells and may play a role in the regeneration of endometrial glands in ectopic locations.[105] It is also an antigenic factor. IGF-1 is an antiapoptotic growth

| Table 155-1 | Cytokines and Growth Factors in Endometriosis | |
|---|---|---|
| Factors | Level in Peritoneal Fluid of Women with Endometriosis | Possible Effects |
| GM-CSF | No difference | Proinflammatory |
| IL-1 | No difference | Stimulates proliferation of fibroblasts<br>Induces differentiation of T, B cells<br>Induces other cytokines and prostaglandins |
| IL-2 | No difference | Stimulates proliferation of T, B cells |
| IL-4 | No difference | Stimulates proliferation of T, B, mast cells<br>Activates macrophages<br>Induces differentiation of B cells |
| IL-5 | No difference | Induces gravity and activation of B cells |
| IL-6 | No difference | Regulates immunocompetent cell growth and differentiation<br>Induces acute phase reaction<br>Stimulates or inhibits cell growth<br>Regulates ovarian steroid production |
| IL-8 | Elevated | Neutrophil chemoattractant, activator<br>Angiogen |
| IL-10 | Elevated | Suppresses IL-1, IFN-γ in T, NK cells |
| TNF-α | No difference | Mediates macrophage cytotoxicity<br>Proinflammatory factor<br>Induces or suppresses growth<br>Immune modulator<br>Angiogen |
| IFN-γ | No difference | Inhibits cell growth/differentiation<br>Induces MHC antigen<br>Activates macrophage, endothelial, NK cells |
| MCP-1 | Elevated | Monocyte chemoattractant<br>Stimulates respiratory burst |
| RANTES | Elevated | Chemoattractant d>monocytes, T cells |
| EGF | No difference | Potent mitogen<br>Possible estromedin (rodents) |
| TGF-β | Elevated | Regulates growth<br>Chemoattractant for monocytes<br>Suppresses NK cells<br>Induces fibroblast growth<br>Induces angiogenesis |
| IGF-1, IGF-2 | No difference | Mitogen glucose metabolism |
| PDGF | Elevated | Mitogen for fibroblasts<br>Chemoattractant d>fibroblasts, monocytes, neutrophils |
| VEGF | Elevated | Angiogen |

EGF, epidermal growth factor; GM-CSF, granulocyte-macrophage colony-stimulating factor; HGF, hepatocyte growth factor; IFN, interferon; IGF, insulin-like growth factor; IL, interleukin; MCP, monocyte chemotactic protein; MHC, major histocompatibility complex; NK, natural killer, PDGF, platelet-derived growth factor; RANTES, regulated upon activation, normal, T-cell expressed and secreted; TGF, transforming growth factor; TNF, tumor necrosis factor; VEGF, vascular endothelial growth factor.
Adapted from Giudice LC, Tazuke SI, Swiersz L: Current research in endometriosis. J Reprod Med 43:252–262, 1998.

factor and may enhance cell survival. EGF and IGF mediate estrogen actions and, thus, are probably participants in the pathogenesis of endometriosis.

Angiogenic activity is increased in peritoneal fluid from women with endometriosis.[106] Vascular EGF (VEGF), a potent angiogenic factor, has been found in peritoneal fluid from women with endometriosis, and VEGF levels in the peritoneal fluid correlate directly with the severity of disease.[107] The source of VEGF has not been identified but may be the endometrial cells or mesothelial cells.

## AROMATASE

Recent evidence demonstrates abundant and abnormal expression in endometriotic lesions of aromatase, the key enzyme in estradiol ($E_2$) biosynthesis.[108] This enzyme is rarely expressed in eutopic endometrium of women without disease and is minimally expressed in women with disease.[108] In addition, the enzyme that inactivates $E_2$, 17β hydroxysteroid dehydrogenase-1, is downregulated in endometriotic lesions,[109] thus resulting in increased $E_2$ synthesis locally in endometriotic lesions. This has important consequences with regard to therapies (see the later section on treatment), which are aimed primarily at decreasing circulating $E_2$ as a treatment strategy, as local $E_2$ production would not be treated.[110]

## IMMUNE SYSTEM

Despite the ample evidence that endometriosis is associated with a variety of abnormal immune responses, a causative role for abnormal immune responses in the etiology or progression of endometriosis is only speculative. Direct cytotoxic effects by peripheral and peritoneal natural killer (NK) cells in general and specifically against autologous endometrial cells in vitro are greatly reduced in women with endometriosis in comparison to controls.[111–114] The NK cell activity, however, is partly under the regulation of soluble factors such as cytokines and growth factors, as evidenced by a further decrease in the activity of NK cells with the addition of sera or peritoneal fluid from women with endometriosis.[114,115] In particular, NK cell activity is decreased[112,113,115,116] and endometrial cells are more resistant to NK-mediated cytolysis.[113] Intercellular adhesion molecule-1 (ICAM-1) is important for NK-target cell interactions, including endometrial cell–NK cell interactions. Recent evidence suggests that endometrial cells from women with endometriosis produce more soluble ICAM-1,[117] an antagonist of the NK-target interaction, which may contribute to the relative resistance of endometrial cell destruction by NK cells. These observations support the theory that women with endometriosis have a compromised ability to reject autologous endometrial tissue, for example, in the peritoneal cavity, and thus have an increased risk for the disorder. Whether this resistance to destruction by NK cells is an intrinsic immune dysfunction or a reaction to refluxed endometrial tissue that has been altered by the environment in the peritoneal cavity remains to be determined.[116,118] Of interest, however, is the finding that ectopic endometrium could not be established in the peritoneum of NK-deficient mice.[119]

Alterations in immune function have been described in endometriosis, but the changes are complex and none independently or satisfactorily explains the pathogenesis of this disorder. In addition, it is not clear whether the alteration is the cause of endometriosis or secondary to the inflammatory reaction that endometriosis induces. Further research involving the potential interactions between the immune system, MMPs, and TCDD may be promising.

## MECHANISMS UNDERLYING PAIN AND INFERTILITY

Pelvic pain associated with endometriosis is manifested as dysmenorrhea, dyspareunia, and/or chronic noncyclic pelvic pain.

Sometimes pain is related to tissues or organs, such as bowel or pleura, that are involved with the disease. Symptoms vary with the location of the disease, stage, type of lesion, and depth of invasion.[2,120] The pathogenesis of endometriosis-related pain is believed to include inflammation, pressure, adhesions, neuronal involvement with disease, and increased prostaglandin production by ectopic implants. Red fleshy lesions, for example, produce higher amounts of prostaglandins.[121] Adhesions may cause pain by damage to tissues and subsequent scarring or by damage to nerves and/or blood supply, with the latter resulting in ischemia or hypoxia of the tissues perfused by compromised vessels. The etiology of endometriosis-related pain is important because of the need to address the underlying cause when designing therapies to treat the pain (see the later section on treatment).

With regard to infertility, as many as 30.5% of women with infertility who undergo surgery have endometriosis.[122] Other investigators have found that endometriosis was noted more frequently among women being investigated for infertility (21%) than among those undergoing sterilization (6%).[123] The infertility may be due to a variety of causes, including mechanical factors obstructing the union of oocyte and sperm or obstructing embryo transport, sperm and embryo toxicity, ovulatory and endocrine abnormalities, immunologic abnormalities, and implantation defects.[124] With regard to ovulatory and endocrine abnormalities, there is much controversy about abnormal follicle dynamics, anovulation, hyperprolactinemia, luteal-phase defects, and luteinized unruptured follicle syndrome, as well as an increase in spontaneous abortion in women with endometriosis.[124] The evidence is convincing, however, that peritoneal fluid from women with endometriosis adversely affects sperm motility,[125] sperm velocity,[126] and sperm binding to the zona pellucida in a hemizona assay.[127] Peritoneal fluid from patients with endometriosis significantly reduces the percentage of mouse embryos reaching the blastocyst and hatching stages,[128,129] thus suggesting a direct embryotoxic effect. It is likely that these adverse effects of peritoneal fluid from women with endometriosis on sperm and embryos derive from cytokines from activated macrophages and other immune cells in the peritoneal fluid.[79] In 1994, Lessey and colleagues reported the absence of $\alpha_v\beta_3$ integrin expression on the endometrial epithelium during the window of implantation in approximately 50% of women with minimal to mild disease.[130] Whether this effect is caused by an intrinsic abnormality in the endometrium of women with endometriosis is a result of access to the uterine cavity by peritoneal cytokines and other factors that adversely affect $\alpha_v\beta_3$ expression, or has an underlying immune basis is not clear at this time. A plethora of genes aberrantly expressed in eutopic endometrium from women with versus without endometriosis suggests mechanisms for implantation failure, including genes that are related to embryo toxicity, detoxification of chemicals, immune dysregulation, antibacterial agents, and calcium homeostasis, to name a few.[46]

## DIAGNOSIS

Endometriosis is part of the differential diagnosis of pelvic pain or infertility.[131] Because the extent of disease and the severity of pain symptoms or the duration of infertility are not correlated, however, it is not possible to make a diagnosis of endometriosis solely on the initial symptoms. The gold standard for making the diagnosis is laparoscopy. Serum markers have been evaluated for diagnosing endometriosis and include CA-125,[132,133] placental protein-14,[133–135] and endometrial antibodies.[28,29,136] The specificity and sensitivity of these tests are not high enough, however, to warrant their use in a clinical setting either for diagnosing or for monitoring the disease. With the advent of genomic and proteomic technology, it is likely that minimally invasive tests such as endometrial biopsies and blood tests may be able to assist in the diagnosis of endometriosis.

Imaging techniques, including ultrasonography, computed tomography (CT), and magnetic resonance imaging (MRI), have limited value in diagnosing endometriosis. Ultrasonography is useful in determining the location of a pelvic mass and in distinguishing cystic and solid lesions. Neither it nor the more expensive technique of magnetic resonance imaging offers sufficient specificity for use in clinical practice, however.[137,138]

## THERAPIES

Therapy for endometriosis very much depends on the patient's needs. The natural history of the disease must also be considered because endometriosis in women and baboons undergoes about a 25% spontaneous regression rate and a 65% progression rate.[139,140] Because up to 25% of women have asymptomatic endometriosis, an initial complaint, compromised function of internal organs, or infertility must be present for therapy to be initiated. Therapy may be aimed at removing or ablating the disease, suppressing the disease, and/or addressing pain and fertility therapies adjunctively (Table 155-2).

### MEDICAL

For the treatment of endometriosis-related pelvic pain, the goal of medical therapy is to suppress endogenous $E_2$ in the circulation or locally produced by endometriotic lesions, minimize cyclic menstrual bleeding, and inhibit pain-causing factors within the peritoneal cavity.[141,142] This goal is achieved by a variety of approaches, including danazol (Danocrine) therapy,[143] continuous oral contraceptives,[144,145] long-acting progestins,[142] gonadotropin-releasing hormone (GnRH) agonists,[144] and, recently, aromatase inhibitors[146] usually coupled with nonsteroidal anti-inflammatory drugs (NSAIDs). The mechanism of action of the hormone-based therapies primarily involves inhibition of ovulation and minimization of menstrual blood volume and flow. NSAIDs are a useful adjunct in pain management because of their inhibition of prostaglandin synthesis (see earlier). Most medical therapies achieve relief of symptoms in up to 90% of women. Long-term use of these medications, however, may be limited by their side effects, especially in the case of Danocrine, which has unwanted androgenic side effects. Unusual among the hormonal treatment options, however, is the immunosuppressive effects of danazol, which may add to its efficacy in the treatment of endometriosis.[141] Long-term hypoestrogenism is beneficial for

| Table 155-2 | Therapies for Endometriosis |
|---|---|

Medical
  Hormonal
    Oral contraceptives (noncycling)
    Long-acting progestins (Norplant, Depo-Provera)
    Danocrine
    GnRHa (nafarelin, leuprolide acetate)
  Other
    Nonsteroidal anti-inflammatory drugs
    Immunotherapy
Surgical
  Conservative therapy
    Laparoscopic ablation
    Laparoscopic excision
    Abdominal presacral neurectomy
    Laparoscopic presacral neurectomy
  Definitive therapy
    Hysterectomy/bilateral salpingo-oophorectomy

GnRHa, gonadotropin-releasing hormone agonist.

relief of symptoms and is achieved with GnRH agonists. Since this treatment results in a mostly reversible 13% decrease in bone density over a 6-month interval,[142] "add-back" therapy with low-dose estrogens and progestins has been advocated to reduce the side effects of hypoestrogenism and decreased bone density.[147] Cost limits their widespread use, however. Although most women continue to experience significant relief of pain, when medications are stopped, approximately 30% have recurrence of symptoms within 6 months after therapy.[148,149] New medical treatments for endometriosis are on the horizon and include progesterone receptor modulators, GnRH antagonists, aromatase inhibitors, TNF-α inhibitors, angiogenesis inhibitors, matrix metalloproteinase inhibitors, pentoxifylline (and other general immune modulators), and estrogen receptor β agonists.[150]

Hormonal therapies have not had the success in fertility enhancement that they have had in pain management.[142] Surgical ablation of the disease has more promise than medical therapies in enhancing fertility (see later). Historically, endometriosis-related infertility has been treated with controlled ovarian hyperstimulation coupled with intrauterine insemination, or assisted reproduction. In view of recent observations regarding lack of expression of $\alpha_v\beta_3$ integrin during the window of implantation in approximately 50% of women with endometriosis, it is prudent to determine the integrin (or "receptivity") status of the endometrium before initiating these therapies. If $\alpha_v\beta_3$ is absent, surgical ablation of endometriosis or a 3-month trial of GnRH agonist therapy may restore normal $\alpha_v\beta_3$ expression.[151] Subsequent use of fertility protocols, versus expectant management, would then depend on other factors, such as male factor, patient age, ovarian reserve, and cost.

Due to observations of increased prevalence of autoimmunity and reactivity to environmental and opportunistic allergens in women with endometriosis (see earlier), immunotherapy has recently been entertained.[152] This therapy involves desensitization with low doses of the offending allergen (e.g., *Candida albicans*, estrogen, chemicals, foods) such that the allergic response is reduced or eliminated. Prospective, randomized controlled studies are needed to confirm the efficacy of this therapy.

### SURGICAL

Surgical therapy for endometriosis is primarily by laparoscopy, during which endometriosis is either ablated or excised.[1,153] In women who have successful pain relief, however, symptoms recur in 12% to 54% within a year of therapy.[154] This observation suggests that adjunctive medical therapy be helpful, and indeed both preoperative and postoperative medical therapies have been efficacious.[155] Ovarian endometriomas and extensive disease in the cul-de-sac must be completely resected for successful relief of pain. Presacral neurectomy for the control of pelvic pain is about 80% successful[156] and is usually performed by laparotomy or, in carefully chosen patients, by laparoscopy.[157] Definitive surgery for recalcitrant pelvic pain is total hysterectomy and bilateral salpingo-oophorectomy. This technique may be performed by laparotomy or as a laparoscopically assisted vaginal procedure.

Laparoscopic ablation of minimal/mild endometriosis has been shown to enhance pregnancy rates in a meta-analysis of nonrandomized studies[158] and is significantly better than expectant management, hormonal therapies,[159] or laparotomy.[1] There was sufficient heterogeneity among the studies, however, so two randomized controlled trial were performed. A Canadian study, ENDOCAN, randomized 341 women with stage I or II endometriosis, followed them for 36 weeks postoperatively, and determined that the rate of pregnancy was significantly higher in the surgically treated group (30.7% vs. 17.7%). A second multi-center study, however, performed in Italy with 101 subjects demonstrated a live birthrate of 19.6% in the treatment group and 22.2% in the controls. Combining the results of these two studies into a meta-analysis favors surgical treatment (odds ratio for pregnancy = 1.7; 95% confidence limits = 1.1–2.5).[160] By reducing disease load, the inflammatory response within the pelvis is decreased. Based on known actions of the mitogens, morphogens, chemoattractants, and angiogenic factors within the peritoneal fluid, it is likely that a reduction in these factors will result in an environment that is more favorable for sperm and embryo survival.

## SUMMARY

Endometriosis may be a result of modern advances in the twentieth century, including contraception (decreased frequency of pregnancy and thus greater numbers of menses during a woman's reproductive lifetime), hormonal replacement therapy, and modern industrial development with its attendant immunotoxicants and estrogen-like compounds. Advances in basic and clinical research on the pathophysiology of endometriosis have already begun to direct therapies to minimize pain or maximize fertility. The ultimate therapy for this disorder is prevention, however. Hysterectomy for endometriosis increased dramatically between 1965 and 1984,[161] probably because of an increased awareness of the presence of endometriosis and perhaps because of an increasing incidence of the disorder. A major global effort to minimize environmental toxins, coupled with pharmacologic suppression of menses, would ideally reduce the incidence of this disease. Although this result may be long in coming, patient advocacy, education, and support, coupled with basic and clinical research in endometriosis, should also be high priorities in a national women's health agenda.

## REFERENCES

1. Metzger D: Endometriosis. In Rakel RE (ed): Conn's Current Therapy. Philadelphia, WB Saunders, 1998.
2. Fedele L, Parazzini F, Bianchi S, et al: Stage and localization of pelvic endometriosis and pain. Fertil Steril 53:155–158, 1990.
3. Muzii L, Marana R, Pedulla S, et al: Correlation between endometriosis-associated dysmenorrhea and the presence of typical or atypical lesions. Fertil Steril 68:1922, 1997.
4. Dizerega GS, Barber DL, Hodgen GD: Endometriosis: Role of ovarian steroids in initiation, maintenance, and suppression. Fertil Steril 33:649–653, 1980.
5. Sampson J: Ovarian hematomas of endometrial type (perforating hemorrhagic cysts of the ovary) and implantation adenomas of endometrial type. Boston Med Surg J 186:445, 1922.
6. MacKenzie WF, Casey HW: Animal model of human disease: Endometriosis. Animal model: Endometriosis in rhesus monkeys. Am J Pathol 80:341–344, 1975.
7. Punnonen R, Klemi PJ, Nikkanen V: Postmenopausal endometriosis. Eur J Obstet Gynecol Reprod Biol 11:195–200, 1980.
8. von Rokitansky C: Ueber uterusdrusen-Neubildung in uterus and ovarilsarcomen. Z Gesellschaft Aerzte Wien 37:577–593, 1860.
9. Sampson J: Peritoneal endometriosis due to menstrual dissemination of endometrial tisue into the peritoneal cavity. Am J Obstet Gynecol 14:422–469, 1927.
10. Meyer R: Uber den Stande der frage der Adenomyositis und adenomyome in allgemeinen und insbesondere uber adenomyositis seroepithelialis und adenomyometritis sacromatosa. Zentrab Gynakol 36:745, 1919.
11. Gruenwald P: Origin of endometriosis from the mesenchyme of the coelomic walls. Am J Obstet Gynecol 44:470–474, 1942.
12. Halme J, Hammond MG, Hulka JF, et al: Retrograde menstruation in healthy women and in patients with endometriosis. Obstet Gynecol 64:151–154, 1984.
13. Ayers JW: Utero-tubal hypotonia associated with pelvic endometriosis. Proceedings of the American Fertility Society. Seattle, WA, 1985, p 131.
14. Salamanca A, Beltran E: Subendometrial contractility in menstrual phase visualized by transvaginal sonography in patients with endometriosis. Fertil Steril 64:193–195, 1995.
15. D'Hooghe TM: Clinical relevance of the baboon as a model for the study of endometriosis. Fertil Steril 68:613–625, 1997.
16. Olive DL, Henderson DY: Endometriosis and müllerian anomalies. Obstet Gynecol 69:412–415, 1987.
17. Suginami H: A reappraisal of the coelomic metaplasia theory by reviewing endometriosis occurring in unusual sites and instances. Am J Obstet Gynecol 165:214–218, 1991.
18. Donnez J, Nisolle M, Gillerot S, et al: Rectovaginal septum adenomyotic nodules: A series of 500 cases. Br J Obstet Gynaecol 104:1014–1018, 1997.
19. Halban J: Lymphatic origin of so-called heterotopic adenofibromatosis. Arch Gynakol 124:457–468, 1925.
20. Haney AF, Muscato JJ, Weinberg JB: Peritoneal fluid cell populations in infertility patients. Fertil Steril 35:696–698, 1981.
21. Halme J, Becker S, Wing R: Accentuated cyclic activation of peritoneal macrophages in patients with endometriosis. Am J Obstet Gynecol 148:85–90, 1984.
22. Sidell N, Han SW, Parthasarathy S: Regulation and modulation of abnormal immune responses in endometriosis. Ann N Y Acad Sci 955:159–173; discussion 199–200, 396–406, 2002.
23. Lebovic DI, Mueller MD, Taylor RN: Immunobiology of endometriosis. Fertil Steril 75:1–10, 2001.
24. Dmowski WP: Immunologic aspects of endometriosis. In Diamond MP (ed): Endometrium and Endometriosis. Malden, MA, Blackwell, 1997, pp 174–181.
25. Gleicher N, el-Roeiy A, Confino E, et al: Is endometriosis an autoimmune disease? Obstet Gynecol 70:115–122, 1987.
26. Startseva NV: Clinico-immunological aspects of genital endometriosis. Akush Ginekol (Mosk) 3:23–26, 1980.
27. Kennedy SH, Nunn B, Cederholm-Williams SA, et al: Cardiolipin antibody levels in endometriosis and systemic lupus erythematosus. Fertil Steril 52:1061–1062, 1989.
28. Mathur S, Peress MR, Williamson HO, et al: Autoimmunity to endometrium and ovary in endometriosis. Clin Exp Immunol 50:259–266, 1982.
29. Kennedy SH, Sargent IL, Starkey PM, et al: Localization of anti-endometrial antibody binding in women with endometriosis using a double-labelling immunohistochemical method. Br J Obstet Gynaecol 97:671–674, 1990.
30. Sinaii N, Cleary SD, Ballweg ML, et al: High rates of autoimmune and endocrine disorders, fibromyalgia, chronic fatigue syndrome and atopic diseases among women with endometriosis: A survey analysis. Hum Reprod 17:2715–2724, 2002.
31. Kennedy S: The genetics of endometriosis. J Reprod Med 43:263–268, 1998.
32. Simpson JL, Elias S, Malinak LR, et al: Heritable aspects of endometriosis. I. Genetic studies. Am J Obstet Gynecol 137:327–331, 1980.
33. Moen MH, Magnus P: The familial risk of endometriosis. Acta Obstet Gynecol Scand 72:560–564, 1993.
34. Lamb K, Hoffmann RG, Nichols TR: Family trait analysis: A case-control study of 43 women with endometriosis and their best friends. Am J Obstet Gynecol 154:596–601, 1986.
35. Kennedy S, Hadfield R, Mardon H, et al: Age of onset of pain symptoms in non-twin sisters concordant for endometriosis. Hum Reprod 11:403–405, 1996.
36. Hadfield RM, Yudkin PL, Coe CL, et al: Risk factors for endometriosis in the rhesus monkey (*Macaca mulatta*): A

case-control study. Hum Reprod Update 3:109–115, 1997.

37. Fanton JW, Golden JG: Radiation-induced endometriosis in *Macaca mulatta*. Radiat Res 126:141–146, 1991.

38. Wood DH, Yochmowitz MG, Salmon YL, et al: Proton irradiation and endometriosis. Aviat Space Environ Med 54:718–724, 1983.

39. Presl J: [Endometriosis in monkeys and its relation to radiation exposure]. Cesk Gynekol 58:194–195, 1993.

40. Rier SE, Martin DC, Bowman RE, et al: Endometriosis in rhesus monkeys (*Macaca mulatta*) following chronic exposure to 2,3,7, 8-tetrachlorodibenzo-p-dioxin. Fundam Appl Toxicol 21:433–441, 1993.

41. Cummings AM, Metcalf JL, Birnbaum L: Promotion of endometriosis by 2,3,7,8-tetrachlorodibenzo-p-dioxin in rats and mice: time-dose dependence and species comparison. Toxicol Appl Pharmacol 138:131–139, 1996.

42. Yang JZ, Foster WG: Continuous exposure to 2,3,7, 8-tetrachlorodibenzo-p-dioxin inhibits the growth of surgically induced endometriosis in the ovariectomized mouse treated with high dose estradiol. Toxicol Ind Health 13:15–25, 1997.

43. Koninckx PR, Braet P, Kennedy SH, et al: Dioxin pollution and endometriosis in Belgium. Hum Reprod 9:1001–1002, 1994.

44. De Felip E, Porpora MG, di Domenico A, et al: Dioxin-like compounds and endometriosis: A study on Italian and Belgian women of reproductive age. Toxicol Lett 150:203–209, 2004.

45. Schena M, Shalon D, Davis RW, et al: Quantitative monitoring of gene expression patterns with a complementary DNA microarray. Science 270:467–470, 1995.

46. Kao LC, Germeyer A, Tulac S, et al: Expression profiling of endometrium from women with endometriosis reveals candidate genes for disease-based implantation failure and infertility. Endocrinology 144:2870–2881, 2003.

47. Arimoto T, Katagiri T, Oda K, et al: Genome-wide cDNA microarray analysis of gene-expression profiles involved in ovarian endometriosis. Int J Oncol 22:551–560, 2003.

48. Gogusev J, Bouquet de Joliniere J, Telvi L, et al: Detection of DNA copy number changes in human endometriosis by comparative genomic hybridization. Hum Genet 105:444–451, 1999.

49. Wang Y, Guo SW: Statistical methods for detecting genomic alterations through array-based comparative genomic hybridization (CGH). Front Biosci 9:540–549, 2004.

50. Kosugi Y, Elias S, Malinak LR, et al: Increased heterogeneity of chromosome 17 aneuploidy in endometriosis. Am J Obstet Gynecol 180:792–797, 1999.

51. Giudice LC, Tazuke SI, Swiersz L: Status of current research on endometriosis. J Reprod Med 43:252–262, 1998.

52. Hopwood D, Levison DA: Atrophy and apoptosis in the cyclical human endometrium. J Pathol 119:159–166, 1976.

53. Kokawa K, Shikone T, Nakano R: Apoptosis in the human uterine endometrium during the menstrual cycle. J Clin Endocrinol Metab 81:4144–4147, 1996.

54. Gebel HM, Braun DP, Tambur A, et al: Spontaneous apoptosis of endometrial tissue is impaired in women with endometriosis. Fertil Steril 69:1042–1047, 1998.

55. Witz CA, Cho S, Centonze VE, et al: Time series analysis of transmesothelial invasion by endometrial stromal and epithelial cells using three-dimensional confocal microscopy. Fertil Steril 79(Suppl 1):770–778, 2003.

56. Witz CA: Cell adhesion molecules and endometriosis. Semin Reprod Med 21:173–182, 2003.

57. van der Linden PJ, de Goeij AF, Dunselman GA, et al: Expression of integrins and E-cadherin in cells from menstrual effluent, endometrium, peritoneal fluid, peritoneum, and endometriosis. Fertil Steril 61:85–90, 1994.

58. Matrisian LM: The matrix-degrading metalloproteinases. Bioessays 14:455–463, 1992.

59. Gomez DE, Alonso DF, Yoshiji H, et al: Tissue inhibitors of metalloproteinases: structure, regulation and biological functions. Eur J Cell Biol 74:111–122, 1997.

60. Rodgers WH, Matrisian LM, Giudice LC, et al: Patterns of matrix metalloproteinase expression in cycling endometrium imply differential functions and regulation by steroid hormones. J Clin Invest 94:946–953, 1994.

61. Osteen KG, Bruner KL, Sharpe-Timms KL: Steroid and growth factor regulation of matrix metalloproteinase expression and endometriosis. Semin Reprod Endocrinol 14:247–255, 1996.

62. Salamonsen LA, Woolley DE: Matrix metalloproteinases in normal menstruation. Hum Reprod 11(Suppl 2):124–133, 1996.

63. Rodgers WH, Osteen KG, Matrisian LM, et al: Expression and localization of matrilysin, a matrix metalloproteinase, in human endometrium during the reproductive cycle. Am J Obstet Gynecol 168:253–260, 1993.

64. Marbaix E, Donnez J, Courtoy PJ, et al: Progesterone regulates the activity of collagenase and related gelatinases A and B in human endometrial explants. Proc Natl Acad Sci U S A 89:11789–11793, 1992.

65. Irwin JC, Kirk D, Gwatkin RB, et al: Human endometrial matrix metalloproteinase-2, a putative menstrual proteinase: Hormonal regulation in cultured stromal cells and messenger RNA expression during the menstrual cycle. J Clin Invest 97:438–447, 1996.

66. Schatz F, Papp C, Aigner S, et al: Biological mechanisms underlying the clinical effects of RU486: Modulation of cultured endometrial stromal cell stromelysin-1 and prolactin expression. J Clin Endocrinol Metab 82:188–193, 1997.

67. Saito T, Mizumoto H, Kuroki K, et al: [Expression of MMP-3 and TIMP-1 in the endometriosis and the influence of danazol]. Nippon Sanka Fujinka Gakkai Zasshi 47:495–496, 1995.

68. Kokorine I, Nisolle M, Donnez J, et al: Expression of interstitial collagenase (matrix metalloproteinase-1) is related to the activity of human endometriotic lesions. Fertil Steril 68:246–251, 1997.

69. Sharpe-Timms KL, Penney LL, Zimmer RL, et al: Partial purification and amino acid sequence analysis of endometriosis protein-II (ENDO-II) reveals homology with tissue inhibitor of metalloproteinases-1 (TIMP-1). J Clin Endocrinol Metab 80:3784–3787, 1995.

70. Bruner-Tran KL, Eisenberg E, Yeaman GR, et al: Steroid and cytokine regulation of matrix metalloproteinase expression in endometriosis and the establishment of experimental endometriosis in nude mice. J Clin Endocrinol Metab 87:4782–4791, 2002.

71. Mulayim N, Savlu A, Guzeloglu-Kayisli O, et al: Regulation of endometrial stromal cell matrix metalloproteinase activity and invasiveness by interleukin-8. Fertil Steril 81(Suppl 1):904–911, 2004.

72. Ueda M, Yamashita Y, Takehara M, et al: Gene expression of adhesion molecules and matrix metalloproteinases in endometriosis. Gynecol Endocrinol 16:391–402, 2002.

73. Liu XJ, He YL, Peng DX: Expression of metalloproteinase-9 in ectopic endometrium in women with endometriosis. Di Yi Jun Yi Da Xue Xue Bao 22:467–469, 2002.

74. Chung HW, Lee JY, Moon HS, et al: Matrix metalloproteinase-2, membranous type 1 matrix metalloproteinase, and tissue inhibitor of metalloproteinase-2 expression in ectopic and eutopic endometrium. Fertil Steril 78:787–795, 2002.

75. Ueda M, Yamashita Y, Takehara M, et al: Survivin gene expression in endometriosis. J Clin Endocrinol Metab 87:3452–3459, 2002.

76. Bruner KL, Matrisian LM, Rodgers WH, et al: Suppression of matrix metalloproteinases inhibits establishment of ectopic lesions by human endometrium in nude mice. J Clin Invest 99:2851–2857, 1997.

77. Ramey JW, Archer DF: Peritoneal fluid: Its relevance to the development of endometriosis. Fertil Steril 60:1–14, 1993.

78. Oral E, Arici A: Peritoneal growth factors and endometriosis. Semin Reprod Endocrinol 14:257–267, 1996.

79. Ryan IP, Taylor RN: Endometriosis and infertility: New concepts. Obstet Gynecol Surv 52:365–371, 1997.

80. Fukaya T, Sugawara J, Yoshida H, et al: The role of macrophage colony stimulating factor in the peritoneal fluid in infertile patients with endometriosis. Tohoku J Exp Med 172:221–226, 1994.

81. Fakih H, Baggett B, Holtz G, et al: Interleukin-1: A possible role in the infertility associated with endometriosis. Fertil Steril 47:213–217, 1987.

82. Hill JA, Anderson DJ: Lymphocyte activity in the presence of peritoneal fluid from fertile women and infertile women with and without endometriosis. Am J Obstet Gynecol 161:861–864, 1989.

83. Koyama N, Matsuura K, Okamura H: Cytokines in the peritoneal fluid of patients with endometriosis. Int J Gynaecol Obstet 43:45–50, 1993.

84. Rier SE, Zarmakoupis PN, Hu X, et al: Dysregulation of interleukin-6 responses in ectopic endometrial stromal cells: Correlation with decreased soluble receptor levels in peritoneal fluid of women with endometriosis. J Clin Endocrinol Metab 80:1431–1437, 1995.

85. Tseng JF, Ryan IP, Milam TD, et al: Interleukin-6 secretion in vitro is upregulated in ectopic and eutopic endometrial stromal cells from women with endometriosis. J Clin Endocrinol Metab 81:1118–1122, 1996.

86. Overton C, Fernandez-Shaw S, Hicks B, et al: Peritoneal fluid cytokines and the relationship with endometriosis and pain. Hum Reprod 11:380–386, 1996.

87. Punnonen J, Teisala K, Ranta H, et al: Increased levels of interleukin-6 and interleukin-10 in the peritoneal fluid of patients with endometriosis. Am J Obstet Gynecol 174:1522–1526, 1996.

88. Harada T, Yoshioka H, Yoshida S, et al: Increased interleukin-6 levels in peritoneal fluid of infertile patients with active endometriosis. Am J Obstet Gynecol 176:593–597, 1997.

89. Eisermann J, Gast MJ, Pineda J, et al: Tumor necrosis factor in peritoneal fluid of women undergoing laparoscopic surgery. Fertil Steril 50:573–579, 1988.

90. Halme J: Role of peritoneal inflammation in endometriosis-associated infertility. Ann N Y Acad Sci 622:266–274, 1991.

91. Ryan IP, Tseng JF, Schriock ED, et al: Interleukin-8 concentrations are elevated in peritoneal fluid of women with endometriosis. Fertil Steril 63:929–932, 1995.

92. Arici A, Tazuke SI, Attar E, et al: Interleukin-8 concentration in peritoneal fluid of patients with endometriosis and modulation of interleukin-8 expression in human mesothelial cells. Mol Hum Reprod 2:40–45, 1996.

93. Akoum A, Lemay A, Brunet C, et al: Secretion of monocyte chemotactic protein-1 by cytokine-stimulated endometrial cells of women with endometriosis. Le groupe d'investigation en gynecologie. Fertil Steril 63:322–328, 1995.

94. Akoum A, Lemay A, McColl S, et al: Elevated concentration and biologic activity of monocyte chemotactic protein-1 in the peritoneal fluid of patients with endometriosis. Fertil Steril 66:17–23, 1996.

95. Jolicoeur C, Boutouil M, Drouin R, et al: Increased expression of monocyte chemotactic protein-1 in the endometrium of women with endometriosis. Am J Pathol 152:125–133, 1998.

96. Khorram O, Taylor RN, Ryan IP, et al: Peritoneal fluid concentrations of the cytokine RANTES correlate with the severity of endometriosis. Am J Obstet Gynecol 169:1545–1549, 1993.

97. Hornung D, Ryan IP, Chao VA, et al: Immunolocalization and regulation of the chemokine RANTES in human endometrial and endometriosis tissues and cells. J Clin Endocrinol Metab 82:1621–1628, 1997.

98. Oosterlynck DJ, Meuleman C, Waer M, et al: Transforming growth factor-beta activity is increased in peritoneal fluid from women with endometriosis. Obstet Gynecol 83:287–292, 1994.

99. Halme J, White C, Kauma S, et al: Peritoneal macrophages from patients with endometriosis release growth factor activity in vitro. J Clin Endocrinol Metab 66:1044–1049, 1988.

100. Huang JC, Papasakelariou C, Dawood MY: Epidermal growth factor and basic fibroblast growth factor in peritoneal fluid of women with endometriosis. Fertil Steril 65:931–934, 1996.

101. De Leon FD, Vijayakumar R, Brown M, et al: Peritoneal fluid volume, estrogen, progesterone, prostaglandin, and epidermal growth factor concentrations in patients with and without endometriosis. Obstet Gynecol 68:189–194, 1986.

102. Giudice LC, Dsupin BA, Gargosky SE, et al: The insulin-like growth factor system in human peritoneal fluid: Its effects on endometrial stromal cells and its potential relevance to endometriosis. J Clin Endocrinol Metab 79:1284–1293, 1994.

103. Sbracia M, Zupi E, Alo P, et al: Differential expression of IGF-1 and IGF-2 in eutopic and ectopic endometria of women with endometriosis and in women without endometriosis. Am J Reprod Immunol 37:326–329, 1997.

104. Chang SY, Ho YS: Immunohistochemical analysis of insulin-like growth factor 1, insulin-like growth factor 1 receptor and insulin-like growth factor 2 in endometriotic tissue and endometrium. Acta Obstet Gynecol Scand 76:112–117, 1997.

105. Sugawara J, Fukaya T, Murakami T, et al: Increased secretion of hepatocyte growth factor by eutopic endometrial stromal cells in women with endometriosis. Fertil Steril 68:468–472, 1997.

106. Oosterlynck DJ, Meuleman C, Sobis H, et al: Angiogenic activity of peritoneal fluid from women with endometriosis. Fertil Steril 59:778–782, 1993.

107. Shifren JL, Tseng JF, Zaloudek CJ, et al: Ovarian steroid regulation of vascular endothelial growth factor in the human endometrium: Implications for angiogenesis during the menstrual cycle and in the pathogenesis of endometriosis. J Clin Endocrinol Metab 81:3112–3118, 1996.

108. Zeitoun KM, Bulun SE: Aromatase: a key molecule in the pathophysiology of endometriosis and a therapeutic target. Fertil Steril 72:961–969, 1999.

109. Zeitoun K, Takayama K, Sasano H, et al: Deficient 17β-hydroxysteroid dehydrogenase type 2 expression in endometriosis: Failure to metabolize 17β-estradiol. J Clin Endocrinol Metab 83:4474–4480, 1998.

110. Bulun SE, Zeitoun KM, Takayama K, et al: Molecular basis for treating endometriosis with aromatase inhibitors. Hum Reprod Update 6:413–418, 2000.

111. Steele RW, Dmowski WP, Marmer DJ: Immunologic aspects of human endometriosis. Am J Reprod Immunol 6:33–36, 1984.

112. Vigano P, Vercellini P, Di Blasio AM, et al: Deficient antiendometrium lymphocyte-mediated cytotoxicity in patients with endometriosis. Fertil Steril 56:894–899, 1991.

113. Oosterlynck DJ, Cornillie FJ, Waer M, et al: Women with endometriosis show a defect in natural killer activity resulting in a decreased cytotoxicity to autologous endometrium. Fertil Steril 56:45–51, 1991.

114. Oosterlynck DJ, Meuleman C, Waer M, et al: The natural killer activity of peritoneal fluid lymphocytes is decreased in women with endometriosis. Fertil Steril 58:290–295, 1992.

115. Kanzaki H, Wang HS, Kariya M, et al: Suppression of natural killer cell activity by sera from patients with endometriosis. Am J Obstet Gynecol 167:257–261, 1992.

116. Ho HN, Chao KH, Chen HF, et al: Peritoneal natural killer cytotoxicity and CD25+ CD3+ lymphocyte subpopulation are decreased in women with stage III–IV endometriosis. Hum Reprod 10:2671–2675, 1995.

117. Vigano P, Gaffuri B, Somigliana E, et al: Expression of intercellular adhesion molecule (ICAM)-1 mRNA and protein is enhanced in endometriosis versus endometrial stromal cells in culture. Mol Hum Reprod 4:1150–1156, 1998.

118. Evers JL: The defense against endometriosis. Fertil Steril 66:351–353, 1996.

119. Ramey JW, Booker SS, Kanbour-Shakir A, et al: Inability to establish ectopic endometrium in a natural killer cell–deficient murine model: Immunologic, histologic and histochemical assessment. J Reprod Med 41:807–814, 1996.

120. Cornillie FJ, Oosterlynck D, Lauweryns JM, et al: Deeply infiltrating pelvic endometriosis: Histology and clinical significance. Fertil Steril 53:978–983, 1990.

121. Vernon MW, Beard JS, Graves K, et al: Classification of endometriotic

implants by morphologic appearance and capacity to synthesize prostaglandin F. Fertil Steril 46:801–806, 1986.

122. Ajossa S, Mais V, Guerriero S, et al: The prevalence of endometriosis in premenopausal women undergoing gynecological surgery. Clin Exp Obstet Gynecol 21:195–197, 1994.

123. Mahmood TA, Templeton A: Prevalence and genesis of endometriosis. Hum Reprod 6:544–549, 1991.

124. Grunert CM: Pathogenesis of infertility in endometriosis. In Nezhat CR BG, Nezhat FR, et al (eds): Endometriosis: Advanced Management and Surgical Techniques. New York, Springer-Velag, 1995, pp 45–59.

125. Oak MK, Chantler EN, Williams CA, et al: Sperm survival studies in peritoneal fluid from infertile women with endometriosis and unexplained infertility. Clin Reprod Fertil 3:297–303, 1985.

126. Burke RK: Effect of peritoneal washings from women with endometriosis on sperm velocity. J Reprod Med 32:743–746, 1987.

127. Coddington CC, Oehninger S, Cunningham DS, et al: Peritoneal fluid from patients with endometriosis decreases sperm binding to the zona pellucida in the hemizona assay: A preliminary report. Fertil Steril 57:783–786, 1992.

128. Morcos RN, Gibbons WE, Findley WE: Effect of peritoneal fluid on in vitro cleavage of 2-cell mouse embryos: Possible role in infertility associated with endometriosis. Fertil Steril 44:678–683, 1985.

129. Taketani Y, Kuo TM, Mizuno M: Comparison of cytokine levels and embryo toxicity in peritoneal fluid in infertile women with untreated or treated endometriosis. Am J Obstet Gynecol 167:265–270, 1992.

130. Lessey BA, Castelbaum AJ, Sawin SW, et al: Aberrant integrin expression in the endometrium of women with endometriosis. J Clin Endocrinol Metab 79:643–649, 1994.

131. Murphy AA: Clinical endometriosis. In Yoshinaga K (ed): Endometriosis: Emerging Research and Intervention Strategies, vol 955. New York, New York Academy of Sciences, 2002, pp 1–3.

132. Barbieri RL, Niloff JM, Bast RC Jr, et al: Elevated serum concentrations of CA-125 in patients with advanced endometriosis. Fertil Steril 45:630–634, 1986.

133. Koninckx PR, Riittinen L, Seppala M, et al: CA-125 and placental protein 14 concentrations in plasma and peritoneal fluid of women with deeply infiltrating pelvic endometriosis. Fertil Steril 57:523–530, 1992.

134. Telimaa S, Kauppila A, Ronnberg L, et al: Elevated serum levels of endometrial secretory protein PP14 in patients with advanced endometriosis: Suppression by treatment with danazol and high-dose medroxyprogesterone acetate. Am J Obstet Gynecol 161:866–871, 1989.

135. Cornillie FJ, Lauweryns JM, Seppala M, et al: Expression of endometrial protein PP14 in pelvic and ovarian endometriotic implants. Hum Reprod 6:1411–1415, 1991.

136. Badawy SZ, Cuenca V, Stitzel A, et al: Autoimmune phenomena in infertile patients with endometriosis. Obstet Gynecol 63:271–275, 1984.

137. Arrive L, Hricak H, Martin MC: Pelvic endometriosis: MR imaging. Radiology 171:687–692, 1989.

138. Carbognin G, Guarise A, Minelli L, et al: US and MRI features of pelvic endometriosis. Abdom Imaging 29:609–618, 2004.

139. Mahmood TA, Templeton A: The impact of treatment on the natural history of endometriosis. Hum Reprod 5:965–970, 1990.

140. D'Hooghe TM, Bambra CS, Isahakia M, et al: Evolution of spontaneous endometriosis in the baboon (Papio anubis, Papio cynocephalus) over a 12-month period. Fertil Steril 58:409–412, 1992.

141. Dmowski W: The role of medical management in the treatment of endometriosis. In Nezhat CR, Nezhat FR, et al (eds): Endometriosis: Advanced Management and Surgical Techniques. New York, Springer-Verlag, 1995, pp 229–240.

142. Metzger D: Treatment of infertility associated with endometriosis. In Nezhat CR, Nezhat FR, et al (eds): Endometriosis: Advanced Management and Surgical Techniques. New York, Springer-Verlag, 1995, pp 245–256.

143. Dmowski WP: Danazol-induced pseudomenopause in the management of endometriosis. Clin Obstet Gynecol 31:829–839, 1988.

144. Vercellini P, Trespidi L, Colombo A, et al: A gonadotropin-releasing hormone agonist versus a low-dose oral contraceptive for pelvic pain associated with endometriosis. Fertil Steril 60:75–79, 1993.

145. Vessey MP, Villard-Mackintosh L, Painter R: Epidemiology of endometriosis in women attending family planning clinics. Br Med J 306:182–184, 1993.

146. Ailawadi RK, Jobanputra S, Kataria M, et al: Treatment of endometriosis and chronic pelvic pain with letrozole and norethindrone acetate: A pilot study. Fertil Steril 81:290–296, 2004.

147. Schlaff W: Benefits of hormonal add-back therapy. In Rock J (ed): Current Management of Endometriosis. New York, HP Publishing, 1994, pp 14–19.

148. Dlugi AM, Miller JD, Knittle J: Lupron depot (leuprolide acetate for depot suspension) in the treatment of endometriosis: A randomized, placebo-controlled, double-blind study. Lupron Study Group. Fertil Steril 54:419–427, 1990.

149. Fedele L, Bianchi S, Bocciolone L, et al: Buserelin acetate in the treatment of pelvic pain associated with minimal and mild endometriosis: A controlled study. Fertil Steril 59:516–521, 1993.

150. Olive DL, Lindheim SR, Pritts EA: New medical treatments for endometriosis. Best Pract Res Clin Obstet Gynaecol 18:319–328, 2004.

151. Lessey BA: Implantation defects in infertile women with endometriosis. Ann N Y Acad Sci 955:265–280; discussion 293–265, 396–406, 2002.

152. Ballweg M: Immunotherapy for endometriosis: The science behind a promising new treatment. In Diamond MP (ed): Endometrium and Endometriosis. Cambridge, MA, Blackwell, 1997, pp 367–376.

153. Martin D: Rational for surgical treatment of endometriosis. In Nezhat CR, Nezhat FR, et al (eds): Endometriosis: Advanced Management and Surgical Techniques. New York, Springer-Verlag, 1995, pp 69–76.

154. Candiani GB, Fedele L, Vercellini P, et al: Repetitive conservative surgery for recurrence of endometriosis. Obstet Gynecol 77:421–424, 1991.

155. Buttram V: Rationale for combined medical and surgical treatment of endometriosis. In Nezhat CR, Nezhat FR, et al (eds): Endometriosis: Advanced Mangement and Surgical Techniques. New York, Springer-Verlag, 1995, pp 241–244.

156. Vercellini P, Fedele L, Bianchi S, et al: Pelvic denervation for chronic pain associated with endometriosis: Fact or fancy? Am J Obstet Gynecol 165:745–749, 1991.

157. Perez JJ: Laparoscopic presacral neurectomy: Results of the first 25 cases. J Reprod Med 35:625–630, 1990.

158. Hughes EG, Fedorkow DM, Collins JA: A quantitative overview of controlled trials in endometriosis-associated infertility. Fertil Steril 59:963–970, 1993.

159. Adamson GD, Pasta DJ: Surgical treatment of endometriosis-associated infertility: Meta-analysis compared with survival analysis. Am J Obstet Gynecol 171:1488–1504; discussion 1504–1485, 1994.

160. Olive DL, Pritts EA: The treatment of endometriosis: A review of the evidence. Ann N Y Acad Sci 955:360–372; discussion 389–393, 396–406, 2002.

161. Statistics NCHS: Hysterectomies in the United States, 1965–84. Hyattsville, MD, National Center for Health Statistics, Vital and Health Statistics, 1987, pp 88–1753.

# Female Subfertility: Evaluation and Management

*Bart C. J. M. Fauser and Joop S. E. Laven*

## INTRODUCTION

Infertility is generally defined as the inability to conceive within 1 year of regular unprotected intercourse. Fecundability is the probability of achieving a pregnancy within a given menstrual cycle. Finally, the term *fecundity* represents the capacity of a couple to achieve a live birth. One in every six couples visits a physician because of an unfulfilled wish for children. The 1-year period is chosen arbitrarily and is mainly based on the assessment of the likelihood for pregnancy (Fig. 156-1). Infertility should be viewed as a problem of the couple and, therefore, the medical attention should focus on both partners. Chances are roughly similar for finding some form of reproductive dysfunction in the male as in the female. Abnormalities may also be found in both the male and female partner.

Opposite to what most patients believe, a situation of (absolute) infertility rarely exists. No chance of conception (i.e., sterility) only occurs in rare cases of amenorrhea, bilateral tubal occlusion, or azoospermia. Therefore, the term *subfertility* seems more accurate in describing a condition of diminished natural fertility. Decreased fertility of a given individual may be well compensated for by enhanced fertility of the partner. These couples may generate offspring without difficulty and therefore never visit a doctor. The true clinical challenge is to assess chances for pregnancy, either spontaneously or after infertility treatment, of a given couple visiting an infertility clinic. The proposed management algorithm for a couple may include distinctly different options, ranging from expectant management without intervention, causal therapy, or assisted reproduction as an empiric approach to increasing chances for offspring.

Primary (as opposed to secondary) subfertility involves individuals (or couples) with no previous pregnancy. Today, physicians see many couples in the Western world with different reproductive histories with previous partners (marriages). Although the debate continues as to whether subfertility should be considered a disease, the major impact of involuntary childlessness on psychosocial well-being and quality of life should not be underestimated. According to the World Health Organization (WHO), health should be defined as "a state of complete physical, mental and social well-being and not merely the absence of disease or infirmity." Infertility, therefore, constitutes an unhealthy state. For the benefit of the general public, the clinician should voice clearly and consistently to politicians and health-care providers the message that subfertility should be considered a serious health issue since the majority of people worldwide still have insufficient access to infertility services.

## HISTORY

Infertility care is a relatively young subspecialty that really only started in the early 1960s. The first 2 decades were dominated by the possibilities of endocrine diagnosis and treatments and surgical procedures. Gonadotropin and steroid hormone assays were developed for widespread clinical use, and the synthetic antiestrogen clomiphene citrate and urinary gonadotropins (human menopausal gonadotropin, obtained from postmenopausal women excreting large quantities of pituitary follicle-stimulating hormone [FSH] and luteinizing hormone [LH]) became available for stimulating gonadal function in both males and females. Initial surgical approaches in the female involved wedge resection of polycystic ovaries, followed by microsurgery of endometriotic cysts and uterine myomas, adhesions, and tubal disease, and, more recently, by endoscopic pelvic surgery and hysteroscopy. Surgical approaches in the male have been dominated by varicocele correction in attempts to improve sperm quality. Most of these initial surgical approaches have not proven efficacious when vigorous methods of assessment are applied.[1,2]

The past 2 decades have been dominated by the development of assisted reproductive techniques, chiefly intrauterine insemination (IUI), in vitro fertilization (IVF) in 1979,[3] and intracytoplasmic sperm injection (ICSI) in 1992.[4] These novel in vitro therapeutic strategies, combined with complex ovarian hyperstimulation protocols, have created new possibilities for offspring for thousands of couples with no chances for a child otherwise. These treatments are successful, but have disadvantages in terms of patient discomfort, complications, and high cost. This empiric approach has largely replaced conventional causal therapies, with consequent reduced interest in the mechanisms underlying decreased

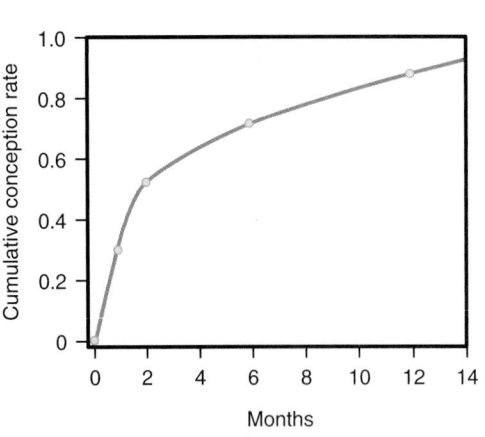

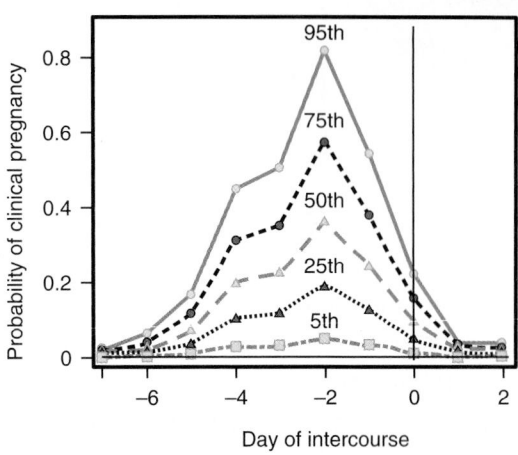

*Figure 156-1* **Left panel,** Cumulative conception rates during the first 12 months of unprotected intercourse. **Right panel,** Probability of a clinical pregnancy relative to the day of intercourse. Day 0 depicts the day of the serum luteinizing hormone (LH) surge. Individual lines depict 5th to 95th percentiles of the total population. (Left panel from Taylor A: ABC of Subfertility: The extent of the problem. Br Med J 327:434–436, 2003. Right panel from Evers JL: Female subfertility. Lancet 360:151–159, 2002.)

fertility, which may have a negative impact on future development of novel causal treatment options. Due to changes in society and the commercial environment in which IVF is usually practiced, we have reached a paradoxical state with overconsumption of infertility therapies in some parts of the Western world and insufficient access to infertility care in many other societies. Fortunately, recent studies demonstrated that IVF should not replace a conventional treatment algorithm.[5,6]

## EPIDEMIOLOGY

In the general population, the highest chance of pregnancy occurs in the first cycle of unprotected intercourse. The maximal probability for a clinical pregnancy is about 30% per cycle, and chances for pregnancy are highest when intercourse takes place 2 days before ovulation[7] (see Fig. 156-1). The likelihood of pregnancy slowly decreases in subsequent cycles, generating a cumulative chance for pregnancy of 60% within three cycles, 70% within six cycles, and around 90% within a year[8] (see Fig. 156-1). Very fertile couples are likely to achieve a pregnancy within the first few cycles,

whereas others will conceive within 12 months (Table 156-1). Moreover, a considerable proportion of couples will still conceive spontaneously after 1 year (Fig. 156-2 and Fig. 156-3). As mentioned previously, a 1-year period has arbitrarily been chosen as the cutoff to define subfertility and justify an infertility workup. Subfertility is described as occurring in around 10% to 15% of the population.

Multiple tendencies interfering with normal fertility have been described, especially: (1) early sexarche and promiscuous sexual behavior (resulting in increased chances for tubal disease due to sexually transmitted disease), (2) postponement of pregnancy and consequently an increased proportion of women older than 30 years of age when offspring is desired, (3) female lifestyle factors (especially obesity and resulting ovarian dysfunction), and (4) environmental and toxic agents (for instance, cigarette smoking inducing accelerated follicle pool depletion). Consequently, more couples will not conceive spontaneously within a year of unprotected intercourse and will, therefore, visit a doctor for subfertility care. Current data suggest that around one in six couples attend an infertility clinic during their reproductive life. Surprisingly, it appears that the prevalence of subfertility in the Western

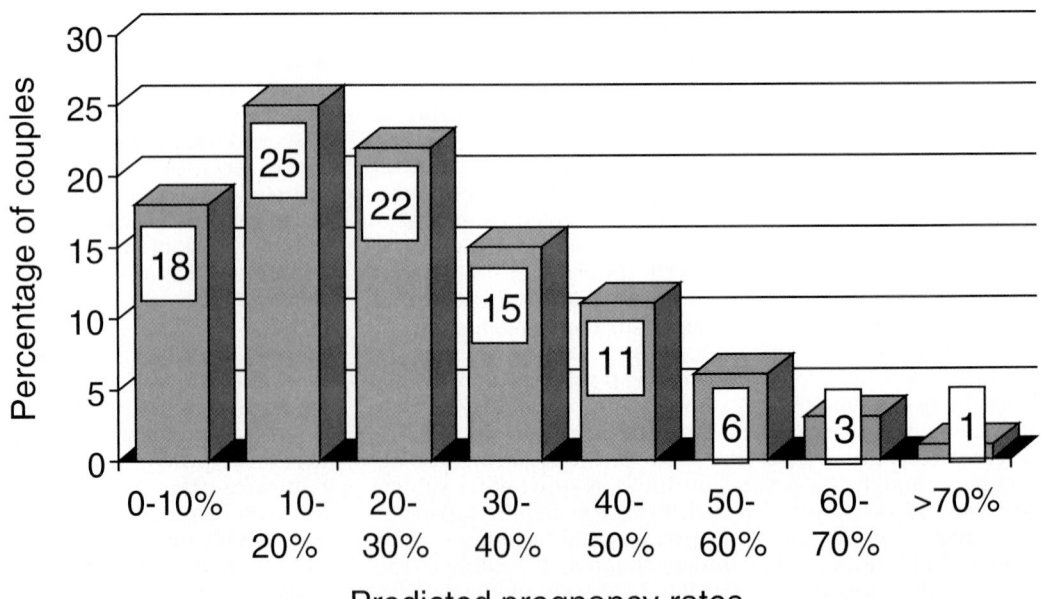

*Figure 156-2* The distribution of pregnancy rates among untreated subfertile couples within the year between intake (defined as having had at least 1 year of unprotected intercourse) and the occurrence of the first pregnancy. (From Eimers JM, te Velde ER, Gerritse R, et al: The prediction of the chance to conceive in subfertile couples. Fertil Steril 61:44–52, 1994.)

| Table 156-1 | Estimated Spontaneous Cumulative Pregnancy Rates in Normal Fertile and Infertile Couples* |

| | Monthly Fecundity Rate | Cumulative Pregnancy Rate | | | |
|---|---|---|---|---|---|
| | | 6 | 12 | 24 | 60 |
| Superfertile | 60% | 100% | | | |
| Normally fertile | 20% | 74% | 93% | 100% | |
| Moderately subfertile | 5% | 26% | 46% | 71% | 95% |
| Severely subfertile | 1% | 6% | 11% | 21% | 45% |
| Infertile | 0% | 0% | 0% | 0% | 0% |

*Rates over a given period of time, under conditions with different monthly fecundity rates.
From Evers JL: Female subfertility. Lancet 360:151–159, 2002.

world remains unaltered over the past 50 years, although more couples have been seeking access to infertility services.[9]

## PATHOGENESIS/CLINICAL FEATURES

According to textbooks, the female factor accounts for approximately 35% of subfertility, the male factor for 35%, and, in about 30% of cases, both male and female factors are involved. In female subfertility, around 30% to 40% of cases involve ovulatory dysfunction, 30% to 40% tubal and pelvic pathology, and 30% other and unexplained causes.[10,11] Clinical data supporting these figures are not robust, however, especially in light of uncertainties regarding causal factors, differences in population, and referral characteristics.

Couples suffering from subfertility usually do not have associated complaints or symptoms. Exceptions are abnormal or absent menstrual bleeding, a history of pelvic inflammatory disease, a ruptured appendix, or testicular injury. The general rule that the more tests you do, the more likely that at least one test will be abnormal by chance certainly also holds true for subfertility. It may not be easy to identify the disease state that is causally related to reproductive failure in a given couple. Classic examples include conditions such as endometriosis or uterine leiomyomas, which were widely believed to induce infertility, until it was found that both these conditions are also prevalent in the general fertile population.

Similar findings apply to the identification of male subfertility. Poor sperm quality (according to World Health Organization criteria) was widely believed to be the cause of infertility in many cases, until more recent studies showed

that diminished sperm qualities can be readily observed in males with children.[12,13] Although criteria for defining abnormal sperm have been revised repeatedly, the predictive power of sperm quality assessment should be viewed with caution in a subfertility population.

Several classes of disease conditions that may underlie female subfertility can be identified, notably: ovulatory dysfunction, mechanical dysfunction, ovarian aging, and unexplained subfertility.

### OVULATORY DYSFUNCTION

Changes in ovarian function are usually presented by extended bleeding intervals (oligomenorrhea) or absence of bleeding (amenorrhea). Amenorrhea is usually associated with a hypoestrogenic status, whereas bleeding in oligomenorrhea may either represent occasional ovulation or breakthrough bleeding due to continued estrogen exposure. In primary amenorrhea, with or without disturbed sexual differentiation, one should consider rare conditions involving abnormal gonadal or uterine development due to (inherited or spontaneous) gene mutations.

Ovulatory dysfunction can be classified in three categories based on FSH and estradiol ($E_2$) hormone assays in peripheral blood.[14,15] Low FSH and $E_2$ indicate a central origin of the abnormality at the level of the brain. Hence, ovaries fail to function normally due to insufficient stimulation by pituitary gonadotropins (WHO group 1). In contrast, the combination of high FSH and low $E_2$ concentrations indicate that the primary defect is at the ovarian level (WHO group 3, i.e., early menopause or premature ovarian failure [POF]). The ovary fails to produce estrogens despite maximal stimulation by endogenous FSH. The third group of patients (WHO group 2) is represented by FSH and $E_2$ levels within the normal range. This heterogeneous group also includes polycystic ovary syndrome (PCOS) characterized by hyperandrogenemia, obesity, and polycystic ovaries.[16,17]

Luteal phase insufficiency has long been believed to be an important factor in subfertility, occurring in up to 14% of infertile patients. However, there is a lack of controlled studies establishing its role in subfertility or the value of any treatment in improving pregnancy rates.[18]

### MECHANICAL DYSFUNCTION

The normal functioning of the reproductive tract is important for undisturbed fertility. Many uterine abnormalities have been associated with infertility or early miscarriage, including congenital uterine malformations, malformations due to fetal exposure to diethylstilbestrol, fibroids (in particular the submucosal, or cornual myomas), polyps, and adhesions related to previous intrauterine procedures.

Normal fertility may also be affected by pelvic adhesions (especially involving the ovaries and fallopian tubes), appendicitis, or intra-abdominal surgery. Abnormal tubal function may be due to occlusion occurring after salpingitis or to previous surgical intervention for the management of ectopic pregnancy or phimosis (interfering with normal oocyte pickup). Peritubal adhesions may interfere with normal tubal motility and, hence, with gamete and zygote transport. Severely damaged tubes may fill with fluid, giving rise to hydrosalpinges.

Endometriosis is a topic of continued controversy related to disease conditions associated with subfertility.[19] Endometriosis is the ectopic localization of endometrial tissue outside the uterine cavity, most commonly in the pelvis; retrograde menstruation may be an important causal factor. Severe forms of endometriosis give rise to adhesions, cyst formation, and reduced fertility chances. In addition, abdominal discomfort and dyspareunia are frequent complaints. Limited data suggest, however, that minimal and mild endometriosis is also prevalent in the general population. Moreover, positive effects

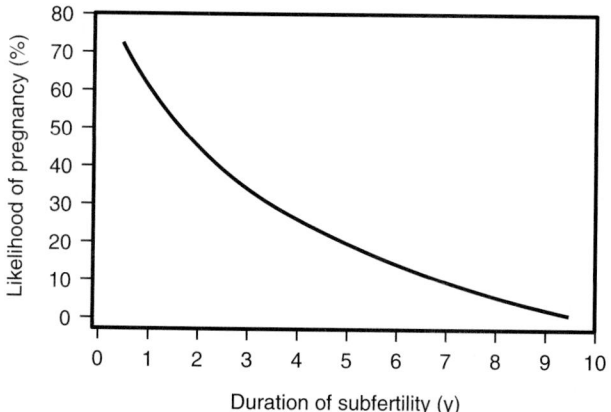

*Figure 156-3* The likelyhood of pregnancy in couples relative to the duration of their subfertility. Note the considerable chance to conceive within the first 3 years of unprotected intercourse. (From Evers JL: Female subfertility. Lancet 360:151–159, 2002.)

of intervention studies using either medication or surgical procedures on subsequent fertility are questionable.[20]

Myomas reportedly occur in 1% to 2.5% of infertile patients without other evident cause of infertility,[21] and removal is thought to improve subsequent pregnancy chances. A systematic literature search involving 106 studies regarding a possible relationship between fibroids and subfertility remained inconclusive, however.[21] A recent meta-analysis of 11 studies showed that only submucous fibroids induced reduced pregnancy and implantation rates.[22] In these women, pregnancy chances could be increased with hysteroscopic myomectomy.

As with many other factors associated with infertility, comparative data on the frequency of similar abnormalities in a matched, fertile population are lacking. In addition, randomized follow-up studies of pregnancy rates comparing intervention versus expectant management are rare, so the efficacy of treatment is uncertain.

## OVARIAN AGING

In many societies around the world, increased participation of females in extended education and careers results in the postponement to a later age of the wish to have a first child. For instance, in the Netherlands the average age of the mother having her first child has risen steadily and is currently 29.5.[23] An increased proportion of women start their first attempts to conceive when they are older than 30. After the age of 30, natural fertility starts to decrease, with a major subsequent decline in fertility after 37 years of age[24] (Fig. 156-4). At the age of 45, chances of having a baby have decreased to almost zero.

Around 20 weeks of female fetal life, initial germ cell mitosis is arrested and the primordial follicle pool reaches its maximum size of around 8 million per ovary. Thereafter, this stock of resting primordial follicles is slowly depleted (by the onset of growth of follicles), falling to 2 million at birth, 0.5 million at menarche (first menstrual period), with final exhaustion of the pool with the last spontaneous menstrual period. Thus, it should be emphasized that only a small proportion (around 10% to 15%) of the initial follicle pool remains when many women initially consider conceiving for the first time.

Menopause marks the definitive end of the reproductive life span, and occurs at the average age of 51, with a range from 40 to 60 years of age. This indicates that exhaustion of the follicle pool takes 50% more time (60 rather than 40 years) in some women compared to others. This also suggests that the association between chronologic age and ovarian aging is poor. Indirect evidence indicates that a fixed time interval exists between the transition from normal fertility into decreased and finally into absent fertility (sterility).[23,25] This means that some women at the age of 35 may already have severely compromised fertility (these women will likewise also present with an early although normal menopause), whereas, for other women of identical age, natural fertility is still completely normal. This latter group of women will probably experience menopause at a later age. The clinical challenge is to assess the reproductive aging status of a given woman. This will help to predict her pregnancy chances more accurately compared to chance assessment based on chronologic age alone. This may help in counseling the patient on expectant management or therapeutic strategies.

The mechanisms underlying reduced natural fertility in relation to ovarian aging are not yet fully elucidated. It has been clearly established that the size of the cohort of growing follicles is diminished and coincides with an increased proportion of chromosomally abnormal oocytes. Changes in follicle cohort size can either be assessed by transvaginal ultrasound or by hormone estimates in peripheral blood, as will be discussed later.

## UNEXPLAINED SUBFERTILITY

The indicated percentage of subfertility of unknown origin is usually around 30%. The reported incidence is very much dependent on the extent of the infertility evaluation, along with the reported incidence of other "known" factors related to subfertility. Again, a clear-cut causal relationship between an abnormal condition as established in initial evaluation and the subfertility is usually absent.

On the other hand, there are many processes involved in natural fertility that cannot be tested properly in a routine clinical setting. These processes involve oocyte maturation and fertilization, embryo transport through the tube and uterine cavity, chromosomal constitution of embryos, apposition and implantation of embryos, and, finally, endometrial receptivity, including regulation of endometrial maturation by steroids produced by the corpus luteum.[26] Moreover, many pregnancies, either under natural conditions or in a subfertile population, may miscarry very early, before the occurrence of regular menses.[27]

## EVALUATION OF THE FEMALE IN THE SUBFERTILE COUPLE

The extent to which basic infertility testing should be performed is extensively debated in the current era, which is dominated by assisted reproductive techniques. Consequently, marked differences exist with regard to the number and type of tests performed.[28,29] Tests are time consuming and costly, and some are not without risks. According to some clinical investigators, results may have little bearing on assisted reproduction outcomes. In a commercial environment where patients have to pay for services, the "customers" may prefer to spend their money on treatment with at least some chances for pregnancy rather than diagnostic procedures with no impact on their chances to conceive.

Many tests are not clearly standardized and reproducibility is therefore limited. The usefulness of infertility tests should be based on the proper evaluation of: (a) sensitivity (the capacity of a test to detect abnormalities); (b) specificity (the chance that an abnormality is actually present if the test gives an abnormal result); (c) invasiveness, complexity, and cost of the test; and, finally, (d) the predictive value of the test.

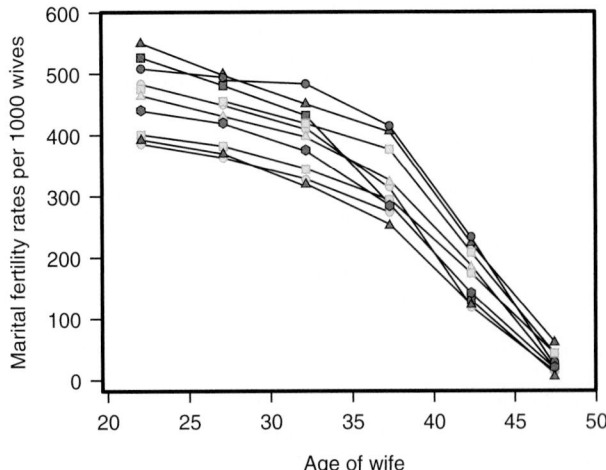

**Figure 156-4** Natural marital fertility rates as a function of age of the woman, indicated for different populations from the sixteenth until the twentieth century (Hutterites, Geneva bourgeoisie, Canada, Normandy, Tunis, Norway, and Iran). (From Menken J, Trussel J, Larsen U, et al: Age and infertility. Science 233:1389–1394, 1986; Schwartz D, Mayaux MJ: Female fecundity as a function of age: Results of artificial insemination in 2193 nulliparous women with azoospermic husbands. Federation CECOS. N Engl J Med 306:404–406, 1982.)

Indeed, there are few studies evaluating the predictive validity of tests, despite widespread use of tests in clinical practice.[9]

Subfertile couples should be seen together. During the initial consultation, the physician should take a full medical history from both partners. Relevant information includes: duration of subfertility, past sexual development, previous relationships as well as children, obstetrical history, previous surgery, abdominal or menstrual discomfort, and sexually transmitted diseases. Moreover, the clinician should counsel the couple regarding the timing of intercourse and fertility chances, effects of lifestyle factors (such as excessive smoking, alcohol intake, caffeine consumption, and exercise), food intake and obesity, and professional hazards.[30] A general physical examination is usually only advised for women.[31–34]

Diagnostic tests that may be performed for the evaluation of subfertile couples include assessment of the normal menstrual cycle, assessment of mechanical factors, assessment of cervical mucus-sperm interaction, and assessment of ovarian aging.

## ASSESSMENT OF THE NORMAL MENSTRUAL CYCLE

Regular menstrual periods suggest normal ovulatory cycles. Ovulations and normal corpus luteum function can be assessed in different ways.[35] The tests are not very good in terms of accuracy and reproducibility, however, nor in the detection of a meaningful and treatable disease condition relevant to subfertility.

### Menstrual Period Chart
This represents the simplest way to document the menstrual cycle pattern. The days of onset and cessation of menses should be recorded on a calendar for several months. A normal menstrual cycle ranges between 25 and 35 days, with a median duration of 28 days.

### Basal Body Temperature (BBT) Chart
Progesterone produced by the corpus luteum has many effects on the central nervous system, including changes in the body temperature set point. Consequently, the daily assessment of body temperature can be used to document a persistent increase in temperature (typically from 36.9°C to 37.1°C) and therefore provide proof of ovulation. A rise in temperature indicates that ovulation and corpus luteum formation has taken place. The length of the second half of the cycle should be at least 10 days. The daily temperature assessments should be performed at the same time during the early morning before the onset of activities. Though performing these tests for several months can be quite stressful to women, it may be helpful for the couple to be aware of the day of ovulation in order to time intercourse to achieve optimal pregnancy chances. However, the BBT is notoriously unreliable.

### Urinary LH Surge
When LH concentrations are high in serum during the midcycle surge, sufficient quantities are excreted into urine to allow its detection. Kits are commercially available for use at home. On average, LH appears in the urine around 12 hours after the onset of the LH surge in the blood and can therefore accurately predict ovulation. This method, again, can help with optimal timing of intercourse.

### Ultrasound
The preovulatory, graafian follicle usually attains a diameter of around 20 mm (ranging from 16 to 24 mm) before rupture and subsequent release of the oocyte. The rupture of the follicle can be established by visualizing the disappearance or decrease in size of the dominant follicle by transvaginal ultrasound. This method is usually reserved for monitoring of ovarian stimulation during infertility therapies, or for the proper timing of a postcoital test or midluteal phase progesterone assay (see the following section).

### Progesterone Assay
Appropriate timing of the assessment of progesterone serum concentrations is crucial and should always be checked in retrospect, especially in women whose cycle length may vary. A level above 2 ng/mL indicates ovulation, although levels between 6 and 25 ng/mL are considered normal and are associated with chances for pregnancy. Some investigators advocate that multiple hormone assays should be performed around the midluteal phase to document an insufficient luteal. The luteal phase may either be reduced in length or insufficient quantities of progesterone may be produced during the luteal phase.

### Endometrial Biopsy
A proportion of cases of subfertility may be related to insufficient endometrial maturation resulting in compromised endometrial receptivity and reduced embryo implantation rates. This condition may be due to an abnormal response of the endometrium or to abnormal steroid biosynthesis by the corpus luteum. The morphology of endometrial tissue obtained by biopsy has been advocated for decades as a routine diagnostic procedure for testing the adequacy of the luteal phase. The Noyes morphology criteria primarily assess whether the endometrium is *in phase* (within 2 days of the actual calculated date). The appropriate timing for a biopsy is still questioned[36] and, as a result, this test has been largely abandoned from the routine infertility workup.

## ASSESSMENT OF MECHANICAL FACTORS

Some type of mechanical factor relevant to subfertility is reported to occur in 10% to 30% of subfertile couples. Several methods exist to establish abnormalities at the level of the uterus, fallopian tubes, or ovary-ampulla complex relevant for in vivo oocyte pickup. Until recently, diagnosis of mechanical abnormalities by hysterosalpingography (HSG) during the early infertility workup and by laparoscopy later in the evaluation have been standard procedures for each patient. Currently, the tendency is toward screening tests to identify women at risk for tubal disease, and the performance of more invasive diagnostic procedures only in those women at increased risk for such abnormalities. The question remains as to what extent any mechanical deviation from normal truly contributes to the subfertility. The clinician should take this reservation seriously, especially in cases of minor abnormalities of the uterine cavity and with presumed unilateral tubal damage.

### Screening by Chlamydia Antibody Testing in Serum
*Chlamydia trachomatis* represents the most common sexually transmitted pathogen in the Western world, with a reported prevalence of infection around 5% to 10%. The majority of these infections remain without symptoms, but around 10% can cause pelvic inflammatory disease.[37] *Chlamydia* acts as an immunogen, giving rise to antibody formation. Immunoglobulin G (IgG) antibodies remain for years in the circulation and can therefore be used as a marker for a past infection. IgG concentrations are reported to be elevated in 30% to 60% of women from subfertile couples. The capacity of IgG antibody levels to predict tuboperitoneal disease (as assessed by laparoscopy) has been evaluated prospectively with acceptable receiver operator characteristic (ROC) curves using titers between 16 and 32[38,39] (Fig. 156-5). In subfertile couples with a relatively good fertility prognosis, a workup strategy starting with screening for *Chlamydia* is an effective approach,[40] and many women will escape the need for more invasive procedures.

### Diagnosis by Hysterosalpingography or Laparoscopy
*Hysterosalpingography*
HSG represents the radiographic visualization of the endocervical canal, the uterine cavity, and the lumen of the fallopian tubes. Both oil- or water-based contrast media are used.

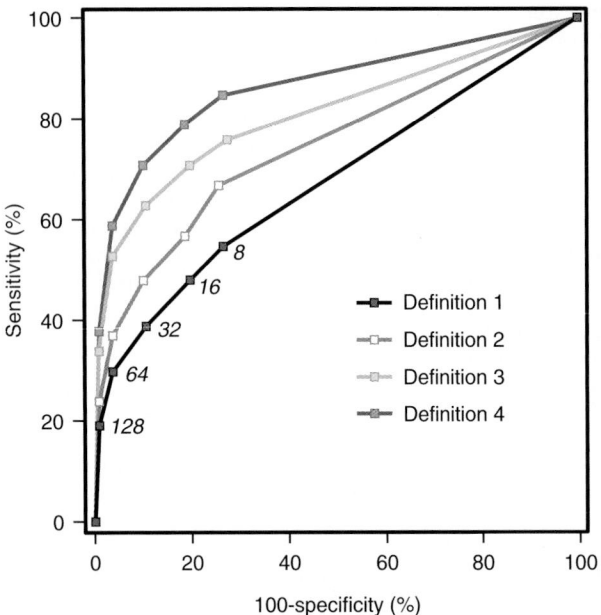

**Figure 156-5** Receiver operating charateristic curves for *Chlamydia* antibody titers using different definitions for tubal factor subfertility. Definition 1: Any periadnexal adhesions and/or proximal or distal occlusion of at least one tube; Definition 2: Extensive periadnexal adhesions and/or proximal or distal occlusion of at least one tube; Definition 3: Extensive periadnexal adhesions and/or distal occlusion of at least one tube; Definition 4: Extensive periadnexal adhesions and/or distal occlusion of both tubes. (From Land JA, Evers JL, Goossens VJ: How to use Chlamydial antibody testing in subfertility patients. Human Reprod 13:1094–1098, 1998.)

The oil-based medium may have the advantage of a minor subsequent increase in spontaneous pregnancy chances, whereas the water-based medium is faster and less painful, and results in improved visibility of minimal abnormalities. Abnormal uterine features that may be observed include: outpouching (due to previous cesarean section or perforation of the uterine wall); filling defect (related to submucous fibroids, polyps, or intrauterine adhesions); or abnormal shape (congenital uterine anomalies such as unicornuate, bicornuate, septate uterus, or uterus didelphys, fetal exposure to diethylstilbestrol, or intrauterine adhesions). In addition, unilateral or bilateral tubal occlusion, with or without hydrosalpinges, may be diagnosed. The occurence of peritubal adhesions may also be suspected based on an abnormal intra-abdominal distribution pattern of contrast medium.

The HSG procedure should be planned during the proliferative, late-follicular phase of the menstrual cycle in order to enable assessment of endometrial development and to avoid an unexpected early pregnancy.[41] This procedure can be quite painful, and an ascending infection with acute salpingitis is the most significant complication, occurring in around 1% to 2%. Preventive antibiotic prophylaxis should be advised in all patients at risk. HSG is reasonably effective in diagnosing tubal occlusion; abnormal results are associated with reduced fecundity rates.[42] An important drawback of this procedure remains the subjective nature of evaluation, rendering the reproducibility of this test poor.

*Laparoscopy*
This procedure is considered the gold standard for the diagnosis of tubal disease and intra-abdominal disorders such as endometriosis and adhesions interfering with normal fertility.[38,42,43] Some authorities feel laparoscopy should be performed before the diagnosis of unexplained subfertility is made. More recent data suggest, however, that the added value of such a procedure in women without a history suggestive of tubal disease and a normal HSG is limited.[44]

Laparoscopy involves the intra-abdominal inspection of the internal genital organs after abdominal insufflation with $CO_2$ of a patient under general anesthesia. Next to the reproductive organs, the appendix should be inspected for infections and the perihepatic region for adhesions suggestive of past chlamydial infections (Fitz-Hugh-Curtis syndrome). In experienced hands, risks associated with this technique are minimal. Attention should be focused toward standardizing the evaluation of the abdominal cavity.

*Other Techniques*
Other recently introduced, more sophisticated techniques to visualize intrauterine, intratubal, or intra-abdominal abnormalities include ultrasound imaging of the uterine cavity after fluid lavage (usually referred to by the acronym HyCoSy) and the endoscopic techniques hysteroscopy, salpingoscopy, falloposcopy, transvaginal hydrolaparoscopy, and microlaparoscopy.[45] Although some of these techniques seem promising, with the focus on reduced patient discomfort and costs, the usefulness of these tools in a standard infertility workup has yet to be established.

## ASSESSMENT OF CERVICAL MUCUS–SPERM INTERACTION

In some mammals such as the horse, semen is ejected directly into the uterus. In contrast, in the human, semen is deposited in the fornix posterior of the vagina. The cervix is believed to play an important role in reproduction by allowing the sperm to enter the uterine cavity.

A number of specific functions of cervical mucus have been identified, including: protection of the sperm from the hostile acidic milieu in the vagina, allowing the sperm to enter the cervix, supporting energy requirements for sperm motility, and filtration of morphologically abnormal sperm. Before ovulation, cervical mucus is produced in large quantities, allowing easy sperm access at the most appropriate moment during the menstrual cycle. The prognostic performance of cervical mucus tests, the incidence of cervical factor subfertility, and the validity of treatment options to correct disturbed cervical mucus–sperm interactions remain highly controversial.

**Postcoital Test**
This test involving the appraisal of the presence of motile sperm in cervical mucus was originally described in 1866 by Sims and reemphasized in 1913 by Huhner. The test should be performed after intercourse during the late follicular phase of the menstrual cycle. There is no agreement regarding the preferred interval between intercourse and the test, nor the cutoff between a normal or abnormal test result. The threshold is somewhere between one and five spermatozoa per high-power magnification (i.e., $10 \times 40$) field. Although the test has been widely applied in Europe, questions accumulate regarding the diagnostic and prognostic power of the test.

A systematic review of 11 well-designed studies indicated that the discriminating ability of the postcoital test is poor, regardless of the applied criteria for normality.[46] A subsequent systematic prospective evaluation indicated that the inclusion of a postcoital test in the routine evaluation of new couples only results in more interventions.[47] Several national and international bodies (such as the American Society of Reproductive Medicine, the European Society of Human Reproduction, and the Royal College of Obstetrics and Gynaecology) currently advise against performing the postcoital test in routine subfertility evaluation. In addition, earlier tests to evaluate the quality of the cervical mucus, along with several in vitro tests of interactions between cervical mucus and sperm have been abandoned.

## ASSESSMENT OF OVARIAN AGING

It is well established that the age of the woman is the most prominent factor in determining pregnancy chances, either spontaneously[24,48] (see Fig. 156-4) or after infertility therapy such as insemination with donor sperm[49] or IVF.[50] As discussed previously, however, chronologic age is only a poor predictor of ovarian aging. Some 35-year-old women may be normally fertile, and expectant management may be the most appropriate option. In contrast, natural conception chances may already be severely compromised in other women of similar age, and the clinician should offer the most effective treatment options without delay. The major challenge of today is to assess the magnitude of ovarian aging on an individual basis.[51,52] Subtle endocrine and ultrasound changes can be observed in women of advanced reproductive age, and recent efforts have focused on the clinical implications of these findings in terms of their ability to predict chances for pregnancy, either spontaneously or after infertility therapies. Several factors appear to predict fertility chances, with improved predictive power by application of multivariate regression analysis. In addition, challenge tests using clomiphene citrate, exogenous FSH, or a GnRH agonist,[53] have been applied in attempts to enlarge endocrine differences and improve the predictive power, but have met with little success.

Initial physiologic studies in normo-ovulatory women have emphasized that the length of the follicular phase is shortened with increasing age, along with elevated early follicular phase serum FSH concentrations. Indeed, baseline FSH is capable of predicting IVF outcome, independent of chronological age.[54] However, a meta-analysis of 21 relevant studies on the predictive value of baseline FSH for IVF outcome concluded that the clinical value is restricted to a small group of patients only[55] (Fig. 156-6). In these women, recent studies showed that the intercycle rise in FSH and inhibin B is decreased and can predict IVF treatment outcome.[56] In addition, a decreased cohort of follicles being recruited can be observed by ultrasound and used as a marker of ovarian aging to predict treatment outcome.[57] A prospective evaluation of 120 women undergoing their first IVF cycle concluded that the antral follicle count is the best single predictor for poor IVF response, with a ROC curve of 0.87. The addition of baseline FSH and inhibin B to the antral follicle number in multivariate analysis further improved the predictive power with

**Table 156-2** Univariate and Multivariate Prediction Models*

| | Odds Ratio | P | ROC AUC |
|---|---|---|---|
| **UNIVARIATE** | | | |
| FSH | 1.40 | < 0.001 | 0.84 |
| Inhibin B | 0.98 | < 0.001 | 0.77 |
| Ovarian follicle # | 0.70 | < 0.001 | 0.87 |
| **MULTIVARIATE** | | | |
| Step 1 (follicle #) | 0.70 | < 0.001 | 0.87 |
| Step 2 (+ inhibin B) | 0.98 | < 0.001 | 0.90 |
| Step 3 (+ FSH) | 1.27 | < 0.007 | 0.92 |

*Involving the capacity of initial screening characteristics to predict poor ovarian response to hyperstimulation in IVF.
AUC, area under the curve; FSH, follicle-stimulating hormone; LH, luteinizing hormone, ROC, receiver operating characteristic.
From Brancsi LF, Broekmans FJ, Eijkemans MJ, et al: Predictors of poor response in IVF: A prospective study comparing basal markers of ovarian reserve. Fertil Steril 77:328–336, 2002.

an ROC of 0.92[56] (Table 156-2). This study also demonstrated that women older than 40 years of age, with a relatively favorable predictive test, still have a reasonable chance to become pregnant after IVF.

Finally, antimüllerian hormone (AMH) is a novel marker associated with very early pre–antral follicle development (just after leaving the resting primordial stage). The hormone has to be measured in serum, and its association with ovarian aging[58] and IVF outcome[59] is being established. It is presently unknown if the inclusion of antimüllerian hormone in the multivariate model will further enhance the predictive power of this test.

### FROM DIAGNOSIS TO PROGNOSIS

In view of the limited capacity of evaluation tests to diagnose a causal condition underlying subfertility, various prospective follow-up studies have evaluated whether specific characteristics could predict chances for a spontaneous pregnancy in

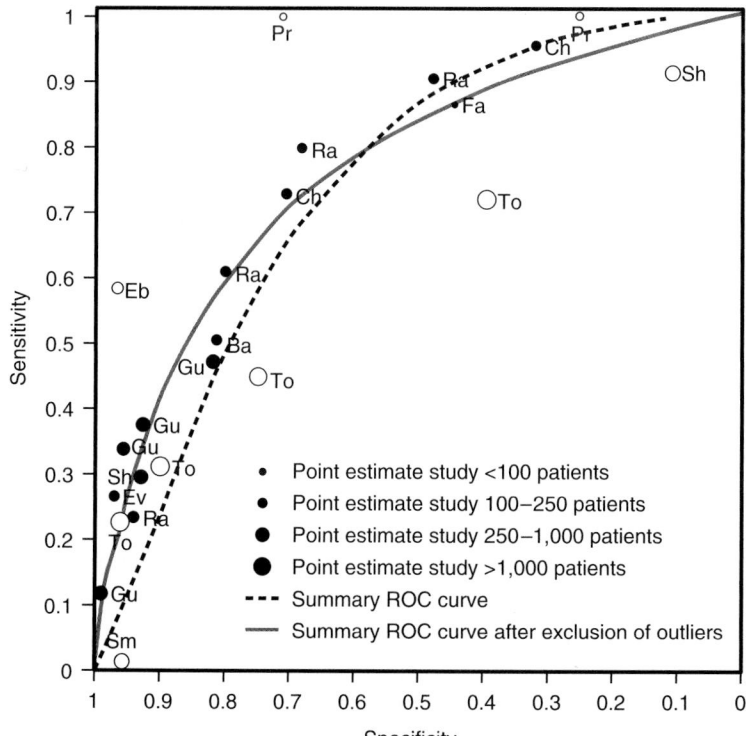

**Figure 156-6** Receiver operating characteristic (ROC) curves of studies reporting on the performance of baseline (cycle days 3–5) FSH to predict poor ovarian response during ovarian hyperstimulation in IVF. Note that the size of different point estimates indicate the number of patients. (From Bancsi L, Broekmans FJ, Mol BW, et al: Performance of basal follicle-stimulating hormone in the prediction of poor ovarian response and failure to become pregnant after in vitro fertilization: A meta-analysis. Fertil Steril 79:1091–1100, 2003.)

these couples. Three studies[60–62] have identified similar factors predicting pregnancy changes (Table 156-3). Despite some minor differences, presumably reflecting differences in the study populations and test interpretation, duration of subfertility, woman's age, sperm quality, and sometimes mechanical factors emerged as factors that may be causally related to reduced fertility.

Application of these prediction models[63] can allow a more accurate assessment of the likelihood of a spontaneous pregnancy in a given couple. This may help in counseling the couple regarding a preferred expectant management or whether (empiric) treatment should be initiated. This approach may also reduce overtreatment since invasive therapies can be avoided with couples who have a favorable likelihood of a spontaneous pregnancy. Interestingly, a well-designed cohort follow-up study concluded that 61% of couples achieved a pregnancy independent of treatment[64] (Fig. 156-7).

## MANAGEMENT OF THE SUBFERTILE COUPLE

The chances that a spontaneous pregnancy will occur after unprotected intercourse for 1 year is around 90%[65] (see Fig. 156-1). Subsequently, when a couple seeks evaluation of subfertility, it is important first to assess the likelihood of a spontaneous pregnancy, before commencing any kind of empiric therapy. As mentioned previously, the age of the woman and the duration of subfertility are the most important factors affecting the future likelihood of conception (see Figs. 156-3 and 156-4 and Table 156-3).

Increasing patient pressure and the financial interest of some infertility centers have led in the industrialized world to a tendency to start infertility treatment prematurely. This contrasts with the observation that there is insufficient access to infertility care for financial reasons in many remaining parts of the world. The approach of comparing spontaneous pregnancy chances in relation to chances after intervention may aid in the proper timing of the initiation of therapies, and therefore prevent overtreatment. This approach is distinctly different from focusing on the highest chances for pregnancy per treatment cycle, which is often used.

It was calculated for Canada in 1995 that the cost of infertility management represents only 0.6% of the annual healthcare budget.[66] The definition of cost-effective infertility care is the achievement of the desired end point at the lowest possi-

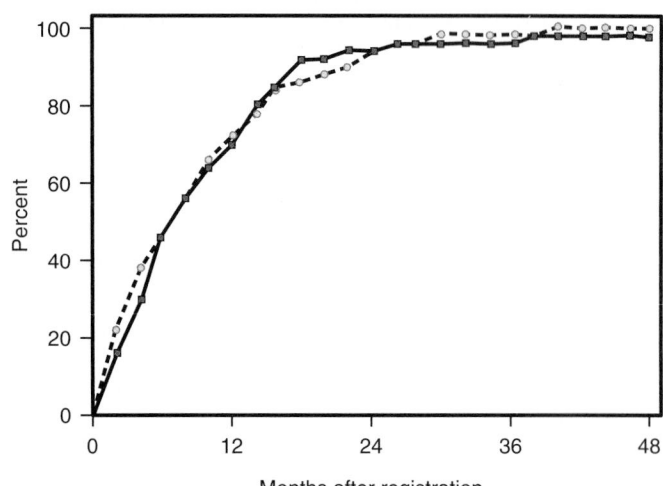

*Figure 156-7* Cummulative distribution of intervals from registration to pregnancy in a large Canadian cohort of 1145 subfertile couples. A distinction is made between treatment-dependent (*circles*) versus treatment-independent pregnancies (*squares*). (From Collins J, Wrixon W, Janes LB: Treatment-independent pregnancy among infertile couples. N Engl J Med 309:1201–1206, 1983.)

ble expenditure of resources.[67] Analysis modeling in the United Kingdom confirmed that IVF is the most cost-effective treatment option for severe tubal factor and minimal endometriosis.[68] Initial cost-effectiveness studies also support the use of IUI and ovarian hyperstimulation before IVF.[69,70] Gradually, a consensus is evolving that healthy live birth (preferably from singleton pregnancies) per started treatment should be the preferred end point.[71] In addition, a systematic evaluation documented that the success rates of infertility therapies are often overstated and that the quality of studies is often questionable.[72]

Anovulation can usually be treated effectively with ovulation induction agents (such as clomiphene citrate, insulin-sensitizing agents, or exogenous gonadotropins) aiming at restoring normal ovarian function (see Chapters 154, 157, and 158). In addition, mechanical factors involving the uterine cavity, tubal function, or oocyte pickup can usually be restored by endoscopic surgery (such as hysteroscopic myomectomy, adhesiolysis, or fimbrioplastia).

The diagnosis of unexplained subfertility can only be made after an appropriate diagnostic infertility workup has established the absence of any abnormalities.[73] As no consensus exists on the extent of testing that should be performed during an infertility workup, however, cases of unexplained subfertility comprise a notoriously heterogeneous group of patients. In many cases of unexplained subfertility or male factor subfertility, patients undergo empiric treatment in order to improve pregnancy chances. Assisted reproduction encompasses various techniques to increase the chances of pregnancy per cycle by basically bringing more gametes closer together. This goal can be achieved by ovarian hyperstimulation, IUI, or IVF.

### OVARIAN HYPERSTIMULATION

Under normal conditions, a cohort of follicles is recruited for ongoing gonadotropin-dependent development during the intercycle rise in FSH. During a limited time interval (the so-called FSH window), FSH concentrations rise above the threshold before declining[74] (Fig. 156-8). The aim of ovarian hyperstimulation is to intervene in the mechanisms regulating single dominant follicle development, in order to mature multiple follicles with generation of multiple oocytes for fertilization either in vivo (after intercourse or IUI) or in vitro

| *Table 156-3* | Multivartiate Prediction Models* | | |
|---|---|---|---|
| | Eimers et al. | Collins et al. | Snick et al. |
| | Tertiary Referral, Single-center (*n* = 996) | National, Multi-center (*n* = 2198) | Primary Care, Isolated Population (*n* = 726) |
| Woman's age | − | + | − |
| Duration of infertility | + | + | + |
| Primary/Secondary infertility | + | + | − |
| Male factor | + | + | − |
| PCT | + | − | + |
| Mechanical factors | − | + | + |
| Anovulation | − | − | + |

*Regarding the capacity of characteristics on initial screening to predict spontaneous pregnancy chances in subfertile couples.
PCT, postcoital test.
From Eimers JM, te Velde ER, Gerritse R, et al: The prediction of the chance to conceive in subfertile couples. Fertil Steril 61:44–52, 1994; Collins JA, Burrows EA, Wilian AR, et al: The prognosis for live birth among untreated infertile couples. Fertil Steril 64:22–28, 1995; Snick HK, Snick TS, Evers JL, et al: The spontaneous pregnancy prognosis in untreated subfertile couples: The Walcheren primary care study. Hum Reprod 12:1582–1588, 1997.

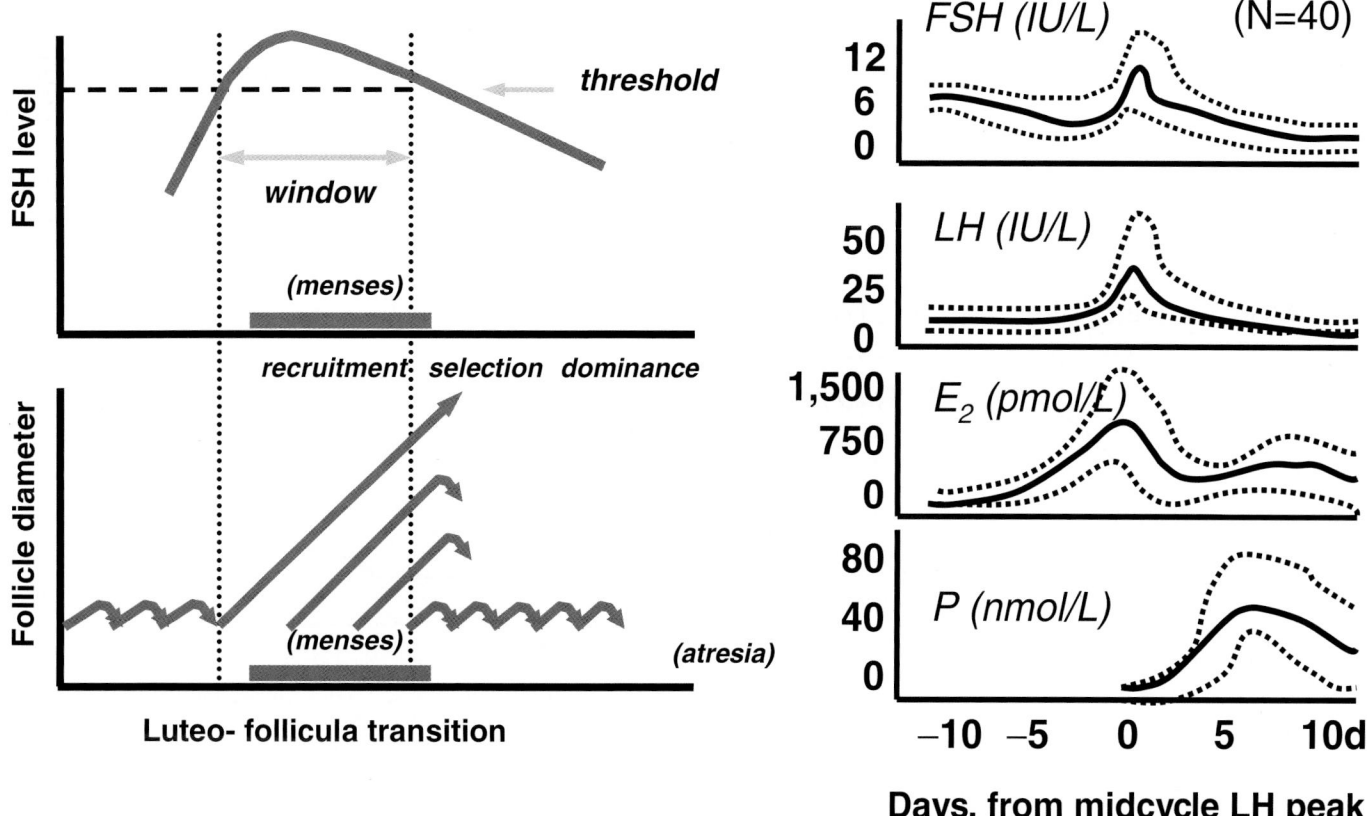

**Figure 156-8   Left panel,** Schematic representation of the intercycle rise in serum follicle-stimulating hormone (FSH) concentrations above a certain level (*threshold*) during a limited time interval (*window*), and follicle growth dynamics (*recruitment, selection,* and *dominance*) during the follicular phase of the normal menstrual cycle. **Right panel,** Variation in serum FSH, luteinizing hormone (LH), estradiol (E₂), and progesterone (P) levels during the normal menstrual cycle in 40 normo-ovulatory women. *Solid lines* indicate median levels whereas dotted lines indicate 5th and 95th percentiles. (From Macklon NS, Fauser BC: Regulation of follicle development and novel approaches to ovarian stimulation for IVF. Hum Reprod Update 6:307–312, 2000.)

(IVF). An increase from 3% to 9% in monthly fecundity rate can be achieved, and a distinct increase in cumulative pregnancy rates can be established over time[75] (Fig. 156-9). Along with a twofold to fourfold increase in pregnancy rate, occurrence of multiple pregnancies and the ovarian hyperstimulation syndrome is increased because of ovarian hyperstimulation. When multiple oocytes are released in vivo, the number fertilized cannot be controlled, and a marked increase in multiple and especially in higher-order multiple pregnancies has occurred[76,77] (Fig. 156-10).

The results of ovarian hyperstimulation are often combined with those of IUI, and few studies allow differentiation between the independent effects of the two[78,79] (Fig. 156-11). Due to low costs and ease of administration, the antiestrogen clomiphene citrate (CC) should be recommended as first-choice medication, despite a limited efficacy. Analysis of 45 reports concluded that the adjusted pregnancy rate per cycle is 5.6% for CC alone compared to 8.3% for CC/IUI, against an estimated background spontaneous pregnancy rate of 1.3%.[80] A meta-analysis concluded that CC resulted in a 2.5 increase in chance per cycle compared to that with no treatment.[81] Finally, a meta-analysis of five trials indicated that exogenous gonadotropins are superior to CC in relation to enhancing pregnancy chances.[82]

### INTRAUTERINE INSEMINATION

The intrauterine insemination (IUI) procedure refers to the positioning of sperm, after a washing procedure in the laboratory, in the uterine cavity just before ovulation. The rationale for IUI treatment with ovulation induction is to increase gamete density at the site of fertilization. Hence, the classic indications for IUI are male (erectile and ejaculatory) or female (vaginism) sexual dysfunction and cervical hostility. IUI combined with "controlled" ovarian hyperstimulation has also been applied in couples suffering from male factor as well as from unexplained infertility.

Renewed interest in IUI reflects evolution of better washing (i.e., gradient or swim-up) techniques to improve the quality of the initial sperm sample. Washing procedures are necessary to remove prostaglandins, infectious agents, and antigenic proteins. Nonmotile cells, either leucocytes or immotile and immature spermatozoa, are also removed. This contributes to better sperm quality, in part by decreased release of cytokines and lymphokines with a subsequent reduction in free oxygen radicals.[83]

IUI is usually performed within 30 to 36 hours after human chorionic gonadotropin (hCG) has been administered or within 20 to 28 hours after the LH surge has been detected.[84] Insemination is usually performed using a small flexible catheter through which a small volume (between 0.3 and 0.5 mL) of washed spermatozoa is delivered into the uterine cavity. When IUI is used to manage fertility problems, single rather than double inseminations should be used.[85]

Ovarian hyperstimulation in IUI cycles can be achieved using CC or exogenous gonadotropins. CC is usually administered during the early or mid-follicular phase (cycle days 2–7 or 5–9) in dosages varying between 100 and 150 mg. Exogenous gonadotropins are used either in a low-dose step-up regimen, or using a fixed dose (i.e., 75 IU daily) throughout the cycle. In the low-dose step-up regimen, the starting dose is 75 IU per day and this dose is increased by 37.5 IU

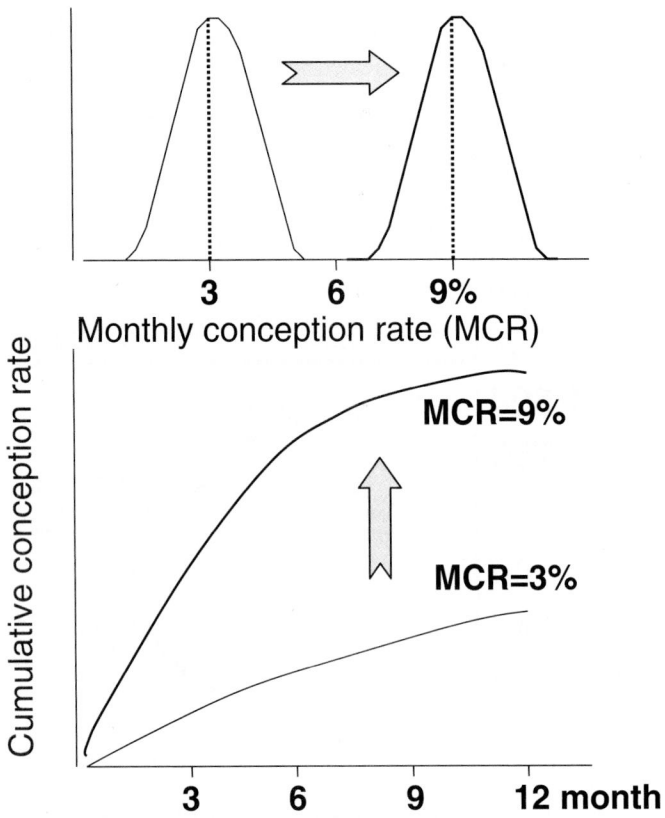

**Figure 156-9**    A shift from 3% to 9% in monthly conception rates due to assisted reproduction results **(top panel)** in a distinct increase in cumulative pregnancy rates in the first 12 months **(bottom panel)**. (From Stovall DW, Guzick DS: Current management of unexplained infertility. Curr Opin Obstet Gynecol 5:228–233, 1993.)

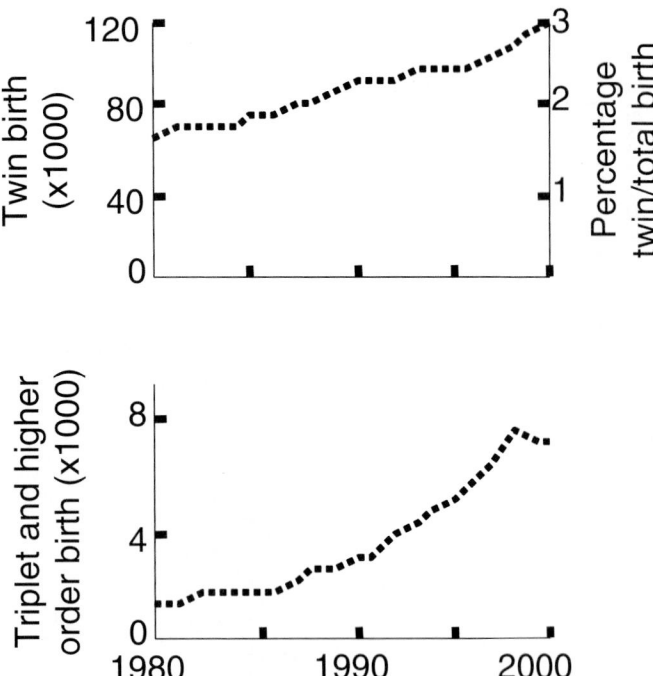

**Figure 156-10**    Twin pregnancy rates **(upper panel)** and triplet and higher-order multiples **(lower panel)** in the United States. Note twin and higher-order births associated with assisted reproductive technology have increased significantly since 1980. Although births resulting from assisted reproductive technology amount to fewer than 1% of all live births, they now account for about a third of all twin births and more than 40% of triplets and higher-number births. (From Hogue CJ: Successful assisted reproductive technology: The beauty of one. Obstet Gynecol 100:1017–1019, 2002.)

after 7 days, when multiple follicle development (defined as more than two follicles measuring 15 mm or more) is not observed. The use of GnRH agonist cotreatment to avoid a premature LH rise is generally not recommended in IUI cycles. Properly designed studies comparing CC with gonadotropins for stimulated IUI cycles are scant, but indicate a similar live birth rate per couple.[81] Using gonadotropins, both step-up and conventional fixed-dose protocols seem equally effective in inducing multiple follicle development. The incidence of ovarian hyperstimulation syndrome was increased using the conventional protocol, however.[86]

The combined use of IUI and hyperstimulation for unexplained subfertility may bypass various subtle barriers, such as minimal sperm abnormalities, sperm–cervical mucus interaction, and the timing of sperm delivery. A meta-analysis of randomized trials comparing FSH/IUI with FSH/timed intercourse for unexplained infertility revealed a common odds ratio for pregnancy of 2.37 (95% confidence interval: 1.43–3.90), suggesting a significant improvement with IUI after ovulation induction in this patient group[78] (Table 156-4). Cost-effectiveness analyses have led to the conclusion that IUI, with or without hyperstimulation, should precede IVF.[69,87] These assessments were made, however, before the advent of the current approaches to minimize costs and complications in IVF by minimal ovarian hyperstimulation[88] and transfer of a reduced number of embryos.[71]

The position of IUI, with or without ovarian hyperstimulation, in the treatment of infertility remains a topic of ongoing debate. Clearly, pregnancy chances increase (especially when IUI is combined with hyperstimulation), but the inherent associated risk is a considerable chance of (higher-order) multiple pregnancies. A large multi-center study in the United States has demonstrated that both IUI and ovarian hyper-

stimulation with FSH have independent effects on the likelihood of pregnancy. An acceptable overall cumulative pregnancy rate of 33% within three cycles was reported. The multiple pregnancy rate was unacceptably high, however, with 20% of pregnancies being twins and 10% triplet or higher-order multiples.[89] A large retrospective analysis in a single European center assessed 1878 pregnancies obtained from IUI combined with gonadotropin hyperstimulation, and reported a 16% twin and 6% higher-order multiple pregnancy rate[90] (see Table 156-4). Finally, a 2-year follow-up in a U.S. infertility center involving 3347 ovarian stimulation cycles found a high multiple pregnancy rate, with an overall pregnancy rate of 30%.[91] Although births resulting from assisted reproduction represent only 1% of all live births in the United States, they now account for 35% of twin births, and for more than 40% of triplet and higher-order multiple births.[76] The adverse impact of multiple births on perinatal morbidity and mortality has been clearly documented. For instance, mortality is increased fivefold in twins and at least sevenfold in higher-order multiples,[92] and risks for cerebral palsy are increased 47-fold in children from triplet pregnancies.[93]

As the pregnancy chances per cycle remain low, it can be calculated that the number needed to treat to benefit from any additional intervention is high. For instance, in comparing FSH and IUI combined versus intracervical insemination alone, it was calculated that 31 treatment cycles are required before there would be one more singleton live birth.[94] Offset against the additional pregnancy are the added costs of medication and frequent ovarian response monitoring. When costs related to multiple pregnancies are also taken into consideration, the conclusion seems justified that the widespread use of ovarian hyperstimulation with exogenous gonadotropins should be discouraged. The real question remains: Will society (especially patients, physicians, and health insurance companies) consider the high rate of multi-

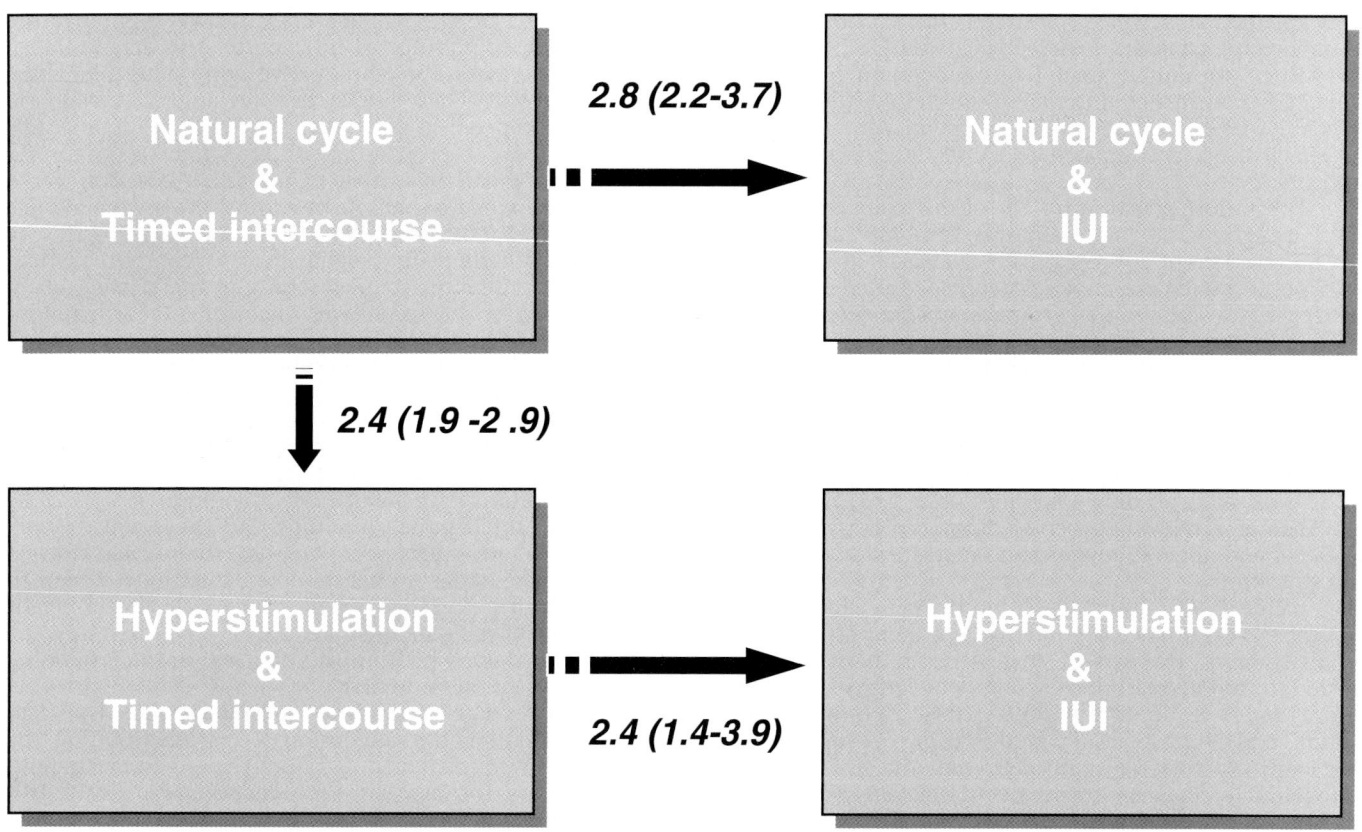

**Figure 156-11** Depicting a Latin-square design to test whether intrauterine insemination (IUI) offers couples with unexplained subfertility benefit over timed intercourse, both in natural cycles and in cycles with ovarian hyperstimulation. Values depict pooled odds ratios and 95% confidence intervals (in parentheses). Note there are two independent significant effects of IUI and ovarian hyperstimulation. (From Hughes EG: The effectiveness of ovulation induction and intrauterine insemination in the treatment of persistent infertility: A meta-analysis. Hum Reprod 12:1865–1871, 1997.)

ple pregnancies an acceptable price to be paid for increased pregnancy chances per cycle?

### IN VITRO FERTILIZATION

The treatment modality of in vitro fertilization (IVF) involves ovarian hyperstimulation, oocyte retrieval, the fertilization of oocytes in vitro (either spontaneously or by intracytoplasmic sperm injection), and the subsequent transfer of embryos into the uterine cavity. This technique is discussed in detail in Chapter 158, and only aspects of IVF relevant to infertility management are discussed here.

IVF was originally designed for the treatment of bilateral tubal occlusion, but, currently, tubal factor only involves a small proportion of indications for IVF. At present, IVF treatment is most often applied in (mild) male factor and unexplained subfertility, with or without previous treatment with IUI or hyperstimulation. A meta-analysis of five relevant trials

| **Table 156-4** | Summary of Four Relevant Studies Concerning Assisted Reproduction Therapies for Unexplained Subfertility | | | | |
|---|---|---|---|---|---|
| **Study** | **Design** | **Comparison** | **Outcomes** | **Note** | |
| Guzick et al. | RCT Multi-center n = 932 | Intracervical insem, IUI +/– hyperstimulation | IUI + hyperstim 3.2 Higher pregnancy chances | Very high multiple PR | |
| Gleicher et al. | Observational Single center n = 3347 cycles, 441 pregnancies | Hyperstimulation | Higher PR in COH and IUI cycles | Very high multiple PR | |
| Goverde et al. | RCT Single center n = 258 couples | IUI, IUI + hyperstim, IVF | IUI more cost effective | High PR in multi-follicular cycles | |
| Tur et al. | Observational Single center n = 1878 pregnancies | Hyperstimulation Heterogeneous | Multiple pregnancies can be predicted | Number of follicles and estradiol | |

IUI, intrauterine insemination; IVF, in vitro fertilization; PR, pregnancy rate; RCT, randomized controlled trial.
From Guzick DS, Carson SA, Coutifaris C, et al: Efficacy of superovulation and intrauterine insemination in the treatment of infertility. National Cooperative Reproductive Medicine Network. N Engl J Med 340:177–183, 1999; Gleicher N, Oleske DM, Tur-Kaspa I, et al: Reducing the risk of high-order multiple pregnancy after ovarian stimulation with gonadotropins. N Engl J Med 343:2–7, 2000; Goverde AJ, McDonnell J, Vermeiden JP, et al: Intrauterine insemination or in-vitro fertilisation in idiopathic subfertility and male subfertility: A randomised trial and cost-effectiveness analysis. Lancet 355:13–18, 2000; Tur R, Barri PN, Coroleu B, et al: Risk factors for high-order multiple implantation after ovarian stimulation with gonadotrophins: Evidence from a large series of 1878 consecutive pregnancies in a single centre. Hum Reprod 16:2124–2129, 2001.

in unexplained subfertility confirmed that no difference in pregnancy rates could be observed when comparing IVF with IUI, with or without ovarian hyperstimulation (odds ratio 1.96; 95% confidence interval: 0.88–4.36).[95] Two separate studies indicated that initial treatment with IVF is not cost effective when compared to a conventional treatment algorithm.[5,6]

Tubal occlusion, constituting one of the major indications for IVF, can give rise to hydrosalpinges. In women undergoing IVF, the presence of hydrosalpinges is associated with early pregnancy loss and poor implantation due to altered endometrial receptivity. Thus, salpingectomy should be offered before IVF when hydrosalpinges are present.[96]

Similarly, endometriosis-associated infertility reduces pregnancy rates. IVF represents an effective means of bypassing the hostile peritoneal environment and anatomic distortion associated with this disease. Pretreatment with GnRH agonists immediately before IVF cycle initiation appears to be beneficial. It is uncertain if only a specific subset or if all patients with endometriosis would benefit from this approach, and the use of endometrial implantation markers may be helpful in this regard.[97]

The incidence of multiple gestation in IVF is easier to control, since its occurrence is primarily dependent on the number of embryos transferred. Increased emphasis is being directed toward decreasing the number of embryos for transfer and, therefore, diminishing the chances of (higher-order) multiple pregnancies. Clearly, studies using appropriate end points such as singleton, term delivered, and live birth rate are required to elucidate further the optimal approach of the empiric treatment of unexplained infertility.[98,99]

## SUMMARY AND FUTURE DEVELOPMENTS

Subfertility should be considered a serious health issue, and the majority of people worldwide still have insufficient access to infertility services. The postponement of pregnancy beyond the age of 30, as observed in the Western world, will give rise to an increased demand for infertility services, because more couples will fail to conceive spontaneously within a year of unprotected intercourse. The major clinical challenge is to assess the reproductive aging status of a given woman. This will help to predict her pregnancy chances more accurately compared to assessment based on chronologic age alone. The use of multivariate models may even further improve the prediction capacity of initial screening for a given couple. The duration of subfertility and a woman's age constitute the most important predictors for chances of achieving a spontaneous pregnancy. This approach should help when counseling couples regarding the relative likelihood of success of expectant management or whether (empiric) treatment should be initiated.

The diagnosis of unexplained subfertility can only be made after an appropriate diagnostic infertility workup has established the absence of any abnormalities. Since no consensus exists with regard to the extent of testing that should be performed, unexplained subfertility represents notoriously heterogeneous group of patients. This condition may include couples with undiagnosed infertility and those with normal fertility for whom pregnancy, purely by chance, has not yet occurred. These patients often undergo empiric treatment in order to improve pregnancy chances per cycle. The inherent disadvantage of such an approach is decreased interest in the diagnostic workup, which impairs progress in understanding the underlying pathophysiology.

When costs related to multiple pregnancies are also taken into consideration, the conclusion seems justified that the widespread use of ovarian hyperstimulation with exogenous gonadotropins for assisted reproduction, especially IUI, should be discouraged. It is easier to control the incidence of multiple gestation with IVF since its occurrence is primarily dependent on the number of embryos transferred. With IVF, increased emphasis is directed toward decreasing the number of embryos for transfer and, therefore, diminishing the chances of (higher-order) multiple pregnancies. Clearly, more cohort follow-up studies, using appropriate end points such as singleton, term delivered, and live birth rate, are required to elucidate further the optimal approach to the empiric treatment of unexplained infertility.

## REFERENCES

1. Johnson NP, Proctor M, Farquhar CM: Gaps in the evidence for fertility treatment: An analysis of the Cochrane Menstrual Disorders and Subfertility Group database. Hum Reprod 18:947–954, 2003.
2. Evers JL, Collins JA: Assessment of efficacy of varicocele repair for male subfertility: A systematic review. Lancet 361:1849–1852, 2003.
3. Edwards RG, Steptoe PC, Purdy JM: Establishing full-term human pregnancies using cleaving embryos grown in vitro. Br J Obstet Gynaecol 87:737–756, 1980.
4. Palermo G, Joris H, Derde MP, et al: Sperm characteristics and outcome of human assisted fertilization by subzonal insemination and intracytoplasmic sperm injection. Fertil Steril 59:826–835, 1993.
5. Soliman S, Daya S, Collins J, et al: A randomized trial of in vitro fertilization versus conventional treatment for infertility. Fertil Steril 59:1239–1244, 1993.
6. Karande VC, Korn A, Morris R, et al: Prospective randomized trial comparing the outcome and cost of in vitro fertilization with that of a traditional treatment algorithm as first-line therapy for couples with infertility. Fertil Steril 71:468–475, 1999.
7. Evers JL: Female subfertility. Lancet 360:151–159, 2002.
8. Bagshawe A, Taylor A: ABC of subfertility: Counselling. Br Med J 327:1038–1040, 2003.
9. Guzick DS: Fertility: Evaluation of the infertile couple. In Barbieri RL (ed): Up to Date: Obstetrics, Gynecology, and Women's Health, 2004.
10. Hull MG, Cahill DJ: Female infertility. Endocrinol Metab Clin North Am 27:851–876, 1998.
11. Templeton A: Infertility and the establishment of pregnancy: Overview. Br Med Bull 56:577–587, 2000.
12. Bostofte E, Bagger P, Michael A, et al: Fertility prognosis for infertile couples. Fertil Steril 59:102–107, 1993.
13. Ombelet W, Wouters E, Boels L, et al: Sperm morphology assessment: Diagnostic potential and comparative analysis of strict or WHO criteria in a fertile and a subfertile population. Int J Androl 20:367–372, 1997.
14. Lunenfeld B, Insler V: Classification of amenorrhoeic states and their treatment by ovulation induction. Clin Endocrinol (Oxf) 3:223–237, 1974.
15. The ESHRE Capri Workshop Group. Anovulatory infertility. Hum Reprod 10:1549–1553, 1995.
16. Laven JS, Imani B, Eijkemans MJ, et al: New approach to polycystic ovary syndrome and other forms of anovulatory infertility. Obstet Gynecol Surv 57:755–767, 2002.
17. Fauser BC: Revised 2003 consensus on diagnostic criteria and long-term health risks related to polycystic ovary syndrome (PCOS): The Rotterdam ESHRE/ASRM-sponsored PCOS Consensus Workshop Group. Hum Reprod 19:41–47, 2004.
18. Karamardian LM, Grimes DA: Luteal phase deficiency: Effect of treatment on pregnancy rates. Am J Obstet Gynecol 167:1391–1398, 1992.
19. Ledger WL: Endometriosis and infertility: An integrated approach. Int J Gynaecol Obstet 64(Suppl 1):S33–S40, 1999.
20. Marcoux S, Maheux R, Berube S: Laparoscopic surgery in infertile women

with minimal or mild endometriosis. Canadian Collaborative Group on Endometriosis. N Engl J Med 337:217–222, 1997.

21. Donnez J, Jadoul P: What are the implications of myomas on fertility? A need for a debate? Hum Reprod 17:1424–1430, 2002.

22. Pritts EA: Fibroids and infertility: A systematic review of the evidence. Obstet Gynecol Surv 56:483–491, 2001.

23. te Velde ER, Pearson PL: The variability of female reproductive aging. Hum Reprod Update 8:141–154, 2002.

24. Menken J, Trussell J, Larsen U: Age and infertility. Science 233:1389–1394, 1986.

25. Nikolaou D, Templeton A: Early ovarian aging: A hypothesis—detection and clinical relevance. Hum Reprod 18:1137–1139, 2003.

26. van der Gaast MH, Beckers NG, Beier-Hellwig K, et al: Ovarian stimulation for IVF and endometrial receptivity: The missing link. Reprod Biomed Online 5(Suppl 1):36–43, 2002.

27. Macklon NS, Geraedts JP, Fauser BC: Conception to ongoing pregnancy: The "black box" of early pregnancy loss. Hum Reprod Update 8:333–343, 2002.

28. Helmerhorst FM, Oei SG, Bloemenkamp KW, et al: Consistency and variation in fertility investigations in Europe. Hum Reprod 10:2027–2030, 1995.

29. Guzick DS: Do infertility tests discriminate between fertile and infertile populations? Hum Reprod 10:2008–2009, 1995.

30. Barbieri RL: Fertility: The initial fertility consultation in couples planning pregnancy. In Barbieri RL (ed): Up to Date: Obstetrics, Gynecology, and Women's Health, 2004.

31. Healy DL, Trounson AO, Andersen AN: Female infertility: Causes and treatment. Lancet 343:1539–1544, 1994.

32. Crosignani PG, Rubin BL: Optimal use of infertility diagnostic tests and treatments. The ESHRE Capri Workshop Group. Hum Reprod 15:723–732, 2000.

33. Rosene-Montella K, Keely E, Laifer SA, et al: Evaluation and management of infertility in women: The internists' role. Ann Intern Med 132:973–981, 2000.

34. Cahill DJ, Wardle PG: Management of infertility. Br Med J 325:28–32, 2002.

35. Welt CK, Taylor AE: Menstrual cycle: Evaluation of the menstrual cycle and timing of ovulation. In Barbieri RL (ed): Up to Date: Obstetrics, Gynecology, and Women's Health, 2004.

36. Insler V: Corpus luteum defects. Curr Opin Obstet Gynecol 4:203–211, 1992.

37. Land JA, Evers JL: Chlamydia infection and subfertility. Best Pract Res Clin Obstet Gynaecol 16:901–912, 2002.

38. Land JA, Evers JL, Goossens VJ: How to use Chlamydia antibody testing in subfertility patients. Hum Reprod 13:1094–1098, 1998.

39. Akande VA, Hunt LP, Cahill DJ, et al: Tubal damage in infertile women: Prediction using chlamydia serology. Hum Reprod 18:1841–1847, 2003.

40. Mol BW, Collins JA, van der Veen, et al: Cost-effectiveness of hysterosalpingography, laparoscopy, and Chlamydia antibody testing in subfertile couples. Fertil Steril 75:571–580, 2001.

41. Richmond JA: Hysterosalpingography. In Lobo RA, Paulson RJ (eds): Mishell's Textbook of Infertility, Contraception, and Reproductive Endocrinology. Malden, MA, Blackwell, 1997, pp 567–579.

42. Mol BW, Collins JA, Burrows EA, et al: Comparison of hysterosalpingography and laparoscopy in predicting fertility outcome. Hum Reprod 14:1237–1242, 1999.

43. Gomel V: Diagnostic laparoscopy in infertility. In Keye W Jr, Chang RJ, Rebar RW, et al (eds): Infertility: Evaluation and Treatment. Philadelphia, WB Saunders, 1995, pp 330–348.

44. Fatum M, Laufer N, Simon A: Investigation of the infertile couple: Should diagnostic laparoscopy be performed after normal hysterosalpingography in treating infertility suspected to be of unknown origin? Hum Reprod 17:1–3, 2002.

45. Surrey ES: Endoscopy in the evaluation of the woman experiencing infertility. Clin Obstet Gynecol 43:889–896, 2000.

46. Oei SG, Helmerhorst FM, Keirse MJ: When is the post-coital test normal? A critical appraisal. Hum Reprod 10:1711–1714, 1995.

47. Oei SG, Helmerhorst FM, Bloemenkamp KW, et al: Effectiveness of the postcoital test: Randomised controlled trial. Br Med J 317:502–505, 1998.

48. Bukman A, Heineman MJ: Ovarian reserve testing and the use of prognostic models in patients with subfertility. Hum Reprod Update 7:581–590, 2001.

49. Schwartz D, Mayaux MJ: Female fecundity as a function of age: Results of artificial insemination in 2193 nulliparous women with azoospermic husbands. Federation CECOS. N Engl J Med 306:404–406, 1982.

50. Templeton A, Morris JK, Parslow W: Factors that affect outcome of in-vitro fertilisation treatment. Lancet 348:1402–1406, 1996.

51. Fauser BC: Follicle pool depletion: Factors involved and implications. Fertil Steril 74:629–630, 2000.

52. Lobo RA: Early ovarian aging: A hypothesis. What is early ovarian aging? Hum Reprod 18:1762–1764, 2003.

53. Elting MW, Kwee J, Schats R, et al: The rise of estradiol and inhibin B after acute stimulation with follicle-stimulating hormone predict the follicle cohort size in women with polycystic ovary syndrome, regularly menstruating women with polycystic ovaries, and regularly menstruating women with normal ovaries. J Clin Endocrinol Metab 86:1589–1595, 2001.

54. Scott MG, Ladenson JH, Green ED, et al: Hormonal evaluation of female infertility and reproductive disorders. Clin Chem 35:620–629, 1989.

55. Bancsi LF, Broekmans FJ, Mol BW, et al: Performance of basal follicle-stimulating hormone in the prediction of poor ovarian response and failure to become pregnant after in vitro fertilization: A meta-analysis. Fertil Steril 79:1091–1100, 2003.

56. Bancsi LF, Broekmans FJ, Eijkemans MJ, et al: Predictors of poor ovarian response in in vitro fertilization: A prospective study comparing basal markers of ovarian reserve. Fertil Steril 77:328–336, 2002.

57. Chang MY, Chiang CH, Chiu TH, et al: The antral follicle count predicts the outcome of pregnancy in a controlled ovarian hyperstimulation/intrauterine insemination program. J Assist Reprod Genet 15:12–17, 1998.

58. de Vet A, Laven JS, de Jong FH, et al: Antimullerian hormone serum levels: A putative marker for ovarian aging. Fertil Steril 77:357–362, 2002.

59. Van Rooij IA, Broekmans FJ, te Velde ER, et al: Serum anti-Mullerian hormone levels: A novel measure of ovarian reserve. Hum Reprod 17:3065–3071, 2002.

60. Eimers JM, te Velde ER, Gerritse R, et al: The prediction of the chance to conceive in subfertile couples. Fertil Steril 61:44–52, 1994.

61. Collins JA, Burrows EA, Wilan AR: The prognosis for live birth among untreated infertile couples. Fertil Steril 64:22–28, 1995.

62. Snick HK, Snick TS, Evers JL, et al: The spontaneous pregnancy prognosis in untreated subfertile couples: The Walcheren primary care study. Hum Reprod 12:1582–1588, 1997.

63. Hunault CC, Habbema JD, Eijkemans MC, et al: Two new prediction rules for spontaneous pregnancy leading to birth among subfertile couples, based on the synthesis of three previous models. Hum Reprod 19:2019–2026, 2004.

64. Collins JA, Wrixon W, Janes LB, et al: Treatment-independent pregnancy among infertile couples. N Engl J Med 309:1201–1206, 1983.

65. Bagshawe A, Taylor A: ABC of subfertility: Counselling. Br Med J 327:1038–1040, 2003.

66. Collins JA, Feeny D, Gunby J: The cost of infertility diagnosis and treatment in Canada in 1995. Hum Reprod 12:951–958, 1997.

67. Gleicher N: Cost-effective infertility care. Hum Reprod Update 6:190–199, 2000.

68. Philips Z, Barraza-Llorens M, Posnett J: Evaluation of the relative cost-effectiveness of treatments for infertility in the UK. Hum Reprod 15:95–106, 2000.

69. Van Voorhis BJ, Sparks AE, Allen BD, et al: Cost-effectiveness of infertility treatments: A cohort study. Fertil Steril 67:830–836, 1997.

70. Garceau L, Henderson J, Davis LJ, et al: Economic implications of assisted reproductive techniques: A systematic review. Hum Reprod 17:3090–3109, 2002.

71. Fauser BC, Bouchard P, Coelingh Bennink HJ, et al: Alternative approaches in IVF. Hum Reprod Update 8:1–9, 2002.

72. Johnson NP, Proctor M, Farquhar CM: Gaps in the evidence for fertility treatment: An analysis of the Cochrane Menstrual Disorders and Subfertility Group database. Hum Reprod 18:947–954, 2003.

73. Aboulghar MA, Mansour RT, Serour GI, et al: Diagnosis and management of unexplained infertility:an update. Arch Gynecol Obstet 267:177–188, 2003.

74. Fauser BC, van Heusden AM: Manipulation of human ovarian function: Physiological concepts and clinical consequences. Endocr Rev 18:71–106, 1997.

75. Stovall DW, Guzick DS: Current management of unexplained infertility. Curr Opin Obstet Gynecol 5:228–233, 1993.

76. Hogue CJ: Successful assisted reproductive technology: The beauty of one. Obstet Gynecol 100:1017–1019, 2002.

77. Jones HW Jr: Total reproductive potential of a single cycle: To include fresh and frozen embryos? Fertil Steril 79:1044, 2003.

78. Hughes EG: The effectiveness of ovulation induction and intrauterine insemination in the treatment of persistent infertility: A meta-analysis. Hum Reprod 12:1865–1872, 1997.

79. te Velde ER, Cohlen BJ: The management of infertility. N Engl J Med 340:224–226, 1999.

80. Guzick DS, Sullivan MW, Adamson GD, et al: Efficacy of treatment for unexplained infertility. Fertil Steril 70:207–213, 1998.

81. Hughes E, Collins J, Vandekerckhove P: Clomiphene citrate for unexplained subfertility in women (Cochrane review). Cochrane Database Syst Rev 49:CD000057, 2000.

82. Athaullah N, Proctor M, Johnson NP: Oral versus injectable ovulation induction agents for unexplained subfertility. Cochrane Database Syst Rev CD003052, 2002.

83. Aitken RJ, Clarkson JS: Cellular basis of defective sperm function and its association with the genesis of reactive oxygen species by human spermatozoa. J Reprod Fertil 81:459–469, 1987.

84. Duran HE, Morshedi M, Kruger T, et al: Intrauterine insemination: A systematic review on determinants of success. Hum Reprod Update 8:373–384, 2002.

85. Cantineau AE, Heineman MJ, Cohlen BJ: Single versus double intrauterine insemination in stimulated cycles for subfertile couples: A systematic review based on a Cochrane review. Hum Reprod 18:941–946, 2003.

86. Sengoku K, Tamate K, Takaoka Y, et al: The clinical efficacy of low-dose step-up follicle stimulating hormone administration for treatment of unexplained infertility. Hum Reprod 14:349–353, 1999.

87. Goverde AJ, McDonnell J, Vermeiden JP, et al: Intrauterine insemination or in-vitro fertilisation in idiopathic subfertility and male subfertility: A randomised trial and cost-effectiveness analysis. Lancet 355:13–18, 2000.

88. Hohmann FP, Macklon NS, Fauser BC: A randomized comparison of two ovarian stimulation protocols with gonadotropin-releasing hormone (GnRH) antagonist cotreatment for in vitro fertilization commencing recombinant follicle-stimulating hormone on cycle day 2 or 5 with the standard long GnRH agonist protocol. J Clin Endocrinol Metab 88:166–173, 2003.

89. Guzick DS, Carson SA, Coutifaris C, et al: Efficacy of superovulation and intrauterine insemination in the treatment of infertility. National Cooperative Reproductive Medicine Network. N Engl J Med 340:177–183, 1999.

90. Tur R, Barri PN, Coroleu B, et al: Risk factors for high-order multiple implantation after ovarian stimulation with gonadotrophins:evidence from a large series of 1878 consecutive pregnancies in a single centre. Hum Reprod 16:2124–2129, 2001.

91. Gleicher N, Oleske DM, Tur-Kaspa I, et al: Reducing the risk of high-order multiple pregnancy after ovarian stimulation with gonadotropins. N Engl J Med 343:2–7, 2000.

92. Suri K, Bhandari V, Lerer T, et al: Morbidity and mortality of preterm twins and higher-order multiple births. J Perinatol 21:293–299, 2001.

93. Stromberg B, Dahlquist G, Ericson A, et al: Neurological sequelae in children born after in-vitro fertilisation: A population-based study. Lancet 359:461–465, 2002.

94. Collins J: Stimulated intra-uterine insemination is not a natural choice for the treatment of unexplained subfertility: Current best evidence for the advanced treatment of unexplained subfertility. Hum Reprod 18:907–912, 2003.

95. Pandian Z, Bhattacharya S, Nikolaou D, et al: The effectiveness of IVF in unexplained infertility: A systematic Cochrane review. 2002. Hum Reprod 18:2001–2007, 2003.

96. Strandell A, Lindhard A, Waldenstrom U, et al: Hydrosalpinx and IVF outcome: Cumulative results after salpingectomy in a randomized controlled trial. Hum Reprod 16:2403–2410, 2001.

97. Surrey ES, Schoolcraft WB: Management of endometriosis-associated infertility. Obstet Gynecol Clin North Am 30:193–208, 2003.

98. Min JK, Breheny SA, MacLachlan V, et al: What is the most relevant standard of success in assisted reproduction? The singleton, term gestation, live birth rate per cycle initiated: The BESST endpoint for assisted reproduction. Hum Reprod 19:3–7, 2004.

99. Heijnen EM, Macklon NS, Fauser BC: What is the most relevant standard of success in assisted repoduction? Consider the whole treatment. Hum Reprod 19:1936–1938, 2004.

# Hyperandrogenism, Hirsutism, and the Polycystic Ovary Syndrome

## David A. Ehrmann, Randall B. Barnes, and Robert L. Rosenfield

In the 5 years that have transpired since publication of the fourth edition of this textbook, significant advances have been made in our understanding of the physiologic and pathophysiologic factors controlling the biosynthesis, secretion, and action of androgens in women. These insights have led to improved methods for the diagnosis and treatment of androgen excess.

In this chapter, we first summarize the normal physiology of androgen production in women. This is followed by a review of the pathogenesis and clinical presentation of disorders leading to androgen excess. Finally, an approach to the diagnosis, differential diagnosis, and therapy of these disorders is provided.

## ANDROGEN PHYSIOLOGY AND PATHOPHYSIOLOGY

### ANDROGEN BIOSYNTHESIS

The sequential enzymatic processing of cholesterol is required to form one of five possible steroid end products, namely progestins, mineralocorticoids, glucocorticoids, androgens, and estrogen (Fig. 157-1)[1,2]

The biosynthesis of androgens is modulated by two key cytochrome P-450 enzymes: cytochrome P-450scc (CYP11A) and cytochrome P-450c17 (CYP-17). The former mediates the chemical reactions involved in cholesterol side chain cleavage and, together with the cholesterol transport enzyme steroidogenic acute regulatory protein, is the rate-determining step for the formation of all steroid hormones in both the adrenal glands and gonads.[1,3] Cytochrome P-450c17 is rate-limiting for the formation of cortisol and sex hormones and its level of expression is absolutely dependent on tropic hormone stimulation. This one enzyme possesses both 17-hydroxylase and 17,20-lyase activities. The first of these two sequential activities is necessary to form cortisol, and both activities are necessary to form the 17-ketosteroids dehydroepiandrosterone (DHEA) and androstenedione, which are, in turn, the precursors of all potent sex steroids. P-450c17 mediates conversion of pregnenolone by a two-step chemical reaction involving 17-hydroxylation (to 17-hydroxypregnenolone) followed by 17,20-lyase activity (to DHEA). Progesterone undergoes parallel reactions: P-450c17 carries out 17-hydroxylation to 17-hydroxyprogesterone, and this, in turn, is converted to androstenedione by 17,20-lyase activity. Whether

P-450c17 is the source of 17,20-lyase activity in this path is unclear. The 17,20-lyase activity of P-450c17 is regulated differently from its 17-hydroxylase activity; phosphorylation of enzyme serine residues and electron transfer enzymes upregulate the lyase activity. $\Delta^5$-isomerase-3$\beta$-hydroxysteroid dehydrogenase (3$\beta$-HSD) and 17$\beta$-HSD are non-P-450 steroidogenic enzymes. 3$\beta$-HSD is required to convert pregnenolone to progesterone and DHEA to androstenedione. In the gonads, androstenedione is the major precursor for both testosterone and estrogen synthesis; it is converted by 17$\beta$-HSD to form testosterone or aromatized by aromatase (cytochrome P-450arom) to form estrone.

Under normal circumstances, the ovaries and adrenal glands contribute nearly equally to testosterone production (Fig. 157-2).[4,5] Approximately half of the total testosterone originates from direct secretion while half is derived from peripheral conversion of secreted 17-ketosteroids. Other tissues, including liver, adipose tissue, and skin, contain the enzymes 3$\beta$-HSD, 17$\beta$-HSD, and P-450arom, which allow for the further processing of steroids synthesized within the adrenal glands and gonads.

### REGULATION OF ANDROGEN SECRETION

Androgens are secreted by both the adrenal glands and ovaries in response to their respective tropic hormones, adrenocorticotropic hormone (ACTH) and luteinizing hormone (LH).[2] Since androgens are, in a sense, byproducts of estradiol and cortisol secretion by the ovary and adrenal gland, respectively, androgen levels in females are not controlled by direct negative feedback by the pituitary gland, as is the case for cortisol and estradiol secretion. Rather, intraglandular paracrine and autocrine mechanisms seem to play a major role in the regulation of androgen secretion by these glands (see discussion that follows and Table 157-1).

#### Adrenal

Adrenal 17-ketosteroid secretion gradually begins during midchildhood as a result of adrenarche, the point at which there is a change in the pattern of the adrenal secretory response to ACTH. There are marked increases in 17-hydroxypregnenolone and DHEA production[6] that lead to DHEA-sulfate (DHEA-S, the sulfated derivative of DHEA) becoming the predominant androgen secreted by the adrenal gland. The conversion of DHEA to DHEA-S is catalyzed by the sulfotransferase SULT2A1.

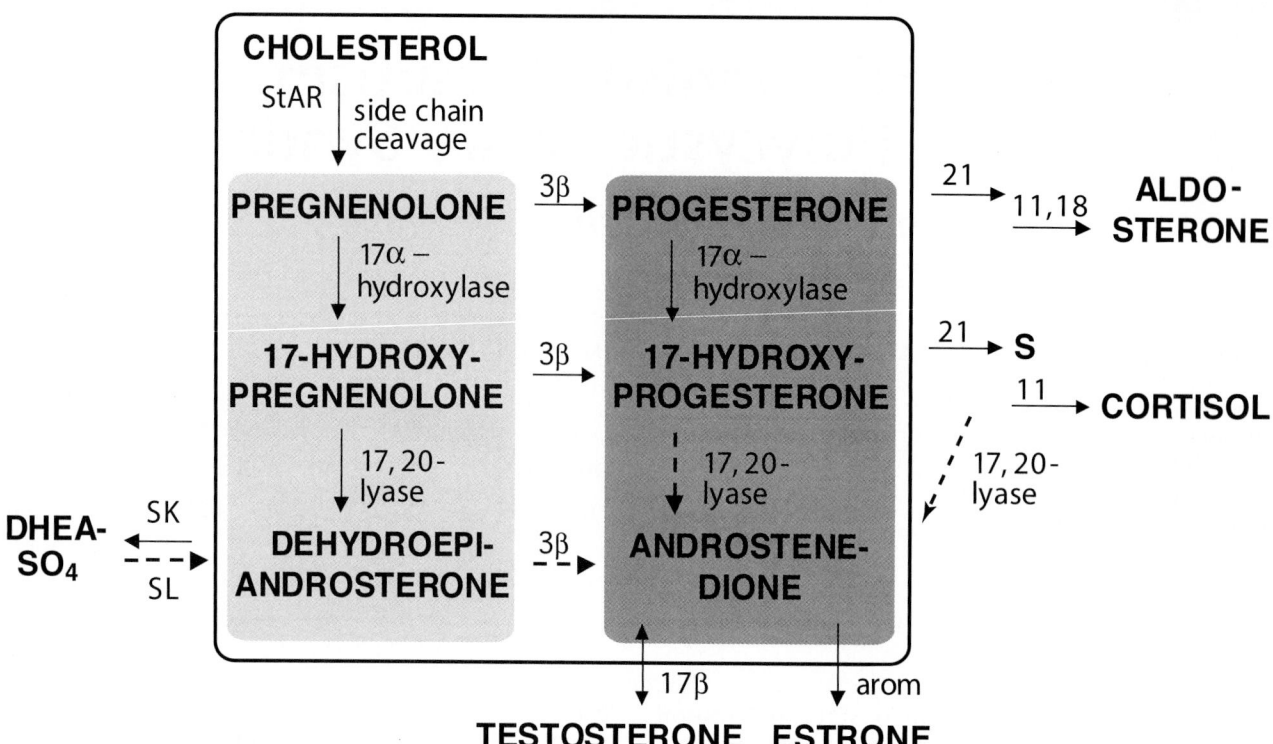

***Figure 157-1*** Outline of the major steroid biosynthetic pathways. The core pathway utilized by the adrenal cortex and ovary is outlined. The Δ5 steroids are shown in light shading; the Δ4 steroids are shown in dark shading. Half of testosterone is formed by peripheral conversion of secreted androstenedione in females. The 17-ketosteroids are formed by cytochrome P-450c17, an enzyme with both 17-hydroxylase and 17,20-lyase activities. StAR, steroidogenic acute regulatory protein; 3β, Δ5isomerase-3β-hydroxysteroid dehydrogenase; 17β, 17β-reductase; 21, 21-hydroxylase; 11,18, 11β-hydroxylase/aldosterone synthase; arom, aromatase; SK, sulfokinase; SL, sulfotransferase. Modified from Ref. 109.

These adrenarchal changes seem to be related to the development of the zona reticularis of the adrenal cortex, an adrenal zone that produces large amounts of DHEA and DHEA-S.[2,6] This zone has low 3β-HSD activity and possesses the sulfokinase activity to sulfate the DHEA that accumulates. DHEA synthesis increases because of a combination of the low 3β-HSD activity and a change, of unknown origin, in the regulation of the 17,20-lyase activity of P-450c17.

The nature of the factor or factors responsible for bringing about the adrenarchal change within the adrenal gland has been the subject of considerable controversy.[2,6,7] Because ACTH levels do not increase in adrenarche but appear to be

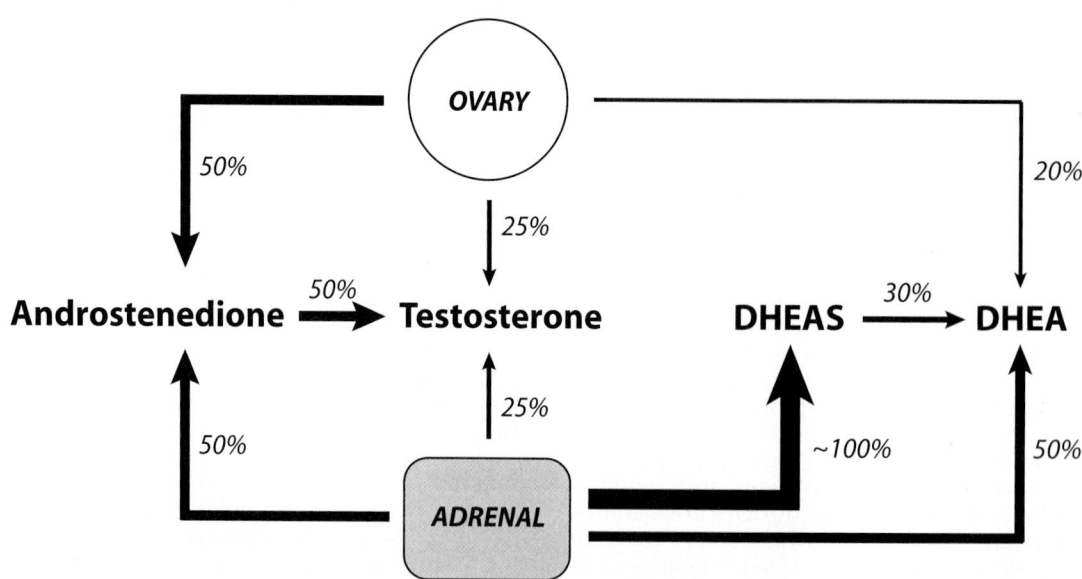

***Figure 157-2*** Relative contribution by the ovary and adrenal glands to circulating androgens and proandrogens in normal women. Approximately 25% of circulating testosterone is derived from the ovary; an equal proportion is of adrenal origin. The remaining 50% of testosterone in the circulation is derived from the conversion of androstenedione which, in turn, is equally contributed to by the adrenal and ovary. The majority of DHEA is of adrenal origin: 50% is directly secreted, while 30% is derived from conversion of DHEA-S. A small proportion (20%) of circulating DHEA comes from ovarian secretion. Finally, DHEA-S is almost entirely derived from direct secretion by the adrenal. Based on data from Ref. 217.

**Table 157-1** Modulators of Theca Cell Androgen Biosynthesis

| Factor | Effect on Theca Cell Androgen Biosynthesis | |
| --- | --- | --- |
| | Stimulation | Inhibition |
| **AUTOCRINE** | | |
| Transforming growth factor-α | | • |
| Transforming growth factor-β | | • |
| Hepatocyte growth factor | | • |
| Keratinocyte growth factor | | • |
| Nerve growth factor | • | |
| **PARACRINE** | | |
| Transforming growth facator-β | | • |
| Activin | | • |
| β–Fibroblast growth factor | | • |
| Tumor necrosis factor-α | | • |
| Interleukin-1β | | • |
| Bone morphogenetic protein-4 | | • |
| Insulin-like growth factor 1 | • | |
| Inhibin | • | |
| Growth differentiation factor-9 | • | |
| **ENDOCRINE** | | |
| Luteinizing hormone | • | |
| Insulin | • | |

Adapted from Ref. 218.

necessary for its development, ACTH is thought to play a "permissive" role in the process.[6] Several substances have been implicated as the putative pituitary hormone responsible for bringing about the adrenarchal change, including "cortical androgen stimulating hormone" and pro-opiomelanocortin-related peptides. The fact that adrenarche represents a change in the steroidogenic response pattern of the adrenal gland to ACTH suggests that potential adrenarche factors may control the growth and differentiation of the zona reticularis and/or regulate steroidogenic enzyme activity, especially the 17,20-lyase activity of P-450c17. Intra-adrenal hormones, such as estradiol,[8] as well as extra-adrenal hormones, such as leptin, have also been postulated as potential adrenarchal factors.[9,10] No single factor or hormone has yet been identified as both necessary and sufficient for the development of adrenarche.

Analogous to the case in the ovary, insulin and insulin-like growth factors (IGFs) may alter the response of adrenal steroids to ACTH.[11] Insulin infusion has been reported to modestly potentiate the 17-ketosteroid response to ACTH, in a pattern compatible with increases in 17-hydroxylase and 17,20-lyase activities, the former more prominently.[12] Insulin excess might explain the enhanced responsiveness of 17-ketosteroids to ACTH in simple obesity. In vitro studies have directly shown that insulin and IGFs upregulate adrenal 17-hydroxylase, 17,20-lyase, and 3β-HSD activities.

**Ovary**

The combined action of LH on theca-interstitial (thecal) cells and of follicle-stimulating hormone (FSH) on ovarian granulosa cells, respectively, is necessary for the development and maintenance of normal ovarian function (Fig. 157-3).[2]

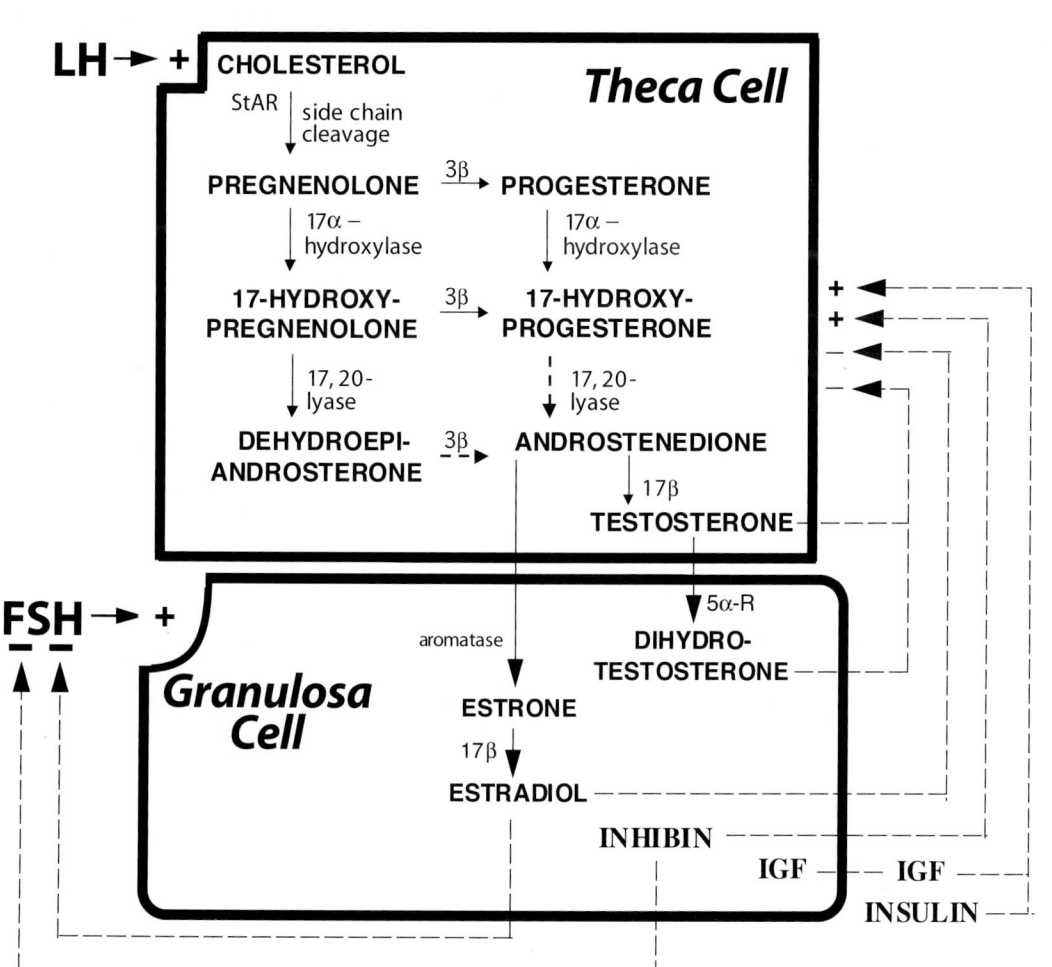

**Figure 157-3** Outline of the organization of the major steroid biosynthetic pathways in the small antral follicle of the ovary, depicted according to the two-gonadotropin, two-cell model of ovarian steroidogenesis. LH stimulates androgen formation within theca cells via the steroidogenic pathway common to the gonads and adrenal glands. FSH regulates estradiol biosynthesis from androgen by granulosa cells. Long-loop negative feedback of estradiol on gonadotropin secretion does not suppress LH at physiologic levels of estradiol. Androgen formation in response to LH appears to be modulated by intraovarian feedback at the levels of 17-hydroxylase and 17,20-lyase, both of which are activities of cytochrome P-450c17. The quantitative importance of androstenedione formation from 17-hydroxyprogesterone (*dotted arrow*) in the intact follicle is unknown. Androgens and estradiol inhibit (*minus signs*) and inhibin, insulin, and insulin-like growth factor 1 (IGF) stimulate (*plus signs*) 17-hydroxylase and 17,20-lyase activities. StAR, steroidogenic acute regulatory protein; 3β, Δ5isomerase-3β-hydroxysteroid dehydrogenase; 17β, 17β-reductase; 21, 21-hydroxylase; 5α-R, 5α-reductase. Modified from Ref. 2.

Androgenic precursors (especially androstenedione) are produced by thecal cells under LH stimulation. These are aromatized to estrogen by FSH-stimulated granulosa cell aromatase activity. Estrogens, acting in concert with FSH and LH, induce granulosa cell growth and follicular maturation. Androgens, in turn, may be involved in the selection of a single follicle for ovulation. As the dominant follicle emerges, both increased amounts of androstenedione and estradiol are secreted, with the ratio favoring estradiol in healthy preovulatory follicles.

Androgens are obligate intermediates in the biosynthesis of estradiol (see Fig. 157-3) and appear to have a dual role in follicular development within the ovary. Intraovarian androgens enhance the initial recruitment of primordial follicles into the growth pool while at the same time they appear to impair the cyclic recruitment of late antral follicles, thus leading to follicular atresia.[13] Atretic follicles are relatively deficient in aromatase activity and, thus, contribute to androgen excess. Therefore, it seems critical for the function of the ovary that the intraovarian androgen concentration be kept at a level that is sufficient for the initial recruitment of primordial follicles and the production of estradiol, which is essential to prevent atresia. It is not known how ovarian androgen secretion is minimized while the formation of estrogen is optimized. We have postulated that androgen excess is normally prevented by the downregulation process whereby excessive or protracted LH stimulation leads to intraovarian desensitization of the responses to LH, primarily at the level of P-450c17.[14]

A number of hormones and growth factors seem to be involved in the intraovarian modulation of P-450c17 steroidogenic responsiveness to LH (see Table 157-1 and Fig. 157-3).[14,15] Desensitization to LH is mediated in part by ovarian steroids. It appears likely that estrogen inhibits this response by a short-loop (paracrine) negative feedback mechanism. Androgens, on the other hand, may well be inhibitory by an autocrine mechanism. These inhibiting modulators seem to be counterbalanced by hormones and growth factors that amplify P-450c17 activities, including insulin, IGF-1,[16,17] and inhibin, as well as numerous other small peptides.[2,14]

## BLOOD LEVELS AND TRANSPORT OF ANDROGENS

The total plasma concentrations of androgens and intermediates in their biosynthesis are shown in Table 157-2. Plasma levels of DHEA-S normally reflect adrenal androgen production, while plasma testosterone and androstenedione levels are accounted for by both ovarian and adrenal androgen secretion. Plasma 17-hydroxyprogesterone, like plasma testosterone and androstenedione, may arise from either the adrenal glands or ovaries. Of the circulating androgens, testosterone is the most important biologically and clinically, because of its relatively high plasma concentration and potency at the target organ level.

Over 96% of the plasma testosterone and structurally related 17β-hydroxysteroids circulate in plasma bound to carrier proteins, with only a small fraction remaining free.[18,19] Sex hormone–binding globulin (SHBG) and albumin are the principal sex steroid–binding proteins in plasma. Although there has been interest in the possibility that albumin-bound testosterone is bioactive, most evidence suggests that it is only the free steroid intermediate that is bioavailable.[20,21] Due to its high binding affinity, SHBG concentration is the major determinant of the fraction of 17β-hydroxysteroids binding to plasma albumin and of the fraction remaining free and biologically active in blood.

SHBG is a glycoprotein synthesized in the liver.[19] Its synthesis is modulated by a number of physiologic and pathologic states that ultimately impact on its plasma concentration: SHBG levels are increased by estrogens and thyroid hormone excess; plasma concentrations are decreased by androgen, glucocorticoid, growth hormone, and insulin.[22] Because SHBG levels are often decreased in hyperandrogenic states and obesity, serum-free testosterone levels are often elevated in women whose total testosterone levels are normal. Consequently, the plasma-free testosterone concentration is more often elevated in women with hirsutism or acne than is the plasma total testosterone concentration, reflecting the truly elevated plasma concentration of bioavailable androgen.[23]

## MECHANISMS OF ANDROGEN ACTION

Testosterone exerts its androgenic effect by binding to the androgen receptor of target tissues. However, the biologic activity of testosterone is dependent in large part on its being converted to dihydrotestosterone (DHT) by 5α-reductase. The formation of DHT from testosterone and other precursors determines, to a significant extent, the expression of androgen action at the level of the pilosebaceous unit.[24,25] DHT is primarily formed by the 5α-reductase activity of target tissues and liver.[26,27] In skin, 5α-reductase activity resides primarily in sebaceous and sweat glands, as well as dermis, rather than in hair itself. Measurement of plasma or urinary 3α-androstanediol glucuronide, a metabolite of DHT, has been touted as a marker of hypersensitivity of the hair follicle to androgen.[26] However, the extent to which this metabolite arises from hepatic or skin 5α-reductase activity is controversial.[28] DHT has greater biologic potency than testosterone due to its higher affinity for and slower dissociation from the androgen receptor.[29] The length of the androgen receptor's CAG repeat, a polymorphism in exon 1, is potentially inversely related to the transactivation efficiency of the androgen receptor.[30]

## CUTANEOUS MANIFESTATIONS OF ANDROGEN EXCESS

Hair can be categorized as either vellus or terminal (Fig. 157-4).[31,32] Vellus hair is fine, soft, and not pigmented, while terminal hair is long, coarse, and pigmented. Virtually

| *Table 157-2* Typical Normal Ranges for Plasma Androgens and Intermediates* | | | | | | | | |
|---|---|---|---|---|---|---|---|---|
| | 17-Hydroxy-pregnenolone (ng/dL) | 17-Hydroxy-progesterone (ng/dL) | 11-Deoxy-cortisol (ng/dL) | Cortisol (µg/dL) | DHEA (ng/dL) | Androstenedione (ng/dL) | Testosterone (ng/dL) | DHEA-S (µg/dL) |
| **Prepubertal, 2–8 yr** | <25–235 | <25–65 | <25–160 | 5–25 | <25–120 | <25–50 | <15 | <40 |
| **Adrenarchal†** | <25–355 | <25–95 | <25–120 | 5–25 | 100–420 | 30–75 | 10–<45 | 40–400 |
| **Adult Female** | 40–360 | 30–130‡ | 30–220 | 5–25 | 100–1000 | 55–200 | 20–75 | 100–400 |

Data from Refs. 219, 220.

*Normal range may differ slightly among laboratories.

†Children with premature adrenarche.

‡17-Hydroxyprogesterone rises in the preovulatory phase to a peak as high as 360 ng/dL in the luteal phase of the cycle.

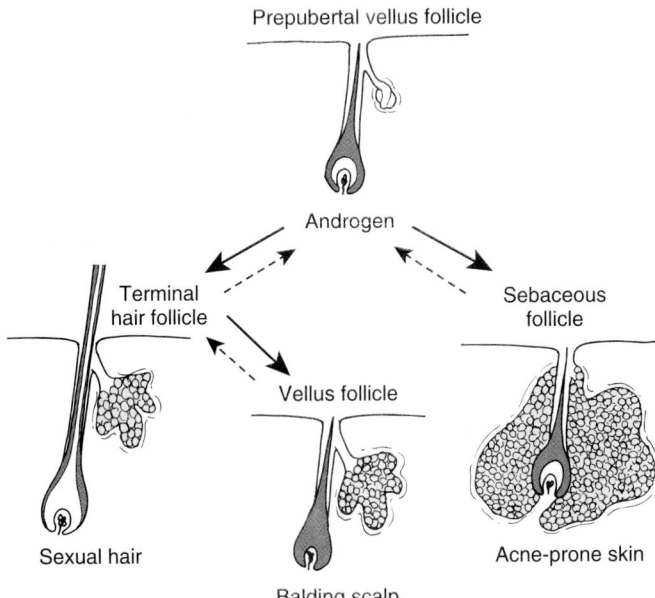

**Figure 157-4** Role of androgen in the development of the pilosebaceous unit. *Solid lines* indicate effects of androgens, *dotted lines* those of antiandrogens. Hairs are depicted only in the anagen (growing) phase of the hair cycle. In conjunction with other regulatory factors, androgens cause the prepubertal pilosebaceous unit in androgen-dependent areas to differentiate into either a sexual hair follicle, in which the vellus hair transforms into a terminal hair, or into a sebaceous follicle, in which the sebaceous component proliferates and the hair remains vellus. In balding scalp (*bracketed area*) terminal hairs not previously dependent on androgen regress to vellus hairs under its influence. Reproduced from Ref. 32.

all hair follicles are associated with sebaceous glands to form pilosebaceous units (PSUs). The growth of the hair follicle of PSU is controlled by as yet uncharacterized induction factors elaborated by the dermal papilla. In target areas, androgens cause the prepubertal PSU to differentiate into either a sexual hair follicle (in which the vellus hair transforms into a terminal hair) or into a sebaceous gland (in which the sebaceous component proliferates and the hair remains vellus). Thus, androgens are necessary for sexual hair and sebaceous gland development. Antiandrogens reverse this process, causing PSUs to revert toward the prepubertal state. Male pattern sexual hair development (for example, mustache and beard) occurs in sites where relatively high levels of androgen are necessary for PSU differentiation. The greater density of terminal hairs in the androgen-sensitive areas of men than women is accounted for by a greater proportion of PSUs with terminal rather than vellus hairs. Male pattern baldness is largely the result of conversion of terminal hair to sebaceous follicles.

Hirsutism is defined as excessive male pattern hair growth in women.[31] Hirsutism must be distinguished from *hypertrichosis*, the term used to describe the excessive growth of androgen-independent hair which is vellus, prominent in nonsexual areas, and most commonly familial or caused by metabolic disorders (for example, thyroid disturbances, anorexia nervosa) or medications (e.g., phenytoin, minoxidil or cyclosporine). In adult white women, hirsutism can be defined by a total score of 8 or more on a modified scale of Ferriman and Gallwey (Fig. 157-5). Thus, it is normal for women to have a few sexual hairs in most "male" areas (such as the upper lip and chin areas).

The cutaneous manifestations of androgen excess include acne and balding in addition to hirsutism.[33] However, these are variably expressed manifestations of hyperandrogenism:

Some patients have hirsutism or acne alone, others both, yet others neither, and balding in a diffuse pattern can be the sole manifestation.

An increase in the plasma-free testosterone concentration underlies half of the cases of mild hirsutism and a third of the cases of persistent mild acne in adolescents.[33] Moderately severe hirsutism or cystic acne is even more likely to be hyperandrogenic.[33,34] However, it must be noted that the amount of sexual hair and sebaceous gland development seems to depend as much on the factors determining sensitivity of the PSUs to androgens as it is dependent on the plasma androgen level itself. At one end of the normal spectrum are women whose PSUs seem "hypersensitive" to normal blood free androgen levels; this seems to account for "idiopathic" hirsutism and acne. At the other end of the spectrum are women whose PSUs are relatively insensitive to androgen; this seems to account for "cryptic" hyperandrogenemia (hyperandrogenism without skin manifestations). In idiopathic hirsutism, an inverse relationship between the hirsutism score and repeat size has been reported[30] and disputed.[35] The former study also claimed that these patients had a skewed pattern of X-inactivation that preferentially methylated (inactivated) the longer of the two alleles, favoring the expression of the shorter and presumably more functional allele.

## HYPERANDROGENIC DISORDERS

Hyperandrogenism arises from abnormal adrenal or ovarian function in most cases, but occasionally from apparent abnormalities in the peripheral formation of androgen. Functional abnormalities (Table 157-3) are much more common than tumors.

### ADRENAL DISORDERS

#### Premature Adrenarche

Normally, the first manifestation of the adrenal or gonadal contributions to androgen production is pubarche, the appearance of pubic hair.[6,36] Premature pubarche refers to the appearance of sexual pubic hairs before 8.5 years of age and is often the result of premature adrenarche.[37,38] That is, some children with the precocious onset of pubic hair have undergone a pubertal amount of maturation of adrenal androgen secretion earlier than normal. In others, premature pubarche represents inordinate sensitivity of sexual hair follicles to normal adrenal androgen levels. The best hormonal indicator of adrenarche is a plasma level of DHEA-S over 40 μg/dL. In children with premature adrenarche, plasma testosterone levels also rise into the early pubertal range and the responses of steroid intermediates to ACTH are typically in between the prepubertal and adult range. The predominant steroids are the $\Delta^5$-3β-steroids, 17-hydroxypregnenolone, and DHEA. Recent data suggest that premature adrenarche may be a risk factor for the subsequent development of polycystic ovary syndrome during adolescence (see Polycystic Ovary Syndrome discussed later in chapter).[39,40] This is particularly true in those patients who have the higher androgen levels and steroid intermediate responses to ACTH greater than those of normal adults, that is, "exaggerated adrenarche" or functional adrenal hyperandrogenism.

The distinction of premature adrenarche from mild (nonclassic) virilizing congenital adrenal hyperplasia (CAH) has been a matter of considerable controversy. On one hand, in some clinics as many as 40% of children presenting with premature pubarche have been diagnosed as having nonclassic CAH due to 21-hydroxylase deficiency.[41,42] This high prevalence is clearly skewed by the presence of patients of ethnic groups with a high prevalence of CAH, such as Ashkenazi Jews and Hispanics, in these clinics. On the other,

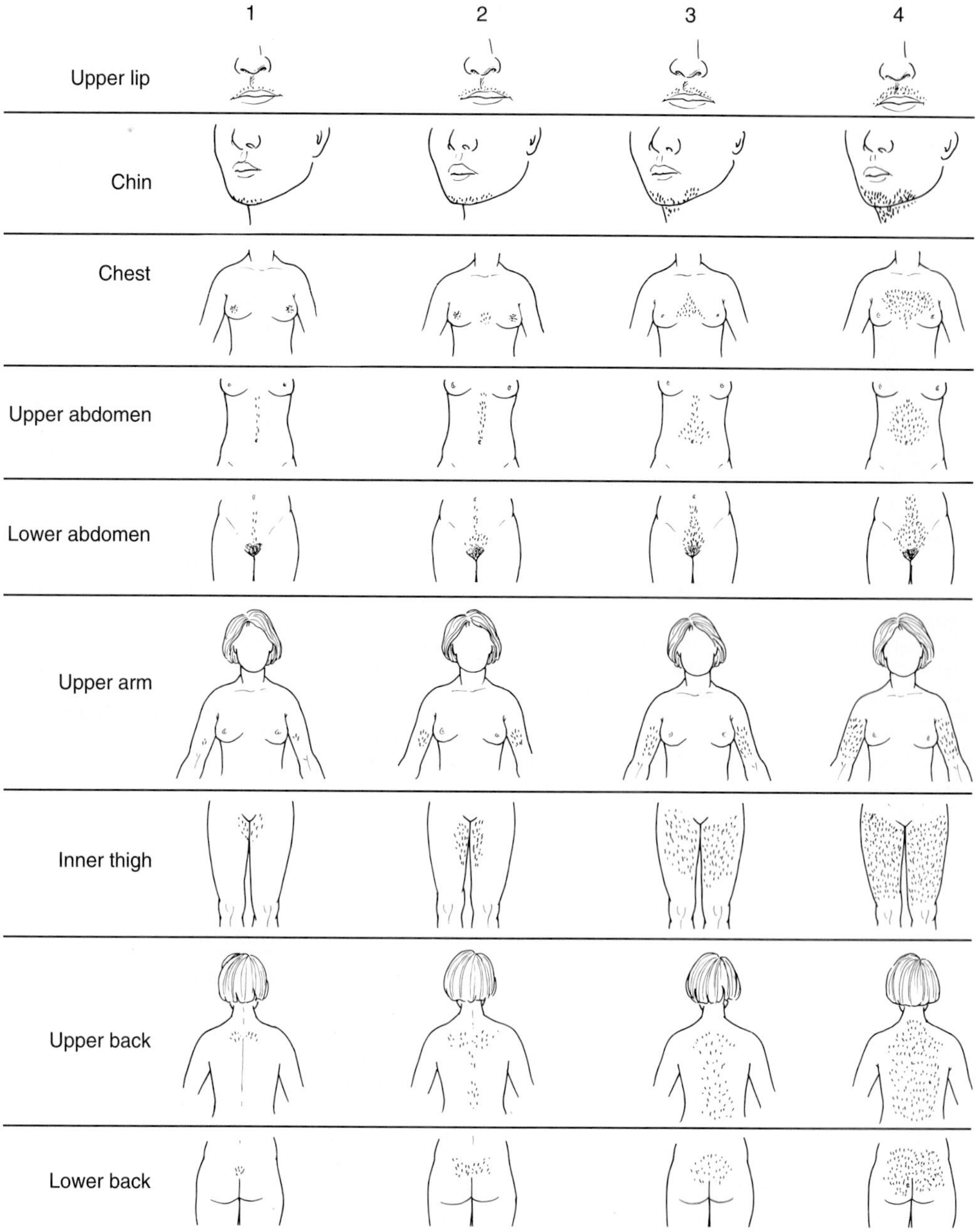

**Figure 157-5** Hirsutism scoring scale of Ferriman and Gallwey. The nine body areas possessing androgen sensitive PSUs are graded from 0 (no terminal hair) to 4 (frankly virile) and the sum totaled. Normal hirsutism score is less than 8. Modified from Ref. 31.

**Table 157-3  Causes of Androgen Excess in Women**

**I. Adrenal Hyperandrogenism**
  A. Premature adrenarche
  B. Functional adrenal hyperandrogenism
  C. Congenital adrenal hyperplasia
  D. Cushing's syndrome
  E. Hyperprolactinemia and acromegaly
  F. Abnormal cortisol action/metabolism
  G. Adrenal neoplasms
**II. Gonadal Hyperandrogenism**
  A. Ovarian hyperandrogenism
    1. Functional ovarian hyperandrogenism/polycystic ovary syndrome
    2. Adrenal virilizing disorders and rests
    3. Ovarian steroidogenic blocks
    4. Syndromes of extreme insulin resistance
    5. Ovarian neoplasms
  B. True hermaphroditism
  C. Pregnancy-related hyperandrogenism.
**III. Peripheral Androgen Overproduction**
  A. Obesity
  B. Idiopathic

much of the dispute centers around the distinction of mild 3β-HSD deficiency from premature adrenarche based on the responses of steroid intermediates to ACTH stimulation. Some investigators have designated Δ⁵-steroid responses greater than those of midpubertal controls as indicating 3β-HSD deficiency, thus concluding that 3β-HSD deficiency is a common cause.[41] It is now clear from molecular genetic studies that 3β-HSD deficiency is rarely the cause of premature pubarche.[43] Table 157-4 shows the typical ranges of steroid intermediate responses to ACTH in normal and prematurely adrenarchal subjects.

**Functional Adrenal Hyperandrogenism**

Functional adrenal hyperandrogenism (FAH) may be defined as glucocorticoid-suppressible, ACTH-dependent 17-ketosteroid excess. So defined, FAH is found in approximately one half of hyperandrogenic females and polycystic ovary syndrome (PCOS) patients (see later discussion).[2,15] This entity has been attributed by some to "exaggerated

**Table 157-4**  Typical Normal Ranges for Steroid Levels Post-ACTH*

| | 17-Hydroxy-pregnenolone (ng/dL) | 17-Hydroxy-progesterone (ng/dL) | 11-Deoxy-cortisol (ng/dL) | Cortisol (μg/dL) | DHEA (ng/dL) | Androstenedione (ng/dL) |
|---|---|---|---|---|---|---|
| **Prepubertal, 2–8 yr** | 130–340 | 80–180 | <25–350 | 13–50 | 45–120 | <25–80 |
| **Adrenarchal†** | 240–1100 | 40–190 | 40–300 | 13–50 | 285–495 | 55–140 |
| **Adult/Female** | 150–1070 | 35–130‡ | 40–200 | 13–50 | 225–1470 | 55–185 |

Data from Refs. 219–222.

*30 min post-ACTH 10 μg/m$^2$ as IV bolus. Values 60 min after 250 μg ACTH are slightly greater.

†Children with premature adrenarche.

‡17-Hydroxyprogesterone rises in the preovulatory phase to a peak as high as 360 ng/dL in the luteal phase of the cycle.

adrenarche" based on the observation that fully one half of women with 17-ketosteroid hyperresponsiveness to ACTH have a pattern of steroid intermediates that resembles an exaggeration of steroid secretion in adrenarche. Typically, there are moderately excessive 17-hydroxypregnenolone and DHEA responses to ACTH together with androstenedione hyperresponsiveness. Occasionally, there are mild abnormalities of 17-hydroxyprogesterone or 11-deoxycortisol in response to ACTH.

Currently, several lines of evidence support the concept that FAH is due to dysregulation of adrenal steroidogenesis. First, the 17-ketosteroid hyperresponsiveness to ACTH can be interpreted as overactivity of 17-hydroxylase/17,20-lyase in the adrenal cortex and is frequently associated with apparent overactivity of these steps in the ovaries. Secondly, the adrenal overproduction of 17-ketosteroids is associated with increased levels of the adrenarche marker DHEA-S in only a minority of cases (approximately 20%). Thirdly, there is evidence of widespread but variable dysregulation of a number of aspects of corticosteroid secretion and metabolism, such as a tendency for hypercortisolism and evidence of increased 11β-HSD activity. In addition, evidence is accumulating that hyperinsulinemia is also related to adrenal dysregulation as it is to ovarian dysregulation.

FAH occurs in approximately 35% of hyperandrogenic women in the absence of ovarian hyperandrogenism. Although the menstrual cycle is normal in two thirds of these patients, in the remainder it is associated with anovulatory symptoms, so some would consider this an adrenal variant of PCOS[44,45] (see Polycystic Ovary Syndrome discussed later). FAH is also found in half of patients with PCOS.

## Congenital Adrenal Hyperplasia

CAH results from an autosomal-recessive defect in the activity of any one of the steroidogenic enzymes necessary for the synthesis of corticosteroid hormones by the adrenal gland (see Fig. 157-1).[46,47] Because of the enzyme defect, the adrenal gland cannot efficiently secrete glucocorticoids (especially cortisol) and mineralocorticoids (primarily aldosterone), or both. There is diminished negative feedback inhibition of ACTH and/or of renin-angiotensin secretion, respectively, which markedly increases the secretion of these trophic hormones and leads to compensatory hyperplasia of the adrenal cortex. The result is defective synthesis of end product, on one hand, and accumulation of steroid precursors proximal to the enzyme defect, on the other. These precursors are subsequently converted to androgen.

Each enzyme deficiency leads to characteristic clinical syndromes and biochemical abnormalities. Virilizing CAH occurs as the result of 21-hydroxylase, 3β-HSD, or 11β-hydroxylase deficiency. In virilizing CAH, inefficient cortisol synthesis is associated with the accumulation of androgenic precursors that produce excessive virilization of female infants with genital ambiguity in the newborn period or hyperandrogenism later in childhood. These disorders may be associated with some degree of altered mineralocorticoid secretion,

mineralocorticoid deficiency with salt wasting in the case of 21-hydroxylase and 3β-HSD deficiency, salt retention with hypertension in the case of 11β-hydroxylase deficiency. CAH due to 21-hydroxylase deficiency accounts for over 90% of the cases of CAH. The classic forms have an overall prevalence in the general population of about 1:12,000.

Nonclassical (late onset or attenuated) 21-hydroxylase deficiency can present as premature pubarche or with peripubertal or postpubertal onset of hirsutism, acne, or amenorrhea. Such nonclassical cases account for about 5% of adult hirsutism in the general population,[15,48] and approximately 10% in adolescents. Additional cases are entirely cryptic; they are discovered serendipitously in family studies and have no clinical manifestations. These nonclassic forms of 21-hydroxylase deficiency CAH have been shown to be due to distinct 21-hydroxylase mutations which cause only mild enzyme deficiencies.[49] Studies of the molecular biology of 21-hydroxylase deficiency have provided important tools for the diagnosis of this condition. The gene for 21-hydroxylase (P450c21) is located on chromosome 6, and DNA probes are now available to detect the most common mutations.

Using ACTH response patterns and molecular genetic techniques, New and her colleagues[49] have shown that the rapid 17-hydroxyprogesterone response to an intravenous bolus of ACTH distinguishes among nonclassic cases and heterozygotes, and normals better than baseline steroid levels. The degree of clinical severity is correlated with the degree of 21-hydroxylase deficiency elucidated by the ACTH test.

Severe 3β-HSD deficiency leads to defective cortisol and mineralocorticoid synthesis, with adrenal insufficiency presenting in the newborn period. Because of deficient synthesis of gonadal Δ$^4$ steroids (including testosterone), affected male infants classically have insufficient virilization with sexual ambiguity. Affected female infants, on the other hand, are often virilized because of the very high levels of the weakly androgenic DHEA and its more androgenic metabolites.[50] When the enzyme deficiency is mild, virilization later in childhood or adolescence may be the first sign of the accumulation of these androgenic precursors.[43,51] The controversy about the distinction of mild 3β-HSD deficiency from simple premature adrenarche was discussed previously.

11β-hydroxylase deficiency classically presents with genital ambiguity in the female and subsequent incomplete sexual precocity in association with hypertension. Atypical cases with late-onset hirsutism without hypertension have been reported but are rare.[52]

## Adrenal Neoplasms

Adrenal tumors can produce androgens and lead to virilization.[53] The diagnosis of adrenal tumor is usually easily made on the basis of the clinical presentation, plasma testosterone, and/or plasma DHEA-S. The presence of DHEA-S values over 600 μg/dL should make one consider adrenal tumor as the cause.[53] However, the pattern of steroid secretion may be atypical. Some adrenal tumors secrete only testosterone and have a degree of gonadotropin dependency.[54]

## Other Adrenal Disorders

Glucocorticoid-suppressible hyperandrogenism may also occur in the setting of hyperprolactinemia and acromegaly. The sequelae of hyperprolactinemia may mimic those of PCOS: Women may present with hirsutism or acne, and menstrual disturbance and galactorrhea are typical, although not necessarily present.[55] Polycystic ovaries and LH hyperresponsiveness may be associated with prolactinoma.[56,57] DHEA and DHEA-S levels are elevated, as is the plasma-free testosterone, in part because of a direct effect of hyperprolactinemia on adrenal cortical function. It is important to note that mild to modest elevations in prolactin levels may be seen in association with the other hormonal disturbances of PCOS. In these instances, it is important to establish that the prolactin elevation is not a consequence of primary hypothyroidism, prolactinoma, or medications.

A number of other causes of adrenal hyperandrogenism may occur, but are relatively rare. These include Cushing's syndrome, glucocorticoid resistance, or excessively rapid cortisol metabolism. Acromegaly may also be associated with either adrenal or ovarian androgenic hyperfunction, possibly because of direct effect of the elevated IGF-1.[58]

## OVARIAN DISORDERS

Most women with androgen excess have ovarian hyperandrogenism as demonstrated by the results of ovarian vein catheterization,[59] dexamethasone suppression testing,[48,59-61] long-term administration of gonadotropin-releasing hormone (GnRH) agonists[62,63] and, more recently, the acute ovarian steroidogenic response to the administration of a GnRH agonist[48,64] or human chorionic gonadotropin (hCG).[65] The causes of gonadal androgen excess in women are listed in Table 157-3, the most common of which is PCOS.

## Polycystic Ovary Syndrome

Despite the fact that 75 years have elapsed since its first description, diagnostic criteria for PCOS remain controversial. Interindividual and temporal variation in presenting signs and symptoms contribute to the difficulties in diagnosing PCOS. An international PCOS consensus workshop group[66] has recently proposed that PCOS can be diagnosed after excluding alternate medical conditions that cause irregular menstrual cycles and androgen excess (see Table 157-3), and then establishing that at least two of the following are present: (1) oligo-ovulation or anovulation, usually manifested as oligomenorrhea or amenorrhea; (2) elevated levels of circulating androgens (hyperandrogenemia) or clinical manifestations of androgen excess (hyperandrogenism); and (3) polycystic ovaries defined by ultrasonography.[67] These criteria recognize that PCOS is a functional disorder in which ovarian hyperandrogenism can occur in the presence or absence of ovarian morphologic changes. That is, polycystic ovaries need not be present to make a diagnosis of PCOS[48] and, conversely, their presence alone does not establish the diagnosis.[68,69]

Women with PCOS will almost always have some aberration in gonadotropin secretion compared to normally cycling women if intensively studied with frequent blood sampling.[70] Because women with PCOS are known to have an increase in LH pulse frequency when compared to normal women,[70] it has been inferred that the GnRH pulse frequency must be accelerated in PCOS. Controversy persists, however, regarding whether this accelerated pulse frequency is primary, that is, an intrinsic abnormality in the GnRH pulse generator, or secondary to the relatively low levels of progesterone resulting from infrequent ovulatory events. Because progestins act to slow the GnRH pulse generator, the lower-than-normal circulating progestin levels in women with PCOS can lead to an acceleration in GnRH pulsatility,[71] an increase in LH, and thus an overproduction of ovarian androgen.

Since gonadotropin concentrations vary over the menstrual cycle and are released into the circulation in a pulsatile fashion, it is felt by many that a single measurement of LH and FSH lack sufficient sensitivity and specificity for making a diagnosis of PCOS.

The symptoms of PCOS usually begin at about the time of initiation of menses (menarche),[72] but postpubertal onset is also seen as a result of environmental modifiers such as weight gain. Pathologic conditions that occur prior to puberty may be harbingers of PCOS. Girls with premature pubertal maturation resulting from the early secretion of adrenal steroids (i.e., premature pubarche) are thought to be at increased risk for subsequent development of PCOS.[73] In addition, an aberrant intrauterine environment has been implicated in the pathogenesis of PCOS in both human and nonhuman primates, particularly with regard to the metabolic components of the disorder.[74-77]

PCOS remains one of the most common hormonal disorders across the life span in women, with a prevalence estimated to be between 5% and 10%.[78-80] Variance in prevalence between populations may reflect the impact of ethnic origin, race, and other environmental factors that can modify the expression of the PCOS phenotype.[81,82]

A number of lines of evidence suggest that PCOS is a heritable disorder.[83-87] Various approaches have been undertaken to try to define a specific genetic etiology.[88,89] Linkage studies, case control studies, and, most recently, microarray analyses of affected target tissues in PCOS[89] have been used to identify likely candidate genes. While a number of candidate genes appear to make modest contributions to the clinical expression of PCOS, no single gene has been confidently identified to play a predominant role in the pathogenesis of PCOS.

Mendelian modes of transmission have been reported and, in rare instances, single gene mutations can give rise to the PCOS phenotype.[90] It has become increasingly evident, however, that PCOS is more likely to be a complex multigenic disorder. Several recent reviews provide a summary of the contributions of the candidate genes implicated in the etiology of PCOS.[88,91,92]

### Clinical Characteristics

Women with classic PCOS present with symptoms of anovulation, hyperandrogenemia, and obesity and are found to have polycystic ovaries.[93-95] Structurally, classic polycystic ovaries are enlarged with a thickened tunica albuginea, thecal hyperplasia, and over 10 follicles, most of which are about 4 to 8 mm in diameter and subcapsular in location. The anovulation is typically expressed as oligomenorrhea or infertility and the hyperandrogenism as hirsutism. About two thirds of these women have anovulatory symptoms, two thirds have hirsutism, and at least one half are obese.

It has long been recognized that women with PCOS are at increased risk for developing type 2 diabetes.[96] Recent studies have found that glucose intolerance (either impaired glucose tolerance or frank diabetes) is evident in approximately 45% of women with PCOS by their fourth decade.[97,98]

The synergistic effects of insulin resistance and obesity were thought to be sufficient to account for the predisposition to diabetes in PCOS. However, it has become clear that once present, elevated glucose levels serve as evidence that the ability of the pancreatic beta cell to compensate for insulin resistance has been exceeded.[99] Indeed, alterations in insulin secretion are demonstrable in PCOS[85,100,101] and these alterations may have a genetic basis,[102] since they are present more often in those women with PCOS who have a first-degree relative with type 2 diabetes.[85]

### Pathogenesis

The pathogenesis of PCOS has been highly controversial.[15,45,94,103-105] Part of the controversy surrounds the issue of whether hyperandrogenism in PCOS arises from adrenal or ovarian sources. In any model, a vicious cycle that perpetuates hyperandrogenism may be established. As a result, the primary abnormality initiating the development of PCOS has been difficult to delineate. Because of the frequent adrenal 17 ketosteroid hyperresponsiveness to ACTH, some investigators believe that PCOS originates as an adrenal disorder during puberty. According to this school of thought, adrenal hyperandrogenism is central to the pathogenesis via a complex cycle of events in which secretion of androstenedione and its peripheral conversion to estrone initiate the syndrome.[45,94] Yen and his coworkers have suggested that exaggerated adrenarche initiates this process. More specifically, increased secretion of androstenedione by the adrenal gland leads to increased concentrations of estrogen, primarily estrone, through its peripheral conversion in adipose and other tissues. The increase in the plasma concentration of estradiol sensitizes the pituitary to secrete excessive LH, resulting in a high LH-to-FSH ratio, which leads to excessive stimulation of ovarian thecal androstenedione production and deficient granulosa cell aromatase activity. The resulting increase in ovarian androgens leads to polycystic ovaries while at the same time contributing further to the circulating pool of androgens, perpetuating the vicious cycle of hyperandrogenism. This theory, while plausible, is not universally accepted for several reasons.[103] Estrone is a weak estrogen and attempts to reproduce gonadotropin secretory abnormalities through exogenous estrone administration have not led to increased LH concentrations. Furthermore, recent studies suggest that there is an important element of ovarian dysfunction that is independent of elevated LH levels.[2]

Eighty percent or more of cases of PCOS appear to arise from abnormal regulation (dysregulation) of ovarian androgen secretion. We found that the vast majority of women with classic PCOS have a characteristic pituitary-gonadal response to testing with an acute GnRH agonist challenge test (Fig. 157-6)[15,64] Their gonadotropin responses often resemble those of males in that they have significantly greater early LH and lesser FSH responses than normal females. They have greater 17-hydroxyprogesterone and, to a lesser extent, androgenic responses than those of normal women. 17-Hydroxypregnenolone and DHEA responses are less consistently elevated, and pregnenolone is not elevated at all in PCOS patients. There is no evidence of a discrete block in the steroidogenic pathway since the responses of all steroids on the pathway from 17-hydroxyprogesterone to estrone and estradiol are normal or elevated. The elevated responses of 17-hydroxyprogesterone and androstenedione, without evidence of a block in the subsequent steroidogenic steps or consistent abnormalities in the earlier steps in the steroidogenic pathway, suggest increased ovarian 17-hydroxylase and 17,20-lyase activities as part of a generalized overactivity of steroidogenesis.[2]

This type of ovarian dysfunction is found in over one half of hyperandrogenic patients[15,48] and can manifest in the absence of LH excess or sonographic abnormalities. The peak response of 17-hydroxyprogesterone to GnRH agonist correlated well with the free testosterone level after dexamethasone suppression of adrenal function, and there was 85% concordance between the two tests. Thus, these tests reflect closely related aspects of ovarian dysfunction.

Abnormal regulation (dysregulation) of ovarian androgen secretion appears to result from escape from desensitization to LH.[2] This seems to be the consequence of abnormal modulation of LH responses by endocrine, paracrine, or autocrine factors, which normally coordinate intraovarian androgen with estrogen production.[15] We have postulated that similar intrinsic abnormalities in the regulation of P-450c17 within

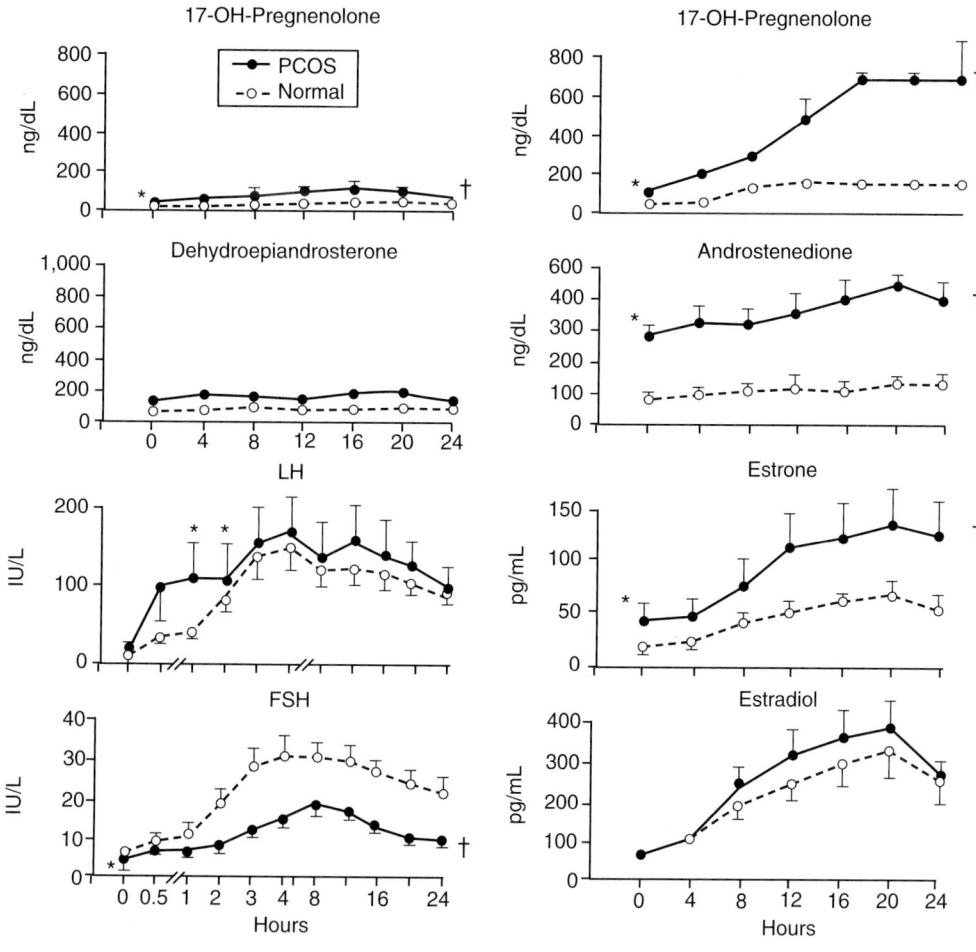

**Figure 157-6** Patterns of response to GnRH agonist (nafarelin) testing in patients with classic PCOS. All subjects were pretreated with dexamethasone to suppress coincident adrenal androgen production. Baseline (0 min) for LH and FSH is the mean of four samples taken over one hour. Nafarelin 100 μg was administered subcutaneously after obtaining the baseline samples. The time scale for the LH and FSH graphs is expanded to demonstrate the early (30–60 min) hyperresponsiveness of LH in PCOS. Substantial and prolonged release of gonadotropins stimulates ovarian steroid secretion within 24 hours. PCOS patients had 17-hydroxyprogesterone (8/8 cases) and androstenedione (6/8) hyperresponsiveness, with no evidence of a steroidogenic block on the pathway to estrogens. PCOS patients differed significantly from normal at designated time points (*) and in peak incremental responses (†). Reproduced from Ref. 2.

the adrenal cortex could explain the coexistence of adrenal 17-ketosteroid hyperresponsiveness to ACTH in one half the cases of PCOS (see earlier discussion of functional adrenal hyperandrogenism).[15]

The cause of the apparent dysregulation of steroidogenesis is unclear. A primary role for LH excess is arguable.[2] When PCOS patients are given a fixed dose of the LH analogue hCG, they have 17-hydroxyprogesterone and androstenedione hyperresponses. In addition, theca cells from polycystic ovaries secrete abnormal amounts of steroids in culture,[106,107] both before and after LH stimulation. Perhaps the most important consideration militating against a primary role of LH excess as a cause of the hyperandrogenism is consideration of the desensitization process. Normal thecal cells are very sensitive to the downregulating effect of LH levels within the physiologic range. Maximal stimulation of 17-hydroxyprogesterone and androstenedione secretion by thecal cells in culture normally occurs at LH concentrations approximating the upper portion of the normal range for follicular phase serum LH levels, and a further increase in LH dosage leads to no further rise. However, both in vivo and in vitro studies suggest that the steroid responses of PCOS do not fall along the normal LH-steroid dose-response curve, but rather seem displaced upward and to the left. Thus, the defect in steroidogenesis appears to be the result of escape from normal downregulation of thecal cell secretion, rather than from overstimulation by LH.

The pattern of steroid secretion is similarly abnormal in those PCOS patients with and without LH excess. Both groups of patients also have an LH-17-hydroxyprogesterone dose-response curve, which is shifted upward and to the left. Therefore, we favor the concept that the fundamental defect underlying the androgen excess of PCOS is ovarian hyperresponsiveness to gonadotropin action because of escape from downregulation. The ovarian dysfunction seems independent of LH excess, although gonadotropins are permissive. The LH excess may intensify the intrinsic ovarian hyperandrogenic dysfunction.

The cause of the apparent escape of theca cells from downregulation is unclear. The cause could be intrinsic or extrinsic to the ovaries. We favor a major role for defects in the intrinsic intraovarian processes by which thecal and granulosa cell function are coordinated. Evidence exists to support an intrinsic defect in theca cell function in response to LH.[48,65,106-108]

IGFs are candidates for being FSH-inducable factors capable of interfering with downregulation of steroidogenesis, and a defect in the IGF system could account for the altered set point of the granulosa cell response to FSH. Inhibin is another FSH-dependent candidate. Recent clinical studies found elevated serum inhibin-B levels in PCOS, which is compatible with the excess numbers of developing ovarian follicles. Since inhibin stimulates androgen synthesis and androgen stimulates inhibin production, there is the potential for a vicious cycle developing within the ovary, which could cause androgen excess and inhibit follicular development. It is theoretically possible that follicular maturation arrest, resulting in a premature commitment of follicles to atresia, may be the primary event leading to PCOS. Atretic follicles are relatively androgenic and hypoestrogenic; this imbalance between the production of androgen and estrogen would be expected to perpetuate the cycle of hyperandrogenism and follicular maturational arrest.

Insulin seems to be a key factor given that hyperinsulinemia amplifies the effect of trophic hormones on steroidogenesis.[2,109] Hyperandrogenism seems to contribute only modestly to insulin resistance. The abnormality of thecal function in PCOS resembles the escape from desensitization, which occurs when normal cells are treated with insulin or IGF. The ovaries in PCOS behave as if responsive to excess insulin or IGFs in a state of resistance to the glucose-metabolic effects of insulin. Alternatively, it has been proposed that ovarian hyperandrogenism may arise from a defect common to both insulin action and ovarian steroid biosynthesis. An increase in phosphorylation of serine residues of the insulin receptor results in resistance to insulin, and serine phosphorylation of P-450c17 upregulates the 17,20-lyase activity of this enzyme.[110] However, insulin abnormalities are variable, and insulin excess is typically moderate, though it can be striking.[85] Therefore, although insulin excess may be a provocative factor, it is rarely the sole factor causing the syndrome.

PCOS may also arise in the setting of frankly virilizing disorders, ovarian steroidogenic blocks, or severe insulin resistance syndromes. Frankly virilizing disorders like poorly controlled virilizing CAH or exogenous androgen administration to transsexual females have been shown to produce the ovarian anatomic changes of Stein-Leventhal syndrome, namely cortical sclerosis, cysts, and hyperthecosis, probably because of the great increase in the intraovarian concentration of androgen.[2] The virilization of classic CAH can also cause functional ovarian hyperandrogenism. Women with virilizing CAH may have polycystic ovaries and high serum LH levels.[111] Adrenal rests of the ovaries, as are found in some cases of CAH, may also mimic PCOS.[112] Ovarian steroidogenic blocks in the pathway to estradiol may on rare occasions cause hyperandrogenism, estrogen deficiency, and multicystic ovaries. This can result from congenital defects in the activity of ovarian 3β-HSD,[64] 17β-HSD,[113] or aromatase[114,115] (see Fig. 157-1). The aromatase mutations reported to date have resulted in congenital virilization with ambiguous genitalia. Virtually every form of extreme insulin resistance, whether due to anti-insulin receptor antibodies, insulin receptor mutations, or postreceptor defects, has been reported to be associated with PCOS.[116] The hyperinsulinemia of these insulin resistance syndromes may cause ovarian hyperandrogenism by acting through the IGF-1 receptor,[16,17,117] although it has been recently shown that a very high level of insulin is capable of acting on the theca cell via its own receptor.[118]

### Ovarian Neoplasms

Virilizing ovarian tumors may be malignant or benign and are frequently suspected on the basis of rapidly progressive virilization, testosterone concentrations over 200 ng/dL, and characteristic ultrasound or computed tomography findings. The most common virilizing ovarian tumor is arrhenoblastoma, which is occasionally gonadotropin-responsive.[61] Ovarian lipid cell tumors are also typically gonadotropin-responsive and dependent, in part, on ACTH as well.[119] Ovarian virilizing tumors typically secrete predominantly androstenedione and are thus characterized by a disproportionate elevation of plasma androstenedione relative to testosterone. Mild elevation of urinary 17-ketosteroid excretion characteristically results.

### Other

Subjects with true hermaphroditism are characterized by the presence of functional testicular and ovarian tissue. This tissue may be separate or it may be combined in the same gonad, in which case it is referred to as an ovotestis. True hermaphrodites occasionally present as menstruating, phenotypic females with signs of androgen excess such as clitoromegaly.[120] The diagnosis can be made by the response to gonadotropin stimulation.[121]

Virilization during pregnancy may be due to androgen hypersecretion by a luteoma or hyperreactio luteinalis.[122] These conditions represent benign hyperplastic thecal luteinization of the ovary, solid and cystic, respectively, which spontaneously regress post partum. Luteomas appear not to be associated with excessive levels of hCG. In contrast, hyperreactio luteinalis is almost always associated with hCG excess. Maternal virilization occurs in 10% to 50% of women with luteomas and in 25% of those with hyperreactio luteinalis.

Fetal virilization is rare owing to placental aromatization of androgen to estrogen.

## PERIPHERAL OVERPRODUCTION OF ANDROGEN

Obesity can cause hyperandrogenemia and amenorrhea, thus mimicking PCOS.[2,123] Because testosterone formation from androstenedione is increased and SHBG is suppressed (due, in part, to the insulin resistance of obesity), testosterone production is increased and the plasma-free testosterone levels are high.[124] Estrone formation from androstenedione is also increased, and estradiol metabolism is diverted to active rather than inactive metabolites.[125]

Less than 10% of our series of hyperandrogenemic women had idiopathic hyperandrogenemia, that is, hyperandrogenemia for which an intensive search revealed no clear adrenal or ovarian source for the androgen excess.[48,109] We suspect that this arises from increased peripheral metabolism of inactive steroid precursors to active androgens. We are left with this diagnosis in chronically hyperandrogenic females who demonstrate normal steroid responses to ACTH, GnRH agonist, and dexamethasone testing. Dexamethasone and estrogen-progestin, alone or in combination, suppress the plasma-free testosterone to normal levels in these cases.

## DIAGNOSIS OF HYPERANDROGENIC STATES

Evaluation of the woman with androgen excess includes an assessment of the pattern and quantity of hair growth. The presence of hirsutism must first be established and differentiated from hypertrichosis (see earlier discussion). The degree of hirsutism may be scored, though imperfectly, by the method of Ferriman and Gallwey (see Fig. 157-5) in which the body areas possessing androgen-sensitive PSUs are graded and summed. A total score of 8 or more is seen in only 5% of premenopausal white women; these women, by definition, are hirsute.

We recommend screening for hyperandrogenemia by measuring blood levels of total and free testosterone, and DHEA-S

(Fig. 157-7). A normal plasma total testosterone does not exclude an important hyperandrogenic disorder, such as virilizing CAH or PCOS. A random value may be misleadingly normal, in part, because of the variation in secretion of androgens and, in part, because a depressed SHBG level may lower the total testosterone while an abnormally great fraction of the total testosterone is free and bioavailable. LH, FSH, androstenedione, and prolactin may also be obtained at the time of initial evaluation.[31] A baseline plasma testosterone level in the male range (over 350 ng/dL; 12 nM) usually indicates a virilizing tumor and a level over 200 ng/dL (7 nM) is suggestive. A basal DHEA-S level over 800 µg/dL (18.5 µM) suggests an adrenal tumor. Ultrasound, computed tomography, or magnetic resonance imaging will usually demonstrate the mass.

It is both costly and impractical to measure many steroids on multiple occasions; a strategy must be used to derive maximal diagnostic information from limited sampling. One approach to accomplish this involves dexamethasone suppression testing (see Fig. 157-7).[31] The dexamethasone androgen-suppression test is performed by obtaining a blood sample before and after administering a "low dose" of dexamethasone: 2.0 mg daily in divided doses by mouth for 4 days (or longer in patients who are very obese or who have relatively high DHEA-S levels). The pattern of response of plasma-free testosterone, DHEA-S, and cortisol segregates patients diagnostically. Normal suppression of androgens is most specifically indicated by a reduction of the plasma-free testosterone into the normal range for dexamethasone-suppressed, non-hirsute women. In our laboratory, dexamethasone suppressibility is considered normal in a perimenarcheal or postmenarcheal female if the plasma-free testosterone is less than 8 pg/mL (27 pmol per liter).[48] Normal adrenal suppression is indicated by a reduction of both DHEA-S and cortisol levels below the normal range for adult controls (<70 and <3 µg/dL, respectively, in our laboratory). Inadequate cortisol suppression indicates Cushing's syndrome, glucocorticoid resistance, or noncompliance. Subnormal suppressibility of free testosterone with normal adrenal suppression is usually due to PCOS. If cortisol is suppressed, the only other considerations

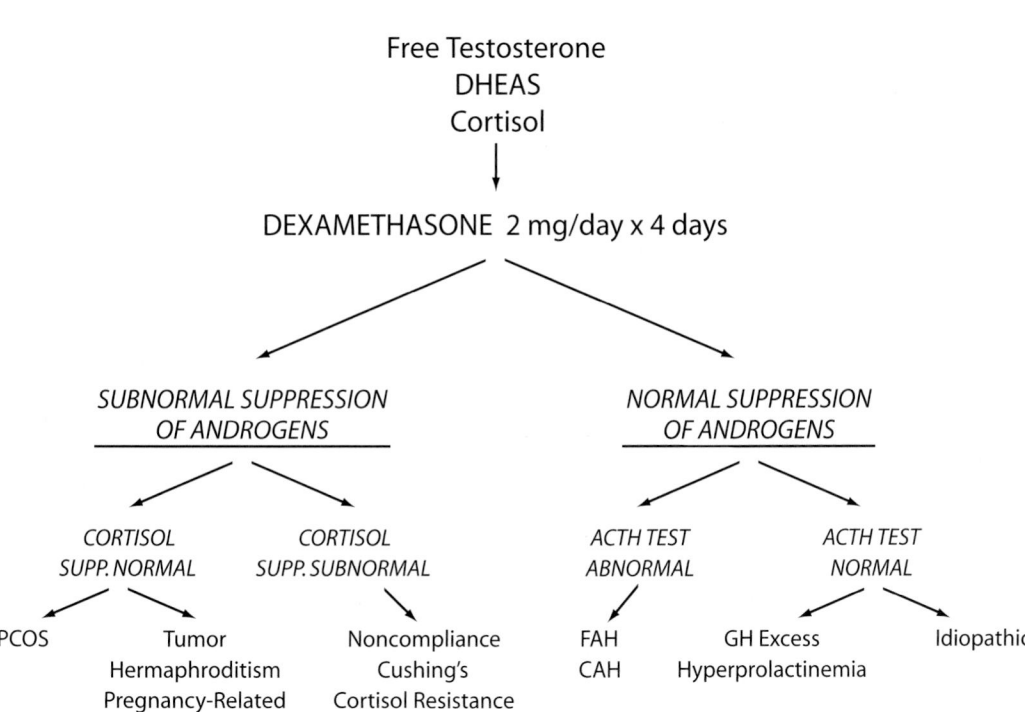

Free Testosterone
DHEAS
Cortisol

↓

DEXAMETHASONE 2 mg/day x 4 days

SUBNORMAL SUPPRESSION OF ANDROGENS

NORMAL SUPPRESSION OF ANDROGENS

CORTISOL SUPP. NORMAL

CORTISOL SUPP. SUBNORMAL

ACTH TEST ABNORMAL

ACTH TEST NORMAL

PCOS

Tumor
Hermaphroditism
Pregnancy-Related

Noncompliance
Cushing's
Cortisol Resistance

FAH
CAH

GH Excess
Hyperprolactinemia

Idiopathic

**Figure 157-7** Algorithm for the differential diagnosis of hyperandrogenemia. The response of the plasma-free testosterone, DHEA-S, and cortisol to DEX for 4 days or more is evaluated. Adult women are typically given 2 mg daily for four days; in those weighing over 100 kg, a dose of 1.0 mg/m² is used. Subnormal suppression of androgens by DEX points toward FOH/PCOS (if both DHEA-S and cortisol suppress normally), tumor, true hermaphroditism, or pregnancy-related androgen excess (if only cortisol suppresses normally), or Cushing's syndrome, cortisol resistance, or noncompliance (if cortisol does not suppress normally). CAH, congenital adrenal hyperplasia; DEX, dexamethasone; FOH, functional ovarian hyperandrogenism; FAH, functional adrenal hyperandrogenism; GH, growth hormone; PCOS, polycystic ovary syndrome. Modified from Ref. 223.

are virilizing tumor, true hermaphroditism, and, in pregnancy, hCG-related disorders.

An elevated serum LH level may be a useful corroborative test. However, elevation of serum LH is not specific for PCOS and approximately one half of women with FOH have levels that are normal.[48] Suppression of plasma-free testosterone after a therapeutic trial of estrogen-progestin may also be confirmatory. However, gonadotropin dependence has been occasionally reported with virilizing ovarian[61] and adrenal[54] tumors.

Ovaries from women with PCOS are sonographically normal in up to one half of cases.[48] Conversely, polycystic ovaries may be found on ultrasound examination of women without PCOS.[126] Therefore, polycystic ovaries are a relatively insensitive and nonspecific finding for the diagnosis of ovarian hyperandrogenism. Indeed, the best ultrasound correlate of ovarian steroidogenic function in hyperandrogenic women is stromal area rather than ovarian area, cyst area, or cyst number.[15,127]

GnRH agonist testing has been used as a means of making a specific diagnosis of PCOS. Our data suggest that a peak 17-hydroxyprogesterone level of 260 ng/dL (7.8 nmol per liter) or more, after the administration of 100 µg nafarelin subcutaneously is virtually diagnostic.[48] A similar peak in 17-hydroxyprogesterone is obtained by the administration of leuprolide at a dose of 10µg/kg body weight.[128] The results of GnRH agonist testing are highly concordant with those obtained by dexamethasone suppression testing.[48]

## TREATMENT OF HYPERANDROGENISM

Women with androgen excess most often seek treatment for reduction of hair growth and/or acne, restoration of menstrual cyclicity, and infertility. In addition, patients are increasingly seeking treatment for the metabolic abnormalities related to PCOS. A "problem-oriented" approach to the treatment of the patient with androgen excess follows (Table 157-5).

### HIRSUTISM AND ACNE

Medical treatment of hirsutism and/or acne in PCOS generally involves reduction of androgen levels or their end-organ effects. This is usually accomplished by the following: (1) suppression of adrenal and/or ovarian androgen production; (2) alteration of binding of androgens to their plasma-binding proteins; (3) impairment of the peripheral conversion of androgen precursors to active androgen; and (4) inhibition of androgen action at the target tissue level.

Combination estrogen-progestin therapy, in the form of an oral contraceptive, is the first line of endocrine treatment for hirsutism and acne, after cosmetic and dermatologic management. The estrogenic component of most oral contraceptives currently in use is either ethinyl estradiol or mestranol. The estrogenic component, in particular, is responsible for the suppression of LH and thus serum androgen levels[129] and also results in a dose-related increase in SHBG,[130] thus lowering the fraction of plasma testosterone that is unbound. Combination therapy has also been demonstrated to decrease DHEA-S levels, perhaps by reducing ACTH levels.[131,132] Estrogens also have a direct, dose-dependent suppressive effect on sebaceous cell function, with a uniform effect on acne at a dose of 100 µg.[133]

The choice of a specific oral contraceptive should be predicated on the progestational component as each progestin has a variably suppressive effect on SHBG levels as well as some androgenic potential. Ethynodiol diacetate has a relatively low androgenic potential while progestins such as norethindrone, norgestrel, and levonorgestrel are particularly androgenic,[134] as can be judged from their attenuation of the estrogen-induced increase in SHBG.[135] The newer generation

of progestins (norgestimate, desogesterel) are virtually nonandrogenic[136] and seem to be well-suited for treatment of hyperandrogenic women.[137] More recently, drospirenone, an analogue of spironolactone that is unique in that it has both antimineralocorticoid and antiandrogenic activities,[138] has been approved for use as the progestational agent in combination with ethinyl estradiol. As such, it holds the potential for use in the treatment of women with PCOS.[139]

Assessment of adequacy of ovarian suppression can be made at the end of the third week after starting treatment; by this time, ovarian androgen suppression is complete.[129] The effect on acne can be expected to be maximal in 1 to 2 months. In contrast, the effect on hair growth may not be evident for 6 months and the maximum effect requires 9 to 12 months due to the length of the hair growth cycle. In most trials, estrogen-progestin therapy alone improves the extent of acne by 50% to 70%.[140] Although similar claims have been made for hirsutism,[141] it is our experience that this treatment typically does little more than arrest progression of hair growth.

GnRH agonists have been reported to be effective in the treatment of hirsutism.[142,143] Their chronic administration suppresses pituitary-ovarian function thus inhibiting both ovarian androgen and estrogen secretion. The addition of dexamethasone (0.5 mg/day) to leuprolide has been reported to further improve the response of some women with PCOS.[62] Because of the concomitant reduction of serum estrogen levels and the attendant, albeit apparently reversible, reductions in bone mineral density observed when GnRH agonists are used alone,[144,145] it appears unwise to use these agents for longer than 6 months. It has been suggested that "add back" therapy, in which combination estrogen-progestin is prescribed in conjunction with a GnRH agonist, may be effective in treating androgen excess without the side effects of hypoestrogenemia.[146]

Adrenal androgens are more sensitive than cortisol to the suppressive effects of glucocorticoids.[147] Therefore, glucocorticoids are the mainstay of treatment of the adrenal androgen excess of CAH, but appear to be less effective in other forms of functional adrenal androgen excess.[148,149] Although glucocorticoids have been reported to restore ovulatory function in PCOS, the extent to which this occurs is highly variable.[150,151]

Prednisone in doses of 5 to 10 mg at bedtime is usually effective in suppressing adrenal androgens while posing minimal risk of the sequelae of glucocorticoid excess. We do not advocate the use of dexamethasone because it is difficult to prevent Cushingoid striae even with doses as low as 0.5 mg daily. DHEA-S levels are used to indicate the degree of adrenal suppression; the target is a level of approximately 70 µg/dL. It has been suggested by some that antiandrogen therapy in the form of cyproterone acetate[152] or spironolactone[149] is at least as effective as glucocorticoid for the treatment of hirsutism due to adrenal androgen excess (see later discussion).

Ketoconazole, a synthetic imidazole antifungal agent, inhibits multiple steps in the biosynthesis of testosterone but acts primarily to inhibit 17-hydroxylase/17,20-lyase and 11β-hydroxylase activities.[153,154] In doses of 400 mg per day for 6 months it has been demonstrated to have a moderate salutary effect on acne and hirsutism, although side effects are relatively frequent and include nausea, dry skin, pruritus, and transaminase elevation.[155]

Cyproterone acetate is the prototypic antiandrogen. It acts mainly by competitive inhibition of the binding of testosterone and DHT to the androgen receptor.[156] In addition, it may act to enhance the metabolic clearance of testosterone by inducing hepatic enzymes. Although not available for use in the United States, cyproterone acetate is an effective treatment for hirsutism and acne[157,158] and is used throughout Canada, Mexico, and Europe. Because of its potent progestational activity and its prolonged half-time, it is administered in a "reverse sequential" manner: cyproterone acetate 50 to

**Table 157-5** Pharmacologic Agents Available for the Treatment of Polycystic Ovary Syndrome and Other Disorders of Androgen Excess in Women

| Agent | Mechanism(s) of Action | Advantages/Disadvantages | Examples | Uses |
|---|---|---|---|---|
| Combination estrogen-progestin | Increase SHBG; suppress LH and FSH; suppress ovarian androgen production | • Restoration of cyclic exposure of endometrium to estrogen-progestin; relatively effective for hirsutism and/or acne<br>• May enhance/aggravate risk of thrombosis, metabolic abnormalities | Ethinyl estradiol; norgestimate (Ortho-Cyclen)<br><br>Ethinyl estradiol; desogesterel (Ortho-Cept) | 1, 2 |
|  | As above with a progestin that acts as an antiandrogen | • Added benefit from antiandrogenic effects of drosperinone, the progestin component | Ethinyl estradiol; drosperinone (Yasmin) |  |
| Antiandrogens | Inhibit androgens from binding to the androgen receptor | • Substantial efficacy in treatment of hirsutism and/or acne<br>• Risk for hyperkalemia (spironolactone) or hepatitis (flutamide) | Cyproterone acetate, spironolactone, flutamide | 1 |
| GnRH agonists | Downregulation of GnRH secretion | • May be beneficial in short-term (<6 mo) use<br>• Long-term use associated with osteopenia | Leuprolide, nafarelin | 1 |
| Glucocorticoids | Suppress ACTH and thus adrenal androgen production | • Effective in lowering adrenal component of androgen excess<br>• Long-term risks include glucose intolerance, insulin resistance, osteopenia, weight gain, etc. | Prednisone, dexamethasone | 1, 2, 3 |
| 5α-reductase inhibitors | Inhibition of 5α-reductase | • Does not specifically target the isoenzyme of 5α-reductase in the pilosebaceous unit | Finasteride (Propecia) | 1 |
| Ornithine decarboxylase inhibitors | Inhibition of ornithine decarboxylase | • Minimal documented efficacy; used topically | Eflornithine HCl (Vaniqa) | 1 |
| Clomiphene citrate | Antiestrogen; acts to induce rise in FSH, LH | • Moderately effective as monotherapy; less effective in obese PCOS patients; increasingly used in conjunction with insulin lowering therapies | Clomiphene citrate (Clomid) | 3 |
| Biguanides | Reduce hepatic glucose production, secondarily lowering insulin levels | • Substantial efficacy in restoration of menstrual cyclicity, less effective for hirsutism; usually associated with initial weight loss | Metformin (Glucophage, Glucophage XR) | 1, 2, 3, 4 |
|  | May have direct effects on ovarian steroidogenesis | • May be associated with untoward gastrointestinal effects |  |  |
| Thiazolidinediones | Enhance insulin action at target tissue level (adipocyte, muscle) | • Extremely effective at lowering levels of insulin and androgens; modest effects on hirsutism | Troglitazone (Rezulin*), pioglitazone (Actos), rosiglitazone (Avandia) | 1, 2, 3, 4 |
|  | Some evidence for direct effects upon ovarian steroidogenesis | • Often associated with weight gain |  |  |

1-Hirsutism and/or acne; 2-oligo/amenorrhea; 3-ovulation induction; 4-insulin lowering therapy.
*No longer available for use. Modified from Ref. 224.

100 mg per day from day 5 to day 15 of the cycle with ethinyl estradiol in a dose of 35 to 50 µg per day from day 5 to day 26 of the cycle.[157] The dose of cyproterone acetate may be reduced incrementally at 6-month intervals. Diane (2 mg of cyproterone acetate with 50 µg of ethinyl estradiol) may be effective in maintaining improvement in milder cases of hirsutism. Side effects of cyproterone acetate include irregular uterine bleeding, nausea, headache, fatigue, weight gain, and decreased libido.

Spironolactone appears to be as effective an antiandrogen as cyproterone acetate in doses of 100 to 200 mg daily.[159,160] It is a potent antimineralocorticoid that was developed as a progestational analogue and has diverse effects on steroid metabolism.[161–164] Although there has been concern about possible toxicity, its side effects are remarkably few; however, patients must be monitored for hyperkalemia and hypotension. Its major side effect is menstrual irregularity when used

alone. Estrogen-progestin should be given in conjunction with spironolactone[165,166] not only for this reason, but to prevent pregnancy because of the danger of feminization of a male fetus.

Flutamide is a potent nonsteroidal antiandrogen without progestational, estrogenic, corticoid, antigonadotropic, or androgenic activity[167] that appears to be efficacious in the treatment of hirsutism. In a 7-month trial of flutamide (250 mg twice daily) in conjunction with an estrogen-progestin, marked improvement in acne, seborrhea, and hirsutism was reported.[168] Concerns about the induction of hepatocellular dysfunction have limited its use.

Finasteride, a 4-aza-steroid, is a competitive inhibitor of type 2 5α-reductase.[169] Although beneficial effects on hirsutism have been reported,[170] the prominence of type 1 5α-reductase in the pilosebaceous unit makes it unlikely to be an optimal form of treatment.

It is important to note that one recent prospective, randomized trial comparing low dose flutamide, finasteride, ketoconazole, and combination cyproterone acetate-ethinyl estradiol demonstrated relative superiority of flutamide and cyproterone acetate-ethinyl estradiol in the treatment of hirsutism.[171] Ultimately, then, the choice of any specific agents must be tailored to the needs of the patient being treated.

## OLIGO/AMENORRHEA AND INFERTILITY

Chronic oligo/anovulation results in persistent stimulation of endometrial tissue by estrogen (mainly estrone). In the setting of PCOS, without the progesterone-induced inhibition of proliferation and differentiation to secretory endometrium that occurs after ovulation, there is an increased risk for endometrial hyperplasia and carcinoma.[172] A threefold increased risk of endometrial cancer in anovulatory women has been reported.[173] Although 5% or fewer of endometrial cancers occur in women under the age of 40 years, the majority have PCOS.[174] Thus, anovulatory women with PCOS are recommended to take progestins to reduce the risk of endometrial hyperplasia or carcinoma.

An endometrial biopsy is suggested if a patient has been anovulatory for 1 year or more[175]; ultrasonography may help to establish risk and need for biopsy. If a progestin is used, it should be given for 12 to 14 days every month to minimize the risk of endometrial hyperplasia.[176,177] The combined estrogen/progestin oral contraceptive pill is particularly beneficial in women with PCOS in that it both inhibits endometrial proliferation and reduces ovarian androgen production, thus ameliorating the consequences of hyperandrogenism.

Clomiphene citrate remains the first line of therapy for ovulation induction in women with PCOS.[178,179] The usual regimen is 50 mg per day for 5 days beginning on cycle day 3 to day 5 following spontaneous or progestin-induced bleeding. The dose can be increased by 50 mg per day (usually to a maximum dose of 200 mg/day) in subsequent cycles if ovulation does not occur (serum progesterone in the luteal phase remains less than 3 ng/mL). Using a graduated regimen of 50 to 200 mg daily for 5 days, ovulation can be induced in about 80% of oligomenorrheic women, of whom approximately one half conceive. In women without other infertility factors, about 88% of those ovulating will eventually conceive with a monthly fecundity rate of 0.22, which is similar to that of fertile women discontinuing the diaphragm.[180] There is a 15% spontaneous abortion rate and a 4% incidence of twins[180,181] associated with the use of clomiphene citrate. Metformin has been reported to reduce the rate of spontaneous pregnancy loss in PCOS (see following discussion).[182]

Those PCOS patients who fail clomiphene therapy will usually require either low dose human recombinant FSH or surgically induced ovulation (i.e., ovarian diathermy). In hyperinsulinemic women with PCOS, lowering insulin levels with either drugs or weight loss may also induce ovulation (see following discussion).

There is no clinical advantage of human menopausal gonadotropins over FSH for induction of ovulation in women with PCOS.[183] In PCOS, stimulation is initiated with 75 IU/day, instead of the standard 150 IU, and patients are maintained on this dose for 1 to 2 weeks. This lower dose lowers the risk of ovarian hyperstimulation syndrome. Gonadotropins are increased at 0.5 ampoule increments (37.5 IU) every 7 days if no follicular growth occurs at the initial dose as determined by ultrasound. Compared to standard gonadotropin therapy, low dose therapy with either FSH or human menopausal gonadotropins in PCOS results in a higher rate of single dominant follicle development, fewer ovulatory follicles at the time of hCG administration, and lower mean estradiol levels.[184-188] Reducing the FSH dose as follicular size increases may further increase the likelihood of monofollicular development.[189,190]

With low dose gonadotropin therapy, about 95% of patients will ovulate with a 55% cumulative pregnancy rate after six cycles.[191] Multiple gestation occurs in only 6% of pregnancies. However, spontaneous abortion rates range from 20% to 35%.[187,191] Downregulating the pituitary-ovarian axis with GnRH agonist prior to initiation of gonadotropin therapy may decrease the likelihood of spontaneous abortion,[192,193] but this has never been confirmed in a randomized trial.

There has been renewed interest in surgically inducing ovulation in women with PCOS using laparoscopy and electrocautery or laser to produce multiple burns in the ovarian capsule. A review of 1124 patients found spontaneous ovulation in 77% and pregnancy in 49% of patients.[194] Most patients ovulated spontaneously following laparoscopic ovulation induction, but some required clomiphene citrate or gonadotropins, which increased the total pregnancy rate to 60%. In PCOS patients with only anovulation and no other infertility factors, a cumulative pregnancy rate of 80%, with about 80% of conceptions occurring within the first 8 months after surgery has been reported.[195] In contrast to gonadotropins, the spontaneous abortion rate after a laparoscopic ovulation induction is only about 15% and multiple pregnancies are uncommon (2.5%).[194,196]

As noted, lowering insulin levels with either weight loss or drugs may induce ovulation in obese, hyperinsulinemic women with PCOS. A modest weight loss of 5% to 10% results in return to regular menses or pregnancy in up to 80% of obese women with PCOS.[179,197] Both metformin and troglitazone have been reported to restore regular menses and induce ovulation in women with PCOS.[198-200] In a randomized trial, obese women with PCOS were significantly more likely to ovulate if they received 1500 mg of metformin daily (34%) rather than placebo (4%: $P < 0.001$) for 35 days.[201] In the subjects who remained anovulatory after 35 days, the metformin treated subjects were significantly more likely to ovulate following clomiphene treatment than were the placebo treated subjects (90% vs. 8%: $P < 0.001$). When troglitazone was administered to women with PCOS either alone or in conjunction with clomiphene citrate, there was a significant enhancement in ovulatory function.[199] Specifically, the ovulation rate per cycle increased from 34.9% with clomiphene citrate alone to 72.7% when troglitazone was coadministered.

Finally, a recent multicenter study[200] in which 305 premenopausal women with PCOS were randomly assigned to treatment with placebo or troglitazone (150 mg/day, 300 mg/day, or 600 mg/day) revealed that ovulatory rates were significantly greater for patients receiving 300 mg and 600 mg than for those receiving placebo. Of PCOS patients treated with 600 mg, 57% ovulated over half of the time compared with 12% of placebo-treated patients. Thus, troglitazone improved the ovulatory dysfunction of PCOS in a dose-related fashion, with a minimum of adverse effects. Although ovulation induction with insulin-lowering therapy has been promising, especially in obese PCOS patients, pregnancy rates and long-term outcomes with such agents remains unknown.

### Treatment of Associated Metabolic Abnormalities: Insulin Resistance and Glucose Intolerance

As noted, weight reduction, when it can be achieved, is an important component in the treatment of PCOS. However, not all women with PCOS are obese, and since the etiology of obesity in PCOS in not known, there is currently no unique weight-loss regimen to target excess adiposity in PCOS. It is generally perceived that a carbohydrate-restricted diet holds advantages over a diet restricted in fat in this population. However, several recent studies designed to address this issue have failed to show a distinct benefit from restriction of calories consumed from carbohydrate rather than from fat.[202,203]

Pharmacologic reduction in insulin levels ameliorates the sequelae of both hyperinsulinemia and hyperandrogenemia. The place of insulin reduction therapies in the treatment of

PCOS should be viewed in the context of all currently available therapies for PCOS, as summarized in Table 157-4. In current clinical practice, three pharmacologic agents have been used to reduce insulin resistance: metformin (a biguanide) and either pioglitazone or rosiglitazone, both of which are thiazolidinediones.

Although metformin has been reported to have direct effects on ovarian steroidogenesis,[204,205] this does not appear to be the primary mechanism responsible for attenuation of ovarian androgen production in women with PCOS. Rather, metformin inhibits hepatic glucose output, necessitating a lower insulin concentration and thereby a reduction in theca cell production of androgen.

It has been difficult to draw conclusions regarding efficacy of metformin in PCOS given that published studies have varied widely in terms of patient characteristics, control for effects of weight change, dose of metformin administered, and outcome measures. In an attempt to address this heterogeneity, data derived from 13 trials in which metformin was administered to 543 participants were subjected to meta-analysis.[206] This analysis showed that when compared to placebo, the odds ratio for ovulation on metformin was 3.88 (CI, 2.25 to 6.69) and that the odds ratio for ovulation was 4.41 (CI, 2.37 to 8.22) for metformin plus clomiphene compared to clomiphene alone. Metformin also had salutary effects on fasting insulin levels, blood pressure, and low-density lipoprotein cholesterol. These effects were judged to be independent of any weight changes associated with metformin, but controversy persists as to whether the beneficial effects of metformin are entirely independent of the weight loss[207] typically seen early in the course of therapy. Finally, the rates of spontaneous miscarriage and gestational diabetes are reportedly lower among PCOS women who conceive while taking metformin.[182,208-210] The long-term effects of metformin in pregnancy are unknown.

The thiazolidinediones improve the action of insulin in the liver, skeletal muscle, and adipose tissue and have but a modest effect on hepatic glucose output. As is the case with metformin,[204,205] this class of compounds has been reported to directly impact ovarian steroid synthesis,[211] although the bulk of evidence indicates that the reduction in insulin levels is responsible for the lowering of circulating androgen concentrations.

When troglitazone was administered to obese women with PCOS, the findings were consistent: insulin resistance, hyperandrogenemia, and glucose tolerance were all significantly improved.[212,213] In addition, troglitazone treatment was associated with a relative improvement in pancreatic β-cell function and a reduction in levels of the prothrombotic factor plasminogen activator inhibitor type 1.[212] Based on these findings, a double-blind, randomized, placebo-controlled study of troglitazone in PCOS was initiated.[200] Subjects were assigned to receive placebo or troglitazone at either 150, 300, or 600 mg per day day for 44 weeks. Among the 305 women who entered the trial, ovulatory rates were significantly greater for those who received 300 or 600 mg of troglitazone compared to those receiving placebo (0.42 and 0.58 vs. 0.32; $P < 0.05$ and 0.0001, respectively). Of PCOS patients treated with 600 mg, 57% ovulated over half of the time compared with 12% of placebo-treated patients. Free testosterone decreased and SHBG increased in a dose-related fashion with troglitazone treatment, and all three troglitazone treatment groups were significantly different from placebo. Nearly all glycemic parameters showed dose-related decreases with troglitazone treatment. Results of subsequent smaller-scale studies using rosiglitazone[214,215] and pioglitazone[216] have been similar, but because of concern regarding use of these agents in pregnancy, they have been less readily adopted for routine use in clinical practice.

## REFERENCES

1. Miller W: Molecular biology of steroid hormone synthesis. Endocr Rev 9:295–318, 1988.
2. Rosenfield R: Ovarian and adrenal function in polycystic ovary syndrome. Endocrinol Metab Clin North Am 28:265–293, 1999.
3. Miller WL: Early steps in androgen biosynthesis: From cholesterol to DHEA. Baillieres Clin Endocrinol Metab 12:67–81, 1998.
4. Abraham G: Ovarian and adrenal contributions to peripheral androgens during the menstrual cycle. J Clin Endocrinol Metab 39:340–346, 1974.
5. Rosenfield RL: Role of androgens in growth and development of the fetus, child, and adolescent. Adv Pediatr 19:171, 1972.
6. Auchus RJ, Rainey WE: Adrenarche—physiology, biochemistry and human disease. Clin Endocrinol (Oxf) 60:288–296, 2004.
7. Grumbach M, Richards C, Conte F, Kaplan S: Clinical disorders of adrenal function and puberty: An assessment of the role of the adrenal cortex in normal and abnormal puberty in man and evidence for an ACTH-like pituitary adrenal androgen stimulating hormone. In James V, Serio M, Giusti C, Martini L (eds): The Endocrine Function of the Human Adrenal Cortex. London, Academic Press, 1978, p 583.
8. Byrne C, Perry Y, Winter J: Kinetic analysis of adrenal 3β-hydroxysteroid dehydrogenase activity during human development. J Clin Endocrinol Metab 60:934, 1985.
9. l'Allemand D, Schmidt S, Rousson V, et al: Associations between body mass, leptin, IGF-I and circulating adrenal androgens in children with obesity and premature adrenarche. Eur J Endocrinol 146:537–543, 2002.
10. Cizza G, Dorn LD, Lotsikas A, et al: Circulating plasma leptin and IGF-1 levels in girls with premature adrenarche: Potential implications of a preliminary study. Horm Metab Res 33:138–143, 2001.
11. Rosenfield RL: Evidence that idiopathic functional adrenal hyperandrogenism is caused by dysregulation of adrenal steroidogenesis and that hyperinsulinemia may be involved [editorial]. J Clin Endocrinol Metab 81:878–880, 1996.
12. Moghetti P, Castello R, Negri C, et al: Insulin infusion amplifies 17a-hydroxycorticosteroid intermediates response to ACTH in hyperandrogenic women: Apparent relative impairment of 17,20-lyase activity. J Clin Endocrinol Metab 81:881–886, 1996.
13. McGee EA, Hsueh AJW: Initial and cyclic recruitment of ovarian follicles. Endocr Rev 21:200–214, 2000.
14. Ehrmann DA: Relation of functional ovarian hyperandrogenism to non-insulin dependent diabetes mellitus. Baillieres Clin Obstet Gynaecol 11:335–347, 1997.
15. Ehrmann D, Barnes R, Rosenfield R: Polycystic ovary syndrome as a form of functional ovarian hyperandrogenism. Endocr Rev 16:322–353, 1995.
16. Cara J, Rosenfield R: Insulin-like growth factor-I and insulin potentiate luteinizing hormone-induced androgen synthesis by rat ovarian theca-interstitial cells. Endocrinology 123:733–739, 1988.
17. Hernandez E, Resnick C, Holtzclaw W, et al: Insulin as a regulator of androgen biosynthesis by cultured rat ovarian cells: Cellular mechanism(s) underlying physiological and pharmacological hormonal actions. Endocrinology 122:2034, 1988.
18. Rosenfield RL, Moll GW Jr: The role of proteins in the distribution of plasma androgens and estradiol. In Molinatti G, Martini L, James V (eds): Androgenization in Women. New York, Raven Press, 1989, p 25.
19. Hammond G: Molecular properties of corticosteroid binding globulin and sex-steroid binding proteins. Endocr Rev 11:65, 1990.
20. Ekins R: Measurement of free hormones in blood. Endocr Rev 11:5, 1990.
21. Moll G Jr, Rosenfield RL: Estradiol inhibition of pituitary luteinizing hormone release is antagonized by serum proteins. J Steroid Biochem 25:308, 1986.

22. Nestler J, Powers L, Matt DW, et al: A direct effect of hyperinsulinemia on serum sex hormone-binding globulin levels in obese women with the polycystic ovary syndrome. J Clin Endocrinol Metab 72:83–89, 1991.

23. Moll G Jr, Rosenfield R: Testosterone binding and free plasma androgen concentrations under physiologic conditions: Characterization by flow dialysis technique. J Clin Endocrinol Metab 49:730–736, 1979.

24. Kaufman F, Gentzschein E, Stanczyk F, et al: Dehydroepiandrosterone and dehydroepiandrosterone sulfate metabolism in human genital skin. Fertil Steril 54:251, 1990.

25. Kuttenn F, Mowszowicz D, Shaison G, Mauvais-Jarvis P: Androgen production and skin metabolism in hirsutism. J Clin Endocrinol Metab 75:83, 1977.

26. Lobo R, Paul W, Gentzsschein E, et al: Production of 3a-androstanediol glucuronide in human genital skin. J Clin Endocrinol Metab 65:711, 1987.

27. Rosenfield RL: Pilosebaceous physiology in relation to hirsutism and acne. Clin Endocrinol Metab 15:341–362, 1986.

28. Rittmaster RA: Androgen conjugates: Physiology and clinical significance. Endocr Rev 14:121–132, 1993.

29. Lubhan DB, Joseph DR, Sullivan PM, et al: Cloning of human androgen receptor complementary DNA and localization to the X chromosome. Science 240:327, 1988.

30. Vottero A, Stratakis C, Ghizzoni L, et al: Androgen receptor-mediated hypersensitivity to androgens in women with nonhyperandrogenic hirsutism: Skewing of X-chromosome inactivation. J Clin Endocrinol Metab:1091–1095, 1999.

31. Ehrmann D, Rosenfield R: An endocrinologic approach to the patient with hirsutism. J Clin Endocrinol Metab 71:1, 1990.

32. Rosenfield RL, Deplewski D: Role of androgens in the developmental biology of the pilosebaceous unit. Am J Med 98:80S–88S, 1995.

33. Reingold SB, Rosenfield RL: The relationship of mild hirsutism or acne in women to androgens. Arch Dermatol 123:209–212, 1987.

34. Marynick SP, Chakmakjian ZH, McCafffree DL, et al: Androgen excess in cystic acne. N Engl J Med 308:981, 1983.

35. Legro R, Shahbahrami B, Lobo R, Kovacs B: Size polymorphisms of the androgen receptor among female Hispanics and correlation with androgenic characteristics. Obstet Gynecol 83(5 Pt 1):701–706, 1994.

36. Saenger P, Dimartino-Nardi J: Premature adrenarche. J Endocrinol Invest 24:724–733, 2001.

37. Rosenfield RL: Normal and almost normal variants of precocious puberty. Premature pubarche and premature thelarche revisited. Horm Res 41:7–13, 1994.

38. Rosenfield RL, Qin K: Normal adrenarche. In Rose BD (ed): UpToDate (CD). Wellesley, MA, UpToDate, 1998.

39. Ibanez L, Dimartino-Nardi J, Potau N, Saenger P: Premature adrenarche—normal variant or forerunner of adult disease? Endocr Rev 21:671–696, 2000.

40. Ibañez L, Potau N, Francois I, deZegher F: Precocious pubarche, hyperinsulinism, and ovarian hyperandrogenism. J Clin Endocrinol Metab 83:3558–3562, 1998.

41. Temeck J, Pang S, Nelson C, New M: Genetic defects of steroidogenesis in premature pubarche. J Clin Endocrinol Metab 64:609, 1987.

42. Oberfield S, Mayes D, Levine L: Adrenal steroidogenic function in a Black and Hispanic population with precocious pubarche. J Clin Endocrinol Metab 70:76, 1990.

43. Pang S: Congenital adrenal hyperplasia. Bailliere's Clin Obstet Gynaecol 11:281, 1997.

44. Lobo R: The role of the adrenal in polycystic ovary syndrome. Semin Reprod Endocrinol 2:251–262, 1984.

45. McKenna T: Current concepts: Pathogenesis and treatment of polycystic ovary syndrome. N Engl J Med 318:558–562, 1988.

46. Miller WL: Congenital adrenal hyperplasia in the adult patient. Adv Intern Med 44:155–173, 1999.

47. White P, New M, Dupont B: Congenital adrenal hyperplasia. N Engl J Med 316:1519, 1987.

48. Ehrmann D, Rosenfield R, Barnes R, et al: Detection of functional ovarian hyperandrogenism in women with androgen excess. N Engl J Med 327:157–162, 1992.

49. New M: Steroid 21-hydroxylase deficiency (congenital adrenal hyperplasia). Am J Med 98(Suppl A):2S–8S, 1995.

50. Cara J, Moshang T Jr, Bongiovanni A, Marx B: Elevated 17-hydroxyprogesterone and testosterone in a newborn with 3β-hydroxysteroid dehydrogenase deficiency. N Engl J Med 313:618, 1985.

51. Rosenfield R, Rich B, Wolfsdorf JE, et al: Pubertal presentation of congenital? Δ5-β-hydroxysteroid dehydrogenase deficiency. J Clin Endocrinol Metab 51:345–353, 1980.

52. Joehrer K, Geley S, Strasser-Wozak E, et al: CYP11B1 mutations causing non-classic adrenal hyperplasia due to 11beta-hydroxylase deficiency. Hum Mol Genet 6:1829–1834, 1997.

53. Lee P, Winter R, Green O: Virilizing adrenocortical tumors in childhood: Eight cases and a review of the literature. Pediatr 70:129, 1985.

54. Werk E, Sholiton L, Kaalejs L: Testosterone-secreting adenoma under gonadotropin control. N Engl J Med 289:767, 1973.

55. Glickman SP, Rosenfield RL, Bergenstal RM, Helke J: Multiple androgenic abnormalities, including elevated free testosterone, in hyperprolactinemic women. J Clin Endocrinol Metab 55:251, 1982.

56. Futterweit W, Krieger D: Pituitary tumors associated with hyperprolactinemia and polycystic ovary disease. Fertil Steril 31:608–613, 1979.

57. Monroe S, Levine L, Chang J, et al: Prolactin-secreting pituitary adenomas. V. J Clin Endocrinol Metab 52:1171, 1981.

58. Lim N, Dingman J: Androgenic adrenal hyperfunction in acromegaly. N Engl J Med 271:1189, 1964.

59. Kirschner M, Zucker I, Jesperson D: Idiopathic hirsutism–an ovarian abnormality. N Engl J Med 294:637–640, 1976.

60. Abraham G, Maroulis G, Buster J, et al: Effect of dexamethasone on serum cortisol and androgen levels in hirsute patients. Obstet Gynecol 47:395–402, 1976.

61. Hatch R, Rosenfield R, Kim M, Tredway D: Hirsutism: Implications, etiology, and management. Am J Obstet Gynecol 140:815–830, 1981.

62. Rittmaster R, Thompson D: Effect of leuprolide and dexamethasone on hair growth and hormone levels in hirsute women: The relative importance of the ovary and the adrenal in the pathogenesis of hirsutism. J Clin Endocrinol Metab 70:1096–1102, 1990.

63. Chang R, Laufer L, Meldrum D, et al: Steroid secretion in polycystic ovary disease after ovarian suppression by a long-acting gonadotropin-releasing hormone agonist. J Clin Endocrinol Metab 56:897–903, 1983.

64. Barnes R, Rosenfield R, Burstein S, Ehrmann D: Pituitary-ovarian responses to nafarelin testing in the polycystic ovary syndrome. N Engl J Med 320:559–565, 1989.

65. Gilling-Smith C, Story H, Rogers V, Franks S: Evidence for a primary abnormality of thecal cell steroidogenesis in the polycystic ovary syndrome. Clin Endocrinol 47:93–99, 1997.

66. Revised 2003 consensus on diagnostic criteria and long-term health risks related to polycystic ovary syndrome (PCOS). Hum Reprod 19:41–47, 2004.

67. Adams J, Polson D, Franks S: Prevalence of polycystic ovaries in women with anovulation and idiopathic hirsutism. Br Med J 293:355–359, 1986.

68. Polson D, Adams J, Wadsworth J, Franks S: Polycystic ovaries—a common finding in normal women. Lancet:870–872, 1988.

69. Michelmore KF, Balen AH, Dunger DB, Vessey MP: Polycystic ovaries and associated clinical and biochemical features in young women. Clin Endocrinol (Oxf) 51:779–786, 1999.

70. Waldstreicher J, Santoro N, Hall J, et al: Hyperfunction of the hypothalamic-pituitary axis in women with polycystic ovarian disease: Indirect evidence for partial gonadotroph desensitization. J Clin Endocrinol Metab 66:165–172, 1988.

71. Eagleson CA, Gingrich MB, Pastor CL, et al: Polycystic ovarian syndrome: Evidence that flutamide restores

sensitivity of the gonadotropin-releasing hormone pulse generator to inhibition by estradiol and progesterone. J Clin Endocrinol Metab 85:4047–4052, 2000.

72. Franks S: Adult polycystic ovary syndrome begins in childhood. Best Pract Res Clin Endocrinol Metab 16:263–272, 2002.

73. Ibanez L, Valls C, Potau N, et al: Polycystic ovary syndrome after precocious pubarche: Ontogeny of the low-birthweight effect. Clin Endocrinol 55:667–672, 2001.

74. Eisner JR, Dumesic DA, Kemnitz JW, Abbott DH: Timing of prenatal androgen excess determines differential impairment in insulin secretion and action in adult female rhesus monkeys. J Clin Endocrinol Metab 85:1206–1210, 2000.

75. Eisner JR, Dumesic DA, Kemnitz JW, et al: Increased adiposity in female rhesus monkeys exposed to androgen excess during early gestation. Obes Res 11:279–286, 2003.

76. Eisner JR, Barnett MA, Dumesic DA, Abbott DH: Ovarian hyperandrogenism in adult female rhesus monkeys exposed to prenatal androgen excess. Fertil Steril 77:167–172, 2002.

77. Abbott DH, Dumesic DA, Franks S: Developmental origin of polycystic ovary syndrome—a hypothesis. J Endocrinol 174:1–5, 2002.

78. Knochenhauer E, Key T, Kahsar-Miller M, et al: Prevalence of the polycystic ovary syndrome in unselected black and white women of the southeastern United States: A prospective study. J Clin Endocrinol Metab 83:3078–3082, 1998.

79. Diamanti-Kandarakis E, Kouli CR, Bergiele AT, et al: A survey of the polycystic ovary syndrome in the Greek island of Lesbos: Hormonal and metabolic profile. J Clin Endocrinol Metab 84:4006–4011, 1999.

80. Asuncion M, Calvo RM, San Millan JL, et al: A prospective study of the prevalence of the polycystic ovary syndrome in unselected Caucasian women from Spain. J Clin Endocrinol Metab 85:2434–2438, 2000.

81. Kauffman RP, Baker VM, DiMarino P, et al: Polycystic ovarian syndrome and insulin resistance in white and Mexican American women: A comparison of two distinct populations. Am J Obstet Gynecol 187:1362–1369, 2002.

82. Williamson K, Gunn A, Johnson N, Milsom S: The impact of ethnicity on the presentation of polycystic ovarian syndrome. Aust N Z J Obstet Gynaecol 41:202–206, 2001.

83. Azziz R, Kashar-Miller MD: Family history as a risk factor for the polycystic ovary syndrome. J Pediatr Endocrinol Metab 13:1303–1306, 2000.

84. Urbanek M, Legro R, Driscoll D, et al: Thirty-seven candidate genes for polycystic ovary syndrome: Strongest evidence for linkage is with follistatin [see comments]. Proc Natl Acad Sci U S A 96:8573–8578, 1999.

85. Ehrmann D, Sturis J, Byrne M, et al: Insulin secretory defects in polycystic ovary syndrome: Relationship to insulin sensitivity and family history of non-insulin dependent diabetes mellitus. J Clin Invest 96:520–527, 1995.

86. Legro RS, Driscoll D, Strauss JF 3rd, et al: Evidence for a genetic basis for hyperandrogenemia in polycystic ovary syndrome. Proc Natl Acad Sci U S A 95:14956–14960, 1998.

87. Kahsar-Miller MD, Nixon C, Boots LR, et al: Prevalence of polycystic ovary syndrome (PCOS) in first-degree relatives of patients with PCOS. Fertil Steril 75:53–58, 2001.

88. Urbanek M, Spielman R: Genetic analysis of candidate genes for the polycystic ovary syndrome. Curr Opin Endocrinol Diabetes 9:492–501, 2002.

89. Wood JR, Nelson VL, Ho C, et al: The molecular phenotype of polycystic ovary syndrome (PCOS) theca cells and new candidate PCOS genes defined by microarray analysis. J Biol Chem 278:26380–26390, 2003.

90. Draper N, Walker EA, Bujalska IJ, et al: Mutations in the genes encoding 11beta-hydroxysteroid dehydrogenase type 1 and hexose-6-phosphate dehydrogenase interact to cause cortisone reductase deficiency. Nat Genet 34:434–439, 2003.

91. Roldan B, San Millan JL, Escobar-Morreale HF: Genetic basis of metabolic abnormalities in polycystic ovary syndrome: Implications for therapy. Am J Pharmacogenomics 4:93–107, 2004.

92. Carmina E: Genetic and environmental aspect of polycystic ovary syndrome. J Endocrinol Invest 26:1151–1159, 2003.

93. Stein I, Leventhal M: Amenorrhea associated with bilateral polycystic ovaries. Am J Obstet Gynecol 29:181–191, 1935.

94. Yen S: The polycystic ovary syndrome. Clin Endocrinol 12:177–208, 1980.

95. Goldzieher M, Green J: The polycystic ovary. I. Clinical and histologic features. J Clin Endocrinol Metab 22:325–338, 1962.

96. Achard C, Thiers J: Le virilisme pilaire et son association a l'insuffisance glycolytique (diabete des femmes a barbe). Bull Acad Natl Med 86:51–64, 1921.

97. Ehrmann DA, Barnes RB, Rosenfield RL, et al: Prevalence of impaired glucose tolerance and diabetes in women with polycystic ovary syndrome. Diabetes Care 22:141–146, 1999.

98. Legro RS, Kunselman AR, Dodson WC, Dunaif A: Prevalence and predictors of risk for type 2 diabetes mellitus and impaired glucose tolerance in polycystic ovary syndrome: A prospective, controlled study in 254 affected women. J Clin Endocrinol Metab 84:165–169, 1999.

99. Polonsky K, Sturis J, Bell G: Non-insulin-dependent diabetes mellitus—a genetically programmed failure of the beta cell to compensate for insulin resistance. N Engl J Med 334:777–783, 1996.

100. Ehrmann DA, Schneider DJ, Sobel BE, et al: Troglitazone improves defects in insulin action, insulin secretion, ovarian steroidogenesis, and fibrinolysis in women with polycystic ovary syndrome. J Clin Endocrinol Metab 82:2108–2116, 1997.

101. Dunaif A, Finegood D: β-cell dysfunction independent of obesity and glucose intolerance in the polycystic ovary syndrome. J Clin Endocrinol Metab 81:942–947, 1996.

102. Colilla S, Cox NJ, Ehrmann DA: Heritability of insulin secretion and insulin action in women with polycystic ovary syndrome and their first degree relatives. J Clin Endocrinol Metab 86:2027–2031, 2001.

103. Barnes R, Rosenfield R: The polycystic ovary syndrome: Pathogenesis and treatment. Ann Intern Med 110:386–399, 1989.

104. Franks S: Polycystic ovary syndrome. N Engl J Med 333:853–861, 1995.

105. Goldzieher J: Polycystic ovarian disease. Clin Obstet Gynecol 16:82, 1973.

106. Wickenheisser JK, Nelson-DeGrave VL, Quinn PG, McAllister JM: Increased cytochrome P450 17alpha-hydroxylase promoter function in theca cells isolated from patients with polycystic ovary syndrome involves nuclear factor-1. Mol Endocrinol 18:588–605, 2004.

107. Nelson VL, Qin Kn KN, Rosenfield RL, et al: The biochemical basis for increased testosterone production in theca cells propagated from patients with polycystic ovary syndrome. J Clin Endocrinol Metab 86:5925–5933, 2001.

108. Gilling-Smith C, Willis D, Beard R, Franks S: Hypersecretion of androstenedione by isolated thecal cells from polycystic ovaries. J Clin Endocrinol Metab 79:1158–1165, 1994.

109. Rosenfield RL: Current concepts of polycystic ovary syndrome. Bailliere's Clin Obstet Gynaecol 11:307–333, 1997.

110. Zhang L-H, Rodriguez H, Ohno S, Miller W: Serine phosphorylation of human P450c17 increases 17,20-lyase activity: Implications for adrenarche and the polycystic ovary syndrome. Proc Natl Acad Sci U S A 92:10619–10623, 1995.

111. Dewailly D, Vantyghem-Haudiquet M, Sainsard C, et al: Clinical and biological phenotypes in late-onset 21-hydroxylase deficiency. J Clin Endocrinol Metab 63:418–423, 1986.

112. Barnes R, Rosenfield R, Ehrmann D, et al: Ovarian hyperandrogenism as a result of congenital adrenal virilizing disorders: Evidence for perinatal masculinization of neuroendocrine function in women. J Clin Endocrinol Metab 79:1328–1333, 1994.

113. Pang S, Softness B, Sweeney W, New M: Hirsutism, polycystic ovarian disease, and ovarian 17-ketosteroid reductase deficiency. N Engl J Med 316:1295–1301, 1987.

114. Conte F, Grumbach M, Ito Y, et al: A syndrome of female pseudohermaphroditism, hypergonadotropic hypogonadism, and multicystic ovaries associated with missense mutations in the gene encoding aromatase (P450arom). J Clin Endocrinol Metab 78:1287–1292, 1994.

115. Morishima A, Grumbach MM, Simpson ER, et al: Aromatase deficiency in a male and female siblings caused by a novel mutation and the physiologic role of estrogens. J Clin Endocrinol Metab 80:3689–3698, 1995.

116. Dunaif A: Insulin resistance and the polycystic ovary syndrome: Mechanism and implications for pathogenesis. Endocr Rev 18:774–800, 1997.

117. Moller D, Flier J: Insulin resistance—mechanisms, syndromes, and implications. N Engl J Med 325:938–948, 1991.

118. Nestler J, Jakubowicz D, de Vargas A, et al: Insulin stimulates testosterone biosynthesis by human thecal cells from women with polycystic ovary syndrome by activating its own receptor and using inositolglycan mediators as the signal transduction system. J Clin Endocrinol Metab 83:2001–2005, 1998.

119. Rosenfield RL, Cohen RM, Talerman A: Lipid cell tumor of the ovary in reference to adult-onset congenital adrenal hyperplasia and polycystic ovary syndrome. J Reprod Med 32:363, 1987.

120. Talerman A, Jarabak J, Amarose AP: Gonadoblastoma and dysgerminoma in a true hermaphrodite with a 46, XX karyotype. Am J Obstet Gynecol 140:475–477, 1981.

121. Pablo-Mendez J, Schiavon R, Diaz-Cueto L, et al: A reliable endocrine test with human menopausal gonadotropins for diagnosis of true hermaphroditism in early infancy. J Clin Endocrinol Metab 83:3523–3526, 1998.

122. Hensleigh PA, Woodruf JD: Differential maternal-fetal response to androgenizing luteoma or hyperreactio luteinalis. Obstet Gynecol Surv 33:262–271, 1978.

123. Diamanti-Kandarakis E, Biergiele A: The influence of obesity on hyperandrogenism and infertility. Obes Rev 2:231–238, 2001.

124. Penttila TL, Koskinen P, Penttila TA, et al: Obesity regulates bioavailable testosterone levels in women with or without polycystic ovary syndrome. Fertil Steril 71:457–461, 1999.

125. Lustig R, Bradlow H, Fishman J: Estrogen metabolism in disorders of nutrition and dietary composition. In Pirke K, Wuttke W, Schweiger U (eds): The Menstrual Cycle and Its Disorders. Berlin, Springer-Verlag, 1989, pp 119–132.

126. Dewailly D: Definition and significance of polycystic ovaries. In Rosenfield R (ed): Bailliere's Clinical Obstetrics and Gynaecology: Hyperandrogenic States and Hirsutism. London, Bailliere Tindall, 1997, pp 349–368.

127. Dewailly D, Duhamel A, Robert Y, et al: Interrelationship between ultrasonography and biology in the diagnosis of polycystic ovarian syndrome. Ann N Y Acad Sci 687:206–216, 1993.

128. Rosenfield R, Perovic N, Ehrmann D, Barnes R: Acute hormonal responses to the gonadotropin releasing hormone agonist leuprolide: Dose-response studies and comparison to nafarelin. J Clin Endocrinol Metab 81:3408–3411, 1996.

129. Givens J, Andersen R, Wiser W: Dynamics of suppression and recovery of plasma FSH, LH, androstenedione and testosterone in polycystic ovarian disease using an oral contraceptive. J Clin Endocrinol Metab 38:727–735, 1974.

130. Mandel F, Geola F, Lu J: Biological effects of various doses of ethinyl estradiol in postmenopausal women. Obstet Gynecol 58:673–679, 1982.

131. Carr B, Parker C, Madden J, et al: Plasma levels of adrenocorticotropin and cortisol in women receiving oral contraceptive steroid treatment. J Clin Endocrinol Metab 49:346–349, 1979.

132. Wild R, Umstot E, Andersen R, Givens J: Adrenal function in hirsutism. II. Effect of an oral contraceptive. J Clin Endocrinol Metab 54:676–681, 1982.

133. Palitz L: Estrogen-progestin in the control of acne in girls. Clin Med 75:43–54, 1968.

134. Brotherton J: Animal biological assessment. In J Brotherton E (ed): Sex Hormone Pharmacology. London, Academic Press, 1976, pp 43–78.

135. Thijssen J: Hormonal and nonhormonal factors affecting sex hormone-binding globulin levels in blood. Ann N Y Acad Sci 538:280–286, 1988.

136. Kuhl H: Comparative pharmacology of newer progestogens. Drugs 51:188–215, 1996.

137. Lucky AW, Henderson TA, Olson WH, et al: Effectiveness of norgestimate and ethinyl estradiol in treating moderate acne vulgaris. J Am Acad Dermatol 37:746–754, 1997.

138. Krattenmacher R: Drospirenone: Pharmacology and pharmacokinetics of a unique progestogen. Contraception 62:29–38, 2000.

139. Guido M, Romualdi D, Giuliani M, et al: Drospirenone for the treatment of hirsute women with polycystic ovary syndrome: A clinical, endocrinological, metabolic pilot study. J Clin Endocrinol Metab 89:2817–2823, 2004.

140. Lemay A, Dewailly S, Grenier R, Huard J: Attenuation of mild hyper-androgenic activity in postpubertal acne by a triphasic oral contraceptive containing low doses of ethinyl estradiol and d,l-norgesterl. J Clin Endocrinol Metab 71:8–14, 1990.

141. Hancock K, Levell M: The use of oestrogen/progestogen preparations in the treatment of hirsutism in the female. J Obstet Gynaecol 81:804–811, 1974.

142. Rittmaster R: Differential suppression of testosterone and estradiol in hirsute women with the superactive gonadotropin-releasing hormone agonist leuprolide. J Clin Endocrinol Metab 67:651–655, 1988.

143. Pazos F, Escobar-Morreale HF, Balsa J, et al: Prospective randomized study comparing the long-acting gonadotropin-releasing hormone agonist triptorelin, flutamide, and cyproterone acetate, used in combination with an oral contraceptive, in the treatment of hirsutism. Fertil Steril 71:122–128, 1999.

144. Sidenius-Johansen J, Juel-Riis B, Hassager C, et al: The effect of a gonadotropin-releasing hormone agonist analog (nafarelin) on bone metabolism. J Clin Endocrinol Metab 67:701–706, 1988.

145. Matta W, Shaw R, Hesp R, Evans R: Reversible trabecular bone density loss following induced hypooestrogenism with the GnRH analogue buserelin in premenopausal women. Clin Endocrinol 29:45–51, 1988.

146. Adashi E: Potential utility of gonadotropin-releasing hormone agonists in the management of ovarian hyperandrogenism. Fertil Steril 53:765–779, 1990.

147. Rittmaster R, Loriaux D, Cutler G: Sensitivity of cortisol and adrenal androgens to dexamethasone suppression in hirsute women. J Clin Endocrinol Metab 61:462–466, 1985.

148. Rittmaster R, Givner M: Effect of daily and alternate day low dose prednisone on serum cortisol and adrenal androgens in hirsute women. J Clin Endocrinol Metab 67:400–403, 1988.

149. Carmina E, Lobo R: Peripheral androgen blockade versus glandular androgen suppression in the treatment of hirsutism. Obstet Gynecol 78:845–849, 1991.

150. Steinberger E, Rodriguez-Rigau L, Weidman E, et al: Glucocorticoid therapy in hyperandrogenism. Balliere's Clin Obstet Gynaecol 4:457–471, 1990.

151. Azziz R, Black VY, Knochenhauer ES, et al: Ovulation after glucocorticoid suppression of adrenal androgens in the polycystic ovary syndrome is not predicted by the basal dehydroepiandrosterone sulfate level. J Clin Endocrinol Metab 84:946–950, 1999.

152. Spritzer P, Billaud L, Thalabard J-C: Cyproterone acetate versus hydrocortisone treatment in late-onset adrenal hyperplasia. J Clin Endocrinol Metab 70:642–646, 1990.

153. Rajfer J, Sikka S, River F, Handelsman D: Mechanism of

inhibition of human testicular steroidogenesis by oral ketoconazole. J Clin Endocrinol Metab 63:1193–1198, 1986.

154. Couch R, Muller J, Perry Y, Winter J: Kinetic analysis of human adrenal steroidogenesis by ketoconazole. J Clin Endocrinol Metab 65:551–555, 1987.

155. Venturoli A, Fabri R, Dal Prato L: Ketoconazole therapy for women with acne and/or hirsutism. J Clin Endocrinol Metab 71:335–339, 1990.

156. Mowszowicz I, Wright F, Vincens M: Androgen metabolism in hirsute patients treated with cyproterone acetate. J Steroid Biochem 20:757–761, 1984.

157. Miller J, Jacobs H: Treatment of hirsutism and acne with cyproterone acetate. Clin Endocrinol Metab 15:373–389, 1986.

158. Miller J, Wojnarowska F, Dowd P: Antiandrogen treatment in women with acne: A controlled trial. Br J Dermatol 114:705–716, 1986.

159. Barth J, Cherry C, Wojnarowska F, Dawber R: Spironolactone is an effective and well tolerated systemic antiandrogen therapy for hirsute women. J Clin Endocrinol Metab 68:966–970, 1989.

160. O'Brien R, Cooper M, Murray R: Comparison of sequential cyproterone acetate versus spironolactone/oral contraceptive in the treatment of hirsutism. J Clin Endocrinol Metab 72:1008–1013, 1991.

161. Edgren R, Elton R: Estrogen antagonisms: Effects of several steroidal spironolactones on estrogen-induced uterine growth in mice. Proc Soc Exp Biol Med 104:664–665, 1960.

162. Camino-Torres R, Ma L, Snyder P: Gynecomastia and semen abnormalities induced by spironolactone in normal men. J Clin Endocrinol Metab 45:255–260, 1977.

163. Serafini P, Lobo R: The effects of spironolactone on adrenal steroidogenesis in hirsute women. Fertil Steril 44:595–599, 1985.

164. Serafini P, Catalino J, Lobo R: The effect of spironolactone on genital skin 5a-reductase activity. J Steroid Biochem 23:191–194, 1985.

165. Givens J: Treatment of hirsutism with spironolactone. Fertil Steril 43:841–843, 1985.

166. Crosby P, Rittmaster R: Predictors of clinical response in hirsute women treated with spironolactone. Fertil Steril 55:1076–1081, 1991.

167. Neri R, Monahan M: Effects of a novel nonsteroidal antiandrogen on canine prostatic hyperplasia. Invest Urol 10:123–130, 1972.

168. Cusan L, Dupont A, Belanger A, et al: Treatment of hirsutism with the pure antiandrogen flutamide. J Am Acad Dermatol 23:462–469, 1990.

169. Liang T, Rasmusson G, Brooks J: Biochemical and biological studies with 4-aza-steroidal 5a-reductase

inhibitors. J Steroid Biochem 19:385–390, 1983.

170. Rittmaster RS: 5alpha-reductase inhibitors. J Androl 18:582–587, 1997.

171. Venturoli S, Marescalchi O, Colombo F, et al: A prospective randomized trial comparing low dose flutamide, finasteride, ketoconazole, and cyproterone acetate-estrogen regimens in the treatment of hirsutism. J Clin Endocrinol Metab 84:1304–1310, 1999.

172. Jafari K, Tavaheri C, Ruiz G: Endometrial adenocarcinoma and the Stein-Leventhal syndrome. Obstet Gynecol 51:97–100, 1978.

173. Coulam C, Annegers J, Kranz J: Chronic anovulation syndrome and associated neoplasia. Obstet Gynecol 61:403–407, 1983.

174. Farhi D, Nosanchuk J, Silverberg S: Endometrial adenocarcinoma in women under 25 years of age. Obstet Gynecol 68:741–745, 1986.

175. Bayer S, DeCherney A: Clinical manifestations and treatment of dysfunctional uterine bleeding. JAMA 269:1823–1828, 1993.

176. Group PTW: Effects of estrogen or estrogen/progestin regimens on heart disease risk factors in postmenopausal women. JAMA 273:199–208, 1995.

177. Woodruff J, Pickar J: Incidence of endometrial hyperplasia in postmenopausal women taking conjugated estrogens (Premarin) with medroxyprogesterone acetate or conjugated estrogens alone. Am J Obstet Gynecol 170:1213–1223, 1994.

178. Messinis I, Milingos S: Current and future status of ovulation induction in polycystic ovary syndrome. Hum Reprod Update 3:235–253, 1997.

179. Barnes R: Diagnosis and therapy of hyperandrogenism. Bailliere's Clin Obstet Gynaecol 11:369–396, 1997.

180. Hammond M, Halme J, Talbert L: Factors affecting the pregnancy rate in clomiphene citrate induction of ovulation. Obstet Gynecol 62:196–202, 1983.

181. Gysler M, March C, Mishell D, Bailey E: A decade's experience with an individualized clomiphene treatment regimen including its effects on the post-coital test. Fertil Steril 37:161–167, 1982.

182. Glueck CJ, Phillips H, Cameron D, et al: Continuing metformin throughout pregnancy in women with polycystic ovary syndrome appears to safely reduce first-trimester spontaneous abortion: A pilot study. Fertil Steril 75:46–52, 2001.

183. Sagle A, Hamilton-Fairley D, Kiddy D, Franks S: A comparative, randomized study of low-dose human menopausal gonadotropin and follicle-stimulating hormone in women with polycystic ovarian syndrome. Fertil Steril 55:56–60, 1991.

184. Buvat J, Buvat-Herbaut M, Marcolin G: Purified follicle-stimulating hormone in polycystic ovary syndrome: Slow administration is safer and more effective. Fertil Steril 52:553–559, 1989.

185. Shoham Z, Patel A, Jacobs H: Polycystic ovarian syndrome: Safety and effectiveness of stepwise and low-dose administration of purified follicle-stimulating hormone. Fertil Steril 55:1051–1056, 1991.

186. Mizunuma H, Takagi T, Yamada K: Ovulation induction by step-down administration of purified urinary follicle-stimulating hormone in patients with polycystic ovarian syndrome. Fertil Steril 55:1195–1196, 1991.

187. Homburg R, Levy T, Ben-Rafael Z: A comparative prospective study of conventional regimen with chronic low-dose administration of follicle-stimulating hormone for anovulation associated with polycystic ovary syndrome. Fertil Steril 63:729–733, 1995.

188. Brzyski R, Grow D, Sims J, Seltman H: Increase in androgen:estrogen ratio specifically during low-dose follicle-stimulating hormone therapy for polycystic ovary syndrome. Fertil Steril 64:693–697, 1995.

189. Hugues J, Cedrin-Durnerin I, Avril C: Sequential step-up and step-down regimen: An alternative method for ovulation induction with follicle-stimulating hormone in polycystic ovarian syndrome. Hum Reprod 11:2581–2584, 1996.

190. van Santbrink E, Fauser B: Urinary follicle-stimulating hormone for normogonadotropic clomiphene-resistant anovulatory infertility: Prospective, randomized comparison between low dose step-up and step-down dose regimens. J Clin Endocrinol Metab 82:3597–3602, 1997.

191. White D, Polson D, Kiddy D: Induction of ovulation with low-dose gonadotropins in polycystic ovary syndrome: An analysis of 109 pregnancies in 225 women. J Clin Endocrinol Metab 81:3821–3824, 1996.

192. Homburg R, Levy T, Berkovitz D: Gonadotropin-releasing hormone agonist reduces the miscarriage rate for pregnancies achieved in women with polycystic ovarian syndrome. Fertil Steril 59:527–531, 1993.

193. Balen A, Tan S, MacDougall J, Jacobs H: Miscarriage rates following in-vitro fertilization are increased in women with polycystic ovaries and reduced by pituitary desensitization with buserelin. Human Reprod 8:959–964, 1993.

194. Campo S: Ovulatory cycles, pregnancy outcome and complications after surgical treatment of polycystic ovary syndrome. Obstet Gynecol Surv 53:297–308, 1998.

195. Amar N, Lachelin G: Laparoscopic ovarian diathermy: An effective treatment for anti-oestrogen resistant anovulatory infertility in women with the polycystic ovary syndrome. B J Obstet Gynaecol 100:161–164, 1993.

196. Donesky B, Adashi E: Surgically induced ovulation in the polycystic ovary syndrome: Wedge resection

revisited in the age of laparoscopy. Fertil Steril 63:439–463, 1995.

197. Kiddy D, Hamilton-Fairley D, Bush A, et al: Improvement in endocrine and ovarian function during dietary treatment of obese women with polycystic ovary syndrome. Clin Endocrinol 36:105–111, 1992.

198. Velazquez E, Acosta A, Mendoza S: Menstrual cyclicity after metformin therapy in polycystic ovary syndrome. Obstet Gynecol 90:392–395, 1997.

199. Hasegawa I, Murakawa H, Suzuki M: Effect of troglitazone on endocrine and ovulatory performance in women with insulin resistance-related polycystic ovary syndrome. Fertil Steril 71:323–327, 1999.

200. Azziz R, Ehrmann D, Legro RS, et al: Troglitazone improves ovulation and hirsutism in the polycystic ovary syndrome: A multicenter, double blind, placebo-controlled trial. J Clin Endocrinol Metab 86:1626–1632, 2001.

201. Nestler J, Jakubowicz D, Evans W, Pasquali R: Effects of metformin on spontaneous and clomiphene-induced ovulation in the polycystic ovary syndrome. N Engl J Med 338:1876–1880, 1998.

202. Stamets K, Taylor DS, Kunselman A, et al: A randomized trial of the effects of two types of short-term hypocaloric diets on weight loss in women with polycystic ovary syndrome. Fertil Steril 81:630–637, 2004.

203. Moran LJ, Noakes M, Clifton PM, et al: Dietary composition in restoring reproductive and metabolic physiology in overweight women with polycystic ovary syndrome. J Clin Endocrinol Metab 88:812–819, 2003.

204. Mansfield R, Galea R, Brincat M, et al: Metformin has direct effects on human ovarian steroidogenesis. Fertil Steril 79:956–962, 2003.

205. Attia G, Rainey W, Carr B: Metformin directly inhibits androgen production in human thecal cells. Fertil Steril 76:517–524, 2001.

206. Lord JM, Flight IHK, Norman RJ: Insulin-sensitizing drugs (metformin, troglitazone, rosiglitazone, pioglitazone, D-chiro-inositol) for polycystic ovary syndrome. Cochrane Database Syst Rev:CD003053, 2003.

207. Crave C, Fimbel S, Lejeune H, et al: Effects of diet and metformin administration on sex hormone-binding globulin, androgens, and insulin in hirsute and obese women. J Clin Endocrinol Metab 80:2057–2062, 1995.

208. Glueck CJ, Goldenberg N, Wang P, et al: Metformin during pregnancy reduces insulin, insulin resistance, insulin secretion, weight, testosterone and development of gestational diabetes: Prospective longitudinal assessment of women with polycystic ovary syndrome from preconception throughout pregnancy. Hum Reprod 19:510–521, 2004.

209. Glueck CJ, Wang P, Goldenberg N, Sieve-Smith L: Pregnancy outcomes among women with polycystic ovary syndrome treated with metformin. Hum Reprod 17:2858–2864, 2002.

210. Glueck CJ, Wang P, Kobayashi S, et al: Metformin therapy throughout pregnancy reduces the development of gestational diabetes in women with polycystic ovary syndrome. Fertil Steril 77:520–525, 2002.

211. Mitwally MF, Witchel SF, Casper RF: Troglitazone: A possible modulator of ovarian steroidogenesis. J Soc Gynecol Investig 9:163–167, 2002.

212. Ehrmann D, Schneider D, Sobel B, et a.: Troglitazone improves defects in insulin action, insulin secretion, ovarian steroidogenesis, and fibrinolysis in women with polycystic ovary syndrome. J Clin Endocrinol Metab 82:2108–2116, 1997.

213. Dunaif A, Scott D, Finegood D, et al: The insulin-sensitizing agent troglitazone improves metabolic and reproductive abnormalities in the polycystic ovary syndrome. J Clin Endocrinol Metab 81:3299–3306, 1996.

214. Ghazeeri G, Kutteh WH, Bryer-Ash M, et al: Effect of rosiglitazone on spontaneous and clomiphene citrate-induced ovulation in women with polycystic ovary syndrome. Fertil Steril 79:562–566, 2003.

215. Belli SH, Graffigna MN, Oneto A, et al: Effect of rosiglitazone on insulin resistance, growth factors, and reproductive disturbances in women with polycystic ovary syndrome. Fertil Steril 81:624–629, 2004.

216. Romualdi D, Guido M, Ciampelli M, et al: Selective effects of pioglitazone on insulin and androgen abnormalities in normo- and hyperinsulinaemic obese patients with polycystic ovary syndrome. Hum Reprod 18:1210–1218, 2003.

217. Burger HG: Androgen production in women. Fertil Steril 77 (Suppl 4):S3–S5, 2002.

218. Magoffin D: The role of the ovary in the genesis of hyperandrogenism. In Leung P, Adashi E (eds): The Ovary, 2d ed. San Diego, CA: Elsevier, 2004, pp 513–522.

219. Lashansky G, Saenger P, Fishman K, et al: Normative data for adrenal steroidogenesis in a healthy pediatric population: Age- and sex-related changes after adrenocorticotropin stimulation. J Clin Endocrinol Metab 73:674–686, 1991.

220. Rosenfield RL, Lucky AW: Acne, hirsutism, and alopecia in adolescent girls. Endocrinol Metab Clin North Am 22:507–532, 1993.

221. Rich B, Rosenfield R, Lucky A, et al: Adrenarche: Changing adrenal response to adrenocorticotropin. J Clin Endocrinol Metab 52:1129–1134, 1981.

222. Lucky A, Rosenfield R, McGuire J, et al: Adrenal androgen hyperresponsiveness to ACTH in women with acne and/or hirsutism: Adrenal enzyme defects and exaggerated adrenarche. J Clin Endocrinol Metab 62:840–848, 1986.

223. Rosenfield R: The Ovary and Female Maturation. Philadelphia, Saunders, 1996.

224. Ehrmann DA, Rychlik D: Pharmacologic treatment of polycystic ovary syndrome. Semin Reprod Med 21:277–283, 2003.

# CHAPTER 158

# Ovulation Induction and Assisted Reproduction

## *Efstratios M. Kolibianakis, Paul Devroey, and André C. Van Steirteghem*

**INTRODUCTION**
Definitions
When Should Ovulation Induction Be Performed?

**MODES OF OVULATION INDUCTION**
Ovulation Induction with Clomiphene Citrate
Alternate Medications for Ovulation Induction
Ovulation Induction Using GnRH
Ovulation Induction with Gonadotrophins

**ASSISTED REPRODUCTION**
Intrauterine Insemination
In Vitro Fertilization
Social Aspects and Ethical Problems in Assisted Reproduction

## INTRODUCTION

The reproductive period in women is characterized by their ability to ovulate. Ovulation, the release of an oocyte in the peritoneal cavity, follows rupture of a dominant follicle, developed in response to stimulation by endogenous gonadotrophins. In the presence of normal fallopian tubes, the released oocyte will be able to interact with spermatozoa ascending the female genital tract. This may lead to the production of the zygote and establishment of pregnancy if implantation occurs. When ovarian activity is disrupted, no ovulation takes place and, as a consequence, achievement of pregnancy is not feasible.

### DEFINITIONS

Ovulation induction refers to exogenous direct or indirect stimulation of the ovary with the aim of alleviating subfertility due to anovulation.

Ovulation induction should be differentiated from *reestablishment of ovulation*, which occurs after treatment of conditions interfering with the normal function of the hypothalamic-pituitary-ovarian (HPO) axis. These include weight and eating disorders, thyroid dysfunction, hyperprolactinemia, or excess exercise.

It should also be differentiated from *enhancement of ovulation*. This is usually performed in ovulatory women with unexplained infertility in the hope of increasing the probability of pregnancy.

More important, ovulation induction must be differentiated from superovulation for in vitro fertilization (IVF), in which the aim of ovarian stimulation is to induce multifollicular development. This leads to the retrieval of multiple oocytes and thus allows the selection of the morphologically best embryo(s) for replacement. In IVF, follicular rupture is not necessary as oocytes are collected by transvaginal aspiration.

### WHEN SHOULD OVULATION INDUCTION BE PERFORMED?

Ovulation induction is performed in conditions in which the primary cause leading to anovulation cannot be corrected, as in the World Health Organization (WHO) I classification of women with hypothalamic disorders such as Kallmann's syndrome or with isolated gonadotrophin deficiency. It is also carried out in women in whom the pathophysiology of the underlying disease is not entirely clear and thus specific treatment is not available, as in the WHO II classification of women with polycystic ovary syndrome (PCOS). The anovulation in these categories of patients is managed in the context of their disease. In women with resistant ovary syndrome, premature ovarian failure, or Turner's syndrome (WHO III), ovulation induction is not feasible.

## MODES OF OVULATION INDUCTION

Ovulation induction can be accomplished by altering the function of the HPO axis to increase the production of endogenous gonadotrophins (WHO II women) using clomiphene citrate or letrozole, by stimulating the hypophysis with gonadotrophin releasing hormone (GnRH) (WHO I patients) or by injecting gonadotrophins (WHO I patients, WHO II patients).

### OVULATION INDUCTION WITH CLOMIPHENE CITRATE

The introduction of clomiphene citrate (CC) in clinical practice in 1961 signified a major breakthrough in reproductive endocrinology. Clomiphene citrate, a racemic mixture of zuclomiphene and enclomiphene citrate, is the treatment of choice for WHO II patients.

#### Mechanisms of CC Action
In humans, CC acts as both an agonist and antagonist of estrogen receptor.[1] CC displaces estrogen by occupying hypothalamic estrogen nuclear receptors for a prolonged period. Estrogen receptor replenishment is also inhibited, resulting in simulation of a hypoestrogenic state that prevents the negative feedback effect of endogenous estrogen. This results, in turn, in an altered pattern of hypothalamic GnRH release and increased gonadotrophin secretion, leading to follicular development and ovulation. After CC administration in anovulatory women, an increase in pulse amplitude of gonadotrophins is observed.[2] Evidence supports a direct effect of CC on the pituitary, where it possibly acts as an estrogen agonist, enhancing GnRH-stimulated gonadotrophin release.[3] The role of CC at the ovarian level is more controversial, with evidence existing for both a stimulatory[4] and an inhibitory effect.[5]

#### Administration Scheme of CC
An initial dose of 50 mg is administered for 5 days starting from day 2 to 5 of the menstrual cycle in a graded incremen-

2983

tal scheme. An earlier administration of CC might simulate the earlier rise in follicle-stimulating hormone (FSH) in ovulatory cycles. Nevertheless, no differences were reported in terms of ovulation, pregnancy, or spontaneous miscarriage rates, after initiation of CC treatment on different days of the menstrual cycle (day 2–5).[6]

If ovulation occurs, usually between days 14 and 19 of the CC cycle, a progesterone increase is observed, suggesting the formation of a functional corpus luteum. Couples are instructed to have frequent intercourse for a week starting on day 5 after discontinuation of CC.

If an excessive ovarian response to CC occurs, as might be expected in PCOS patients, either the dose or the duration of treatment can be decreased to 25 mg or 3 days, respectively, in the next cycle. Among the patients who ovulate with CC, about 63% will do so after the initial dose of 50 mg[7] (Fig. 158-1). There is no need to increase the dose of CC if conception does not occur in an ovulatory cycle, as pregnancy is expected to occur with successive cycles. If ovulation does not occur in consecutive cycles, the maximum daily dosage of CC is probably 100 mg, a dose approved by the Food and Drug Administration in the United States for 5 days of use and recommended by the British Fertility Society.[8] Seventy-four percent of all ovulations as well as 73.6% of all pregnancies achieved after increasing doses of CC in consecutive cycles are expected to occur with doses of up to 100 mg[9] (Table 158-1). A daily dose of CC of more than 100 mg confers little benefit, while the possibility of enhancing undesirable effects on cervical mucus and/or endometrium is increased.

**Results of Treatment with CC**　A significant improvement in the occurrence of ovulation has been observed in oligoovulatory women subjected to CC treatment (common odds ratio, 6.82; 95% confidence interval [CI], 3.92–11.85).[10] However, although 70% to 85% of patients will ovulate with CC, only 40% to 45% of patients achieve pregnancy.[11] This discrepancy between ovulation and conception rates might be attributed to nonreliable confirmation of ovulation, the presence of additional infertility factors, and early discontinuation of treatment. The cumulative conception rate in couples with no other factors contributing to subfertility rises with six to nine successive cycles to 70% to 75%,[12,13] approaching the pregnancy rate observed in the normal population.

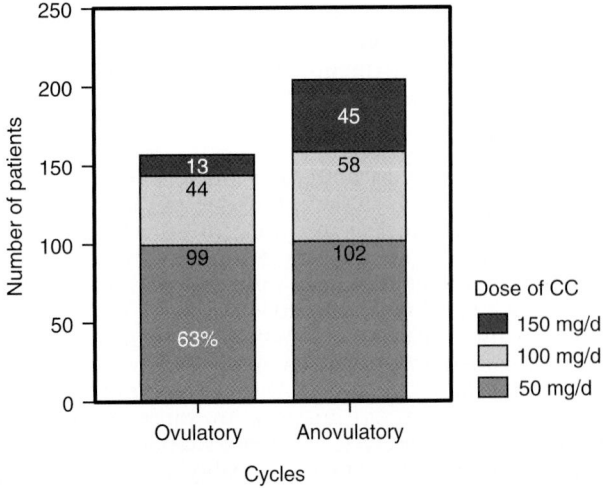

**Figure 158-1**　Distribution of normogonadotrophic oligomenorrheic or amenorrheic infertile women who do or do not ovulate after clomiphene citrate (CC) treatment in incremental daily doses of 50, 100, and 150 mg for 5 subsequent days. (Adapted from Imani B, Eijkemans MJ, te Velde ER, et al: Predictors of patients remaining anovulatory during clomiphene citrate induction of ovulation in normogonadotropic oligoamenorrheic infertility. J Clin Endocrinol Metab 83:2361–2365, 1998.)

| Dose (mg) | No. Ovulated | Total Ovulating %* | No. Pregnancies | Total Pregnancies %† |
|---|---|---|---|---|
| 50 | 190 | 52.1 | 102 | 52.8 |
| 100 | 80 | 21.9 | 40 | 20.7 |
| 150 | 45 | 12.3 | 19 | 9.8 |
| 200 | 25 | 6.9 | 17 | 8.8 |
| 250 | 18 | 4.9 | 12 | 6.2 |
| 250 + hCG (10,000 IU) | 7 | 1.9 | 3 | 1.6 |

**Table 158-1**　Dose-Related Response to Clomiphene Citrate Initiation of Ovulation

*Proportion of the total number of ovulations achieved at each dose of clomiphene citrate (CC) in consecutive cycles.
†Proportion of the total number of pregnancies achieved at each dose of CC in consecutive cycles.
Adapted from Gysler M, March CM, Mishell DR Jr, et al: A decade's experience with an individualized clomiphene treatment regimen including its effect on the postcoital test. Fertil Steril 37:161–167, 1982.

**Resistance to CC**　A discernible difference in describing CC-treated populations is seen between CC resistance (failure to ovulate under the maximum allowable dose of CC) and CC failure (failure to conceive after a certain number of ovulatory cycles). CC resistance occurs in about 15% to 30% of patients and is associated with obesity, hyperandrogenemia, amenorrhea, and increased ovarian volume.[14] Administration of gonadotrophins in these patients will result in ovulation in about 50% of cases; however, it remains an expensive approach accompanied by potentially serious complications.

Alternatively, in CC-resistant patients, addition of dexamethasone to the CC regime has been shown to result in high rates of ovulation and pregnancy.[15] In addition, the coadministration of metformin with CC in PCOS patients results in a significantly higher ovulation rate as compared with CC alone (odds ratio, 4.41; 95% CI, 2.37–8.22).[16] Metformin may also improve endocrine abnormalities such as hyperinsulinemia and hyperandrogenemia present in PCOS patients. Opioid receptor blockers alone or in combination with CC have also been used successfully in anovulatory patients resistant to CC, indicating the inhibitory action of endogenous opioids on GnRH secretion.[17] Adequate monitoring of a CC-stimulated cycle will identify patients who remain anovulatory despite follicular maturation and progressive increments in estradiol levels. In such cases, accurately timed human chorionic gonadotropin (hCG) administration may confer benefit in inducing ovulation.

**Effect of CC at the Periphery**　The effect of CC on cervical mucus as well as on endometrium quality is debatable. Inadequate endometrial development, as reflected in endometrial thickness assessed by ultrasound, may adversely affect implantation and result in biochemical pregnancy in patients undergoing ovulation induction with CC.[18] Ultrasonographic findings from the endometrium do not correlate directly with histological findings, however, while the association between endometrial thickness and pregnancy achievement in CC-treated cycles is not uniformly accepted.[19]

**Side Effects of CC**　CC may result in multiple follicular development and thus in multiple pregnancies not related to zygotic cleavage. Multiple follicular development resulting from increased gonadotrophin levels in the early follicular phase occurs in 35% to 60% of CC cycles compared to a 5% to 10% occurrence in the general population, whereas the reported multiple pregnancy rate in the literature ranges from 8% to 13%, of which the majority are twins. The need for monitoring CC cycles using ultrasound scans and serum endocrinology should therefore be emphasised. Although the occurrence of ovarian hyperstimulation syndrome (OHSS) is very rare, mild ovarian enlargement and cyst formation may occur with CC treatment. In addition, CC treatment has been associated with infrequent side effects such as hot flashes, visual side effects, abdominal distension, breast discomfort, nausea, and vomiting.

## ALTERNATE MEDICATIONS FOR OVULATION INDUCTION

### Tamoxifen
Both CC and tamoxifen are nonsteroidal estrogen receptor modulators that share a structural homology. Tamoxifen can induce ovulation with efficiency comparable to CC.[20] Tamoxifen is administered as a 20-mg dose in the early follicular phase of the cycle and, in contrast with CC, has been reported to improve cervical mucous scores in women with an abnormal postcoital test.[21]

### Letrozole
Letrozole, the best known of the aromatase inhibitors, appears to be a promising alternative for ovulation induction.[22] Its safety, however, needs to be confirmed. The aromatase enzyme is a cytochrome P-450 protein that catalyzes the aromatization of C19 androgens into estrogens. Induction of ovulation by letrozole is thought to be mediated through an increased secretion of gonadotrophins resulting from inhibition of estrogen-negative feedback on the hypothalamus. Enhancement of the sensitivity of granulosa cells to FSH through an increase in androgen production may also play a role. The dose of letrozole for ovulation induction is 2.5 mg daily from day 3 to day 7 of the cycle.

## OVULATION INDUCTION USING GnRH

Women with hypogonadotropic hypogonadism (HH) are characterized by reduced hypothalamic or pituitary function. If pituitary function is intact, GnRH treatment can lead to ovulation and establishment of pregnancy. Stimulation with GnRH maintains the normal pituitary-ovarian feedback mechanisms, as rising levels of estradiol inhibit endogenous FSH secretion, allowing the development of a single dominant follicle.

GnRH is administered intravenously (IV) or subcutaneously (SC) in pulses every 60 to 90 minutes at a dose of 15–20 µg SC or 5–10 µg IV. If the patient fails to respond, the dose may be increased by 5 µg increments. hCG can be used to trigger final oocyte maturation and follicular rupture. The luteal phase can be supported with progesterone/hCG, or, alternatively, the ensuing corpus luteum can be stimulated by continuing the GnRH infusion after ovulation.

GnRH is an effective treatment, with an 80% to 93% cumulative pregnancy rate reported after six treatment cycles.[23] Moreover, it is more frequently associated with monofollicular development compared with gonadotrophins, and thus leads to a low multiple pregnancy rate (4% to 5%). Although safe and inexpensive, ovulation induction with GnRH requires administration of the medication through the infusion pump for several weeks, resulting in decreased patient compliance and acceptance. Side effects are minimal and mainly due to local irritation from the pump needle or thrombophlebitis in cases of IV administration.

## OVULATION INDUCTION WITH GONADOTROPHINS

Gonadotrophins are used for ovulation induction in patients with hypogonadotropic hypogonadism in whom the HPO axis cannot be stimulated to produce endogenous gonadotrophins. In addition, they are used for women in the WHO II category for whom ovulation induction with CC or letrozole has failed. Currently available gonadotrophin preparations are derived from the urine of postmenopausal women or are synthesized by recombinant technology, having replaced those originating from pregnant mares and human pituitaries.

### Conventional Step-Up Protocol
Gonadotrophins can be administered according to a conventional step-up protocol in which stimulation is initiated with 75 IU/day and the dose is increased by 75 IU if no response occurs after 7 days. The response to treatment is judged by monitoring estradiol levels. Homburg and colleagues reported a cumulative pregnancy rate of 82% after six treatment cycles.[24] This approach, although effective, is associated with an increased chance of multiple follicular development, increasing the probability of multiple pregnancy to 34% and that of ovarian hyperstimulation syndrome (OHSS) to 4.6%.[25]

### Low-Dose Step-Up Protocol
Alternatively, a low-dose step-up protocol can be used, especially in patients prone to multifollicular development as in PCOS. Stimulation starts with 75 IU/day, although lower starting doses have been applied, and remains unchanged for 14 days. If no response is observed, the dose can be increased by 37.5 IU/day. After each increase, the dose remains constant for 7 days.

Several studies have examined the use of a low-dose step-up protocol to avoid the occurrence of multiple pregnancies; the collective results appear in Table 158-2.[26] The comparison of low-dose step-up protocol with a conventional step-up protocol has shown that pregnancy rates are at least equal, while the probability of multifollicular development and multiple pregnancies appears to be decreased.[24]

### Step-Down Protocol
The step-down protocol is a more physiologic approach simulating the events of a normal follicular phase in which FSH levels decline as estradiol levels rise. An initial dose of 150 IU is followed by two reducing steps (37.5 IU each) based on sonographic criteria to a final daily dose of 75 IU, which is sustained until hCG administration.

A comparison between the low-dose step-up and the step-down protocol showed that monofollicular development is present in a significantly higher proportion of cases in the step-down protocol (88% vs. 56%, respectively) after a shorter duration of stimulation (9 days vs. 18 days, respectively).[27]

### Which Type of Gonadotrophin Should be Used for Ovulation Induction?
No conclusive data currently exist on the type of gonadotrophin to be used for ovulation induction.[28–30] In hypogonadotropic patients, it appears that luteinizing hormone (LH) is necessary for optimal stimulation of follicle development and estradiol synthesis.[31] Utilization of human menopausal gonadotrophins (HMG) in HH patients results in 90% conception rates after 6 months of treatment.[32] This is far higher than the success of ovulation induction with gonadotrophins in women in the WHO II category. It should

| Table 158-2 | A Summary of Results of Published Series of Low Starting Dose FSH Therapy for Women with PCOS | |
|---|---|---|
| | No. (%) | Range (%) |
| Patients | 717 | |
| Cycles completed | 1391 | |
| Clinical pregnancies | 280 (40%) | 21–45 |
| Fecundity/cycle | 20% | 12–24 |
| Uniovulatory cycle | 69% | 54–88 |
| OHSS | 0.14% | 0–2.4 |
| Multiple pregnancies | 5.7% | 0–14.1 |

FSH, follicle-stimulating hormone; OHSS, ovarian hyperstimulation syndrome; PCOS, polycystic ovary syndrome.
Adapted from Homburg R, Howles CM: Low-dose FSH therapy for anovulatory infertility associated with polycystic ovary syndrome: Rationale, results, reflections and refinements. Hum Reprod Update 5:493–499, 1999.

be noted, however, that HH patients represent a minority of the patients seeking treatment for anovulation.

### Chance of Singleton Live Birth after Ovulation Induction Using CC or in CC-resistant Patients Using Gonadotrophins

Eijkemans and colleagues[33] prospectively studied 240 consecutive anovulatory patients (WHO II) who had not been treated previously. Patients underwent six cycles with CC before switching to gonadotrophins if no pregnancy ensued, or three cycles of CC if they remained anovulatory. Stimulation with gonadotrophins was performed according to step-down protocol. Singleton live birth resulted in 56% of women, while the cumulative pregnancy rate leading to singleton live birth was 50% and 71% after 12 and 24 months, respectively. The cumulative chance of pregnancy increased to 74% when multiple pregnancies were included (7% of all births).

### GnRH Analogues in Ovulation Induction

A Cochrane review[34] was performed to assess the value of GnRH agonist pretreatment in combination with FSH/HMG for ovulation induction in WHO II women with ovulatory dysfunction. No evidence suggesting a benefit of GnRH agonist pretreatment in pregnancy rates could be demonstrated, whereas there was a tendency for an increased risk of OHSS associated with the use of GnRH agonists. Pretreatment with GnRH for ovulation induction should probably not be recommended as a standard treatment for WHO II patients.

Preliminary experience with the use of GnRH antagonists starting from day 1 of stimulation for ovulation induction, which led to an ongoing pregnancy rate of 27.8% in PCOS patients, appears to be promising.[35]

### Ovulation Induction and Multiple Pregnancies

Several studies have shown[36,37] that at least one third of twin pregnancies and the majority of the triplet or high-order gestations can be attributed to ovulation induction. This is probably an underestimation of its true contribution to the occurrence of multiple pregnancies, as no reporting system on the use of ovulation-inducing drugs not associated with IVF is available.

Currently, the positions of professional societies (Society for Assisted Reproductive Technology [SART], American Society for Reproductive Medicine [ASRM], and Society for Reproductive Endocrinology and Infertility [SREI] coincide in that there are insufficient data to apply regulations such as practice guidelines to avoid multiple pregnancies from ovulation induction. Multifollicular development during ovulation induction has been treated by converting the cycle to IVF. This allows control of the number of embryos to be transferred. The current availability of GnRH antagonists increases the odds of successful conversion to IVF,[38] although a proportion of patients are reluctant to follow such an approach. In these patients, preovulatory follicular reduction may have a role.[39] Multifetal reduction is acceptable only if the physician has done all that is possible to prevent the occurrence of multiple pregnancies; and it is certainly not preventive in nature while being associated with its own risks.

## ASSISTED REPRODUCTION

Assisted reproduction, or assisted reproductive technology (ART), refers to a spectrum of techniques that aim at enhancing the human reproductive potential, resulting in the delivery of a healthy child. The previous section of this chapter dealt with induction of ovulation, which is used in couples with dysovulation problems. Subfertility due to a cervical factor, male factor, or unidentified causes can be managed by intrauterine insemination (IUI) alone or in combination with enhancement of ovulation. If this approaches fail to result in pregnancy, the alternative is IVF.

After the first delivery from IVF in 1978, a wide armamentarium of techniques has been developed by altering or expanding the concept of the original method.[40] In parallel, several alternative stimulation protocols (use of GnRH agonists or GnRH antagonists) and newer safer medications (recombinant FSH [r-FSH], recombinant LH [r-LH], and recombinant hCG [r-hCG] were introduced for ovarian superovulation to ensure the availability of female gametes for IVF.

### INTRAUTERINE INSEMINATION

In IUI, sperm is transferred into the uterus around the time of ovulation. Facilitation of fertilization is achieved by enhancing the number and the quality of the spermatozoa reaching the fallopian tubes, and may be combined with an increase in the number of oocytes ovulated. This is achieved by semen preparation that removes seminal fluid and selects spermatozoa with progressive motility and by ovarian stimulation, respectively. Alternative methods of insemination include intravaginal, intracervical, pericervical using a cap, intratubal, or direct intraperitoneal insemination. Intrauterine insemination, however, appears to be the preferred method in most studies.[41,42]

Timing of IUI is an important factor that may affect its success. This is due to the fact that spermatozoa probably survive for a shorter period after IUI, since they are not deposited in the cervical crypts, as is the case after intercourse. Moreover, data from in vitro studies suggest that the life span of the oocyte in vivo, during which fertilization can occur, is probably short. In timing ovulation, the onset of the LH rise is a more accurate criterion than the LH peak itself. Insemination is performed the day after the initiation of LH surge or 36 hours after administration of hCG.

IUI can be performed with a husband's or donor's sperm. IUI with donor sperm is used not only in cases of severe male factor infertility, but also in heterosexual single women or lesbian couples.[43]

A significantly higher fecundity rate at 1 month is present when IUI is compared to sexual intercourse (21.2% vs. 3.9%) in women with cervical factor infertility during a natural cycle.[44] On the other hand, in couples with male subfertility, IUI significantly improves the probability of conception compared with timed intercourse, both in natural cycles and in cycles in which enhancement of ovulation is performed.[45] Currently, the minimum number of spermatozoa in the ejaculate in the presence of which IUI should be attempted is not known, although IUI success seems to be impaired with less than 5% normal spermatozoa and an inseminating motile count of less than $1 \times 10^6$. Performing double intrauterine insemination in the same cycle[46] has not been shown to result in an increased probability of conception as compared to single intrauterine insemination.[47]

### Semen Preparation for Assisted Reproduction

Semen preparation for assisted reproduction aims at separating motile sperm from nonmotile, dead sperm, cell debris, and prostaglandins, as well as at initiating capacitation and concentrating motile sperm in a small volume of culture medium. Methods of semen preparation include straight centrifugation and washing, glass wool filtration, swim-up, use of Sephadex columns, and discontinuous or continuous gradients.[48]

### IN VITRO FERTILIZATION

#### Collection of Gametes for IVF
*Female Gametes*
Currently, the method of choice for collecting female gametes is by the transvaginal route via ultrasound visualization.[49] Local anesthesia can be used successfully in the majority of cases. Light vaginal hemorrhage may occur in 8.6% of patients. More severe and rare complications may result from

inadvertent puncture of iliac vessels or pelvic infection by inoculation of vaginal flora intraperitoneally or by bowel injury.

Laparoscopic retrieval of oocytes used originally by Steptoe and Edwards is still performed in cases where ovaries are inaccessible vaginally, or in the case of gamete intrafallopian transfer (GIFT) where laparoscopy is necessary for placing the gametes in the fallopian tube. Other methods for oocyte collection such as through the abdominal wall and the bladder or via the urethral route are no longer performed.

### Male Gametes

The standard procedure for collecting semen involves masturbation into a sterile glass or plastic flask. In cases of retrograde ejaculation, spermatozoa may be collected in urine preprocessed with sodium bicarbonate to adjust urinary pH to 7. In patients suffering from impotence caused by spinal paralysis in the segments T11–L2, ejaculation can be induced by vibration or by electroejaculation, which is effective in 90% of patients.

In cases of azoospermia, several collection techniques have been used, including microsurgical sperm aspiration from the epididymis (MESA), percutaneous sperm aspiration from the epididymis (PESA), biopsy and sperm extraction from the testicle (TESE), and testicular fine-needle sperm aspiration (TEFNA).

In MESA, several incisions into the epididymis may be required before sperm is found. During TESE, the number of tissue samples removed depends on the origin of azoospermia. Usually, in obstructive azoospermia, one tissue sample is enough, whereas in nonobstructive azoospermia, multiple tissue samples may be required. In nonobstructive azoospermia, focal spermatogenesis appears to be present and sperm can be retrieved in about 50% of cases.

PESA and TEFNA are less invasive techniques and are performed more rapidly and without the costly equipment required for TESE and MESA. The numbers of recovered spermatozoa appear to be lower than those present after the use of the more invasive procedures; however, at present there is insufficient evidence to recommend any specific sperm retrieval technique for azoospermic men undergoing intracytoplasmic sperm injection (ICSI).[50]

## Genetic Origin of the Gametes

### Sperm Donation

Where retrieval of sperm is not possible, sperm donation represents a realistic solution for achievement of pregnancy. It involves a genetic dissociation between husband and offspring, however, which may result in psychological stress and ethical dilemmas for the couple. Donated sperm is usually via anonymous donors. Sperm donors are screened for human immunodeficiency virus (HIV), hepatitis B and C, syphilis, *Chlamydia*, cytomegalovirus (CMV), cystic fibrosis, fragile X syndrome, and any known hereditary disorders in the family. Donated sperm is cryopreserved and used after thawing, after quarantine of donors for a period of 6 months.

### Oocyte Donation

Oocyte donation has made childbearing possible in women previously thought to be untreatable. Women who request egg donation are those with premature menopause (occurring spontaneously, after surgical castration or induced by chemo- or radiotherapy) as well as women with resistant ovary syndrome. An additional group consists of women who repeatedly show poor ovarian response to stimulation or absence of fertilization with husband or donor semen, or who carry a genetic disease that can be transmitted to the offspring.

Oocyte donation involves egg retrieval from the donor, insemination with semen from the recipient's husband, in vitro culture, and transfer of cleaved embryos into the recipient's uterus. According to the 1997 ASRM/SART registry,

donor oocytes were used in approximately 9% of all ART cycles in the United States.

Steroid substitution therapy is mandatory in agonadal women to simulate the endocrine environment of the natural cycle. In women with ovarian function, replacement of embryos can take place in a natural cycle, after mild ovarian stimulation in cases of dysovulation or, alternatively, these women can be downregulated with GnRH agonists and then given exogenous steroids as in the case of agonadal women.

Oocyte donors undergo a detailed medical and social history and screening for karyotype abnormalities, cystic fibrosis, fragile X syndrome, as well as for previous viral (hepatitis B and C, HIV, and CMV) and treponemal infection. Donors are usually matched to recipients on the basis of skin color and ethnic origin only.

The age of the oocyte donor is a significant predictor of pregnancy success.[51] Pregnancies resulting from oocyte donation are associated with an increased risk compared with IVF pregnancies, although most oocyte recipients experience a favorable pregnancy outcome.[52]

Egg donation may impose risks on the donor's health. These include development of OHSS, the occurrence of complications during oocyte retrieval, and the potential association of repeated ovarian stimulation with development of ovarian cancer.

An alternative source of oocytes for donation is egg-sharing, in which women undergoing IVF donate part of their oocytes to an anonymously matched recipient in exchange for subsidized treatment. Donors in an egg-sharing program are not exposed to risks other than those pertaining to hormonal treatment and oocyte retrieval, which represent their only way of becoming parents using their own genetic material. Egg-sharing is an efficient method reported to result in three deliveries for every five oocyte retrievals.[53]

### Gamete Donation: The Risk of Consanguinity

Inadvertent consanguinity can result from gamete donation. Guidelines on therapeutic donor insemination and oocyte donation, published by the American Society for Reproductive Medicine, have advised an arbitrary limit of no more than 25 pregnancies per sperm or oocyte donor in a population of 800,000 in order to minimize such a risk.

## The Insemination Method

Alternative methods for inseminating oocytes were developed in response to significantly lower fertilization rates present after IVF in couples with male infertility. Partial zona dissection (PZD) provided encouraging results, but was accompanied by an increased occurrence of polyspermy. Subzonal insemination (SUZI) was then developed, involving injection of spermatozoa into the perivitelline space. The benefits of this were debatable, and results of both PZD and SUZI were inconsistent. Intracytoplasmic sperm insemination (ICSI) was introduced in 1992 and offered couples with severe male infertility and those with fertilization failure after conventional IVF a realistic chance of parenthood.[54] With the advent of ICSI, both SUZI and PZD were abandoned.

Fertilization failure after ICSI is rare (3% of all ICSI cycles) and is mainly due to defective oocyte activation. ICSI is performed with ejaculated, epididymal, or testicular sperm fresh or thawed after cryopreservation. The injection of precursors of mature spermatozoa (from men in whom mature sperm forms cannot be identified) into oocytes is considered experimental. It is not clear whether ICSI should be preferred to IVF in cases of non–male factor subfertility.[55] In couples with moderate male factor infertility, ICSI is a more efficient technique in terms of fertilization, but not in comparison with high insemination concentration IVF.[56]

Insemination of oocytes in both IVF and ICSI is carried out 2 to 4 hours after oocyte retrieval. In conventional IVF, after sperm preparation, approximately 5000 to 20,000 motile spermatozoa are placed in a 25 µL microdrop under quality-controlled paraffin oil. In ICSI, the cumulus-oocyte complexes are denuded from their cumulus cells using a solution of hyaluronidase followed by pipetting. Only metaphase II oocytes are used for injection. A single spermatozoon is aspirated tail-first into a sharp tipped glass pipet, and injected centrally into the cytoplasm of the oocyte stabilized by a suction pipet. Eighteen to 20 hours after insemination, the oocytes are examined under an inverted microscope. The presence of two pronuclei and the extrusion of the second polar body is considered evidence of normal fertilization.

The European Society for Human Reproduction and Embryology (ESHRE) reported pregnancy rates of 24.2% and 26.1% per oocyte retrieval for IVF and ICSI, respectively.[57] Miscarriage rates reported by SART in 1999 were similar for ICSI and IVF (17.6% vs. 16.7%), whereas ICSI did not appear to impose any additional obstetrical risk to the developing fetus over conventional IVF.[58]

ICSI, on the other hand, can result in an increased risk of chromosomal aberrations, mainly due to the underlying parental risk of abnormality and not to the ICSI procedure itself.[59] ICSI can allow the transmission of microdeletions in the azoospermia factor (AZF) region of the Y chromosome, present in infertile men with nonobstructive azoospermia. In these cases, genetic counseling is mandatory before ICSI treatment. The majority of the studies performed addressing the issue of congenital malformations after ICSI showed no increased rate of malformations. Moreover, based on the available evidence, it appears that the psychomotor development of children born after ICSI is normal.[59]

### Embryo Culture

Culture conditions for IVF initially relied on a single medium, either Earle's Balanced Salt Solution or a complex medium such as Ham's Nutrient Medium F10. Subsequently, specific media for human embryo culture until the cleavage stage were developed,[60,61] and development until the blastocyst stage became feasible by using coculture and, recently, sequential media.[62]

#### Duration of Embryo Culture

For several years, embryo transfer was performed at the cleavage stage (day 2–3 after fertilization). The development of sequential media made extended culture (to day 5–6 after fertilization) feasible without the need for coculture, which is not totally safe. Blastocyst development varies considerably, ranging from 28% to 46%.[63] By analyzing several randomized control trials, it appears that extended culture and transfer at the blastocyst stage do not improve pregnancy or implantation rates over culture and transfer of embryos at the cleavage stage.[63–64] Moreover, blastocyst transfer appears to be associated with an increased incidence in the rate of monozygotic twinning.

### Enhancing the Implantation Potential of Human Embryos

Several methods have been developed to disrupt artificially the zona pellucida, the glycoprotein coat surrounding the embryo. These include partial zona dissection, zona drilling, zona thinning through the use of acid tyrodes, proteinases, piezon vibrator manipulators, and lasers. The premise behind these methods, known as assisted hatching techniques, is that failure of implantation might be partially related to an inability of the blastocyst to escape from its zona pellucida. A meta-analysis of studies involving 2752 women provided no evidence that assisted hatching has an impact on live birth rate.[65]

### Preimplantation Genetic Diagnosis

Preimplantation genetic diagnosis (PGD) allows for the identification of embryos with a specific genetic disease present in the parents, including those with structural or numeral chro-

mosomal aberrations. Therefore, it can be used both as a means of preventing genetic disease and of eliminating the transfer of abnormal embryos that will not lead to establishment of pregnancy or delivery of a healthy child. Currently, the advantages of PGD for aneuploidy screening to increase the probability of implantation have not been demonstrated. PGD has also been used to enable parents of a child affected by a disease to generate a "savior sibling" who may serve as a donor of hematopoietic stem cells or other tissues for the sick sibling.[66] PGD for gender selection is performed in the cases of X-linked diseases, whereas its use to satisfy a couple's desire for gender selection is highly controversial.

Preimplantation genetic diagnosis requires an embryo biopsy during which one or two blastomeres are removed at the eight-cell stage on day 3 after fertilization through an opening created in the zona pellucida. This is achieved by using laser, Tyrodes solution, or slicing with a sharp pipet. The blastomeres removed are in turn analyzed by using polymerase chain reaction (PCR) or fluorescent in situ hybridization (FISH). PCR is used to identify specific DNA sequences that include the mutation of interest by using specific primers for that mutation, by digestion with restriction enzymes, or by heteroduplex analysis. FISH is used to assess the ploidy status of an embryo or structural aberrations by using chromosome-specific probes. Identification of all 46 chromosomes is possible through comparative genome hybridization. The method is complex, however, and has not been introduced into regular clinical practice. After FISH or PCR, diagnosed embryos are replaced into the uterus on day 5 after fertilization. Analysis of the first and second polar body, which are byproducts of the first and the second meiotic division, is also possible. In the case of the first polar body, however, analysis will only give information about maternal genetic material and may lead to misdiagnosis of heterozygous genetic defects.

### Type of Embryo Transfer

Embryo transfer is one of the most critical steps in IVF. Regardless of the effort paid to patient selection, stimulation protocol, and embryo culture conditions, inefficient embryo transfer will not result in pregnancy. Transcervical intrauterine transfer is the most widely used technique and also the least invasive. Embryos are transferred in a small volume of culture medium through the cervical canal close to the uterine fundus by using various types of catheters. Ultrasound-guided embryo transfer is a variation of this technique. A meta-analysis of randomized controlled trials (RCTs) comparing ultrasound-guided transfer with conventional embryo transfer showed a significant improvement in ongoing pregnancy rates with the use of ultrasound guidance of the transfer catheter.[67] The exact mechanism for the improvement in ongoing pregnancy rate is not clear, although confirming a correct positioning of the catheter tip is probably important.

Male and female gametes can be transferred into the fallopian tube(s) through laparoscopy or via the cervix using the technique called GIFT, which, as noted previously, stands for gamete intrafallopian transfer. A major disadvantage of GIFT is the lack of information regarding fertilization, which can be easily gained through conventional transfer at later stages of development. Alternative invasive transfer techniques involve transfer at the pronuclear stage (PROST), tubal pre-embryo transfer (TPET), tubal embryo stage transfer (TEST), and tubal embryo transfer (TET). Collectively, these techniques are known as zygote intrafallopian transfer (ZIFT). The rationale for applying GIFT and ZIFT is based on the assumption that the fallopian tube represents a better environment than the laboratory for fertilization/embryo development. Refinement of laboratory techniques and improvement in implantation rates with conventional intrauterine transfer rendered these invasive methods less attractive, however. A meta-analysis of published randomized trials comparing ZIFT and intrauterine ET showed that there is no difference in implantation and pregnancy rates between the two methods.[68]

## Cryopreservation

Cryopreservation was applied to humans for the first time in the late 1970s, and the first pregnancy was reported by Trounson and Mohr in 1983.[69] Refinement of cryopreservation protocols has made the achievement of pregnancy feasible from frozen-thawed human oocytes, two pronuclei (2-pn) zygotes, cleavage stage embryos, and blastocysts, thereby establishing cryopreservation as an essential part of IVF.

Cryopreservation of human embryos has several clinical benefits, among which the most important is probably the cost-effective increase of IVF pregnancy rates.[70] This occurs despite an adverse effect of cryopreservation on the implantation potential of human embryos. Cryopreservation can, in addition, facilitate synchronization between donors and recipients or allow for storage of cryopreserved donated embryos. Available evidence suggests that there are no adverse consequences in babies born after embryo cryopreservation, although larger studies are necessary to reach solid conclusions.

Alternatively, oocyte cryopreservation could be used in a donation program or an IVF program.[71] Although oocyte freezing is still not widely available, it can be valuable for cancer patients about to undergo chemotherapy and can assist in overcoming religious or ethical objections to embryo freezing.

## Superovulation for IVF
### Gonadotrophins
The source of gonadotrophins used at present in assisted reproduction is either the urine from postmenopausal women or recombinant technology. Urinary gonadotrophins are at present in the form of HMG, purified or highly purified FSH, containing small amounts of LH (<1%). Urinary FSH preparations can potentially transfer various donor medications or biologically active proteins. The absence of contaminating proteins in r-FSH preparations allows for subcutaneous administration and improved patient tolerance. Moreover, recombinant methods produce relatively unlimited gonadotrophin amounts and batch-to-batch consistency is enhanced compared to urinary preparations.

Currently, there is no evidence of a difference between HMG and r-FSH with regard to ongoing pregnancy rate and live birth.[72] In a meta-analysis comparing r-FSH and urinary-derived FSH gonadotrophins (HMG, urinary purified FSH [FSH-P], and highly purified FSH [FSH-HP]) in an IVF/ICSI program, no differences in clinical pregnancy rate could be shown.[73]

### GnRH Analogues
Suppression of endogenous gonadotrophin secretion is achieved through the use of long-acting GnRH analogues, the synthesis of which became possible after isolation of the GnRH decapeptide in 1971. Pituitary downregulation has decreased the number of women for whom the IVF cycle had to be canceled due to premature luteinization to 2 in 100. Two types of GnRH analogues are currently available: GnRH agonists and GnRH antagonists.

GnRH agonists bind to the pituitary receptor and initially induce release of FSH and LH ("flare") over several days. Subsequently, internalization of the GnRH agonist receptor occurs, and LH and FSH secretion falls to low levels. GnRH antagonists act through a different mechanism, and bind competitively to GnRH receptors, preventing the action of endogenous GnRH pulses on the pituitary. Secretion of gonadotrophins is decreased within hours of antagonist administration and the "flare" is avoided. Moreover, discontinuation of GnRH-antagonist treatment results in a rapid and predictable recovery of the pituitary-gonadal axis.

The beneficial effect of GnRH agonists in enhancing the chance of pregnancy was confirmed by one of the first meta-analyses in reproductive medicine.[74] The use of agonists, how-ever, was also accompanied by several disadvantages such as an initial increase in the secretion of gonadotropins (flare) and the need for a prolonged treatment period before desensitization occurred. This resulted in increased cost of treatment and also in associated menopausal symptoms after gonadotrophin suppression. In addition, delayed recovery of pituitary responsiveness after discontinuation of agonist treatment complicated luteal phase support. Finally, the occurrence of OHSS in GnRH agonist protocols was not infrequent. Various modifications of the long agonist protocol were proposed to simplify treatment and further improve IVF outcome. These included the short protocol or the ultrashort protocol, but pregnancy rates were not as high as those that were obtained using the long protocol.[75]

The first generations of GnRH antagonists were associated with allergic reactions, but continuing modifications of the chemical structure led to two molecules free of histaminic side effects: Ganirelix (Organon, Oss, Netherlands) and Cetrorelix (ASTA-Medica, Frankfurt/M, Germany). Antagonist protocols were developed involving either multiple[76] or single administration[77] of the antagonist and both simulated the natural cycle by administering the antagonist only during the late follicular phase. In the multiple dose protocol, the antagonist was given continuously, starting 5 days after stimulation with gonadotrophins until the day of hCG administration. The minimal dose shown to prevent the occurrence of premature LH surge was 0.25 mg.[78,79] In the single-dose protocol, 3 mg of GnRH antagonist given on day 7 of a menstrual cycle with an already adequate ovarian response was shown to prevent a premature LH surge.[80] If hCG was delayed more than 4 days from a single antagonist dose, which was considered to be a protected period for premature LH rise, Cetrorelix (0.25 mg daily) could be given.

## Complications in IVF
### Multiple Pregnancies
It has been estimated that approximately one third of the increase in multiple births since the 1980s can be attributed to a shift in maternal age distribution. This is due to the fact that older women are more likely to have a multiple birth in spontaneous conceptions. The other two thirds, however, are attributed to IVF/ICSI and ovulation induction. At least 25% of all pregnancies after IVF/ICSI are twin pregnancies, and close to 40% of all babies born after ART are born as part of a twin pair.[81] Transfer of a single embryo into the uterus can obviously eliminate multiple pregnancies from IVF/ICSI. Elective single embryo transfer has been performed successfully,[82] whereas its universal application in women younger than age 36 in the first and second trial remains low. Prevention of multiple pregnancies, including twins, must be considered as a major challenge for all ART programs.

### Ovarian Stimulation and Cancer
A possible association between the use of fertility drugs and the risk of developing specific cancers could not be convincingly demonstrated in a recent systematic review of available epidemiologic studies.[83]

### Ovarian Hyperstimulation Syndrome
Ovarian hyperstimulation syndrome (OHSS) is a dramatic iatrogenic complication of ovarian stimulation and, in its severe form, occurs in 0.2% to 0.5% of IVF attempts. Patients with PCOS are particularly prone to develop OHSS. The physiopathologic mechanisms responsible for the development of OHSS are not yet clear, but may include overproduction of vascular endothelial growth factor (VEGF). OHSS can be a life-threatening complication as, in its severe form, it is accompanied by ascites, pleural effusion, electrolyte imbalance, and hypovolemia with hypotension and oliguria. Milder forms are characterized by weight gain, abdominal discomfort, and enlarged ovaries.

Prevention of OHSS has been attempted by canceling the cycle; proceeding to oocyte retrieval, but not to embryo transfer, with cryopreservation of available embryos; administration of albumin during oocyte retrieval; or administration of glucocorticoids. Altering the signal for final oocyte maturation (using GnRH agonist or rLH instead of hCG) and/or coasting (withholding stimulation until estradiol levels normalize) are the most commonly used measures.

Treatment of OHSS is mainly supportive and based on the knowledge that the syndrome will gradually resolve. Prophylaxis for venous thromboembolism is given if the patient is hospitalized, weight is recorded daily, and monitoring of fluid input and output is performed. If ascetic fluid causes considerable discomfort to the patient, it can be removed by vaginal puncture.

## SOCIAL ASPECTS AND ETHICAL PROBLEMS IN ASSISTED REPRODUCTION

The potential for genetic dissociation of the offspring from one or both of its parents as well as the right of a single woman or a lesbian couple to decide when and how to conceive raise important questions about the psychological development of the children, and long-term follow-up studies are necessary. The age limit above which assisted reproduction should not be offered is also debatable; any considerations about age and ART should apply equally to both sexes.

In addition, although the need to use surrogacy (i.e., a woman genetically unrelated to the conceptus to carry out the pregnancy and deliver the child for the benefit of the genetic parents) is understandable, fears of unwanted commercialization have limited its acceptance to a few countries only. On the other hand, although there is an immense potential for solving several medical problems through cloning, its use for reproductive purposes through asexual means has raised serious legal, religious, and social problems.

The development of IVF in the past 25 years has been a rich source of debate, probably more so than in any other medical field. This has gradually transformed attitudes to ART and led to the establishment of legislation in several countries.

## REFERENCES

1. Adashi EY: Clomiphene citrate: Mechanism(s) and site(s) of action—a hypothesis revisited. Fertil Steril 42:331–344, 1984.
2. Kettel LM, Roseff SJ, Berga SL, et al: Hypothalamic-pituitary-ovarian response to clomiphene citrate in women with polycystic ovary syndrome. Fertil Steril 59:532–538, 1993.
3. Adashi EY, Hsueh AJ, Bambino TH, et al: Disparate effect of clomiphene and tamoxifen on pituitary gonadotropin release in vitro. Am J Physiol 240:E125–E130, 1981.
4. Kessel B, Hsueh AJ: Clomiphene citrate augments follicle-stimulating hormone-induced luteinizing hormone receptor content in cultured rat granulosa cells. Fertil Steril 47:334–340, 1987.
5. Laufer N, Reich R, Braw R, et al: Effect of clomiphene citrate on preovulatory rat follicles in culture. Biol Reprod 27:463–471, 1982.
6. Wu CH, Winkel CA: The effect of therapy initiation day on clomiphene citrate therapy. Fertil Steril 52:564–568, 1989.
7. Imani B, Eijkemans MJ, te Velde ER, et al: Predictors of patients remaining anovulatory during clomiphene citrate induction of ovulation in normogonadotropic oligoamenorrheic infertility. J Clin Endocrinol Metab 83:2361–2365, 1998.
8. Balen A: Anovulatory infertility and ovulation induction. Policy and Practice subcommittee of the British Fertility Society. Hum Reprod 12:83–87, 1997.
9. Gysler M, March CM, Mishell DR Jr, et al: A decade's experience with an individualized clomiphene treatment regimen including its effect on the postcoital test. Fertil Steril 37:161–167, 1982.
10. Hughes E, Collins J, Vandekerckhove P: Clomiphene citrate for ovulation induction in women with oligo-amenorrhoea. Cochrane Database Syst Rev, CD000056, 2000.
11. The ESHRE Capri Workshop: Female infertility: Treatment options for complicated cases. European Society for Human Reproduction and Embryology. Hum Reprod 12:1191–1196, 1997.
12. Imani B, Eijkemans MJ, te Velde ER, et al: Predictors of chances to conceive in ovulatory patients during clomiphene citrate induction of ovulation in normogonadotropic oligoamenorrheic infertility. J Clin Endocrinol Metab 84:1617–1622, 1999.
13. Imani B, Eijkemans MJ, te Velde ER, et al: A nomogram to predict the probability of live birth after clomiphene citrate induction of ovulation in normogonadotropic oligoamenorrheic infertility. Fertil Steril 77:91–97, 2002.
14. Imani B, Eijkemans MJ, te Velde ER, et al: Predictors of patients remaining anovulatory during clomiphene citrate induction of ovulation in normogonadotropic oligoamenorrheic infertility. J Clin Endocrinol Metab 83:2361–2365, 1998.
15. Isaacs JD Jr, Lincoln SR, Cowan BD: Extended clomiphene citrate (CC) and prednisone for the treatment of chronic anovulation resistant to CC alone. Fertil Steril 67:641–643, 1997.
16. Lord JM, Flight IH, Norman RJ: Metformin in polycystic ovary syndrome: Systematic review and meta-analysis. Br Med J 327:951–953, 2003.
17. Roozenburg BJ, van Dessel HJ, Evers JL, et al: Successful induction of ovulation in normogonadotrophic clomiphene resistant anovulatory women by combined naltrexone and clomiphene citrate treatment. Hum Reprod 12:1720–1722, 1997.
18. Dickey R, Olar T, Taylor S, et al: Relationship of biochemical pregnancy to pre-ovulatory endometrial thickness and patttern in patients undergoing ovulation induction. Hum Reprod 8:327–330, 1993.
19. Kolibianakis EM, Zikopoulos K, Fatemi H, et al: Endometrial thickness cannot predict ongoing pregnancy achievement in cycles stimulated with clomiphene citrate for intrauterine insemination. Reprod Biomed Online 8:115–118, 2004.
20. Boostanfar R, Jain JK, Mishell DR Jr, et al: A prospective randomized trial comparing clomiphene citrate with tamoxifen citrate for ovulation induction. Fertil Steril 75:1024–1026, 2001.
21. Roumen FJ, Doesburg WH, Rolland R: Treatment of infertile women with a deficient postcoital test with two antiestrogens: clomiphene and tamoxifen. Fertil Steril 41:237–243, 1984.
22. Fatemi H, Kolibianakis EM, Tournaye H, et al: Clomiphene citrate vs letrozole for ovarian stimulation: A pilot study. Reprod Biomed Online 7:543–546, 2003.
23. Homburg R, Eshel A, Armar NA, et al: One hundred pregnancies after treatment with pulsatile luteinising hormone releasing hormone to induce ovulation. Br Med J 298:809–812, 1989.
24. Homburg R, Levy T, Ben-Rafael Z: A comparative prospective study of conventional regimen with chronic low-dose administration of follicle-stimulating hormone for anovulation associated with polycystic ovary syndrome. Fertil Steril 63:729–733, 1995.
25. Hamilton-Fairley D, Franks S: Common problems in induction of ovulation. Baillieres Clin Obstet Gynaecol 4:609–625, 1990.
26. Homburg R, Howles CM: Low-dose FSH therapy for anovulatory infertility associated with polycystic ovary syndrome: Rationale, results, reflections

and refinements. Hum Reprod Update 5:493–499, 1999.

27. van Santbrink EJ, Fauser BC: Urinary follicle-stimulating hormone for normogonadotropic clomiphene-resistant anovulatory infertility: Prospective, randomized comparison between low dose step-up and step-down dose regimens. J Clin Endocrinol Metab 82:3597–3602, 1997.

28. Aboulghar MA, Mansour RT, Serour GI, et al: Recombinant follicle-stimulating hormone in the treatment of patients with history of severe ovarian hyperstimulation syndrome. Fertil Steril 66:757–760, 1996.

29. Bayram N, van Wely M, van Der Veen F: Recombinant FSH versus urinary gonadotrophins or recombinant FSH for ovulation induction in subfertility associated with polycystic ovary syndrome. Cochrane Database Syst Rev, CD002121, 2001.

30. Nugent D, Vandekerckhove P, Hughes E, et al: Gonadotrophin therapy for ovulation induction in subfertility associated with polycystic ovary syndrome. Cochrane Database Syst Rev, CD00410, 2000.

31. Fauser BC: Follicular development and oocyte maturation in hypogonadotrophic women employing recombinant follicle-stimulating hormone: The role of oestradiol. Hum Reprod Update 3:101–108, 1997.

32. Fluker MR, Urman B, Mackinnon M, et al: Exogenous gonadotropin therapy in World Health Organization groups I and II ovulatory disorders. Obstet Gynecol 83:189–196, 1994.

33. Eijkemans MJ, Imani B, Mulders AG, et al: High singleton live birth rate following classical ovulation induction in normogonadotrophic anovulatory infertility (WHO 2). Hum Reprod 18:2357–2362, 2003.

34. Hughes E, Collins J, Vandekerckhove P: Gonadotrophin-releasing hormone analogue as an adjunct to gonadotropin therapy for clomiphene-resistant polycystic ovarian syndrome (Cochrane Review). In Cochrane Library 4, 2003. Chichester, UK, John Wiley & Sons.

35. Elkind-Hirsch KE, Webster BW, Brown CP, et al: Concurrent ganirelix and follitropin beta therapy is an effective and safe regimen for ovulation induction in women with polycystic ovary syndrome. Fertil Steril 79:603–607, 2003.

36. Bergh T, Ericson A, Hillensjo T, et al: Deliveries and children born after in-vitro fertilization in Sweden 1982–95: A retrospective cohort study. Lancet 354:1579–1585, 1999.

37. Derom C, Derom R, Vlietinck R, et al: Iatrogenic multiple pregnancies in East Flanders, Belgium. Fertil Steril 60:493–496, 1993.

38. Fatemi H, Platteau P, Albano C, et al: Case report: Rescue IVF and coasting with the use of a GnRH antagonist after ovulation induction. Reprod Biomed Online 5:273–275, 2002.

39. Albano C, Platteau P, Nogueira D, et al: Avoidance of multiple pregnancies after ovulation induction by supernumerary preovulatory follicular reduction. Fertil Steril 76:820–822, 2001.

40. Steptoe PC, Edwards RG: Birth after the reimplantation of a human embryo. Lancet 2:366, 1978.

41. Williams DB, Moley KH, Cholewa C, et al: Does intrauterine insemination offer an advantage to cervical cap insemination in a donor insemination program? Fertil Steril 63:295–298, 1995.

42. Guzick DS, Carson SA, Coutifaris C, et al: Efficacy of superovulation and intrauterine insemination in the treatment of infertility. National Cooperative Reproductive Medicine Network. N Engl J Med 340:177–183, 1999.

43. Ferrara I, Balet R, Grudzinskas JG: Intrauterine insemination with frozen donor sperm: Pregnancy outcome in relation to age and ovarian stimulation regime. Hum Reprod 17:2320–2324, 2002.

44. Check JH, Spirito P: Higher pregnancy rates following treatment of cervical factor with intrauterine insemination without superovulation versus intercourse: The importance of a well-timed postcoital test for infertility. Arch Androl 35:71–77, 1995.

45. Cohlen BJ, Vandekerckhove P, te Velde ER, Habbema JDF: Timed intercourse versus intrauterine insemination with or without ovarian hyperstimulation for subfertility in men (Cochrane Review). In Cochrane Library 4, 2003. Chichester, UK, John Wiley & Sons.

46. Ragni G, Maggioni P, Guermandi E, et al: Efficacy of double intrauterine insemination in controlled ovarian hyperstimulation cycles. Fertil Steril 72:619–622, 1999.

47. Cantineau AEP, Heineman MJ, Cohlen BJ: Single versus double intrauterine insemination (IUI) instimulated cycles for subfertile couples (Cochrane Review). In Cochrane Library 4, 2003. Chichester, UK, John Wiley & Sons.

48. Henkel RR, Schill WB: Sperm preparation for ART. Reprod Biol Endocrinol 1:108, 2003.

49. Schulman JD, Dorfmann A, Jones S, et al: Outpatient in vitro fertilization using transvaginal oocyte retrieval and local anesthesia. N Engl J Med 312:1639, 1985.

50. Van Peperstraten AM, Proctor ML, Phillipson G, Johnson NP: Techniques for surgical retrieval of sperm prior to ICSI for azoospermia (Cochrane Review). In Cochrane Library 4, 2003. Chichester, UK, John Wiley & Sons.

51. Cohen MA, Lindheim SR, Sauer MV: Donor age is paramount to success in oocyte donation. Hum Reprod 14:2755–2758, 1999.

52. Soderstrom-Anttila V, Tiitinen A, Foudila T, et al: Obstetric and perinatal outcome after oocyte donation: Comparison with in-vitro fertilization

pregnancies. Hum Reprod 13:483–490, 1998.

53. Kolibianakis EM, Tournaye H, Osmanagaoglu K, et al: Outcome for donors and recipients in two egg-sharing policies. Fertil Steril 79:69–73, 2003.

54. Van Steirteghem AC, Liu J, Joris H, et al: Higher success rate by intracytoplasmic sperm injection than by subzonal insemination: Report of a second series of 300 consecutive treatment cycles. Hum Reprod 8:1055–1060, 1993.

55. van Rumste MME, Evers JLH, Farquhar CM: Intra-cytoplasmic sperm injection versus conventional techniques for oocyte insemination during in vitro fertilization in patients with non-male subfertility (Cochrane Review). In Cochrane Library 4, 2003. Chichester, UK, John Wiley & Sons.

56. Tournaye H, Verheyen G, Albano C, et al: Intracytoplasmic sperm injection versus in vitro fertilization: A randomized controlled trial and a meta-analysis of the literature. Fertil Steril 78:1030–1037, 2002.

57. Nygren KG, Andersen AN: Assisted reproductive technology in Europe, 1999: Results generated from European registers by ESHRE. Hum Reprod 17:3260–3274, 2002.

58. Bonduelle M, Liebaers I, Deketelaere V, et al: Neonatal data on a cohort of 2889 infants born after ICSI (1991–1999) and of 2995 infants born after IVF (1983–1999). Hum Reprod 17:671–694, 2002.

59. Retzloff MG, Hornstein MD: Is intracytoplasmic sperm injection safe? Fertil Steril 80:851–859, 2003.

60. Menezo Y, Testart J, Perrone D: Serum is not necessary in human in vitro fertilization, early embryo culture, and transfer. Fertil Steril 42:750–755, 1984.

61. Quinn P, Kerin JF, Warnes GM: Improved pregnancy rate in human in vitro fertilization with the use of a medium based on the composition of human tubal fluid. Fertil Steril 44:493–498, 1985.

62. Gardner DK: Mammalian embryo culture in the absence of serum or somatic cell support. Cell Biol Int 18:1163–1179, 1994.

63. Kolibianakis EM, Devroey P: Blastocyst culture facts and fiction. Reprod Biomed Online 5:285–293, 2002.

64. Blake D, Proctor M, Johnson N, Olive D: Cleavage stage versus blastocyst stage embryo transfer in assisted conception (Cochrane Review). In Cochrane Library 4, 2003. Chichester, UK, John Wiley & Sons.

65. Edi-Osagie ECO, Hooper L, McGinlay P, Seif MW: Effect(s) of assisted hatching on assisted conception (IVF & ICSI) (Cochrane Review). In Cochrane Library 4, 2003. Chichester, UK, John Wiley & Sons.

66. Verlinsky Y, Rechitsky S, Schoolcraft W, et al: Preimplantation diagnosis for Fanconi anemia combined with HLA matching. JAMA 285:3130–3133, 2001.

67. Buckett WM: A meta-analysis of ultrasound-guided versus clinical touch embryo transfer. Fertil Steril 80:1037–1041, 2003.

68. Habana AE, Palter SF: Is tubal embryo transfer of any value? A meta-analysis and comparison with the Society for Assisted Reproductive Technology database. Fertil Steril 76:286–293, 2001.

69. Trounson A, Mohr L: Human pregnancy following cryopreservation, thawing and transfer of an eight-cell embryo. Nature 305:707–709, 1983.

70. Kolibianakis EM, Zikopoulos K, Devroey P: Implantation potential and clinical impact of cryopreservation: A review. Placenta 24(Suppl B):S27–S33, 2003.

71. Porcu E: Oocyte freezing. Semin Reprod Med 19:221–230, 2001.

72. Van Wely M, Westergaard LG, Bossuyt PMM, Van der Veen F: Human menopausal gonadotropin versus recombinant follicle stimulation hormone for ovarian stimulation in assisted reproductive cycles (Cochrane Review). In Cochrane Library 4, 2003. Chichester, UK, John Wiley & Sons.

73. Al-Inany H, Aboulghar M, Mansour R, et al: Meta-analysis of recombinant versus urinary-derived FSH: An update. Hum Reprod 18:305–313, 2003.

74. Hughes EG, Fedorkow DM, Daya S, et al: The routine use of gonadotropin-releasing hormone agonists prior to in vitro fertilization and gamete intrafallopian transfer: A meta-analysis of randomized controlled trials. Fertil Steril 58:888–896, 1992.

75. Daya S. Gonadotrophin-releasing hormone agonist protocols for pituitary desensitization in in vitro fertilization and gamete intrafallopian transfer cycles (Cochrane Review). In Cochrane Library 4, 2003. Chichester, UK, John Wiley & Sons.

76. Diedrich K, Diedrich C, Santos E, et al: Suppression of the endogenous luteinizing hormone surge by the gonadotrophin-releasing hormone antagonist Cetrorelix during ovarian stimulation. Hum Reprod 9:788–791, 1994.

77. Olivennes F, Fanchin R, Bouchard P, et al: The single or dual administration of the gonadotropin-releasing hormone antagonist Cetrorelix in an in vitro fertilization–embryo transfer program. Fertil Steril 62:468–476, 1994.

78. Albano C, Smitz J, Camus M, et al: Comparison of different doses of gonadotropin-releasing hormone antagonist Cetrorelix during controlled ovarian hyperstimulation. Fertil Steril 67:917–922, 1997.

79. The Ganirelix Dose-Finding Study Group: A double-blind, randomized, dose-finding study to assess the efficacy of the gonadotrophin-releasing hormone antagonist ganirelix (Org 37462) to prevent premature luteinizing hormone surges in women undergoing ovarian stimulation with recombinant follicle stimulating hormone (Puregon). Hum Reprod 13:3023–3031, 1998.

80. Olivennes F, Alvarez S, Bouchard P, et al: The use of a GnRH antagonist (Cetrorelix) in a single dose protocol in IVF-embryo transfer: A dose finding study of 3 versus 2 mg. Hum Reprod 13:2411–2414, 1998.

81. Land JA, Evers JL: Risks and complications in assisted reproduction techniques: Report of an ESHRE consensus meeting. Hum Reprod 18:455–457, 2003.

82. Gerris J, De Neubourg D, Mangelschots K, et al: Prevention of twin pregnancy after in-vitro fertilization or intracytoplasmic sperm injection based on strict embryo criteria: A prospective randomized clinical trial. Hum Reprod 14:2581–2587, 1999.

83. Klip H, Burger CW, Kenemans P, et al: Cancer risk associated with subfertility and ovulation induction: A review. Cancer Causes Control 11:319–344, 2000.

*Anna Glasier*

## INTRODUCTION

Almost everyone in the developed world uses contraception at some time in their lives. Most men will use a condom and many women will take the oral contraceptive pill. All doctors should be aware that most men and women have a sexual life, and that for women it puts them at risk of pregnancy. Contraception is of particular relevance to endocrinologists since many endocrine diseases affect reproductive function and vice versa. Endocrinologists, even if not infertility specialists, should have some knowledge of reproduction and of the methods available to prevent it.

### CONTRACEPTIVE USE

Contraceptive prevalence has increased dramatically in the past 30 years. In the year 2000, between 75% and 84% of women of reproductive age who were married or in union and living in the industrialized world were using contraception. Mainly as a result of contraceptive use, the total fertility rate (TFR) in the more developed world is below 2.1, the rate at which population growth stops. In 2001, the TFR in the United States fell to 2.034 (Table 159-1).[1] Demographic change itself has an impact on contraceptive use. The average age of first intercourse has fallen (in the United Kingdom, it has stabilized for both men and women at 16 years), and the average age of first childbirth has risen to almost 30 in many developed countries. Not only married and cohabiting couples use contraception. According to the National Survey of Family Growth (NSFG), 64% of all women in the United States aged 15 to 44 were using a method of contraception in 1995[2] (compared with 56% in 1982 and 60% in 1988).

Patterns of contraceptive use vary across the world, and contraceptive choice depends on numerous factors. In the United States in 1995, over 38% of couples were sterilized, 27% were using the pill, and 20% were using condoms. Fewer than 1% of women in the United States use an intrauterine device (IUD). By contrast, sterilization is much less common and IUD use much more common in France[3] and Sweden,[4] and many more women in France use the pill compared to women in either the United States or Sweden (Table 159-2).

Not only do patterns of contraceptive use vary between countries, but they also vary in the same country between different age groups and stages of life. In the United States, only 12% of women aged 35 to 39 used the combined pill in 1995 compared with 27% of women aged 15 to 44. Patterns also vary according to ethnicity and race, marital status and fertility intentions, education and income. In the United States in 1995, for example, 19% of black teenagers used Depo-Provera compared with only 8% of white teenagers.

Despite the widespread use of contraception, unintended pregnancy is common. Although the decline in population growth is largely due to contraceptive use, no country has achieved low fertility rates without access to abortion. In the United States, the abortion rate in 2001 was 45 out of 1000 women of reproductive age, compared with around 15 in England and only 5 in the Netherlands. In 1995, 5% of sexually active women of reproductive age not planning pregnancy were not using contraception. In a national survey of 10,683 women in the United States having an abortion in 2000–2001, 54% claimed to be using contraception in the month of conception, 28% were using condoms, and 14% were using the pill.[5] Women who were not using a method (46%) perceived themselves at low risk of pregnancy (33%) and/or had concerns about side effects or had experienced past problems with contraception (32%).

Currently available reversible methods of contraception fall into two broad categories: hormonal and nonhormonal. Certain issues are common to all methods.

### EFFICACY AND EFFECTIVENESS

The effectiveness of a method of contraception is judged by the failure rates associated with its use. Failure rates for currently available methods are shown in Table 159-3.[6] The rates are estimated from U.S. studies and show the percentage of couples who experience an accidental pregnancy during the first year of use of each method. The effectiveness of a contraceptive depends on its mode of action and how easy it is to use. Pregnancy rates during perfect use of a method reflect its efficacy. If a method prevents ovulation in every cycle in every woman, it should have an efficacy of 100%, since, if there is no egg, there can be no conception. Only if a mistake is made or the method is used inconsistently will a pregnancy occur. The contraceptive implant Implanon inhibits ovulation for 3 years. There have been no pregnancies reported when Implanon has been correctly inserted. The combined pill is very effective at preventing ovulation, but only if taken correctly. Pregnancy rates for perfect use are around 1 in 1000; failures are due to incomplete inhibition of ovulation,

| Table 159-1 | Total Fertility Rate and Contraceptive Prevalence of Selected Countries | | |
|---|---|---|---|
| | | Contraceptive Prevalence (%) | |
| Country | TFR | All Methods | Modern Methods |
| USA | 2.0 | 76 | 72 |
| Canada | 1.5 | 75 | 75 |
| UK | 1.6 | 72 | 71 |
| Switzerland | 1.4 | 82 | 78 |
| Italy | 1.2 | 60 | 39 |
| China | 1.7 | 83 | 83 |

TFR, total fertility rate.

especially among women who metabolize the pill rapidly. Inhibition of ovulation depends, however, on the pill being taken daily for 21 days followed by a pill-free interval (PFI) of only 7 days. If pills are missed or the PFI prolonged— that is, imperfect use—ovulation can occur. Unless a method is independent of compliance, use is rarely perfect and the effectiveness (as opposed to efficacy) of a method is reflected by pregnancy rates during typical use (see Table 159-3). Pregnancy rates are still often described by the Pearl Index, the number of unintended pregnancies divided by the number of women years of exposure to the risk of pregnancy while using the method. Failure rates of most methods decrease with time, however, since women most prone to failure fall pregnant early after beginning to use a method. With time, a cohort of couples still using a method increasingly comprises couples unlikely to fall pregnant (because they are good at using the method or are infertile). So the longer the cohort is followed, the lower the pregnancy rate is likely to be. Furthermore, failure rates in most clinical trials are often underestimated because all the months of use of the method are taken into account when calculating failure rates, regardless of whether or not intercourse has occurred during that cycle. For long-acting methods of contraception such as IUDs and implants, the pregnancy rate with time (cumulative pregnancy rate) is informative.

## COMPLIANCE

Many couples using contraception often do so inconsistently and/or incorrectly. Inconsistent or incorrect use accounts for the difference between perfect and typical use failure rates. Some methods are easier to use than others. The IUD, intrauterine system (IUS), and implants are inserted and

| Table 159-2 | Contraceptive Use in the United States (1995), France (2000), and Sweden (1994) among Women Aged 15–44 Years | | |
|---|---|---|---|
| Method | USA [%] | France [%] | Sweden [%] |
| Sterilization | 38.6 | 4.5 | 4.2 |
| Female | 27.7 | 4.5 | 2.7 |
| Male | 10.9 | 0 | 1.5 |
| Pill | 26.9 | 45.8 | 25.0 |
| Implant | 1.3 | Not available | Not available |
| Injection | 3.0 | Not available | 1.7 |
| IUD | 0.8 | 16.1 | 17.1 |
| Diaphragm | 1.9 | <1 | <1 |
| Condom | 20.4 | 7.5 | 17.2 |
| NFP | 2.3 | — | 5.0 |
| Withdrawal | 3.0 | — | 2.3 |

IUD, intrauterine device; NFP, natural family planning.

removed by a health professional and are entirely independent of compliance for efficacy; their failure rates are accordingly very low (see Table 159-3) and typical and perfect use rates are almost the same. Imperfect use with these methods is usually due to provider error—undetected uterine perforation during IUD insertion, for example. Progestogen-only injectables last 12 weeks but still demand the motivation and organizational skills required to attend for repeat doses. Compliance with oral contraception is not easy. In one study, 47% of women reported missing one or more pills per cycle and 22% reported missing two or more pills per cycle.[7] In a study using electronic diaries to record compliance, 63% of women missed one or more pills in the first cycle of use, and 74% in the second cycle.[8] Poor compliance with and discontinuation of oral contraceptives together account for approximately 700,000 unintended pregnancies in the United States each year. Typical use failure rates are even higher with methods of contraception that rely on correct use with every act of intercourse (condoms, diaphragms, withdrawal, and natural family planning).

## DISCONTINUATION RATES

In an international review of discontinuation rates after 1 year of use of hormonal contraception, rates varied from 19% (for Norplant) to 62% (the combined pill).[9] Discontinuation rates are higher for methods that do not require removal by a health professional, as is clear from Table 159-3, which shows the percentage of couples in the United States still using each method at the end of 1 year. In the United States, 40% of married women and 61% of unmarried women using a reversible method of contraception change it in the course of 2 years.[10] Many (especially those with more years of education) change from a less effective method to a more effective method. In a study of women presenting for emergency contraception in the United Kingdom and followed up for 1 year, use of oral contraception increased from 13% to more than 50%.[11] Adolescents are particularly likely to discontinue their contraceptive methods. In one study, 50% discontinued during the first 3 months of use.[12] Reasons for discontinuation are often associated with perceived risks and real or perceived side effects. In the international review,[9] the most common reason for discontinuation was bleeding dysfunction. In a Swedish study following up 656 women for 10 years,[13] between 28% and 35% of women (depending on age) stopped taking the oral contraceptive pill because of fear of harmful side effects; 13% to 17% of women who had used the pill stopped because of menstrual dysfunction, 15% to 20% because of weight increase, and 14% to 21% because of side effects associated with mood change. Continuation rates are often regarded as a surrogate for acceptability of a method. This is simplistic. A multitude of factors determine acceptability, and continuation of a method may only reflect that method being the best of a bad lot.

## CONTRAINDICATIONS

Pharmaceutical companies list endless cautions, warnings, and contraindications in their contraceptive product labels. Most contraceptive users are young and medically fit and can use any available method safely. A few medical conditions, however, are associated with theoretical increased health risks with certain contraceptives, either because the method adversely affects the condition (the combined pill, for example, may increase the risk of a woman with diabetes developing cardiovascular complications) or because the condition or its treatment affects the contraceptive (some anticonvulsants interfere with the efficacy of the combined pill). Since most trials of new contraceptive methods deliberately exclude subjects with serious medical conditions, there is little direct evidence on which to base sound prescribing advice. In an attempt to produce a set of international norms for providing

**Table 159-3** Percentage of Women Experiencing an Unintended Pregnancy with Use of Contraception

| Method (1) | % of Women Experiencing an Unintended Pregnancy within the First Year of Use | | % of Women Continuing Use at One Year[3] (4) |
|---|---|---|---|
| | Typical Use[1] (2) | Perfect Use[2] (3) | |
| No method[4] | 85 | 85 | |
| Spermicides[5] | 29 | 15 | 42 |
| Withdrawal | 27 | 4 | 43 |
| Periodic abstinence | 25 | | 51 |
| Calendar | | 9 | |
| Ovulation method | | 3 | |
| Symptothermal[6] | | 2 | |
| Postovulation | | 1 | |
| Cap[7] | | | |
| Parous women | 32 | 26 | 46 |
| Nulliparous women | 16 | 9 | 57 |
| Sponge | | | |
| Parous women | 32 | 20 | 46 |
| Nulliparous women | 16 | 9 | 57 |
| Diaphragm[7] | 16 | 6 | 57 |
| Condom[8] | | | |
| Female (reality) | 21 | 5 | 49 |
| Male | 15 | 2 | 53 |
| Combined pill and minipill | 8 | 0.3 | 68 |
| Evra patch | 8 | 0.3 | 68 |
| NuvaRing | 8 | 0.3 | 68 |
| Depo-Provera | 3 | 0.3 | 56 |
| Lunelle | 3 | 0.05 | 56 |
| IUD | | | |
| No method[4] | 85 | 85 | |
| Spermicides[5] | 29 | 15 | 42 |
| Progestasert (progesterone T) | 2.0 | 1.5 | 81 |
| ParaGard (copper T) | 0.8 | 0.6 | 78 |
| Mirena (LNG-IUS) | 0.1 | 0.1 | 81 |
| Norplant and Norplant-2 | 0.05 | 0.05 | 84 |
| Female sterilization | 0.5 | 0.5 | 100 |
| Male sterilization | 0.15 | 0.10 | 100 |

**Emergency contraceptive pills**: Treatment initiated within 72 hours after unprotected intercourse reduces the risk of pregnancy by at least 75%.[9]

**Lactational amenorrhea method**: LAM is a highly effective, *temporary* method of contraception.[10]

[1] Among *typical* couples who initiate use of a method (not necessarily for the first time), the percentage who experience an accidental pregnancy during the first year if they do not stop use for any other reason. Estimates of the probability of pregnancy during the first year of typical use for spermicides, withdrawal, periodic abstinence, the diaphragm, the male condom, the pill, and Depo-Provera are taken from the 1995 National Survey of Family Growth, corrected for underreporting of abortion; see the text for the derivation of estimates for the other methods.

[2] Among couples who initiate use of a method (not necessarily for the first time) and who use it *perfectly* (both consistently and correctly), the percentage who experience an accidental pregnancy during the first year if they do not stop use for any other reason. See the text for the derivation of the estimate for each method.

[3] Among couples attempting to avoid pregnancy, the percentage who continue to use a method for 1 year.

[4] The percentages becoming pregnant in columns (2) and (3) are based on data from populations where contraception is not used and from women who cease using contraception in order to become pregnant. Among such populations, about 89% become pregnant within 1 year. This estimate was lowered slightly (to 85%) to represent the percentage who would become pregnant within 1 year among women now relying on reversible methods of contraception if they abandoned contraception altogether.

[5] Foams, creams, gels, vaginal suppositories, and vaginal film.

*Continued*

[6] Cervical mucus (ovulation) method supplemented by calendar in the pre-ovulatory and basal body temperature in the postovulatory phases.

[7] With spermicidal cream or jelly.

[8] Without spermicides.

[9] The treatment schedule is one dose within 120 hours after unprotected intercourse, and a second dose 12 hours after the first dose. Both doses of Plan B can be taken at the same time. Plan B (1 dose is 1 white pill) and Preven (1 dose is 2 blue pills) are the only dedicated products specifically marketed for emergency contraception. The Food and Drug Administration has, in addition, declared the following 17 brands of oral contraceptives safe and effective for emergency contraception: Ogestrel or Ovral (1 dose is 2 white pills); Alesse, Lessina, or Levlite (1 dose is 5 pink pills); Levlen or Nordette (1 dose is 4 light-orange pills); Cryselle, Levora, Low-Ogestrel, or Lo/Ovral (1 dose is 4 white pills); Tri-Levlen or Triphasil (1 dose is 4 yellow pills); Portia or Trivora (1 dose is 4 pink pills); Aviane (1 dose is 5 orange pills); and Empresse (1 dose is 4 orange pills)

[10] To maintain effective protection against pregnancy, however, another method of contraception must be used as soon as menstruation resumes, the frequency or duration of breastfeeds is reduced, bottle feeds are introduced, or the baby reaches 6 months of age.

Reproduced with permission from Trussel J: Contraceptive failure. In Hatcher RA, Trussell J, Stewart F, et al (eds): Contraceptive Technology, 18th ed. New York, Ardent Media 2004, pp 226–227.

LNG-IUS, levonorgestrel-intrauterine system.

contraception to women and men with a range of medical conditions that may contraindicate one or more contraceptive methods, the World Health Organization (WHO) has developed a system of medical eligibility criteria (MEC) for contraceptive use.[14] Using evidence-based systematic reviews,[15] the document classifies conditions into one of four categories. Category 1 includes conditions for which there is no restriction for the use of the method, whereas category 4 includes conditions that represent an unacceptable health risk if the contraceptive method is used (absolutely contraindicated). Classification of a condition as category 2 indicates that the method may generally be used but more careful follow-up is required. Category 3 conditions are those for which the risks of the combined oral contraceptive (COC) generally outweigh the benefits (relatively contraindicated). Provision of a method to a woman with a category 3 condition requires careful clinical judgment since use of that method is not recommended unless there is no acceptable alternative. The document is available on the Internet at www.who.int/reproductive-health/publications/MEC_3/Index.htm, and a system is in place to incorporate new data into the guidelines as it becomes available. Category 3 and 4 conditions for the IUD, COC, and progestogen-only contraceptive (POC) are summarized in Tables 159-4, 159-5, and 159-6, respectively.

## HEALTH BENEFITS

Most couples use contraception for more than 30 years. Additional health benefits beyond pregnancy prevention offer significant advantages and influence acceptability. In a nationwide sample of 943 women in the United States, satisfaction with oral contraception was most likely among women aware of the noncontraceptive benefits of the pill and who experienced few side effects.[16]

Existing combined hormonal methods improve menstrual bleeding patterns and alleviate dysmenorrhea, acne, and sometimes premenstrual syndrome (PMS). The combined pill reduces the risk of ovarian and endometrial cancer. Increasing numbers of women choose the levonorgestrel-releasing intrauterine system (LNG-IUS) and Depo-Provera (depot medroxyprogesterone acetate [DMPA]) because of the amenorrhea they confer. Perimenopausal women appreciate the facility to continue using the LNG-IUS into the menopause when it can be used to deliver the progestogen component of

## Table 159-4 WHO Medical Eligibility Criteria: Conditions Classified as Categories 3 and 4 for Combined Oral Contraceptives

**CATEGORY 3 CONDITIONS**
Breastfeeding 6 weeks to 6 months postpartum
Before 3 weeks after childbirth (bottlefeeding)
Smoking < 15 cigarettes/day and > age 35
Adequate controlled hypertension
Blood pressure > 140/90
Severe hyperlipidemia
Nonfocal migraine and > age 35
Past breast cancer—5 years without recurrence
Current or medically treated gallbladder disease
Past COC-related cholestasis
Mild cirrhosis

**CATEGORY 3/4 CONDITIONS**
Multiple risk factors for cardiovascular disease
Diabetes with retinopathy, nephropathy, neuropathy, or other vascular disease of more than 20 years' duration.

**CATEGORY 4 CONDITIONS**
Breastfeeding < 6 weeks postpartum
Smoking > 15 cigarettes/day and > age 35
Blood pressure > 160/100
Hypertension with vascular disease
History of, or current DVT
Major surgery with prolonged immobilization
History of, or current MI
History of stroke
Complicated valvular heart disease
Focal migraine
Current breast cancer
Severe cirrhosis
Liver tumors

COC, combined oral contraceptives; DVT, deep venous thrombosis; MI, myocardial infarction.
From Ref. 14.

## Table 159-5 WHO Medical Eligibility Criteria: Conditions Classified as Categories 3 and 4 for Copper IUDs

**CATEGORY 3 CONDITIONS**
With 48 hours and 4 weeks of childbirth
Benign gestational trophoblastic disease
Initiation of an IUD in the presence of ovarian cancer
Increased risk of STI
High risk of HIV
HIV-positive
AIDS
Continuation in the presence of pelvic tuberculosis

**CATEGORY 4 CONDITIONS**
Puerperal sepsis
Immediate post septic abortion
Anatomical abnormalities or fibroids that distort the uterine cavity
Initiation of an IUD before evaluation of unexplained vaginal bleeding
Malignant gestational trophoblastic disease
Initiation in the presence of cervical cancer
Initiation in the presence of endometrial cancer
Initiation with current PID or PID within the last 3 months
Continuation of an IUD in the presence of current PID
Current purulent arthritis, gonorrhea, chlamydia
Initiation with known pelvic tuberculosis

AIDS, acquired immunodeficiency syndrome; HIV, human immunodeficiency virus; IUD, intrauterine device; PID, pelvic inflammatory disease; STI, sexually transmitted infection.
From World Health Organization: Improving Access to Quality Care in Family Planning: Medical Eligibility Criteria for Contraceptive Use. Geneva, WHO, 2004.

## Table 159-6 WHO Medical Eligibility Criteria: Conditions Classified as Categories 3 and 4 for Progestogen-Only Contraceptives

| Condition | POP | DMPA | Nor | LNG-IUS |
|---|---|---|---|---|
| Breastfeeding < 6 weeks | 3 | 3 | 3 | - |
| Before 4 weeks postpartum | - | - | - | 3 |
| Puerperal sepsis | - | - | - | 4 |
| Post septic abortion | - | - | - | 4 |
| Distorted uterine cavity | - | - | - | 4 |
| Multiple risk factors for arterial cardiovascular disease | - | 3 | - | - |
| Blood pressure > 160/100 | - | 3 | - | - |
| Hypertension with vascular disease | - | 3 | - | - |
| Current DVT/PE | 3 | 3 | 3 | 3 |
| Current or history of IHD—initiation | - | 3 | - | - |
| Current or history of IHD—continuation | 3 | 3 | 3 | 3 |
| Stroke—initiation of method | - | 3 | - | - |
| Stroke—continuation of method | 3 | 3 | 3 | - |
| Focal migraine—continuation of method | 3 | 3 | 3 | 3 |
| Unexplained unevaluated vaginal bleeding | - | 3 | 3 | - |
| Benign trophoblastic disease | - | - | - | 3 |
| Malignant trophoblastic disease | - | - | - | 4 |
| Current breast cancer | 4 | 4 | 4 | 4 |
| Past breast cancer | 3 | 3 | 3 | 3 |
| PID current | - | - | - | 4 |
| STI current | - | - | - | 4 |
| Increased risk of STI | - | - | - | 3 |
| High risk of, or HIV or AIDS | - | - | - | 2 |
| Complicated diabetes | - | 3 | - | - |
| Active viral hepatitis | 3 | 3 | 3 | 3 |
| Severe cirrhosis | 3 | 3 | 3 | 3 |
| Liver tumors | 3 | 3 | 3 | 3 |

DMPA, Depo-Provera; DVT, deep venous thrombosis; HIV, human immunodeficiency virus; LNG-IUS, levonorgestrel-intrauterine system; IHD, ischemic heart disease; PE, pulmonaryembolism; PID, pelvic inflammatory disease; POP, progestogen-only pill; STI, sexually transmitted infection. Nor, Norplant; LNG-IUS, levonorgestrel-intrauterine system.
From World Health Organization: Improving Access to Quality Care in Family Planning: Medical Eligibility Criteria for Contraceptive Use. Geneva, WHO, 2004.

hormone replacement therapy (HRT). Barrier methods, particularly condoms, protect against sexually transmitted infections, including cervical cancer. When contraceptives are being used for their beneficial side effects or in the management of a medical problem such as menorrhagia, the risk-benefit ratio changes.

## NONHORMONAL METHODS

### NATURAL FAMILY PLANNING

Although few couples in the United States use the methods of so-called natural family planning (NFP), in some parts of the world, these methods are common. All involve avoidance of intercourse during the fertile period of the cycle ("periodic abstinence"). Methods differ in the way in which they recognize the fertile period. The simplest is the calendar or rhythm method in which the fertile period is calculated according to the length of the normal menstrual cycle. The mucus or Billings method relies on identifying changes in the quantity and quality of cervical and vaginal mucus. As circulating estrogens increase with follicle growth, the mucus becomes clear and stretchy, allowing the passage of sperm. With ovulation, and in the presence of progesterone, mucus becomes opaque, sticky, and much less stretchy or disappears altogether. Intercourse must stop when fertile-type mucus is identified and can start again when infertile type mucus is recognized. Progesterone secretion is also associated with a rise in basal body temperature (BBT) of about 0.5°C. The BBT method is thus able to identify the end of the fertile period. Other signs and symptoms such as ovulation pain, position of cervix, and degree of dilatation of the cervical os can be used to help define the fertile period. (For a detailed review of NFP methods, see reference 17.)

Many couples find periodic abstinence difficult. Failure rates of natural methods are high (see Table 159-3) mostly due to rule breaking. Perfect use of the mucous method is associated with a failure rate of only 3.4%. There is no evidence that accidental pregnancies occurring among NFP users, which are conceived with aging gametes, are associated with a higher risk of congenital malformations.

The lactational amenorrhea method (LAM) is used during breastfeeding. Amenorrhea during breastfeeding provides more than 98% protection from pregnancy in the first 6 months postpartum, if the mother is fully or nearly fully breastfeeding and has not yet experienced vaginal bleeding after the 56th day postpartum. Guidelines for LAM advise that, as long as the baby is younger than 6 months old, a woman can rely on breastfeeding alone as a contraceptive method until she menstruates or until she starts to give her baby significant amounts of food other than breast milk.[18] Prospective studies of LAM confirm its effectiveness.[19]

### BARRIER METHODS

The male condom is cheap, widely available without involving health professionals, and, apart from occasional allergic reactions, is free from side effects. Polyurethane condoms were developed to overcome the disadvantages of traditional latex condoms (allergic reactions, impaired sensation during intercourse, short shelf life in certain storage conditions, and weakening with oil-based lubricants). None has yet proved as effective for contraception,[20] but polyurethane condoms offer an alternative for people with latex sensitivity. A recent report from the U.S. National Institutes of Health (NIH) concluded that condoms are effective in preventing sexually transmitted infection (STI).[21] Use of the condom has increased significantly in the past decade as a result of concern over the spread of human immunodeficiency virus (HIV) and acquired immunodeficiency syndrome (AIDS).

Female barrier methods are much less popular. The diaphragm and cervical cap must be fitted by a health professional and do not confer the same degree of protection from STI. The female condom covers the mucous membranes of the vagina and vulva and is more effective in preventing STI, but has a high failure rate and low acceptability.

Spermicide alone is not recommended for prevention of pregnancy as it is only moderately effective. Nonoxynol 9 (N-9) is a spermicidal product sold as a gel, cream, foam, film, or pessary for use with diaphragms or caps. Many male condoms are lubricated with N-9. In response to recent data suggesting that frequent use of N-9 might increase the risk of HIV transmission, WHO recommends that women who have multiple daily acts of intercourse or who are at high risk for HIV infection should not use N-9. For women at low risk for HIV infection, N-9 is probably not unsafe. Since there is no evidence that lubricating male condoms with N-9 improves efficacy, such condoms should no longer be promoted.[22]

### INTRAUTERINE DEVICE

The intrauterine device is a safe, effective, and long-acting method of contraception.[23] In the United States in the 1970s, some 10% of couples used the IUD; currently, it accounts for less than 1% of contraceptive use. The decline in use resulted mainly from the reports of a number of septic maternal deaths among women using the Dalkon Shield.[24] The IUD has remained an important method in many other countries in the developed and developing world (see Table 159-2) and has, if anything, undergone a revival since the introduction of the LNG device Mirena. The copper IUD is an extremely cheap method of contraception even in the United States where the cost of the device and its insertion is high. The only device currently available in the United States, the TCu 380A, is licensed for use of 10 years' duration, but it is effective for at least 12 years.

#### Efficacy

In a study involving 7159 women years of use of the TCu 380A, the cumulative pregnancy rate after 8 years was 2.2 per 100 women years, not significantly different from that of female sterilization.[25]

#### Mechanism of Action

The mechanism of action of the IUD has long been controversial. There is evidence that the copper ions are toxic to gametes and that the viability of both sperm and egg are impaired, inhibiting fertilization. The presence of an IUD in the uterus, however, is associated with a local inflammatory response in the endometrium sufficient to prevent implantation should fertilization occur.[26] In reality, the IUD probably acts both before and after fertilization.[27]

#### Safety and Side Effects

The IUD is inserted using an aseptic technique, with or without local anesthetic (in parous women, anesthesia is rarely required). *Perforation* occurs in fewer than 1 in 1000 insertions. If recognized within a few weeks, the IUD can usually be retrieved laparoscopically before adhesions form around it. For this reason, routine follow-up is recommended 4 to 6 weeks after insertion, which should be delayed in breastfeeding women until at least 4 weeks after delivery. *Expulsion* occurs in approximately 1 in 20 women, most commonly within the first 3 months of use and usually during menstruation. Women can be taught to feel for the tail of the device to check that it is still present after menstruation. *Menorrhagia* is the most common side effect associated with IUD use and the most common reason for discontinuation. Periods tend to last a couple of days more in addition to being heavier. *Dysmenorrhea* is also more likely to occur among IUD users.

## Ectopic Pregnancy

Since the IUD does not inhibit ovulation, it does not prevent ectopic pregnancy as well as methods that inhibit ovulation. Nonetheless, ectopic pregnancy is rare: 0.02 per 100 women years compared with 0.3 to 0.5 for women not using contraception.[28]

## Pelvic Infection and Infertility

Although a concern in the past, the balance of evidence suggests that use of an IUD is not associated with infertility.[29] A meta-analysis undertaken by WHO suggested an increased risk of pelvic infection only in the first 20 days after insertion.[30] After the first month, the risk of upper genital tract infection is small.[29] A recent case control study has demonstrated that whereas STI is associated with an increased risk of tubal infertility, previous IUD use is not.[31] Many studies have investigated pregnancy rates after IUD removal; the vast majority have demonstrated no impairment of fertility. A recent systematic review[32] highlights the lack of quality evidence identifying the risk of pelvic infection after IUD insertion in the presence of an STI. A sexual history should be taken from every woman before IUD insertion, however. Routine screening for *Chlamydia trachomatis* and *Neisseria gonorrhoeae* is only indicated in population groups in which prevalence of infection is high. Under these conditions, if screening is not readily available, prophylactic antibiotics may be given before insertion, but are not recommended routinely as they have not been shown to be of benefit.[33]

# HORMONAL CONTRACEPTION

There are two categories of hormonal contraception: combined and progestogen only. Until very recently, combined hormonal contraception was only available as an oral preparation—the pill. Combined injectables, the contraceptive patch, and the vaginal ring now offer an increased range in modes of administration. Progestogen-only contraception is available through oral, injectable, implantable, and intrauterine delivery systems. Long-acting delivery systems have the theoretical advantage of providing constant release rates of steroid hormone (compared with daily administration) and also avoid the first-pass effect through the liver, enabling lower doses of steroids to be used.

## COMBINED HORMONAL CONTRACEPTIVES

### Mode of Action

Combined hormonal contraceptives inhibit follicle development and ovulation. The 7-day break between courses of pills, patches, and rings allows the resumption of follicular growth, which may continue to ovulation if the contraceptive method is restarted late. Endometrial atrophy and an alteration of cervical mucous characteristics impair implantation and sperm transport, respectively.

### Delivery Systems
#### Oral

The COC pill is by far the most popular method of hormonal contraception. Classically taken for 21 days out of every 28, with a withdrawal bleed occurring during the pill-free interval, almost all available preparations contain ethinyl estradiol (EE, commonly 30–35 µg/day) in combination with a synthetic progestogen. Natural progesterone is inactive orally. Over the years, the pharmaceutical industry has developed a variety of progestogens, which differ mainly in their affinity for the androgen receptor. Screeds have been written about the benefits of one progestogen over another in terms of "androgenic side effects" (such as acne, mood change, bloating) and cycle control. In reality, there is little evidence for any differential effects, and cycle control (regular withdrawal bleeds at the scheduled time without any bleeding or spotting in between) is determined largely by the dose of estrogen. One or two brands of COC contain antiandrogens rather than a classical progestogen, and preexisting symptoms of hyperandrogenicity, particularly acne and hirsutism, are probably better controlled by these pills. The most recent addition to the list of progestogens is drospirenone (a derivative of spironolactone), which is not only antiandrogenic, but also has antimineralocorticoid effects. A combined pill containing drospirenone (Yasmin) is said to be associated with less weight gain than pills with older progestogens, although the effect, if any, is not clinically significant.[34]

In an attempt to reduce the cardiovascular risks of the combined pill, the dose of estrogen has been reduced over the years and pills are now available that contain only 15 µg/day EE.[35] Very low doses of EE are associated with an increased incidence of breakthrough bleeding and are almost certainly at the lower limit of effective ovulation inhibition. The PFI can be decreased to only 4 days to reduce the risk of failure with very low dose pills. In the United States, a preparation of 20 µg/day EE (Mircette) provides only 2 days of placebo after 5 days of 10 µg/day.[36] This preparation is associated with less ovarian follicle development in the 7 days between "active pills."

Pills are available as monophasic, biphasic, or triphasic preparations in which the dose of both steroids stays the same throughout the 21 days of use, or changes once (biphasic) or twice (triphasic). There is no evidence for any benefit of biphasic or triphasic pills, which tend to be more expensive. Recognizing the increased desirability of amenorrhea, a COC with 84 days of active pills followed by a 7-day interval during which a withdrawal bleed occurs has recently been launched in the United States (Seasonale).[37]

#### Transdermal

Although transdermal hormone replacement therapy has been available for years, it was not until 2003 that the first contraceptive patch was marketed. One preparation is available, a 20 cm$^2$ patch delivering 20 µg EE and 150 µg/day norelgestromin (17-deacetyl norgestimate) daily. Each patch lasts 7 days, three patches are used consecutively with a placebo or patch-free interval in week 4 when a withdrawal bleed occurs. Contraceptive protection lasts for up to 10 days, allowing for errors in changing the patch. In a randomized trial comparing the patch with a COC, effectiveness was not significantly different; the overall Pearl Index for the patch was 1.24 per 100 women years and for the COC was 2.18.[38] In a large nonrandomized trial, four of the six pregnancies that occurred were in women weighing over 90 kg, suggesting that efficacy may be reduced among heavier women.[39] After the first few cycles of use, bleeding patterns and side effects are similar to those associated with the combined pill. Self-reported "perfect use" was significantly better with the patch (88%) than with the pill (78%) in the randomized trial, although whether this is so with use outside a clinical trial remains to be seen.

#### Vaginal Ring

A combined contraceptive vaginal ring (Nuvaring, Organon) releasing 15 µg of EE and 120 µg of etonorgestrel is now licensed in the United States and in much of Europe. The ring is made of soft ethylene-vinyl-acetate (EVA) copolymer and has an outer diameter of 54 mm and a cross-sectional diameter of 4 mm. Designed to last for 3 weeks, a 7-day ring-free interval is associated with bleeding patterns that appear superior to those associated with a COC. In a comparison with a COC containing 30 µg of EE and 150 µg of levonorgestrel (Microgynon 30; Schering) the incidence of irregular bleeding in the Nuvaring was significantly less (1.9% versus 38.8%).[40] In all other respects, including efficacy, the ring is no different from the pill; however, there may be advantages in terms of demands on compliance.

## Injectable

A monthly combined injectable contraceptive (CIC) contains 25 mg medroxyprogesterone acetate and 5 mg estradiol cypionate (Lunelle Pharmacia).[41] Injections are administered intramuscularly every 28 days. Bleeding patterns and efficacy are comparable with the COC. Bleeding episodes can be anticipated 18 to 22 days after injection and are induced by a decline in estrogen concentrations to 50 pg/mL or less. Approximately 70% of women experience one bleeding episode per month, with only 4% experiencing amenorrhea over three treatment cycles.

## Safety and Side Effects

Presently, there are very limited data on the long-term safety of the CIC, patch, and vaginal ring. Although it may be tempting to extrapolate from studies of hormone replacement therapy patches and assume that the risk of venous thromboembolism (VTE) may be less with a method that avoids the first pass through the liver, it seems sensible to assume that the risks are similar for all methods. In the WHO Medical Eligibility Criteria,[14] the patch and ring are treated like the pill. Since the estrogens in CICs may be less potent than ethinyl estradiol, however, the side effects and their magnitude may be different. The CIC is positioned somewhere between POC and COC in terms of medical eligibility. For example, smoking more than 15 cigarettes a day is a category 4 condition for the COC, but a category 3 condition for a CIC.

The combined pill is extremely safe. In a Royal College of General Practitioners (RCGP) 25-year follow-up of 46,000 women in the United Kingdom, the overall risk of death from any condition was the same for COC users and nonusers.[42] Among current and recent (within 10 years) users, the COC was associated with an increased risk of death from only two conditions: cervical cancer (relative risk [RR] 2.5) and cerebrovascular disease (RR 1.9).

### Minor Side Effects

The combined pill is associated with a variety of minor side effects probably common to all combined hormonal contraceptives regardless of delivery system. Nausea (rarely persistent), breakthrough bleeding, chloasma, and breast tenderness are all attributable to the steroid hormones. Mood change and loss of libido are but two of a list of common complaints less clearly related to the drugs. Combined hormonal contraception is not associated with weight gain, although weight gain is a very common reason given for discontinuation (73% of British women of all ages quoted weight gain as being a disadvantage of the pill[43]). Most women gain weight with time. A study of weight changes among Brazilian women of reproductive age using nonhormonal contraception demonstrated a mean increase of 2.8 kg over 5 and 3.9 kg over 7 years.[44]

### Hypertension

Pooled data[45] from four large phase 2 clinical trials suggest that the COC has a negligible effect on blood pressure.

### Venous Thromboembolism

There is a three- to fivefold increase in the risk of VTE associated with COC use, which is apparently independent of the dose of estrogen (and definitely so if it is below 50 µg). COCs containing the progestogens gestodene and desogestrel are probably associated with twice the risk of VTE than pills containing levonorgestrel or norethisterone.[46] Although often attributed to confounding or bias, there is some biological plausibility for this differential risk. Whichever progestogen is used, the absolute risk of VTE is small (15/100,000 women years for pill users compared with 5/100,000 for nonusers), and much less than that associated with pregnancy (60/100,000 women years). The risk appears to be greatest during the first year of use of the COC (perhaps due to the unmasking of inherited thrombophilias such as factor V Leiden) and disappears within 3 months of stopping. Screening for known thrombophilias is not cost effective and, although asking about a family history of VTE is routine when prescribing the pill, this too fails to detect most women at risk of VTE.

### Myocardial Infarction

The relationship between COC use and myocardial infarction (MI) is controversial. Though there is widespread agreement that there is an increased risk of MI among women who smoke or have hypertension, some studies have demonstrated an increased risk among normotensive nonsmokers and other studies have not. One recent study from the Netherlands showed a relative risk of 2.8 (95% confidence interval [CI]; 1.3–6.3) among women with no known risk factors.[47] Another case control study from the United Kingdom showed no significant association between COC use and MI.[48] In a recent meta-analysis of 23 studies, the adjusted odds ration of MI was 2.48 (95% CI; 1.91–3.22) for current COC users compared to those who had never used.[49] The risk among past users was not significantly increased. The risk of MI was significant for users of second-generation COCs, but not third-generation pills. There was also a dose response relationship with EE, with pills containing 20 µg EE associated with no increase in risk. The risk of MI was significantly increased by smoking (odds ratio [OR] 9.3; 95% CI; 3.89–22.23) compared with nonsmokers (many other studies have shown this[50]) and for women with a history of hypertension (OR 9.9; 95% CI; 1.83–53.53) and hypercholesterolemia (OR 2.08; 95% CI; 1.5–2.9). The absolute risk of MI in women of reproductive age, even those with known risk factors, is extremely small, however.[15]

### Stroke

Use of the COC increases the risk of ischemic stroke twofold; however, the risk of hemorrhagic stroke is unchanged.[51] Smoking and hypertension increase the risk of stroke by 3 to 10 times. Stroke is rare, however, in women of reproductive age.

### Migraine

Women with focal migraine who use the COC may have an increased risk of ischemic stroke.[52] Focal migraine is therefore a category 4 condition and the COC is contraindicated.

### Breast Cancer

COC use has long been thought to be associated with an increased risk of breast cancer. A meta-analysis[53] of data from over 53,000 women with breast cancer and 100,000 controls, published in 1996, showed a relative risk of 1.24 (95% CI; 1.15–1.33). The increased risk takes 10 years to decline to that of nonusers. A more recent case control study[54] involving 8000 women suggested no increased risk of breast cancer (RR 1.0; 95% CI; 0.8–1.3); however, the upper limit of the confidence interval was in keeping with the much larger meta-analysis. The risk of breast cancer appears to be independent of the dose of EE and of the duration of use and is not influenced by family history or age at first use. In the RCGP study, no increase in the risk of death from breast cancer was detected.[42]

### Cervical Cancer

The COC is associated with an increased risk of squamous carcinoma of the cervix, but it is often suggested that the association may be simply the result of inadequate adjustment in the epidemiologic studies for sexual behavior. In a meta-analysis of 10 case control studies published in 2002,[55] among women with persistent infection with human papilloma virus (HPV), use of hormonal contraception for more than 5 years was associated with an increased relative risk of cervical cancer of 2.8. Hormonal contraceptive use for longer than 10 years increased the relative risk to 4.0. Most of the women were likely to have been using the COC.

## Liver Cancer

COC use is associated with an increased risk of liver cancer, but only in populations with a high rate of hepatitis B infection. Among others, the absolute risk of liver cancer is extremely small.

## PROGESTOGEN-ONLY CONTRACEPTIVES

The progestogen-only contraceptive (POC) is available in a variety of delivery systems. The injectable preparations deliver a high dose of hormone, whereas the oral preparation, implants, and intrauterine systems deliver much lower doses (Table 159-7).

### Mode of Action

The mode of action depends on the dose of hormone. High doses (injectables) inhibit follicle development and ovulation completely; alter the characteristics of cervical mucus, interfering with sperm transport; and cause endometrial changes including atrophy. Intermediate doses (the subdermal implant Implanon and the pill Cerazette) inhibit ovulation but allow follicular development, whereas very low doses (classical progestogen-only pills, intrauterine delivery systems, and the implants Norplant and Jadelle) inhibit ovulation only inconsistently and rely mainly on their effect on cervical mucus.

### Delivery Systems

#### Oral

The oral POC (progestogen-only pill, POP or mini-pill) has been available for more than 40 years, but is little used in most parts of the world. It offers a pill to women with contraindications to estrogen, such as breastfeeding, diabetes with complications, and migraine. Until recently, all available POPs contained second-generation progestogens at a dose that inhibited ovulation inconsistently. In 2002, a POP containing 75 μg of desogestrel per day, a dose sufficient to inhibit ovulation in almost every cycle, was introduced in Europe.[56] All POPs are designed to be taken daily without a break. Bleeding patterns depend on the degree of suppression of ovarian activity. If normal ovulation occurs consistently, a woman will experience menstrual bleeds at a frequency characteristic of her normal cycle. If both ovulation and follicle development are completely suppressed, amenorrhea will result. If ovulation or follicular development sufficient to stimulate endometrial growth occurs irregularly, bleeding will be erratic and unpredictable.

#### Injectable

Only one preparation of injectable POC is available in the United States, depot medroxyprogesterone acetate (DMPA, Depo-Provera), administered intramuscularly every 12 weeks. The dose is sufficient to inhibit all ovarian activity. Some 80% of women become amenorrheic after 1 year of use, but a small number will have persistent heavy and prolonged bleeding.

The recent development of a micronized subcutaneous preparation, similar in all respects to the existing preparation, will allow self-injection, which may further increase acceptability for many women.

#### Implants

The first contraceptive implant to become available (in 1983 in Finland) was Norplant, six Silastic capsules containing a total of 216 mg of crystalized levonorgestrel. Circulating levels of levonorgestrel are around 80 μg/day during the first 8 weeks and decline slowly to 25 to 30 μg/day at 60 months. Jadelle comprises two silicone rods releasing levonorgestrel at a similar rate. Jadelle and Norplant are virtually identical in terms of efficacy and side effects. Implanon, a single rod containing 68 mg 3-keto-desogestrel (a metabolite of desogestrel), provides contraception for 3 years. The initial release rate of 60 to 70 μg/day falls gradually to around 25 to 30 μg/day at the end of 3 years. All three implants are inserted subdermally on the inner aspect of the upper arm. Although not difficult to insert, removal can be troublesome, particularly if the implants are inserted subcutaneously rather than subdermally. Implanon is preloaded into a sterile disposable inserter, making insertion and removal much easier.

#### Intrauterine Systems

The progesterone T is a device made of an EVA copolymer, the stem of which contains 38 mg of progesterone released at a rate of 65 μg/day. It is only available in the United States. The LNG-IUS (Mirena) has a T-shaped plastic frame with a reservoir on the vertical stem containing 52 mg of levonorgestrel, releasing 20 μg/day. It is available worldwide. Intrauterine concentrations of levonorgestrel are 1000 times higher than those associated with subdermal implants. Marked endometrial atrophy occurs. The dose of levonorgestrel has a minimal effect on ovarian activity; most women continue to ovulate.

### Safety and Side Effects

*Unpredictable, unscheduled vaginal bleeding* is the most common side effect of all low-dose POCs and the most common reason for discontinuation. Although incomplete suppression of ovarian activity is partly the cause, a local effect on the endometrium of the continuous administration of progestogens also probably contributes. Erratic bleeding occurs in around 70% of users of progestogen-only implants and around 40% of POP users. In the first 3 to 6 months after insertion of Mirena, spotting is common and can be persistent. By the end of 1 year, most women have very light, short, and infrequent bleeding episodes. Although the administration of estrogens will usually stop the unscheduled bleeding with the POC, this is only a temporary solution and not one open to women with contraindications to estrogen. If the bleeding pattern is unacceptable (for some women, the advantages of the method outweigh the inconvenience of unpredictable bleeding), a different contraceptive method must be sought.

**Table 159-7** Progestogen-Only Methods of Contraception

| Method | Type of Progestogen | Dose | Duration of Use | Mode of Delivery |
|---|---|---|---|---|
| DMPA (Depo-Provera) | Medroxyprogesterone ac | 150 mg | 12 weeks | IM injection |
| Net-en | Norethisterone enanthate | 200 mg | 8 weeks | IM injection |
| Norplant | Levonorgestrel | 25–80 μg | 5 years | Subdermal implant |
| Jadelle | Levonorgestrel | 25–80 μg | 5 years | Subdermal implant |
| Implanon | Etonorgestrel | 25–70 μg | 3 years | Subdermal implant |
| Mirena | Levonorgestrel | 20 μg/day | 5 years | Intrauterine |
| Progestasert | Progesterone | 65 μg/day | 1 year | Intrauterine |
| Cerazette | Desogstrel | 75 μg/day | Daily | Oral |

IM, intramuscular.

*Amenorrhoea* occurs in up to 10% of women using the POP and levonorgestrel implants, 20% of IUD users, 25% of Mirena users, and 80% of women using Depo-Provera. Most women consider amenorrhea a positive side effect, although for some, it may prove unacceptable. Counseling before initiation about bleeding disturbances, including amenorrhea, improves continuation rates.

*Return to fertility* occurs within days of cessation of all POC methods except injectables. The delay following discontinuation of DMPA is well recognized, but pregnancy rates eventually reach those associated with cessation of other methods.

*Ectopic* pregnancy is listed in many older textbooks as a side effect of the POP due to the theoretical effect of progestogens on tubal motility. The best data are for Norplant and show no increased risk compared with women not using contraception.

*The metabolic side effects of progestogens* are said to be associated with a range of common minor symptoms including acne, hirsutism, headache, mood change, and weight gain or bloating. Although collectively accounting for more than 10% of discontinuations of POCs, all are common complaints among women not using contraception. Depo-Provera may be associated with more significant weight increase[57] than other POCs, but concerns about an increased risk of depression are probably unfounded.

### Ovarian Cysts

The incomplete suppression of ovarian activity is a recipe not only for erratic bleeding, but also for the development of ovarian follicular cysts. These occur in 20% of women using the POP and Mirena. They are almost always asymptomatic.

### Cancer

In the large meta-analysis reporting a relative risk of 1.24 for use of the COC,[53] an increased relative risk of breast cancer for both oral and injectable progestogen-only methods of contraception (RR 1.17 for both) was demonstrated, although for injectables this was not statistically significant. There are much fewer data for POP than for COC, and women with risk factors for breast cancer may be preferentially prescribed POC. Recent anxieties about the contribution of progestogens to the increased risk of breast cancer associated with hormone replacement therapy have not yet spread to progestogen-only contraceptives. There is no evidence for any increased risk of other cancers and indeed some evidence to suggest a reduction in the risk of endometrial cancer.

### Cardiovascular Disease Including VTE

There is no evidence for an increase in the risk of stroke, myocardial infarction, or VTE in association with POC.[58] An association between VTE and progestogen used for the treatment of gynecologic conditions such as anovulatory dysfunctional uterine bleeding[59] is likely to be due to prescriber bias since the COC, often the method of choice, is contraindicated in women with known risk factors for VTE. A very weak association between use of Norplant and hypertension[60] may be due to observer bias.

### Gallbladder Disease

A weak association between use of Norplant and gallbladder disease has been described,[60] but there is no evidence of any association with other POCs.

### Bone Mineral Density

No study has demonstrated any adverse effect of progestogen-only implants on bone mineral density (BMD). It is unlikely, therefore, that use of oral or intrauterine POC would be harmful. Injectable methods, however, deliver high doses of progestogen, suppressing ovarian activity and causing hypoestrogenism, and there have been concerns that their use may increase the risk of osteoporosis.[61] A recent meta-analysis of 12 data sets demonstrated a decreased average BMD among current users of DMPA, but BMD was within one standard deviation of the mean for nonusers.[62] Loss of BMD seems to stabilize after 4 years and is reversed after discontinuation of DMPA. A recent prospective study suggested that even if DMPA is used up to the menopause, the effect on BMD is small and may be associated with an attenuation in immediate menopausal bone loss because the estrogen-sensitive component of bone has already been lost.[63] The data for most women then are reassuring. Concern remains about adolescents who use DMPA since use of the method before peak bone mass is achieved may be harmful.[64] DMPA certainly is associated with BMD loss in teenagers using DMPA compared with those using no contraception, but further research on the clinical significance of this observation is required. Few adolescents use any method of contraception for long periods of time so the concern may be more theoretical than practical. Moreover, the benefits in terms of pregnancy prevention with this easy-to-use method outweigh any theoretical concerns. Although there is a case for caution in prescribing DMPA to women with known existing risk factors for osteoporosis, there is no evidence to support the use of add-back estrogen, which makes it an expensive and complicated method of contraception unsuitable for women with contraindications to estrogen.

## INITIATION OF HORMONAL CONTRACEPTION AND FOLLOW-UP

The vast majority of women who use hormonal contraception do not have any medical problems and they are young. Providers need to recognize the very few who may be at risk of the rare but serious complications of hormonal contraception. Mostly, providers should rely on identifying women who have other risk factors associated with the conditions of concern (e.g., cardiovascular disease or breast cancer) and either informing them of the increased risks or advising them not to use hormonal contraception. Taking a careful history (including family history) and observing obvious physical characteristics (like obesity) provide a lot of useful information. In the United States, detailed physical examination (including breast and pelvic examinations) and a variety of blood tests (such as the measurement of serum cholesterol) have become routine before starting a women on a hormonal method of contraception. These tests and examinations are often repeated annually. The contraceptive consultation is often seen as an opportunity to undertake other screening procedures and there is a danger that these too become part of routine screening for hormonal contraception.

The WHO distinguishes between examinations and investigations that are essential for safe prescribing of contraception from those that are commonly done but which "do not contribute substantially to safe and effective use of the contraceptive method."[65]

## EMERGENCY CONTRACEPTION

Emergency contraception (EC) is defined as any drug or device that is used after intercourse to prevent pregnancy. It is used most commonly after unprotected intercourse or after intercourse during which a condom burst or slipped.

Two hormonal EC preparations are available in the United States: Preven (two doses of a combination of ethinyl estradiol [100 µg] and levonorgestrel [0.5 mg]) and Plan B (two doses of levonorgestrel alone [0.75 mg each]). Both regimens recommend taking the first dose within 72 hours of intercourse and the second 12 hours after the first. Recent data suggest that the two doses of levonorgestrel can be taken at the same time without compromising efficacy. Levonorgestrel appears to be more effective than the Yuzpe regimen (estrogen and progestin) and, as it contains no estrogen, side effects, such as nausea and vomiting, are much less common. IUD insertion is sometimes used as an alternative to hormonal EC if a woman presents more than 72 hours after intercourse but before 5 days after ovulation (for a review, see reference 66).

## Mode of Action

The mechanism of action of hormonal EC is not completely understood.[67] There is good evidence that both the Yuzpe regimen and levonorgestrel inhibit or delay ovulation. Ovulation inhibition is less likely the nearer to ovulation that either drug is taken.[68] Taken 5 days before ovulation, both methods will delay or inhibit ovulation in most women; but taken 2 days before ovulation, both methods are much less effective. That both methods appear more effective if taken within 24 hours of intercourse than if taken later is consistent with this observation. Evidence for an effect on the endometrium that might inhibit implantation is poor for both hormonal methods. The IUD diminishes the viability of gametes and the number of sperm reaching the fallopian tube, but if it is inserted after fertilization has occurred, it works by inhibiting implantation.

## Efficacy

The efficacy of emergency contraception is described in terms of the number of potential pregnancies prevented, based on calculating the risk of pregnancy for the day of the cycle on which intercourse occurred.[69] This is difficult to calculate because many users are of unproven fertility; the information about cycle length, date of last period, and timing of intercourse is often vague or incorrect; and it is impossible to know precisely when, in relation to ovulation, treatment has been given. Data suggest that the Yuzpe regimen and levonorgestrel prevent 75% to 85% of expected pregnancies. The IUD is even more effective and probably prevents over 95% of pregnancies.

## Contraindications

There are no absolute contraindications to hormonal EC. For women at risk of STI (category 3), IUD insertion should be covered with a broad-spectrum antibiotic.

## Side Effects

**Nausea and Vomiting**  Up to 60% of women complain of nausea and up to 16% vomit after the Yuzpe regimen; 23% of women taking levonorgestrel complain of nausea. Nausea and vomiting may decrease compliance.

**Breast Tenderness**  The high dose of estrogen in the Yuzpe regimen may result in breast tenderness for a day or two.

**Changes in the Next Menstrual Cycle**  Almost 30% of women will experience a delay of more than 3 days in the onset of the next menstrual period. Some will menstruate early. For most women, however, menses will come at the expected time.

**Teratogenicity**  There is no evidence that either of the hormonal EC methods are teratogenic if pregnancy occurs or if given inadvertently to a woman who is already pregnant.

## REFERENCES

1. Population Reference Bureau: 2003 World Population Data Sheet. Available at www.prb.org.
2. Piccinino LJ, Mosher WD: Trends in contraceptive use in the United States: 1982–1995. Fam Plann Perspect 30:4–10, 46, 1998.
3. Bajos N, Leridon H, Gowlard H, et al; the COCON Group: Contraception: From accessibility to efficiency. Hum Reprod 18:994–999, 2003.
4. Oddens BJ, Milsom I: Contraceptive practice and attitudes in Sweden 1994. Acta Obstet Gynecol Scand 75:932–940, 1996.
5. Jones RK, Darroch JE, Henshaw SK: Contraceptive use among US women having abortions in 2000–2001. Perspect Sex Reprod Health 34:294–303, 2002.
6. Trussel J: Contraceptive Failure. In Hatcher RA, Trussell J, Stewart F, et al (eds): Contraceptive Technology, 18th ed. New York, Ardent Media (in press).
7. Rosenberg A, Waugh MS: Causes and consequences of oral contraceptive non-compliance. Am J Obstet Gynecol 180:276–279, 1999.
8. Potter L, Oakley D, de Leon-Wong E, Canamanr R: Measuring compliance among oral contraceptive users. Fam Plann Perspect 28:154–158, 1996.
9. D'Arcangues C, Odlind V, Fraser IS, In Alexander MJ, D'Arcangues C (eds): Steroid Hormones and Uterine Bleeding. Washington, AAAS, 1992, pp 81–105.
10. Grady WR, Bill JOG, Klepinger DH: Contraceptive method switching in the United States. Perspect Sex Reprod Health 34:135–145, 2002.
11. Glasier A, Baird DT: The effects of self-administering emergency contraception. N Engl J Med 339:1–4, 1998.
12. Emans SJ, Grace E, Woods ER, et al: Adolescent's compliance with the use of oral contraceptives. JAMA 257:3377–3381, 1987.
13. Larsson G, Blohm F, Sundell G, et al: A longitudinal study of birth control and pregnancy outcome among women in a Swedish population. Contraception 56:6–16, 1997.
14. World Health Organization: Improving Access to Quality Care in Family Planning: Medical Eligibilty Criteria for Contraceptive Use, 3d ed. Geneva, WHO Reproductive Health and Research, 2004. Available on the web at www.who.int/reproductive-health/publications/index.htm.
15. Curtis KM, Chrisman CE, Peterson HB, for the WHO Programme for Mapping Best Practices in Reproductive Health: Contraception for women in selected circumstances. Obstet Gynecol 99:1100–1112, 2002.
16. Rosenburg MJ, Waugh MS, Meehan TE: Use and misuse of oral contraceptives: Risk indicators for poor pill taking and discontinuation. Contraception 51:283–288, 1995.
17. Flynn AM: Natural methods of Contraception. Matern Child Health 16:148–153, 1991.
18. Labbok M, Koniz-Booher P, Cooney K, et al: Guidelines for Breastfeeding in Family Planning and Child Survival Programs. Washington, DC, Institute for Studies in Natural Family Planning, 1990.
19. Perez A, Labbok M, Queenan J: Clinical study of the lactational amenorrhoea method for family planning. Lancet 339:968–969, 1992.
20. Steiner MJ, Dominik R, Rountree W, et al: Contraceptive effectiveness of a polyethylene condom and a latex condom: A randomised controlled trial. Obstet Gynecol 101:539–547, 2003.
21. Cates W Jr: The NIH Condom Report: The glass is 90% full. Fam Plann Perspect 33:231–233, 2001.
22. World Health Organization Reproductive Health Research. Available at www.who.int/reproductive-health/rtis/N9_meeting_report.
23. Fortney JA, Feldblum PJ, Raymond EG: Intrauterine devices: The optimal long-term contraceptive method? J Reprod Med 44:269–274, 1999.
24. Hubacher D: The checkered history and bright future of intrauterine contraception in the United States. Perspect Sex Reprod Health 34:98–103, 2002.
25. United Nations Development Programme/United Nations Population Fund/World Health Organization/World Bank Special Programme of Research: Long-term reversible contraception: 12 years of experience with the Tcu380A and Tcu220C. Contraception 56:341–352, 1997.
26. Sheppard B: Endometrial morphological changes in IUD users: A review. Contraception 36:1–10, 1987.
27. Standford JB, Mikolajczyk RT: Mechanisms of action of intrauterine devices: Update and estimation of postfertilization effects. Am J Obstet Gynecol 187:1699–1708, 2002.
28. Sivin I: Dose and age-dependent ectopic pregnancy risks with intrauterine contraception. Obstet Gynecol 78:291–298, 1991.

29. Grimes D: Intrauterine device and upper-genital-tract infection. Lancet 356:1013–1019, 2000.

30. Farley TNM, Rosenberg MJ, Rowe PJ, et al: Intrauterine contraceptive devices and pelvic inflammatory disease: An international perspective. Lancet 339:758–788, 1992.

31. Hubacher D, Lara-Ricalde R, Taylr DJ, et al: Use of copper intra-uterine devices and the risk of tubal infertility among nulligravid women. N Engl J Med 345:561–567, 2001.

32. Grimes DA: Intrauterine devices and infertility: Sifting through the evidence. Lancet 358:6–7, 2001.

33. Sinei SKA, Schulz KF, Lamptey PR, et al: Preventing IUCD-related pelvic infection: The efficacy of prophylactic doxycycline at insertion. Br J Obstet Gynecol 97:412–419, 1990.

34. Foidart JM, Wuttke W, Bouw GM, et al: A comparative investigation of contraceptive reliability, cycle control and tolerance of two monophasic oral contraceptives containing either drospirenone or desogestrel. Eur J Contracept Reprod Health Care 5:124–113, 2000.

35. Fruzetti F, Genazzani AR, Ricci C, et al: A 12-month clinical investigation with a 24-day regimen containing 15 μg ethinyloestradiol plus 60 μg gestodene with respect to haemostasis and cycle control. Contraception 63:303–307, 2001.

36. Killick SA, Fitzgerald C, Davis A: Ovarian activity in women taking an oral contraceptive containing 20 μg ethinyl estradiol and 150 μg desogestrel: Effects of low estrogen doses during the hormone-free interval. Am J Obstet Gynecol 179:S18–S24, 1998.

37. Anderson FD, Hait H, the Seasonale-301 Study Group: A Multi-center, randomized study of an extended cycle oral contraceptive. Contraception 68:89–96, 2003.

38. Audet MC, Moreau M, Koltun WD, et al; the ORTHO/EVRA Study Group: Evaluation of contraceptive efficacy and cycle control of a transdermal contraceptive patch vs an oral contraceptive: A randomized controlled trial. JAMA 285:2347–2354, 2001.

39. Zieman M, Guillebaud J, Weisberg E, et al: Contraceptive efficacy and cycle control with the Ortho Evra/Evra transdermal system: The analysis of pooled data. Fertil Steril 77(Suppl 2):S13–S18, 2002.

40. Bjarnadottir RJ, Tuppurainen M, Killick SR: Comparison of cycle control with a combined contraceptive vaginal ring and oral levonorgestrel/ethinyl estradiol. Am J Obstet Gynecol 186:389–395, 2002.

41. Kaunitz AM, Garceau RJ, Cromie MA; Lunelle Study Group: Comparative safety, efficacy and cycle control of Lunelle monthly contraceptive injection (medroxyprogesterone acetate and estradiol cypionate injectable suspension) and Ortho-Novum 7/7/7 oral contraceptive (norethindrone/ethinyl estradiol triphasic). Contraception 60:179–187, 1999.

42. Beral V, Hermon C, Kay C, et al: Mortality associated with oral contraceptive use: 25 year follow up of a cohort of 46,000 women from Royal College of General Practitioners' oral contraception study. Br Med J 318:96–100, 1999.

43. Oddens BJ, Visser AP, Verner HM, et al: Contraceptive use and attitudes in Great Britain. Contraception 496:73–86, 1994.

44. Hassan DF, Petta CA, Aldrighi JM, et al: Weight variation in a cohort of women using copper IUD for contraception. Contraception 68:27–30, 2003.

45. Endrikat J, Gerlinger C, Cronin M, et al: Blood pressure stability in a normotensive population during intake of monophasic oral contraceptive pills containing 20 μg ethinyl oestradiol and 75 μg desogestrel. Eur J Contracept Reprod Health Care 6:159–166, 2001.

46. Skegg DCG: Third generation oral contraceptives. Br Med J 321:190–191, 2000.

47. Tanis BC, Van der Bosch MAAJ, Kemmeren JM, et al: Oral contraceptives and the risk of myocardial infarction. N Engl J Med 345:1787–1793, 2001.

48. Dunn N, Thorogood M, Faragher B, et al: Oral contraceptives and myocardial infarction: Results of the MICA case control study. Br Med J 318:1579–1584, 1999.

49. Khader YS, Rice J, John L, Abueita O: Oral contraceptive use and risk of myocardial infarction: A meta-analysis. Contraception 68:11–17, 2003.

50. Vessey M, Painter R, Yeates D: Mortality in relation to oral contraceptive use and cigarette smoking. Lancet 362:185–191, 2003.

51. World Health Organization: Cardiovascular Disease and Steroid Hormone Contraception: Report of a WHO Scientific Group. WHO Technical Report Series No 877. Geneva, WHO, 1998.

52. Chang CL, Donaghy M, Poulter NR, for the WHO Collaborative Study of Cardiovascular Disease and Steroid Hormone Contraception: Migraine and stroke in young women: Case-control study. Br Med J 318:13–18, 1999.

53. The Collaborative Group on Hormonal Factors in Breast Cancer: Breast cancer and hormonal contraceptives: A collaborative re-analysis of individual data on 53,297 women with breast cancer and 100,239 women without breast cancer from 54 epidemiological studies. Lancet 347:1717–1727, 1996.

54. Marchbanks PA, McDonald JA, Wilson HG, et al: Oral contraceptives and the risk of breast cancer. N Engl J Med 346:2025–2032, 2002.

55. Moreno V, Bosch FX, Munoz N, et al, for the International Agency for Research on Cancer (IARC) Multicentric Cervical Cancer Study Group: Effect of oral contraceptives on risk of cervical cancer in women with human papillomavirus infection: The IARC multicentric case-control study. Lancet 359:1085–1092, 2002.

56. Rice CF, Killick SR, Dieben T, et al: A comparison of the inhibition of ovulation achieved by desogestrel 75 μg and levonorgestrel 30 μg daily. Hum Reprod 14:982–985, 1999.

57. Bahamondes L, Del Castillo S, Tabares G, et al: Comparison of weight increase in users of depot medroxyprogesterone acetate and copper IUD up to 5 years. Contraception 64:223–225, 2001.

58. World Health Organization Collaborative Study of Cardiovascular Disease and Steroid Hormone Contraception: Cardiovascular disease and use of oral and injectable progestogen-only contraceptives and combined injectable contraceptives: Results of an international multicentre case-control study. Contraception 57:315–324, 1998.

59. Vasilakis C, Jick H, del Mar Melero-Montes M: Risk of idiopathic venous thromboembolism in users of progestogens alone. Lancet 354:1610–1611, 1999.

60. International Collaborative Post-Marketing Surveillance of Norplant: Post-marketing surveillance of Norplant contraceptive implants: II. Non-reproductive health. Contraception 63:187–209, 2001.

61. Westhoff C: Depot-medroxyprogesterone acetate injection (Depo-Provera): A highly effective contraceptive option with proven long term safety. Contraception 68:75–87, 2003.

62. Banks E, Berrington A, Casabonne D: Overview of the relationship between use of progestogen-only contraceptives and bone mineral density. Br J Obstet Gynecol 108:1214–1221, 2001.

63. Cundy T, Cornish J, Roberts H, Reid IR: Menopausal bone loss in long-term users of depot medroxyprogesterone acetate contraception. Am J Obstet Gynecol 186:978–983, 2002.

64. Cromer BA: Bone mineral density in adolescent and young adult women on injectable or oral contraception. Curr Opin Obstet Gynecol 15:353–357, 2003.

65. World Health Organization: Improving Access to Quality Care in Family Planning: Selected Practice Recommendations. Geneva, WHO Reproductive Health and Research, 2002. Available at www.who.int/reproductive-health/publications/index.htm.

66. Westhoff C: Emergency contraception. N Engl J Med 349:1830–1835, 2003.

67. Croxatto HB, Devoto L, Durand M, et al: Mechanism of action of hormonal preparations of emergency contraception: A review of the literature. Contraception 63:111–121, 2001.

68. Croxatto HB, Fuentalba B, Brache V, et al: Effects of the Yuzpe regimen, given during the follicular phase on ovarian function. Contraception 65:121–128, 2002.

69. Trussel J, Ellertson C, Dorflinger L: Effectiveness of the Yuzpe regimen of emergency contraception by cycle day of intercourse: Implications for mechanism of action. Contraception 67:167–171, 2003.

# Female Sexual Dysfunction

## Kathleen E. Walsh and Laura Berman

## INTRODUCTION

Regardless of age or gender, sexuality is one of the most important quality of life issues. Throughout individuals' lives, the expressions of their need for intimacy change continually. These expressions are influenced by a variety of social, psychological, environmental, religious, and physical factors (Table 160-1). The female sexual response involves a unique and complex set of factors that are different from those of males. The approach to female patients and their sexual function should remain separate from the approach taken with males. A woman's emotional intimacy with her partner can have a strong influence on her need and ability to find and respond to sexual stimuli. For many women, their physiologic response to sexual stimuli is frequently less of a factor to a meaningful sexual encounter than is their emotional response. Assessment for possible physiologic barriers to a healthy and satisfying sexual life, however, should be completed for every woman. A comprehensive approach, addressing both the physiologic and psychological factors, is instrumental to the evaluation of female patients with sexual complaints.

## EPIDEMIOLOGY

Sexual dysfunction has been recognized as a common medical problem in both sexes and in all age groups. The prevalence of female sexual dysfunction is a topic that has generated extensive discussions in medical and lay communities alike. Data from the National Health and Social Life Survey (NHSLS), a study of adult sexual behavior in the United States, found that sexual dysfunction (SD) is more prevalent in women (43%) than in men (31%). The survey included 1749 women between the ages of 18 and 59 years old. Younger women and those with poor physical or emotional health had more sexual complaints than did older women. Older women, however, had more complaints with genital lubrication.[1] In a study involving 329 women, aged 18 to 73, a self-administered standardized sexual function questionnaire identified 38.1% with anxiety or inhibition during sexual activity, 16.3% lacked sexual pleasure and 15.4% had difficulty achieving orgasm.[2]

The Yale midlife study included interviews with 130 postmenopausal women; 68% of the women reported having sexual problems. Specific complaints included vaginal dryness (58%), dyspareunia (39%), and a decrease in clitoral sensitivity (36%), orgasmic intensity (35%), and orgasmic frequency (29%).[3]

## FEMALE SEXUAL RESPONSE CYCLE

To assess and treat female sexual problems adequately, it is imperative to understand and appreciate the female sexual response cycle. Masters and Johnson characterized the female sexual response cycle in 1966, identifying four consecutive phases: excitement, plateau, orgasm, and resolution.[4] In 1974, Kaplan identified a three-phase model, which included desire, arousal, and orgasm.[5] In both of these cycles, excitement or sexual desire is depicted as a spontaneous force that by itself stimulates sexual arousal. Recently, Basson proposed a five-phase model focusing on intimacy. In this model, the desire to enhance intimacy is seen as the driving force of the female sexual response cycle. The cycle begins with the basic needs for intimacy, which include mutuality, respect, and communication. When these needs are met, a woman will seek out and will be more receptive to sexual stimuli. A woman's intimacy is enhanced and the cycle strengthened if there is an overall positive emotional and physical interaction.[6]

## CLASSIFICATION OF FEMALE SEXUAL DYSFUNCTION

In 1998, the American Foundation of Urologic Disease (AFUD) Consensus Panel classified female sexual dysfunction into four areas: desire, arousal, orgasmic, and sexual pain disorders.[7]

**(1) Hypoactive Sexual Desire Disorder** Hypoactive sexual desire disorder is the persistent or recurring deficiency (or absence) of sexual fantasies, thoughts, and/or receptivity to sexual activity, which causes personal distress. The cause may be either physiologic, psychological, or a combination of both. Physiologic etiologies such as hormonal abnormalities, neurogenic conditions, or vascular conditions can contribute to low sexual desire. Hypoactive sexual desire disorder can also be a psychologically or emotionally based problem that is influenced by a history of sexual abuse or trauma, depression, and anxiety. Lack of desire can be secondary to

**Table 160-1** Major Factors Influencing Sexual Function

Personal experiences
Family
Friends
Religion
Education
Psychological conditions
Physical diseases/conditions
Medications
Menopause/aging
Partner sexual function
Quality of relationship
Infertility

substance abuse, particularly drug and alcohol abuse, resulting in problems of dependency and lack of self-esteem.

Uneven desire in a relationship can have a significant impact on arousal. Feelings of anger, resentment, hostility, or disappointment can occur in one or both partners, resulting in a withdrawal from the intimate relationship.

**(2) Sexual Arousal Disorder**   Arousal disorder is the persistent or recurring inability to attain or maintain adequate sexual excitement, causing personal distress. It may be experienced as a lack of subjective excitement or a lack of genital (lubrication/swelling) or other somatic responses. Physiologically, a woman may have diminished vaginal/clitoral blood flow and sensation secondary to vascular disease, pelvic surgery or trauma, or medication side effects. These conditions may occur secondary to psychological factors as well. Some women may experience poor body image, promoting increased self-consciousness in sexual situations and therefore an inhibited response. Additional psychological barriers to adequate arousal include low self-esteem, lack of confidence, stress, and/or anxiety.

**(3) Orgasmic Disorder**   Orgasmic disorder is the persistent or recurrent difficulty, delay in, or absence of attaining orgasm, following sufficient sexual stimulation and arousal, that causes personal distress. Orgasmic disorder may be a primary (never achieved orgasm) or a secondary condition (was able to achieve orgasm at one point in time, but now no longer able). Primary orgasmic disorder is typically caused by emotional trauma or sexual abuse. It can also be due to a woman's lack of awareness of her own body, including areas of arousal and methods of stimulation. Secondary orgasmic disorder is thought to be often a result of neurogenic or vascular conditions, hormonal abnormalities, or medications (Table 160-2).

**Table 160-2** Common Medications with Sexual Side Effects

| Class | Examples |
| --- | --- |
| **Antihypertensives** | Diuretics |
| | Adrenergic antagonists |
| | β-Blockers |
| | Calcium-channel blockers |
| **Chemotherapeutic** | Alkylating agents (cyclophosphamide) |
| **Central nervous system agents** | Anticholinergics |
| | Anticonvulsants |
| | Antidepressants |
| | Antipsychotics |
| | Narcotics |
| | Sedatives/anxiolytics |
| **Medications affecting hormone levels** | Antiandrogens (cimetidine, spironolactone) |
| | Antiestrogens (tamoxifen, raloxifen) |
| | Oral contraceptives |

Orgasmic disorder can also be situational. This refers to the woman who can experience orgasm in some circumstances (e.g., masturbation), but not in other situations. Situational orgasmic disorder, while often associated with a trauma history, is also commonly related to emotional stressors and relationship conflicts. Coital orgasmic disorder is another type of anorgasmia commonly experienced by women. It is the inability to achieve orgasm from intercourse without added sexual stimulation. It is estimated that only 30% of women experience orgasm regularly from sexual intercourse. Many women who describe themselves as anorgasmic, in fact, experience coital anorgasmia. The majority of heterosexual women and their partners believe that they should be able to obtain orgasm through sexual intercourse. This belief, when held by either partner, can cause significant stress, disappointment, and apprehension toward sexual activity.

**(4) Sexual Pain Disorders**   Sexual pain disorders include dyspareunia (genital pain with intercourse), vaginismus (involuntary muscle spasms of the outer third of the vagina), and other conditions (genital pain caused by noncoital sexual stimulation). Other etiologic explanations for sexual pain disorder include previous obstetric or gynecologic trauma to the genitalia, radiation atrophy, and inflammation or infection of the urinary tract and/or rectum. Pelvic floor disorders can also cause pain with sexual activity. Disorders of the pelvic floor include incontinence, cystocele, rectocele, enterocele, and vaginal and uterine prolapse. Older women are at increased risk for pelvic floor disorders because of muscular and vascular changes associated with age and childbirth.

Psychological concerns such as fear, anxiety, and intimacy issues can play a significant role in patients presenting with dyspareunia. Interpersonal conflict can be a primary contributing factor in approximately 30% of the cases of dyspareunia. These relationships are often characterized by poor communication, with particular difficulty in discussing sex and emotions. Psychological pressure to "perform" sexually can also be present, especially when sexual intercourse is the primary source of sexual pleasure and coital orgasm is a measure of a successful or intimate sexual encounter.

## HORMONAL INFLUENCE ON FEMALE SEXUAL DYSFUNCTION

### TESTOSTERONE

The mean circulating level of testosterone gradually decreases with age. Testosterone levels in a 20-year-old female are approximately two times greater than in a 40-year-old. Testosterone is carried in the peripheral blood bound to sex hormone–binding globulin (SHBG). Only 1% to 2% of total testosterone circulates unbound, and the nonbound (free) testosterone is biologically active. In women who have undergone a bilateral oophorectomy, testosterone and androstenedione levels decrease by 50%. Dehydroepiandrosterone (DHEA) and dehydroepiandrosterone sulfate (DHEA-S) levels also decrease with age, which further contributes to the decline in testosterone.[8] Low levels of testosterone are associated with decreased sexual arousal, libido, sexual responsiveness, genital sensation, and orgasm.[9,10]

There is no direct regulator, stimulator, or feedback mechanism of androgen production in women. An increase in ovarian activity or adrenal activity has been shown to cause a rise in androgen production.[11] Conditions such as hypopituitarism, adrenal insufficiency, anorexia nervosa, exercise-induced amenorrhea, and premature ovarian failure can cause androgen deficiency. Lower androgen levels can also occur in women taking exogenous corticosteroids and in women with chronic illness. Oral administration of hormones that elevate SHBG levels and reduce bioavailable androgens can place women at risk of androgen deficiency. Increased levels of estradiol, as with the oral contraceptive pill or hormone replacement therapy (HRT), can increase SHBG, which, in turn, decreases biologically available testosterone.[12,13] Methods used to measure testosterone vary significantly. The most sensitive measurement of testosterone availability would be testing "free" or unbound testosterone levels, but commercial assays for free testosterone are inconsistent. Many investigators prefer to use the free testosterone index, which is the calculated ratio of testosterone to SHBG.

## ESTROGEN

In premenopausal women, the ovaries are the principal source of estrogen. More than 60% is estradiol secreted directly by the ovaries, and the remainder is estrone derived from extraglandular conversion of androstenedione. After menopause, the ovarian contribution is reduced and extraglandular formation of estrone from adrenal androstenedione predominates.[14]

Circulating estradiol levels affect both the peripheral and central nervous system, influencing nerve transmission. In a study involving postmenopausal women, estrogen replacement improved clitoral and vaginal vibration and pressure thresholds to premenopausal levels.[15] The vasoprotective and vasodilatory effects of estrogen have also been demonstrated. Estrogen replacement therapy has been shown to increase vaginal, clitoral, and urethral arterial flow in postmenopausal women.[16] Low estradiol levels are associated with thinning of mucosal epithelium, atrophy of vaginal wall smooth muscle, and an increase in vaginal pH. The less acidic environment within the vaginal canal can lead to vaginal infections, incontinence, urinary tract infections, and sexual dysfunction.[17] Levels of estradiol below 50 pg/mL have been directly correlated with increased sexual complaints.[18]

## PATHOGENESIS

Current evidence suggests that up to 50% of cases of sexual dysfunction may have some type of organic component. Conditions that have been associated with sexual dysfunction can be categorized as vascular, hormonal, neurogenic, musculogenic, psychogenic, and due to medications (Table 160-3).

## VASCULAR

Sexual dysfunction secondary to diabetes, cardiovascular disease, hypertension, peripheral vascular disease, and tobacco abuse has been demonstrated in males with erectile dysfunction.[19,20] Several of these conditions can lead to diminished iliohypogastric/pudendal arterial blood flow. In females, this is termed *clitoral* and *vaginal vascular insufficiency syndrome*.[21] Decreased genital blood flow can lead to impairment in both vascular and muscular tissues. This can lead to symptoms of vaginal dryness, decreased sensation and arousal, and dyspareunia. Pelvic fractures, blunt trauma, surgical disruption, radiation, or chronic perineal pressure all have the potential to lead to diminished vaginal and clitoral blood flow and, thus, sexual dysfunction.

## HORMONAL

Menopause, surgical or medical castration, premature ovarian failure, dysfunction of the hypothalamic-pituitary axis, and chronic birth control use are the most common causes of primary endocrine abnormalities in women. Estrogen and testosterone levels play a significant role in regulating female sexual function. A decrease in estrogen levels is associated with adverse neurovascular events affecting vaginal, clitoral, and urethral tissues.[22] Low testosterone levels in females have

**Table 160-3  Medical Risk Factors Associated with Sexual Dysfunction**

**NEUROLOGIC**
Parkinson's disease
Multiple sclerosis
Cerebral vascular accident
Epilepsy
Spinal cord injuries

**VASCULAR**
Diabetes mellitus
Hypertension
Peripheral vascular disease

**ENDOCRINE**
Hypogonadism
Hyperprolactinemia
Hypo/hyperthyroidism
Lipid disorders

**MUSCULOGENIC**
Pelvic floor muscle hyper/hypotonicity

**PSYCHOGENIC**
Depression
Anxiety/obsession-compulsive disorder
Social stressors
Religious inhibitions
Posttraumatic sexual experiences
Dysfunctional attitudes about sex

**OTHER**
Autoimmune disorders
Bowel disease (colostomy)
Bladder disease (incontinence, cystitis)
Skin disorders (contact dermatitis, eczema)

**MEDICATIONS**
(see Table 160-2)

been associated with a decline in sexual arousal, genital stimulation, libido, and orgasm.[23]

## NEUROGENIC

Neurogenic sexual dysfunction can occur in women with injury and/or disease of the central or peripheral nervous system. In a study examining the impact on spinal cord injury and orgasm in 68 premenopausal women, it was reported that less than 50% were able to achieve orgasm, compared with 100% of able-bodied women.[24] A questionnaire-based assessment of sexual function in 120 women (aged 30–46) with Parkinson's disease reported that bowel and bladder dysfunction secondary to the disease and/or medications had a negative impact on sexual function. In addition, 84% of the women had a decrease in libido and 55% had a decrease in intercourse.[25] Studies involving women with diabetes and multiple sclerosis report increased complaints of excessive fatigue, diminished genital sensation, limited sexual desire, decreased vaginal lubrication, and an increased time to reach orgasm.[26,27]

## MUSCULOGENIC

The pelvic floor musculature is composed of the levator ani and perineal membrane, which influence female responsiveness during sexual activity. The perineal membrane consists of the bulbocavernous and ischiocavernosus muscles. These muscles contract both voluntarily and involuntarily, intensifying sexual arousal and orgasm. The levator ani muscles are involved in modulating motor responses during vaginal receptivity and orgasm. Hyper- and hypotonicity in the muscles can occur secondary to trauma (surgery, radiation, childbirth) and aging. This can cause vaginal hypoanesthesia, coital anorgasmia, or urinary incontinence during sexual intercourse or orgasm. Hypertonicity of the levator ani muscles can cause sexual pain disorders such as vaginismus, which leads to dyspareunia.[28]

## PSYCHOGENIC

Despite the presence or absence of organic disease, psychological issues can significantly affect sexual function. In every woman with a sexual complaint, there are relationship, emotional, and medical factors occurring simultaneously and interacting with one another in a nonlinear fashion. From the relationship standpoint, partner sexual dysfunction, lack of communication, relationship conflict, and lack of information about sexual stimulation can all impact on a woman's sexual response. When a woman is struggling with a sexual function complaint, it may create conflict in the relationship, which then cycles back to affect her function negatively.[29] Additional mood disorders and psychological stressors include depression, low self-esteem, anxiety, obsessive-compulsive disorder, chronic stress, and history of sexual abuse, all of which can negatively impact a woman's sexual function.[30,31]

## MEDICATIONS

While many prescription medications have been implicated in causing sexual dysfunction, those most frequently recognized are the antihypertensives, antidepressants, and antipsychotic medications (see Table 160-2).[32] Research is limited on medications and substances believed to cause female sexual dysfunction compared to studies on male impotence. Many articles present only subjective evidence or case reports for medications causing sexual dysfunction in women.

## DIAGNOSIS AND TREATMENT

All women are at risk for sexual dysfunction. Not all women, however, approach their clinician for evaluation. It is important to remember that, in many ways, a sexual problem is no different from any other medical problem. Therefore, the line of questioning can follow the same principles (Table 160-4). Once information is obtained, a thorough physical examination, including a pelvic examination, should be completed. In women who are suspected of having hormonal abnormalities, particularly postmenopausal, the following baseline laboratory tests should be considered: total testosterone, free testosterone, follicle-stimulating hormone (FSH), luteinizing hormone (LH), estradiol, DHEA, SHBG, and prolactin.

In those patients in whom an underlying medical condition has been diagnosed, treatment to correct or control progression should be completed. Consideration should be given to discontinuation of any medication suspected of contributing to sexual dysfunction or, if possible, switching to an alternative medication. For patients with a component of psychogenic dysfunction, referral should be made to a psychotherapist with expertise in sexual dysfunction. There are identifiable "psychosexual red flags" that necessitate appropriate therapy referral (Table 160-5).

## MEDICATIONS: HORMONES

### Estrogen

Medical management of sexual dysfunction in women has focused on hormonal treatment. Both estrogen and testosterone are being used alone and in combination. In postmenopausal women, estrogen replacement has been found to improve clitoral and vaginal sensitivity, increase libido, restore vibratory and pressure thresholds, and decrease symptoms of vaginal dryness and pain during intercourse.[33] Estrogen is available in several forms including oral pill, dermal patch, vaginal ring, and cream. The vaginal ring is a therapeutic option for women with breast cancer who are unable to take oral or transdermal estrogen. Several novel estrogen preparations are under study. New modes of delivery of estrogens, such as intranasal estrogen and estrogen gel, appear promising.[34,35] A low-dose combination estradiol ethinyl ($E_2$)/norethindrone acetate NETA ($E_2$/NETA) patch is also being investigated.[36]

Estrogen, especially when begun early in menopause, has been shown to be beneficial in the prevention and treatment of osteoporosis. Estrogen replacement therapy has also been shown to reduce the risk for colon cancer, but not rectal cancers.[37] Postmenopausal estrogen replacement, with or without progestin therapy, has a generally favorable impact on lipids, improves endothelial function, and has anti-inflammatory and antioxidant effects. However, recent results from two large randomized studies, the Heart and Estrogen/Progestin Replacement Study (HERS) and the Women's Health Initiative (WHI) study suggest potential health risks in postmenopausal women taking estrogen/progestin and estrogen alone. HERS reported that there may be a transitory increase in coronary risk after starting hormone therapy in women with established coronary heart disease, and a decreased risk thereafter.[38] The WHI study involved several different randomized clinical trials. The estrogen/progestin trial included 16,608 postmenopausal women, aged 50 to 79 years. This trial was terminated early because of the increased risk of coronary artery disease, breast cancer, ischemic stroke, and venous thromboembolic disease.[39–41] The estrogen-only arm of the study, which included

---

| **Table 160-4** Sexual Dysfunction Clinical Assessment Questioning |
| --- |
| 1. Clarification of the sexual problem. (e.g., Can you tell me more about it? What are all the sexual symptoms? Which symptom came first?) |
| 2. How long has the problem been occurring? (primary = lifelong, or secondary = following a period of "normal" sexual functioning) |
| 3. Is the problem present in all situations? (global; e.g., with all partners, different locations, positions) or only in certain situations (situational; e.g., only at home, late evening hours) |
| 4. Is there anything that makes the situation better (e.g., going away to a hotel for the weekend, positioning)? Is there anything that makes it worse (e.g., menstrual cycle; partner or self expectations)? |
| 5. How is it affecting the patient's relationship with her partner (e.g., current intimate relationship, partner's reaction to problem)? |
| 6. What is the motivation for evaluation and treatment (e.g., dissolving of marriage/partnership, reached a "breaking point")? |
| 7. Does the partner have any sexual problems (e.g., low libido, male impotence)? |
| 8. Any prior assessment or treatment for problem? What was the outcome? |
| 9. What are the patient's thoughts regarding possible causes for the problem? |
| 10. What is the patient's medical, surgical, and psychological history? |

---

| **Table 160-5** Psychosexual Red Flags for Further Assessment* |
| --- |
| The couple experiences relationship conflicts (e.g., lack of intimacy). |
| The symptoms are lifelong, not acquired. |
| The symptoms are situational (e.g., don't exist when stress is removed or when with another partner). |
| The patient has a history of sexual abuse or trauma. |
| The patient has a psychiatric history. |
| The patient has a history of or is presently experiencing depression, anxiety, and/or stress. |
| The partner has a sexual dysfunction. |

*None of these factors guarantee that the problem is psychosexually based, but they do suggest a need for further clarification by a trained sex therapist.

10,739 postmenopausal women, aged 50 to 79 years, with prior hysterectomy, was discontinued in February 2004 because of the increased risk of ischemic stroke.[42]

## Testosterone

Decreased testosterone levels can be seen in women with premature ovarian failure and after natural, surgical, or post chemotherapy-induced menopause.

Testosterone supplementation has been shown to improve mood and well-being in premenopausal and naturally or surgically induced postmenopausal women.[43,44]

Currently, there are no U.S. Food and Drug Administration (FDA)-approved androgen therapies for female sexual dysfunction. There are, however, several testosterone products in use for "off label" therapy. For replacement purposes, testosterone is available in oral pill form, sublingual form, dermal patch, and cream. Oral methyltestosterone is available in the United States either alone or in combination with estrogen (Estratest). In postmenopausal women who experience low libido, dyspareunia, or lack of vaginal lubrication, testosterone is usually prescribed in combination with low-dose estrogen. Until long-term safety data become available, however, it seems wise to consider the contraindications of the low-dose estrogen preparations to be the same as those of the traditional preparations. The transdermal testosterone patch is under clinical investigation. Preliminary results have been promising.[45,46]

Side effects of testosterone use that need to be monitored in women include weight gain, clitoral enlargement, increased facial hair, and hypercholesterolemia. Measurement of testosterone levels (free and total) before and after therapy, lipid panels, and liver function tests are recommended.[47,48]

## INVESTIGATIONAL MEDICATIONS AND DEVICES

Secondary to the increase in both clinical and biologic research in female sexual dysfunction, several new medications

| Table 160-6 | Investigation Medications and Devices |
|---|---|

Phosphodiesterase ($PDE_5$) inhibitor
Topical alprostadil/prostaglandin (PGE-1)
α-1 and α-2 Adrenergic antagonist
Vasoactive intestinal peptide (VIP)
Apomorphine
α Melanocyte stimulating hormone
Serotonin 5-HT(1A), 5-HT(2A) agonists
Sacral nerve stimulator

and devices are now being investigated for both pre- and postmenopausal women (Table 160-6).

## SUMMARY

Female sexual dysfunction is a multicausal medical problem. Evaluation of the patient should include a comprehensive and collaborative effort by a physician and psychologist. Although there are physiologic similarities between males and females, the complexity of female sexual dysfunction remains distinct from that of a man. The context in which a woman experiences her sexuality, regardless of age, is equally if not more important than the physiologic outcome she experiences. It is imperative that issues regarding how a woman views her sexuality be addressed *before* beginning medical therapy or determining treatment efficacies. There is a need for the development of well-organized, randomized, controlled studies on appropriate assessment and successful intervention for sexual dysfunction in women. Investigational drugs and devices may play a small, but crucial, role in the search for safe and effective treatment options.

## REFERENCES

1. Laumann EO, Paik A, Rosen RC: Sexual dysfunction in the United States: Prevalence and predictors. JAMA 281:537–544,1999.
2. Sarrel PM, Whitehead MI: Sex and menopause: Defining the issues. Maturitas 7:217–224, 1985.
3. Rosen RC, Taylor JF, Leiblum SR, et al: Prevalence of sexual dysfunction in women: Results of a survey study of 329 women in an outpatient gynecological clinic. J Sex Marital Ther 19:171–188, 1993.
4. Masters EH, Johnson VE: Human Sexual Response. Boston, Little, Brown, 1966.
5. Kaplan HS: The New Sex Therapy. London, Baillière Tindall, 1974.
6. Basson R. Using a different model for female sexual response to address women's problematic low sexual desire. J Sex Marital Ther 27:395–403, 2001.
7. Basson R, Berman J, Burnett A, et al: Report of the international consensus development conference on female sexual dysfunction: Definitions and classifications. J Urol 183:888–893, 2000.
8. Burger HG: Androgen production in women. Fertil Steril 77(Suppl 4):3–5, 2002.
9. Talakoub L, Munarriz R, Hoag L, et al: Epidemiological characteristics of 250 women with sexual dysfunction who

presented for initial evaluation. J Sex Marital Ther 28(Suppl 1):217–224, 2002.
10. Davis S: Testosterone deficiency in women. J Reprod Med 46(Suppl 3):291–296, 2001.
11. Rittmaster RS: Clinical relevance of testosterone and dihydrotestosterone metabolism in women. Am J Med 98:(Suppl 1A):17–21, 1995.
12. Burger HG, Dudley EC, Hopper JL, et al: The endocrinology of menopausal transition: A cross-sectional study of population-based sample. J Clin Endocrinol Metab 80:3537–3547, 1995.
13. Davis SR, Burger HG: Androgens and the postmenopausal woman. J Clinical Endocrinol Metab 81:2759–2764, 1996.
14. Simpson ER, Davis SR: Minireview: Aromatase and the regulation of estrogen biosynthesis—some new perspectives. Endocrinology 142:4589–4594, 2001.
15. Sarrel P, Dobay B, Wiita B: Estrogen and estrogen-androgen replacement in postmenopausal women dissatisfied with estrogen-only therapy: Sexual behavior and neuroendocrine response. J Reprod Med 43:847–856, 1998.
16. Sarrel PM: Ovarian hormones and vaginal blood flow: Using laser doppler velocimetry to measure effects in a clinical trial of post-menopausal

women. Int J Impot Res 10:S91–S93, 1998.
17. Caillouette JC, Sharp CF Jr, Zimmerman GJ, Roy S: Vaginal pH as a marker for bacterial pathogens and menopausal status. Am J Obstet Gynecol 176:1270–1275, discussion 1275–1277, 1997.
18. Sarrel PM: Sexuality and menopause. Obstet Gynec 75(Suppl 4):26S–30S, 1990.
19. Benet AE, Melman A: The epidemiology of erectile dysfunction. Urol Clin North Am 22:699–709, 1995.
20. Kaiser FE, Korenman SG: Impotence in diabetic men. Am J Med 85:147–152, 1988.
21. Goldstein I, Berman JR: Vasculogenic female sexual dysfunction: Vaginal engorgement and clitoral erectile insufficiency syndromes. Int J Impot Res 10(Suppl 2):S84–S90, discussion S98–S101, 1998.
22. Berman JR, Berman LA, Werbin TJ, et al: Clinical evaluation of female sexual function: Effects of age and estrogen status on subjective and physiologic sexual responses. Int J Impot Res 11(Suppl 1):S31–S38, 1999.
23. Minto CL, Liao KL, Conway GS, Creighton SM: Sexual function in women with complete androgen insensitivity syndrome. Fertil Steril 80:157–164, 2003.

24. Sipski ML, Alexander CJ, Rosen RC: Sexual response in women with spinal cord injuries: Implications for our understanding of the able-bodied. J Sex Marital Ther 25:11–22, 1999.

25. Sakakibara R, Shinotoh H, Uchiyama T, et al: Questionnaire-based assessment of pelvic organ dysfunction in Parkinson's disease. Auton Neurosci 92:76–85, 2001.

26. Le Mone P: The physical effects of diabetes on sexuality in women. Diabetes Educ 22:361–366, 1996.

27. McCabe MP, McKern S, McDonald E, Vowels LM: Changes over time in sexual and relationship functioning of people with multiple sclerosis. J Sex Marital Ther 29:305–321, 2003.

28. Mallett VT, Bump RC: The epidemiology of female pelvic floor dysfunction. Curr Opin Obstet Gynecol 6:308–312, 1994.

29. Meston, CM: The psychophysiological assessment of female sexual function. J Sex Educ Ther 25:6–16, 2000.

30. Aksaray G, Yelken B, Kaptanoglu C, et al: Sexuality in women with obsessive compulsive disorder. J Sex Marital Ther 27:273–277, 2001.

31. Clayton AH: Recognition and assessment of sexual dysfunction associated with depression. J Clin Psych 62(Suppl 3):5–9, 2001.

32. Finger WW, Lund M, Slagle MA: Medications that may contribute to sexual disorders: A guide to assessment and treatment in family practice. J Fam Pract 44:33–43, 1997.

33. Collins A, Landgren BM: Reproductive health, use of estrogen and experience of symptoms in postmenopausal women: A population based study. Maturitas 20:101–11, 1994.

34. Lopes P, Rozenberg S, Graaf J, et al: Aerodiol versus the transdermal route: Perspectives for patient preference. Maturitas 38(Suppl 1):S31–S39, 2001.

35. Panay N, Toth K, Pelissier C, Studd J: Dose ranging studies of a novel intranasal estrogen replacement therapy. Maturitas 38(Suppl 1):S15–S22, 2001.

36. Travassos de Figueiredo A, Amelia Sobreira Gomes M, Clapauch R: Comparison of gel and patch estradiol replacement in Brazil, a tropical country. Maturitas 36:69–74, 2000.

37. Burkman RT, Collins JA, Greene RA: Current perspectives on benefits and risks of hormone replacement therapy. Am J Obstet Gynecol 185(Suppl 2):S13–S23, 2001.

38. Vittinghoff E, Shlipak MG, Varosy PD, et al: Risk factors and secondary prevention in women with heart disease: The Heart and Estrogen/Progestin Replacement Study. Ann Intern Med 138:81–89, 2003.

39. Manson JE, Hsia J, Johnson KC, et al: Estrogen plus progestin and the risk of coronary heart disease. N Engl J Med 349:523–534, 2003.

40. Chlebowski RT, Hendrix SL, Langer RD, et al; WHI Investigators: Influence of estrogen plus progestin on breast cancer and mammography in healthy postmenopausal women: The Women's Health Initiative Randomized Trial. JAMA 289:3243–3253, 2003.

41. Wassertheil-Smoller S, Hendrix SL, Limacher M, et al; WHI Investigators: Effect of estrogen plus progestin on stroke in postmenopausal women: The Women's Health Initiative: A randomized trial. JAMA 289:2673–2684, 2003.

42. Anderson GL, Limacher M, Assaf AR, et al; Women's Health Initiative Steering Committee: Effects of conjugated equine estrogen in postmenopausal women with hysterectomy: The Women's Health Initiative randomized controlled trial. JAMA 291:1701–1712, 2004.

43. Goldstat R, Briganti E, Tran J, et al: Transdermal testosterone therapy improves well-being, mood, and sexual function in premenopausal women. Menopause 10:390–398, 2003.

44. Davis SR, Tran J: Testosterone influences libido and well being in women. Trends Endocrinol Metab 12:33–37, 2001.

45. Shifren JL, Braunstein GD, Simon JA, et al: Transdermal testosterone treatment in women with impaired sexual function after oophorectomy. New Eng J Med 343:682–688, 2000.

46. Mazer NA: New clinical applications of transdermal testosterone delivery in men and women. J Control Release 65:303–315, 2000.

47. Basaria S, Dobs AS: Safety and adverse effects of androgens: How to counsel patients. Mayo Clin Proc 79(Suppl 4):S25–S32, 2004.

48. Bachmann G, Bancroft J, Braunstein G, et al: Female androgen insufficiency: The Princeton consensus statement on definition, classification, and assessment. Fertil Steril 77:660–665, 2002.

# Premenstrual Syndrome

## Nancy E. Reame

DEFINITION
  Diagnostic Considerations
PATHOPHYSIOLOGY
  PMS as a Reproductive Endocrine Disorder
  PMS as an Affective Disorder
  PMS as a Disorder of Neuroactive Steroid Action

TREATMENT APPROACHES

FUTURE DIRECTIONS IN PMS RESEARCH

## DEFINITION

Although premenstrual symptoms such as bloating, acne, breast pain, and constipation accompany cyclic ovulation in up to 80% of reproductive-age women, in some 30% to 40% of these cases, the cluster of postovulatory molimina are so debilitating or extensive or coupled with fatigue and mood swings as to require some form of self-medication or health-care treatment for relief.[1–3] Premenstrual syndrome (PMS), first described by Frank in 1931, includes a heterogenous group of both physical and psychological symptoms that are present on a reccuring basis during the late luteal phase of each menstrual cycle. Central to the diagnosis is that symptoms disappear in the follicular phase. Thus, it is the timing, duration, and severity of symptoms, not the symptoms per se, that distinguish PMS as a distinct medical disorder.[4] An emotional/behavioral component, such as depressed mood, anxiety, lability, or irritability, which markedly interferes with normal activities and leads to a significant deterioration of interpersonal relationships must be present to meet the criteria for premenstrual dysphoric disorder (PMDD; Table 161-1). Recognized since 1994 by the American Psychiatric Association (APA) as an emerging psychiatric disorder,[5,6] this is the most severe form of PMS, with an estimated lifetime prevalence of 2% to 10% in child-bearing women.[7–10] When the degree of social burden and lowered quality of life is taken into account, the prevalence of clinically significant dysphoric PMS is estimated to be at least double these rates.[10]

In 2000, the American College of Obstetricians and Gynecologists (ACOG) published a practice bulletin on the topic of PMS that used a similar set of criteria for diagnosis and outlined recommendations for the treatment of clinically significant (severe) premenstrual syndrome.[11] Both the ACOG and the APA's DSM-IV (*Diagnostic and Statistical Manual of Mental Disorders, Fourth Edition*) criteria require the presence of at least one moderate to severe affective symptom and functional impairment. The overlap between severe PMS and PMDD has been estimated to be approximately 79%.[6,12] Outside the United States, controversy continues as to whether PMDD is indeed a unique psychiatric entity separate from other mental disorders. A British government panel recently noted that because PMDD is only included in the DSM-IV appendix, it should still be considered in need of further validation.

### DIAGNOSTIC CONSIDERATIONS

Although symptom type, duration, and intensity vary from woman to woman, Reid[13] has described the typical course of PMS as follows: Approximately 1 week before the next menses, the woman experiences the onset of breast tenderness, abdominal bloating, fatigue, weepiness, and depression. These symptoms increase in severity as menses approaches and are compounded by insomnia, food cravings, hyperactivity, irritability, and anxiety, which may lead to marital discord, social isolation, and work absenteeism. The symptoms quickly abate with the first day or two of menses, but dysmenorrhea may actually prolong the physical distress and fatigue.

Because of the heterogeneity of the symptom architecture, there is much controversy about whether subtypes of PMS exist. Dalton[14] was the first to propose that a premenstrual magnification of symptoms that never fully subside during the follicular phase constitutes a unique entity separate from PMS (Fig. 161-1). Others argue that the absence of a symptom-free interval in the follicular phase develops eventually in all women with intractable PMS, arising from chronic guilt, low self-esteem, and emotional turmoil over erratic behavior and emotional outbursts during the premenstruum.[4] In clinical practice, many women seeking treatment for PMS complaints have an underlying psychological or medical condition. Women attending PMS clinics have been found to have brain tumors, anemia, leukemia, thyroid dysfunction, gastrointestinal disorders, and pelvic tumors including endometriosis.[15] Approximately 8% of women complaining of PMS have a medical disorder with premenstrual flare-ups, such as migraine headaches, hypothyroidism, or diabetes.[16] There is a high incidence of psychiatric disorders with premenstrual exacerbation in patients with PMS.[17,18]

Given that the diagnosis of PMS is frequently one of exclusion and relies heavily on prospective charting for a minimum of two cycles to confirm patient complaints, it is not surprising that most women by definition fail to meet the medical standard for "pure" PMS. There are at least three different daily diaries that have been developed to operationalize the PMDD diagnostic criteria.[19–21] In one study of 519 patients in a primary care setting, a premenstrual symptom screening tool was shown to be an efficient complement to the clinical history for identifying those women most likely to demonstrate PMDD profiles with two cycles of daily symptom charting.[22] In patients seeking treatment, the subjective reporting of symptom severity may be the most useful clinical diagnostic indicator[23] and captures the greatest number of symptomatic women.[24]

Apart from the appropriate tests to rule out other medical conditions (e.g., complete blood count [CBC] for anemia and leukemia, thyroid-stimulating hormone [TSH] for hypothyroidism), there is no endocrine test that helps in establishing the diagnosis in most circumstances. In hysterectomized women, a serum progesterone assessment at the time of peak

**Table 161-1** Diagnostic Criteria for Premenstrual Dysphoric Disorder (PDDD)

A. During most, if not all menstrual cycles, symptoms must occur during the week before menses and remit a few days after onset of menses. Five of the following symptoms must be present and at least one must be (1), (2), (3), or (4).
   (1) Markedly depressed mood
   (2) Marked anxiety
   (3) Marked affective lability
   (4) Persistent and marked irritability
   (5) Decreased interest in usual activities
   (6) Difficulty in concentrating
   (7) Marked lack of energy
   (8) Marked change in appetite, overeating, or food cravings
   (9) Hypersomnia or insomnia
   (10) Sense of being overwhelmed or out of control
   (11) Other physical symptoms, e.g., breast tenderness and headaches
B. Symptoms must markedly interfere with work, school, usual activities, or relationships
C. Symptoms must not merely be an exacerbation of another mood disorder
D. Criteria A, B, and C must be confirmed by prospective daily ratings for at least two cycles.

Adapted with permission from the Diagnostic and Statistical Manual of Mental Disorders, Fourth edition (DSM-IV). Copyright © 1994 American Psychiatric Association.

symptoms may help determine symptom synchronicity with the luteal phase.[15] Acute ovarian suppression with agents such as GnRH (gonadotropin-releasing hormone) agonists or danazol to induce a temporary hypogonadal state has been proposed as a potential diagnostic tool to discriminate severe PMS from major depression with comorbid premenstrual symptoms.[15,17]

Apart from the occurrence of ovulatory menstrual cycles, the only clear risk factor to be associated with PMS in multiple studies is a higher prevalence of prior psychiatric disorders, especially major depression.[18] Twin studies have suggested a genetic component to its incidence, with an estimated heredity of 30% to 35%,[25–27] although family environment may also predispose. In one survey, 70% of daughters of affected mothers were themselves PMS sufferers, whereas 63% of daughters of unaffected mothers were symptom free.[28] A worsening of PMS symptom severity as women age has been reported anecdotally, but this has not been consistently observed in epidemiologic surveys[7] or in blinded clinical studies.[29,30] However, women with a prior history of premenstrual dysphoria are likely to experience depression at the time of menopause.[31]

## PATHOPHYSIOLOGY

### PMS AS A REPRODUCTIVE ENDOCRINE DISORDER

Over the last 25 years, a number of endocrine and metabolic abnormalities have been implicated in the etiology of PMS and have served as the basis for numerous clinical investigations of potential treatment remedies. Most of the pathophysiologic mechansims proposed either directly or indirectly relate to the effects of the ovarian steroids on various organ systems including central nervous system (CNS) function. Given that receptors for estradiol and progesterone have been discovered throughout the body and most recently in many regions of the brain, the idea that PMS represents a generalized "steroid" response of target organs on a monthly basis is not without support.[32]

There is substantial clinical evidence for a prominent role for ovarian hormones in the etiology of PMS. PMS-like symptoms are reproduced in some women taking oral contraceptives or at menopause with hormone replacement therapy.[33] PMS symptoms have been shown to persist after hysterectomy if the ovaries are retained,[34] but are eliminated during spontaneous anovulatory cycles, during pregnancy, or by drugs that suppress ovulation, such as danazol[35] and GnRH agonists.[36] These kinds of interventions have led to the use of hysterectomy and bilateral oophorectomy as a last resort treatment for women with intractable symptoms.[37,38]

An elegant study by researchers at the National Institute for Mental Health (NIMH) helped clarify the effect of luteal phase progesterone on symptomatology in PMS patients.[39] To do this, they used RU486, the progesterone receptor blocker that disrupts progesterone action on the endometrium and induces menses within 72 hours. In this study, women with PMS were randomly given placebo or RU486 1 week after ovulation with or without human chorionic gonadotropin (hCG) to maintain serum progesterone levels despite the onset of menses. In the group receiving RU486 alone, premenstrual mood symptoms were not abolished, despite the truncation of the luteal phase and induction of a follicular phase hormonal milieu. Because the resetting of the menstrual cycle failed to influence symptom profiles in most subjects, the investigators concluded that endocrine events prior to the mid-luteal phase trigger PMS dysphoria. The same group also demonstrated that in 10 of 18 PMS patients who remitted after ovarian suppression with gonadotropin-releasing hormone (GnRH) agonist therapy, negative mood symptoms could be reintroduced with the separate addition of either

*Figure 161-1* Symptom profiles across the menstrual cycle for premenstrual dysphoric disorder **(A)** and premenstrual exacerbation of an underlying medical or psychological disorder **(B).** (From Pearlstein TB: Hormones and depression: What are the facts about premenstrual syndrome, menopause, and hormone replacement therapy? Am J Obstet Gynecol 173(2):647.)

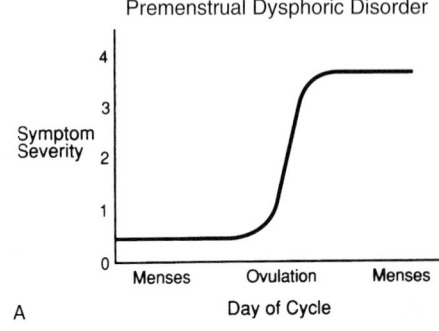
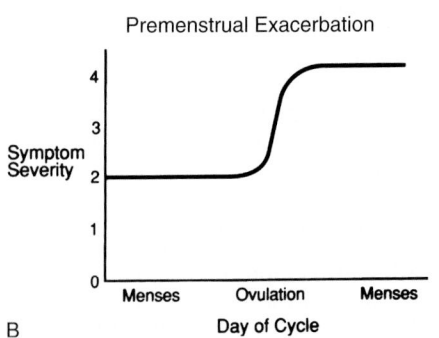

estrogen or progesterone at physiologic concentrations (Fig. 161-2).[40] This finding for the first time implicates follicular or periovulatory changes in sex steroid secretion as mediators of luteal phase symptoms.

Despite the theoretical importance of reproductive hormones in the cause of PMS, the majority of studies have failed to demonstrate differences in absolute concentrations,[40,41] metabolite activity,[42] or pulsatile secretion[43] in ovulatory subjects with PMS compared to asymptomatic, fertile volunteers. Indeed, although a number of pharmacologic challenges and clinical screening tests have been evaluated and some differences between PMS patients and normal volunteers have been occasionally observed (Table 161-2), no specific neuroendocrine marker has been identified as a useful clinical tool for the diagnosis of PMS. In the NIMH study by Schmidt and colleagues,[40] normal volunteers showed no mood perturbations with either hormone manipulation, further supporting the view that PMS sufferers respond abnormally to normal plasma concentrations of gonadal steroids.

## PMS AS AN AFFECTIVE DISORDER

Most investigators have turned from the ovary to the brain in search of an etiology for PMS. The theory of the menstrual cycle as a *zeitgeiber*, or synchronizer of psychopathology, has been proposed, although a number of psychiatric disorders fail to demonstrate significant menstrual cycle entrainment.[44] It has been argued that PMS has a common link with endogenous depression based on evidence of increased prevalence of prior depressive episodes in women with PMS, common neurotransmitter and chronobiologic abnormalities, and its successful treatment with antidepressants and light therapy.[45] Unlike patients with major depressive disorder, however, stimulated hypothalamic-pituitary-adrenal (HPA) axis activity in PMS patients appears to be blunted rather than enhanced as evidenced by reduced cortisol, adrenocorticotropic hormone (ACTH), and arginine vasopressin secretion during graded treadmill exercise challenges compared to normal volunteers.[46]

Alternatively, women with severe PMS also resemble patients with panic disorder as demonstrated by similar responses to provocative stimuli (see Table 161-2) and therapeutic benefit from the antianxiolytic buspirone.[16,18] However, these abnormalities can be induced in both phases of the menstrual cycle, thus countering the idea that a luteal phase–specific factor, active within the central nervous system, serves as the mediator of premenstrual psychopathology. Thus, PMS vulnerability may more likely be a "hardwired" trait rather than a state-related phenomenon. It is noteworthy that some 20% of placebo-treated subjects in double-blind studies demonstrate sustained improvement in PMS symptoms (at least 50% reduction in symptom scores) for 3 months, indicating the importance of nondrug factors in clinical care.[47]

## PMS AS A DISORDER OF NEUROACTIVE STEROID ACTION

The failure to identify gross aberrations in plasma concentrations of the reproductive hormones has led investigators to search for a common link between the dynamic neuroendocrine secretory events that characterize the menstrual cycle and the neurobiology of behavior and mood states. Estrogen and progesterone are known to have manifold neuroregulatory effects that vary over the reproductive cycle. In the rat, sex steroids regulate both opiate and serotonin receptor densities in multiple brain regions.[48–52] Several small positron emission tomography (PET) studies have demonstrated that estrogen treatment in postmenopausal women can variably enhance serotonin 2A receptor binding in conjunction with changes in mood and cognition in numerous brain regions.[50–52]

Progesterone metabolites alter the conformation and functional characteristics of the γ-aminobutyric acid (GABA) receptor family in a similar fashion as barbiturates.[53] In primates, levels of β-endorphins in hypophyseal portal blood increase progressively from mid to late follicular phase and are highest in the mid-luteal phase when circulating levels in plasma of both gonadal steroids are maximal. β-Endorphin levels subsequently decrease during menses or as a result of ovariectomy and are reversed by replacement with estradiol ($E_2$) and progesterone (P).[54,55] In humans, both menopause

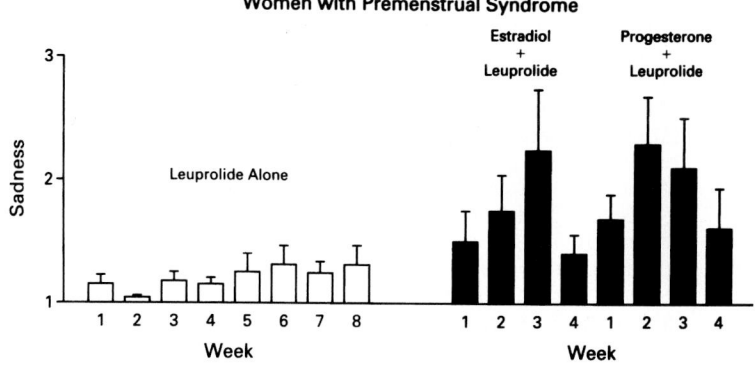

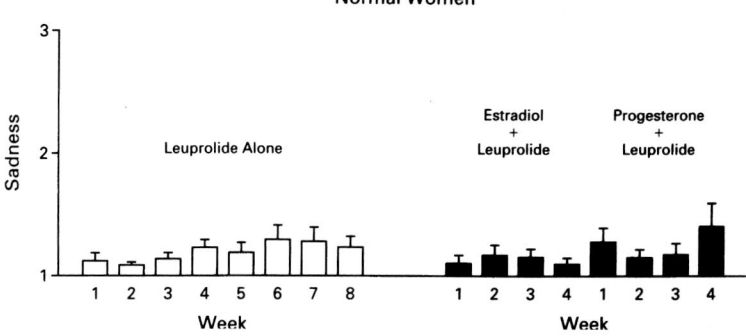

*Figure 161-2*  Negative mood can be artificially induced in patients with premenstrual syndrome *(top panel)* but not controls *(bottom)* when either estradiol or progesterone is added to GnRH agonist treatment. (From Schmidt PJ, Nieman LK, Danaceau MA, et al: Differential behavioral effects of gonadal steroids in women with and in those without premenstrual syndrome. New Engl J Med 338:213. Copyright © 1998, Massachusetts Medical Society.)

**Table 161-2** Dynamic Tests of Neurobiologic Function That Distinguish PMS Patients from Normal Volunteers in Both the Follicular and Luteal Phase of the Menstrual Cycle

Blunted neuroendocrine response after serotonin agonists (l-tryptophan, buspirone, fenfluramine, and m-Chlorophenylpiperazine)
Panic attack in response to $CO_2$ inhalation or sodium lactate infusion
Phase-advanced offset of melatonin secretion and decreased slow-wave sleep
Phase-advanced basal body temperature nadir
Blunted hypothalamic-pituitary-adrenal response to luteal phase exercise

Summarized from Mortola[16], Pearlstein perstyle[18], and Roca et al.[46]

and oophorectomy appear to reduce endogenous opiate tone of the hypothalamus, evidenced by the abolishment of naloxone-induced release of luteinizing hormone (LH) or prolactin, an effect that is reversed by treatment with E2 or P.[56,57]

These kinds of intriguing relationships between the gonadal steroid milieu and central neurotransmitter activity have spawned an acceleration of work aimed at nonclassical actions of estrogen and progesterone as neuroactive steroids. Both are synthesized in the gonads, adrenal cortex, and central nervous system and believed to modulate stress, mood, and sexual activity in animals and humans.[58] The most promising evidence that sex steroids serve as plausible neuromodulators of PMS dysphoria relate to their interaction with the endogenous opioids, GABA, and serotonin systems of the brain.

### Opioid Withdrawal Hypothesis

Central opioid peptide activity was one of the first CNS neurotransmitter systems to be implicated and studied intensively for its relationship to PMS. In 1981, Reid and Yen proposed that many of the symptoms of PMS could be accounted for by an abnormal or excessive response to the transient luteal phase rise and fall of hypothalamic opioid activity,[4] shown to modulate the pulsatile release of GnRH and, in turn, LH.[54,59] They and others suggested that the withdrawal of high central opioid activity prior to menses disinhibits opioid-sensitive norandrenergic neurons, resulting in such dysphoric symptoms as irritability, insomnia, food cravings, anxiety, and hypersensitivity to pain, symptoms similar to those induced by morphine withdrawal in normal volunteers.[60]

Attempts to detect significant aberrations in opioid regulation of the neuroreproductive axis of patients with PMS have met with limited success. Facchinetti and colleagues[61] suggested that central opioid tone was dampened in this disorder based on their observations of blunted LH responsiveness to the opiate antagonist naloxone, as well as faster LH pulse frequencies in the mid-luteal phase in PMS patients compared to normal controls.[62] However, differences in LH pulse frequency and amplitude between the patient and control groups were small and secretory characteristics were within the normal range of variability previously reported for normal, asymptomatic women.[61] In addition, the authors noted that the presence of secondary psychiatric disorders in the PMS group may have confounded their results. Later studies of pulsatile gonadotropin and progesterone secretion across the cycle in patients with the exclusive diagnosis of PMS failed to demonstrate any differences compared to normal volunteers, thus challenging the view that the neuroregulation of the menstrual cycle in women with PMS is markedly altered.[63,64]

Studies of peripheral concentrations of β-endorphins in women with PMS versus normal volunteers have also yielded conflicting evidence for differences in levels between groups and across cycle phases.[65-67] Evidence that most of the peripheral β-endorphin is secreted from the pituitary gland[68] and the finding that peripheral β-endorphin levels do not correlate with cerebral mu-opioid binding in any brain region of healthy female volunteers,[69] supports the view that peripheral measures of β-endorphin may not be useful as markers of CNS activity.

Despite these ambiguous findings, therapeutic effects of naltrexone, the orally active opiate antagonist, have been reported in a placebo-controlled, double-blind study of PMS patients.[70] When administered for 3 months during mid-cycle only, there was significant improvement with active medication. As reviewed by Severino and Moline,[71] however, significant changes in individual symptoms were not reported and the mechanism for a late luteal phase effect is not clear, given the time course of the administration and the loss of opioid receptor blockade by 24 hours after dosage. More recent evidence from PET scan studies of mu-opioid receptor binding densities in young healthy women during the follicular phase suggests that a number of non-hypothalamic opioid networks involved in higher order cognitive, mood, and behavior functions are influenced by sex steroids.[69]

### GABA Agonist Effects

Estrogen and progesterone are considered anxiolytic steroids that have been implicated in PMS as possible endogenous barbiturate-like modulators of central GABA receptors.[48] In the rat, both estrogen and progesterone enhance GABA receptor-mediated chloride ion conductance in cultured hippocampal and spinal cord neurons, and induce behavioral effects in vivo similar to the barbiturates and benzodiazepines. Two 3-α-hydroxysteroid metabolites of progesterone, allopregnenolone and pregnenolone, bind with high affinity to the GABA receptor complex in the CNS.[72] In healthy volunteers, significant fatigue and compromised memory were experienced 2 hours after an oral dose of 1.2 g progesterone, which produced levels greater than 95 nmol/L of allopregnenolone and pregnenolone.[73] Conversely, supraphysiologic levels of 5-α and 5-β pregnenolone produced after daily administration of 300 mg oral progesterone in PMS patients failed to reduce premenstrual anxiety beyond that of placebo.[74] An age-related decline in allopregnenolone occurs in men, but in women, menopause has no effect on circulating levels.[75] Although cyclic elevations have been observed during the luteal phase of the normal menstrual cycle in both metabolites, evidence that patients with PMS show aberrations in peripheral levels is inconclusive.[40,76-78] Modest correlations have been reported between allopregnenolone levels and PMS symptoms[78] as well as treatment responses to antidepressants in PMDD patients.[79]

### Serotonin Dysregulation

The most consistent body of work suggests that PMS results from a dysregulation of the serotonin system A number of plasma and urinary markers of the serotonergic system have been shown to fluctuate with the stage of the menstrual cycle and to be abnormal in women with PDD.[17,80] m-Chlorophenylpiperazine (m-CPP) has been used as a probe for testing serotonergic function in patients with PMS with conflicting results.[80,81] In one controlled study, m-CPP administration during the luteal phase resulted in an acute improvement of PMS symptoms. As plasma cortisol and ACTH responses to m-CPP were blunted in both follicular and luteal phases in PMS patients compared to controls, the investigators concluded that dysregulation of the HPA axis either directly or via serotonin control of the HPA axis was involved in PMS.[81]

The most compelling evidence for serotonin dysregulation as the underlying cause of PMS comes from the outcomes of multisite, clinical trials of agents that selectively inhibit serotonin reuptake.[82,83] The marked symptom improvement observed within the first 2 weeks at doses lower than needed for antidepressant effects has led investigators to suspect a different mechanism of action other than postsynaptic transmission regulation (Fig. 161-3).[83]

## TREATMENT APPROACHES

A number of reviewers have examined the efficacy of various pharmacologic agents, medical interventions, and complementary/alternative therapies in the treatment of PMS.[12,15,82,84–91] A major challenge in the development of treatment options has been the need to demonstrate symptom improvement over and above the significant placebo response, which has been as high as 60% for up to three cycles in some trials.[13] Thus, the discovery that selective serotonin reuptake inhibitors (SSRIs) demonstrate clear superiority over placebo has been viewed as a real breakthrough in symptom management.[83] In a 2002 meta-analysis of 31 randomized controlled trials,[88] it was concluded that there is now very good evidence to support the use of SSRIs in the management of severe PMS. Moreover, a secondary analysis showed that these agents were as effective in treating physical as well as behavioral symptoms, although withdrawals due to side effects were 2.5 times more likely in the active treatment groups than in the controls. There were no significant differences between trials funded by pharmaceutical companies and those independently funded.

Although there are no data to suggest that one SSRI is superior to another, sertraline, a second-generation SSRI agent with fewer side effects, has demonstrated efficacy.[92] Intermittent luteal-phase dosing beginning at mid-cycle has now been shown to be as effective as daily medication when tested for up to six cycles.[93] Recently, it has been reported that long-acting, slow release 90-mg fluoxetine was effective when given intermittently orally once a week at 14 and 7 days prior to menses.[94] In the United States, both fluoxetine (Prozac, Sarafem) and sertraline (Zoloft) are FDA approved with specific indications for PMDD.

Although SSRIs are now considered the first line of treatment for PMDD and severe PMS, some 40% of patients will not respond or find side effects intolerable.[90,95] The most common adverse effects include insomnia, gastrointestinal disturbances, and fatigue.[88,96] In women with moderate to severe premenstrual symptoms and no other current major psychiatric or physical diagnosis, response to SSRI therapy cannot be differentiated by demographic or medical history factors; although high "background" symptoms present in the postmenstrual week predicted poorer treatment response.[97]

There are now several reports of alterations in ovulation and menstrual cycle length associated with short-term SSRI use in women. Elevated prolactin levels, inhibition of hypothalamic GnRH, or reduced estrogen metabolism due to fluoxetine inhibition of CYP34A have all been proposed as possible serotonin-related mechanisms underlying these variable responses.[98–101]

Table 161-3 summarizes efficacy results of the most popular treatment regimens when tested for the ability to produce overall symptom improvement in well-designed clinical trials. It should be noted that treatment efficacy varies depending on the nature of the symptom: Breast tenderness appears especially responsive to danazol; SSRIs show their most robust effects on the negative affect symptoms of PDD; and GnRH agonists work best for PMS patients with debilitating physical symptoms. Despite the questionable value of progesterone as a therapeutic agent, it continues to be among the most frequently prescribed treatments for PMS. A 2001 Cochrane Library database review of the world's literature demonstrated that only 3 of 15 published reports of progesterone treatments were adequately designed to meet conventional clinical trial standards. Although the meta-analysis showed a very small positive effect for oral progesterone, the odds ratio of 1.3 compared to 6.9 for selective serotonin reuptake inhibitors led the reviewers to conclude there was clear evidence of a lack of clinical utility for women with PMS.[102] In contrast to most oral contraceptive regimens, the new low-dose birth

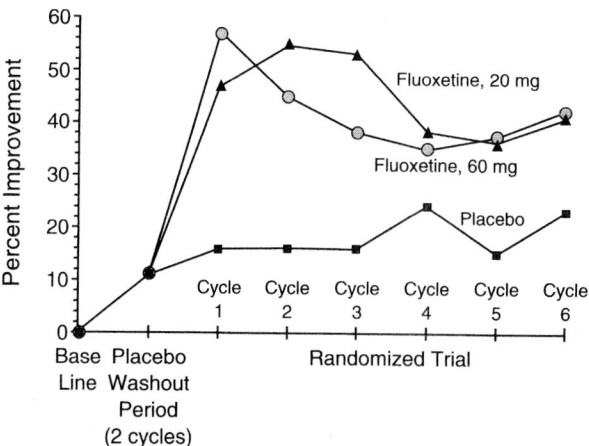

**Figure 161-3** The effects of two different doses of fluoxetine and placebo treatment on percent improvement in luteal phase symptom scores. (From: Steiner M, Steinberg S, Stewart D, et al: Fluoxetine in the treatment of premenstrual dysphoria. New Engl J Med 332:1529. Copyright © 1998, Massachusetts Medical Society.)

| *Table 161-3* | **Clinical Trial Outcomes for the Most Common PMS Therapies** |
|---|---|

**A. TREATMENTS PROVEN CONSISTENTLY SUPERIOR TO PLACEBO IN MULTIPLE STUDIES**
SSRIs (fluoxetine, sertroline; both daily and cyclic luteal phase regimens)
GnRH agonists and other ovulation suppressants

**B. TREATMENTS NOT CONSISTENTLY SUPERIOR TO PLACEBO IN CLINICAL TRIALS**
Progesterone (injection, vaginal, oral)
Oral contraceptives, synthetic progestins
Thyroid hormone
Lithium
Bromocryptine
Alprazolam
Evening primrose oil
Spironolactone
Tricyclic antidepressants

**C. PROMISING TREATMENTS IN NEED OF FURTHER STUDY**
Calcium
Vitamin B6
Nutritional pharaceuticals
Exercise
Magnesium
Mefenamic acid
Vitamin E
Sleep deprivation and light therapy
St. John's Wort
Chasteberry
Yasmin oral contraceptive (low-dose estrogen with drospirenone, the spironolactone analogue/progestin)

Summarized from reviews by Stevenson and Ernst[91], Wyatt et al.[102], Reid[15], Rapkin[87], Girman et al.[89], and Mitwally et al.[90]

control pill, Yasmin, containing estrogen and the progestin drospirenone, a spironolactone analogue, which binds antagonistically to the androgen receptor, shows promise in reducing PMS symptoms in two clinical trials to date.[87,103]

Even for those agents shown to be consistently superior to placebos in alleviating symptoms, expense is a major consideration given the chronic nature of the disorder. Moreover, the side effects associated with GnRH agonists (hypoestrogenism) and danazol (androgenicity) are significant barriers to acceptability for many patients even for short-term therapy. Although the doses used of fluoxetine and sertroline are well tolerated and lower than needed to treat depression, no data are available on long-term efficacy and eventual drug resistance with chronic or intermittent, cyclic therapy for many years. A 2004 government panel has raised concerns about the safety and potential for developmental toxicity of SSRIs in pediatric populations (under age 18), breastfeeding mothers, and women of reproductive age.[104] Although fluoxetine at 20 mg (the dose recommended for PMS) has a comparable safety profile in both adults and children, and the FDA recently approved it for use in 7- to 17-year-olds, the balance of risks and benefits for the use of sertraline in children was judged unfavorable in the United Kingdom (www.mhra.gov.uk). To what extent the presence of fluoxetine in breast milk contributes to the lower infant size of nursing, treated mothers[105,106] is a matter of current controversy, and its use during pregnancy or breastfeeding is not recommended. These considerations are important for PMDD patients, given the frequency of severe PMS in adolescent populations and the likelihood that oral contraceptives may exacerbate symptoms in some individuals.

Depending on whether the woman with PMS presents to her gynecologist, psychiatrist, family practice physician, or nurse practitioner, treatment may target either the elimination of the symptom trigger (i.e., suppression of ovulation), the correction of the neurotransmitter "vulnerability" (by use of serotonergic antidepressants), or the improvement of general health, nutrition, and well-being.

Further studies are needed to confirm initially promising results reported for supplemental calcium, magnesium, vitamin B6, vitamin E, St. John's wort, mefenamic acid, and chasteberry (see Table 161-3). Because of the potential effects on hormones and possible interactions with neurotransmitters and the P450 enzyme system, it is recommended that the use of many of these agents be avoided during pregnancy or breastfeeding, or in combination with such medications as antidepressants or protease inhibitors.

A number of nonpharmacologic therapies have demonstrated some efficacy for moderate to severe PMS.[85,87,89,91] These include exercise, cognitive-behavioral strategies, support groups, acupuncture, biofeedback, reflexology, sleep deprivation, light therapy, and combined, lifestyle modifications. With the exception of light therapy,[107,108] few of these therapies have been adequately assessed in multiple, rigorous clinical trials. Regardless of the treatment approach, it is important to note that patient expectations, environmental stimuli, and cultural context may all have significant effects on the degree of symptom relief.[66]

## FUTURE DIRECTIONS IN PMS RESEARCH

Although small clinical studies have uncovered a backdrop of CNS abnormalities and negative psychosocial characteristics that distinguish PMS patients, future studies are needed to determine their true prevalence and relevance to the pathogenesis and subsequent morbidity arising from chronic PMS. Because of the chronic nature of PMS, there is a clear need to assess the long-term efficacy and safety of the most promising of the SSRI agents. The public's growing interest in vitamins, herbal remedies, botanicals, and nontraditional medical therapies has accelerated the pace of scientific scrutiny of these products.

No one has yet been able to explain how normal events in the menstrual cycle trigger dysphoric symptoms in some women but not in the majority. Reviewers have noted that lifestyle stresses, history of sexual abuse, and negative psychological traits such as a sense of learned helplessness contribute significantly to a PMS vulnerability,[109] but to what extent these characteristics are predisposing or occur in response to PMS remains to be determined. Certainly, further insights into the etiology and optimum treatment of PMS will be revealed as new discoveries uncover the molecular actions of estrogen and progesterone binding in the emotional and cognitive centers of the brain and their relationship to dysphoric mood states.

## REFERENCES

1. Hylan TR, Sundell K, Judge R: The impact of premenstrual symptomatology on functioning and treatment-seeking behavior: Experience from the United States, United Kingdom and France. J Womens Health (Larchmt) 8:1043–1052, 1999.
2. Singh B, Berman B, Simpson R, Annechild A: Incidence of premenstrual syndrome and remedy usage: A national probability sample study. Altern Ther Health Med 4:75–79, 1998.
3. Mortola J: Premenstrual syndrome: Pathophysiologic considerations. N Engl J Med 338:256–257, 1998.
4. Reid RL, Yen SSC: Premenstrual syndrome. Am J Obstet Gynecol 139:85–104,1981.
5. American Psychiatric Association: Diagnostic and Statistical Manual of Mental Disorders, Fourth Edition. Washington, DC, American Psychiatric Association, 1994.
6. Freeman EW: Premenstrual syndrome and premenstrual dysphoric disorder: Definitions and diagnosis.

Psychoneuroendocrinology 28(Suppl 3): 25–37, 2003.
7. Ramcharan S, Love EJ, Fick GH, Goldfien A: The epidemiology of premenstrual symptoms in a population-based sample of 2650 women: Attributable risk and risk factors. J Clin Epidemiol 45:377–392, 1992.
8. Rivera-Tova AD, Frank E: Late luteal phase dysphoric disorder in young women. Am J Psychiatry 147:1634–1636, 1990.
9. Wittchen HU, Becker E, Lieb R, Krause P: Prevalence, incidence and stability of premenstrual dysphoric disorder in the community. Psychol Med 32:119–132, 2002.
10. Halbreich U, Borenstein J, Pearlstein T, Hahn LS: The prevalence, impairment, impact and burden of premenstrual dysphoric disorder (PMS, PMDD). Psychoneuroendocrinology 28(Suppl 3):1–23, 2003.
11. American College of Obstetricians and Gynecologists (ACOG): Premenstrual

Syndrome. Washington, DC, ACOG, 2000.
12. Freeman EW, Rickels K, Sondheimer SJ, Polansky M: A double-blind trial of oral progesterone, alprazolam, and placebo in treatment of severe premenstrual syndrome. JAMA 274:51–57, 1995.
13. Reid RL: Endogenous opiate peptides and premenstrual syndrome. Semin Reprod Endocrinol 5:191–197, 1987.
14. Dalton K: The Premenstrual Syndrome and Progesterone Therapy. Southam, England, Camelot, 1984.
15. Reid R: Premenstrual syndrome, ch 10, pp 1–16. Endotext.com (April 17, 2002) www.endotext.org/female/female10/female10htm.
16. Mortola JF: Premenstrual syndrome. Trends Endocrinol Metab 7:184–189, 1996.
17. Freeman EW, Sondheimer SJ, Rickels K: Gonadotropin releasing hormone agonist in the treatment of premenstrual symptoms with and without ongoing dysphoria:

A controlled study. Psychopharmacol Bull 33:303–309, 1997.

18. Pearlstein, TB: Hormones and depression: What are the facts about premenstrual syndrome, menopause, and hormone replacement therapy? Am J Obstet Gynecol 173:646–653, 1995.

19. Endicott J, Harrison W: The daily record of severity of problems. 1992. Available from Dr. Endicott, New York State Psychiatric Institute Biometrics Unit, 722 W 168th St, New York, NY 10032.

20. Freeman EW, DeRubeis RJ, Rickels K: Reliability and validity of a daily diary for premenstrual syndrome. Psychiatry Res 65:97–106, 1996.

21. Steiner M, Steiner DL, Steinberg S, et al: The measurement of premenstrual mood symptoms. J Affect Disord 53:269–273, 1999.

22. Steiner M, Macdougal M, Brown E: The premenstrual symptoms screening (PSSt) for clinicians. Arch Women Ment Health 6:203–209, 2003.

23. Angst J, Sellaro R, Merikangas KR, Endicott J: The epidemiology of perimenstrual psychological symptoms. Acta Psychiatr Scand 104:110–116, 2001.

24. Smith MJ, Schmidt PJ, Rubinow DR: Operationalizaing DSM-IV criteria for PMDD: Selecting symptomatic and asymptomatic cycles for research. J Psychiatr Res 37:75–83, 2003.

25. Condon JT: The premenstrual syndrome: A twin study. Br J Psychiatry 162:481–486, 1993.

26. Kendler KS, Silberg JI, Neale MC, et al: Genetic and environmental factors in the aetiology of menstrual, premenstrual and neurotic symptoms: A population-based twin study. Psychol Med 22:85–100, 1992.

27. Kendler KS, Karkowski LM, Corey LA, Neale MC: Longitudinal population-based twin study of retrospectively reported premenstrual symptoms and lifetime major depression. Am J Psychiatry 155:1234–1240, 1998.

28. Kantero RL, Widholm O: Correlations of menstrual traits between adolescent girls and their mothers. Acta Obstet Gynecol Scand 14(Suppl):30–42, 1977.

29. Reame NE, Kelch RP, Beitins IZ, et al: Psychobiologic sequelae of ovulation in women over 40. Fertil Steril (Suppl):S12, 1993.

30. Freeman EW, Rickels K, Schweizer E, Ting T: Relationships between age and symptom severity among women seeking medical treatment for premenstrual symptoms. Psychol Med 25:309–315, 1995.

31. Stewart D, Boydell KM: Psychological distress during menopause: Associations across the reproductive life cycle. Int J Psychiatry Med 23:157–162, 1993.

32. MacDonald PC, Dombroski RA, Casey ML: Recurrent secretion of progesterone in large amounts: An endocrine/metabolic disorder unique to younger women? Endocr Rev 12:372–401, 1991.

33. Hammarback S, Backstrom T, Holst J, et al: Cyclical mood changes as in the premenstrual tension syndrome during sequential estrogen-progestogen postmenopausal replacement therapy. Acta Obstet Gynecol Scand 64:393–397, 1985.

34. Backstrom CT, Boyle H, Baird DT: Persistence of symptoms of premenstrual tension in hysterectomized women. Br J Obstet Gynaecol 88:530–536, 1981.

35. Gilmore DH, Hawthorn RJS, Hart DM: Treatment of the premenstrual syndrome: A double-blind placebo controlled cross-over study using danazol: J Obstet Gynecol 318:22, 1989.

36. Muse KN, Cetel NS, Futterman LA, Yen SSC: The premenstrual syndrome: effects of medical ovariectomy. N Engl J Med 311:1345–1349, 1984.

37. Casper RT, Hearn MT: The effect of hysterectomy and bilateral oophorectomy on women with severe premenstrual syndrome. Am J Obstet Gynecol 162:105–109, 1990.

38. Casson P, Hahn P, VanVugt DA, Reid RL: Lasting response to ovariectomy in severe intractable premenstrual syndrome. Am J Obstet Gynecol 162:99–102, 1990.

39. Schmidt PJ, Nieman LK, Grover GN, et al: Lack of effect of induced menses on symptoms in women with premenstrual syndrome. N Engl J Med 324:1174, 1991.

40. Schmidt PJ, Nieman LK, Danaceau MA, et al: Differential behavioral effects of gonadal steroids in women with and in those without premenstrual syndrome. N Engl J Med 338:209–216, 1998.

41. Rubinow DR, Hoban MC, Grover GN, et al: Changes in plasma hormones across the menstrual cycle in patients with menstrually related mood disorder and in control subjects. Am J Obstet Gynecol 158:5–11, 1988.

42. Schmidt PJ, Purdy RH, Moore PH Jr, et al: Circulating levels of anxiolytic steroids in the luteal phase in women with premenstrual syndrome and in control subjects. J Clin Endocrinol Metab 79:1256–1260, 1994.

43. Reame NE, Marshall JC, Kelch RP: Pulsatile LH secretion in women with premenstrual syndrome: Evidence for normal neuroregulation of the menstrual cycle. Psychoneuroendocrinology 17:205–213, 1992.

44. Schmidt PJ, Rubinow DR: Parallels between premenstrual syndrome and psychiatric illness. In Smith S, Schiff I (eds): Modern Management of Premenstrual Syndrome. New York, WW Norton, 1993, pp 71–81.

45. Parry BL, Haynes P: Mood disorders and the reproductive cycle. J Gend Specif Med 3:53–58, 2000.

46. Roca CA, Schmidt PJ, Altemus M, et al: Differential menstrual cycle regulation of hypothalamic-pituitary-adrenal axis in women with premenstrual syndrome and controls. J Clin Endocrinol Metab 88:3057–3063, 2003.

47. Freeman EW, Rickels K: Characteristics of placebo responses in medical treatment of premenstrual syndrome. Am J Psychiatry 156:1403–1408, 1999.

48. Weiland NG, Wise PM: Estrogen and progesterone regulate opiate receptor densities in multiple brain regions. Endocrinology 126:804–808, 1990.

49. Biegon A, Bercovitz H, Samuel D: Serotonin receptor concentration during the estrous cycle of the rat. Brain Res 187:221–225, 1980.

50. Kugaya A, Epperson CN, Zoghbi S, et al: Increase in prefrontal cortex serotonin2A receptors following estrogen treatment in postmenopausal women. Am J Psychiatry 160:1522–1524, 2003.

51. Smith YR, Zubieta J: Neuroimaging of aging and estrogen effects on central nervous system physiology. Fertil Steril 76(4):651–659, 2001.

52. Moses-Kolko EL, Berga SL, Greer PJ, et al: Widespread increases of cortical serotonin type 2A receptor availability after hormone therapy in euthymic postmenopausal women. Fertil Steril 80(3):554–559, 2003.

53. Majewska MD, Harrison NL, Schwartz RD, et al: Steroid hormone metabolites are barbiturate-like modulators of the GABA receptor. Science 232:1004–1007, 1986.

54. Wehrenberg WB, Wardlaw SL, Frantz AG, Ferin M: Beta-endorphin in hypophyseal portal blood: Variations throughout the menstrual cycle. Endocrinology 111:879–881, 1982.

55. Wardlaw SH, Wehrenberg WB, Ferin M, et al: Effects of sex steroids on b-endorphin in hypophyseal portal blood. J Clin Endocrinol Metab 57:1107–1110, 1983.

56. Reid RL, Quigley ME, Yen SSC: The disappearance of opioidergic regulation of gonadotropin secretion in postmenopausal women. J Clin Endocrinol Metab 57:1107–1110, 1983.

57. Shoupe D, Montz FJ, Lobo RA: The effects of estrogen and progestin on endogenous opioid activity in oophorectomized women. J Clin Endocrinol Metab 60:178–183, 1985.

58. Mellon SH: Neurosteroids: Biochemistry, modes of action, and clinical relevance. J Clin Endocrinol Metab 78:1003–1008, 1994.

59. Ropert JF, Quigley ME, Yen SSC: Endogenous opiates modulate pulsatile luteinizing hormone release in humans. J Clin Endocrinol Metab 52:583–585, 1981.

60. Halbreich U, Endicott J: Possible involvement of endorphin withdrawal or imbalance in specific premenstrual syndromes and postpartum depression. Med Hypotheses 7:1045–1058, 1981.

61. Facchinetti F, Martignoni E, Sola D, et al: Transient failure of central opioid tonus and premenstrual symptoms. J Reprod Med 33:633–638, 1988.

62. Facchinetti F, Genazzani AD, Martignoni E, et al: Neuroendocrine correlates of premenstrual syndrome: Changes in the pulsatile pattern of plasma LH. Psychoneuroendocrinology 15:269–277, 1990.

63. Reame N, Sauder SE, Kelch RP, Marshall JC: Pulsatile gonadotropin secretion during the human menstrual cycle: Evidence for altered frequency of gonadotropin-releasing hormone secretion. J Clin Endocrinol Metab 59(2):328–337, 1984.

64. Lewis LL, Greenblatt Em, Rittenhouse CA, et al: Pulsatile release patterns of luteinizing hormone and progesterone in relation to symptom onset in women with premenstrual syndrome. Fertil Steril 64:288–292, 1995.

65. Chuong CJ, Coulam CB, Kao PC, et al: Neuropeptide levels in premenstrual syndrome. Fertil Steril 44:760–765, 1985.

66. Facchinetti F, Martignoni E, Petraglia F, et al: Premenstrual fall of plasma b-endorphin in patients with premenstrual syndrome Fertil Steril 47:570–573, 1987.

67. Taskin O, Gokdeniz R, Yalcinoglu A, et al: Placebo-controlled cross-over study of effects of tibolone on premenstrual symptoms and peripheral b-endorphin concentrations in premenstrual syndrome. Hum Reprod 13:2402–2405, 1998.

68. Frederickson RCA, Geary LE: Endogenous opioid peptides: Review of physiological, pharmacological and clinical aspects. Prog Neurobiol 19:19–69, 1982.

69. Smith YR, Zubieta JK, del Carmen MG, et al: Brain opioid receptor measurements by positron emission tomography in normal cycling women: Relationship to luteinizing hormone pulsatility and gonadal steroid hormones. J Clin Endocrinol Metab 83:4498–4505,1998.

70. Chuong CJ, Coulam CB, Bergstrahl EJ, et al: Clinical trial of naltrexone in premenstrual syndrome. Obstet Gynecol 72:332–336, 1988.

71. Severino SK, Moline ML: Premenstrual Syndrome: A Clinician's Guide. New York, Guilford, 1988.

72. Paul SM, Purdy RH: Neuroactive steroids. FASEB J 6:2311–2322, 1992.

73. Freeman EW, Purdy RH, Coutifaris C, et al: Anxiolytic metabolites of progesterone: correlation with mood and performance measures following oral progesterone administration to healthy female volunteers. Neuroendocrinology 58:478–484, 1993.

74. Vanselow W, Dennerstein L, Greenwood KM, de Lignieres B: Effect of progesterone and its 5 alpha and 5 b metabolites on symptoms of premenstrual syndrome according to route of administration. J Psychosom Obstet Gynaecol 17:29–38, 1996.

75. Genazzani AR, Petraglia F, Bernardi F, et al: Circulating levels of allopregnenolone in humans: Gender, age, and endocrine influences. J Clin Endocrinol Metab 83:2099–2103, 1998.

76. Wang M, Seippel L, Purdy RH, Backstrom T: Relationship between symptom severity and steroid variation in women with premenstrual syndrome: Study of serum pregnenolone sulfate, 5alpha-pregnan-3,20-dione and 3alpha-hydroxy-5alpha-pregnan-20-one. J Clin Endocrinol Metab 81:1076–1082, 1996.

77. Rapkin AJ, Morgan M, Goldman L, et al: Progesterone metabolite allopregnenolone in women with premenstrual syndrome. Obstet Gynecol 90:709–714, 1997.

78. Girdler SS: Allopregnenolone levels and reactivity to mental stress in premenstrual dysphoric disorder. Biol Psychiatry 49:788–797, 2001.

79. Freeman EW: Allopregnenolone levels and symptom improvement in severe premenstrual syndrome. J Clin Psychopharmacol 22:516–520, 2002.

80. Halbreich U, Tworek H: Altered serotonergic activity in women with dysphoric premenstrual syndromes. Int J Psychiatry Med 23:1–27, 1993.

81. Su TP, Schmidt PJ, Danaceau M, et al: Effect of menstrual cycle phase on neuroendocrine and behavioral responses to the serotonin agonist m-chlorophenylpiperazine in women with premenstrual syndrome and controls. J Clin Endocrinol Metab 82:1220–1228, 1997.

82. Yonkers KA: Treatment of premenstrual dysphoric disorder. Current Review of Mood and Anxiety Disorders 1(3):215–237, 1997.

83. Steiner M, Steinberg S, Stewart D, et al: Fluoxetine in the treatment of premenstrual dysphoria. New Engl J Med 332:1529–1534, 1995.

84. Mortola JF: From GnRH to SSRIs and beyond: Weighing the options for drug therapy in premenstrual syndrome. Medscape Women's Health eJournal 2(5), 1997. Available at: http://www.medscape.com/viewarticle/408871.

85. Pearlstein T: Nonpharmacologic treatment of premenstrual syndrome. Psychiatr Ann 26:590–954, 1996.

86. Pearlstein TB, Jain N, Zlotnick C, et al: Dysphoric disorders in women: A case of premenstrual syndrome. Medscape Women's Health eJournal 3(5), 1998. Available at: http://www.medscape.com/viewarticle/405402.

87. Rapkin A: A review of treatment of premenstrual syndrome and premenstrual dysphoric disorder. Psychoneuroendocrinology 3:39–53, 2003.

88. Wyatt KM, Dimmock PW, O'Brien PMS: Selective serotonin reuptake inhibitors for premenstrual syndrome. Cochrane Database Syst Rev 4:CD001396, 2002.

89. Girman A, Lee R, Kligler B: An integrative medicine approach to premenstrual syndrome. Am J Obstet Gynecol 188(5 Suppl):S56–S65, 2003.

90. Mitwally MF, Kahn LS, Halbreich U: Pharmacotherapy of premenstrual syndromes and premenstrual dysphoric disorder: Current practices. Expert Opin Pharmacother 3(11):1577–1590, 2002.

91. Stevinson C, Ernst E: Complementary/alternative therapies for premenstrual syndrome: A systematic review of randomized controlled trials. Am J Obstet Gynecol 185(1):227–325, 2001.

92. Yonkers KA, Halbriech U, Freeman E, et al: the Sertraline Premenstrual Dysphoric Collaborative Study Group: Symptomatic improvement of premenstrual dysphoric disorder with sertraline treatment: A randomized controlled trial. JAMA 278:983–988, 1997.

93. Young SA, Hurt PH, Benedek DM, Howard RS: Treatment of premenstrual dysphoric disorder with sertraline during the luteal phase: A randomized, double-blind, placebo-controlled, crossover trial. J Clin Psychiatry 59:76–80, 1998.

94. Miner C, Brown E, McCray S, et al: Weekly luteal phase dosing with enteric-coated fluoxetine 90 mg in premenstrual dysphoric disorder: A randomized, double-blind, placebo-controlled clinical trial. Clin Ther 24:417–433, 2002.

95. Freeman EW, Rickels K, Sondheimer SJ, Polansky M: Differential response to antidepressants in women with premenstrual syndrome/premenstrual dysphoric disorder: A randomized controlled trial. Arch Gen Psychiatry 56:932–930, 1999.

96. Dimmock PW, Wyatt KM, Jones PW, Obrian PM: Efficacy of selective serotonin-reuptake inhibitors in premenstrual syndrome: A systematic review. Lancet 356:1131–1136, 2000.

97. Freeman EW, Sondheimer SJ, Polansky M, Garcia-Espagna B: Predictors of response to sertraline treatment of severe premenstrual syndromes. J Clin Psychiatry 61(8):579–584, 2000.

98. Strain SL: Fluoxetine-initiated ovulatory cycles in two clomiphene-resistant women. Am J Psychiatry 151(4):620, 1994.

99. Menkes DB, Taghavi E, Mason PA, Howard RC: Fluoxetine's spectrum of action in premenstrual syndrome. Int Clin Psychopharmacol 8(2):95–102, 1993.

100. Steiner M, Korzekwa M, Lamont J, Wilkins A: Intermittent fluoxetine dosing in the treatment of women with premenstrual dysphoria. Psychopharmacol Bull 33(4):771–774, 1997.

101. Urban RJ, Veldhuis JD: A selective serotonin reuptake inhibitor, fluoxetine hydrochloride, modulates the pulsatile release of prolactin in postmenopausal women. Am J Obstet Gynecol 164(1 Pt 1):147–152, 1991.

102. Wyatt K, Dimmock P, Jones P, et al: Efficacy of progesterone and progestogens in management of premenstrual syndrome: Systematic review. Br Med J 323:776–780, 2001.

103. Parsey KS, Pong A: An open-label, multicenter study to evaluate Yasmin, a low-dose combination oral contraceptive containing drospirenone, a new progestogen. Contraception 61:105–111, 2000.

104. Center for the Evaluation of Risks to Human Reproduction National Toxicology Program, US Dept of Health and Human Services: Draft

Report: NTP–CERHR Expert Panel Report on the Reproductive and Developmental Toxicity of Fluoxetine, November 12, 2003. Available at: *http://cerhr.niehs.nih.gov/news/fluoxetine.*

105. Chambers CD, Anderson PO, Thomas RG, et al: Weight gain in infants breastfed by mothers who take fluoxetine. Pediatrics 104(5):e61, 1999.

106. Wisner KL, Gelenberg AJ, Leonard H, et al: Pharmacologic treatment of depression during pregnancy. JAMA 282:1264–1269, 1999.

107. Parry BL, Udell C, Elliott JA, et al: Blunted phase-shift responses to morning bright light in premenstrual dysphoric disorder. J Biol Rhythms 12:443–456, 1997.

108. Lam RW, Carter D, Misri S, et al: A controlled study of light therapy in women with late luteal phase dysphoric disorder. Psychiatry Res 86:185–192, 1999.

109. Smith S: Treatment for the Physical Symptoms of Premenstrual Syndrome. In Smith S, Schiff I (eds): Modern Management of Premenstrual Syndrome. New York, WW Norton, 1993, pp 112–119.

# Mechanisms of Menopause and the Menopausal Transition

## Alison Silverberg and Nanette Santoro

## INTRODUCTION

In 1850, Colombat de L'Isere, discussing the "Change of Life," wrote: "Compelled to yield to the power of time, women now cease to exist as for the species, and henceforward live only for themselves."[1] Why do human females, alone among primates, survive for so long after reproductive capacity ceases with menopause? In 1957, Williams introduced this evolutionary phenomenon as the "stopping early hypothesis,"[2] later to be known as the "grandmother hypothesis."[3] Kristen Hawkes of the University of Utah first coined the grandmother hypothesis in 1997. It is an evolutionary explanation of the menopause, which supports the idea that the fitness of a population is maximized if women stop reproducing and help to raise their grandchildren instead. By provisioning grandchildren, grandmothers ensure their children's survival, boost their daughters' fertility, and improve the chances that their own genes are passed on. Continued investment in already existing children and grandchildren could increase the average lifetime reproductive success to a larger degree than a woman's increasingly risky own reproduction as she grows older. The grandmother hypothesis suggests that natural selection favors menopause, because only grandmothers who are not busy feeding their own children have time to provision grandchildren, as well as long life and perhaps even close family ties.

Women's attitudes toward menopause range from neutral to positive, and ethnic groups within the United States vary slightly in their attitudes toward menopause and aging.[4] Many women embrace this period of their lives when the fear of pregnancy is gone and monthly bleeding is over.

## STAGING REPRODUCTIVE AGING

The World Health Organization (WHO), as well as the Council of Affiliated Menopause Societies (CAMS), assembled in 1996 and 1999, respectively, in an attempt to standardize the terminology of the menopausal transition.[5,6] Commonly accepted terms, including *premenopause, perimenopause, menopausal transition,* and *climacteric,* were thought to be too vague to be useful. In July 2001, the Stages of Reproductive Aging Workshop (STRAW) was held to address the absence of a relevant staging system for female reproductive aging and to discuss the confusing current nomenclature for the premenopause.[7]

This group recommended a revised nomenclature as follows (Fig. 162-1):

*Menopause*: This is the anchor point that is defined after 12 months of amenorrhea following the final menstrual period (FMP) and which reflects a near complete but natural decrease in ovarian hormone secretion.

*Menopausal transition*: Stages –2 (early) and –1 (late) encompass the menopausal transition and are defined by menstrual cycle and endocrine changes. The menopausal transition begins with variation in menstrual cycle length in a woman who has a monotropic follicle-stimulating hormone (FSH) rise and ends with the FMP (not able to be recognized until after 12 months of amenorrhea).

*Postmenopause*: Stages +1 (early) and +2 (late) encompass the postmenopause. The early postmenopause is defined as 5 years since the FMP. (The participants agreed this interval is relevant because it encompasses a further dampening of ovarian hormone function to a permanent level as well as accelerated bone loss.) Stage +1 was further subdivided into segment *a*, the first 12 months after the FMP, and segment *b*, the next 4 years. Stage +2 has a definite beginning but its duration varies, since it ends with death. Further divisions may be warranted as women live longer and more information is accumulated.

*Perimenopause*: This word literally means "about or around the menopause." It begins with stage –2 and ends 12 months after FMP. *The climacteric* is a popular but vague term used synonymously with perimenopause. Generally speaking, the term *menopausal transition* is preferred over *perimenopause* and *climacteric*.

## EPIDEMIOLOGY

Most estimates of age at natural menopause are based on samples of Caucasian women in Western societies. In one large, comprehensive, prospective cohort study of middle-aged Caucasian women in the United States (the Massachusetts Women's Health Study [MWHS]) the age at natural menopause occurred at 51.3 years,[8] confirming prior reports.[9] The Study of Women's Health Across the Nation (SWAN), a multicenter, multiethnic, community-based cohort study of women and the menopausal transition, reported the overall median age at natural menopause to be 51.4 years, after adjustment for other factors.[10] Studies performed outside the United States suggest that Africans,[11] African-Americans,[12] and Hispanics of Mexican descent[13] experience menopause at an earlier age than Caucasian women, as opposed to Japanese[14] and Malaysian[15] women who report a similar median age of menopause to women of European descent.

**STAGES/NOMENCLATURE OF NORMAL REPRODUCTIVE AGING IN WOMEN**
Recommendations of Stages of Reproductive Aging Workshop (STRAW), Park City, Utah USA, July 2001

Final menstrual period
(FMP)

**Figure 162-1** This chart describes a working model of the female reproductive life span, including but not limited to the menopausal transition. The final menstrual period (FMP) is indicated at time 0, and the menopausal transition (stages −2 through 0) encompasses the onset of increased menstrual irregularity and/or skipped menses up to the FMP. Note that intermittent elevations in early follicular phase FSH (follicle-stimulating hormone) are detectable before the onset of any clinical sign of the transition (stage −3), and that the FMP is not defined until 1 year without menses has elapsed. (Reprinted with permission from Soules MR, Sherman S, Parrott, E, et al: Executive summary: Stages of Reproductive Aging Workshop (STRAW). Fertil Steril 76:874–878, 2001.)

| Stages: | −5 | −4 | −3 | −2 | −1 | 0 | +1 | +2 |
|---|---|---|---|---|---|---|---|---|
| Terminology: | Reproductive | | | Menopausal transition | | | Postmenopause | |
| | Early | Peak | Late | Early | Late* | | Early* | Late |
| | | | | Perimenopause | | | | |
| Duration of stage: | Variable | | | Variable | | 1 yr | 4 yrs | Until demise |
| Menstrual cycles: | Variable to regular | Regular | | variable cycle length (> 7 days different from normal) | ≥ 2 skipped cycles and an interval of amenorrhea (≥ 60 days) | Amen × 12 mos | None | |
| Endocrine: | normal FSH | ↑ FSH | | ↑ FSH | | ↑ FSH | | |

*Stages most likely to be characterized by vasomotor symptoms    ↑ = elevated

Late menopause is defined as an FMP that occurs after 54 years, and early menopause occurs at age 40 to 45. Both are present in about 5% of women. Approximately 1% of women experience hypergonadotropic amenorrhea or premature ovarian failure (POF) before age 40. There are many factors that affect natural menopause age (Table 162-1).

Lower educational attainment and unemployment have been independently associated with earlier age at menopause[10,16-18] and may be markers for elevated biopsychosocial stress. Women who are separated, divorced, or widowed have been shown to have an earlier menopause than women who are married.[10] Age at natural menopause for parous women has been reported to occur significantly later than for nulliparous women.[10,12,16,19,20] Gold and colleagues[10] and Cramer and colleagues[21] observed a trend of increasing age at menopause with increasing number of live births and that prior use of oral contraceptives was associated with earlier age at natural menopause; however, others have found an assocation between oral contraceptive use and a slight prolongation of reproductive life span.[12,22] The proposed mechanism by which parity and use of oral contraceptives may result in later age at natural menopause is by reducing ovulatory cycles earlier in life and thus preserving oocytes longer, resulting in later menopause.[10] Some studies show that women with a lower body mass index (BMI) experience an earlier menopause[23] although other studies have not confirmed this finding.[10,12]

Genetic factors may influence the timing of menopause. The blepharophimosis gene, located on chromosome 3,[24] and X chromosome deletions such as the POF1 and POF2 genes[25] have been shown to predispose women to an earlier menopause. In one study by Tibiletti and colleagues, pedigree analysis revealed a dominant pattern of inheritance of early menopause and POF through maternal or paternal relatives; since POF and early menopause have been shown to share the same genetic features, they may actually be a variable expression of the same genetic disease.[26] Fragile X syndrome premutation carriers are prone to premature menopause.[27] The *Pvu II* polymorphic allele for estrogen receptor-α has been associated with a slightly earlier age at natural menopause and a twofold increase in risk for hysterectomy.[28]

Environmental toxicants may play a role in early menopause. There is a large body of literature showing that current smokers tend to experience menopause at an earlier age (1–2 years) than nonsmokers[9,10,16,29] and possibly have a shorter menopausal transition.[8] It has been shown that polycyclic hydrocarbons in cigarette smoke are toxic to ovarian follicles,[30] and potentially lead to their loss and thus an earlier menopause in smokers. Irradiation and chemotherapy with alkylating cytotoxics are also implicated as causes for early menopause.[31] Evidence suggests that galactose consumption through the ingestion of high-lactose dairy foods

**Table 162-1  Etiologic Factors in Early Menopause**

Race/ethnicity
Parity
Prior oral contraceptive use
Socioeconomic status
  Lower educational attainment
  Marital status
  Stress
Familial/genetic factors
  Blepharophimosis gene
  POF1/POF2 gene
  Fragile X syndrome
  *Pvu II* polymorphic allele
Environmental toxins
  Smoking
  Chemotherapy
  Irradiation
  Galactose consumption
BMI (body mass index)
Depression

From Colombat de L'Isere M (1850): Diseases of Women. American edition translated by Meigs CD. Cited in Ricci JV: One Hundred Years of Gynaecology, 1800–1900. Philadelphia, Blakiston, 1945, p 532.

may be a dietary risk factor and that galactose metabolism, as measured by galactose-1-phosphate uridyl transferase, may be a genetic risk factor for early menopause.[32]

Harlow and colleagues observed that women with a history of medically treated depression had a 20% increased rate of entering perimenopause sooner compared with women with no depression history, after adjustment for age, parity, age at menarche, education, cigarette smoking, and body mass index.[33]

Epidemiology gives answers about populations, whereas clinical medicine deals with patient samples and individuals. For example, in population-based studies,[8] there is no global increased prevalence of depression associated with the menopause transition. In clinical samples,[34] however, depression around menopause has been reported to increase. Symptomatology varies among women, and the distinction between populations versus individuals needs to be made when evaluating epidemiologic factors related to menopause.

## PATHOGENESIS

The basis of reproductive senescence in women is oocyte/follicle depletion in the ovary. Developmentally, a women attains her peak oocyte complement at 20 weeks' gestational age.[35] Between 20 and 40 weeks' gestation, two thirds of a woman's oocyte complement is lost and total oocyte counts drop from a mean of about 6–8 million to 1–2 million.[36] The most massive wave of atresia (rate of follicle loss) a woman ever experiences happens before she is born. At the onset of puberty, the germ cell mass has reduced to 300,000 to 500,000 units.[37] Subsequent reproductive aging consists of a steady loss of oocytes through atresia or ovulation and does not necessarily occur at a constant rate.

Atresia is an apoptotic process. During the 35 to 40 years of reproductive life, 400 to 500 oocytes will be selected for ovulation. By menopause, only a few hundred follicles remain.[37] The relatively wide age range (42–58 years) for menopause in normal women seems to indicate that women are either endowed with a highly variable number of oocytes or the rate of oocyte loss varies greatly.[7]

All levels of follicular loss are influenced by molecular genetics. Genetic modifiers of oocyte/follicle endowment, development, and atresia have been shown to play a major role in the mouse ovary.[38] The KIT receptor, present on oocyte and theca cells in ovarian follicles, and its ligand, KIT LIGAND, produced by granulosa cells, are encoded at the *Kit* gene and *Mgf* gene, respectively. Mutations in these genes alter the expresssion of KIT and KIT LIGAND proteins, resulting in alterations in granulosa cell proliferation and/or oocyte growth in mice.[39] Growth and differentiation factor-9 (GDF-9), a growth factor that is secreted by oocytes in growing ovarian follicles, has been shown to promote growth, development, and survival of human ovarian follicles in organ culture.[40] Finally, FOXL2 (forkhead transcription factor gene) is thought to be a highly conserved regulator of vertebrate ovarian development and has been implicated as an etiologic factor in the ovarian failure present in patients with blepharophimosis ptosis epicanthus inversus syndrome (BPES).[41] Interestingly, FOX03 shunts follicles through development at a more rapid pace and causes follicle depletion by promoting presumptive development and apoptosis.[42] Furthermore, genetic modifiers indicate that there are acquired ways to change the size of the follicle pool.

Concurrent with the loss of ovarian follicles as a woman transitions to menopause are hormonal changes in the hypothalamic-pituitary-ovarian axis. FSH is an established indirect marker of follicular activity; as follicle numbers decline, FSH levels increase.[43] An elevated level is often the first clinically measurable sign of reproductive aging. Large cross-sectional studies have observed a progressive, quantitative rise in FSH with age.[44]

In the late reproductive years, initial elevations in FSH are most prominent in the early follicular phase of the menstrual cycle, but are intermittent and do not occur in every cycle.[45] This increase is first detectable some years before there are any clinical indications of approaching menopause.[43] The rise in FSH appears to be a result of a decline in inhibin B, a dimeric protein that reflects the fall in ovarian follicle numbers. In reproductive life, inhibin serves to inhibit FSH selectively by binding to receptors on the anterior pituitary.[46] Estradiol is stable or even elevated during the earlier menopause transition (Fig. 162-2), though closer to the final menstrual period,

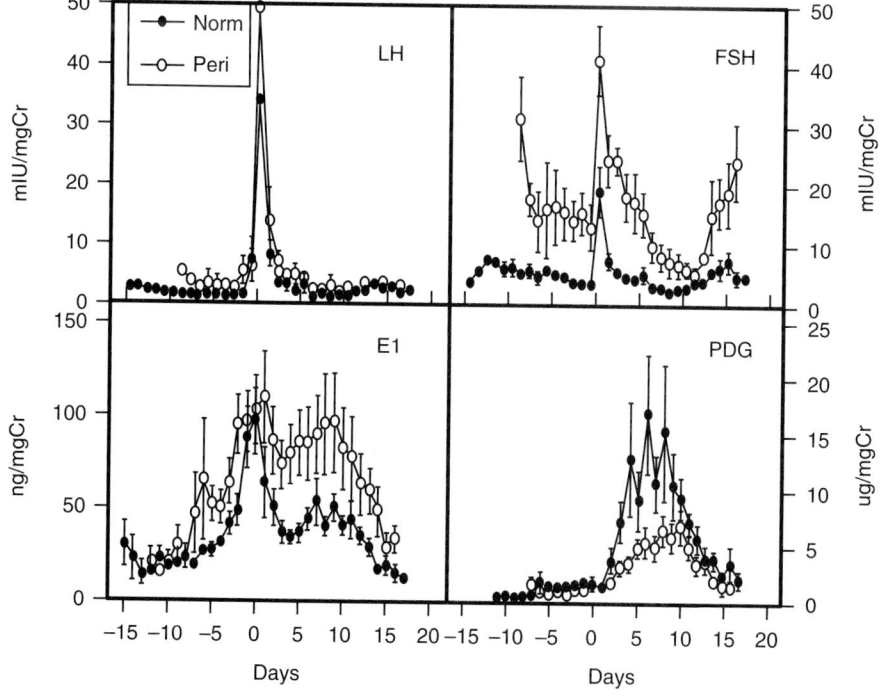

EARLY TRANSITION HORMONE PATTERNS

*Figure 162-2* Urinary reproductive hormone patterns in a group of 11 midreproductive-age (norm, age 19–38) and 11 late reproductive-age (peri, age 43–52) women having ovulatory cycles. Note that, in late reproductive-age women, FSH (follicle-stimulating hormone) is consistently elevated throughout the cycle, estradiol metabolite excretion (estrone conjugates, or E1c) is overall elevated, and progesterone metabolites (pregnanediol glucuronide, or PDG) are decreased compared to the midreproductive-age women. LH, luteinizing hormone. (Reprinted with permission from Santoro N, Banwell T, Tortoriello D, et al: Effects of aging and gonadal failure on the hypothalamic-pituitary axis in women. Am J Obstet Gynecol 178:732–741, 1998.)

a decline is clearly observed.[47] These findings are consistent with erratic follicular development and dysregulation of folliculogenesis.[48–50]

While FSH and estradiol vary near menopause, steroidogenic enzymes appear to be completely absent in the postmenopausal ovary after all functional follicles are lost.[51] Between the ages of 20 and 40 years, concentrations of total testosterone have been reported to fall about 50%.[52] This age-related decline does not change further during the transition years.[53] Similarly, dehydroepiandrosterone (DHEA) and its sulfate (DHEA-S) decline with age.[54,55] Because circulating sex hormone–binding globulin (SHBG) decreases across the menopausal transition, free androgen levels actually rise as indicated by a small increase in free androgen index (T ÷ SHBG × 100).[53]

Androstenedione, which remains relatively stable during the transition, is converted to estrone in extraglandular tissue. This accounts for almost all the estrogen in circulation after menopause. When ovulation stops, concurrent with a woman's FMP, the serum progesterone levels are invariably low.[56] Plasma luteinizing hormone (LH) eventually increases, although at a slower rate than FSH.

## CLINICAL FEATURES (FIG.162-3)

Impending menopause is clinically evident with menstrual cycle changes. A normal menstrual cycle ranges anywhere from every 21 to 35 days.[57] Anovulatory cycles become more common as women progress through the menopause transition, and cycle lengths become increasingly variable. An analysis of prospectively kept menstrual calendars has shown that cycle lengths rise in mean length to more than 35 days during the last 10 cycles before cessation of menses. After reaching this level, cycles decrease in length for some and continue to increase for others.[58]

Women who have skipped more than 3 but less than 12 menses are very likely (estimated probability, 0.93) to stop menstruating within the next 4 years.[59] A woman older than 45, whose difference between the lengths of the longest and shortest cycle is longer than 42 days, has fewer than 20 cycles remaining before her final menstrual period.[58]

*Dysphoric mood* is a common complaint in the early menopause transition and is reported less frequently in the later phases.[60] Menstrual migraines peak during the transitional years,[61] as well as often unrecognized hot flashes around menses.[62] In the early menopause, breast soreness-tenderness is significantly more common, but, as the menopause transition progresses, more hypoestrogenic symptoms such as hot flashes, vaginal dryness, and night sweats occur with greater frequency.[63]

Neuromuscular symptoms have been found to be stable throughout the menopausal transition, suggesting that other events in a midlife woman's life (i.e., life stress, acute and chronic illnesses) account for the common complaint of joint pains.[64]

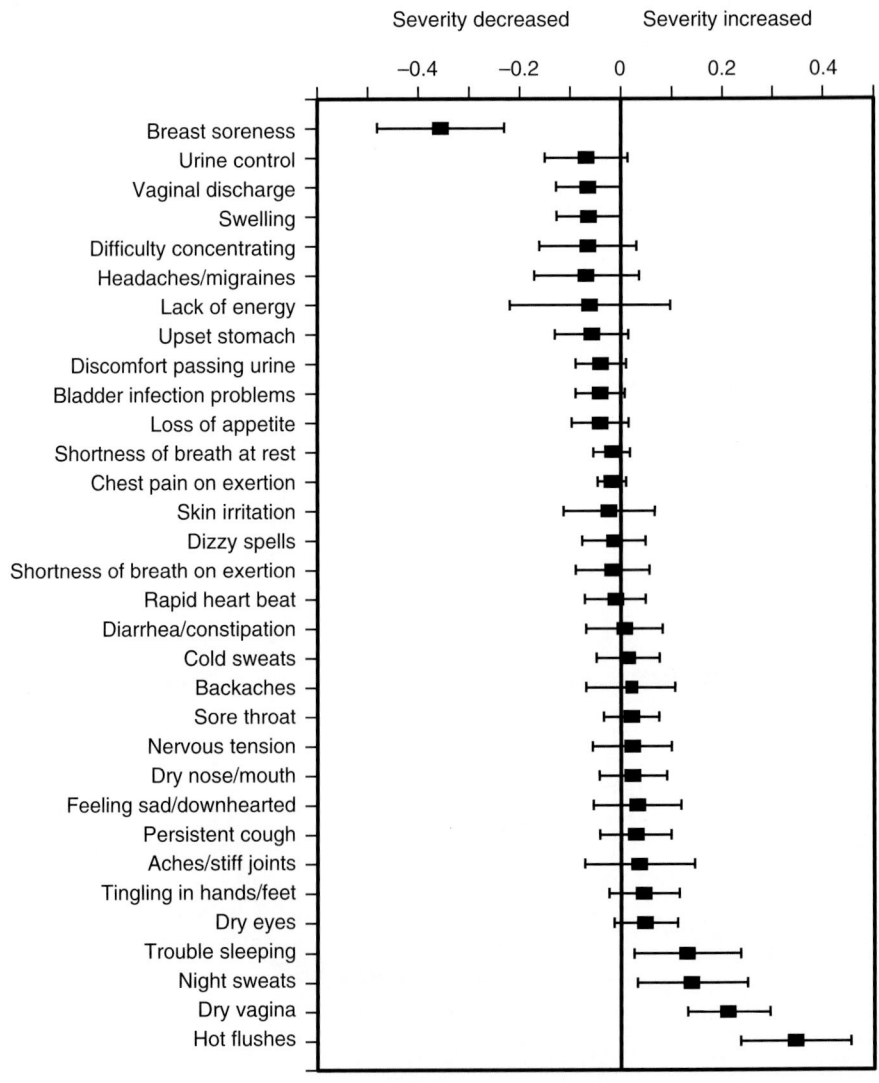

**Figure 162-3** The net change in a series of menopause associated symptoms before and after the final menstrual period (FMP). Data from 172 women's serial observations are from the Melbourne Women's Health Study, a longitudinal study of the menopause transition. Note that most symptoms do not demonstrate significant change in severity across the transition. (Reprinted with permission from Dennerstein L, Lehert P, Burger H, et al: Mood and the menopause transition. J Nerv Ment Dis 187:685–691, 1999.)

Hot flashes are considered a hallmark symptom of the menopausal transition.[65] Hot flashes are commonly defined as transient periods of intense heat in the upper arms and face, often followed by flushing of the skin and profuse sweating. Many hot flashes are followed by chills and can be accompanied by palpitations and a sense of anxiety.[66] Approximately 40% to 70% of menopausal women experience hot flashes, and 10% to 20% of these women obtain medical attention for treatment of their hot flashes.[67] Most midlife women will experience hot flashes for several months up to 5 years, but some will have hot flashes for up to 30 years.[66] Although the etiology of hot flashes is not entirely clear, studies have suggested that changes in core body temperature regulation, changes in endogenous hormone levels, or both are associated with the onset of hot flashes.[65] Hot flashes negatively impact the quality of life for women by causing sleep disturbance, which often results in fatigue, irritability, forgetfulness, acute physical discomfort, and negative effects on work.[68,69]

## REPRODUCTIVE AND SOMATIC AGING

Reproductive aging is confounded by somatic aging. All women do not age at the same rate. When interpreting menopausal data, we have to take the overall aging backdrop into account.

Menopause has historically been regarded as a primary ovarian event, with associated changes in pituitary gonadotropin secretion occurring secondary to the decline in ovarian sex steroid and protein production. Increasing evidence suggests, however, that aging is associated with dynamic changes in the hypothalamic and pituitary components of the reproductive axis that are independent of changes in gonadal hormone secretion. Using gonadotropin free α subunit (FAS) as a surrogate marker of gonadotropin-releasing hormone (GnRH) pulse frequency in postmenopausal women, Hall and colleagues demonstrated a 35% decline in GnRH pulse frequency between the fifth and eighth decades with aging, providing evidence of slowing of the hypothalamic GnRH pulse generator activity.[70] Other studies in which LH was used as a marker for GnRH secretion have shown variable results. Although estimates of pulse frequency were lower than in the previously stated study, Rossmanith and coworkers showed a decline in LH pulse frequency with age when comparing naturally postmenopausal women aged 49–57 years and 78–87 years.[71] Santoro and colleagues did not observe different patterns of LH secretion in postmenopausal women who were compared to young women with premature ovarian failure, but older women were much more readily suppressed by exogenous estradiol.[72] Whether these age-related changes in GnRH pulse frequency are due to lesser secretion of GnRH or to changes in pituitary responsiveness to GnRH is uncertain. Using prematurely menopausal women as controls allows separation of the process of ovarian failure from the hypothalamic-pituitary changes accompanying aging.

The *somatopause* begins before the menopause with aging. Twenty-four-hour GH secretion decreases in women before the onset of estrogen deficiency, and insulin-like growth factor 1 (IGF-1) levels in adults decline progressively with age.[73] Since IGF-1 is a cofactor for FSH action, there may be additional gonadal compromise imposed by reduced somatotrophic axis function.[74] Body composition changes, including an increase in body fat in the visceral/abdominal compartment and a decrease in lean body mass, as well as adverse changes in lipoproteins, a relative increase in insulin resistance, and a reduction in aerobic capacity are thought to be secondary to the changes in the somatotrophic axis.[75]

Like other endocrine systems, aging is associated with significant changes in the anatomy of the thyroid gland and modifications in the physiology of the hypothalamic-pituitary-thyroid axis. Direct age-related changes should be distinguished from indirect alterations caused by other physiologic and pathologic states that occur with age. The subtle changes in the hypothalamic-pituitary-thyroid axis suggest a decreased hypothalamic stimulation of thyroid function.[76] The thyroid-stimulating hormone (TSH) nocturnal surge may be lost with increasing age, thus providing evidence for hypothalamic dysfunction.[77] Moreover, thyroid hormone clearance decreases with age, which explains the reduced daily replacement doses of thyroxine in elderly hypothyroid subjects.[78]

With aging, minimal and mean cortisol plasma concentrations increase, with no alteration in pulsatile frequency, and the diurnal amplitude of cortisol and adrenocorticotropic hormone (ACTH) relative to the 24-hour mean of hormones shows an age-related decline.[79] In addition, the evening cortisol quiescent period is shortened in the elderly, suggesting increasingly impaired circadian function in aging.

In relation to bone loss and aging around the menopausal transition, SWAN reported that in premenopausal and early perimenopausal women, higher FSH concentrations were positively associated with greater bone turnover before the last menstrual period as assessed by higher serum osteocalcin and urinary N-telopeptide of type I collagen concentrations.[80] SWAN also showed that serum FSH was inversely correlated with bone mineral density (BMD) and that BMD tended to be lower in women in the late perimenopause or early postmenopause versus the early perimenopause.[81] Finally, SWAN found that more sport and home physical activity, as compared to work and active living activity, was statistically significantly associated with greater BMD,[82] suggesting the importance of preserving activity in middle-aged women.

Cognitive function declines with age. Studies on young, oophorectomized animals serve as classic endocrine ablation-replacement models to support a role for estrogen in decreasing cerebral ischemia and Alzheimer's disease. While aging predicts cognitive decline, leisure activity mitigates those effects. In a prospective, cohort study, Verghese and coworkers found that reading and playing board games were associated with a reduced risk of dementia and Alzheimer's disease.[83] In the Nun Study, nuns that exhibited complex, verbal skills early in life maintained cognitive function longer as they aged and were protected against the development of Alzheimer's disease.[84] Although hormone therapy has been associated with a decreased risk of dementia, neither the Women's Health Initiative nor the Heart and Estrogen/progestin Replacement Study (HERS) reported effects of hormone therapy on cognition and dementia.

The aging process is associated with predictable anatomic and physiologic alterations in the cardiovascular system. The cardiac mass increases approximately 1 to 1.5 g yearly.[85] There is a gradual increase in the circumference of all four cardiac valves.[86] Studies that have excluded subjects with hypertension show consistent increases in left ventricular wall thickness in conjunction with reduced diastolic compliance,[87,88] and the duration of the contraction of the myocardium is prolonged. Histologic changes detected in the vasculature include increased intimal thickness, elastin fragmentation, and increased collagen content of the arterial wall. Finally, the natural history of heart disease is generally adversely affected by age.[89] None of these changes are abruptly affected by menopause; all are gradual.

## DIAGNOSIS

Despite the epidemiologic trend of elevated FSH and decreased estradiol with progression through the transition, measurement of FSH, inhibin, and estradiol provides at best an unreliable guide to the menopausal status of an individual woman.[43,90] A more rational approach to diagnosing menopause would include an assessment of the longitudinal symptoms of a woman who presents with perimenopausal complaints.[91] Hormone profiles correlate well with symptoms and cycle features.[92] Thus, if a woman is older than 45 years old, has a recent disruption in her menstrual pattern and symptoms suggestive of transient hypoestrogenemia, it is likely that she has entered her menopausal transition.[60]

That being said, the clinician should take care to rule out other pathologies that can be masked by the common complaints associated with the menopausal transition. At minimum, a screening TSH level should be performed, as menstrual irregularity can be the only manifestation of thyroid dysfunction. Women with a prior history of depression appear to be at excess risk for menopause-related depression,[74,93] and, therefore, screening for depression may be indicated. Many women experience dysphoric mood and a loss of "wellness" during the transition, and these syndromes should be formally distinguished from the more severe and life-threatening risk that clinical depression poses. Atypical hot flashes can be due to nonestrogen-related causes including new-onset diabetes with autonomic dysfunction, carcinoid, and pheochromocytoma.[62] Poor sleep can be secondary to nonestrogen-related causes, for example, sleep apnea. Women who appear to be entering the menopausal transition earlier than age 40 years should have a more extensive workup, including screening appropriate for patients with premature ovarian failure.[94]

## TREATMENT

It is important to emphasize short-term and long-term therapeutic goals with patients when discussing treatment options during and after the menopausal transition. It is also important to separate these issues because short-term (defined herein as <5 years) and long-term (≥5 years) benefits and harms may differ.[95] During counseling about hormone therapy (HT), both physicians and patients are often confused about how to interpret the literature in individual cases. The role of short-term therapy for symptom relief is considerably less confusing, since the benefits are immediate and often large in magnitude.

### SHORT-TERM THERAPY

Some women sail through menopausal transition without notice, others are miserable, and the majority have symptoms that are somewhat bothersome. Women may visit their physician because they have symptoms they suspect are related to menopause and desire a validation of their complaints, others desire treatment, and some want general information about menopause. In each situation, it is helpful to allow the patient to dictate her primary concerns before recommending therapy. Choosing the best treatment option for an individual woman involves knowledge of the risks and benefits of each treatment.

Vasomotor symptoms can be disabling. Behavioral techniques can be beneficial. Encouraging patients to wear layered clothing that can be added or removed easily can help a woman maintain control of her core body temperature. Changes in dietary habits such as avoiding spicy foods and reducing caffeine and excess alcohol intake, which can cause flushing, can be beneficial. Patients should be told that regular physical activity, a balanced diet, and stress reduction (particularly paced breathing) may be of additional help in decreasing vasomotor flushing.

Pharmacologic options are available. Hormones remain the most effective option, resulting in 80% to 90% reduction in hot flashes. More than 40 randomized controlled trials of oral and transdermal estrogen have reported a reduction in the severity of vasomotor symptoms, and estrogen was effective in doses lower than the usual 0.625 mg of equine estrogen or equivalent.[96] Transdermal estradiol[97-99] and intranasal 17-beta estradiol spray[100-102] are also effective in reducing hot flashes. Transdermal administration of estrogen is recommended in postmenopausal women with hypertriglycemia because this treatment has little effect on lipid metabolism. Serum estradiol levels in women on parenteral estrogen should be maintained at appropriate levels (i.e., 61–122 pg/mL) to be beneficial and not be excessively high in order to prevent side effects.[103] To increase the rate of compliance, selection of the most appropriate regimen of HT (dose, route of administration, and schedule) for the needs of each individual is important.

The most promising second-line treatment to date is in the class of newer antidepressants, which act by selectively inhibiting serotonin reuptake. Research suggests that venlafaxine provides approximately 60% reduction in hot flashes,[104] and in low doses is effective in the management of hot flashes in cancer survivors.[105] In a randomized, double-blind, placebo-controlled, parallel group study comparing paroxetine controlled release to placebo, there was a greater than 60% median reduction in hot flashes in the paroxetine-treated group compared with 37% in the placebo group.[106]

Oral tibolone has been reported to be as effective as other forms of HT (i.e., estradiol valerate or conjugated estrogens) in reducing vasomotor symptoms.[107-109] Veralipride has also been shown to be more efficient than placebo in the treatment of postmenopausal hot flashes.[110] Depomedroxyprogesterone acetate[111] and megestrol acetate[112] can be effective alternatives to estrogen therapy for vasomotor symptoms in selected menopausal patients. Both oral[113] and transdermal clonidine[114] may be beneficial to some patients.

For women who prefer alternative therapies, there is a limited body of scientific information in English about botanicals. The use of soy/isoflavone products may have some benefits. In one study, women given a soy protein supplement with 40 mg of protein and 76 mg of isoflavones had a 45% reduction in vasomotor symptoms compared with 30% reduction in controls who received a placebo.[115] Although limited evidence on black cohosh exists, there appears to be a positive effect on sleep disturbances, mood disturbances, and hot flashes.[116] In a randomized, double-blind, placebo-controlled study of the use of evening primrose oil (gamma-linolenic acid [GLA]) in the treatment of vasomotor symptoms during menopause, the women had significant improvement in the maximum number of nighttime flushes; however, GLA provided no benefits beyond those seen with placebo.[117] Finally, in a double-blind controlled clinical trial using a daily dose of 4.5 g of dong quai, dong quai and placebo both reported a 25% reduction in hot flashes.[118] There is a relative lack of literature supporting its clinical use, but vitamin E at doses up to 800 IU daily has demonstrated efficacy in some studies, and its cost-to-benefit ratio can be evaluated for patients on an individualized basis. While most alternative therapies appear to lack the potential to cause harm, they can be expensive. Open-ended usage is not indicated.

There are at least nine randomized controlled trials that have shown estrogen (oral, transdermal, or vaginal) improves urogenital symptoms. Topical estrogens (cream, tablet, or ring) appear to be better than systemic estrogens for relieving vaginal dryness and dyspareunia, while avoiding high circulating levels. Vaginal lubricants such as Replens and Astroglide are also effective for women with dyspareunia who wish to avoid hormones.

As stated earlier, menstrual irregularities are common during the menopausal transition. Management options include cycling with oral contraceptive pills, as long as there are no contraindications (i.e., smokers, migraines with aura[119]). Birth control pills and the newer nonoral methods (such as monthly rings and patches) are effective for regulation of menses, mood lability, and contraception. Women taking oral contraceptives during the menopausal transition may experience adverse symptoms during the pill-free interval of 7 days, however, and limiting or eliminating the pill-free interval may result in improved symptom profiles.[120] Another option includes adding either transdermal (i.e., 25–50 mcg) or oral estradiol during the pill-free week. In women who do not need contraception, hormone replacement therapy can be considered; however, the patient must understand that short-term use of HT for the prevention of menstrual irregularities during the menopausal transition is not the same as HT for long-term prevention of future disease. With combined continuous administration of HT, breakthrough bleeding may occur at any time. With cyclic regimens, women will continue to experience monthly bleeding. Therefore, it is the patient who must ultimately decide which symptoms are more bothersome when choosing a HT regimen that is right for her. Finally, in women whose chief complaint is menstrual irregularities, the Mirena IUD is an option that will decrease menstrual flow as long as there is no uterine pathology. Furthermore, before initiating therapy for irregular bleeding during the menopausal transition, uterine pathology must be appropriately ruled out.

## LONG-TERM HT FOR THE PREVENTION OF CHRONIC CONDITIONS

### Cardiovascular Disease

Observational studies have suggested that combined hormone replacement therapy (HRT) is beneficial for the primary prevention of heart disease. When given orally, it reduces low-density lipoprotein (LDL) cholesterol by 10%, raises high-density lipoprotein (HDL) cholesterol by 10%, and raises triglycerides by 20%.[96] For many years, these findings, along with a lack of clinical trial evidence on cardiovascular risks and benefits, were viewed as an incentive to recommend HT. The major findings of the Women's Health Initiative (WHI), a primary prevention trial on 16,608 healthy postmenopausal women, changed the perspective on this issue. After 5.2 years (average duration) of daily combined HRT or placebo, a small but significant increased risk for nonfatal heart attacks was observed.[121] Although coronary heart disease mortality was not increased, the risk for heart disease was 29% higher for women taking combined HRT compared to those on placebo. In other words, among 10,000 healthy, postmenopausal women with a uterus who are taking combined estrogen plus progestin, according to the WHI, 7 more will have a heart attack in the first year of use. Subsequent analysis of the data demonstrated no significant difference in cardiovascular morbidity or mortality in hormone users versus nonusers. When counseling patients today on the primary prevention of heart disease, it is important to emphasize that combined HRT has not been shown to lead to cardiovascular health benefits. This finding has major epidemiologic implications, in that the largest single determinant of long-term public health benefit for HRT was its impact on cardiovascular disease. Even a small positive impact would translate into many lives saved were HRT usage to become widespread, or even considered "standard of care" as a preventive medication. In the absence of any current demonstration of cardiovascular benefit, the rationale for most women to remain on hormone therapy after their symptoms have subsided is meager.

For secondary prevention of heart disease, the most widely quoted study in clinical practice for aid in management is the HERS. The results of HERS indicated that women with known coronary heart disease (CHD) who were randomized to conjugated equine estrogen and medroxyprogesterone acetate had a 52% increased risk of myocardial infarction during the first year of use and increased CHD deaths during the first 3 years of use.[122] After 6.8 years of follow-up in HERS II, there was no difference in primary or secondary CHD events among estrogen users.[123] Again, for secondary prevention of heart disease, there is no clinical benefit to HRT. As a result, the American Heart Association supports discontinuing treatment in the event of an acute event in a woman who is currently using HT.[124]

In addition to a lack of benefit on heart disease, HT may also play a role in recurrent thrombotic events. The WHI reported an increased risk for stroke after 5 years of HT use[121] and, in agreement with previous studies, a higher risk of thromboembolism in the first year of HRT use, which diminishes thereafter to approximately a twofold increased risk.[121,125,126] This translates into 8 more strokes and 8 more pulmonary emboli per 10,000 women ages 50 to 79 years taking estrogen and progestin for 1 year.

In light of the findings of recently reported clinical trials, most organizations with guidelines on postmenopausal HT have revised their recommendations. The American College of Obstetricians and Gynecologists,[127] the North American Menopause Society,[128] and the American Heart Association[129] now specifically recommend against the use of HT for the primary prevention or secondary prevention of cardiovascular disease. Since cardiovascular disease is a more common cause of morbidity and mortality for women than osteoporosis and cancer combined, efforts to identify patients at risk and recommendations on lifestyle modifications, diet, and other pharmacotherapy (i.e., β-blockers, aspirin, ACE [angiotensin-converting enzyme] inhibitors, and statins) are of proven benefit and have been studied as preventive agents suitable for long-term treatment.

### Bone Health

There are many factors that increase a woman's risk for bone fractures. Nonmodifiable risk factors include age, family history, personal history of osteoporotic fracture, and early menopause. Modifiable risk factors include weight (increased risk in thin women), excess alcohol consumption, current smoking, low calcium intake, vitamin D deficiency, sedentary lifestyle, and low bone density.

Peak bone mass is achieved around age 25 and is maximized by an adequate calcium intake, physical activity (weight-bearing, muscle-building, and balance exercises), and avoiding smoking. If adequate dietary calcium is unattainable, which is often the case, calcium supplementation should be given to a reach a dose of 1200 to 1500 mg each day. Clinical trials have shown that calcium with vitamin D (600–800 IU/day) can reduce fracture risk, while calcium with estrogen allows better bone preservation than estrogen alone. Vitamin D is often not necessary, however, since most women obtain enough through sunlight. Weight-bearing exercise stimulates osteoblasts to form new bone.[130] In menopausal women, weight-bearing exercise for 22 months was shown to result in a 6.1% increase in bone density of the lumbar spine,[131] and the benefits of exercise have been demonstrated into the ninth decade of life and persist only when they are continued.[132] Since lifestyle modifications have been shown to improve bone density in young women and prevent fractures in older women, these inexpensive and safe treatment recommendations should be included in every routine health maintenance examination.

Pharmacotherapy is necessary for women who are at high risk for fracture in the future and in women with established osteoporosis. Estrogen replacement therapy is the primary preventive and therapeutic modality for hypoestrogenic women with osteoporosis, and should be offered as the first line of therapy. Many randomized clinical trials have demonstrated that HT increases bone density at the hip, lumbar spine, and peripheral sites. Observational studies have also demonstrated reductions in fractures of the vertebrae, and possibly hip, in women on HT. A meta-analysis of 22 trials of estrogen reported an overall 27% reduction in nonvertebral fractures, taking into account that the quality of individual studies varied.[133] HERS and HERS II found no reduction in hip, wrist, vertebral, or total fractures with hormone therapy.[126] The WHI is the first randomized controlled trial to demonstrate reduction of hip fracture risk with estrogen use,[121] and risk reductions were also reported for vertebral and other osteoporotic fractures. Finally, the U.S. Preventive Services Task Force (USPSTF) concluded that there is good evidence that HT increases BMD and fair to good evidence that it reduces fractures, despite its overall unfavorable risk/benefit profile.[134]

Raloxifene is a *selective estrogen receptor modulator* (SERM), a term that defines compounds that are mixed estrogen receptor agonist. Raloxifene, the only SERM that the U.S. Food and Drug Administration (FDA) has approved, has demonstrated efficacy in prevention of osteoporosis and treatment of established bone demineralization.[135] Raloxifene shares some of the risks of estrogen but avoids others. It appears to cause a dramatic reduction in incident breast cancer, but increases the risks of thromboembolism in a manner similar to estrogen.[136] Its long-term safety profile is currently being established.

For women with established osteoporosis who cannot or prefer not to take estrogen, other pharmacologic modalities are available. Alendronate, a bisphosphonate that has been demonstrated to increase BMD and reduce fracture rate in menopausal women with osteoporosis, is FDA-approved for the prevention (5 mg daily) and treatment (10 mg daily or 70 mg weekly) of osteoporosis. It must be taken in the morning with 8 ounces of water, 30 minutes before taking any food or beverage because it is poorly absorbed by the gastrointestinal (GI) tract, and the woman must remain in the upright position to minimize its gastrointestinal side effects. Risedronate is more potent and has fewer upper gastrointestinal side effects than alendronate, and reduces the incidence of fractures in osteoporotic women.

Calcitonin inhibits bone resorption and can be delivered intranasally (one spray in each nostril) at a dose of 200 IU daily. It has been demonstrated to increase bone mass and reduce risk of vertebral fractures.[137,138] Although fluoride, which stimulates osteoblasts to produce new bone, has been demonstrated to improve bone density and decrease fracture risk,[139] there is insufficient evidence to support its safety and efficacy for the treatment of osteoporosis.[140] Finally, parathyroid hormone is not approved by the FDA for the treatment of osteoporosis.

Despite the demonstration of increased and unexpected risks associated with exogenous estrogen, it is clearly the least expensive long-term preventive and treatment modality available for osteoporosis today. In the post WHI era, many women are reluctant to take hormones. The FDA did not withdraw the indication of bone protection from estrogen, however. As our elderly population is growing, women not suffering from breast cancer and heart disease are at increased risk for fractures, and hormones are both beneficial and inexpensive, and may be particularly applicable in very low doses.[141] With the advent of a diverse armamentarium of effective agents, early detection, prevention, and treatment of osteoporosis with standardized screening techniques, alternate dosing of hormones and other medications, and close follow-up will most likely become commonplace.

## SUMMARY

Menopause represents an irreversible point in a woman's life after which ovarian follicle function definitively ceases. A series of ovarian, endocrine, and central nervous system events accompany the menopause transition. These events are associated with unique symptomatology and may acutely change a woman's risk for development of disease. Temporizing treatments are usually indicated in the perimenopausal period to assist women in coping with adverse physical symptoms and transient dysphoric mood. The clinician is constantly challenged to determine which symptoms and adverse health markers are occurring as a function of aging, and which are occurring as a function of menopause. Once a woman becomes postmenopausal, the hypoestrogenic background becomes a primary consideration in her subsequent development of osteoporosis, a disease that is becoming more prevalent as the population ages. Again, the clinician is challenged in the postmenopausal period to recognize that postmenopause is not a monolithic physiologic state, and that the aging changes continue to occur and may well challenge the appropriate therapeutic approaches for disease prevention and disease treatment. In the near future, better-defined guidelines for duration of therapies, a better understanding of the genetic contributions to risks for diseases of aging, and enhanced understanding of ovarian physiology can all be expected to improve the diagnostic and therapeutic accuracy of endocrinology as it is applied to the health of women.

## REFERENCES

1. Colombat de L'Isere M (1850): Diseases of Women. American edition translated by Meigs CD. Cited by Ricci JV: One Hundred Years of Gynaecology 1800–1900. Philadelphia, Blakiston,1945, p 532.
2. Hawkes K, O'Connell JF, Jones NG, et al: Grandmothering, menopause, and the evolution of human life histories. Proc Natl Acad Sci U S A 95:1336–1339, 1999.
3. Williams, G: Evolution 11:398–411, 1957.
4. Sommer B, Avis N, Meyer P, et al: Attitudes toward menopause and aging across ethnic/racial groups. Psychosom Med 61:863–875, 1999.
5. WHO Scientific Group: Research on Menopause in the 1990s: Report of a WHO Scientific Group. WHO Technical Report Series 866. Geneva, WHO, 1996.
6. Utian, WH: The International Menopause Society, Menopause-related terminology definitions. Climacteric 2:284–286, 1999.
7. Soules MR, Sherman S, Parrott, E, et al: Executive summary: Stages of Reproductive Aging Workshop (STRAW). Fertil Steril 76:874–878, 2001.
8. McKinlay SM, Brambilla DJ, Posner JG, et al: The normal menopause transition. Am J Hum Biol 4:37–46, 1992.
9. McKinlay SM, Bifano NL, McKinlay JB: Smoking and age at menopause in women. Ann Intern Med 103:350–356, 1985.
10. Gold EB, Bromberger J, Crawford S, et al: Factors associated with age at natural menopause in a multiethnic sample of midlife women. Am J Epidemiol 153:865–874, 2001.
11. Frere G: Mean age at menopause and menarche in South Africa. S Afr J Med Sci 36:21–24, 1971.
12. Bromberger JT, Matthews KA, Kuller LH, et al: Prospective study of the determinants of age at menopause. Am J Epidemiol 145:124–133, 1997.
13. Garcia VA, Nava LE, Malacara JM: La edad de la menopausia en lo poblacion urbana de la ciudad de Len Gto [in Spanish]. Rev Invest Clin 39:329–332, 1987.
14. Tamada T, Iwasake H: Age at natural menopause in Japanese women. Nippon Sanka Fujinka Gakkai Zasshi 47:947–952, 1995.
15. Ismael NN: A study of the menopause in Malaysia. Maturitas 19:205–209, 1994.
16. Torgerson DJ, Avenell A, Russell IT: Factors associated with onset of menopause in women aged 45–49. Maturitas 19:83–92, 1994.
17. Luoto R, Kaprio J, Uutela A: Age at natural menopause and sociodemographic status in Finland. Am J Epidemiol 139:64–76, 1994.

18. vanNoord PAH, Dubas JS, Dorland M, et al: Age at natural menopause in a population-based screening cohort: The role of menarche, fecundity, and lifestyle factors. Fertil Steril 68:95–102, 1997.

19. Stanford JL, Harge P, Brinton LA, et al: Factors influencing the age at natural menopause. J Chronic Dis 40:995–1002, 1987.

20. Whelan EA, Sandler DP, McConnaughey DR, et al: Menstrual and reproductive characteristics and age at natural menopause. Am J Epidemiol 131:625–632, 1990.

21. Cramer DW, Xu H, Harlow BL: Does "incessant" ovulation increase risk for early menopause? Am J Obstet Gynecol 172:568–573, 1995.

22. Hardy R, Kuh D: Reproductive characteristics and the age at inception of the peri-menopause in a British national cohort. Am J Epidemiol 149:612–620, 1999.

23. Willett W, Stampfer MJ, Bain C, et al: Cigarette smoking, relative weight, and menopause. Am J Epidemiol 117:651–658, 1983.

24. Crisponi L, Deiana M, Loi A, et al: The putative forkhead transcription factor FOXL2 is mutated in blepharophimosis/ptosis/epicanthus inversus syndrome. Nat Genet 27:159–166, 2001.

25. Anasti JN: Premature ovarian failure: An update. Fertil Steril 70:1–15, 1998.

26. Tibiletti MG, Testa G, Vegetti W, et al: The idiopathic forms of premature menopause and early menopause show the same genetic pattern. Hum Reprod 14:2731–2734, 1999.

27. Allingham-Hawkins DJ, Babul-Hirji R, Chitayat D, et al: Fragile X premutation is a risk factor for premature ovarian failure: The International Collaborative POF in Fragile study—preliminary data. Am J Med Genet 83:322–325, 1999.

28. Weel AE, Utterlinden AG, Westendorp IC, et al: Estrogen receptor polymorphism predicts the onset of natural and surgical menopause. J Clin Endocrinol Metab 84:3146–3150, 1999.

29. Cooper G, Sandler DP, Bohlig M: Active and passive smoking and the occurrence of natural menopause. Epidemiology 10:771–773, 1999.

30. Mattison DR, Thorgiersson SS: Smoking and industrial pollution and their effects on menopause and ovarian cancer. Lancet 1:187–188, 1978.

31. Vermeulen A: Environment, human reproduction, menopause, and andropause. Environ Health Perspect 101:91–100, 1993.

32. Cramer DW: Epidemiologic aspects of early menopause and ovarian cancer. Ann N Y Acad Sci 592:363–375, 1990.

33. Harlow BL, Wise LA, Otto MW, et al: Depression and its influence on reproductive endocrine and menstrual cycle markers associated with per menopause: The Harvard Study of Moods and Cycles. Arch Gen Psychiatry 60:29–36, 2003.

34. Campbell S, Whitehead M: Oestrogen therapy and the menopausal transition. Clin Obstet Gynaecol 4:31–47, 1977.

35. Baker TG: A quantitative and cytological study of germ cells in human ovaries. Proc R Soc London 158:417–33, Series B: Biological Sciences, 1963.

36. Zapantis G, Santoro N: Ovarian ageing and the menopause transition. Best Pract Res Clin Obstet Gynaecol 16:263–276, 2002.

37. Speroff L, Glass RH, Kase NG: Clinical Gynecologic Endocrinology and Infertility. Baltimore, Lippincott Williams & Wilkins, 1999, p 116.

38. Canning J, Takai Y, Tilly JL: Evidence for genetic modifiers of ovarian follicular endowment and development from studies of five inbred mouse strains. Endocrinology 144:9–12, 2003.

39. Reynaud K, Cortvrindt R, Smitz J, et al: Alterations in ovarian function of mice reduced amounts of KIT receptor. Reproduction 121:229–237, 2001.

40. Hreinsson JG, Scott JE, Rasmussen C, et al: Growth differentiation factor-9 promotes the growth, development, and survival of human ovarian follicles in organ culture. J Clin Endocrinol Metab 87:316–321, 2002.

41. Loffler, KA, Zarkower D, Koopman P: Etiology of ovarian failure in blepharophimosis ptosis epicanthus inversus syndrome: FOXL2 is a conserved, early-acting gene in vertebrate ovarian development. Endocrinology 144:3237–3243, 2003.

42. Richards JS, Sharma SC, Falendar AE, Lo YH: Expression of FKIIR, FKIIRL1, and AFX genes in the rodent ovary: Evidence for regulation by IGF-1, estrogen, and the gonadotropins. Mol Endocrinol 16:580–599, 2002.

43. Burger HG, Dudley EC, Robertson DM, et al: Hormonal changes in the menopause transition. Recent Prog Horm Res 57:257–275, 2002.

44. Ahmed-Ebbiary NA, Lenton EA, Cooke ID: Hypothalamic-pituitary ageing: Progressive increases in FSH and LH concentrations throughout the reproductive life in regularly menstruating women. Clin Endocrinol 41:199–206, 1994.

45. Klein NA, Soules MR: Endocrine changes of the peri menopause [review]. Clin Obstet Gynecol 41:912–920, 1998.

46. Robertson DM, Burger HG: Reproductive hormones: Ageing and the perimenopause. Acta Obstet Gynecol Scand 81:612, 2002.

47. Longscope C, Franz C, Morello C, et al: Steroid and gonadotropin levels in women during the perimenopausal years. Maturitas 8:189–196, 1986.

48. Brown JB, Harrisson P, Smith MA, et al: Correlations between the mucus symptoms and the hormonal markers of fertility throughout reproductive life. Melbourne, Ovulation Method Research Centre of Australia, Advocate Press, 1981.

49. Metcalf MG, Donald RA, Livesey JH: Pituatary-ovarian function in normal women during the menopausal transition. Clin Endocrinol 14:245–255, 1981.

50. Metcalf MG, Donald RA: Fluctuating ovarian function in a perimenopausal woman. N Z Med J 89:45–47, 1979.

51. Couzinet B, Meduri G, Lecce MG, et al: The postmenopausal ovary is not a major androgen-producing gland. J Clin Endocrinol Metab 86:5060–5066, 2001.

52. Zumoff B, Straw GW, Miller LK, et al: Twenty-four hour mean plasma testosterone concentration declines with age in normal premenopausal women. J Clin Endodcrinol Metab 80:1429–1430, 1995.

53. Burger HG, Dudley EC, Cui J, et al: A prospective longitudinal study of serum testosterone, dehydroepiandrosterone sulfate, and sew hormone–binding globulin levels through the menopause transition. J Clin Endocrinol Metab 85:2832–2838, 2000.

54. Carlstrom K, Brody S, Lunell NO, et al: Dehydroepiandrosterone sulphate and dehydroepiandrosterone in serum: Differences related to age and sex. Maturitas 10:297–306, 1988.

55. Lasley BL, Santoro N, Randolf JF, et al: The relationship of circulating dehydroepiandrosterone, testosterone, and estradiol to stages of the menopausal transition and ethnicity. J Clin Endocrinol Metab 87:3760–3767, 2002.

56. Rannevik G, Jeppsson S, Johnell O, et al: A longitudinal study of the peri menopausal transition: Altered profiles of steroid and pituitary hormones, SHBG, and bone mineral density. Maturitas 21:103–113, 1995.

57. Treloar AE, Boynton R, Behn BG, et al: Variation of the human menstrual cycle through reproductive life. Int J Fertil 12:77–126, 1967.

58. Taffe J, Dennerstein L: Menstrual patterns leading to the final menstrual period. Menopause 9:32–40, 2002.

59. Taffe J, Garameszegi C, Dudley E, et al: Determinants of self related menopause status. Maturitas 27:223–229, 1997.

60. Bromberger JT, Meyer PM, Kravitz HM, et al: Psychologic distress and natural menopause: A multicenter community study. Am J Public Health 91:1435–1442, 2001.

61. Lipton RB, Goadsby P, Silberstein SD: Classification and epidemiology of headache. Clin Cornerstone 1:1–10, 1999.

62. Santoro N, Miller Valery T: Menopause and the postmenopausal state. Curr Med 1:423–428, 1998.

63. Dennerstein L, Dudley EC, Hopper JL, et al: A prospective population-based study of menopausal symptoms. Obstet Gynecol 96:351–358, 2000.

64. Mitchell ES, Woods NF: Symptom experiences of midlife women: Observations from the Seattle Midlife Women's Health Study. Maturitas 25:1–10, 1996.

65. Whiteman MK, Staropoli CA, Benedict JC, et al: Risk factors for hot flashes in midlife women. J Womens Health 12:459–472, 2003.

66. Kronenberg F, Downey JA: Thermoregulatory physiology of menopausal hot flashes: A review. Can J Physiol Pharmacol 65:1312, 1987.

67. Schwingl PJ, Hulka BS, Harlow SD: Risk factors for menopausal hot flashes. Obstet Gynecol 64:29, 1994.

68. Oldenhave A, Jaszmann IJ, Haspels AA, et al: Impact of climacteric on well-being: A survey based on 5213 women 39 to 60 years old. Am J Obstet Gynecol 168:772, 1993.

69. Hollander LE, Freeman EW, Sammel Berlin JA, et al: Sleep quality, estradiol levels, and behavioral factors in late reproductive age women. Obstet Gynecol 98:391, 2001.

70. Hall JE, Lavoie HG, Marsh EE, et al: Decrease in gonadotropin-releasing hormone pulse frequency with aging in postmenopausal women. J Clin Endocrinol Metab 85:1794–1800, 2000.

71. Rossmanith WG, Scherbaum WA, Lauritzen C: Gonadotropin secretion during aging in postmenopausal women. Neuroendocrinology 54:211–218, 1991.

72. Santoro N, Banwell T, Tortoriello D, et al: Effects of aging and gonadal failure on the hypothalamic-pituitary axis in women. Am J Obstet Gynecol 178:732–741, 1998.

73. Wilshire GB, Loughlin JS, Brown JR, et al: Diminished function of the somatotrophic axis in older reproductive-aged women. J Clin Endocrinol Metab 80:608–613, 1995.

74. Santoro N: The menopause transition: An update. Hum Reprod Update 8:155–160, 2002.

75. Cummings DE, Merriam GR: Age-related changes in growth hormone secretion: Should the somatopause be treated? Semin Reprod Endocrinol 17:311–325, 1999.

76. Leitol H, Behrends J, Brabant G: The thyroid axis in ageing. Novartis Found Symp 242:193–204, 2002.

77. Monzani F, Del Guerra P, Caraccio N, et al: Age-related modifications in the regulation of the hypothalamic-pituitary-thyroid axis. Horm Res 46:107–112, 1996.

78. Mooradian AD: Normal age-related changes in thyroid hormone economy. Clin Geriatr Med 11:159–169, 1995.

79. Deuscle M, Gotthardt U, Weber B, et al: With aging in humans the activity of the hypothalamus-pituitary-adrenal system increases and its diurnal amplitude flattens. Life Sci 61:2239–2246, 1997.

80. Sowers MR, Greendale GA, Bondarenko I, et al: Endogenous hormones and bone turnover markers in pre- and perimenopausal women: SWAN. Osteoporos Int 14:191–197, 2003.

81. Sowers MR, Finkelstein JS, Ettinger B, et al: Study of Women's Health Across the Nation: The association of endogenous hormone concentrations and bone mineral density measures in pre- and perimenopausal women of four ethnic groups: SWAN. Osteoporos Int 14:44–52, 2003.

82. Greendale GA, Huang MH, Wang Y, et al: Sport and home physical activity are independently associated with bone density. Med Sci Sports Exerc 35:506–512, 2003.

83. Verghese J, Lipton RB, Katz MJ, et al: Leisure activities and the risk of dementia in the elderly. N Engl J Med 348:2508–2516, 2003.

84. Lemonick MD, Park A: The Nun study. Time 157:54–59, 62, 64, 2001.

85. Linzbach AJ, Akuamoa-Boateng E: Die Alternsveranderungen des menschlichen Herzens [in German]. I Das Herzgewicht im Alter Klin Wochenschr 51:156–163, 1973.

86. Kitzman DW, Scholz DG, Hagen PT, et al: Age-related changes in normal human hearts during the first 10 decades of life. Part II (Maturity): A quantitative anatomic study of 765 specimens from subjects 20 to 99 years old. Mayo Clin Proc 63:137–146, 1988.

87. Spirito P, Maron BJ: Influence of aging on Doppler echocardiographic indices of left ventricular diastolic function. Br Heart J 59:672–679, 1988.

88. Sartori MP, Quinones MA, Kuo LC: Relation of Doppler-derived left ventricular filling parameters to age and radius/thickness ratio in normal and pathologic states. Am J Cardiol 59:1179–1182, 1987.

89. Duncan AK, Vittone J, Fleming KC, et al: Cardiovascular disease in elderly patients. Mayo Clinic Proc 71:184–196, 1996.

90. Burger HG: Diagnostic role of follicle stimulating hormone (FSH) measurements during the menopause transition: An analysis of FSH, oestradiol and inhibin. Eur J Endocrinol 130:38–42, 1994.

91. Lobo RA: Treatment of the Postmenopausal Woman: Basic and Clinical Aspects, 2d ed. Philadelphia, Lippincott Williams & Wilkins, 1999, p 67.

92. Burger HD, Dudley EC, Hooper JL, et al: The endocrinology of the menopausal transition: A cross-sectional study of a population-based sample. J Clin Endocrinol Metab 80:3537–3545, 1995.

93. Dennerstein L, Lehert P, Burger H, et al: Mood and the menopause transition. J Nerv Ment Dis 187:685–691,1999.

94. Kim TJ, Anasti JN, Flack MR, et al: Routine endocrine screening for patients with karyotypically normal spontaneous premature ovarian failure. Obstet Gynecol 89:777–779, 1997.

95. Nelson HD, Humphrey LL, Nygren P, et al: Postmenopausal hormone replacement therapy: Scientific review. JAMA 287:591–597, 2002.

96. Best clinical practices. In the International Position Paper on Women's Health and Menopause: A Comprehensive Approach. National Heart, Lung, and Blood Institute, NIH Office of Research on Women's Health, Giovanni Lorenzini Medical Science Foundation. 2002, pp 1–32.

97. Utian WH, Burry KA, Archer DF, et al: Efficacy and safety of low, standard, and high doses of an estradiol transdermal system (Esclim) compared with placebo on vasomotor symptoms in highly symptomatic menopausal patients. The Esclim Study Group. Am J Obstet Gynecol 181:71–79, 1999.

98. Rovati LC, Setnikar I, Genazzani AR: Dose-response efficacy of a new estradiol transdermal matrix patch for 7-day application: A randomized, double-blind, placebo-controlled study. Italian Menopause Research Group. Gynecol Endocrinol 14:282–291, 2000.

99. De Aloysio D, Rovati LC, Giacovelli G, et al: Efficacy on climacteric symptoms and safety of low dose estradiol transdermal matrix patches. A randomized, double-blind placebo-controlled study. Arzneimittelforschung 50:293–300, 2000.

100. Lopes P, Rozenberg S, Graaf J, et al: Aerodiol versus the transdermal route: Perspectives for patient preference. Maturitas 15(Suppl 1):S31–S39, 2001.

101. Ozsoy M, Oral B, Ozsoy D: Clinical equivalence of intranasal estradiol and oral estrogen for postmenopausal symptoms. Int J Gynaecol Obstet 79:143–146, 2002.

102. Rozenbaum H, Chevallier O, Moyal M, et al: Efficacy and tolerability of pulsed estrogen therapy: A 12-week double-blind placebo-controlled study in highly symptomatic postmenopausal women. Aerodiol study group. Climacteric 5:249–258, 2002.

103. Steingold KA, Laufer L, Chetkowski RJ, et al: Treatment of hot flashes with transdermal estradiol administration. J Clin Endocrinol Metab 61:627–632, 1985.

104. Baroton D, Loprinzi C, Wahner-Roedler D: Hot flashes: Aetiology and management. Drugs Aging 18:597–606, 2001.

105. Loprinzi CL, Pisansky TM, Fonseca R, et al: Pilot evaluation of venlafaxine hydrochloride for the therapy of hot flashes in cancer survivors. J Clin Oncol 16:2377–2381, 1998.

106. Stearns V, Beebe KL, Iyengar M, et al: Paroxetine controlled release in the treatment of menopausal hot flashes: A randomized controlled trial. JAMA 289:2827–2834, 2003.

107. Landgren MB, Bennink HJ, Helmond FA, et al: Dose-response analysis of effects of tibolone on climacteric symptoms. BJOG 109:1109–1114, 2002.

108. Al-Azzawi F, Wahab M, Habiba M, et al: Continuous combined hormone replacement therapy compared with tibolone. Obstet Gynecol 93:258–264, 1999.

109. Hammar M, Christau S, Nathorst-Boos J, et al: A double-blind, randomized trial comparing the effects of tibolone and continous combined hormone replacement therapy in postmenopausal women with menopausal symptoms. Br J Obstet Gynaecol 105:904–911, 1998.

110. Boulot P, Viala JL: A multicenter comparison of veralipride versus placebo in the vasomotor flushes of menopause: An evaluation of the prolonged effect. Rev Fr Gynecol Obstet 83:823–827, 1988.

111. Bullock JL, Massey FM, Gambrell RD Jr: Use of medroxyprogesterone acetate to prevent menopausal symptoms. Obstet Gynecol 46:165–168, 1975.

112. Quella SK, Loprinzi C, Sloan JA, et al: Long term use of megestrol acetate by cancer survivors for the treatment of hot flashes. Cancer 82:1784–1788, 1998.

113. Pandya KJ, Raubertas RF, Flynn PJ, et al: Oral clonidine in postmenopausal patients with breast cancer experiencing tamoxifen-induced hot flashes: A University of Rochester Cancer Center Community Clinical Oncology Program study. Ann Intern Med 16:788–793, 2000.

114. Nagamani M, Kelver ME, Smith ER: Treatment of menopausal hot flashes with transdermal administration of clonidine. Am J Obstet Gynecol 156:561–565, 1987.

115. Albertazzi P, Pansini F, Bonaccorsi G, et al: The effect of dietary soy supplementation on hot flushes. Obstet Gynecol 91:6–11, 1998.

116. Warnecke G: Influence of a phytopharmaceutical on climacteric complaints. Die medizinische Welt 36:871–874, 1985.

117. Chenoy R, Hussain S, Tayob Y, et al: Effect of oral gamolenic acid from evening primrose oil on menopausal flushing. Br Med J 308:501–503, 1994.

118. Hirata JD, Swiersz LM, Zell B, et al: Does dong quai have estrogenic effects in postmenopausal women? A double-blind, placebo-controlled trial. Fertil Steril 68:981–986, 1997.

119. Tietjen GE: The relationship of migraines and stroke. Neuroepidemiology 19:13–19, 2000.

120. Sulak PJ, Bressman BE, Waldrop E, et al: Extending the duration of active oral contraceptive pills to manage hormone withdrawal symptoms. Obstet Gynecol 89:179–183, 1997.

121. Writing Group for the Women's Health Initiative Investigators: Risks and benefits of estrogen plus progestin in healthy postmenopausal women. JAMA 228:321–333, 2002.

122. Hulley S, Grady D, Bush T, et al: Randomized trial of estrogen plus progestin for secondary prevention of coronary heart disease in postmenopausal women. Heart and Estrogen/progestin Replacement Study (HERS) Research Group. JAMA 280:605–613, 1998.

123. Grady D, Herrington D, Bittner V, et al: Cardiovascular disease outcomes during 6.8 years of hormone therapy. JAMA 288:49–57, 2002.

124. Mosca L, Collins P, Herrington DM, et al: Hormone replacement therapy and cardiovascular disease. Circulation 104:499–503, 2001.

125. Miller J, Chan BKS, Nelson HD: Postmenopausal estrogen replacement and risk of venous thromboembolism: A systemic evidence review and meta-analysis for the US Preventive Services Task Force. Ann Intern Med 136:680–690, 2002.

126. Hulley S, Furberg C, Barrett-Connor E, et al: Noncardiovascular disease outcomes during 6.8 years of hormone therapy: Heart and Estrogen/progestin Replacement Study follow–up (HERS II). JAMA 288:58–66, 2002.

127. American College of Obstetricians and Gynecologists: Guidelines for Women's Health Care, 2d ed. Washington, DC, American College of Obstetricians and Gynecologists, 2002, pp 130–133, 171–176, 314–318.

128. North American Menopause Society (NAMS): Report from the NAMS Advisory Panel on Postmenopausal Hormone Therapy. Available at *www.menopause.org.*

129. American Heart Association: Q & A about hormone replacement therapy. Available at *http://216.185.112.5/ presenter.jhtml?identifier=3004068.*

130. Gutin B, Kasper MJ: Can vigorous exercise play a role in osteoporosis prevention? A review. Osteoporos Int 2:55–69, 1992.

131. Dalsky GP, Stocke KS, Ehsani AA, et al: Weight-bearing exercise training and lumbar bone mineral content in postmenopausal women. Ann Intern Med 108:824–828, 1988.

132. Fiatarone MA, Marks EC, Ryan ND, et al: High-intensity strength training in nonagenarians: Effects on skeletal muscle. JAMA 263:3029–3034, 1990.

133. Togerson DJ, Bell-Syer SE: Hormone replacement therapy and prevention of no vertebral fractures: A meta-analysis of randomized trials. JAMA 285:2891–2897, 2001.

134. U.S. Preventive Services Task Force: Postmenopausal hormone replacement therapy for primary prevention of chronic conditions: Recommendations and rationale. Ann Intern Med 137:834–839, 2002.

135. Ettinger B, Black DM, Mitlak BH, et al: Reduction of vertebral fracture risk in postmenopausal women with osteoporosis treated with raloxifene: Results from a 3-year randomized clinical trial. Multiple Outcomes of Raloxifene Evaluation (MORE) Investigators. JAMA 282:637–645, 1999.

136. Goldstein SR, Siddhanti S, Ciaccia AV, et al: A pharmacological review of selective oestrogen receptor modulators. Hum Reprod Update 6:212–224, 2000.

137. Overgaard K, Hansen MA, Jensen SB, et al: Effect of salcatonin given intranasal on bone mass and fracture rates in established osteoporosis: A dose-response study. Br Med J 305:556–561, 1992.

138. Rico H, Hernandez ER, Revilla M, et al: Salmon calcitonin reduces vertebral fracture rate in postmenopausal crush fracture syndrome. Bone Miner 16:131–138, 1992.

139. Pak CYC, Sakhaee K, Piziak V, et al: Slow-release sodium fluoride treatment on the fracture rate in postmenopausal women with osteoporosis. N Engl J Med 322:802–809, 1990.

140. American Medical Association: Drug Evaluations Annual. Chicago, AMA, 1995.

141. Prestwood KM, Kenny AM, Kleppinger A, et al: Ultralow-dose micron zed 17beta-estradiol and bone density and bone metabolism is older women: A randomized controlled trail. JAMA 290:1042–1048, 2003.

# CHAPTER 163

# Ovarian Tumors with Endocrine Manifestations

## Gary L. Keeney

**OVARIAN TUMORS ASSOCIATED WITH STEROID HORMONE ABNORMALITIES**
Sex Cord–Stromal Cell Tumors
Steroid Cell Tumors
Gonadoblastoma
Tumors with Functioning Stroma

**GONADOTROPIN-SECRETING TUMORS**
Germ Cell Tumors

**SPECIALIZED TERATOMAS WITH HORMONE PRODUCTION**
Struma Ovarii
Carcinoid

Strumal Carcinoid
Teratoma Containing Pituitary Adenoma

**TUMORS WITH ECTOPIC HORMONE PRODUCTION**

**TUMOR-LIKE CONDITIONS WITH ENDOCRINE MANIFESTATIONS**
Solitary Follicular Cyst and Corpus Luteum Cyst
Polycystic Ovarian Syndrome
Stromal Hyperplasia and Hyperthecosis
Massive Ovarian Edema
Pregnancy Luteoma, Hyperreactio Luteinalis, and Large Solitary Luteinized Follicular Cyst of Pregnancy and Puerperium

## OVARIAN TUMORS ASSOCIATED WITH STEROID HORMONE ABNORMALITIES

Ovarian tumors with overt endocrine manifestations constitute less than 5% of all ovarian neoplasms and less than 10% of all malignant ovarian tumors. These tumors may produce the steroid hormones directly or produce a steroid nucleus, which can then be converted to the functioning compound elsewhere. Ovarian tumors probably produce hormones at a higher subclinical rate, as evidenced by increased maturation on the vaginal smears of postmenopausal women with ovarian cancers[1] and increased total urinary estrogens in 50% of women with surface epithelial tumors.[2] The stroma associated with many of these tumors has cells closely resembling those seen in functioning sex cord–stromal tumors.[3]

Most ovarian tumors with endocrine manifestations are associated with overproduction of steroid hormones. Estrogens are most commonly produced, but androgens and, rarely, progesterone and corticosteroids are also produced. Some tumors with specialized tissue, such as thyroid or pituitary cells, produce specific secretory products.

### SEX CORD–STROMAL CELL TUMORS

Sex cord–stromal cell tumors include all neoplasms that contain granulosa cells, theca cells, Sertoli cells, and Leydig cells singly or in combination.[3] Granulosa cells and Sertoli cells arise from the sex cords. Theca cells, Leydig cells, and fibroblasts arise from the supporting stroma. The cellular elements often differentiate in an ovarian direction (granulosa cells, theca cells, or both) or in a testicular direction (Sertoli cells, Leydig cells, or both). These two groups of tumors are the tumors most frequently associated with endocrine manifestations.[3,4]

#### Granulosa Cell Tumors

Granulosa cell tumors may be composed exclusively of granulosa cells or have a significant component of theca cells and fibroblasts.[3,5,6] Granulosa cell tumors account for approximately 1.5% of all ovarian tumors[7] and for 6% of malignant ovarian tumors.[8] Approximately three fourths are associated with hyperestrinism, but rare cases are androgenic.[9,10] Five percent of granulosa cell tumors occur before the onset of puberty and approximately three fourths of these are

associated with isosexual pseudoprecocity, accounting for 3% to 10% of all cases of sexual precocity.[11,12] The remaining cases of granulosa cell tumors occur most often in the postmenopausal age group. A specific pattern of granulosa cell tumors occurring in the first two decades of life has been referred to as juvenile granulosa cell tumors. These have been a associated with Ollier's disease (endochondromatosis) and Maffucci's syndrome (endochondromatosis and hemangiomatosis).[5,13–16] Granulosa cell tumors are associated with elevated estrogen, inhibin, and follicle-regulation protein levels.[17–19] Ten percent present with abdominal pain due to tumor rupture.[5]

Granulosa cell tumors are unilateral in 95% of cases. The tumor is usually palpable on pelvic or abdominal examination. In approximately 10% of patients, the tumor is not discovered until the ovary is sectioned by the pathologist.[20] These tumors vary greatly in size.[21] Approximately 11% are 5 cm or less in diameter, 38% range from 6 to 10 cm, 24% from 11 to 15 cm, and 27% are more than 15 cm.[5,22] The appearance varies from uniformly solid to large unilocular or multilocular cystic tumors.

Microscopically, granulosa cell tumors are composed of granulosa cells with or without a stromal component of fibroblasts, theca cells, or lutein cells. Various patterns are seen, with two or more coexisting in the same lesion. The microfollicular pattern with Call-Exner bodies is the most characteristic pattern. Other patterns include macrofollicular, trabecular, insular, solid tubular, gyriform, and water silk (moiré). The single best diagnostic criterion is the finding of the characteristic nuclei. The nuclei are typically pale, round-oval to angular, and often haphazardly oriented to each other. They are often grooved. Less well-differentiated forms of granulosa cell tumors have been called diffuse or sarcomatoid and may resemble a round cell sarcoma. Typical granulosa cells may be difficult to find in these patterns. Some patterns of granulosa cell tumors may mimic ovarian carcinoma, particularly the endometrioid type.[23]

The histology of juvenile granulosa cell tumors is distinctive.[12,24–28] Low-power examination shows sheets and nodular aggregates of granulosa cells with scattered varying-sized follicles containing eosinophilic or basophilic secretions. The tumor cells lack the grooved nuclei seen in the adult granulosa cell tumor.

Most granulosa cell tumors are estrogenic. Approximately 80% of tumors arising in prepubertal girls are associated with isosexual pseudoprecocity. After the removal of a functioning tumor, withdrawal bleeding typically occurs in 1 to 2 days, and regular menses follow shortly. Ten percent of granulosa cell tumors have extended beyond the ovary, usually into the pelvis, at the time of diagnosis. When stage I tumors recur, it is usually in the pelvis. Distant metastases are rare. Most recurrences in adult granulosa cell tumors are after 5 years. There are reported recurrences as late as 20 to 30 years. Juvenile granulosa cell tumors tend to recur within 2 to 3 years, and if they do recur, they tend to have a more aggressive course.[12]

The preferred treatment for stage I granulosa cell tumors in postmenopausal woman is total hysterectomy and bilateral salpingo-oophorectomy. Younger women who wish to maintain fertility may be treated with unilateral salpingo-oophorectomy if the disease has not spread beyond the ovary. Recurrent disease is usually managed surgically. Radiation and chemotherapy have been used with varying success.[29,30] The prognosis for granulosa cell tumors is good. The 10-year survival rate ranges from 90% to 95%. There is a progressive decline in survival with longer follow-up.[5,6] The most important factor in determining prognosis is tumor stage. Ruptured tumors and tumors with a high degree of nuclear atypia tend to behave more aggressively.

## Thecomas and Fibromas

Thecomas and fibromas occur approximately one third as commonly as granulosa cell tumors and at an older average age of 59 years.[31] It is unusual to see these tumors before puberty.[32-34] Fibromas are composed of fibroblasts of ovarian stromal origin and are nonfunctional. Thecomas are composed of theca cells and typically contain abundant lipid. These patients often demonstrate estrogenic manifestations.[35-37] Tumors with mixed ovarian stromal fibroblasts and theca differentiation seldom have estrogenic manifestations.

Most thecomas range in size from 5 to 10 cm in diameter. The cut surface is solid and yellow or white with yellow flecks. Microscopically, thecomas show ill-defined masses of rounded vacuolated cells with abundant lipid. Luteinized thecomas show similar features but also contain lutein cells, singly or in nests. Luteinized thecomas are estrogenic in approximately one half of cases and virilizing in approximately 10% of cases.[38,39]

Thecomas are bilateral in 3% of cases.[37] A few cases of malignant thecomas have been reported in the literature. However, many of these likely represent fibrosarcomas or diffuse granulosa cell tumors.[40]

Another rare tumor in this group is the sclerosing stromal cell tumor. In contrast to fibromas and thecomas, this tumor usually presents in the first three decades.[41,42] Microscopically, there are alternating areas of hypo- and hypercellularity and a prominent hemangiopericytoma-like vascular pattern. The cellular component ranges from fibroblasts to lipid-laden cells.[42] Some of these tumors have been associated with estrogen and androgen secretion.[43,44]

## Sertoli-Stromal Cell Tumors

Sertoli-stromal cell tumors (androblastomas) contain Sertoli cells, Leydig cells, and indifferent stromal cells or all three in varying proportions with varying degrees of differentiation.[3,45-47] These tumors account for less than 0.2% of ovarian neoplasms.[47-49] They are often seen in the early reproductive age group but may be encountered at any age. The average age is 25 years.[47] Approximately one half of the patients present with hirsutism or virilization. After removal of the tumor, menses usually return to normal in approximately 4 weeks and hirsutism improves. Clitoral enlargement and deepening of the voice are less likely to regress.

Occasional patients have estrogen-related manifestations.[47] Plasma testosterone levels are always elevated in virilized patients, ranging from 1.2 to 7.0 ng/mL (4.2–24.2 nmol/L).[50] Some tumors have been associated with elevated α-fetoprotein levels but not to the extent seen in ovarian yolk sac tumors.[51]

The diameter of Sertoli-stromal cell tumors is variable, averaging 10 cm. They are usually firm, lobulated, and yellow to tan. A cystic component may be present. Hemorrhage and necrosis are uncommon except in poorly differentiated tumors.

On microscopic examination, Sertoli-stromal cell tumors have been divided into five categories: well-differentiated, tumors of intermediate differentiation, poorly differentiated (sarcomatoid), tumors with heterologous elements, and retiform type. Well-differentiated tumors are composed of hollow or solid tubules filled or lined by Sertoli cells. The intervening stroma contains variable numbers of Leydig cells.[46] These cells may contain Reinke's crystals, the specific cytoplasmic inclusion seen in testicular Leydig cells. Tumors of intermediate differentiation have a lobulated appearance with densely cellular areas divided by relatively acellular fibrous bands. The cellular areas may have well-defined islands and cords or ill-defined masses of Sertoli cells. Leydig cells are best demonstrated at the periphery of the cellular nodules. Poorly differentiated Sertoli-stromal cell tumors may resemble poorly differentiated carcinoma or sarcoma. Areas showing mature Sertoli cells and Leydig cells must be present to make the diagnosis of Sertoli-stromal cell tumor. Tumors with heterologous elements account for 20% of Sertoli-stromal cell tumors.[46] The most common heterologous component is mucinous epithelium of the gastrointestinal type.[52] The mucinous epithelium is usually benign but may be borderline or malignant.[52,53] Approximately one fourth of heterologous tumors have foci of immature skeletal muscle, cartilage, or both.[52,54] When such foci are extensive, the prognosis is poor. Retiform Sertoli-stromal cell tumors have tubules and papillary projections that simulate the rete testis.[55,56] Sometimes the complexity of the papilla raises the possibility of an epithelial malignancy.

Sertoli-stromal cell tumors may also be composed exclusively of either Sertoli cells or Leydig cells in various degrees of differentiation. Pure Sertoli cell tumors may contain lipid and be associated with estrogenic manifestations. Tumors composed of Leydig cells may arise directly from the hilar cells (hilar Leydig cells).

Sertoli-stromal cell tumors are treated with salpingo-oophorectomy. In younger patients wishing to maintain fertility, unilateral salpingo-oophorectomy may be considered provided there is no evidence of contralateral involvement or extraovarian disease.

The overall 5-year survival rate for patients with Sertoli-stromal cell tumors is approximately 80%. The prognosis varies greatly with tumor stage and degree of differentiation.[47] Most tumors are stage I. Well-differentiated Sertoli-stromal cell tumors are benign. Poorly differentiated Sertoli-stromal cell tumors are aggressive, with only a 41% survival rate. Intermediate differentiated tumors have an 89% survival rate and heterologous tumors, an 81% survival rate. Recurrences usually occur within the first year and are rare after 5 years.

## Sex Cord Tumor with Annular Tubules

The sex cord–stromal tumor with annular tubules is associated with Peutz-Jeghers syndrome in one third of cases[57] and rarely with minimal deviation adenocarcinoma (adenoma malignum) of the cervix.[58,59] When associated with Peutz-Jeghers syndrome, these tumors are usually an incidental, microscopic, multifocal finding, bilaterally in ovaries removed for another reason.[60,61] Patients without Peutz-Jeghers syndrome typically present with a palpable mass and 40% have clinical manifestations of hyperestrinism.

These tumors are composed of simple and complex ringlike solid tubular structures. Some cells lining the tubules contain Charcot-Böttcher bundles of filaments demonstrated by electron microscopy.[62] These are thought to represent Sertoli cell differentiation. Other areas more closely resemble granulosa cell tumor.

The incidental tumors associated with Peutz-Jeghers syndrome are considered benign. The larger tumors may metastasize to lymph nodes. In one case, a woman had repeated lymph node metastasis over a 22-year period. The recurrences were associated with marked elevation of müllerian-inhibiting substance in the plasma. Inhibin and progesterone levels were also elevated.[63]

## STEROID CELL TUMORS

Steroid cell tumors are composed of cells that have morphologic features of steroid hormone–producing cells.[3,64] Patients are virilized in almost one half of the cases, but evidence of endocrine function is often absent. Rarely, these tumors are associated with estrogenic changes or Cushing's syndrome. Steroid cell tumors are separated into three categories depending on the cell of origin.

### Steroid Cell Tumors, Not Otherwise Specified (Lipid Cell Tumor)

Steroid cell tumors, not otherwise specified, are the most common tumors in the steroid cell tumor category, accounting for approximately two thirds of cases.[64] They may occur at any age, with an average age of 43 years. They are usually virilizing[64] but may be estrogenic or unassociated with endocrine manifestations. Rare cases occurring in children have been associated with isosexual pseudoprecocity. Some tumors in this group have caused unequivocal Cushing's syndrome.[64–66]

Most tumors are unilateral, solid, and mutinodular, averaging 8.5 cm in diameter.[64] The color depends on the amount of lipid present in the cells. Tumors with a large amount of intracytoplasmic lipid are yellow and those that are lipid free are dark brown or black. Larger tumors may have areas of hemorrhage and necrosis.

Microscopically, cells are arranged in a diffuse pattern, nests, or columns and cords separated by a rich vascular network. The typical tumor cell is polygonal and medium to large in size and has slightly granular to eosinophilic cytoplasm. Some tumors show moderate to marked cytologic atypia.

In a review of cases at the Armed Forces Institute of Pathology, Taylor and Norris[67] found that at least one fourth of these tumors were clinically malignant. In the large series of Hayes and Scully,[64] 36% were clinically malignant. Malignancy is more common in postmenopausal than premenopausal women. The most reliable pathologic features of malignancy are two or more mitotic figures per 10 high-power fields (92% malignant), necrosis (86% malignant), maximal diameter of 7 cm or greater (78% malignant), hemorrhage (77% malignant), and grade 2 to 3 nuclear atypia (64% malignant).

Chemotherapy for malignant steroid cell tumors has limited success. Some patients have responded well to gonadotropin-releasing hormone agonist therapy.[68]

### Stromal Luteoma

The term *stromal luteoma* is applied to small steroid cell tumors that lie within the ovarian stroma and presumably arise from it.[69] These account for approximately 25% of steroid cell tumors. They occur over a wide age range, with an average age of 58 years.[69] Approximately 60% are estrogenic and 12% are androgenic.

Microscopic examination shows a rounded nodule of lutein-type cells growing in nests and cords. The stroma is usually sparse. Some large steroid cell tumors may be of stromal origin, but the specific diagnosis cannot be made when the tumor is no longer confined to the ovarian stroma. These tumors are benign.

### Leydig (Hilar) Cell Tumors

The Leydig cell nature of a steroid cell tumor can be proved only by the identification of Reinke's crystals in the cytoplasm by light or electron microscopic examination.[70] Only 35% to 40% of testicular Leydig cell tumors contain Reinke's crystals on light microscopic examination. Because Leydig cells cannot be otherwise differentiated from lutein cells or adrenal cortical cells, it is reasonable to assume that a number of steroid cell tumors, not otherwise specified, are Leydig cell tumors. Leydig cell tumors situated in the hilum of the ovary are referred to as hilar cell tumors.[70–72]

Hilar cell tumors occur at an average age of 58 years. They cause hirsutism and virilization in 75% of cases.[70] The androgenic manifestations are often of long duration and contrast with those seen in patients with Sertoli-Leydig cell tumors, which usually are more abrupt. Most hilar cell tumors are benign.

Leydig cell tumors, nonhilar type, range from 1 to 15 cm in diameter, with most being less than 5 cm. They are usually unilateral. The cut surface is brown, orange, or yellow. On microscopic examination, the cells grow in sheets, cords, or nests. Individual tumor cells are indistinguishable from those seen in steroid cell tumors but with the added feature of Reinke's crystals. These 10- to 20-μm crystals are slender rod-like bodies with rounded square or tapering ends. Leydig cell tumors have also been uniformly benign.

## GONADOBLASTOMA

Gonadoblastoma is a rare tumor that occurs almost exclusively in children or young adults with an underlying gonadal disorder.[73,74] The most common disorders associated with this tumor are 46,XY pure gonadal dysgenesis and mixed gonadal dysgenesis. Occasional patients have had Turner's syndrome or true hermaphroditism. Eighty percent of the patients are phenotypic females who are usually masculinized to some extent. Clinical and biochemical evidence suggests that the Leydig-like cells of the tumor are capable of androgen production causing virilization. In vitro evidence of estrogen production had been reported, and a few patients have experienced hot flashes after removal of the tumor.[74] Calcification can be so extensive in these tumors that they may be seen on a pelvic radiograph.

The gross appearance varies according to the presence or absence of an associated malignant germ cell tumor and calcification. The tumors may be soft and fleshy or firm and cartilaginous, flecked with calcification, or totally calcified. Pure gonadoblastomas are usually less than 8 cm in diameter and 25% are microscopic. Those with an associated malignant germ cell tumor component are larger. Tumors are bilateral in one third of cases, and less often the opposite gonad contains a malignant germ cell tumor with no evidence of an underlying gonadoblastoma. The gonad in which a gonadoblastoma develops is unknown in 60%, an abdominal or inguinal testis in 20%, and a gonadal streak in 20% of cases.

The characteristic microscopic appearance is of discrete cellular aggregates composed of an intimate admixture of germ cells, sex cord, and sometimes stromal cells. The germ cells are similar to those of ovarian dysgerminoma. The sex cord elements have the appearance of immature Sertoli or granulosa cells. Extensive deposition of basement membrane material, calcification, or overgrowth by a malignant germ cell tumor may greatly alter this basic pattern. The most common associated malignant germ cell component is germinoma (80%). Other malignant germ cell components (yolk sac tumor, embryonal carcinoma, choriocarcinoma) may be present.[73,74] Gonadoblastoma without an invasive germ cell tumor component is clinically benign, but due to the high frequency (~60%) of an associated malignant germ cell tumor component, it should be regarded as an in situ malignant germ cell tumor and removed. The contralateral gonad is at risk because these tumors are bilateral in one third of cases. Many gonadoblastomas are found incidentally on a biopsy specimen obtained to establish the diagnosis of a sexual disorder. Twenty-five percent of patients with gonadal dysgenesis and a Y chromosome have been reported to have gonadoblastoma or other malignant germ cell tumor, and routine gonadectomy is recommended for patients with this disorder. In gonads containing only gonadoblastoma, the survival rate is 100%. If an invasive malignant germ cell tumor component is present, the prognosis assumes that of the germ cell tumor in its pure form.

### TUMORS WITH FUNCTIONING STROMA

In tumors with functioning stroma, the neoplastic cells stimulate the tumor or residual normal ovarian stroma to become hormonally active.[3,75–82] This phenomenon can be seen in primary tumors and tumors metastatic to the ovaries. The evidence of functioning stroma can be the appearance of an endocrine disorder that regresses after removal of the tumor, abnormal preoperative levels of steroid hormones, the presence of cells resembling steroid-producing cells in the tumor stroma, and recovery of steroids from the tumor tissue.

Some ovarian tumors with functioning stroma occur in virilized pregnant women, suggesting that human chorionic gonadotropin (hCG) is a factor in stromal stimulation.[3,75–82] Most ovarian tumors with functioning stroma occur in nonpregnant patients, and hCG produced by the tumor likely plays a role in stromal stimulation. A number of ovarian carcinoma types have been associated with elevated serum hCG levels.[83] Immunoperoxidase stains also show epithelial staining.[84]

### GONADOTROPIN-SECRETING TUMORS

#### GERM CELL TUMORS

Choriocarcinoma is a malignant germ cell tumor composed of cytotrophoblasts and syncytiotrophoblasts without the presence of chorionic villi. Choriocarcinoma of the ovary is usually metastatic from another site or is gestation related. Pure choriocarcinoma of germ cell origin is rare and usually a component of another malignant germ cell tumor.[3,85–88] The germ cell origin of choriocarcinoma is acceptable only if the tumor develops before puberty or is associated with another germ cell tumor type. Patients are usually younger than the age of 20 years and present with abdominal enlargement and pain. Serum hCG levels are elevated and may cause isosexual pseudoprecocity in children, and menstrual abnormalities, rapid breast enlargement, and occasionally colostrum secretion in adults. Serum levels of hCG, placental lactogen, estrogens, and androgens may be elevated.

Germ cell choriocarcinoma is not as responsive to chemotherapy as gestational choriocarcinoma. The tumors are rapidly progressive with distant metastasis. Combination chemotherapy with methotrexate, dactinomycin, and chlorambucil has produced prolonged remissions in some patients.

Other malignant germ cell tumors, most notably embryonal carcinoma, polyembryoma, and dysgerminoma, may have scattered syncytiotrophoblastic cells capable of producing clinically significant quantities of hCG.[78,89–92]

## SPECIALIZED TERATOMAS WITH HORMONE PRODUCTION

### STRUMA OVARII

In struma ovarii, the main component of the teratoma is thyroid-type tissue. This is the most common monodermal teratoma,[93,94] with a peak incidence in the fifth decade of life. The most common symptom is a pelvic mass. Patients may have Meigs' syndrome[95] and occasionally hormonal manifestations due to peripheral luteinization.[96] Rare cases have caused or contributed to the development of hyperthyroidism, and enlargement of the thyroid has been reported in 15% of cases.

Grossly, the thyroid tissue is usually solid and is brown or greenish-brown. There may be an associated dermoid cyst, mucinous or serous cystadenoma, and, rarely, a Brenner tumor. Microscopically, a struma may resemble normal thyroid tissue or have changes similar to those of a thyroid adenoma. In some cases, typical thyroid follicles may be sparse and the lesion confused with another tumor type.[94] Although 5% to 10% of reported strumas have been considered malignant, only 40% have been associated with extraovarian spread. Occasionally, vascular invasion and a papillary carcinoma pattern are observed. Less than 5% of strumas have had a malignant clinical course, with metastasis reported to the lungs, bones, liver, and brain.[3,97,98] Occasionally, struma implants on the peritoneum as benign-appearing nodules of thyroid tissue (peritoneal strumosis). Despite being considered "malignant," the course is indolent.

Most strumas are adequately treated by oophorectomy. If the tumor is greater than 5 cm in diameter or has solid foci on microscopic examination, radiologic examination of the lungs and bones and scanning with iodine are indicated to rule out possible metastases. Treatment with thyroidectomy and iodine-131 should be considered for malignant struma ovarii.[99]

### CARCINOID

Carcinoids are the second most common type of ovarian monodermal teratoma. They are divided into insular and trabecular pure carcinoid tumors, strumal carcinoids, and mucinous carcinoids.[3,60,100–102] Only the primary insular and metastatic insular forms have been accompanied by the carcinoid syndrome. In the largest series of metastatic carcinoids involving the ovary, 40% were associated with the carcinoid syndrome.[101] Patients ranged in age from early reproductive to postmenopausal, and a pelvic mass was usually present. Patients with the carcinoid syndrome are usually older than 50 years of age and have larger tumors. With tumor removal, the clinical symptoms of carcinoid syndrome disappear.[60]

All primary carcinoid tumors are unilateral. They may be pure but often have a dermoid cyst component. The contralateral ovary may also contain a dermoid cyst. The insular carcinoid is characterized by discrete cellular masses and rests separated by fibromatous stroma. The peripheral cells of the islands often contain reddish-brown argentaffin granules visible on routine staining. The trabecular carcinoid has long, wavy, parallel one- to two-cell thick ribbons of cells. The eosinophilic cytoplasm contains argyrophilic granules.

One third of reported cases of primary insular carcinoid have been associated with manifestations of carcinoid syndrome. These need to be distinguished from metastatic carcinoid tumor. This can be difficult at the time of surgery because the primary tumor in the bowel may be small and difficult to find. Features favoring metastatic disease include the presence of a bowel carcinoid tumor, extraovarian metastasis, bilateral ovarian disease, multiple tumor nodules in the ovarian parenchyma, and persistence of carcinoid syndrome after oophorectomy.

Primary ovarian carcinoid tumors are adequately treated by unilateral oophorectomy in young women wishing to maintain fertility. Total abdominal hysterectomy and bilateral salpingo-oophorectomy is preferable when fertility is not the issue. Only a small percentage of reported cases of primary insular carcinoid have a malignant course.

## STRUMAL CARCINOID

Strumal carcinoids are characterized by the presence of both struma and carcinoid typically intimately admixed.[3,102–105] Either component may predominate. Most cases are associated with a teratomatous component, but they may present in pure form. Almost all reported patients have been between 30 and 60 years of age. The gross appearance varies depending on whether the strumal, carcinoid, or teratomatous component predominates. The tumors are unilateral.

Microscopically, the carcinoid component exhibits a trabecular pattern in one half of the cases, a mixed trabecular-insular pattern with the trabecular component predominating in most of the remainder, and rarely a pure insular pattern. The thyroid component usually has the appearance of normal thyroid tissue or that of follicular adenoma. Argyrophilic granules are typically present within the cells, forming trabeculae and lining the thyroid follicles. Argentaffin granules are present in one half of the tumors. Strumal carcinoid tumors rarely metastasize.

## TERATOMA CONTAINING PITUITARY ADENOMA

Rarely, pituitary tissue is found in ovarian teratomas. Two reported cases secreted adrenocorticotropic hormone and caused Cushing's syndrome.[106] A case of a prolactin-secreting adenoma causing hyperprolactinemia has also been reported.[107]

## TUMORS WITH ECTOPIC HORMONE PRODUCTION

A variety of ovarian tumors has been associated with hypercalcemia. The most common types are small cell and clear cell carcinoma. Small cell carcinoma occurs almost exclusively in young women, with an average age of 24 years.[108–110] The nature of the neoplastic cells and the hypercalcemia factor that they produce are unknown. Three small cell carcinomas of the hypercalcemic type have occurred in sisters, two in cousins, and two in a mother and daughter, suggesting some cases may be familial.[108–110]

Biochemically documented Cushing's syndrome has been seen in cases of steroid cell tumor.[111–114] Rarely, other cell types have been associated with Cushing's syndrome, including endometrioid carcinoma,[115] poorly differentiated adenocarcinoma,[116] a malignant Sertoli cell tumor,[117] a trabecular carcinoid,[118] and a tumor resembling atypical carcinoid of lung origin.[119]

Various mucinous tumors (cystadenoma, borderline, and carcinoma) have caused Zollinger-Ellison syndrome.[119–129] Gastrin-containing cells were identified immunohistochemically in the cyst lining in some cases. Gastrin has also been demonstrated in the cyst fluid.

Hypertension related to hormone secretion by an ovarian tumor has been reported.[130–135] In eight cases, the hypertension was associated with a renin-secreting tumor, hyperreninism, and secondary hyperaldosteronism. In three cases, an aldosterone-secreting tumor resulted in primary hyperaldosteronism and low or normal plasma renin levels. Elevated aldosterone levels were present in one case in which renin was not measured. Most of the tumors were sex cord–stromal tumors or steroid (lipid) cell tumors.

## TUMOR-LIKE CONDITIONS WITH ENDOCRINE MANIFESTATIONS

### SOLITARY FOLLICULAR CYST AND CORPUS LUTEUM CYST

Solitary follicular and corpus luteum cysts may occur at any time during the reproductive age. Generally, they are less than 4 cm in diameter and are asymptomatic. Cyst formation is thought to result from continuous gonadotropin stimulation of the developing follicle without the mid-cycle surge of luteinizing hormone. Most follicular cysts involute spontaneously. Occasionally, they may rupture, bleed, and present with abdominal pain. Follicular cysts may be associated with menstrual irregularities. Cysts that fail to involute may require surgery to exclude a neoplastic process. Steroid contraceptives may cause more rapid cyst involution.[136]

Solitary cysts rarely develop in utero or during childhood.[11] They may be associated with sexual precocity that reverses after cyst removal. Autonomous follicular cysts may be a component of McCune-Albright syndrome (polyostotic fibrous dysplasia, café-au-lait spots, and other endocrine abnormalities).[137]

Solitary cysts occurring outside of pregnancy typically are less than 8 cm in diameter and are lined by granulosa cells, theca cells, or a combination of both.

### POLYCYSTIC OVARIAN SYNDROME

Polycystic ovarian syndrome (Stein-Leventhal syndrome) is characterized by enlarged ovaries with multiple small follicular cysts just beneath the surface.[138–140] The superficial cortex is thickened and whitened. The central portion of the ovary has homogeneous stroma with rare or absent evidence of previous ovulation.[3,141,142]

The syndrome usually begins in the postmenarchal years but occasionally follows pregnancy or withdrawal from oral contraceptives.[143] Patients do not ovulate, are infertile, and have menstrual disturbances. They are often hirsute and obese. Due to continuous estrogen stimulation, the endometrium may show changes ranging from those of the proliferative phase to hyperplasia and adenocarcinoma.[144] Adenocarcinomas arising in this clinical setting tend to be low grade and minimally invasive. Some cancers have been cured by curettage and progestational stimulation.[145]

Polycystic ovarian syndrome is a clinicopathologic syndrome, and the pathologic findings described previously, in and of themselves, do not warrant a specific diagnosis. Polycystic ovaries may be seen in children, normal pubertal girls, girls in the second decade with hypothyroidism,[146] and some women with adrenal hyperplasia.[147,148]

### STROMAL HYPERPLASIA AND HYPERTHECOSIS

Stromal hyperplasia is characterized by the abnormal proliferation of ovarian stroma without the presence of lutein cells.[3,149–152] The process primarily involves the medulla but is often present in the cortex as well. Stromal hyperplasia usually occurs in perimenopausal women but may be seen at any time after puberty. Stromal hyperthecosis is characterized by proliferation of ovarian stroma with lutein cells scattered singly or in nests.[3,71] Stromal hyperthecosis may be associated with clinical features identical to those of polycystic ovary syndrome. Occasional cases have shown marked virilization[3,71] accompanied by obesity, hypertension, and decreased glucose tolerance. Sometimes these patients have developed endometrial hyperplasia and adenocarcinoma.[153] The clinical symptoms usually evolve gradually, but the onset may be abrupt, mimicking that of an androgenic tumor.[154] There has been association of insulin resistance, sometimes accompanied by diabetes, acanthosis nigricans, and hyperandrogenism.[155–158]

The ovaries of stromal hyperplasia and hyperthecosis range from slightly enlarged to masses as large as 7 cm. On the cut surface, the medulla and sometimes the cortex are replaced by solid white to yellow stroma. In younger women, multiple follicular cysts and white collagenization of the outer cortex are seen. Usually both ovaries are involved. Resection of the affected ovaries results in regression of the clinical manifestations.[159–161] Wedge resection is usually ineffective.

## MASSIVE OVARIAN EDEMA

Rarely, children and young women present with unilateral or bilateral ovarian enlargement and markedly edematous stroma.[162–167] Massive ovarian edema was first described by Kalstone and colleagues.[168] The age range is from 6 to 33 years, with an average age of 21 years. Three fourths of patients have presented with abdominal pain. Some patients have presented with disorders of menstruation, evidence of androgen excess, or both.

The ovarian enlargement is usually unilateral and torsion of the ovarian pedicle is present in approximately one half of cases. The size ranges from 8 to 35 cm, averaging 11.5 cm in diameter. The ovarian surface is usually opaque and white, and the cut surface is edematous. Microscopically, the edematous hypocellular stroma surrounds entrapped follicles and their derivatives. Lutein cells are present in the edematous areas in 40% of cases and are presumably responsible for the hormonal manifestations.

There are two theories on the pathogenesis. One is that repeated intermittent torsion results in edema. The edema is thought to stimulate the production of stromal cells. The other theory is that the primary process is stromal hyperplasia that enlarges the ovary and predisposes it to torsion and edema.

## PREGNANCY LUTEOMA, HYPERREACTIO LUTEINALIS, AND LARGE SOLITARY LUTEINIZED FOLLICULAR CYST OF PREGNANCY AND PUERPERIUM

Pregnancy luteoma is characterized by the presence of single or multiple nodules composed of lutein cells.[169,170] They are usually incidentally encountered at the time of cesarean section or tubal ligation near the termination of pregnancy. Approximately 80% of the cases are associated with multiparity, and the majority of patients are black.[171] In approximately 25% of cases, there is evidence of overproduction of androgens.[172,173] Female infants born to masculinized mothers may also be virilized.[173] The lesions are bilateral in one third of cases and multiple in almost one half. The nodules range from microscopic to more than 20 cm in diameter. On sectioning, the lesions are well circumscribed and red brown, and foci of hemorrhage are common. Microscopic examination shows a diffuse proliferation of large lutein cells intermediate in size between normal granulosa lutein cells and theca lutein cells. The lack of intracellular lipid, numerous mitotic figures, and the common presence of multiple lesions help distinguish these from other tumors in the steroid cell category. Pregnancy luteomas are benign and regress spontaneously after the termination of pregnancy.[174] Their occurrence during pregnancy suggests a role for hCG in their pathogenesis. However, the rarity of pregnancy luteomas in association with hydatidiform moles and choriocarcinoma,[171] which are accompanied by high levels of hCG, and the almost exclusive recognition of the lesions during the third trimester when hCG levels are lower,[175,176] suggest that other factors play a role in their development.

Hyperreactio luteinalis is characterized by bilateral marked enlargement of the ovaries by multiple thin-walled cysts.[177–180] Occasionally, hemorrhage into the cysts and rarely torsion or rupture with intra-abdominal bleeding occur. Hyperreactio luteinalis may be detected during any trimester of pregnancy and is usually associated with an abnormality of pregnancy, particularly hydatidiform mole and choriocarcinoma, but occasionally erythroblastosis fetalis and multiple gestation.[181,182] They may also be iatrogenic, complicating the administration of clomiphene citrate or gonadotropins for induction of ovulation.[181–183] Symptoms are usually lacking but if present include abdominal pain, swelling, and occasionally virilization.[184] Microscopic examination reveals multiple large follicular cysts, often with marked edema of the intervening stroma. The theca and granulosa cells lining the cysts are enlarged, hyperplastic, and luteinized. The process usually regresses after termination of pregnancy.

Several cases of unilateral solitary luteinized follicular cyst have been detected during pregnancy or puerperium.[185–187] These cysts are large (average diameter, 25 cm) and may cause abdominal swelling. The cysts are unilocular and thin walled and contain watery fluid. On microscopic examination, the cyst is lined by lutein cells, which often vary greatly in size and shape. Foci of bizarre hyperchromatic nuclei may be present.

## REFERENCES

1. Rubin DK, Frost JK: The cytologic detection of ovarian cancer. Acta Cytol 7:191–195, 1963.
2. Rome RM, Fortune DW, Quinn MA, Brown JB: Functioning ovarian tumors in postmenopausal women. Obstet Gynecol 57:705–710, 1981.
3. Scully RE, Young RH, Clement PB: Tumors of the ovary, maldeveloped gonads, fallopian tube, and broad ligament. In Atlas of Tumor Pathology. Washington, DC, Armed Forces Institute of Pathology, 1996.
4. Young RH, Scully RE: Ovarian sex cord-stromal tumors: Recent advances and current status. Clin Obstet Gynecol 11:93–134, 1984.
5. Stenwig JT, Hazekamp JT, Beecham JB: Granulosa cell tumors of the ovary: A clinicopathological study of 118 cases with long term follow-up. Gynecol Oncol 7:136–152, 1979.
6. Bjorkholem E, Silversward C: Prognostic factors in granulosa cell tumors. Gynecol Oncol 11:261–274, 1981.
7. Hodgson JE, Dockerty MB, Mussey RD: Granulosa cell tumor of the ovary: A clinical and pathologic review of sixty-two cases. Surg Gynecol Obstet 81:631–642.
8. Bennington JL, Ferguson BR, Haber SL: Incidence and relative frequency of benign and malignant ovarian neoplasms. Obstet Gynecol 32:627–632, 1968.
9. Nakashima N, Young RH, Scully RE: Androgenic granulosa cell tumors of the ovary: A clinicopathologic analysis of 17 cases and review of the literature. Arch Pathol Lab Med 108:786–791, 1984.
10. Norris HJ, Taylor HB: Virilization associated with cystic granulosa cell tumors. Obstet Gynecol 34:629–635, 1969.
11. Liapi C, Evain-Brion D: Diagnosis of ovarian follicular cysts from birth to puberty: A report of twenty cases. Acta Paediatr Scand 76:91–96, 1987.
12. Young RH, Dickersin GR, Scully RE: Juvenile granulosa cell tumor of the ovary. A clinicopathologic analysis of 125 cases. Am J Surg Pathol 8:575–596, 1984.
13. Vassal G, Flamant F, Cailaud JM, et al: Juvenile granulosa cell tumor of the ovary in children: A clinical study of 15 cases. J Clin Oncol 6:990–995, 1988.
14. Velasco-Oses A, Alonso-Alvaro A, Blanco-Pozo A, Nogales FF Jr: Ollier's disease associated with ovarian juvenile granulosa cell tumor. Cancer 62:222–225, 1988.
15. Tamini HK, Bolen JW: Enchondromatosis (Ollier's disease) and ovarian juvenile granulosa cell tumor. Cancer 53:1605–1608, 1984.
16. Tanaka Y, Sasaki Y, Nishihira H, et al: Ovarian juvenile granulosa cell tumor associated with Maffucci's syndrome. Am J Clin Pathol 97:523–527, 1992.
17. Rodgers KE, Marks JF, Ellefson DD, et al: Follicle regulatory protein: A novel marker for granulosa cell cancer

patients. Gynecol Oncol 40:381–387, 1990.

18. Lappohn RE, Burger HG, Bouma J, et al: Inhibin as a marker for granulosa-cell tumors. N Engl J Med 321:790–793, 1989.

19. Nishida M, Jimi S, Haji M, et al: Juvenile granulosa cell tumor in association with a high serum inhibin level. Gynecol Oncol 40:90–94, 1991.

20. Fathalla MF: The occurrence of granulosa and theca tumors in clinically normal ovaries. Br J Obstet Gynaecol 74:279–282, 1967.

21. Fox H, Agrawal K, Langley FA: A clinicopathologic study of 92 cases of granulosa cell tumor of the ovary with special reference to the factors influencing prognosis. Cancer 35:231–241, 1975.

22. Norris HJ, Taylor HB: Prognosis of granulosa-theca tumors of the ovary. Cancer 21:255–263, 1968.

23. Young RH, Prat J, Scully RE: Ovarian endometrioid carcinomas resembling sex cord-stromal tumors: A clinicopathologic analysis of 13 cases. Am J Surg Pathol 6:513–522, 1982.

24. Biscotti CV, Hart WR: Juvenile granulosa cell tumors of the ovary. Arch Pathol Lab Med 113:40–46, 1989.

25. Roth LM, Nichols TR, Ehrlich CE: Juvenile granulosa cell tumor: A clinicopathologic study of three cases with ultrastructural observations. Cancer 44:2194–2205, 1979.

26. Lack EE, Perez-Atayde AR, Murthy ASK, et al: Granulosa theca cell tumors in premenarchal girls. A clinical and pathologic study of ten cases. Cancer 48:1846–1854, 1981.

27. Young RH, Scully RE: Sex cord-stromal, steroid cell, and other ovarian tumors with endocrine, paraendocrine, and paraneoplastic manifestations. In Kurman RJ (ed): Blaustein's Pathology of the Female Genital Tract. New York, Springer-Verlag, 1994, pp 783–847.

28. Zaloudek C, Norris HJ: Granulosa tumors of the ovary in children: A clinical and pathologic study of 32 cases. Am J Surg Pathol 6:503–512, 1982.

29. Wolf JK, Mullen, J, Eifel PJ, et al: Radiation treatment of advanced or recurrent granulosa cell tumor of the ovary. Gynecol Oncol 73:35–41, 1999.

30. Savage P, Constenla D, Fisher C, et al: Granulosa cell tumours of the ovary: Demographics, survival and the management of advanced disease. Clin Oncol (R Coll Radiol) 10:242–245, 1998.

31. Dockerty MB, Masson JC: Ovarian fibromas: A clinical and pathologic study of 283 cases. Am J Obstet Gynecol 47:741–752, 1944.

32. Junaid TA, Nkposong EO, Kolawole TM: Cutaneous meningiomas and an ovarian fibroma in a 3-year-old girl. J Pathol 108:165–167, 1972.

33. Martins SM, Klinger OJ: Bilateral ovarian fibromas occurring before the menarche. Am J Obstet Gynecol 89:386–390, 1964.

34. Bower JF, Erickson ER: Bilateral fibromas in a 5-year-old girl. Am J Obstet Gynecol 99:880–882, 1967.

35. Banner EA, Dockerty MB: Theca cell tumors of the ovary: A clinical and pathologic study of 23 cases (including 13 new cases) with a review. Surg Gynecol Obstet 81:234–242, 1945.

36. Sternberg WH, Gaskill CJ: Theca-cell tumors: With a report of 12 new cases and observations on the possible etiologic role of ovarian stromal hyperplasia. Am J Obstet Gynecol 59:575–587, 1950.

37. Bjorkholem E, Silversward C: Theca-cell tumors: Clinical features and prognosis. Acta Radiol Oncol 19:241–244, 1980.

38. Zhang J, Young RH, Arseneau J, Scully RE: Ovarian stromal tumors containing lutein or Leydig cells (luteinized thecomas and stromal Leydig cell tumors): A clinicopathological analysis of fifty cases. Int J Gynecol Pathol 1:270–285, 1982.

39. Roth LM, Sternberg WH: Partly luteinized theca cell tumor of the ovary. Cancer 51:1697–1704, 1983.

40. Waxman M, Vuletin JC, Urcuyo R, Belling CG: Ovarian low grade stromal sarcoma with thecomatous features: A critical reappraisal of the so-called "malignant thecoma." Cancer 44:2206–2217, 1979.

41. Marelli G, Carinelli S, Mariani A, et al: Sclerosing stromal tumor of the ovary: Report of eight cases and review of the literature. Eur J Obstet Gynecol Reprod Biol 76:85–89, 1998.

42. Chalvardjian A, Scully RE: Sclerosing stromal tumors of the ovary. Cancer 31:664–670, 1973.

43. Cashell AW, Cohen ML: Masculinizing sclerosing stromal tumor of the ovary during pregnancy. Gynecol Oncol 43:281–285, 1991.

44. Duska LR, Flynn C, Goodman A: Masculinizing sclerosing stromal cell tumor in pregnancy: Report of a case and review of the literature. Eur J Gynaecol Oncol 19:441–443, 1998.

45. Young RH, Scully RE: Ovarian Sertoli cell tumors: A report of 10 cases. Int J Gynecol Pathol 2:349–363, 1984.

46. Young RH, Scully RE: Well-differentiated ovarian Sertoli-Leydig cell tumor: A clinico-pathologic analysis of 23 cases. Int J Gynecol Pathol 3:277–290, 1984.

47. Young RH, Scully RE: Ovarian Sertoli-Leydig cell tumors: A clinicopathologic analysis of 207 cases. Am J Surg Pathol 9:543–569, 1985.

48. Zaloudek C, Norris HJ: Sertoli-Leydig tumors of the ovary: A clinicopathologic study of 64 intermediate and poorly differentiated neoplasms. Am J Surg Pathol 8:405–418, 1984.

49. Roth LM, Anderson MC, Govan ADT, et al: Sertoli-Leydig cell tumors: A clinicopathologic study of 34 cases. Cancer 48:187–197, 1981.

50. Meldrum DR, Abreham GE: Peripheral and ovarian venous concentration of various hormones in virilizing ovarian tumors. Obstet Gynecol 53:36–43, 1979.

51. Gagnon S, Tetu B, Silva EG, McCaughey WT: Frequency of alpha fetoprotein production by Sertoli-Leydig cell tumors of the ovary: An immunohistochemical study of eight cases. Mod Pathol 2:63–67, 1989.

52. Prat J, Toung RH, Scully RE: Ovarian Sertoli-Leydig cell tumors with heterologous elements (II): Cartilage and skeletal muscle. Cancer 50:2465–2475, 1982.

53. Waxman M, Damjanov I, Alpert L, Sardinsky T: Composite mucinous ovarian neoplasms associated with Sertoli-Leydig and carcinoid tumors. Cancer 47:2044–2052, 1981.

54. Guerard MJ, Ferenczy A, Arguelles MA: Ovarian Sertoli-Leydig cell tumor with rhabdomyosarcoma: An ultrastructural study. Ultrastruct Pathol 3:347–358, 1982.

55. Roth LM, Slayton RE, Brady LW, et al: Retiform differentiation in ovarian Sertoli-Leydig cell tumors: A clinicopathologic study of six cases from a gynecologic oncology group study. Cancer 55:1093–1098, 1985.

56. Talerman A: Ovarian Sertoli-Leydig cell tumor (androblastoma) with retiform pattern: A clinicopathologic study. Cancer 60:3056–3064, 1987.

57. Scully RE: Sex cord tumor with annular tubules: A distinctive ovarian tumor of the Peutz-Jeghers syndrome. Cancer 25:1107–1121, 1970.

58. Young RH, Welch WR, Dickersin GR, Scully RE: Ovarian sex cord tumor with annular tubules: Review of 74 cases including 27 with Peutz-Jeghers syndrome and four with adenoma malignum of the cervix. Cancer 50:1384–1402, 1982.

59. McGowan L, Young RH, Scully RE: Peutz-Jeghers syndrome with adenoma malignum of cervix: A report of two cases. Gynecol Oncol 10:125–133, 1980.

60. Robboy SJ, Norris HJ, Scully RE: Insular carcinoid primary in the ovary: A clinicopathologic analysis of 48 cases. Cancer 36:404–418, 1975.

61. Anderson MC, Rees DA: Gynandroblastoma of the ovary. Br J Obstet Gynaecol 82:68–73, 1975.

62. Tavassoli FA, Norris HJ: Sertoli tumors of the ovary: A clinicopathologic study of 28 cases with ultrastructural observations. Cancer 46:2282–2297, 1980.

63. Gustafson ML, Lee MM, Scully RE, et al: Müllerian inhibiting substance as a marker for ovarian sex cord tumor. N Engl J Med 326:466–471, 1992.

64. Hayes MC, Scully RE: Ovarian steroid tumors, not otherwise specified: A report of 63 cases. Am J Surg Pathol 11:835–845, 1987.

65. Marieb HJ, Spangler S, Kashgarian M, et al: Cushing's syndrome secondary to ectopic cortisol production by an ovarian carcinoma. J Clin Endocrinol Metab 57:737–740, 1983.

66. Young RH, Scully RE: Ovarian steroid cell tumors associated with Cushing's syndrome: A report of three cases. Int J Gynecol Pathol 6:40–48, 1987.

67. Taylor HB, Norris HJ: Lipid cell tumors of the ovary. Cancer 20:1953–1962, 1967.

68. Brewer CA, Shevlin DS: Encouraging response of an advanced steroid-cell tumor to GnRH agonist therapy. Obstet Gynecol 92:661–663, 1998.

69. Hayes MC, Scully RE: Stromal luteoma of the ovary: A clinicopathological analysis of 25 cases. Int J Gynecol Pathol 6:313–321, 1987.

70. Paraskevas M, Scully RE: Hilus cell tumor of the ovary: A clinicopathological analysis of 12 Reinke crystal-positive and 9 crystal-negative cases. Int J Gynecol Pathol 8:299–310, 1989.

71. Honore LH, Chari R, Mueller HD, et al: Postmenopausal hyperandrogenism of ovarian origin: A clinicopathologic study of four cases. Gynecol Obstet Invest 34:52–56, 1992.

72. Sternberg WH: The morphology, endocrine function, hyperplasia and tumors of the ovarian hilus cells. Am J Pathol 25:493–521, 1949.

73. Scully RE: Neoplasia associated with anomalous sexual development. Pediatr Adolesc Endocrinol 8:203–217, 1981.

74. Scully RE: Gonadoblastoma: A review of 74 cases. Cancer 25:1340–1356, 1970.

75. McDonald PC, Grodin JM, Edman CD, et al: Origin of estrogen in a postmenopausal woman with a non-endocrine tumor of the ovary and endometrial hyperplasia. Obstet Gynecol 47:644–650, 1976.

76. Quinn MA, Baker H, Rome R, et al: Response of a mucinous ovarian tumor of borderline malignancy to human chorionic gonadotropin. Obstet Gynecol 61:121–126, 1983.

77. Rutgers JL, Scully RE: Functioning ovarian tumors with peripheral steroid cell proliferation: A report of 24 cases. Int J Gynecol Pathol 5:319–337, 1986.

78. Case records of the Massachusetts General Hospital. N Engl J Med 286:594–600, 1972.

79. Besch PK, Byron RC, Barry RD, et al: Testosterone synthesis by a Brenner tumor: II. In vitro biosynthetic steroid conversion of a Brenner tumor. Am J Obstet Gynecol 86:1021–1026, 1963.

80. Hamwi GJ, Byron RC, Besch PK, et al: Testosterone synthesis by a Brenner tumor: I. Clinical evidence of masculinization during pregnancy. Am J Obstet Gynecol 86:1015–1020, 1963.

81. Conner TB, Ganis FM, Levin HS: Gonadotropin-independent Krukenberg tumor causing virilization during pregnancy. J Clin Endocrinol 28:198–214, 1968.

82. Verhoeven ATM, Mastboom JL, Van Leusden H, Van Der Velden W: Virilization in pregnancy coexisting with an (ovarian) mucinous cystadenoma: A case report and review of virilizing ovarian tumors in pregnancy. Obstet Gynecol Surv 28:597–622, 1973.

83. Mahlck CG, Grankvist K, Kjellgren O, Backstrom T: Human chorionic gonadotropin, follicle stimulating hormone, and luteinizing hormone in patients with epithelial ovarian carcinoma. Gynecol Oncol 36:219–225, 1990.

84. Matias-Guiu X, Prat J: Ovarian tumors with functioning stroma. An immunohistochemical study of 100 cases with human chorionic gonadotrophin monoclonal and polyclonal antibodies. Cancer 65:2001–2005, 1990.

85. Kurman RJ, Norris HJ: Malignant mixed germ cell tumors of the ovary. Obstet Gynecol 48:579–589, 1976.

86. Gershenson DM, Del Junco G, Copeland LJ, Rutledge FN: Mixed germ cell tumors of the ovary. Obstet Gynecol 64:200–206, 1984.

87. Axe S, Klein VR, Woodruff JD: Choriocarcinoma of the ovary. Obstet Gynecol 66:111–114, 1985.

88. Jacobs AS, Newland JR, Green RK: Pure choriocarcinoma of the ovary. Obstet Gynecol Surv 37:603–609, 1982.

89. Ueda G, Hamanaka N, Hayakawa K, et al: Clinical, histochemical, and biochemical studies of an ovarian dysgerminoma with trophoblasts and Leydig cells. Am J Obstet Gynecol 114:748–754, 1972.

90. Takeda A, Ishizuka T, Goto T, et al: Polyembryoma of ovary producing alpha-fetoprotein and HCG: Immunoperoxidase and electron microscopic study. Cancer 49:1878–1889, 1982.

91. Kurman RJ, Norris HJ: Embryonal carcinoma of the ovary: A clinicopathologic entity distinct from endodermal sinus tumor resembling embryonal carcinoma of the adult testis. Cancer 38:2420–2433, 1976.

92. Zaloudek C, Tavassoli F, Norris HJ: Dysgerminoma with syncytiotrophoblastic giant cells: A histologically and clinically distinctive subtype of dysgerminoma. Am J Surg Pathol 5:361–367, 1981.

93. Young RH: New and unusual aspects of ovarian germ cell tumors. Am J Surg Pathol 17:2110–2124, 1993.

94. Szyfelfbein WM, Young RH, Scully RE: Struma ovarii simulating ovarian tumors of other types. Am J Surg Pathol 19:21–29, 1995.

95. Kempers RD, Dockerty MB, Hoffman DL, Bartholomew LG: Struma ovarii-ascitic, hyperthyroid, and asymptomatic syndromes. Ann Intern Med 72:883–893, 1970.

96. Pardo-Mindan FJ, Vazquez JJ: Malignant struma ovarii: Light and electron microscopic study. Cancer 51:337–343, 1983.

97. Rosenblum NG, LiVolsi VA, Edmonds PR, Mikuta JJ: Malignant struma ovarii. Gynecol Oncol 32:224–227, 1989.

98. Willemse P, Oosterhuis JW, Aalders JG, et al: Malignant struma ovarii treated with ovariectomy, thyroidectomy, and 131-I administration. Cancer 60:178–182, 1987.

99. DeSimone CP, Lele SM, Modesitt SC: Malignant struma ovarii: A case report and analysis of cases reported in the literature with focus on survival and $I^{131}$ therapy. Gynecol Oncol 89:543–548, 2003.

100. Young RH, Prat J, Scully RE: Ovarian Sertoli-Leydig cell tumors with heterologous elements (I). Gastrointestinal epithelium and carcinoid: A clinicopathologic analysis of thirty-six cases. Cancer 50:2448–2456, 1982.

101. Robboy SJ, Scully RE, Norris HJ: Carcinoid metastatic to the ovary: A clinicopathologic analysis of 35 cases. Cancer 33:798–811, 1974.

102. Robboy SJ, Scully RE: Strumal carcinoid of the ovary: An analysis of 50 cases of a distinctive tumor composed of thyroid tissue and carcinoid. Cancer 46:2019–2034, 1980.

103. Snyder RR, Tavassoli FA: Ovarian strumal carcinoid: Immunohistochemical, ultrastructural, and clinicopathologic observations. Int J Gynecol Pathol 5:187–201, 1986.

104. Stagno PA, Petras RE, Hart WR: Strumal carcinoids of the ovary: An immunohistochemical and ultrastructural study. Arch Pathol Lab Med 111:440–446, 1987.

105. Ulbright TM, Roth LM, Ehrlich CE: Ovarian strumal carcinoid: An immunocytochemical and ultrastructural study of two cases. Am J Clin Pathol 77:622–631, 1982.

106. Axiotis CA, Lippes HA, Merino MJ, et al: Corticotroph cell pituitary adenoma within an ovarian teratoma. Am J Surg Pathol 11:218–224, 1987.

107. Palmer PE, Bogojavlensky S, Bhan AK, Scully RE: Prolactinoma in wall of ovarian dermoid cyst with hyperprolactinemia. Report of a case. Obstet Gynecol 75:540–543, 1990.

108. Dickersin GR, Kline IW, Scully RE: Small cell carcinoma of the ovary with hypercalcemia: A report of 11 cases. Cancer 49:188–197, 1982.

109. Abeler V, Kjorstad KE, Nesland JM: Small cell carcinoma of the ovary: A report of six cases. Int J Gynecol Pathol 7:315–329, 1988.

110. Young RH, Oliva EO, Scully RE: Small cell carcinoma of the ovary, hypercalcemic type. Am J Surg Pathol 18:1102–1116, 1994.

111. Donovan JT, Otis CN, Powell JL, Cathcart HK: Cushing's syndrome secondary to malignant lipoid cell tumor of the ovary. Gynecol Oncol 50:249–253, 1993.

112. Adeyemi SD, Grange AO, Giwa-Osagie OF, Elesha SO: Adrenal rest tumor of the ovary associated with isosexual precocious pseudopuberty and cushingoid features. Eur J Pediatr 145:236–238, 1986.

113. Marieb HJ, Spangler S, Kashgarian M, et al: Cushing's syndrome secondary to ectopic cortisol production by an ovarian carcinoma. J Clin Endocrinol Metab 57:737–740, 1983.
114. Young RH, Scully RE: Ovarian steroid cell tumors associated with Cushing's syndrome: A report of three cases. Int J Gynecol Pathol 6:40–48, 1987.
115. Crawford SM, Pyrah RD, Ismail SM: Cushing's syndrome associated with recurrent endometrioid adenocarcinoma of the ovary. J Clin Pathol 47:766–768, 1994.
116. Parsons V, Rigby B: Cushing's syndrome associated with adenocarcinoma of the ovary. Lancet 182:992–994, 1958.
117. Nichols J, Warren JC, Mantz FA: ACTH-like secretion from carcinoma of the ovary. JAMA 182:713–718, 1962.
118. Schlaghecke R, Kreuzpaintner G, Burrig KF, et al: Cushing' syndrome due to ACTH-production of an ovarian carcinoid. Klin Wochenschr 67:640–644, 1989.
119. Brown H, Lane M: Cushing's and malignant carcinoid syndromes from ovarian neoplasm. Arch Intern Med 115:490–494, 1965.
120. Garcia-Villanueva M, Figuerola NB, del Arbol LR, Ortiz M: Zollinger-Ellison syndrome due to a borderline mucinous cystadenoma of the ovary. Obstet Gynecol 75:549–551, 1990.
121. Boixeda D, Roman AL, Pascasio JM, et al: Zollinger-Ellison syndrome due to gastrin-secreting ovarian cystadenocarcinoma: Case report. Acta Chir Scand 156:409–410, 1990.
122. Matson P, Mackem S, Norton J, et al: Ovarian carcinoma as a cause of Zollinger-Ellison syndrome: Natural history, secretory products, and response to provocative tests. Gastroenterology 97:468–471, 1989.
123. Heyd J, Livni N, Herbert D, et al: Gastrin-producing ovarian cystadenocarcinoma: Sensitivity to secretin and SMS 201-995. Gastroenterology 97:464–467, 1989.
124. Primrose JN, Maloney M, Wells M, et al: Gastrin-producing ovarian mucinous cystadenoma: A cause of Zollinger-Ellison syndrome. Surgery 104:830–833, 1988.
126. Morgan DR, Wells M, MacDonald RC, Johnston D: Zollinger-Ellison syndrome due to a gastrin secreting ovarian mucinous cystadenoma: Case report. Br J Obstet Gynaecol 92:867–869, 1985.
126. Julkunen R, Partanen S, Salaspuro M: Gastrin-producing ovarian mucinous cystadenoma. J Clin Gastroenterol 5:67–70, 1983.
127. Bollen E, Lamers C, Jansen J, et al: Zollinger-Ellison syndrome due to a gastrin-producing ovarian cystadenocarcinoma. Br J Surg 68:776–777, 1981.
128. Long LTI, Barton TK, Draffin R, et al: Conservative management of the Zollinger-Ellison syndrome: Ectopic gastrin production by an ovarian cystadenoma. JAMA 243:1837–1839, 1980.
129. Cocco AE, Conway SJ: Zollinger-Ellison syndrome associated with ovarian mucinous cystadenoma. N Engl J Med 293:485–486, 1975.
130. Fox R, Eckford S, Hirschowitz L, et al: Refractory gestational hypertension due to a renin-secreting ovarian fibrothecoma associated with Grolin's syndrome. Br J Obstet Gynaecol 101:1015–1017, 1994.
131. Kulkarni JN, Mistry RC, Kamant MR, et al: Autonomous aldosterone-secreting ovarian tumor. Gynecol Oncol 37:284–289, 1990.
132. Tetu B, Lebel M, Camilleri J: Renin-producing ovarian tumor: A case report with immunohistochemical and electron-microscopic study. Am J Surg Pathol 12:634–640, 1988.
133. Korzets A, Nouriel H, Steiner Z, et al: Resistant hypertension associated with a renin-producing ovarian Sertoli cell tumor. Am J Clin Pathol 85:242–247, 1986.
134. Todesco S, Terrible Z, Borsatti A, Mantero F: Primary aldosteronism due to a malignant ovarian tumor. J Clin Endocrinol Metab 41:809–819, 1975.
135. Ehrlich EN, Dominguez OV, Samuels LT, et al: Aldosteronism and precocious puberty due to an ovarian androblastoma (Sertoli cell tumor). J Clin Endocrinol Metab 23:358–367, 1963.
136. Spanos WJ: Preoperative hormonal therapy of cystic adnexal masses. Am J Obstet Gynecol 116:551–554, 1973.
137. Mauras N, Blizzard RM: The McCune-Albright syndrome. Acta Endocrinol 113(Suppl 279):207–217, 1986.
138. Goldzieher JW: Polycystic ovarian disease. Fertil Steril 35:371–394, 1981.
139. Givins JR: Hirsutism and hyperandrogenism. Adv Intern Med 21:221–247, 1976.
140. Yen S: The polycystic ovarian syndrome. Clin Endocrinol 12:177–208, 1980.
141. Milewicz A, Silber D, Mielecki T: The origin of androgen synthesis in polycystic ovary syndrome. Obstet Gynecol 62:601–604, 1983.
142. Franks S: Polycystic ovary syndrome: A changing perspective. Endocrinology 3:87–120, 1989.
143. Beaconsfield P, Dick R, Ginsburg J, Lewis P: Amenorrhea and infertility after the use of oral contraceptives. Surg Gynecol Obstet 138:571–575, 1974.
144. Coulam CB, Annegers JF, Kranz JS: Chronic anovulation syndrome and associated neoplasia. Obstet Gynecol 61:403–407, 1983.
145. Fechner RE, Kaufman RH: Endometrial adenocarcinoma in Stein-Leventhal syndrome. Cancer 34:444–452, 1974.
146. Lindsay AN, Voorhes ML, Macgillivray MH: Multicystic ovaries detected by sonography in children with hypothyroidism. Am J Dis Child 134:588–592, 1980.
147. Benedict PH, Cohen RB, Cope O, Scully RE: Ovarian and adrenal morphology in cases of hirsutism or virilism and Stein-Leventhal syndrome. Fertil Steril 13:380–395, 1962.
148. Chrousos GP, Loriaux L, Mann DL, Cutler GB: Later onset 21-hydroxylase deficiency mimicking idiopathic hirsutism or polycystic ovarian disease. N Engl J Med 272:1189–1194, 1965.
149. Boss JH, Scully RE, Wegner KH, Cohen RB: Structural variations in the adult ovary-clinical significance. Obstet Gynecol 25:747–764, 1965.
150. Novak ER, Mohler DI: Ovarian stromal changes in endometrial cancer. Am J Obstet Gynecol 65:1099–1110, 1953.
151. Schneider GT, Bechtel M: Ovarian cortical stromal hyperplasia. Obstet Gynecol 8:713–719, 1956.
152. Woll E, Hertig AT, Smith G, Johnson LC: The ovary of endometrial carcinoma. Am J Obstet Gynecol 56:617–633, 1948.
153. Case records of the Massachusetts General Hospital: Case 85. N Engl J Med 267:1311–1317, 1962.
154. Fienberg R: Ovarian estrogenic tumors and diffuse estrogenic thecomatosis in postmenopausal colporrhagia. Am J Obstet Gynecol 76:851–860, 1958.
155. Taylor SI, Dons RF, Hernandez E, et al: Insulin resistance associated with androgen excess in women with autoantibodies to the insulin receptor. Ann Intern Med 97:851–855, 1982.
156. Imperato-McGinley J, Peterson RE, Sturla E, et al: Primary amenorrhea associated with hirsutism, acanthosis nigricans, dermoid cysts of the ovary and a new type of insulin resistance. Am J Med 65:389–395, 1978.
157. Bar RS, Muggeo M, Roth J, et al: Insulin resistance, acanthosis nigricans and normal insulin receptors in a young woman: Evidence for a post receptor defect. J Clin Endocrinol Metab 47:620–625, 1978.
158. Kahn CR, Flier JS, Bar RS, et al: The syndromes of insulin resistance and acanthosis nigricans: Insulin receptor disorders in man. N Engl J Med 294:739–745, 1976.
159. Dunaif BL, Hoffman AR, Scully RE, et al: The clinical, biochemical and ovarian morphologic features in women with acanthosis nigricans and masculinization. Obstet Gynecol 66:545–552, 1985.
160. Dennefors BL, Janson PO, Knutson F, et al: Steroid production and responsiveness to gonadotropin in isolated stromal tissue of human postmenopausal ovaries. Am J Obstet Gynecol 136:997–1002, 1980.
161. Judd HL, Scully RE, Herbst AL, et al: Familial hyperthecosis: Comparison of endocrinologic and histologic findings with polycystic ovarian disease. Am J Obstet Gynecol 117:976–982, 1973.

162. van den Brule F, Bourque J, Gaspard UJ, Hustin JF: Massive ovarian edema with androgen secretion: A pathological and endocrine study with review of the literature. Horm Res 41:209–214, 1994.

163. Roberts CL, Weston MJ: Bilateral massive ovarian edema: A case report. Ultrasound Obstet Gynecol 11:65–67, 1998.

164. Yuce K, Yucel A, Tanir M, et al: Massive bilateral ovarian edema: Report of 2 cases. Eur J Gynaecol Oncol 19:305–307, 1998.

165. Bychkov V, Kijek M: Massive ovarian edema: Four cases and some pathogenetic considerations. Acta Obstet Gynecol Scand 66:397–379, 1987.

166. Chervenak FA, Castadot MJ, Wiederman J, Sedlis A: Massive ovarian edema: Review of world literature and report of two cases. Obstet Gynecol Surv 35:677–684, 1980.

167. Roth LM, Deaton RL, Sternberg WH: Massive ovarian edema: A clinicopathologic study of five cases including ultrastructural observations and review of the literature. Am J Surg Pathol 3:11–21, 1979.

168. Kalstone CE, Jaffe RB, Abell MR: Massive edema of the ovary simulating fibroma. Obstet Gynecol 34:564–571, 1969.

169. Norris HG, Taylor HB: Nodular theca-lutein hyperplasia of pregnancy (so-called "pregnancy luteoma"): A clinical and pathologic study of 15 cases. Am J Clin Pathol 47:557–566, 1967.

170. Sternberg WH, Barclay DL: Luteoma of pregnancy. Am J Surg Obstet Gynecol 95:165–194, 1966.

171. Garcia-Bunuel R, Berek JS, Woodruff JD: Luteomas of pregnancy. Obstet Gynecol 45:407–414, 1975.

172. Cohen DA, Daughaday WH, Welden VV: Fetal and maternal virilization associated with pregnancy. Am J Dis Child 136:353–356, 1982.

173. Hensleigh PA, Woodruff JD: Differential maternal-fetal response to androgenizing luteoma or hyperreactio luteinalis. Obstet Gynecol Surv 33:262–271, 1978.

174. Malinak LR, Miller GV: Bilateral multicentric luteomas of pregnancy associated with masculinization of a female infant. Am J Obstet Gynecol 91:251–259, 1965.

175. Pastorfide GB, Foldstein DP, Kosasa TS, Levesque L: Serum chorionic gonadotropin activity after molar pregnancy, therapeutic abortion, and term delivery. Am J Obstet Gynecol 118:293–294, 1974.

176. MacDonald HN, Buckler J, Scott JS: Human chorionic gonadotropin levels during and after labour. Br J Obstet Gynaecol 81:371–373, 1974.

177. Montz FJ, Schlaerth JB, Morrow CP: The natural history of theca lutein cysts. Obstet Gynecol 72:247–251, 1988.

178. Girpiard DP, Barclay DL, Collins CG: Hyperreactio luteinalis: Review of the literature and report of 2 cases. Obstet Gynecol 23:513–252, 1964.

179. Curry SL, Hammond CB, Tyrey L, et al: Hydatidiform mole: Diagnosis, management, and long-term followup of 347 patients. Obstet Gynecol 45:1–8, 1975.

180. Caspi E, Schreyer P, Bukovsky J: Ovarian lutein cysts in pregnancy. Obstet Gynecol 42:388–398, 1973.

181. Aboulghar MA, Mansour RT, Serour GI, et al: Ultrasonically guided vaginal aspiration of ascites in the treatment of severe ovarian hyperstimulation syndrome. Fertil Steril 53:933–935, 1990.

182. Borenstein R, Elhalah U, Lunenfeld B, et al: Severe ovarian hyperstimulation syndrome: A reevaluated therapeutic approach. Fertil Steril 51:791–795, 1989.

183. Schenker JG, Weinstein D: Ovarian hyperstimulation syndrome: A current survey. Fertil Steril 30:255–268, 1978.

184. Judd HL, Bernirschke K, Devane G, et al: Maternal virilization developing during twin pregnancy: Demonstration of excess ovarian androgen production associated with theca lutein cysts. N Engl J Med 288:118–122, 1973.

185. Albukerk JN, Berlin M: Unilateral lutein cyst in pregnancy. N Y State J Med 76:259–261, 1976.

186. Kott MM, Schmidt WA: Massive postpartum corpus luteum cyst: A case report. Hum Pathol 12:468–470, 1981.

187. Clement PB, Scully RE: Large solitary luteinized follicular cyst of pregnancy and puerperium. Am J Surg Pathol 4:431–438, 1980.

# PART 16

# ENDOCRINOLOGY OF THE BREAST

# Hormonal Control of Breast Development

## Jose Russo, Richard J. Santen, and Irma H. Russo

HYPOTHALAMIC-PITUITARY INFLUENCES, OVARIAN FUNCTION, AND BREAST DEVELOPMENT

ADOLESCENCE

THE MATURE BREAST
Nulliparous Women
Parous Women

PATTERN OF DISTRIBUTION OF CELLS POSITIVE FOR ESTROGEN AND PROGESTERONE RECEPTORS IN RELATION TO PROLIFERATING CELLS IN THE MAMMARY GLAND

DISTRIBUTION OF PROLIFERATING CELLS IN RELATION TO THE PRESENCE OF STEROID RECEPTORS AND THEIR COACTIVATORS

THE MENOPAUSAL BREAST

GENOMIC DIFFERENCES BETWEEN LOBULAR STRUCTURES

## HYPOTHALAMIC-PITUITARY INFLUENCES, OVARIAN FUNCTION, AND BREAST DEVELOPMENT

In the nonpregnant female, mammary gland development is rigorously controlled by the ovary. Although puberty is often considered to be the point of initiation of ovarian function, the development of gonadal function, in fact, evolves gradually.[1] The complex regulatory mechanisms controlling ovarian function involve gonadotropin-releasing hormone (GnRH), luteinizing hormone (LH), follicle-stimulating hormone (FSH), the ovarian peptides inhibin, activin, and follistatin, as well as growth hormone (GH) and prolactin.[2] The ovary is active during late fetal development and for a short time after birth, but becomes relatively quiescent until the onset of puberty. At that time, ductal elongation and branching begin under the influence of estradiol as well as GH.[3,4] Although its exact mechanism of action is unclear, GH directly stimulates ductal growth in hypophysectomized-ovariectomized rats, and might act as well through its local mediator, insulin-like growth factor 1 (IGF-1). Normal duct development, however, requires the presence of estrogen and progesterone acting through their respective steroid receptors present in the mammary gland. Estradiol acts locally to stimulate DNA synthesis and promote bud formation, probably through an estrogen receptor (ER) mediated effect. Prolactin plays an additional role, but its specific actions are not fully understood. The response of the mammary gland to these complex hormonal and metabolic interactions results in developmental changes that permanently modify both the architecture and the biologic characteristics of the gland.[3,4] The mammary gland, in turn, responds selectively to given hormonal stimuli, depending on specific topographic differences in gland development, which modulate the expression of either cell proliferation or differentiation.

## ADOLESCENCE

Although the main changes occurring in the mammary gland are initiated at puberty, development continues during adulthood. The final histomorphometry of the gland varies greatly from woman to woman.[3] Mammary gland development can be defined by the external appearance of the breast or by determination of mammary gland area, volume, degree of branching, or level of differentiation of the gland, such as lobule type formation.[5]

The adolescent period begins with the first signs of sexual change at puberty and terminates with sexual maturity. Thelarche, defined as the initial clinical appearance of a breast bud, occurs at an average age of 11.2 (0.7 standard deviation) in white and 1 year earlier in African-American females.[6,7] With the approach of puberty, the rudimentary mammae begin to show growth activity both in the glandular tissue and in the surrounding stroma.[3–5] Glandular increase is due to the growth and division of small bundles of primary and secondary ducts (Fig. 164-1). These grow and divide in two ways. One involves repeated bifurcation of existing ducts, a process called "dichotomous" from the Greek word dichotomos or "to divide into two parts." The other involves localized buds on an expanding ductular base, a process called "sympodial" from Greek syn + podion base (Fig. 164-2).

The ducts grow, divide, and form club-shaped terminal end buds. The structures give origin to new branches, twigs, and small ductules or alveolar buds (see Fig. 164-2). We have coined the term alveolar bud to identify those structures that are morphologically more developed than the terminal end bud but yet more primitive than the terminal structure of the mature structure, which is called an acinus. Alveolar buds cluster around a terminal duct, forming the type 1 lobule or virginal lobule (Fig. 164-3). Each cluster is composed of approximately 11 alveolar buds. Lobule formation in the female breast occurs within 1 to 2 years after onset of the first menstrual period. Full differentiation of the mammary gland is a gradual process taking many years, and in some cases, if pregnancy does not supervene, is never attained.

## THE MATURE BREAST

Study of normal breast tissue in adult women identifies two additional and more mature types of lobules, designated types 2 and 3 (Figs. 164-4 and 164-5). The transition from type 1 to the more mature types 2 and 3 represents a gradual process, with sprouting of an increased number of new alveolar buds. In type 2 and 3 lobules, these are now called ductules; they

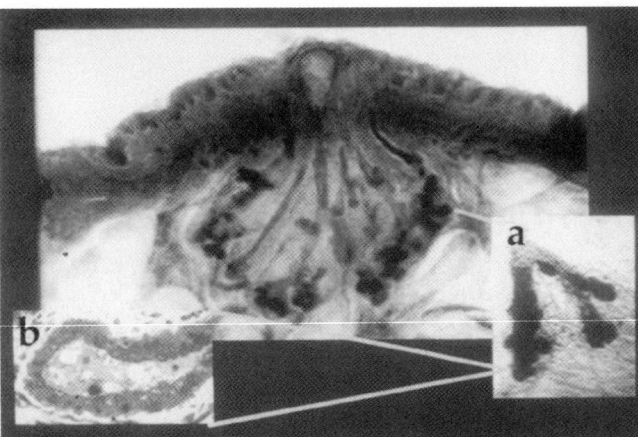

**Figure 164-1** Mammary gland of human female at birth formed by several excretory ducts, ending in terminal ducts. **A,** Detail of the inset showing the club-shaped terminal end bud from which lengthening and further divisions of the virginal ducts originate. **B,** Cross-section at the level shown in *a*; the duct is limed by the two layers of cells. Proliferation takes place chiefly in the basal cells. The inner cells have secretary properties from which the "witch milk" is formed. Toluidine blue ×25.

increase in number from approximately 11 in the type 1 lobule to 47 in the type 2 lobule and 80 in type 3 (Fig. 164-6 and Table 164-1). The increase in number results in a concomitant increase in size of the lobules and a reduction in size of each individual structure.[3,8]

### NULLIPAROUS WOMEN

In nulliparous women, breast tissue contains more undifferentiated structures, such as terminal ducts and type 1 lobules, although occasional type 2 and 3 lobules are seen. This pattern remains constant throughout the reproductive years unless pregnancy ensues. Type 2 lobules are present in moderate numbers during the early reproductive years, but sharply decrease after age 23, whereas the number of type 1 lobules remains significantly higher. This observation suggests that a certain percentage of type 1 lobules might have progressed to type 2 lobules, but the number of type 2 lobules

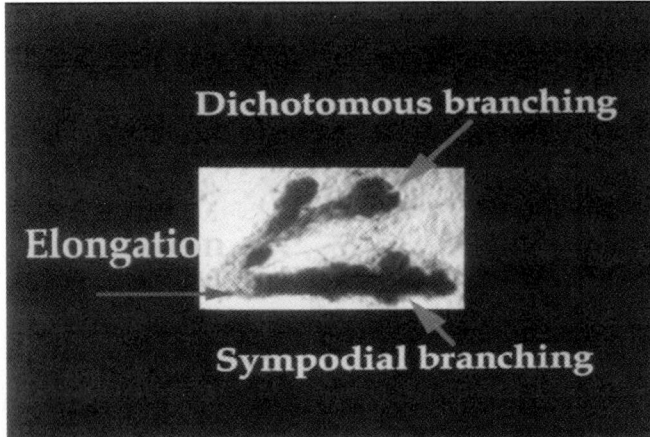

**Figure 164-2** Before the onset of puberty in human females, the ducts grow and divide in a dichotomous and sympodial basis; a ball-shaped end bud sprouts from the duct, and new branches and twigs develop from the terminal and lateral end buds. Toluidine blue ×25.

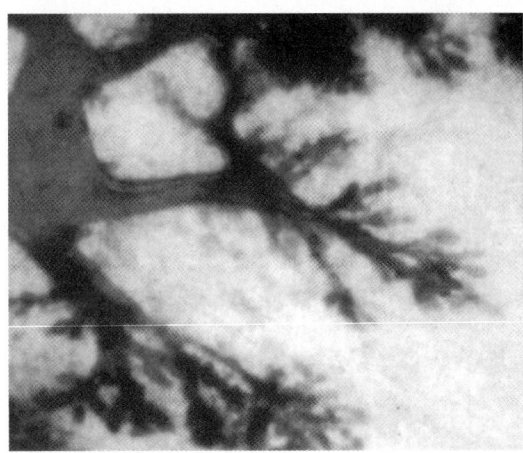

**Figure 164-3** Whole mount preparation of breast tissue of an 18-year-old nulliparous woman showing lobules type 1. Toluidine blue ×25.

progressing to type 3 is significantly lower than it is in parous women.

### PAROUS WOMEN

In this group, the predominant structure is the most differentiated lobule (i.e., type 3). The number of type 3 structures peaks during the early reproductive years and decreases after the fourth decade of life. A history of parity between the ages of 14 to 20 years correlates with a significant increase in the number of type 3 lobules that remain present as the predominant structure until the age of 40. At that time, the number of type 3 lobules decreases, due to their involution to predominantly type 1 lobules (Fig. 164-7).[9]

### PATTERN OF DISTRIBUTION OF CELLS POSITIVE FOR ESTROGEN AND PROGESTERONE RECEPTORS IN RELATION TO PROLIFERATING CELLS IN THE MAMMARY GLAND

Even though the breast is influenced by a myriad of hormones and growth factors,[10–17] estrogens are considered to play a major role in promoting the proliferation of both the normal and the neoplastic breast epithelium.[18–24] Estrogens

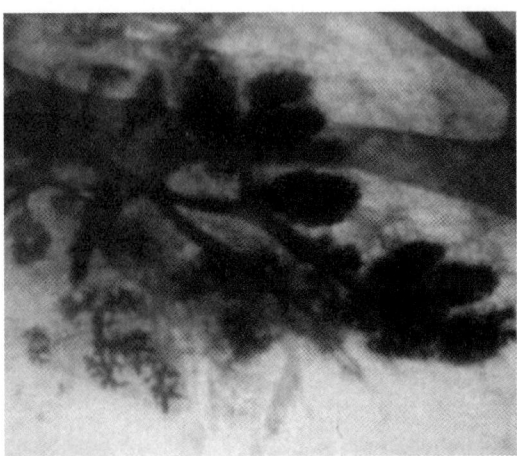

**Figure 164-4** Whole mount preparation of human breast tissue of a 24-year-old nulliparous woman showing lobules type 2. Toluidine blue ×25.

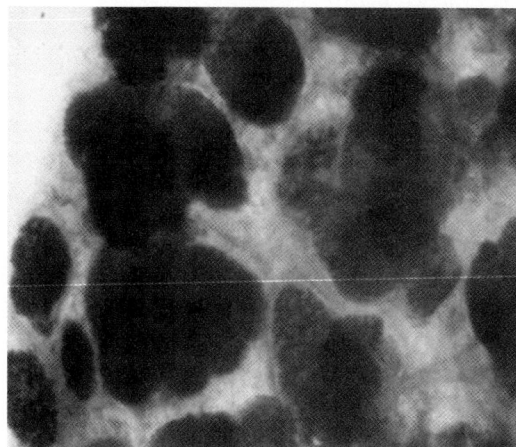

**Figure 164-5**  Whole mount preparation of human breast tissue of a 35-year-old parous woman containing lobules type 3. Toluidine blue ×25.

| Table 164-1 | Characteristics of the Lobular Structures of the Human Breast | | |
|---|---|---|---|
| **Structure** | Lobular Area[a] (μm²) | No. of Ductules/ Lobule[b] | No. of Cells/ Cross-section[c] |
| **Lob 1** | 48 ± 44 | 11.2 ± 6.3 | 32.4 ± 14.1 |
| **Lob 2** | 60 ± 26 | 47.0 ± 11.7 | 13.1 ± 4.8 |
| **Lob 3** | 129 ± 49 | 81.0 ± 16.6 | 11.0 ± 2.0 |

[a]Student's T-tests were done for all possible comparisons. Lobular areas showed significant differences between lob 1 vs. lob 3 and lob 2 vs. lob 3 ($P < 0.005$).
[b]The number of ductules per lobule was different ($P < 0.01$) in all the comparisons.
[c]The number of cells per cross-section was significantly different in ductules of lob 1 vs. 2 and 3. ($P < 0.01$).
(Reprinted with permission from Russo J, et al, Breast Cancer Res Treat 23:211–218, 1992.)

could influence the proliferative activity of mammary epithelial cells by at least three different mechanisms: direct receptor-mediated[19,25–32] stimulation; indirect autocrine/paracrine loops[22,23]; or interruption of negative feedback factors (i.e., the effect of estrogen to remove one or more inhibitory factors present in the serum[21,33]). Unfortunately, none of these mechanisms has been precisely defined with regard to their role in the normal development and differentiation of the breast, or the initiation and progression of the neoplastic process.

A greater degree of complexity emerged recently with the cloning of a gene encoding a second type of ER, the ER-β. This receptor is present in the mouse, rat, and human and has an affinity for estradiol similar to that of the classical ER (now identified as ER-α). In addition, it has now become possible to localize modulators of ER and progesterone receptor (PR) function in tissue. ER and PR mediated transcription often involves binding of coactivators to the transcription complex, a mechanism that enhances receptor function. One of these coactivators, steroid receptor coactivator 1 (SRC-1), has been cloned and can be localized with specific antibodies. Knockout of SRC-1 causes decreased growth and development of the uterus, prostate, testis, and mammary gland.[34] Examination of its localization in mammary tissue can provide insight into the local regulation of ER functionality.[35] These new findings have prompted a reevaluation of the estrogen signaling system in mammary tissue.[36–38]

Cell proliferation is indispensable for the normal growth and development of the breast. The fact that the normal epithelium contains receptors for both estrogen and progesterone lends support to the receptor-mediated mechanism as

a major player in the hormonal regulation of breast development. The essential role of ER-α and PR in mammary gland development has recently been confirmed by knockout mice lacking functional receptors. ER-α knockout mice display grossly impaired ductal epithelial proliferation and branching. PR knockout mice display significant ductal development but decreased arborization and absence of alveolar differentiation.[39,40]

Clinical studies have defined the relationship of cell proliferation to estrogen and progesterone production by correlation with phases of the menstrual cycle in women. The breast epithelium of sexually mature, normally cycling women does not exhibit maximal proliferation during the follicular phase of the menstrual cycle[14–18,41–46] when estrogens reach peak levels of 200 to 300 pg/mL and progesterone is less than 1 ng/mL. Maximal proliferative activity occurs during the luteal phase, when progesterone reaches levels of 10 to 20 ng/mL and estrogen levels are two- to threefold lower than during the follicular phase.[47] In breast cells grown

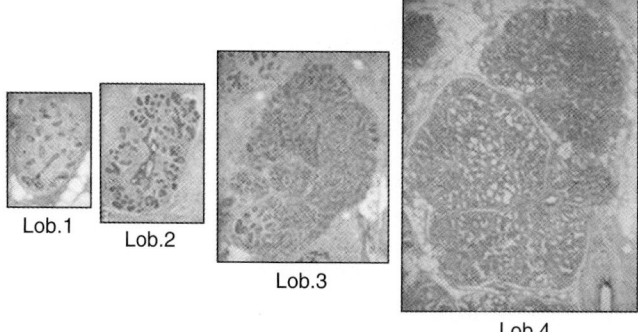

**Figure 164-6**  Lobules type 1, 2, 3, and 4 taken at the same magnification (×2.5) and stained with hematoxylin and eosin (H&E).

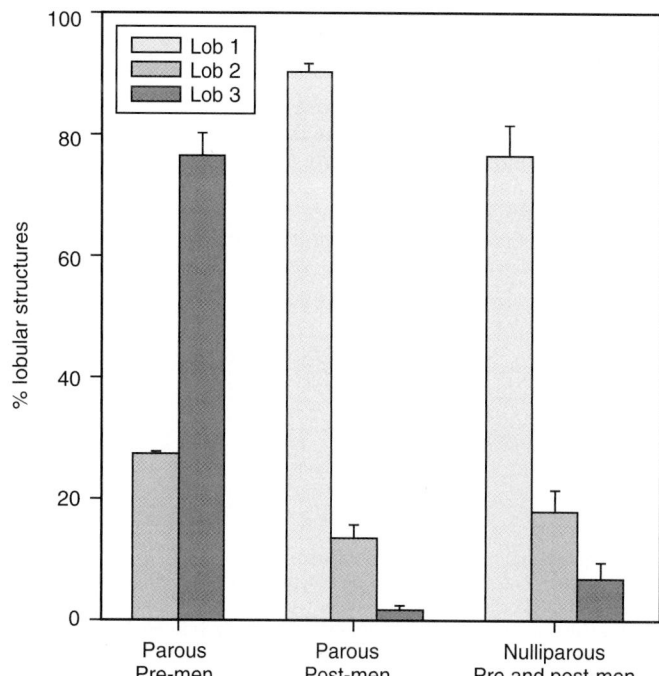

**Figure 164-7**  Percentage of lobule type structures in the breast of premenopausal (Pre-Men) and postmenopausal (Post-Men) parous women, and pre- and postmenopausal (Pre- & Post-Men) nulliparous women. Lobules type 1 (lob 1), type 2 (lob 2), and type 3 (lob 3).

in vitro, or when breast tissues are implanted in athymic nude mice, however, estrogens alone stimulate cell proliferation and progesterone has no effect, or even inhibits cell growth.[22,25,45,46]

Our studies of the proliferative activity of the mammary epithelium in both rodents and humans have demonstrated that cell division varies with the degree of differentiation of the mammary parenchyma.[10–13,18,48–50] In women, the highest level of cell proliferation is observed in the undifferentiated type 1 lobules (lob l) which are present in the breasts of young nulliparous subjects.[10–13,18] The progressive differentiation of type 1 lobules into type 2 and 3 results in a concomitant reduction of the proliferative activity of the mammary epithelium.[9–13] Further differentiation into type 4 lobules, characteristic of breast tissue during end of pregnancy and during lactation, further lowers the rate of proliferation.

Understanding of the relationship between lobular differentiation, cell proliferation, and hormone responsiveness of the mammary epithelium is just beginning. An important finding is that ER-$\alpha$ and progesterone receptor (PR) content in the lobular structures of the breast is directly proportional to the rate of cell proliferation. Proliferation and receptor content is maximal in the undifferentiated type 1 lobule and decreases progressively in types 2, 3, and 4.

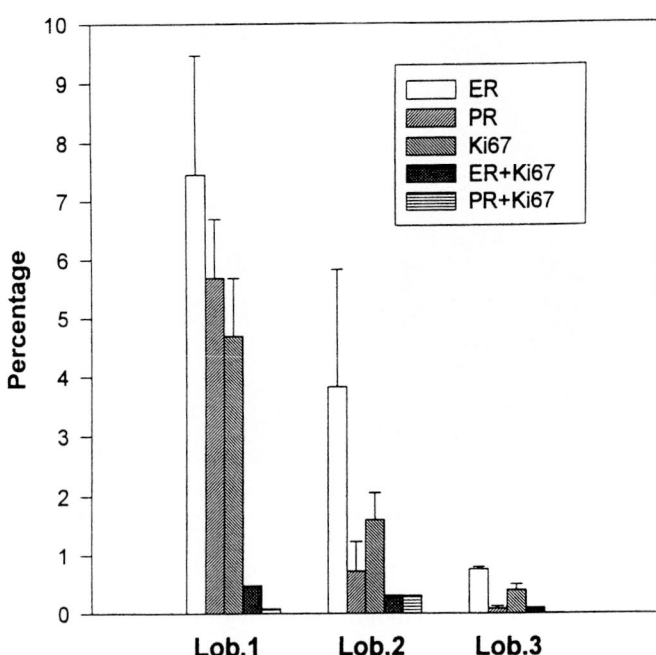

**Figure 164-8** Percentage of cells positive for estrogen receptor (ER), progesterone receptor (PR), Ki67, and both ER and Ki67 (ER+Ki67) or PR and Ki67 (PR+Ki67) (ordinate). Cells were quantitated in lobules type 1 (lob 1), type 2 (lob 2), and type 3 (lob 3) of the breast (abscissa).

## DISTRIBUTION OF PROLIFERATING CELLS IN RELATION TO THE PRESENCE OF STEROID RECEPTORS AND THEIR COACTIVATORS

Use of Ki67 immunohistochemical techniques allows detection of proliferating cells in tissue. The highest percentage of positive cells occurs in type 1 lobules (Fig. 164-8 and Table 164-2); a threefold lower percentage is found in type 2 lobules and a 10-fold decrement in type 3 (see Figs. 164-8 and 164-9A and B, and Table 164-2). The proliferating cells are almost exclusively found in the epithelium lining ducts and lobules, whereas only occasional positive cells are found in the myoepithelium, or in the intralobular and interlobular stroma. The same pattern of reactivity is observed in tissue sections incubated with the ER and PR antibodies. Positive cells are found exclusively in the epithelium with type 1 lobules containing the highest number of positive cells. Their number decreases progressively in type 2 and 3 lobules (see Fig. 164-8 and Table 164-2).

Use of double staining procedures for Ki67 and ER or PR has allowed quantitation in the same tissue sections of the spatial relationship between proliferating and receptor positive cells. This can be done with techniques using two colors or by immunofluorescent methodology (data are shown in Table 164-2). The percentage of ER- and PR-positive cells in type 1

lobules does not differ significantly, 7.5% and 5.7%, respectively. In type 2 lobules, the percentage of ER- and PR-positive cells is reduced to 3.8% and 0.7%, respectively; and in type 3, their numbers become negligible. There are similarities in the relative percentages of Ki67-, ER-, and PR-positive cells and the progressive reduction in the percentage of positive cells as the lobular differentiation progresses. However, those cells positive for Ki67 are not the same that reacted positively for ER or PR (see Fig. 164-9A and B). Very few cells, less than 0.5% in type 1 lobules and even fewer in type 2 and 3, appear positive for both Ki67 and ER (Ki67+ER). Double reactivity with this technique is identified by the darker staining of the nuclei, which appear dark purple-brown. The percentage of cells exhibiting double labeling with Ki67 and PR antibodies (Ki67+PR) in type 1 lobules is lower than the percentage of double-labeled ER-positive cells.

The content of ER and PR in the normal breast tissue, as detected immunocytochemically, varies with the degree of lobular development in a linear relationship with the rate of

**Table 164-2** Distribution of Ki67-, ER-, and PR-positive Cells in the Lobular Structures of the Human Breast

| Lobule Type | No. Cells | Ki67 | ER | PR | Ki67+ER | Ki67+PR |
|---|---|---|---|---|---|---|
| Lob 1 | 19,339[a] | 4.72 ± 1.00[d,e] | 7.46 ± 2.88[h] | 5.70 ± 1.36[k] | 0.48 ± 0.28[n] | **0.09** ± 0.01[o] |
| Lob 2 | 8,490[b] | 1.58 ± 0.45[f] | 3.83 ± 2.44[i] | 0.73 ± 0.57[l] | 0.31 ± 0.21 | 0.28 ± 0.27 |
| Lob 3 | 17,750[c] | 0.40 ± 0.18[g] | 0.76 ± 0.04[j] | 0.09 ± 0.04[m] | 0.01 ± 0.01 | 0.01 ± 0.01 |

ER, estrogen receptor; PR, progesterone receptor.
[a]Total number of cells counted in lobules type 1 (Lob 1) in breast tissue samples of 12 donors;
[b]Total number of cells counted in lobules type 2 (Lob 2) in breast tissue samples of 5 donors;
[c]Total number of cells counted in lobules type 3 (Lob 3) in breast tissue samples of 3 donors.
[d]Proliferative activity determined by the percentage cells Ki67 positive, expressed as the mean ± standard deviation. Differences were significative in [e]lob 1 vs. [f]lob 2 (t = 1.98 $P < 0.05$), [g]lob 2 vs. [g]lob 3 (t = 2.27 $P < 0.04$), and [e]lob 1 vs. [g]lob 3 (t = 2.56 $P < 0.01$).
ER-positive cells were significantly different in [h]lob 1 vs. [i]lob 2 (t = 2.04 $P < 0.05$) and [j]lob 3 (t = 2.50 $< 0.02$)
PR-positive cells were significantly different in [k]lob 1 vs. [l]lob 2 (t = 2.27 $P < 0.05$), and [k]lob 1 vs. [m]lob 3 (t = 2.60 $< 0.031$).
[n]Percentage of cells positive for both Ki67 and ER, expressed as the mean ± standard deviation.
[o]Percentage of cells positive for both Ki67 and PR, expressed as the mean ± standard deviation.

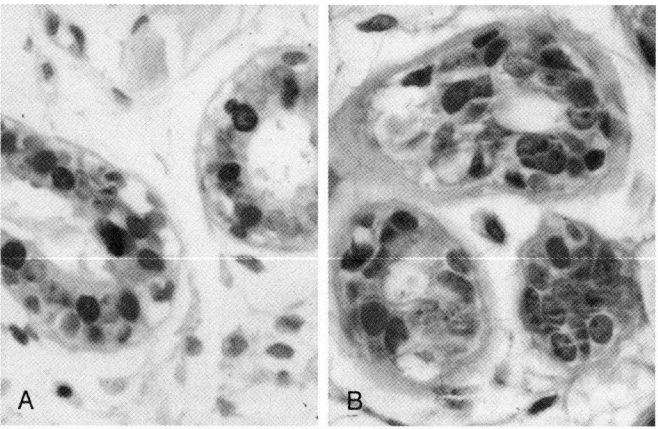

*Figure 164-9* Lob I ductules of the human breast. **A,** The single-layered epithelium lining the ductule contains Ki67-positive cells (brown nuclei), and ER-positive cells (red-purple nuclei) (×40). **B,** the single-layered epithelium lining the ductule contains brown Ki67-positive cells, and red-purple PR-positive cells. Sections were stained with DAB/alkaline phosphatase-vector red, with light hematoxylin counterstain and photographed at ×40. (See Color Plate.)

cell proliferation of the same structures. The utilization of a double-labeling immunocytochemical technique has allowed the determination whether the receptor-positive cell population is the same population that is proliferating (i.e., Ki67-positive cells). Clearly, this was not the case as was also reported by other authors.[44] The findings that proliferating cells are different from those that are ER and PR positive support data that indicate that estrogen controls cell proliferation by an indirect mechanism. A likely explanation is that ER-positive cells respond to estrogen with an increase in growth factor production, which acts in a paracrine fashion on neighboring ER-negative cells. This paracrine phenomenon has also been demonstrated using supernatants of estrogen-treated ER-positive cells that stimulate the growth of ER-negative cell lines in culture and in vivo in nude mice bearing ER-negative breast tumor xenografts.[51,52] A paracrine mechanism can also explain inhibition of cellular proliferation. ER-positive cells treated with antiestrogens secrete transforming growth factor-α (TGF-α), which inhibits the proliferation of ER-negative cells.[29]

The proliferative activity and the percentage of ER- and PR-positive cells are highest in type 1 lobules in comparison with types 2 to 4 composing the normal breast. These findings provide a mechanistic explanation for the higher susceptibility of these structures to transformation by chemical carcinogens in vitro,[53,54] supporting as well the observation that type 1 lobules are the site of origin of ductal carcinomas.[55] The relationship between ER-positive and ER-negative breast cancers is not clear, however.[56–58] It has been suggested that either ER-negative breast cancers result from the loss of the ability of the cells to synthesize ER during clinical evolution of ER-positive cancers, or that ER-positive and ER-negative cancers are different entities.[56,58] It is postulated that type 1 lobules contain at least three cell types: ER-positive cells that do not proliferate, ER-negative cells that are capable of proliferating, and a small proportion of ER-positive cells that can proliferate as well (Fig. 164-10). Therefore, estrogen might stimulate ER-positive cells to produce a growth factor, which, in turn, stimulates neighboring ER-negative cells capable of proliferating (see Fig. 164-10). In the same fashion, the small proportion of cells that are ER positive and can proliferate could be the source of ER-positive tumors. The possibility exists as well that the ER-negative cells convert to ER-positive cells. The conversion of ER-negative to ER-positive cells has been reported.[59,60] The newly discovered ER-β opens the possibility that those cells traditionally considered to be ER-α negative might be ER-β positive.[36–37] It has recently been found that ER is expressed during the immortalization and transformation of ER-negative human breast epithelial cells, supporting the hypothesis of conversion from a negative to a positive receptor cell.[61]

The findings that proliferating cells in the human breast are different from those that contain steroid hormone receptors explain many of the in vitro data.[62–65] Of interest are a series of observations regarding ER and cell proliferation. ER-positive MCF-7 cells respond to estrogen treatment with increased cell proliferation. Enhanced expression of the receptor by transfection also increases the proliferative response to estrogen.[62,66] When ER-negative cells such as MDA-MB 468 and others are transfected with the ER, however, estrogen then inhibits cell growth.[63–67] Although the negative effect of estrogen on those ER-negative cells transfected with the receptor has been interpreted as an interference of the transcription factor used to maintain estrogen independent growth,[66] there is no definitive explanation for

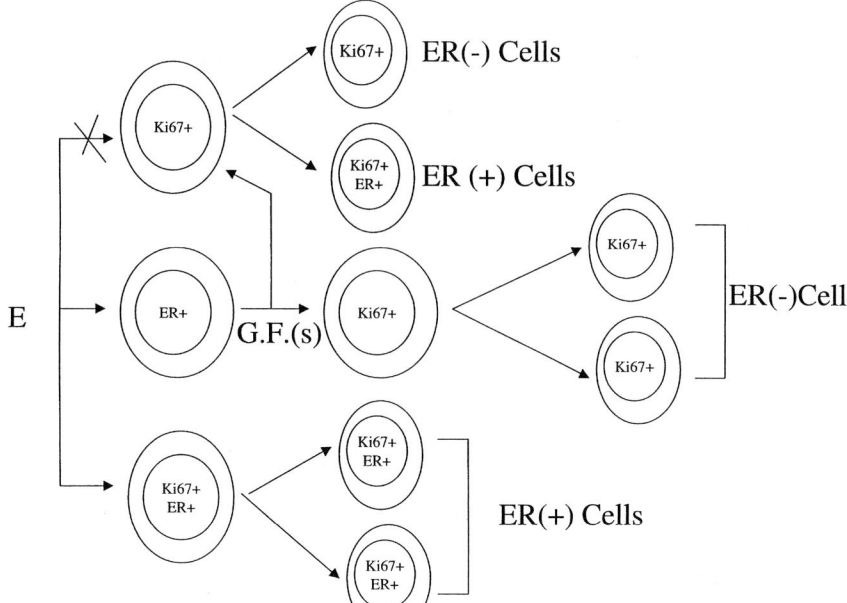

*Figure 164-10* Schematic representation of the postulated pathways of estrogen actions on breast epithelial cells. Cells expressing three different phenotypes might be present in the epithelium: Estrogen receptor (ER)—negative Ki67-positive cells that are capable of proliferating, ER-positive cells that do not proliferate, and a small proportion of ER- and Ki67-positive cells. Estrogen might stimulate ER-positive cells to produce a growth factor (GF) that in turn stimulates neighboring ER-negative cells capable of proliferating. ER+Ki67-positive cells can proliferate and could be stimulated by estrogen to originate ER-positive daughter cells or probably tumors. ER-negative cells may convert to ER-positive cells during neoplastic transformation.

their lack of survival, but it can be explained by the finding that proliferating and ER-positive cells are two separate populations. Further support is the finding that, when type 1 lobules of normal breast tissue are placed in culture, they lose the ER-positive cells, indicating that only proliferating cells that are also ER negative can survive and that these constitute the stem cells.[67,68]

Until recently, it was believed that estrogens acted through a single nuclear estrogen receptor that transcriptionally activated specific target genes. There is mounting evidence, however, that a membrane receptor coupled to alternative second messenger signaling mechanisms[69,70] is also operational, and may stimulate the cascade of events leading to cell proliferation. This knowledge suggests that ER-$\alpha$ negative cells found in the human breast may respond to estrogens through this or other pathways. Although more studies need to be done in this direction, it is clear that paracrine mechanisms are important in mediating cellular proliferation. In the normal breast, the proliferating and steroid hormone receptor positive cells are different. This finding opens new possibilities for clarifying the mechanisms through which estrogens might act on the proliferating cells to initiate the cascade of events leading to cancer.

An additional complexity arises on examination of the cell specific localization of steroid receptor coactivators in mammary tissue. Steroid receptor coactivators, such as SRC-1, enhance the transcriptional capabilities of both the ER and PR. Our recent studies demonstrate that SRC-1 is segregated in distinct subsets of cells within the epithelium of the estrogen-responsive rat mammary gland. This finding is in contrast to findings in the stroma, where significant numbers of cells coexpressed both ER-$\alpha$ and SRC-I (Fig. 164-11). These findings highlight the need to explore further whether stromal-epithelial interactions might be important in the human breast.[71-75] Prior studies have shown that, in the uterus and prostate, receptors in stroma tissue are necessary for epithelial proliferation. In those organs, growth factors made by stroma in response to estrogens and androgens regulate the proliferation of epithelial cells. Although the presence of estrogen receptors in the stroma of human mammary tissue has not been established, further studies are required to understand fully the potential stromal-epithelial interactions in the breast. This is particularly pertinent because of the demonstration that stromal tissue can synthesize estrogen through the aromatase enzyme in human breast. The estrogen produced locally in stroma may then act in a paracrine fashion on surrounding epithelial cells.[71-75]

With development of proliferative benign breast lesions, the relationship between the presence of ER-$\alpha$ positive cells and proliferation appears to change. The first abnormality of proliferation to appear is called the hyperplastic unfolded lobule (HUL). HUL lesions are associated with a substantial enlargement of the lobules abutting normal ducts.[76] The percentage of ER-positive cells in these lesions increases to 80% from that found in normal benign epithelium (30%), with Ki67 labeling index of 6.7% in HUL lesions versus 1.6% ($P < 0.001$) in the normal epithelium. These recent findings suggest that hyperplastic breast abnormalities may be associated with conversion from paracrine to endocrine regulation of cell growth.[77,78]

## THE MENOPAUSAL BREAST

The menopause occurs at an average age of 51 when the ovaries stop synthesizing estradiol and amenorrhea ensues. The years leading up to the final menstrual period constitute the perimenopause.[10] Many women ovulate irregularly during the perimenopausal transition. After menopause, the breast regresses both in nulliparous and parous women. This involutionary process is manifested by an increase in the

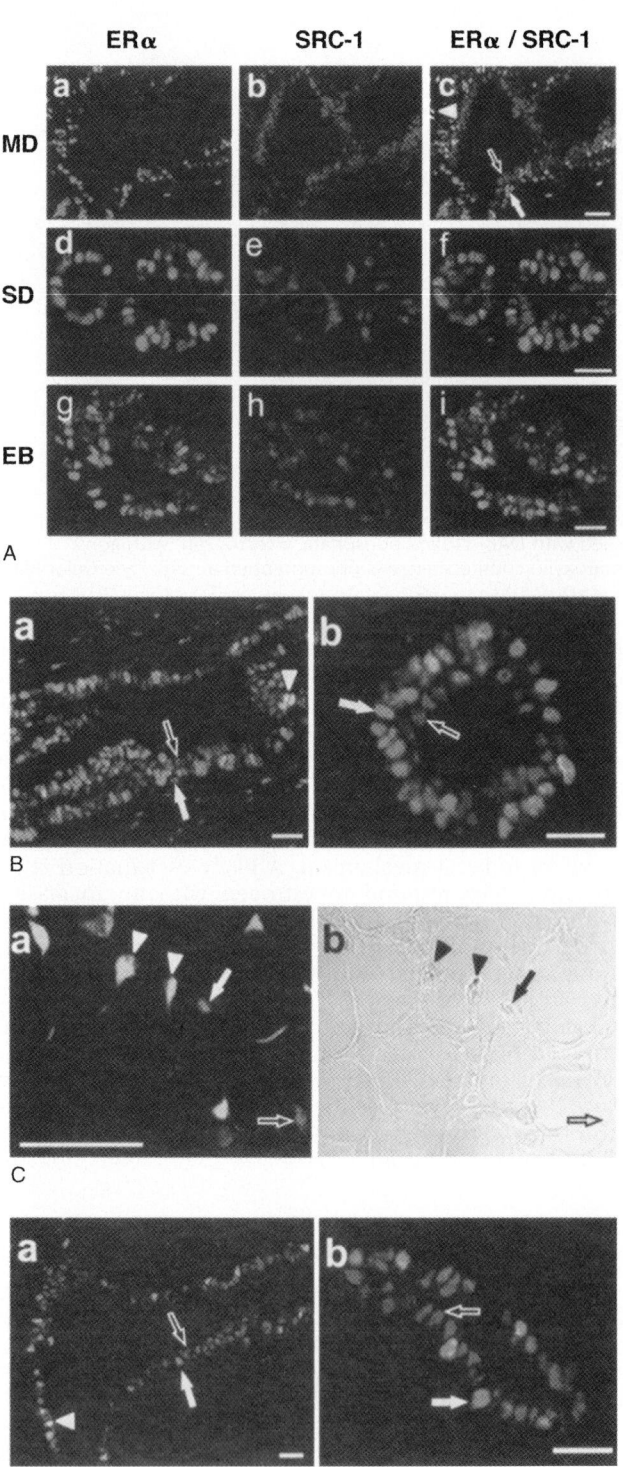

**Figure 164-11** Segregation of steroid receptor coactivator 1 (SRC-1) expression from ER-$\alpha$-positive cells as illustrated by dual fluorescence labeling of SRC-1 and ER-$\alpha$. **A,** mammary glands from 3-week-old virgin female rats were stained simultaneously for SRC-1 (*b, e,* and *h;* red) and ER-$\alpha$ (*a, d,* and *g;* green). Green and red images were superimposed (*c, f,* and *i*). Main duct (MD), small duct (SD), and end bud (EB) are shown. **B,** The discrete distribution pattern of ER-$\alpha$ (green) and SRC-1 (red) was confirmed with the combination of two different antibodies (*a* and *b*). **C,** Stroma expressing ER-$\alpha$ alone (green), SRC-1 alone (red), or both (yellow). The phase contrast image from *a* is shown in *b*. **D,** Staining from 10-week-old virgin female rat mammary gland also demonstrated the segregation of SRC-1 from ER-$\alpha$ in epithelial cells. *Solid arrow,* Cells expressing only ER-$\alpha$; *open arrow,* cells expressing only SRC-1; *solid arrowhead,* cells expressing both ER-$\alpha$ and SRC-1. (*Bar = 100 μm.*) (See Color Plate.)

number of type 1 lobules and a concomitant decline in type 2 and type 3 lobules. At the end of the fifth decade of life, the breasts of both nulliparous and parous women contain predominantly type 1 lobules (see Fig. 164-7). These observations led us to conclude that the understanding of breast development requires a horizontal study in which all the different phases of growth are taken into consideration. For example, the analysis of breast structures at a single given point, for instance, age 50 years, might lead one to conclude that the breasts of both nulliparous and parous women are identical (see Fig. 164-7). The phenomena occurring in prior years, however, might have imprinted permanent changes on breast biology. This would affect the potential of the breast for neoplasm, but would be no longer morphologically observable. Thus, from a quantitative point of view, the regressive phenomenon occurring in the breast at menopause differs in nulliparous and parous women. It should be recalled that in nulliparous breasts, the predominant structure is the type 1 lobule, which comprises 65% to 80% of the total lobule type components, a percentage independent of age. Type 2 lobules represent 10% to 35%, and type 3, only 0% to 5% of the total lobular population. In breasts of premenopausal parous women, on the other hand, the predominant lobular structure is the type 3 lobule, which comprises 70% to 90% of the total lobule component. At menopause, the type 3 lobules have declined in number, and the relative proportion of the three lobule types are similar to those observed in nulliparous women. These observations led us to conclude that early parous women truly underwent lobule differentiation, which was evident at a younger age, whereas nulliparous women seldom reached the lobule type 3 and never the lobule type 4 stages (see Figs. 164-6 and 164-12).

## GENOMIC DIFFERENCES BETWEEN LOBULAR STRUCTURES

To better understand normal human breast development and each stage of lobular differentiation, we have applied the established cDNA microarray technique, which can reveal the expression of thousand of genes simultaneously.[79] We have determined the genomic signature between normal human breast type 1 lobules (lob 1) and type 3 lobules (lob 3), which represent two distinct structures present in nulliparous and

parous premenopausal women, respectively. We found that lob 3 has a gene expression profile significantly different from that of lob 1. When we applied a cutoff value of greater than or equal to twofold upregulation or less than or equal to 50% downregulation, a total of 111 genes, including 63 genes upregulated and 48 genes downregulated, showed expression changes in lob 3 compared with lob 1. Considering the limited numbers of samples examined and the existing intersubject variations, we only selected 47 genes that are changed over a fivefold range (Tables 164-3 and 164-4). These genes have putative functions in a variety of cellular processes. Interestingly, there are more growth factors and cell receptors downregulated than upregulated in lob 3, which indicates lob 3 is less proliferative than lob 1. Most of the extracellular matrix genes are downregulated in lob 3, and are implicated in the differentiation of epithelial cells. Only one caspase family member directly related to cell apoptosis-caspase 4 is upregulated fivefold in lob 3.

Although it is difficult to discuss in detail all the possible functional roles of each one of the genes differentially expressed in lob 3 versus lob 1, it is of interest to note that the RhoE gene is amplified 9.44-fold in the lob 3 of the parous breast. This gene belongs to a small G protein superfamily that consists of the Ras, Rho, Rab, Arf, Sarl, Rheb, and Ran families.[80–83] In vivo, RhoE is found exclusively in the GTP-bound form, suggesting that, unlike previously characterized small GTPases, RhoE may be normally maintained in an activated state.[81] This could be an important function, considering that this gene might remain expressed even after involution of lob 3 to lob 1 in the postmenopausal state.

The other gene that is significantly overexpressed (average 10.4-fold) in the lob 3 is the protein tyrosine phosphatase (PPTPCAAXI or PRL-1). This gene encodes a unique nuclear protein-tyrosine phosphatase,[84–87] which is regulated by a mechanism different from those of other immediate-early genes such as c-fos and c-jun.[84] This gene has been shown to be upregulated in villus but not crypt enterocytes, and in confluent differentiated but not undifferentiated cells.[88,89]

IGF-binding protein-3 (IGFBP-3) is significantly overexpressed in lob 3 when compared with lob 1 of the breasts of premenopausal women. This gene codes a specific binding protein for the insulin-like growth factors. IGFBP-3 modulates the mitogenic and metabolic effects of IGFs, and forms a ternary complex with IGF-1 or IGF-2 and a 85-kilodalton

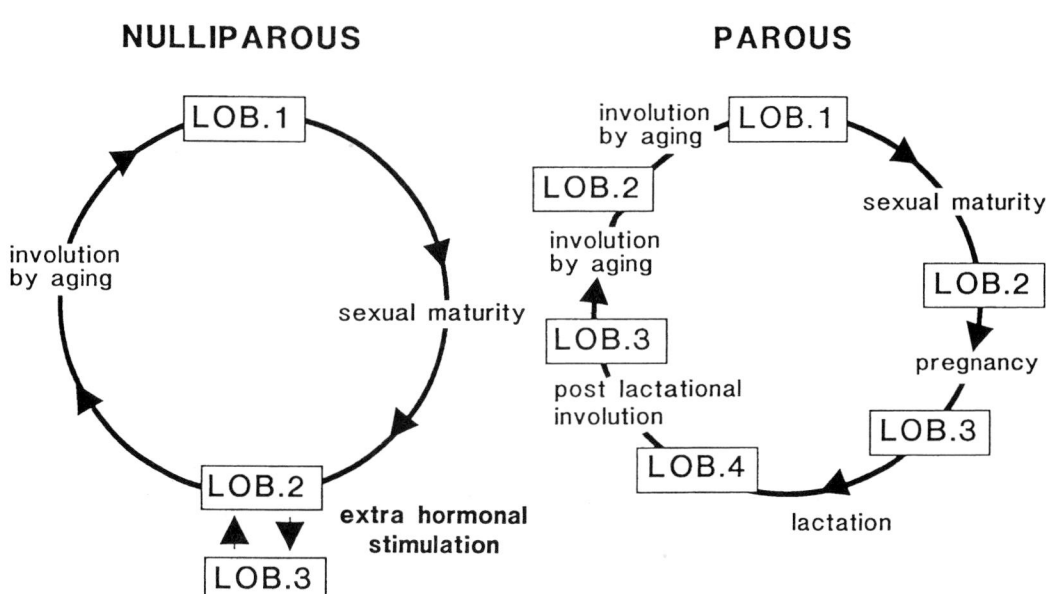

**NULLIPAROUS**

**PAROUS**

**Figure 164-12** Schematic representation of breast development based on relative percentage of lobules present. Nulliparous women's breasts contain primarily lobules type 1 (lob 1) with some progression to type 2 (lob 2), and only minimal formation of lobules type 3 (lob 3). Parous women undergo a complete cycle of development through the formation of lobules type 4 (lob 4), which later regress. (Reproduced with permission from Russo J, Rivera R, Russo IH: Influence of age and parity on development of the human breast. Breast Cancer Res Treat 23:211–218, 1992.)

**Table 164-3** Upregulated Genes in Human Lob 3 in Comparison with Lob 1

| Gene/Protein Name | Swissprot # | Function | Pair 1 | Pair 2 | Pair 3 | Average |
|---|---|---|---|---|---|---|
| STAT2 | P52630 | Transcription | 5.54 | 1.55 | 10.7 | 5.93 |
| PIG7 | Q99732 | Tumor suppressor | 1.51 | 2.64 | 15.92 | 6.69 |
| SAP102 | Q92796 | Tumor suppressor | 3.08 | 6.37 | 9.81 | 6.42 |
| PCNA | P12004 | Cyclin | 3.69 | 4.27 | 7.55 | 5.17 |
| Lipocalin 2 | P80188 | Signaling | 1.46 | 6.44 | 10.91 | 5.97 |
| IGFBP3 | P17936 | Hormone | 15.67 | 0.42 | 2.13 | 6.07 |
| Platelet basic protein | P02775 | Growth factor | ND | 1.08 | 13.82 | 7.45 |
| VEGF | P15692 | Growth factor | 3.44 | 2.14 | 53.80 | 19.8 |
| RhoE | P52199 | G protein | 12.29 | 1.42 | 14.61 | 9.44 |
| p21-rac2 | P15153 | G protein | 2.49 | 2.51 | 12.58 | 5.85 |
| p21-rac1 | P15154 | G protein | 3.51 | 1.19 | 14.08 | 6.26 |
| GNBP gamma-10 | P50151 | G protein | 11.22 | 1.88 | 9.79 | 7.63 |
| PRL-1 | O00648 | Phosphatase | 7.24 | 3.06 | 21.01 | 10.4 |
| Caspase-4 precursor | P49662 | Apoptosis | 5.14 | 2.61 | 7.61 | 5.12 |
| MMP-7 | P09237 | Metalloproteinase | 8.14 | 7.08 | 3.71 | 6.31 |
| Inosine phosphorylase | P00491 | Metabolism | 6.14 | 3.25 | 10.36 | 6.58 |
| LDHA | P00338 | Metabolism | 5.84 | 1.59 | 8.5 | 5.31 |
| Cytosolic superoxide dismutase 1 | P00441 | Xenobiotic metabolism | 1.6 | 1.6 | 17.98 | 7.06 |
| HSC70-interacting protein | P50502 | Chaperone | 1.36 | 0.51 | 17.27 | 6.38 |
| CD9 antigen | P21926 | Cell antigen | ND | 5.26 | 55.51 | 30.9 |
| Integrin beta 6 | P18564 | Cell adhesion | 6.37 | 1.53 | 7.23 | 5.04 |
| Integrin beta 4 | P16144 | Cell adhesion | 0.47 | 1.51 | 15.33 | 5.66 |
| BENE | Q13021 | Unclassified | 2.77 | 8.71 | 9.79 | 7.09 |

ND, no data.

glycoprotein acid-labile subunit.[90,91] IGFBP-3 may also play more active, IGF-independent roles in growth regulation of cancer cells.[89,92] IGFBP-3 protein levels are developmentally regulated and influenced by a number of hormonal stimuli both in vitro and in vivo.[93] P53 may regulate apoptosis in tumor cells via transactivation of the IGFBP-3 gene.[94] We have found (data not shown) that IGBP-3 could be modulated by human chorionic gonadotropin (hCG)s and be one important pathway in the differentiation effect of this hormone in the mammary gland. Its expression in the lob 3 is a new finding that requires further investigation. We also found that two tumor suppressor genes, SAP102 and PIG7, are upregulated in lob3. SAP102 is a postsynaptic protein.[95] PIG7 is induced by p53 gene.[96] Another gene product that was upregulated in the lob 3 was lipocalin 2. Lipocalins are mainly extracellular carriers of lipophilic molecules, though exceptions with properties such as prostaglandin synthesis and protease inhibition are observed for specific lipocalins. The influence of the extracellular lipocalins on intracellular cell regulation events is not fully understood, but several of the lipocalin ligands are also well-known agents in cell differentiation and proliferation.[97] Recently, lipocalin 2 has been attributed to have a role in the growth regulatory effects of estrogen in normal breast epithelium.[98]

**Table 164-4** Downregulated Genes in Human Breast Lob 3 in Comparison with Lob 1

| Gene/Protein Name | Swissprot # | Function | Pair 1 | Pair 2 | Pair 3 | Average |
|---|---|---|---|---|---|---|
| STAT1 | P42224 | Transcription | 0.15 | 0 | 0.27 | 0.14 |
| IGFBP4 | P22692 | Signaling | 0.14 | 0 | 0.07 | 0.07 |
| IGFBP5 | P24593 | Signaling | 0 | 0 | 0 | 0 |
| Smoothened homologue | Q99835 | Signaling | 0.16 | 0 | 0.35 | 0.17 |
| BMP1 | P13497 | Growth factor | 0.16 | 0.13 | 0.19 | 0.16 |
| CTGF | P29279 | Growth factor | 0 | 0 | 0 | 0 |
| GASP | Q14393 | Growth factor | 0.12 | 0 | 0 | 0.04 |
| VEGFB | P49765 | Growth factor | 0 | 0 | 0 | 0 |
| PDGFRB | P09619 | Cell receptor | 0 | 0 | 0 | 0 |
| p125 | Q01831 | Stress response | 0 | 0 | 0 | 0 |
| Interleukin-14 precursor | P40222 | Interleukin | 0.14 | 0 | 0.28 | 0.14 |
| Interleukin-3 precursor | P08700 | Interleukin | 0 | 0 | 0 | 0 |
| Monocyte ARG-serpin | P05120 | Protease inhibitor | 0 | 0 | 0 | 0 |
| MMP15 | P51511 | Metalloproteinase | 0 | 0 | 0 | 0 |
| BIGH3 | Q15582 | Microfilament | 0.27 | 0.02 | 0.28 | 0.19 |
| Polycystin precursor | P98161 | Cell adhesion | 0.09 | 0.34 | 0 | 0.14 |
| Wnt-5A | P41221 | Cell communication | 0 | 0.06 | 0.21 | 0.09 |
| PGS1 | P21810 | Extracellular matrix | 0.06 | 0 | 0.03 | 0.03 |
| Collagen 4 alpha 2 | P08572 | Extracellular matrix | 0.37 | 0.17 | 0 | 0.18 |
| Collagen 6 alpha 1 | Q14041 | Extracellular matrix | 0.13 | 0.01 | 0.13 | 0.09 |
| Collagen 6 alpha 2 | Q13909 | Extracellular matrix | 0 | 0 | 0 | 0 |
| Collagen 6 alpha 3 | P12111 | Extracellular matrix | 0.25 | 0 | 0.11 | 0.12 |
| Collagen 8 alpha 1 | P27658 | Extracellular matrix | 0 | 0 | 0 | 0 |
| Collagen 11 alpha 2 | P13942 | Extracellular matrix | 0 | 0 | 0 | 0 |

Some genes may also have an important role in the differentiation pattern of the mammary gland, which, in turn, could influence their susceptibility to carcinogenesis, although the changes in the level of expression were less than fivefold. For example, G.T mismatch-specific thymine DNA glycosylase (TDG), which upregulated 3.6-fold in lob 3, is capable of recognizing G.T and G.U mismatches in DNA and initiating their restoration to G.C base pairs through a base excision repair.[99,100] Activated TDG might decrease C-T transition mutations at CpG sites, especially in p53 gene. We also found TDG is upregulated by hCG treatment in MCF-10F cells (unpublished data). Since human tumors including breast cancers contain a high proportion of C-T transition mutations, TDG upregulated in lob 3 might be an important protective factor against carcinogenesis. In our previous study, we also found that mammary-derived growth inhibitor (MDGI), which suppresses carcinogenesis in transformed human breast cancer cells,[101] was also upregulated in lob 3.[102] MDGI may have a role in normal cell differentiation through suppressing cell proliferation and/or inhibiting carcinogenesis by the same mechanism.

Of interest is the observation that there was no difference between lob 1 and lob 3 in the expression of cytoskeletal proteins such as cytokeratins 8, 18, and 19, which are overexpressed in tumor cells.[103] Known genes that are overexpressed in breast cancer, such as HER-2/neu[104] and mucin[105,106] were not expressed in any of the lobular structures. Other genes, such as fibroblast growth factor-1 (FGF-1),[104] IGF-1-binding protein-2,[107,108] and Zinc-(X-2-glycoprotein, which are generally up- or downregulated in the neoplastic process, were not differentially expressed in the lob 3 versus lob 1.

Differentially expressed genes occur during normal human breast lobular differentiation and these changes might persistently modify the susceptibility to carcinogenesis. Since cells derived from the differentiated lob 3 are resistant to growing in vitro and do not express transformation phenotypes on carcinogen treatment, as cells from lob 1 do,[53,54] the final biological significance of the genes found in the process of differentiation of the breast, the persistence of their expression during postmenopausal involution, and how they are regulated by the reproductive history of the woman are not known.

## REFERENCES

1. Edwards RG, Howles CM, Macnarnee C: Clinical endocrinology of reproduction. In Baulieu, E-E, Kelly PA (eds): Hormones: From Molecules to Disease. New York, Chapman & Hall, 1990, pp 457–476.
2. Strauss J, Msueh AJW: Ovarian hormone synthesis. In Marshall JC (ed): Endocrinology. Philadelphia, Saunders, 2001, pp 2043–2052.
3. Russo J, Russo IH: Development of human mammary gland. In Neville MC, Daniel CW (eds): The Mammary Gland: Development, Regulation, and Function. Plenum, New York, 1987, pp 67–93.
4. Dabelow A: die Milchdruse. In Bargmann W (ed): Handbuch der Mikroskopischen Anatomic des Menchen, Vol 3, Part 3, Haut and Sinnes Organs. Berlin, Springer-Verlag, 1957, pp 277–485.
5. Tanner JM (ed): The development of the reproductive system. In Growth at Adolescence. Oxford, Blackwell Scientific, 1962, pp 28–39.
6. Roche AF, Wellens R, Attie KM, Siervogel RM: The timing of sexual maturation in a group of US white youths. J Ped Endocrinol Metab 8:11–18, 1995.
7. Herman-Giddens ME, Slora EJ, Wasserman RC, et al: Secondary sexual characteristics and menses in young girls seen in office practice: A study from the Pediatric Research in Office Settings Network. Pediatrics 99:505–512, 1997.
8. Russo J, Tay LK, Russo IH: Differentiation of the mammary gland and susceptibility to carcinogenesis. Breast Cancer Res Treat 2:5–73, 1982.
9. Russo J, Rivera R, Russo IH: Influence of age and parity on the development of the human breast. Breast Cancer Res Treat 23:211–218, 1992.
10. Russo J, Russo IH: Role of hormones in human breast development: The menopausal breast. In Wren BG (ed): Progress in the Management of Menopause. London, Parthenon, 1997, pp 184–193.
11. Russo IH, Russo J: Role of hormones in cancer initiation and progression. J Mammary Gland Biol Neoplasia 3:49–61, 1998.
12. Russo J, Russo IH: Role of differentiation in the pathogenesis and prevention of breast cancer. Endocr Relat Cancer 4:7–21, 1997.
13. Calaf G, Alvarado ME, Bonney GE, et al: Influence of lobular development on breast epithelial cell proliferation and steroid hormone receptor content. Int J Oncol 7:1285–1288, 1995.
14. Lippman ME, Dickson RB, Gelmann EP, et al: Growth regulation of human breast carcinoma occurs through regulated growth factor secretion. J Cell Biochem 35:1–16, 1987.
15. Meyer JS: Cell proliferation in normal human breast ducts, fibroadenomas, and other duct hyperplasias, measured by nuclear labeling with tritiated thymidine. Hum Pathol 8:67–81, 1977.
16. Masters JRW, Drife JO, Scarisbrick JJ: Cyclic variations of DNA synthesis in human breast epithelium. J Natl Cancer Inst 58:1263–1265, 1977.
17. Ferguson DJP, Anderson TJ: Morphologic evaluation of cell turnover in relation to the menstrual cycle in the "resting" human breast. Br J Cancer 44:177–181, 1981.
18. Russo J, Russo IH: Estrogens and cell proliferation in the human breast. J Cardiovasc Pharmacol 28:19–23, 1996.
19. Kumar V, Stack GS, Berry M, et al: Functional domains of the human estrogen receptor. Cell 51:941–951, 1987.
20. King RJB: Effects of steroid hormones and related compounds on gene transcription. Clin Endocrinol 36:1–14, 1992.
21. Soto AM, Sonnenschein C: Cell proliferation of estrogen-sensitive cells: The case for negative control. Endocr Rev 48:52–58, 1987.
22. Huseby RA, Maloney TM, McGrath CM: Evidence for a direct gowth-stimulating effect of estradiol on human-MCF-7 cells in vitro. Cancer Res 144:2654–2659, 1987.
23. Huff KK, Knabbe C, Lindsey R, et al: Multihormonal regulation of insulin-like growth factor-1-related protein in MCF-7 human breast cancer cells. Mol Endocrinol 2:200–208, 1988.
24. Dickson RB, Huff KK, Spencer EM, Lippman ME: Introduction of epidermal growth factor related polypeptides by 17beta-estradiol in MCF-7 human breast cancer cells. Endocrinol 118:138–142, 1986.
25. Katzenellenbogen BS, Kendra KL, Norman MJ, Berthois Y: Proliferation, hormonal responsiveness and estrogen receptor content of MCF-7 human breast cancer cells growth in the short-term and long-term absence of estrogens. Cancer Res 47:4355–4360, 1987.
26. Petersen OW, Hoyer PE, van Deurs B: Frequency and distribution of estrogen receptor positive cells in normal, nonlactating human breast tissue. Cancer Res 47:5748–5751, 1987.
27. Jacquemier JD, Hassouin J, Torente M, Martin PM: Distribution of estrogen and progesterone receptors in healthy tissue adjacent to breast lesions at various stages: Immunohistochemical study of 107 cases. Breast Cancer Res Treat 15:109–117, 1990.
28. McGuire W, Carbone P, Vollmer R (eds): Estrogen Receptors in Human Breast Cancer. New York, Raven, 1975.
29. Dickson R, Lippman M: Control of human breast cancer by estrogen, growth factors and oncogenes. In Lipman ME, Dickson RB (eds): Estrogen Receptors in Human Breast Cancer. New York, Raven, 1975.
30. Wittliff IL: Steroid-hormone receptors in breast cancer. Cancer 53:630–643, 1984.
31. Watts CKW, Handel ML, King RJB, Sutherland RL: Oestrogen receptor gene structure and function in breast cancer.

J Steroid Biochem Mol Biol 41:5293–5536, 1992.

32. Aakvaag A, Utaacker E, Thorsen T, et al: Growth control of human mammary cancer cells (MCF-7 cells) in culture: Effect of estradiol and growth factors in serum containing medium. Cancer Res 50:7806–7810, 1990.

33. Dell'aquilla ML, Pigott DA, Bonaquist DL, Gaffney EV: A factor from plasma derived human serum that inhibits the growth of the mammary cell line MCF-7: Characterization and purification. J Natl Cancer Inst 72:291–298, 1984.

34. Xu J, Qiu Y, DeMayo FJ, et al: Partial hormone resistance in mice with disruption of the steroid receptor co-activator-1 (SRC-1) gene. Science 279:1922–1925, 1998.

35. Shim W-S, DiRenzo J, DeCaprio JA, et al: Segregation of steroid receptor coactivator-I from steroid receptors in mammary epithelium. Proc Natl Acad Sci U S A 96:208–213, 1999.

36. Kuiper GGJM, Enmark E, Pelto-Huikko M, et al: Cloning of a novel estrogen receptor expressed in rat prostate and ovary. Proc Natl Acad Sci U S A 93:5925–5930, 1996.

37. Byers M, Kuiper GGJM, Gustaffson J-A, Park-Sarge OK: Estrogen receptor beta mRNA expression in rat ovary down-regulation by gonadotropins. Mol Endocrinol 11:172–182, 1997.

38. Vladusic EA, Homby AE, Guerra-Vladusic FK, Lupu R: Expression of estrogen receptor beta messenger RNA variant in human breast cancer. Cancer Res 58:210–214, 1998.

39. Lubahn DB, Moyer JS, Golding TS, et al: Alteration of reproductive function but not prenatal sexual development after insertional disruption of the mouse estrogen receptor gene. Proc Natl Acad Sci U S A 90:11162–11166, 1993.

40. Bocchinfuso WP, Korach KS: Mammary gland development and tumerigenesis in estrogen receptor knockout mice. J Mammary Gland Biol Neoplasia 2:323–334, 1997.

41. Longacre TA, Bartow SA: A coffelative morphologic study of human breast and endometrium in the menstrual cycle. Am J Surg Pathol 10:382–393,1986.

42. Going JJ, Anderson TJ, Battersby S: Proliferative and secretary activity in human breast during natural and artificial menstrual cycles. Am J Pathol 130:193–204, 1988.

43. Potten CS, Watson RJ, Williams GT: The effect of age and menstrual cycle upon proliferative activity of the normal human breast. Br J Cancer 58:163–170, 1988.

44. Clark RB, Howell A, Potter CS, Anderson E: Dissociation between steroid receptors expression and cell proliferation in the human breast. Cancer Res 57:4987–4991, 1997.

45. Laidlaw U, Clark RB, Howell A, et al: Estrogen and progesterone stimulate proliferation of normal human breast tissue implanted in athymic nude mice. Endocrinology 136:164–171, 1995.

46. Clarke RB, Howell A, Anderson E: Estrogen sensitivity of normal human breast tissue in vivo and implanted into athymic nude mice: Analysis of the relationship between estrogen-induced proliferation and progesterone receptor expression. Breast Cancer Res Treat 45:121–183, 1997.

47. Goodman HM: Basic Medical Endocrinology. New York, Raven, 1994, pp 288–290.

48. Russo J, Russo IH: Influence of differentiation and cell kinetics on the susceptibility of the rat mammary gland to carcinogenesis. Cancer Res 40:2677–2687, 1980.

49. Russo J, Romero AL, Russo IH: Architectural pattern of the normal and cancerous breast under the influence of parity. J Cancer Epidemiol Prev 3:219–224, 1994.

50. Russo J, Russo IH: Biology of disease: Biological and molecular bases of mammary carcinogenesis. Lab Invest 57:112–137, 1987.

51. Clarke R, Dickson RB, Lippman ME: Hormonal aspects of breast cancer: Growth factors, drugs and stromal interactions. Crit Rev Oncol Hematol 12:1–23, 1992.

52. Knabbe C, Lippman ME, Wakefield LM, et al: Evidence that transforming growth factor β is a hormonally regulated negative growth factor in human breast cancer cells. Cells 48:417–428, 1987.

53. Russo J, Reina D, Frederick J, Russo IH: Expression of phenotypical changes by human breast epithelial cells treated with carcinogens in vitro. Cancer Res 48:2837–2857, 1988.

54. Russo J, Calaf G, Russo IH: A critical approach to the malignant transformation of human breast epithelial cells. Crit Rev Oncog 4:403–417, 1993.

55. Russo J, Gusterson, BA, Rogers A, et al: Biology of the disease: Comparative study of human and rat mammary tumorigenesis. Lab Invest 62:244–278, 1990.

56. Habel LA, Stamford JL: Hormone receptors and breast cancer. Epidemiol Rev 15:209–219, 1993.

57. Harlan LC, Coates RJ, Block G: Estrogen receptor status and dieting intakes in breast cancer patients. Epidemiology 4:25–31, 1993.

58. Moolgavkar SH, Day NE, Stevens RG: Two-stage model for carcinogenesis: Epidemiology of breast cancer in females. J Natl Cancer Inst 65:559–569, 1980.

59. Kodama F, Green GL, Salmon SE: Relation of estrogen receptor expression to clonal growth and antiestrogen effects on human breast cancer cells. Cancer Res 45:2720–2724, 1985.

60. Podhajcer OL, Bravo-AL, Sorin I, et al: Determination of DNA synthesis, estrogen receptors, and carcinoembryonic antigen in isolated cellular subpopulations of human breast cancer. Cancer 58:720–729, 1986.

61. Hu YF, Lau KM, Ho SM, Russo J: Increased expression of estrogen receptor beta in chemically transformed human breast epithelial cells. Int J Oncol 12:1225–1228, 1998.

62. Foster JS, Wimalasena J: Estrogen regulates activity of cyclin-dependent kinases and retinoblastoma protein phosphorylation in breast cancer cells. Mol Endocrinol 10:488–498, 1996.

63. Wang W, Smith R, Burghardt R, Safe SH: 17β estradiol–mediated growth inhibition of MDA-MB 468 cells stably transfected with the estrogen receptor: Cell cycle effects. Mol Cell Endocrinol 133:49–62, 1997.

64. Izvenson AS, Jordan VC: Transfection of human estrogen receptor (ER) CDNA into ER negative mammalian cell lines. J Steroid Biochem Mol Biol 51:229–239, 1994.

65. Weisz A, Bresciani F: Estrogen regulation of proto-oncogenes coding for nuclear proteins. Crit Rev Oncog 4:361–388, 1993.

66. Zajchowski DA, Sager R, Webster L: Estrogen inhibits the growth of estrogen receptor negative, but not estrogen receptor-positive, human mammary epithelial cells expressing a recombinant estrogen receptor. Cancer Res 53:5004–5011, 1993.

67. Pilat MJ, Christman JK, Brooks SC: Characterization of the estrogen receptor transfected MCF-10A breast cell line 139B6. Breast Cancer Res Treat 37:253–266, 1996.

68. Calaf G, Tahin Q, Alvarado ME, et al: Hormone receptors and cathepsin D levels in human breast epithelial cells transformed by chemical carcinogens. Breast Cancer Res Treat 29:169–177, 1993.

69. Aronica SM, Kraus WL, Katzenellenbogen BS: Estrogen action via the CAMP signaling pathway: Stimulation of adenylate cyclase and CAMP regulated gene transcription. Proc Natl Acad Sci U S A 91:8517–8521, 1994.

70. Pappos TC, Gametahu B, Watson CS: Membrane estrogen receptors identified by multiple antibody labeling and impeded-ligand binding FASEB J 9:404–410, 1994.

71. Santner SJ, Pauley RJ, Tait L, et al: Aromatase activity and expression in breast cancer and benign breast tissue stromal cells. J Clin Endocrinol Metab 82:200–208, 2997.

72. Cunha GR, Hom YK: J Mammary Gland Biol Neoplasia 1:21–35, 1996.

73. Cunha GR, Young P, Hom YK, et al: Elucidation of a role for stromal steroid hormone receptors in mammary gland growth and development using tissue recombinants. J Mammary Gland Biol Neoplasia 2:393–402, 1997.

74. Hayward SW, Rosen MA, Cunha GR: Stromal-epithelial interactions in the normal and neoplastic prostate. Br J Urol 79(Suppl 2):18–26, 1997.

75. Cooke PS, Buchanan DL, Young P, et al: Stromal estrogen receptors mediate mitogenic effects of estradiol on uterine epithelium. Proc Natl Acad Sci U S A 94:6535–6540, 1997.

76. Allred DC, Mohgsin SK, Fuqua SAW: Histological and biological evolution of human premalignant breast disease. Endocr Relat Cancer 8:47–61, 2001.

77. Allred DC, Mohsin SK, Medina D: Estrogen receptor and proliferation are elevated and deregulated in hyperplastic unfolded lobules. Proceedings of the San Antonio Breast Cancer Symposium. Breast Cancer Res Treat 82(Suppl 1;abstract 1036):S179, 2003.

78. Golewale NH, Bhandare D, Ramakrishnan K, et al: Estrogen receptor alpha expression in normal breast epithelium (NBE) and hyperplasia in breast cancer cases and controls. Proceedings of the San Antonio Breast Cancer Symposium. Breast Cancer Res Treat 82(Suppl 1;abstract 258):S60, 2003.

79. Patriotis PC, Querec TD, Gruver BN, et al: ArrayExplorer, a program in Visual Basic for robust and accurate filter CDNA array analysis. Biotechniques 31:866–868, 2001.

80. Hall A: Rho GTPases and the actin cytoskeleton. Science 279:509–514, 1998.

81. Foster R, Hu KQ, Lu Y, et al: Identification of a novel human Rho protein with unusual properties: GTPase deficiency and in vivo farnesylation. Mol Cell Biol 6:2689–2699, 1996.

82. Wilde C, Chhatwal GS, Schmalzing G, et al: A novel C3-like ADP-ribosyltransferase from Staphylococcus aureus modifying RhoE and Rnd3. J Biol Chem 276:9537–9540, 2001.

83. Guasch RM, Scambler P, Jones GE, Ridley AJ: RhoE regulates actin cytoskeleton organization and cell migration. Mol Cell Biol 18:4761–4771, 1998.

84. Diamond RH, Cressman DE, Laz TM, et al: PRL-1, a unique nuclear protein tyrosine phosphatase, affects cell growth. Mol Cell Biol 14:3752–3762, 1994.

85. Kong W, Swain GP, Li S, Diamond RH: PRL-I, PTPase expression is developmentally regulated with tissue-specific patterns in epithelial tissues. Am J Physiol Gastrointest Liver Physiol 279:G613–G621, 2000.

86. Peng Y, Du K, Ramirez S, et al: Mitogenic up-regulation of the PRL-I protein-tyrosine phosphatase gene by Egr-1: Egr-I activation is an early event in liver regeneration. J Biol Chem 274:4513–4520, 1999.

87. Takano S, Fukuyama H, Fukumoto M, et al: PRL-1, a protein tyrosine phosphatase, is expressed in neurons and oligodendrocytes in the brain and induced in the cerebral cortex following transient forebrain ischemia. Brain Res Mol Brain Res 40:105–115, 1996.

88. Rundle CH, Kappen C: Developmental expression of the murine Prl-I protein tyrosine phosphatase gene. J Exp Zool 283:612–617, 1999.

89. Peng Y, Genin A, Spinner NB, et al: The gene encoding human nuclear protein tyrosine phosphatase, PRL-1: Cloning, chromosomal localization, and identification of an intron enhancer. J Biol Chem 273:17286–17295, 1998.

90. Baxter RC: Signaling pathways involved in antiproliferative effects of IGFBP-3: A review. J Clin Pathol Mol Pathol 54:145–148, 2001.

91. Phillips LS, Pao CI, Villafuerte BC: Molecular regulation of insulin-like growth factor-I and its principal binding protein, IGFBP-3. Prog Nucleic Acid Res Mol Biol 60:195–265, 1998.

92. Oh Y: IGFBPs and neoplastic models: New concepts for roles of IGFBPs in regulation of cancer cell growth. Endocrine 7:111–113, 1997.

93. Cubbage ML, Suwanichku A, Powell DR: Insulin-like growth factor binding protein-3: Organization of the human chromosomal gene and demonstration of promoter activity. J Biol Chem 265:12642–12649, 1990.

94. Coverley JA, Baxter RC: Phosphorylation of insulin-like growth factor binding proteins. Mol Cell Endocrinol 128:1–5, 1997.

95. El-Husseini AE, Topinka JR, Lehrer-Graiwer JE, et al: Ion channel clustering by membrane-associated guanylate kinases: Differential regulation by N-terminal lipid and metal binding motifs. J Biol Chem 275:23904–23910, 2000.

96. Zhu J, Jiang J, Zhou W, et al: Differential regulation of cellular target genes by p53 devoid of the PXXP motifs with impaired apoptotic activity. Oncogene 18:2149–2155, 1999.

97. Bratt T: Lipocalins and cancer. Biochim Biophys Acta 1482:318–326, 2000.

98. Seth P, Porter D, Lahti-Domenici J, et al: Cellular and molecular targets of estrogen in normal human breast tissue. Cancer Res 62:4540–4544, 2002.

99. Neddermann P, Jiricny J: Efficient removal of uracil from G.U mispairs by the mismatch-specific thymine DNA glycosylase from Hela cells. Proc Natl Acad Sci U S A 91:1642–1646, 1994.

100. Waters TR, Swann PF: Kinetics of the action of thymine DNA glycosylase. J Biol Chem 273:20007–20014, 1998.

101. Huynh HT, Larsson C, Narod S, Pollak M: Tumor suppressor activity of the gene encoding mammary-derived growth inhibitor. Cancer Res 55:2225–2231, 1995.

102. Hu YF, Russo IH, Ao X, Russo J: Mammary-derived growth inhibitor (MDGI) cloned from human breast epithelial cells is expressed in fully differentiated lobular structures. Int J Oncol 11:5–11, 1997.

103. Brotherick I, Robson CN, Bronell DA: Cytokeratin expression in breast cancer: Phenotypic changes associated with disease progression. Cytometry 32:301–308, 1998.

104. Welch DR, Wei LL: Genetic and epigenetic regulation of human breast cancer progression and metastasis. Endocr Relat Cancer 5:155–197, 1998.

105. Aoki R, Tanaka S, Haruma K, et al: MUC-1 expression as a predictor of the curative endoscopic treatment of submucosally invasive colorectal carcinoma. Dis Colon Rectum 41:1262–1272, 1998.

106. Segal Eiras A, Croce MV: Breast cancer associated mucin: A review. Allergol Immunopathol 25:176–181, 1997.

107. Manni A, Badger B, Wei L, et al: Hormonal regulation of insulin-growth factor 11 and insulin growth factor binding protein expression by breast cancer cells in vivo: Evidence for epithelial stromal iteractions. Cancer Res 54:2934–2942, 1994.

108. Nickerson T, Zhang J, Pollak M: Regression of DMBA-induced breast carcinoma following ovariectomy is associated with increase expression of genes encoding insulin growth factor biding proteins. Int J Oncol 14:987–990, 1999.

# Benign Breast Disorders

## *Richard J. Santen*

## NORMAL PHYSIOLOGY

Current knowledge regarding prepubertal breast development and function and the process of full breast maturation during the adult years is reviewed in Chapter 164.[1] Briefly summarized, estradiol and progesterone levels increase to initiate breast development at the time of puberty. A complex treelike structure results, which comprises 5 to 10 primary milk ducts originating at the nipple, 20 to 40 segmental ducts, and 10 to 100 subsegmental ducts ending in glandular units called *terminal duct lobular units* (TDLUs).[2] Cells comprising the TDLUs proliferate more rapidly than other breast components and are believed to represent the site of origin of cancer.[3] Full breast maturation, a process enhanced by pregnancy, evolves over several years and results in lobules with diminished proliferation.[1] In the adult breast, TDLUs undergo cyclic changes during the menstrual cycle with an increased rate of cell proliferation during the luteal phase and apoptotic cell death during the follicular.[4] As a result of this and other factors, breast size may increase by as much as 15% during the luteal phase of the cycle. At menopause, the total number of lobules diminishes, but this process is reversed by estrogen/progestin therapy.[1,5]

### SPECTRUM OF CHANGES IN THE NORMAL BREAST

Until the past decade, benign breast disorders were considered to fall into a general category called *fibrocystic disease*.[6] The signs and symptoms of fibrocystic breast disease are so common, however, that the term *fibrocystic changes* is now preferred.[7] Autopsy series report the presence of "fibrocystic disease," defined as the presence of microcysts and macrocysts or epithelial hyperplasia, in 50% to 60% of women, whereas clinical studies report the prevalence of "fibrocystic disease" to be 8.8%.[8] As a reflection of these histologic changes, some degree of breast nodularity ("lumpy bumpy consistency") on physical examination encompasses the broad range of normal findings. Breast pain is also common, with nearly 60% of healthy women experiencing cyclic breast pain prior to the onset of menses.

The new term *fibrocystic changes* rather than "fibrocystic disease" serves to emphasize that most women with breast pain, lumpy breasts, or nodules do not have a disease and are at no increased risk of breast cancer. On the other hand, the term *fibrocystic changes* is not specific and does not describe histologic changes of varying structures. For this reason, European investigators have introduced the term *ANDI*, "**A**berrations of **N**ormal **D**evelopment and **I**nvolution," to describe the spectrum of fibrocystic changes.[9] While useful, the ANDI classification attributes many changes in the late reproductive period to involution, a concept not experimentally validated.

## CLASSIFICATION

A modification of the ANDI classification describes the spectrum of benign breast disorders and focuses on specific breast components (Fig. 165-1). Pertinent parameters include the age of the patient, the tissue component involved, the histologic changes present, and the spectrum of findings ranging from "normal," to "aberrant," to "disease process." Distinction of "aberrant" from "disease process" is arbitrary but useful for the clinician and patient as a means to focus the educational process and to provide a framework for evaluation and treatment. This descriptive classification divides age-related findings into those involving the early, middle, and late reproductive periods; describes changes involving glandular, ductal, and stromal elements; and considers the spectrum of normal, aberrant, and disease-related processes.

During the *early reproductive period*, cyclic hormonal changes commonly result in mild breast pain and tenderness as a result of hormonal stimulation of normal glandular elements. Glandular components of the breast may also respond to hormonal stimuli in an exaggerated fashion with the development of single or multiple fibroadenomas. These consist of lobular units that grow to larger than normal size and contain both epithelial and stromal elements. Fibroadenomas range in size from slightly larger than normal single lobular units containing glandular and associated stromal tissue (not true fibroadenomas) to larger and more discrete, palpable lesions (true fibroadenomas). Autopsy series report a prevalence of 15% to 23% of fibroadenomas, whereas clinical studies find a cumulative incidence of only 2.2%.[8] The natural history of fibroadenomas is for transient growth followed by quiescence or regression. Actuarially, 46% regress by 5 years and 69% at 9 years.[10] When fibroadenomas are giant (>5 cm)

# SPECTRUM OF BENIGN BREAST PROBLEMS

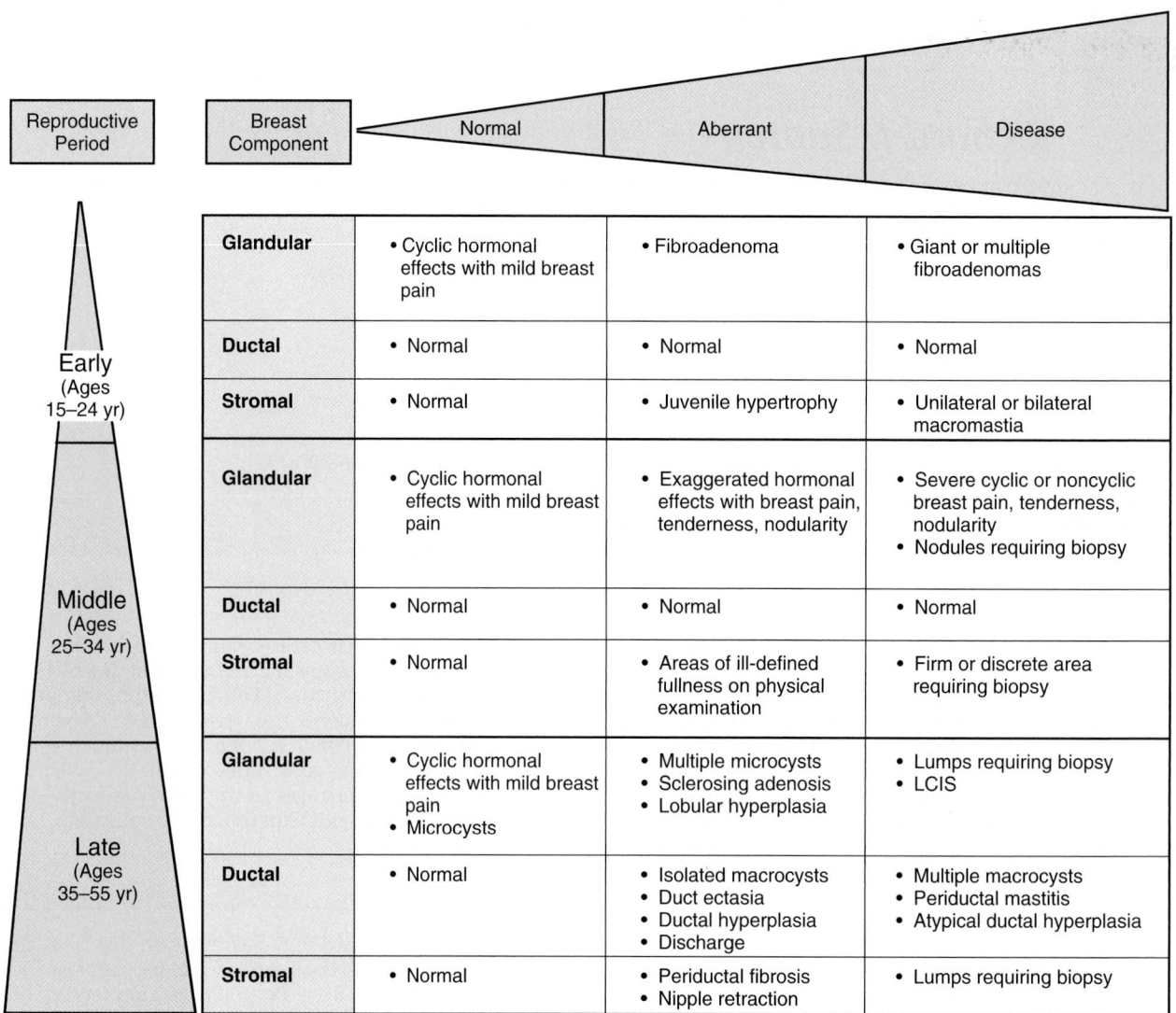

| Reproductive Period | Breast Component | Normal | Aberrant | Disease |
|---|---|---|---|---|
| **Early** (Ages 15–24 yr) | Glandular | • Cyclic hormonal effects with mild breast pain | • Fibroadenoma | • Giant or multiple fibroadenomas |
| | Ductal | • Normal | • Normal | • Normal |
| | Stromal | • Normal | • Juvenile hypertrophy | • Unilateral or bilateral macromastia |
| **Middle** (Ages 25–34 yr) | Glandular | • Cyclic hormonal effects with mild breast pain | • Exaggerated hormonal effects with breast pain, tenderness, nodularity | • Severe cyclic or noncyclic breast pain, tenderness, nodularity<br>• Nodules requiring biopsy |
| | Ductal | • Normal | • Normal | • Normal |
| | Stromal | • Normal | • Areas of ill-defined fullness on physical examination | • Firm or discrete area requiring biopsy |
| **Late** (Ages 35–55 yr) | Glandular | • Cyclic hormonal effects with mild breast pain<br>• Microcysts | • Multiple microcysts<br>• Sclerosing adenosis<br>• Lobular hyperplasia | • Lumps requiring biopsy<br>• LCIS |
| | Ductal | • Normal | • Isolated macrocysts<br>• Duct ectasia<br>• Ductal hyperplasia<br>• Discharge | • Multiple macrocysts<br>• Periductal mastitis<br>• Atypical ductal hyperplasia |
| | Stromal | • Normal | • Periductal fibrosis<br>• Nipple retraction | • Lumps requiring biopsy |

**Figure 165-1** Classification of the spectrum of benign breast problems. LCIS, lobular carcinoma in situ. (Adapted from Hughes LE, et al: Aberrations of normal development and involution (ANDI): A new perspective on pathogenosis and nomenclature of benign breast disease. Lancet 2:1316–1319, 1987.)

or multiple, these lesions are considered to be part of a disease process. Ductal abnormalities are exceedingly rare in the early reproductive period. Stromal hyperplasia may occur and produces juvenile breast hypertrophy or, rarely, the more significant problems of unilateral or bilateral macromastia (enlargement of breast tissue beyond what is considered normal).

During the *middle reproductive years,* glandular breast tissue continues to undergo changes in response to cyclic increments in estradiol and progesterone concentrations, and mild breast pain occurs in up to 60% of women. The process may progress to an aberrant and then to a disease state depending on the degree of pain, tenderness, and nodularity. This process of glandular change is called adenosis. Ductal changes remain uncommon in the middle reproductive period. Stromal hyperplasia may occur, which results in areas of ill-defined fullness on physical examination or in firm areas requiring biopsy, a process called mazoplasia. When this process is present, patients usually present with upper outer quadrant breast pain and an indurated axillary tail.

During the *late reproductive period,* glandular tissue may become hyperplastic with sclerosing adenosis or lobular hyperplasia. The hyperplastic glandular lesions may progress

to palpable or mammographically detectable abnormalities requiring biopsy. LCIS (lobular carcinoma in situ) may be found when these lesions are biopsied. The junctions between glandular tissue and ducts may undergo cellular alterations to form cysts. Multiple macrocysts may occur, originating in ductal tissue at the interface of the terminal duct lobular unit.

Ductal tissue may also undergo hyperplastic change with an increase in the number of ductal cells but without changes in the normality of their appearance, a process called usual ductal hyperplasia (UDH). The lobules may hypertrophy and unfold, a process called hyperplastic ductal unfolding.[3,11] With progression, atypical ductal hyperplasia (ADH) or ductal carcinoma in situ (DCIS) may ensue. In some women, the ducts undergo ectasia, a process characterized by distention of subareolar ducts and presence within them of lipidlike, yellow-orange material with crystalline round and oval structures. Penetration of the duct wall by this material produces acute focal inflammatory changes in the surrounding tissues. Spontaneous resolution may occur, but residual fibrosis and nodule formation may persist. Periductal mastitis, a condition thought to be more frequent in cigarette smokers, represents a more chronic and extensive inflammatory process.[12] Abnormalities of ductal secretion may result in discharge of clear, cloudy, blue, green, or black aqueous material. Finally, stromal hyperplasia can result in periductal fibrosis and nipple retraction and in palpable lesions requiring biopsy.

## THE ANDI CLASSIFICATION SYSTEM AND "FIBROCYSTIC CHANGE"

All of the findings generally considered to be fibrocystic changes are incorporated into the ANDI classification, but, in addition, lesions with progression to the pathologic stage such as giant or multiple fibroadenomas, typical or atypical ductal hyperplasia, and sclerosing adenosis are included. The usual features of fibrocystic changes are considered under the categories of normal or aberrant. In the middle and late reproductive periods, stromal hyperplasia and cyst formation represent changes that occur commonly and do not usually progress sufficiently to be considered a disease process. Some degree of cyst formation and stromal hyperplasia may occur in 50% to 60% of normal women, particularly those in their middle and late reproductive periods.[8] Higher prevalence is associated with late menopause, use of hormone replacement therapy, thin body composition, high level of education, and high socioeconomic status.[8] The mean age of women with cyst formation is 44.5 plus or minus 5.7 years.[13]

## ETIOLOGY OF BENIGN BREAST DISORDERS

Recent cytogenetic studies have demonstrated frequent loss of allelic heterozygosity (LOH) in proliferative breast lesions and suggest that these represent benign adenomas. In order for LOH to be detected, a group of cells with loss of chromosomal material must have undergone clonal expansion, a characteristic of adenomas. Additional findings supporting the concept of clonality are nonrandom inactivation of the X chromosome and the presence of DNA amplification, aneuploidy, and point mutations in benign lesions. Based on these considerations, an appropriate new terminology for benign breast lesions would be typical and atypical mammary adenomas rather than UDH and ADH.[14]

Systematic assessment of benign breast lesions has documented a high frequency of multifocality and LOH of different DNA loci in separate lesions. Based on these findings, investigators consider that certain patients with these lesions may have an underlying disorder that predisposes them to development of multiple lesions. Recently, this predisposition has been termed the *mutator phenotype*, but it was originally called a *field effect*.[5] Multifocality of the associated benign hyperplastic lesions is most apparent in breast tissue from women with coexisting cancer, but also is seen in those without.[14] Examination of tissue adjacent to an invasive breast cancer or in the contralateral breast reveals one or more additional hyperplastic lesions in 40% of patients, most of which contain LOH at different loci than observed in the tumor itself.[14–19] In women with ADH but without breast cancer, half this number will have additional lesions with LOH.

The nature of the "mutator phenotype" in most patients is unknown, but could represent disordered processes involved in cellular proliferation, DNA repair, estradiol synthesis or degradation, metabolism of procarcinogens to carcinogens, regulation of apoptosis, or other cellular events. Known examples of a mutator phenotype include loss of the normal p53 gene in the Li-Fraumeni syndrome and aberrations of PTEN in Cowden's syndrome and a DNA repair enzyme in the ataxia-telangiectasia syndrome. Suggested causes of the mutator phenotype in other patients include abnormalities in enzymes involved in steroid synthesis or metabolism, such as the CYP-17 gene, inheritance of a low catechol *O*-methyltransferase (COMT) phenotype, and overexpression of the estrogen synthase (aromatase) enzyme.[20–24]

These defects could enhance local concentrations of estrogen and result in an increased rate of cell division and chances for mutations to develop. Alternatively, increased production of depurinating catecholamine metabolites of estradiol could result and directly cause mutations. As another possibility, defects causing the mutator phenotype could alter the processing of environmental carcinogens.[25]

The "mutator phenotype" concept would explain many of the findings from recent cytogenetic studies in patients with breast disease.[15] For example, one would predict that the finding of atypical lobular or ductal hyperplasia in an individual patient would put her at greater risk for developing breast cancer (Fig. 165-2). One of the original hyperplastic lesions might directly evolve into cancer, but others might not progress further. Accordingly, some original lesions would be related cytogenetically to subsequent cancer and others would not. Based on the "mutator" hypothesis, cancers might arise in the opposite as well as the ipsilateral breast in women with UDH or ADH and the original lesion would not necessarily predict the type of breast cancer found. Epidemiological studies have found this to be true, namely that patients with ADH or ALH are at increased risk for breast cancer in the same or opposite breast and that these patients have an increased risk of ductal and lobular as well as tubular, mucinous, or other histologic types of cancer.

A corollary of the "mutator phenotype" hypothesis is that a relationship might exist between specific benign hyperplastic lesions and anatomically proximate cancers. For example, as a result of the accumulation of unrepaired mutations, usual ductal hyperplasia might gain additional mutations and progress first to atypical ductal hyperplasia, then to carcinoma in situ, and finally to frank invasive cancer (see Fig. 165-2).[26] This process would be sequential and involve multiple mutational "hits" with repetitive expansion of parent and daughter clones. Populations of cells with increasing proliferative potential or reduced capability of undergoing apoptosis or cell death would result from this stochastic or random process.

Substantial recent data[14] characterizing the genetic makeup of benign hyperplastic lesions support both the presence of a mutator phenotype and progression of specific hyperplastic lesions to frank cancer. Microdissection of hyperplastic and normal breast tissue from histologic sections, amplification of the DNA present, and analysis of specific genetic abnormalities allow a precise comparison of the genetic makeup of neighboring benign and malignant lesions. As predicted by the "mutator phenotype" hypothesis, a random series of genetic abnormalities with differing mutations in each hyperplastic lesion would be anticipated and, indeed, recent observations confirm this expectation. Furthermore, the hypothesis that a single hyperplastic lesion progresses to cancer would be supported by the finding of identical mutations in the invasive cancer and the hyperplastic lesion immediately adjoining it. Systematically collected data reveal that 80% to 90% of hyperplastic lesions contain DNA mutations similar to those in the contiguous tumors.[14]

See Figure 165-2 for a diagrammatic illustration of how the "mutator phenotype" would result in the lesions found clinically.[15] Some tissue in the breast would develop usual ductal or lobular hyperplasia, but would not undergo further genetic mutations. Additional lesions would progress from this step to atypical hyperplasia, but no further. A small number would undergo additional "hits" or genetic mutations and progress to in situ cancer or invasive cancer. As shown by the arrows, lesions progressing from one step to the next would be genetically similar, as found by LOH studies. Others would be genetically distinct as a reflection of their independent derivation. This concept would explain why patients with invasive breast cancer have an increased incidence of associated DCIS, LCIS, ADH, and UDH. This concept has important implications since identification of specific mutator

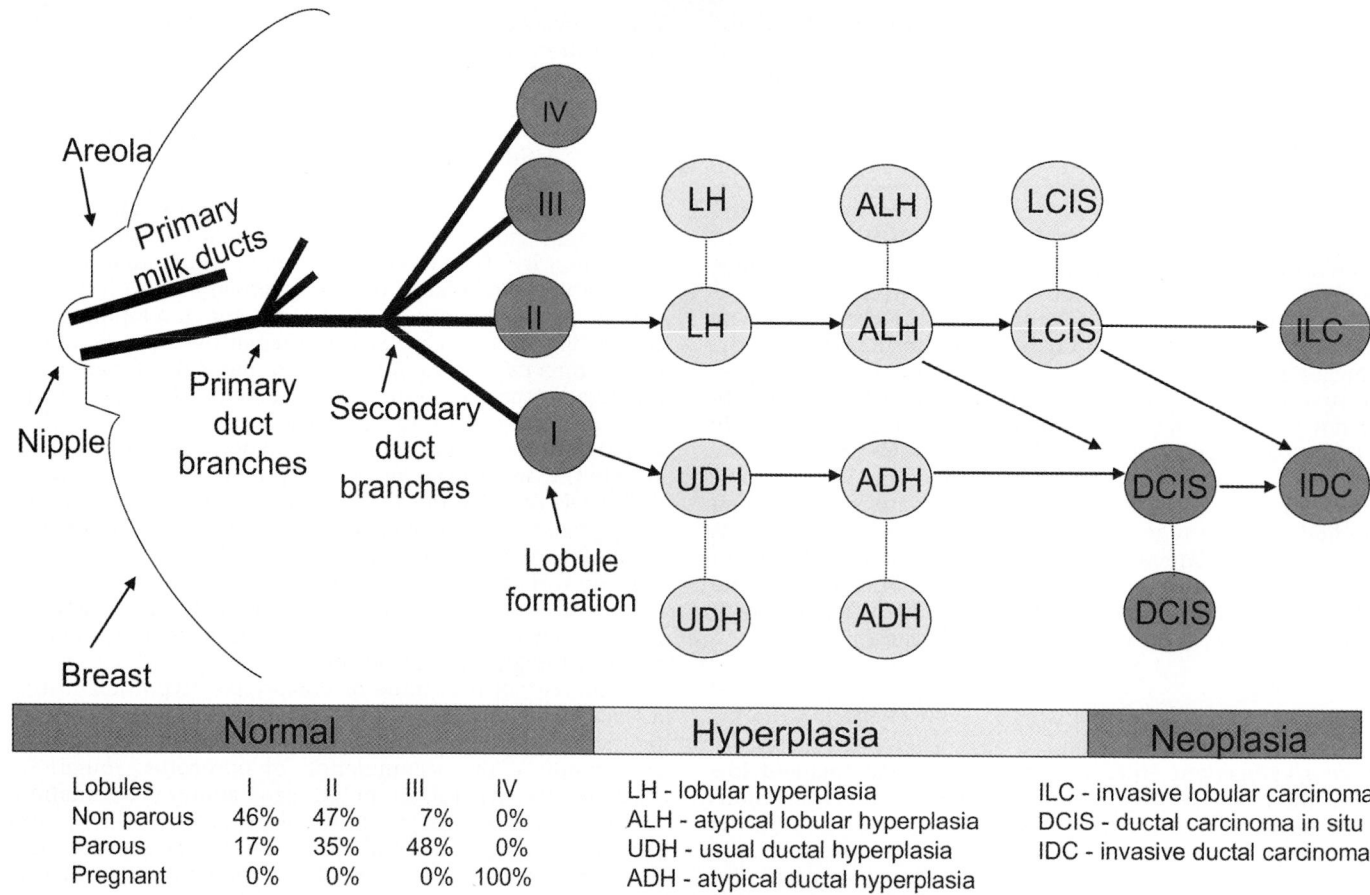

| | | | | | LH - lobular hyperplasia | ILC - invasive lobular carcinoma |

| Normal | | | | | Hyperplasia | Neoplasia |
|---|---|---|---|---|---|---|
| Lobules | I | II | III | IV | LH - lobular hyperplasia | ILC - invasive lobular carcinoma |
| Non parous | 46% | 47% | 7% | 0% | ALH - atypical lobular hyperplasia | DCIS - ductal carcinoma in situ |
| Parous | 17% | 35% | 48% | 0% | UDH - usual ductal hyperplasia | IDC - invasive ductal carcinoma |
| Pregnant | 0% | 0% | 0% | 100% | ADH - atypical ductal hyperplasia | |
| | | | | | LCIS - lobular carcinoma in situ | |

*Figure 165-2* Diagrammatic representation of the progression of benign breast lesions to cancer. Primary and secondary duct structures branch and ultimately end in lobules. As described in Chapter 164, lobules are classified as types I, II, III, and IV depending on their biologic and histologic characteristics. The percent of each in nonparous, parous, and pregnant women is shown. With an increasing number of mutations, lesions develop that are increasingly more abnormal. For example, normal lobular cells may progress to LH (lobular hyperplasia), atypical lobular hyperplasia (ALH), lobular carcinoma in situ (LCIS), and invasive lobular carcinoma (ILC). Other cells can progress to usual ductal hyperplasia (UDH), atypical ductal hyperplasia (ADH), ductal carcinoma in situ (DCIS), and invasive ductal carcinoma (IDC). However, ALH and LCIS may also progress to the respective ductal lesions. Earlier lesions such as LH or UDH may either undergo further progression or remain stable. At any given time, lesions may develop on a serial pathway whereby each precursor lesion evolves directly into a more abnormal lesion (e.g., UDH to ADH) or on parallel pathways whereby other precursor lesions undergo progression parallel to those in other cells.

phenotypes would allow more targeted means to prevent breast cancer.

## SPECIFIC GENETIC ALTERATIONS ASSOCIATED WITH BENIGN BREAST DISEASE

Extensive molecular genetic studies have now described progression of abnormalities in breast lesions spanning the spectrum from normal to DCIS or LCIS. Figure 165-3 summarizes a large body of data and indicates a progressive increase in rate of cell proliferation, percentage of aneuploid cells, ratio of estrogen receptor-α (ER-α) to estrogen receptor-β (ER-β), an increase in expression of transforming growth factor alpha (TGF-α), and the appearance of c-erb-B2 in lesions of ducal carcinoma in situ and particularly those with a comedo appearance.[26] In a recent study, presence of aberrant p53 protein increased the relative risk of breast cancer by 2.55[27] whereas the presence of c-erb-B2 was associated with no increased risk.[28]

## HORMONAL INFLUENCE ON BENIGN BREAST DISORDERS

Hormonal events appear to play a role in the etiology of benign lesions as evidenced by clinical observations in women receiving estrogens and antiestrogens. In postmenopausal women receiving estrogens with or without progestins for longer than 8 years, the prevalence of benign breast lesions is increased by 1.70-fold (95% confidence interval [CI]: 1.06–2.72).[29] The antiestrogen tamoxifen, when used for breast cancer prevention, is associated with a 28% (relative risk [RR]: 0.72, 95% CI: 0.65–0.79) reduction in prevalence of benign breast lesions, including adenosis, cysts, duct ectasia, and hyperplasia.[30] Increments in estradiol and progesterone during the luteal phase of the menstrual cycle enhance the number of cells undergoing cell division.[4] This and associated effects on cellular function probably result in the mild cyclic breast pain experienced by 60% of normal women[31,32] and increased lumpiness during the luteal phase. Few studies have addressed the potential etiologic causes of cyst formation, stromal hyperplasia, or fibrocystic changes. While hormonal influences are possible, a number of factors such as caffeine ingestion and iodine deficiency have been suggested but not proven.[33,34]

## CLINICAL FEATURES OF BENIGN BREAST DISORDERS

The clinician is confronted with four separate problems in benign breast disorders: breast pain, nipple discharge, lumps, and risk of breast cancer.

# Progression from a Benign to a Malignant Lesion

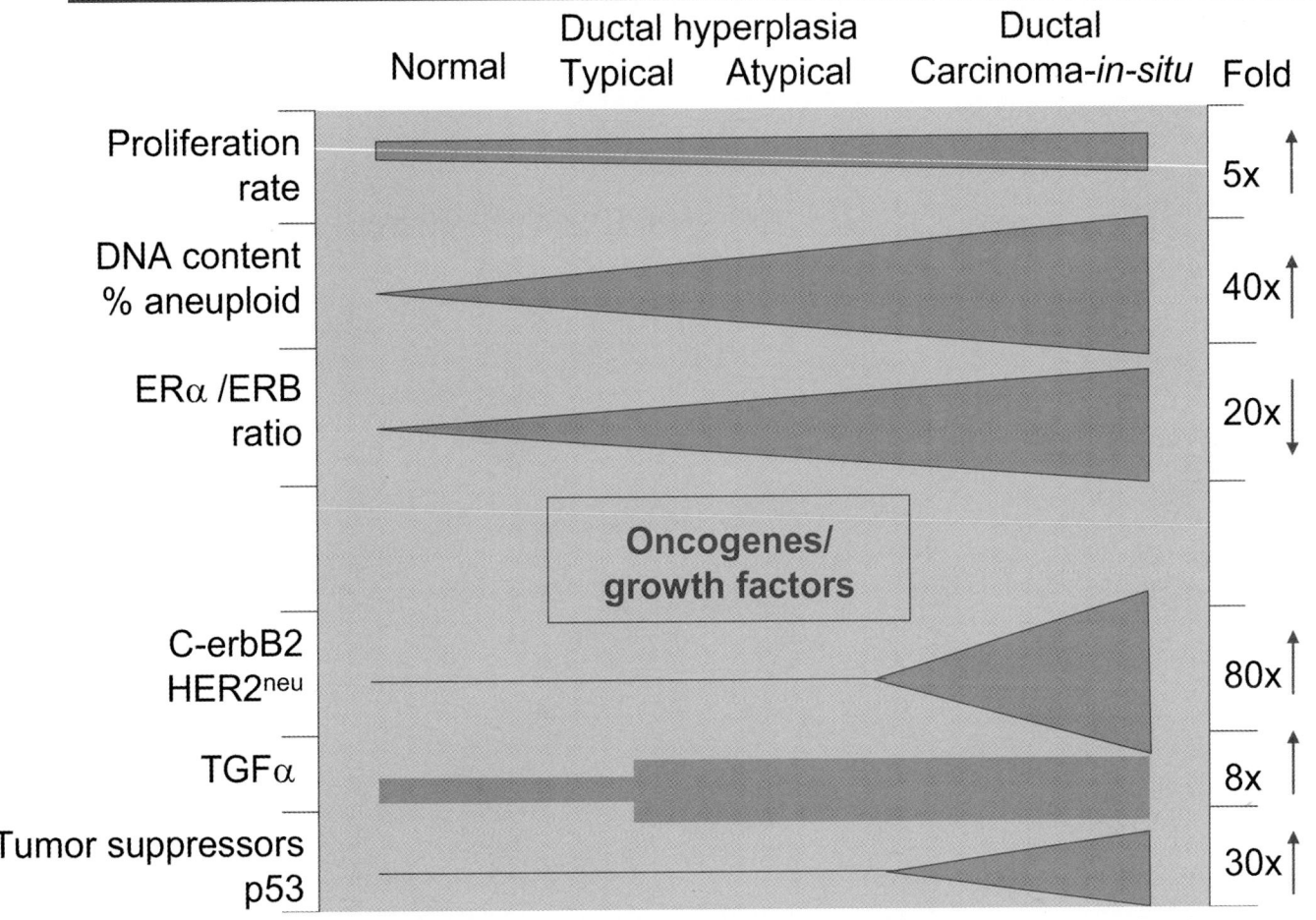

**Figure 165-3** Progression from a benign to a malignant lesion probably represents the accumulation of an increasing number of genetic mutations, as evidenced by a compilation of several recent studies. The proliferation rate increases fivefold when comparing benign breast tissue with carcinoma in situ. The DNA content, as represented by aneuploidy (i.e., DNA with greater or less DNA than expected for the presence of 46 chromosomes) increases 40-fold between normal breast tissue and carcinoma in situ. The content of estrogen receptor-α (ER-α) increases and estrogen receptor-β (ER-β) decreases such that the ER-α/ER-β ratio increases with greater degree of abnormality of lesion. The oncogene transforming growth factor-α (TGF-α) increases concomitantly with the appearance of hyperplasia. Finally, the oncogene c-erb-B2/HER2-neu and mutations of the tumor suppresser p53 increase only in ductal carcinoma in situ.

## BREAST PAIN

Breast pain can be divided into two subcategories: cyclic and noncyclic (Table 165-1).[35]

*Cyclic breast pain* usually occurs during the late luteal phase of the menstrual cycle with resolution at onset of menses[35,36] and may occur in association with the premenstrual syndrome or independently.[31,37,38] A recent study of 1171 healthy American women indicated that 11% experience moderate to severe cyclic breast pain and 58%, mild discomfort.[31,32] Breast pain interfered with usual sexual activity in 48% and with physical (37%), social (12%), and school (8%) activity in others. A role for caffeine, iodine deficiency, alterations in fatty acid levels in the breast, fat intake in the diet, and psychological factors in the etiology of breast pain remains unproven.[8,33,34]

*Noncyclic breast pain* is unrelated to the menstrual cycle. Detection of focal tenderness is helpful diagnostically and suggests a tender cyst, rupture through the wall of an ectatic duct, or a particularly tender area of breast nodularity. Acute enlargement of cysts and periductal mastitis may cause severe, localized pain of sudden onset.

Pain may be mistakenly attributed to the breast when it actually arises from the chest wall. Pain localized to a limited area and characterized as burning or knifelike in nature suggests this possibility. Chest wall pain comprises four distinct subtypes: localized lateral chest wall, diffuse lateral chest wall, radicular from cervical arthritis, and Tietze's syndrome.

## NIPPLE DISCHARGE

This symptom directs 6.8% of referrals to specialists for breast concerns. Although particularly distressing to women, only 5% are found to have serious underlying pathology.[39] Discharge is considered pathologic if spontaneous, arising from a single duct, persistent or troublesome, and containing gross or occult blood. Age is an important factor with respect to risk of malignancy. In one series, 3% of women younger than age 40, 10% between 40 and 60, and 32% older than 60 with nipple discharge as their only symptom were found to have a malignancy.[40]

## FOCAL AND DIFFUSE BREAST LUMPS

Detected by palpation or routine mammography, discrete lesions represent different entities in women younger than age 30, 30 to 50, and older than 50 (see Table 165-1). On a statistical basis, 9 in 10 new nodules are benign. Diffuse

**Table 165-1** Classification of Common Benign Breast Disorders in Women

**PAIN**

*BREAST PAIN*

| | |
|---|---|
| Cyclic | Hormonal stimulation of normal breast lobules prior to menses |
| Noncyclic | Stretching of Cooper's ligaments |
| | Pressure from a brassiere |
| | Fat necrosis from trauma |
| | Hydradenitis suppurativa |
| | Focal mastitis |
| | Periductal mastitis |
| | Cyst |
| | Mondor's disease (thrombophlebitis of breast veins) |

*NONBREAST PAIN*

| | |
|---|---|
| Chest wall pain | Tietze's syndrome (costochondritis) |
| | Localized lateral chest wall pain |
| | Diffuse lateral chest wall pain |
| | Radicular pain from cervical arthritis |
| Non–chest wall pain | Gallbladder disease |
| | Ischemic heart disease |

**NIPPLE DISCHARGE**

*GALACTORRHEA*

| | |
|---|---|
| Arising from multiple ducts bilaterally | Hyperprolactinemia from pituitary tumor, hypothyroidism, drugs (see list in standard textbooks) |

*NONGALACTORRHEA*

| | |
|---|---|
| One duct | Papilloma |
| Bloody, occult blood, serosanguineous | Ductal carcinoma in situ |
| | Paget's disease of breast |
| Multiple ducts | Fibrocystic changes |
| Nonbloody | Duct ectasia |
| Bilateral | |
| Expressible | |
| Green, blue, yellow, black, or clear discharge | |

**DISCRETE SOLITARY LUMP**

*<AGE 30*

| | |
|---|---|
| Firm, rubbery | Most common lesion: fibroadenoma |

*AGE 30–50*

| | |
|---|---|
| Firm, discrete | Most common lesions: UDH, ADH, ALH, cyst, fibrocystic change |

*>AGE 50*

| | |
|---|---|
| Firm, discrete | Most common lesions: cyst, DCIS, invasive cancer |

**DIFFUSE LUMPINESS**

*"LUMPY-BUMPY"*

| | |
|---|---|
| Absence of discrete lump | Fibrocystic changes |

ADH, atypical ductal hyperplasia; ALH, atypical lobular hyperplasia; DCIS, ductal carcinoma in situ; UDH, usual ductal hyperplasia.

lumpiness is commonly found on physical examination and is associated histologically with fibrocystic changes.

### INCREASED BREAST CANCER RISK

A major consideration for women is whether they have a higher than normal risk of developing breast cancer. Certain breast lesions are associated with no increased risk of subsequent breast cancer (Fig. 165-4). These include fibrocystic changes, noncomplex fibroadenoma without associated proliferative changes, apocrine metaplasia, duct ectasia, stromal fibrosis, adenosis (including florid), and solitary papillomas.[41–45] Some investigators believe that macrocysts impart a higher risk of subsequent breast cancer, but this is controversial.[13] Other lesions are associated with a 1.5- to 2-fold greater risk of development of breast cancer over a 20-year period of follow-up[41–44] and are characterized by an increased rate of cellular proliferation. Usual ductal hyperplasia without atypia (UDH or typical hyperplasia) represents the most common type. Epithelial cells lining the basement membrane of ducts increase but retain typical benign cellular features and vary in

size and shape. Lobular tissue can also undergo hyperplastic change with increased fibrous tissue and interspersed glandular cells, a lesion called *sclerosing adenosis*. When multiple areas of papilloma form, diffuse papillomatosis[44] is present. Complex fibroadenomas[46] are defined as lesions containing cysts greater than 3 mm in diameter as well as components of sclerosing adenosis, epithelial calcification, or papillary apocrine changes. This entity imparts a 1.5- to 2-fold increased risk of breast cancer when proliferative changes surround the glandular tissue.

The spectrum of benign lesions extends to those with an even higher risk of later breast cancer development. ADH imparts a fourfold increased risk of breast cancer if sporadic and a sixfold greater risk in patients with a strong family history of breast cancer.[43] When the volume of atypical tissue increases, the lesions are no longer called benign but are classified as carcinoma in situ. Lobular tissue may also undergo atypical hyperplasia, which imparts an increased risk of subsequent breast cancer although the magnitude is not as precisely defined as for ADH.[45] The relative risk of development of invasive cancer when DCIS and LCIS are present is increased 10- to 12-fold (see Fig. 165-4).

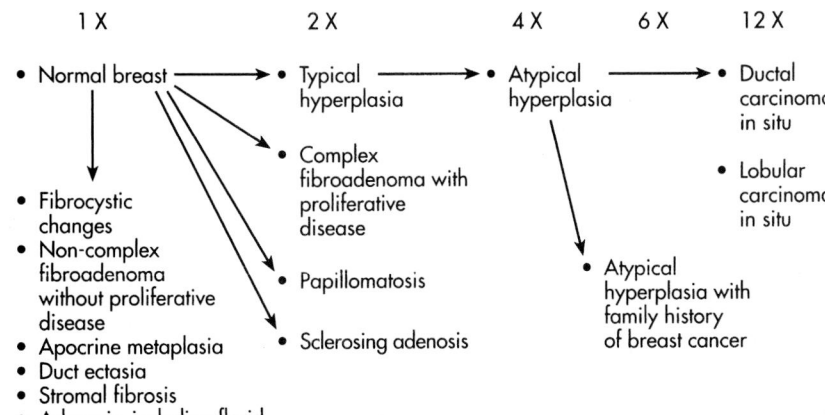

1 X
2 X
4 X
6 X
12 X
Normal breast
Typical hyperplasia
Atypical hyperplasia
Ductal carcinoma in situ
Complex fibroadenoma with proliferative disease
Lobular carcinoma in situ
Fibrocystic changes
Non-complex fibroadenoma without proliferative disease
Apocrine metaplasia
Duct ectasia
Stromal fibrosis
Adenosis, including florid
Solitary papilloma
Papillomatosis
Sclerosing adenosis
Atypical hyperplasia with family history of breast cancer

*Figure 165-4* The relative risk of the later development of invasive breast cancer with specifically defined benign breast lesions and carcinoma in situ. Interestingly, with each of these lesions, the breast cancer that develops many years later usually involves a different area of the breast than that of the initial lesion.

Enhanced mammographic density represents another factor associated with increased breast cancer risk (Fig. 165-5).[47–50] The breast density classification system originally reported by Wolfe and colleagues has now been superceded by that of Boyd and colleagues.[47,48,50,51] Utilizing data from a study involving 45,000 screening mammograms in Canada,[50] Boyd and coworkers described a spectrum of breast density with six categories representing the percent of the breast containing radio-opaque tissue as opposed to fat. Computerized densitometry techniques validate the reproducibility of defining categories and the degree of inter-observer agreement.[52] These studies demonstrated a striking correlation between breast density and breast cancer risk determined prospectively. In the highest density category, a fivefold increased risk of breast cancer was found (see Fig. 165-5). This is to be compared with the twofold increased risk found with UDH and fourfold with nonfamilial ADH.[41] Changes in breast density were associated with histologic findings. Those with high density breasts revealed a high prevalence of benign breast lesions such as UDH or ADH.[48] Two aspects of these findings impart practically important information: (1) the presence of high breast density makes it more difficult to read mammograms

Relative Risk
0
1
2
3
4
5
6
1
1.2
2.2
2.4
3.4
5.3
None
<10%
10 – 25%
25 – 50%
50-75%
>75%
Categories of % Breast Density

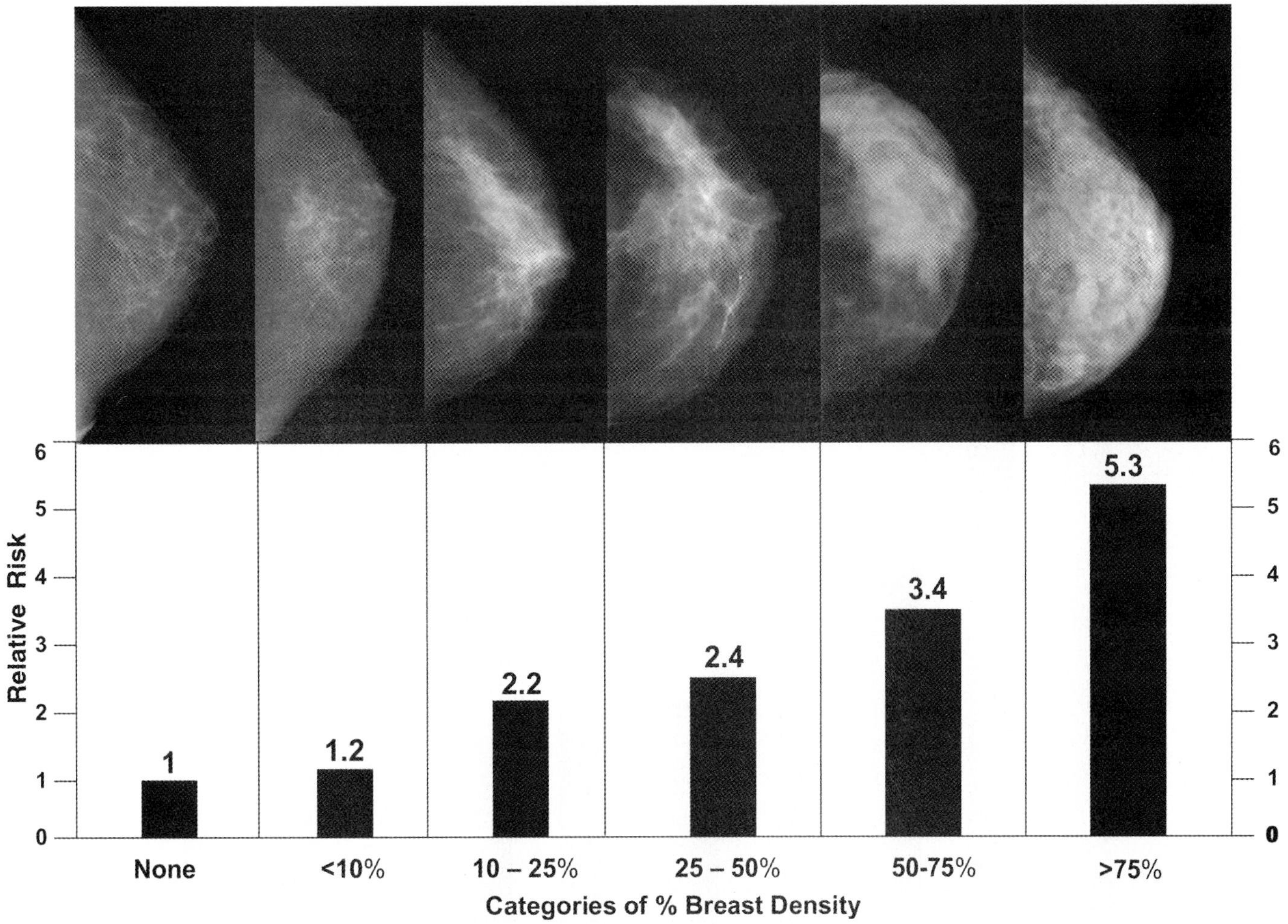

*Figure 165-5* The degree of breast density, classified by Boyd and colleagues into the six categories shown, correlates with the relative risk of developing breast cancer. (Classification from Boyd NF, Lookwood GA, Byng JW, et al: Mammographic density and breast cancer risk. Cancer Epidemiol Biomarkers Prev 7:1133–1144, 1998.

and decreases the sensitivity of finding breast cancer; and (2) there is an increased risk of breast cancer associated with increased breast density.

Epidemiologic studies reveal a number of additional hormone-related factors that are associated with an increased risk of breast cancer.[53,54] Figure 165-6 illustrates the rank order of risk associated with the various factors reported.[55] Of particular importance are recent data from a pooled analysis of nine studies reporting the relationship between hormone levels and breast cancer risk.[54] These findings convincingly demonstrated that free plasma estradiol measurements in postmenopausal women predict the risk of breast cancer more effectively than an low-density lipoprotein (LDL)-cholesterol measurement predicts the risk of heart disease.[56]

### Risk Prediction Tools

Two practical methods to assess breast cancer risk, based on the Gail and Claus models, are available. On request, the National Cancer Institute provides a "risk disk" based on the Gail model; access to this tool is also available online[57–59] (*http://bcra.nci.nih.gov/bcr*). Clinical parameters utilized include number of first-degree relatives with breast cancer (mother, sister, or daughter), age at birth of first living child, age of menarche, number of breast biopsies, and presence or absence of atypical hyperplasia. Strong but uncommon risk factors such as carrying the BrCa1 or BrCa2 gene or being of Ashkenazi Jewish heritage are not included. This program is useful to estimate the 5-year and lifetime risk of breast cancer in women with benign breast disease who wish to know their individual risks of developing breast cancer. The Claus model is particularly applicable to women with a family history of breast cancer since it includes information regarding second-degree relatives whereas the Gail model does not.[57–59] Better risk prediction tools that incorporate breast density, bone density, plasma estradiol and androgen levels, and obesity as well as factors used in the Gail model are urgently needed.

### CLINICAL EVALUATION

A detailed history and physical examination precisely define symptoms and systematically evaluate the entire breast and chest wall with focus on areas involving the patient's symptoms (Table 165-2).

### *DIAGNOSTIC STUDIES*

"Triple evaluation" of lumps includes palpation, imaging, and biopsy. Mammography is required for evaluation of discrete palpable lesions in women older than 40; ultrasound provides an optional substitute between ages 30 and 40, whereas ultrasound is preferred in those younger. Round dense lesions on mammography often represent cystic fluid, which requires ultrasonography (± aspiration) to distinguish solid from cystic lesions. Radiographically or ultrasonically directed core biopsy (or, less commonly, excisional biopsy) provides highly discriminative information regarding the presence or absence of malignancy. The exact role of magnetic resonance imaging (MRI) and digital mammography in evaluating breast lesions is currently being determined. Galactography (ductography) is useful for detection of focal lesions in a single duct. Though controversial and being reevaluated, cytology of nipple

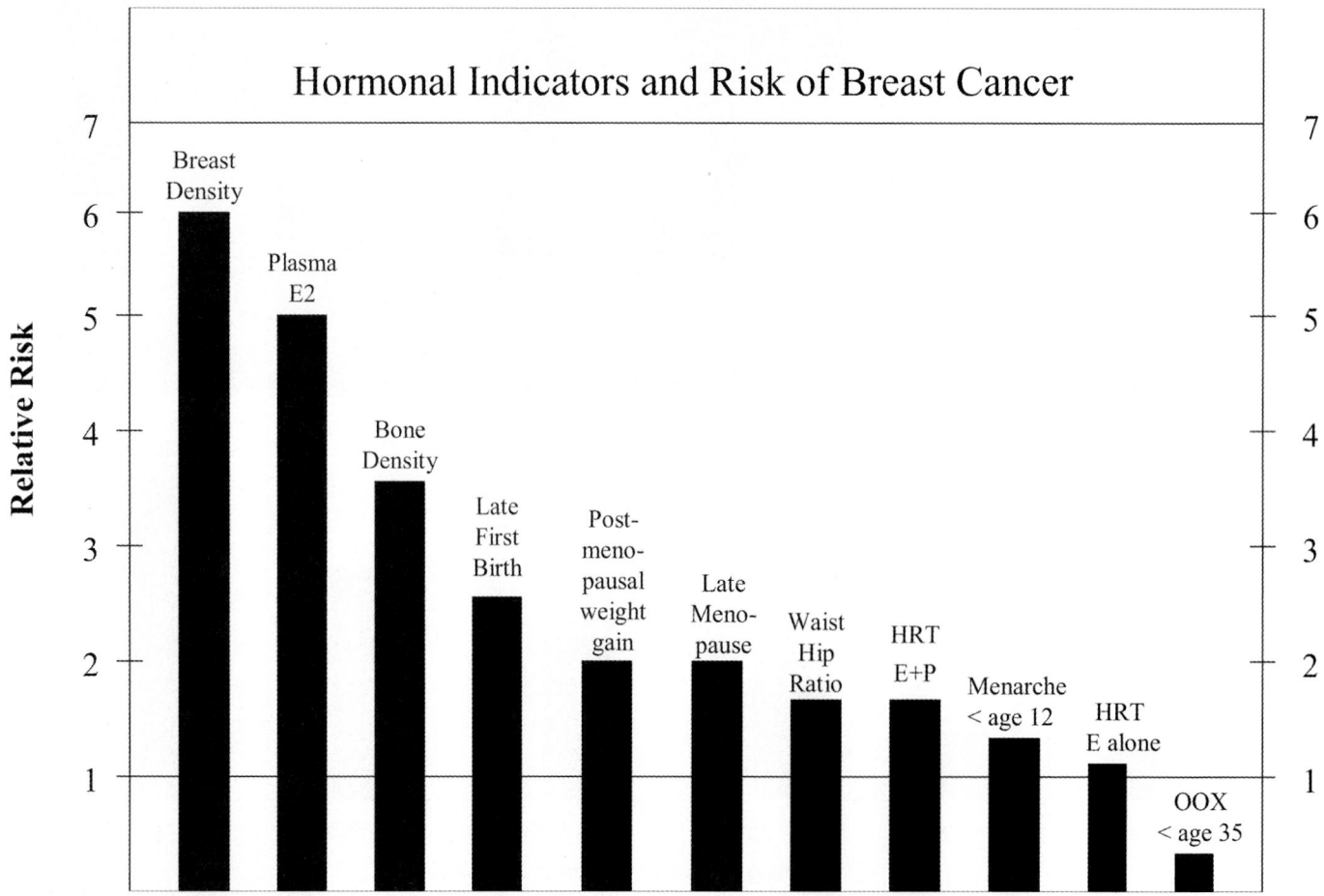

*Figure 165-6*   Relative risk of breast cancer as a function of several factors related to long-term exposure to estradiol. E, estrogen; E2 estradiol; HRT, hormone replacement therapy; OOX, oophorectomy; P, progesterone. (Reprinted from Santen RJ: Endocrine-responsive cancer. In Larsen PR, Kronenberg HM, Melmed S, Polansky KS (eds): Williams Textbook of Endocrinology, 10th ed. Philadelphia, WB Saunders, 2003, p 1798.)

**Table 165-2**    Clinical Examination

**HISTORY**
Characterize symptoms.
Identify breast cancer risk factors.
  Age
  Age of menarche
  Age of first live birth
  Number of relatives with breast cancer
  Number of previous breast biopsies
  Presence of atypical hyperplasia or lobular carcinoma in situ on
    previous breast biopsy
  Amount of weight gain after menopause
  Current weight and height
  Bone density results
  Age of menopause if menopausal—duration of use of
    estrogen/progestin therapy if menopausal

**PHYSICAL EXAMINATION**
Palpate four breast quadrants in sitting and lying position.
  Identify discrete lumps.
  Determine if doughy consistency with vague nodularity consistent
    with fibrocystic changes.
  In women < age 30, determine if discrete lesion with distinctly
    marginated borders consistent with fibroadenoma.
Examine overlying skin, areola, axilla.
Determine degree of symmetry.
  Asymmetry suggests underlying pathology.
Examine nipple and seek to elicit discharge.
  Determine if galactorrhea.
  Determine if from one or multiple ducts.
  Determine if viscous, watery, serosanguineous, grossly bloody,
    clear, blue-black or green.
  Determine if occult blood present
Seek to elicit chest wall pain
  costochondral junctions (Tietze's syndrome)
  lateral chest wall
    Examine with patient lying on side at 90 degrees to move
      breast away from chest wall.
    Compare pain elicited by squeezing breast tissue versus
      palpation of the chest wall.

discharge is thought to be of limited value. Two studies involving more than 1300 patients found that sensitivity for malignancy ranged from only 35% to 47%.[39] Current studies are evaluating use of nipple aspirate and ductal lavage as means of early detection of breast cancer.[60]

## TREATMENT

Detailed algorithms for management of breast pain, lumps, and discharge have been published previously.[61] They are available to the interested reader, but are beyond the scope of this chapter.

### CYCLIC BREAST PAIN

The major management issue is to decide whether or not to treat. In the absence of a mass or discharge, those with mild symptoms are reassured regarding absence of serious pathology and a graded treatment approach is recommended for the others.[62] In 85% of women, treatment is not necessary and watchful waiting considered acceptable after alleviating anxiety regarding fear of malignancy. For the remaining 15%, one can recommend medical therapy based on evidence from clinical trials.

#### Evidence of Efficacy of Various Treatments
Recommendations regarding treatment are ideally based on valid scientific evidence of efficacy. Unfortunately, the majority of reports describing relief of cyclic mastalgia are from nonrandomized studies and are of questionable validity since

up to 40% of women experience improvement from a placebo.[63] However, several well-designed, randomized, controlled, double-blind, crossover trials have examined the efficacy of medical therapy for cyclic mastalgia. A summary of these studies allows categorization of therapies as definitely effective, definitely ineffective, possibly effective, and insufficiently studied. (For classification as *definitely effective*, two or more randomized trials are required. For the category *possibly effective*, one randomized trial must be positive in some respect, but others may be negative. For the category *definitely ineffective*, prospective trials must be uniformly negative. For the category *insufficiently studied*, only one randomized trial, either negative or positive is available.) The drugs proven to be definitely effective in reducing the severity of breast pain include danazol, bromocriptine, and tamoxifen[64] (Table 165-3).[65–67] Three studies reported the efficacy of evening primrose oil, but another more recent one did not. Several studies also demonstrate greater improvement in breast nodularity and in tenderness with these agents than with placebo.

Vitamin E is considered definitely ineffective based on three randomized controlled trials.[68–70] Therapies such as iodine[34] and vaginal progesterone[71] are considered possibly effective based on one randomized trial showing efficacy but no confirmatory second trial. Those drugs insufficiently studied include medroxyprogesterone acetate and progesterone, which have been shown to be ineffective in one trial each, but have not been studied further.[72,73] One randomized study of low-fat diet reported beneficial results, but no other randomized studies have examined this.[74] The data on avoidance of caffeine is also considered insufficient to evaluate. One randomized controlled trial reported a significant reduction in nodularity in patients with reduced caffeine intake, but the improvement was minimal and the observer not blinded to the caffeine avoidance group.[75] Another randomized trial demonstrated no benefit.[76]

Several other therapies have not been examined in randomized controlled trials, but are based on physiologic principles. Observational studies have reported relief of pain with precise fitting of a bra to provide support for pendulous breasts.[77] Another therapy involves use of gonadotropin-releasing hormone (GnRH) agonist analogues to lower luteinizing hormone, follicle-stimulating hormone, and estradiol levels and to create a temporary postmenopausal state.[78] Onset of menopause is known to reduce the frequency of breast pain. Based on anecdotal observations (personal communication), reduction of the dosage of estrogens in postmenopausal women or addition of an androgen to estrogen replacement therapy (e.g., Estrotest tablets) appears to be beneficial in reducing breast pain. Androgenic progestins, given alone or as a component of birth control pills, can also antagonize the effects of estrogen on breast tissue and have been reported in observational studies to relieve breast pain.[61] Use of such agents has been associated with a decreased incidence of "benign breast disease" in epidemiologic studies. Further studies are needed to evaluate the effects of birth control pills containing a low estrogen dosage and high androgenic progestin on the incidence and severity of breast pain.

#### Relative Efficacy of Various Therapies
No large randomized, controlled studies have compared the relative efficacy of danazol, bromocriptine, evening primrose oil, and tamoxifen. Noncontrolled observations with use of these agents in large specialized clinics suggests that danazol and tamoxifen are most effective followed by bromocriptine and evening primrose oil (Fig. 165-7).[62] Another large observational experience found Danazol the most effective therapy.[79] One small randomized study suggested that danazol is more effective than bromocriptine.[80] In another trial, 10 mg of tamoxifen was as effective as 20 mg of tamoxifen given daily[67] and the 70% frequency of responders (see Fig. 165-7) suggested efficacy equal to that of danazol.

**Table 165-3** Studies Evaluating Clinical Effectiveness

| Therapy | Number Evaluable | Months | Dose | Decrease in Cyclic Pain | Decrease in Nodularity | Decrease in Tenderness | Reference |
|---|---|---|---|---|---|---|---|
| **DEFINITELY EFFECTIVE** | | | | | | | |
| Danazol (or gestrinone)* | 25 | 2 | 400 mg | Yes ($P < .005$) | Yes ($P < .005$) | NE | 64 |
| | 21 | 3 | 200–400 | Yes ($P < .001$) | Yes ($P < .01$) | Yes ($P < .05$) | 97 |
| | 30 | 3 | 100–200 | Yes ($P < .001$) | Yes ($P < .01$) | NE | 98 |
| | 38 | 3 | 400 | Yes ($P < .001$) | NE | NE | 99 |
| | 21 | 3 | 300 | Yes ($P =$ NS) | NE | Yes ($P =$ NS) | 100 |
| | 80 | 3 | 400 | Yes ($P < .001$) | Yes ($P < .001$) | Yes ($P < .001$) | 101 |
| | 158 | 1 | 200 | Yes ($P < .05$) | Yes ($P < .01$) | Yes ($P < .01$) | 102 |
| | 125 | 3 | 2.5 mg* twice weekly | Yes ($P < .005$) | Yes ($P < .002$) | Yes ($P < .005$) | 103 |
| Bromocriptine | 21 | 3 | 3.75 | Yes ($P < .05$) | Yes ($P < .01$) | Yes ($P < .001$) | 104 |
| | 10 | 2 | 2.5 | Yes ($P < .02$) | NE | NE | 105 |
| | 31 | 3 | 5.0 | Yes ($P < .01$) | No ($P =$ NS) | Yes ($P < .01$) | 106 |
| | 40 | 3 | 5.0 | Yes ($P < .01$) | Yes ($P < .01$) | Yes ($P < .01$) | 107 |
| | 19 | 3 | 5.0 | Yes (NE) | NE | No | 100 |
| | 38 | 3 | 5.0 | Yes ($P < .05$) | Yes ($P < .01$) | Yes ($P < .05$) | 108 |
| | 187 | 3 | 5.0 | Yes ($P < .023$) | NE | Yes ($P < .04$) | 109 |
| Evening primrose oil (linoleic acid) | 41 | 3 | 3000 mg | Yes ($P < .05$) | Yes ($P < .02$) | Yes ($P < .02$) | 110 |
| | 54 | 3 | Not specified | Yes ($P < .05$) | NE | Yes ($P < .02$) | 111 |
| | 37 | 4 | 2 (0.6 mL q.d.s.) | Yes ($P < .02$) | Yes ($P < .05$) | Yes ($P < .01$) | 112 |
| | 120 | 6 | 3000 mg | No ($P =$ NS) | NE | NE | 113 |
| Tamoxifen | 60 | 6 | 20 | Yes ($P < .025$) | NE | NE | 114 |
| | 36 | 6 | 10 | Yes ($P < .01$) | NE | NE | 115 |
| **DEFINITELY INEFFECTIVE** | | | | | | | |
| Vitamin E | 62 | 2 | 600 IU | No ($P =$ NS) | No ($P =$ NS) | NE | 116 |
| | 128 | 2 | 150 IU | | Composite score of all 3 parameters | | |
| | | | 300 IU | | No response ($P =$ NS) | | |
| | | | 600 IU | | | | |
| | 83 | 3 | 600 IU | | Composite score of pain and tenderness | | 117 |
| **POSSIBLY EFFECTIVE** | | | | | | | |
| Iodine | 56 | 6 | 0.17–0.09 mg I$_2$/kg | Yes ($P < .001$) | Yes ($P < .001$) | NE | 118 |
| Vaginal progesterone | 80 | 6 | 4 g days 10–25 | Yes ($P < .01$) | No ($P =$ NS) | Yes ($P < .01$) | 119 |
| Caffeine avoidance | 140 | 4 | NA | NE | Yes ($P < .001$)† | NE | 120 |
| | 56 | 4 | NA | No | No | No | 121 |
| Low-fat diet | 19 | 6 | NA | Yes ($P < .002$) | Probable ($P = .07$) | Yes ($P < .001$) | 122 |
| **INSUFFICIENTLY STUDIED** | | | | | | | |
| Progestins | | | | | | | |
| MPA | 18 | 3 | 20 mg | No | No | NE | 123 |
| Progesterone cream | 25 | 3 | 5 g day 10 to start of menses | No | No | NE | 124 |

* Gestrinone is an agent that acts almost identically to Danazol.
†Decrease of 25%; observer not blinded to treatment group.
MPA, medroxyprogesterone acetate; NA, not available; NE, not evaluated; NS, not significant; q.d.s., four times daily.

## Mechanisms of Action of Therapies

Danazol is believed to reduce estrogen production by inhibiting luteinizing hormone and follicle-stimulating hormone secretion and acts as a weak androgen to inhibit stimulatory hormonal effects on the breast. Bromocriptine lowers prolactin levels and may act on other dopaminergic receptor sites to effect pain relief. Preliminary studies reported abnormal fatty acid profiles and reduced levels of metabolites of linoleic acid in the serum of women with mastalgia.[81] Evening primrose oil contains predominantly linoleic acid, which could act to ameliorate this deficiency. Tamoxifen acts to antagonize the stimulatory effects of estradiol on glandular breast tissue.

## Practical Treatment Strategy for Cyclic Breast Pain

The treatment of breast pain requires a rational strategy. An initial educational process explains several aspects of the evaluation, treatment, and underlying risks imparted by the findings.

The clinician informs patients that breast cancers are not usually painful and that a minority of women with breast pain have breast cancer; that decisions about screening mammography depend on the patient's age and other considerations; and that breast pain is not merely a psychological or psychiatric problem[82,83] but occurs in a majority of normal women.

The evaluation undertaken depends on the age of the patient and nature of clinical findings. Mammography is obtained routinely in women older than 40 if clearly defined or nondiscrete areas of fullness or lumpiness are palpable. Mammography or ultrasound are utilized in those between age 30 and 40. The goal is to reassure the patient that breast cancer is not present. In those younger than 30, clinical judgment dictates mammography or ultrasonography for all clearly defined lesions and usually repeat examination in those with less well-defined lesions or generalized lumpiness. Reexamination early in the menstrual cycle allows palpation

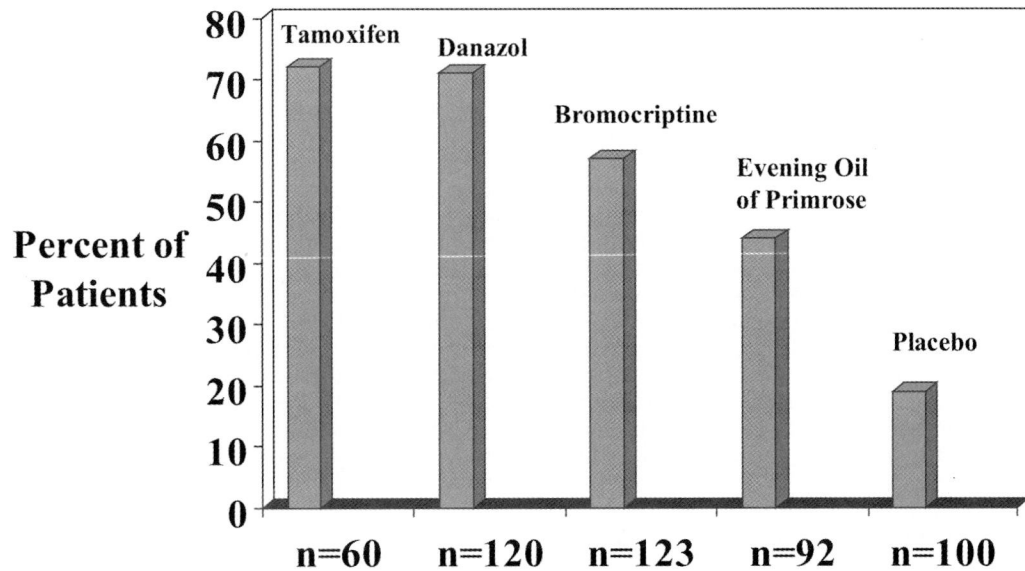

*Figure 165-7* Clinically reported comparative responses to various therapies for breast pain. Only a limited number of controlled trials have compared one therapy with another. Consequently, the data in this figure represent comparative experience with danazol, evening primrose oil, and bromocriptine in a large clinic using similar evaluative techniques and subjects for each agent (see Table 165-3). Data regarding tamoxifen is from another large clinic specializing in benign breast disorders and utilizing similar evaluation methodology.

when glandular tissue is under a lesser degree of hormonal stimulation.

Eighty-five percent of women do not wish treatment for breast pain after they have been reassured that no serious underlying problem such as breast cancer is present. Initial recommendations then include use of a soft bra (or well-fitted bra if pendulous breasts) and mild analgesics such as acetaminophen, nonsteroidal anti-inflammatory agents, or aspirin. Although diuretics have commonly been advised if the breast pain occurs in conjunction with the premenstrual syndrome, the efficacy of this approach has never been substantiated and its use is to be discouraged. Focal lesions with a trigger point may be aspirated if found to be cystic on ultrasound and are quite tender.

Patients are asked to fill out a pain scale diary for 2 months to document cyclicity of pain and to limit their consumption of caffeine. At least one third of women obtain a placebo effect from any directed measure and some may be benefited pharmacologically from a reduction in caffeine. This advice is given in the absence of supporting data regarding efficacy, but with the understanding that this therapy is not harmful.

Only 5% to 10% of women with breast pain seek further treatment. For their management, a graded approach involves initial use of therapies that are associated with few side effects. For this reason, a common next step involves use of linoleic acid in the form of evening primrose oil, 1 to 3 grams daily (2 to 6 capsules of 500 mg each). This is a prescription medication in some countries (Efamast, Scotia Pharmaceuticals), but available as a natural substance without prescription in the United States. Patients are advised that beneficial effects take place slowly with substantial pain relief at 3 months and further relief with longer duration of therapy.[84] A study by Mansel and colleagues reported 18% improvement at 1 month and 32% at 4 months, and another by Wilkins found 4% improvement at 1 month and 35% at 5 months. Minimal if any side effects are observed. The clinician can start those not responding on either tamoxifen or danazol, with tamoxifen now the preferred agent of the author of this chapter. Tamoxifen is started at a dosage of 20 mg daily with taper over a 6-month period. Danazol is started at 100 mg twice daily for 1 month. Responders are tapered to 100 mg daily for 2 months and then 100 mg every other day or days 14 to 18 of the menstrual cycle[85] for a total of 6 to 9 months. Barrier contraception is advised. Tamoxifen usage is uncommonly associated with deep venous thrombophlebitis and pulmonary emboli. Endometrial cancer has been observed, but only in

postmenopausal women. Side effects of danazol include acne, facial oiliness or mild hirsutism, weight gain, and irregular menses or amenorrhea. Bromocriptine is now rarely used because of side effects of nausea, dizziness, feelings of malaise, and mood changes. Seventy percent can expect complete or substantial relief of pain, nodules, and breast tenderness with either tamoxifen or danazol. Fifty percent relapse upon cessation of medication, but respond to a second course.

A sequential approach is used in women refractory to the first therapeutic modality. In a large series of 126 patients who did not respond to their first hormonal therapy, 57% responded to second-line and 25% to third-line therapies.[86]

Preliminary experience is available with use of medical oophorectomy with GnRH agonists to reduce estrogen production as treatment of breast pain.[78] Because of the risk of osteopenia, this approach should be limited to those with severe pain unresponsive to other measures.

A range of other approaches have been advocated for relief of cyclic breast pain. These include use of iodine,[34] androgenic progestins,[87] vaginal progesterone,[71] and low-fat diet[74] (see Table 165-3). Support in the literature for these maneuvers is either preliminary, conflicting, or negative. Before additional data are available, physicians may wish to try these approaches with the knowledge that their use is not substantiated. Particularly intriguing is the concept that iodine deficiency causes fibrocystic lesions in rodents and that iodine, but to a lesser extent iodide, caused relief of breast pain in two large uncontrolled trials and in one placebo-controlled trial.[34]

The effects of oral contraceptives on breast pain are largely unknown. Observations from a decade ago suggest that the frequency of fibrocystic changes decreases with prolonged use of oral contraceptives as a result of the progestin component.[8] On this basis, European investigators suggest that high doses of 19-nor-progestins such as norlutate (10 mg daily) can reduce breast pain.[88] One study also suggests that 19-nor-progestins can reduce the risk of breast cancer in patients treated long term.[89] Oral contraceptives containing moderate amounts of 19-nor-progestins may also be beneficial for the same reason, but further data are required on this issue. A reasonable approach in women already taking oral contraceptives is to switch them to a preparation containing the smallest possible dose[90] of estrogen, 20 mcg of ethinyl estradiol, and a moderate amount of a 19-nor-progestin such as Lo-Estrin 1:20.

Postmenopausal women may complain of breast pain while receiving hormone replacement. Reduction in estrogen dosage can be beneficial in relieving breast pain in these patients. Anecdotal observations in the author's clinic suggest that a combination of estrogen and androgen such as half-strength Estrotest (methyltestosterone plus 0.625 mg Premarin) is effective in relieving breast pain. Raloxifene may also be substituted for estrogen if the primary therapeutic goal is prevention of osteoporosis. Mastectomy is rarely used as a treatment for severe mastalgia unresponsive to medical therapy; some experts consider this never to be warranted.

### NONCYCLIC PAIN

When truly arising from the breast, this type of pain is managed similarly to cyclic pain. However, a musculoskeletal etiology is present in 40% of women referred to specialized mastalgia clinics for pain thought to arise in the breast. Factors associated with chest wall pain include physical exertion and repetitive work. Two thirds of women with diffuse chest wall pain respond to topical nonsteroidal anti-inflammatory drugs (NSAIDs) or to systemic NSAIDs if topical therapy is not available.[91] Of the remaining patients, 85% gain temporary or permanent relief from an anaesthetic/steroid combination injected into the tender site.[91]

### FOCAL BREAST LESIONS

Careful examination distinguishes solitary, discrete, dominant masses from vague nodularity, thickening, or asymmetry. Practice guidelines of the Society of Surgical Oncology[92] recommend the following evaluation for discrete breast lumps. In women younger than 35, all discrete palpable lesions require referral to a surgeon. If vague nodularity, thickening, or asymmetry is present, the clinician repeats the examination after one or two menstrual cycles approximately 1 to 2 weeks after the menstrual period. If the abnormality resolves, the patient

is reassured and if not, referred to a surgeon. Breast imaging may be appropriate. In women older than 35 with a dominant mass, a diagnostic mammogram is obtained and the patient is referred to a surgeon. For possible gross cysts, the clinician performs needle aspiration and discards if nonbloody. If the same cyst persistently refills, the clinician obtains a diagnostic mammogram and refers to a surgeon. If the original needle aspiration is bloody, the physician obtains cytology, orders a mammogram, and refers to a surgeon.

Usual practice requires "triple evaluation" with palpation, mammography, and biopsy in women older than 40 with discrete masses. In women between 30 and 40, mammography may be omitted if ultrasound and biopsy yield definitive information. Many but not all surgeons omit biopsy in women younger than 30 with lesions characteristic of fibroadenoma on ultrasound and elect to follow carefully with serial ultrasound assessment. Surgical excision is required for lesions with ADH since more complete resection often changes the diagnosis to DCIS.

### DISCHARGE

The presence of a palpable mass, positive mammogram, or positive ultrasound in association with discharge warrants the evaluation detailed for a mass. A practical algorithm[93] divides discharge into two categories: nongalactorrhea and galactorrhea (Fig. 165-8). Galactorrhea is defined as milk production more than 1 year after weaning or in any nulligravid or menopausal women. Work-up for galactorrhea includes measurement of prolactin and thyroid-stimulating hormone (TSH) levels and appropriate endocrinologic evaluation and treatment if elevated (see Chapter 27). Nongalactorrheic discharge is considered to be ductal in origin and is subclassified as arising from a single or from multiple ducts. When verified

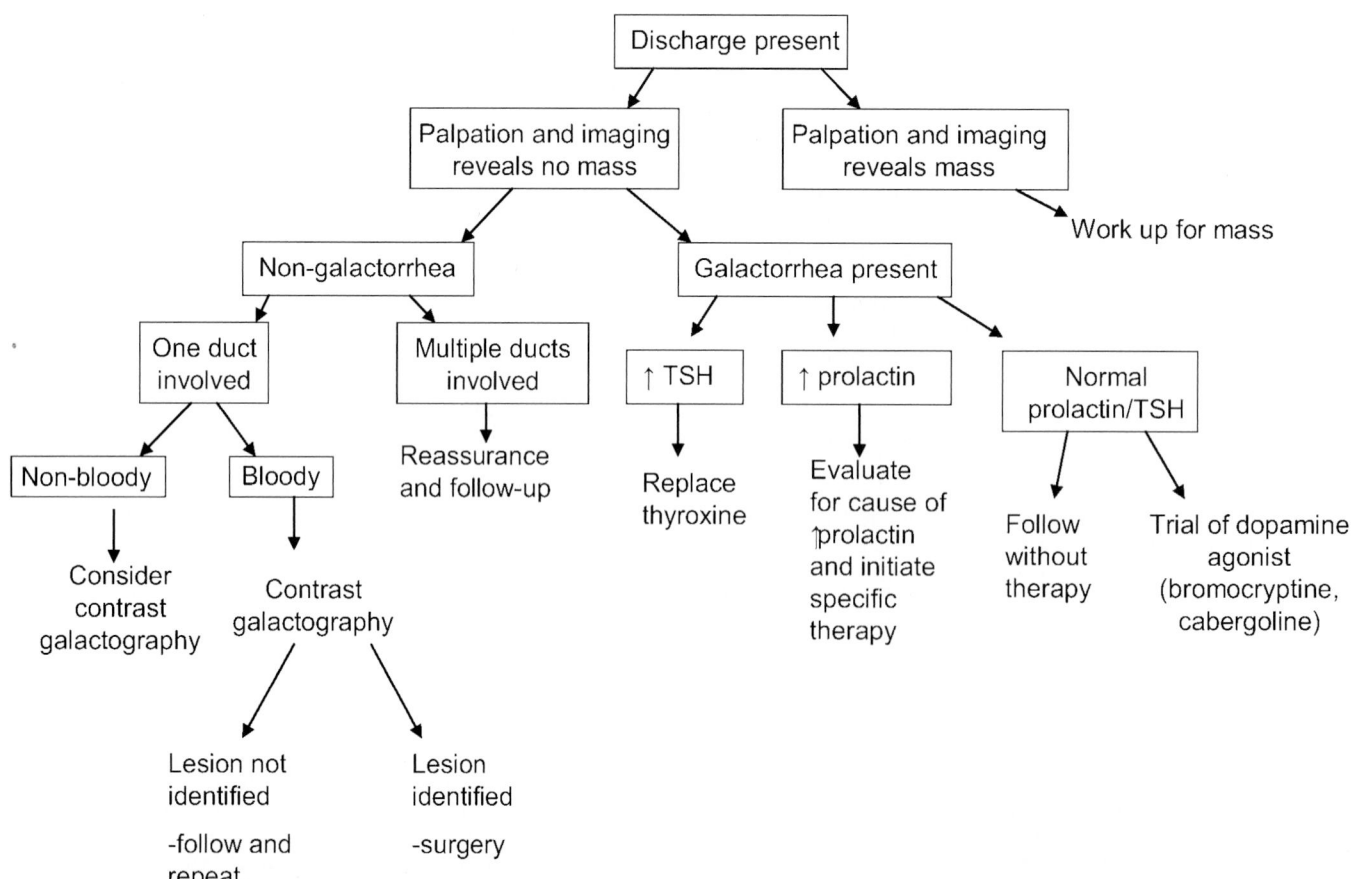

**Figure 165-8** Algorithm for evaluating patient with complaint of nipple discharge.

to come from one duct, and particularly if grossly bloody or positive on occult testing, further workup is needed. Contrast galactography with cannulation and insertion of dye into the single duct emitting blood at the nipple allows demonstration of a space-occupying lesion in the duct. Direct examination of the ducts using a mini-fiberoptic endoscope (ductoscopy) is currently being evaluated in research centers. If a lesion is present, surgical exploration allows removal of pathologic lesions and cessation of discharge. Multiduct discharge that is clear, serous, green-black, or nonbloody requires only reassurance. Blood arising predominantly from one or two ducts should be evaluated further.

## BREAST CANCER PREVENTION

Patients with benign breast lesions imparting an increased risk of breast cancer can be offered tamoxifen as a prevention strategy. The risk of breast cancer is determined using the Gail model (or in women with a strong family history, the Claus model) and the benefits versus risks of tamoxifen evaluated.[57–59] Risk factors not included in the Gail or Claus models include degree of breast density, plasma-free estradiol levels, bone density, weight gain after menopause, and obesity.[53,94] Current recommendations suggest that clinicians should inform premenopausal women with a 5-year risk of breast cancer of greater than 1.67% and no contraindications to tamoxifen about the possibility of taking tamoxifen for 5 years.[95] Postmenopausal women with no uterus and similar risk factors are also candidates. A recent overview has shown a 50% reduction of the relative risk of breast cancer with tamoxifen, but benefits may be offset by increased risks of thromboembolic phenomena, endometrial cancer, and maturation of cataracts.[59] An ongoing trial (the Star trial) is addressing whether raloxifene might be preferable to tamoxifen.[96]

## REFERENCES

1. Russo J, Santen RJ, Russo IH: Hormonal control of breast development. In De Groot LJ, Jameson JL (eds): Endocrinology. Philadelphia, WB Saunders, 2001, pp 2181–2188.
2. Osborne MP: Breast anatomy and development. In Harris JR, Lippman ME, Morrow M, Osborne CK (eds): Diseases of the Breast. Philadelphia, Lippincott Williams & Wilkins, 2000, pp 1–13.
3. Alpers CE, Wellings SR: The prevalence of carcinoma in situ in normal and cancer-associated breasts. Hum Pathol 16:796–807, 1985.
4. Potten CS, Watson RJ, Williams GT, et al: The effect of age and menstrual cycle upon proliferative activity of the normal human breast. Br J Cancer 58:163–170, 1988.
5. Russo J, Russo IH: Role of hormones in human breast development: The menopausal breast. In Birkhaüsen MH(ed): Progress in Management of Menopause. London, Parthenon, 1997, pp 184–193.
6. Love SM, Gelman RS, Silen W: Sounding board: Fibrocystic "disease" of the breast—a nondisease? N Engl J Med 307:1010–1014, 1982.
7. Drukker BH: Fibrocystic change of the breast. Clin Obstet Gynecol 37:903–915, 1994.
8. Goehring C, Morabia A: Epidemiology of benign breast disease, with special attention to histologic types. Epidemiol Rev 19:310–327, 1997.
9. Hughes LE, Mansel RE, Webster DJ: Aberrations of normal development and involution (ANDI): A new perspective on pathogenesis and nomenclature of benign breast disorders. Lancet 2:1316–1319, 1987.
10. Dent DM, Cant PJ: Fibroadenoma. World J Surg 13:706–710, 1989.
11. Wellings SR, Jensen HM, Marcum RG: An atlas of subgross pathology of the human breast with special reference to possible precancerous lesions. J Natl Cancer Inst 55:231–273, 1975.
12. Bundred NJ, Furlong A, El-Nakib L, Knox F: The aetiology of periductal mastitis. In Mansel RE (ed): Recent Developments in the Study of Benign

Breast Disease. London, Parthenon, 1997, pp 209–214.
13. Costantini L, Bucchi L, Dogliotti L, et al: Cohort study of women with aspirated gross cysts of the breast: An update. In Mansel RE (ed): Recent Developments in the Study of Benign Breast Disease. London, Parthenon, 1994, pp 227–239.
14. O'Connell P, Pekkel V, Fuqua SA, et al: Analysis of loss of heterozygosity in 399 premalignant breast lesions at 15 genetic loci. J Natl Cancer Inst 90:697–703, 1998.
15. Euhus DM, Cler L, Shivapurkar N, et al: Loss of heterozygosity in benign breast epithelium in relation to breast cancer risk. J Natl Cancer Inst 94:858–860, 2002.
16. Boone CW, Kelloff GJ, Freedman LS: Intraepithelial and postinvasive neoplasia as a stochastic continuum of clonal evolution, and its relationship to mechanisms of chemopreventive drug action. J Cell Biochem 17G (Suppl):14–25, 1993.
17. Ringberg A, Palmer B, Linell F: The contralateral breast at reconstructive surgery after breast cancer operation: A histopathological study. Breast Cancer Res Treat 2:151–161, 1982.
18. Egan RL: Multicentric breast carcinomas: Clinical-radiographic-pathologic whole organ studies and 10-year survival. Cancer 49:1123–1130, 1982.
19. Simkovich AH, Sclafani LM, Masri M, Kinne DW: Role of contralateral breast biopsy in infiltrating lobular cancer. Surgery 114:555–557, 1993.
20. Chenevix-Trench G, Spurdle AB, Gatei M, et al: Dominant negative ATM mutations in breast cancer families. J Natl Cancer Inst 94:205–215, 2002.
21. Yager JD, Liehr JG: Molecular mechanisms of estrogen carcinogenesis. Annu Rev Pharmacol Toxicol 36:203–232, 1996.
22. Jefcoate CR, Liehr JG, Santen RJ, et al: Tissue-specific synthesis and oxidative metabolism of estrogens. J Natl Cancer Inst Monogr 27:95–112, 2000.
23. Liehr JG: Is estradiol a genotoxic mutagenic carcinogen? Endocr Rev 21:40–54, 2000.

24. Schultz LB, Weber BL: Recent advances in breast cancer biology. Curr Opin Oncol 11:429–434, 1999.
25. Keshava N, Mandava U, Kirma N, Tekmal RR: Acceleration of mammary neoplasia in aromatase transgenic mice by 7,12-dimethylbenz[a]anthracene. Cancer Lett 167:125–133, 2001.
26. Berardo MD: Biologic characteristics of premalignant and preinvasie breast disease. In O'Connell P, Katzenellenbogen BS, Pasqualini JR, Allred DC (eds): Hormone-Dependent Cancer. New York, Marcel Dekker, 2002.
27. Allred DC, Hilsenbeck SG: Biomarkers in benign breast disease: Risk factors for breast cancer. J Natl Cancer Inst 90:1247–1248, 1998.
28. Rohan TE, Hartwick W, Miller AB, Kandel RA: Immunohistochemical detection of c-erbB-2 and p53 in benign breast disease and breast cancer risk. J Natl Cancer Inst 90:1262–1269, 1998.
29. Rohan TE, Miller AB: Hormone replacement therapy and risk of benign proliferative epithelial disorders of the breast. Eur J Cancer Prev 8:123–130, 1999.
30. Tan-Chiu E, Wang J, Costantino JP, et al: Effects of tamoxifen on benign breast disease in women at high risk for breast cancer. J Natl Cancer Inst 95:302–307, 2003.
31. Ader DN, South-Paul J, Adera T, Deuster PA: Cyclical mastalgia: Prevalence and associated health and behavioral factors. J Psychosom Obstet Gynaecol 22:71–76, 2001.
32. Ader DN, Shriver CD: Cyclical mastalgia: Prevalence and impact in an outpatient breast clinic sample. J Am Coll Surg 185:466–470, 1997.
33. Minton JP, Abou-Issa H: Nonendocrine theories of the etiology of benign breast disease. World J Surg 13:680–684, 1989.
34. Ghent WR, Eskin BA, Low DA, Hill LP: Iodine replacement in fibrocystic disease of the breast. Can J Surg 36:453–460, 1993.
35. Preece PE, Mansel RE, Bolton PM, et al: Clinical syndromes of mastalgia. Lancet 2:670–673, 1976.

36. Khan SA, Apkarian AV: The characteristics of cyclical and noncyclical mastalgia: A prospective study using a modified McGill Pain Questionnaire. Breast Cancer Res Treat 75:147–157, 2002.

37. Goodwin PJ, Miller A, Del Giudice ME, Ritchie K: Breast health and associated premenstrual symptoms in women with severe cyclic mastopathy. Am J Obstet Gynecol 176:998–1005, 1997.

38. Kessel B: Premenstrual syndrome: Advances in diagnosis and treatment. Obstet Gynecol Clin North Am 27:625–639, 2000.

39. Ambrogetti D, Berni D, Catarzi S, Ciatto S: The role of ductal galactography in the differential diagnosis of breast carcinoma [Italian]. Radiol Med (Torino) 91:198–201, 1996.

40. Seltzer MH, Perloff LJ, Kelley RI, Fitts WT Jr: The significance of age in patients with nipple discharge. Surg Gynecol Obstet 131:519–522, 1970.

41. Is "fibrocystic disease" of the breast precancerous? Arch Pathol Lab Med 110:171–173, 1986.

42. London SJ, Connolly JL, Schnitt SJ, Colditz GA: A prospective study of benign breast disease and the risk of breast cancer. JAMA 267:941–944, 1992.

43. Dupont WD, Page DL: Relative risk of breast cancer varies with time since diagnosis of atypical hyperplasia. Hum Pathol 20:723–725, 1989.

44. Ciatto S, Andreoli C, Cirillo A, et al: The risk of breast cancer subsequent to histologic diagnosis of benign intraductal papilloma follow-up study of 339 cases. Tumori 77:41–43, 1991.

45. Page DL, Kidd TE Jr, Dupont WD, et al: Lobular neoplasia of the breast: Higher risk for subsequent invasive cancer predicted by more extensive disease. Hum Pathol 22:1232–1239, 1991.

46. Dupont WD, Page DL, Parl FF, et al: Long-term risk of breast cancer in women with fibroadenoma. N Engl J Med 331:10–15, 1994.

47. Boyd NF, Lockwood GA, Byng JW, et al: Mammographic densities and breast cancer risk. Cancer Epidemiol Biomarkers Prev 7:1133–1144, 1998.

48. Boyd NF, Jensen HM, Cooke G, et al: Mammographic densities and the prevalence and incidence of histological types of benign breast disease. Reference Pathologists of the Canadian National Breast Screening Study. Eur J Cancer Prev 9:15–24, 2000.

49. Byrne C, Schairer C, Brinton LA, et al: Effects of mammographic density and benign breast disease on breast cancer risk (United States). Cancer Causes Control 12:103–110, 2001.

50. Boyd NF, Byng JW, Jong RA, et al: Quantitative classification of mammographic densities and breast cancer risk: Results from the Canadian National Breast Screening Study. J Natl Cancer Inst 87:670–675, 1995.

51. Wolfe JN, Saftlas AF, Salane M: Mammographic parenchymal patterns and quantitative evaluation of mammographic densities: A case-control study. Am J Roentgenol 148:1087–1092, 1987.

52. Freedman M, San Martin J, O'Gorman J, et al: Digitized mammography: A clinical trial of postmenopausal women randomly assigned to receive raloxifene, estrogen, or placebo. J Natl Cancer Inst 93:51–56, 2001.

53. Hulka BS, Moorman PG: Breast cancer: Hormones and other risk factors. Maturitas 38:103–113, 1928.

54. The Endogenous Hormones and Breast Cancer Collaborative Group: Endogenous sex hormones and breast cancer in postmenopausal women: Reanalysis of nine prospective studies. J Natl Cancer Inst 94:606–616, 2002.

55. Santen RJ: Endocrine responsive cancer. In Larsen PR, Kronenberg HM, Melmed S, Polansky KS (eds): Williams Textbook of Endocrinology. Philadelphia, WB Saunders, 2002, pp 1797–1833.

56. Santen RJ: Risk of breast cancer with progestins: Critical review of data. Steroids 68:953–964, 2003.

57. McTiernan A, Kuniyuki A, Yasui Y, et al: Comparisons of two breast cancer risk estimates in women with a family history of breast cancer. Cancer Epidemiol Biomarkers Prev 10:333–338, 2001.

58. Gail MH, Brinton LA, Byar DP, et al: Projecting individualized probabilities of developing breast cancer for white females who are being examined annually. J Natl Cancer Inst 81:1879–1886, 1989.

59. Gail MH, Costantino JP, Bryant J, et al: Weighing the risks and benefits of tamoxifen treatment for preventing breast cancer. J Natl Cancer Inst 91:1829–1846, 1999.

60. Klein P, Glaser E, Grogan L, et al: Biomarker assays in nipple aspirate fluid. Breast J 7:378–387, 2001.

61. Santen RJ, Cerilli LA, Harvey JA: The breast: Gynecomastia and benign breast disease in women. In Besser GM, Thorner MO (eds): Comprehensive Clinical Endocrinology, 3d ed. Spain, Mosby, 2002, pp 585–612.

62. Gateley CA, Miers M, Mansel RE, Hughes LE: Drug treatments for mastalgia: 17 years experience in the Cardiff Mastalgia Clinic. J R Soc Med 85:12–15, 1992.

63. Ader DN, Shriver CD: Update of clinical and research issues in cycl\ical mastalgia. Breast J 4:25–32, 1998.

64. Dhont M, Delbeke L, van Eyck J, Voorhoof L: Danazol treatment of chronic cystic mastopathy: A clinical and hormonal evaluation. Postgrad Med J 55(Suppl):70, 1979.

65. Fentiman IS, Caleffi M, Brame K, et al: Double-blind controlled trial of tamoxifen therapy for mastalgia. Lancet 1:287–288, 1986.

66. Messinis IE, Lolis D: Treatment of premenstrual mastalgia with tamoxifen. Acta Obstet Gynecol Scand 67:307–309, 1988.

67. Fentiman IS, Caleffi M, Hamed H, Chaudary MA: Dosage and duration of tamoxifen treatment for mastalgia: A controlled trial. Br J Surg 75:845–846, 1988.

68. Ernster VL, Goodson WH III, Hunt TK, et al: Vitamin E and benign breast "disease": A double-blind, randomized clinical trial. Surgery 97:490–494, 1985.

69. London RS, Sundaram GS, Murphy L, et al: The effect of vitamin E on mammary dysplasia: A double-blind study. Obstet Gynecol 65:104–106, 1985.

70. Meyer EC, Sommers DK, Reitz CJ, Mentis H: Vitamin E and benign breast disease. Surgery 107:549–551, 1990.

71. Nappi C, Affinito P, Di Carlo C, et al: Double-blind controlled trial of progesterone vaginal cream treatment for cyclical mastodynia in women with benign breast disease. J Endocrinol Invest 15:801–806, 1992.

72. Maddox PR, Harrison BJ, Horobin JM, et al: A randomised controlled trial of medroxyprogesterone acetate in mastalgia. Ann R Coll Surg Engl 72:71–76, 1990.

73. McFadyen IJ, Raab GM, MacIntyre CC, Forrest AP: Progesterone cream for cyclic breast pain. Br Med J 298:931, 1989.

74. Boyd NF, McGuire V, Shannon P, et al: Effect of a low-fat high-carbohydrate diet on symptoms of cyclical mastopathy. Lancet 2:128–132, 1988.

75. Ernster VL, Mason L, Goodson WH III, et al: Effects of caffeine-free diet on benign breast disease: A randomized trial. Surgery 91:263–267, 1982.

76. Allen SS, Froberg DG: The effect of decreased caffeine consumption on benign proliferative breast disease: A randomized clinical trial. Surgery 101:720–730, 1987.

77. Wilson MC, Sellwood RA: Therapeutic value of a supporting brassiere in mastodynia 2116. Br Med J 2:90, 1976.

78. Hamed H, Caleffi M, Chaudary MA, Fentiman IS: LHRH analogue for treatment of recurrent and refractory mastalgia. Ann R Coll Surg Engl 72:221–224, 1990.

79. Wetzig NR: Mastalgia: A 3 year Australian study. Aust N Z J Surg 64:329–331, 1994.

80. Hinton CP, Bishop HM, Holliday HW, et al: A double-blind controlled trial of danazol and bromocriptine in the management of severe cyclical breast pain. Br J Clin Pract 40:326–330, 1986.

81. Gateley CA, Maddox PR, Pritchard GA, et al: Plasma fatty acid profiles in benign breast disorders. Br J Surg 79:407–409, 1992.

82. Patey DH: Two common non-malignant conditions of the breast: The clinical features of cystic disease and the pain syndrome. Br Med J 1:96–99, 1949.

83. Preece PE, Mansel RE, Hughes LE: Mastalgia: Psychoneurosis or organic disease? Br Med J 1:29–30, 1978.

84. Mansel RE, Pye JK, Hughes LE: Effects of essential fatty acids on cyclical mastalgia and non-cyclical disorders. In Horrobin DE (ed): Omega-6 Essential Fatty Acids: Pathophysiology and Roles in Clinical Medicine. New York, Wiley-Liss, 1990, pp 557–566.

85. Fenn NJ: Current treatment of mastalgia. In Mansel RE (ed): Recent Developments in the Treatment of Benign Breast Disease. London, Parthenon, 1997, pp 135–142.

86. Gateley CA, Maddox PR, Mansel RE, Hughes LE: Mastalgia refractory to drug treatment. Br J Surg 77:1110–1112, 1990.

87. Mauvais-Jarvis P: Mastodynia and fibrocystic disease. Curr Ther Endocrinol Metab 3:280–284, 1988.

88. Colin C, Gaspard U, Lambotte R: Relationship of mastodynia with its endocrine environment and treatment in a double blind trial with lynestrenol. Arch Gynakol 225:7–13, 1978.

89. Plu-Bureau, Le MG, Sitruk-Ware R, et al: Progestogen use and decreased risk of breast cancer in a cohort study of premenopausal women with benign breast disease. Br J Cancer 70:270–277, 1994.

90. BeLieu RM: Mastodynia. Obstet Gynecol Clin North Am 21:461–477, 1994.

91. Kollias J: Topical non-steroidal anti-inflammatory gel for diffuse chest wall pain in mastalgia patients. In Mansel RE (ed): Recent Developments in the Study of Benign Breast Disease. London, Parthenon, 1997, pp 119–128.

92. Morrow M, Bland KI, Foster R: Breast cancer surgical practice guidelines. Society of Surgical Oncology practice guidelines. Oncology (Huntington) 11:877–881, 1997.

93. Falkenberry SS: Nipple discharge. Obstet Gynecol Clin North Am 29:21–29, 2002.

94. Clemons M, Goss P: Estrogen and the risk of breast cancer. N Engl J Med 344:276–285, 2001.

95. Chlebowski RT, Collyar DE, Somerfield MR, Pfister DG: American Society of Clinical Oncology technology assessment on breast cancer risk reduction strategies: Tamoxifen and raloxifene. J Clin Oncol 17:1939–1955, 1999.

96. Pappas SG, Jordan VC: Chemoprevention of breast cancer: Current and future prospects. Cancer Metastasis Rev 21:311–321, 2002.

97. Mansel RE, Wisbey JR, Hughes LE: Controlled trial of the antigonadotropin danazol in painful nodular benign breast disease. Lancet 1:928–930, 1982.

98. Doberl A, Tobiassen T, Rasmussen T: Treatment of recurrent cyclical mastodynia in patients with fibrocystic breast disease. A double-blind placebo-controlled study—The Hjorring project. Acta Obstet Gynecol Scand Suppl 123:177–184, 1984.

99. Gorins A, Perret F, Tournant B, et al: A French double-blind crossover study (danazol versus placebo) in the treatment of severe fibrocystic breast disease. Eur J Gynaecol Oncol 5:85–89, 1984.

100. Hinton CP, Bishop HM, Holliday HW, et al: A double-blind controlled trial of danazol and bromocriptine in the management of severe cyclical breast pain. Br J Clin Pract 40:326–330, 1986.

101. Ramsey-Stewart G: The treatment of symptomatic benign breast disease with danazol. Aust NZ J Obstet Gynaecol 28:299–304, 1988.

102. Yayoi E, Senoo T, Izuo M, et al: Clinical trial of danazol in benign breast disease. In Mansel RE (ed): Recent Developments in the Study of Benign Breast Disease. London, Parthenon, 1997, pp 143–154.

103. Peters F: Multicentre study of gestrinone in cyclical breast pain. Lancet 339:205–208, 1992.

104. Mansel RE, Preece PE, Hughes LE: A double blind trial of the prolactin inhibitor bromocriptine in painful benign breast disease. Br J Surg 65:724–727, 1978.

105. Blickert-Toft M, Anderson AN, Hendriksen OB, Mygind T: Treatment of mastalgia with bromocriptine: A double-blind cross-over study. Br Med J 1:237, 1979.

106. Durning P, Sellwood RA: Bromocriptine in severe cyclical breast pain. Br J Surg 69:248–249, 1982.

107. Nazli K, Syed S, Mahmood MR, Ansari F: Controlled trial of the prolactin inhibitor bromocriptine (Parlodel) in the treatment of severe cyclical mastalgia. Br J Clin Pract 43:322–327, 1989.

108. Mansel RE, Preece PE, Hughes LE: Treatment of cyclical breast pain with bromocriptine. Scot Med J 25 (suppl):65–70, 1980.

109. Mansel RE, Dogliotti L: European multicentre trial of bromocriptine in cyclical mastalgia. Lancet 335:190–193, 1990.

110. Preece PE, Hanslip JI, Gilbert L: Evening primrose oil (Efamol) for mastalgia. In Horrobin DF (ed): Clinical Uses Of Essential Fatty Acid. Montreal, Eden, 1982, pp 147–154.

111. Pashby NL, Mansel RE, Hughes LE, et al: A clinical trial of evening primrose oil in mastalgia. Br J Surg 68:801, 1981.

112. Mansel RE, Pye JK, Hughes LE: Effects of essential fatty acids on cyclical mastalgia and non-cyclical disorders. In Horrobin DE (ed): Omega-6-Essential Fatty Acids: Pathophysiology and Roles in Clinical Medicine. New York, Wiley-Liss, 1990, pp 557–566.

113. Blommers J, de Lange-de Klerk ES, Kuik DJ, et al: Evening primrose oil and fish oil for severe chronic astalgia: A randomized, double-blind, controlled trial. Am J Obstet Gynecol 187:1389–1394, 2002.

114. Fentiman IS, Caleffi M, Hamed H, Chaudary MA: Dosage and duration of tamoxifen treatment for mastalgia: A controlled trial. Br J Surg 75:845–846, 1988.

115. Fentiman IS, Caleffi M, Brame K, et al: Double-blind controlled trial of tamoxifen therapy for mastalgia. Lancet 1:287–288, 1986.

116. Ernster VL, Goodson WH III, Hunt TK, et al: Vitamin E and benign breast "disease": A double-blind, randomized clinical trial. Surgery 97:490–494, 1985.

117. London RS, Sundaram GS, Murphy L, et al: The effect of vitamin E on mammary dysplasia: A double-blind study. Obstet Gynecol 65:104–106, 1985.

118. Ghent WR, Eskin BA, Low DA, Hill LP: Iodine replacement in fibrocystic disease of the breast. Can J Surg 36:453–460, 1993.

119. Nappi C, Affinito P, Di Carlo C, et al: Double-blind controlled trial of progesterone vaginal cream treatment for cyclical mastodynia in women with benign breast disease. J Endocrinol Invest 15:801–806, 1992.

120. Ernster VL, Mason L, Goodson WH III, et al: Effects of caffeine-free diet on benign breast disease: A randomized trial. Surgery 91:263–267, 1982.

121. Allen SS, Froberg DG: The effect of decreased caffeine consumption on benign proliferative breast disease: A randomized clinical trial. Surgery 101:720–730, 1987.

122. Body NF, McGuire V, Shannon P, et al: Effect of a low-fat high-carbohydrate diet on symptoms of cyclical mastopathy. Lancet 2:128–132, 1988.

123. Maddox PR, Harrison BJ, Horobin JM, et al: A randomised controlled trial of medroxyprogesterone acetate in mastalgia. Ann R Coll Surg Engl 72:71–76, 1990.

124. McFadyen IJ, Raab GM, MacIntyre CC, Forrest AP: Progesterone cream for cyclic breast pain. Br Med J 298:931, 1989.

# Endocrine Management of Breast Cancer

## William J. Gradishar and V. Craig Jordan

Breast cancer is diagnosed in approximately 180,000 patients in the United States each year.[1] Even more striking is the prevalence of breast cancer in the general population, which exceeds other solid tumors such as lung cancer, colon cancer, and prostate cancer.[1] Not only are a large number of new diagnoses of breast cancer made each year, but an enormous number of breast cancer survivors also remain at risk of recurrence of the disease or development of a new primary breast cancer.

Since 1970, breast cancer treatment has improved significantly, with more effective therapy now available for the treatment of advanced disease and better adjuvant therapy for the eradication of microscopic disease. Systemic treatment options that are available to patients with breast cancer include chemotherapy, hormonal therapy, and biologic therapy.[2] In addition, results from chemoprevention studies now offer risk-reduction strategies for women with an elevated risk to develop the disease.[3] This chapter focuses on advances in the use of endocrine agents for the treatment of early and advanced stage breast cancer

## HISTORICAL PERSPECTIVE AND BACKGROUND

The relationship between endocrine manipulation and breast cancer was first established more than 100 years ago. In 1896, Beatson[4] demonstrated that removal of the ovaries from a premenopausal woman with advanced breast cancer resulted in tumor regression. A few years later, Boyd[5] reported that approximately one third of premenopausal women with metastatic breast cancer would show objective evidence of tumor regression after undergoing surgical oophorectomy, and these women gained approximately 1 year of additional life. DeCourmellers[6] demonstrated a similar effect on breast cancer by irradiating the ovaries. Block[7] later showed that the effect of radiation on ovarian function correlated with estrogen production reaching basal levels several months after treatment.

Once synthetic corticosteroids became available in the 1950s, other forms of endocrine ablation became feasible, including surgical adrenalectomy and hypophysectomy.[8,9] Tumor responses were reported in 30% to 40% of patients undergoing these procedures, but the associated morbidity and mortality rates were unacceptably high.[8,9] Eventually, medical therapies for inducing adrenalectomy with drugs such as aminoglutethimide were identified.[10] Although much of the early work focused on ways to achieve estrogen deprivation, Haddow[11] demonstrated that high-dose estrogen therapy resulted in tumor regression in postmenopausal women with advanced breast cancer. However, the use of additive endocrine therapy was also not without significant toxicity for patients.

Through a series of elegant experiments, Jensen and Jacobsen[12] hypothesized that an estrogen receptor (ER) must be present in estrogen target tissues, such as the uterus, vagina, and pituitary. Ultimately, the ER protein was isolated and characterized as an extractable protein from estrogen target tissues by Toft and colleagues.[13] These findings led to the development of ER assays that could be used to predict which patients with metastatic breast cancer would respond to endocrine manipulation.[14] In a random population of patients with metastatic breast cancer, 30% to 35% will respond to endocrine manipulation, whereas 55% to 60% of patients with tumors known to be ER positive benefit from endocrine manipulation.[14,15]

Additional insight into the biology of breast cancer was provided by identification and characterization of the progesterone receptor (PgR), which was determined to be an estrogen-regulated protein that can be synthesized only if the ER is functional.[16] The ability to characterize a given tumor for the presence of ER or PgR led to the ability to predict the probability that a given patient would respond to endocrine manipulation.[17,18] Several studies have shown that older patients in whom breast cancer is diagnosed were more likely to express ER than were younger patients.[18,19] One study found that 44% of breast cancer patients in the 40 to 49 year age group express ER, whereas 69% of patients 70 years or older do so.[19] Similarly, Witliff[18] showed that 72% of premenopausal and 83% of postmenopausal patients with breast cancer express ER. These data suggest that most patients with metastatic breast cancer are candidates for endocrine therapy at some point in the course of their disease. Similarly, as discussed later, the majority of patients diagnosed with early stage breast cancer benefit from the addition of endocrine therapy, either alone or in conjunction with chemotherapy.[20,21]

In 1958, MER-25, the first nonsteroidal antiestrogen, was developed, but because of central nervous system toxicity and relatively low potency, further development was discontinued.[22] Tamoxifen, the antiestrogenic, pure *trans* isomer of a substituted triphenylethylene (Fig. 166-1), was initially developed as a potential postcoital contraceptive but was eventually shown to induce ovulation in subfertile women.[23–26] Fortunately, preliminary clinical studies of tamoxifen in patients with metastatic breast cancer showed antitumor activity, which led to its development as a treatment of breast cancer.[27–29]

The use of tamoxifen as a treatment for breast cancer heralded the modern era of endocrine therapy and was responsible for the exploration of other strategies that eventually resulted in the clinical development of now widely used therapeutic agents, such as the selective aromatase inhibitors[30,31] and the selective estrogen receptor downregulator fulvestrant.[32,33]

## ENDOCRINE THERAPY IN PATIENTS WITH METASTATIC BREAST CANCER

General recommendations for endocrine therapy in patients with metastatic breast cancer can be reasonably based on several clinical factors: ER- and/or PgR-positive tumors, asymptomatic metastatic disease, predominantly bone or soft-tissue disease, and a long disease-free interval since the original diagnosis.[34] Several caveats related to endocrine therapy must be considered before making specific treatment recommendations.

1. Approximately one third of unselected patients with metastatic disease will respond to any type of endocrine therapy (e.g., surgical ablative therapy, antiestrogens, aromatase inhibitors, progestins). Patients with tumors determined to be ER/PgR positive have a 60% to 80% chance of benefiting from endocrine manipulation (disease stability or tumor regression), and the duration of response is approximately 12 to 18 months.[17,18] Patients with predominantly bone and/or soft-tissue disease and/or a long disease-free interval are also those who are likely to have tumors that are ER and/or PgR positive.[34,35]

2. Patients who respond to one endocrine therapy are likely to respond to another endocrine therapy.[36–40] However, as with chemotherapy, the likelihood of response to subsequent endocrine therapy decreases with each maneuver and the duration of benefit also shortens. Wilson[38] reported that second-line therapy (e.g., adrenalectomy, hypophysectomy, aminoglutethimide, estrogens, androgens, progestins) after first-line therapy with tamoxifen or oophorectomy achieved a 19% to 38% response rate. More recent experience with selective aromatase inhibitors following tamoxifen, tamoxifen following an aromatase inhibitor, or selective estrogen receptor downregulators following an aromatase inhibitor demonstrates a clinical benefit rate (CBR) as high as 70% (disease regression or disease stability) with additional endocrine therapy at the time of disease progression.[39,40]

3. Reassessment of the ER/PgR status of a tumor is a reasonable consideration at the time of disease recurrence if it can be done with minimal morbidity. Approximately 20% to 25% of tumors originally determined to be ER positive were found to be ER negative at the time of recurrence.[41,42] The International Breast Cancer Study Group found that some patients who had been classified as ER negative based on assessment of the primary tumor had ER-positive recurrences.[43] False-negative results of the ligand-binding assay were not sufficient to explain these cases, which consisted almost exclusively of patients with late relapses (>3 years) and a high content of ER. These findings suggest that clonal selection in vivo may result not only in the loss of ER but also in an apparent gain of ER because of the emergence of ER-positive clones from a predominantly ER-negative tumor at initial diagnosis.[43]

4. Tumor flare or symptoms related to the cancer may be exacerbated at the initiation of endocrine therapy. This phenomenon has been observed with tamoxifen, progestins, estrogens, and androgens, although it occurs in less than 10% of cases.[44–49] Exacerbation of bone pain in a patient with known bone metastases is one of the most common clues. In addition, an increase in the level of tumor markers, increased alkaline phosphatase, or worsening of abnormalities on a bone scan has also been observed.[44–46,49] These symptoms tend to occur within hours to days of starting therapy and resolve within days to weeks. The endocrine therapy should be continued, and efforts should be directed at palliating symptoms (e.g., analgesics, even short-term steroids).

5. For patients receiving endocrine therapy at the time of disease progression who do not have rapidly progressing disease, consideration should be given to discontinuing the current endocrine therapy without immediately starting another endocrine therapy. Withdrawal responses have been observed with tamoxifen, progestins, estrogens, and androgens.[50] To date, withdrawal responses have not been described with the new selective estrogen receptor downregulator, fulvestrant, and only once with the new selective aromatase inhibitor exemestane.[51] Although the precise mechanism underlying the withdrawal response has not been fully defined, compounds that were once antagonistic to tumor growth may have over time become agonists for tumor growth.[52]

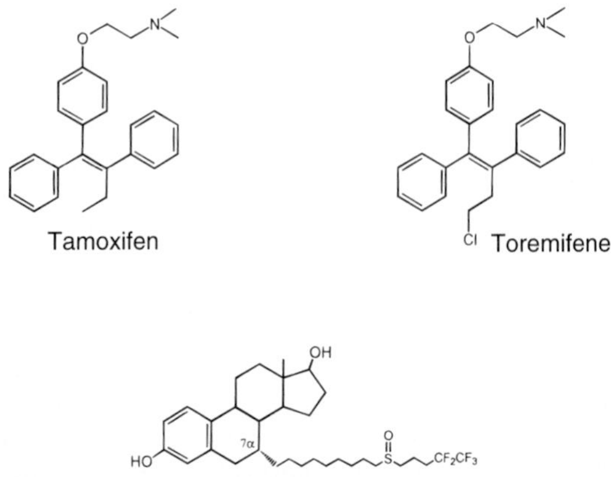

### MECHANISMS OF ACTION OF ENDOCRINE THERAPY

Most endocrine therapies are believed to act on tumor growth by reducing the synthesis of estrogen or by interfering with the action of estrogen at the level of the tumor cell. In addition, less well defined mechanisms of action include modulation of autocrine growth factors, direct cytotoxicity, apoptosis, and cell-cycle arrest.[34,53]

Surgical ablative procedures act by directly or indirectly reducing the synthesis of estrogen in the ovary and adrenals, whereas aromatase inhibitors interfere with the peripheral conversion of steroid precursors into estrogen.[30,33,53–55] In contrast, antiestrogens act at the cellular level principally by interfering with the action of estrogen on the ER.[56] The selective estrogen

**Figure 166-1** Structure of currently available antiestrogens (tamoxifen, toremifene) and the selective estrogen receptor downregulator fulvestrant.

receptor downregulator fulvestrant downregulates the expression of the estrogen receptor.[33] The mechanism of action of additive endocrine therapies such as progestins, androgens, and estrogens remains poorly defined. The choice of endocrine therapy in a given patient is influenced by menopausal status and previous endocrine therapy as outlined here.

## ANTIESTROGENS

### TAMOXIFEN

The antitumor effect of tamoxifen is mediated primarily through the ER.[56-60] Binding of estradiol or any estrogen to the nuclear ER produces a change in the shape of the protein complex and exposes the DNA-binding domain. The activated receptor complex then dimerizes, releases heat shock proteins, and binds to an estrogen response element located in the promoter region of the estrogen-responsive genes. Once bound to the estrogen response element, the estrogen-ER complex acts an anchor for other transcription factors or coactivation proteins that, when assembled and associated with RNA polymerase, produce a transcription complex. The estrogen-responsive gene is then transcribed and subsequently translated to proteins involved in either growth or differentiation responses, such as PgR synthesis.[56]

The tamoxifen-ER complex, unlike the estrogen-ER complex, is unable to signal DNA transcription.[61-66] The tamoxifen-ER complex is incompletely converted to the fully activated form and cannot bind the appropriate coactivators. As a result, the complex is only partially active in initiating the programmed series of events necessary to initiate gene activation. Furthermore, tamoxifen has other actions potentially not mediated through the ER that may contribute to its antitumor effect (e.g., antiangiogenesis, inhibition of calmodulin).[67]

Tamoxifen is an appropriate first-line endocrine therapy for all stages of breast cancer and has been shown to reduce the risk of breast cancer in high-risk populations of women.[3] Tamoxifen is currently approved for the treatment of metastatic breast cancer in postmenopausal women, ER-positive metastatic breast cancer in premenopausal women, chemoprevention, and metastatic breast cancer in men. Tamoxifen is also approved as an adjuvant therapy, either alone or after chemotherapy for early stage, hormone receptor–positive breast cancer in premenopausal and postmenopausal women. More recently, tamoxifen has been approved for treatment of women with ductal carcinoma in situ after breast surgery and radiation.[68] In addition, tamoxifen is indicated to reduce the incidence of breast cancer in women at high risk of breast cancer.[68]

Clinical trials evaluating tamoxifen in postmenopausal women with advanced breast cancer have reported response rates of 15% to 53%, with a median duration of response of 20 months.[69,70] Patient characteristics that predict a response to tamoxifen are similar to those of other endocrine therapies. Tumors expressing ER have up to a 50% probability of responding to tamoxifen as compared with less than 10% in patients with ER-negative tumors. Tamoxifen has been shown to be equally effective in inducing tumor responses as other forms of endocrine therapy; however, tamoxifen was associated with less toxicity compared with older endocrine therapies.[34,70] The few published phase II clinical trials of tamoxifen treatment in premenopausal women with ER-positive metastatic breast cancer report response rates between 20% and 45%, with a median duration of response of 2.5 to 36 months.[69,70] For patients with tumors expressing both ER and PgR, a CBR as high as 75% has been reported.[71] Small, randomized clinical trials comparing tamoxifen with oophorectomy in premenopausal patients with metastatic disease show no statistically significant difference in the overall response rate between the two treatments.[71,72]

### Toxicity of Tamoxifen

The most common adverse effect reported in relation to tamoxifen therapy is vasomotor instability, manifested by hot flashes, facial flushing, tachycardia, and sweating.[73,74] These symptoms are reported in 15% to 20% of premenopausal and postmenopausal patients and typically decrease in intensity and frequency over time. Amenorrhea can occur in as many as 40% of premenopausal women.[75-77] Visual disturbances caused by cataract formation, optic neuritis, retinopathy, or macular edema rarely occur.[78] Thromboembolic events can occur in 1% to 2% of patients treated with tamoxifen.[79] Tamoxifen therapy has been associated with an increased incidence of endometrial carcinoma.[80-82] Several analyses of available data have concluded that the incidence of endometrial carcinoma is modestly increased as a result of receiving tamoxifen (2/1000 tamoxifen-treated women per year versus 1/1000 women per year for the normal female population).[83] This potential toxicity is more relevant to patients receiving tamoxifen as adjuvant therapy or as a chemopreventive agent.

### TOREMIFENE

Toremifene or chlorotamoxifen (Fareston) is approved for the treatment of metastatic breast cancer (see Fig. 166-1). The recommended daily dose is 60 mg administered orally. Toremifene and tamoxifen produce the same estrogen-like effects on the histology of the postmenopausal endometrium. Several phase II trials of toremifene in previously untreated, postmenopausal patients with advanced breast cancer have shown tumor response rates of 21% to 68%.[84] Several randomized trials have compared toremifene with tamoxifen in postmenopausal patients with advanced breast cancer. The largest trial, conducted in patients with ER-positive or unknown tumors, showed similar tumor response rates and median time to disease progression (TTP) in the two treatment arms.[85] The toxicity profile and quality-of-life assessments were also similar in the two treatment arms. Several phase II clinical trials evaluating toremifene in patients with advanced breast cancer, after disease progression with tamoxifen, showed low overall response rates.[86-90] This observation suggests cross-resistance between the two drugs and implies that toremifene is an alternative to tamoxifen as therapy for metastatic breast cancer. Although claims have been made that toremifene may be associated with fewer side effects, particularly in the uterus, compelling laboratory or clinical evidence is lacking.[91]

## SELECTIVE ESTROGEN RECEPTOR DOWNREGULATORS

### FULVESTRANT

Selective estrogen receptor downregulators, unlike mixed agonist/antagonist compounds such as tamoxifen and toremifene, have a different molecular mode of action.[32,33,92-95] Fulvestrant (Faslodex) binds to the ER with affinity similar to that of estrogen, but it causes destabilization of the ER dimer and enhanced ER degradation (see Fig. 166-1). The drug has proved effective against tamoxifen-resistant and tamoxifen-stimulated tumors in vitro and in vivo.[96] Animal experiments also show that fulvestrant causes complete block of endometrial and myometrial proliferation.[97,98] The potential advantages of complete estrogen blockade in patients include more complete and/or longer lasting clinical responses, activity in tumors that have become resistant to tamoxifen therapy, and lack of uterine complications. The potential disadvantages of complete estrogen blockade include exacerbation of menopausal symptoms, reduced bone mineral density, vaginal dryness, and lipid changes. The efficacy and safety of fulvestrant were initially evaluated in a study in which 19 postmenopausal women with tamoxifen-resistant metastatic breast cancer received 250 mg fulvestrant intramuscularly once monthly until tumor progression.[99] Objective responses were observed in 67% of patients who progressed while receiving treatment with tamoxifen, and in 70% of women who relapsed after treatment with adjuvant tamoxifen. Response duration of as long as 33 months was observed in five patients, and no significant adverse events were reported.[99]

Two phase III trials have been published that demonstrate that fulvestrant is at least as effective as the selective aromatase inhibitor anastrozole in postmenopausal women with tamoxifen-resistant advanced breast cancer.[100,101] In the North American trial, 400 postmenopausal women with progressive disease after antiestrogen adjuvant therapy or first-line endocrine therapy for advanced disease were randomized (double-blind design) to monthly fulvestrant (250 mg intramuscularly) or anastrozole (1 mg/day orally).[101] After a median follow-up period of 16.8 months, fulvestrant was at least as effective as anastrozole with respect to TTP, time to treatment failure (TTF), and objective response rate (ORR). Assessments of quality of life, early withdrawal rates, and adverse event rates were similar between the two treatment groups. Injection site reactions, none of which were serious, occurred in approximately 25% of patients in either treatment group.

In the international trial, 451 postmenopausal patients were randomized to receive open-label fulvestrant (250 mg monthly intramuscularly) or anastrozole (1 mg/day orally).[100] After a median follow-up of 14.4 months, fulvestrant was equivalent to anastrozole in terms of TTP, TTF, ORR, and quality of life. The adverse event rate was similar to that in the North American trial, and few patients withdrew because of toxicity. An extended follow-up analysis of the data from these two pivotal trials evaluated the duration of response in those patients attaining an objective response with either anastrozole or fulvestrant. The mean duration of response for fulvestrant was 35% longer than for anastrozole in the North American study[101] and 27% longer in the international study.[100] The combined analysis of both studies revealed that fulvestrant-treated patients had a 30% greater mean duration of response compared with anastrozole-treated patients. These studies demonstrate that fulvestrant is at least as effective and an equally well-tolerated compound as the aromatase inhibitor anastrozole.

More recently, the results of a phase III trial comparing fulvestrant with tamoxifen for the treatment of metastatic breast cancer in postmenopausal women previously untreated with endocrine therapy have been reported.[102] In this double-blind, randomized trial, 587 patients were assigned to either fulvestrant (250 mg intramuscularly monthly) or tamoxifen (20 mg/day). At a median follow-up of 14.5 months, there was no significant difference between fulvestrant and tamoxifen for the primary end point of TTP (median TTP, 6.8 and 8.3 months, respectively). In patients with hormone receptor–positive tumors, fulvestrant had efficacy and tolerability similar to those of tamoxifen.[102] Fulvestrant is currently approved by the U.S. Food and Drug Administration for the treatment of hormone receptor–positive metastatic breast cancer in postmenopausal women with disease progression after antiestrogen therapy.

## AROMATASE INHIBITORS

The aromatase enzyme is the rate-limiting step in the conversion of androgens to estrogens.[103] Aromatase is an enzyme complex containing a cytochrome P-450 hemoprotein and a flavoprotein, nicotinamide-adenine dinucleotide phosphate P-450 reductase.[103] The cytochrome P-450 catalyzes a series of three hydroxylations of the androgen substrates androstenedione and testosterone. Because the aromatase cytochrome

P-450 has little homology to other P-450 enzymes, it has been assigned to a separate gene family designated CYP19.

The major substrates for the aromatase enzyme are androstenedione and testosterone, both produced principally in the adrenal glands and to a lesser degree in the ovaries.[104,105] Aromatase expression has also been demonstrated in the stromal compartment of some human breast tumors.[106–108] This finding suggests that some breast tumors may have an innate ability to synthesize estrogen, thereby stimulating growth locally.[109] Whether this finding is clinically relevant remains unknown. The aromatase enzyme selectively catalyzes only the production of estrogens, whereas other similar enzymes govern the production of other steroid hormones, including glucocorticoids, androgens, and mineralocorticoids. The optimal way to decrease estrogen production is to *selectively* target the aromatase enzyme without inhibiting the activity of the other enzyme systems.

In premenopausal women, the most important site of aromatase expression is the ovary. Other sites of aromatase enzyme expression include adipose tissue, liver, muscle, placenta, and hair follicles. In the ovaries of premenopausal women, follicle-stimulating hormone (FSH) stimulates the granulosa cell compartment to synthesize more aromatase, whereas luteinizing hormone (LH) stimulates the theca cell compartment to synthesize androstenedione, the substrate for aromatase.[110] In premenopausal women, inhibition of ovarian aromatase is incomplete because decreased estradiol synthesis signals the pituitary to increase FSH and LH secretion. The reflex increase in gonadotropins overcomes the inhibition of aromatase enzyme in the ovary.[111,112] As a result, strategies to reduce estrogen synthesis by affecting the aromatase enzyme system are more successful in postmenopausal women, in whom the primary source of estrogen production is the extraovarian conversion of adrenal androstenedione to estrone. In postmenopausal women, the ovaries also secrete a small amount of androstenedione, so precise measurement of estradiol will reveal slightly higher levels in women who undergo natural menopause compared with patients who undergo oophorectomy.[113]

Aromatase inhibitors are of two general types: type I, referred to as suicide inhibitors, and type II, or competitive inhibitors.[30,114] Once a suicide inhibitor binds the aromatase enzyme, the sequence of hydroxylations is initiated, but the hydroxylations produce a covalent bond between the enzyme and inhibitor that irreversibly blocks the activity of the enzyme. After exposure to a suicide inhibitor, aromatase enzyme activity can be restored only with new enzyme synthesis.[30,114] Suicide inhibitors include formestane and exemestane. Competitive inhibitors *reversibly* bind to the active enzyme site, and either no enzyme activity is triggered or it has no effect. The inhibitor can dissociate from the binding site to allow renewed competition between the inhibitor and substrate (i.e., androstenedione) for binding to the active binding site. For the effect of a competitive inhibitor to persist, a constant concentration of the inhibitor in excess of the substrate must be present.[30,114] Available competitive inhibitors include aminoglutethimide (nonselective), anastrozole, and letrozole.

As a general rule, aromatase inhibitors are used to treat breast cancer in postmenopausal women. In premenopausal women, the use of aromatase inhibits would result in a compensatory increase in gonadotropins to reverse the block in estrogen biosynthesis in the ovary.[111,112]

### COMPETITIVE AROMATASE INHIBITORS

#### Aminoglutethimide

Aminoglutethimide was the first widely used aromatase inhibitor for the treatment of advanced breast cancer. It causes a medical adrenalectomy by blocking cholesterol side chain cleavage and thereby leading to a decrease in adrenal steroid synthesis. In addition, inhibition of the peripheral aromatase system by aminoglutethimide results in decreased conversion of androstenedione to estrogens (Fig. 166-2).[115] Adrenal synthesis of cortisol is inhibited by the action of aminoglutethimide, which can lead to clinical features of Addison's disease, including skin rash, fatigue, lethargy, ataxia, and orthostatic hypotension.[112,115] As a result, aminoglutethimide was usually administered with a supplemental corticosteroid such as hydrocortisone.

The results of numerous clinical trials involving the combination of aminoglutethimide and replacement steroids show response rates of 20% to 56% in previously untreated patients with advanced breast cancer.[10,112] The median duration of response is 11 to 12 months. Although described as untreated, many of the patients in these early trials had previously received androgens, estrogens, or oophorectomy. Patients with ER-positive tumors had higher response rates (56%) than patients with ER-negative tumors (12%). Additionally, patients with sites of disease predominantly in the skin, soft tissues, and bone were most likely to respond to aminoglutethimide.[34,112] A prospective, randomized clinical trial conducted by the Eastern Cooperative Oncology Group demonstrated response rates of 45% in patients treated with aminoglutethimide versus 27% in patients treated with tamoxifen.[116] Survival in both groups of patients was identical; however, toxicities were more common and severe in patients treated with aminoglutethimide. Although the antitumor effect of aminoglutethimide is equivalent to that of antiestrogens and progestins, its unfavorable toxicity profile

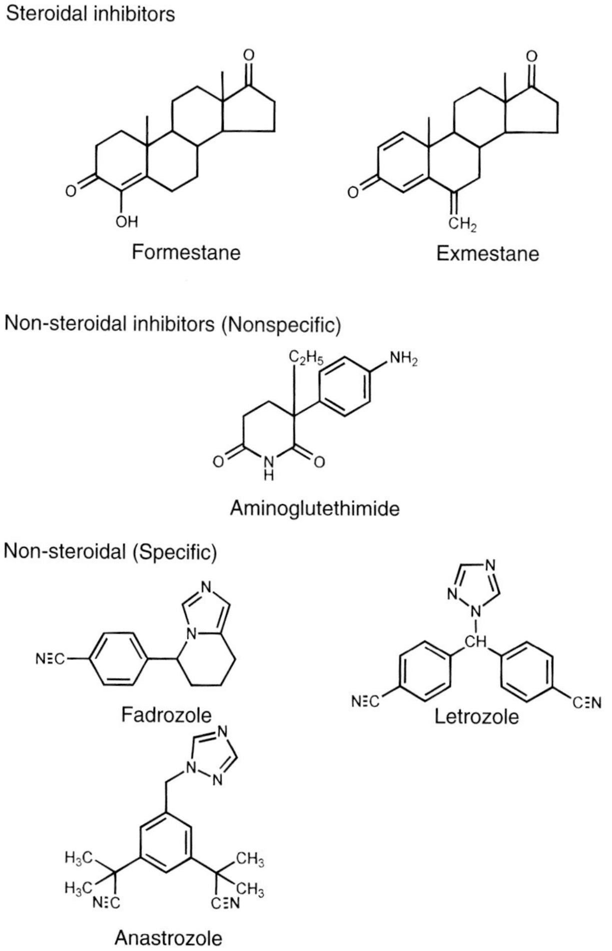

*Figure 166-2* The structure of currently available aromatase inhibitors.

and the development of more selective aromatase inhibitors have relegated it to historical interest.

### Anastrozole/Letrozole

Both anastrozole (Arimidex) and letrozole (Femara) are potent, orally administered, nonsteroidal selective aromatase inhibitors approved as first-line treatment of ER-positive metastatic breast cancer in postmenopausal women (See Fig. 166-2).

In animal studies, anastrozole was selective for the aromatase enzyme while not inhibiting enzymes in the adrenal gland that control other pathways such as mineralocorticoid or glucocorticoid synthesis. For all doses of anastrozole evaluated in phase I studies, the drug was well tolerated and did not affect cortisol or aldosterone secretion at baseline or in response to adrenocorticotropic hormone.[117-120] Consequently, glucocorticoid or mineralocorticoid replacement therapy is not required with anastrozole (or letrozole) treatment.

The results from two mature phase III clinical trials demonstrated that anastrozole is superior to progestins in postmenopausal patients with metastatic breast cancer in whom progressive disease developed after treatment with tamoxifen.[121] Patients who received anastrozole had a statistically significant survival advantage over patients receiving megestrol acetate (22% relative reduction in mortality). Patients receiving anastrozole had a longer median time to death (26.7 months) than did patients receiving megestrol acetate (22.5 months).[121] Although gastrointestinal side effects were more common with anastrozole, it was not associated with the weight gain or dyspnea observed in patients treated with megestrol acetate. The recommended daily dose of anastrozole is 1 mg.

The approval of anastrozole as first-line therapy was based on the results of two randomized, double-blind studies comparing anastrozole with tamoxifen in postmenopausal women with hormone receptor–positive or unknown metastatic breast cancer.[122-124] One trial was conducted outside North America and accrued 668 patients, of whom approximately 45% were known to have ER-positive and/or PgR-positive breast cancer, and 55% had unknown receptor status.[122] With a median follow-up of 19 months, the ORR (33%) and the CBR (56%) were equivalent between the two treatment groups. The TTPs were also equivalent in the two groups (8.2 and 8.3 months, respectively).

The other trial was conducted in North America and accrued 353 patients.[124] Unlike the international trial, 89% of patients in the North American trial were known to have ER-positive and/or PgR-positive tumors, and only 11% had receptor unknown status. Although the objective tumor response rates were equivalent between the two treatment groups, the CBR favored those receiving anastrozole (59.1% versus 45.6%). In addition the TTF was 11.1 months for patients treated with anastrozole and 5.6 months for patients treated with tamoxifen.

Phase I/II clinical trials of letrozole showed that both the 0.5- and 2.5-mg doses of letrozole suppressed circulating levels of estrogen by more than 90%[125] and that both doses were clinically effective.[126] Two randomized phase III clinical trials compared letrozole (0.5 or 2.5 mg/day) with megestrol acetate (160 mg/day). In the first of these trials, 551 patients were randomized to three treatment arms. Patients treated with 2.5 mg/day letrozole attained a 24% overall response rate compared with 16% and 13% in patients treated with 160 mg megestrol acetate or 0.5 mg letrozole, respectively.[127] Patients treated with 2.5 mg/day letrozole also had a longer median duration of response compared with patients treated with 160 mg megestrol acetate (33 months versus 18 months, $P = 0.009$, letrozole versus megestrol acetate, respectively). There was no statistical difference in TTP and overall survival between patients treated with letrozole and megestrol acetate; however, TTP and overall survival were superior for those receiving letrozole 2.5 mg/day compared with those receiving

0.5 mg/day. An identically designed trial involving 602 patients failed to show that letrozole treatment was associated with a superior response rate compared with megestrol acetate or that there was a dose-response rate with letrozole favoring the 2.5-mg/day dose. Instead, patients receiving 0.5 mg/day letrozole had superior TTP and TTF compared with patients receiving megestrol acetate. Similar to the anastrozole trials, letrozole was well tolerated and was associated with less weight gain and dyspnea than reported with megestrol acetate.[127]

In another large trial, 555 postmenopausal women with tamoxifen-resistant advanced breast cancer were randomized to letrozole (0.5 or 2.5 mg/day) or aminoglutethimide (250 mg twice daily).[128] Patients treated with letrozole achieved a higher response rate than did patients treated with aminoglutethimide: 2.5 mg/day letrozole, 19.5%; 0.5 mg/day letrozole, 16.7%; and aminoglutethimide, 12.4%. Patients treated with the higher dose of letrozole attained a small but statistically significant improvement in TTP and overall survival (28 months versus 20 months) when compared with patients treated with aminoglutethimide.[128] The recommended daily dose of letrozole is 2.5 mg.

Fadrozole (see later) (1 mg twice daily) has also been compared with 1 mg/day letrozole in postmenopausal patients with metastatic breast cancer.[129] Of 157 randomized patients, 80% had received previous antiestrogen therapy. The ORR and CBR were superior for patients treated with letrozole (ORR: 31% versus 13%, $P = 0.011$; CBR: 50% versus 35%). The median TTP was 211 days in the letrozole group and 113 days in the fadrozole (no signficance). Adverse events were reported in a similar number of patients in both groups.

The results of a large, randomized clinical trial comparing letrozole with tamoxifen as first-line therapy for postmenopausal patients with metastatic disease has been reported.[130] Previous adjuvant tamoxifen therapy was allowed as long as disease recurrence did not develop while receiving tamoxifen or within 12 months of completing adjuvant tamoxifen therapy. A total of 916 patients were randomized. The TTP and TTF were identical, both showing a statistically significant improvement favoring treatment with letrozole (9.6 months) over tamoxifen (6.1 months). The improvement in TTP was similar whether patients previously received adjuvant tamoxifen or not.

The ORR was also superior for patients receiving letrozole compared with those receiving tamoxifen (30% versus 20%, $P = 0.0006$).[130] In addition, the CBR also favored patients who received letrozole (49% versus 39%). At the time of disease progression, approximately 50% of patients crossed over the other endocrine agent. Although there was not a difference in overall survival rate at a median of 32 months, a survival analysis at 1 and 2 years demonstrated a significant increase in survival rate favoring patients treated with letrozole (1 year: 83% versus 75%, $P = 0.004$; 2 years: 64% versus 58%, $P = 0.02$). There were no differences in toxicity between the two treatment arms, but, interestingly, there were fewer thromboembolic events in patients receiving letrozole (1% versus 2%). The data from this trial strongly support the use of letrozole as first-line therapy of metastatic disease in postmenopausal patients with breast cancer.

The results of a randomized trial comparing letrozole with anastrozole in postmenopausal patients with metastatic breast cancer were recently reported.[131] A total of 713 patients who had progressed on tamoxifen were randomized to letrozole (2.5 mg/day) or anastrozole (1 mg/day). Less than 50% of patients in the trial were known definitively to have ER-positive and/or PgR-positive breast cancer. The primary end point of the study was the TTP. The results presented indicate a modestly higher ORR for letrozole (19.1%) compared with anastrozole (12.3%). There was no difference between the two agents in terms of the CBR, TTP, or overall survival.[131] The data from this trial support the use of either nonsteroidal aromatase inhibitor as second-line therapy after disease progression on tamoxifen.

## SUICIDE INHIBITORS

### Formestane

Formestane (Lentaron), or 4-hydroxyandrostenedione, is a steroidal inhibitor that is approved outside the United States for the treatment of advanced breast cancer in postmenopausal women (see Fig. 166-2). Formestane has poor oral bioavailability and is generally administered as an intramuscular injection.[132] A schedule of 250 mg intramuscularly every 2 weeks inhibits peripheral aromatization by 85% and suppresses estradiol levels by 65%.[133] Several reports indicate that this administration schedule results in tumor ORRs as high as 40% and stable disease status in an additional 14% to 29% of patients.[134-136] Formestane has been compared with tamoxifen as first-line therapy for metastatic disease in postmenopausal patients who have previously received adjuvant therapy.[137] The ORRs were similar for the two agents. Intramuscular administration of the drug can be associated with injection abscesses, and inadvertent intravenous injection has been associated with anaphylactoid reactions.[135] A clinical trial involving 547 patients comparing formestane with megestrol acetate in patients previously treated with tamoxifen demonstrated similar response rates, TTFs, and overall survival benefit between the two treatment arms.[138]

### Exemestane

Exemestane (Aromasin) is a steroidal aromatase inhibitor developed for oral use. After a 25-mg/day oral dose of exemestane, plasma levels of estrone, estradiol, and estrone sulfate were found to be suppressed by 94.5%, 92.2%, and 93.2%, respectively.[139] An ORR of 13% was observed in 91 patients in whom progressive disease developed after treatment with megestrol acetate and tamoxifen.[140] An additional 17% of patients maintained stable disease for longer than 6 months. Patients who had become refractory to 25 mg/day exemestane did not respond to 100 mg/day.[140]

A large international trial comparing exemestane with megestrol acetate in tamoxifen-refractory metastatic disease demonstrated the superiority of exemestane.[141] A total of 769 patients were randomized. The ORR was higher in patients receiving exemestane compared with megestrol acetate (15% versus 12.4%) as was the CBR. These differences were not statistically different between the two treatment groups, but the median TTP (4.7 months versus 3.8 months) and median overall survival (not reached versus 28 months) were statistically superior for patients receiving exemestane. In general, these clinical trials have shown exemestane to be well tolerated. Grade 3 or 4 weight gain was more common in patients receiving megestrol acetate. A large international trial comparing exemestane with tamoxifen as first-line endocrine therapy in postmenopausal women with advanced breast cancer showed a higher objective response rate for patients treated with exemestane compared with tamoxifen (45% vs. 30%). The median progression-free survival (PFS) was 9.95 months for patients treated with exemestane compared with 5.72 months for patients treated with tamoxifen.[141a]

The nonsteroidal and steroidal aromatase inhibitors do not appear to be completely cross-resistant to one another. In a report by Lonning and colleagues,[142] 105 patients previously treated with nonsteroidal aromatase inhibitors, other than aminoglutethimide, received treatment with the steroidal aromatase inhibitor exemestane. An ORR of 5% was observed, but an additional 20% of patients maintained a stable disease status for 6 months or longer. Bertelli and colleagues[143] confirmed that patients treated initially with letrozole or anastrozole had a CBR of 25% with subsequent exemestane treatment. For those patients initially treated with exemestane ($n = 10$), the CBR for subsequent anastrozole or letrozole treatment was 40%. Although these experiences are limited, the data suggest that a small fraction of patients may benefit from the alternative class of aromatase inhibitors at the time of disease progression.

## PROGESTINS

The progestins were a commonly used class of drugs for the treatment of hormone receptor–positive breast cancer; however, with the introduction of the selective aromatase inhibitors and fulvestrant, they are less commonly used today and usually as third- or fourth-line endocrine therapy. Megestrol acetate and medroxyprogesterone acetate are the progestins most widely used to treat advanced breast cancer. Only megestrol acetate has been approved by the U.S. Food and Drug Administration for the treatment of advanced breast cancer in the United States. Selective aromatase inhibitors have replaced the progestins as second-line therapy in metastatic breast cancer after treatment with an anti-estrogen because of evidence that treatment with selective aromatase inhibitors improves survival when compared with treatment with a progestin.[121,127,128,141] In addition, the toxicity profile of newer endocrine agents are superior to the progestins.

Megestrol acetate is an oral active progesterone derivative with better gastrointestinal absorption and bioavailability than is the case with medroxyprogesterone acetate.[144] A standard oral dose of megestrol acetate (160 mg/day) results in blood levels 5 to 10 times higher than those detected after oral medroxyprogesterone (1000 mg/day). Because of its poor oral bioavailability, medroxyprogesterone is generally administered intramuscularly and is used outside the United States.

In unselected postmenopausal women with advanced breast cancer, megestrol acetate has produced objective tumor response rates of approximately 30%, results similar to those of other endocrine therapies.[145,146] A clinical trial comparing the antitumor effect of standard-dose (160 mg/day) with high-dose (800 mg/day) megestrol acetate reported a higher response rate, longer time to relapse, and improved survival in patients treated with the higher dose of megestrol acetate.[147] However, the increased daily dose of megestrol acetate was associated with decreased levels of patient function and increased levels of distress. Almost one half of the patients receiving the higher dose of megestrol acetate gained 20 lb and also had a higher incidence of thromboembolic disease than did patients receiving standard-dose megestrol acetate. Randomized clinical trials comparing megestrol acetate with tamoxifen, amino-glutethimide, or selective aromatase inhibitors report similar antitumor effects[148,149]; however, progestin therapy is often associated with undesired weight gain (18%–50%) and a 4% to 5% risk of thromboembolism.[147,150]

## LUTEINIZING HORMONE-RELEASING HORMONE AGONISTS

Castration was first reported as an effective therapy for metastatic breast cancer more than 100 years ago, at a time when hormones had not been characterized. Several different means of causing ovarian ablation or ovarian suppression have been studied in the interim: surgical oophorectomy, radiation-induced ablation of the ovaries, and, more recently, medical therapy with luteinizing hormone–releasing hormone (LHRH) agonists, such as goserelin acetate (Zoladex).[151]

LHRH is produced by the hypothalamus and stimulates the release of LH and FSH from the anterior pituitary, which in turn stimulates the ovaries to synthesize estrogen and progesterone. Under normal conditions, LHRH is released in a pulsatile manner and results in pulsatile release of LH and FSH.

Continuous administration of an LHRH agonist overstimulates the LHRH receptors and causes an initial increase in LH and FSH. However, after 1 to 2 weeks, desensitization of the LHRH receptors leads to decreased release of FSH and LH.[152] The ovaries respond by decreasing the synthesis of estrogen, and within 4 weeks of starting therapy with an LHRH agonist, circulating estrogen levels are at a postmenopausal level.[152] Unlike the other ways of causing castration, serum estradiol levels return to normal within 4 weeks of discontinuing use of an LHRH agonist.[152]

Goserelin acetate is the only LHRH agonist approved by the U.S. Food and Drug Administration for the treatment of metastatic breast cancer in premenopausal and peri-menopausal women. It is administered as a monthly subcutaneous injectable implant (3.6 mg) that provides continuous release of the drug. Response rates ranging from 28% to 60% have been reported from phase II clinical trials of goserelin acetate in premenopausal women with metastatic breast cancer.[151,153–156] In a randomized trial of premenopausal women with metastatic disease that compared goserelin acetate with surgical oophorectomy, with or without tamoxifen, no significant differences in response rates or survival were detected between treatment arms.[157] A more recent analysis of four randomized clinical trials comparing treatment with an LHRH agonist (goserelin or buserelin) alone with tamoxifen plus an LHRH agonist in premenopausal patients with advanced breast cancer demonstrated improvement in outcome for patients who received combined endocrine therapy.[158] With a median follow-up of 6.8 years, there was a significant survival benefit, progression-free survival benefit, and superior overall response rate in favor of combined treatment. These findings support the use of combined endocrine therapy in premenopausal women with metastatic breast cancer.

The toxicities reported in women receiving goserelin acetate are those consistent with a menopausal state, including hot flashes, loss of libido, vaginal dryness, and decreased bone mineral density. Other LHRH agonists under investigation include buserelin and triptorelin. The role of LHRH agonists as adjuvant therapy for early stage breast cancer, either alone or in addition to chemotherapy and/or other endocrine therapies, is the subject of ongoing clinical trials.

## ADJUVANT ENDOCRINE THERAPY OF BREAST CANCER

### TAMOXIFEN

A meta-analysis of systemic adjuvant therapy for early stage breast cancer (Oxford Overview) confirmed that tamoxifen reduces the odds of breast cancer recurrence by 25% and the risk of death from breast cancer by 16% when compared with patients not treated with tamoxifen.[21] The benefit produced by tamoxifen was more significant in postmenopausal women, in whom the annual odds of breast cancer recurrence and death were reduced by 29% and 20%, respectively.[21] The relative benefit of tamoxifen was the same whether patients were axillary node positive or node negative, but the absolute benefit was of greater magnitude in patients with the greatest risk of recurrence (i.e., axillary node positive).[21] The magnitude of benefit derived from adjuvant tamoxifen therapy also depended on whether a tumor was ER positive or ER negative. The annual odds of recurrence were reduced by 13% in patients with ER-poor tumors and by 32% in patients with ER-positive tumors. Similarly, the reduction in the annual odds of death was 11% and 21% in patients with ER-poor and ER-positive tumors, respectively. In postmenopausal women with ER-positive tumors, tamoxifen reduced the annual odds of recurrence and death by 36% and 23%, respectively, when compared with patients with ER-negative tumors, in whom the annual odds of recurrence and death were reduced by only 16%. ER-positive patients younger than 50 years who are treated with adjuvant tamoxifen have a significant reduction in the odds of death that is comparable with that in patients older than 50 years who are treated with adjuvant tamoxifen and similar to the reduction in the annual odds of death detected in patients younger than 50 who are treated with adjuvant chemotherapy.[21]

It is important to point out that the Oxford Overview analysis of breast cancer adjuvant clinical trials[21] confirmed several principles defined in the laboratory[56,159,160]: (1) tamoxifen blocks estrogen binding to the ER, so a patient with an ER-positive tumor is more likely to respond; (2) long-term early treatment in animal models produces a more complete antitumor effect than does short-term treatment, so long-term adjuvant therapy should be superior to short-term adjuvant therapy; and (3) tamoxifen prevents rat mammary carcinogenesis, so the drug should reduce the incidence of primary breast cancer. It is well established that tamoxifen is effective in premenopausal and postmenopausal women, 5 years of adjuvant treatment is superior to 1 or 2 years of treatment, and 5 years of adjuvant treatment reduces the incidence of contralateral breast cancer by 47%.[21]

The concerns regarding the side effects related to tamoxifen therapy (described previously), disease recurrence in some patients even after 5 years of tamoxifen therapy, and the emerging data related to the activity of new aromatase inhibitors as treatment for metastatic disease came together to provide a rationale to evaluate strategies of incorporating the aromatase inhibitors into the adjuvant therapy of early stage breast cancer.

### Duration of Tamoxifen

The optimal duration of tamoxifen therapy in the adjuvant setting has been addressed by several clinical trials and considered in the Oxford Overview analysis.[21,69,161] The Oxford Overview analysis stratified patients according to tamoxifen therapy administered for less than 2, 2, and more than 2 years. Although the Oxford Overview analysis does not answer the question regarding the optimal duration of tamoxifen treatments, the greatest reduction in the risk of recurrence and death was seen in patients treated with tamoxifen for longer than 2 years.[21] It is now clear that 5 years of therapy is superior to shorter durations of therapy in terms of reducing the risk of recurrence and death. It is also true for the reduction in incidence of contralateral breast cancer.

The benefit of tamoxifen therapy for longer than 5 years has been addressed in three studies comparing 5 years of tamoxifen therapy with 10 years or indefinite therapy.[161] The results of these trials do not show additional clinical benefit from adjuvant tamoxifen treatment longer than 5 years.[161] In addition, preclinical experiments suggest that prolonged tamoxifen therapy may actually produce an agonist effect in breast cancer cells.[162]

An important observation bearing on the duration of treatment is the fact that patients who stop taking tamoxifen at 5 years continue to accrue survival benefit. Two international trials, the Adjuvant Tamoxifen Treatment Offer More (aTTom) and Adjuvant Tamoxifen Longer Against Shorter (ATLAS), are evaluating the impact of duration of adjuvant tamoxifen therapy beyond 5 years.[163] These trials may become less important as the standard of care evolves to incorporate the aromatase inhibitors into adjuvant therapy, either instead of tamoxifen or sequenced with tamoxifen (see later). Only additional clinical trials of longer duration can address this issue, but decades of patient follow-up will be necessary before sufficient data are available.

Holli,[164] on behalf of the Finnish Breast Cancer Group, reported the results of a clinical trial comparing tamoxifen with toremifene in the adjuvant setting. A total of 1480 postmenopausal patients were accrued to the trial, in which patients received either tamoxifen (20 mg/day for 3 years) or toremifene (40 mg/day for 3 years). The side effect profiles were similar in both treatment groups, and with a median follow-up of 4.4 years, toremifene was determined not to be inferior to tamoxifen in terms of reducing the risk of disease recurrence.[164] Recently, the International Breast Cancer Study Group reported on more than 1000 postmenopausal patients randomized to tamoxifen or toremifene. The analysis confirmed that toremifene is a safe and valid alternative to tamoxifen in patients with early stage breast cancer.[165] It is possible that toremifene has fewer estrogenic effects than tamoxifen, as evidenced by the trend toward fewer thromboembolic events and bone fractures in patients receiving toremifene.

### AROMATASE INHIBITORS AS FIRST-LINE ADJUVANT THERAPY

Based on multiple large clinical trials demonstrating the superiority of aromatase inhibitors over tamoxifen in the advanced disease setting, both anastrozole and letrozole were approved as first-line therapy for metastatic disease. Small, underpowered pilot studies with aminoglutethimide in the adjuvant setting were started more that 20 years ago.[166] Although the number of patients in these studies was small, these reports suggested reductions in the number of relapses and deaths. The ATAC (Arimidex and Tamoxifen Alone or in Combination) trial was the first large randomized trial to compare a third-generation aromatase inhibitor with tamoxifen and to evaluate the utility of the two drugs in combination.[167] The ATAC trial accrued 9366 postmenopausal women with hormone receptor–positive or unknown disease. The primary end points of the study were disease-free survival (DFS) and safety/tolerability with secondary end points of overall survival, distant recurrence, and secondary nonbreast primaries. In the latest update of the data from this trial, with a median follow-up of 47 months, there was a significant reduction in the risk of first event (recurrence, contralateral breast cancer, death).[168] The 3-year DFS was 85% in the tamoxifen arm compared and 87% in the anastrozole arm ($P = 0.03$) In addition, there was a 44% proportional reduction in the risk of contralateral breast cancer in the anastrozole group. To date, there is no difference in overall survival between the groups. The patients treated with anastrozole had an increased risk of bone fractures and a higher incidence of musculoskeletal complaints but demonstrated a decreased incidence of cardiovascular events, endometrial cancer, and vaginal bleeding. Based on these findings, the U.S. Food and Drug Administration granted accelerated approval for use of anastrozole as adjuvant therapy in 2002.

Although the ATAC trial provided data regarding the efficacy and tolerability of aromatase inhibitor therapy, there remained questions about whether the data were sufficiently compelling to justify the routine use of anastrozole as first-line therapy in the adjuvant setting. In 2002, the American Society of Clinical Oncology Health Services Research Committee convened an expert panel to conduct a technology assessment on the adjuvant use of aromatase inhibitors. The recommendations were initially published in 2002[169] and updated in 2003.[170] The panel concluded that 5 years of tamoxifen remains the gold standard for the adjuvant treatment of hormone-responsive breast cancer. The American Society of Clinical Oncology panel did find the data reported in the ATAC trial to be promising but insufficient to change standard practice. They recommended that anastrozole be considered in postmenopausal women with an absolute or relative contraindication to tamoxifen. These recommendations were based on a number of considerations, most importantly, the short duration of follow-up in most women. At the time of the updated analysis, 3000 women had been observed for more than 4 years, but fewer than 400 had been followed for more than 5 years, which is the duration of tamoxifen associated with the most benefit. In addition, although statistically significant, the difference seen in DFS was small. At the time of the analysis, there were very few total events with only an absolute difference of 59 events between the anastrozole and tamoxifen groups. This corresponds with an absolute difference in DFS of 2%. Although formal survival analysis will not be performed until there is a predetermined number of events, the preliminary data do not demonstrate an overall survival benefit in the patients receiving anastrozole.

Uncertainty also remains regarding the potential long-term toxicity associated with anastrozole in an otherwise well patient population. Tamoxifen has a well-established short- and long-term toxicity profile based on data gathered over 3 decades. There are longer follow-up data available in the metastatic setting with aromatase inhibitors, but these data are based on significantly shorter treatment durations. Although aromatase inhibitors appear to have decreased short-term side effects compared with tamoxifen, the long-term toxicity is unknown. The acute toxicities that have been documented, predominantly musculoskeletal complaints and bone fractures, may be compounded as treatment duration increases. Because of the profound estrogen depression seen with this class of drugs, other long-term effects may yet emerge including an effect on cognitive dysfunction.

### SEQUENTIAL ADJUVANT TAMOXIFEN AND AROMATASE INHIBITOR THERAPY

The ATAC trial provided supporting evidence for the incorporation of anastrozole into the adjuvant treatment of breast cancer. The ATAC trial also investigated the concurrent use of anastrozole and tamoxifen and found the combination to be no better than tamoxifen alone.[167,168]

A small study evaluated the strategy of switching patients from tamoxifen to the older aromatase inhibitor aminoglutethimide.[171] A total of 380 postmenopausal women who had received tamoxifen for 3 years were randomized to continuing tamoxifen for 2 more years or to discontinuing tamoxifen and switching to aminoglutethimide to complete 5 years of therapy. At a median follow-up of 61 months, there was no difference between the two groups in terms of DFS, but there did appear to be a benefit in terms of overall survival and breast cancer–specific survival in the patients treated with aminoglutethimide.

A subsequent trial led by the same group of investigators evaluated the same question but used anastrozole rather than aminoglutethimide.[172] In this trial, 448 patients who had received tamoxifen for more than 2 years were randomized to continue tamoxifen for a total of 5 years or to switch to anastrozole for the same period. At a median follow-up of 36 months, there was a statistically significant improvement in event-free survival and progression-free survival for the patients who received the sequence of tamoxifen followed by anastrozole. There was a trend toward an improved overall survival that was not statistically significant. These data are not sufficiently mature to justify switching the majority of tamoxifen-treated patients to a nonsteroidal aromatase inhibitor before completing 5 years of tamoxifen.

Another recent trial reported on the strategy of switching patients from tamoxifen to the steroidal aromatase inhibitor exemestane.[173] In this trial, 2362 postmenopausal women receiving tamoxifen as adjuvant therapy were randomly assigned to switching to exemestane after 2 or 3 years of tamoxifen or continuing tamoxifen for 5 years. With a median survival of 30.6 months, there was a 32% risk reduction in first events (recurrence, contralateral breast cancer, death) in the exemestane group. This corresponded with an absolute benefit in DFS of 4.7%. There was no statistically significant difference in overall survival between the groups.[173]

Although more than 5 years of tamoxifen therapy has not conferred an improvement in clinical outcome compared with 5 years of therapy, the addition of an aromatase inhibitor after 5 years of tamoxifen therapy has been proposed as a way of exploiting the benefits of both agents.[174] The NCI MA17 trial investigated the effectiveness of adding 5 years of letrozole therapy in postmenopausal women who had completed 5 years of tamoxifen compared with 5 years of tamoxifen alone.[174] The primary end point of the study was DFS. A total of 5187 patients who had discontinued tamoxifen less than 3 months before enrollment were randomized. At the first analysis, with a median follow-up of 2.4 years, the 4-year DFS was 93% in the letrozole group and 87% in the placebo group.[174] This difference was statistically significant ($P < 0.001$), and the study was terminated according to stopping rules that had been incorporated into the study. An analysis of adverse events revealed that arthralgias were more common in the letrozole group and there was a trend toward increased osteoporosis. The letrozole-treated patients had a decreased risk of vaginal bleeding and a significant decrease in contralateral breast cancers. In an unplanned subset analysis, there appeared to be benefit in both node-negative and node-positive women with a hazard ratio for recurrence of 0.47 in the node-negative group and 0.60 in the node-positive group.

Because the MA17 study was terminated early, several important questions remain unanswered. Although the study demonstrated an improvement in DFS in the letrozole group, there was not a corresponding improvement in overall survival.[174] The survival curves may have separated at a later time point in follow-up, but because of the study termination and inevitable crossover, interpretable survival data may never be available. Furthermore, at the time of study termination, none of the patients had completed the planned 5 years of letrozole, leaving the question of optimal therapy duration unanswered. In addition, there remains uncertainty about long-term toxicity, with particular concern regarding loss of bone density and implications about future risk of fractures. Because of these uncertainties, longer follow-up of this data set will be necessary before the benefits and risks of sequential therapy can fully be appreciated. A plan is in place to randomize patients receiving letrozole for 5 years to no further therapy or 5 additional years of letrozole. This study will address the efficacy and toxicity of very long durations of adjuvant therapy with an aromatase inhibitor.

### THE OPTIMAL SEQUENCE OF AVAILABLE ENDOCRINE AGENTS

The increasing number of endocrine agents available for the treatment of advanced breast cancer has led to the question of whether endocrine agents should be used in a particular sequence for optimal patient benefit. Further complicating this issue is the emerging evidence that the aromatase inhibitors are now becoming more widely used as adjuvant endocrine therapy for patients with early stage breast cancer. The old paradigm held that tamoxifen was not only the optimal adjuvant endocrine agent, but the only endocrine agent that should be used for treatment of early stage breast cancer. Recent, large, randomized clinical trials in early stage breast cancer have shown that aromatase inhibitors reduce the risk of disease recurrence compared with tamoxifen or that the sequential use of an aromatase inhibitor following tamoxifen is superior to tamoxifen alone.[167,168,172–174] The implication of these data in the near future is that at the time of disease recurrence, many patients will have already been exposed to two of the most active endocrine agents available for the treatment of advanced breast cancer. The clinical dilemma will then be to select among the available agents for the first treatment of metastatic disease.

For those patients previously treated with both tamoxifen and a nonsteroidal aromatase inhibitor, there are limited data on the efficacy of subsequent endocrine therapy. Lonning and colleagues[142] and Carlini and colleagues[175] reported a CBR of 24% (n = 241) and 43% (n = 21), respectively, for exemestane treatment after both tamoxifen and a nonsteroidal aromatase inhibitor. Perey and colleagues[176] reported on the experience with fulvestrant after treatment with both tamoxifen and a nonsteroidal aromatase inhibitor. In this small phase II experience, 11 of 32 patients (34%) attained clinical benefit. As more data emerge supporting the use of aromatase inhibitors in the adjuvant setting, these trials and others that are under way should help define the optimal treatment strategy for those patients who subsequently develop disease progression.

## CONCLUSIONS

The development of endocrine therapy for the treatment and prevention of breast cancer has evolved dramatically over the past 100 years. Most patients with an established diagnosis of breast cancer will receive some form of endocrine therapy during the clinical course of their disease. Table 166-1 presents an algorithm for the use of endocrine agents in patients with metastatic breast cancer, assuming initial treatment with either an antiestrogen or an aromatase inhibitor.

The advances made in the treatment of breast cancer have been based on a greater understanding of the biology of the disease. Going forward, endocrine therapy holds the promise of greater impact on improving efficacy in patients with advanced disease, reducing the risk of recurrence in patients with early stage breast cancer, and preventing the development of breast cancer in women at risk of developing the disease.

**Table 166-1** Sequential Endocrine Therapy

| | Premenopausal | Postmenopausal |
|---|---|---|
| First-line | Tamoxifen or ovarian ablation or combination | Tamoxifen or aromatase inhibitor or fulvestrant |
| Second-line | Aromatase inhibitor (must be postmenopausal or continue luteinizing hormone–releasing hormone agonist) | Aromatase inhibitors or fulvestrant |
| Third-line | Fulvestrant or aromatase inhibitor | Progestins, androgens, or high-dose estrogen |
| Fourth-line | Progestins, androgens, or high-dose estrogen | Recycle |
| Fifth-line | Recycle | |

## REFERENCES

1. Jemal A, Tiwari RC, Murray T, et al: Cancer statistics, 2004. CA Cancer J Clin 54:8–29, 2004.
2. Hudis CA: Current status and future directions in breast cancer therapy. Clin Breast Cancer 4(Suppl 2):S70–S75, 2003.
3. Fisher B, Costantino JP, Wickerham DL, et al: Tamoxifen for prevention of breast cancer: Report of the National Surgical Adjuvant Breast and Bowel Project P-1 Study. J Natl Cancer Inst 90:1371–1388, 1998.
4. Beatson G: On the treatment of inoperable cases of carcinoma of the mammary. Suggestions for a new method of treatment, with illustrative cases. Lancet 2:104–107, 162–165, 1896.
5. Boyd S: An oophorectomy in cancer of the breast. Br Med J 2:1161–1167, 1900.
6. DeCourmellers F: La radiotherapie indirecte, ou dirigée par les correlations organiques. Arch Elect Med 32:264, 1922.
7. Block G: Estrogen excretion following operative and irradiation castration in cases of mammary cancer. Surgery 43:415–422, 1958.
8. Santen RJ, Worgul TJ, Samojlik E, et al: A randomized trial comparing surgical adrenalectomy with aminoglutethimide plus hydrocortisone in women with advanced breast cancer. N Engl J Med 305:545–551, 1981.
9. Huggins C, Dao T: Adrenalectomy and oophorectomy in the treatment of advanced carcinoma of the breast. JAMA 151:1388–1394, 1953.
10. Santen RJ, Worgul TJ, Samojlik E, et al: A randomized trial comparing surgical adrenalectomy with aminoglutethimide plus hydrocortisone in women with advanced breast cancer. N Engl J Med 305:545–551, 1981.
11. Haddow A: Stilbesterol for advanced breast cancer. Br Med J 2:393–398, 1944.
12. Jensen E, Jacobson H: Basic guides to the mechanism of estrogen action. Recent Prog Horm Res 18:387–414, 1962.
13. Toft D, Shyamala G, Gorski J: A receptor molecule for estrogens: Studies using a cell free system. Proc Natl Acad Sci U S A 57:1740–1743, 1967.
14. Jensen E, Block G, Smith S, et al: Estrogen receptors and breast cancer response to adrenalectomy. Natl Cancer Inst Monogr 34:55–70, 1971.
15. McGuire W, Carbone P, Vollmer E: Estrogen Receptors in Breast Cancer. New York, Raven, 1975.
16. Horwitz K, McGuire K: Specific progesterone receptors in human breast cancer. Steroids 25:497–505, 1975.
17. McGuire WL, Chamness GC, Fuqua SA: Estrogen receptor variants in clinical breast cancer. Mol Endocrinol 5:1571–1577, 1991.
18. Witliff J: Steroid-hormone receptors in breast cancer. Cancer 53:630–643, 1984.
19. Allegra J: Role of hormone receptors in determining treatment of breast cancer. In The Management of Breast Cancer through Endocrine Therapies. Amsterdam, Excerpta Medica, 1984, pp 1–13.
20. Goldhirsch A, Wood WC, Gelber RD, et al: Meeting highlights: Updated international expert consensus on the primary therapy of early breast cancer. J Clin Oncol 21:3357–3365, 2003.
21. Early Breast Cancer Trialists' Group: Tamoxifen for early breast cancer: An overview of the randomised trials. Early Breast Cancer Trialists' Collaborative Group. Lancet 351:1451–1467, 1998.
22. Lerner L: The first non-steroidal antioestrogen-MER-25. In Sutherland R, Jordan VC (eds): Non-steroidal Antioestrogens: Molecular Pharmacology and Antitumour Activity. Sydney, Academic, 1981, pp 1–16.
23. Harper M, Walpole A: Contrasting endocrine activities of cis and trans isomers in a series of substituted triphenylethylenes. Nature 212:87, 1966.
24. Harper M, Walpole A: A new derivative of triphenylethylene: Effect on implantation and mode of action in rats. J Reprod Fertil 13:101–119, 1967.
25. Bedford G, Richardson D: Preparation and identification of cis and trans isomers of a substituted triarylethylene. Nature 212:733–734, 1966.
26. Williamson J, Ellis J: The induction of ovulation by tamoxifen. J Obstet Gynaecol Br Commonw 80:844–847, 1973.
27. Ward H: Antioestrogen therapy for breast cancer: A trial of tamoxifen at two dose levels. Br Med J 1:13–14, 1973.
28. Cole M, Jones C, Todd I: The treatment of advanced carcinoma of the breast with the antineoplastic agent tamoxifen (ICI 46,474)-a series of 96 patients. Adv Antimicrob Antineoplast Chemother 2:529–531, 1972.
29. Cole M, Jones C, Todd I: A new antioestrogenic agent late in breast cancer: An early clinical appraisal of ICI 46,474. Br J Cancer 25:270–275, 1971.
30. Johnston SR, Dowsett M: Aromatase inhibitors for breast cancer: Lesions from the laboratory. Nat Rev Cancer 3:821–831, 2003.
31. Buzdar AU: Aromatase inhibitors in breast cancer therapy. Clin Breast Cancer 4(Suppl 2):S84–S88, 2003.
32. Cheung KL, Robertson JF: Fulvestrant. Expert Opin Investig Drugs 11:303–308, 2002.
33. Osborne CK, Wakeling A, Nicholson RI: Fulvestrant: An oestrogen receptor antagonist with a novel mechanism of action. Br J Cancer 90(Suppl 1):S2–S6, 2004.

34. Gradishar WJ, Jordan VC: Endocrine Therapy of Breast Cancer. In Bland KI, Copeland EM (eds): The Breast: Comprehensive Management of Benign and Malignant Disease, 3d ed, vol 2. Philadelphia, Saunders/Elsevier Science, 2004, pp 1367–1394.

35. Rozencweig M, Heuson J: Breast cancer: Prognostic factors and clinical evaluation. In Staquet M (ed): Cancer Therapy: Prognostic Factors and Criteria of Response. New York, Raven, 1975.

36. Iveson TJ, Ahern J, Smith IE: Response to third-line endocrine treatment for advanced breast cancer. Eur J Cancer 4:572–574, 1993.

37. Rose C, Mouridsen H: Preferred sequence of endocrine therapies in advanced breast cancer. In Santen R, Juhos E (eds): Endocrine-Dependent Breast Cancer: Critical Assessment of Recent Advances. Bern, Switzerland, Hans Huber, 1988, p 81.

38. Wilson A: Response in breast cancer to a second-line therapy. Rev Endocr Relat Cancer 14:5–11, 1983.

39. Ingle JN: Sequencing of endocrine therapy in postmenopausal women with advanced breast cancer. Clin Cancer Res 10:362S–367S, 2004.

40. Carlson RW: Sequencing of endocrine therapies in breast cancer-integration of recent data. Breast Cancer Res Treat 75(Suppl 1):S27–S35, 2002.

41. Kuukasjarvi T, Kononen J, Helin H, et al: Loss of estrogen receptor in recurrent breast cancer is associated with poor response to endocrine therapy. J Clin Oncol 14:2584–2589, 1996.

42. Spataro V, Price K, Goldhirsch A, et al: Sequential estrogen receptor determinations from primary breast cancer and at relapse: Prognostic and therapeutic relevance. The International Breast Cancer Study Group (formerly Ludwig Group). Ann Oncol 3:733–740, 1992.

43. Spataro V, Goldhirsch A: Breast cancer: Relevance of estrogen receptor determination at relapse. J Clin Oncol 15:862, 1997.

44. Cech P, Block JB, Cone LA, Stone R: Tumor lysis syndrome after tamoxifen flare. N Engl J Med 315:263–264, 1986.

45. Clarysse A: Hormone-induced tumor flare. Eur J Cancer Clin Oncol 21:545–547, 1985.

46. Vogel CL, Schoenfelder J, Shemano I, et al: Worsening bone scan in the evaluation of antitumor response during hormonal therapy of breast cancer. J Clin Oncol 13:1123–1128, 1995.

47. Greenwald ES: Megestrol acetate flare. Cancer Treat Rep 67:405, 1983.

48. Otteman LA, Long HJ: Hypercalcemic flare with megestrol acetate. Cancer Treat Rep 68:1420–1421, 1984.

49. Plotkin D, Lechner JJ, Jung WE, Rosen PJ: Tamoxifen flare in advanced breast cancer. JAMA 240:2644–2646, 1978.

50. Wiebe VJ, Osborne CK, Fuqua SA, DeGregorio MW: Tamoxifen resistance in breast cancer. Crit Rev Oncol Hematol 14:173–188, 1993.

51. Bhide SA, Rea DW: Metastatic breast cancer response after exemestane withdrawal: a case report. Breast 13:66–68, 2004.

52. Sipila PE, Wiebe VJ, Hubbard GB, et al: Prolonged tamoxifen exposure selects a breast cancer cell clone that is stable in vitro and in vivo. Eur J Cancer 15:2138–2144, 1993.

53. Ellis MJ, Hayes DF: Improving hormonal therapy for breast cancer. Breast 3(Suppl):57–68, 1997.

54. Miller WR: Fundamental research leading to improved endocrine therapy for breast cancer. J Steroid Biochem 27:477–485, 1987.

55. Miller WR: Aromatase inhibitors and breast cancer. Cancer Treat Rev 23:171–187, 1997.

56. Jordan VC, Gradishar WJ: Molecular mechanisms and future uses of antiestrogens. Mol Aspects Med 18:167–247, 1997.

57. Green S, Chambon P: The oestrogen receptor from perception to mechanism. In Parker M (ed): Nuclear Hormone Receptors. New York, Academic, 1991, pp 15–38.

58. Wolf D, Fuqua S: Mechanisms of action of antiestrogens. Cancer Treat Rev 21:247–271, 1995.

59. Jordan V, Koerner S: Tamoxifen (ICI 46 474) and the human carcinoma 8S estrogen receptor. Eur J Cancer 11:205–206, 1975.

60. Jordan V, Dowse L: Tamoxifen as an antitumor agent: Effect on oestrogen binding. J Endocrinol 68:297–303, 1976.

61. Tate A, Greene G, Desombre E, et al: Differences between estrogen and antiestrogen-estrogen receptor complexes identified with an antibody raised against the estrogen receptor. Cancer Res 44:1012–1018, 1984.

62. Martin P, Berthoise Y, Jensen E: Binding of antiestrogen exposes an occult antigenic determinant in the human estrogen receptor. Proc Natl Acad Sci U S A 85:2533–2537, 1988.

63. Pham T, Elliston J, Nawaz Z, et al: Antiestrogens can establish nonproductive receptor complexes and alter chromatin structure at target enhancers. Proc Natl Acad Sci U S A 88:2135–3129, 1991.

64. Tzukerman M, Esty A, Santiwso-Mere D, et al: Human estrogen receptor transactivational capacity is determined by both cellular and promoter context and mediated by two functionally distinct intramolecular regions. Mol Endocrinol 8:21–30, 1994.

65. McDonnell D, Clemm D, Hermann T, et al: Analysis of estrogen receptor function reveals three distinct classes of antiestrogens. Mol Endocrinol 9:659–669, 1995.

66. Allan G, Leng X, Tsai S, et al: Hormone and antihormone induce distinct conformational changes which are central to steroid receptor activation. J Biol Chem 267:19513–19520, 1992.

67. Colletta A, Benson J, Baum M: Alternative mechanisms of action of antiestrogens. Breast Cancer Res Treat 31:5–9, 1994.

68. Clemons M, Danson S, Howell A: Tamoxifen ("Nolvadex"): A review. Cancer Treat Rev 28:165–180, 2002.

69. Osborne CK: Tamoxifen in the treatment of breast cancer. N Engl J Med 339:1609–1618, 1998.

70. Jaiyesimi IA, Buzdar AU, Decker DA, Hortobagyi GN: Use of tamoxifen for breast cancer: Twenty-eight years later. J Clin Oncol 13:513–529, 1995.

71. Buchanan RB, Blamey RW, Durrant KR, et al: A randomized comparison of tamoxifen with surgical oophorectomy in premenopausal patients with advanced breast cancer. J Clin Oncol 4:1326–1330, 1986.

72. Ingle JN, Krook JE, Green SJ, et al: Randomized trial of bilateral oophorectomy versus tamoxifen in premenopausal women with metastatic breast cancer. J Clin Oncol 4:178–185, 1986.

73. Fisher B, Costantino J, Redmond C, et al: A randomized clinical trial evaluating tamoxifen in the treatment of patients with node-negative breast cancer who have estrogen-receptor-positive tumors. N Engl J Med 320:479–484, 1989.

74. Cummings FJ, Gray R, Davis TE, et al: Adjuvant tamoxifen treatment of elderly women with stage II breast cancer. A double-blind comparison with placebo. Ann Intern Med 103:324–329, 1985.

75. Manni A, Pearson OH: Antiestrogen-induced remissions in premenopausal women with stage IV breast cancer: Effects on ovarian function. Cancer Treat Rep 64:779–785, 1980.

76. Margreiter R, Wiegele J: Tamoxifen (Nolvadex) for premenopausal patients with advanced breast cancer. Breast Cancer Res Treat 4:45–48, 1984.

77. Planting AS, Alexieva-Figusch J, Blonk-v.d.Wijst J, van Putten WL: Tamoxifen therapy in premenopausal women with metastatic breast cancer. Cancer Treat Rep 69:363–368, 1985.

78. Nayfield SG, Gorin MB: Tamoxifen-associated eye disease. A review. J Clin Oncol 14:1018–1026, 1996.

79. Meier CR, Jick H: Tamoxifen and risk of idiopathic venous thromboembolism. Br J Clin Pharmacol 45:608–612, 1998.

80. Assikis VJ, Jordan VC: Tamoxifen and endometrial cancer: From experiment to patient. Recent Results Cancer Res 140:61–71, 1996.

81. Fisher B, Costantino JP, Redmond CK, et al: Endometrial cancer in tamoxifen-treated breast cancer patients: Findings from the National Surgical Adjuvant Breast and Bowel Project (NSABP) B-14. J Natl Cancer Inst 86:527–537, 1994.

82. Fisher B: Commentary on endometrial cancer deaths in tamoxifen-treated breast cancer patients. J Clin Oncol 14:1027–1039, 1996.

83. Jordan VC, Assikis VJ: Endometrial carcinoma and tamoxifen: Clearing up a controversy. Clin Cancer Res 1:467–472, 1995.

84. Vogel CL: Phase II and III clinical trials of toremifene for metastatic breast cancer. Oncology (Huntingt) 12:9–13, 1998.

85. Hayes DF, Van Zyl JA, Hacking A, et al: Randomized comparison of tamoxifen and two separate doses of toremifene in postmenopausal patients with metastatic breast cancer. J Clin Oncol 13:2556–2566, 1995.

86. Ebbs SR, Roberts J, Baum M: Response to toremifene (Fc-1157a) therapy in tamoxifen failed patients with breast cancer. Preliminary communication. J Steroid Biochem 36:239, 1990.

87. Hindy I, Juhos E, Szanto J, Szamel I: Effect of toremifene in breast cancer patients. Preliminary communication. J Steroid Biochem 36:225–226, 1990.

88. Jonsson PE, Malmberg M, Bergljung L, et al: Phase II study of high dose toremifene in advanced breast cancer progressing during tamoxifen treatment. Anticancer Res 11:873–875, 1991.

89. Pyrhonen S, Valavaara R, Vuorinen J, Hajba A: High dose toremifene in advanced breast cancer resistant to or relapsed during tamoxifen treatment. Breast Cancer Res Treat 29:223–228, 1994.

90. Vogel CL, Shemano I, Schoenfelder J, et al: Multicenter phase II efficacy trial of toremifene in tamoxifen-refractory patients with advanced breast cancer. J Clin Oncol 11:345–350, 1993.

91. Tomas E, Kauppila A, Blanco G, et al: Comparison between the effects of tamoxifen and toremifene on the uterus in postmenopausal breast cancer patients. Gynecol Oncol 59:261–266, 1995.

92. Gibson MK, Nemmers LA, Beckman WC Jr, et al: The mechanism of ICI 164,384 antiestrogenicity involves rapid loss of estrogen receptor in uterine tissue. Endocrinology 129:2000–2010, 1991.

93. Wakeling AE, Bowler J: Novel antioestrogens without partial agonist activity. J Steroid Biochem 31:645–653, 1988.

94. Wakeling AE, Dukes M, Bowler J: A potent specific pure antiestrogen with clinical potential. Cancer Res 51:3867–3873, 1991.

95. Dauvois S, Danielian PS, White R, Parker MG: Antiestrogen ICI 164,384 reduces cellular estrogen receptor content by increasing its turnover. Proc Natl Acad Sci U S A 89:4037–4041, 1992.

96. Gottardis MM, Ricchio ME, Satyaswaroop PG, Jordan VC: Effect of steroidal and nonsteroidal antiestrogens on the growth of a tamoxifen-stimulated human endometrial carcinoma (EnCa101) in athymic mice. Cancer Res 50:3189–3192, 1990.

97. Dukes M, Waterton JC, Wakeling AE: Antiuterotrophic effects of the pure antioestrogen ICI 182,780 in adult female monkeys (Macaca nemestrina): Quantitative magnetic resonance imaging. J Endocrinol 138:203–210, 1993.

98. Dukes M, Chester R, Yarwood L, Wakeling AE: Effects of a non-steroidal pure antioestrogen, ZM 189,154, on oestrogen target organs of the rat including bones. J Endocrinol 141:335–341, 1994.

99. Howell A, DeFriend D, Robertson J, et al: Response to a specific antioestrogen (ICI 182780) in tamoxifen-resistant breast cancer. Lancet 345:29–30, 1995.

100. Howell A, Robertson JF, Quaresma Albano J, et al: Fulvestrant, formerly ICI 182,780, is as effective as anastrozole in postmenopausal women with advanced breast cancer progressing after prior endocrine treatment. J Clin Oncol 20:3396–3403, 2002.

101. Osborne CK, Pippen J, Jones SE, et al: Double-blind, randomized trial comparing the efficacy and tolerability of fulvestrant versus anastrozole in postmenopausal women with advanced breast cancer progressing on prior endocrine therapy: Results of a North American trial. J Clin Oncol 20:3386–3395, 2002.

102. Howell A, Robertson JF, Abram P, et al: Comparison of fulvestrant versus tamoxifen for the treatment of advanced breast cancer in postmenopausal women previously untreated with endocrine therapy: A multinational, double-blind, randomized trial. J Clin Oncol 22:1605–1613, 2004.

103. Simpson ER, Merrill JC, Hollub AJ, et al: Regulation of estrogen biosynthesis by human adipose cells. Endocr Rev 10:136–148, 1989.

104. Hemsell D, Grodin G, Breuner P, et al: Plasma precursors of estrogen II: Correlation of the extent of conversion of plasma androstenedione to estrone with age. J Clin Endocrinol Metab 38:476–479, 1974.

105. Grodin J, Sitteri P, MacDonald P: Sources of estrogen production in postmenopausal women. J Clin Endocrinol Metab 36:207–214, 1973.

106. Reed M: The role of aromatase in breast tumors. Breast Cancer Res Treat 30:7–17, 1994.

107. Miller WR, Mullen P, Sourdaine P, et al: Regulation of aromatase activity within the breast. J Steroid Biochem Mol Biol 61:193–202, 1997.

108. Miller WR, Mullen P, Telford J, Dixon JM: Clinical importance of intratumoral aromatase. Breast Cancer Res Treat 49(Suppl):27–37, 1998.

109. Abul H, Iverson R, Kiang D: Aromatization of androgens by human breast cancer. Steroids 33:215–222, 1979.

110. Richards JS, Hickey GJ, Chen SA, et al: Hormonal regulation of estradiol biosynthesis, aromatase activity, and aromatase mRNA in rat ovarian follicles and corpora lutea. Steroids 50:393–409, 1987.

111. Santen RJ: Clinical use of aromatase inhibitors: Current data and future perspectives. J Enzyme Inhib 4:79–99, 1990.

112. Santen RJ, Manni A, Harvey H, Redmond C: Endocrine treatment of breast cancer in women. Endocr Rev 11:221–265, 1990.

113. Samojlik E, Veldhuis JD, Wells SA, Santen RJ: Preservation of androgen secretion during estrogen suppression with aminoglutethimide in the treatment of metastatic breast carcinoma. J Clin Invest 65:602–612, 1980.

114. Brodie A: Aromatase, its inhibitors and their use in breast cancer treatment. Pharmacol Ther 50:537–548, 1993.

115. Santen RJ, Misbin RI: Aminoglutethimide: Review of pharmacology and clinical use. Pharmacotherapy 1:95–120, 1981.

116. Gale KE, Andersen JW, Tormey DC, et al: Hormonal treatment for metastatic breast cancer. An Eastern Cooperative Oncology Group Phase III trial comparing aminoglutethimide to tamoxifen. Cancer 73:354–361, 1994.

117. Dowsett M, Lonning PE: Anastrozole-a new generation in aromatase inhibition: Clinical pharmacology. Oncology 54:11–14, 1997.

118. Geisler J, King N, Dowsett M, et al: Influence of anastrazole (Arimidex), a selective, non-steroidal aromatase inhibitor, on in vivo aromatisation and plasma oestrogen levels in postmenopausal women with breast cancer. Br J Cancer 74:1286–1291, 1996.

119. Hortobagyi GN, Buzdar AU: Anastrozole (Arimidex), a new aromatase inhibitor for advanced breast cancer: Mechanism of action and role in management. Cancer Invest 16:385–390, 1998.

120. Jonat W: Clinical overview of anastrozole-a new selective oral aromatase inhibitor. Oncology 54:15–18, 1997.

121. Buzdar AU, Jonat W, Howell A, et al: Anastrozole versus megestrol acetate in the treatment of postmenopausal women with advanced breast carcinoma: Results of a survival update based on a combined analysis of data from two mature phase III trials. Arimidex Study Group. Cancer 83:1142–1152, 1998.

122. Bonneterre J, Thurlimann B, Robertson JF, et al: Anastrozole versus tamoxifen as first-line therapy for advanced breast cancer in 668 postmenopausal women: Results of the Tamoxifen or Arimidex Randomized Group Efficacy and Tolerability study. J Clin Oncol 18:3748–3757, 2000.

123. Bonneterre J, Buzdar A, Nabholtz JM, et al: Anastrozole is superior to tamoxifen as first-line therapy in hormone receptor positive advanced breast carcinoma. Cancer 92:2247–2258, 2001.

124. Nabholtz JM, Buzdar A, Pollak M, et al: Anastrozole is superior to tamoxifen as first-line therapy for advanced breast cancer in postmenopausal women: Results of a North American multicenter randomized trial. Arimidex Study Group. J Clin Oncol 18:3758–3768, 2000.

125. Dowsett M, Jones A, Johnston SRD, et al: In vivo measurement of aromatase inhibition by letrozole (CGS 20267) in postmenopausal patients with breast cancer. Clin Cancer Res 1:1511–1515, 1995.

126. Ingle JN, Johnson PA, Suman VJ, et al: A randomized phase II trial of two dosage levels of letrozole as third-line hormonal therapy for women with metastatic breast carcinoma. Cancer 80:218–224, 1997.

127. Dombernowsky P, Smith I, Falkson G, et al: Letrozole, a new oral aromatase inhibitor for advanced breast cancer: Double-blind randomized trial showing a dose effect and improved efficacy and tolerability compared with megestrol acetate. J Clin Oncol 16:453–461, 1998.

128. Gershanovich M, Chaudri HA, Campos D, et al: Letrozole, a new oral aromatase inhibitor: Randomised trial comparing 2.5 mg daily, 0.5 mg daily and aminoglutethimide in postmenopausal women with advanced breast cancer. Letrozole International Trial Group (AR/BC3). Ann Oncol 9:639–645, 1998.

129. Tominaga T, Adachi I, Sasaki Y, et al: Double-blind randomised trial comparing the non-steroidal aromatase inhibitors letrozole and fadrozole in postmenopausal women with advanced breast cancer. Ann Oncol 14:62–70, 2003.

130. Mouridsen H, Gereshanovich M, Sun Y, et al: Superior efficacy of letrozole versus tamoxifen as first-line therapy for postmenopausal women with advanced breast cancer: Results of a phase III study of the International Letrozole Breast Cancer Group. J Clin Oncol 19:2596–2606, 2001.

131. Rose C, Vtoraya O, Pluzanska A, et al: An open randomised trial of second-line endocrine therapy in advanced breast cancer. Comparison of the aromatase inhibitors letrozole and anastrozole. Eur J Cancer 39:2318–2327, 2003.

132. Cunningham D, Powles TJ, Dowsett M, et al: Oral 4-hydroxyandrostenedione, a new endocrine treatment for disseminated breast cancer. Cancer Chemother Pharmacol 20:253–133.

133. Dowsett M: Aromatase inhibition: Basic concepts, and the pharmacodynamics of formestane. Ann Oncol 5(Suppl):3–5, 1994.

134. Coombes RC, Hughes SW, Dowsett M: 4-Hydroxyandrostenedione: A new treatment for postmenopausal patients with breast cancer. Eur J Cancer 12:1941–1945, 1992.

135. Dowsett M, Cunningham DC, Stein RC, et al: Dose-related endocrine effects and pharmacokinetics of oral and intramuscular 4-hydroxyandrostenedione in postmenopausal breast cancer patients. Cancer Res 49:1306–1312, 1989.

136. Pickles T, Perry L, Murray P, Plowman P: 4-Hydroxyandrostenedione-further clinical and extended endocrine observations. Br J Cancer 62:309–313, 1990.

137. Perez Carrion R, Alberola Candel V, Calabresi F, et al: Comparison of the selective aromatase inhibitor formestane with tamoxifen as first-line hormonal therapy in postmenopausal women with advanced breast cancer. Ann Oncol 5(Suppl):19–24, 1994.

138. Freue M, Kjaer M, Boni C, et al: Open comparative trial of formestane versus megestrol acetate in postmenopausal patients with advanced breast cancer previously treated with tamoxifen. Breast 9:9–16, 2000.

139. Geisler J, King N, Anker G, et al: In vivo inhibition of aromatization by exemestane, a novel irreversible aromatase inhibitor, in postmenopausal breast cancer patients. Clin Cancer Res 4:2089–2093, 1998.

140. Jones S, Vogel C, Arkhipov A, et al: Multicenter, phase II trial of exemestane as third-line hormonal therapy of postmenopausal women with metastatic breast cancer. Aromasin Study Group. J Clin Oncol 17:3418–3425, 1999.

141. Kaufmann M, Bajetta E, Dirix LY, et al: Exemestane is superior to megestrol acetate after tamoxifen failure in postmenopausal women with advanced breast cancer: Results of a phase III randomized double-blind trial. The Exemestane Study Group. J Clin Oncol 18:1399–1411, 2000.

141a. Paridaens R, Therasse P, Dirix L, et al: First line hormonal treatment for metastatic breast cancer with exemestane ortamoxifen in post-menopausal patients—A randomized phase III trial of the EORTC Breast Group. J Clin Oncol 22:515(abstract), 2004.

142. Lonning PE, Bajetta E, Murray R, et al: Activity of exemestane in metastatic breast cancer after failure of nonsteroidal aromatase inhibitors: A phase II trial. J Clin Oncol 18:2234–2244, 2000.

143. Bertelli G, Garrone O, Merlano M: Sequential use of aromatase inactivators and inhibitors in advanced breast cancer [abstract 238]. Proc Am Soc Clin Oncol 21:60a, 2002.

144. Miller AA, Becher R, Schmidt CG: Plasma concentrations of medroxyprogesterone acetate and megestrol acetate during long-term follow-up in patients treated for metastatic breast cancer. J Cancer Res Clin Oncol 114:186–190, 1988.

145. McGuire WL, Johnson PA, Muss HB, Osborne CK: Megestrol acetate in breast cancer—A panel discussion. Breast Cancer Res Treat 14:33–38, 1989.

146. Pronzato P, Brema F, Amoroso D, et al: Megestrol acetate: Phase II study of a single daily administration in advanced breast cancer. Breast Cancer Res Treat 17:51–54, 1990.

147. Muss HB, Case LD, Capizzi RL, et al: High-versus standard-dose megestrol acetate in women with advanced breast cancer: A phase III trial of the Piedmont Oncology Association. J Clin Oncol 8:1797–1805, 1990.

148. Lundgren S, Gundersen S, Klepp R, et al: Megestrol acetate versus aminoglutethimide for metastatic breast cancer. Breast Cancer Res Treat 14:201–206, 1989.

149. Muss HB, Wells HB, Paschold EH, et al: Megestrol acetate versus tamoxifen in advanced breast cancer: 5-year analysis-a phase III trial of the Piedmont Oncology Association. J Clin Oncol 6:1098–1106, 1988.

150. Sedlacek SM: An overview of megestrol acetate for the treatment of advanced breast cancer. Semin Oncol 15:3–13, 1988.

151. Blamey RW, Jonat W, Kaufmann M, et al: Goserelin depot in the treatment of premenopausal advanced breast cancer. Eur J Cancer 28A:810–814, 1992.

152. Nicholson RI, Walker KJ, Walker RF, et al: Review of the endocrine actions of luteinising hormone-releasing hormone analogues in premenopausal women with breast cancer. Horm Res 32:198–201, 1989.

153. Bajetta E, Zilembo N, Buzzoni R, et al: Goserelin in premenopausal advanced breast cancer: Clinical and endocrine evaluation of responsive patients. Oncology 51:262–269, 1994.

154. Brambilla C, Escobedo A, Artioli R, et al: Medical castration with Zoladex: A conservative approach to premenopausal breast cancer. Tumori 77:145–150, 1991.

155. Dixon AR, Robertson JF, Jackson L, et al: Goserelin (Zoladex) in premenopausal advanced breast cancer: Duration of response and survival. Br J Cancer 62:868–870, 1990.

156. Kaufmann M, Jonat W, Schachner-Wunschmann E, et al: The depot GnRH analogue goserelin in the treatment of premenopausal patients with metastatic breast cancer— A 5-year experience and further endocrine therapies. Cooperative German Zoladex Study Group. Onkologie 14:22–24, 26–28, 30, 1991.

157. Boccardo F, Rubagotti A, Perrotta A, et al: Ovarian ablation versus goserelin with or without tamoxifen in pre- and perimenopausal patients with advanced breast cancer: Results of a

multicentric Italian study. Ann Oncol 5:337–342, 1994.

158. Klijn JG, Blamey RW, Boccardo F, et al: Combined tamoxifen and luteinizing hormone-releasing hormone (LHRH) agonist versus LHRH agonist alone in premenopausal advanced breast cancer: A meta-analysis of four randomized trials. J Clin Oncol 19:343–353, 2001.

159. Jordan VC: The past, present, and future of selective estrogen receptor modulation. Ann N Y Acad Sci 949:72–79, 2001.

160. Jordan VC: Selective estrogen receptor modulation: A personal perspective. Cancer Res 61:5683–5687, 2001.

161. Peto R: Five years of tamoxifen—or more? J Natl Cancer Inst 88:1791–1793, 1996.

162. Hodges LC, Cook JD, Lobenhofer EK, et al: Tamoxifen functions as a molecular agonist inducing cell cycle-associated genes in breast cancer cells. Mol Cancer Res 1:300–311, 2003.

163. Bryant J, Fisher B, Dignam J: Duration of adjuvant tamoxifen therapy. J Natl Cancer Inst Monogr 30:56–61, 2001.

164. Holli K: Tamoxifen versus toremifene in the adjuvant treatment of breast cancer. Eur J Cancer 38(Suppl 6):S37–S38, 2002.

165. International Breast Cancer Study Group: Toremifene and tamoxifen are equally effective for early-stage breast cancer: first results of International Breast Cancer Study Group Trials 12-93 and 14-93. Ann Oncol 15:1749–1759, 2004.

166. Jones AL, Powles TJ, Law M, et al: Adjuvant aminoglutethimide for postmenopausal patients with primary breast cancer: Analysis at 8 years. J Clin Oncol 10:1547–1552, 1992.

167. Baum M, Budzar AU, Cuzick J, et al: Anastrozole alone or in combination with tamoxifen versus tamoxifen alone for adjuvant treatment of postmenopausal women with early breast cancer: First results of the ATAC randomised trial. Lancet 359:2131–2139, 2002.

168. Baum M, Buzdar A, Cuzick J, et al: Anastrozole alone or in combination with tamoxifen versus tamoxifen alone for adjuvant treatment of postmenopausal women with early-stage breast cancer: Results of the ATAC (Arimidex, Tamoxifen Alone or in Combination) trial efficacy and safety update analyses. Cancer 98:1802–1810, 2003.

169. Winer EP, Hudis C, Burstein HJ, et al: American Society of Clinical Oncology technology assessment on the sue of aromatase inhibitors as adjuvant therapy for women with hormone receptor-positive breast cancer: Status report 2002. J Clin Oncol 20:3317–3327, 2002.

170. Winer EP, Hudis C, Burstein HJ, et al: American Society of Clinical Oncology Technology Assessment Working Group update: Use of aromatase inhibitors in the adjuvant setting. J Clin Oncol 21:2597–2599, 2003.

171. Boccardo F, Rubagotti A, Amoroso D, et al: Sequential tamoxifen and aminoglutethimide versus tamoxifen alone in the adjuvant treatment of postmenopausal breast cancer patients: Results of an Italian cooperative study. J Clin Oncol 19:4209–4215, 2001.

172. Boccardo F, Rubagotti A, Amoroso D, et al: Anastrozole appears to be superior to tamoxifen in women already receiving adjuvant tamoxifen treatment [abstract 3]. Breast Cancer Res Treat 82(Suppl 1):S6, 2003.

173. Coombes RC, Hall E, Gibson LJ, et al: A randomized trial of exemestane after two to three years of tamoxifen therapy in postmenopausal women with primary breast cancer. N Engl J Med 350:1081–1089, 2004.

174. Goss PE, Ingle JN, Martino S, et al: A randomized trial of letrozole in postmenopausal women after five years of tamoxifen therapy for early-stage breast cancer. N Engl J Med 349:1793–1802, 2003.

175. Carlini P, Ferretti G, Di Cosimo S, et al: Is there a benefit by the sequence anastrozole-formestane for postmenopausal metastatic breast cancer women? J Steroid Biochem Mol Biol 86:107–109, 2003.

176. Perey L, Thurlimann B, Hawle H, et al: Fulvestrant as hormonal treatment in postmenopausal patients with advanced breast cancer progressing after treatment with tamoxifen and aromatase inhibitors [abstract 249]. Breast Cancer Res Treat 76:S72, 2002.

# MALE REPRODUCTION

# Functional Morphology of the Testis

## Jeffrey B. Kerr and David de Kretser

## MACROSCOPIC ORGANIZATION

The testis is covered on its anterolateral and medial surfaces by apposed serous membranes that form a closed cavity termed the *tunica vaginalis*, an isolated outpocketing of the peritoneum reflecting the retroperitoneal origin of the testis. In adults, the testis is 4 to 5 cm long (15–35 mL) and of firm consistency. Posteriorly, the testis is associated with the epididymis and spermatic cord, the latter incorporating the ductus deferens, together with neurovascular structures running to the testis.[1] Nerves (autonomics from the renal and abdominal aortic plexuses) and vessels exit and enter the testis through a thick (1 mm), fibrous connective tissue capsule deep to the tunica vaginalis, termed the *tunica albuginea*, which is semitransparent in many species but opaque in the human testis due to the abundance of collagen fibers. Entering the testis posteriorly, the testicular artery descends to the inferior pole just deep to the tunica albuginea and gives rise to the region termed the *tunica vasculosa*. In the human testis, the main stem of the artery ascends beneath the anterior surface before smaller branches penetrate the parenchyma. Incisions into the medial and lateral aspects of the upper pole of the tunica albuginea of the human testis are least likely to encounter a major arterial branch.[2] Posteriorly, the tunica albuginea is thickened and projects into the parenchyma of the testis to form the mediastinum, a honeycomb-like structure through which the rete testis links the seminiferous tubules via the efferent ductules to the epididymis. Numerous imperfect, thin connective tissue septa extend from the tunica albuginea toward the mediastinum, establishing several hundred incomplete pyramidal lobules containing loose connective tissue that supports the seminiferous tubules, the terminal ends of which empty into the mediastinum by straight tubular extensions termed *tubuli recti*. Depending on the species, individual seminiferous tubules may be highly convoluted (e.g., human) or they may form numerous relatively linear segments linked by cranial and caudal hairpin turns as seen in rodent testes.[3]

Spermatozoa and fluid produced by the seminiferous tubules enter the rete testis, a maze of anastomosing corridors within the mediastinum that provide a route toward the epididymis. The morphology of the rete is species specific,[4,5] although three principal zones (Fig. 167-1) have been described: the *septal* rete, which consists of straight tubules that empty into the *mediastinal* rete, a network of anastomosing passages and channels that in turn drain into the *extratesticular* rete, which is characterized by still wider spaces in continuity with the 6 to 12 fine efferent ductules leading to the head of the epididymis.

### COMPOSITION OF THE HUMAN TESTIS

Quantitative histologic studies of the human testis have revealed ethnic differences in the tissue compartments and cell numbers from Chinese, Hispanic, and white backgrounds.[6] These data, using 8 or 12 samples per group from men aged 29 to 30 years, are summarized in part in Figure 167-2. Average testis weights were 13.7, 25.9, and 21 g, respectively; the fraction of the whole testis occupied by the seminiferous epithelium was higher in the Hispanic group at 44% compared with the Chinese (41%) and white (36%) groups, but the total tubule length per testis was not significantly different, ranging from 450 to 620 m. The number of Sertoli cells per testis was lower in Chinese men (350 million) than in the other groups (475 million), but there was no statistical difference in the number of Leydig cells per testis among ethnic groups (125–200 million).

## SPERMATOGENESIS

Spermatogenesis in mammals, including humans, is a complex, dynamic process that depends on the proliferation and maturation of germ cells derived from self-renewing stem cells. In the testis, stem cells maintain a supply of germ cells capable of differentiating into fully formed spermatozoa. The

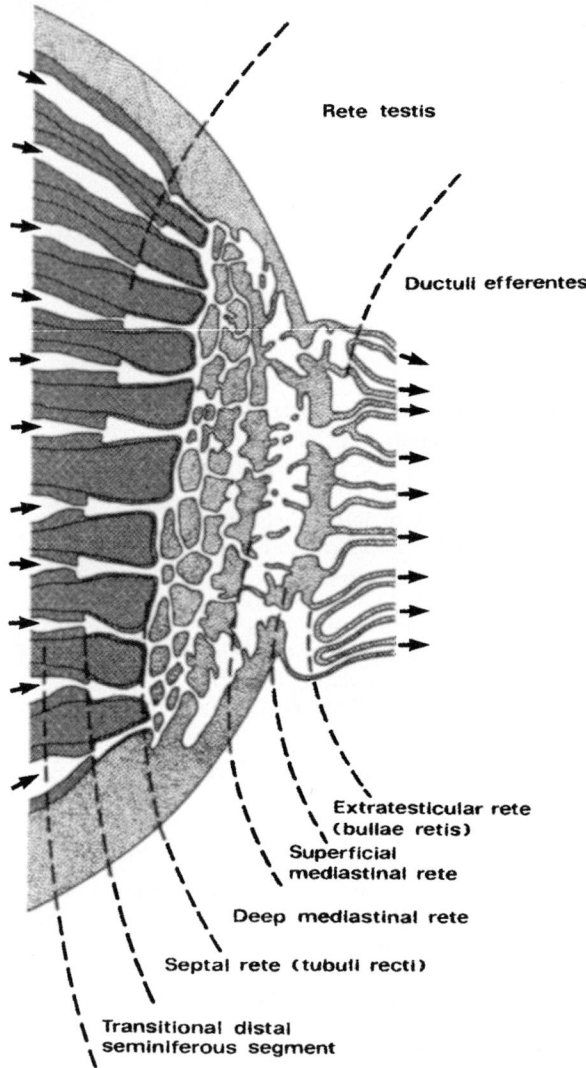

Rete testis

Ductuli efferentes

Extratesticular rete (bullae retis)

Superficial mediastinal rete

Deep mediastinal rete

Septal rete (tubuli recti)

Transitional distal seminiferous segment

*Figure 167-1* Relationship between the seminiferous tubule and the rete testis within the mediastinum. Zones of the rete testis are indicated (From de Kretser DM, Temple-Smith PD, Kerr JB: Anatomical and functional aspects of the male reproductive organs. In Bandhauser K, Frick J [eds]: Handbook of Urology, vol 16. Disturbances in Male Fertility. Berlin, Springer-Verlag, 1982, pp 1–131)

duration of the entire process of spermatogenesis varies between species,[7,8] for example, 35 days in the mouse and hamster, 50 days in the rat, 45 to 65 days in various nonhuman primates,[9,10] and 70 days in humans. In humans, the onset of release of spermatozoa (spermarche) within the testis occurs in the early stages of puberty, at approximately 13.5 years of age,[11] with spermatogenesis continuing throughout life into the eighth and ninth decades.[12] In quantitative terms, the output of spermatozoa in an average adult man is remarkable and equivalent to approximately 1000 new sperm per second, with 150 to $250 \times 10^6$ sperm commonly present in a single ejaculate. Although the morphologic features of spermatogenesis have been studied extensively for more than 50 years, our understanding of how this process is controlled is far from complete. A range of techniques in molecular biology, studies of individual genes and the biologic actions of their products, and specific experimental alterations in endocrine factors associated with spermatogenesis and testicular function continue to provide valuable insight into the genetic and hormonal control of germ cell development.

## SEMINIFEROUS TUBULES

In the human testis, the seminiferous tubules are approximately 200 μm in diameter and occupy approximately two thirds of the parenchymal volume; their total length on average is approximately 600 m per man. Structural support of tubules is provided by peritubular tissue consisting of five to seven layers of myofibroblasts and fibroblasts separated by collagen and extracellular matrix.[13,14] Transport of sperm along the seminiferous tubules toward the rete testis occurs via peristaltic contraction-relaxation of peritubular tissue, a process regulated by the local production and action of vasoconstrictive and vasorelaxant agents such as endothelin, vasopressin, oxytocin, and nitric oxide.[15–17] Peritubular cells are androgen responsive and secrete various proteins capable of modifying the intratubular environment and maintaining interactions between the basement membrane and the seminiferous epithelium.[18–20]

## SEMINIFEROUS EPITHELIUM

Germ cells make up the bulk of the seminiferous epithelium, and their basal-to-luminal arrangement in multiple layers is attributable to the structural support provided by the tall columnar Sertoli cells. The histologic relationship between the nondividing Sertoli cells and the various types of dividing and differentiating germ cells is difficult to appreciate in routine paraffin sections because the cytoplasmic extensions of Sertoli cells between the germ cells are thin and stain poorly with dyes such as hematoxylin and eosin. The complexities of

*Figure 167-2* Comparison of testicular components and cells from Asian, *n* = 12 (**A**); Hispanic, *n* = 8 (**B**); and white, *n* = 12 (**C**) men. (Based on data from quantitative histologic analysis of vascular perfusion-fixed testes from Johnson et al.[114,389])

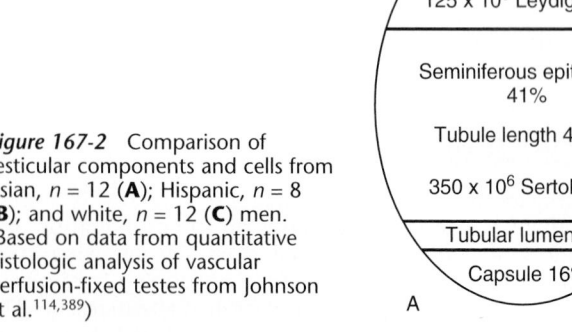

Intertubular space 34%

$125 \times 10^6$ Leydig cells

Seminiferous epithelium 41%

Tubule length 450 m

$350 \times 10^6$ Sertoli cells

Tubular lumen 9%

Capsule 16%

A

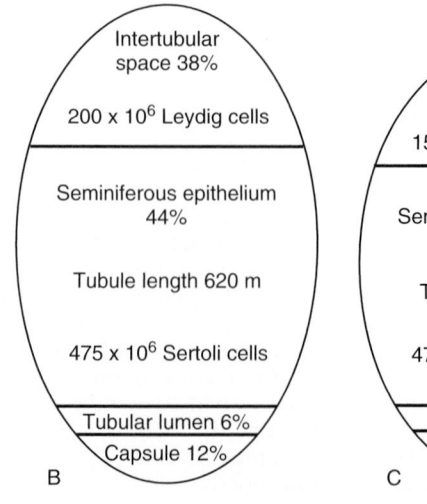

Intertubular space 38%

$200 \times 10^6$ Leydig cells

Seminiferous epithelium 44%

Tubule length 620 m

$475 \times 10^6$ Sertoli cells

Tubular lumen 6%

Capsule 12%

B

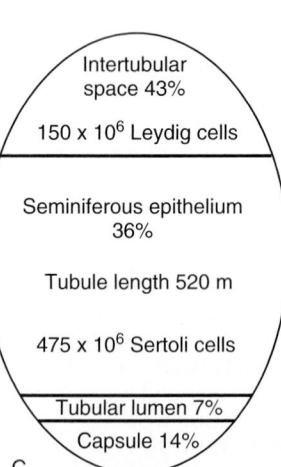

Intertubular space 43%

$150 \times 10^6$ Leydig cells

Seminiferous epithelium 36%

Tubule length 520 m

$475 \times 10^6$ Sertoli cells

Tubular lumen 7%

Capsule 14%

C

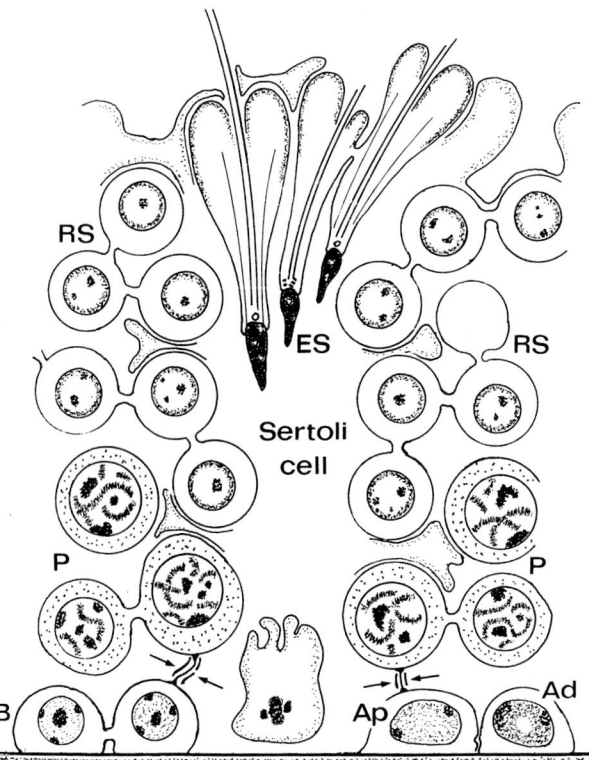

**Figure 167-3** Drawing of the human seminiferous epithelium shows the relationship between the Sertoli cells and the position of germ cells. Type A pale (Ap), A dark (Ad), and B spermatogonia (B) are shown together with primary spermatocytes (P), early round spermatids (RS), and elongating spermatids (ES). Inter–Sertoli cell tight junctions are indicated by *arrows*.

this association have been thoroughly described in ultrastructural studies (see reviews elsewhere[21–24]). As the germ cells progress through spermatogenesis, they are progressively transported apically through the seminiferous epithelium within pockets or recesses of Sertoli cell cytoplasm and ultimately released, as spermatozoa, into the lumen of the seminiferous tubule (Figs. 167-3 to 167-5). Although the histologic appearance of the seminiferous epithelium is fundamentally

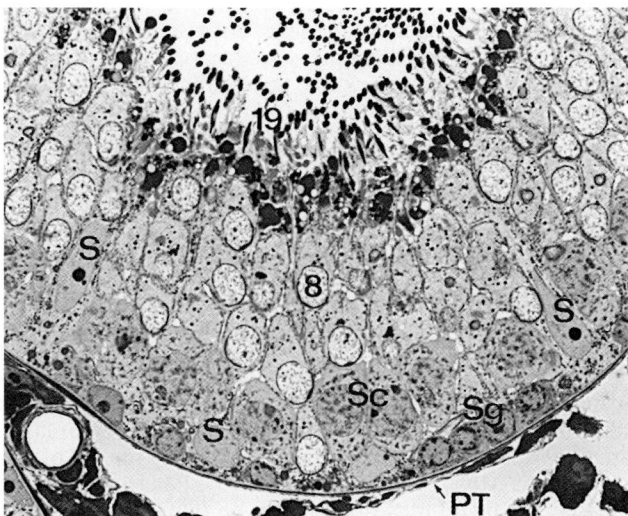

**Figure 167-4** Seminiferous epithelium of the rat testis illustrates Sertoli cell nuclei (S), spermatogonia (Sg), primary spermatocytes (Sc), step 8 spermatids (8), step 19 spermatids (19), and peritubular tissue (PT).

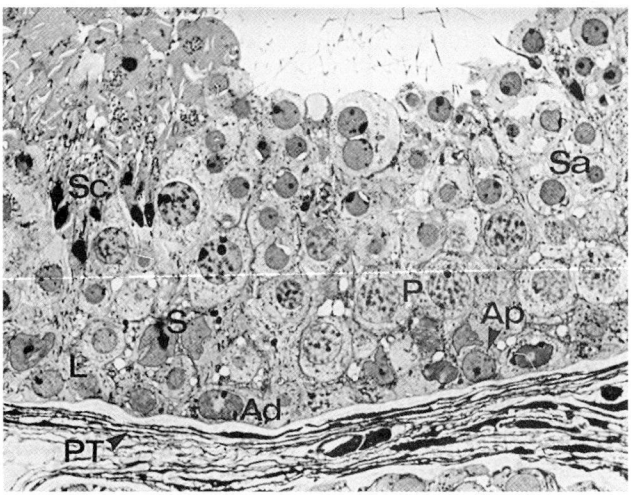

**Figure 167-5** Sequence of germ cell types in human spermatogenesis commencing with a spermatogonium, progressing through an orderly sequence of cell proliferation and maturation and terminating in a mature spermatozoon. Spermatogonia: types A dark (Ad), and B (B); primary spermatocytes: leptotene (L) and pachytene (P); spermatids (Sa, Sc); peritubular tissue (PT).

similar in all mammals, including primates and humans, species variations do occur in the relationships between particular groups or associations of germ cells and the Sertoli cells within defined segments of the seminiferous tubules. These characteristic associations are discussed in the section on the spermatogenic cycle. The complexity of the spermatogenic process is evident from the following considerations: (1) dependence of the seminiferous epithelium on appropriate stimulation of the testis by gonadotropins, steroid hormones (notably androgens), and local paracrine, autocrine, and growth factors; (2) differential expression of genes within germ cells and Sertoli cells; (3) interactions between individual Sertoli cells and the various types of developing germ cells with which they are intimately associated; and (4) maintenance by the Sertoli cells of a unique physiologic environment within the seminiferous tubule that restricts the entry of cells, macromolecules, and immunogenic agents originating from the intertubular tissues and its vasculature. Disturbances or impairment of any one of these parameters may result in disruption or suppression of spermatogenesis and contribute to defects in spermatozoa and/or oligospermia or azoospermia.

## SPERMATOGONIA AS STEM CELLS

In the adult testis, the continuous production of spermatozoa that are released from the seminiferous epithelium requires that successive new generations of germ cells be made available to replenish those that leave the testis. Based on morphologic features and functional data, spermatogenesis in mammals commences with the replication of spermatogonial stem cells, which are associated with the basement membrane of the seminiferous epithelium. Most of our knowledge concerning the identity, relative numbers, and proliferative and maturation capabilities of spermatogonia, together with the factors that control their activities, is based on studies of laboratory species.[25–29] In all mammals studied to date, including primates[30,31] and humans,[32,33] spermatogonia are subdivided into types A and B according to nuclear chromatin patterns in histologic preparations. In mice and rats, intermediate-type spermatogonia are present with morphologic features between those of types A and B. Type A spermatogonia are the stem cells, or cells that are the precursors of all further differentiated germ cells and are capable of prolonged or indefinite production of more of their own kind. Primates and humans show dark and pale type A spermatogonia; the former, which are designated as A dark (Ad), have deeply staining, homogeneous, finely granulated chromatin with a central pale-stained area in the nucleus. Pale type A (Ap) spermatogonia exhibit pale-staining nuclei, no central vacuole-type area, and one or two nucleoli associated with the nuclear membrane. Type B spermatogonia show coarse, deeply stained clumps of heterochromatin subjacent to the nuclear membrane, and a central nucleolus.

As a renewing tissue, the seminiferous epithelium has three cell compartments: (1) self-renewing stem cells, (2) cells that via proliferation amplify the numbers of differentiating cells, and (3) a differentiating compartment in which germ cells are committed to mature into spermatozoa. Type Ad spermatogonia rarely divide in the human testis; they serve as reserve stem cells and only divide and transform into type Ap cells after irradiation or cytotoxic treatment.[25] Type Ap spermatogonia also function as stem cells by self-renewal and by mitotic proliferation into type B spermatogonia.[34] In this sense, Ap cells belong to the amplifying compartment, which also includes type B spermatogonia because the latter divide by mitosis and then progress to become primary spermatocytes. The stability of the genome in germ stem cells is remarkable because in a 50-year-old man, the spermatogonia probably pass through more than 1000 mitotic divisions before they enter the process of meiosis.[35] Spermatocytes belong to the differentiating compartment, and these cells undergo two cell divisions during the process of meiotic maturation and become spermatids destined for transformation into spermatozoa. In humans, the ratio of type Ad, type Ap, and type B spermatogonia and spermatocytes is 1:1:2:4, respectively, and Ad and Ap spermatogonia are arranged in homogeneous groups along the seminiferous tubule[35] (see Fig. 167-4). Within these groups, the spermatogonia form pairs of morphologically identical cells, which suggests that their mitotic behavior is "equivalent," that is, the products of their proliferation are either the same cells or a pair of differentiated spermatogonia.[25,32,33]

The proliferation and differentiation of spermatogonia are regulated by hormones (gonadotropins, androgens [see later]), local growth factors, intercellular paracrine/autocrine factors, and systemic nutrients. They arise from the gonocytes, which are in turn products of the primordial germ cells. Basally located in the seminiferous epithelium, the spermatogonia are partly surrounded by adjacent Sertoli cells, and their contact with the basal lamina places enables the secretory products of peritubular tissues and Leydig cells, hormones, and other factors to influence their function.

Vitamin A is essential for the maintenance of spermatogenesis because vitamin A deficiency in rats and mice results in the arrest of type A spermatogonial proliferation, which is reversed after the administration of either vitamin A or retinoic acid.[26] Interleukin-1α produced by Sertoli cells stimulates the proliferation of differentiating spermatogonia in vivo and in vitro in the rat,[36,37] and similar effects have been reported for insulin-like growth factors, also produced by Sertoli cells.[38] Spermatogonia express the c-kit receptor transmembrane protein, which promotes proliferation of these cells in association with the receptor ligand termed *stem cell factor*, produced by Sertoli cells.[39,40] c-kit is a proto-oncogene associated with the dominant white spotting (W) locus in mice, mutations of which lead to defects in spermatogenesis.[41] Stem cell factor is associated with the Steel (Sl) locus in mice, and mutations can cause deficiencies in germ cell development.[42] c-kit and stem cell factor are also found in the human testis and appear to be abnormally expressed in testicular tissues showing defective spermatogenesis.[43] Other factors affecting spermatogonial proliferation include glia-derived neurotropic factor, neurotropin-3, nerve growth factor, epidermal growth factor, platelet-derived growth factor, and follistatin.[44-49]

Mounting evidence indicates that a number of genes on the human Y chromosome (and perhaps some autosomal genes[50]) are candidates for regulation of spermatogenesis, including the proliferation and/or maturation of spermatogonia.[51] Several loci on the long arm of the Y chromosome, $Y_q$, if lost through microdeletions, are associated with oligozoospermia or azoospermia, and some of the genes within these regions are crucial for spermatogenesis. Two genes, *DAZ* (deleted in azoospermia), and *RBM* (RNA-binding motif), are present in multiple copies, and if these are deleted, azoospermia or severe oligozoospermia will result.[52,53] Both are RNA-binding proteins and are testis specific. *DAZ* maps to the *AZF* region, and *DAZ* transcripts are restricted to the germ line in the testis of humans, Old World monkeys, and apes. In other mammals, it is an autosomally located gene, *DAZL* (*DAZ*-like). *DAZL* genes also occur in humans, mice, monkeys, *Xenopus*, and *Drosophila*; the homology between *DAZ* and *DAZL* is very high.

In recent studies, the heterochromatic and euchromatic gene sequences of the human Y chromosome have been mapped and used to define the male-specific region (MSY) that makes up 95% of the chromosome's length and contains specific sequences called amplicons, which are essential for spermatogenesis.[54] Gene conversion, that is, nonreciprocal recombination within the Y chromosome itself, is as frequent as reciprocal crossing over in autosomes. The MSY euchromatic region is unique to males, approximately 30% of it contains amplicons, whose testis-specific genes are limited or mostly abundant in germ cells, possibly for the purpose of generating unique chromatin configurations. Intra-Y gene conversions may have evolved to conserve testis germ cell gene functions through evolution.[54] As discussed previously, deletions in the MSY region are the most common genetic causes of spermatogenic failure because they arise from homologous rather than nonreciprocal recombinations.[55-57] The MSY region contains palindromic sequences that can result in deletions that excise large regions of DNA containing the copies of *DAZ* and *RBM*. The identified palindromes can result in smaller deletions, and these small deletions are also associated with low sperm counts.[54,57]

Opportunities for the study of spermatogonial stem cell function have become available through the techniques of germ cell transplantation, cryopreservation, and cell culture.[58-62] Successful transplantation of germ cells has been achieved through heterologous or xenologous transfer of cells, in which either rat or hamster germ cells undergo spermatogenic development in recipient mouse testes.[63-66] These studies have shown that not only will mouse Sertoli cells support rat or hamster spermatogenesis, but also the rate of transplanted germ cell development is maintained with the timing characteristic of the donor cells, thus indicating that the rate of germ cell maturation during spermatogenesis is regulated by germ cells alone. Germ cell transplantation in primates has also been reported.[67]

## MEIOSIS

Periodically, at fixed and regular intervals, the type A spermatogonia proceed through a series of mitotic divisions to produce type B spermatogonia that enter the prophase of the first meiotic division to form primary spermatocytes. It is not known how this cell proliferation is initiated or coordinated. Because of incomplete cytokinesis among dividing spermatogonia, spermatocytes remain connected via cytoplasmic bridges, which persist between all subsequent phases of spermatogenesis until mature spermatids (spermatozoa) are released into the tubule lumen. These bridges contribute to the synchronous development of successive generations of germ cells, which are histologically reflected as interconnected cohorts or families of cells. The arrangement in the seminiferous epithelium of several generations of spermatocytes and spermatids creates morphologically distinct combinations or cell associations in given segments of the seminiferous tubules (see later). Recent studies have shown that spermatids linked by these cytoplasmic bridges can share mRNAs.[68]

Spermatocytes are classified as primary or secondary types, both of which respectively undergo the first and second meiotic divisions in which the diploid number of chromosomes (44,XY) is reduced to the haploid number (22,X or 22,Y) characteristic of the spermatid. In human spermatogenesis, meiotic maturation is a lengthy process wherein the earliest or preleptotene primary spermatocytes require approximately 24 days to become early round spermatids.[69] Preleptotene spermatocytes perform DNA synthesis (the last time that DNA synthesis occurs in spermatogenesis); as a result, each chromosome is duplicated and the twin copies are referred to as sister chromatids. The chromosome number remains diploid, but the DNA content is now 4C or twice that found in spermatogonia. This event marks the commencement of prophase 2, which is subdivided into leptotene (thread-type chromosomes), zygotene (paired, homologous, double chromosomes), pachytene (large 20-μm primary spermatocytes with condensed, thickened chromosomes), diplotene (paired chromosomes decondensed and partially separated), and diakinesis (recondensed chromosomes) (Figs. 167-6 and 167-7). Metaphase, anaphase, and telophase follow when daughter cells separate but remain connected by a cytoplasmic bridge and form two haploid secondary spermatocytes containing 2C DNA. Division II of meiosis proceeds promptly (less than 24 hours), but with no DNA replication, to produce two haploid spermatids of 1C DNA content. Thus, four spermatids may be formed from each primary spermatocyte.

Pairing, or synapsis, of maternal and paternal chromosome homologues becomes evident during zygotene and is completed in pachytene, in which close apposition of the entire length of each homologue pair is maintained by a long ladder-like core of proteins termed the *synaptonemal complex*. Genes encoding synaptonemal complex proteins (SCP1) and chromosomal core proteins (COR1) are unique to meiosis.

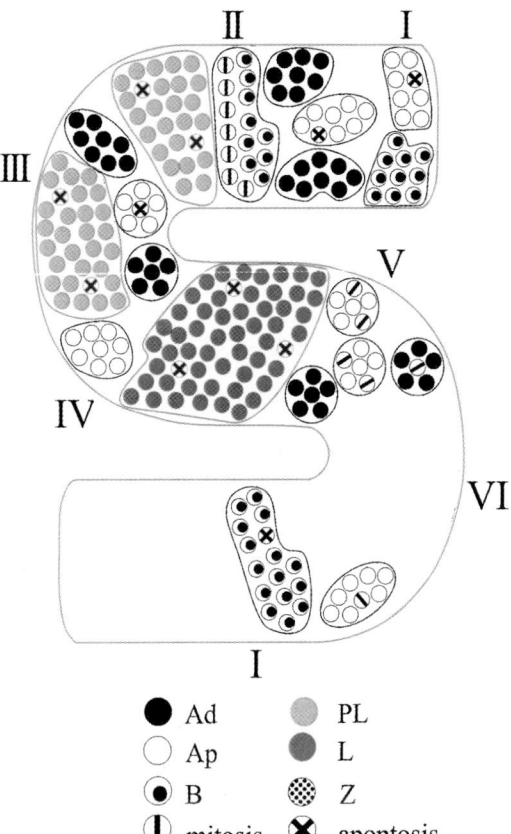

**Figure 167-7** Drawing of a seminiferous tubule illustrates how germ cells lying on or close to the basement membrane are distributed in clusters. For clarity, the arrangements of groups of germ cells are shown in relation to their locations and development as applied to the human testis, in which stages I to VI are depicted in sequence along the tubule. In reality, the stages may exhibit a partial orderly sequence or may occur in random locations. Sertoli cells are not shown. At stages I to II, spermatogonia type A dark (Ad), A pale (Ap), and B (B) occur in the ratio 1:1:2, respectively. Some of these cells die by apoptosis (*cells with crosses*). Type B spermatogonia divide by mitosis (*cells with a bar*) and produce preleptotene spermatocytes (PL), their number double that of type B spermatogonia. Progressing through early meiotic maturation, PL spermatocytes become leptotene (L) and then zygotene (Z) primary spermatocytes, some of which become apoptotic. The Ad and Ap spermatogonia, through longevity or self-renewal, are maintained in clusters, occasionally becoming apoptotic, but at stages V to VI, Ap cells divide mitotically to again supply a new generation of type B spermatogonia at stage I. (Based on data from Clermont[32] and DeRooij and Grootegoed.[28])

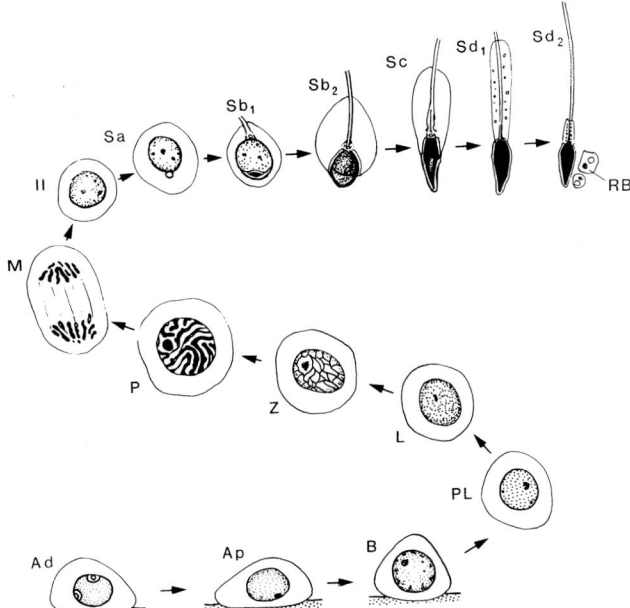

**Figure 167-6** Sequence of germ cell types in human spermatogenesis commencing with a spermatogonium, progressing through an orderly sequence of cell proliferation and maturation and terminating in a mature spermatozoon. Explanation of symbols—spermatogonia: type A dark (Ad), A pale (Ap), and B (B); primary spermatocytes: preleptotene (PL), leptotene (L), zygotene (Z), pachtene (P), and meiotic division (M); secondary spermatocyte (II), spermatids (Sa, Sb$_1$, Sb$_2$, Sc, Sd$_1$, Sd$_2$); residual body (RB).

Heat shock protein (HSP70-2) synthesis occurs after its transcription in leptotene-zygotene spermatocytes and is required for desynapsis of synaptonemal complexes and completion of meiosis I.[70,71] The purpose of pairing is to contribute to genetic reassortment in gametes via exchange of fragments of DNA between maternal and paternal homologues, a process referred to as genetic recombination. Exchange of DNA occurs when the aligned chromosomes in pachytene cross over at locations called chiasmata. Recombination requires endogenously induced breaking and ligation of DNA, mediated by proteins that perform error-free repair of double-strand breaks. These proteins are topoisomerases that are strongly induced in mid-phase primary spermatocytes and conserved from yeast to humans.[72] The random distribution of paternal and maternal sets of chromosomes produced by meiosis I could form more than 8 million genetically different gametes, that is, $2^n$ different gametes, where $n = 23$, the haploid number of chromosomes. Genetic recombination between homologous chromatids greatly increases the number of variants such that gametes from an individual are genetically related but contain slightly different gene sequences based on a common genetic program inherited from their biologic ancestors.

Most DNA synthesis in spermatocytes occurs during the preleptotene (premeiotic) S phase, each replicated chromosome then consisting of two sister chromatids. Indirect evidence of DNA replication during zygotene is available, so these very small segments (~0.1% of genomic DNA) are possibly involved in the alignment of homologues during the establishment of synapsis. DNA synthesis during pachytene has also been reported[73] and is thought to be a DNA repair event associated with the requirements for chromosome crossover. Spermatocytes engage in RNA synthesis, but a proportion of meiotic transcripts are not released from the nucleus to the cytoplasm until diplotene, and constitute a pool of stable mRNA that is translated postmeiotically in spermatids.[74–76] Some of these transcripts provide for enzymes such as lactate dehydrogenase and phosphoglycerate kinase, which are essential for sperm glycolysis, and others encode some proteins used in assembly of the sperm tail during spermiogenesis.

Injection of nuclei of mouse pachytene primary spermatocytes into mature mouse oocytes may result in the formation of viable embryos, with approximately 4% of these embryos developing into normal offspring after embryo transfer.[77] This finding emphasizes the early developmental competence of germ cells but also raises a point of caution for clinical applications because of the high risk of creating conceptuses with severe or lethal developmental abnormalities arising from chromosomal damage, including autosomal aneuploidies.

## SPERMIOGENESIS

Completion of meiotic maturation produces haploid spermatids, which are spherical and approximately 8 μm in diameter and usually located in the inner third of the seminiferous epithelium. There is no further cell division in spermatogen-

esis. As a consequence of incomplete cytokinesis commencing with the proliferation of renewing spermatogonia, numerous spermatids remain connected by cytoplasmic bridges, and this feature may contribute to their synchronized development in particular segments of the seminiferous tubule. Spermiogenesis refers to the complex transformation of round spermatids into spermatozoa (in humans, approximately 65 μm in length), a process requiring 24 days in humans (Fig. 167-8). Maturation of spermatids not involving cell proliferation has been described extensively in morphologic studies,[7,23,24,78,79] and studies using molecular biology techniques are providing new insight into the regulation of gene expression during spermiogenesis.[80–84]

From a functional perspective, spermiogenesis proceeds in three phases, although many of the morphogenetic changes shown by maturing spermatids occur concomitantly, and several are initiated early and evolve throughout the entire process. The first third of spermiogenesis is mainly concerned with formation of the acrosome, the second third with nuclear condensation and elongation, and the final third with completion of various components of the tail. The terminology used to describe the structure of spermatozoa provides a basis from which the phases of spermiogenesis are more readily understood. Each spermatozoon has a head and tail. The head of the human spermatozoon is spatulate in form, flattened, and somewhat pear shaped and contains the condensed nucleus. In rodents, the sperm have a falciform head. The coverings of the spermatid head and the microtubules in the developing tail region are thought to influence nuclear shaping during spermiogenesis. A membrane-bound thin cap, the acrosome, extends from the tip or leading edge of the head and covers approximately 60% of the sperm head. A perinuclear theca attaches the acrosome to the nucleus, and a plasma membrane encloses the entire head.

The tail, also delimited by a plasma membrane, consists of four components: the connecting piece or neck, the middle, the principal piece, and the end piece. The neck, which artic-

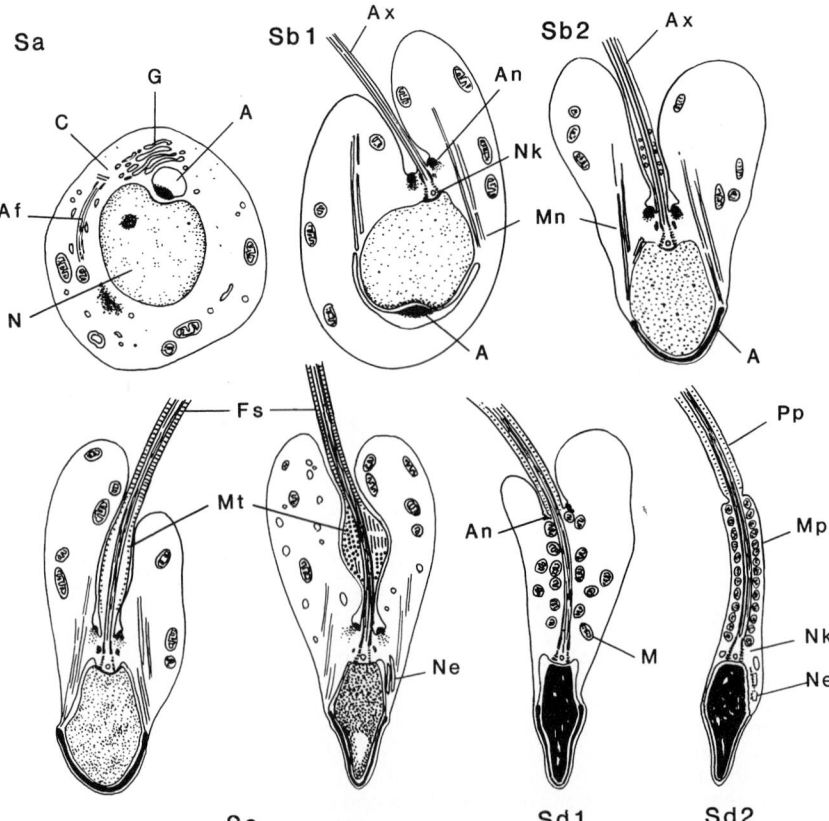

*Figure 167-8* Spermiogenesis in the human testis as noted by electron microscopy. Steps Sa and Sb₁ and Sb₂ correspond to the Golgi and cap phases of cell development, Sb₂ and Sc to the acrosome phase, and Sd to the maturation phase. A, acrosome or acrosomic vesicle; Af, developing axial filament; An, annulus; Ax, axoneme; C, centrioles; Fs, fibrous sheath; G, Golgi complex; M, mitochondria; Mn, manchette; Mp, middle piece; Mt, microtubules in spindle-shaped body; N, nucleus, Ne, redundant nuclear envelope; Nk, neck; Pp, principal piece. (From Kerr JB: Functional cytology of the human testis, Baillieres Clin Endocrinol Metab 6:235–250, 1992.)

ulates with the head, resembles a hollow cone, the base of which is associated with the caudal pole of the nucleus. The sides of the cone consist of nine cross-striated columns continuous with the nine outer dense fibers (ODFs, cytoskeletal elements) of the tail. In the core of the neck, the remnant of the distal centriole anchors the tail to the sperm head and also gives rise to the axial filament, or axoneme, of the tail (nine + two arrangement of microtubules). The companion proximal centriole, which remains intact, is also lodged within the cone, and its axis lies at 90 degrees to the axoneme.

Extending from the neck, the middle piece (~5 μm long) includes the central axoneme, which continues to the end of the tail; the ODFs, which encircle the axoneme, and the sheath of mitochondria, which lies external to the ODFs and terminates at the annulus, a ringlike structure beyond which is the principal piece. The latter (~45 μm long) consists of seven tapering ODFs, ODF-3 and ODF-8 being replaced by longitudinal columns of the fibrous sheath (FS). Specialized structures run circumferentially around the ODFs and join the longitudinal columns. These structures are known as the transverse ribs. Tapering toward its end, the principal piece is devoid of ODFs and the FS and forms the end piece in which the axoneme terminates as disorganized microtubules.

Based on structural alterations of the nucleus and acrosome (see Figure 167-8), spermiogenesis may be subdivided into the Golgi, cap, acrosome, and maturation phases.[24,78–80] In summary, during the first two phases, the Golgi complex contributes to formation of the acrosome (marking the cranial pole of the nucleus), which flattens and progressively covers the anterior aspect of the sperm head. At the opposite pole of the nucleus, the pair of centrioles that have commenced formation of the axoneme lodge in a shallow fossa in the nucleus. In the acrosome phase, the nuclear chromatin begins to condense, and with elongation and remodeling of the nucleus, the species-specific shape of the sperm head is developed. Elongation of the caudal cytoplasm is associated with development of the middle and then the principal piece to form the flagellum. During the maturation phase, most of the spermatid cytoplasm becomes separated from the head and tail and forms several globular masses of residual cytoplasm termed *residual bodies*. Disengagement of the spermatozoa from the seminiferous epithelium at spermiation is marked by retention and engulfment of residual bodies by the Sertoli cells, which dispose of them by phagocytosis.

The regulatory mechanisms associated with spermiogenesis are not well understood and represent a combination of processes in which the microenvironment of the seminiferous epithelium (i.e., the extrinsic biologic actions of hormones, growth factors, and biochemical activities of the Sertoli cell) is a corequisite that modulates gene expression and the synthetic and metabolic activities intrinsic to the developing spermatids. Numerous current studies of the intrinsic processes regulating gene expression in spermiogenesis are focusing on changes in transcription/translation as the nucleus and its chromatin undergo condensation, as well as mechanisms contributing to formation of the tail.

During spermiogenesis, the spermatid nucleus is dramatically reorganized in shape and size and degree of compaction of the chromatin. The DNA in sperm occupies only approximately 5% of the volume of DNA in somatic cells.[85] The basic proteins, the nucleosomal histones of the spermatocytes, are replaced by intermediate proteins (transition proteins) and protamines leading to an extreme condensation of chromatin.

The commencement of spermiogenesis is associated with a massive wave of transcriptional activity involving the activation of a variety of postmeiotic genes in haploid cells.[86] However, translational control of gene expression is important because as the chromatin condenses during the second phase of spermiogenesis, nuclear transcription activities are progressively shut down. The silencing of transcription is achieved by the replacement of histones by protamines

such that the spermatids are almost devoid of histones. The somatic-type histones are thought to be acetylated, causing disassociation with DNA followed by ubiquitination, allowing their removal in favor of transition proteins (TP1, TP2).[87] The latter enhance DNA compaction and may be involved in the repair of DNA breaks that arise during chromatin remodeling.[88] However, TP1 and TP2 mutant mice are fertile, suggesting that these proteins are redundant and that histone replacement and chromatin compaction may proceed independently of transition protein formation.[89,90] The last highly basic proteins associated with the DNA are the protamines (HP1-4 in man), which are transcribed early, but the resulting mRNA is stored (for several days or more) before translation into protein.[76,82,83] These stable mRNAs and possibly numerous others (e.g., those produced during meiotic prophase with translational repression until spermiogenesis) are thought to be stored or bound to specific RNA-binding proteins until translation is required.[91,92] Premature translation of protamine mRNA in transgenic mice causes precocious condensation of nuclear DNA with arrest of final spermiogenesis and infertility.[93] Protamines organize the spermatid genome into very specialized doughnut-shaped chromatin components that are quite distinct from the usual architecture of the nucleosomes,[94] which may be necessary for specific translation activities after fertilization.

It is well known that the acrosome is a modified secretory granule with distinct regional molecular composition and function associated with its membrane and matrix. The acrosome has two biochemical components: a soluble protein compartment and an insoluble acrosomal matrix. Hyaluronidase and dipeptidyl peptidase are found in the soluble phase, whereas proacrosin and proacrosin-binding protein occur in the latter.[95] Soluble proteins are released during acrosome exocytosis, but the matrix proteins remain with the sperm. It is thought that these protein compartments regulate the acrosome reaction and sperm–zona pellucida interaction. Hydrolytic enzymes are bound to the protein matrix, and in the course of fertilization, acrosomal hydrolases are released during the acrosome reaction to allow sperm penetration of the zona surface. The outer acrosomal membrane–associated matrix complex proteins show sequence homology between bovine, primate, human, and mouse spermatozoa.[96] The stability of the outer acrosomal membrane–associated matrix complex during the acrosome reaction suggests that it localizes a hydrolase pool at the sperm-zona binding site and maintains attachment of the sperm to the zona pellucida. Patients with a disorder resulting in failure of acrosome formation are infertile, and the sperm take on a globular shape, the condition being termed *globozoospermia*. Mice with a targeted disruption of the casein kinase II, a catalytic subunit gene, show the absence of the acrosome and globozoospermia.[97]

Details of the genetic basis and molecular biology of the assembly, structure, and function of the sperm tail are emerging and indicate that genetic causes may account for a minor yet significant proportion of male infertility.[84] In mice, males of the *Hst 7* genotype s/t (on proximal chromosome 17 within the t complex) produce abnormal sperm consistent with asthenospermia and sterility. Forward movement of sperm is impaired, the axoneme is disorganized, or the mitochondria of the middle piece are misaligned or interrupted by gaps.[98] Potentially, these studies in mice may be useful for exploring the basis of human asthenospermia.

Several studies have identified some of the proteins composing the neck, the ODFs, and the FS and have enabled cloning of the relevant genes.[81,99–102] The precise function of ODFs is unclear, but their elastic properties and tensile strength may be integral components of proper flagellar motility. Studies of spermiogenesis in the rat and bovine model have shown that expression of genes encoding some of these proteins occurs in early round spermatids and reaches peak levels during the acrosome phase. Some ODF proteins appear to be stored in granulated bodies in the spermatid cytoplasm before their assembly in a proximal-to-distal direction along the axoneme.[81,99] Immunogold-labeling studies with anti-ODF-27 and anti-ODF-84 antibodies have shown localization to the neck of the tail, thus confirming that the segmental columns and basal plate contain cytoskeleton-type proteins similar to those in the flagellum.[99,100]

Immunostaining of elongating spermatids with specific anti–FS antibodies has shown that FS proteins are assembled in a distal-to-proximal direction along the axoneme, eventually meeting and overlapping the ODF assembly within the periaxonemal cytoplasmic compartment.[81] Unlike the association of ODFs within cytoplasmic granular bodies, FS proteins are randomly distributed in the caudal spermatid cytoplasm and then targeted directly along the axoneme to their site of assembly.

An important structural relationship between spermatids and the plasma membrane of Sertoli cells is the attachment of the former, specifically flanking the developing acrosome of elongating spermatids, to regions of ectoplasmic specialization (ES) of the Sertoli cell.[103] In this respect, ESs resemble half of the unique inter–Sertoli cell junctional specializations that form the blood-testis barrier located in the basal region of the seminiferous epithelium (see later). The adhesive properties of ESs facing elongating spermatids are attributable to a complex association of cytoskeletal proteins, including actin, vinculin, integrins, and α-actinin. Ectoplasmic specializations are thought to orient spermatids within the seminiferous epithelium; for example, when step 7 round spermatids in the rat rotate during step 8 of spermiogenesis such that the cranial pole with the developing acrosome faces basally, the caudal cytoplasm then points apically.[7] Adhesion at the interface of the ES and acrosome, shown to be androgen dependent, is also necessary to prevent spermatid detachment from the Sertoli cells.[104] In the immature testis, acquisition of binding between Sertoli cell ESs and post–step 8 spermatids may be dependent on a "primary effect" of follicle-stimulating hormone (FSH)-stimulated maturation of Sertoli cells.[105]

Studies of the developmental competence of spermatids with respect to their capacity to fertilize a mature oocyte and lead to the production of normal, fertile offspring have shown that this ability is achieved early in spermiogenesis. Round spermatid nuclei from mice, with or without cytoplasm, can initiate normal embryo development when electrofused with or injected into oocytes,[106-108] and cryopreserved round spermatids have been used to achieve the same result.[109] These findings indicate that imprinting of parts of the genome necessary for normal embryonic development is accomplished during the initial phases of spermiogenesis.

## GERM CELL DEGENERATION

Germ cell degeneration is common in the testis during its development and in the adult period and is a major factor in determining the efficiency of spermatogenesis in terms of the theoretic versus the observed yield of mature spermatozoa.[28,110,111] Excessive germ cell degeneration is therefore an important determinant of fertility and may arise either in response to external or extratesticular influences (e.g., seasonality, nutrition, therapeutic drugs, environmental agents, infection) or as a result of intrinsic dysfunction of spermatogenesis, the details of which are largely unknown. Depending on the species, as much as 75% of the expected sperm yield is thought to be lost in the normal process of spermatogenesis. Degeneration with death of germ cells is often conspicuous in histologic sections of seminiferous tubules, including human tubules, and is attributable to programmed cell death, or apoptosis, in which activation or suppression of particular genes dictates a cell death or survival pathway. Apoptotic cells occur in most tissues in which a balance between cell proliferation and elimination is required for normal growth and/or

maintenance of the cellular population. In contrast to necrosis, apoptotic cells fragment and form several or numerous condensed bodies that include the pyknotic nucleus, but these bodies do not lyse, instead being phagocytosed by neighboring cells, and in the testis, the Sertoli cells rapidly dispose of these elements. Apoptosis therefore does not normally initiate an inflammatory response. In mice, a growing number of genes have been identified that, if deleted or disrupted, lead to germ cell apoptosis at various phases of spermatogenesis, and most of these genetically altered mice are infertile.[111] A range of proteins termed the *Bcl-2 family*, act to either promote (Bax, Bak, Bcl-x$_s$, Bad proteins) or prevent (Bcl-2, Bcl-x$_L$, Bcl-w, Mcl, Al proteins) apoptosis. These proteins form homodimers or heterodimers with each other, and the balance between them determines whether a cell will enter the apoptotic pathway. The expression of these proteins are developmentally controlled, and disruption of the genes encoding these proteins results in disordered spermatogenesis, often through mechanisms that alter the Sertoli cell–germ cell ratios.[112,113]

Human seminiferous tubules show spontaneous germ cell apoptosis for all phases of spermatogenesis, and its incidence varies with ethnic background.[6,114] The factors triggering apoptosis in an otherwise normal testis remain unknown. Numerous studies in laboratory animals[115-118] and in humans[119,120] have shown that this process is hormonally dependent (gonadotropin and androgen deprivation) and activated in response to heat stress, radiation, antimetabolic agents, cytoskeletal disrupters, cytotoxic agents, and tumor-inducing drugs. The precise causes and significance of germ cell death during spermatogenesis remain unclear, but the emerging details of apoptosis in the testis are consistent with the following speculations[110]: (1) dividing germ cells are deleted if they harbor nonrepaired DNA, (2) spermatocytes are eliminated if after chromosomal exchange in pachytene they contain faulty DNA, and (3) spermatids (or any germ cell) will degenerate if they are overproduced and therefore inadequately supported by Sertoli cells. Maintenance of normal function and numbers of germ cells by control of their survival versus death may be a key factor in the complex organization and synchronization of spermatogenesis.

## GENETIC DEFECTS AND SPERMATOGENESIS

Although a thorough description of how spermatogenesis is affected by specific gene activity is beyond the scope of this chapter, it is worth mentioning that in approximately 60% of men with idiopathic spermatogenic disruption, a genetic cause is suspected.[50,121] Well more than 100 gene mutations are known to cause spermatogenic disruption and fertility defects in mice.[122,123] Random mutations in mice have been generated by the use of chemical mutagens such as ethylnitrosourea or, in the case of embryonic stem cells, with ethylmethanesulfonate,[124] and the mutations resulting in spermatogenic disruption are being identified and providing novel concepts as to the genetic regulation of spermatogenesis. The number of genes affecting fertility/spermatogenesis remains unknown but in *Caenorhabditis elegans*, approximately 12% of genes are expressed in the germ line,[125] and in yeast, 14% of genes are regulated in meiosis.[126] It seems likely that in mice and humans, many more genes remain to be discovered with important functions in spermatogenesis.

## GERM CELL ASSOCIATIONS AND SPERMATOGENIC CYCLE

Coordinated and synchronous development of germ cells occurs within the seminiferous tubule. Cell associations are defined combinations of germ cells present at any moment in a given site of the seminiferous epithelium, an example of which is seen in Figure 167-4. For particular species, these associations are classified by Roman numerals into stages, such as I to XIV for rat, I to XII for the guinea pig, and I to VI for humans.[7,127] If it were possible to observe stages for prolonged periods in living seminiferous tubules, the morphology of each stage in a fixed tubular location would gradually transform into the stage with the structural features of the next Roman numeral. On reaching the highest numbered stage applicable, the germ cell association transforms into stage I and continues thereafter to proceed through successive stages.

The mechanisms underlying this synchronous development are (1) controlled proliferation of spermatogonial stem cells and their production of young spermatocytes, (2) fixed time intervals associated with meiotic maturation of spermatocytes into spermatids and the latter into spermatozoa, (3) coordinated development of cohorts of germ cells linked by cytoplasmic bridges, and (4) interactions between all germ cells and Sertoli cells, which occur in response to transduction of hormonal stimulation of the seminiferous epithelium. In most mammals and nonhuman primates, stages stretch along seminiferous tubules for as long as several millimeters, and when isolated tubules are examined by low-magnification transillumination microscopy, consecutive density patterns may be observed and reflect changes in germ cell number, position, and density. When an identical stage reappears along the length of a tubule, the distance between them is defined as the wave of the seminiferous epithelium. A complete sequence of stages (14 in the rat) requires passage of a species-specific interval (in days) referred to as one cycle of the seminiferous epithelium (12 days in rats and 16 days in humans). Commencing with the proliferation of a spermatogonium, completion of spermatogenesis requires that the germ cell passes through four cycles as it is transformed into a spermatozoon. The orderly, segmental sequence of stages is noted in cross sections of tubules in which the same stage of the seminiferous cycle occupies the entire tubule (see Fig. 167-4; Fig.167-9), but in humans and some primates (baboon, crab-eating macaque, orangutan, chimpanzee),[10,28,33,127] several stages are present in transversely sectioned tubules (see Fig. 167-5). In some selected examples of human seminiferous

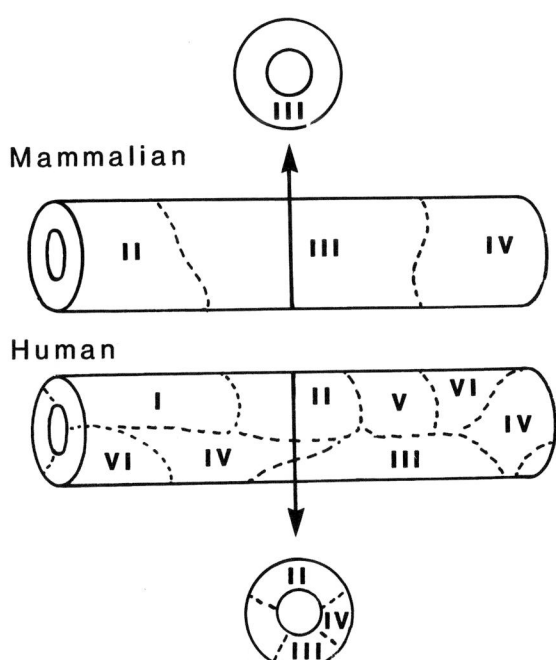

*Figure 167-9* Comparison of the organization of the stages (I–VI) of spermatogenesis in mammals (including numerous primates) and humans. In mammals, the stages occupy longitudinal segments along the seminiferous tubules, whereas in humans, they occur as discrete patches. When transverse sections of tubules are examined, two or more stages are noted in the human seminiferous epithelium.

tubules, the arrangement of developing germ cells follows a series of overlapping helical strips (Fig. 167-10) that gyrate toward the tubule lumen[127] (Fig. 167-11). Other studies have shown that this helical pattern is the exception rather than the rule inasmuch as a partial wave in humans appears to be a random occurrence.[128] The architectural composition stages within human seminiferous tubules vary with the level of efficiency of spermatogenesis. Men with high daily sperm production per gram of testis parenchyma ($7.5 \pm 0.2 \times 10^6$) show more stages per cross-sectional tubule than do men with lower sperm production ($3.6 \pm 0.3 \times 10^6$). Incompleteness of the wave in the human testis may be a variant of the same phenomenon in the rodent testis, in which most (80%) tubules show localized site reversal of the numerical order of stages along the tubules, and as many as nine of these modulations have been noted in a single entire tubule.[127-130]

It should be noted that stages or cell associations classified by cell phenotypes are not of constant length along the longitudinal axis of the seminiferous tubules, either within a particular stage or when comparing different stages. Thus, in the rat testis, stages VII through VIII are normally of greater length compared with other stages,[130] but they also show variable length within individual tubules. Synchrony among germ cells forming a stage is attributed in large part to the morphology of the spermatids that are interconnected by intercellular bridges. Conjoined spermatids (and the germ cell types from which they are derived) are clones that originate from the cell divisions of the spermatogonia and the stem cells in particular. The synchrony of spermatogenesis along the seminiferous tubule is suggested to be the result of the number of spermatogonia that supply spermatocytes to the process of meiosis and the resultant synchronous development of clones of cells joined by intercellular bridges).[131] Recent studies of the fate of isolated germ cells transplanted into testes of the same or different species have demonstrated that recipient seminiferous tubules can support spermatogenesis of the donor germ cells. In one study, the transplanted germ cells established intraluminal mini-seminiferous tubules within the host's tubules, and both donor and host spermatogenic tissue showed synchronous stages.[132] This observation suggests that the local tubule microenvironment in some way regulates the cycle of the seminiferous epithelium. The question of whether it is Sertoli cells or germ cells that control the orderly processes of germ cell proliferation and morphogenesis during spermatogenesis has been resolved by the demonstration that transplanted hamster or rat germ cells can partly or fully complete spermatogenesis in association with the Sertoli cells of the recipient mouse testis.[59,63,65,66] These studies have been extended to transplantation of germ cells to mouse recipients from nonrodent species such as the dog, rabbit, pig, bull, primate, and human.[133-136] Although transplanted germ cells, thought to be spermatogonia, were able to colonize recipient mouse seminiferous tubules and persist there for 6 months, none of them differentiated into more advanced germ cell types. These studies suggest that local factors that support interactions between stem cells and the Sertoli cells are generally species specific and have been preserved in the divergence of particular mammalian species. In contrast to isolated germ cells used for transplantation, xenografts of neonatal or immature testicular tissue from the mouse, pig, lamb, and rhesus monkey into mouse hosts show spermatogenic development resulting in germ cell differentiation and production of fertilization-competent sperm.[137-140] Xenografts exhibit precocious induction of spermatogenesis compared with the normal time frame required for germ cell development, probably due to elevated endogenous gonadotropins in the castrated immunodeficient host mice. Development of rat germ cells supported by mouse Sertoli cells proceeds with the timing characteristic and stage architecture of the rat, not the mouse, thus indicating that germ cells, within a suitable tissue environment, dominate and

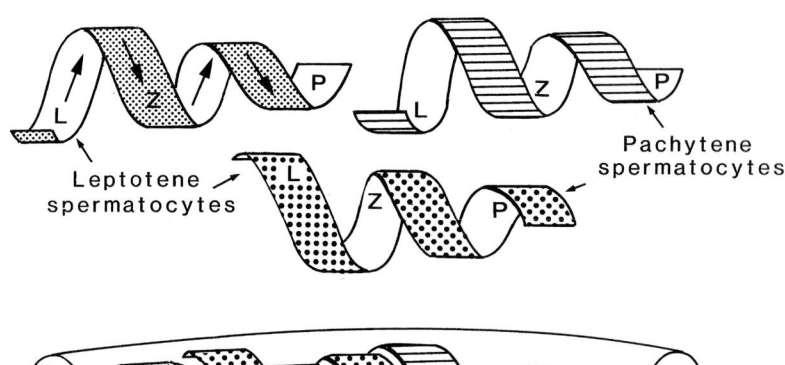

Helical organization pattern
of the human seminiferous epithelium

**Figure 167-10** Helical arrangement of the development of primary spermatocytes of the human testis (leptotene [L], zygotene [Z], pachytene [P]) drawn as strips that overlap and gyrate toward the tubule lumen. This pattern, when apparent, occupies only small segments of the seminiferous tubule; otherwise, the stages of spermatogenesis (I–VI) occur randomly along the tubules.

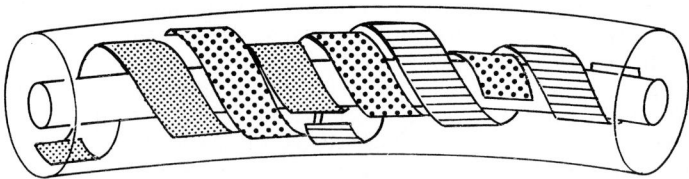

regulate the spermatogenic process; the Sertoli cells appear as passive supportive cells that recognize or tolerate xenogeneic germ cells, provided that donor germ cells and host Sertoli cells share some phylogenetic commonalities.

## POSTNATAL GROWTH OF THE HUMAN TESTIS

Quantitative assessment of seminiferous tubule growth is available for ages 0 to 18 years.[141,142] Testis volume increases

significantly from 0 to 10 years; from 1.1 cm³ (median value of paired testes) in the 0- to 1-year age range to 3 cm³ at ages 5 to 10 years. At 14 to 18 years, median paired testis volume is greatly increased to 23 cm³ and continues to increase to 40 cm³ in an adult group aged 18 to 50 years (Fig. 167-12). Seminiferous tubule length per testis also increases with age, showing a biphasic pattern in the pre- and postpubertal age ranges and reaching a median length of 600 m. The latter figure varies widely between individuals, in some cases, reaching in excess of 1000 m. Until the age of 14 years, the tubule diameter does not appreciably increase from birth (50–60 μm) but thereafter expands to approximately 130 μm in the 14- to 18-year age range and in adults is approximately 200 μm. Other studies from birth to 10 years of age also report no increase in tubule diameter, although the slightly larger size of 70 to 80 μm probably reflects postmortem change before tissue fixation.[143] Growth in the length but not the diameter of the seminiferous tubules in the prepubertal period is consistent with the fact that the testis in childhood is not a quiescent organ but shows a significant increase in the

**Figure 167-11** Representation of stages I through VI of the spermatogenic cycle of the human testis with their complement of germ cells arranged to show how the sequence of development corresponds to the geometry of spirals gyrating conically toward the lumen. In actual tubules, usually two to four stages per cross section are seen, some of which are located at slightly more superficial or deeper levels along the seminiferous tubule. Symbols are as defined in Figure 167-5. (From Kerr JB: Functional cytology of the human testis. Baillieres Clin Endocrinol Metab 6:235–250, 1992.)

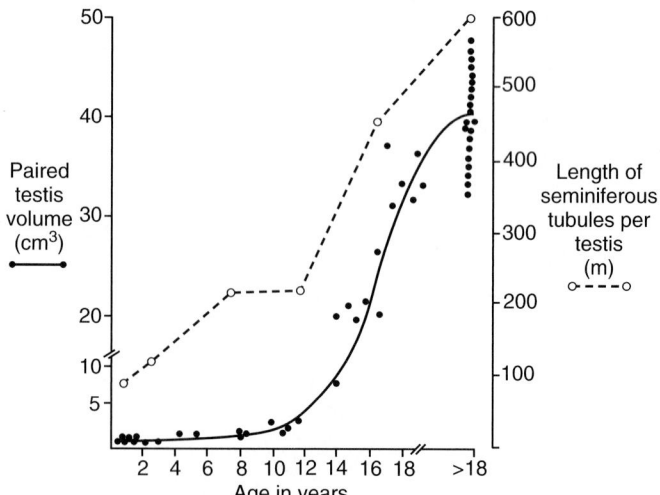

**Figure 167-12** Growth in testis volume and seminiferous tubule length in 50 boys from ages 0 to 18 years. Tissue samples obtained postmortem were fixed and processed in paraffin. Stained sections were analyzed using quantitative histologic methods. (Data based on Muller and Skakkebaek.[141])

total number of germ cells. From 1 to 10 years of age, the total number of germ cells per testis is estimated to increase from 13 to 83 million and grow exponentially after this stage.[141] Much of this cellular growth is attributable to proliferation of the spermatogonia that populate the growing seminiferous tubules by forming colonies that migrate and expand along the length of the tubules.[141,143–145]

## SERTOLI CELLS

Sertoli cells are the only somatic, nondividing cell population within the seminiferous tubules, where they occupy as much as 25% of the volume of the seminiferous epithelium. Because they extend from the basal lamina to the tubule lumen, each of these cells partly or completely surrounds several dozen or more germ cells, for which they provide structural and biochemical support together with local immunologic protection. The literature on Sertoli cells is considerable and detailed[7,8,21] and provides some insight into precisely how Sertoli cells support the process of spermatogenesis.

### SHAPE AND DISTRIBUTION

Sertoli cells resemble the shape of a tree in that they are tall columnar cells resting on the basement membrane and extending lateral and apical cytoplasmic branches from the body or trunk of the cell that overarch the spermatogonia and interdigitate and surround all other germ cells (see Fig. 167-4). By providing physical support to the germ cells, the Sertoli cell must maintain a degree of rigidity while retaining the capacity to change shape in synchrony with the division, enlargement, and metamorphic alterations of germ cells. Attainment of quantitatively normal spermatogenesis in an adult is dependent on an adequate number of Sertoli cells,[146,147] which is achieved by their proliferative activity during growth of the fetal and postnatal testis and is dependent on FSH stimulation.[148,149] Quantitative histologic studies of the human testis have indicated that Sertoli cell numbers may increase until approximately 15 years of age.[150] At its base, each Sertoli cell is in contact with five or six adjacent Sertoli cells, and each cell supports as many as 50 germ cells throughout the depth of the seminiferous epithelium.[22,151]

### BLOOD-TESTIS BARRIER

Where the plasma membranes of adjacent Sertoli cells are apposed in the basolateral regions of the cell, they form special occluding tight junctions (Fig. 167-13), which in freeze-fracture preparations resemble multiple parallel rows of spot fusions forming a band or zone of adhesion around the circumference of the cell.[21] The junctions form the blood-testis barrier and are stabilized by a large number of component proteins[152,153] including subsurface actin filaments, actin-binding protein such as espin,[154] and smooth membranous cisternae.[151] Their unusual position at the base of the seminiferous epithelium is known to subdivide the epithelium into basal and adluminal regions that partition young and more mature germ cells into two distinct anatomic and functional compartments. Spermatogonia and early spermatocytes (up to leptotene) reside within the basal compartment and may be exposed to the biochemical environment maintained by the intertubular tissue. The strategic position of the tight junctions between adjacent Sertoli cells and above these germ cells prevents intercellular transport between Sertoli cells and thus creates an adluminal compartment thought to provide a unique physiologic environment for all other germ cells. Completion of meiotic maturation and spermiogenesis therefore occurs within a special epithelial domain created and regulated by Sertoli cells. Upward displacement of germ cells from the basal to the adluminal compartment is

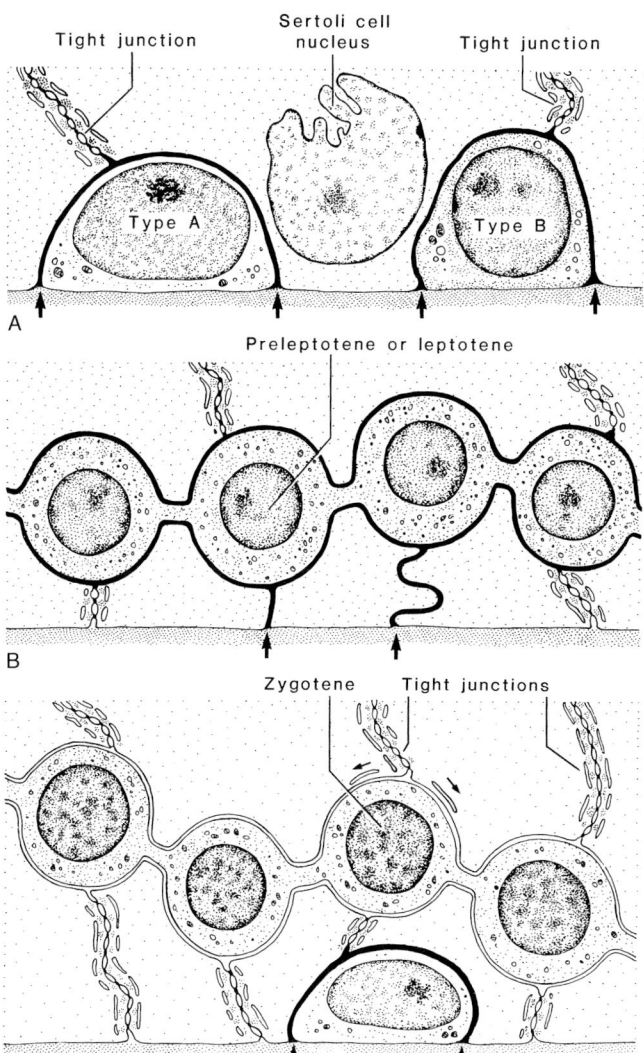

**Figure 167-13** Diagram illustrates the manner in which the cell membranes of adjacent Sertoli cells form the tight occluding junctions that constitute the blood-testis barrier. Also illustrated is how developing germ cells move from the basal to the adluminal compartment of the testis. Passage of tracers through the intercellular space is illustrated *(arrows)*.

achieved by synchronized dissolution and reassembly of tight junctions above and below the migrating germ cells. The blood-testis barrier exists in all animals[7] and is formed during the initiation of spermatogenesis[155] in response to gonadotropic stimulation[156] and the appearance of zygotene-pachytene primary spermatocytes. In the developing human testis, junctional specializations between Sertoli cells are absent until 8 years of age but in the early phase of puberty (11–13 years), the typical inter–Sertoli cell junctions are assembled.[157] These junctions are impermeable to lanthanum penetration and coincide with the appearance from 12 years of age of increasing numbers of spermatocytes, consistent with the establishment of basal and adluminal epithelial compartments.

### PLASTICITY AND LINKS WITH GERM CELLS

Sertoli cells exhibit an elaborate and dynamic cytoskeleton that serves to maintain the columnar shape of the cell, determine the intracellular distribution of organelles, and provide intercellular adhesion with germ cells. The supranuclear regions of the Sertoli cell cytoplasm are supplied with microtubules (chiefly α-tubulin) and the motor proteins dynein and kinesin, which are especially abundant in the crypts surrounding elongating spermatids.[158,159] Together with intermediate filaments,[160] these cytoskeletal elements are believed to influence the shape and position of the germ cells in concert with the spermatogenic cycle. A further component of the cytoskeleton of Sertoli cells is evident at the interface between the plasma membranes of Sertoli cells and germ cells and is identified as an ES. This component appears to be identical to half of the inter–Sertoli tight junction and consists of a dense mat of actin filaments sandwiched between the plasma membrane and a cistern of smooth endoplasmic reticulum.[151,161] Only rarely associated with zygotene primary spermatocytes, they are more frequently observed facing pachytene primary spermatocytes and always occur in association with round and elongating spermatids and form a mantle around the heads of the latter germ cells.[7] The presence of vinculin within these ESs[162] suggests that Sertoli cells adhere to the plasma membrane of germ cells and thus play a role in determining the shape of the elongating sperm head and in adjusting the orientation of the germ cells within the seminiferous epithelium. Translocation of spermatids within the deep recesses created by the Sertoli cells is shown in Figure 167-14. The Sertoli cell microtubular system is especially abundant and may act as an intracellular transport apparatus that moves germ cells by coupling the motor proteins to an intercellular junction in the form of ESs.[159] It is thought that the ES-spermatid association allows microtubule motors within the columnar Sertoli cell cytoplasm to direct the movement of elongating spermatids initially in a basal direction via the microtubule-associated protein kinesin. With further development of the spermatid, particularly as the axoneme lengthens, the microtubule motor protein dynein then translocates the spermatid in the reverse direction toward the apical region of the Sertoli cell. After release of the mature spermatid at spermiation, the disconnected ES fragments may be reassembled in the body of the Sertoli cell cytoplasm where they establish new associations with the next generation of round spermatids. Why it is necessary for elongating spermatids to penetrate into deep Sertoli cell crypts is unknown, but this close association with the surrounding Sertoli cell cytoplasm may assist with stabilization of the long (50 µm)

spermatid tail during its assembly and restructure of its ultimately redundant cytoplasm.

## PHAGOCYTOSIS, ENDOCYTOSIS, AND SECRETION

Sertoli cells phagocytose the excess residual cytoplasm of spermatids shed at spermiation and eliminate degenerating germ cells, which is a naturally occurring phenomenon during spermatogenesis. The residual bodies fuse with endosomes and lysosomes and migrate toward the base of the Sertoli cell.[31] Lysosomal numbers and enzymatic activities vary throughout the spermatogenic cycle[163–166] and serve to dispose of degenerative germ cell products. The endocytosis of tracers such as ferritin has suggested that the lysosomal system also participates in the reduction of excess plasma membrane and absorption of luminal fluid through the apical cytoplasm.[163] Sertoli cells show receptor-mediated endocytosis of macromolecules via their apex and base,[167,168] and recent in vivo and in vitro studies have demonstrated this to be the mechanism by which the Sertoli cells deliver iron to germ cells from the serum.[169] The Sertoli cells in adult males do not divide, and consequently, the complement of Sertoli cells is established at the conclusion of puberty. The proliferative phases for this cell population are in fetal and early postnatal life and are controlled by FSH and activin A,[170,171] and further proliferation takes place during puberty in mammals in which birth and puberty are significantly separated temporally.[150]

## INTERTUBULAR TISSUE

### ORGANIZATION

The region between the seminiferous tubules, termed the *intertubular* or *interstitial tissue*, consists of loose connective tissue, the cellular and extracellular components of which are qualitatively similar in the mammalian testis, although its quantitative composition is species specific.[7,172] The relative proportion of Leydig cells, which synthesize and secrete androgens, chiefly testosterone,[172,173] varies between species usually occupying only 10% to 20% of the intertubular tissue

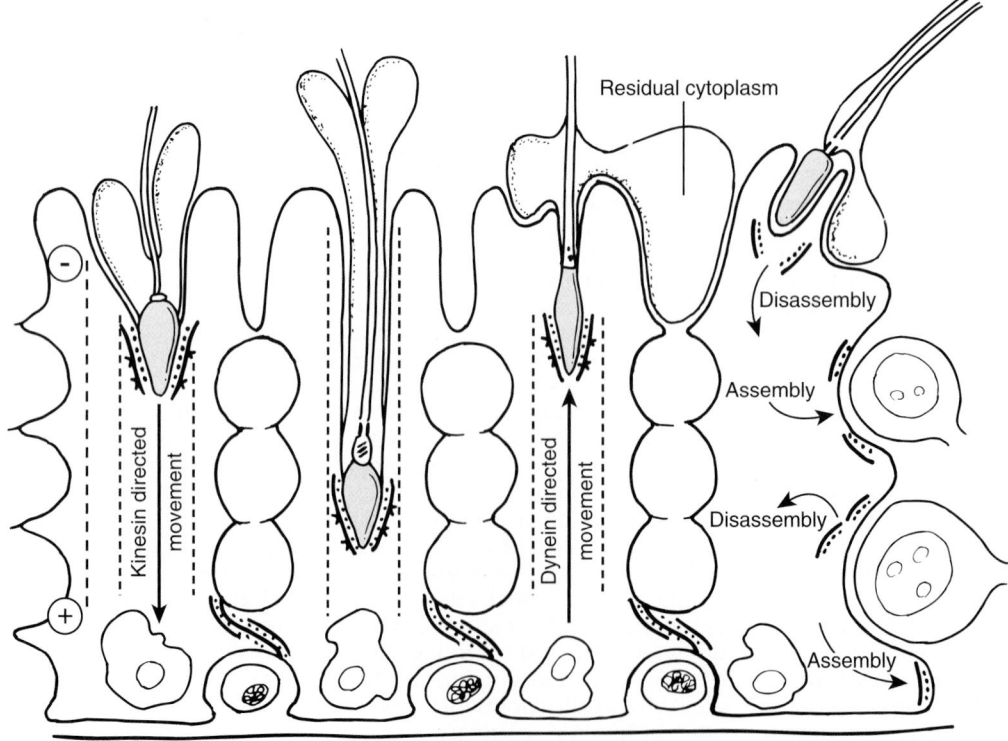

*Figure 167-14* Scheme of spermatid translocation hypothesis shows relationship between ectoplasmic specializations of germ cells and their transport along Sertoli cell microtubules via motor proteins. After spermiation, ectoplasmic specializations disassemble and associate with spermatids. With adluminal migration of early spermatocytes from the basal to the adluminal compartment, the Sertoli ectoplasmic specialization is degraded then reassembled to seal the inter–Sertoli cell tight junctions. (Redrawn from Vogl AW, Pfeiffer DC, Mulholland D, et al: Unique and multifunctional adhesion junctions in the testis: Ectoplasmic specializations. Arch Histol Cytol 63:1–15, 2000.)

(rat, guinea pig, ram, human).[7] Blood vessels occur randomly throughout the intertubular tissue, and capillaries are non-fenestrated. Lymphatic vessels and large lymphatic sinusoids are seen in several rodent species (mouse, rat, guinea pig), in contrast to the human testis, in which these vessels exist only in the main connective tissue septa extending inward from the tunica albuginea.[174] Fibroblasts and macrophages are also found in the intertubular tissue, whereas lymphocytes and mast cells are irregularly distributed and occur more commonly in the region of the tunica vasculosa.

## LEYDIG CELLS

The morphology of Leydig cells in the mammalian testis is typically that of a steroid-secreting cell that produces testosterone.[172,173] Fetal, immature, and adult-type Leydig cells are epithelioid in shape (Fig. 167-15), and their basophilic staining property is attributed to the dominant organelle within their cytoplasm, the smooth endoplasmic reticulum, whose surface provides binding sites for numerous enzymes catalyzing a variety of steroidogenic conversions. The substrate for the synthesis of testosterone is acetate or cholesterol, and the latter is derived from lipoproteins transported into the cell through the involvement of lipoprotein receptors. The subsequent steps in the steroidogenic pathway and its control are discussed below. Leydig cells contain Golgi membranes, microtubules, smooth endoplasmic reticulum, mitochondria with tubular cristae (unique in steroidogenic cells), and small quantities of rough endoplasmic reticulum. The mechanism by which testosterone leaves the Leydig cell remains unclear, and it is assumed that exit occurs via diffusion because typical secretory vacuoles or granules have not been observed. Leydig cells are capable of endocytotic activity via fluid-phase or adsorptive endocytosis, the ingested materials entering the lysosomal pathway.[7]

Peroxisomes have been identified in Leydig cells and contain a sterol carrier protein, which suggests involvement in the intracellular transport of cholesterol to the mitochondria for subsequent side chain cleavage to pregnenolone.[175] Undigested materials appear as lipofuscin pigment granules, which are prevalent in human Leydig cells. Crystals of Reinke, which are composed of globular protein subunits, are frequently noted in human Leydig cells, and although similar crystalline inclusions increase in abundance in the Leydig cells of a seasonally breeding wild rat, their functional significance is unknown.[7]

## INTERSTITIAL CELLS

The intertubular tissue contains macrophages, which have been characterized for several species by histochemical, immunologic, and ultrastructural techniques.[172,176–179] In most species, the ratio of macrophages to Leydig cells is approximately in the range of 1 to 10 or even 50, whereas in the rat testis, they are especially abundant, with one macrophage for every four Leydig cells. Testicular macrophages have different properties to macrophages elsewhere in that their antigen-presenting functions are modified, perhaps providing some explanation as to why tissue allografts or xenografts survive for long periods in the rat testis,[179,180] thus suggesting that the latter represents an immunologically privileged tissue. These issues are discussed below.

The populations of mesenchymal or fibroblast-type cells in the intertubular tissue not only serve as loose connective tissue cells but also as a source of new Leydig cells. These precursor or stem cells are found in peritubular and perivascular locations. They are capable of producing testosterone via luteinizing hormone (LH) stimulation and ultimately differentiate into Leydig cells.[181,182] Studies of the endocrine and paracrine factors that influence the development of Leydig cells are discussed later in this chapter.

## CONTROL OF TESTICULAR FUNCTION

The major factors that control the production of testosterone by Leydig cells and the production of spermatozoa by the seminiferous tubules are the gonadotropic hormones FSH and LH. These two hormones are secreted by the anterior pituitary gland under control of the episodic secretion of gonadotropin-releasing hormone (GnRH) into the pituitary portal vessels. In addition to GnRH, their secretion is controlled by the level of negative feedback from the testis via testosterone and inhibin (see later). Hormonal mechanisms are crucial for normal testicular function, but the appropriate developmental processes must occur to establish the architecture of the testis. Furthermore, once the testis is formed, key cellular processes and interactions are essential to successfully produce normal sperm output. These interactions include the structure-function relationships of the Sertoli and germ cells, control of spermatogonial proliferation, and successful completion of meiosis and the complex cellular transformation that constitutes spermiogenesis. Although cell proliferation may occur normally, recent data indicate that disturbances in the control of cell survival can drastically impair spermatogenesis through an increase in apoptosis.[183]

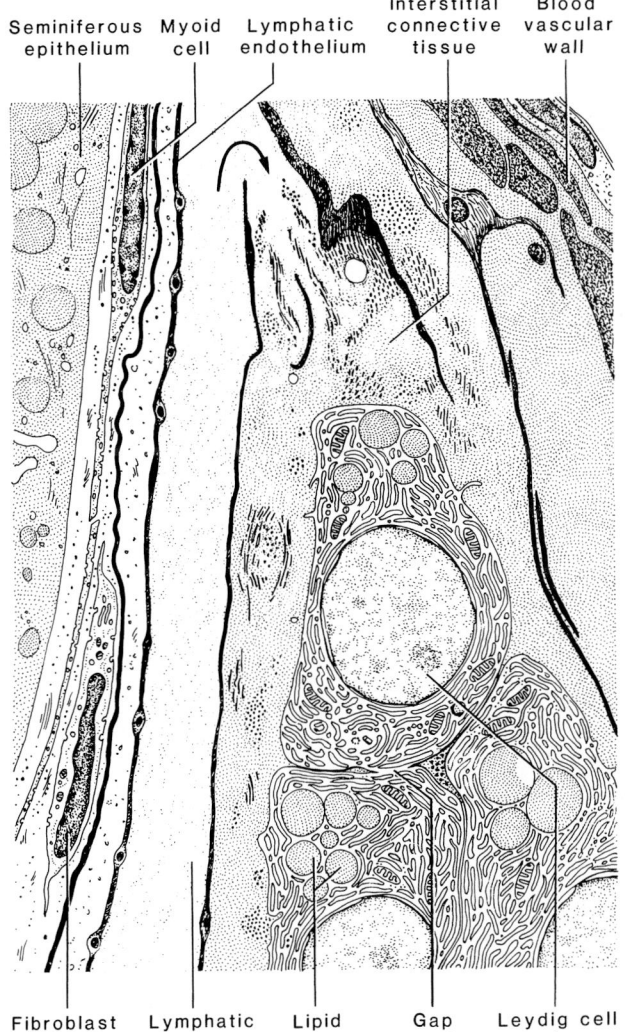

Seminiferous epithelium · Myoid cell · Lymphatic endothelium · Interstitial connective tissue · Blood vascular wall

Fibroblast · Lymphatic vessel · Lipid inclusions · Gap junction · Leydig cell nucleus

*Figure 167-15* Arrangement of the intertubular tissue of the testis. (From de Kretser DM, Kerr JB: The cytology of the testis. In Knobil Z, Neill JD [eds]: The Physiology of Reproduction, 2d ed. New York, Raven, 1994, pp 1177–1290.)

Although it is useful to consider control of the compartments of the testis separately, increasing evidence suggests that their functions are intimately related through known and unknown factors operating through paracrine mechanisms.[184-187] Furthermore, a substantial body of evidence now indicates that the stimulatory action of FSH and LH, the latter through testosterone, on seminiferous tubule function is modulated by local factors. Hormonal control, through the actions of gonadotropic hormones, is considered first, and the interaction between Leydig cells, Sertoli cells, and germ cells in modulating the actions of FSH and LH is considered later in this chapter.

## LEYDIG CELL FUNCTION AND CONTROL

The juxtaposition of the Leydig cells and seminiferous tubules facilitates paracrine mechanisms. Transport of testosterone into the circulation is facilitated through the close proximity of capillaries to Leydig cells. Although a number of naturally occurring steroids have the capacity to exhibit androgen action, testosterone is the major product of Leydig cells and has the most potent androgenic action.[172,173] The adult human testis produces approximately 7 mg of testosterone daily. In addition, the testis produces smaller amounts of weaker androgens, such as androstenedione and dehydroepiandrosterone (DHEA). As discussed later, testosterone exerts its action by binding to specific intracellular androgen receptors, and the weaker androgens, androstenedione and DHEA, have a lower binding affinity for the androgen receptor. The testis also produces small amounts of dihydrotestosterone, which has a very strong affinity for the androgen receptor. In addition to androgens, the testis produces approximately 25% of the total daily production of 17β-estradiol,[188] with the remainder (both estradiol and estrone) being derived by conversion of both testicular and adrenal androgens, such as androstenedione and DHEA, by the enzyme aromatase in peripheral tissues.

### Biosynthetic Pathway

Androgen production by Leydig cells is regulated by LH. Tropic stimulation of Leydig cells may be chronic or acute; the acute effects of hormonal stimuli occur within minutes and are distinct from the chronic effects, which take hours and involve the regulation of genes encoding the steroidogenic enzymes required for biosynthesis.

The major substrate for steroid production by the Leydig cell is cholesterol. To initiate or maintain steroidogenesis, an adequate supply of cholesterol is required and can be derived from two sources. The first consists of an uptake mechanism by which circulating low-density lipoprotein can bind to specific receptors on Leydig cells and, by internalization, provide a ready source of cholesterol. In the rat, Leydig cell receptors for high-density lipoprotein have also been found.[189] The other source of cholesterol is from de novo synthesis from acetate by the Leydig cell. It is likely that the proportion of cholesterol obtained by these two pathways may vary, depending on the species and state of stimulation of the Leydig cells. Some estimates have suggested that more than half of the cholesterol required by the Leydig cells comes from low-density lipoprotein.[190] Conversion of cholesterol to testosterone involves a number of steps that are catalyzed by hemoprotein mixed-function oxidases, which predominantly belong to the cytochrome P-450 family. The steps in the steroidogenic pathway are illustrated in Figure 167-16.

The first step in this pathway is the mobilization of cholesterol from pools of cholesterol esters by a testicular cholesterol ester hydrolase[172,173] and the conversion of cholesterol to pregnenolone. The free cholesterol is transported to mitochondria,

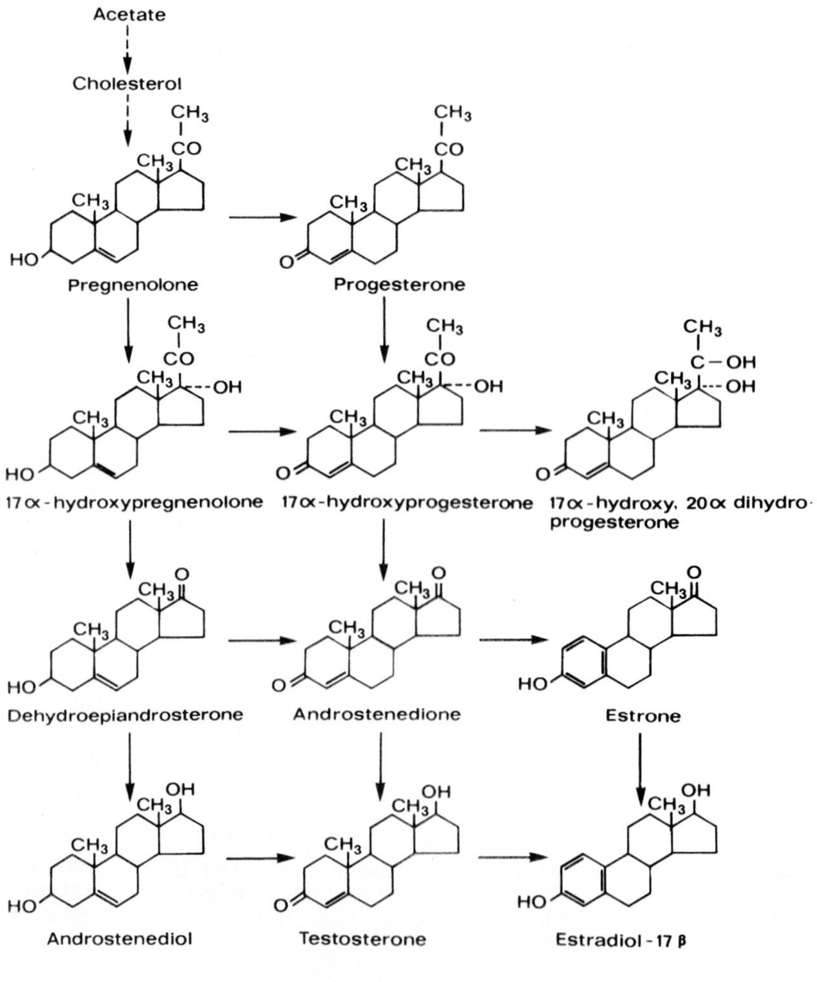

*Figure 167-16* Steroid biosynthetic pathways leading to testosterone and estradiol production.

where it passes from the outer to the inner mitochondrial membrane with the aid of a 30-amino acid steroidogenic activator peptide.[191] The cholesterol side-chain cleavage enzyme, which converts cholesterol to pregnenolone, is located on the inner mitochondrial membrane and catalyzes three separate reactions. Two hydroxylations occur at the C20 and C22 positions and cleavage of the cholesterol side chain at the C20 to C22 carbon bond forms pregnenolone, with the release of the six-carbon compound isocaproic acid. The enzyme catalyzing this reaction is termed *cytochrome P-450scc*. It is likely that stimulation of this reaction is crucial in the regulation of steroidogenesis, with cholesterol substrate being a rate-limiting step. Cytochrome P-450scc is encoded by a single gene that transcribes a single species of mRNA, and the testicular and adrenal enzymes are identical.[192]

Most studies of acute regulation of steroidogenesis were conducted on the adrenal cortex, but the underlying mechanisms are probably the same in all steroidogenic cells, including Leydig cells. Acute production of steroids requires de novo protein synthesis, and a number of candidate proteins have been studied, including sterol carrier protein 2, the peripheral benzodiazepine receptor (PBR), and the steroidogenic acute regulatory protein (StAR). Sterol carrier protein 2 is associated with the intracellular trafficking of cholesterol and is found in liver and steroidogenic cells.[193] The evidence that it is able to effectively transfer cholesterol to the inner mitochondrial membrane in response to acute hormonal stimulation is not convincing, and it is likely that it functions to support steroidogenesis and maintain sterol movement to the mitochondria.

In 1994, Clark and colleagues[194] identified StAR, which has received widespread attention and is a crucial protein involved in acute steroid synthesis. In humans, StAR has been localized to normal and neoplastic cells of the gonads and adrenal cortex, but it is not detected in the placenta.[195] The most convincing evidence for the importance of StAR comes from the study of congenital lipoid adrenal hyperplasia. Mitochondria from the adrenals and gonads of these patients cannot convert cholesterol to pregnenolone, and nonsense mutations of StAR have been identified by sequence analysis.[196] Targeted disruption of the mouse gene encoding StAR supports these findings, and although the mice show sex-specific differences in gonadal involvement, after birth they fail to grow normally and die of adrenal cortical insufficiency.[197]

The role of PBR and its intracellular ligand diazepam-binding inhibitor has been reviewed by Papadopolous.[198] Benzodiazepines regulate chloride channel gating of a γ-aminobutyric acid receptor; benzodiazepine-binding receptors have been identified in the kidney and central nervous system as well as in many peripheral tissues, including steroidogenic cells, where they are localized to the outer mitochondrial membrane. Papadopolous[198] has suggested that hormone stimulation affects the binding of PBR to diazepam-binding inhibitor; a structural change in the PBR follows this alteration in binding affinity and allows the formation of contact sites between the inner and outer mitochondrial membrane, the net result being an increased flux of cholesterol. However, it is not certain that diazepam-binding inhibitor and PBR are directly regulated by tropic hormones, and the precise role of PBR in steroidogenesis requires clarification. The pregnenolone formed may be converted to progesterone through the enzyme 3β-hydroxysteroid hydrogenase (3β-HSD), or it can be hydroxylated at the 17α-position by 17α-hydroxylase. The pathways taken by pregnenolone either through progesterone (the $\Delta^4$ pathway) or through 17α-hydroxypregnenolone (the $\Delta^5$ pathway) may vary between species and the physiologic state of the mammal. In humans, the $\Delta^5$ pathway appears to predominate in both the adult and fetal testis.[199,200]

In following the $\Delta^5$ pathway, pregnenolone is hydroxylated to 17α-hydroxypregnenolone, which subsequently under-

goes cleavage to form the C19 steroid DHEA by the enzyme 17,20-lyase. Both steps appear to be catalyzed by a single microsomal enzyme, cytochrome P-450c17. A single gene on chromosome 10 encodes for this enzyme in both the adrenal and testis.[201,202] Further conversion of DHEA to androstenediol is mediated by the enzyme 17β-HSD, which is a microsomal enzyme that does not belong to the cytochrome P-450 series.[203] There appears to be a single gene for 17β-HSD on chromosome 17.[204]

Conversion of substrates in the $\Delta^5$ pathway to the $\Delta^4$ pathway (see Fig. 167-16) involves the enzyme 3β-HSD. It is possible that more than one copy of the human 3β-HSD gene may exist.[205] In addition to the conversion of pregnenolone to progesterone, 3β-HSD has the capacity to convert other precursors in the $\Delta^5$ pathway to the $\Delta^4$ pathway, namely, the conversion of 17α-hydroxypregnenolone to 17-hydroxyprogesterone, the conversion of DHEA to androstenedione, and the conversion of androstenediol to testosterone.

As indicated earlier, the testis has the capacity to produce 17β-estradiol, and this reaction is catalyzed by the enzyme cytochrome P-450 aromatase. This conversion involves a series of reactions resulting in hydroxylation at C3 and loss of the methyl side chain at C10. Two cytochrome P-450 aromatase genes have been found on chromosome 15.[206]

The testis has the capacity to secrete small amounts of dihydrotestosterone, and the enzyme catalyzing the conversion of testosterone to dihydrotestosterone is 5α-reductase. The testicular level of this enzyme is much lower than that found in genital skin or prostatic tissue. The enzyme encoding human 5α-reductase has been cloned and catalyzes a reduction of the unsaturated C4-C5 double bond of testosterone to form 5α-dihydrotestosterone.[207]

Determination of the cellular localization of these enzymes has been achieved through the localization of cytochrome P-450scc on the inner mitochondrial membrane in the process of conversion of cholesterol to pregnenolone within the mitochondria.[172] Pregnenolone is transported from the mitochondrion to the smooth endoplasmic reticulum, where the remaining enzymes necessary for the conversion of pregnenolone to testosterone are located. Numerous studies have demonstrated that the smooth endoplasmic reticulum gives rise to the microsomal fraction that contains the necessary enzymes.

## REGULATION OF TESTICULAR STEROIDOGENESIS

Control of testosterone production is mediated by the gonadotropin LH through the presence of specific receptors on the surface of Leydig cells.[208] The LH receptor has been isolated, sequenced, and cloned and was shown to be a member of the seven-transmembrane domain G protein–coupled receptor superfamily.[209] Mutations of the receptor have been identified and are classified as inactivating (loss-of-function) or activating (gain-of-function) mutations. In males, constitutively activating mutations in the first and third transmembrane helices of the receptor have been reported to result in precocious puberty.[210–212] Inactivating mutations of the LH receptor, however, have been reported to be associated with familial testicular resistance[213] and male pseudohermaphroditism[214] and occur in the seventh and first transmembrane helices, respectively. Insights into the pivotal role of the LH receptor in relation to Leydig cell steroidogenesis has emerged from studies of Leydig cell function in LH receptor knockout mice.[215] LH/LH receptor signaling is not essential for the differentiation of fetal Leydig cells because testicular testosterone levels in neonate LH receptor knockout and wild-type mice are similar. During postnatal life, mRNA expression of numerous key steroidogenic enzymes in LH receptor knockout mice decreased to undetectable levels. This decrease occurred in parallel with a 97% reduction in testicular testosterone content and the absence of adult type Leydig cells.[215]

One exception was the expression of mRNA for 3β-HSD, which remained detectable in LH receptor knockout mice testes up to adult age. This enzyme is synthesized in mesenchymal and peritubular cells but is not dependent on LH/LH receptor signaling.

Considerable evidence indicates that interaction of LH with its receptor activates the cyclic adenosine monophosphate pathway through a guanosine triphosphate–binding protein.[7,216] Some concern about signal transduction through the protein kinase A pathway existed because LH could stimulate submaximal testosterone production without any significant changes in cyclic adenosine monophosphate concentration.[217] More recent data have suggested the possibility that changes in intracellular calcium concentration may be involved in the action of LH by activating phospholipases in the lipoxygenase pathway.[218] This mechanism would provide an alternative pathway for the control of steroidogenesis in Leydig cells. In addition, changes in calcium may regulate adenylate cyclase via the protein kinase C pathway.[7,216,218]

The action of LH leads to a number of events resulting in the provision of cholesterol substrate and in stimulation of the side-chain cleavage enzyme to convert cholesterol to pregnenolone. This process involves mobilization of cholesterol from cholesterol stores and stimulation of cholesterol ester hydrolase.[173] The resultant production of pregnenolone is rapidly translated into the release of testosterone within 30 to 60 minutes of LH stimulation. This acute response varies in magnitude between species, being very clear in the rat and the ram but less so in humans. A much longer response can be seen after repeated stimuli with LH or after a single injection of human chorionic gonadotropin (hCG), the latter having a considerably longer half-life.[219,220] In experiments using hCG, the initial increase in testosterone peaks within 12 hours, and the levels subsequently decrease to an elevated plateau at 24 hours, again increasing to a peak 48 to 72 hours after the initial injection. This biphasic response of testosterone secretion to hCG stimulation of Leydig cells does not occur with LH and probably results from a number of factors. After acute stimulation of Leydig cells with high doses of LH or hCG, a loss of receptors from the surface of Leydig cells is noted.[221] This loss is also accompanied by refractoriness of the Leydig cells to further LH/hCG stimulation for approximately 48 to 72 hours,[220] probably as a result of the conversion of testosterone to estradiol and feedback inhibition of the 17,20-lyase enzyme.[222] The second phase of testosterone secretion that occurs 72 hours after hCG injection is likely to be due to recovery from this inhibition of steroid biosynthesis, and the long half-life of hCG ensures that after high doses, adequate levels of hCG are still present in the circulation to result in the reactivation of steroid secretion. However, other factors are also likely to play a role because LH and hCG are tropic hormones and their action results in stimulation of a range of enzyme synthesis, cellular hypertrophy, and hyperplasia.[223,224] Thus, in states of chronic Leydig cell stimulation, LH enhances the transcription of genes encoding the range of enzymes in the steroidogenic pathway.[225] In the normal physiologic state, it is unlikely that the phenomenon of downregulation of receptors and refractoriness to further LH stimulation occurs, mainly because LH stimulation of the testis is episodic and pulsatile and results from the pulsatility of GnRH stimulation of the pituitary gland. Nevertheless, increases in pulse frequency can result in augmentation of the testosterone secretory responses, although the size of the LH pulses decreases.[226]

### CONTROL OF SEMINIFEROUS TUBULE FUNCTION

The intimate association of germ cells with Sertoli cells and their dependence on this cell type for survival, which was described earlier in this chapter, emphasize the need to consider the control of spermatogenesis in conjunction with the factors modulating Sertoli cell function. The link between the two populations of cells is amply demonstrated by the wealth of data demonstrating that the spermatogenic output of the mammalian testis is dependent on the number of Sertoli cells in the testis.[146–150,227,228] These studies demonstrate that increasing or decreasing the number of Sertoli cells by neonatal modulation of FSH or thyroxine can increase or decrease the number of Sertoli cells and subsequent adult sperm output.

It is generally agreed that the seminiferous tubule is controlled by FSH and LH, the latter acting via the local secretion of testosterone. However, the specific cell types and processes influenced by these hormones are still debated, particularly the role of FSH in the maintenance of spermatogenesis. Furthermore, increasing evidence indicates that local factors may modulate the actions of FSH and testosterone, and these issues are considered later in this chapter.

### Localization of Receptors

Receptors for FSH in the seminiferous tubules were demonstrated on Sertoli cells and spermatogonia.[229,230] No germ cells other than spermatogonia have been shown to contain FSH receptors.

LH receptors have not been demonstrated on seminiferous tubule cells, and consequently the hormonal requirement of LH for tubule function results from LH stimulation of Leydig cell testosterone production. Several studies have failed to identify receptors for testosterone on germ cells.[231,232] However, functional androgen receptors have been localized to Sertoli cells, Leydig cells, and peritubular cells.[231–234]

Localization of FSH and androgen receptors to Sertoli cells and the absence of these hormonal receptors on germ cells other than spermatogonia emphasize the key role of the Sertoli cell as an intermediary of FSH and androgen action on spermatogenesis. As discussed later, although aspects of Sertoli cell function are clearly controlled by FSH and testosterone, the molecules or mechanisms by which these hormones exert their action on spermatogenesis remain unknown. It has been proposed that the action of androgens on peritubular cells can influence seminiferous tubule function by the production of a protein, P-Mod-S, by peritubular cells under androgen stimulation, that acts by stimulating Sertoli cell inhibin and transferrin production.[235,236] Whether this protein acts directly on germ cells is yet to be established.

In view of the importance of the Sertoli cell as a key intermediary in hormonal action on spermatogenesis, the mechanisms and effects of FSH and androgen action on this cell are considered before discussion of their role in spermatogenesis.

### HORMONAL CONTROL OF SERTOLI CELL FUNCTION

#### Mechanism of Follicle-Stimulating Hormone Action

FSH acts through receptors on Sertoli cells and exerts its actions via the adenylate cyclase–protein kinase system.[237,238] FSH stimulation increases cyclic adenosine monophosphate, which in turn phosphorylates a number of Sertoli cell proteins.[238–240] Evidence has shown that FSH modulates intracellular free calcium levels[241] and, through this mechanism, influences other signal transduction pathways. These processes lead to modification of cellular processes, which in turn alter a number of Sertoli cell functions. This view is consistent with numerous studies demonstrating that FSH stimulates mRNA and protein synthesis by Sertoli cells.[238,242]

Stimulation by FSH, like a number of tropic hormones, results in desensitization of its target tissue, the Sertoli cell, which is made less sensitive to further stimulation. This process involves a loss of receptors,[243] reduced response by adenylate cyclase,[244] and increased phosphodiesterase production.[245,246]

Stimulation of immature Sertoli cell cultures by FSH results in increases in a number of proteins secreted by these cells, such as androgen-binding protein (ABP),[247] transferrin,[248] inhibin,[249] aromatase,[250] and plasminogen activators.[251] Recent data indicate that, in humans, measurements of serum inhibin B concentrations may provide a circulating marker of Sertoli cell function.[252]

Other Sertoli cell functions modulated by FSH stimulation include glucose transport and the conversion of glucose to lactate.[253] The dependence of germ cells on Sertoli cell lactate production is one mechanism by which FSH can indirectly influence germ cell development.[254] FSH, cyclic adenosine monophosphate, and calcium have also been shown to stimulate phosphorylation of cytoskeletal proteins such as vimentin in Sertoli cells, and these actions may be responsible for the morphologic changes induced by FSH in culture.[199,255]

FSH also stimulates immature Sertoli cells to divide mitotically.[148,149] Because the major proliferation of Sertoli cells takes place in late gestation and the early postnatal period in the rat, the adequacy of FSH stimulation during this time significantly influences the total Sertoli cell complement of the adult testis.[146] The specific effects of FSH on the proliferation and maturation of Sertoli cells have been revealed in mouse models, in which the actions of FSH have been studied in the absence of LH.[256] In this study, the gonadotropin-deficient hypogonadal (*hpg*) background was used to investigate gain-of-function effects of human FSH or activated human FSH receptor introduced onto the *hpg* background by cross-breeding. Males transgenic for FSH/*hpg* or FSH receptor/*hpg* showed a twofold increase in Sertoli cell numbers per testis in comparison with age-matched nontransgenic *hpg* testes. Sertoli cells in the transgenic testes showed nuclear morphology characteristic of mature Sertoli cells. FSH/*hpg* males expressing high levels of serum FSH had similar numbers of Sertoli cells per testis to those in wild-type mice. Thus, FSH is capable of stimulating normal Sertoli cell growth independently of the actions of LH. Little is known about the kinetics of Sertoli cell division in other species, but a study in humans demonstrated a fivefold increase in Sertoli cell numbers in the late fetal testis to the age of 10 years.[150]

In adults, Sertoli cells represent a stable cell population. Some studies have emphasized the temporal dependence of some aspects of their function and claimed that the mature Sertoli cell is resistant to FSH stimulation based on the failure of FSH to stimulate Sertoli cell function in whole adult testis preparations.[238] However, Parvinen[257] showed that FSH action is stage dependent, with the highest levels of FSH receptors being found at stage I and FSH-dependent cyclic adenosine monophosphate production being greatest at stages I to III. The failure to demonstrate effects of FSH in the whole testis may have been due to the mixture of responsive and nonresponsive stages of the seminiferous cycle. More recent studies have shown that parameters such as inhibin production by adult seminiferous tubules in culture and by adult Sertoli cells in culture can be stimulated by FSH.[258]

### Mechanism of Androgen Action

The Sertoli cell functions modulated by androgen are beginning to be well defined. In studies of testicular function in which the androgen receptor in Sertoli cells is specifically disrupted, transition of round spermatids to elongating stages is impaired, but earlier steps of meiosis leading to spermatid formation are unaffected.[259] It is possible that one of the actions of androgens on the Sertoli cell is for adhesion of newly formed spermatids to the Sertoli cell plasma membrane. Other studies of selective Sertoli cell androgen knockouts[260] showed impaired spermatocyte development assessed by quantitative histology. The mechanisms by which androgen, acting through the Sertoli cell, are responsible for disruption of meiotic maturation are unknown. In vivo, seminiferous tubule fluid production is disrupted if androgens are removed and is stimulated in hypophysectomized rats treated with testosterone.[261,262] In vitro, testosterone stimulates RNA polymerase II with both a rapid and prolonged phase (3–6 hours).[263] Despite this stimulation, very few of the

well-known Sertoli cell proteins are stimulated by androgens. ABP is one such protein, but androgens either have no effect[244,248] or inhibit factors such as the levels of plasminogen activator[264] or β-nerve growth factor mRNA.[265] Among the proteins stimulated by testosterone are the testins.[266] Studies have shown that depletion of testosterone resulting from Leydig cell destruction by ethane dimethane sulfonate (EDS) caused a 60% reduction in protein synthesis in seminiferous tubules at stage VII of the cycle.[267] Further studies are necessary to identify the nature of these proteins and their role.

Despite the failure of testosterone to stimulate inhibin and transferrin secretion in cultures of immature Sertoli cells, the addition to these cells of P-Mod-S, the androgen-induced protein secreted by peritubular myoid cells, caused significant stimulation of both transferrin and inhibin production.[236] Thus, androgens may exert a dual action on Sertoli cells both directly and indirectly via P-Mod-S. Isolation and characterization of P-Mod-S have shown that it consists of two forms with molecular weights of 56 and 59 kilodaltons.[235]

Although there is no evidence to show that the androgen receptor in the testis differs from that found in other tissues,[268] intratesticular testosterone concentrations are 50 times greater than in peripheral blood, and the levels of testosterone required to maintain spermatogenesis in hypophysectomized rats caused hypertrophy of the prostate and seminal vesicles.[269] The androgen receptor within the testis must be continually saturated, and although 5α-reductase levels in the testis are relatively low when compared with those in the prostate, dihydrotestosterone levels are also sufficiently high to saturate the androgen receptor. What mechanisms are involved in the modulation of androgen action in the presence of saturated receptor sites are unknown, but it is recognized that androgen treatment of immature Sertoli cell cultures stimulates an increase in androgen receptor levels.[270] Evidence that androgen receptors on germ cells are not essential for spermatogenesis has come from studies testing the ability androgen receptor–deficient germ cells to complete spermatogenesis if introduced into testes with normally functioning androgen receptors.[271] Spermatogonia were transplanted from testicular feminized mouse testes (that lack functional androgen receptors) into experimentally azoospermic recipient mouse testes that expressed functional androgen receptors. After 100 or 200 days, donor-derived spermatogenesis was observed in the seminiferous tubules of recipient testes, indicating that androgen receptors do not directly control the gene activity within germ cells required for their proliferation and maturation into fully formed spermatozoa. This finding strongly suggests that androgens regulate spermatogenesis via the Sertoli cells and possibly the peritubular cells.

Recently, experiments using transgenic mice in which the estradiol α receptor was nonfunctional showed that estradiol was required for fluid reabsorption to occur through the efferent ductules.[272] In these mice, the increased back pressure resulted in disruption of spermatogenesis.

## HORMONAL CONTROL OF SPERMATOGENESIS

Despite the absence of FSH and testosterone receptors on germ cells, successful completion of spermatogenesis is under the control of these substances. The relative importance of these two hormones is still unclear, particularly in adults, in whom the requirement for FSH has been questioned. The latter issue arose from the observation that in hypophysectomized rats, testosterone alone could maintain spermatogenesis if commenced immediately after hypophysectomy.

### Initiation of Spermatogenesis

It is generally agreed that successful commencement of spermatogenesis requires both FSH and LH secretion by the pituitary gland. Failure of these hormones to show their pubertal increase is associated with maintenance of the prepubertal state. The progressive increase in FSH and LH during sexual maturation has been documented in humans[273] and in other species.[274] In disorders such as hypogonadotropic hypogonadism (Kallmann's syndrome), in which absence of GnRH stimulation is associated with failure of FSH and LH secretion, treatment with FSH and LH[275] or pulsatile GnRH initiates spermatogenic development.[276] In these studies, subjects fail to achieve normal sperm output, and it has been proposed that this low output results from a subnormal Sertoli cell complement as a result of inadequate FSH stimulation during the neonatal and pubertal phases.[277] In the *hpg* mouse, a model of GnRH deficiency, Singh and colleagues[278] showed that testosterone could initiate spermatogenesis, albeit with a lower than normal sperm output, thus calling into question the need for FSH in the initiation of spermatogenesis. The low sperm output probably results from the absence of the mitogenic stimulus of FSH on Sertoli cells. Furthermore, in several men with inactivating mutations of the FSH receptor, spermatogenesis proceeded to completion, but in most cases, testicular volume and sperm count were impaired.[279] Targeted disruption of the FSH β subunit gene in mice resulted in the maintenance of spermatogenesis, but there was a decrease in total sperm output consistent with a decrease in Sertoli cell number[280] and the "carrying capacity" of the Sertoli cells for germ cells was decreased. Further, targeted disruption of the activin II receptor gene, interfering with the action of activin A, a stimulator of Sertoli cell proliferation in postnatal rats,[171] resulted in the progression of complete spermatogenesis, albeit with decreased germ cell numbers.[281]

Experimental evidence to support the need for a fully functional hypothalamic-hypophyseal unit emerges from the testis regression seen in animals immunized against GnRH.[282] Furthermore, the temporal decrease and increase in FSH and LH that precede seasonal cessation and onset of fertility add further support for this view.

The notion that the role of LH in the control of spermatogenesis is mediated via stimulation of Leydig cell testosterone production is supported by the observation that Leydig cell adenomas in prepubertal boys are associated with stimulation of spermatogenesis in the vicinity of the tumor but not at a distance.[283]

The factors that regulate the neonatal growth of the primate and human testis are less well understood. The neonatal period is associated with FSH and LH secretion and elevation of serum inhibin B and testosterone.[284,285] Germ cell numbers increase threefold in the first 5 months,[141] suggesting a link with the activation of hormone secretion. However, recent studies in pairs of twin marmosets of neonatal testis growth from birth to 6 months of age have shown that treatment of one twin with GnRH antagonist merely attenuated germ cell proliferation[286] with only a 25% reduction compared with the vehicle-treated twin. Thus, the activation of the pituitary-testicular axis in the immediate postnatal period may not have a crucial role in the stimulation of the early steps of germ cell growth and differentiation of gonocytes to spermatogonia. The factors that regulate testis growth in the neonate and infantile primate testis remain unknown.

### Maintenance of Spermatogenesis

In the human and primate testis, a strong case can be made that both FSH and testosterone are required for the maintenance of full spermatogenesis. Immunization of monkeys against FSH either actively[287] or passively[288] was associated with disruption of fertility and a decrease in sperm concentrations, albeit not to zero. Furthermore, patients in whom pituitary tumors interrupted gonadotropin secretion required both FSH and LH to cause a return of fertility.[289]

Several studies by Matsumoto and colleagues[290] have supported the need for FSH but also posed several interesting and unanswered questions. Administration of testosterone to normal men to cause suppression of LH and FSH resulted in a progressive decrease in sperm concentrations to azoospermic or severely oligospermic levels. In this model, they noted that the additional stimulus of LH caused sperm counts to increase, presumably by stimulating intratesticular testosterone concentrations[291]; however, normal sperm concentrations were not achieved. Thus, stimulation of testosterone could, in the absence of detectable FSH, partially restore spermatogenesis. However, in the same model, if FSH were administered instead of hCG, a similar increase in sperm count occurred.[290] This partial restoration of spermatogenesis occurred presumably in association with markedly suppressed endogenous intratesticular testosterone concentrations. As a result of these studies, it is reasonable to conclude that both FSH and LH (testosterone) are required to quantitatively stimulate spermatogenesis in humans.

Studies of spermatogenesis in rodents have questioned the requirement of FSH in view of the capacity of testosterone to initiate and maintain sperm production in mice in which the β subunit of FSH had been knocked out.[280] Furthermore, testosterone had the capacity to restore spermatogenesis in hypophysectomized rats[292] but not quantitatively. More recently, studies have shown that high-dose testosterone can restore spermatogenesis after hypophysectomy-induced regression in rats and monkeys.[293] All these studies suggested that the high local intratesticular concentrations of testosterone achieved by the route of administration were sufficient to maintain spermatogenesis. This view was supported by observations in normal rats: At low doses of testosterone administered by Silastic implants, spermatogenesis was disrupted, but as the testosterone dose was increased, spermatogenesis was maintained despite suppressed LH levels.[294] However, Cunningham and Huckins[295] demonstrated that intratesticular testosterone levels in these rats were only 10% to 20% of normal, which raises doubt about the specific requirement of high intratesticular concentrations of testosterone for the maintenance of spermatogenesis. A number of recent studies using both intact and hypophysectomized rats have reached similar conclusions concerning the concentrations of testosterone within the testis at which spermatogenesis was maintained.[296,297] A detailed dose-response study by Sun and coworkers[269] showed that doses of testosterone required to take spermatogenesis from the suppressed state to the well-maintained range were relatively small. The serum testosterone levels in these animals were equivalent to twice normal and resulted in intratesticular testosterone levels that were 10% to 20% of normal. Although these doses of testosterone were required to maintain spermatogenesis, another androgen-dependent organ, the prostate gland, was grossly hypertrophied by the same levels of testosterone.[269] The differing responses in the prostate and seminiferous epithelium to these doses of testosterone raise questions regarding the nature of the androgen receptors at each site and make it likely that other factors interact with testosterone or its receptors to maintain normal function at one site and yet cause hypertrophy at another.

Most of the studies defining the role of testosterone in the maintenance of spermatogenesis have been relatively short term. In longer term studies extending over 7 to 13 weeks, Sun and coworkers[269] showed that, although testosterone could maintain spermatogenesis in hypophysectomized or intact rats at serum testosterone levels that were approximately twice normal, prolongation of the experiment led to failure of these doses to maintain daily sperm production in the normal range; similar results were also noted by Santulli and associates.[298] These observations suggested that a pituitary factor, which was most likely to be FSH, was involved in the long-term maintenance of spermatogenesis. This possibility is supported by increasing evidence suggesting that high doses of testosterone, rather than suppressing FSH further, actually stimulate FSH secretion.[269,299]

The site at which testosterone exerts its action on spermatogenesis still remains somewhat controversial because of the failure of investigators to use precise quantitative techniques and the use of variable testosterone doses and differing experimental designs. A recent study using morphometric techniques to define the stages of germ cell development that were influenced by testosterone and FSH demonstrated that the transformation of round spermatids to spermatozoa, namely, spermiogenesis, was highly dependent on testosterone, with lower doses of testosterone supporting the survival of round spermatids but higher doses being required to enable these cells to proceed to spermatozoa[300] (Fig. 167-17). Several studies have suggested that the mechanism by which testosterone influences round spermatids involves the production of N-cadherin by the Sertoli cell. This substance may be an integral component of the specialized spermatid–Sertoli cell junctions that are disrupted when testosterone levels decline; as a result of the disruption, spermatids are prematurely sloughed into the lumen of the seminiferous tubules.[301–303]

In addition to the effects on round spermatids, the studies demonstrated that the conversion of spermatogonia to spermatocytes and the latter to round spermatids was also testosterone dependent. Furthermore, by comparing the responses of hypophysectomized and intact rats, these studies strongly suggested that FSH was also likely to be required for the conversion of spermatogonia to spermatocytes, particularly for the conversion of spermatocytes to round spermatids. Others, using the *hpg* mouse model and morphometric techniques, proposed that the most testosterone-sensitive step was the conversion of spermatocytes to spermatids.[278]

The concept that testosterone is an essential requirement for normal formation and maturation of spermatocytes and subsequent supply of early spermatids has been confirmed by

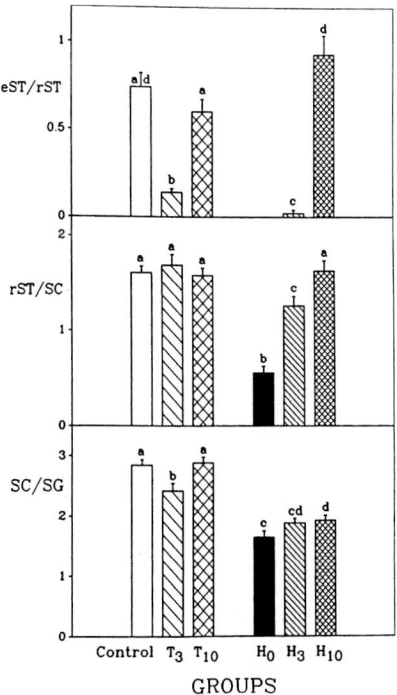

**Figure 167-17** Conversion ratios for spermatogonia (SG) to primary spermatocytes (SC), primary spermatocytes to round spermatids (rST), and round spermatids to elongated spermatids (eST) are shown in intact and hypophysectomized ($H_0$) rats treated for 13 weeks with testosterone-containing Silastic implants of 3 or 10 cm. (From Sun YT, Wreford NG, Robertson DM, de Kretser DM: Quantitative cytological studies of spermatogenesis in intact and hypophysectomized rats: Identification of androgen-dependent stages. Endocrinology 127:1215–1223, 1990. © 1990, The Williams & Wilkins Company, Baltimore.)

studies of mutant mice with a selective knock out of the androgen receptor in Sertoli cells.[260] Spermatogenesis is arrested at the late spermatocyte–early spermatid stage, the latter cell type reduced by 97% compared with wild-type testes. Of the few round spermatids produced, none progressed to the elongating phase. The data suggest that the actions of testosterone on Sertoli cells, through their androgen receptors, is crucial for normal meiotic maturation of spermatocytes, the failure of which results in depletion of spermatids, which in turn are unable to continue their maturation. Identification of the androgen-driven Sertoli cell factors, which are essential for germ cell development remains to be demonstrated. Several recent studies have identified stimulation of spermatogonia as the principal target of FSH action in rodents and primates when gonadotropin deficiency was corrected with the use of recombinant human FSH.[304,305] Furthermore, quantitative studies of germ cell populations in normal men receiving contraceptive doses of testosterone suggested that FSH may have an important role in the maintenance of spermatogonial populations[306] and also suggested that testosterone may have a suppressive effect on spermatogonia, in keeping with recent data in rats[304] and the conclusions reached by Matsumoto.[307] Further studies are clearly required to clarify these issues.

In summary, it is clear that testosterone is an important factor in the maintenance of spermatogenesis despite the absence of receptors on germ cells for this substance. Although still a matter of controversy, it is likely that FSH is required for maintenance of spermatogenesis, but the relative amounts of FSH or testosterone may vary in different pathologic states. The requirement for FSH is more evident in studies using primates and humans.

In addition to androgens and FSH, there is evidence of a requirement for estrogens. Targeted disruption of the estrogen receptor (ER) α gene (*ERKO*) causes changes in spermatogenesis and results in infertility.[308] Hess and colleagues[272] have shown that the infertility is due in part to the lack of ER-α expression in the efferent ductules, which results in a reduction of the absorptive capacity of epithelium. The resultant fluid accumulation results in a disruption of spermatogenesis, in a manner similar to that seen after efferent duct ligation. A clearer picture of the role(s) of the ER-α receptor has come from studies in which germ cells derived from ER-α receptor knockout mouse testes were transplanted into wild-type recipient mouse testes previously depleted of germ cells.[309] After 8 weeks, the recipient mice produced normal offspring when mated with wild-type females. This outcome shows that germ cells do not require ER-α for their maturation or to function in fertilization and suggests that ER knockout males are infertile due to functional disruption of somatic cells.

The testis itself can synthesize estrogen from testosterone via the P-450 aromatase enzyme, which is located in the seminiferous epithelium on germ cells and also Sertoli cells.[310,311] A requirement for local estrogen synthesis in the maintenance but not initiation of spermatogenesis is indicated by the results of targeted disruption of the *cyp*-19 gene. Male mice deficient in aromatase are initially fertile but become increasingly infertile, and spermatogenesis is progressively disrupted. Unlike ER knockout mice, the effects are patchy and due to an arrest in the postmeiotic, early stage of spermiogenesis result in a decrease in the number of round and elongated spermatids. An increase in apoptosis is seen, and abnormal acrosomal development is more frequent.[312] These studies have been extended by the same group[313] to explain why male mice deficient in aromatase are fertile but inevitably experience infertility. Estrogen-type substances in the diet were shown to partially overcome the defects of spermatogenesis associated with the absence of endogenous estrogen, again emphasizing the biologic effects of estrogens in spermatogenesis.

This effect of estrogens in the testis is not exclusively confined to an action through ER-α because another ER, ER-β, has been localized to the rat testis and can mediate a physiologic response to estrogen.[314] In the adult mouse testis, ER-β is localized to Leydig and Sertoli cells, spermatogonia, and most spermatocytes.[315] ER-β proteins detected as isoforms ER-β1 and ER-β2 are widely expressed in the testis and reproductive tissues of the human and primate.[316] The former is chiefly associated with pachytene spermatocytes and round spermatids, whereas the latter is located with Sertoli cells and spermatogonia. The authors speculate that ER-β1 may be required for endogenous estrogen action on the germ cells to which it is localized, but ER-β2 may serve to protect testicular cells from estrogen action. An initial report of mice lacking ER-β shows normal gonadal development, and the young adults (6 weeks) are fully fertile.[317] The effect of age-related abnormalities in gonadal or reproductive tract function warrants further investigation.

## LOCAL CONTROL MECHANISMS

Although the discussion to date has focused on hormonal mechanisms that are involved in the control of spermatogenesis, it is clear that numerous other mechanisms need to be fully operative to enable sperm production to be successfully completed. These processes are only partially understood and have been grouped under the heading of local systems.

### Sertoli Cell Function

Earlier in this chapter, the importance of the number of Sertoli cells in the establishment of total sperm output was discussed. Given the place of the Sertoli cell in the epithelium, the function of these cells appears to be crucial. It is not possible in this chapter to discuss in detail the evidence of this concept, but the following example illustrates this view. As discussed earlier, hypothyroidism in rats at the time of postnatal Sertoli cell division results in an extended period of Sertoli cell proliferation and a resultant increase in total sperm output in the adult rat.[227,228] The hypothyroid state delays some maturational changes in Sertoli cell function and is accompanied by a marked delay in the onset of spermatogenesis.[318] This delay is evidenced by the persistence of gonocytes and impaired movement to the basement membrane, spermatogonial proliferation often occurring in a central location in the tubule, and delayed maturation and poor survival of primary spermatocytes and spermatids. Yet, when the hypothyroidism is reversed, spermatogenesis resumes and ultimately produces an augmented sperm output.

A number of consequences result from structural communications between Sertoli cells; a barrier thus formed is selectively permeable to the entry and exit of some substances, so a unique microenvironment for the developing germ cell populations is provided as well as an immunologic barrier in the testis. Therefore, the Sertoli cells are required to communicate with the germ cells. Specialized cell junctions (tight junctions, gap junctions, and adhering junctions) between Sertoli cell membrane segments that face adjoining germ cell membranes provide structural sites of communication between these cell types, as do the tubulobulbar complexes. It is believed that it is through these sites that germ cells can directly or indirectly influence the function of Sertoli cells and vice versa.

All germ cells, particularly those in the luminal compartment, are dependent on Sertoli cells for survival; therefore, they must influence Sertoli cell function so that adequate provision is made for their development. This influence on Sertoli cell function ensures that the serum proteins, nutrients, hormones, and metabolic activities required for germ cell survival, development, and function are procured at the correct time by the appropriate cell types.

Data providing evidence that these interactions occurred in vivo were initially derived from microscopic examinations showing that Sertoli cell structure changed in a cyclic manner with the stage of the seminiferous epithelium. These studies noted changes in the volume of Sertoli cells, in organization of the cytoplasmic components of the cell, and in the shape and position of the nuclei.[22,166]

Unequivocal evidence that Sertoli cells modulate their secretory functions according to the developmental stage of the germ cells has been provided by the identification of a number of Sertoli cell secretory products, together with the demonstration that their production occurs in a cyclic fashion. Acquisition of much of this knowledge was made possible with the pioneering technique of transillumination-assisted dissection of each individual stage of the seminiferous tubule as developed and modified by Parvinen.[257] More sophisticated techniques of cell isolation and culture have also been used to study specific interactions between germ cells and Sertoli cells in vitro.[319] These techniques have been used to identify Sertoli cell products as binding proteins or transport molecules involved in the delivery of essential chemicals or hormones to the germ cells or as hormones or cytokines thought to have an integral role in the local regulation of seminiferous tubule function.[320,321] Many of these protein products and numerous mRNA species have been shown to be produced in a cyclic manner.

The general metabolic requirements of Sertoli cells can vitally influence germ cell survival, and it was demonstrated that Sertoli cells could produce glucose metabolites such as inositol[322] and pyruvate and lactate.[254] Both pyruvate and lactate are efficient energy sources for germ cells, and it was postulated that Sertoli cells could provide these metabolites to germ cells; furthermore, the transport and metabolism of glucose by Sertoli cells were stimulated by FSH.[253] The means by which the metabolites are then delivered to the germ cells across the physical barriers between germ cells and Sertoli cells remains to be determined.

Other nutritional requirements of germ cells such as essential ions and vitamins are transported from outside the blood-testis barrier to the germ cells via the action of binding or transport proteins. Testicular transferrin is an iron-binding protein that delivers iron to the cell through a receptor-mediated endocytotic process.[323] Transferrin is a secretory product of the Sertoli cell regulated by FSH, and although all cells have transferrin receptors, particularly high concentrations of transferrin receptors have been localized to pachytene spermatocytes.[324] Ceruloplasmin is a binding and transport protein for copper that is thought to act in a manner similar, but not identical, to that of transferrin in the delivery of copper to germ cells.[325] All cells require iron to maintain respiration and cytochrome function, and copper is required as a coenzyme for proteins and ferroxidase. The role of vitamins in the maintenance of testis function has led to numerous studies of vitamin A retinoids. Sertoli cells respond to vitamin A by increased synthesis of secretory products such as transferrin, and retinoid-binding proteins are localized in the Sertoli cells themselves. However, vitamin A is essential for germ cells, and deprivation results in disruption of spermatogenesis,[326] thus suggesting a direct effect on the germ cells themselves. Further support arises from the disrupted sperm production in mice with targeted inactivation of the retinoic acid receptor.[327]

Numerous serum-derived hormones and locally produced factors present in interstitial fluid are required by the germ cell populations in the adluminal compartment but are accessible via the Sertoli cell. Thus, many receptors or binding proteins for these substances are also present on Sertoli cells. Androgens, which are essential for maintenance of the seminiferous epithelium, can enter Sertoli cells by binding to the ABP, both of which are located on the Sertoli cell. ABP was initially thought to transport androgens to the germ cells, but it is now thought to be involved in transporting androgens to the luminal surface of the epithelium and from there to the male reproductive tract, which contains androgen-dependent tissue.[328] Nevertheless, based on observations using transillumination-assisted microdissection of rat seminiferous tubules, ABP production has been shown to be stage specific, which suggests that ABP may have a role in the epithelium that is regulated by the germ cell populations contained within.[329] Production of the androgen receptor is also stage dependent (based on mRNA levels or binding studies) and, as might be expected, the highest levels of receptor binding are detected at stages VII and VIII, which are the most sensitive to the effects of androgen withdrawal.

FSH is another serum-derived hormone that is required for spermatogenesis, and the FSH receptor has been localized to Sertoli cells. Both the level of FSH binding and mRNA receptor levels have been shown to be subject to stage-dependent regulation.[330] Accordingly, a number of Sertoli cell products known to be regulated by FSH have been shown to be produced or localized in a stage-specific manner, for example, inhibin, testibumin, clusterin, and $\alpha_2$-macroglobulin.[185–187,257] $\alpha_2$-Macroglobulin is a protease inhibitor and may be involved in epithelial cell remodeling as well as play a major role in inhibiting the release of sperm through its action on proteases; however, it also binds growth factors or cytokine, such as transforming growth factor beta and interleukin-1$\alpha$, and hence could affect the production and local action of these cytokines in vivo. The stage-specific distribution of other substances, such as sulfated glycoprotein 2, decarboxylase, and cyclic protein 2, would indicate a specific requirement for these products at particular stages of germ cell development (for reviews, see elsewhere[185–187,257]). Because the precise function of some of these substances remains to be determined, it can only be postulated at present that germ cells regulate these Sertoli cell products for this purpose.

Although some hormones or cytokines required by germ cells may be serum derived, a number of substances thought to be involved in Sertoli cell–germ cell interactions are synthesized by the Sertoli cells themselves. Even though these substances may be secreted through the basal surface of the epithelium and into the interstitium and peripheral circulation or secreted apically, they may also act directly on germ cells in the epithelium itself.

### Expansion and Survival of Germ Cell Populations

For successful production of a normal output, several germ cell populations must proliferate, differentiate, and survive. Without a doubt, these events are influenced by the hormones discussed earlier, but emerging data also implicate growth factors and cell survival molecules that regulate the process of apoptosis.

One of the crucial steps is migration and proliferation of the primordial germ cells and their daughter cells termed *gonocytes*. A significant body of evidence indicates that the migration of primordial germ cells and proliferation and survival of spermatogonia are dependent on the secretion of SCF by the Sertoli cell and the presence of its receptor *c-kit* on the relevant cell types. Additionally, a recent study showed that the membrane-bound form of stem cell factor and *c-kit* may be essential for the progression of spermatogonia through meiosis.[331] This example is one of many that will emerge over the ensuing decade to demonstrate the importance of locally produced growth factors and cytokines in mediating the cell-to-cell interactions that are crucial to spermatogenesis. New evidence links glia-derived neurotropic factor, neurotropin-3, nerve growth factor, epidermal growth factor, platelet-derived growth factor, and follistatin with gonocyte or spermatogonial proliferation.[44–49]

### Meiosis

The two cell divisions constituting meiosis involve a number of events that require explicit control. For instance, the pairing of homologous chromosomes to form synaptonemal complexes is an essential step in the process of genetic recombination that allows transfer of DNA between paternal and maternal chromosomes. Cyclins A1, B3, and B2 are involved in progression through different phases of meiosis together with other regulators. Further sister chromatid proteins and DNA mismatch repair proteins are also crucial for progression through meiosis.[72] There is increasing information to suggest that mutations in the genes encoding these proteins cause a disruption of meiosis in mice and human counterparts are being sought. Examples of this approach can be seen from inactivation of the gene encoding HSP70-2 resulting in homozygous males failing to complete the first meiotic division.[332] As the molecular machinery of meiosis is progressively unraveled, examples will emerge from patients that illustrate the result of mutations in genes encoding the proteins that are key steps in this process.

### Spermiogenesis

The steps in the formation of a sperm from its round cell precursor, the haploid round spermatid, represent a fascinating process in cell biology. Development of the sperm tail, the remarkable nuclear changes involving condensation and complexing of DNA, and changes in the relative position of the nucleus, cell organelles, and cytoplasm all pose innumerable questions regarding how these events are controlled. Very few of these control systems are known, but some general mechanisms are becoming clearer. First, because these haploid cells are linked by intercellular bridges arising from incomplete cytokinesis, these clonal units can share RNAs and effectively can use the diploid genome.[68] Second, because of the progressive replacement of histones by protamines and the condensation of chromatin, there is a shutdown of transcription. To ensure that the development of structures during spermiogenesis can proceed, transcription may occur during meiosis and the resultant RNAs are subjected to translational delay. Finally, many genes expressed in postmeiotic cells have alternatively spliced forms that are germ cell specific. As some of the genes controlling these events are identified, examples from patients with specific abnormalities will enable the importance of these mechanisms to be identified. For instance, investigation of these patients with the immotile cilia syndrome has identified structures in the sperm tail that are critical to the mechanisms underlying sperm motility, and the genes encoding these molecules are now being cloned.[333] This knowledge promises better diagnostic and potential therapeutic approaches.

### Cell Survival Mechanisms

The body of knowledge concerning the control of cell survival and the process of cell death (apoptosis) is growing (see earlier discussion). Considerable data indicate that apoptotic processes may underlie the removal of germ cells from the testis during a variety of hormonal manipulations (see the review by Sinha Hikim and Swerdloff[111]). A clear example that shows the importance of this process in spermatogenesis emerged from recent studies of inactivation of the gene encoding bcl-w, a cell survival molecule.[163] These studies showed that the pubertal wave of spermatogenesis almost reached completion, but the entire process collapsed and rendered homozygous male mice infertile with an ultimate phenotype of Sertoli cell–only tubules. The reasons for this phenomenon have emerged from studies of the temporal expression of members of the Bcl2 family of proteins and emphasize the importance of understanding the mechanisms that control the expression of these regulators.[113]

### FEEDBACK CONTROL OF FOLLICLE-STIMULATING HORMONE AND LUTEINIZING HORMONE BY THE TESTIS

The demonstration that FSH and LH secretion by the pituitary gland increases rapidly after castration establishes the existence of negative feedback control by the testis on the production of gonadotropins. Because secretion of FSH and LH is dependent on stimulation of gonadotropins by GnRH, these feedback effects may be exerted at the hypothalamus and result in a change in GnRH secretion or may result from direct action at the pituitary. The demonstration that FSH and LH are cosecreted by most gonadotrophs raises intriguing questions regarding the manner in which stimulatory (GnRH) and inhibitory substances regulate their differential secretion.

## CONTROL OF LUTEINIZING HORMONE SECRETION

Numerous studies have shown that testosterone, estradiol, and dihydrotestosterone exert a negative modulation of LH secretion.[334] Controversy existed regarding whether testosterone could directly exert this action or needed to be metabolized to estradiol or dihydrotestosterone.[335] The demonstration that nonaromatizable androgens could inhibit LH secretion resolved this issue.[336] This careful study by Santen[336] showed that estradiol probably acted at the pituitary by decreasing LH pulse amplitude without changing pulse frequency, whereas testosterone probably acted at the hypothalamus by decreasing pulse frequency without a change in pulse amplitude. In a more recent study, experimental proof of this concept was provided by demonstrating that the pulse frequency of GnRH secretion in portal blood was decreased by the treatment of castrate animals with testosterone.[337] These studies also showed no change in portal blood GnRH secretory patterns during treatment with estradiol, which lowered LH levels by decreasing LH pulse amplitude.

## CONTROL OF FOLLICLE-STIMULATING HORMONE SECRETION

The factors involved in the control of FSH have been a matter of some controversy for many years. This debate has centered on the concept that the steroid hormones testosterone and estradiol could account for the entire negative feedback exerted by the testis on FSH secretion[338] and that there was no need to postulate the presence of a specific FSH feedback substance, namely, inhibin.[339] The existence of inhibin has been established, as discussed in Chapter 140,[340] and this section explores the roles of testosterone and inhibin in the control of FSH secretion.

### Role of Testosterone

Several studies have shown that testosterone can suppress FSH secretion in a number of species when administered at amounts equivalent to or greater than its production rate.[334] When administered to castrate rats, increasing doses of testosterone suppressed both FSH and LH secretion.[340] However, in their study and those of others, the highest doses of testosterone decreased LH to the undetectable range, but FSH levels plateaued in the normal range and could not be suppressed further. More recently, several investigators have shown that at very high doses of testosterone, FSH levels increased,[269,299] thus indicating a complex relationship between testosterone and FSH secretion. Perhaps the most convincing data supporting a physiologic role for testosterone in the control of FSH emerged from experiments in rats in which Leydig cells were destroyed by the cytotoxin EDS. EDS treatment resulted in a rapid decrease in testosterone levels and a rapid increase in FSH concentrations.[341] It is important to note that the FSH levels in these experiments reached only 50% of castrate levels, and it is likely that the continuing feedback control was achieved by inhibin, which was maintained after EDS treatment.[342] In fact, if EDS was given to rats in which induction of cryptorchidism had resulted in increased FSH levels associated with decreased inhibin concentrations, removal of testosterone feedback increased FSH levels to the castrate range.[343] It is clear from this brief summary of a number of papers that testosterone can exert inhibitory control on FSH secretion, but its precise role relative to inhibin may vary according to the physiologic circumstances and the species concerned. In the rat, approximately 50% of the feedback may result from testosterone and 50% from inhibin.

### Role of Inhibin

The isolation, synthesis, and biology of inhibin A and B are described in several important papers[343-353] and discussed in Chapter 140.

In males, several studies have demonstrated that inhibin is produced by immature Sertoli cells in culture.[249,354] mRNAs for the $\alpha$, $\beta_A$, and $\beta_B$ subunits are found in the Sertoli cell, and the predominant form of inhibin in the adult testis is inhibin B because the predominant $\beta$ subunit message in the adult testis was $\beta_B$.[355] Several studies of intact and hypophysectomized rats have suggested that FSH stimulates $\alpha$ subunit production without altering the $\beta$ subunit message.[355,356]

In addition to a Sertoli cell source of inhibin, Leydig cells have now been shown to secrete both immunoreactive and bioactive inhibin.[357] LH stimulation leads to an increase in immunoreactive inhibin but not bioactive inhibin, which raises the possibility that $\alpha$ subunit products may be the result of LH stimulation. The relative contribution of Leydig cells to inhibin secretion is still unclear.

Evidence has also indicated that Sertoli and Leydig cells can produce activin,[358,359] but this activin is likely to have a local role because circulating activin A levels do not decrease after castration.[360] This finding may be of some importance in view of the demonstrated capacity of activin to stimulate spermatogonial mitosis[361] and the presence of activin receptors on primary spermatocytes, round spermatids, and Sertoli cells.[362] Follistatin is also produced in the testis in Sertoli cells, spermatogonia, primary spermatocytes, and round spermatids.[363,364]

The production by the testis of substances that are capable of suppressing or stimulating FSH further complicates our understanding of the mechanisms of feedback control of this gonadotropic hormone. The description of the changes in FSH secretion in rats after EDS treatment provides convincing evidence of a role of inhibin in the control of FSH secretion. Further support for this concept comes from the studies of Dubey and colleagues[365] in primates in which they showed that in arcuate nucleus–lesioned monkeys maintained on a constant GnRH pulse regimen, testosterone could prevent the postcastration increase in LH but not FSH. In subsequent experiments, they demonstrated that partially purified inhibin from porcine follicular fluid could prevent this postcastration increase in FSH secretion.[366]

Finally, recombinant human inhibin A has been shown in rats and rams to specifically suppress FSH with a nadir occurring 6 to 12 hours after administration.[367,368] In fact, doses of inhibin A sufficient to restore levels in castrate rams to normal, in the absence of testosterone, could suppress FSH levels into the normal range.[369]

Isolation of dimers of the $\beta$ subunit of inhibin, called activins,[347,348] which increase FSH levels, have complicated the control of FSH further, especially in view of the presence of $\alpha$ and $\beta$ subunit mRNA in the pituitary gland, particularly in gonadotrophs.[370] That this mRNA functions emerged from the data of Corrigan and colleagues,[371] who showed that a monoclonal antibody to activin B, when added to pituitary cells in culture, causes suppression of FSH secretion. However, in these experiments, they noted that inhibin, when added to these cultures, produced suppression of FSH despite the presence of activin antiserum, thus demonstrating an action of inhibin independent of activin.

Data supporting a role for inhibin in the control of FSH are consistent with the decrease in inhibin secretion by Sertoli cells and the increase in FSH in a number of models of spermatogenic damage such as cryptorchidism[372] and intratesticular glycerol treatment.[373] Recent data using an inhibin B enzyme-linked immunosorbent assay have shown that inhibin B is the principal circulating form of inhibin in males and that levels of serum inhibin B are reduced with testicular damage and are inversely related to FSH.[374,375] The levels of serum inhibin B are a marker of the number of Sertoli cells in the testis, and several studies have shown that there is an inverse relationship between FSH and inhibin B in normal men.[376] It is likely that the actions of activins and follistatin on FSH secretion will be exerted through paracrine actions on the pituitary gland because both activin and follistatin are produced in the pituitary[353] and no physiologically relevant fluctuations are seen during the menstrual cycle. Further studies are required to elicit the exact relationships in different pathophysiologic states.

## CONTROL OF THE IMMUNOLOGIC ENVIRONMENT OF THE TESTIS

The space separating individual seminiferous tubules contains numerous cell types, including Leydig cells, macrophages, and vascular and lymphatic endothelial cells, as well as lymphatic and vascular vessels and fluids. Investigation of local interactions in the interstitium has focused mainly on Leydig cells and has involved regulation of steroidogenesis, mediation of the inflammatory response, or the development of Leydig cells. In the rat, the notion of a functional interaction between Leydig cells and macrophages was suggested by the previous observation that these cells can be observed in intimate association in vivo via specialized points of contact.[377] Local regulation of Leydig cell steroidogenesis was suggested from the demonstration that isolated media from macrophage cultures could stimulate Leydig cell testosterone production in vitro.[378] The stimulatory action of testicular macrophage products on steroidogenesis was specific and not exhibited with peritoneal macrophage products; it was also stimulated by FSH, which can be endocytosed by testicular macrophages.[378] A number of other substances are secreted by macrophages that have the potential to regulate steroidogenesis by Leydig cells, including interleukins. In vitro, these substances are potent regulators of testosterone, but discrepant reports concerning their effects have appeared in the literature. Hence, interleukin-1α has been reported as an inhibitor[379] and as a stimulator of testosterone synthesis.[380–382]

Interleukin-1, tumor necrosis factor-alpha, and interferon-γ are mediators of inflammation, and although macrophage products may be involved in inflammation-like responses in the testis, this response can be induced by hyperstimulation of Leydig cells with hCG.[383] Because hCG binds principally to Leydig cells, it has been suggested that the Leydig cell has a role in mediation of the inflammatory response involving mast cell secretion, infiltration of polymorphonuclear leukocytes, and increased blood flow, capillary permeability, and interstitial fluid accumulation.[384–386] This role was confirmed by the demonstration that selective removal of Leydig cells with the cytotoxic drug EDS prevents the inflammation-like changes induced by hCG administration.[383] These findings suggest that hyperstimulation of Leydig cells in which an inflammatory response is provoked can involve an interaction between Leydig cells and macrophages. The testis is considered to be an immunologically privileged site, and a further consequence of Leydig cell-macrophage interactions is thought to include a role in immunoprotection inasmuch as macrophages in other tissues have been shown to secrete immunosuppressive factors and activate T cells. Therefore, Leydig cells may regulate macrophages by inhibiting antigen-presenting functions and inducing immunosuppressive functions.[387] The nature of these molecules are the subject of studies.[388]

## REFERENCES

1. de Kretser DM, Temple-Smith PD, Kerr JB: Anatomical and functional aspects of the male reproductive organs. In Bandhauer K, Frick J (eds): Handbook of Urology, vol 16. Disturbances in Male Fertility. Berlin, Springer-Verlag, 1982, pp 1–131.
2. Jarrow JP: Intratesticular arterial anatomy. J Androl 11:255–259, 1990.
3. Clermont Y, Huckins C: Microscopic anatomy of the sex cords and seminiferous tubules in growing and adult male albino rats. Am J Anat 108:79–97, 1961.
4. Dym M: The mammalian rete testis—A morphological examination. Anat Rec 186:493–524, 1976.
5. Roosen-Runge EC, Holstein AF: The human rete testis. Cell Tissue Res 189:409–433, 1978.
6. Sinha Hikim AP, Wang C, Lue Y, et al: Spontaneous germ cell apoptosis in humans: Evidence for ethnic differences in the susceptibility of germ cells to programmed cell death. J Clin Endocrinol Metab 83:152–156, 1998.
7. de Kretser DM, Kerr JB: The cytology of the testis. In Knobil E, Neill JD (eds): The Physiology of Reproduction, 2d ed. New York, Raven, 1994, pp 1177–1290.
8. Sharpe RM: Regulation of spermatogenesis. In Knobil E, Neill JD (eds): The Physiology of Reproduction, 2d ed. New York, Raven, 1994, pp 1363–1434.
9. Barr AB: Timing of spermatogenesis in four nonhuman primate species. Fertil Steril 24:381–389, 1973.
10. Smithwick EB, Young LG, Gould KG: Duration of spermatogenesis and relative frequency of each stage in the seminiferous epithelial cycle of the chimpanzee. Tissue Cell 28:357–366, 1996.
11. Nielsen CT, Skakkebaek NE, Richardson DW, et al: Onset of the release of spermatozoa (spermarche) in boys in relation to age, testicular growth, pubic hair, and height. J Clin Endocrinol Metab 62:532–535, 1986.
12. Nieschlag E, Lammers U, Freischem CW, et al: Reproductive functions in young fathers and grandfathers. J Clin Endocrinol Metab 55:676–681, 1982.
13. Davidoff MS, Breucker H, Holstein AF, et al: Cellular architecture of the lamina propria of human seminiferous tubules. Cell Tissue Res 262:253–261, 1990.
14. Holstein AF, Maekawa M, Nagano T, et al: Myofibroblasts in the lamina propria of human seminiferous tubules are dynamic structures of heterogeneous phenotype. Arch Histol Cytol 59:109–125, 1996.
15. Middendorf R, Muller D, Wichers S, et al: Evidence for production and functional activity of nitric oxide in seminiferous tubules and blood vessels of the human testis. J Clin Endocrinol Metab 82:4154–4161, 1997.
16. Filippini A, Tripiciano A, Palombi F, et al: Rat testicular myoid cells respond to endothelin: Characterization of binding and signal transduction pathway. Endocrinology 133:1789–1796, 1993.
17. Pickering BT, Birkett SD, Guldenaar EF, et al: Oxytocin in the testis: What, where and why? Ann N Y Acad Sci 564:198–209, 1989.
18. Skinner MK: Cell-cell interactions in the testis. Endocr Rev 12:45–77, 1991.
19. Skinner MK: Sertoli cell-peritubular myoid cell interactions. In Russell LD, Griswold MD (eds): The Sertoli Cell. Clearwater, FL, Cache River Press, 1993, pp 477–483.
20. Dym M: Basement membrane regulation of Sertoli cells. Endocr Rev 15:102–115, 1994.
21. Fawcett DW: Ultrastructure and function of the Sertoli cell. In Greep RO, Attwood EB (eds): Handbook of Physiology. Washington, DC, American Physiological Society, 1975, pp 21–53.
22. Russell LD, Griswold MD (eds): The Sertoli Cell. Clearwater, FL, Cache River Press, 1993.
23. Holstein AF, Roosen-Runge EC: Atlas of Human Spermatogenesis. Berlin, Grosse, 1981.
24. Kerr JB: Ultrastructure of the seminiferous epithelium and intertubular tissue of the human testis. J Electron Microsc Tech 19:215–240, 1991.

25. Meistrich ML, van Beek M: Spermatogonial stem cells. In Desjardins C, Ewing LL (eds): Cell and Molecular Biology of the Testis. New York, Oxford University Press, 1993, pp 266–295.

26. DeRooij DG, van Dissel-Emiliani FMF: Regulation of proliferation and differentiation of stem cells in the male germ line. In Potten CS (ed): Stem Cells. London, Academic, 1997, pp 283–313.

27. Lin H: The self-renewing mechanism of stem cells in the germline. Curr Opin Cell Biol 10:687–693, 1998.

28. DeRooij DG, Grootegoed JA: Spermatogonial stem cells. Curr Opin Cell Biol 10:694–701, 1998.

29. Meistrich ML, Shetty G: Inhibition of spermatogonial differentiation by testosterone. J Androl 24:135–148, 2003.

30. Clermont Y: Two classes of spermatogonial stem cells in the monkey (Cercopithecus aethiops). Am J Anat 126:57–72, 1969.

31. Clermont Y, Antar M: Duration of the cycle of the seminiferous epithelium and the spermatogonial renewal in the monkey Macaca arctiodes. Am J Anat 136:153–166, 1973.

32. Clermont Y: Dynamics of human spermatogenesis. In Rosemberg E, Paulsen CA (eds): The Human Testis. New York, Plenum, 1970, pp 47–60.

33. Clermont Y: Kinetics of spermatogenesis in mammals. Seminiferous epithelium cycle and spermatogonial renewal. Physiol Rev 52:198–236, 1972.

34. de Rooij DG: Proliferation and differentiation of spermatogonial stem cells. Reproduction 121:347–354, 2001.

35. Clermont Y: Renewal of spermatogonia in man. Am J Anat 118:509–524, 1966.

36. Pollanen P, Soder O, Parvinen M: Interleukin-1α stimulation of spermatogonial proliferation in vitro. Reprod Fertil Dev 1:85–87, 1989.

37. Parvinen M, Soder O, Mali P, et al: In vitro stimulation of stage-specific deoxyribonucleic acid synthesis in rat seminiferous tubule segments by interleukin-1α. Endocrinology 129:1614–1620, 1991.

38. Soder O, Bang P, Wahab A, et al: Insulin-like growth factors selectively stimulate spermatogonial, but not meiosis, deoxyribonucleic acid synthesis during rat spermatogenesis. Endocrinology 131:2344–2350, 1992.

39. Allard EK, Blanchard KT, Boekelheide K: Exogenous stem cell factor (SCF) compensates for altered endogenous SCF expression in 2,5-hexanedione-induced testicular atrophy in rats. Biol Reprod 54:1200–1208, 1996.

40. Blanchard KT, Lee J, Boekelheide K: Leuprolide, a gonadotropin-releasing hormone agonist, reestablishes spermatogenesis after 2,5-hexanedione-induced irreversible testicular injury in the rat, resulting in normalised stem cell factor expression. Endocrinology 139:236–244, 1998.

41. Geissler EN, Ryan MA, Housman DE: The dominant-white spotting (W) locus of the mouse encodes the c-kit proto-oncogene. Cell 55:185–192, 1988.

42. Wittle ON: Steel locus defines new multipotent growth factor. Cell 63:5–6, 1990.

43. Sandlow JI, Fend HL, Cohen MB, et al: Expression of c-KIT and its ligand, stem cell factor, in normal and subfertile human testicular tissue. J Androl 17:403–408, 1996.

44. Meng X, Lindahl M, Hyvonon A, et al: Regulation of cell fate decision of undifferentiated spermatogonia by GDNF. Science 287:1489–1793, 2000.

45. Tadokoro Y, Yomogida K, Hiroshi O, et al: Homeostatic regulation of germinal stem cell proliferation by the GDNF/FSH pathway. Mech Dev 113:29–39, 2002.

46. Cupp AS, Kim GH, Skinner MK: Expression and action of neurotropin-3 and nerve growth factor in embryonic and early postnatal rat testis development. Biol Reprod 63:1617–1628, 2000.

47. Wahab-Wahlgren A, Martinelle N, Holst M, et al: EGF stimulates rat spermatogonial DNA synthesis in seminiferous tubule segments in vitro. Mol Cell Endocrinol 201:39–46, 2003.

48. Basciani S, Mariani S, Arizzi M, et al: Expression of platelet-derived growth factor-A (PDGF-A), PDGF-B and PDGF receptor-alpha and -beta during human testicular development and disease. J Clin Endocrinol Metab 87:2310–2319, 2002.

49. Meehan T, Schlatt S, O'Bryan MK, et al: Regulation of germ cell and Sertoli cell development by activin, follistatin and FSH. Dev Biol 220:225–237, 2000.

50. Lilford R, Jones AM, Bishop DT, et al: Case-control study of whether subfertility in men is familial. Br Med J 309:570–573, 1994.

51. Ruggiu M, Cooke H: Y bind RNA for spermatogenesis? Int J Androl 22:19–27, 1999.

52. Reijo R, Lee T-Y, Sal P, et al: Diverse spermatogenic defects in humans caused by Y chromosome deletions encompassing a novel RNA-binding protein gene. Nat Genet 10:383–392, 1995.

53. Najmabadi H, Huang V, Yen P, et al: Substantial prevalence of microdeletions of the Y chromosome in infertile men with idiopathic azoospermia and oligozoospermia detected using a sequence-tagged site-based mapping strategy. J Clin Endocrinol Metab 81:1347–1352, 1996.

54. Skaletsky H, Kuroda-Kawaguchi T, Minx PJ, et al: The male-specific region of the human Y chromosome is a mosaic of discrete sequence classes. Nature 423:825–837, 2003.

55. Kuroda-Kawaguchi T, Skaletsky H, Brown LG, et al: The AZFc region of the Y chromosome features massive palindromes and uniform recurrent deletions in infertile men. Nat Genet 29:279–286, 2001.

56. Blanco P, Shlumukova M, Sargent CA, et al: Divergent outcomes of intrachromosomal recombination on the human Y chromosome: Male infertility and recurrent polymorphism. J Med Genet 37:752–758, 2000.

57. Repping S, Skaletsky H, Lange J: Recombination between palindromes P5 and P1 on the human Y chromosome causes massive deletions and spermatogenic failure. Am J Hum Genet 71:906–922, 2002.

58. Brinster RL, Zimmermann JW: Spermatogenesis following male germ-cell transplantation. Proc Natl Acad Sci U S A 91:11298–11302, 1994.

59. Russell LD, Franca LR, Brinster RL: Ultrastructure observations of spermatogenesis in mice resulting from transplantation of mouse spermatogonia. J Androl 17:603–614, 1996.

60. Brinster RL, Arvarbock MR: Germ line transmission of donor haplotype following spermatogonial transplantation. Proc Natl Acad Sci U S A 91:11303–11307, 1994.

61. Avarbock MR, Brinster CJ, Brinster RL: Reconstitution of spermatogenesis from frozen spermatogonial stem cells. Nat Med 2:693–696, 1996.

62. Nagano M, Avarbock MR, Leonida EB, et al: Culture of mouse spermatogonial stem cells. Tissue Cell 30:389–397, 1998.

63. Clouthier DE, Avarback MR, Maika SD, et al: Rat spermatogenesis in mouse testes following spermatogonial stem cell transplantation. Nature 381:418–421, 1996.

64. Parriera GG, Ogawa T, Avarback MR, et al: Development of germ cell transplants in mice. Biol Reprod 59:1360–1370, 1998.

65. Franca LR, Ogawa T, Avarback MR, et al: Germ cell genotype controls cell cycle during spermatogenesis in the rat. Biol Reprod 59:1371–1377, 1998.

66. Ogawa T, Dobrinski I, Avarback MR, et al: Xenogeneic spermatogenesis following transplantation of hamster germ cells into mouse testes. Biol Reprod 60:515–521, 1999.

67. Schlatt S, Rosiepen G, Weinbauer GF, et al: Germ cell transfer into rat, bovine, monkey and human testes. Hum Reprod 14:144–150, 1999.

68. Caldwell KA, Handel MA: Protamine transcript sharing among postmeiotic spermatids. Proc Natl Acad Sci U S A 88:2407–2411, 1991.

69. Heller CG, Clermont Y: Kinetics of the germinal epithelium in man. Recent Prog Horm Res 20:545–575, 1964.

70. Eddy EM: Role of heat shock protein HSP70-2 in spermatogenesis. Rev Reprod 4:23–30, 1999.

71. Wu XQ, Gu W, Meng X, Hecht NB: The RNA-binding protein, TB-RBP, is the mouse homologue of translin, a recombination protein associated with chromosomal translocations. Proc Natl Acad Sci U S A 94:5640–5645, 1997.

72. Baarends WM, van der Laan R, Grootegoed JA: DNA repair mechanisms and gametogenesis. Reproduction 121:31–39, 2001.

73. Stubbs L, Stern H: DNA synthesis at selective sites during pachytene in mouse spermatocytes. Chromosoma 93:529–536, 1986.

74. Stern H: The process of meiosis. In Desjardins C, Ewing LL (eds): Cell and Molecular Biology of the Testis. New York, Oxford University Press, 1993, pp 296–331.

75. Grootegoed JA: The testis: Spermatogenesis. In Hillier SG, Kitchener HC, Nielsen JP (eds): Scientific Essentials of Reproductive Medicine. London, WB Saunders, 1996, pp 172–183.

76. Eddy EM, O'Brien DA: Gene expression during mammalian meiosis. In Handel MA (ed): Meiosis and Gametogenesis. San Diego, CA, Academic, 1998, pp 141–200.

77. Kimura Y, Tateno H, Handel MA, et al: Factors affecting meiotic and developmental competence of primary spermatocyte nuclei injected into mouse oocytes. Biol Reprod 59:871–877, 1998.

78. de Kretser DM: Ultrastructural features of human spermiogenesis. Z Zellforsch 98:477–505, 1969.

79. Holstein AF: Ultrastructural observations on the differentiation of spermatids in man. Andrologia 8:157–165, 1976.

80. Clermont Y, Oko R, Hermo L: Cell biology of mammalian spermiogenesis. In Desjardins C, Ewing LL (eds): Cell and Molecular Biology of the Testis. New York, Oxford University Press, 1993, pp 332–376.

81. Oko R: Occurrence and formation of cytoskeletal proteins in mammalian spermatozoa. Andrologia 30:193–206, 1998.

82. Eddy EM: Regulation of gene expression during spermatogenesis. Semin Cell Dev Biol 9:451–457, 1998.

83. Fulcher KD, Mori C, Welch JE, et al: Characterization of Fsc-1 complementary deoxyribonucleic acid for a mouse sperm fibrous sheath component. Biol Reprod 52:41–49, 1995.

84. McLachlan RI, Mallidis C, Ma K, et al: Genetic disorders and spermatogenesis. Reprod Fertil Dev 10:97–104, 1998.

85. Ward SW, Coffey DS: DNA packaging and organization in mammalian spermatozoa: Comparison with somatic cells. Biol Reprod 44:569–574, 1991.

86. Sassone-Corsi P: Unique chromatin remodeling and transcriptional regulation in spermatogenesis. Science 296:2176–2178, 2002.

87. Dadoune JP: Expression of mammalian spermatozoal nucleoproteins. Microsc Res Tech 61:56–75, 2003.

88. Kierszenbaum AL: Transition nuclear proteins during spermiogenesis: Unrepaired DNA breaks not allowed. Mol Reprod Dev 58:357–358, 2001.

89. Yu YE, Zhang Y, Unni E, et al: Abnormal spermatogenesis and reduced fertility in transition nuclear protein 1-deficient mice. Proc Natl Acad Sci U S A 97:4683–4688, 2000.

90. Zhao M, Shirley CR, Yu YE, et al: Targeted disruption of the transition protein 2 gene affects sperm chromatin structure and reduces fertility in mice. Mol Cell Biol 21:7243–7255, 2001.

91. Hecht NB: Post-transcriptional regulation of post-meiotic gene expression. In Hansson V, Levy FO, Tasken K (eds): Signal Transduction in Testicular Cells. Berlin, Springer-Verlag, 1996, pp 123–140.

92. Kleene KC: Patterns of translational regulation in the mammalian testis. Mol Reprod Dev 43:268–281, 1996.

93. Lee K, Haugen HS, Clegg CH, Braun RE: Premature translation of protamine 1 mRNA causes precocious nuclear condensation and arrests spermatid differentiation in mice. Proc Natl Acad Sci U S A 92:12451–12455, 1995.

94. Mills NC, Van NT, Means AR, et al: Histones of rat testis chromatin during early postnatal development and their interactions with DNA. Biol Reprod 17:760–768, 1977.

95. Yoshinaga K, Toshimori K: Organisation and modifications of sperm acrosomal molecules during spermatogenesis and epididymal maturation. Microsc Res Tech 61:39–45, 2003.

96. Olson GE, Winfrey VP, Neff JC, et al: An antigenically related polypeptide family is a major structural constituent of a stable acrosomal matrix assembly in bovine spermatozoa. Biol Reprod 57:325–334, 1997.

97. Xu X, Toselli P, Russell LD, Seldin DC: Globozoospermia in mice lacking the casein kinase II a catalytic subunit. Nat Genet 23:118–121, 1999.

98. Pilder SH, Olds-Clarke P, Orth JM, et al: Hst7: A male sterility mutation perturbing sperm motility, flagellar assembly, and mitochondrial sheath differentiation. J Androl 18:663–671, 1997.

99. Schalles U, Shao X, van der Hoorn FA, et al: Developmental expression of the 84-kDa ODF sperm protein: Localization to both the cortex and medulla of outer dense fibers and to the connecting piece. Dev Biol 199:250–260, 1998.

100. Long CR, Duncan RP, Robl JM: Isolation and characterization of MPM-2-reactive sperm proteins: Homology to components of the outer dense fibers and segmental columns. Biol Reprod 57:246–254, 1997.

101. Turner KJ, Sharpe RM, Gaughan J, et al: Expression cloning of a rat testicular transcript abundant in germ cells, which contains two leucine zipper motifs. Biol Reprod 57:1223–1232, 1997.

102. O'Bryan MK, Loveland KL, Herszfeld D, et al: Identification of a rat testis specific gene encoding a potential rat outer dense fibre protein. Mol Reprod Dev 50:313–322, 1998.

103. Russell LD: Morphological and functional evidence for Sertoli-germ cell relationships. In Russell LD, Griswold MD (eds): The Sertoli Cell. Clearwater, FL, Cache River Press, 1993, pp 365–390.

104. O'Donnell L, McLachlan RI, Wreford NG, et al: Testosterone withdrawal promotes stage-specific detachment of round spermatids from the rat seminiferous epithelium. Biol Reprod 55:895–901, 1996.

105. Cameron DF, Muffly KE, Nazian SJ: Development of Sertoli cell binding competency in the peripubertal rat. J Androl 19:573–579, 1998.

106. Ogura A, Matsuda J, Yanagimachi R: Birth of normal young after electrofusion of mouse oocytes with round spermatids. Proc Natl Acad Sci U S A 91:7460–7462, 1994.

107. Kimura Y, Yanagimachi R: Mouse oocytes injected with testicular spermatozoa or round spermatids can develop into normal offspring. Development 121:2397–2405, 1995.

108. Sasagawa I, Tateno T, Adachi Y, et al: Round spermatids from prepubertal mouse testis can develop into normal offspring. J Androl 19:196–200, 1998.

109. Ogura A, Matsuda J, Asano T, et al: Mouse oocytes injected with cryopreserved round spermatids can develop into normal offspring. J Assist Reprod Genet 13:431–434, 1996.

110. Blanco-Rodriguez J: A matter of life and death: The significance of germ cell death during spermatogenesis. Int J Androl 21:236–248, 1998.

111. Sinha Hikim AP, Swerdloff RS: Hormonal and genetic control of germ cell apoptosis in the testis. Rev Reprod 4:38–47, 1999.

112. Print CG, Loveland K, Gibson L, et al: Apoptosis regulator Bcl-w is essential for spermatogenesis but is otherwise dispensable. Proc Natl Acad Sci U S A 95:12424–12431, 1998.

113. Meehan T, Loveland KL, de Kretser DM, et al: Developmental regulation of the bcl-2 family during spermatogenesis: Insights into the sterility of bcl/w-/-male mice. Cell Death Differ 8:225–233, 2001.

114. Johnson L, Barnard JJ, Rodriguez L, et al: Ethnic differences in testicular structure and spermatogenic potential may predispose testes of Asian men to a heightened sensitivity to steroidal contraceptives. J Androl 19:348–357, 1998.

115. Wang R-A, Nakane PK, Koji T: Autonomous cell death of mouse male germ cells during fetal and postnatal period. Biol Reprod 58:1250–1256, 1998.

116. Yin Y, Hawkins KL, Dewolf WC, et al: Heat stress causes testicular germ cell apoptosis in adult mice. J Androl 18:159–165, 1997.

117. Blanco-Rodriguez J, Martinez-Garcia C: Apoptosis pattern elicited by several apoptogenic agents on the seminiferous epithelium of the adult rat testis. J Androl 19:487–497, 1998.

118. Henrikson K, Kulmala J, Toppari J, et al: Stage-specific apoptosis in the rat seminiferous epithelium: Quantification of irradiation effects. J Androl 17:394–402, 1996.

119. Heiskanen P, Billig H, Toppari J, et al: Apoptotic cell death in the normal and cryptorchid human testis: The effect of human chorionic gonadotropin on testicular cell survival. Pediatr Res 40:351–356, 1996.

120. Erkkila K, Henriksen K, Hirvonen V, et al: Testosterone regulates apoptosis in adult human seminiferous tubules in vitro. J Clin Endocrinol Metab 82:2314–2321, 1997.

121. de Kretser DM, Baker HWG: Infertility in men: Recent advances and continuing controversies. J Clin Endocrinol Metab 84:3443–3450, 1999.

122. Matzuk MM, Lamb DJ: Genetic dissection of mammalian fertility pathways. Nat Cell Biol 4(Suppl):S41–S49, 2002.

123. Cooke HJ, Saunders PTK: Mouse models of male fertility. Nat Rev Genet 3:790–801, 2002.

124. Ward JO, Reinholdt LG, Hartford SA, et al: Toward the genetics of mammalian reproduction: Induction and mapping of gametogenesis mutants in mice. Biol Reprod 69:1615–1625, 2003.

125. Reinke V, Smith HE, Nance J, et al: A global profile of germline gene expression in C. elegans. Mol Cell 6:605–616, 2000.

126. Primig M, Williams RM, Winzeler EA, et al: The core meiotic transcriptome in budding yeasts. Nat Genet 26:415–423, 2000.

127. Kerr JB: Macro, micro and molecular research on spermatogenesis: The quest to understand its control. Microsc Res Tech 32:364–384, 1995.

128. Johnson L, McKenzie KS, Snell JR: Partial wave in human seminiferous tubules appears to be a random occurrence. Tissue Cell 28:127–136, 1996.

129. Schulz W, Rehder U: Organization and morphogenesis of the human seminiferous epithelium. Cell Tissue Res 237:395–407, 1984.

130. Perey B, Clermont Y, Leblond CP: The wave of the seminiferous epithelium in the rat. Am J Anat 108:47–77, 1961.

131. Ren HP, Russell LD: Clonal development of interconnected germ cells in the rat and its relationship to the segmental and subsegmental organization of spermatogenesis. Am J Anat 192:121–128, 1991.

132. Jiang F-X, Short RV: Male germ cell transplantation in rats: Apparent synchronization of spermatogenesis between host and donor seminiferous epithelia. Int J Androl 18:326–330, 1995.

133. Dobrinski I, Avarbock MR, Brinster RL: Transplantation of germ cells from rabbits and dogs into mouse testes. Biol Reprod 61:1331–1339, 1999.

134. Dobrinski I, Avarbock MR, Brinster RL: Germ cell transplantation from large domestic animals into mouse testes. Mol Reprod Dev 56:270–279, 2000.

135. Nagano M, McCarrey JR, Brinster RL: Primate spermatogonial stem cells colonize mouse testes. Biol Reprod 64:1409–1416, 2001.

136. Nagano M, Patrizio P, Brinster RL: Long-term survival of human spermatogonial stem cells in mouse testes. Fertil Steril 78:1225–1233, 2002.

137. Honaramooz A, Snedaker A, Boiani M, et al: Sperm from neonatal mammalian testes grafted in mice. Nature 418:778–781, 2002.

138. Honaramooz A, Li MW, Penedo CT, et al: Accelerated maturation of primate testis by xenografting into mice. Biol Reprod 70:1500–1503, 2004.

139. Dobrinski I, Megee S, Honaramooz A: Xenografting of testis tissue from neonatal ram lambs into mouse hosts accelerates testicular maturation and sperm production. Biol Reprod 68(Suppl):190, 2003.

140. Schlatt S, Honaramooz A, Boiani M, et al: Progeny from sperm obtained after ectopic grafting of neonatal mouse testes. Biol Reprod 68:2331–2335, 2003.

141. Muller J, Skakkebaek NE: Quantification of germ cells and seminiferous tubules by stereological examination of testicles from 50 boys who suffered from sudden death. Int J Androl 6:143–156, 1983.

142. Muller J, Skakkebaek NE: Fluctuations in the number of germ cells during the late foetal and early postnatal periods in boys. Acta Endocrinol 105:271–274, 1984.

143. Paniagua R, Nistal M: Morphological and histometric study of human spermatogonia from birth to the onset of puberty. J Anat 139:535–552, 1984.

144. Chiarini-Garcia H, Russell LD: High-resolution light microscopic characterization of mouse spermatogonia. Biol Reprod 65:1170–1178, 2001.

145. deRooij DG: Proliferation and differentiation of spermatogonial stem cells. Reproduction 121:347–354, 2001.

146. Orth JM, Gunsalus GL, Lamperti AA: Evidence from Sertoli cell-depleted rats indicates that spermatid number in adults depends on numbers of Sertoli cells produced during perinatal development. Endocrinology 122:787–794, 1988.

147. Johnson L, Zane RS, Petty CS, Neaves WB: Quantification of the human Sertoli cell population: Its distribution, relation to germ cell numbers, and age-related decline. Biol Reprod 31:785–795, 1984.

148. Orth JM: Proliferation of Sertoli cells in fetal and postnatal rats: A quantitative autoradiographic study. Anat Rec 203:485–492, 1982.

149. Orth JM: The role of follicle-stimulating hormone in controlling Sertoli cell proliferation in testes of fetal rats. Endocrinology 115:1248–1255, 1984.

150. Cortes D, Muller J, Skakkebaek NE: Proliferation of Sertoli cells during development of the human testis assessed by stereological methods. Int J Androl 10:589–596, 1987.

151. Vogl AW, Soucy LJ: Arrangement and possible functions of actin filament bundles in ectoplasmic specializations of ground squirrel Sertoli cells. J Cell Biol 100:814–825, 1985.

152. Cheng CY, Mruk DD: Cell junction dynamics in the testis: Sertoli-germ cell interactions and male contraceptive development. Physiol Rev 82:825–874, 2002.

153. Toyama Y, Maekawa M, Yuasa S: Ectoplasmic specializations in the Sertoli cell: New vistas based on genetic defects and testicular toxicology. Anat Sci Int 78:1–16, 2003.

154. Bartles JR, Wierda A, Zheng L: Identification and characterization of espin, an actin-binding protein localized to the F-actin rich junctional plaques of Sertoli cell ectoplasmic specializations. J Cell Sci 109:1229–1239, 1996.

155. Setchell BP, Zupp JP, Pollanen P: Blood-testis barrier at puberty. In Parvinen M, Huhtaniemi I, Pelliniemi LJ (eds): Development and Function of the Reproductive Organs. Rome, Serono Symposium Reviews, 1988, no. 14, pp 77–84.

156. de Kretser DM, Burger HG: Ultrastructural studies of the human Sertoli cell in normal men and males with hypogonadotrophic hypogonadism before and after gonadotrophic treatment. In Saxena BB, Beling CG, Gandy HM (eds): Gonadotrophins. New York, Wiley, 1972, pp 640–656.

157. Fuyara S, Kumamoto Y, Sugiyama S: Fine structure and development of Sertoli junctions in human testis. Arch Androl 1:211–219, 1978.

158. Vogl AW: Changes in the distribution of microtubules in rat Sertoli cells during spermatogenesis. Anat Rec 222:34–41, 1988.

159. Vogl AW, Pfeiffer DC, Mulholland D, et al: Unique and multifunctional adhesion junctions in the testis: Ectoplasmic specializations. Arch Histol Cytol 63:1–15, 2000.

160. Paranko J, Kallajoki M, Pelliniemi LJ, et al: Transient coexpression of cytokeratin and vimentin in differentiating rat Sertoli cells. Dev Biol 117:35–44, 1986.

161. Oko R, Hermo L, Hecht NB: Distribution of actin isoforms within cells of the seminiferous epithelium of the rat testis: Evidence for a muscle form of actin in spermatids. Anat Rec 231:63–81, 1991.

162. Pfeiffer DC, Vogl AW: Evidence that vinculin is codistributed with actin bundles in ectoplasmic ("junctional") specializations of mammalian Sertoli cells. Anat Rec 231:89–100, 1991.

163. Morales C, Clermont Y, Nadler NJ: Cyclic endocytic activity and kinetics of lysosomes in Sertoli cells of the rat: A morphometric analysis. Biol Reprod 34:207–218, 1986.

164. Chemes H: The phagocytic function of Sertoli cells: A morphological, biochemical and endocrinological

study of lysosomes and acid phosphatase localization in the rat testis. Endocrinology 119:1673–1681, 1986.

165. Ueno H, Mori H: Morphometrical analysis of Sertoli cell ultrastructure during the seminiferous epithelial cycle in rats. Biol Reprod 43:769–776, 1990.

166. Kerr JB: An ultrastructural and morphometric analysis of the Sertoli cell during the spermatogenic cycle in the rat. Anat Embryol 179:191–203, 1988.

167. Morales C, Clermont Y, Hermo L: Nature and function of endocytosis in Sertoli cells of the rat. Am J Anat 173:203–217, 1985.

168. Rong-Xi D, Djakiew D, Dym M: Endocytic activity of Sertoli cells grown in bicameral culture chambers. Anat Rec 218:306–312, 1987.

169. Petrie RG, Morales CR: Receptor-mediated endocytosis of testicular transferrin by germinal cells of the rat testis. Cell Tissue Res 267:45–55, 1992.

170. Buzzard JJ, Wreford NG, Morrison JR: Marked extension of proliferation of rat Sertoli cells in culture using recombinant human FSH. Reproduction 124:633–641, 2002.

171. Buzzard JJ, Farnworth PG, de Kretser DM, et al: Proliferative phase Sertoli cells display developmentally regulated response to activin A in vitro. Endocrinology 144:474–483, 2003.

172. Christensen AK: Leydig cells. In Hamilton DW, Greep RO (eds): Handbook of Physiology, sect 7, Endocrinology, vol 5, Male Reproductive System. Baltimore, Williams & Wilkins, 1975, pp 57–94.

173. Payne AH, Hardy MP, Russell LD (eds): The Leydig Cell. Vienna, IL, Cache River Press, 1996.

174. Holstein AF, Orlandini GE, Moller R: Distribution and fine structure of the lymphatic system in the human testis. Cell Tissue Res 200:15–27, 1979.

175. Mendis-Handagama SMLC, Zirkin BR, Scallen TJ, et al: Studies on peroxisomes of the adult rat Leydig cell. J Androl 11:270–278, 1990.

176. Miller SC: Localization of plutonium-241 in the testis. An interspecies comparison using light and electron microscope autoradiography. Int J Radiat Biol 41:633–643, 1982.

177. Miller SC, Bowman BM, Rowland HG: Structure, cytochemistry, endocytic activity and immunoglobulin (Fc) receptors of rat testicular interstitial tissue macrophages. Am J Anat 168:1–13, 1983.

178. Hutson JC: Development of cytoplasmic digitations between Leydig cells and testicular macrophages of the rat. Cell Tissue Res 267:385–389, 1992.

179. Pollanen P, Maddocks S: Macrophages, lymphocytes and MHC II antigen in the rat and ram testis. J Reprod Fertil 82:437–445, 1988.

180. Hedger MP: Testicular leucocytes: What are they doing? Rev Reprod 2:38–47, 1997.

181. Jackson AE, O'Leary PC, Ayers MM, de Kretser DM: The effects of ethylene dimethanesulphate (EDS) on rat Leydig cells: Evidence to support a connective tissue origin of Leydig cells. Biol Reprod 35:425–437, 1986.

182. Chemes H, Cigorraga S, Bergada C, et al: Isolation of human Leydig cell mesenchymal precursors from patients with the androgen insensitivity syndrome: Testosterone production and response to human chorionic gonadotropin stimulation in culture. Biol Reprod 46:793–801, 1992.

183. Print CG, Loveland K, Gibson L, et al: Apoptosis regulator Bcl-w is essential for spermatogenesis but is otherwise dispensable. Proc Natl Acad Sci U S A 95:12424–12431, 1998.

184. Sharpe RM: Intratesticular factors controlling testicular function. Biol Reprod 30:29–49, 1984.

185. de Kretser DM: Local regulation of testicular function. Int Rev Cytol 10:89–112, 1987.

186. de Kretser DM: Germ cell-Sertoli cell interactions. Reprod Fertil Dev 2:225–235, 1990.

187. Parvinen M, Vihko KK, Topari J: Cell interactions during the seminiferous epithelial cycle. Int Rev Cytol 104:115–151, 1987.

188. Baird DT, Galbraith A, Fraser IS, Newsam JE: The concentration of oestrone and oestradiol-17 in spermatic venous blood in man. J Endocrinol 57:285–288, 1973.

189. Chen YI, Kraemer FB, Reaven GM: Identification of specific HDL-binding sites in rat testis. J Biol Chem 255:9162–9169, 1980.

190. Freeman DA, Ascoli M: The LDL pathway of cultured Leydig tumour cells. Biochim Biophys Acta 754:72–79, 1983.

191. Mertz LM, Pedersen RC: The kinetics of steroidogenesis activator polypeptide in the rat adrenal cortex. J Biol Chem 264:15274–15279, 1989.

192. Chung B, Matteson KJ, Voutilainen R, et al: Human cholesterol side-chain cleavage enzyme P450 scc: cDNA cloning, assignment of the gene to chromosome 15 and expression in the placenta. Proc Natl Acad Sci U S A 83:8962–8966, 1986.

193. Pollack SE, Furth EE, Kallen CB, et al: Localization of the steroidogenic acute regulatory protein in human tissues. J Clin Endocrinol Metab 82:4243–4251, 1997.

194. Clark BJ, Wells J, King SR, Stocco DM: The purification, cloning, and expression of a novel LH-induced mitochondrial protein in MA-10 mouse Leydig tumor cells: Characterization of the steroidogenic acute regulatory protein (STAR). J Biol Chem 269:28314–28322, 1994.

195. Stocco DM, Clark BJ: Regulation of the acute production of steroids in steroidogenic cells. Endocr Rev 3:221–224, 1996.

196. Lin D, Sugawara T, Strauss III JF, et al: Role of steroidogenic acute regulatory protein in adrenal and gonadal steroidogenesis. Science 267:1828–1831, 1995.

197. Caron KM, Soo SC, Wetsel WC, et al: Targeted disruption of the mouse gene encoding steroidogenic acute regulatory protein provides insights into congenital lipoid adrenal hyperplasia. Proc Natl Acad Sci U S A 94:11540–11545, 1997.

198. Papadopoulos V: Peripheral-type benzodiazepine/diazepam binding inhibitor receptor: Biological role in steroidogenic cell function. Endocr Rev 14:222–240, 1993.

199. Weinsten JJAM, Sunals AGM, Hofman JA, et al: Early time sequence in pregnenolone metabolism to testosterone in homogenates of human and rat testis. Endocrinology 120:1909–1913, 1987.

200. Huhtaniemi I: Studies on steroidogenesis and its regulation in human fetal adrenal and testis. J Steroid Biochem 8:491–497, 1977.

201. Matteson KJ, Picardo-Leonard J, Chung B, et al: Assignment of the gene for adrenal P450c17 (steroid 17α hydroxylase/17,20 lyase) to human chromosome 10. J Clin Endocrinol Metab 63:789–791, 1985.

202. Chung B, Picardo-Leonard J, Haniu M, et al: Cytochrome P450c17 (steroid 17α hydroxylase/17, 20 lyase): Cloning of human adrenal and testis cDNA indicates the same gene is expressed in both tissues. Proc Natl Acad Sci U S A 84:407–411, 1987.

201. Inano H, Ishii-Ohba H, Sugimoto Y, et al: Purification and properties of enzymes related to steroid hormone synthesis. Ann N Y Acad Sci 595:17–25, 1990.

204. Luu-The V, Labrie C, Simard J, et al: Structure of two in tandem 17β human hydroxysteroid dehydrogenase genes. Mol Endocrinol 4:268–275, 1990.

205. Lorence MC, Corbin CG, Kamimura N, et al: Structural analysis of the gene encoding human 3β hydroxysteroid dehydrogenase/delta 5-4 isomerase. Mol Endocrinol 4:1850–1855, 1990.

206. Chen S, Besman MJ, Sparks RS, et al: Human aromatases: cDNA cloning, Southern analysis and assignment of the gene to chromosome 15. DNA 7:27–38, 1988.

207. Andersson S, Russel DW: Structural and biochemical properties of cloned and expressed human and rat steroid 5 alpha reductases. Proc Natl Acad Sci U S A 87:3640–3644, 1990.

208. de Kretser DM, Catt KJ, Paulsen CA: Studies on the in vitro testicular binding of iodinated luteinizing hormone in rats. Endocrinology 88:332–337, 1971.

209. Loosefelt H, Misrahi M, Atger M, et al: Cloning and sequencing of porcine LH-hCG receptor cDNA: Variants lacking transmembrane domain. Science 245:525–528, 1989.

210. Muller J, Gondos B, Kosugi S, et al: Severe testotoxicosis phenotype associated with Asp578:Tyr mutation of the lutrophin/choriogonadotrophin receptor gene. J Med Genet 35:340–341, 1998.

211. Stavrou SS, Zhu YS, Cai LQ, et al: A novel mutation of the human luteinizing hormone receptor in 46XY and 46XX sisters. J Clin Endocrinol Metab 83:2091–2098, 1998.

212. Gromoll J, Partsch CJ, Simoni M, et al: A mutation in the first transmembrane domain of the Lutropin receptor causes male precocious puberty. J Clin Endocrinol Metab 83:476–480, 1998.

213. Latronico AC, Chai Y, Arnhold IJ, et al: A homozygous microdeletion in helix 7 of the luteinizing hormone receptor associated with familial testicular and ovarian resistance is due to both decreased cell surface expression and impaired effector activation by the cell surface receptor. Mol Endocrinol 12:442–450, 1998.

214. Simoni M, Gromoll J, Nieschlag E: Molecular pathophysiology and clinical manifestations of gonadotropin receptor defects. Steroids 63:288–293, 1998.

215. Zhang FP, Pakarainen T, Zhu F, et al: Molecular characterization of postnatal development of testicular steroidogenesis in luteinizing hormone receptor knockout mice. Endocrinology 145:1453–1463, 2004.

216. Dufau ML: Endocrine regulation and communicating functions of the Leydig cell. Annu Rev Physiol 50:483–508, 1988.

217. Dufau ML, Tsuruhara T, Horner KA, et al: Intermediate role of adenosine 3′,5′-cyclic monophosphate and protein kinase during gonadotrophin induced steroidogenesis in testicular interstitial cells. Proc Natl Acad Sci U S A 74:3419–3423, 1977.

218. Cooke BA: Is cyclic AMP an obligatory second messenger for luteinizing hormone? Mol Cell Endocrinol 69:C11–C15, 1990.

219. Hodgson YM, de Kretser DM: Serum testosterone response to single injection of hCG ovine-LH and LHRH in male rats. Int J Androl 5:81–91, 1982.

220. Padron RS, Wischusen J, Hudson B, et al: Prolonged biphasic response of plasma testosterone to single intramuscular injections of human chorionic gonadotrophin. J Clin Endocrinol Metab 50:1100–1104, 1980.

221. Sharpe RM: hCG-induced decrease in availability of rat testis receptors. Nature 264:644–646, 1976.

222. Cigorraga SB, Sorell S, Bator J, et al: Estrogen dependence of a gonadotrophin-induced steroidogenic lesion in rat testicular Leydig cells. J Clin Invest 65:699–705, 1980.

223. Hodgson YM, de Kretser DM: Acute responses of Leydig cells to hCG: Evidence for early hypertrophy of Leydig cells. Mol Cell Endocrinol 35:75–82, 1984.

224. Christensen AK, Peacock KL: Increase in Leydig cell number in testes of adult rats treated chronically with an excess of human chorionic gonadotropin. Biol Reprod 22:383–391, 1980.

225. Waterman MR, Simpson ER: Regulation of steroid hydroxylase gene expression is multifactorial in nature. Recent Prog Horm Res 45:533–566, 1989.

226. Wu FCW, Irby DC, Clarke IJ, et al: Effects of gonadotropin-releasing hormone pulse-frequency modulation on luteinizing hormone, follicle stimulating hormone and testosterone secretion in hypothalamo/pituitary-disconnected rams. Biol Reprod 37:501–510, 1987.

227. Cooke PS, Hess RA, Porcelli J, Meisami E: Increased sperm production in adult rats after transient neonatal hypothyroidism. Endocrinology 129:244–248, 1991.

228. Simorangkir D, Wreford N, de Kretser DM: Increased numbers of Sertoli and germ cells in adult rat testes induced by synergistic action of transient neonatal hypothyroidism and neonatal hemicastration. J Reprod Fertil 104:207–213, 1995.

229. Means AR, Vaitukaitis J: Peptide hormone receptors: Specific binding of ³-FSH to testis. Endocrinology 90:39–46, 1972.

230. Orth J, Christensen AK: Autoradiographic localization of specifically bound ¹²⁵-labelled follicle stimulating hormone on spermatogonia of the rat testis. Endocrinology 103:1944–1951, 1978.

231. Mulder E, Peters MJ, de Vries J, et al: Characterization of a nuclear receptor for testosterone in seminiferous tubules of mature rat testes. Mol Cell Endocrinol 2:171–182, 1975.

232. Sanborn BM, Steinberger A, Tcholakian RK, et al: Direct measurement of androgen receptors in cultured Sertoli cells. Steroids 29:493–502, 1977.

233. Bremner WJ, Millar MR, Sharpe RM: Immunohistochemical localization of androgen receptors in the rat testis: Evidence of a stage dependent expression and regulation by androgens. Endocrinology 135:1227–1234, 1994.

234. Namiki M, Yokokawa K, Okuyama A, et al: Evidence for the presence of androgen receptors in human Leydig cells. J Steroid Biochem Mol Biol 38:79–82, 1991.

235. Skinner MK, Fetterolf PM, Anthony CT: Purification of a paracrine factor, P-Mod-S, produced by testicular peritubular cells that modulates Sertoli cell function. J Biol Chem 25:2884–2890, 1988.

236. Skinner MK, McLachlan RI, Bremner WJ: Stimulation of Sertoli cell inhibin secretion by the testicular paracrine factor P-Mod-S: Mol Cell Endocrinol 66:239–249, 1989.

237. Heindel JJ, Rothenberg R, Robinson GA, et al: LH and FSH stimulation of cyclic AMP in specific cell types isolated from the testes. J Cyclic Nucleotide Res 1:69–79, 1975.

238. Means AR: Biochemical effects of FSH on the testis. In Greep RO, Hamilton DW (eds): Handbook of Physiology, sect 7, Endocrinology, vol 5, Male Reproductive System. Baltimore, Williams & Wilkins, 1975, pp 203–218.

239. Conti M, Toscano MV, Geremia R, et al: Follicle stimulating hormone regulates in vivo phosphodiesterase. Mol Cell Endocrinol 29:79–90, 1983.

240. Ireland ME, Rosenblum BB, Welsh MJ: Two dimensional gel analysis of Sertoli cell protein phosphorylation: Effects of short-term exposure to follicle stimulating hormone. Endocrinology 118:526–532, 1986.

241. Gorczynska E, Handelsman DJ: The role of calcium in follicle-stimulating hormone (FSH) signal transduction in Sertoli cells. J Biol Chem 266:23739–23744, 1991.

242. Dorrington JH, Roller NF, Fritz IB: Effects of follicle stimulating hormone on cultures of Sertoli cell preparations. Mol Cell Endocrinol 3:57–70, 1975.

243. Attramadal H, Le Gac F, Jahnsen T, Hansson V: β Adrenergic regulation of Sertoli cell adenylate cyclase: Desensitization by homologous hormone. Mol Cell Endocrinol 34:1–6, 1984.

244. Le Gac F, Attramadal H, Jahsen T, Hansson V: Studies on the mechanism of follicle stimulating hormone-induced desensitization of Sertoli cell adenyl cyclase in vitro. Biol Reprod 32:916–924, 1985.

245. Conti M, Toscano MV, Petrelli L, et al: Involvement of phosphodiesterase in the refractoriness of the Sertoli cell. Endocrinology 113:1845–1853, 1983.

246. Conti M, Monaco L, Geremia R, Stefanini M: Effect of phosphodiesterase inhibitors on Sertoli cell refractoriness: Reversal of impaired androgen aromatization. Endocrinology 118:901–908, 1986.

247. Hansson V, Reusch E, Trygstad O, et al: FSH stimulation of testicular androgen binding protein. Nature 246:56–58, 1973.

248. Skinner MK, Griswold MD: Secretion of testicular transferrin by cultured Sertoli cells is regulated by hormones and retinoids. Biol Reprod 27:211–221, 1982.

249. Le Gac F, de Kretser DM: Inhibin production by Sertoli cells. Mol Cell Endocrinol 28:487–498, 1982.

250. Dorrington JH, Armstrong DT: Follicle stimulating hormone stimulates estradiol-17β synthesis in cultured Sertoli cells. Proc Natl Acad Sci U S A 72:2677–2681, 1975.

251. Lacroix M, Smith FE, Fritz IB: Secretion of plasminogen activator by Sertoli cell enriched cultures. Mol Cell Endocrinol 9:227–236, 1977.

252. Jensen TK, Andersson AM, Hjollund NHI, et al: Inhibin B as a serum marker of spermatogenesis: Correlation to

differences in sperm concentration and follicle stimulating hormone levels. A study of 349 Danish men. J Clin Endocrinol Metab 82:4059–4063, 1997.

253. Hall PF, Mita M: Influence of FSH on glucose transport by cultured Sertoli cells. Biol Reprod 31:863–869, 1984.

254. Jutte NHPM, Hansen R, Grottegoed JA, et al: FSH stimulation of the production of pyruvate and lactate by rat Sertoli cells may be involved in hormonal regulation of spermatogenesis. J Reprod Fertil 68:219–226, 1983.

255. Spruill WA, Steiner AL, Tres LL, Kierszenbaum AL: Follicle stimulating hormone dependent phosphorylation of vimentin in cultures of rat Sertoli cells. Proc Natl Acad Sci U S A 80:993–997, 1983.

256. Allan CM, Garcia A, Spaliviero J, et al: Complete Sertoli cell proliferation induced by follicle-stimulating hormone (FSH) independently of luteinizing hormone activity: Evidence from genetic models of isolated FSH action. Endocrinology 145:1587–1593, 2004.

257. Parvinen M: Regulation of the seminiferous epithelium. Endocr Rev 3:404–417, 1982.

258. Gonzales GF, Risbridger GP, de Kretser DM: In vitro synthesis and release of inhibin in response to FSH stimulation by isolated segments of seminiferous tubules from normal adult male rats. Mol Cell Endocrinol 59:179–185, 1988.

259. Holdcraft RW, Braun RE: Androgen receptor function is required in Sertoli cells for the terminal differentiation of haploid spermatids. Development 131:459–467, 2004.

260. DeGendt K, Swinnen JV, Saunders PTK, et al: A Sertoli cell-selective knockout of the androgen receptor causes spermatogenic arrest in meiosis. Proc Natl Acad Sci U S A 101:1327–1332, 2004.

261. Jegou B, Le Gac F, Irby D, de Kretser DM: Studies on seminiferous tubule fluid production in the adult rat: Effect of hypophysectomy and treatment with FSH, LH and testosterone. Int J Androl 6:249–260, 1983.

262. Au CL, Irby DC, Robertson DM, de Kretser DM: Effects of testosterone on testicular inhibin and fluid production in intact and hypophysectomized adult rats. J Reprod Fertil 76:257–266, 1986.

263. Lamb DJ, Wagle JR, Tsai YH, et al: Specificity and nature of the rapid steroid stimulated increase in Sertoli cell nuclear RNA polymerase activity. J Steroid Biochem 116:653–660, 1982.

264. Ailenberg M, McCabe D, Fritz IB: Androgens inhibit plasminogen activator activity secreted by Sertoli cells in culture in a two-chambered assembly. Endocrinology 126:1561–1568, 1990.

265. Persson H, Ayer-Le Lievre C, Soder O, et al: Expression of beta-nerve growth factor receptor mRNA in Sertoli cells is down regulated by testosterone. Science 247:704–707, 1990.

266. Cheng CY, Grima J, Stahler MS, et al: Testins are structurally related Sertoli cell proteins whose secretion is tightly coupled to the presence of germ cells. J Biol Chem 264:21386–21393, 1989.

267. Sharpe RM, Maddocks S, Millar M, et al: Testosterone and spermatogenesis. Identification of stage-specific, androgen regulated proteins secreted by adult rat seminiferous tubules. J Androl 13:172–184, 1992.

268. Tan J, Joseph DR, Quarmby VE, et al: The rat androgen receptor primary structure, autoregulation of its messenger ribonucleic acid and immunocytochemical localization of the receptor protein. Mol Endocrinol 2:1276–1285, 1988.

269. Sun YT, Irby DC, Robertson DM, de Kretser DM: The effects of exogenously administered testosterone on spermatogenesis in intact and hypophysectomized rats. Endocrinology 125:1000–1010, 1989.

270. Verhoeven G, Cailleau J: Follicle stimulating hormone and androgens increase the concentration of the androgen receptor in Sertoli cells. Endocrinology 122:1541–1550, 1988.

271. Johnston DS, Russell LD, Friel PJ, et al: Murine germ cells do not require functional androgen receptors to complete spermatogenesis following spermatogonial stem cell transplantation. Endocrinology 142:2405–2408, 2001.

272. Hess RA, Bunick D, Lee KH, et al: A role for oestrogens in the male reproductive tract. Nature 390:509–512, 1997.

273. Boyar RJ, Finkelstein H, Roffwarg S, et al: Synchronization of augmented luteinizing hormone secretion with sleep during puberty. N Engl J Med 287:582–586, 1972.

274. Lee VWK, de Kretser DM, Hudson BH, Wang C: Variations in serum FSH, LH and testosterone levels in male rats from birth to sexual maturity. J Reprod Fertil 42:121–126, 1975.

275. Paulsen CA, Espeland DH, Michals EL: Effects of hCG, HMG, HLH and HGH administration on testicular function. In Rosenberg E, Paulsen CA (eds): The Human Testis. New York, Plenum, 1970, pp 547–562.

276. Finkel DM, Phillips JL, Synder PJ: Stimulation of spermatogenesis by gonadotropins in men with hypogonadotropic hypogonadism. N Engl J Med 313:651–655, 1985.

277. Sheckter CB, McLachlan RI, Tenover JS, et al: Serum inhibin concentrations rise during GnRH treatment of men with idiopathic hypogonadotrophic hypogonadism. J Clin Endocrinol Metab 67:1221–1224, 1988.

278. Singh J, O'Neill C, Handelsman DJ: Induction of spermatogenesis by androgens in gonadotropin-deficient (hpg) mice. Endocrinology 136:5311–5321, 1995.

279. Tapanainen JS, Aittomaki K, Min J, et al: Men homozygous for an inactivating mutation of the follicle stimulating hormone (FSH) receptor gene present variable suppression of spermatogenesis and fertility. Nat Genet 15:205–206, 1997.

280. Kumar TR, Wang Y, Lu N, Matzuk M: Follicle stimulating hormone is required for ovarian follicle maturation but not male fertility. Nat Genet 15:201–204, 1997.

281. Wreford NG, Kumar TR, Matzuk M, de Kretser DM: Analysis of the follicle stimulating hormone (FSH) β subunit knock-out and the activin type II receptor knock-out mice by stereological analysis. Endocrinology 142:2916–2920, 2001.

282. Fraser HM, Gunn A, Jeffcoate SL, Holland DT: Effect of active immunization to luteinizing hormone releasing hormone on serum and pituitary gonadotropins, testes and accessory sex organs in the male rat. J Endocrinol 63:399–401, 1974.

283. Steinberger E, Root A, Ficher M, Smith KD: The role of androgens in the initiation of spermatogenesis in man. J Clin Endocrinol Metab 37:746–751, 1973.

284. Mann DR, Fraser HM: The neonatal period: A critical interval in primate development. J Endocrinol 149:191–197, 1996.

285. Andersson AM, Toppari J, Haavisto AM, et al: Longitudinal reproductive hormones in infants: Peak of inhibin B levels in boys exceeds levels in adult men. J Clin Endocrinol Metab 83:675–681, 1998.

286. Sharpe RM, Fraser HM, Brougham MFH, et al: Role of the neonatal period of pituitary-testicular activity in germ cell proliferation and differentiation in the primate testis. Hum Reprod 18:2110–2117, 2003.

287. Srinath BR, Wickings EJ, Witting C, Nieschlag E: Active immunization with follicle stimulating hormone for fertility control: A 4 1/2 year study in male rhesus monkeys. Fertil Steril 40:110–117, 1983.

288. Murty GSRC, Sheela Rani CS, Moudgal NR, Prasad MRN: Effect of passive immunization with specific antiserum to FSH on the spermatogenic process and fertility of adult male bonnet monkeys (Macaca radiata). J Reprod Fertil 26:147–163, 1979.

289. MacLeod J, Pazianos A, Ray B: The restoration of human spermatogenesis and of the reproductive tract with urinary gonadotropins following hypophysectomy. Fertil Steril 17:7–23, 1986.

290. Matsumoto AM, Karpas AE, Paulsen CA, Bremner WJ: Reinitiation of sperm production in gonadotropin-suppressed normal men by administration of follicle stimulating hormone. J Clin Invest 72:1005–1015, 1983.

291. Matsumoto AM, Paulsen CA, Bremner WJ: Stimulation of sperm production by human luteinizing hormone in gonadotropin-suppressed normal men. J Clin Endocrinol Metab 59:882–887, 1984.

292. Clermont Y, Harvey SG: Duration of the cycle of the seminiferous epithelium of normal hypophysectomized and hypophysectomized-hormone treated albino rats. Endocrinology 76:80–89, 1965.

293. Marshall GR, Wickings EJ, Ludecke DK, Nieschlag E: Stimulation of spermatogenesis in stalk-sectioned rhesus monkeys by testosterone alone. J Clin Endocrinol Metab 57:152–159, 1983.

294. Berndtson WE, Desjardins C, Ewing LL: Inhibition and maintenance of spermatogenesis in rats implanted with polydimethylsiloxane capsules containing various androgens. J Endocrinol 62:125–135, 1974.

295. Cunningham GR, Huckins C: Persistence of complete spermatogenesis in the presence of low intra-testicular concentration of testosterone. Endocrinology 105:177–186, 1979.

296. Sharpe RM: Testosterone and spermatogenesis. J Endocrinol 113:1–2, 1987.

297. Zirkin BR, Santulli R, Awoniyi CA, Ewing LL: Maintenance of advanced spermatogenic cells in the adult rat testis: Quantitative relationships to testosterone concentration within the testis. Endocrinology 124:3043–3049, 1989.

298. Santulli R, Sprando RL, Awoniyi CA, et al: To what extent can spermatogenesis be maintained in the hypophysectomized adult rat testis with exogenously administered testosterone? Endocrinology 126:95–101, 1990.

299. Rea MA, Marshall GR, Weinbauer GF, Nieschlag E: Testosterone maintains pituitary and serum FSH and spermatogenesis in gonadotropin-releasing hormone antagonist suppressed rats. J Endocrinol 108:101–103, 1986.

300. Sun YT, Wreford NG, Robertson DM, de Kretser DM: Quantitative cytological studies of spermatogenesis in intact and hypophysectomized rats: Identification of androgen-dependent stages. Endocrinology 127:1215–1223, 1990.

301. O'Donnell L, McLachlan RI, Wreford N, et al: Testosterone withdrawal promotes stage-specific detachment of round spermatids from the rat seminiferous epithelium. Biol Reprod 55:895–901, 1996.

302. Perryman KJ, Stanton PG, Loveland KL, et al: Hormonal dependency of neural cadherin in the binding of round spermatids to Sertoli cells in vitro. Endocrinology 137:3877–3883, 1996.

303. McLachlan RI, O'Donnell L, Meachem SJ, et al: Identification of specific sites of hormonal regulation in spermatogenesis in rats, monkeys, and man. Recent Prog Horm Res 57:149–179, 2002.

304. Meachem SJ, Wreford NG, Stanton PJ, et al: FSH is important for the initial phase of spermatogenic restoration in adult rats following gonadotrophin suppression. J Androl 19:725–735, 1998.

305. Zhengwei Y, Wreford NG, Schlatt S, et al: GnRH antagonist-induced gonadotropin withdrawal acutely and specifically impairs spermatogonial development in the adult macaque (Macaca fascicularis). J Reprod Fertil 112:139–147, 1998.

306. Zhengwei Y, Wreford NG, Royce P, et al: Stereological evaluation of human spermatogenesis after suppression by testosterone treatment: Heterogeneous pattern of spermatogenic impairment. J Clin Endocrinol Metab 83:1284–1291, 1998.

307. Matsumoto AM: Hormonal control of human spermatogenesis. In Burger HG, de Kretser DM (eds): The Testis, 2d ed. New York, Raven, 1989, pp 181–196.

308. Eddy EM, Washburn TF, Bunch DO, et al: Targeted disruption of the estrogen receptor gene in male mice causes alteration of spermatogenesis and infertility. Endocrinology 137:4796–4805, 1996.

309. Mahato D, Goulding EH, Korach KS, et al: Spermatogenic cells do not require estrogen receptor-a for development or function. Endocrinology 141:1273–1276, 2000.

310. Janulis L, Bahr JM, Hess RA, et al: Rat testicular germ cells and epididymal sperm contain active P450 aromatase. J Androl 19:65–71, 1998.

311. Carreau S, Bilinska B, Levallet J: Male germ cells: A new source of estrogens in the mammalian testis. Ann Endocrinol (Paris) 59:79–92, 1998.

312. Robertson KM, O'Donnell L, Jones MEE, et al: Impairment of spermatogenesis in mice lacking a functional aromatase (cyp 19) gene. Proc Natl Acad Sci U S A 96:7986–7991, 1999.

313. Robertson KM, O'Donnell L, Simpson ER, et al: The phenotype of the aromatase knockout mouse reveals dietary phytoestrogens impact significantly on testis function. Endocrinology 143:2913–2921, 2002.

314. Saunders PTK, Maguire SM, Gaughan J, et al: Expression of oestrogen receptor beta (ERβ) in multiple cell types including some germ cells in the rat testis. J Endocrinol 156:R13–R17, 1997.

315. Zhou Q, Nie R, Prins GS, et al: Localization of androgen and estrogen receptors in adult male mouse reproductive tract. J Androl 23:870–881, 2002.

316. Saunders PTK, Millar MR, MacPherson S, et al: ERbeta 1 and ERbeta 2 splice variant (ERbetacx/beta 2) are expressed in distinct cell populations in the adult human testis. J Clin Endocrinol Metab 87:2706–2715, 2002.

317. Krege JH, Hodgin JB, Couse JF, et al: Generation and reproductive phenotypes of mice lacking estrogen receptor beta. Proc Natl Acad Sci U S A 95:15677–15682, 1998.

318. Simorgangkir DR, Wreford NG, de Kretser DM: Impaired germ cell development in the testis of immature rats with neonatal hypothyroidism. J Androl 18:186–193, 1997.

319. Hadley MA, Djakiew D, Byers SW, Dym M: Polarized secretion of androgen binding protein and transferrin by Sertoli cells grown in bicameral culture system. Endocrinology 120:1097–1103, 1987.

320. Griswold MD: Protein secretions of Sertoli cells. Int Rev Cytol 110:133–156, 1988.

321. Jegou B: The Sertoli cell. Ballieres Clin Endocrinol Metab 6:273–311, 1992.

322. Robinson R, Fritz B: Myoinositol biosynthesis by Sertoli cells and levels of myoinositol biosynthesis enzymes in testis and epididymis. Can J Biochem 57:962–974, 1979.

323. Djakiew D, Griswold MD, Lewis DM, Dym M: Micropuncture studies of receptor-mediated endocytosis of transferrin in the rat epididymis. Biol Reprod 34:691–699, 1986.

324. Morales C, Sylvester SR, Griswold MD: Transport of iron and transferrin synthesis by the seminiferous epithelium of the rat in vitro. Biol Reprod 37:995–1005, 1987.

325. Skinner MK, Griswold MD: Sertoli cells synthesize and secrete a ceruloplasmin-like protein. Biol Reprod 28:1225–1229, 1983.

326. Rich K, de Kretser DM: Effect of differing degrees of distinction of the rat seminiferous epithelium on levels of serum follicle stimulating hormone and androgen binding protein. Endocrinology 101:959–968, 1977.

327. Kastner P, Mark M, Leid M, et al: Abnormal spermatogenesis in RXRβ mutant mice. Genes Dev 10:80–92, 1996.

328. Hagenas L, Ritzen EM, Ploen L, et al: Sertoli cell origin of testicular androgen-binding protein (ABP). Mol Cell Endocrinol 2:239–250, 1975.

329. Linder CC, Heckert LL, Roberts KP, et al: Expression of receptors during the cycle of the seminiferous epithelium. Ann N Y Acad Sci 637:313–321, 1991.

330. Kangasneimi M, Kaipia A, Toppari J, et al: Cellular regulation of follicle-stimulating hormone (FSH) binding in rat seminiferous tubules. J Androl 11:336–343, 1990.

331. Vincent S, Segretain D, Nishikawa S, et al: Stage-specific expression of the kit receptor and its ligand (KL) during male gametogenesis in the mouse: A Kit-KL interaction critical for meiosis. Development 125:4585–4593, 1998.

332. Dix DJ, Allen JW, Collins BW, et al: Targeted disruption of Hsp 70-2 results in failed meiosis, germ cell apoptosis and male infertility. Proc Natl Acad Sci U S A 93:3264–3268, 1996.

333. Afzelius BA, Eliasson R, Johnsen O, Lindholmer C: Lack of dynein arms in immotile human spermatozoa. J Cell Biol 66:225–232, 1975.

334. Sherins RJ, Loriaux DL: Studies on the role of sex steroids in the feedback control of FSH concentrations in men. J Clin Endocrinol Metab 36:886–893, 1973.

335. Naftolin F, Ryan KJ, Petro Z: Aromatization of androstenedione by the diencephalon. J Clin Endocrinol Metab 33:368–370, 1971.

336. Santen RJ: Is aromatization of testosterone to estradiol required for inhibition of luteinizing hormone secretion in man. J Clin Invest 56:1555–1563, 1975.

337. Tilbrook AJ, de Kretser DM, Cummins JT, Clarke IJ: The negative feedback effects of the testicular steroids are predominantly at the hypothalamus in rams. Endocrinology 129:3080–3092, 1991.

338. Decker MH, Loriaux DL, Cutler GB: A seminiferous tubular factor is not obligatory for regulation of plasma follicle-stimulating hormone in the rat. Endocrinology 108:1035–1039, 1981.

339. McCullagh DR: Dual endocrine activity of the testes. Science 76:19–20, 1932.

340. Robertson DM, Foulds LM, Leversha L, et al: Isolation of inhibin from bovine follicular fluid. Biochem Biophys Res Commun 126:220–226, 1985.

341. Jackson CM, Morris ID: Gonadotrophin levels in male rats following impairment of Leydig cell function by ethylene dimethanesulphonate. Andrologia 9:29–32, 1977.

342. de Kretser DM, O'Leary PO, Irby DC, Risbridger GP: Inhibin secretion is influenced by Leydig cells: Evidence from studies using the cytotoxin ethane dimethane sulphonate (EDS). Int J Androl 12:273–280, 1988.

343. O'Leary P, Jackson AE, Averill S, de Kretser DM: The effects of ethane dimethane sulphonate (EDS) on bilaterally cryptorchid rat testes. Mol Cell Endocrinol 45:183–190, 1986.

344. Ling N, Ying SY, Ueno N, et al: Isolation and partial characterization of a Mw 32,000 protein with inhibin activity from porcine follicular fluid. Proc Natl Acad Sci U S A 82:7217–7221, 1985.

345. Mason AJ, Hayflick JS, Esch F, et al: Complementary DNA sequences of ovarian follicular fluid inhibin show precursor structure and homology with transforming growth factor β. Nature 318:659–663, 1985.

346. Forage RG, Ring JM, Brown RW, et al: Cloning and sequence analysis of cDNA species coding for the two subunits of inhibin from bovine follicular fluid. Proc Natl Acad Sci U S A 83:3091–3095, 1986.

347. Vale W, Rivier J, Vaughan J, et al: Purification and characterization of an FSH releasing protein from porcine follicular fluid. Nature 321:776–779, 1986.

348. Ling N, Ying SY, Ueno N, et al: Pituitary FSH is released by a heterodimer of the β subunits of the two forms of inhibin. Nature 321:782–779, 1986.

349. Ueno N, Ling N, Ying SY, et al: Isolation and partial characterization of follistatin: A single-chain Mr35000 monomeric protein that inhibits the release of follicle stimulating hormone. Proc Natl Acad Sci U S A 84:8282–8286, 1987.

350. Robertson DM, Klein R, de Vos FL, et al: The isolation of polypeptides with FSH suppressing activity from bovine follicular fluid which are structurally different to inhibin. Biochem Biophys Res Commun 149:744–749, 1987.

351. Shimasaki S, Koga M, Esch F, et al: Porcine follistatin gene structure supports two forms of mature follistatin produced by alternative splicing. Biophys Biochem Res Commun 152:717–723, 1988.

352. Nakamura T, Takio K, Eto Y, et al: Activin binding protein from rat ovary is follistatin. Science 247:836–838, 1990.

353. Gospodarowicz D, Lau K: Pituitary follicular cells secrete both vascular endothelial growth factor and follistatin. Biochem Biophys Res Commun 165:292–298, 1989.

354. Steinberger A, Steinberger E: Secretion of a FSH-inhibiting factor by cultured Sertoli cells. Endocrinology 99:918–921, 1976.

355. Klaij I, Timmerman MA, Blok LJ, et al: Regulation of inhibin $\beta_B$ subunit mRNA expression in rat Sertoli cells: Consequences for the production of bioactive and immunoactive inhibin. Mol Cell Endocrinol 85:237–246, 1992.

356. Krummen LA, Toppari J, Kim WH, et al: Regulation of testicular inhibin subunit messenger ribonucleic acid levels in vivo: Effects of hypophysectomy and selective follicle-stimulating hormone replacement. Endocrinology 125:1630–1637, 1989.

357. Risbridger GP, Clements J, Robertson DM, et al: Immuno bioactive inhibin and inhibin α subunit expression in rat Leydig cell cultures. Mol Cell Endocrinol 66:119–122, 1989.

358. Lee W, Mason AJ, Schwall R, et al: Secretion of activin by interstitial cells in the testis. Science 243:396–398, 1989.

359. de Winter JP, Vanderstichele HMJ, Timmerman MA, et al: Activin is produced by rat Sertoli cells in vitro and can act as an autocrine regulator of Sertoli cell function. Endocrinology 132:975–982, 1993.

360. McFarlane JR, Foulds LM, Pisciotta A, et al: Measurement of activin in biological fluids by radioimmunoassay, utilizing dissociating agents to remove the interference of follistatin. Eur J Endocrinol 134:481–489, 1996.

361. Mather JP, Attie KM, Woodruff TK, et al: Activin stimulates spermatogonial proliferation in germ cell-Sertoli cell cocultures from immature rat testis. Endocrinology 127:3206–3214, 1990.

362. de Winter JP, Themmen APN, Hoogerbrugge JW, et al: Activin receptor mRNA expression in rat testicular cell types. Mol Cell Endocrinol 83:R1–R8, 1992.

363. Michel U, Albiston A, Findlay JK: Rat follistatin: Gonadal and extragonadal expression and evidence for alternative splicing. Biochem Biophys Res Commun 173:401–407, 1990.

364. Meinhardt A, O'Bryan MK, McFarlane JR, et al: Localization of follistatin in the testis. J Reprod Fertil 112:233–241, 1998.

365. Dubey AK, Zeleznik AJ, Plant TM: In the Rhesus monkey (Macaca mulatta), the negative feedback regulation of follicle stimulating hormone secretion by an action of testicular hormone directly at the level of the anterior pituitary gland cannot be accounted for by either testosterone or estradiol. Endocrinology 121:2229–2237, 1987.

366. Abeyawardene SA, Plant TM: Institution of combined treatment with testosterone and charcoal-extracted follicular fluid immediately after orchidectomy prevents the post castration hypersecretion of follicle stimulating hormone in the hypothalamus-lesioned rhesus monkey (Macaca mulatta) receiving an invariant intravenous gonadotropin releasing hormone infusion. Endocrinology 124:1310–1318, 1989.

367. Tierney ML, Goss NH, Tomkins SM, et al: Physiochemical and biological characterization of recombinant human inhibin A. Endocrinology 126:3268–3270, 1990.

368. Robertson DM, Prisk M, McMaster J, et al: Serum FSH suppressing activity of human recombinant inhibin A in male and female rats. J Reprod Fertil 91:321–328, 1991.

369. Tilbrook AJ, de Kretser DM, Clarke IJ: Human recombinant inhibin A suppresses plasma follicle stimulating hormone to intact levels but has no effect on luteinizing hormone in castrated rams. Biol Reprod 49:779–788, 1993.

370. Roberts V, Meunier H, Vaughan J, et al: Production and regulation of inhibin subunits in pituitary gonadotropes. Endocrinology 124:552–554, 1989.

371. Corrigan AZ, Bilezikjian LM, Carroll RS, et al: Evidence for an autocrine role of activin B within the rat anterior pituitary cultures. Endocrinology 128:1682–1685, 1991.

372. Gonzales GF, Risbridger GP, de Kretser DM: In vivo and in vitro production of inhibin by cryptorchid testes from adult rats. Endocrinology 124:1661–1668, 1989.

373. Weinbauer GF, Behre HM, Fingscheidt U, Nieschlag E: Human follicle stimulating hormone exerts a stimulatory effect on spermatogenesis, testicular size and serum inhibin levels in the gonadotropin-releasing hormone antagonist-treated non human primate (*Macaca fascicularis*). Endocrinology 129:1831–1839, 1991.

374. Anawalt BD, Bebb RA, Matsumoto AM, et al: Serum inhibin B levels reflect Sertoli cell function in normal men and men with testicular dysfunction. J Clin Endocrinol Metab 81:3341–3345, 1996.

375. Anderson RA, Wallace EM, Groome NP, et al: Physiological relationships between inhibin B, follicle stimulating hormone secretion and spermatogenesis in normal men and response to gonadotrophin suppression by exogenous testosterone. Hum Reprod 12:746–751, 1997.

376. Jensen TK, Andersson AM, Hjollund NH, et al: Inhibin B as a serum marker of spermatogenesis: Correlation to differences in sperm concentration and follicle stimulating hormone levels. A study of 349 Danish men. J Clin Endocrinol Metab 82:4059–4063, 1997.

377. Miller SC, Bowman BM, Roberts LK: Identification and characterization of mononuclear phagocytes isolated from rat testicular interstitial tissues. J Leukoc Biol 36:679–687, 1984.

378. Yee JB, Hutson JC: Effects of testicular macrophage-conditioned medium on Leydig cells in culture. Endocrinology 116:268–274, 1985.

379. Calkins JH, Sigel MM, Nankin HR, Lin T: Interleukin-1 inhibits Leydig cell steroidogenesis in primary culture. Endocrinology 123:1605–1610, 1988.

380. Verhoeven G, Kayo J, van Damme J, Billiau A: Interleukin-1 stimulates steroidogenesis in cultured rat Leydig cells. Mol Cell Endocrinol 57:51–60, 1988.

381. Moore C, Moger WH: Interleukin-1α induced changes in androgen and cyclic adenosine 3′,5′-monophosphate release in adult rat Leydig cells in culture. J Endocrinol 129:381–390, 1991.

382. Warren DW, Pasupupeti V, Lu Y, et al: Tumour necrosis factor and interleukin-1 stimulate testosterone secretion in adult rat Leydig cells in vitro. J Androl 11:353–360, 1990.

383. Setchell BP, Rommerts FFG: The importance of the Leydig cells in the vascular response to hCG in the testis. Int J Androl 8:436–440, 1985.

384. Sharpe RM, Doogan DG, Cooper I: Direct effects of a luteinizing hormone-releasing hormone agonist on intratesticular levels of testosterone and interstitial formation in intact male rats. Endocrinology 113:1306–1313, 1983.

385. Sowerbutts SF, Jarvis LG, Setchell BP: The increase in testicular permeability induced by human chorionic gonadotrophin involves 5-hydroxy tryptamine and possibly estrogens, but not testosterone, prostaglandins, histamine or bradykinin. Aust J Exp Biol Med Sci 64:137–147, 1986.

386. Bergh A, Rooth P, Widmark A, Damber J: Treatment of rats with hCG induced inflammation by changes in the testicular circulation. J Reprod Fertil 79:135–143, 1987.

387. Hedger MP, Qin J, Robertson DM, de Kretser DM: Intragonadal regulation of immune system function. Reprod Fertil Dev 2:263–280, 1990.

388. Hedger MP, Nikolic-Paterson DJ, Hutchinson P, et al: Immunoregulatory activity in adult rat testicular interstitial fluid: Roles of interleukin-1 and transforming growth factor-β1. Biol Reprod 58:927–934, 1998.

389. Johnson I, Petty CS, Neaves WB: A comparative study of daily sperm production and testicular composition in humans and rats. Biol Reprod 22:1233–1243, 1980.

# Androgen Action and Pharmacologic Uses

## *David J. Handelsman*

## INTRODUCTION

Testosterone is the principal androgen in the circulation of mature male mammals. An androgen, or male sex hormone, is defined as a substance capable of developing and maintaining masculine sexual characteristics (including the genital tract, secondary sexual characteristics, and fertility) and the anabolic status of somatic tissues. Testosterone and synthetic androgens based on its structure may be used clinically at physiologic doses for androgen replacement therapy and at higher doses for pharmacologic androgen therapy. The principal goal of androgen replacement therapy is to restore a physiologic pattern of androgen exposure to the body. At present, such treatment is restricted to the major natural androgen testosterone and aims to deliver testosterone to replicate physiologic circulating testosterone levels. Thus, an understanding of the normal physiology of testosterone is required as a basis for androgen pharmacology.[1] Pharmacologic androgen therapy exploits the anabolic effects of testosterone or synthetic androgens on muscle, bone, and other tissues as hormonal drugs that are judged on efficacy, safety, and relative cost effectiveness.

## TESTOSTERONE: PHYSIOLOGY

### BIOSYNTHESIS

Testosterone is synthesized by an enzymatic sequence of steps from cholesterol[2] (Fig. 168-1) within the 500 million Leydig cells located in the interstitial (intertubular) compartment, which constitutes approximately 5% of mature testis volume (see Chapter 167 for details).[3] The cholesterol is predominantly formed by de novo synthesis from acetate, although preformed cholesterol either from intracellular cholesterol ester stores or extracellular supply from circulating low-density lipoproteins also contributes.[2] Testosterone biosynthesis involves two multifunctional cytochrome P-450 complexes involving hydroxylations and side-chain scissions (cholesterol side-chain cleavage [C20 and C22 hydroxylation and C20,22 lyase] and 17-hydroxylase/17,20 lyase) together with 3 and 17β-hydroxysteroid dehydrogenases and $\Delta^{4,5}$ isomerase. The highly tissue-selective regulation of the 17,20 lyase activity (active in gonads but inactive in adrenals) independently of 17-hydroxylase activity (active in all steroidogenic tissues) when both activities reside in a single, multifunctional protein remains to be fully explained.

Testicular testosterone secretion is principally governed by luteinizing hormone (LH) through its regulation of the rate-limiting conversion of cholesterol to pregnenolone within Leydig cell mitochondria by the cytochrome P-450 cholesterol side-chain cleavage enzyme complex located on the inner mitochondrial membrane. Cholesterol supply is governed by key proteins including sterol carrier protein 2,[4] which facilitates cytoplasmic transfer of cholesterol to mitochondria as well as steroidogenic acute regulatory protein[5] and peripheral benzodiazepine receptor,[6] which govern cholesterol transport across mitochondrial membrane. All subsequent enzymatic steps are located in the Leydig cell endoplasmic reticulum. The high testicular production rate of testosterone creates both high local concentrations (as much as 1 μg/g tissue) and rapid turnover (200 times per day) of intratesticular testosterone.

### SECRETION

Testosterone is secreted at adult levels during three epochs of male life: transiently during the first trimester of intrauterine life (coinciding with genital tract differentiation), again during neonatal life (with unknown physiologic significance), and continually after puberty to maintain virilization. After middle age, circulating total and free testosterone levels decrease gradually as gonadotrophin and sex hormone–binding globulin (SHBG) levels increase,[7–9] with these trends being exaggerated by the coexistence of chronic illness.[8–12] These changes are attributable to impaired hypothalamic regulation of testicular function[13–17] and Leydig cell attrition[3] and dysfunction,[18,19] so that multiple functional defects are operative throughout the hypothalamic-pituitary-testicular axis.[20,21]

Testosterone and other lipophilic steroids leave the testis by diffusing down a concentration gradient across cell membranes into the bloodstream, with smaller amounts secreted into lymphatics and tubule fluid. After puberty, more than 95% of circulating testosterone is derived from testicular secretion with the remainder arising from metabolic conversion of precursors of low intrinsic androgenic potency such as dehydroepiandrosterone and androstenedione. These weak androgens, predominantly originating from the adrenal cortex, constitute a large reservoir of precursors for extragonadal conversion to bioactive sex steroids in extragonadal tissues including the liver, kidney, muscle, and adipose tissue. Endogenous adrenal androgens contribute negligibly to direct virilization of men,[22] and residual circulating androgens after

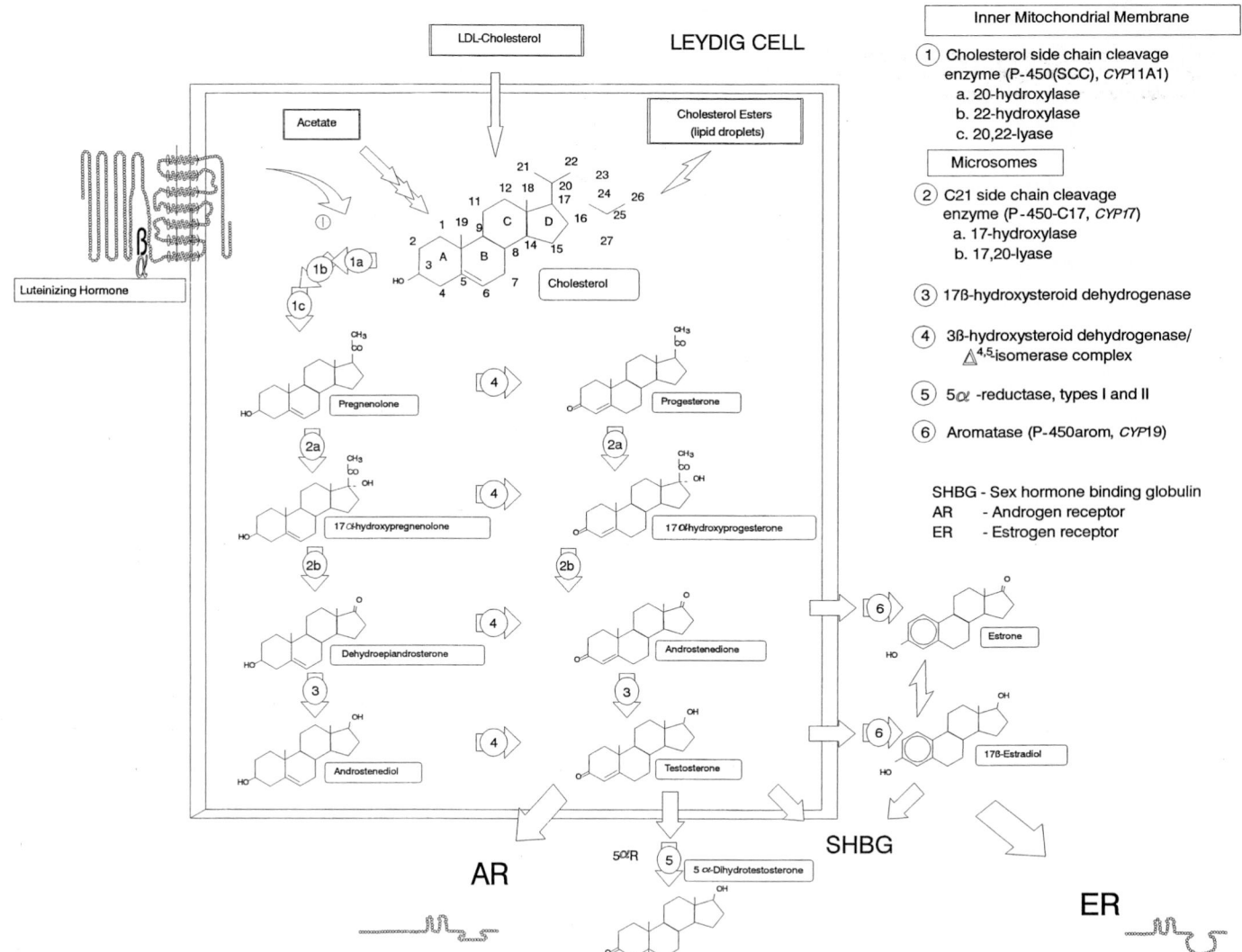

*Figure 168-1* Pathways of testosterone biosynthesis and action. In men, testosterone biosynthesis occurs almost exclusively in mature Leydig cells by the enzymatic sequences illustrated. Cholesterol originates predominantly by de novo synthesis pathway from acetyl coenzyme A with luteinizing hormone (LH) regulating the rate-limiting step, the conversion of cholesterol to pregnenolone within mitochondria, while the remaining enzymatic steps occur in smooth endoplasmic reticulum. The $\Delta^5$ and $\Delta^4$ steroidal pathways are on the left and right, respectively. Testosterone and its androgenic metabolite, dihydrotestosterone, exert biologic effects directly through binding to the androgen receptor and indirectly through aromatization of testosterone to estradiol, which allows action via binding to the estrogen receptor (ER). The androgen and ERs are members of the steroid nuclear receptor superfamily with a highly homologous structure differing mostly in the C-terminal ligand-binding domain. The LH receptor has the structure of a G protein–linked receptor with its characteristic seven-transmembrane spanning helical regions and a large extracellular domain that binds the LH molecule, which is a dimeric glycoprotein hormone consisting of an α subunit common to other pituitary glycoprotein hormones and a β subunit specific to LH. Most sex steroids bind to sex hormone–binding globulin (SHBG), which binds tightly and carries the majority of testosterone in the bloodstream.

medical or surgical castration have minimal biologic effect on androgen-sensitive prostate cancer.[23] Conversely, however, adrenal androgens make a proportionately larger contribution to the much lower circulating testosterone concentrations in children and women (~5%–10% of men) in whom blood testosterone is derived approximately equally from direct gonadal secretion and indirectly from peripheral interconversion of adrenal androgen precursors. Exogenous dehydroepiandrosterone at physiologic replacement doses of 50 mg/day orally[24] is incapable of providing adequate androgen replacement in men but produces hyperandrogenism in women.[25]

Hormone production rates can be calculated from either estimating metabolic clearance rate (from bolus injection or steady-state isotope infusion using high specific-activity tracers) and mean circulating testosterone levels[26] or by estimation of testicular arteriovenous differences and testicular blood flow rate.[27] These methods give consistent estimates of a testosterone production rate of 3 to 10 mg/day using tritiated[28,29] or nonradioactive deuterated[30] tracers with interconversion rates of approximately 4% to dihydrotestosterone (DHT)[29,31] and 0.2% to estradiol[32] under the assumption of steady-state conditions (hours to days). These steady-state methods are a simplification that neglects diurnal rhythm,[33] episodic fluctuation in circulating testosterone levels over shorter periods (minutes to hours) entrained by pulsatile LH secretion,[34] and postural influence on hepatic blood flow.[28] The major known determinants of testosterone metabolic clearance rate are circulating SHBG concentration[35] and hepatic blood flow.[28]

## TRANSPORT

Testosterone circulates in blood at concentrations greater than its aqueous solubility by binding to circulating plasma proteins. Testosterone binds avidly to SHBG, a dimeric glycoprotein of 95 kilodaltons with a single high-affinity androgen binding site and identical with testicular androgen-binding protein.[36] SHBG is secreted by the liver so its circulating levels are particularly influenced by first-pass effects of oral drugs including sex steroids. Circulating SHBG (and thereby total testosterone) concentrations are characteristically decreased (androgens, glucocorticoids) or increased (estrogens, thyroxine) by supraphysiologic hormone concentrations at the liver such as produced by oral administration or by parenteral high-dose injections of hormones. In contrast, endogenous sex steroids and parenteral (nonoral) administration, which maintain physiologic hormone concentrations (transdermal, depot implants), have minimal effects on blood SHBG levels. Other modifiers of circulating SHBG levels include upregulation by acute or chronic liver disease and androgen deficiency and downregulation by obesity, protein-losing states, and genetic SHBG deficiency.[37] Under physiologic conditions, 60% to 70% of circulating testosterone is SHBG bound with the remainder bound to lower affinity, high-capacity binding sites (albumin, $\alpha_1$ acid glycoprotein, transcortin) and 1% to 2% remaining nonprotein bound. According to the free hormone hypothesis,[38–40] the free (nonprotein bound) fraction is the most biologically active with the loosely protein-bound testosterone constituting a larger bioavailable fraction of circulating testosterone. Nevertheless, free and/or bioavailable fractions would have enhanced accessibility not only to sites of bioactivity but also sites of inactivation by degradative metabolism. Hence, the net significance of such derived measures of testosterone depends on empirical clinical evaluation, which is very limited. Free testosterone levels can be measured by the reference methods of tracer equilibrium dialysis or ultrafiltration methods or calculated by a variety of nomograms based on immunoassays of total testosterone and SHBG. Some estimates of free testosterone, notably the direct analogue assay[41–43] and the free testosterone index,[44] are clearly invalid. Overall, the clinical utility of various derived measures of testosterone remain to be established.

Circulating testosterone levels demonstrate distinct circhoral and diurnal rhythms. Circhoral LH pulsatility entrains some pulsatility in blood testosterone levels,[34] although delays in testosterone secretion and buffering effects of the circulating steroid-binding proteins markedly dampens pulsatility of blood testosterone concentrations. Diurnal patterns of morning peak testosterone levels and nadir levels in the afternoon are evident in younger men, although this pattern is lost in some aging men,[33] possibly because of increased circulating SHBG levels, reduced testosterone secretion, and/or neuroendocrine defects.[16] Consequently, it is conventional practice to standardize testosterone measurements to morning blood samples on at least 2 different days.

## METABOLISM

Testosterone undergoes metabolism to both bioactive metabolites and to inactivated oxidized and conjugated metabolites for urinary and/or biliary excretion. A small proportion of circulating testosterone is metabolized to biologically active metabolites in specific target tissues to modulate biologic effects. This includes both an activation pathway converting testosterone to the pure androgen DHT and a diversification pathway whereby the enzyme aromatase produces estradiol capable of activating estrogen receptors (ERs).

The amplification pathway involves conversion of a small fraction (~4%) of circulating testosterone to a more potent androgen, DHT.[29,31] DHT has higher binding affinity to the androgen receptor and three- to 10-fold greater molar potency than testosterone. In vitro, DHT is a more potent androgen than testosterone due to its higher binding affinity[45] and more efficient transactivation of the androgen receptor.[46,47] Testosterone is converted to the most potent natural androgen DHT by the 5α-reductase enzyme that originates from two distinct genes (I and II).[48] Type 1 5α-reductase is expressed in the liver, kidney, skin, and brain, whereas type 2 5α-reductase is characteristically expressed strongly in the prostate but also at lower levels in the skin (hair follicles) and liver.[48] Congenital 5α-reductase deficiency due to mutation of the type 2 enzyme protein[49] leads to a distinctive form of genital ambiguity causing undermasculinization of genetic males, who may be raised as females, but in whom puberty leads to marked virilization including phallic growth and, occasionally, masculine gender reorientation,[50] although prostatic development remains rudimentary.[51] This remarkable natural history reflects the dependence of full development of urogenital sinus derivative tissues on strong expression of 5α-reductase as a local amplification mechanism. This amplification mechanism for androgen action was exploited in developing azasteroid 5α-reductase inhibitors.[52] As the type 2 5α-reductase enzyme results in more than 95% of testosterone entering the prostate being converted to the more potent androgen DHT,[53] blockade of that enzyme with expression largely restricted to the prostate facilitates the inhibition of testosterone action on urogenital sinus tissue derivatives, notably the prostate, without blocking all peripheral androgenic action. DHT circulates at approximately 10% of blood testosterone concentrations, due to spillover from the prostate[54,55] and nonprostatic sources.[56] Genetic mutations disrupting type 2 5α-reductase lead to disorders of sexual differentiation involving the external genitalia and accessory glands originating from the urogenital sinus,[57] which is developmentally dependent on local amplification of testosterone to DHT. By contrast, genetic inactivation of type 1 5α-reductase has no male phenotype in mice, but no analogous human mutations of the type 1 enzyme are yet reported. An important issue is whether eliminating intraprostatic androgen amplification by inhibition of 5α-reductase can prevent prostate disease. A major 10-year chemoprevention study randomizing nearly 19,000 men older than 55 years of age without known prostate disease to daily treatment with an oral 5α-reductase inhibitor, finasteride, or placebo observed a cumulative 25% reduction at 7 years of treatment in early stage, organ-confined, low-grade prostate cancer. Although not designed to determine survival benefit, there was an apparent stage shift toward higher grade, but still organ-confined, cancers, possibly a medication effect on tumor histology. These findings highlight the importance of androgen amplification within the prostate in the origin of cancer during the long latent premalignant phase. Although routine preventive use of prostatic 5α-reductase inhibition is not warranted, novel synthetic androgens refractory to 5α-reductive amplification may have advantages for clinical development.

The diversification pathway of androgen action involves testosterone being converted by the enzyme aromatase to estradiol[32] to activate ERs. Although this involves only a small proportion (~0.2%) of testosterone output, the much higher molar potency (~100-fold versus testosterone) of estradiol makes aromatization a potentially important mechanism to diversify androgen action in various tissues via ER-mediated effects. This diversification pathway of androgen action is governed by the cytochrome P-450 enzyme (CYP19) aromatase.[58,59] In eugonadal men, most (~80%) circulating estradiol is derived from extratesticular aromatization. The biologic importance of aromatization in male physiology is highlighted by the striking developmental defects in bone and other tissues of a man[60] and mouse line[61] with genetic mutations inactivating the ERα. By contrast, genetic inactivation of the ERβ has little effect on male mouse phenotype,[62] but human mutations have not been reported. It is likely that the extent of aromatization varies among tissues contributing to variable local modulation of tissue-specific androgen action. The importance of estrogen to male physiology is further highlighted by reports of men with complete genetic estrogen deficiency due to a nonfunctional mutated aromatase enzyme.[63,64] Men with aromatase deficiency had not only the same phenotype as in estrogen resistance but demonstrated significant bone maturation with estrogen treatment. These observations suggest the importance of aromatization of testosterone to estradiol for the development of some tissues, notably bone. Nevertheless, other observations indicate that androgens and androgen receptors have important additional effects on bone. These include the greater mass of bone in men[65] despite very low circulating estradiol concentrations compared with young women, the failure of *tfm* rats having no functional androgen receptors but normal estradiol and ERs to maintain bone mass of normal males[66] and the ability of a nonaromatizable androgen to increase bone mass in estrogen-deficient women.[67] Further studies are needed to fully understand the significance of aromatization in maintaining androgen action in mature animals.

Testosterone is metabolized to inactive metabolites in the liver, kidney, gut, muscle, and adipose tissue. Inactivation is predominantly by hepatic oxidases (phase I metabolism), notably cytochrome P-450 3A family,[68] leading ultimately to oxidation of most oxygen moieties followed by hepatic conjugation to glucuronides (phase II metabolism), which are rendered sufficiently hydrophilic for renal excretion.

The metabolic clearance rate of testosterone is reduced by increases in circulating SHBG levels[35] or decreases in hepatic blood flow (e.g., posture)[28] or function. Theoretically, drugs that influence hepatic oxidase activity could alter metabolic inactivation of testosterone, but empirical examples are few. Rapid hepatic metabolic inactivation of testosterone leads to both low oral bioavailability[69,70] and short duration of action when injected parenterally.[71] To achieve sustained androgen replacement, these limitations dictate the need for parenteral depot testosterone formulations (e.g., injectable testosterone esters, testosterone implants, transdermal testosterone), oral delivery systems that involve portal bypass (buccal,[72,73] sublingual,[72,74] gut lymphatic,[75]) or synthetic androgens.[76]

## REGULATION

During sexual differentiation early in intrauterine life, Leydig cell testosterone secretion precedes ontogeny of pituitary gonadotropin secretion. Testosterone is required for masculine sexual differentiation and is secreted by fetal Leydig cells autonomously on gonadotropin stimulation in most mammals.[77] Higher primate placenta secretes a chorionic gonadotropin during early fetal life, but whether this drives human fetal Leydig cell steroidogenesis is uncertain,[78] particularly as male sexual differentiation of subprimate mammals does not require a chorionic gonadotropin.[77] After birth, testicular testosterone output is primarily regulated by pituitary LH secretion, which stimulates Leydig cell steroidogenesis via increasing substrate (cholesterol) availability, activating rate-limiting steroidogenic enzymes and cholesterol transport proteins, and enhancing testicular blood flow. LH is a dimeric glycoprotein consisting of an α subunit common to human chorionic gonadotropin (hCG), follicle-stimulating hormone, and thyrotropin-stimulating hormone and a β subunit providing distinctive biologic specificity for each dimeric glycoprotein hormone by virtue of its specific binding to the LH/hCG, follicle-stimulating hormone, or thyrotropin-stimulating hormone receptors.[79] These cell surface receptors are highly homologous members of the heptahelical, G protein–linked family of membrane receptors. Functionally, hCG is a natural, long-acting analogue of LH because their β subunits are nearly identical except that hCG has a C-terminal extension of 31 amino acids containing four O-linked, terminally sialic acid–capped carbohydrate side chains conferring greater resistance to degradation, which prolongs circulating residence time and biologic activity compared with LH.[80] LH receptors are located on Leydig cell surface membranes and use signal transduction mechanisms involving both cyclic adenosine monophosphate[81] and calcium[82] as second messengers to cause protein kinase–dependent protein phosphorylation and DNA transcription, ultimately resulting in testosterone secretion.

Driven by brief episodic bursts of hypothalamic secretion of gonadotropin-releasing hormone (GnRH) into the pituitary portal bloodstream, pituitary gonadotrophs secrete LH episodically in pulses of high amplitude at approximately hourly intervals with little intervening interpulse basal LH secretion so that circulating LH levels are distinctly pulsatile.[83] This pattern maintains Leydig cell sensitivity to LH as more continuous exposure causes desensitization.[2] Additional factors regulating testosterone secretion include paracrine factors originating within the testis to influence Leydig cell function usually via indirect effects on Sertoli cells and blood vessels, respectively.[84] These include inhibin, activin, GnRH, follicle-stimulating hormone, prolactin, prostaglandins $E_2$ and $F_{2\alpha}$, growth hormone, and insulin-like and other growth factors as well as partially uncharacterized factors secreted by Sertoli cells. LH also influences testicular testosterone output by stimulation of Leydig cell secretion of vasoactive factors that promote testicular blood flow.[85]

Testosterone participates in a negative testicular feedback cycle through its inhibition of hypothalamic GnRH and, consequently, pituitary gonadotropin secretion. Such negative feedback involves both testosterone effects on androgen receptors as well as aromatization to estradiol within the hypothalamus. The small proportion (20%) of circulating estradiol directly secreted from the testes means that estradiol derived from the bloodstream is minimally regulated physiologically so that it is unlikely to participate significantly in the acute negative feedback regulation of gonadotropin secretion in men.

## ACTION

The primary mechanism of biologic androgen action is initiated by the binding of testosterone or its analogues to the androgen receptor causing its activation. In addition, testosterone is also converted to its bioactive metabolites, DHT and estradiol. The enzyme 5α-reductase[48] is a local androgen amplification mechanism converting testosterone to the most potent natural androgen, DHT. Further, conversion of testosterone to estradiol by the enzyme aromatase[58] diversifies androgen action by facilitating effects mediated via ERs. The quantitative importance of direct effects on the androgen receptor relative to indirect effects via active metabolites varies between androgens and target tissues, as do the androgenic thresholds and dose-response characteristics for each tissue.

The androgen receptor is specified by a single gene located at Xq11-12 that specifies a protein of 919 amino acids that resides in the nucleus.[86] Androgen binding to the C-terminal hormone-binding domain causes a conformational change in the androgen receptor protein and dimerization to facilitate receptor-binding to segments of DNA featuring a characteristic palindromic motif known as an androgen-response element. Ligand binding leads to shedding of heat shock proteins that act as a chaperone for the unliganded androgen receptor. Specific binding of the dimerized, ligand-bound androgen receptor complex to tandem androgen-response elements initiates gene transcription so that the androgen receptor acts as a ligand-activated transcriptional factor. Androgen receptor transcriptional activation is governed by a large number of coregulators[87] whose tissue distribution and modulation of androgen action remain little understood. Mutations in the androgen receptor are relatively common, leading to a wide spectrum of effects from functionally silent polymorphisms to androgen insensitivity syndromes that have phenotypes proportionate to the variable degree of blockade of androgen action[86] (see also Chapter 169).

## PHARMACOLOGY OF ANDROGENS

### INDICATIONS FOR ANDROGEN THERAPY

Androgen therapy can be classified as physiologic or pharmacologic according to the dose and objectives of treatment. Androgen replacement therapy aims to restore tissue androgen exposure in androgen-deficient men to levels comparable with those of eugonadal men. Using the natural androgen testosterone and a dose limited to one ensuring blood testosterone levels within the eugonadal range, androgen replacement therapy aims to restore the full spectrum of androgen effects while replicating the safety experience of eugonadal men of similar age. Androgen replacement therapy is unlikely to prolong life because androgen deficiency does not shorten life expectancy.[88] In contrast, pharmacologic androgen therapy uses androgens without restriction on androgen type or dose but aiming primarily to produce androgen effects on muscle, bone, brain, or other tissues. In this context, pharmacologic androgen therapy requires evaluation by efficacy, safety, and cost-effectiveness criteria as for any other drug. Many older uses of pharmacologic androgen therapy are now considered second-line therapies as more specific treatments are developed. For example, erythropoietin has largely supplanted androgen therapy for anemia due to marrow or renal failure, whereas better first-line treatments for endometriosis and advanced breast cancer have similarly relegated androgen therapy to a last resort.[89]

### Androgen Replacement Therapy

The main specific clinical indication for testosterone is as androgen replacement therapy for hypogonadal men. The prevalence of male hypogonadism requiring androgen therapy in the general community can be estimated from the known prevalence of Klinefelter syndrome (1.5 to 2.5 per 1000 male births[90]) because Klinefelter syndrome accounts for 35% to 50% of men requiring androgen replacement therapy (Handelsman, unpublished). The estimated prevalence of 5 per 1000 men in the general community makes androgen deficiency the most common hormonal deficiency disorder among men. Although it does not shorten life expectancy,[91] androgen deficiency is associated with preventable morbidity and a suboptimal quality of life. Due to its variable and often subtle clinical features, androgen deficiency remains underdiagnosed, thus denying hypogonadal men simple and effective medical treatment with often striking benefits. Only 25% of men with the distinctive phenotype of Klinefelter syndrome are diagnosed during their lifetime.[92]

Hypogonadism of any cause may require androgen replacement therapy if the deficit in endogenous testosterone production is sufficient to cause clinical and biochemical manifestations of androgen deficiency (see Chapter 170 for details). The clinical features of androgen deficiency vary according to the severity, chronicity, and epoch of life at presentation. These include ambiguous genitalia, microphallus, delayed puberty, sexual dysfunction, infertility, osteoporosis, anemia, flushing, muscular ache, lethargy, lack of stamina or endurance, easy fatigue, or incidental biochemical diagnosis.[93] Because the underlying disorders are mostly irreversible, lifelong treatment is usually required. Androgen replacement therapy can rectify most clinical features of androgen deficiency apart from inducing spermatogenesis.[94] When fertility is required in gonadotropin-deficient men, spermatogenesis can be initiated by treatment with pulsatile GnRH[95] (if pituitary gonadotroph function is intact[96]) or gonadotropins[97] to substitute for pituitary gonadotropin secretion. Either

endogenous LH (stimulated by GnRH) or exogenous hCG act on Leydig cell LH receptors to stimulate endogenous testosterone production. Where spermatogenesis remains persistently suboptimal, follicle-stimulating hormone may subsequently be added.[97] Once fertility is no longer required, androgen replacement therapy usually reverts to the simpler and cheaper use of testosterone while preserving the ability subsequently to reinitiate spermatogenesis by gonadotropin replacement.[97,98]

The potential role for androgen replacement therapy in men with partial or subclinical androgen deficiency states remains to be fully evaluated. Biochemical features of Leydig cell dysfunction, notably persistently elevated LH with low to normal levels of testosterone and/or a high LH/testosterone ratio are observed in aging men,[99] in men with testicular dysfunction associated with male infertility,[100] or after chemotherapy-induced testicular damage.[101,102] Although it is plausible that such features signify mild androgen deficiency, the clinical benefits remain uncertain.[103]

The prospect of ameliorating male aging by androgen therapy has long been of interest and recently been subject to clinical trials. The consensus from population-based cross-sectional[7] and longitudinal studies[8,9] is that circulating testosterone concentrations fall by approximately 1% per annum from mid-life onward, a decrease accelerated by the presence of concomitant chronic disease[7] and associated with decreases in tissue androgen levels.[104] After a number of randomized, placebo-controlled clinical trials aiming to determine whether androgen supplementation ameliorates age-related changes in bone, muscle, and other androgen-dependent tissues, the best available evidence shows no benefits on bone density, muscular strength, or consistent effects on quality of life.[105,106] Other studies have shown small changes only in body composition but no consistent benefits in muscle, bone, or quality of life measures after treatment with testosterone,[107] DHT,[108] or hCG.[109] The Institute of Medicine report concluded that large and longer studies to balance putative benefits with potential long-term risks of accelerating cardiovascular or prostatic disease will be justified only if unequivocal benefit is established by more powerful, short-term studies.[110] At present, androgen treatment for aging men cannot be recommended as routine treatment. Nevertheless, androgen replacement therapy may be used even in older men who have severe androgen deficiency if contraindications such as prostate cancer are excluded.

Hormonal male contraception can be considered a form of androgen replacement therapy because all currently envisaged regimens aiming to suppress spermatogenesis by inhibiting gonadotropin secretion, using testosterone either alone or with a progestin or a GnRH antagonist (see also Chapter 174). As a consequence, exogenous testosterone is required to replace endogenous testosterone secretion.

### Pharmacologic Androgen Therapy

Pharmacologic androgen therapy uses androgens to maximal efficacy within adequate safety limits without regard to androgen class or dose. The objectives of pharmacologic androgen therapy are ideally to improve mortality and morbidity due to an underlying disease. Mortality benefits require that androgens modify the natural history of an underlying disease, a goal not yet achieved for any nongonadal disorder. Morbidity benefits are more realistic in aiming to improve quality of life by enhancing muscle, bone, brain, or other androgen-sensitive function including mood elevation in an adjuvant therapy in nongonadal diseases. Such treatment is judged by the efficacy, safety, and cost-effectiveness standards of other drugs. However, very few studies of pharmacologic androgen therapy fulfill the requirements of adequate study design (randomization, placebo control, objective end points, adequate power, and duration).[89] Pharmacologic androgen therapy has not reduced mortality or altered the natural history of any nongonadal disease but has beneficial effects on morbidity of aplastic anemia (maintaining hemoglobin and reducing transfusion dependence) and anemia of end-stage renal failure as a cheaper alternative to, and synergistic with, erythropoietin and prevents acute episodes of hereditary angioedema and probably chronic urticaria.[89]

Pharmacologic uses of androgens include treatment of anemia due to marrow or renal failure; osteoporosis; ER-positive breast cancer; hereditary angioedema (C1 esterase inhibitor deficiency); immunologic, pulmonary, and muscular diseases (reviewed in Ref. 89). Although these traditional indications for androgen therapy may be surpassed by more specific and effective (and costly) treatments, they usually persist as second-line, empirical therapies for which the lower cost and/or equivalent or synergistic efficacy may still favor androgen therapy in some settings. For historical reasons, pharmacologic androgen therapy has often involved synthetic, orally active 17α-alkylated androgens despite their hepatotoxicity.[111] Other than in treating angioedema, in which direct hepatic effects of 17α-alkyl androgens (rather than androgen action per se) appear to be crucial to increasing circulating C1 esterase inhibitor levels to prevent attacks,[112,113] safer (nonhepatotoxic) testosterone preparations should be favored for long-term clinical use, although the risk-benefit balance may vary according to prognosis.

Many important questions and opportunities remain for androgen therapy in nongonadal disease, but careful clinical trials are essential for proper evaluation. The best opportunities for future evaluation of adjuvant use of androgen therapy in men with nongonadal disease include steroid-induced osteoporosis; wasting due to acquired immunodeficiency syndrome (AIDS) and cancer; and chronic respiratory, rheumatologic, and some neuromuscular diseases. In addition, the role of androgen therapy in recovery and/or rehabilitation after severe catabolic illness such as burns, critical illness, or major surgery is promising but requires more detailed evaluation. Future studies of adjuvant androgen therapy require high-quality clinical data involving randomization and placebo controls as well as finding the optimal dose and a real, rather than surrogate, end point.

An important watershed was the proof by a well-designed, placebo-controlled clinical trial that pharmacologic testosterone doses increase muscular size and strength even in eugonadal men.[114] The clear dose-dependent effects of testosterone on muscle size and strength[115] and body metabolism[116] through and beyond the physiologic range suggest that androgenic effects may be beneficial in reversing the frailty observed in many medical settings. Whether such effects can be applied effectively and safely to improve frailty and quality of life in chronic disease or male aging remains an important unanswered question.

Androgen therapy for human immunodeficiency virus (HIV) has been investigated for its effects on disease-associated morbidity, notably AIDS wasting, but it does not alter the natural history of underlying disease and the objective functional benefits remain modest. The rationale for androgen therapy in AIDS wasting is that body weight loss is an important terminal determinant of survival in AIDS and other fatal diseases,[117] with death estimated to occur when lean body mass reaches 66% of the ideal.[118] This leads to the hypothesis that androgens may delay death by increasing appetite and/or body weight. Several randomized, placebo-controlled studies of androgen therapy in HIV-positive men with AIDS wasting have reported increased lean and decreased fat mass due to testosterone with additive effects from resistance training but inconsistent improvement in quality of life.[119–121] Among HIV-positive men without wasting, there are fewer androgen-induced changes in body composition and no improvement in quality of life.[119,122]

Pharmacologic androgen treatment has been advocated for treatment of estrogen-resistant menopausal symptoms such as loss of energy or libido.[123] The similarity of blood testosterone in women, children, and orchidectomized men indicates that the term *androgen deficiency* is not meaningful in women[124] with normal adrenal function.[125] High-dose androgens suitable for androgen replacement in men[126,127] produce markedly supraphysiologic blood testosterone levels and virilization.[128,129] Lower but still supraphysiologic testosterone doses increase bone density in menopausal women.[130] The efficacy of add-on testosterone therapy for estrogen-resistant menopausal symptoms was evaluated in one randomized, placebo-controlled study of menopausal women.[131] This study demonstrated no overall benefits of transdermal testosterone with a claimed benefit for a post hoc analysis of a subgroup with supraphysiologic blood testosterone concentrations.[132] In addition to the risk of virilization, safety issues concerning androgen effects on cardiovascular disease and hormone-dependent cancers in women remain to be resolved.

### Androgen Misuse and Abuse

Misuse of androgens involves medical prescription without a valid clinical indication, and androgen abuse is the use of androgens for nonmedical purposes. Medical misuse of androgens includes prescribing androgens for male infertility or sexual dysfunction in nonandrogen-deficient men in whom there is no likely benefit. The epidemic of androgen (anabolic steroid) abuse, began in the 1950s, a product of the Cold War,[133,134] and has escalated, being fostered by the rewards of fame and fortune in elite competitive sports. For decades, androgen abuse has been cultivated by underground folklore among athletes and trainers, particularly in power sports and body building, with the belief that "anabolic steroids" enhance sports performance. Based largely on speculation promulgated in pseudoscientific underground publications, this folklore promotes the use of prodigious androgen doses in combination ("stacking") regimens. Although the benefits of androgen abuse for muscular performance were long doubted, based on studies[135,136] and meta-analysis[137] concluding that the claimed performance benefits were primarily a placebo response involving motivation, training, and diet effects, a pivotal randomized, placebo-controlled clinical study showed that supraphysiologic testosterone doses (600 mg testosterone enanthate weekly) for 10 weeks increases muscular size and strength.[114] In well-controlled studies of eugonadal young and older men, testosterone shows strong linear relationships of dose with muscular size and strength throughout and beyond the physiologic range.[138]

Progressively, the epidemic of androgen abuse has spread from elite power athletes to recreational and cosmetic users wishing to augment body building as well as to occupational users who work in security-related professions. As an illicit activity, the extent of androgen abuse in the general community is difficult to estimate, although point estimates of prevalence are more feasible in captive populations such as high schools. The prevalence of self-reported lifetime ("ever") use is estimated to be 66 in the United States,[139] 58 in Sweden,[140] 32 in Australia,[141] and 28 in South Africa[142] per 1000 boys in high school, with a much lower prevalence among girls. Voluntary self-report of androgen abuse understates drug use among weight lifters[143] and prisoners.[144,145] Abusers consume androgens from many sources including veterinary, inert, or counterfeit preparations, obtained mostly through illicit sales by underground networks with a small proportion obtained from compliant doctors. Although highly sensitive urinary drug screening methods for synthetic androgens have been adopted by international sporting bodies and legislation has been introduced by some governments to tightly regulate clinical use of androgens, the epidemic of androgen abuse driven by user demands shows little signs of abating.[146] Most recently, the first illicit nonmarketed designer androgen tetrahydrogestrinone, custom produced for elite athletes to avoid detection, has been identified.[147,148]

Androgen abuse is associated with reversible depression of spermatogenesis and fertility,[149-153] gynecomastia,[154] hepatotoxicity due to 17α-alkylated androgens,[155] HIV and hepatitis from needle sharing,[156-161] local injury and sepsis from injections,[162] overtraining injuries,[163] and mood and/or behavioral disturbances.[164,165] The medical consequences of androgen abuse for the cardiovascular system has been reviewed,[166-168] but only anecdotal reports are available relating to prostate diseases.[169,170] Few controlled clinical studies of the cardiovascular[171-173] or prostatic[174] effects of androgen abuse and no systematic, population-based studies are available, so that the overall risks remain ill defined, although some evidence suggests minimal differences in life expectancy comparing power with other elite athletes.[175] More definitive studies are required, but, at present, largely anecdotal information suggests that serious short-term medical danger is limited considering the extent of androgen abuse, that androgens are not physically addictive,[176,177] and that most androgen abusers eventually discontinue drug use. After cessation of prolonged use of high-dose androgens, recovery of the hypothalamic-pituitary-testicular axis may be delayed for months, creating a transient gonadotropin deficiency state.[153,178,179] This may lead to temporary androgen deficiency symptoms that eventually abate without requiring additional hormonal treatments, which may further delay recovery and perpetuate the drug abuse cycle. The most effective approach for medical intervention to prevent and/or halt androgen abuse is yet to be defined, but educational programs[180] and support and encouragement comparable with those of smoking cessation programs may be appropriate.

## PRACTICAL GOALS OF ANDROGEN REPLACEMENT THERAPY

The goal of androgen replacement therapy is to replicate the physiologic actions of endogenous testosterone, usually for the remainder of life. This requires rectifying the deficit and maintaining androgenic/anabolic effects on bone,[181,182] muscle,[183] blood-forming marrow,[184,185] sexual function,[186,187] and other androgen-responsive tissues. The ideal preparation for long-term androgen replacement therapy should be safe, effective, convenient, and inexpensive with long-acting depot properties due to reproducible, zero-order, release kinetics. Androgen replacement therapy usually employs testosterone rather than synthetic androgens for reasons of safety and ease of monitoring and aims to maintain physiologic testosterone levels.[93] The practical goal of androgen replacement therapy is therefore to maintain stable, physiologic testosterone levels for prolonged periods using convenient depot testosterone formulations that facilitate compliance and avoid either supranormal or excessive fluctuation of androgen levels. The potential for pharmacogenetic tailoring of testosterone replacement dose to an individual's genetic background of androgen sensitivity was suggested in a study demonstrating that prostate growth response to exogenous testosterone for androgen replacement therapy is strongly related to the CAG triplet repeat polymorphism in exon 1 of the androgen receptor.[188] Whether this can be applied to other important androgen-sensitive end points will determine whether the promise of this approach can be fulfilled.

## PHARMACOLOGIC FEATURES OF ANDROGENS

The major features of the clinical pharmacology of testosterone are its short circulating half-life/transit time and low oral bioavailability, both largely attributable to rapid hepatic conversion to biologically inactive oxidized and glucuronidated excretory metabolites. The pharmaceutical development of practical testosterone preparations has been geared to overcoming these limitations. This has led to the development of parenteral depot formulations (injectable, implantable, transdermal), products to bypass the hepatic portal system (sublingual, buccal, gut lymphatic absorption), and orally active synthetic androgens.

Androgens are defined pharmacologically by their binding and activation of the androgen receptor.[86] Testosterone is the model androgen featuring a 19-carbon, four-ring steroid structure with two oxygens (3-keto, 17β-hydroxy) including a $\Delta^4$ nonaromatic A ring. Testosterone derivatives (Fig. 168-2) have been developed to enhance intrinsic androgenic potency, prolong duration of action, and/or improve oral bioavailability of synthetic androgens. Major structural modifications of testosterone include 17β-esterification, 19-nor-methyl, 17α-alkyl, 1-methyl, 7α-methyl, and D-homoandrogens.[189] Recently, the first nonsteroidal androgens, modified from nonsteroidal antiandrogen structures, have been reported.[190,191]

The identification of a single gene and protein for the androgen receptor[192] explains the physiologic observation that, at equivalent doses, all androgens have essentially similar effects.[193] Consequently, the term *anabolic steroid*, referring to an idealized androgen lacking virilizing features but maintaining myotrophic properties, is a false distinction and perpetuates an obsolete terminology. Better understanding of the metabolic activation of androgens via 5α-reduction and aromatization in target tissues has, however, led to the

Pathways of testosterone action

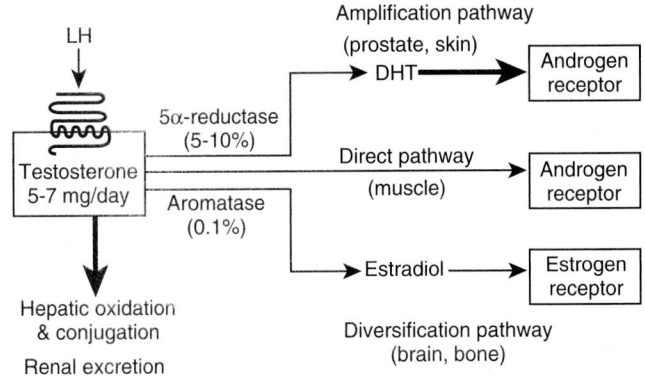

Inactivation pathway

**Figure 168-2** Pathways of testosterone action. In men, most (>95%) testosterone is produced under luteinizing hormone (LH) stimulation through its specific receptor, a heptahelical G protein–coupled receptor located on the surface membrane of the steroidogenic Leydig cells. The daily production of testosterone (5–7 mg) is disposed along one of four major pathways. The direct pathway of testosterone action is characteristic of skeletal muscle in which testosterone itself binds to and activates the androgen receptor. In such tissues, there is little metabolism of testosterone to biologically active metabolites. The amplification pathway is characteristic of the prostate and hair follicle in which testosterone is converted by the type 2 5α-reductase enzyme into the more potent androgen dihydrotestosterone (DHT). This pathway produces local tissue-based enhancement of androgen action in specific tissues according to where this pathway is operative. The local amplification mechanism was the basis for the development of prostate-selective inhibitors of androgen action via 5α-reductase inhibition, the forerunner being finasteride. The diversification pathway of testosterone action allows testosterone to modulate its biologic effects via estrogenic effects that often differ from androgen receptor–mediated effects. The diversification pathway, characteristic of bone and brain, involves the conversion of testosterone to estradiol by the enzyme aromatase, which then interacts with the estrogen receptors α and/or β. Finally, the inactivation pathway occurs mainly in the liver, with oxidation and conjugation to biologically inactive metabolites that are excreted by the liver into the bile and by the kidney into the urine.

concept of designer androgens with tissue-specific actions analogous to the development of synthetic estrogen partial agonists with tissue specificity.[194]

## FORMULATION, ROUTE, AND DOSE

### Unmodified Testosterone

#### Testosterone Implants

Implants of fused crystalline testosterone provide stable, physiologic testosterone levels for as long as 6 months after a single implantation procedure.[195] Typically, four 200-mg pellets are inserted under the skin of the lateral abdominal wall or hip using in-office minor surgery and a local anesthetic. No suture or antibiotic is required, and the pellets are fully biodegradable and thus do not require removal. This old testosterone formulation[196] has nearly ideal depot properties, with testosterone being absorbed by simple dissolution from a solid reservoir into extracellular fluid at a rate governed by the solubility of testosterone in the extracellular fluid. The long duration of action makes it popular among younger androgen-deficient men as reflected by a high continuation rate.[197] The major limitations of this form of testosterone administration are the cumbersome implantation procedure and extrusion of a single pellet after 5% to 10% of procedures. Extrusions are more frequent among men with less subdermal fat and who undertake vigorous physical activities. However, neither surface washing[198] nor antibiotic impregnation[199] nor varying the site of implantation[200] prevents extrusions. Other side effects are rare (bleeding or infection, <1%).[201] Despite its clinical advantages and popularity, the commercial unattractiveness of a simple, nonexclusive technology has limited its marketing availability.

#### Transdermal Testosterone

Delivery of testosterone across the skin has long been of interest.[76] In recent decades, testosterone in adhesive dermal patches and gels has been developed that can maintain physiologic testosterone levels by daily application. The first transdermal patch was developed for application to the scrotum where the thin, highly vascular skin facilitates steroid absorption.[202,203] The scrotal patches are effective for long-term use,[204] and there is minimal skin irritation.[205,206] However, they are relatively large, require shaving for adhesion and disproportionately increase blood DHT levels due to 5α-reduction of testosterone during transdermal passage. Subsequently, a smaller patch for nonscrotal skin was developed[207] that is also effective for long-term use.[208] The smaller size and application to less permeable dermal sites required inclusion of absorption enhancers that cause skin irritation[205,206] of varying severity.[209] This skin irritation may be prevented or ameliorated by topical corticosteroid cream,[210] but discontinuation rates due to dermal intolerance are substantial (10%–20%).

Dermal testosterone[211] or DHT[212,213] gels developed in Europe are now more widely available.[214–217] They must be applied daily on the trunk, and the volatile hydroalcoholic gel base evaporates rapidly and is nonirritating to the skin. A potential problem is the transfer of androgen to the female partner by skin contact,[218] although washing off excess gel after a short time may reduce this risk.[219] Unlike transdermal patches, gels have considerable misuse and abuse potential.

#### Testosterone Microspheres

Suspensions of biodegradable microspheres, consisting of polyglycolide-lactide matrix similar to absorbable suture material and laden with testosterone, can deliver stable, physiologic levels of testosterone for 2 to 3 months after intramuscular injection.[220,221] Recent findings[222] suggest that the practical limitations of microsphere technology such as loading capacity, large injection volumes, and batch variability may be overcome.

### Oral Testosterone

Micronized oral testosterone has low oral bioavailability requiring high daily doses (200–400 mg) to maintain physiologic testosterone levels.[69] This heavy androgen load causes prominent hepatic enzyme induction, although testosterone itself is not hepatotoxic.[223] Although effective in small studies, micronized oral testosterone is little used because it is not commercially available.

Buccal or sublingual delivery of testosterone is an old technology[72] designed to bypass the avid first-pass hepatic metabolism of testosterone that is inevitable with the portal route of absorption. Recent reinventions of this technology include testosterone in a sublingual cyclodextrin formulation[74,224,225] and in a buccal lozenge.[73,226] The multiple daily dosing required by such products to maintain physiologic testosterone levels are drawbacks for long-term androgen replacement, and their acceptability remains to be established. Like all transepithelial (nonparenteral) testosterone delivery systems, disproportionate amounts of testosterone undergo 5α-reduction during local absorption, resulting in higher blood DHT levels than those in eugonadal men. Because intraprostatic DHT is unlikely to be elevated and prostate diseases remain rare among men with genuine androgen deficiency receiving androgen replacement therapy, the higher blood DHT levels do not appear to pose any real risk of accelerating prostate disease.

### Testosterone Esters

#### Injectable

The most widely used testosterone formulation is intramuscular injection of testosterone esters, formed by 17β-esterification of testosterone with fatty acids of various aliphatic and/or aromatic chain lengths, injected in a vegetable oil vehicle. This depot formulation relies on retarded release of the testosterone ester from the oil vehicle injection depot because esters undergo rapid hydrolysis by ubiquitous esterases to liberate free testosterone into the circulation. The pharmacokinetics and pharmacodynamics of androgen esters is therefore primarily determined by ester side-chain length, volume of oil vehicle, and site of injection via hydrophobic physicochemical partitioning of the androgen ester between the hydrophobic oil vehicle and the aqueous extracellular fluid.[227]

Testosterone propionate with a short aliphatic side-chain ester has a brief duration of action requiring injections of 25 to 50 mg at 1- to 2-day intervals for androgen replacement therapy. In contrast, testosterone enanthate has a longer duration of action so that it is routinely administered at doses of 200 to 250 mg per 10 to 14 days for androgen replacement therapy in hypogonadal men.[228–231] Other testosterone esters (cypionate, cyclohexane carboxylate) have virtually identical pharmacokinetics, making them pharmacologically equivalent to testosterone enanthate,[231] the most widely used ester. Mixtures of short- and longer acting testosterone esters are available but lack a convincing rationale and remain far from desirable zero-order kinetics release profiles.

Recent advances have been the development of new injectable testosterone esters including testosterone undecanoate and bucilate. Testosterone undecanoate in an oil vehicle has a strikingly longer (8–12 weeks) duration of action,[232–234] a great advance in depot testosterone products and soon to be marketed. Testosterone bucilate (trans-4-n-butyl cyclohexane carboxylate) is a novel insoluble testosterone ester in an aqueous suspension that produces prolonged slow testosterone release due to steric hindrance of ester side-chain hydrolysis. Although this produces low physiologic levels of testosterone lasting as long as 4 months after injection in nonhuman primates[235] as well as hypogonadal[236] and eugonadal[237] men, product development has not progressed.

#### Oral Testosterone Undecanoate

Oral testosterone undecanoate, a suspension of the ester in 40-mg oil-filled capsules, is administered as 160 to 240 mg in three to four doses per day. The hydrophobic, long aliphatic chain ester in an oil vehicle favors preferential absorption into chylomicrons entering the gastrointestinal lymphatics and largely bypassing hepatic first-pass metabolism during portal absorption[75] but is only absorbed when ingested with food.[238] Testosterone undecanoate has low and erratic oral bioavailability and short duration of action and causes gastrointestinal intolerance. Widely marketed except in the United States, it has well established safety,[239] but its limitations in efficacy make it a second choice,[229,230] unless parenteral therapy must to be avoided (e.g., bleeding disorders, anticoagulation) or a low dose, as for induction of male puberty, must be provided.[240]

### Synthetic Androgens

Most oral androgens are hepatotoxic 17α-alkylated androgens (methyltestosterone, fluoxymesterone, oxymetholone, oxandrolone, ethylestrenol, stanozolol, methandrostenolone, norethandrolone, danazol), which are unacceptable for long-term androgen replacement therapy (Fig. 168-3). The 1-methyl androgen mesterolone is functionally an orally active DHT analogue free of hepatotoxicity but is not used for androgen replacement due to the need for multiple daily dosing and its poorly described pharmacology.[241] Another potent synthetic androgen free of hepatotoxicity, 7α-methyl 19-nortestosterone, is under development as a depot androgen[242] for androgen replacement[243] and male contraception.[244] As a nandrolone derivative, it has tissue-specific selectivity in being susceptible to aromatization but not to amplification by 5α-reduction,[245] thereby representing a forerunner of designer androgens based on metabolite selectivity. The inability of 7α-methyl 19-nortestosterone to maintain bone density in androgen deficient men,[246] possibly due to underdosing rather than an intrinsic feature of this synthetic androgen, illustrates the need for thorough dose titration in different tissues for synthetic androgen that may not possess the full spectrum of testosterone effects.

### Nonsteroidal Androgens

Recently, the development of the first nonsteroidal androgens was reported.[190] Based on structural modifications of the nonsteroidal class of antiandrogens, such compounds offer the possibility of orally active, potent androgens. They would, however, be intrinsically nonaromatizable and, if taken orally, subject to first-pass hepatic metabolism and liable to produce disproportionate androgenic effects on the liver. These features suggest that they have greater potential for development into pharmacologic androgen therapy regimens as tissue-selective androgen partial agonists (SARMs) rather than for androgen replacement therapy in which the full spectrum of testosterone effects including aromatization is required.

The choice of testosterone formulation for androgen replacement therapy depends on physician experience and patient preference, involving factors such as convenience, availability, familiarity, cost, and tolerance of frequent injections. Preparations of testosterone or its esters are favored over synthetic androgens for all androgen applications by virtue of ensured safety and efficacy, ease of dose titration, and assay monitoring. The hepatotoxicity of synthetic 17α-alkylated androgens[111] makes them unsuitable for long-term androgen replacement therapy. This obsolete class of androgen is being progressively withdrawn from marketing and clinical use in most countries.

Cross-over studies indicate that patients prefer formulations with stable testosterone levels and smoother clinical effects (e.g., implants,[230] transdermal patches[247]) to the wide fluctuations in testosterone levels and effects with intramuscular injections of testosterone esters in an oil vehicle.[228,230,248]

There are few well-established formulation or route-dependent differences between various testosterone formulations once adequate doses are administered. As with estrogen replacement, testosterone effects on SHBG may be viewed as manifestations of hepatic overdose[37] so that oral 17α-alkylated androgens and testosterone undecanoate cause prominent lowering of SHBG levels due to marked first-pass hepatic effects, whereas intramuscular testosterone ester injections cause transient decreases that mirror testosterone levels and long-acting depot testosterone formulations (e.g., testosterone buciclate, implants, microspheres) have minimal effects.[221,230,236,249] Long-acting depot testosterone preparations with zero-order release patterns,[195,222,234,236] which are also convenient and affordable, are likely to supplant the present injectable testosterone esters as the mainstays of androgen replacement therapy.

### SIDE EFFECTS OF ANDROGEN THERAPY

Serious adverse effects from androgens are uncommon and are mostly due to either inappropriate treatment (children, women) or the hepatotoxicity of the 17α-alkylated androgens. Virtually all androgenic side effects are rapidly reversible on cessation of treatment apart from inappropriate virilization in children or women in which voice deepening, terminal body hair, or stunting of final height may be irreversible.

### Steroidal Effects

Androgen replacement therapy activates physical and mental activity to enhance mood, behavior, and libido, thereby reversing their impairment during androgen deficiency.[250] In healthy eugonadal men, however, administration of additional androgen has negligible effects on mood or behavior.[251–256] This contrasts with androgen abusers among whom high levels of background psychologic disturbance,[164] drug habituation,[176] and anticipation[257] predispose to behavioral disturbances reported during this form of drug abuse.[250,258] Idiosyncratic hypomanic episodes have been reported in a small minority of young having supraphysiologic doses of testosterone in some[259–261] but not all[251,252,254,255] clinical studies.

Excessive or undesirable androgenic effects may be experienced during androgen therapy due to intrinsic androgenic effects in inappropriate settings (e.g., virilization in women or children). In some untreated hypogonadal men, particularly older men, initiation of androgen treatment with standard doses occasionally produces an intolerable increase in libido and erection frequency. More gradual acclimatization to full androgen doses with counseling of men and their partners may be useful in such situations.

Seborrhea and acne are commonly associated with high blood testosterone levels, particularly among androgen abusers taking injectable testosterone esters. It has a predominantly truncal distribution in men in contrast to the predominantly facial distribution of adolescent acne. Acne is uncommon during androgen replacement therapy, being restricted to a few susceptible individuals treated with intramuscular testosterone esters, probably related to their generation of transient supraphysiologic testosterone concentrations in the days after injection.[228] Acne is rare with depot testosterone products that maintain steady-state physiologic blood testosterone levels. Androgen-induced acne is usually adequately managed with topical measures and/or broad-spectrum antibiotics with a switch to steady-state delivery avoiding supraphysiologic peaks of plasma testosterone. Increased body hair and temporal hair loss or balding may also be seen.

Weight gain reflecting anabolic effects on muscle mass is also common. Gynecomastia is a feature of androgen deficiency in men but may appear during androgen replacement

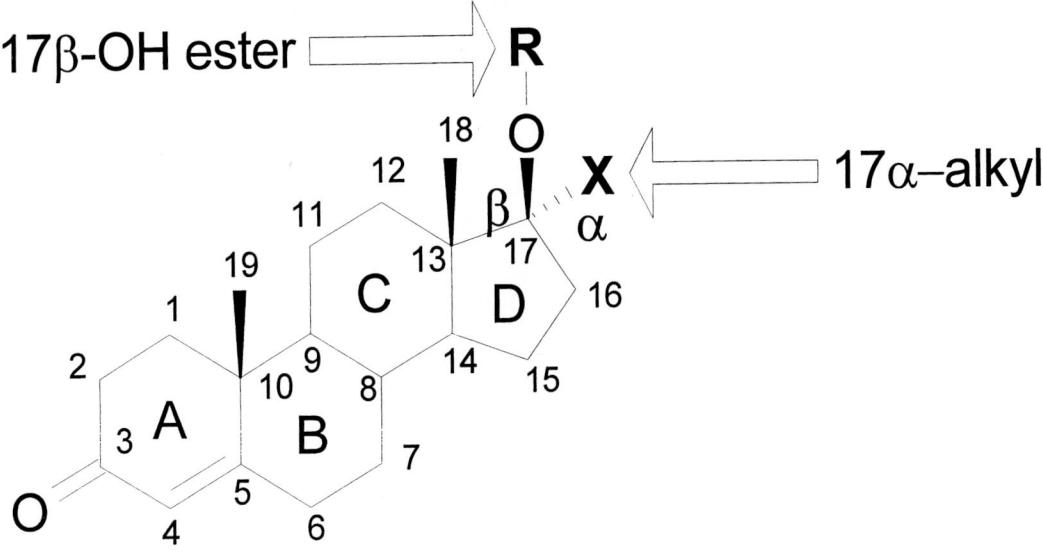

| GENERIC NAME | YEAR of PATENT | R (17β) | X (17α) | OTHER MODIFICATIONS | | |
|---|---|---|---|---|---|---|
| **NATURAL ANDROGENS** | | | | | | |
| Testosterone | | H | H | | | |
| 5αDihydrotestosterone | 1960 | H | H | 4,5-ane | | |
| **UNMODIFIED 17β ESTERS** | | | | | | |
| Testosterone propionate | 1941 | $COCH_2CH_3$ | H | | | |
| Testosterone cypionate | 1956 | $CO(CH_2)_2$— | H | | | |
| Testosterone enanthate | 1958 | $CO(CH_2)_5CH_3$ | H | | | |
| Testosterone undecanoate | 1975 | $CO(CH_2)_9CH_3$ | H | | | |
| Testosterone buciclate | 1987 | CO—$(CH_2)_3CH_3$ | H | | | |
| **MODIFIED ANDROGENS** | | | | | | |
| Methenolone | 1958 | H | H | 4,5-ane | :1,2-ene | :1-$CH_3$ |
| Nandrolone | 1955 | H | H | 19-nor$CH_3$ | | |
| Mesterolone | 1962 | H | H | 4,5-ane | :1α-$CH_3$ | |
| MENT (7α-methyl nandrolone) | 1994 | H | H | 19-nor$CH_3$ | :7α-$CH_3$ | |
| **MODIFIED 17β ESTERS** | | | | | | |
| Methenolone acetate | 1958 | $COCH_3$ | H | 4,5-ane | :1,2-ene | :1-$CH_3$ |
| Nandrolone phenylpropionate | 1959 | $CO(CH_2)_2$—⬡ | H | 19-nor$CH_3$ | | |
| Nandrolone decanoate | 1961 | $CO(CH_2)_8CH_3$ | H | 19-nor$CH_3$ | | |
| **17α ALKYLATION** | | | | | | |
| Methyltestosterone | 1945 | H | $CH_3$ | | | |
| Fluoxymesterone | 1957 | H | $CH_3$ | 9α-F | :11β-OH | |
| Methandrostenolone | 1959 | H | $CH_3$ | 1,2-ene | | |
| Oxandrolone | 1964 | H | $CH_3$ | 4,5-ane | :C2-replaced by O | |
| Oxymetholone | 1959 | H | $CH_3$ | 4,5-ane | :2-methyleneOH | |
| Stanozolol | 1962 | H | $CH_3$ | 4,5-ane | :[2,3-c]pyrazole | :2,3-ene |
| Danazol | 1962 | H | C≡CH | 2,3-ene | :[2,3-d]isoxazole} | |
| Norethandrolone | 1955 | H | $CH_2CH_3$ | 19-nor$CH_3$ | | |
| Ethylestrenol | 1959 | H | $CH_2CH_3$ | 19-nor$CH_3$ | :3-$H_2$ | |

**Figure 168-3** Testosterone and its derivatives. Listed are the androgens in most common clinical use and their structural and chemical relationship to testosterone.

therapy, especially during use of aromatizable androgens such as testosterone that increase circulating estradiol levels at times when androgenic effects are inadequate (e.g., a too low or infrequent dose or unreliable compliance with treatment).

Obstructive sleep apnea causes a mild lowering of blood testosterone concentrations[262] that is rectified by effective continuous positive airway pressure treatment.[263] Although testosterone treatment has precipitated obstructive sleep apnea[264] and has potential adverse effects on sleep in older men,[265] the prevalence of obstructive sleep apnea precipitated by testosterone treatment remains unclear. It appears to be a rare idiosyncratic reaction among younger hypogonadal men, but the risk may be higher among older men because the background prevalence of obstructive sleep apnea increases steeply with age. Hence, screening for obstructive sleep apnea by asking about daytime sleepiness and partner reports of loud and irregular snoring, especially among overweight men with large collar size, is wise for older men starting testosterone treatment, although not routinely required for young men with classic hypogonadism.

### Hepatotoxicity

Hepatotoxicity is a well-recognized but uncommon side effect of 17α-alkylated but not with other androgens.[111] Biochemical hepatotoxicity, involving either a cholestatic or hepatitic pattern, usually abates with cessation of steroid ingestion. Hepatic tumors related to androgen use include peliosis hepatis (blood-filled cysts), adenoma, and carcinoma. Prolonged use of 17α-alkylated androgens, if unavoidable, requires regular clinical examination and biochemical monitoring of hepatic function. If biochemical abnormalities are detected, treatment with 17α-alkylated androgens should cease and safer androgens may be substituted without concern. Where structural lesions are suspected, radionuclide scan, ultrasonography, or abdominal computed tomography scan should precede hepatic biopsy during which severe bleeding may be provoked in peliosis hepatis. Because equally effective and safer alternatives exist, the hepatotoxic 17α-alkylated androgens should not be used for androgen replacement therapy.

### Formulation-Related Effects

Complications related to testosterone formulations are related to mode of administration or idiosyncratic reactions to constituents. Intramuscular injections of oil vehicle may cause local pain, bleeding, or bruising and, rarely, coughing fits or fainting possibly due to oil microembolization.[266] Inadvertent subcutaneous administration of the oil vehicle is highly irritating and may cause pain, inflammation, or even dermal necrosis. Allergy to vegetable oil vehicle of testosterone ester injections (sesame, castor, arachis) is very rare, and even patients allergic to peanuts may tolerate arachis (peanut) oil without incident. Oral testosterone undecanoate frequently causes gastrointestinal intolerance due to the oleic acid suspension vehicle. Testosterone implants may be associated with extrusion of implants or bleeding, infection, or scarring at implant sites.[197] Parenteral injection of newer testosterone esters[236] or biodegradable microspheres[221] involves a large injection volume that may cause discomfort. Nonscrotal transdermal patches frequently cause skin irritation with a significant minority (10%–20%) unable to use truncal patches. Topical steroid–impregnated gels may transfer androgens through topical skin-to-skin contact.[218]

### *MONITORING OF ANDROGEN REPLACEMENT THERAPY*

Monitoring of androgen replacement therapy involves primarily clinical observations to optimize androgen effects (including continuation of treatment) and recognize side effects. Once well established, androgen replacement therapy requires only very limited, judicious use of biochemical

testing or hormone assays. Testosterone and its esters at conventional doses for replacement therapy are sufficiently safe not to require routine toxicologic monitoring. The World Health Organization has developed guidelines for the therapeutic use of androgens in men.[267]

Clinical monitoring depends on observation of serial improvement in the key presenting features of androgen deficiency. Androgen-deficient patients may report subjective improvements in energy, well-being, psychosocial drive, initiative, and assertiveness as well as sexual activity (especially libido and ejaculation frequency), increased sexual hair and muscular strength and endurance. Patients become familiar with their own leading androgen deficiency symptoms, and these appear in predictable sequence and at consistent blood testosterone thresholds for symptoms.[268] Objective and sensitive measures of androgen action are highly desirable but not available for most androgen-responsive tissues.[269] The main biochemical measures available for monitoring of androgenic effects include hemoglobin and trough reproductive hormone (testosterone, LH, follicle-stimulating hormone) levels. Hemoglobin increases by approximately 10% to 20 g/L when the androgen dose is adequate.[184,185] Occasionally, excessive hemoglobin responses may create polycythemia, requiring venesection and/or anticoagulation together with temporary interruption. Because these idiosyncratic reactions appear related to supraphysiologic peak testosterone concentrations, treatment should be resumed with more steady-state testosterone delivery systems, if possible. Circulating testosterone and gonadotropin levels must be considered in relation to time since last testosterone dose. Trough levels (immediately before next scheduled dose) may be helpful in establishing adequacy of depot testosterone regimens. In the presence of normal testosterone, negative feedback on hypothalamic GnRH and pituitary LH secretion (i.e., men with hypergonadotropic hypogonadism), plasma LH levels are elevated in rough proportion to the degree of androgen deficiency. In severe androgen deficiency, virtually castrate LH levels may be present, and, conversely, circulating LH levels provide a sensitive and specific index of tissue testosterone effects.[195,228] Suppression of LH into the eugonadal range indicates adequate androgen replacement therapy, whereas persistent nonsuppression after the first few months of treatment is an indication of inadequate dose or pattern of testosterone levels. In hypogonadotropic hypogonadism, however, impaired hypothalamic-pituitary function diminishes circulating LH levels regardless of androgen effects, so LH levels do not reflect tissue androgenic effects.

Plasma testosterone measurements are of most importance for diagnosis, during initiation, and for evaluating adequacy of treatment. During depot testosterone treatment in which quasi steady-state plasma testosterone levels are achieved, trough plasma testosterone levels may detect patients whose treatment is suboptimal and whose dose and/or treatment interval need modification. Plasma testosterone levels are not helpful for routine monitoring of androgen therapy using any synthetic androgens or oral testosterone undecanoate. Serial evaluation of bone density (especially vertebral trabecular bone) by dual photon absorptiometry at 1- to 2-year intervals may be helpful in verifying the adequacy of tissue androgen effects.[181,182]

Although chronic androgen deficiency protects against prostate disease,[51,270] the prostate of androgen-deficient men receiving androgen replacement therapy is restored to, but does not exceed, age-appropriate norms.[271–273] Between-subject variability in response to testosterone replacement is partly explained by genetic sensitivity to testosterone, which is inversely related to length of the CAG triplet (polyglutamine) repeat polymorphism in exon 1 of the androgen receptor.[188] Furthermore, because endogenous blood testosterone or other androgen concentrations do not predict subsequent development of prostate cancer,[274,275] maintaining physiologic testosterone concentrations should ensure no higher rates of prostate disease than eugonadal men of similar age.[276]

The potential long-term risks for cardiovascular disease of androgen replacement and pharmacologic androgen therapy remain uncertain. Although men have two to three times the prevalence[277] as well as earlier onset and more severe atherosclerotic cardiovascular disease than women, the precise role of blood testosterone and of androgen treatment in this marked gender disparity is still poorly understood.[88,278] Although low blood testosterone concentration is a risk factor for cardiovascular disease and testosterone effects include vasodilation and amelioration of coronary ischemia as well as potentially deleterious effects, it is not possible to predict the net clinical risk-benefit of androgen replacement therapy on cardiovascular disease. Hence, during androgen replacement therapy, it is prudent to aim at maintaining physiologic testosterone concentrations and surveillance of cardiovascular and prostate disease should be comparable with, and no more intensive than, that for eugonadal men of equivalent age.[276] The effects of pharmacologic androgen therapy, in which the androgen dose is not necessarily restricted to eugonadal limits, on cardiovascular and prostate disease are still more difficult to predict, and surveillance then depends on the nature, severity, and life expectancy of the underlying disease.

## CONTRAINDICATIONS AND PRECAUTIONS FOR ANDROGEN REPLACEMENT THERAPY

Contraindications to androgen replacement therapy are prostate or breast cancer, because these tumors may be androgen responsive, and pregnancy, in which transplacental passage of androgens may disturb fetal sexual differentiation. Precautions and/or careful monitoring of androgen use is required in (1) initiating treatment in older men who may experience intolerable changes in libido; (2) competitive athletes who may be disqualified; (3) women of reproductive age, especially those who use their voice professionally, who may become irreversibly virilized; (4) prepubertal children in whom inappropriate androgen treatment risks precocious sexual development and premature epiphyseal closure with compromised final adult height; (5) patients with bleeding disorders or during anticoagulation when parenteral administration may cause severe bruising or bleeding; (6) sex steroid–sensitive epilepsy or migraine; (7) those with cardiac or renal failure or severe hypertension susceptible to fluid overload from sodium and fluid retention; and (8) older men with subclinical obstructive sleep apnea.

## REFERENCES

1. Nieschlag E, Behre HM (eds): Testosterone: Action-Deficiency-Substitution, 2d ed. Berlin, Springer, 1998.
2. Hall PF: Testicular steroid synthesis: organization and regulation. In Knobil E, Neill J (eds): The Physiology of Reproduction. New York, Raven Press, 1988, pp 975–998.
3. Neaves WB, Johnson L, Porter JC, et al: Leydig cell numbers, daily sperm production, and serum gonadotropin levels in aging men. J Clin Endocrinol Metab 55:756–763, 1984.
4. Seedorf U, Ellinghaus P, Roch Nofer J: Sterol carrier protein-2. Biochim Biophys Acta 1486:45–54, 2000.
5. Stocco DM: Tracking the role of a star in the sky of the new millennium. Mol Endocrinol 15:1245–1254, 2001.
6. Papadopoulos V, Amri H, Li H, et al: Structure, function and regulation of the mitochondrial peripheral-type benzodiazepine receptor. Therapie 56:549–556, 2001.
7. Gray A, Berlin JA, McKinlay JB, et al: An examination of research design effects on the association of testosterone and male aging: Results of a meta-analysis. J Clin Epidemiol 44:671–684, 1991.
8. Harman SM, Metter EJ, Tobin JD, et al: Longitudinal effects of aging on serum total and free testosterone levels in healthy men. Baltimore Longitudinal Study of Aging. J Clin Endocrinol Metab 86:724–731, 2001.
9. Feldman HA, Longcope C, Derby CA, et al: Age trends in the level of serum testosterone and other hormones in middle-aged men: Longitudinal results from the Massachusetts male aging study. J Clin Endocrinol Metab 87:589–598, 2002.
10. Nieschlag E, Lammers U, Freischem CW, et al: Reproductive function in young fathers and grandfathers. J Clin Endocrinol Metab 55:676–681, 1982.
11. Handelsman DJ, Staraj S: Testicular size: the effects of aging, malnutrition and illness. J Androl 6:144–151, 1985.
12. Gray A, Feldman HA, McKinlay JB, et al: Age, disease, and changing sex hormone levels in middle-aged men: Results of the Massachusetts Male Aging Study. J Clin Endocrinol Metab 73:1016–1025, 1991.
13. Deslypere JP, Kaufman JM, Vermeulen T, et al: Influence of age on pulsatile luteinizing hormone release and responsiveness of the gonadotrophs to sex hormone feedback in men. J Clin Endocrinol Metab 64:68–73, 1987.
14. Vermeulen A, Desylpere JP, Kaufman JM: Influence of antiopioids on luteinizing hormone pulsatility in aging men. J Clin Endocrinol Metab 68:68–72, 1989.
15. Veldhuis JD, Urban RJ, Lizarralde G, et al: Attenuation of luteinizing hormone secretory burst amplitude as a proximate basis for the hypoandrogenism of healthy aging men. J Clin Endocrinol Metab 75:707–713, 1992.
16. Veldhuis JD: Recent neuroendocrine facets of male reproductive aging. Exp Gerontol 35:1281–1308, 2000.
17. Veldhuis JD, Zwart A, Mulligan T, et al: Muting of androgen negative feedback unveils impoverished gonadotropin-releasing hormone/luteinizing hormone secretory reactivity in healthy older men. J Clin Endocrinol Metab 86:529–535, 2001.
18. Mulligan T, Iranmanesh A, Gheorghiu S, et al: Amplified nocturnal luteinizing hormone (LH) secretory burst frequency with selective attenuation of pulsatile (but not basal) testosterone secretion in healthy aged men: Possible Leydig cell desensitization to endogenous LH signaling—A clinical research center study. J Clin Endocrinol Metab 80:3025–3031, 1995.
19. Mulligan T, Iranmanesh A, Veldhuis JD: Pulsatile iv infusion of recombinant human LH in leuprolide-suppressed men unmasks impoverished Leydig-cell secretory responsiveness to midphysiological LH drive in the aging male. J Clin Endocrinol Metab 86:5547–5553, 2001.
20. Mulligan T, Iranmanesh A, Kerzner R, et al: Two-week pulsatile gonadotropin releasing hormone infusion unmasks dual (hypothalamic and Leydig cell) defects in the healthy aging male gonadotropic axis. Eur J Endocrinol 141:257–266, 1999.
21. Pincus SM, Mulligan T, Iranmanesh A, et al: Older males secrete luteinizing hormone and testosterone more irregularly, and jointly more asynchronously, than younger males. Proc Natl Acad Sci U S A 93:14100–14105, 1996.
22. Oesterling JE, Epstein JI, Walsh PC: The inability of adrenal androgens to stimulate the adult human prostate: An autopsy evaluation of men with hypogonadotropic hypogonadism and panhypopituitarism. J Urol 136:1030–1034, 1986.
23. Prostate Cancer Trialists' Collaborative Group: Maximum androgen blockade in advanced prostate cancer: An overview of the randomised trials. Lancet 355:1491–1498, 2000.
24. Arlt W, Justl HG, Callies F, et al: Oral dehydroepiandrosterone for adrenal androgen replacement: Pharmacokinetics and peripheral conversion to androgens and estrogens in young healthy females after dexamethasone suppression. J Clin Endocrinol Metab 83:1928–1934, 1998.

25. Young J, Couzinet B, Nahoul K, et al: Panhypopituitarism as a model to study the metabolism of dehydroepiandrosterone (DHEA) in humans. J Clin Endocrinol Metab 82:2578–2585, 1997.
26. Gurpide E: Tracer Methods in Hormone Research. New York, Springer, 1975.
27. Setchell BP: The Mammalian Testis. London, Paul Elek, 1978.
28. Southren AL, Gordon GG, Tochimoto S: Further studies of factors affecting metabolic clearance rate of testosterone in man. J Clin Endocrinol Metab 28:1105–1112, 1968.
29. Santner S, Albertson B, Zhang GY, et al: Comparative rates of androgen production and metabolism in Caucasian and Chinese subjects. J Clin Endocrinol Metab 83:2104–2109, 1998.
30. Wang C, Catlin DH, Starcevic B, et al: Testosterone metabolic clearance and production rates determined by stable isotope dilution/tandem mass spectrometry in normal men: Influence of ethnicity and age. J Clin Endocrinol Metab 89:2936–2941, 2004.
31. Ishimaru T, Edmiston WA, Pages L, et al: Splanchnic extraction and conversion of testosterone and dihydrotestosterone in man. J Clin Endocrinol Metab 46:528–533, 1978.
32. Longcope C, Sato K, McKay C, et al: Aromatization by splanchnic tissue in men. J Clin Endocrinol Metab 58:1089–1093, 1984.
33. Bremner WJ, Vitiello MV, Prinz PN: Loss of circadian rhythmicity in blood testosterone levels with aging in normal men. J Clin Endocrinol Metab 56:1278–1281, 1983.
34. Veldhuis JD, King JC, Urban RJ, et al: Operating characteristics of the male hypothalamo-pituitary-gonadal axis: Pulsatile release of testosterone and follicle-stimulating hormone and their temporal coupling with luteinizing hormone. J Clin Endocrinol Metab 65:929–941, 1987.
35. Petra P, Stanczyk FZ, Namkung PC, et al: Direct effect of sex-steroid binding protein (SBP) of plasma on the metabolic clearance rate of testosterone in the rhesus macaque. J Steroid Biochem Mol Biol 22:739–746, 1985.
36. Petra PH: The plasma sex steroid binding protein (SBP or SHBG). A critical review of recent developments on the structure, molecular biology and function. J Steroid Biochem Mol Biol 40:735–753, 1991.
37. von Schoultz B, Carlstrom K: On the regulation of sex-hormone-binding globulin. A challenge of an old dogma and outlines of an alternative mechanism. J Steroid Biochem Mol Biol 32:327–334, 1989.
38. Pardridge WM: Plasma protein-mediated transport of steroid and thyroid hormones. Am J Physiol 252:E157–E164, 1987.
39. Mendel CM: The free hormone hypothesis: A physiologically based mathematical model. Endocr Rev 10:232–274, 1989.
40. Ekins R: Measurement of free hormones in blood. Endocr Rev 11:5–46, 1990.
41. Rosner W: Errors in the measurement of plasma free testosterone. J Clin Endocrinol Metab 82:2014–2015, 1997.
42. Winters SJ, Kelley DE, Goodpaster B: The analog free testosterone assay: Are the results in men clinically useful? Clin Chem 44:2178–2182, 1998.
43. Rosner W: An extraordinarily inaccurate assay for free testosterone is still with us. J Clin Endocrinol Metab 86:2903, 2001.
44. Kapoor P, Luttrell BM, Williams D: The free androgen index is not valid for adult males. J Steroid Biochem Mol Biol 45:325–326, 1993.
45. Kumar N, Crozat A, Li F, et al: 7alpha-methyl-19-nortestosterone, a synthetic androgen with high potency: Structure-activity comparisons with other androgens. J Steroid Biochem Mol Biol 71:213–222, 1999.
46. Deslypere JP, Young M, Wilson JD, et al: Testosterone and 5 alpha-dihydrotestosterone interact differently with the androgen receptor to enhance transcription of the MMTV-CAT reporter gene. Mol Cell Endocrinol 88:15–22, 1992.
47. Zhou ZX, Lane MV, Kemppainen JA, et al: Specificity of ligand-dependent androgen receptor stabilization: Receptor domain interactions influence ligand dissociation and receptor stability. Mol Endocrinol 9:208–218, 1995.
48. Russell DW, Wilson JD: Steroid 5 alpha-reductase: Two genes/two enzymes. Annu Rev Biochem 63:25–61, 1994.
49. Thigpen AE, Davis DL, Milatovich A, et al: Molecular genetics of steroid 5a-reductase 2 deficiency. J Clin Invest 90:799–809, 1992.
50. Imperato-McGinley J, Peterson RE, Gautier T, et al: Androgens and the evolution of male gender identity among male pseudohermaphrodites with 5-a reductase deficiency. N Engl J Med 300:1233–1237, 1979.
51. Imperato-McGinley J, Gautier T, Zirinsky K, et al: Prostate visualization studies in males homozygous and heterozygous for 5-a reductase deficiency. J Clin Endocrinol Metab 75:1022–1026, 1992.
52. Steers WD: 5alpha-reductase activity in the prostate. Urology 58:17–24, 2001.
53. Frick J, Aulitzky W: Physiology of the prostate. Infection 19(Suppl 3):S115–S118, 1991.
54. Gisleskog PO, Hermann D, Hammarlund-Udenaes M, et al: A model for the turnover of dihydrotestosterone in the presence of the irreversible 5 alpha-reductase inhibitors GI198745 and finasteride. Clin Pharmacol Ther 64:636–647, 1998.
55. Miller LR, Partin AW, Chan DW, et al: Influence of radical prostatectomy on serum hormone levels. J Urol 160:449–453, 1998.
56. Toorians AW, Kelleher S, Gooren LJ, et al: Estimating the contribution of the prostate to blood dihydrotestosterone. J Clin Endocrinol Metab 88:5207–5211, 2003.
57. Zhu YS, Katz MD, Imperato-McGinley J: Natural potent androgens: Lessons from human genetic models. Baillieres Clin Endocrinol Metab 12:83–113, 1998.
58. Simpson ER, Zhao Y, Agarwal VR, et al: Aromatase expression in health and disease. Recent Prog Horm Res 52:185–214, 1997.
59. Simpson ER: Sources of estrogen and their importance. J Steroid Biochem Mol Biol 86:225–230, 2003.
60. Smith EP, Boyd J, Frank GR, et al: Estrogen resistance caused by a mutation in the estrogen-receptor gene in a man. N Engl J Med 331:1056–1061, 1994.
61. Lubahn DB, Moyer JS, Golding TS, et al: Alteration of reproductive function but not prenatal sexual development after insertional disruption of the mouse estrogen receptor gene. Proc Natl Acad Sci U S A 90:11162–11166, 1993.
62. Couse JE, Mahato D, Eddy EM, et al: Molecular mechanism of estrogen action in the male: Insights from the estrogen receptor null mice. Reprod Fertil Dev 13:211–219, 2001.
63. Carani C, Zini D, Baldini A, et al: Effects of androgen treatment in impotent men with normal and low levels of free testosterone. Arch Sex Behav 19:223–234, 1990.
64. Bilezikian JP, Morishima A, Bell J, et al: Increased bone mass as a result of estrogen therapy in a man with aromatase deficiency. N Engl J Med 339:599–603, 1998.
65. Seeman E: Growth in bone mass and size—Are racial and gender differences in bone mineral density more apparent than real? J Clin Endocrinol Metab 83:1414–1419, 1998.
66. Vanderschueren D, Van Herck E, Suiker AM, et al: Bone and mineral metabolism in the androgen-resistant (testicular feminized) male rat. J Bone Miner Res 8:801–809, 1993.
67. Need AG, Nordin BEC, Chatterton BE: Double-blind placebo-controlled trial of treatment of osteoporosis with the anabolic steroid nandrolone decanoate. Osteoporos Int 3(Suppl 1):S218–S222, 1993.
68. Nebert DW, Russell DW: Clinical importance of the cytochromes P450. Lancet 360:1155–1162, 2002.
69. Johnsen SG, Bennet EP, Jensen VG: Therapeutic effectiveness of oral testosterone. Lancet ii:1473–1475, 1974.
70. Frey H, Aakvag A, Saanum D, et al: Bioavailability of testosterone in males. Eur J Clin Pharmacol 116:345–349, 1979.
71. Parkes AS: Effective absorption of hormones. Br Med J 371–373, 1938.
72. Lisser H, Escamilla RF, Curtis LE: Testosterone therapy of male eunuchoids. III Sublingual administration of testosterone compounds. J Clin Endocrinol 2:351–360, 1942.

73. Korbonits M, Slawik M, Cullen D, et al: A comparison of a novel testosterone bioadhesive buccal system, striant, with a testosterone adhesive patch in hypogonadal males. J Clin Endocrinol Metab 89:2039–2043, 2004.

74. Wang C, Eyre DR, Clark R, et al: Sublingual testosterone replacement improves muscle mass and strength, decreases bone resorption, and increases bone formation markers in hypogonadal men—A clinical research center study. J Clin Endocrinol Metab 81:3654–3662, 1996.

75. Shackleford DM, Faassen WA, Houwing N, et al: Contribution of lymphatically transported testosterone undecanoate to the systemic exposure of testosterone after oral administration of two andriol formulations in conscious lymph duct-cannulated dogs. J Pharmacol Exp Ther 306:925–933, 2003.

76. Foss GL: Clinical administration of androgens. Lancet i:502–504, 1939.

77. O'Shaughnessy PJ, Baker P, Sohnius U, et al: Fetal development of Leydig cell activity in the mouse is independent of pituitary gonadotroph function. Endocrinology 139:1141–1146, 1998.

78. Gromoll J, Eiholzer U, Nieschlag E, et al: Male hypogonadism caused by homozygous deletion of exon 10 of the luteinizing hormone (LH) receptor: Differential action of human chorionic gonadotropin and LH. J Clin Endocrinol Metab 85:2281–2286, 2000.

79. Chin WW, Boime I (eds): Glycoprotein Hormones: Structure, Synthesis and Biologic Function. Norwell, MA, Serono Symposia, USA, 1990.

80. Muyan M, Furuhashi M, Sugahara T, et al: The carboxy-terminal region of the beta-subunits of luteinizing hormone and chorionic gonadotropin differentially influence secretion and assembly of the heterodimers. Mol Endocrinol 10:1678–1687, 1996.

81. Dufau ML, Catt KJ: Gonadotropin receptors and regulation of steroidogenesis in the testis and ovary. Vitam Horm 36:461–592, 1978.

82. Cooke BA: Is cyclic AMP an obligatory second messenger for luteinizing hormone? Mol Cell Endocrinol 69:C11–C15, 1990.

83. Veldhuis JD, Carlson ML, Johnson ML: The pituitary gland secretes in bursts: appraising the nature of glandular secretory impulses by simultaneous multiple-parameter deconvolution of plasma hormone concentrations. Proc Natl Acad Sci U S A 84:7686–7690, 1988.

84. Skinner MK: Cell-cell interactions in the testis. Endocr Rev 12:45–77, 1991.

85. Maddocks S, Setchell BP: Effect of a single injection of human chorionic gonadotrophin on testosterone levels in testicular interstitial fluid, and in testicular and peripheral venous blood in adult rats. J Endocrinol 121:311–316, 1989.

86. Quigley CA, DeBellis A, Marschke KB, et al: Androgen receptor defects: Historical, clinical and molecular perspectives. Endocr Rev 16:271–321, 1995.

87. Heinlein CA, Chang C: Androgen receptor (AR) coregulators: An overview. Endocr Rev 23:175–200, 2002.

88. Liu PY, Death AK, Handelsman DJ: Androgens and cardiovascular disease. Endocr Rev 24:313–340, 2003.

89. Liu PY, Handelsman DJ: Androgen therapy in non-gonadal disease. In Nieschlag E, Behre HM (eds): Testosterone: Action, Deficiency and Substitution, 3d ed. Berlin, Springer-Verlag, 2004.

90. Sorensen K: Klinefelters Syndrome in Childhood, Adolescence and Youth: A Genetic, Clinical, Developmental, Psychiatric and Psychological Study. Chippenham, Parthenon Publishing, 1987.

91. Nieschlag E, Nieschlag S, Behre HM: Lifespan and testosterone. Nature 366:215, 1993.

92. Bojesen A, Juul S, Gravholt CH: Prenatal and postnatal prevalence of Klinefelter syndrome: A national registry study. J Clin Endocrinol Metab 88:622–626, 2003.

93. Nieschlag E, Behre HM: Pharmacology and clinical uses of testosterone. In Nieschlag E, Behre HM (eds): Testosterone: Action Deficiency Substitution, 2d ed. Berlin, Springer-Verlag, 1998, pp 293–328.

94. Schaison G, Young J, Pholsena M, et al: Failure of combined follicle-stimulating hormone-testosterone administration to initiate and/or maintain spermatogenesis in men with hypogonadotropic hypogonadism. J Clin Endocrinol Metab 77:1545–1549, 1993.

95. Pitteloud N, Hayes FJ, Dwyer A, et al: Predictors of outcome of long-term GnRH therapy in men with idiopathic hypogonadotropic hypogonadism. J Clin Endocrinol Metab 87:4128–4136, 2002.

96. Wang C, Tso SC, Todd D: Hypogonadotropic hypogonadism in severe beta-thalassemia: Effect of chelation and pulsatile gonadotropin-releasing hormone therapy. J Clin Endocrinol Metab 68:511–516, 1989.

97. Liu PY, Gebski VJ, Turner L, et al: Predicting pregnancy and spermatogenesis by survival analysis during gonadotropin treatment of gonadotropin deficient infertile men. Hum Reprod 17:625–633, 2002.

98. Burger HG, de Kretser DM, Hudson B, et al: Effects of preceding androgen therapy on testicular response to human pituitary gonadotropin in hypogonadotropic hypogonadism. Fertil Steril 35:64–68, 1981.

99. Davidson JM, Chen JJ, Crapo L, et al: Hormonal changes and sexual function in aging men. J Clin Endocrinol Metab 57:71–77, 1983.

100. Booth JD, Merriam GR, Clark RV, et al: Evidence for Leydig cell dysfunction in infertile men with a selective increase in plasma follicle-stimulating hormone. J Clin Endocrinol Metab 64:1194–1198, 1987.

101. Howell SJ, Radford JA, Adams JE, et al: The impact of mild Leydig cell dysfunction following cytotoxic chemotherapy on bone mineral density (BMD) and body composition. Clin Endocrinol (Oxf) 52:609–616, 2000.

102. Howell SJ, Radford JA, Smets EM, et al: Fatigue, sexual function and mood following treatment for haematological malignancy: The impact of mild Leydig cell dysfunction. Br J Cancer 82:789–793, 2000.

103. Howell SJ, Radford JA, Adams JE, et al: Randomized placebo-controlled trial of testosterone replacement in men with mild Leydig cell insufficiency following cytotoxic chemotherapy. Clin Endocrinol (Oxf) 55:315–324, 2001.

104. Vermeulen A: Androgens and male senescence. In Nieschlag E, Behre HM (eds): Testosterone: Action Deficiency Substitution. Berlin, Springer-Verlag, 1990, pp 261–276.

105. Snyder PJ, Peachey H, Hannoush P, et al: Effect of testosterone treatment on body composition and muscle strength in men over 65 years of age. J Clin Endocrinol Metab 84:2647–2653, 1999.

106. Snyder PJ, Peachey H, Hannoush P, et al: Effect of testosterone treatment on bone mineral density in men over 65 years of age. J Clin Endocrinol Metab 84:1966–1972, 1999.

107. Gruenewald DA, Matsumoto AM: Testosterone supplementation therapy for older men: Potential benefits and risks. J Am Geriatr Soc 51:101–115, 2003.

108. Ly LP, Jimenez M, Zhuang TN, et al: A double-blind, placebo-controlled, randomized clinical trial of transdermal dihydrotestosterone gel on muscular strength, mobility, and quality of life in older men with partial androgen deficiency. J Clin Endocrinol Metab 86:4078–4088, 2001.

109. Liu PY, Wishart SM, Handelsman DJ: A double-blind, placebo-controlled, randomized clinical trial of recombinant human chorionic gonadotropin on muscle strength and physical function and activity in older men with partial age-related androgen deficiency. J Clin Endocrinol Metab 87:3125–3135, 2002.

110. Liverman CT, Blazer DG (eds): Testosterone and Aging: Clinical Research Directions. Washington, DC, Institute of Medicine, The National Academies Press, Board on Health Sciences Policy, 2004.

111. Ishak KG, Zimmerman HJ: Hepatotoxic effects of the anabolic-androgenic steroids. Semin Liver Dis 7:230–236, 1987.

112. Gelfand JA, Sherins RJ, Alling DW, et al: Treatment of hereditary angioedema with danazol: Reversal of clinical and biochemical abnormalities. N Engl J Med 295:1444–1448, 1976.

113. Agostini A, Cicardi M: Hereditary and acquired C1-inhibitor deficiency: Biological and clinical characteristics in 235 patients. Medicine (Baltimore) 71:206–215, 1992.

114. Bhasin S, Storer TW, Berman N, et al: The effects of supraphysiologic doses of testosterone on muscle size and strength in normal men. N Engl J Med 335:1–7, 1996.

115. Storer TW, Magliano L, Woodhouse L, et al: Testosterone dose-dependently increases maximal voluntary strength and leg power, but does not affect fatigability or specific tension. J Clin Endocrinol Metab 88:1478–1485, 2003.

116. Singh AB, Hsia S, Alaupovic P, et al: The effects of varying doses of T on insulin sensitivity, plasma lipids, apolipoproteins, and C-reactive protein in healthy young men. J Clin Endocrinol Metab 87:136–143, 2002.

117. Grunfeld C, Feingold KR: Metabolic disturbances and wasting in the acquired immunodeficiency syndrome. N Engl J Med 327:329–337, 1992.

118. Kotler DP, Tierney AR, Wang J, et al: Magnitude of body-cell-mass depletion and the timing of death from wasting in AIDS. Am J Clin Nutr 50:444–447, 1989.

119. Bhasin S, Storer TW, Asbel-Sethi N, et al: Effects of testosterone replacement with a nongenital, transdermal system, Androderm, in human immunodeficiency-virus-infected men with low testosterone levels. J Clin Endocrinol Metab 83:3155–3162, 1998.

120. Grinspoon S, Corcoran C, Askari H, et al: Effects of androgen administration in men with the AIDS wasting syndrome. A randomized, double-blind, placebo-controlled trial. Ann Intern Med 129:18–26, 1998.

121. Grinspoon S, Corcoran C, Parlman K, et al: Effects of testosterone and progressive resistance training in eugonadal men with AIDS wasting. A randomized, controlled trial. Ann Intern Med 133:348–355, 2000.

122. Sattler FR, Jaque SV, Schroeder ET, et al: Effects of pharmacological doses of nandrolone decanoate and progressive resistance training in immunodeficient patients infected with human immunodeficiency virus. J Clin Endocrinol Metab 84:1268–1276, 1999.

123. Davis SR, Burger HG: The role of androgen therapy. Best Pract Res Clin Endocrinol Metab 17:165–175, 2003.

124. Bachmann G, Bancroft J, Braunstein G, et al: Female androgen insufficiency: The Princeton consensus statement on definition, classification, and assessment. Fertil Steril 77:660–665, 2002.

125. Arlt W, Callies F, van Vlijmen JC, et al: Dehydroepiandrosterone replacement in women with adrenal insufficiency. N Engl J Med 341:1013–1020, 1999.

126. Greenblatt RB, Barfield WE, Garner JF, et al: Evaluation of an estrogen, androgen, estrogen-androgen combination, and a placebo in the treatment of the menopause. J Clin Endocrinol Metab 10:1547–1558, 1950.

127. Sherwin BB, Gelfand MM: The role of androgens in the maintenance of sexual functioning in oophorectomized women. Psychosom Med 49:397–409, 1987.

128. Urman B, Pride SM, Yuen BH: Elevated serum testosterone, hirsutism, and virilism associated with combined androgen-estrogen hormone replacement therapy. Obstet Gynecol 77:1124–1131, 1991.

129. Baker J: A report on alterations to the speaking and singing voices of four women following hormonal therapy with virilizing agents. J Voice 13:496–507, 1999.

130. Davis SR, McCloud P, Strauss BJG, et al: Testosterone enhances estradiol's effects on postmenopausal bone density and sexuality. Maturitas 21:227–236, 1995.

131. Shifren JL, Braunstein GD, Simon JA, et al: Transdermal testosterone treatment in women with impaired sexual function after oophorectomy. N Engl J Med 343:682–688, 2000.

132. Guzick DS, Hoeger K: Sex, hormones, and hysterectomies. N Engl J Med 343:730–731, 2000.

133. Hoberman JM, Yesalis CE: The history of synthetic testosterone. Sci Am 272:76–81, 1995.

134. Franke WW, Berendonk B: Hormonal doping and androgenization of athletes: A secret program of the German Democratic Republic government. Clin Chem 43:1262–1279, 1997.

135. Haupt HA, Rovere GD: Anabolic steroids: A review of the literature. Am J Sports Med 12:469–484, 1984.

136. Wilson JD: Androgen abuse by athletes. Endocr Rev 9:181–199, 1988.

137. Elashoff JD, Jacknow AD, Shain SG, et al: Effects of anabolic-androgenic steroids on muscular strength. Ann Intern Med 115:387–393, 1991.

138. Herbst KL, Bhasin S: Testosterone action on skeletal muscle. Curr Opin Clin Nutr Metab Care 7:271–277, 2004.

139. Buckley WE, Yesalis CE, Freidl KE, et al: Estimated prevalence of anabolic steroid use among male high school students. JAMA 260:3441–3445, 1988.

140. Nilsson S: Androgenic anabolic steroid use among male adolescents in Falkenberg. Eur J Clin Pharmacol 48:9–11, 1995.

141. Handelsman DJ, Gupta L: Prevalence and risk factors for anabolic-androgenic steroid abuse in Australian secondary school students. Int J Androl 20:159–164, 1997.

142. Lambert MI, Titlestad SD, Schwellnus MP: Prevalence of androgenic-anabolic steroid use in adolescents in two regions of South Africa. S Afr Med J 88:876–880, 1998.

143. Ferenchick GS: Validity of self-report in identifying anabolic steroid use among weightlifters. J Gen Intern Med 11:554–556, 1996.

144. Pope HG, Kouri EM, Powell KF, et al: Anabolic-androgenic steroid use among 133 prisoners. Compr Psychiatry 37:322–327, 1996.

145. Isacsson G, Garle M, Ljung EB, et al: Anabolic steroids and violent crime—An epidemiological study at a jail in Stockholm, Sweden. Compr Psychiatry 39:203–205, 1998.

146. Yesalis CE, Barsukiewicz CK, Kopstein AN, et al: Trends in anabolic-androgenic steroid use among adolescents. Arch Pediatr Adolesc Med 151:1197–1206, 1997.

147. Death AK, McGrath KC, Kazlauskas R, et al: Tetrahydrogestrinone is a potent androgen and progestin. J Clin Endocrinol Metab 89:2498–2500, 2004.

148. Catlin DH, Sekera MH, Ahrens BD, et al: Tetrahydrogestrinone: Discovery, synthesis, and detection. Rapid Commun Mass Spectrom 18:1245–1249, 2004.

149. Holma PK: Effects of an anabolic steroid (metandienone) on spermatogenesis. Contraception 15:151–162, 1977.

150. Knuth UA, Maniera H, Nieschlag E: Anabolic steroids and semen parameters in bodybuilders. Fertil Steril 52:1041–1047, 1989.

151. Turek PJ, Williams RH, Gilbaugh JH, et al: The reversibility of anabolic steroid-induced azoospermia. J Urol 153:1628–1630, 1995.

152. Sorensen M, Ingerslev HJ: Azoospermia in two bodybuilders taking anabolic steroids. Ugeskr Laeger 157:1044–1045, 1995.

153. Gazvani MR, Buckett W, Luckas MJ, et al: Conservative management of azoospermia following steroid abuse. Hum Reprod 12:1706–1708, 1997.

154. Reyes RJ, Zicchi S, Hamed H, et al: Surgical correction of gynaecomastia in bodybuilders. Br J Clin Pract 49:177–179, 1995.

155. Friedl KE: Reappraisal of health risks associated with use of high doses of oral and injectable androgenic steroids. NIDA Res Monogr 102:142–177, 1990.

156. Sklarek HM, Mantovani RP, Erens E, et al: AIDS in a bodybuilder using anabolic steroids [letter]. N Engl J Med 311:1701, 1984.

157. McClain WJ, Bucci KK: Anabolic steroid use as an AIDS risk factor [letter]. Clin Pharm 7:95, 1988.

158. Scott MJ, Scott MJ Jr: HIV infection associated with injections of anabolic steroids [letter]. JAMA 262:207–208, 1989.

159. Nemechek PM: Anabolic steroid users—Another potential risk group for HIV infection [letter]. N Engl J Med 325:357, 1991.

160. Henrion R, Mandelbrot L, Delfieu D: HIV contamination after injections of anabolic steroids [letter]. Presse Med 21:218, 1992.

161. Rich JD, Dickinson BP, Merriman NA, et al: Hepatitis C virus infection related to anabolic-androgenic steroid injection in a recreational weight lifter [letter]. Am J Gastroenterol 93:1598, 1998.

162. Evans NA: Local complications of self administered anabolic steroid injections. Br J Sports Med 31:349–350, 1997.

163. Freeman BJ, Rooker GD: Spontaneous rupture of the anterior cruciate ligament after anabolic steroids. Br J Sports Med 29:274–275, 1995.

164. Pope HG, Katz DL: Affective and psychotic symptoms associated with anabolic steroid use. Am J Psychiatry 145:487–490, 1988.

165. Bahrke MS, Yesalis CE, Wright JE: Psychological and behavioural effects of endogenous testosterone levels and anabolic-androgenic steroids among male. A review. Sports Med 10:303–337, 1990.

166. Rockhold RW: Cardiovascular toxicity of anabolic steroids. Annu Rev Pharmacol Toxicol 33:497–520, 1993.

167. Melchert RB, Welder AA: Cardiovascular effects of androgenic-anabolic steroids. Med Sci Sports Exerc 27:1252–1262, 1995.

168. Sullivan ML, Martinez CM, Gennis P, et al: The cardiac toxicity of anabolic steroids. Prog Cardiovasc Dis 41:1–15, 1998.

169. Roberts JT, Essenhigh DM: Adenocarcinoma of prostate in 40 year old body-builder. Lancet 2:742, 1986.

170. Nakata S, Hasumi M, Sato J, et al: Prostate cancer associated with long-term intake of patent medicine containing methyltestosterone: A case report. Hinyokika Kiyo 43:791–793, 1997.

171. Yeater R, Reed C, Ullrich I, et al: Resistance trained athletes using or not using anabolic steroids compared to runners: Effects on cardiorespiratory variables, body composition, and plasma lipids. Br J Sports Med 30:11–14, 1996.

172. Palatini P, Giada F, Garavelli G, et al: Cardiovascular effects of anabolic steroids in weight-trained subjects. J Clin Pharmacol New Drugs 36:1132–1140, 1996.

173. Dickerman RD, Schaller F, Zachariah NY, et al: Left ventricular size and function in elite bodybuilders using anabolic steroids. Clin J Sports Med 7:90–93, 1997.

174. Jin B, Turner L, Walters WAW, et al: Androgen or estrogen effects on the human prostate. J Clin Endocrinol Metab 81:4290–4295, 1996.

175. Sarna S, Sahi T, Koskenvuo M, et al: Increased life expectancy of world class male athletes. Med Sci Sports Exerc 25:237–244, 1993.

176. Kashkin KB, Kleber HD: Hooked on hormones? An anabolic steroid addiction hypothesis. JAMA 262:3166–3170, 1989.

177. Fingerhood MI, Sullivan JT, Testa M, et al: Abuse liability of testosterone. J Psychopharmacol (Oxf) 11:59–63, 1997.

178. Gill GV: Anabolic steroid induced hypogonadism treated with human chorionic gonadotropin. Postgrad Med J 74:45–46, 1998.

179. Boyadjiev NP, Georgieva KN, Massaldjieva RI, et al: Reversible hypogonadism and azoospermia as a result of anabolic-androgenic steroid use in a bodybuilder with personality disorder. A case report. J Sports Med Phys Fitness 40:271–274, 2000.

180. Goldberg L, Elliot DL, Clarke GN, et al: Effects of a multidimensional anabolic steroid prevention intervention: The Adolescents Training and Learning to Avoid Steroids (ATLAS) program. JAMA 276:1555–1562, 1996.

181. Behre HM, Kliesch S, Leifke E, et al: Long-term effect of testosterone therapy on bone mineral density in hypogonadal men. J Clin Endocrinol Metab 82:2386–2390, 1997.

182. Leifke E, Korner HC, Link TM, et al: Effects of testosterone replacement therapy on cortical and trabecular bone mineral density, vertebral body area and paraspinal muscle area in hypogonadal men. Eur J Endocrinol 138:51–58, 1998.

183. Bhasin S, Storer TW, Berman N, et al: Testosterone replacement increases fat-free mass and muscle size in hypogonadal men. J Clin Endocrinol Metab 82:407–413, 1997.

184. Palacios A, Campfield LA, McClure RD, et al: Effect of testosterone enanthate on hematopoiesis in normal men. Fertil Steril 40:100–104, 1983.

185. Jockenhövel F, Vogel E, Reinhardt W, et al: Effects of various modes of androgen substitution therapy on erythropoiesis. Eur J Med Res 2:293–298, 1997.

186. Davidson JM, Camargo CA, Smith ER: Effects of androgens on sexual behaviour in hypogonadal men. J Clin Endocrinol Metab 48:955–958, 1979.

187. Gooren LJ: Androgen levels and sex functions in testosterone-treated hypogonadal men. Arch Sex Behav 16:463–473, 1987.

188. Zitzmann M, Depenbusch M, Gromoll J, et al: Prostate volume and growth in testosterone-substituted hypogonadal men are dependent on the CAG repeat polymorphism of the androgen receptor gene: A longitudinal pharmacogenetic study. J Clin Endocrinol Metab 88:2049–2054, 2003.

189. Avery MA, Tanabe M, Crowe DF, et al: Synthesis and testing of 17ab-hydroxy-7a methyl-D-homoestra-4,16-dien-3-one: A highly potent orally active androgen. Steroids 55:59–64, 1990.

190. Dalton JT, Mukherjee A, Zhu Z, et al: Discovery of nonsteroidal androgens. Biochem Biophys Res Commun 244:1–4, 1998.

191. Marhefka CA, Gao W, Chung K, et al: Design, synthesis, and biological characterization of metabolically stable selective androgen receptor modulators. J Med Chem 47:993–998, 2004.

192. Lubahn D, Joseph DR, Sullivan PM, et al: Cloning of the human androgen receptor complementary DNA and localisation to the X-chromosome. Science 240:327–330, 1988.

193. Wilson JD: The use and misuse of androgens. Metabolism 29:1278–1295, 1980.

194. Negro-Vilar A: Selective androgen receptor modulators (SARMs): A novel approach to androgen therapy for the new millennium. J Clin Endocrinol Metab 84:3459–3462, 1999.

195. Handelsman DJ, Conway AJ, Boylan LM: Pharmacokinetics and pharmacodynamics of testosterone pellets in man. J Clin Endocrinol Metab 71:216–222, 1990.

196. Deansley R, Parkes AS: Further experiments on the administration of hormones by the subcutaneous implantation of tablets. Lancet ii:606–608, 1938.

197. Handelsman DJ, Mackey MA, Howe C, et al: Analysis of testosterone implants for androgen replacement therapy. Clin Endocrinol (Oxf) 47:311–316, 1997.

198. Kelleher S, Turner L, Howe C, et al: Extrusion of testosterone pellets: A randomized controlled clinical study. Clin Endocrinol 51:469–471, 1999.

199. Kelleher S, Conway AJ, Handelsman DJ: A randomised controlled clinical trial of antibiotic impregnation of testosterone pellet implants to reduce extrusion rate. Eur J Endocrinol 146:513–518, 2002.

200. Kelleher S, Conway AJ, Handelsman DJ: Influence of implantation site and track geometry on the extrusion rate and pharmacology of testosterone implants. Clin Endocrinol 55:531–536, 2001.

201. Handelsman DJ: Clinical pharmacology of testosterone pellet implants. In Nieschlag E, Behre HM (eds): Testosterone: Action Deficiency Substitution, 2d ed. Berlin, Springer, 1998, pp 349–364.

202. Bals-Pratsch M, Knuth UA, Yoon YD, et al: Transdermal testosterone substitution therapy for male hypogonadism. Lancet 2:943–946, 1986.

203. Findlay JC, Place VA, Snyder PJ: Transdermal delivery of testosterone. J Clin Endocrinol Metab 64:266–268, 1987.

204. Bals-Pratsch M, Langer K, Place VA, et al: Substitution therapy of hypogonadal men with transdermal testosterone over one year. Acta Endocrinol (Copenh) 118:7–13, 1988.

205. Jordan WP Jr: Allergy and topical irritation associated with transdermal testosterone administration: A comparison of scrotal and nonscrotal transdermal systems. Am J Contact Dermat 8:108–113, 1997.

206. Jordan WP Jr, Atkinson LE, Lai C: Comparison of the skin irritation

potential of two testosterone transdermal systems: An investigational system and a marketed product. Clin Ther 20:80–87, 1998.

207. Meikle AW, Mazer NA, Moellmer JF, et al: Enhanced transdermal delivery of testosterone across nonscrotal skin produces physiological concentrations of testosterone and its metabolites in hypogonadal men. J Clin Endocrinol Metab 74:623–628, 1992.

208. Arver S, Dobs AS, Meikle AW, et al: Long-term efficacy and safety of a permeation-enhanced testosterone transdermal system in hypogonadal men. Clin Endocrinol (Oxf) 47:727–737, 1997.

209. Bennett NJ: A burn-like lesion caused by a testosterone transdermal system. Burns 24:478–480, 1998.

210. Wilson DE, Kaidbey K, Boike SC, et al: Use of topical corticosteroid pretreatment to reduce the incidence and severity of skin reactions associated with testosterone transdermal therapy. Clin Ther 20:299–306, 1998.

211. Guerin JF, Rollet J: Inhibition of spermatogenesis in men using various combinations of oral progestagens and percutaneous or oral androgens. Int J Androl 11:187–199, 1988.

212. Chemana D, Morville R, Fiet J, et al: Percutaneous absorption of 5a-dihydrotestosterone in man. II. Percutaneous administration of 5a-dihydrotestosterone in hypogonadal men with idiopathic haemochromatosis; clinical, metabolic and hormonal effectiveness. Int J Androl 5:595–606, 1982.

213. Fiet J, Morville R, Chemana D, et al: Percutaneous absorption of 5a-dihydrotestosterone in man. I. Plasma androgen and gonadotrophin levels in normal adult men after percutaneous administration of 5a-dihydrotestosterone. Int J Androl 5:586–594, 1982.

214. Wang C, Iranmanesh A, Berman N, et al: Comparative pharmacokinetics of three doses of percutaneous dihydrotestosterone gel in healthy elderly men—A clinical research center study. J Clin Endocrinol Metab 83:2749–2757, 1998.

215. Swerdloff RS, Wang C, Cunningham G, et al: Long-term pharmacokinetics of transdermal testosterone gel in hypogonadal men. J Clin Endocrinol Metab 85:4500–4510, 2000.

216. Wang C, Swedloff RS, Iranmanesh A, et al: Transdermal testosterone gel improves sexual function, mood, muscle strength, and body composition parameters in hypogonadal men. Testosterone Gel Study Group. J Clin Endocrinol Metab 85:2839–2853, 2000.

217. Rolf C, Kemper S, Lemmnitz G, et al: Pharmacokinetics of a new transdermal testosterone gel in gonadotrophin-suppressed normal men. Eur J Endocrinol 146:673–679, 2002.

218. Delanoe D, Fougeyrollas B, Meyer L, et al: Androgenisation of female partners of men on medroxyprogesterone acetate/percutaneous testosterone contraception. Lancet 1:276, 1984.

219. Rolf C, Knie U, Lemmnitz G, et al: Interpersonal testosterone transfer after topical application of a newly developed testosterone gel preparation. Clin Endocrinol (Oxf) 56:637–641, 2002.

220. Burris AS, Ewing LL, Sherins RJ: Initial trial of slow-release testosterone microspheres in hypogonadal men. Fertil Steril 50:493–497, 1988.

221. Bhasin S, Swerdloff RS, Steiner B, et al: A biodegradable testosterone microcapsule formulation provides uniform eugonadal levels of testosterone for 10–11 weeks in hypogonadal men. J Clin Endocrinol Metab 74:75–83, 1992.

222. Amory JK, Anawalt BD, Blaskovich PD, et al: Testosterone release from a subcutaneous, biodegradable microcapsule formulation (Viatrel) in hypogonadal men. J Androl 23:84–91, 2002.

223. Johnsen SG, Kampmann JP, Bennet EP, et al: Enzyme induction by oral testosterone. Clin Pharmacol Ther 20:233–237, 1976.

224. Stuenkel CA, Dudley RE, Yen SSC: Sublingual administration of testosterone-hydroxyypropyl-b-cyclodextrin inclusion complex simulates episodic androgen release in hypogonadal men. J Clin Endocrinol Metab 72:1054–1059, 1991.

225. Salehian B, Wang C, Alexander G, et al: Pharmacokinetics, bioefficacy, and safety of sublingual testosterone cyclodextrin in hypogonadal men: comparison to testosterone enanthate—A clinical research center study. J Clin Endocrinol Metab 80:3567–3575, 1995.

226. Dobs AS, Hoover DR, Chen MC, et al: Pharmacokinetic characteristics, efficacy, and safety of buccal testosterone in hypogonadal males: A pilot study. J Clin Endocrinol Metab 83:33–39, 1998.

227. Minto C, Howe C, Wishart S, et al: Pharmacokinetics and pharmacodynamics of nandrolone esters in oil vehicle: Effects of ester, injection site and volume. J Pharmacol Exp Ther 281:93–102, 1997.

228. Snyder PJ, Lawrence DA: Treatment of male hypogonadism with testosterone enanthate. J Clin Endocrinol Metab 51:1335–1339, 1980.

229. Cantrill JA, Dewis P, Large DM, et al: Which testosterone replacement therapy? Clin Endocrinol (Oxf) 24:97–107, 1984.

230. Conway AJ, Boylan LM, Howe C, et al: A randomised clinical trial of testosterone replacement therapy in hypogonadal men. Int J Androl 11:247–264, 1988.

231. Behre HM, Nieschlag E: Comparative pharmacokinetics of testosterone

esters. In Nieschlag E, Behre HM (eds): Testosterone: Action Deficiency Substitution, 2d ed. Berlin, Springer, 1998, pp 329–348.

232. Zhang GY, Gu YQ, Wang XH, et al: A pharmacokinetic study of injectable testosterone undecanoate in hypogonadal men. J Androl 19:761–768, 1998.

233. Nieschlag E, Buchter D, Von Eckardstein S, et al: Repeated intramuscular injections of testosterone undecanoate for substitution therapy in hypogonadal men. Clin Endocrinol (Oxf) 51:757–763, 1999.

234. von Eckardstein S, Nieschlag E: Treatment of male hypogonadism with testosterone undecanoate injected at extended intervals of 12 weeks: A phase II study. J Androl 23:419–425, 2002.

235. Weinbauer GF, Marshall GR, Nieschlag E: New injectable testosterone ester maintains serum testosterone of castrated monkeys in the normal range for four months. Acta Endocrinol 113:128–132, 1986.

236. Behre HM, Nieschlag E: Testosterone buciclate (20 Aet-1) in hypogonadal men: Pharmacokinetics and pharmacodynamics of the new long-acting androgen ester. J Clin Endocrinol Metab 75:1204–1210, 1992.

237. Behre HM, Baus S, Kliesch S, et al: Potential of testosterone buciclate for male contraception: Endocrine differences between responders and nonresponders. J Clin Endocrinol Metab 80:2394–2403, 1995.

238. Bagchus WM, Hust R, Maris F, et al: Important effect of food on the bioavailability of oral testosterone undecanoate. Pharmacotherapy 23:319–325, 2003.

239. Gooren LJ: A ten-year safety study of the oral androgen testosterone undecanoate. J Androl 15:212–215, 1994.

240. Butler GE, Sellar RE, Walker RF, et al: Oral testosterone undecanoate in the management of delayed puberty in boys: Pharmacokinetics and effects on sexual maturation and growth. J Clin Endocrinol Metab 75:37–44, 1992.

241. Luisi M, Franchi E: Double-blind group comparative study of testosterone undecanoate and mesterolone in hypogonadal male patients. J Endocrinol Invest 3:305–308, 1980.

242. Suvisaari J, Sundaram K, Noe G, et al: Pharmacokinetics and pharmacodynamics of 7a-methyl-19-nortestosterone after intramuscular administration in healthy men. Hum Reprod 12:967–973, 1997.

243. Sundaram K, Kumar N, Bardin CW: 7a-methyl-19-nortestosterone (MENT): An ideal androgen for replacement therapy. In Bhasin S, Gabelnick HL, Spieler JM, et al (eds): Pharmacology, Biology, and Clinical Applications of Androgens. New York, Wiley-Liss, 1996, pp 493–497.

244. Sundaram K, Kumar N, Bardin CW: 7a-Methyl-nortestosterone (MENT): The optimal androgen for male contraception. Ann Med 25:199–205, 1993.

245. Sundaram K, Kumar N, Monder C, et al: Different patterns of metabolism determine the relative anabolic activity of 19-norandrogens. J Steroid Biochem Mol Biol 53:253–257, 1995.

246. Anderson RA, Wallace AM, Sattar N, et al: Evidence for tissue selectivity of the synthetic androgen 7 alpha-methyl-19-nortestosterone in hypogonadal men. J Clin Endocrinol Metab 88:2784–2793, 2003.

247. Place VA, Atkinson L, Prather DA, et al: Transdermal testosterone replacement through genital skin. In Nieschlag E, Behre HM (eds): Testosterone: Action, Deficiency, Substitution. Berlin, Springer-Verlag, 1990, pp 165–181.

248. Behre HM, Oberpenning F, Nieschlag E: Comparative pharmacokinetics of androgen preparations: Application of computer analysis and simulation. In Nieschlag E, Behre HM, (eds): Testosterone: Action Deficiency Substitution. Berlin, Springer-Verlag, 1990, pp 115–135.

249. Small M, Beastall GH, Semple CG, et al: Alterations of hormone levels in normal males given the anabolic steroid stanozolol. Clin Endocrinol (Oxf) 21:49–55, 1984.

250. Christiansen K: Behavioural correlates of testosterone. In Nieschlag E, Behre HM (eds): Testosterone: Action Deficiency Substitution, 2d ed. Berlin, Springer, 1998, pp 107–142.

251. WHO Task Force on Methods for the Regulation of Male Fertility: Contraceptive efficacy of testosterone-induced azoospermia in normal men. Lancet 336:955–959, 1990.

252. Anderson RA, Bancroft J, Wu FCW: The effects of exogenous testosterone on sexuality and mood of normal men. J Clin Endocrinol Metab 75:1503–1507, 1992.

253. Buena F, Peterson MA, Swerdloff RS, et al: Sexual function does not change when serum testosterone levels are pharmacologically varied within the normal male range. Fertil Steril 59:1118–1123, 1993.

254. Tricker R, Casaburi R, Storer TW, et al: The effects of supraphysiological doses of testosterone on angry behavior in healthy eugonadal men—A clinical research center study. J Clin Endocrinol Metab 81:3754–3758, 1996.

255. WHO Task Force on Methods for the Regulation of Male Fertility: Contraceptive efficacy of testosterone-induced azoospermia and oligozoospermia in normal men. Fertil Steril 65:821–829, 1996.

256. Wu FCW, Farley TMM, Peregoudov A, et al: Effects of testosterone enanthate in normal men: Experience from a multicenter contraceptive efficacy study. Fertil Steril 65:626–636, 1996.

257. Bjorkvist K, Nygren T, Bjorklund AC, et al: Testosterone intake and aggressiveness: Real effect or anticipation? Aggressive Behav 20:17–26, 1994.

258. Archer J: The influence of testosterone on human aggression. Br J Psychiatry 82:1–28, 1991.

259. Su TP, Pagliaro M, Schmidt PJ, et al: Neuropsychiatric effects of anabolic steroids in male normal volunteers. JAMA 269:2760–2764, 1993.

260. Yates WR, Perry PJ, MacIndoe J, et al: Psychosexual effects of three doses of testosterone cycling in normal men. Biol Psychiatry 45:254–260, 1999.

261. Pope HG Jr, Kouri EM, Hudson JI: Effects of supraphysiologic doses of testosterone on mood and aggression in normal men: A randomized controlled trial. Arch Gen Psychiatry 57:133–140, 155–156, 2000.

262. Santamaria JD, Prior JC, Fleetham JA: Reversible reproductive dysfunction in men with obstructive sleep apnea. Clin Endocrinol (Oxf) 28:461–470, 1988.

263. Grunstein RR, Handelsman DJ, Lawrence SJ, et al: Hypothalamic dysfunction in sleep apnea: Reversal by nasal continuous positive airways pressure. J Clin Endocrinol Metab 68:352–358, 1989.

264. Sandblom RE, Matsumoto AM, Scoene RB, et al: Obstructive sleep apnea induced by testosterone administration. N Engl J Med 308:508–510, 1983.

265. Liu PY, Yee BJ, Wishart SM, et al: The short-term effects of high dose testosterone on sleep, breathing and function in older men. J Clin Endocrinol Metab 88:3605–3613, 2003.

266. Mackey MA, Conway AJ, Handelsman DJ: Tolerability of intramuscular injections of testosterone ester in an oil vehicle. Hum Reprod 10:862–865, 1995.

267. Nieschlag E, Wang C, Handelsman DJ, et al (eds): Guidelines for the Use of Androgens in Men. Geneva, Special Programme of Research, Development and Research Training in Human Reproduction of the World Health Organisation, 1992.

268. Kelleher S, Conway AJ, Handelsman DJ: Blood testosterone threshold for androgen deficiency symptoms. J Clin Endocrinol Metab 89:3813–3817, 2004.

269. Mooradian AD, Morley JE, Korenman SG: Biological actions of androgens. Endocr Rev 8:1–28, 1987.

270. Wu JP, Gu FL: The prostate 41-65 years post castration. Chin Med J (Engl) 100:271–272, 1987.

271. Behre HM, Bohmeyer J, Nieschlag E: Prostate volume in testosterone-treated and untreated hypogonadal men in comparison to age-matched normal controls. Clin Endocrinol (Oxf) 40:341–349, 1994.

272. Dobs AS, Meikle AW, Arver S, et al: Pharmacokinetics, efficacy, and safety of a permeation-enhanced testosterone transdermal system in comparison with bi-weekly injections of testosterone enanthate for the treatment of hypogonadal men. J Clin Endocrinol Metab 84:3469–3478, 1999.

273. Jin B, Conway AJ, Handelsman DJ: Effects of androgen deficiency and replacement on prostate zonal volumes. Clin Endocrinol (Oxf) 54:437–445, 2001.

274. Shaneyfelt T, Husein R, Bubley G, et al: Hormonal predictors of prostate cancer: A meta-analysis. J Clin Oncol 18:847–853, 2000.

275. Slater S, Oliver RT: Testosterone: Its role in development of prostate cancer and potential risk from use as hormone replacement therapy. Drugs Aging 17:431–439, 2000.

276. Handelsman DJ: The safety of androgens: Prostate and cardiovascular disease. In Wang C (ed): Male Reproductive Function (Endocrine Updates Series). Boston, Kluwer Academic Publishers, 1998, pp 173–190.

277. Kalin MF, Zumoff B: Sex hormones and coronary disease: A review of the clinical studies. Steroids 55:330–352, 1990.

278. Wu FC, von Eckardstein A: Androgens and coronary artery disease. Endocr Rev 24:183–217, 2003.

# Mutations That Alter Androgen Receptor Function: Androgen Insensitivity and Related Disorders

## Michael J. McPhaul

In vertebrates, androgens control or influence a large number of developmental and homeostatic processes, ranging from the regulation of events critical to the development of the normal male phenotype during embryogenesis to those required for normal function in adults, such as spermatogenesis.[1]

In mammals, two steroids, testosterone and 5α-dihydrotestosterone (DHT), serve as the major circulating androgens. Although these steroids differ only in the presence of a single double bond, in selected circumstances, each has been associated with the control of specific processes, and the actions of both hormones are required to account for the entire spectrum of processes regulated by androgens. This topic remains an area of active investigation, and it remains to be determined how some events are preferentially dependent on the action of testosterone or DHT.[2,3] Despite this diversity of actions, the effects of androgen are exerted via a single androgen receptor (AR) that is encoded on the X chromosome.

In recent years, increasingly detailed information has accumulated regarding the types of genetic defects that disturb the function of the human AR.[1,4] In parallel, extensive work has established a base of information that has permitted the formulations of general models to describe the mechanisms by which steroid receptors mediate their effects on responsive genes. This chapter summarizes the progress that has been made in each of these areas.

## ANDROGENS AND MALE PHENOTYPIC DEVELOPMENT

A great deal of information now exists regarding the process of sexual development in mammals. The studies that have been performed have refined and extended the inferences of Jost, as outlined in Figure 169-1. The complement of sex chromosomes dictates whether the indifferent gonad will develop as a testis or ovary. As a consequence of gonadal differentiation, specific hormones are produced that determine the type of phenotypic development that occurs. In males, the testes begin to secrete testosterone at approximately 9 weeks of development. This hormone and its 5α-reduced derivative, DHT, act to promote the virilization and growth of the internal and external genitalia. During this critical development window, the phallus enlarges and the genital ridges fuse to form the scrotum. In parallel, the wolffian duct structures form the pelvic portion of the urogenital sinus, giving rise to the seminal vesicles and the epididymis. It is important to note that the two androgens present in mammals, testosterone and DHT, are not biologically equivalent. Developmentally, it is clear that although testosterone is capable of mediating the virilization of the internal structures (wolffian duct structures) by itself, the action of DHT is required for the normal virilization of the external genitalia. This conclusion is based on studies of patients defective in 5α-reductase type 2, the isozyme responsible for the formation of DHT in the external genitalia[5-7] as well as on experiments that have examined the effects of treatment of animals with inhibitors of 5α-reductase during development.[8,9]

In addition to the aspects of male development that are affected by the actions of testosterone and DHT, a polypeptide hormone produced by the Sertoli cells of the testes, müllerian-inhibiting substance, acts to induce a regression of the müllerian duct–derived structures, including the uterus and fallopian tubes. The action of this hormone is crucial to the regression of these structures in the normal male, and defects of müllerian-inhibiting substance production or action lead to a form of male pseudohermaphroditism in which the uterus

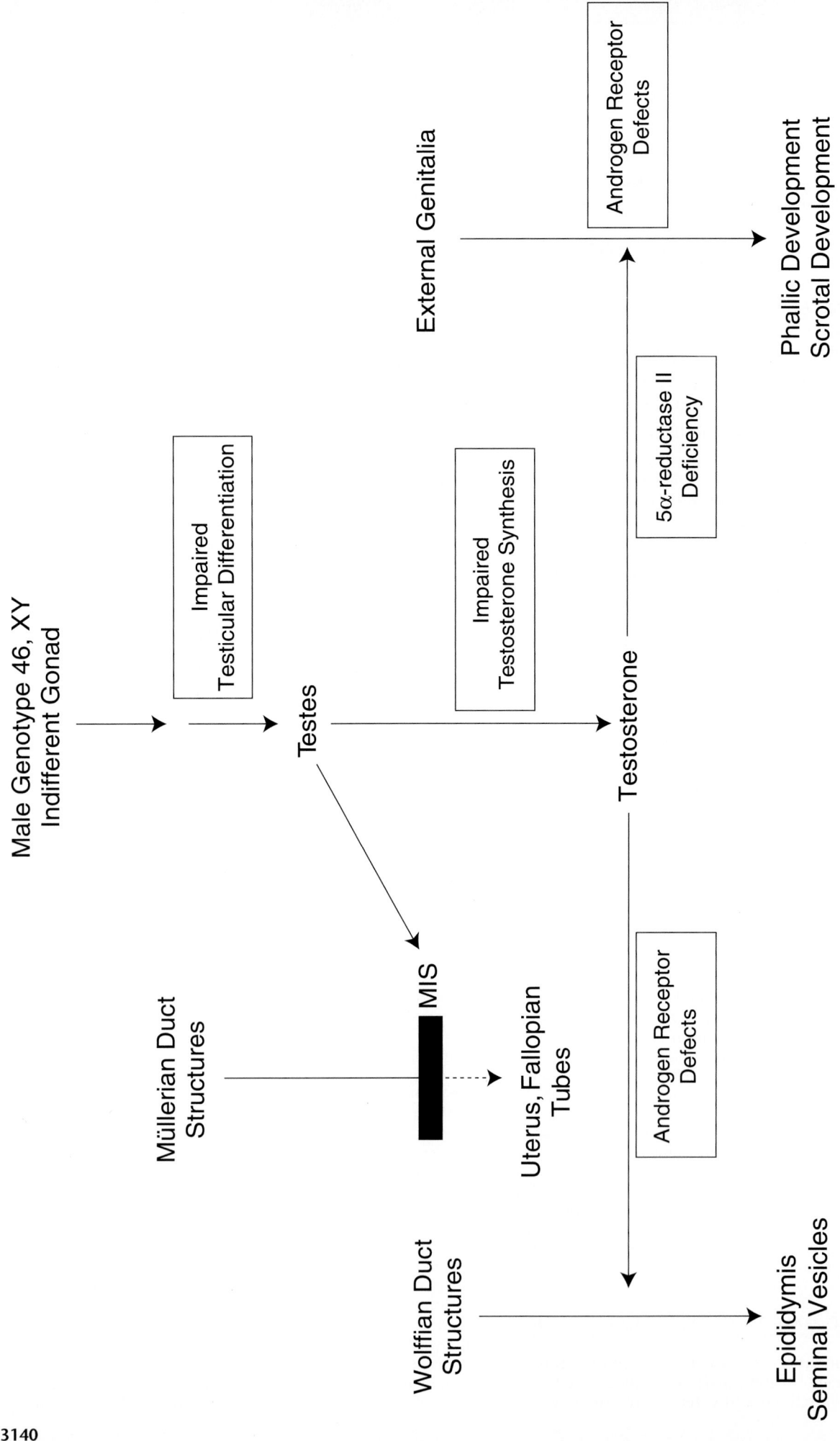

*Figure 169-1* Overview of the pathways of male phenotypic development. According to the paradigm established by Jost, mammalian sexual development is a hierarchical cascade that follows from the establishment of gonadal sex. In this scheme, genes encoded on the human X and Y chromosomes (genotypic sex) dictate the subsequent developmental pathway that is active in the indifferent gonad. Testicular differentiation, occurring as a result of the actions of these genes, results in the synthesis of specific hormones by the developing male gonad (endocrine sex). These products, müllerian-inhibiting substance (MIS) and androgens (testosterone and 5α-dihydrotestosterone), act in concert to direct the morphologic changes that result in the development of the normal male phenotype (phenotypic sex). MIS directs the regression of the müllerian duct structures, such as the uterus and fallopian tubes. Testosterone and 5α-dihydrotestosterone affect the virilization of the wolffian duct structures and the masculinization of the external genitalia. In this regard, it is important to note that defects in the formation of 5α-dihydrotestosterone result in selective defects of virilization of the external genitalia. Androgen receptor (AR) defects, by contrast, can be manifested as defects of virilization of the external genitalia and wolffian duct–derived structures, depending on the degree to which AR function is impaired.

and fallopian tubes persist. A number of reviews describing the endocrine and molecular aspects of sexual development have been published.[1,10]

## STRUCTURE OF THE ANDROGEN RECEPTOR

The AR is a prototypic member of the nuclear receptor (NR) family.[11,12] This gene family includes all the classic steroid receptors as well as a large number of related proteins such as the receptors for thyroid hormone, vitamin D, and retinoic acid. Each member of this family shares particular structural features, including a centrally located DNA-binding domain (DBD), a C-terminal ligand-binding domain (LBD), and a segment at the N terminus that is of variable length. In addition to NRs that bind hormones, such as the steroid hormones, thyroid hormones, and the retinoids, this family contains a number of proteins that share a similar structural organization (Fig. 169-2). Based on the presence of domains resembling LBDs, many of these were suspected to represent potential receptors for ligands that had not been identified ("orphan" receptors). This expectation has been met in recent years as potential ligands have been identified that are capable of modulating the activity of an increasing number of such orphan receptors in functional assays.

Studies of the structure and function of members of the NR family have established that the homologous domains present in these receptor proteins serve similar roles in each. The central DBD is the most highly conserved segment of each of the receptor proteins and is responsible for mediating the contact of the receptor protein with its specific DNA targets. This region is approximately 80 amino acids in length and encodes a series of eight conserved cysteine residues that are organized into two motifs that each serve to coordinate an atom of zinc that is an integral component of each DBD ("zinc finger"). Site-directed mutagenesis performed in a number of laboratories identified specific amino acid residues within the zinc-finger motifs that dictate the specificity as to the DNA sequences that are recognized and that influence the dimerization properties of many of the receptor molecules. These regions were referred to as the P and D boxes (reviewed in Umesono and Evans[13]). The details of these structures and the interactions that they mediate have now been defined for several receptors at the molecular level using nuclear magnetic resonance spectroscopy and crystallographic methods (see later).

The LBD is the portion of the receptor protein that binds ligand with high affinity. Although this segment is not as highly conserved between different family members (compared with the DBDs of the different receptor proteins), considerable homology is evident, even when comparing members of this family that are related only distantly and that serve completely different functions. Deletion mapping of the human AR has demonstrated that the LBD of the

human AR consists of approximately 250-amino acid residues at the C terminus, a structure consistent with the structural requirements defined by deletion and linker-scanning mutagenesis of other steroid receptors. Structural studies have established the crystal structures of the LBDs of normal and mutant ARs.[15–17] These studies have demonstrated that the AR LBD is organized in a fashion that is quite similar to that of other NR family members, composed of an array of α helices that surround a central ligand-binding pocket. As in the structures of other NR family members, it is believed that the position of the terminal helix (helix 12) determines the activity of the AR by regulating the availability of surfaces required for the recruitment of coactivators.

In contrast to the well-defined roles of the DBD and LBD, the function of the N-terminal domain of the NR proteins is less clear. In functional assays using model reporter genes, this portion of the receptor is required for full activity. Unlike mutagenesis studies of the DBD and LBD, experiments to define critical segments of the N terminus required for exerting this effect on receptor function have not identified individual critical amino acids within this segment. Instead, these studies have identified larger regions of the N terminus that are required for full receptor function. It is believed that these results reflect intrinsic properties of the N-terminal segment of the NRs, particularly those steroid receptors that possess large N-terminal domains such as the AR. First, this is believed to reflect a "diffuseness" of the functional components of the AR N terminus that represents the presence of multiple domains within the N terminus that contact ancillary proteins that are required for full function. Alternatively, this requirement may indicate that the structure of the N terminus influences the capacity of the remainder of the receptor to bind hormone or to bind DNA properly. In this regard, it is interesting to note that work by several groups has suggested that the N and C termini of the AR interact with and influence one another[18–20] and that this interaction is an important determinant of AR function in the context of the control of specific sets of genes.[21,22]

The predicted amino acid sequence of the human AR is unusual in that it contains three segments that are composed of direct repeats of single amino acid residues (homopolymeric repeats). These repeat elements, each located within the N terminus of the protein, are not unique to the AR and have been identified in other transcription factors, including other members of the steroid receptor family. Evolutionary studies have suggested that these elements have evolved in primates only relatively recently.[23] Consistent with this suggestion is the fact that such repeated elements are not found in the ARs of other vertebrate species.

The repeated segments of the human AR (see Fig. 169-2) vary considerably in the extent to which they are polymorphic within the population, affect receptor function, and are associated with the appearance or progression of disease. The proline homopolymeric repeat appears to be constant in size

$(Gln)_{20}$          $(Pro)_8$   $(Gly)_{23}$    DNA          LIGAND

**BINDING DOMAINS**

*Figure 169-2*  Schematic of the human androgen receptor (AR). A schematic representation of the predicted amino acid sequence of the human AR is shown. In common with other members of the nuclear receptor family, the AR contains distinct domains responsible for the high-affinity binding of ligand (ligand-binding domain) and target DNA sequences (DNA-binding domain). The AR is among the larger members of the nuclear receptor family, owing to its large N terminus. This region is critical to the function of the AR and contains several elements composed of repeated amino acids. Of these, the glutamine repeat (glutamine homopolymeric segment) is the most polymorphic. Alterations in the length of the glutamine repeat have been linked to the pathogenesis of the X-linked spinal and bulbar muscular atrophy (Kennedy syndrome). Owing to differences in the lengths of these segments, the predicted amino acid sequences of cDNAs encoding the human AR isolated by different groups are of slightly different sizes. The coordinates of Lubahn et al.[14] are employed in the AR mutation database (*http://www.mcgill.ca/androgendb/*) and throughout this chapter.

and instances in which variations in the length of this segment are found have not been reported. Although length polymorphisms have been identified within the glycine homopolymeric repeat, such variations appear to be relatively infrequent.

The relative genetic stability of the glycine and proline repeats contrasts with the polymorphisms of the glutamine homopolymeric domain that have been identified in the normal human population.[18,24,25] These polymorphisms occur with such frequency that they can frequently be employed in family studies to track the inheritance of specific AR alleles. In addition to their importance as potential genetic markers, variations in the length of the glutamine homopolymeric segment of the human AR appear to have important clinical consequences. The pathogenesis of spinal and bulbar muscular atrophy has been traced to an expansion of the glutamine repeat,[26] and a shortening of the glutamine homopolymeric domain has been suggested to identify individuals who are at risk of developing aggressive forms of prostate cancer.[27–32] Additional studies have suggested that variations in the length of the glutamine repeat segment may predict a predisposition to infertility[33–37] and breast cancer.[38–41]

## ASSAYS TO MEASURE THE ABUNDANCE AND FUNCTION OF THE ANDROGEN RECEPTOR

The methods used to detect and study the AR have undergone considerable evolution in the past two decades (Table 169-1). The AR was originally identified and characterized in cells and tissues by measuring the binding of tritiated androgens, such as DHT, in whole-cell or broken-cell preparations. Using these reagents, techniques were developed to measure the affinity of androgen binding by the receptor protein, detect its association with DNA, and characterize its general physical properties. When applied to patient samples, such as genital fibroblast cultures, several groups were able to detect and characterize abnormalities of ligand binding in patients with various forms of androgen resistance.

The isolation of cDNAs encoding the AR and the determination of the predicted primary sequence of the AR permitted the development of specific antibodies that permitted detection of the AR using immunoblot and immunohistochemical assays. Although considerably more sensitive than ligand-binding assays and capable of detecting the AR when ligand is bound, such assays also possess limitations. In most assays, antibodies are unable to distinguish receptor molecules that are capable of binding ligand from those incapable of binding hormone. In addition, the most widely used antibodies have been raised to a limited number of epitopes within the N terminus of the receptor protein, and molecules lacking the epitope recognized by the antibody employed (owing to deletion, degradation, or mutation) will not be detected.

Although measurement of AR levels is an important tool with which to study defects of the AR, it is unable to give insight into the functional capacities of the receptor proteins that are detected. To permit a more direct assessment of normal and mutant ARs, methods have been developed that allow an estimation of the functional activity of normal and mutant ARs. The tests employed are transfection assays in which a gene encoding a measurable enzymatic activity (e.g., chloramphenicol acetyltransferase or luciferase) is placed under the control of an androgen-responsive promoter. A number of different androgen-inducible promoters have been employed in such measurements, including elements derived from the mouse mammary tumor virus, prostate-specific antigen, and probasin promoters. By comparing the induction of the reporter gene by the normal and mutant receptors in this fashion, it is possible to assess the activities of individual mutant receptors in a fashion that is able to evaluate overall function without the need to measure individual properties of the receptor protein (i.e., hormone and DNA binding). Modifications of these assays using adenoviruses to deliver the reporter genes to genital skin fibroblasts can permit a direct assessment of receptor activity in patient samples, such as genital skin fibroblast cultures.[52] Such assays may potentially play a role in the definition of patients in whom defects of AR cofactors or perturbations of cell signaling may be at the root of clinical defects of male development.[52,53]

## COMPONENTS OF ANDROGEN RECEPTOR FUNCTION

The application of ligand binding and cell fractionation techniques established that the non-ligand-bound AR exists in cells as a complex with a number of ancillary proteins, including chaperones such as heat shock proteins 70 and 90.[54,55] The binding of ligand by the receptor results in the "transformation" of the receptor protein, a process that involves dissociation of the associated proteins and the acquisition of the capacity to bind to DNA. The AR undergoes these steps in a fashion that is similar to that described for other members of the steroid receptor family.

Under most conditions, it appears that the human AR is localized predominantly to the nucleus of the cells in which it is expressed. The segments of the AR open reading frame required for this localization have been identified in a number of different laboratories and appear to encompass two distinct regions of the receptor. One is localized within the second zinc finger and the second maps to a region immediately following the second zinc finger.[56,57]

The conformational changes that occur after the binding of ligand have been studied in a number of different ways. Limited proteolysis has proved to be capable of distinguishing different types of ligand-receptor complexes from each other and from non-ligand-bound receptors. Such studies,

| Table 169-1 | Advantages and Limitations of Different Methodologies Available to Detect and Characterize the Androgen Receptor | | |
|---|---|---|---|
| **Assay** | **Advantages** | **Limitations** | **Refs.** |
| Ligand binding | Capable of detecting and quantitating levels of AR | Limited sensitivity; unable to detect alterations of AR that do not affect ligand binding by the AR | 42–44 |
| Immunoblot | Excellent specificity and sensitivity | Unable to distinguish functional from mutant or denatured receptor proteins; unable to detect isoforms or processed forms of the AR, depending on the epitope(s) recognized | 45–47 |
| Reporter gene | Capable of measuring AR function, circumventing the need to know the exact mechanism by which AR function is altered | Influence of the ligand and ligand metabolism; effect of cell context | 48–51 |

AR, androgen receptor.

conducted initially for the progesterone receptor (PR) and glucocorticoid receptor, have now been performed to examine the changes occurring in the conformation of the AR after the binding of AR agonists or antagonists.[58,59] As in studies of the PR and glucocorticoid receptor, distinct conformations appear to result after the binding of AR agonist or antagonist ligands.

For several members of the NR family, inferences made using indirect means have been followed by studies performed using precise spectroscopic methods. Although individual members of the NR family vary considerably in their primary amino acid sequences, it is clear that each has retained basic similarities of 3-dimensional structure. Owing to the complexity of the structures and the difficulty in producing adequate amounts of homogeneous protein, at present detailed structural information is available only for individual domains of the NRs.

From the time of their initial characterizations, the DBDs were identified as being the most highly conserved regions of the NR family members. A great deal of information has been deduced from studies of individual members of the NR family, particularly the glucocorticoid receptor and estrogen receptor. It was recognized in these studies that two individual DBDs bind as a dimer to half-sites of a prototypic palindromic hormone response element in a cooperative fashion. Furthermore, it was established that these small (~80 amino acids) segments of the receptor protein possess the ability to bind to DNA and to discriminate closely related palindromic motifs. Detailed mutagenesis experiments of the DBDs resulted in the mapping of the amino acid residues critical for the dimerization (D box) and for discriminating specific target DNA sequence elements (P box) (reviewed in Umesono and Evans[14]).

The solution of nuclear magnetic resonance and crystal structures of the DBDs of members of the NR family have demonstrated that the conservation of sequence identified at the primary amino acid sequence level extends to the 3-dimensional structures assumed by each. These studies have also elucidated the fashion in which this domain interacts with DNA and is capable of identifying specific target DNA sequences (Fig. 169-3).

Each steroid receptor DBD binds to one half of the palindromic response element often oriented in a head-to-head fashion. The N-terminal α helix of each DBD aligns itself with bases in the major groove of each target DNA half-site. Protein-protein contacts occur between the DBD monomers via residues that constitute the D boxes, and amino acid residues at the tips of both the N-terminal and C-terminal zinc fingers contact the phosphate backbone of the target DNA sequence. In addition, amino acid residues within the boundaries of the P box directly contact bases within the half-sites of target DNA sequences. These latter interactions are believed to contribute to the specificity conferred by residues of the P box that were inferred from mutagenesis studies.[70,71] Modeling of the AR DBD bound to a prototypic palindromic hormone response element has been performed using the coordinates of closely related receptors, such as the glucocorticoid receptor DBD.[72,73] Such modeling suggests that the mechanism of target DNA recognition by the AR is likely to be similar to that described for other members of the NR family, such as the estrogen receptor and glucocorticoid receptor. Interestingly, this head-to-head orientation of the DBD monomers is maintained even when binding to elements that would seem to force a distinctive orientation.[74]

Although structures were first obtained for the DBDs of the NRs, crystal structures of the LBDs of an increasing number of NR family members have been solved.[75-87] Although the available structures represent a divergent group of proteins, each LBD is organized in a similar fashion. The structures of the LBDs of the rat and human ARs bound to agonist have been solved[15-17] and bear the closest similarity to the structure

$$5' - G\ G\ A/T\ A\ C\ A\ nnn\ T\ G\ T\ T\ C\ T\ -\ 3'$$

A

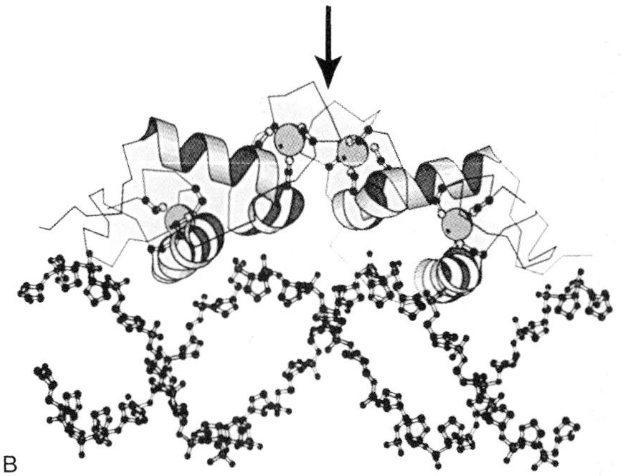

B

**Figure 169-3** Steroid receptor–DNA interactions. **A,** The DNA sequences recognized by the human androgen receptor (AR) are palindromic and are similar in structure to those recognized by related receptors, such as the glucocorticoid and progesterone receptors. Individual half-sites of the response elements are separated by a three-nucleotide interval. **B,** A model of the interaction of steroid receptor DNA-binding domains (DBDs) and a target DNA sequence is depicted as represented by the interaction of the glucocorticoid receptor DBD and its palindromic target DNA sequence.[60] Owing to the palindromic nature of the target DNA sequence and the spacing between the two response element half-sites, two monomers bind to one surface of the DNA helix and make extensive contacts with each other (indicated by the *arrow*). The four gray globes represent the locations of the individual zinc atoms. The interactions depicted here parallel results obtained in other studies of the binding of steroid receptors to target DNA sequences.[61-69] Although crystal structures have not been solved for the AR DBD, the types of interactions depicted here are likely to be applicable to the interaction of the AR DBD and its target DNA sequences as well. (From Freedman LP, Luisi BF: On the mechanism of DNA binding by nuclear hormone receptors: A structural and functional perspective. J Cell Biochem 51:140–150, 1993.)

of the PR (Fig. 169-4). Each consists of a collection of α helices that are organized into three layers. Helices 5, 8, and 9 form a central core, and outer layers are composed of helices 1 and 3 and 7, 10, and 11. The ligand-binding pocket is hydrophobic and surrounded by the framework of α helices composed of helices 3, 5, 7, and 10/11. Direct contacts are made between DHT and residues of helices 3, 4, 5, 7, and 11 and with a residue within the antiparallel beta sheet between helices 5 and 6. As in the structure of the PR, the carboxyl terminal extension of the AR following helix 12 is closely apposed to an antiparallel beta sheet extension that is present between helices 8 and 9. Interestingly, the shapes of the AR LBD differ subtly in the structures complexed to R1881 and DHT, suggesting that significant differences in conformation of the AR LBD, even when bound to ligands with similar physiologic effects.

At present, only a limited number of structures have been published that permit the comparison of a receptor LBD bound to antagonist and to agonist ligands.[81,84,85] Because such structures have not yet been solved for the AR, inferences must be made by comparison with other members of the NR family, particularly the estrogen and glucocorticoid receptors. In the LBD of the estrogen receptor-α bound to estradiol, helix 12, the terminal helix, is positioned over the ligand-binding pocket and is "packed" against helices 3, 5/6, and 11, as shown in Figure 169-4. Of note, helix 12 is

**Figure 169-4**  The binding of agonist and antagonist ligands alters the conformation of the ligand-binding domain (LBD) of steroid receptors. The solution of crystal structures for several members of the nuclear receptor family have permitted conclusions regarding the general structures of this domain in different members of this protein family.[75–85] Although differences are evident between the 3-dimensional structures of each member, certain similarities of structure are evident. In all instances, the LBD is composed of a collection of $\alpha$ helix structures arranged in a "three-layered helix sandwich" surrounding a hydrophobic core. In a limited number of instances, structures of the LBDs of nuclear receptors have been solved when complexed to agonist or antagonist ligands. In such structures, here represented by the estrogen receptor-$\alpha$ complexed to estradiol (**A**) and to raloxifene (**B**),[81] the C-terminal helix (helix 12) assumes distinct conformations (indicated by the *arrows*). This alteration of conformation is believed to underlie the differential recruitment of coactivators and corepressors, which results in the contrasting activities of these two classes of ligands. Similar changes in structures are likely to result from the complexes of other members of the nuclear receptor family, including the androgen receptor, to agonist and to antagonist ligands. **C** and **D**, Two views of the structure of the AR LBD complexed to 5$\alpha$-dihydrotestosterone are shown. The positions of the individual helices and the ligand are labeled. (**A** and **B**: Reprinted with permission from Brzozowski AM, Pike AC, Dauter Z, et al: Molecular basis of agonism and antagonism in the oestrogen receptor. Nature 389:753–758, 1997.)

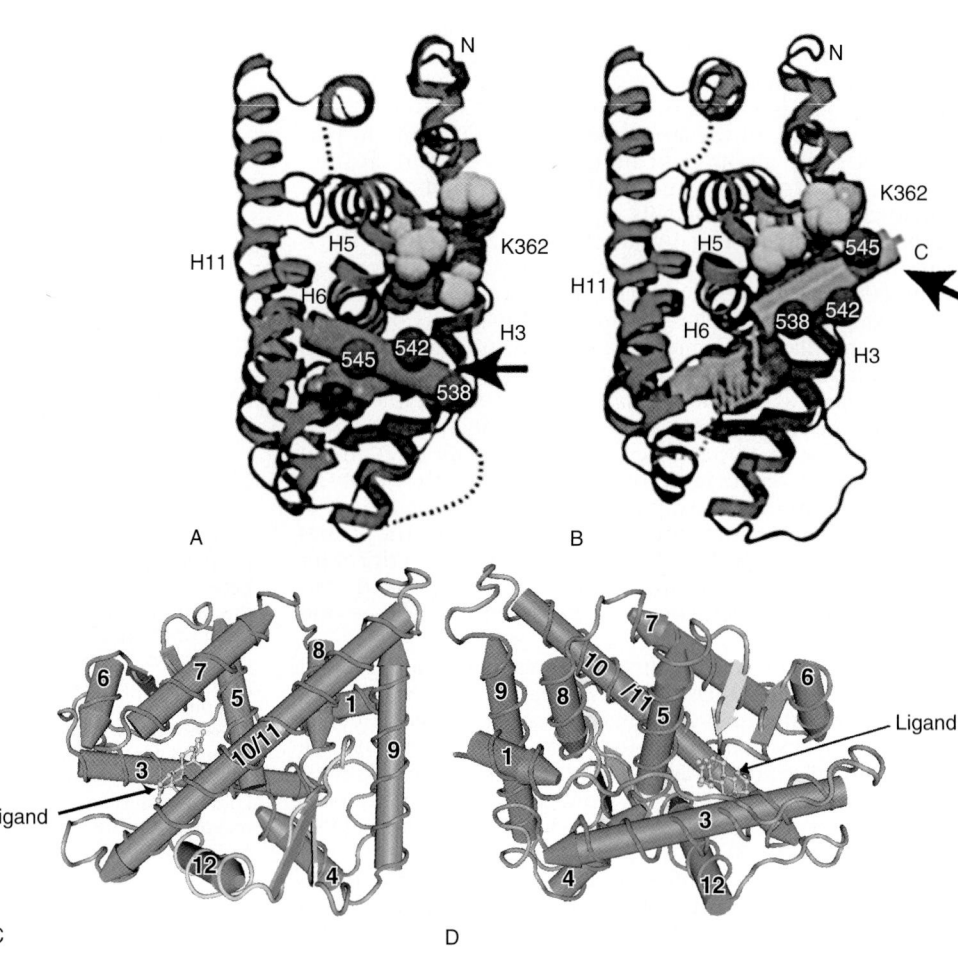

positioned in a similar fashion in the structures of other agonist-bound LBDs that have been analyzed. It is believed that such positioning may well be required for the formation of functional activation function-2 surfaces that are capable of interacting with coactivators. This idea is further reinforced by the recognition that one of the major alterations of structure that is evident in the structure of the estrogen receptor-$\alpha$ and glucocorticoid receptor complexed to antagonist ligands is the dramatic change in the position of helix 12.[81,84] Although these studies have identified changes that may well be functionally critical, different classes of antagonists possess distinctive properties, and additional structures will be required to determine whether the changes observed are general and whether discrete conformations are characteristic of different antagonist classes. Despite these qualifications, it seems likely that the formation of distinctive structures in response to the binding of different classes of ligands represents the physical basis by which coactivators and corepressors are differentially recruited by ligand- and antagonist-bound steroid receptors, respectively. Experiments using phage display libraries have demonstrated that a range of conformations may result even when receptors are complexed to compounds, such as different antiestrogens,[88] that are chemically similar but display functionally distinct activi-

ties. It is not yet clear how readily these concepts will apply to the AR because structures of the AR LBD complexed to antagonist ligands have not yet been solved. Definitive extension of concepts regarding the antagonist- and agonist-bound structures of other NRs to the AR will require the solution of the crystals of the AR complexed to a range of ligands exhibiting antagonistic properties.

## COACTIVATORS AND COREPRESSORS: LINKS TO THE GENERAL TRANSCRIPTION MACHINERY

mRNA is synthesized by RNA polymerase II complexes that contain dozens of individual peptides.[89] The activity and stability of the RNA polymerase II complexes that are formed determine the quantity of RNA that is synthesized from a promoter.

As with the complexes that associate with constitutively active promoters, those that assemble on steroid-responsive promoters contain basal transcription factors as well as peptides that are found preferentially in transcription complexes associated with members of the NR family. These differences in the composition of such complexes are believed to reflect the selective recruitment of proteins that act as links between the individual NR family members and the core components of the transcription apparatus. Two general classes of molecules have been identified: corepressors and coactivators.[90,91] Many of these studies have identified potential coactivators or repressors using methods such as the yeast two-hybrid assay to identify proteins capable of interacting with the NRs.

Corepressor proteins associated with nuclear receptors were discovered during investigations focused on understanding the basis of the inhibitory effects that thyroid hormone receptors exerted on the activity of the thyroid hormone–responsive genes in the absence of ligand.[92,93] Mapping studies of the thyroid hormone and retinoic acid receptors identified segments of the LBDs of the respective receptor proteins capable of mediating this effect. Further studies demonstrated that this property was intrinsic to these regions and that their transfer could confer inhibitory properties when fused to segments of other transcription factors, such as the DBD of the yeast transcription factor GAL4. Independent work in two laboratories identified two proteins, NCoR (NR corepressor) and silencing mediator of retinoic acid and thyroid hormone receptor (SMRT), with substantial homologies at the amino acid sequence level that are capable of interacting with the critical segments of the thyroid and retinoid receptors. Subsequent mapping experiments demonstrated that specific domains of these proteins interact with the receptor proteins and mediate the inhibition of target hormone–responsive genes in the absence of ligand.[94,95] Extensions of these investigations established that the same proteins are critical to the negative influences that are observed on gene expression in many other systems, including the effects of steroid receptor antagonists.[96,97]

In parallel with the identification of corepressors, several groups conducted studies to identify proteins capable of modulating the activities of members of the NR family to activate gene transcription. The first such coactivator was identified by Oñate and coworkers[98] using a two-hybrid assay to identify molecules capable of interacting with the human PR LBD in a ligand-dependent fashion. Experiments conducted in mammalian cells demonstrated that the coexpression of cDNAs encoding steroid receptor coactivator-1 (SRC-1) augmented the activation of a reporter gene by the PR as well as several other members of the NR family. Work in a number of laboratories has identified additional proteins capable of acting as coactivators in transfection assays, many of which share structural similarities to SRC-1.[90,91,99,100] In the case of SRC-1, experiments conducted in vivo have demonstrated the complex roles played in the modulation of target genes by these molecules. Experiments in which the *SRC-1* gene was disrupted indicated that discernible impairment of hormone action could be identified for a number of different axes, including the actions of the androgens and thyroid hormone.[101–112] The apparent functional redundancy that appears to exist for many different NR coactivators is further complicated by observations that suggest that the complement of coactivators expressed differs among individual cell types, even within the same tissue.[113] In addition to general reviews that describe the coactivators that modulate the function of NR family members, the review by Heinlein and Chang[99] outlines the diversity of proteins that have been reported to directly modify the function of the AR.

In addition to corepressors and coactivators, additional higher order components (co-integrators) appear to act to integrate a number of diverse influences. Examples are cyclic adenosine monophosphate response element binding protein (CBP) and its related homologue p300. These proteins interact with a number of different classes of transcription factors and appear to participate in the integration of signals from a variety of pathways, including the effects of coactivators that modulate the activities of members of the NRs[114–119] (see later).

## BIOCHEMICAL FRACTIONATION OF NUCLEAR RECEPTOR COMPLEXES

In parallel with the use of methods such as the two-hybrid screen to identify potential coactivators or corepressors, other investigators sought to identify and characterize proteins using biochemical techniques that copurified with individual NRs or individual receptor domains. The purification of the multiprotein complexes that associate with the thyroid receptor and with the vitamin D receptor LBD demonstrated that distinctive sets of proteins associated with these activated receptor proteins.[120,121] Importantly, these complexes were found to share remarkable similarity to each other, to multiprotein complexes purifying with other transcriptional coactivators, and to the mediator complex defined genetically and biochemically in yeast as a central regulator of gene transcription.[122]

## MODIFICATION OF CHROMATIN STRUCTURE AND UNIFYING CONCEPTS OF GENE REGULATION BY STEROID HORMONES

Despite the complexity that is apparent when considering NR function of the level of coactivators, corepressors, and co-integrators, these protein complexes do not act to modify gene expression by acting on naked DNA but instead exert effects on DNA in its native, chromatinized state. It has been recognized for a considerable time that chromatin remodeling is a critical aspect of transcription regulation and in model steroid hormone–responsive systems, alterations of chromatin structure are closely linked to changes in the activities of responsive genes.[123,124] Considerable information has now been amassed that addresses the mechanisms by which such alterations are effected.

The basis for such models stemmed from the recognition that cyclic adenosine monophosphate response element binding protein (CBP), in addition to functionally integrating the activities of numerous NRs and their associated coactivators, possesses intrinsic histone acetyltransferase activity[125] and acts to recruit the histone acetylase, p300/cyclic adenosine monophosphate response element binding protein–associated factor P/CAF to transcription complexes. These observations suggested that the histone-modifying activities that these complexes possessed might play a direct role in the activation of steroid receptor genes.[126] Such inferences have been reinforced by experiments that have demonstrated the ability of inhibitors of histone deacetylase activity to augment coactivator function measured in vivo.[127]

Based on the concepts emerging from the study of activation by steroid receptors, it was logical to consider whether the inverse, that is, transcriptional repression, might directly involve modification of chromatin structure as well. This became even more plausible as the genes involved in mediating transcriptional repression in yeast and their mammalian counterparts were identified.[128,129] Experiments examining the complexes mediating NR repression in mammalian cells identified many parallels between the yeast and mammalian systems. Both silencing mediator of retinoid and thyroid receptors and NR corepressor were shown to be capable of recruiting repressive complexes containing Sin3A and histone deacetylase. These effects not only related to the activities of the NRs themselves (e.g., the non-ligand-bound thyroid receptor) but also to the activities of steroid receptors when bound to steroid receptor antagonists.[96]

Such experiments have led to the emergence of an integrated model of steroid receptor function (Fig. 169-5) in which the ligand-bound receptor protein binds to specific target sequences and recruits coactivator complexes that possess histone acetyltransferase activity. Recruitment of these

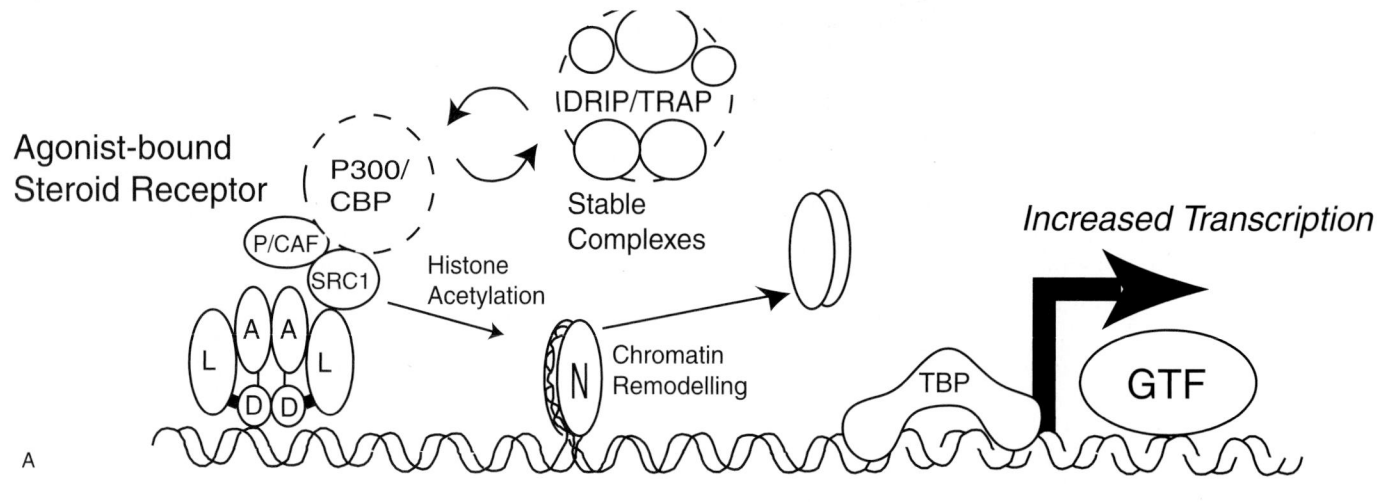

Agonist-bound
Steroid Receptor

DRIP/TRAP

Stable
Complexes

Increased Transcription

P300/
CBP

P/CAF

SRC1

Histone
Acetylation

Chromatin
Remodelling

N

TBP

GTF

L    A  A    L
   D  D

A

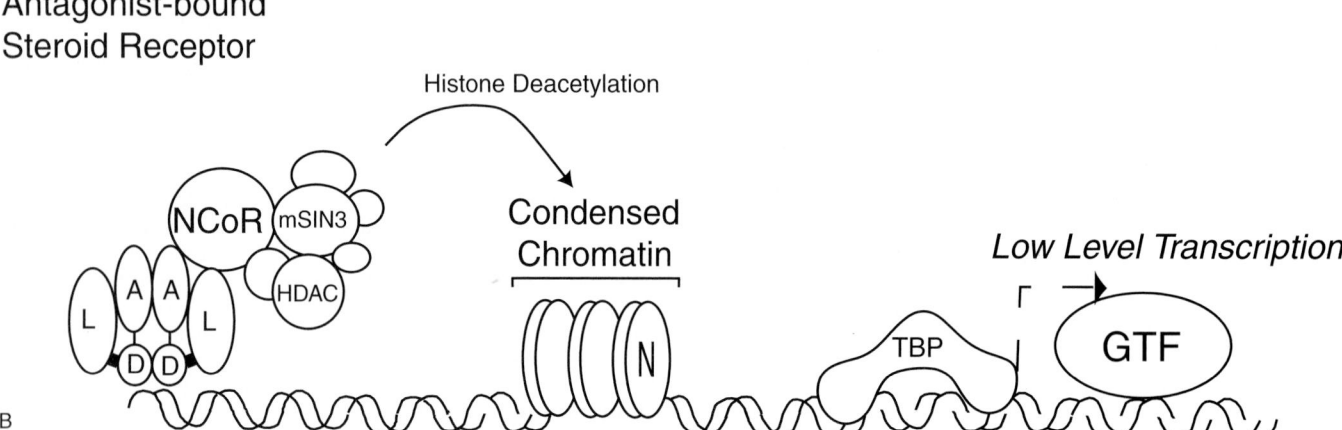

Antagonist-bound
Steroid Receptor

Histone Deacetylation

NCoR    mSIN3

HDAC

L    A  A    L
   D  D

Condensed
Chromatin

N

Low Level Transcription

TBP

GTF

B

**Figure 169-5** Coactivators and corepressors in the action of nuclear receptors. A general model for the activities of coactivators and corepressors in the modulation of the transcription of responsive genes by nuclear receptors is depicted using steroid receptors as representative members of this family. **A,** The binding of an agonist-bound steroid receptor to specific sequences adjacent to the site of transcription initiation of a responsive gene recruits coactivator complexes containing proteins such as steroid receptor coactivator (SRC1), p300/cyclic adenosine monophosphate response element–binding protein, and DRIPs/TRAPs (the order or competition among these different proteins for nuclear receptor binding is unclear at this time). Enzymatic activities contained within these complexes (e.g., histone acetyl transferase) modify the local chromatin structure. In some instances, these modifications may result in large-scale alterations of chromatin organization. These changes make the transcription unit more accessible to the assembly and stability of transcription initiation complexes and results in an increase in the rate of transcription. **B,** The binding of an antagonist to nuclear receptors results in the recruitment of protein complexes containing corepressors such as nuclear receptor corepressor (NCoR) and silencing mediator of retinoic acid and thyroid hormone receptor (SMRT). The enzymatic activities (e.g., deacetylases) associated with these corepressor complexes, which include Sin3 and histone deacetylase (HDAC), leads to a condensation of chromatin structure and a decreased level of gene transcription. A, amino terminus of NR with activation functions; CBP, cyclic adenosine monophosphate response element binding protein; D, DNA binding domain of NR; GTF, general transcription factor; L, ligand-binding domain of NR; N, nucleosome; P/CAF, p300/cyclic adenosine monophosphate response element binding protein–associated factor; TBP, TATA binding protein. (From Zoppi S, Young M, McPhaul MJ: Regulation of gene expression by the nuclear receptor family. In Mason JI (ed): Genetics of Steroid Biosynthesis and Function. New York, Harwood Academic Publisher, 2002, pp 376–403.)

enzymatic activities leads to alterations of local chromatin structure that represent an integral component of the ligand-induced transcription activation. Binding of receptor antagonists, by contrast, leads to the assumption of a distinct conformation by the receptor protein that is capable of recruiting corepressor complexes possessing histone deacetylase activity. The actions of these repressive complexes lead to histone hypoacetylation and gene repression. Although studies to define the involvement of each of these effectors have not been reported for the AR, it is likely that the broad outlines of the pathway defined for related members of the NR family apply to the AR as well.

The diversity of ancillary proteins that have been identified led to debate as to whether this diversity indicated that these proteins that were involved in regulating all genes (e.g., all

those regulated by estrogen or androgen) in parallel or sequential pathways. Although the answer is far from complete, studies have now examined this issue in model cell lines examining the recruitment of specific coactivators and corepressors to the promoter elements controlling the regulation of regulated genes using the chromatin precipitation assay. These studies reveal that selected coactivators and corepressors can be shown to bind to and be released from the sites of gene regulation in response to incubation with hormone in a cyclical fashion.[130,131] Detailed studies of the *PS2* gene, an estrogen-regulated gene in breast cancer cells, suggest that specific classes of proteins are recruited in a specific and hierarchical fashion in complexes that are engaged and exchanged at different points after stimulation with hormone.[132]

## LIGAND-INDEPENDENT ACTIVATION OF THE ANDROGEN RECEPTOR AND ALTERNATE PATHWAYS OF ANDROGEN RECEPTOR SIGNALING

Experiments conducted using the chicken PR demonstrated that under selected experimental conditions steroid hormone receptors could be activated in the absence of their cognate steroid hormone ligand.[133,134] These reports stimulated investigations to determine whether other members of the steroid hormone receptor family, including the AR, could be activated in the absence of ligand.[135–140]

Although it is not clear that ligand-independent regulation of AR function plays an important role in homeostasis or development, it has been proposed that such cross-talk might play a role in some pathologic processes, such as the development and progression of prostate cancer to an androgen-independent state. Investigations by a number of groups have explored this possibility. In some model cell systems, it has been possible to demonstrate cross-talk between the AR signaling pathways and other signaling pathways, such as those employing cyclic adenosine monophosphate.[136,137] In general, these experiments have demonstrated an augmentation of the gene activation that is effected by the AR in response to androgen. Some of the most intriguing experiments in this regard, however, are those that have reported a similar influence of distinct signaling pathways on AR function. In one series of experiments, Craft and colleagues[138] examined the influence of the *her-2/neu* oncogene on the androgen responsiveness of the prostate-specific antigen promoter. The expression of this oncogene has been reported in some studies to be increased during the progression of some models of prostate cancer and could conceivably serve to stimulate growth as well as alter the activation of selective androgen-responsive genes.[138–140] In other models, additional signaling pathways have been demonstrated to augment AR signaling.[141] Signaling by cytokines, such as interleukin-4 and interleukin-6, have been reported to augment the activity of the AR in model systems.[142–145]

In addition to pathways that are capable of modifying the function of NRs, pathways by which steroid receptors can signal that are not immediately dependent on the regulation of gene transcription have been the subject of increasing interest. Such pathways, first explored for the estrogen and glucocorticoid receptors, alter cell function in a time frame that is inconsistent with the regulation at the transcriptional level. Such signaling pathways have now been described for an increasing number of members of the NR pathway, including the AR. The activation of these pathways requires the interaction of the activated NR with intermediary proteins that serve as links to downstream effectors. Although in some instances, the activation of these pathways have been tied to specific biologic responses, in many instances, the physiologic importance of responses mediated through such pathways are as yet undefined.[146–151]

## ANDROGEN INSENSITIVITY: A SPECTRUM OF MALE PHENOTYPIC ABNORMALITIES CAUSED BY DEFECTS OF THE ANDROGEN RECEPTOR

Compared with other members of the NR family, defects of the AR are relatively common. In addition to the relative high frequency of patients exhibiting clinically apparent forms of androgen resistance, the AR is unusual in the wide range of phenotypic abnormalities that have been identified and traced to defects of the AR protein. Several different attributes of the AR appear to contribute to the frequency and diversity of the disorders that have been identified. First, the AR is located on the X chromosome. As such, in normal 46,XY males, only a single AR gene is present. For this reason, in males, any defect of function of the AR in mediating the responses to androgen will result in an abnormality of male phenotypic development (i.e., no second allele is present, as would be true for any autosomal locus). Second, many such defects of virilization are often identified at birth and thus are likely to precipitate a careful investigation of their nature. Finally, although abnormalities of sexual development may be present, it appears that individuals affected by such disorders have a normal or nearly normal life span and are thus available for study.

The range of phenotypic abnormalities is most easily viewed as a spectrum that reflects the extent to which the androgen-mediated processes of male sexual development have been disturbed.

### COMPLETE ANDROGEN INSENSITIVITY (COMPLETE TESTICULAR FEMINIZATION)

In those patients in whom AR function is completely defective, none of the androgen-dependent internal or external male structures develop. This clinical picture has been referred to as complete androgen insensitivity or complete testicular feminization. Such individuals can present at any stage of life: from the neonate period to childhood to early adulthood. In early adulthood, affected individuals may present for evaluation of primary amenorrhea. Infrequently, the birth of an infant with female external genitalia does not agree with expectations based on the results of a karyotype analysis done in the context of amniocentesis. More frequent is the identification of affected individuals during the evaluation and repair of inguinal hernias during infancy. Estimates of the frequency of patients with complete androgen insensitivity within the group of phenotypically female infants with have varied among different reports but are in the range of 1% to 2%. Interestingly, the position of the gonad has been reported to correlate with the degree of androgen insensitivity.[152]

Owing to the inability to respond to androgen, these individuals show no signs of virilization and have normally developed external female genitalia. The normal feminization that is observed at puberty in such patients can be traced to the high circulating levels of androgen, which, although unable to act via the AR, can be aromatized to estrogen. This circulating estrogen binds to the normal ERs present to mediate the feminization that is observed. For this reason, affected individuals appear as normally developed females with normal breast development, although gynecologic examinations will reveal testes located either within the labia majora or within the abdominal cavity. As the endocrine functions of the testes are normal in such patients, müllerian-inhibiting substance is produced and the müllerian-derived structures, the uterus and fallopian tubes, are absent and the vagina is blind ending.

At birth, subjects with complete androgen insensitivity exhibit the phenotype that is a unambiguously female in character (Table 169-2). Unless identified during routine examinations, affected individuals grow and develop normally. At puberty, female secondary sexual characteristics develop with normal breast development owing to the unopposed effects of estrogen. The pubertal growth spurt resembles that observed in women, but the final height is somewhat greater.[153] Bone mineralization also appears to be defective.[154] Pubic axillary hair is reduced or absent in approximately one third of patients, and it absence appears to correlate with the severity of the androgen insensitivity.[152]

The levels of luteinizing hormone (LH) are regulated in a feedback fashion by androgen. Studies in adult subjects with androgen insensitivity have demonstrated that the release of this feedback inhibition results in an increase in LH secretion, caused by increases in both the amplitude and frequency of LH pulses.[155] These increased LH levels drive testicular steroidogenesis, resulting in increased secretion of testosterone

**Table 169-2** Clinical Characteristics of Individuals with Various Forms of Androgen Insensitivity

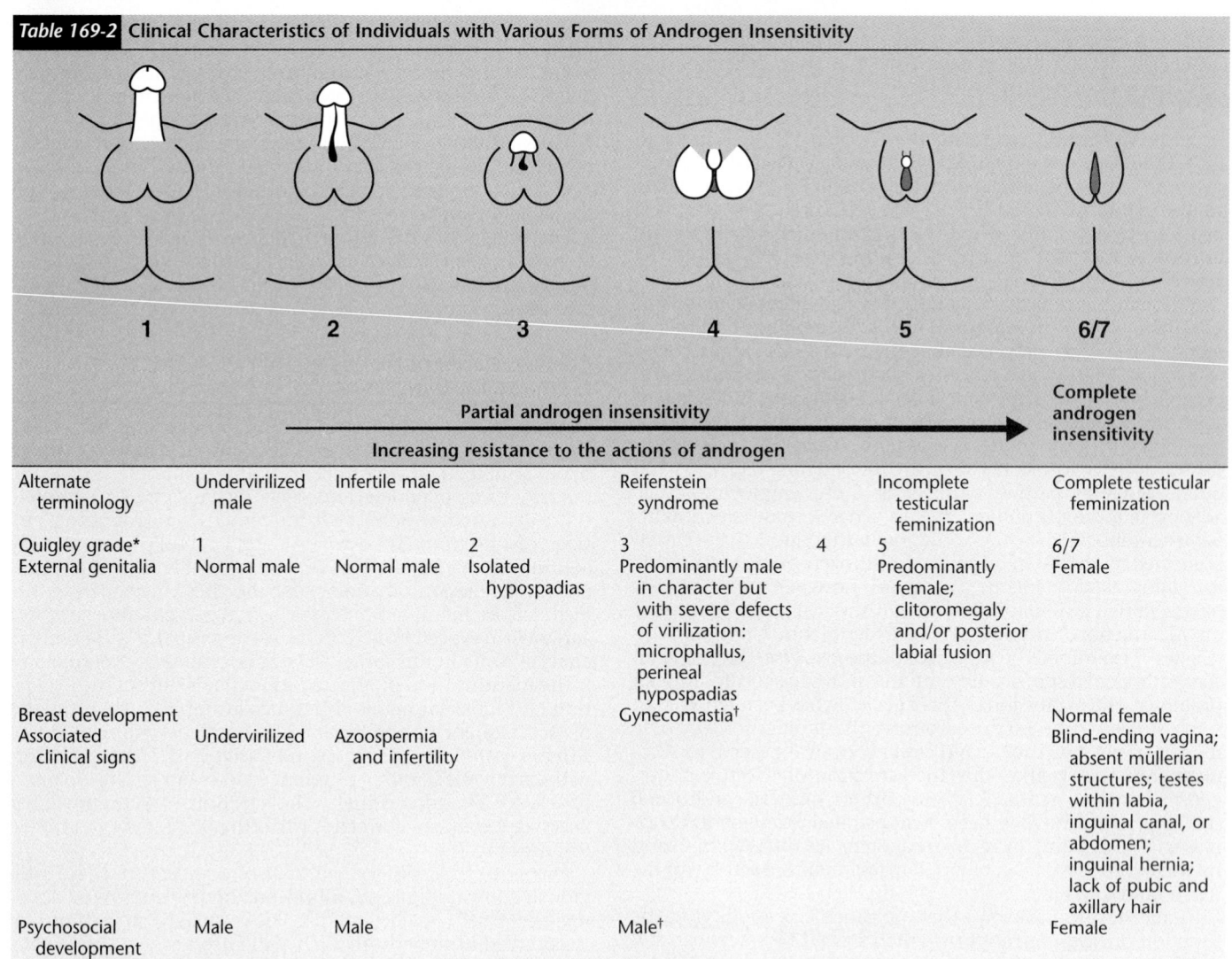

| | 1 | 2 | 3 | 4 | 5 | 6/7 |
|---|---|---|---|---|---|---|
| Alternate terminology | Undervirilized male | Infertile male | | Reifenstein syndrome | Incomplete testicular feminization | Complete testicular feminization |
| Quigley grade* | 1 | | 2 | 3 | 4 | 5 | 6/7 |
| External genitalia | Normal male | Normal male | Isolated hypospadias | Predominantly male in character but with severe defects of virilization: microphallus, perineal hypospadias | Predominantly female; clitoromegaly and/or posterior labial fusion | Female |
| Breast development | | | | Gynecomastia† | | Normal female |
| Associated clinical signs | Undervirilized | Azoospermia and infertility | | | | Blind-ending vagina; absent müllerian structures; testes within labia, inguinal canal, or abdomen; inguinal hernia; lack of pubic and axillary hair |
| Psychosocial development | Male | Male | | Male† | | Female |

*The diagram and grading scale of genitalia development shown are from the adaptation of the Prader virilization scale used in the assessment of congenital adrenal hyperplasia[156] adapted by Quigley et al[4] to the assessment of the degree of masculinization in subjects with androgen insensitivity syndrome. (Reprinted with permission from Quigley CA, Quigley CA, De Bellis A, et al: Androgen receptor defects: Historical, clinical, and molecular perspectives. Endo Reviews 16: 271–321, 1995; Copyright 1995, The Endocrine Society).

†Based on the assessments of Migeon et al.[157] This report indicated that the vast majority of individuals with ambiguous genitalia raised as males reported heterosexual orientations. Importantly, the authors also noted that these data may have not included those individuals with the most profound dissatisfaction with gender assignment and outcome and that AR mutations could be identified in only 6 of 14 individuals with partial androgen insensitivity.

and estradiol. The increased levels of the estradiol observed in affected individuals are derived from both increased secretion of estradiol by the testes and the peripheral conversion of androgen to estrogen.[158,159] In addition to the increased secretion of testosterone, the effect of estrogen to increase levels of circulating testosterone-estradiol binding globulin contributes to the increased levels of circulating testosterone that are observed.[160,161]

Additional complexities may be operative earlier in development. Owing to the decline in maternal estrogen at birth, LH and testosterone increase in the early neonatal period (the neonatal androgen surge).[162] In keeping with such a regulatory loop in normal male infants, it might be anticipated that LH and testosterone levels would be increased, even in childhood. The work of Bouvattier and coworkers[163] has demonstrated that the pattern that is observed is dependent on the degree of androgen insensitivity. In this series of patients, the neonatal surge was detected in subjects with partial androgen insensitivity. By contrast, in patients with complete forms of androgen resistance, the surge was absent, suggesting that the

absence of androgen feedback in early development had subsequent effects on the hypothalamic-pituitary axis that was needed to support the neonatal surge.

The diagnosis of complete androgen insensitivity is suggested by the constellation of clinical features presented by an individual with a female phenotype and a 46,XY karyotype. Additional supporting information may be provided by the family history, which may reveal affected maternal aunts, consistent with an X-linked trait. Endocrine evaluation will reveal elevated testosterone and LH values in the adult. In the pediatric age group, differentiation from other entities, particularly 5α-reductase 2-deficiency and abnormalities in androgen because synthesis is necessary. The measurement of testosterone and DHT after stimulation with human chorionic gonadotropin can be used to establish the normal synthesis of androgens. A number of in vitro and in vivo protocols had been used to assist in the identification of AR defects.

Except for the inability to bear children, patients with complete androgen insensitivity develop and function normally as women. Gonadectomy is recommended, owing to the increased risk of neoplasms within the testes, and estrogen replacement is recommended in such subjects to preserve both mineral density and promote normal breast development.

## PARTIAL ANDROGEN INSENSITIVITY

In cases in which AR function is less completely impaired, a range of intermediate phenotypes can be observed.[1,4] These syndromes have been referred to with a variety of terms, including *Reifenstein syndrome, partial androgen insensitivity,* and *incomplete testicular feminization* (see Table 169-2). Each is characterized by differing degrees of virilization. At one end of the spectrum, affected individuals exhibit phenotypes that are predominantly female, with only minor degrees of virilization present (incomplete testicular feminization). In other instances, a predominantly male phenotype is present, although severe defects of urogenital development are present, such as perineal hypospadias (the Reifenstein phenotype). Some authors have attempted to define a more detailed system with which to categorize patients with partial androgen insensitivity.[4] Finally, at the other end of the phenotypic spectrum from patients with complete forms of androgen resistance are individuals in whom male sexual development is normal or nearly normal but in whom androgen-dependent processes are not normal. In some such patients, only subtle signs of undervirilization, such as gynecomastia, decreased beard and body hair, and small phallus, may be present. In others, defective spermatogenesis appears to be the only manifestation of the associated AR defect.[1]

## ANDROGEN RECEPTOR MUTATIONS AND CLINICAL ANDROGEN RESISTANCE

It is possible to characterize mutations of the AR that cause syndromes of androgen resistance in a number of different ways. As the AR was originally identified and characterized using ligand-binding assays, a great deal of the literature on defects of AR function have focused on the effects that such mutations have on the binding of ligand by the receptor protein. As the sophistication of the analyses of the mutations causing androgen resistance has increased, it is now possible to view these categories from perspectives more directly related to the effects exerted on receptor structure and function.

### MUTATIONS THAT INTERRUPT THE OPEN READING FRAME

A number of mechanisms can result in an interruption of the primary sequence of the human AR: large-scale deletions, small-scale deletions, insertions, and aberrations of AR mRNA splicing. Although each of these is the result of different types of genetic events, in each instance, the predicted mutant AR protein that is produced differs in sequence from that of the normal human AR, either by premature truncation of the receptor protein or by the addition or removal of amino acids from the receptor sequence. Owing to the location of the critical LBDs and DBDs at the C terminus of receptor protein, mutations that result in premature termination of the receptor have a dramatic effect on receptor function when introduced at virtually any position within the primary amino acid sequence. In agreement with the studies of single amino acid substitution mutations (see later), alterations that serve to insert or remove single or multiple amino acids (small insertions or deletions) cause androgen resistance only when occurring within the DNA- or hormone-binding segments of the receptor protein.

### MUTATIONS IN THE DNA-BINDING DOMAIN

In one series, approximately 20% of patients with a clinical picture of androgen resistance and with endocrine studies or

family histories suggesting a defect of the AR did not display discernible abnormalities of ligand binding by the AR in monolayers of patient fibroblasts.[1] This group included patients with complete forms of androgen resistance as well as patients with less complete forms. Such individuals were believed to possess either subtle abnormalities of AR function or to harbor defects in genes other than the AR that were required for normal AR function.

The analyses of the AR genes from a number of such pedigrees have now been reported. In the vast majority of cases, amino acid substitutions are detected within the DBD of the receptor. In the studies of Zoppi et al.,[164] the amino acid substitutions were localized to the DBD of receptor protein in four unrelated subjects with complete or nearly complete forms of androgen resistance. When analyzed using transfection assays in heterologous cells, these mutant receptors were found to bind ligand with normal or nearly normal affinity, in keeping with analyses performed on fibroblasts from the same patients. Functional studies performed in heterologous cells demonstrated that although ligand binding was normal, the mutant ARs were markedly impaired in terms of function (Fig. 169-6A). In vitro experiments found that each of the mutant receptors was unable to bind normally to target DNA sequences. Similar results have been obtained in studies conducted in a number of different laboratories to analyze similar groups of patients with complete or partial forms of androgen resistance.[165-169] In aggregate, these results suggest that the AR defects in this patient group constitute a relatively homogeneous group from a mechanistic standpoint. These mutations alter the structure of the DBD of the receptor and cause androgen insensitivity by interfering with the capacity of the receptor to recognize specific target DNA sequences. It appears that the degree of phenotypic abnormality that is observed has a direct relationship to the extent that DNA binding and receptor function are impaired.

### MUTATIONS IN THE HORMONE-BINDING DOMAIN

Single amino acid substitutions in the LBD represent the most frequent type of mutation that is identified in patients with androgen resistance. These individual amino acid replacements are usually caused by single nucleotide substitution mutations and account for approximately 60% of the mutations identified in patients with clinical defects of androgen action. In a fashion similar to the mutations of the AR DBD, substitution mutations in the LBD have been identified in patients with all the androgen-resistant phenotypes: from complete testicular feminization to those that result in infertility or undervirilization. When categorized based on their effects on the binding of ligand in patient fibroblast samples, the mutations can be divided into two categories: those resulting in the absence of detectable ligand binding and those that cause qualitative abnormalities of ligand binding.

#### Amino Acid Substitutions That Lead to Undetectable Levels of Ligand Binding in Fibroblast Strains
Amino acid substitutions in the LBD of the AR that result in undetectable levels of androgen binding appear to fall into two general classes. The first is infrequent and represents the substitution of amino acid residues in critical segments of the LBD. Presumably, these amino acid substitutions induce major alterations of the structure of the LBD, such that it is no longer capable of interacting with ligand. One well-characterized mutation of this type is the mutant receptor W 739 R described by Marcelli et al.[170] This amino acid substitution replaces a hydrophobic residue within the N-terminal end of helix 5 that would be predicted to make important contacts with the C ring of testosterone.[15-17,171] In addition to considerations of the effects that such changes might have on receptor-ligand interactions, the introduction of a charged residue into this hydrophobic region of the LBD is likely to

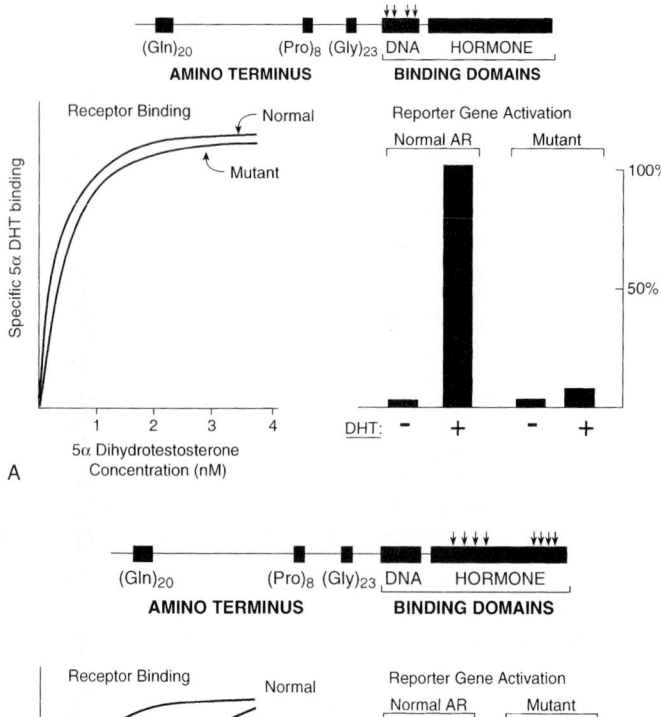

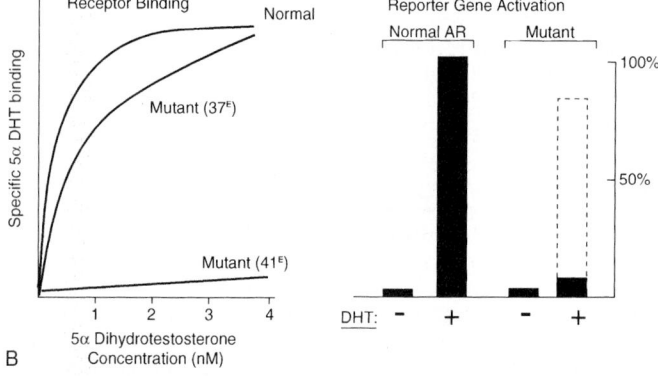

*Figure 169-6* Summary of androgen receptor (AR) mutations and effects on AR function. **A,** The effects of mutations in the DNA-binding domain of the human AR are depicted. These mutations clustered in a small segment of the AR open reading frame (residues 485–520). As depicted (*left panel*), the effects of these mutations are not reflected in assays of ligand binding by the receptor protein. By contrast, when functional assays are applied to such mutant receptors (*right panel*), clear-cut disturbances of function can be detected, compared with the normal AR protein. Although receptor function is dramatically impaired in the example presented here (and would be expected to be associated with a severe clinical defect of androgen action), in other instances mutations within the DNA-binding domain impair receptor function to a lesser degree and are associated with partial forms of androgen resistance. **B,** Amino acid substitutions in the hormone-binding domain can result in two different types of abnormality. Some substitutions completely abrogate the ability of the receptor protein to bind hormone and are completely inactive in functional assays (not shown). Most amino acid substitutions in the hormone-binding domain of the AR have less dramatic effects on the capacity of the receptor protein to bind ligand. In most instances, the receptor retains the ability to bind ligand but does so in a fashion that is qualitatively abnormal (displaying changes in either affinity or stability). An interesting aspect of such qualitatively abnormal receptors is that the amount of ligand binding or functional activity that is measured can be influenced dramatically by the conditions under which such assays are performed. Alterations in the conditions of binding (e.g., temperature, as shown in the *left panel*) or the concentration of ligand that is employed (*dotted lines, right panel*) can have a dramatic effect on the amount of ligand binding or function that is measured. DHT, dihydrotestosterone.

have additional and dramatic effects on the tertiary structure of the ligand-binding pocket. Mutant ARs of this type are incapable of binding hormone and cannot be activated by AR agonists.

Mutant ARs that are completely incapable of binding hormone are rare. Much more frequently, although studies performed in patient fibroblasts indicate that the mutant AR lacks the capacity to bind ligand, when cDNAs encoding such mutant receptors are created and expressed in heterologous cells, they are frequently found to be capable of binding hormone. One such mutant (R774C) was categorized originally as ligand-binding negative, based on the results of monolayer ligand-binding assays to measure AR levels in patient fibroblast samples. When cDNAs encoding the same mutant receptor were created and expressed in heterologous cells, however, ligand binding was clearly detectable, although with altered kinetics and stability of ligand binding.[172] A number of mutant receptors of this type have been described that exhibit the same general type of behavior: relatively normal or nearly normal levels of immunoreactive receptor but with markedly decreased levels of ligand binding.[173] Although at some level, it might appear that this difference reflects differences in the handling or processing of the AR in native and heterologous cells, it is more likely that this apparent discrepancy reflects differences in the level of expression in the two types of cells and the sensitivity of the assays that are employed to analyze the samples.

### Qualitative Abnormalities of Ligand Binding

Analyses of fibroblast samples from some individuals with forms of partial or complete androgen resistance have identified normal levels of AR using monolayer-binding assays. Detailed studies of the kinetics and stability of androgen binding by the receptor protein in some pedigrees revealed that, although the fibroblasts from some such patients expressed normal levels of receptor when analyzed quantitatively, discernible differences were identified when qualitative tests of ligand binding were applied. Such measures included the affinity of ligand binding, the rapidity with which ligand dissociates from the receptor (accelerated ligand dissociation), or increased susceptibility to thermal denaturation.

Although large-scale changes (e.g., created in vitro by mutagenesis) of the N terminus of the AR can result in subtle qualitative abnormalities of ligand binding, virtually all the naturally occurring mutations that cause qualitative abnormalities of ligand binding are single amino acid substitutions and are localized to the LBD of the receptor. Examination of the distribution of the amino acid residues mutated in receptors exhibiting qualitative abnormalities of ligand binding revealed a pattern similar to that observed for substitutions causing absent ligand binding.[174] This finding suggested that the type of receptor defect observed is a direct consequence of the degree to which the structure of the LBD is disrupted. This concept has been reinforced by the study of mutant receptors from pedigrees in which the same amino acid has undergone mutation in different residues. In these instances, it has been possible to show that the replacement of a single residue is capable of resulting in absent ligand binding or qualitative abnormalities of ligand binding, depending on the nature of the amino acid substitution. This is probably most easily seen in the work of Prior and coworkers,[175] in which replacement of arginine 774 by cysteine residue leads to androgen resistance and undetectable ligand binding in patient fibroblasts. Substitution of the same residue by histidine, a more conservative amino acid replacement, leads to normal levels of androgen binding that displays a marked thermal instability in in vitro assays. Other investigators have identified additional pedigrees in which different amino acid substitution mutations lead to differing effects on the binding of ligand by the receptor, depending on the nature of the amino acid substitution.[176–178]

The functional analysis of mutant ARs is not difficult in circumstances in which the receptor protein possesses little or no activity, regardless of the nature of the defect. In this regard, the analysis of qualitatively abnormal ARs poses special challenges because mutant receptors of this class are capable of binding ligand, albeit to varying degrees. For this reason, the cellular environment and the specific ligand that is used to analyze the functional capacity of the receptor protein are critical. This aspect was shown most clearly in the work of Marcelli et al.,[170] who examined the responsiveness of mutant receptors carrying a range of different amino acid substitution mutations in the LBD using several agonist ligands, including DHT, testosterone, and mibolerone (a potent, nonmetabolizable synthetic androgen). Importantly, these experiments were conducted by the introduction of reporter genes and expression plasmids encoding the mutant receptors into a cell strain in which the metabolism of testosterone and DHT is rapid, a circumstance that is similar to the degradation of androgen that occurs in most androgen target tissues in mammals. These experiments demonstrated the varying results that can be obtained and the analysis of qualitatively abnormal receptors, depending on how the analyses are performed. When the physiologic ligands were used to stimulate the mutant receptors, greater deficiencies of function were observed for most of the mutant receptors and testosterone was demonstrated to exert a lesser degree of activity compared with DHT. In all instances, the nonmetabolizable androgen mibolerone was observed to be more potent than either of the two androgens that were subject to metabolic inactivation. Experiments in which pulses of hormone were repeatedly added to maintain high levels of androgen in the cell culture medium demonstrated that increased function could also be observed with repeated additions of the metabolizable androgens.

These results suggested the critical role that the formation of stable hormone-receptor complexes plays in the function of the AR. Alterations of receptor structure that diminish the stability of the hormone-receptor complex will have a major effect on the activity of the ligand-bound receptor protein. These results also demonstrate that the environment in which such analyses are employed can have an important modifying influence on the levels of function that are observed, particularly in response to metabolizable androgens. Finally, these results also indicate that mutant receptors that display qualitative abnormalities of ligand binding can be manipulated pharmacologically, in vitro and potentially in vivo, to achieve more normal levels of receptor function. There exist several instances in which responses have been observed to supraphysiologic levels of androgen, and in most cases, the responses that have been observed have been in patients with qualitative abnormalities of ligand binding.[179,180]

## MUTATIONS THAT CAUSE DECREASED LEVELS OF LIGAND BINDING

It is likely that the types of mutations that cause decreased levels of ligand binding will be quite heterogeneous. Those that have been described to date act principally to affect the level of AR protein that is synthesized.

The first mutation of this type was discovered during analysis of the AR genes of affected subjects in a pedigree with complete androgen insensitivity. Monolayer binding assays of fibroblasts from affected individuals detected measurable, but reduced, levels of a qualitatively normal AR protein.[181] Surprisingly, when immunoblots were performed to analyze samples from the same cell strains using an N-terminal antibody, no detectable immunoreactive AR was detected. Analysis of the nucleotide sequence of the AR gene in affected individuals revealed a single nucleotide substitution within the N terminus of the AR protein that resulted in insertion of a premature termination codon. More detailed analysis using antibodies directed at additional internal epitopes revealed that a shorter form of the AR was synthesized in the mutant fibroblasts, accounting for the residual ligand binding that was detected in monolayer-binding assays. More recent studies have established that the shortened form of the AR (AR-A) is synthesized by internal initiation at methionine 188 and is expressed in normal fibroblasts and tissues, albeit at low levels.[182,183] Studies performed in transfected cells demonstrated that the AR-A isoform displays subtle differences of function on selected response elements, suggesting that phenotype of complete androgen insensitivity that was observed in the original pedigree was due to the expression of a reduced level of AR that possesses a reduced functional capacity.[184] Of note, the genesis of this form of the AR is not without controversy, and others have suggested that this form may derive from proteolysis.[18]

The mutation identified in the partial androgen insensitivity syndrome pedigree analyzed by Choong and colleagues[186] suggests a somewhat different mechanism. Analysis of the AR gene in affected subjects identified a single nucleotide substitution that predicted an amino acid substitution at the second amino acid residue (D2K, lysine residue in place of the normal aspartate residue) of the AR open reading frame. Expression of cDNAs encoding the mutant AR and expression in heterologous cells suggested that the androgen insensitivity syndrome phenotype was due primarily to the reduced levels of AR that were expressed, although it was not possible to examine the effects of this mutation in cultured fibroblasts from affected individuals in this pedigree.

## THE RELATIONSHIP BETWEEN CLINICAL PHENOTYPE AND THE LOSS-OF-FUNCTION MUTATIONS THAT ARE DETECTED IN THE ANDROGEN RECEPTOR GENE OF PATIENTS WITH VARIOUS FORMS OF ANDROGEN RESISTANCE

Although it has been clear for some time that the nature of the AR defect does not directly determine the type of phenotype that is observed, the large number of mutations that has been analyzed makes it possible to draw general conclusions regarding the nature of the relationship between clinical phenotype and AR mutation. First, mutations that cause interruptions of the open reading frame of the AR are invariably associated with a phenotype of complete androgen resistance. This relationship is due to the locations of the conserved, essential DBDs and LBDs at the C terminus of the receptor protein. As a result, mutations that truncate the receptor protein at any point during its synthesis will remove portions of one or both of these important functional domains. Such interruptions of the AR open reading frame can be caused either by premature termination, aberrant splicing, shifts of the reading frame, or deletion of partial or complete exon segments.

Mutations that interrupt of the AR open reading frame invariably lead to complete forms of androgen resistance. By contrast, amino acid substitutions within the AR are capable of causing the complete spectrum of androgen-resistant phenotypes. The degree of clinical resistance that is observed does not appear to correlate with the nature or location of the specific mutation. Instead, the phenotype appears to reflect the level of residual AR function that is expressed in the target tissues themselves. This diminished level of AR function can be caused by alterations in the functional capacity of the receptor protein, its level of expression, or combinations of both factors.

A number of individuals have been identified who carry identical mutations within their AR genes. Although in most instances, these individuals exhibit identical phenotypes, this is not uniformly so. In an analysis performed by Gottlieb et al.,[187] as many as 10% to 15% of cases contained in the AR Mutation Database with identical mutations have been reported to have phenotypes that appear distinctive. It is likely that the extent to which the observed phenotypes agree is dependent on a number of different influences. The first of these is the degree to which AR function is impaired. In those instances in which the levels of AR are greatly diminished or the function of the mutant AR is severely depressed, the phenotype is consistently observed to be that of complete androgen insensitivity. The phenotype that is observed is likely to be more variable when the defect of AR level or function is less severe. In these instances, influences that could serve to accentuate or mitigate the degree of AR dysfunction would be expected to have greater effects on phenotype. In keeping with these expectations, fully one third of families with identical mutations associated with partial forms of androgen insensitivity syndrome showed considerable variation in phenotype.[188]

A number of potential modifiers could contribute to such variations in phenotype, both within and between pedigrees. To this point, only two mechanisms have been explored in any detail, as they pertain to variations in phenotype between pedigrees with identical mutations. The first is one reported by Boehmer and coworkers.[189] This group examined a family in which two children who carried identical mutations (R855H) exhibited substantially different degrees of virilization. Analysis of fibroblast strains established from these two siblings demonstrated higher levels of 5α-reductase expression in the strain established from the sibling with the greater degree of virilization. It was proposed by these authors that differences in the formation of DHT in these two siblings contributed to the different extents to which the two subjects virilized. Because the vast majority of LBD amino acid substitutions can be shown to respond to increased hormone concentrations, these findings may have significance for explaining phenotypic differences in a number of pedigrees.

The second mechanism was first identified in a study conducted by Holterhus and coworkers.[190] In this study, these investigators identified a mutation that led to the insertion of a premature termination codon at amino acid residue 172. This was unexpected because this finding was made in a patient with evidence of virilization (clitoromegaly). Additional studies conducted in fibroblast cultures established that reduced levels of full-length AR were expressed in the patient's fibroblasts. This apparent contradiction was reconciled by the recognition that different populations of fibroblasts were present within the patient's biopsy specimen, reflecting somatic mosaicism. The reduced but detectable AR is derived from the proportion of cells that express the normal AR. This residual AR is believed to mediate the virilization observed in this patient. Of note, this mechanism could cause substantial variations in phenotype that may bear striking contrast to the degree to which AR function is disturbed. In this model, the proportion of mutant AR expressed in the tissues would determine the degree of virilization that results.

Subsequent studies by this same group of investigators have identified additional examples in which somatic mosaicism has apparently contributed to the observed phenotype.[191]

## UNUSUAL ALTERATIONS OF ANDROGEN RECEPTOR FUNCTION: SPINAL AND BULBAR MUSCULAR ATROPHY AND PROSTATE CANCER

The syndromes of androgen insensitivity described previously all result from alterations of the AR protein that impair its function to varying degrees. In addition to these loss-of-function mutations of the AR, spinal and bulbar muscular atrophy, a rare neurodegenerative disorder, has been traced to the expansion of a CAG triplet repeat in the N terminus of the AR.[26] The increased size of this repeat results in the expansion of a glutamine homopolymeric segment within the open reading frame of the AR and is believed to result in the acquisition of new "toxic" properties by the mutant AR protein. A number of different mechanisms have been postulated. In some models, the AR containing the expanded glutamine repeat is cleaved into fragments, which may be important in exerting the observed toxicity.[192-194] In other models, the expanded repeat ARs interfere directly with transcription[195] or other cellular processes, such as axonal transport,[196] leading to the development of a syndrome in which neurons within selected spinal and bulbar nuclei degenerate. An intriguing aspect of this syndrome is the timing of its onset in mid-adulthood. The establishment of mouse models of this disorder promise to permit the elucidation of the pathogenesis of its toxicity.[197] Although male development and fertility are initially normal in these patients, signs of mild androgen resistance, such as gynecomastia, emerge during middle age in parallel with the appearance of neurologic symptoms. The mild androgen resistance that is observed clinically may reflect a modest decrease in AR function or abundance that is caused by the glutamine expansion.

The acquisition of novel functions also appears to characterize the mutations of the AR that have been identified in advanced forms of prostate cancer. Several AR mutations, such as that described in the prostate epithelial cell line LNCaP[198] have been shown to result in a broadened responsiveness of the receptor to different ligands (reviewed in McPhaul[171] and Taplin and Balk[199]). These mutations have been identified most frequently in advanced forms of prostate cancer,[200,201] particularly in patients progressing during therapy with antiandrogens.[202] Whether this relaxed specificity will be found to be characteristic of the mutant ARs that appear as a reflection of endocrine influences during the progression to androgen independence or whether other selective pressures may also lead to the appearance of mutations in the AR remains to be established.

## REFERENCES

1. Griffin JE, McPhaul MJ, Russell DW, Wilson JD: The androgen resistance syndromes: Steroid 5α-reductase 2 deficiency, testicular feminization, and related disorders. In Scriver CR, Beaudet AL, Valle D, Sly WS (eds.): The Metabolic and Molecular Bases of Inherited Disease, vol III, 8th ed. New York, McGraw-Hill, 2001, pp 4117–4146.
2. Wilson JD: Role of dihydrotestosterone in androgen action. Prostate Suppl 6:88–92, 1996.
3. Avila DM, Fuqua SAW, George FW, et al: Identification of genes expressed in the rat prostate that are modulated

differently by castration and finasteride treatment. J Endocrinol 159:403–411, 1998.
4. Quigley CA, Quigley CA, De Bellis A, et al: Androgen receptor defects: Historical, clinical, and molecular perspectives. Endocr Rev 16:271–321, 1995.
5. Russell DW, Wilson JD: Steroid 5 alpha-reductase: Two genes/two enzymes. Annu Rev Biochem 63:25–61, 1994.
6. Wilson JD, Griffin JE, Russell DW: Steroid 5 alpha-reductase 2 deficiency. Endocr Rev 14:577–593, 1993.
7. Russell DW, Berman DM, Bryant JT, et al: The molecular genetics of steroid

5 alpha-reductases. Recent Prog Horm Res 49:275–284, 1994.
8. Imperato-McGinley J, Binienda Z, Arthur A, et al: The development of a male pseudohermaphroditic rat using an inhibitor of the enzyme 5 alpha-reductase. Endocrinology 116:807–812, 1985.
9. George FW, Peterson KG: 5 Alpha-dihydrotestosterone formation is necessary for embryogenesis of the rat prostate. Endocrinology 122:1159–1164, 1988.
10. Quigley CA: Disorders of sex determination and differentiation. In Jameson JL (ed): Principles of Molecular

Medicine. Clifton, NJ, Humana Press, 1998, pp 527–559.

11. Mangelsdorf DJ, Thummel C, Beato M, et al: The nuclear receptor superfamily: The second decade. Cell 83:835–839, 1995.

12. Zoppi S, Young M, McPhaul MJ: Regulation of gene expression by the nuclear receptor family. In Mason JI (ed): Genetics of Steroid Biosynthesis and Function. Harwood Academic Publishers, pp 376–403, 2002.

13. Umesono K, Evans RM: Determinants of target gene specificity for steroid/thyroid hormone receptors. Cell 57:1139–1146, 1989.

14. Lubahn DB, Joseph DR, Sar M, et al: The human androgen receptor: Complementary deoxyribonucleic acid cloning, sequence analysis and gene expression in prostate. Mol Endocrinol 2:1265–1275, 1988.

15. Matias PM, Donner P, Coelho R, et al: Structural evidence for ligand specificity in the binding domain of the human androgen receptor. Implications for pathogenic gene mutations. J Biol Chem 275:6164–6171, 2000.

16. Sack JS, Kish KF, Wang C, et al: Crystallographic structures of the ligand-binding domains of the androgen receptor and its T877A mutant complexed with the natural agonist dihydrotestosterone. Proc Natl Acad Sci U S A 98:904–909, 2001.

17. Matias PM, Carrondo MA, Coelho R, et al: Structural basis for the glucocorticoid response in a mutant human androgen receptor (AR(ccr)) derived from an androgen-independent prostate cancer. J Med Chem 45:439–446, 2002.

18. McPhaul MJ, Marcelli M, Tilley WD, et al: Molecular basis of androgen resistance in a family with a qualitative abnormality of the androgen receptor and responsive to high-dose androgen therapy. J Clin Invest 87:1413–1421, 1991.

19. Wilson LE, Kemppainen JA, Wilson EM: Intermolecular $NH_2$-/carboxyl-terminal interactions in androgen receptor dimerization revealed by mutations that cause androgen insensitivity. J Biol Chem 273:92–101, 1998.

20. Doesburg P, Kuil CW, Berrevoets CA, et al: Functional in vivo interaction between the amino-terminal, transactivation domain and the ligand binding domain of the androgen receptor. Biochemistry 36:1052–1064, 1997.

21. He B, Lee LW, Minges JT: Wilson 2002 EM Dependence of selective gene activation on the androgen receptor NH2- and COOH-terminal interaction. J Biol Chem 277:25631–25639.

22. Chang CY, McDonnell DP: 2002 Evaluation of ligand-dependent changes in AR structure using peptide probes. Mol Endocrinol 16:647–660.

23. Choong CS, Kemppainen JA, Wilson EM: Evolution of the primate androgen receptor—A structural basis

24. Edwards A, Hammond HA, Jin L, et al: Genetic variation at five trimeric and tetrameric tandem repeat loci in four human population groups. Genomics 12:241–253, 1992.

25. Sleddens HF, Oostra BA, Brinkmann AO, et al: Trinucleotide repeat polymorphism in the androgen receptor gene (AR). Nucleic Acids Res 20:1427, 1992.

26. La Spada AR, Wilson EM, Lubahn DB, et al: Androgen receptor gene mutations in X-linked spinal and bulbar muscular atrophy. Nature 352:77–79, 1991.

27. Giovannucci E, Stampfer MJ, Krithivas K, et al: The CAG repeat within the androgen receptor gene and its relationship to prostate cancer. Proc Nat Acad Sci U S A 1997;94:3320–3323.

28. Bratt O, Borg A, Lundgren R, et al: CAG repeat length in the androgen receptor gene is related to age at diagnosis of prostate cancer and response to endocrine therapy, but not to prostate cancer risk. Br J Cancer 81:672–676, 1999.

29. Hsing AW, Gao Y-T, Wu G, et al: Polymorphic CAG and GGN repeat lengths in the androgen receptor gene and prostate cancer risk: A population-based case control study in China. Cancer Res 60: 5111–5116, 2000.

30. Bratt O, Borg A, Kristoffersson U, et al: CAG repeat length in the androgen receptor gene is related to age at diagnosis of prostate cancer and response to endocrine therapy, but not to prostate cancer risk. Br J Cancer 1999;81:672–676.

31. Mir K, Edwards J, Paterson PJ, et al: The CAG trinucleotide repeat length in the androgen receptor does not predict the early onset of prostate cancer. BJU Int 90:573–578.

32. Chang BL, Zheng SL, Hawkins GA, et al: Polymorphic GGC repeats in the androgen receptor gene are associated with hereditary and sporadic prostate cancer risk. Hum Genet 110:22–29, 2002

33. Dowsing AT, Yong EL, Clark M, et al: Linkage between male infertility and trinucleotide repeat expansion in the androgen-receptor gene. Lancet 354:40–43, 1999.

34. Mifsud A, Sim CK, Boettger-Tong H, et al: Trinucleotide (CAG) repeat polymorphisms in the androgen receptor gene: Molecular markers of risk for male infertility. Fertil Steril 75:75–81, 2001.

35. Yong EL, Loy CJ, Sim KS: Androgen receptor gene and male infertility. Hum Reprod Update 9:1–7, 2003.

36. Patrizio P, Leonard DG: Expansion of the CAG trinucleotide repeats in the androgen receptor gene and male infertility: A controversial association. J Androl 22:748–749, 2001.

37. Patrizio P, Leonard DG, Chen KL, et al: Larger trinucleotide repeat size in the androgen receptor gene of infertile men

with extremely severe oligozoospermia. J Androl 22:444–448, 2001.

38. Rebbeck TR, Kantoff PW, Krithivas K, et al: Modification of BRCA1-associated breast cancer risk by the polymorphic androgen-receptor CAG repeat. Am J Hum Genet 64:1371–1377, 1999.

39. Giguere Y, Dewailly E, Brisson J, et al: Short polyglutamine tracts in the androgen receptor are protective against breast cancer in the general population. Cancer Res 61:5869–5874, 2001.

40. Haiman CA, Brown M, Hankinson SE, et al: The androgen receptor CAG repeat polymorphism and risk of breast cancer in the Nurses' Health Study. Cancer Res 62:1045–1049, 2002.

41. Lillie EO, Bernstein L, Ingles SA, et al: Polymorphism in the androgen receptor and mammographic density in women taking and not taking estrogen and progestin therapy Cancer Res 64:1237–1241, 2004.

42. Brown TR, Maes M, Rothwell SW, et al: Human complete androgen insensitivity with normal dihydrotestosterone receptor binding capacity in cultured genital skin fibroblasts: Evidence for a qualitative abnormality of the receptor. J Clin Endocrinol Metab 55:61–69, 1982.

43. Griffin JE, Durrant JL: Qualitative receptor defects in families with androgen resistance: Failure of stabilization of the fibroblast cytosol androgen receptor. J Clin Endocrinol Metab 55:465–474, 1982.

44. Pinsky L, Kaufman M, Summitt RL: Congenital androgen insensitivity due to a qualitatively abnormal androgen receptor. Am J Med Genet 10:91–99, 1981.

45. Zegers ND, Claassen E, Neelen C, et al: Epitope prediction and confirmation for the human androgen receptor: Generation of monoclonal antibodies for multi-assay performance following the synthetic peptide strategy. Biochim Biophys Acta 1073:23–32, 1991.

46. Chang CS, Whelan CT, Popovich TC, et al: Fusion proteins containing androgen receptor sequences and their use in the production of poly- and monoclonal antiandrogen receptor antibodies. Endocrinology 125:1097–1099, 1989.

47. Husmann DA, Wilson CM, McPhaul MJ, et al: Antipeptide antibodies to two distinct regions of the androgen receptor localize the receptor protein to the nuclei of target cells in the rat and human prostate. Endocrinology 126:2359–2368, 1991.

48. Otten AD, Sanders MM, McKnight GS: The MMTV LTR promoter is induced by progesterone and dihydrotestosterone but not by estrogen. Mol Endocrinol 2:143–147, 1988.

49. Ham J, Thomson A, Needham M, et al: Characterization of response elements for androgens, glucocorticoids and progestins in mouse mammary tumour virus. Nucleic Acids Res 16:5263–5276, 1988.

50. Cleutjens KB, van der Korput HA, van Eekelen CC, et al: An androgen response element in a far upstream enhancer region is essential for high, androgen-regulated activity of the prostate-specific antigen promoter. Mol Endocrinol 11:148–161, 1997.

51. Kasper S, Rennie PS, Bruchovsky N, et al: Cooperative binding of androgen receptors to two DNA sequences is required for androgen induction of the probasin gene. J Biol Chem 269:31763–31769, 1994.

52. McPhaul MJ, Schweikert H-U, Allman DR, et al: Assessment of androgen receptor function in genital skin fibroblasts using a recombinant adenovirus to deliver an androgen-responsive reporter gene. J Clin Endocrinol Metab 82:1944–1948, 1997.

53. Adachi M, Takayanagi R, Tomura A, et al: 2000 Androgen-insensitivity syndrome as a possible coactivator disease. N Engl J Med 343:856–862.

54. Fang Y, Fliss AE, Robins DM, et al: Hsp90 regulates androgen receptor hormone binding affinity in vivo. J Biol Chem 271:28697–28702, 1996.

55. Veldscholte J, Berrevoets CA, Brinkmann AO, et al: Anti-androgens and the mutated androgen receptor of LNCaP cells: Differential effects on binding affinity, heat-shock protein interaction, and transcription activation. Biochemistry 31:2393–2399, 1992.

56. Zhou ZX, Sar M, Simental JA, et al: A ligand-dependent bipartite nuclear targeting signal in the human androgen receptor. Requirement for the DNA-binding domain and modulation. J Biol Chem 269:13115–13123, 1994.

57. Jenster G, Trapman J, Brinkmann AO: Nuclear import of the human androgen receptor. Biochem J 293:761–768, 1993.

58. Kuil CW, Berrevoets CA, Mulder E: Ligand-induced conformational alterations of the androgen receptor analyzed by limited trypsinization. Studies on the mechanism of antiandrogen action. J Biol Chem 270:27569–27576, 1995.

59. Kallio PJ, Janne OA, Palvimo JJ: Agonists, but not antagonists, alter the conformation of the hormone-binding domain of androgen receptor. Endocrinology 134:998–1001, 1994.

60. Freedman LP, Luisi BF: On the mechanism of DNA binding by nuclear hormone receptors: A structural and functional perspective. J Cell Biochem 51:140–150, 1993.

61. Baumann H, Paulsen K, Kovacs H, et al: Refined solution structure of the glucocorticoid receptor DNA-binding domain. Biochemistry 32:13463–13471, 1993.

62. Schwabe JW, Neuhaus D, Rhodes D: Solution structure of the DNA-binding domain of the oestrogen receptor. Nature 348:458–461, 1990.

63. Luisi BF, Xu WX, Otwinowski Z, et al: Crystallographic analysis of the interaction of the glucocorticoid receptor with DNA. Nature 352:497–505, 1991.

64. Schwabe JW, Chapman L, Finch JT, et al: The crystal structure of the estrogen receptor DNA-binding domain bound to DNA: How receptors discriminate between their response elements. Cell 75:567–578, 1993.

65. Schwabe JW, Fairall L, Chapman L, et al: The cocrystal structures of two zinc-stabilized DNA-binding domains illustrate different ways of achieving sequence-specific DNA recognition. Cold Spring Harb Symp Quant Biol 58:141–147, 1993.

66. Rastinejad F, Perlmann T, Evans RM, et al: Structural determinants of nuclear receptor assembly on DNA direct repeats. Nature 375:203–211, 1995.

67. Gewirth DT, Sigler PB: The basis for half-site specificity explored through a noncognate steroid receptor-DNA complex. Nat Struct Biol 2:386–394, 1995.

68. Gronemeyer H, Moras D: Nuclear receptors. How to finger DNA. Nature 375:190–191, 1995.

69. Luisi BF, Schwabe JW, Freedman LP: The steroid/nuclear receptors: From three-dimensional structure to complex function. Vitam Horm 49:1–47, 1994.

70. Danielsen M, Hinck L, Ringold GM: Two amino acids within the knuckle of the first zinc finger specify DNA response element activation by the glucocorticoid receptor. Cell 57:1131–1138, 1989.

71. Mader S, Kumar V, de Verneuil H, Chambon P: Three amino acids of the oestrogen receptor are essential to its ability to distinguish an oestrogen from a glucocorticoid-responsive element. Nature 338:271–274, 1989.

72. Lobaccaro JM, Poujol N, Chiche L, et al: Molecular modeling and in vitro investigations of the human androgen receptor DNA-binding domain: Application for the study of two mutations. Mol Cell Endocrinol 116:137–147, 1996.

73. Bruggenwirth HT, Boehmer AL, Lobaccaro JM, et al: Substitution of Ala564 in the first zinc cluster of the deoxyribonucleic acid (DNA)-binding domain of the androgen receptor by Asp, Asn, or Leu exerts differential effects on DNA binding. Endocrinology 139:103–110, 1998.

74. Shaffer PL, Jivan A, Dollins DE, et al: Structural basis of androgen receptor binding to selective androgen response elements. Proc Natl Acad Sci U S A 101:4758–4763, 2004.

75. Wagner RL, Apriletti JW, McGrath ME, et al: A structural role for hormone in the thyroid hormone receptor. Nature 378:690–697, 1995.

76. Renaud JP, Rochel N, Ruff M, et al: Crystal structure of the RAR-gamma ligand-binding domain bound to all-trans retinoic acid. Nature 378:681–689, 1995.

77. Bourguet W, Ruff M, Chambon P, et al: Crystal structure of the ligand-binding domain of the human nuclear receptor RXR-alpha. Nature 375:377–382, 1995.

78. Wurtz JM, Bourguet W, Renaud JP, et al: A canonical structure for the ligand-binding domain of nuclear receptors. Nat Struct Biol 3:206, 1996.

79. Rochel N, Renaud JP, Ruff M, et al: Purification of the human RARgamma ligand-binding domain and crystallization of its complex with all-trans retinoic acid. Biochem Biophys Res Commun 230:293–296, 1997.

80. Klaholz BP, Renaud JP, Mitschler A, et al: Conformational adaptation of agonists to the human nuclear receptor RAR gamma. Nat Struct Biol 5:199–202, 1998.

81. Brzozowski AM, Pike AC, Dauter Z, et al: Molecular basis of agonism and antagonism in the oestrogen receptor. Nature 389:753–758, 1997.

82. Wurtz JM, Egner U, Heinrich N, et al: Three-dimensional models of estrogen receptor ligand binding domain complexes, based on related crystal structures and mutational and structure-activity relationship data. J Med Chem 41:1803–1814, 1998.

83. Williams SP, Sigler PB: Atomic structure of progesterone complexed with its receptor. Nature 393:392–396, 1998.

84. Kauppi B, Jakob C, Farnegardh M, et al: The three-dimensional structures of antagonistic and agonistic forms of the glucocorticoid receptor ligand-binding domain: RU-486 induces a transconformation that leads to active antagonism. Journal of Biological Chemistry 278:22748–22754, 2003.

85. Bourguet W, Vivat V, Wurtz JM, et al: Crystal structure of a heterodimeric complex of RAR and RXR ligand-binding domains Mol Cell 5:289–298, 2000.

86. Bourguet W, Germain P, Gronemeyer H: 2000 Nuclear receptor ligand-binding domains: three-dimensional structures, molecular interactions and pharmacological implications. Trends Pharmacol Sci 21:381–388.

87. Nettles KW, Sun J, Radek JT, et al: Allosteric control of ligand selectivity between estrogen receptors alpha and beta: Implications for other nuclear receptors Mol Cell 13:317–327, 2004.

88. Lisa A, Paige LA, Christensen DJ, et al: Estrogen receptor (ER) modulators each induce distinct conformational changes in ER. Proc Natl Acad Sci U S A 96:3999–4004, 1999.

89. Hampsey M, Reinberg D: RNA polymerase II as a control panel for multiple coactivator complexes. Curr Opin Genet Dev 9:132–139, 1999.

90. Jenster G: Coactivators and corepressors as mediators of nuclear receptor function: An update. Mol Cell Endocrinol 143:1–7, 1998.

91. McKenna NJ, Lanz RB, O'Malley BW: Nuclear receptor coregulators: Cellular and molecular biology. Endocr Rev 20:321–344, 1999.

92. Sap J, Munoz A, Damm K, et al: The c-erb-A protein is a high-affinity receptor for thyroid hormone. Nature 324:635–640, 1986.

93. Weinberger C, Thompson CC, Ong ES, et al: The c-erb-A gene encodes a thyroid hormone receptor. Nature 324:641–646, 1986.

94. Chen JD, Evans RM: A transcriptional co-repressor that interacts with nuclear hormone receptors. Nature 377:454–457, 1995.

95. Horlein AJ, Naar AM, Heinzel T, et al: Ligand-independent repression by the thyroid hormone receptor mediated by a nuclear receptor co-repressor. Nature 377:397–404, 1995.

96. Smith CL, Nawaz Z, O'Malley BW: Coactivator and corepressor regulation of the agonist/antagonist activity of the mixed antiestrogen, 4-hydroxytamoxifen. Mol Endocrinol 11:657–666, 1997.

97. Jackson TA, Richer JK, Bain DL, et al: The partial agonist activity of antagonist-occupied steroid receptors is controlled by a novel hinge domain-binding coactivator L7/SPA and the corepressors N-CoR or SMRT. Mol Endocrinol 11:693–705, 1997.

98. Oñate SA, Boonyaratanakornkit V, Spencer TE, et al: The steroid receptor coactivator-1 contains multiple receptor interacting and activation domains that cooperatively enhance the activation function. J Biol Chem 273:12101–12108, 1998.

99. Heinlein CA. Chang C: Androgen receptor (AR) coregulators: An overview. Endocr Rev 23:175–200, 2002.

100. Shibata H, Spencer TE, Onate SA, et al: Role of co-activators and co-repressors in the mechanism of steroid/thyroid receptor action. Recent Prog Horm Res 52:141–164, 1997.

101. Xu JM, Qiu YH, Demayo FJ, et al: Partial hormone resistance in mice with disruption of the steroid receptor coactivator-1 (Src-1). Gene Sci 279:1922–1925, 1998.

102. Weiss RE, Xu JM, Ning G, et al: Mice deficient in the steroid receptor coactivator 1 (SRC-1) are resistant to thyroid hormone. EMBO J 18:1900–1904, 1990.

103. Takeuchi Y, Murata Y, Sadow P, et al: Steroid receptor coactivator-1 deficiency causes variable alterations in the modulation of (T3regulated) transcription of genes in vivo. Endocrinology 143:1346–1352, 2002.

104. Weiss RE, Gehin M, Xu J, et al: Thyroid function in mice with compound heterozygous and homozygous disruptions of SRC-1 and TIF-2 coactivators: evidence for haploinsufficiency. Endocrinology 143:1554–1557, 2002.

105. Sadow PM, Chassande O, Gauthier K, et al: Specificity of thyroid hormone receptor subtype and steroid receptor coactivator-1 on thyroid hormone action. Am J Physiol Endocrinol Metab 284:E36–E46, 2003.

106. Picard F, Gehin M, Annicotte J, et al: SRC-1 and TIF2 control energy balance between white and brown adipose tissues. Cell. 111:931–941, 2002.

107. Gehin M, Mark M, Dennefeld C, et al: The function of TIF2/GRIP1 in mouse reproduction is distinct from those of SRC-1 and p/CIP. Mol Cell Biol. 22:5923–5937, 2002.

108. Modder UI, Sanyal A, Kearns AE, et al: Effects of loss of steroid receptor coactivator-1 on the skeletal response to estrogen in mice Endocrinology 145:913–921, 2004.

109. Nishihara E, Yoshida-Komiya H, Chan CS, et al: SRC-1 null mice exhibit moderate motor dysfunction and delayed development of cerebellar Purkinje cells. J Neurosci 23:213–222, 2003.

110. Yuan Y, Liao L, Tulis DA, Xu J: Steroid receptor coactivator-3 is required for inhibition of neointima formation by estrogen. Circulation 105:2653–2659, 2002.

111. Zhou G, Hashimoto Y, Kwak I, et al: Role of the steroid receptor coactivator SRC-3 in cell growth. Mol Cell Biol 23:7742–7755, 2003.

112. Jepsen K, Hermanson O, Onami TM, et al: Combinatorial roles of the nuclear receptor corepressor in transcription and development. Cell 102:753–763, 2000.

113. Shim WS, DiRenzo J, DeCaprio JA, et al: Segregation of steroid receptor coactivator-1 from steroid receptors in mammary epithelium. Proc Natl Acad Sci U S A 96:208–213, 1999.

114. Kamei Y, Xu L, Heinzel T, et al: A CBP integrator complex mediates transcriptional activation and AP-1 inhibition by nuclear receptors. Cell 85:403–414, 1996.

115. Chakravarti D, LaMorte VJ, Nelson MC, et al: Role of CBP/P300 in nuclear receptor signalling. Nature 383:99–103, 1996.

116. Smith CL, Oñate SA, Tsai M-J, et al: CREB binding protein acts synergistically with steroid receptor coactivator-1 to enhance steroid receptor-dependent transcription. Proc Natl Acad Sci U S A 93:8884–8888, 1996.

117. Yao TP, Ku G, Zhou N, et al: The nuclear hormone receptor coactivator SRC-1 is a specific target of p300. Proc Natl Acad Sci U S A 93:10626–10631, 1996.

118. Hanstein B, Eckner R, DiRenzo J, et al: p300 is a component of an estrogen receptor coactivator complex. Proc Natl Acad Sci U S A 93:11540–11545, 1996.

119. Aarnisalo P, Palvimo JJ, Janne OA: CREB-binding protein in androgen receptor-mediated signaling. Proc Natl Acad Sci U S A 95:2122–2127, 1998.

120. Rachez C, Lemon BD, Suldan Z, et al: Nuclear receptors require the DRIP complex for ligand-dependent transactivation on chromatin templates. Nature 398:824–828, 1999.

121. Fondell JD, Ge H, Roeder RG: Ligand induction of a transcriptionally active thyroid receptor coactivator complex. Proc Natl Acad Sci U S A 93:8329–8333, 1998.

122. Taatjes DJ, Marr MT, Tjian R: Regulatory diversity among metazoan co-activator complexes Nat Rev Mol Cell Biol 5:403–410, 2004.

123. Smith CL, Htun H, Wolford RG, et al: Differential activity of progesterone and glucocorticoid receptors on mouse mammary tumor virus templates differing in chromatin structure. J Biol Chem 272:14227–14235, 1997.

124. Fryer CG, Archer TK: Chromatin remodelling by the glucocorticoid receptor requires the BRG1 complex. Nature 393:88–91, 1998.

125. Ogryzko W, Schiltz RL, Russanova V, et al: The transcriptional coactivators p300 and CBP are histone acetyltransferases. Cell 87:953–959, 1996.

126. Yang XJ, Ogryzko W, Nishikawa J, et al: A p300/CBP-associated factor that competes with the adenoviral oncoprotein E1A. Nature 382:319–324, 1996.

127. Jenster G, Spencer TE, Burcin MM, et al: Steroid receptor induction of gene transcription: A two-step model. Proc Natl Acad Sci U S A 94:7879–7884, 1997.

128. Wolffe AP: Histone deacetylase: A regulator of transcription. Science 272:371–372, 1996.

129. Yang WM, Inouye C, Zeng Y, et al: Transcriptional repression by YY1 is mediated by interaction with a mammalian homolog of the yeast global regulator RPD3. Proc Natl Acad Sci U S A 93:12845–12850, 1996.

130. Shang Y, Hu X, DiRenzo J, Lazar MA, Brown M: Cofactor dynamics and sufficiency in estrogen receptor-regulated transcription. Cell 103:843–852, 2000.

131. Shang Y, Myers M, Brown M: Formation of the androgen receptor transcription complex. Mol Cell 9:601–610, 2002.

132. Metivier R, Penot G, Hubner MR, et al: Estrogen receptor-[alpha] directs ordered, cyclical, and combinatorial recruitment of cofactors on a natural target promoter. Cell 115:751–763, 2003.

133. Power RF, Mani SK, Codina J, et al: Dopaminergic and ligand-independent activation of steroid hormone receptors. Science 254:1636–1639, 1991.

134. Wagner BL, Norris JD, Knotts TA: The nuclear corepressors NCoR and SMRT are key regulators of both ligand- and 8-bromo-cyclic AMP-dependent transcriptional activity of the human progesterone receptor. Mol Cell Biol 18:1369–1378, 1998.

135. Darne C, Veyssiere G, Jean C: Phorbol ester causes ligand-independent activation of the androgen receptor. Eur J Biochem 256:541–549, 1998.

136. Nazareth LV, Weigel NL: Activation of the human androgen receptor through a protein kinase A signaling pathway. J Biol Chem 271:19900–19907, 1996.

137. Sadar MD: Androgen-independent induction of prostate-specific antigen gene expression via cross-talk between the androgen receptor and protein kinase A signal transduction pathways. J Biol Chem 274:7777–7783, 1999.

138. Craft N, Shostak Y, Carey M, et al: A mechanism for hormone-independent prostate cancer through modulation of androgen receptor signaling by the HER-2/neu tyrosine kinase. Nat Med 5:280–285, 1999.

139. Yeh SY, Lin HK, Kang HY, et al: From HER2/Neu signal cascade to androgen receptor and its coactivators: A novel pathway by induction of androgen target genes through MAP kinase in prostate cancer cells. Proc Nat Acad Sci U S A 96:5458–5463, 1999.

140. Abreu-Martin MT, Chari A, et al: Mitogen-activated protein kinase kinase 1 activates androgen receptor-dependent transcription and apoptosis in prostate cancer. Mol Cell Biol 19:5143–5154, 1999.

141. Gregory CW, Fei X, Ponguta LA, et al: Epidermal growth factor increases coactivation of the androgen receptor in recurrent prostate cancer. J Biol Chem 279:7119–7130, 2004.

142. Corcoran NM, Costello AJ: Interleukin-6: minor player or starring role in the development of hormone-refractory prostate cancer? BJU Int 91:545–553, 2003.

143. Yang L, Wang L, Lin HK, et al: Interleukin-6 differentially regulates androgen receptor transactivation via PI3K-Akt, STAT3, and MAPK, three distinct signal pathways in prostate cancer cells. Biochem Biophys Res Commun 305:462–469, 2003.

144. Debes JD, Schmidt LJ, Huang H, Tindall DJ: P300 mediates androgen-independent transactivation of the androgen receptor by interleukin 6. Cancer Res 62:5632–5636, 2002.

145. Ueda T, Mawji NR, Bruchovsky N, Sadar MD: Ligand-independent activation of the androgen receptor by interleukin-6 and the role of steroid receptor coactivator-1 in prostate cancer cells. J Biol Chem 277:38087–38094, 2002.

146. Coleman KM, Smith CL: Intracellular signaling pathways: Nongenomic actions of estrogens and ligand-independent activation of estrogen receptors. Front Biosci 6:D1379–D1391, 2001.

147. Wyckoff MH, Chambliss KL, Mineo C, et al: Plasma membrane estrogen receptors are coupled to endothelial nitric-oxide synthase through Galpha(i). J Biol Chem 276:27071–27076, 2001.

148. Edwards DP, Wardell SE, Boonyaratanakornkit V: Progesterone receptor interacting coregulatory proteins and cross talk with cell signaling pathways. J Steroid Biochem Mol Biol 83:173–186, 2002.

149. Baron S, Manin M, Beaudoin C, et al: Androgen receptor mediates non-genomic activation of phosphatidylinositol 3-OH kinase in androgen-sensitive epithelial cells. J Biol Chem 279:14579–14586, 2004.

150. Wong CW, McNally C, Nickbarg E, et al: Estrogen receptor-interacting protein that modulates its nongenomic activity-crosstalk with Src/Erk phosphorylation cascade. Proc Natl Acad Sci U S A 99:14783–14788, 2002.

151. Unni E, Shihua S, Bicheng N, et al: Changes in non-genotropic signaling correlate with LNCaP cells transition to androgen-independence. Cancer Res 64:7156–7168, 2004.

152. Barthold JS, Kumasi-Rivers K, Upadhyay J, et al: Testicular position in the androgen insensitivity syndrome: Implications for the role of androgens in testicular descent. J Urol 164:497–501, 2000.

153. Zachmann M, Prader A, Sobel EH, et al: Pubertal growth in patients with androgen insensitivity: Indirect evidence for the importance of estrogens in pubertal growth of girl. J Pediatr 108:694–697, 1986.

154. Marcus R, Leary D, Schneider DL, et al: The contribution of testosterone to skeletal development and maintenance: Lessons from the androgen insensitivity syndrome. J Clin Endocrinol Metab 85:1032–1037, 2000.

155. Boyar RM, Moore RJ, Rosner W, et al: Studies of gonadotropin-gonadal dynamics in patients with androgen insensitivity J Clin Endocrinol Metab 47:1116–1122, 1978.

156. Prader VA: Der Genitalbefund beim Pseudohermaphroditism femininus des kongenitalen adrenogenitalen. Syndroms 3:231–248, 1954.

157. Migeon CJ, Wisniewski AB, Gearhart JP, et al: Ambiguous genitalia with perineoscrotal hypospadias in 46,XY individuals: Long-term medical, surgical, and psychosexual outcome. Pediatrics 110:e31, 2002.

158. MacDonald PC, Madden JD, Brenner PF, et al: Origin of estrogen in normal men and in women with testicular feminization. J Clin Endocrinol Metab 49:905–916, 1979.

159. Guerami A, Griffin JE, Kovacs WJ, et al: Estrogen and androgen production rates in two brothers with Reifenstein syndrome. J Clin Endocrinol Metab 71:247–251, 1990.

160. Imperato-McGinley J, Peterson RE, Gautier T, et al: Hormonal evaluation of a large kindred with complete androgen insensitivity: Evidence for secondary 5 alpha-reductase deficiency. J Clin Endocrinol Metab 54:931–941, 1982.

161. Kelch RP, Jenner MR, Weinstein R, et al: Estradiol and testosterone secretion by human, simian, and canine testes, in males with hypogonadism and in male pseudohermaphrodites with the feminizing testes syndrome J Clin Invest 51:824–830, 1972.

162. Forest MG, Nicolino M, David M, Morel Y: The virilized female: Endocrine background. BJU Int 93(Suppl 3):35–43, 2004.

163. Bouvattier C, Carel J-C, Lecointre C, et al: Postnatal changes of T, LH, and FSH in 46,XY infants with mutations in the AR gene. J Clin Endocrinol Metab 87:29–32, 2002.

164. Zoppi S, Marcelli JP, Griffin JE, et al: Amino acid substitutions in the DNA-binding domain of the human androgen receptor are a frequent cause of receptor-binding positive androgen resistance. Mol Endocrinol 6:409–415, 1992.

165. Beitel LK, Prior L, Vasiliou DM, et al: Complete androgen insensitivity due to mutations in the probable alpha-helical segments of the DNA-binding domain in the human androgen receptor. Hum Mol Genet 3:21–27, 1994.

166. De Bellis A, Quigley CA, Marschke KB, et al: Characterization of mutant androgen receptors causing partial androgen insensitivity syndrome. J Clin Endocrinol Metab 78:513–522, 1994.

167. Sultan C, Lumbroso S, Poujol N, et al: Mutations of androgen receptor gene in androgen insensitivity syndromes. J Steroid Biochem Mol Biol 46:519–530, 1993.

168. Lumbroso S, Lobaccaro JM, Belon C, et al: A new mutation within the deoxyribonucleic acid-binding domain of the androgen receptor gene in a family with complete androgen insensitivity syndrome. Fertil Steril 60:814–819, 1993.

169. Mowszowicz I, Lee HJ, Chen HT, et al: A point mutation in the second zinc finger of the DNA-binding domain of the androgen receptor gene causes complete androgen insensitivity in two siblings with receptor-positive androgen resistance. Mol Endocrinol 7:861–869, 1993.

170. Marcelli M, Zoppi S, Wilson CM, et al: Amino acid substitutions in the hormone-binding domain of the human androgen receptor alter the stability of the hormone receptor complex. J Clin Invest 94:1642–1650, 1994.

171. McPhaul MJ: The androgen receptor in syndromes of androgen insensitivity and in prostate cancer. In Shupnick MA (ed): Gene Engineering and Molecular Models in Endocrinology. Totowa, NJ, Humana Press, 2000, pp 3392–3372.

172. Marcelli M, Tilley WD, Zoppi S, et al: Androgen resistance associated with a mutation of the androgen receptor at amino acid 772 (Arg → Cys) results from a combination of decreased messenger ribonucleic acid levels and impairment of receptor function. J Clin Endocrinol Metab 73:318–325, 1991.

173. Avila DM, Wilson CM, Nandi N, et al: Immunoreactive androgen receptor (AR) in genital skin fibroblasts from subjects with androgen resistance and undetectable levels of AR in ligand binding assays, J Clin Endocrinol Metab 87:182–188, 2002.
174. McPhaul MJ, Marcelli M, Zoppi S, et al: Mutations in the ligand-binding domain of the androgen receptor gene cluster in two regions of the gene. J Clin Invest 90:2097–2101, 1992.
175. Prior L, Bordet S, Trifiro MA, et al: Replacement of arginine 773 by cysteine or histidine in the human androgen receptor causes complete androgen insensitivity with different receptor phenotypes. Am J Hum Genet 51:143–155, 1992.
176. Beitel LK, Kazemi-Esfarjani P, Kaufman M, et al: Substitution of arginine-839 by cysteine or histidine in the androgen receptor causes different receptor phenotypes in cultured cells and coordinate degrees of clinical androgen resistance. J Clin Invest 94:546–554, 1994.
177. Kazemi-Esfarjani P, Beitel LK, Trifiro M, et al: Substitution of valine-865 by methionine or leucine in the human androgen receptor causes complete or partial androgen insensitivity, respectively with distinct androgen receptor phenotypes. Mol Endocrinol 7:37–46, 1993.
178. Ris-Stalpers C, Trifiro MA, Kuiper GG, et al: Substitution of aspartic acid-686 by histidine or asparagine in the human androgen receptor leads to a functionally inactive protein with altered hormone-binding characteristics. Mol Endocrinol 5:1562–1569, 1991.
179. Grino PB, Isidro-Gutierrez RF, Griffin JE: Androgen resistance associated with a qualitative abnormality of the androgen receptor and responsive to high dose androgen therapy. J Clin Endocrinol Metab 68:578–584, 1989.
180. Tincello DG, Saunders PT, Hodgins MB, et al: Correlation of clinical, endocrine and molecular abnormalities with in vivo responses to high-dose testosterone in patients with partial androgen insensitivity syndrome. Clin Endocrinol 46:497–506, 1997.
181. Zoppi S, Wilson CM, Harbison MD, et al: Complete testicular feminization caused by an amino-terminal truncation of the androgen receptor with downstream initiation. J Clin Invest 91:1105–1112, 1993.
182. Wilson CM, McPhaul MJ: A and B forms of the androgen receptor are present in human genital skin fibroblasts. Proc Natl Acad Sci U S A 91:1234–1238, 1994.
183. Wilson CM, McPhaul MJ: A and B forms of the androgen receptor are expressed in a variety of human tissues. Mol Cell Endocrinol 120:51–57, 1996.
184. Gao TS, McPhaul MJ: Functional activities of the A- and B-forms of the human androgen receptor in response to androgen receptor agonists and antagonists. Mol Endocrinol 12:654–663, 1998.
185. Gregory CW, He B, Wilson EM: The putative androgen receptor-A form results from in vitro proteolysis. J Mol Endocrinol 27:109–119, 2001.
186. Choong CS, Quigley CA, French FS, et al: A novel missense mutation in the amino-terminal domain of the human androgen receptor gene in a family with partial androgen insensitivity syndrome causes reduced efficiency of protein translation. J Clin Invest 98:1423–1431, 1996.
187. Gottlieb B, Beitel LK, Trifiro MA: Variable expressivity and mutation databases: The androgen receptor gene mutations database Hum Mutat 17:82–88, 2001.
188. Boehmer AL, Brinkmann O, Bruggenwirth H, et al: Drop SL. Genotype versus phenotype in families with androgen insensitivity syndrome. J Clin Endocrinol Metab 86:151–160, 2001.
189. Boehmer AL, Brinkmann AO, Nijman RM, et al: Phenotypic variation in a family with partial androgen insensitivity syndrome explained by differences in 5alpha dihydrotestosterone availability. J Clin Endocrinol Metab 86:240–246, 2001.
190. Holterhus PM, Bruggenwirth HT, Hiort O, et al: Mosaicism due to a somatic mutation of the androgen receptor gene determines phenotype in androgen insensitivity syndrome. J Clin Endocrinol Metab 82:3584–3589, 1997.
191. Holterhus PM, Wiebel J, Sinnecker GH, et al: Clinical and molecular spectrum of somatic mosaicism in androgen insensitivity syndrome. Pediatr Res 46:684–690, 1999.
192. Wellington CL, Ellerby LM, Hackam AS, et al: Caspase cleavage of gene products associated with triplet expansion disorders generates truncated fragments containing the polyglutamine tract. J Biol Chem 273:9158–9167, 1998.
193. Butler R, Leigh PN, McPhaul MJ, et al: Truncated forms of the androgen receptor are associated with polyglutamine expansion in X-linked spinal and bulbar muscular atrophy. Hum Mol Genet 7:121–127, 1998.
194. Ellerby LM, Hackam AS, Propp SS, et al: Kennedy's disease: Caspase cleavage of the androgen receptor is a crucial event in cytotoxicity. J Neurochem 72:185–195, 1999.
195. McCampbell A, Taylor JP, Taye AA, et al: CREB-binding protein sequestration by expanded polyglutamine. Hum Mol Genet 9:2197–2202, 2000.
196. Szebenyi G, Morfini GA, Babcock A, et al: Neuropathogenic forms of Huntington and androgen receptor inhibit fast axonal transport. Neuron 40:41–52, 2003.
197. Sopher BL, Thomas PS Jr, LaFevre-Bernt MA, et al: Androgen receptor YAC transgenic mice recapitulate SBMA motor neuronopathy and implicate VEGF164 in the motor neuron degeneration. Neuron 41:87–99, 2004.
198. Veldscholte J, Ris-Stalpers C, Kuiper G, et al: A mutation in the ligand binding domain of the androgen receptor of human LNCaP cells affects steroid binding characteristics and response to anti-androgens. Biochem Biophys Res Commun 173:534–540, 1990.
199. Taplin ME, Balk SP: Androgen receptor: a key molecule in the progression of prostate cancer to hormone independence. J Cell Biochem 91:83–90, 2004.
200. Taplin ME, Bubley GJ, Shuster TD, et al: Mutation of the androgen-receptor gene in metastatic androgen-independent prostate cancer. N Engl J Med 332:1393–1398, 1995.
201. Tilley WD, Buchanan G, Hickey TE, et al: Mutations in the androgen receptor gene are associated with progression of human prostate cancer to androgen independence. Clin Cancer Res 2:277–285, 1997.
202. Taplin ME, Bubley GJ, Ko YJ, et al: Selection for androgen receptor mutations in prostate cancers treated with androgen antagonist. Cancer Res 59:2511–2515, 1999.

# Androgen Deficiency Disorders

## Carolyn A. Allan and Robert I. McLachlan

## INTRODUCTION

The Leydig cells of the testis are the site of testosterone biosynthesis, and are intimately related to the seminiferous tubules, which are the source of spermatozoa. Testosterone is secreted under the influence of pituitary luteinizing hormone (LH), whereas follicle-stimulating hormone (FSH) acts directly on the Sertoli cell to promote spermatogenesis. The juxtaposition of Leydig cells and the seminiferous epithelium has functional significance for reproduction, as spermatogenesis is dependent on androgens being present in high local concentration. In many men undergoing investigation for infertility, their defect appears related only to the seminiferous epithelium, as androgen deficiency is not common. There are those with congenital and acquired disorders of spermatogenesis, however, in whom both androgen deficiency and impaired fertility are present. Androgen deficiency can be defined as a lack of adequate androgen-dependent gene expression resulting from defective androgen production and/or action, which results in a diverse range of physiologic and clinical expressions. In this chapter, disorders featuring androgen deficiency have been broadly classified as being of primary testicular origin or being secondary to inadequate gonadotropic stimulation. Systemic disorders and drug therapies that affect testosterone production are discussed separately as they often involve elements of both. The controversial issue of androgen deficiency in the aging male,

the uncertainties that exist with regard to the diagnostic criteria for hypoandrogenism, and the potential benefits and risks of androgen replacement are also reviewed.

## CLINICAL FEATURES OF ANDROGEN DEFICIENCY

The features of androgen deficiency depend on the age of onset and its severity and duration. Intersex disorders and abnormal in utero androgen exposure are dealt with in other chapters. Prepubertal hypoandrogenism manifests as microphallus and testicular maldescent, and, later, with delayed puberty and, because of the failure of closure of the epiphyseal growth plates, excessive long bone growth leading to eunuchoid proportions. The postpubertal onset of testosterone deficiency produces a number of typical features (Table 170-1), although the clinical scenario may vary depending on the rate and extent of the fall in testosterone levels. In some cases, the diagnosis is easily appreciated; however, an affected individual may have a limited number of features of insidious onset that may be overlooked. A striking example of this is the failure to diagnose more than half of all men with Klinefelter syndrome during their lifetime,[1] and yet, almost invariably, comprehensive clinical examination reveals salient features. An important practical indicator is examination of the testes, which should be part of any complete evaluation of male reproductive function.

| Table 170-1 | Clinical Features of Postpubertal Onset Hypoandrogenism |
| --- | --- |

**GENERAL**
Lethargy, fatigue
Decreased strength and/or endurance
Loss of height
Low mood, irritability, poor concentration, impaired short-term memory, tendency to fall asleep
Deteriorating work performance
Headaches
Hot flushes

**ORGAN-SPECIFIC**
Bone: osteopenia, osteoporosis
Muscle: sarcopenia, esp. pectoral girdle
Adipose: increase fat mass
Gynecomastia

**SEXUAL/REPRODUCTIVE**
Decreased libido
Erectile dysfunction (uncommon)

| Table 170-2 | Causes of Hypogonadotropic Hypogonadism |
| --- | --- |

**CONGENITAL HYPOGONADOTROPIC HYPOGONADISM (HH)**
Isolated gonadotropin deficiency
  Idiopathic hypogonadotropic hypogonadism (IHH)
  Kallmann's syndrome
  Non-X-linked
  Partial HH (fertile eunuch syndrome)
Associated with CNS disorders
  Prader-Willi syndrome
  Laurence-Moon-Biedl syndrome
  Möbius' syndrome
  Lowe's syndrome
  Noonan's syndrome
  LEOPARD syndrome
  X-linked ichthyosis
Genetic defects
  GnRH Receptor gene mutations
  FGFR1
  GPR54
  Adrenal hypoplasia congenita
Multiple pituitary hormone deficiency

**ACQUIRED HH**
Organic lesions
  Tumors
    Craniopharyngiomas
    Pituitary adenomas (e.g., prolactinoma, nonfunctioning tumor)
    Meningioma
  Pituitary apoplexy
  Infiltrative disorders
    Sarcoidosis, hemochromatosis, histiocytosis X
  Head trauma
  Leydig cell tumors, choriocarcinoma
  CNS radiation therapy
Systemic disorders affecting the HPT axis
  Critical illness including burns
  Extreme exercise
  Malnutrition (anorexia nervosa)
  Morbid obesity
  Anabolic steroid abuse
  Glucocorticoid excess (endogenous, i.e., Cushing's syndrome/exogenous)
  Narcotics

HPT, hypothalamic-pituitary-testicular.

## HYPOGONADOTROPIC HYPOGONADISM

*Hypogonadotropic hypogonadism (HH)* is the term for disorders in which testicular function is impaired because gonadotropic stimulation is inadequate. Gonadotropin deficiency may occur selectively or may coexist with a deficiency of other pituitary hormones. It may be congenital or acquired and may result from pathology intrinsic to the pituitary gland or from impairment in the hypothalamic control of pituitary gonadotropin secretion. HH may be broadly classified into congenital or acquired disorders (Table 170-2).

### IDIOPATHIC HYPOGONADOTROPIC HYPOGONADISM

Idiopathic hypogonadotropic hypogonadism (IHH) is a heterogeneous disorder with a prevalence of approximately 1 in 10,000. Most cases are sporadic, although X-linked and autosomal forms are recognized.[2,3] Most affected individuals are males, usually presenting as teenagers with deficient sexual maturation. They have a male phenotype because maternal human chorionic gonadotropin (hCG) stimulates the fetal testis to produce testosterone, thereby masculinizing the genitalia. Unilateral or bilateral cryptorchidism and microphallus may occur, however, probably because of relative androgen deficiency in the third fetal trimester. Linear growth and childhood development are normal, but the growth rate falls off in the teenage years because no adolescent growth spurt occurs.[4] In untreated young adults, bone age is delayed in comparison to chronologic age. Severe osteopenia develops[5] because the sex hormone–mediated increase in bone density of adolescence fails to occur. The long bones grow excessively in length due to delayed epiphyseal closure with resultant "eunuchoid body proportions"; that is, the arm span exceeds the height, and the upper-to-lower segment ratio is less than 0.9 (Fig. 170-1). Patients also tend to be tall.[6] Testis volume is variable and ranges from a prepubertal value of less than 4 mL to nearly normal adult size. Gynecomastia is common. Some pubic hair growth is often seen as a result of the production of androgens by the adrenal glands.[7] Psychological problems may occur because of delayed sexual development.

In most cases, the testes have a prepubertal histologic appearance. The seminiferous tubules are small and contain immature Sertoli cells that are round and may be pseudostratified. A few gonocytes with clear cytoplasm and a central nucleolus are present in the center of the seminiferous tubule. The interstitium is composed of loose connective tissue.

Mature Leydig cells are absent, but fibroblast-like precursor cells are found (Fig. 170-2).

Serum testosterone levels in most patients are at the low levels characteristic of prepubertal boys, and serum LH levels are barely detectable even with highly sensitive two-site assays[8,9] (Fig. 170-3). LH secretion is generally apulsatile, but a few low-amplitude fluctuations occur in some patients, which presumably reflect attenuated episodes of gonadotropin-releasing hormone (GnRH) secretion. Prolonged pulsatile administration of GnRH usually induces full pubertal development, thus indicating that most cases of IHH are due to a lack of normal stimulation of the pituitary by endogenous GnRH.[10] The secretion of other pituitary hormones is normal.[11] Growth hormone (GH) secretion is reduced slightly because of the sex steroid deficiency and increases to adult values during treatment with testosterone or hCG.[12]

Other patients have less pronounced clinical signs of hypogonadism and variable testis enlargement, and their signs may be unappreciated until adulthood (see Fig. 170-1C). Basal LH, FSH, and testosterone levels and the gonadotropin response to GnRH stimulation are greater in these men than in men with complete gonadotropin deficiency.[13] Spontaneous LH pulses of reduced amplitude and/or frequency can often be detected in the circulation, sometimes with augmentation during sleep.[13,14] Because of evidence of

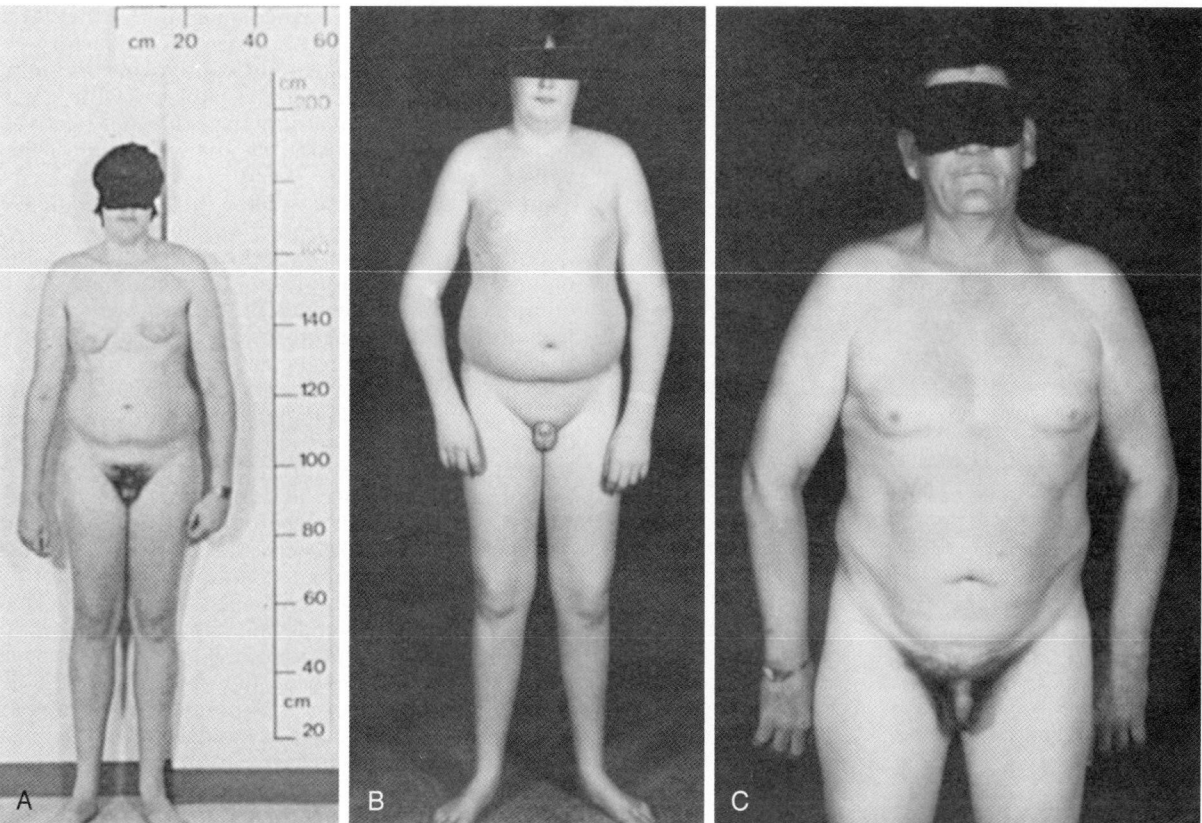

*Figure 170-1* **A**, An 18-year-old male with isolated hypogonadotropic hypogonadism. Note the normal height, long arms and legs, poor muscular development, and prominent gynecomastia. Although his testes and phallus are small, pubic hair is present. It is very unusual for normal boys to have pubic hair growth before the genitalia have begun to develop. **B**, A 13½-year-old boy with underdeveloped genitals, absent pubic hair, and gynecomastia. The normal relationship between genital development and pubic hair growth is preserved, and, in the ensuing year, spontaneous testis growth began, indicative of constitutional delay of puberty. **C**, A 51-year-old man with incomplete gonadotropin deficiency and osteoporosis. He had life-long hypogonadism, including two infertile marriages. His serum testosterone level was 125 ng/dL, and serum luteinizing hormone and follicle-stimulating hormone levels were in the low normal range. His testes were 10 mL in volume.

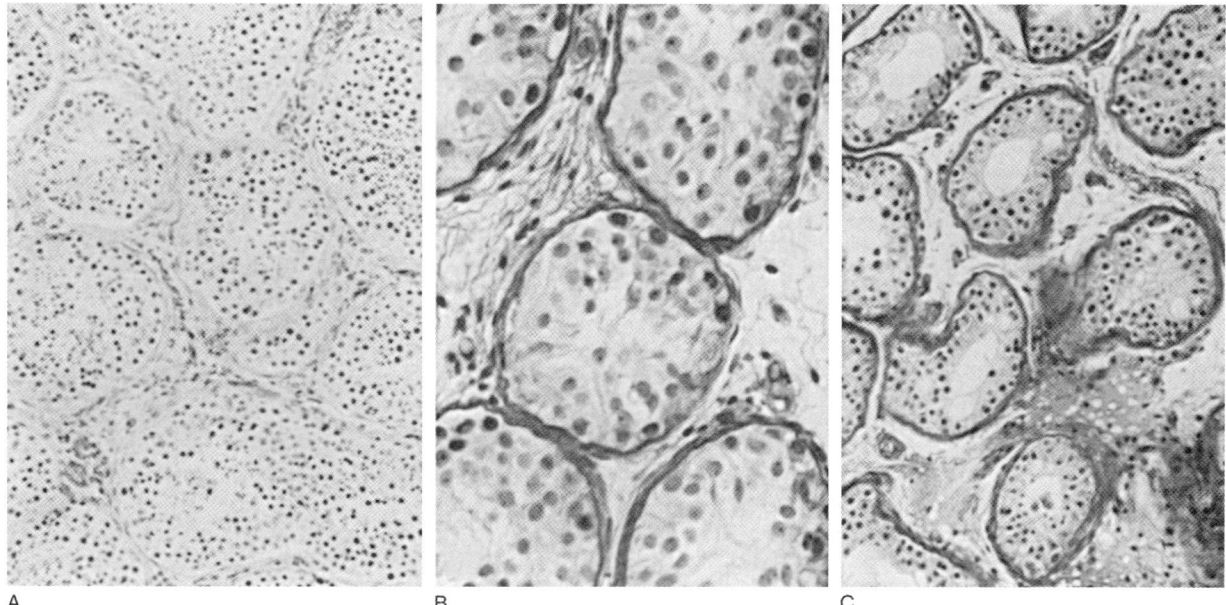

*Figure 170-2* **A**, Parenchyma of a normal adult testis. Seminiferous tubules have a cross-sectional diameter of 150 to 300 μm and are surrounded by a basement membrane and several layers of peritubular myoid cells. Sertoli cells, which extend from the basement membrane to the tubular lumen, have polygonal nuclei located at the basal portion of the cell that contain prominent nucleoli. An organized arrangement of germ cells is present, with various cell types predominating in different portions of the tubule. Spermatozoa predominate in some portions and spermatids in others. Between the seminiferous tubules is loose connective tissue containing single cells and clusters of Leydig cells (hematoxylin-eosin [H&E], ×50). **B**, Testicular biopsy from a patient with isolated hypogonadotropic hypogonadism. The seminiferous tubules are small (mean tubular diameter, 50 μm) and are lined by immature Sertoli cells and spermatogonia. A few primary spermatocytes are also present. The tunica propria is delicate. Interstitial cells are immature and resemble undifferentiated mesenchymal cells (H&E, ×125). **C**, Testicular biopsy from a patient with partial gonadotropin-releasing hormone deficiency. The seminiferous tubules are reduced in diameter (50 to 80 μm) and have incomplete spermatogenesis. Leydig cells are reduced in number (H&E, ×50).

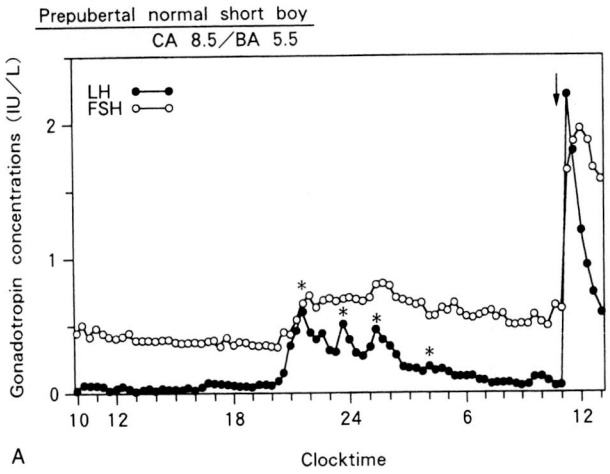

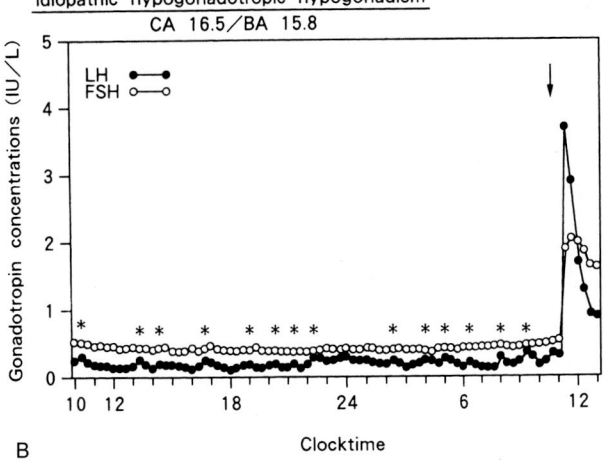

**Figure 170-3** Luteinizing hormone (LH) and follicle-stimulating hormone (FSH) levels in blood samples drawn every 20 minutes for 25 hours beginning at 10:00 A.M. in a prepubertal normal boy (**A**) and an untreated 16½-year-old with hypogonadotropic hypogonadism (**B**). The *arrows* indicate intravenous administration of gonadotropin-releasing hormone at a dose of 25 ng/kg. Plasma LH and FSH levels were measured by DELFIA time-resolved immunofluorometric assays. *Asterisks* indicate pulses scored by the cluster algorithm. BA, bone age; CA, chronologic age. (From Goji K, Tanikaze S: Comparison between spontaneous gonadotropin concentration profiles and gonadotropin response to low-dose gonadotropin-releasing hormone in prepubertal and early pubertal boys and patients with hypogonadotropic hypogonadism: Assessment by using ultrasensitive, time-resolved immunofluorometric assay. Pediatr Res 31:535–539, 1992.)

testis growth and spermatogenesis, but with incomplete androgenization, the term *fertile eunuch* has been applied to these men, but *partial gonadotropin deficiency* is preferred.

## Kallmann's Syndrome

Male hypogonadism with anosmia, first described by Maestre de San Juan in 1856, is now designated as *olfactogenital dysplasia* to emphasize the association between agenesis of the olfactory bulbs and hypogonadism, and the first familial cases were reported by Kallmann and colleagues in 1944.[15] Among affected kindreds, the high male-to-female ratio is consistent with an X-linked trait, although kindreds with apparent autosomal-dominant or -recessive modes of inheritance with variable penetrance are also described.[3] Peripheral leukocyte karyotypes are generally normal.

Anosmia or hyposmia is present in 33% to 50% of men with complete IHH and less frequently in patients with par-

tial IHH. Magnetic resonance imaging (MRI) reveals that the anosmia results from hypoplasia of the olfactory nerves and tracts.[16] Genital, somatic, and neurologic abnormalities may also occur[17–19] (Table 170-3). Subjects with gonadotropin deficiency and anosmia may have affected relatives without anosmia, thus demonstrating that the clinical features are variable.

Immunocytochemical studies in the fetal mouse showed that GnRH neurons migrate from the olfactory placode to the hypothalamus together with the central processes of olfactory nerves.[20] These findings, and the awareness that olfactory bulb development depends on contact between central projections of olfactory neurons and forebrain anlage, suggested that Kallmann's syndrome results from a neuron migration defect. Studies of a 19-week stillborn male fetus from a kindred with apparent Kallmann's syndrome associated with a deletion of the short arm of the X chromosome advanced this hypothesis.[21] Whereas GnRH-containing cells were present in the median eminence and preoptic area of age-matched fetuses, no GnRH cells were found in this fetal brain. Instead, dense clusters of GnRH cells were found in his nose, GnRH-containing fibers terminated abruptly on the cribriform plate, and the olfactory bulbs and tracts were absent. The gene for X-linked Kallmann's syndrome, the KAL gene, is found on the short arm of the X chromosome (Xp22.3). Various mutations in the KAL gene have been found in up to 50% of patients with X-linked Kallmann's syndrome.[22] This gene encodes the protein anosmin, which is homologous with neural cell adhesion proteins and is believed to guide axonal growth. The resulting failure of GnRH neuronal migration leads to profound HH and, consequently, a high frequency of failed sexual development, cryptorchidism, and microphallus. There is also variability in the clinical phenotype related to the same mutation within families.[19,23]

Kallmann's syndrome may be associated with X-linked ichthyosis, which results from steroid sulfatase deficiency (STS gene); this gene is also localized to the pseudoautosomal region of the X chromosome. In these patients, large dark dry scales develop on the trunk and limbs because deficient aryl-sulfatase activity in keratinocytes leads to the accumulation of steroid sulfates. Large Xp deletions may produce a "contiguous gene syndrome" and involve the adjacent KAL gene.[22]

### Non-X-linked HH

It appears that autosomal gene mutations probably account for most familial HH. In one study of 36 familial cases with GnRH deficiency, only 21% could be attributed to X-linkage[18] and, when the data were extended to include surrogate markers of IHH (isolated congenital anosmia and delayed puberty), the X-linked pedigrees comprised 11%, autosomal recessive 25%, and autosomal dominant 64%. Some of these specific

| **Table 170-3** | **Congenital Defects Associated with Kallmann's Syndrome** | |
| --- | --- | --- |
| **Neurologic Defects** | **Genital Defects** | **Somatic Defects** |
| Anosmia | Cryptorchidism | Cleft lip |
| Nystagmus | Microphallus | Cleft palate |
| Sensorineural hearing loss | | Renal agenesis |
| Cerebellar ataxia | | Horseshoe kidney |
| Spastic paraplegia | | Pes cavus |
| Learning disability | | |
| Color blindness | | |
| Synkinesis | | |
| Seizures | | |

genetic defects have been identified, as discussed in the following sections.

## Specific Gene Mutations Causing HH

### GnRH Receptor Gene Mutations

The GnRH receptor gene is located on chromosome 4 and encodes a G protein–coupled 7-transmembrane domain receptor,[24] and mutations result in autosomal-recessive IHH.[25] Impairment of GnRH receptor expression and/or signaling may be complete or partial, the latter allowing some response to GnRH[26] and the resulting phenotype varies from complete HH (cryptorchidism, microphallus, undetectable gonadotropins) to one of partial HH with preserved fertility. GnRH receptor mutations appear to account for less than 2% of IHH cases. Of note is the fact that no mutation or deletion of the GnRH gene itself has been described in man.

### FGFR1 Gene

An autosomal-dominant variant of HH was recently identified from the study of patients with contiguous gene syndromes (including Kallmann's) in which the presence of overlapping deletions at 8p12–p11 led to analysis of the gene encoding fibroblast growth factor receptor-1 (FGFR1).[27] In 129 unrelated Kallmann's patients, heterozygous FGFR1 mutations were found in four familial and eight sporadic cases, consistent with an autosomal-dominant mode of inheritance. One patient born from a consanguineous union had a homozygous missense mutation and was severely affected with cleft palate, agenesis of the corpus callosum, and other defects. The authors suggested that FGFR1 signaling involves the product of the KAL1 gene (anosmin-1) involved in X-linked Kallmann's. In support of this, some patients with FGFR1 mutations had somatic anomalies typical of X-linked Kallmann's such as cleft palate/lip, dental agenesis, and synkinesia. In a recent Japanese study, both KAL1 and FGFR1 mutations were found in Kallmann's syndrome families[19] with a variable expression of HH within families. In addition, the presence of somatic abnormalities varied between subjects with the same mutations, and were evident in members without demonstrable mutations.

### GPR54 Gene

Linkage analysis on chromsome19p13[28] in HH siblings of a large consanguineous family identified a new autosomal-recessive cause of HH involving a 155-bp deletion in GPR54, a G protein–coupled receptor gene. Coincidently, a role for GPR54 in regulating puberty was proposed after detection of a homozygous mutation of this gene in another consanguineous family.[29]

### Adrenal Hypoplasia Congenita

HH may occur in adrenal hypoplasia congenita (AHC), a rare disorder usually seen in neonates, featuring hypotension, hypoglycemia, hyponatremia, and hyperkalemia, which is generally fatal if not treated with glucocorticoids and mineralocorticoids,[30] although other cases present later in childhood. The severity of the HH phenotype is variable, with cryptorchidism sometimes being present. The DAX1 gene, located on Xp21, is responsible for AHC and encodes a member of the orphan nuclear hormone superfamily.[31] DAX1 and a second transcription factor, steroidogenic factor-1 (SF-1), colocalize in the testis, ovary, adrenal cortex, pituitary, and hypothalamus. Null mutations in these genes produce a similar phenotype lacking adrenal glands and gonads, which suggests that the function of DAX1 and SF-1 is interrelated.[32]

Stimulation with pulsatile GnRH usually fails to increase gonadotropin secretion, although responses in some cases suggest an underlying problem with endogenous GnRH production.[33] The existence of a primary testicular defect in some cases is suggested by the failure of hCG to induce normal spermatogenesis.[26]

## CONGENITAL HYPOGONADISM WITH OTHER CENTRAL NERVOUS SYSTEM DISORDERS

In a variety of other syndromes, neurologic abnormalities are associated with hypogonadism (Table 170-4). In some of these conditions, patients may not reach adulthood, and delayed puberty rather than hypogonadism may be present.

The Prader-Willi syndrome (PWS), characterized by neonatal hypotonia, obesity, short stature, small hands and feet, mental retardation, and hypogonadism,[34] is diagnosed mostly in childhood. The prevalence of PWS approximates 1 in 25,000, males and females are affected equally, and most cases are sporadic. Deletions of chromosome 15q of paternal origin are generally present. Subjects often fail to complete puberty spontaneously, although some patients may have early pubarche or, more rarely, precocious puberty. In one study of 42 males, all had cryptorchidism (86% bilateral), with small testes and scrotal hypoplasia being present in 76% and 69%, respectively.[35] Total testosterone levels are low but exceed those of prepubertal boys. Basal LH and FSH concentrations are reduced, and the acute response to GnRH is attenuated.[36] Treatment with clomiphene may stimulate gonadotropin secretion, as may long-term treatment with GnRH.[37] These data suggest suppression of GnRH secretion through an obesity-associated increase in circulating estrogen concentrations, but this mechanism would not explain the findings of cryptorchidism and microphallus, which imply an intrauterine disturbance. Moreover, patients with PWS are GH deficient, with evidence of hypothalamic dysfunction.[38] Cryptorchidism may further damage the testes, which would explain the subnormal testosterone response to long-term treatment with hCG. Testosterone treatment is indicated in selected patients.

Patients with the Laurence-Moon-Biedl syndrome have pigmented retinal dystrophy, obesity, mental retardation, polydactyly, renal structural abnormalities, spastic paraparesis, and hypogonadism.[39] The designation *Bardet-Biedl syndrome* is often used in the absence of spastic paraparesis. The reproductive features are variable and include delayed puberty, microphallus, and, in adulthood, small testes and sterility. Testosterone levels are usually normal, and FSH and LH levels are increased or normal.[40] The disorder is often inherited as an autosomal-recessive trait, but its cause is unknown.

Congenital oculofacial paralysis (Möbius' syndrome) is characterized by cranial nerve paralysis and includes eye movement disorders, seizures, mental retardation, gait disturbance, limb anomalies (Poland's syndrome), and hypogonadism.[41] It is suggested to represent a syndrome of rhombencephalic maldevelopment involving motor nuclei and axons, in addition to traversing long tracts, but feeding

| Table 170-4 | Clinical Syndromes of Hypogonadism and Neurologic Dysfunction |
| --- | --- |

Kallmann's syndrome
Prader-Willi syndrome
Laurence-Moon-Bardet-Biedl syndrome
Möbius' syndrome
Lowe's syndrome
Noonan's syndrome
Multiple lentigenes (LEOPARD) syndrome
Carpenter's syndrome

LEOPARD, lentigenes (multiple), electrocardiographic conduction abnormalities, ocular hypertelorism, pulmonary stenosis, abnormal genitalia, retardation of growth, deafness (sensorineural).

and respiratory problems and poor motor development suggest a regional developmental disorder.[42] Several patients have had documented gonadotropin deficiency.[43]

Lowe's syndrome is a rare X-linked disorder characterized by bilateral congenital cataracts, hypotonia, mental retardation, renal tubular acidosis, and hypogonadism. It is caused by loss-of-function mutations of the OCRL gene, encoding an inositol polyphosphate 5-phosphatase,[44] which leads to abnormal actin cytoskeleton structure and abnormal formation and function of tight and adherens junctions.[45]

Noonan's syndrome features multiple congenital anomalies, including a characteristic facies, valvular heart disease, short stature, and hypogonadism. In one series, 77% of affected males had cryptorchidism.[46] Noonan's syndrome is an autosomal-dominant condition affecting 1 in 1000 to 2500 births; however, 50% of cases are sporadic.[47] In half the patients, the gene has been mapped to chromosome 12[48] and involves missense mutations in the protein-tyrosine-phosphatase, non-receptor-type II (PTPNII) gene that encodes a protein called SHP2. This protein is essential in intracellular signaling pathways involved in development. Cryptorchidism is associated with features of primary testicular failure, including hypospermatogenesis and androgen deficiency,[49] although a patient with idiopathic hypopituitarism and Noonan's syndrome was reported.[50]

The multiple lentigenes (LEOPARD) syndrome is an autosomal disorder characterized by lentigenes (L), electrocardiographic conduction defects (E), ocular hypertelorism (O), pulmonic stenosis (P), abnormal genitalia (A), retarded growth (R), and deafness (D). The clinical features of LEOPARD syndrome are similar to those of Noonan's syndrome. Recently, a different mutation in the PTPNII gene was described, leading to the hypothesis that some PTPNII mutations are associated with the typical Noonan phenotype, but that others are associated with both the Noonan phenotype and features such as multiple lentigines or café-au-lait spots.[51]

Carpenter's syndrome is an autosomal-recessive disorder in which hypogonadism is associated with obesity, acrocephaly, craniosynostosis, and agenesis of the hands and feet.

## IDIOPATHIC PARTIAL HYPOPITUITARISM AND PANHYPOPITUITARISM

HH may occur together with other pituitary hormone deficiencies, most commonly GH deficiency.[52] The sella turcica is often small, and contrast-enhanced MRI reveals a small pituitary gland, a poorly developed pituitary stalk, and superior dislocation of the neurohypophysis.[53] Because of the association with adverse perinatal events, such as breech birth or urgent cesarean birth, trauma to the stalk vasculature has been suggested to cause this syndrome. The presence of micropenis in some patients, however, implies a disturbance that began earlier in gestation and impaired GH responsiveness to GH-releasing hormone stimulation suggests a hypothalamic disorder. Multiple classes of transcription factors determine the development of the anterior gland. One gene, prophet of pit-1 (Prop-1), is important in the development of Pit-1 lineages, that is, somatotrophs, lactotrophs, and thyrotrophs as well as gonadotrophs. Thus, patients with combined gonadotropin, GH, prolactin (PRL), and thyroid-stimulating hormone (TSH) deficiency often have Prop-1 gene mutations.[54] The same Prop-1 mutation may produce a variable phenotype in terms of hormonal deficiencies and their time of onset, underlining the need for continuous follow-up[55] (see Chapters 6 and 16).

## ACQUIRED HYPOGONADOTROPIC HYPOGONADISM

### Mass Lesions of the Sella and Suprasellar Region
Gonadotropin deficiency may result from a space-occupying lesion (including hemorrhage) within the sella that com-presses and destroys the normal pituitary gland, or from a suprasellar lesion that interrupts the nerve fibers bringing GnRH to the hypophyseal portal circulation. In addition to having hypogonadism, these men often have headaches and visual disturbances, which are characteristic symptoms of a cranial base mass lesion, and variable manifestations of panhypopituitarism. Effects of surgery or external beam radiation therapy to the hypothalamus-pituitary may further damage the endocrine function of the pituitary.[56] Pituitary tumors secreting adrenocorticotropic hormone (ACTH) or PRL produce hypogonadism by specific hormonal mechanisms, as described in the following sections.

### Cushing's Syndrome
Decreased libido, erectile dysfunction, and infertility are common complaints among men with Cushing's syndrome resulting from ACTH-producing pituitary adenomas, adrenal tumors, or tumors outside the pituitary that produce ACTH. Serum testosterone levels are usually low, and basal and GnRH-stimulated LH concentrations are frequently suppressed.[57] Increased cortisol production appears to be responsible for the gonadotropin deficiency because adrenalectomy or treatment with mitotane or the glucocorticoid antagonist mifepristone (RU486) restores LH secretion and gonadal function,[58] and because glucocorticoids have been shown to decrease transcriptional activity of the mouse GnRH gene.[59] The action of glucocorticoids to induce aromatase activity in fibroblasts[60] may also contribute to the hypogonadism and gynecomastia. Decreased sex hormone–binding globulin (SHBG) levels further lower the total testosterone concentration. Prolonged glucocorticoid treatment of men with otherwise normal testicular function also produces gonadotropin deficiency.[61] The combination of hypogonadism and hypercortisolemia leads to loss of muscle mass, weakness, and osteopenia.

### Prolactin-Producing Pituitary Adenomas
Men with prolactinomas were often first seen late in the course of their disease with headaches, disturbed vision secondary to enlargement of the pituitary adenoma, and panhypopituitarism.[62,63] Recognition of microprolactinomas because of earlier evaluation of patients with reduced libido and potency, clinical hypogonadism, gynecomastia, or infertility is now common, however. Teenage boys with delayed pubertal development should also be evaluated for prolactinoma.[64] The frequent finding of eunuchoid body proportions in adult men with prolactinomas dates the onset of the tumor to adolescence. In spite of very high levels of prolactin in serum, only about 10% to 20% of men with prolactinomas have galactorrhea,[65] presumably because circulating estrogen levels are too low to stimulate mammary gland growth and development.

Serum testosterone levels are low in 50% to 74% and 73% to 93% of men with micro- and macroprolactinomas, respectively.[65,66] Serum LH levels parallel those of testosterone, and the attenuated pulsatile pattern of LH secretion found[67] indicates that a decline in LH secretion is responsible for the reduced testosterone production. The nature of the defect appears to be in GnRH secretion because pulsatile treatment with GnRH can restore testicular function to normal.[68] Studies using in situ hybridization techniques in rats with experimental hyperprolactinemia have demonstrated a reduction in GnRH mRNA levels per cell and a resulting decline in GnRH receptor concentration. Reduced semen quality can be present and semen volume low, reflecting reduced androgen action on accessory sex glands.[65] Treatment of micro- and macroprolactinomas with dopamine agonists, bromocriptine, and cabergoline suppresses serum prolactin levels into the normal range in 75% to 83% of micro- and macroadenomas,[65,66] with a prompt rise in LH and testosterone concentrations, although maximum testosterone levels may not be achieved for several months. Libido and erectile function usually improve,[69] as does semen quality.[65] In cases in which prolactin levels are not normalized by cabergoline, or in those with large pituitary tumors in whom gonadotroph number is inadequate, serum LH and testosterone production remain low and testosterone treatment is required. If sperm production remains abnormal when prolactinomas are incompletely cured, spermatogenesis can be stimulated with gonadotropins. The finding that sexual dysfunction may not improve with testosterone replacement alone, whereas coadministration of dopamine agonists and testosterone may increase libido and potency,[62] suggests a direct inhibitory action of prolactin on a central nervous system (CNS) center controlling sexual arousal.

## Miscellaneous Causes of Gonadotropin Deficiency

Infiltrative disorders may affect the hypothalamic-pituitary region. Histiocytosis X may involve the basal hypothalamus, as well as the skeleton, skin, and lungs. Diabetes insipidus and GH deficiency appear to be the most common endocrine disturbances,[70] but HH has been reported.[71] Contrast-enhanced MRI may reveal thickening of the pituitary stalk. Sarcoidosis of the hypothalamic-pituitary region is uncommon, but may cause anterior pituitary hormone deficiency, diabetes insipidus, and hyperprolactinemia.[72] Imaging studies may reveal a solid or cystic sellar or suprasellar mass or pituitary stalk thickening.[73]

Gonadotropin deficiency due to sex steroid feedback may occur in men with Leydig cell tumors of the testis[74] or with benign or malignant tumors of the adrenal cortex that produce estradiol or estrone. Gynecomastia may be the initial complaint in these men, and testosterone levels may be reduced.[75] Computed tomography of the adrenal glands and testicular sonography can be used to identify these tumors.

The production of hCG by a choriocarcinoma may increase circulating levels of estrone and estradiol sufficiently to produce gynecomastia and suppress pituitary gonadotropin secretion.[76] hCG also stimulates Leydig cell testosterone production, but the testis may be replaced by tumor or damaged by X-irradiation or chemotherapy, so serum testosterone levels are variable.[77] Secondary HH may also be induced by sex steroid administration (e.g., anabolic steroid abuse) as discussed later.

## SELECTIVE DEFICIENCY OF LUTEINIZING OR FOLLICLE-STIMULATING HORMONE

Naturally occurring mutations of the gonadotropins and their receptors, although rare, provide fascinating insights into their structural and functional relationships.[78] Selective deficiency of LH or FSH is exceedingly rare. A single case has been reported of a man with sexual infantilism, low serum testosterone, and an elevated immunoreactive serum LH level.[79] Unlike patients with testicular failure, however, after stimulation with hCG, the dramatic increase in serum testosterone level was sufficient to produce sexual maturation and even some spermatogenesis. A biologically inactive LH molecule in serum results from a missense mutation in exon 3 of LH-β, which is important in receptor binding and activation of the signal transduction mechanism. This patient was homozygous for the mutant LH-β arising from consanguineous parents.

LH-β sequence variants, representing polymorphisms, were identified when a specific monoclonal antiserum to the LH-α/β dimer was unable to recognize LH in serum and urine.[80] The LH-β variant, caused by two point mutations, was found in 24% of a healthy Finnish population. The variant protein had increased bioactivity in vitro and altered glycosylation, but men with this variant are not hypoandrogenic.

Two cases of isolated FSH deficiency have been described, one with normal serum LH and testosterone[81] and a second

case of an 18-year-old boy with delayed puberty, very small testes, and undetectable serum FSH level before and after stimulation with GnRH, who unexpectedly had a low serum testosterone and elevated LH, suggesting a concomitant defect of Leydig cell function.[82]

Gonadotropin receptor mutations are more common than those of the gonadotropins. Men homozygous for an inactivating mutation in the FSH receptor gene were identified by screening male relatives of affected women with primary ovarian failure.[83] The five men reported were normally virilized, but had small testes and variable sperm concentrations ranging from less than 0.1 to 42 million/mL. In all subjects, serum FSH levels were moderately elevated and inhibin-B levels were reduced, but testosterone levels were normal. Mutations causing activation of the LH receptor gene produce male limited gonadotropin-independent precocious puberty (testotoxicosis) (see Chapter 147), whereas inactivating LH receptor mutations cause Leydig cell hypoplasia with fetal testosterone deficiency, leading to genital ambiguity, as discussed elsewhere.

## TREATMENT OF GONADOTROPIN-DEFICIENT MEN

Androgen deficiency in men with HH is treated with testosterone whenever fertility is not currently desired. In teenagers with congenital HH, androgen treatment stimulates body and facial hair growth, penile enlargement, muscle development, voice deepening, libido and potency, morning erections, and nocturnal emissions, and increases the hematocrit. Androgen treatment stimulates GH production by increasing the amplitude of spontaneous secretory episodes[12] and thereby contributes to the adolescent growth spurt and increase in bone mass.[84] Such physical changes also have an important psychologic impact. Only native testosterone preparations are recommended as they provide full virilization, are nonhepatotoxic, and are aromatizable to estradiol, as appears important for bone health.

Initiation of treatment in adolescents is recommended to begin at a lower dose in order to reduce dose-dependent side effects such as acne and gynecomastia; for example, testosterone cypionate or enanthate can be started at an initial dose of 75 mg monthly and gradually increased to a full replacement dose of 200 mg every 2 weeks over a period of 2 to 3 years. Although published experience is limited, transdermal testosterone patches or hydroalcoholic gels may be an alternative, with initial treatment delivering 2.5 mg daily restricted to overnight application to simulate normal puberty and a gradual increase to full replacement doses of 5 mg daily. Historically, when the differential diagnosis is between IHH and constitutional delay of puberty, androgen treatment was often postponed until 18 years of age to determine the correct diagnosis. Given the decreased peak bone mass that occurs with sex steroid deficiency during the teenage years[85] and the social ridicule to which androgen-deficient teenagers are exposed, it seems more appropriate to begin androgen treatment by 14 to 15 years of age to produce clinical changes and to withdraw therapy sometime thereafter to reevaluate endogenous androgen production.

In HH, hCG can be used as an LH substitute to stimulate testicular testosterone production with effective virilization, and in contrast to treatment with testosterone, also stimulates testicular growth. Generally, doses of 1000 to 1500 IU twice weekly are used because this dose sustains adult serum testosterone levels for 4 to 7 days. For reasons of convenience, this is now administered by subcutaneous, rather than intramuscular, injection, whereby it works equally well. Induction of testicular aromatase during hCG treatment may produce high serum estradiol levels and gynecomastia. Because of cost factors and the need for frequent injections, hCG treatment is usually only initiated when fertility is desired. Treatment with testosterone for many years does not preclude a favorable response to hCG.[86]

Although LH and FSH are both required for quantitatively normal spermatogenesis, selected patients with IHH may produce spermatozoa and successfully impregnate their partners when treated with hCG alone. Potential responders can be identified when the pretreatment testis size is greater than the 3-mL volume characteristic of prepubertal boys; this volume indicates some endogenous gonadotropin secretion and, therefore, partial gonadotropin deficiency (Fig. 170-4).[87] Treatment efficacy is assessed by clinical observation and sequential determination of serum testosterone and semen analysis. Among responders, testes grow to a volume of 12 to 15 mL and spermatozoa usually appear in the ejaculate within 12 months of starting treatment. hCG alone is generally successful in restoring spermatogenesis in men with pituitary or suprasellar tumors that develop postpubertally[88] (Fig. 170-5). hCG alone may also restore sperm production in men with IHH who previously required both hCG and FSH to initiate spermatogenesis.[89]

Most patients with IHH require treatment with FSH as well as hCG to induce spermatogenesis. This group includes patients with complete HH whose pretreatment testis volume is less than 4 mL and men with larger testes at baseline whose testes fail to grow to volumes of 12 to 15 mL with hCG treatment and who remain azoospermic.[87] All men are generally pretreated with hCG for 6 months before adding FSH. Recombinant human FSH is now widely used in favor of urinary-derived products. The usual dose of FSH is 100 to 150 IU subcutaneously three times weekly. With this approach, more than two thirds of men will become sperm positive (>1 million/mL) if treatment is continued for 18 months,[90] and the pregnancy rate may reach 90%.[91] Most pregnancies occur with sperm counts below the normal range of 20 million/mL; indeed, the sperm concentration at the time of conception may be as low as 1 million/mL with the median sperm concentration reported to be only 5 millon/mL.[92]

Impaired Sertoli cell maturation related to an absent or attenuated postnatal surge in gonadotropin secretion, or to the effect of prolonged gonadotropin deficiency before beginning therapy, may limit the testicular response to treatment in adulthood. Patients with IHH and cryptorchidism tend to respond less well to therapy, although unilateral cryptorchidism does not preclude fertility[93] (see Fig. 170-5).

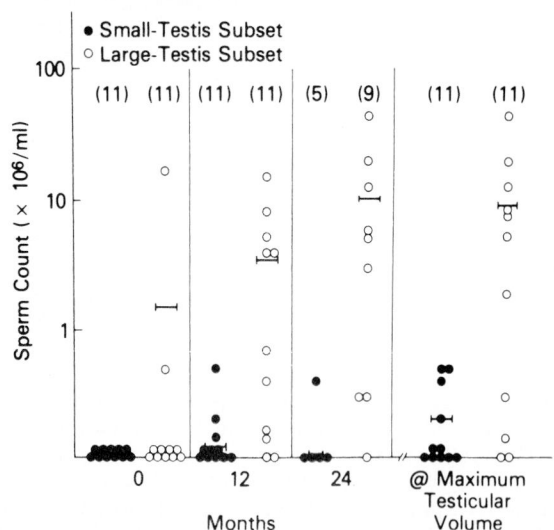

**Figure 170-4** Mean sperm concentration during human chorionic gonadotropin therapy in 22 men with isolated hypogonadotropic hypogonadism (IHH). Men in the small-testis subset (n = 11) had a mean testis volume of 3 mL or less at the start of the study, consistent with complete IHH. (From Burris AS, Robard HW, Winters SJ, Sherins RJ: Gonadotropin therapy in men with isolated hypogonadotropic hypogonadism: The response to human chorionic gonadotropin is predicted by initial testicular size. J Clin Endocrinol Metab 66:1144–1151, 1988.)

Because Kallmann's syndrome is a genetic disorder, the offspring may be affected.

GnRH can also be used to stimulate spermatogenesis in men with GnRH deficiency.[94] Programmable portable infusion pumps provide pulses of GnRH, which, for practical purposes, are given subcutaneously in the abdomen (rather than intravenously) every 2 hours in line with GnRH pulse frequency in normal men. A starting dose of 4 μg per pulse is often used, with increments of 2 μg every 4 weeks if LH and FSH secretions do not rise. Serum testosterone levels are usually in the normal adult range by 6 to 8 weeks. Pulsatile GnRH treatment increases testis size, sometimes dramatically, within

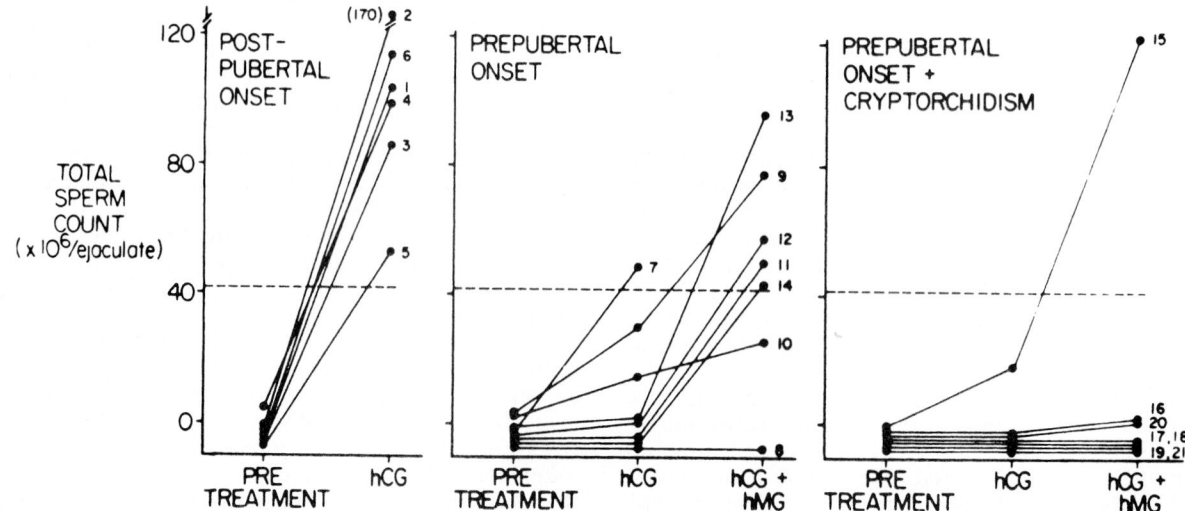

**Figure 170-5** Effects of treatment with human chorionic gonadotropin (hCG) alone and in combination with human menopausal gonadotropin (hMG) on sperm output in men with gonadotropin deficiency (GD). Men with GD of postpubertal onset had pituitary adenomas (two), craniopharyngioma (three), or unknown cause (one). Cryptorchidism (unilateral in six of seven) had been treated in childhood in men with GD of prepubertal onset. (Reprinted by permission from Finkel DM, Phillips JL, Snyder PJ: Stimulation of spermatogenesis by gonadotropins in men with hypogonadotropic hypogonadism. N Engl J Med 313:651–655, 1985. © 1985, Massachusetts Medical Society. All rights reserved.)

3 to 6 months of beginning treatment. As with hCG/FSH treatment, final testicular volume is greater in patients with partial GnRH deficiency, but the testes rarely grow to truly normal adult size. Sperm appear in the ejaculate in approximately two thirds of men treated with pulsatile GnRH, with sperm appearing in the ejaculate after 18 to 139 weeks of treatment. Sperm density is most often in the range of 1 to 10 million/mL in men with complete IHH, but sperm counts may reach 60 to 100 million/mL in men with partial gonadotropin deficiency.

One prospective but nonrandomized study compared hCG/FSH treatment with pulsatile GnRH treatment.[95] Testis size was increased more by GnRH than by hCG/FSH in men with complete IHH, and the time until spermatozoa first appeared in the ejaculate was less for GnRH than for hCG/FSH, 12 versus 20 months. No difference was found in sperm concentration between the two treatment groups, however (Fig. 170-6), and very few subjects were attempting to conceive. A more recent report has confirmed this result.[93] Poor patient compliance can be a limitation of pulsatile GnRH therapy, and allergic reactions[96] and GnRH-binding antibodies[97] may develop. Given the cost, complexity, and inconvenience of pulsatile GnRH therapy, hCG/FSH continues to be recommended as initial therapy, and GnRH is reserved for treatment failures and is generally only available through specialized centers.

For those men achieving a very low sperm count even after prolonged gonadotropin or GnRH therapy, assisted reproduction (specifically, intracytoplasmic sperm injection) provides another avenue for conception. Sperm cryopreservation should be considered after successful induction of spermatogenesis, so as to permit subsequent pregnancies through insemination rather than repeat gonadotropin therapy. If the second pregnancy is planned for shortly thereafter, continuation on hCG alone will probably maintain fertility. Otherwise, gonadotropin treatment should be continued until the beginning of the second trimester to ensure an ongoing pregnancy before reversion back to testosterone replacement therapy.

## PRIMARY TESTICULAR FAILURE

Disorders that damage the testes directly can result from congenital or acquired causes and be reflected by impairment in spermatogenesis and/or hypoandrogenism; the predominant clinical manifestation varies with the etiology (Table 170-5).

**Table 170-5** Causes of Primary Testicular Failure

| Congenital | Acquired |
|---|---|
| Klinefelter's syndrome | Trauma |
| 46,XX male | Torsion |
| Other chromosomal aneuploidies | Orchidectomy |
| Y-chromosome deletions | Orchitis |
| Noonan's syndrome | Chemo/radiotherapy |
| Congenital anorchia | HIV infection |
| Cryptorchidism | Chronic liver disease |
| Myotonic dystrophy | Autoimmune polyglandular failure |
| Hemoglobinopathies | Spinal cord injury |

The testes are usually reduced in size, men are subfertile or sterile, and symptomatic androgen deficiency is relatively common. When testosterone deficiency develops rapidly, as with orchitis, vasomotor symptoms comparable to those of the female climacteric may occur.[98] Elevated FSH and LH levels are markers of primary testicular failure, reflecting damage to the seminiferous tubule and Leydig cell components, respectively. Because the seminiferous tubules are more sensitive to damage than Leydig cells, FSH levels are often increased selectively, although a subtle disturbance in LH secretion is suggested by an exaggerated LH response to stimulation with GnRH.[99]

Gonadotropin production increases because negative feedback inhibition by sex steroids and inhibin B is decreased. The frequency and amplitude of LH secretory episodes are increased in men with testicular failure[100] (Fig. 170-7) and are reduced by testosterone replacement.[101] Direct sampling of GnRH in hypothalamic portal blood in orchiectomized rams reveals that GnRH pulse frequency is regulated by testosterone. The rise in LH pulse frequency that occurs during treatment with aromatase inhibitors or estrogen receptor antagonists implies that estrogens regulate the GnRH pulse generator in men as well.[102]

Increased FSH concentrations in testicular failure are also partly due to increased GnRH secretion; however, inhibin B is now known to be an important testicular regulator of FSH secretion through its action to suppress FSH-β gene expression. Circulating inhibin-B levels are inversely correlated with FSH among normal men,[103] and inhibin-B levels are less than normal in men with testicular failure.[104,105] A further discussion on inhibin B in testicular failure is presented elsewhere.

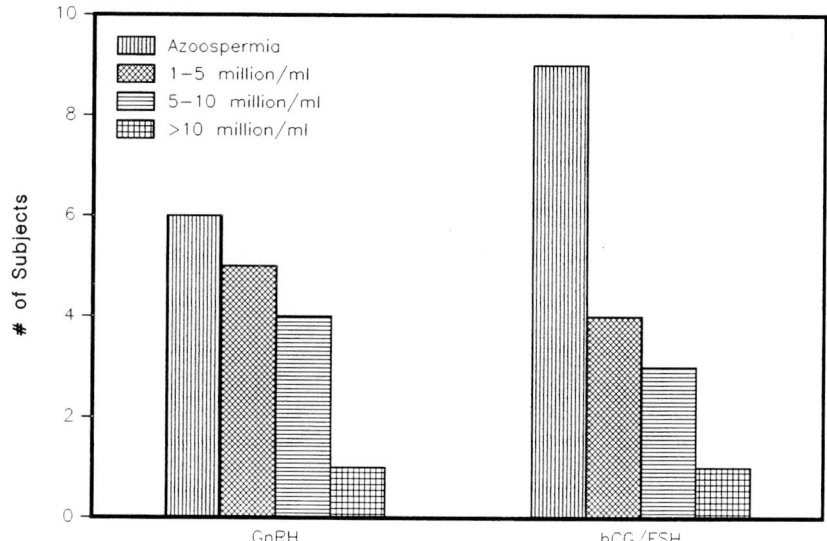

**Figure 170-6** Histogram showing the results of treatment of men with congenital gonadotropin-releasing hormone (GnRH) deficiency with pulsatile GnRH subcutaneously or human chorionic gonadotropin (hCG) human menopausal gonadotropin intramuscularly for 4 to 27 months. FSH, follicle-stimulating hormone. (Data from Schopohl J, Mehltretter G, von Zumbusch R, et al: Comparison of gonadotropin-releasing hormone and gonadotropin therapy in male patients with idiopathic hypothalamic hypogonadism. Fertil Steril 56:1143–1150, 1991.)

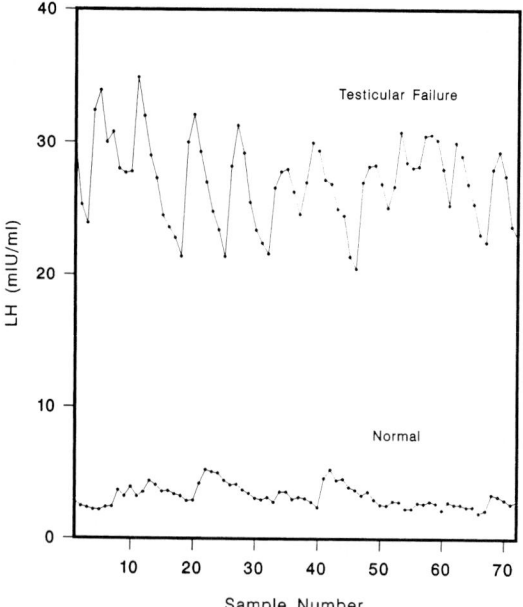

**Figure 170-7** Luteinizing hormone (LH) levels in serum samples drawn every 10 minutes for 12 hours beginning at 8:00 A.M. in a normal adult man aged 21 years and a 35-year-old man with bilateral cryptorchidism.

**Table 170-6** Clinical Features of Patients with Klinefelters Syndrome, Including 47,XXY and Variant Karyotypes

| Feature | Birth | Childhood | Puberty | Adulthood |
|---|---|---|---|---|
| Cryptorchidism | x | | | |
| Microphallus | x | | | |
| Hypospadias | x | | | |
| Somatic anomalies | x | | | |
| Learning disabilities | | x | x | x |
| Behavioral disorders | | x | x | x |
| Tall stature | | | x | x |
| Eunuchoid habitus | | | x | x |
| Delayed puberty | | | x | |
| Small testes | | | x | x |
| Delayed sex characteristics | | | x | x |
| Gynecomastia | | | x | x |
| Infertility | | | | x |
| Impaired libido | | | | x |
| Thyroid dysfunction | | | | x |

## KLINEFELTER SYNDROME

The phenotype of small testes, gynecomastia, a variable degree of eunuchoidism, and increased urinary gonadotropin excretion was recognized by Klinefelter and coworkers in 1942, and the 47,XXY karyotype was identified in 1959. Klinefelter syndrome is a common disorder with a prevalence of 1 in 500 to 640 men.[106] It is estimated that more than 50% of men are not diagnosed and that 90% of those identified are only diagnosed postpubertally, making Klinefelter syndrome the largest single unrecognized (and thus untreated) cause of androgen deficiency in young men.[1] It has clinical manifestations in many systems aside from infertility and androgen deficiency.[107,108]

Nondisjunction during the meiotic division of gametogenesis leads to the formation of spermatozoa containing both X and Y chromosomal material or to 24,XX ova.[109] Southern blotting using DNA probes to detect restriction site polymorphisms of the X chromosome indicates that the additional X is equally likely to be of maternal as of paternal origin.[110] A marked association has been found between advanced maternal age and maternally derived Klinefelter syndrome.[1] The 47,XXY karyotype may also arise from nondisjunction in the early embryo.

The clinical features of 47,XXY males are summarized in Table 170-6. Small testes and phallus and a tall, thin body habitus are clues to the diagnosis of Klinefelter syndrome in childhood, although these findings overlap with findings in normal boys.[111] Poor school performance and behavioral problems may also occur. When the diagnosis of Klinefelter syndrome is made, it is usually in teenage boys who have gynecomastia, incomplete pubertal development, or small testes. Estimates of the prevalence of gynecomastia range from 25% to 88%, depending on the method of examination. Some patients are initially seen in adulthood with similar complaints or with infertility. Virtually all patients with Klinefelter syndrome are azoospermic.[112] Typically, in adults, the seminiferous tubules are sclerotic, although a few tubules may contain Sertoli cells and sparse germ cells (Fig. 170-8), but, in other patients, foci of spermatogenesis and elongated spermatids are seen and allow sperm extraction for assisted reproduction (see later). Spermatogonia are seen in the pre-

pubertal testis and, although some initial testis growth is seen in early puberty, recent data suggest that germ cell depletion accelerates at this time, as serum FSH levels rise with a reciprocal fall in serum inhibin B.[113]

A large portion of 47,XXY men escape diagnosis life-long, presumably because they lack severe symptoms or because the phenotypic clues, especially the markedly reduced testis volumes, have, for whatever reason, escaped recognition. Life span is not affected, but quality of life is reduced due to androgen deficiency and the failure to recognize and address the associated educational and behavioral problems. There are no data about the relative prospects for establishing relationships, but an initial presentation with infertility is common.

Men with Klinefelter syndrome are at increased risk for certain associated medical conditions, although the lifetime risk

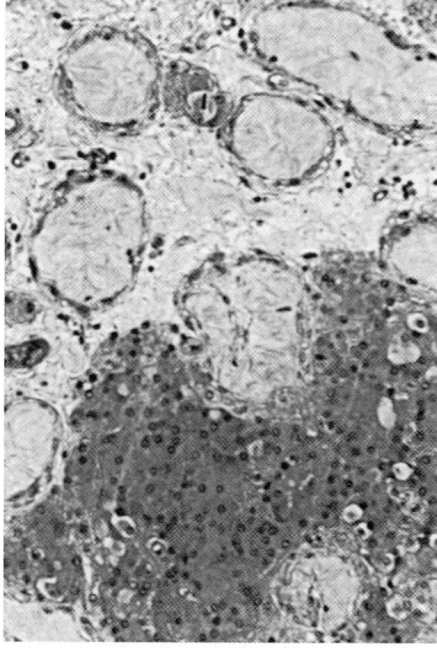

**Figure 170-8** Testicular biopsy from a patient with Klinefelter syndrome. The seminiferous tubules are reduced in diameter and are hyalinized. In many biopsy specimens, however, a few tubules containing Sertoli cells can be identified. The Leydig cells form large clumps between the sclerosed tubules. (Courtesy of CA Paulsen.)

for many is very low. The overall cancer death rate in a British study was increased 1.63-fold, with lung and breast cancer rates being increased.[114] Testicular or extragonadal nonseminomatous germ cell tumors, most often in the mediastinum, have also been described.[115] Immune disorders such as systemic lupus erythematosis, progressive systemic sclerosis, and thyroiditis appear to be more common in men with Klinefelter syndrome than in nonaffected men. Varicose veins and leg ulcers may occur in young adults. Somatic growth may be abnormal, with increased stature and long limbs, even before adolescence. Arm span in adults often exceeds their height, presumably because of delayed epiphyseal fusion. Bone density is reduced in men with the lowest testosterone levels.[116] Lower serum osteocalcin and higher urinary hydroxyproline excretion than in nonaffected men suggests that bone formation is decreased and resorption is increased. Gonadotroph hyperplasia and hypertrophy producing pituitary enlargement and simulating a pituitary adenoma have been reported in a few untreated patients.[117]

Patients with Klinefelter syndrome are prone to intellectual and emotional problems including anxiety and depression.[118] Many demonstrate a cognitive deficit in verbal processing, although nonverbal reasoning is unaffected.[108,119] A 20-year study of 36 unselected Klinefelter syndrome boys and 33 sibling controls showed a verbal cognitive deficit and significant problems in reading, spelling, and mathematics that were evident from early school years, such that, by late adolescence, the Klinefelter syndrome boys were about four grade levels behind. Nonetheless, many boys with Klinefelter syndrome had completed schooling, and a few were also pursuing postsecondary education.[120]

Serum LH and FSH levels are uniformly increased in men with Klinefelter syndrome (Table 170-7), thus indicating Leydig cell as well as seminiferous tubule dysfunction.[121] Serum inhibin-B levels are low or undetectable.[122] Mean serum testosterone levels are reduced, but, importantly, as many as one third of patients have total testosterone levels within the low-normal range. Both the testosterone production rate and the free testosterone concentration are often low, the latter due, in part, to increased SHBG levels, although not all studies have found SHBG to be increased in Klinefelter syndrome.[123] Inadequate Leydig cell function is confirmed by the attenuated testosterone response to hCG stimulation.[124] Leydig cell function declines in men with Klinefelter syndrome as they grow older, as it does in normal men. Serum estradiol levels are generally within the range of normal, although the conversion rate of radiolabeled testosterone to estradiol is greater than normal, perhaps because elevated LH levels stimulate testicular aromatase. The rise in estradiol relative to testosterone secretion may explain the exaggerated PRL response to thyrotropin-releasing hormone administration,[125] as well as the gynecomastia.

| Table 170-7 | Range of Hormone Values in Men with Klinefelter Syndrome versus Healthy Men | |
| --- | --- | --- |
| Hormone | Klinefelter Syndrome | Healthy Men |
| Serum LH (mIU/mL) | 4.25–12.7 (7.8)* | 0.62–2.81 (1.8) |
| Serum FSH (mIU/mL) | 12.1–61.2 (29.4) | 0.51–5.2 (2.7) |
| Plasma testosterone (ng/dL) | 81–849 (316) | 346–1075 (990) |
| Plasma estradiol (pg/mL) | 3–65 (34) | UD–34 (16) |

*Values in parentheses are the population means.
FSH, follicle-stimulating hormone; LH, luteinizing hormone; UD, not detectable.
From Wang C, Baker HWG, Burger HG, et al: Hormonal studies in Klinefelter's syndrome. Clin Endocrinol 4:399–411, 1975.

The decision to institute androgen replacement therapy depends on clinical judgment and biochemical confirmation. There are no controlled studies to provide guidance regarding the timing of testosterone initiation, but most suggest that, having recognized the condition, treatment be initiated during puberty so as to ensure normal progression with peers. Whether this will reduce manifestations such as gynecomastia and provide tangible benefits in term of psychosocial development remains to be established. Follow-up of testosterone-treated patients suggests that androgen replacement is associated with improved mood, school performance, work capacity, strength, libido, and erectile function.[126] Androgen replacement beginning before age 20 may be beneficial in preventing osteoporosis,[127] but earlier treatment may provide further benefit.

Clinical responses and serum testosterone levels, but not gonadotropin levels, should be used to monitor therapy, as testosterone suppresses gonadotropin secretion less effectively in men with Klinefelter syndrome than in normal men.[128] Testosterone treatment occasionally worsens gynecomastia because administered testosterone is aromatized to estradiol. Nearly all men with Klinefelter syndrome are sterile. Testicular sperm have been recovered, however, in about half the nonmosaic men with the syndrome and used to achieve pregnancy using intracytoplasmic sperm injection, with a low incidence of sex chromosomal aneuploidy in the patients' offspring.[129,130]

46,XY/47,XXY mosaicism, the most common cytogenetic variant of Klinefelter syndrome, accounts for approximately 20% of X chromatin–positive patients.[112] The karyotype of cultured skin fibroblasts or testicular cells may reveal a mosaic pattern not identified in peripheral leukocytes. Clinical abnormalities are generally less pronounced and seminiferous tubule damage is less severe in these men.[131] Spontaneous fertility may occur. Males with other sex chromosomal abnormalities, including 48,XXYY, 48,XXXY, and 49,XXXXY, have been reported.[132] These men are more likely to be short and mentally deficient, and to have unusual facies.

### OTHER SEX CHROMOSOME DISORDERS

Approximately 1 per 20,000 phenotypic men has a female (46,XX) sex chromosomal constitution.[133] The phenotype of these men is similar to that of men with Klinefelter syndrome, but short stature and hypospadias are more common. Frequent X-Y recombinations occur during normal male meiosis.[134] A region of the short arm of the Y chromosome, just proximal to the X-Y pairing region, contains a gene, SRY, that codes for a testis-determining factor.[135] Translocation of the SRY DNA sequence to the short arm of an X chromosome occurs in most 46,XX males.[136] About 10% of 46,XX males are SRY-negative, however, which indicates that other genes are required for male sex determination.[137] Absence of the Y genes that influence height may explain the short stature in 46,XX males. Testosterone levels are low, with elevated gonadotropins, and, postpubertally, there is a reduced response to hCG.[138]

The 47,XYY karyotype occurs in 1 per 1000 men; these are phenotypically normal males, but they are often tall and thin. Diagnosis is often incidental when karyotyping is undertaken for unrelated purposes. Testicular function is usually normal and no specific therapy is indicated, although patients with impaired spermatogenesis have been reported.[139] Most 47,XYY men are fertile and produce chromosomally normal 46,XX daughters and 46,XY sons. Preliminary data indicate that the prevalence of chromosomal abnormalities in sperm from 47,XYY men is similar to that of normal men, thus suggesting that the extra Y chromosome is eliminated in germ cells.[140] Psychological problems are increased; the prevalence of this abnormality in mental and mental-penal institute populations is 10-fold greater than in the general population. It has been estimated, however, that these men have only a 1% incidence of criminal behavior as compared with a 0.1% risk for normal men.

## CONGENITAL ANORCHIA

Congenital anorchia (vanishing testis syndrome) is the absence of testicular tissue in 46,XY phenotypic males. The condition is unilateral in 97% of cases and accounts for about 10% of cases in which the testis is absent from the scrotum or inguinal canal. Müllerian structures are absent and wolffian structures are normal, but the ipsilateral vas deferens is often rudimentary and the epididymis is absent. Instead, the vas deferens ends in a fibrovascular bundle that may be calcified and contain iron pigment.[141] Phenotypic males with bilateral anorchia may also be seen; the frequency is reported to be 1 in 20,000 males. Anorchia is a sporadic disorder, and bilateral anorchia has been reported in an identical twin whose brother was normal. Testicular function in the first trimester of fetal life must have been normal in these men, and one hypothesis is that descent into the scrotum is accompanied by testicular torsion. The sequence of the SRY gene, which codes for the testis-determining factor, appears to be normal.[142] At birth, the penis and scrotum are small. Boys with congenital anorchia are distinguished from those with bilateral abdominal cryptorchidism by MRI, laparoscopy, low serum levels of müllerian-inhibiting factor,[143] the failure of serum testosterone levels to increase after stimulation with hCG, or surgical exploration.[144] Inhibin B is undetectable in most boys with congenital anorchia, as in castrates, and may be helpful in determining the presence of intra-abdominal testes.[145] In bilateral anorchia, puberty fails to occur, and serum LH and FSH levels are in the castrate range. Rarely, evidence of limited Leydig cell function is seen, although no testes are found at surgery.[146] Life-long testosterone treatment is begun in the early teenage years. Unilateral anorchia does not require treatment. Testicular prostheses may be indicated for cosmetic or psychological reasons.

## CRYPTORCHIDISM AND SPERMATOGENIC FAILURE

Cryptorchidism is a common congenital anomaly with a prevalence of 2.7% at birth.[147] However, because testicular descent may occur in the newborn, this figure declines to about 1% at 3 months of age, where it remains into adulthood. A rising prevalence of cryptorchidism[147] and striking geographic differences have been reported. A linkage between its occurrence and that of testis cancer, hypospadias, and infertility has been drawn under the unifying concept of the testicular dysgenesis syndrome, in which these conditions are proposed to reflect a developmental disorder involving both genetic and environmental interactions.[148]

Neither the pathogenesis of cryptorchidism nor the impact of surgery or medical therapy on the natural history of this disorder is known with certainty. Men with a past history of cryptorchidism are often infertile, with reduced testicular volumes (even though orchidopexy has almost always been performed in childhood) and elevated serum FSH levels.[149] The results of long-term studies of patients who underwent orchidopexy in the first 2 years of life are awaited. In patients with a history of unilateral cryptorchidism, Leydig cell function is relatively normal with normal total and free testosterone and basal LH levels, but the LH response to GnRH may be exaggerated. High LH and low testosterone levels are common in men with surgically corrected bilateral cryptorchidism.[150] Cryptorchidism is discussed in greater detail elsewhere (see Chapter 171).

Disorders of spermatogenesis represent the leading cause of male infertility and may be described in terms of semen quality or histologic appearance (see Chapter 172). A classic example is the Sertoli cell–only syndrome (SCOS), which is characterized by small testes, azoospermia, and seminiferous tubules devoid of spermatogenic cells, containing only Sertoli cells, and having Leydig cells of normal morphologic appearance.[151] SCOS can arise from a variety of causes including genetic mutations, cryptorchidism, severe injury, chemotherapy or radiotherapy, or mumps orchitis. Other histologic paterns include arrest of spermatogenic development at a particular stage or a global reduction in the number of germ cells (hypospermatogenesis), leading to azoospermia or severe oligospermia.

In many men with spermatogenic disorders, the defect appears limited to the spermatogenic epithelium, as manifest by a falling sperm output and serum inhibin B levels, with a reciprocal rise in serum FSH. In most infertile men, serum LH and testosterone concentrations are normal, but a propensity for lower serum testosterone and high LH levels has long been recognized.[152] A recent study of consecutive infertile men has shown a shift toward lower serum testosterone levels and a rise in serum LH levels, indicating Leydig cell insufficiency; specifically, 12% and 15% of the infertile men had serum testosterone and LH levels below the 2.5 percentile or above the 97.5 percentile of fertile controls, respectively.[153] These data emphasize that infertile men present an at-risk group for androgen deficiency, with a significant minority warranting testosterone replacement at presentation and a need to consider long-term follow-up in borderline cases.

## ORCHITIS

The incidence of mumps has declined dramatically since introduction of the live attenuated mumps vaccine, but mumps orchitis is still common in developing countries. Orchitis typically develops within 1 week of, but may precede, parotitis. Although clinical orchitis is rare in prepubertal boys, orchitis occurs in 15% to 35% of adolescents and adult men infected with the mumps virus, and, in 25%, bilateral orchitis results. In one survey, testicular atrophy and/or azoospermia developed in 22% of men with mumps orchitis.[154] Serum LH and FSH increase markedly[155] and hypoandrogenism and gynecomastia may result. Testicular failure involving both the seminiferous tubules and Leydig cells also occurs occasionally in men with brucellosis, leprosy, syphilis, tuberculosis, nocardiosis, salmonellosis, schistosomiasis, and filariasis.

## TRAUMA, TORSION, AND VASCULAR DISORDERS

Blunt trauma to the testis often leads to testicular atrophy. When injury requires one testis to be removed, the sperm concentration declines slightly and serum LH and FSH levels rise.[156] The vascular insufficiency that accompanies testicular torsion in pubertal boys may also produce hypogonadism.[157] Rapid clinical evaluation and surgical repair after diagnostic confirmation by color flow ultrasonography may prevent testicular loss. The occurrence of infertility and abnormal semen analysis in adulthood despite successful early unilateral surgery suggests that torsion may occur in patients with an underlying disorder of the testes, or that unilateral torsion may damage the contralateral testis.[158] Most patients with polyarteritis have lesions of the internal spermatic artery and histologic evidence of testicular infarcts and hemorrhage with focal degeneration of the seminiferous tubules, but clinical orchitis and hypogonadism are unusual.[159]

## SYSTEMIC DISORDERS THAT AFFECT TESTICULAR FUNCTION

### ILLNESS, EXERCISE, STRESS, AND NUTRIENT DEPRIVATION

Catabolic states such as critical illness,[160] severe burns,[161,162] myocardial infarction,[163] the postoperative phase,[164] and starvation are associated with low serum testosterone, with changes evident within 24 hours[161,165,166] (Fig. 170-9). In addition to physical stress, psychological stress may also reduce testosterone levels.[167] The effects of systemic illness make investigation of the activity of components of the hypothalamic-pituitary-testicular (HPT) axis difficult.

### Severe Illness
Critical illness is associated with profound and prolonged hypoandrogenemia, with Sertoli cell function being less affected.[168] In the acute phase, there may be a rise in gonadotropin levels, suggesting Leydig cell dysfunction,[168] but more prolonged illness is associated with gonadotropin suppression.[160,165] A decrease in LH pulse amplitude that is only partially overcome with exogenous pulsatile GnRH treatment, and the failure of testosterone levels to rise into the normal range are consistent with a combined central and testicular cause of the profound hypoandrogenism.[169,170] Furthermore, as estradiol levels are maintained, it is postulated that this negative feedback may contribute to reduced basal and GnRH-stimulated LH release.[160] Exogenous dopamine or opioid therapy further suppresses GnRH secretion. Although the decrease in serum testosterone has been inversely related to degree of illness[171] and severity of major burns,[162] whether it is predictive of mortality is uncertain.[166,168] A role for testosterone therapy has been studied to a limited degree in men suffering major burns. In small studies, oxandrolone has been shown to promote wound healing[172] and short-term intramuscular testosterone to reduce muscle catabolism,[173] but, as yet, there is no agreement for the use of androgens in the management of severe illness and catabolic states.[174]

### Starvation/Malnutrition
Reduced food intake may contribute to disturbances in testicular function during illness and stress. LH, FSH, and testosterone levels decline within 48 hours of fasting in otherwise healthy men, probably as a result of decreased GnRH secretion.[175,176] The LH and FSH response to GnRH stimulation is increased rather than decreased,[177] and pulsatile treatment with GnRH prevents the fasting-associated decrease in LH and testosterone levels.[178] Whether fasting decreases LH (GnRH) pulse frequency[175,178] and/or pulse amplitude,[176] however, has been controversial.

The severe nutritional deficiency of men with anorexia nervosa is associated with a reduction in serum testosterone and LH to extremely low values, even to the prepubertal range. Dry skin covered with lanugo-type hair, bradycardia, and a distorted attitude toward food and body image may be clues to the diagnosis. In men with severe chronic malnutrition, by contrast, serum testosterone levels are often reduced, but LH levels are normal or increased with equal frequency.[179]

### Exercise
The effects of exercise on the reproductive system depend on its duration, intensity, and factors intrinsic to the subject. Short-term, intensive exercise in men is associated with a 10% to 25% rise in serum testosterone levels.[180] Contributing factors are hemoconcentration and an exercise-related decline in testosterone metabolic clearance because of decreased hepatic blood flow. After several hours of heavy exercise, serum testosterone levels are significantly reduced,[181] and during prolonged, intensive physical exercise with weight loss and sleep deprivation, testosterone concentrations may fall into the profoundly hypogonadal range.[182] Under these conditions, LH deficiency can be clearly documented. In one study, treatment with a GnRH agonist prevented the decline in serum testosterone that followed 4 hours of bicycling, thus implying that short-term exercise suppresses GnRH secretion.[181]

Mean LH, FSH, and testosterone levels, as well as sperm density, motility, and morphology, in endurance athletes, by

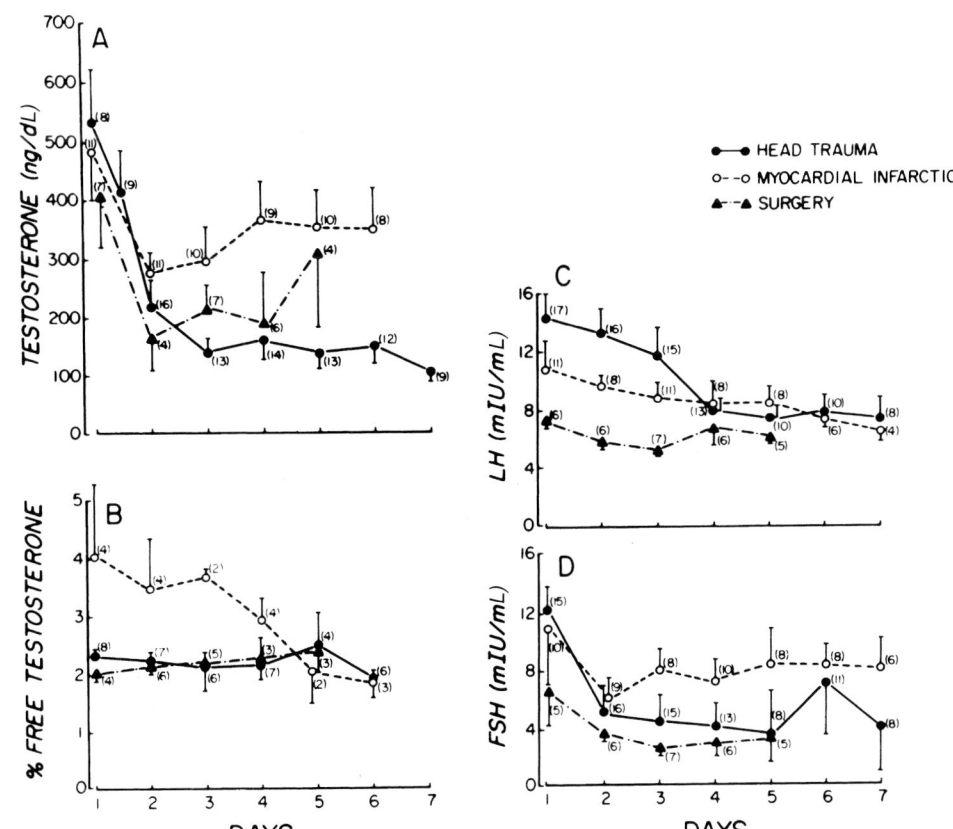

**Figure 170-9** Daily plasma total and percent ultrafilterable testosterone, luteinizing hormone (LH), and follicle-stimulating hormone (FSH) levels in 17 men with traumatic brain injury, 11 men with myocardial infarction, and 7 men undergoing elective surgery. (From Wolff PD, Hamill RW, McDonald JV, et al: Transient hypogonadotropic hypogonadism caused by critical illness. J Clin Endocrinol Metab 60:444–450, 1985.)

contrast, are generally similar to or only slightly less than those of normal men, although some data are conflicting.[183-188] The intensity of training, variable weight loss, and delay between the completion of exercise and blood sampling may explain the varying results. In one study, fewer LH pulses and a reduction in LH pulse amplitude were found in runners, but the physiologic significance of these findings is uncertain because mean LH and testosterone levels were normal.[185] Others found normal pulsatile LH secretion in men who were running at least 50 miles per week and who were 90% to 95% of ideal body weight.[184] Eighteen of 20 marathon runners had a normal semen analysis, but 2 men with body mass index less than 20 kg/m² had oligospermia and a low serum testosterone level.[187] Thus, sustained high-level training producing thinness may cause hypogonadism in men, but, for most, participation in competitive athletics does not significantly impair testicular function.

### Neuropeptides Involved in Mediating the Effects of Stressors

Antigonadotropic activities responsible for suppression of testicular function during stress may include corticotropin-releasing factor (CRF), ACTH, cortisol, PRL, opiate peptides, neuropeptide Y, and interleukin-1 (IL-1). Endogenous CRF and opioid peptides are leading candidates for the inhibition of GnRH secretion during stress.[189] Intraventricular injection of CRF in rodents and primates suppresses GnRH secretion, and CRF antagonists prevent the stress-induced suppression of LH secretion. Opiates likewise reduce gonadotropin secretion, and opiate antagonists appear to increase GnRH secretion. Intraventricular injections of IL-1 in rats decreases LH secretion, and IL-1 antisera or receptor antagonists partially block the suppression of LH secretion that results from intracerebroventricular injection of lipopolysaccharide. In monkeys, evidence indicates that CRF mediates the antigonadotropic effect of IL-1. Leptin secreted by adipocytes acts to regulate GnRH through receptors found in hypothalamic nuclei, and many stimulate neuropeptide Y neurons in the arcuate nucleus.[190] Plasma leptin levels decline with fasting,[191] and in fasted monkeys, as in rodents, suppressed LH and testosterone levels are partly restored by exogenous leptin. In experimentally fasted normal men, exogenous leptin prevented the starvation-induced reduction in LH pulsatility and fall in serum testosterone, indicating a role for this neuropeptide in linking nutrition status and the reproductive system.[192] Finally, the production of cytokines by macrophages may play a role in the hypogonadism of acute and chronic illness, since both interferon γ and tumor necrosis factor-α inhibit rat Leydig cell steroidogenesis and reduce the stimulatory effect of hCG on steroidogenic acute regulatory protein.

### OBESITY

Hypogonadism is often clinically suspected in obese men, and circulating testosterone levels are frequently reduced.[193] Total testosterone levels decrease as body mass index increases, partly because SHBG concentrations are reduced. Hyperinsulinemia resulting from peripheral insulin resistance is known to suppress hepatic SHBG production,[194] and lowering insulin levels with diazoxide increases SHBG.[195] Free and non-SHBG-bound testosterone levels, however, may also decline with massive obesity[196] (Fig. 170-10). Mean serum estrone and estradiol levels may be increased,[197] and increased testosterone to estrogen conversion by aromatase in adipose tissue lowers testosterone levels because gonadotropin pulse amplitude is decreased.[198] In fact, circulating estrone may fall and testosterone may increase with weight loss,[199] but other studies have not confirmed those results.[200] Low gonadotropins together with low testosterone levels suggest a mass lesion of the pituitary or hypothalamus, but, because these findings are anticipated with obesity,

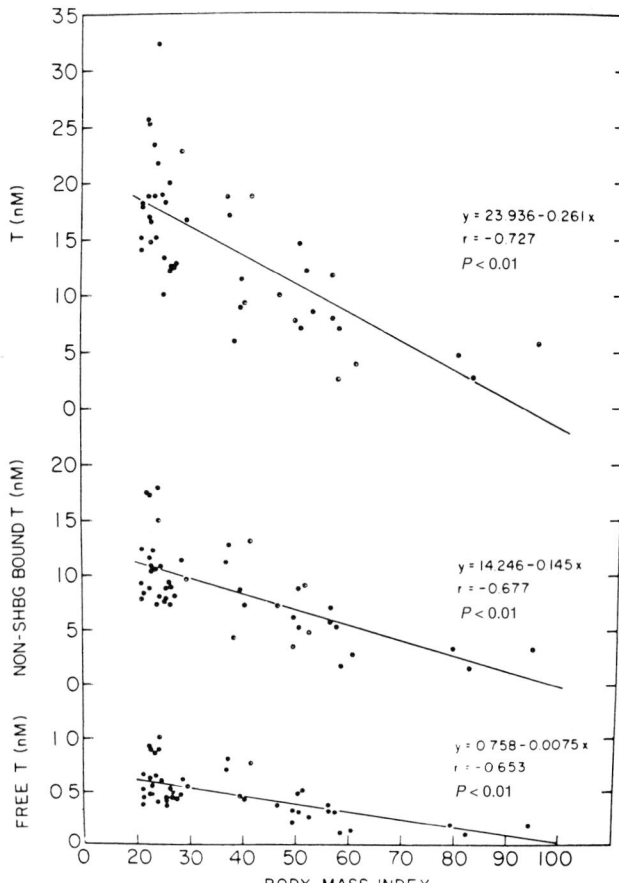

**Figure 170-10**   Relationship between body mass index (kg/m²) and total, non–sex hormone–binding globulin (SHBG) bound and free testosterone (T) levels in 48 healthy male volunteers aged 33.2 ± 12.0 (SD) years. (From Zumoff B, Strain GW, Miller LK, et al: Plasma free and non–sex-hormone-binding-globulin–bound testosterone are decreased in obese men in proportion to their degree of obesity. J Clin Endocrinol Metab 71:929–931, 1990. © 1990, The Endocrine Society.)

caution is advised before beginning an extensive evaluation of pituitary function in obese men. Testosterone treatment of middle-aged men with abdominal obesity reduced visceral fat mass.[201] Morbidly obese hypogonadal men with mutations of the leptin gene who received leptin therapy demonstrated marked weight loss and a restoration of LH pulse amplitude with normalization of serum testosterone levels.[202]

### DIABETES MELLITUS

Low total testosterone and SHBG may be predictive of the development of type 2 diabetes, although these associations are much weaker when controlled for body mass index,[203] and, in eugonadal men, both insulin and glucose are negatively correlated with testosterone.[204] Conversely, in normal men, hypoglycemia leads to suppression of LH and testosterone.[205]

Men with type 2 diabetes may have lower total testosterone levels than those of euglycemic men.[206,207] The level of SHBG is usually low,[207] presumably from obesity and hyperinsulinemia. Total and free testosterone levels, however, remain lower after controlling for body mass index.[206,207]

Rosiglitazone, one of the thiazolidinediones, has been shown to decrease testosterone and DHT biosynthesis in healthy men, but there are no data for diabetic men.[208]

Testosterone levels are generally normal in men with type 1 diabetes; low testosterone levels at the time of diagnosis[209] may reflect the suppressive effects of acute systemic illness on the hypothalamic-pituitary-testicular axis. Poorly controlled type 1 diabetic men have compromised endogenous and GnRH-stimulated LH secretion.[210] Erectile and ejaculatory dysfunction, common in men with diabetes mellitus, is primarily attributable to neural, vascular, and psychological sequelae of the metabolic disturbances; drug therapy may also contribute.

### HUMAN IMMUNODEFICIENCY VIRUS INFECTION

Testicular function is often abnormal in men infected with human immunodeficiency virus 1 (HIV-1).[211] The testes are an early site of HIV infection,[212] and semen may transmit the virus. With progression of disease, spermatogenesis may be reduced or absent, with tubule basement membrane thickening and inflammation.[213] Case reports have also described HIV-associated orchitis from toxoplasmosis, cryptococcosis, tuberculosis, and cytomegalovirus infection. Testosterone levels are normal in healthy HIV-seropositive men, but they are often low in men with acquired immunodeficiciency syndrome (AIDS).[214,215] As illustrated in Figure 170-11, LH levels are usually normal or low but may be increased, which implies that both testicular injury and GnRH deficiency contribute to the testosterone deficiency.[214–217]

HIV-infected men may complain of gynecomastia, decreased libido, loss of body hair, and muscle wasting. The AIDS wasting syndrome, characterized by loss of lean body mass out of proportion to body weight, is associated with decreased survival. Serum total and free testosterone levels are lower in men with HIV who also have AIDS wasting, but substantial overlap is seen between the groups, and whether the low testosterone level is a cause and/or a consequence of the wasting syndrome is controversial. In randomized double-blind placebo-controlled trials, intramuscular testosterone treatment of hypogonadal men with AIDS wasting increased lean body mass, but improvement in strength and exercise performance was variable.[218,219] Replacement with transdermal testosterone produced similar positive effects and increased hemoglobin levels, but CD4+ counts did not change.[220] The results of such studies were determined by the

degree of baseline testosterone deficiency and the dose (physiologic or pharmacologic) of androgen employed. The longer-term effects of these changes on overall physical functioning and quality of life are unknown. Testosterone analogues do not appear to offer any benefit over testosterone.[221]

### RENAL FAILURE

Decreased libido, erectile dysfunction, and gynecomastia are common in men with chronic renal failure, and almost all men are infertile in spite of effective dialysis. The endocrine findings in these men are variable, and the pathophysiology may involve primary and secondary testicular problems.[222] Primary testicular failure is suggested in some men by low serum testosterone and high serum LH levels, and an attenuated testosterone response to hCG stimulation.[223] The LH pulse profile reveals low-amplitude secretory episodes[224] and the difference between the LH response to endogenous and exogenous GnRH suggests reduced GnRH secretion. Chronic illness, poor nutrition, increased production of cortisol, or hyperprolactinemia may each suppress the GnRH signal. Glomerular filtration makes a more important contribution to the metabolism of LH than FSH, such that prolonged LH clearance could explain the elevated LH levels, the delayed LH response to GnRH, and the attenuated LH pulse amplitude.

Erythropoietin therapy may increase testosterone and reduce LH levels by mechanisms that are unclear.[225] Neither peritoneal nor hemodialysis is able to reverse the changes in testosterone levels or sperm production.[222,226] After successful renal transplantation, however, serum testosterone levels and sperm production often increase and LH levels decline. Both before and after transplantation, medications, including antihypertensive drugs, glucocorticoids, and alkylating agents, may contribute to gonadal dysfunction, although renal allograft function remains a more important determinant of testicular function post transplant.[227]

Although erythropoietin now has the major role in the treatment of chronic anemia, androgens have been used in the past for the treatment of anemia, and may produce additional anabolic effects and improved physical function in addition to stimulating hematopoiesis.[228,229] Despite the frequent presence of clinical and biochemical features of androgen deficiency, however, beyond this hematopoietic action, there is no established evidence-based role for androgen treatment in men with chronic renal failure.[230]

In acute renal failure, testosterone levels are decreased with little change to gonadotropin or SHBG levels; the defect appears to be primarily one of hypothalamic dysfunction[231] and is reversible upon restoration of renal function.

### LIVER DISEASE

Hypogonadism is common in men with chronic liver disease. Most studies have been in alcoholic men, among whom gynecomastia, small testes, decreased body hair, and reduced libido and potency are common clinical findings. The hypogonadism in these men is multifactorial.[232] Free and total testosterone levels are usually reduced, and LH and FSH levels are generally increased, suggesting primary testicular failure. Experimental evidence in animals and in cultured Leydig cells indicates that alcohol damages the testes. In men with severe clinical hypogonadism, however, LH and FSH levels may be normal in spite of very low testosterone concentrations, and the LH pulse pattern is suppressed.[233] Moreover, the LH and FSH response to clomiphene stimulation is impaired, whereas the increases in LH and FSH after GnRH administration overlap with normal responses,[232,234] suggesting suppressed GnRH secretion. Increased estrogens, PRL, cortisol, CRF, and IL-1 have been reported in alcoholic cirrhosis, and these hormonal abnormalities, as well as poor nutrition,

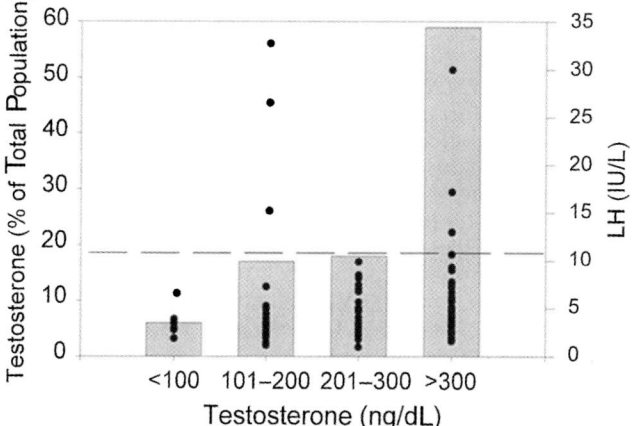

**Figure 170-11** Serum testosterone and luteinizing hormone (LH) levels in HIV-infected men. Data from 108 men were divided into four groups based on the serum testosterone level. Normal values are 300 to 1000 ng/dL. *Dots* represent the serum LH levels, and the *horizontal dashed line* is the upper limit of the LH normal range, which was 11 mIU/mL. Forty-one percent of the men had testosterone levels below 300 ng/dL. Six men had elevated serum LH levels, and 41 of 44 men with low testosterone levels had "inappropriately" normal or low serum LH levels. (Data courtesy of S. Bhasin.)

could inhibit GnRH.[235–237] Additionally, gonadotropin insufficiency may result partly from the ingestion of alcohol.[238] Sustained moderate alcohol intake in healthy older men does not influence total testosterone levels.[239,240]

The prominent feminization often observed in men with alcoholic cirrhosis is explained by reduced testosterone together with increased estrogen production.[241] The adrenal androgen androstenedione is an important estrogen precursor.[242] SHBG is markedly increased in alcoholic liver disease, and because SHBG binds testosterone more avidly than it does estradiol or estrone, the availability to the target tissues of estrogens in relation to testosterone is increased. Increased SHBG may increase the total testosterone level into the normal range when bioavailable testosterone is low. Thus, bioavailable testosterone provides a better estimate of testosterone production in men with alcoholic liver disease than total testosterone does. The reason that SHBG increases is unknown, but may be partly explained by the fact that growth hormone is known to decrease SHBG production, and cirrhosis is associated with growth hormone resistance. Moreover, the SHBG produced by the liver of alcoholic cirrhotics may be abnormally glycosylated, further influencing sex steroid transport and target tissue delivery.[243]

Testosterone levels are also reduced and SHBG is increased in men with nonalcoholic liver failure.[244] Given that gonadotropin levels are normal, the defect may involve both the testes and GnRH production. After liver transplantation, a rise in testosterone and a fall in SHBG levels occur in spite of immunosuppressive therapy.[244]

Selective HH is a common early finding in men with hemochromatosis. Serum testosterone levels are low, but basal LH levels do not rise and LH and FSH responses to GnRH stimulation are blunted or absent.[245] Stainable iron is present in the anterior pituitary gland, especially the gonadotrophs. Unlike in alcoholic liver disease, serum androstenedione, estrone, and SHBG levels are normal and gynecomastia is uncommon[246] (Table 170-8). Although iron is deposited in most endocrine glands, primary glandular failure including of the testis is uncommon. The diabetes mellitus and hepatic cirrhosis that occur in hemochromatosis may also contribute to the endocrine disturbance in these patients.[247] Intensive phlebotomy may reverse the hypogonadism, but results are conflicting.[248,249]

## HEMOGLOBINOPATHIES

### Thalassemia

Homozygous β-thalassemia is associated with pubertal delay, which, in turn, contributes to growth failure and impaired fertility. The anterior pituitary is sensitive, in a dose-dependent fashion, to the effects of iron overload from transfusions and, additionally, MRI may show empty sella, decreased pituitary size, or thinning of the stalk.[250] Gonadotropin levels are reduced both at baseline and after GnRH stimulation.[251] In addition to HH, some men may also have a degree of primary testicular failure due to iron deposition, with a diminished Leydig cell response to hCG.[252] The chemotherapeutic agents associated with bone-marrow transplantation may also directly cause gonadal damage.[253] Serum testosterone levels may be low-normal or overtly subnormal, and SHBG levels are often low. Other contributing factors to the hypogonadism include chronic ill health, chronic hypoxia, low body weight, liver disease, and diabetes mellitus.[254] Hypoandrogenism is an important contributing factor to the osteopenia and osteoporosis associated with thalassemia major.[255] Although hypogonadism is the most common endocrine disorder, seen in up to two thirds of patients,[254] other endocrine manifestations include hypothyroidism, hypoparathyroidism, adrenal insufficiency, growth hormone deficiency, and pancreatic β-cell failure.

### Sickle-Cell Anemia

Pubertal delay is also common in men with sickle-cell anemia. Primary testicular dysfunction has been reported,[256] although others have found that secondary hypogonadism, responsive to clomiphene, may also be present.[257] Both abnormalities may result from vaso-occlusion of small blood vessels. Inhibition of GnRH release due to the effects of stress, pain, and the use of narcotic analgesics also contributes to gonadotropin deficiency. Testosterone levels are reduced when compared to age-matched peers.[258] Gonadal function is preserved in men with sickle-cell trait.[259]

## NEUROLOGIC DISORDERS

Myotonic muscular dystrophy is an autosomal-dominant multisystem disorder in which myotonia is accompanied by weakness, frontal balding, cataracts, cardiac conduction defects, and insulin resistance. Testicular dysfunction is characterized by testicular atrophy, elevated gonadotropins, and defective spermatogenesis. In one study, testicular atrophy was found in two thirds of patients.[260] Serum testosterone levels may be low in some men and the diminished muscle mass is out of proportion to any decrease in serum androgens and although testosterone therapy increases muscle mass, strength is unaffected.[261] Affected patients have an expansion of the CAG trinucleotide repeat, which codes for glutamine, in the 3' region of the myotonin protein kinase gene; the change in this gene alters mRNA production, but the link to impaired testicular function remains undefined.[262]

Men with spinal and bulbar muscular atrophy (Kennedy syndrome) have weakness, muscle atrophy, and fasciculations beginning in the third to fifth decade of life.[263] The weakness progresses, swallowing becomes difficult, and patients may die of aspiration. The lower motor neurons, particularly the anterior horns cells of the spinal cord, are atrophied. Many cases are sporadic, but the disorder is also inherited as an X-linked-recessive trait. Although affected men are initially fertile, gynecomastia, clinical signs of androgen deficiency, and small testes with hypospermatogenesis develop later in life. Serum LH levels are usually increased, which suggests testicular failure, but total testosterone levels are usually normal, a picture of androgen resistance.[264] The knowledge that androgen receptors are present in spinal and bulbar motor neurons led to the proposal of an androgen receptor defect. The condition is associated with an increased CAG triplet

| Table 170-8 | Comparison of the Endocrine Profiles of Men with Cirrhosis of the Liver Caused by Alcoholism or Hemochromatosis | | |
|---|---|---|---|
| Hormone | Alcoholism | Hemochromatosis | Normal Men |
| Testosterone (ng/mL) | 2.78 ± 0.63* | 2.79 ± 0.79* | 5.90 ± 1.20 |
| Androstenedione (ng/mL) | 1.67 ± 0.28*,† | 0.90 ± 0.23* | 1.23 ± 0.10 |
| Estradiol (pg/mL) | 38.0 ± 5.3*,† | 16.2 ± 4.6 | 20.3 ± 3.7 |
| Estrone (pg/mL) | 68.5 ± 17.2*,† | 32.2 ± 4.6 | 26.8 ± 3.1 |
| Cortisol (μg/dL) | 12.5 ± 3.8 | 13.3 ± 2.5 | 11.1 ± 4.2 |
| LH (mIU/mL) | 10.5 ± 3.5*,† | 5.5 ± 2.0* | 21.0 ± 6.5 |
| SHBG (nmol/L) | 80 ± 30* | 35 ± 10 | 25 ± 10 |
| PRL (ng/mL) | 9 ± 4.5 | 3.0 ± 1.5* | 6 ± 2 |

Data are means ± SD for six subjects per group.
*$P < 0.05$ vs. normal men.
†$P < 0.05$, hemochromatosis vs. alcoholism.
LH, luteinizing hormone; PRL, prolactin; SHBG, sex hormone–binding globulin.
Data from Kley HK, Niederau C, Stremmel W, et al: Conversion of androgens to estrogens in idiopathic hemochromatosis: Comparison with alcoholic liver cirrhosis. J Clin Endocrinol Metab 61:1–6, 1985.

repeat coding for a polyglutamine tract in exon 1 of the androgen receptor; disease severity is related to the number of repeats.[265]

Adrenoleukodystrophy is a sex-linked recessive disorder in which very-long-chain fatty acids (VLCFAs) accumulate in cellular membranes, especially in cells with high lipid turnover.[266] In affected children, the accumulation of VLCFAs leads to demyelination of the cerebral hemispheres and to Addison's disease. Adrenomyeloneuropathy is a milder and more slowly progressive form of this disorder, with clinical symptoms beginning in adolescence or young adulthood. Primary testicular insufficiency with a low serum testosterone and elevated serum LH may occur.[267] The gene for adrenoleukodystrophy encodes a 75-kilodalton peroxisomal membrane protein with over 100 missense, nonsense, and splicing mutations having been identified. Peroxisomes in Leydig cells may play a physiologic role in the protein kinase A regulation of testosterone biosynthesis, which would explain the steroidogenic defect in adrenoleukodystrophy.

Temporal lobe epilepsy may be causally associated with hypogonadism; both hyperprolactinemia and gonadotropin deficiency with a blunted response to GnRH have been described.[268] The hypoandrogenemia usually responds to anticonvulsant therapy, but androgen therapy may be required. Successful temporal lobe epilepsy surgery may lead to an increase in serum androgens.[269] Other forms of epilepsy do not appear to be associated with alterations in androgen profiles.

In addition to erectile and ejaculatory dysfunction, spinal cord injury may be associated with an acute decrease in testosterone that returns to baseline over a number of months.[270] Ten years after spinal cord injury, testicular volumes were not different from those of healthy controls, but, even in medically stable men, spinal cord injury was associated with lower testosterone and LH levels than those of healthy men.[271] Postulated mechanisms for this proposed HH include hyperprolactinemia, recurrent urinary tract infections, concomitant medications, or altered central neurotransmitter activity, perhaps related to chronic stress or sleep apnea which is prevalent with spinal cord injury.

Trisomy 21 has been reported to be associated with elevated gonadotropins, although testosterone levels remain normal[272] and a full description of gonadal function is lacking.

## CONGENITAL ADRENAL HYPERPLASIA

Reproductive function in men with congenital adrenal hyperplasia (CAH) is affected to a variable degree. When well controlled on glucocorticoid therapy, boys may progress normally through puberty and have normal reproductive function.[273,274] CAH presents a dual risk to normal testicular function, however. First, inadequate glucocorticoid therapy leading to elevated adrenal steroid secretion may suppress the hypothalamic-pituitary-testicular axis, resulting in reduced testicular volumes and infertility. In support of this concept, serum testosterone levels may be low[274,275] in conjunction with a suppressed LH.[275] Second, clinically palpable testicular tumors occasionally occur in CAH[276] due to hyperplastic nodules of adrenocortical cells (termed *adrenal rests*) growing as a result of excessive ACTH stimulation. Ultrasonographically detectable adrenals rests appear more common in adult men with salt-losing CAH and are associated with spermatogenic problems and subnormal semen quality.[274] Glucocorticoid treatment may suppress these tumors and restore spermatogenesis, but, in other treated patients, there is irreversible damage to the seminiferous tubules with elevated serum FSH levels, and suppression of testosterone and goandotropin levels may occur despite apparent suppression of 17-hydroxyprogesterone levels.[274,275] Despite these risks, some men who have never received glucocorticoids may not suffer adverse reproductive effects.[273]

## THYROID DISEASE

Gynecomastia, a depressed sperm count and/or motility, and sexual dysfunction may develop in hyperthyroid men. Thyroxine stimulates SHBG gene expression, and, therefore, total testosterone levels are sometimes increased because SHBG is increased[277] and the metabolic clearance rate of testosterone is reduced. Basal and GnRH-stimulated LH and FSH levels are elevated, but bioavailable testosterone levels remain subnormal, suggesting a partial adaptation to the increased binding of circulating testosterone to SHBG.[278,279] Increased LH drive stimulates testicular aromatase, and peripheral bioconversion of testosterone to estradiol is increased,[280] thereby elevating plasma estradiol levels. A diminished testosterone response to hCG suggests partial Leydig cell failure or desensitization.[277,279] Abnormal values normalize when euthyroidism is restored.

Men with primary hypothyroidism may experience a decrease in libido among other central nervous system effects. Although total testosterone levels may be reduced, these effects are primarily due to decreased SHBG concentrations.[281] Gonadotropin levels are not elevated and, when present, hyperprolactinemia may contribute to hypogonadotropic hypogonadism.[282] Testicular failure may occur more often than expected in men with primary hypothyroidism, but the patients reported were elderly and levothyroxine treatment did not correct the gonadal dysfunction.[283]

## AUTOIMMUNE DISORDERS

Hypogonadism occurs in 5% to 7% of patients with polyendocrine deficiency types I and II.[284,285] As in other autoimmune disorders, males are less frequently affected than females. Primary testicular failure is generally observed, but gonadotropin deficiency has also been reported.[286] Testicular failure may occur in primary systemic sclerosis[287] or idiopathic retroperitoneal fibrosis.[288] Testicular abnormalities in men with systemic lupus erythematosus have been attributed to treatment with glucocorticoids and chemotherapeutic drugs.[289]

## RESPIRATORY DISORDERS

Obstructive sleep apnea is common in obese men and is associated with sexual dysfunction. Several studies found low testosterone but normal LH levels and concluded that the hormonal findings cannot be explained by obesity alone. The link between obstructive sleep apnea and low testosterone is unclear, with hypoxia and sleep fragmentation possible contributors.[290] Continuous positive airway pressure treatment results in an increase in serum testosterone levels, but this increase also occurs in men with chronic obstructive pulmonary disease of other causes.[291] Conversely, there are concerns that testosterone treatment may worsen sleep apnea[292] by increasing oxygen consumption or reducing the hypoxic respiratory drive. High-dose testosterone increased sleep-related hypoxemia in older men,[293] but no controlled data is available regarding more physiologic dose regimens.

Sexual maturation is delayed in patients with cystic fibrosis, in whom hypoxia, poor nutrition, and hypercortisolemia may decrease GnRH secretion. Men with cystic fibrosis are almost always azoospermic due to congenital bilateral agenesis of the vas deferens and distal epididymis, and absent seminal vesicle. When their lung and gastrointestinal problems are well controlled, however, spermatogenesis is normal and fertility using sperm aspiration and intracytoplasmic sperm injection is possible. Even in men with chronic stable cystic fibrosis not receiving glucocorticoid therapy, total testosterone levels were lower than those of healthy men, however, although generally not to a degree requiring androgen replacement.[294]

## DRUGS THAT ADVERSLY AFFECT ENDOCRINE TESTICULAR FUNCTION

### CYTOTOXIC CHEMOTHERAPY AND RADIOTHERAPY

Chemotherapeutic drugs, particularly alkylating agents (e.g., cyclophosphamide), damage the testis, in particular the germinal epithelium.[295,296] Testicular toxicity is directly proportional to the accumulated dose of drug and manifests as oligospermia or azoospermia, which may be temporary or permanent. Leydig cells may also be affected by the chemotherapy regimens for hematologic, testicular, and other malignancies, and when these agents are used for other disorders such as glomerulonephritis.[296] Indeed, Leydig cell dysfunction was reported in up to 30% of men receiving chemotherapy for hematologic malignancies.[297] Testosterone production may decline, LH concentrations rise, and gynecomastia develop.[298] Even when baseline testosterone levels remain within the normal range, the response to hCG may be impaired.[299] Treatment in adolescence or adulthood is thought to be more damaging than is treatment in childhood.[300] Efforts to protect the testis from damage by suppressing testicular function with gonadal steroids or with GnRH analogues have so far produced disappointing results.[301] Regimens that do not include alkylating agents appear to be less damaging to testicular function[302]; however, Leydig cell dysfunction was dose dependent in a group of men receiving cisplatin for germ cell tumors.[303]

The testis is radiosensitive such that conditioning regimens for bone-marrow transplantation that include total body irradiation are more damaging to the testes than is chemotherapy alone.[299] Leydig cells are more resistant to radiation damage than is the seminiferous epithelium.[302] Doses of 20 to 30 Gy administered prepubertally[304] and in adulthood[305] have resulted in low testosterone and high LH levels. Prepubertal Leydig cells are more radiosensitive than are those of adult men.[306] In addition, central nervous system irradiation that disturbs anterior pituitary hormone secretion further negatively impacts on testicular function.

The role of androgen replacement for men with mild Leydig cell dysfunction is uncertain. Testosterone replacement for 12 months in young men with borderline or low testosterone levels together with elevated LH levels did not show significant effects on bone, body composition, or quality of life.[307]

Gonadotropin deficiency resulting from the effects of acute and chronic illness may explain the testosterone deficiency and oligospermia that sometimes occur in men with Hodgkin's disease before chemotherapy is begun.[308]

### RADIOIODINE

The doses of [131]I employed in the treatment of men with thyroid carcinoma cause some gonadotoxicity,[309] with a dose-dependent but usually transitory impairment of semen quality.[310] There is a transient rise in FSH and a corresponding decline in inhibin B.[311] Plasma testosterone levels were unaffected in two studies using doses of [131]I ranging from 80 to 250 mCi although minor but transient rises in LH levels were seen, suggesting Leydig cell dysfunction.[311,312]

### ANTIANDROGENS

Antiandrogens competitively bind to androgen receptors and/or affect their metabolism. Steroidal antiandrogens may also interact with progesterone and glucocorticoid receptors and may be weak agonists in the absence of testosterone, whereas nonsteroidal antiandrogens tend to be more receptor selective and to lack agonist activity.[313]

Spironolactone, a steroid analogue that binds to mineralocorticoid receptors, also binds to androgen receptors. In addition, it reduces the concentration of the cytochrome P-450/17$\alpha$-hydroxylase/17,20-lyase enzyme complex in testicular microsomes.[314] The result is not only a partial blockade of androgen action, but also a decline in testosterone biosynthesis and an increase in circulating progesterone levels. The fall in circulating testosterone levels leads to increased LH and FSH secretion, which, in turn, restores serum testosterone to normal values, and standard therapeutic regimens are not associated with clinically relevant changes in serum testosterone.[314] Aromatization of testosterone to estradiol is also enhanced and produces gynecomastia; this effect is seen at a dose of 200 mg daily.[315]

Antiandrogens may be used in the treatment of androgen-dependent prostate carcinoma and benign prostatic hyperplasia. Cyproterone acetate is a progestogen that reduces androgen action by inhibiting LH secretion and thereby testosterone biosynthesis, but also acts as an antiandrogen at the receptor level.[316] Flutamide and bicalutamide are nonsteroidal antiandrogens used in combination therapy with GnRH analogues in the treatment of metastatic prostatic carcinoma.[316] These drugs lack androgen agonist activity. Flutamide competes only weakly for androgen receptor binding in vitro and is 2-hydroxylated in vivo for full biologic activity.[317] When the testes are present and no GnRH analogues are taken, flutamide and bicalutamide increase LH and FSH secretion and thereby increase testosterone and estradiol production by blocking testosterone negative feedback.[318] Tender gynecomastia may occur.

The histamine $H_2$ antagonist cimetidine is a competitive antagonist of the androgen receptor[319] and in large doses may produce gynecomastia, breast tenderness, and erectile dysfunction.[320] Although minor changes in testosterone, prolactin, LH, and FSH[321] have been reported, these do not appear to be clinically significant. Concerns regarding reduced sperm counts were not substantiated in controlled trials. Ranitidine does not cause any change in serum androgen levels.[322] Although omeprazole has been linked to gynecomastia and erectile dysfunction, causality has not been clearly proven[323]; neither lansoprezole, pantoprazole, nor rabeprazole has a demonstrable effect on androgen profiles.

### KETOCONAZOLE

Ketoconazole, a synthetic imidazole oral antifungal agent, inhibits cytochrome P-450 (CYP3A4) enzyme systems not only in fungi, but also in the mammalian testis, ovary, adrenal, kidney, and liver.[324] It is a competitive inhibitor of cholesterol side-chain cleavage and 17,20-lyase activity in the testosterone biosynthetic pathway, leading to a dose-dependent reduction in circulating testosterone levels and to an increase in serum 17$\alpha$-hydroxyprogesterone concentrations in men.[325] Serum LH and FSH levels also rise.[326] Because of ketoconazole's short serum half-life, serum testosterone levels may be normal when the drug is administered once daily. High-dose ketoconazole treatment causes gynecomastia.

### 5$\alpha$-REDUCTASE INHIBITORS

Finasteride, a 4-azasteroid inhibitor of type 2 5$\alpha$-reductase isoenzyme activity, competitively inhibits the conversion of testosterone to dihydrotestosterone and is used to treat prostatic hyperplasia and male pattern baldness. At a dose of 1 mg daily (as used for balding), finasteride decreases prostatic and serum dihydrotestosterone levels by approximately 85% and 70%, respectively.[327] A 5-mg daily dose increased prostatic testosterone levels sevenfold, but did not alter serum testosterone,[327] and no changes were seen in basal or GnRH-stimulated LH and FSH levels.[328] Dutasteride, a dual 5$\alpha$-reductase inhibitor, reduced serum dihydrotestosterone levels by 93% and increased serum testosterone by 19%, although levels remained within the normal range after

2 years of treatment.[329] Inhibition of 5α-reductase activity does not appear to influence spermatogenesis adversely.

## SEX STEROIDS

Anabolic androgenic steroids that have been used since the 1950s to enhance muscle strength result in rapid and profound suppression of LH levels that may persist after withdrawal of the androgen (e.g., before drug testing or as part of a program of intermittent withdrawal),[330] resulting in a variable period of secondary HH, the severity and duration of which depends on the type and dose of drug and its duration of use. Spontaneous recovery occurs, but may take in excess of 4 months.[331] Clues to the diagnosis include a history of involvement in "at-risk" activity such as power sports or physical employment, and biochemical features of isolated HH, but a low (rather than high) SHBG level due to the suppression of its hepatic synthesis. Gynecomastia is a common finding and multifactorial in origin. Temporary relief may be achieved through the supervised use of hCG[332] or a gradually reducing dose of testosterone therapy within the setting of a plan of cessation of the drug taking.

Progestogens, such as depot medroxyprogesterone acetate (DMPA), have been used to induce HH in various settings; most recently, such compounds have been used to augment FSH and LH suppression by coadminstration with testosterone as an approach to male hormonal contraception.[333] Due to its long half-life, DMPA may suppress serum LH and testosterone for more than 6 months.

## AMIODARONE AND DIGOXIN

Amiodarone, because of its lipid solubility, produces testicular levels up to 50-fold higher than in peripheral blood. Gynecomastia and elevated plasma gonadotropin levels may occur although free and total testosterone levels remain normal.[334]

Digoxin is associated with a decrease in plasma testosterone levels.[335] Animal data suggest that the decreased production is due to inhibitory effects on cyclic adenosine monophosphate (cAMP) production and attenuated cytochrome P-450 activity in testicular interstitial cells.[336] Even when cardiac status is taken into consideration, libido and erectile dysfunction may be adversely affected by long-term digoxin use,[337] and inhibition of corpus cavernosum smooth muscle contractility in healthy men has been noted.[338]

## HMG-CoA REDUCTASE INHIBITORS

These agents, used to treat hyperlipidemia, have been reported to cause small declines in serum testosterone,[339] although without associated LH rises or change in hCG response,[340] and it is unlikely that these declines are of any clinical significance.

## ANTIEPILEPTIC DRUGS

Impaired libido and/or erectile function are frequently reported by men with epilepsy, and it is proposed that changes in the androgen profile may contribute to this problem. Phenytoin and carbamazepine increase SHBG levels[341] and subsequently lower indices of free or bioavailable testosterone; this effect is more marked with polytherapy. Total testosterone levels may be increased because of the increase in SHBG,[342] and a decrease in the metabolic clearance rate of testosterone has also been reported.[343] LH levels may be increased, particularly with polytherapy, a proposed mechanism being the decreased negative feedback effect of lowered free testosterone.[344] Valproate is thought to have a lesser

impact on sexual function and does not affect SHBG or suppress serum androgens.[345]

## CANNABINOIDS

Gynecomastia has been described in heavy marijuana users. Whether cannabinoids adversely affect testicular function remains uncertain, however, because both suppressed and unchanged serum testosterone levels have been reported.[346–348] Early claims that cannabinoids interact with estrogen receptors have not been substantiated, although marijuana extracts may have contaminants with estrogenic activity.[349] Marijuana and its constituents have also been reported to interact with androgen receptors.[350]

## HEROIN AND METHADONE

Men using long-acting opiates for nonmalignant pain have a dose-dependent reduction in testosterone levels and a high incidence of subnormal total testosterone levels.[351] Almost 90% of men who report normal sexual function before therapy is initiated experience erectile dysfunction or reduced libido with opiate treatment.[351] Heroin addicts have depressed testosterone levels that may return to normal values as methadone is substituted and then withdrawn.[352] The gonadotropin response to GnRH is not different in heroin addicts when compared to controls, suggesting that chronic abuse may depress testicular function at the hypothalamic level.[353]

## THE AGING MALE

### PREVALENCE OF ANDROGEN DEFICIENCY

Male aging is associated with a decline in serum testosterone that begins in the late third decade,[239,354,355] with the absolute rate of decline in total testosterone levels in longitudinal studies varying from 0.11 nM to 0.38 nM per year.[239,356,357] Cross-sectional studies estimate the rate of decline to be 0.5% to 0.8% per year, but the largest longitudinal study of age effect on reproductive hormones reported a 1.6% decline per annum[356] (Fig. 170-12). Overall, there is a 20% to 40% decline in total testosterone levels seen across life in healthy non-obese men.[355,358] As SHBG levels rise with age, approximately 1% to 2% per year,[356,359] the decline in free testosterone is even greater, approximately 2% to 3% per year[356] (see Fig. 170-12).

It is important to recognize, however, that many older men maintain levels comparable to those of healthy young men. Factors other then age may be important determinants of androgen status, including intercurrent ill-health, both acute[360] and chronic,[356] and concurrent medications. Of note, in the Massachusetts Male Aging Study (MMAS), only 26% of men aged 40 years and older were in "apparent good health," defined by the absence of chronic illness, prescription medication, obesity, or excess alcohol consumption,[356] and, after 7 to 10 years, only 18% of men remained so. Importantly, obese men had total testosterone levels 25% lower than their nonobese counterparts.[356] Estimates of the prevalence of androgen deficiency in the aging population are often based on arbitrary cut-off values for total or free serum testosterone, for example, the lower limit of the young male range. The implication of such cut-off values is that replacement therapy is warranted below that level. Whether the decline in testosterone with aging constitutes a true androgen deficiency state worthy of replacement therapy is contentious. Ill-defined terms such as *andropause* or *partial androgen deficiency of aging men (PADAM)* have been popularized and underscore the increasing use of testosterone treatment for a range of ailments prevalent in older men, albeit one without an evidence base. No consensus has been reached regarding such a threshold value or about the relative risks and benefits of therapy.[361]

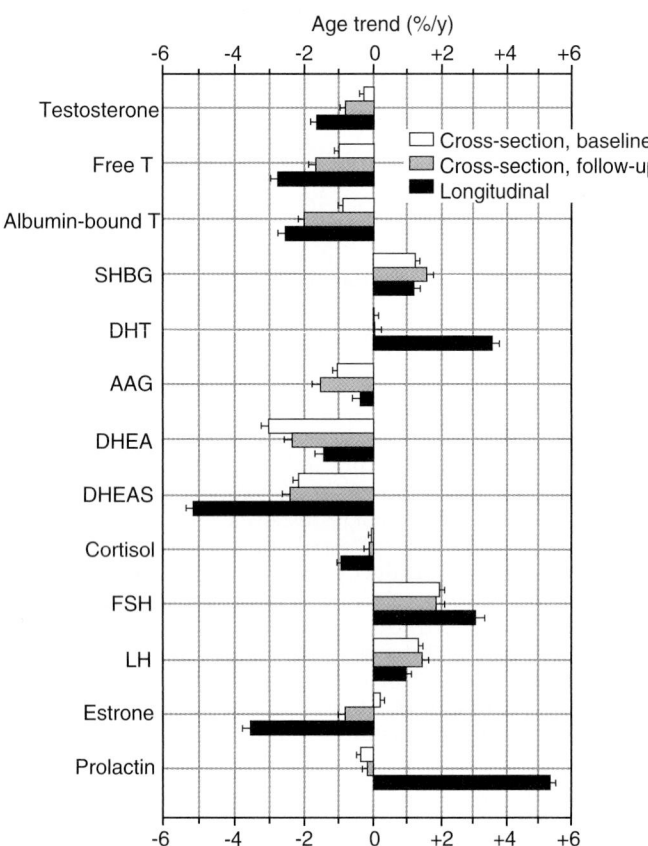

Age trend (%/y)

Testosterone
Free T
Albumin-bound T
SHBG
DHT
AAG
DHEA
DHEAS
Cortisol
FSH
LH
Estrone
Prolactin

☐ Cross-section, baseline
▨ Cross-section, follow-up
■ Longitudinal

*Figure 170-12* Longitudinal trends in reproductive hormones in a cohort of 1156 men aged 40 to 70 years studied between 1987 and 1989 and followed up 7 to 10 years later (the Massachusetts Male Aging Study). (From Feldman HA, Longcope C, Derby CA, et al: Age trends in the level of serum testosterone and other hormones in middle-aged men: Longitudinal results from the Massachusetts Male Aging Study. J Clin Endocrinol Metab 87:589–598, 2002.)

Limitations to determining the prevalence of hypoandrogenism include heterogeneity of study populations (concomitant illness, obesity) and differing assay methods for testosterone levels (total, free estimates). As a result, prevalence estimates vary widely; for example, in institutionalized men aged 46 to 89 years, almost 30% were classified as hypoandrogenemic (defined as total testosterone levels below 10.4 nM).[362] Approximately 20% of ambulant healthy men aged 60 years or older were considered hypoandrogenemic, as defined by total testosterone levels less than 11 nM,[239,363,364] but if a value of less than 8.7 nM was used, this figure fell to only 8%.[364] If free testosterone values were used in the classification, almost one third of men classified as normal according to their total testosterone levels would be redefined as hypoandrogenemic.[365]

### HYPOTHALAMIC-PITUITARY-TESTICULAR AXIS CHANGES

Decreased serum testosterone levels in older men are principally due to a decrease in production, although clearance rates are also slightly reduced.[366] Changes occur at all levels of the hypothalamic-pituitary-testicular (HPT) axis.[367] A primary testicular defect is suggested by reduced Leydig cell number,[368] a reduced testosterone response to hCG stimulation,[369] and a rise in serum LH levels in population studies.[354,356] In one study, the observed rise in LH did not show the expected inverse correlation with testosterone, suggesting an alteration in regulation of the HPT axis.[357] In support of an alteration in GnRH rhythmicity, the diurnal pattern of serum testosterone production may be attenuated as a function of aging,[370,371]

although this finding is not universal.[372] Specific changes in the neuroendocrine pathways in otherwise healthy aging men[367] include a reduction in pulsatile GnRH release,[373] asynchrony between LH release and testosterone secretion,[374] greater sensitivity of LH to the negative feedback effects of testosterone[375] and estradiol,[376] and an attenuation of the amplitude of endogenous LH pulses.[373,377] The pituitary LH response to exogenous GnRH stimulation is inconsistent.[378,379] The end result of these HPT axis changes is that falling testosterone levels in aging men may not elicit a compensatory LH response.[363]

### THE ASSOCIATION BETWEEN CHANGES OF AGING AND ANDROGEN LEVELS

There are similarites between the features of hypoandrogenism and aspects of "normal" male aging (Table 170-9). Moreover, the symptoms of androgen deficiency may be nonspecific. Questionnaires developed to identify aging men with low testosterone levels are neither sufficiently sensitive nor specific enough to be employed as widespread screening tools.[380,381] Additionally, the possibility that such symptoms are of an unrelated etiology must be considered.[382]

Importantly, the observation that there is a correlation between declining testosterone levels and a number of the features of aging does not establish causality. These changes and their relationship to circulating androgen levels are outlined in the following sections.

#### Body Composition
Between the ages of 25 and 70 years, there is, on average, a 12-kg loss of lean body mass and a similar increase in fat mass in men.[383] Muscle mass has been shown to correlate with strength (as measured by dynamometry) in healthy older men,[384] and, in turn, strength has been shown to correlate positively with bioavailable testosterone.[385]

#### Bone
Androgens and estrogens are both important in maintaining bone health in men. Some studies have shown that low bioavailable testosterone levels are correlated with femoral neck bone mineral density in aging men,[386] but most data show that estradiol is the stronger correlate.[387,388] Bioavailable estradiol, but not testosterone, has also been shown to correlate with bone turnover markers in men aged 50 years or older,[389] with bone loss at the forearm in a longitudinal study of men aged 60 to 90 years[390] and with rate of bone loss at the lumbar spine and femoral neck in men aged 55 to 85 years followed for 4 years.[391] In older men subjected to independent withdrawal of estrogen and testosterone, estrogen prevented an increase in bone resorption markers, whereas both hormones played a role in bone formation.[392]

#### Mood and Cognition
An association between reduced testosterone levels and depressed mood in older men is well documented.[393] Epidemiologic data has described an inverse relationship

| **Table 170-9** | Similarites between the Features of Hypoandrogenism and Aspects of "Normal" Male Aging |
|---|---|

Decreasing muscle mass and strength
Increasing adiposity
Loss of bone mineral density, increased fracture risk
Declining libido
Decreasing vigour
Low mood
Poor cognition

between testosterone levels and increasing severity of depression,[394] although other data have found a stronger link with dysthymia than with major depressive illness.[395] Selected parameters of cognitive function have also been related to endogenous testosterone levels[396] and the free testosterone index[397] in healthy older men.

### Libido and Sexual Function

A reduction in sexual desire and function is a frequent accompaniment to male aging,[398] but the extent to which it correlates with testosterone levels is not well defined,[399] particularly when testosterone levels are within the normal young adult range.[400] It has been suggested that this may be due to an apparent threshold effect of testosterone on sexual function within the low-normal range.[401] Erectile dysfunction increases with age, but is predominantly due to neurovascular disease and, across large populations, there is no independent relationship with serum total testosterone.[402]

### Cardiovascular Disease

In contrast to the long-held belief that androgens increase cardiovascular risk, recent observational data suggest that low testosterone levels may confer increased coronary heart disease risk.[403] Critical analyses of the available human and animal studies of the effects of endogenous and exogenous androgens confirm the contradictory nature of our current knowledge.[404,405] Cross-sectional studies of total testosterone in men with coronary heart disease (as determined by clinical events: myocardial infarction, angina, and/or angiography) have either failed to show a relationship or have suggested a negative association.[405] Such a negative association was shown for both total and bioavailable testosterone in men with angiographically determined coronary artery disease.[406] A review of prospective cohort studies involving 3500 middle-aged and older men, with a minimum 5-year follow-up period, showed no association between endogenous testosterone and the development of coronary heart disease.[405] An inverse association between serum testosterone and the presence and progression of aortic atherosclerosis was found after adjusting for multiple cardiovascular risk factors.[403] Furthermore, testosterone is related to many cardiovascular risk factors, having a negative association with hypertension,[407] fasting plasma glucose,[206] hyperinsulinemia,[408] and visceral adiposity,[409] and an uncertain association with high-density lipoprotein (HDL) cholesterol.[410]

### EVIDENCE-BASED DATA REGARDING TESTOSTERONE SUPPLEMENTATION IN AGING MEN

The use of testosterone treatment for symptomatic older men with borderline low testosterone levels presumes that these men will enjoy similar benefits to those seen in younger hypogonadal subjects. Because of the association between the physical changes of aging and serum androgen levels, it has been proposed that testosterone supplementation may attenuate or even reverse age-associated sarcopenia, protect against osteoporosis, enhance the physical strength and mental and psychological well-being of older males, and improve coronary heart disease risk profile. Very few properly conducted randomized, double-blind, placebo-controlled studies have been performed, however.[411] Developing an overview of the results of these studies is made difficult by their use of different doses and formulations of testosterone, varying durations of treatment (3 months to 3 years), and the inclusion of cohorts with a wide range of baseline testosterone levels.[411] One major consideration in reviewing the literature is the difficulty in distinguishing physiologic from pharmocologic androgen action. For example, the consistently reported changes in body composition may represent the effects of supplementing

endogenous testosterone in eugonadal older men rather than the effects of replacement in hypoandrogenism. It should also be borne in mind that the long-term risks of testosterone treatment of older men who are not clearly hypoandrogenic are unknown.

An outline of the major findings from trials involving nonobese, otherwise healthy men, with or without hypoandrogenic symptoms, is shown in Table 170-10. These results are discussed in more detail in the following sections.

### Body Composition

Thirty-six months of testosterone treatment administered to healthy older men increased mean serum testosterone from 12.7 to 21.7 nM and led to a 1.9-kg (4%) increase in lean mass and a 3-kg (14%) decrease in fat mass, but with no demonstrable effect on dynamometric measures of muscle strength, although subjects with the lowest baseline testosterone levels reported that they perceived their physical performance to be improved.[412] A similar change in body composition was seen after 1 year of testosterone supplementation in older eugonadal men,[413,414] and 90 days of treatment in overweight/obese hypogonadal older men.[415] Improvement in muscle strength may be produced in older men when supraphysiologic testosterone levels are achieved.[416] The increase in lean body mass has been linked to a decrease in muscle protein breakdown.[416] Whether the increase in muscle mass results in improved strength or physical function is uncertain, but some short-term benefits are suggested after treatment with testosterone,[413,417] dihydrotestosterone,[418] or hCG.[419]

Further to the reduction in total fat mass that has been consistently demonstrated, regional fat loss may be significant with regard to cardiovascular risk. Intra-abdominal visceral fat loss was seen (on MRI) in nonobese men treated for 6 months with intramuscular testosterone.[420] Similar result have been reported in obese men.[201,421]

### Bone

Overall testosterone may improve bone mineral density (BMD) in men with levels at the lower end of reference range,

| Table 170-10 | Randomized Controlled Trials of Testosterone Supplementation in Aging Men | |
|---|---|---|
| Benefits | Body composition | Lean (muscle) mass ↑ |
| | | Strength and physical function ↑ or ↔ |
| | | Fat mass (including visceral fat) ↓ |
| | Bone | Bone mineral density ↑ (femoral neck and lumbar spine) when baseline T low |
| | | No fracture data |
| | Sexual function | Sexual motivation and performance ↑ (when baseline T low) |
| | | Erectile function ↔ |
| | Mood and cognition | Mood and quality of life ↔ |
| | | Selected aspects of memory ↑ |
| Risks | Prostate | Variable ↑ in PSA (within normal range) |
| | | Prostate size, urine flow ↔ |
| | | Inadequate data on risk of malignancy or development of clinical BPH |
| | Polycythemia | Increasing risk with dose and age |
| | Sleep apnea | Not reported |
| | Cardiovascular | Total or LDL cholesterol and triglycerides ↔ |
| | | Small ↓ in high-density cholesterol |
| | | Surrogate markers for cardiovascular risk ↔ |

BPH, benign prostatic hyperplasia; LDL, low-density lipoprotein; PSA, prostate-specific antigen; T, testosterone.

but there have been no studies powered to examine fracture rates, and there is no concensus as to the role of androgens as antiresorptive agents in eugonadal older men. Testosterone treatment did not improve bone mineral density relative to a vitamin D plus calcium placebo in older men, although, in a post hoc analysis, benefits were seen in those with baseline testosterone levels less than 10.4 nM.[422] Twelve months of transdermal testosterone therapy did not affect bone turnover markers nor increase bone density, but did prevent loss at the femoral neck when compared to placebo.[413] In a similar study of 70 men with testosterone levels less than 12.1 nM, there were increases in lumbar and femoral neck bone mineral density relative to placebo.[423]

### Sexual Function

Most placebo-controlled studies of testosterone replacement assessing sexual function[424] have failed to demonstrate a significant improvement; of note, baseline testosterone values were in low-normal range, consistent with the "threshold-for-sexual-function" theory. Improvement in sexual motivation and performance was reported, relative to placebo, in men with baseline levels less than 10.4 nM receiving 100 mg of testosterone gel daily.[415] A retrospective analysis of older hypogonadal men receiving replacement therapy noted that, although libido was reported to be significantly improved, one third of men did not continue treatment.[425]

Erectile dysfunction in men with low-normal serum testosterone levels is not likely to respond to testosterone supplementation alone. The erectile response in men with borderline low testosterone levels who have previously been resistant to sildenafil may show improvement,[426] however, perhaps by the induction of nitric oxide synthase in the penile vascular endothelium.

### Prostate Health

The limited experience provided by randomized clinical trials (RCTs) testosterone has not shown an excess incidence of prostate cancer,[427] but, importantly, none has been powered for long-term prostate safety, and older men receiving testosterone therapy should be counseled about prostate cancer screening.[427,428] A rise in prostate-specific antigen (PSA) has been reported, although the mean posttreatment PSA levels remained less than 3.0 ng/mL.[413,417,422] Prostate size on examination, urine flow studies, and symptom score, where assessed, have not shown change.

### Well-Being and Cognition

Overall, data have not shown benefits in terms of well-being or cognitive function end points,[412,429,430] but some benefits in spatial and verbal memory were demonstrated when serum testosterone was elevated to supraphysiologic levels.[431] Enhanced spatial memory and working memory were reported in healthy older men when serum testosterone levels were raised into the upper-normal range.[432,433] A small group of elderly men with early cognitive impairment did not show any improvement when treated with intramuscular testosterone for 3 months.[434]

The role of testosterone therapy for middle-aged and older men with depression is uncertain. Two studies of men with major depression and baseline testosterone levels of 9 to 10 nM, found conflicting results, with either no effect[435] or a benefit relative to placebo[436] when serum testosterone levels were raised to supraphysiologic levels.

### TESTOSTERONE THERAPY: MODALITIES, MONITORING, AND POTENTIAL RISKS IN AGING MEN

Testosterone replacement therapy is discussed in detail elsewhere (see Chapter 168). Issues of particular relevance to older men include the choice of testosterone formulation, monitoring, and potential risks, specifically, prostate health (see previous), polycythemia, sleep apnea, altered lipid profiles, and cardiovascular risk.[427]

Implants should be used with caution in older men because of their long duration of action and the problems their removal may present in the event of a coincidental diagnosis of prostate cancer. Anticoagulant therapy, more commonly prescribed in older men, is a contraindication to intramuscular therapy.

Older men appear to be particularly susceptible to polycythemia, with a 5% to 20% rise in hematocrit commonly seen with routine intramuscular therapy.[364] Other testosterone formulations also lead to significant increases in hematocrit and/or hemoglobin,[411,422] making monitoring essential. Whether this increase is dose dependent, as in younger hypogonadal men,[437] is unclear.

Sleep apnea may be exacerbated by exogenous testosterone,[438] perhaps due to an effect on laryngeal muscles. One RCT using physiologic testosterone treatment found no changes in sleep pattern,[422] but short-term supraphysiologic testosterone treatment in older men reduced sleep quality and was not predicted by baseline testosterone levels or sleep pattern.[293] An appropriate history should be taken before initiating therapy and regularly thereafter.

The data pertinent to testosterone treatment in aging men suggest limited effect on lipid profiles, with falls of approximately 10% in total cholesterol and low-density lipoprotein (LDL) cholesterol,[364] although with slightly greater falls in HDL cholesterol. The placebo-controlled studies that used a number of different therapeutic modalities to increase testosterone levels in older men to within the healthy young adult male range also showed minimal effect on total and LDL cholesterol and trigylcerides, although a significant decline in HDL-cholesterol levels has been seen.[411] Randomized controlled trials of testosterone supplementation to date have not been of sufficient duration to determine its effect on the development of cardiovascular disease, and there is only limited information about surrogate markers for coronary heart disease. Vascular reactivity, a noninvasive measure of endothelial function and a recognized marker for atherosclerosis, was not influenced by transdermal testosterone[439] or dihydrotestosterone,[418] although only small numbers of men were studied. Treatment of older men with either dihydrotestosterone or human chorionic gonadotropin did not alter serum inflammatory markers associated with atherosclerosis.[440] Overall, the effects of androgens on hemostatic factors related to cardiovascular risk remain uncertain[441] and may be affected by both the dosage (physiologic versus pharmacologic) and the baseline hormonal status of the subjects. Despite the limitations of current knowledge, analysis of the published data suggests that the use of androgens in older men should not be limited by concerns of increased cardiovascular risk.[405]

Finally, in regard to future research in the field, the extensive 2003 Institute of Medicine report highlighted the limited data that support substantial benefits of testosterone treatment of older men with low-normal T levels and identified a need for coordinated research programs to better define the extent of its potential benefits as a therapeutic agent to address specific problems (frailty, impaired cognition, quality of life).[442] In due course, larger studies powered to assess risk of adverse outcomes, such as prostatic cancer risk, might then be considered.

### Acknowledgments
The authors gratefully acknowledge the significant contributions made by Dr. Stephen J. Winters and the editors of previous editions of this textbook.

# REFERENCES

1. Bojesen A, Juul S, Gravholt CH: Prenatal and postnatal prevalence of Klinefelter syndrome: A national registry study. J Clin Endocrinol Metab 88:622–626, 2003.
2. Seminara SB, Hayes FJ, Crowley WF Jr: Gonadotropin-releasing hormone deficiency in the human (idiopathic hypogonadotropic hypogonadism and Kallmann's syndrome): Pathophysiological and genetic considerations. Endocr Rev 19:521–539, 1998.
3. Hayes F, Pitteloud N: Hypogonadotropic hypogonadism and gonadotropin therapy. In McLachlan RI, DeGroot LJ (eds): Male Reproductive Endocrinology, 2004, www.endotext.org
4. Van Dop C, Burstein S, Conte FA, et al: Isolated gonadotropin deficiency in boys: Clinical characteristics and growth. J Pediatr 111:684–692, 1987.
5. Finkelstein JS, Klibanski A, Neer RM, et al: Osteoporosis in men with idiopathic hypogonadotropic hypogonadism. Ann Intern Med 106:354–361, 1987.
6. Uriarte MM, Baron J, Garcia HB, et al: The effect of pubertal delay on adult height in men with isolated hypogonadotropic hypogonadism. J Clin Endocrinol Metab 74:436–440, 1992.
7. Counts DR, Pescovitz OH, Barnes KM, et al: Dissociation of adrenarche and gonadarche in precocious puberty and in isolated hypogonadotropic hypogonadism. J Clin Endocrinol Metab 64:1174–1178, 1987.
8. Wu FC, Butler GE, Kelnar CJ, et al: Patterns of pulsatile luteinizing hormone and follicle-stimulating hormone secretion in prepubertal (midchildhood) boys and girls and patients with idiopathic hypogonadotropic hypogonadism (Kallmann's syndrome): A study using an ultrasensitive time-resolved immunofluorometric assay. J Clin Endocrinol Metab 72:1229–1237, 1991.
9. Goji K, Tanikaze S: Comparison between spontaneous gonadotropin concentration profiles and gonadotropin response to low-dose gonadotropin-releasing hormone in prepubertal and early pubertal boys and patients with hypogonadotropic hypogonadism: Assessment by using ultrasensitive, time-resolved immunofluorometric assay. Pediatr Res 31:535–539, 1992.
10. Hoffman AR, Crowley WF Jr: Induction of puberty in men by long-term pulsatile administration of low-dose gonadotropin-releasing hormone. N Engl J Med 307:1237–1241, 1982.
11. Lieblich JM, Rogol AD, White BJ, et al: Syndrome of anosmia with hypogonadotropic hypogonadism (Kallmann syndrome): Clinical and laboratory studies in 23 cases. Am J Med 73:506–519, 1982.
12. Liu L, Merriam GR, Sherins RJ: Chronic sex steroid exposure increases mean plasma growth hormone concentration and pulse amplitude in men with isolated hypogonadotropic hypogonadism. J Clin Endocrinol Metab 64:651–656, 1987.
13. Boyar RM, Wu RH, Kapen S, et al: Clinical and laboratory heterogeneity in idiopathic hypogonadotropic hypogonadism. J Clin Endocrinol Metab 43:1268–1275, 1976.
14. Spratt DI, Carr DB, Merriam GR, et al: The spectrum of abnormal patterns of gonadotropin-releasing hormone secretion in men with idiopathic hypogonadotropic hypogonadism: Clinical and laboratory correlations. J Clin Endocrinol Metab 64:283–291, 1987.
15. Kallmann FJ, Schoenfeld WA, Barrera SE: Genetic aspects of primary eunuchoidism. Am J Ment Defic 48:203–236, 1944.
16. Klingmuller D, Dewes W, Krahe T, et al: Magnetic resonance imaging of the brain in patients with anosmia and hypothalamic hypogonadism (Kallmann's syndrome). J Clin Endocrinol Metab 65:581–584, 1987.
17. Schwankhaus JD, Currie J, Jaffe MJ, et al: Neurologic findings in men with isolated hypogonadotropic hypogonadism. Neurology 39:223–226, 1989.
18. Waldstreicher J, Seminara SB, Jameson JL, et al: The genetic and clinical heterogeneity of gonadotropin-releasing hormone deficiency in the human. J Clin Endocrinol Metab 81:4388–4395, 1996.
19. Sato N, Katsumata N, Kagami M, et al: Clinical assessment and mutation analysis of Kallmann syndrome 1 (Kal1) and fibroblast growth factor receptor 1 (FGFR1, or Kal2) in five families and 18 sporadic patients. J Clin Endocrinol Metab 89:1079–1088, 2004.
20. Schwanzel-Fukuda M, Pfaff DW: Origin of luteinizing hormone-releasing hormone neurons. Nature 338:161–164, 1989.
21. Schwanzel-Fukuda M, Bick D, Pfaff DW: Luteinizing hormone-releasing hormone (LHRH)-expressing cells do not migrate normally in an inherited hypogonadal (Kallmann) syndrome. Brain Res Mol Brain Res 6:311–326, 1989.
22. Maya-Nunez G, Zenteno JC, Ulloa-Aguirre A, et al: A recurrent missense mutation in the Kal gene in patients with X-linked Kallmann's syndrome. J Clin Endocrinol Metab 83:1650–1653, 1998.
23. Parenti G, Rizzolo MG, Ghezzi M, et al: Variable penetrance of hypogonadism in a sibship with Kallmann syndrome due to a deletion of the Kal gene. Am J Med Genet 57:476–478, 1995.
24. Stojilkovic SS, Reinhart J, Catt KJ: Gonadotropin-releasing hormone receptors: Structure and signal transduction pathways. Endocr Rev 15:462–499, 1994.
25. de Roux N, Young J, Misrahi M, et al: A family with hypogonadotropic hypogonadism and mutations in the gonadotropin-releasing hormone receptor. N Engl J Med 337:1597–1602, 1997.
26. Caron P, Imbeaud S, Bennet A, et al: Combined hypothalamic-pituitary-gonadal defect in a hypogonadic man with a novel mutation in the Dax-1 gene. J Clin Endocrinol Metab 84:3563–3569, 1999.
27. Dode C, Levilliers J, Dupont JM, et al: Loss-of-function mutations in FGFR1 cause autosomal dominant Kallmann syndrome. Nat Genet 33:463–465, 2003.
28. de Roux N, Genin E, Carel JC, et al: Hypogonadotropic hypogonadism due to loss of function of the Kiss1-derived peptide receptor GPR54. Proc Natl Acad Sci U S A 100:10972–10976, 2003.
29. Seminara SB, Messager S, Chatzidaki EE, et al: The GPR54 gene as a regulator of puberty. N Engl J Med 349:1614–1627, 2003.
30. Peter M, Viemann M, Partsch CJ, et al: Congenital adrenal hypoplasia: Clinical spectrum, experience with hormonal diagnosis, and report on new point mutations of the Dax-1 gene. J Clin Endocrinol Metab 83:2666–2674, 1998.
31. Zanaria E, Muscatelli F, Bardoni B, et al: An unusual member of the nuclear hormone receptor superfamily responsible for X-linked adrenal hypoplasia congenita. Nature 372:635–641, 1994.
32. Wong M, Ikeda Y, Luo X, et al: Steroidogenic factor 1 plays multiple roles in endocrine development and function. Recent Prog Horm Res 52:167–182, discussion 182–164, 1997.
33. Habiby RL, Boepple P, Nachtigall L, et al: Adrenal hypoplasia congenita with hypogonadotropic hypogonadism: Evidence that Dax-1 mutations lead to combined hypothalamic and pituitary defects in gonadotropin production. J Clin Invest 98:1055–1062, 1996.
34. Cassidy SB: Prader-Willi syndrome. J Med Genet 34:917–923, 1997.
35. Crino A, Schiaffini R, Ciampalini P, et al: Hypogonadism and pubertal development in Prader-Willi syndrome. Eur J Pediatr 162:327–333, 2003.
36. Jeffcoate WJ, Laurance BM, Edwards CR, et al: Endocrine function in the Prader-Willi syndrome. Clin Endocrinol (Oxf) 12:81–89, 1980.
37. Bray GA, Dahms WT, Swerdloff RS, et al: The Prader-Willi syndrome: A study of 40 patients and a review of the literature. Medicine (Baltimore) 62:59–80, 1983.
38. Hoybye C: Endocrine and metabolic aspects of adult Prader-Willi syndrome with special emphasis on the effect of growth hormone treatment. Growth Horm IGF Res 14:1–15, 2004.

39. Bray GA: Laurence, Moon, Bardet, and Biedl: Reflections on a syndrome. Obes Res 3:383–386, 1995.

40. Toledo SP, Medeiros-Neto GA, Knobel M, et al: Evaluation of the hypothalamic-pituitary-gonadal function in the Bardet-Biedl syndrome. Metabolism 26:1277–1291, 1977.

41. Kumar D: Moebius syndrome. J Med Genet 27:122–126, 1990.

42. Verzijl HT, van der Zwaag B, Cruysberg JR, et al: Möbius syndrome redefined: A syndrome of rhombencephalic maldevelopment. Neurology 61:327–333, 2003.

43. Brackett LE, Demers LM, Mamourian AC, et al: Moebius syndrome in association with hypogonadotropic hypogonadism. J Endocrinol Invest 14:599–607, 1991.

44. Lin T, Orrison BM, Suchy SF, et al: Mutations are not uniformly distributed throughout the Ocrl1 gene in Lowe syndrome patients. Mol Genet Metab 64:58–61, 1998.

45. Suchy SF, Nussbaum RL: The deficiency of pip2 5-phosphatase in Lowe syndrome affects actin polymerization. Am J Hum Genet 71:1420–1427, 2002.

46. Sharland M, Burch M, McKenna WM, et al: A clinical study of Noonan syndrome. Arch Dis Child 67:178–183, 1992.

47. Saenger P: Editorial: Noonan syndrome: Certitude replaces conjecture. J Clin Endocrinol Metab 87:3527–3528, 2002.

48. Jamieson CR, van der Burgt I, Brady AF, et al: Mapping a gene for Noonan syndrome to the long arm of chromosome 12. Nat Genet 8:357–360, 1994.

49. Theintz G, Savage MO: Growth and pubertal development in five boys with Noonan's syndrome. Arch Dis Child 57:13–17, 1982.

50. Ross JL, Shenkman L: Noonan's syndrome and hypopituitarism. Am J Med Sci 279:47–52, 1980.

51. Legius E, Schrander-Stumpel C, Schollen E, et al: Ptpn11 mutations in LEOPARD syndrome. J Med Genet 39:571–574, 2002.

52. Maghnie M, Triulzi F, Larizza D, et al: Hypothalamic-pituitary dysfunction in growth hormone-deficient patients with pituitary abnormalities. J Clin Endocrinol Metab 73:79–83, 1991.

53. Maghnie M, Genovese E, Villa A, et al: Dynamic MRI in the congenital agenesis of the neural pituitary stalk syndrome: The role of the vascular pituitary stalk in predicting residual anterior pituitary function. Clin Endocrinol (Oxf) 45:281–290, 1996.

54. Deladoey J, Fluck C, Buyukgebiz A, et al: "hot spot" in the Prop1 gene responsible for combined pituitary hormone deficiency. J Clin Endocrinol Metab 84:1645–1650, 1999.

55. Lazar L, Gat-Yablonski G, Kornreich L, et al: Prop-1 gene mutation (r120c) causing combined pituitary hormone deficiencies with variable clinical course in eight siblings of one Jewish Moroccan family. Horm Res 60:227–231, 2003.

56. Littley MD, Shalet SM, Beardwell CG, et al: Hypopituitarism following external radiotherapy for pituitary tumours in adults. Q J Med 70:145–160, 1989.

57. Luton JP, Thieblot P, Valcke JC, et al: Reversible gonadotropin deficiency in male Cushing's disease. J Clin Endocrinol Metab 45:488–495, 1977.

58. Nieman LK, Chrousos GP, Kellner C, et al: Successful treatment of Cushing's syndrome with the glucocorticoid antagonist RU486. J Clin Endocrinol Metab 61:536–540, 1985.

59. Chandran UR, Attardi B, Friedman R, et al: Glucocorticoid repression of the mouse gonadotropin-releasing hormone gene is mediated by promoter elements that are recognized by heteromeric complexes containing glucocorticoid receptor. J Biol Chem 271:20412–20420, 1996.

60. Nawata H, Ono K, Ohashi M, et al: RU486 inhibits induction of aromatase by dexamethasone via glucocorticoid receptor in cultured human skin fibroblasts. J Steroid Biochem 29:63–68, 1988.

61. MacAdams MR, White RH, Chipps BE: Reduction of serum testosterone levels during chronic glucocorticoid therapy. Ann Intern Med 104:648–651, 1986.

62. Carter JN, Tyson JE, Tolis G, et al: Prolactin-screening tumors and hypogonadism in 22 men. N Engl J Med 299:847–852, 1978.

63. Franks S, Jacobs HS, Martin N, et al: Hyperprolactinaemia and impotence. Clin Endocrinol (Oxf) 8:277–287, 1978.

64. Patton ML, Woolf PD: Hyperprolactinemia and delayed puberty: A report of three cases and their response to therapy. Pediatrics 71:572–575, 1983.

65. Colao A, Vitale G, Cappabianca P, et al: Outcome of cabergoline treatment in men with prolactinoma: Effects of a 24-month treatment on prolactin levels, tumor mass, recovery of pituitary function, and semen analysis. J Clin Endocrinol Metab 89:1704–1711, 2004.

66. Pinzone JJ, Katznelson L, Danila DC, et al: Primary medical therapy of micro- and macroprolactinomas in men. J Clin Endocrinol Metab 85:3053–3057, 2000.

67. Winters SJ, Troen P: Altered pulsatile secretion of luteinizing hormone in hypogonadal men with hyperprolactinaemia. Clin Endocrinol (Oxf) 21:257–263, 1984.

68. Bouchard P, Lagoguey M, Brailly S, et al: Gonadotropin-releasing hormone pulsatile administration restores luteinizing hormone pulsatility and normal testosterone levels in males with hyperprolactinemia. J Clin Endocrinol Metab 60:258–262, 1985.

69. De Rosa M, Colao A, Di Sarno A, et al: Cabergoline treatment rapidly improves gonadal function in hyperprolactinemic males: A comparison with bromocriptine. Eur J Endocrinol 138:286–293, 1998.

70. Maghnie M, Bossi G, Klersy C, et al: Dynamic endocrine testing and magnetic resonance imaging in the long-term follow-up of childhood Langerhans cell histiocytosis. J Clin Endocrinol Metab 83:3089–3094, 1998.

71. Braunstein GD, Kohler PO: Endocrine manifestations of histiocytosis. Am J Pediatr Hematol Oncol 3:67–75, 1981.

72. Stuart CA, Neelon FA, Lebovitz HE: Hypothalamic insufficiency: The cause of hypopituitarism in sarcoidosis. Ann Intern Med 88:589–594, 1978.

73. Cannavo S, Romano C, Buffa R, et al: Granulomatous sarcoidotic lesion of hypothalamic-pituitary region associated with Rathke's cleft cyst. J Endocrinol Invest 20:77–81, 1997.

74. Kuhn JM, Mahoudeau JA, Billaud L, et al: Evaluation of diagnostic criteria for Leydig cell tumours in adult men revealed by gynaecomastia. Clin Endocrinol (Oxf) 26:407–416, 1987.

75. Veldhuis JD, Sowers JR, Rogol AD, et al: Pathophysiology of male hypogonadism associated with endogenous hyperestrogenism: Evidence for dual defects in the gonadal axis. N Engl J Med 312:1371–1375, 1985.

76. Stepanas AV, Samaan NA, Schultz PN, et al: Endocrine studies in testicular tumor patients with and without gynecomastia: A report of 45 cases. Cancer 41:369–376, 1978.

77. Saller B, Clara R, Spottl G, et al: Testicular cancer secretes intact human choriogonadotropin (hCG) and its free beta-subunit: Evidence that hCG (+hCG-beta) assays are the most reliable in diagnosis and follow-up. Clin Chem 36:234–239, 1990.

78. Huhtaniemi I: Gonadotrophin actions on the testis: Genotypes and phenotypes of gonadotrophin and gonadotrophin receptor mutations. Endocr Dev 5:81–103, 2003.

79. Weiss J, Axelrod L, Whitcomb RW, et al: Hypogonadism caused by a single amino acid substitution in the beta subunit of luteinizing hormone. N Engl J Med 326:179–183, 1992.

80. Haavisto AM, Pettersson K, Bergendahl M, et al: Occurrence and biological properties of a common genetic variant of luteinizing hormone. J Clin Endocrinol Metab 80:1257–1263, 1995.

81. Lindstedt G, Nystrom E, Matthews C, et al: Follitropin (FSH) deficiency in an infertile male due to FSH-beta gene mutation: A syndrome of normal puberty and virilization but underdeveloped testicles with azoospermia, low FSH but high lutropin and normal serum testosterone concentrations. Clin Chem Lab Med 36:663–665, 1998.

82. Phillip M, Arbelle JE, Segev Y, et al: Male hypogonadism due to a mutation in the gene for the beta-subunit of follicle-stimulating hormone. N Engl J Med 338:1729–1732, 1998.

83. Tapanainen JS, Aittomaki K, Min J, et al: Men homozygous for an inactivating mutation of the follicle-stimulating hormone (FSH) receptor gene present

variable suppression of spermatogenesis and fertility. Nat Genet 15:205–206, 1997.

84. Behre HM, Kliesch S, Leifke E, et al: Long-term effect of testosterone therapy on bone mineral density in hypogonadal men. J Clin Endocrinol Metab 82:2386–2390, 1997.

85. Finkelstein JS, Neer RM, Biller BM, et al: Osteopenia in men with a history of delayed puberty. N Engl J Med 326:600–604, 1992.

86. Burger HG, de Kretser DM, Hudson B, et al: Effects of preceding androgen therapy on testicular response to human pituitary gonadotropin in hypogonadotropic hypogonadism: A study of three patients. Fertil Steril 35:64–68, 1981.

87. Burris AS, Rodbard HW, Winters SJ, et al: Gonadotropin therapy in men with isolated hypogonadotropic hypogonadism: The response to human chorionic gonadotropin is predicted by initial testicular size. J Clin Endocrinol Metab 66:1144–1151, 1988.

88. Finkel DM, Phillips JL, Snyder PJ: Stimulation of spermatogenesis by gonadotropins in men with hypogonadotropic hypogonadism. N Engl J Med 313:651–655, 1985.

89. Johnsen SG: Maintenance of spermatogenesis induced by HmG treatment by means of continuous HcH treatment in hypogonadotrophic men. Acta Endocrinol (Copenh) 89:763–769, 1978.

90. European Metrodin HP Study Group: Efficacy and safety of highly purified urinary follicle-stimulating hormone with human chorionic gonadotropin for treating men with isolated hypogonadotropic hypogonadism. Fertil Steril 70:256–262, 1998.

91. Burris AS, Clark RV, Vantman DJ, et al: A low sperm concentration does not preclude fertility in men with isolated hypogonadotropic hypogonadism after gonadotropin therapy. Fertil Steril 50:343–347, 1988.

92. Liu PY, Gebski VJ, Turner L, et al: Predicting pregnancy and spermatogenesis by survival analysis during gonadotrophin treatment of gonadotrophin-deficient infertile men. Hum Reprod 17:625–633, 2002.

93. Buchter D, Behre HM, Kliesch S, et al: Pulsatile GnRH or human chorionic gonadotropin/human menopausal gonadotropin as effective treatment for men with hypogonadotropic hypogonadism: A review of 42 cases. Eur J Endocrinol 139:298–303, 1998.

94. Whitcomb RW, Crowley WF Jr: Clinical review 4: Diagnosis and treatment of isolated gonadotropin-releasing hormone deficiency in men. J Clin Endocrinol Metab 70:3–7, 1990.

95. Schopohl J, Mehltretter G, von Zumbusch R, et al: Comparison of gonadotropin-releasing hormone and gonadotropin therapy in male patients with idiopathic hypothalamic hypogonadism. Fertil Steril 56:1143–1150, 1991.

96. Popovic V, Milosevic Z, Djukanovic R, et al: Hypersensitivity reaction with intravenous GnRH after pulsatile subcutaneous GnRH treatment in male hypogonadotrophic hypogonadism. Postgrad Med J 64:245–246, 1988.

97. Blumenfeld Z, Frisch L, Conn PM: Gonadotropin-releasing hormone (GnRH) antibodies formation in hypogonadotropic azoospermic men treated with pulsatile GnRH: Diagnosis and possible alternative treatment. Fertil Steril 50:622–629, 1988.

98. Feldman JM, Postlethwaite RW, Glenn JF: Hot flashes and sweats in men with testicular insufficiency. Arch Intern Med 136:606–608, 1976.

99. Mecklenburg RS, Sherins RJ: Gonadotropin response to luteinizing hormone-releasing hormone in men with germinal aplasia. J Clin Endocrinol Metab 38:1005–1008, 1974.

100. Winters SJ, Troen P: A reexamination of pulsatile luteinizing hormone secretion in primary testicular failure. J Clin Endocrinol Metab 57:432–435, 1983.

101. Matsumoto AM, Bremner WJ: Modulation of pulsatile gonadotropin secretion by testosterone in man. J Clin Endocrinol Metab 58:609–614, 1984.

102. Winters SJ, Troen P: Evidence for a role of endogenous estrogen in the hypothalamic control of gonadotropin secretion in men. J Clin Endocrinol Metab 61:842–845, 1985.

103. Jensen TK, Andersson AM, Hjollund NH, et al: Inhibin B as a serum marker of spermatogenesis: Correlation to differences in sperm concentration and follicle-stimulating hormone levels: A study of 349 danish men. J Clin Endocrinol Metab 82:4059–4063, 1997.

104. Anawalt BD, Bebb RA, Matsumoto AM, et al: Serum inhibin B levels reflect Sertoli cell function in normal men and men with testicular dysfunction. J Clin Endocrinol Metab 81:3341–3345, 1996.

105. Wallace EM, Groome NP, Riley SC, et al: Effects of chemotherapy-induced testicular damage on inhibin, gonadotropin, and testosterone secretion: A prospective longitudinal study. J Clin Endocrinol Metab 82:3111–3115, 1997.

106. Smyth CM, Bremner WJ: Klinefelter syndrome. Arch Intern Med 158:1309–1314, 1998.

107. Kamischke A, Baumgardt A, Horst J, et al: Clinical and diagnostic features of patients with suspected Klinefelter syndrome. J Androl 24:41–48, 2003.

108. Simpson JL, de la Cruz F, Swerdloff RS, et al: Klinefelter syndrome: Expanding the phenotype and identifying new research directions. Genet Med 5:460–468, 2003.

109. Thomas NS, Hassold TJ: Aberrant recombination and the origin of Klinefelter syndrome. Hum Reprod Update 9:309–317, 2003.

110. Jacobs PA, Hassold TJ, Whittington E, et al: Klinefelter's syndrome: An analysis of the origin of the additional sex chromosome using molecular probes. Ann Hum Genet 52(Pt 2):93–109, 1988.

111. Caldwell PD, Smith DW: The XXY (Klinefelter's) syndrome in childhood: Detection and treatment. J Pediatr 80:250–258, 1972.

112. Paulsen CA, Gordon DL, Carpenter RW, et al: Klinefelter's syndrome and its variants: A hormonal and chromosomal study. Recent Prog Horm Res 24:321–363, 1968.

113. Wikstrom AM, Raivio T, Hadziselimovic F, et al: Klinefelter syndrome in adolescence: Onset of puberty is associated with accelerated germ cell depletion. J Clin Endocrinol Metab 89:2263–2270, 2004.

114. Swerdlow AJ, Hermon C, Jacobs PA, et al: Mortality and cancer incidence in persons with numerical sex chromosome abnormalities: A cohort study. Ann Hum Genet 65:177–188, 2001.

115. Hasle H, Mellemgaard A, Nielsen J, et al: Cancer incidence in men with Klinefelter syndrome. Br J Cancer 71:416–420, 1995.

116. Horowitz M, Wishart JM, O'Loughlin PD, et al: Osteoporosis and Klinefelter's syndrome. Clin Endocrinol (Oxf) 36:113–118, 1992.

117. Samaan NA, Stepanas AV, Danziger J, et al: Reactive pituitary abnormalities in patients with Klinefelter's and Turner's syndromes. Arch Intern Med 139:198–201, 1979.

118. Sorensen K: Physical and mental development of adolescent males with Klinefelter syndrome. Horm Res 37(Suppl 3):55–61, 1992.

119. Fales CL, Knowlton BJ, Holyoak KJ, et al: Working memory and relational reasoning in Klinefelter syndrome. J Int Neuropsychol Soc 9:839–846, 2003.

120. Rovet J, Netley C, Keenan M, et al: The psychoeducational profile of boys with Klinefelter syndrome. J Learn Disabil 29:180–196, 1996.

121. Wang C, Baker HW, Burger HG, et al: Hormonal studies in Klinefelter's syndrome. Clin Endocrinol (Oxf) 4:399–411, 1975.

122. Christiansen P, Andersson AM, Skakkebaek NE: Longitudinal studies of inhibin B levels in boys and young adults with Klinefelter syndrome. J Clin Endocrinol Metab 88:888–891, 2003.

123. Plymate SR, Leonard JM, Paulsen CA, et al: Sex hormone–binding globulin changes with androgen replacement. J Clin Endocrinol Metab 57:645–648, 1983.

124. Smals AG, Kloppenborg PW, Pieters GF, et al: Basal and human chorionic gonadotropin–stimulated 17-alpha-hydroxyprogesterone and testosterone levels in Klinefelter's syndrome. J Clin Endocrinol Metab 47:1144–1147, 1978.

125. Spitz IM, Zylber E, Cohen H, et al: Impaired prolactin response to thyrotropin-releasing hormone in isolated gonadotropin deficiency and

exaggerated response in primary testicular failure. J Clin Endocrinol Metab 48:941–945, 1979.

126. Nielsen J, Pelsen B, Sorensen K: Follow-up of 30 Klinefelter males treated with testosterone. Clin Genet 33:262–269, 1988.

127. Kubler A, Schulz G, Cordes U, et al: The influence of testosterone substitution on bone mineral density in patients with Klinefelter's syndrome. Exp Clin Endocrinol 100:129–132, 1992.

128. Caminos-Torres R, Ma L, Snyder PJ: Testosterone-induced inhibition of the LH and FSH responses to gonadotropin-releasing hormone occurs slowly. J Clin Endocrinol Metab 44:1142–1153, 1977.

129. Tournaye H, Staessen C, Liebaers I, et al: Testicular sperm recovery in nine 47,XXY Klinefelter patients. Hum Reprod 11:1644–1649, 1996.

130. Palermo GD, Schlegel PN, Sills ES, et al: Births after intracytoplasmic injection of sperm obtained by testicular extraction from men with nonmosaic Klinefelter's syndrome. N Engl J Med 338:588–590, 1998.

131. Gordon DL, Krmpotic E, Thomas W, et al: Pathologic testicular findings in Klinefelter's syndrome. 47,XXY vs 46,XY-47,XXY. Arch Intern Med 130:726–729, 1972.

132. Bloomgarden ZT, Delozier CD, Cohen MP, et al: Genetic and endocrine findings in a 48,XXYY male. J Clin Endocrinol Metab 50:740–743, 1980.

133. de la Chapelle A: The etiology of maleness in XX men. Hum Genet 58:105–116, 1981.

134. Page DC, Brown LG, de la Chapelle A: Exchange of terminal portions of X- and Y-chromosomal short arms in human XX males. Nature 328:437–440, 1987.

135. Sinclair AH, Berta P, Palmer MS, et al: A gene from the human sex-determining region encodes a protein with homology to a conserved DNA-binding motif. Nature 346:240–244, 1990.

136. Fechner PY, Marcantonio SM, Jaswaney V, et al: The role of the sex-determining region Y gene in the etiology of 46,XX maleness. J Clin Endocrinol Metab 76:690–695, 1993.

137. Harley VR, Clarkson MJ, Argentaro A: The molecular action and regulation of the testis-determining factors, SRY (sex-determining region on the Y chromosome) and SOX9 (SRY-related high-mobility group [HMG] box 9). Endocr Rev 24:466–487, 2003.

138. Perez-Palacios G, Medina M, Ullao-Aguirre A, et al: Gonadotropin dynamics in XX males. J Clin Endocrinol Metab 53:254–257, 1981.

139. Ishida H: Studies on pituitary-gonadal endocrine function in patients with male hermaphroditism [author's transl]. Nippon Hinyokika Gakkai Zasshi 70:655–667, 1979.

140. Benet J, Martin RH: Sperm chromosome complements in a 47,XYY man. Hum Genet 78:313–315, 1988.

141. Smith NM, Byard RW, Bourne AJ: Testicular regression syndrome: A pathological study of 77 cases. Histopathology 19:269–272, 1991.

142. Lobaccaro JM, Medlej R, Berta P, et al: PCR analysis and sequencing of the SRY sex determining gene in four patients with bilateral congenital anorchia. Clin Endocrinol (Oxf) 38:197–201, 1993.

143. Lee MM, Donahoe PK, Silverman BL, et al: Measurements of serum müllerian inhibiting substance in the evaluation of children with nonpalpable gonads. N Engl J Med 336:1480–1486, 1997.

144. De Rosa M, Lupoli G, Mennitti M, et al: Congenital bilateral anorchia: Clinical, hormonal and imaging study in 12 cases. Andrologia 28:281–285, 1996.

145. Kubini K, Zachmann M, Albers N, et al: Basal inhibin B and the testosterone response to human chorionic gonadotropin correlate in prepubertal boys. J Clin Endocrinol Metab 85:134–138, 2000.

146. Kirschner MA, Jacobs JB, Fraley EE: Bilateral anorchia with persistent testosterone production. N Engl J Med 282:240–244, 1970.

147. John Radcliffe Hospital Cryptorchidism Study Group: Cryptorchidism: An apparent substantial increase since 1960. Br Med J (Clin Res Ed) 293:1401–1404, 1986.

148. Skakkebaek NE, Rajpert-De Meyts E, Main KM: Testicular dysgenesis syndrome: An increasingly common developmental disorder with environmental aspects. Hum Reprod 16:972–978, 2001.

149. Lee PA, Bellinger MF, Coughlin MT: Correlations among hormone levels, sperm parameters and paternity in formerly unilaterally cryptorchid men. J Urol 160:1155–1157, discussion 1178, 1998.

150. Bramble FJ, Houghton AL, Eccles S, et al: Reproductive and endocrine function after surgical treatment of bilateral crytorchidism. Lancet 2:311–314, 1974.

151. Del Castillo EB, Trabucco A, de la Balze FA: Syndrome produced by absence of the germinal epithelium without impairment of the Sertoli or Leydig cells. J Clin Endocrinol Metab 7:493–502, 1947.

152. De Kretser DM, Burger HG, Fortune D, et al: Hormonal, histological and chromosomal studies in adult males with testicular disorders. J Clin Endocrinol Metab 35:392–401, 1972.

153. Andersson AM, Jorgensen N, Frydelund-Larsen L, et al: Impaired Leydig cell function in infertile men: A study of 357 idiopathic infertile men and 318 proven fertile controls. J Clin Endocrinol Metab 89:3161–3167, 2004.

154. Bennett IL Jr, Petersdorf RG: Treatment of mumps orchitis with adrenal hormones: Report of 23 cases with a note on hepatic involvement in mumps. AMA Arch Intern Med 99:222–233, 1957.

155. Aiman J, Brenner PF, MacDonald PC: Androgen and estrogen production in elderly men with gynecomastia and testicular atrophy after mumps orchitis. J Clin Endocrinol Metab 50:380–386, 1980.

156. Lin WW, Kim ED, Quesada ET, et al: Unilateral testicular injury from external trauma: Evaluation of semen quality and endocrine parameters. J Urol 159:841–843, 1998.

157. Bartsch G, Frank S, Marberger H, et al: Testicular torsion: Late results with special regard to fertility and endocrine function. J Urol 124:375–378, 1980.

158. Hadziselimovic F, Geneto R, Emmons LR: Increased apoptosis in the contralateral testes of patients with testicular torsion as a factor for infertility. J Urol 160:1158–1160, 1998.

159. Dahl EV, Baggenstoss AH, Deweerd JH: Testicular lesions of periarteritis nodosa, with special reference to diagnosis. Am J Med 28:222–228, 1960.

160. Van den Berghe G: Endocrine evaluation of patients with critical illness. Endocrinol Metab Clin North Am 32:385–410, 2003.

161. Semple CG, Robertson WR, Mitchell R, et al: Mechanisms leading to hypogonadism in men with burns injuries. Br Med J (Clin Res Ed) 295:403–407, 1987.

162. Vogel AV, Peake GT, Rada RT: Pituitary-testicular axis dysfunction in burned men. J Clin Endocrinol Metab 60:658–665, 1985.

163. Wang C, Chan V, Tse TF, et al: Effect of acute myocardial infarction on pituitary-testicular function. Clin Endocrinol (Oxf) 9:249–253, 1978.

164. Wang C, Chan V, Yeung RT: Effect of surgical stress on pituitary-testicular function. Clin Endocrinol (Oxf) 9:255–266, 1978.

165. Woolf PD, Hamill RW, McDonald JV, et al: Transient hypogonadotropic hypogonadism caused by critical illness. J Clin Endocrinol Metab 60:444–450, 1985.

166. Luppa P, Munker R, Nagel D, et al: Serum androgens in intensive-care patients: Correlations with clinical findings. Clin Endocrinol (Oxf) 34:305–310, 1991.

167. Schulz P, Walker JP, Peyrin L, et al: Lower sex hormones in men during anticipatory stress. Neuroreport 7:3101–3104, 1996.

168. Dong Q, Hawker F, McWilliam D, et al: Circulating immunoreactive inhibin and testosterone levels in men with critical illness. Clin Endocrinol (Oxf) 36:399–404, 1992.

169. van den Berghe G, Weekers F, Baxter RC, et al: Five-day pulsatile gonadotropin-releasing hormone administration unveils combined hypothalamic-pituitary-gonadal defects underlying profound

hypoandrogenism in men with prolonged critical illness. J Clin Endocrinol Metab 86:3217–3226, 2001.

170. Spratt DI, Bigos ST, Beitins I, et al: Both hyper- and hypogonadotropic hypogonadism occur transiently in acute illness: Bio- and immunoactive gonadotropins. J Clin Endocrinol Metab 75:1562–1570, 1992.

171. Spratt DI, Cox P, Orav J, et al: Reproductive axis suppression in acute illness is related to disease severity. J Clin Endocrinol Metab 76:1548–1554, 1993.

172. Demling RH, Orgill DP: The anticatabolic and wound healing effects of the testosterone analog oxandrolone after severe burn injury. J Crit Care 15:12–17, 2000.

173. Ferrando AA, Sheffield-Moore M, Wolf SE, et al: Testosterone administration in severe burns ameliorates muscle catabolism. Crit Care Med 29:1936–1942, 2001.

174. Spratt DI: Altered gonadal steroidogenesis in critical illness: Is treatment with anabolic steroids indicated? Best Pract Res Clin Endocrinol Metab 15:479–494, 2001.

175. Cameron JL, Weltzin TE, McConaha C, et al: Slowing of pulsatile luteinizing hormone secretion in men after 48 hours of fasting. J Clin Endocrinol Metab 73:35–41, 1991.

176. Veldhuis JD, Iranmanesh A, Evans WS, et al: Amplitude suppression of the pulsatile mode of immunoradiometric luteinizing hormone release in fasting-induced hypoandrogenemia in normal men. J Clin Endocrinol Metab 76:587–593, 1993.

177. Rojdmark S: Increased gonadotropin responsiveness to gonadotropin-releasing hormone during fasting in normal subjects. Metabolism 36:21–26, 1987.

178. Aloi JA, Bergendahl M, Iranmanesh A, et al: Pulsatile intravenous gonadotropin-releasing hormone administration averts fasting-induced hypogonadotropism and hypoandrogenemia in healthy, normal weight men. J Clin Endocrinol Metab 82:1543–1548, 1997.

179. Smith SR, Chhetri MK, Johanson J, et al: The pituitary-gonadal axis in men with protein-calorie malnutrition. J Clin Endocrinol Metab 41:60–69, 1975.

180. Zmuda JM, Thompson PD, Winters SJ: Exercise increases serum testosterone and sex hormone–binding globulin levels in older men. Metabolism 45:935–939, 1996.

181. Kujala UM, Alen M, Huhtaniemi IT: Gonadotrophin-releasing hormone and human chorionic gonadotrophin tests reveal that both hypothalamic and testicular endocrine functions are suppressed during acute prolonged physical exercise. Clin Endocrinol (Oxf) 33:219–225, 1990.

182. Opstad PK: Androgenic hormones during prolonged physical stress, sleep, and energy deficiency. J Clin Endocrinol Metab 74:1176–1183, 1992.

183. Wheeler GD, Wall SR, Belcastro AN, et al: Reduced serum testosterone and prolactin levels in male distance runners. JAMA 252:514–516, 1984.

184. Rogol AD, Veldhuis JD, Williams FA, et al: Pulsatile secretion of gonadotropins and prolactin in male marathon runners: Relation to the endogenous opiate system. J Androl 5:21–27, 1984.

185. MacConnie SE, Barkan A, Lampman RM, et al: Decreased hypothalamic gonadotropin-releasing hormone secretion in male marathon runners. N Engl J Med 315:411–417, 1986.

186. Wheeler GD, Singh M, Pierce WD, et al: Endurance training decreases serum testosterone levels in men without change in luteinizing hormone pulsatile release. J Clin Endocrinol Metab 72:422–425, 1991.

187. Ayers JW, Komesu Y, Romani T, et al: Anthropomorphic, hormonal, and psychologic correlates of semen quality in endurance-trained male athletes. Fertil Steril 43:917–921, 1985.

188. Lucia A, Chicharro JL, Perez M, et al: Reproductive function in male endurance athletes: Sperm analysis and hormonal profile. J Appl Physiol 81:2627–2636, 1996.

189. Rivier C, Rivest S: Effect of stress on the activity of the hypothalamic-pituitary-gonadal axis: Peripheral and central mechanisms. Biol Reprod 45:523–532, 1991.

190. Finn PD, Cunningham MJ, Pau KY, et al: The stimulatory effect of leptin on the neuroendocrine reproductive axis of the monkey. Endocrinology 139:4652–4662, 1998.

191. Sinha MK, Caro JF: Clinical aspects of leptin. Vitam Horm 54:1–30, 1998.

192. Chan JL, Heist K, DePaoli AM, et al: The role of falling leptin levels in the neuroendocrine and metabolic adaptation to short-term starvation in healthy men. J Clin Invest 111:1409–1421, 2003.

193. Glass AR, Swerdloff RS, Bray GA, et al: Low serum testosterone and sex-hormone-binding-globulin in massively obese men. J Clin Endocrinol Metab 45:1211–1219, 1977.

194. Plymate SR, Matej LA, Jones RE, et al: Inhibition of sex hormone–binding globulin production in the human hepatoma (Hep g2) cell line by insulin and prolactin. J Clin Endocrinol Metab 67:460–464, 1988.

195. Pasquali R, Casimirri F, De Iasio R, et al: Insulin regulates testosterone and sex hormone–binding globulin concentrations in adult normal weight and obese men. J Clin Endocrinol Metab 80:654–658, 1995.

196. Zumoff B, Strain GW, Miller LK, et al: Plasma free and non-sex-hormone-binding-globulin-bound testosterone are decreased in obese men in proportion to their degree of obesity. J Clin Endocrinol Metab 71:929–931, 1990.

197. Schneider G, Kirschner MA, Berkowitz R, et al: Increased estrogen production in obese men. J Clin Endocrinol Metab 48:633–638, 1979.

198. Vermeulen A, Kaufman JM, Deslypere JP, et al: Attenuated luteinizing hormone (LH) pulse amplitude but normal LH pulse frequency, and its relation to plasma androgens in hypogonadism of obese men. J Clin Endocrinol Metab 76:1140–1146, 1993.

199. Stanik S, Dornfeld LP, Maxwell MH, et al: The effect of weight loss on reproductive hormones in obese men. J Clin Endocrinol Metab 53:828–832, 1981.

200. Leenen R, van der Kooy K, Seidell JC, et al: Visceral fat accumulation in relation to sex hormones in obese men and women undergoing weight loss therapy. J Clin Endocrinol Metab 78:1515–1520, 1994.

201. Marin P, Holmang S, Jonsson L, et al: The effects of testosterone treatment on body composition and metabolism in middle-aged obese men. Int J Obes Relat Metab Disord 16:991–997, 1992.

202. Licinio J, Caglayan S, Ozata M, et al: Phenotypic effects of leptin replacement on morbid obesity, diabetes mellitus, hypogonadism, and behavior in leptin-deficient adults. Proc Natl Acad Sci U S A 101:4531–4536, 2004.

203. Haffner SM, Shaten J, Stern MP, et al: Low levels of sex hormone–binding globulin and testosterone predict the development of non-insulin-dependent diabetes mellitus in men. MRFIT Research Group. Multiple risk factor intervention trial. Am J Epidemiol 143:889–897, 1996.

204. Seidell JC, Bjorntorp P, Sjostrom L, et al: Visceral fat accumulation in men is positively associated with insulin, glucose, and C-peptide levels, but negatively with testosterone levels. Metabolism 39:897–901, 1990.

205. Oltmanns KM, Fruehwald-Schultes B, Kern W, et al: Hypoglycemia, but not insulin, acutely decreases LH and T secretion in men. J Clin Endocrinol Metab 86:4913–4919, 2001.

206. Barrett-Connor E: Lower endogenous androgen levels and dyslipidemia in men with non-insulin-dependent diabetes mellitus. Ann Intern Med 117:807–811, 1992.

207. Andersson B, Marin P, Lissner L, et al: Testosterone concentrations in women and men with NIDDM. Diabetes Care 17:405–411, 1994.

208. Vierhapper H, Nowotny P, Waldhausl W: Reduced production rates of testosterone and dihydrotestosterone in healthy men treated with rosiglitazone. Metabolism 52:230–232, 2003.

209. Gluud C, Madsbad S, Krarup T, et al: Plasma testosterone and androstenedione in insulin dependent patients at time of diagnosis and during the first year of insulin treatment. Acta Endocrinol (Copenh) 100:406–409, 1982.

210. Lopez-Alvarenga JC, Zarinan T, Olivares A, et al: Poorly controlled type I diabetes mellitus in young men selectively suppresses luteinizing hormone secretory burst mass. J Clin Endocrinol Metab 87:5507–5515, 2002.

211. Sellmeyer DE, Grunfeld C: Endocrine and metabolic disturbances in human immunodeficiency virus infection and the acquired immune deficiency syndrome. Endocr Rev 17:518–532, 1996.

212. Muciaccia B, Uccini S, Filippini A, et al: Presence and cellular distribution of HIV in the testes of seropositive subjects: An evaluation by in situ PCR hybridization. FASEB J 12:151–163, 1998.

213. Dalton AD, Harcourt-Webster JN: The histopathology of the testis and epididymis in AIDS: A post-mortem study. J Pathol 163:47–52, 1991.

214. Croxson TS, Chapman WE, Miller LK, et al: Changes in the hypothalamic-pituitary-gonadal axis in human immunodeficiency virus–infected homosexual men. J Clin Endocrinol Metab 68:317–321, 1989.

215. Dobs AS, Dempsey MA, Ladenson PW, et al: Endocrine disorders in men infected with human immunodeficiency virus. Am J Med 84:611–616, 1988.

216. Wilson LD, Truong MP, Barber AR, et al: Anterior pituitary and pituitary-dependent target organ function in men infected with the human immunodeficiency virus. Metabolism 45:738–746, 1996.

217. Grinspoon S, Corcoran C, Lee K, et al: Loss of lean body and muscle mass correlates with androgen levels in hypogonadal men with acquired immunodeficiency syndrome and wasting. J Clin Endocrinol Metab 81:4051–4058, 1996.

218. Grinspoon S, Corcoran C, Askari H, et al: Effects of androgen administration in men with the AIDS wasting syndrome: A randomized, double-blind, placebo-controlled trial. Ann Intern Med 129:18–26, 1998.

219. Bhasin S, Storer TW, Javanbakht M, et al: Testosterone replacement and resistance exercise in HIV-infected men with weight loss and low testosterone levels. JAMA 283:763–770, 2000.

220. Bhasin S, Storer TW, Asbel-Sethi N, et al: Effects of testosterone replacement with a nongenital, transdermal system, androderm, in human immunodeficiency virus–infected men with low testosterone levels. J Clin Endocrinol Metab 83:3155–3162, 1998.

221. Corcoran C, Grinspoon S: Treatments for wasting in patients with the acquired immunodeficiency syndrome. N Engl J Med 340:1740–1750, 1999.

222. Handelsman DJ: Hypothalamic-pituitary gonadal dysfunction in renal failure, dialysis and renal transplantation. Endocr Rev 6:151–182, 1985.

223. Holdsworth S, Atkins RC, de Kretser DM: The pituitary-testicular axis in men with chronic renal failure. N Engl J Med 296:1245–1249, 1977.

224. Rodger RS, Morrison L, Dewar JH, et al: Loss of pulsatile luteinising hormone secretion in men with chronic renal failure. Br Med J (Clin Res Ed) 291:1598–1600, 1985.

225. Kokot F, Wiecek A, Schmidt-Gayk H, et al: Function of endocrine organs in hemodialyzed patients of long-term erythropoietin therapy. Artif Organs 19:428–435, 1995.

226. Holdsworth SR, de Kretser DM, Atkins RC: A comparison of hemodialysis and transplantation in reversing the uremic disturbance of male reproductive function. Clin Nephrol 10:146–150, 1978.

227. Handelsman DJ, McDowell IF, Caterson ID, et al: Testicular function after renal transplantation: Comparison of cyclosporin A with azathioprine and prednisone combination regimes. Clin Nephrol 22:144–148, 1984.

228. Navarro JF, Mora C, Macia M, et al: Randomized prospective comparison between erythropoietin and androgens in CAPD patients. Kidney Int 61:1537–1544, 2002.

229. Barton Pai A, Chretien C, Lau AH: The effects of nandrolone decanoate on nutritional parameters in hemodialysis patients. Clin Nephrol 58:38–46, 2002.

230. Handelsman DJ, Liu PY: Androgen therapy in chronic renal failure. Baillieres Clin Endocrinol Metab 12:485–500, 1998.

231. Handelsman DJ: Testicular dysfunction in systemic disease. Endocrinol Metab Clin North Am 23:839–856, 1994.

232. Van Thiel DH, Lester R, Sherins RJ: Hypogonadism in alcoholic liver disease: Evidence for a double defect. Gastroenterology 67:1188–1199, 1974.

233. Bannister P, Handley T, Chapman C, et al: Hypogonadism in chronic liver disease: Impaired release of luteinising hormone. Br Med J (Clin Res Ed) 293:1191–1193, 1986.

234. Van Thiel DH, Lester R, Vaitukaitis J: Evidence for a defect in pituitary secretion of luteinizing hormone in chronic alcoholic men. J Clin Endocrinol Metab 47:499–507, 1978.

235. Kirkman S, Nelson DH: Alcohol-induced pseudo-Cushing's disease: A study of prevalence with review of the literature. Metabolism 37:390–394, 1988.

236. Van Thiel DH, McClain CJ, Elson MK, et al: Evidence for autonomous secretion of prolactin in some alcoholic men with cirrhosis and gynecomastia. Metabolism 27:1778–1784, 1978.

237. Gluud C: Testosterone and alcoholic cirrhosis: Epidemiologic, pathophysiologic and therapeutic studies in men. Dan Med Bull 35:564–575, 1988.

238. Gordon GG, Altman K, Southren AL, et al: Effect of alcohol (ethanol) administration on sex-hormone metabolism in normal men. N Engl J Med 295:793–797, 1976.

239. Harman SM, Metter EJ, Tobin JD, et al: Longitudinal effects of aging on serum total and free testosterone levels in healthy men. Baltimore Longitudinal Study of Aging. J Clin Endocrinol Metab 86:724–731, 2001.

240. Sparrow D, Bosse R, Rowe JW: The influence of age, alcohol consumption, and body build on gonadal function in men. J Clin Endocrinol Metab 51:508–512, 1980.

241. Baker HW, Burger HG, de Kretser DM, et al: A study of the endocrine manifestations of hepatic cirrhosis. Q J Med 45:145–178, 1976.

242. Van Thiel DH, Loriaux DL: Evidence for an adrenal origin of plasma estrogens in alcoholic men. Metabolism 28:536–541, 1979.

243. Terasaki T, Nowlin DM, Pardridge WM: Differential binding of testosterone and estradiol to isoforms of sex hormone–binding globulin: Selective alteration of estradiol binding in cirrhosis. J Clin Endocrinol Metab 67:639–643, 1988.

244. Handelsman DJ, Strasser S, McDonald JA, et al: Hypothalamic-pituitary-testicular function in end-stage non-alcoholic liver disease before and after liver transplantation. Clin Endocrinol (Oxf) 43:331–337, 1995.

245. Bezwoda WR, Bothwell TH, Van Der Walt LA, et al: An investigation into gonadal dysfunction in patients with idiopathic haemochromatosis. Clin Endocrinol (Oxf) 6:377–385, 1977.

246. Kley HK, Niederau C, Stremmel W, et al: Conversion of androgens to estrogens in idiopathic hemochromatosis: Comparison with alcoholic liver cirrhosis. J Clin Endocrinol Metab 61:1–6, 1985.

247. Cundy T, Bomford A, Butler J, et al: Hypogonadism and sexual dysfunction in hemochromatosis: The effects of cirrhosis and diabetes. J Clin Endocrinol Metab 69:110–116, 1989.

248. Kelly TM, Edwards CQ, Meikle AW, et al: Hypogonadism in hemochromatosis: Reversal with iron depletion. Ann Intern Med 101:629–632, 1984.

249. Lufkin EG, Baldus WP, Bergstralh EJ, et al: Influence of phlebotomy treatment on abnormal hypothalamic-pituitary function in genetic hemochromatosis. Mayo Clin Proc 62:473–479, 1987.

250. Soliman AT, ElZalabany MM, Ragab M, et al: Spontaneous and GnRH-provoked gonadotropin secretion and testosterone response to human chorionic gonadotropin in adolescent boys with thalassaemia major and delayed puberty. J Trop Pediatr 46:79–85, 2000.

251. Pintor C, Loche S, Puggioni R, et al: Adrenal and testicular function in boys affected by thalassemia. J Endocrinol Invest 7:147–149, 1984.

252. Wang C, Tso SC, Todd D: Hypogonadotropic hypogonadism in severe beta-thalassemia: Effect of chelation and pulsatile gonadotropin-releasing hormone therapy. J Clin Endocrinol Metab 68:511–516, 1989.

253. Raiola G, Galati MC, De Sanctis V, et al: Growth and puberty in thalassemia major. J Pediatr Endocrinol Metab 16(Suppl 2):259–266, 2003.

254. De Sanctis V: Growth and puberty and its management in thalassaemia. Horm Res 58(Suppl 1):72–79, 2002.

255. Anapliotou ML, Kastanias IT, Psara P, et al: The contribution of hypogonadism to the development of osteoporosis in thalassaemia major: New therapeutic approaches. Clin Endocrinol (Oxf) 42:279–287, 1995.

256. Abbasi AA, Prasad AS, Ortega J, et al: Gonadal function abnormalities in sickle cell anemia: Studies in adult male patients. Ann Intern Med 85:601–605, 1976.

257. Landefeld CS, Schambelan M, Kaplan SL, et al: Clomiphene-responsive hypogonadism in sickle cell anemia. Ann Intern Med 99:480–483, 1983.

258. Osegbe DN, Akinyanju OO: Testicular dysfunction in men with sickle cell disease. Postgrad Med J 63:95–98, 1987.

259. Ezeh UO, Modebe O: Is there increased fertility in adult males with the sickle cell trait? Hum Biol 68:555–562, 1996.

260. Vazquez JA, Pinies JA, Martul P, et al: Hypothalamic-pituitary-testicular function in 70 patients with myotonic dystrophy. J Endocrinol Invest 13:375–379, 1990.

261. Griggs RC, Pandya S, Florence JM, et al: Randomized controlled trial of testosterone in myotonic dystrophy. Neurology 39:219–222, 1989.

262. Jansen G, Mahadevan M, Amemiya C, et al: Characterization of the myotonic dystrophy region predicts multiple protein isoform-encoding mRNAs. Nat Genet 1:261–266, 1992.

263. Kennedy WR, Alter M, Sung JH: Progressive proximal spinal and bulbar muscular atrophy of late onset: A sex-linked recessive trait. Neurology 18:671–680, 1968.

264. Dejager S, Bry-Gauillard H, Bruckert E, et al: A comprehensive endocrine description of Kennedy's disease revealing androgen insensitivity linked to CAG repeat length. J Clin Endocrinol Metab 87:3893–3901, 2002.

265. La Spada AR, Wilson EM, Lubahn DB, et al: Androgen receptor gene mutations in X-linked spinal and bulbar muscular atrophy. Nature 352:77–79, 1991.

266. Bezman L, Moser HW: Incidence of X-linked adrenoleukodystrophy and the relative frequency of its phenotypes. Am J Med Genet 76:415–419, 1998.

267. Libber SM, Migeon CJ, Brown FR III, et al: Adrenal and testicular function in 14 patients with adrenoleukodystrophy or adrenomyeloneuropathy. Horm Res 24:1–8, 1986.

268. Spark RF, Wills CA, Royal H: Hypogonadism, hyperprolactinaemia, and temporal lobe epilepsy in hyposexual men. Lancet 1:413–417, 1984.

269. Bauer J, Stoffel-Wagner B, Flugel D, et al: Serum androgens return to normal after temporal lobe epilepsy surgery in men. Neurology 55:820–824, 2000.

270. Morley JE, Distiller LA, Lissoos I, et al: Testicular function in patients with spinal cord damage. Horm Metab Res 11:679–682, 1979.

271. Naderi AR, Safarinejad MR: Endocrine profiles and semen quality in spinal cord injured men. Clin Endocrinol (Oxf) 58:177–184, 2003.

272. Hsiang YH, Berkovitz GD, Bland GL, et al: Gonadal function in patients with Down syndrome. Am J Med Genet 27:449–458, 1987.

273. Urban MD, Lee PA, Migeon CJ: Adult height and fertility in men with congenital virilizing adrenal hyperplasia. N Engl J Med 299:1392–1396, 1978.

274. Cabrera MS, Vogiatzi MG, New MI: Long term outcome in adult males with classic congenital adrenal hyperplasia. J Clin Endocrinol Metab 86:3070–3078, 2001.

275. Stikkelbroeck NM, Otten BJ, Pasic A, et al: High prevalence of testicular adrenal rest tumors, impaired spermatogenesis, and Leydig cell failure in adolescent and adult males with congenital adrenal hyperplasia. J Clin Endocrinol Metab 86:5721–5728, 2001.

276. Cutfield RG, Bateman JM, Odell WD: Infertility caused by bilateral testicular masses secondary to congenital adrenal hyperplasia (21-hydroxylase deficiency). Fertil Steril 40:809–814, 1983.

277. Kidd GS, Glass AR, Vigersky RA: The hypothalamic-pituitary-testicular axis in thyrotoxicosis. J Clin Endocrinol Metab 48:798–802, 1979.

278. Hudson RW, Edwards AL: Testicular function in hyperthyroidism. J Androl 13:117–124, 1992.

279. Abalovich M, Levalle O, Hermes R, et al: Hypothalamic-pituitary-testicular axis and seminal parameters in hyperthyroid males. Thyroid 9:857–863, 1999.

280. Southren AL, Olivo J, Gordon GG, et al: The conversion of androgens to estrogens in hyperthyroidism. J Clin Endocrinol Metab 38:207–214, 1974.

281. Cavaliere H, Abelin N, Medeiros-Neto G: Serum levels of total testosterone and sex hormone binding globulin in hypothyroid patients and normal subjects treated with incremental doses of L-T4 or L-T3. J Androl 9:215–219, 1988.

282. Donnelly P, White C: Testicular dysfunction in men with primary hypothyroidism; reversal of hypogonadotrophic hypogonadism with replacement thyroxine. Clin Endocrinol (Oxf) 52:197–201, 2000.

283. Wortsman J, Rosner W, Dufau ML: Abnormal testicular function in men with primary hypothyroidism. Am J Med 82:207–212, 1987.

284. Neufeld M, Maclaren NK, Blizzard RM: Two types of autoimmune Addison's disease associated with different polyglandular autoimmune (PGA) syndromes. Medicine (Baltimore) 60:355–362, 1981.

285. Dittmar M, Kahaly GJ: Polyglandular autoimmune syndromes: Immunogenetics and long-term follow-up. J Clin Endocrinol Metab 88:2983–2992, 2003.

286. Barkan AL, Kelch RP, Marshall JC: Isolated gonadotrope failure in the polyglandular autoimmune syndrome. N Engl J Med 312:1535–1540, 1985.

287. Nowlin NS, Zwillich SH, Brick JE, et al: Male hypogonadism and scleroderma. J Rheumatol 12:605–606, 1985.

288. Grossman A, Gibson J, Stansfeld AG, et al: Pituitary and testicular fibrosis in association with retroperitoneal fibrosis. Clin Endocrinol (Oxf) 12:371–374, 1980.

289. Vilarinho ST, Costallat LT: Evaluation of the hypothalamic-pituitary-gonadal axis in males with systemic lupus erythematosus. J Rheumatol 25:1097–1103, 1998.

290. Luboshitzky R, Aviv A, Hefetz A, et al: Decreased pituitary-gonadal secretion in men with obstructive sleep apnea. J Clin Endocrinol Metab 87:3394–3398, 2002.

291. Grunstein RR, Handelsman DJ, Lawrence SJ, et al: Neuroendocrine dysfunction in sleep apnea: Reversal by continuous positive airways pressure therapy. J Clin Endocrinol Metab 68:352–358, 1989.

292. Matsumoto AM, Sandblom RE, Schoene RB, et al: Testosterone replacement in hypogonadal men: Effects on obstructive sleep apnoea, respiratory drives, and sleep. Clin Endocrinol (Oxf) 22:713–721, 1985.

293. Liu PY, Yee B, Wishart SM, et al: The short-term effects of high-dose testosterone on sleep, breathing, and function in older men. J Clin Endocrinol Metab 88:3605–3613, 2003.

294. Leifke E, Friemert M, Heilmann M, et al: Sex steroids and body composition in men with cystic fibrosis. Eur J Endocrinol 148:551–557, 2003.

295. Schilsky RL, Lewis BJ, Sherins RJ, et al: Gonadal dysfunction in patients receiving chemotherapy for cancer. Ann Intern Med 93:109–114, 1980.

296. Howell S, Shalet S: Gonadal damage from chemotherapy and radiotherapy. Endocrinol Metab Clin North Am 27:927–943, 1998.

297. Howell SJ, Radford JA, Ryder WD, et al: Testicular function after cytotoxic chemotherapy: Evidence of Leydig cell insufficiency. J Clin Oncol 17:1493–1498, 1999.

298. Friedman NM, Plymate SR: Leydig cell dysfunction and gynaecomastia in adult males treated with alkylating

agents. Clin Endocrinol (Oxf) 12:553–556, 1980.

299. Kauppila M, Viikari J, Irjala K, et al: The hypothalamus-pituitary-gonad axis and testicular function in male patients after treatment for haematological malignancies. J Intern Med 244:411–416, 1998.

300. Rivkees SA, Crawford JD: The relationship of gonadal activity and chemotherapy-induced gonadal damage. JAMA 259:2123–2125, 1988.

301. Morris ID, Shalet SM: Endocrine-mediated protection from cytotoxic-induced testicular damage. J Endocrinol 120:7–9, 1989.

302. Howell SJ, Shalet SM: Effect of cancer therapy on pituitary-testicular axis. Int J Androl 25:269–276, 2002.

303. Gerl A, Muhlbayer D, Hansmann G, et al: The impact of chemotherapy on Leydig cell function in long term survivors of germ cell tumors. Cancer 91:1297–1303, 2001.

304. Brauner R, Czernichow P, Cramer P, et al: Leydig-cell function in children after direct testicular irradiation for acute lymphoblastic leukemia. N Engl J Med 309:25–28, 1983.

305. Giwercman A, von der Maase H, Berthelsen JG, et al: Localized irradiation of testes with carcinoma in situ: Effects on Leydig cell function and eradication of malignant germ cells in 20 patients. J Clin Endocrinol Metab 73:596–603, 1991.

306. Shalet SM, Tsatsoulis A, Whitehead E, et al: Vulnerability of the human Leydig cell to radiation damage is dependent upon age. J Endocrinol 120:161–165, 1989.

307. Howell SJ, Radford JA, Adams JE, et al: Randomized placebo-controlled trial of testosterone replacement in men with mild Leydig cell insufficiency following cytotoxic chemotherapy. Clin Endocrinol (Oxf) 55:315–324, 2001.

308. Vigersky RA, Chapman RM, Berenberg J, et al: Testicular dysfunction in untreated Hodgkin's disease. Am J Med 73:482–486, 1982.

309. Pacini F, Gasperi M, Fugazzola L, et al: Testicular function in patients with differentiated thyroid carcinoma treated with radioiodine. J Nucl Med 35:1418–1422, 1994.

310. Handelsman DJ, Turtle JR: Testicular damage after radioactive iodine (I-131) therapy for thyroid cancer. Clin Endocrinol (Oxf) 18:465–472, 1983.

311. Wichers M, Benz E, Palmedo H, et al: Testicular function after radioiodine therapy for thyroid carcinoma. Eur J Nucl Med 27:503–507, 2000.

312. Hyer S, Vini L, O'Connell M, et al: Testicular dose and fertility in men following I(131) therapy for thyroid cancer. Clin Endocrinol (Oxf) 56:755–758, 2002.

313. Raynaud JP, Ojasoo T: The design and use of sex-steroid antagonists. J Steroid Biochem 25:811–833, 1986.

314. Spironolactone and endocrine dysfunction. Ann Intern Med 85:630–636, 1976.

315. Rose LI, Underwood RH, Newmark SR, et al: Pathophysiology of spironolactone-induced gynecomastia. Ann Intern Med 87:398–403, 1977.

316. Mahler C, Verhelst J, Denis L: Clinical pharmacokinetics of the antiandrogens and their efficacy in prostate cancer. Clin Pharmacokinet 34:405–417, 1998.

317. Kemppainen JA, Lane MV, Sar M, et al: Androgen receptor phosphorylation, turnover, nuclear transport, and transcriptional activation. Specificity for steroids and antihormones. J Biol Chem 267:968–974, 1992.

318. Veldhuis JD, Urban RJ, Dufau ML: Evidence that androgen negative feedback regulates hypothalamic gonadotropin-releasing hormone impulse strength and the burst-like secretion of biologically active luteinizing hormone in men. J Clin Endocrinol Metab 74:1227–1235, 1992.

319. Funder JW, Mercer JE: Cimetidine, a histamine H2 receptor antagonist, occupies androgen receptors. J Clin Endocrinol Metab 48:189–191, 1979.

320. Jensen RT, Collen MJ, Pandol SJ, et al: Cimetidine-induced impotence and breast changes in patients with gastric hypersecretory states. N Engl J Med 308:883–887, 1983.

321. Wang C, Lai CL, Lam KC, et al: Effect of cimetidine on gonadal function in man. Br J Clin Pharmacol 13:791–794, 1982.

322. Knigge U, Dejgaard A, Wollesen F, et al: The acute and long term effect of the H2-receptor antagonists cimetidine and ranitidine on the pituitary-gonadal axis in men. Clin Endocrinol (Oxf) 18:307–313, 1983.

323. Lindquist M, Edwards IR: Endocrine adverse effects of omeprazole. Br Med J 305:451–452, 1992.

324. Sonino N: The use of ketoconazole as an inhibitor of steroid production. N Engl J Med 317:812–818, 1987.

325. Pont A, Williams PL, Azhar S, et al: Ketoconazole blocks testosterone synthesis. Arch Intern Med 142:2137–2140, 1982.

326. Zwart AD, Iranmanesh A, Veldhuis JD: Disparate serum free testosterone concentrations and degrees of hypothalamo-pituitary-luteinizing hormone suppression are achieved by continuous versus pulsatile intravenous androgen replacement in men: A clinical experimental model of ketoconazole-induced reversible hypoandrogenemia with controlled testosterone add-back. J Clin Endocrinol Metab 82:2062–2069, 1997.

327. McConnell JD, Wilson JD, George FW, et al: Finasteride, an inhibitor of 5 alpha-reductase, suppresses prostatic dihydrotestosterone in men with benign prostatic hyperplasia. J Clin Endocrinol Metab 74:505–508, 1992.

328. Rittmaster RS, Lemay A, Zwicker H, et al: Effect of finasteride, a 5 alpha-reductase inhibitor, on serum

gonadotropins in normal men. J Clin Endocrinol Metab 75:484–488, 1992.

329. Andriole GL, Kirby R: Safety and tolerability of the dual 5-alpha-reductase inhibitor dutasteride in the treatment of benign prostatic hyperplasia. Eur Urol 44:82–88, 2003.

330. Alen M, Reinila M, Vihko R: Response of serum hormones to androgen administration in power athletes. Med Sci Sports Exerc 17:354–359, 1985.

331. Ruokonen A, Alen M, Bolton N, et al: Response of serum testosterone and its precursor steroids, SHBG and CBG, to anabolic steroid and testosterone self-administration in man. J Steroid Biochem 23:33–38, 1985.

332. Gill GV: Anabolic steroid induced hypogonadism treated with human chorionic gonadotropin. Postgrad Med J 74:45–46, 1998.

333. Turner L, Conway AJ, Jimenez M, et al: Contraceptive efficacy of a depot progestin and androgen combination in men. J Clin Endocrinol Metab 88:4659–4667, 2003.

334. Dobs AS, Sarma PS, Guarnieri T, et al: Testicular dysfunction with amiodarone use. J Am Coll Cardiol 18:1328–1332, 1991.

335. Stoffer SS, Hynes KM, Jiang NS, et al: Digoxin and abnormal serum hormone levels. JAMA 225:1643–1644, 1973.

336. Lin H, Wang SW, Tsai SC, et al: Inhibitory effect of digoxin on testosterone secretion through mechanisms involving decreases of cyclic AMP production and cytochrome p450scc activity in rat testicular interstitial cells. Br J Pharmacol 125:1635–1640, 1998.

337. Neri A, Aygen M, Zukerman Z, et al: Subjective assessment of sexual dysfunction of patients on long-term administration of digoxin. Arch Sex Behav 9:343–347, 1980.

338. Gupta S, Salimpour P, Saenz de Tejada I, et al: A possible mechanism for alteration of human erectile function by digoxin: Inhibition of corpus cavernosum sodium/potassium adenosine triphosphatase activity. J Urol 159:1529–1536, 1998.

339. Dobs AS, Schrott H, Davidson MH, et al: Effects of high-dose simvastatin on adrenal and gonadal steroidogenesis in men with hypercholesterolemia. Metabolism 49:1234–1238, 2000.

340. Dobs AS, Sarma PS, Schteingart D: Long-term endocrine function in hypercholesterolemic patients treated with pravastatin, a new 3-hydroxy-3-methylglutaryl coenzyme A reductase inhibitor. Metabolism 42:1146–1152, 1993.

341. Duncan S, Blacklaw J, Beastall GH, et al: Antiepileptic drug therapy and sexual function in men with epilepsy. Epilepsia 40:197–204, 1999.

342. Toone BK, Wheeler M, Fenwick PB: Sex hormone changes in male epileptics. Clin Endocrinol (Oxf) 12:391–395, 1980.

343. Wheeler MJ, Toone BK, Dannatt A, et al: Metabolic clearance rate of testosterone in male epileptic patients on anti-convulsant therapy. J Endocrinol 129:465–468, 1991.

344. Macphee GJ, Larkin JG, Butler E, et al: Circulating hormones and pituitary responsiveness in young epileptic men receiving long-term antiepileptic medication. Epilepsia 29:468–475, 1988.

345. Rattya J, Turkka J, Pakarinen AJ, et al: Reproductive effects of valproate, carbamazepine, and oxcarbazepine in men with epilepsy. Neurology 56:31–36, 2001.

346. Kolodny RC, Masters WH, Kolodner RM, et al: Depression of plasma testosterone levels after chronic intensive marihuana use. N Engl J Med 290:872–874, 1974.

347. Mendelson JH, Kuehnle J, Ellingboe J, et al: Plasma testosterone levels before, during and after chronic marihuana smoking. N Engl J Med 291:1051–1055, 1974.

348. Schaefer CF, Gunn CG, Dubowski KM: Letter: Normal plasma testosterone concentrations after marihuana smoking. N Engl J Med 292:867–868, 1975.

349. Sauer MA, Rifka SM, Hawks RL, et al: Marijuana: Interaction with the estrogen receptor. J Pharmacol Exp Ther 224:404–407, 1983.

350. Purohit V, Ahluwahlia BS, Vigersky RA: Marihuana inhibits dihydrotestosterone binding to the androgen receptor. Endocrinology 107:848–850, 1980.

351. Daniell HW: Hypogonadism in men consuming sustained-action oral opioids. J Pain 3:377–384, 2002.

352. Mendelson JH, Mendelson JE, Patch VD: Plasma testosterone levels in heroin addiction and during methadone maintenance. J Pharmacol Exp Ther 192:211–217, 1975.

353. Wang C, Chan V, Yeung RT: The effect of heroin addiction on pituitary-testicular function. Clin Endocrinol (Oxf) 9:455–461, 1978.

354. Baker HW, Burger HG, de Kretser DM, et al: Changes in the pituitary-testicular system with age. Clin Endocrinol (Oxf) 5:349–372, 1976.

355. Leifke E, Gorenoi V, Wichers C, et al: Age-related changes of serum sex hormones, insulin-like growth factor-1 and sex-hormone binding globulin levels in men: Cross-sectional data from a healthy male cohort. Clin Endocrinol (Oxf) 53:689–695, 2000.

356. Feldman HA, Longcope C, Derby CA, et al: Age trends in the level of serum testosterone and other hormones in middle-aged men: Longitudinal results from the massachusetts male aging study. J Clin Endocrinol Metab 87:589–598, 2002.

357. Morley JE, Kaiser FE, Perry HM III, et al: Longitudinal changes in testosterone, luteinizing hormone, and follicle-stimulating hormone in healthy older men. Metabolism 46:410–413, 1997.

358. Deslypere JP, Vermeulen A: Leydig cell function in normal men: Effect of age, life-style, residence, diet, and activity. J Clin Endocrinol Metab 59:955–962, 1984.

359. Field AE, Colditz GA, Willett WC, et al: The relation of smoking, age, relative weight, and dietary intake to serum adrenal steroids, sex hormones, and sex hormone-binding globulin in middle-aged men. J Clin Endocrinol Metab 79:1310–1316, 1994.

360. Impallomeni M, Kaufman BM, Palmer AJ: Do acute diseases transiently impair anterior pituitary function in patients over the age of 75? A longitudinal study of the TRH test and basal gonadotrophin levels. Postgrad Med J 70:86–91, 1994.

361. Bhasin S, Herbst K: Age-related changes in the male reproductive axis. In McLachlan RI, DeGroot LJ (eds): Male Reproductive Endocrinology. 2004, www.endotext.org.

362. Swartz CM, Young MA: Low serum testosterone and myocardial infarction in geriatric male inpatients. J Am Geriatr Soc 35:39–44, 1987.

363. Kaufman JM, Vermeulen A: Declining gonadal function in elderly men. Baillieres Clin Endocrinol Metab 11:289–309, 1997.

364. Tenover JL: Experience with testosterone replacement in the elderly. Mayo Clin Proc 75(Suppl):S77–81, discussion S82, 2000.

365. Morley JE, Patrick P, Perry HM III: Evaluation of assays available to measure free testosterone. Metabolism 51:554–559, 2002.

366. Vermeulen A, Rubens R, Verdonck L: Testosterone secretion and metabolism in male senescence. J Clin Endocrinol Metab 34:730–735, 1972.

367. Veldhuis JD: Recent insights into neuroendocrine mechanisms of aging of the human male hypothalamic-pituitary-gonadal axis. J Androl 20:1–17, 1999.

368. Neaves WB, Johnson L, Porter JC, et al: Leydig cell numbers, daily sperm production, and serum gonadotropin levels in aging men. J Clin Endocrinol Metab 59:756–763, 1984.

369. Harman SM, Tsitouras PD: Reproductive hormones in aging men. I. Measurement of sex steroids, basal luteinizing hormone, and Leydig cell response to human chorionic gonadotropin. J Clin Endocrinol Metab 51:35–40, 1980.

370. Bremner WJ, Vitiello MV, Prinz PN: Loss of circadian rhythmicity in blood testosterone levels with aging in normal men. J Clin Endocrinol Metab 56:1278–1281, 1983.

371. Gupta SK, Lindemulder EA, Sathyan G: Modeling of circadian testosterone in healthy men and hypogonadal men. J Clin Pharmacol 40:731–738, 2000.

372. Diver MJ, Imtiaz KE, Ahmad AM, et al: Diurnal rhythms of serum total, free and bioavailable testosterone and of SHBG in middle-aged men compared with those in young men. Clin Endocrinol (Oxf) 58:710–717, 2003.

373. Mulligan T, Iranmanesh A, Kerzner R, et al: Two-week pulsatile gonadotropin releasing hormone infusion unmasks dual (hypothalamic and Leydig cell) defects in the healthy aging male gonadotropic axis. Eur J Endocrinol 141:257–266, 1999.

374. Veldhuis JD, Iranmanesh A, Godschalk M, et al: Older men manifest multifold synchrony disruption of reproductive neurohormone outflow. J Clin Endocrinol Metab 85:1477–1486, 2000.

375. Winters SJ, Atkinson L: Serum LH concentrations in hypogonadal men during transdermal testosterone replacement through scrotal skin: Further evidence that ageing enhances testosterone negative feedback. The testoderm Study Group. Clin Endocrinol (Oxf) 47:317–322, 1997.

376. Deslypere JP, Kaufman JM, Vermeulen T, et al: Influence of age on pulsatile luteinizing hormone release and responsiveness of the gonadotrophs to sex hormone feedback in men. J Clin Endocrinol Metab 64:68–73, 1987.

377. Veldhuis JD, Urban RJ, Lizarralde G, et al: Attenuation of luteinizing hormone secretory burst amplitude as a proximate basis for the hypoandrogenism of healthy aging in men. J Clin Endocrinol Metab 75:707–713, 1992.

378. Zwart AD, Urban RJ, Odell WD, et al: Contrasts in the gonadotropin-releasing hormone dose-response relationships for luteinizing hormone, follicle-stimulating hormone and alpha-subunit release in young versus older men: Appraisal with high-specificity immunoradiometric assay and deconvolution analysis. Eur J Endocrinol 135:399–406, 1996.

379. Winters SJ, Troen P: Episodic luteinizing hormone (LH) secretion and the response of LH and follicle-stimulating hormone to LH-releasing hormone in aged men: Evidence for coexistent primary testicular insufficiency and an impairment in gonadotropin secretion. J Clin Endocrinol Metab 55:560–565, 1982.

380. Smith KW, Feldman HA, McKinlay JB: Construction and field validation of a self-administered screener for testosterone deficiency (hypogonadism) in ageing men. Clin Endocrinol (Oxf) 53:703–711, 2000.

381. Morley JE, Charlton E, Patrick P, et al: Validation of a screening questionnaire for androgen deficiency in aging males. Metabolism 49:1239–1242, 2000.

382. T'sjoen G, Feyen E, De Kuyper P, et al: Self-referred patients in an aging male clinic: Much more than androgen deficiency alone. Aging Male 6:157–165, 2003.

383. Forbes GB, Reina JC: Adult lean body mass declines with age: Some

longitudinal observations. Metabolism 19:653–663, 1970.

384. Reed RL, Pearlmutter L, Yochum K, et al: The relationship between muscle mass and muscle strength in the elderly. J Am Geriatr Soc 39:555–561, 1991.

385. van den Beld AW, de Jong FH, Grobbee DE, et al: Measures of bioavailable serum testosterone and estradiol and their relationships with muscle strength, bone density, and body composition in elderly men. J Clin Endocrinol Metab 85:3276–3282, 2000.

386. Kenny AM, Prestwood KM, Marcello KM, et al: Determinants of bone density in healthy older men with low testosterone levels. J Gerontol A Biol Sci Med Sci 55:M492–M497, 2000.

387. Amin S, Zhang Y, Sawin CT, et al: Association of hypogonadism and estradiol levels with bone mineral density in elderly men from the Framingham study. Ann Intern Med 133:951–963, 2000.

388. Barrett-Connor E, Mueller JE, von Muhlen DG, et al: Low levels of estradiol are associated with vertebral fractures in older men, but not women: The Rancho Bernardo study. J Clin Endocrinol Metab 85:219–223, 2000.

389. Szulc P, Munoz F, Claustrat B, et al: Bioavailable estradiol may be an important determinant of osteoporosis in men: The Minos study. J Clin Endocrinol Metab 86:192–199, 2001.

390. Khosla S, Melton LJ III, Atkinson EJ, et al: Relationship of serum sex steroid levels to longitudinal changes in bone density in young versus elderly men. J Clin Endocrinol Metab 86:3555–3561, 2001.

391. Gennari L, Merlotti D, Martini G, et al: Longitudinal association between sex hormone levels, bone loss, and bone turnover in elderly men. J Clin Endocrinol Metab 88:5327–5333, 2003.

392. Falahati-Nini A, Riggs BL, Atkinson EJ, et al: Relative contributions of testosterone and estrogen in regulating bone resorption and formation in normal elderly men. J Clin Invest 106:1553–1560, 2000.

393. Seidman SN, Walsh BT: Testosterone and depression in aging men. Am J Geriatr Psychiatry 7:18–33, 1999.

394. Barrett-Connor E, Von Muhlen DG, Kritz-Silverstein D: Bioavailable testosterone and depressed mood in older men: The Rancho Bernardo study. J Clin Endocrinol Metab 84:573–577, 1999.

395. Seidman SN, Araujo AB, Roose SP, et al: Low testosterone levels in elderly men with dysthymic disorder. Am J Psychiatry 159:456–459, 2002.

396. Barrett-Connor E, Goodman-Gruen D, Patay B: Endogenous sex hormones and cognitive function in older men. J Clin Endocrinol Metab 84:3681–3685, 1999.

397. Moffat SD, Zonderman AB, Metter EJ, et al: Longitudinal assessment of serum free testosterone concentration predicts memory performance and cognitive status in elderly men. J Clin Endocrinol Metab 87:5001–5007, 2002.

398. Davidson JM, Chen JJ, Crapo L, et al: Hormonal changes and sexual function in aging men. J Clin Endocrinol Metab 57:71–77, 1983.

399. Vermeulen A: Androgen replacement therapy in the aging male: A critical evaluation. J Clin Endocrinol Metab 86:2380–2390, 2001.

400. Buena F, Swerdloff RS, Steiner BS, et al: Sexual function does not change when serum testosterone levels are pharmacologically varied within the normal male range. Fertil Steril 59:1118–1123, 1993.

401. Hayes FJ: Testosterone: Fountain of youth or drug of abuse? J Clin Endocrinol Metab 85:3020–3023, 2000.

402. Feldman HA, Goldstein I, Hatzichristou DG, et al: Impotence and its medical and psychosocial correlates: Results of the Massachusetts Male Aging Study. J Urol 151:54–61, 1994.

403. Hak AE, Witteman JC, de Jong FH, et al: Low levels of endogenous androgens increase the risk of atherosclerosis in elderly men: The Rotterdam study. J Clin Endocrinol Metab 87:3632–3639, 2002.

404. Liu PY, Death AK, Handelsman DJ: Androgens and cardiovascular disease. Endocr Rev 24:313–340, 2003.

405. Wu FC, Von Eckardstein A: Androgens and coronary artery disease. Endocr Rev 24:183–217, 2003.

406. English KM, Mandour O, Steeds RP, et al: Men with coronary artery disease have lower levels of androgens than men with normal coronary angiograms. Eur Heart J 21:890–894, 2000.

407. Phillips GB, Jing TY, Resnick LM, et al: Sex hormones and hemostatic risk factors for coronary heart disease in men with hypertension. J Hypertens 11:699–702, 1993.

408. Simon D, Charles MA, Nahoul K, et al: Association between plasma total testosterone and cardiovascular risk factors in healthy adult men: The Telecom study. J Clin Endocrinol Metab 82:682–685, 1997.

409. Haffner SM, Valdez RA, Stern MP, et al: Obesity, body fat distribution and sex hormones in men. Int J Obes Relat Metab Disord 17:643–649, 1993.

410. Barrett-Connor EL: Testosterone and risk factors for cardiovascular disease in men. Diabetes Metab 21:156–161, 1995.

411. Allan CA, McLachlan RI: Age-related changes in testosterone and the role of replacement therapy in older men. Clin Endocrinol (Oxf) 60:653–670, 2004.

412. Snyder PJ, Peachey H, Hannoush P, et al: Effect of testosterone treatment on body composition and muscle strength in men over 65 years of age. J Clin Endocrinol Metab 84:2647–2653, 1999.

413. Kenny AM, Prestwood KM, Gruman CA, et al: Effects of transdermal testosterone on bone and muscle in older men with low bioavailable testosterone levels. J Gerontol A Biol Sci Med Sci 56:M266–M272, 2001.

414. Wittert GA, Chapman IM, Haren MT, et al: Oral testosterone supplementation increases muscle and decreases fat mass in healthy elderly males with low-normal gonadal status. J Gerontol A Biol Sci Med Sci 58:618–625, 2003.

415. Steidle C, Schwartz S, Jacoby K, et al: AA2500 testosterone gel normalizes androgen levels in aging males with improvements in body composition and sexual function. J Clin Endocrinol Metab 88:2673–2681, 2003.

416. Ferrando AA, Sheffield-Moore M, Yeckel CW, et al: Testosterone administration to older men improves muscle function: Molecular and physiological mechanisms. Am J Physiol Endocrinol Metab 282:E601–E607, 2002.

417. Sih R, Morley JE, Kaiser FE, et al: Testosterone replacement in older hypogonadal men: A 12-month randomized controlled trial. J Clin Endocrinol Metab 82:1661–1667, 1997.

418. Ly LP, Jimenez M, Zhuang TN, et al: A double-blind, placebo-controlled, randomized clinical trial of transdermal dihydrotestosterone gel on muscular strength, mobility, and quality of life in older men with partial androgen deficiency. J Clin Endocrinol Metab 86:4078–4088, 2001.

419. Liu PY, Wishart SM, Handelsman DJ: A double-blind, placebo-controlled, randomized clinical trial of recombinant human chorionic gonadotropin on muscle strength and physical function and activity in older men with partial age-related androgen deficiency. J Clin Endocrinol Metab 87:3125–3135, 2002.

420. Munzer T, Harman SM, Hees P, et al: Effects of GH and/or sex steroid administration on abdominal subcutaneous and visceral fat in healthy aged women and men. J Clin Endocrinol Metab 86:3604–3610, 2001.

421. Schroeder ET, Singh A, Bhasin S, et al: Effects of an oral androgen on muscle and metabolism in older, community-dwelling men. Am J Physiol Endocrinol Metab 284:E120–E128, 2003.

422. Snyder PJ, Peachey H, Hannoush P, et al: Effect of testosterone treatment on bone mineral density in men over 65 years of age. J Clin Endocrinol Metab 84:1966–1972, 1999.

423. Amory JK, Watts NB, Easley KA, et al: Exogenous testosterone or testosterone with finasteride increases bone mineral density in older men with low serum testosterone. J Clin Endocrinol Metab 89:503–510, 2004.

424. Brill KT, Weltman AL, Gentili A, et al: Single and combined effects of growth hormone and testosterone administration on measures of body composition, physical performance, mood, sexual function, bone turnover, and muscle gene expression in healthy

older men. J Clin Endocrinol Metab 87:5649–5657, 2002.

425. Hajjar RR, Kaiser FE, Morley JE: Outcomes of long-term testosterone replacement in older hypogonadal males: A retrospective analysis. J Clin Endocrinol Metab 82:3793–3796, 1997.

426. Aversa A, Isidori AM, Spera G, et al: Androgens improve cavernous vasodilation and response to sildenafil in patients with erectile dysfunction. Clin Endocrinol (Oxf) 58:632–638, 2003.

427. Rhoden EL, Morgentaler A: Risks of testosterone-replacement therapy and recommendations for monitoring. N Engl J Med 350:482–492, 2004.

428. Snyder PJ: Hypogonadism in elderly men: What to do until the evidence comes. N Engl J Med 350:440–442, 2004.

429. Kenny AM, Bellantonio S, Gruman CA, et al: Effects of transdermal testosterone on cognitive function and health perception in older men with low bioavailable testosterone levels. J Gerontol A Biol Sci Med Sci 57:M321–M325, 2002.

430. Reddy P, White CM, Dunn AB, et al: The effect of testosterone on health-related quality of life in elderly males: A pilot study. J Clin Pharm Ther 25:421–M426, 2000.

431. Cherrier MM, Asthana S, Plymate S, et al: Testosterone supplementation improves spatial and verbal memory in healthy older men. Neurology 57:80–88, 2001.

432. Janowsky JS, Chavez B, Orwoll E: Sex steroids modify working memory. J Cogn Neurosci 12:407–414, 2000.

433. Janowsky JS, Oviatt SK, Orwoll ES: Testosterone influences spatial cognition in older men. Behav Neurosci 108:325–332, 1994.

434. Kenny AM, Fabregas G, Song C, et al: Effects of testosterone on behavior, depression, and cognitive function in older men with mild cognitive loss. J Gerontol A Biol Sci Med Sci 59:75–78, 2004.

435. Seidman SN, Spatz E, Rizzo C, et al: Testosterone replacement therapy for hypogonadal men with major depressive disorder: A randomized, placebo-controlled clinical trial. J Clin Psychiatry 62:406–412, 2001.

436. Pope HG Jr, Cohane GH, Kanayama G, et al: Testosterone gel supplementation for men with refractory depression: A randomized, placebo-controlled trial. Am J Psychiatry 160:105–111, 2003.

437. Jockenhovel F, Vogel E, Reinhardt W, et al: Effects of various modes of androgen substitution therapy on erythropoiesis. Eur J Med Res 2:293–298, 1997.

438. Sandblom RE, Matsumoto AM, Schoene RB, et al: Obstructive sleep apnea syndrome induced by testosterone administration. N Engl J Med 308:508–510, 1983.

439. Kenny AM, Prestwood KM, Gruman CA, et al: Effects of transdermal testosterone on lipids and vascular reactivity in older men with low bioavailable testosterone levels. J Gerontol A Biol Sci Med Sci 57:M460–M465, 2002.

440. Ng MK, Liu PY, Williams AJ, et al: Prospective study of effect of androgens on serum inflammatory markers in men. Arterioscler Thromb Vasc Biol 22:1136–1141, 2002.

441. Winkler UH: Effects of androgens on haemostasis. Maturitas 24:147–155, 1996.

442. Liverman CT, Blazer DG (eds): Testosterone and Aging: Clinical Research Directions. Washington, DC, Institute of Medicine of the National Academies, National Academies Press, 2003.

# Cryptorchidism and Hypospadias

## *John M. Hutson*

## CRYPTORCHIDISM

### INTRODUCTION

Undescended testis, or cryptorchidism, is a very common disorder in males, with approximately 1 in 20 boys undergoing orchidopexy by the time that they reach puberty.[1] There remain unresolved issues about the prognosis for fertility and malignancy risk as well as the optimal time for surgery. In addition, there is controversy about whether some boys have acquired rather than congenital cryptorchidism.

Currently, it is not known whether the dramatic changes in the recommended age for surgery (from 10 to 15 years of age 50 years ago to 6 months old now) will decrease the risk of testicular cancer and infertility. All current treatment, however, is based on the assumption that early orchidopexy will prevent germ cell degeneration in early childhood and hence lead to fewer tumors and improved fertility.

There have been significant advances in understanding the complex embryology of testicular descent, with new theories and experimental evidence to explain the hormonal regulation of major anatomic changes. The classification of cryptorchidism also is changing, with increasing recognition and acceptance of an acquired form. With so much change, not only in the way in which we understand but also treat cryptorchidism, readers need to be aware of current concepts.

### EMBRYOLOGY

The testes descend prenatally from their initial intra-abdominal position on the urogenital ridge into the low-temperature environment of the scrotum via a complex multistage mechanism.[1] Before 7 to 8 weeks of gestation, the gonadal position is similar in both sexes. With the onset of sexual differentiation, the fetal testis begins producing müllerian-inhibiting substance (MIS) [also called antimüllerian hormone (AMH)], from the developing Sertoli cells as well as androgen and insulin-like hormone 3 (also known as relaxin-like factor) from the Leydig cells. These hormones are involved in controlling the descent of the male gonad, which is held by the cranial suspensory ligament at the upper pole and by the genitoinguinal ligament at the lower pole.[2] The genitoinguinal ligament was called the gubernaculum testis by John Hunter in 1762 because it appeared to steer the testis into the scrotum.

During the initial phase of descent, regression of the cranial ligament and thickening of the gubernaculum allow the testis to be held near the inguinal region.[3] By contrast, in the female, the cranial ligament persists, while the gubernaculum remains thin, and holds the ovary higher on the posterior abdominal wall as the fetal abdomen enlarges. The inguinal canal forms by the abdominal wall muscles developing around the caudal, gelatinous end of the gubernaculum. By 15 weeks, the testis is attached by a short, stout, and gelatinous gubernaculum to the future internal inguinal ring, whereas the ovary is higher in the pelvis.[4]

After 20 to 25 weeks, a diverticulum of the peritoneal membrane, known as the processus vaginalis, begins to elongate within the gubernaculum, which retains a central connection with the epididymal tail and the lower pole of the testis. The caudal end of the gubernaculum grows out of the abdominal wall and elongates toward the scrotum, extending the processus vaginalis eventually to the scrotum. Between 25 and 30 weeks, the testis descends rapidly through the inguinal canal and then more slowly across the pubic region and into the scrotum, followed by obliteration of the proximal processus vaginalis.[5] Descent within this peritoneal diverticulum is complete by 35 weeks. The gubernaculum is not anchored to adjacent structures during inguinoscrotal migration but becomes secondarily attached to the scrotum after descent is complete.

The two phases of testicular descent are controlled by different hormones (Fig. 171-1). Gubernacular enlargement in the first phase is stimulated primarily by insulin-like hormone 3, with a possible secondary role for MIS/AMH.[6-9] The caudal attachment of the gubernaculum to the inguinal abdominal wall grows (called the swelling reaction) by proliferation of the embryonic mesenchyme and deposition of extracellular matrix.

Androgens are responsible for regression of the cranial suspensory ligament, but this alone is not sufficient for descent. The swelling reaction of the gubernaculum occurs without androgens.

The second phase of descent with migration of the gubernaculum from the groin to the scrotum appears to be controlled indirectly by androgens, although this remains controversial.[10] The genitofemoral nerve is masculinized by androgens so that the sensory fibers contain calcitonin gene-related peptide, which is released by the nerve endings in the scrotum. Calcitonin gene-related peptide stimulates elongation of the gubernaculum by growth of its tip and also appears to control the direction of migration. Gubernacular growth and testicular descent are inhibited by prenatal exposure to both antiandrogens and estrogens, which may account for the high incidence of cryptorchidism in some places with high levels of estrogen-like molecules in the environment. There

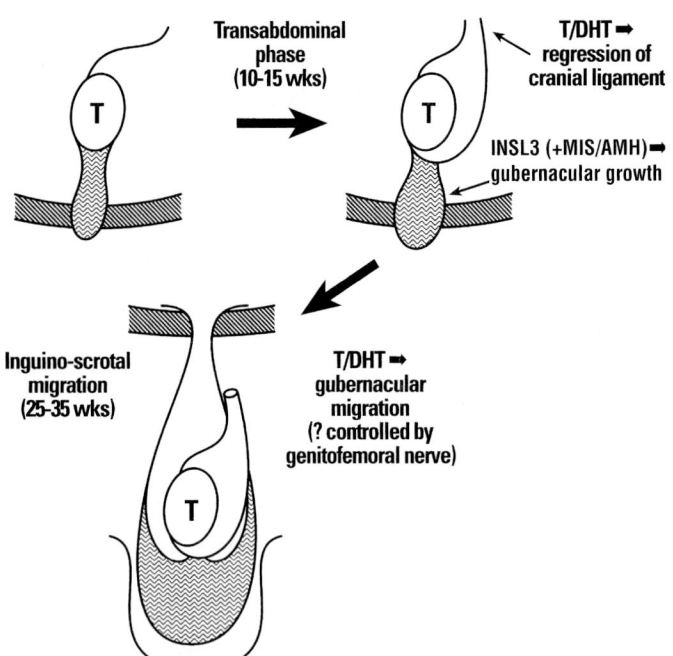

Figure 171-1 Schema of normal testicular descent. The first phase is controlled by insulin-like hormone 3 (INSL3) with auxiliary roles for androgen and müllerian-inhibiting substance/antimüllerian hormone (MIS/AMH). The second phase is controlled by androgen acting indirectly via the genitofemoral nerve and release of calcitonin gene-related peptide. DHT, dihydrotestosterone; T, testosterone.

are also theories suggesting that the second phase of descent may be controlled by sympathetic nerves or direct effects of androgens on the gubernaculum, although the supporting evidence is lacking. It is generally agreed that the physical force needed for elongation of the processus vaginalis is probably provided by the intra-abdominal pressure.

## ETIOLOGY

Any anomaly in either the hormonal control or the anatomic processes in normal testicular descent will cause cryptorchidism.[10,11] Hormonal defects in insulin-like hormone 3[12] or androgenic or MIS/AMH action are identified only rarely, suggesting that mechanical anomalies are more common. These patients may present with rare forms of intersex, with cryptorchidism as part of a complex genital anomaly. The first or transabdominal phase involves little movement of the testis, and this may explain the low frequency (5% to 20%) of intra-abdominal testes. Because the swelling reaction of the male gubernaculum simply holds the testis near the groin as the embryo enlarges, the relative positions of the ovary and testis change, but there is no active movement of the gubernaculum. By contrast, the inguinoscrotal migration phase requires very significant mechanical and anatomic movements, and consequently anomalies are common: More than 60% of testes are found just outside the external inguinal ring, consistent with anomalous or arrested gubernacular migration. Transient deficiency of androgen production in utero, perhaps related to deficiency of gonadotropin production by the fetal pituitary or the placenta,[12] may account for some, particularly where there is intrauterine growth retardation. Anomalies of the genitofemoral nerve also may cause undescended testes; for example, perineal testes may be caused by an anomalous location of the genitofemoral nerve.[1]

Inherited syndromes frequently are associated with cryptorchidism. Hypothalamic dysfunction, connective tissue disorders, neurogenic (e.g., spina bifida anomalies), and mechanical anomalies (e.g., arthrogryposis multiplex congenita) all may cause disruption in testicular descent.[13-15] Cryptorchidism is also common in infants with abdominal wall defects, such as exomphalos or omphalocele, gastroschisis, and exstrophy of the bladder.[16] The body of the epididymis is hypoplastic and frequently is not tightly adherent to the cryptorchid testis.[17] This is more common in high intra-abdominal testes and probably indicates significantly decreased androgen production. Whether epididymal-testicular separation is the cause or the result of cryptorchidism is not known.[18] In addition, its effect on fertility is uncertain, even though the rete testis is nearly always still connected to the head of the epididymis.

Currently, there is a lot of interest in the possible role of environmental estrogens on the frequency of cryptorchidism and hypospadias.[19] Furthermore, there are data on male offspring of mothers treated with diethylstilbestrol, in whom congenital cryptorchidism was a common outcome.[20-22] There are data from animal models to explain diethylstilbestrol exposure, but the role of synthetic or plant estrogenic compounds remains uncertain. It will be some time before we can determine whether environmental estrogens actually cause genital anomalies in the human male.

## CLINICAL PRESENTATION

As many as 4% to 5% of newborn males show cryptorchidism, but this decreases to 1% to 2% by 12 weeks after term, after normal (but postnatal) descent in premature infants and delayed postnatal descent in some term babies. Beyond 12 weeks, spontaneous testicular descent is rare.[23] There are local differences in the frequency reported (e.g., between Denmark and Finland), but this is not being seen elsewhere.[24]

An undescended testis is best defined as a testis that cannot be manipulated to the bottom of the scrotum (with excess tension on the spermatic cord) by 12 weeks of age. Most testes (approximately 85%) are near the neck of the scrotum or just lateral to the external inguinal ring, described by Denis Browne[25] as the superficial inguinal pouch. A few cryptorchid testes are within the inguinal canal, making them impalpable unless they can be squeezed out of the external inguinal ring by compression. Ten percent of testes are intra-abdominal or absent (presumed to be secondary to prenatal testicular torsion). Ectopic cryptorchid testes are rare (less than 5%) and occur in the perineum, prepubic region, thigh, or the contralateral inguinal canal (transverse testicular ectopia).[26]

## ENDOCRINE EFFECTS

In infants with undescended testes, the testosterone and gonadotropin levels are diminished between 1 and 4 months of age compared with normal males.[27] Whether this is a sign of primary endocrinopathy or secondary dysfunction of the testis is unknown. Postnatal increase in testosterone production also is diminished in premature infants, perhaps secondary to inadequate stimulation by chorionic gonadotropin in utero.[28] Despite lower than normal androgen levels between 1 and 4 months of age, there is no apparent anomaly in androgen receptors from gonadal or skin biopsy specimens collected at orchidopexy or in screening the androgen receptor for mutations.[29]

The postnatal secretion of MIS/AMH in infants with cryptorchidism also is deranged. Production of MIS/AMH from Sertoli cells normally increases between 4 and 12 months, but this surge is inhibited in undescended testes.[30,31]

## GERM CELL MATURATION

Germ cells mature postnatally from a primitive gonocyte through a series of steps to primary spermatocytes by 3 to 4 years. This process is perturbed in cryptorchid testes, with failure of transformation of gonocytes into type

A spermatogonia between 4 and 12 months.[32–34] These observations suggest that germ cell deficiency may be secondary to postnatal dysfunction rather than being congenital, as previously thought.[35]

Lack of germ cell transformation could be secondary to postnatal gonadotropin or androgen deficiency[34,36] or, alternatively, may be related to low MIS/AMH levels.[36] Abnormal postnatal maturation of gonocytes could lead to both infertility and malignancy,[37] although some authors propose that there may be congenital carcinoma in situ cells in the cryptorchid testis.[38,39]

## DIAGNOSIS

The aim of clinical examination is to locate the gonad, if palpable, and determine its lowest position without causing traction on the spermatic cord (which probably corresponds to the caudal limit of the tunica vaginalis).[40] In infants, the diagnosis is straightforward because the scrotum is thin and pendulous. Hypoplasia of the hemiscrotum indicates that it does not contain a testis. The inguinal testis is within its tunica vaginalis, which gives it significant mobility. Ultrasonography, computed tomography, and magnetic resonance imaging have been proposed for the diagnosis of the impalpable testis but generally are not contributory because the testis may be absent or concealed by abdominal viscera. A simple and reliable approach is to use laparoscopy, which allows the testis to be located easily or absence of the testis to be confirmed.[41]

## TREATMENT

Hormone therapy remains controversial.[42,43] It is based on the assumption that cryptorchidism is secondary to a deficiency of the hypothalamic-pituitary-gonadal axis. Both human chorionic gonadotropin and luteinizing hormone-releasing hormone therapy have been tried, with success rates of 10% to 50%. Randomized, double-blind, placebo-controlled studies have not shown a more than marginal benefit with either human chorionic gonadotropin or luteinizing hormone-releasing hormone.[44–46] Despite endocrine control of descent, the mechanical factors appear to be too complex for this simple approach to be successful. Hormone treatment may be effective for acquired undescended testes.

Surgical treatment is based on the assumption that early intervention will prevent secondary testicular degeneration caused by high temperature, and this lower temperature is essential for normal postnatal germ cell maturation.[47] Evidence of progressive germ cell loss in the cryptorchid testis after 6 months of age has accumulated over the past 50 years and now suggests that orchidopexy should be considered at 6 months of age or shortly thereafter (?up to 1 to 2 years) because the first signs of abnormal germ cell development can be seen between 4 and 12 months of age.[34] Surgery at this very early age needs a trained pediatric surgeon because the technique is quite different from that for a 5- to 10-year-old boy.[48]

All baby boys need examination at birth to document gonadal position. Those infants without two fully descended testes should be reexamined at 12 weeks, and if a testis is still undescended, the child should be referred to a pediatric surgeon for possible surgical treatment. Orchidopexy is done as an ambulatory procedure, with discharge home a few hours after operation. General anesthesia is supplemented with local or regional analgesia, which will provide pain relief for the first few hours postoperatively.

In adolescents and adults presenting late for treatment, the undescended testis is usually best removed because the risk of malignancy is high and the prognosis for fertility is poor.[49] If a biopsy is done and shows carcinoma in situ, this is also an indication for excision.

## PROGNOSIS

The complication rate after orchidopexy is less than 5% in experienced hands.[48] Wound infection is common in infants secondary to external contamination of the wound, although there is a very low risk of atrophy of the testis, which is greatest when intra-abdominal testes are pulled down under tension. Laparoscopy, with or without ligation of the testicular vessels (Fowler-Stephens procedure),[41,50] shows promise in increasing the success for high intra-abdominal gonads.[41,51,52]

The prognosis for fertility, the primary aim of orchidopexy, remains uncertain.[53–55] An extensive review of the literature has not demonstrated any significant improvement in fertility, either by paternity or sperm count, with surgery between 4 and 14 years.[56] However, now that early germ cell maturation in the first year is known to be deranged, improved fertility might be expected with very early orchidopexy.[33,34] Unfortunately, it will be at least another 10 years before the outcome of this new policy is known.

The risk of malignancy is calculated to be 5 to 10 times greater than normal for a man with a history of unilateral cryptorchidism.[57–60] The risk in a future generation of men who underwent orchidopexy in infancy is unknown at present but is anticipated to be lower than previously. Some clinical features are associated with statistically better outcomes (i.e., fertility and cancer risk) and include a testis near the neck of the scrotum and ascending or retractile testes (see later). Poor prognostic factors are primary testicular or epididymal dysplasia, intra-abdominal or intracanalicular position, associated strangulated inguinal hernia, and (possibly) surgery late in childhood or adolescence.[61]

## ACQUIRED CRYPTORCHIDISM

### RETRACTILE TESTES

Retraction of the testis out of the scrotum secondary to reflex contraction of the cremaster muscle is both normal and common and is involved in temperature control and protection of the testis from trauma. The reflex is absent or weak at birth and becomes more active after 1 year, reaching a peak in 5- to 10-year-old boys.[62]

Many testes are erroneously described as retractile when they can be pulled down into the scrotum during the physical examination but retract out of the scrotum on release. This retractility is assumed to be secondary to cremasteric activity, but an alternative explanation has been proposed recently, which is that retractile testes may be caused by failure of the spermatic cord to elongate with age.[63] Because the distance from the external inguinal ring to the bottom of the scrotum increases with age, the spermatic cord must grow longer to keep the testis in the scrotum. Preliminary evidence suggests that failure of complete obliteration of the processus vaginalis may prevent postnatal elongation of the vas and vessels[64] (Fig. 171-2).

### ASCENDING TESTES

The ascending testis is a special variant of the retractile testis, in which there is delayed postnatal descent of the testis in the first 3 months after birth.[65,66] Follow-up studies suggest that subsequent ascent of the testis is common later in childhood.[67–69] The cause of ascending testes is not resolved, with the only well-documented cause being neuronal dysfunction as seen in children with cerebral palsy.[70] In normal children, the explanation is likely to be persistence of the processus vaginalis, either patent or as a fibrous remnant.[64]

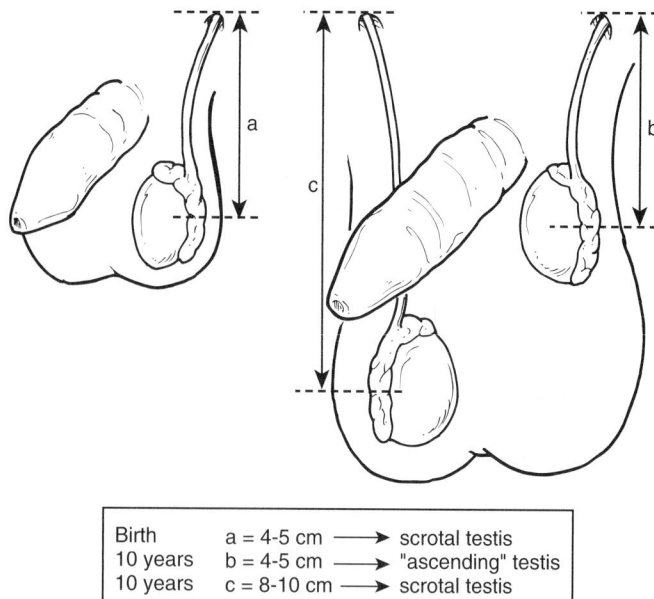

Birth      a = 4-5 cm ⟶ scrotal testis
10 years   b = 4-5 cm ⟶ "ascending" testis
10 years   c = 8-10 cm ⟶ scrotal testis

*Figure 171-2*    Proposed mechanism for development of acquired cryptorchidism. Growth of the pubic bone in the first 5 to 10 years increases the distance from the external inguinal ring to the scrotum from 4 to 5 cm to 8 to 10 cm. Failure of elongation of the spermatic cord will lead to secondary maldescent or ascending testis.

## MANAGEMENT

Both retractile and ascending testes may be names for what is, in effect, acquired cryptorchidism caused by persistence of the processus vaginalis.[68,69,71,72] The normal spermatic cord elongates gradually with growth, and hence acquired cryptorchidism develops insidiously, presenting mostly between 5 and 10 years of age.[73] Orchidopexy is required once the testis can no longer reside spontaneously in the scrotum, and it can be performed in the standard manner or by a scrotal approach.[74,75] Once the fibrous remnant of the processus vaginalis is divided, the testis can reach the scrotum easily.

The prognosis for this special group is probably much better than for congenital cryptorchidism because the testis is normally located in the scrotum during infancy.[76,77] The outcome for malignancy is now thought to be similar to that of normal men.[78] The frequency of acquired cryptorchidism, like the concept itself, remains unknown and controversial but may account for as many as one half of all children coming to orchidopexy.[68,69,73,79]

## HYPOSPADIAS

The primitive phallus begins to enlarge at 8 weeks of gestation in the male in response to fetal androgens. The inner genital folds fuse in the midline, and the endodermal urethral plate canalizes[80] to create the anterior urethra up to the coronal groove, whereas the urethra within the glans forms later by further proliferation of the urethral plate and subsequent canalization. The preputial skin forms from low folds on the dorsum of the shaft at the corona, eventually covering the entire glans.[81]

Failure of urethral fusion leads to hypospadias (from *hypo-* plus Greek *span*, to draw, tear), with secondary deficiency of the ventral prepuce (dorsal hood) and relative deficiency in the growth of the periurethral tissues compared with the

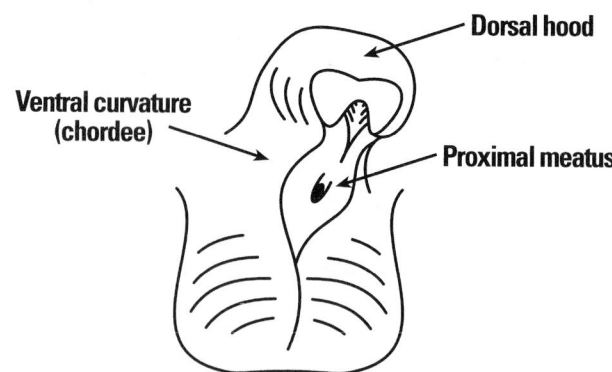

*Figure 171-3*    Proximal hypospadias. Drawing of hypospadias with a urethral meatus on the proximal shaft of the penis. The fusion line in the scrotum bifurcates distally, ending on each side of the ventrally deficient foreskin (dorsal hood). Inadequate growth of the ventral surface of the shaft causes ventral curvature (chordee).

corpora cavernosa, leading to chordee or ventral curvature of the penis[81] (Fig. 171-3).

Hypospadias occurs in 1 in every 100 to 300 boys, depending on the criteria used for diagnosis.[82] Approximately 10% of patients with hypospadias have a sibling or father with the anomaly, suggesting a polygenic inheritance pattern.[83] The severity of the anomaly varies widely, from a perineal opening to an opening on the proximal glans or even chordee with a normal urethral meatus.

Care is needed in diagnosis because some infants with ambiguous genitalia may be diagnosed as having simple hypospadias.[84] Because hypospadias is an anatomic anomaly of anterior urethral development, the rest of the external (and also internal) genitalia should be normal. Patients with ambiguous genitalia, by contrast, have a more extensive genital anomaly, reflecting the failure of all androgen-dependent development. A useful rule of thumb is to assume that any baby with hypospadias and an undescended testis or bifid scrotum should be investigated for intersex, with immediate hormonal, chromosomal, and anatomic studies. Immediate gender assignment as male is quite safe if the scrotum is fused and both testes are descended fully (i.e., androgen-dependent genital development is normal).

Surgical treatment is required to reconstruct the penis in hypospadias.[82] Despite the numerous different surgical techniques available, there are a few principles of management: (1) create an extension to the urethra to bring it to the tip of the glans, allowing normal micturition; (2) correct the chordee to create a straight shaft for normal sexual function; and (3) repair the dorsal hood for cosmetic reasons. (In severe cases, the skin is moved ventrally to create the urethra and elongate the ventral surface; in mild cases, the dorsal hood can be repaired to restore the normal appearance of the foreskin.) Surgery should be completed in infants or young children before school entry, with current trends toward repair in 6- to 18-month-old children.[85] The operation may be done as day surgery but may need prolonged admission with urinary diversion, depending on the severity of the anomaly and the surgeon's preference.

The prognosis for micturition and sexual function is good, with improving cosmetic appearance with newer procedures.[86] However, wound infection, hematoma, urethral breakdown to create a fistula, and stricture continue to be serious problems because the surgery requires significant skill.[87,88]

# REFERENCES

1. Hutson JM, Hasthorpe S, Heyns CF: Anatomical and functional aspects of testicular descent and cryptorchidism. Endocr Rev 18:259–280, 1996.
2. Backhouse KM: The natural history of testicular descent and maldescent. Proc R Soc Med 59:357–360, 1966.
3. van der Schoot P: The name cranial ovarian suspensory ligaments in mammalian anatomy should only be used to indicate the structures derived from the foetal cranial mesonephric and gonadal ligaments. Anat Rec 237:434–438, 1993.
4. England MA: A Colour Atlas of Life Before Birth. Normal Fetal Development. London, Wolfe Medical, 1983, pp 157–167.
5. Heyns CF: The gubernaculum during testicular descent in the human fetus. J Anat 153:93–112, 1987.
6. Nef S, Parada LF: Cryptorchidism in mice mutant for Insl3. Nat Genet 22:95–299, 1999.
7. Zimmermann S, Steding G, Emmen JM, et al: Targeted disruption of the Insl3 gene causes bilateral cryptorchidism. Mol Endocrinol 13:681–691, 1999.
8. Emmen JM, McLasky A, Adham IM, et al: Hormonal control of gubernaculum development during testis descent: Gubernaculum outgrowth in vitro requires both insulin-like factor and androgen. Endocrinology 141:4720, 2000.
9. Kubota Y, Temelcos C, Bathgate RAD, et al: The role of insulin 3, testosterone, MIS and relaxin in rat gubernacular growth. Hum Mol Reprod 8:900–905, 2002.
10. Hutson JM: The gubernaculum in testicular descent and cryptorchidism. Turkish J Pediatr 46(Suppl):3–6, 2004.
11. Husmann DA, Levy JB: Current concepts in the pathophysiology of testicular descent. Urology 46:267–276, 1995.
12. Ferlin A, Simonato M, Bartolini L, et al: The INSL3-LGR8/GREAT ligand-receptor pair in human cryptorchidism. J Clin Endocrinol Metab 88:4273–4279, 2003.
13. Hadziselimovic F, Duckett JW, Snyder HM III, et al: Omphalocele, cryptorchidism, and brain malformations. J Pediatr Surg 22:854–856, 1987.
14. Fallat ME, Hersh JH, Hutson JM: Theories on the relationship between cryptorchidism and arthrogryposis. Pediatr Surg Int 7:271–273, 1992.
15. Hutson JM, Beasley SW, Bryan AD: Cryptorchidism in spina bifida and spinal cord transection: A clue to the mechanism of transinguinal descent of the testis. J Pediatr Surg 23:275–277, 1988.
16. Kaplan LM, Koyle MA, Kaplan GW, et al: Association between abdominal wall defects and cryptorchidism. J Urol 136:645–647, 1986.
17. Johansen TEB: Non-union of testis and epididymis. Scand J Urol Nephrol 22:165–170, 1988.
18. Gill B, Kogan S, Starr S, et al: Significance of epididymal and ductal anomalies associated with testicular maldescent. J Urol 142:556–558, 1989.
19. Fisher JS, Macpherson S, Marchetti N, et al: Human "testicular dysgenesis syndrome": A possible model using in-utero exposure of the rat to dibutyl phthalate. Hum Reprod 18:1383–1394, 2003
20. Goldberg JM, Falcone T: Effect of diethylstilbestrol on reproductive function. Fertil Steril 72:1–7, 1999.
21. Block K, Kardana A, Igarashi P, et al: In utero diethylstilbestrol (DES) exposure alters HOX gene expression in the developing mullerian system. FASEB J 14:1101–1108, 2000.
22. Whitehead ED, Leiter E: Genital abnormalities and abnormal semen analyses in male patients exposed to diethylstilbestrol in utero. J Urol 125:47–50, 1981.
23. John Radcliffe Hospital Cryptorchidism Study Group: Cryptorchidism: A prospective study of 7500 consecutive male births, 1984–8. Arch Dis Child 67:892–899, 1992.
24. Borsen KA, Kaleva A, Main KM, et al: Difference in prevalence of congenital cryptorchidism in infants between two Nordic countries. Lancet 363:1264–1269, 2004.
25. Browne D: The diagnosis of undescended testicle. Br Med J 2:92–97, 1938.
26. Dogruyol H, Balkan E: Perineal ectopic testis. Br J Urol 5:547, 1992.
27. Raivio T, Toppari J, Kaleva M, et al: Serum androgen bioactivity in cryptorchid and noncryptorchid boys during the postnatal reproductive hormone surge. J Clin Endocrinol Metab 88:2597–2599, 2003.
28. Baker BA, Morley R, Lucas A: Plasma testosterone in preterm infants with cryptorchidism. Arch Dis Child 63:1198–1200, 1988.
29. Brown TR, Berkovitz GD, Gearhart JP: Androgen receptors in boys with isolated bilateral cryptorchidism. Am J Dis Child 142:933–936, 1988.
30. Baker ML, Metcalfe SA, Hutson JM: Serum levels of müllerian inhibiting substance in boys from birth to 18 years, as determined by enzyme immunoassay. J Clin Endocrinol Metab 70:11–15, 1990.
31. Yamanaka J, Baker M, Metcalfe SA, et al: Serum levels of Müllerian inhibiting substance in boys with cryptorchidism. J Pediatr Surg 26:621–623, 1991.
32. Huff DS, Hadziselimovic F, Snyder H McC III, et al: Postnatal testicular maldevelopment in unilateral cryptorchidism. J Urol 142:546–548, 1989.
33. Huff DS, Hadziselimovic F, Snyder H McC III, et al: Early postnatal testicular maldevelopment in cryptorchidism. J Urol 146:624–626, 1991.
34. Huff DS, Hadziselimovic F, Snyder HM III, et al: Histologic maldevelopment of unilaterally cryptorchid testes and their descended partners. Eur J Pediatr 152:S10–S14, 1993.
35. Scorer CG, Forrest DM, Dennison WM, et al: Undescended testicle. Br Med J April 30:1359, 1960.
36. Zhou B, Watts LM, Hutson JM: Germ cell development in neonatal mouse testes in vitro requires müllerian inhibiting substance. J Urol 150:613–616, 1993.
37. Hutson JM: Undescended testes. In Stringer MD, Mouriquand PDE, Oldham K, Howard ER (eds): Pediatric Surgery and Urology: Long-Term Outcomes, 2d ed. London, WB Saunders, in press.
38. Giwercman A, Bruun E, Frimodt-Moller C, Skakkebaek NE: Prevalence of carcinoma in situ and other histopathological abnormalities in testes of men with a history of cryptorchidism. J Urol 142:998–1002, 1989.
39. Giwercman A, Muller J, Skakkebaek NE: Carcinoma in situ of the testis: Possible origin, clinical significance, and diagnostic methods. Recent Results Cancer Res 123:21–36, 1991.
40. Beltran-Brown F, Villegas-Alvarez F: Clinical classification for undescended testes: Experience in 1,010 orchidopexies. J Pediatr Surg 23:444–447, 1988.
41. Peters CA. Laparoscopy in pediatric urology. Curr Opin Urol 14:67–73, 2004.
42. Hadziselimovic F: Hormonal treatment of cryptorchidism. N Engl J Med 315:322, 1986.
43. de Muinck Keizer-Schrama SM: Hormonal treatment of cryptorchidism. Horm Res 30:178–186, 1988.
44. Rajfer J, Handelsman DJ, Swerdloff RS, et al: Hormonal therapy of cryptorchidism. A randomized, double-blind study comparing human chorionic gonadotropin and gonadotropin-releasing hormone. N Engl J Med 314:466–470, 1986.
45. deMuinck Keizer-Schrama SM, Hazebroek FWJ, Drop SLS, et al: Double-blind, placebo-controlled study of luteinising-hormone-releasing-hormone nasal spray in treatment of undescended testes. Lancet 1:876–879, 1986.
46. Bica DTG, Hadziselimovic F: Buserelin treatment of cryptorchidism: A randomized, double-blind, placebo-controlled study. J Urol 148:617–621, 1992.
47. Mieusset R, Fonda PJ, Vaysse P, et al: Increase in testicular temperature in case of cryptorchidism in boys. Fertil Steril 59:1319–1321, 1993.
48. Wilson-Storey D, McGenity K, Dickson JAS: Orchidopexy: The younger the better? J R Coll Surg Edinb 35:362–364, 1990.
49. Oh J, Landman J, Evers A, et al: Management of the postpubertal patient with cryptorchidism: An

updated analysis. J Urol 167:1329–1333, 2002.

50. Elder JS: Two-stage Fowler-Stephens orchiopexy in the management of intra-abdominal testes. J Urol 148:1239–1241, 1992.

51. Pintus C, Coppola R, Talamo M, et al: Laparoscopic approach for nonpalpable abdominal testis. Surg Laparosc Endosc 7:156–158, 1997.

52. Cortes D, Thorup JM, Lenz K, et al: Laparoscopy in 100 consecutive patients with 128 impalpable testes. Br J Urol 75:281–287, 1995.

53. Lee PA, Coughlin MT, Bellinger MF. Paternity and hormone levels after unilateral cryptorchidism: Association with pretreatment testicular location. J Urol 164:1697–1701, 2000.

54. Lee PA, Coughlin MT, Bellinger MF: No relationship of testicular size at orchiopexy with fertility in men who previously had unilateral cryptorchidism. J Urol 166:236–239, 2001.

55. Cortes D, Thorup JM, Lindenberg S: Fertility potential after unilateral orchiopexy: Simultaneous testicular biopsy and orchiopexy in a cohort of 87 patients. J Urol 155:1061–1065, 1996.

56. Chilvers C, Dudley NE, Gough MH, et al: Undescended testis: The effect of treatment on subsequent risk of subfertility and malignancy. J Pediatr Surg 21:691–696, 1986.

57. Moller H, Skakkebaek NE: Risks of testicular cancer and cryptorchidism in relation to socio-economic status and related factors: Case-control studies in Denmark. Int J Cancer 66:287–293, 1996.

58. Moller H, Prener A, Skakkebaek NE: Testicular cancer, cryptorchidism, inguinal hernia, testicular atrophy, and genital malformations: Case-control studies in Denmark. Cancer Causes Control 7:264–274, 1996.

59. Muller J, Skakkebaek NE: Cryptorchidism. Curr Ther Endocrinol Metab 6:363–366, 1997.

60. Swerdlow AJ, Higgins CD, Pike MC: Risk of testicular cancer in cohort of boys with cryptorchidism. Br Med J 314:1507–1511, 1997.

61. Stone JM, Cruickshank DG, Sandeman TF, et al: Laterality, maldescent, trauma and other clinical factors in the epidemiology of testis cancer in Victoria, Australia. Br J Cancer 64:132–138, 1991.

62. Farrington GH: The position and retractibility of the normal testis in childhood with reference to the diagnosis and treatment of cryptorchidism. J Pediatr Surg 3:53–59, 1968.

63. Hutson JM: Can undescended testes be acquired? Lancet 341:504, 1993.

64. Clarnette TD, Rowe D, Hasthorpe S, et al: Incomplete disappearance of the processus vaginalis as a cause of ascending testis. J Urol 157:1889–1891, 1997.

65. Mayr J, Rune GM, Holas A, et al: Ascent of the testis in children. Eur J Pediatr 154:893–895, 1995.

66. John Radcliffe Hospital Cryptorchidism Study Group: Boys with late descending testes: The source of patients with "retractile" testes undergoing orchidopexy? Br Med J 293:789–790, 1986.

67. Davey RB: Undescended testes: Early versus late maldescent. Pediatr Surg Int 12:165–167, 1997.

68. Barthold JS, Gonzalez R: The epidemiology of congenital cryptorchidism, testicular ascent and orchiopexy. J Urol 170:2396–2401, 2003.

69. Hack WW, Meijer RW, van der Voort-Doedens LM, et al: Natural course of acquired undescended testis in boys. Br J Surg 90:728–731, 2003.

70. Smith A, Hutson JM, Beasley SW, et al: The relationship between cerebral palsy and cryptorchidism. J Pediatr Surg 24:1303–1305, 1989.

71. Atwell JD: Ascent of the testis: Fact or fiction. Br J Urol 57:474–477, 1985.

72. Robertson JFR, Azmy AF, Cochran W: Assent to ascent of the testis. Br J Urol 61:146–147, 1988.

73. Donaldson KM, Tong SYC, Hutson JM: Prevalence of late orchidopexy is consistent with some undescended testes being acquired. Indian J Pediatr 63:725–729, 1996.

74. Bianchi A, Squire BR: Transscrotal orchiopexy: Orchiopexy revised. Pediatr Surg Int 4:189–192, 1989.

75. Russinko PJ, Siddiq FM, Tackett L, et al: Prescrotal orchiopexy: An alternative surgical approach for the palpable undescended testis. J Urol 170:2436–2438, 2003.

76. Puri P, O'Donnell B: Semen analysis of patients who had orchidopexy at or after seven years of age. Lancet 2:1051–1052, 1988.

77. Nistal M, Paniagua R: Infertility in adult males with retractile testes. Fertil Steril 41:395–403, 1984.

78. Cortes D, Thorup J, Peterson BL: Testicular neoplasia in undescended testes or cryptorchid boys—Does surgical strategy have an impact on the risk of invasive neoplasia? Turkish J Pediatr 46(Suppl):35–42, 2004.

79. Pike MC: Boys with late descending testes: The source of patients with "retractile" testes undergoing orchidopexy? Br Med J 293:789–790, 1986.

80. Penington EC, Hutson JM: The urethral plate—Does it grow into the genital tubercle or with it? Br J Urol Int 89:733–739, 2002.

81. Stephens FD, Smith ED, Hutson JM: Congenital Anomalies of the Kidney, Urinary and Genital Tracts, 2d ed. London, Martin Duniz, 2002.

82. Hadidi AT, Azmy AF. Hypospadias Surgery. Berlin, Springer, 2004.

83. Bauer S, Retik A, Colodny A: Genetic aspects of hypospadias. Urol Clin North Am 8:559, 1981.

84. Tong SY, Donaldson K, Hutson JM: When is hypospadias not hypospadias? Med J Aust 164:153–154, 1996.

85. Mouriquand PD, Mure PY: Current concepts in hypospadiology. Br J Urol Int 93(Suppl 3):26–34, 2004.

86. Baskin LS, Duckett JW: Hypospadias. In Stringer MD, Mouriquand PDE, Oldham KT, Howard ER (eds): Long-Term Outcomes in Pediatric Surgery and Urology. London, WB Saunders, 1998, pp 559–567.

87. Secrest CL, Jordan GH, Winslow BH, et al: Repair of the complications of hypospadias surgery. J Urol 150:1415–1418, 1993.

88. Scherz HC, Kaplan GW, Packer MG, et al: Post-hypospadias repair urethral strictures: A review of 30 cases. J Urol 140:1253–1255, 1988.

# Clinical Management of Male Infertility

## H. W. Gordon Baker

## NATURE AND CAUSES OF MALE INFERTILITY

### DEFINITIONS

Infertility is an inability or reduced ability to produce a pregnancy within a reasonable period of trying, usually 6 to 12 months. Sterility is a total inability to produce a pregnancy, and this may be reversible or irreversible. Subfertility is infertility without an absolute barrier to reproduction that would cause sterility, such as azoospermia. *Hypogonadism* is a nonspecific term for decreased testicular or ovarian function that could include a disorder of gamete production or function or a disorder of sex hormone production or action. Usually, hypogonadism indicates testicular failure associated with androgen deficiency. Primary hypogonadism results from disorders that affect the gonads directly, and secondary hypogonadism results from defective pituitary gonadotropin secretion.

### INCIDENCE AND DISTRIBUTION

The average pregnancy rates in most human communities range from 15% to 40% in the first month and decline in each subsequent month of trying. Approximately 50% of couples conceive a first pregnancy by 3 to 5 months and 85% by 12 months.[1,2] Recently, there appears to have been an increase in pregnancy rates in the first few months of trying, possibly because of a more general awareness in the community of the timing of ovulation and the fertile phase of the menstrual cycle.[3] The 6- to 12-month period used to define infertility means that it afflicts approximately 15% of couples.[1,2,4] Infertility is thus common, the male contribution is substan-

tial, and medical intervention and costs to the community are increasing.[4–6]

Infertility results from female disorders (anovulation, tubal obstruction, or other pathology) in approximately 30%, a male disorder in 30%, and disorders in both partners in 30%. No abnormalities are found in approximately 10%. Because male and female factors frequently coexist, both partners of the infertile couple are investigated and managed together.[7]

### ETIOLOGY AND CLASSIFICATION OF MALE INFERTILITY

At present, the precise cause cannot be determined in most men investigated for infertility.[4,7,8] Relationships between testicular damage, semen quality, and fertility are not strong.[9,10] Even genetic disorders may have marked phenotypic variation. For example, with microdeletions in the long arm of the Y chromosome, testicular histology may show Sertoli-cell-only syndrome, germ cell arrest, or hypospermatogenesis.[11–13] Arising from concerns about toxins in the environment affecting testicular development, a concept of a "testicular dysgenesis syndrome" has arisen that encompasses testicular impairment from hormonal inhibition of the proliferation of Sertoli cell precursors ("endocrine disruption") during fetal life via adverse environmental, dietary, lifestyle, or other influences affecting the mother and resulting in increased risks of cryptorchidism, hypospadias, primary spermatogenic defects, and testicular cancer.[14–16] There is a relationship between abnormal spermatozoa in semen, DNA strand breaks in sperm heads, and markers of apoptosis on sperm that may result from abnormalities of apoptosis or replacement of histones with protamines in the chromatin during spermatogenesis.[17] Effects on embryos and even the health of

**Table 172-1** Classification of Male Infertility by Effectiveness of Medical Intervention to Improve Natural Conception Rate

| Type of Infertility | Frequency (%) |
| --- | --- |
| Untreatable sterility | 12 |
| Primary seminiferous tubule failure | 12 |
| Treatable conditions | 18 |
| Sperm autoimmunity | 7 |
| Obstructive azoospermia | 10 |
| Gonadotropin deficiency | 0.5 |
| Disorders of sexual function | 0.5 |
| Reversible toxin effects | 0.02 |
| Untreatable subfertility | 70 |
| Oligospermia | 35 |
| Asthenospermia and teratospermia | 30 |
| Normospermia with functional defects | 5 |

offspring are also postulated to result from associated reactive oxygen species induced sperm DNA damage.[18,19] Although these pathogenetic mechanisms of male infertility are being investigated, their cause-and-effect relationships are not yet confirmed.

A classification of causes of male infertility based on the effectiveness of treatment is shown in Table 172-1. In this classification, the effectiveness of treatment means medical intervention known or proved by clinical trial to improve the chances of the man producing a conception by coitus or artificial insemination and does not include the use of in vitro fertilization (IVF) or intracytoplasmic sperm injection (ICSI) to bypass the impairment.

## CLINICAL EVALUATION

Patients with irreversible sterility can be separated from those with potentially treatable conditions or subfertility (see Table 172-1), usually with standard clinical evaluation (Table 172-2) and some simple investigations (Table 172-3).

### HISTORY

It cannot be overemphasized that both members of the couple need to be involved in the assessment and discussion of the results. The emotional reaction of the couple to the diagnosis of infertility may interfere with clinical evaluation and management. Intimate information may not be disclosed while the couple is embarrassed, hostile, or confused. Previous sexually transmissible infections or pregnancy may be concealed from the partner.

### Nature and Duration of Infertility

Previous pregnancies and time taken to conceive each pregnancy and duration of infertility are important prognostic factors. The couple may be aware of an infertility-related problem, such as previous undescended testes or orchitis. Some who present with a short duration of infertility may be unaware of the normal human pregnancy rates. The plan for investigation depends on the possibility of finding remediable abnormalities and on the age of the female partner.

**Table 172-2** Clinical Evaluation of the Infertile Man

History of illness or injury affecting testes, pubertal development, sexual performance, fertility
Exposures: occupation, habits
General physical examination
Virilization, body proportions
Scrotal examination, testicular size

**Table 172-3** Basic Investigation of the Infertile Man

Semen analysis
  Semen volume, sperm concentration, motility, morphology, and sperm antibodies
Hormone measurements
  Luteinizing hormone, follicle-stimulating hormone, prolactin, testosterone, sex hormone–binding globulin
Imaging
  Ultrasound of scrotum and rectum, magnetic resonance imaging of pituitary
Testis biopsy
  Needle aspiration: cells or tissue, open

### Family History

The family history should be considered but may not be known because infertility is often not discussed openly.[20] Increasing numbers of chromosomal and genetic causes for male infertility are being discovered (Table 172-4).[21] Some of these cause sterility and are recessive disorders or de novo mutations, and others may only affect fertility slightly so that there may be no family history of infertility. The most important genetic causes include Kallmann's syndrome, myotonic dystrophy, androgen receptor defects, gonadotropin and gonadotropin receptor defects,[22–25] cystic fibrosis and bilateral congenital absence of the vasa,[26–28] and Yq microdeletions.[11,13,29,30] There are many pediatric syndromes that involve hypogonadism or undescended testes in association with ambiguous genitalia, multiple malformations, obesity, or mental retardation, but patients with these generally do not present for management of infertility. Other genetic diseases may be associated with infertility, for example, hemoglobinopathy, Huntington's disease, polycystic kidneys, and mitochondrial disorders.[21] Predispositions to some conditions may also have a genetic basis such as the anatomic variant of the tunica vaginalis, which predisposes to testicular torsion, the association of Young's syndrome with mercury poisoning in infancy and the familial aspects of sperm autoimmunity. Men with sperm autoimmunity have increased frequencies of both family histories of organ-specific autoimmune diseases and autoantibodies to thyroid and gastric parietal cells in their serum.[31,32] Furthermore, brothers of men with poor semen analysis results are more often infertile than expected.[33] Thus, it is postulated that genetic causes or predispositions will be found for most male infertility. However, genetic factors remain unclear for the common types or associations of male infertility: idiopathic oligospermia, asthenospermia, teratospermia or varicocele, and past undescended testes.

### Coital Adequacy and Timing

Information on impotence and ejaculatory disturbances is important because intravaginal deposition of semen near the time of ovulation is crucial for fertility. Infrequent coitus is common in couples seen for infertility. Low libido may result from androgen deficiency, general illness, or a psychological reaction to the infertility.

### Childhood and Pubertal Development

Treatment in childhood for penile or scrotal disorders (e.g., hypospadias, epispadias, urethral valves, undescended testes, inguinal hernia, hydroceles) could be relevant. Sexual maturation may be delayed and incomplete with primary or secondary hypogonadism. There may have been associated growth problems that required treatment. Early puberty and growth resulting in short stature suggest congenital adrenal hyperplasia.[34,35]

### General Health

Any illness, acute or chronic, can impair sperm production in a nonspecific manner.[36] Acute critical illness, such as severe

**Table 172-4** Genetic and Chromosomal Defects in Infertile Men: Known or Suspected

| Function | Defect | Phenotype (Approximate frequency) |
|---|---|---|
| Hormonal regulation | KAL 1 | Kallmann's syndrome, isolated gonadotropin deficiency (1/10,000) |
| | GnRH receptor | |
| | DAX1 | Adrenal hypoplasia congenita (rare) |
| | Steroidogenic enzymes | Congenital adrenal hyperplasia (rare) |
| | Hemochromatosis | Iron deposition in gonadotroph: (1/1000) |
| | FSH-β | Oligospermia (rare) |
| | FSH receptor | Oligospermia (rare) |
| | Androgen receptor | Oligospermia (1/20,000) |
| Spermatogenesis | XXY and variants | Klinefelter syndrome (1/800) |
| | XYY | Oligospermia (1/5000) |
| | Translocations | Oligospermia (1/3000) |
| | Yq microdeletions | Sertoli cell only, oligospermia (1/500) |
| | DMPK CTG ext. | Myotonic dystrophy (1/8000) |
| | INSL3 | Undescended testes (?) |
| Meiosis | Translocations | Germ cell arrest (rare) |
| | ?CREM | Germ cell arrest (?) |
| Spermiogenesis | Fibrous sheath or Axonemal proteins | Dysplasia (1/50,000) |
| | | Immotile cilia (1/50,000) |
| | ? | Absent acrosomes (rare) |
| | ? | Decapitate sperm (rare) |
| | Protamine II | Teratospermia (?) |
| | LDH-x | Asthenospermia (?) |
| Genital tract | CFTR | BCAV (1/2000) |
| | ? | Other obstructions (rare) |
| | APKD | Necrospermia (rare) |
| | Dopamine | Failure of ejaculation |
| | β-Hydroxylase | |
| Sperm-oocyte interaction | | |
| | ? | Disordered zona pellucida–induced acrosome reaction (1/4000) |
| | ? | Defective sperm–pellucida zona binding with normal sperm morphology (rare) |

APKD, adult-onset polycystic kidney disease; BCAV, bilateral congenital absence of the vasa; CFTR, cystic fibrosis trans membrane conductance regulator; CREM, cyclic adenosine monophosphate–response element modulator; DAX1, dosage-sensitive sex reversal, adrenal hypoplasia congenita, critical region on x chromosome gene 1; DMPK CTG, myotomic dystrophy protein kinase gene CTG expression; FSH, follicle-stimulating hormone; GnRH, gonadotropin-releasing hormone; INSL3, insulin-like protein 3; KAL, Kallmann; LDH-x, lactate dehydrogenase-x.

trauma, surgery, myocardial infarction, burns, liver failure, intoxication, and starvation, is often accompanied by suppression of gonadotropin secretion and secondary hypogonadism. In contrast, a primary testicular disorder with elevated gonadotropin levels may occur with chronic illnesses. Increased peripheral conversion of androgens to estrogens may produce some features of feminization such as gynecomastia. The association of hypogonadism and feminization with chronic liver disease is well known. Similar hypogonadism may occur with other chronic illnesses such as chronic anemia, chronic renal failure, rheumatoid arthritis, chronic spinal cord injury, thyroid diseases, Cushing's syndrome, obesity, human immunodeficiency virus (HIV) infection, and neoplasia. Sex hormone–binding globulin levels are increased with some conditions such as cirrhosis and thyrotoxicosis but suppressed with others such as obesity, hypercortisolism, and hypothyroidism.[36] Numerous drugs have side effects on the reproductive system.[36] Heroin addiction and intrathecal narcotic infusions to control chronic pain suppress luteinizing hormone secretion.[37] Fever can cause transient declines of a few months' duration.[38,39] Diabetes mellitus may be associated with impotence in early uncontrolled stages, ejaculatory disorders with autonomic neuropathy, and sperm autoimmunity. Men with renal disease may have infertility of multifactorial origin, including testicular failure from chronic illness, cytotoxic drug exposure, zinc deficiency, and damage to the vasa or penile blood supply during kidney transplantation. However, as with cirrhosis, provided that metabolic decompensation is not severe, semen quality often is adequate for fertility.[36] Epididymal obstruction associated with chronic sinopulmonary disease (Young's syndrome) was diagnosed frequently in Australia and the United Kingdom in the past yet is rare elsewhere.[40] Some cases of Young's syndrome may have been caused by mercury poisoning in child-

hood from calomel-containing teething powders.[41] These were withdrawn from the market in the mid-1950s when it was found that they caused pink disease, and Young's syndrome is seen less commonly. Bronchiectasis and sinusitis are common in men with immotile sperm from cilial defects.[42] Situs inversus may also be present.

*Testicular Symptoms*
Previously undescended testes are common in men being investigated for infertility.[8,43–45] (see Chapter 171). Undescended testes may be associated with other congenital malformations and disorders of testicular hormone production or action during fetal development, such as Kallmann's syndrome, insulin-like factor 3 receptor mutations, androgen receptor mutations or defects of androgen metabolism, and diethylstilbestrol exposure in utero (see Table 172-4).[46,47] In Western countries, this condition is usually treated in early childhood, but whether early surgery reduces the severity of the subsequent spermatogenic disorder is unclear.[45] A testicular dystrophy may cause both the failure of descent and defective sperm production in adult life despite early surgery. It is difficult to explain otherwise how men with unilateral undescended testes are so frequent in the infertile population. Bilateral undescended testes carry a worse outlook for fertility than unilateral undescended testes. Infertility after bilateral treatment was approximately six times more common than in the general population and occurred in approximately half of men, whereas after unilateral treatment, infertility was increased by a factor of two and affected approximately 10%.[44] There may be associated malformation of the epididymides.[48] Rarely, the testes atrophy after surgery because of interference with the blood supply or coincidental torsion

Episodes of severe testicular pain and swelling may result from torsion, orchitis, or epididymo-orchitis and may be followed by loss or atrophy of the testis. Postinflammatory atrophy is particularly frequent with mumps orchitis but rare with other illnesses such as glandular fever and brucellosis. Epididymo-orchitis of bacterial origin is commonly associated with urethritis or urinary tract infections and may follow straining with heavy lifting. Sexually transmitted diseases are important, particularly if there was associated epididymal pain or swelling. Some patients have postgonococcal obstructions in the tails of the epididymides without clear or admitted histories of epididymitis.

Failure of development and a decrease in size of one or both testes are important symptoms of spermatogenic defects. Torsion of the testes may cause atrophy. The vasa may be damaged during hernia repairs and kidney transplantation. Testicular biopsy may inadvertently damage the epididymis, especially if retroversion of the testis is not recognized and the biopsy is performed without taking the testis out of the tunica. Similarly, surgery for torsion, hydroceles, or epididymal cysts may result in the obstruction of the epididymis. Hematomas in the scrotum and infarction of the testes may follow interference with the vascular supply of the testes. Rarely, autoimmune orchitis results from testicular injury or inflammation. Testicular tumors and carcinoma in situ occur with increased frequency in infertile men even without a history of undescended testes.[49,50]

### Iatrogenic Infertility

Vasectomy and Sertoli-cell-only syndrome caused by cytotoxic chemotherapy and radiation therapy for malignant tumors of the testes, leukemia, lymphoma, and serious autoimmune diseases are the most common forms of medically induced infertility.[51-53] Although some treatment regimens only suppress spermatogenesis temporarily, recovery of fertility is unpredictable.[51,53] Alkylating agents, such as cyclophosphamide and busulfan, destroy spermatogonia.[52] Antimetabolites may be used to treat psoriasis, rheumatoid arthritis, or xenograft rejection and can have transient adverse effects on spermatogenesis.[36] Treatment with sulfasalazine for inflammatory bowel disease or arthritis causes a reversible impairment of semen quality.[36,53,54] Cessation of sulfasalazine often results in a marked improvement in semen quality over several months. Many other drugs have real or potential adverse effects on spermatogenesis or sexual performance, including androgens, anabolic agents, estrogens, glucocorticoids, cimetidine, spironolactone, antibacterials (especially nitrofurantoin), antihypertensive drugs, and psychotropic agents. However, these are not common causes of infertility in practice.[36]

### Antispermatogenic Factors

The association of occupational and environmental exposures and reproductive disorders is receiving increasing attention.[55-60] Exposure to heat from frequent sauna baths, vehicle driving, furnaces, and perhaps working outdoors in summer may cause a decline in spermatogenesis.[56,61] Impaired testicular heat exchange from obesity and varicoceles may accentuate the effect. Exposure to chemicals in the workplace or elsewhere, particularly nematocides; organophosphates; estrogens; benzene; and welding, zinc, lead, cadmium, and mercury fumes, may have antispermatogenic effects.[62,63] Various social drugs, including tobacco, alcohol, marijuana, and narcotics, are potentially antispermatogenic, but these usually require heavy use for an adverse effect.[36,64,65] Some addicts have other organ damage, such as cirrhosis, which may further impair testicular function.[36]

### PHYSICAL EXAMINATION

A general physical examination is performed (see Table 172-2) and specific abnormalities are sought in particular circumstances, for example, of the respiratory system with suspected genital tract obstructions or immotile sperm, the prostate for ejaculatory duct obstruction or prostatitis, the endocrine system for hypopituitarism or other defects associated with testicular failure, the nervous system for autonomic neuropathy with coital disorders, optic field defects with pituitary tumors, and hyposmia with Kallmann's syndrome.

### Virilization

Hair distribution varies markedly between men. The loss or reduced growth of facial, pubic, axillary, and body hair is an important feature of androgen deficiency but often is unrecognized by patients. Men may note a reduced frequency of the need to shave. The stages of genital and pubic hair development can be recorded according to the method of Tanner. Eunuchoidal proportions (arm span greater than 5 cm longer than height or pubis-to-floor measurement greater than 5 cm longer than one half the height) result from delayed fusion of the epiphyses and are a good sign of delayed or incomplete puberty in whites or Asians.

### Gynecomastia

Gynecomastia of mild degree is common in men with testicular failure of any cause.[36] Marked gynecomastia may be associated with Klinefelter syndrome, cirrhosis, androgen receptor defects, estrogen-producing tumors, or anabolic steroid abuse and particularly the illicit use of human chorionic gonadotropin. Galactorrhea is rare in men and usually but not always associated with hyperprolactinemia.[66,67]

### External Genitalia

Examination of the penis for the position of the meatus, phimosis, urethral strictures, and Peyronie's disease is important because these may influence the adequacy or completeness of ejaculation. Inadequate penile size appears to be an exceptionally rare cause of infertility.[68]

Examination of the scrotal contents is critical in the evaluation of male infertility. A general approach to the examination is outlined in Figure 172-1. The body of the testes, the head, the body, and the tail of the epididymis and vas are palpated as shown on both sides. Sometimes it is difficult to examine the scrotum thoroughly because of ticklishness or because the scrotum is very tight. Testes may retract into the superficial inguinal region, especially if small. Testes not present in the scrotum may be palpable in the subcutaneous tissue in the groin or, occasionally, in the inguinal canal. Palpable remnants of the vas and epididymis in the scrotum suggest the testis has atrophied completely—the vanishing testis.[69]

#### Orchiometry

The volume of the testis is determined by comparison with an orchidometer (normal: 15–35 mL).[70] In the absence of varicoceles, the right and left testes are approximately equal in size. Testicular volume is related to body size and number of sperm per ejaculate. As seminiferous tubules occupy more than 90% of the volume of the testes, impairment of spermatogenesis is reflected by reduced testicular size. Testicular atrophy suggests severe impairment of spermatogenesis.

#### Testicular Abnormalities

Pain on palpation or excessive tenderness suggests inflammation. Loss of normal testicular sensation may occur with chronic inflammations, neuropathy, or neoplasia. Reduced consistency or softness of the testes is a feature of reduced spermatogenesis. Abnormalities of shape and hard lumps suggest tumors or scars.

#### Epididymal Abnormalities

Palpable abnormalities include congenital absence of the vas or other failures of development, enlargements of the heads or nodules in the tails of the epididymides with obstruction, spermatoceles, and other cysts and tumors. In men with very small testes (<5 mL), small epididymides suggest severe

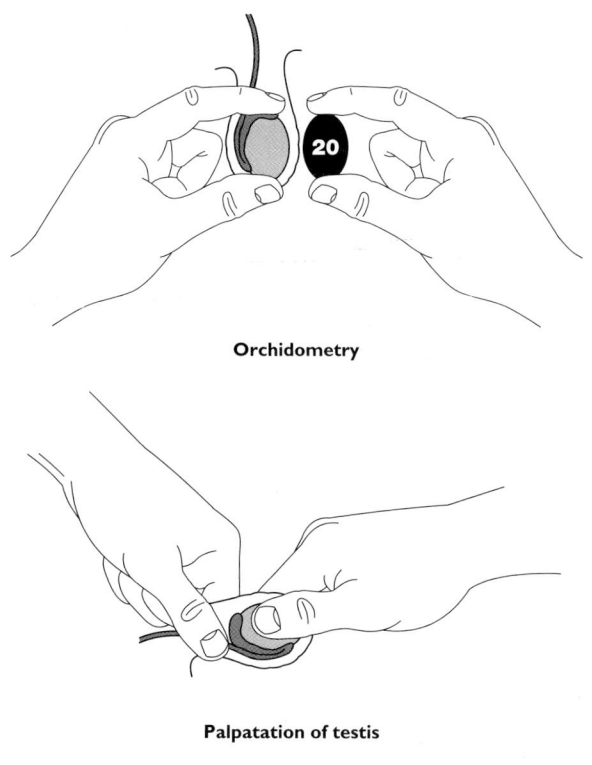

Orchidometry

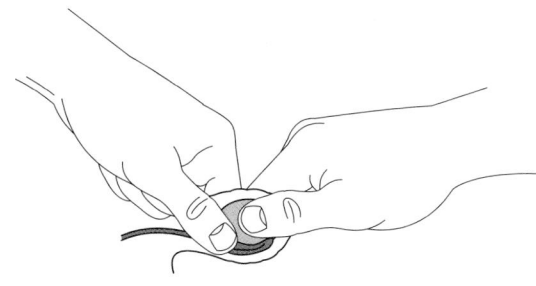

Palpatation of testis

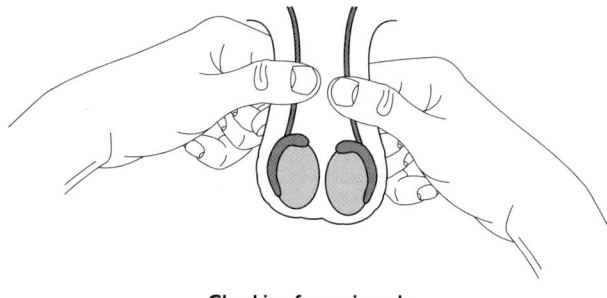

Palpatation of epididymis

Checking for varicocele

*Figure 172-1*  Clinical examination of the scrotum.

androgen deficiency, and normal-size epididymides suggest postpubertal testicular atrophy or a severe seminiferous epithelial disorder, such as Klinefelter syndrome.

### Vasal Abnormalities
Abnormalities of the vas include absence, nodules and gaps with vasectomy, and thickening or beading of the vas with severe postinflammatory scarring as from tuberculosis.

### Miscellaneous Abnormalities
Incidental scrotal findings include scars from surgery, scrotal dermatitis, and pubic fat pads around the genitals in extreme

obesity. Inguinal hernias and lipomas and encysted hydroceles of the cord are palpated above and behind the epididymis. Cysts "hydatids" of the appendix testis or epididymis are typically anterior to the head of the epididymis. Spermatoceles and cysts of the paradidymis are in the head or body of the epididymis. Retroversion of the testes is common: The vas and epididymis are anterior rather than posterior to the testes. Hydroceles of mild degree are common. A tense hydrocele may hide a testicular tumor. Unilateral absence of the vas may be associated with ipsilateral agenesis of the kidney and ureter on the same side. Many of these anomalies have little relationship with infertility.

### Checking for Varicocele
With the man standing up, the scrotum can be inspected for swelling of the pampiniform plexus and a cough or Valsalva impulse seen or palpated by holding the spermatic cords between the thumb and index finger of each hand and elevating the testes toward the external inguinal ring (see Fig. 172-1).[71] This maneuver reduces the risk of confusing contractions of the cremaster muscles with venous impulses. Varicocele size is graded: cough impulse without palpable enlargement of the spermatic cord (grade 1), palpable enlargement (grade 2), and visible enlargement (grade 3). Although predominantly a left-sided condition, varicoceles occasionally may be on the right side.

The accuracy and reproducibility of clinical examination even for structures as accessible as those in the scrotum may not be high. Varicoceles may vary in size from day to day. Even absence of the vasa may be overlooked. With practice, orchidometry can be repeated to within one to two orchidometer sizes.

### SEMEN ANALYSIS AND OTHER INVESTIGATIONS

Investigations are outlined in Table 172-3.

### SEMEN ANALYSIS

The most important laboratory investigation in male infertility is semen analysis. The variables assessed and the methods are in the World Health Organization's laboratory manual for the examination of human semen and sperm–cervical mucous interaction.[72,73] Automation of semen analysis is in progress and should be used in most specialized laboratories soon.[74]

It is crucial that the laboratory is experienced in the performance of semen analyses, participates in quality assurance activities, and has a room nearby for the collection of semen. Semen may be obtained by masturbation or coitus using a special nontoxic condom. Ordinary latex contraceptive condoms are unsatisfactory because the rubber usually immobilizes the sperm.[75] If these methods of collection are not possible, postcoital examination of midcycle cervical mucus may give some information about the likelihood of adequate semen quality if many motile sperm are found. In contrast, a negative postcoital test on its own is of little diagnostic value because conception can occur in the same cycle.[76]

The man should be provided with a wide-mouth, sterile, and nontoxic collection jar and written instructions about collection and delivery to the laboratory specifying a period of abstinence from ejaculation from 2 to 5 days, delivery of the sample to the laboratory within 1 hour of collection, and avoidance of exposure to lubricants or extremes of temperature.

To check for retrograde ejaculation, urine collected immediately after ejaculation is centrifuged and the pellet examined for sperm.

Several semen analyses at intervals of 2 or more weeks are necessary in a man with an abnormality in the first test because of the variability of results (Fig. 172-2). Even with

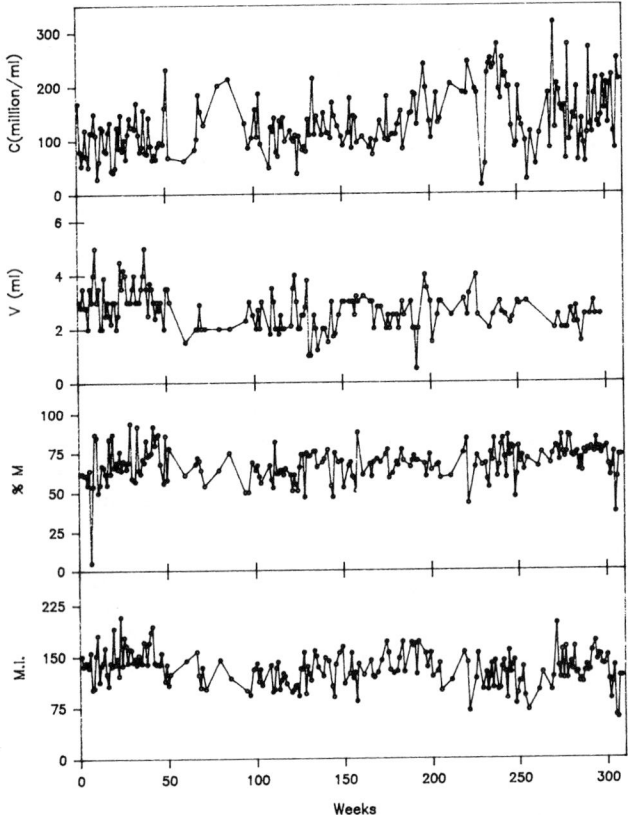

*Figure 172-2* Variability of semen analysis results in a fertile sperm donor. C, sperm concentration; M, total motility; MI, motility index-product of grade and percentage of sperm with progressive motility graded 0 to 3; V, semen volume. (From Mallidis C, Howard EJ, Baker HWG: Variation of semen quality in normal men. Int J Androl 14:99–107, 1991. Used by permission Blackwell Scientific Publications.)

complete collection of samples, there is variability caused by counting error, other technical errors, and differences in the ejaculate from day to day.[72,77] These large variations need to be remembered when interpreting results of semen analysis.

Assays of semen constituents from the accessory glands and testis are available: zinc and acid phosphatase from the prostate, fructose from the seminal vesicles, neutral α-glucosidase, glycerophosphocholine, and L-carnitine from the epididymis and inhibin B from the Sertoli cells. Prostatic fluid is acid (pH approximately 6.0), but the ejaculate is alkaline because of the admixture with seminal vesicle fluid. Semen biochemistry is of limited usefulness in clinical practice. Some examples are given in Table 172-5.

### Immunobead Test

Tests for sperm antibodies should be done routinely on all men being evaluated for infertility because no semen analysis pattern is characteristic of sperm autoimmunity.[31] The immunobead test (IBT) with beads binding to more than 50% of motile sperm is regarded as positive, but there usually is more than 70% to 80% immunoglobulin A (IgA) binding with clinically significant sperm autoimmunity. Tail tip–only IBT binding is not significant.[72] The indirect IBT in which normal donor sperm are exposed to test serum or seminal plasma can be used to test men with too few motile sperm for the direct IBT. An alternative screening method for men with sperm in the semen would be to perform a sperm-mucous penetration test.[72] The mixed antiglobulin reaction test is an alternative to the IBT.[72]

Sperm-mucous penetration tests can be performed by postcoital examination of sperm in cervical mucus collected at mid-cycle or after estrogen treatment (ethinyl estradiol, 50 μg twice daily for 4 days) to produce mucus of equivalent quality.[72] In vitro capillary mucous penetration (Kremer) tests are particularly important for evaluating the significance of sperm autoantibodies; failure of sperm to penetrate more than 2 cm in 1 hour indicates severe sperm autoimmunity with a poor prognosis if untreated.[31]

| *Table 172-5* | Common or Characteristic Patterns of Semen Abnormality | | | | |
|---|---|---|---|---|---|
| Volume (mL) 1–6* | Concentration ($10^6$/mL) >20* | Motility (%) >50 | Normal Morphology (%) >15 | Comment | Cause |
| 0.4 | 0 | — | — | Fructose 1 nmol/L (low) pH 6.5 (low) | Congenital absence of vasa Ejaculatory duct obstruction Partial retrograde ejaculation Testicular failure with androgen deficiency (Spill or incomplete collection) |
| 4.0 | 0 | — | — | Fructose 15 nmol/L | Genital tract obstruction Primary seminiferous tubal failure Secondary seminiferous tubule failure with androgen treatment |
| 3.0 | 100 | 0 | 35 | Live 70% | (Contamination or condom collection) Immotile cilia |
| 3.0 | 100 | 5 | 35 | Live 20% | (Contamination or delayed examination) Necrospermia Sperm autoimmunity |
| 3.0 | 100 | 65 | 0 | Small round heads | Total teratospermia: absent acrosomes |
| 3.0 | 100 | 25 | 10 | Liquefaction delayed Sperm aggregation 2+ Live 40% Polymorphs $1 \times 10^6$/mL | Idiopathic asthenospermia Sperm autoimmunity Prostatitis (Delayed examination) |
| 3.0 | 4 | 30 | 3 | Mixed abnormal morphology | Oligospermia of specific or nonspecific causes |
| 3.0 | <1 | — | — | Motile sperm present | Severe oligospermia of specific or nonspecific causes Primary seminiferous tubule failure Partial genital tract obstruction |

*Normal range.

## Sperm Function Tests
A number of tests of sperm function are available to examine the human fertilization process (Fig. 172-3). These are only performed in specialist laboratories. If simpler approaches or active preparations of zona pellucida (ZP) or sperm receptor proteins become available, they will be widely used to improve the assessment of human sperm. IVF has permitted many conventional and new tests of sperm function to be examined. Groups of sperm variables that are independently significantly related to the proportion of oocytes that fertilize in vitro can be determined by regression analysis.[78] This approach has confirmed the importance of sperm morphology and the ability of sperm to interact with the coverings of the oocyte.

### Human Sperm–Zona Pellucida Binding Ratio Test
Because the number of sperm bound to the ZP is strongly related to the fertilization rate, human sperm–ZP interaction tests have been developed using oocytes that failed to fertilize in vitro.[72,78,79] These oocytes can be used either fresh or after storage in concentrated salt solutions. Because the ZP binding capacity is variable, control (fertile donor) and test sperm are labeled with different fluorochromes (fluorescein and rhodamine). After incubation with equal numbers of control and test sperm, the oocytes are aspirated through a wide bore pipet to dislodge loosely adherent sperm and the numbers of sperm tightly bound to the ZP are counted with a fluorescence microscope. Results are expressed as a ratio of binding to the ZP of test and control sperm for four oocytes.[78] An alternative method is to cut the zonae in half and expose each to test and control sperm (Hemizona assay).[80]

### Human Sperm–Zona Pellucida Penetration Test
It is difficult to determine the number of sperm penetrating the ZP when many sperm are bound to the surface. The sperm bound to the surface of the ZP can be sheared off by repeatedly aspirating the oocyte with a pipet with an internal diameter less than the diameter of the oocyte (120 μm). The sperm penetrating the ZP or perivitelline space can then be counted easily, and the results of this test are the most predictive of fertilization rates with standard IVF.[78]

### Zona Pellucida–Induced Acrosome Reaction Test
Sperm dislodged from the ZP can be stained with a fluorescein-labeled lectin such as pisum sativum agglutinin or an antibody specific for the acrosomal contents to determine the proportion that are acrosome reacted. This test is useful for diagnosing disordered ZP-induced acrosome reaction.[81]

### Human Sperm–Oolemma Binding Ratio Test
Sperm-oolemma binding has been studied in the same way as in the sperm-ZP binding test but using oocytes that have had the ZP removed.[78]

### Interpretation of Semen Analysis Results
Table 172-5 shows various patterns of abnormality of semen quality and their common causes. It is always important to ask whether the result is spurious? Were there any problems with collection? Repeated tests are necessary to establish an average and to determine the variability within an individual man (see Fig. 172-2).

### Variations in Semen Volume and Appearance
Low semen volume suggests incomplete collection, short duration of abstinence from ejaculation before the test, absence or obstruction of the seminal vesicles, or androgen deficiency. High semen volume (>8 mL) may be seen in association with oligospermia but is of little practical significance. Hemospermia is usually is the result of minor bleeding from the urethra, but serious conditions, such as genital tract tumors, must be excluded. Other discoloration of the semen may indicate inflammation of accessory sex organs. The semen may be yellow with jaundice or salazopyrine administration. Defects of liquefaction and viscosity are relatively common and presumably result from malfunction of the accessory sex organs.[7] Although these may cause problems with semen analysis and preparation of sperm for assisted reproductive technology (ART), they are probably of little relevance to fertility. Sperm agglutination is common with sperm autoimmunity but can also occur for other reasons.

### Azoospermia
The total absence of sperm from the semen needs to be confirmed in repeated tests with vigorous centrifugation of the semen and careful examination of the pellet.[72] Rarely, an illness or difficulty with collection will cause transient azoospermia; however, this can also occur for unexplained reasons. With severe spermatogenic disorders and some obstructions, sperm may be present in the semen intermittently. If any live sperm can be found, these can be cryopreserved for intracytoplasmic sperm injection (ICSI).

### Oligospermia
Sperm concentrations of less than 20 million/mL are classified as oligospermic.[72] This figure probably derives mainly from the work of MacLeod and Gold,[82] who found that only 5% of fertile men had sperm concentrations less than 20 million per milliliter. Recent studies of fertile men generally support 20 million per milliliter as a clinically useful figure.[10,83–85] There is a correlation between sperm concentration and other aspects of semen quality, such as the percentage motility and normal morphology. Both motility and morphology are usually poor with oligospermia.

### Asthenospermia
Asthenospermia is defined as a sperm motility less than 50% total or less than 25% with rapid progressive motility.[72] Spurious asthenospermia because of exposure of sperm to rubber (particularly condoms), spermicides, extremes of temperature, or long delays between collection and examination should be excluded before accepting that sperm motility is poor. Low sperm motility is a frequent accompaniment of oligospermia, and there usually is a mixed picture of morphologic defects. It presumably arises because of defective spermiogenesis.

Severe asthenospermia requires evaluation by electron microscopy.[42,86] Specific ultrastructural defects of the axoneme

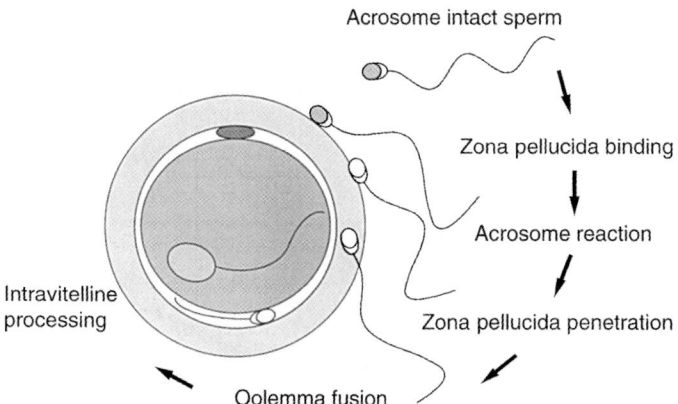

**Figure 172-3** Stages of human fertilization. Spermatozoa swim through the surrounding medium and cumulus mass (not shown) and bind to the surface of the zona pellucida. The acrosome reaction is stimulated by zona proteins and the acrosome-reacted sperm penetrates the zona, enters the perivitelline space, and binds to the oolemma via the equatorial segment. Oocyte processes surround the sperm head, and it enters the ooplasm and decondenses. Infertility could result from defects of any of these processes. For example, abnormal sperm, particularly with defective head morphology, bind poorly to the zona.

Labels in figure:
Acrosome intact sperm
Zona pellucida binding
Acrosome reaction
Zona pellucida penetration
Oolemma fusion
Intravitelline processing

are associated with zero sperm motility or extreme asthenospermia (less than 5% motile sperm) and sterility. Absent dynein arms, other less common axonemal defects, mitochondrial abnormalities, disorganized fibrous sheath or outer dense fibers with stumpy tails, or normal ultrastructure may be found.[42,86] The gene defects in some of these disorders are being discovered.[87] Standard semen analyses of these patients usually show normal sperm concentrations and normal sperm morphology, although some have tail abnormalities at the light microscopic level: short, straight, or thick tails, or midpiece defects. Viability tests help to distinguish this group of patients from those with necrospermia.[88] Patients with structural defects in the sperm that cause complete immotility are untreatable and sterile except for ICSI. Asthenospermia may also be associated with sperm autoimmunity. The causes of other motility defects of moderate degree are unidentified.

### Necrospermia

It is important to distinguish necrospermia from other types of severe asthenospermia because some patients produce pregnancies despite the low sperm motility.[88] Necrospermia is characterized by usually less than 20% to 30% total motility, less than 5% progressive motility, and a viability test less than 30% to 40%, indicating a high proportion of dead sperm. Other causes of severe asthenospermia such as sperm autoimmunity and collection problems must be excluded. Necrospermia may fluctuate in severity, particularly with changes in coital frequency.[88,89] The condition may be caused by defective storage of sperm in the tails of the epididymides or stasis in the genital tract, and it also occurs with chronic spinal cord injury and with adult polycystic kidney disease associated with cysts in the region of the ejaculatory ducts.[90,91] There are ultrastructural features of degeneration in the ejaculated sperm but normal structure of late spermatids in testicular biopsies.[88,90,91] Characteristic of necrospermia is an improvement of sperm motility with increased frequency of ejaculation. Treatment with antibiotics may have a beneficial effect, but this is not proved. The couple should have intercourse once or twice every day for 3 to 4 days up to the time of ovulation.

### Teratospermia

If there is a reduced percentage of sperm with normal morphology assessed by light microscopy, the classification of teratospermia is used.[72] In general, human spermatozoa are very variable in appearance and the microscopic assessment of sperm morphology is highly subjective and difficult to standardize between laboratories. Only a small proportion (<25%) of the motile sperm from fertile men are capable of binding the ZP in vitro, and this zona binding capacity is closely related to the morphology of the sperm head.[92] The morphometric characteristics of the sperm that bind to the ZP may be useful as a standard for sperm morphology.[74,93] Various histologic assessments of morphology have been used. The simplest is to assign defects with a priority in order, head, midpiece, and tail, and to record as normal only those that conform to ideal shape with no defects in any region. In the strict morphology approach, although size measurements are set, the sperm are assessed by eye and those marginally abnormal are assigned abnormal. Differential counts give the proportions of abnormal sperm with large, small, tapered, pyriform, or amorphous heads; normal heads but midpiece defects; or normal heads and midpieces but abnormal tails.[72] Indices based on the average number of defects per spermatozoon are also used (teratospermia index).[72] Automated methods involving image analysis by computer have been developed that could overcome the between-laboratory variability and greatly improve the predictive value of semen analysis for natural conception.[74,93]

Before the introduction of ICSI, the percentage of sperm with normal morphology assessed by strict criteria after washing the sperm and adjusting the concentration to 80 million per milliliter provided one of the most useful predictors of fertilization rates with standard IVF. There was a progressive reduction in oocytes fertilized from 60% to 20% as abnormal morphology increased from less than 70% to more than 95%.[78] Patients with high proportions of sperm with abnormal morphology are now treated by ICSI because of the risk of failure of fertilization with standard IVF. ICSI results are independent of sperm morphology.

It is important to distinguish mixed abnormalities of sperm morphology from those in which all or the majority of sperm show a single uniform defect, such as spherical heads with absence of the acrosomes (globospermia) and pinhead sperm. Pinhead sperm result when the centrioles from which the sperm tails develop are not correctly aligned opposite the developing acrosome. On spermiation, the sperm heads are disconnected from the tails and absorbed during epididymal transit so that there are only sperm tails in the ejaculate, the cytoplasmic droplet on the midpiece giving the pinhead appearance.[86] Both these conditions are extremely rare.

## HORMONE ASSESSMENT

It is not necessary to perform hormone measurements routinely. Follicle-stimulating hormone (FSH) levels in patients with azoospermia, normal testicular volume, and normal virilization may help distinguish genital tract obstruction from a spermatogenic disorder. However, some men with primary seminiferous tubal failure have normal FSH levels. Normal FSH is common with germ cell arrest at the primary spermatocyte stage. Rarely, high FSH levels are seen with normal spermatogenesis.[94,95] Measurement of FSH, luteinizing hormone, and testosterone is useful in men with reduced testicular volume and signs of androgen deficiency to distinguish primary from secondary hypogonadism. Inhibin B measurement may provide additional information about the state of spermatogenesis.[96,97] Isolated FSH deficiency due to mutations in the FSH-β gene have been described.[98,99]

Prolactin should be measured in men with galactorrhea or androgen deficiency and loss of libido.[66,67] Other hormone investigations occasionally are required, for example, thyroid function tests with hyperprolactinemia, 17-hydroxyprogesterone measurements with congenital adrenal hyperplasia, estradiol with liver disease or tumors, human chorionic gonadotropin with tumors and estrogen excess, and pituitary function tests for panhypopituitarism.[36]

## GENETIC STUDIES

Karyotypes are performed in men with clinical evidence of primary testicular failure and small testes to confirm a clinical diagnosis of Klinefelter syndrome in which the karyotype usually is 47,XXY, but there may be higher numbers of X chromosomes or a sex-reversal 46,XX karyotype.[100–103] Although most men with Klinefelter syndrome produce no sperm in the semen, some are oligospermic and very rarely fertile.[103] Also, sperm for ICSI may be obtained by testicular biopsy in as many as 50% of patients.[102,104] Defective spermatogenesis may occur with 47,XYY, but the clinical picture is much less uniform than it is for Klinefelter syndrome.[101] The extra sex chromosome is deleted early in gametogenesis because the sperm, embryos, and children generally have normal karyotypes.[102,103,105,106] However, an increased rate of sex chromosomal and autosomal aneuploidy has been noted in studies of sperm from XXY and XYY men.[104,106] Because of the increased frequency of autosomal abnormalities (reciprocal and robertsonian translocations and inversions in patients with defective spermatogenesis and the risk of transmitting these in the unbalanced form in offspring), karyotypes should be performed before treatment in all men with moderate to severe oligospermia (e.g., average sperm concentrations less than 10 million per milliliter) of primary testicular origin.

Cystic fibrosis gene studies are important for evaluation of patients with congenital absence of the vas and their partners.[26–28] If the woman has a cystic fibrosis gene mutation, preimplantation genetic diagnosis of their embryos can be offered.[28] Microdeletions in the long arm of the Y chromosome have been found in 3% to 15% of men with severe primary spermatogenic disorders.[12,13,29,30] Sons of men with these microdeletions have the same microdeletions.[107] Androgen receptor defects have also been found in some men with unexplained primary spermatogenic disorders. Mutations in the gene impairing androgen receptor activity produce androgen insensitivity, which has a variable phenotypic expression from testicular feminization to otherwise normal males with gynecomastia or hypospermatogenesis and oligospermia.[25] Increases in the number of CAG repeats in exon 1 over approximately 40 are associated with Kennedy disease, progressive spinobulbar atrophy, and men with this condition may be infertile. It is considered that the number of CAG repeats has an inverse effect on the activity of the androgen receptor. Several studies of the CAG repeat numbers in men with primary spermatogenic defects have indicated significant increases in repeat number compared with those in controls, although the numbers of repeats are within the normal range. However, this has not been confirmed in all studies.[25]

Other specific genetic tests and family studies may be indicated on clinical grounds (see Table 172-4), for example, hemochromatosis, Kallmann's syndrome, FSH and FSH receptor mutations, myotonic dystrophy, mitochondrial gene mutations, and defects of sperm ultrastructure.[21,108] At present, it is reasonable to screen all infertile men with otherwise unexplained average sperm concentrations less than 10 million per milliliter for chromosomal disorders by karyotype and Yq microdeletions. All patients should be counseled about the possibility of transmitting known and unknown genetic defects.

### TESTICULAR BIOPSY

Testicular biopsies are necessary to assess spermatogenesis in men with presumed genital tract obstruction. A significant proportion of men with azoospermia, normal testicular size, and normal FSH are found to have severe spermatogenic disorders.[8] Some severe spermatogenic defects may be incomplete, and because ICSI can be performed if sperm can be obtained from the testes, diagnostic testicular biopsies should be offered to men with severe primary testicular failure with persistent azoospermia. If any tubules containing elongated spermatids can be found, it should be possible to perform ICSI. However, if no areas of spermatogenesis to this stage are seen in the diagnostic biopsies there is less chance that more extensive removal of testicular tissue for sperm retrieval from the testes will be successful (see later). Open biopsies may be performed under local or general anesthesia. It is most important that tissue for histology is removed from the testes with minimal damage and placed in a suitable fixative, such as Bouin's or Steive's solution. Standard formalin fixatives destroy the cytoarchitecture. Needle biopsy procedures have become popular, and although many obtain only isolated cells, these cells may be sufficient for diagnosis based on cytology or for flow cytometry assessment. A technique for obtaining small amounts of tissue by needle aspiration biopsy under local anesthesia has been developed (Fig. 172-4) that usually provides sufficient material for a histologic diagnosis of the state of the seminiferous epithelium.[109] The aspiration biopsy techniques do produce some deformation artifacts in the tissue. Provided there is not a severe spermatogenic defect, needle aspiration biopsy is useful for obtaining testicular sperm for ICSI.[110] Complications of this procedure include failure to obtain tissue, particularly with very small or fibrosed testes (<5%), minor bleeding in the skin and testis,

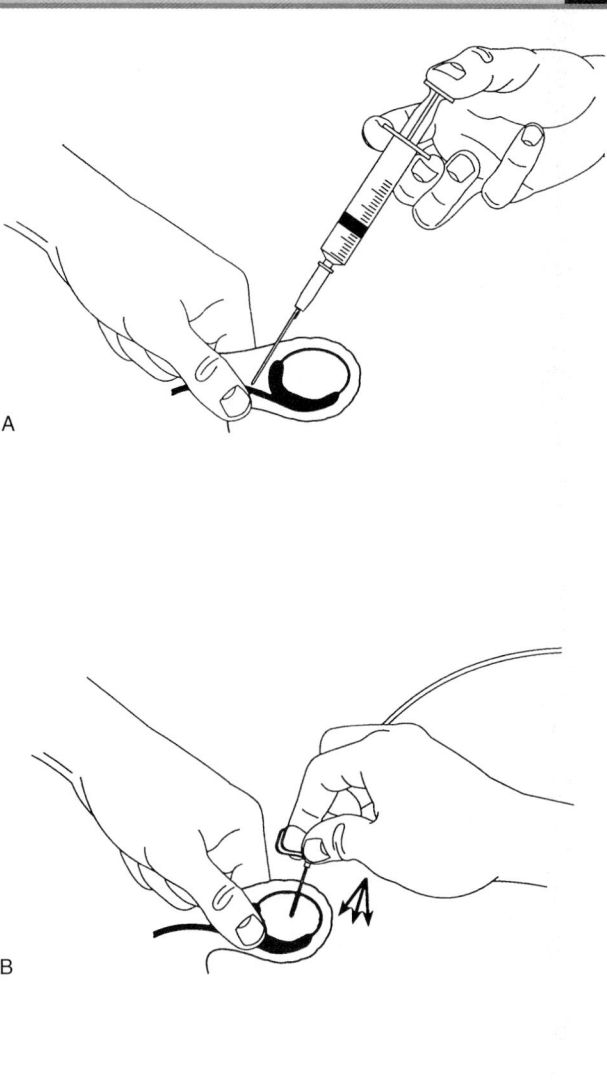

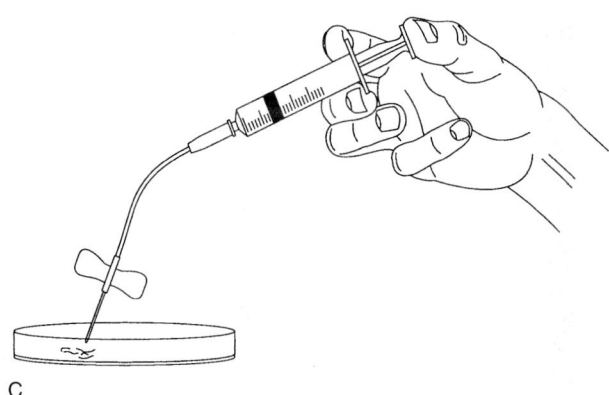

**Figure 172-4** Fine-needle tissue aspiration biopsy of the testis. **A,** Local anesthetic is injected around the vas to block testicular sensation. **B,** Fine-needle tissue aspiration biopsy of the testis. A 21-gauge butterfly needle is inserted into the testis. An assistant applies suction to the needle tubing via a syringe, and the operator makes thrusting movements of the needle into the substance of the testis. The appearance of some tissue fluid in the tubing (1–2 mm) usually indicated adequate tissue has entered the needle. While maintaining the suction, the needle is removed carefully and any seminiferous tubules protruding from the needle are grasped with fine forceps to avoid their falling back into the puncture hole. **C,** Seminiferous tubule sections sucked into the needle are expelled into some culture medium. Portions can be sent for histology or used for extraction of sperm for ICSI by stripping the seminiferous tissue out of the connective tissue membrane of the seminiferous tubule.

and rarely swelling. Some men may faint from anxiety about the procedure. Reactions to the local anesthetic are rare.

For clinical purposes, testicular histology is classified as follows: normal or hypospermatogenesis (all the cellular elements of spermatogenesis are present but in reduced numbers), germ cell arrest (the initial cellular elements of spermatogenesis are present but at a certain stage, the process stops, most often at the primary spermatocytes), Sertoli-cell-only syndrome or germ cell aplasia (the tubules contain Sertoli cells but no germ cells), hyalinization (the cellular elements have disappeared, leaving only thickened seminiferous tubule walls as in Klinefelter syndrome), and immature testis (no gonadotropin stimulation, prepubertal appearance).[111] Examples are shown in Figure 172-5. Other classifications are used in the literature that may cause some confusion, such as partial or incomplete germ cell or maturation arrest and partial germ cell aplasia in which some tubules contain spermatogenesis to the elongated spermatid stage.[112]

## OTHER INVESTIGATIONS

Ultrasonography is useful for checking for tumors in the testes, particularly when the testes are difficult to palpate because of a tense hydrocele. It can also be used to measure testicular size and confirm the presence and nature of cysts or other abnormalities in the scrotum.[113] Doppler blood flow assessment is valuable in assessing a painful swollen testis for torsion or inflammation and for evaluating varicoceles. Other tests of a varicocele, including thermography, technetium scans, and venography, may be performed but, as pointed out later, the value of treating varicoceles to improve fertility is uncertain. Rectal ultrasound may demonstrate cysts in the prostate, enlarged seminal vesicles, or dilated ejaculatory ducts associated with distal genital tract obstructions.[114] Clinical suspicion of the presence of a pituitary tumor should be followed up by appropriate radiology. Abdominal imaging is necessary to check the position of an impalpable testis.

## MANAGEMENT OF SPECIFIC CONDITIONS

This section addresses the management of sperm autoimmunity, male genital tract obstructions, coital disorders, genital tract inflammation, and varicocele. Treatment of gonadotropin deficiency and androgen replacement therapy are covered in Chapters 148 and 170.

## SPERM AUTOIMMUNITY

### Clinical Characteristics

Sperm autoimmunity is present in 6% to 10% of men seen for treatment of infertility.[31,115] Approximately half have spontaneously occurring sperm autoimmunity, and the remainder have associated genital tract obstruction.[116] Autoimmune orchitis with inflammatory cell infiltrates in the testis may follow an episode of epididymo-orchitis or occur spontaneously but is very rare. Men with spontaneously occurring autoimmunity have slightly higher frequencies of family histories of other autoimmune diseases and thyroid and gastric autoantibodies in their serum, suggesting a familial predisposition to develop sperm autoantibodies.[31,32] The types of genital tract obstruction associated with sperm autoimmunity appear to be those that have occurred after puberty, such as postgonococcal epididymitis, vasectomy, or traumatic obstructions. The obstruction may be one sided. Sperm autoimmunity is common in men with persisting infertility after vasectomy reversal.[116] Approximately 70% of men develop sperm antibodies in their serum within 12 months of vasectomy.[116] The presence of these antibodies is a relative adverse factor for the success of achieving a pregnancy after vasovasostomy. Sperm autoimmunity is less common with congenital epididymal obstructions, Young's syndrome, and congenital absence of the vasa.

### Differential Diagnosis

Men with severe sperm autoimmunity must be distinguished from those with low-level sperm autoantibodies that are not relevant to the infertility. The latter have mucous penetration tests that are normal or only marginally impaired.[31] Treatment for the antibodies is not warranted, and other causes of the couple's infertility should be sought. Many patients with low-level sperm antibodies have immunobead binding only to the tail tips or IBT results with less than 70% binding to the sperm heads.[72,117] It is possible that the antibody levels may vary over time, either spontaneously or as a result of relief of obstruction. If there are few or no sperm

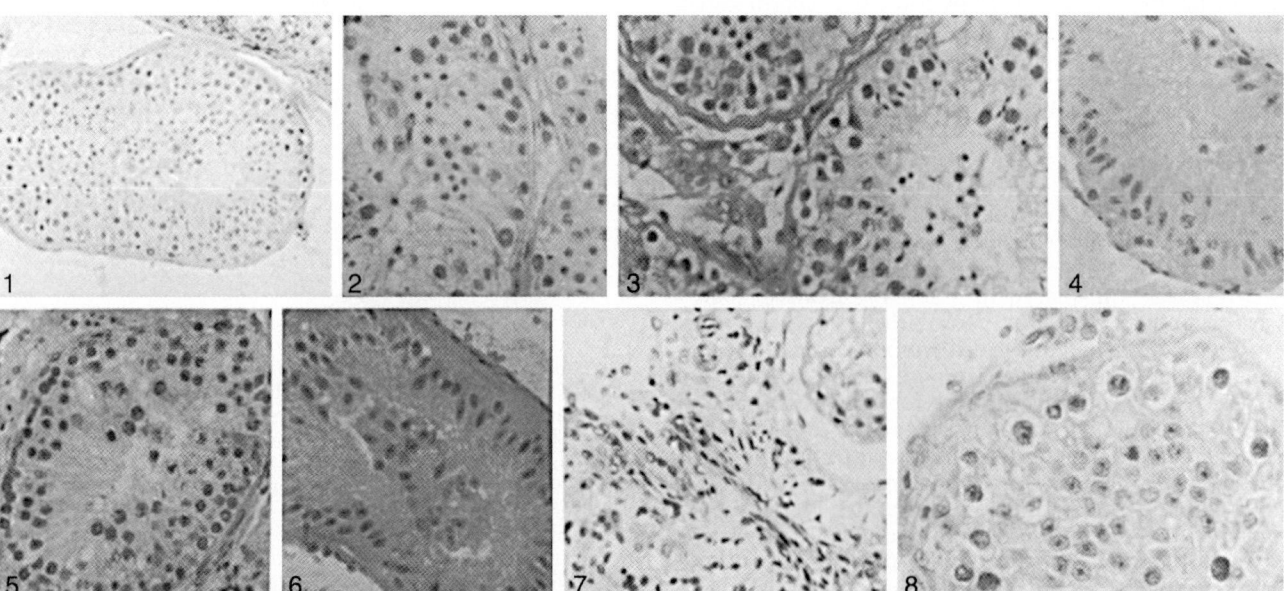

*Figure 172-5* Testicular histology from fine-needle aspiration samples. **1,** Normal (×200); **2,** mild hypospermatogenesis (×500); **3,** moderate hypospermatogenesis; **4,** severe hypospermatogenesis; **5,** germ cell arrest at the primary spermatocyte stage; **6,** Sertoli-cell-only syndrome; **7,** Leydig cell tumor in an undescended testis with hyalinized Sertoli-cell-only tubules; **8,** carcinoma in situ, only transformed spermatogonia and Sertoli cells present.

present in the semen, the main problem is to determine whether the sperm antibodies are the only cause of the problem or whether there is also an obstruction or a spermatogenic disorder.

## Pathophysiology
Despite intense study, much remains unknown about sperm antibodies. Most of the epitopes for the autoantibodies are unknown. The antibodies may be naturally occurring and to sperm coating proteins from the epididymis and nonpeptide antigens.[118] The different patterns of immunobead binding to the sperm surface may result from antibodies binding to different sites or from variations in the total amount of antibodies on the sperm.[72,117] The autoantibodies could enter the genital tract because of defects in the blood-testis barrier or impairment of other mechanisms that make the testis an immunologically privileged organ.[115,119] The antibodies may also be produced by lymphocytes residing in the epithelium of the epididymis.

Sperm antibodies interfere with fertility at several levels: interference with spermatogenesis, sperm agglutination in the male genital tract, reduced sperm motility and mucous penetration, interference with sperm binding to the ZP, the acrosome reaction on the ZP, and penetration of the ZP.[120,121] Sperm antibodies of different immunoglobulin classes can be found in serum, in seminal plasm, and on sperm. Immunoglobulin G and A sperm antibodies, particularly secretory immunoglobulin A, locally produced in the male genital tract, cause the greatest interference with sperm function.[72,117]

## Natural History
In most patients, sperm autoimmunity causes persistent severe infertility. The pregnancy rate for untreated patients is less than 0.5% per month.[31,122] Glucocorticoid treatment usually only produces a transient benefit. Occasionally, sperm autoimmunity may fluctuate in severity. The rare patients who produce pregnancies without treatment appear to have spontaneous improvements with a fall in antibody levels and increased sperm-mucous penetration. Sperm antibodies may decrease after relief of genital tract obstruction, but this may take many months or years to occur.

## Treatment
Most clinicians and patients would choose ICSI as the preferred management.[123] However, glucocorticoid treatment is reasonable when sperm autoimmunity is the only obvious cause for infertility in an otherwise healthy couple who wish to do everything possible to achieve a natural pregnancy and are prepared to accept the risks of the treatment. Although there is a range of opinion, the effectiveness of glucocorticoid treatment for sperm autoimmunity has an evidence base in controlled clinical trials.[115,124] Long-term glucocorticoid treatment is contraindicated if the woman is infertile or the man has other illnesses that increase the risks of serious adverse effects, particularly peptic ulcer disease, hypertension, obesity, or diabetes mellitus. The couple may choose either ICSI or glucocorticoid treatment initially and try the other if the first treatment is unsuccessful. The couple may also pursue donor insemination or accept the infertility.

Various regimens of prednisolone or other glucocorticoid therapy have been used.[115,124] Because a number of cases of aseptic necrosis of the femoral head have been associated with high-dose methylprednisolone, it not used.

### Prednisolone Therapy
Both continuous and intermittent prednisolone therapy regimens have been shown to be effective in placebo-controlled trials, although some small trials have produced negative results.[31,115,124,125] Continuous therapy is 0.75 mg/kg or 50 mg/d given as a single dose each morning with breakfast until

a pregnancy occurs or for a maximum of 4 to 6 months. The intermittent regimen is to give 20 to 25 mg prednisolone each day from days 1 through 10 or days 4 through 14, of the woman's cycle. If the semen quality and mucous penetration have not improved by 3 months, then the dose is doubled and again after 6 months for a maximum of a further 3 months. If it is uncertain whether sperm autoimmunity alone or an associated primary spermatogenic defect or genital tract obstruction is causing severe oligospermia or azoospermia, 50 mg/d prednisolone may be given for 4 to 8 weeks as a therapeutic trial.

### Monitoring
Patients are carefully monitored for improvement in semen quality and adverse effects. Semen tests are performed monthly about the time of the woman's menses. Semen analysis, IBT, and sperm-mucous penetration tests are performed to assess progress. Promising signs are increased sperm concentration, motility, and mucous penetration and decreased IBT binding, particularly immunoglobulin A levels falling to less than 70% binding to the heads of motile sperm.

### Adverse Effects
Adverse effects of prednisolone treatment are common. Insomnia and dyspepsia are frequent early problems. After 2 to 3 months of treatment, cushingoid appearance, muscle weakness, and joint aches are common. Transient decreases in muscle and bone mass and increased fat mass occur. Occasional adverse effects resulting from depressed immunity are herpes zoster or severe folliculitis. Serious adverse effects, such as depression, cataracts, addisonian crisis after cessation of treatment, and aggravation of peptic ulcer disease, are rare. The main serious adverse effect is aseptic necrosis of bone, most commonly the femoral head.[31,115,124,126] This side effect has been described in a number of men being treated for sperm autoimmunity.[126] Heavy alcohol drinking may predispose to it. Patients need to be advised carefully of this adverse effect because it has led to a number of litigation actions. It is also important to remember that other common illnesses, such as asthma and psoriasis, although improved during glucocorticoid treatment, may flare up after withdrawal. Rarely, semen quality deteriorates during glucocorticoid treatment.

### General Management
The couple is advised to have intercourse frequently at the fertile time of the cycle, preferably daily. Semen is cryopreserved if the quality improves because this may be used for artificial insemination or ICSI after cessation of the prednisolone therapy.

### Other Treatments
ICSI is the main alternative treatment.[123] Testosterone suppression of spermatogenesis, artificial insemination by husband (AIH), washing sperm to remove sperm antibodies, antibiotic therapy, and standard IVF or gamete intrafallopian transfer without previous prednisolone therapy are ineffective.[31,115,124] Surgery to relieve obstructions, such as repeat vasovasostomy and vasoepididymostomy, or removal of an orchitic testis could be considered.

### Results
Approximately 50% of men treated with glucocorticoids for sperm autoimmunity have a reduction in sperm antibody levels and an increase in sperm concentration, motility, and mucous penetration.[31,115,124] Pregnancies occur in approximately 25% of couples during a 4- to 6-month course of prednisolone or after a longer period of intermittent prednisolone therapy. Ovulatory disorders, endometriosis, and tubal abnormalities are negative prognostic factors. Artificial insemination may be successful with stored semen from a previous course of prednisolone therapy.[31]

## GENITAL TRACT OBSTRUCTION

### Clinical Characteristics

Most men with genital tract obstruction have azoospermia, normal testicular size, normal virilization, and normal serum FSH levels. However, some have combined obstruction and spermatogenic disorders or partial obstructions and severe oligospermia. There may be a history of an event that caused the obstruction, such as epididymitis with gonorrhea or associated respiratory disease.[8,27,28,38,40,41] Because a few men with normal spermatogenesis have elevated FSH levels and some spermatogenesis may occur in association with a severe spermatogenic disorder, all patients should be offered further investigation.[94,95,110] Sperm antibodies may be present and are an adverse prognostic factor for surgery. In men with congenital absence of the vas or ejaculatory duct obstruction, semen volume, pH, and fructose levels are low. The semen also does not have its characteristic smell and does not form a gel after ejaculation because it contains only prostatic and urethral fluid. The semen characteristics of complete ejaculatory duct obstruction are the same as for bilateral congenital absence of the vasa, but the vasa are present. Rectal ultrasound may show the cause of the obstruction such as a cyst of the prostatic utricle.[114] Some men may have partial or intermittent ejaculatory duct obstruction and may notice the low ejaculate volume. Testicular biopsy is normal or there may be some reduction in spermatogenesis either as a coincidence or as a result of the obstruction, particularly after vasectomy.[127]

### Pathophysiology

Degeneration or failure of development of the wolffian duct structures occurs with cystic fibrosis gene mutations but can be of variable extent.[27,28] Although most often only the heads of the epididymides are palpable some men with bilateral congenital absence of the vasa have parts or all of the epididymides and scrotal vasa present with absent or atrophic pelvic vasa and seminal vesicles. Young's syndrome is now rare. The pathology shows inspissated material in the head of the epididymis, and there are lipid inclusions in the epithelial cells.[38,40,41] As some men had children, the blockage may develop in adulthood. Young's syndrome is not related to cystic fibrosis gene mutations.[28]

Postinflammatory obstructions after gonorrhea typically occur in the tail of the epididymis, whereas nonspecific bacterial inflammation produces more widespread destruction, and tuberculosis usually causes multiple obstructions in the epididymides and vasa. Back pressure blowout obstructions in the epididymis are frequent after vasectomy. Iatrogenic causes of genital tract obstruction include inadvertent epididymectomy during testicular biopsy, vasal damage during hernia repair or pelvic or lower abdominal surgery such as renal transplantation, and ejaculatory duct obstruction from prostatectomy or complicated bladder catheterization.

### Differential Diagnosis

Men with persistent azoospermia, normal testicular size, normal virilization, and normal FSH levels can be assumed to have obstruction until proved otherwise. As many as one third of men with this clinical picture are found to have a serious spermatogenic disorder on testicular biopsy despite the normal serum FSH level.[8] There are rare instances of normal men who show azoospermia on single occasions or over a short period.[7,128] This "spurious azoospermia" must be excluded before surgery is contemplated. Once diagnosis of obstruction is confirmed, it is necessary to determine the feasibility of surgery. Intratesticular and caput-epididymal obstructions have a poor prognosis, but cauda-epididymal and vasal obstructions can often be treated successfully with surgery.[129] Distal obstructions are important to diagnose because they may be reversed at transurethral endoscopy.[114]

Sperm retrieval for ICSI, either from the testis or other part of the genital tract, is an alternative to surgery.[110,130] ICSI is also used when reconstructive surgery is not possible, the female partner has an infertility problem, or the couple cannot wait 6 to 12 months to have a reasonable attempt at conceiving naturally after surgery.

### General Management

Female partners of men with bilateral congenital absence of the vasa should be screened for cystic fibrosis gene abnormalities and the couple counseled accordingly. Preimplantation or prenatal genetic diagnosis may be performed if mutations are found in both partners.[28] The woman should be investigated in detail to ensure her potential fertility before surgery is contemplated in the man. The prognosis of the procedure and the availability of other forms of treatment, including donor insemination, should be discussed realistically with the couple. For ICSI, sperm may be obtained by testicular biopsy or percutaneous sperm aspiration from the epididymis under local anesthesia. If a natural spermatocele is present, usable sperm may be obtained by direct puncture through the scrotal skin. It may be possible to combine vasoepididymostomy with sperm aspiration for cryopreservation or ICSI.

### Epididymal and Vasal Surgery

Treatment of male genital tract obstructions is best undertaken by specialist microsurgeons.[114,129] The testis is exposed and the most proximal (to the testis) level of obstruction determined. A testicular biopsy is obtained, and the patency of the vas is determined by syringing with saline or by vasography. The vas or epididymal tubule is opened proximal to the obstruction, and, if possible, the presence of motile sperm is demonstrated by microscopy. Then microsurgical anastomosis between the ends of the vas or between the vas and the epididymal tubule is undertaken.

#### Results

Vasovasostomy and vasoepididymostomy for caudal blocks produce relatively good results, with 50% to 80% of patients having sperm present in the semen; however, less than half of these produce a pregnancy within the first year.[114,129] There may be continuing obstruction, sperm autoimmunity, or coexisting spermatogenic disorders. The results of vasoepididymostomy for proximal blocks are poor. Although sperm may appear in the semen, pregnancies are extremely uncommon after vasoepididymostomy for caput epididymal blocks. The results of ICSI with testicular or epididymal sperm, fresh or after cryopreservation, are similar to those obtained with sperm from semen.[110]

## COITAL DISORDERS

Male coital disorders important for infertility include impotence, failure of ejaculation, and retrograde ejaculation. Many men have problems with sexual performance after first learning about the infertility, but this usually ameliorates with time. Infrequent and poorly timed intercourse may result from incorrect advice, low libido, or the psychological reaction to infertility.[7]

### Impotence

Impotence may be associated with low libido from androgen deficiency with primary or secondary hypogonadism. (This topic is considered in detail in Chapter 173.) Impotence related to vascular or neurologic abnormalities (diabetic autonomic neuropathy or pelvic nerve damage) is uncommon in men presenting with infertility.[8] Selective impotence at the time of ovulation may indicate psychological problems and ambivalence about having children.

### Failure of Ejaculation

Failure of ejaculation is usual with chronic spinal cord injury and may also be caused by antihypertensive and psychotropic drugs but otherwise is an infrequent cause of infertility in most societies.[131,132] Healthy men who cannot ejaculate with intercourse may be able to produce semen by masturbation, with a vibrator, or other stimulation.

## Retrograde Ejaculation

Retrograde ejaculation occurs when the bladder neck fails to contract at the time of ejaculation so that all or most of the semen passes into the bladder. Usually, there is an obvious cause: prostatic surgery, diabetic neuropathy, pelvic nerve damage, or spinal cord injury. Retrograde ejaculation is diagnosed by the finding of sperm in urine passed after ejaculation.

### Differential Diagnosis

Recognition of a coital disorder is crucial; thus, all infertile patients must discuss their sexual history in detail. Once recognized, the contribution of organic and psychological factors needs to be evaluated.

### General Treatment

An optimistic prognosis can be given, provided that live sperm can be obtained. The couple is advised about the various techniques that might be used for collecting the sperm for AIH or other ART. The woman's potential fertility must be evaluated.

### Specific Treatment

A drug, such as an antihypertensive or a tranquilizer, that may be contributing to the sexual disorder should be stopped temporarily or permanently.[36] Impotence may respond to sex behavior therapy, physical approaches with pumps and rubber occlusion devices to initiate and maintain erections, administration of phosphodiesterase 5 inhibitor, intrapenile injections of vasodilators, and penile implants, but these seldom are needed in men with infertility. Some men with failure of ejaculation or retrograde ejaculation may be able to ejaculate during intercourse with a full bladder or after the administration of phosphodiesterase 5 inhibitor, imipramine, or cholinergic antihistamines, such as brompheniramine or ephedrine.[132] Others require more powerful stimulation with vibrators or electroejaculation.[131,133] If these are unsuccessful, sperm may be collected surgically from the vas, epididymis, or testis.[110]

### Use of Collected Semen

If semen can be obtained by masturbation or by wearing nontoxic condoms to collect nocturnal emissions, the couple can be taught to inseminate samples at home. The timing of ovulation can be determined by calendar and either mucous symptoms or luteinizing hormone surge detected with a urinary luteinizing hormone dipstick kit. Cryopreservation of samples for AIH or ICSI may also be possible.

### Assisted Ejaculation

Ejaculation may be stimulated by applying a vibrator to the underside of the penis near the frenulum of the glans. Vibrators with a 2-mm pitch and frequency of 60 Hz or more are most effective. Men with complete spinal cord injuries below T10 are unlikely to respond and will require electroejaculation. Modern electroejaculation equipment is safe: The probe includes a thermal sensor and proctoscopy is performed before and after the procedure to ensure there are no burns or other damage to the rectum. A balloon catheter in the bladder is used to prevent retrograde ejaculation.[133,134]

Semen obtained by assisted ejaculation from able-bodied men or in the acute stages of spinal cord injuries is often normal.[134] In contrast, with chronic spinal cord injury, there is frequently low volume, high sperm concentration, and poor motility.[131,133] As with necrospermia, repeated ejaculation over several days can improve sperm motility. If the semen quality

is too poor for AIH or the risks associated with electroejaculation are considered unacceptable, aspiration of sperm from the testis and ICSI produces good results. Assisted ejaculation may cause autonomic hyperreflexia with chronic spinal cord injuries above T6.[131,133] The resulting uncontrolled hypertension may cause cerebral hemorrhage. Careful monitoring of blood pressure and prophylactic nifedipine treatment usually prevents serious problems. Men without complete sensory deprivation require general anesthesia for electroejaculation.

### Retrieval of Sperm with Retrograde Ejaculation

Motile sperm may be obtained from the urine after retrograde ejaculation.[135] Urinary pH is adjusted to above 7 and osmolality to between 200 and 400 mOsm/kg by administration of 80 g of sodium bicarbonate and 2.0 to 2.5 L of water daily for 3 days before the expected time of ovulation. On the day of ovulation, the man ejaculates and passes urine. Sperm are recovered from the urine by centrifugation, washed, and resuspended in an IVF culture medium. The final pellet is resuspended in approximately 0.5 mL of culture medium for insemination. It is also possible to cryopreserve the sample obtained. If this method fails, electroejaculation and catheterization of the bladder could be considered.

## EFFECTS OF SYSTEMIC ILLNESS AND REVERSIBLE EXPOSURES TO TOXINS OR DRUGS

A very large number of exposures to agents in the environment, drugs, and illnesses can adversely affect testicular function, but it is rare to find patients in whom such exposures can be confirmed as contributing to male infertility. However, this should always be considered during clinical evaluation. The most commonly encountered problems clinically are impairment of spermatogenesis by salazopyrine used for treatment of inflammatory bowel disease or arthritis, testosterone administration, anabolic steroid abuse, long-term high-dose opiate use, and febrile illnesses causing transient reduction of spermatogenesis. Workplace exposures may be implicated in some patients, but the association is rarely clear-cut enough to advise change of occupation.

### Acute Illnesses

#### Fever

The adverse effect of acute febrile illness on the semen quality is well known but only occasionally seen.[36,38,39] Frequent hot baths or saunas may also have a similar effect. There is a temporary suppression of spermatogenesis that recovers over 3 to 6 months. Whether increased scrotal temperature because of clothing, varicocele, obesity, or environmental temperature contributes to male infertility is controversial.

#### Critical Conditions

Suppression of gonadotropin secretion can occur with critical illness such as hepatic failure, myocardial infarction, head injury, stroke, respiratory failure, congestive cardiac failure, sepsis, burns, starvation, and severe stress, both psychological and physical.[36] Transient decreases occur after drug or alcohol intoxication, anesthesia, and surgery. The reduction in testosterone is proportional to the severity of some of the critical conditions and may predict the likelihood of recovery. There may also be direct effects on the testes and alterations in sex hormone–binding globulin levels. The shutdown of testicular function may be a useful adaptation to illness or starvation. During recovery from the critical condition, pulsatile secretion of gonadotropins increases in a manner reminiscent of the changes with puberty, and gynecomastia may develop.[36]

#### Nutritional Aspects

Starvation is associated with gonadotropin suppression. Specific deficiencies of vitamins and minerals such as B$_{12}$, C, folate, and zinc may affect testicular function, but these are rare in Western countries.[136] Simple obesity may be associated with alterations in the hypothalamic-pituitary-testicular axis and impaired scrotal thermoregulation. The most common changes are increased conversion of androgens to estrogens in peripheral tissues and low sex hormone–binding globulin levels related to insulin resistance. Total testosterone, sex hormone–binding globulin levels and gonadotropin levels may be low and estrogen levels elevated.[36] However, clinical androgen deficiency, estrogen excess, and abnormal semen analysis are not regularly seen in morbidly obese men.

### Chronic Illnesses

Impairment of testicular function is common in uncontrolled or poorly controlled chronic diseases.[36] There are usually elevated gonadotropin levels, indicating a primary testicular defect, but impaired gonadotropin secretion or hyperprolactinemia may occur and changes in sex hormone–binding globulin and aromatization of androgens to estrogens are common. Although this pattern of change in testicular function is a common nonspecific response to chronic illness, the mechanism is obscure. There may be symptoms and signs of androgen deficiency and estrogen excess. Hepatic cirrhosis is one of the classic conditions known to have a profound adverse effect on the male reproductive function. Testicular function may recover after liver transplantation. Similar primary hypogonadism may occur with noncirrhotic liver disease, chronic alcoholism without liver disease, and a variety of chronic diseases without alcoholism: chronic anemias, chronic renal failure, thyroid hyper- or hypofunction, HIV infection, lymphoma, leukemia, advanced metastatic cancers, rheumatoid arthritis, severe cardiac disease, and chronic respiratory disease.

### Effects of Drugs

Drugs may contribute to male infertility by affecting gonadotropin (e.g., steroids, opiates) or prolactin secretion (psychotropic agents), or spermatogenesis (salazopyrine, alkylating agents) or by reducing sexual performance (psychotropic and antihypertensive drugs). Some drugs may also cause gynecomastia (antiandrogens, estrogens).[36,137]

There is currently no place for testosterone treatment of infertile men either continuously for low testosterone levels resulting in primary or secondary testicular failure or as "testosterone rebound" therapy because testosterone suppresses gonadotropin secretion and reduces spermatogenesis. Abuse of androgens is widespread in people hoping to enhance athletic performance or bodybuilding. Some men are seen for infertility from azoospermia or oligospermia as a result. Others have sexual performance problems after stopping the drugs. The abuse may be concealed by the patient. Normal virilization but low testosterone, low sex hormone–binding globulin, and low, normal, or transiently high gonadotropin levels may be seen. Recovery can take several months, particularly after depot anabolic steroids.

Salazopyrine used for bowel disease and arthritis commonly causes spermatogenic defects. Usually, there are poor sperm motility and morphology or oligospermia. The semen may be stained yellow. The antispermatogenic effect is caused by the sulfapyridine in the drug. Stopping the drug results in a recovery of sperm output within a few months provided the patient's health remains good and he does not have an underlying defect of spermatogenesis.

Other drugs and toxins are claimed to have adverse effects on spermatogenesis such as colchicine and anticonvulsants, and some antihypertensive drugs, calcium-channel blockers, and antiparasitic chemotherapeutic drugs may impair sperm motility, capacitation, or the acrosome reaction.[36,137]

### GENITAL TRACT INFLAMMATION

Specific inflammations of the genital tract such as mumps orchitis or gonorrheal epididymitis may cause sterility.

Nonspecific inflammations in the accessory sex organs are more common in men with infertility than in fertile men.[7,138–140] Also, male accessory sex organ inflammation and infertility may be more important in some countries than in others.[7] Symptoms include chronic low back pain, intermittent dysuria, discharges from the penis on straining, and discomfort in the pelvic region or testes after ejaculation or prolonged sexual abstinence. The prostate may be enlarged and tender. The semen may show discoloration, variations in volume, increased viscosity, delayed liquefaction, high pH, sperm agglutination, bacteriospermia, and pyospermia. The bacteria in semen are frequently not pathogens but the commensals of the urethra or skin.[138]

To have more than 1 million polymorphs per milliliter in semen determined by peroxidase reaction or monoclonal antibodies to leukocyte antigens is considered abnormal.[72] Although inflammatory cells could damage sperm by releasing oxygen free radicals or cytokines, bacteria could impair sperm motility, and inflammation could also cause partial genital tract obstruction, the actual contribution of nonspecific genital tract inflammation to male infertility is contentious.[138–141] Routine cultures of semen are not warranted except for sperm donors.

### General Management

Men with clinical evidence of prostatitis require full urologic assessment.[142] Specific infections with pathogenic agents are treated with appropriate agents. It remains unclear what should be done about asymptomatic pyospermia and nonspecific male accessory gland inflammation. Therapeutic trials generally show no benefit from antibacterial therapy on semen quality.[143] Antibiotics or other agents may be used if it is thought that the pyospermia compromises semen quality or that bacteria might contaminate the IVF culture media. Because the organisms commonly implicated in nonspecific genital tract inflammation include *Chlamydia*, *Mycoplasma*, and various bacteria, broad-spectrum antimicrobial therapy is required if treatment it is to be given. Also, many of the standard drugs do not enter inflamed accessory sex organs. Trimethoprim, erythromycin, doxycycline, and norfloxacin are potentially effective.[144] Increased frequency of ejaculation to facilitate drainage of the accessory glands and stress management may also help.

### VARICOCELE

Varicoceles are found in approximately 25% of men being examined for infertility. An additional 15% of men may have a subclinical left varicocele indicated by a faint cough impulse in the spermatic cord or increase in diameter of the veins on ultrasound.[7,8,71,145,146] Varicoceles are also found in fertile men.[64] Varicoceles are more common in tall men and in men with larger testes.[8] They are less frequent in men with severe testicular atrophy, for example, in Kallmann's and Klinefelter syndromes. When there is a moderate to large left varicocele, the left testis is usually smaller than the right testis.

### Pathophysiology

Men with varicoceles generally have poorer semen quality than those without varicoceles.[64,71,145] Thus, varicoceles can have an adverse effect on testicular function. Various theories have been advanced for the effect, including vascular stasis, back pressure, interference with oxygenation, reflux of renal or adrenal products into the pampiniform plexus, and interference with the heat exchange function of the pampiniform plexus, but the precise mechanisms are not clear.[145,146] Varicoceles are usually first noticed at puberty and thereafter may increase in size but remain relatively stable in size throughout the man's lifetime. Symptoms, including swelling and a dragging sensation in the scrotum, are infrequent, and many men with a large varicocele are unaware of its presence.

The sudden appearance of a varicocele in an adult should be taken seriously because it may be a feature of a renal carcinoma with extension into the left renal vein. This well-known clinical association is uncommon.

### Differential Diagnosis

The semen quality in men with varicoceles varies from azoospermic to normal. There is no specific pattern of abnormality with varicocele. Testicular histology is also variable, the only common feature being that the defect in spermatogenesis is more severe on the left side than on the right side. Varicocele may be more of an association rather than an absolute cause of a couple's infertility. Therefore, full evaluation of other aspects of male infertility and of the female partner is necessary.

### Treatment

The value of treatment of varicocele for infertility is controversial.[146-149] One view is that treating varicoceles may not improve fertility; therefore, the varicoceles should only be treated for other reasons, such as symptoms.[9,145,147] The other extreme is the belief that varicocele is the most important treatable cause of male infertility, therefore all varicoceles should be treated even if small.[149-151] In the middle are those who would select cases. When there is an absent, obstructed, or atrophic right testis and all sperm in the semen come from the left testis, treatment of the varicocele may produce a reasonable result.[152]

Treatment of the varicocele involves the venographic obstruction of the incompetent veins or surgery to prevent venous back flow from the abdomen to the pampiniform plexus. Radiographic techniques involve placement of a sclerosant, glue, or coil that promotes clotting in the vein and carry a lower morbidity than surgery under general anesthesia, but there are relatively high failure and recurrence rates.[145,146,150] A variety of operations can be performed for varicocele. In the past, retroperitoneal ligation and division of the testicular veins with or without preservation of the testicular artery and lymphatics was performed. Inguinal and scrotal microsurgical approaches have lower failure, recurrence, and hydrocele rates.[151] Successful venous occlusion will relieve pain and reduce the size of large varicoceles. Whether semen quality and fertility are improved is not certain.

### Results

Because varicoceles are so frequent, treatment of varicocele for infertility became common and several large series were published with claims of high success rates for improving semen and fertility. Floating numerator pregnancy rates averaging 35% (range, 20%–60%) were commonly reported. Regression toward the mean in semen variables, the nature of subfertility, and the need to include time in the denominator of pregnancy rates were ignored.[128] Although there are reports of successful treatment of azoospermic men by varicocelectomy, transient azoospermia may follow a minor illness or occur for unknown reasons, and, thus, such examples do not prove the value of treatment.[151] Most exponents of varicocele treatment regard azoospermia as a bad prognostic sign, especially if the FSH level is elevated.

#### Follow-Up Studies and Controlled Trials

Follow-up studies of groups of treated and untreated patients with varicoceles suggest pregnancies are as frequent without treatment as with treatment of the varicocele.[9,153,154] Attempts have been made to conduct randomized, controlled clinical trials of varicocele treatment. Such trials are difficult because the ideal design with sham operations and blinding, which is so important in controlling for outcomes affected by psychological factors, is not possible. Large trials are also needed: For example, approximately 250 pregnancies are required to have

a high chance of finding a 25% increase in pregnancy rate after treatment significant at the 5% level.[128]

So far, the trials have produced conflicting results. A small prospective, controlled study of percutaneous embolization of the left testicular vein in 17 to 20 year olds showed an increase in testicular volume and sperm concentration in the treated group.[155] Others have reported similar beneficial effects of treatment of varicoceles in adolescents in less well controlled studies. A prospective, randomized, controlled trial of occlusion of the spermatic vein by surgical or angiographic techniques versus follow-up counseling alone for 1 year in 125 couples without other causes of infertility showed no difference in pregnancy rate: 29% and 25%, respectively, at 12 months.[156]

The World Health Organization set up a multicenter controlled trial of Palomo ligation in men with infertility of more than 1-year duration, abnormal semen analyses, a moderate to large left varicocele, and a potentially fertile female partner. Volunteers were randomized to immediate operation or operation delayed for 12 months to provide an untreated control group. One of the participating centers reported their results separately.[157] There was a substantial effect on pregnancy rate. Two pregnancies occurred in 20 couples during the 1 year of observation without treatment compared with 15 pregnancies in 20 couples in the year after the operation. During the year after the operation in the remaining 18 control patients, there were 8 pregnancies. Semen analysis results also improved after the operation. There were another 248 couples in 12 countries in the trial, and there was a less marked but significant improvement, the life table pregnancy rates at 1 year being 35% for the operated group and 17% for the unoperated group (relative pregnancy rate, 2.7; 95% confidence interval, 1.6–4.4). Semen analysis results also improved over the first year in the operated group. In the control patients having the delayed operation, the life table pregnancy rate at 1 year after the operation was 21%. However, there were problems with the World Health Organization trial, particularly with possible irregularities of randomization in some centers early in the trial and high dropout rates, and the results have not yet been published in detail.[145] Also, the pregnancy rates in the control group are lower than expected for untreated subfertile men with varicoceles: approximately 30% produce a pregnancy in 12 months.[9,156]

Thus, although some people remain convinced of the value of treating varicoceles for infertility, it is not easy to demonstrate this unequivocally and the apparent improvements in semen quality and fertility may result from random fluctuations and regression toward the mean.[128,144,151] Although better trials are needed, meta-analyses do not support treatment of varicocele for infertility.[146-148] It is clear that normal fertility is not achieved in a high proportion of patients treated for varicocele. ART is a realistic alternative for most couples who have not conceived after a reasonable time.

## GENERAL MANAGEMENT

This section covers aspects of the management of couples with male infertility not amenable to specific treatment (Table 172-6; Fig. 172-6). A number will conceive during investigation. Others will decide not to continue with medical intervention. Some patients with treatable conditions may choose ICSI instead of treatment or after a treatment has been unsuccessful. However, most couples with male infertility have conditions for which there is no clearly defined and certainly effective treatment.[7,8] In these cases, it is important to discuss the prognosis for a natural pregnancy occurring, the ineffectiveness of treatments, and the availability of IVF and ICSI, donor insemination, and adoption. The investigation of the female partner should be reviewed and abnormalities

| Table 172-6 | Current Management of Subfertility |
|---|---|

Estimate prognosis for natural conception
Discuss doubtful value of "empirical therapies"
Advise of alternatives: donor insemination, adoption, childlessness
Review coital timing
Review female partner's potential fertility
Consider artificial reproductive technology: in vitro fertilization/intra-
    cytoplasmic sperm injection

treated when possible. Patients should be acquainted with the physiology of the menstrual cycle and symptoms of ovulation to help time sexual intercourse over the fertile phase of the cycle.[158] Good health practices should be promoted, particularly cessation of smoking because it reduces fertility in women.[65] The psychological upheaval experienced by the couple should be discussed and additional help offered if necessary. Specialist infertility counselors and patient support groups are particularly valuable in this area.

### PROGNOSIS FOR NATURAL PREGNANCY

A number of factors in addition to semen quality affect the likelihood of natural pregnancies occurring.[1-4,9,74,159-164] Some are obvious, such as female disorders and coital dysfunction. Female age is important because fertility declines after approximately 35 years of age. Duration of infertility is a major factor in most studies: The longer the infertility, the worse the outlook. The prognostic factors found in a study to determine the effect of varicocele surgery were duration of infertility (negative), mean sperm concentration (positive), untreated sperm autoimmunity (negative), ovulatory disorders (negative), occupational group (farmers doing better than other workers), female age (negative), and previous fertility in the couple (positive).[9] Interestingly, varicocele presence and size were positive prognostic factors even though varicocele surgery was not significant. The pregnancy rate curves for different sperm concentration groups are shown in Figure 172-7. A recent study of subfertile patients seen in the late 1990s had similar natural conception rates.[74] Such factors can be used to advise patients about their chances of producing a natural pregnancy over time. The accuracy of prediction is low because the statistically significant factors only explain a small part of the variance (in the study cited previously, approximately 17%). New studies using automated methods for semen analysis reveal the percentage of sperm with characteristics conforming to morphometrics preferred for binding to the ZP, and the straight line velocity, may have better predictive value.[74] However, other factors currently not assessable, such as gamete transport, may have an important bearing on conception and may explain the occurrence of pregnancies in some couples despite severely abnormal semen analysis results. Patients should not be told natural conception is impossible unless there is an absolute barrier to fertility.

### PSYCHOLOGICAL ASPECTS

Infertility causes major trauma to the ego of most patients, but few suffer serious psychological disorders.[165] Many undergo a grief reaction with initial denial of the problem followed by a tendency to blame others and a period of depression before final acceptance of the infertility. The reaction may take years to resolve, and it can threaten the stability of the partnership, interfere with investigation and management of infertility, and lead to futile involvement in expensive "cures" offered by the unscrupulous. Participation in unsuccessful treatments during this phase often is particularly difficult emotionally for the patients. Stresses of ordinary existence are unlikely to influence semen quality.[166] An empa-

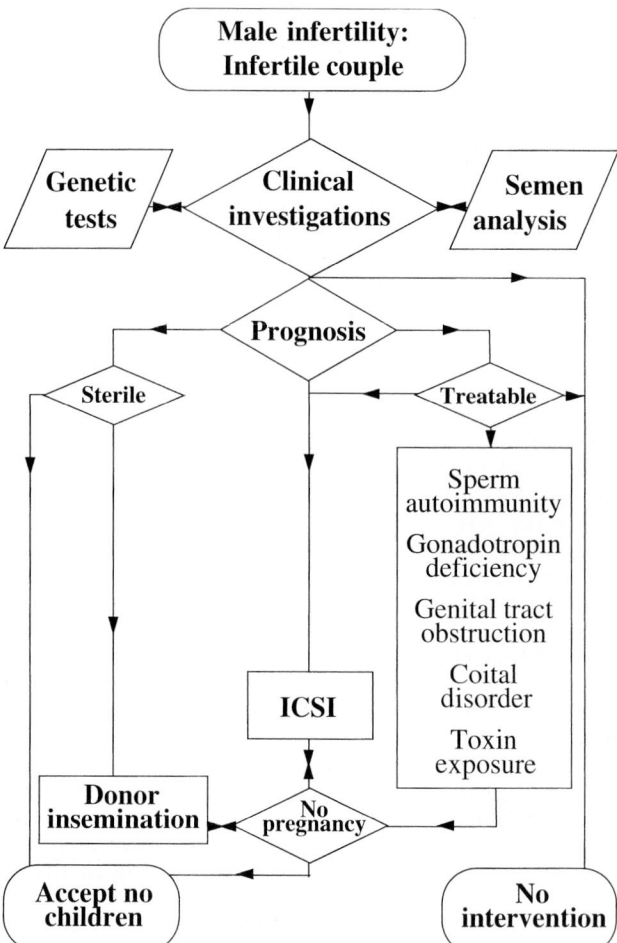

Figure 172-6    Flow chart of management of male infertility.

thetic approach and involvement of independent counselors or self-help infertility groups may assist some couples. In most, the unpleasantness of the psychological reaction subsides with time.

### TIMING OF COITUS

A practical approach is to advise intercourse each day when ovulation might occur. Ovulation can be predicted to occur approximately 14 days before a period is due. Knowing the range of menstrual cycle lengths allows calculation of the days when ovulation is most likely to occur. Symptoms of ovulation including mittelschmerz and mid-cycle mucous changes also help identify the fertile time.[158,167] Temperature charts may be used to indicate the end of the fertile time as the basal body temperature rises after ovulation. Ovulation timing by measurement of estrogen and progesterone metabolites in urine, urine or serum LH levels, or ovarian ultrasonography may also be used.

### GENERAL HEALTH ASPECTS

Although correction of adverse lifestyle factors in the usual man seen for infertility is unlikely to produce normal fertility, healthy living has positive long-term benefits.[15,168] The following are advised: weight reduction for the obese, reduced alcohol intake for the moderate to heavy drinker, avoidance of social drugs including tobacco, avoidance of heat from frequent sauna and spa baths, and management of stress in the workplace, in marriage, and that engendered by the infertility.

## EMPIRICAL TREATMENTS: EVIDENCE-BASED VERSUS UNCONFIRMED TREATMENTS

Treatments of some causes of male infertility are available as discussed previously, but for the majority of patients with abnormal semen analyses, there are no methods of proved effectiveness.[128,169,170] A medical or surgical treatment may become established because it is logical and obviously effective, for example, gonadotropin treatment for Kallmann's syndrome or vasoepididymostomies for postinflammatory obstructions of the tails of the epididymides. However, in other situations in which semen quality is reduced and there is subfertility rather than absolute sterility, it is necessary to demonstrate that the treatment increases semen analysis results and pregnancy rates by a clinically meaningful amount. This evidence-based medicine approach generally requires controlled clinical trials of promising methods. These trials are usually designed to detect a certain magnitude of difference in the primary responses and thus a positive result supports the use of the method. However, if the trial is negative, it merely does not confirm the magnitude of benefit tested; it does not prove the method is of no value. In time, the results of several trials can be combined by meta-analysis to get better estimates of the overall effects of the method.

In the past, many treatments were used in an uncontrolled fashion for defects of sperm production.[128] Androgens have been given to suppress spermatogenesis in the hope that there would be "rebound" improvement after the treatment is stopped.[128,169] Low-dose testosterone or weak androgens, such as mesterolone, have been given in the hope of improving epididymal maturation of sperm. Human chorionic gonadotropin has been given for similar reasons. Antiestrogens have been used to increase gonadotropin secretion or gonadotropins (FSH and human chorionic gonadotropin) given to "stimulate" spermatogenesis.[151] Antibiotics and anti-inflammatory drugs have been given for subtle infections or inflammations in the accessory sex organs. Antioxidants, amino acids, vitamins, herbs, and minerals such as zinc, cold baths, and testicular coolers have been used. There are difficulties with the interpretation of the results of these treatments.[128] Marked improvements in semen quality can occur spontaneously (Fig. 172-8). Semen analysis results also display the phenomenon of regression to the mean: On average, repeated semen analyses improve in men with initially abnormal results.[171] Pregnancy rate data were not analyzed effectively in many early studies. Floating numerator pregnancy rates, in which a percentage of patients pregnant is given without regard for time of exposure, have caused confusion in the infertility literature. Statistical methods for life table analysis and regression analysis with censored data are especially useful for assessing the impact of groups of variables on pregnancy rates, for analysis of prognostic factors, and for testing results of therapeutic trials.[128]

The empirical treatments either have not been submitted to adequately controlled clinical trials, or when they have, the trials have not shown consistently positive results. Meta-analyses have also produced conflicting results, probably because of the variable quality of the trials included in the analyses. Until there is sound evidence of the value of a drug or procedure from controlled therapeutic trials, patients should be advised that none of the empirical methods meet the requirements of evidence-based medicine.

AIH is widely practiced with dubious evidence of efficacy in patients who do not have coital difficulties. Ovulation induction with intrauterine artificial insemination probably does increase the pregnancy rates by increasing the number of oocytes exposed to the sperm.[172,173] Results are lower with timed intercourse and multiple ovulation induction. Generally, the results are poor when the semen analysis is abnormal. Although this may be acceptable in countries where ART is expensive, the risk of multiple pregnancy is substantial. IVF or ICSI would be preferable because the number

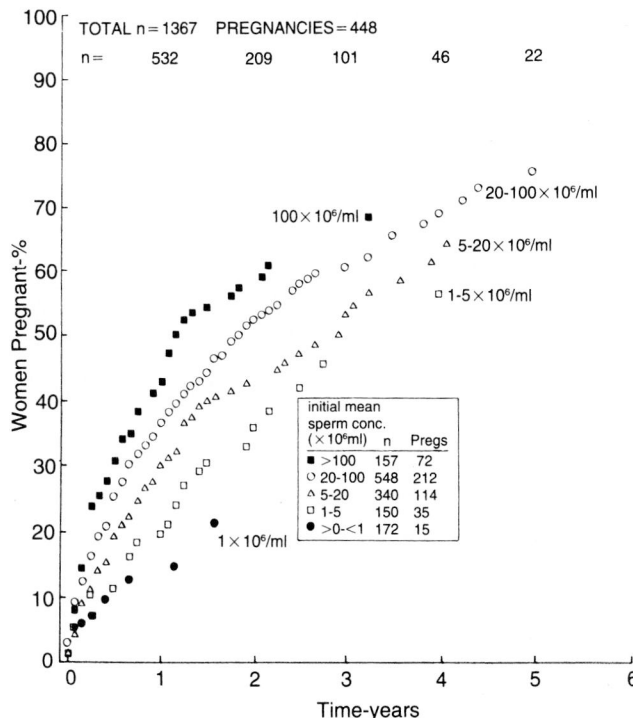

**Figure 172-7** Pregnancy rate curves grouped according to average pretreatment sperm concentration. The number of patients (n) followed each year is shown. The numbers of men and pregnancies in each sperm concentration group are shown in the inset.

of pre-embryos placed in the uterus can be controlled and high multiple pregnancies avoided.[173]

## IN VITRO FERTILIZATION/INTRACYTOPLASMIC SPERM INJECTION FOR MALE INFERTILITY

ICSI has revolutionized the management of male infertility. It involves the injection of a single sperm into the ooplasm (Fig. 172-9).[174–176] ICSI can be used with almost any live sperm with an expectation of results close to those obtained with standard IVF (see Chapter 158) using normal sperm. ICSI may not be needed with mild semen disorders. Provided that more than approximately 2 million motile sperm can be harvested from an ejaculate, IVF can be attempted with an expectation of success close to that of IVF for other indications. The

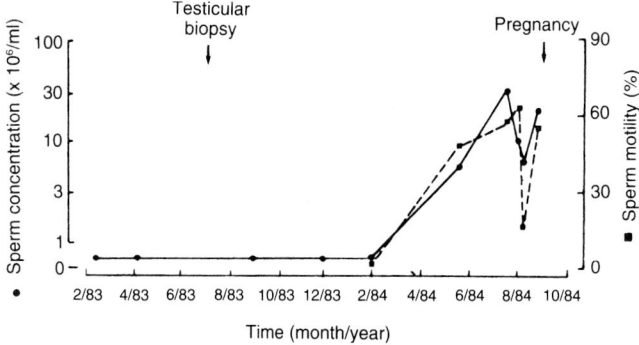

**Figure 172-8** Sperm concentration and motility in a man with severe oligospermia and severe hypospermatogenesis included in a therapeutic trial of clomiphene. Semen quality improved and his wife conceived. He was given the placebo! (Baker HWG: Requirements for controlled therapeutic trials in male infertility. Clin Reprod Fertil 4:13–25, 1986.)

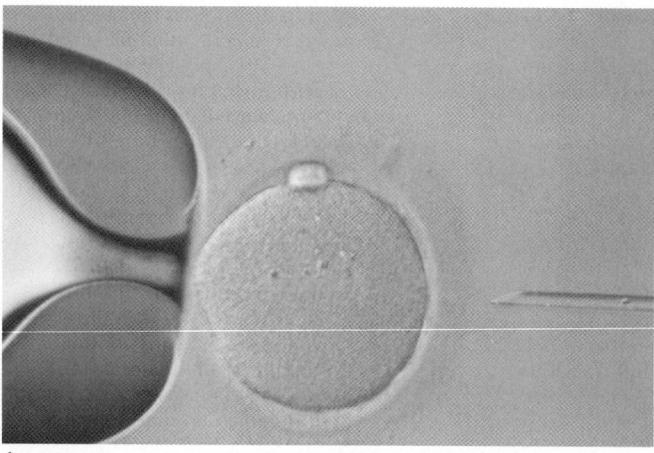

A

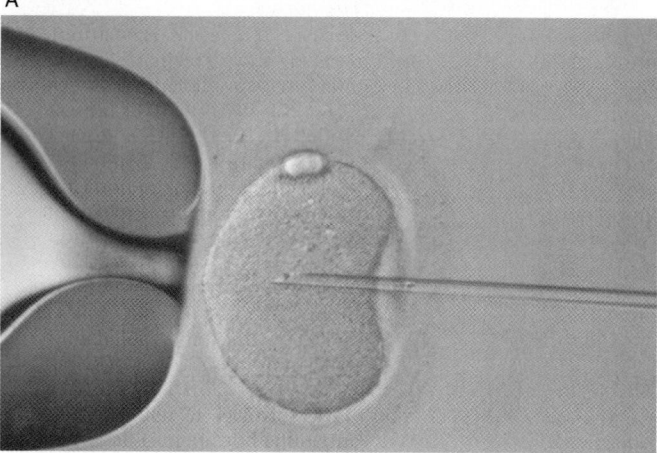

B

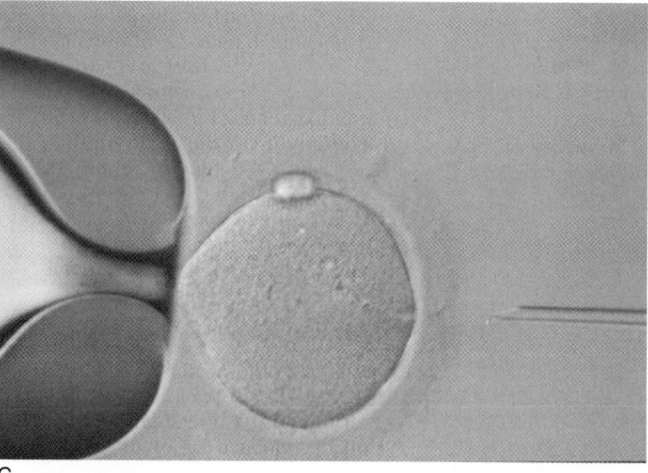

C

*Figure 172-9* Intracytoplasmic sperm injection.

outcome depends particularly on sperm morphology and the ability of the sperm to bind to and penetrate the ZP. ICSI should be offered if there is a chance of failure of fertilization with IVF: less than 2 million motile sperm per ejaculate, less than 5% of sperm with normal morphology, less than 5% of sperm with progressive motility, sperm autoimmunity with positive IBTs and zero sperm-mucous penetration, and defects of sperm-oocyte interaction.

### PREPARATION OF THE PATIENTS

The couple needs to be counseled carefully about the procedures, predicted chance of a live birth, and the possible com-

plications. Special preparation of the man may be required. Trial-run sperm preparations help to identify those patients who have difficulty collecting semen. These patients should practice collections before attending for the IVF procedure. Men with many inflammatory cells in the semen could be treated with antibiotics. Those with low motility or sperm autoimmunity may have better sperm motility with short, 1- to 2-day durations of abstinence. Cryopreserved semen can be used as backup if the fresh semen is particularly poor on the day of ICSI in patients with fluctuating semen abnormalities. This is particularly useful when sperm are present in the semen only intermittently. Those patients who produce an unexpectedly poor sample on the day of IVF should provide a second sample later to supplement the first sample. Electroejaculation or needle biopsy of the testes can be used if the man is unexpectedly unable to collect semen. Patients with genital tract obstruction can have sperm retrieved from the testis or epididymis by needle aspiration.[110]

ICSI also allows patients with severe primary spermatogenic disorders to be treated provided some live sperm or elongated spermatids can be recovered from the semen, testes, or genital tract (Table 172-7). If no sperm can be found in the semen, the likelihood of finding elongated spermatids in the testicular tissue can be estimated by the clinical situation and testicular histology. Perhaps surprisingly, sperm can be found by extensive biopsies in approximately 50% of men with Klinefelter syndrome. Results are good if any tubules with complete spermatogenesis can be seen in diagnostic biopsies. However, if there are no elongated spermatids, the success rate with open biopsies is low: approximately 20% with Sertoli-cell-only syndrome and rarely with germ cell arrest at the primary spermatocyte stage.[177] Yq microdeletions in the AZFa and b regions are also associated with a complete absence of spermatogenesis. Other factors such as hormone levels and testicular size do not seem to be predictive.[178,179] The use of donor sperm should be discussed during preparation of the couple if the outlook is poor.

New testicular biopsy techniques have been developed to maximize the chance of finding sperm while minimizing damage. Microsurgery with examination of exposed testicular tissue under the operating microscope may allow selection of the larger diameter tubules, which are more likely to contain more advanced spermatogenesis.[151] Alternatively, multiple sampling through small holes in the tunica may be used.[180] Large biopsies, particularly at multiple sites, have higher complication rates and will further impair testicular function.[181,182] Generally, repeat open biopsies for sperm collection should be performed only after the patient and testes have recovered from the previous surgery, and this may take several months.

### APPROACHES

The standard approach is to stimulate multiple ovarian follicular development with FSH and collect the oocytes by ultrasound-guided transvaginal needle puncture of the ovaries after administration of human chorionic gonadotropin. ICSI or IVF is performed, and the resulting embryos

| Table 172-7 | Steps in the Management of Severe Primary Seminiferous Tubule Failure |
| --- | --- |

Multiple semen samples at intervals to cryopreserve live sperm for ICSI
Diagnostic needle biopsy: if elongated spermatids found, do testicular biopsy ICSI
If no spermatids seen, consider open testicular biopsy ICSI with donor backup
Donor insemination, adoption, or accept childlessness

ICSI, intracytoplasmic sperm injection.

are transferred into the uterine cavity, usually at the four- to eight-cell or blastocyst stage with cryopreservation of remaining embryos. Although cryopreservation may reduce the implantation potential, frozen and fresh embryos of the same stage and quality produce similar implantation and pregnancy rates.

Biopsy of blastomeres for detection of chromosomal and genetic abnormalities is possible and will increase in use as more conditions causing serious hereditary diseases or defective embryo development are able to be diagnosed.[28]

## SPERM PREPARATION

Various procedures have been developed for sperm preparation for IVF. Most popular is centrifugation on gradients of colloidal silica because this can be performed with high reproducibility. Cryopreserved samples require especially gentle handling, particularly with dilution of the semen cryoprotectant medium with culture medium. Motility, even just an occasional slight twitch of the tail, is preferred in selecting sperm for ICSI. The morphology of the sperm cannot be assessed in detail at the magnification used, but obviously grossly abnormal sperm would be excluded. If no motile sperm can be found, motility stimulation with pentoxifylline or hypoosmotic swelling can be used to show that the sperm are alive.[72,130]

## RESULTS

With IVF and ICSI, 60% of oocytes fertilize and cleave normally over the first 48 hours. Some groups report lower fertilization rates with sperm or elongated spermatids obtained by testicular biopsy of men with severe primary spermatogenic defects.[183] Pregnancy rates for each fresh transfer of 1- or 2-day two or three embryos are approximately 20% to 30% with fetal heart implantation rates of 10% to 20% for women younger than 35 years of age.[184] Implantation and pregnancy rates are approximately 25% lower with cryopreserved embryos. The cumulative live birth rates with transfer of fresh and cryopreserved embryos are approximately 30% to 40% for the first oocyte collection and 60% to 80% by the fourth oocyte collection. Approximately 20% of the pregnancies resulting from transfer of 2-day two embryos are twins.[184] Multiple pregnancy is more frequent if three or more cleave stage embryos or blastocysts are transferred.[185,186] A number of other factors are known to influence the results of IVF/ICSI including embryo quality and particularly female age.[187] Implantation and pregnancy rates decrease and pregnancy losses increase after age 35, mostly due to increasing abnormalities in the oocytes.

## EVALUATION OF FAILED FERTILIZATION

When most or all oocytes fail to fertilize in IVF, the cause is usually defective sperm. Oocytes may not fertilize because of immaturity or abnormality, but this is an unusual cause of total failure of fertilization of all the oocytes retrieved from a woman.[78] Unexpected failures of fertilization should be evaluated by examination of the number of sperm on the ZP and penetrating the ZP: Low numbers usually indicate sperm defects.[78] Low fertilization rates may also result from undiagnosed sperm autoimmunity, the presence of sperm antibodies in maternal serum added to culture media, infected semen, or technical defects in the IVF laboratory. Careful evaluation of the semen quality and screening patients with idiopathic infertility for disordered ZP-induced acrosome reaction before IVF should allow most couples likely to have low fertilization with standard IVF to be directed to ICSI.[78,79] ICSI of unfertilized oocytes with the man's sperm 12 to 24 hours after standard IVF insemination may result in fertilization and pregnancy, but, overall, the results are poor and many

clinics would not perform this "ICSI rescue" procedure. Re-insemination of failed fertilization oocytes with donor sperm is also possible for diagnostic or therapeutic purposes. This procedure is not permitted in some countries.

Individual oocytes may not fertilize with ICSI. In these, the sperm head is often only partially decondensed. Failure of fertilization of all oocytes with ICSI is rare. Globospermic and immotile sperm and sperm from rare patients with severe oligospermia may produce low or zero fertilization rates with ICSI. The sperm head may not decondense or there may be a defect of an oocyte-activating factor from the sperm. Modified ICSI techniques may be successful in artificially activating the oocytes in some of these cases.[188]

## COMPLICATIONS OF IN VITRO FERTILIZATION/INTRACYTOPLASMIC SPERM INJECTION

Potential adverse effects of ART include well-understood conditions in the woman and a variety of possible issues for the offspring. At this stage, the latter are largely unconfirmed or contentious. In general, the outcome and complications of ART are the same for standard IVF and ICSI.[184] The implantation rate, pregnancy wastage, pregnancy complications, perinatal mortality, and risk of congenital abnormalities are no greater than with patients who have IVF for other indications (Table 172-8).

### Risks for the Woman
The ovarian hyperstimulation syndrome is a major risk with gonadotropin stimulation of multiple follicular development. Careful monitoring of the patients is necessary. If many follicles develop, embryo freezing rather than transfer avoids pregnancy and allows the ovaries to recover, reducing the risk of severe complications such as thromboembolism, renal failure, and death. Surgical complications including bleeding and infection from the oocyte collection procedure are rare. There are also small risks of complications from anesthesia and sedation. Maternal complications of pregnancy increase in frequency with multiple pregnancy.[184,185,189,190] Cesarean section is more frequent for singleton ART births (40%) than in the general community (20%).[184] There are also concerns about the ovarian stimulation drugs predisposing to breast or gynecologic cancers.[191]

### Risks for the Child
*Multiple Pregnancy*
The risks of multiple pregnancy for the child, prematurity, low birth weight, increased perinatal mortality and morbidity, less parental attention during childhood, are well known and are being addressed in some countries by reducing the numbers of embryos transferred together.[186,190,192,193]

*Transmission of Genetic and Chromosomal Disorders*
The known genetic risks were covered previously (see Table 172-4). For some conditions, for example, cystic fibrosis and myotonic dystrophy, pre-implantation genetic diagnosis can be used so that only unaffected embryos are transferred. Balanced chromosomal translocations may become unbalanced in embryos and result in miscarriage or rarely in the birth of an abnormal child. Pre-implantation genetic diagnosis may also be used to detect unbalanced chromosomal constitution in the pre-implantation embryo.[176]

*Defects Possibly Associated with Abnormal Spermatogenesis*
The mechanisms involved in the causation of the common forms of male infertility associated with oligospermia, asthenospermia, and teratospermia are not understood. There is a correlation between the production of abnormal sperm with poor morphology and motility and abnormal sperm DNA measured by the variety of techniques including acridine orange fluorescence, sperm chromatin structure assay, and other techniques

**Table 172-8**  Comparison of 8793 Intracytoplasmic Sperm Injection and 22,319 In Vitro Fertilization Pregnancy Outcomes from the Australian Institute of Health and Welfare National Perinatal Statistics Unit and Fertility Society of Australia Database on Assisted Conception in Australia and New Zealand to 1999 and 2000[184]

|  | ICSI (%) | IVF (%) |
|---|---|---|
| **Pregnancy outcome** | | |
| Spontaneous abortion | 18.9 | 20.7 |
| Ectopic pregnancy | 1.9 | 4.2 |
| Live birth | 77.2 | 73.3 |
| **Multiple births** (>20 wk) | | |
| Total | 19.8 | 19.9 |
| Twin | 18.5 | 17.9 |
| Triplet and quadruplets | 1.4 | 2.0 |
| **Preterm birth** (20–36 wk) | | |
| Total | 22.9 | 23.3 |
| Singleton | 11.5 | 13.9 |
| **Low birth weight** (<2.5 kg) | | |
| Total | 26.8 | 27.0 |
| Singleton | 10.4 | 11.4 |
| **Perinatal mortality** (<28 d) | | |
| Total | 2.81 | 3.23 |
| Singleton | 1.67 | 2.26 |
| **Major congenital malformations** | | |
| (live, stillborn, abortions >16 wk) | 2.65 | 2.42 |
| **Sex ratio** | | |
| (male/female) | 105.4 | 109.0 |

All treatments are reported from all assisted reproductive technology centers in Australia and New Zealand since 1979. Australia has high assisted reproductive technology use with approximately 850 treatments per 100,000 women of reproductive age per year. Treatments are covered by national health insurance (Medicare). Comparable rates for all births in Australia are for preterm birth (5.8%), low birth weight (5.2%), and perinatal mortality (0.8%).

for DNA breaks including chromomycin staining, and comet assays.[17,19,194–197] Abnormal sperm produce reactive oxygen species that could damage sperm DNA and result in defects of implantation or pregnancy loss.[19,195] However, the results of ICSI to date do not reveal such problems (see Table 172-8). It is possible that the abnormal sperm with redundant cytoplasm are excluded in natural or assisted fertilization by poor or zero motility and sperm aggregation caused by heavy coating with clusterin.[198]

A two- to sixfold increase in de novo sex chromosomal aneuploidy and structural autosomal defects has been noted with ICSI, probably related to increased rates of chromosomal nondisjunction as a general association with abnormal spermatogenesis.[176,199] Bonduelle and colleagues[200] showed that the rate of de novo chromosomal defects in children was higher after ICSI with sperm from oligospermic men (2.1%) than from normospermic men (0.24%). Tests on sperm show increasing rates of aneuploidy with severity of oligospermia.[199] The results of treatment of patients with Klinefelter syndrome who produce some sperm is also consistent with chromosomal aneuploidy being associated with severe primary spermatogenic disorders in general. An extra X chromosome in a male germ cell results in its death. Spermatogenesis in Klinefelter testes results from nondisjunction with loss of one X chromosome so that a clone of XY spermatogonia results.[105] The increased aneuploidy found in sperm from men with severe primary spermatogenic defects suggests this results from segregation errors during cell division from XY stem spermatogonia as an associated feature of severely compromised spermatogenesis.

### Embryo Defects Possibly Caused by Laboratory Conditions

Laboratory conditions or procedures on gametes could affect embryo development that might influence the health of the child. In domestic animal IVF, there is a syndrome of large offspring that results from stress-induced changes in gene expression that may involve changes in DNA methylation and gene imprinting in embryos cultured to blastocysts.[201] Adverse conditions of culture have been shown experimentally to alter methylation of an imprinted gene in the mouse embryo.[202] Thus, recent reports of conditions such as Beckwith-Weidemann syndrome and Angelman's syndrome in children born from IVF/ICSI procedures are of concern.[203] Increased frequencies of tumors in children born after ART have also been claimed, for example, retinoblastoma, but other studies do not support a general increase in childhood cancer rates.[204]

### Surveillance Studies

Because of concerns about the normality of offspring after ART, a database on the children born in Australia and New Zealand from these procedures was organized by the Fertility Society of Australia and the National Perinatal Statistics Unit (NPSU), and this remains a valuable resource. In this database, the fertilization, implantation, and pregnancy failure rates and congenital malformation rates are no greater with ICSI than with standard IVF (see Table 172-8).[184,205] However, overall results are different from those in the general population: preterm birth (5.8%), low birth weight (5.1%), major congenital malformations (1.74%), and perinatal mortality (0.8%). The differences are partly explained by the high multiple pregnancy rate with IVF and ICSI, and perhaps female age and infertility factors. Closer surveillance and more accurate reporting may also contribute. The lower birth weight has been reported by many groups and does not appear to be explained by the multiple pregnancies because singletons also have a slightly lower birth weight.[206] Initially, there were suggestions that some abnormalities, particularly heart defects, neural tube defects, and brain tumors, may have been more frequent after IVF, but with the greater numbers of babies, this is no longer statistically significant.[184]

After the introduction of ICSI, it was noted that there were many differences in the fertilization process compared with those that occurred by standard IVF.[207] However, the NPSU results on children do not show any clear adverse effect of ICSI compared with IVF. Until 1998, there appeared to be a change in the sex ratio in the NPSU data with an increase in female offspring after ICSI, however, that varies from year to year.[208] The report of a significantly lower IQ score at 1 year of age in male babies from ICSI compared with those from IVF and naturally conceived controls has not been supported in larger studies at later ages.[209,210] Studies of children born as a result of ART have not revealed any consistently associated congenital malformations, but there are data suggesting generally increased congenital malformation rates.[211,212] However, these studies may be biased. For example, if IVF and ICSI babies are examined more thoroughly and reporting to health registers is more complete, the malformation rates may appear higher than for naturally conceived children who are less carefully examined and reported. Even with perfect reporting, differences in malformation rates could be caused by other factors, such as age or health of the mothers, which have not been adequately accounted for in the statistical analysis.

## USE OF DONOR SPERM

Donor insemination is a common method of managing male sterility.[213–216] Sperm banks may be involved in approximately 1 in 200 births in countries where the use of donor sperm is permitted. The main indications for donor insemination are untreatable sterility in the man or when treatments and ICSI for severe or chronic subfertility have failed. The couple may choose donor insemination as the primary method of managing their infertility. Rarely, donor insemination is used because of genetic abnormalities in the man. Donor sperm may also be used in IVF when there is a combination of female infertility and male sterility. Because of the higher pregnancy rates, IVF with donor sperm may be used if donor insemination fails.[215] Donor sperm may also be used in IVF procedures as a backup, for example, when testicular sperm aspiration is to be attempted for severe spermatogenic defects and there is doubt as to whether sperm will be obtained.

## CRYOPRESERVATION OF SEMEN

Donor insemination can be performed in the setting of a specialist infertility clinic with patient counseling, ovulation monitoring, and insemination procedure available.[213,214] Alternatively, the sperm bank may only supply semen for the patient and be separate from the clinics or physicians performing the artificial insemination. Because of the risk of transmission of infectious diseases, particularly HIV and hepatitis B, and also for convenience, donor insemination services now use only cryopreserved semen.[213–215] Semen cryopreservation with glycerol–egg yolk cryoprotectant and either vapor freezing or controlled-rate freezing in plastic straws or vials produces pregnancy rates equal to those with fresh semen.[213] Importantly, cryopreservation allows the semen to be quarantined for 3 to 6 months for donors to be recalled and retested for infectious diseases, particularly HIV, before any is used.

## SELECTION OF DONORS

Prospective donors have their medical and family histories evaluated and a physical examination to exclude the possibility of transmitting serious genetic diseases such as hemoglobinopathies or sexually transmissible infections. Donors sign a lifestyle declaration to indicate that they are not involved in any practices that might expose them to serious infections, such as HIV. There usually is an upper age limit of 40 to 45 years because of the increasing frequency of genetic abnormalities in sperm with age. Semen quality is selected to be in the upper part of the normal range, particularly for concentration and motility.[213,215] The semen is cultured for bacteria and blood is tested for hepatitis and HIV antibodies. The freezing of semen does not appear to cause any increase in the frequency of congenital abnormalities.[213,215]

It is usual to match the physical characteristics of the recipient's husband and the donor including race, complexion, build, height, hair color, and eye color. In addition, blood groups may be matched. In some programs, the recipient couple may be able to choose the donor on other information such as occupation and education. Known donors may also be used; these may be friends or relatives of the infertile couple. In this situation, special counseling of the donors and recipients is necessary. Also, there should be a full workup of the known donor as for an anonymous donor, including cryopreservation and quarantining of the semen.

Donor factors relevant to the success of donor insemination are mainly to do with the quality of the semen. Postthaw motility has the strongest predictive value for high fertilization rates, but sperm morphology, motility, and concentration are also significant.[213,214] Despite selection of high-quality semen, there remains considerable variability in the pregnancy rates between donors. A policy to discard semen from a donor who produces no pregnancy after a certain number (e.g., 20–40) of inseminations is necessary.[214]

## COUNSELING

The special nature of the use of donor sperm needs to be discussed in detail with the couple so that they are fully aware of the implications of having a child by donor.[217] Donor insemination is forbidden in some religions. There may be local legislation or regulations to control the use of donated gametes. In some countries, special laws have been enacted that may either allow or prevent the child from obtaining identifying information about the donor. The legal status of the child may also be specified in various ways. The couple needs to decide how and when to disclose the child's donor sperm origin. What and how much they should tell their friends and relatives about their infertility treatment should also be discussed, as should their reaction to acquaintances questioning the paternity of the child. The possibility that in the future half-siblings may unwittingly find each other and attempt to have children is of concern to some prospective parents and donors. This needs to be discussed carefully and the risks explained in view of the number of pregnancies permitted per donor by the clinic. Studies of donor families in which there has been expert pretreatment counseling, indicate no physical or emotional problems with the children, and greater marital stability than average.[216,217] Some donor offspring resent being told late about their donor conception and not having access to identifying information about the donor.

## PROCEDURES AND RESULTS

The prospective recipients are screened for HIV, hepatitis B and C, rubella immunity, blood group, and genetic conditions if necessary. Tests of tubal patency are performed if the history suggests pelvic pathology. The inseminations are timed to coincide with natural ovulation. Careful monitoring of ovulation and timing of intrauterine insemination of prepared motile sperm suspensions (as for IVF) appear to increase the pregnancy rate. Pregnancy rates are approximately 10% to 25% per month for the first 4 to 6 months and then 5% to 10% thereafter, so that approximately 50% of women are pregnant by 4 to 6 months.[213,215,218] Female age affects the pregnancy rates. Women older than 35 have lower pregnancy rates than those younger than 35, for example, 65% pregnant by 1 year are younger than 35 and 50% pregnant by 1 year are older than 35.[213] Women with subfertile male partners have on average lower pregnancy rates than those with sterile male partners, indicating the presence of female factors contributing to the infertility when the male partner is subfertile.[213] Cumulative pregnancy rates for women who have had more than one pregnancy by donor insemination indicate higher conception rates over the first few months for the second pregnancy, approximately 33% pregnant in the first cycle and 55% by the second cycle.[213]

Multiple ovulation induction and intrauterine insemination may increase the pregnancy rates but at the risk of multiple pregnancy.[218] IVF may be used if no pregnancy has occurred after a reasonable number of inseminations (e.g., 4–12).[215] Live birth pregnancy rates with IVF in such patients are high, and women in good health can be advised that they have an 80% chance of having a child within 2 years.

## PREVENTION OF INFERTILITY

Prevention is difficult because of the lack of understanding of the causes of most types of male infertility.[8,36,219] Mumps orchitis was an uncommon cause of infertility, and childhood immunization for this disease should make it very rare. It is important to recognize that subfertility often is a couple problem, with both partners contributing. Therefore, general factors that would change a society's attitude to childbearing could have an important impact on the frequency of infertility, for example, a trend toward having children at earlier ages. On the other hand, toxins and environmental factors known to cause defects of sperm production, such as heat, dibromochlorobenzine, lead, benzene, ionizing radiation, and microwaves, are probably well controlled by environmental health measures.[14,55,56,61–63]

## PREVENTABLE DISEASES AND CONDITIONS

### Sexually Transmissible Infections

Postgonococcal epididymal obstructions appear to be the most important cause of infertility from sexually transmitted diseases. In countries where gonorrhea is treated promptly, postgonococcal epididymal obstruction is rare. On the other hand, it remains a common preventable cause of infertility in other countries.

### Undescended Testes

Although undescended testes have been sought and treated aggressively over the past 50 years, previously undescended testes remain a common association of male infertility, affecting approximately 7% of the men seen.[8,43–46] It is therefore uncertain whether early surgery for undescended testes has any impact on subsequent fertility. It is possible that the failure of normal descent is a feature of testicular dystrophy and that the sperm production will be poor whether or not the testes are placed in the scrotum. Because men who have had one testis removed usually have semen quality within normal limits, men with a unilateral undescended testis would not be expected to have poor semen unless there was an additional disorder of spermatogenesis in the contralateral descended scrotal testis. Thus, although orchiopexy is important for cosmetic aspects and reducing the risk and improving the ease of checking the testis for malignant change, it is not certain whether early orchiopexy preserves or promotes fertility. Gonadotropin treatment before or after orchiopexy is in trials.[45]

### Varicocele

As discussed previously, the effectiveness of varicocelectomy for sperm defects is controversial. Varicoceles are common and usually appear about the time of puberty. Although some groups believe that varicoceles should be sought actively and treated in adolescence to prevent infertility, this approach could pose a major burden on the health resources because at least 15% of men have varicoceles. Long-term prospective trials are needed.

### Vasectomy

Vasectomy reversal and treatment for continuing infertility after attempted vasectomy reversal are now common.[220] Better counseling about the limited effectiveness of vasectomy reversal is needed. Cryopreservation of semen before vasectomy in men who are uncertain about their need for future fertility should be promoted. Also, cryopreservation of semen after vasectomy reversal, if the quality is adequate, is worthwhile because restenosis of the vasovasostomy sites can occur.

## SEMEN CRYOPRESERVATION BEFORE LOSS OF FERTILITY

Men about to have treatment for malignant conditions may have sperm cryopreserved before commencing chemotherapy or radiotherapy.[53,221,222] Although pretreatment semen quality may be too poor for AIH, ICSI now has improved the outlook for successful pregnancies. Although the risks of having a child with a serious malformation or defect are difficult to estimate, in humans, semen collected during chemotherapy or radiotherapy must not be used because of the likelihood of induced mutations.[223] Other illnesses that require treatment that might cause sterility include nephritis, prostatic disease, rheumatoid arthritis, multiple sclerosis, and inflammatory bowel diseases. Infertile men with conditions such as orchitis or Young's syndrome that might involve progressively declining semen quality should also store any live sperm that can be obtained as insurance for the future. A similar approach could be extended to adolescents with risk factors for infertility such as undescended testes in childhood, testicular torsion, and possibly a family history of infertility or a father with a Yq microdeletion. Although the frozen sperm are only used by a small proportion of men who store semen, the service continues to provide insurance for future fertility.[224] Some groups are offering to cryopreserve prepubertal testicular tissue before potentially sterilizing treatments in the expectation that effective techniques for transplantation or in vitro production of sperm will be developed in the future.[225–227]

## REFERENCES

1. Leridon H: Human Fertility: The Basic Components. Chicago: University of Chicago Press, 1977.
2. Greenhall E, Vessey M: The prevalence of subfertility: A review of the current confusion and a report of two new studies. Fertil Steril 54:978–983, 1990.
3. Joffe M: Time trends in biological fertility in Britain. Lancet 355:1961–1965, 2000.
4. Irvine DS: Epidemiology and aetiology of male infertility. Hum Reprod 13(Suppl 1):33–44, 1998.
5. Shaw LM, Balen A, Lenton E, et al: National Health Service provision for the management of infertility: The case for funding and reorganization of fertility services in the UK. Hum Fertil (Camb) 5:167–174, 2002.
6. Hirsh A: Male subfertility. Br Med J 327:669–672, 2003.
7. Comhaire FH, de Kretser DM, Farley TM, et al: Towards more objectivity in diagnosis and management of male infertility. Int J Androl Suppl 7:1–53, 1987.
8. Baker HWG, Burger HG, de Kretser DM, et al: Relative incidence of etiologic disorders in male infertility. In Santen

RJ, Swerdloff RS (eds): Male Reproductive Dysfunction: Diagnosis and Management of Hypogonadism, Infertility and Impotence. New York, Marcel Dekker, 1986, pp 341–372.
9. Baker HWG, Burger HG, de Kretser DM, et al: Testicular vein ligation and fertility in men with varicoceles. Br Med J 291:1678–1680, 1985.
10. Guzick DS, Overstreet JW, Factor-Litvak P, et al: Sperm morphology, motility, and concentration in fertile and infertile men. N Engl J Med 345:1388–1393, 2001.
11. Skaletsky H, Kuroda-Kawaguchi T, Minx PJ, et al: The male-specific region of the human Y chromosome is a mosaic of discrete sequence classes. Nature 423:825–837, 2003.
12. Krausz C, Forti G, McElreavey K: The Y chromosome and male fertility and infertility. Int J Androl 26:70–75, 2003.
13. Vogt PH: Molecular genetic of human male infertility: From genes to new therapeutic perspectives. Curr Pharm Des 10:471–500, 2004.
14. Toppari J, Larsen JC, Christiansen P, et al: Male reproductive health and environmental xenoestrogens. Environ

Health Perspect 104(Suppl 4):741–803, 1996.
15. Sharpe RM, Franks S: Environment, lifestyle and infertility—An intergenerational issue. Nat Cell Biol 4(Suppl):s33–s40, 2002.
16. Asklund C, Jorgensen N, Kold Jensen T, et al: Biology and epidemiology of testicular dysgenesis syndrome. BJU Int 93(Suppl 3):6–11, 2004.
17. Sakkas D, Seli E, Bizzaro D, et al: Abnormal spermatozoa in the ejaculate: Abortive apoptosis and faulty nuclear remodelling during spermatogenesis. Reprod Biomed Online 7:428–432, 2003.
18. Lewis SE: Importance of mitochondrial and nuclear sperm DNA in sperm quality assessment and assisted reproduction outcome. Hum Fertil (Camb) 5:102–109, 2002.
19. Aitken RJ, Sawyer D: The human spermatozoon—Not waving but drowning. Adv Exp Med Biol 518:85–98, 2003.
20. Van der Avoort IA, Van Golde RJ, Tuerlings JH, et al: Underestimation of subfertility among relatives when using a family history: Taboo bias. J Androl 24:285–288, 2003.

21. Baker HWG: Clinical approach to molecular genetic diagnosis in andrology. In Robaire B, Chemes H, Morales CR (eds): Andrology in the 21st Century. Englewood, NJ, Medimond, 2001, pp 373–382.

22. Conway GS: Clinical manifestations of genetic defects affecting gonadotrophins and their receptors. Clin Endocrinol (Oxf) 45:657–663, 1996.

23. McPhaul MJ: Molecular defects of the androgen receptor. Recent Prog Horm Res 57:181–194, 2002.

24. Huhtaniemi IT: LH and FSH receptor mutations and their effects on puberty. Horm Res 57(Suppl 2):35–38, 2002.

25. Yong EL, Loy CJ, Sim KS: Androgen receptor gene and male infertility. Hum Reprod Update 9:1–7, 2003.

26. Kaplan E, Shwachman H, Perlmutter AD, et al: Reproductive failure in males with cystic fibrosis. N Engl J Med 279:65–69, 1968.

27. Anguiano A, Amos JA, Dean M, et al: Congenital bilateral absence of the vas deferens: A primary genital form of cystic fibrosis. JAMA 267:1794–1797, 1992.

28. Lissens W, Liebaers I: The genetics of male infertility in relation to cystic fibrosis. Baillieres Clin Obstet Gynaecol 11:797–817, 1997.

29. Reijo R, Lee TY, Salo P, et al: Diverse spermatogenic defects in humans caused by Y chromosome deletions encompassing a novel RNA-binding protein gene. Nat Genet 10:383–393, 1995.

30. Najmabadi H, Huang V, Yen P, et al: Substantial prevalence of microdeletions of the Y-chromosome in infertile men with idiopathic azoospermia and oligozoospermia detected using a sequence-tagged site-based mapping strategy. J Clin Endocrinol Metab 81:1347–1352, 1996.

31. Baker HWG, Clarke GN, Hudson B, et al: Treatment of sperm autoimmunity in men. Clin Reprod Fertil 2:55–71, 1983.

32. Baker HWG, Clarke GN, McGowan MP, et al: Increased frequency of autoantibodies in men with sperm antibodies. Fertil Steril 43:438–441, 1985.

33. Lilford R, Jones A, Bishop D: Case-control study of whether subfertility in men is familial. Br Med J 309:570–573, 1994.

34. Wischusen J, Baker HWG, Hudson B: Reversible male infertility due to congenital adrenal hyperplasia. Clin Endocrinol (Oxf) 14:571–577, 1981.

35. Tiitinen A, Valimaki M: Primary infertility in 45-year-old man with untreated 21-hydroxylase deficiency: Successful outcome with glucocorticoid therapy. J Clin Endocrinol Metab 87:2442–2445, 2002.

36. Baker HWG: Reproductive effects of nontesticular illness. Endocrinol Metab Clin North Am 27:831–850, 1998.

37. Pedrazzoni M, Vescovi PP, Maninetti L, et al: Effects of chronic heroin abuse on bone and mineral metabolism. Acta Endocrinol (Copenh) 129:42–45, 1993.

38. MacLeod J, Hotchkiss R: The effect of hyperpyrexia on spermatozoa counts in men. Endocrinology 28:780, 1941.

39. Carlsen E, Andersson AM, Petersen JH, et al: History of febrile illness and variation in semen quality. Hum Reprod 18:2089–2092, 2003.

40. Handelsman DJ, Conway AJ, Boylan LM, et al: Young's syndrome. Obstructive azoospermia and chronic sinopulmonary infections. N Engl J Med 310:3–9, 1984.

41. Hendry WF, A'Hern RP, Cole PJ: Was Young's syndrome caused by exposure to mercury in childhood? Br Med J 307:1579–1582, 1993.

42. Chemes EH, Rawe YV: Sperm pathology: A step beyond descriptive morphology. Origin, characterization and fertility potential of abnormal sperm phenotypes in infertile men. Hum Reprod Update 9:405–428, 2003.

43. Mieusset R, Bujan L, Massat G, et al: Clinical and biological characteristics of infertile men with a history of cryptorchidism. Hum Reprod 10:613–619, 1995.

44. Lee PA, Bellinger MF, Coughlin MT: Correlations among hormone levels, sperm parameters and paternity in formerly unilaterally cryptorchid men. J Urol 160:1155–1157, discussion 1178, 1998.

45. Cortes D, Thorup J, Lindenberg S, et al: Infertility despite surgery for cryptorchidism in childhood can be classified by patients with normal or elevated follicle-stimulating hormone and identified at orchidopexy. BJU Int 91:670–674, 2003.

46. Hutson JM, Hasthorpe S, Heyns CF: Anatomical and functional aspects of testicular descent and cryptorchidism. Endocr Rev 18:259–280, 1997.

47. Ivell R, Hartung S: The molecular basis of cryptorchidism. Mol Hum Reprod 9:175–181, 2003.

48. Barthold JS, Redman JF: Association of epididymal anomalies with patent processus vaginalis in hernia, hydrocele and cryptorchidism. J Urol 156:2054–2056, 1996.

49. Skakkebaek NE, Holm M, Hoei-Hansen C, et al: Association between testicular dysgenesis syndrome (TDS) and testicular neoplasia: Evidence from 20 adult patients with signs of maldevelopment of the testis. APMIS 111:1–9, discussion 9–11, 2003.

50. Forman D, Pike MC, Davey G, et al: Aetiology of testicular cancer— Association with congenital abnormalities, age at puberty, infertility, and exercise. Br Med J 308:1393–1399, 1994.

51. Sandeman T: The effects of X-irradiation on male human fertility. Br J Radiol 39:901–907, 1966.

52. Fairley KF, Barrie JU, Johnson W: Sterility and testicular atrophy related to cyclophosphamide therapy. Lancet 1:568–569, 1972.

53. Kovacs GT, Stern K: Reproductive aspects of cancer treatment: An update. Med J Aust 170:495–497, 1999.

54. Wu FC, Aitken RJ, Ferguson A: Inflammatory bowel disease and male infertility: Effects of sulfasalazine and 5-aminosalicylic acid on sperm-fertilizing capacity and reactive oxygen species generation. Fertil Steril 52:842–845, 1989.

55. Henderson J, Baker HWG, Hanna PJ: Occupation-related male infertility: A review. Clin Reprod Fertil 4:87–106, 1986.

56. Thonneau P, Bujan L, Multigner L, et al: Occupational heat exposure and male fertility—A review. Hum Reprod 13:2122–2125, 1998.

57. Bonde JP, Joffe M, Danscher G, et al: Objectives, designs and populations of the European Asclepios study on occupational hazards to male reproductive capability. Scand J Work Environ Health 25:49–61, discussion 76–78, 1999.

58. Sheiner EK, Sheiner E, Hammel RD, et al: Effect of occupational exposures on male fertility: Literature review. Ind Health 41:55–62, 2003.

59. Coughlin LB, McGuigan JR, Haddad NG: Social class and semen analysis. J Obstet Gynaecol 23:276–277, 2003.

60. Swan SH: Do environmental agents affect semen quality? Epidemiology 14:261–262, 2003.

61. Brown-Woodman PD, Post EJ, Gass GC, et al: The effect of a single sauna exposure on spermatozoa. Arch Androl 12:9–15, 1984.

62. Goldsmith JR: Dibromochloropropane: Epidemiological findings and current questions. Ann N Y Acad Sci 837:300–306, 1997.

63. Joffe M, Bisanti L, Apostoli P, et al: Time to pregnancy and occupational lead exposure. Occup Environ Med 60:752–758, 2003.

64. Handelsman DJ, Conway AJ, Boylan LM, et al: Testicular function in potential sperm donors: Normal ranges and the effects of smoking and varicocele. Int J Androl 7:369–382, 1984.

65. Vine MF: Smoking and male reproduction: A review. Int J Androl 19:323–337, 1996.

66. Baker HWG, Pepperell RJ: Lack of effect of bromocriptine on semen quality in men with normal or slightly elevated prolactin levels. Aust N Z J Obstet Gynaecol 20:158–161, 1980.

67. Strachan MW, Teoh WL, Don-Wauchope AC, et al: Clinical and radiological features of patients with macroprolactinaemia. Clin Endocrinol (Oxf) 59:339–346, 2003.

68. Gebhard P, Johnson A: The Kinsey Data: Marginal Tabulations of the 1938–1963, 1979 Interviews. Philadelphia, Institute for Sex Research 1979, pp 116–120.

69. Smith NM, Byard RW, Bourne AJ: Testicular regression syndrome—A pathological study of 77 cases. Histopathology 19:269–272, 1991.

70. Prader A: Testicular size: Assessment and clinical importance. Triangle 7:240–243, 1966.

71. WHO: The influence of varicocele on parameters of fertility in a large group of men presenting to infertility clinics. World Health Organization. Fertil Steril 57:1289–1293, 1992.

72. WHO: World Health Organization laboratory manual for the examination of human semen and sperm-cervical mucus interaction. Cambridge, Cambridge University Press, 1999.

73. McLachlan RI, Baker HWG, Clarke GN, et al: Semen analysis: Its place in modern reproductive medical practice. Pathology 35:25–33, 2003.

74. Garrett C, Liu DY, Clarke GN, et al: Automated semen analysis: "Zona pellucida preferred" sperm morphometry and straight-line velocity are related to pregnancy rate in subfertile couples. Hum Reprod 18:1643–1649, 2003.

75. Jones DM, Kovacs GT, Harrison L, et al: Immobilization of sperm by condoms and their components. Clin Reprod Fertil 4:367–372, 1986.

76. Kovacs GT, Newman GB, Henson GL: The postcoital test: What is normal? Br Med J 1:818, 1978.

77. Mallidis C, Howard EJ, Baker HWG: Variation of semen quality in normal men. Int J Androl 14:99–107, 1991.

78. Liu DY, Baker HWG: Tests of human sperm function and fertilization in vitro. Fertil Steril 58:465–483, 1992.

79. Liu DY, Garrett C, Baker HWG: Clinical application of sperm-oocyte interaction tests in vitro fertilization-embryo transfer and intracytoplasmic sperm injection. Fertil Steril 82:1251–1263, 2004.

80. Burkman LJ, Coddington CC, Franken DR, et al: The hemizona assay (HZA): Development of a diagnostic test for the binding of human spermatozoa to the human hemizona pellucida to predict fertilization potential. Fertil Steril 49:688–697, 1988.

81. Liu DY, Baker HWG: Disordered acrosome reaction of sperm bound to the zona pellucida: A newly discovered sperm defect with reduced sperm-zona pellucida penetration and reduced fertilization in vitro. Hum Reprod 9:1694–1700, 1994.

82. MacLeod J, Gold R: The male factor in fertility and infertility. VI. Semen quality and certain other factors in relation to ease of conception. Fertil Steril 4:10–33, 1953.

83. Ombelet W, Bosmans E, Janssen M, et al: Semen parameters in a fertile versus subfertile population: A need for change in the interpretation of semen testing. Hum Reprod 12:987–993, 1997.

84. Slama R, Eustache F, Ducot B, et al: Time to pregnancy and semen parameters: A cross-sectional study among fertile couples from four European cities. Hum Reprod 17:503–515, 2002.

85. Andersen AG, Ziebe S, Jorgensen N, et al: Time to pregnancy in relation to semen quality assessed by CASA before and after sperm separation. Hum Reprod 17:173–177, 2002.

86. Zamboni L: The ultrastructural pathology of the spermatozoon as a cause of infertility: The role of electron microscopy in the evaluation of semen quality. Fertil Steril 48:711–734, 1987.

87. O'Bryan MK, Sebire K, Meinhardt A, et al: Tpx-1 is a component of the outer dense fibers and acrosome of rat spermatozoa. Mol Reprod Dev 58:116–125, 2001.

88. Wilton LJ, Temple-Smith PD, Baker HWG, et al: Human male infertility caused by degeneration and death of sperm in the epididymis. Fertil Steril 49:1052–1058, 1988.

89. Correa-Perez JR, Fernandez-Pelegrina R, Aslanis P, et al: Clinical management of men producing ejaculates characterized by high levels of dead sperm and altered seminal plasma factors consistent with epididymal necrospermia. Fertil Steril 81:1148–1150, 2004.

90. Mallidis C, Lim TC, Hill ST, et al: Necrospermia and chronic spinal cord injury. Fertil Steril 74:221–227, 2000.

91. Fang S, Baker HWG: Male infertility and adult polycystic kidney disease are associated with necrospermia. Fertil Steril 79:643–644, 2003.

92. Liu DY, Garrett C, Baker HWG: Low proportions of sperm can bind to the zona pellucida of human oocytes. Hum Reprod 18:2382–2389, 2003.

93. Garrett C, Baker HWG: New fully automated system for the morphometric analysis of human sperm heads. Fertil Steril 63:1306–1317, 1995.

94. Karpas AE, Matsumoto AM, Paulsen CA, et al: Elevated serum follicle-stimulating hormone levels in men with normal seminal fluid analyses. Fertil Steril 39:333–336, 1983.

95. Hauser R, Templesmith PD, Southwick GJ, et al: Fertility in cases of hypergonadotropic azoospermia. Fertil Steril 63:631–636, 1995.

96. Anawalt BD, Bebb RA, Matsumoto AM, et al: Serum inhibin B levels reflect Sertoli cell function in normal men and men with testicular dysfunction. J Clin Endocrinol Metab 81:3341–3345, 1996.

97. de Kretser DM, Hedger MP, Loveland KL, et al: Inhibins, activins and follistatin in reproduction. Hum Reprod Update 8:529–541, 2002.

98. Layman LC, Porto AL, Xie J, et al: FSH beta gene mutations in a female with partial breast development and a male sibling with normal puberty and azoospermia. J Clin Endocrinol Metab 87:3702–3707, 2002.

99. Giltay JC, Deege M, Blankenstein RA, et al: Apparent primary follicle-stimulating hormone deficiency is a rare cause of treatable male infertility. Fertil Steril 81:693–696, 2004.

100. Smyth CM, Bremner WJ: Klinefelter syndrome. Arch Intern Med 158:1309–1314, 1998.

101. Van Assche E, Bonduelle M, Tournaye H, et al: Cytogenetics of infertile men. Hum Reprod 11(Suppl 4):1–24, discussion 25–26, 1996.

102. Tournaye H, Staessen C, Liebaers I, et al: Testicular sperm recovery in nine 47,XXY Klinefelter patients. Hum Reprod 11:1644–1649, 1996.

103. Bourne H, Stern K, Clarke G, et al: Delivery of normal twins following the intracytoplasmic injection of spermatozoa from a patient with 47,Xxy Klinefelters-syndrome. Hum Reprod 12:2447–2450, 1997.

104. Staessen C, Tournaye H, Van Assche E, et al: PGD in 47,XXY Klinefelter's syndrome patients. Hum Reprod Update 9:319–330, 2003.

105. Bergere M, Wainer R, Nataf V, et al: Biopsied testis cells of four 47,XXY patients: Fluorescence in-situ hybridization and ICSI results. Hum Reprod 17:32–37, 2002.

106. Rives N, Simeon N, Milazzo JP, et al: Meiotic segregation of sex chromosomes in mosaic and non-mosaic XYY males: Case reports and review of the literature. Int J Androl 26:242–249, 2003.

107. Silber SJ, Repping S: Transmission of male infertility to future generations: Lessons from the Y chromosome. Hum Reprod Update 8:217–229, 2002.

108. Brugh VM 3rd, Maduro MR, Lamb DJ: Genetic disorders and infertility. Urol Clin North Am 30:143–152, 2003.

109. Mallidis C, Baker HWG: Fine needle tissue aspiration biopsy of the testis. Fertil Steril 61:367–375, 1994.

110. Watkins W, Nieto F, Bourne H, et al: Testicular and epididymal sperm in a microinjection program—Methods of retrieval and results. Fertil Steril 67:527–535, 1997.

111. de Kretser DM, Burger HG, Hudson B: The relationship between germinal cells and serum FSH levels in males with infertility. J Clin Endocrinol Metab 38:787–793, 1974.

112. Sousa M, Cremades N, Silva J, et al: Predictive value of testicular histology in secretory azoospermic subgroups and clinical outcome after microinjection of fresh and frozen-thawed sperm and spermatids. Hum Reprod 17:1800–1810, 2002.

113. Ragheb D, Higgins JL Jr: Ultrasonography of the scrotum: Technique, anatomy, and pathologic entities. J Ultrasound Med 21:171–185, 2002.

114. Fisch H, Kang YM, Johnson CW, et al: Ejaculatory duct obstruction. Curr Opin Urol 12:509–515, 2002.

115. Mazumdar S, Levine AS: Antisperm antibodies: Etiology, pathogenesis, diagnosis, and treatment. Fertil Steril 70:799–810, 1998.

116. Hellema HW, Rumke P: Sperm autoantibodies as a consequence of vasectomy. I. Within 1 year post-operation. Clin Exp Immunol 31:18–29, 1978.

117. Wang C, Baker HWG, Jennings MG, et al: Interaction between human cervical mucus and sperm surface

antibodies. Fertil Steril 44:484–488, 1985.

118. Isojima S, Kameda K, Tsuji Y, et al: Establishment and characterization of a human hybridoma secreting monoclonal antibody with high titers of sperm immobilizing and agglutinating activities against human seminal plasma. J Reprod Immunol 10:67–78, 1987.

119. Imade GE, Baker HWG, de Kretser DM, et al: Immunosuppressive activities in the seminal plasma of infertile men: Relationship to sperm antibodies and autoimmunity. Hum Reprod 12:256–262, 1997.

120. Liu DY, Clarke GN, Baker HWG: Inhibition of human sperm-zona pellucida and sperm-oolemma binding by antisperm antibodies. Fertil Steril 55:440–442, 1991.

121. Shibahara H, Shiraishi Y, Hirano Y, et al: Diversity of the inhibitory effects on fertilization by anti-sperm antibodies bound to the surface of ejaculated human sperm. Hum Reprod 18:1469–1473, 2003.

122. Rumke P, Van Amstel N, Messer EN, et al: Prognosis of fertility of men with sperm agglutinins in the serum. Fertil Steril 25:393–398, 1974.

123. Clarke GN, Bourne H, Baker HWG: Intracytoplasmic sperm injection for treating infertility associated with sperm autoimmunity. Fertil Steril 68:112–117, 1997.

124. Hendry WF, Hughes L, Scammell G, et al: Comparison of prednisolone and placebo in subfertile men with antibodies to spermatozoa. Lancet 335:85–88, 1990.

125. Bals-Pratsch M, Doren M, Karbowski B, et al: Cyclic corticosteroid immunosuppression is unsuccessful in the treatment of sperm antibody-related male infertility: A controlled study. Hum Reprod 7:99–104, 1992.

126. Skinner JA, Mann BS, Carrington RW, et al: Male infertility and avascular necrosis of the femoral head. Ann R Coll Surg Engl 86:15–17, 2004.

127. Hirsch IH, Sedor J, Kulp D, et al: Objective assessment of spermatogenesis in men with functional and anatomic obstruction of the genital tract. Int J Androl 17:29–34, 1994.

128. Baker HWG: Medical treatment for idiopathic male infertility: Is it curative or palliative? Baillieres Clin Obstet Gynaecol 11:673–689, 1997.

129. Schroeder-Printzen I, Diemer T, Weidner W: Vasovasostomy. Urol Int 70:101–107, 2003.

130. Baker G, Bourne H, Edgar DH: Sperm preparation techniques. In Gardner D, Weissman A, Howles C, Shoham Z (eds): Testbook of Assisted Reproductive Techniques Laboratory and Clinical Perspectives. London, Martin Dunitz, 2001, pp 77–87.

131. Sonksen J, Ohl DA: Penile vibratory stimulation and electroejaculation in the treatment of ejaculatory dysfunction. Int J Androl 25:324–332, 2002.

132. Kamischke A, Nieschlag E: Update on medical treatment of ejaculatory disorders. Int J Androl 25:333–344, 2002.

133. Lim TC, Mallidis C, Hill ST, et al: A simple technique to prevent retrograde ejaculation during assisted ejaculation. Paraplegia 32:142–149, 1994.

134. Mallidis C, Lim TC, Hill ST, et al: Collection of semen from men in acute phase of spinal cord injury. Lancet 343:1072–1073, 1994.

135. Mahadevan M, Leeton JF, Trounson AO: Noninvasive method of semen collection for successful artificial insemination in a case of retrograde ejaculation. Fertil Steril 36:243–247, 1981.

136. Wong WY, Thomas CM, Merkus JM, et al: Male factor subfertility: Possible causes and the impact of nutritional factors. Fertil Steril 73:435–442, 2000.

137. Nudell DM, Monoski MM, Lipshultz LI: Common medications and drugs: How they affect male fertility. Urol Clin North Am 29:965–973, 2002.

138. McGowan MP, Burger HG, Baker HWG, et al: The incidence of non-specific infection in the semen in fertile and sub-fertile males. Int J Androl 4:657–662, 1981.

139. Aitken RJ, Baker HWG: Seminal leukocytes—Passengers, terrorists or good Samaritans. Hum Reprod 10:1736–1739, 1995.

140. Weidner W, Krause W, Ludwig M: Relevance of male accessory gland infection for subsequent fertility with special focus on prostatitis. Hum Reprod Update 5:421–432, 1999.

141. Andrade-Rocha FT: *Ureaplasma urealyticum* and *Mycoplasma hominis* in men attending for routine semen analysis. Prevalence, incidence by age and clinical settings, influence on sperm characteristics, relationship with the leukocyte count and clinical value. Urol Int 71:377–381, 2003.

142. Meares E, Stamey T: Bacteriologic localisation patterns in bacterial prostatis and urethritis. Invest Urol 5:492–518, 1968.

143. Baker HWG, Straffon WG, McGowan MP, et al: A controlled trial of the use of erythromycin for men with asthenospermia. Int J Androl 7:383–388, 1984.

144. Comhaire FH, Rowe PJ, Farley TM: The effect of doxycycline in infertile couples with male accessory gland infection: A double blind prospective study. Int J Androl 9:91–98, 1986.

145. Hargreave TB: Varicocele: overview and commentary on the results of the World Health Organisation varicocele trial. In Waites GMH, Frick J, Baker HWG (eds): Current Advances in Andrology. Bologna, Monduzzi Editore, 1997, pp 31–44.

146. Sandlow J: Pathogenesis and treatment of varicoceles. Br Med J 328:967–968, 2004.

147. Evers JL, Collins JA: Assessment of efficacy of varicocele repair for male subfertility: A systematic review. Lancet 361:1849–1852, 2003.

148. Redmon JB, Carey P, Pryor JL: Varicocele—The most common cause of male factor infertility? Hum Reprod Update 8:53–58, 2002.

149. Penson DF, Paltiel AD, Krumholz HM, et al: The cost-effectiveness of treatment for varicocele related infertility. J Urol 168:2490–2494, 2002.

150. Comhaire F, Zalata A, Schoonjans F: Varicocele: Indications for treatment. Int J Androl 18(Suppl 2):67–71, 1995.

151. Hopps CV, Goldstein M, Schlegel PN: The diagnosis and treatment of the azoospermic patient in the age of intracytoplasmic sperm injection. Urol Clin North Am 29:895–911, 2002.

152. Asci R, Sarikaya S, Buyukalpelli R, et al: The outcome of varicocelectomy in subfertile men with an absent or atrophic right testis. Br J Urol 81:750–752, 1998.

153. Nilsson S, Edvinsson A, Nilsson B: Improvement of semen and pregnancy rate after ligation and division of the internal spermatic vein: Fact or fiction? Br J Urol 51:591–596, 1979.

154. Vermeulen A, Vandeweghe M: Improved fertility after varicocele correction: Fact or fiction? Fertil Steril 42:249–256, 1984.

155. Laven JS, Haans LC, Mali WP, et al: Effects of varicocele treatment in adolescents: A randomized study. Fertil Steril 58:756–762, 1992.

156. Nieschlag E, Hertle L, Fischedick A, et al: Update on treatment of varicocele: Counselling as effective as occlusion of the vena spermatica. Hum Reprod 13:2147–2150, 1998.

157. Madgar I, Weissenberg R, Lunenfeld B, et al: Controlled trial of high spermatic vein ligation for varicocele in infertile men. Fertil Steril 63:120–124, 1995.

158. Billings EL, Brown JB, Billings JJ, et al: Symptoms and hormonal changes accompanying ovulation. Lancet 1:282–284, 1972.

159. Bostofte E, Bagger P, Michael A, et al: Fertility prognosis for infertile men: Results of follow-up study of semen analysis in infertile men from two different populations evaluated by the Cox regression model. Fertil Steril 54:1100–1106, 1990.

160. Ayala C, Steinberger E, Smith DP: The influence of semen analysis parameters on the fertility potential of infertile couples. J Androl 17:718–725, 1996.

161. Snick HK, Snick TS, Evers JL, et al: The spontaneous pregnancy prognosis in untreated subfertile couples: The Walcheren primary care study. Hum Reprod 12:1582–1588, 1997.

162. Basso O, Olsen J, Bisanti L, et al: Repeating episodes of low fecundability. A multicentre European study. The European Study Group on Infertility and Subfecundity. Hum Reprod 12:1448–1453, 1997.

163. Zinaman MJ, Brown CC, Selevan SG, et al: Semen quality and human

fertility: A prospective study with healthy couples. J Androl 21:145–153, 2000.

164. Dunson DB, Baird DD, Colombo B: Increased infertility with age in men and women. Obstet Gynecol 103:51–56, 2004.

165. Anderson KM, Sharpe M, Rattray A, et al: Distress and concerns in couples referred to a specialist infertility clinic. J Psychosom Res 54:353–355, 2003.

166. Hjollund NH, Bonde JP, Henriksen TB, et al: Reproductive effects of male psychologic stress. Epidemiology 15:21–27, 2004.

167. Stanford JB, Smith KR, Dunson DB: Vulvar mucus observations and the probability of pregnancy. Obstet Gynecol 101:1285–1293, 2003.

168. Hassan MA, Killick SR: Negative lifestyle is associated with a significant reduction in fecundity. Fertil Steril 81:384–392, 2004.

169. Liu PY, Handelsman DJ: The present and future state of hormonal treatment for male infertility. Hum Reprod Update 9:9–23, 2003.

170. Crosignani PG, Rubin BL: Optimal use of infertility diagnostic tests and treatments. The ESHRE Capri Workshop Group. Hum Reprod 15:723–732, 2000.

171. Baker HWG, Kovacs GT: Spontaneous improvement in semen quality: regression towards the mean. Int J Androl 8:421–426, 1985.

172. Pandian Z, Bhattacharya S, Nikolaou D, et al: The effectiveness of IVF in unexplained infertility: A systematic Cochrane review. 2002. Hum Reprod 18:2001–2007, 2003.

173. Duran HE, Morshedi M, Kruger T, et al: Intrauterine insemination: A systematic review on determinants of success. Hum Reprod Update 8:373–384, 2002.

174. Palermo G, Joris H, Devroey P, et al: Pregnancies after intracytoplasmic injection of single spermatozoon into an oocyte. Lancet 340:17–18, 1992.

175. Harari O, Bourne H, McDonald M, et al: Intracytoplasmic sperm injection—A major advance in the management of severe male subfertility. Fertil Steril 64:360–368, 1995.

176. Devroey P, Van Steirteghem A: A review of ten years experience of ICSI. Hum Reprod Update 10:19–28, 2004.

177. Su LM, Palermo GD, Goldstein M, et al: Testicular sperm extraction with intracytoplasmic sperm injection for nonobstructive azoospermia: Testicular histology can predict success of sperm retrieval. J Urol 161:112–116, 1999.

178. Bohring C, Schroeder-Printzen I, Weidner W, et al: Serum levels of inhibin B and follicle-stimulating hormone may predict successful sperm retrieval in men with azoospermia who are undergoing testicular sperm extraction. Fertil Steril 78:1195–1198, 2002.

179. Bailly M, Guthauser B, Bergere M, et al: Effects of low concentrations of inhibin B on the outcomes of testicular sperm extraction and intracytoplasmic sperm injection. Fertil Steril 79:905–908, 2003.

180. Shah RS: Surgical and non-surgical methods of sperm retrieval. In Hansotia M, Desai S, Parihar M (eds): Advanced Infertility Management. New Delhi, Jaypee Brothers, 2002, pp 253–258.

181. Amer M, Ateyah A, Hany R, et al: Prospective comparative study between microsurgical and conventional testicular sperm extraction in non-obstructive azoospermia: Follow-up by serial ultrasound examinations. Hum Reprod 15:653–656, 2000.

182. Dardashti K, Williams RH, Goldstein M: Microsurgical testis biopsy: A novel technique for retrieval of testicular tissue. J Urol 163:1206–1207, 2000.

183. Vernaeve V, Tournaye H, Osmanagaoglu K, et al: Intracytoplasmic sperm injection with testicular spermatozoa is less successful in men with nonobstructive azoospermia than in men with obstructive azoospermia. Fertil Steril 79:529–533, 2003.

184. Hurst T, Lancaster P: Assisted Conception Australia and New Zealand 1999 and 2000. Assisted Conception Series, vol 6. no 6. Sydney, Australian Institute of Health and Welfare National Perinatal Statistics Unit, 2001, p 73.

185. Wright VC, Schieve LA, Reynolds MA, et al: Assisted reproductive technology surveillance—United States, 2000. MMWR Surveill Summ 52:1–16, 2003.

186. Nyboe Andersen A, Gianaroli L, Nygren KG: Assisted reproductive technology in Europe, 2000. Results generated from European registers by ESHRE. Hum Reprod 19:490–503, 2004.

187. Speirs AL, Baker HWG, Abdullah N: Analysis of factors affecting embryo implantation. Hum Reprod 11:187–191, 1996.

188. Tesarik J, Rienzi L, Ubaldi F, et al: Use of a modified intracytoplasmic sperm injection technique to overcome sperm-borne and oocyte-borne oocyte activation failures. Fertil Steril 78:619–624, 2002.

189. Pinborg A, Loft A, Schmidt L, et al: Maternal risks and perinatal outcome in a Danish national cohort of 1005 twin pregnancies: The role of in vitro fertilization. Acta Obstet Gynecol Scand 83:75–84, 2004.

190. ESHRE: Multiple gestation pregnancy. The ESHRE Capri Workshop Group. Hum Reprod 15:1856–1864, 2000.

191. Venn A, Watson L, Lumley J, et al: Breast and ovarian cancer incidence after infertility and in vitro fertilisation. Lancet 346:995–1000, 1995.

192. Alper MM: In vitro fertilization outcomes: Why doesn't anyone get it? Fertil Steril 81:514–516, 2004.

193. Min JK, Breheny SA, MacLachlan V, et al: What is the most relevant standard of success in assisted reproduction? The singleton, term gestation, live birth rate per cycle initiated: The BESST endpoint for assisted reproduction. Hum Reprod 19:3–7, 2004.

194. Evenson DP, Jost LK, Marshall D, et al: Utility of the sperm chromatin structure assay as a diagnostic and prognostic tool in the human fertility clinic. Hum Reprod 14:1039–1049, 1999.

195. Morris ID, Ilott S, Dixon L, et al: The spectrum of DNA damage in human sperm assessed by single cell gel electrophoresis (Comet assay) and its relationship to fertilization and embryo development. Hum Reprod 17:990–998, 2002.

196. Perreault SD, Aitken RJ, Baker HWG, et al: Integrating new tests of sperm genetic integrity into semen analysis: Breakout group discussion. Adv Exp Med Biol 518:253–268, 2003.

197. Apedaile AE, Garrett C, Liu DY, et al: Flow cytometry and microscopic acridine orange test: Relationship with standard semen analysis. Reprod Biomed Online 8:398–407, 2004.

198. O'Bryan MK, Murphy BF, Liu DY, et al: The use of anticlusterin monoclonal antibodies for the combined assessment of human sperm morphology and acrosome integrity. Hum Reprod 9:1490–1496, 1994.

199. Martin RH, Rademaker AW, Greene C, et al: A comparison of the frequency of sperm chromosome abnormalities in men with mild, moderate, and severe oligozoospermia. Biol Reprod 69:535–539, 2003.

200. Bonduelle M, Van Assche E, Joris H, et al: Prenatal testing in ICSI pregnancies: Incidence of chromosomal anomalies in 1586 karyotypes and relation to sperm parameters. Hum Reprod 17:2600–2614, 2002.

201. Sinclair KD, Young LE, Wilmut I, et al: In-utero overgrowth in ruminants following embryo culture: Lessons from mice and a warning to men. Hum Reprod 15(Suppl 5):68–86, 2000.

202. Doherty AS, Mann MR, Tremblay KD, et al: Differential effects of culture on imprinted H19 expression in the preimplantation mouse embryo. Biol Reprod 62:1526–1535, 2000.

203. Lucifero D, Chaillet JR, Trasler JM: Potential significance of genomic imprinting defects for reproduction and assisted reproductive technology. Hum Reprod Update 10:3–18, 2004.

204. Bruinsma F, Venn A, Lancaster P, et al: Incidence of cancer in children born after in-vitro fertilization. Hum Reprod 15:604–607, 2000.

205. Baker HWG: Marvellous ICSI: The viewpoint of a clinician. Int J Androl 21:249–252, 1998.

206. Schieve LA, Meikle SF, Ferre C, et al: Low and very low birth weight in infants conceived with use of assisted reproductive technology. N Engl J Med 346:731–737, 2002.

207. Hewitson L, Simerly CR, Schatten G: Fate of sperm components during assisted reproduction: Implications for infertility. Hum Fertil (Camb) 5:110–116, 2002.

208. Baker HWG: Is ICSI a safe therapeutic approach for severe male factor infertility? In Robaire B, Chemes H, Morales C (eds): Andrology in the 21st Century. Englewood, NJ, Medimond, 2001, pp 311–315.

209. Bowen JR, Gibson FL, Leslie GI, et al: Medical and developmental outcome at 1 year for children conceived by intracytoplasmic sperm injection. Lancet 351:1529–1534, 1998.

210. Bonduelle M, Ponjaert I, Steirteghem AV, et al: Developmental outcome at 2 years of age for children born after ICSI compared with children born after IVF. Hum Reprod 18:342–350, 2003.

211. Hansen M, Kurinczuk JJ, Bower C, et al: The risk of major birth defects after intracytoplasmic sperm injection and in vitro fertilization. N Engl J Med 346:725–730, 2002.

212. Kurinczuk JJ: Safety issues in assisted reproduction technology. From theory to reality—Just what are the data telling us about ICSI offspring health and future fertility and should we be concerned? Hum Reprod 18:925–931, 2003.

213. Barratt C, Cooke ID: Donor Insemination. Cambridge: Cambridge University Press, 1993.

214. McGowan MP, Baker HWG, Kovacs GT, et al: Selection of high fertility donors for artificial insemination programmes. Clin Reprod Fertil 2:269–274, 1983.

215. Clarke GN, Bourne H, Hill P, et al: Artificial insemination and in-vitro fertilization using donor spermatozoa—A report on 15 years of experience. Hum Reprod 12:722–726, 1997.

216. Kovacs GT, Mushin D, Kane H, et al: A controlled study of the psycho-social development of children conceived following insemination with donor semen. Hum Reprod 8:788–790, 1993.

217. Daniels KR: Toward a family-building approach to donor insemination. J Obstet Gynaecol Can 24:17–21, 2002.

218. Ferrara I, Balet R, Grudzinskas JG: Intrauterine insemination with frozen donor sperm. Pregnancy outcome in relation to age and ovarian stimulation regime. Hum Reprod 17:2320–2324, 2002.

219. Thompson ST: Prevention of male infertility: An update. Urol Clin North Am 21:365–376, 1994.

220. Jequier AM: Vasectomy related infertility: A major and costly medical problem. Hum Reprod 13:1757–1759, 1998.

221. Anserini P, Chiodi S, Spinelli S, et al: Semen analysis following allogeneic bone marrow transplantation. Additional data for evidence-based counselling. Bone Marrow Transplant 30:447–451, 2002.

222. Brougham MF, Kelnar CJ, Sharpe RM, et al: Male fertility following childhood cancer: Current concepts and future therapies. Asian J Androl 5:325–337, 2003.

223. Arnon J, Meirow D, Lewis-Roness H, et al: Genetic and teratogenic effects of cancer treatments on gametes and embryos. Hum Reprod Update 7:394–403, 2001.

224. Audrins P, Holden CA, McLachlan RI, et al: Semen storage for special purposes at Monash IVF from 1977 to 1997. Fertil Steril 72:179–181, 1999.

225. Thomson AB, Campbell AJ, Irvine DC, et al: Semen quality and spermatozoal DNA integrity in survivors of childhood cancer: A case-control study. Lancet 360:361–367, 2002.

226. Hovatta O: Cryopreservation of testicular tissue in young cancer patients. Hum Reprod Update 7:378–383, 2001.

227. Brinster RL: Germline stem cell transplantation and transgenesis. Science 296:2174–2176, 2002.

# Sexual Dysfunction in Men

## Shalender Bhasin and Wayne J. G. Hellstrom

Increasing recognition of the importance of sexual health, powerful demographic trend toward aging of human populations, and availability of effective, oral medications for the treatment of erectile dysfunction in men have contributed to growing interest in issues of men's health, including sexual dysfunction. In a landmark statement, the World Health Organization recognized the important contribution of sexual health to men's quality of life, when it declared sexual health to be a fundamental right of human beings. In a nationwide survey, individuals experiencing low sexual desire or erectile dysfunction (ED) were significantly more likely to report low physical and emotional satisfaction, and low general happiness in their lives than men without sexual problems[1]; thus, sexual dysfunction in men is a significant contributor to distress and impaired quality of life.[2] It is, therefore, ironic that most men with sexual dysfunction are either undiagnosed or suboptimally treated. For instance, Laumann and colleagues[1] found that only 1 out of 10 men who had participated in the National Health and Social Life Survey (NHSLS) and experienced ED had sought medical attention for it. In another survey,[3] 74% of men with ED indicated that they were embarrassed to talk to their doctors about this problem, and another 12% believed that ED was a normal part of human aging. A high index of suspicion, appropriate diagnostic evaluation, and treatment of ED are important for several reasons. ED is often a manifestation of a systemic disorder such as atherosclerotic heart disease, diabetes mellitus, or hypertension, and evaluation may uncover these underlying disorders.[4,5] Second, ED can be effectively treated medically in a vast majority of patients. Third, the patients are often reluctant to bring up this issue, even though they may be experiencing significant distress and relationship difficulties because of ED.

Although the term *sexual dysfunction* is sometimes erroneously used interchangeably with erectile dysfunction, the two are not the same; sexual dysfunction is a global term that includes a wide array of sexual disorders that interfere with an individual's ability to enjoy sexual satisfaction and that cause personal distress.[6,7] In contrast, erectile dysfunction, previously referred to as impotence, is the inability of the man to attain and/or maintain an erection sufficient for satisfactory sexual performance.[8] As the most widely used classification of sexual dysfunction defines the clinical disorder in terms of the specific phase of sexual response cycle in which the individual is experiencing problems, a general understanding of the sexual response cycle is helpful in identifying the subcategories of sexual dysfunction.

## HUMAN SEXUAL RESPONSE CYCLE AND THE FOUR CATEGORIES OF SEXUAL DISORDERS

William Masters and Virginia E. Johnson,[9] in a pioneering effort, described four phases of the physiologic response to sexual stimulation in humans: the excitement phase, the plateau phase, the orgasmic phase, and the resolution phase. During the excitation phase, the heart and breathing rates increase, blood pressure rises, nipples become erect, penis achieves varying degrees of erection, the testes are drawn up, and the skin may undergo a sex flush.[9] This is followed by the plateau phase in which heart rate increases further, sexual pleasure increases, bladder sphincter closes, the muscles at the base of the penis contract rhythmically, and men begin to secrete a small amount of seminal fluid. Achievement of orgasm releases the sexual tension and is associated with contractions of the pelvic muscles and anal sphincter, ejaculation of seminal fluid, and a perception of intense pleasure. The resolution phase is characterized by a period of muscle relaxation, lowering of heart rate and blood pressure, loss of penile erection, and entry into a refractory period in which men are unable to achieve orgasm again.[9]

As abnormalities can exist in each of these phases of the sexual response cycle, there are four categories of sexual disorders[10] (Table 173-1):

1. Hypoactive sexual desire disorder
2. Erectile dysfunction
3. Ejaculatory and orgasmic disorders
4. Disorders of pain

## HYPOACTIVE SEXUAL DESIRE DISORDER

Hypoactive sexual desire disorder is the persistent or recurrent deficiency (or absence) of sexual fantasies and desire for sexual activity that causes marked distress or interpersonal difficulty, and which is not better explained by another disorder, direct physiologic effects of a substance (drug, medication), or general medical condition.[11] On the other hand, sexual aversion disorder refers to the aversion to and/or avoidance of direct genital sexual contact with a partner that causes marked distress or interpersonal difficulty, and which is not better explained by another disorder. A diagnosis of hypoactive sexual desire disorder is appropriate *only* if the person reports "distress or interpersonal difficulty" due to low sexual

**Table 173-1** Classification of Sexual Dysfunction

| Category Disorder | Definition | Specific Clinical Disorders |
|---|---|---|
| Hypoactive sexual desire disorder | Hypoactive sexual desire disorder is the persistent or recurrent deficiency (or absence) of sexual fantasies and desire for sexual activity that causes marked distress or interpersonal difficulty, and which is not better explained by another disorder, direct physiologic effects of a substance (drug, medication), or general medical condition | Disorders of diminished libido; sexual aversion disorder; disorders of increased libido |
| Erectile problems | The consistent or recurrent inability to attain and/or maintain a penile erection sufficient for sexual performance | Erectile dysfunction; priapism, erectile deformity |
| Ejaculatory and orgasmic disorders | Persistent or recurrent difficulty in ejaculating or in achieving orgasm that causes distress and is not explained by another disorder | Premature ejaculation, delayed ejaculation, retrograde ejaculation, inability to ejaculate, failure to achieve and orgasm |
| Disorders of pelvic pain | Persistent or recurrent pelvic pain that interferes with sexual satisfaction and causes distress | Peyronie's disease, pelvic pain of known or unknown origin |

desire.[12–17] Low sexual desire is not necessarily pathologic and, in some circumstances, may be an adaptation to relationship and differentiation issues. For instance, low sexual desire in an individual whose partner or spouse has a serious medical illness may be an appropriate adaptation. Also, "high desire" and "low desire" are different coordinates in the complex geometry of a sexual relationship; these coordinates may change during different phases of an individual's life and relationships.[12–17]

The incidence and prevalence rates of hypoactive sexual desire disorders are unknown. Prevalence is estimated at 5% in men and 22% in women[18]; prevalence increases with age.[15] In addition, hypoactive sexual desire may coexist in men presenting with other sexual disorders.[15] Hypoactive sexual desire disorder is often a multifactorial disorder that can result from androgen deficiency,[19–24] as an adverse effect of medications (selective serotonin reuptake inhibitors [SSRIs], antiandrogens, gonadotropin-releasing hormone [GnRH] analogues, antihypertensives, cancer chemotherapeutic agents, anticonvulsants), systemic illness, depression and other psychological problems secondary to other causes of sexual dysfunction, fear of humiliation,[25,26] or relationship and differentiation problems. Evaluation may lead to detection of (treatable) androgen deficiency. It is important to evaluate and diagnose hypoactive sexual desire disorders because the evaluation may lead to the identification of androgen deficiency or a systemic illness that may have adverse health consequences. Also, hypoactive sexual desire disorder can lead to emotional gridlock and cessation of physical affection between the partners, and can contribute to ED. Low sexual desire may impede or reduce effectiveness of treatments for other sexual dysfunctions.

A structured interview of the couple is the key to determining whether the patient has ED or a sexual desire problem as the primary problem, and whether the couple has a relationship problem. A detailed history and physical examination to rule out systemic illness, depression, and use of drugs is an important first step. Although in theory, the use of self-reported questionnaires can be helpful, the utility and validity of these self-report instruments in clinical practice has not been tested rigorously. Androgen deficiency is an important, treatable cause of hypoactive sexual desire disorder, and should be excluded by measuring serum total testosterone levels.

## ERECTILE DYSFUNCTION

*Sexual dysfunction* is a more general term that also includes libidinal, orgasmic, and ejaculatory dysfunction, in addition to the inability to attain or maintain penile erection.[27] Erectile dysfunction, previously referred to as impotence, is the inability of the male to attain and/or maintain an erection sufficient for satisfactory sexual intercourse.

## PREVALENCE AND INCIDENCE RATES

The current estimates of the prevalence of erectile dysfunction in men are based largely on the results of two cross-sectional studies that used probability sampling techniques, namely the Massachusetts Male Aging Study (MMAS)[28–30] and the NHSLS.[1,31] The MMAS was a cross-sectional, community-based epidemiologic survey that used a random sample of 1709 men, 40 to 70 years of age, in the greater Boston area, who were surveyed first between 1987 and 1989.[28,29] Approximately 50% of these men were resurveyed between 1995 and 1997.[29] This survey revealed a surprisingly high prevalence of erectile dysfunction in men: 52% of men between the ages of 40 and 70 were affected by erectile dysfunction to some degree, 17.2% of surveyed men reported minimal erectile dysfunction, 25.2% moderate erectile dysfunction, and 9.6% complete erectile dysfunction. The NHSLS was a national probability survey of English-speaking Americans, 18 to 59 years of age, living in the United States in 1992.[1,31] In this survey, 7% of men between 18 and 29 years of age, 9% between 30 and 39 years of age, 11% between 40 and 45 years, and 18% between 50 and 59 years reported difficulty in obtaining or maintaining erections.

These two landmark studies and data from several other studies are in agreement that erectile dysfunction is a common problem affecting 20 to 30 million men in the United States alone.[1,28,31,32] The prevalence of erectile dysfunction increases with age; it affects less than 10% of men younger than 45 years of age, but 75% of men over 80 years of age.[28] Men suffering from other medical problems, such as hypertension, diabetes, cardiovascular disease, and end-stage renal disease, have a significantly higher prevalence of erectile dysfunction than healthy men.[27,28]

Longitudinal data on the incidence rates of ED in men are somewhat limited.[30] In the MMAS, the crude incidence rate of ED in white men, 40 to 70 years of age, who were living in the Boston area was 25.9 cases per thousand man-years.[33–37] The incidence rates increased from 12.4 cases per thousand man-years for men 40 to 49 years of age to 29.8 cases per thousand man-years for men 50 to 59 years of age and 46.4 per thousand man-years for men 60 to 69 years of age.[29] In another study, incidence rates were derived from a survey of men who were seen at a preventive medicine clinic between 1987 and 1991. The incidence rates of ED in this study were fewer than 3 cases per thousand man-years among men younger than 45 years of age and 52 cases per thousand man-years among men 65 years of age or older. Based on these estimates of incidence rates, it is likely that there are 600,000 to 700,000 new cases of erectile dysfunction each year in the United States alone. McKinlay predicts that the worldwide prevalence of erectile dysfunction will nearly double in the next 30 years, increasing from 152 million affected men in 1995 to an estimated 322 million men in 2025.[33]

## THE REGULATION OF SEXUAL FUNCTION AND THE PHYSIOLOGY OF PENILE ERECTION

Sexual function is a complex, multicomponent biologic process that comprises central mechanisms for regulation of libido and arousability, as well as local mechanisms for the generation of penile tumescence, rigidity, orgasm, and ejaculation.

### Regulation of Libido

*Webster's New World Dictionary* defines libido as "sexual urge, psychic energy comprising the positive loving instincts and manifested variously at different stages of personality development." The term *libido* is frequently used interchangeably with sexual desire, but libido is a more complex construct, involving sexual thoughts, fantasies, attentiveness to erotic stimuli, and sex-seeking behavior. Although sexual desire in men and women is affected by sense of well-being, satisfaction with relationship, sexual identity, and differentiation issues, and by the occurrence of comorbidities, testosterone is an important regulator of libido. Although androgen-deficient men can achieve penile erections, their overall sexual activity is decreased.[38-43] In a series of pioneering experiments, Davidson and colleagues[41,42] demonstrated that compared to eugonadal men, hypogonadal men had lower self-reported sexual activity, feelings, and thoughts, and fewer spontaneous erections. When hypogonadal men were shown erotic pictures and videos, however, they were able to achieve normal erections. Testosterone replacement for hypogonadal men increased sexual feelings and thoughts, overall sexual activity scores, and the number of spontaneous erections, but did not change erectile response to visual erotic stimulus.[42] Davidson's experiments led to the prevalent dogma that spontaneous, but not stimulus-induced, erections are testosterone dependent, and that testosterone stimulates sexual thoughts and feelings. The concept that libido is testosterone dependent and the local mechanisms for penile erection are androgen independent may be simplistic, however. There is emerging evidence that testosterone is a regulator of nitric oxide synthase activity in the cavernosal smooth muscle.[44,45] Therefore, it is possible that physiologically normal testosterone concentrations might be required for optimum penile rigidity. Orgasm and ejaculation are not androgen dependent and can occur without a full penile erection.

### Mechanisms of Penile Erection

The essential processes that result in penile erection include relaxation of cavernosal smooth muscle, increased blood flow into cavernosal sinuses, and venous occlusion resulting in penile engorgement and rigidity.[46-50] Normal penile erection requires coordinated involvement of intact central and peripheral nervous systems, corpora cavernosa and spongiosa, as well as a normal arterial blood supply and venous drainage.[46-50]

The neural input to the penis is conveyed through sympathetic (T11–L2), parasympathetic (S2–S4), and somatic nerves. Sympathetic and parasympathetic fibers converge in the inferior hypogastric plexus where the autonomic input to the penis is integrated and communicated to the penis through cavernosal nerves. In general, parasympathetic input is proerectile and sympathetic input is inhibitory. The stimuli from the perineum and lower urinary tract are carried to the penis through the sacral reflex arc. Several brain regions including the amygdala, medial preoptic area, paraventricular nucleus of the hypothalamus, and periaqueductal gray matter act coordinately to affect penile erections. The medial preoptic area of the hypothalamus serves as the integration site for the central nervous system control of erections; it receives sensory input from the amygdala and sends impulses to the

paraventricular nuclei of the hypothalamus and the periaqueductal gray matter. Neurons in paraventricular nuclei project on to the thoracolumbar and sacral nuclei associated with erections.

The pudendal artery, a branch of the hypogastric artery, divides into cavernosal, dorsal penile, and bulbourethral arteries. The cavernosal arteries and their branches, the helicine arteries, provide blood flow to the corpora cavernosa.[50] Dilatation of the helicine arteries increases the blood flow and pressure in the cavernosal sinuses (Fig. 173-1).[46,47]

Relaxation of the cavernosal smooth muscle that surrounds the cavernosal sinuses, along with increased blood flow, results in pooling of blood in the cavernosal spaces and penile engorgement. The expanding corpora cavernosa compress the venules against the rigid tunica albuginea, restricting the venous outflow from the cavernosal spaces. This facilitates entrapment of blood in the cavernosal sinuses and achievement of a rigid erection.[46]

The erectile state of the penis is determined by the tone of the corporal smooth muscle cells.[51] When the cavernosal smooth muscle cells are relaxed, the tone is low and the penis is engorged with blood and erect. Conversely, when the cavernosal smooth muscle tone is high, there is predominance of sympathetic neural activity, and the penis is flaccid. The smooth muscle tone in the corpora cavernosa is maintained by agonist-stimulated release of intracellular calcium into the cytoplasm and an influx of calcium through membrane channels (Fig. 173-2). An increase in intracellular calcium through its binding to calmodulin activates myosin light-chain kinase resulting in phosphorylation of myosin light chain, actin-myosin interactions, and muscle contraction. The transmem-

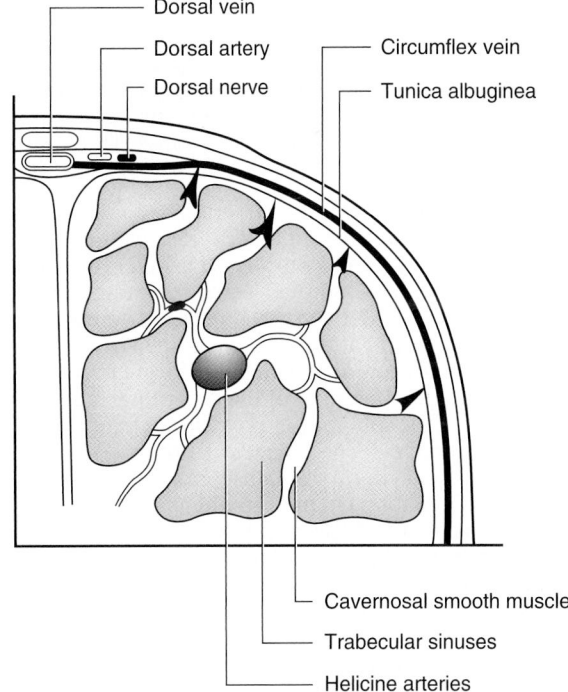

***Figure 173-1*** Penile circulation and anatomy. Penis contains two corpora cavernosa that are made up of trabecular spaces surrounded by cavernosal smooth muscle. The cavernosal arteries and their branches, the helicine arteries, provide blood flow to corpora cavernosa. The sensory innervation to the penis is supplied by the dorsal nerve. The relaxation of cavernosal smooth muscle and increased blood flow result in engorgement of the sinusoidal spaces in the corpora cavernosa. As the corpora cavernosa expand against tunica albuginea, the venous return from the penis is occluded, resulting in entrapment of blood; this imparts rigidity to the enlarged penis. (Adapted and modified from Lue TF: Erectile dysfunction. N Engl J Med 342:1802–1813, 2000.)

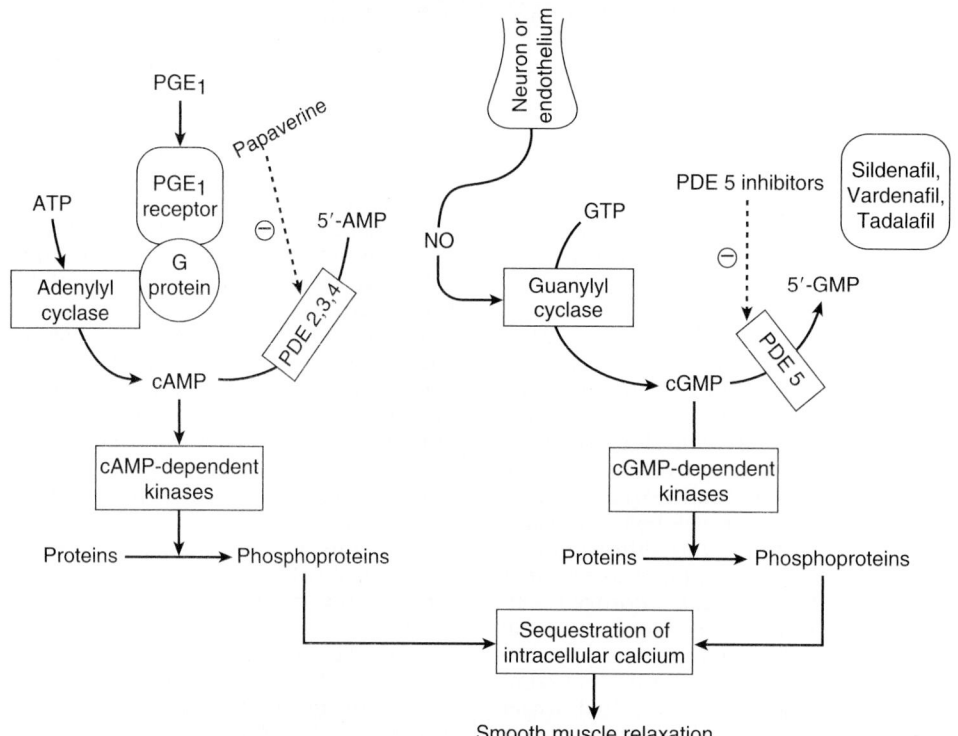

*Figure 173-2* Biochemical mechanisms of penile erection and sites of action of pharmacologic therapies for erectile dysfunction. Penile erections occur as a consequence of cavernosal smooth muscle relaxation, increased blood flow to the penis, and entrapment of blood within the penis. Cavernosal smooth muscle relaxation is regulated by intracellular cAMP and cGMP. These intracellular second messengers, by activating specific protein kinases, cause phosphorylation of specific proteins, resulting in sequestration of intracellular calcium. The resulting decrease in intracellular calcium concentrations causes smooth muscle relaxation. cGMP and cAMP are degraded by a class of enzymes called phosphodiesterases. cAMP is degraded by phosphodiesterase isoforms 2, 3, and 4, whereas cGMP is degraded by phosphodiesterase isoform 5. Sildenafil, vardenafil, and tadalafil are relatively specific inhibitors of phosphodiesterase isoform 5. Nitric oxide, a neurotransmitter, released by nonadrenergic, noncholinergic neurons, stimulates guanylyl cyclase and increases the amount of intracellular cGMP. Prostaglandin $E_1$ (PGE$_1$), by binding to PGE$_1$ receptor stimulates adenylyl cyclase and increases the intracellular concentrations of cAMP. Papaverine, by inhibiting PDE2, -3, and -4 increases the intracellular concentrations of cAMP. ATP, adenosine triphosphate; cAMP, cyclic adenosine monophosphate; cGMP, cyclic guanosine monophosphate; GTP, guanine triphosphate; NO, nitric oxide; PDE, phosphodiesterase. (Adapted and modified from Corbin JD, Francis SH: Molecular biology and pharmacology of PDE5-inhibitor therapy for erectile dysfunction. J Androl 24[Suppl]:S38–S41, 2003.)

brane and intracellular calcium flux in the cavernosal smooth muscle cells is regulated by a number of cellular processes and signaling molecules such as potassium flux through potassium channels, connexin-43-derived gap junctions, norepinephrine, prostaglandin $E_1$ (PGE$_1$), and nitric oxide (see Fig. 173-2).

Movement of potassium ions across the membrane determines the membrane potential of the cavernosal smooth muscle cells; at least four subtypes of potassium channels mediate this potassium efflux.[51] The adjacent smooth cells are interconnected in a syncytium through connexin-43-derived gap junctions.[52–55] Therefore, changes in potassium channel activity in one myocyte affect the membrane potential of adjacent cells, resulting in rapid transmission of electrical and biochemical signaling throughout the syncytium[52–55] (see Fig. 173-2).

The vascular smooth muscle contraction in the corpora cavernosa is regulated by the noradrenergic pathway. Norepinephrine binds to adrenergic receptors, resulting in generation of diacyl glycerol and inositol triphosphate. Diacyl glycerol activates protein kinase C, which inhibits potassium channels, while inositol triphosphate (IP3) increases intracellular calcium and calcium influx through the membrane. The net increase in intracellular calcium promotes actin-myosin interaction, resulting in smooth muscle contraction.

Prostaglandin $E_1$ results in generation of cyclic adenosine monophosphate (cAMP), which activates protein kinase A. Activated protein kinase A stimulates potassium channels resulting in potassium efflux from the cell. In addition, protein kinase A–mediated processes also result in a net decrease in intracellular calcium, favoring smooth muscle cell relax-

ation (see Fig. 173-2). Nitric oxide through activation of intracellular cyclic guanosine monophosphate (cGMP) also decreases intracellular calcium and K+ efflux.

The relaxation of the cavernosal smooth muscle trabeculae is under the regulation of the autonomic nervous system.[46–50,56,57] A number of cholinergic, adrenergic, and noradrenergic noncholinergic mediators regulate cavernosal smooth muscle relaxation. The noradrenergic noncholinergic mediators include vasoactive intestinal peptide, calcitonin gene-related peptide, and nitric oxide. Nitric oxide is derived from the nerve terminals innervating the corpora cavernosa, endothelial lining of penile arteries, and cavernosal sinuses,[46–50,56,57] and is an important biochemical regulator of cavernosal smooth muscle relaxation. Nitric oxide also induces arterial dilatation. The actions of nitric oxide on the cavernosal smooth muscle and the arterial blood flow are mediated through the activation of guanylyl cyclase and the production of cGMP.[46–50,56–58] The latter acts as an intracellular second messenger and causes smooth muscle relaxation by lowering intracellular calcium.[50]

A class of enzymes called cyclic nucleotide phosphodiesterases degrades cGMP and cAMP into inactive forms, and plays an important role in the physiologic control of erection (see Fig. 173-2). Currently, researchers have identified at least 13 different isoforms of cyclic nucleotide phosphodiesterases. These isoforms are widely distributed throughout the body; the predominant isoform of this enzyme in the cavernosal smooth muscle is cyclic nucleotide phosphodiesterase type 5 (PDE5).[46,48,50] Hydrolysis of cGMP by this enzyme results in reversal of the smooth muscle relaxation and reversal of penile erection. Sildenafil, vardenafil, and tadalafil are potent and selective inhibitors of the activity of PDE5, preventing breakdown of cGMP and thereby enhancing penile erection.[59]

## PHYSIOLOGIC, LIFESTYLE, AND PSYCHOSOCIAL CORRELATES AND RISK FACTORS FOR ERECTILE DYSFUNCTION IN MEN

Advancing age is an important risk factor for ED in men: Less than 10% of men younger than 40 and more than 50% of men older than 70 have ED.[1,28,31,32] In both the MMAS and the NHSLS, the prevalence of ED increased with each decade of life.[1,31,32] Similarly, in the Cologne Male Survey,[60] an epidemiologic survey of male sexuality in Germany, there was a remarkable age-related increase in the prevalence of erectile dysfunction from 2.3% in men 30 years of age to 53.4% in men 80 years of age.

Epidemiologic studies indicate that in addition to age, diabetes mellitus, hypertension, medication use, cardiovascular disease, and depression are significant risk factors for ED.[31,32,60] Among the chronic diseases associated with ED, diabetes mellitus is the most important risk factor. In the MMAS, the age-adjusted risk of complete ED was three times higher in men with a history of treated diabetes mellitus than in those without a history of diabetes mellitus.[32] Fifty percent of men with diabetes mellitus will experience ED sometime in the course of their illness. In the MMAS, treated heart disease, treated hypertension, and hyperlipidemia were associated with significantly increased risk of ED.[28,32] Among men with treated heart disease and hypertension, the probability of ED was more than two times greater for smokers than for nonsmokers. Smoking also increases the risk of ED in men taking medications for cardiovascular diseases. Cardiovascular disorders, including hypertension, stroke, coronary artery disease, and peripheral vascular disease, are all associated with increased risk of ED.

Men with severe depression have a greater prevalence of ED than men who are not depressed or those with mild depression.[28] Ninety percent of men with severe depression experience moderate or complete ED compared with 25% of men with mild depression.

Recent epidemiologic surveys have also emphasized lower urinary tract symptoms (LUTS) as a significant risk factor for ED.[60,61] A large-scale, multinational survey conducted in the United States and six European countries systematically investigated the relationship between LUTS and sexual dysfunction in older men.[61] Sexual disorders and their bothersomeness were strongly related to both age and severity of LUTS. The presence and severity of LUTS were independent risk factors for sexual dysfunction in older men, after adjusting for comorbidities such as diabetes, hypertension, cardiac disease, and hypercholesterolemia.[61] These results highlight the clinical importance of evaluating LUTS in patients with sexual dysfunction, and the need to consider sexual issues in the management of patients with benign prostatic hypertrophy.

Several reviews have emphasized the relationship of prescription medications and the occurrence of ED.[10,17,48] In the MMAS, the use of antihypertensives, cardiac medication, and oral hypoglycemic drugs was associated with an increased risk of ED.[28,32] Thiazide diuretics and psychotropic drugs used in the treatment of depression may be the most common drugs associated with ED, simply because of the high prevalence of their use. A variety of drugs, however, including almost all antihypertensives, digoxin, histamine-2 receptor antagonists, anticholinergics, cytotoxic agents, and androgen antagonists, have been implicated in the pathophysiology of ED.

## EVALUATION OF PATIENTS WITH ERECTILE DYSFUNCTION

### History

The diagnostic workup of the patient with erectile dysfunction should start with an evaluation of general health.[48,62]

General medical history should be directed at identifying etiologic factors as well as factors that might affect the selection and response to therapy (Table 173-2). The presence of diabetes mellitus, coronary artery disease, peripheral vascular disease, and hypertension may suggest a vascular cause. History of stroke, spinal cord or back injury, multiple sclerosis, or dementia may point to a neurologic disorder. Also relevant are history of pelvic trauma, prostate surgery, or priapism. Social history must include ascertainment of tobacco use and recreational drug abuse, particularly of cocaine, marijuana, and alcohol. Information about medications, particularly antihypertensives, antiandrogens, antidepressants, and antispsychotic drugs is important because almost a quarter of all cases of impotence can be attributed to medications. Psychiatric illnesses such as depression or psychosis or drugs used to treat these disorders might be associated with sexual dysfunction.

---

**Table 173-2  Diagnostic Evaluation of Erectile Dysfunction**

**HISTORY**

A. Ascertain psychosexual history of:
 1. Sexual beliefs and practices
 2. The strength of marital relationship and marital discord
 3. Depression
 4. Stress
 5. Performance anxiety

B. Ascertain etiologic factors, such as:
 1. The presence of diabetes mellitus, hypertension, end-stage renal disease, peripheral vascular disease
 2. History of spinal cord injury, stroke, or Alzheimer's disease
 3. Prostate or pelvic surgery
 4. Pelvic injury
 5. Concomitant medications such as antihypertensives; antidepressants; antipsychotics; antiandrogens such as flutamide, casadex, cyproterone acetate, and cimetidine; inhibitors of androgen production such as ketoconazole and GnRH agonists
 6. The use of recreational drugs such as alcohol, cocaine, opiates, and tobacco

C. Ascertain factors that might affect choice of therapy and the patient's response to it, such as:
 1. Coexisting coronary artery disease and its symptoms and severity
 2. The use of nitrates for angina
 3. The use of $\alpha$-blockers
 4. Exercise tolerance
 5. The use of vasodilators for hypertension or congestive heart failure
 6. The use of drugs that affect metabolism, such as erythromycin, ketoconazole, and itraconazole

**PHYSICAL EXAMINATION**

 1. Ascertain signs of androgen deficiency such as loss of secondary sex characteristics, eunuchoidal proportions, small testicular volume, or breast enlargement
 2. Neurologic findings of spinal cord lesion, previous stroke, or peripheral neuropathy; genital and peripheral sensation
 3. Palpation of femoral and pedal pulses, and evidence of lower extremity ischemia
 4. Penile examination to exclude Peyronie's disease

**LABORATORY EVALUATION**

Tests that should be performed in most men with ED
 1. Blood counts and chemistries
 2. Fasting blood glucose
 3. Plasma lipids
 4. Serum total testosterone levels*

Tests that may be indicated in a small subset of men, but are not necessary in all patients with ED
 1. Brachial penile blood pressure index
 2. Intracavernosal injection of vasodilator
 3. Duplex ultrasonography
 4. Pelvic arteriography
 5. Cavernosography
 6. Penile tumescence recording

---

ED, erectile dysfunction; GnRH, gonadotropin-releasing hormone.

A detailed sexual history including the nature of relationships, partner expectations, situational erectile failure, performance anxiety, and marital discord should be elicited[4,48] (see Table 173-2). It is important to distinguish between inability to achieve erection, changes in sexual desire, failure to achieve orgasm and ejaculation, and dissatisfaction with the sexual relationship. The physician should inquire about the onset, duration, quality, and duration of erections and presence of nocturnal and early morning erections. The presence of nocturnal or early morning erections with a full bladder indicates that the neurologic and vascular parthways are intact, raising the possibility of psychosocial factors as a basis for the erectile dysfunction. Not uncommonly, psychogenic factors may be rooted in events from the past such as restrictive upbringing, traumatic early sexual experience including sexual abuse, lack of trust, and internal conflict over sexual pleasure because of religious or misguided beliefs.

## Physical Examination

A directed physical examination should assess secondary sex characteristics, the presence or absence of breast enlargement, and testicular volume. An evaluation of femoral and pedal pulses can provide clues to the presence of peripheral vascular disease (see Table 173-2). The neurologic examination focuses on the presence of motor weakness, perineal sensation, anal sphincter tone, and bulbocavernosus reflex. The examination of the penis evaluates for any unusual curvature, palpable plaques, or superficial lesions.

## Self-Reporting Questionnaires

In the last decade, there has been a general shift in most male sexual dysfunction clinics away from expensive, time-consuming, and invasive techniques (e.g., dynamic infusion cavernosometry, penile duplex Doppler ultrasonography, and Rigiscan studies) and toward the use of simple, noninvasive, self-reporting questionnaires. These questionnaires are useful because, for a variety of reasons, many men with ED do not voluntarily come forward to their physicians and state their sexual complaints. Many men with ED feel embarrassed, while others consider ED an inevitable concomitant of the aging process. Some physicians themselves feel uncomfortable discussing issues of such a personal nature; this creates an atmosphere that is not conducive to effective communication. These self-reporting questionnaires can help break the ice and facilitate communication. These instruments are widely available, easy to complete, and can complement or enhance the workup of sexual dysfunction.

The International Index of Erectile Function (IIEF) is a multidimensional scale consisting of 15 questions that address relevant domains of male sexual function, including sexual desire, intercourse satisfaction, orgasmic function, and overall satisfaction.[63–65] It has been validated in several languages, used in many multinational clinical trials, and found to have adequate sensitivity and specificity for detecting treatment-related changes, including response to oral erectogenic agents in men with ED.

Considerable effort has been invested in the development of abbreviated questionnaires that take less time than the International Index of Erectile Dysfunction but more concisely address similar aspects of male sexuality[66] (e.g., Sexual Health Inventory for Men [SHIM]). Erectile Dysfunction Inventory of Treatment Satisfaction (EDITS) was developed to assess satisfaction with ED treatment modalities and impact of patient-partner satisfaction on the continuation of treatment.[67] Brief Sexual Function Inventory (BSFI) is an 11-item scale for men that measures sexual drive, erection, ejaculation, perception of problems, and overall satisfaction; in addition, this instrument has a three-item scale for the female partner to assess the frequency and firmness of erection and satisfaction with sex life.[68]

## Laboratory Tests

The diagnostic evaluation of a man with ED starts with general health evaluation. This may include measurements of hemoglobin, white blood count, blood glucose, aspartate (AST), alanine (ALT), bilirubin, alkaline phosphatase, blood urea nitrogen (BUN), and creatinine.

Measurement of serum total testosterone concentrations can help detect androgen deficiency. Although there is no consensus on this issue, it is important to exclude androgen deficiency in men presenting with ED because androgen deficiency may be a manifestation of serious underlying illness such as a pituitary tumor or human immunodeficiency virus (HIV) infection. In addition, testosterone replacement is desirable in men with androgen deficiency, not just for restoration of sexual function, but also for maintaining bone mineral density, muscle mass, protein metabolism, and a sense of well-being.

If the history, physical examination, and ED questionnaire do not identify any obvious medical concerns needing further workup, then a cost-effective approach is to prescribe a trial of an oral selective phosphodiesterase inhibitor if there are no contraindications (e.g., nitrate use) (Table 173-3).

## Evaluation of Penile Vasculature and Blood Flow

There are several tests that can evaluate the integrity of penile vasculature and blood flow.[48,62] The clinical utility of these tests is limited, however. Of these, the penile brachial blood pressure index is a simple and specific, but not a very sensitive index of vascular insufficiency.[69–72] It is of historic interest and rarely used today.

Intracavernosal injection of a vasoactive agent such as prostaglandin $E_1$ can be as both a diagnostic and potential therapeutic modality.[48,62] This procedure can show whether the patient will respond to this therapeutic modality and facilitate patient education about the procedure and its potential side effects. Failure to respond to intracavernosal injection can raise the suspicion of vascular insufficiency or a venous leak that might need further evaluation and treatment.

Most men with erectile dysfunction do not need duplex color sonography, cavernosography, or pelvic angiography.[48,62] These procedures should be reserved for patients for whom the results of these tests would alter the management or prognosis, and performed only by those with considerable experience in their use. For instance, angiography could be useful in a young man with arterial insufficiency associated with pelvic trauma. Similarly, suspicion of congenital or traumatic venous leak in a young men presenting with erectile dysfunction would justify a cavernosography. In each instance, confirmation of the vascular lesion might lead to consideration of surgery. Duplex ultrasonography can provide a noninvasive evaluation of vascular function.[48]

| Table 173-3 | A Graduated Approach to Treatment of Erectile Dysfunction |
|---|---|

1. All patients and their sexual partners can benefit from and should receive psychosexual counseling.
2. First- and second-line therapies
   Selective phosphodiesterase 5 inhibitors
3. Second-line therapies
   Vacuum devices
   Intraurethral application of prostaglandin $E_1$
4. Third-line therapies that can be used in general medical or endocrine practice but require a urologic backup in the event of complications
   Intracavernosal injection of prostaglandin $E_1$
   Intracavernosal injections of other vasoactive amines
5. Specialized therapies that require urologic consultation
   Penile prosthesis
   Vascular surgery

## Nocturnal Penile Tumescence

Although recording of formal nocturnal penile tumescence (NPT) in a sleep laboratory for successive nights can help differentiate organic from psychogenic impotence, this test is expensive, labor intensive, and not required in most men with erectile dysfunction. In most cases, formal NPT studies are reserved for medical legal documentation.

The introduction of portable Rigiscan devices in 1985 provided clinicians with a reliable means of continuously monitoring penile tumescence and rigidity at home. It is a multicomponent device that the patient wears at bedtime for 2 to 3 nights. It has two wire gauge loops that are placed around the base and tip of the penis that record changes in penile circumference and rigidity. Data is stored and then downloaded via a software program that allows for sophisticated interpretation.

Nocturnal penile tumescence testing is not needed for most patients being evaluated for erectile dysfunction and is recommended only for patients with a high clinical suspicion of psychogenic ED or situational problems, or to document preoperatively poor penile rigidity. For most cases, a careful history eliciting the incidence of nighttime or early morning erections provides a reasonable correlation with formal NPT and Rigiscan studies.[73]

## Diagnostic Tests to Exclude Androgen Deficiency and Hypothalamic-Pituitary Lesions

There is considerable debate about the usefulness and cost effectiveness of hormonal evaluation and the extent to which androgen deficiency should be investigated in men presenting with erectile dysfunction. Of men with ED, 8% to 10% have low testosterone levels; the prevalence of androgen deficiency increases with advancing age.[40,74–79] The prevalence of low testosterone levels is not significantly different between men who present with ED and those in an age-matched population.[74,77] Urologic studies report that 6% to 8% of men with ED have an endocrine basis to their condition. These data are consistent with the proposal that ED and androgen deficiency are two common but independently distributed disorders.[77]

It is important, however, to exclude androgen deficiency in this patient population.[80] Androgen deficiency is a correctable cause of sexual dysfunction and some men with ED and low testosterone levels will respond to testosterone replacement. Hypogonadism might have additional deleterious effects on the individual's health; for instance, hypogonadism might contribute to osteoporosis, loss of muscle mass and function, and increased risk of disability, falls, and fracture. In addition, in cross-sectional epidemiologic studies, low testosterone levels are associated with increased risk of mid-segment obesity,[81,82] insulin resistance,[83,84] type 2 diabetes mellitus,[83,84] and coronary artery disease[85]; however, we do not know whether testosterone replacement can reduce visceral fat and improve insulin sensitivity and cardiovascular risk in middle-aged men with mid-segment obesity. Therefore, regardless of the presence of sexual dysfunction, androgen deficiency needs to be corrected by appropriate hormone replacement therapy. Further, androgen deficiency might be a manifestation of a serious underlying disease such as HIV infection or a hypothalamic-pituitary space-occupying lesion.

In large studies,[74,75,78] only a small fraction of men with erectile dysfunction and low testosterone levels have been found to have space-occupying lesions of the hypothalamic-pituitary region. Elevation of prolactin assists in the identification of the disorders. In one large survey, all of the hypothalamic-pituitary lesions were found in men with serum testosterone levels less than 150 ng/dL.[78] Therefore, the cost effectiveness of the diagnostic workup to rule out an underlying lesion of the hypothalamic-pituitary region can be increased by limiting the workup to men with serum testosterone levels less than 150 ng/dL.

## TREATMENT OF ERECTILE DYSFUNCTION

The selection of the therapeutic modality should be based on the underlying etiology, patient preference (goal-directed approach), the nature and strength of relationship with his sexual partner, and the absence or presence of underlying cardiovascular disease and other comorbid conditions.[48,62] In current practice, it is common to employ a step approach that first utilizes minimally invasive therapies that are easy to use and have fewer adverse effects and progresses to more invasive therapies that may require injections in some circumstances or surgical interventions after the first-line choices have been exhausted (see Table 173-3). The physician should discuss the risks, benefits, and alternatives of all the diagnostic procedures and therapies with the couple. In the execution of good medical practice, treatment of all associated medical disorders should be optimized. In men with diabetes mellitus, efforts to optimize glycemic control should be instituted, although improving glycemic control may not necessarily improve sexual function. In men with hypertension, control of blood pressure should be optimized and, if possible, the therapeutic regimen may need to be modified to remove antihypertensive drugs that impair sexual function. This strategy is not always feasible because almost all antihypertensive agents have been associated with sexual dysfunction; the frequency of this adverse event is less with converting enzyme inhibitors than with other agents.

All patients with ED can benefit from psychosexual counseling.[48,62] Unfortunately, many couples are reluctant to pursue this avenue. When there is latent marital discord, the sensitive and astute clinician needs to direct affected couples appropriately.

### First-Line Therapies

#### Psychosexual Counseling

As Rosen[86] has emphasized, the major goals of psychosexual therapy are to reduce performance anxiety, develop patient's sexual skills and knowledge, modify negative sexual thoughts and attitudes, and improve communication between partners. Counseling can be of benefit in both psychogenic and organic causes of sexual dysfunction[8] (Table 173-4).

Masters and Johnson considered "spectatoring" the adoption of a role in which the individual is focused on sexual performance rather than erotic stimulation, as a major factor in the pathophysiology of psychogenic ED.[86,87] Many experts recommend a "sensate focus" treatment approach in which intercourse is avoided and the couple is encouraged to engage in nongenital, nondemand pleasure-seeking exercises in order to reduce performance anxiety.[88–90]

Involving the partner in the counseling process helps dispel misperceptions about the problem, decreases stress, enhances intimacy and the ability to talk about sex, and increases the chances of successful outcome of therapy.[86,88–90] Counseling sessions are also helpful in uncovering conflicts in relationships, psychiatric problems, alcohol and drug abuse, and significant misperceptions about sex. As both men and women often harbor misinformation and unrealistic expectations

| *Table 173-4* Goals and Targets of Psychosexual Therapy in Men with Erectile Dysfunction |
| --- |
| • Reduce performance anxiety; "sensate focus" rather than "spectatoring" |
| • Identify relationship problems and improve partner communication and intimacy |
| • Cognitive restructuring to modify sexual attitudes and beliefs |
| • Improve couple's repertoire of sexual skills |

Adapted from Rosen RC: Psychogenic erectile dysfunction. Urol Clin North Am 28:269, 2001.

about sexual performance and age-related changes in sexual function, cognitive restructuring techniques are helpful in correcting sexual myths and beliefs. Although psychobehavioral therapy has been claimed to relieve depression and anxiety, there is a striking paucity of outcome data on the effectiveness of this therapeutic modality.

## Selective Phosphodiesterase Inhibitors

**Mechanisms by Which Selective Inhibition of Phosphodiesterase within the Corpora Cavernosa Can Induce Erection** Three classes of enzymes—adenylyl cyclase, guanylyl cyclase, and phosphodiesterases—play an important role in regulating the intracavernosal concentrations of cAMP and cGMP. Phosphodiesterases hydrolyze cAMP and cGMP, thus reducing their concentrations within the cavernosal smooth muscle.[48,91-95] Although phosphodiesterase isoforms 2, 3, 4, and 5 are expressed in the penis, only phosphodiesterase 5 (PDE5) is specific to the nitric oxide (NO)/cGMP pathway in the corpora cavernosa.[96] The phosphodiesterase inhibitors (PDEIs) sildenafil, vardenafil, and tadalafil are relatively selective inhibitors of PDE5.[97-109] These drugs block the hydrolysis of cGMP induced by nitric oxide,[96,110,111] thus promoting cavernosal smooth muscle to relax. Therefore, the action of these drugs requires an intact nitric oxide response, as well as constitutive synthesis of cGMP by the smooth muscle cells of the corpora cavernosa. By selectively inhibiting cGMP catabolism in the cavernosal smooth-muscle cells, PDE5 inhibitors restore the natural erectile response to sexual stimulation, but do not produce an erection in the absence of sexual stimulation.

**Clinical Pharmacology of Orally Active, Selective Phosphodiesterase Inhibitors** Although the three currently available phosphodiesterase inhibitors have some structural similarities, they differ in their selectivity and pharmacokinetics (Table 173-5).

The selectivity of the phosphodiesterase inhibitors is closely related to the adverse effects experienced by the users. The common adverse events of the available PDE5 inhibitors—headache, visual problems, and flush—are related to nonselective inhibition of phosphodiesterase isoforms 6 and 11 in other organ systems.[109] The selectivity of an PDE5 inhibitor is the ratio of its inhibitory potency for phosphodiesterase isoforms other than type 5 relative to its inhibitory potency for PDE5.[109] For PDE6, tadalafil is the most selective and sildenafil is the least selective; for PDE11, vardenafil is the most selective and tadalafil is the least selective.[109] The retinal side effects of sildenafil are related to inhibition of PDE6 in the retina, while muscle aches experienced by a small fraction of men using tadalafil may be related to inhibition of PDE11 in the skeletal muscles.[103,112-114]

**Pharmacokinetics of Phosphodiesterase Inhibitors (see Table 173-5)** After oral administration of sildenafil, peak plasma concentrations are achieved within 30 to 120 minutes, after which plasma concentrations decline with a half-life of

| Table 173-5 | Clinical Pharmacology of Selective PDE5 Inhibitors | | |
|---|---|---|---|
| | **Sildenafil** | **Vardenafil** | **Tadalafil** |
| Commercial name | Viagra | Levitra | Cialis |
| Tmax | 0.5–2.0 hr | 0.7–0.9 hr | 2 hr |
| T½ | 3–4 hr | 4–5 hr | 16.9 hr (young) 21.6 (old) |
| Selectivity (ratio of PDE6/PDE5 IC50) | 11 | 25 | 187 |
| Selectivity (ratio of PDE11/PDE5 IC50) | 780 | 1160 | 5 |
| Onset of erection (min) | 30–60 | 15–45 | 20–30 min |
| Effect of food and alcohol | Cmax decreased | Minimal change | No change |

Sildenafil

Vardenafil

Tadalafil

4 hours.[115,116] Vardenafil achieves peak concentrations within 0.7 to 0.9 hours and has a half-life of 4 to 5 hours. In contrast, peak concentrations of tadalafil are achieved at 2 hours and its half-life of 16.9 hours in young men is significantly longer than the half-lives of sildenafil and vardenafil. The half-life of tadalafil is even longer in older men (21.6 hours) in comparison to young men (16.9 hours). Because of the relatively short half-lives of vardenafil and sildenafil, these drugs should be taken 2 to 4 hours before the planned intercourse; in contrast, because of its longer half-life, tadalifil can be, but does not have to be, taken on demand.

Food, particularly a high-fat meal, and alcohol can delay and decrease the absorption of sildenafil. Early pharmacokinetic studies, however, have not reported changes in maximum serum concentrations or absorption rates of vardenafil or tadalafil due to food or moderate alcohol ingestion.[117]

**Efficacy**    Introduced to the U.S. market in March 1998, sildenafil (Viagra, Pfizer, New York, NY) was the first effective oral agent for the treatment of ED.[59,96,110,111,118–121] The efficacy of all three orally active PDE5 inhibitors has been proven in randomized clinical trials.

The efficacy of sildenafil was demonstrated in a randomized dose-response study[58] in which 532 men with organic, psychogenic, or mixed erectile dysfunction were randomized to receive placebo or 25, 50, or 100 mg of sildenafil for 24 weeks. Subjects on sildenafil performed better in terms of increased rigidity, frequency of vaginal penetration, and maintenance of erection. Increasing doses of sildenafil were associated with higher mean scores for the questions assessing frequency of penetration and maintenance of erections after sexual penetration. In a follow-up dose-escalation study,[59] 329 men were randomly assigned to receive placebo or 50 mg of sildenafil for 12 weeks. At each follow-up, the dose of sildenafil was increased or decreased by 50% depending on the therapeutic response or side effects. For the men receiving sildenafil, 64% of attempts at intercourse were successful, as compared to 22% among the men receiving placebo. The mean number of successful attempts per month was 5.9 for men receiving sildenafil and 1.5 for those receiving placebo. The mean scores for orgasms, intercourse satisfaction, and overall satisfaction domain were also significantly higher in the sildenafil group, as compared to placebo.[59]

In a separate randomized clinical trial, 268 men with diabetes mellitus and ED received either placebo or sildenafil for 12 weeks.[111] Fifty-six percent of men receiving sildenafil reported improved erections compared with 10% of those receiving placebo ($P < 0.001$). The percent of men reporting at least one successful attempt at intercourse was 61% for the sildenafil versus 22% for the placebo group. This study[111] demonstrated that sildenafil is an effective treatment for ED in patients with diabetes mellitus.

In the vardenafil efficacy trials, 5, 10, and 20 mg doses of vardenafil were all superior to placebo in improving erectile function domain scores; the improvements in erectile function scores were dose related. Vardenafil improved rates of vaginal penetration, intercourse success, and overall satisfaction with sexual experience in a broad population of men with erectile dysfunction.

Similarly, in randomized, clinical trials, 2.5, 5, 10, and 20 mg doses of tadalafil were each superior to placebo in improving erectile function domain scores. The beneficial effects of tadalafil were dose related.

PDE5 inhibitors are also effective in men with ED due to a variety of other causes including spinal cord injury and post radical prostatectomy.[119,120] In general, baseline sexual function correlates positively with response to sildenafil, and patients with diabetes mellitus or previous prostate surgery respond less well than patients with psychogenic or vasculogenic ED.[120] Because there is no baseline characteristic that predicts the likelihood of failure to respond to sildenafil

therapy, a therapeutic trial of PDE5 inhibitors is warranted in all patients except in those in whom it is contraindicated.[120]

**Adverse Effects Associated with PDE5 Inhibitors (Table 173-6)**
In clinical trials, the adverse effects reported with greater frequency in men treated with PDE5 inhibitors than in those treated with placebo include headaches, flushing, rhinitis, dyspepsia, and visual disturbances.[122] The occurrence of headache, flushing, and rhinitis, being a direct consequence of nonselective PDE5 inhibition in other organ systems, is related to the administered dose. These drugs do not affect semen characteristics.[123] No cases of priapism were noted in any of the pivotal clinical trials.

**Cardiovascular and Hemodynamic Effects of Sildenafil Citrate (Table 173-7)**    In postmarketing surveillance of adverse events associated with sildenafil use, several instances of myocardial infarction and sudden death were reported.[124–128] Forty-four of the 130 deaths reported by the U.S. Food and Drug Administration from March to November 1998 occurred in temporal relation to the ingestion of sildenafil[124–128]; 16 of these deaths occurred in individuals who were taking nitrates. Because most men presenting with ED also have cardiovascular risk factors, it is unclear whether these events were causally related to the ingestion of sildenafil, underlying heart disease, or both.[127] In a rigorously controlled study,[129] oral administration of 100 mg of sildenafil to men with severe coronary artery disease produced only small decreases in systemic blood pressure and no significant changes in cardiac output, heart rate, coronary blood flow, and coronary artery diameter. In a separate analysis of five randomized, placebo-controlled trials of vardenafil, Kloner and colleagues pooled the data on cardiovascular safety profile. The overall frequency of cardiovascular events was similar in vardenafil-treated men and placebo-treated men. Vardenafil treatment, however, was associated with a mild reduction in blood pressure (4.6 mm Hg decrease in systolic blood pressure) and a small increase in heart rate (2 beats per minute). This led the American Heart Association to conclude that the preexistence of coronary artery disease by itself does not constitute a contraindication for the use of sildenafil.[127]

**Guidelines for the Use of PDE5 Inhibitors in Men with Coronary Artery Disease (see Table 173-7)[127]**    Before prescribing PDE5 inhibitors, it is crucial to assess cardiovascular risk factors. If the patient has hypertension or symptomatic

| *Table 173-6* | Common Adverse Events Associated with the Use of Selective Phosphodiesterase 5 Inhibitors in Men with Erectile Dysfunction | | |
|---|---|---|---|
| **Adverse Effect** | **Sildenafil (%)** | **Vardenafil (%)*** | **Tadalafil (%)†** |
| Headache | 12 | 6 | 8 |
| Flushing | 9 | 10 | 2 |
| Nasal congestion | 2 | 3 | — |
| Dyspepsia | 5 | 3 | 8 |
| Abnormal vision | 3 | — | — |
| Myalgia | 2 | — | 3 |
| Diarrhea | 2 | — | — |
| Back pain | Rare | — | — |
| Rash | 2 | — | — |

*Porst et al: Int J Impot Res 13:192–199, 2001.
†Brock, et al: J Urol, 168:1332–1336, 2002.
Most adverse effects were reported to be mild to moderate in intensity and transient (38). These adverse effects are likely due to nonselective inhibition of phosphodiesterase enzyme isoforms in other tissues.
Adapted from Kuritzky L, Samraj G: How to choose among the PDE5 inhibitors for erectile dysfunction. JAAPA Archive. Available at *http://www.jaapa.com/be_core/journals/j/data/2004/0101/w1004erectdys.html.*

**Table 173-7** American College of Cardiology and American Heart Association Recommendations for the Use of Sildenafil by Men with Cardiac Disease

1. Sildenafil is absolutely contraindicated in men taking long-acting or short-acting nitrate drugs on a regular basis.
2. If the patient has stable coronary artery disease, is not taking long-acting nitrates, and uses short-acting nitrates only infrequently, the use of sildenafil should be guided by careful consideration of risks.
3. All men taking nitrates should be warned about the risks of the potential interaction between nitrates and sildenafil. The patients should also be warned that concurrent recreational use of inhaled nitrates or "poppers" could result in marked hypotension that could be serious or even fatal.
4. Sildenafil is contraindicated within 24 hours of the ingestion of any form of nitrate.
5. In men with preexisting coronary artery disease, the risks of inducing cardiac ischemia during sexual activity should be assessed before prescribing sildenafil. This assessment may include a stress test.
6. Men who are taking a combination antihypertensive medication should be warned about the possibility of sildenafil-induced hypotension. This is of particular concern in men with congestive heart failure who have borderline low blood volume or who are receiving complex regimens that include vasodilators or diuretics.

Adapted from Cheitlin MD, Hutter AM Jr, Brindis RG, et al: Use of sildenafil (Viagra) in patients with cardiovascular disease. Technology and Practice Executive Committee [see comments]. Circulation 99:168–177, 1999 [published erratum in Circulation 100:2389, 1999].

**Table 173-8** Drug-Drug Interactions with PDE5 Inhibitors

PDE5 inhibitors are absolutely contraindicated for men taking these drugs
- Nitrates of any kind

PDE5 inhibitors are relatively contraindicated for men taking these drugs
- α-adrenergic blockers

PDE5 inhibitors should be used cautiously with appropriate dose adjustments in men taking these drugs
- Vasodilators
- Protease inhibitors
- Erythromycin and related macrolides
- Ketoconazole, itraconazole

coronary artery disease, the treatment of those clinical disorders should be addressed first.[48,127] The use of nitrates must be ascertained because PDE5 inhibitors are contraindicated in individuals taking any form of nitrates. PDE5 inhibitors should not be used within 24 hours of the use of nitrates.[127]

As the data on the effects of PDE5 inhibitors on exercise-induced ischemia are limited, it is prudent to warn the patients that sexual activity can induce coronary ischemia in men with preexisting coronary artery disease[128]; these individuals should undergo assessment of their exercise tolerance. One practical way to assess exercise tolerance is to have the patient climb one or two flight of stairs. If the individual can safely climb one or two flights of stairs without angina or excessive shortness of breath, he can likely engage in sexual intercourse with a stable partner without similar symptoms. Exercise testing before prescribing PDE5 inhibitors may be indicated in some men with significant heart disease to assess the risk of inducing cardiac ischemia during sexual activity.[127] In one double-blind, crossover study, vardenafil was shown not to impair the ability of patients with stable coronary artery disease to engage in exercise at levels equivalent to that attained during sexual intercourse. Similarly, each of the three PDE5 inhibitors has been shown not to have significant adverse effects on hemodynamics and cardiac events in carefully selected men with erectile dysfunction who did not have any contraindication for the use of PDE5 inhibitors.[130] None of the PDE5 inhibitors adversely affects total exercise time or time to ischemia during exercise testing in men with stable angina. Tadalafil and vardenafil are contraindicated in men using α-blockers; the sildenafil label also has a precautionary warning for use with α-blockers.

In men with congestive heart failure or those receiving vasodilator drugs or those who are using complex regimens of antihypertensive drugs, blood pressure should be monitored after initial administration of PDE5 inhibitors.[127,131-137]

**Drug-Drug Interactions (Table 173-8)** Sildenafil is metabolized mostly by the P-450 2C9 and the P-450 3A4 pathways.[127] Cimetidine and erythromycin, inhibitors of P-450 3A4, increase the plasma concentrations of sildenafil. Protease inhibitors may also alter the activity of the P-450 3A4 pathway and affect the clearance of sildenafil.[127] Conversely, sildenafil

is an inhibitor of the P-450 2C9 metabolic pathway and its administration could potentially affect the metabolism of drugs metabolized by this system, such as warfarin and tolbutamide.[127] Combined administration of sildenafil and ritonavir in combination results in significantly increased plasma levels of sildenafil than sildenafil given alone.[138] There are similar reactions with other drugs, including saquinavir, erythromycin, and itraconazole. Therefore, the doses of PDE5 inhibitors should be reduced appropriately in men taking protease inhibitors or erythromycin.

Grapefruit juice can alter oral drug pharmacokinetics by different mechanisms. Grapefruit juice given as a single normal amount (e.g., 200–300 mL) or by whole fresh fruit segments can irreversibly inactivate intestinal cytochrome P-450 (CYP) 3A4, thus reducing presystemic metabolism and oral drug bioavailability of PDE5 inhibitors.[139] While the magnitude of this problem in clinical practice is unknown, it seems prudent to warn men who are contemplating the use of PDE5 inhibitors not to ingest more than a small amount of grapefruit juice.

The most serious interactions of PDE5 inhibitors are with the nitrates. The vasodilator effects of nitrates are augmented by PDE5 inhibitors; this also applies to inhaled forms of nitrates such as amyl nitrate or nitrite that are sold under the street name "poppers." Concomitant administration of the two drugs can cause a potentially fatal decrease in blood pressure.[127]

**Therapeutic Regimens** In most men with ED, sildenafil can be started at an initial dose of 25 or 50 mg. If this dose does not produce any adverse effects, the dose can be titrated up to a maximum of 100 mg.[59,127] Further dose adjustments should be guided by the therapeutic response to therapy and occurrence of adverse effects. Typically, unit doses higher than 100 mg are not recommended. To minimize the risk of hypotension and adverse cardiovascular events in association with the use of sildenafil, the American Heart Association has prepared a list of recommendations (see Table 173-3), which should be followed rigorously.[127] Vardenafil is typically started at an initial dose of 10 mg; the dose can be increased to 20 mg or decreased to 5 mg depending on the clinical response and the occurrence of adverse effects. Unit doses of vardenafil higher than 20 mg are not recommended. Tadalafil should be started at an initial unit dose of 10 mg, with further adjustments of dose based on effectiveness and side effects. Tadalafil need not be taken more frequently than once every 48 hours.

In men taking protease inhibitors, particularly ritonavir and indinavir, or other drugs that affect protease metabolism, such as erythromycin, ketoconazole, itranconazole, or large amounts of grapefruit, the doses of PDE5 inhibitors should be reduced; doses greater than 25 mg of sildenafil, 5 mg of vardenafil, or 10 mg of tadalafil are not recommended in patients who are using these drugs.

Sildenafil and vardenafil are taken "on demand" at least 1 hour before sexual intercourse and not more than once in any

24-hour period; because of its longer half-life, tadalafil need not be taken immediately before intercourse.

## Cost-Effectiveness of PDE5 Inhibitor Use for Erectile Dysfunction
A number of studies have evaluated the economic cost of treating ED in men in managed care organizations.[140-142] In one, computer simulation estimated that sildenafil citrate costs about $11,290 per quality adjusted life-year (QALY) that it produces. This amount is less than many other accepted health treatments. Most accepted health treatments cost less than $50,000 to $100,000 per quality adjusted life-year. The cost-effectiveness of sildenafil appears to compare favorably with other accepted medical therapies. There may, however, be many reasons other than cost-effectiveness to explain why insurance companies choose not to cover the cost of Viagra.

These analyses, using a prevalence-based cost of illness approach, have concluded that PDE5 inhibitors and vacuum constriction devices are the most cost effective of all the available therapeutic options in a managed care setting and should be considered first-line strategies.[140-142]

### Testosterone Replacement in Androgen-Deficient Men Presenting with Erectile Dysfunction
Testosterone replacement in healthy, young, androgen-deficient men restores sexual function.[19,23,41,42,143-148] In healthy young men, relatively low normal levels of serum testosterone can maintain sexual function.[19,23,148] In male rats,[147,148] a decrease in serum testosterone concentrations to castrate levels is associated with marked impairment of all measures of mating behavior and testosterone replacement to levels that are at the lower end of the adult male range and normalizes all measures of mating behavior. In general, supraphysiologic doses of testosterone do not further improve sexual function. It is possible that increasing testosterone levels above the physiologic range may increase arousability; however, this has not been conclusively demonstrated.

As previously stated, androgen deficiency and ED are two common, but independently distributed, clinical disorders in middle-aged and older men that often coexist in the same patient. Also as previously noted, among men presenting with ED, 8% to 10% have low testosterone levels.[40,74,75,77,78] The prevalence of low testosterone levels is not significantly different between middle-aged and older men with impotence and those without impotence.[74] Testosterone administration is unlikely to improve sexual function in men with normal testosterone levels. Therefore, indiscriminate use of testosterone replacement in all older men with erectile dysfunction is not warranted. It is important, however, to exclude testosterone deficiency in older men presenting with ED. Androgen deficiency may be a manifestation of an underlying disease such as a pituitary tumor. Additionally, therapies directed just at ED in men will not correct androgen deficiency, which, if left uncorrected, will have deleterious effects on bone, muscle, energy level, and sense of well-being.

Many, but not all, of the impotent men with low testosterone levels experience improvements in their libido and overall sexual activity with androgen replacement therapy.[80,149] The response to testosterone supplementation even in this group of men is variable[74-78] because of the coexistence of other disorders such as diabetes mellitus, hypertension, cardiovascular disease, and psychogenic factors. A meta-analysis[149] of the usefulness of androgen replacement therapy concluded that testosterone administration is associated with greater improvements in sexual function than those associated with placebo in men with erectile dysfunction and low testosterone levels.

ED in middle-aged and older men is often a multifactorial disorder. Common causes of ED in men include diabetes mellitus, hypertension, medications, peripheral vascular disease, psychogenic factors, and end-stage renal disease. Many of these factors often coexist in the same patient. Therefore, it is not surprising that testosterone treatment alone may not improve sexual function in all men with androgen deficiency.

Testosterone treatment does not improve sexual function in impotent men who have normal testosterone levels.[40] It is not known whether testosterone replacement improves sexual function in impotent men with borderline serum testosterone levels.

Although hypogonadal men can achieve erections, testosterone modulates a number of processes that culminate in penile erection. Testosterone regulates NO synthase expression and activity in the cavernosal smooth muscle of rats,[45,150-152] dogs,[153] and rabbits[154,155]; thus, NO synthase expression is lower in cavernosal tissue of castrated rats and is restored by testosterone replacement.[156-161] There is additional evidence that non-NO-dependent pathways may also be androgen sensitive in the erectile response.[156-161] The sensitivity to $\alpha$-adrenergic stimulation is higher in castrated rats than in testosterone-replaced castrated rats.[161]

Androgens support erectile function through a direct effect on the erectile tissue. Castration results in impaired erectile response to central and peripheral stimulation and a decrease in penile tissue concentration of NO synthase–containing nerves[162]; testosterone replacement reverses these abnormalities.[162]

Testosterone has trophic effects in maintaining the mass of the bulbospongiosus and ischiocavernosus muscles; these muscles contribute to the achievement of peak rigidity just before ejaculation. Lowering of testosterone levels is associated with significant atrophy of these muscles and decreased peak rigidity. Testosterone also has trophic effects on the cavernosal tissue. Castration induces apoptosis and testosterone replacement induces cell proliferation and DNA synthesis in the cavernosal tissue of rat penis.[163,164] These data lead us to postulate that testosterone supplementation of androgen-deficient men would increase the mass of cavernosal tissue.

Testosterone regulates blood flow into the penis; the blood flow is reduced in castrated rats, and is restored by testosterone supplementation.[159,160] Furthermore, during ganglionic stimulation, veno-occlusion fails to occur in castrated rats. Thus, androgens not only regulate blood flow into the erectile tissue, but are also necessary for the veno-occlusive mechanisms.[158-160,165] Collectively, these data indicate that testosterone plays an important role in regulating erectile mechanisms at multiple levels.

## Second-Line Therapies
### Vacuum Devices for Inducing Erection
Commercially available vacuum devices consist of a plastic cylinder, a vacuum pump, and an elastic constriction band.[48,62] The plastic cylinder fits over the penis and is connected to a vacuum pump. The negative pressure created by the vacuum within the cylinder draws blood into the penis, producing an erection. An elastic band slipped around the base of the penis traps the blood in the penis, maintaining an erection as long as the rubber band is retained around the base. The constriction band should not be left in place for more than 30 minutes.

These devices are safe, relatively inexpensive, and reasonably effective. They can impair ejaculation, resulting in entrapment of semen, however, and are difficult and awkward for some patients to use. Some couples dislike the lack of spontaneity engendered by the use of these devices. Partner cooperation is usually important for successful use.[166-170]

### Intraurethral Therapies
An intraurethral system for delivery of alprostadil called MUSE (medicated urethral system for erection; VIVUS, Menlo Park, CA) was released in 1997. Alprostadil is a stable, synthetic form of prostaglandin $E_1$, which causes an increase in cAMP levels and a decrease in intracellular calcium, and

thereby promotes cavernosal smooth muscle relaxation and penile erection.

Alprostadil, when applied into the urethra, is absorbed through the urethral mucosa and ventral side of the tunica albuginea into the corpus cavernosum. Intraurethral aprostadil has several advantages over intracavernosal injection of prostaglandin $E_1$; intraurethral administration is easier and adverse effects, particularly penile fibrosis, are less frequent.

Aprostadil is available in 100-, 125-, 250-, and 500-μg strengths. Typically, the initial aprostadil dose of 500 μg is applied in the clinician's office to observe for any changes in blood pressure or urethral bleeding secondary to misapplication of the device into the urethra. Common side effects of transurethral alprostadil are penile pain and urethral burning in up to 30% of patients.[171-173] Initial randomized, placebo-controlled studies reported 40% to 60% success rates, determined as having at least one successful sexual intercourse during a 3-month study period.[171-173] In clinical practice, approximately one third of men using intraurethral aprostadil respond. The use of a constriction device (Actis, VIVUS) at the time of application of transurethral alprostadil has been shown to increase efficacy.

The use of intraurethral aprostadil is associated with penile pain in 32% of men; in addition, its use may cause dizziness, hypotension, and syncope in a small fraction of users. It can also cause mild burning or itching in the vagina of the sexual partner. Intraurethral aprostadil should not be used by men whose partners are pregnant or planning to get pregnant.

*Intracavernosal Injection of Vasoactive Agents (Table 173-9)*
The use of intracavernosal injections of vasoactive agents has been a cornerstone of the medical management of erectile dysfunction since the early 1980s. Patients are taught how to self-inject a vasoactive agent into their corpora cavernosa with a 27- or 30-gauge needle up to three times a week for sexual intercourse. Erections occur typically 15 minutes after intracorporal injection and last 45 to 90 minutes. When appropriately titrated, the success rate of this therapy in producing a rigid erection is 80% to 90%. Early studies with

intracavernosal injection therapy report patient and partner satisfaction rates of 70% and 67%, respectively.

The main adverse effects include penile pain, occurrence of hematoma, formation of corporal nodules, and the possibility of prolonged erections (priapism, if longer than 4 hours). Despite the effectiveness of this approach in producing rigid erections, the majority of patients do not relish injecting a needle into their penis; therefore, it is not surprising that long-term dropout rates approach 60% to 70%.

Three different agents, prostaglandin $E_1$, papaverine, and phentolamine, are commonly used alone or in combination by clinicians who prescribe injection therapy for the treatment of ED. Several formulations of alprostadil ($PGE_1$) are commercially available (Caverject, Pharmacia; Prostin VR, Pharmacia; Edex, Schwarz Pharma). $PGE_1$ binds to $PGE_1$ receptors on the cavernosal smooth muscle cells, stimulates adenylyl cyclase, increases the concentrations of cAMP, and is a powerful smooth muscle relaxant. In one efficacy trial, intracavernosal aprostadil injection resulted in satisfactory sexual performance in over 80% of users. The usual dose is 5 to 20 μg. Common side effects of intracavernosal $PGE_1$ injections include penile pain, fibrosis, and prolonged erections. Priapism occurs less commonly compared with other vasoactive agents.

Papaverine, derived originally from the poppy seed, is a nonspecific phosphodiesterase inhibitor, which increases both intracellular cAMP and cGMP. As a single agent, it is efficacious and inexpensive, and does not need to be refrigerated. It does not cause penile pain, but has a greater propensity to induce priapism and fibrosis with long-term use.

Phentolamine is a competitive $\alpha_1$ and $\alpha_2$ adrenergic antagonist that contributes to smooth muscle relaxation. As a single agent, it is minimally efficacious, but it is commonly used in combination to potentiate the effects of papaverine and/or $PGE_1$.

In an attempt to maximize efficacy and minimize side effects, many clinicians use a combination of $PGE_1$, papavarine, and phentolamine as a tri-mix, which allows the use of a lower dose of each agent. A common mixture contains papavarine, 120 mg (4 mL of 30 mg/mL); phentolamine, 6 mg; and $PGE_1$, 120 μg (6 mL of 20 mg/mL) to make a total volume of 10 mL. The reliable patient can titrate his intracavernosal dose from 0.2 to 0.5 mL to optimize his erectile response.

The biggest concern with intracavernosal injection therapy is priapism (see Table 173-5). In the event the patient develops a prolonged or painful erection with $PGE_1$, either brethane (5 mg) or pseudoephedrine (60 mg), self-administered orally, may be of benefit. If priapism persists longer than 4 hours, patient should be instructed to seek medical care in which aspiration alone or with the injection of an α-adrenergic agent is used to induce detumescence. Vital signs should be closely monitored during this procedure. If this fails, surgical therapy may be indicated to reverse a prolonged erection, otherwise anoxic damage to the cavernosal smooth muscle cells, fibrosis, and permanent ED can occur.

**Third-Line Therapies**
*Penile Prosthesis*
While penile prostheses are considered invasive and costly, for many patients with advanced organic disease who are unresponsive to any contemporary form of therapy, have significant structural disorders of the penis (e.g., Peyronie's disease), or have suffered corporal loss from cancer or traumatic injury prostheses remain a highly effective and predictable method for restoring erectile function.

Penile implants are paired supports that are placed one in each of the two erectile bodies. There are two basic types: hydraulic or fluid filled, referred to as inflatable prostheses; and malleable, semirigid rods, which are bendable and positionable, but always remain firm in the penis.

---

**Table 173-9** | **Checklist before Administering Intracavernosal Therapy**

1. Verify whether there is any contraindication to the use of intracavernosal injection; intracavernosal therapy is not suitable for patients with psychiatric disorders, hypercoagulable states, or sickle-cell disease, or those receiving anticoagulant therapy.
2. Instruct the patient on how to inject the medication, and about the risks of this form of therapy.
3. Before prescribing intracavernosal injections, develop a reliable contingency plan that includes a designated urologist to handle emergencies related to complications of intracavernosal injections such as priapism.
4. Administer the first injection in the physician's office and observe the blood pressure and heart rate response. This provides an excellent opportunity for educating the patient, observing adverse effects, and determining whether the patient will respond to this form of therapy.
5. Adjust the dose of the vasoactive substance to achieve an erection that is sufficient for sexual intercourse, but that does not last more than 30 minutes.
6. Advise the patient that priapism and fibrosis are potential complications of intracavernosal therapy.
7. Advise the patient to compress the injection site after the injection to minimze the risk of hematoma formation and subsequent fibrosis.
8. If the erection does not abate in 30 minutes, instruct the patient to take a tablet of pseudoephedrine or an intracavernosal injection of phenylephrine. If this is not effective, the patient should either call the designated urologist or go to the emergency room.

The inflatable prostheses include the three-piece and the two-piece models. The three-piece model utilizes a reservoir located in the pelvis behind the rectus muscle, a pump in the scrotum, and two inflatable cylinders. The two-piece device has the reservoir and pump combined, located in the scrotum, and two cylinders.

Penile prostheses come in a variety of lengths and girths. The size selected for implantation is determined at the time of surgery when each erectile body is measured. Implantation surgery usually takes less than an hour and in most cases can be done as an outpatient procedure under general or regional anesthesia.

With a number of recent modifications incorporating newer materials and designs, the chance of mechanical malfunction has decreased to 5% to 10% in the first 10 years. Penile prostheses have a higher reliability than any other mechanical device implanted in the human body.[3] The complication that surgeons most fear from prosthesis implantation is infection, which occurs in 1% to 3% of cases, but this can be higher in revision surgery, especially in men with diabetes mellitus.[3]

The total cost of penile prosthesis implantation varies from $3000 to $20,000, depending on the type of device used and the community where the procedure is performed. Health or medical insurance in the United States frequently covers most of this cost if the ED has an organic etiology.

Recent studies have reported that more than 80% of patients and 70% of partners are pleased with their prosthesis and the togetherness that it brings to their relationship.[4,5,174,175]

With an increasing aging population, a growing awareness of ED and the availability of effective treatments, and more general practitioners prescribing oral ED agents, one can anticipate an increasing number of men with severe forms of ED who will need penile prosthesis procedures in the coming years.[174] This speculation is supported by a recent Dain Bosworth industry analysis report projecting an increase in the number of penile implant procedures performed through 2010. There will always be a portion of the impotent population with advanced ED who will be candidates for penile prosthesis implantation.

## Oral Therapeutic Agents under Development

It has been clearly established, in North America at least, that the preferred route of administration for an ED treatment is by mouth. The huge success of sildenafil (Viagra) attests to the insatiable public demand for an effective oral erectogenic agent.

Another central initiator of erection in early development is α-melanocyte-stimulating hormone (α-MSH; Melontan II), which is a nonselective melanocortin agonist. It is recognized to have dopaminergic agonist activity, but, in addition, it has beneficial effects on libido. In a double-blind, placebo-controlled, crossover study, there was significant improvement in Rigiscan events, penile rigidity, and sexual desire in 10 patients with documented ED risk factors. Nausea was the most common adverse event.[176]

PT-141, another synthetic analogue of α-melanocyte-stimulating hormone, is an agonist at melanocortin receptors including the MC3R and MC4R.[177–180] Administration of PT-141 to rats and nonhuman primates results in penile erections. Administration of PT-141 to normal men and to patients with erectile dysfunction resulted in a rapid dose-dependent increase in erectile activity. Efficacy trials of PT-141 are in early stages. Apomorphine, a PDE5 inhibitor, also functions as a dopamine agonist, and acts centrally to initiate erection; its main adverse effect is nausea.

## Gene Therapy and Erectile Dysfunction

Gene therapy can be defined as the introduction of genetic material (RNA or DNA) into an appropriate cell type, thus altering gene expression of that cell in order to produce a therapeutic effect.[181] Gene therapy involves a number of sequential steps: the administration of a desired gene into the body, delivery of the gene to a targeted cell, and expression of the therapeutic product. Recently, there has been an explosion in the amount of basic and clinical research in the field of gene therapy. In the past, gene therapy approaches were used to treat disorders that had an underlying genetic component. Gene therapy has evolved, however, to the point where treatment of any disease process, genetic or acquired, can be theoretically accomplished as long as there exists a target gene, which can effectively restore or supplement defective functions. The goal of gene therapy for ED is to introduce novel genetic material into an appropriate cell in an attempt to restore normal cellular and physiologic function.

Gene therapy has been proposed as a viable treatment option for diseases that have a vascular origin, such as arteriosclerosis, congestive heart failure, and pulmonary hypertension.[181–184] This, by biological extension, suggests that gene therapy may also be employed to treat vascular diseases of the penis; in most cases, ED is a manifestation of vascular disease. One advantage of applying gene therapy for the treatment of ED is the easily accessible external location of the penis.[185,186] Hence, a tourniquet can be placed around the base of the penis and the desired gene can be administered directly into the corpora cavernosa without it entering the systemic circulation. This is a distinct advantage to other gene therapy approaches in which a vector encoding a desired gene is introduced into the systemic circulation. This approach may cause numerous adverse systemic effects, including the gene being introduced into the incorrect organ or vascular bed. This potential adverse effect is minimized when gene therapy vectors are used for treatment of ED, however, because the penis has its own external circulation, allowing a gene to be transferred and localized in one organ, thus lessening the risk of systemic spillover. Determination of the number of cells that must be transfected in order to produce a therapeutic effect is often difficult to determine. In the penis, however, only a small number of cells need to be transfected because the corpus cavernosum smooth muscle cells are interconnected by gap junctions, which allow second messenger molecules and ions to be transferred to a number of interconnected smooth muscle cells, thus causing physiologically relevant changes in erectile function.[186] Moreover, the vascular smooth muscle cells of the penis have a relatively low turnover rate, thus allowing a desired gene to be expressed for long periods of time.

The concept of gene therapy for ED treatment focuses on preventing cavernosal tissue degradation and increasing cavernosal smooth muscle tone. Smooth muscle relaxation is the necessary step to achieving a normal erection. Therefore, molecules, enzymes, or growth factors that influence the signal transduction pathway of corporal smooth muscle relaxation represent potential targets for ED gene therapy. Nitric oxide has been recognized as the principal mediator of penile erection.[187] Other diverse mediators, however, such as the prostaglandins, vasoactive intestinal polypeptide (VIP), and calcitonin gene-related peptide (CGRP), play a role in erectile physiology. Only a few laboratories have utilized the gene therapy approach for the treatment of ED. Garban and associates first demonstrated that gene therapy can be performed in the penis by utilizing naked cDNA, encoding the penile inducible nitric oxide synthase gene leading to physiologic benefit in the aging rat.[188] Christ and colleagues later showed that injection of hSlo cDNA, which encodes the human smooth muscle maxi-K+ channel, into the rat corpora cavernosa can increase gap junction formation and enhance erectile responses to nerve stimulation in the aged rat.[189] More recently, Bivalacqua and colleagues utilized an adenoviral gene transfer approach, in which an adenoviral construct encoding the endothelial nitric oxide synthase (eNOS) and

CGRP genes were shown to reverse age-related erectile dysfunction in rats.[91,183,184,190,191] In these studies, cytomegalovirus and rous sarcoma adenoviruses were utilized, and both eNOS and CGRP expression were sustained for at least 1 month in the corpora cavernosa of the rat penis. Five days after transfection with the AdCMVeNOS or AdRSVeNOS viruses, aged rats had significant increases in erectile function when stimulated by cavernosal nerve stimulation or pharmacologic stimulation with the endothelium-dependent vasodilator acetylcholine, and the type 5 phosphodiesterase inhibitors zaprinast and sildenafil.[91,183,190] Radical pelvic surgery is another common cause of ED due to injury to the cavernosal nerves. Lue and colleagues have demonstrated that intracavernous injection of adeno-associated virus-brain derived neurotrophic factor could improve erectile function after cavernosal nerve injury.[48] This neurotrophic factor purportedly restored neuronal NOS in the major pelvic ganglion, thus enhancing the recovery of erectile function after bilateral cavernous nerve injury. These early but innovative studies provide evidence that in vivo gene transfer can have beneficial physiologic effects on penile erection.

The application of gene therapy for the treatment of ED represents an exciting new field, which still requires a significant amount of basic research before in vivo gene therapy techniques can be applied to humans.

### The Role of Neutraceuticals in the Treatment of Men with Erectile Dysfunction

While the use of neutraceuticals and alternative medicine therapies have always been an important part of people's cultural practices, the passage of the Dietary Supplement and Health Education Act by the U.S. Congress unleashed an explosion of nutraceutical sales in the United States. As these compounds are sold over the counter without the oversight of the usual regulatory systems that control pharmaceutical sales, it is difficult to obtain reliable estimates of their sales volume. There is agreement, however, that the sales of nutraceuticals in this country total billions of dollars. Due to the paucity and, in many instances, complete absence of published, peer-reviewed evidence of efficacy and safety, advertised claims of their potency are not verifiable. In the absence of data from placebo-controlled, randomized trials, the use of these compounds for the medical management of patients with sexual dysfunction is not recommended. Also, the use of over-the-counter nutraceuticals tends to bypass the process of medical evaluation, which is necessary before treatment initiation because it may uncover comorbidities that need treatment.

It is important, however, for the physician to be familiar with what is being sold over the counter for several reasons. First, nutraceuticals and alternative medicine therapies are widely used; in one survey of patients presenting for preanesthesia evaluation, 63% had used a dietary supplement or unapproved herbal product.[192,193] Second, some of the nutraceuticals affect drug metabolism, including the metabolism of PDE5 inhibitors.[194] Some unapproved herbal products may contain organic nitrates whose use in conjunction with PDE5 inhibitors could provoke a serious, life-threatening hypotensive episode. Finally, some dietary supplements may have a legitimate role in treatment of erectile dysfunction and are worthy of further investigation. Thus, L-arginine is a precursor of NO,[195] Ginkgo biloba has been shown to relax cavernosal smooth muscle,[196-201] and ginsenosides (components in extracts of ginseng) enhance the release of NO from endothelial cells.[202] Initial studies with L-arginine, however, have not demonstrated significant hemodynamic improvements or greater improvements in clinical outcomes than placebo. In an uncontrolled study, 76% of men taking 40 to 120 mg of Ginkgo biloba extract reported some improvement in sexual function. Ginkgo biloba inhibits platelet aggregation and may increase the risk of bleeding, especially when used in conjunction with a selective serotonin reuptake inhibitor (SSRI).

## EJACULATORY DISORDERS

Data from a recent national survey highlighted the high prevalence and clinical importance of ejaculatory disorders[31,61,203]; this survey recognized premature ejaculation as the most prevalent sexual disorder in men 18 to 59 years of age. Ejaculatory disorders can also lead to infertility among men.

Ejaculation involves a series of events triggered by central nervous system activation of the sympathetic nervous system that creates an emission containing the semen, the secretions from seminal vesicles, prostate, and bulbourethral glands.[204-208] This emission is ejected out of the urethra by the contractions of the bulbocavernosus and levator ani muscles. The sensation associated with the rhythmic contractions of these pelvic floor muscles is referred to as the orgasm.[204-208] Thus, it is easy to understand how diseases of the central nervous system, autonomic nervous system, damage to the pelvic nerves that carry the sympathetic input to the penis, or damage to the pelvic floor muscles or bladder neck could contribute to ejaculatory problems.[204-208]

Ejaculatory disorders are a heterogeneous group of disorders that includes anejaculation, anorgasmia, delayed ejaculation, retrograde ejaculation, premature ejaculation, and painful ejaculation.[209] Of these, premature ejaculation often due to psychological factors and retrograde ejaculation due to diabetes-associated autonomic neuropathy are the most frequent ejaculatory disorders. Anejaculation is usually due to the lesions involving the nerve supply to the penis as a result of spinal cord injury, pelvic surgery, degenerative diseases, or complications of drugs, such as antihypertensives, antipsychotics, or antidepressants. Retrograde ejaculation is the result of autonomic dysfunction due to autonomic neuropathy associated with diabetes mellitus, sympathectomy, or therapy with adrenergic antagonists, some types of antihypertensives, antipsychotics, or antidepressants, bladder neck incompetence, or urethral obstruction.

### DIAGNOSTIC EVALUATION OF MEN WITH EJACULATORY DISORDERS

The diagnostic workup of men with ejaculatory disorders should include a detailed history of neuropathies, diabetes mellitus, pelvic or vertebral trauma, spinal cord injury, pelvic surgery, and urogenital infections including sexually transmitted diseases.[209-213] The ingestion of drugs such as antihypertensives, antidepressants, and antipsychotics should be verified. Psychosexual history of relationship problems, performance anxiety, expectations, and sexual trauma, especially childhood abuse, should be elicited. Physical examination should focus on verifying the presence of autonomic dysfunction, genital examination, sensitivity of scrotum, testes, and perineum, and cremasteric and deep tendon reflexes. Presence of sperm in the postejaculatory urine can confirm the presence of retrograde ejaculation. Although autonomic neuropathy can be verified by assessing postural change in heart rate and blood pressure, or changes in heart rate and blood pressure in response to Valsalva's maneuver or a cold pressor test, in practice, such tests are rarely necessary beyond demonstration of postural hypotension.

### TREATMENT OF EJACULATORY DISORDERS

The treatment of premature ejaculation usually includes counseling to reduce performance anxiety, couple education, and the use of stop and start technique or topical anesthetics during intercourse to delay ejaculation. There is no evidence from randomized controlled trials, however, that psychosexual counseling is effective over the long range. The use of SSRIs can delay ejaculation and orgasm,[211-213] and these compounds have been used "off-label" for the treatment of premature ejaculation. Although there are few, long-term, placebo-controlled trials of SSRIs for the treatment of premature ejaculation, a number of open-label studies have provided suggestive evidence of their usefulness.[214-222] Empiric application of a multimodal approach that includes counseling, the use of topical anesthetics, and SSRIs can be useful, although it should be recognized that there is no published evidence from randomized controlled trials to demonstrate the efficacy of such an approach.[223,224]

## HELPFUL HINTS FOR THE PRACTICING INTERNIST OR ENDOCRINOLOGIST (TABLE 173-10)

Due to the growing interest in men's sexual health and the high prevalence of sexual dysfunction among men in any general or specialty practice, management of sexual dysfunction can be both intellectually and financially rewarding. Attention to several details can increase efficiency and remuneration. For instance, mailing out a previsit packet that contains questionnaires and forms, having the patient fill out the questionnaires and forms before physician contact, using a standardized algorithm such as that recommended by the Process of Care Expert Panel or World Health Organization can maximize efficiency. Also, delegating several time-consuming tasks, such as patient education and instructions in the use of the therapies, to appropriately trained staff can reduce physician time exposure. It is also fruitful to establish a formal collaborative relationship with a designated urologist who can manage treatment-related complications such as priapism and who is available in the event of such emergencies; this can help allay physician and patient anxiety. Also, as counseling of the couple and psychosexual therapy require skill and time, a collegial relationship with a sex therapist or a clinical psychologist with appropriate training in the management of sexual disorders is always useful. Most patients

with ED are motivated, and providing them access to sources of information, such as brochures, educational pamphlets, videos, answers to frequently asked questions, and websites can not only enhance patient satisfaction, but also reduce physician time exposure.

| *Table 173-10* | Helpful Hints for the Practicing Internist or Endocrinologist |
|---|---|

1. Maximizing efficiency
   a. Mail out a previsit packet containing questionnaires and forms.
   b. Have the patient fill out the questionnaires and forms before physician contact.
   c. Use a standardized algorithm such as that recommended by the Process of Care Expert Panel or WHO; familiarize your staff with the algorithm.
   d. Provide the patient access to sources of information, such as brochures, educational pamphlets, videos, answers to frequently asked questions, and websites, such as *http://www.impotence.org; http://www.nlm.nih.gov; http://www.mayohealth.org; http://www.hon.ch; http://webmd.com;* and *http://www.andrologyaustralia.org.*
2. Appropriate coding to receive reimbursement
   a. Provide comprehensive documentation and code appropriately consistent with the documentation.
   b. Initial visit: 99201–99205, depending on the intensity
   c. Follow-up visit: 99211–99215, depending on the intensity
   d. Code for comorbidities as well as for erectile dysfunction.
3. Train the office staff or a nurse to handle routine operations, such as patient education, mailing out previsit packets, providing drug information and instructions, retrieving laboratory data before the visit, coding appropriately, and distributing patient education material.
4. Build a network of collaborators, including a referral base of primary care providers, urologists, and sex therapists or clinical psychologists with training in counseling couples with sexual problems.

## REFERENCES

1. Laumann EO, Paik A, Rosen RC: The epidemiology of erectile dysfunction: Results from the National Health and Social Life Survey. Int J Impot Res 11(Suppl 1):S60–S64, 1999.
2. Morgentaler A: Male impotence. Lancet 354:1713–1718, 1999.
3. Baldwin K, Ginsberg P, Harkaway RC: Under-reporting of erectile dysfunction among men with unrelated urologic conditions. Int J Impot Res 15:87–89, 2003.
4. National Institutes of Health Consensus Conference: Impotence. NIH Consensus Development Panel on Impotence. JAMA 270:83–90, 1993.
5. Levine LA, Kloner RA: Importance of asking questions about erectile dysfunction. Am J Cardiol 86:1210–1213, A1215, 2000.
6. Shabsigh R: Recent developments in male sexual dysfunction. Curr Psychiatry Rep 2:196–200, 2000.
7. Wyllie MG: The Second International Consultation on Erectile Dysfunction: Highlights from the pharmaceutical industry. BJU Int 92:645–646, 2003.
8. The process of care model for evaluation and treatment of erectile dysfunction. The Process of Care Consensus Panel. Int J Impot Res 11:59–70; discussion 70–54, 1999.

9. Masters WH, Johnson VE: Human Sexual Response. Boston, MA, Little Brown, 1966.
10. Meuleman E: Clinical evaluation and the doctor-patient dialogue. In Jardin A, Wagner G, Khoury S, et al (eds): Erectile Dysfunction. Plymouth, UK, Plymbridge, 2000, pp 115–138.
11. American Psychiatric Association: Diagnostic and Statistical Manual of Mental Disorders. Arlington, VA, American Psychiatric Association, 1994.
12. Rosen RC, Leiblum SR: Hypoactive sexual desire. Psychiatr Clin North Am 18:107–121, 1995.
13. Ponticas Y: Sexual aversion versus hypoactive sexual desire: A diagnostic challenge. Psychiatr Med 10:273–281, 1992.
14. Halvorsen JG, Metz ME: Sexual dysfunction, part I: Classification, etiology, and pathogenesis. J Am Board Fam Pract 5:51–61, 1992.
15. Segraves KB, Segraves RT: Hypoactive sexual desire disorder: Prevalence and comorbidity in 906 subjects. J Sex Marital Ther 17:55–58, 1991.
16. Beck JG: Hypoactive sexual desire disorder: An overview. J Consult Clin Psychol 63:919–927, 1995.
17. Rosen RC: Prevalence and risk factors of sexual dysfunction in men and women. Curr Psychiatry Rep 2:189–195, 2000.
18. Laumann EO, Paik A, Rosen RC: Sexual dysfunction in the United States:

Prevalence and predictors. JAMA 537–544, 1999.
19. Bagatell CJ, Heiman JR, Rivier JE, Bremner WJ: Effects of endogenous testosterone and estradiol on sexual behavior in normal young men. J Clin Endocrinol Metab 78:711–716, 1994 [published erratum in J Clin Endocrinol Metab 78:1520, 1994].
20. Alexander GM, Swerdloff RS, Wang C, et al: Androgen-behavior correlations in hypogonadal men and eugonadal men. I. Mood and response to auditory sexual stimuli. Horm Behav 31:110–119, 1997.
21. Wang C, Eyre DR, Clark R, et al: Sublingual testosterone replacement improves muscle mass and strength, decreases bone resorption, and increases bone formation markers in hypogonadal men: A clinical research center study. J Clin Endocrinol Metab 81:3654–3662, 1996.
22. Alexander GM, Swerdloff RS, Wang C, et al: Androgen-behavior correlations in hypogonadal men and eugonadal men. II. Cognitive abilities. Horm Behav 33:85–94, 1998.
23. Buena F, Swerdloff RS, Steiner BS, et al: Sexual function does not change when serum testosterone levels are pharmacologically varied within the normal male range. Fertil Steril 59:1118–1123, 1993.

24. Wang C, Berman N, Longstreth JA, et al: Pharmacokinetics of transdermal testosterone gel in hypogonadal men: Application of gel at one site versus four sites. A General Clinical Research Center Study. J Clin Endocrinol Metab 85:964–969, 2000.
25. Schover LR, LoPiccolo J: Treatment effectiveness for dysfunctions of sexual desire. J Sex Marital Ther 8:179–197, 1982.
26. LoPiccolo J: Diagnosis and treatment of male sexual dysfunction. J Sex Marital Ther 11:215–232, 1985.
27. Benet AE, Melman A: The epidemiology of erectile dysfunction. Urol Clin North Am 22:699–709, 1995.
28. Feldman HA, Goldstein I, Hatzichristou DG, et al: Impotence and its medical and psychosocial correlates: Results of the Massachusetts Male Aging Study. J Urol 151:54–61, 1994.
29. Johannes CB, Araujo AB, Feldman HA, et al: Incidence of erectile dysfunction in men 40 to 69 years old: Longitudinal results from the Massachusetts Male Aging Study. J Urol 163:460–463, 2000.
30. Lewis RW: Epidemiology of erectile dysfunction. Urol Clin North Am 28:209–216, vii, 2001.
31. Laumann EO, Paik A, Rosen RC: Sexual dysfunction in the United States: Prevalence and predictors. JAMA 281:537–544, 1999.
32. Feldman HA, Johannes CB, Derby CA, et al: Erectile dysfunction and coronary risk factors: Prospective results from the Massachusetts Male Aging Study. Prev Med 30:328–338, 2000.
33. McKinlay JB: The worldwide prevalence and epidemiology of erectile dysfunction. Int J Impot Res 12(Suppl 4):S6–S11, 2000.
34. Derby CA, Araujo AB, Johannes CB, et al: Measurement of erectile dysfunction in population-based studies: The use of a single question self-assessment in the Massachusetts Male Aging Study. Int J Impot Res 12:197–204, 2000.
35. McKinlay JB, Digruttolo L, Glasser D, et al: International differences in the epidemiology of male erectile dysfunction. Int J Clin Pract Suppl 102:35, 1999.
36. Johannes CB, Araujo AB, Feldman HA, et al: Incidence of erectile dysfunction in men 40 to 69 years old: Longitudinal results from the Massachusetts Male Aging Study. J Urol 163:460–463, 2000.
37. Ayta IA, McKinlay JB, Krane RJ: The likely worldwide increase in erectile dysfunction between 1995 and 2025 and some possible policy consequences. BJU Int 84:50–56, 1999.
38. Carani C, Granata AR, Bancroft J, Marrama P: The effects of testosterone replacement on nocturnal penile tumescence and rigidity and erectile response to visual erotic stimuli in hypogonadal men. Psychoneuroendocrinology 20:743–753, 1995.
39. Cunningham GR, Hirshkowitz M, Korenman SG, Karacan I: Testosterone replacement therapy and sleep-related erections in hypogonadal men. J Clin Endocrinol Metab 70:792–797, 1990.
40. Carani C, Zini D, Baldini A, et al: Effects of androgen treatment in impotent men with normal and low levels of free testosterone. Arch Sex Behav 19:223–234, 1990.
41. Davidson JM, Camargo CA, Smith ER: Effects of androgen on sexual behavior in hypogonadal men. J Clin Endocrinol Metab 48:955–958, 1979.
42. Kwan M, Greenleaf WJ, Mann J, et al: The nature of androgen action on male sexuality: A combined laboratory self-report study on hypogonadal men. J Clin Endocrinol Metab 57:557–562, 1983.
43. Salmimies P, Kockott G, Pirke KM, et al: Effects of testosterone replacement on sexual behavior in hypogonadal men. Arch Sex Behav 11:345–353, 1982.
44. Lugg JA, Rajfer J: Drug therapy for erectile dysfunction. American Oncology Association Update 15:290, 1996.
45. Lugg JA, Rajfer J, Gonzalez-Cadavid NF: Dihydrotestosterone is the active androgen in the maintenance of nitric oxide–mediated penile erection in the rat. Endocrinology 136:1495–1501, 1995.
46. Andersson KE, Wagner G: Physiology of penile erection. Physiol Rev 75:191–236, 1995.
47. Christ GJ: The penis as a vascular organ: The importance of corporal smooth muscle tone in the control of erection. Urol Clin North Am 22:727–745, 1995.
48. Lue TF: Erectile dysfunction. N Engl J Med 342:1802–1813, 2000.
49. Lue TF, Tanagho EA: Hemodynamics of erection. In Tanagho EA, Lue TF, McClure RD (eds): Contemporary Management of Impotence and Infertility. Baltimore, Williams & Wilkins, 1988, pp 28–38.
50. Naylor AM: Endogenous neurotransmitters mediating penile erection. Br J Urol 81:424–431, 1998.
51. Melman A, Christ GJ: Integrative erectile biology: The effects of age and disease on gap junctions and ion channels and their potential value to the treatment of erectile dysfunction. Urol Clin North Am 28:217–231, vii, 2001.
52. Christ GJ, Moreno AP, Melman A, Spray DC: Gap junction–mediated intercellular diffusion of Ca2+ in cultured human corporal smooth muscle cells. Am J Physiol 263:C373–C383, 1992.
53. Moreno AP, Campos de Carvalho AC, Christ G, et al: Gap junctions between human corpus cavernosum smooth muscle cells: Gating properties and unitary conductance. Am J Physiol 264:C80–C92, 1993.
54. Campos de Carvalho AC, Roy C, Moreno AP, et al: Gap junctions formed of connexin-43 are found between smooth muscle cells of human corpus cavernosum. J Urol 149:1568–1575, 1993.
55. Tsai H, Werber J, Davia MO, et al: Reduced connexin-43 expression in high grade, human prostatic adenocarcinoma cells. Biochem Biophys Res Commun 227:64–69, 1996.
56. Rajfer J, Aronson WJ, Bush PA, et al: Nitric oxide as a mediator of relaxation of the corpus cavernosum in response to nonadrenergic, noncholinergic neurotransmission. N Engl J Med 326:90–94, 1992.
57. McDonald LJ, Murad F: Nitric oxide and cyclic GMP signaling. Proc Soc Exp Biol Med 211:1–6, 1996.
58. Nehra A, Barrett DM, Moreland RB: Pharmacotherapeutic advances in the treatment of erectile dysfunction. Mayo Clin Proc 74:709–721, 1999.
59. Goldstein I, Lue TF, Padma-Nathan H, et al: Oral sildenafil in the treatment of erectile dysfunction. Sildenafil Study Group [see comments]. N Engl J Med 338:1397–1404, 1998 [published erratum in N Engl J Med 339:59, 1998].
60. Braun M, Wassmer G, Klotz T, et al: Epidemiology of erectile dysfunction: Results of the Cologne Male Survey. Int J Impot Res 12:305–311, 2000.
61. Rosen R, Altwein J, Boyle P, et al: Lower urinary tract symptoms and male sexual dysfunction: The Multinational Survey of the Aging Male (MSAM-7). Eur Urol 44:637–649, 2003.
62. NIH consensus: Impotence. NIH Consensus Development Panel on Impotence. JAMA 270:83–90, 1993.
63. Cappelleri JC, Rosen RC, Smith MD, et al: Diagnostic evaluation of the erectile function domain of the International Index of Erectile Function. Urology 54:346–351, 1999.
64. Rosen RC, Riley A, Wagner G, et al: The International Index of Erectile Function (IIEF): A multidimensional scale for assessment of erectile dysfunction. Urology 49:822–830, 1997.
65. Cappelleri JC, Rosen RC: A comparison of the International Index of Erectile Function and erectile dysfunction studies. BJU Int 92:654, 2003.
66. Rosen RC, Cappelleri JC, Smith MD, et al: Development and evaluation of an abridged, 5-item version of the International Index of Erectile Function (IIEF-5) as a diagnostic tool for erectile dysfunction. Int J Impot Res 11:319–326, 1999.
67. Althof SE, Corty EW, Levine SB, et al: EDITS: Development of questionnaires for evaluating satisfaction with treatments for erectile dysfunction. Urology 53:793–799, 1999.
68. O'Leary MP, Fowler FJ, Lenderking WR, et al: A brief male sexual function inventory for urology. Urology 46:697–706, 1995.
69. Ruutu ML, Virtanen JM, Lindstrom BL, Alfthan OS: The value of basic investigations in the diagnosis of impotence. Scand J Urol Nephrol 21:261–265, 1987.
70. Takasaki N, Kotani T, Miyazaki S, Saitou S: [Measurement of penile brachial index (PBI) in patients with impotence]. Hinyokika Kiyo 35:1365–1368, 1989.

71. Aitchison M, Aitchison J, Carter R: Is the penile brachial index a reproducible and useful measurement? Br J Urol 66:202–204, 1990.

72. Mueller SC, Wallenberg-Pachaly H, Voges GE, Schild HH: Comparison of selective internal iliac pharmaco-angiography, penile brachial index and duplex sonography with pulsed Doppler analysis for the evaluation of vasculogenic (arteriogenic) impotence. J Urol 143:928–932, 1990.

73. Brock G: Tumescence monitoring devices: Past and present. In Hellstrom W (ed): Handbook of Sexual Dysfunction. Lawrence, KS, Allen Press, 1999, pp 65–69.

74. Korenman SG, Morley JE, Mooradian AD, et al: Secondary hypogonadism in older men: Its relation to impotence. J Clin Endocrinol Metab 71:963–969, 1990.

75. Buvat J, Lemaire A: Endocrine screening in 1022 men with erectile dysfunction: Clinical significance and cost-effective strategy [see comments]. J Urol 158:1764–1767, 1997.

76. Carani C, Bancroft J, Granata A, et al: Testosterone and erectile function, nocturnal penile tumescence and rigidity, and erectile response to visual erotic stimuli in hypogonadal and eugonadal men. Psychoneuroendocrinology 17:647–654, 1992.

77. Kaiser FE, Viosca SP, Morley JE, et al: Impotence and aging: Clinical and hormonal factors. J Am Geriatr Soc 36:511–519, 1988.

78. Citron JT, Ettinger B, Rubinoff H, et al: Prevalence of hypothalamic-pituitary imaging abnormalities in impotent men with secondary hypogonadism. J Urol 155:529–533, 1996.

79. Morales A, Johnston B, Heaton P, Lundie M: Testosterone supplementation for hypogonadal impotence: Assessment of biochemical measures and therapeutic outcomes. J Urol 157:849–854, 1997.

80. Hajjar RR, Kaiser FE, Morley JE: Outcomes of long-term testosterone replacement in older hypogonadal males: A retrospective analysis. J Clin Endocrinol Metab 82:3793–3796, 1997.

81. Khaw KT, Barrett-Connor E: Lower endogenous androgens predict central adiposity in men. Ann Epidemiol 2:675–682, 1992.

82. Seidell JC, Bjorntorp P, Sjostrom L, et al: Visceral fat accumulation in men is positively associated with insulin, glucose, and C-peptide levels, but negatively with testosterone levels. Metabolism 39:897–901, 1990.

83. Haffner SM: Sex hormone–binding protein, hyperinsulinemia, insulin resistance and non–insulin-dependent diabetes. Horm Res 45:233–237, 1996.

84. Haffner SM, Shaten J, Stern MP, et al: Low levels of sex hormone–binding globulin and testosterone predict the development of non–insulin-dependent diabetes mellitus in men. MRFIT Research Group. Multiple Risk Factor Intervention Trial. Am J Epidemiol 143:889–897, 1996.

85. Alexandersen P, Haarbo J, Christiansen C: The relationship of natural androgens to coronary heart disease in males: A review. Atherosclerosis 125:1–13, 1996.

86. Rosen RC: Psychogenic erectile dysfunction: Classification and management. Urol Clin North Am 28:269–278, 2001.

87. Abrahamson DJ, Barlow DH, Beck JG, et al: The effects of attentional focus and partner responsiveness on sexual responding: replication and extension. Arch Sex Behav 14:361–371, 1985.

88. Vickers MA Jr, De Nobrega AM, Dluhy RG: Diagnosis and treatment of psychogenic erectile dysfunction in a urological setting: Outcomes of 18 consecutive patients. J Urol 149:1258–1261, 1993.

89. Halvorsen JG, Metz ME: Sexual dysfunction, part II: Diagnosis, management, and prognosis. J Am Board Fam Pract 5:177–192, 1992.

90. Kilmann PR, Boland JP, Norton SP, et al: Perspectives of sex therapy outcome: A survey of AASECT providers. J Sex Marital Ther 12:116–138, 1986.

91. Bivalacqua TJ, Champion HC, Mehta YS, et al: Adenoviral gene transfer of endothelial nitric oxide synthase (eNOS) to the penis improves age-related erectile dysfunction in the rat. Int J Impot Res 12(Suppl 3):S8–S17, 2000.

92. Kim NN, Huang YH, Goldstein I, et al: Inhibition of cyclic GMP hydrolysis in human corpus cavernosum smooth muscle cells by vardenafil, a novel, selective phosphodiesterase type 5 inhibitor. Life Sci 69:2249–2256, 2001.

93. Haning H, Niewohner U, Bischoff E: Phosphodiesterase type 5 (PDE5) inhibitors. Prog Med Chem 41:249–306, 2003.

94. Bischoff E: Potency, selectivity, and consequences of nonselectivity of PDE inhibition. Int J Impot Res 16(Suppl 1):S11–S14, 2004.

95. Kuhn R, Uckert S, Stief CG, et al: Relaxation of human ureteral smooth muscle in vitro by modulation of cyclic nucleotide-dependent pathways. Urol Res 28:110–115, 2000.

96. Boolell M, Allen MJ, Ballard SA, et al: Sildenafil: An orally active type 5 cyclic GMP-specific phosphodiesterase inhibitor for the treatment of penile erectile dysfunction. Int J Impot Res 8:47–52, 1996.

97. Taher A, Meyer M, Stief CG, et al: Cyclic nucleotide phosphodiesterase in human cavernous smooth muscle. World J Urol 15:32–35, 1997.

98. Jeremy JY, Ballard SA, Naylor AM, et al: Effects of sildenafil, a type-5 cGMP phosphodiesterase inhibitor, and papaverine on cyclic GMP and cyclic AMP levels in the rabbit corpus cavernosum in vitro. Br J Urol 79:958–963, 1997.

99. Stief CG, Uckert S, Becker AJ, et al: The effect of the specific phosphodiesterase (PDE) inhibitors on human and rabbit cavernous tissue in vitro and in vivo. J Urol 159:1390–1393, 1998.

100. Moreland RB, Goldstein I, Traish A: Sildenafil, a novel inhibitor of phosphodiesterase type 5 in human corpus cavernosum smooth muscle cells. Life Sci 62:PL309–PL318, 1998.

101. Carter AJ, Ballard SA, Naylor AM: Effect of the selective phosphodiesterase type 5 inhibitor sildenafil on erectile dysfunction in the anesthetized dog. J Urol 160:242–246, 1998.

102. Chuang AT, Strauss JD, Murphy RA, Steers WD: Sildenafil, a type-5 CGMP phosphodiesterase inhibitor, specifically amplifies endogenous cGMP-dependent relaxation in rabbit corpus cavernosum smooth muscle in vitro. J Urol 160:257–261, 1998.

103. Wallis RM, Corbin JD, Francis SH, Ellis P: Tissue distribution of phosphodiesterase families and the effects of sildenafil on tissue cyclic nucleotides, platelet function, and the contractile responses of trabeculae carneae and aortic rings in vitro. Am J Cardiol 83:3C–12C, 1999.

104. Wallis RM: The pharmacology of sildenafil, a novel and selective inhibitor of phosphodiesterase (PDE) type 5. Nippon Yakurigaku Zasshi 114(Suppl 1):22P–26P, 1999.

105. Stief CG, Uckert S, Becker AJ, et al: Effects of sildenafil on cAMP and cGMP levels in isolated human cavernous and cardiac tissue. Urology 55:146–150, 2000.

106. Maggi M, Filippi S, Ledda F, et al: Erectile dysfunction: From biochemical pharmacology to advances in medical therapy. Eur J Endocrinol 143:143–154, 2000.

107. Uckert S, Kuthe A, Stief CG, Jonas U: Phosphodiesterase isoenzymes as pharmacological targets in the treatment of male erectile dysfunction. World J Urol 19:14–22, 2001.

108. Yu G, Mason HJ, Wu X, et al: Substituted pyrazolopyridines as potent and selective PDE5 inhibitors: potential agents for treatment of erectile dysfunction. J Med Chem 44:1025–1027, 2001.

109. Saenz de Tejada I, Angulo J, Cuevas P, et al: The phosphodiesterase inhibitory selectivity and the in vitro and in vivo potency of the new PDE5 inhibitor vardenafil. Int J Impot Res 13:282–290, 2001.

110. Goldstein I: A 36-week, open label, non-comparative study to assess the long-term safety of sildenafil citrate (Viagra) in patients with erectile dysfunction. Int J Clin Pract Suppl 102:8–9, 1999.

111. Rendell MS, Rajfer J, Wicker PA, Smith MD: Sildenafil for treatment of erectile dysfunction in men with diabetes: A randomized controlled trial. Sildenafil Diabetes Study Group [see comments]. JAMA 281:421–426, 1999.

112. Yu G, Mason H, Wu X, et al: Substituted pyrazolopyridopyridazines as orally bioavailable potent and selective PDE5 inhibitors: Potential agents for treatment of erectile dysfunction. J Med Chem 46:457–460, 2003.

113. Seftel AD: Phosphodiesterase type 5 inhibitor differentiation based on selectivity, pharmacokinetic, and efficacy profiles. Clin Cardiol 27:I14–I19, 2004.

114. Crowe SM, Streetman DS: Vardenafil treatment for erectile dysfunction. Ann Pharmacother 38:77–85, 2004.

115. Grossman EB, Swan SK, Muirhead GJ, et al: The pharmacokinetics and hemodynamics of sildenafil citrate in male hemodialysis patients. Kidney Int 66:367–374, 2004.

116. Sussman DO: Pharmacokinetics, pharmacodynamics, and efficacy of phosphodiesterase type 5 inhibitors. J Am Osteopath Assoc 104:S11–S15, 2004.

117. Rajagopalan P, Mazzu A, Xia C, et al: Effect of high-fat breakfast and moderate-fat evening meal on the pharmacokinetics of vardenafil, an oral phosphodiesterase-5 inhibitor for the treatment of erectile dysfunction. J Clin Pharmacol 43:260–267, 2003.

118. Moreland RB, Goldstein I, Traish A: Sildenafil, a novel inhibitor of phosphodiesterase type 5 in human corpus cavernosum smooth muscle cells. Life Sci 62:PL309–PL318, 1998.

119. Giuliano F, Hultling C, el Masry WS, et al: Randomized trial of sildenafil for the treatment of erectile dysfunction in spinal cord injury. Sildenafil Study Group. Ann Neurol 46:15–21, 1999.

120. Jarow JP, Burnett AL, Geringer AM: Clinical efficacy of sildenafil citrate based on etiology and response to prior treatment [see comments]. J Urol 162:722–725, 1999.

121. Dinsmore WW, Hodges M, Hargreaves C, et al: Sildenafil citrate (Viagra) in erectile dysfunction: Near normalization in men with broad-spectrum erectile dysfunction compared with age-matched healthy control subjects. Urology 53:800–805, 1999 [published erratum in Urology 53:1072, 1999].

122. Morales A, Gingell C, Collins M, et al: Clinical safety of oral sildenafil citrate (Viagra) in the treatment of erectile dysfunction. Int J Impot Res 10:69–73, 1998.

123. Aversa A, Mazzilli F, Rossi T, et al: Effects of sildenafil (Viagra) administration on seminal parameters and post-ejaculatory refractory time in normal males. Hum Reprod 15:131–134, 2000.

124. Feenstra J, Drie-Pierik RJ, Lacle CF, Stricker BH: Acute myocardial infarction associated with sildenafil [letter; see comments]. Lancet 352:957–958, 1998.

125. Zusman RM, Morales A, Glasser DB, Osterloh IH: Overall cardiovascular profile of sildenafil citrate. Am J Cardiol 83:35C–44C, 1999.

126. Arora RR, Timoney M, Melilli L: Acute myocardial infarction after the use of sildenafil [letter]. N Engl J Med 341:700, 1999.

127. Cheitlin MD, Hutter AM Jr, Brindis RG, et al: Use of sildenafil (Viagra) in patients with cardiovascular disease. Technology and Practice Executive Committee [see comments]. Circulation 99:168–177, 1999 [published erratum in Circulation 100:2389, 1999].

128. Muller JE, Mittleman A, Maclure M, et al: Triggering myocardial infarction by sexual activity: Low absolute risk and prevention by regular physical exertion. Determinants of Myocardial Infarction Onset Study Investigators [see comments]. JAMA 275:1405–1409, 1996.

129. Herrmann HC, Chang G, Klugherz BD, Mahoney PD: Hemodynamic effects of sildenafil in men with severe coronary artery disease. N Engl J Med 342:1622–1626, 2000.

130. Kloner RA: Novel phosphodiesterase type 5 inhibitors: Assessing hemodynamic effects and safety parameters. Clin Cardiol 27:I20–I25, 2004.

131. Padma-Nathan H, Steers WD, Wicker PA: Efficacy and safety of oral sildenafil in the treatment of erectile dysfunction: A double-blind, placebo-controlled study of 329 patients. Sildenafil Study Group [see comments]. Int J Clin Pract 52:375–379, 1998.

132. Goldenberg MM: Safety and efficacy of sildenafil citrate in the treatment of male erectile dysfunction. Clin Ther 20:1033–1048, 1998.

133. Conti CR, Pepine CJ, Sweeney M: Efficacy and safety of sildenafil citrate in the treatment of erectile dysfunction in patients with ischemic heart disease. Am J Cardiol 83:29C–34C, 1999.

134. Osterloh IH, Collins M, Wicker P, Wagner G: Sildenafil citrate (Viagra): Overall safety profile in 18 double-blind, placebo controlled, clinical trials. Int J Clin Pract Suppl 102:3–5, 1999.

135. Young J: Sildenafil citrate (Viagra) in the treatment of erectile dysfunction: A 12-week, flexible-dose study to assess efficacy and safety. Int J Clin Pract Suppl 102:6–7, 1999.

136. Kloner RA: Cardiovascular risk and sildenafil. Am J Cardiol 86:57F–61F, 2000.

137. McMahon CG, Samali R, Johnson H: Efficacy, safety and patient acceptance of sildenafil citrate as treatment for erectile dysfunction [in process citation]. J Urol 164:1192–1196, 2000.

138. Highleyman L: Protease inhibitors and sildenafil (Viagra) should not be combined. Beta 12:3, 1999.

139. Bailey DG, Dresser GK: Interactions between grapefruit juice and cardiovascular drugs. Am J Cardiovasc Drugs 4:281–297, 2004.

140. McGarvey MR: Tough choices: The cost-effectiveness of sildenafil [editorial; comment]. Ann Intern Med 132:994–995, 2000.

141. Smith KJ, Roberts MS: The cost-effectiveness of sildenafil [see comments]. Ann Intern Med 132:933–937, 2000.

142. Tan HL: Economic cost of male erectile dysfunction using a decision analytic model: For a hypothetical managed care plan of 100,000 members. Pharmacoeconomics 17:77–107, 2000.

143. Skakkebaek NE, Bancroft J, Davidson DW, Warner P: Androgen replacement with oral testosterone undecanoate in hypogonadal men: A double blind controlled study. Clin Endocrinol (Oxf) 14:49–61, 1981.

144. McClure RD, Oses R, Ernest ML: Hypogonadal impotence treated by transdermal testosterone. Urology 37:224–228, 1991.

145. Nankin HR, Lin T, Osterman J: Chronic testosterone cypionate therapy in men with secondary impotence. Fertil Steril 46:300–307, 1986.

146. Arver S, Dobs AS, Meikle AW, et al: Improvement of sexual function in testosterone deficient men treated for 1 year with a permeation enhanced testosterone transdermal system. J Urol 155:1604–1608, 1996.

147. Bhasin S, Fielder T, Peacock N, et al: Dissociating antifertility effects of GnRH-antagonist from its adverse effects on mating behavior in male rats. Am J Physiol 254:E84–E91, 1988.

148. Fielder TJ, Peacock NR, McGivern RF, et al: Testosterone dose-dependency of sexual and nonsexual behaviors in the gonadotropin-releasing hormone antagonist-treated male rat. J Androl 10:167–173, 1989.

149. Jain P, Rademaker AW, McVary KT: Testosterone supplementation for erectile dysfunction: Results of a meta-analysis [in process citation]. J Urol 164:371–375, 2000.

150. Garban H, Marquez D, Cai L, et al: Restoration of normal adult penile erectile response in aged rats by long-term treatment with androgens. Biol Reprod 53:1365–1372, 1995.

151. Vernet D, Cai L, Garban H, et al: Reduction of penile nitric oxide synthase in diabetic BB/WORdp (type I) and BBZ/WORdp (type II) rats with erectile dysfunction. Endocrinology 136:5709–5717, 1995.

152. Chamness SL, Ricker DD, Crone JK, et al: The effect of androgen on nitric oxide synthase in the male reproductive tract of the rat. Fertil Steril 63:1101–1107, 1995.

153. Trigo-Rocha F, Aronson WJ, Hohenfellner M, et al: Nitric oxide and cGMP: Mediators of pelvic nerve-stimulated erection in dogs. Am J Physiol 264:H419–H422, 1993.

154. Holmquist F, Persson K, Bodker A, Anderson KE: Some pre- and postjunctional effects of castration in

rabbit isolated corpus cavernosum and urethra. J Urol 152:1011–1016, 1994.

155. Andersson KE, Holmquist F, Bodker A: Castration enhances NANC nerve-mediated relaxation in rabbit isolated corpus cavernosum. Acta Physiol Scand 146:405–406, 1992.

156. Lewis RW, Mills TM: Effect of androgens on penile tissue. Endocrine 23:101–105, 2004.

157. Dai YT, Stopper V, Lewis R, Mills T: Effects of castration and testosterone replacement on veno-occlusion during penile erection in the rat. Asian J Androl 1:53–59, 1999.

158. Mills TM, Lewis RW: The role of androgens in the erectile response: A 1999 perspective. Mol Urol 3:75–86, 1999.

159. Mills TM, Dai Y, Stopper VS, Lewis RW: Androgenic maintenance of the erectile response in the rat. Steroids 64:605–609, 1999.

160. Mills TM, Lewis RW, Stopper VS: Androgenic maintenance of inflow and veno-occlusion during erection in the rat. Biol Reprod 59:1413–1418, 1998.

161. Reilly CM, Lewis RW, Stopper VS, Mills TM: Androgenic maintenance of the rat erectile response via a non–nitric-oxide-dependent pathway. J Androl 18:588–594, 1997.

162. Heaton JP, Varrin SJ: Effects of castration and exogenous testosterone supplementation in an animal model of penile erection. J Urol 797–800, 1994.

163. Shabsigh R, Raymond JF, Olsson CA, et al: Androgen induction of DNA synthesis in the rat penis. Urology 52:723–728, 1998.

164. Shabsigh R: The effects of testosterone on the cavernous tissue and erectile function. World J Urol 15:21–26, 1997.

165. Fournier GR Jr, Juenemann KP, Lue TF, Tanagho EA: Mechanisms of venous occlusion during canine penile erection: An anatomic demonstration. J Urol 137:163–167, 1987.

166. Witherington R: Vacuum devices for the impotent. J Sex Marital Ther 17:69–80, 1991.

167. Lewis JH, Sidi AA, Reddy PK: A way to help your patients who use vacuum devices. Contemp Urol 3:15–21, 1991.

168. Lewis RW, Witherington R: External vacuum therapy for erectile dysfunction: Use and results. World J Urol 15:78–82, 1997.

169. Ganem JP, Lucey DT, Janosko EO, Carson CC: Unusual complications of the vacuum erection device. Urology 51:627–631, 1998.

170. Morales A: Nonsurgical management options in impotence. Hosp Pract (Off Ed) 28:15–20, 23, 1993.

171. Engelhardt PF, Plas E, Hubner WA, Pfluger H: Comparison of intraurethral liposomal and intracavernosal prostaglandin-E1 in the management of erectile dysfunction. Br J Urol 81:441–444, 1998.

172. Kim ED, McVary KT: Topical prostaglandin-E1 for the treatment of erectile dysfunction [see comments]. J Urol 153:1828–1830, 1995.

173. Peterson CA, Bennett AH, Hellstrom WJ, et al: Erectile response to transurethral alprostadil, prazosin and alprostadil-prazosin combinations. J Urol 159:1523–1527, 1998.

174. Carson CC, Mulcahy JJ, Govier FE: Efficacy, safety and patient satisfaction outcomes of the AMS 700CX inflatable penile prosthesis: Results of a long-term multicenter study. AMS 700CX Study Group. J Urol 164:376–380, 2000.

175. Wilson SK, Cleves MA, Delk JR II: Comparison of mechanical reliability of original and enhanced Mentor Alpha I penile prosthesis. J Urol 162:715–718, 1999.

176. Wessells H, Gralnek D, Dorr, R, et al: Effect of an α-melanocyte stimulating hormone analog on penile erection and sexual desire in men with organic erectile dysfunction. Urology 56:641–646, 2000.

177. Pfaus JG, Shadiack A, Van Soest T, et al: Selective facilitation of sexual solicitation in the female rat by a melanocortin receptor agonist. Proc Natl Acad Sci U S A 101:10201–10204, 2004.

178. Rosen RC, Diamond LE, Earle DC, et al: Evaluation of the safety, pharmacokinetics and pharmacodynamic effects of subcutaneously administered PT-141, a melanocortin receptor agonist, in healthy male subjects and in patients with an inadequate response to Viagra. Int J Impot Res 16:135–142, 2004.

179. Diamond LE, Earle DC, Rosen RC, et al: Double-blind, placebo-controlled evaluation of the safety, pharmacokinetic properties and pharmacodynamic effects of intranasal PT-141, a melanocortin receptor agonist, in healthy males and patients with mild-to-moderate erectile dysfunction. Int J Impot Res 16:51–59, 2004.

180. Molinoff PB, Shadiack AM, Earle D, et al: PT-141: A melanocortin agonist for the treatment of sexual dysfunction. Ann N Y Acad Sci 994:96–102, 2003.

181. Nabel EG, Pompil VJ, Plantz GE, Nabel GJ: Gene transfer and vascular disease. Cardiovasc Res 28:445–455, 1994.

182. Heistad DD, Faraci FM: Gene therapy for cerebral vascular disease. Stroke 27:1688–1693, 1996.

183. Champion HC, Bivalacqua TJ, Hyman AL, et al: Gene transfer of endothelial nitric oxide synthase to the penis augments erectile responses in the aged rat. Proc Natl Acad Sci U S A 96:11648–11652, 1999.

184. Champion HC, Bivalacqua TJ, Toyoda K, et al: In vivo gene transfer of prepro-calcitonin gene-related peptide to the lung attenuates chronic hypoxia-induced pulmonary hypertension in the mouse. Circulation 101:923–930, 2000.

185. Bivalacqua TJ, Hellstrom WJ: Potential application of gene therapy for the treatment of erectile dysfunction. J Androl 22:183–190, 2001.

186. Christ GJ, Melman A: The application of gene therapy to the treatment of erectile dysfunction. Int J Impot Res 10:111–112, 1998.

187. Burnett AL, Lowenstein CJ, Bredt DS, et al: Nitric oxide: A physiologic mediator of penile erection. Science 257:401–403, 1992.

188. Garban H, Marquez D, Magee T, et al: Cloning of rat and human inducible penile nitric oxide synthase: Application for gene therapy of erectile dysfunction. Biol Reprod 56:954–963, 1997.

189. Christ GJ, Rehman J, Day N, et al: Intracorporal injection of hSlo cDNA in rats produces physiologically relevant alterations in penile function. Am J Physiol 275:H600–H608, 1998.

190. Champion HC, Bivalacqua TJ, D'Souza FM, et al: Gene transfer of endothelial nitric oxide synthase to the lung of the mouse in vivo: Effect on agonist-induced and flow-mediated vascular responses. Circ Res 84:1422–1432, 1999.

191. Bivalacqua TJ, Rajasekaran M, Champion HC, et al: The influence of castration on pharmacologically induced penile erection in the cat. J Androl 19:551–557, 1998.

192. Kaye AD, Kucera I, Sabar R: Perioperative anesthesia clinical considerations of alternative medicines. Anesthesiol Clin North Am 22:125–139, 2004.

193. Kaye AD, Clarke RC, Sabar R, et al: Herbal medicines: Current trends in anesthesiology practice: A hospital survey. J Clin Anesth 12:468–471, 2000.

194. Balon R: Ginkgo biloba for antidepressant-induced sexual dysfunction? J Sex Marital Ther 25:1–2, 1999.

195. Marletta MA: Nitric oxide, nitrovasodilators, and L-arginine: An unusual relationship. West J Med 154:107–109, 1991.

196. Moyad MA, Hathaway S, Ni HS: Traditional Chinese medicine, acupuncture, and other alternative medicines for prostate cancer: An introduction and the need for more research. Semin Urol Oncol 17:103–110, 1999.

197. Shen WW, Urosevich Z, Clayton DO: Sildenafil in the treatment of female sexual dysfunction induced by selective serotonin reuptake inhibitors. J Reprod Med 44:535–542, 1999.

198. Adimoelja A: Phytochemicals and the breakthrough of traditional herbs in the management of sexual dysfunctions. Int J Androl 23(Suppl 2):82–84, 2000.

199. Moyad MA: Dietary supplements and other alternative medicines for erectile dysfunction: What do I tell my patients? Urol Clin North Am 29:11–22, vii, 2002.

200. McKay D: Nutrients and botanicals for erectile dysfunction: Examining the evidence. Altern Med Rev 9:4–16, 2004.

201. Moyad MA, Barada JH, Lue TF, et al: Prevention and treatment of erectile dysfunction using lifestyle changes and dietary supplements: What works and what is worthless, part II. Urol Clin North Am 31:259–273, 2004.

202. Achike FI, Kwan CY: Nitric oxide, human diseases and the herbal products that affect the nitric oxide signalling pathway. Clin Exp Pharmacol Physiol 30:605–615, 2003.

203. Brannigan RE: Ejaculatory disorders and lower urinary tract symptoms. Curr Urol Rep 5:280–286, 2004.

204. Marberger H: The mechanisms of ejaculation. Basic Life Sci 4:99–110, 1974.

205. deGroat WC, Booth AM: Physiology of male sexual function. Ann Intern Med 92:329–331, 1980.

206. Yeates WK: Ejaculation and its disorders. Arch Ital Urol Nefrol Androl 62:137–148, 1990.

207. Gil-Vernet JM Jr, Alvarez-Vijande R, Gil-Vernet A, Gil-Vernet JM: Ejaculation in men: A dynamic endorectal ultrasonographical study. Br J Urol 73:442–448, 1994.

208. Argiolas A, Melis MR: The neurophysiology of the sexual cycle. J Endocrinol Invest 26:20–22, 2003.

209. Hendry WF: Disorders of ejaculation: Congenital, acquired and functional. Br J Urol 82:331–341, 1998.

210. Vale J: Ejaculatory dysfunction. BJU Int 83:557–563, 1999.

211. Segraves RT: Male sexual dysfunction and psychoactive drug use: Review of a common relationship. Postgrad Med J 71:227–233, 1982.

212. Segraves RT: Effects of psychotropic drugs on human erection and ejaculation. Arch Gen Psychiatry 46:275–284, 1989.

213. Schiavi RC, Segraves RT: The biology of sexual function. Psychiatr Clin North Am 18:7–23, 1995.

214. Chia S: Management of premature ejaculation: A comparison of treatment outcome in patients with and without erectile dysfunction. Int J Androl 25:301–305, 2002.

215. Rosen RC, Lane RM, Menza M: Effects of SSRIs on sexual function: A critical review. J Clin Psychopharmacol 19:67–85, 1999.

216. Waldinger MD, Berendsen HH, Blok BF, et al: Premature ejaculation and serotonergic antidepressants-induced delayed ejaculation: The involvement of the serotonergic system. Behav Brain Res 92:111–118, 1998.

217. Montejo-Gonzalez AL, Llorca G, Izquierdo JA, et al: SSRI-induced sexual dysfunction: fluoxetine, paroxetine, sertraline, and fluvoxamine in a prospective, multicenter, and descriptive clinical study of 344 patients. J Sex Marital Ther 23:176–194, 1997.

218. Mos J, Mollet I, Tolboom JT, et al: A comparison of the effects of different serotonin reuptake blockers on sexual behaviour of the male rat. Eur Neuropsychopharmacol 9:123–135, 1999.

219. Lane RM: A critical review of selective serotonin reuptake inhibitor–related sexual dysfunction: Incidence, possible aetiology and implications for management. J Psychopharmacol 11:72–82, 1997.

220. Lee HS, Song DH, Kim CH, Choi HK: An open clinical trial of fluoxetine in the treatment of premature ejaculation. J Clin Psychopharmacol 16:379–382, 1996.

221. Stone KJ, Viera AJ, Parman CL: Off-label applications for SSRIs. Am Fam Physician 68:498–504, 2003.

222. Waldinger MD, Olivier B: Utility of selective serotonin reuptake inhibitors in premature ejaculation. Curr Opin Investig Drugs 5:743–747, 2004.

223. Steidle C: Ejaculatory disorders. 2004. Available at *http://www.seekwellness. com/mensexuality/ ejaculatory_disorders. htm.*

224. Colpi GM, Hargreave TB, Papp GK, et al: Guidelines on disorders of ejaculation. 2004. Available at *www.uroweb.nl/files/uploaded_files/2000_ 2010_Disorders_Ejaculat.pdf.*

# CHAPTER 174 Male Contraception

## David J. Handelsman

BACKGROUND

NONHORMONAL METHODS
 Traditional Methods
 Modern Methods

HORMONAL METHODS
 Steroidal Methods

## BACKGROUND

A male contraceptive must reduce the number of fertile sperm in the ejaculate to levels that reliably prevent fertilization.[1] Conception can be prevented by diverting or suppressing sperm output and/or inhibiting sperm fertilizing capacity. So far, all male methods depend on reducing female exposure to sperm by traditional drug and device-free methods (abstinence, withdrawal, nonvaginal intercourse), condoms, and vasectomy. No new male methods were introduced during the twentieth century, contrasting with numerous highly reliable, reversible contraceptive female methods developed over the last 4 decades. Unfortunately, among existing male contraceptive options, the reversible methods are not reliable and the reliable method is not intentionally reversible. Despite these limitations, male involvement in family planning remains extensive. Globally, one third of couples using family planning rely on contraceptive methods requiring active male participation,[2] reflecting the traditional and ongoing reliance of family planning on male involvement. Greater participation by men in sharing the burdens as well as the benefits of effective family planning requires the development of more effective male methods. Despite strong community interest and medical agreement on the need for new, reversible male contraceptives as well as proof that reversible hormonal suppression of gonadal function is equally feasible for men and women,[3,4] commercial development of male contraceptives by the pharmaceutical industry continues to stagnate.[5]

## NONHORMONAL METHODS

### TRADITIONAL METHODS

#### Periodic Abstinence

Although theoretically effective, neither celibacy nor castration is an acceptable or practical contraceptive method. Periodic abstinence, the limiting of sexual intercourse to "safe" days,[6] has high contraceptive efficacy if the rules are followed perfectly, but the failure rates rise steeply with rule breaking.[7] This cost- and device-free method of family planning is used by more than 30 million couples worldwide.[2] The typical use first-year failure rate is approximately 20%.[7] While inherently safe, it has limited acceptability due to low reliability, inflexibility, and interference in the spontaneity of lovemaking.

#### Nonvaginal Ejaculation

Withdrawal is a traditional male method of contraception whereby intercourse culminates in extravaginal ejaculation.[8] Often overlooked as a contraceptive method, it,

together with abortion, was the major preindustrial method of family planning largely responsible for the demographic transition from high to low birthrates in industrial nation states and continues to be used by 40 million couples.[2] This cost- and device-free method has limited reliability in its demanding requirement for skill and self-control. The typical use first-year failure rate is approximately 20%.[7] While safe and reasonably effective for experienced users, interfering with the pleasurability of coitus leads to a correspondingly high failure rate in practice.[9] Other sexual practices that avoid intravaginal ejaculation have also been used traditionally to avoid conception. These include masturbation, oral and anal intercourse, deliberate anejaculation, and retrograde ejaculation.[10]

### Condom

After centuries of use in preventing sexually transmitted infections, condoms are today relied on for contraception by more than 45 million couples.[11] Condoms provide safe, cheap, widely available, user-controlled, and reversible contraception with few side effects. In the case of latex allergy, nonrubber (polyurethane, natural membrane) condoms can be substituted. Latex condoms are moderately effective at preventing pregnancy, with a typical first-year failure rate of 14%.[12] This is higher than the estimated 3% perfect-use failure rate is mainly due to human error, notably misuse or nonuse, rather than mechanical failure (breakage or slippage).[13] The major limitations of condoms for contraception are relatively high failure rates and interference with sexuality. The requirement for regular and correct application during sexual foreplay disturbs the spontaneity of lovemaking and dulls erotic sensation. These aesthetic drawbacks limit the popularity of condoms, especially among stable couples.[14] Latex condoms are perishable through tears or snagging on nails, clothing, or jewelry as well as deterioration from exposure to light, heat, humidity, or organic oils. Polyurethane condoms with improved tactile sensitivity were developed in the 1990s to enhance acceptability,[15] but they have shown marginally inferior efficacy compared with latex condoms in prospective randomized controlled clinical trials.[16] Although the theoretical requirements for condom use to protect against sexually transmitted infections differ from those to prevent pregnancy, in practice, the protections are similar.[17] Laboratory testing of condoms standardizes integrity and durability for strength and leakage and, although viral penetration is not routinely tested, synthetic (latex or polyurethane) but not natural membrane condoms are effective (but not perfect) at preventing passage of prototype human pathogenic viruses.[18] Using a sensitive biochemical prostate-specific antigen (PSA) marker, even after mechanical condom failure (breakage, slippage), vaginal exposure to semen was still reduced by 50% to 80%.[19] There is now interest in developing novel spermicides with virucidal properties, but whether spermicide impregnation improves the contraceptive efficacy of condoms has not been established rigorously. Since noncompliance is the major cause of failure for both methods,[13] their efficacy may not be additive.

## Vasectomy

Vasectomy, used by more than 40 million couples for family planning,[2] varies widely between countries, depending on cultural factors, public education, and availability of male-oriented facilities.[20] For men who have completed their family and are fit for minor surgery, vasectomy is a very safe and highly effective office procedure.[21] Relative contraindications include risks from office-type surgery (bleeding disorders, allergy to local anesthetic) or scrotal pathology (post–inguinal surgery scarring, keloid proneness, active genitourinary or groin infections). Conventional vasectomy, usually performed under local anesthesia via scrotal incisions, excises a segment of vas deferens and interposes a fascial barrier between the occluded cut ends to minimize risk of recanalization.[22] The "no-scalpel" technique[23] further minimizes skin incision and reduces immediate side effects (bleeding, infection) 10-fold to 0.3% compared with conventional vasectomy.[24] Additional studies are needed to determine whether cautery further enhances reliability and whether leaving an open testicular end reduces retrograde pressure-related damage (sperm granuloma, epididymal and testicular damage), thereby better preserving reversibility. Vasectomy is highly effective once sperm are cleared from the distal vas deferens; however, flushing with saline or water during surgery does not accelerate sperm clearance,[25] although nonirritant spermicides may have promise.[26] Additional contraception must continue, ideally until azoospermia is demonstrated or, less reliably, for at least 3 months (or 20 ejaculations).[27] Contraceptive failures are rare; early failures are due to not awaiting sperm clearance or misidentification or duplication of the vas deferens, whereas late failures are due to spontaneous vas recanalization (0.1%). Vasectomy causes no consistent changes in circulating hormones,[28] sexual function, or risk of cardiovascular or other diseases,[29] including prostate, testis, or other cancer.[21,30] Sperm antibodies develop in most vasectomized men but have no known deleterious health effects apart from a debatable role in reducing fertility after vasectomy reversal. Vasectomy is a quick, simple, highly effective, and convenient method of permanent sterilization; its major drawback as a male contraceptive is its limited reversibility. Elective sperm cryostorage is occasionally useful, but may reflect ambivalence about the irreversible intent of vasectomy. The cumulative rate of requests for reversal, mostly prompted by remarriage, is 2.4% at 10 years post vasectomy, but exceeds 10% for young men (younger than 25 years of age at vasectomy),[31] so that requests for, and failed, vasectomy reversal are now a significant cause of male infertility. Following microsurgical vasovasostomy, 80% to 100% have sperm return to the ejaculate ("patency"), but normal sperm output is less common and cumulative conception rate at 12 months is only approximately 50%.[31] Reversibility is better with microsurgery and longer testicular vasal stump,[32] and in younger men with shorter duration since vasectomy[31]; unfavourable predictors include nonmicrosurgical techniques, older age of wife, sperm antibodies,[33] and duration since vasectomy[34] due to long-term epididymal[35] and testicular damage.[34,36] An alternative to surgical vasectomy reversal, either instead of or after failed vasovasostomy, is sperm harvesting (epididymis or testis) in conjunction with in vitro fertilization. Currently, cost-benefit analyses suggest that microsurgical vasovasostomy is more cost effective and safer in both North America[37] and Europe,[38] although optimal management depends on local clinical expertise and access to microsurgery and reproductive technologies.

## MODERN METHODS

### Vas Occlusion

The efficacy, safety, simplicity, and acceptability of vasectomy suggest that a reversible mechanical method of vas occlusion would be an attractive male contraceptive option. Since vasectomy reversal is neither cheap nor widely available, more reversible vas occlusion methods are needed.[39] A nonsurgical, potentially reversible technique involving percutaneous injections of polymers that harden in situ to form occluding plugs that may be removed later to restore fertility was reported,[40] but, despite preliminary positive findings,[41] formal evaluation showed vas occlusion had lower efficacy (inducing azoospermia) than vasectomy.[42] Other technical developments including percutaneous injection of sclerosants and transcutaneous delivery of physical agents (ultrasound, lasers) continue to be developed.

### Heating

It has long been known[43] that even brief elevations of testicular temperature can profoundly suppress spermatogenesis,[44] whereas sustained elevation may contribute to testicular pathology in cryptorchidism, varicocele, and occupational male infertility.[45] Clinical studies evaluating the potential for tight scrotal supports as a practical male contraceptive method[46,47] showed a reversible decrease in sperm output but of inadequate magnitude to serve as reliable contraception. Given the dubious acceptability and safety[48] of heat-induced suppression of sperm output, the feasibility of a male contraceptive method based on testicular heating remains to be established.

### Immunocontraception

Sperm vaccines to interrupt fertility have long been of interest.[49] Sperm express unique epitopes within the immunologically protected adluminal compartment of the seminiferous tubules at puberty, long after the definition of immune self-tolerance, hence explaining their potential autoimmunogenicity. Sperm autoimmunity may contribute to subfertility after vasectomy reversal and in approximately 7% of infertile men without adverse effects on general health apart from focal orchitis. Experimental models for an effective sperm vaccine targeting surface-expressed antigens involved in fertilization have been reported. Yet, practical application requires resolving problems of the large antigenic load requiring virtually complete functional blockade, variability of individual immune responses, restricted access of antibodies into the seminiferous tubules and epididymis, and the risks of autoimmune orchitis or immune-complex disease. The smaller antigenic burden requiring complete neutralization in the female reproductive tract suggests that a sperm vaccine may be more applicable for women.[50]

### Chemical (Nonhormonal) Methods

The rapidly proliferating germinal epithelium is highly susceptible to cytotoxins such as drugs, heat, or ionizing irradiation, which disrupt mitosis and/or meiosis, resulting in inhibition of spermatogenesis, but the mutagenic risk from direct interference with DNA replication precludes their safe use for reversible contraception. The seclusion of functionally immature postmeiotic, haploid sperm during transit through seminiferous tubules and epididymis, however, offers a target for chemical methods of regulating male fertility. A model rapid-onset oral spermicide was provided by the chlorosugars, which showed rapid, irreversible effect on rodent epididymal sperm[51] but proved too toxic for clinical development. Novel leads for male contraceptive development arise from fortuitous observation of existing chemicals (including drugs or natural products), from mechanisms that impair male fertility, or from functional genomic research.[52] Among existing drugs, an orally active spermicide concentrated in semen[53] and drugs inhibiting male fertility,[54] ejaculation,[55] or epididymal sperm function[56] have been identified. Among the numerous plant products and natural medicines reputed to inhibit male fertility, the most widely tested was gossypol, a polyphenolic yellow pigment identified in China as causing epidemic infertility among workers ingesting raw cottonseed oil. In more than 10,000 men, purified gossypol reduced sperm output to less than 4 million/mL in over 98% within 75 days, with suppression maintained by a lower weekly maintenance dose.[57] Although an effective male contraceptive, the systemic toxicity of gossypol and irreversibility precluded further clinical development.[58] Subsequently, extracts of *Tripterygium wilfordii*, a traditional Chinese herbal medicine for rheumatoid arthritis and skin disorders, inhibited fertility and impaired sperm output and function in rodents and men. Studies aiming to characterize triptolide, an active component of the herb, as a potential lead for an orally effective sperm function inhibitor are under way.[59] Possible leads from serendipitous discovery of genes found to be necessary for normal fertility include inhibition of sperm function by ion channel aberration[60,61] or of ductular transport of sperm.[62] Practical clinical development of these promising leads remains well in the future.[52]

## HORMONAL METHODS

A key strategic issue in developing a hormonal male contraceptive is defining the degree of suppression of sperm output required.[63] Two landmark World Health Organization (WHO) studies involving 671 men from 16 centers in 10 countries established the proof of principle that hormonally induced azoospermia provides highly reliable, reversible contraception (Fig. 174-1).[3,4] Among the minority (≈25%) of men who remained severe oligozoospermic (0.1–3 million sperm/mL) using weekly testosterone enanthate injections, contraceptive failure rate (≈8% per annum) was directly proportional to their sperm output. Hence, to achieve effective contraception, azoospermia is analogous to anovulation as a sufficient, but not necessary, requirement. Nevertheless, reliable contraception by modern standards[64] requires uniform azoospermia as the desirable target for male contraceptive regimens.[65] No regimen yet achieves this consistently in all men, although in some Asian countries (e.g., China,[3] Indonesia[66,67]) azoospermia is achieved in close to 100% by a variety of regimens. A study involving 308 Chinese men in six centers has shown that monthly injections of testosterone undecanoate provide a highly effective and reversible contraception.[68] No

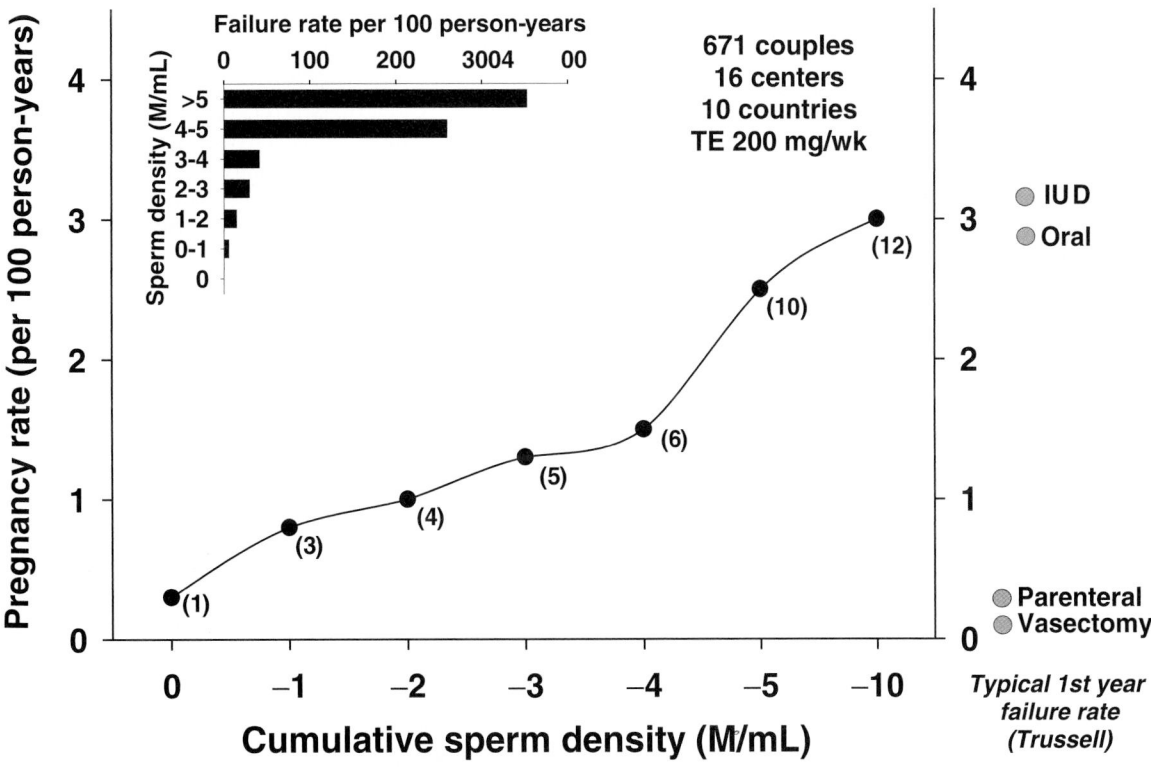

# WHO Male Contraceptive Efficacy Studies 1987-96

*Figure 174-1*   Pooled summary of contraceptive efficacy from two World Health Organization (WHO) male contraceptive efficacy studies where contraceptive failure rate (pregnancy rate) is plotted against the current sperm concentration in the ejaculate. This illustrates a summation of all data pooled from both studies. Data comprise monthly observations of the mean sperm concentration (averaging monthly sperm counts) and whether a pregnancy occurred in that month or not. Pregnancy rate (per 100 person-years, Pearl index) on the Y-axis is plotted against the cumulative sperm density (in million sperm per mL) indicating that contraceptive failure rates are proportional to sperm output. The inset is the same data replotted in discrete sperm concentration bands rather than cumulatively. For comparison, the average contraceptive failure rates in the first year of use of modern reliable contraceptive methods are indicated by *diamond* symbols. IUD, intrauterine device; TE, testosterone enanthate. (From Trussell J, Kost K: Contraceptive failure in the United States: A critical review of the literature. Stud Fam Plann 18:237–283, 1987; Trussell J, Hatcher RA, Cates W, et al: Contraceptive failure in the United States: An update. Stud Fam Plann 21:51–54, 1990; WHO Task Force on Methods for the Regulation of Male Fertility: Contraceptive efficacy of testosterone-induced azoospermia in normal men. Lancet 336:955–959, 1990; and WHO Task Force on Methods for the Regulation of Male Fertility: Contraceptive efficacy of testosterone-induced azoospermia and oligozoospermia in normal men. Fertil Steril 65:821–829, 1996.)

pregnancies were recorded among men who were azoospermic or severely oligozoospermic (<3 million sperm per mL), providing a 95% upper confidence limit of pregnancy (contraceptive failure) rate of 2.5% per annum. The overall failure rate based on suppression of spermatogenesis was more than 4%. The prototype regimen was well tolerated apart from injection site discomfort, due to large oil injection volume (4 mL), and reversible androgenic effects (acne, weight gain, hemoglobin, lipids). Nevertheless, despite these promising findings, non-Chinese men require combination hormonal regimens involving a second gonadotropin-suppressing agent, notably progestins, together with testosterone to ensure adequate spermatogenic suppression. This approach was proven for the depot androgen/progestin combination approach, as no pregnancies were observed among 55 couples during 35.5 person-years of exposure (95% upper limit of failure rate ≈8%) in a study with satisfactory tolerability and reversibility for a prototype regimen.[69] Hormonal methods have proven efficacy and reasonable prospects for safety and pose the most likely opportunity for development in the near future of a practical contraceptive method for men, but progress depends on pharmaceutical company commitment, which has languished.[5]

## STEROIDAL METHODS

### Androgen Alone

Testosterone provides both gonadotropin suppression and androgen replacement, making it an obvious first choice as a single agent for a reversible hormonal male contraceptive. Although the mechanism of androgen-induced, reversible suppression of human spermatogenesis has long been known,[70-73] systematic studies of androgens for male contraception began in the 1970s.[74,75] Feasibility and dose-finding studies,[76] mostly using testosterone enanthate (TE) in an oil vehicle as a prototype, showed that weekly intramuscular injections of 100 to 200 mg TE induce azoospermia in most Caucasian men,[77] but less frequent or lower doses fail to sustain suppression.[78-81] The largest experience with an androgen alone regimen arises from the two WHO studies in which over 670 men from 16 centers in 10 countries received weekly injections of 200 mg TE. In these studies, approximately 60% of non-Chinese and more than 90% of Chinese men became azoospermic and the remainder were severely oligozoospermic.[3,4] The within and between population differences in susceptibility to hormonally induced azoospermia remain largely unexplained,[82] although possibly relevant population differences in reproductive physiology of environmental,[83,84] genetic,[85,86] or uncertain[87] origin have been described. Azoospermia occurs in 3 to 4 months and is maintained consistently during ongoing treatment. After cessation of treatment, sperm reappear within 3 months and normal output by about 6 months. Apart from intolerance of weekly injections, there were few discontinuations due to acne, weight gain, polycythemia, or behavioral effects and these were reversible, as were changes in hemoglobin, testis size, and plasma urea. There was no evidence of liver, prostate, or cardiovascular disorders.[3,4,88]

The pharmacokinetics of testosterone products are crucial for suppressing sperm output. Oral androgens have major first-pass hepatic effects, producing prominent route-dependent effects on hepatic protein secretion (e.g., sex hormone–binding globulin [SHBG], high-density lipoprotein [HDL] cholesterol) and inconsistent bioavailability. Short-acting testosterone products requiring daily or more frequent administration (oral, transdermal patches or gels), which may be acceptable for androgen replacement therapy, are not appropriate for hormonal contraception. Weekly TE injections required for maximal suppression of spermatogenesis[76] are far from ideal[89] and cause supraphysiologic blood testosterone levels, risking both excessive androgenic side effects

and preventing maximal depletion of intratesticular testosterone for optimal efficacy.[90] Other currently available oil-based testosterone esters (cypionate, cyclohexanecarboxylate, propionate) are no improvement over the enanthate ester,[91] and longer-acting depot preparations are needed. Subdermal testosterone pellets sustain physiologic testosterone levels for 4 to 6 months[92] and the newer injectable preparations testosterone undecanoate,[68] testosterone-loaded biodegradable microspheres,[93] and testosterone buciclate[94] currently in development promise 2 to 3 months' duration of action. Depot androgens suppress spermatogenesis faster, at lower doses, and with fewer metabolic side effects than TE injections, but azoospermia is still not achieved uniformly[95]; although this goal is achievable when depot androgens are combined with a depot progestin.[69]

Oral synthetic 17α alkylated androgens such as methyltestosterone,[96] fluoxymesterone,[97] methandienone,[98] and danazol[99,100] suppress spermatogenesis, but azoospermia is rarely achieved and the inherent hepatotoxicity of the 17α alkyl substitutent[101] renders them unsuitable for long-term use. Athletes self-administering supratherapeutic doses of androgens also exhibit suppression of spermatogenesis.[98,102] Synthetic androgens lacking the 17α alkyl substituent have been little studied, although injectable nandrolone esters produce azoospermia in 88% of European men[103,104] whereas oral mesterolone is ineffective.[105] On the other hand, nandrolone hexyloxyphenylpropionate alone was unable to maintain spermatogenic suppression induced by a gonadotropin-releasing hormone (GnRH) antagonist[106] in a prototype hybrid regime (where induction and maintenance treatment differ), whereas testosterone appears more promising.[107] A 7-methyl derivative of nandrolone (MENT), which is partly aromatizable but resistant to 5α reductive amplification of androgenic potency, has been studied as a nonoral androgen for hormonal male contraceptive regimens.[108] While it is prostate-sparing,[109] dose titration to achieve essential androgen replacement at each relevant tissue is more complex than for testosterone and may be difficult to achieve.[110] More potent, synthetic androgens lacking 17α alkyl groups[111,112] remain to be evaluated.

Antiandrogens have been used to inhibit epididymal and testicular effects of testosterone selectively without impeding systemic androgenic effects.[113] Cyproterone acetate, a steroidal antiandrogen with progestational activity, suppresses gonadotropin secretion without achieving azoospermia, but leads to androgen deficiency when used alone.[114] In contrast, pure nonsteroidal antiandrogens lacking androgenic or gestagenic effects such as flutamide, nilutamide, and casodex fail to suppress spermatogenesis when used alone.[115,116] Two studies evaluating the hypothesis that incomplete suppression of spermatogenesis is due to persistence of testicular dihydrotestosterone (DHT) have reported no additional suppression from administration of finasteride, a type II 5α-reductase inhibitor[117,118]; however, as testes express predominantly the type I isoforms,[119] further studies are required to test this hypothesis conclusively.

The safety of androgen administration concerns mainly potential effects on cardiovascular and prostatic disease. As the explanation for the higher male susceptibility to cardiovascular disease is not well understood, the risks of exogenous androgens are not clear.[120,121] In clinical trials, lipid changes are minimal with depot (nonoral) hormonal regimens.[69,95,122,123] Changes in blood cholesterol fractions observed during high hepatic exposure to testosterone and/or progestins, due to either oral first-pass effects or high parenteral doses, have unknown clinical significance, but, in any case, maintenance of physiologic blood testosterone concentrations is the prudent and preferred objective. The real cardiovascular risks or benefits of hormonal male contraception will require long-term surveillance of cardiovascular outcomes.[124]

The long-term effects of exogenous androgens on the prostate also require monitoring since prostatic diseases are both age and androgen dependent. Exposure to adult testosterone levels is required for prostate development and disease.[125-127] The precise relationship of androgens to prostatic disease and, in particular, any influence of exogenous androgens remains poorly understood. There is little direct relationship between blood testosterone levels and the occurrence of prostatic disease in prospective studies of adults.[128] A genetic polymorphism, the CAG (polyglutamine) triplet repeat in exon 1 of the androgen receptor, is an important determinant of prostate sensitivity to circulating testosterone with short repeat lengths leading to increased androgen sensitivity[129]; however, the relationship of the CAG triplet repeat length polymorphism to late-life prostate diseases remains unclear.[130] Among androgen-deficient men, prostate size and prostate-specific antigen (PSA) concentrations are reduced and returned toward normal by testosterone replacement without exceeding age-matched eugonadal controls.[129,131-133] Even self-administration of massive androgen overdosage does not increase total prostate volume or PSA in anabolic steroid abusers, although central prostate zone volumes increase.[134] In situ prostate cancer is common in all populations of older men, whereas rates of invasive prostate cancer differ manyfold between populations, despite similar blood testosterone concentrations. This suggests that early and prolonged exposure to androgens may initiate in situ prostate cancer, but later androgen-independent environmental factors promote the outbreak of invasive prostate cancer. Therefore, it is prudent to maintain physiologic androgen levels with exogenous testosterone, which might then be no more hazardous than exposure to endogenous testosterone. Prolonged surveillance comparable with that for cardiovascular and breast disease in users of female hormonal contraception would be equally essential to monitor both cardiovascular and prostatic disease risk in men receiving exogenous androgens for hormonal contraception.

Extensive experience with testosterone in doses equivalent to replacement therapy in normal men indicates minimal effects on mood or behavior.[3,4,76,135-137] By contrast, extreme androgen doses used experimentally in healthy men can produce idiosyncratic hypomanic reactions in a minority.[138] Aberrant behavior in observational studies of androgen-abusing athletes or prisoners is difficult to interpret, particularly distinguishing genuine androgen effects from the influence of self-selection on underlying psychological morbidity.[139]

### Androgen Combination Regimens

Combination steroid regimens using nonandrogenic steroids (estrogens, progestins) to suppress gonadotropins in conjunction with testosterone for androgen replacement have shown the most promising efficacy with enhanced rate and extent of spermatogenic suppression compared with androgen alone regimens.[122,140,141] Synergistic combinations reduce the effective dose of each steroid, and minimizing testosterone dosage could enhance spermatogenic suppression if high blood testosterone levels counteract the necessary maximal depletion of intratesticular testosterone[142,143] as well as reduce androgenic side seffects.

Progestins are potent inhibitors of pituitary gonadotropin secretion used widely for female contraception and hormonal treatment of disorders such as endometriosis, uterine myoma, and mastalgia. Used alone, progestins suppress spermatogenesis but cause androgen deficiency including impotence,[144,145] so androgen replacement is necessary. Extensive feasibility studies concluded that progestin-androgen combination regimens had promise as hormonal male contraceptives if more potent and durable agents were developed.[76,146] The most detailed information on androgen/progestin regimens derives from studies with medroxyprogesterone acetate (MPA)

combined with testosterone. Monthly injections of both agents or daily oral progestin with dermal androgen gels produce azoospermia in approximately 60% of fertile men of European background, with the remainder having severe oligozoospermia and impaired sperm function.[76,146,147] Nearly uniform azoospermia is produced in men treated with depot MPA and either of two injectable androgens in Indonesian men[66,67] or testosterone depot implants in Caucasian men.[122] Smaller studies with other oral progestins such as levonorgestrel[140,148,149] and norethisterone[150,151] combined with testosterone demonstrate similar efficacy to oral MPA, whereas cyproterone acetate with its additional antiandrogenic activity has higher efficacy in conjunction with TE[141,152] but not oral testosterone undecanoate.[153] Promising findings of highly effective suppression of spermatogenesis are reported with depot progestins in the form of nonbiodegradable implants of norgestrel[154] or etonorgestrel[155] or depot injectable medroxyprogesterone acetate[69,122] or norethisterone enanthate[156] coupled with testosterone. The pharmacokinetics of the testosterone preparation is critical to efficacy of spermatogenic suppression with long-acting depots being most effective, whereas transdermal delivery is less effective than injectable testosterone.[154] Progestin side effects are few and sexual function is maintained by adequate androgen replacement dosage. The metabolic effects depend on the specific regimen, with oral administration and higher testosterone doses exhibiting more prominent hepatic effects such as lowering SHBG and high-density lipoprotein (HDL) cholesterol. After treatment ceases with depletion or withdrawal of hormonal depots, spermatogenesis recovers completely but gradually, consistent with the length (2½ months) of the spermatogenic cycle.

Estradiol augments testosterone-induced suppression of primate spermatogenesis[157] and fertility,[158] but estrogenic side effects (gynecomastia) and modest efficacy at tolerable doses make estradiol-based combinations impractical for male contraception.[159] The efficacy and tolerability of newer estrogen analogues in combination with testosterone remain to be evaluated.

### GnRH Blockade

The pivotal role of GnRH in the hormonal control of testicular function makes it an attractive target for biochemical regulation of male fertility. Blockade of GnRH action by GnRH receptor blockade with synthetic analogues or GnRH immunoneutralization would eliminate luteinizing hormone (LH) and testosterone secretion, requiring testosterone replacement. Many superactive GnRH agonists are used to induce reversible medical castration for androgen-dependent prostate cancer by causing a sustained, paradoxical inhibition of gonadotropin and testosterone secretion and spermatogenesis due to pituitary GnRH receptor downregulation. When combined with testosterone, GnRH agonists suppress spermatogenesis but rarely achieve azoospermia,[142,143,160] being less effective than androgen/progestin regimens. By contrast, pure GnRH antagonists create and sustain immediate competitive blockade of GnRH receptors[161] and, in combination with testosterone, are highly effective at suppressing spermatogenesis. Early hydrophobic GnRH antagonists were difficult to formulate and irritating, causing injection-site mast-cell histamine release. Newer, more potent but less irritating GnRH antagonists produce rapid, reversible, and complete inhibition of spermatogenesis in monkeys[162-164] and men[165,166] when combined with testosterone. The striking superiority of GnRH antagonists may be due to more secure inhibition of gonadotropin secretion and/or depletion of intratesticular testosterone. Due to their highly specific site of action, GnRH analogues have few unexpected side effects. Depot GnRH antagonist plus testosterone formulations suitable for administration at up to 3-month intervals could be promising as a hormonal male contraceptive regimen. The drawback of high cost might be overcome by hybrid regimens using GnRH antagonists to initiate and then switching to more economical steroids for maintenance of spermatogenic suppression.[107] A GnRH vaccine could intercept GnRH in the pituitary-portal bloodstream, preventing its reaching pituitary GnRH receptors. Gonadotropin-selective immunocastration would require androgen replacement in men[167] and pilot feasibility studies in advanced prostate cancer are under way,[168] but the prospects for acceptably safe application for male contraception are doubtful.

### Follicle-Stimulating Hormone Blockade

Selective follicle-stimulating hormone (FSH) blockade theoretically offers the opportunity to reduce spermatogenesis without inhibiting endogenous testosterone secretion. FSH action could be abolished by selective inhibition of pituitary FSH secretion with inhibin[169] or novel steroids,[170] by FSH vaccine,[171] or by FSH receptor blockade with peptide antagonists.[172] Although FSH was considered essential to human spermatogenesis, spermatogenesis and fertility persist in rodents[173-175] and humans[176] lacking FSH bioactivity. Hence, even complete FSH blockade might produce insufficient reduction in sperm output and function required for adequate contraceptive efficacy.[177] In addition to the usual safety concerns with contraceptive vaccines, including autoimmune hypophysitis, orchitis, or immune-complex disease, an FSH vaccine might be overcome by reflex increases in pituitary FSH secretion.

## REFERENCES

1. Anderson RA, Baird DT: Male contraception. Endocr Rev 23:735–762, 2002.
2. United Nations: Levels and trends of contraceptive use as assessed in 1998. New York, Department of International Economic and Social Affairs, 2000.
3. WHO Task Force on Methods for the Regulation of Male Fertility: Contraceptive efficacy of testosterone-induced azoospermia in normal men. Lancet 336:955–959, 1990.
4. WHO Task Force on Methods for the Regulation of Male Fertility: Contraceptive efficacy of testosterone-induced azoospermia and oligozoospermia in normal men. Fertil Steril 65:821–829, 1996.
5. Handelsman DJ: Hormonal male contraception: Lessons from the East when the Western market fails. J Clin Endocrinol Metab 88:559–561, 2003.
6. WHO Task Force on Methods for the Determination of the Fertile Period: A prospective multicentre trial of the ovulation method of natural family planning. III. Characteristics of the menstrual cycle and of the fertile phase. Fertil Steril 40:773–778, 1983.
7. Trussell J, Grummer-Strawn L: Contraceptive failure of the ovulation method of periodic abstinence. Fam Plann Perspect 22:65–75, 1990.
8. Rogow D, Horowitz S: Withdrawal: A review of the literature and an agenda for research. Stud Fam Plann 26:140–153, 1995.
9. Trussell J, Kost K: Contraceptive failure in the United States: A critical review of the literature. Stud Fam Plann 18:237–283, 1987.
10. Potts M, Diggory P: Textbook of Contraceptive Practice, 2d ed. Cambridge, England, Cambridge University Press, 1983.
11. Liskin L, Wharton C, Blackburn R, et al: Condoms: Now More Than Ever. Baltimore, Population Information Program, Johns Hopkins University, 1990.
12. Trussell J, Vaughan B: Contraceptive failure, method-related discontinuation and resumption of use: Results from the 1995 National Survey of Family Growth. Fam Plann Perspect 31:64–72, 93, 1999.
13. Steiner MJ, Cates W Jr, Warner L: The real problem with male condoms is nonuse. Sex Transm Dis 26:459–462, 1999.
14. Grady WR, Klepinger DH, Nelson-Wally A: Contraceptive characteristics: The perceptions and priorities of men and women. Fam Plann Perspect 31:168–175, 1999.
15. Rosenberg MJ, Waugh MS, Solomon HM, et al: The male polyurethane condom: A review of current knowledge. Contraception 53:141–146, 1996.
16. Gallo MF, Grimes DA, Schulz KF: Nonlatex vs. latex male condoms for contraception: A systematic review of randomized controlled trials. Contraception 68:319–326, 2003.
17. Cates W Jr, Steiner MJ: Dual protection against unintended pregnancy and sexually transmitted infections: What is the best contraceptive approach? Sex Transm Dis 29:168–174, 2002.
18. Carey RF, Lytle CD, Cyr WH: Implications of laboratory tests of condom integrity. Sex Transm Dis 26:216–220, 1999.
19. Walsh TL, Frezieres RG, Peacock K, et al: Use of prostate-specific antigen (PSA) to measure semen exposure resulting from male condom failures: Implications for contraceptive efficacy and the prevention of sexually transmitted disease. Contraception 67:139–150, 2003.
20. Liskin L, Benoit E, Blackburn R: Vasectomy: New Opportunities. Baltimore, Population Information Program, Johns Hopkins University, Baltimore, 1992.
21. Schwingl PJ, Guess HA: Safety and effectiveness of vasectomy. Fertil Steril 73:923–936, 2000.
22. Chen-Mok M, Bangdiwala SI, Dominik R, et al: Termination of a randomized controlled trial of two vasectomy techniques. Control Clin Trials 24:78–84, 2003.
23. Li S, Goldstein M, Zhu J, et al: The no-scalpel vasectomy. J Urol 145:341–344, 1991.
24. Sokal D, McMullen S, Gates D, et al: A comparative study of the no scalpel and standard incision approaches to vasectomy in five countries. The Male Sterilization Investigator Team. J Urol 162:1621–1625, 1999.
25. Berthelsen JG: Peroperative irrigation of the vas deferens during vasectomy. Scand J Urol Nephrol 10:100–102, 1976.
26. Wood BL, Doncel GF, Reddy PR, et al: Effect of diltiazem and methylene blue on human sperm motility, viability and cervical mucus penetration: Potential use as vas irrigants at the time of vasectomy. Contraception 67:241–245, 2003.
27. Barone MA, Nazerali H, Cortes M, et al: A prospective study of time and number of ejaculations to azoospermia after vasectomy by ligation and excision. J Urol 170:892–896, 2003.
28. Peng XS, Li FD, Miao ZR, et al: Plasma reproductive hormones in normal and vasectomized Chinese males. Int J Androl 10:471–479, 1987.
29. Petitti DB: Epidemiologic studies of vasectomy. In Zatuchni GI, Goldsmith A, Spieler JM, Sciarra JJ (eds): Male Contraception: Advances and Future Prospects. Philadelphia, Harper & Row, 1986, pp 24–33.
30. Dennis LK, Dawson DV, Resnick MI: Vasectomy and the risk of prostate cancer: A meta-analysis examining vasectomy status, age at vasectomy, and time since vasectomy. Prostate Cancer Prostatic Dis 5:193–203, 2002.
31. Holman CD, Wisniewski ZS, Semmens JB, et al: Population-based outcomes after 28,246 in-hospital vasectomies and 1,902 vasovasostomies in Western Australia. BJU Int 86:1043–1049, 2000.
32. Witt MA, Heron S, Lipshultz LI: The post-vasectomy length of the testicular vasal remnant: A predictor of surgical outcome in microscopic vasectomy reversal. J Urol 151:892–894, 1994.
33. Silber SJ: Microsurgery for vasectomy reversal and vasoepididymostomy. In Zatuchni GI, Goldsmith A, Spieler JM, Sciarra JJ (eds): Male Contraception: Advances and Future Prospects. Philadelphia, Harper & Row, 1986, pp 54–69.
34. Raleigh D, O'Donnell L, Southwick GJ, et al: Stereological analysis of the human testis after vasectomy: Impairment of spermatogenic efficiency with increasing obstructive interval. Fertil Steril 81:1595–1603, 2004.
35. Silber SJ: Epididymal extravasation following vasectomy as a cause for failure of vasectomy reversal. Fertil Steril 31:309–315, 1979.
36. Jarow JP, Budin RE, Dym M, et al: Quantitative pathologic changes in the

human testis after vasectomy: A controlled study. N Engl J Med 313:1252–1256, 1985.

37. Pavlovich CP, Schlegel PN: Fertility options after vasectomy: A cost-effectiveness analysis. Fertil Steril 67:133–141, 1997.

38. Heidenreich A, Altmann P, Engelmann UH: Microsurgical vasovasostomy versus microsurgical epididymal sperm aspiration/testicular extraction of sperm combined with intracytoplasmic sperm injection: A cost-benefit analysis. Eur Urol 37:609–614, 2000.

39. Zhang GY, Wang XH, Chen ZW, et al: Research on male contraception in China. In Waites GMH, Frick J, Baker GWH (eds): Current Advances in Andrology. Bologna, Italy, Monduzzi Editore, 1997, pp 233–239.

40. Zhao S-C: Vas deferens occlusion by percutaneous injection of polyurethane elastomer plugs: Clinical experience and reversibility. Contraception 41:453–459, 1990.

41. Soebadi DM, Gardjito W, Mensink HJ: Intravasal injection of formed-in-place medical grade silicone rubber for vas occlusion. Int J Androl 18(Suppl 1):45–52, 1995.

42. Zambon JV, Barone MA, Pollack AE, et al: Efficacy of percutaneous vas occlusion compared with conventional vasectomy. BJU Int 86:699–705; discussion 705–706, 2000.

43. Moore CR, Oslund R: Experiments on the sheep testis: Cryptorchidism, vasectomy and scrotal insulation. Am J Physiol 67:595–607, 1924.

44. Kandeel FR, Swerdloff RS: Role of temperature in regulation of spermatogenesis and the use of heating as a method for contraception. Fertil Steril 49:1–23, 1988.

45. Thonneau P, Bujan L, Multigner L, et al: Occupational heat exposure and male fertility: A review. Hum Reprod 13:2122–2125, 1998.

46. Mieusset R, Bujan L: The potential of mild testicular heating as a safe, effective and reversible contraceptive method for men. Int J Androl 17:186–191, 1994.

47. Wang C, McDonald V, Leung A, et al: Effect of increased scrotal temperature on sperm production in normal men. Fertil Steril 68:334–339, 1997.

48. Setchell BP: The Parkes Lecture. Heat and the testis. J Reprod Fertil 114:179–194, 1998.

49. Baskin MJ: Temporary sterilization by injection of human spermatozoa: A preliminary report. Am J Obstet Gynecol 24:892–897, 1932.

50. McLaughlin EA, Holland MK, Aitken RJ: Contraceptive vaccines. Expert Opin Biol Ther 3:829–841, 2003.

51. Ford WCL, Waites GMH: Chlorinated sugars: A biochemical approach to the control of male fertility. Int J Androl (Suppl 2):541–564, 1978.

52. Matzuk MM, Lamb DJ: Genetic dissection of mammalian fertility pathways. Nat Cell Biol 4(Suppl):S41–S49, 2002.

53. Vickery BH, Grigg MB, Goodpasture JC, et al: Towards a same-day, orally administered male contraceptive. In Zatuchni GI, Goldsmith A, Spieler JM, Sciarra JJ (eds): Male Contraception: Advances and Future Prospects. Philadelphia, Harper & Row, 1986, pp 271–292.

54. Giwercman A, Skakkebaek NE: The effect of salicylazosulphapyridine (sulphasalazine) on male fertility: A review. Int J Androl 9:38–52, 1986.

55. Kjaergaard N, Kjaergaard B, Lauritsen JG: Prazosin, an adrenergic blocking agent inadequate as male contraceptive pill. Contraception 37:621–629, 1988.

56. van der Spoel AC, Jeyakumar M, Butters TD, et al: Reversible infertility in male mice after oral administration of alkylated imino sugars: A nonhormonal approach to male contraception. Proc Natl Acad Sci U S A 99:17173–17178, 2002.

57. Wu D: An overview of the clinical pharmacology and therapeutic potential of gossypol as a male contraceptive agent and in gynaecological disease. Drugs 38:333–341, 1989.

58. Waites GMH, Wang C, Griffin PD: Gossypol: Reasons for its failure to be accepted as a safe, reversible male antifertility agent. Int J Androl 21:8–12, 1998.

59. Huynh PN, Hikim AP, Wang C, et al: Long-term effects of triptolide on spermatogenesis, epididymal sperm function, and fertility in male rats. J Androl 21:689–699, 2000.

60. Breton S, Smith PJ, Lui B, et al: Acidification of the male reproductive tract by a proton pumping (H+)-ATPase. Nat Med 2:470–472, 1996.

61. Ren D, Navarro B, Perez G, et al: A sperm ion channel required for sperm motility and male fertility. Nature 413:603–609, 2001.

62. Mulryan K, Gitterman DP, Lewis CJ, et al: Reduced vas deferens contraction and male infertility in mice lacking P2X1 receptors. Nature 403:86–89, 2000.

63. Kamischke A, Nieschlag E: Progress towards hormonal male contraception. Trends Pharmacol Sci 25:49–57, 2004.

64. Baird DT, Glasier AF: Hormonal contraception. N Engl J Med 328:1543–1549, 1993.

65. Nieschlag E: Sixth Summit Meeting Consensus: Recommendations for regulatory approval for hormonal male contraception. Int J Androl 25:375, 2002.

66. Pangkahila W: Reversible azoospermia induced by an androgen-progestagen combination regimen in Indonesian men. Int J Androl 44:248–256, 1991.

67. World Health Organization Task Force on Methods for the Regulation of Male Fertility: Comparison of two androgens plus depot-medroxyprogesterone acetate for suppression to azoospermia in Indonesian men. Fertil Steril 60:1062–1068, 1993.

68. Gu YQ, Wang XH, Xu D, et al: A multicenter contraceptive efficacy study of injectable testosterone undecanoate in healthy Chinese men. J Clin Endocrinol Metab 88:562–568, 2002.

69. Turner L, Conway AJ, Jimenez M, et al: Contraceptive efficacy of a depot progestin and androgen combination in men. J Clin Endocrinol Metab 88:4659–4667, 2003.

70. Heckel NJ: Production of oligospermia in a man by the use of testosterone propionate. Proc Soc Exp Biol Med 40:658–659, 1939.

71. McCullagh EP, McGurl FJ: The effects of testosterone propionate on epiphyseal closure, sodium and chloride balance and on sperm counts. Endocrinology 26:377–384, 1940.

72. Heller CG, Nelson WO, Hill IB, et al: Improvement in spermatogenesis following depression of the human testis with testosterone. Fertil Steril 1:415–422, 1950.

73. Heckel NJ, Rosso WA, Kestel L: Spermatogenic rebound phenomenon after administration of testosterone propionate. J Clin Endocrinol Metab 11:235–245, 1951.

74. Reddy PRK, Rao JM: Reversible antifertility action of testosterone propionate in human males. Contraception 5:295–301, 1972.

75. Mauss J, Borsch G, Richter E, et al: Investigations on the use of testosterone oenanthate as a male contraceptive agent: A preliminary report. Contraception 10:281–289, 1974.

76. Patanelli DJ (ed): Hormonal control of fertility. Washington, US Department of Health Education and Welfare (NIH 78-1097), 1977.

77. Matsumoto AM: Effects of chronic testosterone administration in normal men: Safety and efficacy of high dosage testosterone and parallel dose-dependent suppression of luteinizing hormone, follicle-stimulating hormone and sperm production. J Clin Endocrinol Metab 70:282–287, 1990.

78. Cunningham GR, Silverman VE, Thornby J, et al: The potential for an androgen male contraceptive. J Clin Endocrinol Metab 49:520–526, 1979.

79. Steinberger E, Smith KD, Rodriguez-Rigau LJ: Suppression and recovery of sperm production in men treated with testosterone enanthate for one year: A study of a possible reversible male contraceptive. Int J Androl (Suppl 2):748–760, 1978.

80. Swerdloff RS, Palacios A, McClure RD, et al: Male contraception: Clinical assessment of chronic administration of testosterone enanthate. Int J Androl (Suppl 2):731–747, 1978.

81. Paulsen CA: Male contraceptive development: Reexamination of testosterone enanthate as an effective single entity agent. In Patanelli DJ (ed): Hormonal Control of Male Fertility. Washington, Department of Health Education and Welfare (DHEW Publication No [NIH] 78-1097),1978, pp 17–40.

82. Handelsman DJ, Farley TMM, Peregoudov A, et al: Factors in nonuniform induction of azoospermia by testosterone enanthate in normal men. Fertil Steril 63:125–133, 1995.

83. Santner S, Albertson B, Zhang GY, et al: Comparative rates of androgen production and metabolism in Caucasian and Chinese subjects. J Clin Endocrinol Metab 83:2104–2109, 1998.

84. Jin B, Turner L, Zhou Z, et al: Ethnicity and migration as determinants of human prostate size. J Clin Endocrinol Metab 84:3613–3619, 1999.

85. Yu B, Handelsman DJ: Pharmacogenetic polymorphisms of the AR and metabolism and susceptibility to hormone-induced azoospermia. J Clin Endocrinol Metab 86:4406–4411, 2001.

86. Eckardstein SV, Schmidt A, Kamischke A, et al: CAG repeat length in the androgen receptor gene and gonadotrophin suppression influence the effectiveness of hormonal male contraception. Clin Endocrinol (Oxf) 57:647–655, 2002.

87. Johnson L, Barnard JJ, Rodriguez L, et al: Ethnic differences in testicular structure and spermatogenic potential may predispose testes of Asian men to a heightened sensitivity to steroidal contraceptives. J Androl 19:348–357, 1998.

88. Wu FCW, Farley TMM, Peregoudov A, et al: Effects of testosterone enanthate in normal men: Experience from a multicenter contraceptive efficacy study. Fertil Steril 65:626–636, 1996.

89. Mackey MA, Conway AJ, Handelsman DJ: Tolerability of intramuscular injections of testosterone ester in an oil vehicle. Hum Reprod 10:862–865, 1995.

90. McLachlan RI, O'Donnell L, Stanton PG, et al: Effects of testosterone plus medroxyprogesterone acetate on semen quality, reproductive hormones, and germ cell populations in normal young men. J Clin Endocrinol Metab 87:546–556, 2002.

91. Behre HM, Nieschlag E: Comparative pharmacokinetics of testosterone esters. In Nieschlag E, Behre HM (eds): Testosterone: Action Deficiency Substitution, 2d ed. Berlin, Springer, 1998, pp 329–348.

92. Handelsman DJ, Conway AJ, Boylan LM: Pharmacokinetics and pharmacodynamics of testosterone pellets in man. J Clin Endocrinol Metab 71:216–222, 1990.

93. Amory JK, Anawalt BD, Blaskovich PD, et al: Testosterone release from a subcutaneous, biodegradable microcapsule formulation (Viatrel) in hypogonadal men. J Androl 23:84–91, 2002.

94. Behre HM, Baus S, Kliesch S, et al: Potential of testosterone buciclate for male contraception: Endocrine differences between responders and nonresponders. J Clin Endocrinol Metab 80:2394–2403, 1995.

95. Handelsman DJ, Conway AJ, Boylan LM: Suppression of human spermatogenesis by testosterone implants in man. J Clin Endocrinol Metab 75:1326–1332, 1992.

96. McCullagh EP, Rossmiller HR: Methyl testosterone. I. Androgenic effects and production of gynecomastia and oligospermia. J Clin Endocrinol Metab 1:1941.

97. Jones TM, Fang VS, Landau RL, et al: The effects of fluoxymesterone administration on testicular function. J Clin Endocrinol Metab 44:121–129, 1977.

98. Holma PK: Effects of an anabolic steroid (metandienone) on spermatogenesis. Contraception 15:151–162, 1977.

99. Skoglund RD, Paulsen CA: Danazol-testosterone combination: A potentially effective means for reversible male contraception: A preliminary report. Contraception 7:357–365, 1973.

100. Sherins RJ, Gandy HM, Thorslund TW, et al: Pituitary and testicular function studies. I. Experience with a new gonadal inhibitor, 17a-pregn-4-en-20-yno-(2,3-d) isoxazol-17-ol (Danazol). J Clin Endocrinol Metab 32:522–531, 1971.

101. Ishak KG, Zimmerman HJ: Hepatotoxic effects of the anabolic-androgenic steroids. Semin Liver Dis 7:230–236, 1987.

102. Knuth UA, Maniera H, Nieschlag E: Anabolic steroids and semen parameters in bodybuilders. Fertil Steril 52:1041–1047, 1989.

103. Knuth UA, Behre H, Belkien L, et al: Clinical trial of 19-nortestosterone hexoxyphenylpropionate (Anadur) for male fertility regulation. Fertil Steril 44:814–821, 1985.

104. Schurmeyer T, Knuth UA, Belkein L, et al: Reversible azoospermia induced by the anabolic steroid 19-nortestosterone. Lancet 1:417–420, 1984.

105. Schellen TNCM, Beek JMJHA: The influence of high doses of mesterolone on the spermiogram. Fertil Steril 23:712–714, 1972.

106. Behre HM, Kliesch S, Lemcke B, et al: Suppression of spermatogenesis to azoospermia by combined administration of GnRH antagonist and 19-nortestosterone cannot be maintained by this non-aromatizable androgen alone. Hum Reprod 16:2570–2577, 2001.

107. Swerdloff RS, Bagatell CJ, Wang C, et al: Suppression of spermatogenesis in man induced by Nal-Glu gonadotropin releasing hormone antagonist and testosterone enanthate (TE) is maintained by TE alone. J Clin Endocrinol Metab 83:3527–3533, 1998.

108. Sundaram K, Kumar N: 7alpha-methyl-19-nortestosterone (MENT): The optimal androgen for male contraception and replacement therapy. Int J Androl 23(Suppl 2):13–15, 2000.

109. Cummings DE, Kumar N, Bardin CW, et al: Prostate-sparing effects in primates of the potent androgen 7alpha-methyl-19-nortestosterone: A potential alternative to testosterone for androgen replacement and male contraception. J Clin Endocrinol Metab 83:4212–4219, 1998.

110. Anderson RA, Wallace AM, Sattar N, et al: Evidence for tissue selectivity of the synthetic androgen 7 alpha-methyl-19-nortestosterone in hypogonadal men. J Clin Endocrinol Metab 88:2784–2793, 2003.

111. Avery MA, Tanabe M, Crowe DF, et al: Synthesis and testing of 17ab-hydroxy-7a methyl-D-homoestra-4,16-dien-3-one: A highly potent orally active androgen. Steroids 55:59–64, 1990.

112. Sundaram K, Kumar N, Bardin CW: 7a-Methyl-nortestosterone (MENT): The optimal androgen for male contraception. Ann Med 25:199–205, 1993.

113. Prasad MRN, Singh SP, Rajalakshmi M: Fertility control in male rats by continuous release of microquantities of cyproterone acetate from subcutaneous silastic capsules. Contraception 2:165–178, 1970.

114. Wang C, Yeung KK: Use of low-dosage oral cyproterone acetate as a male contraceptive. Contraception 21:245–272, 1980.

115. Chandolia RK, Weinbauer GF, Simoni M, et al: Comparative effects of chronic administration of the non-steroidal antiandrogens flutamide and casodex on the reproductive system of the male rat. Acta Endocr 125:547–555, 1991.

116. Dhar JD, Sety BS: Effect of a nonsteroidal antiandrogen, anadron, on the reproductive system and fertility in male rats. Contraception 42:121–138, 1990.

117. McLachlan RI, McDonald J, Rushford D, et al: Efficacy and acceptability of testosterone implants, alone or in combination with a 5α-reductase inhibitor, for male hormonal contraception. Contraception 62:73–78, 2000.

118. Kinniburgh D, Anderson RA, Baird DT: Suppression of spermatogenesis with desogestrel and testosterone pellets is not enhanced by addition of finasteride. J Androl 22:88–95, 2001.

119. Killian J, Pratis K, Clifton RJ, et al: 5α-Reductase isoenzymes 1 and 2 in the rat testis during postnatal development. Biol Reprod 68:1711–1718, 2003.

120. Wu FC, von Eckardstein A: Androgens and coronary artery disease. Endocr Rev 24:183–217, 2003.

121. Liu PY, Death AK, Handelsman DJ: Androgens and cardiovascular disease. Endocr Rev 24:313–340, 2003.

122. Handelsman DJ, Conway AJ, Howe CJ, et al: Establishing the minimum effective dose and additive effects of depot progestin in suppression of human spermatogenesis by a

testosterone depot. J Clin Endocrinol Metab 81:4113–4121, 1996.
123. Atkinson LE, Chang YL, Snyder PJ: Long-term experience with testosterone replacement through scrotal skin. In Nieschlag E, Behre HM (eds): Testosterone: Action Deficiency Substitution, 2d ed. Berlin, Springer, 1998, pp 364–388.
124. Handelsman DJ: The safety of androgens: Prostate and cardiovascular disease. In Wang C (ed): Male Reproductive Function. Boston, Kluwer, 1998, pp 173–190.
125. Wu JP, Gu FL: The prostate 41–65 years post castration. Chin Med J (Engl) 100:271–272, 1987.
126. Imperato-McGinley J, Gautier T, Zirinsky K, et al: Prostate visualization studies in males homozygous and heterozygous for 5α-reductase deficiency. J Clin Endocrinol Metab 75:1022–1026, 1992.
127. Quigley CA, DeBellis A, Marschke KB, et al: Androgen receptor defects: Historical, clinical and molecular perspectives. Endocr Rev 16:271–321, 1995.
128. Shaneyfelt T, Husein R, Bubley G, et al: Hormonal predictors of prostate cancer: A meta-analysis. J Clin Oncol 18:847–853, 2000.
129. Zitzmann M, Depenbusch M, Gromoll J, et al: Prostate volume and growth in testosterone-substituted hypogonadal men are dependent on the CAG repeat polymorphism of the androgen receptor gene: A longitudinal pharmacogenetic study. J Clin Endocrinol Metab 88:2049–2054, 2003.
130. Nelson KA, Witte JS: Androgen receptor CAG repeats and prostate cancer. Am J Epidemiol 155:883–890, 2002.
131. Behre HM, Bohmeyer J, Nieschlag E: Prostate volume in testosterone-treated and untreated hypogonadal men in comparison to age-matched normal controls. Clin Endocrinol (Oxf) 40:341–349, 1994.
132. Meikle AW, Arver S, Dobs AS, et al: Prostate size in hypogonadal men treated with a nonscrotal permeation-enhanced testosterone transdermal system. Urology 49:191–196, 1997.
133. Jin B, Conway AJ, Handelsman DJ: Effects of androgen deficiency and replacement on prostate zonal volumes. Clin Endocrinol (Oxf) 54:437–445, 2001.
134. Jin B, Turner L, Walters WAW, et al: Androgen or estrogen effects on the human prostate. J Clin Endocrinol Metab 81:4290–4295, 1996.
135. Archer J: The influence of testosterone on human aggression. Br J Psychiatry 82:1–28, 1991.
136. Anderson RA, Bancroft J, Wu FCW: The effects of exogenous testosterone on sexuality and mood of normal men. J Clin Endocrinol Metab 75:1503–1507, 1992.
137. Christiansen K: Behavioural correlates of testosterone. In Nieschlag E, Behre HM (eds): Testosterone: Action Deficiency Substitution, 2d ed. Berlin, Springer, 1998, pp 107–142.
138. Pope HG Jr, Kouri EM, Hudson JI: Effects of supraphysiologic doses of testosterone on mood and aggression in normal men: A randomized controlled trial. Arch Gen Psychiatry 57:133–140; discussion 155–156, 2000.
139. Bahrke MS, Yesalis CE, Wright JE: Psychological and behavioural effects of endogenous testosterone levels and anabolic-androgenic steroids among male: A review. Sports Med 10:303–337, 1990.
140. Bebb RA, Anawalt BD, Christensen RB, et al: Combined administration of levonorgestrel and testosterone induces more rapid and effective suppression of spermatogenesis than testosterone alone: A promising male contraceptive approach. J Clin Endocrinol Metab 81:757–762, 1996.
141. Meriggiola MC, Bremner WJ, Paulsen CA, et al: A combined regimen of cyproterone acetate and testosterone enanthate as a potentially highly effective male contraceptive. J Clin Endocrinol Metab 81:3018–3023, 1996.
142. Bouchard P, Garcia E: Influence of testosterone substitution on sperm suppression by LHRH agonists. Hormone Res 28:175–180, 1987.
143. Behre HM, Nashan D, Hubert W, et al: Depot gonadotropin-releasing hormone agonist blunts the androgen-induced suppression of spermatogenesis in a clinical trial of male contraception. J Clin Endocrinol Metab 74:84–90, 1992.
144. Heller CG, Moore DJ, Paulsen CA, et al: Effects of progesterone and synthetic progestins on the reproductive physiology of normal men. Fed Proc 18:1057–1064, 1959.
145. Frick J, Danner C, Joos H, et al: Spermatogenesis in men treated with subcutaneous application of levonorgestrel and estrone rods. J Androl 2:331–338, 1981.
146. Schearer SB, Alvarez-Sanchez F, Anselmo J, et al: Hormonal contraception for men. Int J Androl (Suppl 2):680–712, 1978.
147. Wu FCW, Aitken RJ: Suppression of sperm function by depot medroxyprogesterone acetate and testosterone enanthate in steroid male contraception. Fertil Steril 51:691–698, 1989.
148. Foegh M: Evaluation of steroids as contraceptives in men. Acta Endocr (Suppl 260):1–48, 1983.
149. Anawalt BD, Bebb RA, Bremner WJ, et al: A lower dosage levonorgestrel and testosterone combination effectively suppresses spermatogenesis and circulating gonadotropin levels with fewer metabolic effects than higher dosage combinations. J Androl 20:407–414, 1999.
150. Lobel B, Olivo JF, Guille F, et al: Contraception in men: Efficacy and immediate toxicity, a study of 18 cases. Acta Urol Belg 57:117–124, 1989.
151. Guerin JF, Rollet J: Inhibition of spermatogenesis in men using various combinations of oral progestagens and percutaneous or oral androgens. Int J Androl 11:187–199, 1988.
152. Meriggiola MC, Bremner WJ, Constantino A, et al: Low dose of cyproterone acetate and testosterone enanthate for contraception. Hum Reprod 13:1225–1229, 1998.
153. Meriggiola MC, Pavani A, Bremner WJ, et al: An oral regimen of cyproterone acetate and testosterone undecanoate for spermatogenic suppression in men. Fertil Steril 68:844–850, 1997.
154. Gonzalo IT, Swerdloff RS, Nelson AL, et al: Levonorgestrel implants (Norplant II) for male contraception clinical trials: Combination with transdermal and injectable testosterone. J Clin Endocrinol Metab 87:3562–3572, 2002.
155. Anderson RA, Kinniburgh D, Baird DT: Suppression of spermatogenesis by etonogestrel implants with depot testosterone: Potential for long-acting male contraception. J Clin Endocrinol Metab 87:3640–3649, 2002.
156. Kamischke A, Heuermann T, Kruger K, et al: An effective hormonal male contraceptive using testosterone undecanoate with oral or injectable norethisterone preparations. J Clin Endocrinol Metab 87:530–539, 2002.
157. Ewing LL, Cochran RC, Adams RJ, et al: Testis function in rhesus monkeys treated with a contraceptive steroid formulation. Contraception 27:347–362, 1983.
158. Lobl TJ, Kirton KT, Forbes AD, et al: Contraceptive efficacy of testosterone-estradiol implants in male rhesus monkeys. Contraception 27:383–389, 1983.
159. Handelsman DJ, Wishart S, Conway AJ: Oestradiol enhances testosterone-induced suppression of human spermatogenesis. Hum Reprod 15:672–679, 2000.
160. Lunn SF, Dixson AF, Sandow J, et al: Pituitary-testicular function is suppressed by an LHRH antagonist but not by an LHRH agonist in the marmoset monkey. J Endocrinol 125:233–239, 1990.
161. Marshall GF, Akhtar FB, Weinbauer GF, et al: Gonadotrophin-releasing hormone (GnRH) overcomes GnRH antagonist-induced suppression of LH secretion in primates. J Endocrinol 110:145–150, 1986.
162. Weinbauer GF, Surmann FJ, Nieschlag E: Suppression of spermatogenesis in a non-human primate (*Macaca fascicularis*) by concomitant gonadotrophin-releasing hormone antagonist and testosterone treatment. Acta Endocr 114:138–146, 1987.
163. Weinbauer GF, Khurshid S, Findscheidt U, et al: Sustained inhibition of sperm production and inhibin secretion by a

gonadotrophin-releasing hormone antagonist and delayed testosterone substitution in non-human primates (*Macaca fascicularis*). Acta Endocr 123:303–310, 1989.

164. Bremner WJ, Bagatell CJ, Steiner RA: Gonadotropin-releasing hormone antagonist plus testosterone: A potential male contraceptive. J Clin Endocrinol Metab 73:465–469, 1991.

165. Tom L, Bhasin S, Salameh W, et al: Induction of azoospermia in normal men with combined Nal-Glu GnRH antagonist and testosterone enanthate. J Clin Endocrinol Metab 75:476–483, 1992.

166. Pavlou SN, Brewer K, Farley MG, et al: Combined administration of a gonadotropin-releasing hormone antagonist and testosterone in men induces reversible azoospermia without loss of libido. J Clin Endocrinol Metab 73:1360–1369, 1991.

167. Simms MS, Scholfield DP, Jacobs E, et al: Anti-GnRH antibodies can induce castrate levels of testosterone in patients with advanced prostate cancer. Br J Cancer 83:443–446, 2000.

168. Talwar GP: Fertility regulating and immunotherapeutic vaccines reaching human trials stage. Hum Reprod Update 3:301–310, 1997.

169. Burger HG: Inhibin. Reproductive Medicine Review 1:1–20, 1992.

170. Wiebe JP, Wood PH: Selective suppression of follicle-stimulating hormone by 3-alpha-hydroxy-4-pregnen-20-one, a steroid found in Sertoli cells. Endocrinology 120:2259–2264, 1987.

171. Moudgal NR, Jeyakumar M, Krishnamurthy HN, et al: Development of male contraceptive vaccine: A perspective. Hum Reprod Update 3:335–346, 1997.

172. Leng N, Grasso P, Reichert LE: D-amino acid substitution of residues 32 to 46 of the glycoprotein hormone common alpha-subunit: Development of a synthetic glycoprotein hormone antagonist. Pept Res 9:188–194, 1996.

173. Singh J, O'Neill C, Handelsman DJ: Induction of spermatogenesis by androgens in gonadotropin-deficient (hpg) mice. Endocrinology 136:5311–5321, 1995.

174. Kumar TR, Wang Y, Lu N, et al: FSH is required for ovarian follicle maturation but not for male fertility. Nat Genet 15:201–204, 1997.

175. Dierich A, Sairam MR, Monaco L, et al: Impairing follicle-stimulating hormone (FSH) signalling in vivo: Targeted disruption of the FSH receptor leads to aberrant gametogenesis and hormonal imbalance. Proc Natl Acad Sci U S A 95:13612–13617, 1998.

176. Tapanainen JS, Aittomaki K, Min J, et al: Men homozygous for an inactivating mutation of the follicle-stimulating hormone (FSH) receptor present variable suppression of spermatogenesis and fertility. Nat Genet 15:205–206, 1997.

177. Nieschlag E: Reasons for abandoning immunization against FSH as an approach to male fertility regulation. In Zatuchni GI, Goldsmith A, Spieler JM, Sciarra JJ (eds): Male Contraception: Advances and Future Prospects. Philadelphia, Harper & Row, 1986, pp 395–400.

# Testicular Tumors with Endocrine Manifestations

## Ewa Rajpert-De Meyts, Jorma Toppari, and Niels E. Skakkebæk

**INTRODUCTION**

**GERM CELL TUMORS**
Epidemiology and Risk Groups
Classification and Histopathologic Aspects
Pathogenesis
Diagnosis and Tumor Markers
Staging, Prognostic Factors, and Management

**SEX CORD–STROMAL TUMORS OF THE TESTIS**
Leydig Cell Hyperplasia and Leydig Cell Tumors
Sertoli Cell Tumors and Sertoli-Leydig Cell Tumors
Juvenile-type and Adult-type Granulosa Cell Tumors
Mixed Sex Cord–Stromal Tumors

**ENDOCRINE DISORDERS RELATED TO TESTICULAR NEOPLASIA**

## INTRODUCTION

Testicular tumors may originate from several cell types that occur in the testis, but in the vast majority of cases, the germ cell is the cell of origin. Since this chapter is focused on tumors with endocrine manifestations, however, somatic cell tumors, known as sex cord–stromal neoplasms, which are less frequent than germ cell tumors but are derived from endocrine active cells, are also considered in detail. In addition, other abnormalities with endocrine significance that are on a boundary between normal and neoplastic growth, such as Leydig cell hyperplasia, as well as the endocrine effects of testicular tumors and their treatment are briefly discussed in this chapter.

## GERM CELL TUMORS

Germ cell tumors account for an estimated 90% to 95% of cases of testicular cancer and are by far the most frequent neoplasms of this organ. They are unique in comparison with other solid tumors for several reasons. First, nearly all germ cell tumors originate early in life and have a common preinvasive precursor that further transforms into overt tumors in young adulthood. The only exceptions to this rule are the rare tumors of infants and the equally rare spermatocytic seminoma of elderly men. Second, germ cell tumors are extremely radiosensitive and chemosensitive, with the exception of highly differentiated mature teratomas that are clinically more benign but also less sensitive to treatment. Finally, the incidence of testicular germ cell cancer has been steadily rising in recent decades, in concert with other abnormalities of the male reproductive tract, but with marked geographic and ethnic differences.[1-3]

### EPIDEMIOLOGY AND RISK GROUPS

The average age-adjusted incidence of testicular germ cell tumors has been markedly increasing among whites, in particular in North America and northwestern Europe, and is now approaching 10 per 100,000 in the countries with the highest incidence, such as Denmark and Switzerland.[1,3] Testicular cancer has thus become the most frequent malignancy among young Caucasian men in Western Europe. Epidemiologic studies have documented that cryptorchidism is a strongly predisposing condition for testicular cancer,[4-7] and revealed an almost identical pattern of risk factors for both diseases. Among risk factors, the following are most frequently reported: low birth weight, premature birth, birth order, high levels of maternal estrogens or bleeding during pregnancy, high maternal age or body weight of the mother, and neonatal jaundice.[8-14] It has been recently demonstrated that the trends in cryptorchidism follow the trends for testicular cancer in Denmark (where the rates for both diseases are among the highest in the world) and in Finland (among the lowest in Europe), thus providing further evidence for a pathogenetic link between the two diseases.[15]

Individuals with developmental abnormalities of the gonads and sex differentiation are at high risk of acquiring germ cell tumors. Conditions with an abnormal karyotype, especially those involving aneuploidy of sex chromosomes (i.e., 45,XO/46,XY) and structural abnormalities of chromosome Y,[16] as well as the androgen insensitivity syndrome,[17] carry a high risk of germ cell neoplasia. An association with testicular germ cell cancer was also reported in Down syndrome.[18,19] Patients with a unilateral testicular germ cell tumor are at increased risk for the development of a new primary testicular tumor in the contralateral testis, with the presence of testicular atrophy increasing the risk.[20]

The first cases of testicular *carcinoma in situ* (CIS), a common preinvasive precursor for germ cell tumors of young adults, were described in patients referred for infertility,[21,22] and recent studies indicated that the two conditions are risk factors for each other. Sperm production in patients with testicular cancer is often markedly lower than in controls, and these patients have significantly decreased offspring sex ratio and lower fertility rates, even prior to development of their tumor.[23-26] The association of poor testicular function, atrophy, maldescent, and abnormal testicular differentiation with testicular germ cell cancer led to a hypothesis that these disorders may be etiologically linked. A new concept called the *testicular dysgenesis syndrome (TDS)*, in which testicular cancer is one of the late consequences of a delayed or impaired fetal/infantile development of the testis, was then proposed.[27] Since then, histologic and clinical studies have provided additional evidence that dysgenetic features, such as tubules with undifferentiated Sertoli cells or hyaline bodies (also visible as microlithiasis in the scrotal ultrasound), are frequently seen in the contralateral biopsies of patients with testicular cancer.[28,29]

### CLASSIFICATION AND HISTOPATHOLOGIC ASPECTS

Germ cell–derived testicular tumors are characterized by a striking variety of morphologic forms; therefore, several classifications exist.[30] Two nomenclatures are the most commonly used: the so-called British classification[31] and the World Health Organization classification.[32] For practical purposes, especially for use by nonpathologists, a simple division into three age groups, modified from the one proposed by Looijenga and Oosterhuis,[33] is clinically most logical (Table 175-1). The first group includes rare germ cell tumors of early childhood (infantile tumors, mainly *mature teratoma* and *yolk sac tumor*). The tumors of adolescents and young adults are most frequent, and these tumors include *seminoma, nonseminomatous tumors,* and *combined tumors.* The combined (mixed) tumors contain elements of seminoma and nonseminomatous tumors, but are clinically treated as nonseminoma. Finally, in older age, *spermatocytic seminoma* is the predominant type of tumor. A characteristic feature of the tumors of young adults is that they originate from CIS,[21] which is most probably a transformed primordial germ cell or gonocyte. The infantile tumors and spermatocytic seminoma are not preceded by CIS and apparently have a different pathogenesis.[34]

A separate type of gonadal germ cell tumor is *gonadoblastoma,* which occurs almost exclusively in children or young individuals with sexual differentiation disorders (both females and males), predominantly those with mixed gonadal dysgenesis (e.g., 45,XO/46,XY).[35] The affected gonad in most cases is abnormal and may contain testicular cordlike structures, ovarian-like elements, or atrophic streak gonad tissues. Gonadoblastoma consists of nests of gonocyte- or CIS-like cells surrounded by stromal cells resembling primitive granulosa cells. The clinical course is usually benign; however, gonadoblastoma can transform into a malignant germ cell tumor. No particular endocrine manifestations of gonadoblastoma have been noted other than the endocrine problems inherent to a background intersex problem.

As far as morphology is concerned, CIS cells resemble gonocytes, or immature germ cells. CIS cells are located inside seminiferous tubules, in the place normally occupied by spermatogonia (Fig. 175-1*A*). Seminoma cells resemble CIS cells and grow as a homogeneous tumor that retains features of germ cells (Fig. 175-1*B*). Seminomas are usually diagnosed in the age group of 25 to 40 years, while nonseminomatous tumors occur in relatively younger men (17–30 years) and usually have a more severe clinical course. Nonseminomas display a variety of histologic forms (embryonic or extraembryonic) ranging from undifferentiated embryonal carcinoma to mature teratoma[30–32] (Fig. 175-1*C*). Among nonseminomatous components, two extraembryonic types deserve special note because of their endocrine activity: *choriocarcinoma,* which resembles gestational trophoblast, produces large

| Table 175-1 | Simplified Classification of Testicular Germ Cell Tumors |
|---|---|

Infantile tumors
  Teratoma (mature)
  Yolk sac tumor
Gonadoblastoma
Tumors of young adult age
  Preinvasive lesion: carcinoma in situ (gonocytoma in situ)
  Seminoma (classic)
  Nonseminoma
    Embryonal carcinoma
    Teratoma
      Mature
      Immature
      With malignant transformation
    Extraembryonic elements
      Choriocarcinoma
      Yolk sac tumor (endodermal sinus tumor)
  Combined tumor (elements of both seminoma and nonseminoma)
Spermatocytic seminoma (spermatocytoma)

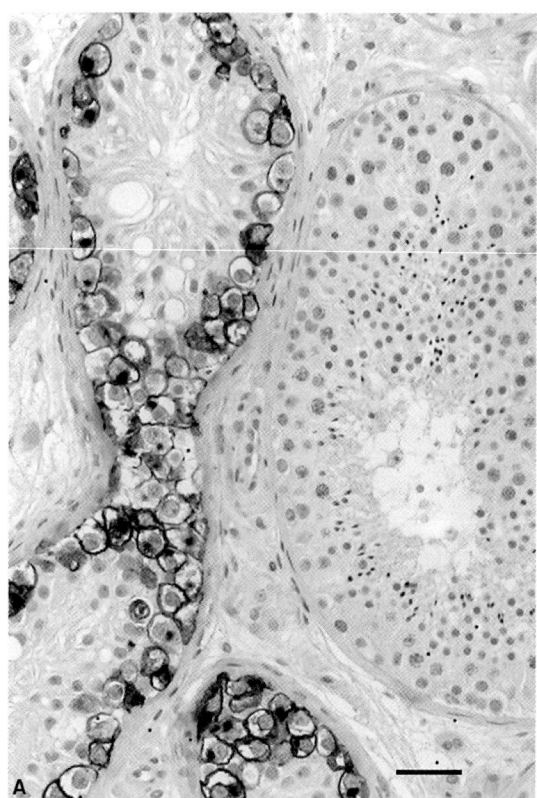

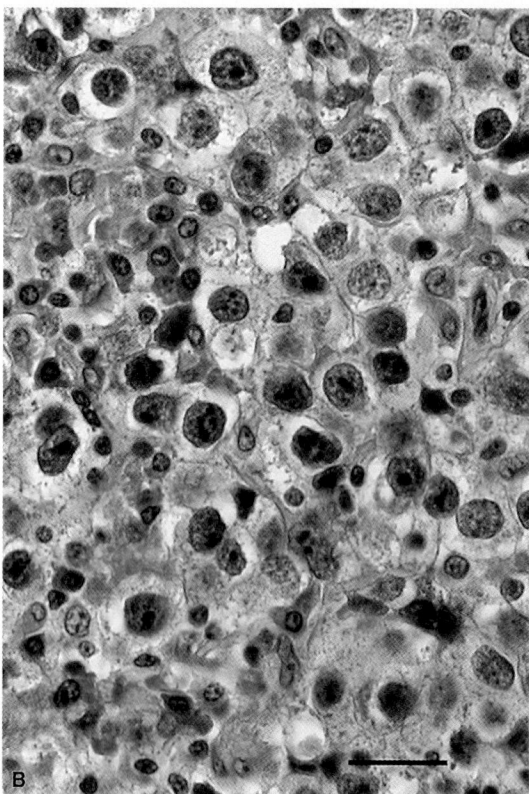

***Figure 175-1*** Histology of the most frequent germ cell neoplasms. Bar, 50 μg. **A,** Preinvasive carcinoma in situ (CIS). CIS cells are stained immunohistochemically with an anti-PLAP (placenta-like alkaline phosphatase) antibody. Note the difference between the CIS-containing tubules and the adjacent larger tubules with normal spermatogenesis. **B,** Seminoma. Tumor cells closely resemble CIS cells and are also positive for PLAP.

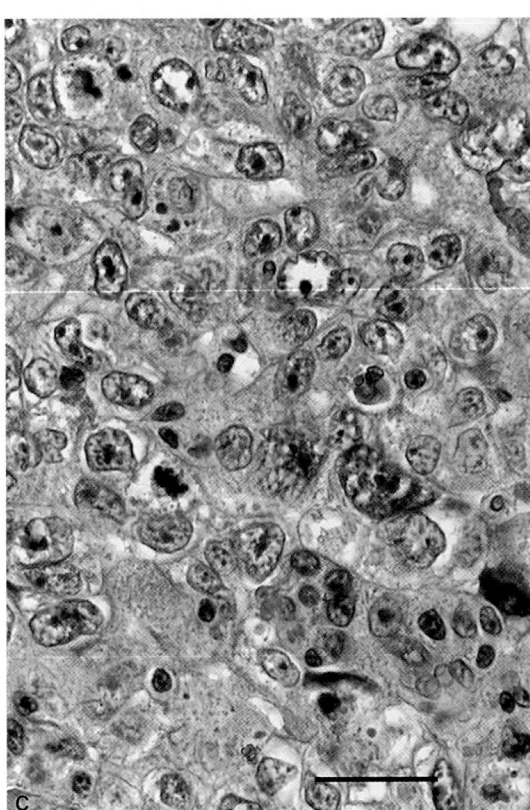

*Figure 175-1, cont'd* **C,** Embryonal carcinoma. Shown here is a component of a nonseminomatous tumor that also contains elements of teratoma.

quantities of human chorionic gonadotropin (hCG); and *yolk sac tumor,* which is similar in morphology to the embryonic yolk sac, secretes α-fetoprotein (AFP).

## PATHOGENESIS

The origin and pathogenesis of testicular germ cell tumors are poorly understood, but there is consensus that the most common tumors of young adults stem from CIS cells.[34,36] The high incidence of testicular cancer in subjects with congenital errors of gonadal development and sexual differentiation, as well as an association of a number of risk factors in the prenatal or perinatal period strongly implicate intrauterine factors in the malignant transformation of germ cells.[11–14] Additional evidence comes from comparative studies of the pattern of expression of various antigens, which is shared between primordial germ cells/gonocytes and CIS cells.[36,37] On the other hand, evidence from epidemiologic studies, in particular, the rising incidence of testicular cancer in well-developed countries but with striking geographic differences, as well as the association with other components of TDS such as cryptorchidism or subfertility suggest a possible influence of environmental factors.[38] Because the rise is strongly associated with the year of birth rather than the age of patients, the unknown environmental factor has to occur prenatally or in early infancy.[39] Observations of wildlife and experiments in laboratory animals exposed to synthetic hormones suggest that a disturbance in the hormonal milieu of the developing gonad, in particular, an imbalance between sex hormones (a relative insufficiency of androgens or estrogenic excess), can disturb the differentiation of early germ cells.[40] This finding gave rise to the hypothesis that a developmental delay or arrest due to an inherited genetic problem (including possible genetic polymorphisms), environmental in utero exposure, or a combination of both can render early fetal germ cells prone to neoplastic transformation.[27,38]

## DIAGNOSIS AND TUMOR MARKERS

Preinvasive CIS is asymptomatic, and clinical diagnosis at this early stage is sporadic, usually in cases of unilateral testicular atrophy or in individuals from high-risk groups. Surgical testicular biopsy is currently the only sure diagnostic procedure for CIS, although some leads to establish methods of noninvasive detection in semen are promising.[41] Testicular dysgenesis is frequently associated with microcalcifications; therefore, scrotal ultrasound revealing testicular microlithiasis may suggest the presence of CIS. If testicular atrophy or other risk factors (e.g., the history of cryptorchidism) are also present, testicular microlithiasis supports an indication for biopsy.[29]

CIS cells are located in the basal compartment of the seminiferous tubules and are thus in communication with the intertubular space. No serum markers for CIS have been discovered to date; however, in cases associated with testicular atrophy, hormonal profiles typical for testicular failure, that is, decreased inhibin B and increased gonadotropin levels may be observed. In the vast majority of cases, CIS progresses to overt tumors unnoticed.

The most common manifestation of an overt testicular cancer is a scrotal mass, with pain reported by only a few patients.[42] In the differential diagnosis, several other conditions have to be considered, such as orchitis, epididymitis, hydrocele, varicocele, and inguinal hernia. Ultrasonographic examination is helpful in these cases. In a small percentage of cases of testicular cancer, the initial symptoms are those of metastatic disease. These symptoms are usually uncharacteristic and may include lumbar pain, a palpable abdominal mass, supraclavicular lymph node enlargement, and, rarely, pulmonary symptoms.

Most overt germ cell tumors secrete protein products that can be detected in circulating blood. These products are known as biochemical serum tumor markers and are helpful in the diagnosis of these tumors. Some excellent immunometric assays have been developed to measure several serum markers.[43] The most important in clinical practice are AFP,[44,45] hCG,[46] and lactate dehydrogenase (LDH, LD-1).[47,48] AFP and hCG are predominantly markers for nonseminomatous tumors, whereas LDH is also produced by seminoma. It is important to remember, however, that germ cell tumors very rarely occur in pure histologic form; for example, the presence of a relatively modest number of giant cells in a seminomatous tumor mass may be sufficient to detect hCG in serum. Nevertheless, very high levels of AFP and hCG are associated with nonseminomas, whereas an increased concentration of LDH in the absence of AFP and hCG is pathognomonic for seminoma. LDH (LD-1) levels in serum tend to be higher in patients harboring tumors with an increased copy number of chromosome 12p, consistent with the genomic location of the LDH gene.[48] Some other markers used for immunohistochemical diagnosis of CIS cells and tumors in tissue sections, such as TRA-1-60[49,50] and placental-like alkaline phosphatase (PLAP),[51] are also detectable in serum and have recently begun to be used in clinical research, but the results are not yet consistent enough to use these assays in routine practice.

## STAGING, PROGNOSTIC FACTORS, AND MANAGEMENT

In general, higher levels of tumor markers tend to be associated with a poorer prognosis of the patient. Careful staging is necessary in each case, however, to determine the most appropriate treatment strategy. In addition to measurements of circulating tumor markers, spread of disease has to be evaluated by various procedures, such as bipedal lymphangiography, thoracic radiography, retroperitoneal computed tomography, or ultrasonography.[52] These procedures help to classify patients into three stages, according to the TNM (tumor, node, metastases) System of the International Union Against Cancer[53]: stage I (disease confined to one or both testicles); IIA (retroperitoneal node metastases, RNM < 2 cm); IIB (RNM ≥ 2 cm but < 5 cm); IIC (RNM > 5 cm); IIIA (supradiaphragmatic node metastases); and IIIB (extranodal metastases, e.g., lung). Other commonly used staging systems have been developed by the American Joint Committee on Cancer Staging, the Royal Marsden Hospital, the Memorial Sloan-Kettering Cancer Center, and Indiana University.[52]

As far as treatment of testicular germ cell tumors is concerned, orchiectomy remains the primary method. Postsurgical management is variable, depending on the histologic type of tumor, stage of disease, and presence of residual retroperitoneal masses. A surveillance strategy for patients in clinical stage I is used in some centers.[54] The most common therapy of disseminated disease after orchiectomy is radiotherapy in association with systemic combination chemotherapy with various cytotoxic drugs such as cisplatin, etoposide, bleomycin, vinblastine, and methotrexate.[55,56] Germ cell tumors are in general highly sensitive to both radiotherapy and chemotherapy, nonseminomas being less sensitive than seminomas. Because of this sensitivity, testicular germ cell cancer has become a model of a highly curable malignant disease, with more than 80% of patients reaching a sustained complete remission.[55]

Monitoring of serum markers is obligatory for accurate prognosis and assessment of treatment, especially in metastatic disease.[57] The rate of decrease in hCG and AFP serum levels (half-life) has a very high prognostic significance for a durable complete response. Various additional biologic prognostic factors have been proposed in recent years, such as the number of copies of isochromosome 12p, the degree of neovascularization, or vascular invasion, and the expression of proto-oncogenes and adhesion proteins,[58-60] but these factors have to be considered only as part of multifactorial analysis in conjunction with the traditional serum markers.[57,60,61] Whatever the parameters used, it is very important to make a dynamic assessment of progress through the early stages of chemotherapy. For details concerning treatment of testicular tumors, the reader should consult specialist oncologic literature.

## SEX CORD–STROMAL TUMORS OF THE TESTIS

In contrast to the adults, in whom sex cord–stromal tumors of the testis are very rare, children develop these tumors in up to 40% of cases of testicular neoplasms.[62-64] These tumors are derived from somatic cells; Leydig cells, Sertoli/granulosa cells, and nearly all of these tumors secrete inhibin A, which is the best serum marker to distinguish them from germ cell–derived neoplasms.[65,66] A classification of sex cord–stromal tumors of the testis[30,67] is presented in Table 175-2.

### LEYDIG CELL HYPERPLASIA AND LEYDIG CELL TUMORS

Leydig cells in adult men are considered to be a terminally differentiated and mitotically quiescent cell type. In various

**Table 175-2** Sex Cord–Stromal Tumors of the Testis

Leydig cell tumors
Sertoli cell tumors
   Large cell calcifying tumor
   Sex cord tumor with annular tubules
   Sclerosing tumor
   Sertoli cell tumors, not otherwise specified
Sertoli-Leydig cell tumors
Juvenile-type granulosa cell tumors
Adult-type granulosa cell tumors
Mixed sex cord–stromal tumors
Unclassified

disorders of testicular function, however, especially those associated with decreased testosterone/luteinizing hormone ratio, variable in size micronodules of Leydig cells are quite common.[68] In certain forms of the so-called Sertoli cell–only syndrome (germinal aplasia or del Castillo syndrome), and in Klinefelter's syndrome, large nodules of Leydig cells can be seen. When the size of a nodule exceeds the diameter of a seminiferous tubule by several-fold, the term *Leydig cell adenoma* is used. Leydig cell adenomas are usually benign and their progression to overt Leydig cell tumors is exceedingly rare.

The mechanism of *Leydig cell hyperplasia* in human males is poorly understood. Disruption of the testicular-pituitary-hypothalamic axis leading to prolonged stimulation of Leydig cells directly by luteinizing hormone or indirectly by gonadotropin-releasing hormone may play a central role.[68] Leydig cell hyperplasia and adenomas can be easily induced in rodents by the administration of estrogens, gonadotropins, and a wide range of chemical compounds. Whether such induction is relevant in humans remains to be elucidated. Mutations that cause constitutive activation of the luteinizing hormone receptor or $G_s$ protein in Leydig cells have been identified only in a small subset of patients, usually children with precocious puberty, and in some cases they have manifested as tumors.[69-71]

*Leydig cell tumors* are found in all age groups, but the peak incidence occurs between 5 and 10 years and between 30 and 35 years of age.[72-74] In children, a Leydig tumor in most cases causes precocious puberty with an enlarged penis, pubic hair, accelerated growth, skin changes, and an adult-type odor of sweat, due to increased secretion of androgens by the tumor. Approximately 10% of boys also have gynecomastia, which is caused by estrogens produced in excess as a result of high aromatase activity in some of the tumors. In adults, adverse hormone effects are found in about half the patients. The excessive androgen secretion does not cause such conspicuous effects as in prepubertal boys and, therefore, gynecomastia is the adverse manifestation that is most common in adult patients (in 20% to 40% of cases).[72] Gynecomastia may be associated with loss of libido, impotence, and infertility.

In children, Leydig cell tumors are always benign and can be treated by surgical enucleation,[63] whereas in adults, malignant tumors have been reported in 10% to 15% of patients. An example of a Leydig cell tumor is shown in Figure 175-2. Metastatic behavior in Leydig cell tumors is associated with the presence of cytologic atypia, necrosis, angiolymphatic invasion, increased mitotic activity, atypical mitotic figures, infiltrative margins, extension beyond testicular parenchyma,

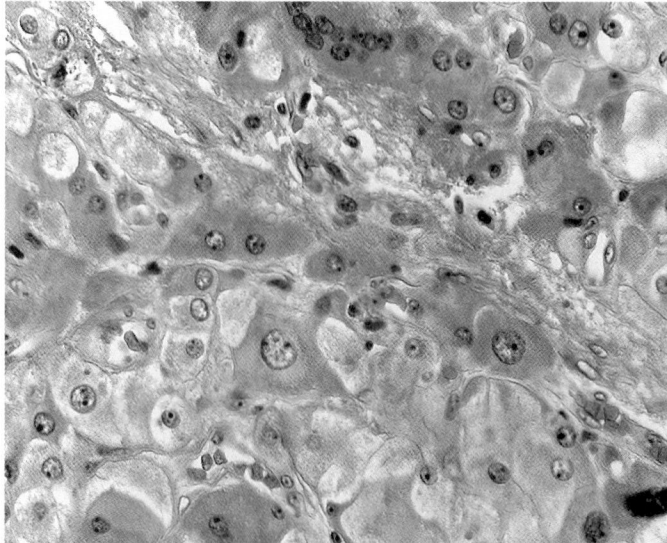

*Figure 175-2* Leydig cell tumor (unilateral) isolated from an 8-year-old boy. Note the heterogeneity and cellular atypia of the Leydig cells.

and DNA aneuploidy.[72,74] Malignant tumors were found to be hormonally inactive in one series of patients.[72] Benign tumors are successfully treated by orchiectomy, whereas an additional retroperitoneal lymphadenectomy should be considered in the cases in which gross or histologic features indicate a likelihood of malignancy.[72] Chronic hyperestrogenism may cause irreversible damage to the remaining testis and, therefore, both permanent infertility and hypoandrogenism.[73] Malignant tumors have been resistant to conventional chemotherapy and irradiation.[75] Survival after the initial diagnosis of malignant Leydig cell tumor ranges from 2 months to 17 years (median, 2 years), and metastases can be found as late as 9 years after diagnosis.[73] Therefore, lifelong follow-up of patients with malignant Leydig cell tumors is necessary.

Excessive secretion of adrenocorticotropic hormone (ACTH) in poorly controlled 21-hydroxylase deficiency or Nelson's syndrome (postadrenalectomy status) may lead to the development of adrenal rests, or hyperplastic interstitial nodules in the testis.[76] These cells secrete androgens, and the condition may therefore resemble Leydig cell hyperplasia or tumor. However, adrenal rests are effectively treated by appropriate glucocorticoid replacement, which may also lead to gradual regression.[77] Obviously, it would be an error to perform an orchiectomy on these patients and, therefore, careful endocrine evaluation, including adrenal hormones and ACTH, is necessary before any testicular tumors are treated surgically. Whenever possible, testis-sparing surgery (nodule enucleation) should be considered in those rare cases.

## SERTOLI CELL TUMORS AND SERTOLI-LEYDIG CELL TUMORS

Sertoli cells are the somatic cells in the seminiferous epithelium that support differentiating spermatogenic cells. Normally, these cells cease proliferation at puberty and function as terminally differentiated cells throughout adulthood. *Sertoli cell tumors* are found in association with multiple neoplasia syndromes, such as the Carney complex[78] and Peutz-Jeghers syndrome.[73] One study documented the presence of multiple foci of proliferating Sertoli cells in young boys, who later developed full-blown Peutz-Jeghers syndrome or Carney complex, thus these proliferations are probably the early intratubular forms of Sertoli cell tumors.[79]

In the *Carney complex*, patients have skin myxomas, heart myxomas, typical skin pigmentations, and adrenal and testicular tumors, among other symptoms.[78] The testicular tumors are large cell calcifying Sertoli cell tumors that are multifocal and bilateral[80] (Fig. 175-3). The tumors often appear at the time of puberty and are in most cases benign. Only one malignant case has been reported in association with the Carney complex, whereas seven other malignant tumors were reported in other patients with large cell calcifying Sertoli cell tumors.[80] The malignant cases were unilateral and solitary. Large cell calcifying Sertoli cell tumors are not usually hormonally active, although elevated levels of serum inhibin have been reported.[66] Other tumors of Carney complex, including Leydig cell tumors, can cause endocrine manifestations.[81] Two genetic loci for the Carney complex has been identified on chromosomes 2p16 and 17q22–24 by Stratakis and colleagues.[82] The genetic loci are different from those in other multiple neoplasia syndromes, including Peutz-Jeghers syndrome.[83] The Carney complex susceptibility gene in chromosome 17 was found to be the type I-alpha regulatory subunit of protein kinase A,[84,85] whereas the gene in chromosome 2 remains to be identified. To reach an early diagnosis of these diseases, clinicians should be aware of the association of large cell calcifying Sertoli cell tumors with other neoplasms, particularly heart myxomas in the Carney complex and gastrointestinal tumors in Peutz-Jeghers syndrome.

Sertoli cell tumors associated with *Peutz-Jeghers syndrome* are sometimes difficult to distinguish from those found in patients with the Carney complex. However, Peutz-Jeghers

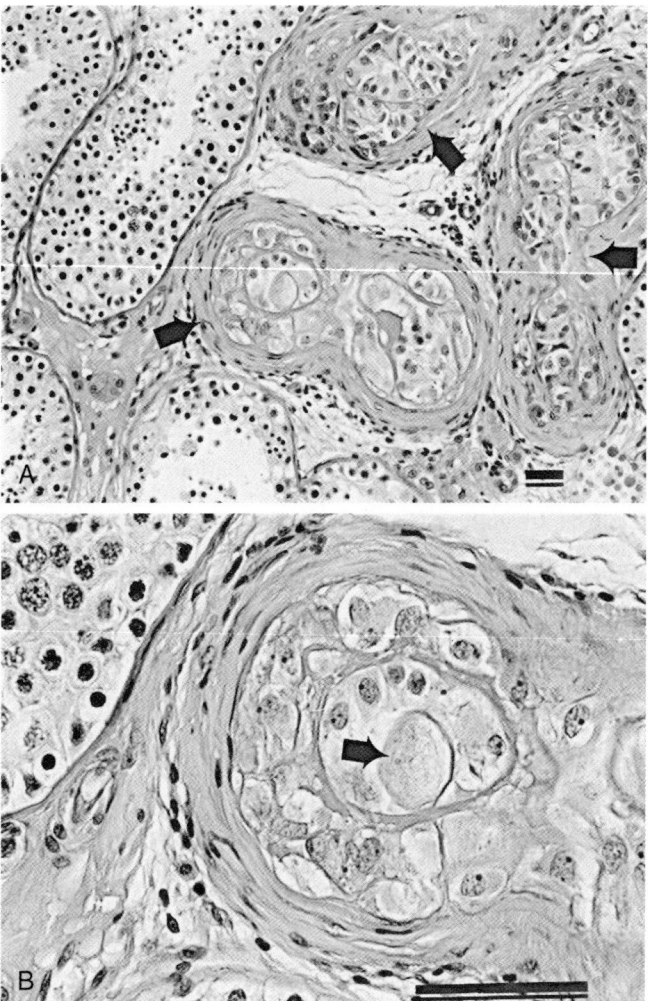

**Figure 175-3**  Large cell calcifying Sertoli cell tumor isolated from a 12-year-old boy. Bar, 50 μm. **A,** The neoplastic seminiferous tubules *(arrows)* contain only large pale Sertoli cells and visible calcifications in the lumen. Adjacent normal tubules show advanced spermatogenesis. **B,** Higher magnification shows detail of the malignant tubule with a typical calcification *(arrow)*.

tumors of the testis also resemble ovarian sex cord tumors with annular tubules.[73] These tumors often express strong aromatase activity and therefore cause gynecomastia.[86] Germline loss-of-function mutations in the STK11/LKB1 gene, which encodes for a serine-threonine kinase, cause the syndrome,[87] although some patients may have other genes affected. How the defect in this putative tumor suppressor gene influences tumorigenesis is not yet known.

*Sclerosing Sertoli cell tumors* are rare and account for only approximately 5% of sex cord–stromal tumors.[88,89] They are not associated with any syndromes. Most of the patients are young adults (median age, 30; range, 18–80 years). Tumors are small, well demarcated, and rarely malignant. No adverse endocrine activity has been reported in these patients.

Many Sertoli cell tumors cannot be classified in any of the aforementioned histopathologic groups and are therefore referred to as *Sertoli cell tumors, not otherwise specified.* These tumors occur primarily in adults; in one series of 60 patients, only four were younger than 20 years.[90] The tumors were always unilateral and occurred in descended testes. Most of the tumors were well circumscribed, but an infiltrative margin was found in four cases. The tumors were hormonally inactive, and gynecomastia developed in only two patients, who also had alcoholic cirrhosis. In the study from the Kiel Paediatric Tumor Registry, 18 pediatric cases were reported, perhaps on a somewhat different histopathologic basis because the age of the patients was very young (median, 4 months; range, 0–14 months).[62] Juvenile Sertoli cell tumors often showed infiltrative growth into adjacent tissue, dense cellularity, and considerable proliferative activity, but after surgical excision no local recurrences or metastases occurred. Thus, these tumors have a good prognosis. Sertoli cell tumors can be treated by orchiectomy, and only in a few cases does retroperitoneal lymphadenectomy have to be considered when malignancy is apparent.[81]

*Sertoli-Leydig cell tumors* are distinguished from pure Sertoli cell tumors by the presence of a prominent stromal component in the former.[90] Leydig cells are difficult to recognize in these tumors. Patients may present with gynecomastia.

## JUVENILE-TYPE AND ADULT-TYPE GRANULOSA CELL TUMORS

*Juvenile-type granulosa cell tumors* are the most common testicular tumors in infants. In the 11 patients reported by Harms and Kock,[62] the diagnosis was made before the age of 3 months. Juvenile granulosa cell tumors have been found in undescended testes, with an abnormal karyotype (e.g., mosaicism XO/XY) and ambiguous genitalia detected in 6 of 26 reported cases of the disease.[62] The distinction between Sertoli cell tumors, not otherwise specified, and juvenile granulosa cell tumors is based on the prominent differentiation into follicles in the latter, in contrast to tubular differentiation in Sertoli cell tumors.[90] The two tumor types share most of the immunohistochemical markers, for example, inhibin. Similar to Sertoli cell tumors, not otherwise specified, juvenile granulosa cell tumors have a good prognosis. In contrast to their ovarian counterparts, testicular juvenile granulosa cell tumors do not show endocrine hyperactivity.

*Adult-type granulosa cell tumors* are comparable to ovarian tumors, but are extremely rare in men, and occur mainly in adults.[73,91] Only some of the patients have manifestations of feminization, primarily gynecomastia, resulting from the hormonal activity of the tumor. Most of the tumors are benign, but malignant cases have also been reported.[91]

## MIXED SEX CORD–STROMAL TUMORS

Sex cord–stromal tumors can contain combinations of Leydig, Sertoli, granulosa, and theca cells and are therefore called *mixed tumors*.[30,73] In addition to inhibin A, which appears to be a common marker for sex cord–stromal tumors, including Leydig cell, Sertoli cell, and juvenile granulosa cell tumors,[65,92] Sertoli cell–derived components can be distinguished by the presence of antimüllerian hormone[93] and GATA-4.[94] Other immunohistochemical markers are reviewed in Ulbright and coworkers.[30] Sex cord–stromal tumors are rare and can occur at any age. They are benign in children, but at least one malignant case has been reported in adults.[95] Most of the patients can be treated by orchiectomy, and lymph node dissection is indicated only in cases with overt malignant features on microscopic examination.[30]

## ENDOCRINE DISORDERS RELATED TO TESTICULAR NEOPLASIA

The most pronounced secondary endocrine symptoms of testicular neoplasia, especially in children and adolescents, are associated with a relative excess of androgens caused by tumors either producing androgens directly, as in Leydig cell tumors, or after stimulation with large amounts of hCG, as is the case for some germ cell tumors. Aromatization of androgens leads, in turn, to a relative excess of estrogens, which is usually manifested as gynecomastia and impairment of spermatogenesis in young adults.[96]

Testicular dysfunction in patients with germ cell cancer is an important clinical problem, especially in view of the fact that the vast majority of these patients are of reproductive age. Patients with testicular neoplasms in general have decreased fertility and poor spermatogenesis even before the overt tumor has developed.[23,25,26,97,98] Abnormalities include oligozoospermia, elevated luteinizing hormone levels, and in some cases smaller testicular volume and microlithiasis in ultrasonic examination.[29] A variable degree of testicular dysgenesis with undifferentiated Sertoli cells and hyaline bodies is often revealed by a testicular biopsy, which may detect the presence of CIS cells in some tubules. Histologic evaluation of contralateral biopsies in patients with an overt unilateral tumor may show a similar picture, with the cumulative presence of histologic symptoms of TDS in about 25% of patients, and a 5% to 8% risk of the presence of CIS cells.[28,97]

Testicular function in patients with testicular neoplasms may be further disturbed by treatment of the neoplastic disease. Radiotherapy and chemotherapy induce severe and dose-dependent impairment in spermatogenesis and secondary androgen deficiency.[97,99,100] Neoplasia-harboring gonads may be more susceptible to radiation-induced damage than normal testes. Refinement of the dosage must be considered in each patient in order to eradicate neoplasia without causing severe hormonal abnormalities. Thus, in general, men treated for testicular cancer require careful counseling about their reproductive function with respect to the chance of recovery of spermatogenesis and fertility and the possible need for androgen replacement therapy and assisted fertility treatment.[99,100]

## REFERENCES

1. Huyghe E, Matsuda T, Thonneau P: Increasing incidence of testicular cancer worldwide: A review. J Urol 170:5–11, 2003.
2. Brown LM, Pottern LM, Hoover RN, et al: Testicular cancer in the United States: Trends in incidence and mortality. Int J Epidemiol 15:164–170, 1992.
3. Adami HO, Bergström R, Möhner M, et al: Testicular cancer in nine northern European countries. Int J Cancer 59:33–38, 1994.
4. Müller J, Skakkebæk NE, Nielsen OH, Græm N: Cryptorchidism and testis cancer: Atypical infantile germ cell followed by carcinoma in situ and invasive carcinoma in adulthood. Cancer 54:629–634, 1984.
5. Giwercman A, Grinsted J, Hansen B, et al: Testicular cancer risk in boys with maldescended testis: A cohort study. J Urol 138:1214–1216, 1987.
6. Campbell HE: Incidence of malignant growth of the undescended testicle. Arch Surg 44:353–369, 1942.
7. Møller H, Prener A, Skakkebæk NE: Testicular cancer, cryptorchidism, inguinal hernia, testicular atrophy, and genital malformations: Case-control studies in Denmark. Cancer Causes Control 7:264–274, 1996.
8. Henderson BE, Benton B, Jing J, et al: Risk factors for cancer of the testis in young men. Int J Cancer 23:598–602, 1979.
9. Depue RH, Pike MC, Henderson BE: Estrogen exposure during gestation and risk of testicular cancer. J Natl Cancer Inst 71:1151–1155, 1983.
10. Beard CM, Melton LJ, O'Fallon WM, et al: Cryptorchidism and maternal estrogen exposure. Am J Epidemiol 120:707–716, 1984.
11. Swerdlow AJ, Huttly SR, Smith PG: Prenatal and familial associations of testicular cancer. Br J Cancer 55:571–577, 1987.
12. Prener A, Hsieh C-C, Engholm G, et al: Birth order and risk of testicular cancer. Cancer Causes Control 3:265–272, 1992.
13. Akre O, Ekbom A, Hsieh C-C, et al: Testicular nonseminoma and seminoma in relation to perinatal characteristics. J Natl Cancer Inst 88:883–889, 1996.

14. Möller H, Skakkebæk NE: Testicular cancer and cryptorchidism in relation to prenatal factors: Case-control studies in Denmark. Cancer Causes Control 8:904–912, 1997.

15. Boisen KA, Kaleva M, Main KM, et al: Difference in the prevalence of congenital cryptorchidism between two Nordic countries. Lancet 363:1264–1269, 2004.

16. Müller J, Skakkebæk NE, Ritzén M, et al: Carcinoma in situ of the testis in children with 54,X/46,XY gonadal dysgenesis. J Pediatr 106:431–436, 1985.

17. Müller J, Skakkebæk NE: Testicular carcinoma in situ in children with androgen insensitivity (testicular feminisation) syndrome. Br Med J 288:1419–1420, 1984.

18. Dexeus FH, Logothetis CJ, Chong C, et al: Genetic abnormalities in men with germ cell tumors. J Urol 140:80–84, 1988.

19. Dieckmann KP, Rube C, Henke RP: Association of Down's syndrome and testicular cancer. J Urol 157:1701–1704, 1997.

20. Harland SJ, Cook PA, Fosså SD, et al: Intratubular germ cell neoplasia of the contralateral testis in testicular cancer: Defining a high risk group. J Urol 160:1353–1357, 1998.

21. Skakkebæk NE: Possible carcinoma-in-situ of the testis. Lancet 2:516–517, 1972.

22. Skakkebæk NE: Carcinoma in situ of the testis: Frequency and relationship to invasive germ cell tumours in infertile men. Histopathology 2:157–170, 1978.

23. Berthelsen JG, Skakkebaek NE: Gonadal function in men with testis cancer. Fertil Steril 39:68–75, 1983.

24. Møller H, Skakkebaek NE: Risk of testicular cancer in subfertile men: Case-control study. Br Med J 318:559–562, 1999.

25. Jacobsen R, Bostofte E, Engholm G, et al: Fertility and offspring sex ratio of men who develop testicular cancer: A record linkage study. Hum Reprod 15:1958–1961, 2000.

26. Jacobsen R, Bostofte E, Engholm G, et al: Risk of testicular cancer in men with abnormal semen characteristics: Cohort study. Br Med J 321:789–792, 2000.

27. Skakkebaek NE, Rajpert-De Meyts E, Main KM: Testicular Dysgenesis Syndrome: An increasingly common developmental disorder with environmental aspects. Hum Reprod 16:972–978, 2001.

28. Hoei-Hansen CE, Holm M, Rajpert-De Meyts E, Skakkebaek NE: Histological evidence of testicular dysgenesis in contralateral biopsies of 218 patients with testicular germ cell cancer. J Pathol 200:370–374, 2003.

29. Holm M, Hoei-Hansen CE, Rajpert-De Meyts E, Skakkebaek NE: Increased risk of carcinoma in situ in patients with testicular germ cell cancer with ultrasonic microlithiasis in the contralateral testicle. J Urol 170:1163–1167, 2003.

30. Ulbright TM, Amin MB, Young RH: Atlas of Tumor Pathology: Tumors of the Testis, Adnexa, Spermatic Cord, and Scrotum. Washington, DC, Armed Forces Institute of Pathology, 1999.

31. Pugh RCB: Pathology of the Testis. Oxford, Blackwell, 1976.

32. Eble J, Sauter G, Epstein JI, Sesterhenn IA (eds): Pathology and Genetics of Tumours of the Male Urinary System and Male Genital Organs. WHO Classification of Tumours. Lyon, IARC Press, 2004.

33. Looijenga LH, Oosterhuis JN: Pathogenesis of testicular germ cell tumours. Rev Reprod 4:90–100, 1999.

34. Skakkebæk NE, Berthelsen JG, Giwercman A, et al: Carcinoma-in-situ of the testis: Possible origin from gonocytes and precursor of all types of germ cell tumours except spermatocytoma. Int J Androl 10:19–28, 1987.

35. Scully RE: Gonadoblastoma: A review of 74 cases. Cancer 25:1340–1356, 1970.

36. Jørgensen N, Rajpert-De Meyts E, Græm N, et al: Expression of immunohistochemical markers for testicular carcinoma in situ by normal human germ cells. Lab Invest 72:223–231, 1995.

37. Rajpert-De Meyts E, Bartkova J, Samson M, et al: The emerging phenotype of the testicular carcinoma in situ cell. APMIS 111:267–279, 2003.

38. Skakkebæk NE, Rajpert-De Meyts E, Jørgensen N, et al: Germ cell cancer and disorders of spermatogenesis: An environmental connection? APMIS 106:3–12, 1998.

39. Bergström R, Adami HO, Möhner M, et al: Increase in testicular cancer incidence in six European countries: A birth cohort phenomenon. J Natl Cancer Inst 88:727–733, 1996.

40. Rajpert-De Meyts E, Skakkebæk NE: The possible role of sex hormones in the development of testicular cancer. Eur Urol 23:54–61, 1993.

41. Giwercman A: Carcinoma in situ of the testis: Screening and management. Scand J Urol Nephrol Suppl 148:1–47, 1992.

42. Richie JP: Advances in the diagnosis and treatment of testicular cancer. Clin Invest 11:670–675, 1993.

43. Bower M, Rustin GJS: Serum tumor markers and their role in monitoring germ cell cancers of the testis. In Vogelzang NT, Scardino PT, Shipley WU, Coffey DS (eds): Comprehensive Textbook of Genitourinary Oncology, 2d ed. Philadelphia, Lippincott Williams & Wilkins, 2000, pp 927–938.

44. Gitlin D, Perricelli A: Synthesis of serum albumin, prealbumin, alpha-fetoprotein, 1-antitrypsin and transferrin by the human yolk sac. Nature 228:995–996, 1970.

45. Grigor KM, Detre SI, Kohn J, Neville AM: Serum alpha foetoprotein levels in 153 male patients with germ cell tumours. Br J Cancer 35:52–58, 1977.

46. Friedman NB, Moore RA: Tumours of the testis. Mil Surg 99:573–579, 1946.

47. Lippert M, Papadopoulos N, Javadpour N: Role of lactate dehydrogenase isoenzymes in testicular cancer. Urology 18:50–53, 1981.

48. von Eyben FE, de Graaff WE, Marrink J, et al: Serum lactate dehydrogenase isoenzyme-1 activity in patients with testicular germ cell tumours correlates with the total number of copies of the short arm of chromosome 12 in the tumour. Mol Genet 235:140–147, 1991.

49. Gels ME, Marrink J, Visser P, et al: Importance of a new tumor marker TRA-1-60 in the follow-up of patients with clinical stage I nonseminomatous testicular germ cell tumors. Ann Surg Oncol 4:321–327, 1997.

50. Lajer H, Daugaard G, Andersson AM, Skakkebaek NE: Clinical use of serum TRA-1-60 as tumor marker in patients with germ cell cancer. Int J Cancer 100:244–246, 2002.

51. Koshida K, Uchibayashi T, Yamamoto H, Hirano K: Significance of placental alkaline phosphatase (PLAP) in the monitoring of patients with seminoma. Br J Urol 77:138–142, 1996.

52. Steele GS, Kantoff PW, Richie JP: Staging and imaging of testis cancer. In Vogelzang NJ, Scardino PT, Shipley WU, Coffey DS (eds): Comprehensive Textbook of Genitourinary Oncology, 2d ed. Philadelphia, Lippincott Williams & Wilkins, 2000, pp 939–949.

53. International Union Against Cancer: TNM Classification of Malignant Tumours, 3d ed. Geneva, IUAC, 1978.

54. Daugaard G, Petersen PM, Roerth M: Surveillance in stage I testicular cancer. AMPIS 111:76–85, 2003.

55. Einhorn LH: Treatment of testicular cancer: A new improved method. J Clin Oncol 11:1777–1781, 1990.

56. Jones RH, Vasey PA: Part I: Testicular cancer—management of early disease. Part II: Testicular cancer—management of advanced disease. Lancet Oncol 4:730–737 (Part I), 738–747 (Part II), 2003.

57. Garzotto M, Nichols CR: Current concepts in risk factor assessment for advanced germ cell cancer. Semin Urol Oncol 19:165–169, 2001.

58. Bosl GJ, Dmitrovsky E, Reuter VE, et al: Isochromosome of chromosome 12: Clinically useful marker for male germ cell tumors. J Natl Cancer Inst 81:874–878, 1989.

59. Olivarez D, Ulbright T, DeRiese W, et al: Neovascularization in clinical stage A testicular germ cell tumor: Prediction of metastatic disease. Cancer Res 54:2800–2802, 1994.

60. George DW, Foster RS, Hromas RA, et al: Update on late relapse of germ cell tumor: A clinical and molecular analysis. J Clin Oncol 21:113–122, 2003.

61. Albers P, Siener R, Kliesch S, et al: Risk factors for relapse in clinical stage I nonseminomatous testicular germ cell tumors: Results of the German Testicular Cancer Study. J Clin Oncol 21:1505–1512, 2003.

62. Harms D, Kock LR: Testicular juvenile granulosa cell and Sertoli cell tumours:

A clinicopathological study of 29 cases from the Kiel Paediatric Tumour Registry. Virchows Arch 430:301–309, 1997.

63. Rushton HG, Belman AB: Testis-sparing surgery for benign lesions of the prepubertal testis. Urol Clin North Am 20:27–37, 1993.

64. Borer JG, Tan PE, Diamond DA: The spectrum of Sertoli cell tumors in children. Urol Clin North Am 27:529–541, 2000.

65. Iczkowski KA, Bostwick DG, Roche PC, Cheville JC: Inhibin A is a sensitive and specific marker for testicular sex cord–stromal tumors. Mod Pathol 11:774–779, 1998.

66. Toppari J, Kaipia A, Kaleva M, et al: Inhibin gene expression in a large cell calcifying Sertoli cell tumour and serum inhibin and activin levels. APMIS 106:101–113, 1998.

67. Cheville JC: Classification and pathology of testicular germ cell and sex cord–stromal tumors. Urol Clin North Am 26:595–609, 1999.

68. Holm M, Rajpert-De Meyts E, Andersson A-M, Skakkebaek NE: Leydig cell micronodules are a common finding in testicular biopsies from men with impaired spermatogenesis and are associated with decreased testosterone/LH ratio. J Pathol 199:378–386, 2003.

69. Shenker A, Laue L, Kosugi S, et al: A constitutively activating mutation of the luteinizing hormone receptor in familial male precocious puberty. Nature 365:652–654, 1993.

70. Iiri T, Herzmark P, Nakamoto JM, et al: Rapid GDP release from Gs alpha in patients with gain and loss of endocrine function. Nature 371:164–168, 1994.

71. Fragoso MC, Latronico AC, Carvalho FM, et al: Activating mutation of the stimulatory G protein (gsp) as a putative cause of ovarian and testicular human stromal Leydig cell tumors. J Clin Endocrinol Metab 83:2074–2078, 1998.

72. Kim I, Young RH, Scully RE: Leydig cell tumors of the testis: A clinicopathologic study of 40 cases and review of the literature. Am J Surg Pathol 9:177–192, 1985.

73. Dilworth JP, Farrow GM, Oesterling JE: Non–germ cell tumors of the testis. Urology 37:399–417, 1991.

74. Cheville JC, Sebo TJ, Lager DJ, et al: Leydig cell tumor of the testis: A clinicopathologic, DNA content, and MIB-1 comparison of nonmetastasizing and metastasizing tumors. Am J Surg Pathol 22:1361–1367, 1998.

75. Bertram KA, Bratlof B, Hodges GF, Davidson H: Treatment of malignant Leydig cell tumor. Cancer 68:2324–2329, 1991.

76. Hamwi GJ, Gwinup G, Mostow JH, Besch PK: Activation of testicular adrenal rest tissue by prolonged excessive ACTH production. J Clin Endocrinol Metab 23:861–869, 1963.

77. Rich MA, Keating MA: Leydig cell tumors and tumors associated with congenital adrenal hyperplasia. Urol Clin North Am 27:519–528, 2000.

78. Carney JA, Gordon H, Carpenter PC, et al: The complex of myxomas, spotty pigmentation, and endocrine overactivity. Medicine (Baltimore) 64:270–283, 1985.

79. Venara M, Rey R, Bergada I, et al: Sertoli cell proliferations of the infantile testis: An intratubular form of Sertoli cell tumor? Am J Surg Pathol 25:1237–1244, 2001.

80. Kratzer SS, Ulbright TM, Talerman A, et al: Large cell calcifying Sertoli cell tumor of the testis: Contrasting features of six malignant and six benign tumors and a review of literature. Am J Surg Pathol 21:1271–1280, 1997.

81. Giglio M, Medica M, De Rose AF, et al: Testicular Sertoli cell tumours and relative subtypes: Analysis of clinical and prognostic features. Urol Int 70:205–210, 2003.

82. Stratakis CA, Carney JA, Lin JP, et al: Carney complex, a familial multiple neoplasia and lentiginosis syndrome: Analysis of 11 kindreds and linkage to the short arm of chromosome 2. J Clin Invest 97:699–705, 1996.

83. Stratakis CA, Kirschner LS, Taymans SE, et al: Carney complex, Peutz-Jeghers syndrome, Cowden disease, and Bannayan-Zonana syndrome share cutaneous and endocrine manifestations, but not genetic loci. J Clin Endocrinol Metab 83:2972–2976, 1998.

84. Kirschner LS, Carney JA, Pack SD, et al: Mutations of the gene encoding the protein kinase A type I-alpha regulatory subunit in patients with the Carney complex. Nat Genet 26:89–92, 2000.

85. Casey M, Vaughan CJ, He J, et al: Mutations in the protein kinase A R1alpha regulatory subunit cause familial cardiac myxomas and Carney complex. J Clin Invest 106:R31–R38, 2000.

86. Hertl MC, Wiebel J, Schäfer H, et al: Feminizing Sertoli cell tumors associated with Peutz-Jeghers syndrome: An increasingly recognized cause of prepubertal gynecomastia. Plast Reconstr Surg 102:1151–1157, 1998.

87. Hemminki A, Markie D, Tomlison I, et al: A serine/threonine kinase gene defective in Peutz-Jeghers syndrome. Nature 391:184–187, 1998.

88. Zukerberg LR, Young RH, Scully RE: Sclerosing Sertoli cell tumor of the testis: A report of 10 cases. Am J Surg Pathol 15:829–834, 1991.

89. Gravas S, Papadimitriou K, Kyriakidis A: Sclerosing sertoli cell tumor of the testis: A case report and review of the literature. Scand J Urol Nephrol 33:197–199, 1999.

90. Young RH, Koelliker DD, Scully RE: Sertoli cell tumors of the testis, not otherwise specified. Am J Surg Pathol 22:709–721, 1998.

91. Jimenez-Quintero LP, Ro JY, Zavala-Pompa A, et al: Granulosa cell tumor of the adult testis: A clinicopathologic study of seven cases and a review of the literature. Hum Pathol 24:1120–1125, 1993.

92. Kommoss F, Oliva E, Bittinger F, et al: Inhibin-alpha CD99, HEA125, PLAP, and chromogranin immunoreactivity in testicular neoplasms and the androgen insensitivity syndrome. Hum Pathol 31:1055–1061, 2000.

93. Rey R, Sabourin JC, Venara M, et al: Anti-Mullerian hormone is a specific marker of Sertoli- and granulosa-cell origin in gonadal tumors. Hum Pathol 31:1202–1208, 2000.

94. Ketola I, Pentikainen V, Vaskivuo T, et al: Expression of transcription factor GATA-4 during human testicular development and disease. J Clin Endocrinol Metab 85:3925–3931, 2000.

95. Eble JN, Hull MT, Warfel KA, Donohue JP: Malignant sex cord–stromal tumor of testis. J Urol 131:546–551, 1984.

96. Morrish DW, Venner PM, Siy O, et al: Mechanisms of endocrine dysfunction in patients with testicular cancer. J Natl Cancer Inst 82:412–418, 1990.

97. Petersen PM, Skakkebæk NE, Rørth M, Giwercman A: Semen quality and reproductive hormones before and after orchiectomy in men with testicular cancer. J Urol 161:822–826, 1999.

98. Jacobsen KD, Fosså SD, Bjoro TP, et al: Gonadal function and fertility in patients with bilateral testicular germ cell malignancy. Eur Urol 42:229–238, 2002.

99. DeSantis M, Albrecht W, Holtl W, Pont J: Impact of cytotoxic treatment on long-term fertility in patients with germ-cell cancer. Int J Cancer 83:864–865, 1999.

100. Petersen PM, Daugaard G, Rørth M, Skakkebæk NE: Endocrine function in patients treated for carcinoma in situ in the testis with irradiation. APMIS 111:93–99, 2003.

# Anabolic Steroids

## *Don H. Catlin*

## PHARMACOLOGY

### DEFINITION

Anabolic androgenic steroids are a class of chemically related steroid hormones that promote both protein anabolism and masculinization. Chemically, they are analogues of testosterone. Pharmacologically, their dominant effect is net synthesis of protein in virtually all tissues that are capable of growth, including male reproductive tissue. Even effects that are commonly referred to as androgenic, for example, regulation of male sexual accessory organs, can be considered to be anabolic; in fact, an androgenic effect has been described as an anabolic effect on sex organs.[1]

Testosterone, other endogenous steroids, and hundreds of synthetic steroids fulfill this definition. The terms *androgen* and *anabolic* are overly simplistic and inadequate, however, because some effects are not easily classified as anabolic or androgenic, and some are clearly neither (e.g., decrease in sex hormone–binding globulin). In fact, a remarkable feature of the anabolic androgenic steroids is their diverse and large number of effects. Virtually all tissues are affected in some manner, and often it is difficult to distinguish between primary and secondary effects. Further, individuals given the same dose show a remarkable variability in response.

Despite intense research efforts, no steroid has been described that is purely anabolic or androgenic. Furthermore, in healthy men, there is no direct evidence for more than one receptor. Thus, the dual ability to promote growth and masculinize is inherent in the same molecule, therefore, the most appropriate designation is anabolic androgenic steroid (AAS). Nevertheless, the term *AAS* is commonly shortened to "anabolic steroid" or "androgenic steroid" depending on the context. "Androgenic" is used for discussions that emphasize sexual differentiation, pubertal changes, virilization, and effects on primary and secondary organs of reproduction. This chapter focuses on anabolic effects and the use of synthetic AASs for conditions other than hypogonadism and related endocrine disease.

### THE ANDROGEN RECEPTOR

The notion of one receptor mediating androgenic effects in male reproductive tissue and another mediating anabolic effects in muscle tissue arose from the observation in experimental animals that some compounds exert anabolic activity and relatively little androgenic activity.[2] The hope of discovering an AAS devoid of androgenic activity fueled a concerted effort to synthesize and test new agents.[1] Since nitrogen balance studies were cumbersome, a simple bioassay was developed that compared, in the same animal, the AAS-induced increases in weight of the prostate and of the levator ani muscle. The anabolic-androgenic ratio was interpreted as an index of relative dissociation of anabolic from androgenic activity.[3] Although this assay did correlate reasonably well with nitrogen retention studies, the validity of the assay was later questioned. In addition, research on specific intracellular enzymes, differences in the affinity of compounds for receptor binding proteins, and differences in levels of receptors in various tissues showed that the diversity of responses could be explained by other mechanisms. Moreover, recent studies provide substantial evidence for only one receptor.

The androgen receptor (AR) has been isolated and characterized,[4] and a cDNA that encodes the AR has been cloned and expressed.[5-7] Defects or single amino acid substitutions in the AR are associated with several diseases.[8] Only one AR type has been discovered by either molecular biologic techniques or receptor-binding studies. The binding characteristics of receptors-isolated from reproductive tissue and from skeletal muscle are identical.[9] Antiandrogens also bind to the AR and compete with testosterone (T) and dihydrotestosterone (DHT) for the binding sites. Perhaps the most convincing evidence for the one-receptor theory is research describing the clinical consequences of androgen receptor disorders and associated molecular biology of the androgen-receptor gene.[10,11]

Most of the effects of AASs are presumed to be mediated, like those of T in tissues that contain AR, which include reproductive organs, brain, kidney, liver, skin, skeletal muscle, cardiac muscle, bone, larynx, thymus, and hematopoietic and lipid tissue. At the subcellular level, the effects are determined by the affinity-binding constant with the AR and molecular details of receptor DNA interaction, transcription, and translation (see Chapter 2). Within the target cell, the effects of AAS are presumed to be influenced by the same mechanisms that control the fate and effects of T. These include enzymes that activate and deactivate T, enzymes that control the activity of receptor androgen interactions, and differences in receptor content.[12,13]

## ABSORPTION, DISTRIBUTION, AND METABOLISM

None of the synthetic nonendogenous AASs have been studied as intensively as T. The synthetic agents are absorbed from the gastrointestinal tract, mucous membranes, skin, and intramuscular depots. In the circulation, most T is loosely bound to albumin, a smaller fraction is tightly bound to sex hormone–binding globulin (SHBG), and some is free. The synthetic agents also bind to SHBG.[9,14] The concentration of AASs and metabolites can be measured in serum and urine, and there are some data on concentration in serum relative to therapeutic effects; however, plasma levels are not commonly used to monitor dosing.

Free T diffuses into cells where it may bind directly to the AR, undergo reduction of the $C_4$-$C_5$ double bond to 5α-DHT by 5α-reductase, or be metabolized further (see Chapter 2). Both T and DHT bind to the same AR,[15] although DHT is more tightly bound, leading to the conclusion that DHT is the most active and potent intracellular androgen.[16] Binding to the AR activates the complex, enabling it to interact specifically with DNA and activate specific genes.[4] Some T is metabolized by aromatase to estradiol, which binds to the estrogen receptor (ER). These important features of T metabolism emphasize that administration of T will result in a mixture of effects mediated by T + AR and/or DHT + AR and estradiol + ER. In some cases, the effects at one receptor may be neutralized or enhanced by effects at the other.

The extent to which the effects of AASs are mediated at both ER and AR is less certain, in part because the metabolism of AASs has not been studied as extensively as that of T. Any synthetic AAS with a δ-4,3-keto function is subject to metabolism by aromatase to the corresponding estrogen. A few estrogen metabolites of AASs have been described in humans, and in vitro studies indicate that many more are likely. Examples of AASs that are not substrates for aromatase are DHT, fluoxymesterone, mesterolone, and oxandrolone.

Receptor-binding studies confirm that ARs derived from muscle tissue or prostate tissue are the same, and that synthetic agents, T, and DHT bind to the same AR.[9] All synthetic AASs undergo extensive metabolism primarily to hydroxylated and 5α- and 5β-reduced metabolites. Most of these are excreted in urine as sulfates or glucuronides. Various metabolites of synthetic AAS have been found in subcellular fractions of target tissues and their binding to AR has been characterized.[17,18] Unlike T, however, 5α-reduced metabolites of 17α-methyl AASs are not more active than the parent compound.

## ROUTE OF ADMINISTRATION AND MOLECULAR STRUCTURE

A fundamental determinant of the magnitude and spectrum of effects produced by AASs is their molecular structure, which, in turn, determines their metabolism, kinetics, optimal routes of administration, and efficacy.

### Oral Administration
The male testis produces approximately 7 mg of T per day. After oral administration of up to 25 mg of T, however, plasma levels do not increase because T is rapidly metabolized during its first pass through the gastrointestinal tract and liver. This led to the design and synthesis of analogues of T that were resistant to metabolism. Of the hundreds of compounds developed and tested, the most resistant to first-pass metabolism are those with a methyl or other alkyl group at $C_{17}$ (Fig. 176-1). Of these, methyltestosterone (MT), methandrostenolone, oxandrolone, oxymetholone, and stanozolol are the orally active AASs used most today. Although some of these are also active via the buccal route of administration, there is little advantage to this route and absorption is highly variable.[19]

Compared to 17α-methylated AAS, methylation at the $C_1$ position (e.g., methenolone and mesterolone) reduces oral potency; nevertheless, these agents are sufficiently resistant to metabolism to be useful by the oral route. Various additions to the ring structure (e.g., fluoxymesterone), substitutions in the A ring (e.g., oxandrolone), or even the addition of a pyrazole ring to the A ring (stanozolol) result in orally active substances with preservation of anabolic and androgenic activity. Danazol, which has both a 2,3-isoxazole group and a $C_{17}$ ethinyl group, is unique, however, in that it is a good inhibitor of gonadotropin secretion and has relatively little androgenic and anabolic activity. Accordingly, danazol is useful in clinical circumstances in which androgenicity is unwanted and inhibition of gonadotropin secretion is desired.

### Parenteral Administration
Parenteral administration of unmodified AAS is neither practical nor efficacious, even though first-pass metabolism is bypassed. Parenterally administered labeled T has a half-life of approximately 1 hour. The formation of an ester in the 17β position, by increasing lipophilicity, markedly influences the duration of action and plasma levels of T and other parenteral AAS. The length of the ester group correlates positively with lipid solubility, plasma half-life, and duration of action. The esterified AAS is commonly prepared in a lipid vehicle (sesame oil) and injected intramuscularly. The ester is slowly released from the site and both the ester and the de-esterified drug may be detected in plasma. The rate-limiting step is release from the site rather than cleavage of the ester.[18] One of the most commonly prescribed AASs is nandrolone (N) (19-nortestosterone) esterified as decanoate (ND) or phenpropionate (NP). The plasma half-life of N after ND and NP administration is approximately 8 and 21 days, respectively.[20]

## CHOICE OF AGENTS AND DOSE

Relative to other classes of drugs, little systematic information is available on comparative dosage, potency, and efficacy of the synthetic AASs. Unfortunately, the effects of AAS on experimental animals are not good predictors of effects in humans.[1] In fact, data from receptor-binding studies with human tissue correlate better with clinical activity than do data from intact experimental animals. For most variables, it is difficult to find clinical studies that provide dose response curves that directly compare one AAS with another. This lack is related to a combination of methodologic difficulties, a limited number of clinical indications, and less stringent regulatory requirements in the past. As a result, dosing regimens are generally based on clinical observation and experience.[1,21] Despite numerous claims of differences between the various 17-alkylated AASs, there are no systematic clinical data that show a clear difference in the relative position of dose response curves for any of the effects.

Conversely, there are now considerable pharmacodynamic and pharmacokinetic data on T enanthate (TE) in healthy 18- to 35-year-old men with weightlifting experience and normal T levels. After suppressing T production with a long-acting gonadotropin-releasing hormone (GnRH) agonist, Bhasin and colleagues[161] administered graded doses of TE (25, 50, 125, 300, and 600 mg per week) and assessed outcomes at baseline and in the 20th week. Dose response relationships were shown for fat free mass (FFM), muscle volume, and muscle strength and power. There were also dose-related changes in hemoglobin, insulin-like growth factor 1 (IGF-1), and plasma

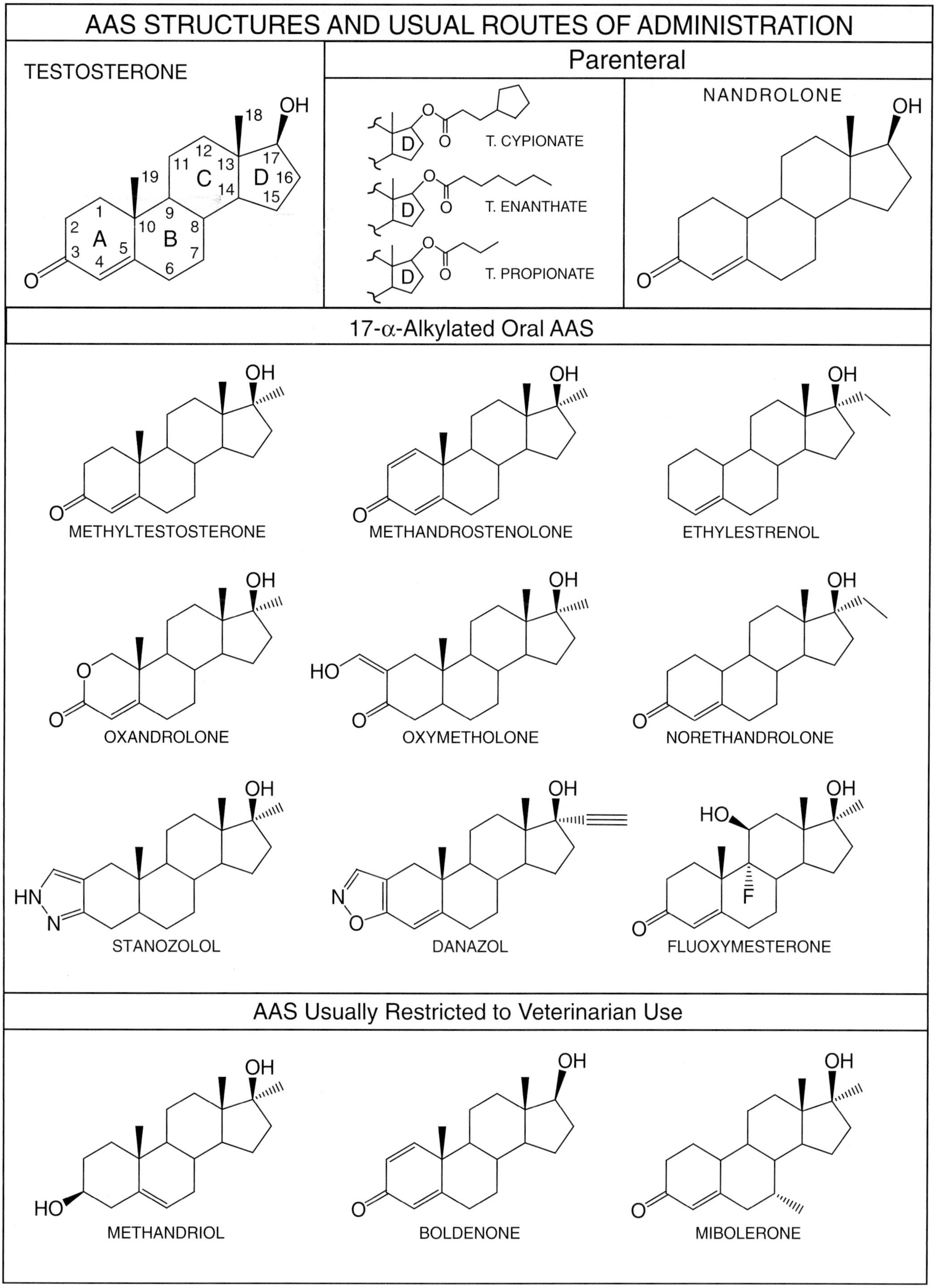

# AAS STRUCTURES AND USUAL ROUTES OF ADMINISTRATION

**Figure 176-1**  Anabolic androgenic steroid (AAS) structures and usual routes of administration. For testosterone (*upper left*), the conventional numbering and lettering system for the carbon atoms and rings, respectively, is shown. For parenteral AASs (*upper right*), the three testosterone esters shown (*upper middle*) are those most commonly prescribed; the most commonly prescribed esters (not shown) of nandrolone (*upper right*) are the phenpropionate and decanoate. The 17α-alkylated, orally active AASs (*middle panel*) have either a methyl group (e.g., methyltestosterone), ethyl group (e.g., ethylestrenol), or ethynyl group (e.g., danazol) on carbon number 17. The veterinarian AASs (*bottom panel*) are typically formulated for parenteral (boldenone) or oral (mibolerone) administration.

high-density lipoprotein (HDL) cholesterol. The data generally conformed to a single log-linear dose response curve. Whether the oral AAS will show dose response relationships when the end points are efficacies in various diseases remains to be determined.

The dose of T esters for replacement in hypogonadal men is approximately 100 mg/week (1.4 mg/kg/week = 0.2 mg/kg/day). Since the synthetic agents are rarely used for hypogonadal syndromes, good comparative data are not available. Higher doses of T, approximately 0.4 to 0.5 mg/kg/day administered weekly, are used in contraception trials where the objective is to suppress follicle-stimulating hormone (FSH), luteinizing hormone (LH)s, and sperm production. In order to achieve an effect equivalent to T esters, it is necessary to administer larger daily doses of oral AASs. The dosing range is extremely broad. Doses as low as 0.05 mg/kg are effective in short stature, and the lowest effective dose has not been established. Typical doses are, in postmenopausal osteoporosis, approximately 0.1 mg/kg/day, and in aplastic anemia, 2 to 3 mg/kg/day. Athletes have used doses of 5 to 7 mg/kg/day. Of the oral agents, stanozolol may be somewhat more potent, and oxymetholone less than the others. Danazol is far less potent. Maximum therapeutic doses recommended by the pharmaceutical manufacturers range from 8 to 30 mg, yet doses of 50 to 400 mg/day are used for aplastic anemia.

T esters, particularly TE, are currently the drug of choice for hypogonadal syndromes. This recommendation is based on a wealth of clinical experience, numerous successful clinical trials with various formulations of T, and advantages of providing the natural hormone and avoiding the hepatotoxicity associated with 17-alkylated AASs. For most other disorders that are treated with oral AASs, the supporting clinical data are not sufficient to distinguish clearly one agent from another. The choice of an agent seems to depend on custom and clinical experience, with the result that oxandrolone is widely used for short stature, nandrolone and oxymetholone for anemia, and stanozolol, methandienone, or ND for osteoporosis.

## EFFICACY IN VARIOUS DISORDERS

### OSTEOPOROSIS

Osteoporosis is a common affliction of older men and women, and its prevalence will probably increase as the population ages. Sex steroids exert a major influence on bone metabolism and homeostasis in men and women.[22,23] Postmenopausal osteoporosis is due to estrogen deficiency and is retarded by estrogen replacement therapy. Serum T levels gradually decline with age and elderly males experience a progressive decline in bone mass. Some develop osteoporosis late in life. The use of antiandrogens such as flutamide in the management of prostate carcinoma results in osteoporosis.[24] In the male, osteoporosis associated with hypogonadism responds to T administration,[25] whereas, in the female, it improves with androgens alone[26,27] or androgens plus estrogens.[28] ARs have been identified in both osteoclast-like and osteoblast-like cells in vitro.[29,30] The osteoclast AR responds to both 5α-DHT and 5β-DHT, whereas only the 5α-isomer is active in other androgen receptor systems. These and other observations stimulated investigations of the effects of anabolic steroids on bone and their role in the management of osteoporosis.

There have been many efficacy studies with nandrolone and stanozolol; however, they have not reported a significant decrease in the incidence of new fractures and their use has largely been abandoned. AASs can increase bone mass in postmenopausal osteoporosis, but their efficacy is modest and the magnitude of the effects is mitigated by virilization and other adverse effects. On average, only 10% of European patients are treated with AAS,[31] and the U.S. Food and Drug Administration

(FDA) has withdrawn support for the use of AAS for osteoporosis. Moreover, there is convincing evidence of efficacy for alternatives such as estrogens, biophosphonates, parathyroid hormone, strontium ranelate, calcitonin, and calcitriol.[32,33]

Tibolone is a complex steroid with unusual metabolic features and activity in the androgen, estrogen, and progestin systems. Its effects appear to be tissue specific and at least two hydroxylated metabolites are active.[34] Clinical trials have shown that loss of bone in the spine and proximal hip can be prevented with tibolone (2.5 mg/day) and that the efficacy primarily involves estrogen receptors.[35,36] Several controlled studies of tibolone in postmenopausal women have shown beneficial results on bone density.[37,38] Significant improvement in density of the lumbar spine, femoral neck, and other sites were reported by all groups and, if measured, the urinary excretion of biochemical markers of bone resorption were decreased.[39] Some subjects withdrew due to unacceptable adverse effects. Two of the groups used two doses of tibolone (1.25 and 2.5 mg/day); one showed no effect of dose, and the other showed superior results for the higher dose. Two 8-year studies of postmenopausal women have shown an increase in bone mineral density and prevention of bone loss.[38,40]

There is some evidence from studies of hypogonadal patients that T and DHT play a role in maintaining healthy bone and correcting osteoporosis. Elderly males with bona fide hypogonadism and accompanying osteoporosis are treated with T esters, agents specific for the primary cause of the osteoporosis or both.[41]

### HEMATOPOIETIC

AASs have been used for many years in the management of patients with aplastic anemia, Fanconi's anemia, and the anemia associated with end-stage renal disease (ESRD). With the availability of recombinant human erythropoietin (EPO), androgens are used less in the treatment of anemia of ESRD. They are still used in aplastic anemia and related disorders.

#### Pharmacology

The use of AASs in the management of various types of bone-marrow failure and anemia arose from observations linking androgens to erythropoiesis. The hemoglobin concentration in boys and girls is the same until puberty.[42] Hypogonadism is associated with reduced red cell mass, which is corrected by replacement therapy, and castration results in a 10% decline in red cell mass.[43] The administration of AAS to eugonadal males and females results in a small but definite increase in hemoglobin and hematocrit.[44]

T and AASs stimulate EPO production,[43] presumably via the kidney. In turn, EPO regulates red blood cell production by stimulating erythroid progenitor cells. In addition, there is experimental evidence that T and various 5β-reduced analogues of T stimulate hemoglobin production directly by a mechanism that is independent of EPO.[45] The stereochemistry of this mechanism is unusual because it is the only instance where anabolics with the 5β configuration mediate an important effect. DHT, the most active metabolite of T, is 5α-DHT. Extracts of cultured human erythroblasts have been found to contain binding sites that share many physicochemical characteristics of typical AR, except the extracts bind 5β-DHT with higher affinity than 5α-DHT.[46] Taken together, it appears that AASs may enhance hemoglobin production by two mechanisms: 5α-AASs acting indirectly via EPO, and possibly by a direct effect of T and/or 5β-steroids on erythropoietic stem cells.

#### Anemia of End-Stage Renal Disease

This anemia is mainly but not entirely due to a deficiency of EPO. Prior to the availability of recombinant human EPO, androgens were used with modest success. Between 30% and 50% of patients respond with an increase in hematocrit of 3 to 5 percentage points.[21] The response rate is greater if AASs are given by the parenteral route and for at least 1 year. Patients with nephrectomies or who require transfusions generally respond poorly. In some patients, hemoglobin levels may remain stable even after discontinuation of the AASs.[21] Parenterally administered esters of T and N are the most efficacious AASs, although several oral agents have produced satisfactory results. Dose response data are not available for the individual agents.

The use of AAS in ESRD has been preempted by EPO, which is highly effective in virtually all patients with ESRD. The possibility of combining EPO and nandrolone decanoate ($\approx$100 mg/week) is under investigation to determine if efficacy equivalent to that of EPO alone can be achieved with smaller and less costly doses of EPO ($\approx$1500 units, 3 times/week). The results have been mixed,[47-50] with EPO generally providing superior efficacy and ND producing significant adverse effects, particularly in females.

### Aplastic Anemia
Nearly 40 years of investigation have established that about half the patients will improve on AAS.[43,51] Patients with severe disease have a poor prognosis even with AASs. The anemia may not improve for 3 to 6 months even though the marrow displays changes earlier. The response often includes improvement in the neutrophil and platelet counts. Because some patients dramatically improve while on AASs, these drugs are often tried even though improvement may be coincidental. An occasional patient will demonstrate marked androgen dependence characterized by blood counts that fluctuate in parallel with drug administration.[52] Ethical considerations preclude a comparison of AAS with placebo; thus, research designs compare AAS with other modes of therapy or they are uncontrolled. It is difficult to draw conclusions regarding the relative efficacy of various AASs. Positive and negative results are reported with virtually all parenteral and oral agents. In the United States, oxymetholone (2–4 mg/kg/day) and ND (1–1.5 mg/kg/week) are used most often. In a large prospective series of trials, 1 mg/kg of fluoxymesterone and norethandrolone provided much greater efficacy than doses of 0.2 mg/kg; and at doses of 1 mg/kg, fluoxymesterone was superior to norethandrolone and stanozolol.[53] A prospective comparison of AAS with bone marrow transplantation (BMT) showed no benefit with oxymetholone or ND, and good results with BMT.[54] If BMT is not a possibility, immunosuppressive therapy with antilymphocyte globulin and cyclosporin A is the preferred treatment.[55] With the advent of BMT and effective immunotherapy, the use of androgens is increasingly limited.

### Other Anemias
Anemias associated with myelofibrosis, myeloid metaplasia, and myelodysplastic syndromes generally respond favorably to AASs.[56,57] In contrast, results with myelodysplastic syndromes have been poor.[51] Preliminary data indicate that AASs increase hemoglobin in patients with paroxysmal nocturnal hemoglobinuria and danazol may decrease the number of crises in sickle-cell disease.[58] Danazol has proved useful in managing autoimmune hemolytic anemia,[59] autoimmune thrombocytopenia,[60] and idiopathic thrombocytopenic purpura.[61,62]

### Hereditary Angioneurotic Edema
Hereditary angioneurotic edema (HANE) is a rare genetic disorder characterized by attacks of mucosal swelling, abdominal pain, and life-threatening obstruction of the upper airways due to indiscriminate activation of the complement system. Type I HANE is due to a deficiency in an inhibitor of $C_1$, a plasma protein that controls the activation of $C_1$. $C_1$ and the remainder of the complement system are not affected. In type II, a $C_1$ inhibitor is present in normal or increased amounts, but it is dysfunctional. The efficacy of 17-alkylated AAS in this disorder is dramatic and unequivocal.[63,64] The levels of $C_1$

inhibitor return to normal in type I and become functional in type II. AASs that have been shown to be effective include stanozolol, MT, oxymetholone, and danazol. Many patients respond to doses of danazol (200 mg/day) that are well tolerated and produce minimal adverse effects.

### Coagulation, Fibrinolysis, and Hemophilia
Reports appear periodically on the effects of oral AASs on the clotting system and blood fibrinolytic activity, and on efficacy in conditions in which enhanced fibrinolytic activity may be beneficial. These investigations find that AASs increase fibrinolytic activity, decrease fibrinogen, and increase plasminogen.[65,66] These effects may be temporary, however, and the agents have not been widely used for their fibrinolytic activity. Danazol increased levels of factors VIII and IX in patients with hemophilia A and B in one account,[67] although others report minimal efficacy and/or insignificant clinical improvement.[68]

## DISORDERS OF GROWTH

### Constitutional Delay of Growth and Puberty
Constitutional delay of growth and puberty (CDGP) is the most common cause of short stature in boys during puberty. In view of the substantial psychological distress associated with CDGP, and despite considerable controversy,[69] both oral AASs and T have been used to initiate the adolescent growth spurt. Proponents of AASs in CDGP consider that efficacy is established if height velocity is increased, ultimate height is not less than predicted height, puberty is not delayed, and there are no unwanted side effects.

These objectives have been achieved with low doses of T or oxandrolone administered alone for 3 months, 6 months, and 12 months or more. Although some reports are retrospective reviews, efficacy is found in prospective randomized studies with a control group[70-73] and/or a placebo group.[70,74-76] Studies that included T and oxandrolone treatment groups showed no differences between the two active treatments. The most common indicator of efficacy is an increase in height velocity during treatment. Final height is similar to the control or placebo group when measured 6 months after treatment. Thus, T or oxandrolone induces a growth spurt; however, the control and placebo groups catch up a few months later, indicating that most cases of CDGP resolve spontaneously. Minimum doses and durations have not been unequivocally established. Oxandrolone accelerated growth with doses as small as 1.25 mg/day for 3 months.[77] T enanthate was considered efficacious in doses of 50 mg per month for 0.8 to 1.7 years.[78]

The most feared complication is that skeletal maturation will be enhanced more than linear growth and that final height will be less than predicted. This has occurred with high doses of oral AASs administered for 1 year or longer.[79-81] Another concern is that AASs may delay progression of puberty due to suppression of gonadotrophins required for T maturation and secretion. Assessments of the effects of AASs on pubertal stage, however, generally find either no effect[80] or slight temporary acceleration,[82] although reduced testicular volume is reported. If AASs are used to treat CDGP, it is essential to emphasize to patients and family that the effect is on short-term growth and not on final height. AASs are not indicated for growth hormone deficiency and have no effect on growth hormone levels in this condition.

### Turner's Syndrome
Virtually 100% of females with Turner's syndrome have short stature together with sexual infantilism, webbing of the neck, and deformity of the elbows. The short stature has been treated with a variety of AASs, T esters, and estrogens, with variable results.[83] The authors of a large multi-center trial recently concluded that human growth hormone alone or in combination

with oxandrolone (0.0625 mg/kg/day) results in a sustained increase in growth rate and a significant increase in adult height for most prepubertal girls with Turner's syndrome.[84]

## MUSCLE-WASTING DISORDERS

### Acquired Immunodeficiency Syndrome

Some patients with acquired immunodeficiency syndrome (AIDS) and AIDS-related complex (ARC) have low serum T, hypogonadism, and weight loss.[85,86] Therefore, studies on the efficacy of T and AAS on body composition and body weight of AIDS patients with weight loss have been carried out. Initially, these involved T patches; now the work focuses on parenteral T and oral AAS.

The 5-mg transdermal patch increased serum free T (FT) and total T in hypogonadal males, but did not result in weight gain or a significant change in lean body mass (LBM).[87] The transscrotal patches used daily for 12 weeks increased serum T and FT, but did not lead to significant changes in body weight.[88] One study utilized women with AIDS, weight loss, and low serum FT; transdermal T patches delivering up to 300 μg/day increased body weight and serum FT.[89]

Three double-blind, placebo-controlled efficacy studies using parenteral T gave encouraging results. T cypionate (200 mg every 2 weeks, for 3 months) improved well-being scores in male patients but did not result in weight gain[90]; however, 300 mg of T enanthate every 3 weeks for 6 months resulted in increases in FFM, LBM, muscle mass, and well-being, but no improvement in body weight.[91] In the most extensive study, T enanthate (100 mg/week) was compared to exercise and placebo in human immunodeficiency virus (HIV)-infected men with low serum T.[92] The T-treated patients gained weight (2.6 kg), LBM, and muscle strength. The patients in the exercise-only group also gained weight. One placebo-controlled study of ND (200 mg/week, 3 weeks) demonstrated reasonable efficacy in HIV.[93]

The 17α-methylated oral AASs also show efficacy against AIDS. Hengge and colleagues[94] gave 50 mg/day of oxymetholone in one study, and 100 and 150 mg/day in the second study.[95] The patients in the single-dose study gained 8 kg in 30 weeks. The weight gain was less impressive (≈3 kg) at the 100 mg/day dose and there was no difference in efficacy between the 100 and 150 mg doses. There was good improvement in quality of life measures for both doses, but liver toxicity was substantial at the higher dose. In a 16-week study that compared two doses of oxandrolone (5 and 15 mg/day), the placebo group continued to lose weight, the 5-mg oxandrolone group maintained their weight, and the 15-mg group gained weight.[96] An interesting experimental design was employed in a placebo-controlled oxandrolone study in which endogenous production was suppressed and normalized with weekly doses of T (100 mg) before oxandrolone (20 mg/day) was administered for 16 weeks and all subjects received supervised and specific exercise training.[93] The placebo and oxandrolone groups showed significant nitrogen retention and gains in LBM, body weight, and strength; moreover, the gains were significantly greater in the oxandrolone group compared to the placebo group.

Considered together, these AIDS efficacy studies establish a role for AAS in the management of AIDS patients with weight loss, with or without hypogonadism. There is the usual trade-off between the hepatotoxicity associated with 17α-methylated oral agents and the inconvenience and discomfort of parenteral agents. The role of nutritional support combined with highly active antiretroviral therapy, however, is currently under very active investigation; thus, the future role of AAS, which seemed clear just a few years ago, is now less certain.

### Burns

Two groups have been investigating the role of oxandrolone, testosterone, and other AASs in the treatment of weight loss and lean body loss from severe burns.[97] Oxandrolone improves protein balance and lean body mass during the catabolic phase of burn injuries.[98,99] Patients treated with oxandrolone (20 mg/day) during the acute phase regain weight and are able to retain it for at least 6 months after discontinuing oxandrolone.[99] These and other studies reveal an increasing role for androgens in the treatment of burn injuries.

### Chronic Obstructive Pulmonary Disease

Patients suffering from chronic obstructive pulmonary disease (COPD) complain mostly of exercise intolerance, and this symptom is largely due to muscle dysfunction. The possible reasons for muscle dysfunction have been described and include disuse atrophy, malnutrition, low serum T, and myopathy secondary to corticosteroids.[100] Two recently reported randomly assigned, placebo-controlled AAS efficacy studies with COPD have produced promising results. In one short-term study, the patients received ND (200 mg in 4 doses over 43 days)[101] and, in the other, 12 mg per day of stanozolol was administered orally for 27 weeks.[102] Both studies included pulmonary rehabilitation training and both reported improvements in the treated groups. In the ND study, FFM improved[101] and, in the stanozolol study, LBM, body mass index (BMI), and anthropometric measure improved but endurance exercise capacity did not.[102] The underlying mechanism of action of AAS, these studies, and other open-label studies[103] are promising and suggest that in the future AASs might play a role in the treatment of COPD.

## ALCOHOLIC HEPATITIS

Since the early 1960s, various AASs including T have been used to treat patients with alcoholic hepatitis under the rationale that positive nitrogen balance and perhaps appetite and well-being will be enhanced. In 1984, a comprehensive multi-center study found that oxandrolone (80 mg/day for 30 days) had no effect on short-term survival, but was associated with a beneficial effect on long-term survival.[104] Most recently, oxandrolone (20 mg/day for 21 days) was associated with short-term benefits as measured by laboratory parameters; however, the overall results appeared to be similar to that provided by parenteral nutrition alone or with oxandrolone.[105,106] Recently, a comprehensive review of five studies that utilized randomized subjects and covered 499 patients concluded that AAS provided no significant benefit on any clinically important measure.[107]

## MISUSE OF ANDROGENS

### EPIDEMIOLOGY

Weightlifters, throwers, and bodybuilders discovered AASs in the early 1960s; by the mid-1970s, misuse spread to elite athletes in aerobic and endurance sports; in the 1980s, misuse spread to university sports and even teenagers experimented with AASs.[108-110] The illegal and secretive nature of the misuse defies efforts to discover its true scope and magnitude. Various testimonials suggest that in the past, virtually all elite athletes in some sports used AASs.[111-114] Classified documents retrieved after the collapse of the German Democratic Republic in 1990 describe an extensive, secret, and deliberate program to enhance the performance of the East German Olympic teams for 30 years by physician-directed use of AASs.[109] Although extensive state-directed doping may have ended, there is no evidence suggesting that doping directed by specific coaches, sports doctors, or "gurus" is decreasing.

Many adolescent users consume AAS in the belief that they will enhance their physical appearance. Surveys estimate that by age 17, 5% to 11% of U.S. males and 0.5% to 2.5% of females have used AASs. A 1991 national household survey based on 32,500 questionnaires showed that there were more than 1 million current or past AAS users in the United States, that more than 300,000 individuals had used AAS in the past year, and that usage began in the teen years.[113] Surveillance data collected in the United States in 2003 showed that 6.1% of adolescents had taken steroid pills or shots without a prescription one or more times and that between 1996 and 1999 steroid use among 10th graders in the United States nearly doubled to 3.5%.[115] The intense media attention focused on popular athletes during these years[116] increased public awareness of muscle-building drugs and raised glorification and emulation issues.

Despite the lack of accurate usage data, it became increasingly obvious that AASs were having a substantial impact on sports. New records became commonplace, anecdotal reports appeared regularly, morbidity reports increased, some females appeared quite masculinized, and well-known athletes tested positive. Sports authorities worldwide took notice and initiated testing programs and extensive educational campaigns. Urine testing for AASs formally began with the 1976 Olympics and has increased in sophistication and number ever since.[117,118] AASs do not enhance performance in the short term. They are taken months before the event and, if testing is anticipated, discontinued 3 to 4 weeks before the scheduled test. Recently, sports authorities have imposed random selection, year-round, short notice (up to 48 hours) testing schedules. These programs are extremely effective deterrents, yet they are complex and difficult to administer.

## DIETARY SUPPLEMENTS

Since the late 1990s, androstenedione, 19-norandrostenedione, 19-norandrostenediol, dehydroepiandrosterone (DHEA), and other steroids have been sold legally over the counter (OTC) in the United States as food supplements. These steroids are heavily promoted to athletes, young adults, and others interested in appearance and physical fitness.[119] Through extensive advertising on the Internet, they are widely available even in countries that classify them as controlled substances. The number of people taking steroid supplements is not known; however, since the lifetime prevalence of illegal AAS use in the United States is 4.9% for male adolescents and 2.4% for females[120] and since OTC steroids are readily available and legal, it is quite likely that the prevalence of steroid supplement use exceeds these numbers. The market for supplements in the United States has been rapidly and greatly expanding. By 1999, the market size was $16 billion and sports supplements accounted for $1.4 billion of that.[121]

The OTC supplement industry was enabled by the Dietary Supplement Health and Education Act of 1994[122] (DSHEA), which made it possible for suppliers and manufacturers to sell any natural product OTC so long as the label made no claims to treat, cure, mitigate, or prevent a disease. In addition, these steroids cannot be regulated under the Anabolic Steroid Control Act of 1990,[123] unless it can be shown that they promote muscle growth in humans and are chemically and pharmacologically similar to T. The latter two criteria are met, but the first would require expensive clinical efficacy studies. Lawmakers are showing some concern and are making moves to amend the DSHEA.

Androstenedione, a steroid hormone, is an immediate precursor to testosterone in the intrinsic synthetic pathways of androgens, and DHEA is an immediate precursor of androstenedione (Fig. 176-2).[124,125] Both are produced by the

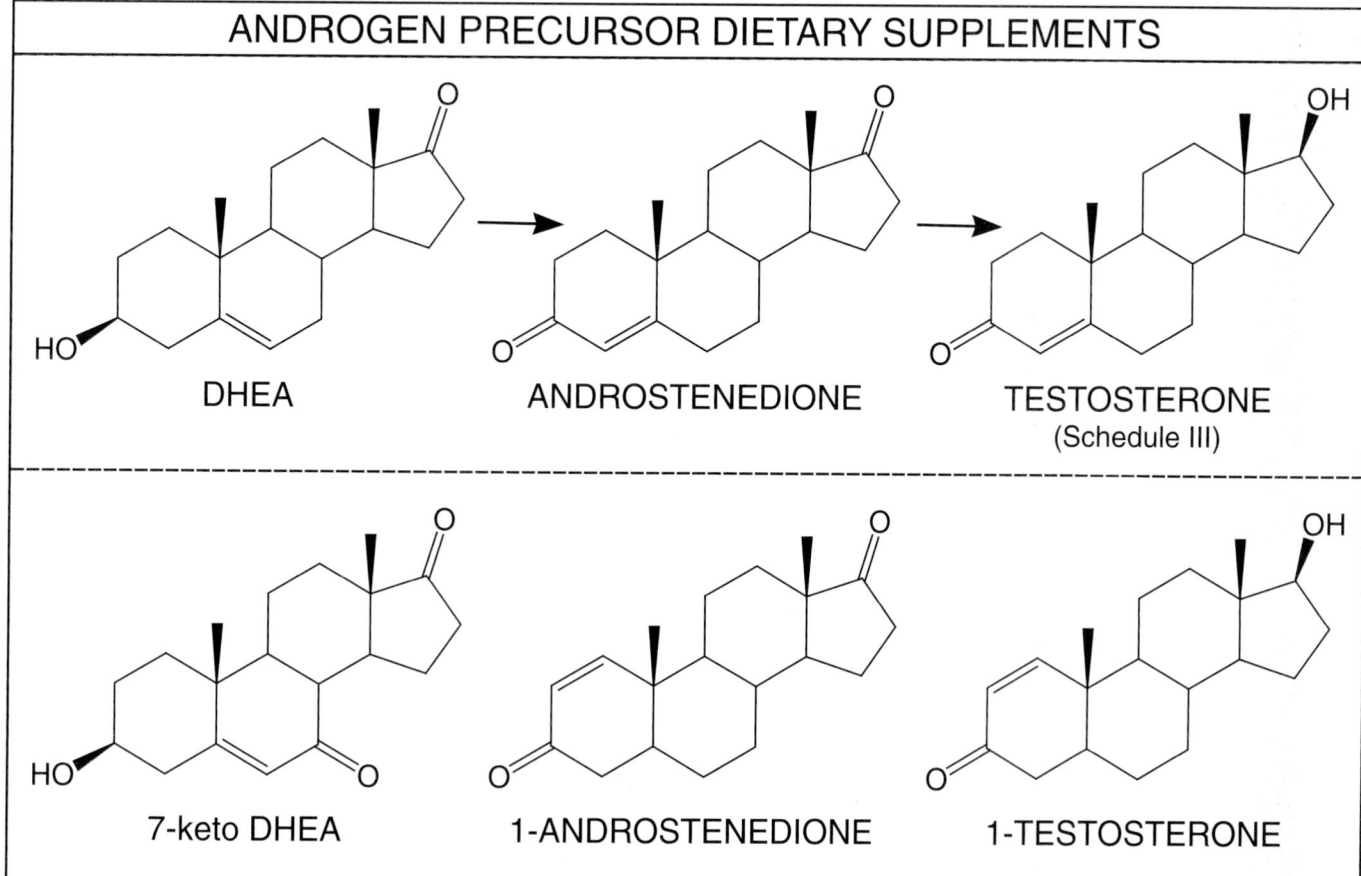

**Figure 176-2** Androgen precursor dietary supplements. Dehydroepiandrosterone (DHEA) is the biosynthetic precursor of androstenedione, itself the biosynthetic precursor of testosterone. DHEA is also an over-the-counter (OTC) dietary supplement. Androstenedione was an OTC dietary supplement until the U.S. Food and Drug Administration banned its sale in 2004. Testosterone is a Schedule III controlled substance. The three OTC supplements (*bottom*) result from minor modifications of the above structures.

adrenal glands and gonads of both sexes and both used to be sold OTC in the United States until March 2004 when the FDA banned the sale of androstenedione. Androstenedione has about 10% of the intrinsic activity of T. Androstenedione is marketed primarily to athletes as a potential anabolic agent. Advertising materials claim that androstenedione improves athletic performance, libido, and quality of life; however, none of these assertions have been demonstrated in peer-reviewed studies. Advocates of DHEA recommend it to prevent the effects of aging and for various chronic conditions such as diabetes and cardiovascular disease, but these claims cannot be verified. DHEA has been shown to reduce body fat in post-menopausal women and normal men.[126,127] Androstenedione is synthesized from DHEA and is converted to T and to estrone.[125] Relative to T, not much is known about the clinical effects or toxicology of androstenedione and DHEA.

DHEA and androstenedione are biosynthetic precursors of T; thus, it is assumed that they will be converted endogenously to T. Supraphysiologic doses of T increase muscle size and strength,[128] and raise serum concentrations of T; thus, there is speculation that orally administered androstenedione or DHEA will have similar anabolic effects. Both oral DHEA and androstenedione (399 mg) increase plasma T in men and women.[129–132] Some studies show no effects of androstenedione on plasma T,[133–135] probably because insufficient doses were administered. Individuals who wish to dope may take hundreds of milligrams of androstenedione. These huge doses might elicit large increases in serum T, more side effects, and a greater potential for anabolic effects. To date, no thorough and comprehensive studies on the performance-enhancing properties of androstenedione or DHEA have been conducted. One limited study showed no efficacy after androstenedione doses of 300 mg/day for 6 of 8 weeks.[133] In another study, there was no change in muscle protein synthesis in six healthy men after 5 days of oral androstenedione (100 mg/day).[136] There are no studies of the effects of 19-norandrostenedione or 19-norandrostenediol on performance.

The use of supplements has added a new and difficult dimension to doping control because their use often leads to positive doping tests. In the early days of doping control, finding 19-norandrosterone in urine virtually signified that the athlete doped with "Deca," the nickname for an oily solution of the decanoate ester of 19-nortestosterone (Deca-Durabolin). That conclusion is no longer tenable, however, since 19-norandrosterone is also a metabolite of 19-norandrostenedione and 19-norandrostenediol.[130,137] Thus, finding 19-norandrosterone in urine is now consistent with administration of any or all of three different AASs, two of which are available OTC. A related issue is that DHEA or androstenedione[137,138] may increase the ratio of testosterone to epitestosterone (T/E) in urine. The T/E is a marker for T administration and laboratories report to the testing authority if the T/E exceeds 6:1. The situation is partially relieved by the development of a specific urine test for androstenedione.[130]

An additional issue with OTC steroids is that many are mislabeled or contain steroids that are not listed on the label. As many as one third of OTC steroids are improperly labeled and may lead to positive doping tests.[130,139] Most sports organizations prohibit the use of all OTC steroids and warn athletes that the only sure way to avoid a positive test from supplements is not to take them. Practically, this is difficult for athletes since protein-containing supplements are an integral part of their nutritional programs. Some adjudication panels find it difficult to sanction an athlete who ingests a supplement obtained from a health food store.

## DRUGS AND DOSING REGIMENS

While there are an infinite variety of regimens, the first-time user typically begins with an oral agent and graduates to parenteral formulations and multiple drugs (stacking). Doses of 25, 100, or even 500 mg/day are consumed for several weeks or months.[108,110,140,141] The most sophisticated regimens include human chorionic gonadotrophin (hCG) to prevent testicular atrophy and antiestrogens to inhibit gynecomastia. Methandienone, stanozolol, oxandrolone, oxymetholone, and MT are the most popular oral AASs. Even veterinarian products such as boldenone and mibolerone are used. Before drug testing was instituted, ND was widely used. Its metabolites are detectable for several months after discontinuation, however, so its use has sharply declined. Parenteral formulations of methenolone, methandienone, and stanozolol clear more rapidly. Use of T esters is rapidly increasing, in part because their use is more difficult to detect.[142] Another disturbing trend is the misuse of other endogenous steroids such as DHT.[143]

## DESIGNER STEROIDS

Late in 2002, the U.S. Department of Justice (DOJ) secretly began investigating a California laboratory (Balco) that was suspected of distributing various drugs to prominent athletes. About a year later, and unbeknownst to DOJ, a coach forwarded a spent syringe to the U.S. Anti-Doping Agency (USADA).

Researchers at an International Olympic Committee–World Anti-Doping Agency (IOC/WADA)-accredited laboratory detected a steroid in the washings of the syringe and deduced its chemical formula from spectra obtained by several types of mass spectrometers. The steroid now known as tetrahydrogestrinone (THG, or 18a-Homo-pregna-4,9,11-trien-17β-ol-3-one) had never before been described, therefore it was not named on the IOC/WADA list of prohibited substances and was not being monitored in urine testing laboratories. The laboratory proved that the syringe contained THG by synthesizing it from gestrinone, further characterizing it by nuclear magnetic resonance (NMR) studies, and showing by mass spectrometry that the synthesized material was identical to material in the syringe.[144] Figure 176-3 shows the chemical structure of THG, its similarity to a steroid that is used to promote muscle mass weight gain in cattle (trenbolone), and how THG can be synthesized by hydrogenating a known progestin (gestrinone). Note that if the hydrogenation step goes too far, norbolethone, another designer steroid, is produced.

At that time, the method used in IOC/WADA laboratories to screen urine for anabolic steroids[117] included a derivatization step to render the steroids volatile and therefore amenable to gas chromatography/mass spectrometry (GC/MS) analysis; however, when THG is derivatized the molecule becomes unstable and disintegrates in the heated environment of the GC/MS. The laboratories were blind to THG because its chemical structure was unknown and derivatized THG was unstable. A new testing strategy was devised to screen urine based on liquid chromatography (LC) combined with two mass spectrometers operating in tandem (LC/MS/MS).[144] This method is perfectly suited to detecting THG and similar molecules, but it adds to the expense of testing.

After THG was synthesized and purified, it was administered to a baboon and the urine collected for pharmacokinetic analyses and metabolite determinations. THG was detectable in baboon urine for 96 hours after both intravenous and intramuscular administration. The serum half-life estimated from urine concentrations is quite short, about 3 hours, and there are many metabolites. In vitro studies establish that THG binds to AR with an affinity similar to that of DHT, and it activates AR-mediated signaling and myogenic differentiation[145] and binds to AR expressed in a yeast-based in vitro bioassay system.[146] These data provide evidence that THG is an androgen.

A few weeks after the syringe appeared, the DOJ and USADA began collaborating on the aspects of the case that

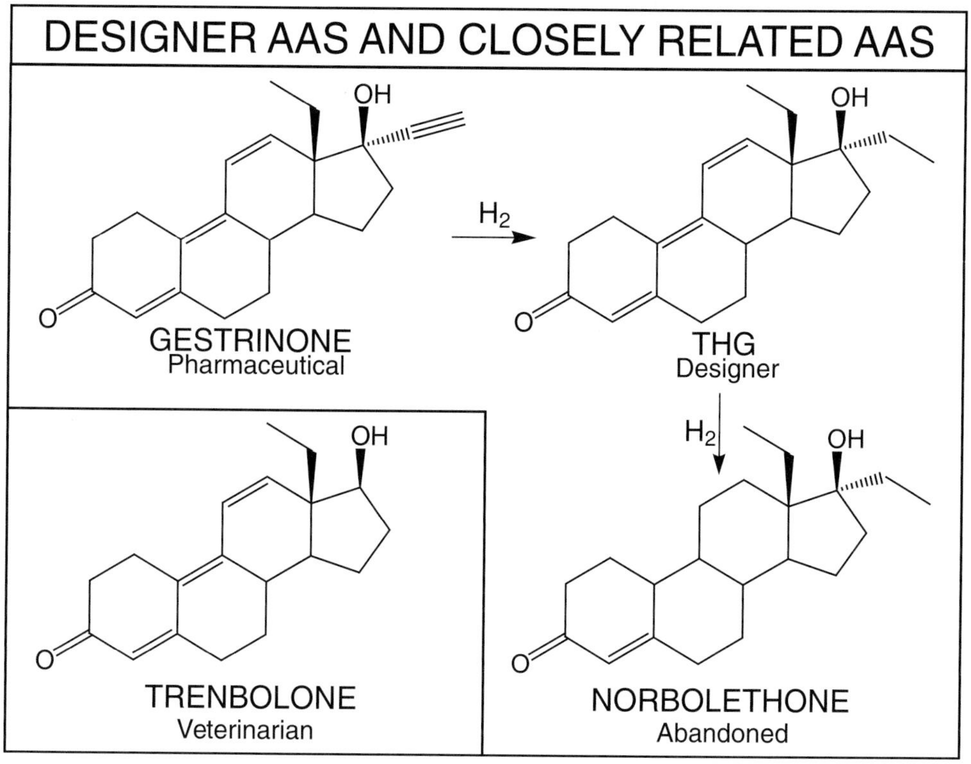

# DESIGNER AAS AND CLOSELY RELATED AAS

**Figure 176-3** Designer anabolic androgenic steroids (AASs) and closely related AASs. Gestrinone is used in Europe to treat endometriosis. Partial hydrogenation yields tetrahydrogestrinone (THG), a designer steroid uncovered in 2003. If the reaction is allowed to continue, further hydrogenation yields norbolethone, an AAS abandoned by the pharmaceutical industry decades before it was found in an athlete's urine sample in 2002. Trenbolone is a potent veterinarian AAS and most of its molecular structure (rings A, B, and C) is identical to those of gestrinone and THG.

involved Olympic athletes. Late in 2003, the USADA announced that THG, the first designer steroid, had been found in the urine of several athletes.[147] In 2004, a federal grand jury handed down a 42-count indictment charging that: "The defendants distributed to athletes a liquid 'The Clear,' aka tetrahydragestinone, aka 'THG' without adequate directions regarding its use in its labeling. The co-conspirators recommended the substance to athletes as a 'designer steroid' or 'steroid-like derivative' which would provide 'steroid-like' effects without causing the athlete to test positive for steroids."[148]

One year before THG was discovered, another steroid, norbolethone, was detected in the urine of an athlete.[149] Technically, norbolethone was not a designer steroid because its structure (see Fig. 176-3) was known,[150] but because it had been under development more than 30 years before and was never marketed for legitimate human use, the IOC/WADA laboratories were not looking for it. It is a member of the gonene class of steroids.[151] Norbolethone may have become interesting to athletes and their associated synthetic chemists because in animal studies its anabolic activity exceeds its androgenic activity by a factor of 20.[152,153] Efficacy studies had been conducted more than 30 years before in children of short stature and in underweight conditions. The reasons why norbolethone was never marketed are not known, but likely relate to animal toxicity studies or adverse side effects noted during efficacy trials.[154–156]

Evidently, the demand for new or undetectable steroids is sufficient to spawn a designer steroid industry. The chemistry of steroids is such that one can easily design many new ones using simple starting materials that are readily available (Fig. 176-4). Due to its secretive and illegal nature, obvious questions such as side effects, dates of introduction, distribution methods, countries involved, sources of starting materials, and many others cannot be answered. THG represents the pure form of a designer steroid, that is, a steroid that has never been described, published, patented, or registered in a chemical database. Norbolethone is a variant or subtype of designer steroid: an abandoned pharmaceutical not monitored by

sports testing laboratories until after it was found in two athlete's urine samples. Although it was a simple matter to add norbolethone to the IOC/WADA list of prohibited substances, by that time the industry had moved on to the next designer steroid, probably THG. Designer steroids are produced outside the pharmaceutical industry; they are not subject to any of the regulations that make drugs safe for humans, and they serve no useful purpose—except for cheaters.

## PHARMACOLOGIC BASIS FOR USE BY ATHLETES

The most widely considered hypothesis is that AASs act via ARs to increase muscle mass, which, in turn, provides greater strength and speed. Other possibilities include an anticatabolic effect mediated by glucocorticoid receptors, increased blood volume, and behavioral or motivational effects mediated by the central nervous system.

### Muscle Androgen Receptors

ARs are found in most human skeletal muscles[157] and, like other ARs, human muscle receptors bind both T and DHT. Skeletal muscle tissue differs from other androgen responsive tissue, however, in that 5α-reductase activity is low[158] and T is present in greater amounts than DHT.[159] Thus, T is the dominant intracellular agonist in muscle. In the experimental animal, the concentration of ARs varies markedly from one muscle group to another, and those with high concentrations respond the most to androgen. This parallels the observation that, in humans, muscles of the upper arm, chest, and back are more responsive than other muscles to AASs.

### Muscle Hypertrophy

Morphometric analysis of human skeletal muscle biopsies performed after a course of AASs or TE reveals an increase in muscle fiber diameter.[160–162] More detailed studies in animals show that AASs increase and castration decreases cross-sectional area and width of muscle fibers. In the normal animal, T produces marked hypertrophy in selected muscles.[163] At the

## POTENTIAL DESIGNER AAS

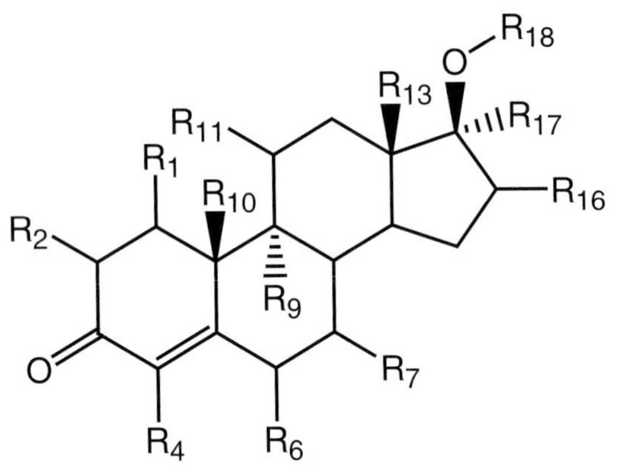

$R_1$: H, CH$_3$
$R_2$: H, CH$_3$, CHOH
$R_4$: H, Cl
$R_6$: H, OH
$R_7$: H, CH$_3$
$R_9$: H, F
$R_{10}$: H, CH$_3$
$R_{11}$: H, OH
$R_{13}$: CH$_3$, C$_2$H$_5$
$R_{16}$: H, OH
$R_{17}$: H, CH$_3$, C$_2$H$_2$, C$_2$H$_5$
$R_{18}$: H, CH$_3$, various esters and ethers

*Figure 176-4* Potential designer anabolic androgenic steroids (AASs). One type of potential designer AAS is a novel molecule created from a known structure by a known modification. The substituents shown (all R$_1$ to R$_{18}$ possibilities) are all found in known compounds. Of the tens of thousands of possible combinations of substituents, only a few are found in known compounds. The rest represent potential designer AASs. In addition, there are many more known basic structures and substituents.

subcellular level, the increased width of muscle fibers is due to an increased number of myofilaments and myofibrils.[164]

### Lean Body Mass
The earliest clinical investigations unequivocally established that hypogonadal men given replacement doses of T undergo positive nitrogen balance accompanied by proportional retention of potassium, phosphates, and sulfates.[165,166] More recent studies of hypogonadal men show that T and AAS increase muscle strength and mass.[167–170] Total body weight and lean body mass (LBM) increase, body fat decreases, and there is growth of muscles particularly in the upper back and shoulder regions. If the enhanced muscle mass hypothesis is correct, then AASs must also increase muscle mass in normal men and women.

There is convincing evidence that supraphysiologic doses of AAS produce supranormal anabolic effects in normal men and women. Using various methods for estimating LBM, increases are observed in nonathletic men,[171,172] athletic men,[128] men older than 65,[173] sedentary women with osteoporosis,[174] and bodybuilders and strength athletes.[175] The increase in LBM appears to depend on the cumulative total dose[176] and is observed with a variety of AASs including T and N esters, methandienone, and stanozolol. Negative studies may not have administered sufficient doses. These studies utilized $^{40}$K estimates of LBM, creatinine excretion, protein synthesis measured by [$^{13}$C] leucine incorporation into muscle, and muscle cross-sectional areas obtained from radiographs.

The most comprehensive studies of body composition reveal that, in addition to an increase in LBM, AASs also decrease body fat.[171,176] The pattern of increased LBM and decreased fat is not found in any other condition, and distinguishes the effects of AAS from that of simple caloric excess, which produces both an increase in fat and LBM.

### Increased Blood Volume
Many clinical studies report that AASs increase body weight, but many do not describe which compartment is affected. In fact, a fraction of the increase in LBM is likely due to fluid retention and/or expanded blood volume[177]; however, muscle hypertrophy accounts for the most substantial portion of the increase. AASs increase red cell mass, and this could contribute to enhanced performance in aerobic sports that depend on delivery of oxygen to muscles, but it is unlikely to affect performance that relies on static strength.

Taken together, studies of muscle morphology, ARs, and body composition provide strong evidence that pharmacologic doses of AAS increase body weight and LBM, and that the increase is due to muscle hypertrophy.

### Glucocorticoid Receptors
One alternative hypothesis that does not require ARs is that AASs promote positive nitrogen balance and muscle growth by acting as an antagonist at glucocorticoid receptors, thereby inhibiting catabolic actions of glucocorticoids.[178] This hypothesis is supported by studies in adrenalectomized-castrated animals[179] and by cell culture experiments showing that, in cells that express AR and glucocorticosteroid receptors (GRs), oxandrolone suppresses glucocorticoid action via a novel type of cross-talk between the receptors.[180]

### Central Nervous System
The role of the central nervous system has not been established. ARs are present in the brain, but their function in adults is unclear. AASs do promote aggressiveness and some athletes feel that enhanced performance is related to aggressiveness and other motivational factors.

### EFFICACY
Assuming that AASs do increase muscle mass, the question is whether this muscle is sufficient to enhance athletic performance. While it is reasonable to speculate that larger muscles are stronger muscles, the relationship between cross-sectional area and strength is complex. Likewise, the relationship between muscle diameter and speed of contraction is complex. Experienced users are completely convinced that AASs enhance performance in both strength and aerobic sports.[108]

Prior to 1996, nearly 30 studies of the effects of AASs on athletic performance of males had been conducted, yet the results do not provide a consensus. Some showed an increase in performance and others did not. Nevertheless, various authors, athletes who use AASs, and sports medicine societies concluded that AASs probably do enhance performance.[141,181,182]

In 1996, a critical study revealed that 600 mg of TE per week for 10 weeks produced significant increases in FFM, muscle size, and muscle strength.[128] This placebo- and exercise-controlled study utilized four groups: placebo alone, T alone, exercise alone, and T plus exercise. The T alone group experienced significant increases in muscle size and strength compared to the placebo alone group, and the effect of T plus exercise on strength, muscle size, and mass was greater than either no-exercise group. Finally, this study overcame the shortcomings of previous studies, which included insufficient total dose, confounding effects of exercise, small numbers of subjects, and lack of statistical power.

## TOXIC AND UNDESIRED EFFECTS

One consequence of the extensive number of effects of AASs is difficulty distinguishing between primary and secondary effects, and between specific AR-mediated and nonspecific effects. Often, a specific AR action is inferred if the action is associated with a particular organ and ARs are present in the tissue. For some effects, supporting data are available from experimental animals treated with AR inhibitors alone and with AASs. There are essentially no systematic data from chronic administration studies that convincingly demonstrate any difference between various oral AASs with respect to the relative position of dose response curves for any of the adverse effects. The agents do differ in potency based on dose, although in equipotent doses the adverse effects are similar. It is not clear if danazol is truly an exception to this.

In the case of endocrine effects involving reproductive organs and secondary sexual characteristics, it is clear that adverse effects of pharmacologic doses are extensions of underlying normal physiologic actions mediated by endogenous AASs at ARs. At the other extreme, the mechanism of AAS-induced cholestatic hepatitis is unknown. Many effects are common to all AASs, although others are only observed with 17-alkylated AASs. In the latter case, one hypothesis is that the alkyl group is the essential element; an alternative is that T and nandrolone esters form more potent estrogenic metabolites than alkylated AASs and that the estrogens neutralize the effect.

### ENDOCRINE EFFECTS AND VIRILIZATION

Except for the management of hypogonadism and male contraception, oral AASs are most often used in pharmacologic doses in circumstances in which the desired effects are anabolic enhancements of bone, muscle, hematopoiesis, or specific proteins. In this context, most endocrine effects are undesired and adverse. In the female, virilization is unavoidable and often limits treatment. The voice is lowered due to enlargement of the larynx and stiffening of the vocal cords. Muscles increase in size and strength. Hair growth is stimulated, particularly on the face, arms, and legs. Females chronically treated with high doses experience clitoral enlargement, breast atrophy, and male pattern baldness.[183] Suppression of gonadotrophins leads to inhibition of ovulation and amenorrhea. In the only clinical descriptions of adverse effects in females who self-administered AASs, many experienced a low voice, menstrual irregularities, breast atrophy, enhanced strength, clitoral enlargement, fluid retention, and increased facial hair.[140] In addition, a report on the systematic administration of AASs to elite athletes in the German Democratic Republic during the 1980s documents many adverse effects of AASs in females.[109]

In the male, high doses of AASs exert control over the hypothalamic-pituitary-testicular axis by inhibiting the release of LH, FSH, and probably GnRH, which progressively leads to oligospermia and aspermia. Testosterone production declines and serum levels of T, FSH, and LH fall. In one study of 97 males who regularly attended gymnasia but were not competitive athletes, 56% reported testicular atrophy and 52% reported gynecomastia.[183] The mechanism of gynecomastia is complex and poorly understood. It has been linked to an imbalance between androgens and estrogens, to various drugs,

and to prolactin[184,185] (see Chapter 11). Prior to puberty, AASs both promote longitudinal bone growth and hasten the closure of the epiphyses. Accordingly, administration of AASs requires scrupulous attention to dose and growth rates, since continual dosing leads to short stature.

Both males and females experience an increase in number, size, and secretions of sebaceous glands. The skin is oily and acne results from obstructed sebaceous glands. Skin atrophy and striae have been noted.[186] Adverse effects of T in contraceptive trials[187] and of AAS among male bodybuilders have been summarized.[160,188,189]

### SERUM PROTEINS AND THYROID FUNCTION

Both natural and synthetic AASs consistently lower plasma concentrations of three binding proteins of hepatic origin: SHBG, thyroxine-binding globulin (TBG), and vitamin D–binding globulin (DBG).[65,189–191] It is not known if these effects are primary or secondary, or if they are due to diminished synthesis, enhanced clearance, or both. Levels of cortisol-binding globulin (CBG) are not consistently altered by AASs. In addition, 17-alkylated AASs elevate plasma levels of haptoglobin, orosomucoid, protein-bound sialic acid, plasminogen, and $\beta$-glucuronidase.[65]

In addition to the decrease in thyroxine-binding globulin, oral AASs also decrease plasma levels of thyroxine ($T_4$) and triiodothyronine.[189,191,192] Free $T_4$ and thyroid-stimulating hormone (TSH) levels are either unchanged or slightly decreased.[189] The administration of AASs is not associated with hyper- or hypothyroidism.

### METABOLIC EFFECTS

AASs increase the basal metabolic rate, although if the rate is calculated per gram of LBM, there is no change.[172] Insulin resistance and diminished glucose tolerance are reported with two 17-alkylated AASs,[193] but not with esters of T or nandrolone.[194,195] Adipose tissue contains ARs, and biopsies performed after a course of AASs reveal a marked decrease in lipoprotein lipase (LPL) activity. Excessive doses result in modest increases in blood pressure due to salt and water retention.

### DECREASE IN HDL CHOLESTEROL

The most predictable and universal adverse effect of oral AASs, and one that has stimulated considerable research, is a decrease in the HDL fraction of cholesterol.[196–198] The HDL-C2 fraction and accompanying A1 are most affected. The fall in HDL cholesterol is shortly preceded by increased activity of hepatic triglyceride lipase activity (HTLA), leading to the hypothesis that the decline is due to induction of HTLA.[197] T and androstenedione also lower HDL cholesterol.[187,199–201] In contrast to the oral AAS, ND is not clearly associated with a decline in HDL cholesterol.[202] In addition, AASs often increase the low-density lipoprotein (LDL) cholesterol fraction, thus the combined effect is an increased LDL/HDL cholesterol ratio. Since a low HDL cholesterol and elevated ratio are risk factors for cardiovascular disease, the possibility that athletes and medical patients have an increased risk for cardiovascular disease has been considered.[196]

Androgens have been implicated in myocardial infarction, atrial fibrillation, stroke, pulmonary embolism, hypertension, cardiomyopathy, sudden death, and other disorders associated with the cardiovacular system; however, there is no uniform hypothesis or mechanism that unites these observations.[203–206] An autopsy was conducted on nine males who died suddenly while consuming high doses of AASs.[207] A myocardial infarction was demonstrated in only one case; thus, except for the temporal relationship between AAS consumption and sudden death, the mechanism for sudden death is not known and apparently does not involve infarction. The many ways by which AASs might influence the cardiovascular system have been reviewed.[208]

## HEPATIC EFFECTS ASSOCIATED WITH C$_{17}$ ALKYLATED AASs

Virtually all AASs alkylated at C$_{17}$ are associated with modest elevations of alanine (ALT) and aspartate (AST) aminotransferases.[209,210] Such elevations are extremely common, probably dose dependent, rarely exceed twice the baseline level, and usually regress even if the AASs are continued.[211] One exception is a bodybuilder who used T, stanozolol, and methylandrostenediol and developed transaminase levels exceeding 5000 IU/L.[212] Although the effects on ALT and AST are considered hepatic in origin and toxic, other tissues could contribute, and many other serum markers of hepatotoxicity are not affected by AASs.

Infrequently, AASs cause cholestatic jaundice characterized by elevated bilirubin, stasis of small bile ducts, and reversal after cessation of AASs.[203,210,213] Cholestatic jaundice is associated with all oral AASs and has not been convincingly linked to esters of T or N. In most reviews, the incidence is a few percent, although in one series 17% developed jaundice.

## NEOPLASIA

### Hepatocellular Adenoma and Carcinoma

AAS administration is associated with a variety of histologic types of hepatic neoplasia, ranging from benign adenoma to histologically malignant adenocarcinoma.[203,214,215] A review of cancer registries and literature surveys discovered 91 androgen-associated tumors, of which 48 were discounted either because of a lack of convincing histology or because they occurred in patients with Fanconi's anemia, which itself is associated with neoplasia.[203] Despite the histologic characteristics of hepatic carcinomas, their clinical behavior is benign: They do not metastasize; they are not associated with elevated γ-fetoprotein; and they usually but not always regress with discontinuation of the AAS.[209,216] The median time of androgen exposure before diagnosis is 5 years and latency is 2 to 30 years. Four cases of hepatic angiosarcoma have been associated with AASs.[217] AASs are not mutagenic in the Ames test.[218]

### Peliosis Hepatis

This unusual lesion is characterized by micro- and macroscopic blood-filled hepatic or splenic cysts. Because of deaths and serious morbidity due to spontaneous bleeding, peliosis hepatis is the most serious complication of AASs.[203] The lesion regresses with discontinuation of the AAS.[219,220] At least 70 cases have been reported, and many of them were being treated with oxymetholone or MT for anemia or hypogonadism.[203] Peliosis hepatis has been reported with all commonly used oral AASs, and to a lesser extent with T and nandrolone esters. Autopsy series report a high incidence of unrecognized peliosis in patients treated with oral AASs.[221]

## PSYCHIATRIC EFFECTS

Most medical patients do not experience remarkable psychiatric effects while receiving AASs, although some report a general sense of well-being and invigoration. AASs have been used to treat depression with variable results[222,223] and less efficacy than tricyclic antidepressants.

The hypothesis that T promotes aggressiveness in males is not supported by very many adverse reports arising from studies of T as a male contraceptive. Furthermore, supraphysiologic doses of T enanthate (600 mg/week) administered to healthy males for 10 weeks did not produce significant changes in mood and anger inventories, or in an observer mood inventory administered to spouses or significant others.[224] A similar study reported marked hypomania in 2 out of 56 subjects.[225]

One study of AAS users found no significant mood disturbances[226]; however, reports of serious behavioral and psychiatric sequelae including aggressiveness, hostility, and even homicide associated with AASs are increasing.[227–229] A structured psychiatric interview of high-dose users found a high incidence of aggressive behavior, affective syndromes, and psychotic symptoms.[230] A double-blind, fixed-order, placebo-controlled study of the effects of placebo, 40 mg MT, 240 mg MT, and placebo withdrawal for 3 days each on mood and behavior in healthy non-AAS users revealed both positive (euphoria, energy, sexual arousal) and negative (irritability, mood swings, violent feelings, hostility) mood changes during high-dose MT.[228] In addition, 1 of the 20 subjects developed acute mania. The possibility that high-dose users develop an addiction with physical dependence and a withdrawal syndrome has been proposed.[231]

## DRUG INTERACTIONS AND CONTRAINDICATIONS

Both AASs and isoretinoin lower HDL cholesterol. The combination has resulted in a profound reduction in HDL cholesterol.[232] Concurrent administration of oral anticoagulants and oral AASs leads to prolonged prothrombin times and life-threatening bleeding.[233] The mechanism of AAS-induced potentiation of anticoagulants does not involve altered pharmacokinetics of the anticoagulant. The combination of MT and imipramine in depressed men led to an acute paranoid state in four of five patients.[234] AASs are contraindicated in prostate cancer, mammary carcinoma in men, and pregnancy, and for individuals who cannot tolerate a change in the quality of their voice.[235]

## TOXICITY PECULIAR TO ATHLETES AND BODYBUILDERS

Injections of AAS into muscle and other soft tissues may produce abscesses and inflammation. Most of these are due to *Staphylococcus*, *Streptococcus*, or *Pseudomonas* and respond to conventional antibiotics. Less commonly, the offending organism is an acid-fast bacilli (*Mycobacterium fortitium*[236] and *Mycobacterium smegmatis*[237]). Needle sharing has been linked to HIV infection, hepatitis B, and hepatitis C in AAS abusers.[237]

Uncommon syndromes associated with AAS use include unilateral mesenteric hypertrophy,[238] mononeuropathies of the upper limbs,[239] popliteal-artery entrapment,[240] and priapism.[241] Individuals with documented use of enormous doses of AASs have experienced an acute abdomen due to extraordinary iliopsoas hypertrophy,[242] ruptured tendons,[243–245] and bleeding esophageal varices secondary to liver disease.[246]

## ONSET, DURATION, AND REVERSIBILITY OF ADVERSE EFFECTS

The onset of hormone suppression may be very rapid. Methyltestosterone, 25 mg/day for 3 days followed by 240 mg/day for 3 more days, led to highly significant declines in serum T, DHT, FSH, and LH.[191] Three days after the 6 days of methyltestosterone, the levels of T and DHT were still low, while FSH and LH had returned to normal.

The hallmarks of reversibility are marked variability and unpredictability. Some effects in some individuals rapidly reverse and others very slowly if at all. At one extreme, diminished height resulting from premature closure of the epiphyses is completely irreversible, while elevated levels of ALT and AST rapidly reverse. Cholestatic jaundice and peliosis hepatis are reversible and, to some extent, hepatic adenoma will regress with discontinuation of AASs. Voice changes are particularly slow to change.[247]

Most of the virilizing effects in females are considered irreversible, although detailed studies are not available. Changes in body composition take many months to subside fully. After a 12-week course of T enanthate, body fat and LBM did not return to baseline for approximately 6 months[248] and, after 1 year of ND, the forearm fat content remained low for at least another 6 months.

Hypogonadotrophic hypogonadism induced by AASs is reversible, although the rate of recovery may be quite slow and depends in part on the particular AAS that was used and the duration of use. For example, following a 2-week course of methandienone (30 mg/day), FSH and LH returned to baseline in 7 days, but T levels were still low after 2 weeks,[249] whereas, after 12 weeks of fluoxymesterone (10–30 mg/day), plasma levels of T were back to normal in 1 to 2 weeks.[250] The esters of nandrolone and T produce the longest lasting effects. In contraception studies with T esters lasting several months, the sperm count may not return to normal for 20 to 30 weeks after drug discontinuation.[251] Athletes taking high doses of N esters frequently experience azoospermia, which may last for more than 20 weeks after drug discontinuation, and plasma levels of FSH, LH, HDL cholesterol, and T take 20 to 50 weeks to recover.[160,252,253] Occasionally, azoospermia may still be present after 1 year without steroids.[254,255] One such case was successfully treated with twice-weekly injections of 10,000 IU of hCG and daily injections of 75 IU of human menopausal gonadotrophin (hMG) for 3 months.[255]

These studies show that the degree of the hypogonadism is highly variable, and the severity may be extreme. LH-releasing hormone and related agents may be justified in the cases that do not respond to conservative management for several months. The time to full recovery is correlated with some combination of the total dose, duration of treatment, and serum half-life of the agent.

## REFERENCES

1. Kopera H: The history of anabolic steroids and a review of clinical experience with anabolic steroids. Acta Endocrinol Suppl (Copenh) 271:11–18, 1985.
2. Landau RL: The metabolic effects anabolic steroids in man. In Kochakian CD (ed): Anabolic-Androgenic Steroids. New York, Springer-Verlag, 1976, pp 45–71.
3. Hershberger LG, Shipley EG, Meyer RK: Myotrophic activity of 19-nortestosterone and other steroids determined by modified levator ani muscle method. Proc Soc Exp Biol Med 83:175–180, 1953.
4. Carson-Jurica MA, Schrader WT, O'Malley BW: Steroid receptor family: Structure and functions. Endocr Rev 11:201–220, 1990.
5. Chang CS, Kokontis J, Liao ST: Molecular cloning of human and rat complementary DNA encoding androgen receptors. Science 240:324–326, 1988.
6. Lubahn DB, Joseph DR, Sar M, et al: The human androgen receptor: Complementary deoxyribonucleic acid cloning, sequence analysis and gene expression in prostate. Mol Endocrinol 2:1265–1275, 1988.
7. Tilley WD, Marcelli M, Wilson JD, et al: Characterization and expression of a cDNA encoding the human androgen receptor. Proc Natl Acad Sci U S A 86:327–331, 1989.
8. McPhaul MJ: Molecular defects of the androgen receptor. J Steroid Biochem Mol Biol 69:315–322, 1999.
9. Saartok T, Dahlberg E, Gustafsson JA: Relative binding affinity of anabolic-androgenic steroids: Comparison of the binding to the androgen receptors in skeletal muscle and in prostate, as well as to sex hormone–binding globulin. Endocrinology 114:2100–2106, 1984.
10. Griffin JE: Androgen resistance: The clinical and molecular spectrum. N Engl J Med 326:611–618, 1992.
11. Strickland AL, French FS: Absence of response to dihydrotestosterone in the syndrome of testicular feminization. J Clin Endocrinol Metab 29:1284–1286, 1969.
12. Roy AK: Regulation of steroid hormone action in target cells by specific hormone-inactivating enzymes. Proc Soc Exp Biol Med 199:265–272, 1992.
13. Evans RM: The steroid and thyroid hormone receptor superfamily. Science 240:889–895, 1988.
14. Pugeat MM, Dunn JF, Nisula BC: Transport of steroid hormones: Interaction of 70 drugs with testosterone-binding globulin and corticosteroid-binding globulin in human plasma. J Clin Endocrinol Metab 53:69–75, 1981.
15. Grino PB, Griffin JE, Wilson JD: Testosterone at high concentrations interacts with the human androgen receptor similarly to dihydrotestosterone. Endocrinology 126:1165–1172, 1990.
16. Wilbert DM, Griffin JE, Wilson JD: Characterization of the cytosol androgen receptor of the human prostate. J Clin Endocrinol Metab 56:113–120, 1983.
17. Toth M, Zakar T: Classification of anabolic steroids using the method of competitive metabolism. Exp Clin Endocrinol 87:125–132, 1986.
18. Berglink EW, Geelen JA, Turpijn EW: Metabolism and receptor binding of nandrolone and testosterone under in vitro and in vivo conditions. Acta Endocrinol Suppl (Copenh) 271:31–37, 1985.
19. Kruskemper HL: Anabolic Steroids. New York, Academic Press, 1968.
20. Belkien L, Schurmeyer T, Hano R, et al: Pharmacokinetics of 19-nortestosterone esters in normal men. J Steroid Biochem 22:623–629, 1985.
21. Neff MS, Goldberg J, Slifkin RF, et al: A comparison of androgens for anemia in patients on hemodialysis. N Engl J Med 304:871–875, 1981.
22. Lafferty FW, Spencer GE, Pearson OH: effects of androgens, estrogens and high calcium intakes on bone formation and resorption in osteoporosis. Am J Med 36:514–528, 1964.
23. Slemenda C, Longcope C, Peacock M, et al: Sex steroids, bone mass, and bone loss: A prospective study of pre-, peri-, and postmenopausal women. J Clin Invest 97:14–21, 1996.
24. Peters CA, Walsh PC: The effect of nafarelin acetate, a luteinizing-hormone–releasing hormone agonist, on benign prostatic hyperplasia. N Engl J Med 317:599–604, 1987.
25. Riggs BL, Jowsey J, Kelly PJ, et al: Effect of sex hormones on bone in primary osteoporosis. J Clin Invest 48:1065–1072, 1969.
26. Johansen JS, Hassager C, Podenphant J, et al: Treatment of postmenopausal osteoporosis: Is the anabolic steroid nandrolone decanoate a candidate? J Bone Miner Res 6:77–86, 1989.
27. Need AG, Horowitz M, Walker CJ, et al: Cross-over study of fat-corrected forearm mineral content during nandrolone decanoate therapy for osteoporosis. Bone 10:3–6, 1989.
28. Sands R, Studd J: Exogenous androgens in postmenopausal women. Am J Med 98:76S–79S, 1995.
29. Colvard DS, Eriksen EF, Keeting PE, et al: Identification of androgen receptors in normal human osteoblast-like cells. Proc Natl Acad Sci U S A 86:854–857, 1989.
30. Pederson L, Kremer M, Judd J, et al: Androgens regulate bone resorption activity of isolated osteoclasts in vitro. Proc Natl Acad Sci U S A 96:505–510, 1999.
31. Dequeker J, Geusens P: Treatment of established osteoporosis and rehabilitation: Current practice and possibilities. Maturitas 12:1–36, 1990.
32. Seeman E, Eisman JA: 7: Treatment of osteoporosis: Why, whom, when and how to treat. The single most important consideration is the individual's absolute risk of fracture. Med J Aust 180:298–303, 2004.
33. Consensus Development Report: Prophylaxis and treatment of osteoporosis. Am J Med 90:107–110, 1991.
34. de Gooyer ME, Oppers-Tiemissen HM, Leysen D, et al: Tibolone is not converted by human aromatase to 7α-methyl-17α-ethynylestradiol (7α-MEE): Analyses with sensitive bioassays for estrogens and androgens and with LC-MSMS. Steroids 68:235–243, 2003.
35. Berning B, Bennink HJ, Fauser BC: Tibolone and its effects on bone: A review. Climacteric 4:120–136, 2001.
36. Kloosterboer HJ: Tibolone: A steroid with a tissue-specific mode of action.

J Steroid Biochem Mol Biol 76:231–238, 2001.

37. Beardsworth SA, Kearney CE, Purdie DW: Prevention of postmenopausal bone loss at lumbar spine and upper femur with tibolone: A 2-year randomised controlled trial. Br J Obstet Gynaecol 106:678–683, 1999.

38. Prelevic GM, Markou A, Arnold A, et al: The effect of tibolone on bone mineral density in postmenopausal women with osteopenia or osteoporosis: 8 years' follow-up. Maturitas 47:229–234, 2004.

39. Studd J, Arnala I, Kicovic PM, et al: A randomized study of tibolone on bone mineral density in osteoporotic postmenopausal women with previous fractures. Obstet Gynecol 92:574–579, 1998.

40. Rymer J, Robinson J, Fogelman I: Effects of 8 years of treatment with tibolone 2.5 mg daily on postmenopausal bone loss. Osteoporos Int 12:478–483, 2001.

41. Jackson JA, Kleerekoper M: Osteoporosis in men: Diagnosis, pathophysiology, and prevention. Medicine 69:137–152, 1990.

42. Krabbe S, Christensen T, Worm J, et al: Relationship between haemoglobin and serum testosterone in normal children and adolescents and in boys with delayed puberty. Acta Paediatr Scand 67:655–658, 1978.

43. Shahidi NT: Androgens and erythropoiesis. N Engl J Med 289:72–80, 1973.

44. Gardner FH, Nathan DG, Piomelli S, et al: The erythrocythaemic effects of androgen. Br J Haematol 14:611–615, 1968.

45. Gordon AS, Zanjani ED, Levere RD, et al: Stimulation of mammalian erythropoiesis by 5β-H steroid metabolites. Proc Natl Acad Sci U S A 65:919–924, 1970.

46. Claustres M, Sultan C: Androgen and erythropoiesis: Evidence for an androgen receptor in erythroblasts from human bone marrow cultures. Horm Res 29:17–22, 1988.

47. Berns JS, Rudnick MR, Cohen RM: A controlled trial of recombinant human erythropoietin and nandrolone decanoate in the treatment of anemia in patients on chronic hemodialysis. Clin Nephrol 37:264–267, 1992.'

48. Gaughan WJ, Liss KA, Dunn SR, et al: A 6-month study of low-dose recombinant human erythropoietin alone and in combination with androgens for the treatment of anemia in chronic hemodialysis patients. Am J Kidney Dis 30:495–500, 1997.

49. Teruel JL, Marcen R, Navarro-Antolin J, et al: Androgen versus erythropoietin for the treatment of anemia in hemodialyzed patients: A prospective study. J Am Soc Nephrol 7:140–144, 1996.

50. Navarro JF, Mora C, Macia M, et al: Randomized prospective comparison between erythropoietin and androgens in CAPD patients. Kidney Int 61:1537–1544, 2002.

51. Ammus SS: The role of androgens in the treatment of hematologic disorders. Adv Intern Med 34:191–208, 1989.

52. Azen EA, Shahidi NT: Androgen dependency in acquired aplastic anemia. Am J Med 63:320–324, 1977.

53. French Cooperative Group for Study of Aplastic Anemia and Refractory Anemias: A comparative study of high and low dose and four different androgens. Scand J Haematol 36:346–352, 1986.

54. Camitta BM, Thomas ED, Nathan DG, et al: A prospective study of androgens and bone marrow transplantation for treatment of severe aplastic anemia. Blood 53:504–514, 1979.

55. Fonseca R, Tefferi A: Practical aspects in the diagnosis and management of aplastic anemia. Am J Med Sci 313:159–169, 1997.

56. Gardner FH, Nathan DG: Androgens and erythropoiesis. 3. Further evaluation of testosterone treatment of myelofibrosis. N Engl J Med 274:420–426, 1966.

57. Besa EC, Nowell PC, Geller NL, et al: Analysis of the androgen response of 23 patients with agnogenic myeloid metaplasia: The value of chromosomal studies in predicting response and survival. Cancer 49:308–313, 1982.

58. Temple JD, Harrington WJ, Ahn YS, et al: Treatment of sickle cell disease with danazol. J Fla Med Assoc 73:847–848, 1986.

59. Ahn YS, Harrington WJ, Mylvaganam R, et al: Danazol therapy for autoimmune hemolytic anemia. Ann Intern Med 102:298–301, 1985.

60. West SG, Johnson SC: Danazol for the treatment of refractory autoimmune thrombocytopenia in systemic lupus erythematosus. Ann Intern Med 108:703–706, 1988.

61. Ahn YS, Harrington WJ, Simon SR, et al: Danazol for the treatment of idiopathic thrombocytopenic purpura. N Engl J Med 308:1396–1399, 1983.

62. Schreiber AD, Chien P, Tomaski A, et al: Effect of danazol in immune thrombocytopenic purpura. N Engl J Med 316:503–508, 1987.

63. Cicardi M, Bergamaschini L, Cugno M, et al: Long-term treatment of hereditary angioedema with attenuated androgens: A survey of a 13-year experience. J Allergy Clin Immunol 87:768–773, 1991.

64. Sim TC, Grant JA: Hereditary angioedema: Its diagnostic and management perspectives. Am J Med 88:656–664, 1990.

65. Barbosa J, Seal US, Doe RP: Effects of anabolic steroids on haptoglobin, orosomucoid, plasminogen, fibrinogen, transferrin, ceruloplasmin, α1-antitrypsin, β-glucuronidase and total serum proteins. J Clin Endocrinol Metab 33:388–398, 1971.

66. Cade JF, Stubbs KP, Stubbs AE, et al: Thrombosis, fibrinolysis and ethylestrenol. Acta Endocrinol Suppl (Copenh) 271:53–59, 1985.

67. Gralnick HR, Rick ME: Danazol increases factor VIII and factor IX in classic hemophilia and Christmas disease. N Engl J Med 308:1393–1395, 1983.

68. Saidi P, Lega BZ, Kim HC, et al: Effect of danazol on clotting factor levels, bleeding incidence, factor infusion requirements, and immune parameters in hemophilia. Blood 68:673–679, 1986.

69. Dannenhoffer R, Crawford JD: Testosterone need questioned [letter]. Pediatrics 71:666–667, 1983.

70. Stanhope R, Buchanan CR, Fenn GC, et al: Double blind placebo controlled trial of low dose oxandrolone in the treatment of boys with constitutional delay of growth and puberty. Arch Dis Child 63:501–505, 1988.

71. Rosenfeld RG, Northcraft GB, Hintz RL: A prospective, randomized study of testosterone treatment of constitutional delay of growth and development in male adolescents. Pediatrics 69:681–687, 1982.

72. Arrigo T, Cisternino M, Luca DF, et al: Final height outcome in both untreated and testosterone-treated boys with constitutional delay of growth and puberty. J Pediatr Endocrinol Metab 9:511–517, 1996.

73. Bergada I, Bergada C: Long term treatment with low dose testosterone in constitutional delay of growth and puberty: Effect on bone age maturation and pubertal progression. J Pediatr Endocrinol Metab 8:117–122, 1995.

74. Wilson DM, McCauley E, Brown DR, et al: Oxandrolone therapy in constitutionally delayed growth and puberty. Bio-Technology General Corporation Cooperative Study Group. Pediatrics 96:1095–1100, 1995.

75. Brown DC, Butler GE, Kelnar CJ, et al: A double blind, placebo controlled study of the effects of low dose testosterone undecanoate on the growth of small for age, prepubertal boys. Arch Dis Child 73:131–135, 1995.

76. Crowne EC, Wallace WH, Moore C, et al: Effect of low dose oxandrolone and testosterone treatment on the pituitary-testicular and GH axes in boys with constitutional delay of growth and puberty. Clin Endocrinol (Oxf) 46:209–216, 1997.

77. Albanese A, Kewley GD, Long A, et al: Oral treatment for constitutional delay of growth and puberty in boys: A randomised trial of an anabolic steroid or testosterone undecanoate. Arch Dis Child 71:315–317, 1994.

78. Richman RA, Kirsch LR: Testosterone treatment in adolescent boys with constitutional delay in growth and development. N Engl J Med 319:1563–1567, 1988.

79. Jackson ST, Rallison ML, Buntin WH, et al: Use of oxandrolone for growth stimulation in children. Am J Dis Child 126:481–484, 1973.

80. Marti-Henneberg C, Niirianen AK, Rappaport R: Oxandrolone treatment of constitutional short stature in boys during adolescence: Effect on linear growth, bone age, pubic hair, and

testicular development. J Pediatr 86:783–788, 1975.

81. Sobel EH, Raymond CS, Quinn KV, et al: The use of methyltestosterone to stimulate growth: Relative influence on skeletal maturation and linear growth. J Clin Endocrinol Metab 16:241–248, 1956.

82. Joss EE, Schmidt HA, Zuppinger KA: Oxandrolone in constitutionally delayed growth, a longitudinal study up to final height. J Clin Endocrinol Metab 69:1109–1115, 1989.

83. Lippe B: Turner syndrome. Endocrinol Metab Clin North Am 20:121–152, 1991.

84. Rosenfeld RG, Frane J, Attie KM, et al: Six-year results of a randomized, prospective trial of human growth hormone and oxandrolone in Turner syndrome. J Pediatr 121:49–55, 1992.

85. Grinspoon S, Corcoran C, Lee K, et al: Loss of lean body and muscle mass correlates with androgen levels in hypogonadal men with acquired immunodeficiency syndrome and wasting. J Clin Endocrinol Metab 81:4051–4058, 1996.

86. Dobs AS, Dempsey MA, Ladenson PW, et al: Endocrine disorders in men infected with human immunodeficiency virus. Am J Med 84:611–616, 1988.

87. Bhasin S, Storer TW, Asbel-Sethi N, et al: Effects of testosterone replacement with a nongenital, transdermal system, Androderm, in human immunodeficiency virus-infected men with low testosterone levels. J Clin Endocrinol Metab 83:3155–3162, 1998.

88. Dobs AS, Cofrancesco J, Nolten WE, et al: The use of a transscrotal testosterone delivery system in the treatment of patients with weight loss related to human immunodeficiency virus infection. Am J Med 107:126–132, 1999.

89. Gold J, High HA, Li Y, et al: Safety and efficacy of nandrolone decanoate for treatment of wasting in patients with HIV infection. AIDS 10:745–752, 1996.

90. Coodley GO, Coodley MK: A trial of testosterone therapy for HIV-associated weight loss. AIDS 11:1347–1352, 1997.

91. Grinspoon S, Corcoran C, Askari H, et al: Effects of androgen administration in men with the AIDS wasting syndrome: A randomized, double-blind, placebo-controlled trial. Ann Intern Med 129:18–26, 1998.

92. Bhasin S, Storer TW, Javanbakht M, et al: Testosterone replacement and resistance exercise in HIV-infected men with weight loss and low testosterone levels. JAMA 283:763–770, 2000.

93. Strawford A, Barbieri T, Van Loan M, et al: Resistance exercise and supraphysiologic androgen therapy in eugonadal men with HIV-related weight loss: A randomized controlled trial. JAMA 281:1282–1290, 1999.

94. Hengge UR, Baumann M, Maleba R, et al: Oxymetholone promotes weight gain in patients with advanced human immunodeficiency virus (HIV-1) infection. Br J Nutr 75:129–138, 1996.

95. Hengge UR, Stocks K, Wiehler H, et al: Double-blind, randomized, placebo-controlled phase III trial of oxymetholone for the treatment of HIV wasting. AIDS 17:699–710, 2003.

96. Berger JR, Pall L, Hall CD, et al: Oxandrolone in AIDS-wasting myopathy. AIDS 10:1657–1662, 1996.

97. Ferrando AA, Sheffield-Moore M, Wolf SE, et al: Testosterone administration in severe burns ameliorates muscle catabolism. Crit Care Med 29:1936–1942, 2001.

98. Wolf SE, Thomas SJ, Dasu MR, et al: Improved net protein balance, lean mass, and gene expression changes with oxandrolone treatment in the severely burned. Ann Surg 237:801–810, 2003.

99. Demling RH, DeSanti L: Oxandrolone induced lean mass gain during recovery from severe burns is maintained after discontinuation of the anabolic steroid. Burns 29:793–797, 2003.

100. Casaburi R: Skeletal muscle dysfunction in chronic obstructive pulmonary disease. Med Sci Sports Exerc 33:S662–S670, 2001.

101. Creutzberg EC, Wouters EF, Mostert R, et al: A role for anabolic steroids in the rehabilitation of patients with COPD? A double-blind, placebo-controlled, randomized trial. Chest 124:1733–1742, 2003.

102. Ferreira IM, Verreschi IT, Nery LE, et al: The influence of 6 months of oral anabolic steroids on body mass and respiratory muscles in undernourished COPD patients. Chest 114:19–28, 1998.

103. Yeh SS, DeGuzman B, Kramer T: Reversal of COPD-associated weight loss using the anabolic agent oxandrolone. Chest 122:421–428, 2002.

104. Mendenhall CL, Anderson S, Garcia-Pont P, et al: Short-term and long-term survival in patients with alcoholic hepatitis treated with oxandrolone and prednisolone. N Engl J Med 311:1464–1470, 1984.

105. Bonkovsky HL, Fiellin DA, Smith GS, et al: A randomized, controlled trial of treatment of alcoholic hepatitis with parenteral nutrition and oxandrolone. I. Short-term effects on liver function. Am J Gastroenterol 86:1200–1208, 1991.

106. Bonkovsky HL, Singh RH, Jafri IH, et al: A randomized, controlled trial of treatment of alcoholic hepatitis with parenteral nutrition and oxandrolone. II. Short-term effects on nitrogen metabolism, metabolic balance, and nutrition. Am J Gastroenterol 86:1209–1218, 1991.

107. Rambaldi A, Iaquinto G, Gluud C: Anabolic-androgenic steroids for alcoholic liver disease. Cochrane Database Syst Rev CD003045, 2003.

108. Catlin DH, Hatton CK: Use and abuse of anabolic and other drugs for athletic enhancement. Adv Intern Med 36:399–424, 1991.

109. Franke WW, Berendonk B: Hormonal doping and androgenization of athletes: A secret program of the German Democratic Republic government. Clin Chem 43:1262–1279, 1997.

110. US Senate Committee on the Judiciary: Proper and improper use of drugs by athletes. (Hearings before the Subcommittee to Investigate Juvenile Delinquency, June 18 and July 12 and 13, 1973.) Washington, DC, US Government Printing Office, 1973, pp 1–843.

111. Kusserow RP: Adolescent Steroid Use. Washington, DC, US Department of Health and Human Services, US Government Printing Office, 1990.

112. Stilger VG, Yesalis CE: Anabolic-androgenic steroid use among high school football players. J Community Health 24:131–145, 1999.

113. Yesalis CE, Kennedy NJ, Kopstein AN, et al: Anabolic-androgenic steroid use in the United States. JAMA 270:1217–1221, 1993.

114. Buckley WE, Yesalis CE III, Friedl KE, et al: Estimated prevalence of anabolic steroid use among male high school seniors. JAMA 260:3441–3445, 1988.

115. Grunbaum JA, Kann L, Kinchen S, et al: Youth risk behavior surveillance—United States, 2003. MMWR Surveill Summ 53:1–96, 2004.

116. Brown WJ, Basil MD, Bocarnea MC: The influence of famous athletes on health beliefs and practices: Mark McGwire, child abuse prevention, and androstenedione. J Health Commun 8:41–57, 2003.

117. Catlin DH, Kammerer RC, Hatton CK, et al: Analytical chemistry at the Games of the XXIIIrd Olympiad in Los Angeles, 1984. Clin Chem 33:319–327, 1987.

118. Corrigan B, Kazlauskas R: Drug testing at the Sydney Olympics. Med J Aust 173:312–313, 2000.

119. Yesalis CE III: Medical, legal, and societal implications of androstenedione use. JAMA 281:2043–2044, 1999.

120. Yesalis CE, Barsukiewicz CK, Kopstein AN, et al: Trends in anabolic-androgenic steroid use among adolescents. Arch Pediatr Adolesc Med 151:1197–1206, 1997.

121. Anonymous: Sports supplement sales rise to $1.4 billion. Nutrition Business Journal 5:5–6, 2000.

122. US Congress: Dietary Supplement Health and Education Act of 1994. Public Law No.103 417:103–104, 1994.

123. US Congress: Anabolic Steroid Control Act. Public Law No.100–200, 1990.

124. Longcope C, Kato T, Horton R: Conversion of blood androgens to estrogens in normal adult men and women. J Clin Invest 48:2191–2201, 1969.

125. Horton R, Tait JF: Androstenedione production and interconversion rates measured in peripheral blood and studies on the possible site of its

conversion to testosterone. J Clin Invest 45:301–313, 1966.

126. Nestler JE, Barlascini CO, Clore JN, et al: Dehydroepiandrosterone reduces serum low density lipoprotein levels and body fat but does not alter insulin sensitivity in normal men. J Clin Endocrinol Metab 66:57–61, 1988.

127. Diamond P, Cusan L, Gomez JL, et al: Metabolic effects of 12-month percutaneous dehydroepiandrosterone replacement therapy in postmenopausal women. J Endocrinol 150(Suppl):S43–S50, 1996.

128. Bhasin S, Storer TW, Berman N, et al: The effects of supraphysiologic doses of testosterone on muscle size and strength in normal men. N Engl J Med 335:1–7, 1996.

129. Young J, Couzinet B, Nahoul K, et al: Panhypopituitarism as a model to study the metabolism of dehydroepiandrosterone (DHEA) in humans. J Clin Endocrinol Metab 82:2578–2585, 1997.

130. Leder BZ, Longcope C, Catlin DH, et al: Oral androstenedione administration and serum testosterone concentrations in young men. JAMA 283:779–782, 2000.

131. Leder BZ, Catlin DH, Longcope C, et al: Metabolism of orally administered androstenedione in young men. J Clin Endocrinol Metab 86:3654–3658, 2001.

132. Leder BZ, Leblanc KM, Longcope C, et al: Effects of oral androstenedione administration on serum testosterone and estradiol levels in postmenopausal women. J Clin Endocrinol Metab 87:5449–5454, 2002.

133. King DS, Sharp RL, Vukovich MD, et al: Effect of oral androstenedione on serum testosterone and adaptations to resistance training in young men: A randomized controlled trial. JAMA 281:2020–2028, 1999.

134. Wallace MB, Lim J, Cutler A, et al: Effects of dehydroepiandrosterone vs androstenedione supplementation in men. Med Sci Sports Exerc 31:1788–1792, 1999.

135. Ballantyne CS, Phillips SM, MacDonald JR, et al: The acute effects of androstenedione supplementation in healthy young males. Can J Appl Physiol 25:68–78, 2000.

136. Rasmussen BB, Volpi E, Gore DC, et al: Androstenedione does not stimulate muscle protein anabolism in young healthy men. J Clin Endocrinol Metab 85:55–59, 2000.

137. Uralets VP, Gillette PA: Over-the-counter anabolic steroids 4-androsten-3,17-dione; 4-androsten-3β,17β-diol; and 19-nor-4-androsten-3,17-dione: Excretion studies in men. J Anal Toxicol 23:357–366, 1999.

138. Bowers LD: Oral dehydroepiandrosterone supplementation can increase the testosterone/epitestosterone ratio. Clin Chem 45:295–297, 1999.

139. Geyer H, Parr MK, Mareck U, et al: Analysis of non-hormonal nutritional supplements for anabolic-androgenic steroids: Results of an international study. Int J Sports Med 25:124–129, 2004.

140. Strauss RH, Liggett MT, Lanese RR: Anabolic steroid use and perceived effects in 10 weight-trained women athletes. JAMA 253:2871–2873, 1985.

141. Haupt HA, Rovere GD: Anabolic steroids: A review of the literature. Am J Sports Med 12:469–484, 1984.

142. Catlin DH, Hatton CK, Starcevic SH: Issues in detecting abuse of xenobiotic anabolic steroids and testosterone by analysis of athletes' urine. Clin Chem 43:1280–1288, 1997.

143. Coutts SB, Kicman AT, Hurst DT, et al: Intramuscular administration of 5α-dihydrotestosterone heptanoate: Changes in urinary hormone profile. Clin Chem 43:2091–2098, 1997.

144. Catlin DH, Sekera MH, Ahrens BD, et al: Tetrahydrogestrinone: Discovery, synthesis, and detection in urine. Rapid Commun Mass Spectrom 18:1245–049, 2004.

145. Jasuja R, Catlin DH, Miller A, et al: Tetrahydrogestrinone (THG) binds to androgen receptor and activates AR-mediated signaling pathway [abstract]. Endrocrine Society, 2004.

146. Death AK, McGrath KC, Kazlauskas R, et al: Tetrahydrogestrinone is a potent androgen and progestin. J Clin Endocrinol Metab 89:2498–2500, 2004.

147. Knight J: Drugs in sport: No dope. Nature 426:114–115, 2003.

148. US Department of Justice: Four individuals charged in bay area with money laundering and distribution of illegal steroids. Washington, DC, US Department of Justice, 2004.

149. Catlin DH, Ahrens BD, Kucherova Y: Detection of norbolethone, an anabolic steroid never marketed, in athletes' urine. Rapid Commun Mass Spectrom 16:1273–1275, 2002.

150. Smith H, Hughes GA, Douglas GH, et al: Totally synthetic (+-)-13alkyl-3-hydroxy and methoxy-gona-1,3,5 (10)-trien-17one and related compounds. Experientia 19:394–396, 1963.

151. Edgren RA: A comparative study of the anabolic and androgenic effects of various steroids. Acta Endocrinol (Copenh) 44(Suppl)87:3–21, 1963.

152. Edgren RA, Smith H: Wy 3475, a new potent orally active anabolic agent. In Martini L, Pecile A (eds): Hormonal Steroids. New York, Academic Press, 1965, pp 161–171.

153. Tomarelli RM, Bernhart FW: Oral anabolic activity of (+/−)-13b,17a-diethyl-17b-hydroxy-gon-4en-3one (norbolethone) in a nitrogen retention assay. Steroids 4:451–456, 1964.

154. LeVann LJ, Cohn RE: Clinical evaluation of norbolethone therapy in stunted growth and poorly thriving children. Int J Clin Pharmacol 6:54–59, 1972.

155. Greenblatt RB, Jungck EC, King GC: Clinical evaluation of a new anabolic steroid. Am J Med Sci 248:317–328, 1964.

156. Albanese AA, Lorenze EJ, Orto LA, et al: Nutritional and metabolic effects of some newer steroids. V. Norbolethone. N Y State J Med 68:2392–2406, 1968.

157. Snochowski M, Saartok T, Dahlberg E, et al: Androgen and glucocorticoid receptors in human skeletal muscle cytosol. J Steroid Biochem 14:765–771, 1981.

158. Krieg M, Smith K, Elvers B: Androgen receptor translocation from cytosol of rat heart muscle, bulbocavernosus/levator ani muscle and prostate into heart muscle nuclei. J Steroid Biochem 13:577–587, 1980.

159. Deslypere JP, Vermeulen A: Influence of age on steroid concentrations in skin and striated muscle in women and in cardiac muscle and lung tissue in men. J Clin Endocrinol Metab 61:648–653, 1985.

160. Alen M, Suominen J: Effect of androgenic and anabolic steroids on spermatogenesis in power athletes. Int J Sports Med 5(Suppl):189–192, 1984.

161. Bhasin S, Woodhouse L, Casaburi R, et al: Testosterone dose-response relationships in healthy young men. Am J Physiol Endocrinol Metab 281:E1172–E1181, 2001.

162. Sinha-Hikim I, Artaza J, Woodhouse L, et al: Testosterone-induced increase in muscle size in healthy young men is associated with muscle fiber hypertrophy. Am J Physiol Endocrinol Metab 283:E154–E164, 2002.

163. Lyons GE, Kelly AM, Rubinstein NA: Testosterone-induced changes in contractile protein isoforms in the sexually dimorphic temporalis muscle of the guinea pig. J Biol Chem 261:13278–13284, 1986.

164. Venable JH: Morphology of the cells of normal, testosterone-deprived and testosterone-stimulated levator ani muscles. Am J Anat 119:271–301, 1966.

165. Kenyon AT, Knowlton K, Sandiford I: A comparative study of the metabolic effects of testosterone propionate in normal men and women and in eunuchoidism. Endocrinology 26:26–45, 1940.

166. Kenyon AT, Knowlton K, Sandiford I: The anabolic effects of the androgens and somatic growth in man. Ann Intern Med 20:632–654, 1944.

167. Bhasin S, Storer TW, Berman N, et al: Testosterone replacement increases fat-free mass and muscle size in hypogonadal men. J Clin Endocrinol Metab 82:407–413, 1997.

168. Snyder PJ, Peachey H, Berlin JA, et al: Effects of testosterone replacement in hypogonadal men. J Clin Endocrinol Metab 85:2670–2677, 2000.

169. Wang C, Swerdloff RS, Iranmanesh A, et al: Effects of transdermal testosterone gel on bone turnover markers and bone mineral density in hypogonadal men. Clin Endocrinol (Oxf) 54:739–750, 2001.

170. Brodsky IG, Balagopal P, Nair KS: Effects of testosterone replacement on muscle mass and muscle protein synthesis in hypogonadal men: A clinical research center study. J Clin Endocrinol Metab 81:3469–3475, 1996.

171. Forbes GB: Human Body Composition: Growth, Aging, Nutrition, and Activity. New York, Springer-Verlag, 1987.

172. Welle S, Jozefowicz R, Forbes G, et al: Effect of testosterone on metabolic rate and body composition in normal men and men with muscular dystrophy. J Clin Endocrinol Metab 74:332–335, 1992.

173. Schroeder ET, Singh A, Bhasin S, et al: Effects of an oral androgen on muscle and metabolism in older, community-dwelling men. Am J Physiol Endocrinol Metab 284:E120–E128, 2003.

174. Aloia JF, Kapoor A, Vaswani A, et al: Changes in body composition following therapy of osteoporosis with methandrostenolone. Metabolism 30:1076–1079, 1981.

175. Forbes GB: The effect of anabolic steroids on lean body mass: The dose response curve. Metabolism 34:571–573, 1985.

176. Forbes GB: Body composition as affected by physical activity and nutrition. Fed Proc 44:343–347, 1985.

177. Hervey GR, Knibbs AV, Burkinshaw L, et al: Effects of methandienone on the performance and body composition of men undergoing athletic training. Clin Sci 60:457–461, 1981.

178. Wilson JD: Androgen abuse by athletes. Endocr Rev 9:181–199, 1988.

179. Mayer M, Rosen F: Interaction of anabolic steroids with glucocorticoid receptor sites in rat muscle cytosol. Am J Physiol 229:1381–1386, 1975.

180. Zhao J, Bauman WA, Huang R, et al: Oxandrolone blocks glucocorticoid signaling in an androgen receptor-dependent manner. Steroids 69:357–366, 2004.

181. American College of Sports Medicine: Position statement on the use of anabolic-androgenic steroids in sports. Med Sci Sports Exerc 19:534–539, 1987.

182. Elashoff JD, Jacknow AD, Shain SG, et al: Effects of anabolic-androgenic steroids on muscular strength. Ann Intern Med 115:387–393, 1991.

183. Korkia P, Stimson GV: Indications of prevalence, practice and effects of anabolic steroid use in Great Britain. Int J Sports Med 18:557–562, 1997.

184. Brody SA, Loriaux DL: Epidemic of gynecomastia among Haitian refugees: Exposure to an environmental antiandrogen. Endocr Pract 9:370–375, 2003.

185. Wilson JD, Aiman J, MacDonald PC: The pathogenesis of gynecomastia. Adv Intern Med 25:1–32, 1980.

186. Scott MJ, Scott MJ: Dermatologists and anabolic-androgenic drug abuse. Cutis 44:30–35, 1989.

187. Wu FC, Farley TM, Peregoudov A, et al: Effects of testosterone enanthate in normal men: Experience from a multicenter contraceptive efficacy study. World Health Organization Task Force on Methods for the Regulation of Male Fertility. Fertil Steril 65:626–636, 1996.

188. Pope HGJ, Katz DL: Psychiatric and medical effects of anabolic-androgenic steroid use: A controlled study of 160 athletes. Arch Gen Psychiatry 51:375–382, 1994.

189. Alen M, Rahkila P, Reinila M, et al: Androgenic-anabolic steroid effects on serum thyroid, pituitary and steroid hormones in athletes. Am J Sports Med 15:357–361, 1987.

190. Malarkey WB, Strauss RH, Leizman DJ, et al: Endocrine effects in female weight lifters who self-administer testosterone and anabolic steroids. Am J Obstet Gynecol 165:1385–1390, 1991.

191. Daly RC, Su TP, Schmidt PJ, et al: Neuroendocrine and behavioral effects of high-dose anabolic steroid administration in male normal volunteers. Psychoneuroendocrinology 28:317–331, 2003.

192. Federman DD, Robbins J, Rall JE: Effects of methyltestosterone on thyroid function, thyroxine metabolism, and thyroxine-binding protein. J Clin Invest 37:1024–1030, 1958.

193. Woodard TL, Burghen GA, Kitabchi AE, et al: Glucose intolerance and insulin resistance in aplastic anemia treated with oxymetholone. J Clin Endocrinol Metab 53:905–908, 1981.

194. Friedl KE, Jones RE, Hannan CJJ, et al: The administration of pharmacological doses of testosterone or 19-nortestosterone to normal men is not associated with increased insulin secretion or impaired glucose tolerance. J Clin Endocrinol Metab 68:971–975, 1989.

195. Hobbs CJ, Jones RE, Plymate SR: Nandrolone, a 19-nortestosterone, enhances insulin-independent glucose uptake in normal men. J Clin Endocrinol Metab 81:1582–1585, 1996.

196. Hurley BF, Seals DR, Hagberg JM, et al: High-density-lipoprotein cholesterol in bodybuilders v powerlifters: Negative effects of androgen use. JAMA 252:507–513, 1984.

197. Applebaum-Bowden D, Haffner SM, Hazzard WR: The dyslipoproteinemia of anabolic steroid therapy: Increase in hepatic triglyceride lipase precedes the decrease in high density lipoprotein2 cholesterol. Metabolism 36:949–952, 1987.

198. Friedl KE, Hannan CJ, Jones RE, et al: High-density lipoprotein cholesterol is not decreased if an aromatizable androgen is administered. Metabolism 39:69–74, 1990.

199. Bagatell CJ, Heiman JR, Matsumoto AM, et al: Metabolic and behavioral effects of high-dose, exogenous testosterone in healthy men. J Clin Endocrinol Metab 79:561–567, 1994.

200. Zmuda JM, Fahrenbach MC, Younkin BT, et al: The effect of testosterone aromatization on high-density lipoprotein cholesterol level and postheparin lipolytic activity. Metabolism 42:446–450, 1993.

201. Brown GA, Vukovich MD, Martini ER, et al: Endocrine responses to chronic androstenedione intake in 30- to 56-year-old men. J Clin Endocrinol Metab 85:4074–4080, 2000.

202. Glazer G, Suchman AL: Lack of demonstrated effect of nandrolone on serum lipids. Metabolism 43:204–210, 1994.

203. Friedl KE: Reappraisal of the health risks associated with the use of high doses of oral and injectable androgenic steroids. NIDA Res Monogr 102:142–177, 1990.

204. McNutt RA, Ferenchick GS, Kirlin PC, et al: Acute myocardial infarction in a 22-year-old world class weight lifter using anabolic steroids. Am J Cardiol 62:164, 1988.

205. Kennedy MC, Lawrence C: Anabolic steroid abuse and cardiac death. Med J Aust 158:346–348, 1993.

206. Sullivan ML, Martinez CM, Gennis P, et al: The cardiac toxicity of anabolic steroids. Prog Cardiovasc Dis 41:1–15, 1998.

207. Fineschi V, Baroldi G, Monciotti F, et al: Anabolic steroid abuse and cardiac sudden death: A pathologic study. Arch Pathol Lab Med 125:253–255, 2001.

208. Liu PY, Death AK, Handelsman DJ: Androgens and cardiovascular disease. Endocr Rev 24:313–340, 2003.

209. Zimmerman HJ: Hormonal derivatives and other drugs used to treat endocrine diseases. In Zimmernann HJ (ed): Hepatotoxicity: The Adverse Effects of Drugs and Other Chemicals on the Liver. New York, Appleton-Century-Crofts, 1978, pp 436–467.

210. Ishak KG, Zimmerman HJ: Hepatotoxic effects of the anabolic/androgenic steroids. Semin Liver Dis 7:230–236, 1987.

211. Wynn V, Landon J, Kawerau E: Studies on hepatic function during methandienone therapy. Lancet 1:69–75, 1961.

212. Stimac D, Milic S, Dintinjana RD, et al: Androgenic/anabolic steroid-induced toxic hepatitis. J Clin Gastroenterol 35:350–352, 2002.

213. Foss GL, Simpson SL: Oral methyltestosterone and jaundice. Br Med J 1:259–263, 1959.

214. Ishak KG: Hepatic neoplasms associated with contraceptive and anabolic steroids. In Lingeman CH (ed): Carcinogenic Hormones. Berlin, Springer-Verlag, 1979, pp 73–128.

215. Kosaka A, Takahashi H, Yajima Y, et al: Hepatocellular carcinoma associated with anabolic steroid therapy: Report of a case and review of the Japanese literature. J Gastroenterol 31:450–454, 1996.

216. Overly WL, Dankoff JA, Wang BK, et al: Androgens and hepatocellular

carinoma in an athlete [letter]. Ann Intern Med 100:158–159, 1984.

217. Falk H, Thomas LB, Popper H, et al: Hepatic angiosarcoma associated with androgenic-anabolic steroids. Lancet 2:1120–1123, 1979.

218. Ingerowski GH, Scheutwinkel-Reich M, Stan HJ: Mutagenicity studies on veterinary anabolic drugs with the Salmonella/microsome test. Mutat Res 91:93–98, 1981.

219. Lowdell CP, Murray-Lyon IM: Reversal of liver damage due to long term methyltestosterone and safety of non-17α-alkylated androgens. Br Med J 291:637, 1985.

220. Nadell J, Kosek J: Peliosis hepatis: 12 cases associated with oral androgen therapy. Arch Pathol Lab Med 101:405–410, 1977.

221. Wakabayashi T, Onda H, Tada T, et al: High incidence of peliosis hepatis in autopsy cases of aplastic anemia with special reference to anabolic steroid therapy. Acta Pathol Jpn 34:1079–1086, 1984.

222. Uzych L: Anabolic-androgenic steroids and psychiatric-related effects: A review. Can J Psychiatry 37:23–28, 1992.

223. Altschule MD: The use of testosterone in the treatment of depression. N Engl J Med 239:1036–1038, 1948.

224. Tricker R, Casaburi R, Storer TW, et al: The effects of supraphysiological doses of testosterone on angry behavior in healthy eugonadal men: A clinical research center study. J Clin Endocrinol Metab 81:3754–3758, 1996.

225. Pope HG Jr, Kouri EM, Hudson JI: Effects of supraphysiologic doses of testosterone on mood and aggression in normal men: A randomized controlled trial. Arch Gen Psychiatry 57:133–140, 2000.

226. Bahrke MS, Yesalis CE, Wright JE: Psychological and behavioural effects of endogenous testosterone levels and anabolic-androgenic steroids among males: A review. Sports Med 10:303–337, 1990.

227. Pope HJ, Katz DL: Homicide and near-homicide by anabolic steroid users. J Clin Psychiatry 51:28–31, 1990.

228. Su TP, Pagliaro M, Schmidt PJ, et al: Neuropsychiatric effects of anabolic steroids in male normal volunteers. JAMA 269:2760–2764, 1993.

229. Choi PY, Pope HGJ: Violence toward women and illicit androgenic-anabolic steroid use. Ann Clin Psychiatry 6:21–25, 1994.

230. Pope HJ, Katz DL: Affective and psychotic symptoms associated with anabolic steroid use. Am J Psychiatry 145:487–490, 1988.

231. Brower KJ, Eliopulos GA, Blow FC, et al: Evidence for physical and psychological dependence on anabolic androgenic steroids in eight weight lifters. Am J Psychiatry 147:510–512, 1990.

232. Hoag GN, Connolly VP, Domke HL: Marked fall in high-density lipoprotein following isotretinoin therapy: Report of a case in a weight lifter on anabolic steroids [letter]. J Am Acad Dermatol 16:1264–1265, 1987.

233. McLaughlin GE, McCarty DJ, Segal BL: Hemarthrosis complicating anticoagulant therapy: Report of three cases. JAMA 196:1020–1021, 1966.

234. Wilson IC, Prange AJ, Lara PP: Methyltestosterone with imipramine in men: Conversion of depression to paranoid reaction. Am J Psychiatry 131:21–24, 1974.

235. Baker J: A report on alterations to the speaking and singing voices of four women following hormonal therapy with virilizing agents. J Voice 13:496–507, 1999.

236. Al Ismail K, Torreggiani WC, Munk PL, et al: Gluteal mass in a bodybuilder: Radiological depiction of a complication of anabolic steroid use. Eur Radiol 12:1366–1369, 2002.

237. Rich JD, Dickinson BP, Flanigan TP, et al: Abscess related to anabolic-androgenic steroid injection. Med Sci Sports Exerc 31:207–209, 1999.

238. Skoura C, Mourouzis C, Saranteas T, et al: Masseteric hypertrophy associated with administration of anabolic steroids and unilateral mastication: A case report. Oral Surg Oral Med Oral Pathol Oral Radiol Endod 92:515–518, 2001.

239. Mondelli M, Cioni R, Federico A: Rare mononeuropathies of the upper limb in bodybuilders. Muscle Nerve 21:809–812, 1998.

240. Lepori M, Perren A, Gallino A: The popliteal-artery entrapment syndrome in a patient using anabolic steroids. N Engl J Med 346:1254–1255, 2002.

241. Kachhi PN, Henderson SO: Priapism after androstenedione intake for athletic performance enhancement. Ann Emerg Med 35:391–393, 2000.

242. Zeiss J, Smith RR, Taha AM: Iliopsoas hypertrophy mimicking acute abdomen in a bodybuilder. Gastrointest Radiol 12:340–342, 1987.

243. Laseter JT, Russell JA: Anabolic steroid-induced tendon pathology: A review of the literature. Med Sci Sports Exerc 23:1–3, 1991.

244. Liow RY, Tavares S: Bilateral rupture of the quadriceps tendon associated with anabolic steroids. Br J Sports Med 29:77–79, 1995.

245. Battista V, Combs J, Warme WJ: Asynchronous bilateral achilles tendon ruptures and androstenediol use. Am J Sports Med 31:1007–1009, 2003.

246. Winwood PJ, Robertson DA, Wright R: Bleeding oesophageal varices associated with anabolic steroid use in an athlete. Postgrad Med J 66:864–865, 1990.

247. Damste PH: Voice change in adult women caused by virilizing agents. J Speech Hear Disord 32:126–132, 1967.

248. Forbes GB, Porta CR, Herr BE, et al: Sequence of changes in body composition induced by testosterone and reversal of changes after drug is stopped [see comments]. JAMA 267:397–399, 1992.

249. Clerico A, Ferdeghini M, Palombo C, et al: Effect of anabolic treatment on the serum levels of gonadotropins, testosterone, prolactin, thyroid hormones and myoglobin of male athletes under physical training. J Nucl Med Allied Sci 25:79–88, 1981.

250. Jones TM, Fang VS, Landau RL, et al: The effects of fluoxymesterone administration on testicular function. J Clin Endocrinol Metab 44:121–129, 1977.

251. Mauss J, Beorsch G, Bormacher K, et al: Effect of long-term testosterone oenanthate administration on male reproductive function: Clinical evaluation, serum FSH, LH, testosterone, and seminal fluid analyses in normal men. Acta Endocrinol (Copenh) 78:373–384, 1975.

252. Schurmeyer T, Knuth UA, Belkien L, et al: Reversible azoospermia induced by the anabolic steroid 19-nortestosterone. Lancet 1:417–420, 1984.

253. Urhausen A, Torsten A, Wilfried K: Reversibility of the effects on blood cells, lipids, liver function and hormones in former anabolic-androgenic steroid abusers. J Steroid Biochem Mol Biol 84:369–375, 2003.

254. van Breda E, Keizer HA, Kuipers H, et al: Androgenic anabolic steroid use and severe hypothalamic-pituitary dysfunction: A case study. Int J Sports Med 24:195–196, 2003.

255. Menon DK: Successful treatment of anabolic steroid-induced azoospermia with human chorionic gonadotropin and human menopausal gonadotropin. Fertil Steril 79(Suppl 3):1659–1661, 2003.

# Gynecomastia

## *Richard J. Santen*

Stimulatory and inhibitory hormones control the growth and differentiation of mammary tissue[1-2] (Fig. 177-1). Estradiol binds to estrogen receptors and stimulates glandular cells in the male breast. Testosterone exerts a generalized inhibitory action on growth and differentiation, perhaps through a specific antiestrogenic action.[2] The balance between stimulatory and inhibitory hormones controls the development and maintenance of breast tissue. Growth hormone, insulin, insulin-like growth factor 1 (IGF-1), and cortisol act permissively, exerting no specific effects, but are required for the activity of other hormones.[1] Regulatory hormones modulate the effects of other factors which, in turn, influence breast growth and differentiation. Thyroxine increases the level of testosterone-estradiol–binding globulin (TeBG). Cortisol and prolactin lower circulating testosterone levels through hypothalamic and testicular effects. The application of these physiologic principles provides a framework for evaluation of gynecomastia on a pathophysiologic basis.

## PHYSIOLOGIC FORMS OF GYNECOMASTIA

### NEWBORN GYNECOMASTIA

The high levels of estradiol and progesterone produced by the mother during fetal life stimulate newborn breast tissue that persists for several weeks after birth in boys. Minimal breast discharge, called "witch's milk," can result.

### PUBERTAL GYNECOMASTIA

Beginning at age 11, approximately 30% of boys develop detectable gynecomastia (i.e., glandular tissue >0.5 cm in diameter). By age 14, gynecomastia is detectable in 65%.[3] While usually bilateral, gynecomastia is unilateral in 20% of cases. Spontaneous regression occurs in the majority of boys after 1 year. Hormonal alterations in pubertal boys with gynecomastia are not found consistently and are variably reported as low free testosterone, increased estradiol, elevated estradiol/testosterone ratio, and increased TeBG levels.[4-9]

### ADULT GYNECOMASTIA

Several studies[10-13] document the prevalence of palpable breast tissue in normal volunteers and in hospitalized patients. One third of normal military recruits have palpable glandular tissue that is between 2 and 4 cm in diameter.[10] Only 4% had tissue that measured greater than 4 cm in

diameter. The percentage gradually increased with age from 17% in men younger than 19 years old to 41% between age 40 and 44.[10] Three other studies[11-13] reported a prevalence of gynecomastia in hospitalized patients, which reached 57% in men between 45 and 59. Even though palpable breast tissue exceeded 2 cm in diameter, these men had minimal awareness of the existence of the condition. As proof of the validity of these studies, one autopsy study confirmed the impression of gynecomastia on physical examination in 60 consecutive cases and ruled out the possibility of pseudogynecomastia (i.e., the presence of subareolar fat tissue only).[13] Another autopsy study independently corroborated the frequency with which gynecomastia occurs.

In 83% of hospitalized men with gynecomastia, breast tissue diameter did not exceed 5 cm.[13] The etiology of this form of physiologic gynecomastia is not clear, but correlative evidence suggests increased aromatase activity. The total amount of aromatase activity in the body increases as a function of body fat, and the percentage of patients with gynecomastia appears to increase as a function of body mass index (Fig. 177-2). Notably, the diameter of breast tissue correlated significantly ($r = 0.52$) with body mass index in a group of 214 well-studied men (Fig. 177-3).[13] Animal models support the concept that aromatase excess causes gynecomastia. Two different transgenic mouse strains with overexpression of aromatase in breast tissue exhibit substantial breast development that mimics gynecomastia in men.[14-15]

## PATHOLOGIC FORMS OF GYNECOMASTIA

Two subtypes of gynecomastia can be distinguished histologically.[16-17] Glandular predominance occurs in 5% to 9% of patients and represents a process of recent hormonal stimulation of glandular elements. Stromal tissue predominates in 32% to 48% and reflects the aftermath of a prior hormonal imbalance with spontaneous resolution.

The distinction between physiologic and pathologic gynecomastia in adult men presents a challenge because of the common presence of breast enlargement in normal men and its association with obesity. An operational definition of pathologic gynecomastia is useful to the clinician in deciding the need for and extent of evaluation. Accordingly, pathologic gynecomastia is arbitrarily defined as: palpable tissue greater than 4 cm in diameter; palpable tissue greater than 2 cm and which is tender; or palpable tissue greater than 2 cm demonstrated to be gradually increasing in diameter on follow-up. True gynecomastia should be distinguished from

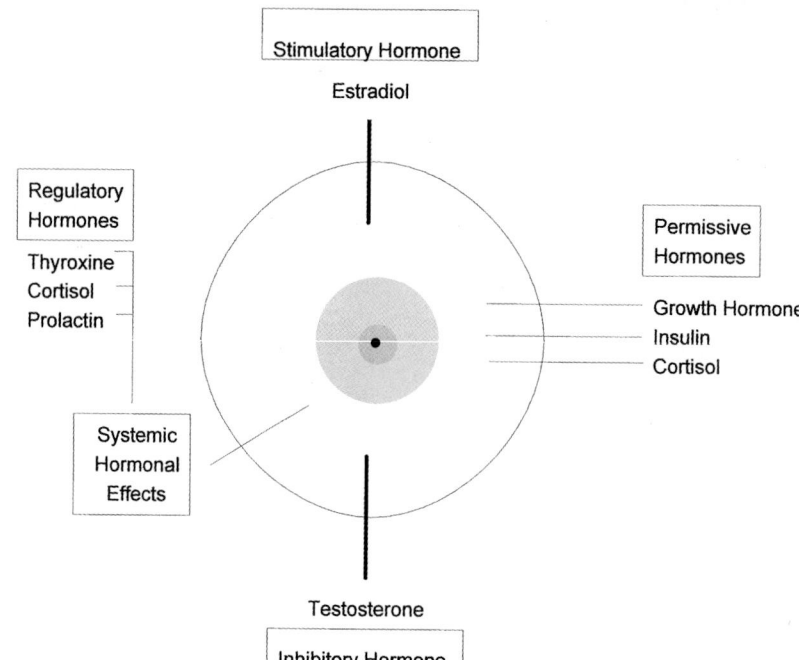

**Figure 177-1**   Diagrammatic representation of the hormones that affect breast tissue growth and differentiation in patients with gynecomastia. This diagram provides a framework for the logical assessment of disorders causing gynecomastia.

pseudogynecomastia (fat tissue present underneath the nipple). Mammography may occasionally be necessary to make this distinction, particularly in obese patients[18-20] (Fig. 177-4). Ultrasonography can also be used but is not considered as sensitive as mammography.[21-24] Gynecomastia is considered physiologic if less than 2 cm in diameter or between 2 and 4 cm but nontender and not enlarging.

A logical approach to the differential diagnosis is based on the physiologic framework represented in Figure 177-1 and Table 177-1. An excess of estradiol, deficiency of testosterone, an imbalance in the ratio of estradiol to testosterone, and abnormalities of regulatory hormones may be responsible for non-drug-related gynecomastia. A multitude of drugs that interact at each of these levels can also cause gynecomastia. The remainder of causes is largely idiopathic or uncertain.

### EXCESS OF ESTRADIOL

#### Tumors

Adrenal tumors may secrete one or several hormones in excess. Adenomas or carcinomas of the adrenal may directly produce large amounts of estradiol.[25-26] Alternatively, the adrenal tumor secretes androstenedione, dehydroepiandrosterone

(DHEA), and dehydroepiandrosterone sulfate (DHEA-S), which are then aromatized in peripheral tissues to estradiol. These patients generally exhibit a rapid onset of gynecomastia in association with hypertension, elevated ketosteroids, elevated DHEA and DHEA-S levels, and an adrenal mass.[27]

Testicular tumors of germ, sex cord, Leydig, or Sertoli cell origin can secrete an excess of estrogen or estrogen precursors. Tumors are large enough to be palpated in approximately half of patients,[28-33] whereas the remainder require detection by testicular ultrasound. Choriocarcinomas of the testis may produce human chorionic gonadotropin (hCG) in situ and stimulate production of both estradiol and testosterone. Ectopic production of hCG by lung, kidney, liver, and gastric carcinomas can also stimulate estradiol production and cause gynecomastia.

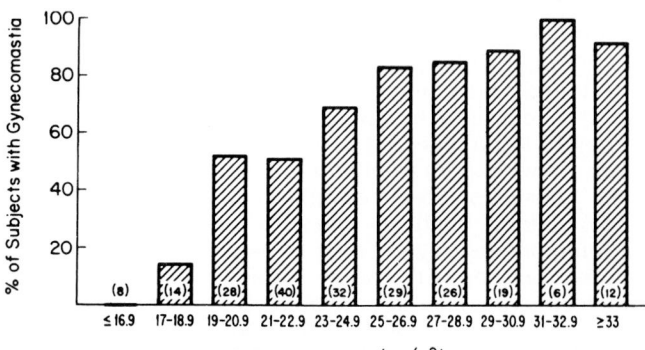

**Figure 177-2**   Correlation of the percentage of subjects with gynecomastia and body mass index. (From Niewoehner CB, Nutall FQ: Gynecomastia in a hospitalized male population. Am J Med 77:633, 1984.)

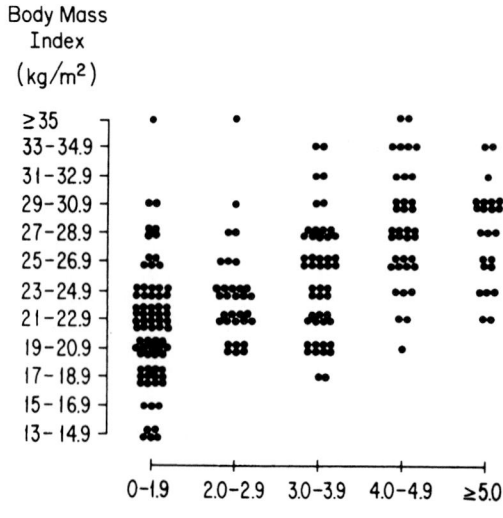

**Figure 177-3**   Correlation of breast tissue diameter with body mass index ($n = 214$, $r = 0.52$, $P < 0.001$). Correlation coefficient was determined by method of least squares. (From Niewoehner CB, Nutall FQ: Gynecomastia in a hospitalized male population. Am J Med 77:633, 1984.)

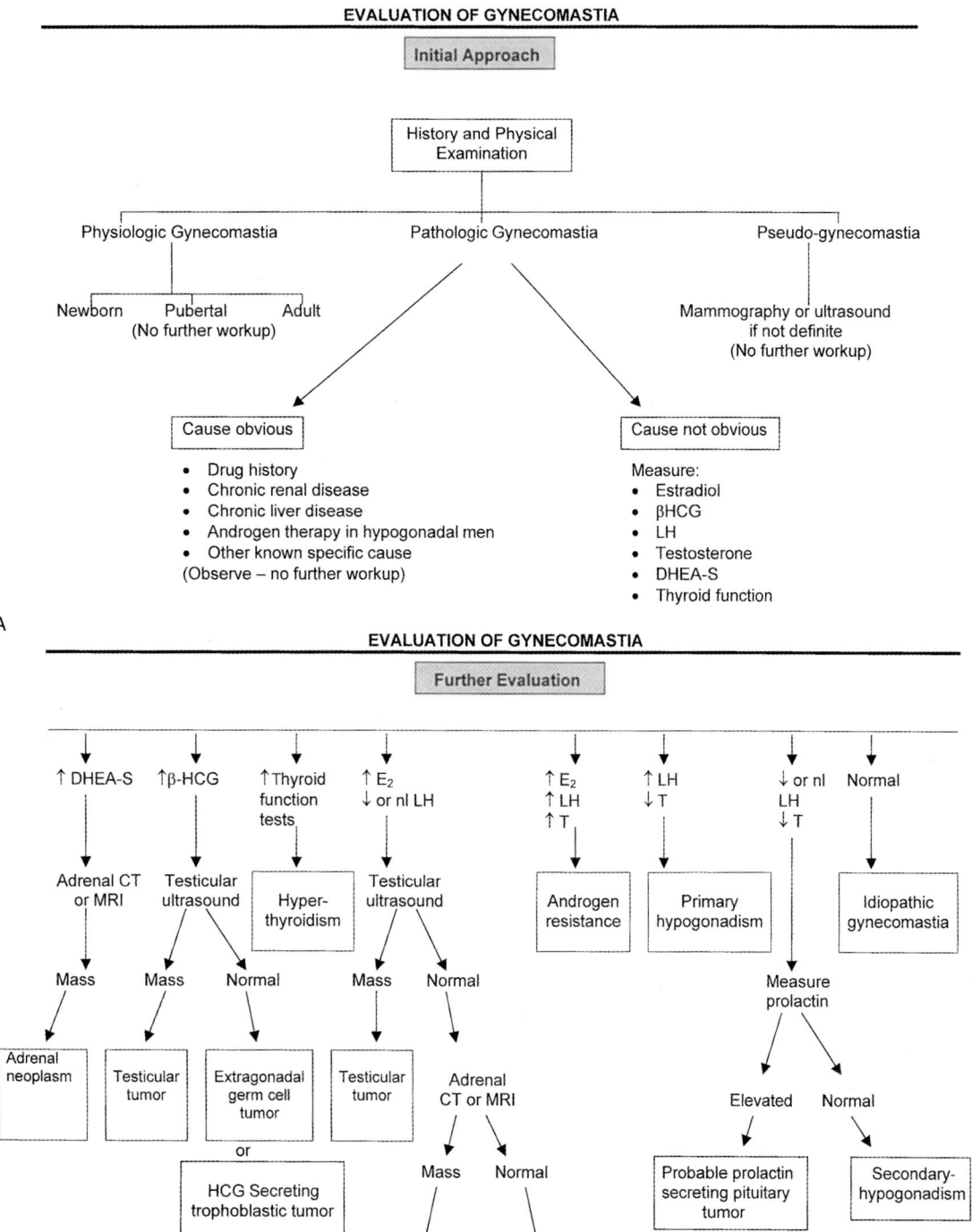

*Figure 177-4* Algorithim depicting evaluation of a patient with gynecomastia. β-hCG, human chorionic gonadotropin-β; CT, computed tomography; CXR, chest X-ray; DHEA-S, dehydroepiandrosterone sulfate; $E_2$, estradiol; LH, luteinizing hormone; MRI, magnetic resonance imaging; nl, normal; T, testosterone. (Adapted from the approach outlined by Braunstein GD: Aromatase and gynecomastia. Endocr Relat Cancer 6:315–324, 1999.)

## Aromatase Excess

Recent studies[34] suggest that overexpression of the aromatase enzyme may be a unifying feature of several clinical causes of gynecomastia (Table 177-2). Obesity and hyperthyroidism are associated with an increase in total body production of aromatase.[35–36] Aromatase also increases with aging, perhaps as a result of the increased percentage of total body fat.[37]

Aromatase excess also explains published reports of familial gynecomastia. Early onset of gynecomastia is the cardinal clinical feature of these patients at presentation. Three families have been demonstrated to have marked overexpression of aromatase with up to 50% systemic conversion of androgens to estrogens.[38–40] Five males in two generations of one family had gynecomastia and 10-fold higher levels of peripheral aromatization than normal. The cause for increased expression of aromatase is unknown. An additional kindred of familial gynecomastia from the time of the eighteenth Egyptian dynasty involved King Tutankhamen, his brother

## Table 177-1  Causes of Pathologic Gynecomastia

**ESTRADIOL EXCESS**
*ESTRADIOL SECRETION*
Adrenal tumors
Sporadic testicular tumors (sex cord, Sertoli, germ cell, Leydig cell)
Testicular tumors associated with familial syndromes (Peutz-Jeghers, Carney complex)
Hepatic tumor with aromatase
Increased aromatase activity (see Table 177-2)

**Exogenous Estrogens or Estrogenic Substances**
Drug therapy with estrogens
Estrogen creams and lotions
Embalming fluid exposure
Delousing powder
Hair oil
Marijuana
Estrogen analogues: digitoxin

*ELEVATED ESTROGEN PRECURSORS: AROMATIZABLE ANDROGENS*
Human chorionic gonadotropin (hCG) excess (eutopic or ectopic)
Exogenous hormones
    Testosterone enanthate
    Testosterone propionate
    Anabolic steroids
    hCG administration

**TESTOSTERONE DEFICIENCY**
Anorchia
Hypogonadotropic syndromes
Drugs or exogenous substances
    Ketoconazole
    Heroin
    Methadone
    Alcohol

**ESTRADIOL/TESTOSTERONE IMBALANCE**
Hypergonadotropic syndromes
Hypogonadotropic hypogonadism syndromes
Primary gonadal diseases
Drugs
    Cytotoxic drug-induced hypogonadism from:
        Busulfan
        Nitrosourea
        Vincristine
        Combination chemotherapy
        Steroid synthesis inhibitory drugs
Androgen resistance
    Complete testicular feminization
    Partial: Reifenstein, Lubs, Rosewater, and Dreyfus syndromes
Androgen antagonistic drugs
    Bicalutamide
    Cimetidine
    Cyproterone acetate
    Flutamide
    Spironolactone
Blockers of 5α-reductase
    Finasteride
Tumor-related: hCG-producing tumors (testis, lung, gastrointestinal tract, etc.)
Hypogonadotropic syndromes
Isolated gonadotropin deficiency, particularly "fertile eunuch syndrome"
Panhypopituitarism
Systemic illnesses
Renal disease
Severe liver disease

**REGULATORY HORMONE EXCESS**
Hyperthyroidism
Acromegaly
Prolactin excess
    Hypothyroidism
    Pituitary tumor
    Drug therapy with:
        Catecholamine antagonists or depleters
        Domperidone
        Haloperidol
        Methyldopa
        Metoclopramide
        Phenothiazines
        Reserpine
        Sulpiride
        Tricyclic antidepressants
Administration of growth hormone
    Cushing's syndrome

**OTHER CAUSES**
    Local trauma
    Hip spica cast
    Chest injury
    Herpes zoster of chest wall
    Post thoracotomy
    Spinal cord injury
    Primary breast tumor
Uncertain causes
Other chronic illnesses
    Renal failure
    Pulmonary tuberculosis
    HIV
    Diabetes mellitus
    Leprosy
    Refeeding gynecomastia
Persistent pubertal macromastia
Idiopathic
Drugs associated with gynecomastia with uncertain mechanisms
    Amiodarone
    Amphetamines
    Auranofin
    Beta blockers
    Calcium channel blockers
    Captopril
    Cyclosporin
    Diazepam
    Diethylproprion
    Enalapril
    Ethionamide
    Etretinate
    Griseofulvin
    Heparin
    Indinavir
    Isoniazide
    Methotrexate
    Metronidazole
    Narcotic analgesics
    Nitrates
    Omeprazole
    Penicillamine
    Phenytoin
    Quinidine
    Sulindac
    Theophyline
    Thiacetazone
    Vitamin E

Smenkhare, his grandfather Amenophis III, and his uncle Akhenaton[41] and could reflect a similar etiology. Familial gynecomastia and mental retardation also have been described in a syndrome linked to the DXS255 region of the X chromosome.[42] Gain of function mutations cause aromatase excess and gynecomastia.[43]

Other familial disorders are associated with gynecomastia and testicular tumors. The Peutz-Jeghers syndrome is associated with aromatase excess, gynecomastia, Sertoli cell tumors, pigmented lesions around the mouth, and colonic carcinoma.[44–45] The testicular tumors contain amounts of aromatase that approach the levels in placenta, whereas levels of

**Table 177-2** Aromatase-Associated Causes of Gynecomastia

I. Increased amount of aromatase enzyme
  A. Increased activity in normal tissue
    1. Obesity
    2. Aging and its associated increase in percentage of fat
  B. Aromatase Dysregulation
    1. Aromatase excess syndrome
      a. Familial
      b. Sporadic
  C. Neoplasms
    1. Eutopic production
      a. Sertoli cell tumors
        i. Isolated
        ii. Peutz-Jegher's syndrome
        iii. Carney complex
      b. Trophoblastic tumors
    2. Ectopic production
      a. Feminizing adrenocortical neoplasms
      b. Hepatocellular carcinoma
      c. Melanoma
II. Mechanism unknown
  A. Idiopthic gynecomastia
  B. Thyrotoxicosis

Adapted with permission from Braunstein GD: Aromatase and gynecomastia. Endocr Relat Cancer 6:315–324, 1999.

aromatizable substrate (i.e., testosterone and androstenedione) in testicular and peripheral vein samples are normal. The amount of aromatase enzyme present is sufficient to convert a large fraction of androgen to estrogen, resulting in estrogen excess. The Carney complex of primary, pigmented, nodular adrenal disease, myxomas, and lentigines is familial and associated with calcified Sertoli cell tumors of the testis.[46]

Several sporadic neoplasms cause gynecomastia through overexpression of aromatase. Isolated Sertoli cell and heptocellular carcinomas may overexpress aromatase, and melanomas contain aromatase and may be associated with gynecomastia.[30–32,47] Choriocarcinomas contain high levels of aromatase as well, which may add to the effects of hCG in inducing gynecomastia.

Idiopathic gynecomastia may also reflect a sporadic increase in aromatase activity. Bulard and coworkers[48] suggested that a mild increase in peripheral aromatase activity might be responsible for gynecomastia in subsets of patients with idiopathic gynecomastia. This conclusion was based on cultures of pubic skin fibroblasts and demonstration of excessive aromatase activity in this tissue. Sasano and colleagues recently provided additional evidence by demonstrating that 11 of 30 cases of gynecomastia had aromatase excess as evidenced by immunochemical assessment of biopsy tissue using a monospecific antiaromatase antibody.[49]

Recent molecular biologic data suggest mechanisms whereby aromatase can be overexpressed. The aromatase gene utilizes nine alternate promoters to regulate transcription. Multiple different enhancers interact with DNA at the promoter sites to stimulate aromatase transcription. The tumors associated with aromatase overexpression commonly utilize promoters that respond to cyclic adenosine monophosphate (cAMP) as an enhancer. Taken together, the studies on tumors suggest a common metabolic abnormality associated with activation of a cAMP-dependent signaling pathway. This gives rise to transcriptional transactivation of aromatase expression via alternate promotors I.3 and II in most tumors overexpressing aromatase.[34]

### Excess Secretion of Precursors of Aromatase
Congenital adrenal hyperplasia, as well as adrenal tumors, may produce gynecomastia through excess production of aromatizable androgens.[50–52]

## Administration of Estrogen and Its Precursors
### Estrogens
Several medications or topical creams provide estrogen or estrogenic substances for absorption and systemic action. Diethylstilbestrol (DES) given to patients with prostatic carcinoma or for other reasons produces a very high rate of gynecomastia.[53] Epidemics of gynecomastia have occurred when an excess of estrogens present in meats was ingested. Regulatory agencies inspect for illegal feeding of diethylstilbestrol or other estrogens to animals prior to slaughter.[54] However, the practice of estrogen use as an anabolic steroid continues in some areas and can result in gynecomastia if residual estrogens in meat remain sufficiently high. Inadvertent ingestion of oral contraceptives by boys from their mother's medicine supply or industrial exposure to oral contraceptives during the manufacturing process can also cause gynecomastia.[55] Other drugs such as digitoxin may have intrinsic estrogenic properties and stimulate breast enlargement.[56] Since this drug is administered to patients with severe systemic illnesses and often liver disease, other factors may be involved in the development of gynecomastia.

Environmental toxins such as embalming fluid may be estrogenic and produce gynecomastia.[57] Unintended exposure to estrogen can occur from coital exposure to women using vaginal estrogen cream or even from women using estrogen-containing cosmetics.[58] Exposure of prepubertal boys to estradiol creams utilized as a cream on their mothers' skin can cause gynecomastia.[59] In France, women distribute estrogen cream over large portions of their body as a means of transdermal estrogen delivery. Gynecomastia in the male partners of these women can occur in this instance as well.

### Estrogen Precursors
Exogenous androgens that can be converted to estrogen through aromatization are a common cause of gynecomastia. Testosterone enanthate and cypionate increase estradiol concentrations substantially[60] and commonly result in transient gynecomastia. This is most common in hypogonadal boys during testosterone treatment, but adult athletes using anabolic steroids and men receiving testosterone as a contraceptive also experience this problem.[60–61] hCG given exogenously to hypogonadal patients raises both testosterone and estradiol levels and may be associated with gynecomastia, but usually only for a transient period of several months.

## ANDROGEN DEFICIENCY

Clinical conditions associated with normal amounts of estradiol secretion but low levels of testosterone are uncommon. Hypogonadotropic patients may have incomplete gonadotropin deficiency and relatively preserved follicle-stimulating hormone (FSH) secretion. Under these circumstances, androgen secretion may be impaired to a greater extent than that of estrogen and gynecomastia may be present. More commonly, this is observed in the "fertile eunuch syndrome" of incomplete gonadotropin deficiency, but patients with panhypopituitarism also may have gynecomastia, presumably due to this mechanism.[62] Fifty percent of anorchic patients also have gynecomastia, perhaps based on absence of testicular androgens but adrenal secretion of aromatizable precursors of estrogen.[63]

## ANDROGEN/ESTROGEN IMBALANCE

### Hypogonadism
Primary gonadal disease is associated with a relative deficiency of androgen secretion and reflex rises in luteinizing hormone (LH) and FSH. The hypergonadotropism stimulates the testes to secrete an excess of estradiol. The resulting alteration of the estradiol/testosterone ratio is causative in producing gynecomastia. Klinefelter's syndrome, with an 85%

prevalence of gynecomastia, is typical of this condition.[62] These patients exhibit a reduction in total serum testosterone, a further reduction in free testosterone, and increases in plasma estradiol, LH, and FSH. All other forms of primary testicular disease, including mumps orchitis, may be associated with gynecomastia on the same basis.[64]

Cytotoxic chemotherapeutic drugs or irradiation frequently produce transient or permanent testicular dysfunction. Treatment of testicular tumors with these drugs caused gynecomastia in 10% of subjects followed prospectively. Gynecomastia after treatment of Hodgkin's disease, lymphomas, or other cancers with chemotherapeutic drugs also occurs.[65–66]

Compromise of androgen secretion on an enzymatic basis alters testosterone/estradiol ratios. Patients with congenital deficiency of 17-ketoreductase, $C_{21}$ hydroxylase, or 3β-ol-dehydrogenase/$\Delta_5$- to $\Delta_4$-isomerase may experience gynecomastia.[50–52] Drugs inhibiting testosterone biosynthesis such as the $C_{17-20}$ lyase inhibitor ketoconazole also commonly produce gynecomastia.[67]

### Androgen Resistance

A number of disorders and drugs result in a lack of tissue responsiveness to androgen.[67–69] Since androgens are generally inhibitory to breast development, these conditions are associated with gynecomastia. In the most extreme instance, complete androgen resistance results in the development of normal to greater than normal breast tissue in a genetic male. Since the hypothalamus and pituitary are also resistant to androgens, LH and testosterone are elevated, resulting in increased estradiol, the aromatized product of testosterone. The combination of estrogen excess and androgen resistance results in the degree of breast development that occurs. In syndromes of partial androgen resistance,[62] a lesser degree of gynecomastia occurs from similar mechanisms. Cloning and sequencing of the androgen receptor have enabled the detection of specific molecular defects in patients with these disorders.[62] Another form of androgen resistance is the Kennedy syndrome, in which the diagnosis is usually delayed until the third to fifth decade. Features include gynecomastia, androgen resistance, androgen receptor mutations, and neurodegenerative findings of symmetrical muscular atrophy, weakness, and fasciculations of the bulbar, facial, and proximal muscles of the extremities.[70]

Several drugs are capable of blocking the tissue effects of androgens by binding to the androgen receptor.[68–69] These agents may also block androgen effects in two other ways: by reducing the inhibitory effects of androgen on breast tissue; and by interrupting negative feedback with resulting increments in LH, testosterone, and the latter's aromatized product, estradiol. Cimetidine acts in this fashion, as do spironolactone, bicalutamide,[71] and flutamide. Recent reports indicate a substantial incidence of gynecomastia in men with prostate cancer treated with flutamide, particularly when given in combination with the 5α-reductase inhibitor finasteride. Androgen resistance induced by the blockade of conversion of testosterone to dihydrotestosterone can by itself also cause gynecomastia.[72] Cyproterone acetate acts predominantly as an antiandrogen, since its progestational actions prevent the reflex rise in LH.[73] Marijuana has also been associated with gynecomastia.[74]

### Systemic Illness

Several systemic illnesses produce gynecomastia through an endocrine mechanism. Patients with chronic renal failure manifest hypogonadal signs and symptoms. Endocrine evaluation reveals high prolactin levels, moderate elevations of LH and FSH, reductions in testosterone levels, and increments in estradiol.[75] These changes reflect several pathophysiologic abnormalities, including delayed peptide hormone clearance, altered gonadotropin negative-feedback set point, and

perhaps primary gonadal dysfunction. This constellation of abnormalities frequently results in chronic gynecomastia.

Chronic liver disease also produces gynecomastia through a number of mechanisms.[76] Increased aromatization of androgens to estrogens occurs in the liver. Alcohol ingestion damages testicular steroidogenic capacity, and a state of hypergonadotropic hypogonadism can ensue. Acute alterations in nutritional state and ingestion of drugs such as spironolactone can further contribute to the gynecomastia. Even though liver disease is commonly believed to cause gynecomastia, one study found gynecomastia as frequently in hospitalized patients with liver disease as in those without.[77]

### REGULATORY HORMONE ABNORMALITIES

Prolactin secretion is modulated by central aminergic neuronal pathways, particularly of the dopaminergic variety. A wide range of drugs with catecholamine antagonistic or depleting actions can stimulate prolactin release. It is unlikely that prolactin alone causes gynecomastia, since many men with very high prolactin levels lack this finding.[78] Prolactin elevations, however, result in reductions of gonadotropin-releasing hormone (GnRH), LH, and testosterone and can alter the balance between testosterone and estradiol. It is in this setting that gynecomastia occurs. While these putative mechanisms are not fully substantiated, a number of drugs with catecholamine-related properties are associated with gynecomastia (see Table 177-1). Prolactin-producing pituitary tumors (i.e., prolactinomas) may also cause gynecomastia through similar mechanisms. Hypothyroidism is another cause of increased prolactin and of gynecomastia. Reductions in serum thyroxine result in an increase in the secretion of thyrotropin-releasing hormone (TRH) and in thyroid-stimulating hormone (TSH). If sufficiently high, TRH can stimulate prolactin as well as TSH secretion through its "cross-talk" properties.

Hyperthyroidism may present with or be associated with breast tenderness and gynecomastia.[79–81] Thyroxine stimulates the production of sex hormone–binding globulin (SHBG), which binds plasma estradiol and increases total serum levels. Because the affinity of SHBG for estradiol is less than that for testosterone, increased estradiol may be available to tissue as a cause of gynecomastia in hyperthyroid men. Increased aromatization of androgens to estrogens also accounts for the increased estradiol levels.[82] In acromegaly, partial gonadotropin deficiency is frequently present. Increased lactotrophic activity (both from growth hormone itself and from the increase in prolactin that occurs in 50% of patients) may contribute to the presence of gynecomastia.

Cushing's syndrome causes gynecomastia, which is probably mediated by several mechanisms. Glucocorticoids directly interfere with testosterone synthesis and induce a state of relative hypogonadism. The increased adipose mass may cause enhanced aromatase activity. Increased aromatizable substrates from the adrenal might also contribute to an increase in local breast or systemic aromatization. Administration of combined IGF-1 and human growth hormone results in gynecomastia as a side effect.

### OTHER CAUSES

#### Drug-Induced

A number of drugs are reported to cause gynecomastia.[83] Documentation does not always involve drug rechallenge, and the causative nature of these associations is not always valid. This review lists several drugs as falling into specific pathophysiologic categories and others whose mechanism is not known (see Tables 177-1 and 177-2).

#### Local Trauma

Trauma to the chest wall is often considered a cause of gynecomastia, although an etiologic relationship is difficult to prove. In 20 of 21 patients of Greene and Howard, unilateral gynecomastia followed unilateral trauma.[84] Traumatic gynecomastia has been reported after thoracotomy, in army recruits wearing military packs, in patients with hip spica casts irritating the chest wall, after herpes zoster infection of the chest wall, and after local chest wall irradiation.[85] Macrophages have recently been shown to contain large amounts of aromatase, which could mediate local formation of estrogen in the breast in response to trauma.[86] Spinal cord injuries may also be associated with gynecomastia.[87]

### Primary Breast Tumor

Carcinoma of the breast occurs in men with 1/100th the frequency observed in women. The firm, irregular, and unilateral nature of the lesion raises suspicion of this diagnosis. Ultrasonography, mammography, and fine-needle aspiration or core biopsy provide means to make the diagnosis if suspected.[88-92] The frequency of breast cancer is increased in patients with Klinefelter's syndrome and gynecomastia,[92] although this has been recently questioned.[92a] A benign tumor of the breast, myofibroblastoma, has been reported in association with bilateral gynecomastia.

### UNCERTAIN CAUSES

After World War II, starved prisoners developed gynecomastia upon refeeding. Starvation suppresses gonadotropin production, and refeeding allows return to normal function. The recovery phase mimics the changes that occur during early puberty. The gynecomastia that ensues is probably also similar to pubertal gynecomastia. This form of gynecomastia is quite frequent and affects patients recovering from chronic illnesses associated with undernutrition. This mechanism is probably responsible for the gynecomastia observed in certain patients with diabetes mellitus, tuberculosis, and perhaps also those with leprosy.[93-94] The finding of gynecomastia in patients with an human immunodeficiency virus (HIV) infection may also fall into this category.[95-96] Men with diabetes mellitus occasionally develop gynecomastia associated with a fibrous inflammatory reaction. Its histopathologic characteristics are a marked chronic periductal and perivascular mastitis with a predominance of B lymphocytes, focal fibrosis, and "epithelioid stromal fibrosis."[97]

### Pubertal Macromastia

The gynecomastia occurring normally at puberty is mild to moderate in degree (i.e., Tanner stage II) and usually resolves spontaneously.[98] Boys with a greater than usual degree of pubertal gynecomastia (i.e., Tanner stages III, IV, and V) experience persistence after puberty. Extensive evaluation usually reveals no hormonal abnormality, and the only effective therapy is surgical. A comprehensive report describes the evaluation of 60 boys with this condition and provides a guide to the frequency of findings. Of the 60 patients, 45 were found to have idiopathic gynecomastia, 8 to have underlying medical disorders (5 neurologic), and 7 to have an endocrine abnormality including the XXY and XY forms of Klinefelter's syndrome, primary testicular failure, partial androgen insensitivity, hepatocellular carcinoma, and increased aromatase activity.[99]

### IDIOPATHIC

The majority of patients referred to an endocrinologist on an outpatient basis will fall into the idiopathic category after careful endocrinologic evaluation.[100] Whether these patients have increased local aromatization of androgens to estrogens in breast tissue, as suggested by Bulard and colleagues,[48] or other causes is unknown.

The study of Carlson[11] provides a guide to expected findings on an inpatient consultation service. He evaluated 68 patients at the Wadsworth Veterans Administration Hospital and found that drugs in conjunction with other illnesses were implicated in 22 and drugs alone in another 20. Other associated conditions included liver disease in nine, refeeding in three, hypogonadism in two, and other miscellaneous disorders (male climacteric, sarcoma, hyperthyroidism, and persistent pubertal gynecomastia) in five. Seven patients were considered to have idiopathic gynecomastia.

### EVALUATION

The clinician must decide when and how extensively to evaluate men with gynecomastia, a condition found in approximately 50% of hospitalized patients.[11-13] Clear indications for extensive evaluation include breast tenderness, rapid enlargement, and eccentric or hard, irregular masses and lesions greater than 4 cm in diameter. Asymptomatic, stable gynecomastia less than 5 cm in diameter, particularly in obese patients, probably requires only a careful history and physical examination for evaluation. In lean subjects, gynecomastia with a breast diameter of 2 to 4 cm should probably be evaluated more extensively.

The appropriate technique for physical examination to detect gynecomastia includes pinching the tissue between thumb and forefinger lateral to the nipple. Ability to "flip an edge" of tissue at the interface of normal and glandular tissue confirms the presence of gynecomastia. Comparison of consistency with that of the fat tissue over the abdomen or along the axillary line is useful. Palpation of tissue with the fingers by pressing over the nipple or lateral to it is an insensitive technique. Mammograms or ultrasound[18-20] can be used to distinguish the presence of fat (pseudogynecomastia) from glandular tissue (see Fig. 177-4). Firm, irregular lesions raise concern about neoplasm, which should be excluded, usually by excisional biopsy.

A detailed medical history directs attention to the following: (1) the time of onset, rate of progression, and degree of pain associated with the gynecomastia; (2) symptoms of androgen deficiency; (3) use of medications and drugs; (4) the presence of diabetes, systemic renal, hepatic, cardiac, or pulmonary disease, and particularly previous malnutrition due to other disorders; (5) symptoms of underlying malignancy, especially testicular; (6) symptoms associated with estradiol, prolactin, growth hormone, cortisol, or thyroxine excess; (7) a history of chest trauma; and (8) family history of gynecomastia. On physical examination, the examiner distinguishes pseudo- from true gynecomastia; determines the percentage of ideal body weight, detects signs of hypogonadism, palpates the testes carefully, and examines for evidence of chronic disease and signs of Cushing's syndrome, hyperthyroidism, acromegaly, and prolactinoma.

If the initial evaluation is unrevealing, and pathologic gynecomastia is present, routine tests in all patients include DHEA-S, estradiol, LH, β-hCG, testosterone, and thyroid function tests. Patients with physiologic gynecomastia are usually followed for 6 months to determine if there is progression in diameter of the palpable breast tissue. If so, the extensive evaluation listed is performed; see Figure 177-4 for an outline of the further studies to be obtained when abnormalities are detected on initial screening and with the resulting diagnoses. The large majority of subjects evaluated in the outpatient setting will fall into the idiopathic category based on results from hormonal evaluation.

### TREATMENT

Management of gynecomastia depends on the clinical circumstances, severity, and presence of pain. The first principle is to stop offending drugs and treat any specific abnormality amenable to therapy. The clinician can reassure boys with pubertal gynecomastia that regression usually occurs after 1 year and at most after 3 years.[3-4] Medical therapy produces reduction in size in a substantial fraction of patients.[101-123] Three nonrandomized studies reported a greater than 20% decrease in size associated with use of the antiestrogen clomiphene citrate in 39 of 53 subjects (74%), but 16 still went on to surgery.[106-108] Two studies reported that the non-aromatizable androgen dihydrotestosterone produced a reduction in 28 of 34 subjects (82%).[113-114] One study examined the effect of danazol on 11 subjects and noted marked or moderate reduction of breast tissue in 10.[111] Finally, the use of the aromatase inhibitor testololactone was associated with reduction in mean breast diameter from 4.4 to 1.7 cm in 20 of 22 subjects.[109]

These studies require cautious interpretation since pubertal gynecomastia resolves spontaneously and placebo controls were not used. As a reflection of this caution, a recent randomized trial compared the aromatase inhibitor anastrozole with placebo in 80 boys with pubertal gynecomastia. The percentage of patients with a response was 38.5% with anastrozole and 31.4% with placebo ($P$ = ns). While the testosterone/estradiol ratio increased to 166% for the anastrozole group, no statistically significant improvement in any parameter was reported in anastrozole-treated patients.[124] This study utilized state-of-the-art methods for conducting a clinical trial and emphasizes the need for a placebo control in any studies of gynecomastia.

Based on these existing data, a prudent approach is to observe for regression and only use medical therapy as a temporizing measure if breast size is substantial, pain is present, or the patient and parents do not elect surgical therapy. While not directly compared, current data would support use of antiestrogens rather than aromatase inhibitors for this purpose. When breast tissue diameter is greater than 5.0 cm and persists for longer than 3 years (persistent pubertal gynecomastia), the only therapeutic option is surgical excision.

In adult men with gynecomastia, specific therapy for causative problems should be used when feasible, and offending drugs discontinued when possible.[125] In men with idiopathic gynecomastia, carefully controlled, randomized studies of medical therapy are limited. Two studies compared tamoxifen with placebo and detected a reduction in size in 10 of 16 men (62%) receiving drug and 1 of 16 with placebo. Pain relief occurred in 9 of 10 men on tamoxifen and 1 of 10 with placebo.[101-102] Three noncontrolled trials reported 6 of 16 (37%) subjects with size reduction and 13 of 15 (87%) with pain relief.[103-105] Two nonrandomized studies examined the effects of danazol in 32 men and found an objective reduction in size in 20 (62%).[111-112] Another study of 55 men receiving danazol reported a significant reduction in mean diameter from 3.70 to 2.05 ($P$ < 0.05).[110] An unpublished study using testololactone found a 47% decrease in mean breast diameter at 6 months in four patients with idiopathic gynecomastia ($P$ < 0.05).[123] Interpretation of these results requires two caveats. One, the studies were not placebo controlled and spontaneous regressions can occur. Two, only the early phase of gynecomastia with glandular and not stromal predominance would be expected to respond to hormonal therapies. The nonaromatizable androgen dihydrotestosterone has been reported to be effective for treating gynecomastia, but experience is limited.[96,113,114]

Based on these data, a trial of tamoxifen may be warranted in patients with recent onset idiopathic gynecomastia. With persistence of glandular enlargement or pain, reduction mammoplasty is occasionally necessary. A highly experienced surgeon should perform this procedure because of the precise sculpturing necessary to produce the desired cosmetic effects.

Treatment of prostate cancer with estrogens, estrogen-containing herbal preparations, or antiandrogens is frequently associated with gynecomastia.[126] A time-honored method of management is to pretreat with low-dose irradiation, which reduces the incidence of gynecomastia and lessens the symptoms.[127]

## REFERENCES

1. Russo J and Santen RJ: Hormonal control of breast development. In DeGroot LJ, Jameson JL (eds): Endocrinology, 4th ed. Philadelphia, WB Saunders, 2004, pp 2181–2188.
2. Casey RW, Wilson JD: Antiestrogenic action of dihydrotestosterone in mouse breast: Competition with estradiol for binding to the estrogen receptor. J Clin Invest 74:2272, 1984.
3. Nydick M, Bustos J, Dale JH Jr, Rawson RW: Gynecomastia in adolescent boys. JAMA 178:449, 1961.
4. Biro FM, Lucky AW, Huster GA, Morrison JA: Hormonal studies and physical maturation in adolescent gynecomastia. J Pediatr 116:450, 1990.
5. Lee PA: The relationship of concentrations of serum hormones to pubertal gynecomastia. J Pediatr 86:212, 1975.
6. LaFranchi SH, Parlow AF, Luppe BM, et al: Pubertal gynecomastia and transient elevation of serum estradiol level. Am J Dis Child 129:927, 1975.
7. Knorr D, Bidlingmaier F: Gynecomastia in male adolescents. J Clin Endocrinol Metab 4:157, 1975.
8. Large DM, Anderson DC: Twenty-four hour profiles of circulating androgens and estrogens in male puberty with and without gynecomastia. Clin Endocrinol (Oxf) 11:505, 1979.
9. Moore DC, Schlaepfor LV, Paunier L, Sizonenko PC: Hormonal changes during puberty: V. Transient pubertal gynecomastia: Abnormal androgen-estrogen ratios. J Clin Endocrinol Metab 58:492, 1984.
10. Nuttal FQ: Gynecomastia as a physical finding in normal men. J Clin Endocrinol Metab 48:338, 1979.
11. Carlson HE: Current concepts: Gynecomastia. N Engl J Med 303:795, 1980.
12. Ley SB, Mozaffarian GA, Leonard JM, et al: Palpable breast tissue versus gynecomastia as a normal physical finding. Clin Res 28:24A, 1980.
13. Niewoehner CB, Nuttal FQ: Gynecomastia in a hospitalized male population. Am J Med 77:633, 1984.
14. Mandava U, Kirma N, Tekmal RR: Aromatase overexpression transgenic mice model: Cell type specific expression and use of letrozole to abrogate mammary hyperplasia without affecting physiology. J Steroid Biochem Mol Biol 79:27–34, 2001.
15. Li X, Warri A, Makela S, et al: Mammary gland development in transgenic male mice expressing human P450 aromatase. Endocrinology 143:4074–4083, 2002.
16. Andersen JA, Gram JB: Male breast at autopsy. Acta Pathol Microbiol Immunol Scand 90:191, 1982.
17. Sandison AT: An autopsy study of the adult human breast. Natl Cancer Inst Monogr 8:77, 1962.
18. Dershaw DD: Male mammography. Am J Roentgenol 146:127, 1986.
19. Rissanen TJ, Makarainen HP, Kallionen MJ, et al: Radiology of the male breast in gynecomastia. Acta Radiologica 33:110, 1992.
20. Appelbaum AH, Evans GF, Levy KR, et al: Mammographic appearances of male breast tissue. Radiographics 19:559–568, 1999.
21. Jackson VP, Gilmore RL: Male breast carcinoma and gynecomastia: Comparison of mammography with sonography. Radiology 149:533, 1986.
22. Gunhan-Bilgen I, Bozkaya H, Ustun EE, Memis A: Male breast disease: Clinical, mammographic, and ultrasonographic features. Eur J Radiol 43:246–255, 2002.
23. Weinstein SP, Conant EF, Orel SG, et al: Spectrum of U.S. findings in pediatric and adolescent patients with palpable breast masses. Radiographics 20:1613–1621, 2000.
24. Evans GF, Anthony T, Turnage RH, et al: The diagnostic accuracy of mammography in the evaluation of

male breast disease. Am J Surg 181:96–100, 2001.

25. Kuhn JM, Lefebvre H, Duparc C, et al: Cosecretion of estrogen and inhibin B by a feminizing adrenocortical adenoma: Impact on gonadotropin secretion. J Clin Endocrinol Metab 87:2367–2375, 2002.

26. Bouraima H, Lireux B, Mittre H, et al: Major hyperestrogenism in a feminizing adrenocortical adenoma despite a moderate overexpression of the aromatase enzyme. Eur J Endocrinol 148:457–461, 2003.

27. Morio H, Terano T, Yamamoto K, et al: Serum levels of dehydroepiandrosterone sulfate in patients with asymptomatic cortisol producing adrenal adenoma: Comparison with adrenal Cushing's syndrome and non-functional adrenal tumor. Endocr J 43:387–396, 1996.

28. Anderson MS, Brogi E, Biller BM: Occult Leydig cell tumor in a patient with gynecomastia. Endocr Pract 7:267–271, 2001.

29. Daniels IR, Layer GT: Testicular tumours presenting as gynecomastia. Eur J Surg Oncol 29:437–439, 2003.

30. Gabrilove JL, Nicholis GL, Mitty HA, et al: Feminizing interstitial cell tumor of the testis: Personal observations and a review of the literature. Cancer 38:1184, 1975.

31. Hendry WS, Garvie WHH, Ah-See AK, et al: Ultrasonic detection of occult testicular neoplasms in patients with gynaecomastia. Br J Radiol 57:571, 1984.

32. Kuhn JM, Mahoudeau JA, Billaud L, et al: Evaluation of diagnostic criteria for Leydig cell tumours in adult men revealed by gynaecomastia. Clin Endocrinol (Oxf) 26:407, 1987.

33. Whitcomb RW, Schimke RN, Kyner JL, et al: Endocrine studies in a male patient with choriocarcinoma and gynecomastia. Am J Med 81:917, 1986.

34. Bulun SE, Noble LS, Takayama K, et al: Endocrine disorders associated with inappropriately high aromatase expression. J Steroid Biochem Mol Biol 61:133, 1997.

35. Schneider G, Kirschner MA, Berkowitz R, Ertel NH: Increased estrogen production in obese men. J Clin Endocrinol Metab 48:633, 1979.

36. Southren AL, Olivo J, Gordan GG, et al: The conversion of androgens to estrogens in hyperthyroidism. J Clin Endocrinol Metab 38:207, 1974.

37. Cleland WH, Mendelson CR, Simpson ER: Effects of aging and obesity on aromatase activity of human adipose cells. J Clin Endocrinol Metab 60:174, 1985.

38. Hemsell DL, Edman CD, Marks JF, et al: Massive extraglandular aromatization of plasma androstenedione resulting in feminization of a prepubertal boy. J Clin Invest 60:455, 1977.

39. Berkowitz GD, Gerami A, Brown TR, et al: Familial gynecomastia with increased extraglandular aromatization of plasma carbon 19-steroid. J Clin Invest 75:1763, 1985.

40. Stratakis CA, Vottero A, Brodie A, et al: The aromatase excess syndrome is associated with feminization of both sexes and autosomal dominant transmission of aberrant P450 aromatase gene transcription. J Clin Endocrinol Metab 83:1348, 1998.

41. Paulshock BZ: Tutankhamen and his brothers: Familial gynecomastia in the eighteenth dynasty. JAMA 244:160, 1980.

42. Wilson M, Mulley J, Gedeon A, et al: New X-linked syndrome of mental retardation, gynecomastia, and obesity is linked to DXS255. Am J Med Gen 40:406, 1991.

43. Shozu M, Sebastian S, Takayama K, et al: Estrogen excess associated with novel gain of function mutations affecting the aromatase gene. N Engl J Med 348:1855–1865, 2003.

44. Coen P, Kulin H, Ballantine T, et al: An aromatase-producing sex-cord tumor resulting in prepubertal gynecomastia. N Engl J Med 324:317–322, 1991.

45. Hertl MC, Wiebel J, Schafer H, et al: Feminizing Sertoli cell tumors associated with Peutz-Jeghers syndrome—an increasingly recognized cause of prepubertal gynecomastia. Plast Reconstr Surg 102:1151, 1998.

46. Carney JA, Young WF Jr: Primary pigmented nodular adrenocortical disease and its associated conditions. Endocrinologist 2:6, 1992.

47. Agarwal VR, Takayama K, Van Wyk JJ, et al: Molecular basis of severe gynecomastia associated with aromatase expression in a fibrolamellar hepatocellular carcinoma. J Clin Endocrinol Metab 83:1797, 1998.

48. Bulard J, Mowszkowicz I, Schaison G: Increased aromatase activity in pubic skin fibroblasts from patients with isolated gynecomastia. J Clin Endocrinol Metab 64:618, 1987.

49. Sasano H, Kimura M, Shizawa S, et al: Aromatase and steroid receptors in gynecomastia and male breast carcinoma: An immunohistochemical study. J Clin Endocrinol Metab 81:3063, 1996.

50. Maclaren NK, Migeon CJ, Raiti S: Gynecomastia with congenital virilizing adrenal hyperplasia (11β-hydroxylase deficiency). J Pediatr 86:579, 1975.

51. Kadair RG, Block MB, Katz FH, et al: "Masked" 21-hydroxylase deficiency of the adrenal presenting with gynecomastia and bilateral testicular masses. Am J Med 62:278, 1977.

52. Frank-Raue K, Raue F, Korth-Schutz S, et al: Clinical features and diagnosis of mild 3-beta-hydroxysteroid dehydrogenase deficiency in men. Dtsch Med Wochenschr 114:331, 1989.

53. Hendrickson DA, Anderson WR: Diethylstilbesterol therapy: Gynecomastia. JAMA 213:468, 1970.

54. Henricks DM, Gray SL, Hoover JLB: Residue levels of endogenous estrogens in beef tissues. J Anim Sci 57:247, 1983.

55. Harrington JM, Stein GF, Rivera RO, et al: The occupational hazards of formulating oral contraceptives: A survey of plant employees. Arch Environ Health 33:12–15, 1978.

56. Rifka SM, Pita JC, Vigersky RA, et al: Interaction of digitalis and spironolactone with human sex steroid receptors. J Clin Endocrinol Metab 46:338, 1977.

57. Finkelstein JS, McCully WF, MacLaughlin DT, et al: The mortician's mystery: Gynecomastia and reversible hypogonadotropic hypogonadism in an embalmer. N Engl J Med 318:961, 1988.

58. DeRaimondo CV, Roach AC, Meador CK: Gynecomastia from exposure to vaginal estrogen cream. N Engl J Med 302:1089, 1980.

59. Felner EI, White PC: Prepubertal gynecomastia: Indirect exposure to estrogen cream Pediatrics 105:E55, 2000.

60. Wu FCW, Farley TMM, Peregoudov A, et al: Effects of testosterone enanthate in normal men: Experience from a multicenter contraceptive efficacy study. World Health Organization Task Force on Methods for the Regulation of Male Fertility. Fertil Steril 65:626–636, 1996.

61. Babigian A, Silverman RT: Management of gynecomastia due to use of anabolic steroids in bodybuilders. Plast Reconstr Surg 107:240–242, 2001.

62. Santen RJ: The testis: Function and dysfunction. In Yen SSC, Jaffe R, Barbieri R: Reproductive Endocrinology: Physiology, Pathophysiology, and Clinical Management, 4th ed. Philadelphia, WB Saunders, 1999, pp 632–668.

63. Mathur R, Braunstein GD: Review. Gynecomastia: Pathomechanisms and treatment strategies. Hormone Res 48:95–102, 1997.

64. Aiman J, Brenner PF, MacDonald PC: Androgen and estrogen production in elderly men with gynecomastia and testicular atrophy after mumps orchitis. J Clin Endocrinol Metab 50:380, 1980.

65. Aki FT, Tekin MI, Ozen H: Gynecomastia as a complication of chemotherapy for testicular germ cell tumors. Urology 48:944, 1996.

66. Harris E, Mahendra P, McGarrigle HH, el al: Gynaecomastia with hypergonadotropic hypogonadism and Leydig cell insufficiency in recipients of high-dose chemotherapy or chemoradiotherapy. Bone Marrow Transplant 28:1141–1144, 2001.

67. Feldman D: Ketoconazole and other imidazole derivatives as inhibitors of steroidogenesis. Endocr Rev 7:409, 1986.

68. Jensen RT, Collen MJ, Pandol SJ, et al: Cimetidine-induced impotence and breast changes in patients with gastric hypersecretory states. N Engl J Med 308:883, 1983.

69. Caminos-Torres R, Ma L, Snyder PJ: Gynecomastia and semen abnormalities induced by spironolactone in normal men. J Clin Endocrinol Metab 5:255, 1977.

70. Berkhoff M, Sturzenegger M, Spiegel R, et al: X-linked bulbospinal muscular atrophy (Kennedy's disease). Schweiz Med Wochenschr 128:817, 1998.

71. Widmark A, Fossa SD, Lundmo P, et al: Does prophylactic breast irradiation prevent antiandrongen induced gynecomastia? Evaluation of 253 patients in the randomized Scandanavian trial SPCG-7/SFUO-3. Urology 61:145–161, 2003.

72. Carlin BI, Seftel AD, Resnick MI, Findlay J: Finasteride induced gynecomastia. J Urol 158:547, 1997.

73. Geller J, Vazakas G, Fruchtman B, et al: The effect of cyproterone acetate on advanced carcinoma of the prostate. Surg Gynecol Obstet 127:748, 1968.

74. Harmon JW, Aliapoulios MA: Marijuana-induced gynecomastia: Clinical and laboratory experience. Surg Forum 25:423, 1974.

75. Emmanouel DS, Lindheimer MD, Katz Al: Pathogenesis of endocrine abnormalities in uremia. Endocr Rev 1:28, 1980.

76. Baker HWG, Burger HG, deKretser DM, et al: A study of the endocrine manifestations of hepatic cirrhosis. Q J Med 45(NS):145, 1976.

77. Cavanaugh J, Niewoehner CB, Nuttal FQ: Gynecomastia and cirrhosis of the liver. Arch Intern Med 150:563, 1990.

78. Frantz AG, Wilson JD: Endocrine disorders of the breast. In Wilson JD, Foster DW (eds): Williams Textbook of Endocrinology, 8th ed. Philadelphia, WB Saunders, 1992, p 953.

79. Becker KL, Winnacker JL, Matthews MJ, et al: Gynecomastia and hyperthyroidism: An endocrine and histological investigation. J Clin Endocrinol 28:227, 1968.

80. Tan YK, Birch CR, Valerio D: Bilateral gynecomastia as the primary complaint in hyperthyroidism. J R Coll Surg Edinb 46:176–177, 2001.

81. Chan WB, Yeung VT, Chow CC, et al: Gyaenecomastia as a presenting feature of thyrotoxicosis. Postgrad Med J 75:229–231, 1999.

82. Southren AL, Olivo J, Gordon GG, et al: The conversion of androgens to estrogens in hyperthyroidism. J Clin Endocrinol Metab 38:207, 1974.

83. Thompson DF, Carter JR: Drug induced gynecomastia. Pharmacotherapy 13:37, 1993.

84. Greene WW, Howard NJ: Relationship of trauma to lesions of male breast. Am J Surg 85:431, 1953.

85. Field JB, Solis RT, Dear WE: Case report: Unilateral gynecomastia associated with thoracotomy following resection of carcinoma of the lung. Am J Med Sci 298:402, 1989.

86. Mor G, Yue W, Santen RJ, et al: Macrophages, estrogen and the microenvironment of breast cancer. J Steroid Biochem Mol Biol 67:403–411, 1998.

87. Heruti RJ, Dankner R, Berezin M, et al: Gynecomastia following spinal cord disorder. Arch Phys Med Rehabil 78:534, 1997.

88. Westenend PJ, Jobse C: Evaluation of fine needle aspiration cytology of breast masses in males. Cancer 96:101–104, 2002.

89. Olsson H, Bladstrom A, Alm P: Male gynecomastia and risk of malignant tumors: A cohort study. BMC Cancer 2:26, 2002.

90. Kapila K, Verma K: Cytomorphological spectrum in gynaecomastia: A study of 389 cases. Cytopathology 13:300–308, 2002.

91. Volpe CM, Raffetto JD, Collure DW, et al: Unilateral male breast masses: Cancer risk and their evaluation and management. Am Surg 65:250–253, 1999.

92. van Geel AN, van Slooten EA, Mavrunac M, Hart AAM: A retrospective study of male breast cancer in Holland. Br J Surg 72:724, 1985.

92a. Hasle H, Mellemgaard A, Neilsen J, Hansen J: Cancer incidence in men with Klinefelter syndrome. Br J Cancer 71:416–420, 1995.

93. Zurbiran S, Gomez-Mont F: Endocrine disturbances in chronic human malnutrition. Vitam Horm 11:97, 1953.

94. Morely JE, Distiller LA, Sagel J, et al: Hormonal changes associated with testicular atrophy and gynecomastia in patients with leprosy. Clin Endocrinol (Oxf) 6:299, 1977.

95. Toma E, Therrien R: Gynecomastia during indinavir antiretroviral therapy in HIV infection. AIDS 12:681, 1998.

96. Beneveniste O, Simon A, Herson S: Successful percutaneous dihydrotestosterone treatment of gynecomastia occurring during highly active antiretroviral therapy: Four cases and a review of the literature. Clin Infect Dis 33:891–893, 2001.

97. Hunfield KP, Basler R, Kronsbein H: Diabetic mastopathy in the male breast—a special type of gynecomastia: A comparative study of lymphocytic mastitis and gynecomastia. Pathol Res Pract 193:197, 1997.

98. Lazala C, Saenger P: Pubertal gynecomastia. J Pediatr Endocrinol Metab 15: 553–560, 2002.

99. Sher ES, Migeon CJ, Berkovitz GD: Evaluation of boys with marked breast development at puberty. Clin Pediatr 37:367, 1998.

100. Ersoz H, Onde ME, Terekeci H, et al: Causes of gynecomastia in young males and factors associated with idiopathic gynecomastia. Int J Androl 25:312–316, 2002.

101. McDermott MT, Hofeldt FD, Kidd GS: Tamoxifen therapy for painful idiopathic gynecomastia. South Med J 83:1283, 1990.

102. Parker LN, Gray DR, Lai MK, Levin ER: Treatment of gynecomastia with tamoxifen: A double-blind crossover study. Metabolism 35:705, 1986.

103. Fairlamb D, Boesen E: Gynaecomastia associated with gonadotropin-secreting carcinoma of the lung. Postgrad Med J 53:269, 1977.

104. Jefferys DB: Painful gynaecomastia treated with tamoxifen. Br Med J 1:1119, 1979.

105. Eversmann T, Moito J, von Werder K: Testosteron- und Ostradiolspiegel bei der gynakomastie des mannes. Dtsch Med Wochenschr 109:1678, 1984.

106. Stepanas AV, Burnet RB, Harding PE, Wise PH: Clomiphene in the treatment of pubertal-adolescent gynecomastia: A preliminary report. J Pediatr 90:651, 1977.

107. Plourde PV, Kulin HE, Santner SJ: Clomiphene in the treatment of adolescent gynecomastia. Am J Dis Child 137:1080, 1983.

108. LeRoith D, Sobel R, Glick SM: The effect of clomiphene citrate on pubertal gynaecomastia. Acta Endocrinol (Copenh) 95:177, 1980.

109. Zachmann M, Eiholzer U, Muritano M, et al: Treatment of pubertal gynaecomastia with testolactone. Acta Endocrinol (Copenh) 279:218, 1986.

110. Jones DJ, Davison DJ, Holt SD, et al: A comparison of danazol and placebo in the treatment of adult idiopathic gynaecomastia: Results of a prospective study in 55 patients. Ann R Coll Surg Engl 72:296, 1990.

111. Buckle R: Danazol therapy in gynaecomastia: Recent experience and indications for therapy. Postgrad Med J 55:71, 1979.

112. Hughes LE, Mansel RE, Webster DJT: The male breast. In Benign Disorders and Disease of the Breast. London, Bailliere Tindall, 1989, p 167.

113. Eberle AJ, Sparrow JT, Keenan BS: Treatment of persistent pubertal gynecomastia with dihydrotestosterone heptanoate. Adolesc Med 109:144, 1986.

114. Kuhn JM, Laudat MH, Roca R, et al: Gynecomasties: Effet due traitement prolonge par la dihydrotestosterone par voie per-cutanee. Presse Med 8:21, 1983.

115. Alagaratnam TT: Treating pubertal gynecomastia. J R Coll Gen Pract 37:178, 1987.

116. Konig R, Schonberger W, Neumann P, et al: Treatment of marked gynecomastia in puberty with tamoxifen. Klin Padiatr 199:389–391, 1987.

117. McDermott M, Hofeldt F, Kidd G: Tamoxifen therapy for painful idiopathic gynecomastia. South Med J 83:1283–1285, 1990.

118. Staiman VR, Lowe FC: Tamoxifen for flutamide/finasteride induced gynecomastia. Urology 50:929–933, 1997.

119. Serels S, Melman A: Tamoxifen as treatment for gynecomastia and mastodynia resulting from hormonal deprivation J Urol 159:1309, 1998.

120. Ting AC, Chow LW, Leung YF: Comparison of tamoxifen with danazol in the management of gynecomastia. Ann Surg 66:38–40, 2000.

121. Beck W, Stubbe P: Excessive gynecomastia in boys: Effective medical treatment using danazol. Monatsschr Kinderheilkd 132:32–37, 1984.

122. Swoboda W, Bohrn E: Steroid treatment of adolescent gynecomastia with danazol. Wien Med Wochenschr 131:127–132, 1981.

123. Braunstein GD: Aromatase and gynecomastia. Endocr Relat Cancer 6:315–324, 1999.

124. Plourde PV, Reiter EO, Hann-Chang J, et al: Safety and efficacy of anastrozole for the treatment of pubertal gynecomastia: A randomized, double blind, placebo controlled trial. J Clin Endocrinol Metab 89:4428–4433, 2004.

125. Gruntmanis U: Treatment of gynecomastia. Curr Opin Investig Drugs 2:643, 2001.

126. Small EJ, Frohlich MW, Bok R, et al: Prospective trial of the herbal supplement PC-SPES in patients with progressive prostate cancer. J Clin Oncol 18:3395–3603, 2000.

127. Dicker PA: The safety and tolerability of low-dose irradiation for the management of gynaecomastia caused by antiandrogen monotherapy. Lancet Oncol 4:30–36, 2003.

# Physiology and Pathophysiology of Androgenetic Alopecia

## Valerie Anne Randall

Androgenetic alopecia, the most frequently occurring form of balding, involves the progressive loss of clearly visible hair on the scalp, particularly in men, in response to circulating androgens. It is also known as male pattern baldness, common baldness, male pattern alopecia, and androgen-dependent alopecia; to the layperson, it is often simply "balding." There are also a range of other nonendocrine causes of scalp baldness or alopecia that can occur in both sexes as well as children; the most common, alopecia areata, a patchy baldness of the scalp or body, which may progress to total scalp or body hair loss, is generally believed to be an autoimmune disease. These fall outside the scope of this book, but have been described elsewhere.[1–3]

Although androgenetic alopecia occurs very frequently and is not life threatening, it has been regarded as an important disorder for many years; the anxieties suffered by ancient Egyptian men were recorded on papyrus 4000 years ago,[4] and Aristotle discussed the importance of "maleness" and the testes in developing androgenetic alopecia in the *Historia Animalum*. This reflects the very significant, although often not now fully appreciated, role of hair in human social and sexual communication, whatever the genetic background or culture; this can be seen in the ritual head shaving of Christian and Buddhist monks and often of prisoners, the standard short haircuts of soldiers, and the religiously uncut hair of Sikhs. As a result, people with hair disorders such as androgenetic alopecia or hirsutism may suffer from marked psychological distress. Numerous cures have been suggested over the years,[5] including the use of goose droppings or arsenic derivatives! It is only recently, however, that there has been sufficient understanding of the cell biology and physiology of the hair follicle, the complex variations in the effects of androgens on follicles depending on their body site, and the actual mechanisms of androgen action to enable the development of more successful modes of control. This chapter considers the normal structure and function of human hair follicles, the various effects of androgens on normal hair growth, the processes of androgenetic alopecia, particularly in men, and possible forms of treatment.

## STRUCTURE AND FUNCTION OF HAIR FOLLICLES

### FUNCTION OF HUMAN HAIR

Hair growth is a specific feature of mammals with important functions in insulation for thermoregulation and camouflage; these often need to be altered in line with seasonal changes (e.g., the thick white winter and short brown summer coat of the arctic fox).[6] Hair also forms an important protective physical barrier and plays a role in social and sexual communication (e.g., the distinctive mane of the male lion); hair follicles are also often specialized as neuroreceptors (e.g., whiskers). Human hair growth is reduced to such an extent that we have been called the "naked ape"[7]; the insulation and camouflage roles have virtually disappeared, although their evolution can be seen in the seasonal patterns of human hair growth[8] and the erection of hairs ("goosebumps") in response to cold. The main functions of human hair are protection and communication; in children, hairs are mainly protective. The eyebrows and eyelashes stop foreign bodies from entering the eyes, and scalp hair may prevent sun damage and physical injury to the scalp and back of the neck or even protect from cold, because the scalp has little adipose tissue.[9,10] The arrival of pubic and axillary hair signals puberty in both sexes,[11–13] and the associated apocrine glands produce secretions yielding odors involved in sexual communication.[4] Mature masculinity is signaled by the generally greater body hair on the chest, upper pubic triangle, and limbs and particularly the beard; this accounts for the significant psychological stress suffered by hirsute women. The beard's involvement in male threatening display behavior[9] may explain the modern custom of removing it daily in the less openly aggressive Western world. Several roles for male pattern baldness have been suggested; these are discussed later.

### STRUCTURE OF THE HAIR AND HAIR FOLLICLE

Outside the skin hairs are thin, flexible tubes of fully keratinized, dead epithelial cells that taper to a point and are very variable in color, length, diameter, and cross-sectional shape. Inside the skin, they are part of the living *hair follicles*, individual cylindrical epithelial downgrowths into the dermis and subcutaneous fat that enlarge at the base to form the *hair bulb* (Fig. 178-1). The hair bulb surrounds the pear-shaped, mesenchyme-derived *dermal papilla*, consisting of specialized fibroblast-type cells, dermal papilla cells, embedded in an extensive extracellular matrix.[15–17] The dermal papilla is the key regulator of the follicle that determines the type of hair produced.[18,19] All cell division of the keratinocytes, which make up the rest of the follicle, takes place in the hair matrix that surrounds the dermal papilla.[15–17] As the keratinocytes move up through the hair bulb and into the thinner part of the follicle, they differentiate into the hair itself (consisting of an outer cuticle, cortex, and inner medulla), the inner root sheath (whose cuticle interdigitates with the hair's, helping it through the skin), and the outer root sheath, which becomes

continuous with the epidermis, preventing entry of microorganisms and water loss. The inner root sheath desquamates around the point where the sebaceous gland duct enters the follicle. The sebum produced by the sebaceous gland coats the hair, making it more waterproof.

## CHANGING THE TYPE OF HAIR PRODUCED—THE HAIR FOLLICLE GROWTH CYCLE

Hairs are produced all over human skin, except for the palms, soles, and lips, like other mammals. Their size and color may vary over an individual's skin; this is particularly obvious in children in whom long, pigmented *terminal* scalp hair contrasts with the tiny, almost colorless *vellus* hair on the face. Many individual mammals also change the type of hair produced on particular areas of the body. This occurs regularly in seasonal changes or with maturity (e.g., the development of

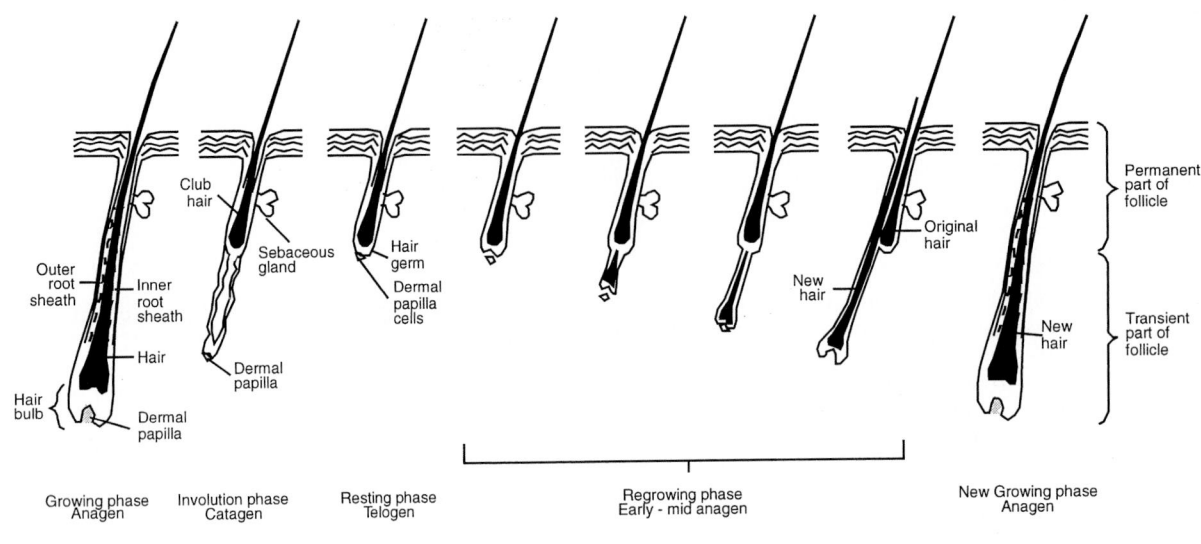

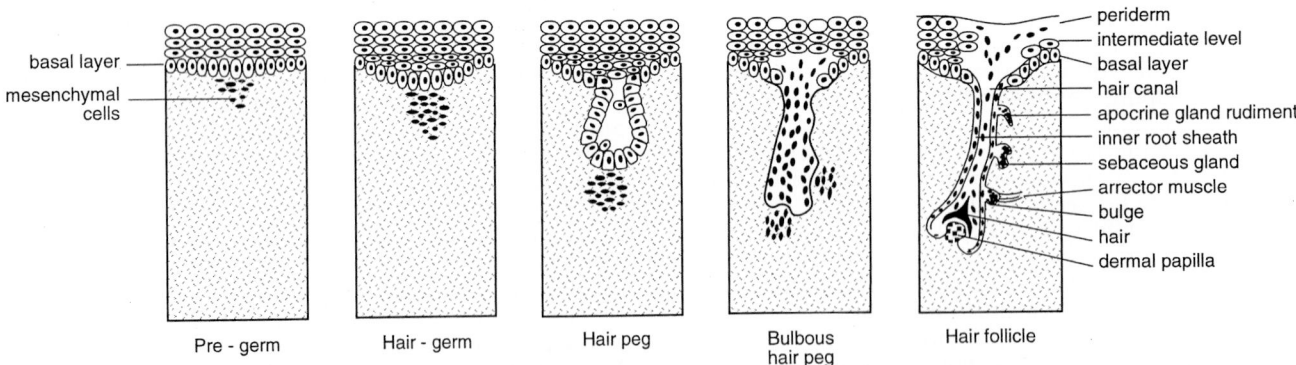

**Figure 178-1**  A diagrammatic comparison of the postnatal hair follicle cycle (*upper diagram*) with the embryogenesis of the hair follicle (*lower diagram*). Hair follicles pass through regular cycles of alternating growth (anagen) and rest (telogen). During growth, the cells of the hair matrix surrounding the dermal papilla divide, move upward, and differentiate into the hair and its outer and inner root sheaths. At the end of anagen, cell division ceases; the dermal papilla shrinks; and the hair becomes fully keratinized, forming a swollen-ended "club" hair. The lower follicle regresses (catagen) and the dermal papilla cells move upward to rest below the bulb with a group of epithelial cells, the hair germ. At the end of telogen, the dermal papilla cells reactivate and move back down into the dermis with keratinocytes to reform a regenerated lower follicle. A new hair is produced and grows up into the existing upper follicle. The original hair is shed, and a new cycle begins. The new hair may be the same as the original one (e.g., in a rodent kept indoors) or may differ (e.g., in the pubis during human puberty). The early stages of anagen appear to mirror the later stages of follicular embryogenesis (*lower diagram*) when interactions between the mesenchyme (presumptive dermal papilla) and epithelial (presumptive follicular keratinocytes) cells result in the formation of the complex follicle. (After Randall VA: Review: Androgens and hair growth. Clin Endocrinol 40:439–457, 1994.)

the lion's mane).[6] In men, dramatic, although quite slow, changes occur during puberty when terminal hairs replace vellus ones in the axillae and pubis in both sexes and on the face, chest, and abdomen.[11–13] The hair follicle possesses a very important and unique mechanism, the hair cycle, to accomplish these changes.[20,21] This involves the destruction of the original lower follicle, and its total regeneration to form another follicle that can produce a hair with different characteristics. In this way, the postnatal hair follicle appears to retain the ability to recapitulate the later stages of follicular embryogenesis throughout life (see Fig. 178-1). It is currently unclear how different a hair can be from its immediate predecessor, because many changes take place over a number of years; for instance, the full production of a beard[22] and ear canal hair[23] in men takes until their 30s and 50s, respectively, and the miniaturization process of male pattern baldness occurs over many years (Fig. 178-2).[24]

Each hair follicle normally undergoes a continual series of active, growing phases called *anagen*, alternating with periods of rest or *telogen*; these are separated at the end of anagen by a brief regression or *catagen* phase[20,21] (see Fig. 178-1). At the end of anagen, cell division halts and the lower part of the hair becomes a fully keratinized *club* hair; the dermal papilla and the lower follicle regress and move up in the skin to settle below the swollen end of the club hair. When telogen ends, the dermal papilla cells reactivate and move back down into the dermis with associated keratinocytes, inside the guidelines of the connective tissue sheath remaining from the previous lower follicle. A new hair bulb is formed, and a new hair grows up into the base of the upper follicle; the existing hair is lost. Previously, the old hair was believed to fall out purely as a passive result of the new hair pushing past it. Recently, a further stage of *exogen*, which involves an active shedding of the old club hair, has been proposed.[25]

There is currently some debate about the origin of the epithelial cells that give rise to the lower follicle. Epithelial stem cells have recently been identified in the bulge area of the outer root sheath below the sebaceous gland,[26] although the traditional view of stem cells in the epithelial germ at the base of the follicle (see Fig. 178-1), the germinative epithelial cells, is supported by coculture studies.[19] The bulge contains stem cells with a wide potency, which are able to replace cells of the epidermis and sebaceous glands as well as the hair follicle.[27,28] It seems likely that both stem cell types are involved in the hair follicle, with the bulge cells as less specialized, higher-order stem cells in line with the hemotpoietic system, possibly providing a source of cells ready to produce the germinative matrix cells for the anagen period of the next hair growth cycle.

The type of hair produced, particularly its length, depends greatly on the length of the anagen phase of the cycle. For example, long scalp hairs are produced by follicles with growing periods of over 3 years,[21,29] whereas those for hair follicles on the finger may last for only 1.5 to 3 months.[29] The cell biology and biochemistry of the local interactions involved in the control processes of the hair cycle are not understood, although there is currently a great deal of interest,[30] with the Holy Grail being the ability to regulate the anagen phase and hence the length of the cycle and final hair length.

## CONTROL OF HAIR GROWTH

### SEASONAL CHANGES IN HUMAN HAIR GROWTH— REQUIREMENT FOR LONG-TERM STUDY OF NEW DRUG TREATMENTS

Hair follicles are under hormonal regulation because of the importance of coordinating alterations in insulative and color properties of an animal's coat to the environment, and changes in the social and sexual communication aspects to the appropriate stage in the life cycle. In mammals, seasonal changes are coordinated to day length and, to a lesser extent, temperature in the same way as seasonal breeding activity. Changes are translated to the follicle via the pineal and hypothalamus-pituitary route, involving gonadal, thyroid, and corticosteroid hormones.[6]

Regular circannual changes in human hair growth have only been fully recognized comparatively recently.[8,31,32] Androgen-dependent beard and thigh hair growth increases significantly in the summer in white Englishmen with indoor occupations[8] and is lowest in January and February. This may reflect changes in circulating androgen levels, because these levels have been reported to rise in European men in the summer.[33–35]

Scalp hair shows a single annual cycle with more than 90% of hairs growing in the spring, falling to about 80% at the end of summer. This is paralleled by an increase in the number of hairs shed per day, which more than doubled[8,31] (see Fig. 178-2). As most people's scalp follicles will be in anagen for at least 2 to 3 years, such a seasonal effect is quite remarkable. It is presently unclear which hormones regulate these seasonal changes. Nevertheless, these observations have a major significance for the investigator, as any new drug or treatment must be studied for at least a year to separate any effects from normal seasonal variations.

SCALP HAIR % ANAGEN

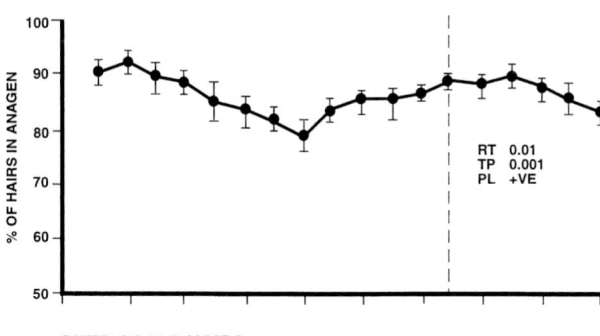

SHED SCALP HAIRS

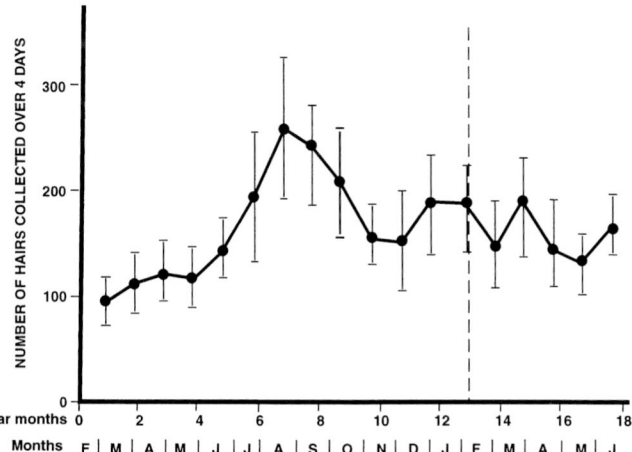

*Figure 178-2*  Human scalp hair growth shows significant seasonal changes. The percentage of hair follicles in anagen (growing) on the scalp decreases (*top*) and the number of hairs shed per day increases in the autumn (*bottom*) in 14 white Englishmen aged 18 to 39. (Mean ± SEM.) This seasonal effect means that clinical investigations of human hair growth need to be carried out over at least a 12-month period. PL, phase length; RT, runs test; TP, turning points; +VE positive. (Data redrawn from Randall VA, Ebling FJG: Seasonal changes in human hair growth. Br J Dermatol 124:146–151, 1991.)

## ANDROGEN REGULATION OF HUMAN HAIR GROWTH

### Paradoxical Effects of Postpubertal Androgens—Ranging from Stimulation of Beard Growth to Balding on the Scalp

Although other hormones (including those of pregnancy, prolactin, melanocyte-stimulating hormone [MSH], and thyroid hormones) have effects on hair growth in men and other species,[36] androgens are the main regulator of human hair growth. One of the first signs of puberty is the gradual replacement of tiny vellus hairs with larger, more pigmented *intermediate* hairs in the pubis and later in the axillae[37,38]; eventually larger and darker terminal hairs are produced (Fig. 178-3). These changes parallel the pubertal rise in plasma androgens that occurs earlier in girls than in boys.[39,40] Later, similar changes occur on the face of young men and this, plus an extended pubic diamond, chest hair, and greater hair on the limbs, readily distinguishes the mature adult man. The changes in all areas are gradual and often progress over many years. Beard growth increases rapidly during puberty, but continues to rise until the man is in his mid-30s,[22] while terminal hair on the chest or auditory canal may not appear until many years after puberty.[23]

In marked contrast to the increased hair production stimulated on many areas of the body, androgens have no obvious effect on many follicles that produce terminal hairs in childhood, such as the eyelashes or many scalp follicles (see Fig. 178-3). Paradoxically, in individuals with a genetic predisposition, androgens promote the gradual transformation of large terminal scalp follicles to tiny vellus ones, causing balding of the scalp, androgenetic alopecia[24,41,42] (see Fig. 178-3). Apart from the role of androgens, the precise mechanisms of these responses within the hair follicle are not well understood, although they are currently the focus of much investigation. What is clear is that the responses are intrinsic to the individual follicle. Not only does the response range from stimulation to inhibition, depending on the body site, but sensitivity to the hormone also varies within clearly defined patterns; facial hair develops first above the mouth and center of the chin in both young men and hirsute women, and regression in androgenic alopecia occurs in a progressive manner.[24] Similarly, female circulating androgen levels are high enough to promote axillary hair growth and the female pubic pattern, but male patterns of body hair require normal male levels.[37–40]

### Mechanism of Androgen Action in Hair Follicles

*Hair Growth in Androgen Insensitivity Syndromes and 5a-reductase Type 2 Deficiency*

The essential requirement for androgens in the paradoxical effects just described (summarized in Fig. 178-3) is shown by

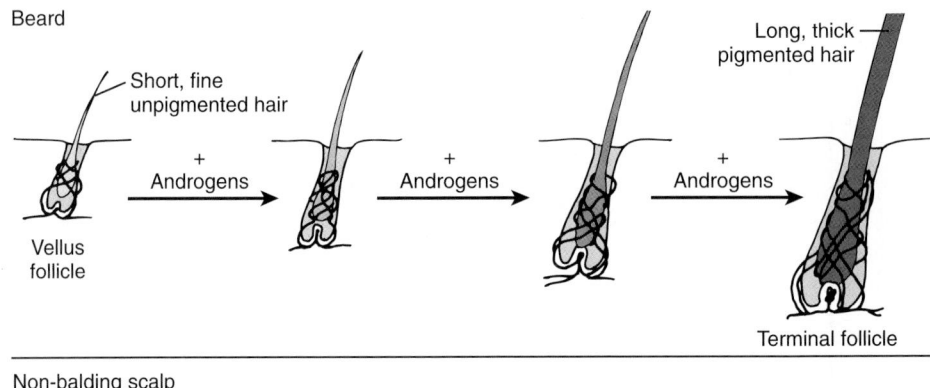

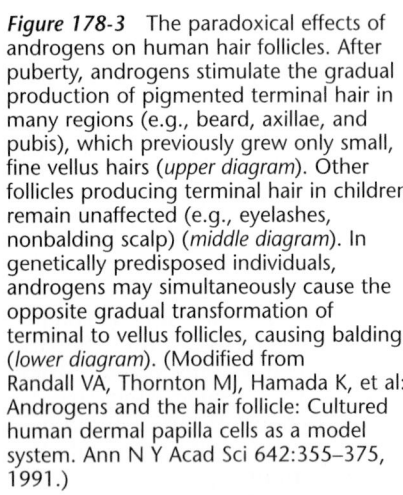

*Figure 178-3* The paradoxical effects of androgens on human hair follicles. After puberty, androgens stimulate the gradual production of pigmented terminal hair in many regions (e.g., beard, axillae, and pubis), which previously grew only small, fine vellus hairs (*upper diagram*). Other follicles producing terminal hair in children remain unaffected (e.g., eyelashes, nonbalding scalp) (*middle diagram*). In genetically predisposed individuals, androgens may simultaneously cause the opposite gradual transformation of terminal to vellus follicles, causing balding (*lower diagram*). (Modified from Randall VA, Thornton MJ, Hamada K, et al: Androgens and the hair follicle: Cultured human dermal papilla cells as a model system. Ann N Y Acad Sci 642:355–375, 1991.)

the absence of any changes in body or scalp hair growth with adulthood in individuals without functional androgen receptors (i.e., with androgen insensitivity syndrome).[43] Individuals with the complete form exhibit no pubic, axillary chest, or beard terminal hair and do not develop androgenetic alopecia (Fig. 178-4).

Although all hair follicles require intracellular androgen receptors to respond to androgens, there appears to be divergence in the requirement for 5α-reductase activity to produce intracellular 5α-dihydrotestosterone for the androgen response.[44] Individuals with 5α-reductase type 2 deficiency do not develop male patterns of body hair growth despite their circulating androgens; they only produce female patterns of pubic and axillary hair along with their masculinized male body shape[45] (see Fig. 178-4). They have not been reported to exhibit male pattern baldness either, but this is more difficult to interpret; for many years, they were said not to suffer from acne, but a later investigation showed normal

sebum production in 5α-reductase deficiency and reported some acne.[46]

Thus, male secondary sexual hair growth appears to require intracellular 5α-reductase type 2 as well as androgen receptors, suggesting the classical mechanism of androgen action via 5α-dihydrotestosterone.[43] Pubic and axillary hair follicles are not only more sensitive to androgens, but also may be using testosterone intracellularly, unless 5α-dihydrotestosterone is being formed by 5α-reductase type 1.[44] Whichever occurs, the mechanism of androgen action appears to differ in the two sorts of follicles, even though androgens are stimulating both follicles.

### Current Model for Androgen Action in the Hair Follicle

The mesenchyme-derived dermal papilla plays an important regulatory role in the follicle, determining the type of hair produced.[18,19] Since, as discussed earlier, hair follicles appear to partially recapitulate embryogenesis during the hair cycle (see Fig. 178-1) and steroids act via the mesenchyme in many developing steroid-dependent tissues,[47] Randall proposed that androgens would act on the other components of the follicle via the dermal papilla.[36,48] This hypothesis, summarized in Figure 178-5, involves circulating androgens entering the dermal papilla via its own blood capillaries. Here they would bind to androgen receptors within the dermal papilla cells of androgen-dependent hair follicles. Whether or not they would first be metabolized intracellularly to 5α-dihydrotestosterone would depend on the site of the follicle; for example, beard follicle cells would first metabolize testosterone with 5α-reductase type 2, but axillary and pubic cells would not.

According to this hypothesis,[36,48,49] after androgens bind to their receptors, the gene expression of the dermal papilla cells alters to modify their production of regulatory factors for the other cell types of the follicle, particularly the keratinocytes and melanocytes (pigment-producing cells). These factors could be soluble growth factors or extracellular matrix proteins.[36,48] Targets could also include the cells of

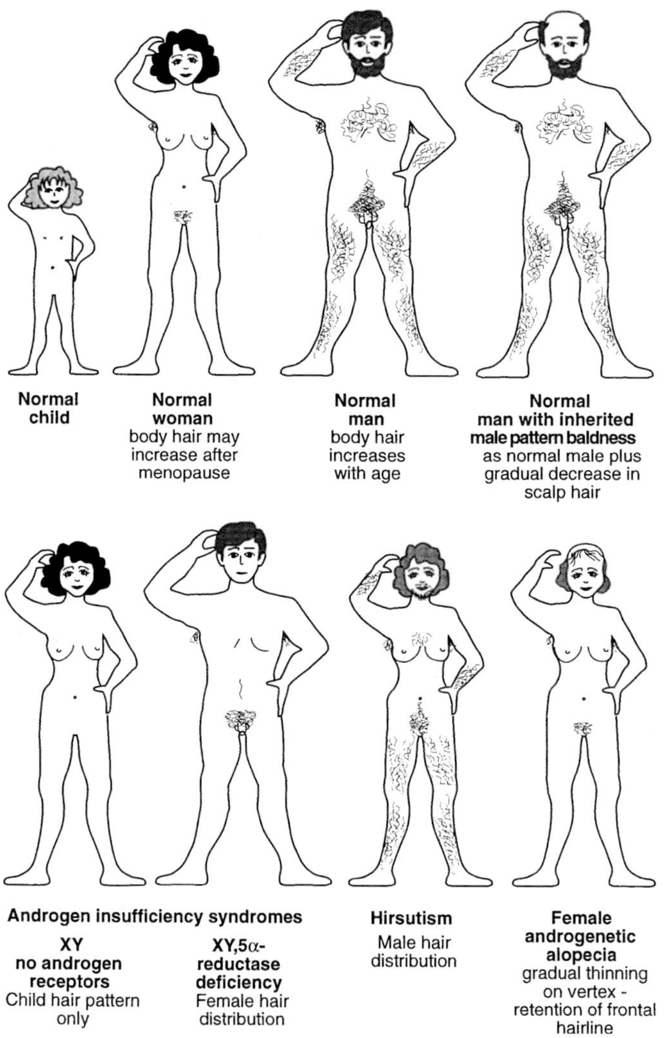

**Figure 178-4** Human hair growth varies with different endocrine conditions. The protective terminal hairs of childhood on the scalp, eyelashes, and eyebrows are augmented during puberty by axillary and pubic hair growth in both sexes, plus beard, chest, and greater body hair in men. None of this occurs without functional androgen receptors and only axillary and pubic hair in the absence of 5α-reductase type 2. In genetically predisposed individuals, androgens may also cause inhibition of scalp hair growth, particularly in men. Raised circulating androgens or idiopathic causes (e.g., increased follicle sensitivity) may lead to hirsutism (i.e., male pattern hair distribution in women). (Modified from Randall VA: Androgens and hair. In Nieschlag E, Behre HM [eds]: Testosterone: Action, Deficiency, Substitution. Berlin, Springer-Verlag, 1998, pp 167–186.)

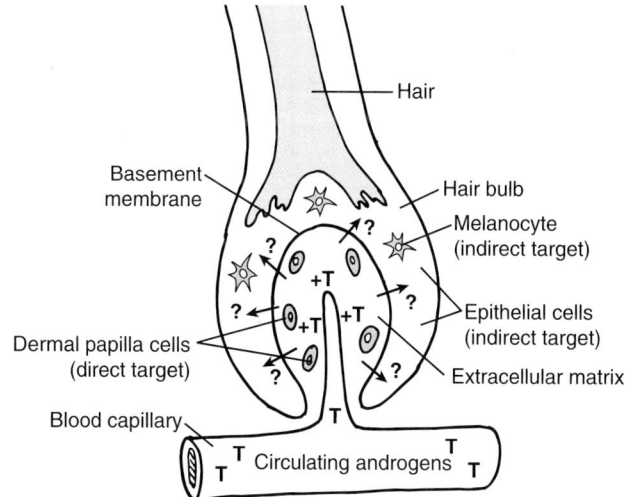

**Figure 178-5** The current model of androgen action in the hair follicle. Androgens from the blood enter the hair follicle via capillaries in the dermal papilla. They are bound by androgen receptors in the dermal papilla cells of androgen-sensitive follicles stimulating an alteration in their production of regulatory paracrine factors; in some follicles, binding to the receptors is preceded by metabolism to 5α-dihydrotestosterone. These paracrine factors then alter the activity of other follicular cells, including keratinocytes and melanocytes. T, testosterone; ?, unknown paracrine factors. (Modified from Randall VA: Androgens and hair. In Nieschlag E, Behre HM [eds]: Testosterone: Action, Deficiency, Substitution. Berlin, Springer-Verlag, 1998, pp 167–186.)

the follicular connective tissue sheath, the melanocytes, the dermal vasculature, and even dermal papilla cells themselves because all these would be altered in the formation of a differently sized or colored hair; beard and scalp dermal papilla cells do produce autocrine stimulatory factors.[50] Therefore, the direct androgen target cells would be the dermal papilla cells, and the other follicular components would be indirectly controlled by androgens. This would seem a realistic model because androgens have such widely differing effects on follicles in different body sites, including whether or not 5α-reductase type 2 is necessary for stimulation of hair growth. It is difficult to conceive of these responses being so well controlled if each target cell in the follicle had to respond to androgens directly.

This hypothesis has now received much experimental support. Androgen receptors have been localized by immunohistochemistry in the dermal papilla and not the keratinocyte cells.[51,52] Cultured dermal papilla cells derived from androgen-sensitive follicles such as beard[53] and balding scalp[54] contain higher levels of specific, saturable androgen receptors than androgen-insensitive, nonbalding scalp in vitro; this has been confirmed by studies using reverse transcription-polymerase chain reaction (RT-PCR).[55] Important corroboration also comes from studies of the metabolism of androgens by cultured dermal papilla cells, because this reflects hair growth in 5α-reductase deficiency (see Fig. 178-3); beard cells produce 5α-dihydrotestosterone,[56,57] but pubic cells do not,[58] corresponding to the absence of beard hair but presence of pubic hair in the patients. Similar results have been obtained examining the gene expression of 5α-reductase type 2 by RT-PCR.[55]

Although the key role of the dermal papilla in the induction of hair follicles and the regulation of the type of hair produced is well established,[19] the lower part of the connective tissue sheath, or dermal sheath, which surrounds the hair follicle and isolates it from the dermis, has recently been shown to form a new dermal papilla and new human hair follicle development in someone of the opposite sex.[59] Cultured dermal sheath cells from the beard hair follicles contain similar levels of androgen receptors to beard dermal papilla cells[60] and balding scalp dermal sheath expresses the mRNA for 5α-reductase type 2, like the dermal papilla.[61] Clearly, the dermal sheath also plays an important role in the hair follicle. This may be as a reserve to replace the key inductive and controlling role of the dermal papilla cells if they are lost. Alternatively, or in addition, it seems highly probable that the dermal sheath cells may respond directly to androgens to facilitate the increase or decrease in size of the sheath or even the dermal papilla in the development of a new anagen follicle; this would enable the new hair follicle to be larger or smaller depending on the follicle's specific response to androgens. These results merit a modification of the model to include a direct action of androgens on the lower dermal sheath too.

The production of growth factors by cultured dermal papilla cells derived from human and rat hair follicles has been investigated by several groups on the basis of the primary role of the dermal papilla, its potential probable role in androgen action, and the retention of hair growth-promoting ability by cultured rat cells.[19] Cultured dermal papilla cells secrete both extracellular matrix factors[62] and soluble, proteinaceous growth factors.[48] Bioassays demonstrate that human cultured dermal papilla cells can secrete soluble, proteinaceous, growth-promoting factors for other dermal papilla cells,[48,50] outer root sheath cells,[63] and transformed epidermal keratinocytes.[64] Importantly, testosterone in vitro altered the mitogenic capacity in line with its effect on hair growth in vivo. Testosterone stimulated beard but not scalp cells to produce greater mitogenic capability for beard dermal papilla cells,[50] outer root sheath cells,[63] and keratinocytes[63]; in marked contrast, testosterone decreased the mitogenic capacity of androgenetic alopecia scalp dermal papilla cells both

from men[64] and the stump-tailed macaque.[65] Research is currently focused on identifying androgen-regulated factors (reviewed in Ref. 66), but, to date, only insulin-like growth factor 1 (IGF-1) has been reported as altered in vitro by androgens.[63] Several other factors have been suggested to play a role in hair growth,[30] but to date only stem cell factor (SCF) is produced in higher amounts by androgen-dependent beard cells than control, nonbalding scalp cells,[67] presumably in response to androgens in vitro. Because SCF is the ligand for the cell surface receptor, c-kit, found on human melanocytes, this may play a role in androgen-potentiated changes in hair pigmentation.

Other factors, which have been implicated in the follicular dermal papilla, include keratinocyte growth factor (KGF) and hepatocyte growth factor (HGF), though many more have been located in the epidermis.[68] The expression of mRNA for the protease nexin-1 in dermal papilla cells is also altered by androgens.[69] This may play a role by altering the amount of extracellular matrix components produced[70] and, therefore, the size of the follicle and hair produced.[71] Recently, dermal papilla cell conditioned media from balding scalp follicles have been shown to inhibit the growth of both human and rodent whisker dermal papilla cells in vitro and delay mouse hair growth in vivo.[72] This suggests the active secretion of an inhibitory factor or factors. A possible candidate is transforming growth factor-β1 (TGF-β1) which has been induced by androgens in balding dermal papilla cells with transfected androgen receptors.[73] TGF-β also inhibits hair follicle growth in vitro[68] and a probable suppressor of TGF-β1 delayed catagen progression in mice in vivo.[74] Further study of such factors should lead to better treatments for androgen-dependent hair follicle disorders, such as androgenetic alopecia or hirsutism.

## ANDROGENETIC ALOPECIA

### PATTERNS OF HAIR LOSS

#### In Men
The gradual replacement of long, pigmented, terminal hairs on the scalp of many adult men by short, pale, vellus hairs occurs in a relatively precise pattern (Fig. 178-6). The progression was first graded by Hamilton[24] from type I, for the prepubertal scalp with terminal hair growth on the forehead and all over the scalp through gradual regression of the frontal hairline and thinning on the vertex, to type VII, where the bald areas have fully coalesced to leave hair only around the back and sides of the head. Hamilton's classification was later modified by Norwood[75] to include variations on the middle grades IIIa, III vertex, IVa, and Va (see Fig. 178-6); this scale has now been used extensively during clinical trials of hair growth promoting agents.

Hamilton's original grading scale[24] was produced after he examined 312 white men and 214 women aged 20 to 89. He reported that after puberty, there was a very common progression of the prepubertal scalp pattern to type II in both sexes (occurring in 96% of men and 79% of women). In addition, most men older than 50 (58%) exhibited at least type V, and further progression tended to occur up to the age of 70.

#### In Women
Interestingly, for a condition usually associated with men, Hamilton's study[24] revealed that, as well as common postpubertal recession to type II, approximately 25% of white women exhibited type IV pattern by age 50, although there was no further development of this balding and no types V to VIII were seen. Some women who had type II frontal recession appeared to return to the prepubertal pattern after 50.

Although the male pattern can occur in women, the progressive diffuse loss of hair from the crown with retention of the frontal hairline described by Ludwig[76] is more common

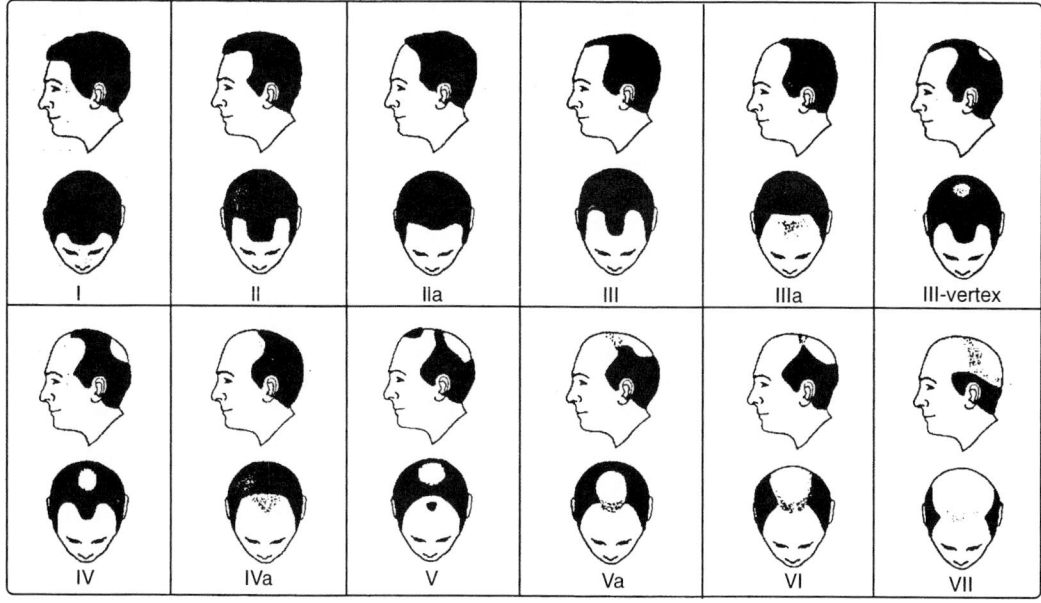

**Figure 178-6** Patterns of hair loss in androgenetic alopecia in men (*upper diagram*) and women (*lower diagram*). Androgens cause a gradual inhibition of hair growth on the scalp in genetically predisposed individuals. This is much more common in men than in women, and the pattern of the hair loss in men differs from that in women. In men, the first signs are generally temporal regression, which spreads backward and joins thinning regions on the vertex to give a bald crown. In women, the front hairline is normally retained, and a general thinning on the vertex gradually becomes more pronounced until the vertex becomes bald. (After Hamilton JB: Patterned loss of hair in man: Types and incidence. Ann N Y Acad Sci 53:708–728, 1951; and Ludwig E: Classification of the types of androgenic alopecia (common baldness) arising in the female sex. Br J Dermatol 97:249–256, 1977.

(see Fig. 178-6). When Venning and Dawber[77] examined 564 women older than 20, they found that 80% of premenopausal women had thinning in the Ludwig pattern types I to III (see Fig. 178-6) and 13% had Hamilton types II to IV. After menopause, the proportion who exhibited the male pattern increased to 37%; although they did not progress beyond Hamilton type IV, some did have marked M-shaped recession at both temples.

### Incidence

Although there are no precise statistics for incidence of androgenetic alopecia within a population, the incidence in whites is high and estimates vary widely. The incidence is often quoted as approaching 100%,[1] although other researchers suggest that about half of men and women older than 40 exhibit androgenetic alopecia.[78] There is a marked variation in incidence among other races, which show much less balding. Hamilton reported that most Chinese retain the prepubertal hairline after puberty and that baldness is less common, less extensive, and starts at a later age.[24] Similarly, Japanese men also begin balding about 10 years later than whites and the incidence is about 1.4 times lower.[79] Four times as many African-Americans as whites also retain a full head of hair.[80] The reason for this racial variation is unclear, but is probably genetic because differences appear to be retained regardless of the individuals' geographic location.

### EFFECTS OF ANDROGENETIC ALOPECIA

#### Functions of Androgenetic Alopecia in Men

Androgenetic alopecia is very common in Homo sapiens,[24] and is also seen in other primates, including the orangutan, chimpanzee, and stump-tailed macaque.[81] This suggests a natural progression of a secondary sexual characteristic rather than a disease. Thinking in comparative biologic terms about human history, marked androgenetic alopecia would clearly identify the surviving older male as a leader, like the silver back of the older male gorilla and the larger antlers on an older deer.[82] Other authors have speculated that the bald patch of an angry older dominant male would flush and look very aggressive to an opponent[83] or give an advantage in hand-to-hand fighting, because there is less accessible hair to pull.[84] Whatever the potential benefit, the reduced incidence of androgenetic alopecia in men of African races[80] suggests evolutionary pressure to retain scalp hair for protection from the sun in the Tropics.

## Negative Effects of Androgenetic Alopecia on Quality of Life

Nowadays in our youth-oriented culture, the association of hair loss with increasing age has negative connotations and because of the importance of hair in human social and sexual communication (discussed earlier), male pattern baldness often causes marked psychological distress and reduction in quality of life, despite not being life threatening or physically painful. Several studies have confirmed the negative effects of hair loss on men[85–90] and women.[91,92] These studies show that others perceive men with visible hair loss as being older, less physically and socially attractive, weaker, and duller; similarly, people with hair loss report a poor self-image, a feeling of being older, and a loss of self-confidence. Although most of these studies focused on people who had already requested medical treatment, a study by Girman and colleagues[90] showed similar perceptions among those who appear more accepting of the condition because they have never sought treatment. Whatever its historical biologic role, androgenetic alopecia reduces the quality of life in the current affluent industrialized world.

## PATHOLOGY

The progressive increase in patterned balding is the result of the gradual transformation of terminal follicles producing the large, thick, pigmented scalp hairs of adolescence and childhood to smaller vellus follicles forming long, colorless vellus hairs (see Fig. 178-3). This is a major change in cell biologic terms, with follicles passing through several cycles before the processes are completed (Fig. 178-7). In the normal scalp, hair follicles are in anagen for most of the time; the average anagen length of 2 to 3 years and telogen of approximately 100 days[21] gives an anagen-to-telogen ratio of about 9:1, although there is some seasonal variation in people living in temperate regions[8] (see Fig. 178-2). While androgenetic alopecia is developing, the anagen phase shortens, producing an increase in the proportion of telogen hairs,[93–95] which can be detected before any balding; it also means that the hairs produced are shorter. Miniaturization of the follicles can also be seen histologically,[93,96] meaning that the hairs produced are also thinner.[94,95] In scalp that appears bald, most of the follicles are very short and small, with occasional resting terminal follicles.

Studies of androgenetic alopecia are complicated by the non-androgen-dependent hair thinning found in those in their 50s, known as *senescent balding*.[97] This also involves a progressive decrease in the number of anagen follicles[98] and hair diameter,[97] but does not normally lead to baldness. Kligman suggested that both forms may occur together and proposed a pronounced inflammatory component in androgenetic alopecia that was not present in senescent baldness.[96] Early indications of inflammatory involvement include focal perivascular degeneration in the lower third of the connective tissue sheath and perifollicular lymphohistiocytic infiltration at the sebaceous gland level[96]; multinucleate giant cells may be seen later.[99] The sclerotic remains of the fibrous sheath can be seen below the shortened follicles as "streamers"[96]; damage to the dermal sheath owing to chronic inflammation may prevent the reformation of terminal hair follicles in long-term alopecia, although this is currently the subject of much debate.

During the miniaturization processes, the follicle's associated arrector pili muscle reduces much more slowly than the follicle,[100] and the sebaceous gland, which is also an androgen-dependent tissue, becomes enlarged.[96] Because the long hairs that are normally coated by the sebum have been lost, the scalp often has an oily, more greasy appearance. Other changes include a reduced blood supply to the follicle[101,102] and nerve networks escaped from follicular support twisting to form a type of encapsulated end organ below the follicle.[103] Whether the reduced blood supply is induced after the reduction in follicle size or precedes it is currently unclear.

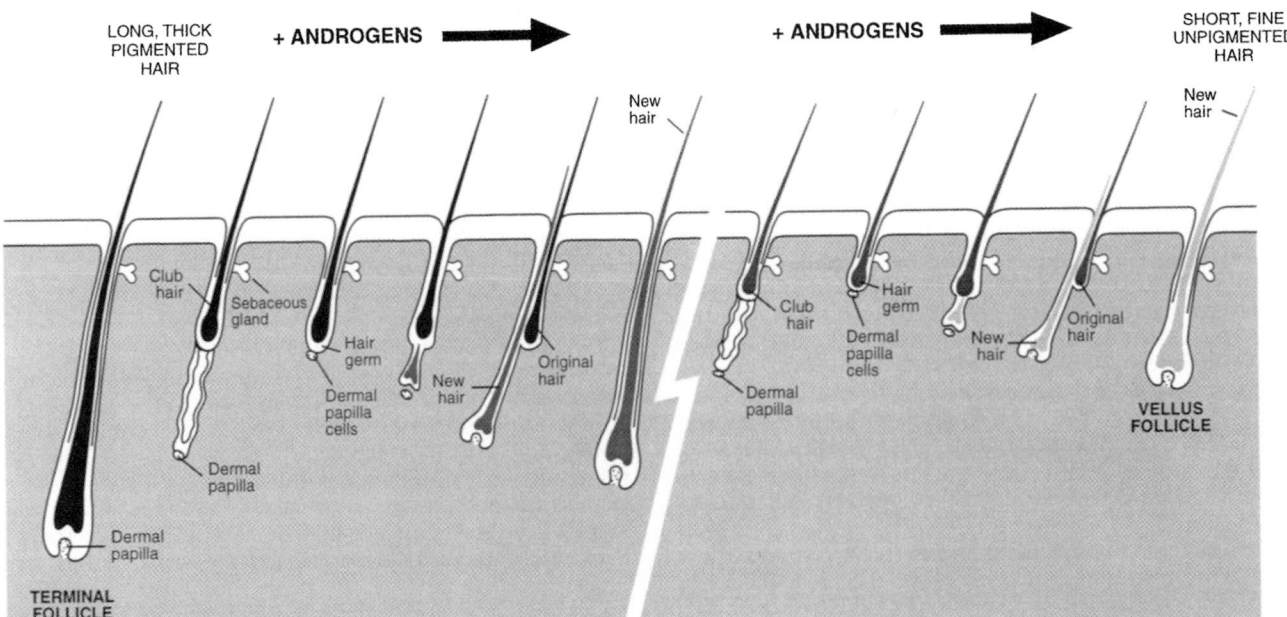

**BALDING SCALP: Androgen sensitive**

*Figure 178-7* Diagram representing the miniaturization processes occurring in response to androgens in the scalp of a person with a genetic predisposition to androgenetic alopecia. The white gap between the two parts of the diagram represents a space for at least one other cycle between the two shown to accommodate these changes in size. Androgens inhibit scalp hair follicles in balding regions by inducing them to produce progressively smaller, finer, and less pigmented hairs until the terminal hairs of childhood and early adulthood are replaced by the vellus hairs of androgenetic alopecia and the area appears bald. Follicles themselves become shorter and finer, but must pass through a full hair cycle, probably a succession of cycles, to accomplish major changes.

## PATHOGENESIS

### Role of Androgens

Androgens are an essential factor in the development of androgenetic alopecia. Hamilton demonstrated that it did not occur in men who had never gone through puberty, and that men castrated after puberty showed no further progression of their baldness, although they did not regain the frontal hairline.[22,41,42] He also analyzed the importance of androgens by giving testosterone propionate replacement therapy to castrated men; this stimulated progressive balding, which halted during temporary withdrawal of the hormone.[41] The importance of androgens is confirmed by the absence of androgenetic alopecia in individuals who are insensitive to androgen and lack functional androgen receptors,[43] the absence of balding in 5α-reductase deficiency,[43] and the regrowth of hair in young balding men given the 5α-reductase inhibitor finasteride.[104]

Despite the widely held belief that baldness is an indicator of increased male sexuality, there is little scientific evidence for this other than the clear link with normal androgen parameters. There was no relationship between androgenetic alopecia and other androgen-regulated parameters, including muscle, bone, and skin or sebum excretion rate and body hair growth in adult men.[105] Normal male testosterone levels have been reported in balding men[106,107] with higher urinary dehydroepiandrosterone (DHEA)[106] or dehydroepiandrosterone sulfate (DHEA-S)[107]; other studies showed raised serum-free testosterone.[108,109] Overall, normal male androgen levels appear to be sufficient to produce androgenetic alopecia; the response obtained appears to be related to the intrinsic response of the follicles.

In women, raised mean circulating levels of androgens, particularly free androgens (that is, not bound to sex hormone–binding globulin), appear to be related to hair loss, although the means from studies are often within the normal ranges for premenopausal women.[110–116] Women who present with androgenetic alopecia also often exhibit polycystic ovarian disease and hirsutism,[116–118] even if the presenting symptom was alopecia without menstrual abnormalities.[116]

### Genetic Involvement

#### Family History

The genetic involvement in androgenetic alopecia is pronounced. Male pattern baldness in men runs in families,[41,119] and Hamilton showed that the balding response to androgen replacement in castrated men depended on their family history; men with no history of balding exhibited no response.[41] This importance of genes fits well with the racial differences discussed earlier. Although there is general acceptance that androgenetic alopecia is an autosomal-dominant trait with variable penetrance,[120] this is based on an early familial analysis, from 1916.[121] No specific gene or set of genes have been identified to date, presumably because of the very high incidence, and a strong argument is easily made for a more complex, polygenic inheritance.[122,123] Interestingly, a very strong correlation in androgenetic alopecia incidence was found in 54 sets of sons and fathers with 81.5% of balding sons having balding fathers (Hamilton-Norwood type III or higher).[123,124] This is greater than expected from an autosomal-dominant inheritance. This strong correlation could implicate a paternally inherited gene, for example, on the Y chromosome, or the involvement of a gene that is capable of being paternally imprinted (that is, preferentially inactivated by methylation of DNA, and so on).

#### Investigation of Specific Genes

A number of genes have recently been investigated for association with androgenetic alopecia. Based on the importance of testosterone metabolism to 5α-dihydrotestosterone in balding and beard growth, as discussed previously, the genes for both type 1 and type 2 5α-reductase genes, the steroid 5α-reductase type 1 (SRD5A1) gene on chromosome 5 and the type 2 (SRD5A2) gene on chromosome 2 have been investigated. No association with androgenetic alopecia was detected with neutral polymorphic markers for type 1 or type 2 in case-control association studies of Australian[125] or Korean (Asian) men.[126]

Known dimorphic and polymorphic markers within the androgen receptor gene are more linked to balding in Caucasian men.[127] The *Stu* I restriction fragment length polymorphism (RFLP) in exon 1 was present in 98% of 54 young balding men and 92% of 392 older balding men, but was also found in 77% of their older, nonbalding controls. When two triplet repeat polymorphisms were examined, the distribution of neither short nor long single triplet repeats of CAG or GAC differed significantly, but the incidence of short/short polymorphic CAG/GGC haplotypes was significantly higher (50% compared to 30%) in balding subjects and short/long was lower (7% rather than 22%), though no significance was stated in the paper. Interestingly, analysis of Spanish girls with precocious puberty, that is, appearance of pubic hair before 8 years old, showed that the mean number of CAG repeats was shorter than controls.[128] Shorter triplet repeat lengths have also been associated with another common androgen-dependent condition, prostate cancer.[129] Whether this has functional significance, such as an increased androgen sensitivity, or simply reflects linkage disequilibrium with a causative mutation is not clear. When the binding capacity for a range of steroids was compared between androgen receptors from balding and nonbalding follicle dermal papilla cells, however, no differences were detected.[54]

Other genes have also been implicated, including a link to one allele of the steroid metabolism gene CYP17 in both women with polycystic ovaries and their brothers with early onset androgenetic alopecia.[130] An interesting connection is severe, early onset androgenetic alopecia in men with the X-linked gene for adrenoleukodystrophy who tend to have low testosterone levels.[131] Recently, the gene for *hairless*, which results in a complete loss of hair,[132] showed a marginally significant correlation with androgenic alopecia with two mutations, but these became insignificant after correction for multiple testing.[133] The situation is not clear at the moment, but further genetic analysis studies focusing on people with advanced balding at an early age should yield important clues soon.

#### Intrinsic Response of Individual Follicles

The paradoxically different effects of androgens on human hair follicles, varying from stimulation of beard follicles, apparent lack of effect on the eyelashes, and inhibition of scalp follicles in a single individual (see Fig. 178-3), clearly demonstrate the intrinsic response of the individual follicle to androgens. This is further emphasized in the range of sensitivity to androgens of scalp follicles, demonstrated by the different rates of progression of the miniaturization processes on different parts of the scalp and the lack of response on the back and sides of the head.

Androgens appear to promote and amplify the individual follicle's genetic programming. This end-organ response is the basis for hair transplant surgery[134]; when "nonbalding" regions of the scalp are transplanted to the balding vertex, they retain their innate lack of androgen response and maintain terminal follicles, while miniaturization progresses in the vertex follicles behind them. Presumably, this different genetic programming occurs during development. The dermis of the frontoparietal scalp (the human balding regions) of the quail chick has been shown to develop from the neural crest, while the occipital/temporal scalp arises from the mesoderm.[135] If this also occurs in human development, it may be involved with the different scalp regional responses to androgens.

Neither androgenetic alopecia[41] nor beard growth[22] is returned to prepubertal levels if men are castrated after puberty, suggesting that the altered gene expression may not need androgen to persist once sufficiently triggered, although it is necessary for further development. On the other hand, male beard growth shows seasonal variation, probably in response to fluctuating hormone levels,[8] antiandrogen treatment with cyproterone acetate causes regression of hirsutism,[136] and finasteride, a 5α-reductase type 2 inhibitor, can cause regrowth in early androgenetic alopecia.[104] This indicates a dependence on androgens to maintain the status quo as well as stimulate progression. The difference between these observations may be caused by the length of time that the androgen effect had been established; for example, if chronic inflammation has caused fibrosis below the shortened, long-standing, balding follicle,[96] it seems much less likely that the follicle could reform a terminal hair follicle, regardless of stimulus.

### Association with Other Diseases

Because androgenetic alopecia is so common in many populations, correlation with other diseases has not been very beneficial. There has been some interest, however, in relating it to other common disorders in men in which androgens may play a role. Generally, the relationship between androgenetic alopecia and coronary heart disease has been inconsistent, and a recent study reported that, when age was taken into account, the levels of coronary risk factors were not significantly different between bald and nonbalding men.[124] Two earlier reports, however, related vertex balding in men younger than 55 to the risk of myocardial infarction in a cross-sectional study[137] and rapidly progressing balding to coronary heart disease in a prospective study.[138] Whether any possible associations indicate a genetic link or dual end-organ increased sensitivity or are due to the psychological stress induced by early balding in the youth-oriented Western culture (discussed earlier) is uncertain. Nevertheless, early or rapidly progressing balding is an easy noninvasive marker, which could prove useful in screening for men with a tendency toward heart disease. A few studies have also explored whether androgenetic alopecia is associated with prostate cancer.[109] The absence of any correlation to date could be due to the case-control study design involving only older men; a prospective study would be necessary to see if there is any correlation.

### Mechanism of Androgen Action in Androgenetic Alopecia

The intrinsic androgen response of scalp hair follicles clearly requires the presence of intracellular androgen receptors since androgenetic alopecia is absent in patients who are insensitive to androgen.[43] The requirement for 5α-reductase is less clear-cut because, although patients with 5α-reductase type 2 deficiency are generally reported not to go bald,[45] their familial tendency toward androgenetic alopecia is often low.

Initial studies on the mechanism of androgen action in skin target tissues focused on extracts of whole skin or plucked hair follicles, but, unfortunately, neither of these are useful systems. The skin contains a range of androgen target tissues that may respond very differently to androgens at the same time, such as the small hair follicles and enlarged sebaceous glands of the face of a woman suffering from acne. Plucked hair follicles do not contain the dermal papilla, the key target in androgen action, because this is retained in the skin, making the results difficult to interpret. Plucked hair follicles from all body sites metabolize testosterone to the less active androstenedione, regardless of the role of 5α-dihydrotestosterone in hair growth in that region, but isolated balding follicles possess higher 5α-reductase activity than nonbalding ones.[139,140] Since the identification of the two forms of 5α-reductase, type 1 activity has been associated with the sebaceous gland and scalp skin after puberty.[141] Interestingly, during a short period

after birth, type 2 is expressed in scalp skin[142]; although its role is unknown, one possibility may be an imprinting function on scalp hair follicles. The strongest evidence for the importance of 5α-reductase type 2 in androgenetic alopecia is the regrowth of terminal hair in some individuals when treated with the 5α-reductase type 2 inhibitor finasteride.[104]

In the current model for androgen action in hair follicles (see Fig. 178-5), androgens act via androgen receptors in the dermal papilla at the base of the hair follicle, altering the production of mitogenic factors that control growth and act on other follicular cell types (discussed previously). Cultured dermal papilla cells contain androgen receptors,[53,54] 5α-reductase, if this is necessary for hair growth in 5α-reductase deficiency patients,[56,57,58] and secrete stimulatory factors for a range of follicular cell types including keratinocytes,[63] other dermal papilla cells,[50] and melanocytes.[67] Interestingly, androgens stimulate the production of mitogenic factors from beard cells[50,63] (i.e., from androgen-potentiated follicles in vivo) while causing inhibition of both human[64] and stump-tailed macque[65] androgenetic alopecia cells. Identification of such factors (discussed earlier) may play an important role in the design of new therapeutic approaches to control androgenetic alopecia.

## TREATMENT

Over the centuries, there have been a wide range of remedies suggested for androgenetic alopecia.[5] Even today, people hit the headlines with their new "cures"; recently, in England, this has included being upside down for some time each day (to increase blood flow to the head) and having a cow lick the balding area regularly. More recognized treatments include wigs and hairpieces, surgery, hormone action modifiers, and nonhormonal therapy.

### Surgery

The principle behind all surgical methods is to capitalize on the different intrinsic responses to androgens by spreading "nonbalding" (i.e., occipital and parietal) terminal follicles over the androgen-sensitive scalp regions.[134] Originally, this was achieved by transplanting small biopsies with several follicles, but this usually now involves variable sized pieces ranging down to micrografts with one or two follicles.[143] Once established, these expensive and painful treatments are long lasting; however, the effect can be marred by the continual natural progression of balding, which may well require further transplants to avoid isolation of the transplanted region.

An alternative approach is scalp expansion, where the central bald skin is removed and the remaining skin is stretched with tissue expanders to cover the gaps[143]; further skin may be removed after the skin has stretched. Skin may also be stretched before any surgery, but the obvious head swelling this involves makes it less popular.

### Hormonal Treatments

#### Antiandrogens

Blocking the androgen receptor with antiandrogens is a theoretically useful approach, but not really practical because antiandrogens would block all androgen actions, with unacceptable side effects on male masculinity and the potential to cause feminization of a male fetus in a pregnant woman. Nevertheless, cyproterone acetate, an antiandrogen with progestational effects, used regularly for hirsutism and acne in Europe and Canada,[136] is also used for androgenetic alopecia in women. Generally, 50 to 100 mg/day is taken in combination with estrogen as oral contraception in premenopausal women. Although there are no large controlled clinical studies, treatment does at least appear to stabilize progression.[144] Spironolactone, an aldosterone antagonist with mild antiandrogenic effects, is often used in the United States, where cyproterone acetate is not available; it seems to have some clinical effect, but does not cause regrowth.[145]

### 5α-Reductase Inhibitors

The most successful current treatment in men is finasteride,[104] a 5α-reductase type 2 inhibitor, which blocks the conversion of testosterone to 5α-dihydrotestosterone.[146] Finasteride was developed for benign prostate hypertrophy, for which it is used at 5 mg/day.[147] In carefully conducted, double-blind clinical trials of 1 mg/day orally in the United States and elsewhere, finasteride slowed the progression of hair loss and promoted hair growth in men younger than 42 with type II to V in 6 to 12 months (Fig. 178-8).[104] Even if hair did not regrow, balding progression was frequently halted. Changing to placebo after 12 months reduced hair counts and balding progressed; as the hormonal trigger and the follicle's ability to respond persist, treatment, like any hormonal therapy, must be maintained. Recently, finasteride has also been shown useful in older men.[148] Whether the inhibitor works centrally or within the balding follicles is unclear because plasma 5α-dihydrotestosterone levels are reduced.[104] However, some improvement in people younger than 40 with early balding with topical applications of 0.005% finasteride suggests a local effect.[149]

A large, prospective, randomized, phase 3 clinical trial of finasteride's potential (5 mg/day) to alter the development of prostate cancer in men older than 54 showed cancer incidence was reduced by about 25%[150,151]; there was minor concern because the reduced number of tumors occurring were more likely to be advanced than on placebo. Nevertheless, finasteride currently offers the most effective treatment for androgenetic alopecia in many men, with a potential protective value against developing prostate cancer, although whether this occurs at the lower hair growth dosage is unknown. Unfortunately, finasteride was not effective in postmenopausal women[152] and its use in premenopausal women is restricted since it may potentially cause hypospadias in a male fetus.

### Nonhormonal Therapy

The most commonly used nonhormonal treatment is minoxidil, initially devised as a vasodilator for use as an antihypertensive drug, which stimulated excessive hair growth as a side effect.[153,154] This provoked major interest in hair follicle biology because vellus follicles were stimulated to form terminal hairs, previously believed impossible. Topical application of minoxidil is used in both men and women, but, again, ceasing treatment leads to balding progression.[153,154] It stimulates regrowth in up to 30%, with only about 10% obtaining complete regrowth, probably due to its acting as a potassium channel regulator.[155] Most success occurs in younger men and in the early stages of balding, that is, Hamilton type V or less. More recently, a stronger topical 5% solution has been licensed for use in men.[156]

## FUTURE DEVELOPMENTS

Androgenetic alopecia is a common, progressive, androgen-dependent hair disorder that often has marked negative effects on the quality of life. There is a great deal of interest among pharmaceutical companies ever since minoxidil demonstrated that terminal hair growth could be stimulated from previously balding follicles. The development of the 5α-reductase type 2 inhibitor finasteride has opened up the use of hormonal treatments in men.

Since finasteride and minoxidil act at different sites, it seems reasonable to predict that their combined effects would be greater; combined treatment produced an additive effect in an animal model using the stump-tailed macaque.[157] The pharmaceutical company interest suggests that further drugs will be developed, both as hormone and biologic response

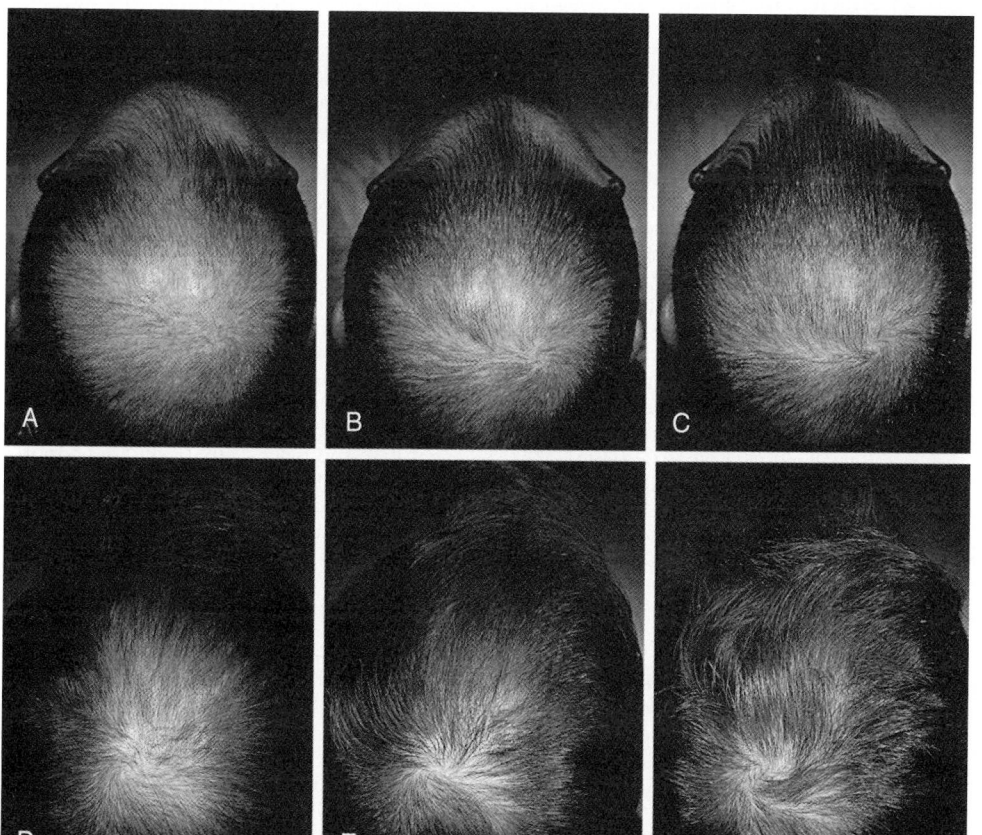

**Figure 178-8**  **A–F,** Oral treatment with the 5α-reductase type 2 inhibitor finasteride promotes hair growth in men 18 to 41 years with Norwood/Hamilton balding stages II vertex, III vertex, or IV or V. Clinical photographs of subjects from the clinical trial of 1 mg/day finasteride. Left photographs (*A* and *D*) show pretreatment values; middle photographs (*B* and *E*) show slight (*upper*) or moderate (*lower*) increased hair growth after 12 months; right (*C* and *F*) photographs exhibit moderately (*upper*) and greatly (*lower*) increased hair growth after 24 months of treatment. (Data from Kaufman et al[104]; photographs provided by Keith Kaufman, MD.)

modifiers. Combined 5α-reductase type 1 and type 2 inhibitors are also a possibility. There is still room for improvement because any current treatment must be taken for as long as the effect is required since the hormone and its target follicles are both still functional.

The culture of human androgenetic alopecia dermal papilla cells should provide a useful model system in which to study the precise parameters of gene expression regulated by androgens.[54,64,100] Identification of such factors could lead to other therapeutic approaches. Topical applications appear the most useful because this should reduce any potential side effects; in the future, this could harness the liposome method shown to deliver compounds into the hair bulb.[158] Overall, in the past 15 years, there have been great improvements in our understanding of hair follicle biology, the mechanism of androgen action in follicles, and ways to treat androgenetic alopecia; the current interest and momentum should produce new ways to control this condition in the not too distant future.

## Acknowledgments

The assistance of Mr. Chris Bowers and Mrs. Jenny Braithwaite with the figures is gratefully acknowledged.

## REFERENCES

1. Dawber RPP, de Berker D, Wojnarowska F: Disorders of hair. In Champion RH, Burton JL, Durns DA (eds): Rook/Wilkinson/Ebling Textbook of Dermatology, 6th ed. Oxford, Blackwell Science, 1998, pp 2869–2973.
2. Camacho F, Randall VA, Price VH (eds): Hair and Its Disorders: Biology, Research and Management. London, Martin Dunitz, 2000
3. Olsen EA (ed): Disorders of Hair Growth: Diagnosis and Treatment. New York, McGraw-Hill, 2003.
4. Giacometti L: Facts, legends and myths about the scalp throughout history. Arch Dermatol 95:629–635, 1967.
5. Lambert G: The Conquest of Baldness: The Wonderful Story of Hair. London, Souvenir, 1961.
6. Ebling FG, Hale PA, Randall VA: Hormones and hair growth. In Goldsmith LA (ed): Biochemistry and Physiology of the Skin, 2d ed. Oxford, Clarendon, 1991, pp 660–690.
7. Morris D: The Naked Ape. London, Jonathan Cape, 1969.
8. Randall VA, Ebling EJG: Seasonal changes in human hair growth. Br J Dermatol 124:146–151, 1991.
9. Goodhart CB: The evolutionary significance of human hair patterns and skin coloring. Adv Sci 17:53–58, 1960.
10. Ebling FJG: The mythological evolution of nudity. J Hum Evol 14:33–41, 1985.
11. Reynolds EL: The appearance of adult patterns of body hair in man. Ann N Y Acad Sci 53:576–584, 1951.
12. Marshall WA, Tanner JM: Variations in pattern of pubertal change in girls. Arch Dis Child 44:291–303, 1969.
13. Marshall WA, Tanner JM: Variations in the pattern of pubertal changes in boys. Arch Dis Child 45:13–23, 1970.
14. Ebling FJG: Hair. J Invest Dermatol 67:98–105, 1976.
15. Montagna W, Van Scott EJ: The anatomy of the hair follicle. In Montagna W, Ellis RA (eds): The Biology of Hair Growth. New York, Academic, 1958, pp 39–64.
16. Hashimoto K: The structure of human hair. Clin Dermatol 6:7–21, 1988.
17. Auber L: The anatomy of follicles producing wool fibers with special reference to keratinization. Trans R Soc Edinb 62:191–254, 1952.
18. Oliver RF, Jahoda CAB: The dermal papilla and maintenance of hair growth. In Rogers GE, Reis PR, Ward KA, et al (eds): The Biology of Wool and Hair. London, Chapman & Hall, 1989, pp 51–67.
19. Jahoda CAB, Reynolds AJ: Dermal-epidermal interactions: Adult follicle-derived cell populations and hair growth. In Whiting DA (ed): Dermatol Clin 14: Update on Hair Disorders. Philadelphia, WB Saunders, 1996, pp 573–583.
20. Dry FW: The coat of the mouse (Mus musculus). J Genet 16:32–35, 1926.
21. Kligman AG: The human hair cycle. J Invest Dermatol 33:307–316, 1959.
22. Hamilton JB: Age, sex and genetic factors in the regulation of hair growth in man: A comparison of Caucasian and Japanese populations. In Montagna W, Ellis RA (eds): The Biology of Hair Growth. New York, Academic, 1958, pp 399–433.
23. Hamilton JB: A secondary sexual character that develops in men but not in women upon aging of an organ present in both sexes. Anat Rec 94:466–467, 1946.
24. Hamilton JB: Patterned loss of hair in man: Types and incidence. Ann N Y Acad Sci 53:708–728, 1951.
25. Stenn K, Parimoo S, Prouty S: Growth of the hair follicle: A cycling and regenerating biological system. In Chuong CM (ed): Molecular Basis of Epithelial Appendage Morphogenesis. Austin, Texas, Laudes, 1998.
26. Cotsarelis G, Sun T, Lavker R: Label-retaining cells reside in the bulge area of the pilosebaceous unit: Implications for follicular stem cells, hair cycle and skin carcinogenesis. Cell 61:1329–1337, 1990.
27. Taylor G, Lehrer MS, Jensen PJ, et al: Involvement of follicular stem cells in forming not only the follicle but also the epidermis. Cell 102:451–461, 2000.
28. Lavker RM, Sun TT, Oshima H, et al: Hair follicle stem cells. J Investig Dermatol Symp Proc 8:28–38, 2003.
29. Saitoh M, Sakamoto M: Human hair cycle. J Invest Dermatol 54:65–81, 1970.
30. Paus R, Müller-Röver S, McKay I: Control of the hair follicle growth cycle. In Camacho FM, Randall VA, Price VH (eds): Hair and Its Disorders: Biology, Pathology and Management. London, Martin Dunitz, 2000, pp 83–94.
31. Orentreich N: Scalp hair replacement in men. In Montagna W, Dobson RL (eds): Advances in Biology of Skin, Vol 9: Hair Growth. Oxford, Pergamon, 1969, pp 99–108.
32. Courtois M, Loussouarn G, Howseau S, et al: Periodicity in the growth and shedding of hair. Br J Dermatol 134:47–54, 1996.
33. Reinberg A, Lagoguey M, Chauffournier JM, Cesselin F: Circannual and circadian rhythms in plasma testosterone in five healthy young Parisian males. Acta Endocrinol 80:732–743, 1975.
34. Smals AGH, Kloppenberg PWC, Benrad THJ: Circannual cycle in plasma testosterone levels in man. J Clin Endocrinol Metab 42:979–982, 1976.
35. Bellastella A, Criscuoco T, Mango A, et al: Circannual rhythms of LH, FSH, testosterone, prolactin and cortisol during puberty. Clin Endocrinol 19:453–459, 1983.
36. Randall VA: Androgens and human hair growth. Clin Endocrinol 40:439–457, 1994.
37. Marshall WA, Tanner JM: Variations in pattern of pubertal change in girls. Arch Dis Child 44:291–303, 1969.
38. Marshall WA, Tanner JM: Variations in the pattern of pubertal changes in boys. Arch Dis Child 45:13–23, 1970.
39. Winter JSD, Faiman C: Pituitary-gonadal relations in male children and adolescents. Pediatr Res 6:125–135, 1972.
40. Winter JSD, Faiman C: Pituitary-gonadal relations in female children and adolescents. Pediatr Res 7:948–953, 1973.
41. Hamilton JB: Male hormone stimulation is a prerequisite and an incitant in common baldness. Am J Anat 71:451–480, 1942.
42. Hamilton JB: Effect of castration in adolescent and young adult males upon further changes in the proportions of bare and hairy scalp. J Clin Endocrinol Metab 20:1309–1318, 1960.
43. McPhaul MJ: Androgen receptors and androgen insensitivity syndromes. In DeGroot LJ, Jameson JL (eds): Endocrinology, 5th ed. Philadelphia, WB Saunders, 2004 (in press).
44. Handelsman DJ: Androgens and androgen action. In DeGroot LJ, Jameson JL (eds): Endocrinology, 5th ed. Philadelphia, WB Saunders, 2004 (in press).
45. Wilson JD, Griffin JE, Russell DW: Steroid 5α-reductase 2 deficiency. Endocr Rev 14:577–593, 1993.
46. Imperato-McGinley J, Gautier T, Cai LQ, et al: The androgen control of sebum

production: Studies of subjects with dihydrotestosterone deficiency and complete androgen insensitivity. J Clin Endocrinol Metab 76:524–528, 1993.

47. Cunha GR: Endocrine actions of the prostate and benign prostatic hypertrophy. In DeGroot LJ, Jameson JL (eds): Endocrinology, 5th ed. Philadelphia, WB Saunders, 2004 (in press).

48. Randall VA, Thornton MJ, Hamada K, et al: Androgens and the hair follicle: Cultured human dermal papilla cells as a model system. Ann N Y Acad Sci 642:355–375, 1991.

49. Randall VA: Androgens and hair: A biological paradox. In Nieschlag E, Behre HM (eds): Testosterone: Action, Deficiency, Substitution, 3d ed. Berlin, Cambridge University Press, 2004.

50. Thornton MJ, Hamada K, Messenger AG, Randall VA: Beard, but not scalp, dermal papilla cells secrete autocrine growth factors in response to testosterone in vitro. J Invest Dermatol 111:727–732, 1998.

51. Choudhry R, Hodgins MB, Van der Kwast TH, et al: Localisation of androgen receptors in human skin by immunohistochemistry: Implications for the hormonal regulation of hair growth, sebaceous glands and sweat glands. J Endocrinol 133:467–475, 1992.

52. Itami S, Kurata S, Sonada T, Takayasu S: Interactions between dermal papilla cells and follicular epithelial cells in vitro: Effect of androgen. Br J Derm 132:527–532, 1995.

53. Randall VA, Thornton MJ, Messenger AG: Cultured dermal papilla cells from androgen-dependent human follicles (e.g., beard) contain more androgen receptors than those from non-balding areas. J Endocrinol 133:141–147, 1992.

54. Hibberts NA, Howell AE, Randall VA: Dermal papilla cells from human balding scalp hair follicles contain higher levels of androgen receptors than those from non-balding scalp. J Endocrinol 156:59–65, 1998.

55. Ando Y, Yamaguchi Y, Hamada K, et al: Expression of mRNA for androgen receptor, 5α-reductase and 17β-hydroxysteroid dehydrogenase in human dermal papilla cells. Br J Derm 141:840–845, 1999.

56. Itami S, Kurata S, Takayasu S: 5α-Reductase activity in cultured human dermal papilla cells from beard compared with reticular dermal fibroblasts. J Invest Dermatol 94:150–152, 1990.

57. Thornton MJ, Liang I, Hamada K, et al: Differences in testosterone metabolism by beard and scalp hair follicle dermal papilla cells. Clin Endocrinol 39:633–639, 1993.

58. Hamada K, Thornton MJ, Liang I, et al: Pubic and axillary dermal papilla cells do not produce 5α-dihydrotestosterone in culture. J Invest Dermatol 106:1017–1022, 1996.

59. Reynolds AJ, Lawrence C, Cserhalmi-Friedman PB, et al: Trans-gender induction of hair follicles. Nature 402:33–34, 1999.

60. Merrick AE, Randall VA, Messenger AG, Thornton MJ: Beard dermal sheath cells contain androgen receptors: Implications for future inductions of human hair follicles. J Invest Dermatol, 2005 (submitted).

61. Asada Y, Sonoda T, Ojiro M, et al: 5α-reductase type 2 is constitutively expressed in the dermal papilla and connective tissue sheath of the hair follicle in vivo but not during culture in vitro. J Clin Endocrinol Metab 86:2875–2880, 2001.

62. Messenger AG, Elliott K, Temple A, Randall VA: Expression of basement membrane proteins and interstitial collagens in dermal papillae of human hair follicles. J Invest Dermatol 96:93–97, 1991.

63. Itami S, Kurata S, Takayasu S: Androgen induction of follicular epithelial cell growth is mediated via insulin-like growth factor I from dermal papilla cells. Biochem Biophys Res Commun 212:988–994, 1995.

64. Hibberts NA, Randall VA: Testosterone inhibits the capacity of cultured cells from human balding scalp dermal papilla cells to produce keratinocyte mitogenic factors. In Van Neste DV, Randall VA (eds): Hair Research for the Next Millennium. Amsterdam, Elsevier Science, 1996, pp 303–306.

65. Obana N, Chang C, Uno H: Inhibition of hair growth by testosterone in the presence of dermal papilla cells from the frontal bald scalp of the post-pubertal stump-tailed macaque. Endocrinology 138:356–361, 1997.

66. Randall VA, Hibberts NA, Thornton MJ, et al: Do androgens influence hair growth by altering the paracrine factors secreted by dermal papilla cells? Eur J Dermatol 11:315–320, 2001.

67. Hibberts NA, Messenger AG, Randall VA: Dermal papilla cells derived from beard hair follicles secrete more stem cell factor (SCF) in culture than scalp cells or dermal fibroblasts. Biochem Biophys Res Commun 222:401–405, 1996.

68. Philpott MP: The roles of growth factors in hair follicles: Investigations using cultured hair follicles. In Camacho F, Randall VA, Price VH (eds): Hair and Its Disorders: Biology, Research and Management. London, Martin Dunitz, 2000, pp 103–113.

69. Sonada T, Asada Y, Kurata S, Takayasu S: The mRNA for protease nexin-1 is expressed in human dermal papilla cells and its level is affected by androgen. J Invest Dermatol 113:308–313, 1999.

70. Randall VA, Hibberts NA, Thornton MJ, et al: The hair follicle: A paradoxical androgen target organ. Horm Res 54:243–250, 2001.

71. Elliot K, Stephenson TJ, Messenger AG: Differences in hair follicle dermal papilla volume are due to extracellular matrix volume and cell number: Implications for the control of hair follicle size and androgen responses. J Invest Dermatol 113:873–877, 1999.

72. Hamada K, Randall VA: Balding scalp dermal papilla cells secrete a soluble factor(s) which delays the onset of anagen in mice in vivo. J Investig Dermatol Symp Proc 8:139, 2003.

73. Inui S, Fukuzato Y, Nakajima T, et al: Identification of androgen-inducible TGF-beta1 derived from dermal papilla cells as a key mediator in androgenetic alopecia. J Investig Dermatol Symp Proc 8:69–71, 2003.

74. Tsuji Y, Denda S, Soma T, et al: A potential suppressor of TGF-β delays catagen progression in hair follicles. J Investig Dermatol Symp Proc 8:65–68, 2003.

75. Norwood OTT: Male pattern baldness: Classification and incidence. South Med J 68:1359–1370, 1975.

76. Ludwig E: Classification of the types of androgenic alopecia (common baldness) arising in the female sex. Br J Dermatol 97:249–256, 1977.

77. Venning VA, Dawber R: Patterned androgenic alopecia. J Am Acad Dermatol 18:1073–1078, 1988.

78. Olsen EA: Androgenetic alopecia. In Olsen EA (ed): Disorders of Hair Growth, Diagnosis and Treatment. New York, McGraw-Hill, 1994, pp 257–283.

79. Takashima I, Iju M, Sudo M: Alopecia androgenetica: Its incidence in Japanese and associated conditions. In Orfanos CE, Montagna W, Stuttgen G (eds): Hair Research Status and Future Aspects. New York, Springer Verlag, 1981, pp 287–293.

80. Setty LR: Hair patterns of the scalp of white and negro males. Am J Phys Anthropol 33:49–55, 1970.

81. Uno H, Imamura K, Pan H: Androgenetic alopecia in the stump-tailed macaque: An important model for investigating the pathology and antiandrogenic therapy of male-pattern baldness. In Camacho F, Randall VA, Price VH (eds): Hair and Its Disorders: Biology, Research and Management. London, Martin Dunitz, 2000, pp 137–151.

82. Croft NJ, Randall VA: The antler of the red deer (Cervus elaphus): An androgen target organ. In Van Neste D (ed): Hair Science and Technology. Brussels, 2003, pp 69–74.

83. Goodhart DB: The evolutionary significance of human hair patterns and skin coloring. Adv Sci 17:53–59, 1960.

84. Ebling FJG: Age changes in cutaneous appendages. J Appl Cosmetol 3:243–250, 1985.

85. Terry RL, Davis JS: Components of facial attractiveness. Percept Mot Skills 42:918, 1976.

86. Cash TF: The psychological effects of androgenetic alopecia in men. J Am Acad Dermatol 26:926–931, 1992.

87. Franzoi SL, Anderson J, Frommelt S: Individual differences in men's perceptions of and reactions to thinning hair. J Soc Psychol 130:209–218, 1990.

88. Maffei C, Fossati A, Reialdi F, Ruia E: Personality disorders and psychopathologic symptoms in patients with androgenetic alopecia. Arch Dermatol 130:868–872, 1994.

89. Wells PA, Willmoth T, Russell RJH: Does fortune favor the bald? Psychological correlates of hair loss in males. Br J Psychol 86:337–344, 1995.

90. Girman CJ, Rhodes T, Lilly FRW, et al: Effects of self-perceived hair loss in a community sample of men. Dermatology 197:223–229, 1998.

91. Cash TF: Psychological effects of androgenetic alopecia on women: Comparisons with balding men and with female control subjects. J Am Acad Dermatol 29:568–575, 1993.

92. Van der Dank J, Passchier J, Knegt-Junk C, et al: Psychological characteristics of women with androgenetic alopecia: A controlled study. Br J Dermatol 125:248–252, 1991.

93. Brun-Falco O, Christophers E: Hair root patterns in male pattern alopecia. In Baccareda-Boy A, Moretti G, Fray JR (eds): Biopathology of Pattern Alopecia. Basel, Kargel, 1968, pp 141–145.

94. Rushton DH, Ramsay ID, Norris MJ, Gilkes JJH: Natural progression of male pattern baldness in young men. Clin Exp Dermatol 16:188–192, 1991.

95. Whiting DA: Diagnostic and predictive value of horizontal sections of scalp biopsy specimens in male pattern androgenetic alopecia. J Am Acad Dermatol 28:755–763, 1993.

96. Kligman AM: The comparative histopathology of male-pattern baldness and senescent baldness. Clin Dermatol 6:108–118, 1988.

97. Ebling FJG: Age changes in cutaneous appendages. J Appl Cosmetol 3:243–250, 1985.

98. Pecoran V, Astore I, Barman JM: The prenatal and postnatal hair cycles in men. In Baccareda-Boy A, Moretti G, Fray JR (eds): Biopathology of Pattern Alopecia. Basel, Kargel, 1968, pp 29–38.

99. Douritz JM, Silvers DN: Giant cells in male pattern alopecia: A histological marker and pathogenic clue. J Cutan Pathol 6:108–113, 1979.

100. Maguire HC, Kligman AM: Common baldness in women. Geriatrics 18:329–334, 1963.

101. Covato F, Morreti G, Bertamino R: In Baccareda-Boy A, Moretti G, Fray JR (eds): Biopathology of Pattern Alopecia. Basel, Kargel, 1968, pp 191–199.

102. Randall VA, Hibberts NA, Hamada K: A comparison of the culture and growth of dermal papilla cells derived from normal and balding (androgenetic alopecia) scalp. Br J Dermatol 134:437–444, 1996.

103. Giacometti L, Montagna W: The nerve fibers in male pattern alopecia. In Baccareda-Boy A, Moretti G, Fray JR (eds): Biopathology of Pattern Alopecia. Basel, Kargel, 1968, pp 208–216.

104. Kaufman KD, Olsen EA, Whiting D, et al: Finasteride in the treatment of men with androgenetic alopecia. J Am Acad Dermatol 39:578–589, 1998.

105. Burton JL, Ben Halim MM, Meyrick G: Male pattern alopecia and masculinity. Br J Dermatol 100:507–512, 1979.

106. Phillipou G, Kirke J: Significance of steroid measurements in male pattern alopecia. Clin Exp Dermatol 6:53, 1981.

107. Pitts RL: Serum elevation of dehydroepiandrosterone sulfate associated with male pattern baldness in young men. J Am Acad Dermatol 16:571–573, 1987.

108. Cipriani R, Ruzza G, Foresta C, et al: Sex hormone binding globulin and saliva testosterone levels in men with androgenetic alopecia. Br J Dermatol 109:249–252, 1983.

109. Denmark-Wahnefried W, Lesko S, Conway MR, et al: Serum androgens: Associations with prostate cancer risk and hair patterning. J Androl 18:495–500, 1997.

110. Buiazzi M, Calandra P: Testosterone elimination in female patients with acne, chronic alopecia and hirsutism. Ital Gen Rev Dermatol 8:241, 1968.

111. Ludwig E: The role of sexual hormones in pattern alopecia. In Baccareda-Boy A, Moretti G, Fray JR (eds): Biopathology of Pattern Alopecia. Basel, Kargel, 1968, pp 50–60.

112. Miller JA, Darley CR, Karkavitsas K, et al: Low sex-hormone binding globulin levels in young women with diffuse hair loss. Br J Dermatol 106:331–336, 1982.

113. De Villez RL, Dunn J: Female androgenic alopecia: The 3α-17β androstanediol glucuronide/sex hormone binding globulin ratio as a possible marker for female pattern baldness. Arch Dermatol 122:1011–1014, 1986.

114. Georgala G, Papasotiriou V, Stavropoulos P: Serum testosterone and sex hormone binding levels in women with androgenic alopecia. Acta Dermatol Venereol (Scand) 66:532–534, 1986.

115. Stickler JH, Algin BG: Androgen excess and hair loss in women. In Azziz R, Nestler JE, Dewailly D (eds): Androgen excess disorders. New York, Lippincot-Raven, 1997, pp 141–147.

116. Cela E, Robertson C, Rush K, et al: Prevalence of polycystic ovaries in women with androgenic alopecia. Eur J Endocrinol 149:439–442, 2003.

117. Futterweit W, Dunaif Y, Yeh H-C, Kingsley P: The prevalence of hyperandrogenism in 109 consecutive female patients with diffuse alopecia. J Am Acad Dermatol 19:831–836, 1988.

118. O'Driscoll JB, Mamtora H, Higginson J, et al: A prospective study of the prevalence of clear-cut endocrine disorders and polycystic ovaries in 350 patients presenting with hirsutism or androgenic alopecia. Clin Endocrinol 4:231–236, 1994.

119. Birch MP, Messenger AG: Genetic factors predispose to balding and non-balding in men. Eur J Dermatol 11:309–314, 2001.

120. Bergfeld WF: Androgenetic alopecia: An autosomal dominant disorder. Am J Med 98:955–985, 1955.

121. Osbourn D: Inheritance of baldness. J Hered 7:347–355, 1916.

122. Kuster W, Happle R: The inheritance of common baldness: Two B or not two B? J Am Acad Dermatol 11:921–926, 1984.

123. Ellis JA, Harrap SB: The genetics of androgenetic alopecia. Clin Dermatol 19:149–154, 2001.

124. Ellis JA, Stebbing M, Harrap SB: Male pattern baldness is not associated with established cardiovascular risk factors in the general population. Clin Sci 100:401–404, 2001.

125. Ellis JA, Stebbing M, Harrap SB: Genetic analysis of male pattern baldness and the 5alpha-reductase genes. J Invest Dermatol 110:849–853, 1998.

126. Ha SJ, Kim JS, Myung JW, et al: Analysis of genetic polymorphisms of steroid 5alpha-reductase type 1 and 2 genes in Korean men with androgenetic alopecia. J Dermatol Sci 31:135–134, 2003.

127. Ellis JA, Stebbing M, Harrap SB: Polymorphism of androgen receptor gene is associated with male pattern baldness. J Invest Dermatol 116:452–455, 2001.

128. Ibanez L, Ong KK, Mongan N, et al: Androgen receptor gene CAG repeat polymorphism in the development of ovarian hyperandrogenism. J Clin Endocrinol Metab 88:3333–3338, 2003.

129. Stanford JL, Just JJ, Gibbs M, et al: Polymorphic repeats in the androgen receptor gene: molecular markers of prostate cancer risk. Cancer Res 57:1194–1198, 1997.

130. Carey AH, Chan KL, Short F, et al: Evidence for a single gene effect causing polycystic ovaries and male pattern baldness. Clin Endocrinol 38:653–658, 1993.

131. Konig A, Happle R, Tchitcherina E, et al: An X-linked gene involved in androgenetic alopecia: A lesson to be learned from adrenoleukodystrophy. Dermatology 200:213–218, 2000.

132. Ahmad W, Faiyaz ul Haque M, Brancolini V, et al: Alopecia universalis associated with a mutation in the human hairless gene. Science 279:720–724, 1998.

133. Hillmer AM, Kruse R, Macciardi F, et al: The hairless gene in androgenetic alopecia: Results of a systematic mutation screening and a family-based association approach. Br J Dermatol 146:601–608, 2002.

134. Orentreich N, Durr NP: Biology of scalp hair growth. Clin Plast Surg 9:197–205, 1982.

135. Ziller C: Pattern formation in neural crest derivatives. In Van Neste D, Randall VA (eds): Hair Research for the Next Millennium. Amsterdam, Elsevier Science, 1996, pp 1–5.

136. Fruzetti F: Treatment of hirsutism: Antiandrogen and 5α-reductase inhibitor therapy. In Azziz R, Nestler JE, Dewailly D (eds): Androgen Excess Disorders in Women. Philadelphia, Lippincott-Raven, 1997, pp 787–797.

137. Lesko SM, Rosenberg L, Shapiro S: A case-control study of baldness in relation to myocardial infarction in men. JAMA 269:998–1003, 1993.

138. Herrera CR, D'Agostino RB, Gerstman BB, et al: Baldness and coronary heart disease rates in men from the Framingham study. Am J Epidemiol 142:828–833, 1995.

139. Schweikert H, Wilson JD: Regulation of human hair growth by steroid hormones. I: Testosterone metabolism in isolated hair. J Clin Endocrinol Metab 40:413–417, 1974.

140. Sawaya ME, Price VH: Different levels of 5α-reductase type I and II, aromatase and androgen receptor in hair follicles of women and men with androgenetic alopecia. J Invest Dermatol 109:296–301, 1997.

141. Chan W, Zouboulis C, Orfanos C: The 5α-reductase system and its inhibitors: Recent development and its perspective in treating androgen-dependent skin disorders. Dermatology 193:177–182, 1996.

142. Thigpen AE, Silver RI, Guileyarlo JM, et al: Tissue distribution and ontogeny of steroid 5α-reductase isoenzyme expression. J Clin Invest 92:903–910, 1993.

143. Unger WP: Innovations in hair transplanting: Progress versus promotion. Adv Dermatol 16:427–450, 2000.

144. Vexiau P, Chaspoux C, Boudou P, et al: Effects of minoxidil 2% vs. cyproterone acetate treatment on female androgenetic alopecia: A controlled, 12-month randomized trial. Br J Dermatol 146:992–999, 2002.

145. Hoffmann R, Happle R: Current understanding of androgenetic alopecia. Part II: Clinical aspects and treatment. Eur J Dermatol 10:410–417, 2000.

146. Shapiro J, Kaufman KD: Use of finasteride in the treatment of men with androgenetic alopecia (male pattern hair loss). J Investig Dermatol Symp Proc 8:20–23, 2003.

147. Whiting DA, Olsen EA, Savin R, et al; Male Pattern Hair Loss Study Group: Efficacy and tolerability of finasteride 1 mg in men aged 41 to 60 years with male pattern hair loss. Eur J Dermatol 13:150–160, 2003.

148. Gormbey GJ, Stener E, Briskewitz RC, et al: The effect of finasteride in men with benign prostate hyperplasia. N Engl J Med 327:1185–1191, 1992.

149. Mazzarella F, Loconsole F, Commisa A, et al: Topical finasteride in the treatment of androgenic alopecia: Preliminary evaluations after a 16-month therapy course. J Dermatol Treat 8:189–192, 1997.

150. Price VH, Roberts JL, Hordinsky M, et al: Lack of efficacy of finasteride in postmenopausal women with androgenetic alopecia. J Am Acad Dermatol 43:768–776, 2000.

151. Thompson IM, Goodman PJ, Tangen CM, et al: The influence of finasteride on the development of prostate cancer. N Engl J Med 349:215–224, 2003.

152. Higgins B, Thompson IM: The Prostate Cancer Prevention Trial: Current status. J Urol 171:S15–S17, 2004.

153. Shapiro J, Price VH: Hair regrowth: Therapeutic agents: Dermatologic therapy. Dermatol Clin 16:341–356, 1998.

154. Dawber R: Update on minoxidil treatment of hair loss. In Camacho F, Randall VA, Price VH (eds): Hair and Its Disorders: Biology, Research and Management. London, Martin Dunitz, 2000, pp 169–173.

155. Messenger AG, Rundegren J: Minoxidil: Mechanisms of action on hair growth. Br J Dermatol 150:186–194, 2004.

156. Olsen EA, Dunlap FE, Funicella T, et al: A randomized clinical trial of 5% topical minoxidil versus 2% topical minoxidil and placebo in the treatment of androgenetic alopecia in men. J Am Acad Dermatol 47:377–385, 2002.

157. Uno H, Imamura K, Pan H: Androgenetic alopecia in the stump-tailed macaque: An important model for investigating the pathology and antiandrogenic therapy of male pattern baldness. In Camacho F, Randall VA, Price VH (eds): Hair and Its Disorders: Biology, Research and Management. London, Martin Dunitz, 2000, pp 137–151.

158. Hoffmann RM, Li LN: The feasibility of targeted selective gene therapy of the hair follicle. Nat Med 1:705–706, 1995.

# Endocrinology of the Prostate and Benign Prostatic Hyperplasia

## Simon W. Hayward, Annemarie A. Donjacour, Neil A. Bhowmick, Axel A. Thomson, and Gerald R. Cunha

INTRODUCTION

DEVELOPMENT AND ADULT FUNCTION OF THE PROSTATE

STEROID HORMONES
Androgen Pathway Mutations

MESENCHYMAL-EPITHELIAL INTERACTIONS

BENIGN PROSTATIC HYPERPLASIA

CONCLUSIONS

## INTRODUCTION

Development of the prostate begins with the growth of prostatic buds from the urogenital sinus at about 10 weeks of fetal development in the human,[1,2] at 19 days of gestation in the rat, and at 17 days in the mouse.[3,4] Testicular androgens act on androgen receptors (ARs) in the urogenital sinus mesenchyme (UGM) to induce epithelial budding, proliferation and differentiation into ductal structures.[5] Prostatic ducts differentiate in a proximal to distal direction (from the urethra to the ductal tip) in the growing prostate. The epithelium undergoes proliferation, ductal branching morphogenesis, cytodifferentiation into luminal and basal subtypes, ductal canalization, and expression of characteristic secretory markers. Concurrent with this process, the UGM proliferates and differentiates into prostatic smooth muscle and interfascicular fibroblasts.[6–8] In adulthood, androgens are believed to act on prostatic smooth muscle (which expresses AR) to maintain a fully differentiated growth-quiescent epithelium, and on the prostatic epithelium to induce and maintain secretory function.[9,10] These events are known to be mediated by the actions of androgens on the stroma of the developing and adult prostate,[11,12] with the role of the epithelial AR apparently being restricted to regulating secretory functions.[13] This clearly suggests that prostate development is mediated by paracrine androgen-regulated factors (andromedins) produced by the mesenchyme and acting on the epithelium. Growth factors are obvious candidate andromedins, however, as is discussed later, present data regarding androgenic regulation of known growth factors are inconclusive.

The presence of many growth factors has been documented in the prostates of humans and other mammals.[14–20] Some growth factors, for example, fibroblast growth factors 7 and 10 (FGF-7 and FGF-10), sonic hedgehog (Shh), and hepatic growth factor (HGF), are prototypic paracrine candidates in that they have expression patterns in which the ligand is restricted to one tissue and the receptor to another.[21–25] For many other growth factors and their receptors, however, there is, as yet, no clearly identified pattern of expression in the different cell types that comprise the prostate.

Growth factors and protein hormones use essentially similar signal transduction mechanisms; however, growth factors have traditionally been considered to act locally, whereas protein hormones act at sites distant from their site of production. It is now clear that many so-called growth factors can be active at sites distant from their production. For example, maternal transforming growth factor β1 (TGF-β1) has been

shown to be capable of crossing the placenta and acting on the fetus.[26] Thus, it is increasingly difficult to determine whether these proteins should be considered hormones or growth factors or whether they belong in both categories with specific roles being defined on a case-by-case basis. Growth factors can act as hormones when their action is endocrine and as growth factors when they have a clearly paracrine or autocrine role. In terms of prostatic biology, a further complication in this area is the revelation that a number of growth factors can stimulate the androgen receptor, leading to transcriptional activation even in the absence of androgens[27] (for a review, see reference 28).

Benign prostatic hyperplasia (BPH) is one of the most common benign proliferative diseases in men. The etiology of BPH requires functional testes and aging. Given sufficient time, the vast majority of men will develop BPH. At age 60, the disease is histologically identifiable in 50% of men and, by age 85 years, is found in 90%, with symptoms occurring in a significant proportion.[29] McNeal has proposed that BPH results from a reawakening of inductive potential in adult prostatic stroma.[30–32] This is believed to result in focalized formation of new ductal architecture in the so-called transition zone of the prostate. This in turn leads to urethral compression and obstruction. One of the central tenets of McNeal's hypothesis is the idea that adult prostatic epithelium retains an ability to respond to inductive signaling with new proliferation and ductal branching morphogenesis, which has been verified for adult rat, mouse, and human prostatic epithelia.[33–35]

This chapter reviews the current state of knowledge of the role of steroid hormones and growth factors in the development and adult maintenance of the prostate and in the genesis of BPH.

## DEVELOPMENT AND ADULT FUNCTION OF THE PROSTATE

Prostatic development has been most widely studied in rats, mice, and dogs, with a limited number of studies of human fetal prostatic development. Thus, much of our knowledge of the endocrinology and physiology of human prostatic development is inferred from animal studies. We know that androgenic stimulation is absolutely required for prostatic development.[36] The development of prostatic tissue is not determined by fetal genetic sex, but rather by exposure to androgens. Both the male and female urogenital sinus (UGS) will form functional prostatic tissue if stimulated by androgens during the appropriate developmental period.[37–39]

In rodents, initial prostatic budding is elicited by prenatal androgenic action. Ductal branching morphogenesis, canalization, and epithelial cytodifferentiation require postnatal androgenic stimulation. In mice and rats, the majority of ductal branching morphogenesis occurs between birth and puberty when circulating androgen levels are extremely low.[40] These early branching events are illustrated in Figure 179-1. At puberty, there is a growth spurt characterized by a large increase in prostatic wet weight but only a small increase in the number of ductal tips.[41] These data indicate that the developing prostate is exquisitely sensitive to low androgen titers for ductal branching morphogenesis and that its response to increased androgen levels at puberty (an increase in wet weight) is separate and discrete from the early ductal branching morphogenesis.

The mesenchymal cells surrounding the UGS are derived from the embryonic mesoderm. These UGM cells are initially fibroblastic, but undergo an orderly differentiation process to form the smooth muscle sheaths of the rodent prostate or the thick sheets of muscle found in human prostate.[42,43] In rats, the first mesenchymal cell marker expressed in UGM is vimentin. This is followed by smooth muscle α-actin, which is widely expressed throughout embryonic UGM.[7] After birth, there is a sequential expression of a number of smooth muscle–specific markers and an associated condensation of the loose mesenchymal tissue into organized muscular sheaths around the epithelial ducts by 20 days postnatal. This process is associated with a downregulation of vimentin in the developing smooth muscle and its localization to the interfascicular fibroblasts of the prostate. The order of the initiation of expression of the various smooth muscle markers is the same in different prostatic lobes in the rat.[7] A similar differentiation pathway also occurs in the developing human prostate (Hayward and Haughney, unpublished data).

The development of the prostatic epithelium occurs concurrently with prostatic stromal maturation. The whole process is dependent on androgenic stimulation. ARs are initially expressed in the UGM and, later in development, are also seen in the developing prostatic epithelium (Fig. 179-2). Androgens act on ARs in the UGM to induce epithelial proliferation, ductal branching morphogenesis, and cytodifferentiation into basal and luminal epithelial subtypes.[11] In turn, the developing prostatic epithelium directs and patterns prostatic smooth muscle differentiation.[35] Neither prostatic epithelium nor prostatic smooth muscle can develop in the absence of the other tissue. It is clear, however, that UGM can induce prostatic differentiation in a number of endodermal epithelia, while many epithelial cells can induce UGM to form smooth muscle.[44–46]

In the human, the prostate is small in childhood, weighing around 2 g. At puberty, it undergoes a phase of exponential growth, increasing in size to about 20 g. This corresponds to the rise in serum testosterone to adult levels. Mean prostatic weight then stabilizes and remains fairly constant until the end of the third decade of life when mean prostatic weight begins to rise slowly.[29] This rise reflects the onset of pathogenesis of BPH.[47] The human prostate is an extremely slow-growing organ. Even during puberty, when the peak rate of prostatic growth is achieved, the gland has a doubling time calculated as 2.76 years.[48] Localized prostatic growth, which occurs during the initiation of BPH nodules, is also extremely slow, with peak doubling times of 4.5 years in 30- to 50-year-old men.[48] This slow rate of growth is balanced by extremely low rates of apoptosis in the normal human prostate.[49,50]

While androgens are commonly thought of as being responsible for prostatic growth, it is important to note that in fact they play a role in both positive and negative regulation of proliferation, with these effects being context dependent. Thus, while androgens are absolutely required for the growth and development of the prostate, and are certainly necessary to maintain a differentiated and functional organ, the normal adult prostate (which exists in the face of adult levels of androgens) is essentially growth quiescent. In addition to their ability to regulate organ size and differentiation, androgens are required to initiate prostatic secretory function at puberty and to maintain it throughout adult life.[51,52]

Adult prostatic epithelium is pseudostratified with tall columnar secretory epithelial cells lining the duct.[53] Basal epithelial cells form a nearly continuous layer in the human, but are sparse in rodents. All luminal epithelial cells express AR (see Fig. 179-2). There is disagreement in the literature about the expression of AR by the basal cells.[54,55]

In the adult, the prostatic stroma is composed principally of smooth muscle cells that express AR. These cells are located immediately subadjacent to the prostatic epithelial basement membrane and, in the human, form thick sheets of muscle throughout the gland. In rodents, the prostatic smooth muscle is organized into thin sheaths around individual prostatic ducts. The thickness of the muscular sheaths varies with prostatic lobe and also with the proximal-distal position along individual ducts (thicker proximally and thinner distally).[7,9] Fibroblasts are interspersed between the smooth muscle cells. Maintenance of adult prostatic morphology is believed to be

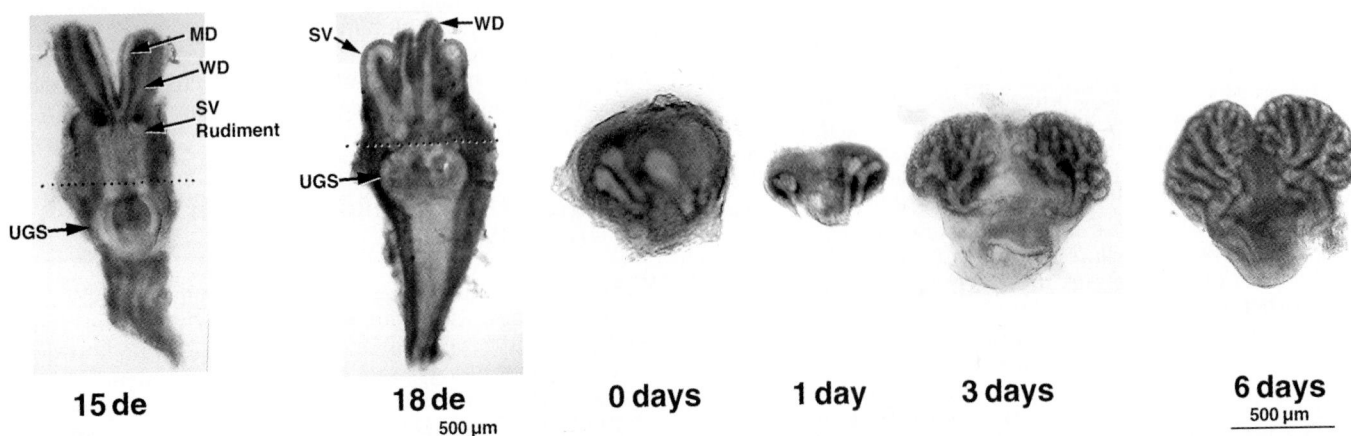

*Figure 179-1* Wholemount images showing the prenatal and early postnatal development of the mouse prostate. At 15 days of embryonic development (15 de), the urogenital sinus (UGS), müllerian duct (MD), and wolffian duct (WD) can be seen. The seminal vesicle (SV) rudiment can be seen as a swelling of the WD. By 18 days of embryonic development (18 de), the developing seminal vesicle is clearly visible. By the day of birth (0 days), the various lobes of the prostate have differentiated. The ventral prostates shown in the four illustrations to the right start as solid epithelial cords that begin to branch within a day of birth (1 day) and continue to branch rapidly over succeeding days (3 days and 6 days).

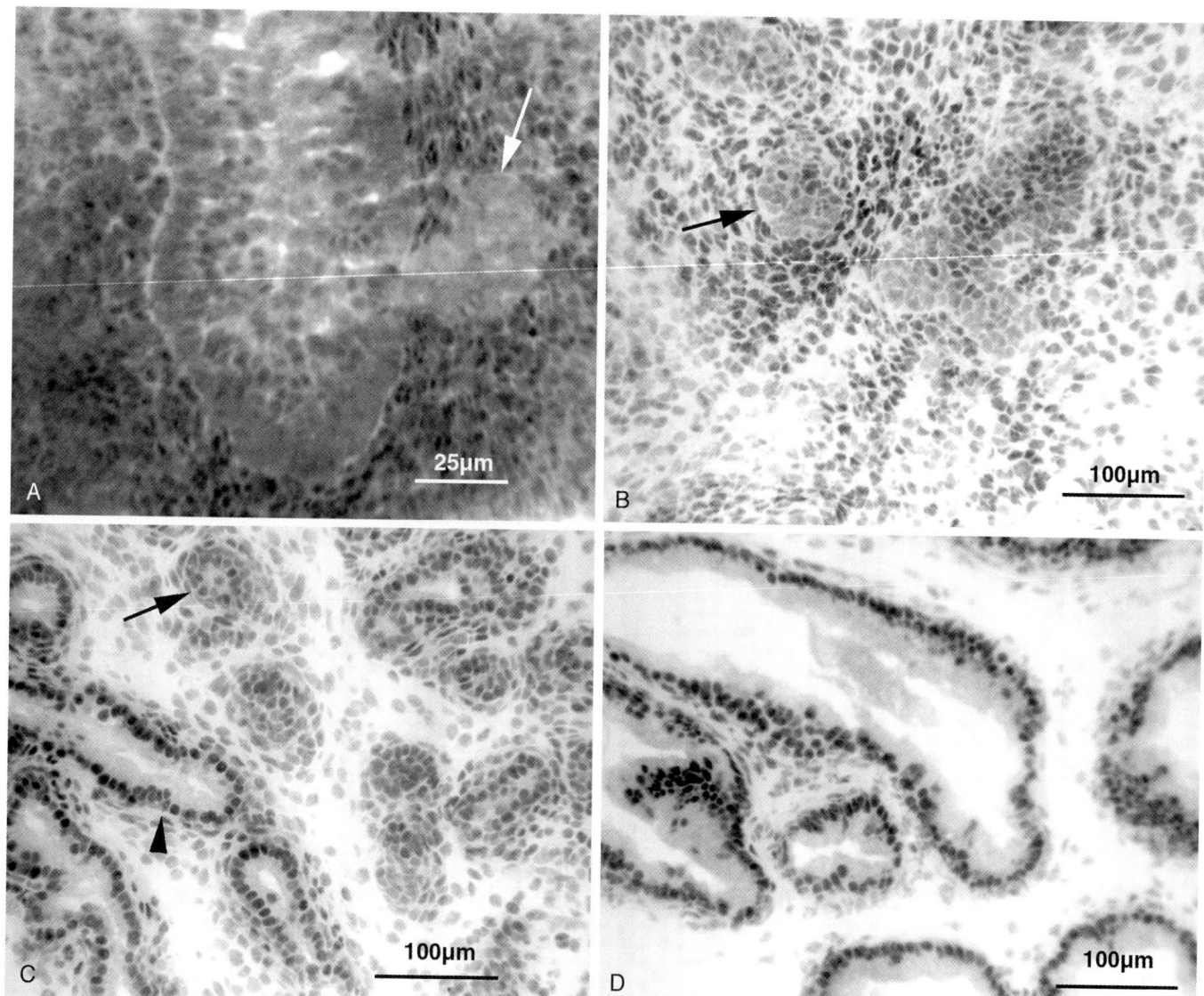

*Figure 179-2*    Expression of the androgen receptor (AR) in the developing rat prostate. **A,** At 19 days of embryonic development, AR staining is seen in the mesenchymal cells surrounding the urogenital sinus epithelium and the developing prostatic bud (*arrow*). **B,** At 2 days postnatal, some staining is evident in the solid epithelial cords (*arrow*), but is more intense in the surrounding mesenchymal cells. **C,** By 9 days postnatal, intense staining is observed in the epithelial cells surrounding canalized ducts (*arrowhead*), but epithelial staining is less intense in solid cords (*arrow*). **D,** In the 20-day postnatal gland, all ducts are canalized. Epithelial staining is intense and the ducts are surrounded by AR-expressing smooth muscle. The fibroblastic stromal cells more distant from the epithelium stain much less intensely.

mediated by androgenic signaling through the ARs of the prostatic smooth muscle. Thus, we have a situation in which androgens act on a fetal mesenchyme to elicit epithelial proliferation and differentiation and on adult smooth muscle to maintain a growth-quiescent state. This illustrates the contextual nature of the interpretation of steroid hormonal signaling.

## STEROID HORMONES

The principal androgen secreted by the testis is testosterone. In the prostate, the biologically active androgen is 5α-dihydrotestosterone (DHT), which is produced by the local reduction of testosterone by the enzyme Δ⁴-3-ketosteroid-5α-reductase (5α-reductase). Two forms of 5α-reductase have been described.[56,57] In the genital tract, the active form appears to be the type 2 5α-reductase gene product, which is localized to both the epithelial and stromal compartments of developing and adult prostates.[58] DHT binds to nuclear androgen receptors that exert their effect on cellular tran-

scription.[59] These ARs are located in both the epithelium and stroma of the adult prostate. As previously described, however, there is a period during embryonic development when ARs are expressed primarily in the mesenchyme.

The links between testicular and prostatic function have been known for many years. John Hunter, writing in 1786 in his "Observations on the glands situated between the rectum and the bladder, called vesiculae seminales," stated, "The prostate and Cowper's glands and those of the urethra which in the perfect male are soft and bulky with a secretion salty to the taste, in the castrated animal are small, flabby, tough and ligermentous and have little secretion." Although Hunter knew nothing about the biochemistry of androgen action, his observations are correct. In an adult, androgenic deprivation leads to loss of secretory function and a reduction in glandular size. The scale of this regression varies, with the species being much more marked in rats and mice (where 80% to 95% of prostatic wet weight can be lost) than in humans. This regression is due to a controlled apoptotic response of the prostatic epithelium.

Apoptosis is a normal, orderly, physiologic process that occurs during embryonic development and tissue homeostasis.[60] It is characterized by blebbing of the plasma membrane, loss of cellular attachment, condensation of the cytoplasm and nucleus, and internucleosomal cleavage of DNA. The dying cells are fragmented into membrane-bound "apoptotic bodies" that are rapidly engulfed by phagocytic cells without eliciting inflammation. Prostatic epithelial apoptosis is triggered by androgen ablation, which elicits a rapid depletion of dihydrotestosterone (DHT) in the prostate. When the DHT concentration falls below that needed to inhibit apoptosis, prostatic ducts start to regress, with a selective loss of secretory epithelial cells.[61] Regression is most extensive in distal regions of prostatic ducts, which may be completely obliterated.[62] The overall process of prostatic epithelial apoptosis is thought to be similar to that of other organs. The unique trigger for apoptosis for the prostate, however, is failure to occupy ARs, which distinguishes apoptosis in the male genital tract from that in all other systems.

While the apoptotic response has been most well studied in the epithelial compartment of the prostate, it should be noted that there are also changes in the prostatic stroma. One of the earliest responses to castration in the rat ventral prostate is a pronounced reduction in blood flow to the gland and apoptosis of the microvasculature of the gland.[63,64] After castration, the stroma of the adult prostate (normally, predominantly smooth muscle) undergoes ordered changes toward a fibroblastic phenotype.[7] If a regressed prostate is subsequently stimulated by androgens, it will respond by undergoing new prostatic development and growth and will ultimately become growth quiescent and secretory. In many animals, including humans and laboratory rodents, the prostate is functional year round and does not normally undergo regression. In some seasonal breeding animals, however, the prostate undergoes a seasonal variation in size in response to fluctuations in androgens.[65] Thus, the ability to regress and regrow may reflect an evolutionary requirement for prostatic function only in the breeding season. There are significant differences in the rates of epithelial apoptosis occurring in the prostates of different species after castration. Much work has been performed on the ventral prostate of the rat, which has one of the highest peak rates of epithelial apoptosis after castration.[66] In contrast, rates in human tissues are much lower, but are still sufficient to account for the destruction of the vast majority of the epithelial cells.[67]

In summary, prostatic budding and branching are dependent on androgens, albeit at low levels. During puberty, androgens rise and the prostate grows significantly and differentiates. The connective tissue begins as loose fibroblastic mesenchyme and differentiates into adult fibromuscular stroma. In the presence of normal endogenous levels of androgens, the adult prostate is an essentially growth-quiescent secretory organ, which has an extremely low rate of both cell proliferation and cell death. In humans, there is an extremely slow overall increase in the mean prostatic weight with age. Under these conditions, the prostatic stroma is principally composed of AR-expressing smooth muscle with a minor fibroblastic component. After castration, the prostate regresses and the stroma changes to a predominantly fibroblastic phenotype that also expresses AR. This regressed prostate will respond to androgenic stimulation by undergoing new growth and differentiation. Thus, the response of the prostate to androgenic stimulation, either growth or growth-quiescence, may be determined by the nature of the stromal cells being stimulated.

Although androgens are the principal male sex hormones, males also produce estrogens. Male fetuses are exposed to estrogenic stimulation in utero and environmental estrogens have been postulated to play a role in congenital urogenital tract defects in males. The classic effect of exogenous estrogens on the adult prostatic is squamous metaplasia.[68] More recently, it has become evident that exogenous estrogenic compounds also affect the developing male genital tract.[69]

This is of particular concern because exposure to exogenous estrogen during development may alter prostatic growth and differentiation and predispose the gland for abnormal function and disease in later life. Indeed, it has been proposed that estrogenization during prostatic development may contribute to the high incidence of BPH and prostatic carcinoma.[70] In laboratory rodents, the effects of estrogen on the developing prostate have been found to be dose dependent. Low doses have been shown to enhance prostatic growth, while high estrogen doses generally have an inhibitory effect on the prostate. Vom Saal and colleagues have shown that low doses (2 ng/g body wt) of estradiol or diethylstilbestrol (DES) administered prenatally increased prostatic weight in adulthood, whereas high doses (200 ng/g body wt) decreased adult prostate weight.[71] An experimental increase in free serum estradiol in male mouse fetuses by 50% induced a 40% increase in the number of prostatic buds and led in adulthood to a twofold increase in levels of prostatic ARs per cell and a 30% increase in prostatic wet weight. As the free-estradiol concentration in serum of male fetuses was increased from two- to eightfold, however, adult prostate weight decreased. These findings suggest that a small increase in estrogen may modulate the action of androgen in regulating prostatic differentiation, resulting in a permanent increase in prostatic ARs and increased prostate size.[71] Thus, the complex mechanisms mediating prostate differentiation and growth can be altered by exposure during fetal life to a very small increase in circulating estrogen, resulting in a permanent, irreversible (imprinted) enlargement of the prostate.

Exposure of developing rats and mice to pharmacologic levels of estrogen generally has an inhibitory effect, resulting in impaired prostatic growth and decreased responsiveness to androgens in adulthood.[72–74] In addition to the changes in growth and morphology, developmental estrogenization also leads to permanent effects on the functional activity of the prostate gland.[75,76] Thus, neonatal exposure to pharmacologic levels of exogenous estrogen elicits long-term alterations in gene expression and molecular defects in the prostate gland.

Santti and coworkers have suggested that the prostatic abnormalities initiated by early exposure to estrogens can lead to preneoplastic lesions as well as tumor formation in aging animals, which has led to the speculation that developmental estrogenization may be a predisposing factor for prostate cancer.[70] Initial studies on male mice and rats exposed prenatally to DES demonstrated squamous metaplasia and dysplasia within the accessory sex glands in aging males.[77–80] These lesions were correlated with increased expression of c-myc.[77] In neonatally estrogenized rats, prostatic hyperplasia, dysplasia, and adenoma formation have been observed at 22 months.[81] Thus, neonatal estrogen imprinting may be a predisposing factor for abnormal prostatic growth and differentiation in adulthood. Estrogenic treatment of whole animals, of course, disrupts the hypothalamic-pituitary axis; however, organ culture experiments suggest that these effects are likely to be a result of direct estrogenic effects on the prostate rather than a consequence of a systemic hormonal disruption.[82]

The probable involvement of estrogens in the etiology of prostatic pathology is further emphasized by studies in adult Noble rats treated chronically with estradiol in combination with testosterone. Such rats sequentially develop prostatic epithelial hyperplasia, dysplasia, and carcinoma in situ and form microscopic prostatic carcinomas.[83,84] Finally, BPH can be induced experimentally in dogs, and the highest incidence of BPH is achieved when androgens are administered in combination with estradiol.[85,86]

Estrogens can elicit effects on the prostate during development as well as in adulthood by acting directly on the prostate or by affecting systemic levels of androgens and other hormones. Direct effects of estrogens on the prostate are mediated by the binding of an estrogenic ligand to the estrogen receptor (ER). Originally, the estrogenic actions were thought to be mediated through a single type of ER. A second receptor was discovered, however, and named ER-β to distinguish it from the original receptor, now termed ER-α. Thus, there are at least two estrogen receptors.[87,88] ER-β, like ER-α, belongs to the steroid receptor super-family, and high levels of ER-β mRNA and protein have been detected in adult prostatic epithelium, but not in prostatic stroma.[88,89] ER-α has been detected in prostatic stroma by a variety of techniques.[90–95] There are data to suggest that ER-α may not normally be expressed in prostatic epithelium.[89] Tissue recombination studies indicate that ER-α is inducible in prostatic epithelial cells.[96]

### ANDROGEN PATHWAY MUTATIONS

#### 5α-Reductase Deficiencies

The prostate responds to testosterone mainly and perhaps entirely through locally produced DHT. Evidence for this is provided by patients suffering from pseudohermaphroditism caused by a congenital 5α-reductase deficiency. While this condition is rare in the general population, a related group of 23 families living in villages in the Dominican Republic carry the trait and have undergone extensive examination. At birth, affected males have feminized external genitalia, including a blind vaginal pouch, and are normally raised as girls. At puberty, their phenotype becomes clearly male. The phallus enlarges to become penis-like, and the voice deepens. Beard growth is scanty, however, and there is no temporal recession of the hairline. The prostate is present in affected individuals, but is very small and does not enlarge even with a significant testosterone surge at puberty. This testosterone surge does masculinize other secondary sex characteristics such as phallus size. The testis, vas deferens, and epididymis of these individuals appear normal.[97–99]

This human condition can be mimicked in rats by prenatal exposure to a 5α-reductase inhibitor.[100] Virilization of the external genitalia and development of the prostate were impaired in treated male offspring, whereas the vas deferens, epididymis, and seminal vesicles were unaffected. A study examining the effects of deletion of the two isoforms of 5α-reductase in transgenic mice showed similar effects, and concludes that testosterone is sufficient for virilization, but that 5α-reductase serves to provide signal amplification.[101] Thus, epidemiologic and experimental studies are in agreement that the prostate does form in the absence of 5α-reductase, but that its growth is severely reduced. It is not clear whether the residual prostatic growth is due to the direct action of testosterone or to very small amounts of DHT that may still be present.

#### Testicular Feminization

Testicular feminization (Tfm) or androgen insensitivity syndrome has been recognized for many years. The first comprehensive description of androgen insensitivity in humans dates from 1953 with a review by Morris of 82 cases of patients with a female phenotype and bilateral testes.[102] Testicular feminization has subsequently been recognized as being caused by mutations in the AR gene (for a review, see reference 103 and more details in Chapters 142 and 169). Since the AR gene is carried on the X chromosome, a single mutation can induce a phenotype in an affected individual. Thus, the AR has one of the longest lists of characterized mutations of any human gene, with more then 200 mutations described. Some of these changes result in complete androgen insensitivity, whereas other mutations may have a range of intermediate phenotypes. In XY humans, complete androgen insensitivity results in a female phenotype with female external genitalia and no pubic hair. All masculine internal genital structures are absent, as are female genitalia with the exception of a shallow vagina. Testes are present and,

although their structure is somewhat abnormal, testosterone is produced at high levels. In mice, an essentially identical phenotype has been identified.[104] The genetic basis for androgen insensitivity in this strain has been determined to be a frameshift mutation in the AR gene.[105] As in the human, Tfm mice are feminized and do not undergo prostatic development. This mouse strain has proved an extremely valuable tool with which to dissect the mechanisms of androgen action in prostatic development.

### MESENCHYMAL-EPITHELIAL INTERACTIONS

The role of mesenchymal-epithelial interactions in mediating androgenic signaling in the developing and adult prostate was established by a series of tissue recombination experiments in which urogenital mesenchyme and epithelium from wild-type and Tfm mice were recombined, as shown in Figure 179-3.[39] These experiments established that ARs are required in the UGM in order for epithelial budding and ductal branching morphogenesis to occur. Epithelial ARs were not required for these processes. In tissue recombinants composed of wild-type UGM and Tfm epithelium, prostatic morphogenesis, growth, and epithelial cytodifferentiation occurred. Prostatic secretory proteins were not expressed, however.[106] These experiments defined some important principles of prostatic biology. The first is that androgenic control of prostatic epithelial proliferation is mediated by ARs in the stromal/mesenchymal tissue layer. The second is that differentiated function (in the case of the prostate secretory activity) requires epithelial ARs. These results demonstrated that interactions between the epithelial and stromal compartments of the prostate are critical in mediating the responses

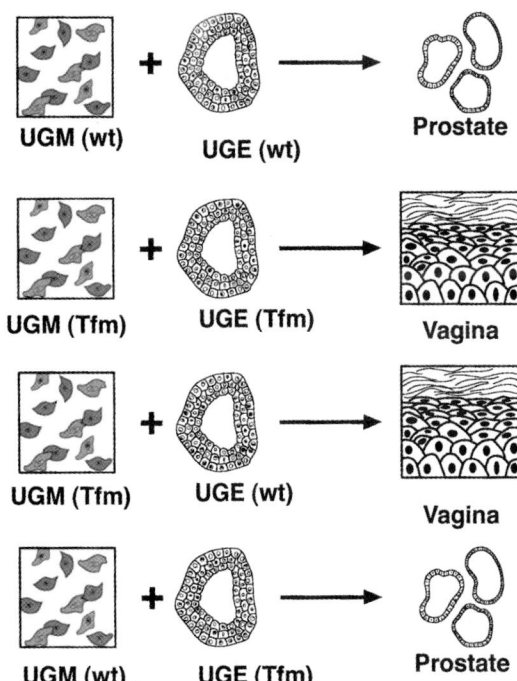

*Figure 179-3* Summary of the results of tissue recombination experiments using urogenital mesenchyme (UGM) and epithelium (UGE) from wild type (+) and androgen receptor–deficient testicular feminized (Tfm) mice. In all cases, the tissue recombinants were grafted beneath the renal capsule of intact athymic male hosts. After 1 month, the hosts were sacrificed and the tissue examined histologically. In all cases, when the mesenchyme was wild type, glandular histology was observed. In the absence of mesenchymal androgen receptors, a multilayered vagina-like histology was observed, irrespective of the androgen receptor status of the epithelium. wt, wild type.

to androgens in the prostate. The manner in which androgens are believed to mediate prostatic development and secretory function is summarized in Figure 179-4. These observations have since been fortified by subsequent experiments examining the role of estrogens and progestins in the female genital tract where, again, regulation of epithelial proliferation is mediated through stromally located steroid receptors. By contrast, differentiated epithelial functions require the presence of epithelial steroid receptors.[107–112]

Stromal-epithelial interactions are also essential for apoptosis during prostatic regression. Androgen withdrawal causes the death of both stromal and epithelial cells. Both of these cell types have ARs in the adult prostate, so, initially, it was not clear whether apoptosis was a direct or indirect response to androgen withdrawal. To distinguish between these two possibilities, Tfm or wild-type bladder epithelium was recombined with wild-type UGM and grown in adult male nude mouse hosts. Both types of tissue recombinants grew and generated ductal structures in response to host androgens.[39] Host mice were then castrated. This elicited an equal apoptotic response in both wild-type and Tfm epithelium. These results show that ARs were required only in the stroma for prostatic epithelial apoptosis.[112] In a general way, this parallels the mechanism controlling epithelial proliferation. It is not known whether prostatic apoptosis results from the withdrawal of a maintenance factor made by the stroma or the result of the induction of a "death signal" by the stroma.

In males, UGM induces prostatic ductal morphogenesis, regulates epithelial proliferation, and specifies expression of prostatic secretory proteins by the epithelium, provided the mesenchyme is associated with an endodermal epithelium,[11] as indicated in Table 179-1. The rodent prostate is composed of well-defined lobar subdivisions (anterior, dorsal, lateral, and ventral prostates), each having unique patterns of ductal branching and each expressing lobe-specific secretory proteins. These lobe-specific morphologic and functional differences in prostatic differentiation appear to be induced by regionally distinct subpopulations of mesenchyme within the UGS. For example, it has been shown that the dorsal and ventral portions of UGM have different inductive properties since only ventral UGM is an effective inducer of ventral prostatic differentiation.[113,114]

Epithelial-mesenchymal interactions are reciprocal in that mesenchyme induces epithelial differentiation, and epithelium induces smooth muscle differentiation in the mesenchyme (see Fig. 179-4). The role of the epithelium as an inducer of smooth muscle differentiation has been demon-strated in studies on the intestine, urinary bladder, uterus, and male genital tract, and is particularly evident in studies on the mouse uterus.[44] Likewise, differentiation and morphologic patterning of smooth muscle in the male urogenital tract is regulated via cell-cell interactions with epithelium. UGM grown by itself in male hosts formed little if any smooth muscle. In contrast, UGM grafted with rat or mouse epithelium from adult prostate or bladder or from embryonic UGS formed prostatic ducts surrounded by actin-positive smooth muscle cells organized into thin sheaths, as is appropriate for the rat prostate.[44] It is notable that rat UGM formed thick sheets of smooth muscle surrounding the epithelial ducts in tissue recombinants composed of rat UGM and human prostatic epithelium.[35] This pattern of smooth muscle (thick layers) is characteristic of human prostate and demonstrates that the human prostatic epithelium not only induced the rat UGM to differentiate into smooth muscle, but also specified the patterning of the smooth muscle. These observations demonstrated that smooth muscle differentiation is induced and spatially patterned by epithelium in both male and female genital tracts, which is consistent with similar findings in the urinary bladder and intestine. Subcutaneous grafts of collagen gels containing human prostatic epithelial cells also affect differentiation and patterning of the stroma. Transplants of adult human prostatic epithelium in collagen gel induced the adult mouse subcutaneous fibroblasts to form smooth muscle sheaths surrounding the epithelium.[115] Similarly, subcutaneous grafts of collagen gels containing fetal rat gut epithelium were able to induce and pattern smooth muscle differentiation from subcutaneous fibroblasts of the host.[116] Growth factors have been widely postulated to act as the mediators of these interactions between the stromal/ mesenchymal and epithelial tissues of the prostate.

The effects of estrogens (like those of androgens) may be elicited in prostatic epithelial cells directly via epithelial ER (α or β) paracrine fashion through ER in stromal cells. For example, studies on estrogenic imprinting, which elicits long-term epithelial consequences, suggest the involvement of stro-mal estrogen receptors.[117] The possibility that certain effects of estrogens on prostatic epithelial cells may be elicited via paracrine mechanisms is further emphasized by recent studies in the mouse uterus and vagina in which mitogenic effects of estradiol on epithelial cells were shown to be mediated by ER-α in stromal cells,[109,118] paralleling the androgenic effects described earlier. Studies of chimeric prostates composed of epithelium and stroma from wild-type and ER-α null mice have shown that estrogen-induced prostatic squamous metaplasia

*Figure 179-4* Summary of the role of androgens in mediating prostatic development and function. **A,** In the developing prostate, androgens induce prostatic growth and differentiation by stimulating the production of mesenchymally derived mitogens and morphogens. In turn, the developing epithelium induces mesenchymal differentiation into prostatic smooth muscle. **B,** In the adult, androgens play two distinct roles. They act on the prostatic smooth muscle to maintain epithelial differentiation and growth quiescence, and they act directly on androgen receptors in the prostatic luminal epithelium to induce secretory activity. The fully differentiated prostatic epithelium is also believed to produce factors that maintain prostatic smooth muscle differentiation.

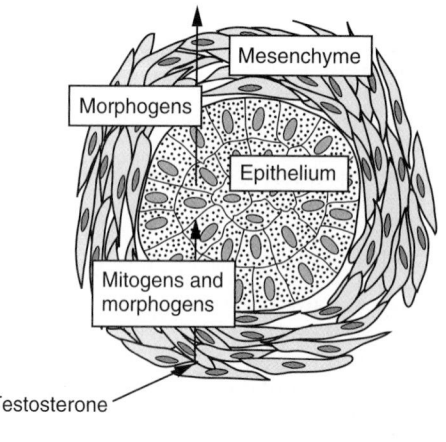

Developing prostate

A

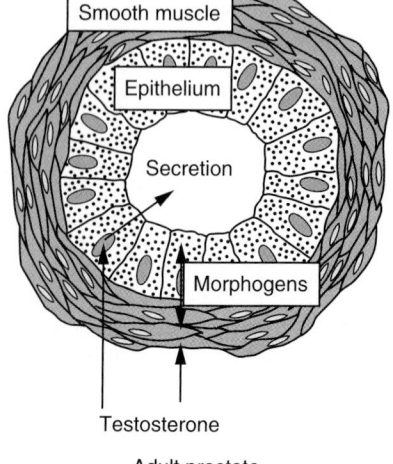

Adult prostate

B

**Table 179-1** Epithelial Characteristics in Prostate, Urinary Bladder, and Heterotypic Urogenital Mesenchyme (UGM) + Bladder Epithelium (BLE) Tissue Recombinants

| | Specimen | | |
|---|---|---|---|
| Type of Analysisor Feature | Bladder | Prostate | UGM + BLE |
| Histology | Transitional | Glandular | Glandular |
| Electron microscopy | Nonsecretory asymmetric membrane | Secretory symmetric membrane | Secretory symmetric membrane |
| Histochemistry | | | |
| Alkaline phosphatase | + | − | − |
| Alcian blue | − | + | + |
| Nonspecific esterase | ± | + | + |
| Prostate antigens | − | + | + |
| Androgen receptors | − | + | + |
| Androgen-dependent DNA synthesis | − | + | + |
| Protein synthesis (2-D gels) | Bladder | Prostate | Prostate-like |
| Prostatic secretory proteins | − | + | + |

Data summarized from Donjacour AA, Cunha GR: Assessment of prostatic protein secretion in tissue recombinants made of urogenital sinus mesenchyme and urothelium from normal or androgen-insensitive mice. Endocrinology 131:2342–2350, 1993; Cunha GR, Fujii H, Neubauer BL, et al: Epithelial-mesenchymal interactions in prostatic development. I. Morphological observations of prostatic induction by urogenital sinus mesenchyme in epithelium of the adult rodent urinary bladder. J Cell Biol 96:1662–1670, 1983; Neubauer BL, Chung LWK, McCormick KA, et al: Epithelial-mesenchymal interactions in prostatic development. II. Biochemical observations of prostatic induction by urogenital sinus mesenchyme in epithelium of the adult rodent urinary bladder. J. Cell Biol. 96:1671–1676, 1983.

occurs only when both the epithelium and stroma are derived from wild-type mice,[96] indicating that ER-α in both tissue compartments plays a role in this process. (For a more complete review of estrogenic effects on the prostate, see reference 119.)

### Growth Factors as Mediators of Mesenchymal-Epithelial Interactions

In the prostate, growth factors are implicated in two distinctly different types of androgen-driven paracrine interactions. The first is the proliferative and differentiative responses that result from the action of androgens on either UGM or the stroma of a regressed prostate after androgen ablation. The second response type is the androgen-dependent maintenance of a growth-quiescent phenotype in the adult prostate. Neither of these end points is simple and straightforward, and it is likely that each is a result of a balance of the effects of various factors. At its simplest, this signaling could be broken down into either proliferative or maintenance phases. McNeal's hypothesis suggests that BPH is a consequence of a reawakening of the proliferative phase in the adult.

In order to determine the nature of specific growth factor effects within the prostate, it is necessary to know the localization of both mRNA and protein for the growth factor of interest and also to know which cells express receptors for the factor. Tenniswood outlined basic mechanisms by which mesenchyme and epithelium may interact in the developing and adult prostate to control gene expression.[120] Advancement in our understanding of the molecules involved in intercellular signaling, in conjunction with gene knockout, knock-in, or transgenic mice, allows analysis of some of the individual signaling molecules involved in prostatic growth and development in vivo. A number of growth factors are well suited, by virtue of the expression and localization of ligand and receptor in the growing gland, as paracrine mediators of mesenchymal-epithelial interactions in the prostate. These included mitogens such as insulinlike growth factor 1 (IGF-1), and a number of members of the FGF family, notably FGF-7 and FGF-10, morphogens such as HGF, and factors such as transforming growth factor betas (TGF-βs), which may act to inhibit proliferation. In addition, Shh, which is made by epithelia, appears to act as a mitogen for mesenchyme.[25] These possible interactions are summarized schematically in Figure 179-5.

The Shh-signaling pathway mediates epithelial-mesenchymal interactions in several tissues during development and disease, and is involved in prostatic growth and differentiation.

Initial studies suggested that Shh was required for prostatic development and might be regulated by androgens.[121,122] More recent studies have shown that Shh is not required for the formation of the prostate, but that it is involved in subsequent growth and patterning.[25,123] The primary cause of prostatic agenesis in Shh knockout mice is androgen insufficiency as a result of a testicular defect.[123] When Shh signaling was disrupted at later stages of prostatic development (in vitro), there was a reduction in organ size, an increase in ductal tip number, and reduced proliferation of ductal tip epithelia, indicating that Shh is involved in prostatic growth. Furthermore, in prostates grown in vitro in the presence of testosterone, inhibition of Shh signaling accelerated the canalization of prostatic

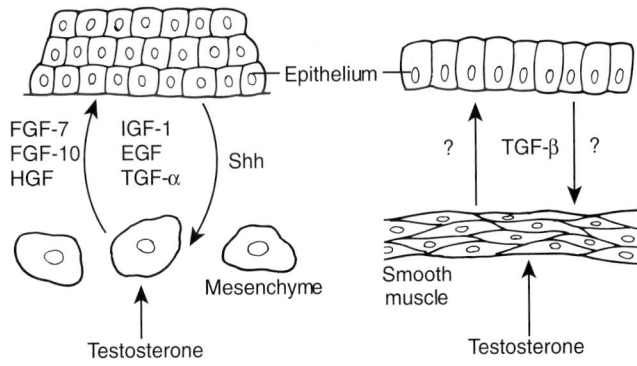

**Figure 179-5** Putative role of some growth factors in stromal-epithelial signaling. A, During prostatic development, androgens act on the mesenchymal cells to elicit prostatic proliferation and ductal branching morphogenesis. Many growth factors may play a role in this process; some, such as hepatic growth factor (HGF), fibroblast growth factor-7 (FGF-7), and FGF-10, are putative mesenchymally derived epithelial mitogens and morphogens. A number of growth factors may act in either or both directions between the two tissues. There may well be epithelially derived factors that exclusively elicit mesenchymal differentiation, with sonic hedgehog (Shh) being a good candidate for this function. In the adult prostate, androgen action on the prostatic smooth muscle maintains a growth-quiescent structure. Transforming growth factor β (TGF-β) family members and other presently unidentified factors may also play a role. EGF, epidermal growth factor; IGF-1, insulin-like growth factor 1.

epithelial ducts and resulted in ducts that showed cribriform morphology. Shh is expressed by prostatic epithelia and its receptor, Patched (Ptc), by the mesenchyme, although it is possible that very low levels of Ptc may be present in the epithelia but undetectable by in situ hybridization. If prostatic epithelia lack the ability to respond directly to Shh signaling, then the abnormalities described previously are likely to be the result of altered mesenchymal signaling (as a result of a lack of Shh activity). This correlates well with the probable involvement of stroma in BPH.[31,43,124] The addition of recombinant Shh to rat ventral prostates grown in vitro caused an expansion of the mesenchyme and showed that Shh is a mitogen for prostatic mesenchyme. Thus, it appears that Shh signaling is not essential for prostatic induction, but is important for prostatic growth, branching, proliferation, and differentiation.

One crucial requirement for ductal growth and branching morphogenesis is that the emerging prostatic buds come into intimate contact with mesenchymal populations rich in the epithelial mitogens and morphogens required for prostatic organogenesis. In this regard, subpopulations of inductive mesenchyme have been described that appear to play critical roles in ductal growth and branching. The ventral mesenchymal pad (VMP) is a peripheral zone of UGM[114] that has an abundance of FGF-10 transcripts and other regulatory molecules. FGF-10 is also localized in a subset of the mesenchymal cells of the other prostatic lobes. Both FGF-7 and FGF-10 are synthesized by mesenchymal and fibroblastic cells and specifically stimulate epithelial cells.[125–127] FGF-7 and FGF-10 signal though the same splice variant of FGF receptor 2 (FGFR2) gene (FGFR2IIIb), which is expressed by epithelial cells.[128] These molecules are thus well suited as paracrine regulators of mesenchymal-epithelial interactions, and are expressed during ductal branching morphogenesis in mesenchyme of the developing salivary gland, mammary gland, prostate, and lung.[22,126,129,130]

The distribution of FGF-10 is much more restricted than FGF-7, both in the number of organs that express FGF-10 as well as in the distribution of FGF-10 within the mesenchyme of those organs. While FGF-7 is expressed in almost all organs of the body, FGF-10 is most abundant in the developing limb, lung, and male reproductive tract, with little FGF-10 expression in other organs. Furthermore, FGF-10 transcripts are generally restricted to a subpopulation of mesenchymal cells, which are associated with active epithelial growth and morphogenesis. Transcripts for FGF-10 are abundant during development and low during adult life, and FGF-10 mRNA levels may be increased in BPH tissue.

Transgenic mice lacking FGF-7 are fertile and their visceral organs have been reported to be normal, though the prostate was not studied specifically.[131] The role of FGF-10 in prostatic development has been examined.[132] FGF-10 null mice die at birth due to lung agenesis,[133,134] and therefore the urogenital sinuses from these mice had to be grown as grafts in adult male nude mice. No prostatic ducts formed in FGF-10 null UGS grafts, though a small number of buds differentiated and produced some prostatic secretory proteins.[132] This indicates that FGF-10 is essential for prostatic growth, but not for the establishment of prostatic epithelial identity and differentiation.

The FGF-10 and FGF-7 genes, as well as the gene for their receptor, do not appear to be directly regulated by androgens in vivo (reviewed in reference 135), yet it is clear that there is androgenic control of the inductive activity of the UGM. Recently, it has been shown that a layer of smooth muscle can control the interaction of nascent prostatic buds with specialized mesenchyme such as the VMP.[136] A layer of smooth muscle forms in females between the VMP and the urethra. This smooth muscle layer is less well developed in males and prostatic buds pass through a gap in the layer to enter the VMP. The smooth muscle is sensitive to the presence of androgens, which are able to modulate smooth muscle differentiation and which lead to sexual dimorphism in this muscle layer. Furthermore, epithelial buds that appear after the smooth muscle layer has formed cannot enter the VMP to develop in response to androgens. These data indicate that smooth muscle can act as a regulator of prostatic organ induction, and that smooth muscle is a barrier preventing prostatic ductal growth.[136]

FGF-3, formerly known as int-2, has also been proposed as a growth factor involved in BPH. Overexpression of FGF-3 under the mouse mammary tumor virus long-term repeat (MMTV LTR) was reported to result in prostatic enlargement.[137] On closer examination, it was found that the ampullary gland was the ductal organ enlarged. The ampullary gland is normally a very small glandular structure that is a diverticulum of the ductus deferens. There is no true glandular human counterpart to this organ. The prostate of the MMTV-FGF-3 mice was normal, even in the face of high levels of transgene expression in the dorso-lateral prostate (DLP).[138] Thus, FGF-3 is unlikely to be an important growth factor in the prostate.

The insulinlike growth factor (IGF) family has been intensively investigated in the prostate in reference to its role in the progression of prostate cancer.[139] There are comparatively few data available on the expression of IGF ligand and receptors in the developing or normal adult human prostate in vivo or in benign hyperplastic growth. There are also no data on the ontogeny of IGF-1 expression in the normal human prostate in vivo, although IGF-1 transcripts have been detected in the stromal component of BPH tissue.[140] IGF-2 is expressed by prostatic stromal cells in culture, with higher levels of transcripts being seen in BPH-derived cultures than in cells derived from normal or tumor tissue.[141] If the ontogeny of IGF-1 and IGF-2 expression is similar in humans and rodents, this observation may reflect a change toward the fetal pattern of expression as would be predicted by McNeal's hypothesis that BPH development is a result of a focal reawakening of inductive potential in the stromal compartment of the adult human prostate.[142] The IGF type 1 receptor has been found in both stromal and epithelial cells of the prostate.[141,143] Guenette and Tenniswood[144] have postulated that IGF signaling is necessary for cell survival in the adult prostate. Thomas and colleagues[145] suggest, however, that loss of IGF signaling (as driven by increased expression of IGF-binding protein 5 [IGFBP-5]) is not a signal for apoptosis but, rather, a consequence of the apoptotic events. Thomas and coworkers also suggest that the elevated expression of this binding protein in the prostatic ducts of castrated animals may serve to inhibit new prostatic ductal growth. A series of in vitro studies by Cohen and Peehl have established that prostate-specific antigen (PSA), a kallikrein proteinase secreted by the luminal cells of the human prostate, can cleave IGFBP-3, thus making IGF-1 biologically available. This implies that PSA expression by human prostate tumors can indirectly induce tumor proliferation (for a review, see reference 139). These studies indicate that the IGF family is an important signaling pathway in the prostate.

TGF-β isoforms (TGF-β1, -β2, and -β3) are physiologic regulators of prostate growth because of their ability to inhibit cell proliferation and mediate apoptosis.[146,147] TGF-βs are secreted by both stromal and epithelial compartments as inactive precursors that have to be proteolytically cleaved in order to bind to their receptors.[148] TGF-βs exert their effects through binding to the TGF-β type 2 receptor and subsequent recruitment of the type 1 receptor for downstream cytoplasmic signaling through multiple parallel signaling pathways.[149] In the prostate, the TGF-β receptors are expressed both in the epithelium (basal and luminal epithelial cells) and in the stroma (fibroblasts, smooth muscle cells, and blood vessels).[150,151]

The coincident increase in TGF-β expression levels and prostate regression associated with androgen removal by castration is well recognized.[150,152] Direct administration of TGF-β1 into rodent prostates will also induce prostate regression, even in the presence of androgens. TGF-β receptor levels are negatively regulated by androgens.[153] TGF-β mRNA and protein are both repressed by androgens in vivo.[146,153,154] At the time of prostate maturation, androgen levels peak to coincide with reduced expression of TGF-β1 and proximal epithelial cell proliferation. After androgen withdrawal, however, the elevation of TGF-β1 expression is capable of inducing apoptotic activity in the epithelial cells of prostates in vivo.[152,155,156] In experiments with transgenic mice, conditional knockout of the TGF-β type 2 receptor in the epithelia and, alternatively, in the stromal fibroblasts indicated a mechanism for the role of TGF-β in prostate regression. The TGF-β type 2 receptor–epithelial knockout mice exhibited prostate regression on androgen ablation much like wild-type mice. In contrast, androgen ablation of mice having TGF-β signaling knocked out in the prostate stromal fibroblasts did not result in elevated epithelial apoptosis or significant prostate regression. Taken together, these observations implicate stromal TGF-β signaling as a mediator of prostate regression after castration by paracrine mechanisms. A possible explanation would be that stromal TGF-β receptors are involved in shutting down prostatic microvasculature, which is known to occur immediately after androgen ablation[63,64] and which probably results in epithelial apoptosis as a secondary effect.

## BENIGN PROSTATIC HYPERPLASIA

BPH is the most common symptomatic tumor-like condition in humans.[157] BPH is rarely identifiable histologically in men younger than 40 years of age. The incidence of the disease increases rapidly with age, however, to around 88% of men by the age of 80. Whilst estimates vary, the number requiring surgical intervention is probably around 30% of men older than 60.[47] The disease appears to be linked to aging and the presence of a functional testis. Cigarette smokers have a lower incidence of surgery for BPH than do nonsmokers, possibly due to decreased serum testosterone and increased estrogens in the smoking population.[158,159]

BPH occurs in humans and dogs. Canine BPH, like its human counterpart, arises with increasing frequency with age and requires a functional testis. Histologic and anatomic differences distinguish canine from human BPH. Human BPH is strongly focal, with distinct nodules of hyperplasia within the gland, whereas the canine disease is usually diffuse, occurring throughout the gland.[160] In the dog, a generalized expansion of the gland is observed; it compresses the rectum, producing constipation. In humans, focal growth of nodules compresses the urethra, resulting in urinary retention.

The exclusive site of human BPH origin is the preprostatic region of the prostate.[161] This is the region immediately distal to the urinary bladder and surrounding the preprostatic sphincter. The preprostatic region is further subdivided into the periurethral and transition zones. The periurethral zone surrounds the urethra within the sleeve of the preprostatic sphincter; the transition zone, in turn, surrounds the sphincter. The principal clinical manifestation of human BPH is urinary retention.

Small early BPH nodules usually form within the transition zone.[161] They occur in a clearly defined area either within or adjacent to the preprostatic sphincter directly lateral or somewhat ventral to the urethral lumen. This represents a sharp focusing of the sites of nodule origin within the prostate into a region comprising about 2% of the total mass of the gland. In prostates with larger, more numerous BPH nodules (generally in older age groups), anatomic focusing is the same, but is not as restricted.

BPH nodules are of several different types with fibrous and or muscular stroma either with or without an epithelial component. Periurethral nodules are often stromal in character or show only a few small glands penetrating from the periphery.

The stroma is described as reminiscent of the embryonic mesenchyme.[161] Transition zone nodules are composed of glandular tissue derived from newly formed small duct branches. They bud off from preexisting ducts, grow into the adjacent stroma, and repeatedly rebranch, creating a new architectural system within the nodule. Individual patients usually have a number of nodes that appear to grow in a coordinated manner.

An important concept that has been identified with the origins of BPH is the reawakening of embryonic inductive potential in BPH stromal cells.[30–32,161] This concept is based on the idea that growth of the prostate results from local interplay of growth factors between the epithelial and stromal elements of the organ under the influence of testicular androgens. The pubertal growth spurt is thought to be mediated by growth-promoting factors under androgenic control. In adulthood, growth-promoting factors are presumably either downregulated or balanced by growth-inhibiting factors. This balance between mitogenic and growth-inhibitory agents stabilizes the size of the prostate in adulthood.[120] A breakdown of this homeostatic balance, however, could lead to localized growth that is characteristic of BPH. This idea enjoys considerable experimental support. For example, it is known that adult prostatic epithelium from rats, mice, and humans can respond to prostatic inductive mesenchyma with new growth and development.[33–35,162] These experimental data, however, still do not address the underlying and, at present, unknown cause of such a stromal to mesenchymal switch. In addition, the specific factors that mediate hyperplastic enlargement of the prostate are presently unknown. It is likely that these will prove to be the same factors involved in normal prostatic growth.

Links between BPH and the testis have long been suspected, being based on the observation that men castrated before the age of 40 do not develop the condition. The Skoptzys, a Russian sect in which the males underwent ritual castration at 35 years, did not suffer from prostatic enlargement.[163,164] Furthermore, it has been shown that the absence of testicular function from a young age, either from castration or hypopituitarism, prevents the occurrence of BPH in elderly men (<55 years). Postmortem examination of 28 such patients showed no histologic evidence of BPH as compared to an age-matched control group in which BPH was found in 50% of the patients.[165]

Other steroids have been implicated in BPH. Work on canine BPH showed that this condition can be induced with androstenediol and with combinations of androstenediol and estradiol. A combined dose of DHT and estradiol was also found to induce canine BPH.[86,160]

In man, levels of serum testosterone drop by about 35% between the ages of 21 and 85 against a constant level of estradiol. Thus, there is a change in the androgen/estrogen ratio, which may be sufficient to promote the growth of BPH. Since these changes are not significant until after the first initiation of the disease, however, their relationship to its induction is questionable.[166] This view is further reinforced by the finding that plasma androgen levels are slightly higher in BPH patients than in age-matched controls, whereas estradiol levels are virtually the same in the two groups.[167] It is known that, in the cynomolgus monkey, the periurethral zone of the prostate is the most sensitive to estrogenic stimulation and, further, that the result of such stimulation is stromal proliferation,[168] suggesting a possible role for estrogens in the genesis of human BPH.

Attempts to inhibit androgens in BPH patients in the late 19th century and in a very limited trial in 1940 were based on castration, a cheap and simple, but understandably unpopular treatment.[47,169] This idea has lived on as a medical rather than surgical approach, with the use of both antiandrogens and luteinizing hormone-releasing hormone (LHRH) agonists to blockade the effects and production, respectively, of androgens.

While producing measurable increases in urine flow in around 50% of patients, this form of treatment does have the problem of associated loss of libido. 5α-Reductase inhibitors have also been used therapeutically.[170-173] Other hormonally based medical approaches have included the blockade of local estrogen production in the prostate by using aromatase inhibitors, the rationale for this being that estrogens produced in the prostatic stroma may play a role in prostatic hyperplasia.[174,175] These compounds have proven clinically useful.[176,177]

A second medical approach to the treatment of BPH has been the use of α-adrenergic receptor antagonists to relax the muscle of the prostate and, thus, improve clinical symptoms.[178] This treatment regimen does not actually slow the growth of the prostate, but does delay the necessity for surgical intervention.[179]

The Medical Therapy of Prostatic Symptoms (MTOPS) trial examined the ability of the 5α-reductase inhibitor finasteride and the α-adrenergic receptor antagonist doxazosin, either singly or in combination, to affect clinical progression of BPH. The findings of the clinical trial show that both drugs given singly were similarly effective in slowing disease progression and delaying surgical intervention. Combination therapy was found to be more effective than either drug given alone.[179]

Historically, the most common method of treating BPH was by open prostatectomy. This procedure has a high morbidity and some mortality associated with it, and requires a long postoperative recovery period. It was, therefore, largely replaced by transurethral resection of the prostate (TURP), which involves physically cutting the obstructing material away from the inside of the urethra using a resectoscope. Although a number of other methods such as balloon dilation, urethral stents, hyperthermia, and local microwave therapy are currently available, TURP remains the surgical intervention of choice for most practitioners. The widespread use of inexpensive and effective medical treatments such as α-adrenergic receptor antagonists as a first line of treatment has moved surgical intervention for BPH to a second-line therapy and has significantly reduced the numbers of TURP surgeries as compared to the situation in the early to mid-1990s.

## CONCLUSIONS

Prostatic endocrinology is extremely complicated. Clearly, the presence of steroids and their receptors is not the single determinant of their mode of action. The effects of a specific steroid depend on the target cell type and the context in which the cell is growing. In the prostate, this is exemplified by the growth response to low levels of androgens in the early stages of prostatic development and in the growth quiescence maintained by high levels of androgens in the adult. This reflects the indirect effects of androgens on epithelial cells, which are mediated through mesenchymal cells during development and smooth muscle cells in the adult. Fibroblastic or mesenchymal cells respond to androgens by producing paracrine factors that promote prostatic epithelial proliferation. Conversely, prostatic smooth muscle responds to androgens by maintaining a differentiated growth-quiescent epithelium. Prostatic epithelial cells depend on growth factors for many of the effects that have traditionally been ascribed to steroid hormones. These factors can act locally (fitting a traditional definition of growth factors) or can be systemic (with actions more akin to traditional protein hormones). In addition, growth factors have been shown to be capable of interacting with AR to initiate transcription in the absence of androgens.

BPH is a disease that is detectable in the vast majority of aging men. First-line treatments for this condition have shifted their focus from surgical to medical approaches during the past decade. There are still many areas of the biology of BPH that are poorly understood. One of the major challenges currently facing researchers is the detection of markers to identify patients whose disease is likely to progress rapidly.

### Acknowledgments
Research support for this chapter was provided by National Institutes of Health Grants DK067049, CA84294, CA89520, CN-15114-MAO, and CN-35115 and by the Medical Research Council of the United Kingdom.

## REFERENCES

1. Kellokumpu-Lehtonen P, Santti R, Pelliniemi LJ: Correlation of early cytodifferentiation of the human fetal prostate and Leydig cells. Anat Rec 196:263–273, 1980.
2. Lowsley OS: The development of the human prostate gland with reference to the development of other structures at the neck of the urinary bladder. Am J Anat 13:299–349, 1912.
3. Raynaud A: The histogenesis of urogenital and mammary tissues sensitive to oestrogens. In Zuckerman S (ed): The Ovary, Vol II. New York: Academic, 1962, pp 179–230.
4. Cunha GR: Epithelio-mesenchymal interactions in primordial gland structures which become responsive to androgenic stimulation. Anat Rec 172:179–196, 1972.
5. Cunha GR, Donjacour AA, Cooke PS, et al: The endocrinology and developmental biology of the prostate. Endocr Rev 8:338–362, 1987.
6. Hayward SW, Baskin LS, Haughney PC, et al: Epithelial development in the rat ventral prostate, anterior prostate and seminal vesicle. Acta Anat (Basel) 155:81–93, 1996.
7. Hayward SW, Baskin LS, Haughney PC, et al: Stromal development in the ventral prostate, anterior prostate and seminal vesicle of the rat. Acta Anat (Basel) 155:94–103, 1996.
8. Hayward SW, Brody JR, Cunha GR: An edgewise look at basal cells: Three-dimensional views of the rat prostate, mammary gland and salivary gland. Differentiation 60:219–227, 1996.
9. Nemeth JA, Lee C: Prostatic ductal system in rats: Regional variation in stromal organization. Prostate 28:124–128, 1996.
10. Cunha GR, Hayward SW, Dahiya R, et al: Smooth muscle–epithelial interactions in normal and neoplastic prostatic development. Acta Anat (Basel) 155:63–72, 1996.
11. Cunha GR, Alarid ET, Turner T, et al: Normal and abnormal development of the male urogenital tract: Role of androgens, mesenchymal-epithelial interactions and growth factors. J Androl 13:465–475, 1992.
12. Sugimura Y, Cunha GR, Bigsby RM: Androgenic induction of deoxyribonucleic acid synthesis in prostatic glands induced in the urothelium of testicular feminized (Tfm/y) mice. Prostate 9:217–225, 1986.
13. Donjacour AA, Cunha GR: Assessment of prostatic protein secretion in tissue recombinants made of urogenital sinus mesenchyme and urothelium from normal or androgen-insensitive mice. Endocrinology 131:2342–2350, 1993.
14. Byrne RL, Leung H, Neal DE: Peptide growth factors in the prostate as mediators of stromal epithelial interaction. Br J Urol 77:627–633, 1996.
15. Cunha GR, Sugimura Y, Foster BA, et al: The role of growth factors in the development and growth of the prostate and seminal vesicle. Biomed Pharmacother 48(Suppl 1):S9–S19, 1994.
16. Djakiew D, Pflug B, Onoda M: Stromal-epithelial paracrine interactions in the neoplastic rat and human prostate. Adv Exp Med Biol 330:185–202, 1993.
17. Peehl DM, Rubin JS: Keratinocyte growth factor: An androgen-regulated mediator of stromal-epithelial interactions in the prostate. World J Urol 13:312–317, 1995.
18. Sherwood ER, Lee C: Epidermal growth factor-related peptides and the epidermal growth factor receptor in

normal and malignant prostate. World J Urol 13:290–296, 1995.

19. Thomson AA, Foster BA, Cunha GR: Analysis of growth factor and receptor mRNAs during development of the rat seminal vesicle and prostate. Development 124:2431–2439, 1997.

20. Timme TL, Truong LD, Slawin KM, et al: Mesenchymal-epithelial interactions and transforming growth factor-beta 1 expression during normal and abnormal prostatic growth. Microsc Res Tech 30:333–341, 1995.

21. Cunha GR, Foster BA, Donjacour A, et al: Keratinocyte growth factor: A mediator of mesenchymal-epithelial interactions in the development of androgen target organs. In Serio L (ed): Sex Hormones and Antihormones in Endocrine Dependent Pathology: Basic and Clinical Aspects. New York, Elsevier, 1994, pp 45–57.

22. Finch PW, Cunha GR, Rubin JS, et al: Pattern of KGF and KGFR expression during mouse fetal development suggests a role in mediating morphogenetic mesenchymal-epithelial interactions. Dev Dyn 203:223–240, 1995.

23. Gherardi E, Sharpe M, Lane K, et al: Hepatocyte growth factor/scatter factor (HGF/SF), the c-met receptor and the behaviour of epithelial cells. Symp Soc Exp Biol 47:163–181, 1993.

24. Thomson AA, Cunha GR: Prostatic growth and development are regulated by FGF10. Development 126:3693–3701, 1999.

25. Freestone SH, Marker P, Grace OC, et al: Sonic hedgehog regulates prostatic growth and epithelial differentiation. Dev Biol 264:352–362, 2003.

26. Letterio JJ, Geiser AG, Kulkarni AB, et al: Maternal rescue of transforming growth factor-beta 1 null mice. Science 264:1936–1938, 1994.

27. Culig Z, Hobisch A, Cronauer MV, et al: Androgen receptor activation in prostatic tumor cell lines by insulin-like growth factor-I, keratinocyte growth factor, and epidermal growth factor. Cancer Res 54:5474–5478, 1994.

28. Culig Z, Hobisch A, Cronauer MV, et al: Regulation of prostatic growth and function by peptide growth factors. Prostate 28:392–405, 1996.

29. Berry SJ, Coffey DS, Walsh PC, et al: The development of human benign prostatic hyperplasia with age. J Urol 132:474–479, 1984.

30. McNeal JE: Origin and evolution of benign prostatic enlargement. Invest Urol 15:340–345, 1978.

31. McNeal JE: The prostate gland: Morphology and pathobiology. Monographs in Urology 4:3–37, 1983.

32. McNeal JE: Morphology and biology of benign prostatic hyperplasia. In Neumann F (ed): Regulation of Androgen Action. Berlin, Congressdruck R Bruckner, 1985, pp 191–197.

33. Norman JT, Cunha GR, Sugimura Y: The induction of new ductal growth in adult prostatic epithelium in response to an embryonic prostatic inductor. Prostate 8:209–220, 1986.

34. Hayashi N, Cunha GR, Parker M: Permissive and instructive induction of adult rodent prostatic epithelium by heterotypic urogenital sinus mesenchyme. Epithelial Cell Biol 2:66–78, 1993.

35. Hayward SW, Haughney PC, Rosen MA, et al: Interactions between adult human prostatic epithelium and rat urogenital sinus mesenchyme in a tissue recombination model. Differentiation 63:131–140, 1998.

36. Price D, Ortiz E: The role of fetal androgens in sex differentiation in mammals. In DeHaan H (ed): Organogenesis. New York: Holt Rinehart & Winston, 1965, pp 629–652.

37. Jost A: Modalities in the action of androgens in the foetus. Res Steroids 3:207–214, 1968.

38. Takeda I, Lasnitzki I, Mizuno T: Analysis of prostatic bud induction by brief androgen treatment in the fetal rat urogenital sinus. J Endocronol 110:467–470, 1986.

39. Cunha GR, Chung LWK, Shannon JM, et al: Stromal-epithelial interactions in sex differentiation. Biol Reprod 22:19–43, 1980.

40. Donjacour AA, Cunha GR: The effect of androgen deprivation on branching morphogenesis in the mouse prostate. Dev Biol 128:1–14, 1988.

41. Sugimura Y, Cunha GR, Donjacour AA: Morphogenesis of ductal networks in the mouse prostate. Biol Reprod 34:961–971, 1986.

42. Hayward SW, Cunha GR, Dahiya R: Normal development and carcinogenesis of the prostate: A unifying hypothesis. Ann N Y Acad Sci 784:50–62, 1996.

43. Hayward SW, Rosen MA, Cunha GR: Stromal-epithelial interactions in the normal and neoplastic prostate. Br J Urol 79(Suppl 2):18–26, 1997.

44. Cunha GR, Battle E, Young P, et al: Role of epithelial-mesenchymal interactions in the differentiation and spatial organization of visceral smooth muscle. Epithelial Cell Biol 1:76–83, 1992.

45. Cunha GR, Fujii H, Neubauer BL, et al: Epithelial-mesenchymal interactions in prostatic development. I. Morphological observations of prostatic induction by urogenital sinus mesenchyme in epithelium of the adult rodent urinary bladder. J Cell Biol 96:1662–1670, 1983.

46. Cunha GR, Lung B, Reese B: Glandular epithelial induction by embryonic mesenchyme in adult bladder epithelium of Balb/c mice. Invest Urol 17:302–304, 1980.

47. Walsh PC: Human benign prostatic hyperplasia: Etiological considerations. Prog Clin Biol Res 145:1–26, 1984.

48. Coffey DS, Berry SJ, Ewing LL: An overview of current concepts in the study of benign prostatic hyperplasia. In Horton R (ed): Benign Prostatic Hyperplasia, vol 2. Washington, DC, US Government Printing Office, 1987, pp 1–14.

49. Isaacs JT, Furuya Y, Berges R: The role of androgen in the regulation of programmed cell death/apoptosis in normal and malignant prostatic tissue. Semin Cancer Biol 5:391–400, 1994.

50. Isaacs JT: Control of cell proliferation and death in the normal and neoplastic prostate: A stem cell model. In Horton R (ed): Benign Prostatic Hyperplasia, vol II. Bethesda, National Institutes of Health, 1985, pp 85–94.

51. Lopes ES, Foster BA, Donjacour AA, et al: Initiation of secretory activity of rat prostatic epithelium in organ culture. Endocrinology 137:4225–4234, 1996.

52. Price D: Normal development of the prostate and seminal vesicles of the rat with a study of experimental postnatal modifications. Am J Anat 60:79–127, 1936.

53. Price D, Williams-Ashman HG: The accessory reproductive glands of mammals. In Young WC (ed): Sex and Internal Secretions, 3d ed. Baltimore, Williams & Wilkins, 1961, pp 366–448.

54. Soeffing WJ, Timms BG: Localization of androgen receptor and cell-specific cytokeratins in basal cells of rat ventral prostate. J Androl 16:197–208, 1995.

55. Prins GS, Birch L: The developmental pattern of androgen receptor expression in rat prostate lobes is altered after neonatal exposure to estrogen. Endocrinology 136:1303–1314, 1995.

56. Andersson S, Berman DM, Jenkins EP, et al: Deletion of steroid 5a-reductase 2 gene in male pseudohermaphroditism. Nature 354:159–161, 1991.

57. Andersson S, Russell DW: Structural and biochemical properties of cloned and expressed human and rat steroid 5a-reductases. Proc Natl Acad Sci U S A 87:3640–3644, 1990.

58. Levine AC, Wang JP, Ren M, et al: Immunohistochemical localization of steroid 5 alpha-reductase 2 in the human male fetal reproductive tract and adult prostate. J Clin Endocrinol Metab 81:384–389, 1996.

59. Brinkmann AO, Blok LJ, de Ruiter PE, et al: Mechanisms of androgen receptor activation and function. J Steroid Biochem Mol Biol 69:307–313, 1999.

60. Kerr JF, Wyllie AH, Currie AR: Apoptosis: A basic biological phenomenon with wide-ranging implications in tissue kinetics. Br J Cancer 26:239–257, 1972.

61. Isaacs JT: Antagonistic effect of androgen on prostatic cell death. Prostate 5:545–557, 1984.

62. Sugimura Y, Cunha GR, Donjacour AA: Morphological and histological study of castration-induced degeneration and androgen-induced regeneration in the mouse prostate. Biol Reprod 34:973–983, 1986.

63. Shabsigh A, Chang DT, Heitjan DF, et al: Rapid reduction in blood flow to the rat ventral prostate gland after castration: Preliminary evidence that androgens influence prostate size by regulating blood flow to the prostate gland and prostatic endothelial cell survival. Prostate 36:201–206, 1998.

64. Buttyan R, Ghafar MA, Shabsigh A: The effects of androgen deprivation on the prostate gland: Cell death mediated by vascular regression. Curr Opin Urol 10:415–420, 2000.

65. Siwela AA, Tam WH: Ultrastructural changes in the prostate gland of a seasonally breeding mammal, the grey squirrel (Sciurus carolinensis, Gmelin). J Anat 138:153–162, 1984.

66. Colombel MC, Buttyan R: Hormonal control of apoptosis: The rat prostate gland as a model system. Methods Cell Biol 46:369–385, 1995.

67. Staack A, Kassis AP, Olshen A, et al: Quantitation of apoptotic activity following castration in human prostatic tissue in vivo. Prostate 54:212–219, 2003.

68. Kroes R, Teppema JS: Development and restitution of squamous metaplasia in the calf prostate after a single estrogen treatment: An electron microscopic study. Exp Mol Pathol 16:286–301, 1972.

69. Newbold RR, McLachlan JA: Neoplastic and non-neoplastic lesions in male reproductive organs following perinatal exposure to hormones and related substances. In Nagasawa H (ed): Toxicity of Hormones in Perinatal Life. Boca Raton, FL, CRC, 1988, pp 89–110.

70. Santti R, Newbold RR, Makela S, et al: Developmental estrogenization and prostatic neoplasia. Prostate 24:67–78, 1994.

71. vom Saal FS, Timms BG, Montano MM, et al: Prostate enlargement in mice due to fetal exposure to low doses of estradiol or diethylstilbestrol and opposite effects at high doses. Proc Natl Acad Sci U S A 94:2056–2061, 1997.

72. Prins GS: Neonatal estrogen exposure induces lobe-specific alterations in adult rat prostate androgen receptor expression. Endocrinology 130:2401–2412, 1992.

73. Naslund MJ, Coffey DS: The differential effects of neonatal androgen, estrogen and progesterone on adult rat prostate growth. J Urol 136:1136–1140, 1986.

74. Rajfer J, Coffey DS: Sex steroid imprinting of the immature prostate: Long-term effects. Invest Urol 16:186–190, 1978.

75. Higgins SJ, Brooks DE, Fuller FM, et al: Functional development of sex accessory organs of the male rat: Use of oestradiol benzoate to identify the neonatal period as critical for development of normal protein-synthetic and secretory capabilities. Biochem J 194:895–905, 1981.

76. Prins GS, Woodham C, Lepinske M, et al: Effects of neonatal estrogen exposure on prostatic secretory genes and their correlation with androgen receptor expression in the separate prostate lobes of the adult rat. Endocrinology 132:2387–2398, 1993.

77. Pylkkanen L, Makela S, Valve E, et al: Prostatic dysplasia associated with increased expression of c-myc in neonatally estrogenized mice. J Urol 149:1593–1601, 1993.

78. McLachlan JA, Newbold RR, Bullock BC: Reproductive tract lesions in male mice exposed prenatally to diethylstilbestrol. Science 190:991–992, 1975.

79. Arai Y: Nature of metaplasia in rat coagulating glands induced by neonatal treatment with estrogen. Endocrinology 86:918–920, 1970.

80. Arai Y: Metaplasia in male rat reproductive accessory glands induced by neonatal estrogen treatment. Experientia 24:180–181, 1968.

81. Prins GS: Developmental estrogenization of the prostate gland. In Naz RK (ed): Prostate: Basic and Clinical Aspects. Boca Raton, FL, CRC, 1997, pp 245–266.

82. Jarred RA, Cancilla B, Prins GS, et al: Evidence that estrogens directly alter androgen-regulated prostate development. Endocrinology 141:3471–3477, 2000.

83. Wang YZ, Wong YC: Sex hormone-induced prostatic carcinogenesis in the Noble rat: The role of insulin-like growth factor-I (IGF-I) and vascular endothelial growth factor (VEGF) in the development of prostate cancer. Prostate 35:165–177, 1998.

84. Leav I, Galluzzi CM, Ziar J, et al: Mitogen-activated protein kinase and mitogen-activated kinase phosphatase-1 expression in the Noble rat model of sex hormone-induced prostatic dysplasia and carcinoma. Lab Invest 75:361–370, 1996.

85. Isaacs JT, Coffey DS: Androgen Metabolism in the prostate: New concepts related to normal and abnormal growth. In Jacobi GH (ed): Antihormone: Bedeutung in der Urologie. Munich, W Zuckschwerdt Verlag, 1981, pp 3–20.

86. Walsh PC, Wilson JD: The induction of prostatic hypertrophy in the dog with androstenediol. J Clin Invest 57:1093–1097, 1976.

87. Kuiper GG, Enmark E, Pelto-Huikko M, et al: Cloning of a novel receptor expressed in rat prostate and ovary. Proc Natl Acad Sci U S A 93:5925–5930, 1996.

88. Kuiper GG, Carlsson B, Grandien K, et al: Comparison of the ligand binding specificity and transcript tissue distribution of estrogen receptors alpha and beta. Endocrinology 138:863–870, 1997.

89. Lau KM, Leav I, Ho SM: Rat estrogen receptor-alpha and -beta, and progesterone receptor mRNA expression in various prostatic lobes and microdissected normal and dysplastic epithelial tissues of the Noble rats. Endocrinology 139:424–427, 1998.

90. Schulze H, Barrack ER: Immunocytochemical localization of estrogen receptors in the normal male and female canine urinary tract and prostate. Endocrinology 121:1773–1783, 1987.

91. Schulze H, Claus S: Histological localization of estrogen receptors in normal and diseased human prostates by immunocytochemistry. Prostate 16:331–343, 1990.

92. Purvis K, Morkas L, Rui H, et al: Estrogen receptors in stromal and epithelial fractions of the ventral prostate of rats. Arch Androl 15:143–151, 1985.

93. Prins GS, Birch L: Neonatal estrogen exposure up-regulates estrogen receptor expression in the developing and adult rat prostate lobes. Endocrinology 138:1801–1809, 1997.

94. Jung-Testas I, Groyer MT, Bruner-Lorand J, et al: Androgen and estrogen receptors in rat ventral prostate epithelium and stroma. Endocrinology 109:1287–1289, 1981.

95. Cooke PS, Young P, Hess RA, et al: Estrogen receptor expression in developing epididymis, efferent ductules and other male reproductive organs. Endocrinology 128:2874–2879, 1991.

96. Risbridger G, Wang H, Young P, et al: Evidence that epithelial and mesenchymal estrogen receptor-alpha mediates effects of estrogen on prostatic epithelium. Dev Biol 229:432–442, 2001.

97. Imperato-McGinley J: 5α Reductase deficiency in man. Prog Cancer Res Ther 31:491–496, 1984.

98. Imperato-McGinley J, Peterson R, Gautier T, et al: Male pseudohermaphroditism secondary to 5 alpha-reductase deficiency. J Steroid Biochem 11:637–645, 1979.

99. Imperato-McGinley J, Guerrero L, Gautier T, et al: Steroid 5α-reductase deficiency in man: An inherited form of pseudohermaphroditism. Science 186:1213–1215, 1974.

100. George F, Peterson K: 5α-Dihydrotestosterone formation is necessary for embryogenesis of the rat prostate. Endocrinology 122:1159–1164, 1988.

101. Mahendroo MS, Cala KM, Hess DL, et al: Unexpected virilization in male mice lacking steroid 5 alpha-reductase enzymes. Endocrinology 142:4652–4662, 2001.

102. Morris JM: The syndrome of testicular feminization in male pseudoermaphrodites. Am J Obstet Gynecol 65:1192–1211, 1953.

103. Quigley CA, De Bellis A, Marschke KB, et al: Androgen receptor defects: Historical, clinical, and molecular perspectives. Endocr Rev 16:271–321, 1995.

104. Ohno S: Major Sex Determining Genes. New York, Springer-Verlag, 1979.

105. He WW, Kumar MV, Tindall DJ: A frameshift mutation in the androgen receptor gene causes complete androgen insensitivity in the testicular-feminized mouse. Nucleic Acids Res 19:2373–2378, 1991.

106. Donjacour AA, Rosales A, Higgins SJ, et al: Characterization of antibodies to androgen-dependent secretory proteins of the mouse dorsolateral prostate. Endocrinology 126:1343–1354, 1990.

107. Kurita T, Lee K-J, Saunders PT, et al: Regulation of progesterone receptors

and decidualization in uterine stroma of the estrogen receptor-α knockout mouse. Biol Reprod 64:271–282, 2001.

108. Buchanan DL, Setiawan T, Lubahn DL, et al: Tissue compartment-specific estrogen receptor participation in the mouse uterine epithelial secretory response. Endocrinology 140:484–491, 1998.

109. Buchanan DL, Kurita T, Taylor JA, et al: Role of stromal and epithelial estrogen receptors in vaginal epithelial proliferation, stratification and cornification. Endocrinology 139:4345–4352, 1998.

110. Kurita T, Lee KJ, Cooke PS, et al: Paracrine regulation of epithelial progesterone receptor and lactoferrin by progesterone in the mouse uterus. Biol Reprod 62:831–838, 2000.

111. Kurita T, Lee KJ, Cooke PS, et al: Paracrine regulation of epithelial progesterone receptor by estradiol in the mouse female reproductive tract. Biol Reprod 62:821–830, 2000 (erratum in Biol Reprod 63:354, 2000).

112. Kurita T, Wang YZ, Donjacour AA, et al: Paracrine regulation of apoptosis by steroid hormones in the male and female reproductive system. Cell Death Differ 8:192–200, 2001.

113. Takeda H, Suematsu N, Mizuno T: Transcription of prostatic steroid binding protein (PSBP) gene is induced by epithelial-mesenchymal interaction. Development 110:273–282, 1990.

114. Timms B, Lee C, Aumuller G, et al: Instructive induction of prostate growth and differentiation by a defined urogenital sinus mesenchyme. Microsc Res Tech 30:319–332, 1995.

115. Hayward SW, Del Buono R, Hall PA, et al: A functional model of human prostate epithelium: The role of androgens and stroma in architectural organisation and the maintenance of differentiated secretory function. J Cell Sci 102:361–372, 1992.

116. Del Buono R, Fleming KA, Morey AL, et al: A nude mouse xenograft model of fetal intestine development and differentiation. Development 114:67–73, 1992.

117. Prins GS, Birch L, Couse JF, et al: Estrogen imprinting of the developing prostate gland is mediated through stromal estrogen receptor alpha: Studies with alphaERKO and betaERKO mice. Cancer Res 61:6089–6097, 2001.

118. Cooke P, Buchanan D, Young P, et al: Stromal estrogen receptors (ER) mediate mitogenic effects of estradiol on uterine epithelium. Proc Natl Acad Sci U S A 94:6535–6540, 1997.

119. Cunha GR, Wang YZ, Hayward SW, et al: Estrogenic effects on prostatic differentiation and carcinogenesis. Reprod Fertil Dev 13:285–296, 2001.

120. Tenniswood M: Role of epithelial-stromal interactions in the control of gene expression in the prostate: An hypothesis. Prostate 9:375–385, 1986.

121. Podlasek CA, Barnett DH, Clemens JQ, et al: Prostate development requires Sonic hedgehog expressed by the urogenital sinus epithelium. Dev Biol 209:28–39, 1999.

122. Lamm ML, Catbagan WS, Laciak RJ, et al: Sonic hedgehog activates mesenchymal Gli1 expression during prostate ductal bud formation. Dev Biol 249:349–366, 2002.

123. Berman D, Desai N, Wang X, et al: Roles for Hedgehog signaling in androgen production and prostate ductal morphogenesis. Dev Biol 267:387–398, 2004.

124. Tuxhorn JA, Ayala GE, Rowley DR: Reactive stroma in prostate cancer progression. J Urol 166:2472–2483, 2001.

125. Igarashi M, Finch PW, Aaronson SA: Characterization of recombinant human fibroblast growth factor (FGF)-10 reveals functional similarities with keratinocyte growth factor (FGF-7). J Biol Chem 273:13230–13235, 1998.

126. Lu W, Luo Y, Kan M, et al: Fibroblast growth factor-10: A second candidate stromal to epithelial cell andromedin in prostate. J Biol Chem 274:12827–12834, 1999.

127. Aaronson SA, Bottaro DP, Miki T, et al: Keratinocyte growth factor: A fibroblast growth factor family member with unusual target cell specificity. Ann N Y Acad Sci 638:62–77, 1991.

128. Miki T, Bottaro DP, Fleming TP, et al: Determination of ligand-binding specificity by alternative splicing: Two distinct growth factor receptors encoded by a single gene. Proc Natl Acad Sci U S A 89:246–251, 1992.

129. Mason IJ, Pace FF, Smith R, et al: FGF-7 (keratinocyte growth factor) expression during mouse development suggests roles in myogenesis, forebrain regionalization and epithelial-mesenchymal interactions. Mech Dev 15:15–30, 1994.

130. Park WY, Miranda B, Lebeche D, et al: FGF-10 is a chemotactic factor for distal epithelial buds during lung development. Dev Biol 201:125–134, 1998.

131. Guo L, Degenstein L, Fuchs E: Keratinocyte growth factor is required for hair development but not for wound healing. Genes Dev 10:165–175, 1996.

132. Donjacour AA, Thomson AA, Cunha GR: FGF-10 plays an essential role in the growth of the fetal prostate. Dev Biol 261:39–54, 2003.

133. Min H, Danilenko DM, Scully SA, et al: Fgf-10 is required for both limb and lung development and exhibits striking functional similarity to Drosophila branchless. Genes Dev 12:3156–3161, 1998.

134. Sekine K, Ohuchi H, Fujiwara M, et al: Fgf10 is essential for limb and lung formation. Nat Genet 21:138–141, 1999.

135. Thomson AA: Role of androgens and fibroblast growth factors in prostatic development. Reproduction 121:187–195, 2001.

136. Thomson AA, Timms BG, Barton L, et al: The role of smooth muscle in regulating prostatic induction. Development 129:1905–1912, 2002.

137. Muller JW, Lee FS, Dickson C, et al: The int-2 gene product acts as an epithelial growth factor in transgenic mice. EMBO J 9:907–913, 1990.

138. Donjacour AA, Thomson AA, Cunha GR: Enlargement of the ampullary gland and seminal vesicle, but not the prostate in int-1/Fgf-3 transgenic mice. Differentiation 62:227–237, 1998.

139. Peehl DM, Cohen P, Rosenfeld RG: The insulin-like growth factor system in the prostate. World J Urol 13:306–311, 1995.

140. Barni T, Vannelli BG, Sadri R, et al: Insulin-like growth factor-I (IGF-I) and its binding protein IGFBP-4 in human prostatic hyperplastic tissue: Gene expression and its cellular localization. J Clin Endocrinol Metab 78:778–783, 1994.

141. Cohen D, Simak R, Fair W, et al: Expression of transforming growth factor-alpha and the epidermal growth factor receptor in human prostate tissues. J Urol 152:2120–2124, 1994.

142. McNeal JE: Relationship of the origin of benign prostatic hypertrophy to prostatic structure of man and other mammals. In Hinman FJ (ed): Benign Prostatic Hypertrophy. New York, Springer-Verlag, 1983, pp 152–166.

143. Cohen P, Peehl DM, Lamson G, et al: Insulin-like growth factors (IGFs), IGF receptors, and IGF-binding proteins in primary cultures of prostate epithelial cells. J Clin Endocrinol Metab 73:401–407, 1991.

144. Guenette RS, Tenniswood M: The role of growth factors in the suppression of active cell death in the prostate: An hypothesis. Biochem Cell Biol 72:553–559, 1994.

145. Thomas LN, Cohen P, Douglas RC, et al: Insulin-like growth factor binding protein 5 is associated with involution of the ventral prostate in castrated and finasteride-treated rats. Prostate 35:273–278, 1998.

146. Kyprianou N, Isaacs JT: Expression of transforming growth factor-beta in the rat ventral prostate during castration-induced programmed cell death. Mol Endocrinol 3:1515–1522, 1989.

147. Martikainen P, Kyprianou N, Isaacs JT: Effect of transforming growth factor-beta 1 on proliferation and death of rat prostatic cells. Endocrinology 127:2963–2968, 1990.

148. Sporn MB, Roberts AB: Transforming growth factor-beta: Recent progress and new challenges. J Cell Biol 119:1017–1021, 1992.

149. Attisano L, Wrana JL: Signal transduction by the TGF-beta superfamily. Science 296:1646–1647, 2002.

150. Wikstrom P, Damber J, Bergh A: Role of transforming growth factor-beta1 in prostate cancer. Microsc Res Tech 52:411–419, 2001.

151. Williams RH, Stapleton AM, Yang G, et al: Reduced levels of transforming growth factor beta receptor type II in human prostate cancer: An immunohistochemical study. Clin Cancer Res 2:635–640, 1996.

152. Brodin G, ten Dijke P, Funa K, et al: Increased Smad expression and activation are associated with apoptosis in normal and malignant prostate after castration. Cancer Res 59:2731–2738, 1999.

153. Kyprianou N, Isaacs JT: Identification of a cellular receptor for transforming growth factor-beta in rat ventral prostate and its negative regulation by androgens. Endocrinology 123:2124–2131, 1988.

154. Kim IY, Ahn HJ, Zelner DJ, et al: Expression and localization of transforming growth factor-beta receptors type I and type II in the rat ventral prostate during regression. Mol Endocrinol 10:107–115, 1996.

155. Hsing AY, Kadomatsu K, Bonham MJ, et al: Regulation of apoptosis induced by transforming growth factor-beta1 in nontumorigenic rat prostatic epithelial cell lines. Cancer Res 56:5146–5149, 1996.

156. Nishi N, Oya H, Matsumoto K, et al: Changes in gene expression of growth factors and their receptors during castration-induced involution and androgen-induced regrowth of rat prostates. Prostate 28:139–152, 1996.

157. Kissane JM: Anderson's Pathology, 9th ed. St. Louis, Mosby, 1989.

158. Kupeli B, Soygur T, Aydos K, et al: The role of cigarette smoking in prostatic enlargement. Br J Urol 80:201–204, 1997.

159. Matzkin H, Soloway MS: Cigarette smoking: A review of possible associations with benign prostatic hyperplasia and prostate cancer. Prostate 22:277–290, 1993.

160. DeKlerk DP, Coffey DS, Ewing LL, et al: Comparison of spontaneous and experimentally induced canine prostatic hyperplasia. J Clin Invest 64:842–849, 1979.

161. McNeal JE: Prostate anatomy and BPH morphogenisis. Prog Clin Biol Res 145:27–54, 1984.

162. Chung LW, Matsuura J, Rocco AK, et al: A new mouse model for prostatic hyperplasia: induction of adult prostatic overgrowth by fetal urogenital sinus implants. Prog Clin Biol Res 145:291–306, 1984.

163. Zuckerman S: Endocrine control of the prostate. Proc R Soc Med 29:1557–1568, 1936.

164. Geller J: Pathogenesis and medical treatment of benign prostatic hyperplasia. Prostate Suppl 2:95–104, 1989.

165. Moore RA: Benign hypertrophy and carcinoma of the prostate: Occurrence and experimental production in animals. Surgery 16:152–167, 1944.

166. Wilson JD: The pathogenesis of benign prostatic hyperplasia. Am J Med 68:745–756, 1980.

167. Vermeulen A, De Sy W: Androgens in patients with benign prostatic hyperplasia before and after prostatectomy. J Clin Endocrinol Metab 43:1250–1254, 1976.

168. Habenicht UF, el Etreby MF: The periurethral zone of the prostate of the cynomolgus monkey is the most sensitive prostate part for an estrogenic stimulus. Prostate 13:305–316, 1988.

169. Huggins C, Stevens R: The effect of castration on benign hypertrophy of the prostate in man. J Urol 43:705–714, 1940.

170. Geller J, Sionit L: Castration-like effects on the human prostate of a 5 alpha-reductase inhibitor, finasteride. J Cell Biochem 164(Suppl):109–112, 1992.

171. Grino P, Stoner E: Finasteride for the treatment and control of benign prostatic hyperplasia: Summary of phase III controlled studies. The Finasteride Study Group. Eur Urol 25:24–28, 1994.

172. Yoshida O, Oishi K, Okada Y, et al: Effect of long-term administration of finasteride (MK-906), an inhibitor of 5 alpha-reductase, in patients with benign prostatic hyperplasia. Hinyokika Kiyo 42:323–331, 1996.

173. Lowe FC, McConnell JD, Hudson PB, et al: Long-term 6-year experience with finasteride in patients with benign prostatic hyperplasia. Urology 61:791–796, 2003.

174. Habenicht UF, el Etreby MF: Rationale for using aromatase inhibitors to manage benign prostatic hyperplasia: Experimental studies. J Androl 12:395–402, 1991.

175. Habenicht UF, Tunn UW, Senge T, et al: Management of benign prostatic hyperplasia with particular emphasis on aromatase inhibitors. J Steroid Biochem Mol Biol 44:557–563, 1993.

176. el Etreby MF: Atamestane: An aromatase inhibitor for the treatment of benign prostatic hyperplasia: A short review. J Steroid Biochem Mol Biol 44:565–572, 1993.

177. Radlmaier A, Eickenberg HU, Fletcher MS, et al: Estrogen reduction by aromatase inhibition for benign prostatic hyperplasia: Results of a double-blind, placebo-controlled, randomized clinical trial using two doses of the aromatase-inhibitor atamestane. Atamestane Study Group. Prostate 29:199–208, 1996.

178. Lepor H: Role of alpha-adrenergic blockers in the treatment of benign prostatic hyperplasia. Prostate Suppl 3:75–84, 1990.

179. McConnell JD, Roehrborn CG, Bautista OM, et al: The long-term effect of doxazosin, finasteride, and combination therapy on the clinical progression of benign prostatic hyperplasia. N Engl J Med 349:2387–2398, 2003.

# Endocrinology of Prostate Cancer

## Gail P. Risbridger and Mark Frydenberg

## INTRODUCTION

In 1941 Huggins and Hodges[1] published a report, "Studies on prostatic cancer," that became a milestone in urology. This publication established the relation of androgenic hormones to carcinoma of the prostate gland and earned the men a Nobel Prize. Specifically, they concluded that cancer of the prostate was activated by androgens, and disseminated carcinoma of the prostate was inhibited by eliminating androgens.[1] Since that landmark article 64 years ago, our understanding of androgen or hormone regulation of prostate cancer has been actively investigated by clinicians and scientists alike. This review focuses on the more recent scientific findings that contribute to this knowledge base, together with a clinical perspective on the topic.

## HORMONAL REGULATION OF NORMAL PROSTATE DEVELOPMENT AND GROWTH

Beginning in the first trimester, the development of the prostate gland is hormonally regulated. In the absence of androgens or receptors for androgens (ARs), the prostate gland does not develop, as illustrated in male patients with complete androgen insensitivity, resulting in testicular feminization. By using Tfm mouse tissues, Cunha and his colleagues[2] conducted a series of elegant tissue-recombination experiments that demonstrated that androgenic effects were elicited through paracrine signaling events, involving mesenchymal–epithelial cell interactions. It is essential that ARs are expressed and functional in the mesenchyme surrounding the epithelial buds that emerge during prostate development. In the absence of ARs in mesenchyme, rather than epithelia, ductal morphogenesis, epithelial proliferation, and columnar cell cytodifferentiation do not occur.[2–4]

At puberty, significant growth of the prostate occurs, and it reaches adult size under the influence of androgens. Peripheral androgens act on normal prostate tissue, through ARs located on stromal cells, to regulate epithelial cell proliferation, differentiation, and death. Normal growth of the prostate is a balance between cellular proliferation and death

and is finely controlled by paracrine growth and differentiation factors that participate in the reciprocal stromal–epithelial cell interactions. For example, androgens acting through AR-positive mesenchyme or stroma regulate the production of androgen-responsive growth and differentiation factors, called andromedins, which in turn induce prostatic epithelial growth. Paracrine signaling events such as these are essential for the maintenance of normal prostate homeostasis, and members of the fibroblast growth factor (FGF) and transforming growth factor β (TGF-β) superfamily of growth factors are implicated in the process.[5,6]

In adulthood, the removal of androgens by castration leads to atrophy and reduction in prostate size, but most important, castrated men do not develop carcinoma of the prostate.[7] With animal models in which androgens can be withdrawn by castration and replaced in a sequential manner, it was possible to show that the atrophic response was reversible, and androgen replacement reactivated prostate growth.[8,9] The potent nature of androgen action in this regard is twofold, and androgens maintain the balance between cell death (apoptosis) and proliferation, as well as stimulating secretory activity of the epithelial cells. Testosterone and dihydrotestosterone (DHT) are equipotent in preventing apoptosis and act through the AR located on the smooth muscle stroma to maintain the growth-quiescent state of the epithelial cells through a range of paracrine factors or andromedins. The reduced metabolite DHT is considered more potent in maintaining secretory activity.[10] The conversion of T to DHT occurs via the action of the enzyme 5α-reductase, located in the stroma, but secretory function of the epithelium is mediated through ARs located on the differentiated columnar epithelium. Hence, the response to DHT may involve a direct action through ARs located on the epithelial cells themselves, but the role of the stroma in providing the more potent ligand for the receptor demonstrates the importance of stromal–epithelial cell interactions for normal balanced growth of the prostate gland.

The prostate gland is responsive to estrogens as well as to androgens. Naturally occurring and synthetic estrogens such as estradiol-17β, diethylstilbestrol (DES), and zeranol induce squamous metaplasia in a large number of animal species as well as humans, including mice, rats, dogs, beef bulls, monkeys, sheep, and goats.[11–22] During fetal human prostate development, squamous metaplasia spontaneously occurs to varying degrees but does not persist long and usually reverts within a month after birth.[23,24] Presumably this is due to the high levels of maternal estrogens to which the fetus is exposed during pregnancy. Nevertheless, these observations, and the plethora of animal studies on the effects of fetal or neonatal estrogen exposure, led to the notion that the prostate gland is sensitive to estrogen hormones at this time, referred to as a period of developmental estrogenization or imprinting.[25] Whether exposure to estrogens during fetal or neonatal life has sustained actions on the prostate is a controversial subject. It remains unclear whether exposure to low or inappropriately high levels of estrogens has long-range consequences related to a change in prostate growth and an increase in the incidence of prostate dysplasia in adulthood.[25,26]

As well as metabolizing testosterone to DHT, the prostate has the capacity to convert androgens to estrogens with the aromatase enzyme. The detection of aromatase activity in human prostate is variable but the aromatase gene is expressed and localized to the stroma.[27–35] Estrogen action is mediated through two receptor subtypes, estrogen receptor-alpha (ER-$\alpha$) and estrogen receptor-beta (ER-$\beta$).[36–39] The capacity to convert androgen to estrogen and the presence of ER subtypes predict a paracrine action of estrogens, similar to that for androgens. Animal studies concur with this prediction. Treatment of ER-$\alpha$- or ER-$\beta$-null mice with the synthetic estrogen DES evoked a response: the induction of squamous metaplasia that is mediated via the ER subtype ER-$\alpha$ rather than ER-$\beta$.[40] A requirement exists for ER-$\alpha$ to be present on the stroma, but in addition, and different from androgens, a requirement exists for epithelial cell ER-$\alpha$.[40]

Overall, normal prostate gland homeostasis involves paracrine signaling events. At the very least, testosterone is locally converted to reduced androgens (such as DHT) or to estrogens, and subsequent actions are mediated through stromal or epithelial ARs or ERs (Fig. 180-1). The importance of reciprocal homeostatic interactions between prostatic stroma and epithelia in adulthood is profound. The levels of cell proliferation and death in each of the cell types are low and in balance and therefore maintain the adult prostate in a growth-quiescent state. Further, this state of growth quiescence and homeostasis occurs when the levels of systemic androgens remain at levels that previously elicited significant growth of the tissues, for example, during pubertal life. A key feature of prostate cancer is the perturbation of these normal stromal–epithelial cell interactions.

## HORMONE-RESPONSIVE GROWTH IN PROSTATE CANCER

### ANDROGENS AND PROSTATE CANCER

Prostate cancer is an androgen-dependent disease that does not occur in eunuchs who are castrated in early life.[7] Initially, prostate cancer is dependent on androgens for growth and differentiation, but ultimately the disease progresses and becomes insensitive or refractory to androgens. During hormone-responsive prostate cancer, significant changes occur to the way in which the tumor cells respond to androgens. As well as paracrine mechanisms of responding to androgens, prostate cancer cells acquire an autocrine mode of androgen action. The tumor cells respond directly to androgens and andromedins (such as growth factors of the TGF or FGF superfamilies) that are produced by, and elicit a response from, the tumor cells themselves. In acquiring this mode of action, the tumor cells obtain a significant growth advantage. Furthermore, evidence exists that the ARs on the tumor cells

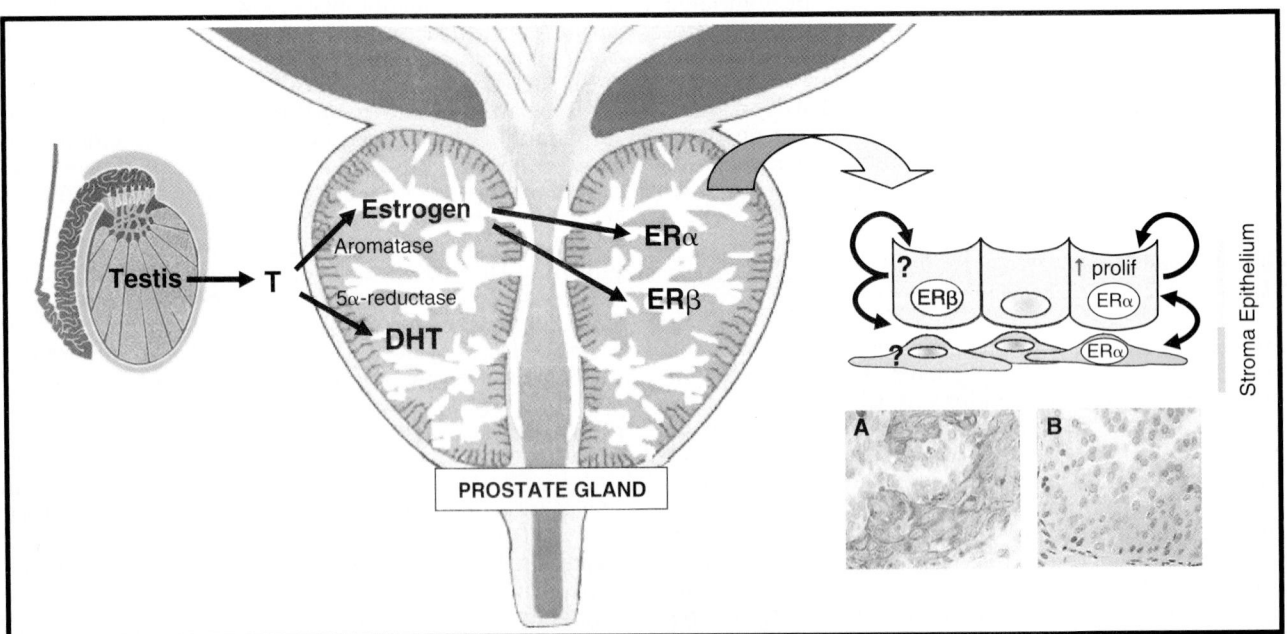

*Figure 180-1* Schematic representation of local estrogen production and receptor-mediated responses in the prostate. Testicular testosterone, secreted into the peripheral circulation, reaches the prostate gland and is further metabolized to more potent androgens (such as dihydrotestosterone; DHT) as well as estrogens by aromatization. The local conversion of testosterone to estrogen provides another level of balance between male and female hormones in addition to that which occurs in the systemic circulation as a result of aging. Within the gland itself, direct responses to estrogens are mediated via hormone receptors present and differentially expressed in the stromal or epithelial cells. The estrogen-receptor subtype ER-$\alpha$ is located in both cell types, but predominantly in the stroma, whereas ER-$\beta$ is located in the prostate epithelium. A proliferative response to estrogen can be identified through the induction of squamous metaplasia (**A**, marked with cytokeratin 10). The epithelial cells that proliferate in response to estrogen are in the basal cell layer (**B**, brown cells marked with proliferating cell nuclear antigen [PCNA], and pink cells marked with cytokeratin 10) and become multilayered, pushing the terminally differentiated cells toward the lumen (**A**). A biologic response that is specifically mediated via ER-$\beta$ remains to be clearly defined.

can be mutated, rendering them responsive to range of steroid ligands and not only to androgens.[41–43]

## THE BALANCE BETWEEN ANDROGENS AND ESTROGENS IN THE AGING MALE

Although the incidence of prostate cancer increases with age and is dependent on androgens, the development of prostate cancer commonly occurs at an age in men when the levels of serum testosterone are declining.[44,45] Although testicular testosterone synthesis and serum testosterone levels decrease in aging men, the levels of estradiol do not and remain unchanged or increase.[44,46–50] Levels of estrogen are thought to be maintained by increased aromatization of adrenal androgens in peripheral adipose tissue, which also tends to increase in the older male.[46,51,52] Therefore, a significant change is found in the ratio of estradiol/testosterone that is temporally related to the onset of prostate disease, including prostate cancer. Epidemiologic evidence provides some further support for this relationship. Serum levels of estrogens in African-American men (who have the highest incidence of prostate cancer in the United States) are significantly higher compared with white American men.[53–56] Conversely, serum levels of estrogens are lower in Japanese men (who are known to have a low risk of prostate cancer) compared with white Dutch men.[57] The age-related shift in the balance of hormones in men, as they become older, also illustrates the gradual nature of the change and the long latency of the disease.

## ROLE OF ESTROGENS IN HORMONE RESPONSIVE PROSTATE CANCER

It is difficult to demonstrate directly a change to the local hormonal milieu that results in a hormone imbalance within the prostate gland. Nevertheless, sufficient evidence exists that when cancer is present, the levels of tissue estrogens are altered, local synthesis of estrogen by aromatization is modified, alternate aromatase gene promoters are utilized, and changes occur in the expression of the ER subtype in the prostate (see Fig. 180-1).

Increased estradiol and estrone levels in prostatic epithelial cells were noted in association with declining DHT levels.[58] The in situ production of estrogen occurs via aromatization and requires expression of the gene encoding aromatase enzyme, *CYP19*.[59] Aromatase gene and protein expression in the prostate gland has been equivocal, and any local actions of estrogens are considered secondary to centrally mediated androgen suppression.[28–32,34,60] The accuracy of laser capture microdissection procedures led to the direct demonstration of aromatase gene expression in normal human prostate tissues and cells. Specifically, aromatase is expressed in stroma, but not in nonmalignant epithelial cells, and the expression pattern changes in prostate cancer so that tumor cells acquire aromatase gene expression, and aromatase messenger RNA (mRNA) and protein become detectable.[35] In stroma from nonmalignant tissue specimens, expression is driven by promoter PII, but after the onset of aromatase expression in the malignant epithelia, different promoter utilization was observed and included promoters I.4 and I.3 in addition to PII. Alternate aromatase promoter use in prostate cancer bears similarity to that in breast cancer when alternate aromatase-promoter transactivation is an important determinant of malignant disease.[61] The significance of the changes to aromatase is twofold. First, the tumor cells have the ability to produce estrogen themselves without the involvement of the stroma, removing any paracrine regulation in this regard. Second, the transactivation of different promoters occurs in response to different growth factors and cytokines, so the overall regulation of aromatase expression is further changed in malignancy.

If the local production of estrogen is modified in prostate cancer, it is reasonable to predict that ER expression is altered. As discussed earlier, the ER-α subtype is thought to mediate the proliferative actions of estrogens and is normally expressed in stroma. Animal studies from the Cunha laboratory implicate ER-α in tumorigenesis. A polymorphism of ER-α was found to be a risk factor for prostate cancer in a Japanese population, further implicating ER-α in the pathogenesis of this human disease. The role of the other receptor subtype ER-β, located mainly on epithelial cells, is not known[62–66]; however, expression of a C-terminal truncated splice variant of ER-β (ER-βcx) is upregulated in high-grade compared with low-grade tumors,[67] and metastases to bone or lymph nodes showed upregulation of ER-β expression.[63] The reason for any of the variations in ER-β or its splice variant in primary tumors or metastases is unclear, and the hypothesis that ER-β is a key determinant of prostate cancer initiation, progression, or metastases remains to be determined.

## ROLE OF ANDROGENS AND ESTROGENS IN HORMONE-RESPONSIVE PROSTATE CANCER

Having established that an overall imbalance or resetting of the hormone balance exists in older men with prostate cancer, it becomes relevant to consider the consequences in terms of prostatic homeostasis. Although the development of prostate cancer is dependent on androgens, the evidence points to a role of estrogens in combination with androgens. As discussed, androgen levels decrease in men as they become older, and the incidence of prostate cancer increases. Animal studies also point to the conclusion that androgens are necessary, but insufficient, to induce tumorigenesis alone. For example, the ARKO mouse is an estrogen-deficient mouse model, and androgen levels are elevated throughout life, but the mice do not develop malignancies of the prostate gland.[68]

Instead, the mechanism of hormonal induction of prostate cancer probably involves both hormones, and some experimental evidence supports this postulate. It is well known that the Noble rat develops precancerous lesions and prostate adenocarcinoma when given estrogens in conjunction with androgens.[56,69,70] Combined hormone treatment of grafted prostatic tissues promotes malignancy in Rb-deficient mouse tissue recombinants.[71] Combined treatment of wild-type mice with high doses of testosterone and estradiol induces prostatic hyperplasia, dysplasia, and carcinoma in situ.[72] Furthermore, an important role for ER-α was deduced from the same treatment of α-ERKO and β-ERKO mice. ER-β knock-out (KO) mice (that express ER-α) developed dysplasia and malignancy comparable to that observed in wild-type mice, but ER-α KO mice did not. These data emphasize the importance of signaling through ER-α, rather than ER-β, during the hormonal induction of prostate cancer.

## STROMAL–EPITHELIAL CELL INTERACTIONS

In considering the imbalance of hormones and the adjustments that occur in hormone-responsive prostate cancer, it is clear that profound alterations to stromal–epithelial cell interactions accompany these changes (Fig. 180-2). The perturbation of normal stromal–epithelial cell interactions is a key feature of prostate cancer, resulting in autocrine growth whereby the tumor cells escape from the regulatory influence of paracrine signals. Whether this is initiated by genetic damage to the epithelial cells or the stromal cells, a sequential disruption in the reciprocal relations leads to a loss of the homeostatic interactions, and a vicious cycle of unregulated growth and differentiation ensues.[73]

The concept that the stroma may play a pivotal role in carcinogenesis has evolved over decades and is based on the observations that the pathology of tumor stroma differs from that of normal stroma.[73,74] In the benign adult human

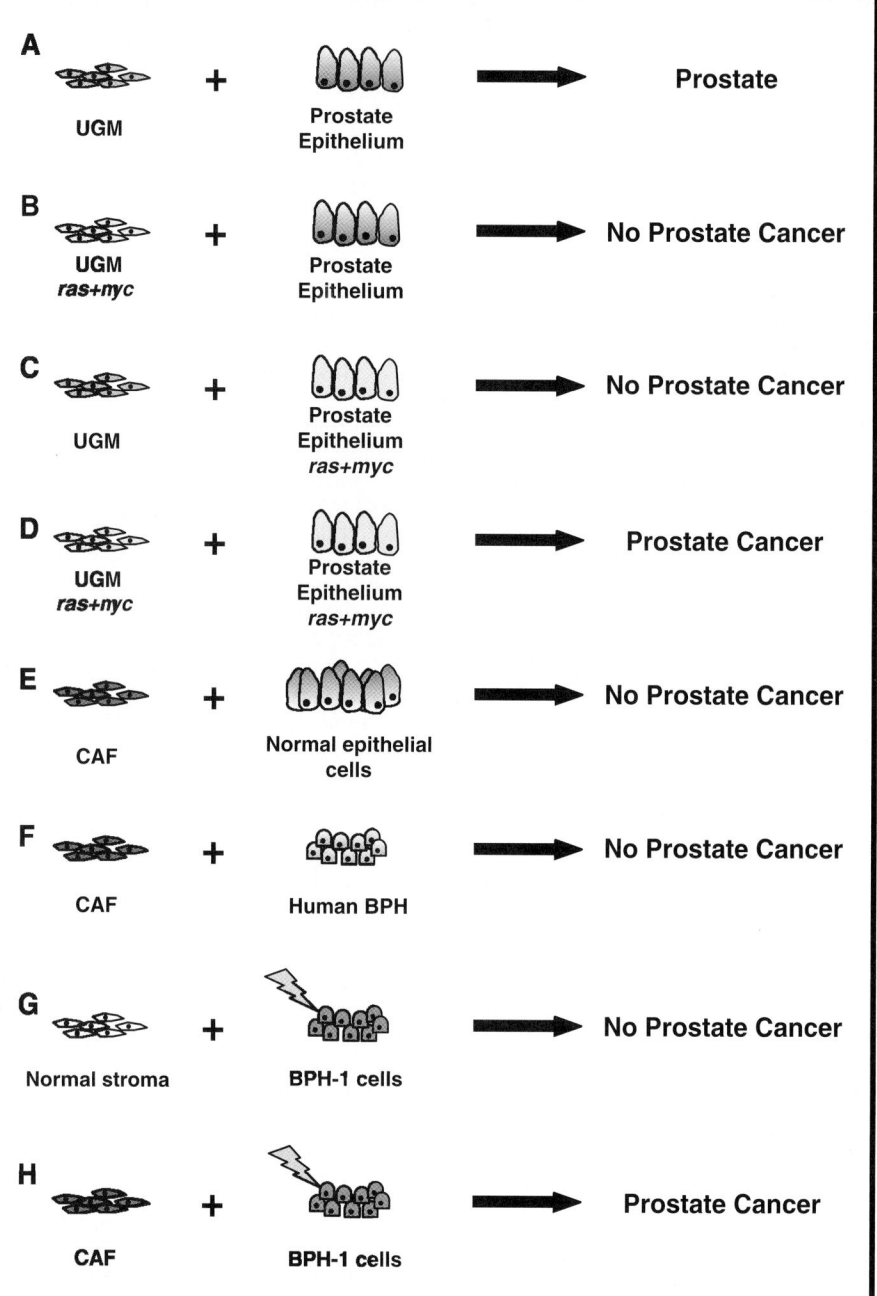

*Figure 180-2* Schematic representation that genetic insults in both of prostate stroma and epithelium contribute to the initiation of prostate cancer. Traditionally, we believed that genetic insult to the prostate epithelium was sufficient to induce prostate cancer. However, more recently, this theory has been challenged by several investigators who provided evidence by using elegant tissue recombination studies that genetic insults to both the epithelium and stroma are required for the initiation of prostate cancer. Classic experiments recombining mouse urogenital mesenchyme (UGM) with prostate epithelium result in the formation of prostate tissue (**A**). With this model, Thompson and colleagues[79] determined the contributions of each cell compartment in the initiation of prostate cancer by using genetically modified mice carrying *myc* and *ras* oncogenes. Tissue recombinants with the oncogenes in either the mesenchyme (**B**) or epithelium (**C**) alone did not result in prostate cancer formation; prostate tumors were observed only when both cell types were infected (**D**). Similar findings were observed by using human prostate cells. Carcinoma-associated fibroblasts (stromal cells surrounding prostate tumors) or normal human prostate stromal cells were used in combination with normal human prostate epithelial cells, human benign prostate hyperplasia (BPH) cells, and BPH-1 cells (immortalized, genetically altered BPH cells). Only when altered stroma cells (carcinoma-associated fibroblast [CAF] cells) were recombined with altered epithelial cells (BPH-1 cells) did prostate tumors form (**H**); in all other cases, no prostate cancer was evident (**E–G**). In combination, all of these studies provide evidence that genetic changes in the stroma, as well as the epithelium, are critical for the

prostate, the stroma consists of smooth muscle actin-positive cells that express ARs and maintain a highly differentiated secretory epithelium under the influence of androgens. In contrast, the stromal cells that surround tumor cells in the prostate are fibroblastic or myofibroblastic and are termed *reactive stroma* or *cancer-associated fibroblasts* (CAFs).[5,75–78] Because the reciprocal interactions between the stroma and epithelia are critical for the maintenance of homeostasis in normal prostate, it was predicted that a change in epithelial and stromal pathology would interfere with or alter these interactions. Not surprisingly then, studies by Thompson and colleagues[79] using tissue-recombination techniques to study the effects of inserting the *myc* and *ras* oncogenes in epithelial or stromal cells showed that carcinomas developed, but only when both the epithelia and stroma were infected. Similarly, human CAFs promote carcinogenesis in combination with immortal, but non-

tumorigenic, human benign prostatic hyperplasia (BPH)-1 human prostate epithelial cells,[78] whereas normal stroma does not. Furthermore, although CAFs can promote carcinogenesis in immortal epithelial cells, they cannot initiate and promote carcinogenesis in normal prostate epithelial cells. Thus, modification to both epithelial and stromal cells is required for conversion and progression to malignancy (see Fig. 180-2).

## MONITORING HORMONE-REGULATED GROWTH IN PROSTATE CANCER BY USING PROSTATE SPECIFIC ANTIGEN

Secretory activity of the mammalian prostate gland is hormonally regulated and in particular prostate-specific antigen (PSA), a proteolytic enzyme belonging to the kallikrein group of serine proteases, is produced by human prostate epithelium. Over the last decade, the assessment of serum PSA has allowed physicians to diagnose prostate cancer earlier in its biologic evolution and led to a subsequent increase in local therapies with the aim of curing the disease.

PSA was initially identified in human seminal plasma,[80] and in the late 1970s, a plasma protein was purified that was prostate specific and identical to that found in semen.[81] Although cancer is often a cause of elevation in serum PSA, other causes include prostatic infarction, prostatitis, ejaculation, vigorous prostate massage but not routine digital rectal examination, and prostatic instrumentation.[82-84] Therapy that alters hormonal status also will affect serum PSA, especially the use of the 5α-reductase inhibitor finasteride, which reliably reduces serum PSA by 50%. The half-life of PSA is 2.2 to 3.2 days, and it can take several weeks for serum PSA to return to baseline after procedures such as prostate biopsy or resection.

In diagnosing cancer, the sensitivity ranges from 63% to 83% and the specificity from 81% to 90% when using PSA of more than 4 µg/L as the cut-off value. Specificity is generally better in the younger age groups, because PSA production from the benign tissue of older men is a confounding variable. As such, recent studies suggested that reducing the cut-off point for younger men is appropriate to increase detection rates from 18% to 36%, while reducing specificity from 98% to 94%.[85] Whether this increases the detection of clinically insignificant cancer is uncertain. Nonetheless, combining digital rectal examination (DRE) with serum PSA appears to give the best screening cancer detection rates, with the combination detecting 27% more cancers than PSA alone, and 34% more than with DRE alone.[86,87] Randomized studies in progress may provide the answers as to whether these screening endeavors will reduce prostate cancer mortality. Some evidence suggests it may, such as the study from Tyrol, Austria, in which men in that state were offered free PSA testing and were encouraged to participate. This study demonstrated a 33% reduction in mortality compared with the expected rate elsewhere in Austria.[88] Whereas many authors suggest this is evidence of the benefit of screening, others claim the causes of the decline in mortality may be due to different variables such as diet and lifestyle factors, attribution bias, and the earlier use of androgen-deprivation therapy (ADT). Other studies showed that despite vastly different rates for PSA screening and testing, the reduction in prostate cancer mortality was similar between the United Kingdom and the United States, and between the Seattle region of the United States and Connecticut. It is clear that the current status of screening remains uncertain.[89] Nonetheless, the introduction of PSA into clinical practice has decreased the incidence of metastatic disease. Many cancers detected today are now potentially curable, and fewer then 20% have been described as pathologically insignificant,[83] although what this constitutes remains debatable.

To improve the positive predictive value of PSA, several strategies were used. These include age-specific reference ranges, PSA velocity, PSA density, free PSA, and, more recently, serum pro-PSA or human kallikreinen 2 (HK2). The use of age-specific ranges improves sensitivity in younger men and specificity in older men. The commonly used cut-offs are less than 2.5 µg/L for 40- to 49-year-old men and less than 3.5 µg/L, less than 4.5 µg/L, and less than 6.5 µg/L for 50- to 59-, 60- to 69-, and 70- to 79-year-old men, respectively. Studies showed an 8% increase in positive biopsies in younger men with these reference ranges, and a 21% reduction in the number of biopsies, while missing only 4% of cancers in older men.[83] Serial PSA determination (PSA velocity) was thought to be valuable in predicting cancer from benign disease, and a PSA change of more than 0.75 µg/L/year was believed to indicate the presence of cancer. Unfortunately, this value is of limited benefit because of the day-to-day variation in serum PSA in any individual. This variability led many to conclude that an isolated elevation in PSA should be confirmed several weeks later before proceeding with biopsy.[82] In addition, the velocity is not easy to calculate and varies depending on the assays used. It does not tend to be used to determine the need for biopsy, although it may indicate the necessity to conduct the procedure. PSA density (the division of serum PSA by prostate volume) was thought to discriminate between cancer and benign tissue, based on the premise that cancer produced more PSA on a volume basis compared with benign tissue. A marked variability is found in the amount of PSA produced by prostate tissue, both benign and malignant, because of the variability in the stromal/epithelial ratios, and this, together with major interobserver variation in the measurement of prostate volume, makes PSA density relatively unreliable. Similar problems emerged when using transition zone PSA density.

More recently attention focused on the various forms of PSA. PSA in the serum is often complexed to $\alpha_1$-antichymotrypsin (ACT) or $\alpha_2$-macroglobulin (A2M). PSA complexed to A2M is not detectable immunologically, as the A2M molecule is large and blocks all epitopes on the surface of PSA. Thus, it is possible to differentiate between free PSA and PSA complexed to ACT, and a percentage of free (%free) PSA can be calculated and expressed. Using a %free PSA cut-off of more than 25%, specificity improves by 20% while maintaining 95% sensitivity.[90] Other assays determine the ratios of complexed PSA that may be less sensitive to DRE and prostate manipulations and can be used as single tests that may be more stable after storage of the specimens. Nonetheless, the %free PSA appears to be the assay in wider clinical use currently and appears particularly useful to assist with the detection of prostate cancer in the lower ranges of 2.5 to 4.0 µg/L.

Human glandular kallikrein belongs to the same family as PSA, shares an 80% homology with PSA, and is prostate specific and androgen dependent. HK2 cleaves PSA from its inactive precursor pro-PSA into active PSA. Studies suggested that this enzyme may be superior in the detection of organ-confined prostate cancer, especially in cancers of higher histologic grade,[91] when serum PSA is less reliable. Early results examining the HK2/free PSA ratio appear promising but require substantial validation and testing before coming into regular use. Studies continue into the use of serum HK2, as well as pro-PSA, which appears to be secreted more by cancerous tissue than by benign tissue. Recent studies suggested an improved specificity for cancer detection comparing percentage of pro-PSA with either %free PSA or total PSA in the 2- to 10-µg/L range.[92]

PSA was found to be a useful tool in the assessment of tumor volume and clinical staging. Although some studies showed little correlation between PSA levels and cancer volume, PSA was used in many nomograms with multivariate analyses, and increasing levels were associated with adverse prognostic factors such as extracapsular extension, seminal vesicle or lymph node involvement, and biochemical progression.[93,94]

PSA is particularly useful after treatment for prostate cancer. Those patients managed expectantly with watchful waiting normally undergo definitive therapy as a result of serial increases in serum PSA. After surgery, an undetectable serum PSA is usually obtained and based on the lowest limit of detection of the particular assay used. Those patients whose PSA did not decrease to undetectable levels, who had a rapid PSA doubling time, and whose PSA was more than 1 µg/L were more likely to have micrometastatic disease and subsequent failure of adjuvant radiotherapy.[95] After radiotherapy, PSA reaches a nadir over a 17- to 32-month period, occasionally with a bounce phenomenon in which it may temporarily increase. Patients will usually demonstrate excellent long-term cancer-specific survivals if PSA levels are less than 0.5 µg/L and the patient does not fail biochemically based on three consecutive increases in PSA above a nadir (i.e., the American Society of Therapeutic Radiology and Oncology [ASTRO] criteria for failure). After ADT, PSA levels can often stratify patients into good and bad prognostic groups. Studies have shown that if PSA is greater than 4 µg/L after 24 to 32 weeks of treatment, median survival is 18 weeks, as compared with 40 weeks if PSA is less than 4 µg/L.[96]

In summary, PSA has revolutionized the way prostate cancer is managed. It is useful in the diagnosis of the disease, but once cancer is diagnosed, is helpful to stage disease clinically, to predict survival after treatment, and is invaluable in disease monitoring after definitive therapy and assisting in determining which adjuvant therapy should be used after failed curative treatment.

## ENDOCRINE THERAPIES FOR HORMONE-RESPONSIVE PROSTATE CANCER

Although hormone therapy in the form of ADT has been used for many decades, the earlier treatment options of bilateral orchidectomy or oral estrogens in the form of oral DES were unacceptable for many men. Studies demonstrated the effectiveness of using these options with a survival advantage if used as early enough, but cardiovascular deaths from the estrogen therapy negated any benefit in survival. As such, it became the standard of care that hormonal therapy was deferred until symptomatic progression occurred. The advent of luteinizing hormone–releasing hormone (LHRH) agonists and oral antiandrogens made immediate hormone therapy more acceptable to many patients, often when they were asymptomatic. It is commonly used for both symptomatic and asymptomatic metastatic disease, as neoadjuvant treatment before radiotherapy, as adjuvant therapy after radiotherapy or surgery for high-risk locally advanced prostate cancer, and for the treatment of PSA-based biochemical failure after definitive therapy.

The issue of whether hormonal therapy should be instituted early or late continues to be a major discussion point in urology. Studies demonstrated the effectiveness of using immediate hormone therapy together with radiotherapy compared with radiotherapy alone, based on 5-year survival figures of 78% and 62%, respectively.[97] Another study to compare these options in locally advanced prostate cancer demonstrated an increase of median survival by more than 3 years with early treatment.[98] Yet another study by the Radiation Therapy Oncology Group demonstrated a survival advantage in using immediate hormonal therapy in those men with high-grade cancers.[99] In contrast, some studies that demonstrated improved progression rates with combined therapy failed to demonstrate survival benefits. Overall consensus opinions suggest that patients with locally advanced or high-grade disease may benefit from a short course of neoadjuvant radiotherapy before the initiation of radiotherapy, and that this should be continued for 2 to 3 years after treatment, based on the results of these studies. These results cannot be extrapolated to patients of lower clinical stage and grade. Similarly, a paucity of data is found regarding the role of ADT combined with prostate brachytherapy, and prospective randomized trials in this area are required.

Survival data on the use of adjuvant immediate hormone therapy after radical prostatectomy were recorded mostly in men with nodal metastatic disease. In the Eastern Cooperative Oncology Group 7887 study, immediate adjuvant therapy was compared with therapy instituted at the time of clinical progression. At a mean follow-up of 7 years, survival was better in the immediate group (85% vs. 65%), with fewer deaths attributed to prostate cancer (6% vs. 31%).[100]

The impact of ADT in the treatment of men with asymptomatic advanced disease was also reported by the Medical Research Council (UK). A survival advantage was seen in men treated with early ADT with M0 but not M1 disease. This benefit was lost with further follow-up, but the early treatment was associated with a reduced rate of pathologic fractures, extraskeletal metastases, spinal cord compression, and ureteral obstruction.[101]

The bicalutamide early prostate cancer (EPC) trial recruited patients from Scandinavia, Europe, and North America. Patients received either bicalutamide, 150 mg, as antiandrogen monotherapy or placebo as adjuvant therapy after either radiotherapy or radical surgery. Although the incidence of progression was lower in the treated group, in some subgroups (those treated with watchful waiting), a trend was noted toward accelerated deaths from cancer in the treated group (25.2% vs. 20.5%). As a result, bicalutamide as monotherapy was withdrawn for this indication in many countries.[102] Ongoing work on the EPC trial will determine what cause-specific survival impact monotherapy has with longer follow-up, in the groups treated with radiotherapy or surgery. Side effects of bicalutamide remain considerable, however, with 38% discontinuing from the medication, mostly because of breast pain, gynecomastia (66% to 72%), asthenia, impotence, hot flashes (all ~9%), and diarrhea and abdominal pain (6%). Therefore, although bicalutamide monotherapy was compared favorably with standard ADT (LHRH agonists or orchiectomy) in locally advanced nonmetastatic prostate cancer, major quality-of-life (QOL) differences are found between the two; less sexual dysfunction is seen with the antiandrogen therapy but greater breast-related complications. All these issues require extensive discussion with the patient so that informed decisions can be made.

A recent study examined the role of early hormone therapy for PSA-only recurrences after radical surgery, which demonstrated that early ADT was an independent predictor of delayed clinical metastases in high-risk cases (those with high-grade cancer or who had a PSA doubling time of <12 months[103] and adverse pathologic stage or a combination of these). Whether this translates into cause-specific survival advantage at this stage is speculative. No evidence now suggests an advantage in either overall or disease-free survival to using neoadjuvant hormonal therapy before radical surgery.

Hormone therapy is now often delivered by depot injections of LHRH agonists. The most recent meta-analysis looked at the role of combined androgen blockade versus monotherapy with LHRH agonists alone. No significant increases in survival were noted for the combination group overall, and combination therapy with flutamide or nilutamide was marginally superior to that with cyproterone acetate.[104] For patients with advanced disease, the initial surge of testosterone that results from the administration of LHRH agonists is well known and can be a major cause of concern in patients with imminent ureteral obstruction or vertebral metastases. A short course of antiandrogen for 2 to 4 weeks should be prescribed before the initiation of LHRH therapy to avoid this flare phenomenon.

Side effects of ADT can be significant, and as such, these QOL issues must be balanced against the potential survival benefits described earlier. Many men treated with ADT describe a loss of libido and erectile dysfunction (ED). Hot flashes frequently occur, associated with profuse sweating, and can interrupt sleep. Other problems include gynecomastia (greatest with antiandrogen use, least with orchidectomy), weight gain, loss of bone mineral density (BMD), anemia, loss of body hair, and decreased cognitive function.[105] In an attempt to reduce treatment-related side effects, intermittent androgen suppression was described, whereby on reaching a nadir in PSA levels, the men discontinue ADT and recommence treatment only when serum PSA increases. The exact PSA at which ADT should be recommenced is not defined conclusively. Several phase II studies demonstrated a lower cost of therapy as well as improved QOL in the "off" cycle. Many phase III studies are under way to determine whether this intermittent regimen produces survival equivalence or advantage over standard continuous therapy.[106]

Osteoporosis as a result of ADT was shown to increase fracture risk in men with prostate cancer. In a study of men who were treated with orchiectomy, 14% had more than one osteoporotic fractures compared with 1% in men with prostate cancer who did not receive ADT. These fractures were more common than either traumatic or pathologic fractures. Other studies demonstrated a risk of 6% to 10% of osteoporotic fractures, associated with the duration of ADT.[107] Most studies confirmed a loss of BMD of 5% to 10% in the first year of ADT, although other factors may play a role, such as vitamin D deficiency or an inadequate calcium intake. Medical castration with estrogens does not lead to osteoporosis, and as bicalutamide monotherapy was shown to lead to increases in serum testosterone and estradiol, it is postulated but not proven that this agent may have a lesser effect on bone metabolism than does standard ADT. Lifestyle modifications should be considered in men undergoing ADT (cessation of smoking, moderation of alcohol intake, regular weight-bearing exercise, supplementary vitamin D and calcium, and consideration of the administration of biphosphonates that act as potent osteoclastic inhibitors).[108] Monitoring BMD is warranted in men undergoing ADT, but prophylactic therapy is not currently recommended. Men with evidence of significant bone loss who are receiving ADT should be treated, and based on current data, zoledronic acid appears the logical choice of therapy because it was shown to increase BMD by 5.6% in a recent study of men taking ADT.[109] In addition, this agent was shown to decrease the risk of skeletal-related events in men with metastatic prostate cancer by 11%.[110] Although the studies were not powered to look at survival, median time to death was longer in the treated arm (546 vs. 464 days). Morbidity with this therapy is limited (fatigue, anemia, myalgia, and pyrexia). Questions of when should treatment begin, how long should it be continued, and the optimal doses and schedules to be used remain largely unanswered, as does the issue of whether prophylactic biphosphonate therapy may prevent or delay the onset of skeletal metastases.

## HORMONE-REFRACTORY GROWTH IN PROSTATE IN PROSTATE CANCER

Despite a variety of endocrine therapies to treat prostate cancer and reduce testosterone levels, these approaches eventually fail and lead to resumption of tumor growth that is independent of hormones (i.e., hormone refractory). The underlying mechanisms of resistance to hormone discontinuation are thought to be due to the adaptation or selection of tumor cells and an accumulation of multiple and sequential changes in DNA structure and gene expression. Prostate tumors are heterogeneous and consist of several types or populations of cancer cells, with differing abilities to respond to hormone ablation. Preexisting *clones* of androgen-independent cells are resistant to hormone withdrawal and can grow in the absence of androgens. Cells that are dependent on androgens for their growth *adapt* by upregulation of survival genes to assist the tumor to grow in a hormone-depleted milieu. Thus, the transition to hormone-refractory growth is a combination of genetic and epigenetic mechanisms involving clonal selection or adaptation to hormone-withdrawal therapy or both.[111-113] At least three main reasons explain the resistance to hormone therapy; DNA-based change to the AR, the activation of alternate growth-factor pathways, and upregulation of survival genes.

### ANDROGEN RECEPTOR

The AR is a key molecule in the progression to hormone-refractory prostate cancer. Overall, it appears that the AR remains active during this phase through a variety of

mechanisms that are aimed at increasing the growth response to lower levels of androgen and to a wider range of compounds. The mechanisms include mutation or amplification of the AR, hypersensitivity to androgen, and alterations in coregulators of AR; some growth factors also can activate AR in the absence of ligand (see Refs. 111, 113, and 114).

Mutations of the AR that effect the ligand-binding domain confer hormone resistance by decreasing the specificity of the AR so that a number of ligands activate AR-regulated genes in androgen-depleted conditions.[115] For example, the point mutation of AR at Thr877Ala in LNCaP cells conferred promiscuity of the AR and was subsequently detected in tumor cells from patients with hormone-refractory prostate cancer.[42,43,116] As well as endogenous steroids (e.g., estrogens, progestins), a number of ligands activate the mutated AR, and in particular, exogenous antiandrogens used in the endocrine ablation therapy. Activation of the AR by antiandrogens is termed *androgen-withdrawal syndrome,* and some patients show reduced PSA levels on termination of hormone-blockade therapy.[116]

A range of other point mutations activate AR in a similar manner,[50,117-119] and a full listing of all known AR mutations in prostate cancer is available on the AR mutation database. Generally, the frequency of AR point mutations is low in hormone-naive prostate tumors, but it increases in hormone-refractory prostate cancer. For example, the point mutation in AR at Thr877Ala was detected in patient tissues after, but not before, therapy and provides another link between the presence of AR mutation and the development of androgen-withdrawal syndrome.[120] As well as those in the primary tumor tissues, mutations of AR also were identified in bone and lymph node metastases.[43,121-124]

*AR gene amplification* or overexpression is believed to permit the tumor cells to respond to low levels of androgen, and amplification occurs at the mRNA and protein levels. Several studies confirmed the early findings; as many as 30% of patients with recurrent tumors showed AR amplification.[64,125-128] An association is found with AR amplification and progression to metastatic disease during hormone withdrawal.[129] However, amplification of the AR occurs only with low frequency and cannot account for the majority of patients with hormone-refractory disease.[126,130]

### HYPERSENSITIVITY TO ANDROGEN

Endocrine ablation reduces serum levels of hormones, but residual androgens might remain effective if the tumor cells become hypersensititve to hormones. To be of any consequence, a significant shift in sensitivity in terms of orders of magnitude would have to occur, rather than severalfold, as exemplified in vitro with tumor cell lines.[131] As well, increased sensitivity to androgens might be achieved by sustained increase in kinase pathway signaling. Activation of Ras/mitogen-activated protein kinase (MAPK) in mutant cells expressing Ras reduced the requirement for androgens, and the tumor cells grew in androgen concentrations that were 1 to 2 orders of magnitude lower than the parental cells.

### ALTERATIONS IN COREGULATORS

Coactivators or corepressors enhance or reduce ligand-dependent activation of ARs, and a change in coactivators leads to hormone-independent tumor growth. Coactivators not only increase the transcription of AR-regulated genes, but they also provide another means to reduce the specificity of the AR by inducing promiscuity and activation with other ligands. For example, the coactivator Ara70 does both; it increases transcriptional activity of AR in cell lines and allows other ligands, such as estradiol, flutamide, and cyproterone acetate, to activate the AR.[132-134]

A number of AR coactivators, such as SRC-1, are upregulated in tumor tissues, consistent with increased sensitivity to androgens.[135] Similarly, a decrease in the expression of corepressors such as nuclear receptor corepressor (NCoR) might lead to hormone resistance.[136,137] Therefore, an imbalance between corepressor and coactivators could lead to increased expression of the nuclear AR and change its ligand-binding specificity.

The critical role of ARs in hormone-refractory prostate cancer was confirmed in an interesting series of expression-profiling experiments in which the AR was unexpectedly, but consistently, upregulated in hormone-resistant xenograft models.[138] Although the increase in receptor levels was modest (three- to fivefold), a number of subsequent effects were consistent with the view that multiple molecular mechanisms of altering ARs leads to resistance to hormone therapy. It was suggested that the AR increase was sufficient to compensate for low levels of androgens, and it was demonstrated that ARs must bind ligand to confer hormone-refractory growth. Nuclear, rather than cytoplasmic, localization of ARs was essential, and deletion of the nuclear localization sequence (NLS) abolished hormone-refractory growth. The higher AR levels converted antagonists, such as cyproterone acetate, bicalutamide, and flutamide, to weak agonists, probably by modifying coactivator assembly, resulting in increased transcriptional activity and induction of the most androgen-sensitive genes. Therefore, more than one molecular event could alter AR expression, leading to a common mechanism of hormone-refractory growth.

### ROLE OF GROWTH FACTORS

The consequences of the changes to AR in hormone-refractory disease include the use of growth factors or cytokines to replace androgens for growth and survival. Either the growth factors or cytokines bypass the use of ARs or they activate the AR, resulting in its becoming transcriptionally active in the absence of any ligand. Growth factors believed to act in this manner include insulin-like growth factor 1 (IGF-1), epidermal growth factor (EGF), and keratinocyte growth factor (KGF)[139] working through activation of one or more of the tyrosine kinase pathways to promote AR activation and hence tumor cell growth.[111,113] Other factors of note in this context include Her2/Neu (erbB2) that activates the AR through MAPK or AKT pathways, interleukin (IL)-6 as well as β-catenin, cyclins E and D1, and Smad3.[140–143] The convergence of the growth factor– and androgen-signaling pathways is another area of research that warrants further investigation to determine the physiological and, ultimately, clinical significance.

### ROLE OF SURVIVAL GENES

In any tissue, the relative balance between cell death and cell survival determines the overall rate of growth. The response to the apoptotic signal is controlled by several gene products that function as antagonists or agonists of apoptosis (e.g., Bcl-2 and Bax, respectively). In particular, Bcl-2 is upregulated in tumors and is believed to protect the cells against apoptosis, thereby adapting them to androgen depletion or withdrawal. Bcl-xl is another antiapoptotic gene from the Bcl-2 family that is expressed at higher levels in androgen-independent tumor cell lines.[111] Clusterin (also known as testosterone-repressed prostate message-2 [TRPM-2] or sulfated glycoprotein-2) is another protein that is usually low in untreated hormone-naive prostate tumor tissues but is significantly upregulated after neoadjuvant hormone therapy,[144] and increased expression closely correlates with higher Gleason score.[145] Together with several other known functions, clusterin has a role in apoptosis, but it has been implicated in both promoting apoptosis and being antiapoptotic (see Ref. 111).

### CLINICAL CONSEQUENCE AND MANAGEMENT OF HORMONE-REFRACTORY PROSTATE CANCER

Although most patients will initially respond to ADT, they will eventually progress to an androgen-independent state, and the median duration of survival, once androgen independence is recognized is approximately 1 year. Although symptoms will eventually develop in most men, initially the development of androgen independence is an asymptomatic increase in serum PSA. Although no evidence exists that secondary hormonal therapies or chemotherapy improves survival, patients and their physicians often pursue treatment. These treatments may have an effect on QOL, and therefore, treatment with relatively nontoxic agents would be preferable in asymptomatic men.

In 1993, PSA responses were seen in men who discontinued the use of the antiandrogen flutamide; 21% of patients had PSA reductions of more than 50%, and although the duration of the response was short (3 to 5 months), on occasions, more lengthy relapses were seen. These responses also were observed after cessation of bicalutamide. The theory to account for this response is that the antiandrogen treatments paradoxically activate mutated ARs, although this theory has been challenged.[146] Second-line hormonal therapies are often also used; however, data on their efficacy are sparse, and most studies demonstrate minimal and often short-lasting effects.[147]

Low-dose corticosteroids decrease adrenal androgen production and were shown to have a palliative effect in advanced prostate cancer by reducing symptoms[148] and to decrease serum PSA levels modestly. Other inhibitors of adrenal androgen production were used, including aminoglutethimide and ketoconazole. Reviews of trials with these agents have shown modest responses in the range of 9% to 15%. More recent studies of ketoconazole at a dose of 400 mg, 3 times daily, showed improved PSA responses in excess of 50%, with the effects clearly being greater than the antiandrogen-withdrawal effect.[147] Duration of response was reported at 8.5 months. Ketoconazole has mild toxicity, including nausea, diarrhea, fatigue, and skin changes. The side effects of aminoglutethimide include fatigue, nausea, rash, hypotension, and ataxia, and, because of its more severe spectrum of toxicity, its use has mostly been replaced by ketoconazole.

Estrogen may have a direct cytotoxic effect and appears to provide responses in androgen-independent disease. Toxicities are once again important, including thromboembolic issues as well as breast swelling and tenderness. Trials using selective ER modulators (raloxifene), as well as aromatase inhibitors, generally had poor results.[149]

The management of more advanced hormone-refractory prostate cancer includes many nonendocrine treatments, which are mostly designed to palliate symptoms. These include chemotherapeutic options, such as mitoxantrone (which is usually administered with corticosteroids), as well as estramustine, which is a synthetic fusion of a nitrogen mustard with estradiol. Recent studies demonstrated the efficacy of the taxane group of chemotherapeutic agents either alone or in conjunction with estramustine.[150] The drug Taxotere (docetaxel) has demonstrated consistent results in phase II studies, with a more than 50% decrease in PSA in 60% of patients, a decrease in measurable disease, and the suggestion of improved survival.[151] It remains the most promising chemotherapeutic agent thus far tested.

Palliative measures require multidisciplinary management including a palliative care team comprising a urologist, radiation oncologist, and medical oncologist. Issues that may require attention include cystoscopy or transurethral resection of the prostate (TURP) for lower urinary tract dysfunction or bleeding; ureteric stenting (retrograde or antegrade) for ureteral obstruction; transfusion for anemia; management of fractures; acute laminectomy or radiotherapy for spinal cord compression; radiotherapy/oral analgesia/radioactive strontium, which are measures often used for the management of bone pain; and laparotomy and colostomy are occasionally needed for severe rectal obstruction. Treatment must always remain patient centered and focused on QOL issues,[152] with support provided at all times for the patient and the family.

## CONCLUSION

Although the incidence of prostate cancer increases with age and is dependent on androgens, the development of prostate cancer commonly occurs at an age in men when the levels of serum testosterone are declining. Instead, a shift in the ratio of estradiol/testosterone is temporally related to the onset of prostate cancer. The peripheral change to the balance between androgens and estrogens in aging men may, in itself, be significant, but local metabolism and hormone action also requires some consideration. The prostate gland is a target organ for androgens as well as for estrogens. Testicular testosterone is metabolized to more potent androgens or estrogens in the gland itself, receptors for both hormone classes are localized to epithelial or stromal cells, and biologic responses can be observed on hormonal stimulation. Therefore, the prostate gland is responsive to changes to the systemic, as well as the local, hormonal milieu. Currently, little is known about specific changes to local hormone balance that might contribute to disease progression, making it difficult to predict the consequences of treatments based on hormone-receptor agonists (especially those for estrogen) or antagonists.

Clinically, the advent of LHRH agonists and oral antiandrogens as a means to induce ADT made immediate hormone therapy more acceptable to many patients. However, the issue of whether hormonal therapy should be instituted early or late continues to be a major discussion point in urology. The extent of the side effects of ADT can be significant, increasing the need to balance QOL against benefits related to increased survival. Further research is required to evaluate fully the side effects such as decreasing BMD, cognitive function, and body hair, together with the onset of gynecomastia, weight gain, and anemia. The development of hormone-refractory disease is a major problem for the patient and clinician. Future research should aim to identify additional endocrine manipulations or alternate treatments; currently the management of more advanced hormone-refractory prostate cancer includes many nonendocrine treatments that are designed mostly to palliate symptoms. Finally, although PSA has changed the face of diagnosis and management of prostate cancer, its continued use will need better refinements for stages of disease progression. Whether this will require new markers to be used with or without PSA tests remains to be discovered.

### Acknowledgments
We thank Sue Godden and Drs. Emma Ball and Renea Taylor for their assistance in the preparation of this review.

## REFERENCES

1. Huggins C, Hodges CV: Studies on prostatic cancer: The effect of castration, of estrogen and of androgen interaction on serum phosphatases in metastatic carcinoma of the prostate. Cancer Res 1:293–297, 1941.
2. Cunha GR, Donjacour AA, Cooke PS, et al: The endocrinology and developmental biology of the prostate. Endocr Rev 8:338–362, 1987.
3. Cunha GR, Young P, Higgins SJ, Cooke PS: Neonatal seminal vesicle mesenchyme induces a new morphological and functional phenotype in the epithelia of adult ureter and ductus deferens. Development 111:145–158, 1991.
4. Cunha GR, Alarid ET, Turner T, et al: Normal and abnormal development of the male urogenital tract: Role of androgens, mesenchymal-epithelial interactions, and growth factors. J Androl 13:465–475, 1992.
5. Hayward SW, Rosen MA, Cunha GR: Stromal-epithelial interactions in the normal and neoplastic prostate. Br J Urol 79(Suppl 2):18–26, 1997.
6. Cunha GR, Rickel W, Thomson A, et al: Hormonal, cellular and molecular regulation of normal and neoplastic prostatic development. (in press)
7. Wu JP, Gu FL: The prostate 41-65 years post castration: An analysis of 26 eunuchs. Chin Med J [English] 100:271–272, 1987.
8. Isaacs JT: Antagonistic effect of androgen on prostatic cell death. Prostate 5:545–557, 1984.
9. Kyprianou N, Isaacs JT: Activation of programmed cell death in the rat ventral prostate after castration. Endocrinology 122:552–562, 1988.
10. Wright AS, Thomas LN, Douglas RC, et al: Relative potency of testosterone and dihydrotestosterone in preventing atrophy and apoptosis in the prostate of the castrated rat. J Clin Invest 98:2558–2563, 1996.
11. Tunn U, Senge T, Schenck B, Neumann F: Biochemical and histological studies on prostates in castrated dogs after treatment with androstanediol, oestradiol and cyproterone acetate. Acta Endocrinol (Copenh) 91:373–384, 1979.
12. Deschamps JC, Ott RS, McEntee K, et al: Effects of zeranol on reproduction in beef bulls: Scrotal circumference, serving ability, semen characteristics, and pathologic changes of the reproductive organs. Am J Vet Res 48:137–147, 1987.
13. Weijman J, Ramaekers FC, Elsinghorst TA, et al: Changing cytokeratin expression patterns in diethylstilbestrol dipropionate-induced metaplastic lesions of the goat prostate. Vet Q 14:2–7, 1992.
14. Andersson H, Tisell LE: Morphology of rat prostatic lobes and seminal vesicles after long-term estrogen treatment. Acta Pathol Microbiol Immunol Scand [A] 90:441–448, 1982.
15. Aumuller G, Funke PJ, Hahn A, et al: Phenotypic modulation of the canine prostate after long-term treatment with androgens and estrogens. Prostate 3:361–373, 1982.
16. Driscoll SG, Taylor SH: Effects of prenatal maternal estrogen on the male urogenital system. Obstet Gynecol 56:537–542, 1980.
17. Habenicht UF, el Etreby MF: The periurethral zone of the prostate of the cynomolgus monkey is the most sensitive prostate part for an estrogenic stimulus. Prostate 13:305–316, 1988.
18. van Kesteren P, Meinhardt W, van der Valk P, et al: Effects of estrogens only on the prostates of aging men. J Urol 156:1349–1353, 1996.
19. Pylkkanen ML, Santti R, Newbold R, McLachlan JA: Regional differences in the prostate of the neonatally estrogenized mouse. Prostate 18:117–129, 1991.
20. Randles JL: Clinical, pathological and histopathological findings in lambs implanted with a growth promoting product containing progesterone and oestradiol. J S Afr Vet Assoc 61:126–127, 1990.
21. Sugimura Y, Cunha GR, Yonemura CU, Kawamura J: Temporal and spatial factors in diethylstilbestrol-induced squamous metaplasia of the developing human prostate. Hum Pathol 19:133–139, 1988.
22. Risbridger GP, Wang H, Frydenberg M, Cunha G: The metaplastic effects of estrogen on mouse prostate epithelium: Proliferation of cells with basal cell phenotype. Endocrinology 142:2443–2450, 2001.

23. Andrews G: The histology of the human foetal and prepubertal prostates. J Anat 85:44–54, 1951.

24. Zondek T, Zondek LH: The fetal and neonatal prostate. In Goland M (ed): Normal and Abnormal Growth of the Prostate. Springfield, IL, Charles C Thomas, 1975, pp 5–28.

25. Prins GS: Developmental estrogenization of the prostate gland. In Naz R (ed): Prostate Basic and Clinical Aspects. New York, CRC Press, 1997, pp 245–263.

26. vom Saal FS, Timms BG, Montano MM, et al: Prostate enlargement in mice due to fetal exposure to low doses of estradiol or diethylstilbestrol and opposite effects at high doses. Proc Natl Acad Sci U S A 94:2056–2061, 1997.

27. Brodie AM, Son C, King DA, et al: Lack of evidence for aromatase in human prostatic tissues: Effects of 4-hydroxyandrostenedione and other inhibitors on androgen metabolism. Cancer Res 49:6551–6555, 1989.

28. Stone NN, Laudone VP, Fair WR, Fishman J: Aromatization of androstenedione to estrogen by benign prostatic hyperplasia, prostate cancer and expressed prostatic secretions. Urol Res 15:165–167, 1987.

29. Kaburagi Y, Marino MB, Kirdani RY, et al: The possibility of aromatization of androgen in human prostate. J Steroid Biochem 26:739–742, 1987.

30. Matzkin H, Soloway MS: Immunohistochemical evidence of the existence and localization of aromatase in human prostatic tissues. Prostate 21:309–314, 1992.

31. Tsugaya M, Harada N, Tozawa K, et al: Aromatase mRNA levels in benign prostatic hyperplasia and prostate cancer. Int J Urol 3:292–296, 1996.

32. Hiramatsu M, Maehara I, Ozaki M, et al: Aromatase in hyperplasia and carcinoma of the human prostate. Prostate 31:118–124, 1997.

33. Smith T, Chisholm GD, Habib FK: Failure of human benign prostatic hyperplasia to aromatise testosterone. J Steroid Biochem 17:119–120, 1982.

34. Negri-Cesi P, Poletti A, Colciago A, et al: Presence of 5alpha-reductase isozymes and aromatase in human prostate cancer cells and in benign prostate hyperplastic tissue. Prostate 34:283–291, 1998.

35. Ellem SJ, Schmitt JF, Pedersen JS, et al: Local aromatase expression in human prostate is altered in malignancy. J Clin Endocrinol Metab 89:2434–2441, 2004.

36. Lau KM, Leav I, Ho SM: Rat estrogen receptor-alpha and -beta, and progesterone receptor mRNA expression in various prostatic lobes and microdissected normal and dysplastic epithelial tissues of the Noble rats. Endocrinology 139:424–427, 1998.

37. Prins GS, Birch L: Neonatal estrogen exposure up-regulates estrogen receptor expression in the developing and adult rat prostate lobes. Endocrinology 138:1801–1809, 1997.

38. Schulze H, Barrack ER: Immunocytochemical localization of estrogen receptors in the normal male and female canine urinary tract and prostate. Endocrinology 121:1773–1783, 1987.

39. Kuiper GG, Enmark E, Pelto-Huikko M, et al: Cloning of a novel receptor expressed in rat prostate and ovary. Proc Natl Acad Sci U S A 93:5925–5930, 1996.

40. Risbridger G, Wang H, Young P, et al: Evidence that epithelial and mesenchymal estrogen receptor-alpha mediates effects of estrogen on prostatic epithelium. Dev Biol 229:432–442, 2001.

41. Veldscholte J, Ris-Stalpers C, Kuiper GG, et al: A mutation in the ligand binding domain of the androgen receptor of human LNCaP cells affects steroid binding characteristics and response to anti-androgens. Biochem Biophys Res Commun 173:534–540, 1990.

42. Veldscholte J, Berrevoets CA, Ris-Stalpers C, et al: The androgen receptor in LNCaP cells contains a mutation in the ligand binding domain which affects steroid binding characteristics and response to antiandrogens. J Steroid Biochem Mol Biol 41:665–669, 1992.

43. Taplin ME, Bubley GJ, Shuster TD, et al: Mutation of the androgen-receptor gene in metastatic androgen-independent prostate cancer. N Engl J Med 332:1393–1398, 1995.

44. Vermeulen A, Rubens R, Verdonck L: Testosterone secretion and metabolism in male senescence. J Clin Endocrinol Metab 34:730–735, 1972.

45. Tenover JL: Testosterone replacement therapy in older adult men. Int J Androl 22:300–306, 1999.

46. Vermeulen A, Kaufman JM, Goemaere S, van Pottelberg I: Estradiol in elderly men. Aging Male 5:98–102, 2002.

47. Baulieu EE: Androgens and aging men. Mol Cell Endocrinol 198:41–49, 2992.

48. Gray A, Berlin JA, McKinlay JB, Longcope C: An examination of research design effects on the association of testosterone and male aging: Results of a meta-analysis. J Clin Epidemiol 44:671–684, 1991.

49. Gray A, Feldman HA, McKinlay JB, Longcope C: Age, disease, and changing sex hormone levels in middle-aged men: results of the Massachusetts Male Aging Study. J Clin Endocrinol Metab 73:1016–1025, 1991.

50. Culig Z, Hobisch A, Cronauer MV, et al: Mutant androgen receptor detected in an advanced-stage prostatic carcinoma is activated by adrenal androgens and progesterone. Mol Endocrinol 7:1541–1550, 1993.

51. Griffiths K: Estrogens and prostatic disease:. International Prostate Health Council Study Group. Prostate 45:87–100

52. Zumoff B, Levin J, Strain GW, et al: Abnormal levels of plasma hormones in men with prostate cancer: Evidence toward a "two-disease" theory. Prostate 3:579–588, 1982.

53. Hill P, Garbaczewski L, Walker AR: Age, environmental factors and prostatic cancer. Med Hypotheses 14:29–39, 1984.

54. Ross R, Bernstein L, Judd H, et al: Serum testosterone levels in healthy young black and white men. J Natl Cancer Inst 76:45–48, 1986.

55. Henderson BE, Bernstein L, Ross RK, et al: The early in utero oestrogen and testosterone environment of blacks and whites: Potential effects on male offspring. Br J Cancer 57:216–218, 1988.

56. Bosland MC: The role of steroid hormones in prostate carcinogenesis. J Natl Cancer Inst Monogr 27:39–66, 2000.

57. de Jong FH, Oishi K, Hayes RB, et al: Peripheral hormone levels in controls and patients with prostatic cancer or benign prostatic hyperplasia: Results from the Dutch-Japanese case-control study. Cancer Res 51:3445–3450, 1991.

58. Krieg M, Nass R, Tunn S: Effect of aging on endogenous level of 5 alpha-dihydrotestosterone, testosterone, estradiol, and estrone in epithelium and stroma of normal and hyperplastic human prostate. J Clin Endocrinol Metab 77:375–381, 1993.

59. Sebastian S, Bulun SE: A highly complex organization of the regulatory region of the human CYP19 (aromatase) gene revealed by the Human Genome Project. J Clin Endocrinol Metab 86:4600–4602, 2001.

60. Harada N, Utsumi T, Takagi Y: Tissue-specific expression of the human aromatase cytochrome P-450 gene by alternative use of multiple exons 1 and promoters, and switching of tissue-specific exons 1 in carcinogenesis. Proc Natl Acad Sci U S A 90:11312–11316, 1993.

61. Chen S, Itoh T, Wu K, et al: Transcriptional regulation of aromatase expression in human breast tissue. J Steroid Biochem Mol Biol 83:93–99, 2002.

62. Horvath LG, Henshall SM, Lee CS, et al: Frequent loss of estrogen receptor-beta expression in prostate cancer. Cancer Res 61:5331–5335, 2001.

63. Leav I, Lau KM, Adams JY, et al: Comparative studies of the estrogen receptors beta and alpha and the androgen receptor in normal human prostate glands, dysplasia, and in primary and metastatic carcinoma. Am J Pathol 159:79–92, 2001.

64. Latil A, Bieche I, Vidaud D, et al: Evaluation of androgen, estrogen (ER alpha and ER beta), and progesterone receptor expression in human prostate cancer by real-time quantitative reverse transcription-polymerase chain reaction assays. Cancer Res 61:1919–9126, 2001.

65. Pasquali D, Rossi V, Esposito D, et al: Loss of estrogen receptor beta expression in malignant human prostate cells in primary cultures and in

prostate cancer tissues. J Clin Endocrinol Metab 86:2051–2055, 2001.

66. Tsurusaki T, Aoki D, Kanetake H, et al: Zone-dependent expression of estrogen receptors alpha and beta in human benign prostatic hyperplasia. J Clin Endocrinol Metab 88:1333–1340, 2003.

67. Fujimura T, Takahashi S, Urano T, et al: Differential expression of estrogen receptor beta (ERbeta) and its C-terminal truncated splice variant ERbetacx as prognostic predictors in human prostatic cancer. Biochem Biophys Res Commun 289:692–699, 2001.

68. McPherson SJ, Wang H, Jones ME, et al: Elevated androgens and prolactin in aromatase-deficient mice cause enlargement, but not malignancy, of the prostate gland. Endocrinology 142:2458–2467, 2001.

69. Noble RL: Production of Nb rat carcinoma of the dorsal prostate and response of estrogen-dependent transplants to sex hormones and tamoxifen. Cancer Res 40:3547–3550, 1980.

70. Leav I, Ho SM, Ofner P, Merk FB, et al: Biochemical alterations in sex hormone-induced hyperplasia and dysplasia of the dorsolateral prostates of Noble rats. J Natl Cancer Inst 80:1045–1053, 1988.

71. Wang Y, Hayward SW, Donjacour AA, et al: Sex hormone-induced carcinogenesis in Rb-deficient prostate tissue. Cancer Res 60:6008–6017, 2000.

72. Wang YZ, Hayward SW, Cao M, et al: Role of estrogen signaling in prostatic hormonal carcinogenesis. J Urol 165:1320, 2001.

73. Cunha GR, Hayward SW, Wang YZ: Role of stroma in carcinogenesis of the prostate. Differentiation 70:473–485, 2002.

74. Grossfeld GD, Hayward SW, Tlsty TD, Cunha GR: The role of stroma in prostatic carcinogenesis. Endocr Relat Cancer 5:253–270, 1988.

75. Hayward SW, Cunha GR, Dahiya R: Normal development and carcinogenesis of the prostate: A unifying hypothesis. Ann N Y Acad Sci 784:50–62, 1996.

76. Tuxhorn JA, Ayala GE, Rowley DR: Reactive stroma in prostate cancer progression. J Urol 166:2472–2483, 2001.

77. Rowley DR: What might a stromal response mean to prostate cancer progression? Cancer Metastasis Rev 17:411–419, 1998.

78. Olumi AF, Grossfeld GD, Hayward SW, et al: Carcinoma-associated fibroblasts direct tumor progression of initiated human prostatic epithelium. Cancer Res 59:5002–5011, 1999.

79. Thompson TC, Timme TL, Kadmon D, et al: Genetic predisposition and mesenchymal-epithelial interactions in ras+myc-induced carcinogenesis in reconstituted mouse prostate. Mol Carcinog 7:165–179, 1993.

80. Hara M, Koyanagi Y, Inoue T, Fukuyama T: [Some physico-chemical characteristics of " -seminoprotein," an antigenic component specific for human seminal plasma: Forensic immunological study of body fluids and secretion, VII]. Nippon Hoigaku Zasshi 25:322–324, 1971.

81. Wang MC, Valenzuela LA, Murphy GP, Chu TM: Purification of a human prostate specific antigen. Invest Urol 17:159–163, 1979.

82. So A, Goldenberg L, Gleave ME: Prostate specific antigen: An updated review. Can J Urol 10:2040–2050, 2003.

83. Polascik TJ, Oesterling JE, Partin AW: Prostate specific antigen: A decade of discovery: What we have learned and where we are going. J Urol 162:293–306, 1999.

84. Hakama M, Stenman UH, Aromaa A, et al: Validity of the prostate specific antigen test for prostate cancer screening: Follow-up study with a bank of 21,000 sera in Finland. J Urol 166:2189–2191; discussion 2191–2192, 2001.

85. Punglia RS, D'Amico AV, Catalona WJ, et al: Effect of verification bias on screening for prostate cancer by measurement of prostate-specific antigen. N Engl J Med 349:335–342, 2003.

86. Catalona WJ, Smith DS, Ratliff TL, et al: Measurement of prostate-specific antigen in serum as a screening test for prostate cancer. N Engl J Med 324:1156–1161, 1991.

87. Brawer MK, Chetner MP, Beatie J, et al: Screening for prostatic carcinoma with prostate specific antigen. J Urol 147:841–845, 1992.

88. Bartsch G, Horninger W, Klocker H, et al: Prostate cancer mortality after introduction of prostate-specific antigen mass screening in the Federal State of Tyrol, Austria. Urology 58:417–424, 2001.

89. Boyle P: Screening for prostate cancer: Have you had your cholesterol measured? BJU Int 92:191–199, 2003.

90. Catalona WJ, Southwick PC, Slawin KM, et al: Comparison of percent free PSA, PSA density, and age-specific PSA cutoffs for prostate cancer detection and staging. Urology 56:255–60, 2000.

91. Haese A, Graefen M, Steuber T, et al: Total and Gleason grade 4/5 cancer volumes are major contributors of human kallikrein 2, whereas free prostate specific antigen is largely contributed by benign gland volume in serum from patients with prostate cancer or benign prostatic biopsies. J Urol 170:2269–2273, 2003.

92. Catalona WJ, Bartsch G, Rittenhouse HG, et al: Serum pro prostate specific antigen improves cancer detection compared to free and complexed prostate specific antigen in men with prostate specific antigen 2 to 4 ng/mL. J Urol 170:2181–2185, 2003.

93. Han M, Partin AW, Zahurak M, et al: Biochemical (prostate specific antigen) recurrence probability following radical prostatectomy for clinically localized prostate cancer. J Urol 169:517–523, 2003.

94. Diblasio CJ, Kattan MW: Use of nomograms to predict the risk of disease recurrence after definitive local therapy for prostate cancer. Urology 62(Suppl 1):9–18, 2003.

95. Duchesne GM, Dowling C, Frydenberg M, et al: Outcome, morbidity, and prognostic factors in post-prostatectomy radiotherapy: An Australian multicenter study. Urology 61:179–183, 2003.

96. Bruchovsky N, Goldenberg SL, Akakura K, Rennie PS: Luteinizing hormone-releasing hormone agonists in prostate cancer: Elimination of flare reaction by pretreatment with cyproterone acetate and low-dose diethylstilbestrol. Cancer 72:1685–1691, 1993.

97. Bolla M, Collette L, Blank L, et al: Long-term results with immediate androgen suppression and external irradiation in patients with locally advanced prostate cancer (an EORTC study): A phase III randomised trial. Lancet 360:103–106, 2002.

98. Granfors T, Modig H, Damber JE, Tomic R: Combined orchiectomy and external radiotherapy versus radiotherapy alone for nonmetastatic prostate cancer with or without pelvic lymph node involvement: A prospective randomized study. J Urol 159:2030–2034, 1998.

99. Pilepich MV, Caplan R, Byhardt RW, et al: Phase III trial of androgen suppression using goserelin in unfavorable-prognosis carcinoma of the prostate treated with definitive radiotherapy: Report of Radiation Therapy Oncology Group Protocol 85-31. J Clin Oncol 15:1013–1021, 1997.

100. Messing EM, Manola J, Sarosdy M, et al: Immediate hormonal therapy compared with observation after radical prostatectomy and pelvic lymphadenectomy in men with node-positive prostate cancer. N Engl J Med 341:1781–1788, 1999.

101. The Medical Research Council Prostate Cancer Working Party Investigators Group: Immediate versus deferred treatment for advanced prostatic cancer: Initial results of the Medical Research Council Trial. Br J Urol 79:235–246, 1997.

102. See WA, Wirth MP, McLeod DG, et al: Bicalutamide as immediate therapy either alone or as adjuvant to standard care of patients with localized or locally advanced prostate cancer: First analysis of the early prostate cancer program. J Urol 168:429–435, 2002.

103. Moul JW, Wu H, Sun L, et al: Early versus delayed hormonal therapy for prostate specific antigen only recurrence of prostate cancer after radical prostatectomy. J Urol 171:1141–1147, 2004.

104. Prostate Cancer Trialists' Collaborative Group: Maximum androgen blockade in advanced prostate cancer: An overview of the randomised trials. Lancet 355:1491–1498, 2000.

105. Higano CS: Side effects of androgen deprivation therapy: Monitoring and minimizing toxicity. Urology 61:32–38, 2003.

106. Pether M, Goldenberg SL: Intermittent androgen suppression. BJU Int 93:258–261, 2004.

107. Smith MR: Osteoporosis during androgen deprivation therapy for prostate cancer. Urology 60:79–85; discussion 86, 2002.

108. Ross RW, Small EJ: Osteoporosis in men treated with androgen deprivation therapy for prostate cancer. J Urol 167:1952–1956, 2002.

109. Higano CS: Management of bone loss in men with prostate cancer. J Urol 170:S59–S63; discussion S64, 2003.

110. Smith MR: Bisphosphonates to prevent skeletal complications in men with metastatic prostate cancer. J Urol 170:S55–S57; discussion S57–S58, 2003.

111. So AI, Hurtado-Coll A, Gleave ME: Androgens and prostate cancer. World J Urol 21:325–437, 2003.

112. Taplin ME, Ho SM: Clinical review 134: The endocrinology of prostate cancer. J Clin Endocrinol Metab 86:3467–3477, 2001.

113. Taplin ME, Balk SP: Androgen receptor: a key molecule in the progression of prostate cancer to hormone independence. J Cell Biochem 91:483–490, 2004.

114. Heinlein CA, Chang C: Androgen receptor in prostate cancer. Endocr Rev 25:276–308, 2004.

115. Sack JS, Kish KF, Wang C, et al: Crystallographic structures of the ligand-binding domains of the androgen receptor and its T877A mutant complexed with the natural agonist dihydrotestosterone. Proc Natl Acad Sci U S A 98:4904–4909, 2001.

116. Demura R, Kubo O, Suzuki T, et al: Demonstration of activin in normal pituitary and in various human pituitary adenomas by immunohistochemistry. Endocr J 43:429–432, 1996.

117. Zhao XY, Malloy PJ, Krishnan AV, et al: Glucocorticoids can promote androgen-independent growth of prostate cancer cells through a mutated androgen receptor. Nat Med 6:703–706, 2000.

118. Fenton MA, Shuster TD, Fertig AM, et al: Functional characterization of mutant androgen receptors from androgen-independent prostate cancer. Clin Cancer Res 3:1383–1388, 1997.

119. Gottlieb B, Lehvaslaiho H, Beitel LK, et al: The Androgen Receptor Gene Mutations Database. Nucleic Acids Res 26:234–238, 1998.

120. Kelly WK: Endocrine withdrawal syndrome and its relevance to the management of hormone refractory prostate cancer. Eur Urol 34(Suppl 3):18–23, 1998.

121. Koivisto P, Kononen J, Palmberg C, et al: Androgen receptor gene amplification: A possible molecular mechanism for androgen deprivation therapy failure in prostate cancer. Cancer Res 57:314–319, 1997.

122. Marcelli M, Ittmann M, Mariani S, et al: Androgen receptor mutations in prostate cancer. Cancer Res 60:944–949, 2000.

123. Taplin ME, Bubley GJ, Ko YJ, et al: Selection for androgen receptor mutations in prostate cancers treated with androgen antagonist. Cancer Res 59:2511–2515, 1999.

124. Newmark JR, Hardy DO, Tonb DC, et al: Androgen receptor gene mutations in human prostate cancer. Proc Natl Acad Sci U S A 89:6319–6323, 1992.

125. Visakorpi T, Hyytinen E, Koivisto P, et al: In vivo amplification of the androgen receptor gene and progression of human prostate cancer. Nat Genet 9:401–406, 1995.

126. Edwards J, Krishna NS, Grigor KM, Bartlett JM: Androgen receptor gene amplification and protein expression in hormone refractory prostate cancer. Br J Cancer 89:552–556, 2003.

127. Linja MJ, Savinainen KJ, Saramaki OR, et al: Amplification and overexpression of androgen receptor gene in hormone-refractory prostate cancer. Cancer Res 61:3550–3555, 2001.

128. Ruizeveld de Winter JA, Janssen PJ, et al: Androgen receptor status in localized and locally progressive hormone refractory human prostate cancer. Am J Pathol 144:735–746, 1994.

129. Brown RS, Edwards J, Dogan A, et al: Amplification of the androgen receptor gene in bone metastases from hormone-refractory prostate cancer. J Pathol 198:237–244, 2002.

130. Visakorpi T, Kallioniemi AH, Syvane AC, et al: Genetic changes in primary and recurrent prostate cancer by comparative genomic hybridization. Cancer Res 55:342–347, 1995.

131. Gregory CW, Johnson RT Jr, Mohler JL, et al: Androgen receptor stabilization in recurrent prostate cancer is associated with hypersensitivity to low androgen. Cancer Res 61:2892–2898, 2001.

132. Miyamoto H, Yeh S, Wilding G, Chang C: Promotion of agonist activity of antiandrogens by the androgen receptor coactivator, ARA70, in human prostate cancer DU145 cells. Proc Natl Acad Sci U S A 95:7379–7384, 1998.

133. Yeh S, Chang C: Cloning and characterization of a specific coactivator, ARA70, for the androgen receptor in human prostate cells. Proc Natl Acad Sci U S A 93:5517–5521, 1996.

134. Fujimoto N, Yeh S, Kang HY, et al: Cloning and characterization of androgen receptor coactivator, ARA55, in human prostate. J Biol Chem 274:8316–8321, 1999.

135. Gregory CW, He B, Johnson RT, et al: A mechanism for androgen receptor-mediated prostate cancer recurrence after androgen deprivation therapy. Cancer Res 61:4315–4319, 2001.

136. Baek SH, Ohgi KA, Rose DW, et al. Exchange of N-CoR corepressor and Tip60 coactivator complexes links gene expression by NF-kappaB and beta-amyloid precursor protein. Cell 110:55–67, 2002.

137. Shang Y, Brown M: Molecular determinants for the tissue specificity of SERMs. Science 295:2465–2468, 2002.

138. Chen CD, Welsbie DS, Tran C, et al: Molecular determinants of resistance to antiandrogen therapy. Nat Med 10:33–39, 2004.

139. Culig Z, Hobisch A, Cronauer MV, et al: Androgen receptor activation in prostatic tumor cell lines by insulin-like growth factor-I, keratinocyte growth factor, and epidermal growth factor. Cancer Res 54:5474–5478, 1994.

140. Grossmann ME, Huang H, Tindall DJ: Androgen receptor signaling in androgen-refractory prostate cancer. J Natl Cancer Inst 93:1687–1697, 2001.

141. Craft N, Shostak Y, Carey M, Sawyers CL: A mechanism for hormone-independent prostate cancer through modulation of androgen receptor signaling by the HER-2/neu tyrosine kinase. Nat Med 5:280–285, 1999.

142. Wen Y, Hu MC, Makino K, et al: HER-2/neu promotes androgen-independent survival and growth of prostate cancer cells through the Akt pathway. Cancer Res 60:6841–6845, 2000.

143. Ueda T, Bruchovsky N, Sadar MD: Activation of the androgen receptor N-terminal domain by interleukin-6 via MAPK and STAT3 signal transduction pathways. J Biol Chem 277:7076–7085, 2002.

144. Jung HS, Francis-West PH, Widelitz RB, et al: Local inhibitory action of BMPs and their relationships with activators in feather formation: Implications for periodic patterning. Dev Biol 196:11–23, 1998.

145. Steinberg J, Oyasu R, Lang S, et al: Intracellular levels of SGP-2 (Clusterin) correlate with tumor grade in prostate cancer. Clin Cancer Res 3:1707–1711, 1997.

146. Small EJ, Vogelzang NJ: Second-line hormonal therapy for advanced prostate cancer: A shifting paradigm. J Clin Oncol 15:382–388, 1997.

147. Oh WK: Secondary hormonal therapies in the treatment of prostate cancer. Urology 60:87–92; discussion 93, 2002.

148. Tannock I, Gospodarowicz M, Meakin W, et al: Treatment of metastatic prostatic cancer with low-dose prednisone: Evaluation of pain and quality of life as pragmatic

indices of response. J Clin Oncol 7:590–597, 1989.

149. Ryan CJ, Small EJ: Role of secondary hormonal therapy in the management of recurrent prostate cancer. Urology 62(Suppl 1):87–94, 2003.

150. Gilligan T, Kantoff PW: Chemotherapy for prostate cancer. Urology 60:94–100; discussion 100, 2002.

151. Khan MA, Carducci MA, Partin AW: The evolving role of docetaxel in the management of androgen independent prostate cancer. J Urol 170:1709–1716, 2003.

152. Clarke NW: The management of hormone-relapsed prostate cancer. BJU Int 92:860–868, 2003.

# PART 18

# ENDOCRINOLOGY OF PREGNANCY

# Implantation and Placental Physiology in Early Human Pregnancy: The Role of the Maternal Decidua and the Trophoblast

## *Ruth B. Lathi, Susan J. Fisher, and Linda C. Giudice*

Implantation in humans is a complex, collaborative process among the fetus, the placenta, and the maternal host. The main goal of this endeavor is to secure attachment of the hemiallogeneic fetus to the uterus, which, in turn, allows for allotransplantation and efficient nutrient transfer from the mother. This complex process is achieved by a complicated molecular dialogue between cells of the offspring and the decidua, involving a variety of cell adhesion molecules, enzymes, enzyme inhibitors, growth factors, immune modulators, angiogenic factors, and their inhibitors. Most of what we think occurs during implantation is derived from in vitro studies and animal models. Transgenic models have been useful in identifying some of the participants in the molecular dialogue among the mother, placenta, and fetus, which may have relevance to human pregnancy. This chapter focuses on a portion of these molecular pathways at the placental-decidual interface in the first half of human pregnancy. Abnormal expression of the molecular components of these pathways, either in the placenta or in the decidua, may lead to clinically significant sequelae, including preeclampsia, intrauterine fetal growth restriction, miscarriage, and infertility. Several related reviews have recently been published focusing on uterine receptivity, paracrine signaling between the embryo and endometrial epithelium or between the trophoblast and the decidua, and placental physiology during the invasive phase of implantation.[1–8]

## UTERINE RECEPTIVITY AND PLACENTAL DEVELOPMENT

The maternal endometrium is selectively receptive to embryo implantation. Endometrial "receptivity" comprises the temporal and spatial endometrial cues that facilitate implantation. In humans, the "window of implantation" is between cycle days 20 to 24.[9] By embryonic day 4, the embryo has differentiated into the inner cell mass, destined to become the fetus, and the trophectoderm, destined to become the placenta.[10,11] At about 6 to 7 days after fertilization, the embryo attaches to the endometrial epithelium and begins the process of intrusion through the epithelial lining of the uterine wall and invasion into the endometrial stroma (Fig. 181-1). The stages of implantation (apposition/attachment, intrusion, invasion) are a consequence of reciprocal interactions between the embryo and the endometrial epithelium. Aberrant expression of specific molecules by embryonic trophectoderm or the uterine epithelium could result in delayed or faulty implantation as well as implantation failure.

Initial trophoblast attachment to the endometrial epithelium involves unique interactions between their apical cell surface membranes,[12] which are mediated by an unusual repertoire of cell adhesion molecules.[13] The unique anatomy of the placenta (Fig. 181-2) is due primarily to differentiation of the organ's specialized epithelial progenitor population, termed *cytotrophoblasts*.[5,14,15] How these cells differentiate determines whether chorionic villi, the placenta's functional units, will float in maternal blood ("floating villi") or anchor the conceptus to the uterine wall ("anchoring villi"). In the former differentiation pathway, cytotrophoblasts differentiate by fusing into multinucleate syncytiotrophoblasts, which primarily function in nutrient, oxygen, and waste exchange at the villus surface. In anchoring villi, cytotrophoblasts also fuse, but many remain as single cells that detach from their basement membrane and aggregate to form cell columns. At the distal ends of these columns, cytotrophoblasts attach to and then deeply invade the decidua (interstitial invasion) and its arterioles (endovascular invasion). Uterine invasion involves cytotrophoblast attachment and migration as well as highly regulated degradation of specific uterine components.[15] Additionally, a subset of cytotrophoblast within the uterine wall replaces the maternal cells that line arterioles and, to a lesser extent, veins. The latter process initiates maternal blood flow to the placenta and changes uterine vessels from high-resistance, low-capacity vessels to a high-capacity, low-resistance circulation. By late second trimester, these vessels are lined exclusively by cytotrophoblasts, and endothelial cells are no longer visible in either the endometrial or the superficial portions of their myometrial segments.[16] If this process is not completed, decreased placental perfusion and relative placental hypoxia ensue, as observed in clinical disorders of placentation and fetal growth, including preeclampsia and intrauterine fetal growth restriction.

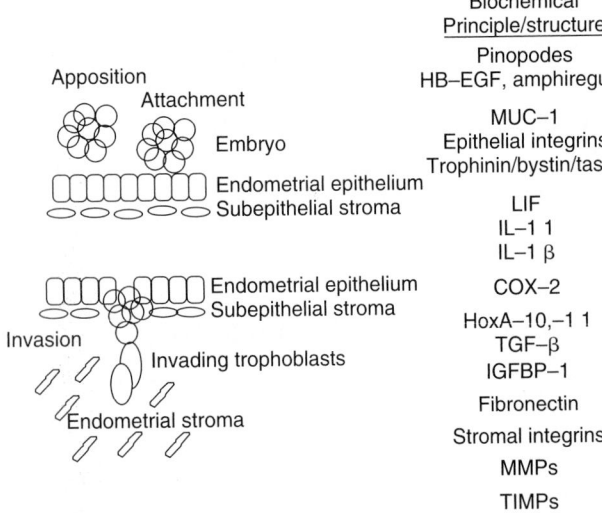

| | Biochemical Principle/structure |
|---|---|
| | Pinopodes |
| | HB–EGF, amphiregulin |
| | MUC–1 |
| | Epithelial integrins |
| | Trophinin/bystin/tastin |
| | LIF |
| | IL–1 1 |
| | IL–1 β |
| | COX–2 |
| | HoxA–10,–1 1 |
| | TGF–β |
| | IGFBP–1 |
| | Fibronectin |
| | Stromal integrins |
| | MMPs |
| | TIMPs |

*Figure 181-1* Schematic of the stages of implantation in humans and principal elements in these stages involving the embryo, the trophoblast, and the decidua.

# APPOSITION AND THE ATTACHMENT PHASE OF IMPLANTATION

## PINOPODES

Pinopodes are structures that are present on the apical surface of endometrial luminal epithelium during the period of uterine receptivity.[17-20] They are thought to be involved in implantation (Fig. 181-3) by mechanisms that involve uptake of macromolecules, withdrawal of uterine fluid, and/or facilitation of blastocyst adhesion to the luminal epithelium.[21] Because of the temporal and spatial pattern of their appearance, pinopodes are markers of the development of uterine receptivity for blastocyst implantation. Scanning electron microscopy shows that 78% of endometrial biopsies obtained from normally cycling women on postovulatory day 6 have pinopodes versus the rare appearance of pinopodes on postovulatory day 2 or 9. Hormonal treatment used to induce ovulation can modify normal development of the endometrium and may have a negative effect on embryonic implantation. For example, only 15% of endometrial biopsies from infertile women undergoing clomiphene citrate therapy or gonadotropin stimulation have pinopodes on postovulatory day 6.[18] These observations support the concept that a

*Figure 181-2* **A,** Diagram of a longitudinal section of an anchoring chorionic villus (AV) at the fetal-maternal interface at about 10 weeks of gestational age. The AV functions as a bridge between the fetal and maternal compartments, whereas floating villi (FV) are suspended in the intervillous space and are bathed by maternal blood. Cytotrophoblasts (CTBs) in AV (zone I) form cell columns (zone II and III). CTBs then invade the uterine interstitium (decidua and first third of the myometrium: zone IV) and maternal vasculature (zone V), thereby anchoring the fetus to the mother and accessing the maternal circulation. Zone designations mark areas in which CTBs have distinct patterns of stage-specific antigen expression. **B,** Diagram of a uterine (spiral) artery in which endovascular invasion is in progress (10 to 18 weeks of gestation). Endometrial and then myometrial segments of spiral arteries are modified progressively. *a,* In fully modified regions, the vessel diameter is large. CTBs are present in the lumen and occupy the entire surface of the vessel wall. A discrete muscular layer (tunica media) is not evident. *b,* Partially modified vessel segments. CTBs and maternal endothelium occupy discrete regions of the vessel wall. In areas of intersection, CTBs appear to lie deep in the endothelium and in contact with the vessel wall. *c,* Unmodified vessel segments in the myometrium. Vessel segments in the superficial third of the myometrium will become modified when endovascular invasion reaches its fullest extent (by 22 weeks), whereas deeper segments of the same artery will retain their normal structure. (Reproduced from Zhou Y, Fisher SJ, Damsky CH: Pre-eclampsia is associated with failure of human cytotrophoblasts to mimic a vascular adhesion phenotype: One cause of defective endovascular invasion in this syndrome? J Clin Invest 99:2152–2164, 1997.)

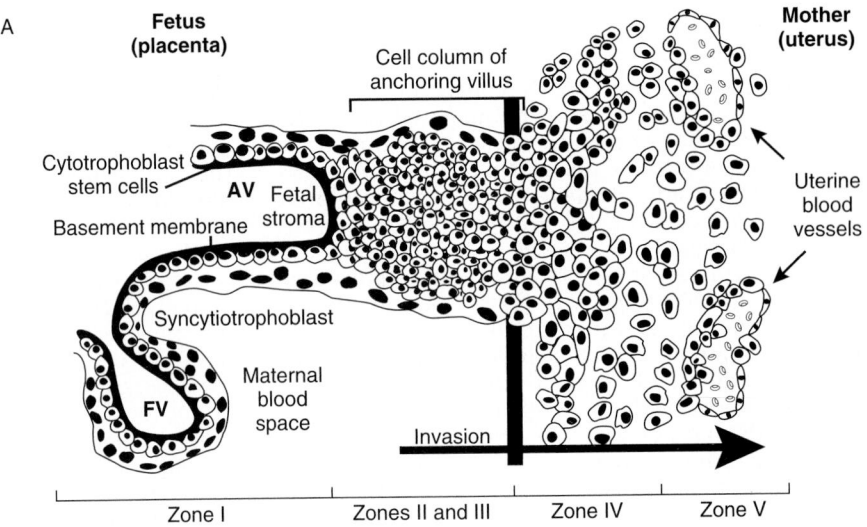

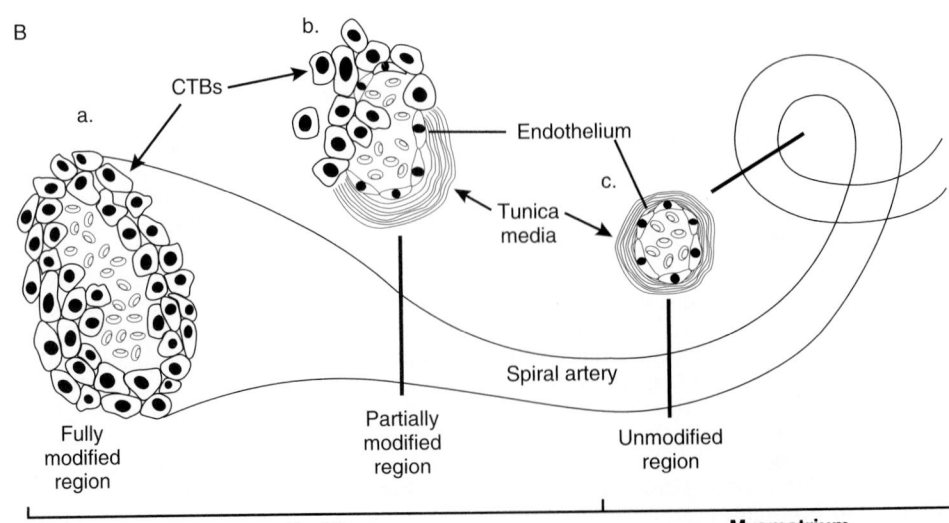

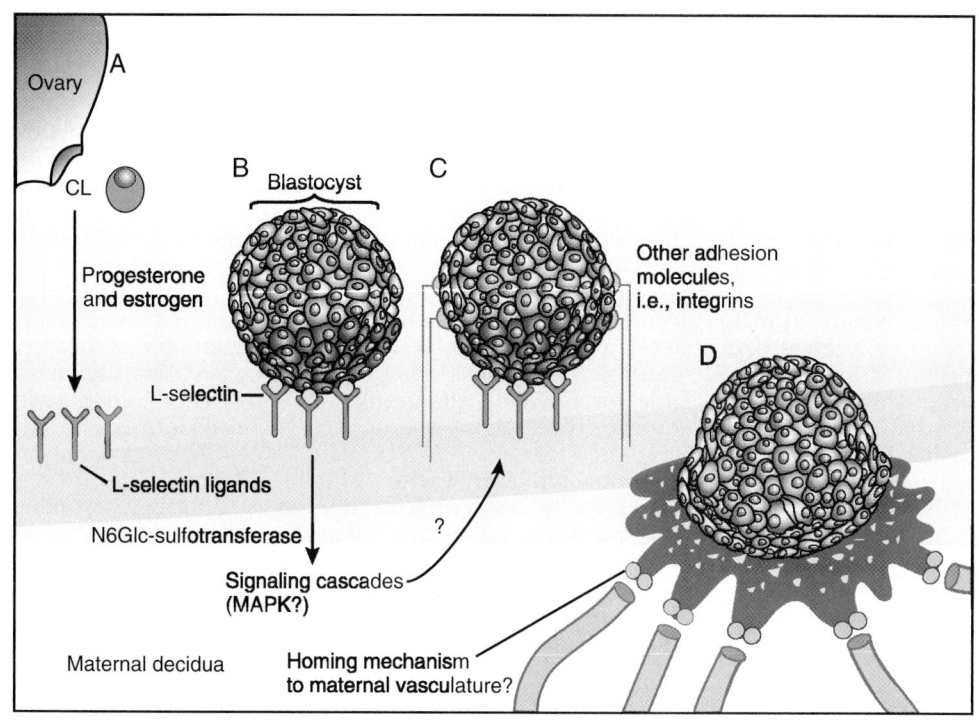

*Figure 181-3* Model of molecular interactions occurring in the early stage of human embryonic implantation (see text). MAPK, mitogen-activated protein kinase. (Reproduced from Genbecev OD, Prakobphol A, Foulk RA, et al: Trophoblast L-selectin-mediated adhesion at the maternal fetal interface. Science 299:405–408, 2003.)

distinct period of endometrial development coincides with the window of implantation. The appearance of pinopodes on the apical surface of endometrial epithelium is associated with increasing serum progesterone concentrations and their regression is associated with the downregulation of the progesterone receptor B.[22]

## CELL ADHESION MOLECULES

Numerous cell adhesion molecules are expressed and highly regulated by the endometrial epithelium (and the embryo) during the window of implantation.[23,24] Given the paramount importance of adhesive interactions to implantation and placentation, these molecules are critical for establishing and maintaining pregnancy. Therefore, their misexpression is often associated with infertility and pregnancy complications.

## MUCINS

Mucins (MUCs) are large, highly glycosylated molecules present on many cell surfaces including the apical side of endometrial epithelial cells. The specialized glycoproteins are thought to play a role in embryo attachment[25] (see Fig. 181-3). Endometrial MUC-1 expression is cycle dependent. In mice, MUC-1 is downregulated on day 4.5, which corresponds to the initial attachment phase of implantation.[26] In this species, MUC-1 may be a barrier to implantation; removal allows the embryo to interact with the apical surface of the endometrial luminal epithelium during the window of implantation. In contrast to the mouse, MUC-1 expression in human endometrium is upregulated during the peri-implantation period[27] and is upregulated by progesterone but downregulated by the human blastocyst in vitro.[28] Additionally, changes in glycosylation of this molecule may permit embryo attachment (Fisher, Carson, and Gerbecev, unpublished results). Specifically, specialized carbohydrate ligands for L-selection expression are upregulated during the window of receptivity. Another mucin, MAG (mouse ascites Golgi), is expressed on the endometrial luminal epithelial surface on cycle days 18 to 19.[29,30] Sixty percent of patients with unexplained infertility have abnormal MAG expression. Thus,

the expression pattern of this molecule may be a clinical marker for uterine receptivity[31] in select patients.

## INTEGRINS

Integrins are ubiquitous transmembrane glycoproteins. Along with immunoglobulin superfamily members, cadherins, and molecules with lectin-like domains, integrins primarily function in cell adhesion.[32] In addition to a transmembrane domain, they have an extracellular region that serves as a receptor for extracellular matrix ligands, including fibronectin, collagen, and laminin.[32] Their specific recognition and binding of extracellular matrix components transmits information to the cytoskeleton that promotes cell adhesion/migration hormone responsiveness and alters gene expression.[33] In the endometrium, integrin expression is both constitutive and cycle dependent.[34-37] Integrins constitutively expressed on endometrial epithelial cells include $\alpha_2\beta_1$, $\alpha_3\beta_1$, and $\alpha_6\beta_4$.[37] These collagen/laminin receptors play a role in cell-substratum adhesion. The fibronectin receptor $\alpha_5\beta_1$ is the only integrin constitutively expressed in the endometrial stroma, where the majority of these heterodimeric receptors are subject to hormonal regulation ($\alpha_1\beta_1$, $\alpha_3\beta_1$, $\alpha_6\beta_1$, $\alpha_v\beta_3$, and $\alpha_v\beta_5$).[35] As to ligands, osteopontin, a secreted protein with immune actions, is capable of binding integrins on the luminal surface of secretory endometrium epithelium as well as the trophectoderm. Interestingly, the molecule is secreted by endometrial glandular epithelium immediately before and during implantation.[38,39]

The presence or absence of individual integrins may serve as a basis for evaluating endometrial function during the window of implantation, as well as a clinical test for uterine receptivity (see Fig. 181-3). In normally menstruating women, the appearance of $\alpha_v\beta_3$ integrin coincides with pinopodes formation during the window of implantation.[40] The absence of endometrial $\alpha_v\beta_3$ may be associated with histologic evidence of delay (i.e., classic luteal-phase ["type I"] defect) or with histologically normal endometrium (i.e., without histologic delay or a "type II defect").[35] The latter finding, which suggests an intrinsic defect in endometrial function, is observed in women with minimal or mild endometriosis,[41] hydrosalpinges,[42] and unexplained infertility.[43] In one study, the presence of $\alpha_v\beta_3$ during the window of implantation positively correlated with in vitro fertilization (IVF) outcome.[44] Because mechanisms regulating $\alpha_v\beta_3$ are not precisely defined, correction of this defect is empiric. Preliminary studies suggest, however, that ovarian suppression or laparoscopic ablation of pelvic endometriosis may restore $\alpha_v\beta_3$ expression in the eutopic endometrium.[45] Endometrial epithelial cells lack functional estrogen receptors and progesterone receptors (PRs) during the window of implantation.[46] The decline in PR is specifically associated with the initiation of $\alpha_v\beta_3$ expression. In infertile women with a type I defect, the loss of PR is delayed, as is the expression of $\alpha_v\beta_3$. Medical therapy normalizes both processes.[35] Although initial reports suggested that testing the endometrium for $\alpha_v\beta_3$ expression during the window of implantation was clinically useful, this finding has been debated in the literature. It is likely that the many and varied causes of failed implantation preclude diagnosis with a single marker. In this context, analysis of a comprehensive panel of molecules whose expression is both positively and negatively coordinated during the implantation window of a normal cycle is likely to be a more successful strategy.

## GROWTH FACTORS AND CYTOKINES

Growth factors and cytokines are expressed in most tissues; however, in the endometrium, expression of many of these molecules is cycle dependent.[47-49] In this location, a subset is differentially expressed during the secretory phase of the cycle, continuing during early pregnancy. Thus, they may play a role in the molecular dialogue between the decidua and conceptus (see Fig. 181-3).

### Epidermal Growth Factor
The epidermal growth factor (EGF) family is composed of EGF, transforming growth factor-α (TGF-α), heparin-binding EGF-like growth factor (HB-EGF), amphiregulin, and betacellulin,[50-54] which interact with EGF receptor.[50] TGF-α stimulates mouse blastocyst development in vitro.[55] In mouse pregnancy, however, EGF mRNA is not detectable in the uterus on the day before implantation, and implantation occurs normally in TGF-α-deficient mice.[55,56] Therefore, HB-EGF and amphiregulin are probably the endogenous ligands stimulating the embryonic EGF receptor during the process of implantation in this species. The HB-EGF gene is expressed in mouse uterine luminal epithelium surrounding the blastocyst just before implantation,[57] and HB-EGF also promotes blastocyst growth, zona hatching, and trophoblast outgrowth in vitro.[57] Another EGF homologue, amphiregulin, expressed in an implantation-specific manner in mouse endometrium, is regulated by progesterone. A transient surge in amphiregulin mRNA expression is observed in association with uterine epithelium on day 4 of pregnancy, with eventual accumulation at sites of blastocyst attachment.[58] EGF stimulates human cytotrophoblast invasion in vitro (see later), which suggests a role for this growth factor system in human pregnancy as well. Recent studies have shown expression of HB-EGF is highly correlated with pinopode formation, with maximal expression by luminal and glandular epithelial cells during the window of implantation and early pregnancy.[59] HB-EGF inhibits apoptosis and promotes an invasive phenotype in trophoblasts.[60,61] Pregnancies complicated by preeclampsia show decreased cytotrophoblast invasion and low HB-EGF levels,[62] underscoring how disordered expression of participants in the implantation process can affect pregnancy outcome. The actions of amphiregulin, and other EGF family members remain to be investigated.

### Colony-Stimulating Factor-1
A role for colony-stimulating factor-1 (CSF-1) in implantation has been underscored by the osteopetrotic (op/op) mouse model,[63] in which mice are homozygous for a naturally occurring null mutation in the CSF gene. Homozygotes are toothless and have multiple skeletal defects, decreased macrophages, and decreased implantation rates and fetal viability. When homozygotes are treated with exogenous CSF-1, their fertility is restored.[64] Thus, CSF-1, produced by uterine epithelium, may interact with the CSF-1 receptor on the trophectoderm and promote blastocyst attachment. CSF-1 has been identified in the glandular and endothelial cells of the human endometrium and the cytotrophoblasts lining the villous core of the first trimester placenta. Its expression is highest in the first trimester.[65] Women with recurrent first trimester miscarriages have lower preconception serum CSF-1 levels as well as lower levels at 8 weeks' gestation than healthy controls.[66] The detection of CSF-1 during gestation supports a role for CSF-1 in the regulation of placental function in humans by autocrine and/or paracrine mechanisms.

### Leukemia Inhibitory Factor
Leukemia inhibitory factor (LIF) is a pleiotropic cytokine that has proliferative and differentiating properties.[67,68] It is expressed in mouse endometrium before ovulation and also on day 4 of pregnancy or pseudopregnancy.[69,70] The role of LIF in murine implantation was shown by using gene targeting and homologous recombination to delete expression of this molecule. Homozygous females produce normal blastocysts that are recoverable by uterine flushing on day 4. Intraperitoneal administration of LIF partially rescues implantation. Furthermore, transfer of embryos from homozygotes to wild-type pseudopregnant females results in normal rates of implantation and pregnancy.[70] Although regulation of maternal endometrial LIF expression and the mechanisms involved in embryonic implantation await elucidation, it is likely that LIF plays an important role in embryonic attachment to the epithelium and, perhaps, intrusion through it. Recent evidence suggests that LIF also plays an important role in the process of decidualization.[71] In humans, LIF is expressed in the endometrial epithelia and stroma as well as in the decidua.[72-74] LIF mRNA, which is preferentially expressed in secretory phase, is threefold higher in glandular epithelia than stroma. Cytokine and steroid hormonal regulation of LIF expression in endometrium[75] supports its importance in the implantation process. As to possible autocrine action, LIF enhances survival of decidualized endometrial stromal cells in vitro, suggesting that this growth factor may protect the stroma from damage during implantation.[76] As to possible paracrine action, LIF promotes cytotrophoblast differentiation along the invasive pathway.[77,78]

Immunostaining for LIF and LIF receptor in the endometrium of healthy fertile women showed that staining of the glandular and apical endometrium peaked when pinopodes were present.[79] Endometrial explants from women with unexplained infertility secrete less LIF than explants from fertile women.[80] This finding suggests a role for LIF in human implantation, although the mechanisms underlying LIF's actions await further investigation.

### Interleukin-1
The interleukin-1 (IL-1) family is composed of IL-1α, IL-1β, IL-1 receptor antagonist (IL-1ra), and one signal-transducing receptor (IL-1R tI).[81] The entire IL system is expressed in human endometrium[82] and in human embryos.[83] Intraperitoneal injection of high levels of IL-1ra on day 3 of murine pregnancy results in a significant decrease in the number of implantation sites (6.7%) as compared with noninjected and buffer-injected animals (59% and 74%, respectively).[84] Fertility is normal, however, in different strains of mice carrying mutations in components of the IL-1 system, including the IL-1R tI.[85] Likewise, absence of the IL-1-converting enzyme, which converts the IL-1β precursor into its active form, does not affect reproduction.[86-88] These observations suggest that IL-1 may not play a key role in implantation or

that redundant mechanisms regulate embryonic attachment. IL-1ra prevents implantation by exerting a negative effect on endometrial expression of integrin $\alpha_4\beta_3$, thought to be important for attachment.[89] A recent study shows that leptin and IL-1 may both stimulate endometrial integrin expression through the leptin receptor (Ob-R).[90]

## CALCITONIN

Calcitonin function is important for calcium homeostasis. In the rat, its mRNA is expressed in endometrial glandular epithelium between days 3 and 5 of pregnancy.[91] Calcitonin expression is regulated by progesterone, and its secretion into the uterine lumen on day 4 suggests that it may be a marker of uterine receptivity.[91] The temporal expression of calcitonin suggests a role in the implantation process, perhaps by altering calcium homeostasis at the implantation site. The effects of calcitonin on calcium signaling may result in redistribution or heightened expression of critical cell adhesion molecules or junctional complexes, thereby preparing the apical cell surface for contact with the trophoblast.[91] Calcitonin gene-related peptide (CGRP) is expressed in human deciduas and glandular cells and its receptor is present in both decidua production and invasive trophoblasts. In vitro data suggest that CGRP stimulates cyclic adenosine monophosphate (cAMP) production in decidual cells and nitric oxide (NO) in trophoblasts.[92]

## HOXA-10

Homeobox (Hox) genes encode highly conserved transcription factors that play important roles in embryonic development. For example, specific Hoxa genes, members of the Hox family, regulate development of the müllerian tract. Hoxa-10 is confined to the uteri of mice and humans,[93] and maternal expression of Hoxa-10 is required for fertility.[94] Specifically, homozygote females with a mutation in Hoxa-10 are either sterile or have small litters. Transfer of embryos from homozygotes to pseudopregnant wild-type foster dams rescues the phenotype, which suggests a deficient uterine environment in the mutant mice. Furthermore, transfer of wild-type embryos into pseudopregnant Hoxa-10-deficient mice did not rescue the phenotype, thus suggesting that adult uterine expression of Hoxa-10 is required during pregnancy. Hoxa-10 is a hormone-regulated endometrial transcription factor that appears to be responsive to both ovarian steroids and relaxin.[95] Additionally, Hoxa-10$^{-/-}$ uteri exhibited decreased decidualization in response to artificial stimuli.[96] These observations are consistent with the observation that, in mice, reducing Hoxa-10 expression before implantation decreases the number of implantation sites, whereas constituitively expressed Hoxa-10 optimizes survival of implanted embryos.[97] In human endometrium, there is a marked increase of epithelial Hoxa-10 mRNA expression in the midsecretory phase. The ability of Hoxa-10 to regulate progesterone production by cultured endometrial cells suggests that this transcription factor plays a role in human implantation as well.[98] The mechanisms underlying Hoxa-10 involvement in normal and abnormal implantation await further investigation.

## CYCLOOXYGENASE-2

Prostaglandins are important regulators of endometrial decidualization and uterine vascular permeability during implantation.[99] Cyclooxygenase (COX), the rate-limiting enzyme in prostaglandin biosynthesis, exists in two isoforms, COX-1 and COX-2. Targeted disruption of the COX-2 but not the COX-1 gene in mice results in the failure of multiple reproductive processes, including ovulation, fertilization, implantation, and decidualization.[100] Expression of LIF or amphiregulin was not compromised in the COX-2-deficient

homozygous mouse, which suggests that COX-2 expression and/or action(s) lies downstream of the actions of these molecules. Although rodent and human implantation processes differ, many similarities exist and many processes would be expected to be conserved from an evolutionary perspective. Thus, whether COX-2 is important in endometrial receptivity in the human is an interesting unanswered question.

## PLACENTATION

### THE PLACENTAL SIDE

#### Integrins and Extracellular Matrix Interactions

During human placentation, a specialized subpopulation of placental cells termed *invasive cytotrophoblasts* invades the decidua. This process attaches the embryo/fetus to the uterus and diverts maternal blood flow to the intervillous space (see Fig. 181-2). Cytotrophoblast acquisition of an invasive phenotype is accompanied by temporally and spatially regulated switching of their integrin repertoire.[101,102] During the first trimester of human pregnancy, $\alpha_6$ integrin expression, which is restricted to cytotrophoblast progenitors, is downregulated as the cells enter the columns of anchoring villi. In this same location, the expression of integrin $\alpha_5\beta_1$ and $\alpha_1\beta_1$ is upregulated.[101] Function perturbation studies using an in vitro model that replicates the in vivo processes demonstrated the functional significance of "integrin switching." The laminin and collagen type IV receptor, $\alpha_1\beta_1$ integrin, promotes invasion, whereas the $\alpha_5\beta_1$ fibronectin receptor inhibits this process.[102] At term, when cytotrophoblasts are no longer invasive, their ability to undergo integrin switching is greatly diminished. In vitro studies show that antiphospholipid antibodies, found in some women with repeated miscarriages and abnormal placentation, decrease $\alpha_1$ and increase $\beta_5$ integrin expression by cytotrophoblasts, supporting the theory of abnormal placentation as a cause for the clinical syndrome seen in these women.[103]

#### Integrins and the Endovascular Trophoblast

In human pregnancy, cytotrophoblasts invade arteries more deeply than veins. By the late second trimester, the former vessels are lined exclusively by cytotrophoblasts; endothelial cells are no longer visible in either the endometrial or the superficial portions of their myometrial segments.[104] Immunohistochemical staining showed that cytotrophoblasts switch from an epithelial phenotype, expressing E-cadherin, to a vascular phenotype, expressing VE-cadherin, as they differentiate and invade the uterus.[16] Antibody-perturbing studies in vitro have underscored functional roles for E- and VE-cadherin expression by cytotrophoblasts. Specifically, E-cadherin restrains invasion, whereas VE-cadherin facilitates the process.[16,105] The invasion was reversed in vitro by incubating cytotrophoblasts with antiphospholipid antibodies, again supporting their negative effect on placentation in a subset of women with recurrent miscarriages, growth restriction, and pre-eclampsia.[103]

### BLOOD FLOW IN NORMAL AND ABNORMAL PLACENTATION

#### Normal Placentation

In normal pregnancy, placental blood flow changes dramatically during early pregnancy. During much of the first trimester, there is little evidence of vascular invasion. Therefore, maternal blood flow to the placenta is minimal. The oxygen pressures of the intervillous space (that is, at the uterine surface) and within the endometrium are estimated to be approximately 18 and 40 mm Hg, respectively, at 8 to 10 weeks of gestation.[106] Afterward, endovascular invasion proceeds rapidly and cytotrophoblasts are in direct contact with blood from maternal spiral arterioles, which could have a mean oxygen pressure as high as 90 to 100 mm Hg. Thus, as cytotrophoblasts invade the uterus during the first half of pregnancy, they encounter a steep, positive oxygen tension gradient, suggesting that oxygen tension might regulate cytotrophoblast proliferation and differentiation along the invasive pathway.

## A Model of Shallow Implantation in Humans

Pre-eclampsia is a pregnancy-specific disorder in the third trimester that is clinically characterized by new-onset maternal hypertension and proteinuria that usually resolves shortly after delivery of the placenta.[107] In this disorder, cytotrophoblast invasion into the decidua and myometrium is shallow, and endovascular invasion does not proceed beyond the terminal portions of the spiral arterioles.[105,108,109] Commonly, most cytotrophoblasts remain at some distance from the spiral arterioles. When endovascular trophoblasts are detected, they display, at a morphologic level, altered interactions with maternal arterioles. Because the endovascular component of invasion fails, maternal vessels are not remodeled into low-resistance, high-capacity structures.[110,111] As a result, the placenta resides in a low oxygen environment (pathologic hypoxia). In the placental bed of pre-eclamptic pregnancies, the absence of adhesion molecule switching is associated with markedly decreased expression of $\alpha_1\beta_1$ and VE-cadherin with persistent expression of E-cadherin.[105,109] In vitro studies demonstrate that under hypoxic conditions, early gestation cytotrophoblasts proliferate and do not undergo the requisite upregulation of $\alpha_1\beta_1$ that facilitates invasion.[112] The evidence to date strongly supports oxygen tension as an important regulator of cytotrophoblast proliferation and differentiation along the invasive pathway. The effects of oxygen tension on the proliferative capacity of cytotrophoblasts could help explain some of the interesting features of normal placental development. Before cytotrophoblast invasion of maternal vessels establishes the uteroplacental circulation ($\leq$10 weeks), the conceptus is in a relatively hypoxic environment. During this period, placental mass increases much more rapidly than that of the embryo. Histologic sections of early-stage pregnant human uteri show bilaminar embryos surrounded by thousands of trophoblast cells. That hypoxia stimulates cytotrophoblasts but not most other cells to undergo mitosis could help account for the discrepancy in size between the embryo and the placenta, which continues well into the second trimester of pregnancy. It is likely that hypoxia, cytokines,[113] and other factors[114] modulate trophoblast expression of adhesion molecules and their receptors and thus regulate cytotrophoblast function at the placental-decidual interface.

## Matrix-Degrading Enzymes and Their Inhibitors

During the invasive phase of implantation, cytotrophoblasts carry out highly localized extracellular matrix proteolysis (by matrix metalloproteinases [MMPs]), as evidenced by the fact that they also express MMP inhibitors[78,101,115–117] (see Fig. 181-3). MMP-2 and MMP-9 are believed to be important in the invasive process.[14,78,116] Among other mechanisms, MMP-9 is upregulated by IL-1$\beta$,[118] one example of the myriad growth factors and cytokines that control MMP production and activation. Additional mechanisms exist for balancing the invasion process. For example, cytotrophoblasts express tissue inhibitors of metalloproteinase (TIMPs) 1 to 3. TIMP-3 is produced by both the trophoblast and the maternal decidua.[119,120] Thus, regulated expression of this inhibitor, as well as the MMPs themselves, could serve to regulate trophoblast invasion of the decidua.

## *THE MATERNAL SIDE*

Although much attention has been focused on the trophoblast, the maternal endometrium also plays a role in accommodating and limiting invasion. In this regard, several complementary mechanisms are at play, including the production of inhibitors of trophoblast differentiation, invasion, inhibition of autocrine or paracrine stimulators of invasion, direct inhibition of invasion, and inhibition of trophoblast-derived matrix-degrading enzymes such as TIMP-3 (see section to follow).

## Enzyme Inhibitors

TIMPs and broad-spectrum protease inhibitors (e.g., $\alpha_2$-macroglobulin) of decidual (and cytotrophoblast) origin are important in limiting cytotrophoblast invasion. Rodent decidua expresses TIMPs,[121] and TIMPs abolish trophoblast invasion in vitro.[118,122] Mice with a null mutation in the TIMP-1 gene, however, have normal fertility,[15] which suggests that TIMP-1 is not a critical inhibitor of trophoblast invasion. In humans, endometrial TIMP-1 and TIMP-2 mRNA expression is not cycle dependent,[123,124] and TIMP-3 appears to play a major role in limiting invasion. TIMP-3 mRNA, which is upregulated by progesterone in vitro, and in vivo in decidualized endometrial stromal cells,[120] is also expressed in the decidua immediately adjacent to the implanting mouse embryo.[125] IL-1$\beta$ inhibits TIMP-3 expression in human decidualized endometrial stromal cells, which suggests that the trophoblast promotes its own invasiveness by inhibiting a maternal restraint on invasion[126] (see Fig. 181-2).

## Extracellular Matrix Proteins

The extracellular matrix probably plays a major role in trophoblast invasiveness because the substratum supports cell adhesion and cell-cell interactions and interactions with the extracurricular matrix also regulate trophoblast invasion. In vitro, decidualized endometrial stromal cells secrete fibronectin and laminin,[127,128] and progestins stimulate fibronectin production by these cells.[128] Laminin production increases during decidualization of rat uterine stromal cells.[129] In human endometrium, laminin is more abundant in secretory than proliferative endometrium, and it increases in early pregnancy.[128] Laminin decreases prolactin and insulin-like growth factor–binding protein 1 (IGFBP-1) production during in vitro decidualization of endometrial stromal cells,[130] suggesting a role in facilitating trophoblast invasion[131] (see later).

Fibronectin is a major secretory product of decidualized endometrial stromal cells.[127] It interacts with specific integrins, including $\alpha_5\beta_1$, which is uniquely expressed by the invading trophoblast, through an arg-gly-asp (RGD) tripeptide motif.[102] Fibronectin inhibits trophoblast invasion in vitro,[102] and RGD-containing peptides inhibit cytotrophoblast attachment to fibronectin-coated culture dishes.[132,133] Thus, cytotrophoblast interactions with fibronectin, through $\alpha_5\beta_1$ integrin, restrain rather than promote invasion. The mechanisms underlying this inhibition are not well understood, but fibronectin may be one of several factors that act by conferring "maternal restraint" on trophoblast invasiveness at the maternal-fetal interface or by conferring endometrial stromal cell receptivity (see Fig. 181-2).

## IGF-2 and IGFBP-1

IGF-2 mRNA is abundantly expressed by the invading cytotrophoblast.[134] Uterine microdialysis experiments in humans have shown that human chorionic gonadotropin (hCG) administration during the secretory phase of the menstrual cycle increases IGFBP-1 production in vivo.[135] In addition, IGF-2 stimulates human trophoblast migration in vitro.[136] IGFBP-1, which has high affinity for the IGFs, primarily inhibits their actions at target cells.[137] IGFBP-1 is a major product of secretory endometrium and decidua in humans,[134,138–142] and maternal serum levels increase during gestation,[143] most likely derived from the decidua.[129,144,145] IGFBP-1 also has IGF-independent actions such as binding to cell membranes and altering cellular motility.[146] Like fibronectin, it contains an RGD sequence (see earlier). Thus, IGFBP-1 is also well situated to interact with the cytotrophoblast to affect the implantation process by IGF-dependent and/or IGF-independent actions. IGFBP-1 competes with endometrial membrane receptors for IGF-1 binding.[147] In choriocarcinoma cells, it also inhibits the binding and biologic activity of IGF-1, suggesting a role in regulating the actions of trophoblast-derived IGF.[148] IGFBP-1 binds to human cytotrophoblasts by mechanisms that include interactions with $\alpha_5\beta_1$ integrin.[133] IGFBP-1 inhibits human cytotrophoblast invasion of decidualized human endometrial stromal cocultures,[133] although it has also been reported to stimulate trophoblast migration in an in vitro Matrigel assay.[136,149] The different results may be due to the fact that the investigator used different sources of trophoblasts (passaged vs. freshly isolated). Overall, the former studies cumulatively suggest that IGFBP-1 interacts with the invading trophoblast and may be one of several "maternal restraints" to curb placental invasion into the maternal host (see Fig. 181-2). Whether an excess of IGFBP-1 at the maternal-fetal interface deters cytotrophoblast invasion and thus causes pregnancy loss or shallow implantation is not certain. IGFBP-1 levels are elevated, however, at the maternal-fetal interface and in the circulation of women with severe pre-eclampsia, a disorder of shallow implantation.[145,150,151] The roles of IGF peptides and IGFBP-1 in normal endometrial development, uterine receptivity and nonreceptivity, occult endometrial defects, and early human pregnancy await further investigation.

## TGF-$\beta_1$

TGF-$\beta_1$ is equally distributed in human endometrial glands and stroma, with the highest levels in secretory endometrium and decidua.[152] The cycle dependence of TGF-$\beta_1$ expression and its abundance in decidua suggest a possible role in implantation.[153,154] TGF-$\beta_1$ inhibits cytotrophoblast proliferation and promotes differentiation to a noninvasive phenotype. Additionally, TGF-$\beta_1$ induces plasminogen activator inhibitor mRNA and TIMP-1 secretion and decreases MMP-2 production in cytotrophoblasts.[155] Since the latent form of TGF-$\beta_1$ is activated by plasmin, it appears that the maternal decidua stores latent TGF-$\beta_1$ in the extracellular matrix, which is activated by trophoblast-derived plasmin. Subsequently, TGF-$\beta_1$ may increase expression of plasminogen activator inhibitor and inhibit trophoblast-derived MMPs (by increasing TIMP-1), thereby limiting trophoblast invasion.[155] In vitro studies demonstrate that TGF-$\beta_1$ produced by first-trimester decidual cells inhibits the invasiveness of first-trimester human trophoblasts by mechanisms that include TIMP-1 induction.[154-156] Together, these data support the role of TGF-$\beta_1$ as a "maternal restraint" on invasion (see Fig. 181-2).

### Gene Expression Profiling in the Endometrium

Since the completion of the human genome project, new high throughput technologies have evolved for profiling the regulation of multiple gene products. These technologies for analyzing DNA, RNA, and protein levels are well positioned to enable a better understanding of the dynamic changes that accompany endometrial maturation and implantation, as well as pregnancy maintenance and failure.[157] Studies comparing human endometrial biopsies during the window of implantation to proliferative endometrium have shown

upregulation of several genes including: apolipoproteins, phospholipase A2, mammaglobin, osteopontin, glycodelin, N-acetyl-6-sulphotransferase, members of the TGF-β-signaling pathway, the IGF system, a variety of immune modulators, antibacterial modulators, metallothioneins, and other genes involved in detoxification and heavy metal availability, members of the Wnt signaling pathway, water and ion transporters, transcription factors, and others.[158] Other studies comparing genes in the window of implantation versus proliferative endometrium[159] or early secretory endometrium[160,161] have many but not all genes in common. This heterogeneity of genes underscores the complexity of processes and factors involved in human implantation and likely involves differences in data analysis as well as patient variability.[162] Similar studies examining the endometrium of women with endometriosis showed that some of the genes that were upregulated during the implantation window of a natural cycle in normal women were not upregulated in women with endometriosis.[163] Examples include IL-15, proline-rich protein, B61, Dickkopf-1, glycodelin, N-acetylglucosamine-6-O-sulfotransferase, G0S2 protein, and purine nucleoside phosphorylase.[163] This type of comparative gene profiling may lead to a better understanding of implantation disorders associated with endometriosis and other causes of implantation failure. Indeed, a particularly striking abnormality is the decreased expression of N-acetylglucosamine-6-0-sulfotransferase in the endometrium of women with endometriosis during the implantation window.[163] This enzyme belongs to a family of sulfotransferases that synthesize high-affinity ligands for L-selectin. Since L-selectin is expressed in the trophectoderm of the implanting blastocyst, implantation failure may result in such circumstances and contribute to the infertility in patients with endometriosis. The application of gene profiling technology in mice, comparing, for example, implantation with interimplantation sites, has demonstrated genes that are differentially regulated during decidualization versus implantation.[153] There are several steps and transformations that occur in the endometrium as it prepares for and participates in implantation. Gene profiling using carefully designed studies and validation tools may help us to understand the complex sequence of events that are required to initiate and maintain pregnancy.

## CONCLUSIONS

Interactions between the trophectoderm of the rapidly developing embryo and the endometrium reflect a molecular coordination that has evolved to ensure survival of the species. Remarkably, there are species-specific and common aspects of implantation that underscore the complexity of the process. The maternal decidua clearly plays a role in accommodating, tolerating, and limiting the invasive trophoblast. The latter undergoes unique changes in integrin and matrix-degrading enzyme expression that appear to be regulated by oxygen tension and a variety of cytokines, with both autocrine and paracrine action. In the future, deeper understanding of trophoblast-decidual interactions will provide the basis for enhancing fertility and implantation success as well as insights for designing novel methods of contraception.

## REFERENCES

1. Smith SK: The menstrual cycle. In Glasser S, Aplin J, Giudice LC, Tabibzadeh S (eds): The Endometrium. London, Taylor & Francis, 2002, pp 73–85.
2. Giudice LC: Implantation and endometrial function. In Fauser BCJM (ed): Reproductive Medicine: Molecular, Cellular and Genetic Fundamentals. New York, Parthenon, 2002, pp 439–465.
3. Lim H, Song H, Paria BC, et al: Molecules in blastocyst implantation: Uterine and embryonic perspectives. Vitam Horm 94:43–76, 2002.
4. Giudice LC: Elucidating human endometrial function in the post-genomic era. Hum Reprod Update 9:223–235, 2003.

5. Genbecev OD, Prakobphol A, Foulk RA, et al: Trophoblast L-selectin-mediated adhesion at the maternal fetal interface. Science 299:405–408, 2003.

6. Wang X, Matsumoto H, Zhao X, et al: Embryonic signals direct the formation of tight junctional permeability barrier in the decidualizing stroma during embryo implantation. J Cell Sci 117:53–62, 2004.

7. Dey S, Lim H, Das SK, et al: Molecular cues to implantation. Endocr Rev 25:341–373, 2004.

8. Aplin JD, Kimber SJ: Trophoblast-uterine interactions at implantation. Reprod Biol Endocrinol 2:48–59, 2004.

9. Anderson TI: Window of uterine receptivity. In Yoshinaga T (ed): Blastocyst Implantation. Boston, Adams, 1990, pp 219–224.

10. Hertig A, Rock JA: A description of 34 human ova within the first 17 days of development. Am J Anat 98:435–494, 1956.

11. Lindenberg S: Experimental studies on the initial trophoblast endometrial interaction. Dan Med Bull 38:371–380, 1991.

12. Denker HW: Endometrial receptivity: Cell biological aspects of an unusual epithelium: A review. Ann Anat 176:53–60, 1994.

13. Kliman HJ, Coutifaris C, Feinberg RF, et al: Implantation: In vitro models utilizing humans. In Yoshinaga K (ed): Blastocyst Implantation. Boston, Adams, 1989, pp 83–91.

14. Fisher SJ, Damsky CH: Human cytotrophoblast invasion. Semin Cell Biol 4:183–188, 1993.

15. Cross JC, Werb Z, Fisher SJ: Implantation and the placenta: Key pieces of the development puzzle. Science 266:1508–1518, 1994.

16. Zhou Y, Fisher SJ, Janatpour M, et al: Human cytotrophoblasts adopt a vascular phenotype as they differentiate: A strategy for successful endovascular invasion? J Clin Invest 99:2139–2151, 1997.

17. Ferenczy A, Richard RM, Agate FJ Jr, et al: Scanning electron microscopy of the human endometrium surface epithelium. Fertil Steril 23:515–521, 1972.

18. Martel D, Frydman R, Glissant M, et al: Scanning electron microscopy of postovulatory human endometrium in spontaneous cycles and cycles stimulated by hormone treatment. J Endocrinol 114:319–324, 1987.

19. Martel D, Monier MN, Roiche D, et al: Hormonal dependence of pinopode formation at the uterine luminal surface. Hum Reprod 6:597–603, 1991.

20. Psychoyos A, Martel D: Receptivite uterine pour l'ovoimplantation et microscopie electronique a balayage. Rech Gynecol 2:116–118, 1990.

21. Psychoyos A, Nikas G: Uterine pinopodes as markers of uterine receptivity. Assist Reprod Rev 4:26–32, 1994.

22. Nardo LG, Sabatini L, Rai R, et al: Pinopode expression during human implantation. Eur J Obstet Gynecol Reprod Biol 101:104–108, 2002.

23. Turpeenniemi-Hujanen T, Feinberg RF, Kauppila A, et al: Extracellular matrix interactions in early human embryos: Implications for normal implantation events. Fertil Steril 64:132–138, 1995.

24. Aplin JD: Adhesion molecules in implantation. Rev Reprod 2:84–93, 1997.

25. Carson DD, Rohde LH, Surveyor G: Cell surface glycoconjugates as modulators of embryo attachment to uterine epithelial cells. Int J Biochem 26:1269–1277, 1994.

26. Surveyor GA, Gendler SJ, Pemberton L, et al: Differential expression of MUC-1 at the apical surface of mouse uterine epithelial cells. FASEB J 7:1151–1157, 1993.

27. Hey NA, Graham RA, Seif MW, et al: The polymorphic epithelial mucin MUC-1 in human endometrium is regulated with maximal expression in the implantation phase. J Clin Endocrinol Metab 78:337–342, 1994.

28. Meseuguer M, Aplin JD, Caballero-Campo P, et al: Human endometrial mucin MUC-1 is up-regulated by progesterone and down-regulated in vitro by the human blastocyst in vitro. Biol Reprod 64:590–601, 2001.

29. Kliman HJ, Feinberg RJ, Schwartz LB, et al: A mucin-like glycoprotein identified by MAG (mouse ascites Golgi) antibodies: Menstrual cycle–dependent localization in human endometrium. Am J Pathol 146:166–181, 1995.

30. Feinberg RF, Kliman HJ: MAG (mouse ascites Golgi) mucin in the endometrium: A potential marker of endometrial receptivity to implantation. In Diamond MP, Osteen KG (eds): Endometrium and Endometriosis. Malden, MA, Blackwell, 1997, pp 131–139.

31. Kliman HJ, Feinberg RJ, Schwartz LB, et al: Patients with unexplained infertility exhibit correctable defects in MAG mucin expression (abstract P-004). Fertil Steril (Suppl):95, 1996.

32. Albelda SM, Buck CA: Integrins and other cell adhesion molecules. FASEB J 4:2868–2880, 1990.

32. Clark EA, Brugge JS: Integrins and signal transduction pathways: The road taken. Science 268:233–239, 1995.

34. Tabibzadeh S: Patterns of expression of integrin molecules in human endometrium throughout the menstrual cycle. Hum Reprod 7:876–882, 1992.

35. Lessey BA, Damjanovich L, Coutifaris C, et al: Integrin adhesion molecules in the human endometrium: Correlation with the normal and abnormal menstrual cycle. J Clin Invest 90:188–195, 1992.

36. Lessey BA, Castlebaum AJ, Buck CA, et al: Further characterization of endometrial integrins during the menstrual cycle and in pregnancy. Fertil Steril 62:497–506, 1994.

37. Lessey BA, Ilesami AO, Sun J, et al: Luminal and glandular endometrial epithelium express integrins differentially throughout the menstrual cycle: Implications for implantation, contraception, and infertility. Am J Reprod Immunol 35:195–204, 1996.

38. Johnson GA, Bunghardt RC, Spencer TE, et al: Ovine osteopontin: II. Osteopontin and $\alpha_v\beta_3$ integrin in the uterus and conceptus during the periimplantation period. Biol Reprod 61:892–899, 1999.

39. Johnson GA, Bazer FW, Jaeger LA, et al: MUC-1, integrin, and osteopontin expression during the implantation cascade in sheep. Biol Reprod 65:820–828, 2001.

40. Nardo LG, Nikas G, Makrigiannakis A, et al: Synchronous expression of pinopodes and $\alpha_v\beta_3$ and $\alpha_4\beta_1$ integrins in the endometrial surface epithelium of normally menstruating women during the implantation window. J Reprod Med 48:355–361, 2003.

41. Lessey BA, Castlebaum AJ, Sawin SJ, et al: Aberrant integrin expression in the endometrium of women with endometriosis. J Clin Endocrinol Metab 79:643–649, 1994.

42. Meyer WR, Castelbaum AJ, Somkuti S, et al: Hydrosalpinges adversely affect markers of endometrial receptivity. Hum Reprod 12:1393–1398, 1997.

43. Lessey BA, Castlebaum AJ, Sawin SJ, et al: Integrins as markers of uterine receptivity in women with primary unexplained infertility. Fertil Steril 63:535–542, 1995.

44. Thomas K, Thomson A, Wood S, et al: Endometrial integrin expression in women undergoing in vitro fertilization and the association with subsequent treatment outcome. Fertil Steril 80:502–507, 2003.

45. Lessey BA, Castlebaum AJ, Somkuti SG, et al: Improvements in pregnancy rates with GnRH agonist in women with infertility, minimal or mild endometriosis, and aberrant $\alpha_v\beta_3$ expression. In Proceedings of the Annual Meeting of the American Society for Reproductive Medicine, 52nd Annual Meeting, Boston, MA, November 2–7, 1996, Abstract O-165, pS82. 1996, S82, pp 1–165.

46. Lessey BA, Killam AP, Metzger DA, et al: Immunohistochemical analysis of human uterine estrogen and progesterone receptors throughout the menstrual cycle. J Clin Endocrinol Metab 6:334–340, 1988.

47. Tabibzadeh S, Sun XZ: Cytokine expression in human endometrium throughout the menstrual cycle. Hum Reprod 7:1214–1221, 1992.

48. Hamovici F, Anderson DJ: Cytokines and growth factors in implantation. Microsc Res Tech 25:201–207, 1993.

49. Giudice LC: Growth factors and growth modulators in human uterine endometrium: Their potential relevance to reproductive medicine. Fertil Steril 61:1–17, 1994.

50. Carpenter G: Receptor for epidermal growth factor and other polypeptide mitogens. Annu Rev Biochem 56:881–914, 1987.

51. Massague J, Pandiella A: Membrane-anchored growth factors. Annu Rev Biochem 62:515–541, 1993.

52. Johnson GR, Kannan B, Shoyab M, et al: Amphiregulin induces tyrosine phosphorylation of the epidermal growth factor receptor and p185[erb B2]. J Biol Chem 268:2924–2931, 1993.

53. Watanabe T, Shintani A, Nakata M, et al: Recombinant human betacellulin. J Biol Chem 269:9966–9973, 1994.

54. Paria BC, Dey SK: Preimplantation embryo development in vitro: Cooperative interactions among embryos and role of growth factors. Proc Natl Acad Sci U S A 87:4756–4760, 1990.

55. Luetteke NC, Qui TH, Peiffer RL, et al: TGF-α deficiency results in hair follicle and eye abnormalities in targeted and waved-1 mice. Cell 73:263–278, 1993.

56. Mann GB, Fowler KJ, Gabriel A, et al: Mice with a null mutation of the TGF-α gene have abnormal skin architecture, wavy hair, and curly whiskers and often develop corneal inflammation. Cell 73:249–261, 1993.

57. Das SK, Wang X, Paria BC, et al: Heparin-binding EGF-like growth factor gene is induced in the mouse uterus temporally by the blastocyst solely at the site of its apposition: A possible ligand for interaction with blastocyst EGF-receptor in implantation. Development 120:1071–1083, 1994.

58. Das SK, Chakraborty I, Paria BC, et al: Amphiregulin is an implantation-specific and progesterone regulated gene in the mouse uterus. Mol Endocrinol 9:691–705, 1995.

59. Leach RE, Khalifa R, Ramirez ND, et al: Multiple roles for heparin-binding epidermal growth factor–like growth factor are suggested by its cell-specific expression during the human endometrial cycle and early placentation. J Clin Endocrinol Metab 84:3355–3363, 1999.

60. Martin KL, Barlow DH, Sargetn IL: Heparin-binding epidermal growth factor significantly improves human blastocyst development and hatching in serum-free medium. Hum Reprod 13:1645–1652, 1998.

61. Leach RE, Kilburn B, Wang J, et al: Heparin-binding EGF-like growth factor regulates human extravillous cytotrophoblast development during conversion to the invasive phenotype. Dev Biol 266:223–237, 2004.

62. Leach RE, Romero R, Kim YM, et al: Pre-eclampsia and expression of heparin-binding EGF-like growth factor. Lancet 360:1215–1219, 2002.

63. Pollard JW, Hunt JS, Wiktor-Jedrzejczak W, et al: A pregnancy defect in the osteopetrotic (op/op) mouse demonstrates the requirement for CSF-1 in female fertility. Dev Biol 148:273–283, 1991.

64. Wiktor-Jedrzejczak W, Urbanowska E, Aukerman S: Correction by CSF-1 of defects in the osteopetrotic op/op mouse suggests local, developmental, and humoral requirements for this growth factor. Exp Hematol 19:1049–1054, 1991.

65. Daiter E, Pampfer S, Yeung YG, et al: Expression of colony-stimulating factor-1 in the human uterus and placenta. J Clin Endocrinol Metab 74:850–858, 1992.

66. Katano K, Matsumoto Y, Ogasawara M, et al: Low serum M-CSF levels are associated with unexplained recurrent abortion. Am J Reprod Immunol 38:1–5, 1997.

67. Hilton DL, Cough NM: Leukemia inhibitory factor: A biological perspective. J Cell Biochem 46:21–24, 1991.

68. Kondera-Anasz Z, Sikora J, Mielczarek-Palacz A: Leukemia inhibitory factor: An important regulator of endometrial function. Am J Reprod Immunol 52:97–105, 2004.

69. Stewart CL, Kaspar P, Brunet LJ, et al: Blastocyst implantation depends on maternal expression of leukemia inhibitory factor. Nature 359:76–79, 1992.

70. Stewart CL: Leukemia inhibitory factor and the regulation of pre-implantation development of the mammalian embryo. Mol Reprod Dev 39:233–238, 1994.

71. Stewart CL, Cullinan EB: Pre-implantation development of the mammalian embryo and its regulation by growth factors. Dev Genet 21:91–101, 1997.

72. Charnock-Jones DS, Sharkey AM, Fenwick P, Smith SK: Leukemia inhibitory factor mRNA concentration peaks in human endometrium at the time of implantation and the blastocyst contains mRNA for the receptor at this time. J Reprod Fertil 101:421–426, 1994.

73. Kojima K, Kanzaki H, Iwai M, et al: Expression of leukemia inhibitory factor in human endometrium and placenta. Biol Reprod 50:882–887, 1994.

74. Cullinan EB, Abbondanzo SJ, Anderson PS, et al: Leukemia inhibitory factor (LIF) and LIF receptor expression in human endometrium suggests a potential autocrine/paracrine function in regulating embryo implantation. Proc Natl Acad Sci U S A 93:3115–3120, 1996.

75. Arici A, Engin O, Attar E, Olive DL: Modulation of leukemia inhibitory factor gene expression and protein synthesis in human endometrium. J Clin Endocrinol Metab 80:1908–1915, 1995.

76. Nakajima S, Tanaka T, Umesaki N, et al: Leukemia inhibitory factor regulates cell survival of normal human endometrial stromal cells. Int J Mol Med 11:353–356, 2003.

77. Nachtigall MJ, Kliman HJ, Feinberg RF, et al: The effect of leukemia inhibitory factor on trophoblast differentiation: A potential role in human implantation. J Clin Endocrinol Metab 81:801–806, 1996.

78. Bischof P, Haenggeli L, Campana A: Effect of leukemia inhibitory factor on human cytotrophoblast differentiation along the invasive pathway. Am J Reprod Immunol 34:225–230, 1995.

79. Aghajanova L, Stavreus-Evers A, Nikas Y, et al: Coexpression of pinopodes and leukemia inhibitory factor, as well as its receptor, in human endometrium. Fertil 79(Suppl 1):808–814, 2003.

80. Hambartsoumian E: Endometrial leukemia inhibitory factor (LIF) as a possible cause of unexplained infertility and multiple failures of implantation. Am J Reprod Immunol 39:137–143, 1998.

81. Dinarello CA: Biology of interleukin-1. FASEB J 2:108–115, 1988.

82. Simon C, Frances A, Pellicer A, et al: Cytokines in implantation. Semin Reprod Endocrinol 13:142–151, 1995.

83. De los Santos MJ, Mercarder A, Frances A, et al: Immunoreactive human embryonic interleukin-1 system and endometrial factors regulating their secretion during embryonic development. Biol Reprod 54:563–574, 1996.

84. Simon C, Frances A, Piquette GN, et al: Embryonic implantation in mice is blocked by interleukin-1 receptor antagonist. Endocrinology 134:521–528, 1994.

85. Abbondanzo SJ, Cullinan EB, McIntyre K, et al: Reproduction in mice lacking a functional type I IL-1 receptor. Endocrinology 137:3598–3601, 1996.

86. Zheng H, Fletcher D, Kozak W, et al: Resistance to fever induction and impaired acute-phase response in interleukin-1β–deficient mice. Immunity 3:9–19, 1995.

87. Kuida K, Lippke JA, Ku G, et al: Altered cytokine export and apoptosis in mice deficient in interleukin-1β converting enzyme. Science 267:2000–2003, 1995.

88. Li P, Allen H, Barerjee S, et al: Mice deficient in IL-1β–converting enzyme are defective in production of mature IL-1β and resistant to endotoxic shock. Cell 80:401–411, 1995.

89. Simon C, Valbuena D, Krussel J, et al: Interleukin-1 receptor antagonist prevents embryonic implantation by a direct effect on the endometrial epithelium. Fertil Steril 70:896–906, 1998.

90. Gonzalez RR, Leary K, Petrozza JC, et al: Leptin regulation of the interleukin-1 system in human endometrial cells. Mol Hum Reprod 9:151–158, 2003.

91. Zhu L-J, Cullinan-Bove K, Polihronis M, et al: Calcitonin is a progesterone-regulated marker that forecasts the receptive state of endometrium during implantation. Endocrinology 139:3923–3934, 1998.

92. Tsatsaris V, Tarrade A, Merviel P, et al: Calcitonin gene-related peptide (CGRP) and CGRP receptor expression at the human implantation site. J Clin Endocrinol Metab 87:4383–4390, 2002.

93. Taylor HS, Vanden Heuvel GB, Igarahi P: A conserved Hox axis in the mouse and human female reproductive system: Late establishment and persistent adult expression of the Hoxa cluster genes. Biol Reprod 57:1338–1345, 1997.

94. Satokata I, Benson GV, Maas RL: Sexually dimorphic sterility phenotypes in Hoxa-10–deficient mice. Nature 374:460–463, 1995.

95. Gui Y, Zhang J, Yuan L, et al: Regulation of Hoxa-10 and its expression in normal and abnormal endometrium. Mol Hum Reprod 5:866–873, 1999.

96. Benson GV, Lim H, Paria BC, et al: Mechanisms of reduced fertility in Hoxa-10 mutant mice: Uterine homeosis and loss of maternal Hoxa-10 expression. Development 12:2687–2696, 1996.

97. Bagot CN, Troy PJ, Taylor HS: Alteration of maternal Hoxa-10 expression by in vivo gene transfection affects implantation. Gene Ther 7:1378–1384, 2000.

98. Taylor HS, Arici A, Olive D, Igarashi P: Hoxa-10 is expressed in response to sex steroids at the time of implantation. J Clin Invest 101:1379–1384, 1998.

99. Chakraborty I, Das SK, Wang J, Dey SK: Developmental expression of the cyclo-oxygenase-1 and cyclo-oxygenase-2 genes in the peri-implantation mouse uterus and their differential regulation by the blastocyst and ovarian steroids. J Mol Endocrinol 16:107–122, 1998.

100. Lim H, Paria BC, Das SK, et al: Multiple female reproductive failures in cyclooxygenase-2–deficient mice. Cell 91:97–208, 1997.

101. Damsky CH, Fitzgerald ML, Fisher SJ: Distribution patterns of extracellular matrix components and adhesion receptors are intricately modulated during first trimester cytotrophoblast differentiation along the invasive pathway, in vivo. J Clin Invest 89:210–222, 1992.

102. Damsky CH, Librach C, Lim KH, et al: Integrin switching regulates normal trophoblast invasion. Development 120:3657–3666, 1994.

103. Di Simone N, Castellani R, Caliandro D, et al: Antiphospholipid antibodies regulate the expression of trophoblast cell adhesion molecules. Fertil Steril 77:905–811, 2002.

104. Zhou Y, Genbacev O, Damsky CH, Fisher SJ: Oxygen regulates human cytotrophoblast differentiation and invasion: Implications for endovascular invasion in normal pregnancy and in pre-eclampsia. J Reprod Immunol 39:197–213, 1998.

105. Zhou Y, Fisher SJ, Damsky CH: Pre-eclampsia is associated with failure of human cytotrophoblasts to mimic a vascular adhesion phenotype: One cause of defective endovascular invasion in this syndrome? J Clin Invest 99:2152–2164, 1997.

106. Rodesch F, Simon P, Donner C, Jauniaux E: Oxygen measurements in endometrial and trophoblast tissues during early pregnancy. Obstet Gynecol 80:283–285, 1992.

107. Freidman SA, Taylor RN, Roberts JM: Pathophysiology of preeclampsia. Clin Perinatol 18:661–682, 1991.

108. Khong TY, De Wolf F, Robertson WB, Brosens IA: Inadequate maternal vascular response to placentation in pregnancies complicated by pre-eclampsia and by small-for-gestational age infants. Br J Obset Gynaecol 93:1049–1059, 1986.

109. Zhou Y, Damsky CH, Chiu K, et al: Pre-eclampsia is associated with abnormal expression of adhesion molecules by invasive cytotrophoblasts. J Clin Invest 91:950–960, 1993.

110. Brosens IA, Robertson WB, Dixon HG: The role of the spiral arteries in the pathogenesis of pre-eclampsia. Obstet Gynecol Annu 1:177–191, 1972.

111. Moodley J, Ramsaroop R: Placental bed morphology in black women with eclampsia. S Afr Med J 75:376–378, 1989.

112. Genbacev O, Joslin R, Damsky CH, et al: Hypoxia alters early gestation human cytotrophoblast differentiation and invasion in vitro and models the placental defects that occur in pre-eclampsia. J Clin Invest 97:540–550, 1996.

113. Conrad KP, Benyo DF: Placental cytokines and the pathogenesis of preeclampsia. Am J Reprod Immunol 37:240–249, 1997.

114. Roberts JM, Taylor RN, Musci TJ, et al: Pre-eclampsia: An endothelial cell disorder. Am J Obstet Gynecol 161:1200–1204, 1989.

115. Fisher SJ, Cui T-Y, Zhang L, et al: Adhesive and degradative properties of human placental cytotrophoblast cells in vitro. J Cell Biol 109:891–902, 1989.

116. Polette M, Nawrocki B, Pintiaux A, et al: Expression of gelatinases A and B and their tissue inhibitors by cells of early and term human placenta and gestational endometrium. Lab Invest 71:838–846, 1994.

117. Bischof P, Campana A: A model for implantation of the human blastocyst and early placentation. Hum Reprod Update 2:252–270, 1996.

118. Librach CL, Werb Z, Fitzgerald ML, et al: 92-kD type IV collagenase mediates invasion of human cytotrophoblasts. J Cell Biol 113:437–449, 1991.

119. Bass KE, Li H, Hawkes SP, et al: TIMP-3 production is up-regulated by human cytotrophoblasts during invasion in vitro (abstract). In Proceedings of the 34th Annual Meeting of the American Society for Cell Biology, San Francisco, 1994, p 353.

120. Higushi T, Kanzaki H, Nakayama H, et al: Induction of tissue inhibitor of metalloproteinase 3 gene during in vitro decidualization of human endometrial stromal cells. Endocrinology 136:4973–4981, 1995.

121. Waterhouse P, Denhardt DT, Kjhokha R: Temporal expression of tissue inhibitors of metalloproteinases in mouse tissues during gestation. Mol Reprod Dev 35:219–226, 1993.

122. Behrendtsen O, Alexander CM, Werb Z: Metalloproteinases mediate extracellular matrix degradation by cells from mouse blastocyst outgrowths. Development 34:447–456, 1992.

123. Rodgers WH, Matrisian LM, Giudice LC, et al: Patterns of matrix metalloproteinase expression in cycling endometrium imply differential functions and regulation by steroid hormones. J Clin Invest 94:946–953, 1994.

124. Hampton AL, Salamonsen LA: Expression of messenger ribonucleic acid encoding matrix metalloproteinases and their tissue inhibitors is related to menstruation. J Endocrinol 141:R1–R3, 1994.

125. Harvey MB, Leco KJ, Arcellana-Panlilio MY, et al: Proteinase expression in early mouse embryos is regulated by LIF and EGF. Development 121:1005–1014, 1995.

126. Huang HY, Wen Y, Irwin JC, et al: Cytokine-mediated regulation of 92-kilodalton type IV collagenase, tissue inhibitor of metalloproteinase-1 (TIMP-1), and TIMP-3 mRNA expression in human endometrial stromal cells. J Clin Endocrinol Metab 83:1721–1729, 1998.

127. Irwin JC, Utian WH, Eckert RL: Sex steroids and growth factors differentially regulate the growth and differentiation of cultured human endometrial stromal cells. Endocrinology 129:2385–2392, 1991.

128. Zhu HH, Huang JR, Mazella J, et al: Progestin stimulates the biosynthesis of fibronectin and accumulation of fibronectin mRNA in human endometrial stromal cells. Hum Reprod 7:141–146, 1992.

129. Glasser SR, Lampelo S, Muniz MI, et al: Expression of desmin, laminin, and fibronectin during in situ differentiation (decidualization) of rat uterine stromal cells. Differentiation 35:132–142, 1987.

130. Brar AK, Frank GR, Richards RG, et al: Laminin decreases PRL and IGFBP-1 expression during in vitro decidualization of human endometrial stromal cells. J Cell Physiol 163:30–37, 1995.

131. Loke YW, Gardner L, Burland K, et al: Laminin in human trophoblast-decidua interaction. Hum Reprod 4:457–463, 1989.

132. Kao L-C, Caltabiano S, Wu S, et al: The human villous cytotrophoblast: Interactions with extracellular matrix proteins, endocrine function, and cytoplasmic differentiation in the absence of syncytium formation. Dev Biol 130:693–702, 1998.

133. Irwin JC, Giudice LC: IGFBP-1 binds to the $\alpha_5\beta_1$ integrin in human cytotrophoblasts and inhibits their invasion into decidualized endometrial stromal cells in vitro. Growth Horm IGF Res 8:21–31, 1998.

134. Han VK, Bassett N, Walton J, et al: The expression of insulin-like growth factor (IGF) and IGF binding protein (IGFBP) genes in the human placenta and membranes: Evidence for IGF-IGFBP interactions at the feto-maternal interface. J Clin Endocrinol Metab 81:2680–2693, 1996.

135. Licht P, Russu V, Lehmeyer S, et al: Molecular aspects of direct LH/hCG effects on human endometrium lesions from intrauterine microdialysis in the human female in vivo. Reprod Biol 1:10–19, 2001.

136. Irving JA, Lala PK: Functional role of cell surface integrins on human trophoblast cell migration: Regulation by TGF-β, IGF-II, and IGFBP-1. Exp Cell Res 217:419–427, 1995.

137. Jones JI, Clemmons DR: Insulin-like growth factors and their binding proteins. Endocr Rev 18:1–31, 1994.

138. Zhou J, Bondy C: Insulin-like growth factor-II and its binding proteins in placental development. Endocrinology 131:1230–1240, 1992.

139. Giudice LC, Irwin JC, Dsupin BA, et al: Insulin-like growth factors (IGFs), IGF binding proteins, and IGFBP protease in human uterine endometrium: Their potential relevance to endometrial cyclic function and maternal-embryonic interactions. In Baxter RC, Gluckmann PD, Rosenfeld RG (eds): The Insulin-like Growth Factors and Their Regulatory Proteins. Amsterdam, Excerpta Medica International Congress Series 1056, 1994, pp 351–361.

140. Rutanen E-M, Koistinen R, Wahlstrom T, et al: Synthesis of placental protein 12 by human decidua. Endocrinology 116:1304–1309, 1985.

141. Rutanen E-M, Koistinen R, Sjoberg J, et al: Synthesis of PP 12 by human endometrium. Endocrinology 118:1067–1071, 1986.

142. Rutanen E-M, Menabawey M, Isaka K, et al: Synthesis of placental protein 12 by decidua from early pregnancy. J Clin Endocrinol Metab 63:675–679, 1986.

143. Rutanen E-M, Koistinen R, Wahlstrom T, et al: Placental protein 12 (PP12) in the human endometrium: Tissue concentration in relation to histology and serum levels of PP12, progesterone, and oestradiol. Br J Obstet Gynaecol 91:377–381, 1984.

144. Rutanen E-M, Bohn H, Seppala M: Radioimmunoassay of placental protein 12: Levels in amniotic fluid, cord blood, and serum of healthy adults, pregnant women, and patients with trophoblastic disease. Am J Obstet Gynecol 144:460–463, 1982.

145. Giudice LC, Martina NA, De Las Fuentes L, et al: Insulin-like growth factor binding protein-1 (IGFBP-1) at the maternal-fetal interface and IGF-I, IGF-II, and IGFBP-1 in the circulation of women with severe pre-eclampsia. Am J Obstet Gynecol 176:751–758, 1997.

146. Jones JI, Gockerman A, Busby WH, et al: IGFBP-1 stimulates cell migration and binds to the $\alpha_5\beta_1$ integrin by means of its arg-gly-asp sequence. Proc Natl Acad Sci U S A 90:10553–10558, 1993.

147. Rutanen E-M, Pekonen F, Makinen T: Soluble 34K binding protein inhibits the binding of insulin-like growth factor I to its receptors in human secretory phase endometrium: Evidence for autocrine/paracrine regulation of growth factor action. J Clin Endocrinol Metab 66:173–180, 1988.

148. Ritvos O, Ranta T, Jalkanen J, et al: IGFBP from human decidua inhibits the binding and biological action of IGF-I in cultured choriocarcinoma cells. Endocrinology 122:2150–2157, 1989.

149. Hamilton GS, Lysiak JJ, Han VKM, Lala PK: Autocrine-paracrine regulation of human trophoblast invasiveness by IGF-II and IGFBP-1. Exp Cell Res 244:147–156, 1998.

150. Than GN, Csaba IF, Szabo DG, et al: Serum levels of placenta-specific tissue protein 12 (PP12) in pregnancies complicated by pre-eclampsia. Arch Gynecol 236:41–45, 1984.

151. Iino K, Sjoberg J, Seppala M: Elevated circulating levels of a decidual protein, placental protein 12, in preeclampsia. Obstet Gynecol 68:58–60, 1986.

152. Chegini N, Zhao Y, Williams RS, et al: Human uterine tissue throughout the menstrual cycle expresses transforming growth factor-β1 (TGF-β1), TGF-β2, TGF-β3, and TGF β type II receptor messenger ribonucleic acid and protein and contains [$^{125}$I]-TGFβ1 binding sites. Endocrinology 235:439–449, 1994.

153. Reese J, Das SK, Paria BC, et al: Global gene expression analysis to identify molecular markers of uterine receptivity and embryo implantation. J Biol Chem 276:44137–44145, 2001.

154. Graham CH, McCrae KR, Lala PK: Molecular mechanisms of controlling trophoblast invasion of the uterus. Trophoblast Res 7:237–250, 1993.

155. Lala PK, Graham CH: Mechanisms of trophoblast invasiveness and their control: The role of proteases and protease inhibitors. Cancer Metastasis Rev 9:369–374, 1990.

156. Graham CH, Lysiak JJ, McCrae KR, et al: Localization of transforming growth factor beta at the human fetal-maternal interface: Role in trophoblast growth and differentiation. Biol Reprod 46:561–572, 1992.

157. Giudice LC: Elucidating endometrial function in the post-genomic era. Hum Reprod Update 9:223–235, 2003.

158. Kao LC, Lobo S, Tulac S, et al: Global gene profiling in human endometrium during the window of implantation. Endocrinology 143:2119–2138, 2002.

159. Borthwick J, Charnock-Jones S, Tom B, et al: Determination of the transcript profile of human endometrium. Mol Hum Reprod 9:19–33, 2003.

160. Carson DD, Lagow E, Thathiah A, et al: Changes in gene expression during the early to mid-luteal (receptive) transition in human endometrium detected by high-density microarray screening. Mol Hum Reprod 8:871–879, 2002.

161. Reisewijk A, Martin J, van Os R, et al: Gene expression profiling of human endometrial receptivity on days LH+2 versus LH+7 by microarray technology. Mol Hum Reprod 9:253–264, 2003.

162. Giudice LC: Microarray expression profiling reveals candidate genes for human uterine receptivity. Am J Pharmacogenomics 2004 (in press).

163. Kao LC, Germeyer A, Tulac S, et al: Expression profiling of endometrium from women with endometriosis reveals candidate genes for disease-based implantation failure and infertility. Endocrinology 144:2870–2881, 2003.

# Placental Hormones

## Samuel Parry and Jerome F. Strauss III

**PROTEIN HORMONES**
Paracrine Interactions between Trophoblastic Cells
Placenta-Specific Patterns of Gene Expression
Hypothalamic-Releasing Hormones
Chorionic Gonadotropin
Chorionic Somatomammotropin and Variant
Growth Hormone

Leptin
Metastin
**STEROID HORMONES**
Progesterone
Estrogens

The human placenta and fetal membranes have a remarkably diverse secretory repertoire, surpassing that of any of the other endocrine organs. These extraembryonic tissues elaborate protein, glycoprotein, steroid hormones, growth factors, and cytokines that control the local environment of the fetus, regulate metabolic activities of the maternal and fetal tissues, and participate in the timing of parturition. The decidua also assumes important endocrine functions during gestation, secreting protein hormones, cytokines, growth factors, and growth factor–binding proteins. Therefore, many of the endocrine changes in the mother, intrauterine compartment, and fetus reflect, in part, the influence of substances derived from the uterus, placenta, and fetal membranes.

Many of the hormones produced by the placenta are identical or similar to hormones secreted by the hypothalamus, pituitary, and gonads. A detailed review of all the hormones and factors produced by the placenta is well beyond the scope of this chapter. We have selected for discussion here those hormones that are unique to the trophoblast or whose synthesis and/or regulation in the placenta is novel.

## PROTEIN HORMONES

### PARACRINE INTERACTIONS BETWEEN TROPHOBLASTIC CELLS

Development of the placenta is largely dependent on the differentiation of cytotrophoblast cells along two pathways.[1,2] In one pathway, extravillous trophoblast cells invade maternal tissues and blood vessels within the decidua and myometrium, anchoring the placenta to the uterine wall. In the other pathway, mononucleated cytotrophoblast cells within the placental villi differentiate into the multinucleated syncytiotrophoblast. Thus, there are two trophoblastic cell phenotypes within placental chorionic villi: mononuclear cytotrophoblast cells that predominate early in gestation but are sparse later in gestation, and the terminally differentiated syncytiotrophoblast that forms a continuous multinuclear layer on the surface of the villi. The syncytiotrophoblast is the major site of protein and steroid production and is in direct contact with maternal blood within the intervillous space. Therefore, most placental hormones are secreted almost exclusively into the maternal circulation. Outside the placenta, the chorion of the fetal membranes contains mononucleated cytotrophoblast cells.

The presence of (1) a number of hypothalamic hormones, such as gonadotropin-releasing hormone (GnRH), corticotropin-releasing hormone (CRH), growth hormone releasing hormone (GHRH), and somatostatin (SRIF, or somatotropin release inhibiting factor), in villous cytotrophoblast; (2) pituitary-like hormones, such as human chorionic gonadotropin (hCG), adrenocorticotropic hormone (ACTH), human growth hormone variant (HGH-V), and human chorionic somatomammotropin (hCS), in the syncytiotrophoblast; and (3) the ability of these "hypothalamic" polypeptides to stimulate or inhibit secretion of their respective pituitary-like hormones by placental tissue in vitro have led to a model of paracrine interactions between cytotrophoblast and syncytiotrophoblast that mimics the hypothalamic-hypophyseal system (Fig. 182-1).[3] Although this model is attractive, the reader should be aware of the notable differences between trophoblastic cells and pituitary cells. Trophoblastic cells are distinguished from the cells of the anterior pituitary in that they do not have large storage granules in which preformed hormone accumulates, ready for acute release in response to a secretogogue.[4] Placental hormones appear to be synthesized and rapidly secreted, possibly through a constitutive pathway.[5] Therefore, many of the factors that have been shown to influence trophoblast hormone production in vitro probably act primarily at the level of hormone synthesis or perhaps control trophoblast differentiation, rather than primarily stimulating exocytosis of granules that contain stored hormone.

### PLACENTA-SPECIFIC PATTERNS OF GENE EXPRESSION

A number of hormones are produced only by cells of the trophoblast lineage and, within the placenta, transcriptional mechanisms appear to regulate differential hormone secretion by trophoblast cell subtypes.[6-9] For example, placental HGH-V differs from pituitary growth hormone (HGH-N, N for normal) by 13 amino acids and predominates in the maternal circulation during the second half of pregnancy. Within the placenta, extravillous trophoblast cells express high levels of hCS messenger ribonucleic acid (mRNA) and low levels of hCG mRNA, which is produced almost exclusively by the syncytiotrophoblast after 6 weeks of gestation.[9,10]

The genetic elements that determine the placenta-specific pattern of gene expression have yet to be fully elucidated. The mechanisms include tissue-specific expression of transcription factors and methylation of key regulatory sequences of placentally expressed genes in extraplacental tissues.[8] Methylation of cytosines prevents binding of transcription factors, and this is thought to be a general mechanism by which genes are silenced. There are, in addition, other mechanisms that govern trophoblastic gene expression, exemplified by the regulation of the α-hCG and β-hCG subunit genes and the genes of the hCS/hGH cluster, including epigenetic

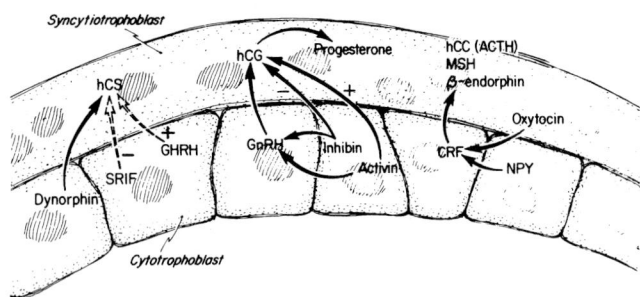

**Figure 182-1** Model for paracrine interactions between cytotrophoblast and syncytiotrophoblast in the control of hCS, hCG, and proopiomelanocortin polypeptide secretion. ACTH, adrenocorticotropic hormone; CRF, corticotropin-releasing factor; GHRH, growth hormone–releasing hormone; GnRH, gonadotropin-releasing hormone; hCC, human chorionic corticotropin; hCG, human chorioic gonadotropin; hCS, human chorionic somatomammotropin; MSH, melanocyte-stimulating hormone; NPY, neuropeptide Y; SRIF, somatotropin release inhibiting factor (somatostatin). (Reprinted with permission from Jaffe RB: Protein hormones of the placenta, decidua, and fetal membranes. In Yen SSC, Jaffe RB [eds]: Reproductive Endocrinology, 3d ed. Philadelphia, WB Saunders, 1991.)

modification (e.g., histone modification) at the hGH locus.[11,12]

The α subunit gene is normally expressed in pituitary gonadotrophs and thyrotrophs and in primate trophoblast cells. The promoter of the α subunit gene contains tandem cyclic adenosine monophosphate (cAMP) response elements (CREs), an upstream regulatory sequence, and a junctional response element (JRE) that specify trophoblastic expression of the α subunit gene.[13–15] The CREs bind CRE-binding proteins and the upsteam regulatory sequence and JRE bind other *trans*-acting factors.[6,13–15] Together, this array of regulatory elements, in conjunction with tissue-specific expression of *trans*-acting factors, endows the promoter of the α subunit gene with trophoblast specificity and maximal activity.[14]

The β-hCG subunit genes evolved from the luteinizing hormone (LH) gene β subunit, and have acquired new regulatory elements that favor their expression in the placenta rather than the pituitary gland.[16] The β subunit genes are also transcriptionally regulated by cAMP, although the β-hCG genes lack CREs. Instead, the major cAMP effects on β-hCG transcription appear to be mediated through two binding sites for the transcription factor Ets-2 in the proximal promoter of the β-hCG5 gene, which is the predominant β-hCG gene expressed in the placenta.[17] The cAMP effects on the β-hCG promoter are largely lost when both Ets-2 binding sites are mutated, although how cAMP is acting remains unclear.[17] Thus, the promoter regions of the α subunit gene and the β-hCG5 gene have little or no sequence identity, but their expression may be synchronized in early pregnancy when production of the intact hormone is vital.

The genes of four members of the placentally expressed hCS/HGH family contain novel sequences that are not present in the pituitary-expressed HGH gene (HGH-N).[18] These unique sequences, when introduced into the promoter of the HGH-N gene, repress its expression in transfected pituitary cells in an orientation-specific manner. In addition, a locus control region (LCR) is located in the 5′-flanking region of the hCS/HGH gene cluster, and the LCR contains pituitary-specific and placenta-specific elements.[11,12] Activation of the pituitary-specific sites by the transcription factor Pit-1 induces extended propagation of histone acetylation, resulting in the creation of a domain of "open" chromatin that is permissive for HGH-N promoter function. Conversely, activation of the placenta-specific sites by Pit-1 induces histone acetylation localized to these LCR sites, and the mechanisms by which

these modifications in the LCR induce promoter activation in the placenta appear to be less linear and might involve long-range looping.[11,12]

Transcriptional mechanisms control not only the production of placenta-specific hormones, but also appear to control trophoblast cellular development from undifferentiated trophectoderm and have ongoing effects regulating hormone production by these specific trophoblast cell subtypes.[8] For example, the transcription factor Hand1 is essential for differentiation of invasive trophoblast cells in mice, and Hand1 also regulates the promoter for the invasive tropholast cell-specific placental lactogen gene, Pl1.[8,19] Conversely, the formation of syncytiotrophoblast in mice is controlled by the Gcm1 transcription factor, and human Gcm1 has been shown to regulate the activity of a placenta-specific enhancer of the aromatase gene, which is expressed specifically in the syncytiotrophoblast.[20] Several other transcription factors also appear to regulate placental development and trophoblast cell subtype-specific hormone production, which ultimately may control end-stage maturation, aging, and programmed death of the trophoblast.[21,22]

## HYPOTHALAMIC-RELEASING HORMONES

### Placental Gonadotropin-Releasing Hormone
The human trophoblast produces gonadotropin-releasing hormone (GnRH), which is a decapeptide that is immunologically and chemically identical to hypothalamic GnRH. Two GnRH peptides, GnRH-1 and GnRH-2, are produced by the placenta.[23,24] Although GnRH-2 binding with its receptor appears to be more resistant to enzymatic degradation than GnRH-1, the functional differences between the two GnRHs in the placenta are not fully understood.[24] Placental GnRH appears to stimulate hCG secretion by the syncytiotrophoblast and may play a role in delaying parturition. In the earliest stages of pregnancy, GnRH-1 and -2 facilitate trophoblast invasion into the maternal uterine wall by upregulating the expression of urokinase-type plasminogen activator and matrix metalloproteinase-2 and -9 in trophoblast cells.[25,26] Later in pregnancy, circulating GnRH levels are significantly higher in women with postterm pregnancies and may be lower in women who develop preterm labor and delivery.[27]

Unlike serum hCG levels, which peak during the first trimester, GnRH mRNA levels in the placenta remain unchanged throughout gestation.[28] GnRH receptor mRNA expression in human trophoblast closely parallels hCG secretion patterns, however, and GnRH receptor gene transcription appears to be regulated by an hCG-activated cAMP pathway.[29] Consequently, human placental explants respond (as measured by hCG secretion) maximally to GnRH stimulation at 9 weeks' gestation, but there is no response in term placenta.[28] Therefore, hCG secretion by the syncytiotrophoblast may be regulated, in part, through an increase followed by a decline in GnRH receptor gene expression from the first trimester to term placenta.

### Placental Corticotropin-Releasing Hormone and Urocortin
Corticotropin-releasing hormone (CRH) is produced by various cell types within the human placenta and is identical to hypothalamic CRH.[30] Immunoreactive CRH in the plasma of nonpregnant women is low, but maternal serum CRH concentrations begin to increase at midgestation and peak during the last 6 to 8 weeks of pregnancy. There is a striking increase (20-fold) in CRH mRNA in the placenta during the last 5 weeks of pregnancy that parallels the increase in CRH peptide in maternal blood.[31] Although CRH receptors are present within the placenta and may modulate paracrine activities, CRH is largely biologically inert in the maternal plasma because it is bound to a binding protein that is produced in the placenta, liver, and brain, and is present at a 10-fold molar excess.[32,33] Thus, the maternal pituitary is not subject to

stimulation by placental CRH. After delivery, maternal plasma CRH levels rapidly decline.

Placental CRH production is regulated by prostaglandins, oxytocin, and cytokines, in a manner that implies a putative role for CRH in labor. Prostaglandin $E_2$ and $F_{2\alpha}$ stimulate CRH release from cultured human placental cells, and CRH stimulates prostaglandin release from amnion and chorionic cells.[30,34-36] Similarly, oxytocin stimulates placental cells to secrete CRH, which then increases the release of immunoreactive oxytocin from placental cells.[37,38] These observations suggest that placental CRH, prostaglandins, and oxytocin interact in a feed-forward regulatory loop that promotes labor. Furthermore, cytokines that have been associated with preterm labor caused by infection stimulate cultured human placental cells to secrete CRH.[37]

In addition to its association with prostaglandins and oxytocin, CRH has biologic activities within the fetus and myometrium that promote labor. Placental CRH stimulates the fetal pituitary to secrete ACTH, which increases the production of dehydroepiandrosterone (DHEA) by the fetal zone of the adrenal gland. In turn, DHEA serves as the primary precursor for placental estriol, which increases myometrial oxytocin receptors and gap junction formation (see discussion to follow).[39] Finally, CRH receptors have been discovered within the myometrium, and stimulatory effects of placental CRH on myometrial contractility have been described.[40] Thus, CRH may have direct and indirect effects that promote parturition, and numerous investigators are using maternal serum CRH levels to predict preterm delivery.

Placental CRH may also promote implantation of the blastocyst in early pregnancy and participate in the fetal response to stress later in gestation. Embryonic trophoblast and maternal decidua produce CRH, which may promote implantation and maintenance of early gestation by killing activated T cells that could otherwise reject the semiallogeneic embryo.[41] In contrast to the usual negative feedback action in the hypothalamus, placental CRH production is increased by glucocorticoids.[42] In experimental sheep models, a reduction in uteroplacental flow and subsequent release of catecholamines triggers CRH release in both the fetus and the placenta.[43] In human gestations complicated by pregnancy-induced hypertension and intrauterine fetal growth restriction, maternal plasma CRH levels are increased when compared to normal controls.[44] Although fetal CRH and ACTH levels do not increase in response to stress, placental CRH may ameliorate fetal hypoxemia by improving uteroplacental blood flow.[45]

Urocortin is a neuropeptide that has approximately 50% sequence homology with CRH. Urocortin binds to CRH receptors and is more potent than CRH in causing vasodilation. Immunoreactive urocortin has been localized in the syncytiotrophoblast and fetal membranes, and it is 25 times more potent than CRH in causing vasodilation of the fetal placental vasculature in vitro.[46,47] The importance of urocortin in modulating placental vascular resistance in vivo and in the fetal response to stress has not been elucidated, however.

## CHORIONIC GONADOTROPIN

### Structure of Chorionic Gonadotropin

Human chorionic gonadotropin (hCG) is the first hormone known to be elaborated by the conceptus. It is a glycoprotein hormone that consists of two dissimilar subunits, α and β, that are joined noncovalently.

The α subunit is a 92-amino acid polypeptide that is common to the pituitary gonadotropins and thryrotropin. The α subunit of hCG contains two asparagine-linked (N-linked) oligosaccharide side chains attached at amino acid residues 52 and 78 (Fig. 182-2). The N-linked oligosaccharide at residue 52 is critical to signal transduction of the hCG hormone, by stimulating cAMP accumulation and steroidogenesis in target cells. The trophoblast secretes two forms of the free α subunit,

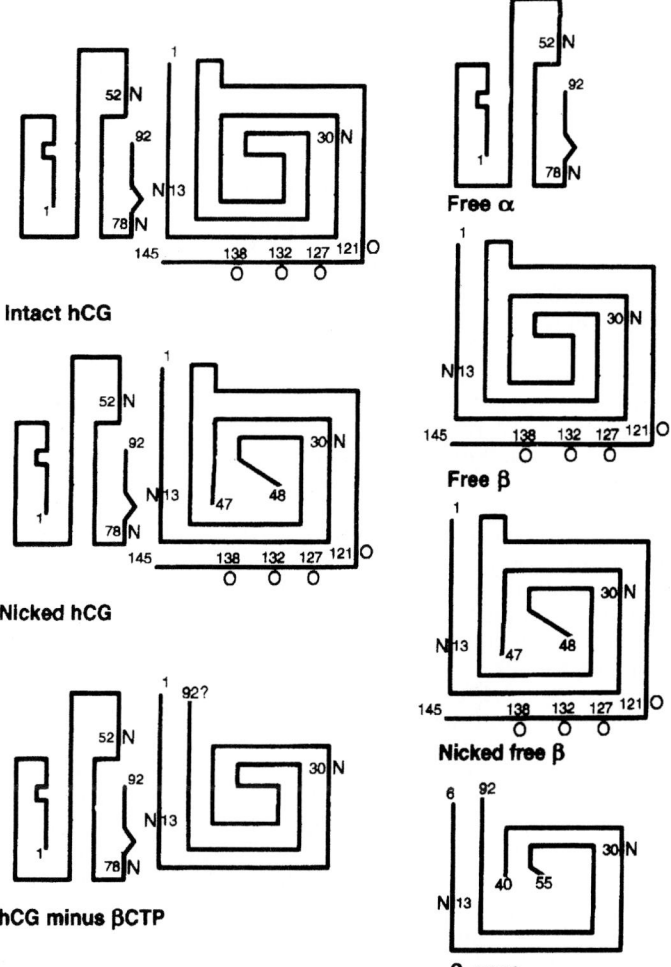

**Figure 182-2** Structures of human chorionic gonadotropin (hCG) subunit molecules identified in biologic fluids. The numbers represent the amino acid residue count. βCTP, β core terminal peptide; N, N-linked glycosylation site; O, O-linked glycosylation site. (Adapted with permission from Bohler H Jr, Cole LA: Human chorionic gonadotropin and related molecules in pregnancy serum and urine. Assist Reprod Rev 3:46, 1993.)

regular free α, which is the same as the α subunit of hCG, and a large free α, which is hyperglycosylated with N-linked oligosaccharides that prevent its combination with β subunit.[48] The majority of free α subunit in the maternal serum is large free α, although no current immunoassays can discriminate between the two forms. The biologic significance of these posttranslational modifications remains to be determined.

The 145-amino acid β-hCG subunit is structurally similar to the 121-amino acid β-LH. The major difference between β-hCG and β-LH is a 24-amino acid C-terminal extension in β-hCG that results from a single base pair deletion and a two base pair insertion that eliminates a termination codon and produces an open reading frame (see Fig. 182-2).[48] The C-terminal peptide contains four serine-linked (O-linked) oligosaccharide chains that markedly increase the half-life of intact hCG in vivo and play an important role in apical targeting of the hCG protein so that it is directed into the maternal circulation.[5] The β subunit also contains two N-linked oligosaccharide chains attached to residues 13 and 30. These N-linked oligosaccharides facilitate β subunit folding, which is the rate limiting step in the secretion of intact hCG.[49]

### Synthesis and Secretion of Chorionic Gonadotropin

The single α subunit gene resides on chromosome 6. The β subunit is encoded by a cluster of six transcriptionally active genes that are located on chromosome 19.[50] Three of the β-hCG genes are expressed at significant levels during pregnancy; all six share extensive (>80%) sequence homology with the LH β subunit gene, which is located in the same region on chromosome 19 and from which the β-hCG genes probably evolved.[50]

The synthesis of hCG is linked to the stages of trophoblastic differentiation.[9,16,50–52] Although α-hCG gene transcription can be detected in cytotrophoblastic cells, synthesis of β-hCG and intact hCG (both subunits in their dimeric form) is restricted to the syncytiotrophoblast after 6 weeks of gestation. The factors responsible for coupling trophoblastic differentiation with the synthesis of hCG have not been identified.

Most of the hCG produced by the syncytiotrophoblast is released into the maternal circulation in a pulsatile fashion. Human chorionic gonadotropin is detectable in the maternal serum 8 to 10 days after ovulation, coinciding with trophoblast formation and implantation of the blastocyst into the uterine wall.[50] Maternal serum hCG levels progressively rise and reach a peak at 9 to 10 weeks' gestation. After 10 weeks of pregnancy, placental secretion of hCG declines to comparatively low levels that are maintained to term. Concentrations of hCG in maternal blood are generally higher in multifetal gestations, reflecting a greater trophoblast mass, and in pregnancies complicated by chromosomal abnormalities. There is no correlation between maternal serum hCG levels and fetal sex or birth weight.

A number of substances may serve as tropic factors for hCG production, including (placental) GnRH, growth factors, and cytokines, by increasing hCG subunit gene transcription or stabilizing hCG subunit mRNAs. As described previously, cAMP, CRE-binding proteins, and other *trans*-acting factors control α subunit transcription by interacting with CREs, JREs, and upstream response elements in a combinatorial fashion.[6,13,14] Placental activins increase placental hCG secretion and may promote placental differentiation, whereas inhibins and follistatin decrease hCG secretion (see discussion to follow).[53] Additionally, trophoblast cells express LH/CG receptors and low levels of hCG may augment its production in an autocrine fashion.[54] Higher levels of hCG and progesterone inhibit hCG production, resulting in lower levels of maternal serum hCG after 10 weeks' gestation. Unidentified intracellular inhibitors probably appear in nonplacental tissues that prevent their expression of β-hCG genes.[16,50,51]

### Metabolism and Clearance of Chorionic Gonadotropin

Free α (regular and large forms) and β subunits and intact hCG are secreted by the trophoblast. The half-life of intact hCG is approximately 24 hours, as compared to 2 hours for LH, a 10-fold difference that is primarily due to the glycosylated C-terminal peptide of the β subunit. The half-lives of the free α and β subunits are approximately 2 and 4 hours, respectively. The majority of hCG and its subunits are cleared through the maternal kidneys at a rate that does not vary throughout gestation.

After secretion, the β-hCG subunit is subject to proteolysis. A single cleavage in the β subunit peptide, most commonly between residues 47 and 48, produces nicked hCG and nicked free β subunit (see Fig. 182-2).[48,55] Nicking of the β subunit markedly reduces its biologic activity. Nicked hCG molecules typically account for 10% to 20% of the hCG molecules present in the maternal serum and urine. Further catabolism of the nicked β subunit in the maternal kidney produces the β-core fragment, which is the terminal degradation product of β-hCG. The β-core fragment is comprised of two peptides, β subunit residues 6 to 40 and residues 55 to 92, held together by five disulfide linkages.[48] Although it is virtually undetectable in the maternal serum, the β-core fragment is the principal β-molecule present in the maternal urine. Thus, the trophoblast secretes intact hCG and free α and

β subunits; nicked and nonnicked forms of hCG and its subunits, as well as β-core fragment, are excreted in the maternal urine (see Fig. 182-2).

### Biologic Activities of Chorionic Gonadotropin

The primary role of hCG in the maternal organism is to serve as a signal to the ovary to maintain the corpus luteum, which would regress if it were not rescued by hCG. Human chorionic gonadotropin acts on the luteal cell LH/CG receptor, which activates adenylyl cyclase and possibly other signal transduction mechanisms to maintain the luteal steroidogenic machinery. Normal doubling time of maternal serum hCG levels, rather than absolute values of hCG, appears to promote rescue of the corpus luteum in early pregnancy.[56] The administration of antisera to hCG in early gestation causes pregnancy termination in primates.

Other roles for hCG have been suggested based on the discovery of LH/CG receptors in the endometrium, myometrium, and the placenta, suggesting that hCG plays a broader role throughout pregnancy than previously believed.[57–59] Stimulation of LH/CG receptors in the endometrium induces decidualization during the luteal phase of the menstrual cycle.[58,59] Within the placenta, hCG regulates the differentiation of cytotrophoblast cells into syncytiotrophoblast.[60] In the fetus, hCG derived from the trophoblast or possibly the fetal kidneys may regulate testicular testosterone production, which drives differentiation of the internal and external genitalia. Although the free hCG subunits are not generally believed to have biologic function, experiments have linked the α subunit to growth of nontrophoblastic tumors and the secretion of prolactin by decidual tissue.[61,62]

### Clinical Applications of Chorionic Gonadotropin Assays

The detection of hCG in the serum or urine serves as the basis of contemporary pregnancy tests. Current serum hCG assays have a sensitivity of approximately 25 IU/L (Third International Standard) and are able to detect pregnancy within 8 to 12 days after ovulation, whereas urine hCG assays generally detect hCG 14 to 18 days after ovulation. Sequential monitoring of quantitative hCG assays provides a biochemical index of growth of the conceptus. For the first 5 to 6 weeks of a normal pregnancy, serum hCG titers double every 1.5 to 2.5 days.[63] This pattern of hCG increase in maternal serum is abnormal in pregnancies that subsequently miscarry or when implantation of the embryo occurs at an ectopic site. In addition, serum hCG measurements may be compared to ultrasound findings in order to determine the location and viability of a pregnancy. An ectopic pregnancy must be considered when a gestational sac cannot be visualized within the uterus by transvaginal ultrasound and the maternal serum hCG titer exceeds 1500 IU/L.[64] Similarly, a missed abortion must be considered when fetal cardiac activity cannot be detected by transvaginal ultrasound and the maternal serum hCG exceeds 9000 IU/L.[64]

Measurements of maternal serum hCG in conjunction with α-fetoprotein, unconjugated estriol, and inhibin-A have been employed in the prenatal diagnosis of chromosomal abnormalities in so-called multiple marker screening. The combination of serum analytes (α-fetoprotein, hCG, unconjugated estriol, and inhibin-A) and maternal age allows detection of approximately 75% of fetuses with Down syndrome, for which the false-positive rate is 5%.[65] Unfortunately, multiple marker screening detects 90% of Down syndrome cases in women aged 35 years and older, but only 25% of cases in women in their early 20s. Because approximately 50% of fetuses with Down syndrome have abnormalities that can be detected by ultrasound, future programs based on various combinations of maternal age, first and second trimester serum markers, and first and second trimester ultrasound findings are undergoing investigation.[66–68]

During the second trimester, elevated hCG (intact, nicked, or free β subunit) is the most sensitive serum marker for Down syndrome. The β-core fragment is also being developed as an efficient urine screening test for Down syndrome.[48] In these pregnancies, elevated α subunit and β subunit hCG mRNA levels in the trophoblast have been discovered, although these genes are not located on chromosome 21.[28] Conversely, maternal serum hCG levels are decreased in pregnancies complicated by trisomy 18, for which screening may also include serum markers and ultrasound.[69]

In addition to screening for fetal aneuploidy, elevated levels of maternal serum and urine hCG have been used to predict adverse pregnancy outcomes associated with uteroplacental insufficiency (pregnancy-induced hypertension, intrauterine fetal growth restriction, and stillbirth).[19,70] Unexplained elevated maternal serum α-fetoprotein levels have also been shown to be associated with adverse pregnancy outcomes. Placental dysfunction and breakdown of the trophoblast barrier are thought to allow greater transfer of hCG and α-fetoprotein into the maternal serum.

Serum hCG measurements are used to diagnose and monitor therapy of gestational trophoblastic disease as well as other hCG-secreting neoplasms. Samples from women with gestational trophoblastic disease contain extremely high levels of nicked hCG and nicked free β subunit, which may lack its C-terminal extension.[55] Therefore, it is important to select an immunoassay that detects these metabolites and avoid the selection of assays that yield relatively frequent false-positive results.[71] In patients with nontrophoblastic tumors, hCG may occasionally be used to monitor therapy. Among testicular tumors, approximately 5% of seminomas and 66% of non-seminoma germ cell tumors screte free β-hCG.[72] Among ovarian tumors, more than one fourth secrete hCG, particularly germ cell tumors.

hCG can normally be detected in the maternal serum or urine up to 4 weeks after delivery at term. Because of the very high levels of hCG in the circulation during the first 10 weeks of pregnancy, hCG may be detected in maternal serum or urine for as many as 10 weeks after pregnancy termination in the first trimester. Outside of pregnancy, immunoreactive hCG has been found in low concentrations (<3 IU/L) in normal men and women, probably secondary to production in the pituitary gland.

### Inhibins, Activins, and Follistatin

The inhibins and activins are glycoproteins that belong to the transforming growth factor beta (TGF-β) family and participate in "fine-tuning" the hypothalamic-pituitary-gonadal secretion of gonadotropins.[73] Inhibins were initially discovered in the gonads and were shown to have an inhibitory effect on pituitary follicle-stimulating hormone (FSH) release.[53] Later, activins and follistatin were discovered in the gonads; activins stimulate FSH release whereas follistatin inhibits pituitary FSH secretion. Specific mRNAs for the inhibins, activins, and follistatin also are expressed in the human placenta, and the respective immunoreactive proteins are localized in small amounts within cytotrophoblast cells and abundantly within the syncytiotrophoblast. Activins stimulate secretion of the placental gonadotropin hCG, whereas inhibins and follistatin inhibit hCG secretion.[53] Mechanisms regulating the placental expression of these hormones have not been elucidated.

Inhibin is a dimeric protein that consists of an α subunit and one of two β subunits (βA or βB, forming inhibin A:αβA and inhibin B:αβB, respectively). Three forms of activin are distinguished by the combination of the two β subunits (activin A:βAβA, activin B:βBβB, and activin AB:βAβB). Follistatin is a single-chain glycoprotein that is present in three isoforms (31 kD, 35 kD, and 38 kD) and is structurally unrelated to the inhibins and activins. No differences in the biologic activities of the different isoforms of these three hormones have been discovered. (For more details, see Chapter 140.)

In addition to their effects on hCG secretion, immunomodulator and embryogenic roles have been proposed for inhibins, activins, and follistatin. Inhibins decrease the release of cytokines from lymphocytes, which may be an important function at the site of trophoblast implantation, whereas activins promote mesodermal differentiation in various animals. Activin receptors are present within the placenta; inhibin and follistatin receptors have not been identified.[74]

Abnormal maternal serum levels of inhibins and activins have been associated with various pregnancy complications. Low maternal serum levels of inhibin A at an early gestational age are associated with an increased risk of miscarriage before the onset of clinical symptoms, whereas elevated levels of inhibin A and activin A may be of value in diagnosis and management of molar pregnancy.[75-78] Pregnant women with pre-eclampsia, fetal growth restriction, and spontaneous preterm labor have elevated serum levels of activin A.[79] During the second trimester of Down syndrome pregnancies, placental and maternal serum inhibin A and activin A levels are 1.5- to 2-fold greater than the normal values.[80] Using two multiples of the median as the discriminatory value, univariate inhibin A analysis can detect 45% of Down syndrome cases at a 5% false-positive rate.[81] Hence, inhibin A measurements have been incorporated into multiple marker screening for fetal aneuploidy, as described previously.[65]

## CHORIONIC SOMATOMAMMOTROPIN AND VARIANT GROWTH HORMONE

### Chorionic Somatomammotropin–Growth Hormone Gene Cluster

The hCS-HGH gene family is represented by five linked genes that are located on human chromosome 17q22-24 (Fig. 182-3). Two HGH and three hCS genes constitute this cluster and are arranged from 5' to 3' as follows: HGH-N (N for normal), hCS-L (L for like), hCS-A (also referred to as hCS-1 or hPL-2), HGH-V (V for variant), and hCS-B (also referred to as hCS-2 or hPL-3).[82] As described earlier, activation of an LCR located upstream from the 5'-border of the hCS-HGH gene cluster appears to control expression of all five genes.[11,12] The hCS-HGH genes and the prolactin gene probably arose from a common ancestral precursor by gene duplication. Thus, the hCS and HGH mRNA sequences are greater than 90% identical, whereas prolactin shares approximately 40% identity with hCS and HGH mRNA.[83] All of the genes contain four introns and their intron-exon boundaries are highly conserved.

The hCS-A and hCS-B genes encode hCS, also called human placental lactogen (hPL). The hCS-A and hCS-B genes encode prehormones that differ at a single amino acid within the signal peptide region, but the mature hormone products are identical.[82] The HGH-N gene encodes pituitary HGH whereas the HGH-V gene encodes placental HGH-V, which differs from HGH-N by nonconservative substitutions at 13-amino acid residues dispersed throughout the protein. The fifth gene, hCS-L, contains a mutation at a splice donor site that interferes with intron processing, resulting in incompletely processed mRNA segments and no known protein products.

Although the amino acid content of the hormones produced by the genes within the hCS-HGH cluster has been conserved, the hCS, HGH, and prolactin receptors are dissimilar. Their extracellular domains demonstrate approximately 20% amino acid sequence identity; the intracellular domains are even less identical. Consequently, hCS binds to the HGH receptor only 1/2300 times as well as HGH.[83] Thus, receptor specificity and variable expression of these receptors in maternal and fetal tissues may delineate the various functions of the individual hormones.

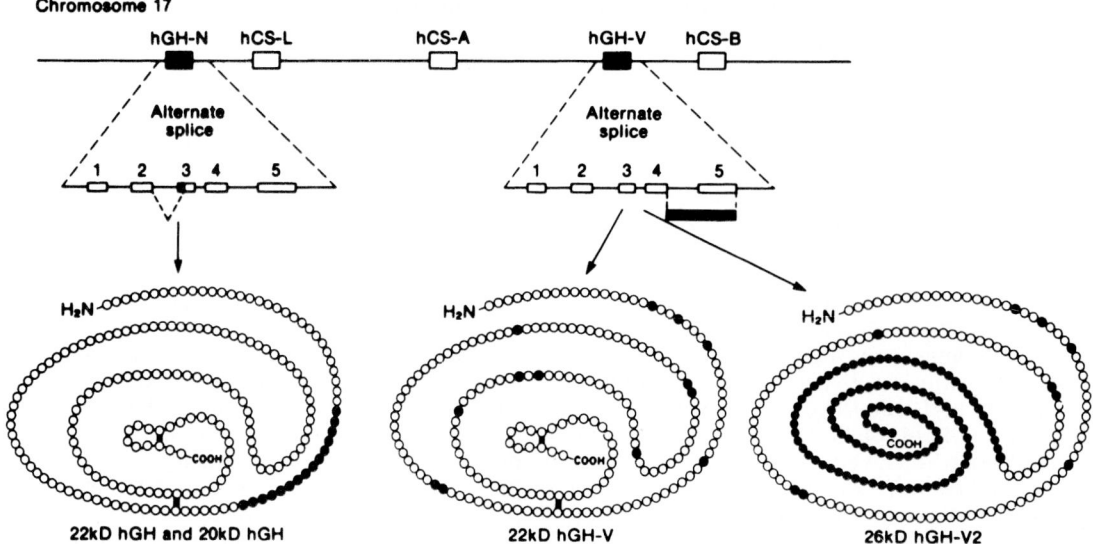

**Figure 182-3** The position of each of the genes in the human growth hormone–human chorionic somatomammotropin (hGH-hCS) gene cluster is represented on the *top line*. The exon-intron structure of the hGH-N (N for normal) and hGH-V (V for variant) genes is shown below the respective genes. The alternatively spliced region at the 5′ end of exon 3 in hGH-N and the 3′ end of exon 4 in hGH-V are both shown as *black rectangles* connected to the gene by *dotted lines*. The 20- and 22-kd hGH-N proteins and the 22- and 26-kd proteins of the hGH-V genes are shown below their respective genes. The 15 amino acids that are deleted in the hGH-N 20-kd protein by usage of the alternative splice site are shown in black in the left protein (hGH-N), the amino acid differences between the 22-kd hGH-N and hGH-V proteins are darkened in the middle protein (hGH-V), and the region of the C-terminus of the hGH-V2 protein that diverges from hGH-V is darkened in the right protein (hGH-V2). The 17.5-kd isoform of hGH-N and the glycosylated 25-kd isoform of hGH-V are not shown. (Adapted with permission from Cooke NE, Emery JG, Ray J, et al: Placental expression of the human growth hormone–variant gene. Troph Res 5:61, 1991.)

## Chorionic Somatomammotropin Structure and Sites of Synthesis

Chorionic somatomammotropin is a nonglycosylated 191-amino acid protein that is produced by the syncytiotrophoblast and extravillous trophoblast cells. It is synthesized with a 26-amino acid signal sequence that is cleaved posttranscriptionally. The hCS hormone is one of the major secretory products of the trophoblast, and is predominantly secreted into the maternal circulation. Concentrations of hCS rise progressively until 34 weeks' gestation and then plateau, reflecting changes in placental mass (Fig. 182-4). Because there is no circadian variation to hCS secretion and it has a short half-life (approximately 15 minutes) in the maternal circulation, hCS has been studied as a biochemical marker of placental function. Although low maternal serum levels of hCS were noted to be associated with fetal growth restriction and fetal distress in earlier studies, subsequent studies failed to substantiate the value of hCS monitoring for detecting fetal complications secondary to uteroplacental insufficiency.[84,85]

## Regulation of Chorionic Somatomammotropin Synthesis and Secretion

The hCS-A and hCS-B genes are transcribed at nearly equal levels during the first 8 weeks of pregnancy, but by term, hCS-A transcripts are approximately fivefold more abundant than hCS-B transcripts. Although the increase in hCS-A mRNA within villous tissue is three to six times greater than the increase in hCS-B mRNA, the stability of hCS-B mRNA is greater. The reader is cautioned, however, that these ratios vary widely among different placentas.[82] Because the two genes encode the same protein, the significance of this differential expression is unknown but may reflect the position of these genes within the hCS/HGH gene cluster and their ability to respond to transcription factors.

Interactions of proteins with enhancer sequences most likely play an integral role in the high levels of placenta-specific production of hCS. For example, the non-tissue-specific transcription factor Sp1 has an overlapping binding site with the pituitary-specific transcription factor Pit-1 in all genes of the hCS/HGH gene cluster.[82] In the pituitary gland, where the Pit-1 concentration is high, it gains access to the HGH-N promoter by outcompeting Sp1. In the placenta, where the concentration of Pit-1 is minimal, however, Sp1 plays a crucial role in binding to upstream hCS promoters and stimulating gene transcription. Placental specificity of hCS expression also may be governed by an enhancer element (CSEn) that is

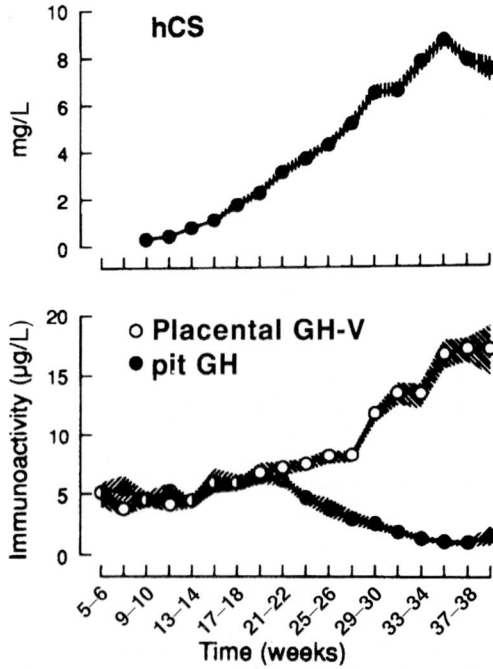

**Figure 182-4** Levels of human chorionic somatomammotropin (hCS; *upper panel*), pituitary growth hormone (pit GH; *solid circles, lower panel*), and placental growth hormone variant (placental GH-V; *open circles, lower panel*) during pregnancy. (Reprinted with permission from Frankenne F, Closset J, Gomez F, et al: The physiology of growth hormones in pregnant women and partial characterization of a placental variant. J Clin Endocrinol Metab 66:1171, 1988.)

located 2 kb downstream from the three hCS genes and gradually activated as syncytiotrophoblast is formed, or by another 1 kb sequence that is located 2 kb upstream from the promoter regions of the hCS and HGH-V genes but is absent from the HGH-N gene.[82,83] This upstream sequence, named "p," is responsible for suppression of expression of hCS genes in the pituitary gland.[18]

Although a variety of secretogogues may enhance hCS secretion, the mature hormone is not stored in secretory granules and it probably is rapidly released after synthesis. Therefore, maternal hormones, such as thyroid hormone, are more likely to regulate hCS synthesis rather than its secretion. A positive thyroid hormone response element has been discovered within the promoter region of hCS, and thyroid hormone appears to upregulate hCS gene expression.[83] There is also some evidence suggesting that GHRH stimulates but SRIF inhibits hCS production by trophoblastic cells.[86] Supporting this hypothesis is the finding that SRIF immunostaining in the placenta is most intense during early pregnancy when hCS production is lowest, and it declines as gestation progresses. SRIF does not, however, inhibit hCS secretion by term placental cells. Similarly, the dopamine agonist bromocriptine, which profoundly suppresses pituitary prolactin secretion, has no effect on maternal hCS levels in early pregnancy. In primate models, estrogen appears to promote morphologic differentiation of cytotrophoblasts into syncytiotrophoblast, which is associated with increased CS expression later in gestation.[87] During the first third of pregnancy, however, estrogen suppresses CS secretion by the syncytiotrophoblast; the physiologic consequences of these estrogen effects are not understood.[88]

A number of observations suggest that placental secretion of hCS is under maternal metabolic regulation; however, the existing data argue that glucose, insulin, amino acids, and lipids are not major short-term regulators of hCS secretion. Prolonged fasting leads to an increase in hCS in maternal serum, but shorter periods of fasting do not affect hCS secretion. Similarly, ingestion of protein- or glucose-rich meals does not have a marked effect on maternal hCS levels. Thus, the effects of maternal hypoglycemia or hyperglycemia on hCS secretion are less important than the effects of hCS on maternal glucose metabolism.

### Biologic Activities of Chorionic Somatomammotropin
The biologic activities of hCS, HGH, and prolactin overlap to some degree, and it is debatable whether hCS is an essential hormone of normal pregnancy.[89] The preponderance of evidence, however, suggests that hCS has metabolic, somatogenic, and lactogenic effects that allow the maternal environment to incur only minimal fluctuations, thereby ensuring the conceptus a continual supply of nutrients.[83]

The diabetogenic effect of pregnancy has been attributed to the actions of hCS, which increases lipolysis and maternal serum levels of free fatty acids, ketones, and glycerol.[83] In the fed state, free fatty acids interfere with insulin-directed entry of glucose into cells. In the fasting state, ketones may cross the placenta and serve as fuel for the fetus. Recent findings, however, suggest that the biologic activities of hCS are not responsible for acute changes in maternal lipolysis and glycemic control. For example, the administration of recombinant chorionic somatomammotropin has no effect on free fatty acid and glucose levels in animal models.[83] Similarly, maternal glucose levels do not appear to regulate hCS secretion acutely. The addition of glucose to placental lobules in vitro does not decrease hCS production, and hypoglycemia in diabetic women does not increase hCS levels in maternal serum.[90,91] Therefore, the integrated role of hCS in modulating maternal metabolism is probably of a chronic nature, over which time hCS dampens swings in nutrient levels that are available to the fetus.

Given the homology between hCS and HGH, there has been considerable interest in the potential role of hCS in fetal growth. Although the effects of hCS in the maternal compartment could have important consequences for fetal growth, its direct role in the fetal compartment may be limited by its concentration, which is 1/50th to 1/100th that of the maternal circulation.[83] During the third trimester of human pregnancy, hCS has been implicated in increasing maternal levels of insulin-like growth factor 1 (IGF-1), which upregulates cellular nutrient uptake, protein and DNA synthesis, and cell replication.[83,92] Fetal fibroblasts also can be stimulated by hCS to release IGF-1. Other evidence suggests that hCS directly upregulates pancreatic islet function, resulting in β-cell proliferation and enhanced insulin secretion.[83,93] These observations are supported by case reports describing fetal growth restriction in pregnancies that lack normal hCS production.[89]

The role of hCS in mammary gland development and function in the perinatal period is unclear. In animal models, recombinant chorionic somatomammotropin significantly increases mammary secretions and DNA content within mammary glands.[83] However, hCS cannot establish lactation in an in vitro system, whereas prolactin can.[94] Thus, the effect of hCS on the mammary gland may be to stimulate cell proliferation but not to enhance milk production.

### Variant Growth Hormone Structure and Sites of Synthesis
The amino acid differences between HGH-V and pituitary-derived HGH-N are largely nonconservative. Hence, their biologic properties may vary significantly, although both hormones affect target cells expressing the GH receptor.[95] The HGH-N gene is alternately spliced into three different mature mRNAs that produce the 22 kd major active HGH-N, a 20 kd variant lacking 15 amino acids from exon 3, and a 17.5 kd variant in which exon 3 is deleted (see Fig. 182-3). Two HGH-V isoforms are generated by alternate splicing of the HGH-V gene. The first isoform, the 22 kd HGH-V, consists of 191 amino acids and an N-glycosylation signal that yields two size variants, one glycosylated (25 kd) and the other nonglycosylated (22 kd).[96] The second isoform, the 26 kd HGH-V2, is derived from alternate splicing of HGH-V pre-RNA that leads to the incorporation of its fourth intron into its fifth exon.[82] This results in the loss of the N-glycosylation site and formation of a hydrophobic tail that anchors HGH-V2 to the membrane of the syncytium.

### Regulation of Variant Growth Hormone Synthesis and Secretion
Early in pregnancy, HGH-N is measurable in the maternal serum and it is secreted in a typical pulsatile fashion. Levels of HGH-V in maternal serum increase as pregnancy progresses, and it becomes the predominant HGH in maternal blood by the second trimester (see Fig. 182-4).[97] The HGH-V hormone stimulates maternal IGF-1 production, which inhibits HGH-N secretion through negative feedback action. Unlike HGH-N, secretion of HGH-V is not modulated by growth hormone releasing hormone and appears to occur at a relatively constant rate. Secretion of HGH-V is inhibited by glucose, and HGH-V is significantly decreased in the maternal circulation in pregnancies with fetal growth restriction.[96] HGH-V and IGF-1 mRNA expression is increased in placentas from pregnancies with fetal growth restriction, however, so the precise role of HGH-V in fetal growth restriction is unclear.[98] Conversely, elevated maternal serum levels of HGH-V in type 1 diabetics are associated with increased levels of IGF-1 and increased birth weights.[99]

Unlike hCS, which is produced throughout the syncytiotrophoblast, HGH-V is produced by a subpopulation of cells within the syncytium and at lower levels than hCS. These findings suggest differential control of the hCS and HGH-V genes, although tissue-specific synthesis of both genes may be governed by the absence or presence of transcription factors (i.e., Sp1, Pit-1) and gene enhancer sequences (see earlier discussion).[83]

## Biologic Activities of Variant Growth Hormone

Placental growth hormone does not appear to have a direct effect on fetal growth (HGH-V is not detectable in the fetal circulation; growth hormone receptors are sparse within the fetus), but it does have clear somatogenic activity.[83] These activities are mediated by maternal IGF-1, a peptide growth factor produced by most tissues that has multiple mitogenic effects on target cells, including increased amino acid transport, increased glucose uptake, enhanced nucleic acid and protein synthesis, and cell replication.[92] Local and hepatic synthesis of IGF-1 is stimulated by HGH-V, and increases in maternal HGH-V levels during pregnancy are paralleled by increases in IGF-1 during the second half of gestation. Hence, HGH-V and IGF-1 promote gluconeogenesis, lipolysis, and anabolism in the maternal liver and other organs, which increases nutrient availability for the fetoplacental unit.[96] Additionally, functional HGH receptors are present on the syncytiotrophoblast, suggesting autocrine and paracrine functions.

## Are Chorionic Somotomammotropin and HGH-V Essential Hormones?

In most cases where the hCS-A, hCS-B, and HGH-V genes were deleted, pregnancy and product were normal.[82] The women had normal glucose tolerance throughout gestation, their offspring were of normal size, and lactation was established after delivery. It should be noted that hormones with similar activities to hCS and HGH-V, such as HGH-N and prolactin, may have subsumed hCS and HGH-V functions. Additionally, the expression of hCS-L has not been explored in these cases. In another report, severe fetal growth restriction resulted from a pregnancy that completely lacked the gene products of hCS-A, hCS-B, and HGH-V.[89] Thus, whether or not hCS and HGH-V are essential for normal pregnancy remains controversial.

## *LEPTIN*

Leptin is the 16-kD protein product of the obese (ob) gene that is secreted by adipose tissue. Leptin appears to be involved in energy homeostasis, and circulating leptin levels have been correlated with adiposity in children and adults. Maternal plasma leptin levels are markedly elevated during pregnancy and leptin production has been detected in the placenta.[100] Although the somatropic properties of leptin are not completely understood, leptin has been shown to stimulate the activity of a key amino acid transporter (system A) in the syncytiotrophoblast.[101] Consequently, elevated umbilical cord levels of leptin have been associated with leptin mRNA expression in the placenta, placental size, and fetal macrosomia, whereas low concentrations of leptin in umbilical cord blood have been associated with fetal growth restriction.[102–105] Dysregulation of leptin metabolism also has been implicated in the pathogenesis of other pregnancy complications, including recurrent miscarriage and preeclampsia.[106–108]

## *METASTIN*

Metastin is a 54-amino acid peptide hormone encoded by a putative metastasis suppressor gene named KISS-1, and metastin has been shown to suppress the motility of melanoma cells. Metastin mRNA and immunoreactivity has been localized within the syncytiotrophoblast, and maternal serum levels of immunoreactive metastin progressively increase throughout pregnancy, falling rapidly after delivery.[109] The transcriptional expression profile of KISS-1 in the placenta suggests that metastin has a role in the invasive and migratory properties of trophoblast cells.[110]

# STEROID HORMONES

The syncytiotrophoblast is the primary site of steroidogenesis, and the capacity of the placenta to produce steroid hormones increases progressively as the placenta grows and the syncytiotrophoblast accumulates. As cytotrophoblastic cells terminally differentiate into syncytiotrophoblast, the intracellular cAMP signaling system is activated, and cAMP causes mRNA levels of all the placental steroidogenic enzymes to increase.[13] As a result, the placental steroids, which are secreted primarily into the maternal circulation, are sufficient to fully support the pregnancy by the eighth week of gestation. The placenta is also a site of steroid hormone metabolism, sheltering the fetus from bioactive maternal steroids.

The human placenta operates in close communication with the developing fetus in the biosynthesis and actions of steroid hormones during pregnancy. For example, the placenta produces progestins and estrogens but cannot synthesize androgens because the enzyme P-450c17 (17α-hydroxylase, 17,20 lyase) is not expressed in the placenta. Therefore, placental estrogen formation depends on a supply of androgen precursors from the fetus and mother. In turn, estrogen stimulates receptor-mediated uptake of low-density lipoproteins (LDLs) and cholesterol side-chain cleavage enzyme (P-450scc) activity within the syncytiotrophoblast, which control the initial steps of progesterone and estrogen synthesis.[111]

Because the placenta is an ephemeral organ that is discarded after delivery, its evolution has likely been driven by unique forces. As a result, placental steroidogenesis has acquired characteristics that distinguish it from steroidogenesis in the adrenal glands and ovaries.[112] For example, the 3β-hydroxysteroid dehydrogenase (3β-HSD) gene expressed in the placenta differs from that expressed in the gonads and the adrenal cortex. Other enzymes, including P-450scc and aromatase (P-450aro), are driven by unique transcription factors acting on *cis* elements in their promoters that differ from those driving expression of these genes in the gonads and adrenal cortex.

## *PROGESTERONE*

### Biosynthesis of Progesterone

All steroid hormones are derived from cholesterol (Fig. 182-5). Progesterone is synthesized in the placenta mainly from cholesterol that is transported by lipoproteins in the maternal circulation. Receptors for low-density lipoproteins, very low-density lipoproteins (VLDLs), and high-density lipoproteins (HDLs) are expressed on the syncytiotrophoblast and mediate uptake of cholesterol. The relative quantitative significance of each of these lipoproteins is not fully determined, although LDLs and VLDLs are probably major sources of cholesterol for the placenta since they are abundant in maternal serum throughout pregnancy.[113] In a subset of pregnant women with familial hypobetalipoproteinemia, progesterone levels were substantially lower than in normal controls, supporting a key role for LDLs in placental progesterone production.[114] Steroidogenic cells can also synthesize cholesterol de novo from acetate, but this pathway is considered to be limited in the placenta.

Within the syncytiotrophoblast, free cholesterol is mobilized into mitochondria. The movement of cholesterol across the mitochondrial membrane is the rate-limiting step of steroidogenesis in most cell types and is facilitated by the steroidogenic acute regulatory protein (StAR).[115] However, StAR is not expressed in the placenta and cholesterol must enter the mitochondria via a StAR-independent pathway.[116] Consequently, mutations in StAR, which result in almost total disruption of adrenal and gonadal steroidogenesis (the syndrome known as congenital lipoid adrenal hyperplasia), do not affect placental steroidogenesis.[117]

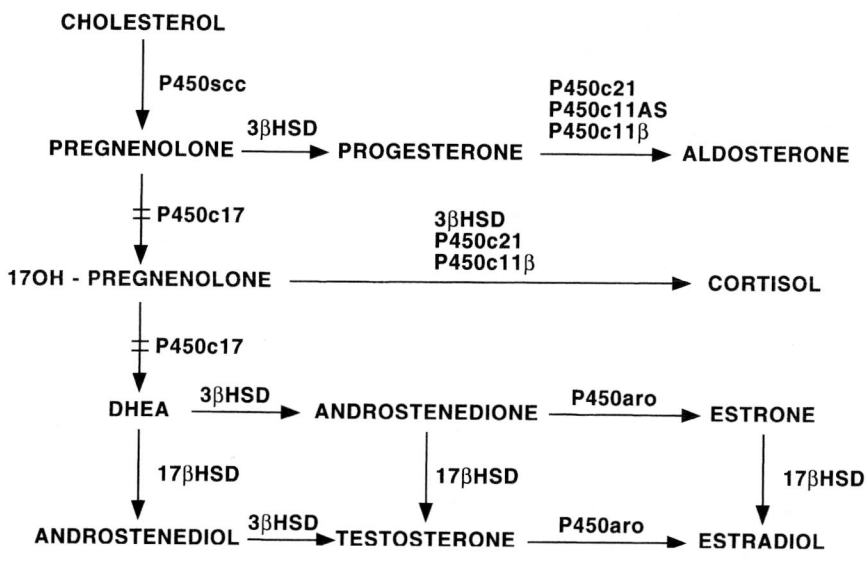

*Figure 182-5* The principal pathways of steroid hormone synthesis. Cholesterol is provided to the placenta by the maternal circulation; dehydroepiandrosterone (DHEA) is primarily derived from the fetal adrenal cortex. The placental deficiency of P-450c17 prevents placental production of 17-hydroxy-pregnenolone (17OH-pregnenolone) and DHEA. HSD, hydroxysteroid dehydrogenase.

Cholesterol is converted to pregnenolone in the inner mitochondrial membrane by the enzymatic activity of P-450scc, which is encoded by a single gene on chromosome 15. This reaction is the rate-limiting step in the synthesis of progesterone by the placenta.[118] cAMP increases P-450scc gene transcription in human trophoblast cells, but the *cis* elements in the P-450scc gene that respond to cAMP stimulation are different from those in the adrenal cortex and gonads.[112] In addition, whereas cholesterol delivery appears to regulate P-450scc activity in other steroidogenic tissues, adrenodoxin reductase, which promotes electron delivery from adrenodoxin to P-450scc, primarily regulates P-450scc activity in the placenta.[119] Finally, *trans*-acting factors (such as steroidogenic factor-1 and Dax-1) that drive transcription of steroidogenic enzymes, including P-450scc, 3β-HSD, and P-450aro, are not present in trophoblastic cells. Thus, mutations in the Dax-1 gene cause X-linked congenital adrenal hypoplasia, but do not affect antenatal development.[112] Unique "placenta-specific" *trans* factors have not yet been identified.

Like all cytochrome P-450 oxidases, P-450scc is energy dependent, requiring the donation of electrons from nicotinamide adenine dinucleotide phosphate (NADPH). This process is mediated by ferredoxin reductase (or adrenodoxin reductase), which donates electrons from NADPH to the iron protein ferredoxin, which then donates them to P-450scc.[120] Mutations in the P-450scc gene have not been described in humans because they presumably would be incompatible with the maintenance of pregnancy secondary to resultant placental progesterone deficiency.

After its formation, pregnenolone is converted into progesterone by 3β-HSD, a typical short-chain dehydrogenase that is encoded by tandemly duplicated genes on chromosome 1 that produce proteins with similar or identical activities.[120] The human 3β-HSD type I gene is expressed in the placenta, whereas the type II gene is expressed in the adrenals and gonads.[121] The two enzymes differ by 12 amino acids, and the placental isoform (3β-HSD-1) more efficiently converts pregnenolone into progesterone. Because P-450c17 is not present in the placenta, almost all of the pregnenolone is converted by 3β-HSD-1 to progesterone. Mutations in the 3β-HSD-1 gene have never been described in humans, probably because inactivating mutations would interrupt placental progesterone synthesis, causing spontaneous abortion.

### Pattern of Placental Progesterone Secretion
The preimplantation embryo does not appear to secrete significant amounts of progesterone, and progesterone secretion by the placenta is generally thought to be insufficient to maintain gestation until approximately 8 weeks of pregnancy (based on the woman's last menstrual period) have passed. Before this time, the corpus luteum is the primary source of progesterone, and its removal before the eighth week can result in spontaneous abortion. In common practice, women who are diagnosed with luteal phase defect (defined as a lag of 2 or more days in histologic development of the endometrium, presumably due to inadequate corpus luteal progesterone secretion), may be supported with progesterone suppositories for the first 8 to 10 weeks of gestation, by which time the placenta has supplanted the corpus luteum as the major source of progesterone.

At term, the placenta produces about 300 mg of progesterone per day in single pregnancies.[112] Eighty-five percent or more of the progesterone produced by the placenta enters the maternal compartment, where serum concentrations range from 100 to 300 μg/L. The principal route of progesterone metabolism is 5α-reduction, followed by hepatic conjugation with sulfuric acid and excretion into bile.

### Actions of Progesterone
The primary function of progesterone is to support pregnancy. It prepares the endometrium for implantation of the embryo, maintains uterine quiescence throughout gestation, and modulates the maternal immune system to prevent rejection of the fetus.

Progesterone suppresses the calcium-calmodulin-myosin light-chain kinase system in uterine smooth muscle, in part by regulating calcium channels and the mobilization of calcium from intracellular stores via regulation of adrenergic receptors.[111] In addition, progesterone inhibits gap junction formation between myometrial cells and upregulates the metabolism of prostaglandins, which are potent uterotonic agents, by prostaglandin dehydrogenase.[122,123] These effects of progesterone appear to be receptor mediated, and can be blocked by the progesterone receptor antagonist RU486 (mifepristone). Antiprogestins such as RU486 have been used as abortifacients, interrupting pregnancy soon after contraception, and can be used to prepare the uterus for parturition, probably by promoting gap junction formation and calcium channel biosynthesis.[124,125] It should be noted that progesterone withdrawal does not precede labor, and RU486 does not normally induce labor by itself later in pregnancy.[124,126] Binding of progesterone receptors to their nuclear response elements is reduced in decidual tissue after labor, however, compared to samples obtained from women preceding labor, which may provide a mechanism for the effective withdrawal of progesterone in human parturition.[127]

Progesterone has been proposed to play a role in the maternal acceptance of the fetal semiallograft by its suppressive actions on lymphocyte toxicity. Specifically, progesterone promotes production of cytokines by lymphocytes that support fetoplacental growth and inhibits the production of cytolytic cytokines.[111]

Despite the varied roles of progesterone in pregnancy, the question of whether placental progesterone production is required for maintenance of human pregnancy remains difficult to answer. The concept that placental progesterone is essential for normal pregnancy is supported by negative data. There are no known informative mutations affecting genes involved in placental progesterone synthesis, including the P-450scc and 3β-HSD genes.[112] Such mutations would prevent placental progesterone synthesis, which appears to be required to achieve a normal gestation.

### Clinical Utility of Progesterone Assays

Early in pregnancy, abnormal gestations, including ectopic pregnancies and abortive gestations, are frequently associated with low maternal serum progesterone levels. The low progesterone values during this time reflect deficient stimulation of the corpus luteum, presumably caused by lower hCG secretion and, to a lesser extent, diminished trophoblast progesterone production. Serum progesterone levels cannot distinguish miscarriage from ectopic pregnancy, but discriminatory levels ranging from 8 ng/mL to 18 ng/mL have been used to differentiate these abnormal gestations from normal intrauterine pregnancies.[128] The sensitivity for values less than the discriminatory value is approximately 90%. The specificity ranges from 85% to 90%. Serum values above 25 ng/mL are considered normal; if values are less than 5 ng/mL, diagnostic uterine evacuation may be performed. Progesterone values between 5 and 25 ng/mL warrant further sonographic evaluation.[129]

## ESTROGENS

### Biosynthesis of Estrogen

The biosynthesis of estrogens during pregnancy involves a complex interplay between the placenta and the fetal adrenal glands (Fig. 182-6). The placenta is capable of carrying out the terminal steps in estrogen synthesis, but is incapable of producing androgens because it does not express P-450c17 (see Fig. 182-5). Thus, the immediate androgen precursors of placental estrogens are provided mainly by the fetal adrenal cortex.

The fetal adrenal cortex is a large organ whose size (approximately 10 g) relative to body weight is 25 times larger than the adult adrenal glands. The fetal zone comprises greater than 85% of the adrenal cortex, but this region involutes after birth. The fetal zone has abundant P-450c17 activity and produces large amounts of DHEA (see Fig. 182-5). However, the fetal zone is relatively deficient in 3β-HSD-2 activity and produces very little progesterone and cortisol. The much smaller definitive zone of the fetal adrenal cortex differentiates after delivery, becoming the zona glomerulosa and, possibly, the zona fasciculata of the adult adrenal gland.[120]

The fetal adrenal gland, which is steroidogenically competent by 8 weeks' gestation, undergoes its greatest period of growth during the first trimester independent of ACTH stimulation. The rapid growth of the fetal adrenal gland during this period may be influenced by other hormones, such as hCG, HGH, or prolactin. Later in pregnancy, however, fetal pituitary hormones are essential for steroidogenesis by the adrenal cortex. Anencephalic fetuses that have poor pituitary development and minimal ACTH production have normal adrenal glands up to 14 or 15 weeks' gestation, but the fetal zone of their adrenal glands undergoes atrophy after 20 weeks' gestation.[130] Additionally, LDL cholesterol levels are elevated in the anencephalic fetus, presumably reflecting the

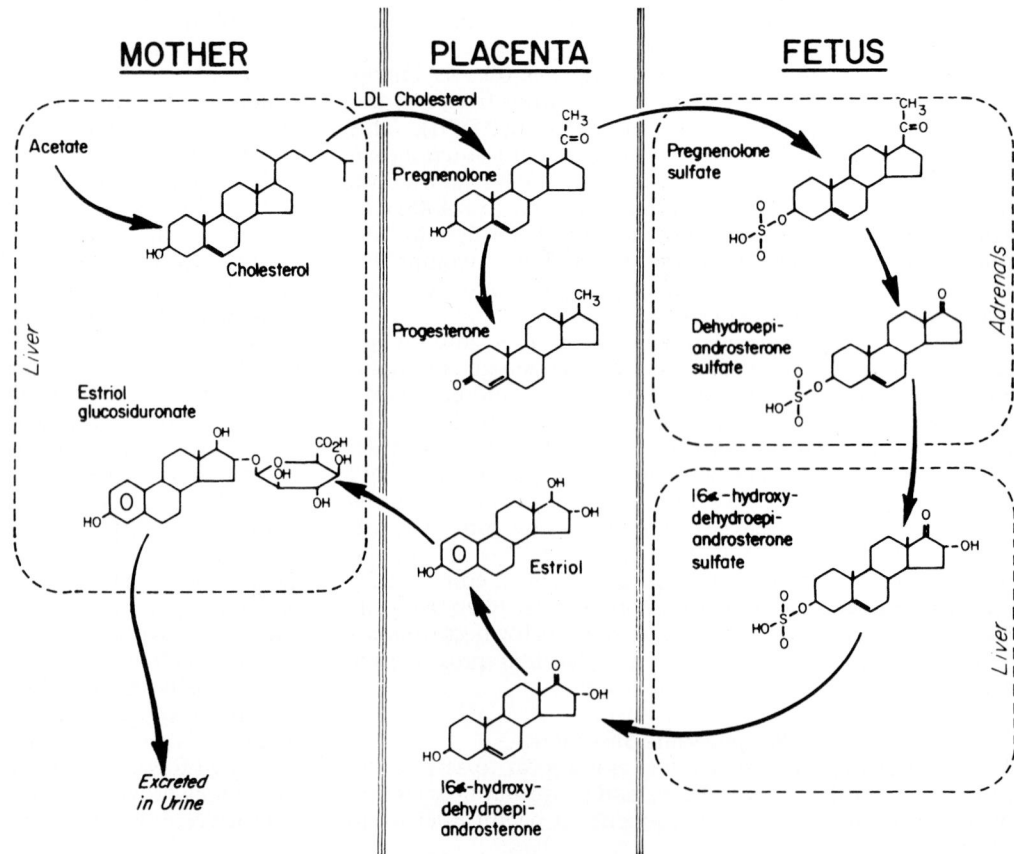

*Figure 182-6* Schematic view of estriol biosynthesis in late pregnancy. (Reprinted with permission from Jaffe RB: Neuroendocrine-metabolic regulation of pregnancy. In Yen SSC, Jaffe RB [eds]: Reproductive Endocrinology, 3d ed. Philadelphia, WB Saunders, 1991.)

diminished metabolism of plasma cholesterol into steroids when the fetal zone is atrophic.

The actions of ACTH in the fetal adrenal glands are mediated by IGF-2, which promotes cell proliferation, and adenylate cyclase, which stimulates steroidogenesis.[131] High levels of ACTH are maintained in the fetal plasma because the adrenal glands have minimal 3β-HSD-2 activity and produce very little cortisol, which normally inhibits pituitary ACTH production. Additionally, placental 11β-HSD-2 inactivates maternal cortisol into cortisone. The net result of these enzymatic activities (3β-HSD-2 and 11β-HSD-2) is fetal cortisol levels that are about 10% to 20% of those found in the maternal circulation.[120]

The steroidogenic capacity of the fetal adrenal cortex is remarkable. These glands convert fetal LDL cholesterol into 100 to 200 mg of steroid per day, which accounts for 90% of the precursor of estriol formed in the placenta at term. The principal steroid product, DHEA, is converted to DHEA-sulfate (DHEA-S) by the abundant steroid sulfotransferase activity of the fetal adrenal.[120] The resulting sulfated compound cannot serve as a substrate for 3β-HSD-2 in the fetal adrenal and it is secreted into the fetal circulation, where it undergoes 16α-hydroxylation in the fetal liver. Only a small fraction of DHEA-S secreted by the adrenal cortex escapes 16α-hydroxlation in the fetal liver.

The resulting 16α-hydroxy-DHEA-S serves as the major substrate for placental sulfatase, 3β-HSD-1, 17β-HSD, and P-450aro to become estriol (E$_3$) (see Fig. 182-5). Much smaller amounts of DHEA-S reach the placenta without undergoing 16α-hydroxylation in the fetal liver, and are converted by 3β-HSD-1, 17β-HSD, and P-450aro into estradiol (E$_2$) or by 3β-HSD-1 and P-450aro (without the action of 17β-HSD) into estrone (E$_1$) (see Fig. 182-5). Because 16α-hydroxy-DHEA-S is much more abundant in the placental circulation than DHEA-S, the resultant ratio of E$_1$:E$_2$:E$_3$ produced by the placenta is approximately 14:5:81.[120]

Male fetuses with X-linked sulfatase deficiency, which is usually caused by gene deletions, cannot convert (16α-hydroxy-) DHEA-S into (16α-hydroxy-) DHEA within the placenta and produce abnormally low amounts of estrogen during pregnancy. These fetuses develop normally and reach term, but may suffer from X-linked ichthyosis after birth. Some reports describe a failure of cervical ripening and the onset of spontaneous labor in this condition.[120] Although these observations suggest that high estrogen levels during late pregnancy are important for the preparation of the reproductive tract for parturition, other enzyme deficiencies that cause diminished placental estrogen production are not associated with failed labor.

The key enzyme in placental estrogen synthesis, P-450aro, is colocalized with sulfatase to the apical (microvillous) surface of the syncytiotrophoblast. This positioning maximizes the ability of these two enzymes to generate estrogen for secretion into the maternal compartment.[112] Aromatase is responsible for converting 19-carbon androgens into 18-carbon estrogens (E$_1$, E$_2$, and E$_3$). Placental P-450aro activity increases substantially as syncytiotrophoblast accumulates, thereby preventing the secretion of androgenic steroids into the maternal compartment and excluding maternal androgens from the fetus. Rare cases of aromatase deficiency have been associated with maternal and fetal virilization, but these fetuses achieve term gestation and undergo normal parturition.

Aromatase is an enzyme complex that is comprised of two polypeptides, the ubiquitous NADPH-cytochrome P-450 reductase and the unique P-450aro, which is encoded by a single-copy gene (CYP19) that spans 75 kb on human chromosome 15. The protein coding sequence of CYP19 is contained within nine exons that are expressed in the placenta, gonads, and adipose tissue. The 5'-untranslated region of the P-450aro gene contains exon 1 and tissue-specific promoter sequences.[112] Putative enhancer elements that are necessary

for trophoblast-specific expression of P-450aro have been described in the 5'-untranslated region between 42 and 501 bp upstream from exon 1.[132] Additionally, regulatory elements within the 5'-flanking region appear to bind inhibitory transcription factors that are expressed in nontrophoblastic cells.[132] Because P-450aro gene expression is induced as cytotrophoblastic cells terminally differentiate into syncytiotrophoblast in vitro, transcription factors that regulate trophoblast differentiation may also be involved with P-450aro expression in the placenta.

At least two of the more than eight different 17β-HSDs are expressed in the placenta. The type I 17β-HSD isoenzyme catalyzes the conversion of the biologically inert estrogen, estrone, to the active estrogen, 17β-estradiol. The type II 17β-HSD isoenzyme is encoded by a distinct gene and oxidizes 17β-estradiol into estrone. Whereas 17β-HSD type I is expressed in the syncytiotrophoblast, the type II isoenzyme is expressed primarily within the endothelial cells of fetal capillaries and placental vessels.[133] The type II isoenzyme is positioned to convert placental estradiol into the inactive estrogen, estrone, reducing the delivery of biologically potent estrogens into the fetal compartment.

### Pattern of Placental Estrogen Secretion

Early in pregnancy, estradiol is the major form of estrogen produced by the maternal ovaries. After the sixth week of gestation, the placenta begins to produce increasing amounts of estrogen that are primarily derived from fetal DHEA-S. After the first trimester, the placenta is the major site of estradiol and estrone synthesis, whereas estriol is produced almost exclusively by the placenta. Estradiol and estrone levels rise progressively in the maternal serum throughout pregnancy and, by term, their concentrations are approximately 15 μg/L and 8 μg/L, respectively. The placental production of estriol parallels the growth of the fetal adrenal cortex and far exceeds that of estradiol and estrone. Unlike estradiol, which is largely bound to sex hormone–binding globulin, estriol is unconjugated in the maternal serum. Thus, estriol is rapidly excreted into the urine (t$_{1/2}$ = 5 to 8 minutes) and its concentration in the maternal serum at term is similar to that of estradiol.

### Actions of Estrogens

Estrogens have been postulated to have a number of important functions in maintaining pregnancy and preparing the reproductive tract for parturition. The rare cases of steroidogenic enzyme deficiencies described previously suggest, however, that a considerable excess of estrogen is produced by the fetoplacental unit and that the physiologic actions of estrogen may be carried out at much lower local concentrations.[111] Because placental estrogen formation is dependent on androgenic precursors (DHEA-S and 16α-hydroxy-DHEA-S) produced by the fetal adrenal, the fetus appears to be ultimately responsible for many of the maternal physiologic effects mediated by estrogen.

Estrogen acts in the trophoblast to stimulate receptor-mediated LDL uptake.[111] Additionally, estrogen enhances placental expression of P-450scc and 11β-HSD-2.[134] Trophoblast 11β-HSD-2 inactivates maternal cortisol, isolating the fetal pituitary and hypothalamus from maternal influence. In turn, fetal ACTH stimulates production of large amounts of DHEA-S and much smaller amounts of cortisol by the fetal adrenal cortex. Fetal cortisol is thought to regulate surfactant biosynthesis, fetal lung maturation, and placental CRH production, which stimulates parturition.[135] Collectively, these observations illustrate the unique interactions between the fetus and the placenta that regulate placental steroidogenesis.

Estrogens also regulate uterine blood flow in nonpregnant and pregnant animals.[111] The maternal spiral arteries within the endometrial and myometrial portions of the uterine wall are invaded by placental trophoblastic cells during the first half of pregnancy, and these vessels become widely dilated and relatively insensitive to regulation via the maternal autonomic nervous system. Instead, humoral factors such as estrogen increase blood flow in the vascular beds of the myometrium and endometrium.[136] The effects of estrogen on uterine blood flow are mediated, in part, by prostanoids. In addition to its effect on uteroplacental blood flow, estrogen has been shown to induce neovascularization within the placenta, possibly by upregulating growth factors such as IGF and vacular endothelial growth factor.[111] These effects of estrogen on the uterine and placental circulations are tonic in nature and do not elicit acute changes in blood flow.

There is strong evidence that estrogen regulates end-of-gestation events, including parturition and lactation. Late in gestation, estrogen activates maternal circadian rhythms that increase oxytocin secretion and induces myometrial gap junction formation that coordinates myometrial contractions.[39] Estrogen also stimulates mammary epithelial cell proliferation in human breast tissue. The mitogenic actions of estrogen on the mammary gland appear to involve the stimulation of growth factors, including IGF-1 and epithelial growth factor. These actions of estrogen are examples of the fetus regulating maternal physiology during pregnancy.

### Clinical Utility of Estrogen Assays
Because estriol is almost exclusively a fetal product that is secreted into the maternal circulation, maternal concentrations of estriol may reflect abnormalities in fetal and placental development. For example, fetal death during the second or third trimester produces a striking drop in maternal estriol concentrations within a few hours. Hence, measurements of plasma unconjugated estriol or urinary total estriol were used for nearly 2 decades as biochemical indices of fetal well-being. Estetrol, which is produced by 15α- and 16α-hydroxylation of estradiol sulfate and DHEA-S in the fetal liver, has also been detected in the maternal serum and used as a marker of fetal well-being. The large intrapatient variability in serum estrogen measurements precludes its clinical usefulness, however, and estriol and estetrol measurements have been replaced by ultrasound technologies (i.e., fetal biophysical profile) as tools to monitor high-risk pregnancies.

In the past 15 years, serum unconjugated estriol levels have been included in prenatal serum screening for Down syndrome and other chromosomal abnormalities. Currently, 90% of women in the second trimester of pregnancy undergo multiple marker screening, which includes measurements of maternal serum α-fetoprotein, unconjugated estriol, inhibin-A, and hCG. Compiled data of 21 studies demonstrate that serum unconjugated estriol levels are low in Down syndrome pregnancies, averaging 0.72 multiples of the median value in normal pregnancies.[81] The inclusion of unconjugated estriol in maternal serum screening raises the detection rate for Down syndrome by approximately 5% to 10%. The pathophysiologic basis for low serum unconjugated estriol levels in Down syndrome is not known, but several theories have been proposed. The fetoplacental unit may be developmentally delayed, resulting in decreased production of estriol and increased production of hCG (reflecting first-trimester values). Other placental secretory products are not decreased in these pregnancies, however. Another possibility is that the fetus may be hyposecretory in these pregnancies, while the placenta is hypersecretory, but this theory has not been substantiated.

Another proposed application of estrogen assays during pregnancy is to predict spontaneous preterm birth. Serum estriol levels generally increase in the weeks preceding labor and salivary levels of estriol closely approximate the level of unconjugated estriol in the maternal serum. Hence, salivary estriol levels have been used to predict preterm birth because they are relatively easy to sample and they do not have wide fluctuations throughout the day as seen with serum assays. A single elevated level of salivary estriol obtained after 22 weeks' gestation has a sensitivity of approximately 40% for predicting spontaneous delivery before 36 weeks' gestation in low-risk and high-risk patients.[137] The positive predictive value in low-risk patients is 14%, however; in high-risk patients, the positive predictive value is 26%.

## REFERENCES

1. Damsky CH, Fitzgerald ML, Fisher SJ: Distribution patterns of extracellular matrix components and adhesion receptors are intricately modulated during first trimester cytotrophoblast differentiation along the invasive pathway, in vivo. J Clin Invest 89:210–222, 1992.
2. Parry S, Holder J, Strauss JF III: Mechanisms of trophoblast-virus interaction. J Reprod Immunol 37:25–34, 1997.
3. Petraglia F, Calza L, Garuti GC, et al: New aspects of placental endocrinology. J Endocrinol Invest 13:353–371, 1990.
4. Morrish DW, Marusyk H, Bhardwaj D: Ultrastructural localization of human placental lactogen in distinctive granules in human term placenta: Comparison with granules containing human chorionic gonadotropin. J Histochem Cytochem 36:193–197, 1988.
5. Jablonka-Shariff A, Garcia-Campayo V, Boime I: Evolution of lutropin to chorionic gonadotropin generates a specific routing signal for apical release in vivo. J Biol Chem 277:879–882, 2002.
6. Knoll BJ: Gene expression in the human placental trophoblast: A model for developmental gene regulation. Placenta 13:311–327, 1992.
7. Salem HT, Menabawey M, Seppala M, et al: Human seminal plasma contains a wide range of trophoblast-"specific" proteins. Placenta 5:413–417, 1984.
8. Cross JC, Anson-Cartwright L, Scott IC: Transcription factors underlying the development and endocrine functions of the placenta. Recent Prog Horm Res 57:221–234, 2002.
9. Tarrade A, Lai Kuen R, Malassine A, et al: Characterization of human villous and extravillous trophoblasts isolated from first trimester placenta. Lab Invest 81:1199–1211, 2001.
10. Lacroix MC, Guibourdenche J, Frendo JL, et al: Human placental growth hormone: A review. Placenta 23(Suppl A):S87–S94, 2002.
11. Kimura AP, Liebhaber SA, Cooke NE: Epigenetic modifications at the human growth hormone locus predict distinct roles for histone acetylation and methylation in placental gene activation. Mol Endocrinol 18:1018–1032, 2004.
12. Ho Y, Liebhaber SA, Cooke NE: Activation of the human GH gene cluster: Roles for targeted chromatin modification. Trends Endocrinol Metab 15:40–45, 2004.
13. Strauss JF III, Kido S, Sayegh R, et al: The cAMP signalling system and human trophoblast function. Placenta 13:389–403, 1992.
14. Budworth PR, Quinn PG, Nilson JH: Multiple characteristics of a pentameric regulatory array endow the human alpha-subunit glycoprotein hormone promoter with trophoblast specificity and maximal activity. Mol Endocrinol 11:1669–1680, 1997.
15. Pittman RH, Clay CM, Farmerie TA, Nilson JH: Functional analysis of the placenta-specific enhancer of the human glycoprotein hormone alpha subunit gene: Emergence of a new element. J Biol Chem 269:19360–19368, 1994.
16. Albanese C, Colin IM, Crowley WF, et al: The gonadotropin genes: Evolution of distinct mechanisms for hormonal control. Recent Prog Horm Res 51:23–58, discussion 59–61, 1996.
17. Ghosh D, Ezashi T, Ostrowski MC, Roberts RM: A central role for Ets-2 in the transcriptional regulation and cyclic adenosine 5'-monophosphate responsiveness of the human chorionic gonadotropin-beta subunit gene. Mol Endocrinol 17:11–26, 2003.

18. Nachtigal MW, Nickel BE, Cattini PA: Pituitary-specific repression of placental members of the human growth hormone gene family: A possible mechanism for locus regulation. J Biol Chem 268:8473–8479, 1993.

19. Chandra S, Scott H, Dodds L, et al: Unexplained elevated maternal serum alpha-fetoprotein and/or human chorionic gonadotropin and the risk of adverse outcomes. Am J Obstet Gynecol 189:775–781, 2003.

20. Yamada K, Ogawa H, Honda S, et al: A GCM motif protein is involved in placenta-specific expression of human aromatase gene. J Biol Chem 274:32279–32286, 1999.

21. Morrish DW, Dakour J, Li H: Life and death in the placenta: New peptides and genes regulating human syncytiotrophoblast and extravillous cytotrophoblast lineage formation and renewal. Curr Protein Pept Sci 2:245–259, 2001.

22. Malassine A, Cronier L: Hormones and human trophoblast differentiation: A review. Endocrine 19:3–11, 2002.

23. White RB, Eisen JA, Kasten TL, Fernald RD: Second gene for gonadotropin-releasing hormone in humans. Proc Natl Acad Sci U S A 95:305–309, 1998.

24. Siler-Khodr TM, Grayson M: Action of chicken II GnRH on the human placenta. J Clin Endocrinol Metab 86:804–810, 2001.

25. Chou CS, Zhu H, MacCalman CD, Leung PC: Regulatory effects of gonadotropin-releasing hormone (GnRH) I and GnRH II on the levels of matrix metalloproteinase (MMP)-2, MMP-9, and tissue inhibitor of metalloproteinase-1 in primary cultures of human extravillous cytotrophoblasts. J Clin Endocrinol Metab 88:4781–4790, 2003.

26. Chou CS, Zhu H, Shalev E, et al: The effects of gonadotropin-releasing hormone (GnRH) I and GnRH II on the urokinase-type plasminogen activator/plasminogen activator inhibitor system in human extravillous cytotrophoblasts in vitro. J Clin Endocrinol Metab 87:5594–5603, 2002.

27. Gohar J, Mazor M, Leiberman JR: GnRH in pregnancy. Arch Gynecol Obstet 259:1–6, 1996.

28. Eldar-Geva T, Hochberg A, deGroot N, Weinstein D: High maternal serum chorionic gonadotropin level in Downs' syndrome pregnancies is caused by elevation of both subunits messenger ribonucleic acid level in trophoblasts. J Clin Endocrinol Metab 80:3528–3531, 1995.

29. Cheng KW, Leung PC: Human chorionic gonadotropin-activated cAMP pathway regulates human placental GnRH receptor gene transcription in choriocarcinoma JEG-3 cells. J Clin Endocrinol Metab 87:3291–3299, 2002.

30. Riley SC, Challis JR: Corticotrophin-releasing hormone production by the placenta and fetal membranes. Placenta 12:105–119, 1991.

31. Frim DM, Emanuel RL, Robinson BG, et al: Characterization and gestational regulation of corticotropin-releasing hormone messenger RNA in human placenta. J Clin Invest 82:287–292, 1988.

32. Saeed BO, Weightman DR, Self CH: Characterization of corticotropin-releasing hormone binding sites in the human placenta. J Recept Signal Transduct Res 17:647–666, 1997.

33. Linton EA, Wolfe CD, Behan DP, Lowry PJ: A specific carrier substance for human corticotrophin releasing factor in late gestational maternal plasma which could mask the ACTH-releasing activity. Clin Endocrinol (Oxf) 28:315–324, 1988.

34. Dibbs KI, Anteby E, Mallon MA, et al: Transcriptional regulation of human placental corticotropin-releasing factor by prostaglandins and estradiol. Biol Reprod 57:1285–1292, 1997.

35. Challis JR, Matthews SG, Van Meir C, Ramirez MM: Current topic: The placental corticotrophin-releasing hormone-adrenocorticotrophin axis. Placenta 16:481–502, 1995.

36. McKeown KJ, Challis JR: Regulation of 15-hydroxy prostaglandin dehydrogenase by corticotrophin-releasing hormone through a calcium-dependent pathway in human chorion trophoblast cells. J Clin Endocrinol Metab 88:1737–1741, 2003.

37. Petraglia F, Sutton S, Vale W: Neurotransmitters and peptides modulate the release of immunoreactive corticotropin-releasing factor from cultured human placental cells. Am J Obstet Gynecol 160:247–251, 1989.

38. Florio P, Lombardo M, Gallo R, et al: Activin A, corticotropin-releasing factor and prostaglandin F2 alpha increase immunoreactive oxytocin release from cultured human placental cells. Placenta 17:307–311, 1996.

39. Nathanielsz PW: Comparative studies on the initiation of labor. Eur J Obstet Gynecol Reprod Biol 78:127–132, 1998.

40. Majzoub JA, McGregor JA, Lockwood CJ, et al: A central theory of preterm and term labor: Putative role for corticotropin-releasing hormone. Am J Obstet Gynecol 180:S232–S241, 1999.

41. Makrigiannakis A, Zoumakis E, Kalantaridou S, et al: Corticotropin-releasing hormone promotes blastocyst implantation and early maternal tolerance. Nat Immunol 2:1018–1024, 2001.

42. Marinoni E, Korebrits C, Di Iorio R, et al: Effect of betamethasone in vivo on placental corticotropin-releasing hormone in human pregnancy. Am J Obstet Gynecol 178:770–778, 1998.

43. Jones CT, Gu W, Parer JT: Production of corticotrophin releasing hormone by the sheep placenta in vivo. J Dev Physiol 11:97–101, 1989.

44. Wolfe CD, Patel SP, Linton EA, et al: Plasma corticotrophin-releasing factor (CRF) in abnormal pregnancy. Br J Obstet Gynaecol 95:1003–1006, 1988.

45. Warren WB, Goland RS: Effects of parturition on corticotropin releasing hormone and products of the pituitary and adrenal in term fetuses at delivery. J Perinat Med 23:453–458, 1995.

46. Leitch IM, Boura AL, Botti C, et al: Vasodilator actions of urocortin and related peptides in the human perfused placenta in vitro. J Clin Endocrinol Metab 83:4510–4513, 1998.

47. Clifton VL, Gu Q, Murphy VE, et al: Localization and characterization of urocortin during human pregnancy. Placenta 21:782–788, 2000.

48. Cole LA: Immunoassay of human chorionic gonadotropin, its free subunits, and metabolites. Clin Chem 43:2233–2243, 1997.

49. Feng W, Matzuk MM, Mountjoy K, et al: The asparagine-linked oligosaccharides of the human chorionic gonadotropin beta subunit facilitate correct disulfide bond pairing. J Biol Chem 270:11851–11859, 1995.

50. Muyan M, Boime I: Secretion of chorionic gonadotropin from human trophoblasts. Placenta 18:237–241, 1997.

51. Chen YH, Chen TM, Hsieh CY: The expression of the human chorionic gonadotropin beta subunit gene depends on negative control. Cell Biochem Funct 14:297–301, 1996.

52. Ringler GE, Strauss JF III: In vitro systems for the study of human placental endocrine function. Endocr Rev 11:105–123, 1990.

53. Petraglia F: Inhibin, activin and follistatin in the human placenta: A new family of regulatory proteins. Placenta 18:3–8, 1997.

54. Lei ZM, Rao CV, Ackerman DM, Day TG: The expression of human chorionic gonadotropin/human luteinizing hormone receptors in human gestational trophoblastic neoplasms. J Clin Endocrinol Metab 74:1236–1241, 1992.

55. Cole LA: hCG, its free subunits and its metabolites: Roles in pregnancy and trophoblastic disease. J Reprod Med 43:3–10, 1998.

56. Alam V, Altieri E, Zegers-Hochschild F: Preliminary results on the role of embryonic human chorionic gonadotrophin in corpus luteum rescue during early pregnancy and the relationship to abortion and ectopic pregnancy. Hum Reprod 14:2375–2378, 1999.

57. Rodway MR, Rao CV: A novel perspective on the role of human chorionic gonadotropin during pregnancy and in gestational trophoblastic disease. Early Pregnancy 1:176–187, 1995.

58. Fanchin R, Peltier E, Frydman R, de Ziegler D: Human chorionic gonadotropin: Does it affect human endometrial morphology in vivo? Semin Reprod Med 19:31–35, 2001.

59. Licht P, Russu V, Lehmeyer S, Wildt L: Molecular aspects of direct LH/hCG effects on human endometrium: Lessons from intrauterine microdialysis in the human female in vivo. Reprod Biol 1:10–19, 2001.

60. Shi QJ, Lei ZM, Rao CV, Lin J: Novel role of human chorionic gonadotropin in differentiation of human cytotrophoblasts. Endocrinology 132:1387–1395, 1993.

61. Kumar S, Talwar GP, Biswas DK: Necrosis and inhibition of growth of human lung tumor by anti-alpha-human chorionic gonadotropin antibody. J Natl Cancer Inst 84:42–47, 1992.

62. Moy E, Kimzey LM, Nelson LM, Blithe DL: Glycoprotein hormone alpha-subunit functions synergistically with progesterone to stimulate differentiation of cultured human endometrial stromal cells to decidualized cells: A novel role for free alpha-subunit in reproduction. Endocrinology 137:1332–1339, 1996.

63. Pittaway DE, Reish RL, Wentz AC: Doubling times of human chorionic gonadotropin increase in early viable intrauterine pregnancies. Am J Obstet Gynecol 152:299–302, 1985.

64. Chard T: Pregnancy tests: A review. Hum Reprod 7:701–710, 1992.

65. Wald NJ, Huttly WJ, Hackshaw AK: Antenatal screening for Down's syndrome with the quadruple test. Lancet 361:835–836, 2003.

66. Chitty LS: Antenatal screening for aneuploidy. Curr Opin Obstet Gynecol 10:91–96, 1998.

67. Wapner R, Thom E, Simpson JL, et al: First-trimester screening for trisomies 21 and 18. N Engl J Med 349:1405–1413, 2003.

68. Nicolaides KH, Heath V, Cicero S: Increased fetal nuchal translucency at 11–14 weeks. Prenat Diagn 22:308–315, 2002.

69. Yankowitz J, Fulton A, Williamson R, et al: Prospective evaluation of prenatal maternal serum screening for trisomy 18. Am J Obstet Gynecol 178:446–450, 1998.

70. Pahal GS, Jauniaux E: Maternal serum biochemical screening for pregnancy complications other than aneuploidy. Curr Opin Obstet Gynecol 9:379–386, 1997.

71. Cole LA, Butler S: Detection of hCG in trophoblastic disease: The USA hCG reference service experience. J Reprod Med 47:433–444, 2002.

72. Braunstein GD, Thompson R, Princler GL, McIntire KR: Trophoblastic proteins as tumor markers in nonseminomatous germ cell tumors. Cancer 57:1842–1845, 1986.

73. Lockwood GM, Muttukrishna S, Ledger WL: Inhibins and activins in human ovulation, conception and pregnancy. Hum Reprod Update 4:284–295, 1998.

74. Schneider-Kolsky ME, Manuelpillai U, Waldron K, et al: The distribution of activin and activin receptors in gestational tissues across human pregnancy and during labour. Placenta 23:294–302, 2002.

75. Luisi S, Florio P, D'Antona D, et al: Maternal serum inhibin A levels are a marker of a viable trophoblast in incomplete and complete miscarriage. Eur J Endocrinol 148:233–236, 2003.

76. Al-Azemi M, Ledger WL, Diejomaoh M, et al: Measurement of inhibin A and inhibin pro-alphaC in early human pregnancy and their role in the prediction of pregnancy outcome in patients with recurrent pregnancy loss. Fertil Steril 80:1473–1479, 2003.

77. Muttukrishna S, Jauniaux E, Greenwold N, et al: Circulating levels of inhibin A, activin A and follistatin in missed and recurrent miscarriages. Hum Reprod 17:3072–3078, 2002.

78. Florio P, Severi FM, Cobellis L, et al: Serum activin A and inhibin A: New clinical markers for hydatidiform mole. Cancer 94:2618–2622, 2002.

79. Florio P, Ciarmela P, Luisi S, et al: Pre-eclampsia with fetal growth restriction: Placental and serum activin A and inhibin A levels. Gynecol Endocrinol 16:365–372, 2002.

80. Dalgliesh GL, Aitken DA, Lyall F, et al: Placental and maternal serum inhibin-A and activin-A levels in Down's syndrome pregnancies. Placenta 22:227–234, 2001.

81. Wald NJ, Kennard A, Hackshaw A, McGuire A: Antenatal screening for Down's syndrome. J Med Screen 4:181–246, 1997.

82. Barrera-Saldana HA: Growth hormone and placental lactogen: Biology, medicine and biotechnology. Gene 211:11–18, 1998.

83. Eberhardt NL, Jiang SW, Shepard AR, et al: Hormonal and cell-specific regulation of the human growth hormone and chorionic somatomammotropin genes. Prog Nucleic Acid Res Mol Biol 54:127–163, 1996.

84. Spellacy WN, Buhi WC, Birk SA: The effectiveness of human placental lactogen measurements as an adjunct in decreasing perinatal deaths: Results of a retrospective and a randomized controlled prospective study. Am J Obstet Gynecol 121:835–844, 1975.

85. Polin JI, Frangipane WL: Current concepts in management of obstetric problems for pediatricians. I. Monitoring the high-risk fetus. Pediatr Clin North Am 33:621–647, 1986.

86. Hochberg Z, Bick T, Perlman R: Two pathways of placental lactogen secretion by cultured human trophoblast. Biochem Med Metab Biol 39:111–116, 1988.

87. Musicki B, Pepe GJ, Albrecht ED: Functional differentiation of placental syncytiotrophoblasts during baboon pregnancy: Developmental expression of chorionic somatomammotropin messenger ribonucleic acid and protein levels. J Clin Endocrinol Metab 82:4105–4110, 1997.

88. Musicki B, Pepe GJ, Albrecht ED: Functional differentiation of the placental syncytiotrophoblast: Effect of estrogen on chorionic somatomammotropin expression during early primate pregnancy. J Clin Endocrinol Metab 88:4316–4323, 2003.

89. Rygaard K, Revol A, Esquivel-Escobedo D, et al: Absence of human placental lactogen and placental growth hormone (HGH-V) during pregnancy: PCR analysis of the deletion. Hum Genet 102:87–92, 1998.

90. Hsieh TT, Chen KC, Hsu JJ, et al: Effects of glucose on placental hormones in the human term placenta in vitro. J Formos Med Assoc 96:309–313, 1997.

91. Bjorklund AO, Adamson UK, Carlstrom KA, et al: Placental hormones during induced hypoglycaemia in pregnant women with insulin-dependent diabetes mellitus: Evidence of an active role for placenta in hormonal counter-regulation. Br J Obstet Gynaecol 105:649–655, 1998.

92. Styne DM: Fetal growth. Clin Perinatol 25:917–938, vii, 1998.

93. Sorenson RL, Brelje TC: Adaptation of islets of Langerhans to pregnancy: Beta-cell growth, enhanced insulin secretion and the role of lactogenic hormones. Horm Metab Res 29:301–307, 1997.

94. Beck P: Lactogenic activity of human chorionic somatomammotropin in Rhesus monkeys. Proc Soc Exp Biol Med 140:183–187, 1972.

95. Silva CM, Kloth MT, Lyons CE, et al: Intracellular signaling by growth hormone variant (GH-V). Growth Horm IGF Res 12:374–380, 2002.

96. Alsat E, Guibourdenche J, Luton D, et al: Human placental growth hormone. Am J Obstet Gynecol 177:1526–1534, 1997.

97. Lonberg U, Damm P, Andersson AM, et al: Increase in maternal placental growth hormone during pregnancy and disappearance during parturition in normal and growth hormone-deficient pregnancies. Am J Obstet Gynecol 188:247–251, 2003.

98. Sheikh S, Satoskar P, Bhartiya D: Expression of insulin-like growth factor-I and placental growth hormone mRNA in placentae: A comparison between normal and intrauterine growth retardation pregnancies. Mol Hum Reprod 7:287–292, 2001.

99. Fuglsang J, Lauszus F, Flyvbjerg A, Ovesen P: Human placental growth hormone, insulin-like growth factor I and II, and insulin requirements during pregnancy in type 1 diabetes. J Clin Endocrinol Metab 88:4355–4361, 2003.

100. Masuzaki H, Ogawa Y, Sagawa N, et al: Nonadipose tissue production of leptin: Leptin as a novel placenta-derived hormone in humans. Nat Med 3:1029–1033, 1997.

101. Jansson N, Greenwood SL, Johansson BR, et al: Leptin stimulates

the activity of the system A amino acid transporter in human placental villous fragments. J Clin Endocrinol Metab 88:1205–1211, 2003.

102. Domali E, Messinis IE: Leptin in pregnancy. J Matern Fetal Neonatal Med 12:222–230, 2002.

103. Jakimiuk AJ, Skalba P, Huterski D, et al: Leptin messenger ribonucleic acid (mRNA) content in the human placenta at term: Relationship to levels of leptin in cord blood and placental weight. Gynecol Endocrinol 17:311–316, 2003.

104. Geary M, Pringle PJ, Persaud M, et al: Leptin concentrations in maternal serum and cord blood: Relationship to maternal anthropometry and fetal growth. Br J Obstet Gynaecol 106:1054–1060, 1999.

105. Lea RG, Howe D, Hannah LT, et al: Placental leptin in normal, diabetic and fetal growth-retarded pregnancies. Mol Hum Reprod 6:763–769, 2000.

106. Sagawa N, Yura S, Itoh H, et al: Possible role of placental leptin in pregnancy: A review. Endocrine 19:65–71, 2002.

107. Poston L: Leptin and preeclampsia. Semin Reprod Med 20:131–138, 2002.

108. Christou H, Serdy S, Mantzoros CS: Leptin in relation to growth and developmental processes in the fetus. Semin Reprod Med 20:123–130, 2002.

109. Horikoshi Y, Matsumoto H, Takatsu Y, et al: Dramatic elevation of plasma metastin concentrations in human pregnancy: Metastin as a novel placenta-derived hormone in humans. J Clin Endocrinol Metab 88:914–919, 2003.

110. Janneau JL, Maldonado-Estrada J, Tachdjian G, et al: Transcriptional expression of genes involved in cell invasion and migration by normal and tumoral trophoblast cells. J Clin Endocrinol Metab 87:5336–5339, 2002.

111. Pepe GJ, Albrecht ED: Actions of placental and fetal adrenal steroid hormones in primate pregnancy. Endocr Rev 16:608–648, 1995.

112. Strauss JF III, Martinez F, Kiriakidou M: Placental steroid hormone synthesis: Unique features and unanswered questions. Biol Reprod 54:303–311, 1996.

113. Wittmaack FM, Gafvels ME, Bronner M, et al: Localization and regulation of the human very low density lipoprotein/apolipoprotein-E receptor: Trophoblast expression predicts a role for the receptor in placental lipid transport. Endocrinology 136:340–348, 1995.

114. Parker CR Jr, Illingworth DR, Bissonnette J, Carr BR: Endocrine changes during pregnancy in a patient with homozygous familial hypobetalipoproteinemia. N Engl J Med 314:557–560, 1986.

115. Stocco DM, Clark BJ: Regulation of the acute production of steroids in steroidogenic cells. Endocr Rev 17:221–244, 1996.

116. Sugawara T, Holt JA, Driscoll D, et al: Human steroidogenic acute regulatory protein: Functional activity in COS-1 cells, tissue-specific expression, and mapping of the structural gene to 8p11.2 and a pseudogene to chromosome 13. Proc Natl Acad Sci U S A 92:4778–4782, 1995.

117. Bose HS, Sugawara T, Strauss JF III, Miller WL: The pathophysiology and genetics of congenital lipoid adrenal hyperplasia. International Congenital Lipoid Adrenal Hyperplasia Consortium. N Engl J Med 335:1870–1878, 1996.

118. Tuckey RC, Kostadinovic Z, Cameron KJ: Cytochrome P450scc activity and substrate supply in human placental trophoblasts. Mol Cell Endocrinol 105:103–109, 1994.

119. Tuckey RC, Headlam MJ: Placental cytochrome P450scc (CYP11A1): Comparison of catalytic properties between conditions of limiting and saturating adrenodoxin reductase. J Steroid Biochem Mol Biol 81:153–158, 2002.

120. Miller WL: Steroid hormone biosynthesis and actions in the materno-feto-placental unit. Clin Perinatol 25:799–817, v, 1998.

121. Rheaume E, Lachance Y, Zhao HF, et al: Structure and expression of a new complementary DNA encoding the almost exclusive 3 beta-hydroxysteroid dehydrogenase/delta 5–delta 4-isomerase in human adrenals and gonads. Mol Endocrinol 5:1147–1157, 1991.

122. Patel FA, Challis JR: Cortisol/progesterone antagonism in regulation of 15-hydroxysteroid dehydrogenase activity and mRNA levels in human chorion and placental trophoblast cells at term. J Clin Endocrinol Metab 87:700–708, 2002.

123. Patel FA, Funder JW, Challis JR: Mechanism of cortisol/progesterone antagonism in the regulation of 15-hydroxyprostaglandin dehydrogenase activity and messenger ribonucleic acid levels in human chorion and placental trophoblast cells at term. J Clin Endocrinol Metab 88:2922–2933, 2003.

124. Baulieu EE: RU486 (mifepristone): A short overview of its mechanisms of action and clinical uses at the end of 1996. Ann N Y Acad Sci 828:47–58, 1997.

125. Chwalisz K, Garfield RE: Antiprogestins in the induction of labor. Ann N Y Acad Sci 734:387–413, 1994.

126. Olson DM, Mijovic JE, Sadowsky DW: Control of human parturition. Semin Perinatol 19:52–63, 1995.

127. Henderson D, Wilson T: Reduced binding of progesterone receptor to its nuclear response element after human labor onset. Am J Obstet Gynecol 185:579–585, 2001.

128. McCord ML, Muram D, Buster JE, et al: Single serum progesterone as a screen for ectopic pregnancy: Exchanging specificity and sensitivity to obtain optimal test performance. Fertil Steril 66:513–516, 1996.

129. Carson SA, Buster JE: Ectopic pregnancy. N Engl J Med 329:1174–1181, 1993.

130. Gray ES, Abramovich DR: Morphologic features of the anencephalic adrenal gland in early pregnancy. Am J Obstet Gynecol 137:491–495, 1980.

131. Mesiano S, Mellon SH, Jaffe RB: Mitogenic action, regulation, and localization of insulin-like growth factors in the human fetal adrenal gland. J Clin Endocrinol Metab 76:968–976, 1993.

132. Kamat A, Alcorn JL, Kunczt C, Mendelson CR: Characterization of the regulatory regions of the human aromatase (P450arom) gene involved in placenta-specific expression. Mol Endocrinol 12:1764–1777, 1998.

133. Moghrabi N, Head JR, Andersson S: Cell type-specific expression of 17 beta-hydroxysteroid dehydrogenase type 2 in human placenta and fetal liver. J Clin Endocrinol Metab 82:3872–3878, 1997.

134. Pepe GJ, Burch MG, Albrecht ED: Estrogen regulates 11 beta-hydroxysteroid dehydrogenase-1 and -2 localization in placental syncytiotrophoblast in the second half of primate pregnancy. Endocrinology 142:4496–4503, 2001.

135. Ni X, Nicholson RC, King BR, et al: Estrogen represses whereas the estrogen-antagonist ICI 182780 stimulates placental CRH gene expression. J Clin Endocrinol Metab 87:3774–3778, 2002.

136. Resnik R, Killam AP, Battaglia FC, et al: The stimulation of uterine blood flow by various estrogens. Endocrinology 94:1192–1196, 1974.

137. Heine RP, McGregor JA, Goodwin TM, et al: Serial salivary estriol to detect an increased risk of preterm birth. Obstet Gynecol 96:490–497, 2000.

# CHAPTER 183

# Fetal and Neonatal Endocrinology

## Delbert A. Fisher

## INTRODUCTION

The intrauterine environment and fetal growth and development are maintained by the interaction of maternal, placental, and fetal hormones and endocrine systems. In addition, a variety of hormones and their metabolites are particularly prominent in the fetus. Some represent ontogeny recapitulating phylogeny, whereas others reflect pathways of hormone inactivation unique to or characteristic of the fetal environment. Fetal growth and development are not dependent on growth hormone and thyroid hormones as in childhood. Rather, a complex interaction of growth factors, acting predominantly by autocrine and paracrine routes, appears to be responsible for the extraordinary rate of growth characteristic of the mammalian fetus.

At parturition, the fetus is faced with the abrupt termination of placental support and rapid transition to the extrauterine environment, in which air breathing, circulatory adjustments, endogenous thermogenesis, free water conservation, and mobilization of energy substrates are required for survival. The adrenal cortex and the autonomic nervous system play key roles in neonatal transitional physiology, but other endocrine systems are required for optimal homeostasis. Understanding the fetal endocrine milieu and neonatal adaptations has contributed importantly to improved management of premature infants, infants of diabetic mothers, infants with abnormal sexual differentiation, and infants with pituitary, thyroid, or parathyroid gland dysfunction. In addition, this understanding allows more effective diagnostic and therapeutic approaches to the compromised fetus.

## PLACENTAL DEVELOPMENT

Fetal metabolic homeostasis and maturation are dependent on placental development and function. The placenta develops in parallel with the fertilized ovum. By 6 to 7 days after conception, the blastocyst consists of an outer layer of trophoblast cells and an inner cell mass destined to become the embryo. By 10 days, the trophoblast cells, implanted in the endometrium, develop two distinct layers: an inner cytotrophoblast layer and an outer layer of continuous cytoplasma, the syncytiotrophoblast. Pockets of cytotrophoblast cells in the mature placenta serve as a reservoir of stem cells for continuing syncytiotrophoblast development.[1,2]

The predominantly syncytiotrophoblastic placenta grows progressively throughout gestation. As the placenta develops, the chorionic villi containing the fetal capillaries extend into the maternal lakes of blood within the maternal decidua. Three layers of fetal tissue separate the fetal from the maternal circulation: the cytotrophoblast-syncytiotrophoblast layer, the fetal mesenchyme layer of extraembryonic connective tissue, and the fetal capillary endothelium. The syncytiotrophoblast is the major site of diffusion between the maternal lakes of blood in the placenta and the fetal capillaries. Placental development is mediated by a proscribed cascade of genetic determinants that program cellular differentiation and function.[3-5] Selected genes shown to be critical for placental development in mice are summarized in Table 183-1.[3]

## PLACENTAL HORMONE TRANSFER AND PRODUCTION

The placenta regulates maternal-fetal molecular and fluid exchange. Thin areas of syncytiotrophoblast adjacent to the fetal capillaries seem specialized for the molecular exchange. Transplacental transfer of molecules may occur via extracellular or transcellular routes. The rate of extracellular transfer is proportional to the size and charge of intercellular channels, as well as the size (roughly correlated with molecular weight) and lipid solubility of the transferred molecule.[1,6] Generally, the placenta is more permeable to lipid-soluble molecules, and this permeability is inversely correlated with molecular weight. Thus, placental transfer decreases with increasing molecular mass, with an upper threshold in the range of 700 to 1200 daltons. Larger hormones have no significant access to the fetal compartment.

Additionally, the human placenta subserves an important endocrine role during fetal development. It is the major source of estrogens and progesterone and synthesizes a variety of protein and peptide hormones and growth factors similar or identical to those secreted from the anterior pituitary or other nonplacental organs.[1,7-23] During pregnancy, the placenta is also a major source of many of the hypothalamic

**Table 183-1  Selected Genes Critical for Placental Development in Mice**

| Process | Genes |
|---|---|
| Implantation | Lif |
| | Ets2 |
| Trophoblast differentation | Hand 1 |
| | Mash 2 |
| | Gem 1 |
| Allantoic differentation | Dnmt 1 |
| Chorioallantoic fusion | Mrj |
| | Vcam 1 |
| | Integrin α4 |
| | Fgfr 2 |
| Villous morphogenesis | Gem 1 |
| | Hsp 90β |
| Placental vascularization | Esx1, Junβ |
| | Arnt |

Modified from Cross JC: Genes regulating embryonic and fetal survival. Theriogenology 55:193–201, 2001.

neuropeptides.[1,24] These diverse hormone and growth factor species are secreted into both the maternal and the fetal circulation. Table 183-2 summarizes the menu of hormones and growth factors produced by the placenta, many of which are reviewed in detail in other chapters.[1,7–24] We are only beginning to understand the roles that these substances play during development, but their contribution to the unique endocrine environment is substantial.

**Table 183-2  Hormones and Growth Factors Produced by the Placenta**

| | |
|---|---|
| Steroid hormones | Renin |
| Estradiol | Sex hormone–binding globulin |
| Estriol | Urocortin |
| Estrone | Neuropeptides |
| Progesterone | CRH |
| Protein and peptide hormones | GHRH |
| Activin | GnRH |
| Adrenomedullin | Neuropeptide Y |
| Angiotensinogen | TRH |
| Calcitonin | PrRP |
| Chorionic gonadotropin | Growth factors |
| Chorionic somatomammotropin | Colony-stimulating factors |
| Chorionic thyrotropin | EGF |
| Follistatin | Endothelin I |
| Placental growth hormone | Erythropoietin |
| Inhibin | Hepatocyte growth factor |
| Leptin | IGF-1 |
| Oxytocin | IGF-2 |
| Pit-1 | IGF-binding proteins 1–6 |
| Placental prolactins | Nerve growth factor |
| Proliferin | Oncomodulin |
| Proopiomelanocortin | PDGF |
| ACTH | Placental growth factor |
| β-Endorphin | TGF-α |
| α/MSH | TGF-β |
| α/β-Lipotropin | Tumor necrosis factor-α |
| PTH-related protein | Vascular endothelial growth |
| Relaxin | factor |

ACTH, adrenocorticotropic hormone; CRH, corticotropin-releasing hormone; EGF, epidermal growth factor; GHRH, growth hormone–releasing hormone; GnRH, gonadotropin-releasing hormone; IGF, insulin-like growth factor; MSH, melanocyte-stimulating hormone; PDGF, platelet-derived growth factor; PrRP, prolactin-releasing peptide; PTH, parathyroid hormone; TGF, transforming growth factor; TRH, thyrotropin-releasing hormone.
Data from references 2–20.

## FETAL ENDOCRINE SYSTEMS

### OVERVIEW

Hormone systems can be classified as shown in Table 183-3. The neuroendocrine hormone systems transduce or convert neural into endocrine information. These include the hypothalamic–anterior pituitary system, the hypothalamic–posterior pituitary system, and the autonomic nervous system. The insulin-glucagon and parathyroid hormone–calcitonin systems function as autonomous endocrine systems in which hormone secretion is regulated largely by local feedback mechanisms. The events of parturition abruptly terminate the period of protected fetal development and precipitate a series of profound metabolic stresses. As indicated earlier, extrauterine survival requires autonomous thermogenesis and alimentation, as well as autonomous respiratory and excretory activities. These activities are largely dependent on the functional state of the endocrine systems, which are critical for extrauterine survival and metabolic homeostasis. The neuroendocrine transducer systems appear to be well developed at birth and function smoothly to defend against the stresses of extrauterine exposure. The autonomous endocrine systems regulating blood sugar and calcium levels, however, are relatively suppressed in utero and must adapt rapidly to the extrauterine environment. Abnormalities related to homeostasis of blood sugar and serum calcium concentrations are relatively frequent in the early neonatal period.

### THE HYPOTHALAMIC–ANTERIOR PITUITARY SYSTEMS

The human fetal forebrain and hypothalamus begin to differentiate by 3 weeks of gestation under control of a series of homeodomain proteins or transcription factors. Our understanding of the number and interactions of these factors is limited, but the availability of modern molecular methods, including mutation analysis, gene transfection, and gene knockout techniques have provided new insights. Mutations of two homeobox genes, sonic hedgehog (Shh) and ZIC2 (a homologue of the *Drosphila* odd-paired gene), have been identified in familial and sporadic holoprosencephaly.[25–26] Hesx1 homeobox gene mutations have been shown in siblings with septo-optic dysplasia involving midline brain defects and pituitary hypoplasia.[27] Other genes involved in hypothalamic development include SF1, Lhx3, and Lhx4; the latter are Lin II, Isl-I, and Mec-3 gene (LIM) class homeodomain factors. A cascade of transcription factors regulates hypothalamic and anterior pituitary development as shown in Figure 183-1. The early pituitary factors, including the Rathke pouch homeobox gene (RPX or Hesx1), program pituitary gland embryogenesis, and targeted disruption of these factors in mice leads to stillbirth or neonatal death.[28,29] The later factors, Prop-1 and Pit-1, program development and function of pituitary cells producing growth hormone (GH), prolactin, thyroid-stimulating hormone beta (TSH-β), and the growth hormone–releasing hormone (GHRH) receptor. Table 183-4 summarizes the human pituitary hormone deficiencies associated with pituitary transcription factor mutations.[29]

Anatomically, the pituitary gland develops from two anlagen: an evagination from the neuroectoderm of the floor of

**Table 183-3  Types of Fetal Endocrine Systems**

| |
|---|
| Neuroendocrine hormone systems |
| Hypothalamus–anterior pituitary–target organs |
| Hypothalamus–posterior pituitary |
| Sympathetic nervous system |
| Autonomous endocrine systems |
| Endocrine-pancreas (insulin-glucagon) |
| Parathyroid gland–thyroid C cells (parathyroid hormone–calcitonin) |

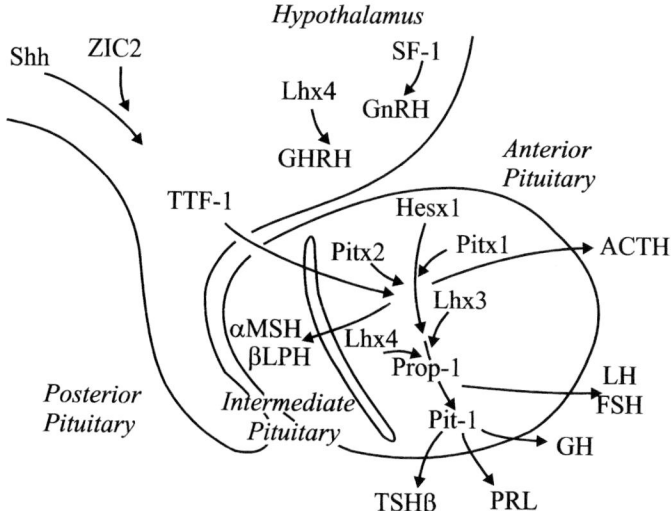

*Hypothalamus*

**Figure 183-1**   Cartoon illustrating the cascade of homeobox genes programming hypothalamic and pituitary embryogenesis and function. Most of this information was derived from gene knockout studies in mice. Shh and Z1C2 are the sonic hedgehog and *Drosophila* odd-paired homologues, mutations of which have been shown to cause human holoprosencephaly. Hesx1 or RPX is the Rathke's pouch homeobox gene critical for anterior pituitary gland embryogenesis. Thyroid transcription factor 1 (TTF-1) knockout leads to pituitary as well as thyroid gland aplasia. Lhx3 and Lhx4 are LIM class homeodomain transcription factors also essential for normal pituitary embryogenesis. Prop-1 and Pit-1 defects in mouse and man lead to a growth hormone (GH), prolactin (PRL), and thyroid-stimulating hormone (TSH) deficiency phenotype. See text and references 25–29. ACTH, adrenocorticotropic hormone; αMSH, alpha melanocyte stimulating hormone; BLPH, beta lipotropic hormone; FSH, follicle-stimulating hormone; GHRH, growth hormone releasing hormone; LH, luteinizing hormone; SF-1, steroidogenic factor-1.

the primitive forebrain and a ventral pouch from the ectoderm of the primitive oral cavity. The latter, Rathke's pouch, is visible by 5 weeks. By 14 weeks, the pituitary gland is morphologically mature, and pituitary-portal blood vessels have begun to develop.[1,29] Maturation and function of the pituitary-portal system continue through 30 to 35 weeks of gestation. The hypothalamic nuclei, median eminence, and supraoptic tract are identifiable by 15 to 18 weeks. Hypothalamic cells and diencephalic fiber tracts for the hypothalamic neuropeptides, somatostatin, corticotropin-releasing hormone (CRH), GHRH, and gonadotropin-releasing hormone (GnRH) are visible by this time, and significant concentrations of thyrotropin-releasing hormone (TRH) and dopamine are detectable.[1,30-32] Secretory granules are present

**Table 183-4   Human Mutations of Pituitary Transcription Factor Genes**

| Gene | Pituitary Hormone Deficiency | Comment |
|---|---|---|
| HESX1 | Panhypopituitarism | Septo-optic dysplasia |
| PITX2 | GH, PRL | Rieger syndrome |
| LHX3 | GH, PRL, TSH, FSH/LH | Rigid cervical spine |
| LHX4 | GH, TSH, ACTH | Cerebellar deformation |
| PROP1 | GH, PRL, TSH | Late FSH/LH/ACTH deficiencies |
| Pit1 | GH, PRL, TSH | |

ACTH, adrenocorticotropic hormone; FSH, follicle-stimulating hormone; GH, growth hormone; LH, lutenizing hormone; PRL, prolactin; TSH, thyroid-stimulating hormone.
From Cohen LE, Radovick S: Molecular basis of combined pituitary hormone deficiencies. Endocr Rev 23:431–442, 2002.

within anterior pituitary cells by 10 to 12 weeks, and pituitary hormones, including GH, prolactin (PRL), TSH, luteinizing hormone (LH), follicle-stimulating hormone (FSH), adrenocorticotropic hormone (ACTH), oxytocin (OT), vasotocin, and vasopressin, can be identified by immunoassay between 10 and 17 weeks. Hormone contents in the pituitary increase progressively, whereas concentrations in fetal serum tend to peak near midgestation and decrease progressively toward term. The exception is serum PRL, concentrations of which increase markedly after 20 weeks' gestation.

Anterior pituitary hormone synthesis and secretion are limited in the first-trimester fetus. During the second trimester, unrestrained release of hypothalamic hormones has been postulated to account for the high fetal circulating levels of anterior pituitary hormones.[31-33] Placental and/or fetal extrahypothalamic production of releasing hormones may also influence release of anterior pituitary hormones during development. During the third trimester, anterior pituitary hormone secretion is progressively modulated, in part because of maturation of inhibitory electrical activity taking place in the neocortex during the latter half of gestation.[31,33] The low levels of serum GH and TSH in anencephalic infants support the view that anterior pituitary hormone secretion is dependent on an intact hypothalamus. The negative feedback control systems for TSH, ACTH, FSH, and LH secretion develop during the latter half of gestation. The control systems for TSH and ACTH secretion seem to be mature or largely so at birth, whereas neuroendocrine control systems for FSH and LH continue to mature during the early weeks, months, and years of extrauterine life.

### Growth Hormone and Prolactin

The fetal pituitary can synthesize and secrete GH by 8 to 10 weeks of gestation. Studies of 9- to 16-week human fetal pituitary cells in culture show a significant response to GHRH and a limited effect of somatostatin, which suggests that the inhibitory action of somatostatin develops late in gestation. This view is substantiated by in vivo studies in sheep showing a failure of somatostatin to inhibit GHRH-stimulated GH release early in the third trimester and maturation of the inhibitory response to somatostatin near term.[31-33] In addition, unrestrained GH secretion may be occurring at the pituitary cell level, and/or the limbic and forebrain inhibitory circuitry that modulates hypothalamic function may be immature. Whatever the mechanisms, control of GH secretion becomes progressively mature during the last half of gestation and the early weeks of postnatal life. Mature responses to sleep, glucose, and levodopa appear during the first 3 months of postnatal life.

The pattern of ontogenesis of fetal plasma PRL differs significantly from that of GH; levels are low until 25 weeks and increase progressively thereafter to high levels at term. In vitro, fetal pituitary cells from midgestation fetuses show limited autonomous PRL secretion, although PRL release increases in response to TRH and decreases in response to dopamine.[31] Estrogen stimulates PRL synthesis and release by pituitary cells, and the increase in fetal plasma PRL concentration in the last trimester parallels the increase in fetal plasma estrogen levels, although lagging by several weeks.[32] Anencephalic fetuses have plasma PRL concentrations in the normal or low-normal range, thus supporting a role for estrogen in stimulating fetal PRL release. In addition, studies in sheep, which demonstrate a similar pattern of fetal plasma PRL levels, indicate that maturation and integration of brain and hypothalamic mechanisms modulating PRL release develop late in gestation and postnatally, which accounts for the delayed postnatal fall in plasma PRL level in the neonate of this species. These data support the view that maturation of brain and hypothalamic control of PRL, like GH, develops late in gestation and during the first months of extrauterine life.[30-33]

## The Fetal Pituitary-Adrenal Axis

Maturation of the fetal adrenal glands is evident by 3 weeks' gestation and is under the control of at least two genes that code for the orphan nuclear receptors SF-1 (steroidogenic factor-1) and DAX-1 (dosage-sensitive sex reversal–AHC critical region on the X chromosome)[34] (Fig. 183-2). These genes show coordinate expression in adrenal cortex, testis, ovary, hypothalamus, and pituitary tissues. Gene knockout of SF-1 in mice leads to adrenal and gonadal agenesis, LH and FSH deficiency, and absence of the hypothalamic ventromedial nucleus.[34] Inactivating mutations of the gene coding for DAX-1 lead to adrenal hypoplasia and gonadotropin deficiency.[35–38] The steroidogenic acute regulatory protein (StAR) is the rate-limiting factor in the regulation of adrenal steroidogenesis; knockout of the gene for StAR in the mouse results in glucocorticoid and mineralocorticoid deficiency and female genitalia in XY animals.[36] In the human fetus, mutations of the gene for StAR cause adrenal hyperplasia and adrenal hormone insufficiency.[36]

Two distinct zones of developing adrenal cortex are distinguishable: an inner fetal zone, which includes most of the glandular cortex, and an outer or definitive zone. Adrenal growth is rapid; cortical mass at term averages 8 g, and the fetal zone accounts for nearly 80% of this mass.[1,36,39] Regulation of fetal adrenal growth and function is complex and depends on a variety of fetal pituitary and placental factors, including CRH, ACTH, insulin-like growth factor 2 (IGF-2), IGF-binding protein-2 (IGFBP-2), and IGFBP-6.[36] The major stimulus to fetal adrenal function is fetal pituitary ACTH.[36,39,40] Although placental human chorionic gonadotropin (hCG) may support

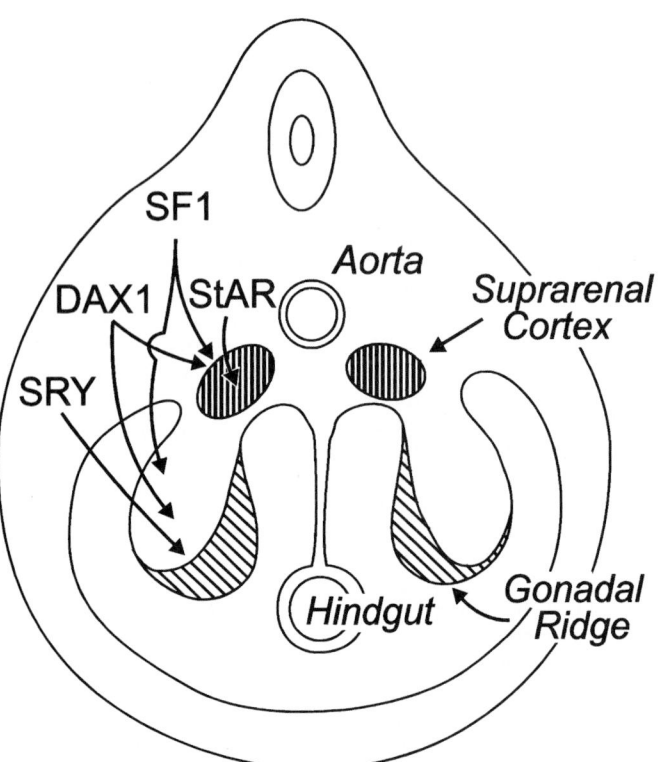

*Figure 183-2* Cartoon showing a cross-section of a 5-week human embryo with location of the adrenal primordia (suprarenal cortices) and gonadal ridges. The homeobox genes known to be programming adrenal and gonadal embryogenesis are indicated. SF-1 is required for testicular and ovarian development while SRY is the single critical regulator of testicular embryogenesis, DAX-1 gene inactivation leads to adrenal hypoplasia. The steroidogenic acute regulatory protein (StAR) is the rate limiting factor for adrenal steroidogenesis. See text and references 34, 35, 37, and 38.

early growth, the involution of the adrenal gland that occurs after 15 weeks in an anencephalic fetus suggests the crucial role of pituitary-derived factors. At midgestation, fetal plasma ACTH levels average 250 pg/mL, and although concentrations decline toward term, fetal ACTH levels exceed those later in life.

Control of fetal ACTH secretion, in turn, is complex. CRH protein has been demonstrated in fetal baboon pituitary, adrenal, liver, kidney, and lung tissues during the last third of gestation. Levels in pituitary are highest (300–500 pg/mg protein); levels in adrenal and lung and liver and kidney tissues average 20–30 and 5–10 pg/mg protein, respectively.[40] CRH knockout in mice leads to neonatal death due to pulmonary hypoplasia, suggesting that CRH-stimulated glucocorticoid production appears essential for normal lung development.[40] Circulating CRH levels are elevated in the fetus and probably result largely from extrahypothalamic and placental sources.[40,41] Arginine vasopressin (AVP) and catecholamines are also significant stimuli for fetal ACTH secretion.[42] Maternal levels of CRH are elevated in the latter half of gestation and continue to rise to values of 0.5 to 1.0 nmol/L at term; levels in nonpregnant women are less than 0.01 nmol/L.[43] This observation may account for the relative lack of suppression of ACTH secretion by cortisol in pregnant females near term. Feedback control of fetal ACTH release is not well characterized in humans. Although exogenous dexamethasone administered in pharmacologic doses to term infants is associated with short-term pituitary-adrenal suppression, a similar phenomenon is not noted in the fetus.[44]

The fetal adrenal expresses the same five steroidogenic apoenzymes as the adult gland: two microsomal enzymes with 17-hydroxylase and 17,20-desmolase (CYP17 or P-450c17) and 21-hydroxylase (CYP21A2 or P-450c21) activities, respectively, plus two mitochondrial cytochrome P-450 enzymes providing cholesterol side-chain cleavage (CYPIIA1 or P-450scc) and C11/C18 hydroxylation of the parent steroid structure (CYP11B1/CYP11B2 or P-450c11/aldosterone synthase). A fifth enzyme, expressed by the smooth endoplasmic reticulum, exhibits both 3β-hydroxysteroid dehydrogenase (3β-HSD) and $\Delta^4$, $\Delta^5$-isomerase activities.[36,39] Quantitative differences in the relative activities of these enzymes are found, however, between cells derived from the fetal versus the definitive zones of the adrenal cortex. Little 3β-HSD is expressed in the fetal zone, which also expresses relatively high steroid sulfotransferase activities.[39] Thus, the major steroid products of the fetal adrenal are dehydroepiandrosterone (DHEA), DHEA sulfate (DHEA-S), pregnenolone sulfate, and several $\Delta^5$-3β-hydroxysteroids. Limited amounts of the $\Delta^5$-3-ketosteroids (such as cortisol or aldosterone) are produced by the fetal zone.[36,39,45] Cholesterol, the major substrate for fetal adrenal steroidogenesis, is derived from circulating low-density lipoprotein (LDL) cholesterol, primarily of hepatic origin. Some de novo adrenal synthesis also occurs.[39]

The major fetal adrenal secretory product, DHEA, converted to 16-OH-DHEA-S by the fetal adrenal and liver, serves largely as a precursor for placental estrogen production. About two thirds of the circulating cortisol in the fetus is derived autonomously from fetal adrenal gland synthesis; the remainder results from transplacental transfer. Fetal cortisol levels are approximately 10% to 20% of the levels found in the adult circulation.[36] Fetal cortisol is rapidly metabolized to inactive cortisone via an 11-HSD expressed in a variety of fetal tissues, with the result that circulating fetal cortisone levels at midgestation are fourfold to fivefold higher than cortisol concentrations.[39] Glucocorticoid receptors are present at midgestation in a variety of fetal tissues, including the placenta, brain, liver, lung, and gut.[46,47] As term approaches, selected fetal tissues express increased levels of 11-ketosteroid reductase activity and are thus able to convert cortisone to cortisol locally. This cortisol serves as an important maturational stimulus to facilitate the fetal extrauterine transition.[48]

In developing mammalian fetal models, all components of the renin-angiotensin system, including renin, angiotensinogen, angiotensins, angiotensin-converting enzyme, and angiotensin II receptors, are present and the genes are generally expressed at higher levels in fetal than postnatal life; in the human metanephric kidney these mRNA species are present by 8 to 9 weeks.[49] Angiotensin II is required for normal kidney morphogenesis and for maintaining the glomerular filtration rate and urine flow in the fetal kidney.[49] The human fetal adrenal gland is capable of aldosterone secretion near term; cord plasma levels of aldosterone exceed maternal levels threefold to fivefold; this increased secretion of aldosterone continues throughout the first year of life.[36,50] Vaginal delivery increases aldosterone levels in both mother and infant, as does maternal salt restriction.[50] In the fetal sheep model, in which late fetal and neonatal aldosterone levels are also high relative to the adult, furosemide stimulates renin but not aldosterone secretion during the last third of gestation; the aldosterone response to furosemide (and renin) is delayed until the neonatal period.[51] The role of the fetal renin-angiotensin-aldosterone system in the fetus is not clear. It has been proposed that rather than modulating renal sodium excretion, the system maintains salt and water homeostasis of amniotic fluid to prevent oligohydramnios.[52] The mechanism(s) for the hyperactivity of the system in the neonatal period is also unclear.

### The Pituitary-Gonadal Axis

Embryogenesis of the gonads, like other endocrine organs, is programmed by genes coding for the male sexual determinant SRY, as well as SF-1 and DAX-1.[34,37,38,53,54] SRY is the single critical regulator of male gonadal differentiation (see Fig. 183-2). SF-1 is also required for testicular and ovarian development and mediates müllerian-inhibiting hormone gene expression and gonadotropin production.[34] SF-1 and DAX-1 are orphan receptors of the steroid-thyroid hormone family of nuclear receptors and appear to interact as heterodimers coordinately involved in the regulation of target genes in the adrenal glands and in hypothalamic gonadotrope cells and the ventromedial hypothalamic nucleus.[34] The menu of genes programming the highly organized pattern of gonadal development and phenotypic sexual differentiation is shown in Table 183-5.[55,56] Developmental events are summarized in Figure 183-3.

Male differentiation of the primitive gonads begins at 7 weeks of gestation, when interstitium and germ cell–containing testicular cords are identifiable.[57,58] Leydig cells are visible during the eighth week and are capable of androgen biosynthesis at that time. By 14 weeks, the fetal testicular mass approximates 20 mg, increasing to 800 mg at term. Female differentiation is also obvious by the seventh week, with the appearance of interstitium and medullary cords containing the oogonia. Primitive granulosa cells are visible by 12 weeks.[57,58] With further maturation, many oogonia degenerate, whereas those surviving undergo the first meiotic division to become primary oocytes. Primordial follicles can be identified at 5 months, and primary follicles, with their thecal cell investment, can be demonstrated by 7 months. The combined ovarian tissue mass approximates 30 mg at 14 weeks and 600 to 700 mg at birth.

In the male fetus, there is an increase in testicular testosterone production, stimulated by the high levels of circulating placental hCG between 10 and 20 weeks.[57,58] Fetal pituitary LH contributes to fetal Leydig cell stimulation, but the predominant gonadotropic effect at this time is hCG. Fetal testosterone stimulates male sexual differentiation of the primitive mesonephric ducts (to form the ductus deferens, epididymis, seminal vesicles, and ejaculatory ducts) and masculinizes the urogenital sinus and external genitalia (to form the prostate gland, phallus, and penile urethra). Enzymatic conversion of testosterone to dihydrotestosterone is necessary

**Table 183-5 Genetic Determinants Mediating Sexual Differentiation**

| Function | Gene |
|---|---|
| Development of indifferent gonad | SF-1 |
| | Lim 1 |
| | WT-1 |
| | GATA4 |
| | DMRT-1 |
| | Lhx9 |
| | Emx2 |
| | DHH |
| Development of testis | DAX-1 |
| | Sry |
| | SOX9 |
| | SF-1 |
| | Dhh |
| | WT-1 |
| | GATA4 |
| | HSP 70 |
| Müllerian duct regression | MIS |
| Development of ovary | Wnt4 |
| | Other? |
| Development of müllerian ducts | Wnt4 |
| Uterus and upper vagina | Wnt7A |
| | Hoxa9, 10, 11, 13 |

MacLaughlin DT, Teixeira J, Donahoe PK: Perspective: Reproductive tract development: New discoveries and future directions. Endocrinology 142:2167–2172, 2001; and Harley VR, Clackson MJ, Argentaro A: The molecular action and regulation of the testis determining factors: SRY (sex determining region of the Y chromosome) and SOX9 (SRY related high mobility group, HMG, Box 9). Endocr Rev 24:466–487, 2003.

for male differentiation of the urogenital sinus and external genitalia.

A critical event in sex determination is the formation of Sertoli cells in the male gonad. These cells produce müllerian-inhibiting substance (MIS, or MIH [müllerian-inhibiting hormone]), which dedifferentiates the primitive müllerian duct system.[59-61] MIS, a glycoprotein approximately 72 kilodalton in size, is a member of the transforming growth factor beta (TGF-β) family produced by Sertoli cells, where MIH gene expression is stimulated by SRY.[62] Production continues throughout gestation, is maximal at the time of müllerian duct regression, and then decreases after birth. MIH also may facilitate testicular descent. In the female fetus, müllerian duct differentiation proceeds in the absence of MIH, and the primitive mesonephric duct system dedifferentiates in the absence of testosterone. In the absence of dihydrotestosterone, the urogenital sinus and external genitalia differentiate to the female phenotype. Gonadal hormones in the fetus also determine sexual differentiation of the developing brain and hypothalamus, programming pulsatile GnRH release and feedback modulation of gonadotropin secretion. Testosterone administration to neonatal female rats ablates cyclic hypothalamic GnRH production; this effect is mediated by local aromatization of testosterone to estradiol.[63,64] In primates and humans, estrogens per se are more effective in this regard; however, androgen receptors and aromatase activity are localized in most brain areas of male and female monkey fetuses by midgestation, so, to date, there are no biochemical differences in male and female fetuses to account for sexual dimorphic programming.[64,65]

### The Pituitary-Thyroid Axis

The thyroid gland is a derivative of the primitive buccopharyngeal cavity and is comprised of two sets of anlagen, a median anlage derived from the pharyngeal floor and paired lateral anlagen from the fourth pharyngeal pouch.[66] At least three homeobox genes are involved in programming thyroid and parathyroid gland development from these anlagen,

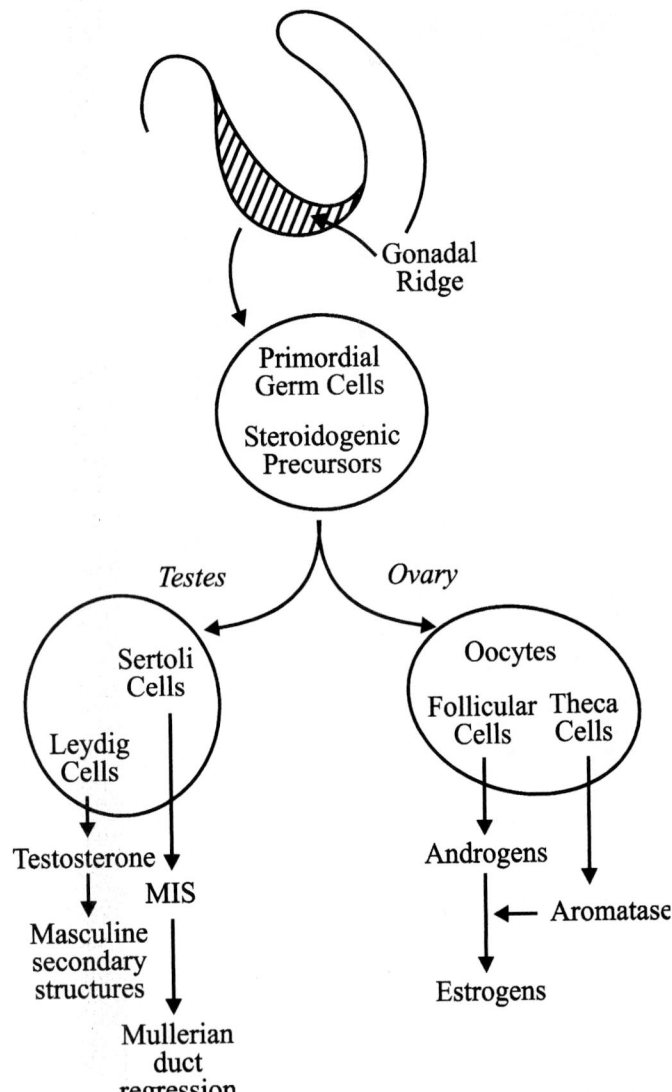

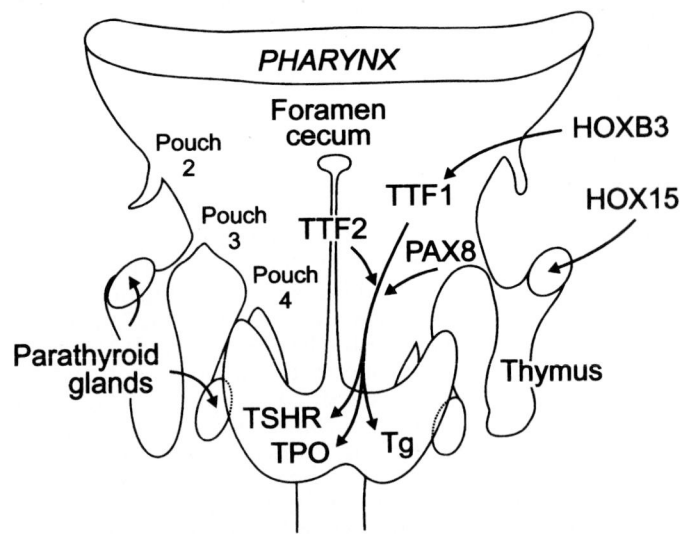

Figure 183-4 Cartoon showing the homeobox genes programming development of the thyroid and parathyroid glands. HOXB3 may be responsible for activation of thyroid transcription factor 1 (TTF1) during early embryogenesis with TTF2 and PAX8 involved in a synergistic cascade programming thyroid gland embryogenesis, descent, and function. These factors are also involved in function of differentiated follicular cells including thyroglobulin (Tg), thyroid peroxidase (TPO), and thyroid-stimulating hormone receptor (TSHR) gene transcription. HOX15 gene knockout in mice causes parathyroid gland aplasia. See text and references 67 and 68.

Figure 183-3 Cartoon summarizing the cellular and hormonal events in sexual differentiation. See text for details. MIS, müllerian-inhibiting substance.

including genes coding for thyroid transcription factor 1 (TTF-1), TTF-2, and PAX-8[67-71] (Fig. 183-4). Studies in mice indicate that knockout of the gene coding for TTF-1 results in pulmonary hypoplasia and thyroid agenesis. Knockout of the mouse gene coding for TTF-2 results in thyroid dysgenesis and cleft palate, whereas mutation of the gene coding for PAX-8 results in thyroid gland hypoplasia and renal anomalies.[67,68,70] Pharyngeal pouch-derived parafollicular C cells are aplastic in the TTF-1 knockout mice but normal in the PAX-8 knockouts.[69] Optimal expression of differentiated postnatal follicular cell function, including normal thyroglobulin, thyroid peroxidase, and TSH receptor activities, requires all three gene effects.[67] Other gene activities, including endothelin and TSH receptor (TSHR) gene activities may also play a role in thyroid gland differentiation.[68,72] Gene mutations involving TTF-1, TTF-2, PAX-8, and TSHR have been described in human neonates with thyroid dysgenesis, but they account for less than 10% of cases.[68]

Thyroid gland embryogenesis is completed by 10 weeks of gestation, at which time colloid formation is demonstrable, and, by 12 weeks, the gland weighs about 80 mg. At term gestation, gland weight approximates 1 g.[73] Pituitary and plasma TSH concentrations increase during the second trimester in the human fetus, coincident with development of the pituitary-portal circulation. The fetal thyroid secretes predomi-nantly thyroxine ($T_4$), and plasma total concentrations increase progressively from low levels at 16 weeks' gestation to plateau values approximating 130 nmol/L at 36 to 38 weeks' gestation, largely because of thyroxine-binding globulin from estrogen-stimulated hepatic production. Circulating free $T_4$ levels also increase progressively because of maturation of thyroidal hormone production.[73-75] These increases in circulating free $T_4$ and TSH levels represent progressive maturation of feed-forward hypothalamic control of TSH secretion, as well as feedback inhibitory effects of thyroid hormones on TSH release. The TSH response to TRH is present by 22 to 24 weeks' gestation, whereas $T_4$ feedback inhibition develops progressively during the third trimester.

$T_4$ can be monodeiodinated to either active 3',3, 5-triiodothyronine ($T_3$) or inactive 3,3',5'-triiodothyronine (reverse $T_3$ [$rT_3$]) by one of the three iodothyronine monodeiodination (MDI) enzymes, type I, type II, or type III.[73-75] Deiodination of the outer (phenolic) ring of $T_4$ to form $T_3$ is catalyzed by either type I or type II MDI. Type I outer ring monodeiodinase is principally expressed in fetal hepatic and renal tissues, whereas type II is expressed in the placenta and in the fetal brain, pituitary, and brown adipose tissues. Type III MDI in fetal placenta, brain, and skin catalyzes deiodination of the inner (tyrosyl) ring of $T_4$ to produce inactive $rT_3$.[74] Fetal thyroid hormone metabolism is characterized by low levels of type I and high levels of type III MDI activity. Thus, in the fetus, $T_4$ is largely converted to $rT_3$, and serum $rT_3$ levels during the third trimester are high, ranging from 2 to 4 nmol/L.[74-76] Fetal serum triiodothyronine ($T_3$) levels remain low until the final weeks of gestation. Plasma $T_3$ levels are less than 0.2 nmol/L before 30 weeks of gestation and then increase slowly to levels averaging 0.7 nmol/L at term.[73,74] The low levels of circulating $T_3$ in the fetus are due to relatively decreased production and increased degradation via type III MDI.

Additionally, sulfated iodothyronine analogues are major thyroid hormone metabolites in the fetus.[74,77] During the last third of gestation in the fetal sheep, average production rates for $T_4$ and metabolites (in μg/kg body weight per day) are as follows: $T_4 = 40$, $rT_3 = 5$, $T_3 = 2$, $T_4$ sulfate = 10, $rT_3$ sulfate = 12, and $T_3$ sulfate = 2. Like $rT_3$, the sulfate metabolites are biologically inactive.[74,77] They serve as substrates for type I MDI and accumulate in serum as a result of increased production in fetal liver and relatively low hepatic type I MDI activity. The sulfate metabolites are not substrates for type III MDI. Significant levels of type II MDI activity are expressed in fetal brain and brown adipose tissue at midgestation (before the near term increase in plasma $T_3$ levels) and provide for local tissue production of $T_3$ during the latter half of gestation.[74,76] Although fetal thyroid development occurs largely independent of maternal influences, limited maternal-to-fetal transport of thyroid hormones occurs and is estimated to supply 20% to 30% of fetal hormone turnover.[74,78] This $T_4$ of maternal origin may serve as an important substrate for local $T_3$ production by type II MDI–expressing tissues (e.g., brain) in the hypothyroid fetus.[73,74]

The physiologic effects of thyroid hormone depend on the expression of functional thyroid hormone receptors (TRs) encoded by the TRα and TRβ genetic loci.[79-81] The genes are differentially expressed as several isoforms mediating both individual and common biologic functions. Both the α and β receptors bind to specific DNA acceptor sites, known as $T_3$ response elements, acting as versatile regulators of gene expression.[79] In mice, the TRα gene is expressed from early stages of embryogenesis preceding TRβ expression, but targeted TRα mutations do not impair embryogenesis.[79] Extensive studies in transgenic and knockout mice have provided insights regarding the relative roles of the TR isoforms in fetal and postnatal growth and development. These studies are summarized in Table 183-6.[79-81] Thyroid hormone receptors have been described in human fetal heart, lung, liver, and brain by the 20th week of gestation, but ontogenic data are largely limited to fetal brain.[82,83] Messenger RNAs (mRNAs) encoding TRα1, α2, β1, and β2 isoforms have been detected in fetal cerebral cortex by 8 to 10 weeks, and immunostaining has revealed TRα1 and α2 protein from week 11.[83] The TR protein expression was largely confined to the pyramidal neurons of the cerebral cortex and Purkinje cells of the cerebellum, and the proportion of cells expressing receptors increased from 10% to 20% during the first trimester to 60% to 80% by the second trimester to 100% during the third trimester.[83]

The size, weight, appearance, behavior, biochemical parameters, extrauterine adaptation, and early neonatal course are usually normal in congenitally hypothyroid infants. The relative lack of signs and symptoms in the athyroid fetus and infant is related in part to the effects of transplacentally acquired maternal $T_4$, which at term provides an estimated 20% of fetal thyroid hormone turnover.[78] In addition, thyroid hormone actions in various tissues are developmentally regulated by the temporal expression of the $T_3$ nuclear receptors, the deiodinase enzymes, and the transcription cofactors that modulate TR activity.[79]

Thyroid hormone is essential for normal central nervous system (CNS) maturation. It regulates a diverse array of processes, including neurogenesis and neural cell migration, neuronal differentiation, dendritic and axonal growth, synaptogenesis, gliogenesis, myelination, and neurotransmitter enzyme synthesis. Thyroid hormone is necessary for normal CNS development early in gestation, before the fetal thyroid gland begins to secrete thyroid hormone at midgestation.[84] The most subtle effect of thyroid hormone on fetal brain development is observed in pregnancies associated with maternal hypothyroxinemia.[84] Even subclinical maternal hypothyroidism has been associated with 5- to 10-point IQ deficits in the offspring. The molecular mechanisms by which thyroid hormone mediates these central nervous effects remain unclear. Aside from a hearing impairment, TRβ knockout mice exhibit neither morphologic or functional abnormalities of brain development nor significant differences in mRNA levels of a number of $T_3$-dependent cerebellar genes.[79] No gross defects in behavior or in myelination have been reported to date in TRα knockout mice. Thus, the major thyroid hormone effects on brain maturation are probably mediated by pathways common to both TR genes.

| Table 183-6 | Thyroid Receptor Isoform Deletion Phenotypes in Mice | | | |
|---|---|---|---|---|
| TR Isoform Deficiency* | Viability | Serum T4 | TSH | Other |
| TRα1 | Viable | ↓ | ↓ | Bradycardia |
| | | | | Hypothermia |
| TRα2 | Viable | | | |
| TRα1 | Lethal | ↓ | ↓ | Thyroid hypoplasia |
| TRα2 | | | | Hypothyroid |
| | | | | Growth retardation |
| | | | | Bone retardation |
| | | | | Intestinal malformation |
| | | | | Impaired lymophocyte maturation |
| TRα1 | Viable | ↓ | N | Hypothermia |
| TRα2 | | | | Intestinal malformation |
| TRΔα1 | | | | Growth retardation |
| | | | | Bone retardation |
| TRβ1 | Viable | ↑ | ↑ | Goiter |
| TRβ2 | | | | Deafness |
| | | | | Defective liver $T_3$ response |
| TRβ2 | Viable | ↑ | ↑ | Goiter |
| TRβ1 | Viable | ↑ | ↑ | Goiter |
| TRβ2 | | | | Deafness |
| TRβ3 | | | | Defective liver $T_3$ response |
| TRα1 | Viable | ↑ | ↑ | Bradycardia |
| TRβ1 | | | | Hypothermia |
| TRβ2 | | | | Goiter |
| | | | | Growth retardation |
| | | | | Bone retardation |
| | | | | Deafness |
| | | | | Female infertility |
| TRα1 | Lethal | ↑ | ↑ | Goiter |
| TRα2 | | | | Growth retardation |
| TRβ1 | | | | Bone retardation |
| TRβ2 | | | | Intestinal malformation |

*Trα2 and TRΔα1 are non-$T_3$-binding isoforms

Forrest D, Vennstrom B: Functions of thyroid hormone receptors in mice. Thyroid 10:41–52, 2000; and Gauthier K, Plateroti M, Harvey CB, et al: Genetic analysis reveals different functions for the products of the thyroid hormone receptor α locus. Mol Cell Biol 21:4748–4760, 2001.

### THE HYPOTHALAMIC–POSTERIOR PITUITARY SYSTEM

AVP is detectable after 10 to 12 weeks of gestation in the human fetal neurohypophysis.[85] By 40 weeks, the level approximates 20% of that in adults. Fetal pituitary oxytocin levels, detectable by 11 to 15 weeks, exceed AVP concentrations by 19 weeks. The AVP-oxytocin ratio falls progressively thereafter. At 11 to 19 weeks of gestation, immunoreactive arginine vasotocin (AVT), characteristic of submammalian species, is found in the human fetal pituitary at approximately two thirds the concentration of AVP and is secreted by cultured human fetal pineal cells during the second trimester.[85,86] In addition, AVT is found in mammalian cerebrospinal fluid, fetal pituitary, and adult pineal gland but not in the adult pituitary. Thus, AVT appears to represent an example of ontogeny recapitulating phylogeny. The role of AVT in mammals is not known, but the hormone is known to bind to and activate AVP receptors.

Little information is available regarding AVP secretion in the human fetus, but considerable data are available in the sheep model. During the final third of gestation, the sheep fetus responds to hemorrhage, hypertonic saline, angiotensin II, and hypoxia with increased AVP secretion, and the inverse relationship of AVP mRNA and pituitary AVP content in the near-term fetal sheep suggests a dynamic AVP synthesis-content feedback relationship.[85,87] The responses to hypertonicity and dehydration in the newborn lamb are quantitatively comparable to the adult responses, whereas the response to hypoxia greatly exceeds that of the adult.[85] Aquaporin-1, aquaporin-2, and aquaporin-3 water channel receptors are present in human fetal and newborn kidney, and the ability of the newborn infant to respond to isotonic dextran or hypertonic saline with appropriate alterations in kidney free-water clearance indicates that human volume and osmolar control systems for AVP secretion are mature at birth.[88,89]

Fetal serum AVP and oxytocin also increase in response to parturition in the human neonate.[85] Newborn serum AVP levels are not increased after cesarean section delivery, whereas oxytocin levels are. Serum levels of AVP in vaginally delivered infants are variable and seem to relate to the degree of fetal stress, probably including hypoxia and head compression. The mechanism for the oxytocin release at birth is not known, but elevated levels after cesarean section delivery indicate that the stimuli for release of AVP and oxytocin differ at the time of parturition.

As noted, the most potent stimulus for AVP release in the fetus is hypoxia, which suggests that AVP in the fetus functions as a stress hormone to sustain cardiovascular homeostasis.[85,87] Hypoxia also stimulates catecholamine release in the fetus, and hypoxia and AVP are known to stimulate pituitary ACTH release.[90,91] AVP is known to function as a corticotropin-releasing factor (CRF) in adults, and the third-trimester ovine fetal pituitary has been shown to respond to CRF and AVP separately and synergistically with regard to ACTH release.[90,91]

Both AVP and AVT evoke antidiuretic effects and inhibit lung fluid production in fetal sheep during the last third of gestation.[85] These actions serve to conserve water for the fetus by inhibiting water loss into amniotic fluid. Maximal renal concentrating ability is limited in the fetus and newborn; however, hypertonic saline administration evokes maximal antidiuresis in the human neonate, whereas isotonic dextran (volume expansion) evokes a maximal water diuresis.[85] Thus, volume and osmolar control of AVP release are mature at birth, and the limitation in renal concentrating ability in the newborn period relates to inherent immaturity of the renal tubules or the aquaporin channels.[88,92]

## THE AUTONOMIC NERVOUS SYSTEM

Functional development of the sympathoadrenal system is critical to both fetal and neonatal adaptation to stress. By 6 weeks of gestation, the primordia of the sympathetic ganglia are discernible.[93] These structures are composed of primitive sympathetic neurons and chromaffin cells that coalesce into paired cell masses along the descending aorta. The paired adrenal medullary masses are well developed by 12 weeks of gestation. Most of the chromaffin tissue in the fetus is present, however, in scattered extramedullary para-aortic paraganglia, the largest of which are termed the *organs of Zuckerkandl*. After birth, these paraganglia gradually atrophy and disappear by 2 to 3 years of age.[93] Both chromaffin cells and sympathetic nerve cells are derived from common neuroectodermal stem cells, and development of these cells is nerve growth factor (NGF) dependent.[94] The role of placental NGF in fetal autonomic nervous system development is unclear.

Catecholamines (epinephrine and norepinephrine) are demonstrable in chromaffin tissue by 15 weeks of gestation, with concentrations increasing to term. Para-aortic tissue contains predominantly norepinephrine as a result of the diminished activity of phenylethanolamine N-methyl transferase (PNMT), which converts norepinephrine to epinephrine.[93] By contrast, epinephrine is the predominant catecholamine secreted by the adrenal medulla. Developmental induction of adrenal medullary PNMT activity occurs in response to

locally elevated glucocorticoid levels derived from surrounding adrenal cortical tissues.[93,95] Before complete splanchnic innervation, which occurs near term, the immature fetus cannot activate catecholamine release via the usual cholinergic mechanisms. The immature fetus does, however, release catecholamines in response to hypoxia. This nonneurally mediated response occurs principally in paraganglionic tissues and results in relatively increased levels of circulating norepinephrine; as maturation continues, the response includes adrenal medullary secretion of epinephrine as well.[95] The physiologic consequences of increased catecholamine secretion differ in the fetus and in adults. The fetus responds with metabolic effects (increased circulating glucose and free fatty acids) and fewer cardiovascular actions, whereas hemodynamic responses predominate in the adult.[93] In the fetus, circulating catecholamines rise acutely in response to maternal hypoglycemia and are accompanied by increases in fetal circulating free fatty acids and glucose.[96] These changes occur in the absence of any demonstrable change in fetal plasma insulin or glucagon levels, which suggests that the fetus may uniquely alter its metabolic environment via activation of the sympathetic-adrenal nervous system.

Basal plasma epinephrine, norepinephrine, and dopamine levels are easily measured during the last third of gestation in fetal sheep, and levels decrease progressively as term approaches. The metabolic clearance of epinephrine increases with gestational age, although the production rate remains unchanged.[97] The fetal sheep responds to maternal exercise or hypoxia with increased catecholamine levels.[98] The human neonate responds to parturition with an increase in plasma epinephrine and norepinephrine concentrations, and these responses are augmented by hypoxia and acidosis.[95,99] The neonate also increases catecholamine levels in response to hypoglycemia or cold exposure.[99,100] Gene knockout studies in mice targeting either tyrosine hydroxylase or dopamine β-hydroxylase produce fetal catecholamine deficiency and midgestation death in 90% of mutant embryos.[101,102] Thus, catecholamines are critical for the maintenance of fetal cardiovascular homeostasis and serve as the major stress hormones in the fetus. They also play an important role in parturition and neonatal adaptation.

Significant increases in fetal circulating catecholamine levels take place during the final hours of labor; logarithmic increases in plasma epinephrine and norepinephrine occur at the time of parturition, coincident with severing the placental circulation, and this response is augmented in the preterm infant.[99] It is likely that this postnatal surge in circulating catecholamines is an integrated response to a variety of stimuli, including head compression, mild asphyxia, tactile stimulation, hypothermia, and afferent baroreceptor activity. The abrupt withdrawal of placental degradation of catecholamines also contributes.

## AUTONOMOUS ENDOCRINE SYSTEMS

### The Fetal Pancreas

Embryogenesis of the pancreas is mediated by a series of homeobox genes in the mouse, including Pdx1, H1xb9, Nkx, PAX-4, PAX-6, IsH, Ngn3, Hnf6, and Beta2.[103,104] Pdx1 gene knockout in the mouse results in pancreatic agenesis; H1xb9 knockout leads to pancreatic hypoplasia; Nkx2.2, Nkx6.1, PAX-4, PAX-6, IsH-1, or Ngn3 knockout results in endocrine cell agenesis or hypogenesis. The Beta 2/neuro D gene knockout in the mouse leads to marked β-cell dysplasia and hypoplasia and early death from diabetes. These factors and perhaps others further downstream program the orderly maturation of pancreatic development and function (Fig. 183-5).

The human fetal pancreas with pancreatic islets, including α and β cells, is present by the eighth week.[105–107] Early in gestation, α cells predominate, whereas β-cell proliferation is programmed during the latter half of gestation. Sulfonylurea

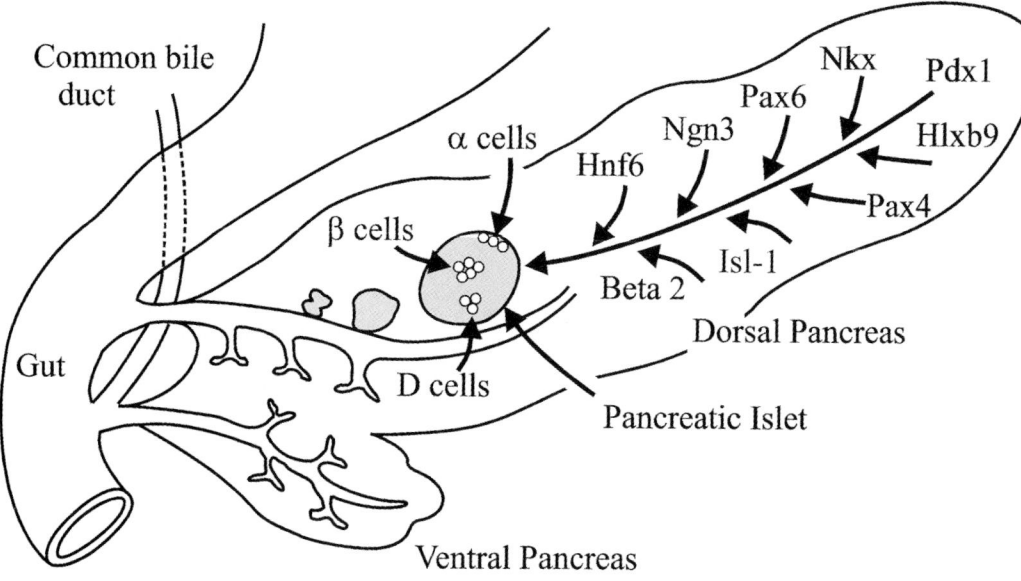

*Figure 183-5* Cartoon showing the homeobox genes programming development of the pancreas and pancreatic islets. PDX1 gene knockout in the mouse leads to pancreatic agenesis while Isl-1 knockout produces islet cell agenesis. PAX4 or PAX6 knockout leads to β-cell or α-cell agenesis or hypogenesis, respectively. Beta 2 gene disruption also produces β-cell hypoplasia. See text and references 103 and 104.

receptor gene expression in fetal mouse pancreas is observed by embryonic day 12 (midgestation), a time roughly comparable to 10 weeks in the human fetus. The β cell is functional by 14 weeks of gestation, and fetal pancreatic insulin content exceeds that of the adult throughout most of gestation. Circulating insulin levels are comparable to those seen in the postprandial adult. Fetal glucose metabolism, however, is largely independent of the glucoregulatory hormones insulin and glucagon.[107,108] In physiologic doses, glucagon does not increase hepatic glucose production, probably because of a paucity of hepatic glucagon receptors in the fetus.[107,108] Insulin receptors are present in a variety of fetal tissues, at levels generally exceeding those of the adult.[107] Downregulation of insulin receptor binding does not occur during fetal hyperinsulinemia, however, in contrast to observations in adult animals.

Acute hypoglycemia or hyperglycemia is not associated with significant alterations in either insulin or glucagon levels. Chronic fetal hyperglycemia does evoke hyperinsulinemia and glucagon suppression, however, and chronic hypoglycemia may inhibit fetal insulin and promote fetal glucagon release.[106,107] Insulin secretion by adult islet cells involves stimulation of adenyl cyclase, with production of cyclic adenosine monophosphate (cAMP) and inhibition of potassium efflux leading to depolarization of the cell membrane and opening of voltage-dependent calcium channels. The relative tachyphylaxis of fetal pancreatic insulin secretion appears to involve immaturity of both systems. Augmentation of the cAMP-generating systems in the fetus is associated with a more robust response of plasma insulin in reaction to hyperglycemia, but calcium channel activation does not occur in fetal islets in response to agents that cause depolarization of adult islet cells.[108] The role of sulfonylurea receptors in the fetal pancreas remains unclear.[109]

In studies involving pregnant sheep, net fetal umbilical glucose uptake from the placenta matches fetal glucose utilization; it is difficult to document fetal hepatic gluconeogenesis under most physiologic conditions,[106,107] which may be explained by the low levels of phosphoenolpyruvate carboxykinase (PEPCK) activity in the fetal liver; PEPCK is the rate-limiting enzyme for gluconeogenesis. Fetal insulin levels are low and relatively insensitive to changes in fetal plasma glucose concentration, but insulin receptor levels are increased in many fetal tissues, and appear to facilitate anabolic deposition of glucose, protein, and fat in fetal tissues. Low levels of circulating glucagon and decreased fetal glucagon receptor binding limit glycogenolysis and catabolism in fetal tissues.

The fetal pancreatic glucagon content at midgestation exceeds that of the adult, but the capacity for glucagon secretion is blunted in the fetus.[106] Hyperglycemia does not suppress fetal plasma glucagon in rats, sheep, or monkeys, and acute hypoglycemia does not stimulate glucagon release in the fetal rat. During the newborn period, the placental source of glucose is abolished, and plasma glucagon levels rise in association with a rapid increase in functionally coupled glucagon receptors. The increase in plasma catecholamines coincident with parturition may be responsible for some of these changes; catecholamines both stimulate glucagon release and inhibit insulin release.[106,107] PEPCK activity also increases during this period. Thus, gluconeogenesis is readily demonstrable in the newborn, where nearly 10% of glucose utilization is accounted for by gluconeogenesis from alanine.[110] Plasma free fatty acid concentrations rise postnatally as a result of the effects of catecholamines and chemical thermogenesis. Oxidation of fatty acids probably provides cofactors (acetyl coenzyme A and the reduced form of nicotinamide adenine dinucleotide) required for gluconeogenesis, as well as spares glucose for utilization by crucially dependent tissues such as the brain.[106,107]

### The Parathyroid Hormone–Calcitonin–Vitamin D System
Parathyroid gland development from the paired third and fourth pharyngeal pouches proceeds in synchrony with thyroid embryogenesis. Mutant mice lacking parathyroid glands and parathyroid hormone (PTH) result from targeted disruption of the homeobox gene HOX15, indicating that this gene functions as part of the gene cascade programming normal thyroid-parathyroid development (see Fig. 183-4).[111] Additional genes involved in parathyroid gland embryogenesis include Gcm2, GATA3, and Tbx1.[112] The pharyngeal pouches are identifiable on the lateral wall of the pharyngeal gut by 4 to 5 weeks of gestation. The third pouches are destined to form the thymus and inferior parathyroid glands, the fourth pouches form the superior parathyroid glands, and the fifth pharyngeal pouches form the paired ultimobranchial bodies, which are incorporated into the thyroid gland during embryogenesis as the perifollicular calcitonin-secreting (C) cells.[113] The parathyroid glands develop between 5 and 15 weeks of gestation and increase from a diameter of less than 0.1 mm at 14 weeks to 1 to 2 mm at birth. Adult glands measure 2 to 5 mm in width and 3 to 8 mm in length. Near term, fetal parathyroid cells are largely composed of inactive chief cells, with only a few intermediate chief cells containing occasional secretory granules. C cells

are particularly prominent in the neonatal thyroid gland, and the calcitonin content is as high as 540 to 2100 mU/g of tissue, values as much as 10 times those observed in the normal adult gland.[113]

Fetal serum calcium levels are maintained by active placental transport involving an adenosine triphosphate (ATP)-dependent calcium pump. Transport occurs across the syncytiotrophoblast, which contains a calcium-binding protein that buffers the calcium ions as they traverse the syncytial cell.[114] The placental calcium pump is stimulated by a mid-molecule portion of the parathyroid hormone related protein (PTHrP) secreted by the fetal parathyroid gland and by other fetal tissues and the placenta, where it may exert a paracrine effect.[115,116] The placenta is impermeable to PTH, PTHrP, and calcitonin, but 25-hydroxyvitamin D and 1,25-dihydroxyvitamin D are transported across the placenta, and free vitamin D levels in fetal blood are similar to or higher than maternal values.[117,118]

Thyroparathyroidectomy in fetal sheep results in a rapid decrease in fetal plasma calcium concentration and loss of the placental calcium gradient.[114,115] In mice, knockout of the gene for PTHrP abolishes the maternal-fetal calcium gradient, and placental transport of calcium is reduced.[116] Placental calcium transport in these models is restored by the midmolecule fragment of PTHrP (amino acids 67–86) but not by PTH or PTHrP fragment 1–34, which activate the PTH/PTHrP receptor.[116,117] Thus, a second, yet unidentified, PTHrP receptor recognizing the PTHrP 67–86 ligand appears to be involved in placental calcium pump activation. Other factors are probably involved in maintenance of fetal serum calcium homeostasis and skeletal development, because knockout of the mouse gene for the PTH/PTHrP receptor also results in hypocalcemia in the presence of normal or increased placental calcium transport.[116] PTH and PTHrP via the PTH/PTHrP receptor presumably modulate fetal skeletal calcium flux, calcium excretion via the fetal kidney, and perhaps reabsorption of calcium from amniotic fluid. PTHrP, and to a lesser degree PTH, play essential roles in fetal bone development and metabolism, as well as fetal calcium homeostasis.[112] PTHrP knockout mice display increased ossification of the basal portion of the skull, long bones, vertebral bodies, and pelvic bones and mineralization of the normally cartilaginous portions of the ribs and sternum; as a result of the latter, the animals die of asphyxiation in the early neonatal period.[119] The skeletal chondrodysplasia is more severe in combined PTH plus PTHrP or PTH/PTHrP receptor gene ablated animals.[112,119] In the mouse model, knockout of the calcitonin gene or the vitamin D receptor gene leads to postnatal osteosclerosis or osteomalacia, respectively; the pups appear normal at birth[120,121] (Table 183-7).

Studies in the fetal sheep model have contributed important observations to our understanding of fetal calcium metabolism. The fetal sheep has low circulating levels of PTH but can increase serum PTH concentrations in response to a fall in serum calcium concentration induced by ethylenediaminetetraacetic acid (EDTA) and can respond promptly to infused calcium with increased serum calcitonin levels.[114] In this model, fetal parathyroidectomy decreases placental calcium transport and lowers fetal serum calcium. Although PTH has no effect on placental calcium transport, PTHrP is present in fetal tissues and placenta and stimulates calcium transport. Nephrectomy in the fetal sheep reduces fetal serum calcium concentrations, and this hypocalcemia can be prevented by prior administration of 1,25-dihydroxyvitamin D. The fetal kidney can produce 1,25-dihydroxyvitamin D, and the placenta contains 1,25-dihydroxyvitamin D receptors, as well as a vitamin D–dependent calcium-binding protein.[117] Dihydroxyvitamin D production in the fetal sheep is sixfold greater than in the maternal ewe. Although not entirely clear, is seems likely that fetal PTH and presumably PTHrP act on the fetal kidney to stimulate 1-hydroxylation of 25-hydroxyvitamin D and that

**Table 183-7** Effects of Knockout of PTH, Calcitonin, and Vitamin D–Related Genes on Fetal Development in Mice

| Gene Knockout | Viability | Other |
|---|---|---|
| PTH | Viable | Decreased cartilage mineralization |
| | | Decreased osteoblast production |
| PTHrP | Neonatal Lethal | Decreased placental calcium transport |
| | | Hypocalcemia |
| | | Parathyroid hyperplasia |
| | | Increased PTH secretion |
| | | Increased osteoblasts and cartilage mineralization |
| | | Chondrodysplasia |
| PTH/PTHrP receptor | Lethal | Fetal growth retardation |
| | | Premature enchondral bone ossification |
| | | Severe chondrodysplasia |
| | | Cardiac anomalies |
| Calcitonin | Viable | Postnatal osteosclerosis |
| Vitamin D receptor | Viable | Postnatal osteomalacia |

PTH, parathyroid hormone; PTHrP, parathyroid hormone related protein. Miao D, He B, Karaplis C, Goltzman D: Parathyroid hormone is essential for normal fetal bone formation. J Clin Invest 109:1173–1182, 2002; Lanske B, Amling M, Neff L, et al: Ablation of the PTHrP gene or the PTH/PTHrP receptor gene leads to distinct abnormalities in bone development. J Clin Invest 104:399–407, 1999; Hoff AO, Catala-Lehnen P, Thomas PM, et al: Increased bone mass in an unexpected phenotype associated with deletion of the calcitonin gene. J Clin Invest 110:1849–1857, 2002; and Amling M, Priemel M, Holzman T, et al: Rescue of the skeletal phenotype of vitamin D receptor ablated mice in the setting of normal mineral ion homeostasis: Formal histomorphometric and biomechanical analyses. Endocrinology 140:4982–4987, 1999.

1,25-dihydroxyvitamin D participates in modulating placental calcium transport. Thus, PTHrP and, to a lesser extent, PTH in the ovine fetus appear to augment maternal-to-fetal calcium transport across the placenta and thus provide for the high rate of bone mineral accretion in the latter half of pregnancy. The high serum calcium concentration, in turn, chronically stimulates fetal calcitonin secretion. Because calcitonin inhibits bone resorption, high blood levels would help promote bone calcium accretion. Placental calcitonin production has also been demonstrated and may contribute as well. These effects are summarized in Figure 183-6.

## FETAL GROWTH

Fetal growth is the net result of a complex interplay of genetic, hormonal, and growth factor effects. The hormones most important for postnatal growth, including T[4], GH, and gonadal steroids, have a limited role in fetal growth.[122–125] The insulin-like growth factors or somatomedins (IGF-1 and IGF-2) play a major role in modulating fetal growth.[123,126–128] Both IGF-1 and IGF-2 are expressed in placental tissue and in a variety of fetal tissues of mesenchymal origin, but they also are identified in tissues of ectodermal and endodermal origin.[123,129] In addition, the type 1 IGF receptor, which mediates most of the biologic actions of the IGFs, is present early in gestation in a wide variety of fetal tissues. Type 2 IGF receptors and insulin receptors are also present in fetal tissues but probably have a limited role in fetal growth.

Transgenic mice with null mutations of IGF-1 or the IGF-1 receptor manifest markedly reduced birth weight, organ hypoplasia, and delayed bone development[123,127] (Table 183-8). IGF-1 receptor–deficient animals and some of the IGF-1 deficient mice die shortly after birth; surviving mice manifest deficient postnatal growth.[123,127] IGF-2-deficient mice also manifest intrauterine growth retardation and delayed bone development but have near-normal postnatal growth because

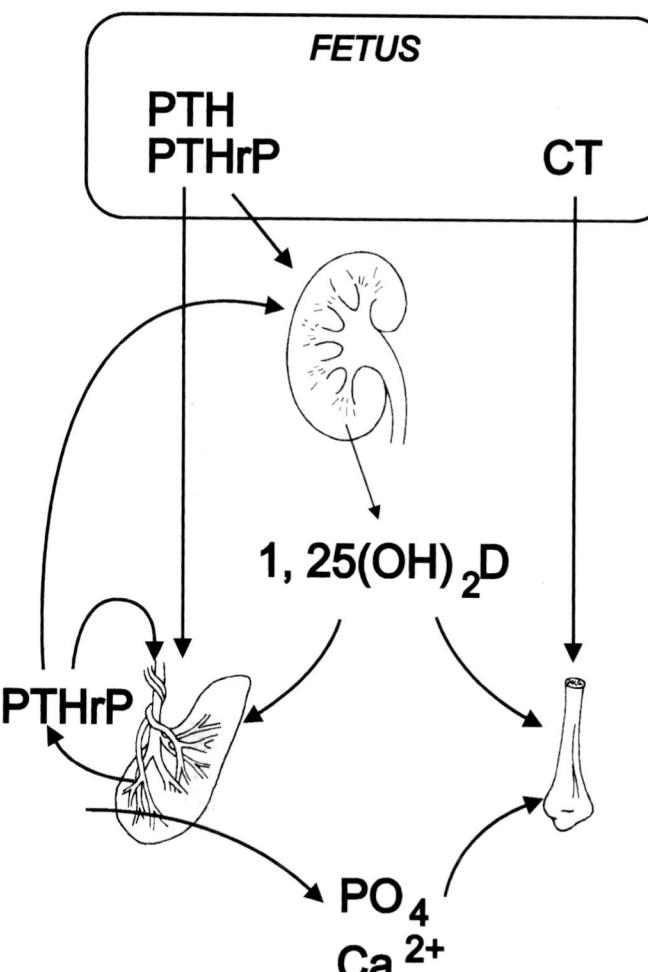

*Figure 183-6* Hormonal modulation of fetal calcium homeostasis. Parathyroid hormone (PTH) and PTH-related peptide (PTHrP) are derived from both fetal parathyroid and placental tissues and stimulate maternal to fetal calcium transport (CT). PTHrP may also stimulate renal 1-hydroxylation of 25(OH) vitamin D, which also acts to promote placental calcium transport.

| Gene Knockout | % Normal Birth Weight | Other Features |
|---|---|---|
| IGF-1 | 60 | Normal placenta<br>Decreased brain size<br>Slow postnatal growth<br>Early death |
| IGF-2 | 60 | Small placenta<br>Normal postnatal growth |
| IGF-1 + IGF-2 | 30 | Small placenta<br>Neonatal death |
| IGF-1 receptor | 45 | Neonatal death |
| IGF-2 receptor | 130 | Large placenta<br>Nonviable |
| IGF-1 + IGF-2 receptors | 100 | Large placenta<br>Normal postnatal growth |
| IGF-1 + IGF-2 + Insulin receptors | 30 | Nonviable |

*Table 183-8* **Features of IGF Knockout Mouse Models**

IGF, insulin-like growth factor. DeLeon DD, Cohen P, Levi IT, Katz LE: Growth factor regulation of fetal growth. In Polin RA, Fox WW, Abman SH (eds): Fetal and Neonatal Physiology, 3d ed. Philadelphia, WB Saunders, 2004, pp 1880–1890.

of IGF-1.[126,128] Pregnancies in mice with fetal IGF-2 deficiency also show impaired placental growth.[128] IGF-2 receptor knockout fetal mice are 30% overweight, suggesting a negative growth-modulating effect of this receptor.[123] The normal growth in fetuses with both IGF-1 and IGF-2 receptor knockout is due to IGF-1 signaling through the insulin receptor since the triple receptor knockout results in severe intrauterine growth retardation and fetal death[123] (see Table 183-8). The effect of knockout of individual IGFBPs in general is minimal, suggesting that there is functional compensation by other members of the family.[123]

The IGFs exert their effects through endocrine and paracrine routes. Circulating IGFBPs are present early in gestation, and total plasma concentrations of the IGFs are high when compared with tissue concentrations. The levels of both IGF-1 and IGF-2 in fetal and cord blood are relatively low, however, in comparison to childhood or adult values.[123,130] The predominant IGF in fetal blood is IGF-2, in keeping with its prominent role in fetal growth. Colocalization of IGF and IGF receptors in growing fetal tissues and the widespread tissue distribution of the IGF and IGF-1 receptor mRNA species suggest an autocrine or paracrine action. In the midgestation fetus, both IGF-1 and IGF-2 are abundant in the gut, liver, kidney, skeletal and cardiac muscle, skin, hematopoietic tissues, lung, and adrenal tissues.[123] The predominant localization of both IGF-1 and IGF-2 mRNA levels to mesenchymal connective tissue around and within these organs suggests their largely paracrine roles on adjacent target cells.[123,129]

Control of IGF production in the fetus differs from that in postnatal life. GH, which stimulates IGF-1 production after birth, has a limited role in fetal IGF production.[122,124] Human somatomammotropin, or placental lactogen (hPL), via unique fetal receptors, stimulates IGF-1 production and DNA synthesis in human fetal muscle cells and fetal fibroblasts.[131,132] Evidence also indicates that insulin may play a role in modulating IGF synthesis in the fetus.[132] The most important factor modulating IGF levels in developing mammals, however, is nutrition. Plasma IGF concentrations are reduced in fetuses of protein-deficient pregnant rats, and IGF-1 levels are reduced in suckling rats deprived of milk.[123] The reduced IGF levels in starved pregnant rats can be reversed by hPL.[133] The available evidence suggests that glucocorticoids limit fetal growth by inhibiting IGF actions at the tissue level.[134]

Insulin has a growth-promoting effect, particularly late in gestation.[123,135] The hyperinsulinemia commonly observed in the fetus of a diabetic mother is associated with augmented body weight and increased body fat deposition. A fetus with pancreatic agenesis and hypoinsulinemia is small and relatively devoid of body fat.[123,132] Insulin infusion to fetal monkeys near term increases body weight, with prominent anabolic effects on the heart, liver, and spleen.[135] Interestingly, homozygosity for a null mutation of the insulin receptor gene in fetal mice leads to early neonatal death with hyperglycemia and ketonemia; birth weight, however, is normal.[136] A homozygous insulin receptor mutation in the human fetus results in leprechaunism in association with intrauterine growth retardation, lack of subcutaneous fat, decreased muscle mass, hirsutism, and early death.[137] Presumably, the difference in growth effect relates to the relatively longer pregnancy in the human species.

Other growth factors also play a role in modulating fetal growth and differentiation.[1,123,138] The epidermal growth factor (EGF)–transforming growth factor alpha (TGF-α) family of growth factors (including neuregulin and amphiregulin), acting through a series of EGF receptors (HER1, HER2, HER3, HER4), is known to stimulate precocious eyelid opening and tooth eruption in neonatal rodents and to stimulate palatal development, gastrointestinal maturation, and lung maturation. These factors probably also play an important role in kidney, liver, thyroid, and adrenal gland growth.[122,138] Maternal salivary gland and plasma EGF concentrations increase fourfold to fivefold in the mouse during pregnancy, and removal of the maternal salivary glands reduces litter size and fetal weight; the administration of exogenous EGF reverses these effects.[139] The mechanism(s) of these EGF effects remains unclear, but an effect on maternal or placental metabolism is likely because the placenta is a rich source of EGF receptors. EGF receptors are present in many fetal tissues early in gestation, and inactivation of the gene encoding the EGF receptor in mice leads to fetal or neonatal death.[140] EGF and EGF precursor RNA have been identified in most fetal tissues or in fetal blood of rodents.[138] Low levels of precursor EGF mRNA have been characterized in tooth, dermis, spleen, and lung tissues of embryonic mice.[141] However, the predominant species of this family of growth factors in the developing fetus and the major fetal ligand for the EGF receptor appears to be TGF-α.[138,142–144] Control of TGF-α production in the fetus is not understood. Thyroid and steroid hormones and GH play a role in the control of EGF production in the neonatal period in rodents but not in the fetus.[138]

Evidence for a role of EGF family growth factors in mammalian central nervous system development is growing.[138,145–147] EGF promotes proliferation of astroglial cells and enhances survival and process outgrowth of selected neuronal cells.[146] EGF, TGF-α, neuregulins, and the receptors EGFR, HER2, and HER4 are widely distributed in the nervous system.[138,145–147] Mice lacking neuregulin, HER2, or HER4 die in utero with cardiac anomalies and developmental anomalies of the forebrain, midbrain, and hindbrain.[148–150] Mice with targeted mutations of HER3 manifest severe neuropathy as a result of the absence of Schwann cells and peripheral nervous system degeneration.[151]

Erythropoietin is produced by the liver during fetal development, and a switch to renal erythropoietin production is seen shortly after birth in sheep and other mammals.[152–154] Postnatal renal erythropoietin production is modulated by oxygen tension in blood and by thyroid hormones and testosterone; oxygen tension also regulates hepatic erythropoietin production in the fetus.[153,154] Thyroid hormone and testosterone regulatory roles become manifest in the neonatal period. Other hematopoietic growth factors, including granulocyte colony–stimulating factor, macrophage colony–stimulating factor, and thrombopoietin, program growth and maturation of precursor cells in fetal bone marrow.[123]

The fibroblast growth factor (FGF) family has been characterized and includes at least seven different FGFs and three receptor species.[123] Achondroplasia is caused by mutation of the FGF3 receptor gene, and FGF2 receptor mutation is associated with craniosynostosis.[123] FGF2 or FGF3 gene knockout in mice produces limb abnormalities, but fetal growth is not impaired.[123] Infusion of FGF into the renal arteries of rats containing a renal subcapsular transplant of a 10-day rat embryo has been shown to stimulate growth of the embryo.[155] The major effects were on tissues of endodermal and mesodermal origin; moreover, FGF antiserum inhibited the growth of endodermal tissue in the transplanted embryos, as well as in some of the mesodermal-derived tissues. Thus, the FGFs appear to have autocrine/paracrine roles in localized organ growth and differentiation, including an essential role in bone growth and maturation.

The NGF family of neurotropic growth factors now includes NGF, brain-derived neurotropic factor (BDNF), neurotropin-3 (NT3), two less well characterized factors, and two receptors, NGF and NGF2 (or Trk).[156–159] NGF is known to stimulate growth and differentiation of the autonomic nervous system in developing rodents. NGF injection in neonatal mice increases the size of the superior cervical ganglia. Selected enzyme activities also increase in response to NGF infusion, including RNA polymerase, ornithine carboxylase, and tyrosine hydroxylase; NGF antiserum injection, by contrast, results in permanent sympathectomy.[156,157] Studies involving induction of autoantibodies of NGF in rats and rabbits have

shown that mothers with high titers to NGF antibody deliver fetuses with significantly impaired autonomic nervous system development.[160,161] NGF is produced by neonatal mouse astroglial cells in tissue culture, is present in developing mouse brain tissue, and, with BDNF and NT3, plays an important role in brain development.[158,162] Thyroid hormones increase NGF, NT3, and BDNF mRNA levels in adult brain tissue.[159]

Other growth factors involved in fetal growth and organ maturation include the TGF-β superfamily, the vascular endothelial growth factor (VEGF) family, and the platelet-derived growth factor (PDGF) family.[163–165] The TGF-β superfamily of extracellular growth factors is comprised of more than 35 members including TGF-β, the bone morphogenic proteins, growth differentiation factors, activins, inhibins, müllerian-inhibiting substance, nodal, and leftys.[163] These ligands activate some 12 transmembrane serine/threonine kinase receptors expressed in a variety of tissues. The family is critical for early embryonic development, left-right asymmetry, heart and vascular system development, craniofacial development, nervous system development, and skeletal morphogenesis, and plays an important role in body composition and growth.[163] Receptor knockouts in mice are generally lethal in utero or during the perinatal period.

The PDGF family is comprised of homo- and heterodimers of PDGFA and B chains encoded by two genes. The ligands activate two receptors α and β distributed in fibroblasts and in smooth muscle, glial, and endothelial cells.[164] PDGFα and/or β knockout in mice is usually lethal or results in postnatal death associated with facial anomalies, spina bifida, skeletal anomalies, lack of pulmonary alveolar septa, and epidermal blistering.[164] During development, VEGF is expressed in almost all tissues.[165] The family includes five isoforms from a single gene and two receptor tyrosine kinases, widely distributed in vascular endothelium. Receptor gene knockout of either receptor in mice is lethal.[165]

It is of interest that a growing number of these factors have been shown to be produced by the placenta. Thus, as is the case with the IGFs, both endocrine and autocrine-paracrine routes of production and action of a variety of growth factors may prove to be important in individual fetal organ development and in overall fetal growth and differentiation.

## ADAPTATION TO EXTRAUTERINE LIFE

Successful transition to extrauterine life requires that the fetus, previously poikilothermic, with the placenta subserving most of its metabolic needs, becomes homeothermic and self-sustaining.[48,166] Crucial integration of a variety of neural and endocrine events is a prerequisite for this transition. The coordinated actions of adrenal cortical and medullary hormones facilitate the early postnatal transition to air breathing, cardiovascular adaptation, glucose homeostasis, and thermogenesis (see Fig. 183-6). A longer-term extrauterine transition requires adaptation to an intermittent substrate supply, which requires activation of the hormonal control systems for maintenance of serum glucose and calcium homeostasis.

### CORTISOL AND CATECHOLAMINE MEDIATED ADAPTATIONS

A modest increase in prenatal, near-term circulating cortisol levels occurs in a variety of primate and other mammalian species as a result of increased fetal adrenal cortisol production and decreased metabolism of cortisol to cortisone.[39,48] Plasma ACTH levels tend to remain stable, although the pulsatility of ACTH secretion may increase during this period. The increase in circulating cortisol concentrations is associated with a variety of physiologic responses. These include (1) induction and maturation of a variety of gut enzymes for nutrient absorption and maturation of gut transport processes, motility, and structure; (2) increased conversion of $T_4$ to $T_3$ by stimulation of hepatic outer ring iodothyronine deiodinase, leading to increased circulating $T_3$ levels; (3) increased epinephrine secretion by sympathetic chromaffin tissue (including adrenal medulla) because of augmented phenylethanolamine transferase activity (which converts norepinephrine to epinephrine); (4) stimulation or maturation of a variety of hepatic enzyme activities; (5) augmented synthesis and secretion of surfactant and maturation of surfactant composition; and (6) increased β-adrenergic receptor density in a variety of tissues, including lung, heart, and brown adipose tissue.[48,167-170] The adaptational effects of the prenatal cortisol surge have led to the current recommendation for prenatal corticosteroid therapy in pregnancies threatened by the risk of preterm delivery. Generally, preterm infants prenatally exposed to augmental glucocorticoid levels have lower overall morbidity and mortality than untreated infants.[171]

As indicated, parturition is also associated with enormous increases in circulating catecholamine levels, which subserve critical extrauterine transitional events. Cord blood norepinephrine levels of 15 nmol/L (2500 pg/mL) and epinephrine values of 2 nmol/L (370 pg/mL) are common after spontaneous delivery of term infants.[93,167,172] These catecholamine levels increase cardiac output and neonatal blood pressure, evoke cardiac ventricular inotropic effects, increase glucagon and decrease insulin secretion, stimulate hepatic glycogenolysis, stimulate brown adipose tissue thermogenesis, increase free fatty acid concentrations, and promote pulmonary adaptation by mobilizing pulmonary fluid and stimulating surfactant synthesis[93,167,172] (Fig. 183-7).

## BROWN ADIPOSE TISSUE THERMOGENESIS

Brown adipose tissue is the major site for newborn thermogenesis.[73,166] The mass of brown adipose tissue peaks at birth and involutes in most species after the first weeks of life. Extirpation of this tissue during fetal life is associated with profound neonatal hypothermia. Regulation of brown adipose tissue function is coordinated through several endocrine systems. Catecholamines, via β-adrenergic receptors, stimulate fatty acid oxidation and thermogenesis; this response is also thyroid hormone dependent.[173,174] Mitochondria in brown adipose tissue express a unique protein, thermogenin (or UCP, uncoupling protein), which uncouples oxidation from subsequent adenosine diphosphate phosphorylation and thereby promotes the release of heat. Thermogenin is $T_3$ dependent; brown adipose tissue expresses an iodothyronine monodeiodinase type II that provides for local $T_3$ production from $T_4$.[173,174] In the ovine fetus, fetal thyroidectomy leads to hypothermia and low plasma free fatty acid concentrations despite increased circulating levels of catecholamines. Thus, thyroid hormones and catecholamines are essential for optimal neonatal thermogenesis and newborn euthermia in the transition to extrauterine life. Placental factors, including adenosine and prostaglandin $E_2$, appear to inhibit the thermogenesis of brown adipose tissue in utero, and umbilical cord cutting thus conditions neonatal hormone-stimulated thermogenesis of brown adipose tissue.[175]

## GLUCOSE HOMEOSTASIS

The abrupt withdrawal of placental glucose transport leads to a prompt fall in plasma glucose immediately after birth. This relative hypoglycemia, along with augmented catecholamine levels largely caused by the absence of placental degradation, stimulates pancreatic glucagon secretion. These early glycogen and catecholamine surges rapidly deplete available hepatic glucagon stores, so maintenance of blood glucose levels in the 12 to 24 hours after birth requires increased hepatic gluconeogenesis. Infants born before term have more severe and prolonged neonatal hypoglycemia because of reduced

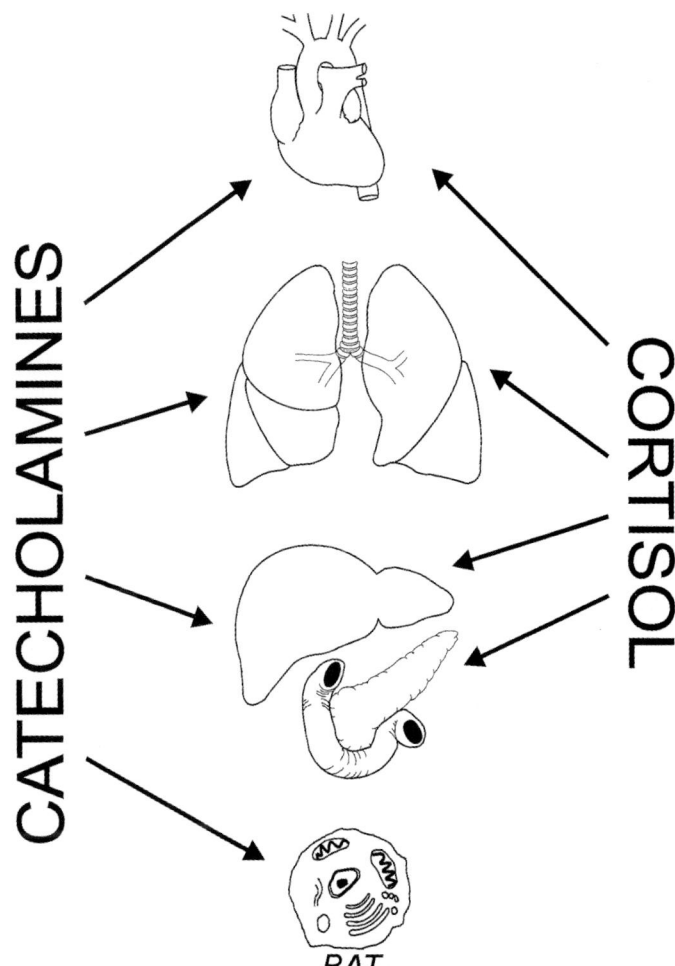

**Figure 183-7** Coordinated effects of cortisol and catecholamines mediate the transition to extrauterine life, promoting extrauterine adaptational changes in cardiovascular, pulmonary, hepatic, and pancreatic function and stimulating brown adipose tissue (BAT) thermogenesis. See text for details.

hepatic glycogen stores and relatively immature hepatic gluconeogenesis.[106,108,176] The insulin-secretory response to hyperglycemia matures in the neonatal period, and healthy term infants achieve adult-like regulation of glucose homeostasis within days of birth. Maturation of glucoregulatory mechanisms is often delayed in premature infants. Relative hyperinsulinemia may occur in the neonatal period in an infant of a diabetic mother, in small-for-gestational-age and/or asphyxiated or severely stressed infants, or in infants with islet β-cell hyperplasia or congenital hyperinsulinism, which may be due to mutation of the sulfonyluria receptor gene.[176] Aggressive treatment is necessary in such infants to avoid central nervous system sequelae.

## CALCIUM HOMEOSTASIS

Neonates must adjust rapidly from a high calcium fetal environment regulated by PTHrP and calcitonin to a low calcium environment regulated by PTH and vitamin D. With placental separation, newborn plasma calcium concentrations fall to values approximating 2.3 mmol/L (9 mg/dL) for total calcium and 1.2 mmol/L (4.8 mg/dL) for ionized calcium.[114,177] Plasma PTH levels are relatively low and minimally responsive to hypocalcemia during the first 2 to 3 days of life. Calcitonin concentrations, already high in cord blood, increase further and remain high for several days after birth.[114,177] The relatively obtunded PTH response and the high calcitonin levels lead to a 2- to 3-day period of transient neonatal hypocalcemia, which inhibits calcitonin secretion and stimulates PTH secretion. In the neonatal lamb, the disappearance of PTHrP is approximately coincident with the time of restoration of calcium levels to the adult range.[114] Calcium homeostasis is also affected in the newborn by a low glomerular filtration rate and reduced renal responsiveness to PTH for several days after birth. These factors limit phosphate excretion and, with high phosphate milk intake, predispose the neonate to hyperphosphatemia.[177] Premature infants tend to have lower PTH and higher calcitonin levels with more immature kidney function, so that neonatal hypocalcemia may be more marked and prolonged. Infants born to mothers with hypercalcemia caused by hyperparathyroidism have a high incidence of symptomatic hypocalcemia. These infants have a more marked suppression of parathyroid function and a more prolonged period of transient hypoparathyroidism in the neonatal period. PTH secretion and calcium homeostasis usually normalize within 1 to 2 weeks in full-term infants, but normalization may require 2 to 3 weeks in small premature infants.

## OTHER HORMONAL ADAPTATIONS

Delivery of the infant and severing of the placental circulation result in abruptly decreased levels of estrogens, progesterone, hCG, and hPL in the newborn. The decrease in estrogens removes a major stimulus to newborn prolactin release, and PRL levels remain low over the next several weeks of life. GH levels are also low in the postnatal period because of delayed hypothalamic-pituitary feedback and control.[30,32,33] These events probably involve changes in GH sensitivity to both GHRH and somatostatin. Newborn IGF levels fall to low values, presumably because of removal of placental hPL stimulation and placental somatomedin production. The dramatic increase in neonatal TSH secretion during the first hour is largely due to the effect of body cooling with extrauterine exposure. The increase in TSH, in turn, increases thyroidal $T_4$ and $T_3$ secretion and enhances thyroidal conversion of peripheral $T_4$ to $T_3$. Increased peripheral outer ring (type I) iodothyronine deiodinase activity increases peripheral $T_4$ to $T_3$ conversion. Neonatal serum TSH levels are reset to lower prevailing extrauterine values, which requires resetting of the thyroid hormone–TSH negative feedback control system. $T_3$ and sulfated iodothyronine production decrease to extrauterine levels by 3 to 4 weeks of age, at which time these hormone concentrations approximate those in adults.[1,74,178]

## REFERENCES

1. Fisher DA: Endocrinology of fetal development. In Larsen PR, Kronenberg AM, Melmed S, Polonsky KS (eds): Williams Textbook of Endocrinology, 10th ed. Philadelphia, WB Saunders, 2003, pp 811–841.
2. Petraglia F, Santuz M, Florio P, et al: Paracrine regulation of the human placenta: Control of hormonogenesis. J Reprod Immunol 39:221–233, 1998.
3. Cross JC: Genes regulating embryonic and fetal survival. Thereogenology 55:193–201, 2001.
4. Rossant J, Cross JC: Placental development: Lessons from mouse mutants. Nat Rev Genet 2:538–548, 2001.
5. Cross JC, Baczyk D, Dobric N, et al: Genes, development and evolution of the placenta. Placenta 24:123–130, 2003.
6. Sibley CP, Boyd RDH: Mechanism of transfer across the human placenta. In Polin RA, Fox WW, Abman SH (eds): Fetal and Neonatal Physiology, 3d ed. Philadelphia, WB Saunders, 2004, pp 111–122.
7. Boguszewski CL, Svensson PA, Jansson T, et al: Cloning of two novel growth hormone transcripts expressed in human placenta. J Clin Endocrinol Metab 83:2878–2885, 1998.
8. Alsat E, Guibourdenche J, Couturier A, Evain-Brion D: Physiological role of human placental growth hormone. Mol Cell Endocrinol 140:121–127, 1998.
9. Petraglia F, Florio P, Gallo R, et al: Human placenta and fetal membranes express human urocortin mRNA and peptide. J Clin Endocrinol Metab 81:3807–3810, 1996.
10. Glynn BP, Wolton A, Rodriguez-Linares B, et al: Urocortin in pregnancy. Am J Obstet Gynecol 179:533–539, 1998.
11. Han VKM, Bassett N, Walton J, Challis JRG: The expression of insulin-like growth factors (IGF) and IGF-binding protein (IGFBP) genes in the human placenta and membranes: Evidence for IGF-IGFBP interactions at the feto-maternal interface. J Clin Endocrinol Metab 81:2680–2693, 1996.
12. Shiraishi S, Nakagawa K, Kimukawa N, et al: Immunohistochemical localization of vascular endothelial growth factor in the human placenta. Placenta 17:111–121, 1996.
13. Kim MJ, Bogic L, Cheung CY, Brace RA: Expression of erythropoietin mRNA, protein and receptor in ovine fetal membranes. Placenta 22:846–851, 2001.
14. Vuorela P, Hatva E, Lymboussaki A, et al: Expression of vascular endothelial growth factor and placental growth factor in human placenta. Biol Reprod 56:489–494, 1997.
15. Jackson D, Linzer DIH: Proliferin transport and binding in the mouse fetus. Endocrinology 138:149–155, 1992.
16. Kauma S, Hayes N, Weatherford S: The differential expression of hepatocyte growth factor and Met in human placenta. J Clin Endocrinol Metab 82:949–954, 1997.
17. Diaz L, Queipo G, Carino C, et al: Biologically active steroid and thyroid hormones stimulate secretion of sex hormone binding globulin by human term placenta in culture. Arch Med Res 28:29–36, 1997.
18. Petraglia F: Inhibin, activin and follistatin in the human placenta: A family of regulatory proteins. Placenta 18:3–8, 1997.
19. Yasui Y, Yamaguchi M, Jikihara H, et al: Expression of prolactin-releasing peptide in human placenta and deciduas. Endocrine J 48:397–401, 2001.
20. Hassink SG, de Lancey E, Sheslow DV, et al: Placental leptin: An important new growth factor in intrauterine and neonatal development? Pediatrics 100:1–6, 1997.
21. Bogic LV, Yamamoto SY, Millar LK, Bryant-Greenwood GD: Developmental regulation of human relaxin genes in the decidua and placenta: Overexpression in the preterm premature rupture of the fetal membranes. Biol Reprod 57:908–920, 1997.
22. Shore VH, Wang TH, Wang CL, et al: Vascular endothelial growth factor, placental growth factor and their receptors in isolated human trophoblast. Placenta 18:657–665, 1997.
23. Marinoni E, Di Iorio R, Letizia C, et al: Immunoreactive adrenomedullin in human fetoplacental tissues. Am J Obstet Gynecol 179:784–787, 1998.
24. Siler-Khodr TM: Endocrine and paracrine function of the human placenta. In Polin RA, Fox WW, Abman SH (eds): Fetal and Neonatal Physiology, 3d ed. Philadelphia, WB Saunders, 2004, pp 122–131.
25. Roessler E, Belloni E, Gaudenz K, et al: Mutations in the human Sonic hedgehog gene cause holoprosencephaly. Nat Genet 14:357–360, 1996.
26. Brown SA, Warburton D, Brown LY, et al: Holoprosencephaly due to mutation in ZIC1, a homologue of drosophila odd paired. Nat Genet 20:180–183, 1998.
27. Dattani MT, Martinez-Barbera JP, Thomas PQ, et al: HESX1: A novel homeobox gene implicated in septo-optic dysplasia. Horm Res 50(Suppl 3): abstract 6, 1998.
28. Mullis PE: Transcription factors in pituitary gland development and their clinical impact on pituitary disease. Horm Res 54:107–119, 2000.

29. Cohen LE, Radovick S: Molecular basis of combined pituitary hormone deficiencies. Endocr Rev 23:431–442, 2002.

30. Grumbach MM, Gluckman PD: The human fetal hypothalamus and pituitary gland: The maturation of neuroendocrine mechanisms controlling secretion of fetal pituitary growth hormone, prolactin, gonadotropins, adrenocorticotropin-related peptides and thyrotropin. In Tulchinsky D, Little AB (eds): Maternal Fetal Endocrinology, 2d ed. Philadelphia, WB Saunders, 1994, pp 193–261.

31. Mulchakey JJ, Di Blasio AM, Martin MC, et al: Hormone production and peptide regulation of the human fetal pituitary gland. Endocr Rev 8:406–425, 1987.

32. Gluckman PD, Pinal CS: Growth hormone and prolactin. In Polin RA, Fox WW, Abman SH (eds): Fetal and Neonatal Physiology, 3d ed. Philadelphia, WB Saunders, 2004, pp 1891–1895.

33. Gluckman PD, Grumbach MM, Kaplan SL: The neuroendocrine regulation and function of growth hormone and prolactin in the mammalian fetus. Endocr Rev 4:363–395, 1981.

34. Ikida Y, Swain A, Weber TH, et al: Steroidogenic factor 1 and DAX-1 localize in multiple cell lineages: Potential links in endocrine development. Mol Endocrinol 10:1261–1272, 1996.

35. Muscatelli F, Strom TM, Walker AP, et al: Mutations in the DAX-1 gene give rise to both X-linked adrenal hypoplasia congenital and hypogonadotropic hypogonadism. Nature 372:672–676, 1994.

36. Miller WL: Steroid hormone biosynthesis and actions in the materno-feto-placental unit. Clin Perinatol 25:799–817, 1998.

37. Goodfellow PN, Lovell-Badge R: Sex and sex determination in mammals. Annu Rev Genet 27:71–92, 1993.

38. Swain A, Zanaria E, Hacker A, et al: Mouse DAX-1 expression is consistent with a role in both adrenal development and sex determination. Nat Genet 12:404–409, 1996.

39. Winter JSD: Fetal and neonatal adrenocortical physiology. In Polin RA, Fox WW, Abman SH (eds): Fetal and Neonatal Physiology, 3d ed. Philadelphia, WB Saunders, 2004, pp 1915–1925.

40. Dotzler SA, Digeronimo RJ, Yoder BA, Siler-Khodr TM: Distribution of corticotropin releasing hormone in the fetus, newborn, juvenile and adult baboon. Pediatr Res 55:120–125, 2004.

41. Thomson M, Smith R: The action of hypothalamic and placental corticotropin releasing factor on the corticotrope. Mol Cell Endocrinol 62:1–12, 1989.

42. Rivier C, Vale W: Neuroendocrine interactions between corticotropin releasing factor and vasopressin on adrenocorticotropic hormone secretion in the rat. In Schrier RW (ed): Vasopressin. New York, Raven, 1985, pp 181–188.

43. Goland RS, Wardlow SL, Blum M, et al: Biologically active corticotropin releasing hormone in maternal and fetal plasma during pregnancy. Am J Obstet Gynecol 159:884–890, 1988.

44. Wilson D, Baldwin R, Ariagno R: A randomized, placebo-controlled trial of dexamethasone on the hypothalamic pituitary adrenal axis in preterm infants. J Pediatr 113:764–768, 1988.

45. Nelson HP, Kuhn RW, Deyman ME, Jaffe RB: Human fetal adrenal definitive and fetal zone metabolism of pregnenolone and corticosterone: Alternative biosynthetic pathways and absence of detectable aldosterone synthesis. J Clin Endocrinol Metab 70:693–698, 1990.

46. Ballard PL: Glucocorticoids and differentiation. In Baxter JD, Rousseau GG (eds): Monographs on Endocrinology, vol 12: Glucocorticoid Action. Berlin, Springer-Verlag, 1979, pp 493–575.

47. Pavlik A, Buresova M: The neonatal cerebellum: The highest level of glucocorticoid receptors in the brain. Brain Res 12:13–20, 1984.

48. Liggins GC: The role of cortisol in preparing the fetus for birth. Reprod Fertil Dev 6:141–150, 1994.

49. Wintour EM: The renin-angiotensin system and the development of the kidney. Trends Endocrinol Metab 8:199–207, 1997.

50. Beitens IZ, Graham GG, Kowarski J, Migeon CJ: Adrenal function in normal infants and in marasmus and kwashiorkor: Plasma aldosterone concentration and aldosterone secretion rate. J Pediatr 84:444–451, 1974.

51. Siegel SR, Fisher DA: Ontogeny of the renin-angiotensin-aldosterone system in the fetal and newborn lamb. Pediatr Res 14:99–102, 1980.

52. Lumbers ER: Functions of the renin-angiotensin-aldosterone system during development. Clin Exp Pharmacol Physiol 22:499–505, 1995.

53. Meeks JJ, Weiss J, Jameson JL: DAX1 is required for testis determination. Nat Genet 34:32–33, 2003.

54. Lalli E, Sassone-Corsi P: DAX1 an unusual orphan receptor at the crossroads of steroidogenic function and sexual differentiation. Mol Endocrinol 17:1445–1453, 2003.

55. MacLaughlin DT, Teixeira J, Donahoe PK: Perspective: Reproductive tract development: New discoveries and future directions. Endocrinology 142:2167–2172, 2001.

56. Harley VR, Clackson MJ, Argentaro A: The molecular action and regulation of the testis determining factors: SRY (sex determining region of the Y chromosome) and SOX9 (SRY related high mobility group, HMG, Box 9). Endocr Rev 24:466–487, 2003.

57. Rey R, Picard JY: Embryology and endocrinology of genital development. Baillieres Clin Endocrinol Metab 12:17–33, 1998.

58. Pelliniemi LJ, Dym M: The fetal gonad and sexual differentiation. In Tulchinsky D, Little AB (eds): Maternal Fetal Endocrinology, 2d ed. Philadelphia, WB Saunders, 1994, pp 298–320.

59. Josso N, Boussin L, Knebelmann B, et al: Antimüllerian hormone and intersex states. Trends Endocrinol Metab 2:227–233, 1991.

60. Behringer RR, Cote RL, Frochik GJ, et al: Abnormal sexual development in transgenic mice chronically expressing müllerian inhibiting substance. Nature 345:167–170, 1990.

61. Donahoe PK, Budzik GP, Trelstad M, et al: Müllerian inhibiting substance: An update. Recent Prog Horm Res 38:279–326, 1992.

62. Haqq CM, King CY, Ukiyama E, et al: Molecular basis of mammalian sexual differentiation: Activation of mullerian inhibiting substance gene expression by SRY. Science 266:1494–1500, 1994.

63. Barraclough CA, Gorski RA: Evidence that the hypothalamus is responsible for androgen-induced sterility in the female rat. Endocrinology 68:68–79, 1961.

64. Naftolin F, Brawer JR: The effect of estrogens on hypothalamic structure and function. Am J Obstet Gynecol 132:758–765, 1978.

65. Sholl SA, Gay RW, Kim KL: 5α-reductase, aromatase and androgen receptor levels in the monkey brain during fetal development. Endocrinology 124:627–634, 1989.

66. Pintar JE: Normal development of the hypothalamic-pituitary-thyroid axis. In Braverman LE, Utiger RD (eds): The Thyroid, 8th ed. Philadelphia, Lippincott, 2000, pp 7–19.

67. Damante G, Tell G, DiLauro R: A unique combination of transcription factors controls differentiation of thyroid cells. Prog Nucl Acid Res Mol Biol 66:307–356, 2001.

68. Van Vliet G: Development of the thyroid gland: Lessons from congenitally hypothyroid mice and men. Clin Genet 63:445–455, 2003.

69. Espinoza CR, Schmitt TL, Lous U: Thyroid transcription factor 1 and Pax8 synergistically activate the promotor of the human thyroglobulin gene. J Mol Endocrinol 27:59–67, 2001.

70. Flamant F, Poguet AL, Plateroti M, et al: Congenital hypothyroid Pax8 mutant mice can be rescued by inactivating the TRα gene. Mol Endocrinol 16:24–32, 2002.

71. Moeller LC, Kimura S, Kusakabet, et al: Hypothyroidism in thyroid transcription factor 1 haploinsufficiency is caused by reduced expression of the thyroid stimulating hormone receptor. Mol Endocrinol 17:2295–2302, 2003.

72. Kurihara Y, Kurihara H, Maemura K, et al: Impaired development of the

thyroid and thymus in endothelin-1 knockout mice. J Cardiovasc Pharmacol 26(Suppl 3):513–516, 1995.

73. Polk DH, Fisher DA: Fetal and neonatal thyroid physiology. In Polin RA, Fox WW, Abman SH (eds): Fetal and Neonatal Physiology, 3d ed. Philadelphia, WB Saunders, 2004, pp 1926–1933.

74. Burrow GN, Fisher DA, Larsen PR: Maternal and fetal thyroid function. N Engl J Med 331:1072–1078, 1994.

75. Fisher DA: Disorders of the thyroid in the newborn and infant. In Sperling MA (ed): Pediatric Endocrinology, 2d ed, Philadelphia, WB Saunders, 2002, pp 161–185.

76. Fisher DA: Thyroid function in premature infants. Clin Perinatol 25:999–1014, 1998.

77. Polk DH, Reviczky A, Wu SY, et al: Metabolism of sulfoconjugated thyroid hormone derivatives in developing sheep. Am J Physiol 266:E892–E896, 1994.

78. Vulsma T, Gons MH, De Viljder JJM: Maternal-fetal transfer of thyroxine in congenital hypothyroidism due to a total organification defect or thyroid agenesis. N Engl J Med 321:13–16, 1989.

79. Forrest D, Vennstrom B: Functions of thyroid hormone receptors in mice. Thyroid 10:41–52, 2000.

80. Gauthier K, Plateroti M, Harvey CB, et al: Genetic analysis reveals different functions for the products of the thyroid hormone receptor α locus. Mol Cell Biol 21:4748–4760, 2001.

81. Abel ED, Moura EG, Ahima RS, et al: Dominant inhibition of thyroid hormone action selectively in the pituitary of thyroid hormone receptor-β null mice abolishes the regulation of thyrotropin by thyroid hormone. Mol Endocrinol 17:1767–1776, 2003.

82. Bernal J, Pekonen F: Ontogenesis of nuclear 3,5,3′ triiodothyronine receptors in human fetal brain. Endocrinology 114:677–679, 1984.

83. Kilby MD, Giltoes N, McCabe C, et al: Expression of thyroid receptor isoforms in the human fetal central nervous system and the effects of intrauterine growth restriction. Clin Endocrinol (Oxf) 53:469–477, 2000.

84. Morreale De Escobar G, Oregon MJ, Escabor Del Rey F: Is neuropsychological development related to maternal hypothyroidism or to maternal hypothyroxinemia? J Clin Endocrinol Metab 85:3975–3987, 2000.

85. Leake RD: The fetal maternal neurohypophysiol system. In Tulchinsky D, Little AB (eds): Maternal Fetal Endocrinology, 2d ed. Philadelphia, WB Saunders, 1994, pp 264–274.

86. Ervin MG, Leake RD, Ross MG, et al: Arginine vasotocin in ovine maternal and fetal blood, fetal urine, and amniotic fluid. J Clin Invest 75:1696–1701, 1985.

87. Zhao X, Nijland MJM, Ervin G, Ross MG: Regulation of hypothalamic arginine vasopressin messenger ribonucleic acid and pituitary arginine vasopressin content in fetal sheep: Effects of acute tonicity alterations and fetal maturation. Am J Obstet Gynecol 179:899–905, 1998.

88. Baum MA, Ruddy MK, Hosselet CA, Harris HW: The perinatal expression of aquaporin-2 and aquaporin-3 in developing kidney. Pediatr Res 43:783–790, 1998.

89. Devuyst O, Burrow CR, Smithe BL, et al: Expression of aquaporins 1 and 2 during nephrogenesis and in autosomal dominant polycystic kidney disease. Am J Physiol 271:F169–F183, 1996.

90. Norman LJ, Challis JRG: Synergism between systemic corticotropin-releasing factor and arginine vasopressin on adrenocorticotropin release in vivo varies as a function of gestational age in the ovine fetus. Endocrinology 120:1052–1058, 1987.

91. Brooks AN, White A: Activation of pituitary adrenal function in fetal sheep by corticotropin-releasing factor and arginine vasopressin. J Endocrinol 124:27–35, 1990.

92. Yasui M, Marples D, Belusa R, et al: Development of urinary concentrating capacity: Role of aquaporin-2. Am J Physiol 271:F461–F468, 1996.

93. Padbury JF: Functional maturation of the adrenal medulla and peripheral sympathetic nervous system. Baillieres Clin Endocrinol Metab 33:689–705, 1989.

94. Aloe L, Levin-Montalcini R: Nerve growth factor–induced transformation of immature chromaffin cells in vivo into sympathetic neurons: Effect of antiserum to nerve growth factor. Proc Natl Acad Sci U S A, 76:1246–1250, 1979.

95. Slotkin TA, Seidler FJ: Adrenomedullary catecholamine release in the fetus and newborn: Secretory mechanisms and their role in stress and survival. J Dev Physiol 10:1–6, 1988.

96. Harwell C, Padbury JF, Anand RS, et al: Fetal catecholamine responses to maternal hypoglycemia. Am J Physiol 259:1126–1130, 1990.

97. Palmer SM, Oakes GK, Lam RW, et al: Catecholamine physiology in the ovine fetus. II. Metabolic clearance of epinephrine. Am J Physiol 246:E350–E355, 1984.

98. Palmer SM, Oakes GK, Champion JA, et al: Catecholamine physiology in the ovine fetus. III. Maternal and fetal response to acute maternal exercise. Am J Obstet Gynecol 149:426–434, 1984.

99. Padbury JF, Martinez AM: Sympathoadrenal system activity at birth: Integration of postnatal adaptation. Semin Perinatol 12:163–172, 1988.

100. Pryds O, Christensen NJ, Friis-Hansen B: Increased cerebral blood flow and plasma epinephrine in hypoglycemic, pretern neonates. Pediatrics 85:172–176, 1990.

101. Zhou QY, Ouaife CJ, Palmiter RD: Targeted disruption of the tyrosine hydroxylase gene reveals that catecholamines are required for mouse fetal development. Nature 374:640–643, 1995.

102. Thomas SA, Matsumoto AM, Palmiter RD: Noradrenaline is essential for mouse fetal development. Nature 374:643–646, 1995.

103. Habener JF, Stoffers DA: A newly discovered role of transcription factors involved in pancreas development and the pathogenesis of diabetes mellitus. Proc Assoc Am Phys 110:12–21, 1998.

104. Edlund H: Pancreatic organogenesis: Developmental mechanisms and implications for therapy. Nat Rev Genet 3:524–532, 2002.

105. Polak M, Bouchareb L, Scharfman R, Czernichow P: Early pattern of differentiation in the human pancreas. Diabetes 49:225–232, 2000.

106. Sperling MA: Carbohydrate metabolism: Insulin and glucagon. In Tulchinsky D, Little AB (eds): Maternal Fetal Endocrinology, 2d ed. Philadelphia, WB Saunders, 1994, pp 380–400.

107. Girard J: Control of fetal and neonatal glucose metabolism by pancreatic hormones. Ballieres Clin Endocrinol Metab 3:817–836, 1989.

108. Aldoretta PW, Carver TD, Hay WW Jr: Maturation of glucose-stimulated insulin secretion in fetal sheep. Biol Neonate 73:375–386, 1998.

109. Hernandez-Sanchez C, Wood TL, LeRoith D: Developmental and tissue specific sulfonylurea receptor gene expression. Endocrinology 138:705–711, 1997.

110. Frazer TE, Karl IE, Hillman LS, Bier D: Direct measurement of gluconeogenesis from $(2,3-^{13}C_2)$-alanine in the human neonate. Am J Physiol 240:E615–E621, 1981.

111. Chisaka O, Capecchi MR: Regionally restricted developmental defects resulting from targeted disruption of the mouse homeobox gene hox 15. Nature 350:473–479, 1991.

112. Miao D, He B, Karaplis C, Goltzman D: Parathyroid hormone is essential for normal fetal bone formation. J Clin Invest 109:1173–1182, 2002.

113. Wolfe HJ, DeLellis RA, Voelkel EF, Tashjian AH Jr: Distribution of calcitonin containing cells in the normal neonatal human thyroid gland: A correlation of morphology and peptide content. J Clin Endocrinol Metab 41:1076–1081, 1975.

114. Care AD: Development of endocrine pathways in the regulation of calcium homeostasis. Baillieres Clin Endocrinol Metab 3:671–688, 1989.

115. Care AD, Abbas SK, Pickard DW, et al: Stimulation of ovine placental transport of calcium and magnesium by mid-molecule fragments of human

parathyroid hormone–related protein. Exp Physiol 75:605–608, 1990.

116. Kovacs CS, Lanske B, Hunzelman JL, et al: Parathyroid hormone–related peptide (PTHrP) regulates fetal-placental calcium transport through a receptor distinct from the PTH/PTHrP receptor. Proc Natl Acad Sci U S A 93:15233–15238, 1996.

117. Moore ES, Langman CB, Fauus MJ, et al: Role of fetal 1,25 dihydroxyvitamin D production in intrauterine phosphorus and calcium homeostasis. Pediatr Res 19:566–569, 1985.

118. Karaplis AC, Luz A, Glowacki J, et al: Lethal skeletal dysplasia from targeted disruption of the parathyroid hormone–related protein gene. Genes Dev 8:277–289, 1994.

119. Lanske B, Amling M, Neff L, et al: Ablation of the PTHrP gene or the PTH/PTHrP receptor gene leads to distinct abnormalities in bone development. J Clin Invest 104:399–407, 1999.

120. Hoff AO, Catala-Lehnen P, Thomas PM, et al: Increased bone mass in an unexpected phenotype associated with deletion of the calcitonin gene. J Clin Invest 110:1849–1857, 2002.

121. Amling M, Priemel M, Holzman T, et al: Rescue of the skeletal phenotype of vitamin D receptor ablated mice in the setting of normal mineral ion homeostasis: Formal histomorphometric and biomechanical analyses. Endocrinology 140:4982–4987, 1999.

122. Itsuro H, Tanaka T: Hormonal regulation of growth and maturation in the effect of hormones on fetal growth. Clin Pediatr Endocrinol 6:57–71, 1997.

123. DeLeon DD, Cohen P, Levi IT, Katz LE: Growth factor regulation of fetal growth. In Polin RA, Fox WW, Abman SH (eds): Fetal and Neonatal Physiology, 3d ed. Philadelphia, WB Saunders, 2004, pp 1880–1890.

124. Styne DM: Fetal growth. Clin Perinatol 25:917–938, 1998.

125. deZegher F, Boehmer ALM, Saggese G, et al: Androgens and fetal growth. Horm Res 50:243–244, 1998.

126. Baker J, Liu JP, Robertson EJ, Efstradiadis A: Role of insulin-like growth factors in embryonic and postnatal growth. Cell 75:73–82, 1993.

127. Liu JKP, Baker J, Perkins AS, et al: Mice carrying null mutations of the genes encoding insulin-like growth factor I and type I IGF receptor. Cell 75:59–72, 1993.

128. DeChiara TM, Efstradiadis A, Robertson EJ: A growth deficiency phenotype in heterozygous mice carrying an insulin-like growth factor II gene disrupted by targeting. Nature 345:78–80, 1990.

129. Han VKM, D'Ercole AJ, Lung PK: Identification of somatomedin (insulin-like growth factor) messenger RNA in the human fetus. Pediatr Res 22:245–249, 1987.

130. Bennett A, Wilson D, Liu F, Nagashima R, et al: Levels of insulin-like growth factors I and II in human cord blood. J Clin Endocrinol Metab 57:609–612, 1983.

131. Freemark M, Comer M: Purification of a distinct placental lactogen receptor, a new member of the growth hormone/prolactin receptor family. J Clin Invest 83:883–889, 1989.

132. Hill DJ, Crace CJ, Strain AJ, Milner RDG: Regulation of amino acid uptake and deoxyribonucleic acid synthesis in isolated human fetal fibroblasts and myoblasts: Effects of human placenta lactogen, somatomedin-C, multiplication stimulating activity, and insulin. J Clin Endocrinol Metab 62:753–760, 1986.

133. Pilistine SJ, Moses AC, Munro HN: Placental lactogen administration reverses the effect of low protein diet on maternal and fetal somatomedin levels in the pregnant rat. Proc Natl Acad Sci U S A 81:5853–5857, 1984.

134. Johnson JW, Mitzner W, Beck JC, et al: Long-term effects of betamethasone in fetal development. Am J Obstet Gynecol 141:1053–1064, 1981.

135. Susa JB, McCormick KL, Widness JA, et al: Chronic hyperinsulinemia in the fetal rhesus monkey: Effects on fetal growth and composition. Diabetes 28:1058–1063, 1979.

136. Accili D, Drago J, Lee EJ, et al: Early neonatal death in mice homozygous for a null allele of the insulin receptor gene. Nat Genet 12:106–109, 1996.

137. Krook A, Brueton L, O'Rahilly S: Homozygous nonsense mutation in the insulin receptor gene in an infant with leprechaunism. Lancet 342:277–278, 1993.

138. Fisher DA, Lakshmanan J: Metabolism and effects of EGF and related growth factors in mammals. Endocr Rev 11:418–442, 1990.

139. Tsutumi O, Oka T: Epidermal growth factor deficiency during pregnancy causes abortion in mice. Am J Obstet Gynecol 156:241–244, 1987.

140. Meittinen PJ, Berger JE, Mesesses T, et al: Epithelial immaturity and multiorgan failture in mice lacking epidermal growth factor receptor. Nature 376:337–341, 1995.

141. Snead ML, Luo W, Oliver P, et al: Localization of epidermal growth factor precursor in tooth and lung during embryonic mouse development. Dev Biol 134:420–429, 1989.

142. Brown PL, Lam R, Lakshmanan J, Fisher DA: Transforming growth factor alpha in the developing rat. Am J Physiol 259:E256–E260, 1990.

143. Freemark M, Comer M: Epidermal growth factor–like transforming growth factor (TGF) activity and EGF receptors in ovine fetal tissues: Possible role for TGF in ovine fetal development. Pediatr Res 22:609–615, 1987.

144. Hemmings R, Langlais J, Falcone T, et al: Human embryos produce transforming growth factors α activity and insulin-like growth factor II. Fertil Steril 58:101–104, 1992.

145. Mazzoni IE, Kemigsberg RL: Effects of epidermal growth factor in the mammalian central nervous system. Drug Dev Res 26:111–128, 1992.

146. Kitchens DL, Snyder EY, Gottlieb DI: FGF and EGF are mitogens for immortalized neural progenitors. J Neurobiol 21:356–375, 1990.

147. Santa-Olalla J, Covarrubias L: Epidermal growth factor, transforming growth factor α, and fibroblast growth factor differentially influence neural precursor cells of mouse embryonic mesencephalon. J Neurosci Res 42:172–183, 1995.

148. Lee KF, Simon H, Chen C, et al: Requirement for neuregulin receptor erbB2 in neural and cardiac development. Nature 378:394–398, 1995.

149. Gassmann M, Casagranda F, Orioli D, et al: Aberrant neural and cardiac development in mice lacking the erbB4 neuregulin receptor. Nature 378:390–394, 1995.

150. Snider WD: Functions of the neurotropins during nervous system development: What the knockouts are teaching us. Cell 77:627–628, 1994.

151. Riethmacher D, Sonnenberg-Riethmacher E, Brinkmann V, et al: Severe neuropathies in mice with targeted mutations in the ErbB3 receptor. Nature 389:725–730, 1997.

152. Sieff CA: Hematopoietic growth factors. J Clin Invest 79:1549–1557, 1987.

153. Zanjani ED, Ascensau JL, McGlave PG: Studies on the liver to kidney switch of erythropoietin production. J Clin Invest 67:1183–1188, 1981.

154. Eckardt KU, Ratcliffe PJ, Tan CC, et al: Age dependent expression of the erythropoietin gene in rat liver and kidneys. J Clin Invest 89:753–760, 1992.

155. Liu L, Nicoll CS: Evidence for a role of basic fibroblast growth factor in rat embryonic growth and differentiation. Endocrinology 123:2027–2031, 1988.

156. Gospodarowicz D: Epidermal and nerve growth factors in mammalian development. Annu Rev Physiol 43:251–263, 1981.

157. Bradshaw RA: Nerve growth factor. Annu Rev Biochem 47:191–216, 1978.

158. Yan Q, Elliott J, Snidor WD: Brain derived neurotropic factor reserves spinal motor neurons from axotomy-induced cell death. Nature 360:753–755, 1992.

159. Giordano T, Pan JB, Casuto D, et al: Thyroid hormone regulation of NGF, NT3, and BDNF RNA in adult rat brain. Brain Res Mol 16:239–245, 1992.

160. Gorin PD, Johnson EM: Effects of exposure to nerve growth factor antibodies on the developing nervous system of the rat: An experimental

autoimmune approach. Dev Biol 80:313–323, 1980.

161. Padbury JF, Lam RW, Polk DH, et al: Autoimmune sympathectomy in fetal rabbits. J Dev Physiol 8:369–376, 1986.

162. Lakshmanan J, Weichsel ME Jr, Tarris R, et al: β Nerve growth factor in developing mouse cerebral cortical synaptosomes: Measurement by competitive radioimmunoassay and bioassay. Pediatr Res 20:391–397, 1986.

163. Chang H, Brown CW, Matzuk MM: Genetic analysis of the mammalian transforming growth factor β superfamily. Endocr Rev 23:787–823, 2002.

164. Stiver SI, Dvorak HF: Vascular permeability factor/vascular endothelial growth factor (VPF/VEGF). J Clin Ligand Assay Society 23:193–205, 2000.

165. Betsholtz C: Functions of the platelet derived growth factor and its receptors deduced from gene inactivation in mice. J Clin Ligand Assay Society 23:206–213, 2000.

166. Gluckman PD, Sizonenko SV, Bassett NS: The transition from fetus to neonate: An endocrine perspective. Acta Paediatr Suppl 428:7–11, 1999.

167. Padbury JF: Functional maturation of the adrenal medulla and peripheral sympathetic nervous system. Baillieres Clin Endocrinol Metab 3:689–705, 1989.

168. Birk E, Iwamoto HS, Heymann M: Hormonal effects on circulating changes during the perinatal period. Ballieres Clin Endocrinol Metab 3:795–815, 1989.

169. Wallace MJ, Hooper SB, Harding R: Effects of elevated fetal cortisol concentrations on the volume, secretion, and absorption of lung liquid. Am J Physiol 269:R881–R887, 1995.

170. Cole TJ, Blendy JA, Monaghan P, et al: Targeted disruption of the glucocorticoid receptor gene blocks adrenergic chromaffen cell development and severely retards lung development. Genes Dev 9:1608–1621, 1995.

171. Ballard RA: Antenatal glucocorticoid therapy: Clinical effects. Monogr Endocrinol 28:137–172, 1986.

172. Padbury JF, Agata Y, Ludlow J, et al: Effect of fetal adrenalectomy on catecholamine release and physiologic adaptation at birth in sheep. J Clin Invest 80:1096–1103, 1987.

173. Polk DH: Thyroid hormone effect on neonatal thermogenesis. Semin Perinatol 12:151–156, 1988.

174. Fisher DA, Polk DH, Wu SY: Fetal thyroid metabolism: A pluralistic system. Thyroid 4:367–371, 1994.

175. Gunn TR, Gluckman PD: Perinatal thermogenesis. Early Hum Dev 42:169–183, 1995.

176. Schwitzgebel VM, Gitelman SE: Neonatal hyperinsulinism. Clin Perinatol 25:1015–1038, 1998.

177. Mimouni F, Tsang RC, Namgung R, Tsang RC: Neonatal calcium, phosphorus and magnesium homeostasis. In Polin RA, Fox WW, Abman SH (eds): Fetal and Neonatal Physiology, 3d ed. Philadelphia, WB Saunders, 2004, pp 323–341.

178. Fisher DA, Nelson JC, Carlton EI, Wilcox RB: Maturation of human hypothalamic-pituitary thyroid function and control. Thyroid 10:229–234, 2000.

# Fuel Homeostasis in the Fetus and Neonate

## *William W. Hay Jr. and Marianne S. Anderson*

**FUEL HOMEOSTASIS IN THE FETUS**
 Fetal Carbohydrate Metabolism
 Fetal Lipid Metabolism
 Fetal Amino Acid Metabolism
 Short- and Long-Term Consequences of Abnormal
 Fetal Nutrient Supply

**FUEL HOMEOSTASIS IN THE NEONATE**
 Glucose Homeostasis in the Newborn
 Neonatal Hyperglycemia
 Postnatal Protein and Amino Acid Metabolism
 Postnatal Energy Metabolism
 Postnatal Lipid Metabolism

## FUEL HOMEOSTASIS IN THE FETUS

The principal metabolic fuels in the fetus are glucose and amino acids. Glucose serves as the main substrate for maintenance energy production and energy storage in glycogen and adipose tissue. Amino acids are also oxidized for maintenance energy production, but their primary role is in protein synthesis and growth. Fatty acids are used primarily for structural components of membranes and for growth of adipose tissue. Glucose and fatty acids are transported from mother to fetus by the placenta according to maternal plasma concentrations. Amino acids are actively transported into the fetus by the placenta. Hormonal regulation of metabolic substrate utilization and anabolism in the fetus, including the effects of insulin and the insulin-like growth factors (IGFs), is important but secondary to the supply of nutrient substrates. Placental metabolism and nutrient transfer to the fetus and placental-fetal metabolic interactions are key regulatory aspects of fetal fuel metabolism. These subjects have been reviewed extensively elsewhere.[1-5] Estimates of carbon supply to the fetus are compared with requirements for energy production and storage in Table 184-1.[5-7]

### FETAL CARBOHYDRATE METABOLISM

Uterine, placental, and fetal glucose uptake rates are directly related to maternal glucose concentration,[8] whereas the partition of uterine glucose uptake into fetal and uteroplacental glucose uptakes is independently regulated by fetal glucose concentration[8,9] (Fig. 184-1). To provide for the increasing glucose requirements of the growing fetus over gestation, fetal glucose concentration decreases relative to that in the mother by progressive development of fetal insulin secretion and growth of insulin-sensitive tissue, thus increasing the transplacental glucose concentration gradient.[10] Placental glucose transport capacity also increases severalfold over the second half of gestation, commensurate with growth of the trophoblast surface area of the placenta and increased expression of GLUT1 and GLUT3 glucose transporter proteins on the trophoblast membranes.[11]

#### Alternative Carbohydrates Produced in the Placenta
The fraction of fetal glucose utilization that acutely produces carbon dioxide is about 0.5 to 0.6[12] (Table 184-2). Thus, carbon substrates other than glucose are required to meet the oxidative requirements imposed by the fetal respiration rate (quantified as the net rate of oxygen consumption). At markedly reduced rates of glucose supply to the fetus, the fetal glucose utilization rate decreases proportionally.[8,13] Under such short-term (hours to days) conditions, fetal oxygen con-

sumption remains near normal, indicating active reciprocal oxidation of other substrates, such as glucose released from glycogen, lactate, amino acids, fatty acids, and keto acids.[14-16] Over longer periods (>2 weeks) of reduced glucose supply, fetal oxygen consumption tends to decrease by up to 25% to 30%. Because the rate of fetal growth decreases at the same time and to the same extent, the reduction in fetal oxygen consumption with prolonged glucose/energy deficiency probably represents the oxidative requirements of the decreased rate of protein synthesis.

### Fetal Glucose Uptake and Utilization
The fetal glucose utilization rate is about 5 to 7 mg/min/kg fetal weight near term, down from values nearly twice as high in midgestation[10,17,18] when fetal growth rate is also about twice as great as that closer to term. Table 184-3 presents estimated utilization rates of glucose in several fetal organs and the remaining carcass of fetal sheep in late gestation. Most organs appear dependent on plasma glucose concentration for their specific rate of glucose uptake, whereas skeletal muscle, heart, and liver develop insulin sensitivity in later gestation.

#### Kinetics of Glucose Utilization in the Fetus
The capacity for glucose utilization in the fetus follows Michaelis-Menton or saturation-limited kinetics.[12] The glucose utilization capacity itself is variable, as increased fetal glucose supply from the placenta increases fetal insulin secretion, which, in turn, augments fetal glucose utilization, limiting further increase in fetal glucose concentration.[18,19] In fetal sheep, plasma glucose and insulin concentrations act independently (i.e., additively) to increase glucose utilization and oxidation proportionally, according to saturation kinetics.[12] Glucose, insulin, or both may promote lipogenesis more than oxidation in the human fetus, which naturally produces adipose tissue in late gestation, similar to adult humans in whom higher rates of glucose utilization are partitioned more into glucose storage (fat and glycogen) than into oxidation. Glucose carbon also contributes significantly to the formation of glycogen in the liver, heart, skeletal muscle, and lung, and to the carbon contained in amino acids and synthesized proteins (DiGiacomo JE et al., unpublished data, 1990). Examples of the fetal metabolic effects of decreased and increased glucose supply to the fetus are shown in Tables 184-4 and 184-5.[1]

### Fetal Insulin Secretion
Glucose-stimulated fetal insulin increases more than fivefold during the second half of gestation in fetal sheep, similar to the evidence for pancreatic development in human fetuses derived from studies of fetal islets in vitro and insulin secretion in preterm infants.[20-22] Fetal insulin secretion can be

**Table 184-1    Estimated Human Fetal Nutrient Substrate Balance in Late Gestation**

|  | Carbon (g/kg/day) | Calories (kcal/kg/day) |
|---|---|---|
| **REQUIREMENT** | | |
| Accretion in carcass: nonfat (human) | 3.2 | 32 |
| Accretion in carcass: fat (human) | 3.5 | 33 |
| Excretion as $CO_2$ | 4.4 | 0 |
| Excretion as urea | 0.2 | 2 |
| Excretion as glutamate | 0.3 | 2 |
| Heat (measured as $O_2$ consumption) | 0.0 | 50 |
| Totals | 11.6 | 119 |
| **UPTAKE** | | |
| Amino acids | 3.9 | 45 |
| Glucose | 3.7 | 26 |
| Lactate | 1.7 | 21 |
| Fatty acids | 1.1–2.2 | 17–34 |
| Totals | 10.4–11.5 | 109–126 |

Data from Battaglia FC, Meschia G: An Introduction to Fetal Physiology. Orlando, FL, Academic, 1986; Hay WW Jr: Fetal requirements and placental transfer of nitrogenous compounds. In Polin RA, Fox WW (eds): Fetal and Neonatal Physiology. Philadelphia, WB Saunders, 1991, pp 431–442; and Sparks JW, Girard J, Battaglia FC: An estimate of the caloric requirements of the human fetus. Biol Neonate 38:113–119, 1980.

modified. Sustained, marked hyperglycemia in fetal sheep[23] and rats,[24,25] for example, actually decreases fetal insulin secretion, which contrasts with the human fetus of a diabetic mother in whom hyperglycemia stimulates fetal insulin secretion.[26] Variability in maternal and, thus, fetal glucose concentration is a principal cause of enhanced fetal insulin secretion. There is a strong tendency among normal pregnant women and women with gestational diabetes to develop increasingly exaggerated, meal-associated hyperglycemia in

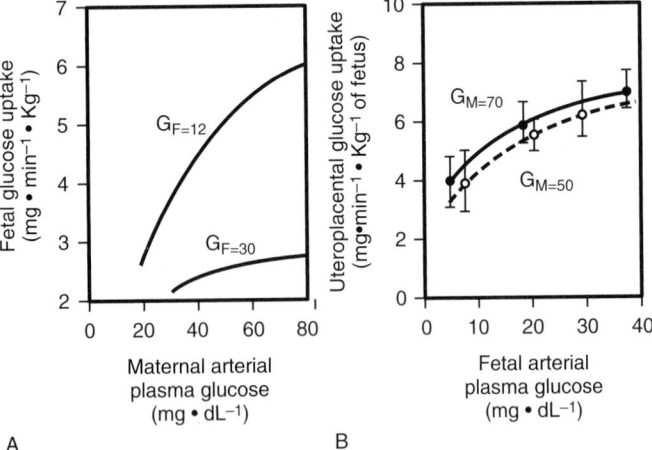

**Figure 184-1    A,** Fetal glucose ($G_F$) uptake (net transfer of glucose from placenta to fetal circulation) plotted against maternal arterial glucose ($G_M$) concentration, showing a saturable dependence of fetal glucose uptake on maternal glucose concentration. This relationship shifts to the left as fetal glucose concentration is decreased, because as fetal glucose concentration decreases relative to that of the mother, the maternal-fetal glucose concentration gradient is increased, which increases the rate of placental-to-fetal glucose transfer. **B,** Net rate of uteroplacental glucose consumption in sheep, showing that although maternal glucose concentration determines glucose entry into the uteroplacenta and fetus, uteroplacental glucose consumption is regulated primarily by the fetal glucose concentration. (Adapted from Hay WW Jr, Molina RD, DiGiacomo JE, et al: Model of placental glucose consumption and transfer. Am J Physiol 258:R569–R577, 1990.)

**Table 184-2    Fetal Carbon Substrate Oxidation in Relation to Fetal Oxygen Consumption ($VO_2$)***

| Substrate | Oxidation Fraction | Carbon for Oxidation (mmol/min/kg) | Fraction for Fetal $VO_2$ |
|---|---|---|---|
| Glucose | 0.55 | 0.09 | 0.29 |
| Lactate | 0.72 | 0.14 | 0.50 |
| Amino acids | 0.30 | 0.03 | 0.09 |
| Total | | 0.26 | 0.88 |

*Estimates derived from data in fetal sheep in late gestation.
Data from Battaglia FC, Meschia G: An Introduction to Fetal Physiology. Orlando, FL, Academic, 1986; Hay WW Jr, DiGiacomo JE, Meznarich HK, et al: Effects of glucose and insulin on fetal glucose oxidation and oxygen consumption. Am J Physiol 256:E704–E713, 1989; Sparks JW, Hay WW Jr, Bonds D, et al: Simultaneous measurements of lactate turnover rate and umbilical lactate uptake in the fetal lamb. J Clin Invest 70:179–192, 1982; Meznarich HK, Hay WW Jr, Sparks JW, et al: Fructose disposal and oxidation rates in the ovine fetus. Q J Exp Physiol 72:617–625, 1987; and Hay WW Jr, Meyers SA, Sparks JW, et al: Glucose and lactate oxidation rates in the fetal lamb. Proc Soc Exp Biol Med 73:553–563, 1983.

**Table 184-3    Metabolic Rates in the Fetus That Account for Glucose Utilization (Based on Data in Fetal Sheep and Estimates for Human Fetuses for Brain)**

|  | Glucose Utilization Rate (mg/min/kg of fetal weight) | % of Total |
|---|---|---|
| Whole fetus (sheep, measured) | 5.0 | 100 |
| Whole fetus (human, estimated) | 6.0–8.0 | 100 |
| Brain (sheep, measured) | 0.8 | 16 |
| Brain (human, estimated) | 4.0 | 50–67 |
| Heart (sheep, measured) | 0.65 | 13 |
| Lungs (sheep, estimated) | 0.1 | 2 |
| Liver (sheep, measured) | 0.1 | 2 |
| Red blood cells (human, estimated) | 0.1 | 2 |
| Carcass/skeletal muscle (estimated sheep) | 3.25 | 65 |
| Total of organs accounted for | | |
| Sheep | 5.0 | 100 |
| Human | 8.2 | 103–137 |

Data from Battaglia FC, Meschia G: An Introduction to Fetal Physiology. Orlando, FL, Academic, 1986; Hay WW Jr: Fetal requirements and placental transfer of nitrogenous compounds. In Polin RA, Fox WW (eds): Fetal and Neonatal Physiology. Philadelphia, WB Saunders, 1991, pp 431–442; and Sparks JW, Girard J, Battaglia FC: An estimate of the caloric requirements of the human fetus. Biol Neonate 38:113–119, 1980.

**Table 184-4    Fetal Responses to Decreased Glucose Supply**

**ACUTE**
Hypoglycemia
Decreased insulin production, secretion, and hypoinsulinemia
Decreased glucose utilization
Increase in the rate of placental glucose transfer to the fetus by increasing the maternal-fetal glucose concentration gradient
Decreased placental lactate production, and fetal lactate uptake and utilization
Substitution of amino acids to maintain oxidative metabolism

**CHRONIC**
Initial increase, then decrease in fetal glucose production
Initial increase in amino acid oxidation, then a return to normal rates
Increased ratio of fetal-to-maternal glucose concentration
Increased ratio of placental glucose consumption to placental glucose transfer

Adapted from Hay WW Jr: Nutrition and development of the fetus: Carbohydrate and lipid metabolism. In Walker WA, Watkins JB, Duggan CP (eds): Nutrition in Pediatrics (Basic Science and Clinical Applications), 3d ed., Hamilton, Ontario, BC Decker, 2003, pp 449–470.

Adapted from Hay WW Jr: Nutrition and development of the fetus:
Carbohydrate and lipid metabolism. In Walker WA, Watkins JB, Duggan CP
(eds): Nutrition in Pediatrics (Basic Science and Clinical Applications), 3d ed.,
Hamilton, BC Decker, 2003, pp 449–470.

late gestation.[27] Furthermore, pulsatile hyperglycemia in fetal
sheep enhances insulin secretion.[28] Fatty acids also stimulate
fetal insulin secretion and their concentrations are increased
in pregnant diabetic women and their fetuses in late gestation, perhaps contributing to augmented insulin secretion,[27]
although short-term lipid infusions into fetal sheep do not
increase glucose-stimulated insulin secretion.[29] Acute and
chronic hypoglycemia decrease fetal glucose and amino acid
stimulated insulin secretion,[30,31] although the independent
roles of decreased glucose per se versus concomitantly
decreased insulin and IGF-1 concentrations have not been
sorted out. Islets of chronically hypoglycemic fetal sheep have
a reduced capacity to secrete insulin, but glucose metabolism
of the islets is unaltered.[32] Islets from nutrient-deprived
intrauterine growth retardation (IUGR) fetuses are not able to
produce adequate amounts of insulin, however, in large measure due to reduced islet number and size.[33] Mechanisms
responsible for these differences are not known; they may
involve the added amino acid and/or oxygen deficiencies,
altered pancreatic β-cell development due to diminished
action of reduced transcription factors, or reduced angiogenesis in the IUGR fetuses.

## Fetal Insulin Action

An acute, sustained increase in fetal insulin concentration,
stimulated either by acute increases in the concentrations of
glucose and/or amino acids or by infusion, augments glucose
utilization in insulin-sensitive tissues.[12] Basal plasma insulin
concentrations, however, appear to have little effect on glucose uptake or metabolism, at least as shown by experiments
in fetal sheep in which an acute decrease of fetal plasma
insulin concentration with somatostatin infusion does not
change fetal glucose concentrations or glucose utilization
rates.[34] By contrast, a chronic decrease in fetal plasma insulin
concentration, either by surgical pancreatectomy or streptozotocin injection into the fetus,[19,35,36] reduces fetal growth
and decreases placental-to-fetal glucose transfer in relation
to fetal hyperglycemia. The hyperglycemia results from
decreased peripheral tissue insulin sensitivity[37] and, thus,
glucose utilization, and from the release of insulin's normal
inhibition of hepatic glucose production.

Insulin is also essential for normal rates of fetal growth,
although growth continues without insulin, just at a slower
rate. Part of this anabolic effect of insulin in the fetus is due
to its augmentation of glucose uptake and utilization by
insulin-sensitive tissues. Insulin also acts to promote amino
acid incorporation into protein synthesis,[38] but not necessarily into oxidation,[39] resulting in increased net protein accretion. There is little effect of insulin to inhibit protein
breakdown in the fetus,[40] and insulin simultaneously
increases the plasma concentration of IGF-binding protein-3
(IGFBP-3), which might serve to attenuate the immediate
anabolic effects of insulin.[41] The anabolic effect of insulin is
enhanced by a separate direct effect of insulin, independent
of glucose: activating the mitogen-activated protein kinase
(MAPK) pathway, which leads to downstream mechanisms
that result in cell growth as well as turnover.[42] In fact, all of
the insulin signal transduction proteins appear to be activated
by insulin in fetal tissues starting as soon as an increase in
plasma insulin concentration occurs.[43] Insulin specifically
regulates protein translation initiation by amino acids in fetal
skeletal muscle and liver via phosphorylation activation of
the phosphatidylinositol kinase (PI 3-kinase)-protein kinase
B (PKB)/Akt-p70 S6 kinase pathway by increasing phosphorylation of 4E-PB1 and eIF4E.eIF4g binding and decreasing
4E-BP1 content associated with eIF4E.[44]

### Effect of Other Hormones on Fetal Glucose Metabolism

Fetal thyroid hormone indirectly enhances fetal glucose utilization by increasing the fetal metabolic rate (oxygen consumption).[45] Changes in fetal plasma cortisol concentrations
during late gestation have little effect on fetal glucose concentrations or on the rates of glucose utilization.[46] Fetal
plasma cortisol concentrations increase in very late gestation,
however, at which time the cortisol-dependent increases in
fetal hepatic glycogen and gluconeogenic enzyme activities
enhance the glucogenic capacity of the fetus and may contribute to the endogenous glucose production observed in
normal fetuses just before term and at the time of delivery.[47]
Such glucose production contributes to acute hyperglycemia,
decreasing fetal glucose uptake from the placenta (due to the
hyperglycemia-produced decrease in the maternal-fetal glucose concentration gradient) but enhancing glucose utilization by the placenta.[48] Infused cortisol in fetal sheep also
inhibits fetal growth, perhaps directly, but at the very least by
increasing fetal glucose production and plasma concentrations and thereby the net uptake of glucose.[49] Glucagon and
circulating catecholamines (adrenal epinephrine and spillover
norepinephrine from peripheral nerve endings) are normally
present in modest concentrations in the fetal plasma, but
they do stimulate fetal glucogenesis when infused into the
fetus—catecholamines at physiologic levels,[50] but glucagon
requiring relatively high concentrations.[51] Like the effects
of increased plasma concentrations of cortisol in the fetus,
increased catecholamine concentrations enhance fetal glucose production directly and by inhibiting insulin secretion
and insulin action.[52]

### Insulin-like Growth Factors and Other Growth Factors

When infused to high physiologic levels, IGF-1 tends to produce lower glucose concentrations in the fetal sheep despite a
simultaneous decrease in insulin concentration, probably by
enhancing glucose utilization.[53] The rate of glucose entry into
the fetal plasma also occurs, probably due to increased glucose transport across the placenta due to the increase in
maternal-fetal glucose concentration gradient produced by
the decrease in fetal glucose concentrations. Studies of these
phenomena are limited and incomplete, however. On balance, it appears that IGF-1 has little or no direct effect on fetal
glucose kinetics.[54] Glucose itself acts at the transcriptional
level to regulate the production and plasma concentrations of
both IGF-1 and IGF-2.[55] Plasma insulin also independently
promotes IGF-1 synthesis.[55,56] These observations indicate
that the supply of glucose regulates fetal IGF-1 production. In

turn, IGF-1 can increase protein synthesis, decrease amino acid oxidation, and inhibit protein breakdown,[56] as does insulin[57]; in fact, IGF-1 and insulin can act synergistically in these situations.[40] Thus, both insulin and IGF-1 indirectly enhance the capacity for glucose to promote fetal nitrogen balance and growth. Circulating concentrations and tissue expression of the IGFs are reduced by undernutrition and deficiency of nutritionally sensitive hormones, such as insulin, thyroxine, and glucocorticoids. In general, the IGF-1 gene is more responsive to these stimuli than the IGF-2 gene. In addition, the effects of the IGFs on fetal growth can be amplified or attenuated by the IGFBPs, which are themselves regulated by nutritional and endocrine signals. The increase in fetal IGFBP-1 expression observed during adverse conditions may attenuate the growth-promoting effects of the IGFs, for example, and thereby contribute to the decline in fetal growth rate found in these circumstances. In contrast, the decrease in the soluble form of the IGF-2 type II receptor during fetal undernutrition may increase availability of plasma IGF-2 and promote tissue differentiation, while maintaining a basal stimulus to fetal growth in the face of low IGF-1 bioavailability. The IGF-2 gene appears to provide the constitutive drive for intrauterine growth (placenta and fetus) via its placental effects and direct paracrine actions on fetal tissue whereas the IGF-1 gene regulates fetal growth in relation to the nutrient supply.[58]

### Fetal Glucose Transporters
Glucose transporter-1 (GLUT1) is found throughout the fetal tissues and on all endothelial cells and probably accounts for the majority of basal tissue glucose uptake from the fetal plasma. GLUT4 is found in the heart, adipose tissue, and skeletal muscle, and its translocation to the cell membrane is promoted by acute increases in fetal plasma insulin concentrations.[43,59] In the fetal sheep, GLUT1 expression is upregulated by hypoglycemia and hypoinsulinemia in skeletal muscle and adipose tissue, in contrast to no change in the brain, and downregulated with hyperglycemia. Insulin-responsive GLUT4 is upregulated by hypoglycemia, but in response to hyperglycemia is initially upregulated and then downregulated in skeletal muscle and adipose tissue. Different studies among species, tissues studied, gestational age, and conditions of glycemia and insulinemia show considerable variability and complexity of the changes in glucose transporter expression during fetal life.[60-67]

### Fetal Glucose Carbon Contribution to Glycogen Formation
Many tissues in the conceptus (fetus plus placenta), including the placenta, brain, liver, lung, heart, and skeletal muscle, produce glycogen over the second half of gestation.[68] Liver glycogen content, which increases with gestation, is the most important store of glycogen for systemic glucose needs in the fetus and neonate, because only the liver contains sufficient glucose-6-phosphatase for release of glucose into the circulation.[69] Skeletal muscle glycogen content increases during late gestation, whereas lung glycogen content decreases with change in cell type, leading to loss of glycogen-containing alveolar epithelium, development of type II pneumocytes, and onset of surfactant production.[70] Cardiac glycogen concentration decreases with gestation, owing to cellular hypertrophy, but cardiac glycogen is essential for postnatal cardiac energy supply and cellular function.[71] Glycogen synthesis by the liver accounts for only a small (<10%) portion of fetal glucose utilization in larger, more slowly growing fetuses (i.e., lamb, monkey, and human).[72]

Net synthesis or degradation of glycogen in the fetus is controlled by the functional balance between glycogen synthase and glycogen phosphorylase. The total content of these two enzymes is relatively constant over gestation. Experimental cortisol depletion reduces whereas cortisol excess by infusion enhances fetal glycogen deposition.[73,74] Fetal hyperglycemia increases fetal glycogen deposition by activating glycogen synthase via increased insulin production and action.[75-77] Glucose also activates phosphorylase, thereby helping to keep glycogen content constant at higher glucose concentrations.[78,79] Glucocorticoid administration to the pregnant animal (rat or monkey) hyperstimulates glycogen synthase and glycogen concentration.[75] Glucose conversion to glycogen is mostly direct, as preliminary studies in fetal sheep show that about 92% to 94% of glycogen formation is from plasma glucose molecules.[80]

Hypoglycemia, glucagon, and cyclic adenosine monophosphate (cAMP) can induce the fetal liver to release glucose from glycogen by activation of phosphorylase.[81,82] Increased glucose-6-phosphatase activity has been found in the fetus after administration of cortisol, glucagon, and cAMP, and in response to fetal hypoglycemia.[77,83]

### Fetal Glucogenesis
There is little glucose production in the fetus under normal conditions[7,18,65,84,86] or in response to short-term (1 to 4 hours) changes in maternal and fetal glucose concentrations or rates of placental-to-fetal glucose transfer. Only after prolonged periods (several days) of decreased fetal glucose supply and sustained fetal hypoglycemia and hypoinsulinemia does fetal glucose production develop significantly.[19,34,35,87] Fetal gluconeogenesis from lactate, amino acids, and glycerol varies considerably among species, but appears in nearly all cases to be a late gestational development regulated by the surge in cortisol production.[88]

## FETAL LIPID METABOLISM

### Placental Lipid Metabolism and Fetal Lipid Supply
The amount and type of fatty acid or complex lipid transported by the placenta varies among species according to the transport capacity of the placenta; it is greatest in the hemochorial placenta of the human.[89] There are many lipid substances in the plasma that are transported across the placenta that are essential to placental and fetal development even if they do not contribute to nutritional or energy metabolism. Also, brown fat is common to all fetuses, even if the neonate is not "fat" with white adipose tissue. Furthermore, many lipid substances entering the fetus are qualitatively different from those taken up by the uterus and uteroplacenta, implying active placental metabolism of individual lipid substances.[90] A schema of placental lipid uptake, metabolism, transport, and metabolic interaction with the fetus is shown in Figure 184-2.[4,90]

Overall, there is a general relationship between the permeability of the placenta to lipids, especially fatty acids, and the adiposity and specific lipid content of various tissues of the fetus.[91-97] Human fetuses develop the most fat of all land mammals, 15% to 18% of body weight at term, at least 50% of which comes from direct placental fatty acid transfer[94-97]; reasons for this unique development of adiposity are not known, but probably relate in part to the relatively high lipid and carbohydrate diet of the mother and the rapid transfer of lipids across the placenta. Experimental studies in animals have shown that fat deposition in the fetus can be enhanced during late gestation after a previous period of nutrient restriction up to midgestation, accompanied by increased mRNA abundance for the receptors of IGF-1 and IGF-2. Increased maternal nutrition in late gestation appears to uniquely enhance brown fat development and the content of uncoupling protein-1 (UCP-1), the UCP that allows for rapid lipid mobilization and energy production after birth.[98]

### Fetal Leptin
Leptin mRNA is detectable in fetal adipose tissue of sheep by approximately 90 days' gestation; abundance of leptin then increases up to term and is closely correlated with fetal

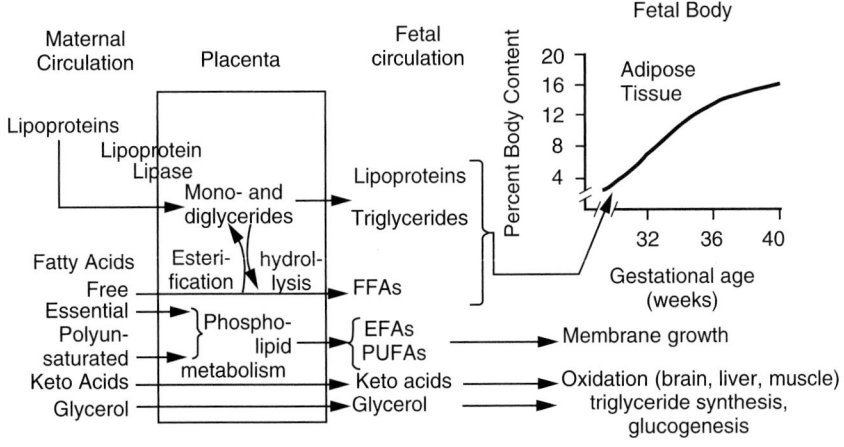

***Figure 184-2*** Schematic of placental-fetal interrelationships in humans for various aspects of placental lipid metabolism, fetal lipid uptake and metabolism, and fetal lipogenesis into adipose tissue. (Adapted from Hay WW Jr: Nutrition and development of the fetus: Carbohydrate and lipid metabolism. In Walker WA, Watkins JB, Duggan CP [eds]: Nutrition in Pediatrics: Basic Science and Clinical Applications, 3d ed. Hamilton, Ontario, BC Decker, 2003, pp 449–470; and Hay WW Jr: Metabolic interrelationships of placenta and fetus. Placenta 16:19–30, 1995.)

weight.[99] This suggests that the production of leptin mRNA is modulated by the increase in size and number of adipocytes that occurs during late gestation in the ovine fetus.[100,101] The rise in leptin could also be due to increasing corticosteroids during late gestation, as these have been shown to stimulate leptin expression transiently both in vitro and in vivo.[102,103] Leptin is also positively regulated by circulating insulin concentrations.[104]

Many studies have measured plasma leptin concentrations in newborn infants; however, the results of these studies have been inconsistent.[105] Clinical studies suggest that plasma leptin remains low throughout gestation, is first detectable by 35 weeks of gestation, and increases toward term in response to the increased abundance of adipose tissue.[106,107] Concentrations have been shown to peak at term in human fetuses, then rapidly decline by day 3 of postnatal age.[108,109] The sympathetic nervous system, cortisol, and thyroid hormones also regulate leptin expression.[110–112] All of these hormones are secreted at birth for the initiation of breathing and thermoregulation.[113]

### Fetal Fatty Acid Utilization

Physiologic changes that develop in the fetus in late gestation and increase nutrient utilization, such as the increase in plasma insulin concentration, act to enhance net maternal-to-fetal fatty acid and lipid transport by increasing fatty acid utilization in the fetus primarily to develop adipose tissue.[7] For example, human maternal venous blood concentrations of fatty acids are directly related to the umbilical artery free fatty acid (FFAs) concentrations and the umbilical vein-artery concentration differences of FFA.[114] Similar observations have been made in the rabbit[96] and the guinea pig,[115] including, in the latter, evidence that experimentally lowering the fetal fatty acid concentration relative to that in the maternal plasma independently increases fatty acid transfer across the placenta.

### Fetal Requirements for Long-Chain Polyunsaturated Essential Fatty Acids

Docosahexaenoic acid (DHA) and arachidonic acid (ARA) are important structural components of the central nervous system. These essential fatty acids are transferred across the placenta, are present in human milk, and are accumulated in the brain and retina during fetal and infant development. The high concentrations of DHA in the retina and of DHA and ARA in the brain gray matter indicate that these fatty acids have important, probably essential roles in retinal and neural development. Animal studies have shown that depletion of DHA from the retina and brain results in reduced visual function and learning deficits. The latter effects may be explained by changes in the membrane bilayer that alter membrane-associated receptors and signal transduction systems, ion channel activity, or direct effects on gene expression. ARA

is essential for normal growth and is critically important through its role in cell signaling and as a precursor to series 2 eicosanoids and series 3 leukotrienes, which also play a role in synaptic transmission. In the fetus, all of the ω-6 and ω-3 fatty acids accumulated by the fetus must originate from the maternal circulation through placental transfer. Although the fetus and preterm infant have significant capacity for production of DHA and ARA from the parent ω-3 α-linolenic acid (18:3ω-3) and ω-6 linoleic acid (18:2ω-6) compounds, respectively, it remains unknown whether this activity is sufficient to produce all of the fetal DHA and ARA requirements throughout gestation. Some clinical studies have indicated that maternal supplementation with DHA can improve subsequent neurodevelopmental outcome in the offspring,[116] although this appears to be a functional development unrelated to measured concentrations of DHA in tissues.[117]

### FETAL AMINO ACID METABOLISM

#### Fetal Amino Acid Uptake

Amino acids are actively concentrated in the trophoblast intracellular matrix by $NA^+/K^+$-ATPase (adenosinetriphosphatase), and $H^+$-dependent transporter proteins at the maternal-facing microvillous membrane of the trophoblast and then transported into the fetal plasma, producing fetal-maternal plasma concentration ratios ranging from 1.0 to more than 5.0.[118] This active transport process is decreased by hypoxia and inhibitors of protein synthesis.[119,120] In vitro studies of trophoblast vesicles and cells have shown that hypoaminoacidemia increases transport,[121] indicating that synthesis of the transporters is, in part, responsible for their functional state, although there is no evidence that this process develops in utero and, in fact, decreased concentrations of transporters have been found in cases of IUGR along with decreased concentrations of amino acids in the fetal plasma.[122] Protein molecules as small as albumin and as large as gamma globulin pass from maternal to fetal plasma by pinocytosis with increasing efficiency as gestational age progresses.[123]

Experimental data in sheep show that net total fetal amino acid uptake accounts for 60% to 70% of carbon requirements for oxidation and for deposition in fetal protein, glycogen, and fat, and 100% of nitrogen requirements.[124,125] The placenta and fetus also interact in a variety of ways to ensure amino acid supply to vital developmental, metabolic, and signaling processes that are unique to fetal growth and development[6] (Fig. 184-3).

#### Fetal Amino Acid Oxidation

Evidence for a relatively high rate of fetal oxidation of amino acids comes from three observations: (1) the excess uptake of amino acids in relation to their rate of deposition in fetal protein[126]; (2) the high rate of fetal urea produc-

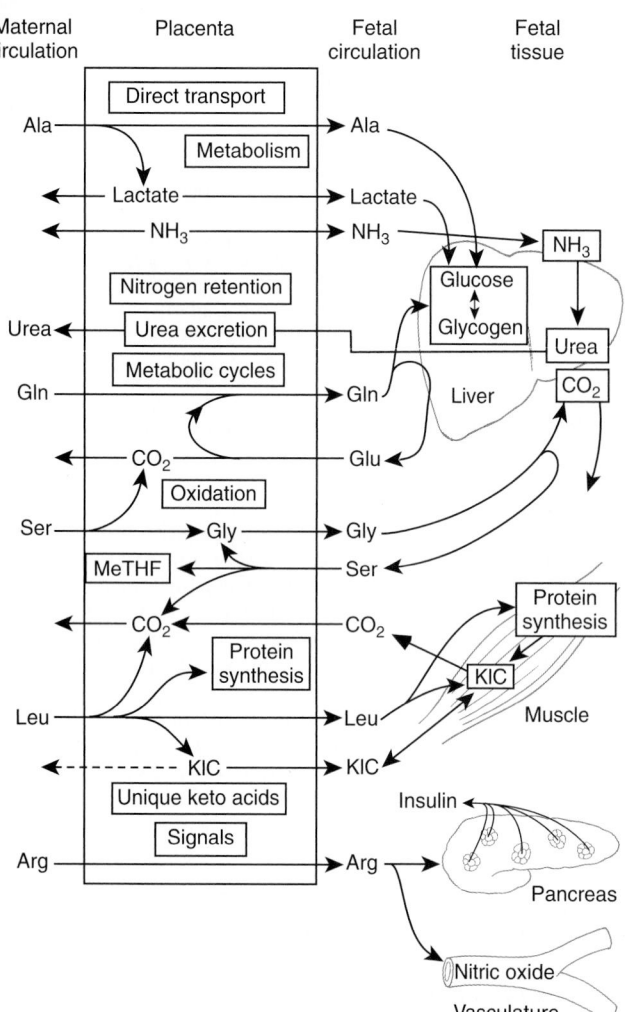

**Figure 184-3** Schematic representation of a variety of placental-fetal metabolic interactions with respect to amino acid uptake by the placenta, metabolism in the trophoblast cells, direct transfer to the fetus, signaling of fetal vascular and metabolic processes, and utilization in fetal tissues. Ala, alanine; Arg, arginine; Gln, glutamine; Glu, glutamate; Gly, glycine; KIC, α-ketoisocaproic acid; Leu, leucine; MeTHF, methyltetrahydrofolate; $NH_3$, ammonia; Ser, serine. (Adapted from Hay WW Jr, Regnault TRH: Fetal requirements and placental transfer of nitrogenous compounds. In Polin RA, Fox WW, Abman SH [eds]: Fetal and Neonatal Physiology, 3d ed. Philadelphia, WB Saunders, 2003, pp 509–527.)

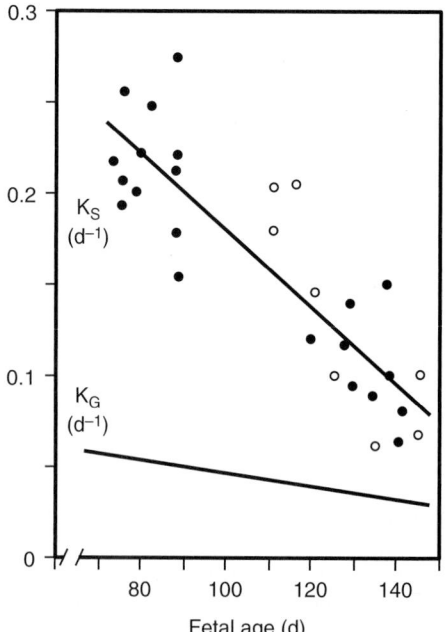

**Figure 184-4** Fractional rate of protein synthesis ($K_S$) over gestation in fetal sheep studied with leucine (*black circles*) and lysine (*open circles*) radioactive tracers compared with the fractional rate of growth ($K_G$) in the lower portion of the figure. (Adapted from Battaglia FC, Meschia G: An Introduction to Fetal Physiology. Orlando, FL, Academic, 1986; Meier PR, Peterson RG, Bonds DR, et al: Rates of protein synthesis and turnover in fetal life. Am J Physiol 240:E320–E324, 1981; and Kennaugh JM, Bell AW, Teng C, et al: Ontogenetic changes in the rates of protein synthesis and leucine oxidation during fetal life. Pediatr Res 22:688–692, 1987.)

### Fetal Protein Synthesis and Turnover

The net fetal uptakes of several nonessential amino acids are less than their total rate of utilization, emphasizing the need for a relatively high rate of fetal amino acid production.[124,125] Protein synthetic rates are also quite high (Fig. 184-4).[130,131] The higher protein synthetic rate in the midgestation fetus is proportional to the higher metabolic rate and glucose utilization rate at that stage of gestation.[132,133] The decrease in protein synthetic rate over gestation is primarily due to the increasing mass of skeletal muscle, which has a relatively lower fractional synthetic rate in late gestation,[134] rather than to anabolic endocrine-paracrine factors such as insulin, pituitary and placental growth hormone, placental lactogen, IGFs (somatomedins), and epidermal growth factors, as most studies suggest an increasing concentration or secretion of these substances as gestation progresses.[135]

### Fetal Skeletal Muscle Amino Acid Metabolism

Skeletal muscle in the fetal sheep has a net uptake of both essential and nonessential amino acids from the circulation,[136] reflecting the relatively high rate of protein synthesis and nitrogen accretion of the fetus. Under hyperinsulinemic conditions in which glucose and amino acids are also infused to maintain normal concentrations, net uptake of most amino acids by skeletal muscle increases, reflecting primarily increased rates of protein synthesis,[38] but not necessarily into oxidation.[39] Protein synthesis is also strongly regulated by the plasma concentration of amino acids. IGF-1 acts similarly to insulin.[40]

### Fetal Protein Metabolism during Maternal Fasting

Glucose utilization increases net protein balance, perhaps simply by substituting its carbon for that of amino acids in the tricarboxylic acid (TCA) cycle, indicating that a positive energy balance and the provision of amino acids allow insulin to promote nitrogen accretion more effectively.[137,138] Thus,

tion[127]; and (3) the direct measurement of labeled $CO_2$ dioxide production and excretion during fetal infusions of carbon-labeled amino acids.[128] The urea production rate in sheep can account for approximately 0.36 g/day/kg of nitrogen excretion (or about 25% of fetal nitrogen uptake in amino acids) and about 0.2 g/day/kg of carbon (about 2% of total fetal carbon uptake, or about 6% of fetal carbon uptake in amino acids).[129] Such fetal urea production rates are large, exceeding term neonatal weight-specific rates, indicating relatively rapid protein turnover and oxidation in the fetus. Direct measurement of fetal amino acid oxidation has been made using carbon-labeled isotopic tracers of selected amino acids (leucine, lysine, alanine, tyrosine, glycine, and serine).[129] Oxidation rates have been calculated for leucine (~25% of utilization), lysine (~10% of utilization), and glycine (~13% of utilization), demonstrating that the oxidation–disposal rate ratio is directly related to the excess umbilical uptake of these amino acids above that required for protein accretion, and to the plasma concentration of the amino acid.[126,130]

despite selective maternal hypoaminoacidemia in pregnant rats,[139] fetal growth under these conditions is reduced only when maternal fasting decreases fetal glucose (energy) supply. Similarly, fetal amino acid concentrations are normal or increased during maternal fasting in pregnant sheep.[140] Under these acute conditions, fetal uptakes of amino acids do not change, indicating either a reduced fetal protein synthetic rate or an enhanced rate of proteolysis.[141,142] In this situation, the leucine oxidation–disposal rate ratio doubles,[128] whereas in acutely fasted pregnant rats, fetal proteolysis is increased but rates of protein synthesis are normal.[143] These animals have relatively normal concentrations of amino acids but markedly reduced glucose concentrations. Prolonged maternal malnutrition, however, with both energy (e.g., glucose) and protein restriction, results in decreased protein synthesis and proteolysis, but, in this case, protein synthesis is reduced to a greater extent.[144] Together, these data support the concept that fetal protein synthesis is dependent on both amino acid and energy supplies, whereas fetal protein catabolism may be more specifically regulated by nonprotein energy substrate supply. Furthermore, certain amino acids released by proteolysis can be oxidized to maintain fetal energy balance at the expense of growth, whereas others contribute to gluconeogenesis to maintain glucose energy requirements.

## SHORT- AND LONG-TERM CONSEQUENCES OF ABNORMAL FETAL NUTRIENT SUPPLY

Fetal overnutrition, principally of glucose and lipid in fetuses of maternal diabetics, produces an obese offspring; such macrosomic infants have a greater chance of becoming obese in childhood, adolescence, and adulthood and of developing insulin resistance and type 2 diabetes mellitus. Interestingly, recent epidemiologic evidence from many studies indicates that the same later life outcomes occur among infants who are born small for gestational age, primarily as a result of IUGR from placental insufficiency.[145–148] In the case of infants of diabetic mothers, exhaustion of insulin production/secretion has been suggested as the cause of earlier failure of insulin release in response to hyperglycemia secondary to obesity and insulin resistance. In the case of IUGR infants, the "thrifty phenotype" hypothesis has been proposed, namely, that poor nutrition in fetal (and early infant) life would be detrimental to the development and function of the pancreatic β cells, which, when coupled with the added insulin resistance of obesity later in life, would lead to type 2 diabetes. Thus, both overweight and underweight at birth are associated with a greater risk for diabetes.[149–151] Problems appear to begin as early as late childhood and early adolescence. Thus, short prepubertal children who had IUGR had increased insulin responses and decreased insulin sensitivity compared with age- and sex-matched children with normal birth weights for age.[152] The highest risks were associated with low birth weight and high fat mass at 8 years of age.[153] Virtually identical findings have been described among Jamaican children aged 7.5 years to 10.5 years.[154] Young adults who were intrauterine growth restricted were found to have increased body fat compared with body mass index (BMI)-matched controls and to have lower insulin-stimulated glucose uptake, which persisted with correction for total body fat and visceral fat.[155] Environmentally caused and genetically determined IUGR appears to have similar effects on growth and development of pancreatic β cells and insulin-sensitive tissues. The expression of the glucose transporter gene (GLUT4) in muscle and fat is impaired in young adults who had IUGR, an effect that could reflect genetic predisposition or be secondary to altered cellular growth and development from nutritional limitation.[156] Similar changes in GLUT4 probably occur in offspring of diabetic mothers, as recent experimental evidence in rats has shown that aberrant insulin-induced GLUT4 translocation develops in fetuses exposed to hyperglycemic dams, and this change predicts glucose intolerance in the offspring later in life.[157] Mechanisms responsible for this aberrant GLUT4 translocation and subsequent glucose intolerance are now under investigation. Two recent studies in IUGR rat offspring have shown impaired oxidative phosphorylation in skeletal muscle and hepatic mitochondria. Defects in skeletal mitochondria might lead to a chronic reduction in the supply of adenosine triphosphate (ATP), compromising energy-dependent GLUT4 translocation, glucose transport, and glycogen synthesis, which contribute to insulin resistance and hyperglycemia of type 2 diabetics.[158] In the liver, impaired mitochondrial oxidative phosphorylation might predispose the IUGR offspring to increased hepatic glucose production by suppressing pyruvate oxidation and increasing gluconeogenesis.[159]

A genetic link between the insulin gene, glucose sensing in the pancreas and other tissues, size at birth, and type 2 diabetes later in life has been provided by several studies. Inheritance of a glucokinase mutation by the fetus has been associated with a reduction in birth weight, and could be linked to the risk of type 2 diabetes,[160] although this defect is rare. In another study in the Avon district of the United Kingdom, expression of the VNTR (variable number of tandem repeats) locus of the insulin gene (INS) was positively associated with length, weight, and head circumference at birth among a selected cohort of newborns.[161] By contrast, this group also described a significant relationship among a variant mitochondrial (i.e., transmitted maternally) DNA, thinness at birth, and the risk of type 2 diabetes in a selected cohort of UK men.[162] These observations are similar to the balance between the paternally expressed fetal growth factor IGF-2 and its maternally expressed receptor; the former promotes fetal growth at the expense of maternal nutrients, whereas the latter constrains fetal growth, protecting the mother.[163]

Increased adrenocortical and adrenomedullary activity also have been noted in IUGR infants,[164–166] and low birth weight is associated with increased plasma cortisol concentrations, which correlates with current blood pressure.[167,168] Thus, cortisol axis activation appears to be a significant development in growth-restricted fetuses that links low birth weight with adult cardiovascular and metabolic disease.[148] Indeed, studies in rats have suggested that glucocorticoid exposure late in pregnancy predisposes the offspring to glucose intolerance in adulthood.[169] Especially important is the type of glucocorticoid. The fetus is normally protected from elevated maternal levels of glucocorticoid by fetoplacental 11β-hydroxysteroid dehydrogenase type 2, which converts active cortisol to inactive cortisone; dexamethasone is a poor substrate for this enzyme and, therefore, more likely to induce changes that mimic fetal undernutrition.[170] The elevation of fetal corticotropin and cortisol levels in IUGR,[171] together with the evidence for an effect of fetal undernutrition on long-term hypothalamic-pituitary-adrenal and adrenomedullary activation,[172] provides a reasonable hypothesis that links fetal growth and development with later life onset of hypertension, central adiposity, and insulin resistance. Appreciation of this possibility adds caution to the perinatal use of steroid therapy.[173]

## FUEL HOMEOSTASIS IN THE NEONATE

After birth, lipid supply to the newborn infant increases dramatically in all species, with the large amount of lipid in milk providing the bulk of carbon for energy production, including the development of gluconeogenesis.[174] Gluconeogenesis and glycogenolysis are essential after birth to provide glucose for critical organ function, particularly of the brain, as glucose supply becomes meal-associated and episodic. Milk protein content and, thus, protein supply vary among species, according to the neonatal growth rate.

## GLUCOSE HOMEOSTASIS IN THE NEWBORN

Basal glucose utilization rates in the term newborn infant are approximately 4 to 6 mg/kg/min,[17] almost twice the weight-specific rate in older children and adults, consistent with their higher metabolic and growth rates. During the first few hours of life, plasma glucose concentrations decrease from the fetal value (range, 50 to 75 mg/dL, or 2.8 to 4.2 mmol/L), which reflects the mother's plasma glucose concentration, to as low as 20 to 30 mg/dL (1.1–1.7 mmol/L) before the infant establishes independent glucose production and normal glucose homeostasis during the next several hours.[175] Increased catecholamine concentrations immediately after birth and the relative hypoglycemia stimulate glucagon secretion. The increased catecholamine and glucagon concentrations inactivate glycogen synthase and activate glycogen phosphorylase, thereby promoting glycogenolysis and inhibiting glycogen synthesis.[106,176,177] Increased cortisol concentrations in late gestation and after birth also upregulate the expression of hepatic glucose-6-phosphatase, allowing the release of hepatic glucose into the circulation to rapidly provide glucose for critical energy needs in the first few hours post partum.[36] Full-term infants have only enough hepatic glycogen to maintain glucose supply for about 10 hours, and preterm and small-for-gestational-age (SGA) infants for much shorter periods; therefore, other mechanisms are required to maintain glucose homeostasis.[178] The increased glucagon-insulin ratio post partum also induces synthesis of the enzymes required for gluconeogenesis, particularly phosphoenolpyruvate carboxykinase (PEPCK), the rate-limiting enzyme for gluconeogenesis. The release of fatty acids from fat stores stimulated by the high catecholamine concentrations and the availability of dietary fatty acids and glycerol (plus amino acids) in the circulation allow the newborn infant some degree of gluconeogenesis by 4 to 6 hours of life.[179] Although enzyme activities do not reach adult levels until 1 to 2 weeks of age, gluconeogenesis rates, even in preterm infants, are sufficient to meet requirements by the first few days of postnatal life.[180]

### Glucose Metabolism and Hypoglycemia in the Newborn

The human brain uses glucose almost exclusively as a substrate for energy metabolism. Cerebral glucose utilization in the fetus and preterm infant accounts for as much as 70% of total body glucose consumption at two-thirds gestation and 90% at full-term gestation.[181] Although alternative fuels such as lactate and ketoacids can be used by the central nervous system (CNS), the initial relative hypoglycemia limits lactate production and, especially in preterm and SGA infants, immature counterregulatory responses to hypoglycemia and lower amounts of adipose tissue limit the availability of fatty acids and ketoacids.

### Incidence, Clinical Presentation, and Diagnosis of Hypoglycemia

The overall incidence of neonatal hypoglycemia is estimated at 1 to 5 per 1000 live births.[182,183] The incidence is increased in defined high-risk groups, varying from 8% among large-for-gestational-age infants of diabetic mothers to 5% to 30% of preterm infants and SGA infants with IUGR. Estimates of incidence are uncertain, however, because of wide variations in the definition of hypoglycemia. From a physiologic standpoint, hypoglycemia occurs when glucose delivery is inadequate to meet glucose demand, and can occur over a relatively broad range of glucose concentrations, depending on the status of the infant. Furthermore, the time at which the blood glucose concentration is measured also affects the value considered "normal," as plasma glucose concentrations in normal term infants decrease precipitously in the first 1 to 2 hours of life and then increase gradually during the next 24 to 48 hours with the onset of feeding and the development of glycogenolysis and gluconeogenesis. Thus, a value considered "low normal" at 2 to 3 hours postnatally could be "hypoglycemic" at 18 hours.

Despite earlier statistical definitions of hypoglycemia, recent studies indicate that the normal lower limit of glucose concentration in newborn infants, preterm or term, should be above approximately 45 to 50 mg/dL (2.5–2.8 mmol/L). A retrospective study by Lucas and colleagues[184] showed increased incidences of mental and motor delays in preterm infants who had repeated glucose concentrations below about 48 mg/dL. A survey study by Srinivasan and coworkers[185] defined a lower 95% confidence interval value of approximately 45 mg/dL by 6 to 12 hours of life, increasing to about 60 mg/dL by the second or third day of postnatal life. Also, a study by Marconi and colleagues[186] showed that, among normal human fetuses from 20 weeks' gestation to term, none had an umbilical venous glucose concentration less than 50 mg/dL. The primary value of targeting such relatively higher lower limits for defining normal glucose concentrations is to encourage the clinician to prevent rather than have to treat hypoglycemia. Also, this practice should help the clinician to consider sooner rather than later the possibility of persistent hypoglycemia due to hyperinsulinism, which is extremely difficult and generally unsuccessful to treat once established. One should not, however, interpret such arbitrary lower limits for normal glucose concentrations as now implying that any concentration of glucose in the newborn infant below a lower limit indicates actual or even potential irreversible neuronal injury. Irreversible neuronal injury only occurs in those infants who have sustained (relatively continuous), prolonged (hours, not minutes) extremely low glucose concentrations associated with seizures and loss of consciousness.[187,188]

Hypoglycemia is often classified as "symptomatic" or "asymptomatic," reflecting the presence or absence of physical signs that accompany low blood glucose concentrations. Most findings are nonspecific and result from the effects of increased circulating catecholamines and sympathetic nervous system discharge as well as of CNS function. These include abnormal respiratory patterns, such as tachypnea, apnea, or respiratory distress; cardiovascular signs, such as tachycardia or bradycardia; and neurologic signs, including jitteriness, lethargy, weak suck, temperature instability, and seizures.

### Etiology of Neonatal Hypoglycemia

Hepatic glycogen stores are limited in preterm infants who have not had adequate substrate supply available for glycogen synthesis. Postterm infants and infants of multiple gestations are also at risk due to the presence of relative placental insufficiency. Infants with asphyxia or hypothermia can have decreased glycogen stores due to stress-induced catecholamines and increased anaerobic metabolism. Infants with increased work of breathing may have normal glycogen stores, but the amount may be inadequate to meet the increased glucose requirements of the respiratory muscles.[189] The development of gluconeogenesis also occurs more slowly in preterm and growth-restricted infants, as does the capacity to increase ketone production in response to hypoglycemia.[189]

Disturbances in neonatal glucose homeostasis also result from a number of endocrine and metabolic disturbances. The most common of these is hyperinsulinism. Infants of diabetic mothers (IDMs) have exaggerated pancreatic insulin secretion in response to a given glucose load compared with non-IDMs.[190] Their relatively high insulin-glucagon ratio inhibits glycogenolysis and lipolysis, the induction of gluconeogenic enzymes, and hepatic glucose production, despite decreasing blood glucose concentrations. Insulin also increases peripheral glucose utilization in insulin-sensitive tissues. The combined effects of increased glucose utilization and inhibition of hepatic glucose production result in hypoglycemia, which may persist for 24 to 72 hours or more before insulin secretion patterns and glucose homeostasis normalize.

Postnatal insulin secretion may be abnormal due to other disorders. Beckwith-Wiedemann syndrome is associated with hyperplasia of multiple organs including the pancreas, with consequent increased insulin secretion.[191] Infants with erythroblastosis fetalis also have increased levels of insulin and an increase in the number of pancreatic β cells.[192] The mechanism is unclear, but one possibility is that glutathione released from hemolyzed red blood cells inactivates insulin in the circulation, triggering more insulin secretion from the pancreatic β cells. Exchange transfusions may exacerbate the risk of insulin-induced hypoglycemia since the blood used is usually preserved with a high concentration of dextrose. Use of β-agonist tocolytic agents is also associated with hyperinsulinemia in the newborn, especially if the agent was used for more than 2 weeks and was discontinued less than 1 week before delivery.[193]

Hypoglycemia that persists for more than 3 to 5 days is uncommon and is most often due to hyperinsulinism.[194] Some infants with IUGR or perinatal asphyxia demonstrate hyperinsulinemia, which may persist for as long as 4 weeks, but such cases are rare, and the underlying mechanisms are unclear.[195] Several types of congenital hyperinsulinism have been described.[196–200] Many of these infants have abnormally increased amounts of pancreatic islet tissue and β cells, including true adenomas (these are quite rare, and can be associated with multiple endocrine neoplasia syndrome type 1), focal islet hyperplasia, and generalized hyperplasia, often called nesidioblastosis (or neoformation of β cells from ductal epithelial cells). The last two conditions have also been found in normal infants, so that the cause of true, persistent hyperinsulinism is excessive insulin secretion, regardless of the amount of islet tissue and β cells that are present. At least six genetic forms of congenital hyperinsulinism have been defined. The autosomal-recessive forms of congenital hyperinsulinism have been linked to defects in the sulfonylurea receptor or $K^+$-ATP channel; these defects maintain relative $K^+$-ATP channel closure and β-cell depolarization, leading to persistent opening of the $Ca^{2+}$ channel, increased intracellular $Ca^{2+}$ concentration, and increased insulin exocytosis. Focal adenomatous lesions of the pancreas result from a random loss of maternal chromosome 11p with its maternally imprinted growth-inhibitory genes or from a single mutation on the short arm of paternal chromosome 11, which has been described in the Ashkenazi Jewish population. Cases in other ethnic groups have been associated with a number of other mutations in the same region. Three autosomal-dominant forms of somewhat milder hyperinsulinemia and hypoglycemia have been described. Two of these involve gain-of-function mutations, one of glucokinase, the enzyme that functions as the glucose sensor in β cells, and the other, representing a syndrome of congenital hyperinsulinemia and asymptomatic hyperammonemia, is associated with mutations in the glutamate dehydrogenase gene, which also regulates ureagenesis in the liver. These dominant disorders differ from the autosomal-recessive forms in that they do not appear to result from abnormal sulfonylurea receptor function. It is very likely that environmental alterations in the sulfonylurea receptor or $K^+$-ATP channel can impose hyperinsulinism on infants who do not have true genetic defects in these protein structures.

Inborn errors of metabolism and endocrine disorders may affect either the availability of gluconeogenic precursors or the function of the enzymes required for hepatic glucose production. These conditions are relatively rare and should be considered only after more common causes have been ruled out.

## Management of the Infant with Hypoglycemia

The key to diagnosing and treating hypoglycemia is frequent and accurate measurement of blood glucose concentrations. Full-term infants with asymptomatic mild hypoglycemia can be treated first with a trial of enteral feeding with milk or formula, providing carbohydrate in the form of lactose, which releases galactose as well as glucose upon hydrolysis in the gut. Galactose has the advantage of producing glycogen directly and not stimulating insulin secretion. Milk and formula also supply protein and fat, which are metabolized more slowly and therefore provide a sustained supply of alternative fuel substrates and substrates for gluconeogenesis. Fatty acids also decrease cellular glucose uptake. Prompt use of intravenous (IV) glucose when repeat preprandial glucose concentrations fail to increase above 40 to 50 mg/dL (2.5–2.8 mmol/L) will avoid further hypoglycemic episodes before each feeding, which appear to be more harmful than an isolated episode.[201]

IV therapy should be used first in symptomatic infants, infants unable to tolerate enteral feedings, and high-risk infants in whom hypoglycemia might be severe or expected to last more than a few hours, for example, preterm infants, SGA infants with IUGR, infants of mothers with poorly controlled diabetes during pregnancy, and infants with underlying causes of hypoglycemia such as sepsis, known or suspected inborn errors of metabolism, endocrine defects, or erythroblastosis. Administration of an initial bolus of dextrose 10% in water, 200 mg/kg (2 mL/kg), should be followed by a continuous infusion of dextrose calculated to deliver 4 to 6 mg/kg/min of glucose, that is, a rate equivalent to the glucose utilization rate of a normal infant.[202] Infants with transient or sustained hyperinsulinemia may require as much as 12 to 15 mg/kg/min of IV glucose to maintain normoglycemia. Usually, infants requiring IV therapy for hypoglycemia should continue with enteral feeding. Failure to wean from IV glucose indicates a more pervasive disorder, such as a metabolic defect or idiopathic hyperinsulinemia.

Several other agents have been used to treat refractory hypoglycemia, most often encountered in one of the hyperinsulinemic states. Corticosteroids (hydrocortisone 5 to 15 mg/kg/day in two or three divided doses, or prednisone 2 mg/kg/day) are associated with decreased peripheral glucose utilization and increased blood glucose concentrations, but they have a variety of other adverse metabolic effects that limit their routine use. Glucagon produces a rapid rise in blood glucose in infants who have adequate glycogen stores, but this is only a transient effect and rebound hypoglycemia frequently occurs. An initial dose of 30 μg/kg may produce a response in some infants, but hyperinsulinemic infants may require a 10-fold higher dose to overcome the effects of high circulating insulin levels and stimulate glycogenolysis. Administration of glucagon is most useful in severely hypoglycemic infants as a temporizing measure until stable IV access can be obtained. Diazoxide will inhibit pancreatic insulin secretion.[203] Somatostatin and its long-acting analogue octreotide also inhibit insulin release, as well as growth hormone and glucagon secretion, and are most often used in infants requiring pancreatectomy for refractory hypoglycemia and hyperinsulinemia.[204] Subtotal (95%) pancreatectomy may be required to manage cases of hyperinsulinemia due to gene mutations or islet cell adenomas. Hypoglycemia recurs, however, in up to one third of these patients, and 40% to 60% develop diabetes mellitus later in life.[190]

## Pathophysiology of Hypoglycemic Brain Injury

Severe hypoglycemia in the newborn is associated with selective neuronal necrosis in multiple brain regions, including the superficial cortex, dentate gyrus, hippocampus, and caudate-putamen.[205] If glucose supply to the brain is not maintained, there may be a decrease in cerebral electrical activity, membrane breakdown with release of FFA, and altered amino acid metabolism, including increased production of glutamate and increased glutamate concentrations in the synaptic cleft. The latter most likely results from a combination of increased glutamate release from presynaptic neurons and decreased ATP-dependent glutamate uptake by glial cells.[206] Glutamate binds to postsynaptic receptors, triggering release of second messengers via the metabotropic glutamate receptors and changes in transmembrane ion fluxes via the ionotropic glutamate receptors. Although there are several types of ionotropic receptors, the N-methyl-D-aspartate (NMDA)-type glutamate receptor, which is associated with an ion channel that transports $Na^+$ and $Ca^{2+}$ into the cell and $K^+$ out of the cell, predominates in the immature brain. Excess activation of the NMDA receptor by glutamate increases cytoplasmic concentrations of $Na^+$ and $Ca^{2+}$ to levels that exceed the capacity of neuronal homeostatic mechanisms, thereby altering transmembrane ion gradients.[207] Hypoglycemia specifically increases the sensitivity of the NMDA receptor to activation by glutamate, which may result in a lower threshold for glutamate-induced excitotoxicity. During hypoglycemia, energy-dependent mechanisms for restoring normal transmembrane gradients of $Na^+$ and $Ca^{2+}$ cannot operate due to the depletion of ATP and phosphocreatine associated with hypoglycemia. Excess $Ca^{2+}$ influx activates cellular phospholipases and proteases, alters mitochondrial metabolism, triggers free-radical formation, changes patterns of synaptic transmission, and may eventually result in selective neuronal necrosis.

Mitochondrial function also plays a significant role in the early events leading to hypoglycemic encephalopathy.[207] Decreased fluxes of substrate through the TCA cycle result in decreased availability of reducing equivalents in mitochondria, leading to incomplete reduction of molecular oxygen within mitochondria, increased formation of oxygen free radicals, and resulting damage to mitochondrial membranes and mitochondrial DNA. Fragmentation of mitochondrial DNA interferes with synthesis of electron transport chain enzymes, impairing the ability of the cell to restore ATP levels and to sequester $Ca^{2+}$ in the cytoplasm. Mitochondrial dysfunction may also contribute to neuronal necrosis by initiating apoptosis. Release of cytochrome c from mitochondria is required to activate the enzymes that trigger apoptosis, and cytochrome c is released as oxidative phosphorylation fails and mitochondrial membrane potential decreases.

Hypoglycemia also exacerbates brain injury during periods of cerebral hypoxia in the immature brain.[208] As in hypoglycemia, cerebral hypoxia is associated with depletion of high-energy phosphates, increased extracellular glutamate concentrations, activation of ionotropic glutamate receptors, and increased intracellular $Na^+$ and $Ca^{2+}$. In addition, anaerobic glycolysis during hypoxia accelerates brain glucose depletion. Studies in immature animals have demonstrated that concurrent hypoglycemia exacerbates hypoxic-ischemic brain injury, possibly by accelerating depletion of high-energy phosphates. Hypoglycemia also abolishes hypoxic vasodilation of cerebral blood vessels, thus impairing compensatory mechanisms that might otherwise improve oxygen delivery to the brain during periods of hypoxemia.

### Clinical Consequences of Hypoglycemia

The long-term effects of neonatal hypoglycemia remain controversial. Repeated episodes of markedly "symptomatic" hypoglycemia, as seen in infants with persistent hyperinsulinism, are often associated with neuronal necrosis and cognitive and motor dysfunction, but almost exclusively when seizures occur.[209] By contrast, most mature infants who experience only one or two brief episodes of hypoglycemia fail to demonstrate significant long-term sequelae. A retrospective study in preterm infants found that, at 18 months of age, those infants with repeated blood glucose values of less than about 48 mg/dL (2.6 mmol/L) during a period of many days had significantly lower scores on standardized tests of mental and motor development and a threefold higher incidence of cerebral palsy than infants who had fewer episodes or those that had experienced a single episode of more severe hypoglycemia. The differences were still significant when other risk factors such as birth weight and intracranial hemorrhage

were taken into account.[184] It cannot be determined from such a retrospective study, however, whether the abnormal outcome was the result of the prolonged, repeated hypoglycemia or other causes that contributed to both the occurrence of repeated hypoglycemia and abnormal development.

### NEONATAL HYPERGLYCEMIA

Hyperglycemia is a major problem among extremely low birth weight (ELBW), preterm infants. Hyperglycemia is generally defined as a whole-blood glucose concentration greater than 120 to 125 mg/dL, or a plasma glucose concentration greater than 145 to 150 mg/dL, regardless of the neonate's gestational age, weight, or postnatal age. The hyperglycemic neonate is usually "asymptomatic" or has signs indicative of other disease processes. Recognizable signs specific to hyperglycemia may include dehydration secondary to osmotic diuresis, weight loss, failure to thrive, fever, glycosuria, ketosis, and metabolic acidosis. More severe signs are particularly common in infants with transient or permanent neonatal diabetes mellitus.[210]

The incidence of hyperglycemia is inversely related to birth weight, ranging from about 2% in infants weighing more than 2000 g to 45% in infants of less than 1000 g, and up to 60% to 80% in ELBW infants weighing less than 750 g.[211-213] There are also significant relationships between hyperglycemia and the initial rates of IV glucose administration and between hyperglycemia and the severity of clinical problems in the neonate.[214] Critically ill neonates on even low rates of glucose infusion have developed hyperglycemia, in part due to the lipid component of parenteral nutrition. Increased plasma FFA concentrations decrease peripheral glucose utilization and inhibit the action of insulin to suppress hepatic glucose production.[215] As a result, insulin concentrations are often paradoxically greater after lipid infusion by the direct effect of fatty acids in promoting insulin secretion.[216,217]

Stress, as measured by increased plasma cortisol concentrations, also appears to be an important risk factor for the development of hyperglycemia, although the cortisol response may be suppressed by hyperglycemia in a negative feedback relationship.[218] Neonates also often develop marked hyperglycemia during and after surgical procedures, due to increased catecholamine release with anesthetic induction and increased cortisol secretion during surgery.[219] Narcotic treatment during and after surgery has decreased the incidence of hyperglycemia, as well as circulating concentrations of epinephrine, glucocorticoids, and glucagon.[220] Epinephrine decreases insulin secretion from the pancreatic $\beta$ cell and interferes with peripheral insulin action. Glucagon promotes glycogenolysis as well as gluconeogenesis by activating PEPCK, the rate-limiting enzyme for gluconeogenesis. Glucocorticoids promote gluconeogenesis by increasing protein breakdown and, thus, the supply of amino acids, and by enhancing hepatic enzyme activity in the gluconeogenic pathway and glucose-6-phosphatase, which releases glucose into the circulation.

An unusual, but important, cause of hyperglycemia in the infant is transient neonatal diabetes mellitus (TNDM).[220] TNDM presents early in postnatal life with weight loss, polyuria, dehydration, glycosuria, and hyperglycemia.[221] When TNDM does not resolve, which rarely happens, it is known as permanent neonatal diabetes mellitus (PNDM).[222] Both conditions are caused by endogenous insulin deficiency secondary to pancreatic $\beta$-cell failure. The pathogenesis is unknown. A family history of diabetes is found in about one third of cases. Infants with familial PNDM have normal glucagon, cortisol, and growth hormone secretion. C peptide concentrations are low, but end-organ insulin receptor sensitivity is normal.

Hyperglycemia may also be due to hepatic and peripheral insulin resistance, resulting in diminished effectiveness of insulin in inhibiting hepatic glucose production and promoting peripheral glucose utilization.[223] Unstressed preterm infants, however, are clearly sensitive to changes in plasma glucose concentration, but proinsulin processing to insulin is partially defective in hyperglycemic, very preterm neonates. Such hyperglycemic preterm neonates are relatively resistant to insulin, as evidenced by the higher insulin concentrations that are needed to achieve euglycemia.[224]

Hyperglycemia is more recalcitrant to control or treatment in stressed preterm infants. In these infants, endogenous glucose production cannot be completely inhibited (no more than 50% to 60%) by any level of insulinemia, whereas only very high concentrations of insulin (>10-fold above normal) enhance peripheral glucose utilization. Preterm neonates also have immature biochemical pathways that incompletely metabolize glucose.[225] Neonatal hyperglycemia has been associated with a wide spectrum of sequelae, ranging from hyperosmolarity to intracranial hemorrhage, although the latter is rare.[226] It remains controversial whether hyperglycemia protects or worsens hypoxic-ischemic neuronal injury. Hyperglycemia helps to maintain cerebral blood flow in the fetal sheep during hypoxia,[227] but observations in neonatal rats have shown that moderate hyperglycemia significantly increases morphologic damage throughout the forebrain with induced ischemic events.[228] The pathophysiology of increased ischemic damage during hyperglycemia is unclear; hypotheses include hyperosmolarity, excessive lactic acidosis,[229] and decreased regional cerebral blood flow.[230] Another potential effect of aggressive glucose administration is steatosis and associated impairment in hepatic triglyceride secretion.[231] Hyperglycemia may also jeopardize respiratory function by lipogenesis, which leads to excessive $CO_2$ production and, potentially, an increase in minute ventilation that could compromise the fragile ELBW or LBW infant.[232,233] Glycosuric neonates have high urinary sodium excretion due to increased filtered sodium load, even with minimal glycosuria.[234]

### Management

Gradual reduction of glucose infusion by 1 to 2 mg/min/kg every 2 to 4 hours usually ameliorates mild to moderate hyperglycemia. Early introduction of IV amino acids, some of which are known insulin secretagogues, has been associated with decreased incidence and severity of hyperglycemia.[235] In addition, such amino acids appear necessary for normal growth and development of the pancreas. At least glutamine and perhaps leucine may also promote insulin action and the disposal of glucose in skeletal muscle. Enteral feeding has been shown as well to promote pancreatic function and the secretion of insulin. Even minimal enteral feeding induces gut production of enteroinsular hormones or incretins, including gastric inhibitory polypeptide and pancreatic polypeptide, which increase insulin secretion by direct actions on the β cells.

Insulin treatment, beginning at 0.02 to 0.05 U/kg/hour, should be reserved until plasma glucose concentrations exceed 250 to 300 mg/dL despite reducing the glucose infusion rate to less than 3 to 4 mg/kg/min.[211,236] Normal infusion rates of potassium are usually sufficient to prevent hypokalemia, but frequent checks of serum potassium concentrations are warranted. Insulin infusion can also produce high plasma concentrations of lactate.[237]

### POSTNATAL PROTEIN AND AMINO ACID METABOLISM

Postnatal protein and amino acid metabolism are primarily important with respect to nutrition of the ELBW infant. Such infants, like their fetal counterparts at the same gestational age, have much higher protein turnover and growth rates than term infants. ELBW infants receiving glucose alone lose in excess of 1.2 g/day/kg of endogenous protein. Provision of amino acids, even if total energy intake is low, spares endogenous protein stores by enhancing the rate of protein synthesis.[238–240] This effect can be augmented by insulin, as proven by

using insulin infusions,[237] but probably also by increased insulin secretion in response to increased amino acid and glucose concentrations. Amino acids and insulin also decrease protein breakdown, although the effect of amino acids alone is less in preterm infants than in term infants.[237,241,242] Providing IV amino acid and energy intakes as low as 1.1 to 1.5 g/day/kg and 30 kcal/day/kg changes protein balance from substantially negative to zero or slightly positive.[243] A higher energy intake decreases proteolysis to some extent, and higher intakes of both protein and energy result in net protein anabolism.[243] At energy intakes above 50 to 60 nonprotein kcal/day/kg, only additional amino acid and/or protein intake increases protein balance significantly, whereas further increases in energy lead to increased adiposity. Despite such evidence, many ELBW infants do not receive even such modest IV amino acid and energy intakes during the first several days of life, virtually assuring, unfortunately, a catabolic state.[244]

Even if total protein intake is adequate, however, a number of factors may limit its utilization. One major factor is an inadequate intake of a single essential (indispensable) amino acid such as threonine or lysine, both of which are low in the plasma of parenterally fed preterm infants compared with the concentrations of these amino acids in the plasma of normal human fetuses of the same gestational age.[245] Insufficient supply of "conditionally essential" amino acids, such as tyrosine, cysteine, taurine, histidine, glycine, glutamine, and arginine, can also limit protein synthesis and balance.[246] A sufficient amount of all "nonessential" amino acids is also required to maintain an appropriately balanced intake of amino acids; otherwise, essential amino acids are diverted to their production and away from protein synthesis.[247–250]

### POSTNATAL ENERGY METABOLISM

Indirect calorimetry has been used to estimate the contribution of carbohydrate and fat to energy metabolism in newborn infants, but such estimates include potential errors in determination of the respiratory exchange ratio (RER) and substrate metabolic interconversions. The assumption that the relation between oxygen consumption and $CO_2$ production is a constant for different rates of substrate utilization is not valid in growing infants. Even the addition of stable isotopes to quantify the carbon substrate used for energy production has limitations. For example, estimates of glucose utilization from respiratory calorimetry and from oxidation of $^{13}C$-glucose are comparable at an RER between 0.76 and 0.90, but the contribution of glucose to energy production is higher than estimates from respiratory calorimetry at an RER of less than 0.76 and less at an RER greater than 0.90. The discrepancy at lower RERs is thought to represent the contribution of gluconeogenesis, which is included as protein oxidation in the RER, whereas the discrepancy at higher RERs is thought to be due to lipogenesis.[251] Indirect calorimetry estimates of energy expenditure of ELBW infants indicate that daily energy expenditure ranges from 60 to 75 kcal/day/kg.[252] The higher energy expenditure of ELBW infants is related, in part, to their higher rates of growth and, hence, greater needs for synthesis of new tissue. ELBW infants can also have higher energy losses from heat and evaporative exchange due to their thin skin and high surface-to-mass ratio. Respiratory distress, sepsis, and some medications (e.g., caffeine, insulin, and dexamethasone) also appear to increase energy expenditure.[253,254]

### POSTNATAL LIPID METABOLISM

Failure to provide sufficient nonprotein energy to the preterm newborn can lead to increased rates of lipolysis and fatty acid oxidation. This may or may not result in breakdown of membrane lipids for oxidation, but it certainly produces a metabolic condition in which essential fatty acids will be oxidized along with other fatty acids in preference to membrane deposition. This could lead to deleterious reduction in the amount and structure of critical membrane development in the brain, potentially leading to abnormal neurologic function and long-term outcome.

### Postnatal Lipid Requirements

Absolute lipid requirements are limited to the requirements for essential fatty acids (EFAs), that is, from 1% to 4% of total energy intake as linoleic acid (LA, 18:2n-6) and approximately 1% of total energy intake as α-linolenic acid (LNA, 18:3n-3). Higher lipid intakes are necessary, however, to achieve total body energy balance and support normal growth. Although lipid makes up about 50% of the nonprotein energy content of both human milk and formulas, both of which contain LA and LNA, customary limitation of enteral intake precludes these sources for early postnatal supply of the EFAs. Parenteral lipid emulsions can also provide nonprotein energy and EFAs. Use of such emulsions in ELBW infants, however, is often delayed or limited by concerns that lipid intolerance—either decreased clearance (increased plasma triglyceride concentrations) or decreased utilization (increased plasma FFA concentrations), both of which are more common in ELBW preterm and IUGR infants—may have adverse effects. These include impaired oxygenation, impaired lung function (ventilation-perfusion ratio), increased risk of lung disease (particularly bronchopulmonary dysplasia), impaired immune function, and increased free bilirubin levels. In addition, clearance of an equivalent amount of triglyceride is slower if infused as a 10% rather than a 20% emulsion because of the interference of phospholipids, which are in relatively greater abundance in the 10% solutions.[255]

The results of studies that have examined the effects of lipid emulsion on the incidence and severity of respiratory morbidity are inconclusive.[256-261] The effect of lipid emulsion on immune function is also uncertain; there is no conclusive evidence of deleterious in vivo effects,[262] but deleterious in vitro effects have been observed. Thus, it is reasonable to anticipate that currently available emulsions might have similar effects. The concern for bilirubin toxicity due to increased plasma unesterified fatty acids is based on the potential for unesterified fatty acids to displace bound bilirubin from albumin, thereby increasing free bilirubin and the risk of bilirubin encephalopathy. Displacement of bilirubin from albumin is minimal, however, at fatty acid–albumin ratios below 4.1, and higher ratios are unlikely. Further, clinical studies have shown that infusion of lipid at rates up to 3 g/day/kg does not increase plasma concentrations of FFA or free bilirubin.[263]

Failure to provide α-linoleic acid results in biochemical signs of deficiency within 72 hours,[264] but this can be prevented by administration of as little as 0.5 g/day/kg of available lipid emulsions. These emulsions do not contain arachidonic acid (AA, 20:4n-6) and docosahexaenoic acid (DHA, 22:6n-3); thus, concerns have been expressed about the availability of sufficient amounts of these fatty acids for the developing CNS. In this regard, plasma, liver, lung, and kidney lipid levels of both AA and DHA fall during infusion of lipid emulsions, although the short-term effects on brain lipid levels are relatively small.[265] The long-term effects of lower intakes of AA and DHA on brain development are unknown, but should be determined, given the large contribution of these EFAs to brain growth and development at early stages of development.

Parenteral lipid emulsions may also lead to abnormal development by producing inappropriate overall fatty acid composition of developing tissues.[266] Currently available emulsions have a very high content of LA and LNA, but a very low content of saturated (16:0) and monounsaturated (18:1) fatty acids, and the balance of the long-chain polyunsaturated fatty acids (LC-PUFAs) shows an excess of n-6 versus n-3 fatty acids, which might lead to abnormal membrane lipid

structure and the production of excess amounts of eicosanoids. There is no consensus about the appropriate range of fatty acids or the LC-PUFAs in plasma (or tissue) lipids despite the importance of dietary fat for membrane lipid composition, a variety of membrane-associated functions, eicosanoid metabolism, CNS development, and the degree of lipid peroxidation and free-radical formation.

### Long-Chain Polyunsaturated Fatty Acids

Some but not all studies have indicated that preterm infants fed human milk and LC-PUFA-supplemented formulas might have better visual development and neurodevelopmental outcomes, at least temporarily, than preterm infants fed unsupplemented formulas.[267-270] The same trend occurs for term infants, who have a higher LC-PUFA status than do preterm infants,[271] although the results are less convincing than for preterm infants.[272-274] Thus, several agencies and individuals have recommended that infant formulas, particularly preterm formulas, be supplemented with DHA and AA.[275-278] The amounts usually suggested are those of human milk. The amounts of LC-PUFAs in milk are variable, however, and seem to reflect the LC-PUFA content of maternal plasma, which, in turn, reflects maternal diet. This suggests that there is no specific mammary gland mechanism for maintaining a narrow range of concentrations of these fatty acids in human milk, making it difficult to determine specific amounts with which to supplement formulas. Furthermore, although DHA is the predominant fatty acid in the retina, retinal DHA content can be maintained by adequate intakes of LNA.[279] Also, although the LU-PUFAs are the predominant n-3 and n-6 fatty acids in the brain, the relationship between the plasma lipid content of these fatty acids (which reflect dietary intake) and the brain content is poorly defined. In fact, data from animal and cell culture studies suggest that the major portion of DHA deposited in the developing brain may be synthesized within the brain.[280,281] Furthermore, LC-PUFAs are precursors of eicosanoids and they enhance as well as depress transcription of genes encoding a number of important metabolic enzymes.[282] Other studies in which DHA was obtained from fish oil have shown slower rates of growth in low-birth-weight (LBW) infants (not all were extremely LBW).[283,284] It is not known whether the level of dietary DHA, the absence of AA, an imbalance of DHA and AA, or some contaminant from the fish oil led to the slower rate of growth.

### Fatty Acid Oxidation and Carnitine Palmitoyltransferase

The postnatal surge in plasma concentrations of long-chain fatty acids (LCFAs) also promotes the development of carnitine palmitoyltransferase-1 (CPT-1), which is essential for the transport of LCFAs across the inner mitochondrial membrane for oxidative metabolism,[285,286] particularly in the heart. Only the CPT-1 isoform activity and gene expression are increased at birth by LCFAs, as the CPT-2 enzyme is already present in the fetus. Both cAMP and LCFAs induce CPT-1 gene transcription in hepatocytes, whereas medium-chain fatty acids do not. This induction is also dependent on relative or absolute insulin deficiency. Neither cAMP nor LCFAs regulate CPT-2 gene expression. Furthermore, it is the LCFAs themselves and not their coenzyme A (CoA) esters that are the metabolic signals for LCFA-induced CPT-1 gene expression. Peroxisome proliferators induce both CPT-1 and CPT-2 gene expression, but, at least for CPT-1, this does not appear to involve a peroxisome-proliferator-activated receptor (PPAR)-dependent mechanism.[287,288] The synthesis of carnitine must also develop as the newborn is weaned from milk, which has a ready supply of carnitine.[289]

The postnatal surge in fatty acid concentrations also changes the fetal pattern of glucose-regulated insulin secretion. In the fetus, glucose and leucine, separately or interactively, increase pancreatic β-cell ATP production, potassium channel closure, calcium channel opening, and insulin exocytosis, whereas glutamine coupled with glucose, in concert with activated acetyl-CoA carboxylase, increases malonyl-CoA production, which inhibits CPT-1 and lipid oxidation.[290] Postnatally, the increase in fatty acid concentrations increases CPT-1 production, and glucose concentration tends to decrease after the placental supply of glucose is removed, resulting in decreased malonyl-CoA production and the oxidation of fatty acids. Insulin secretion is then regulated by meal-associated increases in plasma glucose and amino acid concentrations.

In liver, skeletal muscle, and adipose tissue, fatty acid synthase is active in the fetal state because of the direct simulation by glucose-enhanced production of malonyl-CoA, and in the neonatal period because of the increased supply of fatty acids and triglycerides in the milk diet. These same conditions also enhance ketone production, providing alternative energy sources for the brain. Ketone production is limited by body adipose tissue stores, more so, in fact, than diet. IUGR and ELBW, preterm infants, who have markedly reduced white adipose tissue, also produce much lower concentrations of ketones during both basal and fasting periods during early neonatal life.[291] Because these substrates provide alternative sources for brain energy metabolism, and because these same infants are often hypoglycemic because their gluconeogenic capacity is limited, brain nutrient metabolism in these infants may be markedly compromised, especially when dietary supply is limited due to medical management choices or to actual illnesses.

## Brown Fat Activation

In most mammalian species, brown adipose tissue (BAT) is present before birth and precedes the emergence of white adipose tissue.[292] BAT thermogenesis is triggered by the release of norepinephrine at the surface of brown adipocytes, followed by lipolysis, increase of FFAs, and direct activation of the mitochondrial UCP-1. UCP-1 uncouples adenylate cyclase and ATP production from the outward-to-inward flux of protons across the inner mitochondrial membrane. As a result, heat, rather than ATP, is generated. As evidence, mouse UCP-1 knockouts cannot maintain their body temperature after birth, nor eat a normal amount of food. BAT also expresses leptin, although it is not known how much of the circulating leptin in neonatal plasma is derived from BAT versus white adipose tissue. Leptin is produced by adipose tissue in relation to its mass.[293] Because fatter babies continue to get fatter after they are born as they continue to eat a fat-rich diet,[294] it appears that normal mechanisms by which leptin leads to decreased adipose tissue are developmentally downregulated or inhibited during this critical period of growth. Such mechanisms include activation of neuropeptide Y in the brain, which specifically inhibits appetite and food intake, and increased metabolic rate.

## Acknowledgments

Dr. Hay is supported in part by research grants HD42815, HD28794, and DK52138, training grant HD07186, and GCRC grant RR00069 from the National Institutes of Health. Dr. Anderson is supported by grant KO8DK065079 from the National Institutes of Health.

## REFERENCES

1. Hay WW Jr: Nutrition and development of the fetus: Carbohydrates and lipid metabolism. In Walker WA, Watkins JB (eds): Nutrition in Pediatrics: Basic Science and Clinical Applications, 2d ed. Neuilly-sur-Seine, France, Decker Europe, 1996, pp 364–378.
2. Hay WW Jr: Energy and substrate requirements of the placenta and fetus. Proc Nutr Soc 50:321–336, 1991.
3. Hay WW Jr, Wilkening RB: Metabolic activity of the placenta. In Thorburn GD, Harding R (eds): Textbook of Fetal Physiology. Oxford, Oxford Medical, 1994, pp 30–47.
4. Hay WW Jr: Metabolic interrelationships of placenta and fetus. Placenta 16:19–30, 1995.
5. Battaglia FC, Meschia G: An Introduction to Fetal Physiology. Orlando, FL, Academic, 1986.
6. Hay WW Jr: Fetal requirements and placental transfer of nitrogenous compounds. In Polin RA, Fox WW (eds): Fetal and Neonatal Physiology. Philadelphia, WB Saunders, 1991, pp 431–442.
7. Sparks JW, Girard J, Battaglia FC: An estimate of the caloric requirements of the human fetus. Biol Neonate 38:113–119, 1980.
8. Hay WW Jr, Meznarich HK: Effect of maternal glucose concentration on uteroplacental glucose consumption and transfer in pregnant sheep. Proc Soc Exp Biol Med 190:63–69, 1988.
9. Hay WW Jr, Molina RD, DiGiacomo JE, et al: Model of placental glucose consumption and transfer. Am J Physiol 258:R569–R577, 1990.
10. Molina RD, Meschia G, Battaglia FC, et al: Maturation of placental glucose transfer capacity in the ovine pregnancy. Am J Physiol 261:R697–R704, 1991.
11. Ehrhardt RA, Bell AW: Developmental increases in glucose transporter concentration in the sheep placenta. Am J Physiol 273:R1132–R1141, 1997.
12. Hay WW Jr, DiGiacomo JE, Meznarich HK, et al: Effects of glucose and insulin on fetal glucose oxidation and oxygen consumption. Am J Physiol 256:E704–E713, 1989.
13. DiGiacomo JE, Hay WW Jr: Fetal glucose metabolism and oxygen consumption during sustained maternal and fetal hypoglycemia. Metabolism 39:193–202, 1990.
14. Sparks JW, Hay WW Jr, Bonds D, et al: Simultaneous measurements of lactate turnover rate and umbilical lactate uptake in the fetal lamb. J Clin Invest 70:179–192, 1982.
15. Meznarich HK, Hay WW Jr, Sparks JW, et al: Fructose disposal and oxidation rates in the ovine fetus. Q J Exp Physiol 72:617–625, 1987.
16. Hay WW Jr, Meyers SA, Sparks JW, et al: Glucose and lactate oxidation rates in the fetal lamb. Proc Soc Exp Biol Med 73:553–563, 1983.
17. Kalhan SC, Savin SM, Adam PAJ: Measurement of glucose turnover in the human newborn with glucose-1-13C. J Clin Endocrinol Metab 43:704–707, 1976.
18. Hay WW Jr, Sparks JW, Wilkening RB, et al: Fetal glucose uptake and utilization as functions of maternal glucose concentration. Am J Physiol 246:E237–E242, 1984.
19. Hay WW Jr, Meznarich HK, Fowden AL: Effect of streptozotocin on rates of ovine fetal glucose utilization, oxidation and production in the sheep fetus. Metabolism 38:30–37, 1988.
20. Philipps AF, Carson BS, Meschia G, et al: Insulin secretion in fetal and newborn sheep. Am J Physiol 235:E467–E474, 1978.
21. Carson BS, Philipps AF, Simmons MA, et al: Effects of a sustained fetal insulin infusion upon glucose uptake and oxygenation. Pediatr Res 14:147–152, 1980.
22. Aldoretta PW, Carver TD, Hay WW Jr: Maturation of glucose-stimulated insulin secretion in fetal sheep (abstract). Pediatr Res 35:200A, 1994.
23. Carver TD, Anderson SM, Aldoretta PW, et al: Glucose suppression of insulin secretion in chronically hyperglycemic fetal sheep. Pediatr Res 38:754–762, 1995.
24. Kervran A, Randon J: Development of insulin release by fetal rat pancreas in vitro. Diabetes 29:673–678, 1980.
25. Kervran A, Guillaume M, Jost A: The endocrine pancreas of the fetus of diabetic pregnant rat. Diabetologia 15:387–393, 1978.
26. Cowett RM: Hypoglycemia and hyperglycemia in the newborn. In Polin RA, Fox WW (eds): Fetal and Neonatal Physiology. Philadelphia, WB Saunders, 1992, pp 406–418.
27. Freinkel N, Phelps NL, Metzger BE: Intermediary metabolism during normal pregnancy. In Sutherland HW, Stowers JM (eds): Carbohydrate Metabolism in

Pregnancy and the Newborn. New York, Springer-Verlag, 1979, pp 1–31.

28. Carver TD, Anderson SM, Aldoretta PW, et al: Effect of low-level basal plus marked "pulsatile" hyperglycemia on insulin secretion in fetal sheep. Am J Physiol 271:E865–E871, 1996.

29. Smith DL, Thureen PJ, Hay WW Jr: Effect of short-term fatty acid infusion on glucose and lipid metabolism in late gestation fetal sheep. Pediatr Res 51(Abstr 1790):308A, 2002.

30. Limesand SW, Hay WW Jr: Adaptation of ovine fetal pancreatic insulin secretion to chronic hypoglycemia and euglycemic correction. J Physiol 5471:95–105, 2002.

31. Rozance PJ, Limesand SW, Hay WW Jr: Lysine stimulated insulin secretion in hypoglycemic fetal sheep. Paper presented at the 32nd Aspen Conference on the Newborn, Aspen, Colorado, August 23–25, 2003.

32. Rozance PJ, Limesand SW, Wyckoff M, Hay WW Jr: Correlation between insulin secretion and glucose metabolism in ovine fetal pancreatic islets. Pediatr Res 53:394A, 2003.

33. Limesand SW, Hay WW Jr: A placental insufficiency ovine model of intrauterine growth restriction (PI-IUGR) exhibits reduced β-cell mass. Pediatr Res 53:16A, 2003.

34. DiGiacomo JE, Hay WW Jr: Effect of hypoinsulinemia and hyperglycemia on fetal glucose utilization and oxidation. Am J Physiol 259:E506–E512, 1990.

35. Fowden AL, Hay WW Jr: The effects of pancreatectomy on the rates of glucose utilization, oxidation and production in the sheep fetus. Q J Exp Physiol 73:973–984, 1988.

36. Fowden AL: The endocrine regulation of fetal metabolism and growth. In Gluckman PD, Johnston BM, Nathanielsz PW (eds): Advances in Fetal Physiology: Reviews in Honor of GC Liggins. Ithaca, NY, Perinatology Press, 1989, pp 229–243.

37. Aldoretta PW, Hay WW Jr: Chronic hyperglycemia induces insulin resistance and glucose intolerance in fetal sheep. Pediatr Res 49:307A, 2001.

38. Thureen PJ, Scheer B, Anderson SM, Hay WW Jr: Effect of hyperinsulinemia on amino acid utilization in the ovine fetus. Am J Physiol Endocrinol Metab 279:E1294–E1304, 2000.

39. Davidson LS, Hay WW Jr: Effect of hyperinsulinemia on amino acid utilization independent of glucose metabolism in the ovine fetus. J Investig Med 52:S123, 2004.

40. Lee W-H, Wisniowski P, Ahmed L, et al: Protein anabolic effects of insulin and IGF-I in the ovine fetus. Am J Physiol Endocrinol Metab 284:E748–E756, 2003.

41. Shen W-H, Yang X, Boyle DW, et al: Effects of intravenous insulin-like growth factor-I and insulin administration on insulin-like growth factor–binding proteins in the ovine fetus. J Endocrinol 171:143–151, 2002.

42. Stephens E, Thureen PJ, Goalstone ML, et al: Fetal hyperinsulinemia increases farnesylation of p21 Ras in fetal tissues. Am J Physiol Endocrinol Metab 281:E217–E223, 2001.

43. Anderson MS, Thamotharan M, Kao D, et al: Effects of hyperinsulinemia on fetal ovine signal transduction proteins and glucose transporters in skeletal muscle. Pediatr Res 53:390A, 2003.

44. Shen W-H, Mallon D, Boyle D, Liechty EA: IGF-I and insulin regulate eIF4F formation by different mechanisms in muscle and liver in the ovine fetus. Am J Physiol Endocrinol Metab 283:E593–E603, 2002.

45. Fowden AL, Silver MA: The effects of thyroid hormones on oxygen and glucose metabolism in the sheep fetus during late gestation. J Physiol 482:203–213, 1995.

46. Barnes RJ, Comline RS, Silver M: Effect of cortisol on liver glycogen concentrations in hypophysectomized, adrenalectomized and normal foetal lambs during late or prolonged gestation. J Physiol 275:567–579, 1978.

47. Fowden AL, Comline RS, Silver M: The effects of cortisol on the concentration of glycogen in different tissues in the chronically catheterized fetal pig. Q J Exp Physiol 70:23–32, 1985.

48. Ward JW, Wooding FBP, Fowden AL: Ovine feto-placental metabolism. J Physiol 554:529–541, 2003.

49. Fowden AL, Szemere J, Hughes P, et al: The effects of cortisol on the growth rate of the sheep fetus during late gestation. J Endocrinol 151:97–105, 2003.

50. Padbury JF, Ludlow JK, Ervin MG, et al: Thresholds for physiological effects of plasma catecholamines in fetal sheep. Am J Physiol 252:E530–E537, 1992.

51. Devaskar SU, Ganguli S, Styer D, et al: Glucagon and glucose dynamics in sheep: Evidence for glucagon resistance in fetus. Am J Physiol 246:E256–E265, 1984.

52. Fowden AL, Mundy L, Silver M: Developmental regulation of glucogenesis in the sheep fetus during late gestation. J Physiol 508:937–947, 1998.

53. Liechty EA, Boyle DW, Moorehead H, et al: Glucose and amino acid kinetic response to graded infusion of rhIGH-I in the late gestation ovine fetus. Am J Physiol Endocrinol Metab 277:E537–E543, 1999.

54. Liechty EA, Boyle DW, Moorehead H, et al: Effects of circulating IGF-I on glucose and amino acid kinetics in the ovine fetus. Am J Physiol 271:E177–E185, 1996.

55. Oliver MH, Harding JE, Breier BH, et al: Glucose but not mixed amino acid infusion regulates plasma insulin-like growth factor-I concentrations in fetal sheep. Pediatr Res 34:62–65, 1993.

56. Han VKM, Fowden AI: Paracrine regulation of fetal growth. In Ward RHT, Smith SK, Donnai D (eds): Early Fetal Growth and Development. London, RCOG, 1994, pp 275–291.

57. Liechty EA, Boyle DA, Moorehead H, et al: Effect of hyperinsulinemia on ovine fetal leucine kinetics during prolonged maternal fasting. Am J Physiol 263:E696–E702, 1992.

58. Fowden AL: The insulin-like growth factors and feto-placental growth. Placenta 24:803–812, 2003.

59. He J, Thamotharan M, Devaskar SU: Insulin-induced translocation of facilitative glucose transporters in fetal/neonatal rat skeletal muscle. Am J Physiol Regul Integr Comp Physiol 284:R1138–R1146, 2003.

60. Schroeder RE, Doria-Medina CL, Das UG, et al: Effect of maternal diabetes upon fetal rat myocardial and skeletal muscle glucose transporters. Pediatr Res 41:11–19, 1997.

61. Das UG, Schroeder RE, Hay WW Jr, et al: Chronic hypoglycemia causes time-dependent changes in ovine fetal GLUT 1 and GLUT 4 protein expression (abstract). Pediatr Res 37:60A, 1995.

62. Schroeder RE, Devaskar UP, Trail SE, et al: Effect of maternal diabetes on the expression of genes regulating fetal brain glucose uptake. Diabetes 42:1487–1496, 1993.

63. Das UG, Schroeder RE, Hay WW Jr, et al: Chronic hyperglycemia causes time-dependent changes in ovine fetal GLUT 1 and GLUT 4 protein expression (abstract). Pediatr Res 37:305A, 1995.

64. Das UG, Hay WW Jr, Devaskar SU: Myocardial glucose transporters in fetal sheep are regulated by time-dependent changes in glucose and insulin concentrations (abstract). Pediatr Res 39:26A, 1996.

65. Klip A, Tsakiridis T, Marette A, et al: Regulation of expression of glucose transporters by glucose: A review of studies in vivo and in cell cultures. FASEB J 8:43–53, 1994.

66. Simmons RA, Gounis AS, Shrikar AB, et al: Intrauterine growth retardation: Fetal glucose transport is diminished in lung but spared in brain. Pediatr Res 31:59–63, 1992.

67. Simmons RA, Flozak AS, Ogata ES: Glucose regulates GLUT 1 function and expression in fetal rat lung and muscle in vitro. Endocrinology 132:2312–2318, 1993.

68. Shelley HJ: Glycogen reserves and their changes at birth and in anoxia. Br Med Bull 17:137–143, 1961.

69. Dawkins MJR: Biochemical aspects of developing function in newborn mammalian liver. Br Med Bull 22:28–33, 1961.

70. Shellhase E, Kuroki Y, Emrie PA, et al: Expression of pulmonary surfactant apoproteins in the developing rat lung (abstract). Clin Res 37:208A, 1989.

71. Mott JC: The ability of young mammals to withstand total oxygen lack. Br Med Bull 17:144–148, 1961.

72. Sparks JW: Augmentation of glucose supply. Semin Perinatol 3:141–155, 1979.

73. Zheng Q, Levitsky LL, Fan J, et al: Glycogenesis in the cultured fetal and adult rat hepatocyte is differently

regulated by medium glucose. Pediatr Res 32:714–718, 1992.

74. Fowden AI, Comline RS: The effects of pancreatectomy on tissue glycogen concentrations in the fetal sheep. In Jones CT (ed): Fetal and Neonatal Development. Ithaca, NY, Perinatology Press, 1988, pp 505–508.

75. Sparks JW, Lynch A, Glinsmann WH: Regulation of rat liver glycogen synthesis and activities of glycogen cycle enzymes by glucose, and galactose. Metabolism 25:47–55, 1976.

76. Susa JB, McCormick KL, Widness JD, et al: Chronic hyperinsulinemia in the fetal rhesus monkey: Effects on fetal growth and composition. Diabetes 28:1058–1063, 1979.

77. Glinsmann WH, Eisen HJ, Lynch A, et al: Glucose regulation by isolated near-term monkey liver. Pediatr Res 9:600–604, 1975.

78. Levitsky LL, Paton JB, Fisher DE: Gluconeogenesis from lactate in the chronically catheterized baboon fetus. Biol Neonate 50:97–106, 1986.

79. Levitsky LL, Paton JB, Fisher DE: Lactate and fructose are glycogenic precursors in the chronically catheterized baboon fetus (abstract). Pediatr Res 21:217A, 1987.

80. DiGiacomo JE, Hay WW Jr, Chan L, et al: Determination of pathways of fetal glycogen synthesis by NMR spectroscopy (abstract). Clin Res 37:177A, 1980.

81. Goodner CJ, Thompson DJ: Glucose metabolism in the fetus in utero: The effect of maternal fasting and glucose loading in the rat. Pediatr Res 1:443–451, 1967.

82. Bossi E, Greenberg RE: Sources of blood glucose in the rat fetus. Pediatr Res 6:765–772, 1972.

83. Raiha NCR, Lindroos K: Development of some enzymes involved in gluconeogenesis in human liver. Ann Med Exp Biol Fenn 47:146–150, 1969.

84. Marconi A, Cetin E, Davoli A, et al: An evaluation of fetal glucogenesis in intrauterine growth retarded pregnancies: Steady state fetal and maternal enrichments of plasma glucose at cordocentesis. Metabolism 42:860–864, 1993.

85. Hay WW Jr, Sparks JW, Quissel BJ, et al: Simultaneous measurements of umbilical glucose uptake, fetal utilization rate, and fetal turnover rate of glucose. Am J Physiol 240:E662–E668, 1981.

86. Gleason CA, Rudolph AM: Gluconeogenesis by the fetal sheep liver in vivo. J Dev Physiol 7:184–194, 1985.

87. DiGiacomo JE, Hay WW Jr: Regulation of placental glucose transfer and consumption by fetal glucose production. Pediatr Res 25:429–434, 1989.

88. Fowden AL, Mundy L, Silver M: Developmental regulation of glucogenesis in the sheep fetus during late gestation. J Physiol 508:937–947, 1998.

89. Widdowson EM: Growth and composition of the human fetus and newborn. In Assali NS (ed): Biology of Gestation, vol 2. New York, Academic, 1968, pp 1–48.

90. Coleman RA: Placental metabolism and transport of lipid. Fed Proc 45:2519–2523, 1986.

91. Goldstein R, Levy E, Shafrir E: Increased maternal-fetal transport of fat in diabetes assessed by polyunsaturated fatty acid content in fetal lipids. Biol Neonate 47:343–349, 1985.

92. Stammers JP, Elphick MC, Hull D: Effect of maternal diet during late pregnancy on fetal lipid stores in rabbits. J Dev Physiol 5:395–404, 1983.

93. Elphick MC, Hull D, Sanders RR: Concentrations of free fatty acids in maternal and umbilical cord blood during elective cesarean section. Br J Obstet Gynaecol 83:539–544, 1976.

94. Hummel L, Simmermann T, Wagner H: Quantitative evaluation of the fetal fatty acid synthesis in the rat. Acta Biol Med Ger 37:229–232, 1978.

95. Elphick MC, Hull D: The transfer of free fatty acids across the rabbit placenta. J Physiol (Lond) 264:751–766, 1977.

96. Portman OW, Behrman RE, Soltys P: Transfer of free fatty acids across the primate placenta. Am J Physiol 216:143–147, 1969.

97. Hendrickse W, Stammers JP, Hull D: The transfer of free fatty acids across the human placenta. Br J Obstet Gynaecol 92:945–953, 1985.

98. Symonds ME, Stephenson T: Maternal nutrient restriction and endocrine programming of fetal adipose tissue development. Biochem Soc Trans 319:627-632, 1999.

99. Yuen BSJ, McMillen IC, Symonds ME, Owens PC: Abundance of leptin mRNA in fetal adipose tissue is related to fetal body weight. J Endocrinol 163:R11–R14, 1999.

100. Alexander G: Quantitative development of adipose tissue in foetal sheep. Aust J Biol Sci 31:489–503, 1978.

101. Lonnqvist F, Nordfors L, Jansson M, et al: Leptin secretion from adipose tissue in women. J Clin Invest 99:2398–2404, 1997.

102. De Vos P, Saladin R, Auwerx J, Staels B: Induction of ob gene expression by corticosteroids is accompanied by body weight loss and reduced food intake. J Biol Chem 270:15958–15961, 1995.

103. Forhead AJ, Thomas L, Crabtree J, et al: Plasma leptin concentration in fetal sheep during late gestation: Ontogeny and effect of glucocorticoids. Endocrinology 143:1166–1173, 2002.

104. Devaskar SU, Anthony R, Hay WW Jr: Ontogeny and insulin regulation of fetal ovine white adipose tissue leptin expression. Am J Physiol Regul Integr Comp Physiol 282:R432–R438, 2002.

105. Mostyn A, Keisler DH, Webb R, et al: The role of leptin in the transition from fetus to neonate. Proc Nutr Soc 60:187–194, 2001.

106. Cinaz P, Sen E, Bideci A, et al: Plasma leptin levels of large for gestational age and small for gestational age infants. Acta Paediatr 88:753–756, 1999.

107. Matsuda J, Yokota I, Iida M, et al: Dynamic changes in serum leptin concentrations during the fetal and neonatal periods. Pediatr Res 45:71–75, 1999.

108. Hytinantti T, Koistinen HA, Koivisto VA, et al: Changes in leptin concentration during the early postnatal period: Adjustment to extrauterine life? Pediatr Res 45:197–201, 1999.

109. Schubring C, Siebler T, Kratsch J, et al: Leptin serum concentrations in healthy neonates within the first week of life: Relation to insulin and growth hormone levels, skinfold thickness, body mass index and weight. Clin Endocrinol (Oxf) 51:199–204, 1999.

110. De Vos P, Saladin R, Auwerx J, Staels B: Induction of ob gene expression by corticosteroids is accompanied by body weight loss and reduced food intake. J Biol Chem 270:15958–15961, 1995.

111. Flier JS, Harris M, Hollenberg AN: Leptin, nutrition, and the thyroid: The why, the wherefore, and the wiring. J Clin Invest 105:859–861, 2000.

112. Mostyn A, Rayner DV, Trayhurn P: Effects of adrenaline, noradrenaline and isoprenaline on circulating leptin levels in mice (abstract). Proc Nutr Soc 58:69A, 1998.

113. Symonds ME: Pregnancy, parturition and neonatal development: Interactions between nutrition and thyroid hormones. Proc Nutr Soc 54:329–342, 1995.

114. Thomas CR, Lowy C: Placental transfer of free fatty acids: Factors affecting transfer across the guinea pig placenta. J Dev Physiol 5:323–332, 1983.

115. Dancis J, Jansen V, Kayden JH, et al: Transfer across perfused human placenta. III. Effect of chain length on transfer of free fatty acids. Pediatr Res 8:796–799, 1974.

116. Innis S: Perinatal biochemistry and physiology of long-chain polyunsaturated fatty acids. J Pediatr 143:S1–S8, 2003.

117. DeGroot RHM, Hornstra G, van Houwelingen AC, Roumen F: Effect of α-linolenic acid supplementation during pregnancy on maternal and neonatal polyunsaturated fatty acid status and pregnancy outcome. Am J Clin Nutr 79:251–260, 2004.

118. Smith CH, Moe AJ, Ganapathy V, et al: Nutrient transport pathways across the epithelium of the placenta. Annu Rev Nutr 12:183–206, 1992.

119. Milley JR: Protein synthesis during hypoxia in fetal lambs. Am J Physiol 252:E519–E524, 1987.

120. Milley JR: Uptake of exogenous substrates during hypoxia in fetal lambs. Am J Physiol 254:E572–E524, 1988.

121. Smith CH: Incubation techniques and investigation of placental transport

mechanisms in vitro. Placenta 2(Suppl):163–168, 1981.

122. Cetin I, Ronzoni S, Marconi AM, et al: Maternal concentrations and fetal-maternal concentration differences of plasma amino acids in normal and intrauterine growth-restricted pregnancies. Am J Obstet Gynecol 174:575–583, 1998.

123. Dancis J, Lind J, Oratz M, et al: Placental transfer of proteins in human gestation. Am J Obstet Gynecol 82:167–171, 1961.

124. Lemons JA, Adcock EW III, Jones MD Jr, et al: Umbilical uptake of amino acids in the unstressed fetal lamb. J Clin Invest 58:1428–1434, 1976.

125. Marconi AM, Battaglia FC, Meschia G, et al: A comparison of amino acid arteriovenous differences across the liver, hindlimb and placenta in the fetal lamb. Am J Physiol 257:E909–E915, 1989.

126. Gresham EL, James EJ, Raye JR, et al: Production and excretion of urea by the fetal lamb. Pediatrics 50:372–379, 1972.

127. van Veen LCP, Teng C, Hay WW Jr, et al: Leucine disposal and oxidation rates in the fetal lamb. Metabolism 36:48–53, 1987.

128. Hay WW Jr, Meyers SA, Sparks JW, et al: Glucose and lactate oxidation rates in the fetal lamb. Proc Soc Exp Biol Med 173:553–563, 1983.

129. Battaglia FC, Meschia G: Fetal nutrition. Annu Rev Nutr 8:43–61, 1988.

130. Meier PR, Peterson RG, Bonds DR, et al: Rates of protein synthesis and turnover in fetal life. Am J Physiol 240:E320–E324, 1981.

131. Kennaugh JM, Bell AW, Teng C, et al: Ontogenetic changes in the rates of protein synthesis and leucine oxidation during fetal life. Pediatr Res 22:688–692, 1987.

132. Bell AW, Kennaugh JM, Battaglia FC, et al: Uptake of amino acids and ammonia at mid-gestation by the fetal lamb. Q J Exp Physiol 74:635–643, 1989.

133. Sparks JW: Human intrauterine growth and nutrient accretion. Semin Perinatol 8:74–93, 1984.

134. Waterlow JL, Garlick PJ, Millward DJ: Protein Turnover in Mammalian Tissues and in the Whole Body. Amsterdam, Elsevier/North-Holland, 1978.

135. Milner RDG, Hill DJ: Interaction between endocrine and paracrine peptides in prenatal growth control. Eur J Pediatr 146:113, 1987.

136. Wilkening RB, Boyle DW, Teng C, et al: Amino acid uptake by fetal ovine hindlimb under normal and euglycemic hyperinsulinemic states. Am J Physiol 266:E72–E78, 1994.

137. Liechty EA, Boyle DW, Moorehead H, et al: Increased fetal glucose concentration decreases ovine fetal leucine oxidation independent of insulin. Am J Physiol 265:E617–E623, 1993.

138. Liechty EA, Lemons JA: Changes in ovine fetal hindlimb amino acid metabolism during maternal fasting. Am J Physiol 246:E430, 1984.

139. Domenech M, Gruppuso PA, Nishino VT, et al: Preserved fetal amino acid concentrations in the presence of maternal hypoaminoacidemia. Pediatr Res 20:1071–1076, 1986.

140. Lemons JA, Schreiner RL: Amino acid metabolism in the ovine fetus. Am J Physiol 244:E459–E466, 1983.

141. Lemons JA, Liechty EA: Nitrogen flux across ovine maternal and fetal hindquarters during fasting. J Dev Physiol 9:151–158, 1987.

142. Liechty EA, Denne SC, Lemons JA, et al: Effects of glucose infusion on leucine transamination and oxidation in the ovine fetus. Pediatr Res 30:423–429, 1991.

143. Johnson JD, Dunham T, Skipper BJ, et al: Protein turnover in diseases of the rat fetus following maternal starvation. Pediatr Res 20:1252–1257, 1986.

144. Johnson JD, Dunham T: Protein turnover in tissues of the fetal rat after prolonged maternal malnutrition. Pediatr Res 23:534–538, 1988.

145. Lithell HO, McKeigue PM, Berglund L, et al: Relation of size at birth to non-insulin-dependent diabetes and insulin concentrations in men aged 50–60 years. Br Med J 312:406–410, 1996.

146. Curhan GC, Willett WC, Rimm EB, et al: Birth weight and adult hypertension, diabetes mellitus, and obesity in US men. Circulation 94:3246–3250, 1996.

147. Fall CH, Stein CE, Kumaran K, et al: Size at birth, maternal weight, and type 2 diabetes in South India. Diabet Med 15:220–227, 1998.

148. Levitt NS, Lambert EV, Woods D, et al: Impaired glucose tolerance and elevated blood pressure in low birthweight, nonobese, young South African adults: Early programming of cortisol axis. J Clin Endocrinol Metab 85:4611–4618, 2000.

149. Dabelea D, Pettitt DJ, Hanson RL, et al: Birthweight, type 2 diabetes, and insulin resistance in Pima Indian children and young adults. Diabetes Care 22:944–950, 1999.

150. Fagot-Campagna A, Pettitt DJ, Engelgau MM, et al: Type 2 diabetes among North American children and adolescents: An epidemiological review and a public health perspective. J Pediatr 136:664–672, 2000.

151. Ong KKL, Dunger DB: Thrifty genotypes and phenotypes in the pathogenesis of type 2 diabetes mellitus. J Pediatr Endocrinol Metab 13:1419–1424, 2000.

152. Hofman PL, Cutfield WS, Robinson EM, et al: Insulin resistance in short children with intrauterine growth retardation. J Clin Endocrinol Metab 82:402–406, 1997.

153. Bavdekar A, Yajnik CS, Fall CHD, et al: Insulin resistance syndrome in 8-year old Indian children: Small at birth, big at 8 years, or both? Diabetes 48:2422–2429, 1999.

154. Bennett F, Watson-Brown C, Thame M, et al: Shortness at birth is associated with insulin resistance in prepubertal Jamaican children. Eur J Clin Nutr 56:506–511, 2002.

155. Jaquet D, Gaboriau A, Czernichow P, Levy-Marchal C: Insulin resistance early in adulthood in subjects with intrauterine growth retardation. J Clin Endocrinol Metab 85:1401–1406, 2000.

156. Jaquet D, Vidal H, Hankard R, et al: Impaired regulation of glucose transporter 4 gene expression in insulin resistance associated with in utero undernutrition. J Clin Endocrinol Metab 86:3266–3271, 2001.

157. Thamotharan M, McKnight RA, Thamotharan S, et al: Aberrant insulin-induced GLUT4 translocation predicts glucose intolerance in the offspring of a diabetic mother. Am J Physiol Endocrinol Metab 284:E901–E914, 2003.

158. Selak MA, Storey BT, Peterside IA, Simmons RA: Impaired oxidative phosphorylation in skeletal muscle in growth-retarded rats. Am J Physiol Endocrinol Metab 285:E130–E137, 2003.

159. Peterside IE, Selak MA, Simmons RA: Impaired oxidative phosphorylation in hepatic mitochondria in growth-retarded rats. Am J Physiol Endocrinol Metab 285:E1258–E1266, 2003.

160. Hattersley AT, Beards F, Ballantyne E, et al: Mutations in the glucokinase gene of the fetus result in reduced birthweight. Nat Genet 19:268–270, 1998.

161. Dunger DB, Ong KK, Huxtable SJ, et al: Association of the INS VNTR with size at birth. ALSPAC study team: Avon longitudinal study of pregnancy and childhood. Nat Genet 19:98–100, 1998.

162. Ong KK, Ahmed ML, Emmett PM, et al: The insulin gene VNTR, type 2 diabetes and birth weight. Nat Genet 21:262–263, 1999.

163. Moore T, Haig D: Genomic imprinting in mammalian development: A parental tug-of-war. Trends Genet 7:45–49, 1991.

164. Clark PM, Hindmarsh PC, Schiell A, et al: Size at birth and adrenocortical function in childhood. Clin Endocrinol (Oxf) 45:721–726, 1996.

165. Dalmaz Y, Peyrin L, Dutruge J, Sann L: Neonatal pattern of adrenergic metabolites in urine of small for gestational age and preterm infants. J Neural Transm 49:151–165, 1980.

166. Divers WA, Wilkes MM, Babaknia A, et al: Amniotic fluid catecholamines and metabolites in intrauterine growth retardation. Am J Obstet Gynecol 141:608–610, 1981.

167. Philips DIW, Barker DJP, Fall CHD, et al: Elevated plasma cortisol concentrations: A link between low birth weight and the insulin resistance syndrome? J Clin Endocrinol Metab 83:757–760, 1998.

168. Phillips DI, Walker BR, Reynolds RM, et al: Low birth weight predicts elevated plasma cortisol concentrations in adults from 3 populations. Hypertension 35:1301–1306, 2000.
169. Nyirenda MJ, Lindsay RS, Kenyon CJ, et al: Glucocorticoid exposure in late gestation permanently programs phosphoenolpyruvate carboxykinase and glucocorticoid receptor expression and causes glucose intolerance in adult offspring. J Clin Invest 101:2174–2181, 1998.
170. Leipälä JA, Raivio KO, Sarnesto A, et al: Intrauterine growth restriction and postnatal steroid effects on insulin sensitivity in preterm neonates. J Pediatr 141:472–476, 2002.
171. Goland RS, Josak S, Warren WB, et al: Elevated levels of umbilical cord plasma corticotropin releasing hormone in growth retarded fetuses. J lin Endocrinol Metab 77:1174–1179, 1993.
172. Tenhola S, Martikainen A, Rabiala E, et al: Increased adrenocortical and adrenomedullary hormonal activity in 12-year-old children born small for gestational age. J Pediatr 141:477–482, 2002.
173. Leipälä JA, Raivio KO, Sarnesto A, et al: Intrauterine growth restriction and postnatal steroid effects on insulin sensitivity in preterm neonates. J Pediatr 141:472–476, 2002.
174. Girard J: Gluconeogensis in late fetal and early neonatal life. Biol Neonate 50:237–258, 1986.
175. Heck LJ, Erenberg A: Serum glucose levels in term neonates during the first 48 hours of life. J Pediatr 110:119–122, 1987.
176. Sperling MA, DeLamatar PV, Phelps D, et al: Spontaneous and amino acid stimulated glucagon secretion in the immediate postnatal period: Relation to glucose and insulin. J Clin Invest 53:1159–1164, 1974.
177. Padbury JF, Diakomanolis ES, Hobel CJ, et al: Neonatal adaptation: Sympathoadrenal response to umbilical cord cutting. Pediatr Res 15:1483–1487, 1981.
178. Kalhan S, Saker F: Metabolic and endocrine disorders, part 1: Disorders of carbohydrate metabolism. In Fanaroff AA, Martin RJ (eds): Neonatal-Perinatal Medicine: Diseases of the Fetus and Newborn, 6th ed. St Louis, Mosby–Year Book, 1997, pp 1439–1463.
179. Sunehag AL: The role of parenteral lipids in supporting gluconeogenesis in very premature infants. Pediatr Res 54:480–486, 2003.
180. Ogata ES: Carbohydrate metabolism in the fetus and neonate and altered neonatal glucoregulation. Pediatr Clin North Am 33:35–45, 1986.
181. Gleason CA, Hamm C, Jones MD Jr: Cerebral blood flow, oxygenation, and carbohydrate metabolism in immature fetal sheep in utero. Am J Physiol 256:R1264–R1268, 1989.
182. Williams AF: Hypoglycaemia in the newborn: A review. WHO Reg Publ Eur Ser 5778:1997.
183. Lubchenco LO, Bard H: Incidence of hypoglycemia in newborn infants classified by birth weight and gestational age. Pediatrics 47:831–838, 1971.
184. Lucas A, Morley R, Cole TJ: Adverse neurodevelopmental outcome of moderate neonatal hypoglycaemia. Br Med J 297:1304–1308, 1988.
185. Srinivasan G, Pildes RS, Cattamanchi G, et al: Plasma glucose values in normal neonates: A new look. J Pediatr 109:114–117, 1986.
186. Marconi AM, Paolini C, Buscaglia M, et al: The impact of gestational age and fetal growth on the maternal-fetal glucose concentration difference. Obstet Gynecol 87:937–942, 1996.
187. Stanley CA, Baker L: The causes of neonatal hypoglycemia. N Engl J Med 340:1200–1201, 1999; Stanley CA: Hyperinsulinism in infants and children. Pediatr Clin North Am 44:363–374, 1997.
188. Cornblath M, Hawdon JM, Williams AF, et al: Controversies regarding definition of neonatal hypoglycemia: Suggested operational thresholds. Pediatrics 105:1141–1145, 2002.
189. Hawdon JM, Ward Platt MP, Aynsley-Green A: Patterns of metabolic adaptation for preterm and term infants in the first neonatal week. Arch Dis Child 67:357–365, 1992.
190. Cornblath M, Schwartz R: Hypoglycemia in the Neonate. Disorders of Carbohydrate Metabolism in Infancy, 3d ed. London, Blackwell Scientific, 1991, pp 102–108.
191. Eaton AP, Maurer WF: The Beckwith-Wiedemann syndrome. Am J Dis Child 122:520–525, 1971.
192. Barrett CT, Oliver TK Jr: Hypoglycemia and hyperinsulinism in infants with erythroblastosis fetalis. N Engl J Med 278:1260–1262, 1968.
193. Paran E, Holzberg G, Mazor M, et al: Beta-adrenergic blocking agents in the treatment of pregnancy-induced hypertension. Clin Pharmacol Ther 33:119–123, 1995.
194. Stanley CA: Hyperinsulinism in infants and children. Pediatr Clin North Am 44:363–374, 1997.
195. Collins JE, Leonard JV, Teale D, et al: Hyperinsulinaemic hypoglycaemia in small for dates babies. Arch Dis Child 65:1118–1120, 1990.
196. Glaser B, Kesavan P, Heymann M, et al: Familial hyperinsulinism caused by an activating glucokinase mutation. N Engl J Med 338:226–230, 1998.
197. Stanley CA, Lieu YK, Hsu BYL, et al: Hyperinsulinism and hyperammonemia in infants with regulatory mutations of the glutamate dehydrogenase gene. N Engl J Med 338:1352–1357, 1998.
198. Glaser B, Thornton PS, Herold K: Clinical and molecular heterogenicity of familial hyperinsulinism. J Pediatr 133:801–802, 1998.
199. Verkarre V, Fournet JC, de Lonlay P, et al: Paternal mutation of the sulfonylurea receptor (SUR1) gene and maternal loss of 11p15 imprinted genes lead to persistent hyperinsulinism in focal adenomatous hyperplasia. J Clin Invest 102:1286–1291, 1998.
200. de Lonlay-Debeney P, Poggi-Travert F, Fournet J-C, et al: Clinical features of 52 neonates with hyperinsulinism. N Engl J Med 340:1169–1175, 1999.
201. Hawdon JM, Ward Platt MP, Aynsley-Green A: Prevention and management of neonatal hypoglycaemia. Arch Dis Child 70:F60–F65, 1994.
202. Lillien LD, Pildes RS, Srinivasan G, et al: Treatment of neonatal hypoglycemia with minibolus and intravenous glucose infusion. J Pediatr 97:295–298, 1980.
203. Koch-Weser J: Diazoxide. N Engl J Med 294:1271–1273, 1976.
204. Lamberts SWJ, van der Lely AJ, de Herder WW, et al: Octreotide. N Engl J Med 334:246–254, 1996.
205. Auer RN: Progress review: Hypoglycemic brain damage. Stroke 17:699–708, 1986.
206. Clark GD: Role of excitatory amino acids in brain injury caused by hypoxia-ischemia, status epilepticus, and hypoglycemia. Clin Perinatol 16:459–474, 1989.
207. McGowan JE, Haynes-Laing AG, Mishra OP, et al: The effect of acute hypoglycemia on the cerebral NMDA receptor in newborn piglets. Brain Res 670:283–288, 1995.
208. Vannucci RC, Yager JY: Glucose, lactic acid, and perinatal hypoxic-ischemic brain damage. Pediatr Neurol 8:3–12, 1992.
209. Cornblath M, Schwartz R, Aynsley-Green A, Lloyd JK: Hypoglycemia in infancy: The need for rational definition. A Ciba Foundation Discussion Meeting. Pediatrics 85:834–837, 1990.
210. Fosel S: Transient and permanent neonatal diabetes. Eur J Pediatr 154:944–948, 1995.
211. Binder ND, Raschko PK, Benda GI, et al: Insulin infusion with parenteral nutrition in extremely low birth weight infants with hyperglycemia. J Pediatr 114:273–280, 1989.
212. Louik C, Mitchell AA, Epstein MF, et al: Risk factors for neonatal hyperglycemia associated with 10% dextrose infusion. Am J Dis Child 139:783–786, 1985.
213. Cowett AA, Farrag HM, Gelardi NL, et al: Hyperglycemia in the micropremie: Evaluation of the metabolic disequilibrium during the neonatal period. Prenat Neonatal Med 2:360–365, 1997.
214. Cowett RM, Oh W, Pollak A, et al: Glucose disposal of low birth weight infants: Steady state hyperglycemia produced by constant intravenous glucose infusion. Pediatrics 63:389–396, 1979.

215. Vileisis RA, Cowett RM, Oh W: Glycemic response to lipid infusion in the premature neonate. J Pediatr 100:108–112, 1982.

216. Lilien LD, Rosenfield RL, Baccaro MM, et al: Hyperglycemia in stressed small premature neonates. J Pediatr 94:454–459, 1979.

217. Schalch DS, Kipnis DM: Abnormalities associated with elevated plasma nonesterified fatty acids. J Clin Invest 44:2010–2020, 1965.

218. Srinivasan G, Jain R, Pildes RS, et al: Glucose homeostasis during anesthesia and surgery in infants. J Pediatr Surg 21:718–721, 1986.

219. Anand KJS, Sippell WG, Aynsley-Green A: Randomised trial of fentanyl anesthesia in preterm babies undergoing surgery: Effects on the stress response. Lancet 1:243–248, 1987.

220. Gottschalk ME, Schatz DA, Clare-Salzer M, et al: Permanent diabetes without serological evidence of autoimmunity after transient neonatal diabetes. Diabetes Care 15:1273–1276, 1992.

221. Ferguson AW, Milner RDG: Transient neonatal diabetes in sibs. Arch Dis Child 45:80–85, 1971.

222. Widness JA, Cowett RM, Zeller P, et al: Permanent neonatal diabetes in an infant of an insulin-dependant mother. J Pediatr 100:926–929, 1982.

223. Farrag HM, Nawrath LM, Healy JE, et al: Persistent glucose production and greater peripheral sensitivity to insulin in the neonate vs. the adult. Am J Physiol 272:E86–E93, 1997.

224. Mitanchez-Mokhtari D, Lahlou N, Kieffer F, et al: Both relative insulin resistance and defective islet β-cell processing of proinsulin are responsible for transient hyperglycemia in extremely preterm infants. Pediatrics 113:537–541, 2004.

225. Goldman SL, Hirata T: Attenuated response to insulin in very low birth weight infants. Pediatr Res 14:50–53, 1980.

226. Zarif M, Pildes RS, Vidyasagar D: Insulin and growth-hormone responses in neonatal hyperglycemia. Diabetes 25:428–433, 1976.

227. Murdaugh E, Rosenberg AA: The effect of blood glucose concentration on post-asphyxia cerebral hemodynamics in newborn lambs. Pediatr Res 27:454–459, 1990.

228. Pulsinelli WA, Waldman S, Rawlinson D, et al: Moderate hyperglycemia augments ischemic brain damage: A neuropathologic study in the rat. Neurology 32:1239–1246, 1982.

229. Myers RE: A unitary theory of causation of anoxic and hypoxic brain pathology. Adv Neurol 26:195–213, 1979.

230. Duckrow RB, Beard DC, Brennan RW: Regional cerebral blood flow decreases during hyperglycemia. Ann Neurol 17:267–272, 1985.

231. Quigley EMM, Marsh MN, Shaffer JL, et al: Hepatobiliary complications of total parenteral nutrition. Gastroenterology 104:286–301, 1993.

232. Forsyth JS, Crighton A: Low birthweight infants and total parenteral nutrition immediately after birth: I. Energy expenditure and respiratory quotient of ventilated and non-ventilated infants. Arch Dis Child Fetal Neonatal Ed 73:F4–F7, 1995.

233. Forsyth JS, Murdock N, Crighton A: Low birthweight infants and total parenteral nutrition immediately after birth: III. Randomised study of energy substrate utilisation, nitrogen balance, and carbon dioxide production. Arch Dis Child Fetal Neonatal Ed 73:F13–F16, 1995.

234. Stonestreet BS, Rubin L, Pollak A, et al: Renal functions of low birth weight infants with hyperglycemia and glucosuria produced by glucose infusions. Pediatrics 66:561–567, 1980.

235. Micheli JL, Schutz Y, Junod S, et al: Early postnatal intravenous amino acid administration to extremely low birth weight preterm infants. Semin Neonatal Nutr Metab 2:1–3, 1994.

236. Collins JW, Hoppe M, Brown K, et al: A controlled trial of insulin infusion and parenteral nutrition in extremely low birth weight infants with glucose intolerance. J Pediatr 118:921–927, 1991.

237. Poindexter BB, Karn CA, Denne SC: Exogenous insulin reduces proteolysis and protein synthesis in extremely low birth weight infants. J Pediatr 132:948–953, 1998.

238. Rivera A, Bell E, Bier D: Effect of intravenous amino acids on protein metabolism of preterm infants during the first 3 days of life. Pediatr Res 33:106–111, 1993.

239. Van Goudoever J, Colen T, Wattimena J, et al: Immediate commencement of amino acid supplementation in preterm infants: Effect of serum amino acid concentrations and protein kinetics on the first day of life. J Pediatr 127:458–465, 1995.

240. Van Lingen R, Van Goudoever J, Luijendijk I, et al: Effects of early amino acid administration during total parenteral nutrition on protein metabolism in pre-term infants. Clin Sci 82:199–203, 1992.

241. Poindexter BB, Karn CA, Leitch CA, et al: Amino acids do not suppress proteolysis in premature neonates. Am J Physiol Endocrinol Metab 281:E472–E478, 2001.

242. Poindexter BB, Karn CA, Ahlrichs JA, et al: Amino acids suppress proteolysis independent of insulin throughout the neonatal period. Am J Physiol 272:E592–E599, 1997.

243. Denne S, Karn C, Ahlrichs J, et al: Proteolysis and phenylalanine hydroxylation in response to parenteral nutrition in extremely premature and normal newborns. J Clin Invest 97:746–754, 1996.

244. Reed PJ, Burrin DG, Davis TA, et al: Protein nutrition of the neonate. Proc Nutr Soc 59:87–97, 2000.

245. Thureen PJ, Melara D, Fennessey PV, Hay WW Jr: Effect of low versus high intravenous amino acid intake on very low birth weight infants in the early neonatal period. Pediatr Res 53:24–32, 2003.

246. Rassin DK: Essential and non-essential amino acids in neonatal nutrition. In Raiha NCR (ed): Protein Metabolism during Infancy. New York, Raven, 1994, pp 183–195.

247. Kilani RA, Cole FS, Bier DM: Phenylalanine hydroxylase activity in preterm infants: Is tyrosine a conditionally essential amino acid? Am J Clin Nutr 61:1218–1223, 1995.

248. Keshen TH, Jaksic T, Jahoor F: De novo synthesis of cysteine in premature neonates. Surg Forum 48:639–641, 1997.

249. Heird WC, Hay WW Jr, Helms RA, et al: Pediatric parenteral amino acid mixture in low birth weight infants. Pediatrics 81:41–50, 1988.

250. Wykes LJ, House JD, Ball RO, et al: Aromatic amino acid metabolism of neonatal piglets receiving TPN: Effect of tyrosine precursors. Am J Physiol 267:E672–E679, 1994.

251. Kalhan SC, Denne SC: Energy consumption in infants with bronchopulmonary dysplasia. J Pediatr 116:662–664, 1990.

252. Glamour TS, McCullough AJ, Sauer PJJ, et al: Quantification of carbohydrate oxidation by respiratory gas exchange and isotopic tracers. Am J Physiol 268:E789–E796, 1995.

253. Sauer PJJ, Dane HJ, Visser HKA: Longitudinal studies on metabolic rate, heat loss, and energy cost of growth in low birthweight infants. Pediatr Res 18:254–259, 1984.

254. Wahlig TM, Gatho CW, Boros SJ: Metabolic response of preterm infants to variable degrees of respiratory illness. J Pediatr 124:283–288, 1994.

255. Haumont D, Richelle M, Deckelbaum RJ, et al: Effect of liposomal content of lipid emulsions on plasma lipid concentrations in low birthweight infants receiving parenteral nutrition. J Pediatr 121:759–763, 1992.

256. Alwaidh MH, Shaw BB, Ryan SW: Randomized trial of effect of delayed intravenous lipid administration on chronic lung disease in preterm neonates. J Pediatr Gastroenterol Nutr 22:303–306, 1996.

257. Brownlee KG, Kelly EJ, Ng PC, et al: Early or late parenteral nutrition for the sick preterm neonate. Arch Dis Child 69:281–283, 1993.

258. Cooke RWI: Factors associated with chronic lung disease in preterm infants. Arch Dis Child 66:776–779, 1991.

259. Gilbertson N, Kovar IZ, Cox DJ, et al: Introduction of intravenous lipid administration on the first day of life in the very low birthweight neonate. J Pediatr 119:615–623, 1991.

260. Hammerman C, Arambwo MJ: Decreased lipid intake reduces morbidity in sick premature neonates. J Pediatr 113:1083–1088, 1988.

261. Sosenko IRS, Rodriguez-Pierce N, Bancalari E: Effect of early initiation of intravenous lipid administration on the incidence and severity of chronic lung disease in premature infants. J Pediatr 123:975–982, 1993.

262. Helms RA, Herrod HG, Burckart GJ, et al: E-rosette formation, total T-cells, and lymphocyte transformation in infants receiving intravenous safflower oil emulsion. J Parenter Enteral Nutr 7:541–545, 1983.

263. Rubin M, Naor N, Sirota L, et al: Are bilirubin and plasma lipid profiles of premature infants dependent on the lipid emulsion infused? J Pediatr Gastroenterol Nutr 21:25–30, 1995.

264. Foote KD, Mackinnon MJ, Innis SM: Effect of early introduction of formula versus fat free parenteral nutrition on essential fatty acid status of preterm infants. Am J Clin Nutr 54:93–97, 1991.

265. Friedman Z, Frolich JC: Essential fatty acids and the major urinary metabolites of the E prostaglandins in thriving neonates and in infants receiving parenteral fat emulsions. Pediatr Res 13:932–936, 1979.

266. Innis SM, Sprecher H, Hachey D, et al: Neonatal polyunsaturated fatty acid metabolism. Lipids 34:139–149, 1999.

267. Heird WC, Prager TC, Anderson RE: Docosahexaenoic acid and the development and function of the infant retina. Curr Opin Lipidol 8:12–16, 1997.

268. Simmer K: Longchain polyunsaturated fatty acid supplementation in preterm infants. Cochrane Database Syst Rev 2(CD000375):271, 2000.

269. San Giovanni JP, Parra-Cabrera S, Colditz GA, et al: Meta-analysis of dietary essential fatty acids and long-chain polyunsaturated fatty acids as they relate to visual resolution acuity in health preterm infants. Pediatrics 105:1292–1298, 2000.

270. O'Connor DL, Hall R, Adamkin D, et al: Growth and development in preterm infants fed long-chain polyunsaturated fatty acids: A prospective, randomized controlled trial. Pediatrics 108:359–371, 2001.

271. Foreman-van Drongelen MM, al MD, van Houwelingen AC, et al: Comparison between the essential fatty acid status of preterm and full-term infants, measured in umbilical vessel walls. Early Hum Dev 42:241–251, 1995.

272. Simmer K: Longchain polyunsaturated fatty acid supplementation in infants born at term. Cochrane Database Syst Rev 4(CD000376), 2001.

273. Agostoni C, Trojan S, Bellu R, et al: Neurodevelopmental quotient of healthy term infants at 4 months and feeding practice: The role of long-chain polyunsaturated fatty acids. Pediatr Res 38:262–266, 1995.

274. Birch EE, Garfield S, Hoffman DR, et al: A randomized controlled trial of early dietary supply of long-chain polyunsaturated fatty acids and mental development in term infants. Dev Med Child Neurol 42:174–181, 2000.

275. ESPGAN Committee on Nutrition: Committee report: Comment on the content and composition of lipids in infant formulas. Acta Paediatr Scand 80:887–896, 1991.

276. The British Nutrition Foundation: Unsaturated fatty acids: Nutritional and physiological significance. In The Report of the British Nutrition Foundation's Task Force. Padstow, UK, TJ Press, 1992, pp 63–67.

277. Fats and Oils in Human Nutrition. Rome, Food and Agriculture Organization/World Health Organization, 1994, pp 6–7, 49–55.

278. Makrides M, Neumann MA, Byard RW, et al: Fatty acid composition of brain, retina, and erythrocytes in breast- and formula-fed infant. Am J Clin Nutr 60:189–194, 1994.

279. Rioux FM, Innis SM, Dyer R, et al: Diet-induced changes in liver and bile but not brain fatty acids can be predicted from differences in plasma phospholipid fatty acids in formula- and milk-fed piglets. J Nutr 127:370–377, 1997.

280. Pawlosky R, Barnes A, Salem N Jr: Essential fatty acid metabolism in the feline: Relationship between liver and brain production of long-chain polyunsaturated fatty acids. J Lipid Res 35:2032–2040, 1994.

281. Moore SA, Yoder E, Murphy S, et al: Astrocytes, not neurons, produce docosahexaenoic acid (22:6 omega-3) and arachidonic acid (20:4 omega-6). J Neurochem 56:518–524, 1991.

282. Clarke SD, Jump DB: Dietary polyunsaturated fatty acid regulation of gene transcription. Annu Rev Nutr 14:83–98, 1994.

283. Carlson SE, Cooke RJ, Werkman SH, et al: First year growth of preterm infants fed standard compared to marine oil n-3 supplemented formula. Lipids 27:901–907, 1992.

284. Jensen CL, Prager TC, Fraley JK, et al: Effect of dietary linoleic/alpha-linolenic acid ratio on growth and visual function of term infants. J Pediatr 131:200–295, 1997.

285. Pegorier JP, Chatelain R, Thumelin S, et al: Role of long-chain fatty acids in the postnatal induction of genes coding for liver mitochondrial beta-oxidative enzymes. Biochem Soc Trans 26:113–120, 1998.

286. Stanley CA: Dissecting the spectrum of fatty acid oxidation disorders. J Pediatr 132:384–386, 1998.

287. Pegorier JP, Duee PH, Girard J, et al: Development of gluconeogenesis in isolated hepatocytes from fasting or suckling newborn pigs. J Nutr 112:1038–1046, 1982.

288. Pegorier JP, Ferre P, Leturque A, et al: Metabolic effect of sodium dichloroacetate in the suckling newborn rat. Diabetologia 15:459–463, 1978.

289. Bougneres PF, Saudubray JM, Marsac C, et al: Decreased ketogenesis due to deficiency of hepatic carnitine acyltransferase. N Engl J Med 302:123–124, 1980.

290. Aynsley-Green A, Hawdon AM, Deshpande S, et al: Neonatal insulin secretion: Implications for the programming of metabolic homeostasis. Acta Paediatr Jpn 39(Suppl 1):21–25, 1997.

291. Hawdon JM, Ward Platt MP, Aynsley-Green A: Patterns of metabolic adaptation for preterm and term infants in the first neonatal week. Arch Dis Child 67:357–365, 1992.

292. Nedergaard J, Cannon B: Brown adipose tissue: Development and function. In Polin RA, Fox WW (eds): Fetal and Neonatal Physiology, 2d ed. Philadelphia, WB Saunders, 1997, pp 489–492.

293. Klein S, Coppack SW, Mohamed-Ali V, et al: Adipose tissue leptin production and plasma leptin kinetics in humans. Diabetes 45:984–987, 1996.

294. Sparks JW: Human intrauterine growth and nutrient accretion. Semin Perinatol 8:74–93, 1980.

# Endocrinology of Parturition

## William Gibb and John R. G. Challis

Preterm labor occurs in approximately 8% of all pregnancies in North America, and its incidence has remained relatively unchanged in recent years. It is associated with approximately 70% of all neonatal deaths and more than three quarters of neonatal morbidity.[1] Infants born preterm have an increased incidence of neurologic, metabolic, and respiratory disorders. The cost of caring for very prematurely delivered babies has been estimated at $5 to $6 billion annually in the United States. Although different measures have been advocated as predictors of preterm labor and different treatments have been used to suppress myometrial activity and prevent preterm labor, prediction and prevention of this condition remain a major challenge in clinical practice. This failing stems in large part from a poor understanding of the processes that lead to birth at term and to the myriad causes of preterm labor. Preterm birth may be elective, associated with an underlying infective process, or related to one or more medical variables, including maternal age and history, previous preterm birth, and multiple pregnancies.[1,2] Socioeconomic factors, maternal stress, work habits, and lifestyle have also been recognized as important contributing factors in some cases of preterm birth. The ability to recognize patients with true preterm labor is essential in developing appropriate, scientifically based management strategies. For example, recognition of patients in true preterm labor would allow administration of antenatal glucocorticoids only to those women at risk of delivering prematurely and thereby reduce the risks associated with repeated antenatal corticosteroid treatment. In this chapter, we discuss control of labor at term and examine potential mechanisms that may be associated with premature parturition.

## ACTIVATION AND STIMULATION OF THE UTERUS

In most species, the uterus remains relatively quiescent throughout pregnancy.[3] The contractions that do occur are poorly synchronized and of low amplitude and cause relatively small increases in uterine pressure. This pattern of activity in the sheep, baboon, and rhesus monkey has been called "contractures"; in women, it has been speculated that contractures correspond to Braxton Hicks contractions.[3,4] Importantly, contractures are associated with transient decreases in fetal $PaO_2$, endocrine responses, and mechanical stimulation of the fetus[3] (see discussion to follow). At term, well-coordinated contractions develop in the uterus, and the myometrium becomes highly excitable and generates high-amplitude, high-frequency contractions of labor.[3] The transition of the myometrium from a relatively quiescent state to

an active state has been termed *activation* and is due to the action of substances called uterotrophins. When activation has occurred, the myometrium can respond to various endogenous or exogenous substances (uterotonins) and undergo *stimulation*.[3]

The quiescence of myometrial activity during pregnancy may be referred to as phase 0 of parturition. The phase of activation due to the action of uterotrophins is termed *phase 1*; stimulation by uterotonins, *phase 2*; and postpartum involution of the uterus, *phase 3*. In this sequence, initiation of parturition would correspond to the transition from phase 0 to phase 1 (activation).

During pregnancy, the myometrium is acted on by one or more different inhibitors, which may include progesterone, prostacyclin ($PGI_2$), relaxin, parathyroid hormone–related protein (PTHrP), and nitric oxide (NO).[5,6] PTHrP is synthesized in human myometrium and its secretion is increased by transforming growth factor beta (TGF-$\beta$). PTHrP may act in an autocrine/paracrine fashion through specific receptors to activate the $G_s\alpha$ subunit of G proteins and to increase intracellular levels of cyclic adenosine monophosphate (cAMP).[7] Recent studies found that expression of a cAMP response element modular protein is decreased in the myometrium with advancing gestation and labor.[8] In rats, PTHrP delays the increase in expression of the gap junction associated protein connexin 43 and the oxytocin receptor, which normally occurs at term.[9] NO is a potent endogenous relaxant of uterine smooth muscle that acts through a cyclic guanosine monophosphate (cGMP)–dependent process.[10,11] Nitric oxide synthase (NOS) isoforms have been detected in human fetal membranes and choriodecidua. Several authors have reported a decrease in levels of mRNA-encoding inducible NOS in myometrium collected from patients at term.[11] NOS activity in decidua and myometrium decreases before parturition in a variety of species in a manner consistent with progressive diminution of the inhibitory activity of NO on the uterus. Of particular interest are studies in the rat showing that loss of NOS activity in the myometrium is associated with an increase in NOS activity in the cervix, specifically with increased capacity for NO production by inflammatory cells.[12] The action of NO on the cervix appears to involve cGMP and prostaglandins.[13] These studies suggest a role for NO in cervical effacement and relaxation as the influence of NOS on the myometrium is diminished.

Relaxin is expressed in human fetal membranes, decidua, and placenta, and Bryant-Greenwood and colleagues have argued convincingly that relaxin has a paracrine/autocrine effect on myometrial activity.[14] Relaxin suppresses uterine contractility in a variety of species through elevation of myometrial cAMP levels and inhibition of oxytocin-induced turnover of phosphoinositide.[15] It also increases expression of endothelial-type NOS in the mouse uterus.[16] Relaxin receptors have been localized in the decidua and chorionic trophoblast cells. Relaxin acts through these receptors to upregulate expression of various matrix metalloproteinases and is likely involved in premature rupture of the membranes.[17,18] Similar effects of relaxin occur in the cervix, which suggests that it may contribute to mechanisms of remodeling cervical connective tissue in addition to suppressive actions on the myometrium.[14,19]

Animal models (see later discussion) have provided good evidence for withdrawal of one or more of these inhibitory influences on the myometrium as a prerequisite to the onset of labor.[20] Using DNA microarrays, the pattern of gene expression in the rat uterus indicated that more genes were suppressed than activated at labor.[21] Systemic or local withdrawal of progesterone appears to be a consistent characteristic of parturition in most species, yet progesterone concentrations in maternal peripheral blood do not decrease before parturition in human pregnancy.[20] Recent studies have indicated, however, that there may be functional withdrawal of progesterone action within uterine tissues at term.

It is possible that increased metabolism of progesterone is taking place within intrauterine tissue in a manner that is not reflected in systemic progesterone concentrations. Support for this concept comes from studies on $5\alpha$-reductase-1 knockout mice.[22] These animals do not deliver at the expected time, although some uterine contractility develops in late gestation. The inability to deliver has been related to impaired cervical ripening, suggesting that progesterone withdrawal through metabolism to the inactive $5\alpha$-dihydroprogesterone is necessary for normal cervical ripening.[23] Changes also take place in the relative activities of isoforms of the progesterone receptors PR-A and PR-B that determine receptor-mediated progesterone action on the uterus.[24,25] In the myometrium during human parturition, there are increasing levels of PR-A, a dominant-negative repressor of PR-B that may contribute to functional progesterone withdrawal in this tissue.[26] PR-A dominance in the myometrium of the rhesus monkey at labor has also been proposed to be involved in functional progesterone withdrawal in this species.[27] Declining levels of steroid receptor coactivators may also enhance functional withdrawal of progesterone in the human myometrium and mouse uterus at term, resulting in decreased histone acetylation.[28] TGF-$\beta$ prevents the appearance of progesterone-responsive genes in a number of tissues and could act in this manner in the myometrium or decidua.[29] A recent further suggestion is that progesterone effects in intrauterine tissues may be exerted through the glucocorticoid receptor. Increases in endogenous glucocorticoids occur in late gestation, and by displacing progesterone from the glucocorticoid receptor, glucocorticoid could reverse the activities of progesterone.[30-32]

Increased action of estrogen in the myometrium may be due to increased expression of the estrogen receptor alpha (ER-$\alpha$).[24] The increase in uterine activity at term may occur through withdrawal of inhibitory influences on the myometrium, an increase in stimulus to the myometrium (activation), or a combination of these actions.

It is clear that activation is influenced by the fetal genome.[5,33] Activation may be exerted through different pathways, including a growth pathway that influences stretch of the myometrium, as well as an endocrine pathway. Activation of these pathways results in upregulation of a cassette of contraction-associated proteins (CAPs) in the myometrium.[5,33,34] These proteins include connexin 43, the gap junction protein necessary for the evolution of synchronous uterine contractility, receptors for various uterotonins (prostaglandin receptors, the oxytocin receptor), and ion channel proteins. CAP activation can clearly be induced in animal studies through the stretch pathway, although the magnitude of this effect is regulated by the prevailing endocrine environment. For example, levels of mRNA transcripts encoding connexin 43 and oxytocin receptor were increased in the rat uterus by placing inert tubing within the uterine lumen.[35] This response to stretch was diminished in animals treated with progesterone or in late-gestation unilaterally pregnant animals in which the endogenous systemic progesterone concentration was still high. In contrast, the expression of the mRNA transcripts encoding the PGF$_{2\alpha}$ receptor is temporally associated with progesterone withdrawal, but is not dependent on mechanical stretch.[36] Teleologically, it would make sense that the size, or growth, of the fetus should have some influence on the timing and process of birth, and may explain the higher incidence of preterm birth in multifetal pregnancies

Phase 1 of parturition also depends on endocrine responses resulting from activation of the fetal hypothalamic-pituitary-adrenal (HPA) axis in late pregnancy. Mediators at this stage include changes in estrogen synthesis/action, perhaps in combination with local progesterone withdrawal. Increased production of uterotonins, including oxytocin and prostaglandins, provides stimulation to the uterus in phase 2 of parturition, provided that activation has occurred. Phase 3 is associated with neuroendocrine release of oxytocin, which provides the stimulus for uterine involution. It is evident that understanding the sequence of events is helpful in developing new strategies for preventing preterm labor, on the assumption that such prevention is of benefit to the fetus. More information is needed concerning the reversibility of the processes of activation and the consequences for later stimulation.

## PARTURITION IN ANIMAL MODELS

As already alluded to, rodents, particularly mice and rats, have provided important models to understand the regulation of parturition. In the case of the mouse, many knockout animals have been studied.[37-39] Mice constitutively lacking the gene for prostaglandin H synthase type 1 (PGHS-1) appear to have delayed parturition, and although the young are delivered, viability is reduced.[40] Although oxytocin knockout animals deliver normally, simultaneous deletion of oxytocin and PGHS-1 overcomes the delay in delivery found in the single PGHS-1 knockout animals, but these animals have a protracted labor.[41] Mice lacking the gene for the prostaglandin H synthase type 2 (PGHS-2) enzyme have impaired fertility and implantation and have not been studied in relation to the effects of this null mutation on gestational length.[42,43] Mice lacking PGF receptor (FP) or phospholipase A2 fail to deliver because the corpus luteum does not undergo luteolysis at the appropriate time in late gestation.[44] Luteolysis allows a fall in progesterone to occur, followed by increased expression of oxytocin receptors and parturition. The various knockout studies indicate that many backup systems are acting during labor, as might be expected for such an important evolutionary process. An important limitation with the study of mice and rats as models for human parturition is that, throughout pregnancy, the ovary is the source of progesterone, in contrast to human pregnancy, in which the placenta is the major source. Unlike the human, withdrawal of progesterone through luteolysis is a prerequisite for the onset of parturition in these species.

Of the species that produce progesterone in the placenta, the sheep is the most widely studied animal model. The pioneering studies of Professors Sir Graham (Mont) Liggins and Geoffrey Thorburn in sheep and goat models provided conclusive evidence that, in these species, the fetus triggers the onset of parturition through activation of the fetal HPA axis.[20,45] This event results in increased output of cortisol from the fetal adrenal gland. Evidence in support of this hypothesis is substantial. Thus, in sheep, lesions of the paraventricular nucleus of the hypothalamus, fetal hypophysectomy or adrenalectomy, or pituitary stalk section results in prolonged gestation, whereas infusion of adrenocorticotropic hormone (ACTH) or glucocorticoid into the fetus results in premature delivery.[45] Importantly, glucocorticoid-infused lambs had pulmonary maturation at a stage in gestation when they would not otherwise have been viable. Thus, a single signal from the fetal adrenal, cortisol, simultaneously promotes the maturation of fetal organ systems required for extrauterine survival and initiates the process of birth.[45]

An increase in glucocorticoid concentration in the fetal circulation appears to be a consistent characteristic of late intrauterine life across all species examined.[46] This increase is associated with increases in the concentrations of ACTH in the fetal circulation.[47] In fetal sheep, this HPA activation during pregnancy appears to result from a progressive rise in levels of mRNA encoding both corticotropin-releasing hormone (CRH) in the parvocellular region of the paraventricular nucleus of the fetal hypothalamus and pro-opiomelanocortin, the precursor of ACTH in the pars distalis of the fetal pituitary.[48] The concurrent increase in ACTH and cortisol in the fetal circulation occurs despite the potential for negative feedback of cortisol at the level of the hypothalamus and pituitary. Mechanisms that prevent negative feedback from occurring in the fetus include a decrease in the concentration of glucocorticoid receptor in the paraventricular nucleus during late gestation, which reduces the potential for negative feedback. In addition, fetal cortisol stimulates expression of its own high-affinity binding protein, corticosteroid-binding globulin, which is secreted into the circulation and maintains a relatively low free cortisol concentration.[48,49]

Fetal ACTH acts on the adrenal to increase the number of ACTH receptors and upregulate expression of key steroidogenic enzymes, especially P-450c17, which is necessary for cortisol biosynthesis. Expression of this enzyme is very low in the fetal adrenal at midgestation and is then dramatically upregulated after 125 days at the time of the rise in plasma cortisol before parturition (145–150 days).[48,50]

These general principles may be extended to an understanding of fetal adrenal function in the primate. In humans and in subhuman primates, however, the fetal adrenal cortex is divided into an outer adult zone that produces predominantly aldosterone, an inner fetal zone that is relatively deficient of the enzyme 3β-hydroxysteroid dehydrogenase (3β-HSD) and, therefore, secretes large amounts of the $\Delta^5$ C-19 steroid dehydroepiandrosterone sulfate (DHEA-S), and a transitional zone interposed between the adult and fetal cortex, which is thought to produce cortisol.[51-53] ACTH stimulates steroidogenesis in each region of the gland and recent studies have shown that CRH, possibly of placental origin (see later), also stimulates DHEA-S and cortisol production by the fetal adrenal.[54-56] Fetal ACTH secretion may be relatively suppressed by the negative feedback of glucocorticoid derived from the maternal circulation after transplacental transfer. In late gestation, increased activity of 11β-HSD type 2 in the primate placenta leads to increased conversion of maternal cortisol to cortisone, which is biologically inactive.[57] The fetal hypothalamic-pituitary unit then escapes negative feedback, and fetal ACTH concentrations rise. In the primate, DHEA and DHEA-S from the fetal zone of the fetal adrenal gland are aromatized in the placenta to form estrogen. The sheep placenta also aromatizes C-19 steroids to produce estrogen, and some of these C-19 steroids may be generated in the fetal adrenal cortex. In late gestation, however, the C-19 steroid substrates are generated predominantly within the trophoblast tissue of the placenta itself, under the influence of the prepartum rise in fetal adrenal cortisol.[45] Thus, in both primate and sheep pregnancy, there is clearly a functional fetal-placental unit. The critical difference is that the primate fetal adrenal secretes C-19 precursors de novo for placental

aromatization whereas the sheep fetal adrenal secretes cortisol, which upregulates P-450c17 in the placenta, and it is then the placenta that produces the C-19 precursor steroids for estrogen biosynthesis.

The action of fetal cortisol in the sheep placenta leads to decreased output of progesterone, increased output of estrogen, and increased expression of PGHS-2.[45,58] In turn, output of $PGE_2$ into the fetal circulation and $PGF_{2\alpha}$ into the maternal circulation is increased. Recent studies have suggested that the primary mechanism of action of cortisol is upregulation of prostaglandin synthesis via increased expression of PGHS-2 in the fetal placenta.[59] Although cortisol infusion increases expression of PGHS-2 in the fetal placenta, the expression of the PGE synthase is not altered.[60] The $PGE_2$ produced, in turn, increases expression of P-450c17, which results in a pattern of decreased progesterone and increased estrogen synthesis.[34] The increased estrogen production is then responsible for the increase in $PGF2_\alpha$ production by the maternal intrauterine tissues. There would therefore appear to be a temporal and tissue-specific progression of prostaglandin synthesis from fetal trophoblast to maternal intrauterine tissues. This pattern of expression also holds true for prostaglandin synthesis during normal labor at term.[61] Recent studies, in which estradiol was infused at 121 days, gestation resulted in preterm delivery via stimulation of $PGF_{2\alpha}$, with no changes placental P-450c17 or PGHS-2 expression in the fetal placenta,[62] which is also consistent with the proposed model.

Activation of the fetal HPA axis occurs in response to an adverse intrauterine environment, for example, hypoxemia.[48] With hypoxemia, concentrations of circulating ACTH are increased. Increased levels of mRNA-encoding CRH are found in the fetal paraventricular nucleus, as well as increased levels of mRNA-encoding pro-opiomelanocortin in the fetal pituitary pars distalis. Fetal cortisol rises in association with increased expression of fetal adrenal steroidogenic enzymes, particularly in sustained hypoxemia in older fetuses. This elevation of cortisol, in addition to promoting organ maturation and premature delivery, may also be inhibitory to the growth of many fetal organs, in part by suppressing expression of insulin-like growth factor 2 (IGF-2). Recent studies have also highlighted the potential of preterm labor to be caused by insults occurring long before the actual delivery. Undernutrition around the time of conception caused premature activation of the HPA axis and subsequent preterm delivery in about 50% of the fetuses from undernourished dams.[63]

## THE PRIMATE FETUS AND PARTURITION

In the monkey, it is clear that the length of "placental pregnancy" is prolonged considerably after removal of the fetus.[64] Levels of C-19 estrogen precursors increase in the circulation of the intact fetal monkey during late pregnancy, in parallel with cortisol and mimicking the changes in cortisol that occur in fetal sheep. Infusion of androstenedione to pregnant monkeys 80% of the way through gestation results in premature birth, which is inhibited by concurrent infusion of an aromatase inhibitor.[65] This finding suggests that the androstenedione effect is dependent on conversion to estrogen. Systemic estrogen infusion fails, however, to induce premature delivery, which led the authors to conclude that estrogen is active in a paracrine/autocrine fashion at or near its site of production. Thus, in both primates and sheep, evidence links the fetal HPA axis and the placenta, through the provision of C-19 steroids and synthesis of estrogen, in the mechanisms leading to parturition. Recent studies have suggested that in primates, cortisol, potentially of fetal origin, acts in additional ways to promote delivery.[5,34] Evidence is accumulating that glucocorticoids stimulate prostaglandin output in trophoblast-derived tissues, particularly fetal membranes in late human gestation, by upregulating prostaglandin synthesis and by decreasing rates of prostaglandin metabolism. In addition, glucocorticoids upregulate expression of CRH in the human placenta, and CRH, in turn, serves as a stimulus to prostaglandin production in intrauterine structures and the production of estrogen precursors and cortisol by the fetal adrenal.

Thus, lessons learned from animal models have substantial applicability to the processes of human labor. Clearly, details differ among species. The overall pattern of change is similar, however, and one anticipates that further understanding of the activation mechanisms in human parturition will come about through comparative investigation.

## PROSTAGLANDINS AND PARTURITION

Prostaglandins have long been associated with the labor process, at term and preterm. Prostaglandins appear to contribute to the transition from phase 1 to phase 2, rather than initiating the labor process. Whether they are obligatory for labor can be debated, and no definitive evidence is available from knockout experiments (see previous discussion). Prostaglandins are formed from membrane phospholipids through the obligate precursor arachidonic acid.[66] Hydrolysis of arachidonic acid from phosphatidylethanolamine and phosphatidylinositol occurs through the action of one or more isozymes of phospholipase C or phospholipase $A_2$. Arachidonic acid may be metabolized through different lipoxygenase pathways to form leukotrienes and hydroxyeicosatetraenoic acids and through the cyclooxygenase pathway to form prostaglandins. Early studies suggested that arachidonic acid metabolism is preferentially directed toward lipoxygenase products during human pregnancy, but that a progressive switch to cyclooxygenase products occurs at the time of labor.

PGHS-1 and PGHS-2 are separate gene products.[66,67] PGHS-2 is induced through a variety of cytokines and growth factors and, paradoxically, in human amnion and chorion, PGHS-2 is upregulated by glucocorticoids. Endoperoxides are then converted through specific synthases to form $PGE_2$, $PGF_{2\alpha}$, and $PGI_2$. The major metabolizing enzyme for prostaglandins includes a nicotinamide adenine dinucleotide ($NAD^+$)-dependent (type 1) 15-hydroxyprostaglandin dehydrogenase (PGDH), the activity of which results in the formation of 15-keto and 13,14-dihydro-15-keto compounds, which have reduced biologic activity.[68] This step may be important in preventing biologically active prostaglandin derived from amnion and/or chorion from reaching the underlying decidua and myometrium during most of pregnancy. Failure of this inactivation process in chorion may be one cause of preterm labor.

Prostaglandins act through specific receptors, including four main subtypes of $PGE_2$ receptors (EP1–EP4) and one main subtype of $PGF_{2\alpha}$ receptor (FP).[69] There are also a number of isoforms of each receptor generated by alternate splicing. In the case of the EP3 receptor, for example, there are at least eight isoforms. EP1 and EP3 receptors mediate contraction of smooth muscle by increasing calcium utilization and inhibiting the formation of intracellular cAMP. EP2 and EP4 receptors promote smooth muscle relaxation. Differential regulation of these receptors may contribute to altered patterns of myometrial contractility in the course of gestation.[70] Regional differences in receptor expression could lead to contraction of the uterine fundus at term, with simultaneous relaxation of the lower segment and cervix to allow passage of the fetus. It has been suggested recently that precocious expression of FP in the myometrium may be involved in preterm labor.[71]

### PROSTAGLANDINS IN HUMAN LABOR

Prostaglandins may have a number of effects during human labor. They act to cause cervical ripening, stimulate matrix metalloproteinase expression, which can promote membrane rupture, and can both stimulate and relax myometrium. Prostaglandin concentrations increase in the amniotic fluid prior to the onset of labor, and there is increased PGHS activity in amnion and chorion with advancing gestation and labor. This increase is due principally to increased expression of PGHS-2. Generation of prostaglandins in human intrauterine tissues is discretely compartmentalized.[5,34,72] In amnion, PGHS activity predominates, $PGE_2$ is the major prostaglandin formed, and levels of PGHS-2 but not PGHS-1 mRNA and protein increase at preterm and term labor.[73,74] In addition, the membrane-bound PGE synthase (mPGES) levels did not change with labor. Decidua expresses both synthesizing and some metabolizing enzyme, but little overall change occurs in the capacity for prostaglandin synthesis with labor. Decidual prostaglandin production may, in fact, result from constitutive expression of PGHS-1 rather than induction of PGHS-2. In chorion, PGHS and PGDH mRNA are both expressed, but prostaglandin metabolism predominates. For much of pregnancy, PGDH in chorion trophoblasts forms a metabolic barrier preventing the passage of prostaglandins generated within the amnion or chorion from reaching the underlying decidua and/or myometrium. Thus, at term, the synthetic activity of amnion/chorion would need to exceed the metabolic potential of chorionic trophoblasts. Some patients in preterm labor have a relative deficiency of PGDH in chorion, and it has been suggested that this deficiency might allow prostaglandins generated within amnion or chorion in response to a variety of stimuli to pass unmetabolized to the underlying decidua and myometrium and provoke uterine contractility.[75]

Information on prostaglandin synthesis in myometrium is confusing, in part because of the difficulty of obtaining appropriate tissue for examination. Some workers have reported increased PGHS-2 mRNA levels in myometrium at labor, whereas others have reported decreases. In myometrial samples obtained from the lower segment, there was no significant change in the levels of PGHS-1 or PGHS-2 during labor at term or preterm.[76] PGDH activity decreased, however, during labor. In addition, it should be noted that PGHS-2 is required for production of $PGI_2$ (an inhibitory prostaglandin), as well as $PGE_2$ and $PGF_{2\alpha}$, and, recently, the PGI synthase expression was found to decrease in the myometrium with advancing gestation, although there was no change in the expression of PGE synthase.[77] Taken together, these studies would be consistent with a decrease in the inhibitory $PGI_2$ and a decrease in metabolism of prostaglandins resulting in increases in local levels of stimulatory prostaglandins within the myometrium during labor. Furthermore, if regional differences in prostaglandin synthase activity occur at the time of labor, measurements made on tissue obtained from the lower segment may not be representative of changes observed in the fundal region. Also, in vitro studies with isolated human myometrial cells indicate that stretch upregulated expression of PGI synthase, resulting in increased $PGI_2$ levels, but had no effect on $PGE_2$ or $PGF_{2\alpha}$ levels.[78]

PGHS-2 mRNA localizes to amniotic epithelial cells, as well as subepithelial mesenchymal cells, including fibroblasts.[74] These cells also express the glucocorticoid receptor.[79] In culture, glucocorticoids upregulate PGHS-2 mRNA and protein in amnion cells, particularly in amnion fibroblasts, and increase their output of $PGE_2$.[80-82] These data are consistent with the direct effect of glucocorticoids on PGHS expression in amnion fibroblasts. There is conflicting evidence in the literature as to whether glucocorticoids inhibit or stimulate expression of PGHS-2 in the epithelial cells.[83,84] It remains a possibility that glucocorticoids have a biphasic effect on PGHS-2 expression in these cells. Many studies have shown stimulation of prostaglandin production by cell types from human fetal membranes in response to different agonists and antagonists.[72] It should be remembered that virtually all these studies have been performed with cells maintained in vitro for varying periods and that potential agonists have been added in isolation rather than in the combination that would be present in vivo. Thus, extrapolation from in vitro studies to the in vivo situation must be made with caution. Other effectors of increased prostaglandin production include agents that increase the availability of free calcium, epidermal growth factor, platelet-activating factor, and activators of protein kinase A, including catecholamines.[72] The upstream regulatory region of the gene for PGHS-2 has been cloned and sequenced, and a number of potential regulatory elements in the 5' flanking region have been identified.[66] These elements include a C/EBP motif, AP2 and SP1 sites, nuclear factor-κB (NF-κB) sites, and a cAMP response element (CRE) motif. It is likely that growth factors such as platelet-derived growth factor (PDGF) stimulate PGHS-2 synthesis through functional CREs. However, it should be noted that β-sympathomimetic drugs also stimulate increases in cAMP and increase the output of prostaglandins from uterine tissue in vitro and in vivo.[85] Thus, the reduced efficacy of these drugs in suppressing uterine activity may, in part, be associated with their stimulation of prostaglandins, the uterotonins whose effects the β-agonists are designed to overcome. Importantly, sequences corresponding to a glucocorticoid response element (GRE) have also been identified within the PGHS-2 promoter region,[86] but it is not known whether the stimulatory effect of glucocorticoids described previously is mediated through interaction with this response element. The effects of glucocorticoids may be exerted through the upregulation of a trophoblast-specific product or by interaction with the NF-κB system. NF-κB has been localized in the fetal membranes[87] and shown to be required for activation of PGHS-2 expression in amnion-derived WISH cells,[88] which have been used extensively as models for the less accessible amnion epithelial cells. Transfection studies with human amnion cells have suggested that NF-κB may be involved in functional progesterone withdrawal in this tissue during labor.[89]

## PROSTAGLANDIN METABOLISM

The major enzyme regulating the metabolism of primary prostaglandins is an NAD⁺-dependent (type 1) PGDH.[68] PGDH mRNA, protein, and activity localize to chorion trophoblasts in human fetal membranes. Levels of PGDH mRNA, protein, and activity are lower in at-term spontaneous labor than in elective cesarean section, which suggests a facilitory role in the labor process. They are significantly reduced in a proportion of women in idiopathic preterm labor without infection and are substantially reduced further in many patients in preterm labor with an underlying infective process.[75,90] Loss of PGDH expression is specific for chorion, and levels of PGDH activity in placental tissue from the same groups of patients were similar. Loss of PGDH activity in infection is associated with reduced numbers of chorionic trophoblast cells. In idiopathic preterm labor, chorion trophoblasts are present, but PGDH expression and activity are reduced. Regional differences in expression of PGDH are seen within the human uterus.[91] At labor, the activity of PGDH in chorion trophoblasts overlying the internal os was dramatically reduced in comparison to levels of PGDH expression in chorion adjacent to the placenta or midway between these sites. We have speculated that this difference in PGDH expression might allow prostaglandins generated within amnion and chorion in the lower segment to escape metabolism in chorion at the time of labor and to effect effacement and dilatation of the cervix. It is possible that specific downregulation of PGDH in lower segment membranes could occur in response to bacteria and elevated levels of cytokines in the vagina and/or cervix.

It appears that regulation of PGDH is multifactorial. In vitro studies have clearly demonstrated that glucocorticoids inhibit PGDH activity and decrease levels of PGDH mRNA. Synthetic progestins increase PGDH expression and inhibitors of progesterone action such as RU486 (mifepristone) or inhibitors of progesterone synthesis such as trilostane all decrease PGDH activity.[92] These studies point, therefore, to a tonic role for locally produced progesterone in maintaining basal levels of PGDH expression. Added progesterone was able to reverse the inhibitory effect of trilostane and, in equimolar concentrations, progesterone partially reversed the inhibitory effect of cortisol. These results imply that in vivo, through normal pregnancy, regulation of PGDH expression may reflect a balance between the activities of progesterone and glucocorticoid. It has been proposed that this may occur by competition for binding to the glucocorticoid receptor, although it is also possible that the progesterone receptor is involved in the regulation of PGDH.[32,93,94] Whatever the explanation, it demonstrates that glucocorticoids may be acting as antiprogesterones in the same fashion as they regulate placental CRH production (see discussion to follow). Cortisone, in addition to cortisol, was also found to decrease PGDH activity in chorion because of its conversion to cortisol by the 11β-HSD-1 present in this tissue. The 11β-HSD-1 activity in chorion also increases with advancing gestation, and in vitro studies have shown that it is stimulated by prostaglandins.[95-97] Taken together, these findings would provide a feed-forward mechanism for increased prostaglandin production in the fetal membranes at term.[5,98] Cortisol can stimulate PGHS-2 expression and decrease PGDH expression, resulting in increased prostaglandin production, which could then stimulate the 11β-HSD-1 activity resulting in increased cortisol and further increases in prostaglandin production.

Cytokines such as interleukin-1 (IL-1) also downregulate PGDH expression.[99-101] Thus, proinflammatory cytokines increase PGHS-2 and decrease PGDH expression,[102,103] which may then result in an explosive increase in prostaglandin production in preterm labor associated with infection (see discussion to follow).

## CYTOKINES AND PARTURITION

It is well established that a considerable proportion of preterm labor associated with increased prostaglandin production occurs in the presence of an underlying infective process.[2,72] Infection may be associated with 30% to 40% of cases of preterm labor. Concentrations of lipoxygenase and PGHS products are elevated in the amniotic fluid of patients with infection, as are levels of cytokines, including IL-1β, IL-6, and tumor necrosis factor.[2] Administration of cytokines to animal models provokes premature birth, and cytokines and eicosanoids interact and accelerate each other's production in a cascade fashion.[72] Studies by Romero and colleagues,[2] in particular, have suggested that, in the presence of an ascending bacterial infection, organisms can pass between the membranes and reach the amniotic cavity. Bacterial organisms may release phospholipases that initiate the formation of arachidonic acid and hence the prostaglandin cascade. Additionally, these organisms release endotoxins, including lipopolysaccharide, that act on cell types such as macrophages to provoke prostaglandin or cytokine release. These cytokines, in turn, act on amnion or decidual stromal cells to produce prostaglandins. In cultured human myometrial cells, IL-1β induces calcium transients and also stimulates PGHS-2 expression, which can be attenuated by interferon gamma.[104] Cytokines may also cause the release of other uterotonins, including oxytocin and CRH from myometrium, decidua, membranes, and/or placenta, and these compounds may then affect the myometrium directly or indirectly as a further step in this process.

IL-1 and IL-6 are potent stimulators of PGHS-2 mRNA and prostaglandin output from amnion, chorion, and decidual cells.[72] Recent studies have shown, however, that anti-inflammatory cytokines such as IL-10 attenuate the effects of IL-1 in promoting PGHS-2 mRNA accumulation.[105] There is strong evidence to suggest that increased cytokine production within the intrauterine tissues is involved in both preterm and term parturition, and this has recently been reviewed.[102,103] Increased expression of cytokines occurs in the fetal membranes and decidua both in term and preterm labor and is particularly evident in the presence of intrauterine infection. There is increased IL-1α production in placental and fetal membranes, and IL-1β production by the membranes and decidua is increased with labor.[102] Cytokines in the fetal membranes and decidua not only increase expression of PGHS-2, but also decrease expression of PGDH, which may result in a marked increase in the production of active prostaglandins by these tissues. Recent studies have also shown that tumor necrosis factor-alpha (TNF-α) increases expression of mPGES but not the cytosolic form of the enzyme in chorion and placental trophoblast cultures.[106] In infection, mPGES was increased in placenta but decreased in the fetal membranes. Together with prostaglandins, cytokines may be responsible for stimulating production of matrix metalloproteinases (MMPs) in the membranes that are involved in membrane rupture. Also, locally produced cytokines may regulate collagenase expression in the cervix and be involved in cervical ripening. Interestingly, cytokines involved in cervical ripening may be derived from inflammatory cells that have invaded the tissue.[107-109] Recent cDNA array studies have identified clusters of inflammation-associated genes upregulated with labor both at term and preterm and, in a suppression subtractive hybridization study with human myometrium at term, a number of genes with immune regulatory and inflammatory roles were found to be upregulated.[110]

## STRESS AND CORTICOTROPIN-RELEASING HORMONE

Placental CRH is believed to have an important role in term and preterm labor.[25,111-113] CRH mRNA is present in placental tissue and decidua in increasing amounts during human pregnancy, and it gives rise to increased concentrations of CRH peptide within the placenta and an exponential increase in CRH concentrations in maternal peripheral plasma.[114] The bioactivity of this circulating maternal CRH is diminished by the presence in maternal blood of a high-affinity CRH-binding protein. This binding protein blocks the action of CRH in promoting ACTH release from pituitary cells and, in vitro, inhibits CRH effects on prostaglandin production from uterine tissues.[114] At term, CRH-binding protein concentrations fall, apparently in response to the concurrent rise in total CRH concentration; thus, "free" CRH increases dramatically at this time.[115]

CRH has been localized to syncytiotrophoblasts of the floating villi, intermediate trophoblasts, and the chorionic trophoblast layer of the membranes.[116] CRH output in vitro is decreased by NO and progesterone and stimulated by prostaglandins, cytokines, vasopressin, and glucocorticoids.[30,114] The stimulation by glucocorticoids overcomes the inhibitory effect of progesterone, indicating they are acting as an antiprogesterone in this system, resulting in functional withdrawal of progesterone. In vitro studies with human placenta have shown that cAMP is involved in the stimulation of CRH expression by glucocorticoids and the CRE in the CRH promoter is necessary for this stimulation to occur.[117,118] Glucocorticoids also stimulate placental CRH output in vivo. Thus, in two independent studies, plasma CRH concentrations were elevated within 24 hours of the administration of antenatal synthetic glucocorticoids given to promote fetal lung maturity.[119,120] As discussed earlier, CRH and corticosteroids increase PGHS-2 expression and glucocorticoids decrease PGDH activity. CRH also stimulates the fetal adrenal

to produce androgens[56] that can be metabolized by the placenta to form estrogens, which may then act to stimulate the synthesis of CAPs. It is therefore not surprising that transient elevations in uterine activity have been reported after the administration of synthetic corticosteroid, at least in patients with multiple gestations.[121,122]

Recent studies have shown a clear correlation between maternal perceived stress, anxiety and depression, and preterm labor.[123-125] In stress, women have increased concentrations of CRH in maternal plasma.[123] These high values of CRH predict preterm labor, even as early as 20 to 24 weeks of gestation, and presumably occur in relation to upregulated maternal adrenocortical activity.[123,126] The fetus also responds to stress such as hypoxemia in utero with HPA activation and increased adrenal cortisol output. It has been suggested that fetal cortisol reaches the placenta, where it upregulates expression of placental CRH.[50] In turn, placental CRH stimulates placental ACTH, and potentially both these neuropeptides may act as vasodilators through an NO cyclic guanosine triphosphate (GTP)–dependent pathway. If this activity fails to correct fetal hypoxemia, sustained elevations of fetal glucocorticoid provoke further CRH output, prostaglandin production, estrogen production, and premature delivery.

It is likely that this scenario provides an explanation for some instances of preterm labor. CRH has been proposed to be effective as a placental clock regulating the timing of parturition. CRH in maternal plasma has been reported to be elevated in women at risk of preterm labor in the absence of underlying infection.[127] Between 28 and 36 weeks' gestation, but not 24 and 28 weeks' gestation, maternal plasma CRH concentrations were found to be higher in women with a diagnosis of preterm labor who went on to delivery within 24 to 48 hours than in patients with the same diagnosis of preterm labor but in whom delivery did not occur until term.[127]

Some reports have suggested that CRH synergizes with oxytocin and/or prostaglandins to stimulate myometrial contractility.[114] We discussed earlier that activation of PGHS-2 can occur through a CRE within the promoter sequence and that CRH could upregulate PGHS-2 by increasing the activity of protein kinase A. CRH and urocortin (a CRH-related peptide) are synthesized within the myometrium itself and, therefore, autocrine and paracrine actions of CRH and related peptides may be important in the regulation of the myometrium. CRH could also act as a myometrial relaxant. Recent studies have shown that within the lower segment myometrium, CRH type 1 receptor (CRH-R1) predominates. Levels of mRNA for CRH-R1 increased in lower segment myometrium from patients in labor, both at term and preterm.[128] In vitro studies with cultured human myometrial cells found that CRH but not urocortin II increases nitric oxide synthase and cGMP production, which may act to relax myometrium.[129] The CRH type 2 receptor (CRH-R2) is also expressed in the myometrium, and treatment of myometrial cells with urocortin II stimulated phosphorylation of the myosin light chain.[130] It is possible that the use of different transduction pathways might allow CRH to inhibit lower segment uterine contractility while stimulating contractile activity in the fundal region of the uterus.[113] At present, however, no definitive information concerning these mechanisms is available.

## OXYTOCIN

Oxytocin has long been established as a potent uterotonin.[114,131,132] In oxytocin null mice, however, there is normal delivery, although the pups die postpartum due to the inability of the mother to eject milk.[133,134] This would indicate that oxytocin production is not an absolute requirement for delivery in this species. In the human, oxytocin is present in maternal and fetal blood during late gestation, and secretion within these two compartments occurs independently. Mean oxytocin concentrations rise progressively with the course of labor, and a high-amplitude spurt of oxytocin is released into maternal blood at the time of labor.[114] The modest changes in oxytocin concentration, however, are offset by a more dramatic increase in oxytocin receptor numbers in the myometrium and decidua from patients at term labor and in preterm labor.[114] This marked increase in uterine oxytocin receptor concentration at term occurs in all species studied, including sheep, rabbits, and rodents.[135] These changes in oxytocin receptor numbers can be reproduced experimentally by estrogen treatment in vitro and by uterine stretch.[136] In vivo, the estrogen that brings about this effect could be derived systemically or generated locally within choriodecidual tissue.[137,138]

Mitchell and Chibbar have shown that choriodecidual tissue also produces oxytocin and that the rate of oxytocin mRNA synthesis increases at the time of parturition.[137] A similar increase is seen in the oxytocin receptor population. These changes are promoted, in vitro, by estrogen and inhibited by administration of the estrogen receptor antagonist tamoxifen.[139,140] Oxytocin metabolism does not change in chorion or decidual tissue in relation to labor, which suggests that increases in concentration reflect de novo synthesis. Oxytocin promotes uterine contractility by increasing the myometrial intracellular free calcium concentration through increasing calcium entry and release of calcium from intracellular stores. These effects are secondary to an increase in phosphoinositide turnover and generation of inositol 1,4,5-triphosphate (IP3). The oxytocin receptor couples to phospholipase C through a GTP-binding protein to promote calcium mobilization.[15] This pathway can be inhibited by activation of protein kinase A, thus indicating that cAMP-dependent phosphorylation at a step involving coupling of the GTP-binding protein to phospholipase C can antagonize the stimulatory effect on IP3 formation by oxytocin. Thus, there may be critical interactions between these two pathways. The oxytocin receptor has also been shown to be sensitive to homologous desensitization during human labor.[141] In the human fetal membranes and decidua, oxytocin also stimulates prostaglandin production and may therefore have a dual action, by increasing uterotonins within the uterus and acting directly on the myometrium to stimulate contraction.

## PHARMACOLOGIC MANAGEMENT OF PRETERM LABOR

The recent improvements in our understanding of the physiology and pathophysiology of term and preterm labor as described in previous sections have provided a rational basis for the development of drugs to manage preterm labor. The oxytocin receptor antagonist atosiban prevents uterine contractions in a number of species including humans. A number of clinical trials have been carried out and it would appear that atosiban is as efficacious as the β-agonist ritodrine, and was safer.[142,143] Inhibition of prostaglandin synthesis is an alternative way of diminishing production of uterotonins. Recently, because of the apparent importance of the type 2 PGHS isoform, rather than the type 1 isoform in prostaglandin production at labor, inhibitors specific for the former enzyme have received considerable interest. For example, ongoing studies are being carried out using meloxicam in chronically instrumented animal models to determine the likelihood of potential side effects, particularly in the fetus.[144] There are also some limited studies in humans. The fetal side effects of nimesilide were found to be similar to indomethacin and sulindac.[145] Recent studies have also raised the possibility of using a specific PGF-receptor antagonist to prevent preterm delivery.[146] Ongoing studies with the ovine model indicate that this receptor may be a potential target for tocolysis.[71] In animal models, inhibitors of CRH action prolong pregnancy, but this effect is more likely to occur at the level of the fetal pituitary than at the level of the myometrium. It will be necessary to resolve the potential divergence of stimulatory and inhibitory effects of CRH on the myometrium before attempting to inhibit its activity. The potential role of CRH, with measures of estriol and fibronectin, as a marker of preterm labor, however, continues to offer promise as part of a mix of indicators that may be of clinical value. Pharmacologic regulation of PGDH activity may lead to ways of regulating cervical function and, potentially, to ways of regulating levels of bioactive prostaglandins produced within the membranes that are capable of reaching the underlying decidua and myometrium. Trials involving NO donors as inhibitors of myometrial activity continue to offer promise of efficacy, but the different activities of NO on the myometrium and cervix will need to be considered. At present, however, the major concerns remain first to identify pregnancies in which fetal compromise is such that delivery is a preferred option to the fetus remaining in a hostile uterine environment and, second, to identify patients in true preterm labor as opposed to those who are not. Such identification will then allow antenatal corticosteroid treatment of patients actually in preterm labor rather than repeated administration of corticosteroids to patients who may not be in preterm labor but are undergoing episodes of uterine contractility during an otherwise normal pregnancy.

### Acknowledgments
Work in the authors' laboratories was supported by grants from the Canadian Institutes for Health Research.

## REFERENCES

1. Creasy R: Preventing preterm birth. N Engl J Med 325:727–729, 1991.
2. Romero R, Avila C, Brekus C: The role of systemic and intrauterine infection in preterm parturition. Ann N Y Acad Sci 622:355–375, 1991.
3. Nathanielsz P, Binlenda Z, Wimsatt J: Patterns of myometrial activity and their regulation in the pregnant monkey. In McNellis D, Challis J, MacDonald P (eds): The Onset of Labor: Cellular and Integrative Mechanisms. Ithaca, NY, Perinatology Press, 1987, p 359.
4. Lye S: Initiation of parturition. Anim Reprod Sci 42:495, 1997.
5. Challis J, Matthews S, Gibb W, Lye S: Endocrine and paracrine regulation of birth at term and preterm. Endocr Rev 21:514–550, 2000.
6. Al-Matubsi H, Eis A, Brodt-Eppley J, et al: Expression and localization of the contractile prostaglandin F receptor in pregnant rat myometrium in late gestation, labour and postpartum. Biol Reprod 65:1029–1037, 2001.
7. Morimoto T, Devora G, Mibe M: Parathyroid hormone–related protein and human myometrial cells: Action and regulation. Mol Cell Endocrinol 129:91–99, 1997.
8. Bailey J, Phillips R, Pollard A, et al: Characterization and functional analysis of cAMP response element modulator protein and activating transcription factor 2 (ATF2) isoforms in the human myometrium during pregnancy and labor: Identification of a novel ATF2 species with potent transactivation properties. J Clin Endocrinol Metab 87:1717–1728, 2002.
9. Mitchell J, Ting T, Wong S, et al: Parathyroid hormone–related protein treatment of pregnant rat delays the increase in connexin 43 and oxytocin receptor expression in the myometrium. Biol Reprod 69:556–562, 2003.
10. Dennes W, Slater D, Bennett P: Nitric oxide synthase mRNA expression in human fetal membranes: A possible role in parturition. Biochem Biophys Res Commun 233:276–278, 1997.
11. Bansal R, Goldsmith P, He Y: A decline in myometrial nitric oxide synthase expression is associated with labor and delivery. J Clin Invest 99:2502–2508, 1997.

12. Chwalisz K, Garfield R: Regulation of the uterus and cervix during pregnancy and labor: Role of progesterone and nitric oxide. Ann N Y Acad Sci 828:238–253, 1997.

13. Ekerhovd E, Weijdegard B, Brannstrom M, et al: Nitric oxide induced cervical ripening in the human: Involvement of cyclcic guanosine monophosphate, prostaglandin F(2alpha) and prostaglandin E2. Am J Obstet Gynecol 186:745–750, 2002.

14. Bryant-Greenwood G, Yamomoto S, Bogic L: Relaxin: A role in the premature rupture of the fetal membranes independent of infection. In Charleston S (ed): Preterm Birth: Etiology, Mechanisms and Prevention. Birmingham, University of Alabama, 1997.

15. Sanborn B, Qian A, Ku C: Mechanisms regulating oxytocin receptor coupling to phospholipase C in rat and human myometrium. Adv Exp Med Biol 395:469–479, 1995.

16. Bani D, Baccari M, Nistri S, et al: Relaxin up-regulates the nitric oxide biosynthetic pathway in the mouse uterus: Involvement in the inhibition of myometrial contractility. Endocrinology 140:4434–4441, 1999.

17. Tashima L, Yamamoto S, Yasuda M, et al: Decidual relaxins: Gene and protein up-regulation in preterm premature rupture of the membranes by complementary DNA arrays and quantitative immunocytochemistry. Am J Obstet Gynecol 187:785–797, 2002.

18. Bryant-Greenwood G, Millar L: Human fetal membranes: Their preterm premature rupture. Biol Reprod 63:1575–1579, 2000.

19. Goldsmith L, Palejwala S, Weiss G: The role of relaxin in preterm labor. In Charleston S (ed): Preterm Birth: Etiology, Mechanisms and Prevention. Birmingham, University of Alabama, 1997.

20. Liggins G, Thorburn G: Initiation of parturition. In Lamming G (ed): Marshall's Physiology of Reproduction, vol 3. London, Chapman & Hall, 1994, pp 863–1002.

21. Girotti M, Zingg H: Gene expression profiling of rat uterus at different stages of parturition. Endocrinology 144:2254–2265, 2003.

22. Mahendroo M, Cala K, Russell D: 5α-Reduced androgens play a key role in murine parturition. Mol Endocrinol 10:380–392, 1996.

23. Mahendroo M, Porter A, Russell D, Word R: The parturition defect in steroid 5alpha-reductase type 1 knockout mice is due to impaired cervical ripening. Mol Endocrinol 13:981–992, 1999.

24. Mesiano S, Chan E, Fitter J, et al: Progesterone withdrawal and estrogen activation in human parturition are coordinated by progesterone receptor a expression in the myometrium. J Clin Endocrinol Metab 87:2924–2930, 2002.

25. Smith R, Mesiano S, McGrath S: Hormone trajectories leading to human birth. Regul Pept 108:159–164, 2002.

26. Pieber D, Allport V, Hills F, et al: Interactions between progesterone receptor isoforms in myometrial cells in human labour. Mol Hum Reprod 7:875–879, 2001.

27. Haluska G, Wells T, Hirst J, et al: Progesterone receptor localization and isoforms in myometrium, decidua, and fetal membranes from rhesus macaques: Evidence for functional progesterone withdrawal at parturition. J Soc Gynecol Investig 9:125–136, 2002.

28. Condon J, Jeyasuria P, Faust J, et al: A decline in the levels of progesterone receptor coactivators in the pregnant uterus at term may antagonize progesterone receptor function and contribute to the initiation of parturition. Proc Natl Acad Sci 100:9518–9523, 2003.

29. Casey M, MacDonald P: TGF-β inhibits progesterone-induced enkephalinase expression in human endometrial stromal cells. J Clin Endocrinol Metab 81:4022–4027, 1996.

30. Karalis K, Goodwin G, Majzoub J: Cortisol blockade of progesterone: A possible molecular mechanism involved in the initiation of human labor. Nat Med 2:556–560, 1996.

31. Majzoub J, Karalis K: Placental corticotropin-releasing hormone: Function and regulation. Am J Obstet Gynecol 180:S242–S246, 1999.

32. Patel F, Challis J: Cortisol/progesterone antagonism in regulation of 15-hydroxyprostaglandin dehydrogenase activity and mRNA levels in human chorion and placental trophoblast cells at term. J Clin Endocrinol Metab 87:700–708, 2002.

33. Lye S, Mitchell J, Nashman N, et al: Role of mechanical signals in the onset of term and preterm labor. Front Horm Res 27:165–178, 2001.

34. Challis J, Lye S, Gibb W: Prostaglandins and parturition. Ann N Y Acad Sci 828:254–267, 1997.

35. Ou C-W, Orsino A, Lye S: Expression of connexin-43 and connexin-26 in the rat myometriun during pregnancy and labor is differentially regulated by mechanical and hormonal signals. Endocrinology 138:5398–5407, 1997.

36. Ou C, Chen Z, Qi S, Lye S: Expression and regulation of the messenger ribonucleic acid encoding the prostaglandin F(2alpha) receptor in the rat myometrium during pregnancy and labor. Am J Obstet Gynecol 182:919–925, 2000.

37. Kimura T, Ogita K, Kusui C, et al: What knockout mice can tell us about parturition. Rev Reprod 4:73–80, 1999.

38. Gross G, Imamura T, Muglia L: Gene knockout mice in the study of parturition. J Soc Gynecol Investig 7:88–95, 2000.

39. Muglia L: Genetic analysis of fetal development and parturition control in the mouse. Pediatr Res 47:437–443, 2000.

40. Langenback R, Morham S, Tiano H: Prostaglandin synthase 1 gene disruption in mice reduces arachidonic acid-induced inflammation and indomethacin-induced gastric ulceration. Cell 83:483, 1995.

41. Gross G, Imamura T, Luedke C: Opposing actions of prostaglandins and oxytocin determine the onset of murine labor. Proc Natl Acad Sci U S A 95:11871–11875, 1998.

42. Morham S, Langenbach R, Loftin C: Prostaglandin synthase 2 gene disruption causes severe renal pathology in the mouse. Cell 83:473–482, 1995.

43. Lim H, Paria B, Das S: Multiple fetal reproductive failures in cyclooxygenase-2-deficient mice. Cell 91:197–208, 1997.

44. Sugimoto Y, Yamasaki A, Segi E: Failure of parturition in mice lacking the prostaglandin F receptor. Science 277:681–683, 1997.

45. Thorburn G, Liggins G: Role of the fetal pituitary adrenal axis and placenta in the initiation of parturition. In Lamming G (ed): Marshall's Physiology of Reproduction, vol 3. London, Chapman & Hall, 1994, p 1003.

46. Fowden A, Li J, Forhead A: Glucocorticoids and preparation for life after birth. Proc Nutr Soc 57:113–122, 1998.

47. Norman L, Lye S, Wlodek M: Changes in pituitary responses to synthetic ovine corticotrophin-releasing factor in fetal sheep. Can J Physiol Pharmacol 63:1398–1403, 1985.

48. Matthews S, Challis J: Regulation of the hypothalamo-pituitary-adrenocortical axis in fetal sheep. Trends Endocrinol Metab 7:239–246, 1996.

49. Challis J, Sloboda D, Matthews S, et al: Fetal hypothalamic-pituitary adrenal (HPA) development and activation as a determinant of the timing of birth, and of postnatal disease. Endocr Res 26:489–504, 2000.

50. Challis J, Brooks A: Maturation and activation of hypothalamic-pituitary-adrenal function in sheep. Endocr Rev 10:182–204, 1989.

51. Jaffe R, Mesiano S, Smith R, et al: The regulation and role of fetal adrenal development in human pregnancy. Endocr Res 24:19–26, 1998.

52. Ratcliffe J, Nakanishi M, Jaffe R: Identification of definitive and fetal zone markers in the human fetal adrenal gland reveals putative developmental genes. J Clin Endocrinol Metab 88:3272–3277, 2003.

53. Coulter C, Jaffe R: Functional maturation of the primate fetal adrenal in vivo: 3. Specific zonal localization and developmental regulation of CYP21A2 (P450c21) and CYP11B1/CYP11B2 (P450c11/aldosterone synthase) lead to integrated concept of zonal and temporal steroid biosynthesis. Endocrinology 139:144–150, 1998.

54. Parker CJ, Stankovic A, Goland R: Corticotropin-releasing hormone stimulates steroidogenesis in cultured human adrenal cells. Mol Cell Endocrinol 155:19–25, 1999.

55. Chakravorty A, Mesiano S, Jaffe R: Corticotropin-releasing hormone stimulates P450 17alphahydroxylase/17,20-lyase in human adrenal cells via protein kinase C. J Clin Endocrinol Metab 84:3732–3738, 1999.

56. Smith R, Mesiano S, Chan E-C, et al: Corticotropin-releasing hormone directly and preferentially stimulates dehydroepiandrosterone sulfate secretion by human fetal adrenal cortical cells. J Clin Endocrinol Metab 83:2916–2920, 1998.

57. Pepe G, Albrecht E: Central integrative role of oestrogen in the regulation of placental steroidogenic maturation and the development of the fetal pituitary-adrenocortical axis in the baboon. Hum Reprod Update 4:406–419, 1998.

58. Thorburn G, Challis J: Endocrine control of parturition. Physiol Rev 59:863–918, 1979.

59. Whittle W, Holloway A, Lye S, et al: Prostaglandin production at the onset of ovine parturition is regulated by both estrogen-independent and estrogen dependent pathways. Endocrinology 141:3783–3790, 2000.

60. Martin R, Whittle W, Holloway A, et al: Ontogeny and regulation of ovine placental prostaglandin E2 synthase. Biol Reprod 67:868–873, 2002.

61. Gyomorey S, Lye S, Gibb W, Challis J: Fetal to maternal progression of prostaglandin H2 synthase-2 expression in ovine intrauterine tissues during the course of labor. Biol Reprod 62:797–805, 2000.

62. Wu WX, Ma XH, Coksaygan T, et al: Prostaglandin mediates premature delivery in pregnant sheep induced by estradiol at 121 days of gestational age. Endocrinology 145:1444–1452, 2004.

63. Bloomfield F, Oliver M, Hawkins P, et al: A periconceptional nutritional origin of noninfectious preterm birth. Science 300:606, 2003.

64. Nathaniels P, Figueroa J, Honnebier M: In the rhesus monkey placental retention after fetectomy at 121 to 130 days' gestation outlasts the normal duration of pregnancy. Am J Obstet Gynecol 166:1529–1535, 1992.

65. Mecenas C, Guissani D, Owing J: Production of premature delivery in pregnant rhesus monkeys by androstenedione infusion. Nat Med 2:443–448, 1996.

66. Smith W, DeWitt D: Prostaglandin endoperoxide H synthases-1 and -2. Adv Immunol 62:167–215, 1996.

67. Hla T, Neilson K: Human cyclooxygenase-2 cDNA. Proc Natl Acad Sci U S A 89:7384–7388, 1992.

68. Matuso M, Ensor C, Tai H-H: Characterization of the generic structure and promoter of the mouse NAD-dependent 15-hydroxyprostaglandin dehydrogenase gene. Biochem Biophys Res Commun 235:582–586, 1997.

69. Negishi M, Sugimoto Y, Ichikawa A: Molecular mechanisms of adverse actions of prostanoid receptors. Biochim Biophys Acta 1259:109–119, 1995.

70. Myatt L, Lye S: Expression, localization and function of prostaglandin receptors in myometrium. Prostaglandins Leukot Essent Fatty Acids 70:137–148, 2004.

71. Olson D, Zaragoza D, Shallow M, et al: Myometrial activation and preterm labor: Evidence supporting a role for the prostaglandin F receptor: A review. Placenta 24:S47–S54, 2003.

72. Mitchell M, Trautman M: Molecular mechanisms regulating prostaglandin action. Mol Cell Endocrinol 93:C7–C10, 1993.

73. Hirst J, Teixiera F, Zakar T: Prostaglandin endoperoxide-H synthase-1 and -2 messenger ribonucleic acid levels in human amnion with spontaneous labor onset. J Clin Endocrinol Metab 80:517–523, 1995.

74. Gibb W, Sun M: Localization of prostaglandin H synthase type 2 protein and mRNA in term human fetal membranes and decidua. J Endocrinol 150:497–503, 1996.

75. Sangha R, Walton J, Ensor C: Immunohistochemical localization, mRNA abundance and activity of 15-hydroxyprostaglandin dehydrogenase in placenta and fetal membranes during term and preterm labor. J Clin Endocrinol Metab 78:982–989, 1994.

76. Giannoulias D, Patel F, Holloway A, et al: Differential changes in 15-hydroxyprostaglandin dehydrogenase and prostaglandin H synthase (types I and II) in human pregnant myometrium. J Clin Endocrinol Metab 87:1345–1352, 2002.

77. Giannoulias D, Holloway A, Sun M, et al: Expression of prostaglandin 1 (2) synthase, but not prostaglandin E synthase, changes in myometrium of women at term pregnancy. J Clin Endocrinol Metab 87:5274–5282, 2002.

78. Korita D, Sagawa N, Itoh H, et al: Cyclic mechanical stretch augments prostacyclin production in cultured human uterine myometrial cells from pregnant women: Possible involvement of up-regulation of prostacyclin synthase expression. J Clin Endocrinol Metab 87:5209–5219, 2002.

79. Sun M, Ramirez M, Challis J: Immunohistochemical localization of the glucocorticoid receptor in human fetal membranes and decidua at term and preterm delivery. J Endocrinol 149:243–248, 1996.

80. Zakar T, Olson D: Dexamethasone stimulates arachidonic acid conversion to prostaglandin E2 in human amnion cells. J Dev Physiol 12:269–272, 1989.

81. Economopoulos P, Sun M, Purgina B: Glucocorticoids stimulate prostaglandin H synthase type 2 (PGHS-2) in the fibroblast cells in human amnion cultures. Mol Cell Endocrinol 117:141–147, 1996.

82. Mitchell M, Lytton F, Varticovski L: Paradoxical stimulation of both lipocortin and prostaglandin production in human amnion cells by dexamethasone. Biochem Biophys Res Commun 151:137–141, 1988.

83. Whittle W, Gibb W, Challis J: Characterization of human amnion epithelial and mesenchymal cells; the cellular expression, activity and glucocorticoid regulation of prostaglandin output. Placenta 21:394–401, 2000.

84. Blumenstein A, Hansen WR, DeVal D, Mitchell MD: Differential regulation in human amnion epithelial and fibroblast cells of prostaglandin E2 production and prostaglandin H synthase-2 mRNA expression by dexamethasone but not tumor necrosis factor-α. Placenta 21:210–217, 2000.

85. Warrick C, Skinner K, Mitchell B: Relation between cyclic AMP and prostaglandin output by dispersed cells from human amnion and decidua. Am J Obstet Gynecol 153:66–71, 1985.

86. Tazawa R, Xu X-M, Wu K, Wang L-H: Characterization of the genomic structure, chromosomal location and promoter of human prostaglandin H synthase-2 gene. Biochem Biophys Res Commun 203:190–199, 1994.

87. Yan X, Sun M, Gibb W: Localization of nuclear factor-κB (NFκB) and inhibitory factor-κB (IκBs) in human fetal membranes and decidua at term and preterm delivery. Placenta 23:288–293, 2002.

88. Allport V, Slater D, Newton R, Bennet P: NK-kappaB and AP-1 are required for cyclo-oxygenase 2 gene expression in amnion epithelial cell line (WISH). Mol Hum Reprod 6:561–565, 2000.

89. Allport V, Pieber D, Slater D, et al: Human labour is associated with nuclear factor-kappaB activity which mediates cyclo-oxygenase-2 expression and is involved with the "functional progesterone withdrawal." Mol Hum Reprod 7:581–586, 2001.

90. van Meir C, Matthews S, Kierse M: 15-Hydroxyprostaglandin dehydrogenase (PGDH): Implications in preterm labor with and without ascending infection. J Clin Endocrinol Metab 82:969–976, 1997.

91. van Meir C, Matthews S, Ramirez M: Chorionic prostaglandin catabolism is decreased in the lower uterine segment with term labor. Placenta 18:109–114, 1997.

92. Patel F, Clifton V, Chwalisz K: Steroidal regulation of prostaglandin dehydrogenase activity and expression in human term placenta and choriodecidua in relation to labor. J Clin Endocrinol Metab 84:291–299, 1999.

93. Greenland K, Jantke I, Jenatschke S, et al: The human NAD+dependent 15-hydroxyprostaglandin dehydrogenase gene promoter is controlled by Ets and activating protein 1 transcription factors and progesterone. Endocrinology 141:581–597, 2000.

94. Patel F, Funfer M, Challis J: Mechanism of cortisol/progesterone antagonism in the regulation of 15-hydroxyprostaglandin dehydrogenase activity and messenger

ribonucleic acid levels in human chorion and placental trophoblast cells at term. J Clin Endocrinol Metab 88:2922–2933, 2003.

95. Alfaidy N, Xiong Z, Myatt L, et al: Prostaglandin F2α potentiates cortisol production by stimulating 11β-hydroxysteroid dehydrogenase 1: A novel feedback loop that may contribute to human labour. J Clin Endocrinol Metab 86:5585–5592, 2001.

96. Alfaidy N, Li W, MacIntosh T, et al: Late gestation increase in 11-beta-hydroxysteroid dehydrogenase 1 expression in human fetal membranes: A novel intrauterine source of cortisol. J Clin Endocrinol Metab 88:5033–5038, 2003.

97. Alfaidy N, Li W, MacIntosh T, et al: Late gestation increase in 11-beta-hydroxysteroid dehydrogenase 1 expression in human fetal membranes: A novel intrauterine source of cortisol. J Clin Endocrinol Metab 88:5033–5038, 2003.

98. Gibb W, Challis J: Mechanisms of term and preterm birth. J Obstet Gynaecol Can 24:874–883, 2002.

99. Brown N, Alvi S, Elder M, et al: Interleukin-1beta and bacterial endotoxin change the metabolism of prostaglandins E2 and F2alpha in intact term fetal membranes. Placenta 19:625–630, 1998.

100. Mitchell M, Goodwin V, Mesnage S, Keelan J: Cytokine-induced coordinate expression of enzymes of prostaglandin biosynthesis and metabolism: 15-Hydroxyprostaglandin dehydrogenase. Prostaglandins Leukot Essent Fatty Acids 62:1–5, 2000.

101. Pomini F, Patel F, Mancuso S, Challis J: Activity and expression of 15-hydroxyprostaglandin dehydrogenase in cultured chorionic trophoblast and villous trophoblast cells and in chorionic explants at term with and without spontaneous labor. Am J Obstet Gynecol 182:221–226, 2000.

102. Bowen J, Chamley L, Keelan J, Mitchell M: Cytokines of the placenta and extra-placental membranes: Roles and regulation during human pregnancy and parturition. Placenta 23:257–273, 2002.

103. Keelan J, Blumenstein M, Helliwell R, et al: Cytokines, prostaglandins and parturition: A review. Placenta 24:S33–S46, 2003.

104. Hertelendy F, Molnar M, Romero R: Inteferon gamma antagonizes interleukin-1beta-induced cyclooxygenase-2 expression and prostaglandin E(2) production in human myometrial cells. J Soc Gynecol Investig 9:215–219, 2002.

105. Pomini F, Caruso A, Challis J: Interleukin-10 modifies the effects of interleukin-1β and tumor necrosis factor-α on the activity and expression of prostaglandin H synthase-2 and the NAD+-dependent 15-hydroxyprostaglandin dehydrogenase in cultured term

human villous trophoblast and chorion trophoblast cells. J Clin Endocrinol Metab 84:4645–4651, 1999.

106. Premyslova M, Li W, Alfaidy N, et al: Differential expression and regulation of microsomal prostaglandin E(2) synthase in human fetal membranes and placenta with infection and in cultured trophoblast cells. J Clin Endocrinol Metab 88:6040–6047, 2003.

107. Osman I, Young A, Ledingham M, et al: Leukocyte density and pro-inflammatory cytokine expression in human fetal membranes, decidua, cervix and myometrium before and during labour at term. Mol Hum Reprod 9:41–45, 2003.

108. Yellon S, Mackler A, Kirby M: The role of leukocyte traffic and activation in parturition. J Soc Gynecol Investig 10:323–338, 2003.

109. Kelly R: Inflammatory mediators and cervical ripening. J Reprod Immunol 57:217–224, 2002.

110. Chan E, Fraser S, Yin S, et al: Human myometrial genes are differentially expressed in labor: A suppression subtractive hybridization study. J Clin Endocrinol Metab 87:2435–2441, 2002.

111. Smith R: The timing of birth. Sci Am 280:68–75, 1999.

112. McLean M, Smith R: Corticotrophin-releasing hormone and human parturition. Reproduction 121:493–501, 2001.

113. Hillhouse E, Grammatopoulos D: Role of stress peptides during human pregnancy and labour. Reproduction 124:323–329, 2002.

114. Petraglia F, Florio P, Nappi C: Peptide signaling in human placenta and membranes: Autocrine, paracrine, and endocrine mechanisms. Endocr Rev 17:156–186, 1996.

115. McLean M, Bisits A, Davies J: A placental clock controlling the length of human pregnancy. Nat Med 1:460–463, 1995.

116. Riley S, Walton J, Herlick J: The localization and distribution of corticotropin-releasing hormone in the human placental and fetal membranes throughout gestation. J Clin Endocrinol Metab 72:1001–1007, 1991.

117. Cheng Y-H, Nicholson R, King B, et al: Glucocorticoid stimulation of corticotropin-releasing hormone gene expression requires a cyclic adenosine 3′,5′-monophosphate regulatory element in human primary placental cytotrophoblast cells. J Clin Endocrinol Metab 85:1937–1945, 2000.

118. Cheng Y-H, Nicholson R, King B, et al: Corticotropin-releasing hormone gene expression in primary placental cells is modulated by cyclic adenosine 3′,5′-monophosphate. J Clin Endocrinol Metab 85:1239–1244, 2000.

119. Mariononi E, Korebrits C, Di Iorio R, et al: Effect of betamethasone in vivo on placental corticotrophin-releasing hormone (CRH) in human pregnancy. Am J Obstet Gynecol 178:770–778, 1998.

120. Korebrits C, Yu D, Ramirez M: Antenatal glucocorticoid administration increases corticotrophin-releasing hormone (CRH) in maternal plasma. Br J Obstet Gynaecol 105:556–561, 1998.

121. Elliott J, Radin T: The effect of corticosteroid administration on uterine activity and preterm labor in high order multiple gestations. Obstet Gynecol 85:250–254, 1995.

122. Yeshaya A, Orvieto R, Ben-Shem E, et al: Uterine activity after betamethasone administration for the enhancement of fetal lung maturation. Eur J Obstet Gynecol Reprod Biol 67:139–141, 1996.

123. Hobel C, Dunkel-Schetter C, Roesch S, et al: Maternal plasma corticotropin-releasing hormone associated with stress at 20 weeks' gestation in pregnancies ending in preterm delivery. Am J Obstet Gynecol 180:S257–S263, 1999.

124. Lockwood C: Stress-associated preterm delivery: The role of corticotropin-releasing hormone. Am J Obstet Gynecol 180:S264–S266, 1999.

125. Dayan J, Creveuil C, Herlicoviez M, et al: Role of anxiety and depression in the onset of spontaneous preterm labor. Am J Epidemiol 155:293–301, 2002.

126. Hobel CJ, Dunkel-Schetter C, Roesch S: Maternal stress as a signal to the fetus. Prenatal and Neonatal Medicine 3:116–120, 1998.

127. Korebrits C, Ramirez M, Watson L: Maternal CRH as a predictor of impending preterm birth. J Clin Endocrinol Metab 83:1585–1591, 1998.

128. Stevens M, Challis J, Lye S: Corticotropin-releasing hormone receptor subtype 1 is significantly up-regulated at the time of labor in the human myometrium. J Clin Endocrinol Metab 83:4107–4115, 1998.

129. Aggelidou E, Hillhouse E, Grammatopoulos D: Up-regulation of nitric oxide synthase and modulation of the guanylate cyclase activity by corticotropin-releasing hormone but not urocortin II or urocortin III in cultured human pregnant myometrial cells. Proc Natl Acad Sci U S A 99:3300–3305, 2002.

130. Karteris E, Hillhouse E, Grammatopoulos D: Urocortin II is expressed in human pregnant myometrial cells and regulates myosin light chain phosphorylation: Potential role of the type-2 corticotropin-releasing hormone receptor in the control of myometrial contractility. Endocrinology 145:890–900, 2004.

131. Chard T, Hudson T, Edwards C: Release of oxytocin and vasopressin by the human fetus during labor. Nature 243:352–354, 1971.

132. Chard T: Fetal and maternal oxytocin in human parturition. Am J Perinatol 2:145–152, 1989.

133. Young W, Shepard E, Amico J: Deficiency in mouse oxytocin prevents milk ejection, but not fertility or

parturition. J Neuroendocrinol 8:847–853, 1996.

134. Nishimori K, Young L, Guo Q, et al: Oxytocin is required for nursing but is not essential for parturition or reproductive behavior. Proc Natl Acad Sci U S A 93:11699–11704, 1996.

135. Blanks A, Thornton S: The role of oxytocin in parturition. Br J Obstet Gynaecol 110:46–51, 2003.

136. Mitchell B, Schmid B: Oxytocin and its receptor in the process of parturition. J Soc Gynecol Investig 8:122–133, 2001.

137. Mitchell B, Chibbar R: Synthesis and metabolism of oxytocin in late gestation in human decidua. Adv Exp Med Biol 395:365–380, 1995.

138. Mitchell B, Fang X, Wong S: Oxytocin: A paracrine hormone in the regulation of parturition? Rev Reprod 3:113–122, 1998.

139. Chibbar R, Wong S, Miller F, Mitchell B: Estrogen stimulates oxytocin gene expression in human fetal membranes and decidua. J Clin Endocrinol Metab 80:567–572, 1995.

140. Chibbar R, Wong S, Miller F, Mitchell B: Estrogen stimulates oxytocin gene expression in human chorio-decidua. J Clin Endocrinol Metab 80:567–572, 1995.

141. Phaneuf S, Rodriguez Linares B, TambyRaja R, et al: Loss of myometrial oxytocin receptors during oxytocin-induced and oxytocin-augmented labour. J Reprod Fertil 120:91–97, 2000.

142. Moutquin J, Sherman D, Cohen H, et al: Double-blind randomized, controlled trial of atosiban and ritodrine in the treatment of preterm labor: A multicentre effectiveness and safety study. Am J Obstet Gynecol 182:1191–1199, 2000.

143. Lamont R: The development and introduction of anti-oxytocic tocolytics. Br J Obstet Gynaecol 110:108–112, 2003.

144. McKeown K, Challis J, Small C, et al: Altered fetal pituitary-adrenal function in the ovine fetus treated with RU486 and meloxicam, an inhibitor of prostaglandin synthase-II. Biol Reprod 63:1899–1904, 2000.

145. Sawdy R, Lye S, Fisk N, Bennet P: A double-blind randomised study of fetal side effects during and after the short-term maternal administration of indomethacin, sulindac, and nimesulide for the treatment of preterm labor. Am J Obstet Gynecol 188:1046–1051, 2003.

146. Peri K, Quiniou C, Hou X, et al: THG113: A novel selective FP antagonist that delays preterm labor. Semin Perinatol 26:389–397, 2002.

# Diabetes Mellitus and Pregnancy

## Boyd E. Metzger, Lisa P. Purdy, and Richard L. Phelps

## INTRODUCTION

Pregnancy is a diabetogenic physiologic event. Particularly in late gestation, insulin requirements of women with diabetes increase, and overt diabetes may develop in women with previously undiagnosed glucose intolerance. In others, a transitory asymptomatic impairment in glucoregulation may be unmasked. These diabetogenic aspects of pregnancy are associated with maternal and fetal complications and may have long-term consequences as well. The fetal complications do not occur when the father is the only diabetic parent, and thus, they appear to be distinct from the genetic aspects of diabetes. They are linked instead to alterations in the maternal environment to which the developing conceptus is exposed. The implications for pregnancies in which diabetes mellitus (DM) antedates pregnancy (preexisting DM) or is first recognized during the present pregnancy (gestational DM [GDM]) are discussed in subsequent sections.

## HISTORY

Before the discovery of insulin, pregnancy in a woman with DM was little more than a medical curiosity. The few women with DM who survived adolescence were often infertile. Those who conceived frequently underwent therapeutic abortion in view of the alarmingly high rates of both maternal (25%) and perinatal (40% to 50%) mortality present at the time. After therapy with insulin became available, increasing numbers of women with diabetes reached adulthood with little impairment in fertility. Maternal mortality was soon reduced to levels present in nondiabetic women. A comparable reduction in fetal wastage did not occur until much later. In the 1940s, perinatal loss rates of 40% continued to be reported. In the 1950s and 1960s, pioneering efforts based on the premise that fetal survival is linked to control of maternal diabetes reduced the rates of fetal loss to 10% to 15%. Further improvements followed the development of technologies for (1) monitoring the integrity of the fetoplacental unit, (2) documenting maternal metabolic control more accurately (i.e., self-monitoring of capillary blood sugar), and (3) sophisticated management of neonatal morbidity. In many centers, rates of perinatal loss in diabetic pregnancies (except for those related to major congenital malformations) now approach those of the general obstetric population. Thus, attention has increasingly focused on neonatal morbidity and the potential effects of maternal diabetes on the offspring in later life. For historical perspective, see a review by Gabbe and Graves.[1]

The criteria of O'Sullivan and Mahan for diagnosing GDM[2] were initially established to identify women at high risk for developing diabetes in later years. Subsequently, programs to diagnose GDM systematically were motivated by a desire to detect pregnancies at risk for perinatal morbidity so that caregivers could intervene to reduce such morbidity. Globally acceptable diagnostic criteria and strategies for detecting GDM were not forthcoming. Consequently, for about 3 decades, much controversy has existed regarding the medical/obstetrical significance of GDM and the cost effectiveness of its detection and treatment. The Hyperglycemia & Adverse Pregnancy Outcome (HAPO) Study that is currently under way should help to resolve some of these issues.

## EPIDEMIOLOGY

Preexisting DM complicates 0.2% to 0.5% of pregnancies,[3] with half or more of the pregnancies complicated by type 2 DM rather than type 1. GDM may be present in an additional 1.4% to 15.7%, depending on the population studied and the diagnostic criteria used.[4] These rates are likely to increase because of the epidemic of obesity and diabetes in younger age groups and minority populations. A recent study from California revealed an increase in the incidence of GDM from 5.1% in 1991 to 7.4% in 1997.[5]

## PATHOGENESIS

### *METABOLIC EFFECTS OF PREGNANCY*

The metabolic alterations of pregnancy do not occur with equal intensity throughout gestation. Rather, a temporal progression is seen in which increasing demands for insulin (insulin resistance) parallel the growth of the conceptus. In the immediate postpartum period, the profound insulin resistance dissipates rapidly. These metabolic perturbations and their temporal associations suggest that they derive from the conceptus.[6]

Serial estimates of insulin sensitivity before and during pregnancy in women with normal carbohydrate metabolism indicate a slight reduction in insulin sensitivity by 12 to 14 weeks,[7] further decline by the end of the second trimester, reaching a 40% to 60% decline during the third trimester.[7-10] Catalano and colleagues[7] found modest improvement in insulin sensitivity at 12 to 14 weeks in women with GDM when compared with their state of insulin resistance before pregnancy. This improvement was followed by progression to severe insulin resistance in late gestation that was equal to or greater than that in subjects with normal glucose tolerance. Women with type 1 DM who are in optimal metabolic control before conception do not have an increase in insulin requirement during the first trimester and may even require some reduction in dosage because of hypoglycemia at the end of the first and beginning of the second trimester (Fig. 186-1).

The insulin resistance is not due to a reduction in insulin binding to hepatic and skeletal muscle receptors, suggesting that it is secondary to altered postreceptor factors. GLUT4 transporter number is normal in human skeletal muscle in pregnancy[11] but reduced in adipose tissue in normal and GDM pregnancies.[12] Shao and colleagues[13] found that insulin-stimulated tyrosine kinase activity is inhibited by increased levels of cell membrane glycoprotein-1, which shifts phosphorylation from tyrosine to serine/threonine.

Only a modest, if any, increase in insulin secretion occurs in response to glucose during early pregnancy. Conversely, insulin secretion in response to oral or intravenous glucose in the last trimester of pregnancy is approximately 1.5 to 2.5 times greater than that seen in nongravid conditions[6] and is accompanied by islet cell hyperplasia. Insulin does not cross the placenta, although some is bound there.[14] Although the human placenta is small in proportion to total maternal mass, it actively degrades insulin and moderately increases insulin clearance in normal pregnancy and GDM.[10,15] The product of β-cell secretion is primarily insulin and not a disproportionate amount of proinsulin or intermediates, which have substantially less activity than insulin.

The mediators of increased insulin secretion and insulin resistance are not entirely clear. A number of studies suggest that progesterone, acting separately or in concert with estrogens, has direct β-cell cytotropic actions. When the two sex steroids are administered to nonpregnant animals in appropriate molar concentration ratios, effects on plasma insulin and fuel storage in liver and adipose tissue similar to those seen in normal pregnancy are observed without significantly affecting skeletal muscle sensitivity to insulin.[16] Gestational hormones such as human chorionic somatomammotropin (hCS), the placental growth hormone variant, and growth factors may facilitate this adaptation to the insulin resistance of pregnancy. During the latter half of pregnancy, circulating levels of hCS, estrogen, and progesterone reach maximal plasma concentrations with increasing placental mass.[6] The concentration of pituitary growth hormone decreases,[17] but the increasing level of the growth hormone variant (hGH-V) of placental origin may offset the decline.[17] Prolactin also increases throughout gestation and contributes to the insulin resistance. Free cortisol levels increase, but the diurnal variations are maintained[18] despite the presence of placental corticotropin and corticotropin-releasing factor. The combined effect of these hormonal changes is to oppose insulin at peripheral (muscle and adipose tissue) and hepatic sites. Currently, potential roles of tissue necrosis factor-α,[19] cytokines, and leptin[20] are being investigated.

### Utilization of Maternal Fuels by the Conceptus

Fetal nutrient utilization is covered in detail in Chapter 184. Only topics that are relevant to maternal diabetogenesis or changes that arise as a consequence of diabetes during pregnancy are considered here.

The placenta is the conduit through which the conceptus continuously draws maternal fuel for its metabolic and biosynthetic needs, and glucose is the major source of its metabolic energy. In addition, glucose or three-carbon intermediates derived from glucose (lactate) are precursors for glycogen, glycoproteins, and the glyceride-glycerol in triglycerides and phospholipids of the conceptus. Glucose utilization rates as high as 6 mg/kg/min have been estimated in the human fetus at term,[21] in contrast to glucose turnover of 2 to 3 mg/kg/min in normal adults. Glucose delivery across the placenta occurs by facilitated diffusion, and maternal glucose usually exceeds fetal glucose concentration by 10 to 20 mg/dL (0.6 to 1.1 mmol/L).

In the third trimester, growth of the human fetus requires the net placental transfer of approximately 54 mmol of nitrogen per day.[22] Furthermore, amino acids may be used in the conceptus for oxidative energy. Although quantitative measurements of nitrogen requirement for fetal growth in humans are not available, it is clear that the fetus exerts an unremitting drain on maternal nitrogen reserves.

Although maternal triglyceride represents the largest reserve fuel depot, it can directly support the metabolic needs of the conceptus only to a limited extent. Triglycerides cross the placental barrier poorly, and the net transfer of free fatty acids (FFAs) to the fetus may be limited. Glycerol can be transferred across the placenta readily, but its contribution in nonruminant mammalian species is probably small. Ketones, formed in the maternal liver through oxidation of FAs, readily cross the placenta and are present in the fetal circulation in concentrations approaching those in maternal blood.[23] The enzymes necessary for ketone oxidation are present in

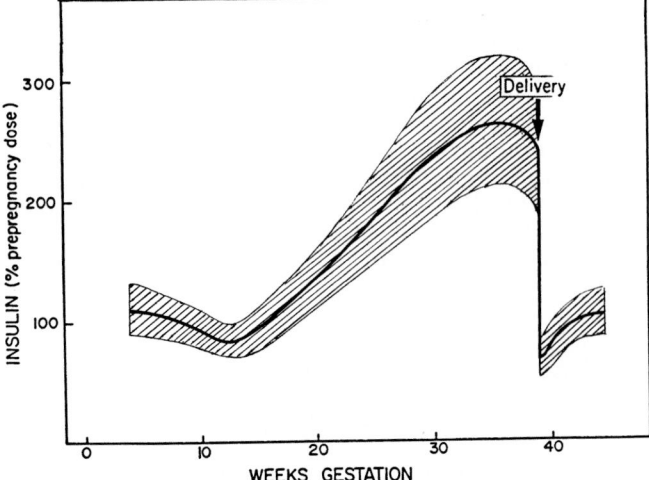

*Figure 186-1* Schematic representation of changing insulin requirements over the course of pregnancy and after delivery in pregestational diabetes mellitus. (Adapted from Phelps RL, Metzger BE, Freinkel N: Medical management of diabetes in pregnancy. In Sciarra J (ed): Gynecology and Obstetrics, vol 3. Philadelphia, Harper & Row, 1988, pp 1–16, with permission.)

the human fetus. When fetal tissues, including the brain, are incubated in vitro with concentrations of ketones similar to those present during fasting, substantial oxidation of ketones is seen even in the presence of alternative fuels (i.e., fasting concentrations of glucose, lactate, and amino acids).[23] Oxidation of ketones lessens that of the other fuels and may "spare" them for biosynthetic disposition or other pathways in the fetus.[24] However, the diversion to the metabolism of ketones during the period of active cell replication in fetal life may have adverse consequences. Ketones inhibit pyrimidine and purine synthesis in developing brain cells in the rat fetus[24] and, at high concentrations, disrupt organogenesis in rodent embryos in culture.[25] Controversial epidemiologic evidence suggested that maternal ketonuria during human pregnancy may be followed by a reduction in the intelligence quotient (IQ) of the offspring in childhood.[26] Rizzo and coworkers[27] reported an inverse association between increased plasma FFAs and β-hydroxybutyrate concentrations in the second and third trimesters of pregnancy and intellectual development of offspring at age 2 to 5 years.

### Circulating Concentrations of Nutrient Fuels
#### In Normal Pregnancy
Normal women have a decrease in the concentration of fasting plasma glucose (FPG) during pregnancy. The greatest decline in 10- to 12-hour overnight FPG occurs early in gestation,[28] well before the high rate of glucose turnover in the conceptus can account for an increase in total glucose turnover. Severely obese women do not show the expected decline of FPG during pregnancy.[28] A lower FPG persists during late gestation despite relatively higher postmeal glucose levels. Basal concentrations of plasma glycerol and FFAs do not change until late gestation, at which time, significant elevations occur, and transition to the metabolic profile characteristic of the fasting state is accelerated in association with mounting lipolysis and insulin resistance.[29] Progressive increases occur in all major lipid fractions, including triglycerides, cholesterol, and phospholipids.[16] Total plasma amino acid concentrations also decline in early pregnancy and persist throughout gestation.[30] The reasons for these changes are unknown. The suppressive effects of insulin on plasma amino acids are well known and could account for this finding. However, in later gestation, release of amino acids from skeletal muscle is less restrained by insulin, at least in pregnant rats. This finding suggests that during this time of insulin resistance, increased fetal removal, as opposed to impaired muscle release, may play a primary role in sustaining maternal hypoaminoacidemia.[31]

#### In Gestational Diabetes Mellitus
Basal and postprandial levels of glucose, FFAs, triglycerides, and amino acids tend to exceed those of normal pregnant control subjects.[32] The alterations tend to persist after dietary intervention, with the extent of the abnormalities paralleling the severity of the GDM.[32] Branched-chain amino acids, which are exquisitely sensitive to insulin and often altered in obesity and other insulin-resistant states, are the most consistently disturbed.[32] The propensity to "accelerated starvation" (e.g., a more rapid decline in circulating glucose concentration in association with a greater increase in FFAs and ketones) in women with GDM is similar to that found in women with normal glucose homeostasis.[33]

### In Women with Preexisting Diabetes Mellitus
In pregnant women in whom type 1 DM is well controlled, few disturbances in plasma lipids (FFAs, cholesterol, and triglycerides) have been found, and individual lipoprotein fractions have little change in their lipid content.[34] The greatest departures from the norm during pregnancy occur in plasma glucose profiles; plasma amino acid concentrations also may be markedly disturbed. Changes in amino acids and indices of

glycemic control (blood glucose self-monitoring records and hemoglobin $A_{1c}$ levels) are poorly correlated, especially in late pregnancy.[35] Lipids tend to be altered more extensively in pregnant women with type 2 DM, with higher total plasma triglycerides and an increased triglyceride content of very-low-density lipoproteins.[34] The cholesterol content of high-density lipoproteins may be decreased when compared with levels in normal pregnancy or in pregnant women with type 1 DM.[34] The relative roles of obesity and diabetes in the development of these lipid aberrations remain to be defined. Studies of amino acid metabolism in type 2 DM in pregnancy have not been reported.

### MATERNAL METABOLISM AND PREGNANCY OUTCOME

The pioneering hypothesis advanced by Pedersen[36] a half century ago stated that maternal hyperglycemia leads to fetal hyperinsulinism, which is responsible for macrosomia and neonatal morbidity. Extensive experimental and clinical evidence indicates that metabolic disturbances in the mother contribute to virtually all the adverse effects of DM on the offspring.[6,37,38] The importance of alterations in other metabolic fuels, in addition to glucose, was recognized later.[32] Freinkel[6] emphasized the temporal relations between a metabolic insult and the adverse outcome expected ("fuel-mediated teratogenesis") and postulated that the altered intrauterine environment of diabetes can have life-long as well as perinatal consequences.[6,37] The key features of the hypotheses of Pedersen and Freinkel are schematically integrated in Figure 186-2.

### Congenital Malformations and Early Fetal Loss
Increased risks of congenital malformations and spontaneous abortions in diabetic pregnancies are linked to metabolic control at conception.[6,38] Good control during the period of organogenesis may reduce the prevalence of these adverse outcomes.[38] Risk of spontaneous abortion increases in direct proportion to hemoglobin $A_{1c}$ concentration measured shortly before or after conception.[39,40] The specific relation between metabolic control and risk of congenital malformations has been more difficult to define. In the National

## PEDERSEN/FREINKEL HYPOTHESES

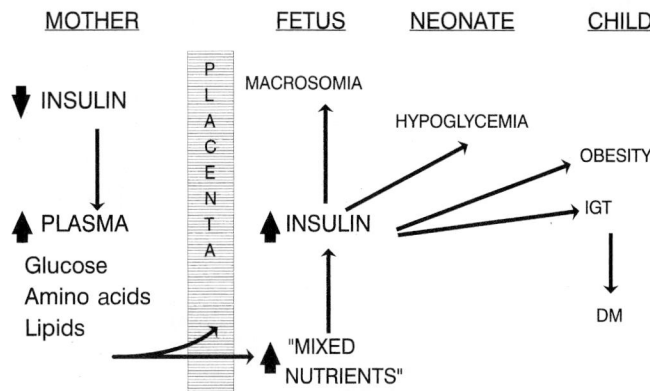

Figure 186-2 Effect of maternal fuels on fetal development. The classic hyperglycemia-hyperinsulinemia hypothesis of Pedersen[36] has been modified to show the contribution of other insulin-responsive maternal fuels, besides glucose. All of these fuels can influence the growth of the fetus and the maturation of its insulin secretion. As indicated here, altered fetal nutrients and enhanced insulin secretion are associated with consequences that extend well beyond the neonatal period. (From Silverman BL, Purdy LP, Metzger BE: The intrauterine environment: Implications for the offspring of diabetic mothers. Diabetes Rev 4:21–35, 1996, with permission.)

Institutes of Health–supported Diabetes in Early Pregnancy Study, major congenital malformations were more common in the women with DM enrolled within 21 days of conception (4.9%) than in the nondiabetic control group (2.1%; $P = 0.027$).[41] However, most of the subjects were in good to fair control, and an association with glycemic control could not be established. Greene and associates[40] found a prevalence of congenital malformation of about 5% until initial hemoglobin $A_{1c}$ concentrations were in excess of 10 to 12 SD of the mean control value (poor control). Beyond that, the risk of malformations increased steeply (Fig. 186-3). Several groups reported that improving control of DM before conception[42] reduces rates of major congenital malformations to those expected in the general obstetric population. In populations in which most pregnancies in women with diabetes are planned, congenital malformations have declined to rates similar to those of the general population.[43]

In vivo and in vitro animal models suggest that diabetic embryopathy is multifactorial.[44] Oxidative stress, increased generation of free radicals, disruption of signaling pathways, or a combination of these have been implicated.[45,46] When tight metabolic control is restored, levels of circulating "serum factors" that may mediate embryopathy decline more slowly than hyperglycemia and hyperketonemia.[25,44] Hypoglycemia also is potentially teratogenic.[47] Thus, measurements of blood glucose or hemoglobin $A_{1c}$ may not fully reflect the "toxicity" of the maternal environment for the fetus. This lack of specificity is reflected in the fact that 60% to 70% of offspring of mothers with first-trimester hemoglobin $A_{1c}$ levels indicative of poor metabolic control are normally developed at birth.[40] Consequently, neither the precise degree of glycemic control nor the interval over which good control must be maintained to achieve optimal outcome is known.[38]

### Disturbances of Fetal Growth

Development of macrosomia (traditionally defined as birth weight >4000 g or above the 90th percentile for gestational age) is the quintessential fulfillment of the Pedersen hypothesis and a frequent complication of pregnancies complicated by DM and GDM. Increased adiposity is the primary component of the macrosomia. Infants of diabetic mothers may have up to twice the body fat content of infants of normal mothers. Skin-fold measurements may be used to document adiposity at birth and reflect maternal metabolic regulation.[48] However, skin-fold measurements are difficult to standardize and are seldom used in routine clinical assessment.[48] Adiposity tends to be prominent in the shoulder region, enhancing risks for cesarean delivery, shoulder dystocia, and birth trauma.[49] Increased fat

content was reported in infants of mothers with GDM even with total body weight identical to that of controls.[50] Asymmetrical growth is the hallmark of diabetic fetopathy. In addition to hypertrophy of subcutaneous fat, other organs responsive to insulin (e.g., the heart and liver) may be larger, whereas insulin-insensitive tissues such as the brain are of normal size. Thickness of fetal humeral soft tissue[51] or cheek-to-cheek dimensions[52] can be used to detect asymmetrical growth caused by maternal diabetes. Buchanan and colleagues[53] use abdominal circumference that is greater than the 75th percentile to identify pregnancies at higher risk for macrosomia and target them for intensive therapy with insulin.

Fetal hyperinsulinemia may develop early in gestation, well before adipose tissue develops. Morphometric studies of the pancreas from fetuses of mothers with diabetes demonstrated islet hypertrophy and hyperplasia during the second trimester. In vitro studies with the pancreas from aborted fetuses indicated that insulin secretion was increased as early as 16 weeks' gestation in poorly controlled diabetes.[54] We observed a stronger association between fetal islet function near term or at birth and metabolic control in the second trimester (hemoglobin $A_{1c}$ concentration) than in the third trimester.[55] Visceromegaly and fat accumulation also resulted from insulin administration to normal fetal monkeys (via implanted insulin pumps) without concurrent infusion of additional nutrients.[56] Once initiated, β-cell overactivity may promote development of macrosomia, even without sustained elevations in nutrient fuels. Finally, the development of fetal hyperinsulinemia in pregnancies with mild GDM (normal FPG) indicates that the fetal β cell is sensitive to minimal alteration in its nutrient environment.[57,58] Alterations of multiple nutrient fuels[55] may contribute to premature activation of fetal islet function and increases in insulin-like growth factors (IGFs).[59]

Historically, intrauterine growth restriction (IUGR) was a common finding in offspring of type 1 diabetic mothers. This was thought to be secondary to maternal vascular disease, resulting in "uteroplacental insufficiency."[36] Now, growth restriction is rarely seen except in pregnancies complicated by hypertension or diabetic nephropathy. Poor metabolic control in early pregnancy may retard growth irreparably, even without associated birth defects.[60]

### Anthropometric and Metabolic Development

Previously, a high prevalence of obesity was reported in offspring of diabetic mothers,[61] without documentation of metabolic status during intrauterine development. Pettitt and colleagues[62] found a correlation in Pima Indian mothers between the 2-hour response to oral glucose during pregnancy and the occurrence of obesity in their offspring. Moreover, the risk of obesity was not limited to those whose birth weight was increased.[61,63] Greater relative weight for height was reported at age 4 years in the offspring of diabetic mothers whose control was "poor" rather than "good" during the index pregnancy.[64] In a prospective long-term follow-up study of offspring of diabetic mothers, our group at Northwestern University found that macrosomia of offspring disappeared by age 1 year. However, by age 8 years, obesity was highly prevalent; nearly half had a weight greater than the 90th percentile.[61,65] These studies also suggested that fetal islet function may predict long-term anthropometric development. Relative obesity at ages 6 to 8 years was significantly correlated with insulin secretion in utero (amniotic fluid insulin content at 32 to 34 weeks' gestation).[65]

In Pima Indians, by age 20 to 24 years, type 2 DM is present in 45.5% of offspring of "diabetic" mothers, 8.6% in offspring of "prediabetic" mothers, and 1.4% of offspring of "nondiabetic" mothers.[66] The differences remain after adjustment for diabetes in the father, age at onset of diabetes in either parent, and obesity in the offspring (Fig. 186-4). The authors concluded, "The intrauterine environment is an

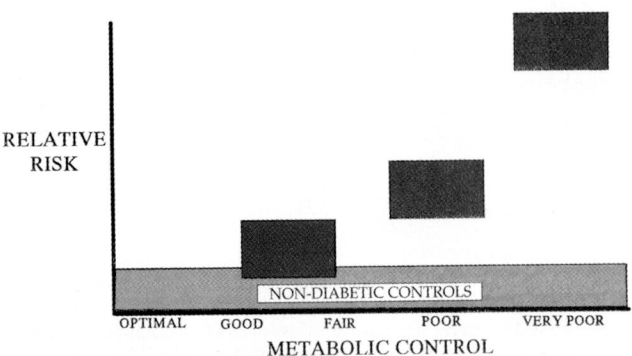

*Figure 186-3*  Schematic representation of the relation between control of maternal diabetes in the first trimester of pregnancy (period of organogenesis) and the risk for congenital malformations in the offspring. Note that some risk may be present even with good control, but it increases dramatically only with very poor control of diabetes.

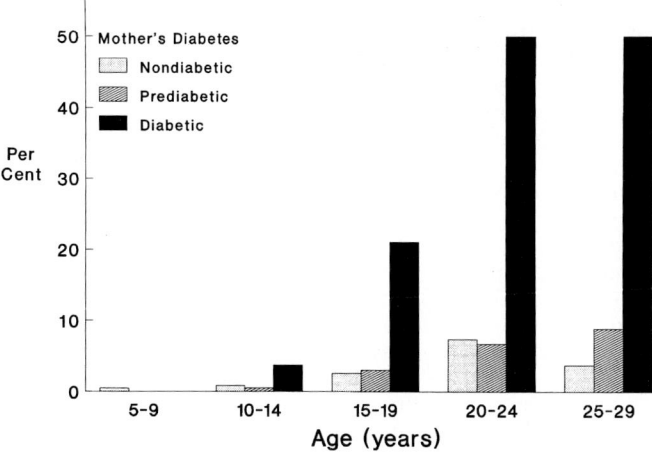

*Figure 186-4*  Age-specific prevalence of non-insulin-dependent diabetes mellitus (plasma glucose > 200 mg/dL 2 hours after oral glucose) in offspring of Pima Indian women without diabetes mellitus *(open bars)*, those developing diabetes only subsequent to pregnancy *(hatched bars)*, or those with diabetes during pregnancy *(solid bars)*. (Adapted from Pettitt DJ, Aleck KA, Baird HR, et al: Congenital susceptibility to NIDDM: Role of intrauterine environment. Diabetes 37:622–628, 1988, with permission.)

important determinant of the development of diabetes and that its effect is in addition to effects of genetic factors."[66] The offspring of diabetic mothers enrolled in the Northwestern University long-term follow-up had a high prevalence of impaired glucose tolerance (IGT),[67] particularly during puberty. IGT developed at similar rates in the offspring of mothers with GDM and preexisting DM. Excessive insulin secretion in utero was a strong predictor of IGT in childhood, independent of degree of obesity.[67] The observations summarized indicate that in offspring of diabetic mothers, nature (genetic factors) and nurture (intrauterine metabolic environment) may interact in predisposing to obesity and type 2 DM.

## DIAGNOSIS AND CLASSIFICATION

### CLASSIFICATION

We advocate the scheme outlined in Table 186-1 for the classification of carbohydrate intolerance during pregnancy. It is based on recommendations of an American Diabetes Association "Expert Committee,"[68] in concert with recommendations of the Fourth International Workshop Conference on GDM.[69]

### Gestational Diabetes Mellitus

GDM is subclassified to distinguish between those with FPG values within the normal range for pregnancy (i.e., <95 mg/dL [5.3 mmol/L]) and those with values exceeding the limits of normal (i.e., ≥95 mg/dL [5.3 mmol/L]). Patients are often seen that had GDM in a previous pregnancy but had no postpartum evaluation of glucose metabolism. Others may have had impaired fasting glucose or IGT postpartum, but not DM. From the perspective of proper classification and epidemiology, the diagnosis of GDM should not be assigned such patients. However, for purposes of clinical management, it is appropriate to stratify them on the basis of FPG (see earlier) and to designate them as class $A_1$, previous GDM, or as class $A_2$, previous GDM.

| Table 186-1 | Classification of Carbohydrate Intolerance during Pregnancy |
|---|---|
| **Class** | **Classification Criteria*** |
| **GESTATIONAL DIABETES MELLITUS (GDM)** | Carbohydrate intolerance of varying degrees of severity that is recognized for the first time during the present pregnancy. Diagnosis as per Tables 186-2 and 186-3<br>Antepartum subclassification on basis of values for fasting plasma glucose (FPG) |
| GDM class $A_1$ | Fasting glucose normal for pregnancy: venous plasma < 95 mg/dL (5.3 mmol/L) |
| GDM class $A_2$ | Fasting glucose exceeds normal for pregnancy: venous plasma ≥ 95 mg/dL (5.3 mmol/L) on at least two occasions |
| | ***Postpartum reclassification***<br>Evaluation as recommended by ADA Expert Committee & 4th International Workshop Conference on GDM<br>FPG ≥ 126 mg/dL (7.0 mmol/L) × 2 = Diabetes mellitus<br>FPG 110–125 mg/dL (6.1–6.9 mmol/L) = Impaired fasting glucose<br>FPG < 110 mg/dL: Perform OGTT (75g)<br>   Normal glucose tolerance: 2-hr value < 140 mg/dL (7.8 mmol/L). Classify "previous abnormality of glucose tolerance (GDM)"<br>   Impaired glucose tolerance: 2-hr value 140–199 mg/dL (7.8–11.0 mmol/L)<br>   Diabetes mellitus: 2-hr value ≥ 200 mg/dL (11.1 mmol/L) |
| **PREVIOUS GDM** | Abnormality of glucose tolerance in a previous pregnancy, without diabetes mellitus having been diagnosed post partum (postpartum glucose tolerance test normal, impaired, or not performed) |
| Class $A_1$ previous GDM<br>Class $A_2$ previous GDM | (See above for fasting plasma glucose parameters) |
| **PREGESTATIONAL DIABETES MELLITUS** | Diabetes mellitus diagnosed according to criteria of ADA Expert Committee when not pregnant |
| Diabetes mellitus type 1 | |
|   Uncomplicated | Absence of retinopathy, nephropathy, neuropathy, coronary artery disease, or hypertension |
|   Complicated | Presence of one or more of the above (see below for designations and definitions)† |
| Diabetes mellitus type 2 | |
|   Uncomplicated | As for type 1 diabetes |
|   Complicated | As for type 1 diabetes |

*Classification is based on prevailing practice in authors' center and the recommendations of the American Diabetes Association's Expert Committee and the 4th International Workshop Conference on Gestational Diabetes.[68,69,98]

†BDR, background diabetic retinopathy; PDR, proliferative diabetic retinopathy; NEPH, diabetic nephropathy defined as ≥0.5 g protein in 24-hr urine collection and/or serum creatinine consistently ≥1.2 mg/dL (≥106 mol/L); NEUR, neuropathy, defined as known gastroparesis when not pregnant, orthostatic hypotension, or sensory abnormalities in lower extremities detected at bedside examination; CAD, coronary artery disease diagnosed by history, electrocardiogram (ECG), or stress ECG; HTN, hypertension, defined as blood pressure ≥ 140/90 mm Hg consistently. (Designations are appended to primary diagnosis as appropriate [e.g., diabetes mellitus type 2 uncomplicated; diabetes mellitus type 1; BDR, NEPH]).

## Preexisting Diabetes

Historically, the White classification[70] was devised to predict pregnancy risk based on age at onset and duration of diabetes, in combination with microvascular or macrovascular complications. In the present era, fetal loss is uncommon, and the degree of metabolic control throughout pregnancy and the presence or absence of vascular complications, independent of maternal age or duration of DM, are more specific predictors of maternal or fetal morbidity. Therefore, we no longer use the "White classification"; instead, we designate pregnancies in women with DM as uncomplicated (no known vascular or neuropathic complications) or complicated (one or more complications). Abbreviations for the specific complication(s) are added as a postscript. We subdivide patients with preexisting DM into those with presumed type 1 or type 2 DM. Hare[71] proposed a similar, although not identical, classification. In the next several paragraphs, we briefly discuss the interrelations between pregnancy and specific complications of diabetes.

### Retinopathy

Diabetic retinopathy may worsen during gestation. The risk is present primarily in women with active proliferative changes or severe preproliferative retinopathy. Patients with mild background retinopathy or inactive laser-treated proliferative disease rarely experience progression of consequence. An association has been found between worsening retinopathy during pregnancy and the severity of hyperglycemia at enrollment[72,73] and the magnitude of improved glycemic control achieved in the first half of gestation.[72] This worsening during pregnancy may be analogous to the transient deterioration observed in nonpregnant subjects after the initiation of "tight" control of diabetes.[74] Data from the Diabetes Control and Complications Trial[74] indicate that pregnancy per se adds independently to the risk of transient progression of retinopathy and that the increased risk of progression may continue during the first postpartum year. Hypertension in pregnancy also is associated with progression of diabetic retinopathy.[75] Regardless of the mechanisms involved, women with preexisting retinopathy should be advised of the potential for deterioration and the need for close ophthalmologic follow-up before conception, during pregnancy, and in the postpartum period. Although photocoagulation therapy can be used effectively during gestation, those with active proliferative disease should be advised to postpone pregnancy until photocoagulation treatment has stabilized the retinal condition.

### Nephropathy

Diabetic nephropathy (24-hour urine protein ≥0.5 g or reduced creatinine clearance) increases risks for both the mother and offspring.[76] Worsening proteinuria (twofold to threefold increase), hypertension, premature labor, and a need for early induction are common outcomes. Most women experience little permanent effect on renal function despite transient but substantial increases in proteinuria.[76,77] Occasionally, patients experience deterioration in renal function that continues in the postpartum period.[78,79] Whether this decline is related to pregnancy or reflects the natural progression of renal impairment is uncertain. Several reports suggest that patients with moderate or severe nephropathy in early pregnancy (serum creatinine ≥1.4 mg/dL [124 mol/L]) are at risk for an accelerated decline in glomerular filtration during pregnancy and a greater likelihood of permanent worsening of renal function, although the postpartum rate of decline may be similar to that before pregnancy.[78,79] The increased glomerular filtration rate (GFR) and afferent arteriolar vasodilation of pregnancy may be maladaptive for those with preexisting renal disease. Ureteral hypomotility with vesicoureteral reflux, consequent physiologic hydronephrosis, and increased urinary nutrient content also increase risk for urinary tract infections and pyelonephritis. These factors may contribute to worsening renal function in pregnancy, and hypertension and urinary tract infections should be monitored carefully and treated aggressively. Regardless of whether pregnancy per se accelerates its progression, patients with nephropathy are frequently unaware of its presence and uninformed of its future health implications. This subject should be fully addressed in the preconception evaluation.

### Neuropathy

Diabetic neuropathy is commonly found in patients with long-standing diabetes. Little is known about the effect of pregnancy on progression of diabetic neuropathy. However, autonomic neuropathy may contribute to maternal morbidity and adverse pregnancy outcome.[80,81] Gastroparesis may result in marked glucose lability, inadequate nutrition, and maternal pulmonary aspiration. Bladder dysfunction may increase risk for urinary tract infection and worsening renal function.

### Cardiovascular Disease

Both systolic and diastolic blood pressure may increase in pregnancy in type 1 diabetic women.[82] In dated studies, myocardial infarction was associated with 50% mortality.[83,84] An increased risk for myocardial infarction and congestive heart failure also is found in the postpartum period.

## DIAGNOSIS OF GESTATIONAL DIABETES MELLITUS

### Screening

Gestational diabetes is generally asymptomatic and usually requires a glucose tolerance test (GTT) for diagnosis. Testing all women for GDM at the first obstetric appointment and serially throughout pregnancy is not cost effective in most populations. However, those with undiagnosed DM or IGT before conception have hyperglycemia in the first trimester and may benefit from early diagnosis and initiation of therapy. Therefore, it is important to have a comprehensive strategy for GDM diagnosis that is tailored to the population served. Participants in the Fourth International Workshop Conference on Gestational Diabetes Mellitus recommended that an assessment of risk for GDM as outlined in Table 186-2 be performed during the first prenatal visit.[69] In the authors' opinion, "universal blood glucose testing" should continue to be performed unless the patient population includes a sizable proportion of women who qualify as low risk. Two points from Table 186-2 deserve emphasis. First, it is critical that women be defined as "low risk" only if they have *all of the low-risk characteristics*. Second, those who are identified as "high risk" should have their initial blood glucose testing at the first prenatal visit. If normal, they are to be retested at 24 to 28 weeks' gestation. Women at "average risk" should receive a glucose challenge test (GCT) for the first time at 24 to 28 weeks' gestation. Those with values of 140 mg/dL (7.8 mmol/L) or more go on to a diagnostic oral glucose tolerance test (OGTT). This threshold requires performance of an OGTT in 14% to 16% of women in populations that are at average risk for GDM,[85] and identifies approximately 80% of women with GDM. The yield of GDM can be increased by about 10% if the screening threshold is reduced to 130 mg/dL (7.2 mmol/L), but to achieve this improved sensitivity, an OGTT must be performed in 23% to 25% of women.[85] Repeated screening also will increase the yield of GDM,[86] but the cost effectiveness is low except in groups at very high risk.

Except in groups at particularly high risk, a two-step screening procedure is used in North America. Step one, a 50-g oral GCT is given without regard to time of day or time of the last meal. Venous plasma glucose is measured 1 hour later. Screening results as high as 240 mg/dL do not preclude the necessity for confirmation with an OGTT.[87] It is important that glucose measurements be made on serum or plasma with certified laboratory techniques. Although measurement of

**Table 186-2** Screening Strategy for Detecting GDM[69]

| GDM risk assessment: | Should be ascertained at the first prenatal visit |
|---|---|
| **Low risk** | Blood glucose testing not routinely required if **all** of the following characteristics are present |
| | Member of an ethnic group with a low prevalence of GDM |
| | No known diabetes in first-degree relatives |
| | Age <25 years |
| | Weight normal before pregnancy |
| | No history of abnormal glucose metabolism |
| | No history of poor obstetric outcome |
| **Average risk** | Perform blood glucose testing at 24–28 weeks by using either |
| | Two-step procedure: 50-g glucose challenge test (GCT) followed by a diagnostic oral glucose tolerance test in those meeting the threshold value in the GCT (see text for details) |
| | One-step procedure: Diagnostic oral glucose tolerance test performed on all subjects (see text for details) |
| **High risk** | Perform blood glucose testing as soon as feasible, by using the procedures described above |
| | If GDM is not diagnosed, blood glucose testing should be repeated at 24–28 weeks, or at any time a patient has symptoms or signs that are suggestive of hyperglycemia |

GDM, gestational diabetes mellitus.

capillary blood glucose with portable meters and reagent strips is convenient and rapid, a within-test variability of 10% to 15% markedly reduces both the sensitivity and specificity of this approach.[69] Measurements of random blood glucose,[88] hemoglobin $A_{1c}$,[89] or fructosamine[90] also are not sufficiently sensitive for screening purposes.[69] Although more palatable, screening with alternative agents such as jelly beans may be less sensitive in detecting GDM.[91] Second-trimester amniocentesis for amniotic fluid insulin demonstrates reasonable sensitivity for early diagnosis of GDM,[57,92] but is invasive and potentially has adverse consequences.

### Diagnosis

Patients with an abnormal GCT receive a 3-hour 100-g OGTT, interpreted according to the criteria of O'Sullivan and Mahan[2] (extrapolated to venous plasma from whole blood). Controversy exists about optimal conversion of Somogyi-Nelson whole blood glucose values originally measured by O'Sullivan and Mahan into equivalent plasma glucose concentrations. When the National Diabetes Data Group (NDDG) developed the classification and diagnosis of DM in 1979,[93] the AutoAnalyzer colorimetric, ferricyanide-based analytic method for glucose was the "gold standard." Currently, glucose assays are primarily enzymatic (glucose oxidase or hexokinase). Carpenter and Coustan[94] derived values for interpretation of a 100-g OGTT that more accurately extrapolates the O'Sullivan results to glucose oxidase–based methods. This results in lower plasma glucose values for the diagnosis of GDM than those recommended by the NDDG and about a 50% increase in the number of women with a diagnosis of GDM.[5] Several studies found that pregnancy-associated complications occurred in equal frequency in the additional pregnancies defined as GDM with the plasma glucose cut-off values recommended by Carpenter and Coustan and those cases that also met the higher NDDG criteria.[95–97]

Consequently, the American Diabetes Association endorsed the Carpenter-Coustan translation of the O'Sullivan-Mahan criteria for interpretation of the 100-g OGTT. The cut-off values for the 100-g OGTT recommended by O'Sullivan and Mahan, by the NDDG, and by Carpenter and Coustan, are given in Table 186-3. The American Diabetes Association also approved criteria for interpretation of a 2-hour 75-g OGTT that are identical to the Carpenter and Coustan levels used in the 100-g OGTT.[98] These criteria are loosely based on studies of populations in the United States, Europe, Brazil, and Australia,[69,99,100] but lack validation from perinatal outcomes in a large number of pregnancies.

Some investigators believe that undesirable pregnancy effects are common in women with plasma glucose levels during the OGTT that are lower than those currently used in the United States for the diagnosis of GDM. Others strongly contend that adverse perinatal outcomes in GDM result primarily from other factors (obesity, advanced maternal age, the metabolic syndrome) rather than mild hyperglycemia. The ongoing National Institutes of Health and American Diabetes Association–funded study, Hyperglycemia & Adverse Pregnancy Outcome (HAPO), is designed to provide data from 15 centers in 9 countries relating degree of hyperglycemia to adverse perinatal outcome to develop criteria for a 75-g 2-hour glucose test.[101] In our opinion, caregivers should continue to apply the diagnostic criteria that they presently use until results from studies such as HAPO define the specific relation between maternal glycemia and adverse pregnancy outcome.

### HETEROGENEITY OF GESTATIONAL DIABETES MELLITUS

All forms of diabetes first recognized in pregnancy are defined as GDM. However, patients with GDM exhibit substantial phenotypic and genotypic heterogeneity. Based on clinical features and follow-up studies, GDM is commonly regarded as a precursor of type 2 DM.

#### Phenotypic Heterogeneity

Substantial heterogeneity has been observed among women with GDM in age, weight, severity of carbohydrate intolerance, and insulin secretion.[102] Those that have GDM are older and heavier than their "normal" counterparts, yet span the age and weight spectrum of the obstetric population. FPG levels tend to increase in GDM in parallel with the degree of obesity, but lean women with elevated FPG levels are frequently encountered. Fasting plasma immunoreactive insulin (IRI) is greater in obese subjects of both control and GDM groups (except in GDM subjects with elevated FPG).[102] Controlling for the effects of age and weight indicates that the short-term (15-minute) and long-term (3-hour integrated) IRI response is

**Table 186-3** Diagnosis of GDM 100-g Oral Glucose Load*

| | O'Sullivan-Mahan Whole Blood[†] Somogyi-Nelson (mg/dL)[†] | NDDG Plasma[93] AutoAnalyzer (mg/dL)[†] | Carpenter-Coustan Plasma[94] Glucose Oxidase (mg/dL)[†] |
|---|---|---|---|
| **Fasting** | 90 | 105 | 95 |
| **1 hr** | 165 | 190 | 180 |
| **2 hr** | 145 | 165 | 155 |
| **3 hr** | 125 | 145 | 140 |

*The test should be performed in the morning after an overnight fast of at least 8 hours but not more than 14 hours and after at least 3 days of unrestricted diet (≥150 g carbohydrate per day) and physical activity. The subject should remain seated and should not smoke throughout the test.
†Two or more of the values for glucose concentrations must be met or exceeded for a positive diagnosis.

attenuated in both obese and lean women with GDM, and the insulinopenia is most pronounced when the fasting plasma glucose level is elevated.[102] A small number of gravida with GDM display well-preserved IRI responses to oral glucose.[102] Similar heterogeneity exists with respect to the first and second phases of IRI secretion in response to intravenous glucose in GDM.[8] Insulin response to mixed meals also is heterogeneous in markedly obese patients with GDM. Severe insulin resistance is characteristic of late normal pregnancy, and several reports indicated that on average, subjects with GDM are even more resistant.[8,9,103] In some studies, the issue is confounded by differences in age and weight and potentially by the effects that even mild fasting hyperglycemia may exert on insulin sensitivity.

*Genotypic Heterogeneity*

Such heterogeneity has been suggested in GDM from finding an increased frequency of human leukocyte antigen (HLA) haplotypes (see Ref. 4 for a review) that are associated with risk of type 1 DM in comparison to the haplotypes of racially matched controls. The prevalence of glutamic acid decarboxylase (GAD) or islet cell antibodies in women with GDM varies with the methods used and populations studied.[4,104,105] Together, the reports suggest a higher prevalence of islet cell antibodies in white women with GDM and elevated FPG at diagnosis. Genotypic heterogeneity also is postulated from studies that found HLA-DQβ restriction endonuclease fragments or HLA antigens DR3 and DR4 present with increased frequency in pregnant women with GDM.[106,107] In another report, an excess of restriction fragment length polymorphisms in regions flanking the insulin receptor were found to be significantly associated with GDM risk in blacks and non-Hispanic whites.[108] These and other findings suggest that the population with GDM may include some patients with slowly evolving type 1 DM. A retrospective review from Copenhagen concurred and noted that a higher than expected number of women with type 1 DM had the onset during pregnancy.[109]

Racial and ethnic group differences in the prevalence of GDM have been observed that are not fully accounted for by differences in maternal age or obesity.[110,111] However, specific genetic or environmental factors mediating predisposition to GDM remain to be defined. DM associated with mutations of mitochondrial DNA[112,113] may be initially discovered as GDM. Maturity-onset diabetes of the young (MODY), another uncommon and atypical form of type 2 DM, also can be manifested as GDM.[114] To date, specific diabetic genetic factors have been demonstrated in only a small fraction of women with GDM. However, detailed, systematic genetic studies looking for associations in large populations of women with GDM have not been completed.

## TREATMENT OF DIABETES MELLITUS DIAGNOSED BEFORE PREGNANCY

The ultimate goal for pregnancies complicated by diabetes is the delivery of a healthy baby at term. Complications for the mother or baby may arise from medical, obstetric, or neonatal factors. To encourage optimal attainment of this goal, we continue to advocate management based on a team approach that includes an internist/diabetologist, obstetrician/perinatologist, pediatrician/neonatologist, nurse-educator, dietitian, and where needed, social worker, especially for cases with maternal complications. Women whose diabetes is not in good control undergo intensive management from these outpatient teams. From the time of initial presentation onward, this entails (1) control of diabetes established as rapidly as possible; (2) ophthalmologic examination, tests of renal function, and cardiovascular evaluation (when appropriate); (3) educational reinforcement (diet, blood glucose monitoring, administration of insulin, etc.); and (4) addressing

medical, psychosocial, financial, and other implications of diabetes in pregnancy. Women with GDM who require insulin are managed like those with preexisting DM.

### PRECONCEPTION PLANNING

Education about the special issues related to pregnancy (impact of diabetic complications, metabolic control and adverse pregnancy outcome, family planning, contraception) should begin when young women with diabetes achieve fertility. At the preconception visit, assessment includes determination of vascular complications, measurement of hemoglobin $A_{1c}$, 24-hour creatinine clearance, quantitative urinary protein, and thyroid-stimulating hormone (TSH). Before gestation, prescribed medications such as angiotensin-converting enzyme (ACE) inhibitors, angiotension receptor blockers (ARBs), thiazolidinediones, and 3-hydroxy-3-methylglutaryl coenzyme A (HMG-CoA) reductase inhibitors should be discontinued, substituting other appropriate medications, such as antihypertensive agents where needed. Supplemental intake of folic acid, 0.8 mg daily, is now routinely recommended to reduce risks for neural tube defects, although the potential benefit in diabetes has not been demonstrated. Lifestyle factors such as smoking and alcohol use should be addressed. Pregnancy should not be discouraged on genetic grounds. Long-term follow-up of the offspring of persons with type 1 DM indicated a prevalence of type 1 DM of 1.3% in the offspring of diabetic mothers and in 6.1% in the offspring of diabetic fathers.[115] Short- and long-term consequences of inadequately controlled maternal diabetes for the offspring should be reviewed. The potential impact of pregnancy on maternal diabetes complications and the time commitment needed to attain optimal control before conception and throughout gestation should be discussed.

As indicated in the discussion of Congenital Malformations and Early Fetal Loss, clinical and experimental evidence indicates that the risks of these events in diabetic pregnancies are linked to disturbances in maternal metabolism around the time of conception.[6,38] Furthermore, control of maternal diabetes during the period of organogenesis may reduce the prevalence of these adverse outcomes.[38] This possibility makes a compelling case for establishing "tight" control of diabetes before conception.

The preceding considerations have led us to advise prospective mothers to attain stable, near-normal glycemic control before pregnancy and during the period of organogenesis. Striving for complete normalization may lead to frequent hypoglycemia in some women, which we attempt to minimize. For patients with more than minimal retinopathy who are in poor control, we recommend slow but steady correction of hyperglycemia over a period of several months before conception, in the hope of preventing deterioration in retinal status. Patients are reassured that with careful adherence to medical and obstetric treatment plans, the chances of a favorable outcome are excellent for both the mother and baby. Unfortunately, in the United States, most women with known preexisting DM still fail to begin intensive management of diabetes before their pregnancy,[43] despite extensive professional and patient educational efforts for more than a decade.

### Diet

Diabetes does not alter the broad dietary recommendations for pregnancy, except that complex carbohydrates should be substituted for "free" sugars. Because of the heightened propensity to accelerated starvation, carbohydrate is not restricted to less than 180 to 200 g/day (unless systematic monitoring for ketonuria is performed), and intake should be distributed during the day to avoid periods of fasting in excess of 5 to 6 hours. The proportion of the daily diet given at specific times can be individualized (within the preceding constraints) according to patient preference and also may be manipulated to stabilize metabolic control. Patients who have stabilized other aspects of their treatment regimen and have demonstrated a capacity to manipulate their diet further on a personal basis can often use "carbohydrate counting" effectively to achieve optimal control while maintaining greater flexibility in their lifestyle. However, day-to-day consistency is helpful to attain optimal control and rapidly recognize the changing insulin needs as pregnancy proceeds.

Dietary prescriptions are individualized and, if necessary, modified over the course of gestation. Although they were developed for the general population, we apply the Institute of Medicine of the National Academy of Sciences guidelines concerning optimal weight gain during gestation[116] to patients with DM. It is recommended that weight gain be proportional to the degree of adiposity (based on body mass index [BMI; weight/height$^2$]) in the mother before conception. This may range from as little as a 15-lb (7-kg) gain in the very obese to as much as 40 lb (18 kg) for underweight women. Downward estimates also have been made in the caloric cost of singleton pregnancy: from an extra 250 to 280 kcal/day (1050 to 1180 kJ/day) to an extra 100 to 150 kcal/day (420 to 630 kJ/day) in the second and third trimesters.[117]

If weight has been stable, we continue the calorie content of the prepregnancy diet for early gestation or prescribe 32 kcal/kg ideal body weight (IBW) (135 kJ/kg). This amount is advanced to 35 to 38 kcal/kg IBW (145 to 160 kJ/kg) at 14 to 16 weeks' gestation, depending on appetite and the early pattern of weight gain. Variations of up to 25% to 30% in total calories may be necessary to attain optimal weight gain as described earlier. Advice concerning the macronutrient content varies considerably. The diets used in the Northwestern Diabetes in Pregnancy Program are constituted as 45% carbohydrate, 18% protein, and 37% fat. Some advocate large amounts of protein (1.5 to 2.0 g/kg IBW) and carbohydrate (50% to 55%), with fat amounting to less than 30% of the total calories. Other centers restrict total carbohydrate intake to facilitate control of postprandial glycemia. In such cases, a reciprocal increase in fat intake takes place. This increase in fat intake during gestation is associated with adverse effects on rodent offspring vascular responsiveness to acetylcholine.[118] A pressing need exists for research on the perinatal and long-term consequences of alterations in dietary composition in pregnancy in normal-weight and in obese human subjects, as well as in pregnancy complicated by DM.

## Insulin

Optimal therapy necessitates individualization. Basal insulin is administered in the form of NPH, given 1 to 3 times daily, with regular insulin or rapid-acting analogues (lispro, aspart) given before meals. An insufficient number of reports are available on the use of insulin glargine, a relatively peakless basal insulin of longer duration, during pregnancy to formulate an assessment of risks related to its use. In nonpregnant patients, the use of glargine, rather than NPH, has reduced the frequency of overnight and between-meal hypoglycemia. After subcutaneous injection, profiles of insulin analogues more closely mimic those of secreted insulin in normal subjects and are preferred for avoiding postprandial hyperglycemia and later hypoglycemia. Concerns that the use of insulin lispro may cause progression of diabetic retinopathy were raised in anecdotal reports but not confirmed in larger studies.[119] In some cases, lispro or aspart insulin must be supplemented with regular insulin to prevent hyperglycemia before the next meal because of the short duration of the insulin analogue.

For women with type 1 DM, multiple-dose regimens are optimal. The short-acting insulin dose varies depending on the blood glucose values measured postprandially and just before injection. Patients use individually tailored algorithms that are revised periodically. More frequent injections permit greater flexibility in responding to the capricious fluctuations in blood glucose concentration that occur in some women.

Patients who are successfully using infusion pumps (continuous subcutaneous insulin infusion [CSII]) at the time of referral continue such therapy. Insulin-pump initiation requires a steep learning curve, and we rarely initiate its use in pregnancy unless the patient is strongly motivated.

Patients with type 2 DM who retain some endogenous insulin can often be managed with a combination of short-acting (regular, lispro, or aspart insulin) and intermediate-acting (NPH) insulin administered before breakfast and supper ("mixed/split" regimen). Blood glucose levels are usually quite stable, provided that no dietary lapses occur, and dosages are altered every 1 to 2 weeks after review of capillary blood sugar values measured by the patient.

Our goal is premeal capillary blood glucose levels of 65 to 85 mg/dL (3.6 to 4.7 mmol/L) and 1- and 2-hour postprandial levels lower than 130 to 140 mg/dL (7.2 to 7.8 mmol/L) and 110 to 120 mg/dL (6.1 to 6.7 mmol/L), respectively, throughout gestation. In some cases, glycemic goals cannot be achieved consistently without recurrent severe hypoglycemia, which does pose potentially serious hazards for the mother. In such cases, normoglycemia should not be relentlessly pursued. In contrast to findings in experimental animal and in vitro models of adverse effects of hypoglycemia on the embryo in early pregnancy,[47] maternal hypoglycemia during the latter two thirds of pregnancy does not appear to be harmful to the fetus.[120]

During the first trimester, aggressive efforts to achieve tight control in those with suboptimal control before gestation may contribute to a risk for significant hypoglycemia. This can be compounded by "morning sickness" and erratic caloric intake, leading to both hyperglycemia and hypoglycemia. Patients previously in good, stable control may experience some decrease in insulin requirement late in the first trimester, followed by a twofold to threefold increase by the middle of the third trimester. The greatest rate of change typically occurs between 20 and 30 weeks of gestation (see Fig. 186-1). Dosing requirements are relatively stable in weeks 32 to 38, with only modest changes required from week to week. Some decline in nocturnal insulin dosing is commonly noted in the 1 to 2 weeks before delivery. The challenge of therapy is to modify the insulin dosage in a timely fashion in parallel with these fluctuations in insulin sensitivity while maintaining optimal glycemic control.

## Exercise

Patients who engage in moderate regular physical exercise are not discouraged from continuing it during pregnancy, provided that they have no obstetric contraindications. Periods of exercise, however, must be integrated into the diabetes treatment regimen to minimize disruptions in blood sugar control, particularly hypoglycemia.

## MONITORING CONTROL OF DIABETES

### Blood Glucose

We recommend self-monitoring of capillary blood glucose levels by all women treated with insulin during pregnancy. A certified diabetes educator gives initial instruction, with follow-up at each clinic visit (every 1 to 2 weeks). There, patients are observed while measuring capillary blood sugar when venous blood is drawn for plasma glucose measurements in the laboratory. The results provide verification of monitoring skills and proper functioning of the monitoring equipment. Blood sugar is measured before each meal and at bedtime, and at least twice weekly, all patients also obtain values 1 or 2 hours after each meal. Measurement of postprandial levels is necessary to determine the appropriate diet or dose of insulin lispro and may more accurately reflect fuel delivery to the fetus than measuring only fasting values.[121] The level of blood glucose before a meal is of utility in selecting doses of regular and intermediate-acting insulin for the next interval.

When postprandial hyperglycemia persists despite normalization of premeal blood glucose, adjustments in analogue insulin, meal size, frequency of feedings, or a combination of these may be of benefit. Monitoring urine glucose is unnecessary.

## Ketones

Measurement of blood (β-hydroxybutyrate) or urine (acetone) ketones is useful to detect inadequate dietary intake, particularly of carbohydrates, and to provide warning of impending metabolic decompensation. Accordingly, patients are asked to monitor blood or urine ketones in the first morning specimen each day, during periods of acute illness, and when premeal capillary blood sugar values exceed 200 to 250 mg/dL (11.1 to 13.9 mmol/L). Urine ketone values that are "Moderate" or "Large" or blood concentrations greater than 0.4 to 0.5 mmol/L must be addressed by a call to a caregiver, unless the finding is transient.

## Hemoglobin A$_{1c}$

Measurements of hemoglobin A$_{1c}$ are obtained at enrollment and at 4- to 8-week intervals until term. As noted earlier, values in the first or early second trimester provide a general indication of the risk of fetal loss and major congenital malformations[38] and help guide decisions about management. Serial assessments provide affirmation for patients that their efforts to achieve better control of diabetes are effective. A disparity between hemoglobin A$_{1c}$ concentrations and blood glucose measurements may signal errors in glucose-monitoring technique or, rarely, falsification of results. Other factors (hemolysis, hemoglobinopathies, variations in analytic technique) can alter the values of hemoglobin A$_{1c}$ appreciably and render such measurements of limited value. In such cases, serial measurements of fructosamine or glycosylated albumin may provide analogous information.

### OBSTETRIC SURVEILLANCE

The goals of obstetric management are to permit pregnancy to be carried to term and to accomplish vaginal delivery unless maternal or fetal health becomes compromised. Ultrasonography is the primary tool used to (1) document viability and confirm gestational age in early pregnancy (6 to 12 weeks), (2) detect malformations, and (3) monitor fetal growth, particularly in the third trimester. Ultrasound examinations are usually performed in the first trimester, at 18 to 20 weeks' gestation (alternatives for management can be considered if severe congenital anomalies are found), and every 3 to 4 weeks in the third trimester for fetal growth assessment.[122] The incidence of neural tube defects is greatly increased in pregnancies complicated by poorly controlled diabetes. The extent to which folic acid supplementation can reduce the risk in fetuses of women with diabetes is unknown. Accordingly, even those who have received folic acid supplementation before conception should be offered maternal serum α-fetoprotein testing at 15 to 20 weeks' gestation. This test may detect 80% to 90% of open neural tube defects and increase the detection of other anomalies including gastroschisis, renal agenesis, Down syndrome, and trisomy 18.

Reassurance of fetal well-being by noninvasive monitoring techniques permits most pregnancies to be carried to term. The biophysical test most commonly used is the nonstress test (NST). Two or more accelerations of fetal heart rate in response to spontaneous fetal activity in 20 minutes of continuous fetal heart monitoring is predictive of fetal well-being. If the NST is nonreactive, further evaluation is undertaken with a biophysical profile. Some use the biophysical profile as the primary mode of fetal surveillance. Modeled after the Apgar score, the biophysical profile assesses five parameters (NST plus fetal activity, fetal breathing activity,

fetal tone, and the volume of amniotic fluid determined by fetal observation with ultrasound). Serial fetal testing may be initiated as soon as the fetus is viable in a highly complicated pregnancy but no later than 32 weeks, even in a pregnancy progressing normally.[122]

Surveillance for pregnancy complications occurs at each prenatal visit on a weekly basis from week 32. Preeclampsia, with an abrupt increase in blood pressure and proteinuria greater than 300 mg in 24 hours, is increased in women with diabetes, particularly if they have evidence of vasculopathy. The diagnosis is more difficult to make in women with nephropathy. Hospitalization is required for close supervision, with immediate delivery at or near term. Amniocentesis to confirm fetal pulmonary maturity is performed only if preterm delivery is anticipated.[122]

### DELIVERY AND PUERPERIUM

During spontaneous or induced labor, the objectives of medical management are to maintain plasma glucose in the physiologic range (70 to 120 mg/dL [3.9 to 6.7 mmol/L]) and to prevent ketosis. Intravenous glucose is administered at 5 to 10 g/hour by a constant-infusion pump. Other intravenous fluids are devoid of glucose. Capillary blood sugar is measured every 1 to 4 hours. The glucose infusion may be delayed by 1 to 2 hours when hyperglycemia is present at entry, and insulin administration may be withheld temporarily if the blood glucose level is less than 70 mg/dL (3.9 mmol/L). Patients with type 1 diabetes are treated with small doses of short-acting subcutaneous insulin (lispro, aspart, or regular) every 3 to 6 hours,[123] or by continuous intravenous infusion of regular insulin at rates of 0.02 to 0.04 U/hr/kg of body weight (1.4 to 2.8 U/hr in a 70-kg woman), or by CSII in patients with an insulin pump. Those with type 2 diabetes often do not require insulin with this regimen. Optimal maternal glucose control in the third trimester reduces the risk for neonatal hypoglycemia when cord glucose is elevated at delivery.

Elective cesarean deliveries, performed for standard obstetric indications, are scheduled early in the morning when possible. If so, neither insulin nor glucose is administered if the blood sugar level before the procedure is between 70 and 140 mg/dL (3.9 to 7.8 mmol/L). Glucose, insulin, or both are given when blood sugar levels are outside this range or the procedure is delayed substantially.

Insulin requirements usually decline dramatically immediately after delivery (often by 50% to 90%; see Fig. 186-1). After several days, insulin requirements usually return to levels similar to those present before pregnancy. Women who wish to breast-feed are maintained at or above their antepartum caloric intake. Because of the potential for oral agents to be secreted in breast milk and cause hypoglycemia in the infant, they are not prescribed for patients with type 2 diabetes if they wish to breast-feed. Those who do not breast-feed are returned immediately to a diet appropriate for nongravid women (30 to 32 kcal/kg IBW [125 to 135 kJ/kg]). All patients are encouraged to use the diabetes management skills they acquired during gestation.

## TREATMENT OF GESTATIONAL DIABETES MELLITUS

### RATIONALE FOR TREATMENT: ASSOCIATED RISKS

#### Morbidities

The risks of perinatal loss and neonatal morbidity are increased when GDM is undetected or treated casually.[124] In many centers, however, women with GDM receive dietary advice, some form of blood sugar monitoring, and treatment with insulin if hyperglycemia persists.[69,98] Moreover, pregnancies complicated by GDM are designated "high risk," which leads to more-intensive obstetric supervision, itself a form of intervention.[69] With such approaches, little if any increase in perinatal loss occurs in GDM, and the frequency of neonatal morbidity (such as hypoglycemia, hypocalcemia, polycythemia, and hyperbilirubinemia) may decrease toward levels found in the general population.[125]

### Congenital Malformations

The risk of congenital anomalies is not increased in most pregnancies with GDM.[126] However, it is now clear that women with GDM who have a degree of fasting hyperglycemia that is diagnostic of DM also have an increased risk of birth defects that is proportional to the severity of their hyperglycemia. This conclusion is supported by studies carried out in the Latino population of Los Angeles, where the prevalence of both GDM and type 2 DM is high.[127] In reality, many of the women with diagnostically elevated FPG probably have had previously undiagnosed DM before pregnancy; however, it is being identified for the first time during pregnancy as GDM. Thus, identifying pregnancies at risk and achieving better care before conception remain major challenges.

### Fetal Hyperinsulinism

Offspring of mothers with GDM remain at risk for fetal hyperinsulinemia, consequent increased fetal adiposity, and often excess fetal size (macrosomia), which increases the likelihood of birth trauma and operative delivery.[69,125] In addition, many studies indicate that the maternal metabolic abnormalities seen in gestational and preexisting diabetes have long-term consequences on weight, pancreatic function, and neurologic development of the offspring (see Anthropometric and Metabolic Development).

### DIET

The objectives of dietary management and the approaches used for GDM are the same as already discussed for normal pregnancy and preexisting DM. Adjustments are made to the initial prescription (35 to 38 kcal/kg IBW [145 to 160 kJ/kg]) as needed to maintain weight gain within the range appropriate for the subject's prepregnancy weight.[116] Several "isocaloric" modifications of the standard diet have been investigated. A reduction in carbohydrate content to 30% to 40% has caused less postprandial hyperglycemia[128] but is associated with an increased fat or protein content or both. The effects on maternal amino acid, ketone, and lipid levels and on long-term outcomes for the offspring are not known. When the daily dietary intake is ingested as multiple small meals (six or seven), postprandial glycemic peaks are reduced.[129] However, fasting levels may not be achieved before the next meal, and mean 24-hour glucose may not differ from the standard approach (three meals plus bedtime snack). Safety, efficacy, and long-term outcomes need further study.

### Hypocaloric Diet

Because caloric restriction in obese nonpregnant subjects with type 2 DM can reduce insulin resistance and correct hyperglycemia, use of a hypocaloric diet in obese women with GDM is appealing. Moderate caloric restriction (25% to 35% below standard diets) results in some correction of hyperglycemia.[130–132] Monitoring plasma β-hydroxybutyrate would be critical to determine fetal safety of this therapy. Some,[132] but not all,[131] groups have noted a reduction in fetal weight in these subjects; however, larger numbers in controlled trials are needed to evaluate immediate and long-term safety and the efficacy of this approach. Knopp and associates[130] also examined metabolic responses to a more severe (50%) reduction in caloric intake in obese women with GDM. Mean 24-hour glucose, fasting insulin, and triglyceride levels declined

substantially; however, plasma β-hydroxybutyrate concentrations increased more than twofold, and ketonuria increased substantially. Until more data are available on the effects of such treatment on perinatal and long-term outcomes, caloric restriction of this magnitude should be considered experimental.

### EXERCISE

Although concern has been expressed about increasing uterine contractility, IUGR, prematurity, fetal bradycardia, and ketonuria in association with exercise, physically active, well-conditioned women have routinely engaged in exercise during pregnancy without apparent adversity. Moreover, cardiovascular fitness training outside of pregnancy is known to increase insulin sensitivity and glucose disposal by recruitment of glucose transporter proteins, thus making exercise an attractive therapeutic possibility in GDM.[133] Studies using arm ergometry[134] or a recumbent bicycle[135] found moderate exercise to be safe and effective in reducing fasting and postprandial blood glucose levels in women with GDM. Others failed to see better glycemic control with the use of moderate exercise.[136] Further studies of exercise programs in GDM are in progress.

### INSULIN

The precise place for insulin therapy in GDM remains difficult to define.[69] It is generally agreed that a woman with overt hyperglycemia diagnostic of DM (FPG ≥ 126 mg/dL [7.0 mmol/L]) should start insulin immediately because the perinatal risks are like those for patients with preexisting diabetes. However, the risk of perinatal loss does not appear to be appreciably increased in the majority with GDM given the excellent obstetric care presently available. Primary emphasis is now focused on preventing perinatal morbidity and potential adverse long-term sequelae. Prevention of macrosomia and the morbidity associated with it has received the greatest attention.

When insulin is used, 0.5 to 1.4 U/kg of body weight per day is required to maintain fasting and premeal glucose concentrations between 65 and 90 mg/dL (3.6 to 5.0 mmol/L) and 1- or 2-hour postprandial values of less than 130 to 140 mg/dL (7.2 to 7.8 mmol/L) or 110 to 120 mg/dL (6.1 to 6.7 mmol/L), respectively. A "mixed/split" insulin regimen is generally used, although multiple injections may provide greater flexibility in management.[137]

### Glycemic Guidelines for Initiating Therapy

When FPG > 105 mg/dL (5.8 mmol/L) on two successive determinations after a brief trial of diet, insulin therapy is initiated. Insulin administration when FPG ranges 95 to 104 mg/dL (5.3 to 5.7 mmol/L) is more controversial. Although no data from controlled trials have identified ideal glycemic targets for the prevention of fetal risk, evidence presented at the Fourth International Workshop Conference on GDM suggests that reducing maternal capillary blood glucose concentrations to 130 to 140 mg/dL or less (7.2 to 7.8 mmol/L) at 1 hour, or 110 to 120 mg/dL or less (6.1 to 6.7 mmol/L) 2 hours after meals, or both, may reduce the risk of excessive fetal growth.[69] However, even when these thresholds are exceeded after dietary or exercise therapies are initiated, only a minority of infants will incur an excess of perinatal morbidity. Operationally, the challenge is to identify pregnancies in which therapy with insulin can reduce the risk. Such distinction is important because treatment with insulin is labor intensive, thus potentially increasing the cost of management substantially. Defining the metabolic threshold for initiation of insulin treatment and the therapeutic goals solely by blood glucose values also is potentially problematic because other maternal nutrients in addition to glucose likely affect fetal growth.[32,37,55,56]

Recent studies examining blood sugars in normal pregnant women have found glucose levels lower than previously expected,[32] with mean glucose levels of 78.3 mg/dL at 38 weeks and mean postprandial glucose levels never exceeding 105.2 mg/dL at 1 or 2 hours.[138] Even in these nondiabetic women, the postprandial glucose measurements correlated with fetal abdominal circumference. However, centers that have attempted more stringent control have suggested that the risk of small-for-gestational age (SGA) neonates may be increased.[139]

## Other Criteria for Initiating Therapy

Various approaches have been used to identify pregnancies at highest risk for fetal hyperinsulinemia or overgrowth or both and to serve as criteria for insulin treatment. Weiss and coworkers[51] use elevated amniotic fluid insulin levels (which reflect fetal hyperinsulinemia) to determine the need for insulin therapy and have reported good fetal outcomes in uncontrolled trials. Fetal ultrasound to measure shoulder soft tissue[51] or abdominal circumference[53,140] has been used to stratify the risk for macrosomia. Those with abdominal circumference less than the 75th percentile were not at increased risk. Those with abdominal circumference at the 75th percentile or higher were considered at risk, and intensive insulin therapy in these patients eliminated that risk. The long-term outcomes associated with the application of these methods must be evaluated further because risk of obesity and glucose intolerance in the offspring is not dependent on the presence of macrosomia at birth.[63] The hypothesis that a relatively low hemoglobin $A_{1c}$ concentration can identify a subgroup of patients who may be treated by diet therapy alone with no excess risk of fetal complications also warrants further investigation.[141]

## ORAL MEDICATIONS

Sulfonylureas are not presently approved for use in pregnant women in the United States. They have the capacity to stimulate fetal insulin secretion directly should they cross the placenta. It has been reported that glyburide passively transfers across the term placenta to 1% to 2% of maternal concentrations,[142] and in a clinical trial was as efficacious as insulin in regulating glycemia, while resulting in lower rates of maternal hypoglycemia. Neonatal outcomes of macrosomia, neonatal hypoglycemia, and cord serum insulin concentration were comparable to those for insulin-treated pregnancies.[143] The extent of this small transplacental transfer on long-term outcome in offspring has yet to be determined, and more studies are required before glyburide should be generally considered as an alternative therapy for GDM.

Metformin is frequently used to enhance fertility in patients with polycystic ovary syndrome (PCOS). Some have advocated its continuation through the first trimester in hope of reducing the risk of miscarriage and GDM.[144] However, metformin crosses the placenta, and controlled clinical trials of metformin during pregnancy in women with PCOS have not been performed. Metformin therapy has been used later in pregnancy in South Africa for years,[145] but detailed, controlled studies were not performed. However, in a single study of a cohort of women with GDM or type 2 DM treated with metformin, sulfonylureas, or insulin during the third trimester, the metformin group demonstrated a higher prevalence of preeclampsia and perinatal mortality.[146]

Safety of thiazolidinedione or α-glucosidase therapy in pregnancy has not been examined.

## METABOLIC SURVEILLANCE

All patients with GDM are asked to monitor blood or urinary ketones before breakfast and dinner to detect possible deficiencies in dietary carbohydrate. Fasting and 1-hour postprandial plasma glucose measurements are obtained at outpatient visits to monitor for deteriorating glucose tolerance requiring treatment with insulin and to assess the accuracy of glucose self-monitoring, if performed. All insulin-treated patients monitor fasting and premeal capillary blood glucose levels to guide adjustment of insulin doses and include measurements of 1- or 2-hour postprandial glucose concentrations at least twice weekly. Debate exists regarding use of postmeal versus premeal glucose levels to determine insulin doses.[147] Participants in the Fourth International Workshop Conference on GDM concluded that glucose self-monitoring appears to be superior to glucose monitoring performed only at clinic visits for the detection of glucose concentrations that may warrant intensification of therapy beyond standard dietary management,[69] but they stopped short of recommending its use by all women with GDM. We recommend its use in subjects who may gain an incentive to achieve better adherence to diet and lifestyle recommendations.

## DELIVERY AND PUERPERIUM

Therapeutic goals for the management of gestational diabetes during labor and delivery are the same as those outlined previously for women with preexisting DM. Insulin therapy is rarely required to maintain intrapartum normoglycemia in women with GDM. The vast majority of patients requiring antepartum insulin therapy can discontinue it at delivery.

## Postpartum Follow-Up

At the time of diagnosis of GDM, one cannot reliably distinguish between evolving type 1 or type 2 DM and glucose intolerance that will subside in the postpartum period. Thus, reclassification and long-term follow-up after pregnancy are essential. Early reports of O'Sullivan[2,148] and subsequent studies[149–153] established that GDM identifies women at high risk for the later development of DM. Postpartum studies demonstrated that women with previous GDM continue to have insulin resistance and impaired insulin secretion.[154] In some of these subjects, abnormalities of glucose tolerance antedate the index pregnancy, but they cannot be identified retrospectively.[155]

Certain features that can be identified during the index pregnancy or at early postpartum testing can detect those at high risk to progress to DM after pregnancy.[148–153] These features include the severity of glucose intolerance at diagnosis, early gestational age at diagnosis, obesity, relative insulinopenia, family history of maternal diabetes, and racial/ethnic origin. In long-term follow-up, with multiple logistic regression, it was found that the severity of antepartum hyperglycemia (fasting and 2-hour values) and relative insulinopenia (lower basal insulin levels and blunted acute-phase insulin response to oral glucose) are independently associated with the presence of DM in the early postpartum period. Obesity and blunted integrated insulin response were independent variables in those in whom DM subsequently developed up to 5 years after the diagnosis of GDM.[149,153] The other prognostic factors are probably mediated through one or more of the independent factors noted earlier. Women identified with GDM based on the Carpenter-Coustan criteria also are at higher risk for postpartum development of DM.[156] A subsequent pregnancy also increases the risk of conversion to DM in women with a history of GDM.[157]

The high incidence of abnormal postpartum glucose tolerance in women with GDM makes a compelling case for early and continuing follow-up. The algorithm for postpartum surveillance that was recommended by the Fourth International Workshop Conference on GDM is outlined in Table 186-1.[69] Patient education concerning the risk of development of DM and its complications is paramount. Those with persistent glucose intolerance or DM should receive appropriate counseling and therapy. Individuals with normal postpartum OGTT need annual fasting or postload glucose testing and should be aware that glucose intolerance may recur before or during any future pregnancy. Excellent intervention trials from Finland[158] and the United States[159,160] were successful in preventing or delaying the onset of DM in high-risk subjects, including women with previous GDM using lifestyle intervention or medication (metformin or troglitazone). Features of the metabolic syndrome including hypertension, elevated triglycerides, and low high-density lipoprotein cholesterol (HDL-C) are frequently found in women with a history of GDM.[161,162] This is particularly prevalent in GDM with preeclampsia.[163] Circulating concentrations of asymmetrical dimethyl-L-arginine (ADMA), an endogenous inhibitor of nitric oxide synthase, are increased in individuals at risk for cardiovascular disease and are found at higher levels in women with a history of GDM.[164] Abnormal endothelial relaxation to acetylcholine also has been demonstrated in women with a history of GDM.[165,166] In light of these risks and the potential benefits that may accrue, it is prudent to advise patients to maintain IBW and exercise regularly. Further studies in this population will be important in defining the pathogenesis of type 2 DM and strategies to prevent or delay its development.

### Contraception

The importance of good preconception care should be reinforced in the postpartum period. Contraception choices include intrauterine devices, low-dose combination oral contraceptive or transdermal delivery systems, and progestin-only depot preparations. Barrier methods have a failure rate of 5% per year. If possible, avoid the use of high-dose synthetic estrogen/progestin oral contraceptives and progestin-only oral contraceptives, as they may exacerbate insulin resistance.

## CONCLUSIONS

The extensive experimental and clinical evidence summarized in this chapter indicates that metabolic disturbances in the mother mediate or contribute to virtually all the adverse effects of DM on the offspring. As Freinkel[6] proposed, the stage(s) of pregnancy during which a metabolic insult occurs determines the kind of adverse outcome for which the pregnancy is at risk ("fuel-mediated teratogenesis"). Furthermore, it is clear that the potential adverse consequences of the altered intrauterine environment of diabetes are not confined to the perinatal period. For example, the predisposition to obesity and altered glucoregulation can have life-long implications. It is anticipated that optimal metabolic control beginning before conception and continuing throughout gestation can minimize the risk of an adverse outcome in the offspring, both perinatally and in the long term.

## REFERENCES

1. Gabbe SG, Graves CR: Management of diabetes mellitus complicating pregnancy. Obstet Gynecol 102:857–868, 2003.
2. O'Sullivan JB, Mahan CM: Criteria for the oral glucose tolerance test in pregnancy. Diabetes 13:278–285, 1964.
3. Connell FA, Vadheim C, Emanuel I: Diabetes in pregnancy: A population based study of incidence, referral for care and perinatal mortality. Am J Obstet Gynecol 151:598–603, 1985.
4. Metzger BE, Cho NH, Brickman WJ: The rising tide of diabetes mellitus: Implications for women of all ages. In Reece EA, Coustan DR, Gabbe SG (eds): Diabetes in Women, 3d ed. Philadelphia, Lippincott Williams & Wilkins, 2004, pp 9–26.
5. Ferrara A, Kahn HS, Quesenberry CP, et al: An increase in the incidence of gestational diabetes mellitus: Northern California, 1991-2000. Obstet Gynecol 103:526–533, 2004.
6. Freinkel N: The Banting Lecture 1980: Of pregnancy and progeny. Diabetes 29:1023–1035, 1980.
7. Catalano PM, Tyzbir ED, Wolfe RR, et al: Carbohydrate metabolism during pregnancy in control subjects and women with gestational diabetes. Am J Physiol 264:E60–E67, 1993.
8. Buchanan TA, Metzger BE, Freinkel N, Bergman RN: Insulin sensitivity and β-cell responsiveness to glucose during late pregnancy in lean and moderately obese women with normal glucose tolerance or mild gestational diabetes. Am J Obstet Gynecol 162:1008–1014, 1990.
9. Catalano PM, Tyzbir ED, Roman NM, et al: Longitudinal changes in insulin release and insulin resistance in nonobese pregnant women. Am J Obstet Gynecol 165:1667–1672, 1991.
10. Catalano PM, Huston L, Amini SB, Kalhan SC: Longitudinal changes in glucose metabolism during pregnancy in obese women with normal glucose tolerance and gestational diabetes mellitus. Am J Obstet Gynecol 180:903–916, 1999.
11. Garvey WT, Maianu L, Hancock JA, et al: Gene expression of GLUT4 in skeletal muscle from insulin-resistant patients with obesity, IGT, GDM and NIDDM. Diabetes 41:465–475, 1992.
12. Okuno S, Mawda Y, Yamaguchi Y, et al: Expression of GLUT4 glucose transporter mRNA and protein in skeletal muscle and adipose tissue from rats in late pregnancy. Biochem Biophys Res Commun 191:405–412, 1993.
13. Shao J, Catalano PM, Yamashita H, et al: Decreased insulin receptor tyrosine kinase activity and plasma cell membrane glycoprotein-1 overexpression in skeletal muscle from obese women with gestational diabetes mellitus (GDM): Evidence for increased serine/threonine phosphorylation in pregnancy and GDM. Diabetes 49:603–610, 2000.
14. Posner BI: Insulin metabolizing enzyme activities in human placental tissue. Diabetes 22:552–563, 1973.
15. Catalano PM, Drago NM, Amini SB: Longitudinal changes in pancreatic β-cell function and metabolic clearance rate of insulin in pregnant women with normal and abnormal glucose tolerance. Diabetes Care 21:403–408, 1998.
16. Kalkhoff RK, Kissebah AH, Kim HJ: Carbohydrate and lipid metabolism during normal pregnancy: Relationship to gestational hormone action. Semin Perinatol 2:291–307, 1978.
17. Eriksson L, Frankenne F, Eden S, et al: Growth hormone 24-h serum profiles during pregnancy: Lack of pulsatility for the secretion of the placental variant. Br J Obstet Gynaecol 96:949–953, 1989.
18. Nolten WE, Lindheimer MD, Rueckert PA, et al: Diurnal patterns and regulation of cortisol secretion in pregnancy. J Clin Endocrinol Metab 51:466–472, 1980.
19. Kirwan JP, Hauguel-DeMouzon S, Challier JC, et al: TNF-alpha is a predictor of insulin-resistance in human pregnancy. Diabetes 51:2207–2213, 2002.
20. Highman TJ, Friedman JE, Huston LP, et al: Longitudinal changes in maternal serum leptin concentrations, body composition, and resting metabolic rate in pregnancy. Am J Obstet Gynecol 178:1010–1015, 1998.
21. Page EW: Human fetal nutrition and growth. Am J Obstet Gynecol 104:378–387, 1969.
22. Young M: Placental transfer of glucose and amino acids. In Camerini-Davalos RA, Cole HS (eds): Early Diabetes in Early Life. New York, Academic Press, 1975, pp 237–242.
23. Shambaugh GE III, Mrozak SC, Freinkel N: Fetal fuels. I. Utilization of ketones by isolated tissues at various stages of maturation and maternal nutrition during late gestation. Metabolism 26:623–636, 1977.
24. Shambaugh GE III, Angulo MC, Koehler RR: Fetal fuels. VII. Ketone bodies inhibit the synthesis of purines in fetal rat brain. Am J Physiol 247:E111–E117, 1984.

25. Freinkel N, Cockroft DL, Lewis NJ, et al: The 1986 McCollum Award Lecture: Fuel-mediated teratogenesis during early organogenesis: The effects of increased concentrations of glucose, ketones, or somatomedin inhibitor during rat embryo culture. Am J Clin Nutr 44:986–995, 1986.

26. Berendes HW: Effect of maternal acetonuria on IQ of offspring. In Camerini-Davalos RA, Cole HS (eds): Early Diabetes in Early Life. New York, Academic Press, 1975, pp 135–140.

27. Rizzo T, Metzger BE, Burns WJ, Burns KC: Correlations between antepartum maternal metabolism and intelligence of offspring. N Engl J Med 325:911–916, 1991.

28. Mills JL, Jovanovic L, Knopp R, et al: Physiological reduction in fasting plasma glucose concentration in the first trimester of normal pregnancy: The Diabetes in Early Pregnancy Study. Metabolism 47:1140–1144, 1998.

29. Metzger BE, Ravnikar V, Vilesis R, et al: Accelerated starvation and the skipped breakfast in late normal pregnancy. Lancet 1:588–592, 1982.

30. Shoengold DM, DeFiore RH, Parlett RC: Free amino acids in plasma throughout pregnancy. Am J Obstet Gynecol 131:490–499, 1978.

31. Rushakoff RJ, Kalkhoff RK: Effects of pregnancy and sex steroid administration on skeletal muscle metabolism in the rat. Diabetes 30:545–550, 1981.

32. Metzger BE, Phelps RL, Freinkel N, et al: Effects of gestational diabetes on diurnal profiles of plasma glucose, lipids and individual amino acids. Diabetes Care 3:402–409, 1980.

33. Buchanan TA, Metzger BE, Freinkel N: Accelerated starvation in late pregnancy: A comparison between obese women with and without gestational diabetes mellitus. Am J Obstet Gynecol 162:1015–1020, 1990.

34. Hollingsworth DR, Grundy SM: Pregnancy-associated hypertriglyceridemia in normal and diabetic women: Differences in insulin-dependent and non-insulin dependent, and gestational diabetes. Diabetes 31:1092–1097, 1988.

35. Kalkhoff RK, Kandaraki E, Morrow PG, et al: Relationship between neonatal birth weight and maternal plasma amino acid profiles in lean and obese nondiabetic women and in type I diabetic women. Metabolism 37:234–239, 1988.

36. Pedersen J: The Pregnant Diabetic and Her Newborn: Problems and Management. Baltimore, Williams & Wilkins, 1977.

37. Freinkel N, Metzger BE: Pregnancy as a tissue culture experience: The critical implications of maternal metabolism for fetal development. In Elliot K, O'Connor M (eds): Pregnancy Metabolism, Diabetes and the Fetus. CIBA Foundation Symposium No. 63. Amsterdam, Exerpta Medica, 1979, pp 3–23.

38. Metzger BE, Buchanan TA (eds): From research to practice: Diabetes and birth defects: Insights from the 1980s, prevention in the 1990s. Diabetes Spectrum 3:150–184, 1990.

39. Mills JL, Simpson JL, Driscoll SG, et al: The NICHHD-Diabetes in Early Pregnancy Study: Incidence of spontaneous abortion among normal women and insulin-dependent diabetic women whose pregnancies were identified within 21 days of conception. N Engl J Med 319:1617–1623, 1988.

40. Greene MF, Hare JW, Cloherty JP, et al: First trimester hemoglobin A$_1$ and risk for major malformations and spontaneous abortion in diabetic pregnancy. Teratology 39:225–231, 1989.

41. Mills JL, Knopp RH, Simpson JL, et al: The NICHD Diabetes in Early Pregnancy Study: Lack of relation of increased malformation rates in infants of diabetic mothers to glycemic control during organogenesis. N Engl J Med 318:671–676, 1988.

42. Ray JG, O'Brien TE, Chan WS: Preconception care and the risk of congenital anomalies in the offspring of women with diabetes mellitus: A meta-analysis. Q J Med 94:435–444, 2001.

43. Herman WH, Janz NK, Becker MP, Charron-Prochownik D: Diabetes and pregnancy: Preconception care, pregnancy outcomes, resource utilization and costs. J Reprod Med 44:33–38, 1999.

44. Buchanan TA, Denno KM, Sipes GF, Sadler TW: Diabetic teratogenesis: In vitro evidence for a multifactorial etiology with little contribution from glucose per se. Diabetes 43:656–660, 1999.

45. Strieleman PJ, Connors MA, Metzger BE: Phosphoinositide metabolism in the developing conceptus: Effects of hyperglycemia and scyllo-inositol in rat embryo culture. Diabetes 41:989–997, 1992.

46. Eriksson UJ, Borg LAH: Diabetes and embryonic malformations: Role of substrate-induced free-oxygen radical production for dysmorphogenesis in cultured rat embryos. Diabetes 42:411–419, 1993.

47. Buchanan T, Schemmer JK, Freinkel N: Embryotoxic effects of brief maternal insulin-hypoglycemia during organogenesis in the rat. J Clin Invest 78:643–649, 1986.

48. Catalano PM, Thomas AJ, Huston LP, Fung CM: Effect of maternal metabolism on fetal growth and body composition. Diabetes Care 21(Suppl 2):B85–B90, 1998.

49. Elliot JP, Garite TJ, Freeman RK: Ultrasonic prediction of fetal macrosomia in diabetic patients. Obstet Gynecol 60:159–164, 1982.

50. Catalano PM, Thomas A, Huston-Presley L, Amini SB: Increased fetal adiposity: A very sensitive marker of abnormal in utero development. Am J Obstet Gynecol 189:1698–1704, 2003.

51. Landon MB, Sonek J, Foy P, et al: Sonographic measurement of fetal humeral soft tissue thickness in pregnancy complicated by GDM. Diabetes 40(Suppl 2):66–70, 1991.

52. Abramowicz JS, Sherer DM, Woods JR Jr: Ultrasonographic measurement of cheek-to-cheek diameter in fetal growth disturbances. Am J Obstet Gynecol 162:405–408, 1993.

53. Schaefer-Graf UM, Kjos SL, Fauzan OH, et al: A randomized trial evaluating a predominantly fetal growth-based strategy to guide management of gestational diabetes in Caucasian women. Diabetes Care 27:297–302, 2004.

54. Reiher H, Fuhrmann K, Noack S, et al: Age-dependent insulin secretion of the endocrine pancreas in vitro from fetuses of diabetic and nondiabetic patients. Diabetes Care 6:446–451, 1983.

55. Metzger BE: Biphasic effects of maternal metabolism on fetal growth: The quintessential expression of "fuel mediated teratogenesis." Diabetes 40(Suppl 2):99–105, 1991.

56. Susa JB, Neave C, Sehgal P, et al: Chronic hyperinsulinemia in the fetal rhesus monkey: Effects of physiologic hyperinsulinemia on fetal growth and composition. Diabetes 33:656–660, 1984.

57. Weiss PAM, Hofmann HM, Winter RR, et al: Diagnosis and treatment of gestational diabetes according to amniotic fluid insulin levels. Arch Gynecol 239:81–91, 1986.

58. Ogata ES, Freinkel N, Metzger BE, et al: Perinatal islet function in gestational diabetes: Assessment by cord plasma C-peptide and amniotic fluid insulin. Diabetes Care 3:425–429, 1980.

59. Verhaeghe J, Van Bree R, Van Herck E, et al: C-peptide, insulin-like growth factors I and II and insulin-like growth factor binding protein-1 in umbilical cord serum: Correlations with birth weight. Am J Obstet Gynecol 169:89–97, 1993.

60. Pedersen JL, Molsted-Pedersen L: Early fetal growth delay detected by ultrasound marks increased risk of congenital malformation in diabetic pregnancy. Br Med J 283:269–271, 1981.

61. Silverman BL, Purdy LP, Metzger BE: The intrauterine environment: Implications for the offspring of diabetic mothers. Diabetes Rev 4:21–35, 1996.

62. Pettitt DJ, Baird HR, Aleck KA, et al: Excessive obesity in offspring of Pima Indian women with diabetes during pregnancy. N Engl J Med 308:242–245, 1983.

63. Pettitt DJ, Knowler WC, Bennett PH, et al: Obesity in offspring of diabetic Pima Indian women despite normal birth weight. Diabetes Care 10:76–80, 1987.

64. Gerlini G, Arachi S, Gori MG, et al: Developmental aspects of the offspring of diabetic mothers. Acta Endocrinol

(Copenh) 112(Suppl 277):150–155, 1986.

65. Silverman BL, Rizzo T, Green OC, et al: Long-term prospective evaluation of offspring of diabetic mothers. Diabetes 40(Suppl 2):121–125, 1991.

66. Pettitt DJ, Aleck KA, Baird HR, et al: Congenital susceptibility for NIDDM: Role of intrauterine environment. Diabetes 37:622–628, 1988.

67. Silverman BL, Cho NH, Metzger BE: Impaired glucose tolerance in adolescent offspring of diabetic mothers: Relationship to fetal hyperinsulinism. Diabetes Care 18:611–618, 1995.

68. Kahn R, Expert Committee on the Diagnosis and Classification of Diabetes Mellitus: Report of the Expert Committee on the Diagnosis and Classification of Diabetes Mellitus. Diabetes Care 20:1183–1197, 1997.

69. Metzger BE, Coustan DR, Organizing Committee: Summary and recommendations of the Fourth International Workshop—Conference on Gestational Diabetes Mellitus. Diabetes Care 21(Suppl 2):B161–B167, 1998.

70. White P: Pregnancy complicating diabetes. Am J Med 7:609–616, 1949.

71. Hare JW: Complicated diabetes complicating pregnancy. Baillieres Clin Obstet Gynaecol 5:3449–3467, 1991.

72. Phelps RL, Sakol P, Metzger BE, et al: Changes in diabetic retinopathy during pregnancy. Correlations with regulation of hyperglycemia. Arch Ophthalmol 104:1806–1810, 1986.

73. Chew EY, Mills JL, Metzger BE, et al: Metabolic control and progression of retinopathy: The diabetes in early pregnancy study. Diabetes Care 18:631–637, 1995.

74. Diabetes Control and Complications Trial Research Group: Effect of pregnancy on microvascular complications in the diabetes control and complications trial. Diabetes Care 23:1084–1091, 2000.

75. Rosenn B, Miodovnik M, Kranias G, et al: Progression of diabetic retinopathy in pregnancy: Association with hypertension in pregnancy. Am J Obstet Gynecol 166:1214–1218, 1992.

76. Reece EA, Coustan DR, Hayslett JP, et al: Diabetic nephropathy: Pregnancy performance and fetomaternal outcome. Am J Obstet Gynecol 159:56–66, 1988.

77. McCance DR, Traub AI, Harley JM, et al: Urinary albumin excretion in diabetic pregnancy. Diabetologia 32:236–239, 1989.

78. Biesenbach G, Stoeger H, Zazgornik J: Influence of pregnancy on progression of diabetic nephropathy and subsequent requirement of renal replacement therapy in female type I diabetic patients with impaired renal function. Nephrol Dial Transplant 7:105–109, 1992.

79. Purdy LP, Hantsch CE, Molitch ME, et al: Effect of pregnancy on renal function in patients with moderate-to-severe diabetic renal insufficiency. Diabetes Care 19:1067–1074, 1996.

80. Macleod AF, Smith SA, Sonksen PH, Lowy C: The problem of autonomic neuropathy in diabetic pregnancy. Diabetic Med 7:80–82, 1990.

81. Airaksinen KEJ, Anttila LM, Linnaluoto MK, et al: Autonomic influence on pregnancy outcome in IDDM. Diabetes Care 13:756–761, 1990.

82. Siddiqi T, Rosenn B, Mimouni F, et al: Hypertension during pregnancy in insulin-dependent diabetic women. Obstet Gynecol 77:514–519, 1991.

83. Hare JW, White P: Pregnancy in diabetes complicated by vascular disease. Diabetes 26:953–955, 1977.

84. Reece EA, Egan JFX, Coustan DR, et al: Coronary artery disease in diabetic pregnancies. Am J Obstet Gynecol 154:150–151, 1986.

85. Coustan DR, Nelson C, Carpenter MW, et al: Maternal age and screening for gestational diabetes: A population-based study. Obstet Gynecol 73:557–561, 1989.

86. Super DM, Edelberg SC, Philipson EH, et al: Diagnosis of gestational diabetes in early pregnancy. Diabetes Care 14:288–294, 1991.

87. Shivvers SA, Lucas MJ: Gestational diabetes: Is a 50-g screening result >200 mg/dL diagnostic? J Reprod Med 44:685–688, 1999.

88. Nasrat AA, Johnstone FD, Hasan SAM: Is random plasma glucose an efficient screening test for abnormal glucose tolerance in pregnancy? Br J Obstet Gynaecol 95:855–860, 1988.

89. Cousins L, Dattel BJ, Hollingsworth DR, Zettner A: Glycosylated hemoglobin as a screening test for carbohydrate intolerance in pregnancy. Am J Obstet Gynecol 150:455–460, 1984.

90. Roberts AB, Baker JR, Metcalf P, Mullard C: Fructosamine compared with a glucose load as a screening test for gestational diabetes. Obstet Gynecol 76:773–775, 1990.

91. Lamar ME, Kuehl TJ, Cooney AT, et al: Jelly beans as an alternative to a fifty-gram glucose beverage for gestational diabetes screening. Am J Obstet Gynecol 181:1154–1157, 1999.

92. Carpenter MW, Canick JA, Star J, et al: Fetal hyperinsulinism at 14-20 weeks and subsequent gestational diabetes. Obstet Gynecol 87:89–93, 1996.

93. National Diabetes Data Group: Classification and diagnosis of diabetes mellitus and other categories of glucose intolerance. Diabetes 28:1039–1057, 1979.

94. Carpenter MW, Coustan DR: Criteria for screening tests for gestational diabetes mellitus. Am J Obstet Gynecol 159:768–773, 1982.

95. Sermer M, Naylor CD, Gare DJ, et al: Impact of increasing carbohydrate intolerance on maternal-fetal outcomes in 3637 women without gestational diabetes. Am J Obstet Gynecol 173:146–156, 1995.

96. Rust OA, Bofill JA, Andrew ME, et al: Lowering the threshold for the diagnosis of gestational diabetes. Am J Obstet Gynecol 175:961–965, 1996.

97. Deerochanawong C, Putiyanun C, Wongsuryrat M, et al: Comparison of the National Diabetes Data Group and World Health Organization criteria for detecting gestational diabetes mellitus. Diabetologia 39:1070–1073, 1996.

98. American Diabetes Association: Gestational diabetes mellitus. Diabetes Care 27(Suppl 1):S88–S90, 2004.

99. Schmidt MI, Duncan BB, Reichelt AJ, et al: Gestational diabetes mellitus diagnosed with a 2-h 75-g OGTT and adverse pregnancy outcomes. Diabetes Care 24:1151–1155, 2001.

100. Weiss PAM, Haeusler M, Kainer F, et al: Toward universal criteria for gestational diabetes: Relationships between seventy-five and one hundred gram glucose loads and between capillary and venous glucose concentrations. Am J Obstet Gynecol 178:830–835, 1998.

101. HAPO Study Cooperative Research Group: The hyperglycemia and adverse pregnancy outcome (HAPO) study. Intl J Gynaecol Obstet 78:69–77, 2002.

102. Freinkel N, Metzger BE: Gestational diabetes: Problems in classification and implications for long-range prognosis. In Vranic M, Hollenberg CH, Steiner G (eds): Comparison of Type I and Type II Diabetes: Similarities and Dissimilarities in Etiology, Pathogenesis and Complications. New York, Plenum, 1985, pp 47–64.

103. Buchanan TA, Catalano PM: The pathogenesis of GDM: Implications for diabetes after pregnancy. Diabetes Rev 3:584–601, 1995.

104. Catalano PM, Tyzbir ED, Sims EAH: Incidence and significance of islet cell antibodies in women with previous gestational diabetes. Diabetes Care 13:478–482, 1990.

105. Buschard K, Buch I, Molsted-Pedersen L, et al: Increased incidence of true type I diabetes acquired during pregnancy. Br Med J 294:275–279, 1987.

106. Owerbach D, Carnegie S, Rich C, et al: Gestational diabetes mellitus is associated with HLA-DQb-chain DNA endonuclease fragments. Diabetes Res 6:109–112, 1987.

107. Mawhinney H, Hadden DR, Middleton D, et al: HLA antigens in asymptomatic diabetes: A 10-year follow-up study of potential diabetes in pregnancy and gestational diabetes. Ulster Med J 48:166–172, 1979.

108. Ober C, Xiang K-S, Thisted RA, et al: Increased risk for gestational diabetes mellitus associated with insulin receptor and insulin-like growth factor II restriction fragment length polymorphisms. Genet Epidemiol 6:559–569, 1989.

109. Buschard K, Buch I, Molsted-Pedersen L, et al: Increased incidence of true type I diabetes acquired during pregnancy. Br Med J 294:275–279, 1987.

110. Beischer NA, Oats JN, Henry OA, et al: Incidence and severity of gestational diabetes mellitus according to country of birth in women living in Australia. Diabetes 40(Suppl 2):35–38, 1991.

111. Green JR, Schumacher LB, Pawson IG, et al: Influence of maternal body habitus and glucose intolerance on birth weight. Obstet Gynecol 78:235–240, 1991.

112. Maassen JA, Kadowaki T: Maternally inherited diabetes and deafness: A new diabetes subtype. Diabetologia 39:375–382, 1996.

113. Gebhart SSP, Shoffner JM, Koontz D, et al: Insulin resistance associated with maternally inherited diabetes and deafness. Metabolism 45:526–531, 1996.

114. Ellard S, Beards F, Allen LI, et al: A high prevalence of glucokinase mutations in gestational diabetic subjects selected by clinical criteria. Diabetologia 43:250–253, 2000.

115. Warram JH, Krolewski AS, Gottlieb MS, Kahn CR: Differences in risk of insulin-dependent diabetes in offspring of diabetic mothers and diabetic fathers. N Engl J Med 311:149–152, 1984.

116. Committee on Nutritional Status during Pregnancy and Lactation, Food and Nutrition Board, Institute of Medicine, National Academy of Sciences: Nutrition During Pregnancy, Part I: Weight Gain. Washington, DC, National Academy Press, 1990, pp 10–13.

117. Durnin JVGA: Energy requirements of pregnancy. Diabetes 40(Suppl 2):152–156, 1991.

118. Koukkou E, Ghosh P, Lowy C, Poston L: Offspring of normal and diabetic rats fed saturated fat in pregnancy demonstrate vascular dysfunction. Circulation 98:2899–2904, 1998.

119. Buchbinder A, Miodovnik M, McElvy S, et al: Is insulin lispro associated with the development or progression of diabetic retinopathy during pregnancy? Am J Obstet Gynecol 183:1162–1165, 2000.

120. Roversi GD, Garginlo M, Nicolini U, et al: A new approach to the treatment of diabetic pregnant women. Am J Obstet Gynecol 135:567–576, 1979.

121. Combs CA, Gunderson E, Kitzmiller JL, et al: Relationship of fetal macrosomia to maternal postprandial glucose control during pregnancy. Diabetes Care 15:1251–1257, 1992.

122. Oats JN: Obstetrical management of patients with diabetes in pregnancy. Baillieres Clin Obstet Gynaecol 5:395–411, 1991.

123. Haigh SE, Tevaarwerk GJM, Harding PEG, Hurst C: A method for maintaining normoglycemia during labor and delivery in insulin-dependent diabetic women. Can Med Assoc J 126:487–490, 1982.

124. Pettitt DJ, Knowler WC, Baird HR, Bennett PH: Gestational diabetes: Infant and maternal complications of pregnancy in relation to third-trimester glucose tolerance in Pima Indians. Diabetes Care 3:458–464, 1980.

125. Hod M, Merlob P, Friedman S, et al: Gestational diabetes mellitus: A survey of perinatal complications in the 1980s. Diabetes 40(Suppl 2):74–78, 1991.

126. Kalter H: The non-teratogenicity of gestational diabetes. Paediatr Perinat Epidemiol 12:456–458, 1998.

127. Schaefer UM, Songster G, Xiang A, et al: Congenital malformations in offspring of women with hyperglycemia first detected during pregnancy. Am J Obstet Gynecol 177:165–171, 1997.

128. Peterson CM, Jovanovic-Peterson L: Percentage of carbohydrate and glycemic response to breakfast, lunch and dinner in women with gestational diabetes. Diabetes 40(Suppl 2):172–174, 1991.

129. Jovanovic-Peterson L, Peterson CM: Dietary manipulation as a primary treatment strategy for pregnancies complicated by diabetes. J Am Coll Nutr 9:320–325, 1990.

130. Knopp RH, Magee MS, Raisys V, Benedetti T: Metabolic effects of hypocaloric diets in management of gestational diabetes. Diabetes 40(Suppl 2):165–171, 1991.

131. Algert S, Shragg P, Hollingsworth DR: Moderate caloric restriction in obese women with gestational diabetes. Obstet Gynecol 65:487–491, 1985.

132. Dornhorst A, Nichols JSD, Probst F, et al: Caloric restriction for the treatment of gestational diabetes. Diabetes 40(Suppl 2):161–164, 1991.

133. Artal R: Exercise: The alternative therapeutic intervention for gestational diabetes. Clin Obstet Gynecol 46:479–487, 2003.

134. Jovanovic-Peterson L, Durak EP, Peterson CM: Randomized trial of diet versus diet plus cardiovascular conditioning on glucose levels in gestational diabetes. Am J Obstet Gynecol 161:415–419, 1989.

135. Bung P, Artal R, Khodiguian N, Kjos S: Exercise in gestational diabetes: An optional therapeutic approach? Diabetes 40(Suppl 2):182–185, 1991.

136. Lesser K, Gruppuso P, Terry R, Carpenter MW: Exercise fails to improve postprandial glycemic excursion in women with gestational diabetes. J Matern Fetal Med 5:211–217, 1996.

137. Nachum Z, Ben-Shlomo I, Weiner E, Shalev E: Twice daily versus four times daily insulin dose regimens for diabetes in pregnancy: Randomised controlled trial. Br Med J 319:1223–1227, 1999.

138. Parretti E, Mecacci F, Papini M, et al: Third-trimester maternal glucose levels from diurnal profiles in nondiabetic pregnancies: Correlation with sonographic parameters of fetal growth. Diabetes Care 24:1319–1323, 2001.

139. Langer O, Levy J, Brustman L, et al: Glycemic control in gestational diabetes mellitus: How tight is tight enough: Small for gestational age versus large for gestational age? Am J Obstet Gynecol 161:646–653, 1989.

140. Bochner CJ, Medearis AL, Williams J, et al: Early third trimester ultrasound screening in gestational diabetes to determine the risk of macrosomia and labor dystocia at term. Am J Obstet Gynecol 157:703–708, 1987.

141. Agarwal MM, Hughes PF, Punnose J, et al: Gestational diabetes screening of a multiethnic, high risk population using glycated proteins. Diabetes Res Clin Pract 51:67–73, 2001.

142. Elliott BD, Schenker S, Langer O, et al: Comparative placental transport of oral hypoglycemic agents in humans: A model of human placental drug transfer. Am J Obstet Gynecol 171:653–660, 1994.

143. Langer O, Conway DL, Berkus MD, et al: A comparison of glyburide and insulin in women with gestational diabetes. N Engl J Med 343:1134–1138, 2000.

144. Glueck CJ, Wang P, Kobayashi S, et al: Metformin therapy throughout pregnancy reduces the development of gestational diabetes in women with polycystic ovary syndrome. Fertil Steril 77:520–525, 2002.

145. Coetzee EJ, Jackson WPU: Metformin in management of pregnant insulin-independent diabetics. Diabetologia 16:241–245, 1979.

146. Hellmuth E, Damm P, Molsted-Pedersen L: Oral hypoglycemic agents in 118 diabetic pregnancies. Diabet Med 17:507–511, 2000.

147. De Veciana M, Major CA, Morgan MA, et al: Postprandial versus preprandial blood glucose monitoring in women with gestational diabetes mellitus requiring insulin therapy. N Engl J Med 333:1237–1241, 1995.

148. O'Sullivan JB: The interaction between pregnancy, diabetes, and long-term maternal outcome. In Reece EA, Coustan DR (eds): Diabetes Mellitus in Pregnancy: Principles and Practice. New York, Churchill Livingstone, 1988, pp 575–585.

149. Metzger BE, Bybee DE, Freinkel N, et al: Gestational diabetes mellitus: Correlations between the phenotypic and genotypic characteristics of the mother and abnormal glucose tolerance during the first year postpartum. Diabetes 34(Suppl 2):111–115, 1985.

150. Grant PT, Oats JN, Beischer NA: The long-term follow-up of women with gestational diabetes. Aust N Z J Obstet Gynaecol 26:17–22, 1986.

151. Buchanan TA, Xiang A, Kjos SL, et al: Gestational diabetes: Antepartum characteristics that predict postpartum glucose intolerance and type 2 diabetes in Latino women. Diabetes 47:1302–1310, 1998.

152. Damm P, Kuehl C, Bertelsen A, Molsted-Pedersen L: Predictive factors for the development of diabetes in women with previous gestational diabetes mellitus. Am J Obstet Gynecol 167:607–616, 1992.

153. Metzger BE, Cho NH, Roston SM, Radvany R: Prepregnancy weight and antepartum insulin secretion predict glucose tolerance five years after gestational diabetes mellitus. Diabetes Care 16:1598–1605, 1993.

154. Byrne MM, Sturis J, O'Meara NM, Polonsky KS: Insulin secretion in insulin-resistant women with a history of gestational diabetes. Metab Clin Exp 44:1067–1073, 1995.

155. Harris MI: Gestational diabetes may represent discovery of preexisting glucose intolerance. Diabetes Care 11:402–411, 1988.

156. Kaufmann RC, Schleyhahn FT, Huffman DG, Amankwah KS: Gestational diabetes diagnostic criteria: Long-term maternal follow-up. Am J Obstet Gynecol 172:621–625, 1995.

157. Peters RK, Kjos SL, Xiang A, Buchanan TA: Long-term diabetogenic effect of single pregnancy in women with previous gestational diabetes mellitus. Lancet 347:227–230, 1996.

158. Tuomilehto J, Lindstrom J, Eriksson JG, et al: Prevention of type 2 diabetes mellitus by changes in lifestyle among subjects with impaired glucose tolerance. N Engl J Med 344:1343–1350, 2001.

159. Diabetes Prevention Program Research Group: Reduction in the incidence of type 2 diabetes with lifestyle or metformin. N Engl J Med 346:393–403, 2002.

160. Buchanan TA, Xiang AH, Peters RK, et al: Preservation of pancreatic beta-cell function and prevention of type 2 diabetes by pharmacological treatment of insulin resistance in high-risk Hispanic women. Diabetes 51:2796–2803, 2002.

161. Pallardo F, Herranz L, Garcia-Ingelmo T, et al: Early postpartum metabolic assessment in women with prior gestational diabetes. Diabetes Care 22:1053–1058, 1999.

162. Kousta E, Lawrence NJ, Godsland IF, et al: Insulin resistance and beta-cell dysfunction in normoglycemic European women with a history of gestational diabetes. Clin Endocrinol 59:289–297, 2003.

163. Barden AE, Beilin LJ, Ritchie J, et al: Does a predisposition to the metabolic syndrome sensitize women to develop pre-eclampsia? J Hypertens 17:1307–1315, 1999.

164. Mittermayer F, Mayer BX, Meyer A, et al: Circulating concentrations of asymmetrical dimethyl-L-arginine are increased in women with previous gestational diabetes. Diabetologia 45:1372–1378, 2002.

165. Knock GA, McCarthy AL, Lowy C, Poston L: Association of gestational diabetes with abnormal maternal vascular endothelial function. Br J Obstet Gynaecol 104:229–234, 1997.

166. Hu J, Norman M, Wallensteen M, Gennser G: Increased large artery stiffness and impaired acetylcholine induced skin vasodilatation in women with previous gestational diabetes mellitus. Br J Obstet Gynaecol 105:1279–1287, 1998.

# Diagnosis and Treatment of Thyroid Disease during Pregnancy

## Susan J. Mandel

## BACKGROUND AND HISTORICAL PERSPECTIVE

Thyroid diseases occur commonly in women of reproductive age and are well-described complications of reproductive dysfunction, pregnancy, and the puerperium.[1-6] Historically, in Egyptian and Roman times, an enlarging thyroid gland was viewed as a positive sign of pregnancy in younger women,[7-9] but it remains controversial whether significant goiter is an acceptable physiologic accompaniment of pregnancy. The spectrum of thyroid disease in pregnancy is similar to that in the normal female population (Table 187-1). Some cases of thyrotoxicosis are attributed to the thyroid-stimulating action of human chorionic gonadotropin (hCG) or related molecules.[10,11] On average, 1 in 20 women experience postpartum thyroiditis (PPT).[12] The clinical manifestations of thyroid disease overlap those of normal pregnancy, and results of traditional tests of thyroid and metabolic status may be abnormal because of pregnancy itself.[13-15] Furthermore, fetal considerations influence thyroid diagnostic protocols and therapy for women of reproductive age and pregnant women.[16] Fortunately, improved assays for free thyroid hormones and thyroid-stimulating hormone (TSH)[16-19] permit accurate assessment of thyroid status in pregnancy.[17-20] The availability of effective therapy, in conjunction with close clinical follow-up and monitoring, generally ensures a safe pregnancy for the mother and largely ameliorates the fetal morbidity and mortality resulting from spontaneous abortion, intrauterine growth retardation, stillbirth, and neonatal death.[16]

Pregnancy itself may be viewed as a euthyroid state amid the complex changes in endocrine (including thyroid) and cardiovascular physiology that characterize gestation.[13,14,21-24] Pregnancy can have a favorable effect on the course of maternal autoimmune thyroid disorders, although the tendency is for exacerbation postpartum.[25,26] This favorable effect is due to generalized suppression of humoral and cell-mediated immunity during gestation, which is itself an example of a successful allograft bearing a complement of maternal antigens.[27-31] The loss of immune suppression with delivery often results in a rebound during the postpartum period. Herein, we focus on thyroid problems in reproduction and of the mother during and after delivery, including the effects of thyroid disease and treatment on the fetus and changes in maternal thyroid function during normal pregnancy.

## THYROID DISEASE AND REPRODUCTION

Thyroid disease has been implicated in several reproductive disorders, including menstrual abnormalities, infertility, hyperprolactinemia, and pregnancy wastage.[1] Whether reproductive status has an effect on the risk of thyroid disease for women is not clear.

### HYPOTHYROIDISM

#### Menstruation and Fertility

Overt hypothyroidism (myxedema) may be accompanied by amenorrhea and anovulation and is sometimes associated with elevated concentrations of prolactin (PRL) or galactorrhea or an enlarged sella turcica.[32-36] Increased production of thyrotropin-releasing hormone (TRH) could account for TSH and PRL hypersecretion. Another proposed mechanism is a defect in hypothalamic dopamine turnover, which would also explain the observation of increased luteinizing hormone levels.[37-39] Ovulatory defects, increased PRL, and galactorrhea are thought to be reversible with thyroxine replacement therapy in severe hypothyroidism. Mild hypothyroidism may be associated with menorrhagia.[40] Anovulatory cycles and luteal-phase dysfunction contribute to infertility and may accompany mild or subclinical hypothyroidism.[41-44] Subclinical hypothyroidism may also be associated with slight elevations in serum PRL.[45-47] Studies in infertile women with mild hypothyroidism have also found increased PRL responses to metoclopramide challenge.[41,46,48] Contrary to earlier reports,[41,45] treatment of latent hyperprolactinemia in hypothyroidism with dopamine agonists is not effective in improving pregnancy rates.[48] An ovarian hyperstimulation syndrome (multiple giant follicular cysts) with normal PRL and gonadotropin levels has been reported in a patient with primary hypothyroidism[49]; thyroxine therapy resulted in cyst involution.

#### Miscarriage

In some patients, recurrent abortions have been attributed to the presence of hypothyroidism.[50] An earlier study that assessed thyroid function by butanol-extractable iodine reported a higher rate of spontaneous abortions in hypothyroid women than in pregnant euthyroid controls.[51] Up to a twofold increase in abortions has been reported with overt

| *Table 187-1* | Thyroid Disorders in Pregnancy |
|---|---|
| Goiter and thyroid nodules | Simple (nontoxic) goiter |
| | Thyroiditis |
| | Colloid nodular disease |
| | Iodine deficiency disorders |
| | Simple (true) cyst |
| | Papillary carcinoma |
| | Follicular neoplasms |
| Hyperthyroidism | Graves' disease (autoimmune thyrotoxicosis) |
| | Subacute (painful) thyroiditis |
| | Lymphocytic (painless) thyroiditis |
| | Toxic adenoma |
| | Toxic multinodular goiter |
| | Inappropriate thyroid-stimulating hormone secretion |
| | Metastatic follicular carcinoma (rare) |
| | Thyrotoxicosis factitia |
| | Iodine-induced thyrotoxicosis |
| | Gestational trophoblastic neoplasia |
| | Hyperemesis gravidarum (human chorionic gonadotropin mediated) |
| Hypothyroidism | Hashimoto's thyroiditis |
| | Primary myxedema |
| | Postablative hypothyroidism |
| | Surgical hypothyroidism |
| Postpartum thyroiditis | Thyrotoxicosis |
| | Hypothyroidism |

hypothyroidism.[52] In some cases, lower serum thyroxine ($T_4$) levels may be due to a fall in thyroxine-binding globulin (TBG) associated with declining estrogen levels in a nonviable pregnancy rather than being due to the presence of hypothyroidism.[16] Adequate thyroxine replacement for women with either mild or overt hypothyroidism in early pregnancy results in term deliveries in over 90%. However, failure to achieve a normal serum TSH level during pregnancy has been reported to be associated with term deliveries in only 20% of women.[53] These and other studies suggest that thyroxine replacement therapy improves early pregnancy outcome even when significant hypothyroidism is present.[50,52,54,55]

Six recent studies have reported a doubling of the spontaneous miscarriage rate early in gestation among women who have serum antithyroid antibodies (either anti–thyroid peroxidase [TPO] or antithyroglobulin) detected in the first trimester.[56-61] Most of these antibody-positive women who miscarry have normal thyroid function. Furthermore, the presence of antithyroid antibodies in the first trimester is not correlated with that of anticardiolipin antibodies, which are known to be associated with pregnancy loss.[56] The mechanism linking thyroid autoimmunity and miscarriage is not known. It may be a marker either for more generalized activation of the immune system or for subtle changes in maternal/fetal thyroid metabolism. In addition, among women undergoing in vitro fertilization, although the presence of antithyroid antibodies does not alter pregnancy rate, the miscarriage rate is significantly higher, as reported in a recent study by Poppe and colleagues.[62] Whether thyroxine therapy is helpful in this situation is not known. In small observational studies, some groups have reported that intravenous immunoglobulin therapy may result in a higher proportion of live births in this population[63-66] and one study reported that euthyroid antibody–positive women treated with Armour thyroid had an even higher pregnancy success rate than those who received intravenous immunoglobulin.[66] Such results are promising and need to be investigated in larger, randomized controlled clinical trials.

### Premenstrual Syndrome
It had been suggested that mild hypothyroidism, defined by isolated elevation of serum TSH levels or even an exaggerated TSH response to TRH, is associated with premenstrual syndrome (PMS) in a significant proportion of cases.[67,68] This finding was not confirmed in a prospective study of patients with PMS and age-matched controls.[69] There would now seem to be little basis for associating PMS with thyroid dysfunction or for recommending thyroxine replacement therapy in this condition.

### THYROTOXICOSIS

Mild to moderate thyrotoxicosis does not necessarily affect fertility.[16] Such thyrotoxic women remain ovulatory and have a normal chance of becoming pregnant.[32] Severe thyrotoxicosis may be accompanied by oligoamenorrhea or amenorrhea.[1] The exact mechanism, however, is not known. Hyperthyroidism is a hyperestrogenic state, in part caused by increased conversion of weak androgens to estrogen.[70] Gonadotropin levels may be elevated with loss of the midcycle luteinizing hormone surge[71] yet remain responsive to exogenous gonadotropin-releasing hormone (GnRH).[72,73] Nutritional, weight, and psychological changes in thyrotoxicosis may also contribute to menstrual dysfunction.[74] Only severe thyrotoxicosis is likely to be associated with an increased risk of spontaneous abortion.[75] Women with thyrotoxicosis in early pregnancy are usually already treated or will be treated, and adequate control data for untreated thyrotoxicosis during gestation are lacking. Adequate treatment of thyrotoxicosis should restore fertility and menstruation and reduce any early pregnancy wastage.

### REPRODUCTIVE STATUS AND THYROID DISEASE

Epidemiologic studies of thyroid disease, including autoimmune thyroid disease, nodular thyroid disease, and thyroid carcinoma, indicate a high prevalence among women, typically those in their late-reproductive or postreproductive years.[76,77] This high prevalence suggests possible influences of sex hormones on the development of thyroid disease. Experimentally, autoimmune thyroiditis in rats and chickens is modulated by exposure to estrogens and androgens, androgens having a protective effect.[78,79] Estrogen exposure leads to a reduction in suppressor/cytotoxic T cells that may permit an increase in autoantibody synthesis.[80] A case-control study of 89 patients with autoimmune thyroiditis (Hashimoto's disease) found no association of thyroiditis with parity.[81] However, a longer reproductive span (early menarche and/or late menopause) was associated with a twofold to threefold increased relative risk of euthyroid or hypothyroid Hashimoto's disease. A prospective study in pregnancy from an area of marginally low iodine intake reported that a greater number of pregnancies and increased parity were associated with an increased prevalence of nodular thyroid disease and goiter in women with thyroid autoimmunity, or in women with a past history of thyroid disease, compared to controls.[82] These changes were independent of maternal age, biochemical thyroid status, or evidence of thyroid autoimmunity. Iodide levels in the population may have played a role.

### THYROID STATUS IN PREGNANCY

### THYROID PHYSIOLOGY

#### Basal Metabolic Rate
The basal metabolic rate increases 15% to 20% between 4 and 8 months' gestation.[13] Most of this increase is due to oxygen consumption by the fetoplacental unit; the balance is accounted for by the changes in cardiovascular physiology accompanying pregnancy.[23] Difficulty distinguishing the true basal metabolic rate, which could be a useful indicator of thyroid function status, from total metabolism in

the setting of pregnancy mitigates against its use for diagnosis.

## Iodine Economy

Glomerular filtration rates increase 50% in pregnancy and result in a sustained increase in iodide clearance.[13] Reduced tubular reabsorption of iodide by the kidneys may also contribute to increased renal clearance.[83] Plasma inorganic iodide levels may fall as a result. Similar changes in renal iodide clearance have been observed in women treated with diethylstilbestrol postpartum.[83] Additionally, iodide readily crosses the placenta (Table 187-2), with a reported fetal-maternal gradient of 5:1 suggesting an active transport process.[84,85] Iodide accumulates in the fetal thyroid primarily after 90 days' gestation.[86-90] Lactation is another source of iodide loss in the mother.[91] This iodide loss during pregnancy has implications for maternal and fetal thyroid hormone economy in view of the major problems still encountered with endemic iodine deficiency disorders on a global basis.[92-94] In many geographic areas outside North America, iodide intake is marginal, that is, an average intake of less than 100 µg/day.[82,83,95] Goiter is unlikely to develop unless plasma inorganic iodide levels are less than 0.08 µg/dL.[96] Levels are considerably higher in North America, with no differences in iodide balance reported in pregnant versus nonpregnant women.[97] Although such studies are now contraindicated, previous measurements of thyroid radioiodine uptake have shown increases in pregnancy that depend on changes in plasma inorganic iodide and thyroid-stimulating activity.[13,86-89,98,99] These studies used $^{123}$I. In some cases, $^{131}$I treatment was inadvertently given to thyrotoxic pregnant women.

Therefore, to compensate for this increased iodine loss during pregnancy, the recommended daily intake of iodine for pregnant women is 150 µm.[100] The most recent National Health and Nutrition Examination Survey in the United States reported a substantial increase in the number of women with a low urinary iodine excretion (<50 µm per gram of creatinine) over the last 20 years (from <1% to 5%).[101] A recent survey by the author of two pharmacies found that 60% of prescription prenatal vitamins do not contain iodine. This should raise the awareness of the obstetrician if a patient is felt to be at risk for iodine deficiency.

## Serum Thyroid Hormones and Protein Binding

Circulating TBG concentrations double in pregnancy as a result of estrogen stimulation of hepatic production[102] and a reduction in clearance of TBG secondary to sialylation.[103] Transthyretin (prealbumin) and albumin levels are reduced.[104-106] As a result, total serum thyroxine ($T_4$), triiodothyronine ($T_3$), and reverse $T_3$ levels are frankly elevated in pregnancy because of increased hormone-TBG binding[9,104-113]; binding to transthyretin and albumin is reduced.[105] The increase in total $T_4$ during gestation is predictable, with a suggested adjustment of the nonpregnant reference range by a factor of 1.5.[114] Indirect estimates of

### Table 187-2 Placental Transfer and Fetal Thyroid Function

| Without difficulty | Some transfer |
|---|---|
| Iodides | $T_4$ |
| Thionamides | $T_3$ |
| Thyroid autoantibodies | Little or no transfer |
| TRH | TSH |

$T_3$, triiodothyronine; $T_4$, thyroxine; TRH, thyrotropin-releasing hormone; TSH, thyroid-stimulating hormone.
Modified from Burrow GN: Thyroid diseases in pregnancy. In Burrow GN, Oppenheimer JH, Volp JR (eds): Thyroid Function and Disease. Philadelphia, WB Saunders, 1989, p 292.

free thyroid hormone status using the resin $T_3$ uptake test may be reduced because of increased TBG, and the free thyroxine ($FT_4$) index calculated from the resin $T_3$ uptake test and total serum $T_4$ generally remains within normal limits.[17] However, this technique does not yield a particularly accurate estimate of free hormone status when TBG concentrations are greatly increased.[115] Women with congenital TBG deficiency show little TBG rise or change in serum $T_4$ in pregnancy.[116,117] At the same time, hypothyroid patients receiving low-dose replacement therapy fail to increase protein-bound iodine ($T_4$) after estrogen therapy even though $T_4$-binding capacity, or TBG, is increased.[107] This finding indicates that an increase in $T_4$ production is required during normal pregnancy, along with increased binding capacity. It is now well recognized that many hypothyroid women require an increase of 25% to 40% in thyroxine dosage during pregnancy. However, studies of $T_4$ turnover in pregnant and estrogen-treated women (done 4 decades ago) yielded normal results: around 90 µg/day.[118] Although fractional $T_4$ turnover is reduced, the absolute amount remains normal or increased because of the increase in total $T_4$. The discrepancy between these studies has not been resolved. Glinoer and colleagues recently observed that serum $T_4$ and $T_3$ concentrations failed to increase as much during pregnancy as predicted by the measured increase in serum TBG[119] (Fig. 187-1). Thus, a state of relative hypothyroxinemia was observed, accompanied by a slight increase in serum TSH levels within the normal range in later pregnancy. Serum thyroglobulin levels also increased during pregnancy and returned to normal by 6 weeks postpartum.[82,119,120] These data are derived from one of the largest groups of pregnant women studied longitudinally and cross-sectionally during pregnancy, albeit in an area of marginal iodide intake.

Early studies of free thyroid hormone concentrations during pregnancy suggest that they remain within normal limits.[105,112,121,122] Results from longitudinal studies reveal significant fluctuations in free thyroid hormone levels throughout pregnancy, although these concentrations also generally remain within normal reference limits.[19,104-106,119,122-124] $FT_4$ and $FT_3$ levels may be slightly increased in the first trimester between 6 and 12 weeks and fall progressively to lower normal or borderline low levels by the third trimester, and TBG saturation is reduced (Fig. 187-2). This pattern is consistent regardless of the $FT_4$ assay method used (dialysis, ultrafiltration, gel filtration and adsorption, or free hormone immunoassay).[19,125] Thus, reductions in free thyroid hormone levels in late pregnancy seem to be a real phenomenon unaccountable for by changes in serum albumin, nonesterified fatty acids, or TBG.[19,104,106] The physiologic relevance of these observations is unclear. The $T_3/T_4$ ratio is increased in the third trimester.[105] $T_4$ bound to transthyretin or albumin is a possible precursor for $T_3$ production.[104] Increased binding of $T_4$ and $T_3$ to monocyte nuclear receptors has been reported in human pregnancy.[126] Unfortunately, except for the equilibrium dialysis $FT_4$ assay, none of the other commercial assays have reported trimester-specific and method-specific reference ranges during pregnancy. The commercially available automated $FT_4$ assays that use two-step or labeled antibody methodologies are protein sensitive and are therefore affected by the pregnancy-induced changes in serum albumin or TBG.[127-129] Consequently, no universal absolute $FT_4$ value can be used to define a low serum $FT_4$ level across methodologies.[130] It has been suggested that the normal range for the serum total $T_4$ level during pregnancy is 1.5 times the nonpregnant reference range.[114] Until validated pregnancy reference ranges are available for serum $FT_4$ assays, the serum total $T_4$ level may be more reliable to use during pregnancy.

Recent studies have measured the concentration of $T_3$ sulfate during gestation. Although maternal levels are not

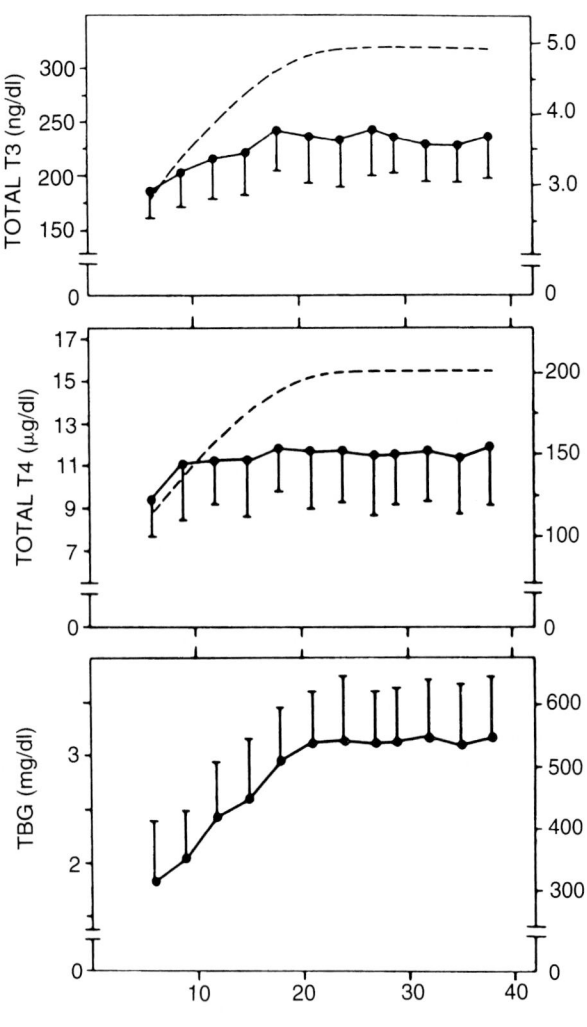

*Figure 187-1* Serum thyroxine (T₄), triidothyronine (T₃), and thyroxine-binding globulin (TBG) as a function of gestational age. Each point gives the mean value (±1 SD) of determinations performed at the initial evaluation, pooled for 3 weeks, between 5 and 28 weeks (*n* = 510), and again for samples obtained between 28 and 39 weeks (*n* = 355). The latter samples include both late initial evaluations and the second series of determinations at 30 to 33 weeks. Each point represents an average of 72 individual determinations. The *dashed lines* illustrate the theoretic curves of $T_3$ and $T_4$ concentrations required to yield the average molar ratios of $T_4$/TBG and $T_3$/TBG that correspond to nonpregnant reference subjects (0.37 for $T_4$/TBG and 0.0089 for $T_3$ TBG with a molecular weight of 57 kDa for TBG). (From Glinoer D, De Nayer P, Bourdoux P, et al: Regulation of maternal thyroid during pregnancy. J Clin Endocrinol Metab 71:276. © 1990 by The Endocrine Society.)

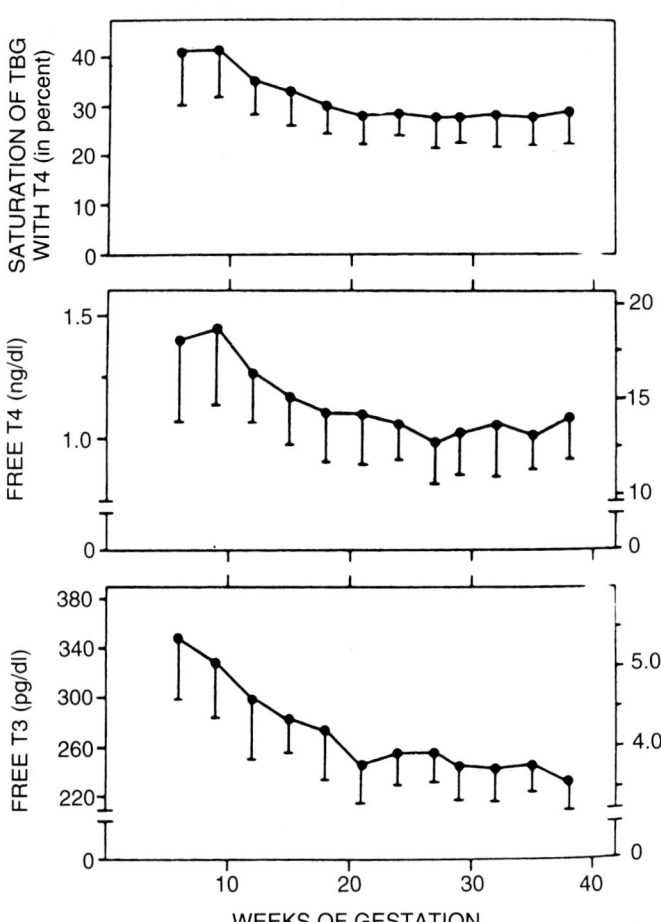

*Figure 187-2* Serum free thyroxine (T₄) and triiodothyronine (T₃) concentrations and thyroxine-binding globulin (TBG) saturation as a function of gestational age. TBG saturation by T₄ corresponds to the molar T₄/TBG ratio expressed as a percentage and was calculated for each individual set of data. Each point gives the mean values (±1 SD) of determinations performed at the initial evaluation, pooled as indicated in Figure 187-1. Each point represents an average of 72 individual determinations for TBG saturation, 64 for free T₄, and 24 for free T₃. (From Glinoer D, De Nayer P, Bourdoux P, et al: Regulation of maternal thyroid during pregnancy. J Clin Endocrinol Metab 71:276. © 1990 by The Endocrine Society.)

elevated, fetal and neonatal levels are generally higher than adult levels. This difference may represent alterations in either production or metabolism in the fetus, but the biologic significance of $T_3$ sulfate during pregnancy is not clear.[131,132]

## Thyroid Stimulation and Regulation
The histologic picture of the thyroid gland during pregnancy is one of active stimulation. Columnar epithelium can be seen lining hyperplastic follicles.[133] Radioactive iodine uptake by the thyroid in pregnancy is responsive to thyroid hormone administration, as shown by $T_3$ suppression testing.[98,99] Some studies suggest reduced sensitivity in terms of radioiodine suppression or a reduction in serum protein-bound iodine after $T_3$ administration in late gestation.[134,135]

The increase in maternal $T_4$ production that occurs in normal gestation is most evident from clinical observations of thyroxine-replaced hypothyroid women who require a 25% to 45% dosage increase in order to maintain normal serum TSH levels in pregnancy.[136] Furthermore, the findings of relative hypothyroxinemia and slightly increased serum TSH levels during pregnancy in women from areas of borderline iodine sufficiency (<100 μm/day) support the view that pregnancy constitutes a stress for the maternal thyroid by stimulating thyroid hormone production.[137]

### Human Chorionic Gonadotropin
With the recognition that trophoblastic hyperthyroidism is due to the thyromimetic actions of hCG,[11,138–144] interest has recently focused on the possibility that hCG is a physiologic regulator of thyroid function in early pregnancy.[105,119,121,122,145–148] Clinically, hCG levels peak in pregnancy at 50 to 100 times $10^3$ IU/L between 6 and 12 weeks; this peak correlates with reduced TSH levels in the first trimester[119,146] (Fig. 187-3). Levels decline thereafter and are undetectable by a few weeks postpartum. An overall increase in thyromimetic activity in the sera of women during early pregnancy may be due to hCG as determined by immunoadsorption studies using hCG monoclonal antibodies.[147,148]

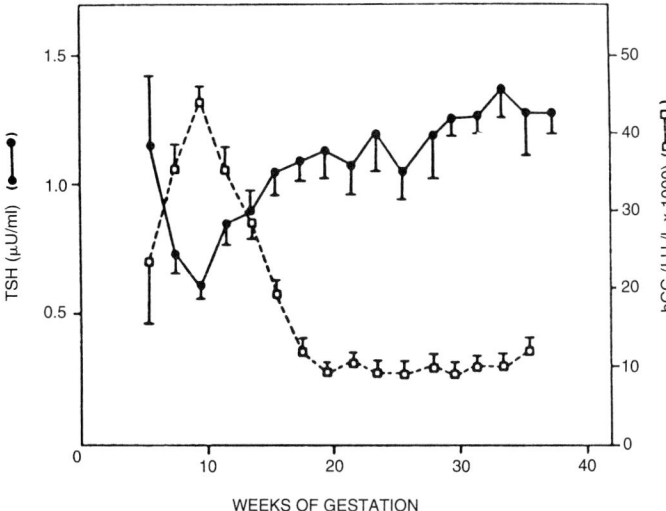

*Figure 187-3* Serum thyroid-stimulating hormone (TSH) and human chorionic gonadotropin (hCG) as a function of gestational age. Serum hCG was determined at the initial evaluation and TSH at the initial evaluation and during late gestation. The symbols give the mean value (±SE) for samples pooled for 2 weeks of gestation. Each point corresponds to an average of 33 determinations for hCG and 49 for TSH. (From Glinoer D, De Nayer P, Bourdoux P, et al: Regulation of maternal thyroid during pregnancy. J Clin Endocrinol Metab 71:276. © 1990 by The Endocrine Society.)

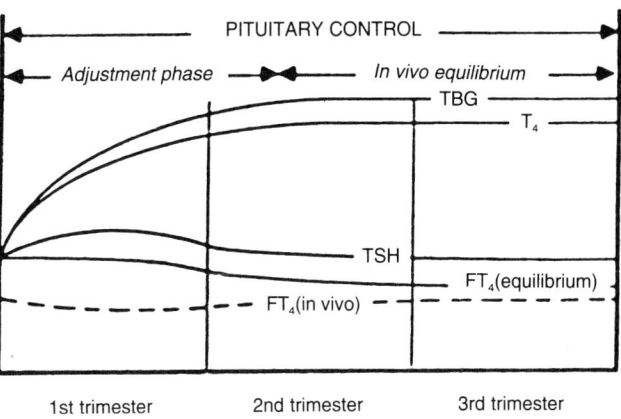

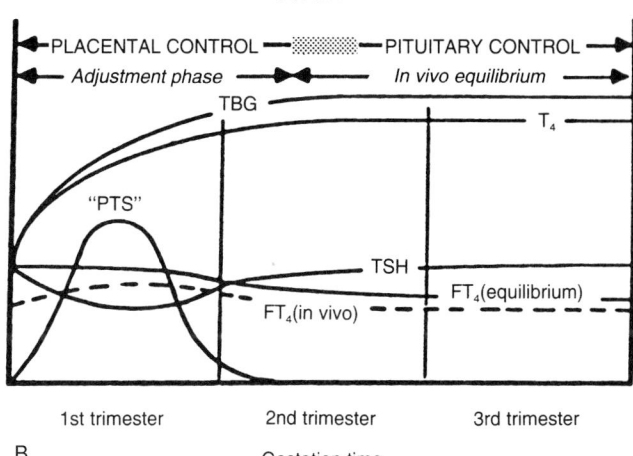

*Figure 187-4* **A,** Conventional model of maternal thyroid gland control throughout pregnancy if based on the traditional hypothalamic/pituitary feedback mechanism. **B,** Hypothetic model of maternal thyroid gland control throughout pregnancy if a putative "placental thyroid stimulator" (PTS), possibly human chorionic gonadotropin, assumes regulatory control over maternal thyroid secretion. FT$_4$, free T$_4$; T$_4$, thyroxine; TBG, thyroxine-binding globulin; TSH, thyroid-stimulating hormone. (From Ballabio M, Poshyachinda M, Ekins RP: Pregnancy-induced changes in thyroid function: Role of human chorionic gonadotropin as a putative regulator of maternal thyroid. J Clin Endocrinol Metab 73:824. © 1991 by The Endocrine Society.)

Ekins and colleagues have effectively argued that an alternative control system such as hCG may regulate maternal thyroid activity in early pregnancy, when the most important changes in TBG and T$_4$ secretion occur, to ensure an adequate supply of thyroid hormones to the placenta and embryo[146,149,150] (Fig. 187-4B). This view is opposed to the conventional model of thyroid gland control, which predicts a temporary decline in FT$_4$ during early pregnancy as TBG rapidly increases (Fig. 187-4A).

Experimentally, in vitro studies show that hCG binds to TSH receptor (TSHR), as assessed by radioreceptor assays using porcine and human thyroid membranes incubated with [125]I-TSH,[151-154] stimulates adenylate cyclase activity and cyclic adenosine monophosphate (cAMP) generation, and enhances T$_3$ secretion in human and porcine thyroid slices.[155] More recently, hCG has been shown to stimulate growth, iodide uptake, and cAMP generation in the rat thyroid cell line FRTL5.[147,148,156-158] Species differences[159,160] and microheterogeneity of hCG molecules through pregnancy and in gestational trophoblastic diseases may account for the variable thyrotropic activities reported.[146-148,154-156,161-163] However, with reported TSH bioactivity of up to 0.7 μU/U hCG,[154,156] the hCG levels obtained in early pregnancy could produce a noticeable thyrotropic effect and it has been reported that up to 9% of pregnant women may have an isolated subnormal serum TSH level in the first trimester.[164]

*Other Factors Resulting in Thyroid Stimulation*
There are several other possible explanations for this increased thyroid stimulation and each may have relative importance at different times in gestation. In early pregnancy, the serum concentration of TBG increases rapidly and more thyroid hormone may be needed to saturate binding sites. Glomerular filtration rate increases, resulting in increased iodide clearance. Later, with placental growth, there is increased metabolism of T$_4$ to its inactive metabolite reverse T$_3$ by the high levels of placental type III deiodinase.[165] In addition, there is transplacental passage of maternal T$_4$.[166] Lastly, there may be alterations in the volume of distribution of thyroid hormone because of both gravid physiology and the fetal/placental unit.

## THYROID FUNCTION AND THE FETUS

The fetal hypothalamic-pituitary-thyroid axis develops autonomously and has been extensively studied in the human, sheep, and rat.[84,85,167-169] A number of agents and maternal factors may affect fetal thyroid function, depending on whether they cross the placenta (see Table 187-2).

### Placental Transfer
*Thyrotropin-Releasing Hormone/Thyroid-Stimulating Hormone*
The placenta is impermeable to TSH but permeable to TRH, although endogenous maternal levels are probably too low to influence fetal thyroid function.[84] Pituitary and serum TSH in the fetus may be under the control of pancreatic TRH before the maturation of hypothalamic TRH after 20 weeks' gestation.[170-174] Injection of TRH in the mother is accompanied by increased cord serum TSH, T$_4$, and T$_3$ levels, thus indicating that endogenous TSH stimulates the fetal thyroid.[175] This action of TRH has been used experimentally for the prevention of respiratory distress syndrome in premature neonates.[176] Experimental human and animal data suggest a role of thyroid hormones in pulmonary surfactant synthesis.[177,178]

## Thyroid Hormones

Before the onset of human fetal thyroid gland function at 10 to 12 weeks' gestation,[86–90] any requirement for thyroid hormone would be met by the maternal supply. This point is controversial. The presence of human fetal tissue thyroid hormones and receptors before 12 to 18 weeks, when fetal serum $T_4$ production increases, is consistent with an early requirement for thyroid hormones from the mother.[179] The placenta has generally been viewed as a substantial barrier to thyroid hormone transfer, in part because of preferential 5-monodeiodination of $T_4$ to reverse $T_3$.[84,168]

Studies in rats have provided good evidence for transfer of maternal thyroid hormones to the fetus in early and late pregnancy, which may be important for early brain development and later brain growth and neuronal differentiation.[180–185] $T_4$ is more important than $T_3$, although the latter remains the major biologically active hormone via local or systemic $T_4$-to-$T_3$ conversion catalyzed by 5-monodeiodinase. In humans and sheep, maternal thyroid hormones have more limited access to the fetal circulation.[168] However, the apparent normality of sporadic congenitally hypothyroid infants at birth indicates the role of maternal thyroid hormones.[186] The devastating effects of maternal and fetal/neonatal thyroid hormone deficiency in endemic cretinism in humans underscores the overall importance of thyroid hormones to the fetus.[92–94] Fortunately, this problem does not seem to occur in areas where iodine intake is just marginal,[95] but concern remains with respect to any effect of maternal hypothyroxinemia on early fetal brain development and the effects on progeny.[149,150,179,187–189] Early studies suggested limited transfer of $T_4$ and $T_3$ across the placenta in humans in the later part of pregnancy and at term,[135,190–195] with $T_3$ crossing more readily than $T_4$. Vulsma and colleagues have convincingly demonstrated maternal-to-fetal $T_4$ transfer in neonates born with a complete organification defect. These infants have subnormal fetal $T_4$ concentrations when compared with normal newborns, but their levels are approximately 40% of the maternal concentration.[166] Because of their absolute inability to produce thyroid hormone, this $T_4$ must be maternal in origin.

The nonhalogenated thyroid hormone analogue 3,5-dimethyl-3'-isopropyl-L-thyroxine crosses the placenta more readily than $T_4$ and $T_3$ do and has been shown to alleviate maternal and fetal hypothyroidism and goiter induced in rats and monkeys and hypothyroidism in pregnant ewes but not cretinism in the lambs.[93,196,197] On balance, the evidence proves that placental transfer of thyroid hormones occurs and that maternal thyroid hormones play a role in fetal development.

## Iodide

Iodide is actively transported to the fetus.[84] The fetal and neonatal thyroid is susceptible to iodine-induced hypothyroidism and goiter with excessive exposure.[168,198,199] This complication can occur after intravenous, oral, mucosal, or topical exposure and absorption in the mother,[200] after amniography,[201] and as a result of postnatal topical absorption,[202] as well as through breast milk.[203] A number of pregnant women have been treated with amiodarone, an antiarrhythmic drug containing 75 mg of iodine per 200-mg dose that partially crosses the placenta and increases maternal and fetal iodide levels.[204] Although thyroid function may remain normal, case reports have described fetal or neonatal goiter, hypothyroidism, or hyperthyroxinemia in association with maternal amiodarone therapy.[205–207]

### Diagnosis of Fetal Thyroid Disorders In Utero

The possibility of thyroid disease in the fetus is usually considered because of maternal thyroid disease. Hyperthyroidism is generally encountered in the setting of maternal Graves' disease, and hypothyroidism is associated with fetal thyroid maldevelopment, iodine deficiency disorders, thyroid autoimmunity, and maternal drug therapy.[208–210] In hypothyroidism, a fetal goiter may be visible on ultrasound,[211] or the radiographic appearance of distal femoral or proximal tibial epiphyses may be delayed.[212,213] The latter has limited clinical application. Measurement of $T_4$ and TSH in serum collected by percutaneous umbilical cord sampling (cordocentesis)[169] is currently the most reliable means of diagnosing hypothyroidism[214] or hyperthyroidism in utero.[215] This technique probably has advantages over measurement of thyroid hormones or TSH in amniotic fluid,[216–218] although the fetus incurs risk with the procedure. The fetus can absorb thyroid hormones injected into amniotic fluid, and such therapy has been used successfully in the treatment of hypothyroidism and goiter in utero.[214,219] Intramuscular thyroxine injection in utero has also been described in the treatment of hypothyroidism,[220] but is probably less desirable than the amniotic fluid route.

## GOITER AND PREGNANCY

Goiter has historically been associated with pregnancy, but its incidence and prevalence vary with the geographic area and iodine status of the general population. Up to 70% of pregnant women in Scotland and Ireland were considered on clinical grounds (visible and palpable thyroid gland) to have a goiter versus 38% of nonpregnant controls.[221,222] No cumulative influence of successive pregnancies was observed, inasmuch as goiters were seen in 39% of nulliparous women and 35% of nonpregnant parous women. These studies are from areas of relatively low iodine intake. A comparative study in Iceland, an area of iodine sufficiency, showed a lower basal prevalence of goiter (20%) and no increase in the incidence of goiter in pregnancy.[223] Similar results are reported in studies from North America,[224,225] which has led some authors to suggest that goiter in pregnancy is a myth.[226] Most goiters during pregnancy in North America are related to autoimmune thyroid disease, colloid nodular disease, or thyroiditis.

Ultrasonography has added a quantitative perspective to the assessment of goiter in pregnancy. In Denmark, an area of marginal iodine intake, a 30% increase in thyroid volume has been documented between 18 and 36 weeks' gestation.[227] Volume returned to baseline postpartum, and no evidence of thyroid dysfunction or thyroid autoimmunity was apparent. Only 25% of the women actually had a goiter on clinical grounds. Serum thyroglobulin levels were also increased during pregnancy.[228] Only a 13% increase in thyroid volume was reported in a North American study.[229] The largest longitudinal and cross-sectional study of thyroid volume in pregnancy involved over 600 women from Belgium, another area of marginal iodine intake.[119] Seventy percent of the women had a 20% or greater increase in thyroid volume during pregnancy, although only 9% had a significant goiter as defined by thyroid volume in excess of 23 mL. Thyroid volume showed positive correlations with higher serum thyroglobulin levels and increased serum $T_3/T_4$ ratio. No correlation was seen with urine iodide excretion and there was a negative correlation with serum TSH levels. The latter may have been due to the influence of hCG during pregnancy. The same authors from Belgium prospectively studied preexisting mild thyroid abnormalities through pregnancy and noted a significant goitrogenic effect and also an increase in the incidence and prevalence of thyroid nodules.[82] Many of these nodules were subclinical and detected only on thyroid ultrasound. Serum thyroglobulin levels were disproportionately increased in women with goiters and nodules when compared with controls and pregnant women with autoimmune thyroid disease or a history of previous thyroid abnormalities. The authors further suggested that previous pregnancies were a significant risk factor for goiter and thyroid nodules. This same risk was also suggested in a study from the Netherlands.[230] It should be noted that an increase in thyroid volume during pregnancy does not necessarily denote increased mitotic activity; since increased colloid volume, cell hypertrophy, inflammation, or increased thyroid blood flow could account for some of the enlargement.

No evidence of adverse effects on fetal development or neonatal thyroid function has been seen in these studies from areas of marginal iodine uptake.[82,95,119] Nor does there appear to be any increased risk of neonatal thyroid dysfunction in goitrous, iodine-sufficient areas.[231] This finding contrasts with results from areas with endemic iodine deficiency.[92–94,232] Maternal smoking has been shown to be a risk factor for neonatal thyroid enlargement, as determined ultrasonographically.[233] Neonatal thyroid volume correlated with cord serum thyroglobulin and thiocyanate levels, but no evidence of neonatal thyroid dysfunction was found.

## THYROTOXICOSIS IN PREGNANCY

### INCIDENCE AND ETIOLOGY

All forms of thyroid disease are more common in women than in men, and thyrotoxicosis is not a rare event during pregnancy. It occurs in about 2 of every 1000 pregnancies. Autoimmune thyrotoxicosis, or Graves' disease, the most common cause of thyrotoxicosis in pregnant women, accounts for about 90% of cases. Toxic adenomas or nodular goiters are much less common in this age group. Other causes of thyrotoxicosis in pregnancy include gestational trophoblastic neoplasia[11,143] and hyperemesis gravidarum (see Table 187-1).

#### Gestational Thyrotoxicosis
A spectrum of hCG-induced hyperthyroidism occurs during pregnancy, and this entity has recently been referred to as "gestational thyrotoxicosis."[234–236] This disorder differs from Graves' disease in several ways: (1) nonautoimmune origin, with negative antithyroid and anti–TSHR antibodies; (2) absence of large goiter; and (3) resolution in almost all patients after 20 weeks.[234]

Findings range from an isolated subnormal serum TSH concentration (approximately 9% of pregnancies[164]) to elevations of free thyroid hormone levels in the clinical setting of hyperemesis gravidarum. Systematic screening of 1900 consecutive pregnant women in Belgium demonstrated low TSH and elevated $FT_4$ in 2.4%, half of whom had weight loss, lack of weight gain, or unexplained tachycardia.[236]

Hyperemesis gravidarum, or pernicious nausea and vomiting in pregnancy, is usually associated with weight loss and fluid and electrolyte disturbances. Its manifestation and diagnosis can be complicated because other causes of severe nausea and vomiting in pregnancy must be excluded (Table 187-3). In women with hyperemesis gravidarum, suppressed TSH levels may occur in 60%, with elevated $FT_4$ levels in almost 50%.[235–239] Serum hCG concentrations correlated with $FT_4$ levels and inversely with TSH determinations. The magnitude of the deviation from normal values increased

with the severity of nausea and vomiting.[164,240] Furthermore, thyroid-stimulating activity, as measured by adenylate cyclase activity per international unit of hCG, is reported to be greater in women with hyperemesis gravidarum than in those with occasional or no vomiting.[234]

Similar thyroid hormone changes and emetic symptoms may be present in multiple gestations, which are associated with higher peak and more sustained hCG levels.[241] In addition, a recent case report further supports the concept of hCG-induced thyrotoxicosis. A woman with recurrent gestational thyrotoxicosis and her mother with the same obstetric history were found to have a missense mutation in the extracellular domain of TSHR that caused a twofold to threefold increase in cAMP generation in transfected COS-7 cells when exposed to hCG as compared with wild-type receptor.[239] This genetic mutation induced hyperresponsiveness to hCG, and thyrotoxicosis.

Gestational thyrotoxicosis is transient and usually resolves within 10 weeks of diagnosis.[242] Treatment with antithyroid drugs is controversial,[235,243,244] but may not be needed if the condition is clinically mild. The clinician may consider antithyroid drug therapy for patients with hyperemesis who remain symptomatic after 20 weeks' gestation and continue to have elevated thyroid hormone concentrations and suppressed TSH levels.

### DIAGNOSIS

The clinical diagnosis of mild to moderate hyperthyroidism is not easy and may be much more difficult during pregnancy. Hyperdynamic symptoms and signs are common in normal pregnant women and include anxiety, heat intolerance, tachycardia, and warm, moist skin. Laboratory tests may support a suspicion of thyrotoxicosis, but confirmation may be difficult. The ocular changes of thyroid ophthalmopathy or pretibial myxedema do not indicate whether Graves' thyrotoxicosis is active. A resting pulse above 100 that is not decreased by Valsalva's maneuver is strongly suggestive of thyrotoxicosis.

Despite the difficulty in interpretation of thyroid function tests because of the elevated TBG concentration during pregnancy, the diagnosis of hyperthyroidism in pregnant women depends on the laboratory. A sensitive TSH determination with a value less than 0.01 mU/L[245,246] and an elevated serum $FT_4$ or total $T_4$ concentration above pregnancy reference values is diagnostic. This illustrates the need for the manufacturers of the commercial $FT_4$ assays to report trimester-specific and method-specific reference ranges during pregnancy. As noted, during the first trimester the serum TSH may be low in response to an increase in hCG concentration.[119]

If the diagnosis is not clear-cut, one can usually wait 3 to 4 weeks and repeat the thyroid function tests because pregnant women tolerate mild to moderate thyrotoxicosis without difficulty in most instances. Determination of maternal TSHR antibodies can be helpful in a prognostic sense to alert the physician to the possibility of fetal or neonatal thyrotoxicosis.

### TREATMENT

Once the diagnosis of thyrotoxicosis is established in a pregnant woman, therapy should be instituted. Treatment of thyrotoxicosis in a pregnant woman is limited to antithyroid drug therapy or surgery because radioactive iodine is contraindicated.[247–249] If [131]I treatment is inadvertently given to a woman in early pregnancy, the effects may be blocked with iodide administration. Maternal and fetal or neonatal hypothyroidism are potential consequences of [131]I administration in pregnancy. Plasmapheresis has been used in the treatment of thyrotoxicosis in pregnancy but is of limited value.[250]

**Table 187-3  Causes of Severe Nausea and Vomiting in Pregnancy**

Hyperemesis gravidarum
Small bowel obstruction
Gastroenteritis
Pyelonephritis
Gastroesophageal reflux disease
Thyrotoxicosis
Peptic ulcer disease
Adrenal insufficiency
Cholecystitis
Diabetic ketoacidosis
Pancreatitis
Psychologic disorders

## Thionamide Therapy

The thionamides propylthiouracil, methimazole, and carbimazole have all been prescribed for the treatment of thyrotoxicosis during pregnancy. Carbimazole, which is metabolized to methimazole, is used mainly in Europe. All these agents cross the placenta and are also secreted in breast milk.[251] The serum half-lives of propylthiouracil and methimazole are 1 hour and 5 hours, respectively.[252–256] These two antithyroid drugs have been used interchangeably. Thionamides block the synthesis but not the release of thyroid hormone. Propylthiouracil does have the potential additional advantage of partially blocking the conversion of $T_4$ to $T_3$. The clinical response thus depends on the depletion of previously synthesized hormone. With either propylthiouracil or methimazole, the typical patient will note some improvement after 1 or 2 weeks and may approach euthyroidism after 6 to 8 weeks, with no difference in the median time to lowering the $FT_4$ index to appropriate pregnant levels.[257]

If minor drug reactions occur, the thionamides may be interchanged, but cross-sensitivity is seen in about half the patients.[258] The most common reactions include fever, nausea, skin rash, pruritus, and metallic taste.[259] Transient leukopenia, not an uncommon reaction to thionamide therapy, occurs in about 12% of adults.[259,260] This association may be complicated because mild leukopenia is not uncommon in untreated Graves' disease.[252] This mild leukopenia is not a sign of agranulocytosis, which occurs in about 0.5% of patients, usually develops within 12 weeks of the onset of therapy, and may be an autoimmune phenomenon.[261–264] Hepatitis and vasculitis have also been reported as side effects of thionamide therapy,[265–267] but these complications have not been reported in utero.

Additionally, the possibility has been raised that methimazole is associated with the development of aplasia cutis of the scalp in the treated mother's offspring.[268–272] Although a statistically significant increase in the rate of aplasia cutis may not occur in infants born to mothers receiving methimazole as opposed to sporadic incidence, because no cases have been reported in babies born to propylthiouracil-treated mothers, some endocrinologists recommend propylthiouracil as initial therapy during pregnancy.[273] In addition, perhaps of greater concern than aplasia cutis are recent descriptions of methimazole embryopathy, including choanal atresia, tracheal-esophageal fistulae, and hypoplastic nipples.[174] When considering the significance of all of these reports, it must be emphasized that there are no case reports of aplasia cutis or other congenital anomalies in association with propylthiouracil (PTU) exposure even though PTU is the preferred drug therapy of hyperthyroidism in pregnancy in the United States.

The goal of antithyroid drug therapy is to gain control of the maternal thyrotoxicosis and maintain the maternal serum $FT_4$ or total $T_4$ concentration in the high normal range for pregnancy (for total $T_4$, 1.5 times the nonpregnant reference range).[114] This approach minimizes the incidence of transient hypothyroidism in newborns.[248] Propylthiouracil is usually started at doses sufficient to control the hyperthyroidism, and the dose may be increased after 4 weeks if necessary to gain control of the thyrotoxicosis. Some women may require high doses (up to 450 mg/day of PTU) for this purpose and must be carefully monitored. Doses of this magnitude may cause fetal hypothyroidism, and may justify a change in therapy to surgery. The need for larger doses may correlate with low serum concentrations of PTU[274] and could be caused by the documented individual variability in serum propylthiouracil profiles after an oral dose[275] or poor compliance with the medication. Total $T_4$ or $FT_4$ and sensitive TSH determinations should be done monthly during pregnancy and the dose of thionamide decreased to maintain maternal serum thyroid hormone levels in the upper normal range for pregnancy. Since there are predictable changes in total serum $T_4$ levels during pregnancy, it may be more reliable to titrate maternal antithyroid therapy to total $T_4$ target levels (maintain at ~1.5 times the upper limit of the nonpregnant range) until pregnancy specific normative ranges are provided for the $FT_4$ assays. If a requirement for higher doses of PTU continues and effects on the fetus are a concern, the clinician should consider thyroid surgery.

## β-Adrenergic Blockers

If it is necessary to give drugs to a pregnant woman, they should be the least toxic agents possible. For this reason, the use of β-adrenergic blocking drugs has been advocated for the treatment of pregnant women with hyperthyroidism.[276] β-Blockers have been used in large numbers of pregnant women to treat hypertension without apparent significant side effects.[277–279] However, intrauterine growth retardation with a small placenta, impaired response to anoxic stress, postnatal bradycardia, and hypoglycemia have been reported in the offspring of mothers receiving these agents, indicating caution in their use.[280–282] β-Blockers are particularly useful for rapid control of the β-adrenergic manifestations of thyrotoxicosis such as tremor and tachycardia. Propranolol, 20 to 40 mg three or four times a day, or atenolol, 50 to 100 mg/day, is usually adequate to control the maternal heart rate at 80 to 90 beats per minute. Esmolol, an ultra-short-acting cardioselective β-blocker given intravenously, controlled the heart rate in a pregnant woman with hyperthyroidism who required emergency surgery and was unresponsive to large doses of propranolol.[283] Current practice is to control hyperthyroidism with antithyroid drugs and to add β-blockers only in exceptional cases.

## Surgery

In pregnant thyrotoxic women with poor compliance or if maternal or fetal toxicity from antithyroid drug therapy is a concern, subtotal thyroidectomy may be advised.[284,285] Thyrotoxicosis needs to be controlled medically before subtotal thyroidectomy can be performed. This treatment includes antithyroid drugs, β-blockers, and possibly short-term use of oral iodides.[286] A useful clinical parameter of control is a resting heart rate of 80 to 90 beats per minute. Because of concern about spontaneous abortion, surgery is often delayed until after the first trimester. The small but real anesthetic and surgical risk is probably greater than the risks associated with thionamide therapy.[287,288] Although surgical complications of recurrent laryngeal nerve paralysis and hypoparathyroidism are rare in patients treated by an accomplished surgeon, they occasionally occur and are difficult to treat.

### PREGNANCY OUTCOME

Maternal thyrotoxicosis significantly increases morbidity in both the fetus and the mother. The prevalence of low-birth-weight offspring is higher, with a trend toward increased neonatal mortality.[52,289] Whether fetal wastage is increased in established pregnancy is not clear. In one study of 57 thyrotoxic pregnancies, the fetal wastage rate was 8.4%, which compares favorably with the estimated overall fetal wastage rate of 17% in normal women, including spontaneous abortion.[75] Very early spontaneous abortions could easily be missed in thyrotoxic women. The suggestion of a higher incidence of minor congenital malformations has been reported in the children of thyrotoxic women who were untreated during the first trimester of pregnancy,[290] but this finding has not been confirmed by others.[257] Only one study has reported Down syndrome to occur more frequently in children born to women with hyperthyroidism.[291] Preterm delivery, perinatal mortality, and maternal congestive heart failure were markedly increased in untreated and inadequately treated thyrotoxic patients in a retrospective study of 60 pregnant women with hyperthyroidism admitted to an inner-city hospital over a 12-year period.[292] Women with newly diagnosed thyrotoxicosis during pregnancy had a higher incidence of morbidity and mortality than did women in whom the condition was diagnosed and treated before conception. Socioeconomic conditions might have played a role in the severity of hyperthyroidism or poor outcomes, but treatment of thyrotoxicosis is indicated nonetheless. These patients are at risk for congestive heart failure because the hyperdynamic state of thyrotoxicosis is superimposed on the increased cardiac output of normal pregnancy.[293] Management of diseases such as diabetes mellitus is also complicated in a pregnant woman with thyrotoxicosis, causing erratic glycemic control, and a need for increased insulin.[294]

### Fetal and Neonatal Thyrotoxicosis
Fetal hyperthyroidism complicates pregnancies in 1% of women with either active or treated Graves' disease, including those who have become hypothyroid after radioactive iodine therapy. These women have thyroid-stimulating immunoglobulins that, like other immunoglobulins such as IgG, cross the placenta.[295] In high enough concentration, they may cause fetal or neonatal thyrotoxicosis. Maternal IgG antibodies, particularly subclasses 1 and 3, and thyroid autoantibodies are able to cross the placenta after 20 weeks' gestation[295,296] by micropinocytosis after IgG binding to Fc receptors on the syncytiotrophoblast. Maternal levels are indicative of the degree of fetal exposure and the potential for fetal thyroid stimulation.[297]

Measurement of maternal thyroid receptor antibody levels (thyroid-stimulating antibodies and TSH-binding inhibiting immunoglobulins) may provide prognostic information about the development of fetal Graves' disease.[298-300] At present, thyroid receptor antibodies can be measured only by radioreceptor assay or in functional assays of biologic stimulation.[168,301] These antibodies may have stimulating or blocking activity resulting in neonatal hyperthyroidism or hypothyroidism.[210,298,302,303] Alternating neonatal hyperthyroidism and hypothyroidism have been described in the same patient.[304] The diagnosis of fetal hyperthyroidism should be considered if persistent fetal tachycardia (>180 beats per minute) without beat-to-beat variation is present, sometimes with fetal growth restriction. The diagnosis is strengthened by the ultrasound documentation of a goiter and confirmed by cordocentesis if considered necessary after discussion of the potential risks.[305] The pathology of fetal thyrotoxicosis includes goiter, visceromegaly, adenopathy, and pulmonary hypertension.[306] Maternal therapy with propylthiouracil, 150 mg/day, may decrease the fetal heart rate to the normal range (120–160 beats per minute) within 2 weeks.[297,307] Maternal thyroid hormone levels should be monitored regularly, with thyroxine supplementation if hypothyroxinemia occurs. Thyroid receptor antibody levels usually decline progressively toward term,[304,308] and the antithyroid drug dose can be lowered to 50 to 75 mg/day or even discontinued with titration to the fetal heart rate and growth. In women with persistent elevations of thyroid receptor antibodies at term,[309,310] however, neonatal hyperthyroidism may result and require continued antithyroid drug therapy after birth. In addition, the presence of TSH-binding inhibiting immunoglobulins in cord blood is highly predictive of the development of neonatal hyperthyroidism.[309-312] If the mother has been treated with antithyroid drugs during pregnancy, the manifestations of neonatal thyrotoxicosis may be delayed until 5 to 10 days of life when the pharmacologic effect of the transplacentally acquired antithyroid drug has cleared.[311] The neonate may become irritable and have feeding problems. Other manifestations include proptosis, goiter, and failure to thrive. In severe cases, congestive heart failure, jaundice, and thrombocytopenia may occur and can cause significant mortality.[313,314] Usually, the disease runs a self-limited course over a period of several months.[168] Treatment is indicated temporarily with iodides, β-blockers, and antithyroid drugs. As maternal antibody levels decrease over the first 3 months of life, treatment can generally be discontinued.[312]

In addition, infants with central hypothyroidism have been reported born to mothers with uncontrolled Graves' disease. LaFranchi and colleagues hypothesized that these infants are exposed to high levels of thyroid hormone in utero, which results in fetal TSH suppression and eventual central hypothyroidism.[311,315]

### LACTATION
Until the last decade, lactation was strongly discouraged in women receiving thionamide therapy. The doctrine against lactation in women receiving antithyroid drug therapy originated in a 1948 report stating that the concentration of thiouracil measured 2 hours after ingestion was three times higher in breast milk than in serum.[316] Over the last 20 years, several studies have both examined the extent of secretion of propylthiouracil and methimazole in breast milk and evaluated the thyroid function of infants nursed by mothers taking these drugs. Propylthiouracil is more tightly protein bound than methimazole and, therefore, the mean milk-to-serum concentration ratio is lower for propylthiouracil, approximately 0.67,[317] than for methimazole, for which the ratio is 1.0.[318,319] Therefore, the mean total amount of methimazole excreted in breast milk is higher than that of propylthiouracil (0.14% vs. 0.025%[317,318]).

Four studies have prospectively evaluated whether antithyroid therapy affects the thyroid function of breastfed infants. Thyroid function remained unaffected in 171 infants whose mothers received daily doses of either 50 to 300 mg of propylthiouracil, 5 to 20 mg of methimazole, or 5 to 15 mg of carbimazole for periods ranging from 3 weeks to 8 months.[317,320-322] In fact, serum TSH and $T_4$ levels remained normal even in six women in whom elevated serum TSH levels (19 mU/L and 120 mU/L) developed while receiving propylthiouracil.[322] Therefore, although the number of infants monitored is small, breastfeeding while continuing antithyroid drugs may be contemplated as long as the doses are less than 300 mg daily for propylthiouracil and 20 mg daily for methimazole. It is important to remember that these antithyroid drugs have other nonthyroidal effects such as agranulocytosis, and no data are available on the possible occurrence of such effects in infants nursed by mothers taking these drugs.

## HYPOTHYROIDISM IN PREGNANCY

### MATERNAL HYPOTHYROIDISM

#### Incidence and Etiology
Hypothyroidism is encountered more often in pregnancy than is hyperthyroidism.[9,26,52] The main causes are related to thyroid autoimmunity: Hashimoto's thyroiditis, primary myxedema, and postablative hypothyroidism in Graves' disease (see Table 187-1). In most women, the hypothyroidism has been already diagnosed and treated before pregnancy. A recent population survey identified 2.5% of pregnant women as having compensated hypothyroidism based on elevated serum TSH levels, and 0.3% were overtly hypothyroid with a reduced $FT_4$ concentration or $T_4$/TBG ratio.[323] Thyroid microsomal and peroxidase antibodies were positive in 60% to 90% of all the hypothyroid subjects versus 11% of controls. Serum TSH was positively correlated with thyroid antibody titers and maternal age. No data were available on pregnancy outcome. A similar prevalence of hypothyroidism and thyroid autoimmunity has been found in previous studies during pregnancy[52,188,189] and in a community survey in nonpregnant women.[324]

Evidence of thyroid autoimmunity is seen in other autoimmune endocrine disorders such as insulin-dependent (type 1) diabetes mellitus,[325] including during pregnancy.[326] Up to

40% of diabetic women are thyroid-antibody positive and up to 10% are mildly hypothyroid with elevated TSH levels. Hypothyroidism does not appear to progress in pregnancy unless proteinuria develops, in which case overt hypothyroidism may ensue.[327] The hypothyroidism may result from increased urinary loss of thyroid hormones with proteinuria in conjunction with the preexisting impaired thyroid reserve.[328] Thyroxine therapy in this situation is appropriate but may result in an increase in insulin requirements. On the other hand, glucose intolerance is found more often in euthyroid pregnant women with thyroid antibodies.[329]

A significant proportion of patients with primary myxedema have TSHR-blocking antibodies; these antibodies are thought to play an etiologic role in the hypothyroidism.[330] Antibodies that stimulate TSHR may be present in patients with postablative hypothyroidism caused by Graves' disease or Hashimoto's thyroiditis, as discussed earlier.

### Diagnosis

Clinical assessment of thyroid status in pregnancy is imprecise. Normal pregnancy symptoms such as lethargy and weight gain may be suggestive of hypothyroidism. Paresthesias resulting from median nerve compression (carpal tunnel syndrome) are seen in both hypothyroidism and pregnancy. Delayed relaxation of deep tendon reflexes (pseudomyotonia) is a good clinical sign of hypothyroidism if present, but pregnancy is also listed as one of its causes.[331] Signs of myxedema such as decreased body temperature, periorbital edema, swelling, thick tongue, and hoarse voice should be apparent in pregnancy but can be confused with the features of preeclampsia and lead to a delayed diagnosis of the hypothyroidism.[332–334] Goiter may be present, but its absence does not detract from a diagnosis of hypothyroidism. The most sensitive indicator of primary hypothyroidism in pregnancy is an elevated serum TSH level.[9,323] Unfortunately, there are no reliable trimester-specific serum TSH reference ranges for pregnancy. Based on changes during normal pregnancy, there is a consensus that the serum TSH reference range for the first trimester should be lower than for nonpregnant women. Until pregnancy normative data are available, a serum TSH level of 2.5 mIU/L is an appropriate conservative upper TSH limit for first trimester pregnancy.[61] Future studies that better define trimester-specific TSH ranges in iodine-sufficient, antithyroid-antibody-negative pregnant women without hyperemesis gravidarum will be critical. The presence of TPO antibodies indicates a probable autoimmune etiology. Hypothalamic or pituitary hypothyroidism is rarely encountered; its presence is suggested by low $FT_4$ with normal or slightly elevated TSH.[330]

Currently, there are no recommendations for universal screening of women before or during pregnancy for thyroid dysfunction. There are both political and medical implications of this type of screening program, which has not been endorsed by any public health or professional society. In the absence of recommendations for universal screening, women belonging to the high-risk populations for development of hypothyroidism during pregnancy should have measurement of serum TSH preferably prior to pregnancy or in early gestation. Those women at higher risk include women with a history of autoimmune thyroid disease or positive antithyroid antibodies, other autoimmune disorders, a family history of autoimmune thyroid disease, a goiter, prior thyroid surgery (decreased thyroid reserve), or a history of head or neck irradiation (potential for decreased thyroid reserve). In addition, clinicians must monitor *all* thyroxine-replaced hypothyroid women during pregnancy, with dosage adjustment based on pregnancy normative data.

### Treatment

If clinical hypothyroidism is diagnosed during pregnancy, thyroxine therapy should be initiated at 2 μg/kg/day, a dose slightly higher than the replacement dose for a nonpregnant woman, which is usually well tolerated in these otherwise healthy individuals. Serum TSH and $FT_4$ determinations should be repeated in a month's time and the $T_4$ dose adjusted accordingly, with these parameters maintained within normal limits for pregnancy. Women in whom subclinical hypothyroidism is diagnosed may be treated with lower thyroxine dosages.

Nine studies have documented that most thyroxine-replaced hypothyroid women require a dosage increase during pregnancy.[136,335–343] Such increases may be seen more frequently now that hypothyroidism is treated with relatively lower $T_4$ doses than in the past.[344] Kaplan has reported that women with hypothyroidism caused by Hashimoto's thyroiditis may be less likely to need an increased thyroxine dose than those who are hypothyroid after treatment with [131]I or thyroidectomy (47% vs. 76%).[338] The average dosage increment for those with Hashimoto's disease (28 μg/day) is less than the increment for those with previous thyroid ablation (50 μg/day). Although these studies have been retrospective, the increased requirement may occur as early as 4 to 8 weeks' gestation. Furthermore, among women with normal initial serum TSH concentrations in early pregnancy, an elevated level will later develop in 30%.[338] A similar increased $T_4$ requirement was also seen in pregnant patients with a history of thyroid carcinoma who were taking suppressive doses of thyroxine.[344] Several explanations for the increased thyroxine requirement during pregnancy are possible. The volume of $T_4$ distribution may be altered by the mass of the fetal-placental unit, and serum $T_4$ pools increase as TBG levels rise. In addition, $T_4$ metabolism may be accelerated because of transplacental passage and degradation.[165]

The clinician should advise hypothyroid women receiving thyroxine therapy to have their serum TSH concentration tested early in the first trimester, with dosage adjustment to maintain a normal TSH level if necessary. If a dosage change occurs, a serum TSH test should be repeated 4 to 6 weeks later. Even if the initial serum TSH concentration is normal, it should be retested at 8- to 10-week intervals inasmuch as 30% may later require a dose change. After delivery, the thyroxine dosage can be lowered to the preconception level, with serum TSH testing 6 weeks postpartum. Thyroxine-treated women with subclinical hypothyroidism may not require a dosage increase. Patients should be instructed to separate thyroxine ingestion by 4 hours from that of prenatal vitamins containing iron and iron supplements, calcium supplements, and soy milk, all of which can interfere with thyroxine absorption.[345–347]

### Pregnancy Outcome

Although hypothyroidism has a negative impact on pregnancy, numerous reports over the last 100 years have documented hypothyroid women carrying their pregnancies to term.[348–358] Early studies reported up to a 20% incidence of perinatal mortality and congenital malformations associated with maternal hypothyroxinemia[50–52] (that is, untreated or inadequately treated hypothyroidism), with up to 60% of surviving children having evidence of impaired mental or physical development.[188,189] An increase in congenital malformations was seen even in infants of women considered to have adequate thyroxine replacement therapy. However, the biochemical assessment of thyroid hormone status in these studies was imprecise. In more recent studies, patients were well characterized with respect to the degree of hypothyroidism and the adequacy of thyroxine replacement therapy.[357,358] Still, untreated or inadequately treated overtly hypothyroid women experienced up to a 40% incidence of anemia, preeclampsia, placental abruption, and postpartum hemorrhage; 30% of the neonates were small for gestational age; and a 10% incidence of perinatal mortality and congenital anomalies was noted. Women with untreated subclinical hypothyroidism (elevated serum TSH only) had approximately one third the incidence of these problems, and in both groups it appeared that maternal and fetal outcomes were improved with adequate thyroxine therapy.[357] A recent study focusing on gestational hypertension reported a 15% incidence in women with subclinical hypothyroidism and a 22% incidence in those with overt disease versus 7.6% in the general population. Among women who were inadequately treated and remained hypothyroid, preeclampsia occurred in 66% and resulted in premature delivery.[359]

Even without increased rates of placental abruption or gestational hypertension, however, two recent studies have found that fetal distress and fetal death may occur more frequently in hypothyroid women.[360,361] Wasserstrum and coworkers found that the likelihood of fetal distress, defined as an abnormal heart rate during labor, was significantly higher in women with overt hypothyroidism (56%) detected during gestation, especially if the serum TSH level remained elevated at term, compared to women with only mild TSH elevations (3%).[360] In a screening study from Maine in the United States, an elevated serum TSH greater than 6 mIU/L at 15 to 18 weeks' gestation was associated with a higher rate of fetal death (3.8%) compared to euthyroid women (0.9%).[361]

Most studies reporting gestational complications of hypothyroidism have consisted of populations in which, on average, the initial antenatal visit was between 16 and 20 weeks' gestation—less than optimal prenatal care. These women often had other medical problems that could be associated with adverse fetal outcome. However, the consistency of findings across several studies supports a contributing causal role of hypothyroidism. The common finding throughout these observational studies is that complication rates are related not only to the severity of hypothyroidism at presentation, but also to the adequacy of thyroxine therapy for the remainder of the gestational period. Abalovich and colleagues correlated the pregnancy outcomes of 51 women found to hypothyroid in the first trimester with the adequacy of subsequent thyroxine therapy.[53] Regardless of whether the initial diagnosis was overt or subclinical hypothyroidism, those with normalization of serum TSH levels had term pregnancies (93%), except for two preterm deliveries (7%). However, only 21% of those with inadequate thyroxine therapy had term deliveries; 67% had spontaneous abortions and 12% had preterm deliveries.[53] In this as in other studies,[358-360] appropriate thyroxine therapy may ameliorate some of the adverse outcomes even if thyroid hormone deficiency is detected during pregnancy. A population-based case-control study found no overall relationship between a history of maternal hypothyroidism, thyroxine therapy, and total birth defects.[362]

### NEONATAL HYPOTHYROIDISM

The incidence of congenital hypothyroidism is 1 per 3000 to 4000 live births, with most cases having primary hypothyroidism.[168,186] Any delay in thyroxine treatment beyond 4 to 6 weeks reduces the chance of normal development and future intellectual performance.[212,363-366] Because clinical diagnosis is imprecise, the solution has been mass neonatal screening programs to measure a heel-prick blood sample drawn between 3 and 5 days postpartum for either TSH alone or thyroxine, with subsequent TSH measurement on samples with the lowest decile $T_4$ values.[136,332,333,335,367] Maternal thyroid autoimmunity may play a role in transient neonatal hypothyroidism as a result of transplacental passage of TSHR antibodies that block thyroid function, growth, or both in utero or postpartum.[208-210,367-371] This transient hypothyroidism accounts for up to 10% of cases of congenital hypothyroidism. Familial forms are also recognized.[298,303,368] The main risk seems to be a maternal history of primary myxedema rather than goitrous Hashimoto's disease.[209] Most cases of congenital hypothyroidism are considered sporadic and likely to be permanent, however. A proportion of them

may also be due to maternal autoimmunization[372,373] or may be associated with maternal TSHR antibodies that inhibit thyroid growth or function[374-376] or with cytotoxic antibodies.[377,378] Antibodies to thyroglobulin or TPO are probably not causal in the hypothyroidism.[379] Endemic cretinism has also been associated with the finding of maternal thyroid growth-blocking antibodies,[380] but this association has yet to be widely confirmed.

In any event, neonatal hypothyroidism, including transient cases,[381] must be treated with thyroxine.[366] The risk of developmental problems may already be increased if maternal hypothyroxinemia has occurred during pregnancy.[382,383] Treatment in cases of suspected transient hypothyroidism may be withdrawn after 2 or 3 years to assess for thyroid recovery.

## POSTPARTUM THYROID DISEASE

Thyroid dysfunction is a well-recognized complication of the puerperium,[5,6] and it follows that close surveillance of mothers with thyroid disease or a history of thyroid disease should be continued after delivery. Although Graves' thyrotoxicosis and Hashimoto's thyroiditis tend to improve in later pregnancy, a relapse often occurs postpartum[25,26,384-386] and may be transient or protracted. The reason for relapse at this time is most likely the rebound in immune surveillance that occurs postpartum.[27-31] TPO antibodies often increase postpartum in Hashimoto's disease and Graves' disease, but correlation of TSHR antibody status and the onset or relapse of thyrotoxicosis has been relatively weak.[387] Rarely, postpartum thyroid dysfunction is associated with hypothalamic-pituitary disease as part of pituitary failure in Sheehan's syndrome or lymphocytic hypophysitis.[388-390] Transient isolated thyrotropin deficiency in the postpartum period has been described.[390] Most often, thyroid dysfunction in the puerperium is part of the spectrum of postpartum thyroiditis (PPT), which differs significantly in terms of its pathogenesis, treatment, and outcome from the aforementioned disorders. Otherwise, diagnosis and treatment of thyroid disease in the postpartum period are as outlined earlier and subject to the usual precautions relevant to pregnancy or breastfeeding.

### POSTPARTUM THYROIDITIS

PPT is now well recognized as a distinct variant of silent (painless) thyroiditis[391] associated with thyroid autoimmunity and transient thyroid dysfunction (hypothyroidism[392] and/or hyperthyroidism[393]). Since the first modern descriptions of PPT over 15 years ago, much has been learned about the pathophysiology, clinical course, treatment, and outcome of this disorder.[12,394-408]

#### Clinical Features
The incidence of PPT averages 5%,[12] with a range as low as 1% to 2%[397,398,407] to as high as 10% to 15%.[399,400] A summary of PPT surveys and the changes in thyroid antibody levels during and after pregnancy are shown in Table 187-4 and Figure 187-5, respectively. Diagnostic measures for PPT are highlighted in Table 187-5.

*Thyrotoxic Phase*
Typically, 70% of women experience a transient period of thyrotoxicosis with onset between 6 weeks and 3 months postpartum and lasting 1 to 2 months before spontaneously resolving. A goiter develops in 50% of cases. Thyrotoxic symptoms are usually milder than in Graves' disease and may be overlooked or attributed to the adjustment to motherhood. Fatigue and palpitations may be prominent. Hypertension is occasionally seen.[409,410] Specific tests to detect biochemical thyrotoxicosis are the same as those generally used in pregnancy. A caveat is that some patients in whom

**Table 187-4** Summary of Postpartum Thyroiditis Surveys

| Feature | No. (%) of Patients | | |
| --- | --- | --- | --- |
| | Nikolai et al.[399] | Jansson et al.[404] | Amino et al.[406] |
| No. screened | 238 | 460 | 507 |
| No. affected | 16 (6.7) | 30 (6.5) | 28 (5.5) |
| Transient thyrotoxicosis | 7 (2.9) | 8 (1.7) | 13 (2.6) |
| Followed by transient hypothyroidism | 3 (1.3) | 2 (0.2) | 7 (1.4) |
| Transient hypothyroidism | 3 (1.3) | 20 (4.3) | 7 (1.4) |
| Persistent hypothyroidism | 3 (1.3) | 0 | 1 (0.2) |
| Positive MCHA titer | | | |
| Affected women | 15/27 (56) | 23/30 (77) | 25/28 (89) |
| Unaffected women | 4/40 (10) | 21/430 (4.9) | 37/479 (7.7) |
| Family history of thyroid disease | | | |
| Affected women | 14/27 (52)* | ND | † |
| Unaffected women | 22/125 (18)* | ND | † |

*Difference highly significant (*P* < 0.001)
†Family history difference not significant; numbers not given.
MCHA, microsomal hemagglutinin antibody; ND, not done.
From Nikolai TF, Turney SL, Roberts RC: Postpartum lymphocytic thyroiditis. Prevalence, clinical course, and long-term follow up. Arch Intern Med 147:221, 1987. © 1987 by The American Medical Association.

PPT develops have antibodies to $T_4$ and $T_3$, which may give spuriously high or low results for total or free thyroid hormone levels depending on the immunoassay method used.[411] TPO antibodies are usually present, higher titers being associated with more severe disease and a greater risk of subsequent hypothyroidism.[404]

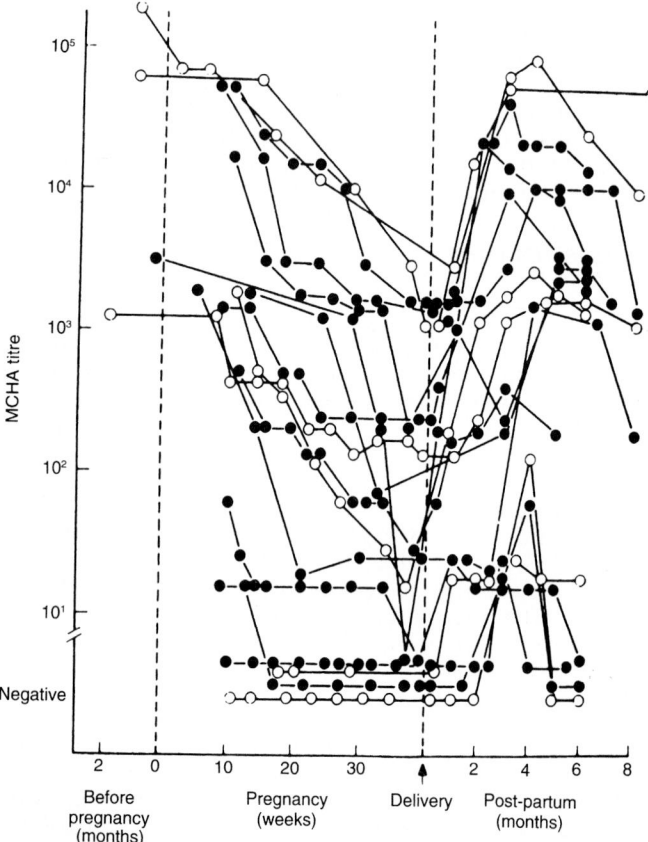

**Figure 187-5** Sequential changes in serum antithyroid antibodies (MCHA) during pregnancy and after delivery in patients with Graves' disease (*black dots*) and autoimmune thyroiditis (*open dots*). (From Amino N, Kuro R, Tanizawa O, et al: Changes in serum antithyroid antibodies during and after pregnancy in autoimmune thyroid diseases. Clin Exp Immunol 31:30, 1978.)

It is important to distinguish between thyrotoxicosis caused by PPT and that caused by Graves' disease. Radioactive iodine uptake in the thyroid readily differentiates the two, being elevated in Graves' disease and reduced or absent in thyrotoxic PPT. Other causes of reduced radioactive iodine uptake include iodine-induced thyrotoxicosis and iatrogenic thyrotoxicosis secondary to thyroid hormone administration. Special consideration must be given to nursing mothers, who should interrupt breastfeeding, while continuing to express milk, for 1 to 3 days after tracer doses of technetium 99m or [123]I.[412,413]

When symptoms of PPT are more severe, the differential diagnosis includes postpartum psychotic depression (postpartum psychosis). Typically, this condition occurs earlier than PPT, 1 to 2 weeks after delivery, and is less common, 1 per 1000 deliveries.[414] Although hyperthyroxinemia and impaired TSH responses to TRH may be seen in patients with acute psychiatric disorders,[415] thyrotoxicosis has not been confirmed in women with postpartum psychosis.[416,417] Thyroid antibodies are typically negative in those with postpartum psychosis.

*Hypothyroid Phase*
Most commonly, with or without symptoms or documentation of a preceding episode of thyrotoxicosis, primary hypothyroidism occurs 3 to 6 months postpartum. Symptoms of lethargy, cold intolerance, and impaired memory and concentration are typically mild. An increase in depressive

**Table 187-5** Diagnostic Measures in Postpartum Thyroiditis

| Investigation | Results |
| --- | --- |
| Thyroid function tests | TSH suppressed, $FT_4$ or $FT_3$ elevated in thyrotoxicosis; TSH increased, $FT_4$ normal or low in hypothyroidism |
| Thyroid autoantibodies | Positive result indicates autoimmune thyroid disorder; higher titers associated with hypothyroidism |
| Isotope uptake and scan (thyrotoxicosis only) | Low or absent uptake and scan in PPT; increased uptake and scan in Graves' disease |
| TSH receptor antibodies (thyrotoxicosis only, not routine) | Negative in PPT; positive in Graves' disease |

$FT_3$, free triiodothyronine; $FT_4$, free thyroxine; PPT, postpartum thyroiditis; TSH, thyroid-stimulating hormone.

symptomatology and depression scores has been reported in patients with PPT hypothyroidism as compared with euthyroid postpartum controls.[418–420] Up to 20% of patients were considered mildly depressed based on symptom scores, although the results did not achieve statistical significance.[419] Moreover, depressed mood related to the course of hypothyroidism and positive thyroid antibodies was seen more often in women with postpartum depression.[420,421] It has not yet been proved that postpartum hypothyroidism is a major cause of postpartum depression, however. Hypothyroidism should be considered in patients with later postpartum depression because treatment with thyroid hormone may result in clinical improvement.

Although spontaneous recovery is usual by 10 to 12 months postpartum, 15% to 20% of women remain permanently hypothyroid and the development of permanent hypothyroidism is correlated with antibody titer and the severity of the hypothyroid phase of PPT.[422,423] A high prevalence of organification defects and susceptibility to iodine-induced hypothyroidism is observed after PPT.[424] The risk of recurrence after subsequent pregnancies is up to 70%.[425]

### Predisposing Factors

The major risk factor for the development of PPT is, of course, the postpartum state. The condition may also occur after miscarriage or abortion[395,397,406] and has recently been described after pregnancy losses as early as 5 to 6 weeks' gestation.[426] Women with a personal or family history of thyroid disease are also at increased risk, specifically those with Hashimoto's thyroiditis. Thyroid autoantibody levels decline during pregnancy, and both TPO antibody titer and time of detection during gestation reflect disease risk. The presence of TPO antibodies in the first trimester is associated with a 30% to 35% incidence of PPT,[427,428] whereas PPT may develop in two thirds of women who remain TPO-antibody positive 2 days postpartum.[418,429,430] The presence of other endocrine autoimmune disorders, particularly type 1 diabetes mellitus, is associated with an increase in thyroid autoimmunity and PPT.[325,326] White and Asian women, as opposed to blacks, may be at increased risk of PPT,[418] as are cigarette smokers.[405] Maternal age, parity, presence of a goiter, breastfeeding, and infant birth weight have not been associated with an increased risk of PPT.[405] It is controversial whether the sex of the infant has any association with PPT.[405,406] On the other hand, a lower ponderal index[325] and reduced early neonatal growth rate[427] have been reported in association with maternal thyroid-antibody positivity in pregnancy and the subsequent development of PPT. Maternal thyroid function was normal in the women during these pregnancies. Iodide exposure may also be a risk factor for the development of PPT,[431,432] although a similar incidence of PPT is seen in geographic areas with high[406] and low[407] iodine intake.

It has been suggested that all pregnant women be screened for thyroid antibodies during pregnancy to predict the risk of PPT.[402] Whether such practice would truly be cost-effective is unclear.[418] It would seem reasonable to screen those with a previous episode of PPT or other thyroid and autoimmune disorders and women with a history of postpartum psychiatric disturbance.

### Pathophysiology

The immune injury to the thyroid gland in PPT is mediated by humoral and cellular mechanisms. A rebound in the immune response is thought to exacerbate autoimmune thyroid disease postpartum.[27–31,384,433] A decline in serum cortisol levels at this time may also be important.[434]

### Genetics

The risk of PPT developing has been associated with HLA haplotypes B8, DR3, DR4, DR5, DRW3, DRW8, and DRW9.[422,435–439] The relative risk is increased twofold to fivefold. The risk of PPT

is reduced in association with the HLA-DR2 haplotype.[422] The variability in HLA haplotypes associated with PPT risk may be due to geographic and population differences. Also, as proposed by DeGroot and Quintans, it is the interaction of genetics along with immune dysfunction and environmental factors that contributes to the clinical expression of autoimmune thyroid disorders.[440]

### Humoral Mechanisms

TPO antibodies reflect disease activity in PPT. Total IgG concentrations are elevated in women with PPT.[441,442] Thyroid antibodies are predominantly associated with IgG subclasses 1 and 4.[442–444] A nonspecific increase in anti-DNA antibodies is seen in postpartum relapses of thyroid autoimmune disorders, including the thyrotoxic phase of PPT.[445]

### Cellular Mechanisms

Thyroid cytolytic activity resulting from T-cell or killer-cell attack[432,440] may be important in the release of thyroid hormones in PPT, as opposed to thyroid antibodies, which serve as markers of the disease process.[444] A significant increase in circulating large peripheral granular lymphocytes having killer-cell and cytotoxic activity has been reported in women with PPT as opposed to euthyroid controls or patients with Graves' disease.[446] Others found no differences in natural-killer-cell activity between postpartum euthyroid controls and patients with PPT,[447] although both groups showed a relative increase in comparison to the reduced killer-cell activity found immediately postpartum. Similarly, these and other investigators showed no change in antibody-dependent cell-mediated cytotoxicity in PPT.[446,447] Analysis of circulating lymphocyte subsets showed an increase in activated T cells with helper-inducer activity in PPT,[448] opposite the findings in Graves' thyrotoxicosis. Stagnaro-Green and colleagues prospectively studied T-cell phenotypes during pregnancy and postpartum and found that women in whom PPT developed had higher ratios of CD4$^+$ to CD8$^+$ T cells throughout gestation than did unaffected women, and therefore exhibited a lesser degree of immunosuppression.[428] Another study reported no change in peripheral blood lymphocytes in PPT but observed an increase in intrathyroidal activated B lymphocytes and T cells with helper-inducer activity.[449] Overall, the cellular mechanisms involved in the pathogenesis of PPT, although undoubtedly important, remain relatively poorly defined.

### Treatment

Treatment of the hyperthyroid phase of PPT is often unnecessary. The thyrotoxicosis is typically mild and self-limited. In more severe cases, β-blockers may provide symptomatic relief of tremor, hyperkinesis, palpitations, and anxiety symptoms. Antithyroid drugs and radioactive iodine have no role in the treatment of PPT during the hyperthyroid phase because thyrotoxicosis results from hormone release rather than synthesis by the thyroid gland. (PTU could be used to decrease $T_4$ to $T_3$ conversion in severe hyperthyroidism.) Symptomatic hypothyroidism should be treated with thyroid hormone replacement, but this therapy can usually be withdrawn after 6 months or at a year postpartum, followed by reevaluation of thyroid function after 6 weeks with measurement of serum TSH. Thyroid hormone therapy may also be useful in patients with PPT and depression who have evidence of hypothyroidism.

## THYROID NODULES AND CARCINOMA DURING PREGNANCY

Ultrasonographic data suggest that thyroid nodules appear more frequently in multiparous women.[82,230,450] These studies have been conducted in areas with lower iodine intake than found in the United States, however. Thyroid radioisotope scanning is contraindicated in the workup of a patient with a thyroid nodule during pregnancy, and although ultrasound provides excellent definition of anatomy, it is relatively nonspecific in terms of thyroid histology or pathology. If a nodule is clinically palpable, the diagnosis, including the diagnosis of papillary carcinoma,[451,452] can be made most specifically by fine-needle aspiration biopsy (FNAB).[453]

Cancer per se is relatively uncommon in pregnancy; it is generally held that pregnancy has little effect on the development or progression of thyroid carcinoma and that thyroid carcinoma has little effect on pregnancy outcome.[454,455] Not all authorities agree. Some authors have reported an increased prevalence of neoplasia in thyroid nodules initially discovered during pregnancy, assessed by FNAB as being suspicious or diagnostic of thyroid cancer, and subsequently operated on during or after pregnancy.[452] Forty percent of these highly selected cases showed thyroid epithelial cell malignancy, and the total incidence of neoplasia (including follicular adenomas) was up to 80%. An isolated report describes a pregnancy with an apparent exacerbation of quiescent follicular carcinoma and distant bone metastasis and hypercalcemia.[455] In another series of 39 patients who had FNAB during pregnancy, however, over 60% had benign cytologic results and histology confirmed neoplasia in only 20%, half of whom had benign adenomas and the others, papillary thyroid cancer.[456] Although theoretically important, the roles of estrogens, thyroid stimulators and other growth factors, and immunosuppression on the development or progression of thyroid neoplasia during pregnancy remain largely unknown.[457] In addition, several authors have reported that the prognosis of patients with papillary and follicular cancers diagnosed during pregnancy does not differ from that in nonpregnant women with respect to disease stage, recurrence, or mortality.[458–460]

Although surgery for nodules that are suspicious for or diagnostic of thyroid cancer may be safely performed during the mid-trimester, some authors recommend delay until the postpartum period.[451,461] One might consider surgery during pregnancy if thyroid cancer is diagnosed early in gestation and if the nodule is enlarging by mid-pregnancy. In fact, the anxiety caused by the diagnosis of cancer by FNAB often mandates operation. For pregnant women in whom thyroid cancer is diagnosed, long-term outcomes do not differ in those undergoing surgery during pregnancy and those operated on postpartum.[458,459,462]

The diagnosis and treatment of clinically apparent thyroid nodules with FNAB and surgery may be pursued in pregnancy. It seems prudent to maintain close clinical follow-up and ensure adequate thyroid hormone replacement and suppression in patients with a history of thyroid carcinoma and to assess disease control and stability before pregnancy. Although no studies have systematically investigated the appropriate timing of pregnancy after high-dose radioactive iodine therapy for ablation of normal thyroid remnants or suspected residual disease, most endocrinologists recommend waiting 6 months or more before attempting conception.[463]

## REFERENCES

1. Thomas R, Reid RL: Thyroid disease and reproductive dysfunction: A review. Obstet Gynecol 70:789, 1987.
2. Crotti A: Simple goiter and pregnancy. In Crotti A (ed): Thyroid and Thymus. Philadelphia, Lea & Febiger, 1918, p 170.
3. Crotti A: Exophthalmic goiter in pregnancy. In Crotti A (ed): Thyroid and Thymus. Philadelphia, Lea & Febiger, 1918, p 367.
4. Seitz L: Trans Dtsch Ges Gynecol 1:213, 1913.
5. Gull W: On a cretinoid state supervening in adult life in women. Trans Clin Soc London 7:180, 1874.
6. Robertson HEW: Lassitude, coldness, and hair changes following pregnancy, and their response to thyroid extract. Br Med J 2:93, 1948.
7. Medvei VC: A History of Endocrinology. Boston, MTP, 1982, p 58.
8. Belchetz PE: Thyroid disease in pregnancy. Br Med J 294:264, 1987.
9. Rodin A, Rodin A: Thyroid disease in pregnancy. Br J Hosp Med 41:234, 1989.
10. Lazarus JH, Othman S: Thyroid disease in relation to pregnancy. Clin Endocrinol 34:91, 1991.
11. Rajatanavin R, Chailurkit L, Srisupandit S, et al: Trophoblastic hyperthyroidism: Clinical and biochemical features in five cases. Am J Med 85:237, 1988.
12. Gerstein HC: How common is postpartum thyroiditis? A methodological overview of the literature. Arch Intern Med 150:1397, 1990.
13. Abdoul-Khair SA, Crooks J, Turnbull AC, et al: The physiologic changes in thyroid function during pregnancy. Clin Sci 27:195, 1964.

14. Mussey RD: The thyroid gland and pregnancy. Am J Obstet Gynecol 36:529, 1938.
15. Smith SCH, Bold AM: Interpretation of in vitro thyroid function tests in pregnancy. Br J Obstet Gynaecol 90:532, 1983.
16. Burrow GN: Thyroid diseases in pregnancy. In Burrow GN, Oppenheimer JH, Volp JR (eds): Thyroid Function and Disease. Philadelphia, WB Saunders, 1989, p 292.
17. Becks GP, Burrow GN: Thyroid function tests: Recent developments. Med North Am 3:2503, 1987.
18. Ekins R: Measurement of free hormones in blood. Endocr Rev 11:5, 1990.
19. Wiersinga WM, Vet T, Berghout A, et al: Serum free thyroxine during pregnancy: A meta-analysis. In Beckers C, Reinwein D (eds): The Thyroid and Pregnancy. Stuttgart, Germany, Shattauer, 1991, p 79.
20. Nicoloff JT, Spencer CA: The use and misuse of sensitive thyrotropin assays. J Clin Endocrinol Metab 72:553, 1990.
21. Kalkhoff RK, Kissebah AH, Kim HJ: Carbohydrate and lipid metabolism during normal pregnancy: Relation to gestational hormone fraction. In Merkoty IR, Adam PAF (eds): The Diabetic Pregnancy: A Perinatal Perspective. New York, Grune & Stratton, 1979.
22. Burrow GN: Pituitary and adrenal disorders. In Burrow GN, Ferris TF (eds): Medical Complications during Pregnancy, 3d ed. Philadelphia, WB Saunders, 1988, p 254.
23. McAnultry JH, Metcalfe J, Ueland K: 1988—Cardiovascular disease. In Burrow GN, Ferris TF (eds): Medical Complications during Pregnancy, 3d ed.

Philadelphia, WB Saunders, 1988, p 180.
24. Burwell CS: Circulating adjustments to pregnancy. Am J Obstet Gynecol 36:529, 1954.
25. Salvi M, How J: Pregnancy and autoimmune thyroid disease. Endocrinol Metab Clin North Am 16:431, 1987.
26. Amino N, Tanizawa O, Mori H, et al: Aggravation of thyrotoxicosis in early pregnancy and after delivery in Graves' disease. J Clin Endocrinol Metab 55:108, 1982.
27. Amino N, Tanizawa O, Miyai K, et al: Changes in serum immunoglobulins during pregnancy. Obstet Gynecol 52:115, 1978.
28. Beer AE, Billingham RE: Immunobiology of mammalian reproduction. Adv Immunol 14:1, 1971.
29. Froelich CJ, Goodwin JS, Bankhurst AD, et al: Pregnancy, a temporary fetal graft of suppressor cells in autoimmune disease? Am J Med 69:329, 1980.
30. Lewis JE, Coulam CB, Moore SB: Immunologic mechanisms in the maternal-fetal relationship. Mayo Clin Proc 61:655, 1986.
31. Scott RM, How J, Gerrie LM, et al: Serum levels of pregnancy associated $\alpha_2$-glycoprotein during pregnancy in autoimmune thyroid disease: Relationship to disease activity. Clin Exp Immunol 59:564, 1985.
32. Goldsmith R, Sturgis S, Lerman J, et al: Menstrual pattern in thyroid disease. J Clin Endocrinol Metab 12:846, 1952.
33. Honbo KS, VanHerle AJ, Kellet KA: Serum prolactin in untreated primary hypothyroidism. Am J Med 64:782, 1978.

34. Kleinberg DL, Noel G, Frantz AG: Galactorrhea: A study of 235 cases. N Engl J Med 296:589, 1977.

35. Yamada T, Tsuki T, Ikerjiri K, et al: Volume of sella turcica in normal patients and in patients with primary hypothyroidism. J Clin Endocrinol Metab 42:817, 1976.

36. Heyburn PJ, Gibby OM, Hourihan M, et al: Primary hypothyroidism presenting as amenorrhea and galactorrhea with hyperprolactinemia and pituitary enlargement. Br Med J 292:1660, 1986.

37. Feek CM, Sawers JSA, Brown NS, et al: Influence of thyroid status on dopaminergic inhibition of thyrotropin and prolactin secretion. J Clin Endocrinol Metab 51:585, 1980.

38. Kramer M, Kauschansky A, Genel M: Adolescent secondary amenorrhea: Association with hypothalamic hypothyroidism. Pediatrics 94:300, 1979.

39. Scanlon MF, Chan V, Heath M, et al: Dopaminergic control of thyrotropin α-subunit, thyrotropin β-subunit, and prolactin in euthyroidism and hypothyroidism: Dissociated responses to dopamine receptor blockade with metoclopramide in hypothyroid subjects. J Clin Endocrinol Metab 53:360, 1981.

40. Willansky DL, Greisman B: Early hypothyroidism in patients with menorrhagia. Am J Obstet Gynecol 160:673, 1989.

41. Bohnet HG, Fieldlerk, Leidenberger FA: Subclinical hypothyroidism and infertility. Lancet 2:1278, 1981.

42. Del Pozo E, Wyss H, Tolis G, et al: Prolactin and deficient luteal function. Obstet Gynecol 53:282, 1979.

43. Gerhard I, Becker T, Eggert-Kruse W, et al: Thyroid and ovarian function in infertile women. Hum Reprod 6:338, 1991.

44. Louvet JP, Gouarre M, Saladin AM, et al: Hypothyroidism and anovulation. Lancet 1:1032, 1979.

45. Peillon F, Vincens M, Cesselin F, et al: Exaggerated prolactin response to thyrotropin-releasing hormone in women with anovulatory cycles: Possible role of endogenous estrogen and effect of bromocriptine. Fertil Steril 37:530, 1982.

46. Lombardi G, Iodice M, Miletto P, et al: Prolactin and TSH-response to TRH and metoclopramide before and after therapy in subclinical hypothyroidism. Neuroendocrinology 43:676, 1986.

47. Seki K, Kato K: Increased thyroid-stimulating hormone response to thyrotropin-releasing hormone in hyperprolactinemic women. J Clin Endocrinol Metab 61:1138, 1985.

48. Gerhard I, Eggert-Kruse W, Merzoug K, et al: Thyrotropin-releasing hormone (TRH) and metoclopramide testing in infertile women. Gynecol Endocrinol 5:15, 1991.

49. Rotmensch S, Scommegna A: Spontaneous ovarian hyperstimulation syndrome associated with hypothyroidism. Am J Obstet Gynecol 160:1220, 1989.

50. Greenman GW, Gabrielson MA, Howard-Flanders I, et al: Thyroid dysfunction in pregnancy: Fetal loss and follow-up of evaluation of surviving infants. N Engl J Med 267:426, 1962.

51. Jones W, Man E: Thyroid function in human pregnancy. VI. Premature deliveries and reproduction failures of pregnant women with low serum butanol-extractable iodines: Maternal serum TBG and TBPA capacities. Am J Obstet Gynecol 104:909, 1969.

52. Niswander KR, Gordon M, Berendes HW: The women and their pregnancies. In The Collaborative Perinatal Study of the National Institutes of Neurological Disease and Stroke. Philadelphia, WB Saunders, 1972, p 239.

53. Abalovich M, Gutierrez S, Alcaraz G, et al: Overt and subclinical hypothyroidism complicating pregnancy. Thyroid 12:63, 2002.

54. Winikoff D, Malinek M: The predictive value of thyroid test profile in habitual abortion. Br J Obstet Gynaecol 82:760, 1975.

55. White A: The effect of thyroid and ovarian gland extracts in cases of previous miscarriage and stillbirth. Br Med J 1:90, 1924.

56. Stagnaro-Green A, Roman SH, Cobin R, et al: Detection of at-risk pregnancy by means of highly sensitive assays for thyroid autoantibodies. JAMA 264:1422, 1990.

57. Lejeune B, Grun JP, de Nayer P, et al: Antithyroid antibodies underlying thyroid abnormalities and miscarriage or pregnancy induced hypertension. Br J Obstet Gynaecol 100:669, 1993.

58. Singh A, Dantas ZN, Stone SC, Asch RH: Presence of thyroid antibodies in early reproductive failure: Biochemical versus clinical pregnancies. Am Soc Reprod Med 63:277, 1995.

59. Glinoer D, Fernandez-Soto D, Bourdoux P, et al: Pregnancy in patients with mild thyroid abnormalities: Maternal and neonatal repercussions. J Clin Endocrinol Metab 73:421, 1991.

60. Iijima T, Tada H, Hidaka Y, et al: Effects of autoantibodies on the course of pregnancy and fetal growth. Obstet Gynecol 90:364, 1997.

61. Bagis T, Gokcel A, Saygili ES: Autoimmune thyroid disease in pregnancy and the postpartum period: Relationship to spontaneous abortion. Thyroid 11:1049, 2001.

62. Poppe K, Glinoer D, Tournaye H, et al: Assisted reproduction and thyroid autoimmunity: An unfortunate combination? J Clin Endocrinol Metab 88:4149, 2003.

63. Kiprov DD, Nachtigall RD, Weaver RC, et al: The use of intravenous immunoglobulin in recurrent pregnancy loss associated with combined alloimmune and autoimmune abnormalities. Am J Reprod Immunol 36:228, 1996.

64. Sher G, Maassarani G, Zouves C, et al: The use of combined heparin/aspirin and immunoglobulin G therapy in the treatment of in vitro fertilization patients with antithyroid antibodies. Am J Reprod Immunol 9:223, 1998.

65. Stricker RB, Steinleitner A, Bookoff CN, et al: Successful treatment of immunologic abortion with low-dose intravenous immunoglobulin. Fertil Steril 73:536, 2000.

66. Vaquero E, Lazzarin N, Carolis D, et al: Mild thyroid abnormalities and recurrent spontaneous abortion: Diagnostic and therapeutic approach. Am J Reprod Immunol 43:204, 2000.

67. Brayshaw ND, Brayshaw DD: Thyroid hypofunction in premenstrual syndrome. N Engl J Med 315:1486, 1986.

68. Roy-Byrne PP, Rubinow DR, Hoban MC, et al: TSH and prolactin response to TRH in patients with premenstrual syndrome. Am J Psychiatry 144:480, 1987.

69. Casper RF, Patel-Christopher A, Powell AM: Thyrotropin and prolactin responses to thyrotropin releasing hormone in premenstrual syndrome. J Clin Endocrinol Metab 68:608, 1989.

70. Southern AL, Olivio J, Gorelon GG, et al: The conversion of androgens to estrogen in hyperthyroidism. J Clin Endocrinol Metab 38:207, 1974.

71. Akande E, Hockaday T: Plasma luteinizing hormone levels in women with thyrotoxicosis. J Endocrinol 53:173, 1972.

72. Distiller L, Sayel J, Morley J: Assessment of pituitary gonadotropin reserve using luteinizing releasing hormone in states of altered thyroid function. J Clin Endocrinol Metab 40:512, 1975.

73. Tanaka T, Tamai H, Kuma K, et al: Gonadotropin response to luteinizing hormone releasing hormone in hyperthyroid patients with menstrual disturbances. Metabolism 30:323, 1981.

74. Roger J: Menstruation and systemic disease. N Engl J Med 259:676, 1958.

75. Mussey RD: Hyperthyroidism complicating pregnancy. Mayo Clin Proc 14:205, 1939.

76. Amino N: Autoimmunity and hypothyroidism. In Lazarus JH, Hall R (eds): Hypothyroidism and Goiter. London, WB Saunders, 1988, p 591.

77. Rojeski MT, Gharib H: Nodular thyroid disease: Evaluation and management. N Engl J Med 313:428, 1985.

78. Gause WC, Marsh JA: Effects of testosterone on the development of autoimmune thyroiditis in two strains of chicken. Clin Immunol Immunopathol 36:10, 1985.

79. Ansar Ahmed S, Young PR, Penhale WJ: Beneficial effect of testosterone in the treatment of chronic autoimmune thyroiditis in rats. J Immunol 136:143, 1986.

80. Talal N, Ansar Ahmed S: Immunomodulation by hormones: An area of growing importance. J Rheumatol 14:191, 1987.

81. Phillips DIW, Lazarus JH, Butland BK: The influence of pregnancy and reproductive span on the occurrence of autoimmune thyroiditis. Clin Endocrinol 32:301, 1990.

82. Glinoer D, Fernandez Soto M, Bourdoux P, et al: Pregnancy in patients with mild thyroid abnormalities: Maternal and neonatal repercussions. J Clin Endocrinol Metab 73:421, 1991.

83. Beckers C: Iodine economy in and around pregnancy. In Beckers C, Reinwein D (eds): The Thyroid and Pregnancy. Stuttgart, Germany, Schattauer, 1991, p 25.

84. Roti E, Gnudi A, Braverman LE: The placental transport, synthesis and metabolism of hormones and drugs which affect thyroid function. Endocr Rev 4:131, 1983.

85. Roti E: Regulation of thyroid-stimulating hormone (TSH) secretion in the fetus and neonate. J Endocrinol Invest 11:145, 1988.

86. Evans TC, Kretschmar RM, Hodges RE, et al: Radioiodine uptake studies of the human fetal thyroid. J Nucl Med 8:157, 1967.

87. Johnson JR: Fetal thyroid dose from intake of radioiodine by the mother. Health Physics 43:573, 1955.

88. Hodges RE, Evans TC, Bradbury JT, et al: The accumulation of radioactive iodine by human fetal thyroid. J Clin Endocrinol Metab 15:661, 1955.

89. Chapman EM, Corner GW, Robinson D, et al: The collection of radioactive iodine by human fetal thyroid. J Clin Endocrinol 8:717, 1948.

90. Fisher DA, Dussault J: Development of the mammalian thyroid gland. In Greer MA, Solomon DH (eds): Handbook of Physiology: Endocrinology. III. Baltimore, Williams & Wilkins, 1974, p 21.

91. Gushurst CA, Mueller JA, Green JA, et al: Breast milk iodide: Reassessment in 1980. Pediatrics 73:354, 1984.

92. Hetzel BS: Progress in the prevention and control of iodine-deficiency disorders. Lancet 2:266, 1987.

93. Hetzel BS, Mano MT: A review of experimental studies of iodine deficiency in fetal development. J Nutr 119:145, 1989.

94. Hetzel BS: Iodine deficiency disorders and their eradication. Lancet 2:1136, 1983.

95. Delange F, Burgi H: Iodine deficiency disorders in Europe. Bull World Health Organ 67:317, 1989.

96. Alexander WD, Koutras DA, Crooks J, et al: Quantitative studies of iodine metabolism in thyroid disease. Q J Med 31:281, 1966.

97. Dworkin HJ, Jacquez JA, Beirewaltes WH: Relationship of iodine ingestion to iodine excretion in pregnancy. J Clin Endocrinol Metab 26:1329, 1966.

98. Halnan KE: Radioiodine uptake of the human thyroid in pregnancy. Clin Sci 17:281, 1958.

99. Pochin EE: The iodine uptake of the human thyroid throughout the menstrual cycle and in pregnancy. Clin Sci 11:441, 1952.

100. Smallridge RC, Ladenson PW: Hypothyroidism in pregnancy: Consequences to neonatal health. J Clin Endocrinol Metab 86:2349, 2001.

101. Hollowell JG, Staehling NW, Hannon WH, et al: 1998 Iodine nutrition in the United States. Trends and public health implications: Iodine excretion data from National Health and Nutrition Examination Surveys I and III. J Clin Endocrinol Metab 83:3401 (1971–1974, 1988–1994).

102. Glinoer D, Gershengorn MC, Dubois A, et al: Stimulation of thyroxine-binding globulin synthesis by isolated rhesus monkey hepatocytes after in vivo 8-estradiol administration. Endocrinology 100:807, 1977.

103. Ain KB, Mori Y, Refetoff S: Reduced clearance of thyroxine binding globulin (TBG) with increased sialylation: A mechanism for estrogen-induced elevation of serum TBG concentration. J Clin Endocrinol Metab 65:686, 1987.

104. Ball R, Freeman DB, Holmes JC, et al: Low-normal concentrations of free thyroxine in late pregnancy; physiological fact, not technical artefact. J Clin Chem 35:1891, 1989.

105. Guillaume J, Schussler GC, Goldman J, et al: Components of the total serum thyroxine during pregnancy: High free thyroxine and blunted thyrotropin (TSH) response to TSH-releasing hormone in the first trimester. J Clin Endocrinol Metab 60:678, 1985.

106. Price A, Griffiths H, Morris BW: A longitudinal study of thyroid function in pregnancy. Clin Chem 35:275, 1989.

107. Engbring NH, Engstrom WW: Effects of estrogen and testosterone on circulating thyroid hormone. J Clin Endocrinol Metab 19:783, 1959.

108. Robbins J, Nelson JH: Thyroxine-binding by serum protein in pregnancy and in the newborn. J Clin Invest 37:153, 1958.

109. Skjoldebrand L, Brundin J, Carlstrom A, Pettersson T: Thyroid associated components in serum during normal pregnancy. Acta Endocrinol 100:504, 1982.

110. Man EB, Reid WA, Hellegers AE, et al: Thyroid function in human pregnancy. III. Serum thyroxine-binding prealbumin (TBPA) and thyroxine-binding globulin (TBG) of pregnant women aged 14 through 43 years. Am J Obstet Gynecol 103:338, 1969.

111. Oppenheimer JH: Role of plasma proteins in the binding, distribution and metabolism of thyroid hormones. N Engl J Med 278:1153, 1968.

112. Osathanondh R, Tulchinsky D, Chopra IJ: Total and free thyroxine and triiodothyronine in normal and complicated pregnancy. J Clin Endocrinol Metab 42:98, 1976.

113. Whitworth AS, Midgley JEM, Wilkins TA: A comparison of free $T_4$ and the ratio of total $T_4$ to $T_4$-binding globulin in serum through pregnancy. Clin Endocrinol 17:307, 1982.

114. Demers LM, Spencer CA: NACB guidelines: Laboratory medicine practice guidelines: Laboratory support for the diagnosis and monitoring of thyroid disease. Thyroid 13:11, 2003.

115. Wilke TJ: A challenge of several concepts of free thyroxine index for assessing thyroid status in patients with altered thyroid-binding protein capacity. Clin Chem 29:56, 1983.

116. Nikolai TF, Seal US: X-chromosome linked familial decrease in thyroxine binding globulin activity. J Clin Endocrinol Metab 26:835, 1966.

117. Premachandra BN, Gossain VV, Perlstein IB: Effect of pregnancy on thyroxine binding globulin (TBG) in partial TBG deficiency. Am J Med Sci 274:189, 1977.

118. Dowling JT, Appleton WG, Nicoloff JT: Thyroxine turnover during human pregnancy. J Clin Endocrinol Metab 27:1749, 1967.

119. Glinoer D, De Nayer P, Bourdoux P, et al: Regulation of maternal thyroid during pregnancy. J Clin Endocrinol Metab 71:276, 1990.

120. Rasmussen NG, Hornnes PJ, Hegedus L, et al: Serum thyroglobulin during the menstrual cycle, pregnancy and postpartum. Acta Endocrinol 121:168, 1989.

121. Harada A, Hershman JM, Reed AW, et al: Comparison of thyroid stimulators and thyroid hormone concentrations in the sera of pregnant women. J Clin Endocrinol Metab 48:793, 1979.

122. Yamamoto T, Amino N, Tanizawa O, et al: Longitudinal study of serum thyroid hormones, chorionic gonadotropin and thyrotropin during and after normal pregnancy. Clin Endocrinol 10:459, 1979.

123. Pachiarotti A, Martino E, Bartalena L, et al: Serum thyrotropin by ultrasensitive immunoradiometric assay and free thyroid hormones in pregnancy. J Endocrinol Invest 9:185, 1986.

124. Weeke J, Dybkjaer L, Granlie K, et al: A longitudinal study of serum TSH, and total and free iodothyronines during normal pregnancy. Acta Endocrinol 101:531, 1982.

125. Gow SM, Kellett HA, Seth J, et al: Limitations of new thyroid function tests in pregnancy. Clin Chim Acta 152:325, 1985.

126. Kvetny J, Poulsen HK: Nuclear thyroxine and 3,5,3'-triiodothyronine receptors in human mononuclear blood cells during pregnancy. Acta Endocrinol 105:19, 1984.

127. VanRaaij JMA, Vermatta-Miedema SH, Schonk CM, et al: Energy requirements of pregnancy in the Netherlands. Lancet 2:953, 1987.

128. Calvo R, Obregon MJ, Riuz de Ona C, et al: Thyroid hormone economy in pregnant rats near term: A physiological animal model of non-thyroidal illness? Endocrinology 126:10, 1990.

129. Sapin R, d'Herbomez M: Free thyroxine measured by equilibrium dialysis and nine immunoassays in sera with various serum thyroxine-binding capacities. Clin Chem 49:1531, 2003.

130. d'Herbomez M, Forzy G, Gasser F, et al: Clinical evaluation of nine free thyroxine assays: Persistent problems in particular populations. Clin Chem Lab Med 41:942, 2003.

131. Chopra IJ, Wu S, Teco GNC, Santini F: A radioimmunoassay for measurement of 3,5,3'-triiodothyronine sulfate: Studies in thyroidal and nonthyroidal diseases, pregnancy, and neonatal life. J Clin Endocrinol Metab 75:189, 1992.

132. Santini F, Cortelazzi D, Baggiani AM, et al: A study of the serum 3,5,3'-triiodothyronine sulfate concentration in normal and hypothyroid fetuses at various gestational stages. J Clin Endocrinol Metab 76:1583, 1993.

133. Stoffer RP, Koeneke IA, Chesky VE, et al: The thyroid in pregnancy. Am J Obstet Gynecol 74:300, 1957.

134. Werner SC: The effect of triiodothyronine administration on the elevated protein-bound iodine level in human pregnancy. Am J Obstet Gynecol 75:1193, 1958.

135. Raiti S, Holsman GB, Scott RL, et al: Evidence for placental transfer of triiodothyronine in human beings. N Engl J Med 277:456, 1967.

136. Mandel SJ, Larsen PR, Seely EW, et al: Increased need for thyroxine during pregnancy in women with primary hypothyroidism. N Engl J Med 323:91, 1990.

137. Glinoer D, Delange F, Laboureur I, et al: Maternal and neonatal thyroid function at birth in an area of marginally low iodine intake. J Clin Endocrinol Metab 75:800, 1992.

138. Kenimer JC, Hershman JM, Higgins HP: The thyrotropin in hydatidiform moles in human chorionic gonadotropin. J Clin Endocrinol Metab 40:482, 1975.

139. Valdalem JL, Pirens G, Hennen G, et al: Thyroliberin and gonadoliberin tests during pregnancy and the puerperium. Acta Endocrinol 86:695, 1977.

140. Ylikorkala O, Kivinen S, Reinila M: Serial prolactin and thyrotropin responses to thyrotropin-releasing hormone throughout normal human pregnancy. J Clin Endocrinol Metab 48:288, 1979.

141. Burrow GN, Polackwich R, Donabedian R: The hypothalamic-pituitary-thyroid axis in normal pregnancy. In Fisher DA, Burrow GN (eds): Perinatal Thyroid Physiology and Disease. New York, Raven, 1975, p 1.

142. Chan BY, Swaminanthan R: Serum thyrotropin concentration measured by sensitive assays in normal pregnancy. Br J Obstet Gynaecol 95:1332, 1988.

143. Desai RK, Norman RJ, Jialal I, et al: Spectrum of thyroid function abnormalities in gestational trophoblastic neoplasia. Clin Endocrinol 29:583, 1988.

144. Cave WT Jr, Dunn JT: Choriocarcinoma with hyperthyroidism: Probable identity of the thyrotropin with human chorionic gonadotropin. Ann Intern Med 85:60, 1976.

145. Pekonen F, Alfthan H, Stenman UH, et al: Human chorionic gonadotropin (HCG) and thyroid function in early human pregnancy: Circadian variation and evidence for intrinsic thyrotropic activity of HCG. J Clin Endocrinol Metab 66:853, 1988.

146. Ballabio M, Poshyachinda M, Ekins RP: Pregnancy-induced changes in thyroid function: Role of human chorionic gonadotropin as a putative regulator of maternal thyroid. J Clin Endocrinol Metab 73:824, 1991.

147. Yoshikawa N, Nishikawa M, Horimoto M, et al: Thyroid stimulating activity in sera of normal pregnant women. J Clin Endocrinol Metab 69:891, 1989.

148. Kinmura M, Amino N, Tamaki H, et al: Physiologic thyroid activation in normal pregnancy is induced by circulating HCG. Obstet Gynecol 75:775, 1990.

149. Ekins R: Roles of serum thyroxine binding proteins and maternal thyroid hormones in fetal development. Lancet 1:1129, 1985.

150. Ekins R, Sinha A, Ballabio M, et al: Role of maternal carrier proteins in the supply of thyroid hormones to the feto-placental unit: Evidence of a feto-placental requirement for thyroxine. In Delange F, Fisher DA, Glinoer D (eds): Research in Congenital Hypothyroidism. New York, Plenum, 1989, p 45.

151. Carayon P, Lefort G, Nisula B: Interaction of human chorionic gonadotropin and human luteinizing hormone with human thyroid membranes. Endocrinology 106:1907, 1980.

152. Davies TF, Taliadouros GS, Catt KJ, et al: Assessment of urinary thyrotropin-competing activity in choriocarcinoma and thyroid disease: Further evidence for human chorionic gonadotropin interacting at the thyroid cell membrane. J Clin Endocrinol Metab 49:353, 1979.

153. Silverberg J, O'Donnel J, Sugenaya A, et al: Effect of human chorionic gonadotropin on human thyroid tissue in vitro. J Clin Endocrinol Metab 46:420, 1978.

154. Carayon P, Amir S, Nisula B, et al: Effect of carboxypeptidase digestion of the human chorionic gonadotropin molecule on its thyrotropic activity. Endocrinology 108:1891, 1981.

155. Mann K, Schneider N, Hoermann R: Thyrotropic activity of acidic isoelectric variants of human chorionic gonadotropin from trophoblastic tumors. Endocrinology 118:1558, 1986.

156. Hershman JM, Lee HY, Sugawara M, et al: Human chorionic gonadotropin stimulates iodide uptake, adenylate cyclase and deoxyribonucleic acid synthesis in cultured rat thyroid cells. Endocrinology 67:74, 1988.

157. Davies TF, Platzer M: HCG-induced TSH receptor activation and growth acceleration in FRTL-5 cells. Endocrinology 118:2149, 1986.

158. Ballabio M, Sinha AK, Ekins RP: Thyrotropic activity of crude HCG in FRTL-5 rat thyroid cells. Acta Endocrinol 116:479, 1987.

159. Amir SM, Eudo K, Osathanoudh R, et al: Divergent responses by human and mouse thyroids to human chorionic gonadotropin in vitro. Mol Cell Endocrinol 39:31, 1985.

160. Pekary AE, Azukizawa M, Hershman JM: Thyroidal responses to human chorionic gonadotropin in the chicken and rat. Horm Res 17:36, 1983.

161. Uchimura H, Nagataki S, Ito K, et al: Inhibition of the thyroid adenylate cyclase response to thyroid-stimulating immunoglobulin G by crude and asialo-human choriogonadotropin. J Clin Endocrinol Metab 55:347, 1982.

162. Amir S, Shimohigahsi Y, Carayon P, et al: Role of carbohydrate moiety of the human chorionic gonadotropin molecule in its thyrotropic activity. Arch Biochem Biophys 229:170, 1984.

163. Fein HG, Rosen SW, Weintraub BD: Increased glycosylation of serum human chorionic gonadotropin and subunits from eutopic and ectopic sources: Comparison with placental and urinary forms. J Clin Endocrinol Metab 50:1111, 1980.

164. Goodwin TM, Montoro M, Mestman JH, et al: The role of chorionic gonadotropin in transient hyperthyroidism of hyperemesis gravidarum. J Clin Endocrinol Metab 75:1333, 1992.

165. Burrow GN, Fisher DA, Larsen PR: Maternal and fetal thyroid function. N Engl J Med 331:1072, 1994.

166. Vulsma T, Gous MH, De Vijlder JJM: Maternal-fetal transfer of thyroxine in congenital hypothyroidism due to a total organification defect or thyroid agenesis. N Engl J Med 321:13, 1989.

167. Fisher DA, Dussault JH, Sack J, Chopra IJ: Ontogenesis of hypothalamic-pituitary-thyroid function in man, sheep and rat. Recent Prog Horm Res 33:59, 1977.

168. Fisher DA, Polk DH: Development of the thyroid. Baillieres Clin Endocrinol Metab 3:627, 1989.

169. Thorpe-Beeston JG, Nicolaides KH, Felton CV, et al: Maturation of the secretion of thyroid hormone and thyroid-stimulating hormone in the fetus. N Engl J Med 324:532, 1991.

170. Greenberg AH, Czernichow P, Reba RC, et al: Observations on the maturation of thyroid function in early fetal life. J Clin Invest 49:1790, 1970.

171. Koivusalo F: Evidence of thyrotropin releasing hormone activity in autopsy pancreata from newborns. J Clin Endocrinol Metab 5:734, 1981.

172. Leduque P, Aratan-Spire S, Czernichow P, et al: Ontogenesis of thyrotropin releasing hormone in human fetal pancreas. J Clin Invest 78:1028, 1986.

173. Polk DH, Reviczky AL, Lam RW, et al: Thyrotropin releasing hormone: Effect of thyroid status on tissue concentrations in fetal sheep. Clin Res 36:203, 1988.

174. DiGianantonio E, Schaefer C, Mastroiacova PP, et al: Adverse effects of prenatal methimazole exposure. Teratology 64:262, 2001.

175. Roti E, Gundi A, Braverman LE, et al: Human cord blood concentrations of thyrotropin, thyroglobulin and iodothyronines after maternal administration of thyrotropin-releasing hormone. J Clin Endocrinol Metab 53:813, 1981.

176. Robertson B: Pathology and pathophysiology of neonatal surfactant deficiency ("respiratory distress syndrome," "hyaline membrane disease"). In Robertson B, van Golde LMG, Batenburg JJ (eds): Pulmonary Surfactant. Amsterdam, Elsevier, 1984, p 383.

177. Smith BT: Pulmonary surfactant during fetal development and neonatal adaptation: Hormonal control. In Robertson B, van Golde LMG, Batenburg JJ (eds): Pulmonary Surfactant. Amsterdam, Elsevier, 1984, p 357.

178. Devaskar U, Nitta K, Szewczyk K, et al: Transplacental stimulation of functional morphological fetal rabbit lung maturation: Effect of thyrotropin-releasing hormone. Am J Obstet Gynecol 1567:460, 1987.

179. Bernal J, Pekonen F: Ontogenesis of the nuclear 3,5,3'-triiodothyronine receptor in the human fetal brain. Endocrinology 114:677, 1984.

180. Calvo R, Obregon MJ, Ruiz de Ona C, et al: Congenital hypothyroidism as studied in rats: Crucial role of maternal thyroxine but not 3,5,3'-triiodothyronine in the protection of the fetal brain. J Clin Invest 86:889, 1990.

181. Morreale de Escobar G, Obregon MJ, Escobar del Rey F: Maternal-fetal thyroid hormone relationships and the fetal brain. Acta Med Austriaca 15:66, 1988.

182. Morreale de Escobar G, Obregon MJ, Ruiz de Ona C, et al: Comparison of maternal to fetal transfer of 3,5,3'-triiodothyronine versus thyroxine in rats. Acta Endocrinol 120:20, 1989.

183. Ruiz de Ona C, Obregon MJ, Escobar del Rey F, et al: Developmental changes in rat brain 5'-deiodinase and thyroid hormones in the fetal period. Pediatr Res 24:588, 1988.

184. Vaccari A: Teratogenic mechanisms of dysthyroidism in the central nervous system. Prog Brain Res 73:71, 1988.

185. Morreale de Escobar G, Calvo R, Obregon MJ, et al: Contribution of maternal thyroxine to fetal thyroxine pools in normal rats near term. Endocrinology 126:2765, 1990.

186. Illig R: Congenital hypothyroidism. J Clin Endocrinol Metab 8:49, 1979.

187. Ferreiro B, Bernal J, Goodyear G, et al: Estimation of nuclear thyroid hormone receptor saturation in human fetal brain and lung during early gestation. Endocrinology 67:853, 1988.

188. Man EB, Jones WS, Holden RH, et al: Thyroid function in human pregnancy. VIII. Retardation of progeny aged 7 years: Relationships to maternal age and maternal thyroid function. Am J Obstet Gynecol 111:905, 1971.

189. Man EB, Brown JF, Serunian SA: Maternal hypothyroxinemia: Psychoneurological deficits of progeny. Ann Clin Lab Sci 21:227, 1991.

190. Dussault J, Row VV, Lickrish G, et al: Studies of serum triiodothyronine concentration in maternal and cord blood. J Clin Endocrinol Metab 29:595, 1969.

191. Fisher DA, Lehman H, Lackey C: Placental transport of thyroxine. J Clin Endocrinol Metab 24:393, 1964.

192. Grumbach MM, Werner SC: Transfer of thyroid hormones across the human placenta at term. J Clin Endocrinol Metab 16:1392, 1956.

193. Carr EA, Bierwaltes WH, Raman G, et al: The effect of maternal thyroid function on fetal thyroid function and development. J Clin Endocrinol Metab 19:1, 1959.

194. Kearns JE, Hutson W: Tagged isomers and analogs of thyroxine: Their transmission across the human placenta and other studies. J Nucl Med 4:453, 1963.

195. Myant NB: Passage of thyroxine and triiodothyronine from mother to fetus in pregnant women. Clin Sci 17:75, 1958.

196. Comite F, Burrow GN, Jorgensen EC: Thyroid hormone analogues and fetal goiter. J Clin Endocrinol Metab 102:1670, 1978.

197. Bachrach LK, Kudlow JE, Silverberg JDH, et al: Treatment of ovine cretinism in utero with 3,5-dimethyl-3'-isopropyl-L-thyronine. Endocrinology 111:132, 1982.

198. Penel C, Rognoni JB, Pastiani P: Thyroid autoregulation. Am J Physiol 16:E165, 1987.

199. Theodoropoulos T, Braverman LE, Vagenakis AG: Iodine-induced hypothyroidism. Science 205:502, 1979.

200. Mahillon I, Peers W, Bourdoux P, et al: Effects of vaginal douching with povidone-iodine during early pregnancy on the iodine supply to mother and fetus. Biol Neonate 56:210, 1989.

201. Stubbe P, Heidemann P, Schurnbrand P, et al: Transient congenital hypothyroidism after amniofetography. Eur J Pediatr 135:97, 1980.

202. Smerdley P, Boyages SC, Wu D, et al: Topical iodine-containing antiseptics and neonatal hypothyroidism in very low birth weight infants. Lancet 2:661, 1989.

203. Danziger Y, Pertzelan A, Mimouni M: Transient congenital hypothyroidism after topical iodine in pregnancy and lactation. Arch Dis Child 62:295, 1987.

204. Rey E, Bachrach LK, Burrow GN: Effects of amiodarone during pregnancy. Can Med Assoc J 136:959, 1987.

205. DeWolf D, DeSchepper J, Verhaaren H, et al: Congenital hypothyroid goiter and amiodarone. Acta Paediatr Scand 77:616, 1988.

206. Tubman R, Jenkins J, Lim J: Neonatal hyperthyroxinemia associated with maternal amiodarone therapy. Ir J Med Sci 157:243, 1988.

207. Widehorn J, Bhandari AK, Bughi S, et al: Fetal and neonatal adverse effects profile of amiodarone treatment during pregnancy. Am Heart J 122:1162, 1991.

208. Dussault JH, Rousseau F: Immunologically mediated hypothyroidism. Endocrinol Metab Clin North Am 16:417, 1987.

209. Tamaki H, Amino N, Aozasa M, et al: Effective method for prediction of transient neonatal hypothyroidism in infants born to mothers with chronic thyroiditis. Am J Perinatol 6:296, 1989.

210. Matsuura N, Konishi J: Transient hypothyroidism in infants born to mothers with chronic thyroiditis: A nationwide study of 23 cases. Endocrinol Jpn 37:369, 1990.

211. Perelman AH, Johnston RL, Clemons RD, et al: Intrauterine diagnosis and treatment of fetal goitrous hypothyroidism. J Clin Endocrinol Metab 71:618, 1990.

212. Glorieux J, Desjardins M, Letarte J, et al: Useful parameters to predict eventual mental outcome of hypothyroid children. Pediatr Res 24:6, 1988.

213. Virtanen M, Perheentupa J: Bone age at birth: Method and effect of hypothyroidism. Acta Paediatr Scand 78:412, 1989.

214. Davidson KM, Richards DS, Schatz DA, et al: Successful in utero treatment of fetal goiter and hypothyroidism. N Engl J Med 324:543, 1991.

215. Wenstrom KD, Weiner CP, Williamson RA, et al: Prenatal diagnosis of fetal hyperthyroidism using funipuncture. Obstet Gynecol 76:513, 1990.

216. Chopra IJ, Crandall BF: Thyroid hormones and thyrotropin in amniotic fluid. N Engl J Med 293:740, 1975.

217. Yoshida K, Sakurada T, Takahashi T, et al: Measurement of TSH in human amniotic fluid. Clin Endocrinol 25:313, 1986.

218. Hollingsworth DR, Alexander NM: Amniotic fluid concentrations of iodothyronines and thyrotropin do not reliably predict fetal thyroid status in pregnancies complicated by maternal thyroid disorders or

anencephaly. J Clin Endocrinol Metab 57:349, 1983.

219. Lightner ES, Fisher DA, Giles H, et al: Intra-amniotic injections of thyroxine to a human fetus. Am J Obstet Gynecol 127:487, 1977.

220. VanHerle AJ, Young RT, Fisher DA, et al: Intrauterine treatment of a hypothyroid fetus. J Clin Endocrinol Metab 40:474, 1975.

221. Crooks J, Abdoul-Khair SA, Turnbull AC, et al: The incidence of goiter during pregnancy. Lancet 2:334, 1966.

222. Drury MI: Hyperthyroidism in pregnancy. J R Soc Med 79:317, 1986.

223. Crooks J, Tulloch MI, Turnbull AC, et al: Comparative incidence of goiter in pregnancy in Iceland and Scotland. Lancet 2:625, 1964.

224. Long TJ, Felice ME, Hollingsworth DR: Goiter in pregnant teenagers. Am J Obstet Gynecol 152:670, 1985.

225. Murray TK: Goiter in Canada. Can J Public Health 68:431, 1977.

226. Levy RP, Newman DM, Rejali LS, et al: The myth of goiter in pregnancy. Am J Obstet Gynecol 137:701, 1980.

227. Rasmussen NG, Hornnes PJ, Hegedus L: Ultrasonographically determined thyroid size in pregnancy and postpartum: The goitrogenic effect of pregnancy. Am J Obstet Gynecol 160:1216, 1989.

228. Pedersen KM, Borlum KG, Knudson PR, et al: Urinary iodine excretion is low and serum thyroglobulin high in pregnant women in parts of Denmark. Acta Obstet Gynecol Scand 67:413, 1988.

229. Nelson M, Wickus GG, Caplan RH, et al: Thyroid gland size in pregnancy. J Reprod Med 32:888, 1987.

230. Struve C, Ohlen S: The influence of previous pregnancies on the prevalence of goitre and thyroid nodules in women without clinical evidence of thyroid disease. Dtsch Med Wochenschr 115:1050, 1990.

231. Gaitan E, Cooksey RC, Meydrech EF, et al: Thyroid function in neonates from goitrous and non-goitrous iodine-sufficient areas. J Clin Endocrinol Metab 69:359, 1989.

232. Liu JL, Zhuang ZJ, Cao XM: Changes in thyroid, cerebral cortex and bones of therapeutically aborted fetuses from endemic goiter region supplied with iodized salt for 5 years. Chin Med J 101:133, 1988.

233. Chanoine JP, Toppet V, Bourdoux P, et al: Smoking during pregnancy: A significant cause of neonatal thyroid enlargement. Br J Obstet Gynaecol 98:65, 1991.

234. Kimura M, Amino N, Tamaki H, et al: Gestational thyrotoxicosis and hyperemesis gravidarum: Possible role of HCG with higher stimulating activity. Clin Endocrinol 38:345, 1993.

235. Goodwin TM, Hershman JM: Hyperthyroidism due to inappropriate production of human chorionic gonadotropin. Clin Obstet Gynecol 40:32, 1997.

236. Glinoer D, Merck AG, European Thyroid Symposium: Thyroid hyperfunction during pregnancy. Thyroid 8:859, 1998.

237. Chin RKH, Lao TTH: Thyroxine concentration and outcome of hyperemetic pregnancies. Br J Obstet Gynaecol 95:507, 1988.

238. Lao TT, Chin RKH, Panesar NS, et al: Observations on thyroid hormones in hyperemesis gravidarum. Asia Oceania J Obstet Gynaecol 14:449, 1988.

239. Rodien P, Bremont C, Sanson ML, et al: Familial gestational hyperthyroidism caused by a mutant thyrotropin receptor hypersensitive to human chorionic gonadotropin. N Engl J Med 339:1823, 1998.

240. Mori M, Amino N, Tamaki H, et al: Morning sickness and thyroid function in normal pregnancy. Obstet Gynecol 72:355, 1988.

241. Grun JP, Meuris S, De Nayer P, Glinoer D: The thyrotrophic role of human chorionic gonadotrophin (HCG) in the early stages of twin (versus single) pregnancies. Clin Endocrinol 46:719, 1997.

242. Goodwin TM, Montoro M, Mestman JH: Transient hyperthyroidism and hyperemesis gravidarum: Clinical aspects. Am J Obstet Gynecol 167:648, 1992.

243. Dozeman R, Kaiser FE, Case O, et al: Hyperthyroidism appearing as hyperemesis gravidarum. Arch Intern Med 143:2202, 1983.

244. Kirshon B, Lee W, Cotton DB: Prompt resolution of hyperthyroidism and hyperemesis gravidarum after delivery. Obstet Gynecol 71:1032, 1988.

245. de los Santos ET, Mazzaferri EL: Sensitive thyroid-stimulating hormone assays: Clinical applications and limitations. Compr Ther 14:26, 1988.

246. Bassett F, Cresswell J, Eastman CJ, et al: Diagnostic value of thyrotropin concentrations in serum as measured by a sensitive immunoradiometric assay. Clin Chem 32:461, 1986.

247. Burrow GN: The management of thyrotoxicosis in pregnancy. N Engl J Med 313:562, 1985.

248. Momotani N, Noh J, Oyanagi H, et al: Antithyroid drug therapy for Graves' disease during pregnancy, optimal regimen for fetal thyroid status. N Engl J Med 315:24, 1986.

249. Pekonen F, Lamberg B-A: Thyrotoxicosis during pregnancy. Ann Chir Gynaecol 67:165, 1978.

250. Derksen RHWM, van de Wiel A, Poortman J, et al: Plasma-exchange in the treatment of severe thyrotoxicosis in pregnancy. Eur J Obstet Gynecol Reprod Biol 18:139, 1984.

251. Mutjaba Q, Burrow GN: Treatment of hyperthyroidism in pregnancy with propylthiouracil and methimazole. Obstet Gynecol 46:282, 1975.

252. Cooper DS, Saxe VC, Meskell M, et al: Acute effects of propylthiouracil (PTU) on thyroidal iodide organification and peripheral iodothyronine deiodination: Correlation with serum PTU levels

measured by radioimmunoassay. J Clin Endocrinol Metab 54:101, 1982.

253. Cooper DS, Bode HH, Nath B, et al: Methimazole pharmacology in man: Studies using a newly developed radioimmunoassay for methimazole. J Clin Endocrinol Metab 58:473, 1984.

254. Sitar DS, Abu-Bakare A, Gardiner RJ: Propylthiouracil disposition in pregnancy and postpartum women. Pharmacology 25:57, 1982.

255. Skellern GG, Knight BI, Otter M, et al: The pharmacokinetics of methimazole in pregnant patients after oral administration of carbimazole. Br J Clin Pharmacol 9:145, 1980.

256. Marchant B, Brownlie BEW, Hart DM, et al: The placental transfer of propylthiouracil, methimazole and carbimazole. J Clin Endocrinol Metab 45:1187, 1977.

257. Wing DA, Millar LK, Koonings PP, et al: A comparison of propylthiouracil versus methimazole in the treatment of hyperthyroidism in pregnancy. Am J Obstet Gynecol 170:90, 1994.

258. Amrhein JA, Kenny FM, Ross D: Granulocytopenia, lupus-like syndrome, and other complications of propylthiouracil therapy. J Pediatr 76:54, 1970.

259. Jackson IMD: Management of thyrotoxicosis. J Maine Med Assoc 66:224, 1975.

260. Wing ES Jr, Asper SP Jr: Observations on the use of propylthiouracil in hyperthyroidism with special reference to long-term treatment. Bull Johns Hopkins Hosp 90:152, 1952.

261. Bilezikian SB, Lalei U, Tsan M-F, et al: Immunological reactions involving leukocytes. III. Agranulocytosis induced by antithyroid drugs. Johns Hopkins Med J 138:124, 1976.

262. Wall JR, Fang SL, Kuroki T, et al: In vitro immunoactivity to propylthiouracil, methimazole, and carbimazole in patients with Graves' disease: A possible cause of antithyroid drug–induced agranulocytosis. J Clin Endocrinol Metab 58:868, 1984.

263. Weitzman SA, Stossel TP, Desmond M: Drug-induced immunological neutropenia. Lancet 1:1068, 1978.

264. Tajiri J, Noguchi S, Murakami T, et al: Antithyroid drug–induced agranulocytosis. Arch Intern Med 150:621, 1990.

265. Romaldini JH, Bromberg N, Werner RS, et al: Comparison of effects of high and low dosage regimens of antithyroid drugs in the management of Graves' hyperthyroidism. J Clin Endocrinol Metab 57:563, 1983.

266. Safani MM, Tatro DS, Rudd P: Fatal propylthiouracil-induced hepatitis. Arch Intern Med 142:838, 1982.

267. Vasily DB, Tyler WB: Propylthiouracil-induced cutaneous vasculitis: Case presentation and review of the literature. JAMA 23:458, 1980.

268. Milham S: Scalp defects in infants of mothers treated for hyperthyroidism with methimazole or carbimazole during pregnancy. Teratology 32:231, 1985.

269. Stephan MJ, Smith DW, Ponzi JW, et al: Origin of scalp vertex aplasia cutis. J Pediatr 101:850, 1982.

270. Van Dijke CP, Heydendael RJ, De Kleine MJ: Methimazole, carbimazole and congenital skin defects. Ann Intern Med 106:60, 1987.

271. Bachrach LK, Burrow GN: Aplasia cutis congenita and methimazole. Can Med Assoc J 130:1264, 1984.

272. Frieden IJ: Aplasia cutis congenita: A clinical review and proposal for classification. J Am Acad Dermatol 14:646, 1986.

273. Mandel SJ, Brent GA, Larsen PR: Review of antithyroid drug use during pregnancy and report of a case of aplasia cutis. Thyroid 4:129, 1994.

274. Sato K, Mimura H, Kato S, et al: Serum propylthiouracil concentration in patients with Graves' disease with various clinical courses. Acta Endocrinol 104:189,1983.

275. Gardner DF, Cruikshank DP, Hays PM, et al: Pharmacology of propylthiouracil (PTU) in pregnant hyperthyroid women: Correlation of maternal PTU concentrations with cord serum thyroid function tests. J Clin Endocrinol Metab 62:217, 1986.

276. Bullock JL, Harris RL, Young R: Treatment of thyrotoxicosis during pregnancy with propranolol. Am J Obstet Gynecol 121:242, 1975.

277. Rubin PC: Current Concepts: Beta-blockers in pregnancy. N Engl J Med 305:1323, 1981.

278. Rubin PC, Butters L, Clark DM, et al: Placebo-controlled trial of atenolol in treatment of pregnancy-associated hypertension. Lancet 1:431, 1983.

279. Sandstrom BL: Antihypertensive treatment with the adrenergic beta-receptor blocker metoprolol during pregnancy. Gynecol Invest 9:195, 1978.

280. Gladstone GR, Hordof A, Gersony WM: Propranolol administration during pregnancy: Effects on the fetus. J Pediatr 86:962, 1975.

281. Habib A, McCarthy JS: Effects on the neonate of propranolol administration during pregnancy. J Pediatr 91:808, 1977.

282. Pruyn SC, Phelan JP, Buchanan GC: Long-term propranolol therapy in pregnancy: Maternal and fetal outcome. Am J Obstet Gynecol 135:485, 1979.

283. Isley WL, Dahl S, Gibbs H: Use of esmolol in managing a thyrotoxic patient needing emergency surgery. Am J Med 89:122, 1990.

284. Worley RJ, Crosby WM: Hyperthyroidism during pregnancy. Am J Obstet Gynecol 119:150, 1974.

285. Innerfield R, Hollander CS: Thyroidal complications of pregnancy. Med Clin North Am 61:67, 1977.

286. Momotani N, Hisaoka T, Noh J, et al: Effects of iodine on thyroid status of fetus versus mother in treatment of Graves' disease complicated by pregnancy. J Clin Endocrinol Metab 75:738, 1992.

287. Brodsky JF, Cohen EN, Brown BW Jr, et al: Surgery during pregnancy and fetal outcome. Am J Obstet Gynecol 138:1165, 1980.

288. Weingold AB: Surgical diseases in pregnancy. Clin Obstet Gynecol 26:793, 1983.

289. Mitsuda N, Tamaki H, Amino N, et al: Risk factors for developmental disorders in infants born to women with Graves' disease. Obstet Gynecol 80:359, 1992.

290. Momotani N, Ito K, Hamada N, et al: Maternal hyperthyroidism and congenital malformation in the offspring. Clin Endocrinol 20:695, 1984.

291. Dinani S, Carpenter S: Down's syndrome and thyroid disorder. J Ment Defic Res 34:187, 1990.

292. Davis LE, Lucas MJ, Hankins GDV, et al: Thyrotoxicosis complicating pregnancy. Am J Obstet Gynecol 160:63, 1989.

293. Easterling TR, Schmucker BC, Carlson KL, et al: Maternal hemodynamics in pregnancies complicated by hyperthyroidism. Obstet Gynecol 78:348, 1991.

294. Bruner JP, Landon MB, Gabbe SG: Diabetes mellitus and Graves' disease complicated by maternal allergies to antithyroid drugs. Obstet Gynecol 72:443, 1988.

295. Pitcher-Willmott RW, Hindocha P, Wood CBS: The placental transfer of IgG subclasses in human pregnancy. Clin Exp Immunol 41:308, 1980.

296. Ewin DL, McGregor AM: Pregnancy and autoimmune thyroid disease. Trends Endocrinol Metab 1:296, 1990.

297. Fisher DA: Fetal thyroid function: Diagnosis and management of fetal thyroid disorders. Clin Obstet Gynecol 40:16, 1997.

298. Matsuura N, Yamada Y, Nohara Y, et al: Familial neonatal transient hypothyroidism due to maternal TSH-binding inhibitor immunoglobulins. N Engl J Med 303:738, 1980.

299. Mitsuda N, Tamaki H, Amino N, et al: Risk factors for developmental disorders in infants born to women with Graves' disease. Obstet Gynecol 80:359, 1992.

300. Tamaki H, Amino N, Aozasa M, et al: Universal predictive criteria for neonatal overt thyrotoxicosis requiring treatment. Am J Perinatol 5:152, 1988.

301. McKenzie JM, Zakarija M: The clinical use of thyrotropin receptor antibody measurements. J Clin Endocrinol Metab 69:1093, 1989.

302. Clavel S, Madec AM, Bornet H, et al: Anti–TSH-receptor antibodies in pregnant patients with autoimmune thyroid disorder. Br J Obstet Gynaecol 97:1003, 1990.

303. Iseki M, Shimizu YM, Oikawa T, et al: Sequential serum measurements of thyrotropin binding inhibition immunoglobulin G in transient familial neonatal hypothyroidism. J Clin Endocrinol Metab 57:384, 1983.

304. Zakarija M, McKenzie JM, Hoffman WH: Prediction and therapy of intrauterine and late onset neonatal hyperthyroidism. J Clin Endocrinol Metab 62:368, 1986.

305. Bruinse HW, Vermeulen-Meiners C, Wit JM: Fetal therapy for thyrotoxicosis in nonthyrotoxic pregnant women. Fetal Ther 3:152, 1988.

306. Page DV, Brady K, Mitchell J, et al: The pathology of intrauterine thyrotoxicosis: Two case reports. Obstet Gynecol 72:479, 1988.

307. Wallace C, Couch R, Ginsberg J: Fetal thyrotoxicosis: A case report and recommendations for prediction, diagnosis, and treatment. Thyroid 5:125, 1995.

308. Mortimer RH, Tyack SA, Galligan JP, et al: Graves' disease in pregnancy: TSH receptor binding inhibiting immunoglobulins and maternal and neonatal thyroid function. Clin Endocrinol 32:141, 1990.

309. Tamaki H, Amino N, Takeoka K, et al: Prediction of later development of thyrotoxicosis or central hypothyroidism from the cord serum TSH level in neonates born to mothers with Graves' disease. J Pediatr 115:318, 1989.

310. Zakarija M, McKenzie JM: Pregnancy-associated changes in the thyroid-stimulating antibody of Graves' disease and the relationship to neonatal hyperthyroidism. J Clin Endocrinol Metab 57:1036, 1983.

311. Tamaki H, Amino N, Takeoka K, et al: Prediction of later development of thyrotoxicosis of central hypothyroidism from the cord serum thyroid-stimulating hormone level in neonates born to mothers with Graves' disease. J Pediatr 115:318, 1989.

312. Skuza KA, Sills IN, Stene M, Rapaport R: Prediction of neonatal hyperthyroidism in infants born to mothers with Graves' disease. J Pediatr 128:264, 1996.

313. Houck JA, Davis RE, Sharma HM: Thyroid stimulating immunoglobulin as a cause of recurrent intrauterine fetal death. Obstet Gynecol 71:1018, 1988.

314. Delange F: Effect of maternal thyroid function during pregnancy on fetal development. In Beckers C, Reinwein D (eds): The Thyroid and Pregnancy. Stuttgart, Germany, Schattauer, 1991, p 7.

315. Mandel S, Hanna C, LaFranchi S: Thyroid function of infants born to mother with Graves' disease. J Pediatr 117:169, 1990.

316. Williams RH, Kay GA, Jandorf BJ: Thiouracil, its absorption, distribution,

and excretion. J Clin Invest 23:613, 1943.

317. Kampmann JP, Hansen JM, Johansen K, Helweg J: Propylthiouracil in human milk: Revision of a dogma. Lancet 1:736, 1980.

318. Johansen K, Andersen AN, Kampmann JP, et al: Excretion of methimazole in human milk. Eur J Clin Pharmacol 23:39, 1982.

319. Cooper DS, Bode HH, Nath B, et al: Methimazole pharmacology in man: Studies using a newly developed radioimmunoassay for methimazole. J Clin Endocrinol Metab 58:473, 1984.

320. Lamberg BA, Ikonen E, Österlund K, et al: Antithyroid treatment of maternal hyperthyroidism during lactation. Clin Endocrinol 21:81, 1984.

321. Momotani N, Yamashita R, Yoshimoto M, et al: Recovery from foetal hypothyroidism: Evidence for the safety of breast-feeding while taking propylthiouracil. Clin Endocrinol 31:591, 1989.

322. Azizi F, Khoshniat M, Bahrainian M, Hedayati M: Thyroid function and intellectual development of infants nursed by mothers taking methimazole. J Clin Endocrinol Metab 85:3233, 2000.

323. Klein RZ, Haddow JE, Faix JD, et al: Prevalence of thyroid deficiency in pregnant women. Clin Endocrinol 35:41, 1991.

324. Tunbridge WMG, Evered D, Hall R, et al: The spectrum of thyroid disease in a community: The Wickham survey. Clin Endocrinol 7:481, 1977.

325. Gray RS, Dorsey DQ, Seth J, et al: Prevalence of subclinical thyroid failure in insulin dependent diabetes. J Clin Endocrinol Metab 50:1034, 1980.

326. Bech K, Hoier-Madsen M, Feldt-Rasmussen U, et al: Thyroid function and autoimmune manifestations in insulin-dependent diabetes mellitus during and after pregnancy. Acta Endocrinol 124:534, 1991.

327. Jovanovic-Peterson L, Peterson CM: De novo clinical hypothyroidism in pregnancies complicated by type I diabetes, subclinical hypothyroidism and proteinuria. Am J Obstet Gynecol 104:909, 1989.

328. Gavin LA, McMahon FA, Laske JN, et al: Alterations in serum thyroid hormones and thyroxine binding globulin in patients with nephrosis. J Clin Endocrinol Metab 46:125, 1978.

329. Hornnes PJ, Rasmussen N, Hegedus L, et al: Glucose tolerance and incidence of pancreatic islet cell antibodies in pregnancy in women with thyroid autoantibodies. Horm Metab Res 23:122, 1991.

330. Amino N: Autoimmunity and hypothyroidism. J Clin Endocrinol Metab 2:591,1988.

331. Dillon RS: Disorders of the thyroid gland. In Dillon RS (ed): Handbook of Endocrinology, 2. Philadelphia, Lea and Febiger, 1980, p 297.

332. Mizgala L, Lao TT, Hannah ME: Hypothyroidism presenting as hypothermia following pre-eclampsia at 23 weeks gestation: Case report and review of the literature. Br J Obstet Gynaecol 98:221, 1991.

333. Patel S, Robinson S, Bidgood RJ, et al: A pre-eclampsia–like syndrome associated with hypothyroidism during pregnancy. Q J Med 79:435, 1991.

334. Lao TT, Chin RHK, Swaminanthan R: Thyroid function in pre-eclampsia. Br J Obstet Gynaecol 95:880, 1988.

335. Tamaki H, Amino N, Takeoka K, et al: Thyroxine requirement during pregnancy for replacement therapy of hypothyroidism. Obstet Gynecol 76:230, 1990.

336. Pekonen F, Teramo K, Ikonen E, et al: Women on thyroid hormone therapy: Pregnancy course, fetal outcome and amniotic fluid thyroid hormone level. Obstet Gynecol 63:635, 1984.

337. Reinwein D, Jaspers C, Kirbas C, et al: Thyroxine substitution during pregnancy. In Beckers C, Reinwein D (eds): The Thyroid and Pregnancy. Stuttgart, Germany, Schattauer, 1991, p 115.

338. Kaplan MM: Monitoring thyroxine treatment during pregnancy. Thyroid 2:147, 1992.

339. Girling JC, de Swiet M: Thyroxine dosage during pregnancy in women with primary hypothyroidism. Br J Obstet Gynaecol 99:368, 1999.

340. McDougall IR, Maclin N: Hypothyroid women need more thyroxine when pregnant. J Fam Pract 41:238, 1995.

341. Caixas A, Albareda M, Garcia-Patterson A, et al: Postpartum thyroiditis in women with hypothyroidism antedating pregnancy. J Clin Endocrinol Metab 84:4000, 1999.

342. Abalovich M, Gutierrez S, Alcaraz G et al : Overt and subclinical hypothyroidism complicating pregnancy. Thyroid 12:63, 2002.

343. Chopra IJ, Baber K: Treatment of primary hypothyroidism during pregnancy: Is there an increase in thyroxine dose requirement in pregnancy? Metabolism 52:122, 2003.

344. Stock JM, Surks MI, Oppenheimer JH: Replacement dosage of L-thyroxine in hypothyroidism: A re-evaluation. N Engl J Med 290:529, 1974.

345. Campbell NR, Hasinoff BB, Stalts H, et al: Ferrous sulfate reduces thyroxine efficacy in patient with hypothyroidism. Ann Intern Med 117:1010, 1992.

346. Singh N, Singh PN, Heshman JM: Effect of calcium carbonate on the absorption of levothyroxine. JAMA 283:2822, 2000.

347. Bell DS, Ovalle F: Use of soy protein supplement and resultant need for increased dose of levothyroxine. Endocr Pract 7:193, 2001.

348. Tamaki H, Amino N, Takeoka K, et al: Thyroxine requirement during pregnancy for replacement therapy of hypothyroidism. Obstet Gynecol 76:230, 1990.

349. Townsend CW: A pregnant cretin. Arch Pediatr 14:20, 1897.

350. Hodges RE, Hamilton HE, Keitel WC: Pregnancy in myxedema. Arch Intern Med 90:863, 1952.

351. Echt CR, Doss JF: Myxedema in pregnancy: Report of 3 cases. Obstet Gynecol 22:615, 1963.

352. Lachelin GCL: Myxedema and pregnancy: A case report. J Obstet Gynaecol Br Commonw 7:77, 1970.

353. Anderson MM, Beales DL: Myxedema in pregnancy. J Obstet Gynaecol Br Commonw 7:74, 1970.

354. Baylan P, Frury MI: Pregnancy in untreated hypothyroidism. Ir J Med Sci 148:10, 1979.

355. Kennedy AL, Montgomery DAD: Hypothyroidism in pregnancy: Review. Br J Obstet Gynaecol 85:225, 1978.

356. Balen AH, Kurtz AB: Successful outcome of pregnancy with severe hypothyroidism: Case report and literature review. Br J Obstet Gynaecol 97:536, 1990.

357. Davis LE, Leveno KJ, Cunningham FG: Hypothyroidism complicating pregnancy. Obstet Gynecol 72:108, 1988.

358. Montoro M, Collea JV, Frasier SD, et al: Successful outcome of pregnancy in hypothyroid women. Ann Intern Med 94:31, 1986.

359. Leung AS, Millar LK, Koonings PP, et al: Perinatal outcome in hypothyroid pregnancies. Obstet Gynecol 81:349, 1993.

360. Wasserstrum N, Anania CA: Perinatal consequences of maternal hypothyroidism in early pregnancy and inadequate replacement. Clin Endocrinol 42:353, 1995.

361. Allan WC, Haddow JE, Palomaki GE, et al: Maternal thyroid deficiency and pregnancy complications: Implications for population screening. J Med Screen 7:127, 2000.

362. Khoury MJ, Becerra JE, d'Almada PJ: Maternal thyroid disease and risk of birth defects in offspring: A population-based case-control study. Pediatr Perinat Epidemiol 3:402, 1989.

363. Rovet J, Ehrlich R, Sorbara D: Intellectual outcome in children with fetal hypothyroidism. J Pediatr 110:700, 1987.

364. New England Congenital Hypothyroidism Collaborative: Neonatal hypothyroidism screening: Status of patients at six years of age. J Pediatr 107:915, 1985.

365. New England Congenital Hypothyroidism Collaborative: Elementary school performance of children with congenital hypothyroidism. J Pediatr 116:27, 1990.

366. Fisher DA, Foley BL: Early treatment of congenital hypothyroidism. Pediatrics 83:785, 1989.

367. New England Congenital Hypothyroidism Collaborative: Characteristics of infantile hypothyroidism discovered on neonatal screening. J Pediatr 104:539, 1984.

368. Coakley JC, Francis I, Gold H, et al: Transient primary hypothyroidism in the newborn: Experience of the Victorian neonatal thyroid screening program. Aust Paediatr J 25:25, 1989.

369. Cho BY, Shong YK, Lee HK, et al: Transient neonatal hypothyroidism due to transplacental transfer of maternal immunoglobulins that inhibit TSH binding, TSH-induced cAMP increases and cell growth. Endocrinol Jpn 35:819, 1988.

370. Takasu N, Mori T, Koizumi Y, et al: Transient neonatal hypothyroidism due to maternal immunoglobulins that inhibit thyrotropin-binding and post-receptor processes. J Clin Endocrinol Metab 59:142, 1984.

371. Root AW: The role of maternal autoimmune thyroid disease in neonatal hypothyroidism. Am J Dis Child 146:1029, 1992.

372. Blizzard RM, Chandler RW, Landing BH, et al: Maternal autoimmunization to thyroid as a probable cause of athyreotic cretinism. N Engl J Med 263:327, 1960.

373. Sutherland JM, Esselborn VM, Burket RL, et al: Familial non-goitrous cretinism apparently due to maternal antithyroid antibody. N Engl J Med 263:336, 1960.

374. Van der Gaag RD, Drexhage HA, Dussault JH: Role of maternal immunoglobulin blocking TSH-induced growth in sporadic forms of congenital hypothyroidism. Lancet 1:246, 1985.

375. Dussault JH, Bernier D: $^{125}$I uptake by FRTL5 cells: A screening test to detect pregnant women at risk of giving birth to hypothyroid infants. Lancet 2:1029, 1985.

376. Brown RS, Keating P, Mitchell E: Maternal thyroid-blocking immunoglobulins in congenital hypothyroidism. J Clin Endocrinol Metab 70:1341, 1990.

377. Bogner U, Graters AH, Sigle B, et al: Cytotoxic antibodies in congenital hypothyroidism. J Clin Endocrinol Metab 68:671, 1989.

378. Orgiazzi J, Rodien P, Morel Y, et al: Thyroid autoimmune disorders and pregnancy. In Beckers C, Reinwein D (eds): The Thyroid and Pregnancy. Stuttgart, Germany, Schattauer, 1991, p 45.

379. Dussault JH, Letarte J, Guyda H, et al: Lack of influence of thyroid antibodies on thyroid function in the newborn and on a mass screening program. J Pediatr 96:385, 1980.

380. Boyages SC, Halpern JP, Maberly GF, et al: Endemic cretinism: Possible role for thyroid autoimmunity. Lancet 2:529, 1989.

381. Francis G, Riley W: Congenital familial transient hypothyroidism secondary to transplacental thyrotropin-blocking autoantibodies. Am J Dis Child 141:1081, 1987.

382. Pharoah POD, Conolly KJ, Ekins RP, et al: Maternal thyroid hormone levels in pregnancy and the subsequent cognitive and motor performance of the children. Clin Endocrinol 21:265, 1984.

383. Bonet B, Herrera E: Differential response to maternal hypothyroidism during the first and second half of gestation in the rat. Endocrinology 122:450, 1986.

384. Amino N, Kuro R, Tanizawa O, et al: Changes in serum antithyroid antibodies during and after pregnancy in autoimmune thyroid diseases. Clin Exp Immunol 31:30, 1978.

385. Nelson JC, Palmer FJ: A remission of goitrous hypothyroidism during pregnancy. J Clin Endocrinol Metab 40:383, 1975.

386. Jansson R, Dahlberg PA, Winsa B, et al: The postpartum period constitutes an important risk for the development of clinical Graves' disease in young women. Acta Endocrinol 116:321, 1987.

387. Tamaki H, Amino N, Aozasa M, et al: Serial changes in thyroid-stimulating antibody and thyrotropin binding inhibitor immunoglobulin at the time of postpartum occurrence of thyrotoxicosis in Graves' disease. J Clin Endocrinol Metab 65:324, 1988.

388. Asa SL, Bilbao JM, Kovacs K, et al: Lymphocytic hypophysitis of pregnancy resulting in hypopituitarism: A distinct clinicopathologic entity. Ann Intern Med 96:166, 1981.

389. Kumar S: Isolated thyroid stimulating hormone deficiency following childbirth. Proc R Soc Med 59:1281, 1966.

390. Merenich JA, McDermott MT, Kidd GS: Transient isolated thyrotropin deficiency in the postpartum period. Am J Med 86:361, 1989.

391. Papetrou PD, Jackson IMD: Thyrotoxicosis due to silent thyroiditis. Lancet 1:361, 1975.

392. Amino N, Miyai K Onishi I, et al: Transient hypothyroidism after delivery in autoimmune thyroiditis. J Clin Endocrinol Metab 42:296, 1976.

393. Ginsberg J, Walfish PG: Post-partum transient thyrotoxicosis with painless thyroiditis. Lancet 1:1125, 1977.

394. Singer PA, Gorsky JE: Familial postpartum transient hyperthyroidism. Arch Intern Med 145:240, 1985.

395. Amino N, Miyai K, Kuro R, et al: Transient postpartum hypothyroidism: Fourteen cases with autoimmune thyroiditis. Ann Intern Med 87:155, 1977.

396. Fein HG, Goldman JM, Weintraub BD: Postpartum lymphocytic thyroiditis in American women: A spectrum of thyroid dysfunction. Am J Obstet Gynecol 138:504, 1980.

397. Freeman R, Rosen H, Thysen B: Incidence of thyroid dysfunction in an unselected postpartum population. Arch Intern Med 146:1361, 1986.

398. Lervang HH, Pryds O, Ostergaard Kristensen HP: Thyroid dysfunction after delivery: Incidence and clinical course. Acta Med Scand 222:369, 1987.

399. Nikolai TF, Turney SL, Roberts RC: Postpartum lymphocytic thyroiditis: Prevalence, clinical course, and long-term follow-up. Arch Intern Med 147:221, 1987.

400. Dailey GE: Recurrent postpartum transient hyperthyroidism. Ann Intern Med 90:719, 1979.

401. Walfish PG, Chan JYC: Postpartum hyperthyroidism. J Clin Endocrinol Metab 14:417, 1985.

402. Ramsay I: Postpartum thyroiditis: An underdiagnosed disease. Br J Obstet Gynaecol 93:1121, 1986.

403. Goldman JM: Postpartum thyroid dysfunction. Arch Intern Med 146:1296, 1986.

404. Jansson R, Dahlberg PA, Karlsson F: Postpartum thyroiditis. Baillieres Clin Endocrinol Metab 2:619, 1988.

405. Fung HYM, Kologlu M, Collison K, et al: Postpartum thyroid dysfunction in Mid Glamorgan. Br Med J 296:241, 1988.

406. Amino N, Mori H, Iwatani Y, et al: High prevalence of transient post-partum thyrotoxicosis and hypothyroidism. N Engl J Med 306:849, 1982.

407. Jansson R, Bernander S, Karlsson A, et al: Autoimmune thyroid dysfunction in the postpartum period. J Clin Endocrinol Metab 58:681, 1984.

408. Wilson R, McKillop JH, Walker JJ, et al: The incidence of clinical thyroid dysfunction in an unselected group of pregnant and postpartum women. Scot Med J 35:170, 1990.

409. White WB, Andreoli JW: Painless postpartum thyroiditis seen initially as severe hypertension. Am J Obstet Gynecol 148:346, 1984.

410. White WB, Andreoli JW: Severe, accelerated postpartum hypertension associated with hyperthyroxinemia. Br J Obstet Gynaecol 93:1297, 1986.

411. Rhys J, Othman S, Parkes AB, et al: Interference in thyroid function tests in postpartum thyroiditis. Clin Chem 37:1397, 1991.

412. Romney BM, Nickoloff EL, Esser PD, et al: Radionuclide administration to nursing mothers: Mathematically derived guidelines. Radiology 160:549, 1986.

413. Dydek GJ, Blue PW: Human breast milk excretion of iodine-131 following diagnostic and therapeutic administration to a lactating patient with Graves' disease. J Nucl Med 29:407, 1988.

414. Robinson GE, Stewart DE: Postpartum psychiatric disorders. Can Med Assoc J 134:31, 1986.

415. Spratt DI, Pont A, Miller MB, et al: Hyperthyroxinemia in patients with acute psychiatric disorders. Am J Med 74:41, 1982.

416. Stewart DE, Addison AM, Robinson GE, et al: Thyroid function in psychosis following childbirth. Am J Psychiatry 145:1579, 1988.

417. Jansson R: Autoimmune thyroiditis: A clinical epidemiological and immunological study with special reference to transient aggravation in the postpartum period [thesis]. Acta Univ Ups 492:1, 1984.

418. Hayslip CC, Fein HG, O'Donnell VM, et al: The value of serum antimicrosomal antibody testing in screening for symptomatic postpartum thyroid dysfunction. Am J Obstet Gynecol 159:203, 1989.

419. Harris B, Fung H, Johns S, et al: Transient post-partum thyroid dysfunction and postnatal depression. J Affect Disord 17:243, 1989.

420. Pop VJM, de Rooy HAM, Vadar HL, et al: Postpartum thyroid dysfunction and depression in an unselected population. N Engl J Med 324:1815, 1991.

421. Harris B, Othman S, Davies JA, et al: Association between postpartum thyroid dysfunction and thyroid antibodies and depression. Br Med J 305:152, 1992.

422. Tachi J, Amino N, Tamaki H, et al: Long-term follow-up and HLA association in patients with postpartum hypothyroidism. J Clin Endocrinol Metab 66:480, 1988.

423. Othman S, Phillips DIW, Parkes AB, et al: A long-term follow-up of postpartum thyroiditis. Clin Endocrinol 32:559, 1990.

424. Roti E, Minelli R, Gardini E, et al: Impaired intrathyroidal organification and iodine-induced hypothyroidism in euthyroid women with a previous episode of postpartum thyroiditis. J Clin Endocrinol Metab 73:958, 1991.

425. Lazarus JH: Postpartum thyroiditis. Thyroid Int 5:3–9, 1996.

426. Marqusee E, Hill JA, Mandel SJ: Thyroiditis after pregnancy loss. J Clin Endocrinol Metab 82:2455, 1997.

427. Bech K, Hertel J, Rasmussen NG, et al: Effect of maternal thyroid autoantibodies and postpartum thyroiditis on the fetus and neonate. Acta Endocrinol 125:146, 1991.

428. Stagnaro-Green A, Roman SH, Cobin RH, et al: A prospective study of lymphocyte-initiated immunosuppression in normal pregnancy: Evidence of a T-cell etiology for postpartum thyroid dysfunction. J Clin Endocrinol Metab 74:645, 1992.

429. Solomon BL, Fein HG, Smallridge RC: Usefulness of antimicrosomal antibody titers in the diagnosis and treatment of postpartum thyroiditis. J Fam Pract 36:177, 1993.

430. Feldt-Rasmussen U, Hoier-Madsen M, Rasmussen NG, et al: Antithyroid peroxidase antibodies during pregnancy and postpartum: Relation to postpartum thyroiditis. Autoimmunity 6:211, 1990.

431. Kampe O, Jansson R, Karlsson FA: Effects of L-thyroxine and iodide on the development of autoimmune postpartum thyroiditis. J Clin Endocrinol Metab 70:1014, 1990.

432. Bech K: Importance of cytolytic activity and dietary iodine in the pathogenesis of postpartum thyroiditis. Allergy 43:161, 1988.

433. Sridama V, Pacini F, Yan SL, et al: Decreased levels of helper T cells: A possible cause of immunodeficiency in pregnancy. N Engl J Med 307:352, 1982.

434. Takasu N, Komiya I, Nagasawa Y, et al: Exacerbation of autoimmune thyroid dysfunction after unilateral adrenalectomy in patients with Cushing's syndrome due to an adrenocortical adenoma. N Engl J Med 322:1708, 1990.

435. Thompson C, Farid NR: Postpartum thyroiditis and goitrous Hashimoto's thyroiditis are associated with HLA-DR4. Immunol Lett 11:301, 1985.

436. Vargas MT, Briones-Urbina R, Gladman D, et al: Antithyroid microsomal autoantibodies and HLA-DR5 are associated with postpartum thyroid dysfunction: Evidence supporting an autoimmune pathogenesis. J Clin Endocrinol Metab 67:327, 1988.

437. Kologlu M, Fung H, Darke C, et al: Postpartum thyroid dysfunction and HLA status. Eur J Clin Invest 20:56, 1990.

438. Jansson R, Safwenberg J, Dahlberg PA: Influence of the HLA-DR4 antigen and iodine status on the development of autoimmune postpartum thyroiditis. J Clin Endocrinol Metab 60:168, 1985.

439. Pryds O, Lervang HH, Ostergaard-Kristensen HP, et al: HLA-DR factors associated with postpartum hypothyroidism: An early manifestation of Hashimoto's thyroiditis? Tissue Antigens 30:34, 1987.

440. DeGroot LJ, Quintans J: The causes of autoimmune thyroid disease. Endocr Rev 10:537, 1989.

441. Jansson R, Karlsson FA, Linde A, et al: Postpartum activation of autoimmunity: Transient increase of total IgG levels in normal women and in women with autoimmune thyroiditis. Clin Exp Immunol 70:68, 1987.

442. Weetman AP, Fung HYM, Richards CJ, et al: IgG subclass distribution and relative functional affinity of thyroid microsomal antibodies in postpartum thyroiditis. Eur J Clin Invest 20:133, 1990.

443. Jansson R, Thompson PM, McLachlan FC, et al: Association between thyroid microsomal antibodies of subclass IgG-1 and hypothyroidism in autoimmune postpartum thyroiditis. Clin Exp Immunol 63:80, 1986.

444. Briones-Urbina R, Parkes AB, Bogner U, et al: Increase in antimicrosomal antibody–related IgG1 and IgG4 and titers of antithyroid peroxidase antibodies but not antibody dependent cell-mediated cytotoxicity in post-partum thyroiditis with transient hyperthyroidism. J Endocrinol Invest 13:879, 1990.

445. Tachi J, Amino N, Iwatani Y, et al: Increase in antideoxyribonucleic acid antibody titer in postpartum aggravation of autoimmune thyroid disease. J Clin Endocrinol Metab 67:1049, 1988.

446. Iwatani Y, Amino N, Tamaki H, et al: Increase in peripheral large granular lymphocytes in postpartum autoimmune thyroiditis. Endocrinol Jpn 35:447, 1988.

447. Hayslip CC, Baker JR, Wartofsky L, et al: Natural killer cell activity and serum autoantibodies in women with postpartum thyroiditis. J Clin Endocrinol Metab 66:1089, 1988.

448. Chan JYC, Walfish PG: Activated (Ia+) T-lymphocytes and their subsets in autoimmune thyroid diseases: Analysis by dual laser flow microfluorocytometry. J Clin Endocrinol Metab 62:403, 1986.

449. Jansson R, Totterman TH, Sallstrom J, et al: Intrathyroidal and circulating lymphocyte subsets in different stages of autoimmune postpartum thyroiditis. J Clin Endocrinol Metab 58:942, 1984.

450. Struve CW, Haupt S, Ohlen S: Influence of frequency of previous pregnancies on the prevalence of thyroid nodules in women without clinical evidence of thyroid disease. Thyroid 3:7, 1993.

451. Rosen IB, Walfish PG: Pregnancy as a predisposing factor in thyroid neoplasia. Arch Surg 121:1287, 1986.

452. Fukada K, Hachisuga T, Sugimori H, et al: Papillary carcinoma of the thyroid occurring during pregnancy. Acta Cytol 35:725, 1991.

453. Goldman MH, Tisch B, Chattock AG: Fine needle biopsy of a solitary thyroid nodule arising during pregnancy. J Med Soc N J 80:525, 1986.

454. Orr JW, Shingleton A: Cancer in pregnancy. Curr Probl Cancer 8:3, 1983.

455. Hod M, Sharony R, Friedman S, et al: Pregnancy and thyroid carcinoma: A review of incidence, course and prognosis. Obstet Gynecol Surv 44:774, 1989.

456. Tan GH, Gharib H, Goellner JR, et al: Management of thyroid nodules in pregnancy. Arch Intern Med 156:2317, 1996.

457. Laitinen K: Life-threatening laryngeal edema in a pregnant woman previously treated for thyroid carcinoma. Obstet Gynecol 78:937, 1991.

458. Asteris GT, DeGroot L: Thyroid cancer: Relationship to radiation exposure and to pregnancy. J Reprod Med 4:209, 1976.

459. Moosa M, Mazzaferri EL: Outcome of differentiated thyroid cancer diagnosed on pregnant woman. J Clin Endocrinol Metab 82:2862, 1997.

460. McTiernan AM, Weiss NS, Daling JR: Incidence of thyroid cancer in women in relation to reproductive and hormonal factors. Am J Epidemiol 120:423, 1984.

461. Rosen IB, Walfish PG, Nikore V: Pregnancy and surgical thyroid disease. Surgery 98:1135, 1985.

462. Herzon FS, Morris DM, Segal MN, et al: Coexistent thyroid cancer and pregnancy. Arch Otolaryngol Head Neck Surg 120:1191, 1994.

463. Balan KK, Critchley M: Outcome of pregnancy following treatment of well-differentiated thyroid cancer with $^{131}$iodine. Br J Obstet Gynaecol 99:1021, 1992.

# Endocrinology of Lactation

## David L. Kleinberg

## INTRODUCTION

All mammals have mammary glands that produce milk to nourish their young. The importance of lactation for the propagation of the species was recognized as far back as biblical times. In the Sabbath section of the Talmud, there is a story of a man who successfully took over the role of nursing his infant child after his wife died suddenly. Lactation begins in the postpartum period, the mammary glands having been prepared for lactation during gestation under the influence of the hormones of pregnancy. Suckling and the influence of hormones, especially prolactin (PRL) and oxytocin, maintain adequate milk production. This chapter briefly outlines the endocrinology of mammary development through lactation and discusses various clinical aspects of lactation and nursing.

## MORPHOLOGIC AND FUNCTIONAL DEVELOPMENT OF THE BREAST

### NEONATAL DEVELOPMENT

Rodents and humans are born with mammary fat pads that contain small glandular anlagen. The glandular anlagen undergo development and differentiation in response to appropriate hormones and growth factors at specific stages of life. The postpartum phases are puberty, pregnancy, lactation, and involution. Our understanding of fetal development of the mammary gland is derived primarily from studies in rodents. At approximately 12 days of gestation, ectodermal buds develop on the ventral body wall of embryonic mice. The embryonic mammary mesenchyme induces these structures from the epidermis both morphologically and functionally.[1–4] The ectodermal buds extend into mesenchyme, and together these two elements form the structure that will eventually become the mature mammary gland, consisting of glands in a mammary fat pad. The mammary fat pad, which, importantly, also interacts with the epithelial elements of the mammary gland during later phases of development, matures independently of the mammary mesenchyme.[1] In the mouse, androgen receptors (ARs) can be detected in the mammary mesenchyme by day 13. It is through these ARs that testos-

terone or dihydrotestosterone can induce regression of the mammary glands in male mice.[5]

In humans, mammary development begins at 4 weeks of embryonic life and continues until delivery.[6] At birth, many human fetuses of both sexes have prominent nipples because of the influence of the hormones of pregnancy on the glandular anlagen, and some have nipple secretions known as "witch's milk." This secretory activity generally subsides within 3 to 4 weeks.

### PUBERTAL DEVELOPMENT

A surge of estrogen starts the process of normal mammary development in early puberty. Development from immature ducts to the adult female mammary gland occurs by a process called *ductal morphogenesis*. This process entails development of structures called *terminal end buds*, which are multilayered club-shaped structures in which active cell division takes place. Under hormonal influence, these terminal end buds form and then extend and penetrate into the surrounding fat pad, leaving in their wake a network of hollow ducts that will eventually drain secretory products of glands though the teat.[7,8] The different stages of mammary development in the mouse are depicted in Figure 188-1. In the human, terminal end buds give rise to alveolar buds in lobules. They are at least two cell layers thick. True single-cell-thick alveoli capable of forming milk do not develop until pregnancy.[6]

#### Estrogen
Although the process of mammary development requires estrogen, which acts directly on the mammary gland,[9] estrogen alone is not sufficient for mammary development. The pituitary gland,[10–12] and specifically growth hormone (GH), is essential for normal mammary development.[13]

#### Growth Hormone
Mammary development does not take place in the absence of a pituitary gland, and mammary development does not occur in animal models deficient in GH (e.g., Ames and Snell dwarfs). Lyons[13] initially suggested that GH was responsible for pubertal mammary development and that PRL was responsible for glandular development during pregnancy. Studies from our own laboratory established that it was

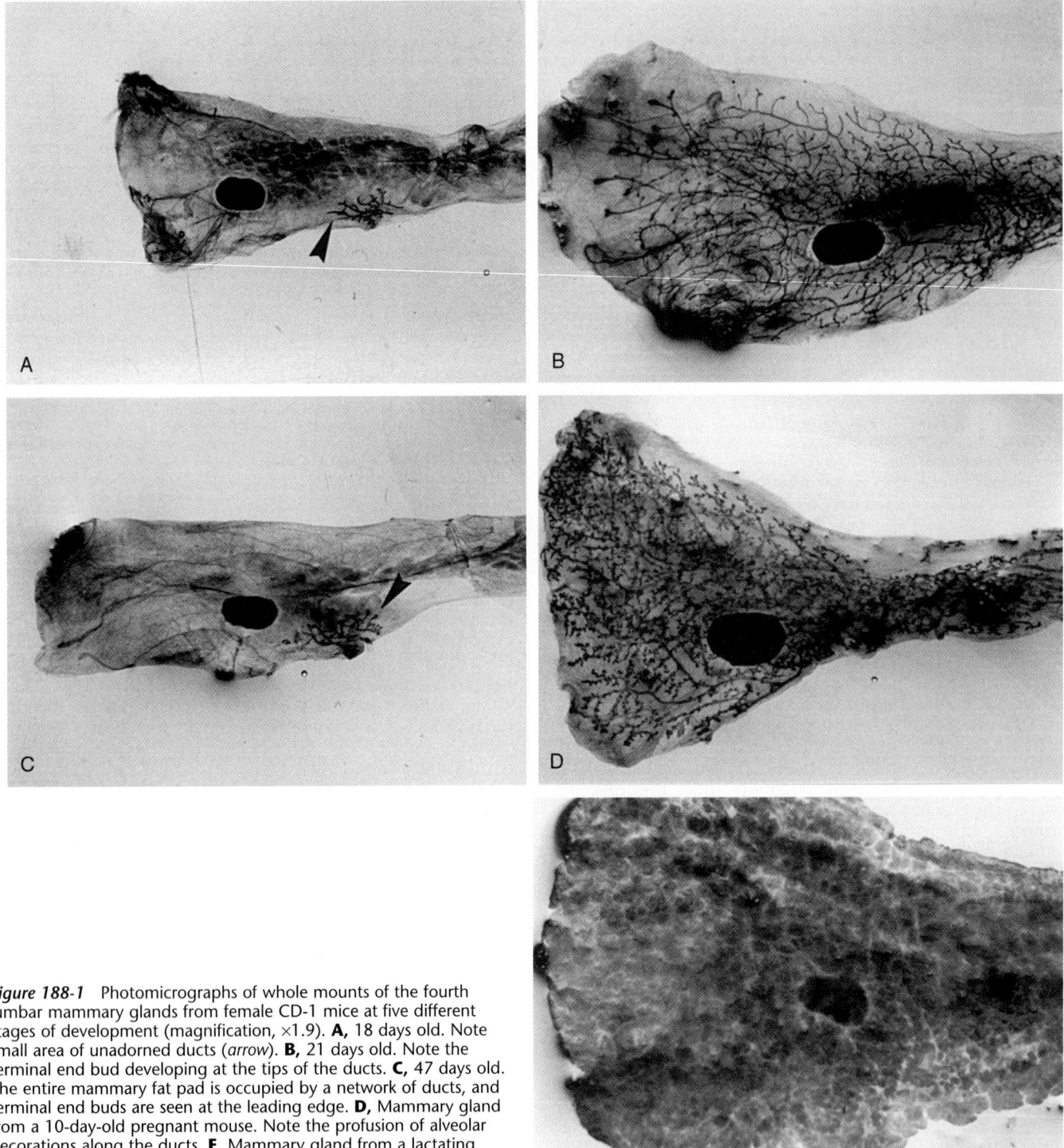

***Figure 188-1*** Photomicrographs of whole mounts of the fourth lumbar mammary glands from female CD-1 mice at five different stages of development (magnification, ×1.9). **A,** 18 days old. Note small area of unadorned ducts (*arrow*). **B,** 21 days old. Note the terminal end bud developing at the tips of the ducts. **C,** 47 days old. The entire mammary fat pad is occupied by a network of ducts, and terminal end buds are seen at the leading edge. **D,** Mammary gland from a 10-day-old pregnant mouse. Note the profusion of alveolar decorations along the ducts. **E,** Mammary gland from a lactating mouse 7 days postpartum. The gland itself is larger and is filled with alveoli containing milk.

indeed GH, working through local GH receptors in the mammary gland, that synergizes[14,15] with estrogen to induce this phase of mammary development. GH permits estrogen to act by a process that is still incompletely understood. The ability of GH to stimulate estrogen receptors (ERs) in the mammary gland may be one of several explanations for this interaction.[16] GH appears to act on stromal elements of the mammary gland[17] to stimulate induction of insulin-like growth factor-1 (IGF-1), which, in turn causes gland development by a paracrine mechanism (Fig. 188-2).

### Insulin-like Growth Factor-1

That IGF-1 is the physiologic mediator of GH action in mammary development is supported by a number of experimental observations, including: (1) IGF-1 mimics the activity of GH in mammary development in hypophysectomized, gonadectomized animals[18,19]; (2) GH stimulates IGF-1 messenger RNA (mRNA) within the mammary gland[17,19,20]; and (3) IGF-1 treatment, but not GH treatment, reverses the deficiency in mammary development in mice lacking the ability to produce IGF-1.[21]

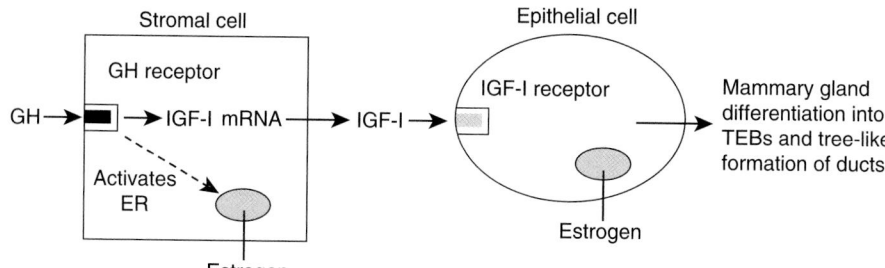

**Figure 188-2** Schematic model of effects of growth hormone, insulin-like growth factor-1, and E$_2$ in early mammary development.

## Progesterone

Until recently, the action of progesterone in mammary gland development and maintenance has been thought to be mainly on alveolar structure development during pregnancy and the luteal phase. Between puberty and eventual pregnancy, the mammary gland is a relatively quiescent organ. However, cyclic proliferative changes occur during the luteal phase of the menstrual cycle, because of the influence of progesterone.[22] Progestins also induce similar structural changes.[23,24] Recent work from our laboratory demonstrated that progesterone also can enhance the action of IGF-1 in experimental ductal morphogenesis. Although it is not clear that progesterone actually participates in ductal morphogenesis physiologically, these studies show that it has the capability of doing so. In early pregnancy, progesterone synergizes with IGF-1 and estradiol to form alveolar structures that will eventually become true alveoli that produce milk (Fig. 188-3).

### Other Hormones and Growth Factors

Contrary to previous concepts,[25,26] an independent effect of PRL on pubertal mammary development has not been demonstrated. Lactogens in the absence of somatotropic activity do not stimulate experimental pubertal mammary development in hypophysectomized, oophorectomized rats[14,15] and mice, and probably monkeys.[27] However, highly lactogenic growth hormones are more potent than nonlactogenic hormones in stimulating formation of terminal end buds,[15] suggesting that, like estrogen and progesterone, PRL might enhance the action of GH-induced IGF-1 on ductal morphogenesis.

Both epidermal growth factor (EGF)[28-30] and transforming growth factor α[31,32] are capable of stimulating formation of terminal end buds, and transforming growth factor β inhibits end bud formation and ductal growth.[33] It is possible that inhibition of ductal formation is developmentally important. However, it is uncertain whether any of these factors is physiologically important in the process of mammary development.

## GROSS ANATOMY OF THE HUMAN MAMMARY GLAND

Anatomically, the human breast is made up of a fat pad with 10 to 15 glandular lobules coursing through it, each of which is drained by a single duct, ending in the nipple (Fig. 188-4).[34-36] A description of the stages of pubertal mammary development according to the stages of Tanner is found in Chapter 142.

## PREPARATION FOR LACTATION

During pregnancy, the mammary gland is exposed to a wide variety of protein and steroid hormones,[36] some of which are produced by the placenta, and others, by the pituitary gland, ovaries, corpus luteum, and adrenal glands or the ovaries in concert with the adrenal glands.[37] They include PRL,[38-40] GH,[39-41] placental lactogen,[42] GH variant,[41,43,44] relaxin,[45]

estrogen and progesterone, glucocorticoids, and C$_{19}$-steroids. Whereas the somatotropic and mammotropic hormones of placental origin are capable of affecting the mammary glands during pregnancy, GH and PRL of pituitary origin are thought to be the most important. Some GH-deficient animal models have no mammary development during puberty (e.g., Lit$^-$/lit$^-$) but are able to nurse after several pregnancies. This suggests that placental hormone production (e.g., placental lactogen,

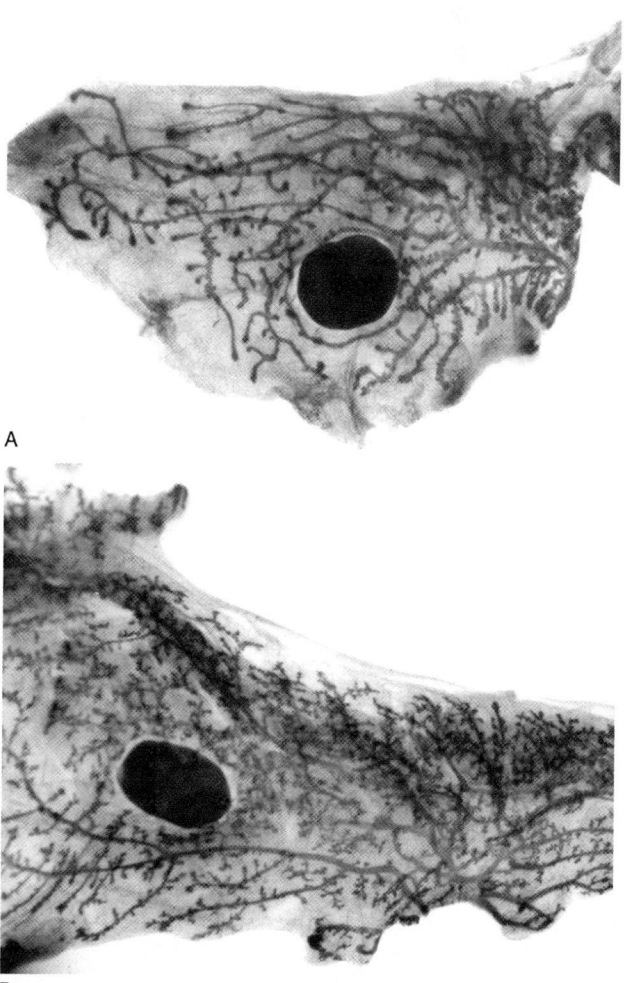

A

B

**Figure 188-3** Photomicrographs of whole mounts of the fourth lumbar mammary glands from female rats that were hypophysectomized and oophorectomized at age 21 days. **A,** Represents 5 days of treatment with des (1-3) insulin-like growth factor-1 (IGF-1) in pellets and E$_2$ administered via Silastic tubing. Note extensive ductal morphogenesis with terminal end buds (TEBs) and some side decorations. **B,** des (1-3) IGF-I + E$_2$ + Pg. The addition of Pg leads to development of true alveoli, as seen in pregnancy.

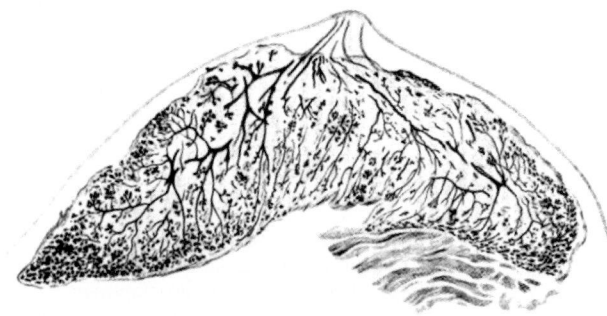

*Figure 188-4* Drawing of a cut through the mammary gland of a 19-year-old woman showing glandular structures that will drain milk through the nipple. (Reprinted from Dabelow A: Die Milchdrüse. In Möllendorff W (ed): Handbuch der Mikroskopischen Anatomie Des Menschen. Berlin, Springer-Verlag, 1957, p 337, with permission.)

GH variant) can replace pituitary hormone production in preparing the mammary gland for lactation in these animals. The potential contribution of placental hormones to mammary development during pregnancy has been well described.[42]

## Anatomic Changes

Under the control of PRL, progesterone, estradiol, and GH-stimulated IGF-I, alveolar elements proliferate in number and begin to produce milk proteins and colostrum in late pregnancy. Vorherr[46] previously described the anatomic changes during pregnancy in humans. In the first trimester, terminal ductal sprouting is followed by lobulo-alveolar formation, which begins at 3 to 4 weeks of gestation. Epithelial buds invade and replace the surrounding fat pad. It is not until the end of the first trimester that true alveoli form. During the second trimester, glandular elements further proliferate, and secretory products begin to appear in the lumina of alveoli. During the third trimester, fat droplets appear within alveolar cells, enlarging glands become filled with colostrum, and the mammary fat pad is overtaken by these elements. It is interesting that only a minority of pregnant women have actual expressible milk production during pregnancy, which is most likely due to inhibitory effects of estradiol and progesterone on PRL-induced milk production.[47-50]

## Effect of Prolactin

During pregnancy, PRL is required for formation of both milk and alveoli, and serum PRL concentrations increase to a mean of 207 ng/mL.[38] In the absence of PRL, formation of alveolar structures is impaired, as demonstrated in mice with targeted disruption of the PRL gene.[51] The mechanisms of action of PRL in this phase of mammary development have been extensively studied. That PRL acts by binding to cell-membrane receptors of mammary gland cells was first established by Kelly and coworkers.[52,53] In the absence of this receptor, which is a member of the cytokine-receptor superfamily,[54] PRL fails to achieve a biologic response. Homozygous PRL receptor (PRL-R) knockout mice are infertile, and therefore, studies on lactation are not possible.[55] However, heterozygous animals have given us some insight into the role of PRL-R in lactation. These animals have normal pregnancies but are unable to nurse their first litters, presumably because of inadequate receptors for PRL after the first but not subsequent pregnancies. PRL appears to induce a cellular response through induction of protein tyrosine phosphorylation, and activation of JAK2 kinase and STAT5.[56,57] STAT5 is one of the substrates of JAK2. Phosphorylation of STAT5 mediates the transcriptional activation of the β-casein gene. See the reviews by Hynes and colleagues[57] and Goffin and colleagues[58] for further details. The result is differentiation from less mature

glandular structures to extensive growth of mature alveoli capable of a secretory response.[59] The effect of PRL added to medium bathing organ cultures of mammary glands from mid-pregnant mice can be seen in Figure 188-5.[60]

## Effect of Placental Prolactin

Ever since it became known that PRL exists in humans as a hormone separate from GH[60,61] and the subsequent purification and development of a radioimmunoassay for PRL,[62-64] the action of this hormone as a mammogen during pregnancy and its source have been carefully studied. Tyson and colleagues[38] determined that PRL concentrations increase throughout gestation with a return to normal serum concentrations by 7 days postpartum. Simultaneously, they found that amniotic fluid PRL levels were 100 times those of maternal or fetal blood, which suggested the possibility that PRL might be produced by the placenta. Although PRL is produced by the decidua, the primary source of PRL that affects the mammary gland is the pituitary, which undergoes hyperplasia of lactotrophs.[39,40]

## Effect of Progesterone

PRL and estrogen do not act alone to produce mammary development during pregnancy; they also require the presence of progesterone. This assertion is supported by the observation that the mammary glands of mice lacking progesterone recep-

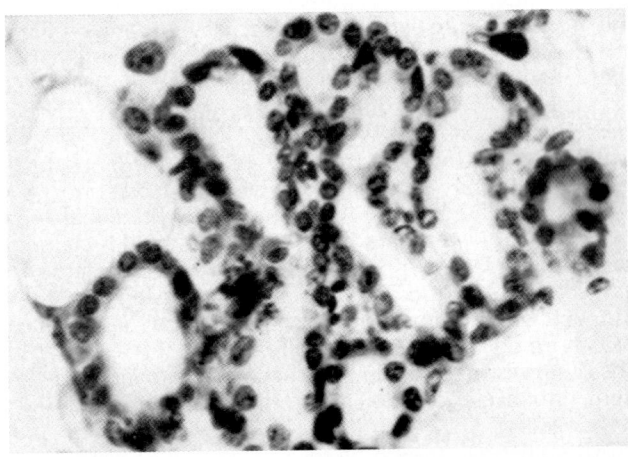

A

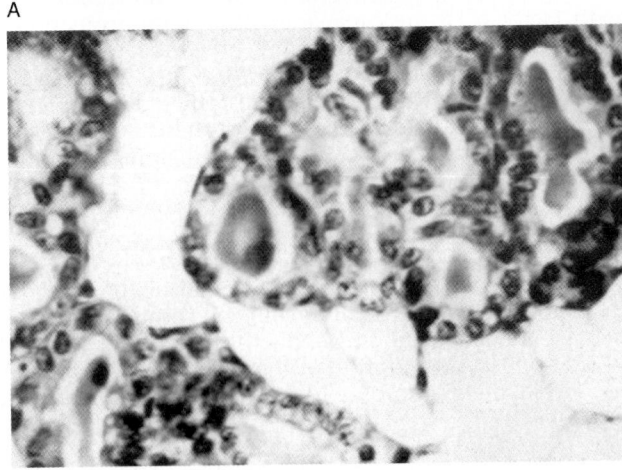

B

*Figure 188-5* **A,** Mouse breast tissue after incubation without prolactin in the medium. Note the absence of intraluminal secretory material. ×430. **B,** Mouse breast tissue after incubation with prolactin at a concentration of 50 ng/mL. Abundant secretory material is present in the lumina. ×430. (Reprinted from Kleinberg DL, Frantz AG: Human prolactin: Measurement in plasma by in vitro bioassay. J Clin Invest 50:1559–1560, 1971, with permission.)

tors (PRs) do not undergo lobulo-alveolar development when they are transplanted into PR-sufficient mice being treated with hormones that ordinarily do cause lobulo-alveolar changes.[65] Furthermore, PR knockout mice do not develop lobulo-alveolar structures when given estrogen and progesterone, although their mammary glands look normal during puberty.[66] Whereas progesterone is known to inhibit casein production during pregnancy, little is known about the mechanism of action of progesterone in lobulo-alveolar development.[48–50]

### Effect of Insulin-like Growth Factor-1

It is likely that GH-induced IGF-1 continues to be essential for mammary development during pregnancy. This assertion is based on experiments that show that IGF-1 and estrogen are required for progesterone to stimulate mammary development that resembles the mammary gland during pregnancy (see Fig. 188-3).

## LACTATION

### INITIATION OF LACTATION

As both estrogen and progesterone inhibit the lactogenic activity of PRL[47,48] and both decrease abruptly postpartum, their absence or reduction provides a trigger for active lactation. Both PRL and oxytocin are stimulated by this process.[67,68] At 3 weeks postpartum, progesterone is unmeasurable, and estradiol is present in mean 24-hour concentrations of 61 pg/mL. After parturition, milk production becomes more active because of reduced inhibition of steroid hormones, suckling, and the influence of lactogens. Suckling is essential for continued lactation, because of its distant effect on hormone production and because it empties the mammary gland of milk.[6,69] Accumulation of milk first causes milk-filled distended mammary glands but eventually has an inhibitory effect on further milk synthesis unless the milk is emptied. That, in part, explains why a certain level of nursing activity is necessary for successful nursing.

### STAGES OF MILK PRODUCTION

In humans, stage I of lactogenesis occurs from mid-pregnancy until delivery, during which time the mammary gland produces substances such as lactose and α-lactalbumin in concentrations high enough to be detected in blood,[70,71] and lipids and other milk products can be identified in the alveoli. Stage II of lactogenesis occurs after parturition and in the first 4 postpartum days. In late pregnancy, mature colostrum can be detected in the gland, but no active lactation is present because of the inhibitory actions of progesterone and probably estrogen. This stage lasts until after parturition, when mature milk is available to the infant. At about 40 hours after delivery, the volume of milk produced by the breast increases copiously and is known as the "coming in" of milk. The process of lactation begins at that point and is continued under the influence of suckling, PRL, and oxytocin.

### EFFECT OF PROLACTIN

Noel and coworkers[72] and later other groups[73–75] demonstrated that suckling and breast stimulation causes 8.5-fold increases in serum PRL in actively nursing mothers. They also showed that the milk "let-down" phenomenon was not associated with an increase in PRL.[72] As nursing continues, PRL concentrations decrease, but each suckling episode continues to cause an increase in serum PRL. When PRL was measured frequently during nursing episodes, Johnston and Amico[73] found that mean serum concentrations were 162 ng/mL at 2 to 4 weeks postpartum, 130 ng/mL at 5 to 14 weeks, and

77 ng/mL at 15 to 24 weeks. Nunley and colleagues[74] noted similar levels of PRL at 3 weeks and 3 months postpartum. The reason that milk production continues actively despite lower PRL levels has not been ascertained. However, Howie and colleagues[76] reported that although PRL is essential for milk production, the milk yield was not closely correlated with the height of the serum PRL. PRL maintains milk production by a complicated molecular biologic process discussed earlier.[77,78]

### EFFECT OF INSULIN-LIKE GROWTH FACTOR-1

The evidence that IGF-1 is or may be important in lactation is that transgenic mice that overexpress IGF-1 have hyperplastic glands during lactation and fail to undergo adequate involution. They are hyperplastic because IGF-1 inhibits apoptosis.[79,80] IGF-binding protein 5 (IGFBP-5) is thought to inhibit physiologically the action of IGF-1 in lactational involution.[81,82]

### EFFECT OF OXYTOCIN

In addition to increasing serum PRL levels, suckling stimulates release of oxytocin from the posterior pituitary with each episode. The signal is neuronally transmitted to the supraoptic and paraventricular nuclei of the hypothalamus, causing a pulsatile release of oxytocin from the posterior pituitary by complex mechanisms that are still not fully understood.[68,83–86] Mean serum levels of oxytocin have been found to be 0.7 mU/mL at baseline and 5.9 mU/mL during suckling. The release of oxytocin often occurs 3 to 10 minutes before the tactile stimulus of suckling (the milk let-down phenomenon).[68,87,88] Either the baby's cry or restlessness or the mother making preparations for nursing can trigger milk let-down.[89] Unlike PRL, oxytocin responses to suckling do not decline as nursing continues for up to 6 months, and those mothers who breastfeed exclusively had significantly higher mean stimulated oxytocin levels during late versus early lactation.[73] Oxytocin has long been known to work by inducing contraction of the myoepithelial cells, thereby causing milk ejection.[45] This hormone also was recently shown by Wagner and colleagues[90] to have important effects on alveolar proliferation during lactation. Mice deficient in oxytocin are unable to nurse their young, but administration of oxytocin permits the dams to nurse. Furthermore, no proliferation of alveolar structures is seen in response to suckling in deficient animals. In contrast, active proliferation was found in wild-type controls. Thus, oxytocin is very important in the process of lactation, not only because of its well-known effect on milk ejection but also because it appears to synergize with PRL in gland formation. Oxytocin also increases blood flow to the mammary gland. The vasoactive peptides VIP and calcitonin gene–related peptide also are known to induce mammary blood flow.[79]

### LACTATIONAL INVOLUTION

When no longer nursing or nursing infrequently, the lactating mammary gland undergoes a process of atrophy of glandular lobules due to apoptosis, with a desmoplastic reaction and fat infiltration.[91] The mammary gland after lactation regresses but has more glandular elements than it would have if pregnancy and lactation had not taken place.

### COMPOSITION OF MILK

Mother's milk is a complex substance containing all the nutrients necessary for neonates during the first 4 months of life. Whether mother's milk alone, without other nutrients, is sufficient thereafter is a matter of controversy.[92] Unlike nourishing a developing fetus, in which placental transfer depends on the mother's nutritional status, the composition of mother's milk in humans remains relatively stable and usually adequate even during periods of inadequate food intake in humans. However, some substances, such as the B vitamins and selenium, are profoundly affected by diet. In other species (e.g., rodents and dairy cows), dietary restriction does alter milk quality and content.[93]

The biochemistry of milk formation is essentially the same in all mammals. However, composition of milk differs among species, at different stages of lactogenesis in the same individual, and among individuals of the same species. The milk produced during pregnancy is high in sodium, chloride, certain milk proteins (α-lactalbumin and whey acidic proteins), and immunoglobulins.[94,95] At the time of parturition, the secretory product of the breast is called colostrum. It, too, is richer in proteins, including immunoglobulins, than mature mother's milk.[96] Therefore, premature infants are fed milk that is richer in proteins and salt but poorer in lactose.[97] During the first 4 postpartum days, the composition of milk changes as milk volume increases (Fig. 188-6).[98] After approximately 5 to 10 days, mature milk is produced copiously, and the quality is maintained. However, when milk composition was analyzed longitudinally during copious production of milk in stage II lactogenesis, increases were noted in lactose, glucose, pH, and ionized calcium and decreases in protein, sodium, potassium, chloride, and calcium over the first 6 months.[99] By 2 to 3 weeks of active lactation, milk production increases to a mean of approximately 800 mL/day. Milk composition also changes when daily milk volume decreases below 400 mL.[100]

Milk composition also is different in different species. Table 188-1 compares cow's milk with that of humans.

Milk contains an enormous number of other substances that may or may not have important physiological effects in the infant. Virtually every hormone and growth factor has been found in milk.[101-107] An example of a growth factor that has a known physiological effect on the infant is EGF. This growth factor has been shown to enhance intestinal growth in neonatal rats.[104,107] Another example is tumor necrosis factor-α, which is thought to enhance the motility of human milk macrophages.[103] IGF-1 concentrations also are significantly increased in human milk during the first to sixth postpartum weeks. Corps and colleagues[102] suggested that IGF-1 might be responsible for the increase in milk volume noted during this period.

Milk also contains vitamins and minerals that are clearly important for nutrition. Human milk is said to prevent infant tetany, which typically occurs only in formula-fed infants.[108,109] This could be due to the presence of parathyroid hormone–like peptide that is produced in mammary tissue in response to PRL,[110,111] to vitamin D,[112,113] and to an increase in calcium and phosphorus in human milk.[108] A nitrogen-containing polysaccharide in mother's milk favors growth of the *Lactobacillus bifidus*, which confers a protective effect against enteropathogenic organisms such as *Escherichia coli*.[114] Transfer of immunoglobulin A (IgA) to milk was discussed earlier, as was the appearance of whole immune cells in milk.

## MEDICATIONS AND ALCOHOL IN MILK

Milk also contains substances that may not be healthful or advantageous. The teratogenic effects of thalidomide in infants heightened awareness of potential dangers of medications during pregnancy and lactation. Thus, it is easier to caution mothers either to avoid medications while nursing or to stop nursing to avoid adverse effects of the medications. Although virtually all medications are found in mother's milk, most do not cause adverse events in the children when used with caution.[115] Even some that do, such as morphine, which can impair oxytocin release,[116] are not considered by some to be totally contraindicated during nursing.[115] The American Academy of Pediatrics (AAP) publishes a list of

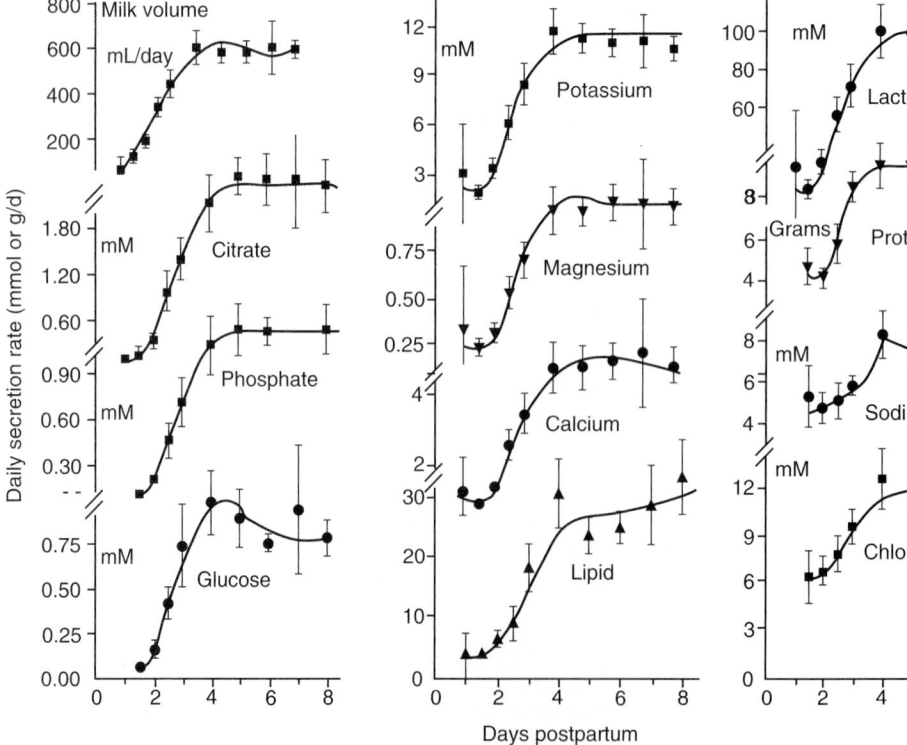

**Figure 188-6** The rate of secretion of milk volume and macronutrients in milk during the first 8 postpartum days. Data were derived from a study of 12 multiparous women who weighed their infants before and after every feed for the first 7 postpartum days and gave frequent milk samples (9). These data illustrate the high level of coordination required to produce milk of consistent composition during early lactation. (Reprinted from Neville MC, Morton J: Physiology and endocrine changes underlying human lactogenesis II. J Nutr 131:3006S, 2001, with permission.)

**Table 188-1** Comparison of the Macronutrient Contents of Human and Bovine Milk

| Component | Human Milk | Bovine Milk |
|---|---|---|
| Carbohydrates | | |
| Lactose | 7.3 g/dL | 4.0 g/dL |
| Oligosaccharides | 1.2 g/dL | 0.1 g/dL |
| Proteins | | |
| Caseins | 0.2 g/dL | 2.6 g/dL |
| α-Lactalbumin | 0.2 g/dL | 0.2 g/dL |
| Lactoferrin | 0.2 g/dL | Trace |
| Secretory IgA | 0.2 g/dL | Trace |
| β-Lactoglobulin | 0 | 0.5 g/dL |
| Milk lipids | | |
| Triglycerides | 4.0% | 4.0% |
| Phospholipids | 0.04% | 0.04% |
| Minerals and other ionic constituents | | |
| Sodium | 5.0 mmol/L | 15 mmol/L |
| Potassium | 15.0 mmol/L | 43 mmol/L |
| Chloride | 15.0 mmol/L | 24 mmol/L |
| Calcium | 7.5 mmol/L | 30 mmol/L |
| Magnesium | 1.4 mmol/L | 5 mmol/L |
| Phosphate | 1.8 mmol/L | 11 mmol/L |
| Bicarbonate | 6.0 mmol/L | 5 mmol/L |

Data from Neville MC: Mammary gland biology and lactation: A short course. Presented at the International Society for Research in Human Milk and Lactation, Plymouth, NH, 1997; based on data from Neville MC, Allen JC, Watters C: The mechanisms of milk secretion. In Neville MC, Neifert MR (eds): Lactation: Physiology, Nutrition and Breast-Feeding. New York, Plenum Press, pp 49–102, with permission.

**Table 188-2** Classification of Classes of Drugs and Compounds for Potential Use in Nursing Mothers

1. **Cytotoxic drugs that may interfere with cellular metabolism in infant:** e.g., suppressants, cyclophosphamide, cyclosporin, methotrexate
2. **Drugs of abuse that can affect infants:** e.g., amphetamines, cocaine, heroin, marijuana
3. **Radioactive compounds that require temporary cessation during breast feeding:** e.g., I[131] (12–14 days), I[125] (12 days), technetium[99] (3 days) (part of a list of nine compounds)
4. **Drugs for which the effect on nursing infants is unknown but may be of concern:** e.g., antianxiety drugs, antidepressants, antipsychotics, others including amiodarone, chloramphenicol, metronidazole (part of a list of 35 drugs)
5. **Drugs that have been associated with significant side effects in some nursing infants:** e.g., acebutalol, 5-aminosalicyclic acid, atenolol, bromocriptine, aspirin, clemastine, ergotamine, lithium, phenindone, phenobarbital, sulfasalazine (part of a list 12 drugs)
6. **Maternal medication usually compatible with breastfeeding:** e.g., acetaminophen, acyclovir, amoxicillin, cascara, chlorothiazide, cimetidine, cisplatin, digoxin, diltiazem, enalapril, gentamicin, ibuprofen, isoniazid, ketoconazole, meperidine, naproxen, phenytoin, prednisone, oral contraceptives (part of a list of 173 medications)
7. **Food and environmental agents:** e.g., aspartame (dangerous in phenylketonuria), chocolate (possible irritability), fava beans, lead, mercury, methylmercury, silicone, vegetarian diet can cause signs of $B_{12}$ deficiency (part of a list of 19 agents)

Adapted from American Academy of Pediatrics: The transfer of drugs and other chemicals into human milk. Pediatrics 108:776–789, 2001, with permission.

hundreds of drugs and other chemicals that are found in milk.[117,118] They divide these drugs into categories listed in Table 188-2. Other publications also considered the utility and risk of taking various medications while nursing.[115,119] Many of them can have deleterious effects on infants, but not all are contraindicated.[117,120,121] For example, methimazole has been given to thyrotoxic mothers without apparent effect on the infant's thyroid function.[122]

When prescribing medications, one must consider whether the benefits of nursing outweigh the potential risks to the infant. These or other sources should be referred to when recommending medications to nursing mothers. Overall, most experts, including the AAP, consider breastfeeding very important and generally urge mothers to continue even if medications are taken. Timing medication use can sometimes reduce exposure to the infants.

Alcohol consumed by nursing mothers also may be excreted into milk. Within 30 to 60 minutes after nursing mothers took small amounts of alcohol (0.3 g/kg body weight), ethanol appeared in milk at levels sufficient to confer an alcoholic odor, according to a "panel of experts." During that study, the infants drank significantly less milk.[94] Whether the reduced milk intake was a manifestation of the heightened epicurean senses of the babies or they fell asleep because of the alcohol and slept through the whole night was not determined.

## PATHOGENS IN MILK

Human immunodeficiency virus-1 (HIV-1), and probably other pathogens, can be transmitted from mothers to infants via milk.[92]

## BENEFITS OF MOTHER'S MILK

Human breast milk has been shown to reduce the incidence or severity of diarrhea and otitis media and other infections in infants.[68,123–130] Howie and colleagues[131] found that the incidence of gastrointestinal infections was significantly reduced in infants who were breastfed for at least 13 weeks when compared with that in formula-fed babies. The protective effect persisted even if lactation was not continued past 13 weeks. It also has been asserted that preterm infants fed mother's milk had higher developmental scores at age 18 months and higher intelligence at age 7.5 to 8 years.[132] A number of reports suggest that breastfeeding reduces breast cancer,[133,134] but others have not been confirmatory.[135,136] As both PRL and oxytocin enhance bonding activity, this too is an advantage of breastfeeding.[137]

## FORMATION OF MILK

The following discussion is based largely on reviews by Neville and her colleagues.[35,71,93,138] Formation of milk occurs by means of five separate transcellular pathways by which components of milk are secreted into the alveolar lumen (Fig. 188-7). These include: (I) exocytosis, (II) fat synthesis and secretion, (III) secretion of ions and water, and (IV) transcytosis of immunoglobulins and other substances from the interstitial space. A fifth pathway (V) is the paracellular pathway. The major components of milk are lactose; milk fat; proteins, including casein, lactoferrin, IgA, α-lactalbumin, and many others; and minerals and water. A large number of minor components also found in milk can be very important for the infant's health.

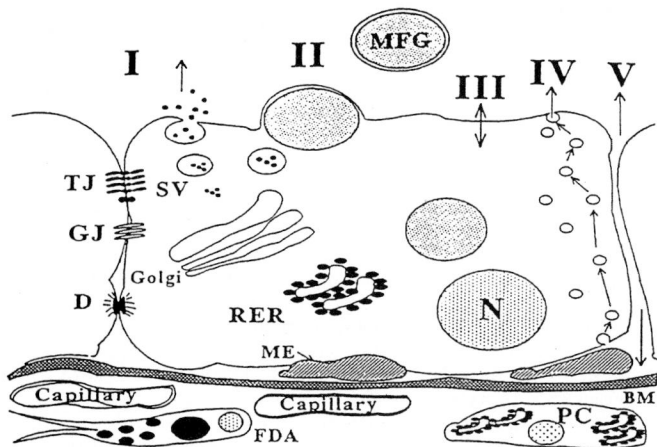

**Figure 188-7** The pathways for milk synthesis and secretion by the mammary epithelial cell. **I**, Exocytosis of milk protein, lactose, and other components of the aqueous phase in Golgi complex–derived secretory vesicles. **II**, Milk fat secretion via the milk fat globule. **III**, Direct movement of monovalent ions, water, and glucose across the apical membrane of the cell. **IV**, Transcytosis of components of the interstitial space. **V**, The paracellular pathway for plasma components and leukocytes. Pathway V is open only during pregnancy, involution, and in inflammatory states such as mastitis. SV, secretory vesicle; RER, rough endoplasmic reticulum; BM, basement membrane; MFG, milk fat globule; N, nucleus; PC, plasma cell; FDA, fat-depleted adipocyte; TJ, tight junction; GJ, gap junction; D, desmosome; ME, myoepithelial cell. (From an updated version of the figure by Neville MC: Mammary gland biology and lactation: A short course. Presented at the International Society for Research in Human Milk and Lactation, Plymouth, NH, 1997, with permission.)

Pathway I represents exocytosis, a process through which most of the components of the aqueous phase of milk are secreted. These include proteins, lactose, and water, all of which are transported in secretory vesicles to the alveolar lumen. Pathway II represents secretion of triglycerides. Triglycerides are first synthesized in the smooth endoplasmic reticulum, subsequently coalescing into large droplets, and finally becoming enveloped in the plasma membrane where they become part of milk in the form of the milk fat globule. In pathway III, direct movement of ions, water, and glucose occurs across the apical membrane. Pathway IV represents transcytosis, a process that allows intact proteins to enter milk. For example, IgA is synthesized in plasma cells in the mammary gland and elsewhere. After binding to receptors in the alveolar cell, the protein/receptor complex is transferred to the apical membrane, and the extracellular portion of the receptor is cleaved and secreted together with IgA. Finally, pathway V is passage of substances between rather than through alveolar cells. During lactation, the tight junctions between alveolar cells are relatively impermeable. They are more open during pregnancy and involution, and in patients with mastitis, when substances from plasma are found in milk, and milk in plasma. When the junctions are open, a higher concentration of sodium and chloride is found in milk.[139] Whole leukocytes also may pass through the tight junctions and become part of breast milk.[140,141]

## INVOLUTION

With menopause and a reduction in estrogen and progesterone, the mammary gland involutes, losing the true glandular structures and terminal end buds and lobules that result from the influence of these hormones.[6,69,138] However, the system of ducts that developed during puberty and thereafter is maintained.

## BREASTFEEDING

In addition to a breast capable of producing milk, breastfeeding requires a nipple that can be grasped by the baby as well as an intact nerve supply to the nipple. Stimulation of sensory nerves in the nipple leads to activation of the hypothalamic/pituitary axis, resulting in oxytocin release (responsible for milk let-down) and PRL release (responsible for milk production). Also essential to breastfeeding, once nursing begins, is the frequent emptying of the mammary gland to continue PRL and oxytocin stimulation and prevent inhibition of milk formation.[142]

The presence of an inverted nipple does not automatically prevent a woman from nursing her baby. A series of Hoffman's prenatal exercises, as well as plastic shields, can help to evert the nipple.[142] Careful attention must be paid to preparation and care of the nipple.[142] Plastic surgeons must take special care to spare the nerves innervating the mammary gland because they are intricately involved in the process of lactation.[143] A discussion of nursing techniques is outside the purview of this chapter; see several papers by Neifert and colleagues.[142,144]

In recent years in the United States and elsewhere, a trend has been noted toward an increased percentage of mothers breastfeeding their babies.[145] Nevertheless, nearly half of all mothers fail to meet their own breastfeeding goals, and many give up breastfeeding altogether.[146] Poor education and preparation by hospitals, doctors, and families have been blamed for this inordinately high failure rate. An anecdotal report of reduced glandular activity in three women who failed to produce adequate milk to nourish their young despite concerted efforts, confirmed by a technique called diaphanography,[147] suggests that specific problems with nursing are not associated with one's psychological state.

## DISORDERS OF NURSING

I find it hard to believe that so few true pathological problems with lactation have been uncovered. Could it be that we have not studied this process adequately?

### Agalactia

Inability to lactate because of a specific hormonal problem is a relatively rare event. In Sheehan's syndrome, inability to breastfeed results because of a deficiency in PRL secretion. This disorder was more common in the earlier part of this century when the syndrome was first described. Recently, Kauppila and colleagues[148] described a patient with isolated PRL deficiency of unknown etiology who was unable to nurse her babies after each of two pregnancies. Whether she had a form of Sheehan's syndrome is not known. In most other forms of pituitary insufficiency, including postpartum hypophysitis, pituitary tumors, and radiation-induced pituitary injury, serum PRL is elevated, whereas the other pituitary hormones become deficient. In recent years, abnormalities in genes that control PRL secretion have been recognized. Abnormalities in the *Pit-1* gene, which controls secretion of GH and thyroid-stimulating hormone (TSH) in addition to PRL, have been identified. At least one patient with this problem has been reported unable to nurse.[149] Very recently, mutations in the *PROP1* gene were found to cause familial combined pituitary hormone deficiency, including deficiency in gonadotropin secretion, but no definite problem with lactation was reported.[149]

It is unclear whether clinically significant cases of oxytocin deficiency result in an inability to nurse. Patients with central diabetes insipidus may have relatively normal concentrations of oxytocin.[150,151] This is thought to be because oxytocinergic neurons are more resistant to destruction by trauma than are vasopressinergic neurons in both mice and humans.[68,85,90] In the Prader-Willi syndrome, a reduced number of oxytocin neurons are found, but it is unclear whether this deficiency results in an inability to produce milk.[152] One might expect a deficiency in milk let-down, which is an oxytocin-stimulated event, if oxytocin were truly deficient. Whereas true oxytocin deficiency is rare, problems with milk let-down occur more frequently.[153]

### Breast Engorgement

This common problem can sabotage the process of breast-feeding. If milk is not adequately removed, breast engorgement occurs between postpartum days 2 and 5. The infant will have difficulty suckling on the nipple if it is engorged, which further complicates the problems associated with engorgement, such as pain.[142] Milking by hand or breast pump can help alleviate the problem, as can attempts to improve milk let-down, such as warm compresses before nursing. In addition, intranasal oxytocin has been reported to benefit some mothers.[142,154]

### Sore Nipples

Sore nipples are a common reason for early discontinuation of breastfeeding. It is said that proper positioning of the infant's mouth and proper positioning of the infant can prevent soreness.[153] A thin layer of lanolin-based cream applied to the nipple after feeding and avoiding prolonged non-nutritive nursing also can reduce soreness. Monilial infections also can contribute to soreness and can affect both mother and infant. With inadequate milk let-down, the infant must nurse longer and more vigorously to get an adequate amount of milk. If milk drips from both breasts after the infant suckles for a minute or two, or if a tingling sensation is felt in the nipple accompanied by increased fullness, it is likely the mother is experiencing milk let-down.

Painful breastfeeding has recently been described in 12 patients with Raynaud's phenomenon of the nipple.[155] They all reported extremely painful breastfeeding, with symptoms precipitated by cold temperatures and blanching and other color changes of the nipple. The pain was relieved in 6 with nifedipine.

### Lactation Mastitis

Mastitis is most frequently caused by *Staphylococcus aureus*, sometimes methicillin resistant. *E. coli* and *Streptococcus* species also may cause mastitis. Sometimes cultures of milk grow only normal flora. Mastitis occurs in from 2% to 33% of nursing mothers, often within the first 7 weeks of breastfeeding.[156] Local redness in a wedge-shaped area and tenderness typically occur, often accompanied by fever and chills. Abscesses occur in a minority. To treat, continued nursing or breast emptying is advised to avoid milk stasis. A 10-day course of antibiotics is often advised.[153] Breast emptying or no intervention other than breast support also is sometimes advised. See articles by Melnikow and Bedinghaus[153] and Barbosa-Chesnik and colleagues[156] for more details about the practical management of mastitis during breastfeeding.

## LACTATIONAL AMENORRHEA

Lactational amenorrhea is the oldest form of birth control. Frequent breastfeeding significantly reduces fertility and serves as a means for population control. For example, women of the !Kung hunter-gatherer people in Africa produce a mean of 4.7 live children during their reproductive years. Their children suckle frequently throughout the day, about four times an hour, and at will during the night.[157] In contrast, the Hutterites of North America have a mean of 10.6 children in their lifetimes. Their children nurse according to a rigid schedule, are introduced to supplemental feedings within a few months of birth, and are weaned within a year. In addition, the Hutterites do not practice other forms of birth control. In highly developed societies, lactational amenorrhea is a contraceptive option, but alternative forms of birth control also are readily available. In Edinburgh, the mean time for resumption of menses in women who breast-fed their children was only 28 weeks, and the first ovulation occurred at a mean of 34 weeks.[97] Early postpartum cycles in most women are anovulatory.[158] Glasier and McNeilly[97] postulated that the anovulation is due to abnormal pulsatile secretion of luteinizing hormone (LH). The experience in developed societies is in sharp contrast to the experience of the !Kung women and is clearly due to the difference in suckling frequency.

A possible explanation for lactational amenorrhea is that hyperprolactinemia, by a short feedback loop, inhibits LH pulsatility via an effect on gonadotropin-releasing hormone (GnRH) secretion.[159,160] As suggested earlier, amenorrhea during breastfeeding correlates with the frequency of suckling episodes. Because PRL levels decrease as nursing continues, one must question whether continued lactational amenorrhea is due to continued hyperprolactinemia. Kremer and colleagues,[161] who measured postpartum LH and PRL pulsatility in lactating and nonlactating mothers, found that LH was unmeasurable at postpartum day 7 in both groups and measurable but low in nursing mothers as compared with nonnursing ones at postpartum day 28. Although they found a negative correlation between LH and PRL, their study did not further determine the mechanism by which LH was suppressed.

### DRUG-INDUCED INCREASE IN MILK YIELD

A number of drugs have been used to increase milk production in mothers not producing enough milk to nourish their young. Aono and colleagues[162] found that sulpiride significantly increased milk yield in women during the first 5 postpartum days. Other investigators reported similar findings.[163] Metoclopramide[164–166] and domperidone,[167] which have a mechanism of action similar to that of sulpiride, also increase milk yield. I believe that the use of dopamine antagonists to stimulate PRL release and consequently milk yield is ill advised because of potential side effects of these drugs in the suckling infant. However, the risks of exposing an infant to dopamine antagonists may be unavoidable if the mother requires such drugs for treatment of a mental condition such as schizophrenia.[168,169]

GH also has shown some clinical utility in stimulating milk production in nursing mothers. A study of the effects of human GH on milk yield in 10 nursing mothers[170] showed that GH treatment is associated with an increase in milk yield compared with that in controls. However, it is unclear whether the effect of GH was due to its intrinsic lactogenicity property or to a somatotropic action.

Oxytocin, which participates in milk let-down, thereby bringing milk closer to the nipple for more immediate use by the child, also has been given to nursing mothers. Luhman[171] found that the infants of mothers receiving intranasal oxytocin consumed significantly more milk than did control infants, but that this increased milk consumption was not translated into increased infant weight gain. Others have not noted an improvement in milk yield with oxytocin treatment.[163]

At present, available data do not support the routine use of any of these drugs to improve milk yield.

## REFERENCES

1. Cunha GR: Role of mesenchymal-epithelial interactions in normal and abnormal development of the mammary gland and prostate [Review]. Cancer 74:1030–1044, 1994.
2. Sakakura T, Nishizuka Y: Mezenchyme-dependent morphogenesis and epithelium-specific cytodifferentiation in mouse mammary gland. Science 194:1439–1441, 1976.
3. Sakakura T: The mammary gland: Development, regulation and function. In Neville MC, Daniel CW (eds): Mammary Embryogenesis. New York, Plenum Press, 1987, pp 37–66.
4. Kratochwil K: Organ specificity in mesenchymal induction demonstrated in the embryonic development of the mammary gland of the mouse. Dev Biol 20:46–71, 1969.
5. Kratochwil K, Schwartz P: Tissue interaction in androgen response of embryonic mammary rudiment of mouse: Identification of target tissue for testosterone. Proc Natl Acad Sci U S A 73:4041–4044, 1976.
6. Russo J, Russo IH: Development of the human mammary gland. In Neville MC, Daniel CW (eds): The Mammary Gland. New York, Plenum Press, 1987, pp 67–93.
7. Daniel CW, Silberstein GB: Postnatal development of the rodent mammary gland. In Neville MC, Daniel CW (eds): The Mammary Gland. New York, Plenum Press, 1987, pp 3–36.
8. Humphreys RC: Programmed cell death in the terminal endbud. J Mammary Gland Biol Neoplasia 4:213–220, 1999.
9. Silberstein GB, Van Horn K, Shyamala G, et al: Essential role of endogenous estrogen in directly stimulating mammary growth demonstrated by implants containing pure antiestrogens. Endocrinology 134:84–90, 1994.
10. Gardner WU, White A: Mammary growth in hypophysectomized male mice receiving estrogen prolactin. Proc Soc Exp Biol Med 48:590–592, 1941.
11. Reece RP, Turner CW, Hill RT: Mammary gland development in the hypophysectomized albino rat. Proc Soc Exp Biol Med 34:204–217, 1936.
12. Lewis AA, Gomez ET, Turner CW: Mammary gland development with mammogen I in the castrated and the hypophysectomized rat. Endocrinology 30:37–47, 1942.
13. Lyons WR: Hormonal synergism in mammary growth. Proc R Soc (Lond) 149:303–325, 1958.
14. Kleinberg DL, Ruan W, Catanese V, et al: Non-lactogenic effects of growth hormone on growth and insulin-like growth factor-1 messenger ribonucleic acid of rat mammary gland [published erratum appears in Endocrinology 127:1977, 1990]. Endocrinology 126:3274–3276, 1990.
15. Feldman M, Ruan WF, Cunningham BC, et al: Evidence that the growth hormone receptor mediates differentiation and development of the mammary gland. Endocrinology 133:1602–1608, 1993.
16. Feldman M, Ruan W, Tappin I, et al: The effect of GH on estrogen receptor in the rat mammary gland. J Endocrinol 163:515–522, 1999.
17. Walden PD, Ruan WF, Feldman MM, et al: Evidence that the mammary gland fat pad mediates the action of growth hormone in mammary gland development. Endocrinology 139:659–662, 1998.
18. Ruan W, Newman CB, Kleinberg DL: Intact and aminoterminally shortened forms of insulin-like growth factor I induce mammary gland differentiation and development. Proc Natl Acad Sci U S A 89:10872–10876, 1992.
19. Ruan W, Catanese V, Wieczorek R, et al: Estradiol enhances the stimulatory effect of insulin-like growth factor-1 (IGF-1) on mammary development and growth hormone-induced IGF-1 messenger ribonucleic acid. Endocrinology 136:1296–1302, 1995.
20. Kleinberg DL, Ruan WF, Catanese V, et al: Non-lactogenic effects of growth hormone on growth and insulin-like growth factor-1 messenger ribonucleic acid of rat mammary gland. Endocrinology 126:3274–3276, 1990.
21. Ruan W, Powell-Braxton L, Kopchick JJ, et al: Evidence that insulin-like growth factor 1 and growth hormone are required for prostate gland development. Endocrinology 140:1984–1989, 1999.
22. Longacre TA, Bartow SA: A correlative morphologic study of human breast and endometrium in the menstrual cycle. Am J Surg Pathol 10:382–393, 1986.
23. Anderson TJ, Battersby S, King RJB, et al: Oral contraceptive use influences resting breast proliferation. Hum Pathol 20:1139–1144, 1989.
24. Clarke CL, Sutherland RL: Progestin regulation of cellular proliferation. Endocr Rev 11:266–301, 1990.
25. Nandi S: Endocrine control of mammary-gland development and function in the C3 11/HE Crgl mouse. J Natl Cancer Inst 21:1039–1062, 1958.
26. Topper YJ, Freeman CS: Multiple hormone interactions in the developmental biology of the mammary gland. Physiol Rev 60:1049–1106, 1980.
27. Kleinberg DL, Niemann W, Flamm E, et al: Primate mammary development: Effects of hypophysectomy, prolactin inhibition and growth hormone administration. J Clin Invest 75:1943–1950, 1985.
28. Kleinberg DL, Todd J: Evidence that human growth hormone is a potent lactogen in primates. J Clin Endocrinol Metab 51:1009–1015, 1980.
29. Coleman S, Silberstein GB, Daniel CW: Ductal morphogenesis in the mouse mammary gland: Evidence supporting a role for epidermal growth factor. Dev Biol 127:304–315, 1988.
30. Tonelli QJ, Sorof S: Epidermal growth factor requirement for development of cultured mammary gland. Nature 285:250–252, 1980.
31. Snedeker SM, Brown CF, DiAugustine RP: Expression and functional properties of transforming growth factor alpha and epidermal growth factor during mouse mammary gland ductal morphogenesis. Proc Natl Acad Sci U S A 88:276–280, 1991.
32. Valverius EM, Bates SE, Stampfer MR, et al: Transforming growth factor α production and epidermal growth factor receptor expression in normal and oncogene transformed human mammary epithelial cells. Mol Endocrinol 3:203–214, 1989.
33. Daniel CW, Silberstein GB, Van Horn K, et al: TGF-beta 1-induced inhibition of mouse mammary ductal growth: Developmental specificity and characterization. Dev Biol 135:20–30, 1989.
34. Dabelow A: Die Milchdrüse. In Möllendorff W (ed): Handbuch der Mikroskopischen Anatomie Des Menschen. Berlin, Springer-Verlag, 1957, pp 277–485.
35. Vorherr H: Morphology of the mature female breast. In Vorherr H (ed): The Breast. New York, Academic Press, 1974, pp 20–70.
36. Neville MC: Physiology of lactation. Clin Perinatol 26:251–279, 1999.
37. Pepe GJ, Albrecht ED: Actions of placental and fetal adrenal steroid hormones in primate pregnancy. Endocr Rev 16:608–648, 1995.
38. Tyson JE, Hwang P, Guyda H: Studies of prolactin secretion in human pregnancy. Am J Obstet Gynecol 113:14–20, 1972.
39. Scheithauer BW, Sano T, Kovacs KT, et al: The pituitary gland in pregnancy: A clinicopathologic and immunohistochemical study of 69 cases. Mayo Clin Proc 65:461–474, 1990.
40. Goluboff LG, Ezrin L: Effect of pregnancy on the somatotroph and the prolactin cell of the human adenohypophysis. J Clin Endocrinol 29:1533–1538, 1969.
41. Frankenne F, Closset J, Gomez F: The physiology of growth hormones (GHs) in pregnant women and partial characterization of the placental GH variant. J Clin Endocrinol Metab 66:1171–1180, 1988.
42. Thordarson G, Talamantes F: Role of the placenta in mammary gland development and function. In Neville MC, Daniel CW (eds): The Mammary Gland: Development, Regulation and Function. New York, Plenum Press, 1987, pp 459–498.
43. Frankenne F, Rentier-Delrue F, Scippo ML: Expression of the growth hormone variant gene in human placenta. J Clin Endocrinol Metab 64:635–637, 1987
44. MacLeod JN, Worsley I, Ray J: Human growth hormone-variant is a biologically active somatogen and

lactogen. Endocrinology 128:1298–1302, 1991.

45. Leite V, Cowden EA, Friesen HG: Endocrinology of lactation and nursing: Disorders of lactation. In DeGroot LJ (ed): Endocrinology, 3d ed. Philadelphia, WB Saunders, 1995, pp 2224–2233.

46. Vorherr H: Hormonal and biochemical changes of pituitary and breast during pregnancy. Semin Perinatol 3:193–198, 1979.

47. Kleinberg DL, Todd J, Babitsky G: Inhibition by estradiol of the lactogenic effect of prolactin in primate mammary tissue: Reversal by antiestrogens (LY 15678 and tamoxifen). Proc Natl Acad Sci U S A 80:4144–4148, 1983.

48. Graham JD, Clarke CL: Physiological action of progesterone in target tissues. Endocr Rev 18:502–519, 1997.

49. Davis JW, Wikman-Coffelt J, Eddington CL: The effect of progesterone on biosynthetic pathways in mammary tissue. Endocrinology 91:1011–1019, 1972.

50. Topper YJ, Freeman CS: Multiple hormone interactions in the developmental biology of the mammary gland. Physiol Rev 60:1049–1106, 1980.

51. Horseman ND, Zhao W, Montecino-Rodriguez E, et al: Defective mammopoiesis, but normal hematopoiesis, in mice with targeted disruption of the prolactin gene. EMBO J 16:6926–6935, 1997.

52. Friesen HG: Prolactin and growth hormone receptors: Regulation and characterization. Fed Proc 38:2610, 1979.

53. Kelly PA, Posner BI, Tsushima T, et al: Studies of insulin, growth hormone and prolactin binding: Ontogenesis, effects of sex and pregnancy. Endocrinology 95:532–539, 1974.

54. Bazan JF: Structural design and molecular evolution of a cytokine receptor superfamily. Proc Natl Acad Sci U S A 87:6934–6938, 1990.

55. Bole-Feysot C, Goffin V, Edery M, et al: Prolactin (PRL) and its receptor: Actions, signal transduction pathways and phenotypes observed in PRL receptor knockout mice. Endocr Rev 19:225–268, 1998.

56. Gao J, Hughes JP, Auperin B, et al: Interactions among JANUS kinases and the prolactin (PRL) receptor in the regulation of a PRL response element. Mol Endocrinol 10:847–856, 1996.

57. Hynes NE, Cella N, Wartmann M: Prolactin mediated intracellular signaling in mammary epithelial cells. J Mammary Gland Biol Neopl 2:19–27, 1997.

58. Goffin V, Kelly PA: The prolactin/growth hormone receptor family: Structure/function relationships. J Mammary Gland Biol Neopl 2:7–17, 1997.

59. Das R, Vonderhaar BK: Prolactin as a mitogen in mammary cells. J Mammary Gland Biol Neopl 2:29–39, 1997.

60. Kleinberg DL, Frantz AG: Human prolactin: Measurement in plasma by in vitro bioassay. J Clin Invest 50:1557–1568, 1971.

61. Frantz AG, Kleinberg DL: Prolactin: Evidence that it is separate from growth hormone in human blood. Science 170:745–747, 1970.

62. Hwang P, Guyda H, Friesen HG: Purification of human prolactin. J Biol Chem 247:1955–1958, 1972.

63. Friesen HG: The discovery of human prolactin: A very personal account. Clin Invest Med 18:66–72, 1995.

64. Frantz AG, Kleinberg DL, Noel GL: Studies on prolactin in man. Recent Prog Horm Res 28:527–598, 1972.

65. Humphreys RC, Lydon J, O'Malley BW, et al: Mammary gland development is mediated by both stromal and epithelial progesterone receptors. Mol Endocrinol 11:801–811, 1997.

66. Lydon JP, DeMayo FJ, Funk CR, et al: Mice lacking progesterone receptor exhibit pleiotrophic reproductive abnormalities. Genes Dev 9:2266–2278, 1995.

67. Insel TR, Young L, Wang Z: Central oxytocin and reproductive behaviours. Rev Reprod 2:28–37, 1997.

68. Robinson AG, Verbalis JG: Posterior pituitary gland. In Larsen PR, Kronenberg HM, Melmed S, et al (eds): Williams Textbook of Endocrinology, 10th ed. Philadelphia, Saunders, 2003, pp 281–329.

69. Vorherr H: Galactopoiesis, galactosecretion, and onset of lactation. In Vorherr H (ed): The Breast. New York, Academic Press, 1974, 71–127.

70. Kleinberg DL: Human-lactalbumin: Measurement in serum and in breast cancer organ culture by radioimmunoassay. Science 190:276–278, 1975.

71. Neville MC, Morton J, Umemura S: Lactogenesis: The transition from pregnancy to lactation. Pediatr Clin North Am 48:35–52, 2001.

72. Noel GL, Suh HK, Frantz AG: Prolactin release during nursing and breast stimulation in postpartum and nonpostpartum subjects. J Clin Endocrinol Metab 38:413–423, 1974.

73. Johnston JM, Amico JA: A prospective longitudinal study of the release of oxytocin and prolactin in response to infant suckling in long term lactation. J Clin Endocrinol Metab 62:653–657, 1986.

74. Nunley WC, Urban RJ, Kitchin JD: Dynamics of pulsatile prolactin release during the postpartum lactational period. J Clin Endocrinol Metab 72:287–293, 1991.

75. Diaz S, Seron-Ferre M, Cardenas H, et al: Circadian variation of basal plasma prolactin, prolactin response to suckling, and length of amenorrhea in nursing women. J Clin Endocrinol Metab 68:946–955, 1989.

76. Howie PW, McNeilly AS, McArdle T, et al: The relationship between suckling-induced prolactin response and lactogenesis. J Clin Endocrinol Metab 50:670–673, 1980.

77. Rosen JM, Woo SLC, Comstock JP: Regulation of casein messenger RNA during the development of the rat mammary gland. Biochemistry 14:2895–2903, 1975.

78. Lee KF, Atiee SH, Henning SJ, et al: Relative contribution of promoter and intragenic sequences in the hormonal regulation of rat -casein transgenes. Mol Endocrinol 3:447–453, 1989.

79. Eriksson M, Lundeberg T, Uvnas-Moberg K: Studies on cutaneous blood flow in the mammary gland of lactating rats. Acta Physiol Scand 158:1–6, 1996.

80. Hadsell DL, Greenberg NM, Fligger JM, et al: Targeted expression of des(1-3) human insulin-like growth factor 1 (IGF-1) in transgenic mice influences mammary gland development and IGF-binding protein expression. Endocrinology 136:321–330, 1996.

81. Wilde CJ, Knight CH, Flint DJ: Control of milk secretion and apoptosis during mammary involution. J Mammary Gland Biol Neoplasia 4:129–136, 1999.

82. Tonner E, Allan G, Shkreta L, et al: Insulin-like growth factor binding protein-5 (IGFBP-5) potentially regulates programmed cell death and plasminogen activation in the mammary gland. Adv Exp Med Biol 480:45–53, 2000.

83. Neumann I, Koehler E, Landgraf R, et al: An oxytocin receptor antagonist infused into the supraoptic nucleus attenuates intranuclear and peripheral release of oxytocin during suckling in conscious rats. Endocrinology 134:141–148, 1994.

84. Brown D, Moos F: Onset of bursting in oxytocin cells in suckled rats. J Physiol 503:625–634, 1997.

85. Young WS, III, Shepard E, DeVries AC, et al: Targeted reduction of oxytocin expression provides insights into its physiological roles. Adv Exp Med Biol 449:231–240, 1998.

86. Crowley WR, Armstrong WE: Neurochemical regulation of oxytocin secretion in lactation. Endocr Rev 13:33–65, 1992.

87. Font de Mora, Brown M: AIB1 is a conduit for kinase-mediated growth factor signaling to the estrogen receptor. Mol Cell Biol 20:5041–5047, 2000.

88. Yokoyama Y, Ueda T, Irahara M, et al: Releases of oxytocin and prolactin during breast massage and suckling in puerperal women. Eur J Obstet Gynecol Reprod Biol 53:17–20, 1994.

89. McNeilly AS, Robinson IC, Houston MJ, et al: Release of oxytocin and prolactin in response to suckling. Br Med J (Clin Res Ed) 286:257–259, 1983.

90. Wagner KU, Young WS, Liu X, et al: Oxytocin and milk removal are required for post partum mammary-gland development. Genes Funct 1:233–244, 1997.

91. Neuenschwander S, Schwartz A, Wood TL, et al: Involution of the lactating mammary gland is inhibited by the IGF system in a transgenic mouse model. J Clin Invest 97:2225–2232, 1996.

92. Neville MC, Allen JC, Watters C: The mechanisms of milk secretion. In Neville MC, Neifert MR (eds): Lacation: Physiology, Nutrition and Breast-Feeding. New York, Plenum Press, 1983, pp 49–102.

93. Neville MC: Anatomy and physiology of lactation. Pediatr Clin North Am 48:13–34, 2001.

94. Mennella JA, Beauchamp GK: The transfer of alcohol to human milk: Effects on flavor and the infant's behavior. N Engl J Med 325:981–985, 1991.

95. Hartmann PE: Changes in the composition and yield of the mammary secretion of cows during the initiation of lactation. J Endocrinol 59:231–247, 1973.

96. Fleet IR, Goode JA, Hamon MH, et al: Secretory activity of goat mammary glands during pregnancy and the onset of lactation. J Physiol 251:763–773, 1975.

97. Glasier A, McNeilly AS: Physiology of lactation. Baillieres Clin Endocrinol Metab 4:379–395, 1990.

98. Neville MC, Morton J: Physiology and endocrine changes underlying human lactogenesis II. J Nutr 131:3005S–3008S, 2001.

99. Allen JC, Keller RP, Archer P, et al: Studies in human lactation: Milk composition and daily secretion rates of macronutrients in the first year of lactation. Am J Clin Nutr 54:69–80, 1991.

100. Neville MC, Allen JC, Archer PC, et al: Studies in human lactation: milk volume and nutrient composition during weaning and lactogenesis. Am J Clin Nutr 54:81–92, 1991.

101. Koldovsky O, Thornburg W: Hormones in milk. J Pediatr Gastroenterol Nutr 6:172–196, 1987.

102. Corps AN, Brown KD, Rees LH, et al: The insulin-like growth factor I content in human milk increases between early and full lactation. J Clin Endocrinol Metab 67:25–29, 1988.

103. Mushtaha AA, Schmalstieg FC, Hughes TK: Chemokinetic agents for monocytes in human milk: Possible role of tumor necrosis factor-α. Pediatr Res 25:629–633, 1989.

104. Berseth CL: Enhancement of intestinal growth in neonatal rats by epidermal growth factor in milk. Am J Physiol 253:G662–G665, 1987.

105. Wilson BC, Summerlee AJS: Effects of exogenous relaxin on oxytocin and vasopressin release and the intramammary pressure response to central hyperosmotic challenge. J Endocrinol 141:75–80, 1994.

106. Peaker M, Fleet IR, Davis AJ, et al: The effects of relaxin on the response of intramammary pressure and mammary blood flow to exogenous oxytocin in the goat. Exp Physiol 80:1047–1052, 1995.

107. Brown CF, Teng CT, Pentecost BT: Epidermal growth factor precursor in mouse lactating mammary gland

alveolar cells. Mol Endocrinol 3:1077–1083, 1989.

108. Oppe TE, Redstone D: Calcium and phosphorus levels in healthy newborn infants given various types of milk. Lancet 1:1045–1048, 1968.

109. Baum D, Cooper L, Davies PA: Hypocalcaemic fits in neonates. Lancet 1:598, 1968.

110. Thiede MA: The mRNA encoding a parathyroid hormone-like peptide is produced in mammary tissue in response to elevations in serum prolactin. Mol Endocrinol 3:1443–1447, 1989.

111. Budayr AA, Halloran BP, King JC: High levels of parathyroid hormone-like protein in milk. Proc Natl Acad Sci U S A 86:7183–7185, 1989.

112. Brommage R, Jarmagin K, DeLuca HF: 1,25-Dihydroxyvitamin $D_3$ normalizes maternal food consumption and pup growth in rats. Am J Physiol 246E:227–231, 1984.

113. Robinson CJ, Spanos E, James MF: Role of prolactin in vitamin D metabolism and calcium absorption during lactation in the rat. J Endocrinol 94:443–453, 1982.

114. Jelliffe DB: Unique properties of human milk (remarks on some recent developments). J Reprod Med 14:133–137, 1975.

115. Della-Giustina K, Chow G: Medications in pregnancy and lactation. Emerg Med Clin North Am 21:585–613, 2003.

116. Lindow SW, Hendricks MS, Nugent FA, et al: Morphine suppresses the oxytocin response in breast-feeding women. Gynecol Obstet Invest 48:33–37, 1999.

117. American Academy of Pediatrics CoD: Transfer of drugs and other chemicals into human milk. Pediatrics 84:924–936, 1989.

118. American Academy of Pediatrics Committee on Drugs: Transfer of drugs and other chemicals into human milk. Pediatrics 108:776–789, 2001.

119. Niebyl JR: Antibiotics and other anti-infective agents in pregnancy and lactation. Am J Perinatol 20:405–414, 2003.

120. Ressel G: AAP updates statement for transfer of drugs and other chemicals into breast milk. Am Fam Physician 65:979–980, 2002.

121. Auerbach KG: Breastfeeding and maternal medication use. J Obstet Gynecol Neonatal Nurs 28:554–563, 1999.

122. Azizi F: Effect of methimazole treatment of maternal thyrotoxicosis on thyroid function in breast-feeding infants. J Pediatr 128:855–858, 1996.

123. Beaudry M, Dufour R, Marcoux S: Relation between infant feeding and infections during the first six months of life. J Pediatr 126:191–197, 1995.

124. Duncan B, Ey J, Holberg CJ, et al: Exclusive breast-feeding for at least 4 months protects against otitis media. Pediatrics 91:867–872, 1993.

125. Frank AL, Taber LH, Glezen WP, et al: Breast-feeding and respiratory virus infection. Pediatrics 70:239–245, 1982.

126. Popkin BM, Adair L, Akin JS, et al: Breast-feeding and diarrheal morbidity. Pediatrics 86:874–882, 1990.

127. Wright AL, Holberg CJ, Taussig LM, et al: Relationship of infant feeding to recurrent wheezing at age 6 years. Arch Pediatr Adolesc Med 149:758–763, 1995.

128. Ellestad-Sayed J, Coodin FJ, Dilling LA, et al: Breast-feeding protects against infection in Indian infants. Can Med Assoc J 120:295–298, 1979.

129. Anderson GH: The effect of prematurity on milk composition and its physiological basis. Fed Proc 43:2438–2442, 1984.

130. Kovar MG, Serdula MK, Marks JS, et al: Review of the epidemiologic evidence for an association between infant feeding and infant health. Pediatrics 74:615–638, 1984.

131. Howie PW, Forsyth JS, Ogston SA, et al: Protective effect of breast feeding against infection. Br Med J 399:11–16, 1990.

132. Victora CG, Smith PG, Vaughan JP: Evidence for protection by breast-feeding against infant deaths from infectious diseases in Brazil. Lancet 2:319–322, 1987.

133. Lucas A, Morley R, Cole TJ: Breast milk and subsequent intelligence quotient in children born preterm. Lancet 339:261–264, 1992.

134. McTiernan A, Thomas DB: Evidence for a protective effect of lactation on risk of breast cancer in young women. Am J Epidemiol 124:353–358, 1986.

135. Byers T, Graham S, Rzepka T, et al: Lactation and breast cancer, evidence for a negative association in premenopausal women. Am J Epidemiol 121:664–674, 1985.

136. Kvale G, Hench I: Lactation and cancer risk: Is there a relation specific to breast cancer? J Epidemiol Community Health 42:30–37, 1987.

137. Melmed S, Kleinberg D: Anterior pituitary. In Larsen PR, Kronenberg HM, Melmed S, et al (eds): Williams Textbook of Endocrinology, 10th ed. Philadelphia, Saunders, 2003, pp 177–279.

138. Salazar H, Tobon H, Josimovich JB: Developmental, gestational and postgestational modifications of the human breast. Clin Obstet Gynecol 18:113–137, 1975.

139. Van de Perre P, Simonon A, Msellati P: Postnatal transmission of human immunodeficiency virus type I from mother to infant: A prospective cohort study in Kigali, Rwanda. N Engl J Med 325:593–598, 1991.

140. Morton JA: The clinical usefulness of breast milk sodium in the assessment of lactogenesis. Pediatrics 93:802–806, 1994.

141. Lin Y, Xia L, Turner JD, et al: Morphological observation of neutrophil diapedesis across bovine

mammary gland epithelium in vitro. Am J Vet Res 56:203–207, 1995.

142. Neifert MR, Seacat JM: Medical management of successful breast-feeding. Pediatr Clin North Am 33:743–762, 1986.

143. Farina MA, Newby BG, Alani HM: Innervation of the nipple-areola complex. Plast Reconstr Surg 66:497–501, 1980.

144. Neifert MR: Routine management of breast feeding. In Neville MC, Neifert MR (eds): Lactation: Physiology, Nutrition and Breast Feeding. New York, Plenum Press, 1983, pp 273–302.

145. Martinez GA, Nalezienski JP: 1980 update: The recent trend in breast feeding. Pediatrics 67:260–263, 1981.

146. Starling J, Fergusson DM, Horwood LJ, et al: Austr Pediatr 15:271–274, 1979.

147. Brown KH, Robertson AD, Akhtar NA: Lactational capacity of marginally nourished mothers: Infants' milk nutrient consumption and patterns of growth. Pediatrics 78:920–927, 1986.

148. Kauppila A, Chatelain P, Kirkinen P, et al: Isolated prolactin deficiency in a woman with puerperal alactogenesis. J Clin Endocrinol Metab 64:309–312, 1987.

149. Wu W, Cogan JD, Pfaffle RW, et al: Mutations in PROP1 cause familial combined pituitary hormone deficiency. Nat Genet 18:147–149, 1998.

150. Blackett PR, Seif SM, Altmiller DH, et al: Case report: Familial central diabetes insipidus: vasopressin and nicotine stimulated neurophysin deficiency with subnormal oxytocin and estrogen stimulated neurophysin. Am J Med Sci 286:42–46, 1983.

151. Shangold MM, Freeman R, Kumaresan P, et al: Plasma oxytocin concentrations in a pregnant woman with total vasopressin deficiency. Obstet Gynecol 61:662–667, 1983.

152. Swaab DF: Prader-Willi syndrome and the hypothalamus. Acta Paediatr Suppl 423:50–54, 1997.

153. Melnikow J, Bedinghaus JM: Management of common breast-feeding problems. J Fam Pract 39:56–64, 1994.

154. Soderqvist G, Isaksson E, von Schoultz B, et al: Proliferation of breast epithelial cells in healthy women during the menstrual cycle. Am J Obstet Gynecol 176:123–128, 1997.

155. Anderson JE, Held N, Wright K: Raynaud's phenomenon of the nipple: A treatable cause of painful breastfeeding. Pediatrics 113:e360–e364, 2004.

156. Barbosa-Cesnik C, Schwartz K, Foxman B: Lactation mastitis. JAMA 289:1609–1612, 2003.

157. Short RV: Breast feeding. Sci Am 250:35–41, 1984.

158. Glasier A, McNeilly AS, Howie PW: Fertility after childbirth: Changes in serum gonadotrophin levels in bottle and breast feeding women. Clin Endocrinol 19:493–501, 1983.

159. Bohnet HG, Dahlen HG, Wuttke W, et al: Hyperprolactinemic anovulatory syndrome. J Clin Endocrinol Metab 42:132–143, 1976.

160. Lachelin GCL, Abu-Fadil S, Yen SSC: Functional delineation of hyperprolactinemic amenorrhea. J Clin Endocrinol Metab 44:1163–1174, 1977.

161. Kremer JA, Borm G, Schellekens LA, et al: Pulsatile secretion of luteinizing hormone and prolactin in lactating and nonlactating women and the response to naltrexone. J Clin Endocrinol Metab 72:294–300, 1991.

162. Aono T, Shioji T, Aki K: Augmentation of puerperal lactation by oral administration of sulpirides. J Clin Endocrinol Metab 48:478–482, 1979.

163. Ylikorkala O, Kauppila A, Kivinen S, et al: Treatment of inadequate lactation with oral sulpiride and buccal oxytocin. Obstet Gynecol 63:57–60, 1984.

164. Guzman V, Toscano G, Canales ES, et al: Improvement of defective lactation by using oral metoclopramide. Acta Obstet Gynecol Scand 58:53–55, 1979.

165. Gupta AP, Gupta PK: Metoclopramide as a lactogogue. Clin Pediatr 24:269–272, 1985.

166. Kauppila A, Anunti P, Kivinen S, et al: Metoclopramide and breast feeding: Efficacy and anterior pituitary responses of the mother and the child. Eur J Obstet Gynecol Reprod Biol 19:19–22, 1985.

167. Petralgia F, De Leo V, Sardelli S, et al: Domperidone in defective and insufficient lactation. Eur J Obstet Gynecol Reprod Biol 19:281–287, 1985.

168. Suri RA, Altshuler LL, Burt VK, et al: Managing psychiatric medications in the breast-feeding woman. Medscape Women's Health 3:1–16, 1998.

169. Patton SW, Misri S, Corral MR, et al: Antipsychotic medication during pregnancy and lactation in women with schizophrenia: Evaluating the risk. Can J Psychiatry 47:959–965, 2002.

170. Gunn AJ, Gunn TR, Rabone DL, et al: Growth hormone increases breast milk volumes in mothers of preterm infants. Pediatrics 98:279–282, 1996.

171. Luhman L: The effect of intranasal oxytocin on lactation. Obstet Gynecol 21:713–717, 1963.

# Gestational Trophoblastic Neoplasms

## Charles B. Hammond and John T. Soper

## INTRODUCTION

The prognosis for patients with choriocarcinoma and related trophoblastic diseases has improved dramatically since the 1950s. Cure rates now exceed 90%, even in patients with metastases.[1-4] These tumors also are interesting in their relations to a variety of endocrinologically active substances. Although systemic chemotherapy has provided the major breakthrough in treatment of these neoplasms, more recent investigations suggest that combination chemotherapy and adjunctive use of surgery and irradiation also can be useful.[2-4] More data have accrued to suggest that chemotherapeutic toxicity can be dramatically reduced by altering drug regimens.[3] Finally, new agents and approaches are being used with some success in patients whose disease is resistant to more traditional therapy.

This chapter deals with trophoblastic diseases of gestational origin only. Histologically similar tumors of nongestational origin, such as primary ovarian or testicular tumors, are omitted because of differences in derivation, treatment, and prognosis. Gestational trophoblastic neoplasia (GTN) is used to define the spectrum of disease that has "benign" hydatidiform mole (a premalignant lesion) at one extreme, and at the other, the highly malignant choriocarcinoma. Such diseases indeed form a continuum, and to understand and adequately manage a patient with one of these conditions requires knowledge of the entire group. In this chapter, we focus on the endocrine aspects of these tumors, but we hope to provide at least an overview of their diagnosis and treatment.

## HISTORY

Recognition of GTN dates to antiquity, when Hippocrates described hydatidiform mole. In 1895, Marchand[5] correctly demonstrated that gestational choriocarcinoma is a sequela of pregnancy. The secretion of human chorionic gonadotropin (hCG) in the urine of patients with GTN was confirmed by Zondek et al.[6] in the late 1920s.

Progress in the past 50 years toward clarification of the spectrum and biologic significance of GTN has been based on the observations of many. Biologic, immunologic, and radioimmunologic assays for hCG have steadily improved in sensitivity and accuracy. Detailed clinical/pathologic correlations in the 1940s and 1950s provided the basis for current concepts of the enigmatic pathology of GTN.[7,8] The first report of chemotherapeutic treatment occurred in 1956 by Li and others[7] at the National Institutes of Health of a patient who had sustained remission for metastatic choriocarcinoma with the use of methotrexate. Efforts since that time by Ross, Odell, Hertz, Lewis, Brewer, Lurain, Bagshawe, Morrow, Goldstein, Berkowitz, and many others have resulted in improvement in survival rates, reduction of toxicity, and individualization of therapy.

## EPIDEMIOLOGY

The incidence of GTN shows marked geographic variation.[8] Hydatidiform mole occurs in 1 in 1000 to 2000 pregnancies in reports from Western countries, whereas in the Far East, the incidence ranges as high as 1 in 125 pregnancies.[9] Environmental factors may be responsible for some of the difference, inasmuch as the incidence of hydatidiform mole in Asian women in Hawaii is decreased in relation to the incidence in Western women.[10] Spontaneous remission (no progression to malignancy) after evacuation of hydatidiform mole occurs in 80% to 90% in most series. Women at both age extremes of reproductive life appear to be at increased risk for molar pregnancy, but age and parity seem unrelated to malignant sequelae.

Recurrent hydatidiform mole is unusual but can occur in 1% to 3% of cases, as well as with different spouses. Choriocarcinoma follows 1 in 20,000 to 40,000 normal pregnancies in the United States. The antecedent pregnancy for choriocarcinoma is hydatidiform mole in approximately 50% of cases, normal pregnancy in 25%, abortion or miscarriage in 20% to 22%, and ectopic pregnancy in 2% to 3%. The role of diet, drugs, viruses, radiation, and toxins in the genesis of GTN is still undefined.

## PATHOLOGY CLASSIFICATION

GTN should be considered a spectrum of histopathologic conditions, including the premalignant hydatidiform mole and the malignant forms of invasive mole and choriocarcinoma (Table 189-1). Other conditions, such as trophoblastic pseudotumor and syncytial endometritis,[11–13] share some of the features of GTN but probably have only modest malignant potential. Further to add to the complexity, hydatidiform mole exists in both complete and partial forms that differ in histology, cytogenetics, and malignant potential. Finally, histologic criteria alone are insufficient to predict the clinical malignancy outcome of an individual case of hydatidiform mole. Innocuous-looking moles can have an aggressive, fulminating malignant course, whereas anaplastic, markedly proliferating hydatidiform moles can undergo spontaneous regression.[12,13]

### COMPLETE HYDATIDIFORM MOLE

A triad of histologic features is present in complete hydatidiform mole, including generalized diffuse hyperplasia of both cytotrophoblast and syncytiotrophoblast elements, edema of the chorionic villi, including central cistern formation, and reduction of fetal vessels. These features result in the macroscopic description of hydatidiform mole as a mass resembling a "bunch of grapes" (Figs. 189-1 and 189-2). The embryo is absent because of resorption before development of the cardiovascular system.

Marked variability in the amount of trophoblastic proliferation and cytologic atypia of the trophoblast is seen in patients with complete moles. Although systems have been designed to categorize the amount of trophoblastic proliferation and relate this proliferation to clinical behavior after molar evacuation, several studies have documented that these relations are not a reliable guide to the clinical behav-

| Table 189-1 | Clinical Spectrum of Gestational Trophoblastic Neoplasia |
|---|---|

Benign
    Hydatidiform mole: complete
    Hydatidiform mole: partial or transitional
    Hydropic degeneration of villi in blighted ovum
Malignant
    Nonmetastatic
        Persistent hydatidiform mole
        Chorioadenoma destruens (invasive mole)
        Choriocarcinoma
    Metastatic
        Good prognosis
        Poor prognosis
            Pretreatment serum hCG >40,000 mIU/mL
            Duration of symptoms >4 mo
            Liver or brain metastases
            Significant prior unsuccessful chemotherapy
            Prior term gestation

hCG, human chorionic gonadotropin.

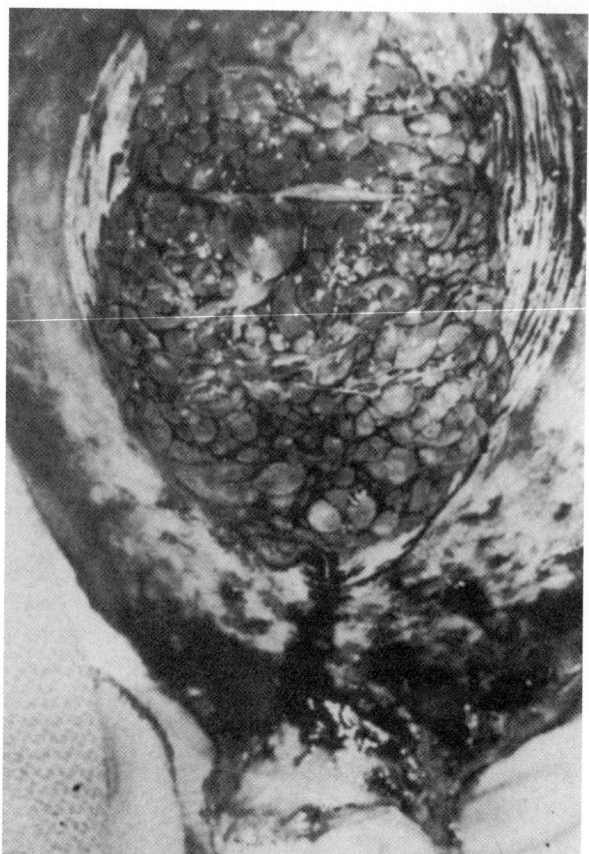

**Figure 189-1** Hysterectomy specimen showing a primary hydatidiform mole in situ.

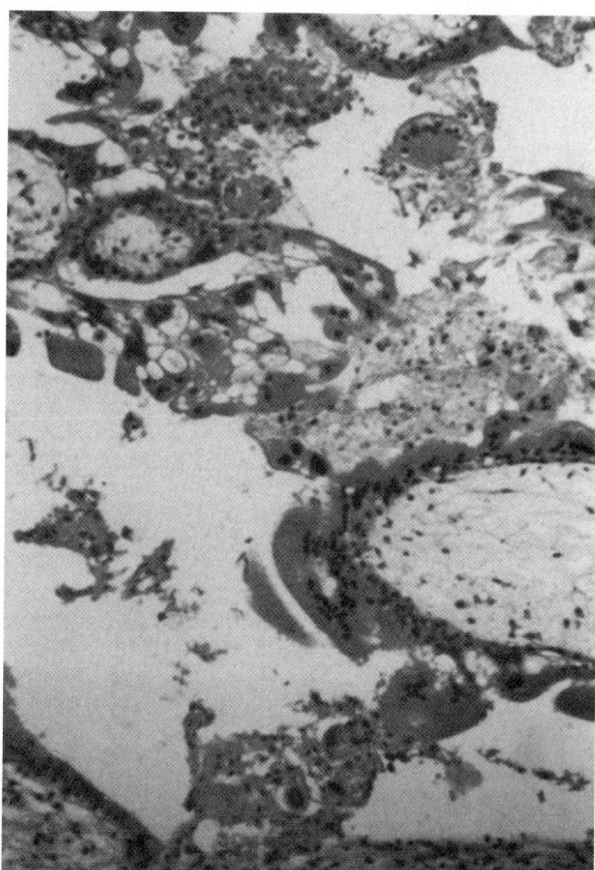

**Figure 189-2** Microscopic view of a complete, primary hydatidiform mole. Trophoblastic tissue is abundant and covers the abnormal villous structure (hematoxylin/eosin, ×40). (Courtesy of Cheryl Szpak, M.D.)

ior of a mole for an individual patient. Therefore, management is based on the pattern of hCG regression after molar evacuation.

## INVASIVE HYDATIDIFORM MOLE

Invasive hydatidiform moles are characterized by pathologic features of complete hydatidiform mole in conjunction with invasion beyond the normal placentation site directly into the myometrium, often penetrating into the venous system.[14] The histologic diagnosis of invasive mole is now rarely made because most patients with such diseases are often treated without resorting to hysterectomy. The diagnosis of myometrial invasion is extremely difficult to make by analysis of uterine curettage tissue. Imaging, such as arteriogram or magnetic resonance scan, can suggest the diagnosis of invasive hydatidiform mole but it is seldom of value because administration of chemotherapy is usually based on hCG regression patterns rather than a specific diagnosis of myometrial invasion. Invasive moles often produce symptoms of uterine subinvolution and bleeding. Local penetration through the myometrium may result in uterine rupture and massive intraperitoneal hemorrhage. Distant metastasis, rare for this form, may result in pulmonary symptoms or hemorrhage from lower genital implants.

Although invasive moles act clinically in a manner similar to that of malignancy, the natural history of invasive mole can include spontaneous remission. However, chemotherapy is used to treat all patients who have an increasing hCG level after evacuation of hydatidiform mole without distinguishing patients with invasive moles from those with choriocarcinoma.

## PARTIAL HYDATIDIFORM MOLE

Cytogenetic study of complete and partial hydatidiform mole has established that partial hydatidiform moles are usually derived from a triploid conceptus. Histologic features include scalloping of the villi with trophoblastic inclusions within chorionic villi. The embryo usually survives much longer than in complete moles (some to term), but embryonic death generally occurs at approximately 8 weeks' gestational age. A prior study confirmed that partial hydatidiform moles are frequently underdiagnosed.[15] Because the hydropic changes of the villi are not clinically evident and evidence of fetal tissue persists, partial moles are most often clinically diagnosed as a "missed abortion" until adequate histologic or cytogenetic studies or both are performed. Follow-up of patients with partial hydatidiform mole should be identical to that of patients with complete mole.

## CYTOGENETICS OF COMPLETE AND PARTIAL MOLAR SYNDROMES

Complete moles result from diandric diploidy; the egg is usually fertilized by a single sperm and loses the maternal haploid 23,X genetic component by an unknown mechanism. If the paternal haploid set of 23,X chromosomes is reduplicated, the normal component of 46 chromosomes is reestablished.[16,17] Zygotes with a 46,YY genotype are nonviable and not clinically recognized. Approximately 5% of complete moles apparently arise from dispermic fertilization of an empty oocyte, which can result in either a 46,XY or a 46,XX genotype. Although some studies have suggested that dispermic moles are even more prone to malignant sequelae, this conclusion has not been validated. The issue is further confused by failure to differentiate invasive moles from choriocarcinoma because of treatment of patients without a histologic diagnosis. Partial moles result from dispermic fertilization of an egg, with retention of the maternal haploid set, resulting in diandric triploidy.[15–18]

## GESTATIONAL CHORIOCARCINOMA

Gestational choriocarcinoma is a malignant transformation of molar tissue or a de novo lesion arising spontaneously from the placenta of a term "normal" pregnancy, a spontaneous abortion, or even an ectopic gestation. It is characterized by a dimorphic population of cytotrophoblast and syncytiotrophoblast elements. Varying amounts of pleomorphism and anaplasia are present; in the absence of a clinical history, the histopathology may be misinterpreted in biopsies of metastatic sites as undifferentiated carcinoma or sarcoma (Fig. 189-3). Chorionic villi are not present, even in primary uterine sites of disease. If villous structures are identified, even in metastatic deposits, the histologic diagnosis is invasive mole.

Gestational choriocarcinoma, similar to other forms of normal and abnormal trophoblast, readily invades blood vessels and produces metastases via hematogenous routes of dissemination. The embolic metastatic sites have a tendency to outgrow their blood supply rapidly and to produce central necrosis that can result in massive local hemorrhage.[19] Secretion of hCG is retained by the vast majority of gestational choriocarcinomas because the tumor is derived from elements of both cytotrophoblast and syncytiotrophoblast.[19] This tumor marker correlates well with the volume of disease, except in a few cases of drug-resistant disease, and is a sensitive marker for response to chemotherapy.[19] Gestational choriocarcinoma usually progresses rapidly, and metastatic disease is usually fatal without treatment.

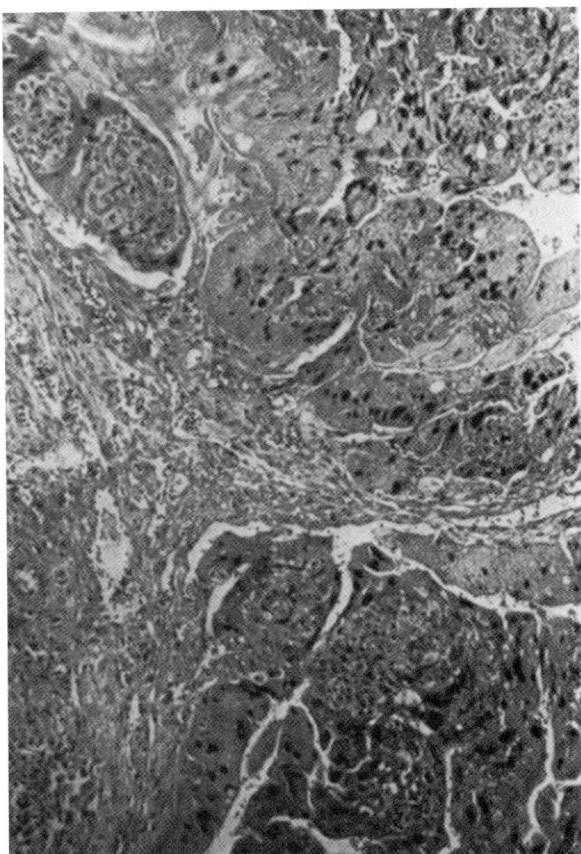

*Figure 189-3* Choriocarcinoma with infiltrating multinucleated cells of the syncytiotrophoblast adjacent to the sheetlike proliferation of cytotrophoblast (hematoxylin/eosin, ×325). (Courtesy of Cheryl Szpak, M.D.)

## ENDOCRINOLOGY

The advances made in the last 3 decades, particularly introduction of various assays for sensitive and precise measurement of protein and steroid hormones, have been applied to patients with trophoblastic disease. The malignant trophoblast retains the ability to produce hCG, thyrotropic hormone (thyrotropin), human placental lactogen (hPL), and the sex steroids that characterize normal placental tissue. Each of these compounds is briefly reviewed as it relates to GTN.

### HUMAN CHORIONIC GONADOTROPIN

Virtually all forms of GTN secrete hCG in proportion to the amount of trophoblastic tissue present, with the exception of placental-site trophoblastic tumors and the possible exception of some cases of drug-resistant malignant GTN, in which hCG can be localized in only a few tumor cells. Both the ability to measure physiologic levels of hCG and the development of effective chemotherapy have contributed to the high cure rates of patients with GTN.

The glycoprotein hormone hCG has significant structural similarities to the glycoprotein hormones produced by the pituitary[20,21] (see Chapter 139). It is composed of two distinct glycopeptide subunits that are noncovalently bound, similar to human luteinizing hormone (hLH), follicle-stimulating hormone (FSH), and thyroid-stimulating hormone (TSH). The α subunits of all four glycoprotein hormones are essentially identical.[21] The β subunits, although sharing structural similarity, differ sufficiently to impart specific biologic activity to the intact (α-β) hormone. Approximately 80% of the amino acid sequences are identical in the β subunits of hCG and LH.[22] The active binding site for gonadotropin receptors results from conformational changes that require association of the α and β subunits together. It is unknown whether the active site involves configuration only within the hormone-specific β subunit or requires a combination of sites on both subunits. Modification of as few as two amino acid groups in the α subunit can cause significant loss of biologic potency without a conformational change in the hormone.

### Radioimmunoassays of Human Chorionic Gonadotropin-β

The development of polyclonal antibodies specific to multiple epitopes present on the β subunit chain of hCG resulted in the development of radioimmunoassay (RIA) competitive-binding procedures used to quantitate hormone concentrations in small amounts of body fluids.[23] With the development of sensitive and specific RIA techniques, hCG levels could be detected with a sensitivity approximately 100-fold greater than that of bioassay methods. Until recently, RIA procedures using polyclonal anti-β antibodies were the method of choice for monitoring gestational trophoblastic disease.

The technical aspects of the β subunit polyclonal RIA were reviewed by Vaitukaitis.[24] It is important to realize that the β subunit RIA does not distinguish between free β subunit and whole-molecule β subunit fragments. However, because the free β subunit is more rapidly cleared from the circulation, the molecular species measured by RIA during normal pregnancy consists of intact hCG.[24] The results reflect the combined immunologic activity of both intact hCG and its free β subunit, which exaggerates total hCG values in patients with GTN, depending on the amount of free subunit present. Furthermore, β subunit RIAs performed with this technique do not exclude high levels of hLH and can detect measurable antigenic activity in situations in which serum hLH levels are markedly elevated, such as menopause.[23] Therefore, sensitivity is limited below a level of approximately 5 mIU/mL.

### Immunoradiometric Assays

Immunoradiometric sandwich assays (IRMAs) also use radioactive isotopes to quantitate the reaction between hormone antigens and antibodies. However, differences in technique yield slightly different results. In RIAs, the quantitated hormone competes with radiolabeled hormone for binding to a limited number of antibody sites.[24] In IRMAs, antibodies are present in excess; it is the antibody that is labeled rather than the hormone.[21-25] Most systems use monoclonal antibodies specific for isolated α and β subunits in sequence to perform the assay, whereas a few use monoclonal antibodies directed against epitopes only on the β subunit. Antibodies against one site are fixed to the solid phase to bind hormone from the biologic fluid, which effectively concentrates the hormone. Antibodies against the other site carry the radioactive label. IRMAs are slightly more sensitive than RIAs, but they also are more specific. Because binding to both subunits is required for quantitation, some methods identify only intact hormone or associated partial α-β fragments that include antibody-binding sites on each subunit fragment.[21,24,25] Although free subunits may react with their respective antibodies, only the combined subunits link the radiolabeled antibodies to the solid phase and are measured when monoclonal antibodies to the different subunits are used for capture and labeling.

### Nonradioactive Immunoassay

Immunoassays that are not dependent on radioactive isotopes offer several advantages over RIA and IRMA in regard to handling and disposal of radioactive materials. Therefore, both enzyme-linked immunosorbent assays (ELISAs) and fluoroimmunoassays have been developed.[21,26,27] Although ELISA methods can be used for quantitative hCG measurements, sensitivity and specificity appear to be worse than those with RIA or IRMA techniques, particularly in the lower ranges of hCG.[21] A technique of fluoroimmunoassay for serum hCG uses a two-site sandwich method with monoclonal antibodies directed against α and β subunits. Although fundamentally similar to the two-site IRMA sandwich techniques, the labeling antibodies are labeled with a rare earth element (europium) that forms a highly fluorescent chelate. A sensitivity of approximately 1 mIU/mL has been achieved, along with the ability to quantitate hCG over a large range.[26] Our experience in using fluoroimmunoassay to monitor patients with malignant GTN suggests that it provides values that are virtually parallel to results achieved with RIA.

### Measurement of Abnormal Human Chorionic Gonadotropin in Patients with Gestational Trophoblastic Neoplasms

Patients with malignant GTN may produce a variety of abnormal forms of hCG, degraded hCG, or uncombined α and β particles that can be detected in serum or urine. These entities include nicked forms of hCG that are cleaved between β subunit residues 47 and 48 or 44 and 45; nicked hCG that is missing the β subunit C terminus; free β or α subunit; and the β core fragment, a degraded form of free β subunit that is roughly one fourth the size of intact hCG.[25-28]

Assays directed against free α and β subunits have been investigated over the past decade. Because these hCG molecules are incomplete, they have little or no biologic activity.

Although Nishimura and associates[29] and Quigley and coworkers[30] reported data suggesting an association between abnormal clearance of free α subunit and poor outcome in GTN, other studies have found little value in measuring free α subunit with no clear relation between the detection of free α subunit and unfavorable disease outcome. Unfortunately, the value of measuring free α subunit is confounded by cross-reactivity with α subunit of pituitary origin.

Measurement of free β subunit in patients with GTN was delayed because of difficulties in discriminating between free subunit and intact hCG. The development of monoclonal antibodies against β subunit epitopes that are concealed when the β unit is associated with the α unit has allowed direct quantitation of free β subunit of hCG. Among patients undergoing evacuation of hydatidiform mole, Khazaeli and associates[31] found a higher free β subunit/total hCG ratio among those in whom persistent disease develops than in those who undergo spontaneous remission. Other studies by the same investigators suggested that patients treated with chemotherapy for malignant GTN have a high risk of failure of primary chemotherapy if the free β subunit/hCG ratio is elevated early in the course of the disease. However, Berkowitz and colleagues[32] were unable to correlate free β ratios with disease outcome in patients undergoing evacuation of hydatidiform mole. Further studies are needed to clarify the value of free β subunit monitoring.

The relation of nicked forms of hCG and the β core fragment to the biologic behavior of GTN has not been established. However, Cole[33] has emphasized the pitfalls in using sandwich monoclonal assays that identify only intact whole hCG molecules when monitoring patients with GTN. Sera from patients with normal pregnancy have predominantly intact hCG, and different hCG assays produce similar hCG measurements. In contrast, sera from patients with GTN have much more heterogeneous species of hCG, which results in wide interassay variation in estimation of hCG levels. Anti-α/anti-β sandwich assays, in particular, which detect only intact hCG with or without intact hCG containing nicked hCG, result in lower values with occasional false-negative values when compared with hCG-β RIA.

As our understanding of hCG metabolism in normal gestations and GTN evolves, it is likely that a panel of assays will be used to quantitate total hCG and free subunit or abnormal fragment levels for monitoring patients with GTN. Alternatively, different assays might be used to evaluate patients before therapy, during active treatment, and during remission of their disease. Despite the limitations of the current assays described earlier, hCG remains the model tumor marker for human neoplasms.

## "Phantom hCG"

Rarely, women are initially seen with persistently elevated hCG levels but are subsequently found to have a false-positive hCG assay result, sometimes after receiving chemotherapy or surgery for presumed malignant GTN. Most patients with "phantom hCG" have low-level hCG elevations,[33,34] but occasionally values as high as 200 to 300 mIU/mL have been recorded. The false-positive hCG values result from interference with the hCG immunometric sandwich assays caused by nonspecific heterophile antibodies in the patients' sera.[34] Many of these patients have an undefined previous pregnancy event and do not have radiographic evidence of metastatic disease. Serial hCG values usually do not substantially vary, despite often-prolonged observation, and usually do not change with therapeutic interventions such as surgery or chemotherapy.[33,34]

"Phantom hCG" also may be seen after evacuation of a hydatidiform mole or after a clearly defined pregnancy event, such as an ectopic pregnancy. It should be suspected if hCG values plateau at relatively low levels and do not respond to therapeutic maneuvers such as methotrexate given for a presumed persistent mole or ectopic pregnancy. Evaluation should include evaluation of serum hCG by using a variety of assay techniques at different dilutions of patient serum, combined with a urinary hCG level if the serum level is greater than 60 mIU/mL.[33,34] False-positive hCG assays usually will not be affected by serial dilution of patient sera and will have markedly different values with different assay techniques, with the majority of assays reflecting undetectable hCG.[33,34] Heterophile antibodies are not excreted in the urine; therefore, urinary hCG values will not be detectable if they are the cause of serum hCG elevation.[34] Other techniques are available to inactivate or strip the patient's serum of heterophile

antibodies. It is important to exclude the possibility of "phantom hCG" before subjecting these patients to hysterectomy or chemotherapy for trophoblastic disease.

## THYROTROPIC HORMONE

Hyperthyroidism is a well-recognized complication of hydatidiform mole, with clinical symptoms occurring in 3% to 5% of patients.[8] A spectrum from mild chemical hyperthyroidism to florid thyrotoxicosis has been observed, generally when an unevacuated mole was initially noted. Malignant GTN is less often associated with significant hyperthyroidism. Pregnancy itself is associated with elevation of serum thyroxine and protein-bound iodine levels, although free thyroxine levels should be in the normal range. Thyroid-binding globulin is increased in normal pregnancy, which leads to a corresponding increase in thyroxine-binding sites. Galton and colleagues[35] observed that among 20 patients with unevacuated molar pregnancy, nearly all had chemical evidence of hyperthyroidism, but none was symptomatic. The hyperthyroid state generally clears soon after molar evacuation or the institution of therapy for GTN.

Previous studies by Anderson and colleagues[36] of eight patients with choriocarcinoma and thyrotoxicosis showed a direct correlation between serum thyroxine and hCG levels, which suggests that hCG itself may have thyrotropic activity in GTN. Herschman[37] compared biologically active thyrotropin in patients with GTN and found that it differed from pituitary TSH and long-acting thyroid stimulator in molecular weight and duration of activity. Chorionic thyrotropin contains no immunoglobulin G (IgG), which further distinguishes it from long-acting thyroid stimulator. Nisela and Taliadourous[38] used the mouse thyroid bioassay to study five patients with hyperthyroidism and GTN. The characteristics of chorionic thyrotropin were identical to those of hCG, which supports the theory that hCG is a weak stimulator of thyroid function. Extremely high levels of hCG are usually seen when clinical hyperthyroidism is observed in GTN. However, recurrence of clinical or laboratory evidence of hyperthyroidism is rare in GTN, even with repeated elevation of hCG levels.

## HUMAN PLACENTAL LACTOGEN

hPL is a placental hormone with lactogenic, luteotropic, and growth-promoting properties. Its molecular mass is approximately 30,000 daltons, and it is composed of hydrogen-bound/linked dimers. Partial immunologic cross-reactivity occurs with both prolactin and growth hormone. hPL is made in relatively massive quantities by the normal placenta and is absent in the nonpregnant state. The serum half-life of hPL is short, approximately 20 minutes. hPL also has been detected in the serum of male patients with malignant germ cell tumors containing choriocarcinoma.[39]

The usefulness of hPL in the management of GTN is limited. We have not found that hPL determinations in GTN are routinely indicated in the clinical management of individual patients.

## STEROID HORMONES

Production of the high levels of estrogen that characterize normal pregnancy is dependent on an intact fetal/placental unit. De novo synthesis of cholesterol from acetate does not occur in the placenta, so fetal or maternal precursors must be provided for steroid synthesis. The fetal adrenal gland is the major source, particularly of androstenedione and dehydroepiandrosterone sulfate (DHEA-S). More than 90% of serum estriol and estetrol in pregnancy is derived by placental conversion of fetal adrenal precursors. Therefore, estrogen levels in complete hydatidiform moles that lack a fetus are predictably lower than those in normal pregnancy, but higher than those in the nonpregnant state.[40] In vitro studies of molar tissue or choriocarcinoma that provides precursor DHEAS confirm the ability of GTN-derived trophoblasts to produce estrogen.[41] Conversion to estrogen seems to be more rapid in malignant GTN, so dedifferentiation of enzymatic potential in choriocarcinoma does not seem to occur.[42]

Marked elevation of serum progesterone occurs in normal pregnancy. Molar pregnancies tend to have even higher progesterone levels, particularly between 12 and 20 weeks' gestation.[43] The presence of theca lutein cysts in hydatidiform mole, a reflection of ovarian hyperstimulation by excess hCG, also is associated with higher serum progesterone levels and suggests a direct relation between hCG and progesterone production. Evacuation of molar pregnancy is followed by a rapid reduction in progesterone levels, and good response to chemotherapy in malignant GTN may be heralded by a decrease in progesterone. No relation exists between the level of 17-hydroxyprogesterone and nausea and vomiting in pregnancy or hydatidiform mole.

## DIAGNOSIS AND MANAGEMENT OF PRIMARY HYDATIDIFORM MOLE

Vaginal bleeding is the most common initial symptom in patients with complete moles and often results in anemia. As many as half of all patients with complete hydatidiform mole will have uterine enlargement consistent with a pregnancy larger by 4 weeks than expected for gestational age as a result of expansion of the uterus by both molar tissue and intrauterine bleeding. Unilateral or bilateral ovarian enlargement (>5 cm) produced by theca lutein cysts is clinically detected in approximately 25% to 35% of patients with complete hydatidiform mole and is usually associated with hCG levels above 100,000 mIU/mL. Pre-eclampsia and hyperemesis each occurs in approximately 25% of patients with complete mole. Most patients with these symptoms also usually have markedly elevated hCG values. The development of pregnancy-induced hypertension before 24 weeks' gestation is almost diagnostic of molar pregnancy. Increases in thyroid hormones are frequently diagnosed in patients with complete hydatidiform moles, but clinical hyperthyroidism is detected in fewer than 10%. Patients with complete moles have an approximately 20% incidence of clinically threatening "malignant" sequelae after evacuation, with 10% to 25% of these patients having metastatic disease.[44]

Management and surveillance of partial and complete molar gestations are similar. After the diagnosis has been confirmed, usually by pelvic ultrasound, evaluation of a patient with a molar gestation is directed to stabilizing the patient for evacuation. Preoperative evaluation consists of a complete physical examination, baseline serum hCG level, chest radiograph, hematologic profile, renal and liver function tests, and thyroid function tests. If the uterus is enlarged to a gestational size of more than 14 to 16 weeks or the patient has pregnancy-induced hypertension, arterial blood gas levels should be obtained preoperatively because respiratory insufficiency will develop in many of these patients after evacuation. A baseline ultrasound examination should be obtained to confirm the diagnosis and to screen for the presence of a fetus or theca lutein cysts.

## EVACUATION OF HYDATIDIFORM MOLE

Techniques now in use for evacuation of hydatidiform mole include cervical dilatation with suction curettage (D&C) and hysterectomy. However, most complete hydatidiform moles can be safely evacuated with suction D&C regardless of uterine size. If the patient desires sterilization, hysterectomy with

the mole in situ is our preferred method of evacuation. Hysterectomy offers the advantage of simultaneous evacuation of hydatidiform mole and sterilization for women who desire no further childbearing. Evacuation by hysterectomy decreases the risk of malignant sequelae to approximately 3.5% from the 20% anticipated after evacuation with D&C. However, hysterectomy does *not* totally eliminate the potential for malignant sequelae, and all women must be monitored by hCG levels after hysterectomy.

### THECA LUTEIN CYSTS

Clinically evident (>5 cm) theca lutein cysts of the ovary are detected in approximately 25% to 35% of women with hydatidiform mole, with additional smaller cysts often detected with ultrasound alone.[8] Ovarian enlargement usually correlates with marked elevation of serum hCG levels greater than 100,000 mIU/mL. Histologically and physiologically, these levels are similar to those seen after iatrogenic ovarian hyperstimulation produced by exogenous gonadotropin/hCG administration for induction of ovulation. Although theca lutein cysts are usually detected before molar evacuation, they may develop within the first week after evacuation. The mean time for disappearance of theca lutein cysts is approximately 8 weeks.

Theca lutein cysts are associated with an increased incidence of postmolar malignant sequelae, with some reporting a 75% incidence of postmolar sequelae among women with bilateral theca lutein cysts. Although theca lutein cysts usually regress spontaneously with decreasing hCG levels after molar evacuation, secondary enlargement will develop in approximately 30% in response to the increasing hCG levels associated with postmolar GTN. Occasionally, these cysts will persist for several months after remission of hCG levels has been achieved.

### MANAGEMENT OF COEXISTENT FETUS AND HYDATIDIFORM MOLE

Rare cases of twin pregnancies consisting of a coexistent normal fetus and a complete or partial mole have been reported. It is important that all cases suggesting these entities be carefully studied to avoid confusion with a partial hydatidiform mole. In twin gestations complicated by a mole, close inspection reveals two placentas, with a normal placenta attached to the fetus and a separate molar gestation; partial moles may have a fetus but have diffuse molar changes throughout the single placenta. Twin gestations complicated by a hydatidiform mole have an estimated incidence of only 1 per 22,000 to 100,000 pregnancies. Early reports failed to distinguish between partial or complete moles; most completely reported cases have involved twin pregnancies complicated by complete moles.

Steller and associates[45] reviewed 14 previously reported cases of coexistent normal fetuses and complete moles and added 8 cases from the New England Trophoblastic Disease Center. Ultrasound correctly suggested the diagnosis in 13 (68%) of 19 patients, and 5 of the remaining 6 had abnormalities of the placenta that were initially misinterpreted as placental hematomas. Five (23%) fetuses survived, and no fetal anomalies were reported. In comparison to a control group of patients with singleton complete moles, patients with multiple pregnancies complicated by complete moles had a significantly longer estimated gestational age at evacuation, larger uterine size, and higher pre-evacuation hCG levels than did those with singleton complete moles.[45]

We have been involved in the care of several women in whom the differential diagnosis has included placental hematoma, partial hydatidiform mole, or twin gestations with coexistent mole and normal pregnancy. In these circumstances, we recommend thorough obstetric ultrasonography to rule out fetal malformations and to fully characterize the placenta.

When the diagnosis of twin viable conceptus/molar gestation is confirmed, however, experience to guide management is limited. The patient should be counseled that she has an increased risk of pregnancy-induced hypertension, bleeding, or other complications of pregnancy that will mandate termination of the gestation. She must be cautioned about a risk for malignant sequelae requiring chemotherapy that probably increases with increasing length of gestation.[45] Balanced against these concerns should be the observation that a significant proportion of multiple gestations complicated by mole can result in a viable fetus and that all patients reported to date have been cured of their malignant postmolar GTN with chemotherapy.[45] Although preferred management would consist of early pregnancy termination, a fully informed patient can participate in the decision to monitor a multiple gestation complicated by hydatidiform mole in the hope of delivering a viable fetus.

Approximately 15% to 20% of primary molar pregnancies will progress to malignant disease (Table 189-2). Surveillance using serial quantitative serum hCG levels is the only reliable means for early detection of malignant sequelae after evacuation of hydatidiform mole.[8] One of any number of sensitive assays with polyclonal or monoclonal antibodies to either whole-molecule hCG or total (free and bound) hCG-β fragments can be used. A baseline level should be obtained within 48 hours of evacuation and serial levels at 1-week intervals until normal hCG levels are obtained. Levels should then be monitored at 1- to 2-month intervals to ensure that spontaneous remission is sustained beyond 6 to 12 months. Although some have recommended that patients with partial hydatidiform moles can stop surveillance after remission of hCG levels has been achieved, the approximately 3% to 4% incidence of malignant sequelae after evacuation of partial moles is of concern. We generally recommend at least 3 to 6 months of normal hCG levels in these patients before surveillance is discontinued.

It is rare for postmolar GTN to result in reelevation of serum hCG levels after more than 6 months of normal hCG levels without an intercurrent pregnancy. Virtually all cases of postmolar GTN reported in adequately monitored patients have occurred within the first 6 months after evacuation. Therefore, we believe that a minimum of 6 months of hCG remission should be recommended for patients before attempting pregnancy after evacuation of a complete hydatidiform mole.

Patients should use contraception in the intervals between hCG monitoring until sustained remission has been documented. This practice avoids confusion caused by an elevated hCG level associated with an intercurrent pregnancy. We routinely recommend the use of oral contraceptives with a low estrogen content, unless the woman has specific contraindications to their use.

## DIAGNOSIS OF POSTMOLAR GESTATIONAL TROPHOBLASTIC NEOPLASMS

Postmolar GTN will develop in approximately 15% to 20% of patients undergoing evacuation of a complete hydatidiform mole. Approximately 70% to 90% of these cases consist of histologically defined persistent or invasive moles, whereas 10% to 30% are choriocarcinoma. Because the historical mortality for patients with invasive moles ranged around 20%, most investigators in the United States have used inclusive or liberal criteria for initiating chemotherapy in patients after evacuation of hydatidiform mole in an attempt to reduce the morbidity caused by local proliferation, infection, and hemorrhage and to prevent mortality from local disease or systemic metastasis.[46] The vast majority of patients are therefore treated on the basis of hCG-level regression patterns without a further firm histologic diagnosis.

Criteria for the diagnosis of malignant postmolar GTN include plateaued or progressively increasing hCG values; histologic evidence of invasive mole, choriocarcinoma, or placental-site trophoblastic tumor; or evidence of metastatic disease.[46] Most American centers will administer chemotherapy to patients who exhibit a plateau of serial hCG values. Additionally, some investigators have recommended basing institution of therapy on persistence of detectable hCG at some arbitrary interval after molar evacuation.

We recommend that patients with hydatidiform mole have therapy instituted according to the following criteria: increase in hCG level; plateau in hCG level (±10%) for three or more consecutive weekly measurements; appearance of metastases; or histologic evidence of choriocarcinoma, placental-site trophoblastic tumor, or invasive mole. As noted earlier, we will individualize the indications for treating reliable patients with low hCG plateaus. In Great Britain, where patients with hydatidiform moles are monitored by a centralized registry system and therapeutic decisions are made by a few experienced physicians, more conservative guidelines for treating patients with postmolar GTN may be practical. In the United States, however, where patient follow-up may not be as reliable and management of moles is decentralized, it is prudent to use more liberal guidelines for institution of therapy. Using these criteria, we have continued to treat approximately 20% of our patients after molar evacuation.

## PREGNANCY AFTER HYDATIDIFORM MOLE

Most women treated for hydatidiform mole are in their prime reproductive years, and many desire future childbearing. In one report of a large series of women whose reproductive outcomes were studied after evacuation of complete hydatidiform moles,[47] the risk for stillbirth, prematurity, spontaneous abortion, and congenital malformation was similar to that in the general population. Recurrent molar gestations were observed in 1.3% of patients. Other series also reported an increased risk for repetitive complete and partial moles ranging between 1% and 2%. Furthermore, the risk of a third molar gestation increases to 28% after a second mole.

Therefore, after a woman has had a molar pregnancy, she should be reassured regarding the probable normal outcome of future pregnancies, but she should be aware of the increased risk of a subsequent molar gestation. We recommend obtaining an ultrasound scan early in pregnancy to confirm a normal gestational sac, combined with a chest radiograph to screen for occult metastasis from choriocarcinoma masked by the increase in hCG level associated with pregnancy. The placenta or products of conception should be examined histologically

**Table 189-2** Incidence of Malignant Gestational Trophoblastic Neoplasia after Molar Evacuation

| Authors | No. of Patients | Percentage of Patients Treated | Percentage of Treated Patients with Metastatic Gestational Trophoblastic Disease |
|---|---|---|---|
| Delfs[71] | 119 | 9 | — |
| Brewer et al.[72] | 51 | 22 | 9 |
| Goldstein[73] | 116 | 20 | 22 |
| Bagshawe et al.[74] | 280 | 6 | — |
| Curry et al.[8] | 347 | 20 | 17 |
| Morrow et al.[75] | 121 | 26 | 12 |
| Hatch et al.[76] | 212 | 32 | 18 |
| Schlaerth et al.[77] | 77 | 36 | 25 |
| Kohorn[78] | 127 | 27 | 6 |
| Lurain et al.[79] | 738 | 19 | 15 |

at the time of delivery or pregnancy evacuation. Additionally, an hCG level should be obtained 6 to 8 weeks after delivery of any future pregnancy to exclude the rare occurrence of choriocarcinoma.

## MALIGNANT TROPHOBLASTIC DISEASE

### DIAGNOSIS

GTN is a clinical spectrum with various benign and malignant pathologic manifestations. As noted, in 15% to 20% of patients after a molar pregnancy, careful monitoring of serial hCG levels in the follow-up period will permit a prompt diagnosis of malignancy. More difficulty is encountered in the diagnosis of malignant GTN after nonmolar pregnancies, and prolonged delays in initiation of therapy are not unusual. Prolonged, irregular bleeding after term delivery should suggest the possibility of choriocarcinoma, and serum hCG should be measured. Because choriocarcinoma follows term pregnancy so rarely, more than 75% of this group will have widespread metastases or very high hCG levels or both because of delay in diagnosis. Diagnosis of malignant GTN after abortion or ectopic pregnancy also may involve a long delay.

In an effort to provide uniformity to the diagnosis of postmolar GTN, International Federation of Obstetrics and Gynecology (FIGO) conducted workshops among a variety of groups. The current FIGO requirements for making a diagnosis of postmolar GTN are as follows[48]:

1. Four values or more of plateaued hCG (±10%) over a period at least 3 weeks; days 1, 7, 14, and 21
2. An increase of hCG of 10% or greater for three values or more over a period of at least 2 weeks; days 1, 7, and 14
3. The histologic diagnosis of choriocarcinoma
4. Persistence of hCG beyond 6 months after mole evacuation

The level and duration for observation of the hCG plateau would be determined at the discretion of the treating physician. Observation of hCG level plateau for longer than 3 weeks was permitted because this does not have an adverse effect on patient survival.

The majority of centers in the United States also will treat patients if metastases are identified on examination or radiographic studies. Some pulmonary metastases result from deportation of trophoblast during molar evacuation, and identification of pulmonary nodules in a postevacuation chest radiograph might not indicate true malignant behavior. Bagshawe and coworkers,[49] reporting the results of a centralized system for monitoring patients after evacuation of hydatidiform mole in the United Kingdom, stated that patients with pulmonary nodules were followed up conservatively and treatment decisions were based on hCG regression patterns. Although the overall results from this policy were excellent, outcome for patients with pulmonary metastases was not detailed. In the United States, where care is decentralized and most patients are followed up by general obstetrician/gynecologists after evacuation of hydatidiform mole, identification of metastases is included as an indication for initiation of therapy.

Other factors involved in the natural history of malignant GTN may obscure the diagnosis. The primary uterine focus may regress, and D&C may not reveal trophoblastic tissue while metastatic sites continue to grow. The clinical features may be dominated by the effect of metastases and include hemoptysis, cerebrovascular accident, or gastrointestinal hemorrhage. Progression of malignant GTN may be delayed for 10 to 20 years after the last pregnancy for reasons not presently understood. The presence of an undiagnosed metastatic tumor in a woman of reproductive age should mandate the exclusion of malignant GTN by sensitive hCG

testing because this tumor is one of the few curable malignant neoplasms in this circumstance.

### CLINICAL STAGING

Once the diagnosis of malignant GTN is established by histology or by hCG testing, staging studies are performed to evaluate sites of metastases, and the general medical condition of the patient is determined (Table 189-3). Computed tomography is currently performed in all cases. Bagshawe[50] depends on an hCG serum–to–cerebrospinal fluid ratio of 60:1 or less to indicate central nervous system (CNS) involvement, but others primarily use computed tomography/magnetic resonance imaging to detect CNS involvement. Repeated D&C seems to have little effect on the management of postmolar GTN unless bleeding of consequence is present. Therefore, we prefer to reserve secondary D&C for patients who experience significant uterine bleeding immediately before or during chemotherapy.

Laparoscopy, craniotomy, and thoracotomy are rarely justified to obtain tissue to establish the primary diagnosis of malignant GTN because clinical decisions related to this diagnosis can be made on the basis of elevated hCG levels coupled with radiographic evidence of metastatic disease after excluding pregnancy. Consideration of the possibility of GTN in these settings would render most of these diagnostic surgical procedures unnecessary, even though the exact histology of the metastatic lesions is not determined.

Although we have found that most patients at high risk for metastases from malignant GTN have radiographic evidence of pulmonary metastases, we remain reluctant to recommend a less than complete radiographic evaluation before initiation of treatment. Selection of the initial therapy and subsequent survival are largely dependent on identification of poor-prognosis factors in patients with metastatic disease.

### Classification and Staging of Malignant Gestational Trophoblastic Neoplasms

Since the original identification by workers at the National Cancer Institute (NCI) of favorable and adverse prognostic factors correlating with single-agent treatment of patients with malignant GTN, several classification and staging systems

| Table 189-3 | Staging Studies for Malignant Gestational Trophoblastic Neoplasia |
|---|---|

1. History and physical examination
2. Blood studies
   CBC, differential, platelet count
   Serum electrolytes, BUN, glucose, creatinine, bilirubin, AST, ALT, LDH, alkaline phosphatase, $Ca^{2+}$, $PO_4$
   Blood type and Rh
   Thyroid panel
   HLA phenotype, patient and consort (optional)
3. Urinalysis
4. Papanicolaou smear
5. Chest roentgenography, PA and lateral; tomography if indicated
6. Brain CT (radionuclide scan if CT unavailable)
7. Abdominal CT with contrast (liver scan if CT unavailable)
8. Pelvic ultrasonography
9. Intravenous pyelography
10. Serum hCG or 24-hour urine hCG (quantitative)

Consider also

11. Lumbar puncture for CSF hCG level
12. Selective arteriography
13. Anti-hCG- or anti-HLA-tagged antibody scan

ALT, alanine aminotransferase; AST, aspartate aminotransferase; BUN, blood urea nitrogen; CBC, complete blood count; CSF, cerebrospinal fluid; CT, computed tomography; hCG, human chorionic gonadotropin; HLA, human leukocyte antigen; LDH, lactate dehydrogenase; PA, posteroanterior.

have been described for evaluating patients with this disease. Three systems are frequently used to classify patients with malignant GTN: the recently modified FIGO staging system, the clinical classification system that is based on prognostic factors that correlated with success or failure of single-agent therapy in the original NCI studies, and the World Health Organization (WHO) prognostic index scoring system. Unlike standard staging systems, all three systems allow reevaluation of previously treated patients when secondary treatment is given. They also do not specify radiographic studies that can be used for assignment of stage or category of disease. This text cannot expound the various merits of these systems; such can be found elsewhere.

In our staging system, patients with gestational trophoblastic disease are divided into three categories: nonmetastatic, low-risk/good-prognosis metastatic, and high-risk/poor-prognosis metastatic disease (see Table 189-1).[3] Essentially all patients with nonmetastatic GTN can be cured with initial single-agent chemotherapy; therefore, they are not assigned to a prognostic category and are initially treated with single-agent chemotherapy, usually methotrexate alternating with its antidote citrovorum factor.[51] The presence of any single high-risk factor in a patient with metastatic GTN places her in the high-risk/poor-prognosis metastatic GTN category.[52] A similar system is used at the Memorial Sloan–Kettering Cancer Center, which, however, subdivides patients into low-, moderate-, and high-risk groups based on criteria used in the clinical classification system.[52] This system recognizes that patients who have high pretherapy hCG levels or long duration of disease as the only prognostic risk have a lesser risk of failure than do patients with metastases involving the brain or liver or both or those for whom prior chemotherapy had failed.

The main virtue of the clinical classification system is that it allows prompt identification of patients who would be likely to be cured by simple forms of chemotherapy and identifies patients who would be unlikely to be cured with single-agent treatment.[53]

Because of its simplicity and known correlation with risk for failure of initial single-agent therapy, we prefer to use the clinical classification system to determine primary therapy for individual patients (Table 189-4). Patients in the nonmetastatic and good-prognosis metastatic groups have a uniformly favorable outcome when treated with primary single-agent regimens, whereas those with poor-prognosis metastatic disease are less likely to respond to single-agent regimens and should be initially treated with multiagent therapy. If therapy of intermediate intensity is shown to be efficacious for patients in an intermediate-risk category or if high-intensity

therapy is proved more effective than current regimens for the treatment of high-risk patients, the more complex FIGO staging or WHO prognostic index scoring systems may have an advantage.[54]

## THERAPY FOR NONMETASTATIC GESTATIONAL TROPHOBLASTIC NEOPLASMS

Since the introduction of methotrexate chemotherapy for malignant GTN, most centers have reported almost 100% cure rates for patients with nonmetastatic disease treated with single-agent regimens. Therefore, we do not use prognostic factors to alter our treatment of patients without evidence of some metastatic disease at the time of pretherapy metastatic survey.

Methotrexate and dactinomycin have been the principal agents used for the treatment of nonmetastatic GTN; however, 5-fluorouracil and oral etoposide have recently been used with excellent results. Despite the high level of success with primary chemotherapy, hysterectomy is still used in the treatment of selected patients with nonmetastatic GTN and should be considered in those who desire concurrent sterilization. Currently, many centers are investigating options of chemotherapy that would retain a high remission rate for this disease while reducing toxicity and cost. The reader is referred elsewhere for details of chemotherapeutic regimens and outcomes, but cure rates of nearly 100% are now expected.[51]

### General Management
Our general approach to the management of patients with nonmetastatic GTN is to use either the weekly methotrexate or the 8-day methotrexate/folinic acid regimen as initial chemotherapy and to reserve dactinomycin for salvage therapy.[54] Patients who do not desire preservation of fertility are offered total abdominal hysterectomy during the first cycle of chemotherapy. Treatment is continued until normal hCG values are obtained, and an additional cycle of chemotherapy is given as maintenance therapy. Monitoring during therapy and after remission of hCG levels is discussed subsequently.

## THERAPY FOR METASTATIC GESTATIONAL TROPHOBLASTIC NEOPLASMS

### Management of Low-Risk/Good-Prognosis Metastatic Gestational Trophoblastic Neoplasms
Most patients with low-risk/good-prognosis metastatic GTN by the clinical classification criteria have low- or medium-risk WHO prognostic index scores. Dating from a 1965 article by Ross and associates,[55] who reported a 95% complete remission rate in women with metastatic GTN who had short duration of disease and low hCG levels, many investigators have reported excellent results with either methotrexate or dactinomycin as initial therapy for patients with low-risk/good-prognosis metastatic GTN. In general, remission rates for 5-day cycles of either agent are comparable, and patients for whom initial therapy with one agent fails can usually be salvaged with the alternative single agent.

Soper and colleagues[51] reported a retrospective review of 52 patients with good-prognosis metastatic GTN treated with the 5-day methotrexate regimen. None of their patients underwent surgical intervention during primary chemotherapy. Based on hCG level criteria, resistance developed in 10 (19%); no new sites of metastatic disease developed in any of the patients, and all but 1 were salvaged with alternative single-agent regimens. A pretherapy hCG level above 10,000 mIU/mL was associated with an increased risk of drug resistance. An additional 11 (21%) had therapy changed because of toxicity. Very conservative criteria were used as a threshold for changing therapy because of toxicity, however, inasmuch as grade 4 hematologic toxicity developed in only 6% of patients.[56] Overall, cure in this category approaches 100%.

---

**Table 189-4  Clinical Classifications of Malignant Gestational Trophoblastic Neoplasia**

I. Nonmetastatic GTN: No evidence of disease outside the uterus, not assigned to a prognostic category
II. Metastatic GTN: Any metastases
  A. Good-prognosis metastatic GTN
    1. Short duration (<4 mo)
    2. Low hCG level (<40,000 mIU/mL serum hCG-β)
    3. No metastases to the brain or liver
    4. No antecedent term pregnancy
    5. No prior chemotherapy
  B. Poor-prognosis metastatic GTN: Any high-risk factor
    1. Long duration (>4 mo since last pregnancy)
    2. High pretreatment hCG level (>40,000 mIU/mL serum hCG-β)
    3. Brain or liver metastases
    4. Antecedent term pregnancy
    5. Prior chemotherapy

GTN, gestational trophoblastic neoplasia; hCG, human chorionic gonadotropin.

## Surgery for Low-Risk Metastatic Gestational Trophoblastic Neoplasms

In part because of the dismal results of treatment with surgical therapy alone for metastatic choriocarcinoma, results of combined medical and surgical therapy have been reported only sporadically. Hammond and colleagues[57] reviewed a series of patients treated for malignant GTN at our center and reported on hysterectomy applied to therapy for patients with good-prognosis metastatic GTN. Approximately 13% of 40 patients with good-prognosis metastatic disease treated initially with chemotherapy required hysterectomy to achieve sustained remission. Additionally, patients who underwent primary hysterectomy and chemotherapy required an average of only 3.8 cycles of chemotherapy versus 5.9 cycles in patients treated primarily with chemotherapy. Therefore, it is reasonable to combine primary hysterectomy with chemotherapy in patients with limited extrauterine metastasis who desire sterilization.

## General Management of Low-Risk Metastatic Gestational Trophoblastic Neoplasms

Our recommended approach to patients with low-risk/good-prognosis metastatic GTN is based on no high-risk prognostic factors by clinical criteria; initial single-agent therapy is a reasonable option, but a higher failure rate with primary therapy should be anticipated when compared with that in patients who have nonmetastatic disease. We generally use 5-day intramuscular methotrexate as the initial chemotherapeutic regimen, with dactinomycin reserved for treatment failures. Patients who have failed two single-agent regimens are considered to have high-risk disease and receive multiagent chemotherapy. Hysterectomy is offered to patients who do not desire preservation of child-bearing capacity. Therapy is continued until normal hCG values are obtained. Maintenance chemotherapy is given after remission of hCG levels and consists of one or two cycles, depending on the amount of therapy required to achieve remission. Monitoring during therapy and after remission of hCG levels is discussed later.

## Management of High-Risk/Poor-Prognosis Metastatic Gestational Trophoblastic Neoplasms

As previously noted, from our center we reported that patients with metastatic GTN who had one or more high-risk/poor-prognosis factors, rather than waiting for drug resistance to single-agent therapy before initiating multiagent treatment, benefited from initial multiagent chemotherapy.[52] Subsequently, most American centers have used multiagent chemotherapy to treat patients with high-risk metastatic GTN based largely on the clinical classification system discussed previously.[53-57] Options and results of therapy are beyond the scope of this chapter, but overall, they approach 85% cure. Such multiagent chemotherapy is now a standard approach, with etoposide/methotrexate/dactinomycin and cyclophosphamide/vincristine (EMA-CO) being our first-line approach.

## High-Risk Sites of Metastatic Gestational Trophoblastic Disease

### Central Nervous System Metastasis

Bagshawe assigned CNS involvement the highest level of risk among metastatic sites.[50] Although the vast majority of patients with CNS involvement have lung or liver involvement or both, a few series have reported CNS metastases in patients who did not have evidence of identifiable metastatic disease elsewhere.

Based in part on work by Brace,[58] who reported a significant incidence of CNS control with the use of whole-brain irradiation in patients receiving single-agent methotrexate in the early National Institutes of Health experience, we previously incorporated whole-brain radiation therapy into the primary treatment of patients with brain metastasis. Three thousand cGy has been administered concurrent with methotrexate/actinomycin D/cyclophosphamide (MAC) chemotherapy delivered in 10 equal fractions. The overall survival rate for patients treated in this fashion is 50%, with rates of 70% to 89% in patients treated for primary CNS metastases versus only about 20% to 30% for those who receive salvage treatment for brain metastases. Others have used whole-brain radiotherapy in conjunction with EMA-CO chemotherapy and have not reported unusual toxicity,[59] and in the future, such radiotherapy may not be required for optimal results.

Patients with CNS metastases of GTN are at risk for neurologic compression caused by cerebral edema and acute hemorrhage into these highly vascular and often centrally necrotic lesions. We routinely administer dexamethasone throughout the course of whole-brain radiation therapy in an effort to minimize cerebral edema. Neurosurgical consultation is obtained early in the course of treatment, in the event that surgical decompression or extirpation is required. Surgical extirpation is generally reserved for patients who demonstrate neurologic decompensation or those who require salvage therapy for recurrent CNS metastases of malignant GTN. Although CNS metastasis of malignant GTN constitutes a poor-prognosis factor in this disease entity, the excellent survival rate of patients treated for primary brain metastases of GTN stands in sharp contrast to the grim outlook for patients with brain metastases from other sites of malignancy.

### Hepatic Metastases

Metastases to the liver are identified in approximately 2% to 8% of patients being evaluated for primary therapy for metastatic GTN.[60-64] Involvement of the liver constitutes a poor-prognosis factor, as evidenced by 40% to 50% survival rates for patients with primary involvement at this site and dismal survival rates in patients in whom liver metastases develop while they are being treated for drug-resistant disease. Optimal management of hepatic metastases has not been established. Hepatic metastases tend to be highly vascular, and death is frequently caused by catastrophic intra-abdominal hemorrhage. In an effort to minimize this risk, we previously used approximately 2000-cGy whole-liver irradiation in conjunction with combination chemotherapy.[62] Toxicity did not prohibit the administration of chemotherapy with this approach. Barnard and associates[63] reported that postirradiation hepatitis developed in only 1 of 13 patients treated with combined therapy. However, salvage was not enhanced by the combination therapy; thus, it does not appear that such therapy is worthwhile.

Selective hepatic embolization or ligation has been reported to control hemorrhage from hepatic metastases.[63,64] Others have advocated direct infusion of chemotherapy into the hepatic artery, without yet reporting their results. Bakri and coworkers, who used cisplatin/etoposide/dactinomycin chemotherapy and no adjuvant radiation therapy, reported survival in five (63%) of eight patients with liver metastases. We have used EMA-CO or similar chemotherapy with high-dose methotrexate systemic infusion (500 to 1000 mg/m$^2$) in a few patients and have not observed hemorrhage from liver metastases. However, the experience is too small to draw strong conclusions regarding the optimal therapy for these very high-risk patients.

### Other High-Risk Metastases

Metastatic GTN has been reported to involve virtually every organ in various studies. However, metastases to the kidneys, gastrointestinal tract, and other organs occurred at a lower frequency than did those to the brain, vagina, or lungs in a series of women being evaluated for primary chemotherapy for malignant GTN.[50] Bagshawe[50] considered renal and gastrointestinal metastases as intermediate in risk between pulmonary or vaginal metastases and brain metastases, but survival data to justify this ranking were not presented.

Gastrointestinal metastases may be manifested as multiple submucosal metastases along the intestine that result in chronic gastrointestinal bleeding or may be caused by direct invasion from pelvic disease. Unless significant gastrointestinal hemorrhage is noted from a single focus of disease, these patients do not usually require surgery and can be successfully treated with chemotherapy alone. In our experience, all five patients with gastrointestinal or intra-abdominal metastases who received primary therapy and did not have liver or brain metastases were cured.[65]

Renal metastasis occurred in 1.3% of 154 women who came to our center for primary therapy and in 14% of 42 patients referred for salvage therapy for metastatic GTN. Only 3 of 8 patients survived, all of whom received primary therapy and had unilateral renal metastasis and limited systemic metastases involving the lungs only. The role of nephrectomy or radiation therapy in the treatment of patients with renal metastases is unclear. Six of our patients with renal metastases underwent nephrectomy, and three survived. Nephrectomy should be considered in the treatment of patients with unilateral renal involvement and limited disease involving the lungs, but it may not contribute to survival in cases with extensive systemic metastases. Irradiation of both kidneys is unlikely to achieve significant disease control for patients with bilateral metastases, given the low radiation tolerance of the kidneys (<2000 cGy); however, unilateral renal metastases might be treated with irradiation.

### Drug-Resistant Disease

Patients with high-risk metastatic GTN for whom failed primary chemotherapy has failed are extremely challenging and have a very poor prognosis. The details of previous therapy must be reviewed completely to identify potentially active agents that have not been used. Surgical extirpation of drug-resistant foci of disease must be considered in patients with limited systemic metastases.

Before cisplatin and etoposide were available, salvage regimens for patients for whom MAC-type regimens failed were rarely successful.[59,66] The CHAMOMA regimen (cyclophosphamide/hydroxyurea/Adriamycin [doxorubicin]/methotrexate/Oncovin [vincristine]/melphalan/actinomycin D) was used as salvage therapy at our center through 1985, with an apparent improvement in results in comparison to previous single-agent and combination regimens.[67,68] Although cisplatin/vinblastine/bleomycin was reported by Azab and associates[69] to produce high complete remission rates among their patients with drug-resistant GTN, others have observed few remissions with this regimen without including surgical resection.

### Coordination of Therapy

It should be stressed that the results cited earlier for treatment of patients with high-risk/poor-prognosis metastatic GTN are from centers that specialize in the treatment of women with this disease. We strongly believe that all women with high-risk/poor-prognosis disease should be treated in consultation with a trophoblastic disease center or by an individual who is experienced in the management of patients with malignant GTN and can coordinate all aspects of therapy.

## MONITORING OF PATIENTS DURING AND AFTER THERAPY FOR MALIGNANT GESTATIONAL TROPHOBLASTIC NEOPLASMS

Patients being treated with chemotherapy for malignant GTN should be monitored at least weekly with sensitive assays for serum hCG-β. Rottmensch and colleagues[70] reported that women treated for nonmetastatic malignant gestational trophoblastic disease (GTD) have a log-linear clearance of serum hCG levels after initiation of treatment. In our experience, patients with low-risk metastatic GTN exhibit a pattern of hCG regression similar to that of patients who respond to methotrexate regimens. A 1-log reduction in hCG is observed between the first and second weeks of chemotherapy.[56] In general, we will consider a change in regimen if less than a 25% reduction in hCG is seen or if the level increases after a single course of therapy.[56] Chemotherapy should be continued beyond the first normal hCG level in an attempt to reduce the development of recurrent GTN. Remission is defined as three normal hCG levels over a 14-day period. After completion of chemotherapy, patients are monitored with serial hCG values at 2-week intervals for the first 3 months after completion of chemotherapy and at least monthly for the first year of surveillance. Although it is rare for recurrent disease to develop more than 1 year after remission, we recommend monitoring hCG values at 6-month intervals indefinitely. Late recurrences have been reported several years after completion of treatment.

## SUMMARY

The last several decades have seen GTN move from one of the most universally fatal neoplasms to one of the most likely to be cured, even when metastatic. The intriguing relation of this disease to endocrinologically active substances also has made it one of the most interesting.

## REFERENCES

1. Hammond CB, Borchert L, Tyrey L, et al: Treatment of metastatic trophoblastic disease: Good and poor prognosis. Am J Obstet Gynecol 115:451–457, 1973.
2. Hammond CB, Hertz R, Ross GT, et al: Primary chemotherapy for nonmetastatic gestational trophoblastic neoplasms. Am J Obstet Gynecol 98:71–78, 1967.
3. Hammond CB, Parker RT: Diagnosis and treatment of trophoblastic disease: A report from the Southeastern Regional Center. Obstet Gynecol 35:132–143, 1970.
4. Ross GT, Goldstein DP, Hertz R, et al: Sequential use of methotrexate and actinomycin D in treatment of metastatic choriocarcinoma and related trophoblastic diseases in women. Am J Obstet Gynecol 92:223–229, 1967.

5. Ober WB, Fass FO: The early history of choriocarcinoma. J Hist Med Allied Sci 16:49–73, 1961.
6. Ashheim S, Zondek B: Hypophysenvorderlappenhormon und ovarial hormon im harn von schwangeren. Klin Wochenschr 6:1322, 1927.
7. Li MC, Hertz R, Spencer DB: Effect of methotrexate therapy under choriocarcinoma and chorioadenoma. Proc Soc Exp Biol Med 93:361–366, 1956.
8. Curry SL, Hammond CB, Tyrey L, et al: Hydatidiform mole: Diagnosis, management and long-term follow up of 347 patients. Obstet Gynecol 45:1–8, 1975.
9. Teoh ES, Dawood MY, Ratnam SS: Epidemiology of hydatidiform mole in Singapore. Am J Obstet Gynecol 110:415–421, 1971.

10. Jacobs PA, Hunt PA, Matsuura JS, et al: Complete and partial hydatidiform mole in Hawaii: Cytogenetics, morphology and epidemiology. Br J Obstet Gynaecol 89:258–266, 1982.
11. Kurman RJ, Scully RE, Norris HJ: Trophoblastic pseudotumor of the uterus: An exaggerated form of "syncytial endometritis" simulating a malignant tumor. Cancer 38:1214–1226, 1976.
12. Rosenshein NB, Wijnen H, Woodruff JD: Clinical importance of the diagnosis of trophoblastic pseudotumors. Am J Obstet Gynecol 136:635–638, 1981.
13. Hammond CB, Lewis JL Jr: Gestational trophoblastic neoplasms. In Sciarra JJ (ed): Gynecology and Obstetrics, vol 4, Gynecologic Oncology. Philadelphia, Harper & Row, 1984, pp 1–28.
14. Lurain J, Brewer JL: Invasive mole. Semin Oncol 9:174, 1982.

15. Jacobs PA, Szulman AE, Funkhouser J, et al: Human triploidy: Relationship between paternal origin of the additional haploid complement and development of partial hydatidiform mole. Ann Hum Genet 46:223, 1982.

16. Kajii T, Ohama K: Androgenetic origin of hydatidiform mole. Nature 268:633, 1977.

17. Sruti U, Szulman AE, O'Brien S: Dispermic origin and clinical outcome of three complete hydatidiform moles with 46,XY karyotype. Am J Obstet Gynecol 144:84, 1982.

18. Lawler SD, Fisher RA, Pickthall VJ, et al: Genetic studies on hydatidiform moles, I: The origin of partial moles. Cancer Genet Cytogenet 5:309, 1982.

19. Mazur MT, Kurman RJ: Choriocarcinoma and placental site tumor. In Szulman AE, Buchsbaum HJ (eds): Gestational Trophoblastic Disease. New York, Springer-Verlag, 1987, p 45.

20. Morgan FJ, Birken S, Canfield RE: The amino acid sequence of human chorionic gonadotropin: The α subunit and β subunit. J Biol Chem 250:5247, 1975.

21. Tyrey L: Human chorionic gonadotropin assays and their uses. Obstet Gynecol Clin North Am 15:457, 1988.

22. Birken S: Chemistry of human choriogonadotropin. Ann Endocrinol (Paris) 45:297, 1984.

23. Vaitukaitis JL, Braunstein GD, Ross GT: A radioimmunoassay which specifically measures human chorionic gonadotropin in the presence of human luteinizing hormone. Am J Obstet Gynecol 113:751, 1972.

24. Vaitukaitis JL: Radioimmunoassay of human choriogonadotropin. Clin Chem 31:1749, 1985.

25. Hussa RO, Rinke ML, Schweitzer PG: Discordant human chorionic gonadotropin results: Causes and solutions. Obstet Gynecol 65:211, 1985.

26. Lougren T, Hemmila I, Pettersson K, et al: Time-resolved fluorometry in immunoassays. In Collins WP (ed): Alternative Immunoassays. New York, John Wiley & Sons, 1985, p 205.

27. Pettersson K, Siitari H, Hemmila L, et al: Time-resolved fluoroimmunoassay of human choriogonadotropin. Clin Chem 29:60, 1983.

28. Cole LA, Kohorn EL, Kim GS: Detecting and monitoring trophoblastic diseases. New perspectives on measuring human chorionic gonadotropin levels. J Reprod Med 39:193, 1994.

29. Nishimura R, Ashitaka Y, Tokjo S: The clinical evaluation of the simultaneous measurements of human chorionic gonadotropin (hCG) and its alpha subunit in sera of patients with trophoblastic diseases. Endocrinol Jpn 26:575, 1979.

30. Quigley MM, Tyrey L, Hammond CB: Utility of assay of alpha subunit of human chorionic gonadotropin in management of gestational trophoblastic malignancies. Am J Obstet Gynecol 138:545, 1980.

31. Khazaeli MB, Hedayat MM, Hatch KD, et al: Radioimmunoassay of free beta-subunit of human chorionic gonadotropin as a prognostic test for persistent trophoblastic disease in molar pregnancy. Am J Obstet Gynecol 155:320, 1986.

32. Berkowitz R, Ozturk M, Goldstein DP, et al: Human chorionic gonadotropin and free subunits' serum levels in patients with partial and complete hydatidiform moles. Obstet Gynecol 74:212, 1989.

33. Cole LA: Phantom hCG and phantom choriocarcinoma. Gynecol Oncol 71:325, 1998

34. Rotmensch S, Cole LA: False diagnosis and needless therapy of presumed malignant disease in women with false-positive human chorionic gonadotropin concentrations. Lancet 355:712, 2000

35. Galton MA, Ingbar SH, Jimenez-Fonseca J, et al: Alterations in thyroid hormone economy in patients with hydatidiform mole. J Clin Invest 50:1345–1354, 1971.

36. Anderson NR, Lokich JJ, McDermott WV, et al: Gestational choriocarcinoma and thyrotoxicosis. Cancer 44:304–306, 1979.

37. Herschman JM: Hyperthyroidism induced by trophoblastic thyrotropin. Mayo Clin Proc 47:913–918, 1972.

38. Nisela BC, Taliadourous GS: Thyroid function in gestational trophoblastic neoplasia: Evidence that the thyrotropic activity of chorionic gonadotropin mediates the thyrotoxicosis of choriocarcinoma. Am J Obstet Gynecol 138:77–85, 1980.

39. Frantz AG, Rabkin MT, Frieson H: Human placental lactogen in choriocarcinoma of the male: Measurements by radioimmunoassay. J Clin Endocrinol Metab 25:1136–1139, 1965.

40. Odell WD, Hertz R, Lipsett MB, et al: Endocrine aspects of trophoblastic neoplasms. Clin Obstet Gynecol 10:290–302, 1967.

41. Van Leusden H, Villee CA: Formation of estrogens by hydatidiform mole in vitro. J Clin Endocriol Metab 26:842–846, 1966.

42. Barlow JJ, Goldstein DP, Reid DE: A study of in vivo estrogen biosynthesis and production rates in normal pregnancy, hydatidiform mole and choriocarcinoma. J Clin Endocrinol Metab 27:1028–1034, 1967.

43. Dawood MY: Progesterone concentrations in the serum of patients with intact and aborting hydatidiform moles. Am J Obstet Gynecol 119:911–918, 1974.

44. Bahar AM, el-Ashnei MC, Senthilselvan A: Hydatidiform mole in the elderly: Hysterectomy or evacuation. Int J Obstet Gynecol 29:233, 1989.

45. Steller MA, Genest DR, Bernstein MR, et al: Natural history of twin pregnancy with complete hydatidiform mole and coexistent fetus. Obstet Gynecol 83:35, 1994.

46. Kohorn EI: Evaluation of the criteria used to make the diagnosis of nonmetastatic gestational trophoblastic neoplasia. Gynecol Oncol 348:1139, 1991.

47. Berkowitz RS, Golstein DP, Bernstein MR, et al: Subsequent pregnancy outcomes in patients with molar pregnancies and gestational trophoblastic tumors. J Reprod Med 32:680, 1987.

48. Kohorn EI: The new FIGO 2000 staging and risk factor scoring system for gestational trophoblastic disease: Description and critical assessment. Int J Gynecol Cancer 11:73, 2000.

49. Bagshawe KD, Dent J, Webb J: Hydatidiform mole in England and Wales 1973-1983. Lancet 2:673, 1986.

50. Bagshawe KD: Risk and prognostic factors in trophoblastic neoplasia. Cancer 38:1373, 1976.

51. Soper JT, Lewis JL Jr, Hammond CB: Gestational trophoblastic disease. In Hoskins WJ, Parez CA, Young RC (eds): Principles and Practice of Gynecologic Oncology, 2d ed. Philadelphia, Lippincott-Raven, 1997, pp 1039–1077.

52. Hammond CB, Borchert LG, Tyrey L, et al: Treatment of metastatic trophoblastic disease: Good and poor prognosis. Am J Obstet Gynecol 115:4, 1973.

53. Lurain JR, Brewer JI, Torok EE, et al: Gestational trophoblastic disease: Treatment results at the Brewer Trophoblastic Disease Center. Obstet Gynecol 60:354, 1982.

54. Soper JT: Staging and evaluation of gestational trophoblastic disease. Clin Obstet Gynecol 46:47, 2003.

55. Ross GT, Goldstein DP, Gertz R, et al: Sequential use of methotrexate and actinomycin D in the treatment of metastatic choriocarcinomas and related trophoblastic tumors in women. Am J Obstet Gynecol 93:223, 1965.

56. Soper JT, Clarke-Pearson DL, Berchuck A, et al: 5-Day methotrexate for women with metastatic gestational trophoblastic disease. Gynecol Oncol 54:76, 1994.

57. Hammond CB, Weed JC Jr, Currie JL: The role of operation in the current therapy of gestational trophoblastic disease. Am J Obstet Gynecol 136:844, 1980.

58. Brace KC: The role of irradiation in the treatment of metastatic trophoblastic disease. Radiology 91:540, 1968.

59. Schinck JC, Singh DK, Rademaker AW, et al: Etoposide, methotrexate, actinomycin D, cyclophosphamide, and vincristine for the treatment of metastatic high-risk gestational trophoblastic disease. Obstet Gynecol 80:817, 1992.

60. Yordan EL Jr, Schlaerth J, Gaddis O, et al: Radiation therapy in the management of gestational choriocarcinoma metastatic to the central nervous system. Obstet Gynecol 69:627, 1987.

61. Miller JM Jr, Surwit EA, Hammond CB: Choriocarcinoma following term pregnancy. Obstet Gynecol 53:207, 1979.

62. Heaton GE, Matthews TH, Christopherson WH: Malignant trophoblastic tumors with massive hemorrhage presenting as liver primary: A report of two cases. Am J Surg Pathol 10:342, 1986.

63. Barnard DE, Woodward KT, Yancy SG, et al: Hepatic metastases of choriocarcinoma: A report of 15 patients. Gynecol Oncol 25:73, 1986.

64. Grumbine FC, Rosenschein NB, Brewerton MD, et al: Management of liver metastasis from gestational trophoblastic neoplasia. Am J Obstet Gynecol 137:959, 1980.

65. Soper JT, Clarke-Pearson DL, Hammond CB: Metastatic gestational trophoblastic disease: Prognostic factors in previously untreated patients. Obstet Gynecol 71:338, 1988.

66. Lewis JL Jr: Treatment of metastatic trophoblastic neoplasms. Am J Obstet Gynecol 136:163, 1979.

67. Weed JC Jr, Barnard DE, Currie JL, et al: Chemotherapy with modified Bagshawe protocol for poor prognosis metastatic trophoblastic disease. Obstet Gynecol 59:377, 1982.

68. DuBeshter B, Berkowitz RS, Goldstein DP, et al: Vinblastine, cisplatin and bleomycin as salvage therapy for refractory high-risk metastatic gestational trophoblastic disease. J Reprod Med 34:189, 1989.

69. Azab M, Droz JO, Theodore C, et al: Cisplatin, vinblastine and bleomycin in combination in the treatment of resistant high-risk gestational trophoblastic tumors. Cancer 64:1189, 1989.

70. Rottmensch J, Rosenchein N, Donehower R, et al: Plasma methotrexate levels in patients with gestational trophoblastic regimens. Am J Obstet Gynecol 148:730, 1984.

71. Delfs E: Chorionic gondatropin determinations with hydatidiform mole and choriocarcinoma. Ann N Y Acad Sci 80:125, 1957.

72. Brewer JI, Torok EE, Webster A, et al: Hydatidiform mole: A follow up regimen for identification of invasive mole and choriocarcinoma and for selection of patients for treatment. Am J Obstet Gynecol 101:557, 1968.

73. Goldstein DP: The chemotherapy of gestational trophoblastic disease: Principles of clinical management. JAMA 220:209, 1972.

74. Bagshawe KD, Wilson H, Dublon P, et al: Follow up after hydatidiform mole: Studies using radioimmunoassays for urinary human chorionic gonadotropin (hCG). J Obstet Gynaecol Br Commonw 80:461, 1973.

75. Morrow CP, Kletzky OA, DiSaia PJ, et al: Clinical and laboratory correlates of molar pregnancy and trophoblastic disease. Am J Obstet Gynecol 128:424, 1977.

76. Hatch KD, Shingleton HM, Austi JM Sr: Southern Regional Trophoblastic Disease Center, 1972-1977. South Med J 71:1334, 1978.

77. Schlaerth JB, Morrow CP, Kletzky OA, et al: Prognostic characteristics of serum human chorionic gonadotropin for regression following molar pregnancy. Obstet Gynecol 58:478, 1981.

78. Kohorn EI: Hydatidiform mole and gestational trophoblastic disease in southern Connecticut. Obstet Gynecol 59:78, 1982.

79. Lurain JR, Brewer JI, Torok EE, et al: Natural history of hydatidiform mole after primary evacuation. Am J Obstet Gynecol 145:591, 1983.

# Hormonal Changes and Endocrine Testing in Pregnancy

## *Mark E. Molitch*

Pregnancy alters normal physiology and endocrine testing in a number of ways as a result of a variety of factors (Table 190-1). Pregnancy results in an expansion of plasma and red blood cell volume; predominance of the former causes a mild hemodilution of substances present in the blood. The increase in plasma volume begins at about 6 to 8 weeks' gestation, and the maximum volume is about 40% increased by 30 to 34 weeks.[1] The increase in plasma volume is accompanied by an increase in cardiac output of 30% to 50%, initially caused by an increase in stroke volume and subsequently by an increase in heart rate.[2,3] Along with the increase in cardiac output is an increase in renal plasma flow and glomerular filtration rate (GFR) of similar proportions. The increase in GFR is apparent by week 4, and between the 6th and 12th weeks of gestation increases to about 140% to 150% of the nonpregnant state.[4–6] The GFR increases by another 10% over the remainder of the second trimester, stabilizes in the third trimester, and sometimes falls in the last 4 weeks of gestation.[6,7] These changes in GFR may result in altered clearance of various hormones and, thus, changes in their serum and urinary levels.

Renal tubular function is also altered, which is important with respect to glucose, in that tubular reabsorption of glucose is decreased, with a consequent low tubular maximum for glucose transport and significant glycosuria despite normal plasma glucose levels.[8] Although the tubular handling of bicarbonate is normal, because of the mild hyperventilation and respiratory alkalosis present during gestation, serum bicarbonate levels are generally decreased, the normal levels being 18 to 22 mEq/L. Thus, a patient suspected of having alcoholic or diabetic ketoacidosis normally has a lower bicarbonate value, and confirmation of the acidotic state with arterial blood gas measurements is crucial. Tubular reabsorption of sodium is increased substantially due to numerous factors, including the increased GFR, increased progesterone production by the placenta, increased concentrations of aldosterone and cortisol, and exaggerated postural effects.[6]

Hormone production by the placenta may have profound effects on other hormonal systems. Estradiol levels increase 100-fold, beginning at about 6 to 8 weeks of gestation[9] (Fig. 190-1). These elevated estrogen levels cause an increase in concentration of the hormone-binding globulins thyroxine-binding globulin (TBG), corticosteroid-binding globulin, and sex hormone–binding globulin. Measurements of the total bound plus free hormone are therefore increased, although free hormone levels are only minimally affected (see discussion to follow). Estrogens also have a direct stimulatory effect on pituitary lactotrophs, causing them to increase production of prolactin (PRL). A number of peptide hormones are produced by the placenta, including human chorionic gonadotropin (hCG), chorionic somatomammotropin (placental lactogen), placental growth hormone (GH) variant, chorionic thyrotropin, chorionic adrenocorticotropic hormone (ACTH), chorionic corticotropin-releasing hormone (CRH), chorionic gonadotropin-releasing hormone, and chorionic somatostatin (see Chapter 182). Although most of these peptides do not interfere with normal circulating blood levels of the hormones present before gestation, some do. For example, the placental GH variant appears to have a negative feedback action in suppressing pituitary GH secretion. Also, placental CRH may influence pituitary ACTH secretion. Although hCG does not affect the pituitary, its structure is so similar to luteinizing hormone (LH) that it cross-reacts in some LH assays; this fact may cause diagnostic problems if unanticipated, and the similarity of its structure to thyroid-stimulating hormone (TSH) may cause activation of the TSH receptor, resulting in hyperthyroidism under some circumstances. The placenta can also produce 1,25-dihydroxyvitamin D, which may have importance in calcium homeostasis during pregnancy.

Placental estrogen, progesterone, lactogen, and possibly the GH variant also function as counterregulatory hormones with respect to insulin and cause insulin resistance and accelerated lipolysis. These phenomena are dealt with fully in Chapter 183.

The placenta produces enzymes that may affect normal endocrine function. Placental vasopressinase is so potent that the production rate of vasopressin in normal individuals must increase substantially to maintain normal levels. In patients with mild, subclinical diabetes insipidus (DI), the accelerated metabolism of vasopressin may make this subclinical condition manifest.

This chapter reviews the changes in normal physiology that occur during pregnancy and result in altered hormone levels that may create diagnostic difficulties when attempting to evaluate endocrine disorders in pregnant patients. Specific aspects of pregnancy as it interacts with intermediary metabolism and diabetes mellitus are dealt with in other chapters (see also Chapters 184 and 186).

| Table 190-1 | Changes in Normal Physiology That May Affect Endocrine Tests |
|---|---|

**CARDIOVASCULAR**
Increased plasma and RBC volume
Increased cardiac output
   Lowered "osmostat" for vasopressin release and thirst

**RENAL**
Increased GFR and renal plasma flow
   Increased hormone and substrate clearance
Altered renal tubular function
   Decreased $T_m$ for glucose

**PLACENTAL HORMONE PRODUCTION**
Increased estrogen and progesterone production
   Increased hormone-binding globulin production
   Stimulation of pituitary lactotrophs
Production of peptide hormones
   ACTH, CRH, GnRH, hCG, GH variant, hPL, cTSH, PRL

**PLACENTAL ENZYME PRODUCTION**
Vasopressinase

ACTH, adrenocorticotropic hormone; CRH, corticotropin-releasing hormone; cTSH, chronic thyroid-stimulating hormone; GFR, glomerular filtration rate; GH, growth hormone; GnRH, gonadotropin-releasing hormone; hCG, human chorionic gonadrotropin; hPL, human placental lactogen; PRL, pro-lactin; RBC, red blood cell; $T_m$, maximum renal tubular excretory capacity.

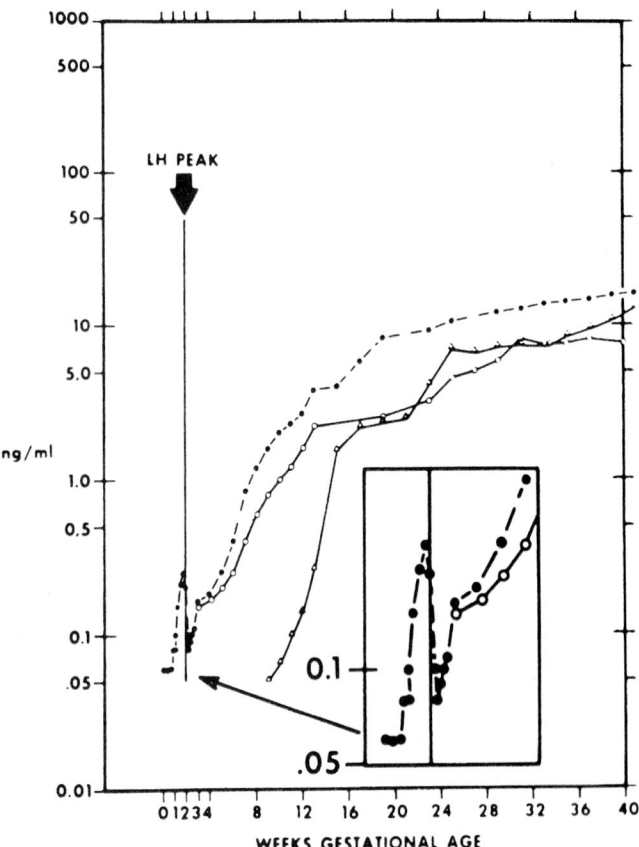

**Figure 190-1** Maternal serum levels of unconjugated estrone ($E_1$), estradiol ($E_2$), and estriol ($E_3$) from the last menstrual flow through a conceptual cycle to term pregnancy. The *points* represent mean steroid hormone levels compiled from four separate studies. LH, luteinizing hormone. (From Buster JE, Abraham GE: The applications of steroid hormone radioimmunoassays to clinical obstetrics. Obstet Gynecol 46:489–499, 1975. Reprinted with permission from the American College of Obstetricians and Gynecologists.)

# PITUITARY

## PROLACTIN

### Changes in Prolactin Physiology during Pregnancy

Estrogens produced by the placenta stimulate lactotroph DNA synthesis and mitotic activity, PRL mRNA levels, and PRL synthesis.[10,11] Progesterone has also been shown to stimulate PRL secretion.[12] During pregnancy, a progressive rise occurs in serum PRL levels[13] (Fig. 190-2) that parallels an increase in the size and number of pituitary lactotroph cells.[14,15] By term, PRL levels may be increased 10-fold to levels over 200 ng/mL.[15] These elevated PRL levels found at term prepare the breast for lactation. Thus, the finding of amenorrhea associated with hyperprolactinemia could well be due to pregnancy and not due to pathologic hyperprolactinemia.

It should be noted that PRL identical to pituitary PRL is also produced by the human decidua during pregnancy and causes high amniotic fluid PRL levels.[16] This decidual PRL is not present in maternal blood, however, and its physiologic role may be limited to regulation of water and ion transport across extraembryonic membranes.[16] The placenta makes another hormone called placental lactogen (also known as chorionic somatomammotropin) that has lactogenic activity but is more structurally related to GH than to PRL and also does not contribute to blood PRL levels during pregnancy.[16]

### Prolactinomas

The normal pituitary enlarges during pregnancy, predominantly as a result of hyperplasia of the PRL-producing lactotroph cells.[14,15] A magnetic resonance imaging (MRI) scan performed during pregnancy often reveals an enlarged pituitary because of this hyperplasia, but careful review of the scan shows no evidence of a pituitary tumor.[17] The finding of an enlarged sella during pregnancy, however, may not be due only to normal lactotroph hyperplasia, but could also be due to the stimulatory effect of pregnancy on a preexisting prolactinoma (Fig. 190-3). In a series of cases collected from the literature composed of 246 patients with prolactinomas who became pregnant, it was found that the risk of significant tumor enlargement was 1.6% for microadenomas, 15.5% for macroadenomas that had not been subjected to prior treatment by surgery or irradiation, and 4.3% for macroadenomas that had been subjected to prior surgery and/or irradiation (Table 190-2).[18] Subsequently, three series totaling an additional 117 women with microadenomas and 60 women with macroadenomas have been reported.[19–21] When these series[18–21] are combined, 5 of the 363 women (1.4%) with microadenomas and 22 of the 84 women (26.2%) with macroadenomas without prior surgery or irradiation had

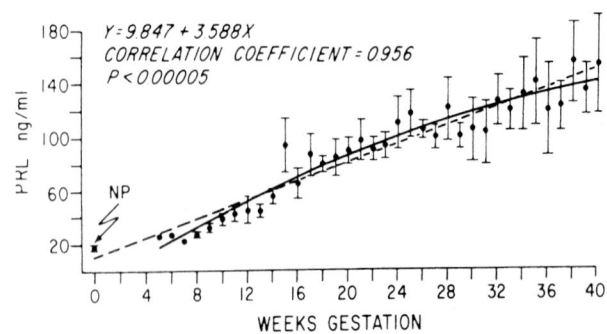

**Figure 190-2** Mean ± SEM (n = 4) serum prolactin (PRL) concentrations measured serially at weekly intervals as a function of the duration of gestation. The *dashed line* represents the linear regression, and the *solid line* represents second-order regression. NP, nonpregnant PRL value. (From Rigg LA, Lein A, Yen SCC: Pattern of increase in circulating prolactin levels during human gestation. Am J Obstet Gynecol 129:454–456, 1977.)

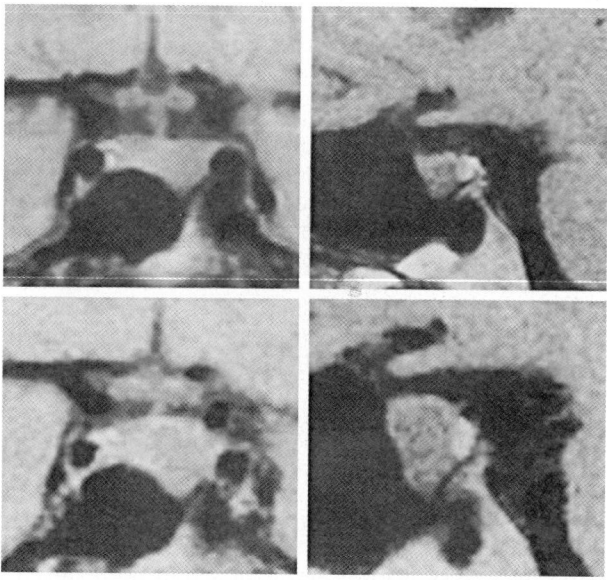

*Figure 190-3*  Magnetic resonance imaging scans with coronal *(left)* and sagittal *(right)* views demonstrating enlargement of a prolactin-secreting macroadenoma *(above)* before pregnancy and *(below)* in the third trimester of pregnancy. The patient had been complaining of increasing headaches.

symptoms of tumor enlargement (headaches or visual disturbances or both); 67 women with macroadenomas had been treated with irradiation or surgery before pregnancy and only 2 (3%) had symptomatic tumor enlargement during gestation.

### Lymphocytic Hypophysitis

Pituitary enlargement during pregnancy may also be due to lymphocytic hypophysitis. Lymphocytic hypophysitis is characterized by massive infiltration of the pituitary by lymphocytes and plasma cells with destruction of the normal parenchyma. The disorder is thought to have an autoimmune basis. Most cases occur in association with pregnancy, and women are seen during pregnancy or post partum either with symptoms of varying degrees of hypopituitarism or with symptoms related to the mass lesion, such as headaches or visual field defects. Mild hyperprolactinemia and DI may also be found. On a computed tomography (CT) scan or MRI, a sellar mass is found that may extend in an extrasellar fashion and cause visual field defects. The condition is usually confused with a pituitary tumor and, in fact, cannot be distinguished from a tumor except by biopsy. By virtue of the hypopituitarism that it produces, lymphocytic hypophysitis can also be clinically confused with Sheehan's syndrome post partum, except that these women have no history of obstetric hemorrhage.[22,23] The diagnosis of lymphocytic hypophysitis should be entertained in women with symptoms of hypopituitarism and/or mass lesions of the sella during pregnancy or post partum, especially in the absence of a history of obstetric hemorrhage. Evaluation of pituitary function is war-

ranted, as well as CT or MRI. If PRL levels are only modestly elevated (<150 ng/mL) in the presence of a large mass, the diagnosis is unlikely to be an enlarging prolactinoma and more likely to be hypophysitis or a nonsecreting tumor.[22,23] Furthermore, there seems to be a particular predilection for loss of ACTH secretion, and deaths have occurred when this has gone untreated.[23]

### *GROWTH HORMONE*

#### Changes in Growth Hormone Physiology during Pregnancy

In the second half of pregnancy, pituitary GH secretion falls and a GH variant made by the syncytiotrophoblastic epithelium of the placenta increases in the circulation[24,25] (Fig. 190-4). The episodic secretion of pituitary GH is replaced by constant,

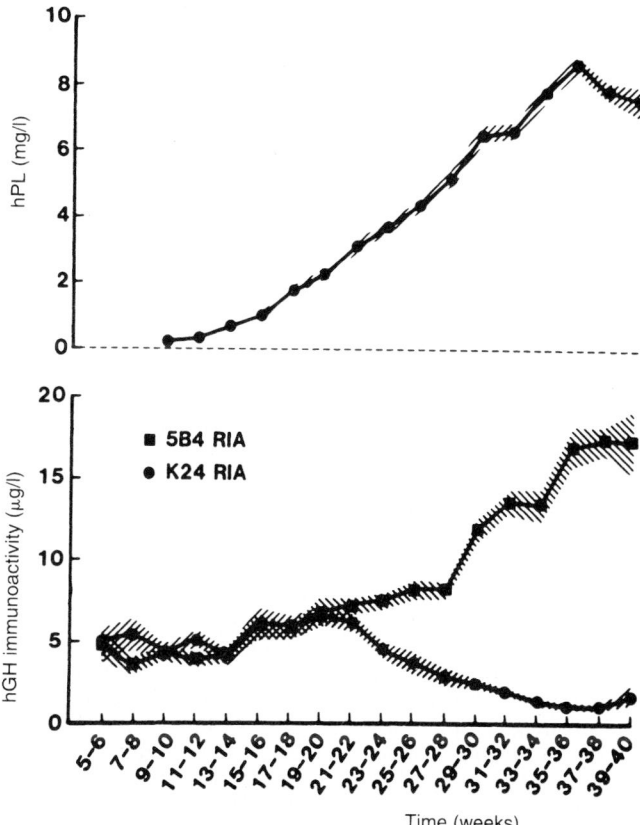

*Figure 190-4*  Mean (±SD) serum growth hormone (GH) and placental lactogen levels in women throughout pregnancy. The 5B4 radioimmunoassay (RIA) antibody is specific for the GH placental variant, whereas the K24 RIA antibody is specific for pituitary GH. Note the rise in serum levels of the GH placental variant coinciding with the fall in serum levels of pituitary GH. (From Frankenne F, Closset J, Gomez F, et al: The physiology of growth hormones [GHs] in pregnant women and partial characterization of the placental GH variant. J Clin Endocrinol Metab 66:1171–1180. © 1978, The Endocrine Society.)

| *Table 190-2* Effect of Pregnancy on Prolactinomas | | | |
|---|---|---|---|
| **Tumor Type** | **Prior Therapy** | **Number** | **Symptomatic Enlargement*** |
| Microadenomas | None | 363 | 5 |
| Macroadenomas | None | 84 | 22 |
| Macroadenomas | Yes | 67 | 2 |

*Requiring intervention: surgery or bromocriptine.
Adapted, by permission, from Molitch ME: Management of pituitary tumors in pregnancy. Growth Horm IGF Res 13:S38–S44, 2003.

nonpulsatile secretion of this variant at the rather high levels of 10 to 20 ng/mL.[25,26] Production of the placental variant is accompanied by decreased production of normal pituitary GH, presumably because of negative feedback effects. Evidence in favor of this feedback effect of placental GH on pituitary GH secretion includes the fact that in patients with acromegaly who have autonomous GH secretion and who become pregnant, both forms of GH persist in the blood throughout pregnancy.[27]

The GH variant differs from pituitary GH by 13 amino acids and has similar somatogenic but less lactogenic bioactivity than pituitary GH does,[28] a reflection of differences in binding to somatogenic versus lactogenic GH receptors.[29] On the other hand, the placental GH variant binds equipotently with pituitary GH to the high-affinity GH-binding protein, which is thought to be the extracellular domain of the GH receptor,[30] and in the second half of pregnancy, overall GH bioactivity is considerably elevated, as measured by a radioreceptor assay.[31] Most reports have demonstrated considerably elevated insulin-like growth factor 1 (IGF-1) levels during pregnancy, commensurate with the elevated GH variant levels measured by radioimmunoassay and radioreceptor assay.[32,33] The GH variant also has activity similar to that of normal pituitary GH with respect to carbohydrate and lipid metabolism.[34]

At present, the physiologic significance of the change in the source of circulating GH during pregnancy is not known. However, the elevated levels of the placental variant with elevated levels of IGF-1 may account for the coarsening of features occasionally seen in some pregnant women, and such women may be suspected of having acromegaly. It is not clear whether these elevated placental GH variant levels contribute to the insulin resistance of pregnancy. Lack of the GH variant does not affect fetal growth,[35] but simultaneous loss of HPL and the GH variant has been reported to cause severe intrauterine growth retardation but an otherwise normal baby.[36]

### Acromegaly

Standard immunoassays for GH cannot usually distinguish between normal pituitary GH and the placental GH variant and may consequently give misleading results with respect to assessment of pituitary GH secretion during the latter half of pregnancy. Basal levels of the variant are considerably higher than normal, nonpregnant GH levels and may therefore erroneously indicate excessive pituitary GH secretion. Special immunoassays using antibodies that recognize specific epitopes on the two hormones[26] or an immunoradiometric assay (IRMA)[27] are necessary to distinguish normal from placental GH. When such specific assays are not available, it may be necessary to wait until infant delivery to assess pituitary GH secretion accurately because placental GH variant is undetectable within 24 hours.[26] However, two differences between placental GH variant secretion and pituitary GH secretion in acromegaly may allow a distinction to be made during pregnancy: (1) pituitary GH secretion in acromegaly is highly pulsatile, with 13 to 19 pulses per 24 hours,[37,38] whereas secretion of GH variant in pregnancy is nonpulsatile[26]; and (2) in acromegaly, about 70% of patients have a GH response to thyrotropin-releasing hormone (TRH),[39] whereas the placental GH variant does not respond to TRH.[27]

Actual reports of pregnancies in acromegalic patients are uncommon,[19,27,40–42] perhaps because about 40% of such patients are hyperprolactinemic.[39] Indeed, correction of the hyperprolactinemia with bromocriptine may be necessary to permit ovulation and conception in these patients.[40] It is possible that, in a patient in whom acromegaly is initially diagnosed during pregnancy, the finding of hyperprolactinemia may be due to the stimulated production of PRL by normal lactotrophs and not to tumor production. Only two patients with tumors secreting GH have been reported to have enlargement of their tumors, with a resultant visual field defect in one during pregnancy[19,41]; neither tumor cosecreted PRL.

### VASOPRESSIN

#### Changes in Vasopressin Physiology during Pregnancy

The primary regulator of vasopressin secretion is the osmolality of plasma, which is sensed by osmoreceptors (see Chapter 30). The osmotic threshold for vasopressin release in nonpregnant subjects is about 280 to 285 mOsm/kg, with a normal range of 275 to 290 mOsm/kg. Thirst is generally stimulated at a plasma osmolality level about 5 mOsm/kg above that for vasopressin release, a level near which maximum concentration of urine will already have been achieved.

Pregnancy is associated with lowering of the "osmostat," the set point for serum osmolality, by about 10 mOsm/kg.[6] The decline in plasma osmolality begins by the time of the first missed menstrual period and gradually decreases until the 10th week of gestation, after which little further change occurs[43] (Fig. 190-5). Pregnant women experience thirst and release vasopressin at lower levels of serum osmolality than

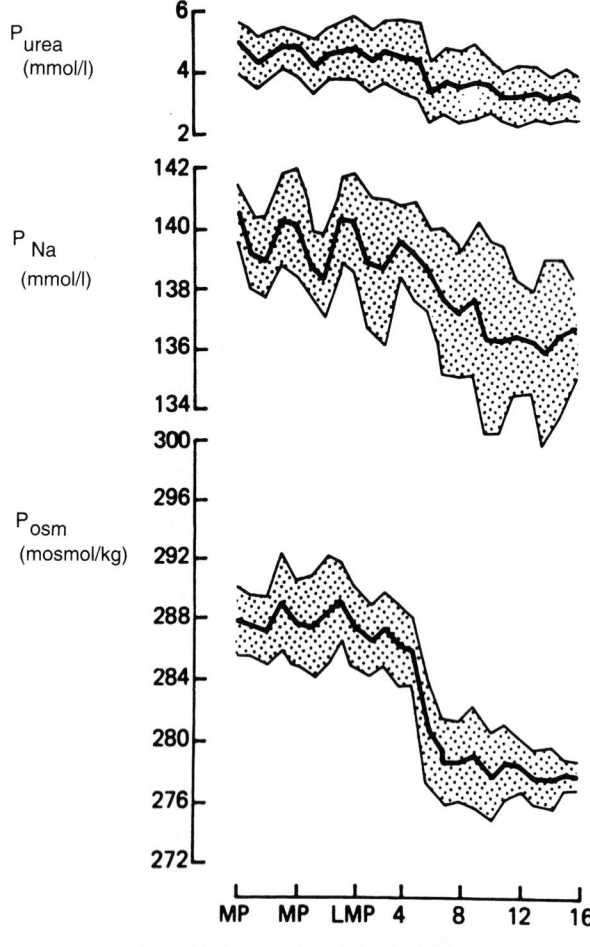

**Figure 190-5** Mean values (±SD) for plasma urea (Purea), sodium (PNa), and osmolality (Posmol) measured at weekly intervals from before conception to the first trimester in nine women with a successful obstetric outcome. LMP, last menstrual period; MP, menstrual period. (From Davison JM, Vallotton MB, Lindheimer MD: Plasma osmolality and urinary concentration and dilution during and after pregnancy: Evidence that lateral recumbency inhibits maximal urinary concentrating ability. Br J Obstet Gynaecol 88:472–479, 1981.)

do nonpregnant individuals to maintain this lower osmolality[44] (Fig. 190-6). A water load will suppress vasopressin secretion appropriately and result in dilute urine and excretion of this water load, thereby maintaining this lower osmolality.[44,45] This reset osmostat results in lowering of serum sodium by about 4 to 5 mEq/mL.[43,45] The physiologic basis for this reset osmostat is not clear. Experiments in humans, however, have shown that hCG injected into nonpregnant women lowers their osmostat by 5 mOsm/kg.[46] Furthermore, a case has been described in which a woman with a hydatidiform mole had a lower osmostat that returned to normal only when hCG levels in the serum finally became undetectable 40 days after evacuation of the mole.[46] Evidence from rat studies and from human studies in which pregnant women were immersed in water to expand the central blood volume suggests that a decreased "effective" blood volume does not play a role in this resetting of the osmostat.[45]

The placenta produces vasopressinase, a cystine aminopeptidase that rapidly inactivates vasopressin. Vasopressinase levels increase 1000-fold between the 4th and 38th weeks of gestation.[47] How much this increase in vasopressinase activity contributes to the increased clearance of endogenous vasopressin during pregnancy is not clear, however.[47] The placenta itself is also able to metabolize vasopressin.[48] Overall, the combination of increased vasopressinase levels and increased placental metabolism of vasopressin results in a twofold to fourfold increased metabolic clearance rate for vasopressin.[47,48]

### Diabetes Insipidus

In a patient with preexisting DI, this increased metabolism of vasopressin during pregnancy results in worsening of the DI.[6,49–51] Thus, patients with mild DI treated with either increased fluids or chlorpropamide will probably experience considerable worsening. Women being treated with pitressin tannate in oil or lysine vasopressin spray may also experience such worsening. The vasopressin analogue dDAVP (desmopressin) is not affected by vasopressinase, and a number of women have been treated quite satisfactorily with this medication.[49,52,53] Rarely, asymptomatic women will experience symptomatic DI only during pregnancy.[54]

When polyuria or polydipsia develops in a pregnant patient, the finding of lower than expected serum sodium levels should not, therefore, exclude the diagnosis of DI.[45,49] Testing for DI (see Chapter 30) in a pregnant woman should be performed with the woman in the sitting position because the lateral recumbent position results in an inhibition of maximal urinary concentrating ability.[45] The increased metabolism of vasopressin also limits the rise in plasma vasopressin levels during testing, especially in the last trimester.[44,46] Therefore, the levels of vasopressin and osmolality used in nomograms for nonpregnant patients cannot be used for pregnant ones, and an extrapolation from Figure 190-6 can be used. When obtained for vasopressin measurement during pregnancy, blood should be drawn into syringes containing orthophenanthroline (0.1 mL in a 10-mL syringe) to inactivate vasopressinase activity and then rapidly transferred to chilled heparinized tubes, centrifuged in the cold, and extracted within 3 hours.[44,47]

One recent important finding in women with transient DI of pregnancy is the simultaneous occurrence of acute fatty liver of pregnancy in some patients. Kennedy and colleagues reported six such cases seen at 35 to 39 weeks of gestation with nausea, vomiting, and polyuria, and preeclampsia was diagnosed in four.[55] In four cases, polyuria developed before delivery and in two it developed post partum. All six had complete resolution of their DI and liver abnormalities by the fourth week post partum. Three additional cases of transient DI of pregnancy associated with mild transaminase abnormalities were reported by Hamai and coworkers.[56] It has been hypothesized that the acute liver dysfunction in these patients reduces the degradation of vasopressinase, thereby increasing vasopressinase levels even more than usual with yet greater clearance of vasopressin.[55] Thus, women in whom DI develops very late in gestation should also be screened for liver function abnormalities.

### THYROID HORMONES AND THYROID REGULATION

#### Changes in Normal Thyroid Physiology during Pregnancy
A number of changes occur in the thyroid and in levels of thyroid hormones during pregnancy.[57] It is widely believed that a goiter commonly develops during pregnancy. This belief stems from uncontrolled early observations and the fact that most such studies were done in iodine-deficient regions. In iodine-replete areas, no increase in the frequency of goiters is noted during pregnancy.[58] In a study of Belgian women with borderline iodine status, thyroid volume was found to increase about 18% during pregnancy,[59] a change that would not be clinically apparent. Of 309 pregnant adolescents evaluated by Long and colleagues, 18 were found to have goiters: 2 had Graves' disease and were hyperthyroid; 3 had Hashimoto's thyroiditis, 1 being hyperthyroid; and 4 had subacute thyroiditis, 1 being hyperthyroid.[60] The other 9 with goiters were thought to have simple nontoxic goiters. Thus, although thyroid volume does increase slightly during pregnancy, perhaps because of relative iodine deficiency and/or the stimulatory effect of hCG (see discussion to follow), the presence of a palpable goiter in iodine-replete areas indicates significant disease in about 50% of patients and should always be evaluated. In one third of patients found to have goiters, an increase in size of 17% to 55% may be expected over the course of gestation.[59]

Renal clearance of iodine is increased because of the increased GFR that occurs with pregnancy. When iodine intake is marginal, this increased loss may result in iodine deficiency.[57]

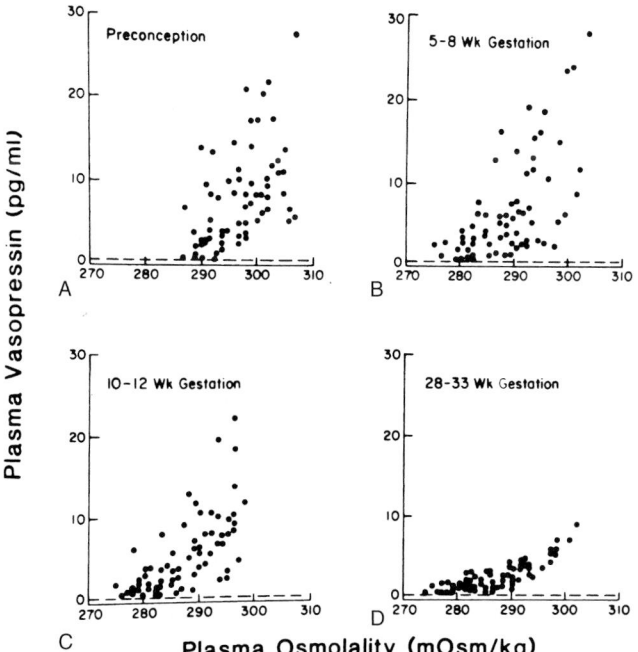

*Figure 190-6*  Relationship of plasma arginine vasopressin (PAVP) to plasma osmolality (Posmol) during a 2-hour hypertonic saline infusion in eight women studied serially before and during pregnancy. Each *point* is an individual plasma determination. *Dashed lines* indicate the lower limit of detection for AVP. (From Lindheimer MD, Barron WM, Davison JM: Osmoregulation of thirst and vasopressin release in pregnancy. Am J Physiol 257:F159–F169, 1989.)

Even in the absence of hypothyroidism, the total body iodine pool becomes decreased, and radioactive iodine uptake is therefore increased.[61] Radioactive iodine is, of course, contraindicated during pregnancy because the placenta is freely permeable to iodine and the fetal thyroid is 20 to 50 times more avid for iodine than the maternal thyroid.[62] The tracer dose used in these studies is so small, however, that it is not sufficient to cause concern if given inadvertently during pregnancy.[62] Generally, the iodine in iodized salt and prenatal vitamins prevents iodine deficiency. Excessive iodine ingestion is to be avoided, however, because it crosses the placenta and may cause neonatal goiter.

The fetal thyroid and the fetal hypothalamic-pituitary-thyroid axis develop independently of maternal thyroid status (see Chapter 183). At 11 to 12 weeks of gestation, the fetal thyroid begins to concentrate iodine. In addition to iodine, the placenta is freely permeable to medications used to treat hyperthyroidism, such as propylthiouracil, methimazole, and propranolol; triiodothyronine ($T_3$) and TSH cross the placenta only minimally.[57] Thyroxine ($T_4$) crosses the placenta in somewhat larger (although still small) amounts and, late in gestation, large doses are able to ameliorate the effects of hypothyroidism in infants with congenital hypothyroidism caused by enzyme defects or agenesis of the thyroid.[57,63]

Bioassayable thyroid-stimulating activity in serum is increased in the first trimester as a result of the intrinsic thyroid-stimulating activity of hCG.[57,64-66] The hCG may cause increased $T_4$ and $T_3$ levels, as well as a transient hyperthyroidism associated with hyperemesis gravidarum (see discussion to follow). The markedly elevated levels of hCG seen in trophoblastic neoplasms may also cause hyperthyroidism.[67,68] A human chorionic thyrotropin with little thyroid-stimulating activity may also be made by the placenta, but it probably plays no physiologic role.[57]

### Alterations in Thyroid Function Tests during Pregnancy

The basal metabolic rate is increased by about 15% to 20% during pregnancy, about 70% to 80% of the increment being attributable to the placenta and fetus and the remainder to increased maternal cardiac output.[69] This test is rarely done at present.

$T_4$ is about 75% bound to TBG, 10% to 15% bound to albumin, and 10% to 15% bound to transthyretin (prealbumin); only about 0.04% is unbound or "free." The increased estrogens of the placenta result in increased TBG levels in the blood because of increased production by hepatocytes,[70] as well as decreased degradation from altered glycosylation.[71] The increased TBG levels result in increased bound $T_4$ measurements, beginning by 4 to 6 weeks of gestation[57,64] (Fig. 190-7). The metabolic activity of the hormones correlates best with free hormone levels and free $T_4$ levels have been reported to be unchanged,[72] increased,[64] or decreased[57] during pregnancy, although they usually remain within the normal range[57,64] (see Fig. 190-7). These differences may relate to relative iodine deficiencies in the populations studied[57] and the stage of pregnancy that is being assessed.[57,64] Free $T_4$ levels are minimally elevated or in the high normal range in the first trimester and then fall back toward baseline and even below baseline, in parallel with changes in hCG[57] (Fig. 190-8). Free $T_4$ levels may actually fall and TSH levels rise in the last trimester in those with significant iodine deficiency.[59]

$T_4$ turnover is increased during pregnancy,[73] and in patients receiving thyroxine replacement, TSH levels should be checked each trimester to determine whether the dose needs to be increased.[74] In one study, 75% of patients needed to increase their thyroxine doses during pregnancy[74] (Fig. 190-9). $T_3$ is bound to TBG with somewhat less affinity than $T_4$ is, but the same increase in total $T_3$ measurements is seen as with $T_4$ during pregnancy.[57,64] TSH levels are minimally decreased

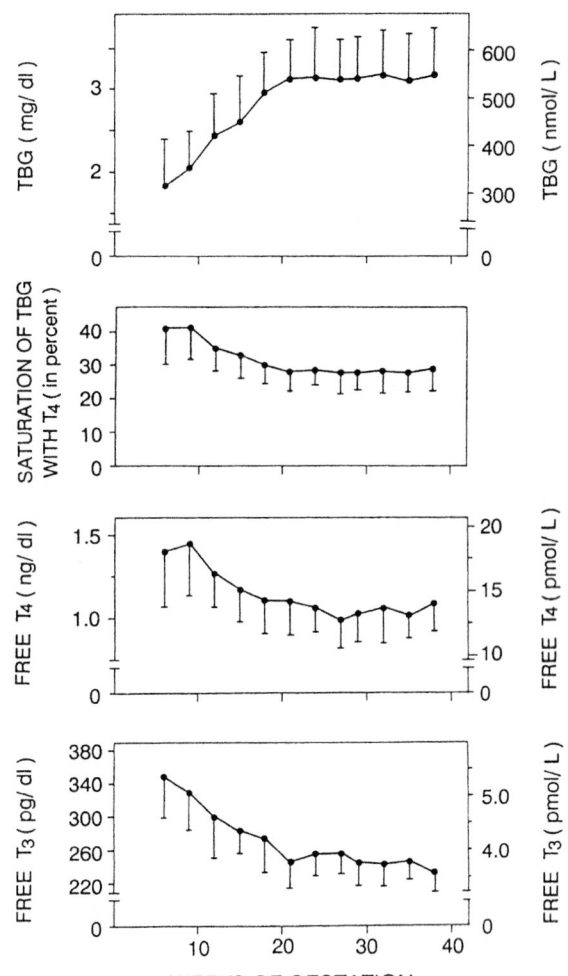

**Figure 190-7** Data collected in 606 normal pregnancies in Brussels are illustrated, showing the progressive rise in serum thyroxine-binding globulin (TBG) during the first part of gestation, accompanied by a progressive decrease in the free $T_4$ index (saturation level of TBG by $T_4$), and free $T_4$ and $T_3$ concentrations. Brussels being in an area with a restricted iodine intake, the quantitative reduction in free hormone concentrations observed in the second part of gestation is more pronounced than in areas without iodine deficiency. $T_3$, triiodothyronine; $T_4$, thyroxine. (Reproduced with permission from Glinoer D: Thyroid regulation during pregnancy. In Delange F, Dunn JT, Glinoer D [eds]: Iodine Deficiency in Europe: A Continuing Concern. NATO ASI Series (vol 241). New York, Plenum, pp 181–190; © 1993, Plenum Publishing Corp.)

during the first trimester of pregnancy (see Fig. 190-8), possibly because of the increased free $T_4$ levels.[57,64]

### HYPERTHYROIDISM

Because of the hyperdynamic state of pregnancy, the clinical diagnosis of hyperthyroidism may prove difficult. The features of tachycardia, warm skin, systolic flow murmurs, and heat intolerance are common to both. Even the finding of a goiter may not be specific. Weight loss, a marked tachycardia, eye signs, and a bruit over the thyroid are more suggestive of hyperthyroidism.[75] Infiltrative dermopathy and ophthalmopathy are specific for Graves' disease but do not indicate the degree of hyperthyroidism.

The changes in thyroid hormones already discussed may cause further diagnostic difficulty. Because of the elevation of TBG in blood, total $T_4$ and $T_3$ levels are elevated. In normal

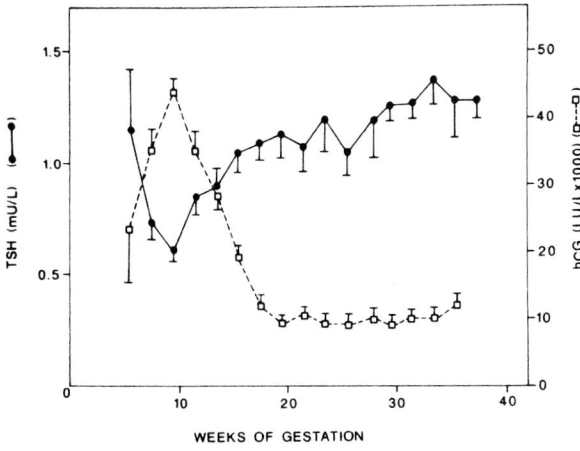

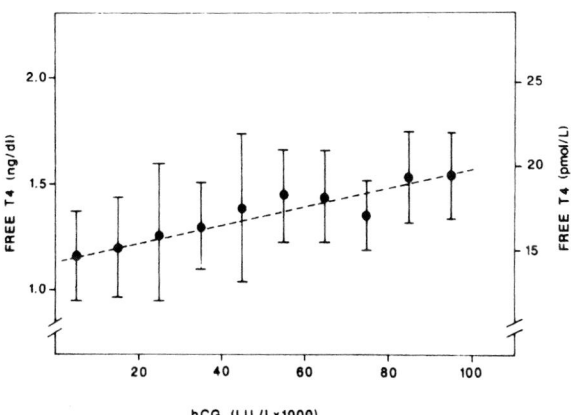

**Figure 190-8** Serum thyroid-stimulating hormone (TSH) and human chorionic gonadotropin (hCG) as a function of gestational age in 606 healthy pregnant women. Between 8 and 14 weeks' gestation, the changes in hCG and TSH levels are mirror images of each other, and there is a significant negative correlation between the individual TSH and hCG levels ($P < 0.001$). Each point gives the mean value (± SE) of individual determinations pooled for 2 weeks. *Lower graph,* scattergram of free thyroxine ($T_4$) levels in relation to hCG concentrations in the first half of gestation. Each point represents the mean (± 1 SD) free $T_4$ values, determined between 6 and 20 weeks, plotted for 10,000 IU/L increments in hCG. The *dashed line* indicates the linear regression curve ($P < 0.001$). (Reproduced with permission from Glinoer D, DeNayer P, Bourdoux P, et al: Regulation of maternal thyroid during pregnancy. J Clin Endocrinol Metab 71:276–287, 1990; © 1990, The Endocrine Society.)

pregnancy, early in the first trimester, however, free $T_4$ levels may also be mildly elevated in some assays,[64] and TSH levels may be suppressed to below the level of detectability with older assays and below normal with the newer, ultrasensitive assays because of the high levels of free $T_4$ and hCG (see previous discussion). TSH will not be very low with these newer assays in pregnancy,[76] as in typical hyperthyroidism,[76] however, which makes TSH the critical assessment when other levels are borderline. It is important to make the diagnosis of hyperthyroidism accurately and carefully because untreated hyperthyroidism clearly has adverse consequences on fetal outcome.[75,76]

Most cases of hyperthyroidism in pregnancy are due to Graves' disease and to antibodies that stimulate the TSH receptor.[75,76] These antibodies cross the placenta and may cause neonatal hyperthyroidism in 2% to 10% of women with active disease during pregnancy.[76–79] The European Thyroid Association has recommended that TSH-receptor antibodies should be measured in the last trimester and, if levels are high, then the neonate should be followed carefully for the development of hyperthyroidism.[77] Rarely, these antibodies may cause intrauterine fetal hyperthyroidism and the thionamides used to treat the mother may cross the placenta and cause fetal hypothyroidism. Some centers have advocated screening the susceptible developing fetus with transvaginal fetal thyroid ultrasounds,[80] measurement of thyroid hormone levels in amniotic fluid samples,[81] and even umbilical blood sampling,[82] but these approaches have not yet gained widespread acceptance.

### Hyperthyroidism and Hyperemesis Gravidarum
Nausea and vomiting may occasionally be the predominant symptoms in patients with hyperthyroidism. Conversely, in pregnancy, the severe nausea and vomiting that sometimes occur in the first trimester, known as hyperemesis gravidarum, may be associated with biochemical hyperthyroidism.[75,76] Elevated $T_4$ and $T_3$ levels may be found transiently in up to one third of subjects with hyperemesis gravidarum, but only about 10% to 20% of such patients manifest clinical thyrotoxicosis.[83–85] The overall prevalence of clinical hyperthyroidism in association with hyperemesis gravidarum is about 2% to 3% of pregnancies in Europe, 0.3% of pregnancies in Japan, but 11% of pregnancies in Hong Kong.[76] The increased thyroid hormone levels are due to stimulation by hCG; serum hCG levels are increased by about 50% in subjects with elevated free $T_4$ levels and correlate with the free $T_4$ levels.[84] On the other hand, hCG levels overlap considerably with those of normal individuals, so some authors have postulated that in these particular cases associated with transient hyperthyroidism, the hCG may have some structural variation resulting in increased biologic activity.[86]

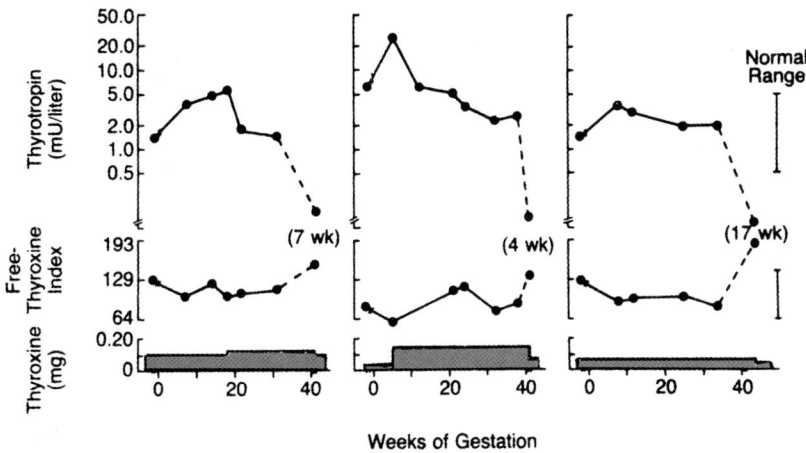

**Figure 190-9** Representative patterns of changes in thyroid function and thyroxine dose during pregnancy in women with hypothyroidism. The *left-hand* and *middle* panels show the results for two women who required an increased dose of thyroxine during pregnancy. The *right-hand* panel shows the results for a woman whose thyroxine dose was not changed during pregnancy. The normal ranges for serum thyrotropin and the free thyroxine index are indicated by the *vertical bars* on the right side of the figure. The *discontinuity marks* indicate the beginning and end of pregnancy. The *dashed line* represents the change between the last gestational and the first postpartum values (the number of weeks post partum is noted in parentheses). (Reproduced, by permission, from Mandel SJ, Larsen PR, Seely EW, Brent EA: Increased need for thyroxine during pregnancy in women with primary hypothyroidism. N Engl J Med 323:91–96, 1990; © 1990, Massachusetts Medical Society. All rights reserved.)

The link between the elevated hCG and vomiting may be the hCG-induced increase in estradiol.[87] A very rare cause of recurrent gestational hyperthyroidism occurring in families has been found to be a missense mutation in the extracellular domain of the TSH receptor; this receptor was more sensitive than the wild-type receptor to hCG and occurred with normal rather than elevated levels of hCG.[88]

In most patients, free T₄ levels fall to normal over a period of 6 to 133 days (mean, 35.1 days) while still pregnant,[84] generally paralleling the fall in hCG levels (Fig. 190-10). Therefore, patients with hyperemesis and elevated free T₄ and T₃ levels present a considerable diagnostic dilemma. In prior studies, TSH levels in patients thought to be hyperthyroxinemic were not usually suppressed,[83] but this result may have been due to the cross-reactivity of very high levels of hCG in those TSH assays. With newer, highly sensitive, more specific TSH assays, TSH levels are undetectable in women who become truly thyrotoxic.[85] Most patients with Graves' disease will have some symptoms that predate the pregnancy, whereas most patients with hyperthyroidism associated with hyperemesis have no goiter and generally no eye findings.[75,76] Due to the increased maternal and fetal morbidity associated with untreated hyperthyroidism, it appears to be safest to administer antithyroid drugs to any woman with symptomatic hyperthyroidism or those in whom thyroid hormone levels do not spontaneously revert to normal over a period of 1 to 3 weeks and in whom TSH levels are suppressed below detectability in a highly sensitive assay. Careful follow-up and adjustment of medications may allow withdrawal of antithyroid medication in those with transient hormonal abnormalities.

## HYPOTHYROIDISM

The clinical picture of spontaneous hypothyroidism developing during pregnancy may be confusing because of the tendency of pregnancy to cause tachycardia, fatigue, warm skin, and heat intolerance. Other typical findings of hypothyroidism should gradually become apparent, however, such as muscle cramps, excessive fatigue, dry skin, and so forth.[76] The elevated TBG levels may cause total T₄ levels to be normal, but free T₄ levels will be low and TSH levels will be elevated. As noted earlier, previously established replacement doses of thyroxine may need to be increased[74] because of the increased

clearance of thyroxine during pregnancy. This has been shown to be critically important, as even subclinical degrees of maternal hypothyroidism have been recently shown to be associated with impairment of subsequent infant intellectual development.[89,90] Because these effects may occur even with subclinical hypothyroidism in the first trimester, routine screening of all pregnant women at their first prenatal visit has been advocated.[91] Some advocate treatment with thyroxine even for women with TSH levels still within the normal range but between 2 and 4 mU/L.[76]

## ADRENAL CORTEX

### GLUCOCORTICOSTEROIDS AND GLUCOCORTICOSTEROID REGULATION

#### Changes in Adrenal Physiology during Pregnancy

Cortisol levels increase progressively over the course of gestation, with a twofold to threefold increase by term[92-97] (Fig. 190-11). Most of the elevation in cortisol levels is due to the estrogen-induced increase in cortisol-binding globulin (transcortin) levels,[92,95-97] but the biologically active "free" fraction in serum is elevated threefold as well.[92,96-98] This increase is reflected in twofold to threefold elevations in urinary free cortisol levels.[99,100] The increased corticosteroid-binding globulin results in a prolonged cortisol half-life in plasma, but the cortisol production rate is also increased.[101,102] Urinary 17-hydroxycorticosteroid levels are decreased, however, because of a decrease in the excretion of cortisol tetrahydro metabolites.[101,102] Cortisol can cross the placenta and the major direction of transfer is from mother to fetus.[103] However, the presence in the placenta and in many fetal tissues of high concentrations of the enzyme type 2 11β-hydroxysteroid dehydrogenase, which converts cortisol to cortisone, protects the fetus from these high maternal levels of cortisol.[104] Deficiencies in this enzyme, which resulting in high fetal glucocorticosteroid exposure, have been hypothesized to retard intrauterine fetal growth and may even program the fetus for the subsequent development of hypertension in adult life.[105]

ACTH levels have been variously reported as being normal,[106] suppressed,[96] and elevated[93,107] early in gestation. During pregnancy, a progressive rise is followed by a final

*Figure 190-10* Changes in plasma total thyroxine concentration in 20 subjects with hyperemesis on admission (A) and during the course of their pregnancy. The *interrupted line* represents the mean (±SD) value seen in normal pregnancy. PN, postnatal. (From Swaminathan R, Chin RK, Lao TTH, et al: Thyroid function in hyperemesis gravidarum. Acta Endocrinol 120:155–160, 1989.)

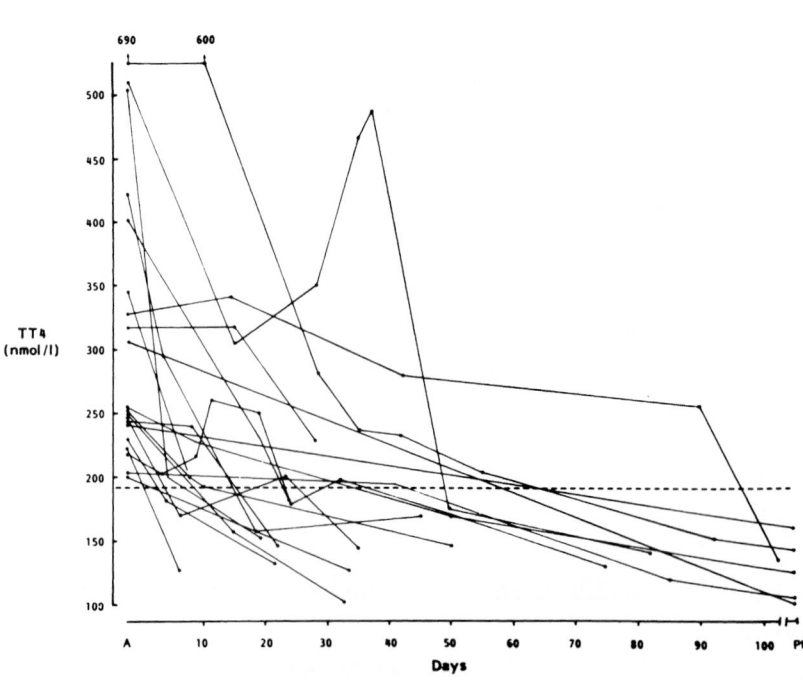

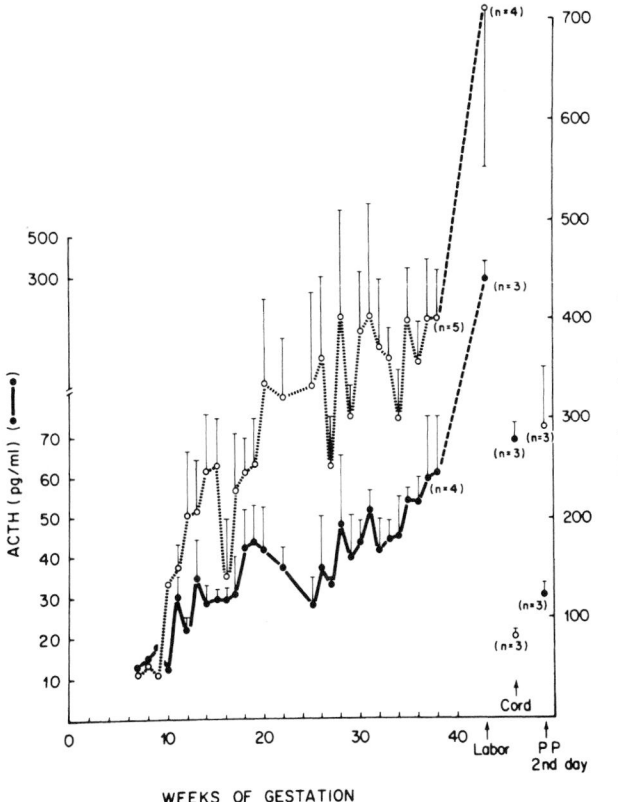

WEEKS OF GESTATION

*Figure 190-11* Plasma concentration of adrenocorticotropic hormone (ACTH) and cortisol during normal pregnancy. Blood samples were obtained weekly at 8 to 9 A.M. from five normal pregnant women and from three women during labor and on the second postpartum day. In addition, umbilical cord plasma was obtained from the newborn infants of three of these subjects. The mean plasma concentrations for ACTH are denoted by the *solid circles*, whereas plasma cortisol levels are denoted by *open circles*. The *vertical bars* correspond to the magnitude of the standard error of the mean. (From Carr BR, Parker CR Jr, Madden JD, et al: Maternal plasma adenocorticotropin and cortisol relationships throughout human pregnancy. Am J Obstet Gynecol 139:416–422, 1981.)

surge of ACTH and cortisol levels during labor[93,94,106] (see Fig. 190-11). ACTH does not cross the placenta,[108] but is manufactured by the placenta[106,109] (see Chapter 182). The amount of ACTH in serum that is due to placental versus pituitary origin at various stages of gestation is not known. The ACTH secretion pattern is pulsatile and strongly correlated with cortisol, however, with both maintaining diurnal variation, suggesting that most of the circulating ACTH derives from the pituitary.[110]

CRH is also produced by the placenta[111] (see Chapter 182) and is released into maternal plasma,[112] where levels gradually increase over the course of the second and third trimesters and peak during labor and delivery.[113,114] This CRH is bioactive and may release ACTH, both from the placenta, in a paracrine fashion,[109,115] and from the maternal pituitary,[116] although the latter has not been absolutely proved. The rise in CRH over the course of gestation and delivery is highly correlated with the rise in ACTH and cortisol levels, thus implying cause and effect.[116,117] Analysis of values obtained from frequent sampling show poor correlation of peripheral CRH with ACTH levels, however, and the high correlation of ACTH and cortisol levels, along with persistent diurnal variation of ACTH and cortisol but no diurnal variation for peripheral CRH levels, casts doubt on the role of placental CRH in the minute-to-minute regulation of ACTH secretion.[110] Other

biologic effects of placental CRH include vasodilation of uterine arteries and regulation of placental blood flow.[118]

Neither ACTH[111] nor CRH production by the placenta[111] is suppressible in vitro with exogenous glucocorticosteroids. In some in vitro studies, CRH production is actually increased by exogenous glucocorticosteroids.[119,120] These findings of the lack of suppressibility of placental ACTH and CRH production by glucocorticosteroids correlate well with the in vivo findings that ACTH and cortisol levels are not normally suppressed in the third trimester, as shown in one patient with unchanging ACTH levels during treatment with 10 mg/day of prednisone at term[93] and by nonsuppressible urinary free cortisol values in six women who underwent a standard low-dose (2 mg/day for 3 days) dexamethasone test during the last trimester.[106] In one study, however, betamethasone was shown to be capable of suppressing ACTH and cortisol, but not CRH levels very early in the third trimester (26 to 30 weeks).[121] In another study, overnight dexamethasone (1 mg) suppression tests showed normal cortisol suppression in seven normal women at unspecified portions of the second and third trimesters.[122] Thus, based on limited studies, it appears that CRH levels are nonsuppressible throughout the last trimester, but that ACTH and cortisol levels become nonsuppressible only in the latter part of the third trimester. No studies in normal pregnant women have been performed with high-dose dexamethasone.

### Cushing's Syndrome

The diagnosis of Cushing's syndrome should be made during pregnancy because, untreated, the condition is associated with high fetal mortality and increased prematurity, as well as maternal hypertension, preeclampsia, and myopathy.[123,124] Although fewer than 100 cases of Cushing's syndrome during pregnancy have been reported,[105,123–130] it is apparent that the distribution of causes of Cushing's syndrome is different in pregnancy. Less than 50% are due to pituitary adenomas, a like number are due to adrenal adenomas, and 10% are due to adrenal carcinomas. Interestingly, in many cases, Cushing's syndrome first became manifest or exacerbated during the pregnancy, with improvement after parturition. It has been speculated that in some cases of Cushing's disease, the unregulated placental CRH was instrumental in causing this pregnancy-induced exacerbation.[123,124]

Diagnosis of Cushing's syndrome during pregnancy may be quite difficult. Both may be associated with weight gain in a central distribution, fatigue, edema, emotional upset, glucose intolerance, and hypertension. The striae associated with the weight gain and increased abdominal girth are usually white in normal pregnancy and red or purple in Cushing's syndrome. Hirsutism and acne may point to excessive androgen production.

As can be inferred from the laboratory findings described, biochemical evaluation of Cushing's syndrome in pregnant women is not straightforward. The finding of a greatly elevated total serum cortisol level, increased serum and urinary free cortisol levels, and increased ACTH levels can be compatible with normal pregnancy, as well as with Cushing's syndrome. For example, the early morning plasma cortisol has been reported at 14.9 ± 3.4 (SEM) µg/dL at 11 weeks and 35.2 ± 9.0 µg/dL at 26 weeks' gestation in normal pregnancies.[105] Furthermore, at least in the latter part of the third trimester, these elevated levels are nonsuppressible by low-dose dexamethasone. In pregnant patients reported with Cushing's disease, plasma cortisol levels are minimally suppressed with 2 days of low-dose dexamethasone, but are suppressed quite well with the high dose.[125] In pregnant patients with adrenal adenomas, plasma cortisol is also not suppressed with high-dose dexamethasone,[130] as expected. Basal ACTH levels have been reported to be normal in two patients with Cushing's disease during pregnancy.[125,126] Similarly, normal ACTH levels have been reported, however, in patients with adrenal adenomas.[130,131] These "normal" rather than suppressed levels of

ACTH in patients with adrenal adenomas may be due to production of ACTH by the placenta or nonsuppressible stimulation of pituitary ACTH by placental CRH (see previous discussion). Thus, the presence of "normal" levels of ACTH may be quite misleading in the differential diagnosis of Cushing's syndrome during pregnancy. Most helpful in distinguishing Cushing's syndrome from the hypercortisolism of pregnancy is the finding of a persistent diurnal variation in elevated levels of total and free serum cortisol during normal pregnancy,[95,98,132] a finding characteristically absent in all forms of Cushing's syndrome (see Chapter 124).

Little experience has been reported with newer techniques such as CRH stimulation testing or petrosal venous sinus sampling in diagnosing Cushing's disease during pregnancy. CRH testing during late gestation has the potential hazard of inducing premature labor because CRH has been shown to potentiate the contractile response of pregnant myometrium to oxytocin and has been implicated in participating in the process of parturition.[133] CRH stimulation tests have been shown to elicit normal ACTH responses in the early second trimester, however, but to elicit no ACTH response in the late third trimester in normal pregnancies.[116,134] Thus, the finding of a blunted ACTH response to CRH would be more in favor of simple pregnancy than Cushing's disease, in which hyperresponsiveness to CRH is generally seen. Indeed, Ross and colleagues found the typical exaggerated ACTH response to CRH in a woman with Cushing's disease, and this patient had no ill effects from such testing.[128] In addition, CRH testing during petrosal sinus sampling was performed without ill effects by Pinette and coworkers in a woman at 14 weeks' gestation,[135] but catheterization was performed via the direct internal jugular vein approach rather than the femoral vein approach to minimize fetal irradiation.

When biochemical evidence points to the presence of Cushing's syndrome and to a pituitary or adrenal origin, radiologic imaging becomes necessary. The pituitary volume is often increased during pregnancy (see previous discussion), and pituitary CT or MRI may yield a false-positive finding. Careful review of the MRI findings, however, may indicate a focal abnormality in a patient with a tumor as opposed to the diffusely enlarged, homogeneous gland seen with pregnancy (see earlier). Often, an adrenal mass will be visible on ultrasound.[136] Usually, however, CT or MRI of the pituitary or adrenal will be necessary, especially to detect masses with a width less than 3.0 cm.[136] With the techniques and equipment available at present, CT and MRI appear to be about equal in detecting adrenal masses.[136] Because MRI may be safer during pregnancy, it may be the technique of choice for localizing the mass. Most adrenal lesions are unilateral, so localization is important.

## Adrenal Insufficiency

Adrenal insufficiency is uncommon during pregnancy.[105,137] Most of the morbidity is due to glucocorticosteroid lack in the mother, as the fetus produces sufficient cortisol from its own adrenals.[105] As in the nonpregnant state, adrenal insufficiency in a pregnant woman is usually due to autoimmune destruction. Adrenal insufficiency caused by infiltrative diseases, such as tuberculosis, fungal diseases, and metastatic cancer, is much less common. Although new adrenal insufficiency currently is seen most commonly in patients with human immunodeficiency virus (HIV),[138] such patients are often infertile. Rarely, bilateral adrenal hemorrhage may occur in association with surgery or anticoagulant use and is usually manifested as an acute adrenal crisis characterized by fever, abdominal or flank pain, vomiting, confusion, and hypotension.[139]

Patients commonly have fatigue, anorexia, nausea, vomiting, weight loss, depression, and nonspecific abdominal pain.[105,137] Obviously, it may be difficult to sort out the features of fatigue, nausea, and vomiting during the first trimester, but

persistence of these symptoms should at least trigger a screening diagnostic evaluation. Patients with primary adrenal insufficiency and normal pituitaries respond by increasing ACTH and lipotropin secretion, which results in increased pigmentation in skin creases, scars, and mucous membranes. Similar increased pigmentation may also be seen during normal pregnancy, however.[140] On examination, patients will usually display evidence of orthostatic hypotension. Mild cases may go undetected during pregnancy, only to go into adrenal crisis with the stress of labor or another illness such as urinary tract infection or dehydration from excessive sun exposure.[137,141] In some cases, severe adrenal insufficiency may not develop until the postpartum period, possibly because of maintenance of maternal cortisol levels by fetal adrenal production.[142] Maternal adrenal insufficiency has been associated with intrauterine growth retardation in some cases.[141,142]

Laboratory features of adrenal insufficiency include hyperkalemia secondary to aldosterone deficiency, hyponatremia resulting from an inability to excrete free water by the kidney because of glucocorticosteroid deficiency, mild azotemia, eosinophilia, and lymphocytosis. Fasting hypoglycemia may also be present. Fasting hypoglycemia may also be seen during normal pregnancy, however, especially in the first trimester. Basal cortisol levels may appear "normal," but are really inappropriately low when corrected for the stage of gestation. The finding of an inappropriately normal or low cortisol level with a substantially elevated ACTH level makes the diagnosis of primary and not secondary adrenal insufficiency. A stimulation test with Cortrosyn (synthetic $ACTH_{1-24}$), 250 μg, should be performed immediately after obtaining the preceding baseline measurements without waiting for the results. In primary adrenal insufficiency, a second cortisol level obtained 60 minutes later will show an inadequate increment (i.e., less than a doubling of the basal level and/or an increase to greater than 18 μg/dL in nonpregnant individuals [see Chapter 121]; normal values have not been established for pregnant women). In patients with suspected pituitary disease as the cause of the adrenal insufficiency, the cortisol and ACTH responses to insulin-induced hypoglycemia should be obtained, with the same parameters used for normal as those given here for the ACTH stimulation test. Because of the insulin resistance associated with pregnancy, a dose of 0.15 or 0.20 U/kg of insulin may be needed to induce hypoglycemia instead of the standard 0.1 U/kg. Standard metyrapone testing (750 mg every 4 hours for six doses) has also been performed during pregnancy, and 75% of normal pregnant subjects showed diminished responses, whereas the other 25% had normal responses.[143] Therefore, such testing does not appear to be valid during pregnancy.

## ALDOSTERONE AND RENIN REGULATION

### Changes in Aldosterone and Renin Physiology during Pregnancy

During pregnancy, blood pressure falls, reaches a nadir at about 28 weeks, and then gradually returns to close to prepregnancy levels by term.[144] This fall in blood pressure is accompanied by an increase in heart rate, which increases by 20 to 25 beats per minute by week 32.[144] Plasma renin activity increases fourfold by 8 weeks and then increases only minimally over the subsequent 32 weeks of gestation (Fig. 190-12), whereas plasma renin substrate (angiotensinogen) levels increase fourfold over the course of the first 20 weeks of gestation and then increase only minimally over the subsequent 20 weeks of gestation.[144,145] Angiotensin II levels double early in pregnancy and are eventually increased threefold to fourfold by term.[145] Similar increases occur in plasma aldosterone levels (Fig. 190-13), a 5-fold increase occurring by 16 weeks and ultimately a 7- to 10-fold elevation occurring by term.[122,144-148] This increase in plasma aldosterone levels is reflected in a 7-fold elevation

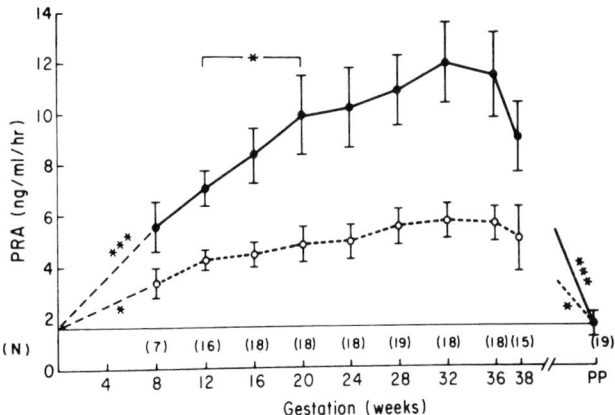

*Figure 190-12* Sequential changes in plasma renin activity (PRA) (—•—) and in PRA normalized to the postpartum substrate values (—○—) (mean ± SE) throughout pregnancy ($^cP < 0.05$; $^{ccc}P < 0.001$). (From Wilson M, Morganti AA, Zervondakis I, et al: Blood pressure, the renin-aldosterone system and sex steroids throughout normal pregnancy. Am J Med 68:97–104, 1980.)

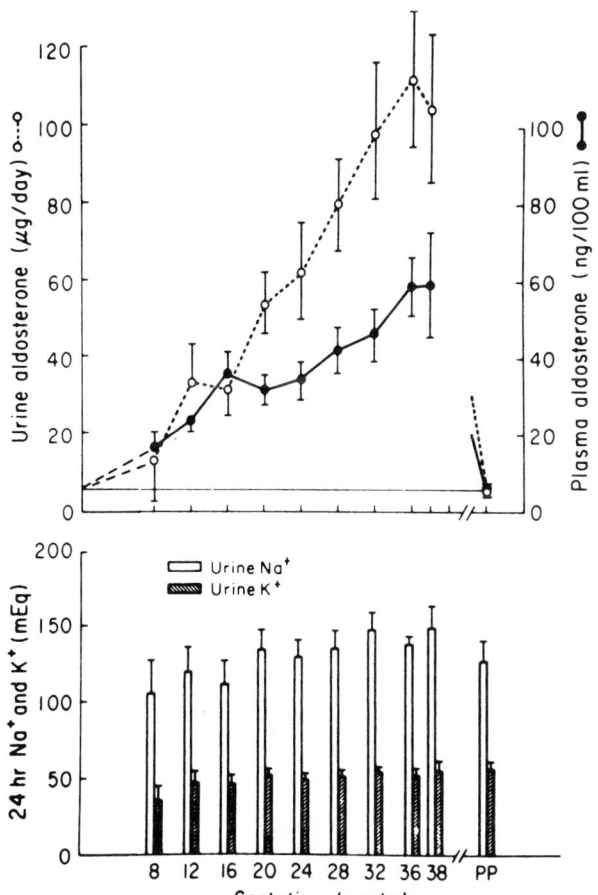

*Figure 190-13* Sequential changes throughout pregnancy in plasma aldosterone, urine aldosterone, urinary sodium, and potassium (mean ± SE). (From Wilson M, Morganti AA, Zervondakis I, et al: Blood pressure, the renin-aldosterone system and sex steroids throughout normal pregnancy. Am J Med 68:97–104, 1980.)

in urinary aldosterone levels by 12 weeks and ultimately a 20- to 25-fold elevation by term.[144] In contrast, in pregnant women with gestational hypertension, plasma renin activity levels are higher than in normotensive nonpregnant women, but do not increase during the pregnancy, whereas aldosterone levels are stable until the last trimester, when they rise.[149] Significant correlation has been demonstrated between plasma aldosterone and plasma renin activity; plasma progesterone, plasma estriol, and plasma estradiol levels; and urine aldosterone levels.[144] Furthermore, plasma renin substrate also correlates with estradiol levels.[144] Individual levels of urinary sodium and potassium did not correlate with aldosterone or plasma renin activity.[144] Wilson and colleagues calculated that about 50% of plasma renin activity was due to the increased renin substrate concentration, but that the remaining 50% represented a real increase in renin concentration.[144] This activation of the renin-angiotensin-aldosterone axis during pregnancy has been hypothesized to be caused by the fall in blood pressure, which may be due to vasodilatation secondary to decreased vascular responsiveness to angiotensin II[150] and decreased vascular resistance caused by altered prostaglandins.[151] The high progesterone levels from placental production also partially block aldosterone action, preventing kaliuresis and hypokalemia.[152,153]

### Primary Hyperaldosteronism
Primary hyperaldosteronism has been rarely reported in pregnant women.[154–156] Whereas the elevated aldosterone levels found in patients with these tumors are similar to those found in pregnancy, in hyperaldosteronism, plasma renin activity should be suppressed rather than elevated as normally found in pregnancy. Reported patients in whom simultaneous renin and aldosterone levels were determined during pregnancy had markedly elevated levels of aldosterone with low renin levels.[154,155]

In addition to measuring simultaneous plasma aldosterone and renin levels, diagnostic testing may also involve determining whether the aldosterone levels can be suppressed by salt loading or the administration of exogenous mineralocorticoid (see Chapter 132). During normal pregnancy, basal elevated aldosterone levels also fall normally with such maneuvers,[148,152] so these maneuvers can be of diagnostic utility. Pregnant patients with aldosteronomas who were put through such testing failed to demonstrate normal suppressibility of aldosterone levels.[155] If the results of baseline renin and aldosterone levels or suppression tests are equivocal and/or CT or MRI does not suggest unilateral disease, it has been recommended that patients be treated medically until delivery, when more definitive isotope scanning can be done and when aldosterone and renin levels should fall.[154] Spironolactone, the aldosterone antagonist generally used for such treatment, can cross the placenta. Because spironolactone is a potent antiandrogen, it may cause abnormal development of the genitalia[157] and is thus contraindicated during pregnancy. There is no published experience with the use of the new aldosterone antagonist, eplerenone, during pregnancy.

A rare variant of hyperaldosteronism, referred to as glucocorticosteroid-remediable aldosteronism is characterized by severe hypertension, hypokalemia, volume expansion, and suppressed plasma renin activity, but is due to a chimeric gene duplication that results from an unequal crossing over between the 11β-hydroxylase and aldosterone synthase genes.[158] A recent review of 35 pregnancies in 16 women with this disorder showed relatively modest adverse consequences, consisting primarily of pregnancy-associated blood pressure aggravation in 39%, a slight decrease in infant birth weight and an increased cesarean section rate.[158] Interestingly, an activating mutation of the mineralocorticoid receptor has recently been reported to be one of the causes of pregnancy-exacerbated hypertension.[159]

## ADRENAL MEDULLA

### PHEOCHROMOCYTOMAS

Pheochromocytomas are uncommonly found during pregnancy. The maternal mortality rate from undiagnosed pheochromocytoma is about 50%; this rate falls to 10% to 20% if the diagnosis is made ante partum.[105,160-164] The fetal loss rate is almost halved if the diagnosis is made during pregnancy.[105] Catecholamines cross the placenta only minimally[163]; therefore, the fetus appears to be unaffected by the high maternal levels. Some element of hypoxia may be present, however, as a result of vasoconstriction of the uterine vascular bed.[164] Because of this high maternal and fetal mortality in undiagnosed and untreated patients, it is critical to make the diagnosis ante partum.

Symptoms may be vague, or classic symptoms may be seen and be due to the episodic secretion of catecholamines, as in the nonpregnant state (see Chapter 130). Some patients may have episodes that are very infrequent and, therefore, the first suspicion of pheochromocytoma may occur with a blood pressure rise during the induction of anesthesia or during labor or surgery. Failure to recognize this possibility may result in death of the patient.[165] Some patients have sudden shock appearing spontaneously or induced by anesthesia or labor and delivery.[162]

Extra-adrenal tumors, which represent about 10% of cases, may provoke paroxysmal symptoms after particular activities. A frequent site is the organ of Zuckerkandl, located at the bifurcation of the aorta, and the enlarging uterus may cause pressure on such a tumor, with hypertensive episodes occurring after changes in position, uterine contractions, fetal movement, and Valsalva's maneuvers.[166] Although about 10% of pheochromocytomas are found to be malignant, this frequency appears to be considerably less when the diagnosis is made in a pregnant woman because only four such cases have been reported.[167] Hereditary syndromes may also be important and patients whose pheochromocytomas were initially diagnosed during pregnancy have been reported who later were found to have multiple endocrine neoplasia type 2[168] and von Hippel–Lindau syndrome.[169] In patients with neurofibromatosis, pheochromocytomas occur in about 2% of those with subcutaneous nodules, but, as opposed to multiple endocrine neoplasia 2 (MEN2) and von Hippel–Lindau, the pheochromocytomas are not almost always bilateral.[170]

A key consideration in diagnosing pheochromocytoma during pregnancy is differentiation from preeclampsia. Onset of hypertension in the first two trimesters is, of course, not characteristic of preeclampsia. Careful evaluation reveals the absence of proteinuria, edema, or hyperuricemia. Urinary and plasma epinephrine and norepinephrine levels are normal in uncomplicated pregnancy,[171,172] as well as in preeclampsia.[173,174] Urinary and plasma catecholamines, however, are twofold to fourfold elevated for more than 24 hours after a seizure in eclampsia.[173,174] Therefore, to make a diagnosis in a woman not having eclampsia, measurement of 24-hour urinary collections for vanillylmandelic acid and fractionated metanephrines and catecholamines can be used as for nonpregnant patients (see Chapter 130). Stimulation tests have been associated with fetal demise, and their use has been discouraged.[105]

Once the diagnosis is made biochemically, efforts should be made to localize the tumor. Both CT and MRI are excellent for detecting the presence of tumors, but MRI has been preferred during pregnancy because of the lack of exposure of the fetus to ionizing radiation.[175] Recently, [131]I-metaiodobenzylguanidine scanning has proven quite useful in localizing tumors (see Chapter 130). It should be noted, however, that false-negative results occur with this technique. Isotopic scanning

is, in general, contraindicated during pregnancy,[62] and its use has not been reported during pregnancy.

## PARATHYROID GLANDS

### CALCIUM AND CALCIUM REGULATION

#### Changes in Calcium Metabolism during Pregnancy

About 25 to 30 g of calcium are transferred from the mother to the fetus during gestation, about 300 mg/day being transferred in the third trimester.[176-178] In addition to the net transfer of calcium from the mother to the fetus, a net loss of calcium into the urine results in a 24-hour urinary calcium value that may be more than 600 mg[179-181] (Fig. 190-14). In some series, over 20% of women had urinary calcium levels greater than 350 mg/24 hours.[179,180] The hypercalciuria is, in part, due to the increased glomerular filtration, but is primarily due to increased gastrointestinal absorption of calcium, that is, absorptive hypercalciuria, probably caused by the increase in 1,25-dihydroxyvitamin $D_3$ levels[181] (see discussion to follow). Total serum calcium levels decrease modestly from about 2.4 to about 2.2 mmol/L, in parallel with a fall in serum albumin from about 4.7 to 3.2 g/dL.[182,183] Ionized calcium levels, however, remain unchanged[177,178,182-186] (Fig. 190-15).

A number of changes in maternal calcium homeostasis occur during pregnancy that prevent the mother from going into markedly negative calcium balance from the increased urinary and fetal calcium losses.[176-178] The primary adaptational event appears to be an increase in circulating 1,25-dihydroxyvitamin D levels[178,185,187-190] (see Fig. 190-15), whereas 25-hydroxyvitamin D levels remain unchanged.[185,187,189] Levels of vitamin D–binding protein also increase during gestation, but it appears that both the bound and free fractions of 1,25-dihydroxyvitamin D increase by 50% to 100%.[187,190] Although this increased formation of 1,25-dihydroxyvitamin D has been thought to be

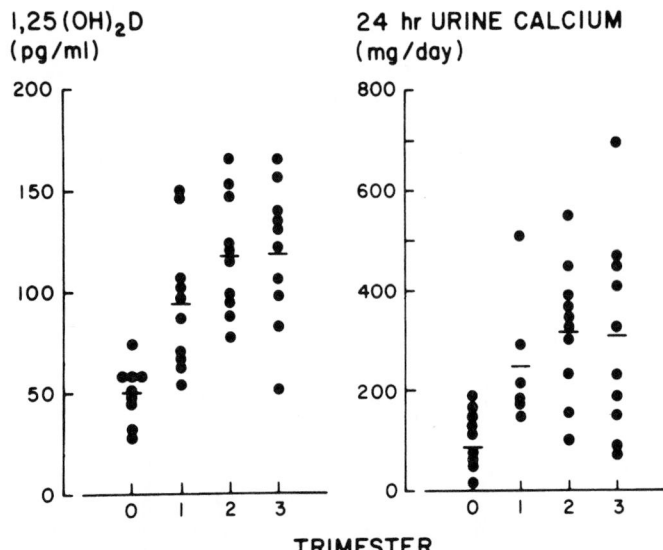

**Figure 190-14** Circulating 1,25-dihydroxyvitamin D concentration and 24-hour calcium excretion during pregnancy by trimester. The values for both determinations were significantly increased *(P < 0.05)* during pregnancy (trimesters 1–3) when compared with postpartum values (trimester 0). The *horizontal bars* represent mean values. The upper normal limit for plasma 1,25-dihydroxyvitamin D is 66 pg/mL. (From Gertner JM, Couston DR, Kliger AS, et al: Pregnancy as state of physiologic absorptive hypercalciuria. Am J Med 81:451–456, 1986.)

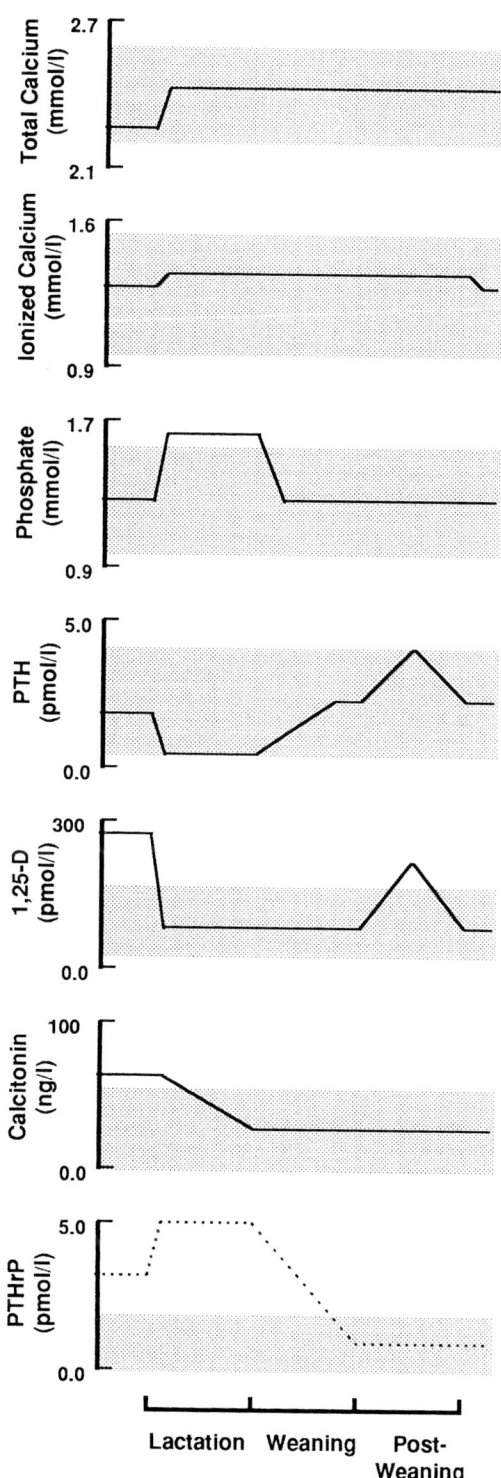

*Figure 190-15* Schematic illustration of the longitudinal changes in calcium, phosphate, and calcitropic hormone levels that occur during human pregnancy. Normal adult ranges are indicated by the *shaded areas*. Data have been compiled from the following sources: total calcium (9), ionized calcium (14–19), phosphate (14, 17, 26, 27), PTH (11, 14–16, 27, 44), 1,25-dihydroxyvitamin D (15, 41, 57–59), calcitonin (14, 34, 36, 37, 86–89), and PTHrP (44, 111). The progression in PTHrP levels has been depicted by a *dashed line* to reflect that the data are less complete. PTH, parathyroid hormone; PTHrP, parathyroid hormone–related peptide. (From Kovacs CS, Kronenberg HM: Maternal-fetal calcium and bone metabolism during pregnancy, puerperium, and lactation. Endocr Rev 18:832–872, 1997; © 1997, The Endocrine Society.)

due to the 30% to 50% increase in parathyroid hormone (PTH) levels found in some series,[182,183,189] PTH levels have been reported as being decreased in other series.[180,184–186] These discrepancies in PTH results may be due to differences in various assays in their detection of PTH cleavage products, whose clearance will increase along with the increased GFR.[178,180] When the biologic effect of PTH is determined by measuring nephrogenous cyclic adenosine monophosphate (cAMP) levels, this activity is normal despite lowered immunoreactive PTH levels in serum.[180] When intact PTH is measured by a two-site IRMA, it has generally been found to decrease modestly into the low-normal range during the early part of pregnancy with a rise to the mid-normal range by term.[177,178,185,186]

Although the kidney is the predominant site of 1-hydroxylation in the formation of 1,25-dihydroxy-vitamin D, a significant amount of 1-hydroxylation of 25-hydroxyvitamin D also occurs in the placenta.[188] 1,25-Dihydroxyvitamin D levels are increased during pregnancy in nephrectomized rats.[191] In humans with pseudohypoparathyroidism, in whom the renal response to PTH is reduced, serum calcium and 1,25-dihydroxyvitamin D levels are normal during pregnancy as a result of placental production,[192,193] but the levels are not increased as in normal pregnancy. It thus appears that the increased levels of 1,25-dihydroxyvitamin D are primarily due to increased maternal renal 1-hydroxylase activity and this activity is likely due to increased levels of parathyroid hormone–related peptide (PTHrP) found in pregnancy.[177,178] PTHrP has been implicated in the majority of cases of the hypercalcemia of malignancy.[194] It is also produced by the placenta, amnion, decidua, umbilical cord, and breast tissue, however.[177,178] PTHrP is present in very high concentrations in breast milk and is thought to play a paracrine role in the regulation of milk calcium content[195] and may also be important in embryogenesis.[176] Elevated levels of PTHrP have reported to cause hypercalcemia during lactation in some women and found to maintain normal to high serum calcium levels in one hypoparathyroid woman during lactation so that she could stop calcium and vitamin D supplements.[196]

### Hypercalcemia

Most patients found to be hypercalcemic are asymptomatic, the condition being discovered on routine screening with a multichannel autoanalyzer.[197–199] It is now uncommon for patients to seek medical attention because of renal calculi, peptic ulcer disease, bone disease, or mental dysfunction, especially women of reproductive age. Rarely, the diagnosis is made in the mother only post partum after an evaluation is done because of hypocalcemia in the neonate.[198,199] The neonatal hypocalcemia is due to placental transfer of the elevated calcium with suppression of the fetal parathyroid glands. At delivery, calcium transfer stops, but the involuted parathyroid glands cannot maintain adequate calcium levels. Rarely, severe hypercalcemia (hypercalcemic crisis) may develop and be manifested as rapidly progressive anorexia, nausea, vomiting, weakness, fatigue, dehydration, and stupor.[197,198] Pancreatitis due to the hyperparathyroidism has also been reported.[198,199] More common clinical findings include hypertension, nausea, and vomiting. The latter two may be mistaken for hyperemesis gravidarum.[197–199] In general, pregnancy has an ameliorating affect on the hypercalcemia because of shunting of calcium from the mother to the fetus. The mother may experience dramatic worsening and even hypercalcemic crisis post partum when such shunting is lost.[199]

Because total serum calcium levels decrease, as previously discussed, the finding of a serum calcium level that is only slightly elevated or that is even at the upper limit of normal may indicate significant hypercalcemia. Ionized calcium levels are helpful in establishing the diagnosis of hypercalcemia because they remain normal during pregnancy. During pregnancy, immunoreactive PTH levels have been reported as being normal, low, or elevated (see previous discussion), depending on the assay used, but even when they have been reported as being elevated, the increase was only 30% to 50%.

Therefore, the finding of a markedly elevated PTH level in the setting of a pregnant hypercalcemic woman would indicate the presence of hyperparathyroidism. The finding of low-normal PTH levels in a pregnant hypercalcemic woman necessitates an investigation for the other myriad causes of hypercalcemia (see Chapters 76 to 78).

## REFERENCES

1. Brown MA: Sodium and plasma volume regulation in normal and hypertensive pregnancy: A review of physiology and clinical implications. Clin Exp Hypertens 7:265–282, 1988.
2. Lee W, Rokey R, Cotton DB: Noninvasive maternal stroke volume and cardiac output determinations by pulsed Doppler echocardiography. Am J Obstet Gynecol 158:505–510, 1988.
3. Robson S, Hunter S, Boys RJ, et al: Serial study of factors influencing changes in cardiac output during human pregnancy. Am J Physiol 256:H1060–H1065, 1989.
4. Dunlop W: Serial changes in renal haemodynamics during normal human pregnancy. Br J Obstet Gynaecol 88:1–9, 1981.
5. Davison JM, Noble MCB: Serial changes in 24 hour creatinine clearance during normal menstrual cycles and the first trimester of pregnancy. Br J Obstet Gynaecol 88:10–17, 1981.
6. Lindheimer MD, Davison JM, Katz AI: The kidney and hypertension in pregnancy: 20 exciting years. Semin Nephrol 21:173–189, 2001.
7. Davison JM, Dunlop W, Ezimokhai M: 24-Hour creatinine clearances during the third trimester of normal pregnancy. Br J Obstet Gynaecol 87:106–109, 1980.
8. Davison JM, Lovedale C: The excretion of glucose during normal pregnancy and after delivery. J Obstet Gynaecol Br Commonw 81:30–34, 1974.
9. Buster JE, Abraham GE: The applications of steroid hormone radioimmunoassays to clinical obstetrics. Obstet Gynecol 46:489–499, 1975.
10. Vician L, Shupnik MA, Gorski J: Effects of estrogen on primary ovine pituitary cell cultures: Stimulation of prolactin secretion, synthesis, and preprolactin messenger ribonucleic acid activity. Endocrinology 104:736–743, 1979.
11. Maurer RA: Relationship between estradiol, ergocryptine, and thyroid hormone: Effects on prolactin synthesis and prolactin messenger ribonucleic acid levels. Endocrinology 110:1515–1520, 1982.
12. Rakoff JS, Yen SSC: Progesterone induced acute release of prolactin in estrogen primed ovariectomized women. J Clin Endocrinol Metab 47:918–921, 1978.
13. Rigg LA, Lein A, Yen SSC: Pattern of increase in circulating prolactin levels during human gestation. Am J Obstet Gynecol 129:454–456, 1977.
14. Goluboff LG, Ezrin C: Effect of pregnancy on the somatotroph and the prolactin cell of the human adenohypophysis. J Clin Endocrinol Metab 29:1533–1538, 1969.
15. Scheithauer BW, Sano T, Kovacs KT, et al: The pituitary gland in pregnancy: A clinicopathologic and immunohistochemical study of 69 cases. Mayo Clin Proc 65:461–474, 1990.
16. Soares MJ, Faria TN, Roby KF, Deb S: Pregnancy and the prolactin family of hormones: Coordination of anterior pituitary, uterine and placental expression. Endocr Rev 12:402–423, 1991.
17. Elster AD, Sanders TG, Vines FS, Chen MYM: Size and shape of the pituitary gland during pregnancy and post partum: Measurement with MR imaging. Radiology 181:531–535, 1991.
18. Molitch ME: Pregnancy and the hyperprolactinemic woman. N Engl J Med 312:1364–1370, 1985.
19. Kupersmith MJ, Rosenberg C, Kleinberg D: Visual loss in pregnant women with pituitary adenomas. Ann Intern Med 121:473–477, 1994.
20. Rossi AM, Vilska S, Heinonen PK: Outcome of pregnancies in women with treated or untreated hyperprolactinemia. Eur J Obstet Gynecol Reprod Biol 63:143–146, 1995.
21. Musolino NRC, Bronstein MD: Prolactinomas and pregnancy. In Bronstein MD (ed): Pituitary Tumors and Pregnancy. Norwell, Mass, Kluwer, 2001, pp 91–108.
22. Thodou E, Asa SL, Kontogeorgos G, et al: Lymphocytic hypophysitis: Clinicopathological findings. J Clin Endocrinol Metab 80:2302–2311, 1995.
23. Gillam M, Molitch ME: Lymphocytic Hypophysitis. In Bronstein MD (ed): Pituitary Tumors and Pregnancy. Norwell, Mass, Kluwer, 2001, pp 131–148.
24. Frankenne F, Rentier-Delrue F, Scippo M-L, et al: Expression of the growth hormone variant gene in the human placenta. J Clin Endocrinol Metab 64:635–637, 1987.
25. Frankenne F, Closset J, Gomez F, et al: The physiology of growth hormones (GHs) in pregnant women and partial characterization of the placental GH variant. J Clin Endocrinol Metab 66:1171–1180, 1988.
26. Eriksson L, Frankenne F, Eden S, et al: Growth hormone 24-h serum profiles during pregnancy: Lack of pulsatility for the secretion of the placental variant. Br J Obstet Gynaecol 96:949–953, 1989.
27. Beckers A, Stevenaert A, Foidart J-M, et al: Placental and pituitary growth-hormone secretion during pregnancy in acromegalic women. J Clin Endocrinol Metab 71:725–731, 1990.
28. MacLeod JN, Worsley I, Ray J, et al: Human growth hormone-variant is a biologically active somatogen and lactogen. Endocrinology 128:1298–1302, 1991.
29. Ray J, Okamura H, Kelly PA, et al: Human growth hormone-variant demonstrates a receptor binding profile distinct from that of normal pituitary growth hormone. J Biol Chem 265:7939–7944, 1990.
30. Baumann G, Davila N, Shaw M, et al: Binding of human growth hormone (GH)-variant (placental GH) to GH-binding proteins in human plasma. J Clin Endocrinol Metab 73:1175–1179, 1991.
31. Daughaday WH, Trivedi B, Winn HN, Yan H: Hypersomatotropism in pregnant women, as measured by a human liver radioreceptor assay. J Clin Endocrinol Metab 70:215–221, 1990.
32. Wilson DM, Bennett A, Adamson GD, et al: Somatomedins in pregnancy: A cross-sectional study of insulin-like growth factors I and II and somatomedin peptide content in normal human pregnancies. J Clin Endocrinol Metab 55:858–869, 1982.
33. Caufriez A, Frankenne F, Enlert Y, et al: Placental growth hormone as a potential regulator of maternal IGF-I during human pregnancy. Am J Physiol 258:E1014–E1019, 1990.
34. Goodman HM, Tai L-R, Ray J, et al: Human growth hormone variant produces insulin-like and lipolytic responses in rat adipose tissue. Endocrinology 129:1779–1783, 1991.
35. Simon P, Decoster C, Brocas H, et al: Absence of human chorionic somatomammotropin during pregnancy associated with two types of gene deletion. Hum Genet 74:235–238, 1986
36. Rygaard K, Revol A, Esquivel-Escobedo D, et al: Absence of human placental lactogen and placental growth hormone (HGH-V) during pregnancy: PCR analysis of the deletion. Hum Genet 102:87-92, 1998.
37. Barkan AL, Stred SE, Reno K, et al: Increased growth hormone pulse frequency in acromegaly. J Clin Endocrinol Metab 69:1225–1233, 1989.
38. Hartman ML, Veldhuis JD, Vance ML, et al: Somatotropin pulse frequency and basal concentrations are increased in acromegaly and are reduced by successful therapy. J Clin Endocrinol Metab 70:1375–1384, 1990.
39. Hanew K, Kokubun M, Sasaki A, et al: The spectrum of pituitary growth hormone responses to pharmacological

stimuli in acromegaly. J Clin Endocrinol Metab 51:292–297, 1980.

40. Herman-Bonert V, Seliverstov M, Melmed S: Pregnancy in acromegaly: Successful therapeutic outcome. J Clin Endocrinol Metab 83:727–731, 1998.

41. Okada Y, Morimoto I, Ejima K, et al: A case of active acromegalic woman with a marked increase in serum insulin-like growth factor-1 levels after delivery. Endocr J 44:117–120, 1997.

42. Fassnacht M, Capeller B, Arlt W, et al: Octreotide LAR treatment throughout pregnancy in an acromegalic woman. Clin Endocrinol 55:411–415, 2001

43. Davison JM, Vallotton MB, Lindheimer MD: Plasma osmolality and urinary concentration and dilution during and after pregnancy: Evidence that lateral recumbency inhibits maximal urinary concentrating ability. Br J Obstet Gynaecol 88:472–479, 1981.

44. Davison JM, Gilmore EA, Durr J, et al: Altered osmotic thresholds for vasopressin secretion and thirst in pregnancy. Am J Physiol 246:F105–F109, 1984.

45. Lindheimer MD, Barron WM, Davison JM: Osmoregulation of thirst and vasopressin release in pregnancy. Am J Physiol 257:F159–F169, 1989.

46. Davison JM, Shiells EA, Philips PR, Lindheimer MD: Serial evaluation of vasopressin release and thirst in human pregnancy: Role of chorionic gonadotropin in the osmoregulatory changes of gestation. J Clin Invest 81:798–806, 1988.

47. Davison JM, Shiells EA, Barron WM, et al: Changes in the metabolic clearance of vasopressin and of plasma vasopressinase throughout human pregnancy. J Clin Invest 83:1313–1318, 1989.

48. Landon MJ, Cspas DK, Shiells EA, Davison JM: Degradation of radiolabeled arginine vasopressin ($^{125}$I-AVP) by the human placenta perfused in vitro. Br J Obstet Gynaecol 95:488–492, 1988.

49. Durr JA: Diabetes insipidus in pregnancy. Am J Kidney Dis 9:276–283, 1987.

50. William DJ, Metcalfe KA, Skingle L, et al: Pathophysiology of transient cranial diabetes insipidus during pregnancy. Clin Endocrinol 38:595–600, 1993.

51. Soule SG, Monson JP, Jacobs HS: Transient diabetes insipidus in pregnancy—a consequence of enhanced placental clearance of arginine vasopressin. Hum Reprod 10:3322–3324, 1995.

52. Kallen BAJ, Carlsson SS, Bengtsson BKA: Diabetes insipidus and use of desmopressin (Minirin) during pregnancy. Eur J Endocrinol 132:144–146, 1995.

53. Ray JG: DDAVP use during pregnancy: An analysis of its safety for mother and child. Obstet Gynecol Surv 53:450-455, 1998.

54. Iwasaki Y, Oiso Y, Kondo K, et al: Aggravation of subclinical diabetes insipidus during pregnancy. N Engl J Med 324:522–526, 1991.

55. Kennedy S, Hall PM, Seymour AE, Hague WM: Transient diabetes insipidus and acute fatty liver of pregnancy. Br J Obstet Gynaecol 101:387–391, 1994.

56. Hamai Y, Fujii T, Nishina H, et al: Differential clinical course of pregnancies complicated by diabetes insipidus which does, or does not, pre-date the pregnancy. Hum Reprod 12:1816–1818, 1997.

57. Glinoer D: The regulation of thyroid function in pregnancy: Pathways of endocrine adaptation from physiology to pathology. Endocr Rev 18:404–433, 1997.

58. Berghout A, Wiersinga W: Thyroid size and thyroid function during pregnancy: An analysis. Eur J Endocrinol 138:536–542, 1998.

59. Glinoer D, Soto MF, Bourdoux P, et al: Pregnancy in patients with mild thyroid abnormalities: Maternal and neonatal repercussions. J Clin Endocrinol Metab 73:421–427, 1991.

60. Long TJ, Felice ME, Hollingsworth DR: Goiter in pregnant teenagers. Am J Obstet Gynecol 152:670–674, 1985.

61. Halnan KE: The radioiodine uptake of the human thyroid in pregnancy. Clin Sci 17:281–290, 1958.

62. Brent RL: The effect of embryonic and fetal exposure to x-ray, microwaves, ultrasound, magnetic resonance, and isotopes. In Barron WM, Lindheimer MD (eds): Medical Disorders of Pregnancy. St. Louis, Mosby, 1991, pp 568–604.

63. Vulsma T, Gons MH, de Vijlder JJM: Maternal-fetal transfer of thyroxine in congenital hypothyroidism due to a total organification defect or thyroid agenesis. N Engl J Med 321:13–16, 1989.

64. Harada K, Hershman JM, Reed AW, et al: Comparison of thyroid stimulators and thyroid hormone concentrations in the sera of pregnant women. J Clin Endocrinol Metab 48:793–797, 1979.

65. Yoshikawa N, Nishikawa M, Horimoto M, et al: Thyroid-stimulating activity in sera of normal pregnant women. J Clin Endocrinol Metab 69:891–895, 1989.

66. Kimura M, Amino N, Tamaki H, et al: Physiologic thyroid activation in normal early pregnancy is induced by circulating hCG. Obstet Gynecol 75:775–778, 1992.

67. Higgins HP, Hershman JM, Kenimer JG, et al: The thyrotoxicosis of hydatidiform mole. Ann Intern Med 83:307–311, 1975.

68. Rajatanavin R, Chailurkit LO, Srisupandit S, et al: Trophoblastic hyperthyroidism: Clinical and biochemical features of five cases. Am J Med 85:237–241, 1988.

69. Burrow GN: Thyroid diseases. In Burrow GN, Ferris TF (eds): Medical Complications during Pregnancy, 3d ed. Philadelphia, WB Saunders, 1988, pp 224–253.

70. Glinoer D, Gershengorn MC, Dubois A, Robbins J: Stimulation of thyroxine-binding globulin synthesis by isolated rhesus monkey hepatocytes after in vivo β-estradiol administration. Endocrinology 100:807–813, 1977.

71. Ain KB, Mori Y, Refetoff S: Reduced clearance rate of thyroxine-binding globulin (TBG) with increased sialylation: A mechanism for estrogen-induced elevation of serum TBG concentration. J Clin Endocrinol Metab 65:686–696, 1987.

72. Osathanondh R, Tulchinsky D, Chopra IJ: Total and free thyroxine and triiodothyronine in normal and complicated pregnancy. J Clin Endocrinol Metab 42:98–104, 1976.

73. Dowling JT, Appleton WG, Nicoloff JT: Thyroxine turnover during human pregnancy. J Clin Endocrinol 27:1749–1750, 1967.

74. Mandel SJ, Larsen PR, Seely EW, Brent GA: Increased need for thyroxine during pregnancy in women with primary hypothyroidism. N Engl J Med 323:91–96, 1990.

75. Mestman JH: Hyperthyroidism in pregnancy. Clin Obstet Gynecol 40:45–64, 1997.

76. Glinoer D: Management of hypo- or hyperthyroidism during pregnancy. Growth Horm IGF Res 13:S45–S54, 2003.

77. Laurberg P, Nygaard B, Glinoer D, et al: Guidelines for TSH-receptor antibody measurements in pregnancy: Results of an evidence-based symposium organized by the European Thyroid Association. Eur J Endocrinol 139:584–586, 1998.

78. Peleg D, Cada S, Peleg A, Ben-Ami M: The relationship between maternal serum thyroid-stimulating immunoglobulin and fetal and neonatal thyrotoxicosis. Obstet Gynecol 99:1040–1043, 2002.

79. Smith C, Thomsett M, Choong C, et al: Congenital thyrotoxicosis in premature infants. Clin Endocrinol 54:371–376, 2001.

80. Cohen O, Pinhas-Hamiel O, Sivan E, et al: Serial in utero ultrasonographic measurements of the fetal thyroid: A new complementary tool in the management of maternal hyperthyroidism in pregnancy. Prenat Diagn 23:740–742, 2003.

81. Singh PK, Parvin CA, Gronowski AM: Establishment of reference intervals for markers of fetal thyroid status in amniotic fluid. J Clin Endocrinol Metab 88:4175–4179, 2003.

82. Nachum Z, Rakover Y, Weiner E, Shalev E: Graves' disease in pregnancy: Prospective evaluation of a selective invasive treatment protocol. Am J Obstet Gynecol 189:159–165, 2003.

83. Lao TT, Chin RKH, Chang AMZ: The outcome of hyperemetic pregnancies complicated by transient hyperthyroidism. Aust N Z J Obstet Gynaecol 27:99–101, 1987.

84. Swaminathan R, Chin RK, Lao TTH, et al: Thyroid function in hyperemesis gravidarum. Acta Endocrinol 120:155–160, 1989.

85. Goodwin TM, Montoro M, Mestman J: Transient hyperthyroidism and hyperemesis gravidarum: Clinical aspects. Am J Obstet Gynecol 167:648–652, 1992.

86. Kimura M, Amino N, Tamaki H, et al: Gestational thyrotoxicosis and hyperemesis gravidarum: Possible role of hCG with higher stimulating activity. Clin Endocrinol 38:345–350, 1993.

87. Goodwin TM, Montoro M, Mestman JH, et al: The role of chorionic gonadotropin in transient hyperthyroidism of hyperemesis gravidarum. J Clin Endocrinol Metab 75:1333–1337, 1992.

88. Rodien P, Bremont C, Sanson M-LR, et al: Familial gestational hyperthyroidism caused by a mutant thyrotropin receptor hypersensitive to human chorionic gonadotropin. N Engl J Med 339:1823–1826, 1998.

89. Haddow JE, Palomaki GE, Allan WC, et al: Maternal thyroid deficiency during pregnancy and subsequent neuropsychological development of the child. N Engl J Med 341:549–555, 1999.

90. Pop VJ, Kuijpens JL, van Baar AL, et al: Low maternal free thyroxine concentrations during early pregnancy are associated with impaired psychomotor development in infancy. Clin Endocrinol 50:149–155, 1999.

91. Klein RZ, Mitchell ML: Maternal hypothyroidism and cognitive development of the offspring. Curr Opin Pediatr 14:443–446, 2002.

92. Rosenthal HE, Slaunwhite WR Jr, Sandberg AA: Transcortin: A corticosteroid-binding protein of plasma: X. Cortisol and progesterone interplay and unbound levels of these steroids in pregnancy. J Clin Endocrinol 29:352–367, 1969.

93. Genazzani AR, Fraioli F, Hurlimann J, et al: Immunoreactive ACTH and cortisol plasma levels during pregnancy: Detection and partial purification of corticotrophin-like placental hormone: The human chorionic corticotrophin. Clin Endocrinol 4:1–14, 1975.

94. Carr BR, Parker CR Jr, Madden JD, et al: Maternal plasma adrenocorticotropin and cortisol relationships throughout human pregnancy. Am J Obstet Gynecol 139:416–422, 1981.

95. Demey-Ponsart E, Foidart JM, Sulon J, Sodoyez JC: Serum CBG, free and total cortisol and circadian patterns of adrenal function in normal pregnancy. J Steroid Biochem 16:165–169, 1982.

96. DeMoor P, Steeno O, Brosens I, et al: Data on transcortin activity in human plasma as studied by gel filtration. J Clin Endocrinol 26:71–78, 1966.

97. Doe RP, Dickinson P, Zinneman HH, et al: Elevated nonprotein-bound cortisol (NPC) in pregnancy, during estrogen administration and in carcinoma of the prostate. J Clin Endocrinol 29:757–766, 1969.

98. Nolten WE, Lindheimer MD, Rueckert PA, et al: Diurnal patterns and regulation of cortisol secretion in pregnancy. J Clin Endocrinol Metab 51:466–472, 1980.

99. Murphy BE: Clinical evaluation of urinary cortisol determinations by competitive protein-binding radioassay. J Clin Endocrinol 28:343–348, 1968.

100. Burke CW, Roulet F: Increased exposure of tissues to cortisol in late pregnancy. Br Med J 1:657–659, 1970.

101. Cohen M, Stiefel M, Reddy WJ, et al: The secretion and disposition of cortisol during pregnancy. J Clin Endocrinol 18:1076–1092, 1958.

102. Migeon CJ, Kenny FM, Taylor FH: Cortisol production rate: VIII. Pregnancy. J Clin Endocrinol Metab 28:661–666, 1968.

103. Beitins IZ, Bayard F, Anges IG, et al: The metabolic clearance rate, blood production, interconversion and transplacental passage of cortisol and cortisone in pregnancy near term. Pediatr Res 7:509–519, 1973.

104. Stewart PM, Rogerson FM, Mason JI: Type 2 11beta-hydroxysteroid dehydrogenase messenger ribonucleic acid and activity in human placenta and fetal membranes: Its relationship to birth weight and putative role in fetal adrenal steroidogenesis. J Clin Endocrinol Metab 80:885–890, 1995.

105. Hadden DR: Adrenal disorders of pregnancy. Endocrinol Metab Clin North Am 24:139–151, 1995.

106. Rees LH, Burke CW, Chard T, et al: Possible placental origin of ACTH in normal human pregnancy. Nature 254:620–622, 1975.

107. Genazzani AR, Felber JP, Fioretti P: Immunoreactive ACTH, immunoreactive human chorionic somatomammotrophin (HCS) and 11-OH steroids plasma levels in normal and pathological pregnancies. Acta Endocrinol 83:800–810, 1977.

108. Allen JP, Cook DM, Kendall JW, et al: Maternal-fetal ACTH relationship in man. J Clin Endocrinol Metab 37:230–234, 1973.

109. Petraglia F, Sutton S, Vale W: Neurotransmitters and peptides modulate the release of immunoreactive corticotropin-releasing factor from cultured human placental cells. Am J Obstet Gynecol 160:247–251, 1989.

110. Magiakou MA, Mastorakos G, Rabin D, et al: The maternal hypothalamic-pituitary-adrenal axis in the third trimester of human pregnancy. Clin Endocrinol 44:419–428, 1996.

111. Shibisaki T, Odagiri E, Shizume K, Ling N: Corticotropin-releasing factor–like activity in human placental extracts. J Clin Endocrinol Metab 55:384–386, 1982.

112. Sasaki A, Liotta AS, Luckey MM, et al: Immunoreactive corticotropin-releasing factor is present in human maternal plasma during the third trimester of pregnancy. J Clin Endocrinol Metab 59:812–814, 1984.

113. Sasaki A, Shinkawa O, Margioris AN, et al: Immunoreactive corticotropin-releasing hormone in human plasma during pregnancy, labor and delivery. J Clin Endocrinol Metab 64:224–229, 1987.

114. Campbell EA, Linton EA, Wolfe CDA, et al: Plasma corticotropin-releasing hormone concentrations during pregnancy and parturition. J Clin Endocrinol Metab 65:1054–1059, 1987.

115. Margioris A, Grino M, Protos P, et al: Corticotropin-releasing hormone and oxytocin stimulate the release of placental proopiomelanocortin peptides. J Clin Endocrinol Metab 66:922–926, 1988.

116. Sasaki A, Shinkawa O, Yoshinaga K: Placental corticotropin-releasing hormone may be a stimulator of maternal pituitary adrenocorticotropic hormone secretion in humans. J Clin Invest 84:1997–2001, 1989.

117. Okamoto E, Takai T, Makino T, et al: Immunoreactive corticotropin-releasing hormone, adrenocorticotropin and cortisol in human plasma during pregnancy and delivery and postpartum. Horm Metab Res 21:566–572, 1989.

118. Mastorakos G, Ilias I: Maternal and fetal hypothalamic-pituitary-adrenal axes during pregnancy and postpartum. Ann N Y Acad Sci 997:136–149, 2003.

119. Robinson BG, Emanuel RL, Frim DM, Majzoub JA: Glucocorticosteroid stimulates expression of corticotropin-releasing hormone gene in human placenta. Proc Natl Acad Sci U S A 85:5244–5248, 1988.

120. Jones SA, Brooks AN, Challis JRG: Steroids modulate corticotropin-releasing hormone production in human fetal membranes and placenta. J Clin Endocrinol 68:825–830, 1989.

121. Goland RS, Wardlaw SL, Blum M, et al: Biologically active corticotropin-releasing hormone in maternal and fetal plasma during pregnancy. Am J Obstet Gynecol 159:884–890, 1988.

122. Nolten WE, Lindheimer MD, Oparil S, Ehrlich EN: Desoxycorticosterone in normal pregnancy: I. Sequential studies of the secretory patterns of desoxycorticosterone, aldosterone, and cortisol. Am J Obstet Gynecol 132:414–420, 1978.

123. Aron DC, Schnall AM, Sheeler LR: Cushing's syndrome and pregnancy. Am J Obstet Gynecol 162:244–252, 1990.

124. Buescher MA, McClamrock HD, Adashi EY: Cushing syndrome in pregnancy. Obstet Gynecol 79:130–137, 1992.

125. Casson IF, Davis JC, Jeffreys RV, et al: Successful management of Cushing's disease during pregnancy by transsphenoidal adenectomy. Clin Endocrinol 27:423–428, 1987.

126. Semple CG, McEwan H, Teasdale GM, et al: Recurrence of Cushing's disease in pregnancy: Case report. Br J Obstet Gynaecol 92:295–298, 1985.

127. Bevan JS, Gough MH, Gillmer MDG, et al: Cushing's syndrome in pregnancy: The timing of definitive treatment. Clin Endocrinol 27:225–233, 1987.

128. Ross RJ, Chew SL, Perry L, et al: Diagnosis and selective cure of Cushing's disease during pregnancy by transsphenoidal surgery. Eur J Endocrinol 132:722–766, 1995.

129. Chico A, Manzanares JM, Halperin I, et al: Cushing's disease and pregnancy. Eur J Obstet Gynecol Reprod Biol 64:143–146, 1996.

130. Guilhaume B, Sanson ML, Billaud L, et al: Cushing's syndrome and pregnancy: Aetiologies and prognosis in 22 patients. Eur J Med 1:38–39, 1992.

131. Pricolo VE, Monchik JM, Prinz RA, et al: Management of Cushing's syndrome secondary to adrenal adenoma during pregnancy. Surgery 108:1072–1078, 1990.

132. Cousins L, Rigg L, Hollingsworth D, et al: Qualitative and quantitative assessment of the circadian rhythm of cortisol in pregnancy. Am J Obstet Gynecol 145:411–416, 1983.

133. Quartero HWP, Fry CH: Placental corticotrophin releasing factor may modulate human parturition. Placenta 10:439–443, 1989.

134. Schulte HM, Weisner D, Allolio B: The corticotrophin releasing hormone test in late pregnancy: Lack of adrenocorticotrophin and cortisol response. Clin Endocrinol 33:99-106, 1990.

135. Pinette MG, Pan YQ, Oppenheim D, et al: Bilateral inferior petrosal sinus corticotropin sampling with corticotropin-releasing hormone stimulation in a pregnant patient with Cushing's syndrome. Am J Obstet Gynecol 171:563–564, 1994.

136. Suzuki Y, Sasagawa SH, Izumi T, et al: The role of ultrasonography in the detection of adrenal masses: Comparison with computed tomography and magnetic resonance imaging. Int Urol Nephrol 32:303–306, 2001.

137. Ambrosi B, Barbetta L, Morricone L: Diagnosis and management of Addison's disease during pregnancy. J Endocrinol Invest 26:698–702, 2003.

138. Mayo J, Collazos J, Martinez E, Ibarra S: Adrenal function in the human immunodeficiency virus-infected patient. Arch Intern Med 162:1095–1098, 2002.

139. Xarli VP, Steele AA, Davis PJ, et al: Adrenal hemorrhage in the adult. Medicine 57:211–221, 1978.

140. Aronson IK, Halaska B: Dermatologic diseases. In Barron WM, Lindheimer MD (eds): Medical Disorders of Pregnancy. St. Louis, Mosby, 1991, pp 534–550.

141. O'Shaughnessy RW, Hackett KJ: Maternal Addison's disease and fetal growth retardation. J Reprod Med 29:752–756, 1984.

142. Drucker D, Shumak S, Angel A: Schmidt's syndrome presenting with intrauterine growth retardation and postpartum addisonian crisis. Am J Obstet Gynecol 149:229–230, 1984.

143. Beck P, Eaton CJ, Young IS, Kupperman HS: Metyrapone response in pregnancy. Am J Obstet Gynecol 100:327–330, 1968.

144. Wilson M, Morganti AA, Zervoudakis I, et al: Blood pressure, the renin-aldosterone system and sex steroids throughout normal pregnancy. Am J Med 68:97–104, 1980.

145. Weir RJ, Brown JJ, Fraser R, et al: Relationship between plasma renin, renin-substrate, angiotensin II, aldosterone and electrolytes in normal pregnancy. J Clin Endocrinol Metab 40:108–115, 1975.

146. Smeaton TC, Andersen GJ, Fulton IS: Study of aldosterone levels in plasma during pregnancy. J Clin Endocrinol Metab 44:1–7, 1977.

147. Bay WH, Ferris TF: Factors controlling plasma renin and aldosterone during pregnancy. Hypertension 1:410–415, 1979.

148. Brown MA, Sinosich MJ, Saunders DM, Gallery EDM: Potassium regulation and progesterone-aldosterone interrelationships in human pregnancy: A prospective study. Am J Obstet Gynecol 155:349–353, 1986.

149. Elsheikh A, Creatsas G, Mastorakos G, et al: The renin-aldosterone system during normal and hypertensive pregnancy. Arch Gynecol Obstet 264:182–185, 2001.

150. Gant NF, Daley GL, Chand S, et al: A study of angiotensin II pressor response throughout primigravid pregnancy. J Clin Invest 52:2682–2689, 1973.

151. Lindheimer MD, Katz AI: The kidney and hypertension in pregnancy. In Brenner BM, Rector FC Jr (eds): The Kidney, 4th ed. Philadelphia, WB Saunders, 1991, pp 1551–1595.

152. Ehrlich EN, Lindheimer MD: Effects of administered mineralocorticoids on ACTH in pregnant women: Attenuation of kaliuretic influence of mineralocorticoids during pregnancy. J Clin Invest 51:1301–1309, 1972.

153. Quinkler M, Meyer B, Oelkers W, Diederich S: Renal inactivation, mineralocorticoid generation, and 11β-hydroxysteroid dehydrogenase inhibition ameliorate the antimineralocorticoid effect of progesterone in vivo. J Clin Endocrinol Metab 88:3767–3772, 2003.

154. Webb JC, Bayliss P: Pregnancy complicated by primary hyperaldosteronism. South Med J 90:243–245, 1997.

155. Robar CA, Poremba JA, Pelton JJ, et al: Current diagnosis and management of aldosterone-producing adenomas during pregnancy. Endocrinologist 8:403–408, 1998.

156. Okawa T, Asano K, Hashimoto T, et al: Diagnosis and management of primary aldosteronism in pregnancy: Case report and review of the literature. Am J Perinatol 19:31–36, 2002.

157. Tremblay RR: Treatment of hirsutism with spironolactone. J Clin Endocrinol Metab 15:363–371, 1986.

158. Wyckoff JA, Seely EW, Hurwitz S, et al: Glucocorticosteroid-remediable aldosteronism and pregnancy. Hypertension 35:668–672, 2000.

159. Geller DS, Farhi A, Pinkerton N, et al: Activating mineralocorticoid receptor mutation in hypertension exacerbated by pregnancy. Science 289:119–123, 2000.

160. Harper MA, Murnaghan GA, Kennedy L, et al: Phaeochromocytoma in pregnancy: Five cases and a review of the literature. Br J Obstet Gynaecol 96:594–606, 1989.

161. Botchan A, Hauser R, Kupfermine M, et al: Pheochromocytoma in pregnancy: Case report and review of the literature. Obstet Gynecol Surv 50:321–327, 1995.

162. Ahlawat SK, Jain S, Kumari S, et al: Pheochromocytoma associated with pregnancy: Case report and review of the literature. Obstet Gynecol Surv 54:728–737, 1999.

163. Thiery M, Derom RMJ, van Kets HE, et al: Pheochromocytoma in pregnancy. Am J Obstet Gynecol 97:21–29, 1967.

164. Griffith MI, Felts JH, James FM, et al: Successful control of pheochromocytoma in pregnancy. JAMA 229:437–439, 1974.

165. Cross DA, Meyer JS: Postoperative deaths due to unsuspected pheochromocytoma. South Med J 70:1320–1323, 1977.

166. Levin N, McTighe A, Abdel-Aziz MIE: Extra-adrenal pheochromocytoma in pregnancy. Md State Med J 32:377–379, 1983.

167. Ellison GT, Mansberger JA, Mansberger AR Jr: Malignant recurrent pheochromocytoma during pregnancy: Case report and review of the literature. Surgery 103:484–489, 1988.

168. Tewari KS, Steiger RM, Lam ML, et al: Bilateral pheochromocytoma in pregnancy heralding multiple endocrine neoplasia syndrome IIA: A case report. J Reprod Med 46:385–388, 2001.

169. Kothari A Bethune M, Manwaring J, et al: Massive bilateral phaeochromocytomas in association with Von Hippel Lindau syndrome in pregnancy. Aust N Z J Obstet Gynaecol 39:381–384, 1999.

170. Bryant J, Farmer J, Kessler LJ, et al: Pheochromocytoma: The expanding genetic differential diagnosis. J Natl Cancer Inst 95:1196–1204, 2003.

171. Zuspan FP: Urinary excretion of epinephrine and norepinephrine during pregnancy. J Clin Endocrinol 30:357–360, 1970.

172. Tunbridge RDG, Donnai P: Plasma noradrenaline in normal pregnancy and in hypertension of late pregnancy. Br J Obstet Gynaecol 88:105–108, 1981.

173. Zuspan FP: Adrenal gland and sympathetic nervous system response in eclampsia. Am J Obstet Gynecol 114:304–311, 1972.

174. Khatun S, Kanayama N, Hossain B, et al: Increased concentrations of plasma epinephrine and norepinephrine in patients with eclampsia. Eur J Obstet Gynecol 74:103–109, 1997.

175. Greenberg M, Moawad AH, Wieties BM, et al: Extraadrenal pheochromocytoma: Detection during pregnancy using MR imaging. Radiology 161:475–476, 1986.

176. Kohlmeier L, Marcus R: Calcium disorders of pregnancy. Endocrinol Metab Clin North Am 24:15–39, 1995.

177. Hosking DJ: Calcium homeostasis in pregnancy. Clin Endocrinol 45:1-6, 1996.

178. Kovacs CS, Kronenberg HM: Maternal-fetal calcium and bone metabolism during pregnancy, puerperium, and lactation. Endocr Rev 18:832–872, 1997.

179. Howarth AT, Morgan DB, Payne RB: Urinary excretion of calcium in late pregnancy and its relation to creatinine clearance. Am J Obstet Gynecol 129:499–502, 1977.

180. Gertner JM, Couston DR, Kliger AS, et al: Pregnancy as state of physiologic absorptive hypercalciuria. Am J Med 81:451–456, 1986.

181. Maikranz P, Holley JL, Parks JH, et al: Gestational hypercalciuria causes pathological urine calcium oxalate supersaturation. Kidney Int 36:108–113, 1989.

182. Pitkin RM, Reynolds WA, Williams GA, et al: Calcium metabolism in normal pregnancy: A longitudinal study. Am J Obstet Gynecol 133:781–787, 1979.

183. Rasmussen N, Rolich A, Hornnes PJ, Hegedus L: Serum ionized calcium and intact parathyroid hormone levels during pregnancy and postpartum. Br J Obstet Gynaecol 97:857–862, 1990.

184. Whitehead M, Lane G, Young O, et al: Interrelations of calcium-regulating hormones during normal pregnancy. Br Med J 283:10–12, 1981.

185. Seely EW, Brown EM, DeMaggio DM, et al: A prospective study of calciotropic hormones in pregnancy and post partum: Reciprocal changes in serum intact parathyroid hormone and 1,25-dihydroxyvitamin D. Am J Obstet Gynecol 176:214–217, 1997.

186. Davis OK, Hawkins DS, Rubin LP, et al: Serum parathyroid hormone (PTH) in pregnant women determined by an immunoradiometric assay for intact PTH. J Clin Endocrinol Metab 67:850–852, 1988.

187. Bouillon R, van Assche FA, van Baelen H, et al: Influence of the vitamin D–binding protein on the serum concentration of 1,25-dihydroxyvitamin $D_3$: Significance of the free 1,25-dihydroxyvitamin $D_3$ concentration. J Clin Invest 67:589–596, 1981.

188. Gray TK, Lowe W, Lester GE: Vitamin D and pregnancy: The maternal-fetal metabolism of vitamin D. Endocr Rev 2:264–274, 1981.

189. Reddy GS, Norman AW, Willis DM, et al: Regulation of vitamin D metabolism in normal human pregnancy. J Clin Endocrinol Metab 56:363–370, 1983.

190. Wilson SG, Retallack RW, Kent JC, et al: Serum free 1,25-dihydroxyvitamin D and the free 1,25-dihydroxyvitamin D index during a longitudinal study of human pregnancy and lactation. Clin Endocrinol 32:613–622, 1990.

191. Weissman Y, Vargas A, Duckett G, et al: Synthesis of 1,25-dihydroxyvitamin D in the nephrectomized pregnant rat. Endocrinology 103:1992–1996, 1978.

192. Breslau NA, Zerwekh JE: Relationship of estrogen and pregnancy to calcium homeostasis in pseudohypoparathyroidism. J Clin Endocrinol Metab 62:45–51, 1986.

193. Zerwekh JE, Breslau NA: Human placental production of 1,25-dihydroxyvitamin $D_3$: Biochemical characterization of production in normal subjects and patients with pseudohypoparathyroidism. J Clin Endocrinol Metab 62:192–196, 1986.

194. Papp AE, Stewart AF: Parathyroid hormone-related protein: A peptide of diverse physiologic functions. Trends Endocrinol Metab 4:181–186, 1993.

195. Lettre L, Grill B, Martin TJ: Hypercalcemia in pregnancy and lactation associated with parathyroidhormone-related peptide. N Engl J Med 328:666–667, 1993.

196. Mather KJ, Chik CL, Corenblum B: Maintenance of serum calcium by parathyroid hormone-related peptide during lactation in a hypoparathyroid patient. J Clin Endocrinol Metab 84:424–427, 1999.

197. Mestman JH: Parathyroid disorders of pregnancy. Semin Perinatol 22:485–496, 1998.

198. Kort KC, Schiller HJ, Numann PJ: Hyperparathyroidism and pregnancy. Am J Surg 177:66–68, 1999.

199. Schnatz PF, Curry SL: Primary hyperparathyroidism in pregnancy: Evidence-based management. Obstet Gynecol Surv 57:365–376, 2002.

# ENDOCRINE TUMOR SYNDROMES

# Multiple Endocrine Neoplasia Type 1

## Rajesh V. Thakker

## INTRODUCTION

Multiple endocrine neoplasia (MEN) is characterized by the occurrence of tumors involving two or more endocrine glands within a single patient.[1–3] The disorder has previously been referred to as multiple endocrine adenopathy[4] or the pluriglandular syndrome.[5] However, glandular hyperplasia and malignancy may also occur in some patients, and the term *multiple endocrine neoplasia* is now preferred.[6,7] Two major forms of MEN are recognized and referred to as type 1 and type 2, and each form is characterized by the development of tumors within specific endocrine glands (Table 191-1). Thus, combined occurrence of tumors of the parathyroid glands, the pancreatic islet cells, and the anterior pituitary is characteristic of MEN1, which is also referred to as *Wermer's syndrome*.[8] In addition to these tumors, adrenal cortical tumors, carcinoid, facial angiofibromas, collagenomas, and lipomatous tumors have been described in patients with MEN1.[3,9] However, in MEN2, which is also called *Sipple's syndrome*,[10] medullary thyroid carcinoma (MTC) occurs in association with pheochromocytoma, and three clinical variants referred to as MEN2A, MEN2B, and MTC-only are recognized[11–13] (see Chapter 192). In MEN2A, which is the most common variant, the development of MTC is associated with pheochromocytoma and parathyroid tumors. However, in MEN2B, parathyroid involvement is rare, and the occurrence of MTC and pheochromocytoma is found in association with a marfanoid habitus, mucosal neuromas, medullated corneal fibers, and intestinal autonomic ganglion dysfunction leading to megacolon. In the variant MTC-only, MTC appears to be the sole manifestation of the syndrome. Although MEN1 and MEN2 usually occur as distinct and separate syndromes, in some patients, tumors that are associated with both MEN1 and MEN2 may occasionally develop. For example, patients suffering from islet cell tumors of the pancreas and pheochromocytoma[14–16] or from acromegaly and pheochromocytoma[17,18] have been described, and MEN in these patients may represent an "overlap" syndrome.[13,14] All these forms of MEN either may be inherited as autosomal-dominant syndromes[19,20] or may occur sporadically; that is, without a family history.[1–3] However, this dis-tinction between sporadic and familial cases may sometimes be difficult, because in some sporadic cases, a family history may be absent because the parent with the disease may have died before symptoms developed.

The detailed clinical and biochemical features of each of these individual hormone syndromes, together with their respective treatments, have been reviewed in other chapters. This chapter discusses individual hormone syndromes in the context of MEN1 and reviews the molecular genetic basis of MEN1.

## HISTORICAL ASPECTS

Patients with MEN1 are characterized by the combined occurrence of tumors of the parathyroid glands, pancreatic islet cells, and anterior pituitary gland. The first occurrence of such multiple endocrine tumors was described in a patient with acromegaly whose autopsy revealed the presence of an anterior pituitary tumor and enlarged parathyroid glands.[21] Pancreatic islet cell tumors were subsequently observed in association with parathyroid and pituitary tumors,[22,23] and a familial occurrence was suggested by the finding of these tumors in two sisters.[24] Further case reports revealing the triad of parathyroid, pancreatic islet cell, and anterior pituitary tumors in individual patients led to the recognition of a unifying disorder,[4] and a familial basis was demonstrated by documenting its occurrence in a father and daughter of one family[25,26] and in a father and four daughters of another family.[7] An autosomal-dominant mode of inheritance was proposed[8] and established by further family studies that demonstrated inheritance of the syndrome in five generations with equal frequency in male and female subjects.[27]

It was proposed that these tumors, which occurred in several different endocrine glands, had a common neuroectodermal origin[28,29] within cells that were capable of amine precursor uptake and decarboxylation (APUD). However, the parathyroids, which are involved in most patients with MEN1, were found to have cytochemical characteristics that differed from those of APUD cells.[30] In addition, consideration

| Type (Chromosomal Location) | Tumors | Gene: Most Frequently Mutated Codons |
|---|---|---|
| MEN1 (11q13) | Parathyroids | *MEN 1* |
|  | Pancreatic islets | 83/84, 4-bp del (≈4%) |
|  | Gastrinoma | 119, 3-bp del (≈3%) |
|  | Insulinoma | 209-211, 4-bp del (≈8%) |
|  | Glucagonoma | 418, 3-bp del (≈4%) |
|  | VIPoma | 514-516, del or ins (≈7%) |
|  | Pituitary (anterior) | Intron 4 ss, (≈10%) |
|  | Prolactinoma |  |
|  | Somatotrophinoma |  |
|  | Corticotrophinoma |  |
|  | Nonfunctioning |  |
|  | Associated tumours |  |
|  | Adrenal cortical |  |
|  | Carcinoid |  |
|  | Lipoma |  |
|  | Angiofibromas |  |
|  | Collagenomas |  |
| MEN2 (10 cen-10q11.2) |  |  |
| MEN2A | MTC | *ret* |
|  | Pheochromocytoma | 634, missense, |
|  | Parathyroid | e.g., Cys → Arg (≈85%) |
| MTC only | MTC | *ret* |
|  |  | 618, missense (>50%) |
| MEN2B | MTC | *ret* |
|  | Pheochromocytoma | 918, Met→ Thr |
|  | Associated abnormalities | (>95%) |
|  | Mucosal neuromas |  |
|  | Marfanoid habitus |  |
|  | Medullated corneal nerve fibers |  |
|  | Megacolon |  |

**Table 191-1** Multiple Endocrine Neoplasia Syndromes and Their Characteristic Tumors and Associated Genetic Abnormalities

Autosomal-dominant inheritance of the MEN syndromes has been established.

Cen, centromere; del, deletion; ins, insertion; MTC, medullary thyroid carcinoma; PPoma, pancreatic polypeptide–secreting tumor; VIPoma, vasoactive intestinal polypeptide–secreting tumor.

Adapted from Thakker RV: Multiple endocrine neoplasia—syndromes of the twentieth century. J Clin Endocrinol Metab 83:2617–2620, © 1998. The Endocrine Society.

of the embryologic development of the three major endocrine glands involved in MEN1 revealed that they do not derive from the neuroectoderm. Thus, the parathyroids are thought to not be of neuroectodermal origin but are instead thought to derive from the pharyngeal pouch endoderm, and the origin of pancreatic islet cells from neuroectoderm remains controversial.[31,32] The anterior pituitary, unlike the posterior pituitary, is not of neuroectodermal origin but from Rathke's pouch, which is not derived from the endoderm of the foregut but from the ectoderm anterior to the stomodeal membrane.[33] Thus, a neuroectodermal origin and a role for the APUD system in the etiology of MEN1 tumors appeared unlikely.[30] Studies using the methods of molecular biology[2,34] revealed that the *MEN 1* gene was likely to be a tumor suppressor gene[35-37] located on chromosome 11q13.[38-40] Further posi-

tional cloning[41] studies identified the *MEN 1* gene,[42,43] which is ubiquitously expressed and encodes a protein designated MENIN, which consists of 610 amino acids.[42] MENIN has been shown to be predominantly a nuclear protein that interacts with a number of proteins, which are involved in transcriptional regulation, genome stability, and cell division.[44,45]

## CLINICAL FINDINGS AND TREATMENT

The incidence of MEN1 has been estimated from randomly chosen postmortem studies to be 0.25%[5,46] and to be 1% to 18% among patients with primary hyperparathyroidism,[47-50] 16% to 38% among patients with gastrinomas,[51,52] and less than 3% among patients with pituitary tumors.[53-56] The disorder affects all age groups, with a reported age range of 5 to 81 years, with clinical and biochemical manifestations of the disorder having developed in 80% and more than 98% of patients, respectively, by the fifth decade.[3,9,27,40,57-62] The clinical manifestations of MEN1 are related to the sites of tumors and to their products of secretion. In addition to the triad of parathyroid, pancreatic, and pituitary tumors (Fig. 191-1), which constitute the major components of MEN1, adrenal cortical tumors, carcinoid, facial angiofibromas, collagenomas, and lipomatous tumors have also been described.[2,3,9,62,63] A patient may be considered to have MEN1 if two of the three principal MEN1-related tumors affecting the parathyroids, pancreatic islets, and anterior pituitary have occurred; familial MEN1 refers to a family in which one individual has at least two of the three principal MEN1-related tumors, plus

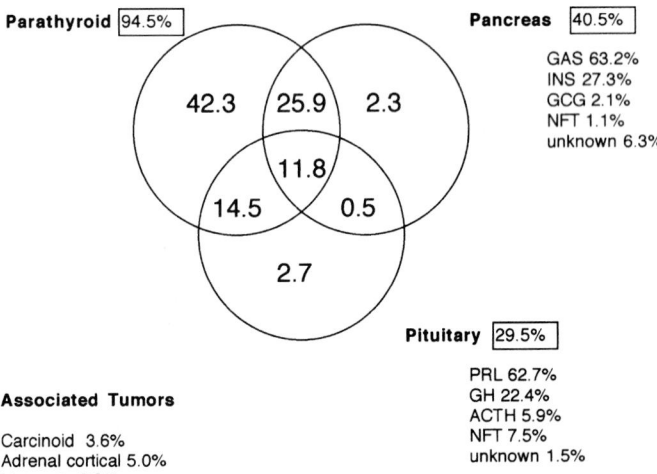

**Parathyroid** 94.5%

**Pancreas** 40.5%
GAS 63.2%
INS 27.3%
GCG 2.1%
NFT 1.1%
unknown 6.3%

42.3  25.9  2.3
11.8
14.5  0.5
2.7

**Pituitary** 29.5%
PRL 62.7%
GH 22.4%
ACTH 5.9%
NFT 7.5%
unknown 1.5%

**Associated Tumors**

Carcinoid 3.6%
Adrenal cortical 5.0%
Lipomata 0.9%
Facial angiofibromas 88.0%
Collagenomas 72%

**Figure 191-1** Schematic representation of the distribution of 384 multiple endocrine neoplasia type 1 (MEN1) tumors in 220 patients with MEN1. The proportions of patients in whom parathyroid, pancreatic, or pituitary tumors occurred are shown in the respective boxes; for example, 94.5% of patients had a parathyroid tumor. The Venn diagram indicates the proportions of patients with each combination of tumors; for example, 37.7% (25.9% + 11.8%) of patients had both a parathyroid and a pancreatic tumor, whereas 2.3% of patients had a pancreatic tumor only. In addition to these tumors observed in one series,[9] multiple facial angiofibromas were observed in 88% of 32 patients and collagenomas in 72% of these patients.[55] The hormones secreted by each of these tumors are indicated: ACTH, adrenocorticotropic hormone; GAS, gastrin; GCG, glucagon; GH, growth hormone; INS, insulin; NFT, nonfunctioning tumor; PRL, prolactin. Parathyroid tumors represent the most common form of MEN1 tumors and occur in approximately 95% of patients, with pancreatic islet cell tumors occurring in about 40% and anterior pituitary tumors occurring in around 30%. (Adapted from Trump D, Farren B, Wooding C, et al: Clinical studies of multiple endocrine neoplasia type 1 (MEN1) in 220 patients. Q J Med 89:653–669, 1996, with permission.)

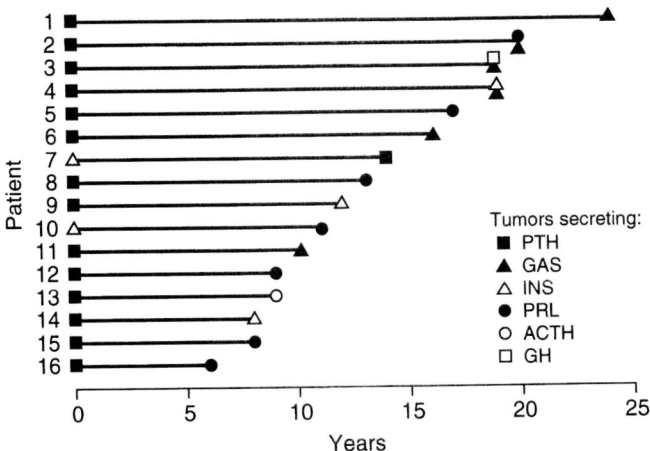

**Figure 191-2** Order of tumor development in 16 patients with multiple endocrine neoplasia type 1 (MEN1). The interval between occurrence of the first tumor (time, 0 years) and subsequent tumors in each patient is shown. Parathyroid tumors were the first manifestation of MEN1 in 14 (88%) of 16 patients, and in the remaining 2 patients, insulinomas represented the first manifestation of MEN1. The interval for occurrence of the subsequent tumors ranged from 6 to 24 years in patients 16 and 1, respectively, and no correlation was found between the interval and tumor types. Abbreviations for the hormones secreted by each tumor are as indicated in Figure 191-1. PTH, parathyroid hormone. (From Trump D, Farren B, Wooding C, et al: Clinical studies of multiple endocrine neoplasia type 1 (MEN1) in 220 patients. Q J Med 89:653–669, 1996, with permission.)

one or more first-degree relatives with at least one of the three principal tumors.[3,62] Parathyroid tumors are the first manifestation of MEN1 in more than 85% of patients (Fig. 191-2), and in the remaining fewer than 15% of patients, the first manifestation may be an insulinoma or a prolactinoma.[3,9,40,60–62] Combinations of these affected glands and their pathologic features (for example, hyperplasia or single or multiple adenomas of the parathyroid glands) have been reported to differ in members of the same family[9,40,59–62] (Fig. 191-3) and even between identical twins.[64,65] MEN1 is inherited as an autosomal-dominant disorder in such families, but a nonfamilial (i.e., sporadic)[3,9] form may have developed in 8% to 14% of patients with MEN1, and molecular genetic studies have confirmed the occurrence of *de novo* mutations of the *MEN 1* gene in approximately 10% of patients with MEN1.[66] In the absence of treatment, these tumors have been observed to be associated with an earlier mortality in patients with MEN1.[67–69]

## PARATHYROID TUMORS

Primary hyperparathyroidism is the most common feature of MEN1 and occurs in approximately 95% of all patients with MEN1.[3,9,40,59–61,70–72] Patients may have asymptomatic hypercalcemia, nephrolithiasis, osteitis fibrosa cystica, vague symptoms associated with hypercalcemia (e.g., polyuria, polydipsia, constipation, or malaise), or occasionally peptic ulcers (see Chapter 193). Biochemical investigations reveal hypercalcemia, usually in association with raised circulating parathyroid hormone (PTH) concentrations. The hypercalcemia is usually mild, and severe hypercalcemia resulting in crisis or parathyroid cancers is a rare occurrence.[58,59] Additional differences in the primary hyperparathyroidism of patients with MEN1, as opposed to those without MEN1, include an earlier age at onset (20 to 25 years vs. 55 years) and an equal male/female ratio (1:1 vs. 1:3). Primary hyperparathyroidism in patients with MEN1 is unusual before the age of 15 years, and the age of conversion from being unaffected to being affected has been observed to be between 20 and 21 years in some individuals.[9]

Surgical removal of the abnormally overactive parathyroids in patients with MEN1 is the definitive treatment, but it is controversial whether to perform subtotal or total parathyroidectomy and whether it should be performed at an early or late stage. Minimally invasive parathyroidectomy is not recommended,[62] as all four parathyroid glands are usually affected with multiple adenomas or hyperplasia,[59,62,73–77] although this histologic distinction may be difficult,[78] and parathyroidectomy for primary hyperparathyroidism in patients with MEN1 has been associated with a high failure rate.[75–77,79,80] Subtotal parathyroidectomy has resulted in persistent or recurrent hypercalcaemia, within 10 to 12 years after surgery, in 40% to 60% of patients, and in hypocalcemia requiring long-term therapy with vitamin D or its active metabolite calcitriol in 10% to 30% of patients with MEN1.[62,76,77,79,80] These rates are markedly higher than those observed for parathyroidectomies in patients who do not have MEN1, in whom recurrent hypercalcemia occurs in 4% to 16% and hypocalcemia in 1% to 8% of patients.[79,81]

To avoid neck reexploration, which is difficult, and to improve the treatment of primary hyperparathyroidism in patients with MEN1, total parathyroidectomy with autotransplantation of parathyroid tissue in the forearm has been performed.[82–85] Both fresh and cryopreserved parathyroid tissue has been used for autotransplantation. The use of cryopreserved parathyroid tissue allows confirmation of hypoparathyroidism in the patient before autotransplantation, but unfortunately, only 50% of parathyroid grafts survive cryopreservation. The use of fresh parathyroid tissue for autotransplantation in the forearm results in viable grafts that secrete PTH. However, the presence of functioning autotransplanted parathyroid tissue leads to recurrent hypercalcemia in more

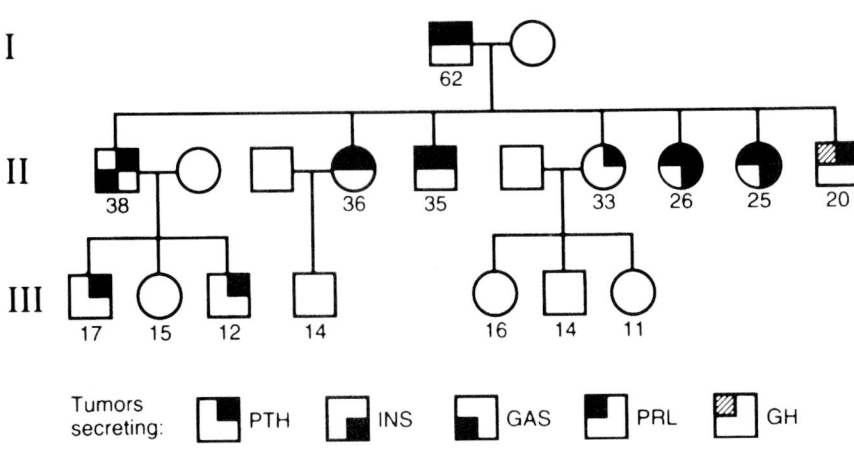

**Figure 191-3** Variable expression of multiple endocrine neoplasia type 1 (MEN1) tumors within a family. In this family, the grandfather (generation I) had parathyroid tumors (PTH) and a prolactinoma (PRL). All of his seven affected children (generation II) had parathyroid tumors, and three daughters and one son also had prolactinomas, whereas another son had a somatotrophinoma secreting growth hormone (GH). In addition, two of his daughters had insulinomas (INS), whereas a son had gastrinomas (GAS). Two grandsons (generation III), who are 17 and 12 years old, have parathyroid tumors, which are the first manifestation of MEN1. Males (*squares*), females (*circles*), unaffected (*open symbol*), and affected (*shaded quadrant*) members are shown. The age in years is indicated below for each individual.

than 50% of patients with MEN1, and surgical removal of transplanted grafts has been required. Thus, management of primary hyperparathyroidism in patients with MEN1 is difficult; parathyroid surgery in these patients is associated with a higher prevalence of persistent or recurrent hypercalcemia. Total parathyroidectomy, which would prevent such recurrence, has therefore been suggested as treatment of primary hyperparathyroidism in MEN1, with the resultant life-long hypocalcemia being treated with oral calcitriol (1,25-dihydroxyvitamin D). However, the management of hypoparathyroidism can be challenging in some patients, even with the use of vitamin D and calcium replacement. One recommendation is that parathyroidectomy be reserved for symptomatic hypercalcemic patients with MEN1 and that asymptomatic hypercalcemic patients with MEN1 not have parathyroid surgery but have regular assessment for the onset of symptoms and complications, at which time total parathyroidectomy, together with a possible transcervical, near-total thymectomy, should be undertaken. The type of surgery (i.e., subtotal or total parathyroidectomy, with or without autotransplantation of parathyroid tissue) and its timing need careful consideration, and factors such as the surgical experience, the availability of facilities for long-term regular serum calcium monitoring, the accessibility of calcitriol (or vitamin D analogues), and the preferences of the patient should be taken into account.

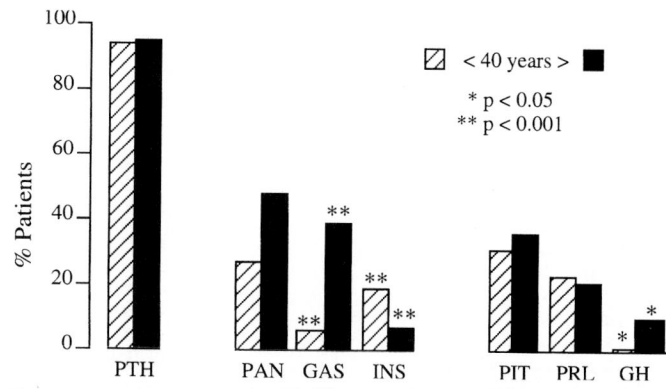

**Figure 191-4** Development of 370 multiple endocrine neoplasia type 1 (MEN1) tumors before (*hatched columns*) and after (*solid columns*) 40 years of age in 220 affected individuals. The proportion of patients with parathyroid tumors (PTH), all pancreatic tumors (PAN), gastrinomas (GAS), insulinomas (INS), all pituitary tumors (PIT), prolactinomas (PRL), and somatotrophinomas secreting growth hormone (GH) is shown for each group. Gastrinomas and somatotrophinomas occurred more often in those older than 40 years, whereas insulinomas occurred more often in those younger than 40 years. (Adapted from Trump D, Farren B, Wooding C, et al: Clinical studies of multiple endocrine neoplasia type 1 (MEN1) in 220 patients. Q J Med 89:653–669, 1996, with permission.)

## PANCREATIC TUMORS

The incidence of pancreatic islet cell tumors (see Chapter 193) in patients with MEN1 varies from 30% to 80% in different series.[9,27,59,73,86] Most of these tumors (see Table 191-1) produce excessive amounts of hormone (for example, gastrin, insulin, glucagon, or vasoactive intestinal polypeptide [VIP]), and are associated with distinct clinical syndromes, although some may remain nonfunctional or nonsecretory (see Fig. 191-1). These pancreatic islet cell tumors have an earlier age at onset in patients with MEN1 than in patients without MEN1.[9]

### Gastrinoma

Zollinger and Ellison[87] initially described two patients in whom non–β islet cell tumors of the pancreas were associated with recurrent peptic ulceration and marked gastric acid production, and gastrin was subsequently extracted from such tumors.[88,89] The association of recurrent peptic ulceration, marked gastric acid production, and non–β islet cell tumors of the pancreas is referred to as the *Zollinger-Ellison syndrome*. Gastrin-secreting tumors (gastrinomas) represent more than 50% of all pancreatic islet cell tumors in patients with MEN1[9,59,60,71] (see Fig. 191-1), and approximately 20% of patients with gastrinomas will have MEN1.[62,90] Gastrinomas, which may also occur in the duodenal mucosa,[91] are the major cause of morbidity and mortality in patients with MEN1, and the prognosis is worse in patients with pancreatic primary tumors, metastases, ectopic Cushing's syndrome, or markedly elevated plasma gastrin concentrations.[92] Most MEN1 gastrinomas are malignant and will have metastasized in patients before a diagnosis is established.[93,94] Gastrinomas occur more often in patients with MEN1 who are older than 40 years[9] (Fig. 191-4), and recurrent severe multiple peptic ulcers, which may perforate, and cachexia are major contributors to the high mortality.[67,68,92] Patients with Zollinger-Ellison syndrome may also suffer from diarrhea and steatorrhea. The diagnosis is established by demonstration of a raised fasting serum gastrin concentration in association with increased basal gastric acid secretion.[95] Occasionally, intravenous provocative tests[96] with either secretin (2 U/kg) or calcium infusion (4 mg $Ca^{2+}$/kg/hr for 3 hours) are required to distinguish patients with Zollinger-Ellison syndrome from other patients with hypergastrinemia, such as those

with antral G-cell hyperplasia. However, in patients with MEN1, Zollinger-Ellison syndrome does not appear to occur in the absence of primary hyperparathyroidism,[60,97] and hypergastrinemia has also been reported to be associated with hypercalcemia.[98] Thus, the diagnosis of Zollinger-Ellison syndrome may be difficult in some patients with MEN1.

Medical treatment of patients with MEN1 and Zollinger-Ellison syndrome is directed toward reducing basal acid output to less than 10 mmol/L, and such reduced acid output may be achieved by parietal cell $H^+$-$K^+$-adenosine triphosphatase (ATPase) inhibitors (e.g., omeprazole or lansoprazole), which have proved efficacious and become the drugs of choice for gastrinomas.[99,100] Some patients may also require additional treatment with the histamine $H_2$ receptor antagonists cimetidine or ranitidine.[100-102] The role of surgery in the treatment of gastrinomas in patients with MEN1 is controversial.[62,94,100,103-106] The ideal treatment for a nonmetastatic gastrinoma situated in the pancreas is surgical excision of the gastrinoma.[103,104] In addition, duodenal gastrinomas, which occur more frequently in patients with MEN1, have been treated successfully with surgery.[91] However, in most patients with MEN1, gastrinomas are frequently multiple or extrapancreatic, and with the exception of duodenal gastrinomas, surgery has often not been successful.[86,106-109] For example, the results of a recent study[106] revealed that only 16% of patients with MEN1 were free of disease immediately after surgery, and at 5 years, this number had decreased to 6%; the respective outcomes in patients without MEN1 were better, at 45% and 40%. Given these findings, the majority of physicians and about 50% of surgeons recommended a nonsurgical management for gastrinomas in MEN1.[62] The use of tumor-localization studies involving ultrasonography, endoscopic ultrasonography, computed tomography (CT), nuclear magnetic resonance imaging (MRI), selective abdominal angiography, venous sampling, or somatostatin-receptor scintigraphy demonstrated that these techniques may sometimes help to improve the surgical success rate.[106,110-115] For example, transhepatic selective venous gastrin sampling in one study demonstrated that patients with MEN1 had either diffuse gastrin secretion from multiple pancreatic sites or localized gastrin secretion from a single region.[110] The combined use of intra-arterial calcium injections with hepatic venous gastrin sampling has also been shown to help determine the location of gastrinomas.[115] The patients in whom gastrin secretion was localized benefited from resection of the gastrinoma by partial pancreatectomy and required no drug therapy postoperatively. Total gastrectomy is rarely undertaken now and would perhaps be considered only for persistently noncompliant patients.[95] Treatment of disseminated gastrinomas is difficult, and chemotherapy with streptozotocin and 5-fluorouracil,[86,116] hormonal therapy with octreotide or lanreotide, which are human somatostatin analogues,[117] hepatic artery embolization,[118] administration of human leukocyte interferon,[86,119] and removal of all resectable tumor[120] have all been successful occasionally.

### Insulinoma

These β islet cell tumors that secrete insulin represent 10% to 30% of all pancreatic tumors (see Fig. 191-1) in patients with MEN1.[3–9,61,73,86] Insulinomas also occur in association with gastrinomas in 10%[9,61,121,122] of patients with MEN1, and the two tumors may arise at different times. Insulinomas occur more often in patients with MEN1 who are younger than 40 years (see Fig. 191-4), and many of them arise in individuals younger than 20 years,[9] whereas in patients without MEN1, insulinomas generally occur in those older than 40 years.[3,9] Insulinomas may be the first manifestation of MEN1 in 10% of patients (see Fig. 191-2), and approximately 4% of patients with insulinomas will have MEN1.[90] Patients with an insulinoma present with hypoglycemic symptoms that develop after a fast or exertion and improve after glucose intake (see Chapters 62 and 193). The most reliable test is a supervised 72-hour fast, and biochemical investigations reveal increased plasma insulin concentrations in association with hypoglycemia.[123] Circulating concentrations of C peptide and proinsulin, which are also increased, are useful in establishing the diagnosis. It also is important to demonstrate an absence of sulfonylureas in the plasma and urine samples obtained during the investigation of the hypoglycemia. Medical treatment, which consists of frequent carbohydrate meals and diazoxide or octreotide, is not always successful, and surgery is the optimal treatment. Most insulinomas are multiple and small, and preoperative localization with endoscopic ultrasonography, CT scanning, or celiac axis angiography, preoperative and perioperative percutaneous transhepatic portal venous sampling, selective intra-arterial stimulation with hepatic venous sampling, and intraoperative direct pancreatic ultrasonography have been undertaken to improve the success rate of surgery.[86,114,124–128] Surgical treatment, which ranges from enucleation of a single tumor to a distal pancreatectomy or partial pancreatectomy, has been curative in many patients.[86,103,124] Chemotherapy consisting of streptozotocin, 5-flurouracil, and doxorubicin or hepatic artery embolization has been used for metastatic disease.[117,118,129]

### Glucagonoma

These α islet cell, glucagon-secreting, pancreatic tumors, occur in fewer than 3% of patients with MEN1[9,69,130–135] (see Fig. 192-1). The characteristic clinical manifestations of a skin rash (necrolytic migratory erythema), weight loss, anemia, and stomatitis may be absent, and the presence of the tumor may have been detected in an asymptomatic patient with MEN1 undergoing pancreatic imaging or detected by glucose intolerance and hyperglucagonemia[9,135] (see Chapter 193). The tail of the pancreas is the most frequent site for glucagonomas, and surgical removal is the treatment of choice. However, treatment may be difficult because approximately 50% to 80% of patients have metastases at the time of diagnosis.[134,135] Medical treatment with somatostatin analogues (e.g., octreotide or lanreotide), or chemotherapy with streptozotocin, and 5-fluorouracil, or dimethyltriazeno-imidazole carboxamide (DITC) has been successful in some patients, and hepatic artery embolization has been used to treat metastatic disease.[136,137]

### VIPoma

Patients with vasoactive intestinal peptide (VIP)omas, which are VIP-secreting pancreatic tumors, develop watery diarrhea, hypokalemia, and achlorhydria (see Chapter 193). This clinical syndrome has been referred to as the *Verner-Morrison syndrome*,[138] the *WDHA syndrome*,[139] or the *VIPoma syndrome*.[140] VIPomas have been reported in only a few patients with MEN1,[60,138,141–143] and the diagnosis is established by excluding laxative and diuretic abuse, by confirming a stool volume in excess of 0.5 to 1.0 L/day during a fast, and by documenting a markedly increased plasma VIP concentration. Surgical management of VIPomas, which are mostly located in the tail of the pancreas, has been curative. However, in patients with unresectable tumor, treatment with somatostatin analogues such as octreotide and lanreotide,[117,143] streptozotocin with 5-fluorouracil,[144] corticosteroids,[145] indomethacin,[146] metoclopramide,[147] and lithium carbonate[148] has proved beneficial, and hepatic artery embolization has been useful for the treatment of metastases.

### PPoma

These tumors, which secrete pancreatic polypeptide (PP), are found in a large number of patients with MEN1.[57,149,150] No pathologic sequelae of excessive PP secretion are apparent, and the clinical significance of PP is unknown, although the use of serum PP measurements has been suggested for the detection of pancreatic tumors in patients with MEN1.[150,151] Many PPomas may have been unrecognized or classified as nonfunctioning tumors[152] (see Fig. 191-1). The management of these nonfunctioning pancreatic islet cell tumors in the asymptomatic patient is controversial.[62] Thus, one recommendation is to undertake surgery irrespective of tumor size once an unequivocal biochemical diagnosis is made, and another recommendation is to undertake surgery if the imaged tumor is 1 cm or larger,[94,96] whereas another recommendation is to undertake surgery only if the tumor is larger than 3 cm or is growing.[105] When considering these recommendations, it is important to consider that occult metastatic disease (i.e., tumors not detected by imaging investigations) is likely to be present in a substantial proportion of these patients at the time of presentation.[104]

### Somatostatinoma

Somatostatin, which inhibits growth hormone secretion, has been demonstrated to be present in the gastrointestinal tract, particularly in the pancreatic islets.[153–155] Pancreatic tumors secreting somatostatin are associated with the somatostatinoma syndrome, which is characterized by hyperglycemia, cholelithiasis, low acid output, steatorrhea, diarrhea, abdominal pain, anemia, and weight loss.[156,157] Although 7% of pancreatic islet cell tumors in MEN1 secrete somatostatin, the somatostatinoma syndrome does not appear to have been reported in any patient with MEN1, a finding that may possibly reflect the inhibitory action of somatostatin on endocrine cell proliferation and secretion.

### GHRHoma

GHRHomas, or tumors that secrete growth hormone-releasing hormone (GHRH), have been reported in some patients with MEN1,[158,159] and it is estimated that approximately 33% of patients with GHRHomas will have other MEN1–related tumors. GHRHomas may be diagnosed by finding elevated serum concentrations of growth hormone and GHRH. More than 50% of GHRHomas occur in the lung, 30% occur in the pancreas, and 10% are found in the small intestine.[159,160]

## PITUITARY TUMORS

The incidence of pituitary tumors in patients with MEN1 varies from 15% to 90% in different series.[9,27,56,59,73] and about two thirds of these are microadenomas (diameter <1 cm). Approximately 60% of MEN1-associated pituitary tumors secrete prolactin (see Fig. 191-1), fewer than 25% secrete growth hormone, 5% secrete adrenocorticotrophic hormone, and the remainder appear to be nonfunctioning, with some secreting glycoprotein subunits.[9,53,71,90,161-166] Prolactinomas may be the first manifestation of MEN1 in fewer than 10% of patients, and somatotrophinomas occur more often in patients older than 40 years[9] (see Fig. 191-4). Fewer than 3% of patients with anterior pituitary tumors will have MEN1.[9,53-55] The clinical manifestations of these tumors in patients with MEN1 are similar to those in patients without MEN1 and depend on the hormone secreted and the size of the pituitary tumor. Thus, patients may have symptoms of hyperprolactinemia (e.g., amenorrhea, infertility, and galactorrhea in women and impotence in men), or have acromegaly, or Cushing's disease. In addition, enlarging pituitary tumors may compress adjacent structures such as the optic chiasm or normal pituitary tissue and cause bitemporal hemianopia or hypopituitarism, respectively. Treatment of pituitary tumors in patients with MEN1 is similar to that in patients without MEN1 and consists of medical therapy or selective hypophysectomy by the transsphenoidal approach if feasible, with radiotherapy being reserved for residual unresectable tumor.

## ASSOCIATED TUMORS

Patients with MEN1 may have tumors involving tissues other than the parathyroids, pancreas, and pituitary. Thus, carcinoid, adrenal cortical tumors, facial angiofibromas, collagenomas, thyroid tumors, and lipomatous tumors (see Fig. 191-1) have been described in association with MEN1.[2,3,9]

### Carcinoid Tumors

Carcinoid tumors, which occur in more than 3% of patients with MEN1 (see Fig. 191-1), may be inherited as an autosomal-dominant trait in association with MEN1.[9,162,167] The carcinoid tumor may be located in the bronchi,[168] the gastrointestinal tract,[168-172] the pancreas,[173] or the thymus.[162,174,175] Bronchial carcinoids in patients with MEN1 occur predominantly in women (male/female ratio, 1:4), whereas thymic carcinoids occur predominantly in men, with cigarette smokers having a higher risk for these tumors.[174,175] The course of thymic carcinoids in MEN1 appears to be particularly aggressive, and CT or MRI is recommended for the early detection of thymic and bronchial carcinoids.[62] Most patients are asymptomatic and do not have the flushing attacks and dyspnea associated with the carcinoid syndrome, which usually develops after the tumor has become malignant and metastasized to the liver.[176] Gastric carcinoids, of which the type II gastric enterochromaffin-like (ECL) cell carcinoids (ECLomas) are associated with MEN1 and the Zollinger-Ellison syndrome, may be detected incidentally at the time of gastric endoscopy for dyspeptic symptoms in MEN1 patients.[176-178] These tumors are usually multiple and smaller than 1.5 cm.[179] Little is known about their malignant potential,[176] but treatment with somatostatin analogues, such as octreotide or lanreotide, has resulted in regression of these ECLomas.[180]

### Adrenocortical Tumors

The incidence of asymptomatic adrenocortical tumors in patients with MEN1 has been reported to be as high as 40%.[27,73,130,181,182] Most of these tumors, which may include cortical adenomas, hyperplasia, multiple adenomas, nodular hyperplasia, or carcinomas, are nonfunctioning.[9,130,181,182] However, functioning adrenocortical tumors in patients with MEN1 have been documented to cause hypercortisolemia and Cushing's syndrome,[9,130,181] as well as primary hyperaldosteronism, as in Conn's syndrome.[183-186]

### Lipomas

Subcutaneous lipomas may occur in more than 33% of patients with MEN1,[27,63,170] and frequently they are multiple.

In addition, visceral pleural or retroperitoneal lipomas may occur in patients with MEN1.

### Facial Angiofibromas and Collagenomas

A study of 32 patients with MEN1 revealed the occurrence of multiple facial angiofibromas in 88% of patients and collagenomas in 72%.[63] MEN1 angiofibromas were clinically and histologically identical to those observed in patients with tuberous sclerosis, with the exception that in patients with MEN1, angiofibromas were also present on the upper lip and vermilion border of the lip, which are areas not involved in tuberous sclerosis. These cutaneous findings, which occur with a higher frequency in patients with MEN1, may provide a useful means for possible presymptomatic diagnosis[63] of MEN1 in the relatives of a patient with MEN1. However, it is important to note that combined occurrence of MEN1 and tuberous sclerosis has been observed.[187]

### Thyroid Tumors

Thyroid tumors consisting of adenomas, colloid goiters, and carcinomas have been reported to occur in more than 25% of patients with MEN1.[27,73] However, the prevalence of thyroid disorders in the general population is high, and it has been suggested that the association of thyroid abnormalities in patients with MEN1 may be incidental and not significant.

## MOLECULAR GENETICS

### MODELS OF TUMOR DEVELOPMENT

The development of tumors may be associated with mutations or inappropriate expression of specific normal cellular genes, which are referred to as *proto-oncogenes*.[2,37,188-190] Two types of oncogenes, *dominant* and *recessive*, have been described. Activation of *dominant* oncogenes leads to transformation of the cells containing them, and examples include the chromosomal translocations associated with the occurrence of chronic myeloid leukemia[191,192] and Burkitt's lymphoma.[193] In these conditions, mutations that lead to activation of the oncogene are dominant at the cellular level, and therefore only one copy of the mutated gene is required for the phenotypic effect. Such dominantly acting oncogenes may be assayed in cell culture by first transferring them into recipient cells and then scoring the numbers of transformed colonies, a technique referred to as the *transfection assay*. However, in some inherited neoplasms, such as retinoblastoma, which may also arise sporadically,[194] tumor development is associated with two recessive mutations that inactivate oncogenes, and these mutations are referred to as *recessive oncogenes*. In the inherited tumors, the first of the two recessive mutations is inherited via the germ cell line and is present in all the cells. This recessive mutation is not expressed until a second mutation, within a somatic cell, causes loss of the normal dominant allele. The mutations causing the inherited and sporadic tumors are similar, but the cell types in which they occur are different. In inherited tumors, the first mutation occurs in the germ cell, whereas in sporadic tumors, both mutations occur in the somatic cell. Thus, the risk of tumor development in an individual who has not inherited the first germ-line mutation is much smaller because both mutational events must coincide in the same somatic cell. In addition, the apparent paradox that the inherited cancer syndromes are due to recessive mutations but dominantly inherited at the level of the family may be explained: in individuals who have inherited the first recessive mutation, loss of the single remaining wild-type allele is almost certain to occur in at least one of the large number of cells in the target tissue. This cell will be detected because it forms a tumor, and almost all individuals who have inherited the germ-line mutation will express the disease, even though they inherited a single copy of the recessive gene.[1,189] This model involving two (or more) mutations in the development of tumors is known as the "two-hit" or Knudson's hypothesis.[195,196] The normal function of these recessive oncogenes appears to be regulation of cell growth and differentiation, and these genes have also been referred to as *anti-oncogenes*, *tumor suppressor genes*, or *gatekeeper genes*.[37,188–190] An important feature that has facilitated investigation of these genetic abnormalities is that loss of the remaining allele (i.e., the "second hit") often involves large-scale loss of chromosomal material.[2,34] This second hit may be detected by comparing DNA sequence polymorphisms in leukocytes and tumor obtained from a patient and observing loss of heterozygosity (LOH) in the tumor (Fig. 191-5).

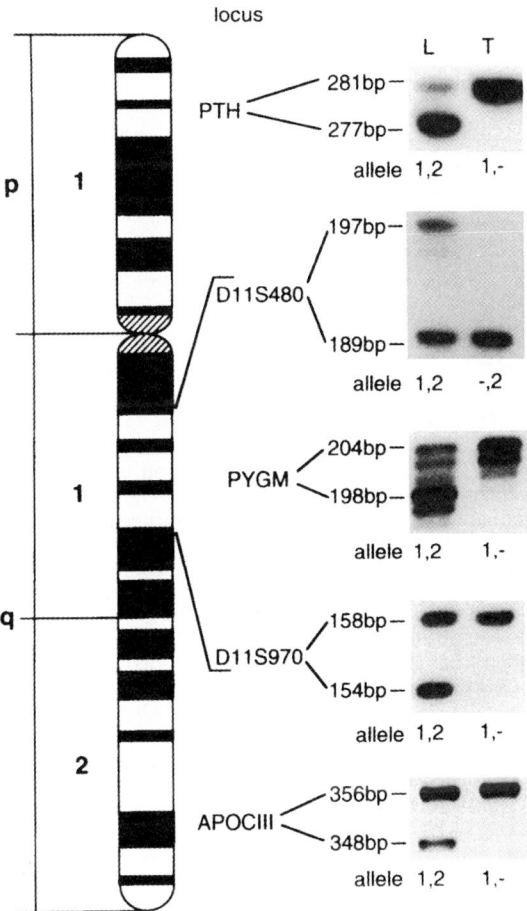

*Figure 191-5* Loss of heterozygosity (LOH) involving polymorphic loci from chromosome 11 in a parathyroid tumor from a patient with familial multiple endocrine neoplasia type 1 (MEN1). The microsatellite polymorphisms obtained from the patient's leukocyte (L) and parathyroid tumor (T) DNA at the *PTH, D11S480, PYGM, D11S970,* and *APOCIII* loci are shown. These microsatellite polymorphisms have been identified with specific primers for each of the loci that have been localized to chromosome 11 and are shown juxtaposed to their regions of origin on the short (p) and long (q) arms of chromosome 11. The microsatellite polymorphisms are assigned alleles (see Fig. 191-6). For example, *D11S480* yielded a 197-bp product (allele 1) and a 189-bp product (allele 2) after polymerase chain reaction amplification of leukocyte DNA, but the tumor cells have lost the 197-bp product (allele 1) and are hemizygous (alleles –, 2). Similar losses of alleles are detected by using the other DNA markers, and an extensive loss of alleles involving the whole of chromosome 11 is observed in the parathyroid tumor of this patient with MEN1. In addition, the complete absence of bands suggest that this abnormality has occurred within all the tumor cells studied and indicates a monoclonal origin for this MEN1 parathyroid tumor. (From Pang JT, Thakker RV: Multiple endocrine neoplasia type 1. Eur J Cancer 30:1961–1968, 1994, with permission.)

## IDENTIFICATION OF THE MEN 1 *GENE AND MUTATIONS*

The gene causing MEN1 was localized to chromosome 11q13 by genetic mapping studies that investigated MEN1-associated tumors for LOH (see Fig. 191-5) and by segregation studies in families with MEN1[38–40,197,198] (Fig. 191-6). The results of these studies, which were consistent with Knudson's model for tumor development,[195,196] indicated that the *MEN 1* gene represented a putative tumor-suppressor gene.[38–40] Further genetic mapping studies defined a less than 300-kb region as the minimal critical segment that contained the *MEN 1* gene, and characterization of genes from this region led to identification in 1997 of the *MEN 1* gene,[42,43,199,200] which consists of 10 exons with a 1830-bp coding region (Fig. 191-7) that encodes a novel 610-amino acid protein referred to as MENIN.[42] The minimal promoter region is located within a few 100 bp upstream of exon 2, and a region further upstream, which contains a series of cis-regulatory sequences, modulates the activity of this minimal promoter, whose expression also depends on the cell type.[201,202] The minimal promoter region does not appear to contain any specific functioning transcription factor sites (e.g., a TATA box). However, binding sites for the SP1 transcriptional factor and nuclear factor (NF) 1 are located in both promoter regions, together with a recognition site for nuclear factor-κB (NF-κB).[201,202] Overexpression of MENIN in an inducible cell-culture system decreased *MEN 1* promoter activity, whereas downregulation of *MEN 1* expression by RNA interference resulted in a compensatory activation of promoter activity.[201] Thus, expression of the *MEN 1* gene is regulated by a feedback mechanism that involves its own protein product, MENIN.[201,202]

Mutations of the *MEN 1* gene (see Fig. 191-7; Fig. 191-8) have been identified, and the total number of germ-line mutations of the *MEN 1* gene that have been detected[42,43,66,176,203–254] in patients with MEN1 is more than 650 (see Fig. 191-7). Approximately 22% are nonsense mutations, around 45% are frameshift deletions or insertions, 8% are in-frame deletions or insertions, 7% are splice-site mutations, and approximately 18% are missense mutations (Fig. 191-9).[224] More than 10% of the *MEN 1* mutations arise *de novo* and may be transmitted to subsequent generations.[66,200,219] It also is important to note that between 5% and 10% of patients with MEN1 may not harbor mutations in the coding region of the *MEN 1* gene,[42,43,66,203,215,221,224,225] and that these individuals may have whole gene deletions[255] or mutations in the promoter or untranslated regions, which remain to be investigated. One study showed that approximately 33% of patients who do not have mutations within the coding region have large deletions involving complete exons.[256] Such abnormalities will not be easily detected by DNA sequence analysis.

Most (75%) of the *MEN 1* mutations are inactivating[224] and are consistent with those expected in a tumor-suppressor gene.[189] The mutations not only are diverse in their types but are also scattered (see Fig. 191-7) throughout the 1830-bp coding region of the *MEN 1* gene with no evidence for clustering as observed in MEN2[12] (see Table 191-1). However, some of the mutations have been observed to occur several times in unrelated families (see Fig. 191-7 and Table 191-2). Mutations at nine sites in the *MEN 1* gene may account for 18.2% to 36.6% of all the germ-line mutations (see Table 191-2). Of these nine types of mutations, five are deletional and insertional mutations involving codons 83 and 84 (nt359 del 4), 119 (Lys[K]119 del), 209 to 211 (nt 738 del 4) (Fig. 191-10), 418 (Asp [D] 418 del), and codons 514 to 516 (nt 1656-7 del or ins C); one is a novel acceptor splice site in intron 4, and three are nonsense mutations (Arg96Stop, Arg460Stop, and Arg527Stop).[225] These mutations at these nine different sites could be considered to represent potential "hot" spots (see Tables 191-1 and 191-2). Such deletional and insertional hot spots may be associated with DNA sequence repeats, which may consist of long tracts of either single nucleotides or shorter elements ranging from dinucleotides to octanucleotides.[66] The DNA sequences in the

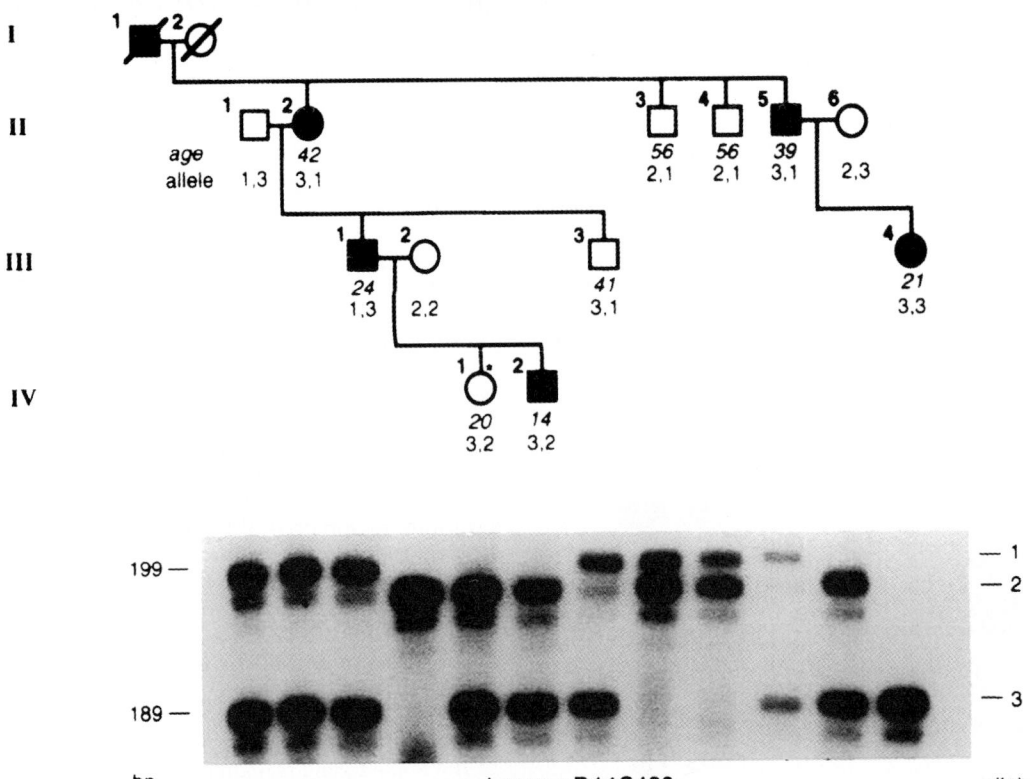

**Figure 191-6** Segregation of *D11S480,* a polymorphic locus from chromosome 11q13 (see Fig. 191-5), and multiple endocrine neoplasia type 1 (MEN1) in a family. Genomic DNA from the family members (**upper panel**) was used with $\gamma$ [$^{32}$P]-adenosine triphosphate (ATP) for polymerase chain reaction (PCR) amplification of the polymorphic repetitive element (CA)$_n$ at this locus.[2,34] The PCR amplification products were separated on a polyacrylamide gel and detected by autoradiography (**lower panel**); the products ranged in size from 189 to 199 bp. Alleles were designated for each PCR product and are indicated on the right. For example, individuals II.1, II.2, and III.1 have two pairs of bands on autoradiography. The upper pair of bands is designated allele 1 and the lower pair of bands is designated allele 3; these three individuals are therefore heterozygous (alleles 1, 3). A pair of bands for each allele is frequently observed in the PCR detection of microsatellite repeats. The upper band in the pair is the "true" allele, and the lower band in the pair is its associated "shadow," which results from slipped-strand mispairing during PCR. Segregation of these bands and their respective alleles together with the disease can be studied in the family members whose alleles and ages are shown. In some individuals, inheritance of paternal and maternal alleles can be ascertained; the paternal allele is shown on the left. Individuals are represented as unaffected male (*open square*), affected male (*solid square*), unaffected female (*open circle*), and affected female (*solid circle*). Individual II.2 is affected and heterozygous (alleles 3, 1), and examination of her affected child (III.1), grandchild (IV.2), sibling (II.5), and niece (III.4) reveals inheritance of allele 3 with the disease. The unaffected individuals II.3, II.4, and III.3 have not inherited this allele 3. However, the daughter (IV.1) of individual III.1 has inherited allele 3 but remains unaffected at age 20 years; this may be either a representation of age-related penetrance (see Fig. 191-9) or a recombination between the disease and *D11S480* loci. In this family, the disease and *D11S480* loci are cosegregating in eight of the nine children, but in one individual (IV.1), assuming 100% penetrance (see later) in early childhood, recombination is observed. Thus, *MEN 1* and *D11S480* are cosegregating in eight of nine of the meioses and not segregating in one of nine meioses, and the likelihood that the two loci are *linked* at $\theta$ = 0.11, that is, 11% recombination, is $(8/9)^8 \times (1/9)^1$. If the disease and the *D11S480* loci were not linked, the disease would be associated with allele 1 in half (1/2) of the children and with allele 3 in the remaining half (1/2) of the children, and the likelihood that the two loci are *not* linked is $(1/2)^9$. Thus, the odds ratio in favor of linkage between the *MEN 1* and *D11S480* loci at $\theta$ = 0.11 in this family is $(8/9)^8 \times (1/9)^1 \div (1/2)^9 = 22.17{:}1$, and the LOD score (i.e., $\log_{10}$ of the odds ratio favoring linkage) = 1.34 (i.e., $\log_{10}$ 22.17). A LOD score of +3, which indicates a probability in favor of linkage of 1000:1, establishes linkage. LOD scores from individual families also can be summated, and such studies revealed that the peak LOD score between the *MEN 1* and *DS11S480* loci was greater than +3, thereby establishing linkage between the *MEN 1* and *D11S480* loci.[309]

vicinity of codons 83 and 84 in exon 2, and codons 209 to 211 (see Fig. 191-10) in exon 3, contain CT and CA dinucleotide repeats, respectively, flanking the 4-bp deletions; this finding would be consistent with a replication-slippage model in which misalignment of the dinucleotide repeat takes place during replication, followed by excision of the 4-bp single-stranded loop.[66] A similar replication-slippage model may also be involved at codons 118 and 119, each of which consists of AAG nucleotides encoding a lysine (K) residue. The deletions and insertions of codon 516 involve a poly(C)$_7$ tract, and a slipped-strand mispairing model also is the most likely mechanism to be associated with this mutational hot spot.[66] Thus, the *MEN 1* gene appears to contain DNA sequences that may render it susceptible to deletional and insertional mutations.

Correlations between *MEN 1* mutations and clinical manifestations of the disorder appear to be absent. For example, a detailed study of five unrelated families with the same 4-bp deletion in codons 209 and 211 (Table 192-3) revealed a wide range of MEN1-associated tumors[20,66]; all affected family members had parathyroid tumors, but members of families 1, 3, 4, and 5 had gastrinomas, whereas members of family 2 had insulinomas. In addition, prolactinomas occurred in members of families 2, 3, 4, and 5 but not in family 1, which was affected with carcinoid tumors. Another study of seven unrelated families with the same $g{\rightarrow}a$ novel acceptor splice-site mutation in intron 4 revealed a similarly wide range of MEN1-associated tumors and a lack of genotype/phenotype correlation.[225] The apparent lack of genotype/phenotype correlation, which contrasts with the situation in MEN2 (see Table 191-1),[12] together with the wide diversity of mutations in the 1830-bp coding region of the *MEN 1* gene, makes mutational analysis for diagnostic purposes in MEN1 time consuming and expensive.[20]

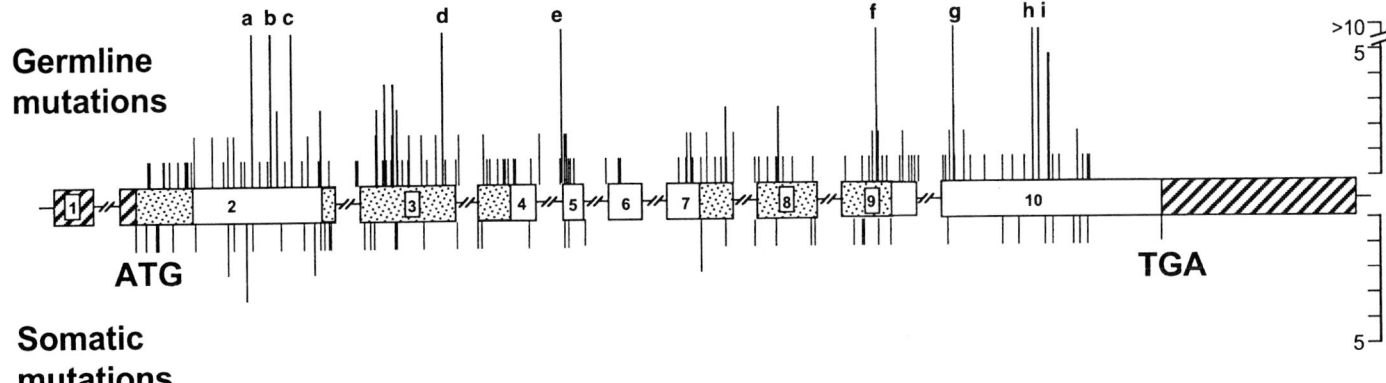

*Figure 191-7*   Schematic representation of the genomic organization of the multiple endocrine neoplasia type 1 (*MEN 1*) gene illustrating germ-line and somatic mutations. The human *MEN 1* gene consists of 10 exons that span more than 9 kb of genomic DNA and encodes a 610-amino acid protein.[42] The 1.83-kb coding region is organized into 9 exons (exons 2–10) and 8 introns (indicated by a *line* but not to scale). The sizes of the exons (*boxes*) range from 88 to 1312 bp, and that of the introns range from 41 to 1564 bp. The start (ATG) and stop (TGA) sites in exons 2 and 10, respectively, are indicated. Exon 1, the 5′ part of exon 2, and the 3′ part of exon 10 are untranslated (indicated by the *hatched boxes*). The promoter region is located within a few 100-bp upstream of exon 2.[201,202] The locations of the three domains formed by codons 1 to 40 (exon 2), 139 to 242 (exons 2, 3, and 4), and 323 to 428 (exons 7, 8, and 9) that interact with JunD are indicated by the *stippled black boxes*. The sites of the 653 germ-line mutations are indicated by the *vertical lines* above the gene, and the sites of 194 somatic mutations are represented below the gene. The number of times that mutations have occurred are indicated (scale shown on the right), and a total of 847 *MEN 1* mutations are represented. Nine sites (a to i) have been frequently involved with mutations (see Table 191-2). These are a, codons 83–84; b, codon 98; c, codons 118–119; d, codons 209–211; e, nt 5168 (intron 4); f, codon 418; g, codon 460; h, codons 514–516; and i, codon 527. The germ-line mutations occurring at these sites represent 27.7% of all of the 653 germ-line mutations. (Adapted from Pannett AAJ, Thakker RV: Multiple endocrine neoplasia type 1 (MEN1). Endocr Rel Cancer 6:449–473, 1999, with permission.)

More than 90% of tumors from MEN1 patients have LOH (see Fig. 191-5), and this has generally been taken as evidence that the *MEN 1* gene acts as a tumor-suppressor gene, consistent with Knudson's two-hit hypothesis.[38–40,195,196] However, this LOH represents only one mechanism by which the second hit may occur, with the other mechanisms being intragenic deletions and point mutations. MEN1 tumors (e.g., parathyroids, insulinoma, and lipoma) that do not have LOH have been shown to harbor different somatic and germ-line mutations of the *MEN 1* gene (see Fig. 191-10),[257] and this is consistent with the Knudson two-hit hypothesis.[196]

### MEN 1 *MUTATIONS IN SPORADIC NON-MEN1 ENDOCRINE TUMORS*

Parathyroid, pancreatic islet cell, and anterior pituitary tumors may occur either as part of MEN1 or more commonly as sporadic, nonfamilial tumors. Tumors from patients with MEN1 have been observed to harbor the germ-line mutation together with a somatic LOH involving chromosome 11q13,[38–40,197,198] or point mutations (see Fig. 191-10), as expected from Knudson's model[195,196,257] and the proposed role of the *MEN 1* gene as a tumor suppressor. However, LOH involving chromosome 11q13, which is the location of *MEN 1*, has also been observed in 5% to 50% of sporadic endocrine tumors, thus implicating the *MEN 1* gene in the etiology of these tumors.[197,198] Somatic *MEN 1* mutations (see Fig. 191-7; Fig. 191-11) have been detected in 18% of sporadic parathyroid tumors (total number, *n* = 452),[257–262] 38% of gastrinomas (*n* = 105),[263–266] 14% of insulinomas (*n* = 43),[261,264] 57% of VIPomas (*n* = 7),[261,263] 16% of nonfunctioning pancreatic tumors (*n* = 32),[267] 60% of glucagonomas (*n* = 5),[267] 2.0% of adrenal cortical tumors (*n* = 83),[222] 35% of bronchial carcinoid tumors (*n* = 26),[204–206] 3.5% of anterior pituitary adenomas (*n* = 167),[211,219,268] 10% of angiofibromas (*n* = 19),[269] and 28% of lipomas (*n* = 8).[270] These 164 somatic mutations are scattered throughout the 1830-bp coding region (see Fig. 191-7), and 18% are nonsense mutations, 40% are frameshift deletions or insertions, 6% are in-frame deletions or insertions, 6% are donor splice-site mutations, and 30% are missense mutations (see Fig. 191-9).[224] A comparison of the locations of the somatic and germ-line mutations revealed a higher frequency (43% [somatic] vs. 27% [germline]; $P < 0.001$) of somatic mutations in exon 2, but the significance of this observation[224,271] in the context of the Knudson two-hit hypothesis[195,196] remains to be elucidated. The tumors harboring a somatic *MEN 1* mutation had chromosome 11q13 LOH as the other genetic abnormality, or "hit," consistent with Knudson's hypothesis. These studies[204,210,211,222,257–261,263–270] indicate that although inactivation of the *MEN 1* gene may have a role in the etiology of some sporadic endocrine tumors, the involvement of other genes, for example, the *GNAS1* gene encoding the G protein–stimulatory α subunit,[198,272,273] with major roles in the etiology of such sporadic endocrine tumors,[274] is highly likely.

### MEN 1 *MUTATIONS IN HEREDITARY ENDOCRINE DISORDERS*

The role of the *MEN 1* gene in the etiology of other inherited endocrine disorders, in which either parathyroid or pituitary tumors occur as an isolated endocrinopathy, has been investigated by mutational analysis. *MEN 1* mutations have been reported in 16 families with isolated hyperparathyroidism (FIHP),[209,214,218,220,223] and 44% of these are missense mutations, and fewer than 38% are nonsense or frame-shift mutations, which would result in a truncated and likely inactivated protein. This contrasts significantly ($P < 0.01$) with the situation in MEN1 patients in whom more than 75% of the germ-line mutations are protein-truncation and about 15% are missense mutations (see Fig. 191-9). These observations are consistent with a more likely association between missense mutations and the milder FIHP variant, but it is important to note that the mutations associated with FIHP are also scattered throughout the coding region and not clustered, a situation that is similar to that found for germ-line *MEN 1* mutations (see Fig. 191-7). Furthermore, the occurrence of protein-truncating mutations in FIHP patients and particularly deletions, such as the 4 bp, involving codons 83–84 (see Table 191-2), which are identical to those observed in MEN1 patients, makes it difficult to establish an unequivocal phenotype/genotype correlation. However, the sole occurrence of parathyroid tumors in these families that harbor *MEN 1* mutations that are similar to those found in families with MEN1 is remarkable, and the mechanisms that determine the altered

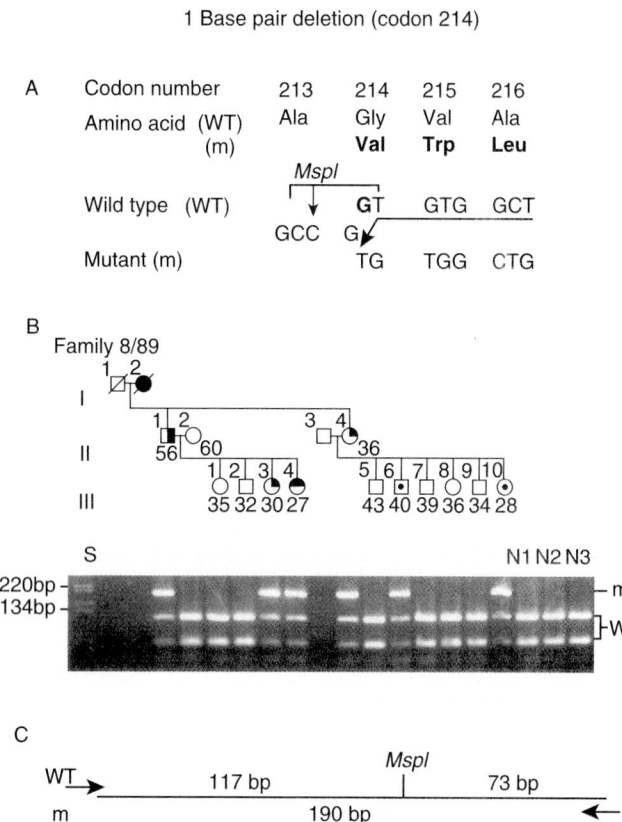

**Figure 191-8**   Detection of mutation in exon 3 in family 8/89 by restriction enzyme analysis. DNA sequence analysis of individual II.1 revealed a 1-bp deletion at the second position (GGT) of codon 214 **(A)**. The deletion has caused a frameshift that continues to codon 223 before a stop codon (TGA) is encountered in the new frame. The 1-bp deletion results in the loss of an *MspI* restriction enzyme site (C/CGG) from the normal (wild-type, WT) sequence **(A)**, and this finding has facilitated detection of this mutation in the other affected members (II.4, III.3, and III.4) of this family **(B)**. The mutant (m) polymerase chain reaction product is 190 bp, whereas the WT products are 117 and 73 bp **(C)**. The affected individuals were heterozygous, and the unaffected members were homozygous for the WT sequence. Individuals III.6 and III.10, who are 40 and 28 years old, respectively, are mutant gene carriers who are clinically and biochemically normal because of the age-related penetrance of this disorder (see Fig. 191-14). These individuals would still require screening (see Fig. 191-13) by clinical, biochemical, and radiologic assessment because they still have a residual risk (i.e., 100% – age-related penetrance) of 2% and >13%, respectively, of tumors developing by age 60 years. Individuals are represented as male (*square*); female (*circle*); unaffected (*open*); affected with parathyroid tumors (*solid upper right quadrant*), gastrinoma (*solid lower right quadrant*), or prolactinoma (*solid upper left quadrant*); and unaffected mutant gene carriers (*dot in the middle of the open symbol*). Individual I.2, who is dead but was known to be affected (tumor details not known), is shown as a *solid symbol*. The age is indicated below for each individual at diagnosis or at the time of the last biochemical screening. The standard size marker (S) in the form of the 1-kb ladder is indicated. Cosegregation of this mutation with *MEN 1* in family 8/89 and its absence in 110 alleles from 55 unrelated normal individuals (N1-3 shown) indicate that it is not a common DNA sequence polymorphism. (Adapted from Bassett JHD, Forbes SA, Pannett AAJ, et al: Characterisation of mutations in patients with multiple endocrine neoplasia type 1 (MEN1). Am J Hum Genet 62:232–244, 1998, with permission.)

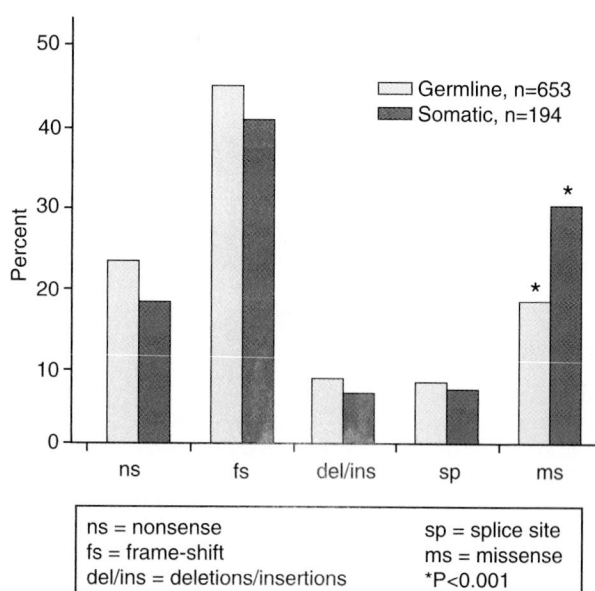

**Figure 191-9**   Frequency of germ-line and somatic *MEN 1* mutations. A total of 653 germ-line mutations and 194 somatic mutations have been reported,[224,225] and these are of diverse types (e.g., nonsense, frameshifts, deletions, insertions, splice-site, and missense mutations). The frequencies of each type of mutation in the germ-line and somatic groups are similar, with the exception of the missense mutations, which are found more frequently in tumors (i.e., the somatic group).[271]

phenotypic expressions of these mutations remain to be elucidated. Mutational analysis studies in another inherited isolated endocrine tumor syndrome, that of familial isolated acromegaly, have not detected abnormalities of the *MEN 1* gene,[215,219,221] even though segregation analysis in one family indicated that the gene was likely to be located on chromosome 11q13.[275] However, nonsense mutations (Tyr312Stop and Arg460Stop) have been detected[203,275,276] in MEN1 families with the *Burin* or prolactinoma variant[162,203] which is characterized by a high occurrence of prolactinomas and a low occurrence of gastrinomas.[276]

### FUNCTION OF MEN 1 PROTEIN (MENIN)

Initial analysis of the predicted amino acid sequence encoded by the *MEN 1* gene did not reveal homologies to any other proteins, sequence motifs, signal peptides, or consensus nuclear localization signal,[42] and thus the putative function of the protein (MENIN) could not be deduced. However, studies based on immunofluorescence, Western blotting of subcellular fractions, and epitope tagging with enhanced green fluorescent protein revealed that MENIN was located primarily in the nucleus.[277] Furthermore, enhanced green fluorescent protein-tagged MENIN deletional constructs identified at least two independent nuclear localization signals that were located in the C-terminal quarter of the protein[277] (Fig. 191-12). Interestingly, the truncated *MEN 1* proteins that would result from the nonsense and frameshift mutations, if expressed, would lack at least one of these nuclear localization signals (see Figs. 191-7 and 191-12). MENIN is predominantly a nuclear protein in nondividing cells, but in dividing cells, it is found in the cytoplasm.[277] The function of MENIN still remains to be elucidated, but it has been shown to interact with a number of proteins[278,279] that are involved in transcriptional regulation,[44,280–284] genome stability,[285–287] and cell division[288] (see Fig. 191-12). Thus, in transcriptional regulation, MENIN has been shown to interact with the activating protein-1 (AP-1), transcription factors JunD[44] and C-Jun,[280] and to suppress Jun-mediated transcriptional activation[289–291];

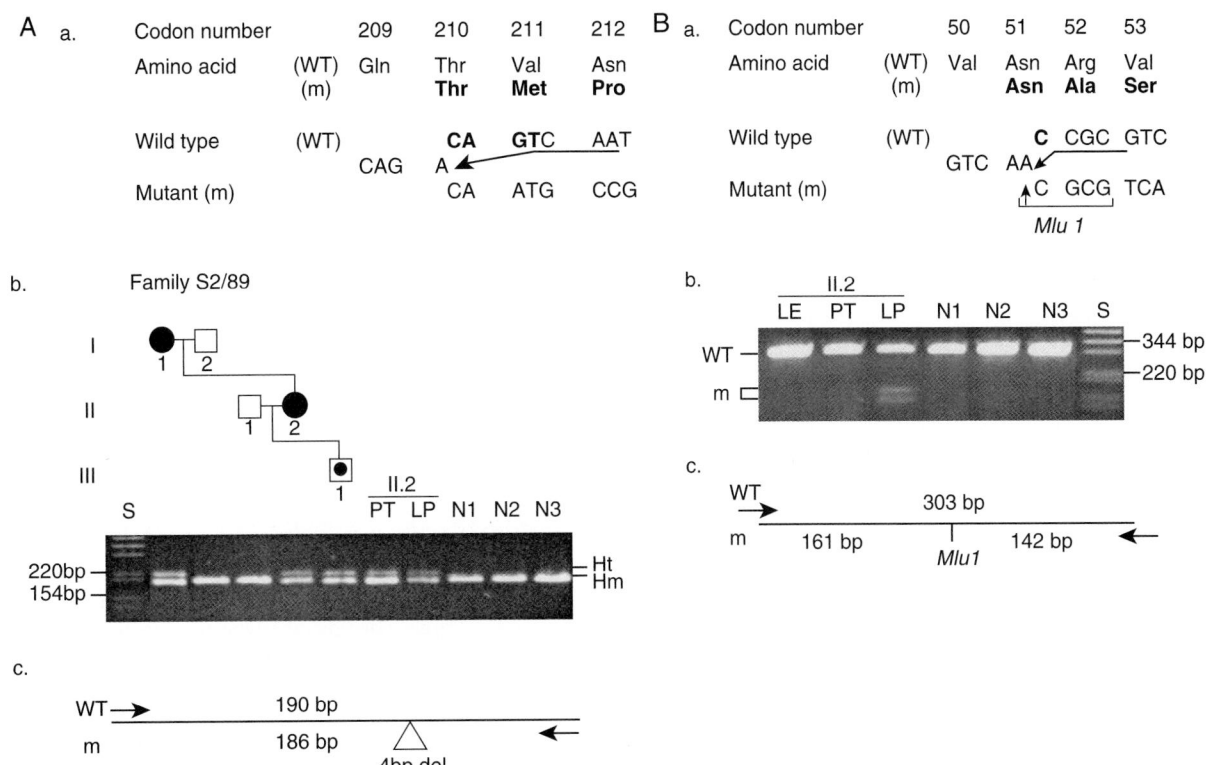

***Figure 191-10*** The detection of germ-line and somatic mutations in a lipoma from a multiple endocrine neoplasia type 1 (MEN1) patient. DNA sequence analysis of the lipoma (LP) from individual II.2 revealed two mutations, one germline **(A)** and one somatic **(B)**. **A,** The germ-line mutation consisted of a 4-bp deletion (CAGT) involving codons 210 and 211, which is one of the nine frequently occurring mutations (see Table 191-2). The mutation is predicted to result in a frameshift with the introduction of 11 missense amino acids followed by a premature stop at codon 222 (a). After polymerase chain reaction (PCR) amplification of the mutation, the PCR products result in the formation of homoduplexes (Hm) and heteroduplexes (Ht), which facilitate the detection of the mutation in the family members and in a parathyroid tumor (PT) and lipoma (LP) from individual II.2 by agarose gel electrophoresis (b and c). The absence of this 4-bp deletion in 110 alleles from 55 unrelated normal individuals (N1–N3 shown) established that this was not a common sequence polymorphism. **B,** The somatic mutation in the lipoma (LP) from individual II.2 consisted of a 1bp deletion (C) at codon 51. The mutation resulted in the gain of an *Mlu*I restriction enzyme site, which facilitated the detection of the mutation (b and c) and the demonstration of its absence in the leukocytes (LE) and parathyroid tumor (PT) from individual II.2, and in 55 normal individuals (N1–N3 shown). After PCR amplification and *Mlu*I digestion, a 303-bp product was obtained for the wild-type (WT) allele, whereas two products of 161-bp and 142-bp were obtained for the mutant (m) alleles, which were resolvable by agarose gel electrophoresis (b and c). Individual I.1 had parathyroid tumors and a gastrinoma; II.2 had parathyroid tumors, prolactinoma, and lipoma; and individual III.1, who is 18 years old, is asymptomatic and biochemically normal, represents a carrier (dot in the middle of symbol) for the MEN1 mutation. There is an age-related penetrance for MEN1 (see Fig. 191-14). *Squares,* males; *circles,* females; *open symbols,* unaffected; *solid symbols,* affected.

members (e.g., p50, p52, and p65) of the NF-κB family of transcriptional regulators to repress NF-κB-mediated transcriptional activation[281]; members of the Smad family, Smad3 and the Smad 1/5 complex, to inhibit the transforming growth factor-β (TGF-β)[282] and the bone morphogenetic protein-2 (BMP-2) signaling pathways,[283] respectively; Runx2, also called cbfa1, which is a common target of TGF-β and BMP-2 in differentiating osteoblasts[292]; and the mouse placental embryonic (pem) expression gene, which encodes a homeobox-containing protein.[284] A role for MENIN in controlling genome stability has been proposed because of its interactions with: a subunit of replication protein (RPA2), which is a heterotrimeric protein required for DNA replication, recombination, and repair[285]; the FANCD2 protein, which is involved in DNA repair and mutations of which result in the inherited cancer-prone syndrome of Fanconi's anemia[293]; the tumor metastases suppressor NM23H1/nucleoside diphosphate kinase, which induces guanosine triphosphate (GTP)ase activity[286,287]; and the glial fibrillary acidic protein (GFAP) and vimentin, which are involved in the intermediate filament network.[294] Finally, the interaction between MENIN and the nonmuscle myosin II-A heavy chain (NMHC II-A) indicates that MENIN has a role in regulating cell division, as NMHC II-A is thought to participate in mediating alterations in cytokinesis and cell shape during cell division.[288] Additional studies have shown that the interaction of MENIN with JunD may be mediated by a histone deacetylase–dependent mechanism,[295] and that MENIN uncouples ELK-1, Jun-D, and C-Jun phosphorylation from mitogen-activated protein kinase (MAPK) activation.[296] The functional role of MENIN as a tumor suppressor also has been investigated, and studies in human fibroblasts have revealed that MENIN acts as a repressor of telomerase activity via hTERT (a protein component of telomerase).[297] Furthermore, overexpression of MENIN in the human endocrine pancreatic tumor cell line (BONI) resulted in an inhibition of cell growth[298] that was accompanied by upregulation of JunD expression but downregulation of δ-like protein 1/preadipocyte factor-1, proliferating cell nuclear antigen, and QM/Jif-1, which is a negative regulator of C-Jun.[298] These findings of growth suppression by MENIN also are observed in other cell types. Thus, expression of MENIN in renin-angiotensin-aldosterone system (RAS)-transformed NIH3T3 cells partially suppressed the RAS-mediated tumor phenotype *in vitro* and *in vivo*,[298] and overexpression of MENIN in CHO-IR cells also suppressed insulin-induced AP-1 transactivation, and this was accompanied by an inhibition of C-Fos induction at the transcriptional level.[299] In contrast, depletion of MENIN in human fibroblasts resulted in their immortalisation.[297] Thus, MENIN

**Table 191-2** Six Frequently Involved *MEN 1* Germ-line Mutation Sites

| Mutation* | Location† Codons | Location† Exon | Frequency (%)‡ n = 71 | Frequency (%)‡ n = 440 |
|---|---|---|---|---|
| del 4bp, nt359 | 83–84 | 2 | 4.2 | 5.2 |
| del 3bp, Lys | 118–119 | 2 | 2.8 | 1.8 |
| del 4bp, nt738 | 209–211 | 3 | 8.5 | 2.5 |
| g→a, nt5168 | ss | Intron 4 | 9.9 | 1.0 |
| del 3bp, Asp | 418 | 9 | 4.2 | 2.3 |
| del/ins C, nt1656-7 | 514–516 | 10 | 7.0 | 5.4 |
| TOTAL | | | 36.6 | 18.2 |

*del, deletion; ins, insertion; bp, base pair; nt, nucleotide.
†Site of mutation referring to codons involved and their exons, or splice site (ss) and intron.
‡Frequencies calculated on 71 mutations from one report,[225] or on 440 mutations from data on different reports.[224] These frequencies, when calculated using the reported 653 germ-line mutations, are similar and are as follows: codons 83–84, 5.7%; codons 118–119, 1.7%; codons 209–211, 3.4%; nt5168 (intron 4), 2.3%; codons 418, 2%; codons 514–516, 7.0%; total, 22.1%. In addition, three other sites appear to have frequent nonsense mutations; these are Arg96Stop (1.5%), Arg460Stop (2.4%), and Arg527Stop (1.7%).
Adapted from Turner JJ, Leotlela PD, Pannett AA, et al: Frequent occurrence of an intron 4 mutation in multiple endocrine neoplasia type 1. J Clin Endocrinol Metab 87:2688–2693, 2002, with permission.

**Table 191-3** Multiple Endocrine Neoplasia Type 1–Associated Tumors in Five Unrelated Families with a 4-bp Deletion at Codons 209 and 211

| Tumors | Family 1 | 2 | 3 | 4 | 5 |
|---|---|---|---|---|---|
| Parathyroid | + | + | + | + | + |
| Gastrinoma | + | – | + | + | + |
| Insulinoma | – | + | – | – | – |
| Glucagonoma | – | – | – | – | + |
| Prolactinoma | – | + | + | + | + |
| Carcinoid | + | – | – | – | – |

+, presence; –, absence of tumors.
Adapted from Thakker RV: Multiple endocrine neoplasia—syndromes of the twentieth century. J Clin Endocrinol Metab 83:2617–2620, © 1998. The Endocrine Society.

appears to have a large number of functions through interactions with proteins,[45] and these mediate alterations in cell proliferation.

## MOUSE MODEL FOR MEN 1

Mouse models for MEN 1 have been generated through homologous recombination (i.e., knockout) of the mouse *Men 1* gene. The mouse *Men 1* gene consists of an 1833-bp

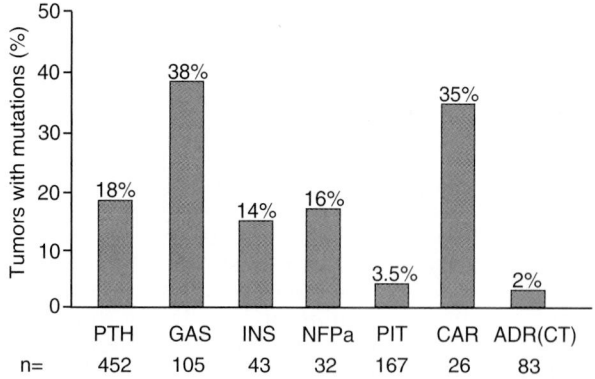

**Figure 191-11** Frequencies of multiple endocrine neoplasia type 1 (*MEN1*) somatic mutations in nonfamilial (i.e., sporadic) tumors from non-MEN1 patients. The number of tumors studied is indicated for each group. Thus, *MEN 1* somatic mutations were observed in 18% of sporadic parathyroid (PTH) tumors; 38% of gastrinomas (GAS); 14% of insulinomas (INS); 16% of nonfunctioning pancreatic islet cell tumors (NFPs); 3.5% of anterior pituitary (PIT) tumors, which were prolactinomas, somatotrophinomas and nonfunctioning tumors; 35% of carcinoid tumors, which were either of bronchial or thymic origin; and 2% of adrenal cortical tumors (ADR[CT]). In addition, *MEN1* somatic mutations have been observed in 57% of vasoactive intestinal peptide (VIP)omas (n = 7), 60% of glucagonomas (n = 5), 28% of lipomas (n = 7), 10% of angiofibromas (n = 19), and 2.5% of melanomas (n = 40) (not shown).

open reading frame that encodes a 611–amino acid protein.[300,301] Thus, the mouse menin protein contains one more amino acid residue than the human MENIN, and this is a glycine at codon 528. However, the mouse and human coding regions have 89% and 96% identities of the nucleotide and amino acid sequences, respectively, indicating a high degree of evolutionary conservation. One mouse knockout model for MEN 1 was generated by introducing a floxed PGK-neomycin cassette into intron 2 and a third loxP site into intron 8, thereby deleting exons 3 to 8 in one allele.[302] Heterozygous mice (+/−), when adult (9 to 16 months of age), developed parathyroid dysplasia, adenomas, and carcinomas; pancreatic islet cell tumors that contained insulin; anterior pituitary tumors that contained prolactin; and adrenal cortical carcinomas.[302] The tumors, which had LOH at the *Men 1* locus, were not associated with any serum biochemical abnormalities, such as hypercalcemia or hypoglycemia, but those +/− mice developing pancreatic islet cell tumors or hyperplasia were found to have elevated serum insulin concentrations.[302] Another mouse knockout model has been generated by deleting exon 3,[303] and heterozygous mice (+/−), when adults, were found to develop parathyroid adenomas and carcinomas; pancreatic islet cell tumors that consisted of insulinomas, gastrinomas, or glucagonomas; and anterior pituitary tumors that consisted of prolactinomas or somatotrophinomas.[303] These +/− mice also developed tumors of the thyroid, Leydig cells, ovarian stroma, and mammary glands.[303] Thus, heterozygous (+/−) mice from these two different types of knockouts provide a model for the human MEN1 disease. However, in another study, heterozygous mice (+/−) surprisingly died as embryos in late gestation, with some mice developing omphaloceles.[304] Homozygous (−/−) mice from two studies[304,305] have been reported to die in utero at embryonic days 11.5 to 13.5. In one study, these −/− mice were developmentally delayed and significantly smaller, and 20% of them developed craniofacial abnormalities.[304] The craniofacial abnormalities have been shown to be due to dysplasia of the membranous skull bones, and this developmental pathway involves the BMP-2 signaling pathway.[283,305] In another study, −/− mice were smaller and developed extensive hemorrhage and edema. In addition, many of these −/− mice had abnormalities of the neural tube, heart, and liver. Thus, many −/− mice had a failure of the closure of the neural tube, myocardial hypotrophy with a thin intraventricular septum, and decreased hepatic cellularity, which was associated with an altered organization and enhanced apoptosis.[305] These results from the −/− mice reveal an important role for the *Men 1* gene in the embryonic development of multiple organs.

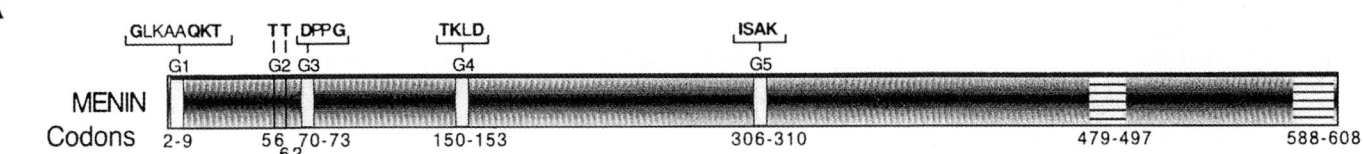

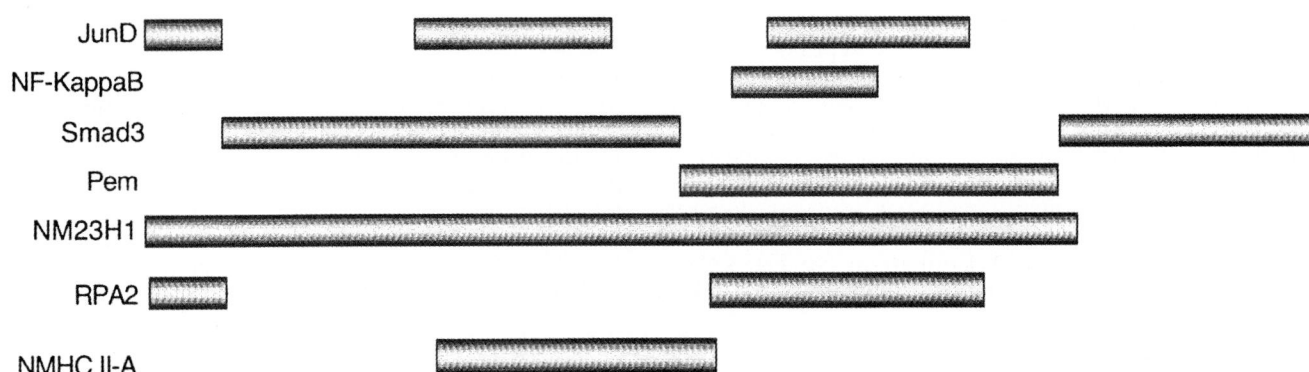

*Figure 191-12*  Schematic representation of the amino acid sequence of MENIN together with the regions that interact with other proteins. **A,** MENIN has two nuclear localization signals (*horizontally hatched boxes*) at codons 479–497 and 588–608,[225]), and five putative guanosine triphosphatase (GTPase) sites (G1–G5)[287] (*open boxes*), whose consensus sequences are shown above, with the conserved amino acid residues shown in bold. **B,** MENIN regions that likely interact with JunD (codons: 1–40, 139–242, 323–428)[46]; nuclear factor- κB (NF-κB) (codons: 305–381)[281]; Smad3 (codons: 40–278–610)[282]; placenta and embryonic expression, Pem (codons: 278–476)[284]; NM23H1 (codons: 1–486)[286]; a subunit Replication protein A (RPA2) (codons: 1–40, 286–448)[285]; and NMHC II-A (codons 154–306) are indicated by the *boxes with gradient shading*. The regions of MENIN that interact with Runx2,[292] FANCD2,[293] GFAP[294] and vimentin[294] remain to be determined.[278,279] (Adapted from Leotlela P, Jauch A, Holtgreve-Grez H, et al: Genetics of neuroendocrine and carcinoid tumors. Endocr Rel Cancer 10:437–450, 2003, with permission.)

## CIRCULATING GROWTH FACTOR

Tumor development in MEN1 may be associated with a circulating growth factor that is mitogenic for parathyroid cells[306] and has similarities to basic fibroblast growth factor (bFGF).[307] This observation is of interest because initial genetic mapping studies of *MEN 1* revealed linkage between *MEN 1* and the oncogene *INT2*,[40,308] which encodes an FGF. Although subsequent genetic-mapping studies that revealed recombination between *MEN 1* and *INT2* excluded *INT2* as the gene causing MEN1,[199,200,309] the finding of this circulating mitogenic growth factor in the plasma of patients with MEN1 may be of importance in further elucidating the etiology of these tumors. The circulating growth factor that was identified in the plasma of patients with MEN1 by *in vitro* studies was detected with the use of bovine parathyroid cells maintained in a long-term culture system.[306] Plasma from patients with MEN1 stimulated these bovine parathyroid cells to rapidly incorporate [³H]thymidine and to proliferate. This plasma mitogenic activity was markedly reduced by heat, acid, and dithiothreitol treatment, which indicated that the stimulatory properties may be due to protein-containing disulfide bonds. Gel-filtration analysis demonstrated the mitogenic activity to be within a single peak in a region between bovine serum albumin and ovalbumin, thereby indicating that the protein has a molecular mass in the range of 50,000 to 55,000 daltons. This mitogenic factor was demonstrated to be a factor distinct from other growth factors, such as epidermal growth factor, platelet-derived growth factor, nerve growth factor, FGF, insulin-like growth factor 1 (IGF-1), and TGF-β and was shown to not be an autocrine product from the parathyroid glands themselves. Additional studies

revealed that the parathyroid mitogenic factor had similarities to bFGF, in contrast to its acidic counterpart, and that the mitogenic factor appeared to act as a tumor angiogenic factor by stimulating endothelial cells.[307] The parathyroid mitogenic factor appeared to be specific for parathyroid cells and did not stimulate activity in anterior pituitary or pancreatic islet cells.[306,310] However, plasma bFGF-like immunoreactivity was found to decrease after surgery for pituitary tumor and after initiation of bromocriptine therapy, thereby indicating that this plasma mitogenic factor may originate from the pituitary.[311] These findings require further study to elucidate the specific role of this circulating growth factor in the development of MEN1 tumors.[310]

## SCREENING IN MEN1

MEN1 is inherited as an autosomal-dominant disorder in most patients.[9] Occasionally, MEN1 may arise sporadically (i.e., without a family history), although it may be difficult to make the distinction between sporadic and familial forms[1,2]; in some cases, a family history may be absent because the parent with MEN1 is not available and may have already died before any manifestations developed, and other cases may be due to *de novo* mutations, which will be transmitted in an autosomal-dominant manner in future generations.[66,203,221] MEN1 is an uncommon disorder, but because of its autosomal-dominant inheritance, the finding of MEN1 in a patient has important implications for other family members; first-degree relatives have about a 50% risk of development of the disease.[9,59] Screening for MEN1 in patients involves the *detection of tumors* and *ascertainment of the germ-line genetic state*, that is, normal or mutant gene carrier.[62] Detection of tumors entails clinical, biochemical, and radiologic investigations for MEN1-associated tumors in patients.[9] The characterization of the *MEN 1* gene[42,43] has facilitated identification of individuals who have mutations and hence a high risk of acquiring the disease (see Figs. 191-7 and 191-8).

### GENETIC ANALYSIS

Molecular genetic analysis for MEN1 either by detecting mutations (see Fig. 191-8) or by performing segregation studies using linked markers (see Fig. 191-6) is useful in identifying individuals who are mutant carriers and thus have a high risk of tumor development.[2,34,312,313] The advantages of DNA analysis are that it requires a single blood sample and does not in theory need to be repeated because the analysis is independent of the age of the individual and provides an objective result. Such mutational analysis may be undertaken in children within the first decade because tumors have developed in some children by the age of 5 years,[27] and appropriate intervention in the form of biochemical testing or treatment or both has been considered.[46] However, the great diversity,[224] together with the widely scattered locations of the *MEN 1* mutations (see Fig. 191-7) and a lack of genotype/phenotype correlation (see Table

191-3), make such mutational screening time consuming, arduous, and expensive.[20] Nevertheless, an integrated program of both mutational analysis, to identify mutant gene carriers, and biochemical screening, to detect the development of tumors, is of advantage[62,312] and used by many centers. Thus, a DNA test identifying an individual as a mutant gene carrier is likely to lead not to immediate medical or surgical treatment but to earlier and more frequent biochemical and radiologic screening, whereas a DNA result indicating that an individual is not at risk will lead to a decision for no further clinical investigations (Fig. 191-13).[62] Thus, the identification of *MEN 1* mutations may be of help in the clinical management of patients and their families with this disorder.

### DETECTION OF MEN1 TUMORS

Biochemical screening for the development of MEN1 tumors in asymptomatic members (see Figs. 191-8 and 191-13) of families with MEN1 is of great importance in as much as earlier diagnosis and treatment of these tumors may help reduce morbidity and mortality.[46,62,67,68] The age-related penetrance (i.e., the proportion of gene carriers manifesting symptoms or signs of the disease by a given age) has been ascertained[66] (Fig. 191-14), and the mutation appears to be nonpenetrant in those younger than 5 years. Thereafter, the mutant *MEN 1*

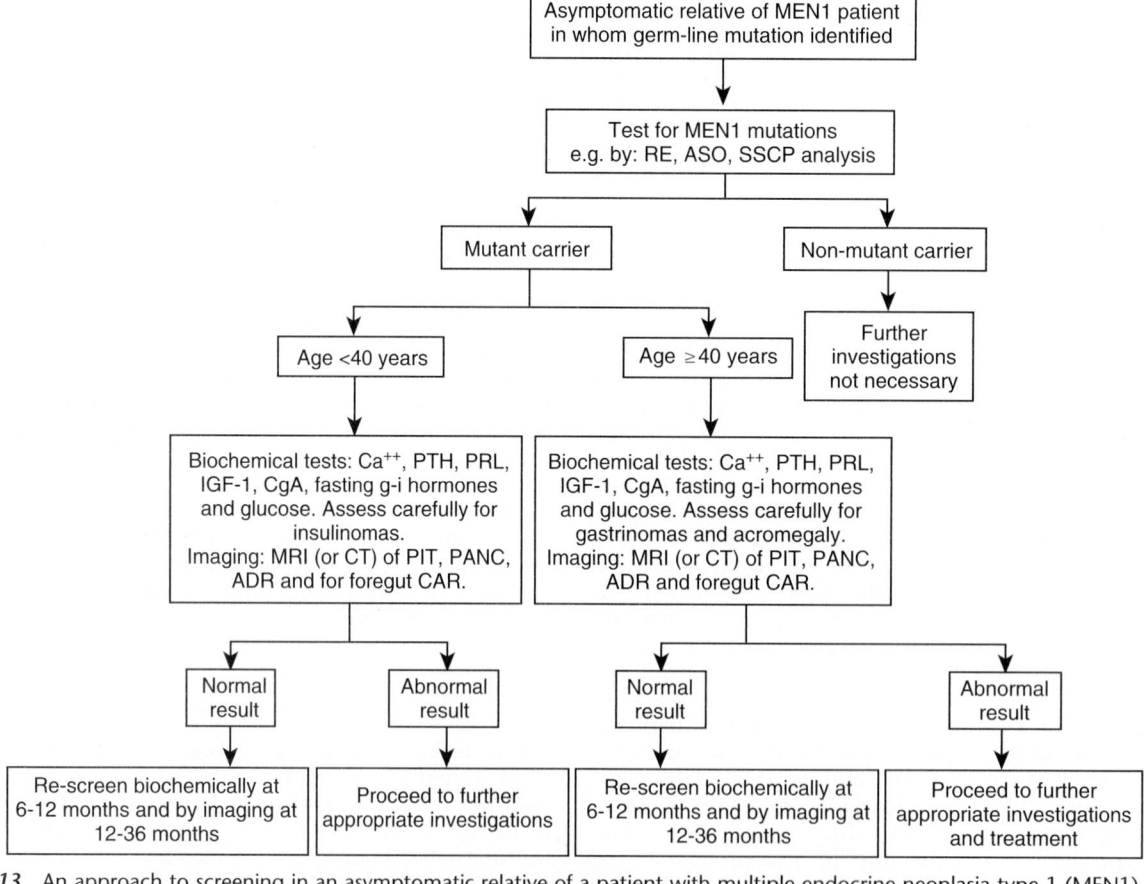

**Figure 191-13** An approach to screening in an asymptomatic relative of a patient with multiple endocrine neoplasia type 1 (MEN1). The relative should have first undergone clinical evaluation for MEN1-associated tumors to establish that the individual is asymptomatic. Relatives who are symptomatic, who should also have a test for *MEN 1* mutations, should proceed to appropriate investigations and management. If mutational analysis for *MEN 1* is not available, then this protocol could be adapted for first-degree relatives.[9] The *MEN 1* mutation may be identified directly by DNA sequence analysis or by restriction enzyme (RE) (see Fig. 191-8) analysis, allele-specific oligonucleotide (ASO) hybridization,[66,198] or another method such as single-stranded conformational polymorphism (SSCP) analysis.[66] The use of mutational analysis and such screening methods in children is controversial and varies in different countries. It has been suggested that nonessential genetic testing in a child who is not old enough to make important long-term decisions be deferred.[313] However, the finding that a child from a family with MEN1 does not have any *MEN 1* mutations removes the burden of repeated clinical, biochemical, and radiologic investigations and enables health resources to be more effectively directed toward those children who are *MEN 1* mutant gene carriers. The approaches to genetic testing and screening in MEN1 vary in different countries.

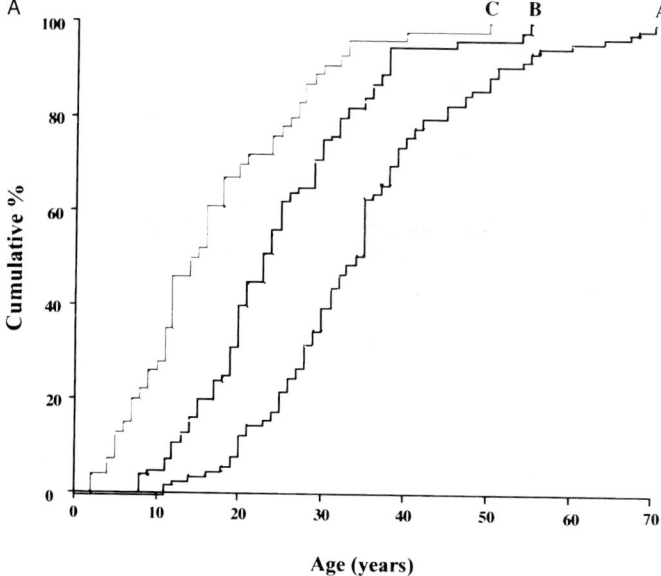

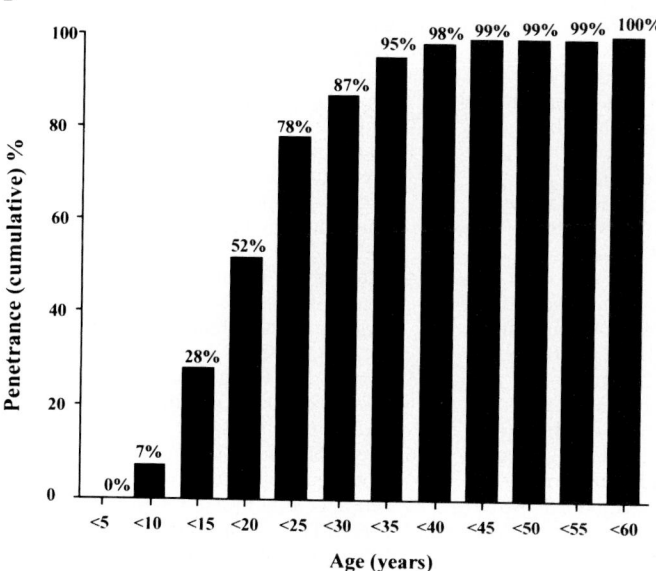

*Figure 191-14*  Age distributions **(A)** and age-related penetrance **(B)** of multiple endocrine neoplasia type 1 (MEN1) determined from an analysis of 174 mutant gene carriers. **A,** The age distributions were determined for three groups of *MEN 1* mutant gene carriers from 40 families in whom mutations were detected.[66] The 91 members of group A had symptoms, whereas the 40 members of group B were asymptomatic and detected by biochemical screening. The 43 members of group C represent individuals who are *MEN 1* mutant gene carriers (see Fig. 191-8) and who remain asymptomatic and biochemically normal. The ages included for members of groups A, B, and C are those at the onset of symptoms, at the finding of the biochemical abnormality, and at the last clinical and biochemical evaluation, respectively. Groups B and C contained members who were significantly younger than those in group A ($P < 0.001$). The younger age of the group C mutant gene carriers is consistent with an age-related penetrance for MEN1, which was calculated **(B)** for the first five decades. The age-related penetrance (i.e., the proportion of mutant gene carriers with manifestations of the disease by a given age) increased steadily from 7% in the group younger than 10 years to 52%, 87%, 98%, 99%, and 100% by the ages of 20, 30, 40, 50, and 60 years, respectively. The residual risk (100% – age-related penetrance) for the development of MEN1 tumors in asymptomatic mutant gene carriers who are biochemically normal would then be 93%, 48%, 13%, 2%, and 1% at the ages of 10, 20, 30, 40, and 50 years, respectively. (From Bassett JHD, Forbes SA, Pannett AAJ, et al: Characterization of mutations in patients with multiple endocrine neoplasia type 1 (MEN1). Am J Hum Genet 62:232–244, 1998, with permission.)

gene has a high penetrance, being greater than 50% penetrant by 20 years of age and greater than 95% penetrant by 40 years.[66] Screening for MEN1 tumors is difficult because the clinical and biochemical manifestations in members of any one family are not uniformly similar[9,40–59] (see Figs. 191-3, 191-8, and 191-10). Attempts to screen for the development of MEN1 tumors in the asymptomatic relatives of an affected individual have depended largely on measuring the serum concentrations of calcium, gastrointestinal (g–i) hormones (e.g., gastrin), and prolactin, as well as on radiologic imaging of the abdomen and pituitary.[2,39,59–62,314] Parathyroid overactivity causing hypercalcemia is almost invariably the first manifestation of the disorder and has become a useful and easy biochemical screening investigation.[9,59–62] In addition, hyperprolactinemia, which may be asymptomatic, may represent the first manifestation in fewer than 10% of patients and may thus also be a useful and easy biochemical screening investigation.[9,62] Pancreatic involvement in asymptomatic individuals has been detected by estimating the fasting plasma concentrations of gastrin, PP, and glucagon and by abdominal imaging.[9,46,62,135] However, one study has shown that a stimulatory meal test is a better method for detecting pancreatic disease in individuals who have no demonstrable pancreatic tumors by CT.[314] An exaggerated increase in serum gastrin or PP or both proved to be a reliable early indicator for the development of pancreatic tumors in these individuals.

At present, it is suggested that individuals at high risk for MEN1 (i.e., mutant gene carriers) undergo biochemical screening (see Fig. 191-13) at least once per annum and also have baseline pituitary and abdominal imaging (e.g., MRI or CT), which should then be repeated at 1- to 3-year intervals.[62] Screening should commence in early childhood because the disease has developed in some individuals by the age of 5 years,[27,46,62] and it should continue for life because the disease has not developed in some individuals until the eighth decade.[46,57,61,62] The screening history and physical examination should be directed toward eliciting the symptoms and signs of hypercalcemia, nephrolithiasis, peptic ulcer disease, neuroglycopenia, hypopituitarism, galactorrhea and amenorrhea in women, acromegaly, Cushing's disease, and visual field loss and the presence of subcutaneous lipomas, angiofibromas, and collagenomas.[3,9,62] Biochemical screening (see Fig. 191-13) should include estimations of serum calcium ($Ca^{++}$), PTH, gastrointestinal (g–i) hormones (e.g., gastrin, insulin with a fasting glucose, glucagon, VIP, and PP), chromogranin A (CgA), prolactin (PRL), and IGF-1 in all individuals,[62] and more specific endocrine-function tests should be undertaken in individuals who have symptoms or signs suggestive of a clinical syndrome. Radiologic screening should include an MRI (or CT scanning) of the pancreas (PANC), adrenals (ADR), and pituitary (PIT), initially as a baseline and then every 1 to 3 years, as well as imaging for foregut carcinoids (CAR).[62]

## CONCLUSIONS

Combined clinical and laboratory investigations of MEN1 have resulted in an increased understanding of this disorder, which may be inherited as an autosomal-dominant condition. Defining the features of each disease manifestation in MEN1 has improved patient management and treatment and has also facilitated a screening protocol to be instituted. Application of the techniques of molecular biology has enabled identification of the gene causing MEN1 and detection of mutations in patients. The function of the protein encoded by the *MEN 1* gene has been shown to involve regulation of transcription, genome stability, and cell division, but much still remains to be elucidated. The availability of an MEN1 mouse model that develops the endocrine tumors associated with MEN1 will greatly help in future studies aimed at defining the function of MENIN and also in investigating new treatments. In addition, these recent advances have facilitated the identification of mutant *MEN 1* gene carriers who are at high risk for development of this disorder and thus require regular and biochemical and radiologic screening to detect the development of endocrine tumors.

## Acknowledgment

I am grateful to the Medical Research Council (UK) for support; to P. T. Christie, J. T. Pang, A.A.J. Pannett, and B. Harding for help in preparation of some of the figures; and to Mrs. Tracey Walker for typing the manuscript.

## REFERENCES

1. Thakker RV, Ponder BA: Multiple endocrine neoplasia. Baillieres Clin Endocrinol Metab 2:1031–1067, 1988.
2. Thakker R: Multiple endocrine neoplasia type 1 (MEN1). In DeGroot LJBG, Besser M, Burger HG, et al (eds): Endocrinology, 3d ed. Philadelphia, WB Saunders, 1995, pp 2815–2831.
3. Marx SJ: Multiple endocrine neoplasia type 1. In Vogelstein B (ed): Genetic Basis of Human Cancer. New York, McGraw-Hill, 1998, pp 489–506.
4. Underdahl LO, Woolner LB, Black BM: Multiple endocrine adenomas: Report of 8 cases in which the parathyroids, pituitary and pancreatic islets were involved. J Clin Endocrinol Metab 13:20–47, 1953.
5. Berdjis CC: Pluriglandular syndrome, II: Multiple endocrine adenomas in man: A report of five cases and a review of literature. Ophthalmologica 15:288–311, 1962.
6. Steiner AL, Goodman AD, Powers SR: Study of a kindred with pheochromocytoma, medullary thyroid carcinoma, hyperparathyroidism and Cushing's disease: Multiple endocrine neoplasia, type 2. Medicine (Baltimore) 47:371–409, 1968.
7. Wermer P: Multiple endocrine adenomatosis: Multiple hormone-producing tumors, a familial syndrome. Clin Gastroenterol 3:671–684, 1974.
8. Wermer P: Genetic aspects of adenomatosis of endocrine glands. Am J Med 16:363–371, 1954.
9. Trump D, Farren B, Wooding C, et al: Clinical studies of multiple endocrine neoplasia type 1 (MEN1). Q J Med 89:653–669, 1996.
10. Sipple J: The association of pheochromocytoma with carcinoma of the thyroid gland. Am J Med 31:163–166, 1961.
11. Ponder BA: Clinical expressions of multiple endocrine neoplasia type 2. In Vogelstein B (ed): The Genetic Basis of Human Cancer. New York, McGraw-Hill, 1998, pp 486–487.
12. Gagel RF: Ret protooncogene mutations in multiple endocrine neoplasia type 2. In Bilezikian JP (ed): Principles of Bone Biology. San Diego, Academic Press, 1996, pp 799–780.
13. Schimke RN: Multiple endocrine neoplasia: How many syndromes? Am J Med Genet 37:375–383, 1990.
14. Tateishi R, Wada A, Ishiguro S, Ehara M, et al: Coexistence of bilateral pheochromocytoma and pancreatic islet cell tumor: Report of a case and review of the literature. Cancer 42:2928–2934, 1978.
15. Carney JA, Go VL, Gordon H, et al: Familial pheochromocytoma and islet cell tumor of the pancreas. Am J Med 68:515–521, 1980.
16. Zeller JR, Kauffman HM, Komorowski RA, Itskovitz HD: Bilateral pheochromocytoma and islet cell adenoma of the pancreas. Arch Surg 117:827–830, 1982.
17. Kahn MT, Mullon DA: Pheochromocytoma without hypertension: Report of a patient with acromegaly. JAMA 188:74–75, 1964.
18. Miller GL, Wynn J: Acromegaly, pheochromocytoma, toxic goiter, diabetes mellitus, and endometriosis. Arch Intern Med 127:299–303, 1971.
19. McKusick V: Mendelian Inheritance in Man. Baltimore, Johns Hopkins University Press, 1998.
20. Thakker RV: Multiple endocrine neoplasia: Syndromes of the twentieth century. J Clin Endocrinol Metab 83:2617–2620, 1998.
21. Erdheim J: Zur normalen und pathologischen histologie der glandular thyreoidea, und hypophysis. Beitr Pathol Anat Allergy 33:158–236, 1903.
22. Cushing H: The Pathological Findings in Four Autopsied Cases of Acromegaly with a Discussion of Their Significance. New York, Rockefeller Institute of Medicine Research Monograph, 1927.
23. Lloyd P: A case of hypophyseal tumor with associated tumor-like enlargement of the parathyroids and islands of Langerhans. Bull Johns Hopkins Hosp 45:1–14, 1929.
24. Rossier P: Familiare erkrankung innersekretorischer Drusen kombiniert mit ulkuskrankheit. Schweiz Med Wochenschr 69:985–990, 1939.
25. Moldawer MP: Case records of the Massachusetts General Hospital, case 39501. N Engl J Med 249:990–993, 1953.
26. Moldawer MP, Nardi GL, Raker JW: Concomitance of multiple adenomas of the parathyroids and pancreatic islets with tumor of the pituitary: A syndrome with a familial incidence. Am J Med Sci 228:190–206, 1954.
27. Ballard HS, Fame B, Hartsock RJ: Familial Multiple Endocrine Adenoma-Peptic Ulcer Complex. Medicine (Baltimore) 43:481–516, 1964.
28. Pearse AG: Common cytochemical and ultrastructural characteristics of cells producing polypeptide hormones (the APUD series) and their relevance to thyroid and ultimobranchial C cells and calcitonin. Proc R Soc Lond B Biol Sci 170:71–80, 1968.
29. Pearse AG: The cytochemistry and ultrastructure of polypeptide hormone-producing cells of the APUD series and the embryologic, physiologic and pathologic implications of the concept. J Histochem Cytochem 17:303–313, 1969.
30. Le Douarin NM: Developmental relationship between the neural crest and the polypeptide-hormone secreting cells. In The Neural Crest. London, Cambridge University Press, 1982, pp 91–107.
31. Pictet RL, Rall LB, Phelps P, Rutter WJ: The neural crest and the origin of the insulin-producing and other gastrointestinal hormone-producing cells. Science 191:191–192, 1976.
32. Le Douarin NM, Teillet MA: The migration of neural crest cells to the wall of the digestive tract in avian embryo. J Embryol Exp Morphol 30:31–48, 1973.
33. Weichert RF 3rd: The neural ectodermal origin of the peptide-secreting endocrine glands: A unifying concept for the etiology of multiple endocrine adenomatosis and the inappropriate secretion of peptide hormones by nonendocrine tumors. Am J Med 49:232–241, 1970.
34. Thakker RV: The molecular genetics of the multiple endocrine neoplasia syndromes. Clin Endocrinol (Oxf) 38:1–14, 1993.
35. Varmus HE: The molecular genetics of cellular oncogenes. Annu Rev Genet 18:553–612, 1984.
36. Friend SH, Dryja TP, Weinberg RA: Oncogenes and tumor-suppressing genes. N Engl J Med 318:618–622, 1988.
37. Fearon ER: Human cancer syndromes: Clues to the origin and nature of cancer. Science 278:1043–1050, 1997.
38. Larsson C, Skogseid B, Oberg K, et al: Multiple endocrine neoplasia type 1 gene maps to chromosome 11 and is lost in insulinoma. Nature 332:85–87, 1988.
39. Friedman E, Sakaguchi K, Bale AE, et al: Clonality of parathyroid tumors in familial multiple endocrine neoplasia type 1. N Engl J Med 321:213–218, 1989.
40. Thakker RV, Bouloux P, Wooding C, et al: Association of parathyroid tumors in multiple endocrine neoplasia type 1 with loss of alleles on chromosome 11. N Engl J Med 321:218–224, 1989.
41. Collins FS: Positional cloning: Let's not call it reverse anymore. Nat Genet 1:3–6, 1992.
42. Chandrasekharappa SC, Guru SC, Manickam P, et al: Positional cloning of the gene for multiple endocrine neoplasia-type 1. Science 276:404–407, 1997.
43. The European Consortium on MEN1: Identification of the multiple endocrine neoplasia type 1 (MEN1) gene. Hum Mol Genet 6:1177–1183, 1997.

44. Agarwal SK, Guru SC, Heppner C, et al: Menin interacts with the AP1 transcription factor JunD and represses JunD-activated transcription. Cell 96:143–152, 1999.

45. Leotlela PD, Jauch A, Holtgreve-Grez H, Thakker RV: Genetics of neuroendocrine and carcinoid tumors. Endocr Relat Cancer 10:437–450, 2003.

46. Lips CJ, Vasen HF, Lamers CB: Multiple endocrine neoplasia syndromes. Crit Rev Oncol Hematol 2:117–184, 1984.

47. Brandi ML, Marx SJ, Aurbach GD, Fitzpatrick LA: Familial multiple endocrine neoplasia type I: A new look at pathophysiology. Endocr Rev 8:391–405, 1987.

48. Christensson T: Familial hyperparathyroidism. Ann Intern Med 85:614–615, 1976.

49. Jackson CE, Boonstra CE: The relationship of hereditary hyperparathyroidism to endocrine adenomatosis. Am J Med 43:727–734, 1967.

50. Uchino S, Noguchi S, Sato M, et al: Screening of the Men1 gene and discovery of germ-line and somatic mutations in apparently sporadic parathyroid tumors. Cancer Res 60:5553–5557, 2000.

51. Bardram L, Stage JG: Frequency of endocrine disorders in patients with the Zollinger-Ellison syndrome. Scand J Gastroenterol 20:233–238, 1985.

52. Farley DR, van Heerden JA, Grant CS, et al: The Zollinger-Ellison syndrome: A collective surgical experience. Ann Surg 215:561–569; discussion 569–570, 1992.

53. Scheithauer BW, Laws ER Jr, Kovacs K, et al: Pituitary adenomas of the multiple endocrine neoplasia type I syndrome. Semin Diagn Pathol 4:205–211, 1987.

54. Schaaf L, Greschner M, Geissler W, et al: The importance of multiple endocrine neoplasia syndromes in differential diagnosis. Klin Wochenschr 68:669–672, 1990.

55. Corbetta S, Pizzocaro A, Peracchi M, et al: Multiple endocrine neoplasia type 1 in patients with recognized pituitary tumors of different types. Clin Endocrinol (Oxf) 47:507–512, 1997.

56. Carty SE, Helm AK, Amico JA, et al: The variable penetrance and spectrum of manifestations of multiple endocrine neoplasia type 1. Surgery 124:1106–1113; discussion 1113–1114, 1998.

57. Gelston AL, Delisle MB, Patel YC: Multiple endocrine adenomatosis type I: Occurrence in an octogenarian with high levels of circulating pancreatic polypeptide. JAMA 247:665–666, 1982.

58. Shepherd JJ: Latent familial multiple endocrine neoplasia in Tasmania. Med J Aust 142:395–397, 1985.

59. Marx SJ, Vinik AI, Santen RJ, et al: Multiple endocrine neoplasia type I: Assessment of laboratory tests to screen for the gene in a large kindred. Medicine (Baltimore) 65:226–241, 1986.

60. Benson L, Ljunghall S, Akerstrom G, Oberg K: Hyperparathyroidism presenting as the first lesion in multiple endocrine neoplasia type 1. Am J Med 82:731–737, 1987.

61. Vasen HF, Lamers CB, Lips CJ: Screening for the multiple endocrine neoplasia syndrome type I: A study of 11 kindreds in The Netherlands. Arch Intern Med 149:2717–2722, 1989.

62. Brandi ML, Gagel RF, Angeli A, et al: Guidelines for diagnosis and therapy of MEN type 1 and type 2. J Clin Endocrinol Metab 86:5658–5671, 2001.

63. Darling TN, Skarulis MC, Steinberg SM, et al: Multiple facial angiofibromas and collagenomas in patients with multiple endocrine neoplasia type 1. Arch Dermatol 133:853–857, 1997.

64. Bahn RS, Scheithauer BW, van Heerden JA, et al: Nonidentical expressions of multiple endocrine neoplasia, type I, in identical twins. Mayo Clin Proc 61:689–696, 1986.

65. Flanagan DE, Armitage M, Clein GP, Thakker RV: Prolactinoma presenting in identical twins with multiple endocrine neoplasia type 1. Clin Endocrinol (Oxf) 45:117–120, 1996.

66. Bassett JH, Forbes SA, Pannett AA, et al: Characterization of mutations in patients with multiple endocrine neoplasia type 1. Am J Hum Genet 62:232–244, 1998.

67. Wilkinson S, Teh BT, Davey KR, et al: Cause of death in multiple endocrine neoplasia type 1. Arch Surg 128:683–690, 1993.

68. Doherty GM, Olson JA, Frisella MM, et al: Lethality of multiple endocrine neoplasia type I. World J Surg 22:581–586; discussion 586–587, 1998.

69. Burgess JR, Greenaway TM, Shepherd JJ. Expression of the MEN-1 gene in a large kindred with multiple endocrine neoplasia type 1. J Intern Med 243:465–470, 1998.

70. Majewski JT, Wilson SD: The MEA-I syndrome: An all or none phenomenon? Surgery 86:475–484, 1979.

71. Eberle F, Grun R: Multiple endocrine neoplasia, type I (MEN I). Ergeb Inn Med Kinderheilkd 46:76–149, 1981.

72. Marx SJ, Spiegel AM, Levine MA, et al: Familial hypocalciuric hypercalcemia: The relation to primary parathyroid hyperplasia. N Engl J Med 307:416–426, 1982.

73. Croisier JC, Azerad E, Lubetzki J: Polyendocrine adenomatosis (Wermer's syndrome) Apropos of a personal case: Review of the literature. Sem Hop 47:494–525, 1971.

74. Lamers CB, Froeling PG: Clinical significance of hyperparathyroidism in familial multiple endocrine adenomatosis type I (MEA I). Am J Med 66:422–424, 1979.

75. Kraimps JL, Duh QY, Demeure M, Clark OH: Hyperparathyroidism in multiple endocrine neoplasia syndrome. Surgery 112:1080–1086; discussion 1086–1088, 1992.

76. Hellman P, Skogseid B, Juhlin C, et al: Findings and long-term results of parathyroid surgery in multiple

endocrine neoplasia type 1. World J Surg 16:718–722; discussion 722–723, 1992.

77. van Heerden JA, Kent RB 3rd, Sizemore GW, et al: Primary hyperparathyroidism in patients with multiple endocrine neoplasia syndromes: Surgical experience. Arch Surg 118:533–536, 1983.

78. Black WC 3rd, Utley JR: The differential diagnosis of parathyroid adenoma and chief cell hyperplasia. Am J Clin Pathol 49:761–775, 1968.

79. Rizzoli R, Green J 3rd, Marx SJ: Primary hyperparathyroidism in familial multiple endocrine neoplasia type I: Long-term follow-up of serum calcium levels after parathyroidectomy. Am J Med 78:467–474, 1985.

80. Prinz RA, Gamvros OI, Sellu D, Lynn JA: Subtotal parathyroidectomy for primary chief cell hyperplasia of the multiple endocrine neoplasia type I syndrome. Ann Surg 193:26–29, 1981.

81. Rudberg C, Akerstrom G, Palmer M, et al: Late results of operation for primary hyperparathyroidism in 441 patients. Surgery 99:643–651, 1986.

82. Wells SA Jr, Ellis GJ, Gunnells JC, et al: Parathyroid autotransplantation in primary parathyroid hyperplasia. N Engl J Med 295:57–62, 1976.

83. Wells SA Jr, Farndon JR, Dale JK, et al: Long-term evaluation of patients with primary parathyroid hyperplasia managed by total parathyroidectomy and heterotopic autotransplantation. Ann Surg 192:451–458, 1980.

84. Saxe AW, Brennan MF: Reoperative parathyroid surgery for primary hyperparathyroidism caused by multiple-gland disease: Total parathyroidectomy and autotransplantation with cryopreserved tissue. Surgery 91:616–621, 1982.

85. Mallette LE, Blevins T, Jordan PH, Noon GP: Autogenous parathyroid grafts for generalized primary parathyroid hyperplasia: Contrasting outcome in sporadic hyperplasia versus multiple endocrine neoplasia type I. Surgery 101:738–745, 1987.

86. Grama D, Skogseid B, Wilander E, et al: Pancreatic tumors in multiple endocrine neoplasia type 1: Clinical presentation and surgical treatment. World J Surg 16:611–618; discussion 618–619, 1992.

87. Zollinger RM, Ellison EH: Primary peptic ulcerations of the jejunum associated with islet cell tumors of the pancreas. Ann Surg 142:709–723; discussion 724–728, 1955.

88. Gregory RA, Grossman MI, Tracy HJ, Bentley PH: Nature of the gastric secretagogue in Zollinger-Ellison tumors. Lancet 2:543–544, 1967.

89. Gregory RA, Tracy HJ, French JM, Sircus W: Extraction of a gastrin-like substance from a pancreatic tumor in a case of Zollinger-Ellison syndrome. Lancet 1:1045–1048, 1960.

90. Metz D: Multiple endocrine neoplasia type 1: Clinical features and management. In Bilezikian JP (ed): The Parathyroids. New York, Raven, 1994, pp 591–636.

91. Pipeleers-Marichal M, Somers G, Willems G, et al: Gastrinomas in the duodenums of patients with multiple endocrine neoplasia type 1 and the Zollinger-Ellison syndrome. N Engl J Med 322:723–727, 1990.

92. Yu F, Venzon DJ, Serrano J, et al: Prospective study of the clinical course, prognostic factors, causes of death, and survival in patients with long-standing Zollinger-Ellison syndrome. J Clin Oncol 17:615–630, 1999.

93. Townsend CM Jr, Thompson JC: Gastrinoma. Semin Surg Oncol 6:91–97, 1990.

94. Lowney JK, Frisella MM, Lairmore TC, Doherty GM: Pancreatic islet cell tumor metastasis in multiple endocrine neoplasia type 1: Correlation with primary tumor size. Surgery 124:1043–1048; discussion 1048–1049, 1998.

95. Wolfe MM, Jensen RT: Zollinger-Ellison syndrome: Current concepts in diagnosis and management. N Engl J Med 317:1200–1209, 1987.

96. Wiedenmann B, Jensen RT, Mignon M, et al: Preoperative diagnosis and surgical management of neuroendocrine gastroenteropancreatic tumors: General recommendations by a consensus workshop. World J Surg 22:309–318, 1998.

97. Betts JB, O'Malley BP, Rosenthal FD: Hyperparathyroidism: A prerequisite for Zollinger-Ellison syndrome in multiple endocrine adenomatosis type 1: Report of a further family and a review of the literature. Q J Med 49:69–76, 1980.

98. Thompson MH, Sanders DJ, Grund ER: The relationship of the serum gastrin and calcium concentrations in patients with multiple endocrine neoplasia type I. Br J Surg 63:779–783, 1976.

99. McArthur KE, Collen MJ, Maton PN, et al: Omeprazole: Effective, convenient therapy for Zollinger-Ellison syndrome. Gastroenterology 88:939–944, 1985.

100. Jensen RT: Management of the Zollinger-Ellison syndrome in patients with multiple endocrine neoplasia type 1. J Intern Med 243:477–488, 1998.

101. Deveney CW, Stein S, Way LW: Cimetidine in the treatment of Zollinger-Ellison syndrome. Am J Surg 146:116–123, 1983.

102. Jensen RT, Collen MJ, McArthur KE, et al: Comparison of the effectiveness of ranitidine and cimetidine in inhibiting acid secretion in patients with gastric hypersecretory states. Am J Med 77:90–105, 1984.

103. Thompson NW: Management of pancreatic endocrine tumors in patients with multiple endocrine neoplasia type 1. Surg Oncol Clin North Am 7:881–891, 1998.

104. Skogseid B, Oberg K, Eriksson B, et al: Surgery for asymptomatic pancreatic lesion in multiple endocrine neoplasia type I. World J Surg 20:872–876; discussion 877, 1996.

105. Cadiot G, Vuagnat A, Doukhan I, et al: Prognostic factors in patients with Zollinger-Ellison syndrome and multiple endocrine neoplasia type 1: Groupe d'Etude des Neoplasies Endocriniennes Multiples (GENEM and groupe de Recherche et d'Etude du Syndrome de Zollinger-Ellison (GRESZE). Gastroenterology 116:286–293, 1999.

106. Norton JA, Fraker DL, Alexander HR, et al: Surgery to cure the Zollinger-Ellison syndrome. N Engl J Med 341:635–644, 1999.

107. Delcore R Jr, Hermreck AS, Friesen SR: Selective surgical management of correctable hypergastrinemia. Surgery 106:1094–1100; discussion 1100–1102, 1989.

108. Sheppard BC, Norton JA, Doppman JL, et al: Management of islet cell tumors in patients with multiple endocrine neoplasia: A prospective study. Surgery 106:1108–1117; discussion 1117–1118, 1989.

109. Ruszniewski P, Podevin P, Cadiot G, et al: Clinical, anatomical, and evolutive features of patients with the Zollinger-Ellison syndrome combined with type I multiple endocrine neoplasia. Pancreas 8:295–304, 1993.

110. Thompson NW, Bondeson AG, Bondeson L, Vinik A: The surgical treatment of gastrinoma in MEN I syndrome patients. Surgery 106:1081–1085; discussion 1085–1086, 1989.

111. Wise SR, Johnson J, Sparks J, et al: Gastrinoma: The predictive value of preoperative localization. Surgery 106:1087–1092; discussion 1092–1093, 1989.

112. Termanini B, Gibril F, Reynolds JC, et al: Value of somatostatin receptor scintigraphy: A prospective study in gastrinoma of its effect on clinical management. Gastroenterology 112:335–347, 1997.

113. Cadiot G, Lebtahi R, Sarda L, et al: Preoperative detection of duodenal gastrinomas and peripancreatic lymph nodes by somatostatin receptor scintigraphy: Groupe d'Etude Du Syndrome De Zollinger-Ellison. Gastroenterology 111:845–854, 1996.

114. Bansal R, Tierney W, Carpenter S, et al: Cost effectiveness of EUS for preoperative localization of pancreatic endocrine tumors. Gastrointest Endosc 49:19–25, 1999.

115. Turner JJ, Wren AM, Jackson JE, et al: Localization of gastrinomas by selective intra-arterial calcium injection. Clin Endocrinol (Oxf) 57:821–825, 2002.

116. Moertel CG, Hanley JA, Johnson LA: Streptozocin alone compared with streptozocin plus fluorouracil in the treatment of advanced islet-cell carcinoma. N Engl J Med 303:1189–1194, 1980.

117. Kvols LK, Buck M, Moertel CG, et al: Treatment of metastatic islet cell carcinoma with a somatostatin

analogue (SMS 201-995). Ann Intern Med 107:162–168, 1987.

118. Carrasco CH, Chuang VP, Wallace S: Apudomas metastatic to the liver: Treatment by hepatic artery embolization. Radiology 149:79–83, 1983.

119. Eriksson B, Oberg K, Alm G, et al: Treatment of malignant endocrine pancreatic tumors with human leucocyte interferon. Lancet 2:1307–1309, 1986.

120. Norton JA, Doppman JL, Collen MJ, et al: Prospective study of gastrinoma localization and resection in patients with Zollinger-Ellison syndrome. Ann Surg 204:468–479, 1986.

121. Croisier JC, Lehy T, Zeitoun P: A2 cell pancreatic microadenomas in a case of multiple endocrine adenomatosis. Cancer 28:707–713, 1971.

122. Peurifoy JT, Gomez LG, Thompson JC: Separate pancreatic gastrin cell and beta-cell adenomas: Report of a patient with multiple endocrine adenomatosis type 1. Arch Surg 114:956–958, 1979

123. Eastman RC: Hypoglycemia. In Moore W (ed): Diagnostic Endocrinology. Toronto, BC Decker, 1990, pp 183–191.

124. Demeure MJ, Klonoff DC, Karam JH, et al: Insulinomas associated with multiple endocrine neoplasia type I: The need for a different surgical approach. Surgery 110:998–1004; discussion 1004–1005, 1991.

125. Doppman JL, Miller DL, Chang R, et al: Insulinomas: Localization with selective intraarterial injection of calcium. Radiology 178:237–241, 1991.

126. Doherty GM, Doppman JL, Shawker TH, et al: Results of a prospective strategy to diagnose, localize, and resect insulinomas. Surgery 110:989–96; discussion 996–997, 1991.

127. Grant CS, van Heerden J, Charboneau JW, et al: The value of intraoperative ultrasonography. Arch Surg 123:843–848, 1988.

128. O'Shea D, Rohrer-Theurs AW, Lynn JA, et al: Localization of insulinomas by selective intraarterial calcium injection. J Clin Endocrinol Metab 81:1623–1627, 1996.

129. Broder L: Chemotherapy of malignant insulinomas with streptozotocin. Proc 8th Intl Congr Diabetes 314:714–727, 1974.

130. Burgess JR, Harle RA, Tucker P, et al: Adrenal lesions in a large kindred with multiple endocrine neoplasia type 1. Arch Surg 131:699–702, 1996.

131. Croughs RJ, Hulsmans HA, Israel DE, et al: Glucagonoma as part of the polyglandular adenoma syndrome. Am J Med 52:690–698, 1972

132. Tiengo A, Fedele D, Marchiori E, et al: Suppression and stimulation mechanisms controlling glucagon secretion in a case of islet-cell tumor producing glucagon, insulin, and gastrin. Diabetes 25:408–412, 1975.

133. Leclere J, Vicari F, Laurent J, et al: [Islet cell tumor with diarrhea and diabetes

(glucagonoma?) associated with hyperparathyroidism: Long-term results of local-regional treatment with streptozotocin]. Ann Endocrinol (Paris) 38:153–154, 1977.

134. Stacpoole PW, Jaspan J, Kasselberg AG, et al: A familial glucagonoma syndrome: Genetic, clinical and biochemical features. Am J Med 70:1017–1026, 1981.

135. Bassett JH: Glucagonomas in multiple endocrine neoplasia type 1. J Endocrinol 152:68, 1997.

136. Strauss GM, Weitzman SA, Aoki TT: Dimethyltriazenoimidazole carboxamide therapy of malignant glucagonoma. Ann Intern Med 90:57–58, 1979.

137. Marynick SP, Fagadau WR, Duncan LA. Malignant glucagonoma syndrome: Response to chemotherapy. Ann Intern Med 93:453–454, 1980.

138. Verner JV, Morrison AB: Islet cell tumor and a syndrome of refractory watery diarrhea and hypokalemia. Am J Med 25:374–380, 1958.

139. Marks IN, Bank S, Louw JH: Islet cell tumor of the pancreas with reversible watery diarrhea and achlorhydria. Gastroenterology 52:695–708, 1967.

140. Bloom SR, Polak JM, Pearse AG: Vasoactive intestinal peptide and watery-diarrhoea syndrome. Lancet 2:14–16, 1973.

141. Brown CH, Crile G Jr: Pancreatic adenoma with intractable diarrhea, hypokalemia, and hypercalcemia. JAMA 190:30–34, 1964.

142. Burkhardt A: The Verner-Morrison syndrome: The clinical picture and pathologic anatomy. Klin Wochenschr 54:1–11, 1976.

143. Long RG, Barnes AJ, Adrian TE, et al. Suppression of pancreatic endocrine tumor secretion by long-acting somatostatin analogue. Lancet 2:764–767, 1979.

144. Kahn CR, Levy AG, Gardner JD, et al: Pancreatic cholera: Beneficial effects of treatment with streptozotocin. N Engl J Med 292:941–945, 1975.

145. Kingham JG, Dick R, Bloom SR, Frankel RJ: Vipoma: Localisation by percutaneous transhepatic portal venous sampling. Br Med J 2:1682–1683, 1978.

146. Jaffe BM, Kopen DF, DeSchryver-Kecskemeti K, et al: Indomethacin-responsive pancreatic cholera. N Engl J Med 297:817–821, 1977.

147. Long RG, Bryant MG, Yuille PM, et al: Mixed pancreatic apudoma with symptoms of excess vasoactive intestinal polypeptide and insulin: Improvement of diarrhoea with metoclopramide. Gut 22:505–511, 1981.

148. Pandol SJ, Korman LY, McCarthy DM, Gardner JD: Beneficial effect of oral lithium carbonate in the treatment of pancreatic cholera syndrome. N Engl J Med 302:1403–1404, 1980.

149. Friesen SR, Kimmel JR, Tomita T: Pancreatic polypeptide as screening marker for pancreatic polypeptide apudomas in multiple endocrinopathies. Am J Surg 139:61–72, 1980.

150. Skogseid B, Oberg K, Benson L, et al: A standardized meal stimulation test of the endocrine pancreas for early detection of pancreatic endocrine tumors in multiple endocrine neoplasia type 1 syndrome: Five years experience. J Clin Endocrinol Metab 64:1233–1240, 1987.

151. Lamers CB, Diemel CM: Basal and postatropine serum pancreatic polypeptide concentrations in familial multiple endocrine neoplasia type I. J Clin Endocrinol Metab 55:774–778, 1982.

152. Takahashi H, Nakano K, Adachi Y, et al: Multiple nonfunctional pancreatic islet cell tumor in multiple endocrine neoplasia type I: A case report. Acta Pathol Jpn 38:667–682, 1988.

153. Bloom SR, Polak JM, West AM: Somatostatin content of pancreatic endocrine tumors. Metabolism 27(9 Suppl 1):1235–1238, 1978.

154. Guillemin R: Some thoughts on current research with somatostatin. Metabolism 27(9 Suppl 1):1453–1461, 1978.

155. Lundbaek K: Somatostatin: Clinical importance and outlook. Metabolism 27(9 Suppl 1):1463–1469, 1978.

156. Krejs GJ, Orci L, Conlon JM, et al: Somatostatinoma syndrome: Biochemical, morphologic and clinical features. N Engl J Med 301:285–292, 1979.

157. Soga J, Yakuwa Y: Somatostatinoma/inhibitory syndrome: A statistical evaluation of 173 reported cases as compared to other pancreatic endocrinomas. J Exp Clin Cancer Res 18:13–22, 1999.

158. Asa SL, Singer W, Kovacs K, et al: Pancreatic endocrine tumour producing growth hormone-releasing hormone associated with multiple endocrine neoplasia type I syndrome. Acta Endocrinol (Copenh) 115:331–337, 1987.

159. Sano T, Yamasaki R, Saito H, et al: Growth hormone-releasing hormone (GHRH)-secreting pancreatic tumor in a patient with multiple endocrine neoplasia type I. Am J Surg Pathol 11:810–819, 1987.

160. Sano T, Asa SL, Kovacs K: Growth hormone-releasing hormone-producing tumors: Clinical, biochemical, and morphological manifestations. Endocr Rev 9:357–373, 1988.

161. Prosser PR, Karam JH, Townsend JJ, Forsham PH: Prolactin-secreting pituitary adenomas in multiple endocrine adenomatosis, type I. Ann Intern Med 91:41–44, 1979.

162. Farid NR, Buehler S, Russell NA, et al: Prolactinomas in familial multiple endocrine neoplasia syndrome type I: Relationship to HLA and carcinoid tumors. Am J Med 69:874–880, 180.

163. Maton PN, Gardner JD, Jensen RT: Cushing's syndrome in patients with the Zollinger-Ellison syndrome. N Engl J Med 315:1–5, 1986.

164. Gaitan D, Loosen PT, Orth DN: Two patients with Cushing's disease in a kindred with multiple endocrine neoplasia type I. J Clin Endocrinol Metab 76:1580–1582, 1993.

165. Hershon KS, Kelly WA, Shaw CM, et al: Prolactinomas as part of the multiple endocrine neoplastic syndrome type 1. Am J Med 74:713–720, 1983.

166. Bidart JM, Baudin E, Troalen F, et al: Eutopic and ectopic production of glycoprotein hormones alpha and beta subunits. Ann Endocrinol (Paris) 58:125–128, 1997.

167. Duh QY, Hybarger CP, Geist R, et al: Carcinoids associated with multiple endocrine neoplasia syndromes. Am J Surg 154:142–148, 1987.

168. Williams ED, Celestin LR: The association of bronchial carcinoid and pluriglandular adenomatosis. Thorax 17:120–127, 1963.

169. Fisher ER, Hicks J: Further pathologic observations on the syndrome of peptic ulcer and multiple endocrine tumors. Gastroenterology 38:458–466, 1960.

170. Snyder N 3rd, Scurry MT, Deiss WP. Five families with multiple endocrine adenomatosis. Ann Intern Med 76:53–58, 1972.

171. Rode J, Dhillon AP, Cotton PB, et al: Carcinoid tumour of stomach and primary hyperparathyroidism: A new association. J Clin Pathol 40:546–551, 1987.

172. Cadiot G, Laurent-Puig P, Thuille B, et al: Is the multiple endocrine neoplasia type 1 gene a suppressor for fundic argyrophil tumors in the Zollinger-Ellison syndrome? Gastroenterology 105:579–582, 1993.

173. Lee C: Carcinoid tumor of the pancreas causing the diarrheogenic syndrome: Report of a case combined with multiple endocrine neoplasia type 1. Surgery 99:123–129, 1980.

174. Teh BT, McArdle J, Chan SP, et al: Clinicopathologic studies of thymic carcinoids in multiple endocrine neoplasia type 1. Medicine (Baltimore) 76:21–29, 1997.

175. Teh BT, Zedenius J, Kytola S, et al: Thymic carcinoids in multiple endocrine neoplasia type 1. Ann Surg 228:99–105, 1998.

176. Bordi C, Falchetti A, Azzoni C, et al: Aggressive forms of gastric neuroendocrine tumors in multiple endocrine neoplasia type I. Am J Surg Pathol 21:1075–1082, 1997.

177. Bordi C, D'Adda T, Azzoni C, Ferraro G: Pathogenesis of ECL cell tumors in humans. Yale J Biol Med 71:273–284, 1998.

178. Gibril F, Reynolds JC, Lubensky IA, et al: Ability of somatostatin receptor scintigraphy to identify patients with gastric carcinoids: A prospective study. J Nucl Med 41:1646–1656, 2000.

179. Rindi G: Gastric carcinoids and neuroendocrine carcinomas:

Pathogenesis, pathology and behaviour: Clinicopathologic analysis of 205 cases. World J Surg 20:158–172, 1996.

180. Tomassetti P, Migliori M, Caletti GC, et al: Treatment of type II gastric carcinoid tumors with somatostatin analogues. N Engl J Med 343:551–554, 2000.

181. Skogseid B, Larsson C, Lindgren PG, et al: Clinical and genetic features of adrenocortical lesions in multiple endocrine neoplasia type 1. J Clin Endocrinol Metab 75:76–81, 1992.

182. Skogseid B, Rastad J, Gobl A, et al: Adrenal lesion in multiple endocrine neoplasia type 1. Surgery 118:1077–1082, 1995.

183. Raker JW, Hanneman PH, Graf WS: Coexisting primary hyperparathyroidism and Cushing's syndrome. J Clin Endocrinol Metab 22:273–280, 1962.

184. Dluhy RG, Williams GH: Primary aldosteronism in a hypertensive acromegalic patient. J Clin Endocrinol Metab 29:1319–1324, 1969.

185. Fertig A, Webley M, Lynn JA: Primary hyperparathyroidism in a patient with Conn's syndrome. Postgrad Med J 56:45–47, 1980.

186. Beckers A, Abs R, Willems PJ, et al: Aldosterone-secreting adrenal adenoma as part of multiple endocrine neoplasia type 1 (MEN1): Loss of heterozygosity for polymorphic chromosome 11 deoxyribonucleic acid markers, including the MEN1 locus. J Clin Endocrinol Metab 75:564–570, 1992.

187. Ilgren EB, Westmoreland D: Tuberous sclerosis: Unusual associations in four cases. J Clin Pathol 37:272–278, 1984.

188. Vogelstein B, Kinzler KW: The multistep nature of cancer. Trends Genet 9:138–141, 1993.

189. Brown MA, Solomon E: Studies on inherited cancers: Outcomes and challenges of 25 years. Trends Genet 13:202–206, 1997.

190. Kinzler KW, Vogelstein B: Cancer-susceptibility genes: Gatekeepers and caretakers. Nature 386:761–763, 1997.

191. de Klein A, van Kessel AG, Grosveld G, et al: A cellular oncogene is translocated to the Philadelphia chromosome in chronic myelocytic leukaemia. Nature 300:765–767, 1982.

192. Kurzrock R, Gutterman JU, Talpaz M: The molecular genetics of Philadelphia chromosome-positive leukemias. N Engl J Med 319:990–998, 1988.

193. Dalla-Favera R, Bregni M, Erikson J, et al: Human c-myc oncogene is located on the region of chromosome 8 that is translocated in Burkitt lymphoma cells. Proc Natl Acad Sci U S A 79:7824–7837, 1982.

194. Hansen MF, Cavenee WK: Retinoblastoma and the progression of tumor genetics. Trends Genet 4:125–128, 1988.

195. Knudson AG Jr: Mutation and cancer: statistical study of retinoblastoma.

Proc Natl Acad Sci U S A 68:820–823, 1971.

196. Knudson AG Jr, Strong LC, Anderson DE: Heredity and cancer in man. Prog Med Genet 9:113–158, 1973.

197. Bystrom C, Larsson C, Blomberg C, et al: Localization of the MEN1 gene to a small region within chromosome 11q13 by deletion mapping in tumors. Proc Natl Acad Sci U S A 87:1968–1972, 1990.

198. Thakker RV, Pook MA, Wooding C, et al: Association of somatotrophinomas with loss of alleles on chromosome 11 and with gsp mutations. J Clin Invest 91:2815–2821, 1993.

199. The European Consortium on MEN1: Construction of a 1.2-Mb sequence-ready contig of chromosome 11q13 encompassing the multiple endocrine neoplasia type 1 (MEN1) gene. Genomics 44:94–100, 1997.

200. Debelenko LV, Emmert-Buck MR, Manickam P, et al: Haplotype analysis defines a minimal interval for the multiple endocrine neoplasia type 1 (MEN1) gene. Cancer Res 57:1039–1042, 1997.

201. Zablewska B, Bylund L, Mandic SA, et al: Transcription regulation of the multiple endocrine neoplasia type 1 gene in human and mouse. J Clin Endocrinol Metab 88:3845–3851, 2003.

202. Fromaget M, Vercherat C, Zhang CX, et al: Functional characterization of a promoter region in the human MEN1 tumor suppressor gene. J Mol Biol 333:87–102, 2003.

203. Agarwal SK, Kester MB, Debelenko LV, et al: Germline mutations of the MEN1 gene in familial multiple endocrine neoplasia type 1 and related states. Hum Mol Genet 6:1169–1175, 1997.

204. Debelenko LV, Brambilla E, Agarwal SK, et al: Identification of MEN1 gene mutations in sporadic carcinoid tumors of the lung. Hum Mol Genet 6:2285–2290, 1997.

205. Gortz B, Roth J, Krahenmann A, et al: Mutations and allelic deletions of the MEN1 gene are associated with a subset of sporadic endocrine pancreatic and neuroendocrine tumors and not restricted to foregut neoplasms. Am J Pathol 154:429–436, 1999.

206. Fujii T, Kawai T, Saito K, et al: MEN1 gene mutations in sporadic neuroendocrine tumors of foregut derivation. Pathol Int 49:968–973, 1999.

207. Mayr B, Apenberg S, Rothamel T, et al: Menin mutations in patients with multiple endocrine neoplasia type 1. Eur J Endocrinol 137:684–687, 1997.

208. Mayr B, Brabant G, von zur Muhlen A: Menin mutations in MEN1 patients. J Clin Endocrinol Metab 83:3004–3005, 1998.

209. Shimizu S, Tsukada T, Futami H, et al: Germline mutations of the MEN1 gene in Japanese kindred with multiple endocrine neoplasia type 1. Jpn J Cancer Res 88:1029–1032, 1997.

210. Toliat MR, Berger W, Ropers HH, et al: Mutations in the MEN I gene in

sporadic neuroendocrine tumours of gastroenteropancreatic system. Lancet 350:1223, 1997.

211. Zhuang Z, Ezzat SZ, Vortmeyer AO, et al: Mutations of the MEN1 tumor suppressor gene in pituitary tumors. Cancer Res 57:5446–5451, 1997.

212. Bartsch D, Kopp I, Bergenfelz A, et al: MEN1 gene mutations in 12 MEN1 families and their associated tumors. Eur J Endocrinol 139:416–420, 1998.

213. Chico A, Gallart L, Mato E, et al: A novel germline mutation in exon 5 of the multiple endocrine neoplasia type 1 gene. J Mol Med 76:837–839, 1998.

214. Fujimori M, Shirahama S, Sakurai A, et al: Novel V184E MEN1 germline mutation in a Japanese kindred with familial hyperparathyroidism. Am J Med Genet 80:221–222, 1998.

215. Giraud S, Zhang CX, Serova-Sinilnikova O, et al: Germ-line mutation analysis in patients with multiple endocrine neoplasia type 1 and related disorders. Am J Hum Genet 63:455–467, 1998.

216. Kishi M, Tsukada T, Shimizu S, et al: A large germline deletion of the MEN1 gene in a family with multiple endocrine neoplasia type 1. Jpn J Cancer Res 89:1–5, 1998.

217. Sakurai A, Shirahama S, Fujimori M, et al: Novel MEN1 gene mutations in familial multiple endocrine neoplasia type 1. J Hum Genet 43:199–201, 1998.

218. Sato M, Matsubara S, Miyauchi A, et al: Identification of five novel germline mutations of the MEN1 gene in Japanese multiple endocrine neoplasia type 1 (MEN1) families. J Med Genet 35:915–919, 1998.

219. Tanaka C: Analysis of loss of heterozygosity on chromosome 11 and infrequent inactivation of MEN1 gene in sporadic pituitary adenomas. J Clin Endocrinol Metab 33:2631–2263, 1998.

220. Teh BT, Esapa CT, Houlston R, et al: A family with isolated hyperparathyroidism segregating a missense MEN1 mutation and showing loss of the wild-type alleles in the parathyroid tumors. Am J Hum Genet 63:1544–1549, 1998.

221. Teh BT, Kytola S, Farnebo F, et al: Mutation analysis of the MEN1 gene in multiple endocrine neoplasia type 1, familial acromegaly and familial isolated hyperparathyroidism. J Clin Endocrinol Metab 83:2621–2626, 1998.

222. Gortz B, Roth J, Speel EJ, et al: MEN1 gene mutation analysis of sporadic adrenocortical lesions. Int J Cancer 80:373–379, 1999.

223. Poncin J, Abs R, Velkeniers B, et al: Mutation analysis of the MEN1 gene in Belgian patients with multiple endocrine neoplasia type 1 and related diseases. Hum Mutat 13:54–60, 1999.

224. Pannett AA, Thakker RV: Multiple endocrine neoplasia type 1. Endocr Relat Cancer 6:449–473, 1999.

225. Turner JJ, Leotlela PD, Pannett AA, et al. Frequent occurrence of an intron

4 mutation in multiple endocrine neoplasia type 1. J Clin Endocrinol Metab 87:2688–2693, 2002.

226. Asteria C, Faglia G, Roncoroni R, et al: Identification of three novel menin mutations (c.741delGTCA, c.1348T>C, c.1785delA) in unrelated Italian families affected with multiple endocrine neoplasia type 1: Additional information for mutational screening. Hum Mutat 17:237, 2001.

227. Bergman L, Teh B, Cardinal J, et al: Identification of MEN1 gene mutations in families with MEN1 and related disorders. Br J Cancer 3:1009–1014, 2000.

228. Cetani F, Pardi E, Cianferotti L, et al: A new mutation of the MEN1 gene in an Italian kindred with multiple endocrine neoplasia type 1. Eur J Endocrinol 140:429–433, 1999.

229. Dackiw AP, Cote GJ, Fleming JB, et al: Screening for MEN1 mutations in patients with atypical endocrine neoplasia. Surgery 126:1097–1103; discussion 1103–1104, 1999.

230. Dwarakanathan AA, Zwart S, Oathus RC: Isolated familial hyperparathyroidism with a novel mutation of the MEN1 gene. Endocr Pract 6:268–270, 2000.

231. Hai N, Aoki N, Matsuda A, et al: Germline MEN1 mutations in sixteen Japanese families with multiple endocrine neoplasia type 1 (MEN1). Eur J Endocrinol 141:475–480, 1999.

232. Hai N, Aoki N, Shimatsu A, et al: Clinical features of multiple endocrine neoplasia type 1 (MEN1) phenocopy without germline MEN1 gene mutations: analysis of 20 Japanese sporadic cases with MEN1. Clin Endocrinol (Oxf) 52:509–518, 2000.

233. Hai N, Muto G, Okamoto H, et al: A novel germline mutation of the MEN1 gene, L259del, in a patient with sporadic multiple endocrine neoplasia type 1 (MEN1). Jpn J Clin Oncol 31:125–127, 2001.

234. Hamaguchi K, Nguyen DC, Yanase T, et al: Novel germline mutations of the MEN1 gene in Japanese patients with multiple endocrine neoplasia type 1. J Hum Genet 44:43–47, 1999.

235. Honda M, Tsukada T, Tanaka H, et al: A novel mutation of the MEN1 gene in a Japanese kindred with familial isolated primary hyperparathyroidism. Eur J Endocrinol 142:138–143, 2000.

236. Jakobovitz-Picard O, Olchovsky D, Berezin M, et al: Mutation analysis of the MEN1 gene in Israeli patients with MEN1 and familial isolated hyperprolactinemia. Hum Mutat 16:269, 2000.

237. Kakizawa T, Sakurai A, Ikeo Y, et al: Novel deletional mutation of the MEN1 gene in a kindred with multiple endocrine neoplasia type 1. Clin Genet 58:61–63, 2000.

238. Karges W, Ludwig L, Kessler H, et al: Menin mutations in the diagnosis and prediction of multiple endocrine neoplasia type 1. Langenbecks Arch Surg 383:183–186, 1998.

239. Karges W, Jostarndt K, Maier S, et al: Multiple endocrine neoplasia type 1 (MEN1) gene mutations in a subset of patients with sporadic and familial primary hyperparathyroidism target the coding sequence but spare the promoter region. J Endocrinol 166:1–9, 2000.

240. Kassem M, Kruse TA, Wong FK, et al: Familial isolated hyperparathyroidism as a variant of multiple endocrine ncoplasia type 1 in a large Danish pedigree. J Clin Endocrinol Metab 85:165–167, 2000.

241. Kishi M, Tsukada T, Shimizu S, et al: A novel splicing mutation (894-9 G → A) of the MEN1 gene responsible for multiple endocrine neoplasia type 1. Cancer Lett 142:105–110, 2000.

242. Komminoth P: A 5178-9g: A splice donor site mutation in intron 4 of the MEN1 gene causing multiple endocrine neoplasia type 1. Int J Cancer 87:306–367, 2000.

243. Kytola S, Villablanca A, Ebeling T, et al: Founder effect in multiple endocrine neoplasia type 1 (MEN1) in Finland. J Med Genet 38:185–189, 2001.

244. Matsubara S, Sato M, Ohye H, et al: Detection of a novel nonsense mutation of the MEN1 gene in a familial multiple endocrine neoplasia type 1 patient and its screening in the family members. Endocr J 45:653–657, 1998.

245. Miyauchi A, Sato M, Matsubara S, et al: A family of MEN1 with a novel germline missense mutation and benign polymorphisms. Endocr J 45:753–759, 1998.

246. Morelli A, Falchetti A, Martineti V, et al: MEN1 gene mutation analysis in Italian patients with multiple endocrine neoplasia type 1. Eur J Endocrinol 142:131–137, 2000.

247. Mutch MG, Dilley WG, Sanjurjo F, et al: Germline mutations in the multiple endocrine neoplasia type 1 gene: Evidence for frequent splicing defects. Hum Mutat 13:175–185, 1999.

248. Namihira H, Sato M, Miyauchi A, et al: Different phenotypes of multiple endocrine neoplasia type 1 (MEN1) in monozygotic twins found in a Japanese MEN1 family with MEN1 gene mutation. Endocr J 47:37–43, 2000.

249. Ohye H, Sato M, Matsubara S, et al: A novel germline mutation of multiple endocrine neoplasia type 1 (MEN1) gene in a Japanese MEN1 patient and her daughter. Endocr J 46:325–329, 1999.

250. Sato M, Miyauchi A, Namihira H, et al: A newly recognized germline mutation of MEN1 gene identified in a patient with parathyroid adenoma and carcinoma. Endocrine 12:223–226, 2000.

251. Tsukada T, Kishi M, Obara T, Yamaguchi K: An intronic splicing mutation of the MEN1 gene. Int J Cancer 87:305–307, 2000.

252. Valdes N, Perez de Nanclares G, et al: Multiple endocrine neoplasia type 1 (MEN1): Clinical heterogeneity in a large family with a nonsense mutation in the MEN1 gene (Trp471Stop). Clin Endocrinol (Oxf) 50:309–313, 1999.

253. Miedlich S, Lohmann T, Schneyer U, et al: Familial isolated primary hyperparathyroidism: A multiple endocrine neoplasia type 1 variant? Eur J Endocrinol 145:155–160, 2001.

254. Burgess JR, Nord B, David R, et al: Phenotype and phenocopy: The relationship between genotype and clinical phenotype in a single large family with multiple endocrine neoplasia type 1 (MEN1). Clin Endocrinol (Oxf) 53:205–211, 2000.

255. Abe T, Yoshimoto K, Taniyama M, et al: An unusual kindred of the multiple endocrine neoplasia type 1 (MEN1) in Japanese. J Clin Endocrinol Metab 85:1327–1330, 3000.

256. Cavaco BM, Domingues R, Bacelar MC, et al: Mutational analysis of Portuguese families with multiple endocrine neoplasia type 1 reveals large germline deletions. Clin Endocrinol (Oxf) 56:465–473, 2002.

257. Pannett AA, Thakker RV: Somatic mutations in MEN type 1 tumors, consistent with the Knudson "two-hit" hypothesis. J Clin Endocrinol Metab 86:4371–4374, 2001.

258. Heppner C, Kester MB, Agarwal SK, et al: Somatic mutation of the MEN1 gene in parathyroid tumours. Nat Genet 16:375–378, 1997.

259. Carling T: Parathyroid MEN1 gene mutations in relation to clinical characteristics of non-familial primary hyperparathyroidism. J Clin Endocrinol Metab 83:2951–2954, 1998.

260. Farnebo F, Teh BT, Kytola S, et al: Alterations of the MEN1 gene in sporadic parathyroid tumors. J Clin Endocrinol Metab 838:2627–2630, 1998.

261. Shan L, Nakamura Y, Nakamura M, et al: Somatic mutations of multiple endocrine neoplasia type 1 gene in the sporadic endocrine tumors. Lab Invest 78:471–475, 1998.

262. Ludwig L, Schleithoff L, Kessler H, et al: Loss of wild-type MEN1 gene expression in multiple endocrine neoplasia type 1-associated parathyroid adenoma. Endocr J 46:539–544, 1999.

263. Wang EH, Ebrahimi SA, Wu AY, et al: Mutation of the MENIN gene in sporadic pancreatic endocrine tumors. Cancer Res 58:4417–4420, 1998.

264. Zhuang Z, Vortmeyer AO, Pack S, et al: Somatic mutations of the MEN1 tumor suppressor gene in sporadic gastrinomas and insulinomas. Cancer Res 57:4682–4686, 1997.

265. Cupisti K, Hoppner W, Dotzenrath C, et al: Lack of MEN1 gene mutations in 27 sporadic insulinomas. Eur J Clin Invest 30:325–329, 2000.

266. Mailman MD, Muscarella P, Schirmer WJ, et al: Identification of MEN1 mutations in sporadic enteropancreatic neuroendocrine tumors by analysis of paraffin-embedded tissue. Clin Chem 45:29–34, 1999.

267. Hessman O, Lindberg D, Skogseid B, et al: Mutation of the multiple endocrine neoplasia type 1 gene in nonfamilial, malignant tumors of the endocrine pancreas. Cancer Res 58:377–379, 1998.

268. Prezant TR, Levine J, Melmed S: Molecular characterization of the men1 tumor suppressor gene in sporadic pituitary tumors. J Clin Endocrinol Metab 83:1388–1391, 1998.

269. Boni R, Vortmeyer AO, Pack S, et al: Somatic mutations of the MEN1 tumor suppressor gene detected in sporadic angiofibromas. J Invest Dermatol 111:539–540, 1988.

270. Vortmeyer AO, Boni R, Pak E, et al: Multiple endocrine neoplasia 1 gene alterations in MEN1-associated and sporadic lipomas. J Natl Cancer Inst 90:398–399, 1998.

271. Pannett AA: Meta-analysis of 31 studies reporting 344 mutations in the multiple endocrine neoplasia type 1 (MEN1) gene [Abstract]. J Bone Miner Res 14:S321, 1999.

272. Landis CA, Masters SB, Spada A, et al: GTPase inhibiting mutations activate the alpha chain of Gs and stimulate adenylyl cyclase in human pituitary tumours. Nature 340:692–696, 1989.

273. Lyons J, Landis CA, Harsh G, et al: Two G protein oncogenes in human endocrine tumors. Science 249:655–659, 1990.

274. Thakker RV: Molecular genetics of parathyroid disease. Endocrinol Diabetes 3:521–528, 1996.

275. Gadelha M: Localization of the isolate familial somatotropinoma gene to a 7.4Mb region at chromosome 11q13 by allelotype and haplotype analysis [Abstract]. Endocr Soc 88:276, 1999.

276. Olufemi SE, Green JS, Manickam P, et al: Common ancestral mutation in the MEN1 gene is likely responsible for the prolactinoma variant of MEN1 (MEN1Burin) in four kindreds from Newfoundland. Hum Mutat 11:264–269, 1998.

277. Guru SC, Goldsmith PK, Burns AL, et al: Menin, the product of the MEN1 gene, is a nuclear protein. Proc Natl Acad Sci U S A 95:1630–1644, 1998.

278. Agarwal SK, Lee Burns A, Sukhodolets KE, et al: Molecular pathology of the MEN1 gene. Ann N Y Acad Sci 1014:189–198, 2004.

279. Poisson A, Zablewska B, Gaudray P: Menin interacting proteins as clues toward the understanding of multiple 279:40267–40275 endocrine neoplasia type 1. Cancer Lett 189:1–10, 2003.

280. Yumita W, Ikeo Y, Yamauchi K, et al: Suppression of insulin-induced AP-1 transactivation by menin accompanies inhibition of c-Fos induction. Int J Cancer 103:738–744, 2003.

281. Heppner C, Bilimoria KY, Agarwal SK, et al: The tumor suppressor protein menin interacts with NF-kappaB proteins and inhibits NF-kappaB-mediated transactivation. Oncogene 20:4917–4925, 2001.

282. Kaji H, Canaff L, Lebrun JJ, et al: Inactivation of menin, a Smad3-interacting protein, blocks transforming growth factor type beta signaling. Proc Natl Acad Sci U S A 98:3837–3842, 2001.

283. Sowa H, Kaji H, Canaff L, et al: Inactivation of menin, the product of multiple endocrine neoplasia type 1 gene, inhibits the commitment of multipotential mesenchymal stem cells into the osteoblast lineage. J Biol Chem 23:21058–21069, 2003.

284. Lemmens IH, Forsberg L, Pannett AA, et al: Menin interacts directly with the homeobox-containing protein Pem. Biochem Biophys Res Commun 286:426–431, 2001.

285. Sukhodolets KE, Hickman AB, Agarwal SK, et al: The 32-kilodalton subunit of replication protein A interacts with menin, the product of the MEN1 tumor suppressor gene. Mol Cell Biol 23:493–509, 2003.

286. Ohkura N, Kishi M, Tsukada T, et al: Menin, a gene product responsible for multiple endocrine neoplasia type 1, interacts with the putative tumor metastasis suppressor nm23. Biochem Biophys Res Commun 282:1206–1210, 2001.

287. Yaguchi H, Ohkura N, Tsukada T, et al: Menin, the multiple endocrine neoplasia type 1 gene product, exhibits GTP-hydrolyzing activity in the presence of the tumor metastasis suppressor nm23. J Biol Chem 277:38197–38204, 2002.

288. Obungu VH, Lee Burns A, Agarwal SK, et al: Menin, a tumor suppressor, associates with nonmuscle myosin II-A heavy chain. Oncogene 22:6347–6358, 2003.

289. Hirai SI, Ryseck RP, Mechta F, et al: Characterization of junD: A new member of the jun proto-oncogene family. EMBO J 8:1433–1439, 1989.

290. Ryder K, Lanahan A, Perez-Albuerne E, et al: jun D, a third member of the jun gene family. Proc Natl Acad Sci U S A 86:1500–1503, 1989.

291. Pfarr CM, Mechta F, Spyrou G, et al: Mouse JunD negatively regulates fibroblast growth and antagonizes transformation by ras. Cell 76:747–760, 1994.

292. Sowa H, Kaji H, Hendy GN, et al: Menin is required for BMP-2- and TGF-beta-regulated osteoblastic differentiation through interaction with Smads and Runx2. J Biol Chem 279:40267–40275, 2004.

293. Jin S, Mao H, Schnepp RW, et al: Menin associates with FANCD2, a protein involved in repair of DNA damage. Cancer Res 63:4204–4210, 2003.

294. Lopez-Egido J, Cunningham J, Berg M, et al: Menin's interaction with glial fibrillary acidic protein and vimentin suggests a role for the intermediate filament network in regulating menin activity. Exp Cell Res 278:175–183, 2002.

295. Gobl AE, Berg M, Lopez-Egido JR, et al: Menin represses JunD-activated transcription by a histone deacetylase-dependent mechanism. Biochim Biophys Acta 1447:51–56, 1999.

296. Gallo A, Cuozzo C, Esposito I, et al: Menin uncouples Elk-1, JunD and c-Jun phosphorylation from MAP kinase activation. Oncogene 21:6434–6445, 2002.

297. Lin SY, Elledge SJ: Multiple tumor suppressor pathways negatively regulate telomerase. Cell 113:881–889, 2003.

298. Stalberg P, Grimfjard P, Santesson M, et al: Transfection of the multiple endocrine neoplasia type 1 gene to a human endocrine pancreatic tumor cell line inhibits cell growth and affects expression of JunD, delta-like protein 1/preadipocyte factor-1, proliferating cell nuclear antigen, and QM/Jif-1. J Clin Endocrinol Metab 89:2326–2337, 2004.

299. Kim YS, Burns AL, Goldsmith PK, et al: Stable overexpression of MEN1 suppresses tumorigenicity of RAS. Oncogene 18:5936–5942, 1999.

300. Stewart C, Parente F, Piehl F, et al. Characterization of the mouse Men1 gene and its expression during development. Oncogene 17:2485–2493, 1998.

301. Bassett JH, Rashbass P, Harding B, et al: Studies of the murine homolog of the multiple endocrine neoplasia type 1 (MEN1) gene, men1. J Bone Miner Res 14:3–10, 1999.

302. Crabtree JS, Scacheri PC, Ward JM, et al. A mouse model of multiple endocrine neoplasia, type 1, develops multiple endocrine tumors. Proc Natl Acad Sci U S A 98:1118–1123, 2001.

303. Bertolino P, Tong WM, Galendo D, et al: Heterozygous Men1 mutant mice develop a range of endocrine tumors mimicking multiple endocrine neoplasia type 1. Mol Endocrinol 17:1880–1892, 2003.

304. Scacheri PC, Crabtree JS, Novotny EA, et al: Bidirectional transcriptional activity of PGK-neomycin and unexpected embryonic lethality in heterozygote chimeric knockout mice. Genesis 30:259–263, 2001.

305. Bertolino P, Radovanovic I, Casse H, et al: Genetic ablation of the tumor suppressor menin causes lethality at mid-gestation with defects in multiple organs. Mech Dev 120:549–560, 2003.

306. Brandi ML, Aurbach GD, Fitzpatrick LA, et al: Parathyroid mitogenic activity in plasma from patients with familial multiple endocrine neoplasia type 1. N Engl J Med 314:1287–1293, 1986.

307. Zimering MB, Brandi ML, deGrange DA, et al: Circulating fibroblast growth factor-like substance in familial multiple endocrine neoplasia type 1. J Clin Endocrinol Metab 70:149–154, 1990.

308. Bale SJ, Bale AE, Stewart K, et al: Linkage analysis of multiple endocrine neoplasia type 1 with INT2 and other markers on chromosome 11. Genomics 4:320–322, 1989.

309. Pang JT, Lloyd SE, Wooding C, et al: Genetic mapping studies of 40 loci and 23 cosmids in chromosome 11p13-11q13, and exclusion of mu-calpain as the multiple endocrine neoplasia type 1 gene. Hum Genet 97:732–741, 1996.

310. Marx SJ, Sakaguchi K, Green J 3rd, et al: Mitogenic activity on parathyroid cells in plasma from members of a large kindred with multiple endocrine neoplasia type 1. J Clin Endocrinol Metab 67:149–153, 1988.

311. Zimering MB, Katsumata N, Sato Y, et al: Increased basic fibroblast growth factor in plasma from multiple endocrine neoplasia type 1: Relation to pituitary tumor. J Clin Endocrinol Metab 76:1182–1187, 1993.

312. Larsson C, Shepherd J, Nakamura Y, et al: Predictive testing for multiple endocrine neoplasia type 1 using DNA polymorphisms. J Clin Invest 89:1344–1349, 1992.

313. American Society of Human Genetics Board of Directors, American College of Medical Genetics Board of Directors: Points to consider: Ethical, legal, and psychosocial implications of genetic testing in children and adolescents. Am J Hum Genet 57:1233–1241, 1995.

314. Skogseid B, Eriksson B, Lundqvist G, et al: Multiple endocrine neoplasia type 1: A 10-year prospective screening study in four kindreds. J Clin Endocrinol Metab 73:281–287, 1991.

# Multiple Endocrine Neoplasia Type 2

## Ana O. Hoff and Robert F. Gagel

## DEFINITIONS

*Multiple endocrine neoplasia type 2A* (MEN2A) is an autosomal-dominant genetic syndrome that includes medullary thyroid carcinoma (MTC), pheochromocytoma, and hyperparathyroidism (Table 192-1). MEN2B is an autosomal-dominant genetic syndrome that includes MTC, pheochromocytoma, multiple mucosal neuromas, and a marfanoid habitus. *Familial medullary thyroid carcinoma-only syndrome* (FMTC) refers to a variant of MEN2A in which MTC is the only clinical manifestation. Two other variants of MEN2A are shown in Table 192-1.

## HISTORICAL PERSPECTIVE

It was a chance autopsy observation by John Sipple in 1961 that led to the association of thyroid carcinoma and pheochromocytoma.[1] It was left to others to define the nature of the thyroid tumor (MTC),[2,3] its derivation from the parafollicular C cell,[4,5] and the nature of the hereditary syndrome, and to separate this polyglandular syndrome from the other major hereditary tumor syndrome MEN1[6] (see Chapter 191). During this *descriptive phase,* the clinical features of bilateral and multicentric MTC, bilateral pheochromocytomas, and hyperparathyroidism (MEN2A) were first delineated.[7–9] It was also during this period that the association of MTC, pheochromocytoma, and multiple mucosal neuromas (MEN2B) was first reported and differentiated from MEN2A.[10,11]

Isolation and characterization of the hypocalcemic peptide calcitonin and the realization that it was produced in large quantities by MTC introduced a second period in our understanding of this clinical syndrome, the *prospective screening phase.* The realization that provocative tests for calcitonin release and measurement of serum or urine catecholamines could be used to identify gene carriers early in the course of the clinical syndrome laid the groundwork for identification of hyperplasia of C cells or the adrenal medulla as precursor lesions[12–14] and the prevention of death from metastatic MTC or pheochromocytoma.

The resurrection of genetic-linkage techniques in the early 1980s and their application to MEN2 led to mapping of a *MEN2* locus on chromosome 10 in 1987[15,16] and the beginning of the current *genetic phase.* Identification of *RET* proto-oncogene mutations in 1993, characterization of each of the clinical MEN2 variants, and the development of specific guidelines for the clinical use of genetic information has transformed management of this clinical syndrome.

## INCIDENCE AND DISTRIBUTION

MEN2-related syndromes are uncommon, with probably fewer than 1500 kindreds worldwide.[17] Multiple affected families have been reported in North and South America, Australia, Europe, and South Africa, most thought to be transmitted by colonists from European countries. Few cases of MEN2 have been reported in Asia, except for Japan, where many families exist.[18] Little information is available regarding the incidence in native Africans, although African-American families are affected in the United States. The earliest deduced case of this disease occurred in approximately 1730,[19] and other examples from the eighteenth century exist.[20] The MEN2 syndromes have received attention far beyond their frequency because of their fascinating clinical features, their importance as a model for genetic malignancy, their unique molecular causation, and the insight that they have provided into the development of components of the endocrine and neurologic systems.

## PATHOPHYSIOLOGY AND IDENTIFICATION OF *RET* PROTO-ONCOGENE MUTATIONS

Parafollicular or calcitonin-producing cells (C cells) are dispersed within the parenchyma of the thyroid gland. These neuroendocrine cells migrate from the neural crest in early embryonic life to a position adjacent to the thyroid follicle. C cells are characteristically distributed within the thyroid gland, with the greatest concentrations located at the juncture of the upper third and lower two thirds of each lobe of the

**Table 192-1** Multiple Endocrine Neoplasia Type 2

MEN2A
  Medullary thyroid carcinoma (100%)
  Pheochromocytoma (50%)
  Parathyroid neoplasia (10%–20%)
  Variants of MEN2A
    MEN2A with cutaneous lichen amyloidosis
MEN2A or familial medullary thyroid carcinoma with Hirschsprung's
  disease
  Familial medullary thyroid carcinoma
MEN2B
  Medullary thyroid carcinoma (100%)
  Pheochromocytoma (50%)
  Absence of parathyroid disease
  Marfanoid habitus
  Intestinal ganglioneuromatosis and mucosal neuromas

thyroid gland along a hypothetic superior-to-inferior central axis (Fig. 192-1). The precise sequence of gene expression that leads to the spatial distribution of C cells in the thyroid gland is unclear, although evidence exists that the mammalian homologue of Achaete-Scute (MASH-1)[21] and the RET receptor[22] play important roles. Histologic definition of a normal C-cell population has been difficult, in part because of the variation in C-cell population within the thyroid gland and the belief that several genetic or pathophysiologic determinants of C-cell number may exist. For example, increased numbers of C cells have been identified in such diverse conditions as autoimmune thyroiditis[23] and hyperparathyroidism.[24]

The adrenal chromaffin cell is thought to migrate from neural crest tissue,[25] although this point has not been established as clearly as for the C cell. These cells uniquely express the enzyme norepinephrine N-methyltransferase (PNMT) and are capable of converting norepinephrine to epinephrine. Differentiation of the adrenal chromaffin cell is a complex process that is dependent on several signaling pathways including transforming growth factor (TGF)-$\beta_2$, TGF-$\beta_3$, bone morphogenic protein (BMP)-4,[26] and several members of the neurotropin receptor family.[27,28] An earlier literature suggesting that glucocorticoids are important in differentiation of the adrenal medulla[29] appears to be incorrect or at least incomplete.[26] A transcription factor, MASH-1, is an important

regulator of normal chromaffin cell differentiation. Mice deficient in this transcription factor have a reduced number of adrenal chromaffin cells, and those present have a reduced amount of tyrosine hydroxylase, necessary for catecholamine synthesis.[30] Deletion of the RET receptor in mice has little effect on development of the adrenal medulla,[31,32] although evidence has accumulated that expression of this receptor is necessary for PNMT expression, epinephrine production, and development of a neuronal phenotype.[31,33] It is therefore not completely surprising that activating mutations of *RET* cause increased production of epinephrine (discussed later in the section on MEN2-related pheochromocytoma).

The normal C cell synthesizes and secretes calcitonin, a peptide hormone important in the regulation of osteoclast function. Hyperplasia of C cells is associated with increased production and release of calcitonin and a change in the pattern of differential RNA processing that results in production of the alternative product, calcitonin gene–related peptide[34] (reviewed in Chapter 72). It is not known whether the increased calcitonin production results exclusively from the increased cell number or is related to increased expression of a cell-specific transcription factor that is a member of the helix-loop-helix family of transcription factors.[35–37] Measurement of serum calcitonin basally and after a provocative test has been used to detect C-cell hyperplasia.[38,39] Carcinoembryonic antigen is normally produced by C cells[40] and by medullary thyroid carcinoma[41]; the serum concentration of carcinoembryonic antigen correlates roughly with tumor mass and provides an independent method of monitoring the mass of MTC. Chromogranin A[42] and somatostatin[43,44] are two other peptides frequently produced by normal C cells and by MTC. Neither is specific for MTC, and therefore these two peptides have not been used extensively to diagnose or monitor patients with MTC.

The primary event in the development of neoplasia is clonal expansion of the C, adrenal medullary, and parathyroid cell populations. The initiating event in MEN2 and in approximately 25% of cases of sporadic MTC is an activating mutation of the *RET* proto-oncogene, a gene that encodes a tyrosine kinase receptor. Identification of these mutations and the RET-receptor system is a fascinating story that has relevance not only to MEN2 but also to several other genetic conditions that affect the nervous system.

The *RET* proto-oncogene was discovered in 1985 by Takahashi and coworkers.[45,46] Several years later, Italian investigators discovered a transforming sequence in papillary thyroid carcinoma,[47–49] a tumor derived from thyroid follicular cells, and showed it to be a naturally occurring rearrangement of *RET*. Subsequently, multiple different rearrangements have been identified in papillary thyroid carcinoma and are thought to be important in its genesis.[50–52]

Efforts to map the causative gene for MEN2 were initiated in the early 1980s and led to identification of a centromeric chromosome 10 locus in 1987.[16,53] Subsequent mapping efforts narrowed the region to include the *RET* gene, and in 1993, Mulligan and coworkers discovered mutations of the *RET* proto-oncogene,[54] observations that were subsequently confirmed by Donis-Keller and others.[55]

The *RET* proto-oncogene encodes a tyrosine kinase receptor. Together with a second extracellular protein, GFRα-1 (*Glial Cell-Derived Neurotrophic Factor Family Receptor-α-1*), it forms a receptor complex for glial cell–derived neurotrophic factor (GDNF),[56] a small peptide discovered because of its ability to prevent neuronal cell death.[57] The recognition that GDNF was a ligand for the RET/GFRα-1-receptor complex arose from a series of parallel but independent murine investigations in which the genes for RET[58] and GDNF[59–61] were deleted by homologous recombination techniques. The RET knockout mouse has a distinctive phenotype that includes failure of normal gastrointestinal neuronal (leading to a Hirschsprung-like phenotype) and kidney development. The

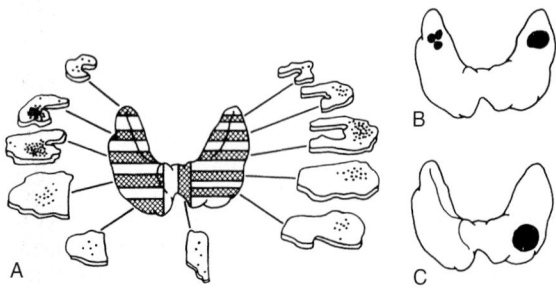

**Figure 192-1** Distribution of C cells in the thyroid gland. **A,** Reconstruction of the distribution of C cells in the thyroid gland. The greatest concentration of C cells occurs at the junction of the upper third and lower two thirds of the gland. This distribution explains the characteristic location of hereditary medullary thyroid carcinoma. **B,** Hereditary medullary thyroid carcinoma is almost always bilateral, although the extent of involvement may not be equal. **C,** Sporadic medullary thyroid carcinoma is most commonly a unilateral process that may develop at any location within the thyroid gland. (**A,** Adapted from Wolfe HJ, Voelkel EF, Tashjian AH Jr: Distribution of calcitonin containing cells in the normal adult human thyroid gland: A correlation of morphology with peptide content. J Clin Endocrinol Metab 38:688–694, 1974, with permission. **B** and **C,** From Grauer A, Raue F, Gagel RF: Changing concepts in the management of hereditary and sporadic medullary thyroid carcinoma. Endocrinol Metab Clin North Am 19:613–635, 1990, with permission.)

## RET Codons Mutated and Genotype-Phenotype Correlations

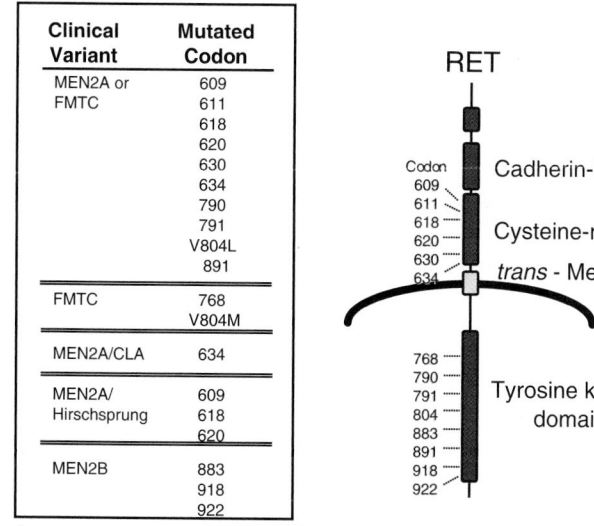

| Clinical Variant | Mutated Codon |
|---|---|
| MEN2A or FMTC | 609 |
| | 611 |
| | 618 |
| | 620 |
| | 630 |
| | 634 |
| | 790 |
| | 791 |
| | V804L |
| | 891 |
| FMTC | 768 |
| | V804M |
| MEN2A/CLA | 634 |
| MEN2A/ Hirschsprung | 609 |
| | 618 |
| | 620 |
| MEN2B | 883 |
| | 918 |
| | 922 |

A

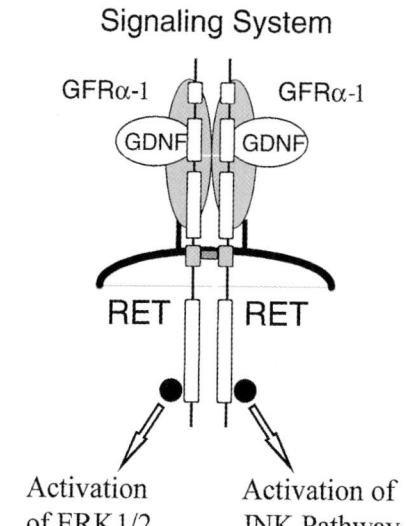

The GDNF/GFRα-1/RET Signaling System

B

**Figure 192-2** **A,** The *RET* proto-oncogene is a tyrosine kinase receptor (**right**). Germ-line mutations of both the extracellular (cysteine-rich) and intracellular (tyrosine kinase) domains cause hereditary medullary thyroid carcinoma (MTC). The clinical variants associated with germ-line mutations of specific codons are shown on the **left**. MEN2A, multiple endocrine neoplasia type 2A; FMTC, familial MTC; MEN2A/CLA, MEN2A and cutaneous lichen amyloidosis variant; MEN2A/Hirschsprung, MEN2A and Hirschsprung's disease; V804L, Val804Leu; and V804M, Val804Met. **B,** The glial cell–derived neurotrophic factor (GDNF)/glial cell–derived neurotrophic factor receptor-α (GFRα)/RET signaling system. GDNF binds to a receptor complex consisting of GFRα and RET. Autophosphorylation of RET results in activation of at least two distinct kinase pathways (ERK1/ERK2 [extracellular signal-regulated kinase] and JNK [c-Jun NH$_2$-terminal kinase]). These pathways are linked to growth, differentiation, and antiapoptotic effects in cell types expressing this complex.

recognition that GDNF was a ligand for RET grew out of the identification of a nearly identical phenotype in the *RET*- and GDNF-deficient mice. The third component of this receptor system, GFRα-1,[62] was identified by investigators seeking to identify a receptor for GDNF; the importance of this extracellular protein was subsequently verified by the finding of a phenotype in the GFRα-1 knockout identical to that found in the RET and GDNF knockouts.[63,64]

The RET/GFRα-1-receptor system is normally activated by GDNF.[65] The GFRα-1 extracellular component is tethered to the plasma membrane and interfaces with RET to function as a receptor for GDNF. Interaction of GDNF with the receptor complex causes dimerization, autophosphorylation of a specific subset of tyrosine residues, and activation of ERK1/ERK2 (extracellular signal–regulated kinase) and JNK (c-Jun NH$_2$-terminal kinase) downstream pathways[66] (Fig. 192-2). Several discrete functions have been established for the receptor complex. The first is to cause normal neuronal and kidney development. The best understood is the interaction between the developing GDNF-expressing renal mesoderm and the ureteral bud where RET is expressed. Absence of either GDNF or RET results in failure of ureteral bud invasion into the developing renal mesoderm,[67] which leads to failure of collecting system development. Addition of a tiny pellet containing GDNF to the kidney derived from the RET-deficient mouse in vitro leads to normalization of ureteral branching.[67] In the gastrointestinal tract, it is thought that RET-expressing neural crest invades the developing gastrointestinal tract in response to temporal and spatial expression of GDNF. Failure of normal RET, GDNF, or GFRα-1 expression leads to a Hirschsprung phenotype.[68] The second function of the receptor system is an antiapoptotic or anti–cell death effect.[69] A component of the neuronal invasion of the gastrointestinal tract may be inhibition of neuronal cell death by this receptor system. Finally, growth-stimulatory functions of the receptor system are mediated through the tyrosine kinase receptor and

its downstream signaling cascade. It is by activation of these growth-stimulatory pathways that mutant RET is thought to cause neoplastic transformation in MEN2.[70–72]

Subsequent studies have demonstrated a total of four ligands (GDNF, artemin, persephin, neuturin) and at least four variants of GFRα (GFRα-1, GFRα-2, GFRα-3, and GFRα-4).[73] Pairing of RET with one of the four GFRα variants creates specificity for one of the four TGF-β-like ligands.[74] This receptor family has broad importance for normal neuronal, kidney, and neuroendocrine cell development.[75]

## THE CLINICAL SYNDROMES

### MULTIPLE ENDOCRINE NEOPLASIA TYPE 2A

MEN2A is the association of MTC, pheochromocytoma, and hyperparathyroidism inherited as an autosomal-dominant trait. The clinical features in the fully developed form of this syndrome include the presence of bilateral thyroid masses, manifestations of pheochromocytoma, and, less commonly, hyperparathyroidism (see Table 192-1). Other clinical features include diarrhea, renal stones, and the potential for sudden death related to elevated levels of catecholamines.

#### Medullary Thyroid Carcinoma

MTC is generally bilateral and multicentric and is set on a background of generalized C-cell hyperplasia. Most commonly, the tumor appears as a chalky-white lesion within the upper portion of each lobe of the thyroid gland (see Fig. 192-1). The tumors are frequently multifocal, a finding thought to represent expansion of individual clones of cells rather than intrathyroidal metastasis[62] (Fig. 192-3).

The onset of prospective screening with provocative calcium or pentagastrin tests in the early 1970s led to the identification of C-cell hyperplasia as a precursor lesion for MTC.[76]

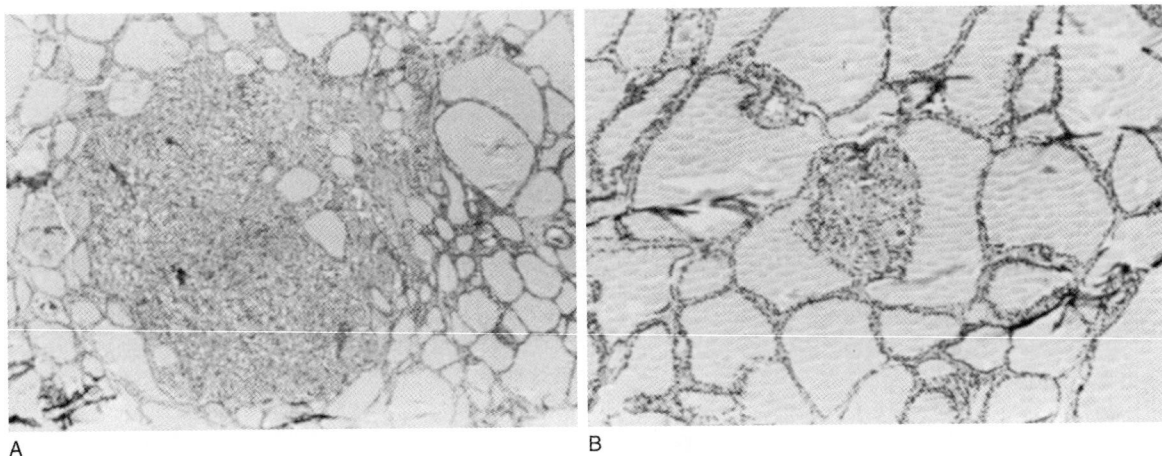

*Figure 192-3* Histologic features of hereditary medullary thyroid carcinoma. **A,** Nodular C-cell hyperplasia displacing an entire thyroid follicle. **B,** Microscopic medullary thyroid carcinoma.

The progression from normal through hyperplasia, nodular hyperplasia, and microscopic and macroscopic carcinoma appears to occur over a number of years. Little is known about the age of initiation of clonal expansion, although C-cell hyperplasia has been observed in gene carriers as young as 3 years. Metastasis has been described in patients with microscopic MTC.[77]

The biologic behavior of MTC in MEN2A is variable. Metastasis to local lymph nodes occurs frequently with tumors larger than 1 cm. Although metastasis may be present, the tumor pursues a relatively indolent course in 80% of affected individuals. In about 5% to 10% of patients, the tumor pursues a more aggressive course, which can include early metastasis and death.[78,79] Some kindreds have a familial pattern of tumor aggressiveness; in others, one or two members will display an aggressive pattern of tumor behavior against a general background of benignity. This characteristic has allowed MEN2A to remain undetected in some families over several generations, with the result that newly discovered kindreds continue to appear with some regularity.[80–82] The characteristics of aggressive tumor behavior include early bone, pulmonary, or liver metastasis; loss of expression of the calcitonin gene; or a switch to production of calcitonin gene–related peptide, the alternatively produced product of the calcitonin gene. Distant metastasis occurs most commonly to liver, lung, and bone. Death is usually attributable to metastatic disease causing local airway obstruction or to liver and lung metastases. The presence of metastatic disease in the liver may or may not be a poor prognostic feature; a number of patients with hepatic metastasis have survived several decades.[83,84]

Diarrhea may be the initial complaint in patients with MTC. At first the diarrhea may be a minor complaint, but with increasing tumor burden, the patient may have 10 to 20 stools per day. Unlike diarrhea associated with islet cell tumors, the stools are not usually voluminous.[85] The etiology of the diarrhea is unclear, although it is believed to be caused by a humoral factor produced by the tumor. Flushing has been observed in patients with MTC.

Another clinical finding associated with MTC is ectopic adrenocorticotropic (ACTH) syndrome (see Chapter 195). The clinical syndrome is most frequently seen in patients with a large primary tumor or with metastatic MTC.[86] Detailed analysis of MTC suggests that most express the pro-opiomelanocortin gene,[87] but the peptide precursor is processed to produce ACTH in only a few tumors. The clinical features of hypercorticism may be subtle (muscle weakness, edema, and mild centripetal obesity). Clinicians should be aware of this clinical syndrome because patients with MTC and ectopic

ACTH production may do well for long periods if the hypercorticism is controlled (see Chapter 195).

## Pheochromocytoma

Clinically detectable pheochromocytoma will develop in approximately 50% of known gene carriers, although autopsy studies suggest that a larger percentage of gene carriers have abnormalities of the adrenal medullae.[12,88] It is generally believed that the adrenal medullary cell, like the C cell, passes through a hyperplastic stage before the development of multicentric pheochromocytoma. It seems likely that the histologic abnormalities in the adrenal medulla occur in parallel with those observed in the C cell, although clinically apparent pheochromocytomas are only rarely detected before the diagnosis of C-cell abnormalities.

### Unique Features of Pheochromocytomas Associated with MEN2A
Pheochromocytoma in MEN2A is generally limited to the adrenal gland. The occasional exception may be explained by the presence of ectopic adrenal rest tissue or rare neoplastic changes in nonadrenal chromaffin tissue, producing paragangliomas.[89] The pheochromocytomas are usually multicentric and set on a background of diffuse adrenal medullary hyperplasia.[12,88] Although malignant pheochromocytoma in MEN2A is rare,[90–92] capsular invasion is observed frequently. No correlation has been found between capsular invasion and recurrence of the tumor.

Pheochromocytoma associated with MEN2A can be differentiated from sporadic pheochromocytoma by several unique features. The first is relative overproduction of epinephrine by the tumor. The earliest biochemical abnormality is an increase in plasma or urine epinephrine[84,93–96] (Fig. 192-4). This may be caused by the positive regulation of PNMT by RET,[31] increasing methylation of norepinephrine to produce epinephrine. A clinical observation that may be attributable to this biochemical finding is the relative lack of hypertension in patients with early pheochromocytomas and the predominance of β-adrenergic-like symptoms such as palpitations, tachycardia, and nervousness. In contrast, sporadic pheochromocytomas or those associated with von Hippel-Lindau syndrome are more commonly norepinephrine-producing tumors (see Fig. 192-4).[96] It also recently was shown that plasma metanephrine is a reliable indicator of pheochromocytoma in MEN2A, perhaps as sensitive as the measurement of plasma or urine catecholamines.[96] Rarely, adrenal medullary hyperplasia may be associated with symptoms suggestive of pheochromocytoma but with few or no detectable abnormalities of catecholamines. Larger pheochromocytomas also are characterized by overproduction of norepinephrine, although the

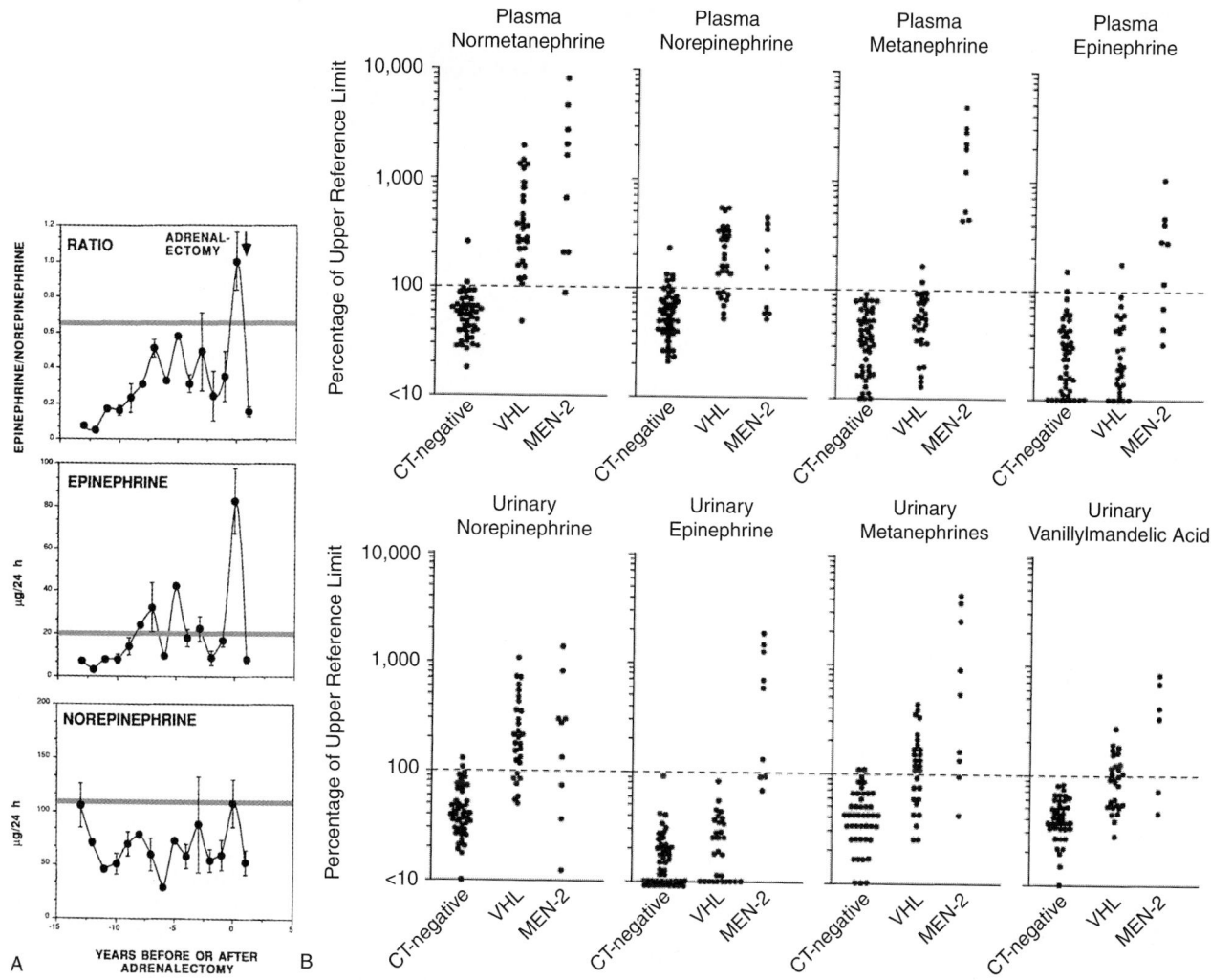

**Figure 192-4** **A,** Mean 24-hour urinary norepinephrine and epinephrine excretion and the ratio of epinephrine-to-norepinephrine excretion in 11 prospectively screened patients subsequently proved to have pheochromocytoma. Each value is the mean of values in 11 prospectively screened patients before adrenalectomy. The *horizontal line* shows the upper limit of normal. To convert epinephrine values to nanomoles, multiply by 5.458; to convert norepinephrine values to nanomoles, multiply by 5.911. **B,** Plasma concentrations of normetanephrine, norepinephrine, metanephrine, and epinephrine **(upper panels)** and urinary excretion of norepinephrine, epinephrine, metanephrine, and vanillylmandelic acid **(lower panels).** Values are expressed as percentages of the upper reference limit for each test. Data on individual patients are shown for three groups of patients with von Hippel-Lindau disease and multiple endocrine neoplasia type 2 (MEN2) as follows: patients with von Hippel-Lindau disease or MEN2 in whom a pheochromocytoma was ruled out on the basis of normal computed tomography (CT-negative), patients with von Hippel-Lindau disease who had histologically verified pheochromocytomas (VHL), and patients with MEN2 who had histologically verified pheochromocytomas (MEN2). Values for patients with pheochromocytoma were determined when the tumors were first identified by CT. The *dotted horizontal line* represents the upper reference limit for each test. The scales are logarithmic. (**A,** Data from Gagel RF, Tashjian AH Jr, Cummings T, et al: The clinical outcome of prospective screening for multiple endocrine neoplasia type 2A: An 18-year experience. N Engl J Med 318:478–484, 1988. **B,** Data from Eisenhofer G, Lenders JWM, Linehan WM, et al: Plasma normetanephrine and metanephrine for detecting pheochromocytoma in von Hippel-Lindau disease and multiple endocrine neoplasia type 2. N Engl J Med 340:1872–1879, 1999, with permission.)

ratio of epinephrine to norepinephrine remains increased.[84] Hypertension may be a clinical problem in patients with larger tumors. Sudden death related to pheochromocytoma occurred with some frequency in kindreds before routine prospective screening, and in some kindreds, was as common a cause of death as medullary thyroid carcinoma.

### Hyperparathyroidism

Hyperparathyroidism occurs in 15% to 20% of patients with the fully developed form of MEN2A. Parathyroid hyperplasia is the most common histologic abnormality; when parathyroid adenomas are found, they are generally set against a background of hyperplasia.[7,8] The clinical features of hyperparathyroidism do not differ from those associated with sporadic hyperparathyroidism (see Chapter 77). Unlike MEN1, in which hyperparathyroidism is generally the first manifestation of the syndrome, hyperparathyroidism in MEN2 rarely

occurs during the early phases of the syndrome. In addition, prospective screening of families with MEN2A led to the finding that hyperparathyroidism or early MTC did not develop in children who underwent thyroidectomy for C-cell hyperplasia during a 10- to 15-year follow-up period.[84] Whether the failure of hyperparathyroidism to develop in thyroidectomized children is related to partial removal of parathyroid tissue at the time of thyroid surgery and reflects an inadequate follow-up period or is related to removal of a growth stimulus by total thyroidectomy is unclear. In some families, hyperparathyroidism occurs early and is a prominent part of the syndrome.[97]

### The MEN2A/Cutaneous Lichen Amyloidosis Variant

At least 20 kindreds have been identified in which MEN2A is associated with the development of a pruritic skin lesion over the upper part of the back[98,99] (Fig. 192-5A, Table 192-1). The

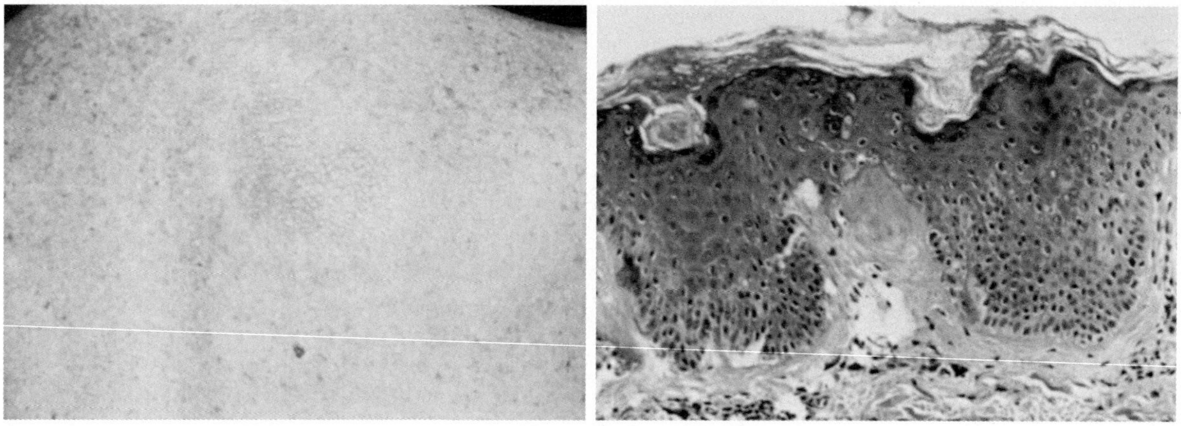

*Figure 192-5* **A,** Characteristic cutaneous feature of lesion of cutaneous lichen amyloidosis. Patients with this lesion complain of intermittent pruritus and burning in the area of the skin lesion. **B,** Characteristic histologic features of cutaneous lichen amyloidosis showing deposition of amyloid at the interface between the dermis and epidermis. (Reproduced from Gagel RF, Levy ML, Donovan DT, et al: Multiple endocrine neoplasia type 2a associated with cutaneous lichen amyloidosis. Ann Intern Med 111:802–806, 1989, with permission.)

first manifestation of the skin lesion is intermittent pruritus. The onset of pruritus generally precedes the development of a visible skin lesion by several years. The fully developed skin lesion has a lichenoid-papular appearance and may be unilateral or bilateral. Amyloid deposition analogous to that found in cutaneous lichen amyloidosis is found in more advanced lesions (Fig. 192-5*B*).

## Familial Medullary Thyroid Carcinoma

FMTC is another variant of MEN2A without other manifestations of MEN2A (see Table 192-1).[100,101] The clinical characteristics of MTC in FMTC do not differ substantially from those of MEN2A, although the observation has been made that the FMTC variant is less aggressive. One viewpoint is that the FMTC-only syndrome is MEN2A but with a later onset of neoplasia, which makes it less likely that pheochromocytoma will develop during a normal lifetime.

## *MULTIPLE ENDOCRINE NEOPLASIA TYPE 2B*

The association of MTC, pheochromocytoma, mucosal neuromas, a marfanoid body habitus, and the absence of hyperparathyroidism has been classified as MEN2B. Although it was described earlier, it was Williams and colleagues who compiled the several components into a distinct clinical syndrome.[10] Most cases of this clinical syndrome are thought to represent new mutations because of failure to find evidence of disease in parents, although germ-line transmission of the disease with an autosomal-dominant pattern of inheritance has been described in several kindreds.[102–104]

## Medullary Thyroid Carcinoma and Pheochromocytoma in MEN2B

Development of MTC in MEN2B is thought to follow a pattern of progression similar to that described for MEN2A, but with a few differences. C-cell hyperplasia and microscopic carcinoma, in general, develop much earlier in MEN2B. Children have been described with metastatic MTC shortly after birth.[105,106] Death related to complications of metastatic MTC may occur before onset of the third decade, although a larger experience that includes several multigenerational families suggests that the prognosis in an individual patient may be better than previously considered.[104,107] Pheochromocytomas in MEN2B occur in more than 50% of affected individuals and also may develop at an early age. The clinical manifestations of pheochromocytoma do not differ substantially from those observed in MEN2A.

## Mucosal Neuromas and Other Clinical Features of MEN2B

The most striking phenotypic feature of MEN2B is the presence of multiple mucosal neuromas. The presence of multiple neuromas located on the tongue tip, within the lips, and on the eyelids makes for a characteristic facies identifiable even in childhood[108] (Fig. 192-6). Mucosal neuromas exist throughout the gastrointestinal tract (see Table 192-1). Gastrointestinal symptoms are the second most common reason for recognition of this syndrome.[109] Children and adults will frequently have complaints of increased gas, abdominal pain, and, occasionally, obstruction or pseudo-obstruction caused by neuromatous tissue. Obstructive symptoms combined with diarrhea caused by MTC can produce a puzzling clinical syndrome characterized by alternating obstructive symptoms and diarrhea. It is important to exclude an anatomic cause of obstruction and, where possible, debulk the mass of MTC to reduce diarrhea. Abdominal exploration is generally indicated only in patients with proven obstruction. Gastrointestinal neuromas associated with MEN2B can be confused with Hirschsprung's disease, a condition also caused by mutations of the *RET* proto-oncogene.[110]

Hyperparathyroidism is rare in MEN2B.[111] Other clinical features frequently found in this syndrome include a marfanoid habitus with long, thin arms, an altered upper-to-lower body ratio, long fingers, hyperextensible joints, and slipped femoral epiphyses.[112]

MEN2A and MEN2B have been viewed as two separate syndromes, but molecular studies have demonstrated that both occur as a result of mutations of the *RET* proto-oncogene. The identification of a mother with MEN2B and two children with MTC, one with the characteristic MEN2B phenotype and the second with no phenotypic features of MEN2B, suggests that the mucosal neuroma phenotype may not be 100% penetrant.[113] Reports of corneal nerve thickening, a finding associated with MEN2B, in kindreds with MEN2A[114] or FMTC,[115] provide additional evidence for overlap.

## SCREENING FOR MEN2A

The primary goal of screening for MEN2 is to identify and treat the several manifestations of MEN2 before they become life threatening. A secondary goal is to provide genetic counseling to family members about the potential for transmission to the next generation. These goals become closely intertwined because family decisions regarding the next generation are

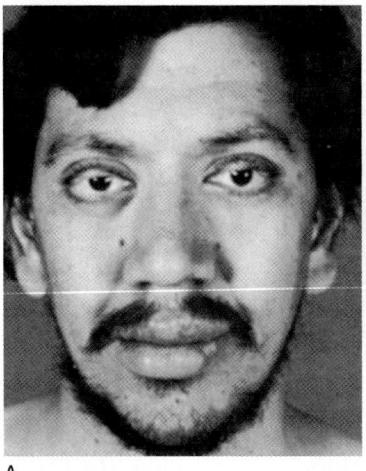
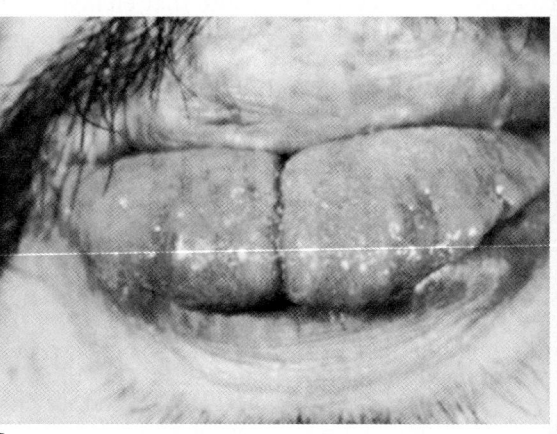
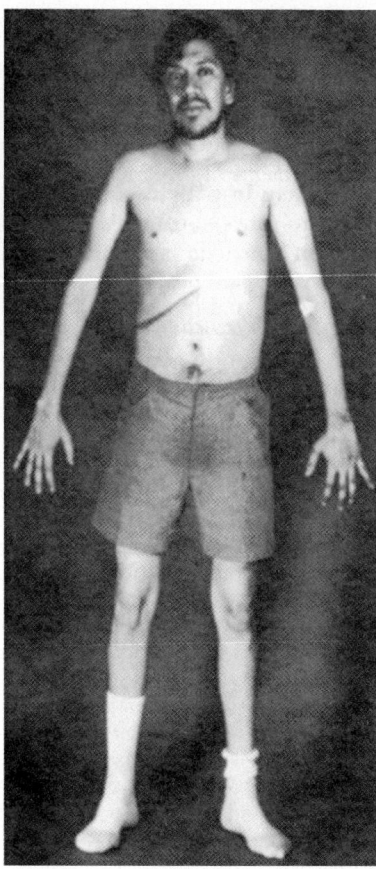

*Figure 192-6* Characteristic facies with thickened lips and eyelids in a patient with multiple endocrine neoplasia (MEN) type 2B. Note that this patient had extensive reconstructive surgery on the left side of his lower lip **(A)** and the tip of his tongue **(B)** during childhood in an attempt to excise the neuromas. **C,** The marfanoid features of MEN2B, including the long arms, thin fingers, and altered body ratio. The abdominal scar resulted from removal of a unilateral pheochromocytoma.

based largely on experience in the current generation. The two life-threatening manifestations of MEN2 are metastasis from MTC and sudden death caused by pheochromocytoma. A 30-year experience with prospective screening now makes it reasonable to believe that death or serious morbidity caused by these manifestations can be prevented in most patients.

## MEDULLARY THYROID CARCINOMA

Measurement of serum calcitonin basally and after a provocative test was the preferred method for diagnosis of MTC in MEN2 until genetic testing was introduced approximately 10 years ago; calcitonin assay remains a useful test for confirming the diagnosis and for follow-up of patients who have been treated. The sensitivity and specificity of the test are enhanced by the use of a provocative stimulus of calcitonin release, such as calcium,[116] pentagastrin,[117] or a combination of the two.[118] The provocative stimulus results in a rapid (within 2 to 10 minutes) increase in serum calcitonin concentration.

The experience with pentagastrin (or combined calcium/pentagastrin) testing over the past 2 decades indicates it is a reliable but not overly sensitive predictor of C-cell abnormalities. The test is performed by the injection of pentagastrin, 0.5 μg/kg, over a 5- to 10-second period, generally in the fasting state. The serum calcitonin level is measured basally and 2, 5, 10, and 15 minutes after the injection, although measurement of basal and 2- and 5-minute samples will reduce the cost of the test without affecting its sensitivity. The normal range is defined for each specific calcitonin assay: Normal values for immunoassays show pentagastrin-stimulated values less than 30 pg/mL for women and 110 pg/mL for men[119]; two-site immunoassays show stimulated values that are generally less than 30 pg/mL for both male and female patients.[120] The major objections from patients to

use of the test are several unpleasant side effects, including nausea, substernal tightness, flushing, tingling of the extremities, and the urge to void; these symptoms usually subside within 2 to 3 minutes of injection and are of variable severity. The patient should be warned of these side effects before the pentagastrin injection and be reassured of their transient nature. In my experience, no serious side effects have occurred when pentagastrin has been used for prospective screening in children. Anecdotal reports have described hypotension and flushing in patients with a significant tumor mass; pentagastrin testing in patients with a sizable tumor mass generally provides no additional information. Currently, pentagastrin is not manufactured in the United States, and calcium stimulation has replaced pentagastrin in situations in which a provocative test is still required.[116]

## PHEOCHROMOCYTOMA

The goal of screening for pheochromocytoma is to identify and treat excess catecholamine production before the development of life-threatening manifestations. Experience over the past 2 decades indicates this can be accomplished by simple screening techniques repeated at regular intervals. A careful history is important and may provide the earliest clue to the presence of an adrenal medullary abnormality. Each suspected gene carrier should be queried annually about the presence of palpitations, nervousness or attacks of jitteriness, headaches, or other unusual vascular symptoms. Screening for excessive catecholamine production can be accomplished by annual measurement of fractionated catecholamines (epinephrine and norepinephrine) in a 12- to 24-hour urine collection or measurement of plasma catecholamines. The earliest indication of increased adrenal medullary mass is an increase in the 12- to 24-hour excretion of epinephrine and an increase in the ratio of epinephrine to norepinephrine in this collection (see Fig. 192-4*A*) or an elevated basal plasma epinephrine level.[121] We have adopted an 8- to 12-hour urine collection for fractionated catecholamines as a compromise measure that most patients find acceptable. A recent report suggests that plasma metanephrine may be equally sensitive for diagnostic purposes[96] (see Fig. 192-4*B*). Measurement of vanillylmandelic acid is not useful for detection of pheochromocytoma.[84]

Screening for pheochromocytoma should begin by age 6 years. Adrenal medullary hyperplasia or pheochromocytoma has been described in the 10- to 12-year age range,[84] and a 13-year-old child had hypertensive encephalopathy caused by a large pheochromocytoma.[122] Parents should be instructed to be alert for symptoms of headache or jitteriness in children. Screening should be intensified during the child-bearing years, which are also the peak years for diagnosis of pheochromocytoma in this syndrome.

Several radiographic studies have been used for the diagnosis of pheochromocytoma in MEN2. Preoperative evaluation with either computed tomography or magnetic resonance imaging is important to define surgical anatomy and determine bilaterality. Considerable controversy has developed over the use of [$^{131}$I]-labeled metaiodobenzylguanidine for the diagnosis of pheochromocytoma in MEN2.[123] Although most investigators agree that this radioisotope is a very sensitive indicator of adrenal medullary hyperfunction, it may be too sensitive and result in the detection of adrenal medullary hyperplasia (which is likely to be present in most gene carriers older than 20 years) before a significant increase in the production of catecholamines has occurred.[124] This technique may be useful to identify the rare extra-adrenal pheochromocytoma in a patient with catecholamine abnormalities and no identifiable adrenal abnormality.[125] Arteriography is almost never indicated in the management of pheochromocytoma associated with MEN2 and should be performed only after the administration of adrenergic receptor antagonists (see Chapter 130).

## HYPERPARATHYROIDISM

Screening for hyperparathyroidism in MEN2 is straightforward. Measurement of the serum calcium concentration every other year after age 10 years is adequate for early diagnosis.[84,97,126] The finding of an elevated serum calcium level should prompt measurement of serum intact parathyroid hormone. Pheochromocytoma is a rare cause of hypercalcemia in MEN2 and should be excluded before parathyroid gland exploration.[84] Other, more common causes of hypercalcemia should be excluded by a careful history and physical examination and additional laboratory tests when appropriate (see Chapter 77).

## SCREENING FOR MEN2B

Evidence indicates that MTC will develop in most patients with MEN2B at an early age. Metastatic carcinoma has been described in children with MEN2B as young as 3 months. Because of this early expression of MTC, all agree that thyroidectomy should be performed at the earliest possible age in children with phenotypic features of MEN2B. It also is possible that the mucosal neuroma phenotype may not be 100% penetrant, thus making it mandatory to screen (genetic analysis or calcitonin testing) all children born to a parent with MEN2B.[113]

## MOLECULAR GENETICS

### RET PROTO-ONCOGENE MUTATIONS IN MEN2A AND -2B

*RET* proto-oncogene mutations that cause MEN2 can be arbitrarily divided into extracellular and intracellular

domain mutations.[120] The most common mutations are those that change a cysteine in the extracellular domain to another amino acid. Mutations of six codons (609, 611, 618, 620, 630, and 634) have been identified, and several other unusual mutations result in insertions or deletions in this region.[127–129] Almost all these mutations cause receptor dimerization and autophosphorylation and lead to activation of downstream ERK1/ERK2 and JNK pathways.[70–72] The most commonly mutated codon is 634, which accounts for almost 80% of mutations in MEN2.[17] Mutations at codons 609, 611, 618, 620, and 630 account for approximately 15% of all mutations.[55] Intracellular codons that are mutated in MEN2 include codons 768,[127,130] 790, 791,[131] 804,[130] 883,[132–135] 891,[115,136] 918,[137] and 922.[17] Fewer than 25 families each have been described for codons 768, 790, 791, 804, and 891. The most common intracellular mutation is a Met918Thr coding change that is found in approximately 5% of all patients with MEN2.[136] The codon 918 mutation causes receptor autophosphorylation in the absence of dimerization and activation of the ERK1/ERK2 and JNK pathways, as well as a different set of downstream substrate proteins.[70,71,138]

## GENOTYPE-PHENOTYPE CORRELATION

The collection of clinical information on almost 500 families with hereditary MTC by the *RET* consortium has provided a broad overview of the clinical phenotype associated with specific mutations.[17] Table 192-2 provides a summary of this information and is based not only on the consortium report but also on numerous subsequent publications and presentations. Several points are important. First, a codon 634 germ-line *RET* mutation with any amino acid substitution is most commonly associated with MEN2A or Sipple's syndrome. Second, codon 883, 918, or 922 germ-line *RET* mutations are associated with MEN2B. Third, germ-line mutations of the other extracellular cysteine residues (609, 611, 618, 620, and 630) may be associated with either FMTC or MEN2A. Fourth, codon 768 and Val804Met have been associated only with FMTC. Finally, intracellular mutations at codon 790, 791,[131] Val804Leu,[139] and Ser891Ala[140] have been associated with either FMTC or MEN2A. It is important to recognize that experience is limited with mutations at some of these codons. For example, only five kindreds had been reported with a codon 891 mutation,[115,137] and the sixth report included one patient with pheochromocytoma, expanding the clinical phenotype to include MEN2A.[140] Some of the unique variants of MEN2 have particular codon associations. For example, all reported cases of MEN2A/cutaneous lichen amyloidosis have a codon 634 mutation, although we have seen a single case of MEN2B with a codon 918 mutation and a nonpruritic upper back lesion seemingly identical to that seen in the MEN2A/cutaneous lichen amyloidosis variant. Individuals with the MEN2A/Hirschsprung variant have been found to have codon 609, 618, or 620 (exon 10) *RET* mutations.[80,123,141,142] Interestingly, screening of kindreds with Hirschsprung's disease has uncovered individuals or families with codon 609 and 620 mutations identical to those seen in MEN2,[143] which has led some to recommend that all individuals with Hirschsprung's disease be screened for an exon 10 (codons 609, 618, and 620) mutation to exclude MEN2. The status of the thyroid glands in these kindreds has not been reported,[143] although it is generally recommended that individuals with these mutations be screened for MTC.

De novo mutations of the *RET* proto-oncogene causing MEN2 are uncommon but have been reported.[80,144,145] Most are codon Cys634Arg substitutions, the most common mutation found in patients with hereditary MTC. Children born to an individual with a de novo mutation are considered to be at risk for the development of MEN2.

**Table 192-2** Mutations of the *RET* Proto-oncogene Associated with Multiple Endocrine Neoplasia Type 2 and Hereditary Medullary Thyroid Cancer

| Affected Codon/Exon | Amino Acid Change, Normal → Mutant | Nucleotide Change, Normal → Mutant | Clinical Syndrome | % of Total |
|---|---|---|---|---|
| 609/10 | Cys→Arg | TGC→CGC | MEN2A/FMTC | 0–1 |
|  | Cys→Gly | TGC→GGC |  |  |
|  | Cys→Tyr | TGC→TAC |  |  |
| 611/10 | Cys→Ser | TGC→AGC | MEN2A/FMTC | 2–3 |
|  | Cys→Arg | TGC→CGC |  |  |
|  | Cys→Gly | TGC→GGC |  |  |
|  | Cys→Tyr | TGC→TAC |  |  |
|  | Cys→Phe | TGC→TTC |  |  |
|  | Cys→Trp | TGC→TGG |  |  |
| 618/10 | Cys→Ser | TGC→AGC | MEN2A/FMTC | 3–5 |
|  | Cys→Arg | TGC→CGC |  |  |
|  | Cys→Gly | TGC→GGC |  |  |
|  | Cys→Tyr | TGC→TAC |  |  |
|  | Cys→Ser | TGC→TCC |  |  |
|  | Cys→Phe | TGC→TTC |  |  |
| 620/10 | Cys→Ser | TGC→AGC | MEN2A/FMTC | 6–8 |
|  | Cys→Arg | TGC→CGC |  |  |
|  | Cys→Gly | TGC→GGC |  |  |
|  | Cys→Tyr | TGC→TAC |  |  |
|  | Cys→Ser | TGC→TCC |  |  |
|  | Cys→Phe | TGC→TTC |  |  |
|  | Cys→Trp | TGC→TGG |  |  |
| 630/11 | Cys→Tyr | TGC→TAC | MEN2A/FMTC | 0–1 |
|  | Cys→Ser | TGC→TCC |  |  |
|  | Cys→Phe | TGC→TTC |  |  |
| 634/11 | Cys→Ser | TGC→AGC | MEN2A | 80–90 |
|  | Cys→Arg | TGC→CGC |  |  |
|  | Cys→Gly | TGC→GGC |  |  |
|  | Cys→Tyr | TGC→TAC |  |  |
|  | Cys→Ser | TGC→TCC |  |  |
|  | Cys→Phe | TGC→TTC |  |  |
|  | Cys→Trp | TGC→TGG |  |  |
| 634, 635/11 | Cys Arg→Trp Gly | TGC CGC→TGG GGC | MEN2A |  |
| 635/11 | Thr Ser Cys Ala insertion | ACGAGCTGTGCC | MEN2A |  |
| 637/11 | Cys Arg Thr insertion | TGCCGCACG | MEN2A |  |
| 768/13 | Glu→Asp | GAG→GAC | FMTC |  |
| 790/13 | Leu→Phe | TTG→TTC | MEN2A/FMTC |  |
|  | Leu→Phe | TTG→TTT |  |  |
| 791/13 | Tyr→Phe | TAT→TTT | FMTC |  |
| 804/14 | Val→Met | GTG→ATG | MEN2A/FMTC |  |
|  | Val→Leu | GTG→TTG |  |  |
| 804, 806/14 | Val Tyr→Met Cys | GTG TAC→ATG TGC | MEN2B |  |
| 883/15 | Ala→Phe | GCT→TTT | MEN2B |  |
| 891/15 | Ser→Ala | TCG→GCG | MEN2A/FMTC |  |
| 918/16 | Met→Thr | ATG→ACG | MEN2B |  |
| 922/16 | Ser→Tyr | TCC→TAC | MEN2B |  |

FMTC, familial medullary thyroid cancer.
These mutations were collected from multiple sources, including published references, the Human Gene Mutation Database (*www.UWCM.AC.UK/search/mg/allgenes*), meeting presentations, and the author's experience. The identification of approximately one newly mutated codon per year suggests that this table will be incomplete at the time of publication.

## GENETIC SCREENING FOR MEN2

*RET* proto-oncogene mutational analysis has quickly become the "gold standard" for decision making in the management of MEN2 and FMTC.[146,147] Unlike many other genetic disorders in which the identification of a specific mutation provides useful information about pathogenesis and excludes unaffected family members from further screening, identification of a *RET* mutation in a known kindred will, in most cases, lead to thyroidectomy based on the test result. It is important to provide genetic counseling to individuals before obtaining a genetic test. The discussion should include the fundamentals of autosomal-dominant inheritance, an outline of the clinical features of the syndrome, and the types of screening and therapy available. Other issues such as potential genetic discrimination as it relates to health insurance and employment also should be discussed.*

*Families of affected individuals may or may not respond positively to the suggestion for genetic screening. It is important, however, to apprise the family of the genetic risks. To aid in this process, we have developed a pamphlet that describes the major features of this syndrome in simple terms. Affected individuals are encouraged to distribute this pamphlet to other first-degree relatives. This information source for family members is frequently more effective in soliciting enthusiasm for screening than is an attempt by a physi-

cian to contact family members directly. A family meeting can provide a nonthreatening forum for hesitant family members to gain information about the disease and screening protocols. A copy of this pamphlet may be obtained from the University of Texas M.D. Anderson Cancer, Department of Endocrine Neoplasia website at *www.mdanderson.org/departments/endocrinology*. Availability of genetic testing for MEN2 can be obtained from the website: *www.genetests.org*.

The high level of genotype-phenotype correlation and the limited number of codons that cause this syndrome have made mutational analysis of the *RET* proto-oncogene straightforward. The approach used by almost all laboratories is direct DNA sequencing, frequently automated.[148] Analysis of three exons (10, 11, and 16) identifies more than 95% of known mutations causing MEN2 or FMTC.[17] The addition of exons 13, 14, and 15 in the screening process increases the proportion identified to more than 98%. In the United States, genetic testing is readily available through commercial sources (see *www.genetests.org*). In rare kindreds, no *RET* mutation has been identified; experience over the past 5 years indicates that reevaluation when new mutations are discovered will eventually lead to the identification of a *RET* mutation in most. Because of the potential for false-positive or false-negative test results, it is important to repeat the analysis on a DNA sample obtained from a separate blood collection before making a decision to perform thyroidectomy or exclude family member from further screening. The availability of genotype-phenotype correlative information has led to the development of codon-specific recommendations that are outlined later.

## CLINICAL MANAGEMENT OF KINDREDS WITH MEN2A OR MEN2B

### MEDULLARY THYROID CARCINOMA

#### Management in Children

Increasingly, the decision to perform a thyroidectomy for early C-cell abnormalities is based on genetic testing. Although the data are far from complete, a framework is emerging for clinical management of hereditary MTC that is based on the clinical behavior of tumors in patients with specific mutations. It is important to recognize that deaths from MTC have been identified in kindreds with all codon mutations, with the exception of codons 790 and 791, with which experience is limited to fewer than 15 kindreds.[131] Despite these observations, it is clear that biologic behavior correlates in general with specific mutations. One indicator of the relative transforming potential of individual mutations is provided by the earliest age at which MTC has been identified in a child with a particular mutation (Fig. 192-7).[149] Although this data set is flawed in several ways, it is nonetheless the best indicator currently available to compare the relative

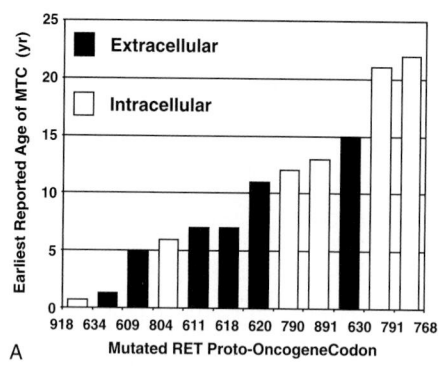

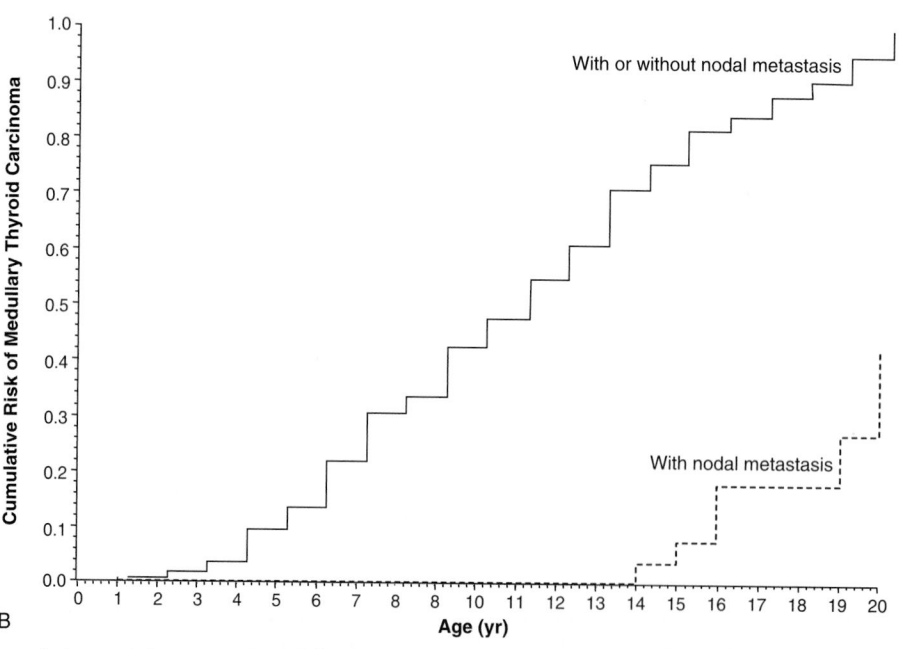

**Figure 192-7**  **A,** Earliest reported age at the onset of medullary thyroid carcinoma (MTC) according to the *RET* mutation (Reprinted from Cote JG, Gagel RF: Lessons learned from the management of a rare genetic cancer. N Engl J Med 349:1566–1568, 2003, with permission). **B,** Cumulative risk of medullary thyroid carcinoma among carriers of codon 634 germ-line *RET* mutations, according to the presence or absence of nodal metastases and age (Reprinted from the Machens A, Niccoli-Sire P, Hoegel J, et al: Early malignant progression of hereditary medullary thyroid cancer. N Engl J Med 349:1517–1525, 2003, with permission.)

aggressiveness of these tumors. A more detailed analysis of 130 European patients who underwent prophylactic thyroidectomy for codon 634 mutations demonstrated that lymph node metastasis was not identified before age 14 years.[150] This is an important report, because it likely represents the largest compilation of age-specific histology that will ever be collected in this disease. However, the breadth of this report, encompassing several European countries (EUROMEN study group), also is its weakness. The thyroidectomies were performed in many different centers; it is difficult to determine how many lymph nodes were removed and how carefully they were examined for microscopic metastasis. No long-term data are available at this time. The report of a 6-year-old child with a codon 634 mutation and local metastasis[77,151] and numerous examples of microscopic MTC identified before age 6 years highlight the need for a broader and longer-term perspective, a point highlighted in the EUROMEN report and consensus statements.[147,150]

It is important to recognize that the biologic behavior of a specific mutation may be modified by genetic background or the acquisition of a somatic mutation. Although no specific examples can be provided in which genetic background (the inheritance of a second cancer-causing gene) has been shown to affect the behavior of MTC, such examples almost certainly exist and will be identified in the future. Multiple reports have described the acquisition of a somatic mutation within MTC that changes the biologic behavior of the tumor. The most commonly cited example is the somatic acquisition of a codon Met918Thr mutation,[132,152] a specific codon change that is associated with a more virulent phenotype.[153,154] Until a more complete picture emerges regarding these background genetic effects, any recommendation scheme should be considered tentative. What follows is an attempt to provide the reader with an overview of current thinking regarding clinical management of children with specific mutations. They have arbitrarily been divided into highest-, higher-, and intermediate-risk codons.[147] It is important to recognize that genetic malignancy is difficult to cure with surgical techniques. Nature is not always neat in its placement and distribution of specific cell/tissue types, and numerous reports exist of failure of prophylactic surgery in hereditary neoplasia. Thyroid surgery is further complicated by the fact that total thyroidectomy is rarely total, and in those cases in which it is, the incidence of hypoparathyroidism increases. Thus, what follows is the MEN2 community's best effort at providing guidance that incorporates not only genetic information, but also experience derived from the past 25 years of prospective screening.

### Highest Risk
Children with MEN2B or codon 883, 918, and 922 mutations or both should have total thyroidectomy and central lymph node dissection performed within the first 6 months, preferably within the first month of life. Metastasis may develop within the first year of life,[105,106] and in most cases, more extensive node dissection may be appropriate.

### High Risk
Children with any codon 611, 618, 620, 630, 634, or 891 mutation should have total thyroidectomy performed before age 5 years.[147,149] Microscopic carcinoma in children with codon 634 mutations has been reported in children as young as 1 year. The finding of lymph node metastasis in children younger than 6 years[77] suggests that lymph node dissection of the central compartment also should be considered routinely,[155,156] although complete consensus has not been reached on this point. Most surgeons favor the performance of central lymph node dissection during the primary operative procedure because of the higher morbidity associated with reentry into the central compartment during a second procedure, but this option should be balanced against the higher rate of hypoparathyroidism and recurrent laryngeal

nerve damage associated with primary central node dissection. Some have advocated central node dissection combined with removal of all parathyroid tissue and transplantation to the nondominant forearm as a method of preventing hypoparathyroidism.[155-157] Currently, no data support the use of radioactive iodine to ablate residual thyroid tissue, and some are concerned that radiation exposure could enhance the rate of mutation in any residual C cells. Long-term (20-year) follow-up studies of children with codon 634 mutations who had total thyroidectomy performed in their teenage years indicate that 50% to 85% remain disease free after total thyroidectomy based on pentagastrin testing.[84,158] It is clear, however, that some of these young patients, now 40 to 50 years old, have evidence of metastasis. The recent recognition that MTC occurs with some frequency in children younger than 6 years argues persuasively for earlier intervention, although proof that earlier intervention will alter the outcome awaits the results of long-term studies in this group of patients.

### Intermediate Risk
Children with codon 609, 768, 790, 791, or 804 mutations should have total thyroidectomy performed. The biologic behavior of MTC in patients with mutations in these codons is variable, but in general, it grows more slowly, and MTC develops at a later age than observed with the high-risk mutations. It is important, however, to recognize that lymph node metastasis and death from MTC have been observed for each of these mutations except codons 790 and 791. Attempts to develop consensus on the management of children with these mutations have been unsuccessful, and management strategies vary from a recommendation for management similar to that for high-risk mutations, to total thyroidectomy at the time of the first calcium or pentagastrin test abnormality, to total thyroidectomy by age 10 years. Several collaborative groups are trying to gather more information about the biologic behavior and clinical outcomes in patients with these rare mutations. It is clear that some kindreds with a rare mutation have never had an identifiable death caused by MTC, and such families resist early thyroidectomy. The most important point to consider in the counseling of such a family is whether an adequate number of affected individuals in the family have been identified to draw meaningful conclusions about biologic behavior. A well-known phenomenon in these kindreds is a pattern of general benignity with superimposition of an occasional aggressive MTC on this pattern, which complicates any rational decision-making process.

### Management of Established MTC
Total thyroidectomy is mandatory for the treatment of hereditary MTC because of the bilateral and multicentric nature of the disease. Metastatic disease to the lymph nodes of the central compartment of the neck is seen in a high percentage of patients with an MTC larger than 1 cm, which makes central lymph node dissection at the time of primary surgery mandatory in this group of patients.[159-162] Although extensive lymph node dissection without proof of metastasis at the time of primary surgery may seem overly aggressive, abundant experience indicates that surgical cure is possible, even in individuals with local nodal metastasis.[159,161] The decision to extend the surgical procedure to include the mediastinum at the time of primary surgery is controversial because of the potential for surgical morbidity and the absence of well-documented cures after surgery.[163] However, it should be pointed out that the natural drainage patterns for the central lymph nodes of the neck make the superior mediastinum one of the logical places to search for metastatic MTC.[164]

Finally, before consideration of thyroid surgery, individuals suspected of having hereditary disease should have measurements of urine catecholamines or other appropriate studies to exclude pheochromocytoma. If a pheochromocytoma is found, surgical removal should be performed before thyroid surgery (see Chapter 130).

## Management of Apparently Sporadic MTC

In individuals with MTC and no history to suggest hereditary disease (apparently sporadic MTC), it is important to perform total thyroidectomy and central lymph node dissection for several reasons. First, even sporadic MTC may be multifocal, and intrathyroidal metastasis is not uncommon. Second, the finding of characteristic C-cell hyperplasia in the lobe contralateral to the tumor may provide evidence for a familial form of the disease. Finally, removal of the entire thyroid gland and performance of central node dissection will simplify subsequent localization procedures if calcitonin levels are elevated postoperatively.[165]

Perhaps the most controversial subject in the management of MTC is whether reoperation has therapeutic value in patients with persistent elevation of the serum calcitonin concentration after an adequate primary operation. At present, data are scarce, but the most optimistic results suggest that 15% to 20% of patients who have no detectable disease when assessed with radiographic techniques can be rendered calcitonin negative by meticulous neck lymph node dissection.[159,161,162,164,166] Before consideration of such extensive surgery, it is important thoroughly to exclude metastatic disease in the lung, liver, and bone with appropriate radiologic techniques.[161,163,167,168] It is uncommon to find imageable disease by any imaging technique currently available, including radionuclide techniques, when serum CT values are lower than 100 pg/mL.[159]

A question asked frequently is whether the family of a patient with apparently sporadic MTC should be screened for hereditary MTC, especially when a careful history fails to turn up any evidence of familial MTC. The key point to be considered in responding to this question is how good is a family history for excluding hereditary disease. Results from multiple studies now demonstrate that 6% to 7% of patients with apparently sporadic MTC have germ-line mutations of the *RET* proto-oncogene.[80–82,144,169] Many of these reports came from academic centers where it is likely family history was considered in assignment of "sporadic" to these medullary thyroid carcinomas. Thus, a compelling case can be made for *RET* analysis in all patients with apparently sporadic MTC. The goal of such screening is to identify kindreds with hereditary MTC and screen members for *RET* mutations during childhood, thereby improving the probability of a curative outcome with total thyroidectomy. Similarly, if an individual with apparently sporadic MTC has a negative genetic test, it is possible to provide the family with reassurance that the probability of hereditary disease is less than 0.2%.[80]

## *PHEOCHROMOCYTOMA*

The goal of prospective screening for pheochromocytoma is to identify pheochromocytomas or adrenal medullary hyperplasia at a point before the development of significant neurologic or cardiovascular manifestations. A patient with a proven pheochromocytoma should be started on a regimen of combined α- and β-adrenergic antagonists with or without α-methyltyrosine for 1 to 3 weeks before surgery (see Chapter 130). The longer periods of blockade are reserved for patients with hypertension and vasoconstriction with presumed reduction in intravascular volume. The most common problems during the removal of small pheochromocytomas detected by prospective screening include tachycardia and intermittent hypertension during tumor manipulation. Hypertension, cardiac arrhythmias, and postoperative vascular collapse, particularly in patients inadequately blocked preoperatively, may occur in patients with large pheochromocytomas.

The introduction of laparoscopic adrenalectomy combined with high-resolution computed tomography or magnetic resonance imaging has had a profound effect on the management of hereditary pheochromocytoma.[170] Current imaging techniques provide almost as much information about adrenal abnormalities as visual examination does. Therefore, most physicians and surgeons who treat this disease obtain high-quality imaging of the adrenal glands and perform unilateral adrenalectomy for a unilateral pheochromocytoma via a laparoscopic approach. Although it is likely that a second operation will be required to remove an apparently unaffected adrenal gland, 8 to 10 years may pass before a second operation is required.[84,97,171,172] It is more difficult to perform bilateral adrenalectomy via laparoscopy because of the necessity to reposition the patient during surgery. As a result, some surgeons recommend a staged procedure; others recommend bilateral adrenalectomy via an anterior abdominal approach. Large pheochromocytomas not easily removed laparoscopically should be removed through a standard flank or anterior approach. It is generally agreed that gene carriers in the rare kindred with a family history of adrenal medullary malignancy have bilateral adrenalectomy at some point during the first or second decade of life or at least be imaged frequently.[90,91]

Adrenal insufficiency associated with bilateral adrenalectomy in MEN2 patients has become a significant concern because of at least 4 deaths caused by adrenal insufficiency. Before the recognition of MEN2 as a clinical syndrome by Sipple in 1961, approximately half of the deaths in gene carriers could be reasonably attributed to a pheochromocytoma (sudden death or stroke associated with hypertension). Since the greater recognition of pheochromocytoma and the application of simple screening techniques, death caused by pheochromocytoma has become rare in those screened. The subtle shift in risk from that associated with pheochromocytoma to that associated with adrenal insufficiency has resulted in a resurgence of interest in cortical-sparing adrenalectomy, a technique first developed several decades ago in which only the adrenal medulla is removed and cortical tissue is left intact.[173] Recent reports document the feasibility of this approach, although the recurrence rate for pheochromocytoma is higher because of residual medullary tissue.[92,174,175] Certainly, this approach should be considered for patients who live long distances from emergency medical facilities, individuals who are in an occupation in which adrenal insufficiency would exclude them from employment, or patients in whom compliance with medication is a problem. Patients who undergo bilateral adrenalectomy should wear a MedicAlert-type bracelet or necklace and be instructed to seek early medical attention for symptoms of adrenal insufficiency.

Screening for pheochromocytoma should be conducted before pregnancy or, if not possible, early in pregnancy. Deaths during childbirth have occurred in MEN2, and family histories include occasional mention of maternal death associated with childbirth.[176,177] After careful consideration of the risks to the fetus and mother, including the size of the tumor and its probable capacity for causing arrhythmia and sudden death, the physician will, in most cases, opt for removal of a pheochromocytoma at a suitable time during pregnancy.

## *HYPERPARATHYROIDISM*

The development of hyperparathyroidism is uncommon in prospectively screened, affected children treated with thyroidectomy. In those in whom hyperparathyroidism does develop, recurrence rates are much lower than observed in MEN1. Therefore, most surgeons treating this disease will remove only glands found to be enlarged at the time of surgery. In unusual kindreds in whom primary hyperparathyroidism is a prominent manifestation of the clinical syndrome, consideration should be given to total removal of parathyroid tissue with implantation into the nondominant forearm, an approach frequently used in patients with MEN1.[97,178,179] Such an approach eliminates the necessity for repetitive neck exploration. Identification of candidates for this type of procedure can be accomplished only by careful review of the clinical course of hyperparathyroidism in other family members.

## MOLECULAR AND CYTOGENETIC ABNORMALITIES FOUND IN MEN2 TUMORS

Recent studies indicate that loss of the normal RET allele or an increase in copy number of the mutant RET allele may be an important component in transformation of the C cell. A significant percentage of MEN2-related tumors have evidence for loss of the normal RET allele or trisomy 10 with duplication of the mutant RET chromosome.[180,181] In addition, the TT cell line, a model of hereditary MTC in which codon 634 RET mutation occurs, has a tandem duplication of the mutant RET locus.[182] The implication is that RET functions as a tumor-suppressor gene and that a loss of the normal copy or an imbalance created by higher levels of expression of the mutant RET causes transformation. In this regard, RET joins a growing number of tyrosine kinases, including MET[183] and kRAS,[184] in which this mechanism has been identified.

Ample evidence also indicates consistent loss of specific chromosomal regions. These include chromosome 1p or 22,[185,186] and cytogenetic evidence suggests abnormalities of chromosomes 3p and 9.[187] Evidence indicates that expression of trkA, trkB, and trkC tyrosine kinase receptors may be important. Ongoing investigation indicates that trkB but not trkA or trkC is expressed in C-cell hyperplasia, whereas in MTCs, trkC is expressed, and trkB is suppressed. Expression of trkB was associated with lower levels of vascular endothelial growth factor.[188]

## THE FUTURE

The identification of activating mutations of the RET proto-oncogene as the cause for 99.8% of hereditary MTC and at least 25% of sporadic MTC and the recent treatment successes with tyrosine kinase inhibitors for other activating mutations[189-191] has stimulated development of tyrosine kinase inhibitors that specifically target RET. Gleevec, the first of the tyrosine kinase inhibitors to achieve clinical usefulness, also has activity in MTC. Unfortunately, the apoptotic-promoting effects of this compound in MTC may not be achievable at concentrations tolerated by humans.[192,193] However, strategies that combine gleevec with other compounds may have merit. The homology between the tyrosine kinase domains of RET and the epidermal growth factor receptor, the latter a target of considerable pharmaceutical interest, has further facilitated the identification of a group of small organic molecules that inhibit the kinase domain of RET. The vascular endothelial growth factor receptor (VEGFR) family may be another potential target. Medullary thyroid carcinomas are vascular tumors, and evidence exists that this receptor family may have an important role in the evolution of the tumor.[188,194-196]

Hereditary MTC in many respects is an optimal tumor type to study. The malignancy develops over years or decades, affording an opportunity for pharmacologic intervention.[197] Some of these tyrosine kinase inhibitors are in preclinical studies[198,199]; others have passed through phase I testing and are now entering phase II or pilot studies for treatment of MTC associated with RET mutations.[200,201] Although there is no certainty that targeting a single kinase will alter the course of this disease, experience with other malignancies with a monogenic etiology suggests that such approach may be effective.

## REFERENCES

1. Sipple JH: The association of pheochromocytoma with carcinoma of the thyroid gland. Am J Med 31:163–166, 1961.
2. Hazard JB: The C-cells (parafollicular cells) of the thyroid gland and medullary thyroid carcinoma: A review. Am J Pathol 88:214, 1977.
3. Hazard JB, Hawk WA, Crile G Jr: Medullary (solid) carcinoma of the thyroid: A clinicopathologic entity. J Clin Endocrinol Metab 19:152–161, 1959.
4. Williams ED, Brown CL, Doniach I: Pathological and clinical findings in a series of 67 cases of medullary carcinoma of the thyroid. J Clin Pathol 19:103–113, 1966.
5. Williams ED: Histogenesis of medullary carcinoma of the thyroid. J Clin Pathol 19:114–118, 1966.
6. Steiner AL, Goodman AD, Powers SR: Study of a kindred with pheochromocytoma, medullary carcinoma, hyperparathyroidism and Cushing's disease: Multiple endocrine neoplasia, type 2. Medicine 47:371–409, 1968.
7. Melvin KEW, Tashjian AH Jr, Miller HH: Studies in familial (medullary) thyroid carcinoma. Recent Prog Horm Res 28:399–470, 1972.
8. Keiser HR, Beaven MA, Doppman J, et al: Sipple's syndrome: Medullary thyroid carcinoma, pheochromocytoma, and parathyroid disease. Ann Intern Med 78:561–579, 1973.

9. Jackson CE, Frame B: Relationship of hyperparathyroidism to multiple endocrine adenomatosis. Birth Defects 7:66–68, 1971.
10. Williams ED: A review of 17 cases of carcinoma of the thyroid and phaeochromocytoma. J Clin Pathol l8:288–292, 1965.
11. Williams ED, Pollock DJ: Multiple mucosal neuromata with endocrine tumours: A syndrome allied to Von Recklinghausen's disease. J Pathol Bacteriol 91:71–80, 1966.
12. DeLellis RA, Wolfe HJ, Gagel RF, et al: Adrenal medullary hyperplasia: A morphometric analysis in patients with familial medullary thyroid carcinoma. Am J Pathol 83:177–196, 1976.
13. Carney JA, Sizemore GW, Tyce GM: Bilateral adrenal medullary hyperplasia in multiple endocrine neoplasia, type 2: The precursor of bilateral pheochromocytoma. Mayo Clin Proc 50:3–10, 1975.
14. Wolfe HJ, Melvin KEW, Cervi-Skinner SJ, et al: C-cell hyperplasia preceding medullary thyroid carcinoma. N Engl J Med 289:437–441, 1973.
15. Simpson NE: The exploration of the locus or loci for the syndromes associated with medullary thyroid cancer (MTC) on chromosome 10. In Brandi ML, White R (eds): Hereditary Tumors. New York, Raven Press, 1991, pp55–67.
16. Mathew CG, Chin KS, Easton DF, et al: A linked genetic marker for multiple

endocrine neoplasia type 2A on chromosome 10. Nature 328:527–528, 1987.
17. Eng C, Clayton D, Schuffenecker I, et al: The relationship between specific RET proto-oncogene mutations and disease phenotype in multiple endocrine neoplasia type 2. International RET mutation consortium analysis. JAMA 276:1575–1579, 1996.
18. Yamamoto M, Takai S, Miki T, et al: Close linkage of MEN2A with RBP3 locus in Japanese kindreds. Hum Genet 82:287–288, 1989.
19. Telenius-Berg M, Berg B, Hamberger B, et al: Impact of screening on prognosis in the multiple endocrine neoplasia type 2 syndromes: Natural history and treatment results in 105 patients. Henry Ford Hosp Med J 32:225–231, 1984.
20. Lindskog S, Ahlman H, Illerskog A, et al: [Phenotypic expression of a mutation in MEN 2A documented in a family in the western part of Sweden]. Lakartidningen 98:3690–3601, 3694–3695, 2001.
21. Sippel RS, Carpenter JE, Kunnimalaiyaan M, et al: The role of human achaete-scute homolog-1 in medullary thyroid cancer cells. Surgery 134:866–871; discussion 871–873, 2003.
22. Lindahl M, Timmusk T, Rossi J, et al: Expression and alternative splicing of mouse Gfra4 suggest roles in endocrine cell development. Mol Cell Neurosci 15:522–533, 2000.
23. Lukacs G, Sapy Z, Gyory F, et al: Distribution of calcitonin-containing

parafollicular cells of the thyroid in patients with chronic lymphocytic thyroiditis: A clinical, pathological and immunohistochemical study. Acta Chir Hung 36:204–206, 1997.

24. Livolsi VA, Feind CR: Incidental medullary thyroid carcinoma in sporadic hyperparathyroidism. Am J Clin Pathol 71:595–599, 1979.

25. Lallier TE: Cell lineage and cell migration in the neural crest. Ann N Y Acad Sci 615:158–171, 1991.

26. Huber K, Combs S, Ernsberger U, et al: Generation of neuroendocrine chromaffin cells from sympathoadrenal progenitors: Beyond the glucocorticoid hypothesis. Ann N Y Acad Sci 971:554–559, 2002.

27. Schober A, Wolf N, Huber K, et al: TrkB and neurotrophin-4 are important for development and maintenance of sympathetic preganglionic neurons innervating the adrenal medulla. J Neurosci 18:7272–7284, 1998.

28. Schober A, Minichiello L, Keller M, et al: Reduced acetylcholinesterase (AChE) activity in adrenal medulla and loss of sympathetic preganglionic neurons in TrkA-deficient, but not TrkB-deficient, mice. J Neurosci 17:891–903, 1997.

29. Anderson DJ: Molecular control of cell fate in the neural crest: The sympathoadrenal lineage. Annu Rev Neurosci 16:129–158, 1993.

30. Huber K, Bruhl B, Guillemot F, et al: Development of chromaffin cells depends on MASH1 function. Development 129:4729–4738, 2002.

31. Allmendinger A, Stoeckel E, Saarma M, et al: Development of adrenal chromaffin cells is largely normal in mice lacking the receptor tyrosine kinase c-Ret. Mech Dev 120:299–304, 2003.

32. Burau K, Stenull I, Huber K, et al: c-Ret regulates cholinergic properties in mouse sympathetic neurons: Evidence from mutant mice. Eur J Neurosci 20:353–362, 2004.

33. Forander P, Broberger C, Stromberg I: Glial-cell-line-derived neurotrophic factor induces nerve fibre formation in primary cultures of adrenal chromaffin cells. Cell Tissue Res 305:43–51, 2001.

34. Rosenfeld MG, Amara SG, Roos BA, et al: Altered expression of the calcitonin gene associated with RNA polymorphism. Nature 290:63–65, 1981.

35. Peleg S, Abruzzese RV, Cote GJ, et al: Transcription of the human calcitonin gene is mediated by a C cell-specific enhancer containing E-box-like elements. Mol Endocrinol 4:1750–1757, 1990.

36. de Bustros A, Lee RY, Compton D, et al: Differential utilization of calcitonin gene regulatory DNA sequences in cultured lines of medullary thyroid carcinoma and small-cell lung carcinoma. Mol Cell Biol 10:1773–1778, 1990.

37. Tverberg LA, Russo AF: Regulation of the calcitonin/calcitonin gene-related peptide gene by cell-specific synergy between helix-loop-helix and octamer-binding transcription factors. J Biol Chem 268:15965–15973, 1993.

38. Melvin KEW, Miller HH, Tashjian AH Jr: Early diagnosis of medullary carcinoma of the thyroid gland by means of calcitonin assay. N Engl J Med 285:1115–1120, 1971.

39. Hennessey JF, Gray TK, Cooper CW, et al: Stimulation of thyrocalcitonin secretion by pentagastrin and calcium in 2 patients with medullary thyroid carcinoma of the thyroid. J Clin Endocrinol Metab 36:200–203, 1973.

40. Kodama T: Identification of carcinoembryonic antigen in the C-cell of the normal thyroid. Cancer 45:98, 1980.

41. DeLellis RA, Rule AH, Spiler I, et al: Calcitonin and carcinoembryonic antigen as tumor markers in medullary thyroid carcinoma. Am J Clin Pathol 70:587–594, l978.

42. Deftos LJ, Woloszczuk W, Krisch I, et al: Medullary thyroid carcinomas express chromogranin A and a novel neuroendocrine protein recognized by monoclonal antibody HISL-19. Am J Med 85:780–784, 1988.

43. Gagel RF, Palmer WN, Leonhart K, et al: Somatostatin production by a human medullary thyroid carcinoma cell line. Endocrinology 118:1643–1651, 1986.

44. Modigliani E, Alamowitch C, Cohen R, et al: The intratumoral immunoassayable somatostatin concentration is frequently elevated in medullary thyroid carcinoma: Results in 34 cases. Cancer 65:224–228, 1990.

45. Takahashi M, Ritz J, Cooper GM: Activation of a novel human transforming gene, ret, by DNA rearrangement. Cell 42:581–588, 1985.

46. Takahashi M, Cooper GM: Ret transforming gene encodes a fusion protein homologous to tyrosine kinases. Mol Cell Biol 7:1378–1385, 1987.

47. Bongarzone I, Pierotti MA, Monzini N, et al: High frequency of activation of tyrosine kinase oncogenes in human papillary thyroid carcinoma. Oncogene 4:1457–1462, 1989.

48. Donghi R, Sozzi G, Pierotti MA, et al: The oncogene associated with human papillary thyroid carcinoma (PTC) is assigned to chromosome 10 q11-q12 in the same region as multiple endocrine neoplasia type 2A (MEN2A). Oncogene 4:521–523, 1989.

49. Grieco M, Santoro M, Berlingieri MT, et al: PTC is a novel rearranged form of the ret proto-oncogene and is frequently detected in vivo in human thyroid papillary carcinomas. Cell 60:557–563, 1990.

50. Santoro M, Melillo RM, Carlomagno F, et al: Molecular mechanisms of RET activation in human cancer. Ann N Y Acad Sci 963:116–121, 2002.

51. Santoro M, Carlomagno F, Hay ID, et al: Ret oncogene activation in human thyroid neoplasms is restricted to the papillary cancer subtype. J Clin Invest 89:1517–1522, 1992.

52. Pierotti MA, Vigneri P, Bongarzone I: Rearrangements of RET and NTRK1 tyrosine kinase receptors in papillary thyroid carcinomas. Recent Results Cancer Res 154:237–247, 1998.

53. Simpson NE, Kidd KK, Goodfellow PJ, et al: Assignment of multiple endocrine neoplasia type 2A to chromosome 10 by linkage. Nature 328:528–530, 1987.

54. Mulligan LM, Kwok JB, Healey CS, et al: Germ-line mutations of the RET proto-oncogene in multiple endocrine neoplasia type 2A. Nature 363:458–460, 1993.

55. Donis-Keller H, Dou S, Chi D, et al: Mutations in the RET proto-oncogene are associated with MEN2A and FMTC. Hum Mol Genet 2:851–856, 1993.

56. Treanor JJ, Goodman L, de Sauvage F, et al: Characterization of a multicomponent receptor for GDNF [see comments]. Nature 382:80–83, 1996.

57. Lin LF, Doherty DH, Lile JD, et al: GDNF: A glial cell line-derived neurotrophic factor for midbrain dopaminergic neurons. Science 260:1130–1132, 1993.

58. Schuchardt A, D'Agati V, Larsson-Blomberg L, et al: Defects in the kidney and enteric nervous system of mice lacking the tyrosine kinase receptor Ret. Nature 367:380–383, 1994.

59. Durbec P, Marcos-Gutierrez CV, Kilkenny C, et al: GDNF signalling through the Ret receptor tyrosine kinase [see comments]. Nature 381:789–793, 1996.

60. Moore MW, Klein RD, Farinas I, et al: Renal and neuronal abnormalities in mice lacking GDNF. Nature 382:76–79, 1996.

61. Sanchez MP, Silos-Santiago I, Frisen J, et al: Renal agenesis and the absence of enteric neurons in mice lacking GDNF. Nature 382:70–73, 1996.

62. Jing S, Wen D, Yu Y, et al: GDNF-induced activation of the Ret protein tyrosine kinase is mediated by GDNFR-α, a novel receptor for GDNF. Cell 85:1113–1124, 1996.

63. Enomoto H, Araki T, Jackman A, et al: GFR alpha1-deficient mice have deficits in the enteric nervous system and kidneys. Neuron 21:317–324, 1998.

64. Heuckeroth RO, Enomoto H, Grider JR, et al: Gene targeting reveals a critical role for neurturin in the development and maintenance of enteric, sensory, and parasympathetic neurons [see comments]. Neuron 22:253–263, 1999.

65. Robertson K, Mason I: The GDNF-RET signalling partnership. Trends Genet 13:1–3, 1997.

66. Chiariello M, Visconti R, Carlomagno F, et al: Signalling of RET receptor tyrosine kinase through the C-Jun NH$_2$-terminal protein kinases (JNKs): Evidence for a divergence of the erks and jnks pathways induced by RET. Oncogene 16:2435–2445, 1998.

67. Pichel JG, Shen L, Sheng HZ, et al: Defects in enteric innervation and kidney development in mice lacking GDNF. Nature 382:73–76, 1996.

68. Durbec PL, Larsson-Blomberg LB, Schuchardt A, et al: Common origin and developmental dependence on c-ret of subsets of enteric and sympathetic neuroblasts. Development 122:349–358, 1996.

69. Clarkson ED, Zawada WM, Freed CR: GDNF reduces apoptosis in dopaminergic neurons in vitro. Neuroreport 7:145–149, 1995.

70. Asai N, Iwashita T, Matsuyama M, et al: Mechanisms of activation of the ret proto-oncogene by multiple endocrine neoplasia 2A mutations. Mol Cell Biol 15:1613–1619, 1995.

71. Santoro M, Carlomagno F, Romano A, et al: Activation of RET as a dominant transforming gene by germline mutations of MEN2A and MEN2B. Science 267:381–383, 1995.

72. Xing S, Smanik PA, Oglesbee MJ, et al: Characterization of ret oncogenic activation in MEN2 inherited cancer syndromes. Endocrinology 137:1512–1519, 1996.

73. Sariola H, Saarma M: Novel functions and signalling pathways for GDNF. J Cell Sci 116:3855–3862, 2003.

74. GFRa Nomenclature Committee: Nomenclature of GPI-linked receptors for the GDNF ligand family. Neuron 19:485, 1997.

75. Airaksinen MS, Saarma M: The GDNF family: Signalling, biological functions and therapeutic value. Nat Rev Neurosci 3:383–294, 2002.

76. Wolfe HJ, DeLellis RA: Familial medullary thyroid carcinoma and C-cell hyperplasia. Clin Endocrinol Metab 10:351–365, 1981.

77. Graham SM, Genel M, Touloukian RJ, et al: Provocative testing for occult medullary carcinoma of the thyroid: Findings in seven children with multiple endocrine neoplasia type IIa. J Pediatr Surg 22:501–503, 1987.

78. Kakudo K, Carney JA, Sizemore GW: Medullary carcinoma of thyroid: Biologic behavior of the sporadic and familial neoplasm. Cancer 55:2818–2821, 1985.

79. Saad MF, Ordonez NG, Rashid RK, et al: Medullary carcinoma of the thyroid: A study of the clinical features and prognostic factors in 161 patients. Medicine 63:319–342, 1984.

80. Wohllk N, Cote GJ, Bugalho MMJ, et al: Relevance of RET proto-oncogene mutations in sporadic medullary thyroid carcinoma. J Clin Endocrinol Metab 81:3740–3745, 1996.

81. Decker RA, Peacock ML, Borst MJ, et al: Progress in genetic screening of multiple endocrine neoplasia type 2A: Is calcitonin testing obsolete? Surgery 118:257–264, 1995.

82. Komminoth P, Kunz EK, Matias-Guiu X, et al: Analysis of RET proto-oncogene point mutations distinguishes heritable from nonheritable medullary thyroid carcinomas. Cancer 76:479–489, 1995.

83. Samaan NA, Schultz PN, Hickey RC: Medullary thyroid carcinoma: Prognosis of familial versus sporadic disease and the role of radiotherapy.

J Clin Endocrinol Metab 67:801–805, 1988.

84. Gagel RF, Tashjian AH Jr, Cummings T, et al: The clinical outcome of prospective screening for multiple endocrine neoplasia type 2a: An 18-year experience. N Engl J Med 318:478–484, 1988.

85. Isaacs P, Whittaker SM, Turnberg LA: Diarrhea associated with medullary carcinoma of the thyroid. Gastroenterology 67:521–526, l974.

86. Deftos LJ, Murray SS, Burton DW, et al: A cloned chromogranin A (CgA) cDNA detects a 2.3Kb mRNA in diverse neuroendocrine tissues. Biochem Biophys Res Commun 137:418–423, 1986.

87. Hoppener JW, Steenbergh PH, Moonen PJ, et al: Detection of mRNA encoding calcitonin, calcitonin gene related peptide and proopiomelanocortin in human tumors. Mol Cell Endocrinol 47:125–130, 1986.

88. Webb TA, Sheps SG, Carney JA: Differences between sporadic pheochromocytoma and pheochromocytoma in multiple endocrine neoplasia, type 2. Am J Surg Pathol 4:121–126, 1980.

89. Lips CJ, Minder WH, Leo JR, et al: Evidence of multicentric origin of the multiple endocrine neoplasia syndrome type 2a (Sipple's syndrome) in a large family in the Netherlands: Diagnostic and therapeutic implications. Am J Med 64:569–578, 1978.

90. Sisson JC, Shapiro B, Beierwaltes WH: Scintigraphy with I-131 MIBG as an aid to the treatment of pheochromocytomas in patients with the multiple endocrine neoplasia type 2 syndromes. Henry Ford Hosp Med J 32:254–261, 1984.

91. Casanova S, Rosenberg-Bourgin M, Farkas D, et al: Phaeochromocytoma in multiple endocrine neoplasia type 2 A: Survey of 100 cases. Clin Endocrinol (Oxf) 38:531–537, 1993.

92. Lee JE, Curley SA, Gagel RF, et al: Cortical-sparing adrenalectomy for patients with bilateral pheochromocytoma. Surgery 120:1064–1070; discussion 1070–1071, 1996.

93. Miyauchi A, Masuo K, Ogihara T, et al: Urinary epinephrine and norepinephrine excretion in patients with medullary thyroid carcinoma and their relatives. Nippon Naibunpi Gakkai Zasshi 58:1505–1516, 1982.

94. Hamilton BP, Landsberg L, Levine RJ: Measurement of urinary epinephrine in screening for pheochromocytoma in multiple endocrine neoplasia type II. Am J Med 65:1027–1032, 1978.

95. Gagel RF, Melvin KE, Tashjian AH Jr, et al: Natural history of the familial medullary thyroid carcinoma-pheochromocytoma syndrome and the identification of preneoplastic stages by screening studies: A five-year report. Trans Assoc Am Physicians 88:177–191, 1975.

96. Eisenhofer G, Lenders JW, Linehan WM, et al: Plasma normetanephrine and

metanephrine for detecting pheochromocytoma in von Hippel-Lindau disease and multiple endocrine neoplasia type 2. N Engl J Med 340:1872–1879, 1999.

97. Cance WG, Wells SA Jr: Multiple endocrine neoplasia type IIa. Curr Probl Surg 22:1–56, 1985.

98. Gagel RF, Levy ML, Donovan DT, et al: Multiple endocrine neoplasia type 2a associated with cutaneous lichen amyloidosis. Ann Intern Med 111:802–806, 1989.

99. Nunziata V, Giannattasio R, di Giovanni G, et al: Hereditary localized pruritus in affected members of a kindred with multiple endocrine neoplasia type 2A (Sipple's syndrome). Clin Endocrinol 30:57–63, 1989.

100. Houdent C, Avronsart B, Dubuisson M, et al: Familial medullary thyroid cancer: Contribution of genealogy and genetics to the study of two families. Presse Med 19:549–552, 1990.

101. Farndon JR, Leight GS, Dilley WG, et al: Familial medullary thyroid carcinoma without associated endocrinopathies: A distinct clinical entity. Br J Surg 73:278–281, 1986.

102. Lairmore TC, Howe JR, Korte JA, et al: Familial medullary thyroid carcinoma and multiple endocrine neoplasia type 2B map to the same region of chromosome 10 as multiple endocrine neoplasia type 2A. Genomics 9:181–192, 1991.

103. Norum RA, Lafreniere RG, O'Neal LW, et al: Linkage of the multiple endocrine neoplasia type 2B gene (MEN2B) to chromosome 10 markers linked to MEN2A. Genomics 8:313–317, 1990.

104. Sizemore GW, Carney JA, Gharib H, et al: Multiple endocrine neoplasia type 2B: Eighteen-year follow-up of a four-generation family. Henry Ford Hosp J 40:236–244, 1992.

105. Moyes CD, Alexander FW: Mucosal neuroma syndrome presenting in a neonate. Dev Med Child Neurol l9:518–534, 1977.

106. Samaan NA, Draznin MB, Halpin RE, et al: Multiple endocrine syndrome type IIb in early childhood. Cancer 68:1832–1834, 1991.

107. Vasen HFA, van der Feltz M, Raue F, et al: The natural course of multiple endocrine neoplasia type IIb: A study of 18 cases. Arch Intern Med 152:1250–1252, 1992.

108. Rashid M, Khairi MR, Dexter RN, et al: Mucosal neuroma, pheochromocytoma and medullary thyroid carcinoma: Multiple endocrine neoplasia type 3. Medicine (Baltimore) 54:89–112, 1975.

109. Carney JA, Go VL, Sizemore GW, et al: Alimentary-tract ganglioneuromatosis: A major component of the syndrome of multiple endocrine neoplasia, type 2b. N Engl J Med 295:1287–1291, 1976.

110. Gabriel SB, Salomon R, Pelet A, et al: Segregation at three loci explains familial and population risk in

Hirschsprung disease. Nat Genet 31:89–93, 2002.

111. Carney JA, Roth SI, Heath H III, et al: The parathyroid glands in multiple endocrine neoplasia type 2b. Am J Pathol 99:387–398, 1980.

112. Carney JA, Bianco AJJ, Sizemore GW, et al: Multiple endocrine neoplasia with skeletal manifestations. J Bone Joint Surg [Am] 63:405–410, 1981.

113. Sciubba JJ, D'Amico E, Attie JN: The occurrence of multiple endocrine neoplasia type IIb, in two children of an affected mother. J Oral Pathol 16:310–316, 1987.

114. Kinoshita S, Tanaka F, Ohashi Y, et al: Incidence of prominent corneal nerves in multiple endocrine neoplasia type 2A. Am J Ophthalmol 111:307–311, 1991.

115. Dang GT, Cote GJ, Schultz PN, et al: A codon 891 exon 15 RET proto-oncogene mutation in familial medullary thyroid carcinoma: A detection strategy. Mol Cell Probes 13:77–79, 1999.

116. Parthemore JG, Bronzert D, Roberts G, et al: A short calcium infusion in the diagnosis of medullary thyroid carcinoma. J Clin Endocrinol Metab 39:108–111, 1974.

117. Hennessey JF, Wells SA, Ontjes DA, et al: A comparison of pentagastrin injections and calcium infusion as provocative agents for the detection of medullary carcinoma of the thyroid. J Clin Endocr Metab 39:487–495, 1974.

118. Wells SA Jr, Baylin SB, Linehan WM, et al: Provocative agents and the diagnosis of medullary carcinoma of the thyroid gland. Ann Surg 188:139–141, 1978.

119. Gharib H, Kao PC, Heath H III: Determination of silica-purified plasma calcitonin for the detection and management of medullary thyroid carcinoma: Comparison of two provocative tests. Mayo Clin Proc 62:373–378, 1987.

120. Niccoli P, Wion-Barbot N, Caron P, et al: Interest of routine measurement of serum calcitonin: Study in a large series of thyroidectomized patients: The French Medullary Study Group. J Clin Endocrinol Metab 82:338–341, 1997.

121. Vistelle R, Grulet H, Gibold C, et al: High permanent plasma adrenaline levels: A marker of adrenal medullary disease in medullary thyroid carcinoma. Clin Endocrinol 34:133–138, 1991.

122. Jadoul M, Leo JR, Berends MJ, et al: Pheochromocytoma-induced hypertensive encephalopathy revealing MEN-IIa syndrome in a 13-year old boy: Implications for screening procedures and surgery. Horm Metab Res Suppl 21:46–49, 1989.

123. Mulligan LM, Eng C, Attie T, et al: Diverse phenotypes associated with exon 10 mutations of the RET proto-oncogene. Hum Mol Genet 3:2163–2167, 1994.

124. Yobbagy JJ, Levatter R, Sisson JC, et al: Scintigraphic portrayal of the syndrome of multiple endocrine neoplasia type-2B. Clin Nucl Med 13:433–437, 1988.

125. Miyauchi A, Matsuzaka F, Kuma K, et al: Diagnosis of adrenal medullary diseases in patients with sporadic or hereditary medullary thyroid carcinoma: A report of 37 cases with 8-year follow-up study. Nippon Geka Gakkai Zasshi 88:1423–1429, 1987.

126. Heath H III, Sizemore GW, Carney JA: Preoperative diagnosis of occult parathyroid hyperplasia by calcium infusion in patients with multiple endocrine neoplasia, type 2a. J Clin Endocrinol Metab 43:428–435, 1976.

127. Eng C, Smith DP, Mulligan LM, et al: A novel point mutation in the tyrosine kinase domain of the RET proto-oncogene in sporadic medullary thyroid carcinoma and in a family with FMTC. Oncogene 10:509–513, 1995.

128. Pigny P, Bauters C, Wemeau JL, et al: A novel 9-base pair duplication in RET exon 8 in familial medullary thyroid carcinoma. J Clin Endocrinol Metab 84:1700–1704, 1999.

129. Da Silva AM, Maciel RM, Da Silva MR, et al: A novel germ-line point mutation in RET exon 8 (Gly(533)Cys) in a large kindred with familial medullary thyroid carcinoma. J Clin Endocrinol Metab 88:5438–5443, 2003.

130. Bolino A, Schuffenecker I, Luo Y, et al: RET mutations in exons 13 and 14 of FMTC patients. Oncogene 10:2415–2419, 1995.

131. Berndt I, Reuter M, Saller B, et al: A new hot spot for mutations in the ret protooncogene causing familial medullary thyroid carcinoma and multiple endocrine neoplasia type 2A. J Clin Endocrinol Metab 83:770–774, 1998.

132. Eng C, Thomas GA, Neuberg DS, et al: Mutation of the RET proto-oncogene is correlated with RET immunostaining in subpopulations of cells in sporadic medullary thyroid carcinoma. J Clin Endocrinol Metabol 83:4310–4313, 1998.

133. Gimm O, Marsh DJ, Andrew SD, et al: Germline dinucleotide mutation in codon 883 of the RET proto-oncogene in multiple endocrine neoplasia type 2B without codon 918 mutation. J Clin Endocrinol Metabol 82:3902–3904, 1997.

134. Marsh DJ, Learoyd DL, Andrew SD, et al: Somatic mutations in the RET proto-oncogene in sporadic medullary thyroid carcinoma. Clin Endocrinol 44:249–257, 1996.

135. Smith DP, Houghton C, Ponder BA: Germline mutation of RET codon 883 in two cases of de novo MEN2B. Oncogene 15:1213–1217, 1997.

136. Hofstra RM, Fattoruso O, Quadro L, et al: A novel point mutation in the intracellular domain of the ret protooncogene in a family with medullary thyroid carcinoma. J Clin Endocrinol Metabol 82:4176–4178, 1997.

137. Hofstra RM, Landsvater RM, Ceccherini I, et al: A mutation in the RET proto-oncogene associated with multiple endocrine neoplasia type 2B and sporadic medullary thyroid carcinoma. Nature 367:375–376, 1994.

138. Xing S, Furminger TL, Tong Q, et al: Signal transduction pathways activated by RET oncoproteins in PC12 pheochromocytoma cells. J Biol Chem 273:4909–4914, 1998.

139. Nilsson O, Tisell LE, Jansson S, et al: Adrenal and extra-adrenal pheochromocytomas in a family with germline RET V804L mutation [Letter]. JAMA 281:1587–1588, 1999.

140. Jimenez C, Habra MA, Huang SC, et al: Pheochromocytoma and medullary thyroid carcinoma: A new genotype-phenotype correlation of the RET protooncogene 891 germline mutation. J Clin Endocrinol Metab 89:4142–4145, 2004.

141. Borst MJ, Van Camp JM, Peacock ML, et al: Mutational analysis of multiple endocrine neoplasia type 2A associated with Hirschsprung's disease. Surgery 117:386–391, 1995.

142. Decker RA, Peacock ML, Watson P: Hirschsprung disease in MEN2A: Increased spectrum of RET exon 10 genotypes and strong genotype-phenotype correlation. Hum Mol Genet 7:129–134, 1998.

143. Angrist M, Bolk S, Thiel B, et al: Mutation analysis of the RET receptor tyrosine kinase in Hirschsprung disease. Hum Mol Genet 4:821–830, 1995.

144. Zedenius J, Wallin G, Hamberger B, et al: Somatic and MEN2A de novo mutations identified in the RET proto-oncogene by screening of sporadic MTCs. Hum Mol Genet 3:1259–1262, 1994.

145. Mulligan LM, Eng C, Healey CS, et al: A de novo mutation of the RET proto-oncogene in a patient with MEN2A. Hum Mol Genet 3:1007–1008, 1994.

146. Eng C: Seminars in medicine of the Beth Israel Hospital, Boston: The RET proto-oncogene in multiple endocrine neoplasia type 2 and Hirschsprung's disease. N Engl J Med 335:943–951, 1996.

147. Brandi ML, Gagel RF, Angeli A, et al: Guidelines for diagnosis and therapy of MEN type 1 and type 2. J Clin Endocrinol Metab 86:5658–5671, 2001.

148. Gagel RF, Cote GJ, Martins Bugalho MJ, et al: Clinical use of molecular information in the management of multiple endocrine neoplasia type 2A. J Intern Med 238:333–341, 1995.

149. Cote GJ, Gagel RF: Lessons learned from the management of a rare genetic cancer. N Engl J Med 349:1566–1568, 2003.

150. Machens A, Niccoli-Sire P, Hoegel J, et al: Early malignant progression of

hereditary medullary thyroid cancer. N Engl J Med 349:1517–1525, 2003.

151. Gill JR, Reyes-Mugica M, Iyengar S, et al: Early presentation of metastatic medullary carcinoma in multiple endocrine neoplasia, type IIA: Implications for therapy. J Pediatr 129:459–464, 1996.

152. Eng C, Mulligan LM, Healey CS, et al: Heterogeneous mutation of the RET proto-oncogene in subpopulations of medullary thyroid carcinoma. Cancer Res 56:2167–2170, 1996.

153. Zedenius J, Larsson C, Bergholm U, et al: Mutations of codon 918 in the RET proto-oncogene correlate to poor prognosis in sporadic medullary thyroid carcinomas. J Clin Endocrinol Metab 80:3088–3090, 1995.

154. Schilling T, Burck J, Sinn HP, et al: Prognostic value of codon 918 (ATG—>ACG) RET proto-oncogene mutations in sporadic medullary thyroid carcinoma. Int J Cancer 95:62–66, 2001.

155. Wells SA Jr, Chi DD, Toshima K, et al: Predictive DNA testing and prophylactic thyroidectomy in patients at risk for multiple endocrine neoplasia type 2A. Ann Surg 220:237–247; discussion 247–250, 1994.

156. Wells SA Jr, Donis-Keller H: Current perspectives on the diagnosis and management of patients with multiple endocrine neoplasia type 2 syndromes. Endocrinol Metab Clin North Am 23:215–228, 1994.

157. Skinner MA, Norton JA, Moley JF, et al: Heterotopic autotransplantation of parathyroid tissue in children undergoing total thyroidectomy. J Pediatr Surg 32:510–513, 1997.

158. Skinner MA, Wells SA Jr: Medullary carcinoma of the thyroid gland and the MEN2 syndromes. Semin Pediatr Surg 6:134–140, 1997.

159. Fleming JB, Lee JE, Bouvet M, et al: Surgical strategy for the treatment of medullary thyroid carcinoma. Ann Surg 230:697–707, 1999.

160. Moley JF, DeBenedetti MK: Patterns of nodal metastases in palpable medullary thyroid carcinoma: Recommendations for extent of node dissection. Ann Surg 229:880–887; discussion 887–888, 1999.

161. Moley JF, Debenedetti MK, Dilley WG, et al: Surgical management of patients with persistent or recurrent medullary thyroid cancer. J Intern Med 243:521–526, 1998.

162. Dralle H, Scheumann G, Proye C, et al: The value of lymph node dissection in hereditary medullary thyroid carcinoma: A retrospective, European, multicentre study. J Intern Med 238:357–361, 1995.

163. Evans DB, Fleming JB, Lee JE, et al: The surgical treatment of medullary thyroid carcinoma. Semin Surg Oncol 16:50–63, 1999.

164. Tisell L, Hansson G, Jansson S, et al: Reoperation in the treatment of asymptomatic metastasizing medullary thyroid carcinoma. Surgery 99:60–66, 1986.

165. Raue F, Winter J, Frank RK, et al: Diagnostic procedure before reoperation in patients with medullary thyroid carcinoma. Horm Metab Res Suppl 21:31–34, 1989.

166. Buhr HJ, Lehnert T, Raue F: New operative strategy in the treatment of metastasizing medullary carcinoma of the thyroid. Eur J Surg Oncol 16:366–369, 1990.

167. Moley JF, Dilley WG, DeBenedetti MK: Improved results of cervical reoperation for medullary thyroid carcinoma. Ann Surg 225:734–740; discussion 740–743, 1997.

168. Tung WS, Vesely TM, Moley JF: Laparoscopic detection of hepatic metastases in patients with residual or recurrent medullary thyroid cancer. Surgery 118:1024–1029; discussion 1029–1030, 1995.

169. Eng C, Mulligan LM, Smith DP, et al: Low frequency of germline mutations in the RET proto-oncogene in patients with apparently sporadic medullary thyroid carcinoma. Clin Endocrinol 43:123–127, 1995.

170. Brunt LM, Lairmore TC, Doherty GM, et al: Adrenalectomy for familial pheochromocytoma in the laparoscopic era. Ann Surg 235:713–720; discussion 720–721, 2002.

171. Tibblin S, Dymling JF, Ingemansson S, et al: Unilateral versus bilateral adrenalectomy in multiple endocrine neoplasia IIA. World J Surg 7:201–208, 1983.

172. Jansson S, Tisell LE, Fjalling M, et al: Early diagnosis of and surgical strategy for adrenal medullary disease in MEN II gene carriers. Surgery 103:11–18, 1988.

173. van Heerden JA, Sizemore GW, Carney JA, et al: Bilateral subtotal adrenal resection for bilateral pheochromocytomas in multiple endocrine neoplasia, type IIa: A case report. Surgery 98:363–366, 1985.

174. Neumann HP, Bender BU, Reincke M, et al: Adrenal-sparing surgery for phaeochromocytoma. Br J Surg 86:94–97, 1999.

175. Neumann HP, Reincke M, Bender BU, et al: Preserved adrenocortical function after laparoscopic bilateral adrenal sparing surgery for hereditary pheochromocytoma. J Clin Endocrinol Metab 84:2608–2610, 1999.

176. Moraca Kvapilova L, Op de Coul AA, Merkus JM: Cerebral haemorrhage in a pregnant woman with a multiple endocrine neoplasia syndrome (type 2A or Sipple's syndrome). Eur J Obstet Gynecol Reprod Biol 20:257–263, 1985.

177. Chodankar CM, Abhyankar SC, Deodhar KP, et al: Sipple's syndrome (multiple endocrine neoplasia) in pregnancy: Case report. Aust N Z J Obstet Gynaecol 22:243–244, 1982.

178. Koch CA, Huang SC, Moley JF, et al: Allelic imbalance of the mutant and wild-type RET allele in MEN2A-associated medullary thyroid carcinoma. Oncogene 20:7809–7811, 2001.

179. Mallette LE, Blevins T, Jordan PH, et al: Autogenous parathyroid grafts for generalized primary parathyroid hyperplasia: Contrasting outcome in sporadic hyperplasia versus multiple endocrine neoplasia type I. Surgery 101:738–745, 1987.

180. Wells SA Jr, Ellis GJ, Gunnells JC, et al: Parathyroid autotransplantation in primary parathyroid hyperplasia. N Engl J Med 195:57–62, 1976.

181. Huang SC, Koch CA, Vortmeyer AO, et al: Duplication of the mutant RET allele in trisomy 10 or loss of the wild-type allele in multiple endocrine neoplasia type 2-associated pheochromocytomas. Cancer Res 60:6223–6226, 2000.

182. Huang SC, Torres-Cruz J, Pack SD, et al: Amplification and overexpression of mutant RET in multiple endocrine neoplasia type 2-associated medullary thyroid carcinoma. J Clin Endocrinol Metab 88:459–463, 2003.

183. Zhuang Z, Park WS, Pack S, et al: Trisomy 7-harbouring non-random duplication of the mutant MET allele in hereditary papillary renal carcinomas. Nat Genet 20:66–9, 1998.

184. Zhang Z, Wang Y, Vikis HG, et al: Wild type Kras2 can inhibit lung carcinogenesis in mice. Nat Genet 29:25–33, 2001.

185. Takai S, Tateishi H, Nishisho I, et al: Loss of genes on chromosome 22 in medullary thyroid carcinoma and pheochromocytoma. Jpn J Cancer Res 78:894–898, 1987.

186. Mathew CG, Smith BA, Thorpe K, et al: Deletion of genes on chromosome 1 in endocrine neoplasia. Nature 328:524–526, 1987.

187. Cooley LD, Elder FF, Knuth A, et al: Cytogenetic characterization of three human and three rat medullary thyroid carcinoma cell lines. Cancer Genet Cytogenet 80:138–149, 1995.

188. McGregor LM, McCune BK, Graff JR, et al: Roles of trk family neurotrophin receptors in medullary thyroid carcinoma development and progression. Proc Natl Acad Sci U S A 96:4540–4545, 1999.

189. Druker BJ, Talpaz M, Resta DJ, et al: Efficacy and safety of a specific inhibitor of the BCR-ABL tyrosine kinase in chronic myeloid leukemia. N Engl J Med 344:1031–1037, 2001.

190. Joensuu H, Roberts PJ, Sarlomo-Rikala M, et al: Effect of the tyrosine kinase inhibitor STI571 in a patient with a metastatic gastrointestinal stromal tumor. N Engl J Med 344:1052–1056, 2001.

191. Lynch TJ, Bell DW, Sordella R, et al: Activating mutations in the epidermal growth factor receptor underlying responsiveness of non-small-cell lung cancer to gefitinib. N Engl J Med 350:2129–2139, 2004.

192. Skinner MA, Safford SD, Freemerman AJ: RET tyrosine kinase and medullary thyroid cells are unaffected by clinical doses of STI571. Anticancer Res 23:3601–3606, 2003.

193. Cohen MS, Hussain HB, Moley JF: Inhibition of medullary thyroid carcinoma cell proliferation and RET phosphorylation by tyrosine kinase inhibitors. Surgery 132:960–966; discussion 966–967, 2002.

194. Takekoshi K, Isobe K, Yashiro T, et al: Expression of vascular endothelial growth factor (VEGF) and its cognate receptors in human pheochromocytomas. Life Sci 74:863–871, 2004.

195. Salmenkivi K, Heikkila P, Liu J, et al: VEGF in 105 pheochromocytomas: Enhanced expression correlates with malignant outcome. APMIS 111:458–464, 2003.

196. Hung CJ, Ginzinger DG, Zarnegar R, et al: Expression of vascular endothelial growth factor-C in benign and malignant thyroid tumors. J Clin Endocrinol Metab 88:3694–3699, 2003.

197. Wells SA, Nevins JR: Evolving strategies for targeted cancer therapy: Past, present, and future. J Natl Cancer Inst 96:980–981, 2004.

198. Cuccuru G, Lanzi C, Cassinelli G, et al: Cellular effects and antitumor activity of RET inhibitor RPI-1 on MEN2A-associated medullary thyroid carcinoma. J Natl Cancer Inst 96:1006–1014, 2004.

199. Strock CJ, Park JI, Rosen M, et al: CEP-701 and CEP-751 inhibit constitutively activated RET tyrosine kinase activity and block medullary thyroid carcinoma cell growth. Cancer Res 63:5559–5563, 2003.

200. Carlomagno F, Vitagliano D, Guida T, et al: ZD6474, an orally available inhibitor of KDR tyrosine kinase activity, efficiently blocks oncogenic RET kinases. Cancer Res 62:7284–7290, 2002.

201. Traxler P, Allegrini PR, Brandt R, et al: AEE788: A dual family epidermal growth factor receptor/ErbB2 and vascular endothelial growth factor receptor tyrosine kinase inhibitor with antitumor and antiangiogenic activity. Cancer Res 64:4931–4941, 2004.

# Gastrointestinal Hormones and Tumor Syndromes

## *Shahrad Taheri, Mohammad A. Ghatei, and Stephen R. Bloom*

## INTRODUCTION

Apart from being the largest endocrine organ in the body, the gastrointestinal endocrine system holds a special place in endocrinology because the concept of blood-borne biochemical communication between tissues was first realized through elegant physiologic experiments carried out on the gut. Indeed, the first hormones to be discovered were gut peptides: secretin in 1902 and gastrin (gastric secretin) in 1905.[1–3] The early gut hormones were named based on their observed physiology and before their full biochemical structures were elucidated. It is now known that gut hormones are peptides that not only regulate the processes of digestion but also many physiologic processes outside the gut.

Several complex processes, mediated by peptide hormones, the enteric nervous system, and extrinsic nerves, regulate the absorption of nutrients from the gut. The functional contribution of the gastrointestinal endocrine system is (1) regulation of the mechanical processes of digestion, (2) regulation of the chemical and enzymatic processes of digestion, (3) control of postabsorptive processes involved in the assimilation of digested food and central nervous system (CNS) feedback regulating intake, and (4) effects on the growth and development of the gastrointestinal tract. An understanding of this system has been made possible by sensitive and specific techniques that have allowed isolation, purification, and localization of gut peptides and their receptors.[2] Molecular techniques increasingly complement more traditional techniques of radioimmunoassay and immunocytochemistry. In particular, gene manipulation studies in rodents are increasingly used to answer fundamental questions about the functions of gut peptides and their receptors. Using these techniques, gut peptides and their receptors have been detected in other tissues such as the CNS (e.g., brain-gut peptides), have been chemically isolated before their physiologic actions were studied (e.g., neuropeptide tyrosine [NPY]), and have been detected in nonmammalian species before being sought and characterized in mammals (e.g., bombesin, gastrin-releasing peptide [GRP]). It has been possible to synthesize peptide and nonpeptide agonists and antagonists for use in physiologic experiments, but the promise of the therapeutic use of these compounds remains to be realized.[4]

Gut peptide hormones and neurotransmitters are single-chain polypeptides that are grouped together into families based on their structures (e.g., gastrin, cholecystokinin [CCK])

(Table 193-1). Different peptides may be derived from the same precursor peptide through tissue-specific posttranslational processing (e.g., glucagon, glucagon-like peptide-1 [GLP-1]) or from the same gene through differential splicing (e.g., calcitonin gene-related peptide [CGRP], calcitonin). Peptide precursor molecules undergo several intracellular modification steps, which may include signal peptide cleavage, tyrosine sulfation, dibasic cleavage, removal of basic residues, and C-terminal amidation.[5] Sorting of peptides into secretory granules depends on structural domains within their molecule.

Gut peptides have a wide range of actions in different tissues. These actions depend on where the peptide is secreted, when it is secreted, and where its receptors are located. In the gut, they may act in an autocrine, paracrine, or endocrine fashion or as neurotransmitters and neuromodulators (neurocrine) (Fig. 193-1). Gut peptides act through seven transmembrane G protein–coupled receptors. The existence of different receptor subtypes and coupling to different second messenger mechanisms allow specificity and variability in the action of these peptides. Recently, there has been great interest in orphan G protein–coupled receptors, which are receptors whose endogenous ligands are unknown.[6] The reverse pharmacology technique is used to identify endogenous ligands for these receptors. This strategy involves challenging cultured cells expressing the orphan receptor on their surface with chromatographically purified extracts from tissues and monitoring receptor activation through measurement of changes in second messengers, ionic fluxes, or pH. This process has resulted in the identification of several peptides including the orexins and ghrelin.[6–8]

Most gut peptides are released in response to meals, with the degree of release depending on meal type and size. This allows appropriate responses to ingested food. The circulating half-lives of gut peptide hormones are usually brief (Fig. 193-2), with the peptides usually being broken down by circulating enzymes and metabolized and excreted by the liver and kidney. Circulating levels of gut peptides vary with different gastrointestinal diseases; this may be due to abnormal changes in release from the damaged bowel or adaptive compensatory changes in the remaining healthy bowel.

The gut contains a diffuse population of endocrine cells, some of which communicate with, and are sensitive to, changes in the chemical environment of the gut lumen such as pH and amino acids (open-type cells). Other endocrine

**Table 193-1** Gastrointestinal Regulatory Peptides and Related Peptides

| | |
|---|---|
| **Gastrin/CCK family** | **Secretin family** |
| Gastrin | Secretin |
| CCK | Proglucagon-derived peptides |
| **Pancreatic polypeptide family** | Glucagon |
| Pancreatic polypeptide | Glucagon-like peptide-1 |
| Peptide YY | Glucagon-like peptide-2 |
| Neuropeptide Y | Glicentin/enteroglucagon |
| **Tachykinin family** | Oxyntomodulin |
| Substance P | Gastric inhibitory peptide |
| Neurokinin A and B | VIP and related peptides |
| **Neurotensin and related** | VIP |
| **peptides** | Peptide histidine isoleucine |
| Neurotensin | Peptide histidine methionine |
| Xenopsin | Pituitary adenylate cyclase– |
| Xenin | activating peptide |
| | Growth hormone releasing |
| **Bombesin and related** | hormone |
| **peptides** | **Others** |
| Bombesin | Somatostatin |
| Gastrin-releasing peptide | Motilin and ghrelin |
| Neuromedin B and C | Galanin |
| **CGRP and related peptides** | Endothelin |
| CGRP | Chromogranins |
| Calcitonin | Opioid peptides |
| Adrenomodulin | Trefoil peptides |
| Amylin | Guanylins |
| | Neuromedin-U |
| | Cocaine and amphetamine–related |
| | transcript |
| | Orexins |

CCK, Cholecystokinin; CGRP, calcitonin gene-related peptide; VIP, vasoactive intestinal peptide.

cells (closed-type) lie within the gut wall and may perform other functions (paracrine, sensitive to stretch, trophic). These endocrine cells are constantly generated from stem cells. Their diffuse distribution allows accurate monitoring and modification of digestive processes. In addition to endocrine cells, there is a wide variety of peptide-producing neuronal cells within the gut. Several markers are used to identify neuroendocrine cells in the gut. These include chromogranins, secretogranins, neuron-specific enolase, and subtilase preprotein convertases. Although several markers are shared with neurons, gastrointestinal endocrine cells are of endodermal origin.[9]

This chapter aims to briefly describe the major gastrointestinal regulatory peptides, which have been divided into those that subserve predominantly hormonal and paracrine actions and those that act mainly as neurotransmitters. The final section deals with the rare gastrointestinal neuroendocrine tumors and their syndromes.

## PHYSIOLOGY

### HORMONES

#### Gastrin and Cholecystokinin

Because of their structural similarity and the fact that gastrin and CCK act at the same receptors, these two peptides have been placed in their own family. The receptors for gastrin and CCK are CCK1 and CCK2. CCK1 (also CCK-A) is predominantly the receptor for CCK, while CCK2 (also CCK-B/gastrin) has affinity for both peptides but is predominantly the gastrin receptor because gastrin circulates at much higher (10–100×) concentrations than CCK.

#### Gastrin

Gastrin is the major hormonal stimulus to gastric acid secretion. The main sites of gastrin synthesis are in the upper small intestine and, in open-type G cells, in the gastric antrum.[5] Gastrin immunoreactivity and/or gene expression have also been observed in the CNS and peripheral nervous system, the pituitary and adrenal glands, the acrosome of spermatogenic cells and the genital tract, the respiratory tract, and several common tumors.[3]

Gastrin exists in several molecular forms, which are the cleavage products of preprogastrin, a 101-amino acid peptide. Preprogastrin is modified to progastrin (by the cotranslational removal of a 21-amino acid hydrophobic N-terminal signal

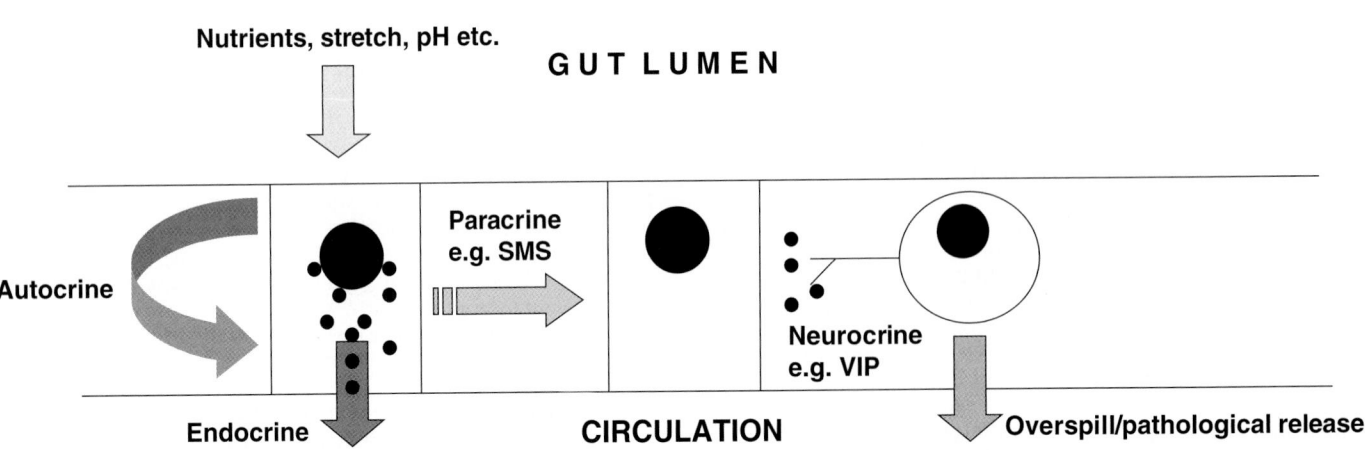

**Figure 193-1** Communication in the gastrointestinal endocrine system. Gastrointestinal endocrine cells respond to nutrients (open-type cells) and/or stretch (closed-type cells). They may release peptides into the circulation to affect distant cells (endocrine), into the interstitial fluid to affect themselves (autocrine), or other nearby cells (paracrine) (e.g., somatostatin [SMS]). Cells in the gut may be stimulated by or influence local neurons (neurocrine effect). Neurotransmitter peptides may be released at very low levels into the circulation (spillover) and at high levels mainly in pathologic states (e.g., vasoactive intestinal peptide [VIP] in VIPomas).

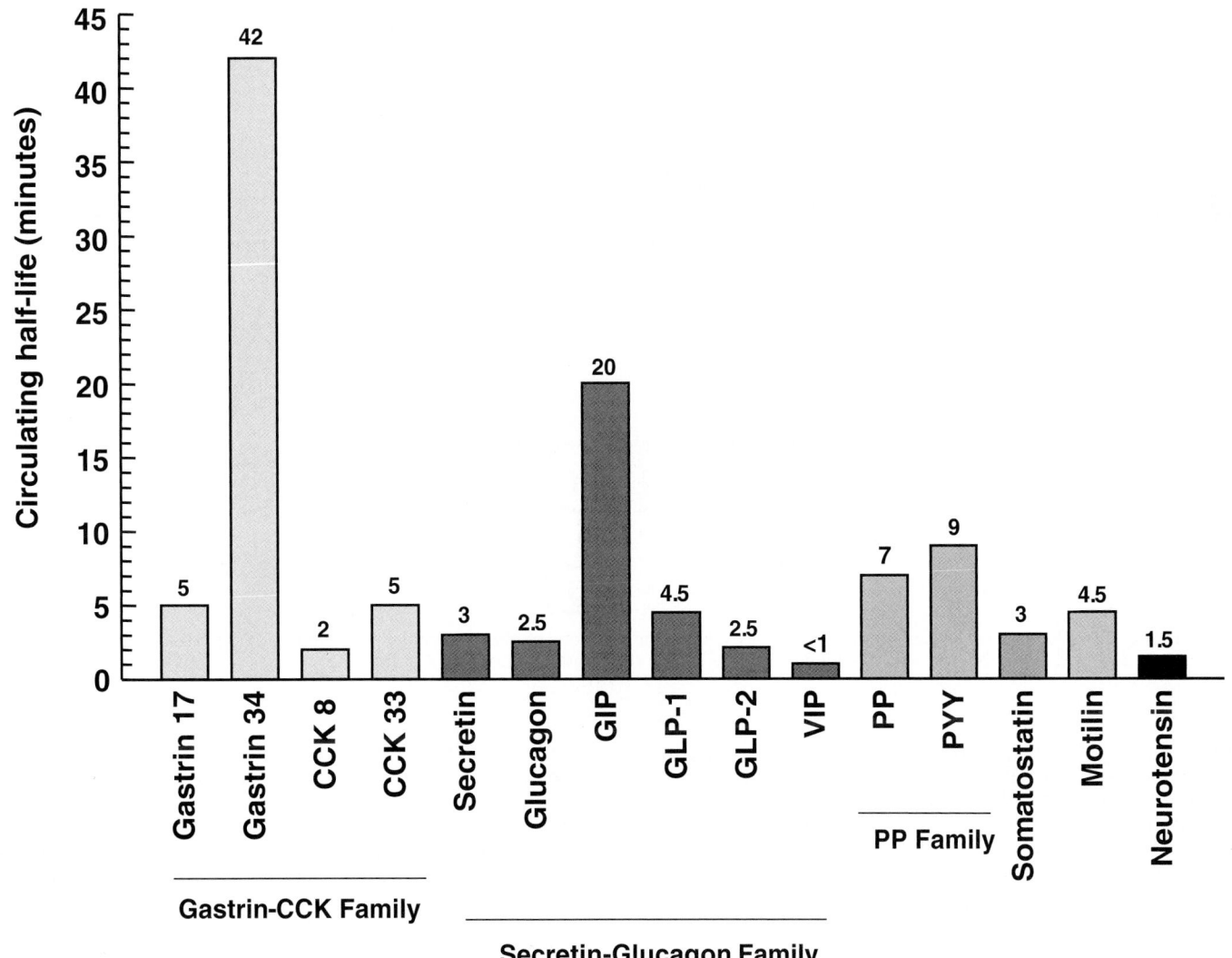

*Figure 193-2*  The circulating half-lives of gastrointestinal hormones. CCK, cholecystokinin; GIP, gastric inhibitory peptide; GLP, glucagon-like peptide; PP, pancreatic polypeptide; PYY; peptide YY.

peptide), which is then further processed into the three major circulating forms of gastrin, with N termini of variable lengths: gastrin-34, gastrin-17, and gastrin-14. Other circulating, but low concentration, gastrins include gastrin-6, gastrin-52, and gastrin-71.[10] Larger intermediate molecular forms, without gastric acid secreting capability, have been described including Gly-extended gastrin (Gly-gastrin), found in significant quantities in human colon cancers, which may affect cellular proliferation, possibly through an as yet unidentified receptor. Full biologic activity of gastrin resides in the C-terminal peptide and requires α-amidation of the C-terminal phenylalanine. Both gastrin and CCK end in the same pentapeptide but differ in that the tyrosine in position 7 of the C terminus is sulfated in CCK (Fig. 193-3). Approximately half of the gastrins in humans are sulfated, but, unlike CCK, sulfation of gastrin does not appear to affect biologic activity. Gastrin-17 is the predominant gastrin in tissue extracts from the stomach and duodenum. Both gastrin-34 and gastrin-17 are biologically active, with gastrin-17 being the predominant form in the circulation after a meal. Plasma gastrin levels are increased in achlorhydria (pernicious anemia, atrophic gastritis), treatment with antisecretory drugs such as protein pump inhibitors, G-cell hyperplasia, antral remnant after gastric surgery, infection with *Helicobacter pylori*, and renal failure (Table 193-2). Hypercalcemia can result in increased gastrin

levels; therefore, hyperparathyroidism needs to be excluded first in patients with multiple endocrine neoplasia type 1 (MEN1) before a diagnosis of gastrinoma is made.

The synthesis and release of gastrin are under the control of humoral and local factors as well as the autonomic nervous system. The predominant regulation is the presence of amino acids, particularly aromatic amino acids, and proteins in the lumen of the stomach, which, along with gastric distension, stimulate gastrin secretion. The vagus nerve not only stimulates gastrin secretion but also has a direct effect on acid secretion, with vagotomy resulting in increased serum gastrin and decreased acid secretion in the stomach. Postganglionic vagal fibers also release GRP, which potently stimulates gastrin secretion. The adrenergic nervous system can also influence gastrin release.[11] Gastrin secretion is inhibited when the pH of the stomach falls below pH 3; this is mediated through the paracrine action of somatostatin released from neighboring antral D cells. The effect of somatostatin on G cells may be to both decrease transcription of the gastrin gene and increase the rate of gastrin mRNA turnover. Reciprocal changes in somatostatin and gastrin gene expression have been demonstrated in response to the proton pump inhibitor omeprazole and to achlorhydria. Several peptides, including enterogastrones (factors released by the intestine that decrease gastric acid secretion and motility), act through somatostatin to reduce gastrin

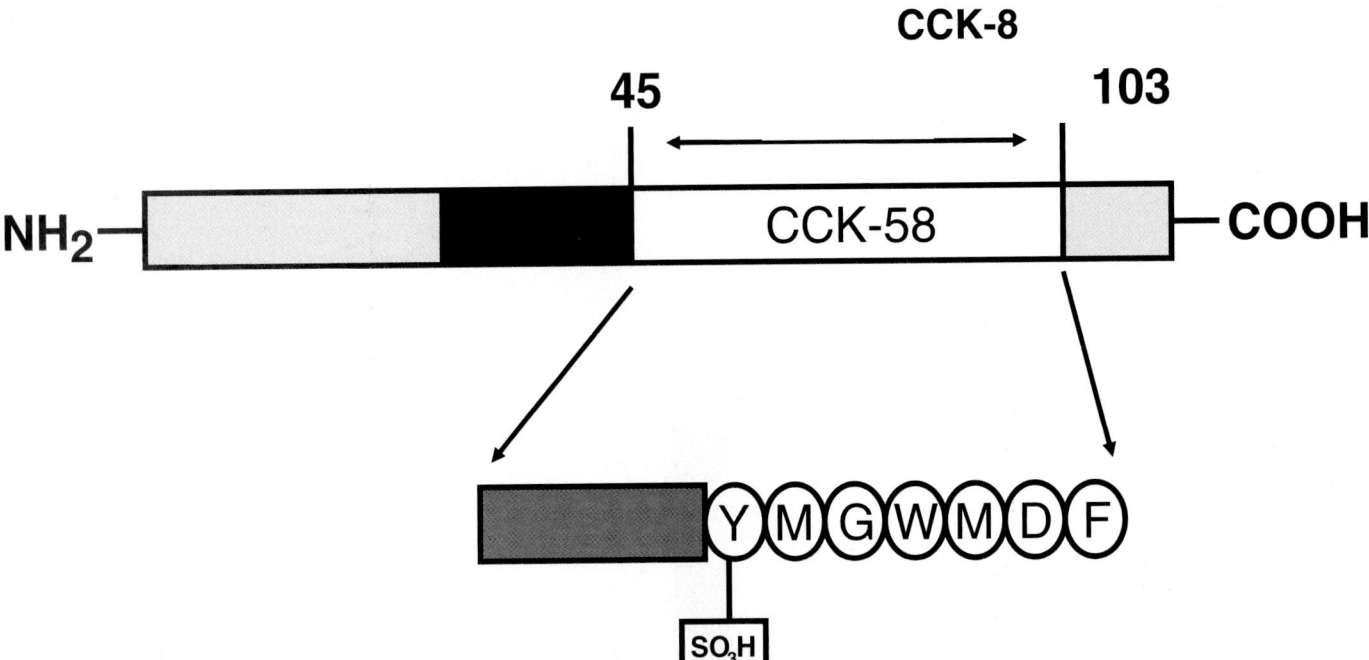

*Figure 193-3* The structural organization of preprocholecystokinin and positions of bioactive cholecystokinin (CCK) peptides in this structure. Both gastrin and CCK end in the same pentapeptide but differ in that the tyrosine in position 7 of the C terminus is sulfated in CCK.

release. Proposed enterogastrones include vasoactive intestinal polypeptide (VIP), CGRP, glucogen, GLP-1, secretin, gastric inhibitory peptide ([GIP], see later), and CCK. Although CCK indirectly inhibits gastric acid secretion through CCK1 receptors on D cells, it may stimulate acid secretion via CCK2 receptors, thus explaining contradictory experimental results.

| Table 193-2 | Causes of Increases of Some Commonly Measured Gut Hormones |
|---|---|
| **Hormone** | **Causes of Increased Plasma Concentration** |
| General | Postabsorptive state |
| | Renal failure |
| | Hepatic failure |
| | Stress |
| Gastrin | Drugs: H$_2$ antagonists, proton pump inhibitors |
| | *Helicobacter pylori* infection |
| | Pernicious anemia |
| | Hypercalcemia |
| | Intestinal resection |
| | Inflammatory bowel disease |
| | Antral remnant |
| | Gastrinoma |
| Glucagon | Drugs: oral contraceptives, Danazol |
| | Diabetes mellitus |
| | Hypoglycemia |
| | Familial hyperglucagonemia |
| | Glucagonoma |
| Pancreatic polypeptide | Inflammatory bowel disease |
| | Other neuroendocrine tumors |
| | PPoma |
| | Elderly |
| | Pernicious anemia |
| Somatostatin | Somatostatinoma |
| VIP | VIPoma |
| | Hepatic cirrhosis |
| | Bowel ischemia |

VIP, vasoactive intestinal peptide.

Galanin inhibits gastrin secretion independently of somatostatin. Beer, wine, and coffee stimulate gastrin secretion independently of alcohol and caffeine.

The neural and endocrine mechanisms involved in gastric acid secretion have been studied in detail (Fig. 193-4). Parietal cells have three stimulatory receptors: histamine (H$_2$), acetylcholine (M3), and gastrin (CCK2) receptors. Histamine and acetylcholine directly stimulate acid secretion, but previous histamine stimulation is required for gastrin action. The major endocrine cells involved in gastric acid secretion are the enterochromaffin-like (ECL) cells of the gastric fundus, the G cells of the antrum, and D cells of the fundus and antrum.

ECL cells release histamine, which stimulates acid secretion via H$_2$ receptors. Gastrin binding to CCK2 receptors on ECL cells results in changes in intracellular calcium (acute effect), upregulation of histidine decarboxylase (intermediate effect), and ECL cell proliferation (chronic effect). Other stimulatory receptors on ECL cells have been described: β$_3$-adrenergic, peptidergic, and cytokine receptors. Inhibitory receptors include receptors for somatostatin and peptide YY (PYY). Somatostatin, therefore, inhibits acid secretion by acting at several sites: parietal cells, G cells, and ECL cells. Fundal D cells are in turn stimulated by gastrin and acetylcholine.

Gastrin gene knockout mice and CCK2 receptor gene knockout mice have reduced basal and stimulated gastric acid secretion. The reduction in stimulated acid secretion is only partially restored by gastrin replacement, raising the possibility that gastrin is important in the development of acid secretory mechanisms.[12] As expected, basal acid secretion is elevated in gastrin-overexpressing mice.[12]

Gastrin has proliferative effects, as demonstrated by the development of ECL hyperplasia and carcinoids following proton pump inhibitor treatment. The risk of gastric carcinoid tumors in response to proton pump inhibitors, however, is low in humans. Gastrin also causes parietal cell proliferation. Further evidence of the trophic actions of gastrin has been provided by the study of animals with targeted disruption of gastrin and CCK2 receptor genes and from animals overexpressing progastrin.[13-15] Gastrin mRNA, resulting in the production of sulfated gastrin, has been observed in fetal

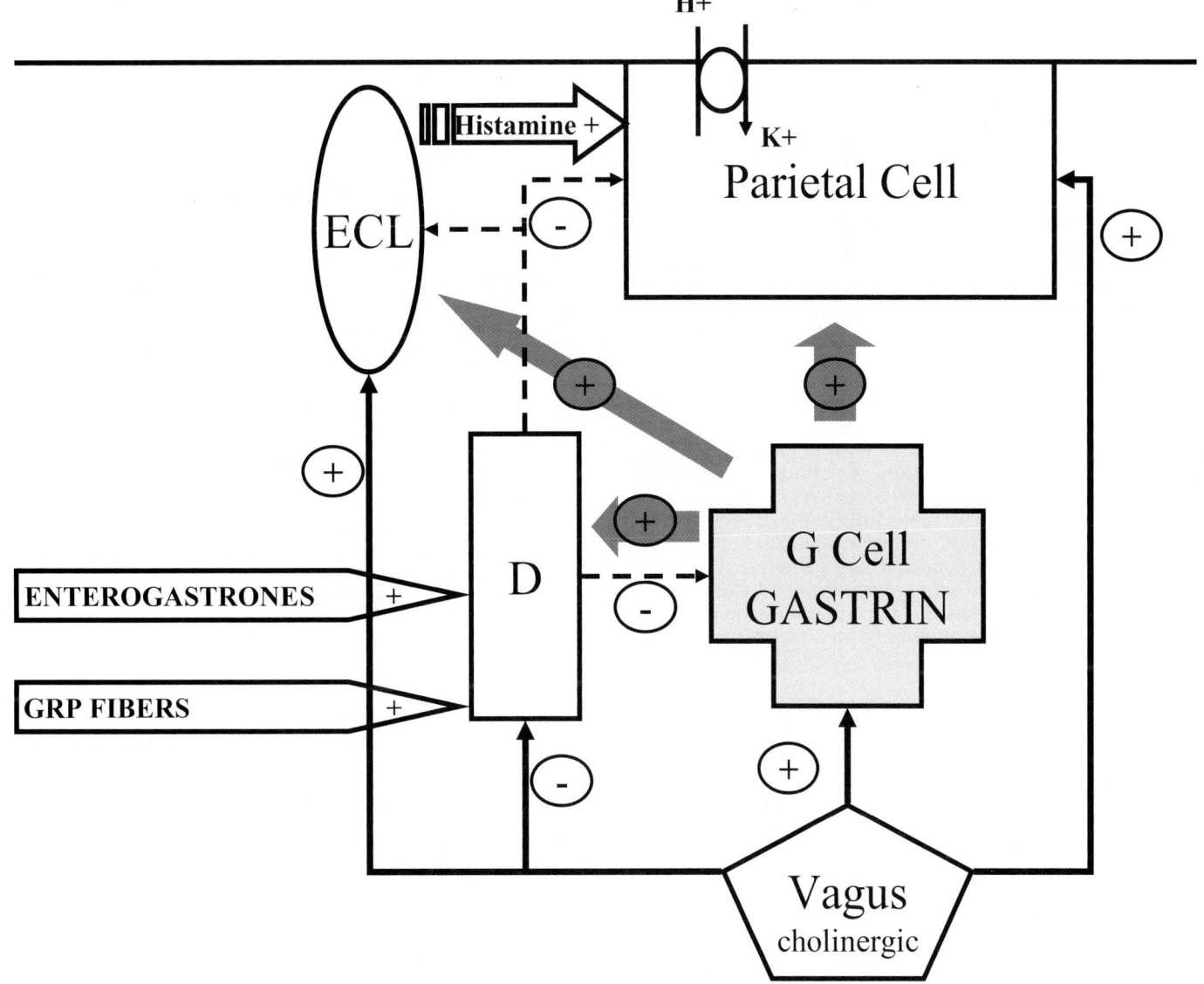

*Figure 193-4*   The control of gastric acid secretion. Multiple stimulatory and inhibitory mechanisms regulate gastric acid secretion. See text for details. ECL, enterochromaffin-like; D, D cell; GRP, gastrin-releasing peptide.

pancreatic cells, explaining the occurrence of pancreatic gastrinomas. Sulfated gastrin may function as a paracrine CCK-like peptide in the developing fetus. Gastrin may also have a role in the developing colon. There is great interest in the use of neutralizing the effects of gastrin through vaccination of patients with gastrointestinal tumors.

### Cholecystokinin
CCK was discovered as a factor that stimulated gallbladder contraction. It is now known to have other effects both in the gut and other tissues. It is secreted by open-type cells (I cells), which are most densely located in the small intestine and gradually decrease in number toward the large intestine. CCK is a brain-gut peptide found in the CNS and peripheral nervous system where it acts as neurotransmitter. Centrally, it has a wide distribution but is particularly concentrated in the hypothalamus and areas of the brain involved in pain perception (where it may act as an antiopioid peptide). Peripherally, it is a neurotransmitter in the myenteric and submucosal plexuses of the large intestine. CCK peptides have also been detected in corticotrophs, the C cells of the thyroid, the adrenal medulla, and the acrosome of developing and mature spermatozoa. Unlike gastrin, the CCK gene is expressed only in rare neuroendocrine tumors and sarcomas. Measurement of circulating CCK by radioimmunoassay has been difficult for several reasons including low blood concentrations (approximately 1 pmol/L basally), the existence of several biologically active molecular forms, and cross-reactivity with gastrin.

CCK is the product of a 115-amino acid precursor. Several molecular forms of CCK have been described (see Fig. 193-3) of which the octapeptide of CCK (CCK8), consisting of the C-terminal eight amino acids of CCK and the most abundant form of CCK in the CNS, is the most potent small peptide of CCK isolated. CCK8, CCK58, CCK33, and CCK39 have all been identified in significant amounts in human plasma. The differential processing of CCK in the CNS and gut is mediated by prohormone convertases. Prohormone convertase-1 appears to be the major processing enzyme in the gut, whereas prohormone convertase-2 is more important in the brain. Peripherally, CCK acts through CCK1 receptors. CCK receptors have been detected in the gut, pancreas, CNS and peripheral nervous system, and lymphocytes. Several CCK receptor antagonists are available.[4]

The predominant stimulus to CCK release is the presence of breakdown products of fat and protein in the upper small intestine, specifically fatty acids of 10 to 18 carbon atoms, and aromatic-aliphatic amino acids. The CCK response is greater for unsaturated versus saturated fats. The release of CCK in response to nutrients occurs independently of vagal innervation. The mechanism by which CCK is released in response to nutrients appears to involve CCK-releasing factors.[16] The pancreas may stimulate CCK release through a 61-amino acid "monitor" peptide involved in the luminal feedback mechanisms underlying pancreatic enzyme secretion in the small intestine.[17] Bile salts may have an inhibitory effect on CCK release as severe obstructive cholestasis or ingestion of cholestyramine increases plasma CCK levels. The bombesin family of peptides acts via bombesin receptors on CCK cells to stimulate CCK release. Adrenergic receptors on CCK cells are also stimulatory.

The strongest evidence of the hormonal action of CCK is stimulation of gallbladder contraction, which is abolished by CCK1 receptor antagonists. Other actions of CCK, such as pancreatic enzyme secretion, may be purely neural or have both neural and endocrine actions. Cholinergic innervation appears to be the major stimulant of pancreatic enzyme secretion, with CCK making a smaller contribution. CCK may have important trophic effects on normal and neoplastic tissues as CCK antagonists inhibit duodenal and pancreatic DNA synthesis in the rat after refeeding, and repeated CCK administration causes hypertrophy and hyperplasia of the pancreas. Otsuka Long-Evans Tokushima fatty rats, which have a congenital lack of expression of CCK1 receptors, have reduced pancreas sizes.

It has been observed that peripheral insulin levels in response to oral glucose intake are higher than in response to an equivalent intravenous dose. The intestine therefore releases factors that sensitize pancreatic beta cells via the enteroinsular axis. This has been named the glucoincretin effect (Fig. 193-5). It is as yet unclear whether CCK is also a physiologic glucoincretin. CCK receptors have been detected in pancreatic islets, and both in vitro and in vivo studies have suggested that CCK stimulates insulin secretion. However, CCK1 receptor blockade has failed to show a direct incretin effect of CCK in humans but has shown that CCK may be important in the secretion of pancreatic polypeptide (PP).

CCK delays gastric emptying in several species; this effect may be mediated through the vagus nerve. Endogenous CCK may also play a role in gastric acid secretion and in the control of lower esophageal sphincter pressure. Other reported gastrointestinal actions of CCK include acceleration of intestinal transport, postprandial reduction in cephalically stimulated anteroduodenal activity, and increased colonic transport.

Exogenous CCK decreases meal size in animals and humans. Blockade of peripheral CCK1 receptors increases appetite, suggesting that CCK may act peripherally as part of the meal termination signal. The peripheral actions of CCK on food intake occur via CCK1 receptors on vagal afferents, which relay this message to satiety centers in the hypothalamus. Peripherally administered CCK has been shown to act synergistically with leptin to reduce food intake in mice.[18] Otsuka Long-Evans Tokushima fatty rats, which lack CCK1 receptors, are hyperphagic and obese.[19] In the brain, CCK has also been implicated in inhibition of food intake, nociception, dopamine regulation, memory, anxiety, sleep, sexual behavior, and modulation of hormones such as gonadotropin-releasing hormone and luteinizing hormone.

Unlike gastrin, there are no clinical syndromes associated with CCK hypersecretion. CCK has been linked to gastrointestinal motility disorders (e.g., constipation, irritable bowel syndrome), pancreatic disorders (e.g., pancreatitis, pancreatic tumor growth), and satiety disorders (e.g., obesity, anorexia). Although CCK has been linked to these disorders, there are

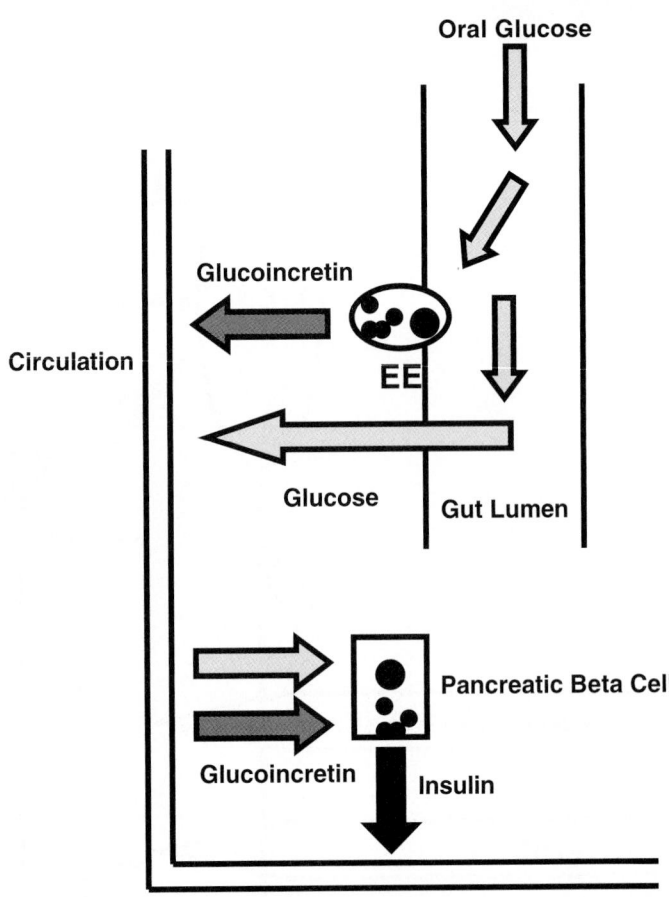

**Figure 193-5** The glucoincretin effect. Oral glucose results in a greater insulin response compared with the same amount of glucose given intravenously. This is because glucose in the gut stimulates glucoincretin hormones that augment insulin secretion. EE, enteroendocrine cell.

few conditions in which a pivotal role for CCK has been unequivocally established.

### Secretin

Secretin, the first hormone to be described, was discovered by Bayliss and Starling in 1902.[1] It is secreted by the S cells of the upper duodenum and jejunum and is a 27-amino acid linear peptide with a helical configuration. Secretin belongs to the secretin-glucagon family of peptides (see Table 193-1). Secretin receptors belong to the secretin family of G protein–coupled receptors.[20,21] Other members of this family include receptors for the secretin family of peptides and receptors for CGRP, parathyroid hormone (PTH), and corticotropin-releasing hormone.

The major stimulus to secretin secretion is the presence of acid in the duodenum. Secretin is released when the pH of duodenal contents falls below 4.5 and has a circulating half-life of 2 to 3 minutes. Patients with achlorhydria have secretin deficiency, whereas hypersecretinemia occurs in Zollinger-Ellison syndrome (ZES). Fatty acids, bile salts, alcohol, and liquorice also stimulate secretin secretion but to a lesser degree. Secretin-releasing factors may be involved in the secretin response to luminal contents. Secretin release is inhibited by somatostatin and is suppressed in conditions associated with intestinal mucosal atrophy (e.g., celiac disease).

Secretin is the principal hormonal stimulant of pancreatic and biliary water and bicarbonate secretion; CCK potentiates this effect. It may also contribute to pancreatic enzyme secretion. The role of secretin in pancreatic islet physiology and normal pancreatic exocrine growth remains controversial. High concentrations of secretin may contribute to secretion of pepsinogen, inhibition of gastric acid secretion (via somatostatin), and postprandial gastric emptying (enterogastrone effect). Other reported actions of supraphysiologic doses of secretin include the stimulation of bicarbonate secretion and epidermal growth factor from Brunner's glands, stimulation of bile secretion and colonic mucus, and inhibition of lower esophageal sphincter tone.

## Gastric Inhibitory Polypeptide

GIP, also called glucose-dependent insulinotropic polypeptide, is secreted by mucosal K cells, which are predominantly found in the duodenum and jejunum and to a lesser extent in the ileum and colon. GIP is one of the largest peptides of the secretin family, consisting of 42-amino acid residues. It is released into the circulation after a mixed meal and also after ingestion of glucose, fat, or amino acids. Fat ingestion appears to be a more potent stimulator of GIP secretion than carbohydrate in humans. The peak concentrations are achieved after 30 to 60 minutes, although this is delayed as long as 2 hours after ingestion of fat. GIP receptors have been detected in many tissues, including pancreatic β cells, the brain, heart, pituitary, adrenal glands, and adipose tissue. GIP is cleaved by the enzyme dipeptidyl peptidase IV (DP IV), which also hydrolyses GLP-1 and peptide histidine methionine. As expected, levels of GIP are increased in DP IV gene knockout mice.

There are conflicting results regarding the role of GIP as a physiologic enterogastrone because supraphysiologic doses are required for this effect in humans. An important action of GIP is its role as a glucoincretin (see Fig. 193-5). GIP receptor gene knockout mice (GIPR[-/-]) are glucose intolerant.[22] It is likely that GIP acts in concert with GLP-1, and perhaps other peptides, to stimulate insulin secretion. GIPR[-/-] and GLP-1 double incretin receptor knockout mice have increased glucose intolerance and reduced insulin responses to oral (but not intraperitoneal) glucose than either knockout alone.[23] Administration of a GIP receptor antagonist has been shown to reduce postprandial insulin release in conscious rats.

The GIP response is absent, and the insulin response is blunted in patients with jejunoileal bypass for morbid obesity. GIP has been implicated in the disordered insulin secretion of several diseases, including chronic pancreatitis, cirrhosis, and Turner's syndrome. Secretion of GIP is enhanced in type 2 diabetes mellitus, but, unlike GLP-1, there is little response to exogenous GIP. Loss of GIP sensitivity may be a genetic predisposing factor for diabetes mellitus. The role of DP IV–resistant GIP and GIP receptor manipulation in the treatment of diabetes remains to be determined.

GIP has been reported to act on adipose tissue and may have an important role in lipid metabolism. It enhances fatty acid synthesis, lipoprotein lipase activity, and incorporation of free fatty acids into triglycerides. Several case reports of adrenocorticotropic hormone–independent, but food-dependent Cushing's syndrome have suggested that GIP may stimulate adrenal corticosteroid secretion through GIP receptors.[24] GIP may also have a role in body weight regulation since GIP receptor knockout mice (GIPR[-/-]) are resistant to diet-induced obesity. These mice appear to preferentially oxidize triglycerides. When leptin-deficient ob/ob mice were crossed with GIPR[-/-], the severity of obesity was reduced.[25]

## Peptide Products of Glucagon Gene

Glucagon is a 29-amino acid residue peptide secreted by α cells of pancreatic islets. It is a major hormone involved in glucose homeostasis. The mRNA of the glucagon precursor preproglucagon is expressed in the pancreas, intestine, and brain and gives rise to proglucagon, a 160-amino acid residue peptide. Proglucagon is differentially processed in tissues[26] (Fig. 193-6) such that it gives rise to glucagon, glicentin-related pancreatic peptide, and a large major fragment in the pancreas, whereas in intestinal L cells, it gives rise to GLP-1, GLP-2, and glicentin-enteroglucagon. Glicentin-enteroglucagon, in turn, gives rise to glicentin-related pancreatic peptide and oxyntomodulin, whereas GLP-1 is further processed to GLP-1 (7-36) amide, GLP-1 (9-36) amide (a GLP-1 antagonist), and GLP-1 (7-37). Proglucagon in the hypothalamus is processed in a similar fashion to intestinal L cells.

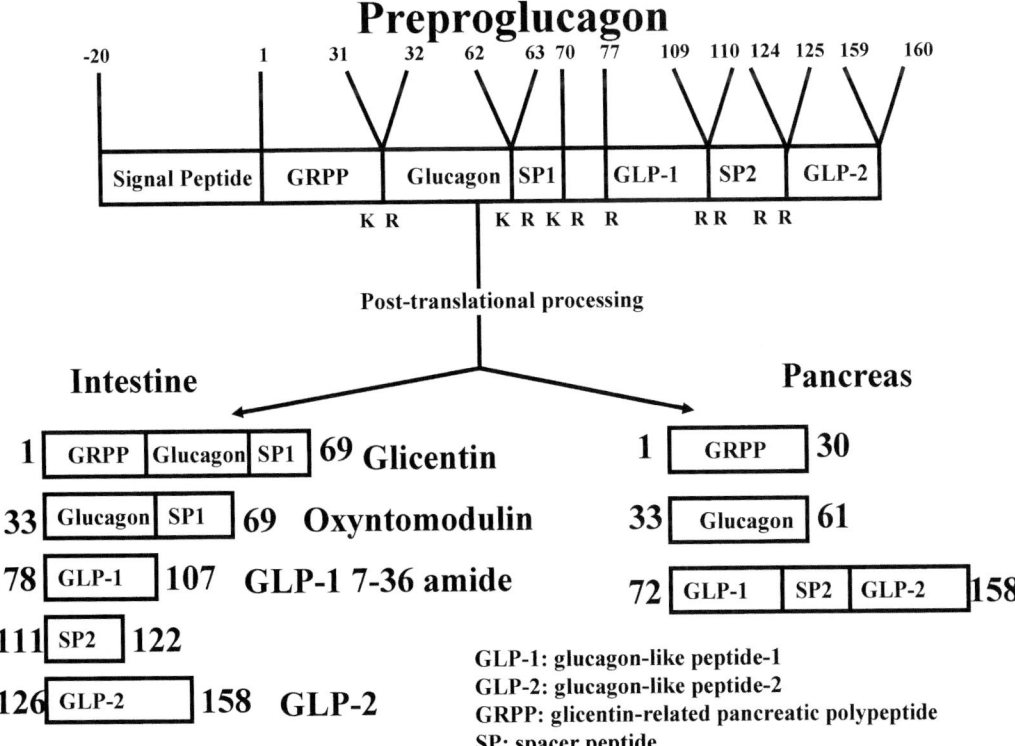

Figure 193-6  Posttranslational processing of proglucagon in the mammalian pancreatic α cell and small intestinal L cell. In the pancreas, the major products are glicentin-related pancreatic peptide, glucagon, and a C-terminal fragment containing the sequence of GLP-1 and GLP-2. In the L cell, the main products are glicentin (or enteroglucagon), oxyntomodulin, GLP-1 (7-36) amide, and GLP-2.

GLP-1: glucagon-like peptide-1
GLP-2: glucagon-like peptide-2
GRPP: glicentin-related pancreatic polypeptide
SP: spacer peptide

Proglucagon-derived gut peptides are secreted by open-type L cells in the mucosa of the ileum and colon. A subpopulation of these cells also synthesize and secrete PYY. Proglucagon-derived gut peptides are secreted rapidly in response to mixed meals containing lipids and carbohydrates. Nonabsorbable sugars do not stimulate release of proglucagon-derived gut peptides. It is as yet unclear whether L cells are capable of sugar absorption and can couple absorption and secretion or receive signals from neighboring enterocytes. Several hormones and neurotransmitters, such as GIP, GRP, substance P, leptin, and neurokinin A (NKA), have been implicated in the regulation of proglucagon-derived gut peptide release.

GLP-1 is a C-terminal amidated 30-amino acid peptide and is the major hormone responsible for the incretin effect. Both in vitro and in vivo studies have shown that GLP-1 is the most potent insulinotropic hormone known and that it greatly potentiates glucose-induced insulin secretion. The GLP-1 receptor antagonist exendin (9-39) (derived from the venom of the Gila monster, *Heloderma suspectum*) has been shown to reduce the insulin response to intestinal glucose in rats and humans. Targeted disruption of the GLP-1 receptor gene in mice results in glucose intolerance and basal hyperglycemia.[27] GLP-1 inhibits glucagon secretion indirectly through stimulation of somatostatin release. The effects of GLP-1 on glucagon and insulin secretion are glucose dependent with little effect observed at glucose levels of approximately less than 3 mmol/L.[28] Exogenous GLP-1 can normalize blood glucose levels in type 2 diabetes mellitus. Some patients, however, have an impaired response to GLP-1. This, in combination with increased activity of the GLP-1-degrading enzyme DP IV, may contribute to the impaired incretin response in type 2 diabetes. GLP-1 has a half-life of only 4 minutes when administered intravenously and 30 to 60 minutes when administered subcutaneously. The study of the actions of GLP-1 on glucose metabolism is a promising area for the discovery of new treatment options for diabetes mellitus. Currently developed drugs include stable GLP-1 receptor agonists (exendin-4 [Exenatide]) and DP IV inhibitors (LAF237).[29]

It is perhaps surprising that the GLP-1 response to nutrient intake is much faster than expected because L cells are most dense in the ileum and are not immediately exposed to nutrients. Although there are fewer L cells in the duodenum, these cells may be responsible for the rapid GLP-1 response to nutrients. The early L-cell response in the rat appears to be mediated by GIP, but in humans, infusion of GIP does not stimulate GLP-1 release, suggesting the existence of other factors (e.g., GRP).

GLP-1 is an enterogastrone (see earlier). It also inhibits pancreatic exocrine secretion, which may be secondary to its effect on gastric emptying. Gastric emptying is more rapid in obese patients who have reduced levels of postprandial GLP-1.[30] GLP-1 almost completely inhibits vagally mediated (sham feeding–induced) gastric acid secretion, an effect that is completely lost after vagotomy. GLP-1 receptors in the circumventricular region of the brain may be responsible for this effect through central interaction with the autonomic nervous system. GLP-1 levels increase markedly in response to ileal infusion of nutrients, suggesting that GLP-1 may contribute to the ileal brake effect (i.e., endocrine inhibition of upper gastrointestinal motility and secretion elicited by the presence of nutrients in the distal small intestine[31]). This may occur in combination with PYY, which is costored with GLP-1 in some intestinal L cells. Centrally, GLP-1 is a potent satiety factor.[32] Administration of GLP-1 into the third ventricle in rats reduces food intake. This effect is inhibited by the GLP-1 antagonist exendin (9-39).

No physiologic actions of enteroglucagon or glicentin have been demonstrated in humans, although initially a trophic action was postulated. GLP-2, usually released in response to nutrients, however, is likely to be an important growth factor in the intestine.[33,34] Circulating GLP-2 levels are elevated in response to gut injury. This hormone may therefore prove to be important in the treatment of intestinal injury. Oxyntomodulin consists of the whole glucagon sequence extended at its C terminus by a basic octapeptide. It inhibits gastric acid secretion and motility and has been shown to promote glucose production from hepatocytes. These effects occur at pharmacologic doses, suggesting that oxyntomodulin may act via receptors for GLP-1 and glucagon at which it has weak agonist activity. Rodent and human studies suggest that oxyntomodulin may have a role in satiety.[35]

### Motilin

Motilin is a 22-amino acid peptide that is found in open-type M cells, which are present in the epithelium throughout the small intestine but are most dense in the duodenum and proximal jejunum.[36,37] Motilin immunoreactivity is also found in the muscle layers of the intestine and has been detected in the large intestine, with the exception of the cecum, and in the gallbladder and biliary tract.

Although other gut hormones are released in response to the presence of nutrients in the gut, motilin release in humans is not only influenced by ingestion of a meal (stimulated potently by fat intake but inhibited by carbohydrate) but also occurs, in a cyclic manner, during the interdigestive state. The cyclic release of motilin is associated with phase III of the migrating motor complex. In fact, motilin induces phase III contractions in the stomach and associated phenomena such as contraction of the lower esophageal sphincter, sphincter of Oddi, and gallbladder, and inhibition of gastric and pancreatic enzyme secretion. Atropine abolishes the cyclic release of motilin, suggesting a cholinergic regulatory mechanism, which, in dogs, appears to be through local nonvagal neurons. In dogs, plasma motilin levels are increased by bombesin, decreased by somatostatin (and perhaps pancreatic polypeptide), and abolished by food ingestion and insulin. Motilin appears to stimulate M cells, resulting in a positive feedback loop. The motor effect of motilin on interdigestive motility is suppressed by a meal, duodenal acidification, somatostatin, pentagastrin, and CCK. The abolition of phase III contractions by atropine and 5-hydroxytryptamine antagonists suggests that cholinergic and serotoninergic mechanisms are substrates for motilin action. Other reported actions for motilin vary among species and include effects on small intestinal water and salt absorption, colonic motility, gastric emptying, and pancreatic endocrine secretion. Although the physiologic role of phase III contractions appears to be the prevention of the buildup of gut secretions ("housekeeping" role) and keeping the gut "warmed up" for the next meal, the physiologic role of motilin released in response to a meal, as seen in humans, has not yet been determined. The prokinetic effect of macrolide antibiotics such as erythromycin is mediated via the motilin receptor. Exploration of these drugs and their analogues for use in conditions such as diabetic gastroparesis is promising.

### Ghrelin

Until the discovery of ghrelin in 1999[8] as the endogenous ligand for the growth hormone (GH) secretagogue receptor, no motilin-like peptides had been described. Although motilin and ghrelin have only 36% homology, prepromotilin and preproghrelin are almost identical. In addition, the motilin receptor belongs to GH secretagogue receptor family. Ghrelin is a 28-amino acid peptide synthesized predominantly in X/A-like cells in the oxyntic mucosa of the stomach.[38] It is also found in smaller quantities in the intestine, pancreas, kidney, testis, pituitary, lung, hypothalamus, lymphocytes, and placenta.[39] Ghrelin has also been detected in several neoplastic tissues including intestinal carcinoid tumors.

The existence of an endogenous GH secretagogue, other than GH-releasing hormone, has long been suspected, based

## Acylated Human Ghrelin

*Figure 193-7* The structure of acylated human ghrelin. Ghrelin is the first hormone to be shown to have an acyl group that is essential for its biologic activity.

on the ability of small synthetic peptide and nonpeptide molecules, called GH secretagogues, to stimulate GH secretion via a receptor other than the GH-releasing hormone receptor. This receptor, GH secretagogue receptor-1a,[40] is found in the pituitary and several brain regions including the hypothalamus, and was an "orphan" until the discovery of ghrelin. There are two prominent ghrelin ligands for the GH secretagogue R-1a: the 28-amino acid acylated ghrelin and acylated Des-Gln14-ghrelin. Acylation is essential for biologic activity (Fig. 193-7). Circulating ghrelin is predominantly nonacylated (i.e., not active at the receptor). The currently available radioimmunoassays measure total (active + inactive) ghrelin; therefore, complete interpretation of the biologic role of measured ghrelin is at present difficult. Ghrelin appears to bind to high-density lipoprotein in the circulation.[41]

Circulating ghrelin levels are sexually dimorphic. Ghrelin secretion appears to occur in response to nutrients in the stomach rather than stretch. High levels of circulating ghrelin in fasting rats rapidly returned to baseline by filling the stomach with 50% glucose, but stomach distension with an equal volume of water had no effect on plasma ghrelin.[42]

Ghrelin has multiple functions (Fig. 193-8). An important role is in the regulation of appetite with its primary action being through the hypothalamus. GH secretagogues have been shown to stimulate food intake. Acute administration of small doses of ghrelin, either systemically or directly into the brain, dramatically increase food intake in rats.[43] Long-term systemic administration of ghrelin to rodents results in weight gain and increased fat mass.[42] Ghrelin causes similar weight gain in GH-deficient dwarf rats, suggesting an action

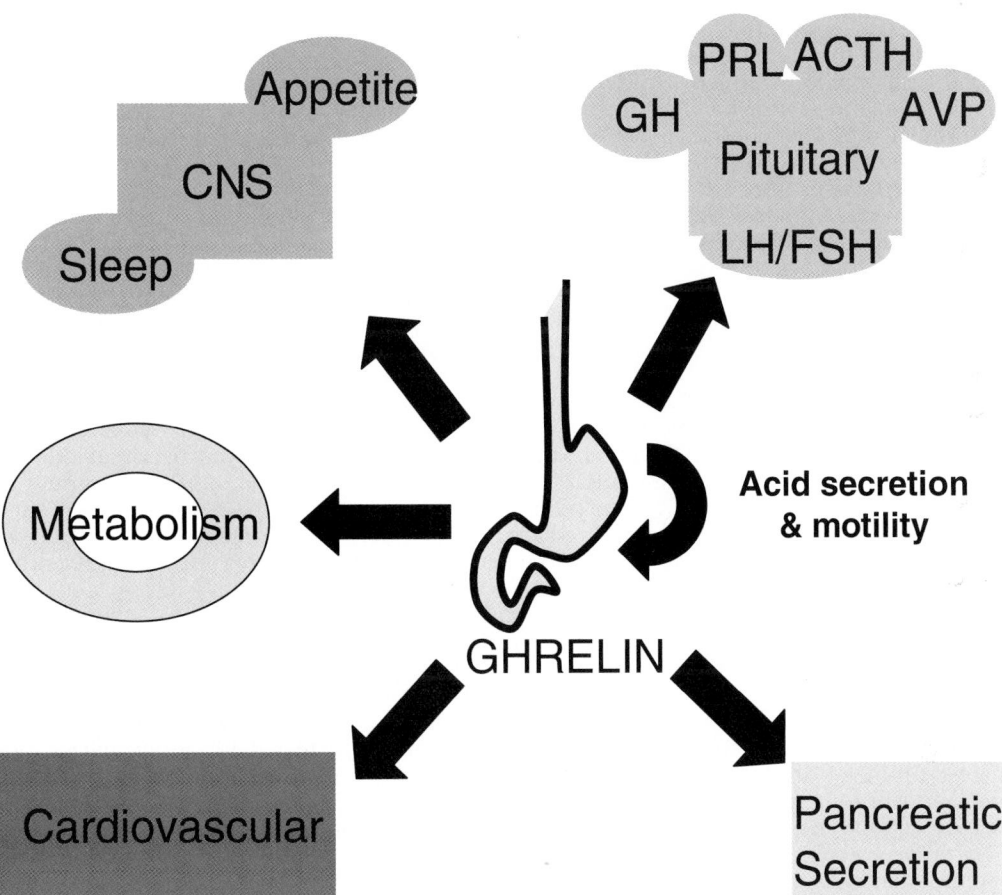

*Figure 193-8* The multiple functions of ghrelin. ACTH, adrenocorticotropic hormone; AVP, arginine vasopressin; CNS, central nervous system; FSH, follicle-stimulating hormone; GH, growth hormone; PRL, prolactin.

independent of GH stimulation. Ghrelin also appears to have effects on energy expenditure. Calorimetry suggests that administration of ghrelin causes an increase in the respiratory quotient.[42]

Plasma ghrelin levels increase before meals, whereas systemic ghrelin infusion results in hunger.[44] High levels of ghrelin are observed in Prader-Willi syndrome, which is associated with voracious appetite.[45] Gastric bypass surgery for treatment of obesity results in almost undetectable ghrelin levels.[46] Interestingly, ghrelin levels are higher with short sleep duration independent of sex, age, and body mass index, suggesting that high ghrelin levels resulting in hunger may be responsible for the observed association between short sleep duration and obesity.[47] Ghrelin knockout mice do not have a phenotype supporting its role in appetite regulation; this may be due to compensatory changes and the existence of redundant feeding circuits. Although the role of ghrelin in appetite regulation has been much studied, its role in other physiologic mechanisms (see Fig. 193-8) are likely to provide novel understanding of several important biologic processes and pathophysiologic responses.

## Somatostatin

Somatostatin was first isolated from the ovine hypothalamus and exists as somatostatin-14 (14 amino acids) and somatostatin-28 (28 amino acids), which are the cleavage products of the same precursor peptide. It is found in a variety of tissues. In the gut, somatostatin is found in endocrine D cells of gastric and duodenal epithelia and extrinsic and intrinsic neurons of the intestinal myenteric and submucosal plexuses. Somatostatin-14 predominates in gastric and pancreatic D cells, whereas the N-terminal extended somatostatin-28 predominates in intestinal mucosal cells. Somatostatin, which has a short half-life in the circulation, appears to function as a hormone and paracrine agent and as a neurotransmitter. It is released in response to a mixed meal. The mechanisms by which luminal stimuli result in somatostatin secretion are not fully understood but may involve CGRP from afferent neurons in the stomach. Other peptides that influence somatostatin release are gastrin, CCK, and bombesin, which are stimulatory, and the secretin family of peptides, which are inhibitory. Somatostatin release is stimulated by β-adrenergic agonists but is inhibited by cholinergic agents.

Somatostatin is a universal inhibitor. Perhaps the best described paracrine action of somatostatin is its inhibition of gastric acid secretion through its action on G cells, ECL cells, and parietal cells. Somatostatin also mediates the action of other enterogastrones on gastric function. Other inhibitory actions include effects on motility, intestinal and pancreatic secretion, release of gut peptides (including itself [autocrine]), intestinal nutrient and electrolyte transport, growth and proliferation, and splanchnic blood flow. Somatostatin may also modify food intake. Five somatostatin receptor subtypes ($sst_{1-5}$), which are G protein–coupled receptors, have been cloned.[48,49] Multiple somatostatin receptor subtypes may be expressed by the same cell.

Synthetic somatostatin analogues such as octreotide primarily act on $sst_2$ receptors. These have been used successfully in the treatment of several conditions, including neuroendocrine tumors, and acromegaly.[50,51] Longer-acting analogues and preparations are likely to replace octreotide, which has a short half-life requiring multiple daily subcutaneous injections[52] (Fig. 193-9). With longer-acting somatostatin analogues and preparations, however, breakthrough of symptoms may occur that can be treated with the shorter-acting octreotide. Side effects of somatostatin-based treatments include malabsorption, steatorrhea, and gallstone formation (usually asymptomatic). Radiolabeled octreotide scanning is routinely used for the localization of neuroendocrine and other tumors. Novel radiolabeled somatostatin analogues that bind a greater number of receptor subtypes than octreotide

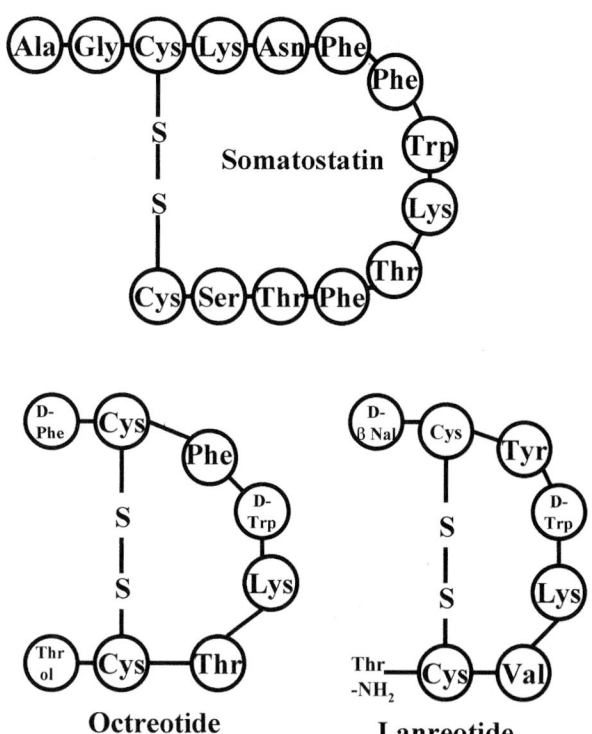

**Figure 193-9**  Amino acid sequences and structures of somatostatin-14 and the synthetic octapeptide somatostatin analogues octreotide and lanreotide. The synthetic analogues preferentially bind somatostatin receptor subtypes $sst_2$ and $sst_5$. In neuroendocrine tumors, octreotide is usually given subcutaneously two or three times daily. Depot forms of octreotide (Sandostatin LAR), administered every 4 weeks, and lanreotide (Somatvline LA), administered every 2 weeks, have recently become available for clinical use.

are currently being evaluated for the treatment of neuroendocrine and other tumors.[53,54] The study of antineoplastic actions of somatostatin may prove useful in the treatment of a number of tumors.

## Neurotensin

Neurotensin (NT) is a tridecapeptide isolated from the bovine hypothalamus. A number of NT-related peptides have been discovered and include neuromedin N, xenopsin, and xenin. The highest concentrations of NT, released from N cells, have been observed in the ileal mucosa, with smaller amounts detected in the jejunum and duodenum. NT immunoreactivity has also been detected in enteric neurons. The gut contains most of the NT in the body, with the remainder being mainly in the brain, particularly in the hypothalamus and pituitary. The most potent stimulator of NT is fat, and it has been proposed that NT mediates the gastrointestinal effects observed after fat ingestion, such as reduction in gastric emptying. Vagal and nonvagal mechanisms (e.g., neurally released bombesin) are involved in NT release. NT release is inhibited by somatostatin. Enhanced NT release is seen in patients with dumping syndrome and after jejunoileal bypass. Elevated concentrations of NT have been detected in the plasma of patients with VIPomas.

A number of biologic actions have been attributed to NT and include vasodilation, increased histamine release from mast cells, inhibitory effects on gastric motility and gastric acid secretion, stimulation of the exocrine and endocrine pancreas, effects on intestinal motility and secretion, and inhibition of blood flow to adipose tissue. PP release invariably follows NT infusion; therefore, NT may play a role in the enteropancreatic polypeptide axis. NT infusion stimulates glucagon, but inhibits insulin release. Intracerebroventricular (ICV) injection of NT has been shown to have several effects, including the inhibition of food intake, but the physiologic relevance of these central effects is unclear. NT may have growth-regulatory functions in the pancreas and colon, with neurotensin receptors detected in several cancer tissues.[55]

## Peptide YY

Peptide tyrosine tyrosine (PYY), a 36-amino acid peptide, is a member of the pancreatic polypeptide family of peptides, including PP and NPY (all named because of the presence of a C-terminal tyrosine). All three peptides have a C-terminal amide (essential to biologic activity) and a hairpin-like structure. The PYY gene is very close to the PP gene on chromosome 17q21.1. PYY immunoreactive cells are found throughout the mucosa of the terminal ileum, colon, and rectum. Partial colocalization of PYY with GLP-1 in L cells has been observed. Small amounts of PYY have been detected in the pancreas where it is colocalized with glucagon. The main physiologic stimulus to PYY release is ingestion of a meal, particularly fat. PYY levels increase at least 50-fold after consumption of a meal and remain elevated for several hours thereafter. The level of PYY achieved is proportional to meal size. Vagal activity contributes little to PYY secretion. PYY receptors are coupled to adenylate cyclase in an inhibitory manner.

PYY is an enterogastrone; this action may be mediated through the inhibition of gastric vagal innervation. PYY reduces intestinal motility, gallbladder contraction, and pancreatic exocrine secretion (a pancreatone). PYY is a potent inhibitor of intestinal fluid and electrolyte secretion.[56] Intravenous infusion of PYY in humans causes a long-lasting reduction in intestinal secretion induced by VIP. PYY is a mediator of the ileal brake. Patients with intestinal resection but without colonic continuity (i.e., with jejunostomy) have a low fasting and a reduced postprandial PYY response, whereas patients with colonic continuity (no jejunostomy) have high fasting PYY values with a normal postprandial increase.[57] This suggests that PYY may act as a "colonic brake," slowing the transit of food in patients with colonic continuity. High plasma PYY levels have been reported in tropical sprue, chronic pancreatitis, and dumping syndrome, with low values detected in patients who have had a colectomy. PYY may have a role in the regulation of cell growth in the intestinal epithelium.

Peptide YY may have a role in induction of satiety. Administration of PYY to both rodents and humans reduces food intake.[58,59] The satiety effects of PYY may be mediated through the inhibitory presynaptic Y2 receptor in the hypothalamus. Obese subjects have lower circulating PYY levels, but remain responsive to its satiety effects.

## Pancreatic Polypeptide

PP is a 36-amino acid peptide closely related to PYY and NPY. The receptors for this family of peptides are G protein–coupled receptors.[60] The Y4 receptor is the endogenous PP receptor. In humans, high levels of Y4 receptor mRNA have been detected in the colon, small intestine, and pancreas, whereas in rats, high levels are found in the testis and lung. Pancreatic F cells, found at the periphery of islets, are the primary source of PP. PP has also been isolated from the antrum and upper duodenum of dogs. In plasma, PP is found as a dimer with a half-life of 6 to 7 minutes. PP is released in a biphasic manner. The first phase is mainly under vagal control with plasma levels rising rapidly after ingestion of a meal. This phase is abolished in diabetic autonomic neuropathy. The second phase, which is longer lasting, is due to stimulation by ingested nutrients, particularly amino acids. This phase is mediated by cholinergic and adrenergic pathways that form the enteropancreatic reflex. Gut distension, CCK, bombesin, gastrin, GRP, neuromedin B and C, and motilin stimulate PP secretion, whereas somatostatin is an inhibitor. PP is also released in response to insulin-induced hypoglycemia. Several neuroendocrine tumors, including gastrinomas, glucagonomas, and insulinomas, secrete PP, in addition to the peptides with which they are associated. Elevated plasma PP is therefore a nonspecific tumor marker in these conditions.

Exogenous PP increases gastric acid secretion, but at high doses, it can inhibit CCK-induced acid secretion. PP, PYY, and NPY have similar potencies in inhibiting pancreatic and biliary secretion. The action of PP on pancreatic secretion is indirect and appears to be its most physiologic effect. PP slows gastric and upper intestinal motility and decreases gallbladder activity. It stimulates glycogenolysis and reduces lipolysis in adipocytes. PP has been implicated in hyperglycerolemia, hypercholesterolemia, and reduction in free fatty acid levels. Centrally, PP is not as widely distributed as NPY and, unlike NPY, produces only a modest increase in food intake (see below). Peripheral PP may regulate vagal activity by acting on the brain stem.

## Chromogranins and Secretogranins

The chromogranins and secretogranins are a family of acidic secretory proteins found in the large "dense-cored" vesicles of secretory granules of endocrine cells and neurons, being stored together with many different peptide hormones and neuropeptides.[61] They are often used as markers for secretory granules of endocrine and neuronal cells.[62] The major proteins belonging to this family are chromogranin A (CgA), chromogranin B, and secretogranin II (chromogranin C).

All members of the chromogranin family have dibasic residues and calcium binding sites. CgA and chromogranin B contain a disulfide-bonded loop structure near their N termini, a structure that is absent in secretogranin II. CgA is very hydrophilic and has abundant charged, mostly acidic, amino acids that act as multiple proteolytic processing sites. CgA binds calcium with moderate affinity at multiple sites and aggregates in the presence of the cation.

Several functions have been proposed for CgA. Within the cell, it may participate in the modulation of proteolytic processing of peptides and as a nucleus for the aggregation of peptides to form dense core vesicles. Extracellularly, CgA is a precursor of biologically active peptides such as pancreastatin, chromostatin, vasostatin, and parastatin. Pancreastatin inhibits pancreatic insulin and glucagon secretion. It also suppresses gastrin secretion and parathyroid hormone secretion from parathyroid cells. Chromostatin inhibits the release of catecholamines from adrenal medulla cells. A peptide, which may be derived from CgA, has been described with sequence homology to N-terminal residues 1-40 of human CgA.[63] This peptide inhibits secretion of parathyroid hormone–related protein, calcitonin, and stimulated CGRP. Peptide derivatives of secretogranin, such as secretoneurin, have also been described.

Circulating CgA is highly stable, and several radioimmunoassay are available for its measurement.[64] In neuroendocrine (particularly carcinoid) tumors, there is a clear correlation between circulating CgA levels and tumor burden, with the highest levels seen in metastatic disease. Serum CgA is usually elevated with glucagonomas, somatostatinomas, and VIPomas. Interestingly, elevated CgA levels can occur with only small gastrinomas and may be derived from hyperplastic ECL cells; therefore, its role as a marker in gastrinoma is less clear. CgA is most useful as a marker in nonfunctioning neuroendocrine tumors and may be a useful marker for pheochromocytomas.[65] CgA levels decline with somatostatin treatment of neuroendocrine tumors. Severe renal failure can result in high CgA levels comparable with levels detected with neuroendocrine tumors. The peptide GAWK (chromogranin B 420-493) is also a useful marker for neuroendocrine tumors.[66]

## NEUROTRANSMITTERS

### Vasoactive Intestinal Polypeptide and Related Peptides

VIP is a 28-amino acid peptide isolated from the porcine intestine and shown to induce systemic vasodilation. It belongs to a group of peptides that include peptide histidine isoleucine, peptide histidine methionine, and pituitary adenylate cyclase–activating peptide (PACAP). Peptide histidine methionine, the human form of peptide histidine isoleucine, and its C-terminal extended version, peptide histidine valine, are derived from the same precursor as VIP (preproVIP). VIP is a neurotransmitter found in intrinsic neural elements throughout the alimentary tract from the esophagus to the rectum and in salivary glands and the pancreas. VIP is also found throughout the CNS, in the lung, and in the urogenital tract. PACAP exists as a 38-amino acid (PACAP-38) and a 27-amino acid (PACAP-27) peptide. It is most abundant in the hypothalamus and has also been detected in the adrenal gland and the testis. PACAP, peptide histidine methionine, and peptide histidine isoleucine are also neurotransmitters and neuromodulators in the enteric nervous system. VIP and PACAP are localized in the same neurons in humans and dogs but occur in distinct neurons in other species. VIP and PACAP share two common G protein–coupled receptors, VPAC1 and VPAC2, whereas PACAP has an additional specific receptor, PAC1. VIP receptors have been detected in the intestinal mucosa, muscularis mucosae, smooth muscle of submucosal arterioles, circular and longitudinal muscles of the muscularis externa, the myenteric plexus, and abdominal lymph nodes. They have also been detected in rat and human brain-derived cells, the lung of many species including humans, the rat pancreas, and several tumors. Iodine 123-VIP receptor scanning has been used clinically for localization of small adenocarcinomas and several gut neuroendocrine tumors.

VIP in the plasma is likely to represent spillover of VIP from local nerve terminals in the gut (see Fig. 193-1) and has a half-life of less than a minute because the liver rapidly degrades it. VIP levels are usually undetectable in plasma with any significantly increased levels, suggesting the existence of a VIP-secreting tumor. Tissue concentrations of VIP are low in conditions in which there is denervation, such as Hirschsprung's disease and Chagas' disease.

VIP is a major inhibitory neurotransmitter in the gut: It induces relaxation of the lower esophageal sphincter, the sphincter of Oddi, and the anal sphincter. It mediates the descending relaxation of the peristaltic reflex and may be involved in reflex vasodilation in the small intestine. Coreleased VIP and PACAP appear to act on neurons and muscle cells to regenerate nitric oxide. Nitric oxide may itself be coreleased from these neurons. VIP is a potent stimulus to intestinal secretion by inhibiting sodium reabsorption and stimulating chloride secretion. In the pancreas and liver, VIP promotes secretion of bicarbonate. The inhibitory action of VIP on gastric acid secretion is mediated via somatostatin. VIP and PHI have been shown to stimulate insulin and glucagon release. VIP released from glial cells may be a neurotrophic factor. VIP stimulates the growth of several tumor cells such as non–small cell lung cancer cells while inhibiting others, such as colonic adenocarcinoma cells. It inhibits mitogen-activated proliferation of T cells by inhibiting interleukin-2 production, suggesting a role in immune function. In the pituitary and adrenal, VIP stimulates the secretion of prolactin and catecholamines, respectively. VIP and PACAP also have roles in several hypothalamic-pituitary-adrenal axes.[67]

PACAP appears to have similar actions to those of VIP in the gut.[68] It stimulates pancreatic secretion of fluid, bicarbonate, and protein in rats; this effect may be mediated by release of both CCK and secretin.[69] PACAP also stimulates catecholamine secretion from the adrenal and may be a regulator of pancreatic insulin secretion. In the CNS, it has been suggested that PACAP released from retinal afferents may be a daytime regulator of the biologic clock.[70]

### Bombesin and Related Peptides

Bombesin is a C-terminal amidated tetradecapeptide originally isolated from skin extracts of the European frog *Bombina bombina*. Bombesin-related peptides include GRP, neuromedin B, and neuromedin C. GRP is a 27-amino acid peptide and has an identical C-terminal α-amidated heptapeptide to bombesin. Neuromedin B and neuromedin C are both decapeptides. Neuromedin C is identical to the C-terminal decapeptide of GRP (GRP 18-27). GRP has been detected in the fundus, antrum, jejunum, terminal ileum, colon, pancreas, lung, and CNS and peripheral nervous system of most mammalian species. GRP and neuromedin C are widely distributed in the brain, spinal cord, and enteric nervous system.

In the gut, GRP, acting mainly as a neurotransmitter, is a potent stimulator of several other gut peptides such as gastrin, CCK, PP, PYY, enteroglucagon, motilin, somatostatin, insulin, and glucagon. GRP, released from postganglionic vagal fibers, stimulates gastrin and somatostatin release. It may also stimulate gastric acid secretion independently of gastrin, but this effect is limited by its stimulation of somatostatin release (see Fig. 193-4). Intravenous GRP stimulates CCK in humans and increases pancreatic enzyme release. This effect is augmented by the direct action of GRP on the pancreas through intrapancreatic nerves. Intravenous GRP stimulates gallbladder contraction, probably through CCK release.

Bombesin and GRP may be important in normal and neoplastic growth of tissues. GRP is synthesized by a large number of neuroendocrine tumors of the lung (small cell carcinoma and carcinoids) and thyroid and by other neuroendocrine cells. High-affinity bombesin and GRP-binding sites have been detected in gastric and colon cancers. GRP receptors in colonic carcinoma may be aberrantly expressed because they are not found in normal colonic tissue. Several GRP analogues are being evaluated for tumor imaging,[71] and targeted cytotoxicity and immunotherapy based on GRP are under investigation.[72,73]

Bombesin and GRP stimulate smooth muscle contraction in most peripheral tissue preparations studied. GRP has been implicated in gastric, intestinal, and gallbladder muscle contraction. Receptors with affinity for either GRP or neuromedin B, or both, have been detected on gastrointestinal smooth muscle cells and on cholinergic and noncholinergic neurons of the myenteric plexus. GRP may therefore either directly stimulate smooth muscle contraction in the gut or act indirectly through neurons in the myenteric plexus.

Peripherally injected bombesin or GRP may extend the postprandial meal interval, the time between the end of one meal to the beginning of the next meal.[74] The delay in gastric emptying and gastric secretion induced by bombesin or GRP may contribute to this effect. Intracerebroventricular injection of bombesin also induces satiety in rats. Central administration of bombesin or GRP inhibits gastric acid secretion independently of the vagus nerve, but its effects on slowing gastric emptying and intestinal and colonic transit may be vagally mediated.

### Calcitonin Gene-Related Peptides

CGRP is a 37-amino acid neuropeptide.[75] It belongs to a group of peptides that also includes calcitonin, adrenomedullin, and amylin. These peptides have a 6-amino acid ring structure (seven for calcitonin) formed by an intramolecular disulfide bond close to the N terminus. They are also C-terminally amidated. CGRP is the product of tissue-specific differential splicing of the calcitonin or CGRP mRNA. Two calcitonin genes have been isolated that encode two different forms of CGRP: CGRP-α and CGRP-β. Human CGRP-β is encoded by its own unique gene and differs from CGRP-α by three amino acids. CGRP, a potent vasodilator, has been detected in many tissues and body fluids. It acts as a neurotransmitter in the enteric nervous system, where CGRP-β is the only form.[76] CGRP-α acts as a neurotransmitter in extrinsic afferent neurons of the gut.

CGRP has effects on gut motility, blood flow, and secretion. The prominent motor action of CGRP is muscle relaxation through a direct effect on smooth muscle cells. CGRP is a potent inhibitor of gastric acid secretion through gastric somatostatin release. Somatostatin also mediates the inhibitory effect of CGRP on pancreatic exocrine secretion. The effects of CGRP on pancreatic endocrine secretion and intestinal ion and fluid transport vary among species. CGRP, acting as a nonadrenergic, noncholinergic transmitter, causes mesenteric arterial dilation. Ablation of primary afferent neurons containing CGRP aggravates experimental mucosal injury, whereas intragastric capsaicin, which stimulates afferent fibers, is protective.[77] Furthermore, close arterial injection of CGRP is also protective. CGRP may therefore have an important function in the response to injurious stimuli.[78]

Amylin (previously islet amyloid polypeptide) is composed of 37 amino acids. It is predominantly synthesized in pancreatic β cells (where it is cosecreted with insulin) but is also expressed in the stomach, intestine, hypothalamus, lung, and several neuroendocrine tumors. Its name derives from its original isolation from pancreatic amyloid deposits. Circulating amylin levels increase in response to meal (carbohydrate and protein) ingestion. In the gut, amylin acts as a paracrine enterogastrone, dose-dependently delaying gastric emptying and reducing gastric acid secretion. Amylin protects gastric mucosa from ulceration.[79] Peripherally, it also increases insulin sensitivity of skeletal muscle. The amylin analogue pramlintide is currently being explored as an adjunct in the treatment of diabetes mellitus. Pramlintide slows gastric emptying and suppresses glucagon secretion to delay and reduce the entry of glucose into the circulation. Peripheral or central administration of amylin reduces food intake. Peripherally, amylin appears to augment the anorectic effects of other peptides such as CCK.[80] Thus, an additional potential benefit of amylin and its analogue is weight loss.[81,82]

The study of the cloned receptor for CGRP (calcitonin-like receptor, previously calcitonin receptor-like receptor) has revolutionized our understanding of G protein–coupled receptors. Unlike classic G protein–coupled receptors (e.g., adrenoceptors), the ligand specificity of calcitonin-like receptor is dependent on the expression of different receptor activity–modifying proteins (RAMPs).[83,84] Expression of calcitonin-like receptor with RAMP-1 results in ligand specificity for CGRP, whereas expression with RAMP-2 or -3 results in specificity for adrenomedullin.[79] One of the functions of RAMPs is to transport receptors to the cell surface. Another protein that may be involved in optimal receptor function is receptor component protein.[84] The calcitonin receptor is not dependent on RAMPs to bind calcitonin, but its association with RAMPs results in receptors with high affinity for amylin and variable affinity for CGRP. The various combinations of receptors with modifying proteins allow coexpression of receptors with affinity for different peptides from the calcitonin group.

## Tachykinins

The tachykinins (the largest known peptide family) include the undecapeptide substance P, and the decapeptides NKA and neurokinin B.[85,86] These peptides share the C-terminal pentapeptide sequence-Phe-X-Gly-Leu-Met-$NH_2$, where -X- is an aromatic or hydrophobic residue. Substance P and NKA are the major tachykinins in the gut. They are derived from larger precursor peptides, the preprotachykinins (PPTs), which are encoded by two different genes. The *TAC1* (PPT-A) gene encodes both substance P and NKA, whereas the *TAC2* (PPT-B) gene encodes only neurokinin B. The primary RNA transcript of TAC1 (PPT-A) is alternatively spliced to four different mRNAs: α-PPT, β-PPT, γ-PPT, and δ-PPT. All PPT mRNAs can be translated into substance P, whereas sequences coding for NKA are only found in β-PPT and γ-PPT mRNA. A novel PPT gene has recently been identified (TAC4, PPT-C) that encodes

a new tachykinin called hemokinin 1.[87–89] Tachykinins are found throughout the peripheral nervous system and CNS, including the sensory organs, respiratory tract, skin, and urogenital tract. In the gut, they are primarily expressed in intrinsic enteric neurons and extrinsic primary afferent nerve fibers. In the guinea pig, tachykinins are cotransmitters in cholinergic enteric neurons. Three G protein–coupled receptors for tachykinins have been cloned: $NK_1$, $NK_2$, and $NK_3$ receptors. All three receptors have all three tachykinins as full agonists, but $NK_1$ receptors are substance P preferring, $NK_2$ receptors are NKA preferring, and $NK_3$ receptors are neurokinin B preferring.

Tachykinins are vasoactive peptides that can have both vasodilator and vasoconstrictor activities depending on the species and the vascular bed studied. The activation of all three tachykinin receptors may result in vasoconstriction, whereas vasodilatation appears to be mediated by $NK_1$ receptors. Tachykinins can both stimulate and inhibit motility in the gut depending on the type and site of activated tachykinin receptors. Activated $NK_1$ receptors on interstitial cells of Cajal and $NK_2$ receptors on gut smooth muscle cells result in facilitation of motor activity. $NK_3$ receptors, confined to enteric neurons, predominantly mediate cholinergic contraction of intestinal musculature. However, some activated $NK_1$ and $NK_3$ receptors, present on inhibitory pathways in the enteric nervous system, result in inhibition of motor activity and peristalsis through release of the inhibitory transmitters VIP and nitric oxide. Extrinsic afferent neurons expressing substance P are sensitive to tissue irritation, inflammation, and injury. These neurons may participate in several reflexes involved in the gastrointestinal motor response to injury. The actions of tachykinins on pancreatic function remain to be clarified.

Changes in the expression of tachykinins and their receptors have been described in many pathologic conditions. Several experimental models of gut inflammation have shown increased synthesis and release of tachykinins.[90] Upregulation and ectopic expression of $NK_1$ receptors in blood vessels and lymphoid tissue have been observed in intestinal samples from patients with inflammatory bowel disease.[91] Tachykinins may also participate in secretory reactions of the gut to injury and are closely associated with immune cells in the gut.[92] $NK_2$ receptors may mediate visceral hypersensitivity and pain. Pharmacologic manipulation of tachykinins and their receptors may in the future contribute to the treatment of conditions associated with gut injury and inflammation. Tachykinins are commonly found in gut carcinoids and may contribute to some of the symptoms of carcinoid patients such as flushing.

## Neuropeptide Y

NPY is a 36-amino acid peptide that is widespread in the CNS and peripheral nervous system, where it is often colocalized with norepinephrine. High concentrations of NPY are found in the hypothalamus, caudate nucleus, putamen, amygdala, and cortical areas. In the gut, NPY is a neurotransmitter that is extensively expressed in intrinsic myenteric and submucous neurons throughout the enteric nervous system and in extrinsic sympathetic neurons. In the rat, 98% of the submucous NPY-positive neurons also express VIP along the small intestine, whereas in the descending colon, their number and proportion are variable. VIP and NPY are often copackaged and coreleased, even though their actions are antagonistic. NPY neurons are also found in the pancreas. Any NPY detected in the circulation, as in patients with pheochromocytomas, is likely to involve neuronal spillover.

NPY is a powerful vasoconstrictor acting mainly through the Y1 receptor. It exerts numerous inhibitory effects in the gastrointestinal tract. It attenuates epithelial anion and fluid secretion in the small intestine and descending colon in vitro. Intravenous NPY infusion has been shown to have an antisecretory effect when hypersecretion is prestimulated with prostaglandin $E_2$. PYY and NPY are similarly inhibitory on gut motility. NPY in the CNS has been implicated in a wide range of behaviors and biologic functions, including food intake and energy homeostasis, anxiety, memory, seizures, circadian rhythms, alcohol intake, cardiovascular regulation, and anterior pituitary hormone release.[93–95]

## Galanin

Galanin is a 30-amino acid C-terminal amidated peptide. Galanin-like immunoreactivity and galanin mRNA have been detected in the CNS, the pituitary, and neural structures within the gut, pancreas, adrenal, and thyroid. Galanin acts through three receptors called GALR-1, GALR-2, and GALR-3.[96,97] In the gut, galanin-like immunoreactivity, which often coexists with VIP and other neurotransmitters, has been observed in the mucosa, circular and longitudinal muscle layers, and the myenteric and submucosal plexuses. Galanin-like immunoreactivity has also been detected in the vagal innervation of the gut. Any galanin detected in the circulation, such as galanin after sympathetic activation, is likely to be a spillover of neuronal galanin (see Fig. 193-1).

In the gut and pancreas, galanin has several effects, although there are differences among the various species studied. Endogenous galanin may contribute to the physiologic regulation of gastric acid secretion via its action on gastrin cells, parietal cells, or both. Galanin has inhibitory actions on pancreatic exocrine secretion and ion transport in the intestine. The effects of galanin on motility vary particularly among species, with both inhibitory and stimulatory effects reported. In humans, intravenous administration of galanin delays gastric emptying and increases the cecum-to-colon transit time. These effects appear to be either direct or via a neuromodulatory effect on the release of excitatory neurotransmitters such as acetylcholine and substance P. Galanin reduces the release of many gut peptides, including insulin, gastrin, PYY, PP, NT, somatostatin, and enteroglucagon. In the rat, central injection of galanin into the paraventricular nucleus inhibits insulin release, suggesting the involvement of a central mechanism. Galanin in the pituitary has a role in GH and prolactin secretion. A galanin-like peptide has been discovered recently that may have a role in coupling reproductive function to energy balance.[98]

## OTHER GUT PEPTIDES

Opioid peptides are involved in gut motility, have antisecretory actions, and may contribute to gastric acid secretion.[99] The vasoconstrictor endothelin-1[100] has been implicated in the pathophysiology of gut ischemia in endotoxic shock.[101] Loss-of-function mutations of the gene encoding the endothelin-B receptor or its ligand, endothelin-3, cause Hirschsprung's disease.[102] Trefoil peptides appear to be important in protecting the gut against injury and maintenance of mucosal integrity.[103] Guanylin and uroguanylin, isolated as endogenous ligands of the receptor for *Escherichia coli* heat-sensitive enterotoxin, stimulate chloride, bicarbonate, and water secretion in the intestine while inhibiting sodium reabsorption.[104] These peptides are also natriuretic, suggesting the existence of an enterorenal axis. Cocaine- and amphetamine-regulated transcript peptide has been detected throughout the gastrointestinal tract, adrenal, and hypothalamus and shown to be involved in the central regulation of food intake.[105,106] Neuromedin U is a neurotransmitter in the enteric nervous system that has effects on intestinal muscle contraction and ion transport.[107,108] Centrally, neuromedin U has been reported to affect satiety. The orexins have also been reported to exist in the gastrointestinal tract, but their most important role is the regulation of wakefulness in the CNS.[109,110] Many other peptides have been discovered in the gut whose physiologic actions remain to be determined.

## NEUROENDOCRINE TUMORS

Gastroenteropancreatic neuroendocrine tumors are rare in clinical practice but, as with most other tumors, are more common in autopsy series. These tumors can be subdivided into functioning and nonfunctioning tumors. Functioning tumors, which generally have a better prognosis, release peptide hormones into the circulation and are usually associated with defined tumor syndromes. These tumors may release several peptides, but not all these peptides produce clinically detectable effects. Furthermore, a tumor producing one peptide may produce another at a later date that may result in a different clinical syndrome. Frequently, it is the effects of the peptide products of these tumors that initially cause patients the most discomfort. Later in the course of the disease, the clinical picture is dominated by tumor bulk. Nonfunctioning tumors may secrete various peptides (e.g., pancreatic polypeptide) but are not associated with described syndromes. Most gastroenteropancreatic tumors are malignant but slow-growing, thus allowing prolonged survival. Although several genes have been associated with neuroendocrine tumorigenesis, mutations in the MEN1 tumor suppressor gene (chromosome 11q13, see Chapter 191) is the most common genetic predisposition. Approximately 25% of tumors occur as part of MEN1, notably gastrinomas and nonfunctioning tumors. Somatic mutations in the *MEN1* gene are also observed in as many as one third of sporadic gastrinomas. Neuroendocrine tumorigenesis follows a common path with other tumors: hyperplasia, dysplasia, neoplasia (well differentiated, progressing to lesser degrees of differentiation), and metastasis. Unlike other tumors, however, progression through these stages is slow. As tumors become less differentiated, they develop the potential to secrete other peptides that may result in a clinical tumor syndrome different from the presenting syndrome.

The diagnosis of gastroenteropancreatic neuroendocrine tumors can be challenging.[111,112] For example, the differential diagnosis of secretory diarrhea, of which a VIP-secreting tumor (VIPoma) is a rare cause, comprises a large number of conditions (Table 193-3). In addition, the characteristic rash of a glucagonoma can easily be mistaken for another more common rash such as pustular psoriasis. Once the diagnosis is suspected, the correct set of biochemical, radiologic, and endoscopic investigations has to be selected to reach a final diagnosis. These investigations will also provide information regarding prognosis and further management. Prognosis cannot be made through histologic techniques alone,[113] but proliferation indices such as Ki67 are useful. An important

### Table 193-3 Differential Diagnosis of Secretory Diarrhea

| | |
|---|---|
| Drugs | Laxatives |
| Infection | *Escherichia coli* |
| | Cholera |
| GEP tumors | Carcinoids |
| | VIPomas |
| | Gastrinoma |
| | Medullary carcinoma of thyroid |
| Congenital | Structural abnormalities |
| | Immunoglobulin A deficiency |
| | Dysautonomia |
| | Choroidorrhea |
| Other | Systemic mastocytosis |
| | Basophilic leukemia |
| | Idiopathic |

Clinical history should identify patients with infections. Carcinoids are associated with flushing, diarrhea, wheeziness, and high urinary 5-hydroxyindoleacetic acid levels. Diarrhea of gastrinomas responds to proton pump inhibitors. Systemic mastocytosis results in elevated mast cell tryptase. GEP, gastroenteropancreatic.

question to answer is whether a tumor is resectable because, at present, only complete surgical removal of a solitary tumor offers a chance of cure. If surgical cure is not possible, then measures are required for controlling the patient's symptoms as well as growth of the tumor. These include surgical tumor debulking, drugs (e.g., antisecretory drugs for gastrinomas and somatostatin analogues for VIPomas), tumor embolization techniques, cytotoxic chemotherapy, treatment with radiolabeled somatostatin analogues, interferon therapy, and liver transplantation.

## GASTRINOMA (ZOLLINGER-ELLISON SYNDROME)

In 1955, Zollinger and Ellison[114] described the syndrome of extreme hypersecretion of gastric acid and intractable peptic ulceration secondary to a non-β islet cell pancreatic tumor. Subsequently, it was shown that these tumors secrete the hormone gastrin and that as many as one third of gastrinomas, or ZES, occur in patients with MEN1[115] (see Chapter 191). ZES is an uncommon syndrome of ectopic hormone secretion with an annual incidence of one per million. The mean age at onset of symptoms is 50 years with a slight male preponderance. The majority of gastrinomas are pancreatic with 20% to 40% occurring in the duodenum. Sporadic duodenal tumors are usually solitary and are less than 1 cm in diameter. In patients with MEN1, gastrinomas are usually multiple and are associated with pancreatic microadenomas. As many as 50% of patients have metastases at the time of diagnosis.

Patients with ZES classically presented with intractable peptic ulceration and its complications, such as perforation, hemorrhage, and stricture formation. With the widespread use of proton pump inhibitors, complicated peptic ulcer disease, however, is now a less common presentation. Proton pump inhibitors now tend to delay diagnosis.[116] Reflux esophagitis is more common, as is diarrhea caused by the action of acid on intestinal enzymes and mucosa. ZES should be suspected in patients with refractory peptic ulcer disease and esophagitis, patients with duodenal ulceration but without H. pylori infection, patients with chronic secretory diarrhea that responds to acid antisecretory medications, and patients with peptic ulcer disease and a pancreatic tumor.[117] Since there is an association with MEN1, a detailed family history is essential, as is vigilance for the manifestations of MEN1 in patients with ZES.

Once the diagnosis of ZES is suspected, the next step is to demonstrate elevated fasting serum gastrin levels off all acid antisecretory medications (14 days for $H^+$-$K^+$ ATPase inhibitors and 3 days for $H_2$ blockers). There is a danger of peptic ulcer perforation with stopping of antisecretory medications, and in high-risk cases, very high gastrin levels (>250 pmol/L) on proton pump inhibitors may indicate gastrinoma. Gastric acid output is then measured, which is usually greater than 15 mEq/hr in patients without previous acid-reducing surgery and greater than 5 mEq/hr in patients with previous acid-reducing surgery. In patients whose investigations are borderline despite strong clinical suspicion of ZES, a secretin stimulation test is carried out in which 2 U/kg of secretin is given intravenously and fasting gastrin levels are measured at 2, 5, 10, and 20 minutes; in the presence of gastrinoma, gastrin levels should be increased by at least 50%. This test has a sensitivity as high as 85% for gastrinoma. The secretin test distinguishes ZES from other conditions associated with gastric acid hypersecretion. Because H. pylori may be associated with hypergastrinemia and hyperchlorhydria, it should be eradicated before any other assessment. Patients with ZES may have manifestations of MEN1 at presentation or develop these later. Therefore, serum calcium and parathyroid hormone levels, as well as baseline pituitary function, should be assessed.

Tumor localization is carried out to identify patients without metastatic disease who may be cured by surgery.[118]

Radiolabeled octreotide scanning is most useful for identifying the primary tumor and metastases.[119-121] Magnetic resonance imaging with short tau inversion-time inversion-recovery sequences appears to be the next sensitive imaging modality for identifying hepatic metastases but is poor at imaging the primary tumor. Small tumors can be detected using endoscopic ultrasound or selective arterial angiography in combination with computed tomography scanning. Intra-arterial secretin, given during angiography, may also aid in localization. This has now been replaced by intra-arterial calcium.[122] In the presence of tumor, hormone levels should double 30 seconds after calcium injection into an artery supplying the tumor. Normal response is a reduction in hormone levels. If all attempts at localization of a solitary primary tumor fail, then surgical exploration is carried out in conjunction with intraoperative ultrasound, duodenal transillumination, and duodenotomy.

Treatment of ZES involves symptomatic control, which can be achieved with acid antisecretory medications (particularly $H^+$-$K^+$ ATPase inhibitors) at doses titrated to the patient's response and aimed to reduce gastric acid secretion to less than 10 mEq/hr (5 mEq/hr in patients with previous acid-reducing surgery) for the hour before the next dose of the drug. Rarely, somatostatin analogues or gastric surgery is required. For solitary tumors, surgery offers the possibility of cure, whereas for metastatic disease, somatostatin analogues, debulking surgery, interferon treatment, cytotoxic chemotherapy, hepatic tumor embolization (Fig. 193-10), and liver transplantation have been attempted. Generally, cytotoxic chemotherapy is most useful in rapidly growing tumors. Several combinations have been tried for neuroendocrine tumors.[123,124] Interferon is not commonly used because of side effects including flulike illness, chronic fatigue, and autoimmune phenomena. With gastrinomas, treatment success can be assessed using serial fasting gastrin measurements and imaging techniques. Other gut hormones are measured regularly in case a second syndrome develops at a later date. Calcium levels are particularly useful because of the association of ZES with MEN1 and because of the possibility of development of parathyroid hormone receptor–related protein secretion from these tumors. Elevated calcium levels in parathyroid hormone–related protein–secreting tumors can be controlled by regular bisphosphonates, hepatic tumor embolization, or surgical tumor debulking.

### VIPoma

The VIPoma, or Verner-Morrison syndrome, was originally described as a syndrome that included the association of watery diarrhea, hypokalemia, and achlorhydria with a pancreatic tumor.[125,126] Ninety percent of VIPomas are pancreatic with the remainder associated with childhood ganglioneuroblastomas and tumors in other tissues. VIPomas account for 2% to 7% of gastroenteropancreatic neuroendocrine tumors and have an annual incidence of one per 10 million population. The mean age at presentation is 49 years with a slight female preponderance. The majority of pancreatic VIPomas occur in the body and tail of the pancreas. VIPomas, of which 61% are malignant, are usually solitary (average diameter of 1–7 cm), and 37% to 68% have metastasized at the time of presentation, typically to the liver and regional lymph nodes. Metastases to the kidneys, lungs, stomach, and mediastinum have also been reported. VIPomas can occur as part of the MEN1 syndrome (see Chapter 191).

The symptomatology and biochemical abnormalities of VIPoma syndrome reflect the physiologic effects of VIP and its related peptides.[127] Secretory diarrhea (see Table 193-3) with large potassium, bicarbonate, and chloride losses, in conjunction with relaxation of the anal sphincter, can result in loss of large volumes of fluid (>3 L but can be as much as 20 L). This can be exacerbated by the vasodilator effects of VIP, together

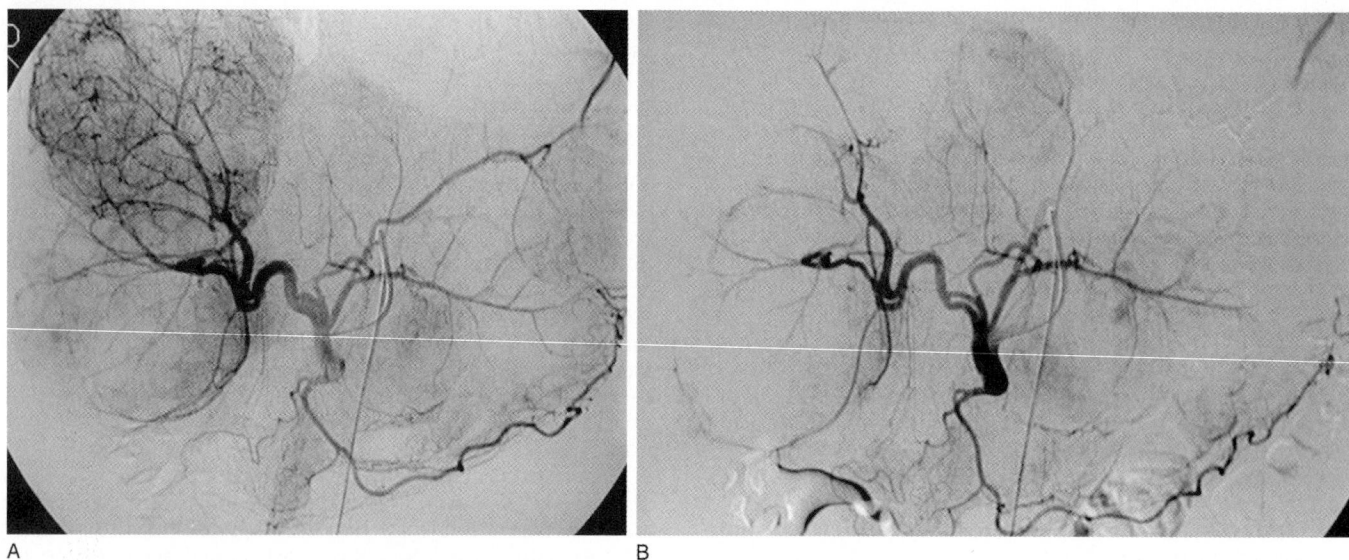

**Figure 193-10** **A,** Hepatic arteriogram in a patient with a metastatic gastroenteropancreatic neuroendocrine tumor. There are multiple liver metastases, with a large one being highly vascular. **B,** Hepatic arteriogram in the same patient after hepatic artery embolization, with inert microspheres demonstrating the disappearance of blood flow to several metastases and particularly to the large, highly vascular metastasis. Hepatic tumor embolization is contraindicated if the portal vein is not patent because blood supply to the normal liver parenchyma is compromised. Also, if more than 50% of the liver is occupied by tumor, there is a danger of fulminant hepatic failure with embolization. Patients selected for embolization are well hydrated and treated with intravenous octreotide and aprotinin; this prevents the sudden release and activity of vasoactive tumor peptides that may result in a severe life-threatening hypotensive crisis. Broad-spectrum antibiotics are also given. Side effects of embolization include fever, which, if prolonged, requires exclusion of hepatic abscess formation using abdominal ultrasound or computed tomography. (Courtesy of Dr. K. Meeran.)

resulting in hemodynamic collapse. The diarrhea may be intermittent, thus delaying the diagnosis by an average of 3 years. The hypokalemia results from intestinal losses and secondary hyperaldosteronism. Other associated abnormalities include achlorhydria or hypochlorhydria, hypomagnesemia, hypercalcemia, glucose intolerance, and mild diabetes. Approximately 20% of patients exhibit flushing of the head and trunk associated with a patchy erythematous rash.

The diagnosis of the VIPoma syndrome involves establishment of the existence of secretory diarrhea, which is isotonic, and persistent despite a 48- to 72-hour fast. A fasting plasma VIP concentration of greater than 200 pg/mL then confirms the diagnosis. The levels of peptide histidine methionine, PP, and NT may also be elevated. Several provocative tests, such as the pentagastrin test, have been recommended but are not routinely used. ZES can be distinguished from VIPoma syndrome by the presence of gastric acid hypersecretion, the absence of metabolic acidosis, and minimal loss of potassium in the stool. Ganglioneuroblastomas may secrete epinephrine and norepinephrine, resulting in increased urinary catecholamines. VIPomas can be localized by ultrasound, computed tomography, and radiolabeled somatostatin receptor scintigraphy. Angiography and transhepatic venous sampling may be required if other methods have not been helpful. Exploratory laparotomy, in conjunction with intraoperative receptor-based scintigraphy or ultrasound, is carried out for small tumors not detected by other means.

The initial treatment of VIPoma syndrome depends on how severely the patient is affected and involves replacement of fluid and electrolytes. Severely affected patients may require invasive monitoring and management in an intensive care unit. The diarrhea can be controlled by somatostatin analogues because somatostatin not only inhibits the actions of VIP but also has independent inhibitory actions on intestinal secretion. Tachyphylaxis to the actions of somatostatin analogues may occur. Glucocorticoids, phenothiazines, prostaglandin synthesis inhibitors (e.g., indomethacin), and lithium carbon-

ate may be tried as second-line agents. If surgical removal is possible, then this presents the best chance of a cure. Surgical debulking of incurable disease is sometimes helpful in symptom control. Combination chemotherapy with 5-fluorouracil and streptozotocin has been shown to be effective, but further evidence of the use of other chemotherapeutic agents is awaited.[128] Treatment with antibodies against VIP may prove useful in the future.

### GLUCAGONOMA SYNDROME

Glucagonomas, which are mostly of pancreatic origin, synthesize and secrete glucagon and other products of the pre-proglucagon gene. These tumors have an estimated annual incidence of 1 in 20 million, with a marginal female preponderance, and invariably present in adulthood. As many as 80% of tumors are sporadic, with the remainder associated with MEN1. More than 70% of patients have metastases at the time of diagnosis. The most dramatic feature of the syndrome is the characteristic necrolytic migratory erythematous rash[129] (Fig. 193-11). This usually starts in the groin and perineum and migrates to the distal extremities. The lesions are erythematous patches, which become increased and may be associated with bullae. These lesions break down and gradually heal, often leaving areas of hyperpigmentation, only to recur at another site. Mucosal membrane involvement may result in stomatitis, cheilitis, and glossitis. Skin biopsies are nondiagnostic. The cause of the rash is unknown, but several possibilities, such as the direct action of glucagon on the skin, amino acid deficiency, fatty acid deficiency, and zinc deficiency, have been proposed.[130] Other manifestations of the glucagonoma syndrome include impaired glucose tolerance and occasionally mild diabetes, progressive weight loss, diarrhea, venous thrombosis and pulmonary embolism, nail dystrophy, normocytic normochromic anemia, and neuropsychiatric symptoms. Paraneoplastic syndromes such as optic atrophy have been reported.

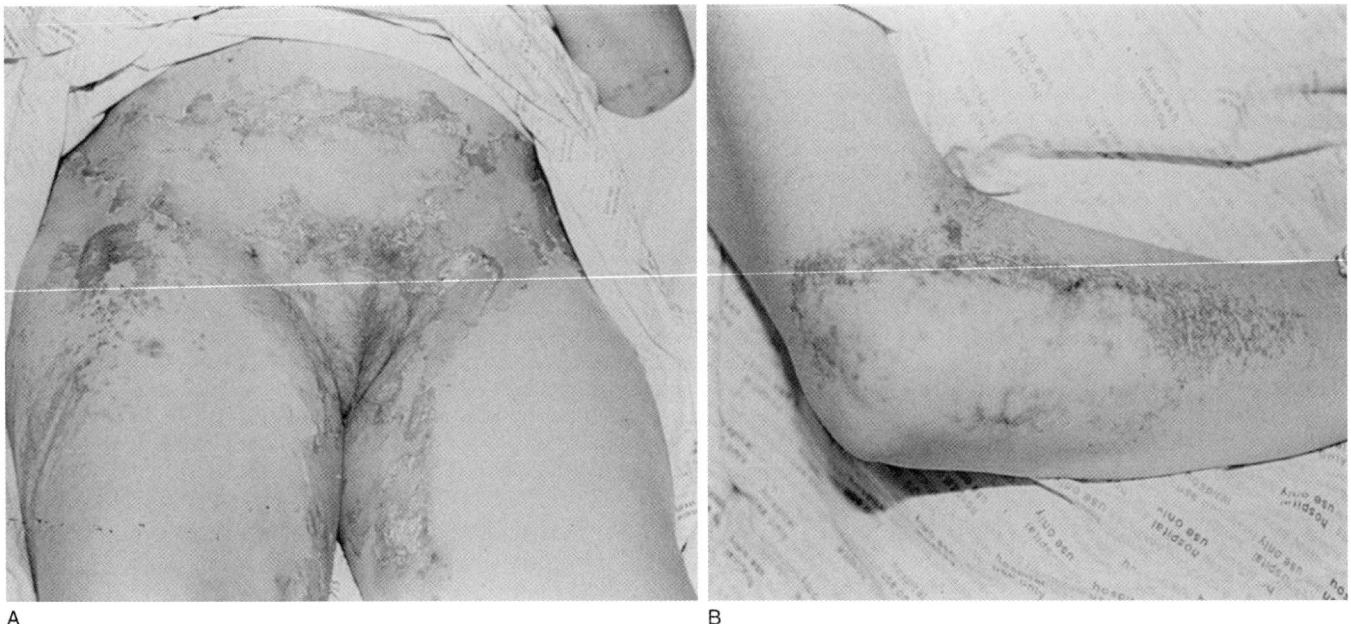

*Figure 193-11*   Necrolytic migratory rash of glucagonoma affecting the perineum (**A**) and the arm (**B**). (Courtesy of Dr. K. Meeran.)

The diagnosis of the glucagonoma syndrome is based initially on clinical grounds and the demonstration of elevated plasma glucagon levels. Glucagon levels are usually increased 10- to 20-fold, which excludes other causes of increased glucagon levels such as trauma, burns, sepsis, diabetic ketoacidosis, renal and hepatic failure, use of danazol and oral contraceptives, prolonged fasting, and Cushing's syndrome (see Table 193-2). Because the majority of the tumors are large and metastatic, they can be identified using techniques such as ultrasound and computed tomography scanning. However, somatostatin receptor scintigraphy is the best modality for identifying the extent of metastatic disease. Localized solitary tumors should be surgically excised. The glucagonoma rash responds well to somatostatin analogue therapy and to oral and topical zinc. Aspirin therapy has been advocated in view of the thromboembolic complications, and insulin is occasionally required for mild diabetes. Palliative treatments for metastatic disease include somatostatin analogue therapy (with long-acting somatostatin analogues being increasingly used), hepatic artery embolization of metastases, debulking surgery, and cytotoxic chemotherapy.

## SOMATOSTATINOMA

Somatostatinomas[131] are extremely rare, with an estimated annual incidence of approximately 1 in 40 million. The tumors are usually pancreatic, but some arise in the duodenum. Somatostatinomas can occur as part of the MEN1 syndrome. Approximately 50% of duodenal somatostatinomas occur in association with neurofibromatosis type 1, in which the tumors are usually periampullary and may be associated with pheochromocytoma. Pancreatic tumors present late with hepatic metastases while local effects identify duodenal tumors earlier and usually before the development of the tumor syndrome, which is characterized by the triad of cholelithiasis, diabetes, and steatorrhea. Hypoglycemia has occasionally been described, possibly secondary to larger molecular forms of somatostatin having a greater inhibitory effect on counterregulatory hormones than on insulin. Cosecretion of adrenocorticotropic hormone may result in Cushing's syndrome. Other features of the syndrome include weight loss, postprandial fullness, hypochlorhydria, and ane-

mia. Somatostatin levels are increased by more than 10-fold in pancreatic tumors, with much lower levels observed with the smaller duodenal tumors. Localization is carried out using ultrasound and computed tomography scanning, with endoscopic ultrasound being useful for duodenal tumors. Treatment is mainly surgical, and palliative treatment is along the same lines as that described for other gastrointestinal neuroendocrine tumors.

## OTHER HORMONES AND MALIGNANCY

Gastrointestinal endocrine tumors have been described that secrete parathyroid hormone–related protein (causing hypercalcemia), adrenocorticotropic hormone (resulting in Cushing's syndrome), and GH-releasing hormone (resulting in acromegaly), either alone or in association with gastrointestinal hormone tumor syndromes (see Chapter 195). A few patients have been described with "enteroglucagonoma" syndrome[132] associated with intestinal villous hypertrophy. These patients have highlighted the importance of GLPs in the maintenance of intestinal mucosal integrity. It is now known that GLP-2 is the major mediator involved. Numerous other peptides have been found either in the plasma or in tissue from endocrine tumors of the gastrointestinal tract, including PP, NPY, NT, neuromedin B, CGRP, bombesin, and motilin, but these have not been associated with specific clinical syndromes.

## THE ROLE OF SURGERY IN NEUROENDOCRINE TUMORS

Surgery provides a cure for any localized neuroendocrine tumor. This should be considered even for small slow-growing tumors because it may alleviate symptoms secondary to hormone hypersecretion. Curative resection of liver metastases is increasingly considered in patients with fewer than five liver metastases and sufficient hepatic reserve.[133,134] Liver transplantation has been performed in patients with multiple metastases, but its role remains to be explored. Tumor debulking may provide relief from both pressure- and hormone-related symptoms. Cryosurgery, causing metastasis necrosis, may also be useful.

## FUTURE DIRECTIONS

Because gastrointestinal neuroendocrine tumors are rare, their diagnosis and management should be confined to specialist centers. Collaboration between specialist centers will allow an accurate database of patients for improving our understanding of these tumors. Further understanding of the pathogenesis of these tumors is also necessary to guide evidence-based treatment, in particular, for the development of chemotherapeutic regimens. The role of chemoembolization of metastases requires further clarification. Larger multicenter controlled trials involving larger patient groups will establish the role of promising novel treatments such as radiolabeled somatostatin analogues.[135]

## REFERENCES

1. Bayliss WM, Starling EH: The mechanism of pancreatic secretion. J Physiol 28:325–335, 1902.
2. Holst JJ, Fahrenkrug J, Stadil F, et al: Gastrointestinal endocrinology. Scand J Gastroenterol Suppl 216:27–38, 1996.
3. Rehfeld JF: The new biology of gastrointestinal hormones. Physiol Rev 78:1087–1108, 1998.
4. Betancur B, Azzi M, Rostene W: Nonpeptide antagonists of neuropeptide receptors: Tools for research and therapy. Trends Pharmacol Sci 18:372–386, 1997.
5. Sawada M, Dickinson CJ: The G cell. Annu Rev Physiol 59:273–298, 1997.
6. Taheri S, Bloom S: Orexins/hypocretins: Waking up the scientific world. Clin Endocrinol (Oxf) 54:421–429, 2001.
7. Sakurai T, Amemiya A, Ishii M, et al: Orexins and orexin receptors: A family of hypothalamic neuropeptides and G protein-coupled receptors that regulate feeding behavior. Cell 92:573–585, 1998.
8. Kojima M, Hosoda H, Date Y, et al: Ghrelin is a growth-hormone-releasing acylated peptide from stomach. Nature 402:656–660, 1999.
9. Schonhoff SE, Giel-Moloney M, Leiter AB: Minireview: Development and differentiation of gut endocrine cells. Endocrinology 145:2639–2644, 2004.
10. Rehfeld JF, Bundgaard JR, Goetze JP, et al: Naming progastrin-derived peptides. Regul Pept 120:177–183, 2004.
11. Walsh JH: Gastrin. In Walsh JH, Dockray GJ (eds): Gut Peptides. New York, Raven Press, 1994, pp 75–122.
12. Samuelson LC, Hinkle KL: Insights into the regulation of gastric acid secretion through analysis of genetically engineered mice. Annu Rev Physiol 65:383–400, 2003.
13. Koh TJ, Goldenring JR, Ito S, et al: Gastrin deficiency results in altered gastric differentiation and decreased colonic proliferation in mice. Gastroenterology 113:1015–1025, 1997.
14. Langhans N, Rindi G, Chiu M, et al: Abnormal gastric histology and decreased acid production in cholecystokinin-B/gastrin receptor-deficient mice. Gastroenterology 112:280–286, 1997.
15. Wang TC, Koh TJ, Varro A, et al: Processing and proliferative effects of human progastrin in transgenic mice. J Clin Invest 98:1918–1929, 1996.

16. Liddle RA: Regulation of cholecystokinin secretion by intraluminal releasing factors. Am J Physiol G319–G327, 1995.
17. Miyasaka K, Funakoshi A: Luminal feedback regulation, monitor peptide, CCK-releasing peptide and CCK receptors. Pancreas 16:277–283, 1998.
18. Barrachina MD, Martinez V, Wang LW, et al: Synergistic interaction between leptin and cholecystokinin to reduce short-term food intake in lean mice. Proc Natl Acad Sci U S A 94:10455–10460, 1997.
19. Bi S, Moran TH: Actions of CCK in the controls of food intake and body weight: lessons from the CCK-A receptor deficient OLETF rat. Neuropeptides 36:171–181, 2002.
20. Ulrich CD, Holtmann M, Miller LJ: Secretin and vasoactive intestinal peptide receptors: Members of a unique family of G protein-coupled receptors. Gastroenterology 114:382–397, 1998.
21. Chey WY, Chang TM: Secretin, 100 years later. J Gastroenterol 38:1025–1035, 2003.
22. Miyawaki K, Yamada Y, Yano H, et al: Glucose intolerance caused by a defect in the entero-insular axis: A study in gastric inhibitory polypeptide receptor knockout mice. Proc Natl Acad Sci U S A 96:14843–14847, 1999.
23. Hansotia T, Baggio LL, Delmeire D, et al: Double incretin receptor knockout (DIRKO) mice reveal an essential role for the enteroinsular axis in transducing the glucoregulatory actions of DPP-IV inhibitors. Diabetes 53:1326–1335, 2004.
24. Chabre O, Liakos P, Vivier J, et al: Cushing's syndrome due to gastric inhibitory polypeptide-dependent adrenal adenoma: Insights into hormonal control and adrenocortical tumorigenesis. J Clin Endocrinol Metab 83:3134–3143, 1998.
25. Miyawaki K, Yamada Y, Ban N, et al: Inhibition of gastric inhibitory polypeptide signaling prevents obesity. Nat Med 8:738–742, 2002.
26. Holst JJ: Enteroglucagon. Annu Rev Physiol 59:257–271, 1997.
27. Scroochi L, Brown TJ, MacLusky N, et al: Glucose intolerance but normal satiety in mice with a null mutation in the glucagon-like peptide 1 receptor gene. Nat Med 2:1254–1258, 1996.
28. Ahren B: Glucagon-like peptide-1 (GLP-1): A gut hormone of potential interest in the treatment of diabetes. Bioessays 20:642–651, 1998.

29. Ahren B, Landin-Olsson M, Jansson PA, et al: Inhibition of dipeptidyl peptidase-4 reduces glycemia, sustains insulin levels, and reduces glucagon levels in type 2 diabetes. J Clin Endocrinol Metab 89:2078–2084, 2004.
30. Ranganath LR, Beety JM, Morgan LM, et al: Attenuated GLP-1 secretion in obesity: Cause or consequence? Gut 38:916–919, 1996.
31. Spiller R, Trotman I, Higgins B, et al: The ileal brake-inhibition of jejunal motility after ileal fat perfusion in man. Gut 25:365–374, 1984.
32. Turton MD, O'Shea D, Gunn I, et al: A role for glucagon-like peptide-1 in the central regulation of feeding. Nature 379:69–72, 1996.
33. Drucker DJ, Erlich P, Asa SL, et al: Induction of intestinal epithelial proliferation by glucagon-like peptide 2. Proc Natl Acad Sci U S A 93:7911–7916, 1996.
34. Ghatei MA, Goodlad RA, Taheri S, et al: Proglucagon-derived peptides in intestinal epithelial proliferation: Glucagon-like peptide-2 is a major mediator of intestinal epithelial proliferation in rats. Dig Dis Sci 46:1255–1263, 2001.
35. Cohen MA, Ellis SM, Le Roux CW, et al: Oxyntomodulin suppresses appetite and reduces food intake in humans. J Clin Endocrinol Metab 88:4696–4701, 2003.
36. Itoh Z: Motilin and clinical application. Peptides 18:593–608, 1997.
37. Poitras P: Motilin. In Walsh JH, Dockray GJ (eds): Gut Peptides. New York, Raven Press, 1994, pp 261–304.
38. Date Y, Kojima M, Hosoda H, et al: Ghrelin, a novel growth hormone-releasing acylated peptide, is synthesized in a distinct endocrine cell type in the gastrointestinal tracts of rats and humans. Endocrinology 141:4255–4261, 2000.
39. Korbonits M, Goldstone AP, Gueorguiev M, Grossman AB: Ghrelin—a hormone with multiple functions. Front Neuroendocrinol 25:27–68, 2004.
40. Howard AD, Feighner SD, Cully DF, et al: A receptor in pituitary and hypothalamus that functions in growth hormone release. Science 273:974–977, 1996.
41. Beaumont NJ, Skinner VO, Tan TM, et al: Ghrelin can bind to a species of high density lipoprotein associated with paraoxonase. J Biol Chem 278:8877–8880, 2003.

42. Tschop M, Smiley DL, Heiman ML: Ghrelin induces adiposity in rodents. Nature 407:908–913, 2000.

43. Wren AM, Small CJ, Ward HL, et al: The novel hypothalamic peptide ghrelin stimulates food intake and growth hormone secretion. Endocrinology 141:4325–4328, 2000.

44. Wren AM, Seal LJ, Cohen MA, et al: Ghrelin enhances appetite and increases food intake in humans. J Clin Endocrinol Metab 86:5992–5995, 2001.

45. Cummings DE, Clement K, Purnell JQ, et al: Elevated plasma ghrelin levels in Prader Willi syndrome. Nat Med 8:643–644, 2002.

46. Cummings DE, Weigle DS, Frayo RS, et al: Plasma ghrelin levels after diet induced weight loss or gastric bypass surgery. N Engl J Med 346:1623–1630, 2002.

47. Taheri S, Lin L, Austin D, et al: Short sleep duration is associated with reduced leptin, elevated ghrelin, and increased body mass index (BMI). PLoS Med 1:e62.

48. Patel YC, Greenwood MT, Panetta R, et al: The somatostatin receptor family. Life Sci 57:1249–1265, 1995.

49. Olias G, Viollet C, Kusserow H, et al: Regulation and function of somatostatin receptors. J Neurochem 89:1057–1091, 2004.

50. Lamberts SWJ, Van der Lely A-J, De Herder WW, et al: Octreotide. N Engl J Med 334:246–252, 1996.

51. Geoghegan J, Pappas TN: Clinical uses of gut peptides. Ann Surg 225:145–154, 1997.

52. De Herder WW, Hofland LJ, Van der Lely A-J, et al: Peptide receptors in gut endocrine tumors. Ballieres Clin Gastroenterol 10:571–587, 1996.

53. Kaltsas G, Rockall A, Papadogias D, et al: Recent advances in radiological and radionuclide imaging and therapy of neuroendocrine tumours. Eur J Endocrinol 151:15–27, 2004.

54. Kaltsas GA, Besser GM, Grossman AB: The diagnosis and medical management of advanced neuroendocrine tumors. Endocr Rev 25:458–511, 2004.

55. Reubi JC, Waser B, Fries H, et al: Neurotensin receptors: A new marker for human ductal pancreatic adeno-carcinoma. Gut 42:546–550, 1998.

56. Cox HM: Peptidergic regulation of intestinal ion transport—a major role for neuropeptide Y and pancreatic polypeptide. Digestion 59:395–399, 1998.

57. Nightingale JMD, Kamm MA, van der Sijp JRM, et al: Gastrointestinal hormones in short bowel syndrome. Peptide YY may be the "colonic brake" to gastric emptying. Gut 39:267–272, 1996.

58. Batterham RL, Cowley MA, Small CJ, et al: Gut hormone PYY(3-36) physiologically inhibits food intake. Nature 418:650–654, 2002.

59. Batterham RL, Cohen MA, Ellis SM, et al: Inhibition of food intake in obese subjects by peptide YY3-36. N Engl J Med 349:941–948, 2003.

60. Berglund MM, Hipskind PA, Gehlert DR: Recent developments in our understanding of the physiological role of PP-fold peptide receptor subtypes. Exp Biol Med (Maywood) 228:217–244, 2003.

61. Taupenot L, Harper KL, O'Connor DT: The chromogranin-secretogranin family. N Engl J Med 348:1134–1149, 2003.

62. Rindi G, Leiter AB, Kopin AS, et al: The "normal" endocrine cell of the gut: Changing concepts and new evidences. Ann N Y Acad Sci 1014:1–12, 2004.

63. Deftos LJ, Hogue-Angeletti R, Chalberg C, et al: PTHrP secretion is stimulated by calcitonin and inhibited by chromogranin A peptides. Endocrinology 125:563–565, 1989.

64. Ardill JE, Erikkson B: The importance of the measurement of circulating markers in patients with neuroendocrine tumours of the pancreas and gut. Endocr Relat Cancer 10:459–462, 2003.

65. Nobels FRE, Kwekkeboom DJ, Bouillon R, et al: Chromogranin A: Its clinical value as marker of neuroendocrine tumors. Eur J Clin Invest 28:431–440, 1998.

66. Sekiya K, Ghatei MA, Salahuddin MJ, et al: Production of GAWK (chromogranin-B 420-493)-like immunoreactivity by endocrine tumors and its possible diagnostic value. J Clin Invest 83:1834–1842, 1989.

67. Nussdorfer GG, Malendowicz LK: Role of VIP, PACAP and related peptides in the regulation of hypothalamo-pituitary-adrenal axis. Peptides 19:1443–1467, 1998.

68. Lauff JM, Modlin IM, Tang LH: Biological relevance of pituitary adenylate cyclase-activating polypeptide (PACAP) in the gastrointestinal tract. Regul Pept 84:1–12, 1999.

69. Lee ST, Lee KY, Li P, et al: Pituitary adenylate cyclase-activating peptide stimulates pancreatic secretion via secretin and cholecystokinin releases. Gastroenterology 114:1054–1060, 1998.

70. Kawaguchi C, Tanaka K, Isojima Y, et al: Changes in light-induced phase shift of circadian rhythm in mice lacking PACAP. Biochem Biophys Res Commun 310:169–175, 2003.

71. Varvarigou A, Bouziotis P, Zikos C, et al: Gastrin-releasing peptide (GRP) analogues for cancer imaging. Cancer Biother Radiopharm 19:219–229, 2004.

72. Moody TW, Mantey SA, Pradhan TK, et al: Development of high affinity camptothecin-bombesin conjugates that have targeted cytotoxicity for bombesin receptor-containing tumor cells. J Biol Chem 279:23580–23589, 2004.

73. Gibbs J, Henderson RP, Rushing PA: Prolongation of the postprandial intermeal interval by gastrin-releasing peptide1-27 in spontaneously feeding rats. Peptides 19:175–177, 1998.

74. Zhou J, Chen J, Mokotoff M, et al: Bombesin/gastrin-releasing peptide receptor: A potential target for antibody-mediated therapy of small cell lung cancer. Clin Cancer Res 9:4953–4960, 2003.

75. Wimalawansa SJ: Calcitonin gene-related peptide and its receptors: Molecular genetics, physiology, pathophysiology and therapeutic potentials. Endocr Rev 17:533–585, 1996.

76. Mulderry PK, Ghatei MA, Spokes RA, et al: Differential expression of α-CGRP and β-CGRP by primary sensory neurons and enteric autonomic neurons of the rat. Neuroscience 25:195–205, 1988.

77. Holzer P: Calcitonin gene-related peptide. In Walsh JH, Dockray GJ (eds): Gut Peptides. New York, Raven Press, 1994, pp 493–524.

78. Holzer P: Implications of tachykinins and calcitonin gene-related peptide in inflammatory bowel disease. Digestion 59:269–283, 1998.

79. Samonina GE, Kopylova GN, Lukjanzeva GV, et al: Antiulcer effects of amylin: a review. Pathophysiology 11:1–6, 2004.

80. Bhavsar S, Watkins J, Young A: Synergy between amylin and cholecystokinin for inhibition of food intake in mice. Physiol Behav 64:557–561, 1998.

81. Maggs D, Shen L, Strobel S, et al: Effect of pramlintide on A1C and body weight in insulin-treated African Americans and Hispanics with type 2 diabetes: A pooled post hoc analysis. Metabolism 52:1638–1642, 2003.

82. Reda TK, Geliebter A, Pi-Sunyer FX: Amylin, food intake, and obesity. Obes Res 10:1087–1091, 2002.

83. McLatchie LM, Fraser NJ, Main JM, et al: RAMPs regulate the transport and ligand specificity of the calcitonin-receptor-like receptor. Nature 393:333–339, 1998.

84. Poyner DR, Sexton PM, Marshall I, et al: International Union of Pharmacology. XXXII. The mammalian calcitonin gene-related peptides, adrenomedullin, amylin, and calcitonin receptors. Pharmacol Rev 54:233–246, 2002.

85. Otsuka M, Yoshioka K: Neurotransmitter functions of mammalian tachykinins. Physiol Rev 73:229–308, 1993.

86. Severini C, Improta G, Falconieri-Erspamer G, et al: The tachykinin peptide family. Pharmacol Rev 54:285–322, 2002.

87. Zhang Y, Lu L, Furlonger C, et al: Hemokinin is a hematopoietic-specific tachykinin that regulates B lymphopoiesis. Nat Immunol 1:392–397, 2000.

88. Page NM, Bell NJ, Gardiner SM, et al: Characterization of the endokinins: Human tachykinins with

cardiovascular activity. Proc Natl Acad Sci U S A 100:6245–6250, 2000.

89. Kurtz MM, Wang R, Clements MK, et al: Identification, localization and receptor characterization of novel mammalian substance P-like peptides. Gene 296:205–212, 2002.

90. Holzer P, Holzer-Petsche U: Tachykinins in the gut. II. Roles in neural excitation, secretion and inflammation. Pharmacol Ther 73:219–263, 1997.

91. Mantyh CR, Vigna SR, Bollinger RR, et al: Differential expression of substance P receptors in patients with Crohn's disease and ulcerative colitis. Gastroenterology 109:850–860, 1995.

92. Maggi CA: The effects of tachykinins on inflammatory and immune cells. Regul Pept 70:75–90, 1997.

93. Woldbye DPD, Larsen PJ: The how and Y of eating. Nat Med 4:671–672, 1998.

94. Grundmar L, Bloom SR (eds): Neuropeptide Y and Drug Development. London, Academic Press, 1997.

95. Cowen MS, Chen F, Lawrence AJ: Neuropeptides: Implications for alcoholism. J Neurochem 89:273–285, 2004.

96. Floren A, Land T, Langel U: Galanin receptor subtypes and ligand binding. Neuropeptides 34:331–337, 2000.

97. Wynick D, Bacon A: Targeted disruption of galanin: New insights from knock-out studies. Neuropeptides 36:132–144, 2002.

98. Gottsch ML, Clifton DK, Steiner RA: Galanin-like peptide as a link in the integration of metabolism and reproduction. Trends Endocrinol Metab 15:215–221, 2004.

99. Dockray GJ: Opioid peptides. In Walsh JH, Dockray GJ (eds): Gut Peptides. New York, Raven Press, 1994, pp 473–492.

100. Ghatei MA, Takahashi K, Kirkland SC, et al: Endothelin. In Walsh JH, Dockray GJ (eds): Gut Peptides. New York, Raven Press, 1994, pp 389–400.

101. Oldner A, Wanecek M, Goiny M, et al: The endothelin receptor antagonist bosentan restores gut oxygen delivery and reverses intestinal mucosal acidosis in porcine endotoxin shock. Gut 42:696–702, 1998.

102. Gariepy CE, Williams SC, Richardson JA, et al: Transgenic expression of the endothelin-B receptor prevents congenital intestinal aganglionosis in a rat model of Hirschsprung disease. J Clin Invest 102:1092–1101, 1998.

103. Taupin D, Podolsky DK: Trefoil factors: Initiators of mucosal healing. Nat Rev Mol Cell Biol 4:721–732, 2003.

104. Semrad CE: Guanylin: Where it's at! Why it's there. Gastroenterology 113:1036–1037, 1997.

105. Couceyro P, Paquet M, Koylu E, et al: Cocaine and amphetamine-regulated transcript (CART) peptide immunoreactivity in myenteric plexus neurons of the rat ileum and co-localization with choline acetyltransferase. Synapse 30:1–8, 1998.

106. Kristensen P, Judge ME, Thim L, et al: Hypothalamic CART is a new anorectic peptide regulated by leptin. Nature 393:72–76, 1998.

107. Nandha KA, Bloom SR: Neuromedin U-an overview. Biomed Res 14(Suppl 3):71–76, 1993.

108. Brighton PJ, Szekeres PG, Willars GB: Neuromedin U and its receptors: Structure, function, and physiological roles. Pharmacol Rev 56:231–248, 2004.

109. Kirchgessner AL: Orexins in the brain-gut axis. Endocr Rev 23:1–15, 2002.

110. Taheri S, Zeitzer JM, Mignot E: The role of hypocretins (orexins) in sleep regulation and narcolepsy. Annu Rev Neurosci 25:283–313, 2002.

111. Taheri S, Meeran K: Islet cell tumours: diagnosis and medical management. Hosp Med 61:824–829, 2000.

112. Barakat MT, Meeran K, Bloom SR: Neuroendocrine tumours. Endocr Relat Cancer 11:1–18, 2004.

113. Bishop AE, Polak JM: Pathology. Ballieres Clin Gastroenterol 10:555–569, 1996.

114. Zollinger RM, Ellison EH: Primary peptic ulceration of the jejunum associated with islet cell tumors of the pancreas. Ann Surg 142:709–728, 1955.

115. Jensen RT: Gastrinoma. Ballieres Clin Gastroenterol 10:673–696, 1996.

116. Corleto VD, Annibale B, Gibril F, et al: Does the widespread use of proton pump inhibitors mask, complicate and/or delay the diagnosis of Zollinger-Ellison syndrome? Aliment Pharmacol Ther 15:1555–1561, 2000.

117. Jensen RT: Gastrinoma. Ballieres Clin Gastroenterol 10:673–696, 1996.

118. Ricke J, Klose KJ, Mignon M, et al: Standardisation of imaging in neuroendocrine tumours: Results of a European Delphi process. Eur J Radiol 37:8–17, 2001.

119. Modlin IM, Tang LH: Approaches to the diagnosis of gut neuroendocrine tumors: The last word (today). Gastroenterology 112:583–590, 1997.

120. Kaltsas G, Rockall A, Papadogias D, et al: Recent advances in radiological and radionuclide imaging and therapy of neuroendocrine tumours. Eur J Endocrinol 151:15–27, 2004.

121. Kaltsas GA, Besser GM, Grossman AB: The diagnosis and medical management of advanced neuroendocrine tumors. Endocr Rev 25:458–511, 2004.

122. Turner JJ, Wren AM, Jackson JE, et al: Localization of gastrinomas by selective intra-arterial calcium injection. Clin Endocrinol (Oxf) 57:821–825, 2002.

123. Moertel CG, Kvols LK, O'Connell MJ, Rubin J: Treatment of neuroendocrine carcinomas with combined etoposide and cisplatin. Evidence of major therapeutic activity in the anaplastic variants of these neoplasms. Cancer 68:227–232, 1991.

124. Kaltsas GA, Mukherjee JJ, Isidori A, et al: Treatment of advanced neuroendocrine tumours using combination chemotherapy with lomustine and 5-fluorouracil. Clin Endocrinol (Oxf) 57:169–183, 2002.

125. Bloom SR, Polak JM, Pearce AGE: Vasoactive intestinal peptide and watery diarrhoea syndrome. Lancet 2:14–16, 1973.

126. Park SK, O'Doriso MS, O'Dorisio TM: Vasoactive intestinal polypeptide-secreting tumours: Biology and therapy. Ballieres Clin Gastroenterol 10:673–696, 1996.

127. Taheri S, Ghatei MA, Bloom SR: Vasoactive intestinal polypeptide (VIP). In Crishton T (ed): Wiley Encyclopedia of Molecular Medicine. New York. John Wiley & Sons, 2002, pp 3344–3346.

128. Bejetta E, Rimassa L, Carnaghi C, et al: 5-Fluorouracil, dacarbazine and epirubicin in the treatment of patients with neuroendocrine tumors. Cancer 83:372–378, 1998.

129. Bloom SR, Polak JM: Glucagonoma syndrome. Am J Med 82:25–36, 1987.

130. Frankton S, Bloom SR: Glucagonomas. Ballieres Clin Gastroenterol 10:673–696, 1996.

131. Kreijs GJ, Orci L, Conlon JM, et al: Somatostatinoma syndrome. N Engl J Med 301:285–292, 1979.

132. Bloom SR: An enteroglucagon tumor. Gut 13:520–523, 1972.

133. Jaeck D, Oussoultzoglou E, Bachellier P, et al: Hepatic metastases of gastroenteropancreatic neuroendocrine tumors: Safe hepatic surgery. World J Surg 25:689–692, 2001.

134. Yao KA, Talamonti MS, Nemcek A, et al: Indications and results of liver resection and hepatic chemoembolization for metastatic gastrointestinal neuroendocrine tumors. Surgery 130:677–682, 2001.

135. Virgolini I, Britton K, Buscombe J, et al: In- and Y-DOTA-lanreotide: Results and implications of the MAURITIUS trial. Semin Nucl Med 32:148–155, 2002.

# Carcinoid Syndrome

## Barbro Eriksson and Kjell Öberg

## INTRODUCTION

This chapter provides an overview of carcinoid tumors, with presentation of the old and new classifications of these tumors, as well as a short description of molecular genetics, tumor biology, and clinical presentation. The main focus of the chapter will be a detailed description of the clinical features of carcinoid syndrome with biochemical background and treatment modalities.

## HISTORY

In 1888 Otto Lubarsch[1] first described the microscopic features of a patient with multiple carcinoids of the ileum, but regarded them as carcinomas. However, Ransom[2] is given credit for the first description of a carcinoid of the ileum in 1890. The term *carcinoid* was used first by Oberndorfer[3] in 1907 to describe tumors that behaved in a more indolent fashion than typical adenocarcinomas. The recognition of carcinoid as endocrine-related tumors was outlined by Gosset and Masson[4] in 1914. They noted that the tumors arise from chromaffin cells at the base of the crypts of Lieberkühn. These chromaffin cells, or Kulchitsky's cells, exhibit characteristics of amine precursor uptake and decarboxylation (APUD). In 1953, Lembeck[5] demonstrated the presence of serotonin in carcinoid tumors, and Thorson and coworkers[6] in 1954 provided the first description of flushing, diarrhea, right-sided heart failure, and increased urinary levels of 5-hydroxyindoleacetic acid (5-HIAA) in association with carcinoid tumors. In 1963, Williams and Sandler[7] classified carcinoids according to their embryonic site of origin as foregut carcinoids (respiratory tract, stomach, duodenum, biliary system, and pancreas), midgut carcinoids (small bowel, appendix, cecum, and proximal colon), and hindgut carcinoids (distal colon, sigmoid, and rectum). In 1986, Norheim and coworkers[8] described the release of tachykinins from carcinoid tumors and their significance in carcinoid flush.

## EPIDEMIOLOGY

The incidence of carcinoid tumors varies with gender and race. The most recent studies indicate an overall incidence for all carcinoid tumors of about 2.1/100,000 per year in both the United States and Europe.[9,10] However, recent data from Modlin and Sandor[9] indicate a higher incidence in black males, with an incidence of 4.2/100,000 per year. A majority of these carcinoids are of the gastric type. In autopsy series from Sweden, an incidence of 8.4/100,000 has been reported, but that series included a number of appendiceal carcinoids, which are usually not clinically significant and are detected only incidentally.[11] The female/male ratio was 1:1, and the median age at diagnosis was 55 to 60 years in different subtypes of carcinoids. The incidence of the carcinoid syndrome has been reported to be between 0.5/100,000 and 0.7/100,000.[9-12]

A newly performed 5-decade analysis of 13,705 carcinoid tumors revealed that, within the gastrointestinal (GI) tract, most carcinoid tumors occurred in the small intestine (42%), rectum (27%), and stomach (8.7%). Bronchopulmonary carcinoids constitute 25.3%.[9] The best 5-year survival rates were recorded for patients with rectal (88.3%), bronchopulmonary (73.5%), and appendiceal (71.0%) carcinoids. The most common type, the midgut carcinoid, had 5-year survival rates of 64% for localized, 72.5% for regional, 44.1% for distant metastases, and 60.8% for all stages. In 12.9% of all patients with carcinoid tumors, distant metastases are evident at the time of diagnosis. This study is the first comprehensive analysis of carcinoid tumors and shows that the overall incidence of carcinoids appears to have increased over the past 30-year period, in particular for gastric and rectal carcinoids. Pathologists are now able to recognize early and unusual forms or poorly differentiated variants of these tumors. The report also indicates that previous decisions on the benignity of carcinoid tumors can be questioned.

## PATHOGENESIS

The neuroendocrine (NE) cell system consists of neuronal and epithelial cells. They synthesize peptide hormones and biogenic amines (Fig. 194-1). The nerve fibers form the large peptidergic and adrenergic autonomic nervous system. The epithelial NE cells form, to a great extent, the parenchyma of the classic endocrine glands. Nevertheless, most of them occur as disseminated cells in the mucosa of the respiratory and alimentary tracts. Basically, NE cells can appear in all solid organs, the skin, and all mucous membranes of the body.[13,14] Both phylogenetically and ontogenetically, the NE cells originate from the nervous system. The hormonal peptides and biogenic amines are synthesized in the endoplasmic reticulum of the NE cells packed in the Golgi apparatus and stored in the secretory granules of the cytoplasm. Peptide hormones and neuropeptides are contained mainly within the so-called large dense core vesicles (LDCVs). Amines are packed within synaptic-like microvesicles (SLMVs).[15] The stored hormones and amines are released via exocytosis to the blood or sometimes intraluminally into the gut.[16,17] The nerve cells of the NE system rarely undergo hyperplasia or neoplastic transformation or both. In contrast, the epithelial NE cells—both those in the endocrine glands and those disseminated in the mucous membranes and the skin—can form hyperplastic tumorlike nodules and genuine neoplastic growths.[12,14] As in most of the other neoplasms of the body, the etiology and pathogenesis are essentially unknown in the carcinoid tumors. However, genetic abnormalities induce cell growth as a result of overstimulation by hormones and growth factors that are known to be responsible for the initiation of NE hyperplasia and development.[18,19] Certain people are predisposed to the tumor because of inherited genetic alterations, such as in multiple endocrine neoplasia (MEN) type 1 families as well as in the von Hippel–Lindau syndrome.[20,21] The course of the NE neoplastic diseases varies to a considerable extent. Assessment of the degree of malignancy of individual NE tumors can be difficult. The main tools for the assessment are comprehensive histopathologic and immunohistochemical examinations combined with a medical history. In particularly difficult cases, electron microscopy must be included. Particular attention is paid to the size of the tumor, its depth of invasion, the growth pattern of the neoplastic cells, as well as their degree of differentiation and proliferation rates. Both lymphatic and hematogenous spread of metastases can occur in carcinoids. Thus, metastatic lesions can appear in most organs and tissues. However, the predominant pattern is spread to the regional lymph nodes and later to the liver, bones, and the brain. The neoplastic parenchymal cells retain their ability to produce peptide hormones and biogenic amines. Thus, metastatic carcinoids give rise to clinical

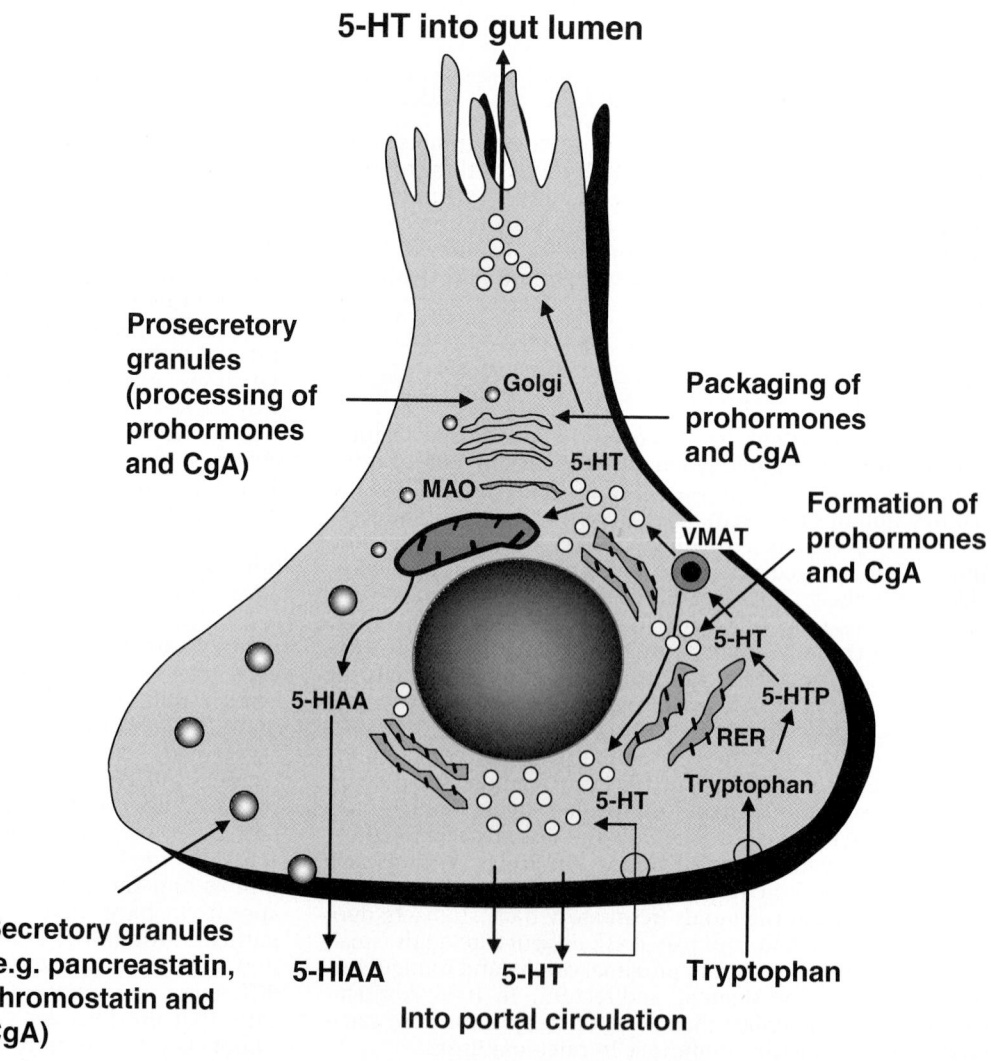

# The neuroendocrine cell

*Figure 194-1* Schematic illustration of tryptophan metabolism in a neuroendocrine cell (enterochromaffin [EC]-cell).

symptoms of hormone overproduction.[12,18,20,21] The proteins in the secretory granules of virtually all the NE cells consist predominantly of the glycoprotein, chromogranin A, which is secreted in to the blood together with hormones and amines. When an NE tumor develops, the levels of chromogranin A in the blood are usually elevated. Chromogranin A measurements in the blood also can be used to follow the course of the disease. The enterochromaffin cells (EC cells) responsible for development of carcinoid tumors of the midgut contain vesicular monoamine transporter 1 (VMAT-1), whereas vesicular monoamine transporter 2 (VMAT-2) is expressed in histamine-producing enterochromaffin-like (ECL) cells of the stomach.[22] Another common biologic feature of NE cells is that they often contain somatostatin and other peptide receptors on the cell surface. This fact provides an opportunity for both scintigraphic diagnosis and therapy.

## CLASSIFICATION

Carcinoid tumors have been traditionally classified according to their embryonic origin into foregut, midgut, or hindgut carcinoids.[23] This classification from 1963 by Williams and Sandler has been debated, and a new classification system has emerged. In 2000, the World Health Organization (WHO) revised the histopathologic classification system of gastroenteropancreatic (GEP) NE tumors. It was decided that the almost 100-year-old concept of carcinoid is no longer adequate to cover the entire structural and biologic spectra of the disseminated NE system neoplasms. Instead, the general terms *neuroendocrine tumor* and *neuroendocrine carcinoma* were introduced. Based on a combination of the classic growth and microscopic structural criteria and the value of the immunohistochemistry using the proliferation index (PI) Ki67 or the conventional mitotic index, benign NE tumors are distinguished from those with uncertain malignant potential and from NE neoplasms displaying low-grade and high-grade malignancy (i.e., highly and poorly differentiated NE carcinomas, respectively).[23]

Thus, for the GEP NE neoplasms, the current classification is:

1. Well-differentiated endocrine tumor (PI <2%)
2. Well-differentiated endocrine carcinoma (PI >2% but <15%)
3. Poorly differentiated endocrine carcinoma (PI >15%)
4. Mixed exocrine/endocrine tumors
5. Tumor-like lesions

As a rule, an NE tumor belonging to group 1 shows all the classic structural features of a benign neoplasm. It is small (<2 cm), well delineated, mostly restricted to the mucosa and the submucosa, displaying no angioinvasion, and being composed of highly differentiated NE cells with a PI <2%. Typical examples are a classic carcinoid of in the tip of the appendix or an incidentally detected trabecular carcinoid of the lower rectum. Some ileal "classic" carcinoids also belong to this group of neoplasms.

The neoplastic lesions of group 2 are usually larger than 2 cm, display widely invasive growth, often have angioinvasion, but are still composed of highly differentiated NE cells with a PI slightly greater than 2%. Typical examples are an ileal classic carcinoid, when discovered by means of clinical symptoms and some so-called foregut carcinoids (lung carcinoids). The NE tumors of group 3 represent a neoplasm with all the characteristic features of a highly malignant carcinoma, being large with extensive angioinvasion (and metastases), and composed of neoplastic NE cells that display severe atypia and a PI high above 15%. Typical examples are the small cell ("oat cell") carcinomas of the bronchi.

Histologic classification is based largely on characteristic cytochemical staining. Carcinoid tumors are routinely stained with antibodies to chromogranin A, synaptophysin, and neuron-specific enolase (NSE; NE markers). The NE tumors belonging to the midgut region, so-called classic carcinoids, also are stained for serotonin. Besides staining with the specific NE markers described earlier, current histopathologic analysis should include staining for the proliferation marker Ki67 and, if possible, also for the expression of somatostatin receptors, which are particularly important for decisions about future treatment. Carcinoid tumors exhibit substantial differences in terms of genotype and phenotype. NE tumors of the foregut area, mainly pulmonary, frequently show losses of chromosome 11q, which represent a characteristic alteration of these tumors.[24] Both typical and atypical carcinoids of the lungs show loss of heterozygosity at 11q13, a region that harbors the *MEN1* gene. Atypical carcinoids also show loss of heterozygosity as at 3p14-p21.3. Tumor biology parameters such as CD44, nM-23, and Ki67 may provide valuable prognostic information and help to identify the patients at risk of disease-related death.[25] Recent studies show that carcinoid tumors of the lung and GI tract may develop via different molecular pathways. Inactivation of several different tumor-suppressor genes on chromosome 18 may be important for the biologic behavior of the GI tumors.[26] Analysis of rectal carcinoids reveals no abnormalities in proliferation, but impaired apoptosis. Transforming growth factor alpha (TGF-α) and epithelial growth factor receptor (EGFR) autocrine mechanisms have been implicated. Poorly differentiated carcinoid tumors demonstrated frequent loss of heterozygozity for *p21, DCC,* and *APC* tumor-suppressor genes.[27] Expression of thyroid transcription factor 1 may indicate a bronchial origin of the carcinoid.[28] Familial midgut carcinoids are rare, but bronchial carcinoids may be part of the MEN1 syndrome.[29]

## CLINICAL FEATURES OF CARCINOID TUMORS

NE tumors of the foregut region usually have a low serotonin/5-hydroxytryptamine (5-HT) content and often secrete precursors of 5-HT such as 5-hydroxytryptophan (5-HTP) but also histamine and a multitude of polypeptide hormones.[30] Such polypeptide hormones include corticotropin-releasing factor (CRF), adrenocorticotropin (ACTH), growth hormone–releasing hormone (GHRH), antidiuretic hormone (ADH), gastrin, somatostatin, glucagon, tachykinins, and chromogranin A. The carcinoid syndrome is sometimes seen in patients with a lung carcinoid with secretion of serotonin, 5-HTP, or histamine.[31,32] Midgut carcinoids are responsible for the majority of patients with the classic carcinoid syndrome.[32,33] They contain peptides and amines and secrete serotonin, tachykinins, and chromogranin A. Hindgut NE tumors only rarely have a carcinoid syndrome, but they contain GI hormones such as chromogranin A, pancreatic polypeptide, peptide YY, and somatostatin.

## THE CARCINOID SYNDROME

The classic carcinoid syndrome includes flushing (80%), diarrhea (70%), abdominal pain (40%), valvular heart disease (40% to 45%), teleangiectasia (25%), wheezing (15%), and pellagra-like skin lesions (5%).[32-34] The carcinoid syndrome, first described in 1954 by Thorson and coworkers,[6] has the following features: A malignant carcinoid of the small intestine with metastases to the liver, valvular disease of the right side of the heart (pulmonary stenosis and tricuspid insufficiency without septal defects), peripheral vasomotor symptoms, bronchial constriction, and an unusual type of cyanosis. One year later, Dr. William Bean[35] gave this colorful description of the carcinoid syndrome:

> This witch's brew of unlikely signs and symptoms, intriguing to the most fastidious connoisseur of clinical esoterica—the

skin underwent rapid and extreme changes resembling in clinical miniature the fecal phantasmagoria of the aurora borealis.

Lembeck[5] had already in 1953 demonstrated the presence of serotonin in carcinoid tumor, and most of the symptoms of the carcinoid syndrome were ascribed to the release of serotonin. In 1986, the release of tachykinins from carcinoid tumors and the significance of the carcinoid flush were reported.[8]

## FLUSHING

Four different types of flushing have been described in the literature. The first type (Fig. 194-2) is the diffuse, erythematous flush, usually affecting the face, neck, and upper chest (i.e., normal flushing area). This flush is commonly of short duration, lasting from 1 to 5 minutes, and is related to early stages of malignant midgut carcinoids. The second type (Fig. 194-3) is violaceous flush, which affects the same areas of the body and has roughly the same time course or sometimes lasts a little longer. These patients also may have facial telangiectasia. This flush is related to the later stages of malignant midgut carcinoids and is normally not felt by the patients because they have become accustomed to the flushing reaction. The third type (Fig. 194-4) is prolonged flushing, lasting for hours up to several days. It sometimes involves the whole body and is associated with profuse lacrimation, swelling of the salivary glands, hypotension, and facial edema. These symptoms are usually associated with malignant bronchial carcinoids. Finally, the fourth type (Fig. 194-5) of flushing reaction is bright red, patchy flushing, which is seen in patients with chronic atrophic gastritis and ECLomas (derived from

*Figure 194-3* Patient with midgut carcinoid with chronic flushing (type 2) and characteristic telangiectasia of the nose.

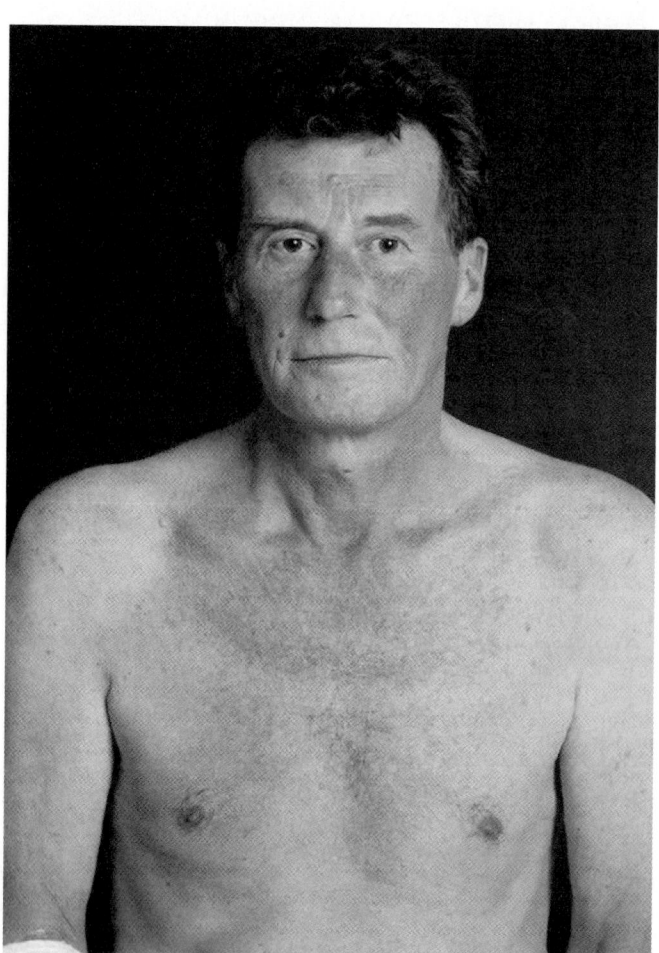

*Figure 194-2* Patient with midgut carcinoid and a typical flush (type 1).

enterochromaffin-like cells) of the gastric mucosa with evidence of increased histamine production.[31–36]

The facial flushing associated with carcinoid tumors should be distinguished from other causes of flushes (see Tables 194-1 to 194-4).The carcinoid flush is provoked by spicy food, alcohol, physical and psychological stress, and is often worse in the morning. Patients with idiopathic flushes usually have a long history of flushing, starting rather early in life and sometimes with a family history without occurrence of a tumor. Menopausal flushes usually involve the whole body and might be related to release of calcitonin gene–related peptide (CGRP) with transient vasodilation, a so-called dry flush. Another type of menopausal symptom is the wet flush, which includes epinephrine-induced sweating.[37,38] Proposed mediators of flushing in the menopause are CGRP, histamine, prostaglandins, serotonin, lysyl-bradykinin, and substance P. Estrogen is known to have an impact on the production and release of different signaling substances such as noradrenaline and β-endorphin. Low estrogen levels cause lower β-endorphin activity, which in turn enhances the release of gonadotropin-releasing hormone (GnRH), which gives rise to high luteinizing hormone (LH) levels.[39] Postmenopausal women in whom a true carcinoid syndrome is developing can tell the difference between the two types of flushes. Sometimes patients with medullary thyroid carcinoma have brief flushes provoked by alcohol. In patients with watery diarrhea, hypokalemia, achlorhydria

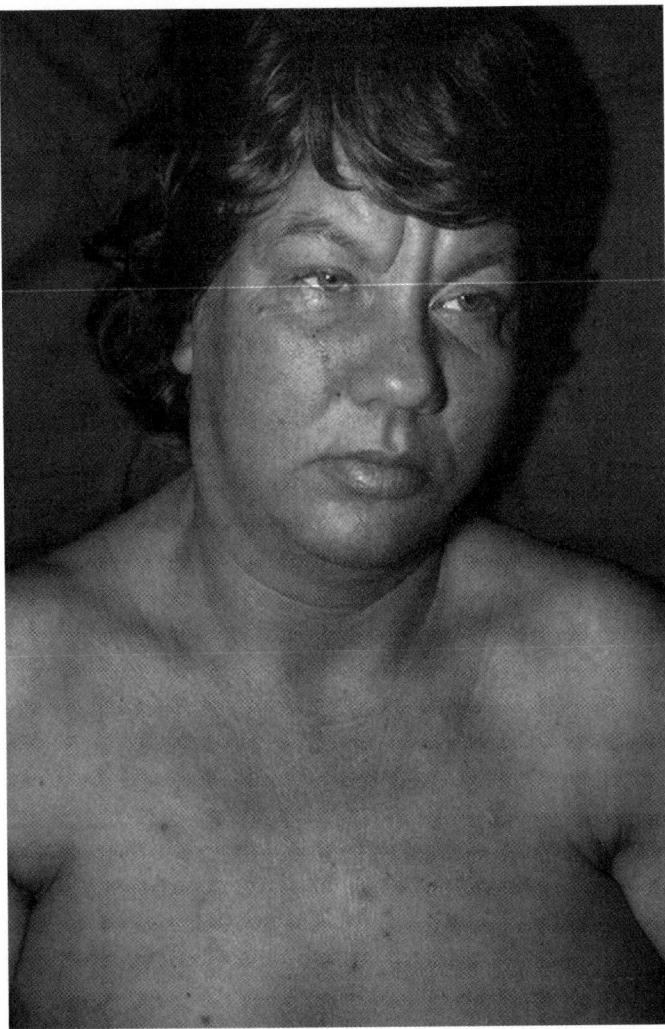

**Figure 194-4** Patient with a lung carcinoid with production of histamine as well as serotonin. Notice the lacrimation and swollen lips in addition to the flush (type 3).

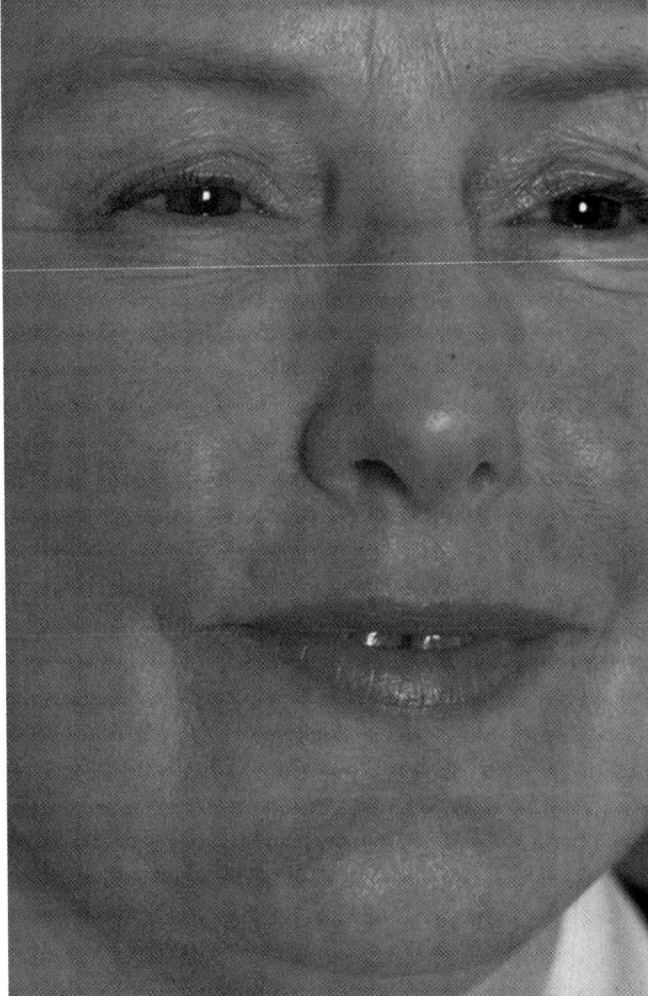

**Figure 194-5** Patient with gastric carcinoid (enterochromaffin-like [ECL]-oma) with histamine production and typical bright-red flushing (type 4).

| *Table 194-1* Flushing Reaction: Differential Diagnosis |
| --- |
| Menopause |
| Carcinoid syndrome |
| Mastocytosis |
| Medullary thyroid carcinoma |
| WDHA syndrome (watery diarrhea, hypokalemia, achlorhydria) |
| Pheochromocytoma |
| Neurologic disorders |
| Drugs |
| Food |
| Ethanol |
| Idiopathic |

| *Table 194-2* Drugs Causing Flushes |
| --- |
| Bromocriptine |
| Tamoxifen |
| Nicotinic acid |
| Opiates |
| Calcium channel blockers |
| Ketoconazole |
| Chlorpromazine |
| Cephalosporin |

| *Table 194-3* Food Causing Flushes |
| --- |
| Spicy food |
| Glutamate |
| Sodium nitrate |
| Sulfites |
| Hot beverages |

| *Table 194-4* Neurologic Disorders Causing Flushes |
| --- |
| Anxiety |
| Migraine |
| Parkinson's disease |
| Spinal cord lesions |
| Brain tumors |

syndrome (WDHA; vasoactive intestinal peptide [VIP]omas), a purple-red constant flushing of the whole body may develop. This flushing reaction is related to the vasodilator effects of VIP. Flushes seen in mastocytosis are related to release of histamine from mast cell granules. Mastocytosis is a rare disease of mast cell proliferation that occurs both cutaneously and systemically.[40,41] In addition to the content of histamine and heparin, the mast cell granules contain arachidonic acid, which can be released and metabolized to prostaglandin $D_2$ ($PGD_2$). Involvement of skin in mastocytosis causes urticaria pigmentosa, which is present in 99% of all mastocytosis (Darier's sign). The diagnosis is based on urinary histamine metabolite determination, urinary $PGD_2$ metabolites, and a tissue biopsy.[42]

The exact cause of flushing in the carcinoid syndrome is not yet fully elucidated. It was previously thought to be related to excess production of serotonin, but some patients with high levels of serotonin do not have any flushing, and serotonin antagonists such as methysergide, cyproheptadine, and ketanserin have little effect on the flushing.[32,33,36,43] In a study from our group in which we measured the release of tachykinins (neuropeptide K and substance P) during flushing provoked by pentagastrin or alcohol, a clear correlation was found between the onset and intensity of the flushing reactions and the release of tachykinins. Furthermore, when the release of the tachykinins was blocked by prestimulatory administration of octreotide, very little or no flushing was observed in the same patient. Others also reported tachykinins as possible mediators of the carcinoid flush.[44,45] Another mediator of the flushing reaction may be bradykinin, which also has been shown to be released during provoked flushing.[34,46] Histamine may be a mediator of the flushes seen in both lung carcinoids and gastric carcinoids. Tachykinins, bradykinins, and histamine are known vasodilators, and somatostatin analogues may relieve flushing by reducing circulating levels of these agents.[47] An interesting theory by Furchgott and Zawadski[48] is that indirect vasodilation is mediated by endothelium-derived relaxing factor or nitric oxide released by 5-HTP during platelet activation and may be a possible cause of flushing.[48]

## DIARRHEA

Diarrhea occurs in 30% to 80% of patients with the carcinoid syndrome. Its pathophysiology is poorly understood but is probably multifactorial. A variety of tumor products, including serotonin, tachykinins, histamine, kallikrein, and prostaglandins can stimulate peristalsis, electromechanical activity, and tone in the intestine. A secretory diarrhea may occur.[49,50] Malabsorption may result from intestinal resections, lymphangiectasia secondary to mesenteric fibrosis, bacterial overgrowth secondary to a tumor partially obstructing the small bowel, or rapid intestinal transit. Increased secretion by the small bowel, malabsorption, or accelerated transit may overwhelm the normal storage and absorptive capacity of the proximal colon and result in diarrhea, which may be aggravated if the reabsorptive function of the colon is impaired.[51] In patients with increased urinary 5-HIAA and carcinoid syndrome, the transit time in the small bowel and colon is increased in comparison with that of normal subjects; the volume of the ascending colon is smaller than that in normal subjects, and the postprandial colonic tone is markedly increased. These findings indicate that, in patients in whom the carcinoid syndrome is associated with diarrhea, major alterations in gut motor function occur that affect both the small intestine and colon.[52] Because many patients with carcinoid tumors undergo wide resection of the small intestine at an earlier stage, they may be affected by the symptoms of short bowel syndrome.

## CARCINOID HEART DISEASE

Carcinoid heart disease occurs in 57% to 77% of patients with the carcinoid syndrome but is hemodynamically significant in a much smaller percentage (< 15%). The carcinoid heart lesions are characterized by plaquelike fibrous and cardiac thickening that classically involves the right side of the heart (approximately 10% affecting the left side). The finding of new collagen beneath the endothelium of the endocardium is almost pathognomonic for carcinoid heart disease. Echocardiography can demonstrate early lesions in about 70% of patients with carcinoid syndrome, whereas routine clinical examination detects them in only 10% to 15%.[53–57] Currently, carcinoid heart disease is a rare event, probably due to earlier diagnosis of carcinoid tumors, but also because of more effective treatment, such as somatostatin analogues and alpha interferons, which block the release of substances causing the fibrosis. The most common lesion is tricuspid insufficiency, followed by tricuspid stenosis, pulmonary regurgitation, and pulmonary stenosis. Patients with carcinoid heart disease have significantly higher 5-HIAA levels and tachykinin levels, suggesting that these substances released into the circulation might play a role.[53] The precise mechanism behind the fibrosis in the right side of the heart has not been established, but it occurs mainly in patients with liver metastases, who usually also have carcinoid syndrome. Substances inducing fibrosis are thought to be released directly into the right side of the heart and then neutralized or degraded through the pulmonary circulation, because rather few patients have similar lesions on the left side. However, patients with lung carcinoid occasionally displayed the same fibrotic changes on the left side. The TGF-β family of growth factors is upregulated in carcinoid fibrous plaques on the right side of the heart, and these growth factors are known to participate in matrix formation and collagen deposition.[58] The substances that induce TGF-β locally are not known, but both serotonin and tachykinins might be involved. Another possible mediator might be insulin-like growth factor 1 (IGF-1), which is released from carcinoid tumor cells. Treatment with somatostatin analogues downregulates circulating IGF-1 and may prevent further development of carcinoid heart disease (clinical observations).

## BRONCHIAL CONSTRICTION

True asthma is rare in patients with carcinoid syndrome. The causative agent for bronchial constriction is not known, but both tachykinins and bradykinins have been suggested as mediators. These agents can constrict smooth muscle in the respiratory tract and also cause local edema in the airways.[59,60]

## OTHER MANIFESTATIONS OF THE CARCINOID SYNDROME

Fibrotic complications other than heart lesions may be found in patients with carcinoid tumors. These include intra-abdominal and retroperitoneal fibrosis, occlusion of the mesenteric arteries and veins, Peyroni's disease of the penis, and carcinoid arthropathy. Intra-abdominal fibrosis can lead to intestinal adhesions and bowel obstruction and is indeed a more frequent cause of bowel obstruction than is the primary carcinoid tumor. Retroperitoneal fibrosis can result in ureteral obstruction that impairs kidney function and sometimes requires treatment with ureteral stents. Narrowing and occlusion of arteries and veins by fibrosis is potentially life threatening. Ischemic loops of small bowel occasionally have to be removed, which ultimately causes short bowel syndrome. Other rare features of the carcinoid syndrome are pellagra-like skin lesions with hyperkeratosis and pigmentation, myopathy, and sexual dysfunction.[61,62]

## DIAGNOSIS OF CARCINOID TUMORS AND THE CARCINOID SYNDROME

### BIOCHEMICAL DIAGNOSIS

In all types of carcinoid tumors, high levels of chromogranin A, pancreatic polypeptide (PP), and α and β human chorionic gonadotropin subunits may be found.[25,30,63–67] Patients with NE tumors of the midgut carcinoids have increased

5-HT production, and elevated 5-HT levels can be measured directly in the plasma or indirectly via the 5-HT metabolite, 5-HIAA, in the urine (Fig. 194-6).[30] Elevated 24-hour urinary 5-HIAA levels have 73% sensitivity and 100% specificity in predicting the presence of a carcinoid tumor of the midgut area. Patients with foregut carcinoids rarely secrete 5-HT but may release ACTH, GHRH, histamine, and high levels of chromogranin A.[25] Patients with hindgut carcinoids rarely have elevated levels of tumor markers, even in the presence of metastatic tissues. However, increased levels of PP and chromogranin A are found in a majority of these patients.[68] Plasma chromogranin A is increased in more than 80% of patients with NE GI tumors and is the best general tumor marker (Fig. 194-7). It also appears to correlate with tumor load and can therefore be used to predict prognosis, particularly in patients with classic midgut carcinoids.[33] Elevation of chromogranin A levels can precede radiographic evidence of occurrence in different types of GI NE tumors. This may prove useful in diagnosis; chromogranin A may be elevated in 93% of patients with metastatic pulmonary carcinoid.[25] The sensitivity and specificity are approximately 92% and 96%, respectively, which is better than for neuron-specific enolase (NSE) or α–human chorionic gonadotropin (hCG) testing.[69] False-positive tests can occur in patients with reduced kidney function or inflammatory bowel disease. It must be remembered that treatment with somatostatin analogues can reduce the levels of chromogranin A but do not necessarily reduce the tumor mass.

Measurement of 5-HIAA in the urine is very sensitive for a patient with a classic midgut carcinoid.[30] Collection of urine should be performed during diet restriction, taking away bananas, chocolate, tea, coffee, walnuts, and spicy food (see Table 194-4). Measurement of urine 5-HIAA for diagnosis of carcinoid tumor is the predominant biochemical analytic procedure. However, urinary and platelet measurement of serotonin in cells may give additional information.[30] In some studies, platelet serotonin levels were more sensitive than urinary 5-HIAA and urinary serotonin levels and were not affected by the patient's diet, as are 5-HIAA levels.[30] Elevation of 5-HIAA can occur in malabsorption states and in a number of other conditions. Foregut carcinoids tend to produce an atypical carcinoid syndrome with increased plasma 5-HTP but not serotonin, because they lack the appropriate decarboxylase, resulting in normal urinary 5-HIAA levels. However, some of the 5-HTP is decarboxylated in the intestine and

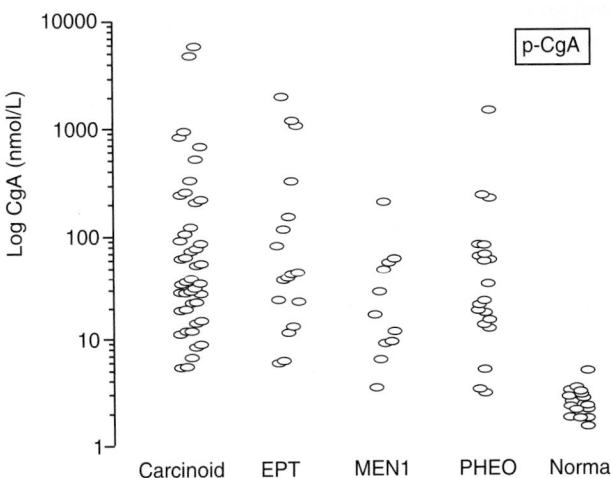

**Figure 194-7** Plasma levels of chromogranin A in patients with carcinoids, patients with endocrine pancreatic tumors (EPTs), patients with multiple endocrine neoplasia type 1 (MEN1), pheochromocytoma (PHEO), and normal controls.

other tissues, and many of these patients have slightly elevated U-5HT or 5-HIAA levels.[30] Tables 194-5 and 194-6 summarize factors that interfere with determination of urinary 5-HIAA.

## IMAGING PROCEDURES

Many radiologic techniques have been used to localize and image carcinoid tumors. However, their utility is dependent on tumor size and location.[70,71] [[111]In]-trisodium zinc diethylenetriaminepentaacetate (DTPA)-octreotide is now used routinely to stage carcinoid tumor and to monitor patients to detect tumor regrowth or new occurrences of metastasis (Fig. 194-8).[70-76] Bronchial carcinoids are detected by computed tomography (CT) or magnetic resonance imaging (MRI), which can be combined with fine-needle aspiration cytology.[70,71] Bronchoscopy also can demonstrate the presence of a bronchial carcinoid. Positron emission tomography with radiolabeled [[11]C]5-HTP may be useful in detecting midgut as well as bronchial carcinoid tumors (Fig. 194-9).[77] Malignant carcinoids with high proliferation capacity might be detected with fluorodeoxyglucose–positron emission

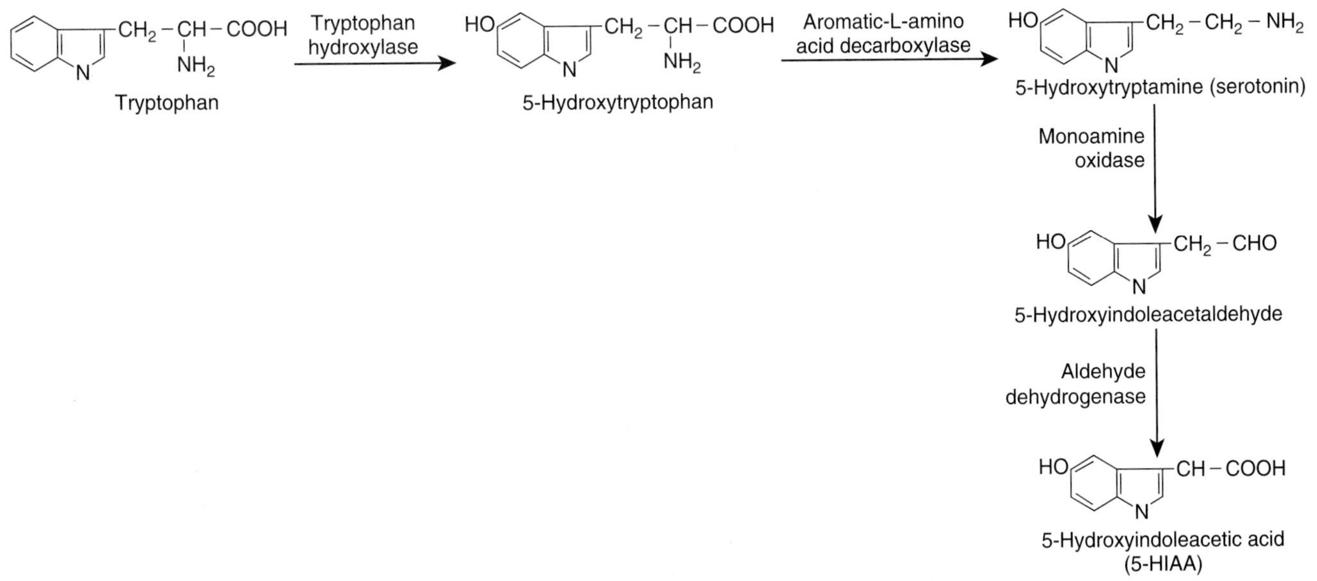

**Figure 194-6** Schematic drawing of the serotonin synthesis.

**Table 194-5** Factors That Produce False-Positive Results

Foods
- Banana
- Chocolate
- Coffee
- Tea
- Walnuts
- Avocado
- Pecan
- Pineapple
- Plum

Drugs
- Fluorouracil
- L-Dopa
- Melphalan
- Salicylates
- Caffeine
- Acetaminophen
- Reserpine

**Table 194-6** Factors That Cause False-Negative Results

Corticotropin
P-chlorophenylalanine
Heparin
Chlorpromazine
Imipramine
Methyldopa
Monoamine oxidase inhibitors
Phenothiazine

tomography (FDG-PET).[78] Gastric carcinoids are usually diagnosed with endoscopy or endosonography, which should be combined with CT scanning of the abdomen. In general, midgut carcinoid tumors, regardless of their functional status, are diagnosed when they have already metastasized. Scintigraphy with [¹¹¹In]-DTPA-octreotide is currently the investigation of choice and is used for staging and identification of the primary lesions.[75] Somatostatin receptor scintigraphy has an 83% diagnostic accuracy and positive predictive value of 100%. It also can identify lesions that are not seen with other imaging modalities. Transabdominal ultrasound identifies approximately a fourth of small bowel carcinoids and the majority of liver metastases, and it also may be used to guide percutaneous biopsies of liver tumors. CT and MRI are less sensitive than somatostatin-receptor scintigraphy and identify only approximately 50% of primary tumors.[70,71] For patients with hindgut tumors, somatostatin-receptor scintigraphy shows high sensitivity, although these tumors also can be localized with endoscopic ultrasonography or MRI. [¹³¹I]metaiodobenzyl guanidine (MIBG) has been used for localization and treatment of carcinoid tumors. However, the sensitivity is lower than that of [¹¹¹In]-DTPA-octreotide.[79]

### DIAGNOSTIC ALGORITHM FOR CARCINOID TUMORS

The diagnostic algorithm for carcinoid tumors is shown in Figure 194-10.

## TREATMENT OF CARCINOID FLUSH

Depending on the type and stage of the tumor causing the carcinoid flush, different therapeutic strategies can be chosen.

### SURGERY

In patients with the carcinoid flush, curative surgical procedures can be performed on tumors located within the bronchus, stomach (ECL-omas), ovary, or testis, because these tend to spread locally, without distant metastases. In general, carcinoid tumors that release bioactive substances directly into the systemic circulation tend to produce early symptoms, resulting in early detection and possibility of cure.

The majority of patients with the carcinoid flush are first seen with multiple liver metastases of a midgut carcinoid, but still surgery should be considered, because debulking large liver metastases may reduce hormonal symptoms and facilitate medical treatment.[80]

### HEPATIC ARTERY EMBOLIZATION

Because NE tumors are highly vascularized tumors deriving most of the blood supply from the hepatic artery, patients with liver metastases may undergo hepatic artery emboliza-

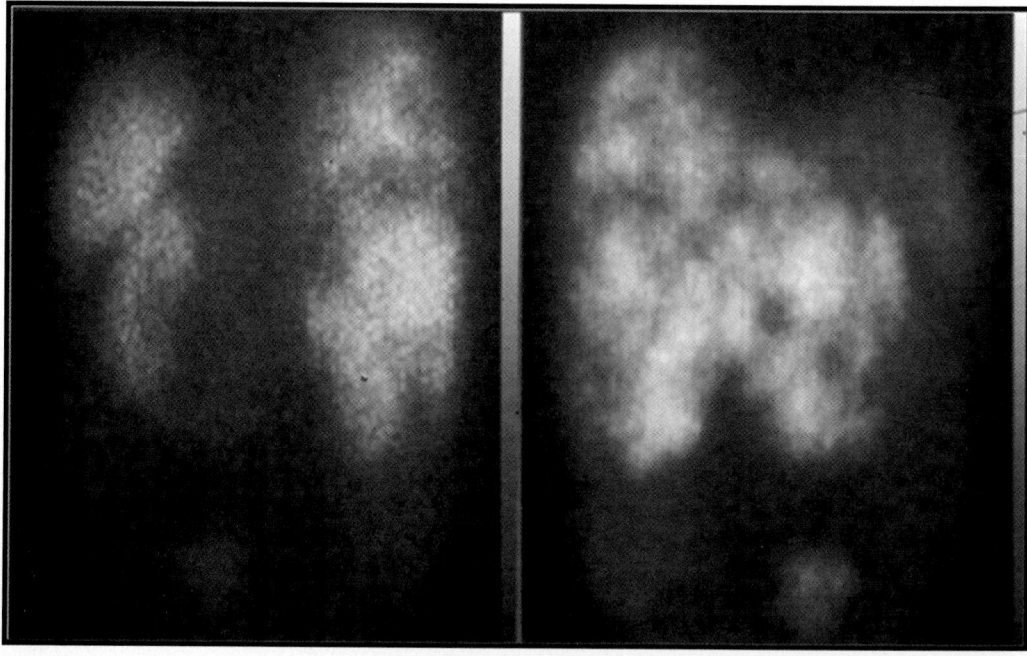

*Figure 194-8* Patient with midgut carcinoid with liver metastases. Notice the increased tracer uptake in the mesenteric root, representing lymph nodes.

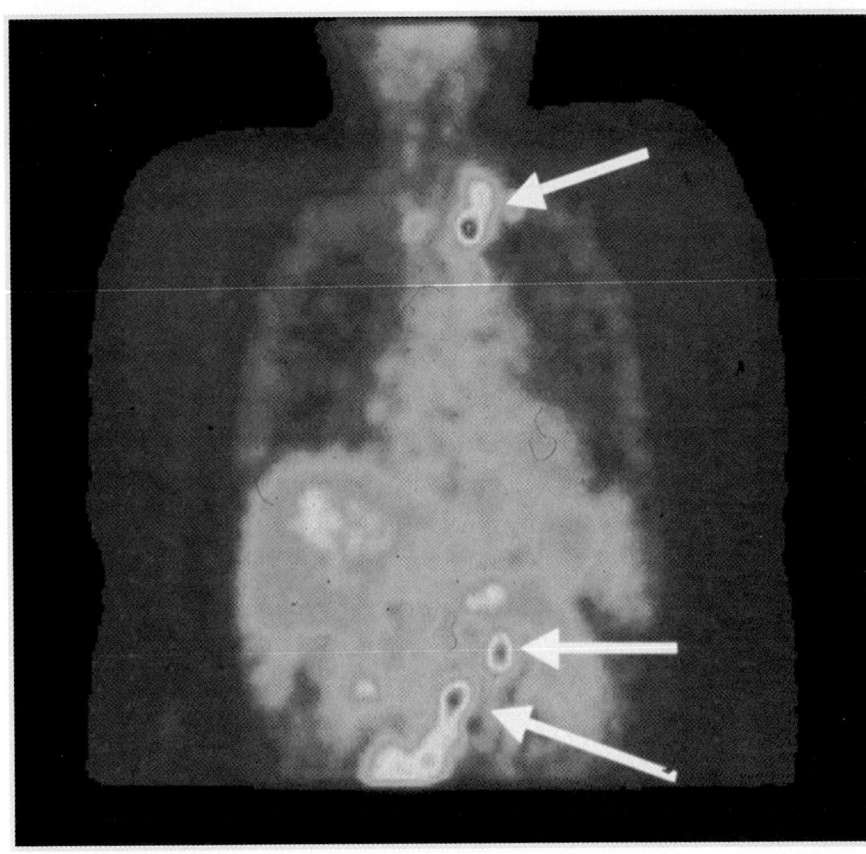

*Figure 194-9*  Patient with carcinoid and lymph node metastases (*arrows*) detected by [$^{11}$C]5-hydroxytryptamine (HTP) positron emission tomography (PET) but with no other method.

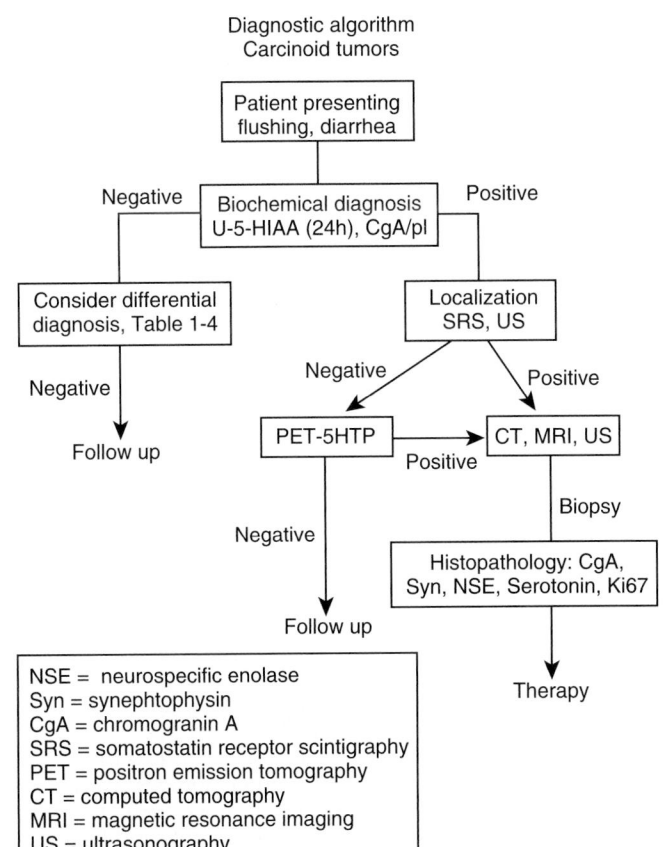

*Figure 194-10*  Diagnostic algorithm for the carcinoid syndrome.

Diagnostic algorithm
Carcinoid tumors

Patient presenting flushing, diarrhea

Biochemical diagnosis U-5-HIAA (24h), CgA/pl

Negative → Consider differential diagnosis, Table 1-4 → Negative → Follow up

Positive → Localization SRS, US

Negative → PET-5HTP

Positive → CT, MRI, US

PET-5HTP Positive → CT, MRI, US

Negative → Follow up

Biopsy → Histopathology: CgA, Syn, NSE, Serotonin, Ki67 → Therapy

NSE = neurospecific enolase
Syn = synephtophysin
CgA = chromogranin A
SRS = somatostatin receptor scintigraphy
PET = positron emission tomography
CT = computed tomography
MRI = magnetic resonance imaging
US = ultrasonography

tion. The rationale is the dual blood supply of normal liver, receiving 25% of its blood supply from the hepatic artery, whereas 75% is supplied by the portal vein. Peripheral embolization is usually preferred, because it can be repeated.

Symptomatic and biochemical responses (40% to 90%) can be prompt (within hours to days), more frequent than radiologic responses (15% to 40%).[80-82] Side effects include the postembolic syndrome with pain, fever, nausea, leukocytosis, and increases in liver enzymes in 50% to 90%. Severe complications are seen in 10% of patients (e.g., renal failure, liver necrosis, intestinal ischemia, cholecystitis), and the mortality rate is 3% to 7%.[81,82]

In light of the significant toxicity, patient selection is important. Severe carcinoid heart disease and impaired liver function are contraindications to performing the procedure.

### RADIOFREQUENCY ABLATION

Radiofrequency ablation can be used to reduce the tumor burden in the liver. Usually, patients with smaller lesions (<4 cm) and a limited number of liver metastases (fewer than eight) are chosen. It can be performed at laparotomy, laparoscopically, or percutaneously.

Symptomatic improvement can be achieved in 95% of the patients, and a partial decrease in tumor markers is observed in 65% in the largest series. During a median follow-up of 1.6 years, 41% of patients showed no progression. In experienced hands, the mortality and morbidity are low (5%).[83]

### SOMATOSTATIN ANALOGUES

Native somatostatin reduces symptoms in patients with the carcinoid syndrome.[47] However, its use is limited by its short half-life (~2 minutes). With the availability of synthetic long-acting somatostatin analogues, octreotide (half-life, 90 minutes)[84] and lanreotide, subcutaneous treatment can be given.[85] Long-acting somatostatin analogues are now the drugs of choice to control the symptoms of the carcinoid syndrome, including flush.[86–98]

Somatostatin analogues bind to specific somatostatin receptors (sst1–5)[99–102] on the tumor cells and are present in 80% to 90% of NE tumors.[103,104] Sst2 is believed to mediate the biochemical response via cyclic adenosine monophosphate (cAMP), resulting in decreased secretion. Octreotide was the first somatostatin analogue. It came into clinical use in the early 1980s, and it decreases the release of serotonin and neuropeptide K (NPK) and other peptide markers by a direct action on tumor cells.

Octreotide scintigraphy (Octreoscan), based on the presence of somatostatin receptors in 80% to 90% of tumors, has been used diagnostically for localization and staging.[104] Octreoscan-positive tumors express sst2, which has been shown to predict sensitivity to somatostatin analogue treatment.[105] However, some patients with Octreoscan-negative tumors respond symptomatically, suggesting direct effects of somatostatin analogues on peripheral target organs (intestine, skin).

In a meta-analysis of 62 published studies,[106] octreotide controlled symptoms in more than 80% of patients. If doses of more 400 μg/day are given, flushing is controlled in more than 89% of patients. About 70% of patients have a biochemical response (i.e., >50% reduction in U-5-HIAA), whereas fewer than 10% of patients show a significant tumor reduction. As maintenance treatment, octreotide is given subcutaneously two to three times a day at doses of 50 to 500 μg. Individual responses vary, and some patients may require more than 3000 μg/day. Forty percent of patients escape from control after a median of 5 months, with the remaining patients having sustained control for up to 2.5 years.

In patients with life-threatening carcinoid crises (profound hypotension with flushing), somatostatin analogues can be given intravenously (octreotide, 100 to 200 μg/hour), which usually relieves the crises.[107–109] Somatostatin analogues also should be given to prevent the development of such carcinoid crises during interventional procedures, including surgery, anesthesia, chemotherapy, or stress.

Slow-release formulations of somatostatin analogues obviate the need for multiple daily injections. These include octreotide-LAR,[110] lanreotide autogel[111] (every 4 weeks), and lanreotide-PR[89] (every 10 to 14 days), given intramuscularly. These agents seem to be as effective as nondepot formulations at controlling symptoms.

Initial mild side effects, subsiding within a few days to weeks, occur in 40% to 50% of patients.[86,89,112] Pain at the injection site and effects related to the GI tract (abdominal discomfort in >50% and nausea in 15%) are most common but rarely necessitate the discontinuation of treatment. Long-term side effects include the development of biliary sludge or gallstones in more than 50% of patients, but fewer than 7% have symptoms.[113] Steatorrhea may be a problem in some patients and may necessitate pancreatic enzyme replacement. More uncommon side effects are hypokalemia and bradycardia.

## INTERFERON ALPHA

Interferon alpha was introduced in the treatment of midgut carcinoids in the early 1980s.[114] It exerts several direct effects on tumor cells (i.e., blocking the cell cycle in the $G_1$/S phase, inhibition of angiogenic factors, and inhibition of protein and hormone synthesis).

In several different studies, the average symptomatic response rate is 40% to 60%, biochemical responses (>50 reduction in U-5-HIAA) are seen in 30% to 60%, and tumor reduction (>50%) in 10% to 15%. Flushing has been reported to improve in 50% to 70% of patients.[115–122]

Initially, human leukocyte interferon was used, but today mainly recombinant interferon alpha is used (Intron-A, Roferon). The dose should be individually titrated in each patient. Low to moderate doses should be used, because no dose/response relation exists. The dose of regular interferon alpha should be 3 to 5 million units (MU) 3 to 5 times per week subcutaneously. Pegylated interferon alpha also is available as long-acting once-weekly formulations (Peg-Introna, Pegasys). The exact dose of pegylated interferon has not been established.

Interferon treatment is associated with more side effects than are somatostatin analogues.[115–122] Most patients experience flulike symptoms and fever during the first 3 to 4 days. The most severe side effects are chronic fatigue (in 30% to 75% of patients) and mental depression (5% to 10% of patients). Other side effects are bone marrow suppression and increased liver enzymes in 10% to 30%, which do not require interruption of treatment. Development of autoimmune disorders such as systemic lupus erythematosus (SLE) syndrome, myositis, and vasculitis necessitates discontinuation of treatment, whereas autoimmune thyroiditis does not. History of manic-depressive disease, SLE, rheumatoid arthritis, and psoriasis are contraindications to interferon treatment.

## COMBINATION OF SOMATOSTATIN ANALOGUES AND INTERFERON ALPHA

Because of their separate tumoristatic effect and ability to control symptoms, the combination of octreotide and interferon alpha has been studied in patients for whom monotherapy with interferon alone[123] or octreotide alone[92,124] does not control the disease. Hormonal symptoms, including flush, were more effectively controlled, and biochemical response rates were achieved in 77%, 72%, and 75% of patients. No objective tumor regression was observed. However, in the latter study, the combination caused inhibition of tumor growth and stabilization over a median period of 12 months in 67% of patients.

## OTHER SYMPTOMATIC THERAPIES

Before the introduction of somatostatin analogues and interferon in the treatment of NE tumors, other drugs, mainly agents inhibiting serotonin synthesis or serotonin antagonists were used to control symptoms, including flush. Parachlorophenylalanine, which blocks the conversion of tryptophan to 5-HTP, relieves diarrhea and improves flushing in some patients, but the side effects make it intolerable for long-term treatment.[125] The $5\text{-}HT_1$ and $5\text{-}HT_2$ cyproheptadine (Periactin) and ketanserin frequently decrease diarrhea but usually do not decrease the flushing.[126,127] The $5\text{-}HT_3$-receptor antagonists (ondansetron, tropisetron, alosetron) usually control diarrhea and occasionally flushing.[128]

In foregut carcinoids (gastric and bronchial) with a histamine-mediated flush, histamine $H_1$- and $H_2$-receptor antagonists can be effective in controlling the so-called "atypical carcinoid syndrome," which includes severe flushing and swelling of the face, lacrimation, and diarrhea.[129] Somatostatin analogues also are often required.

Prednisone, in doses of 20 to 30 mg/day, gives occasional relief in some cases with severe flushing.

## RADIOLABELED SOMATOSTATIN ANALOGUES

During the last few years, treatment with radiolabeled somatostatin analogues as "tumor-targeted" therapy has been introduced. Initially, the same isotope as in octreotide scintigraphy (i.e., $^{111}$In) was used,[130] but recently other isotopes, which can deliver higher irradiation doses to the tumors, such as $^{90}$Y and $^{177}$Lu, have been used.[131] Although the exact role and timing of this treatment is not yet established, prompt symptomatic and some biochemical and antitumoral effects have been reported.

## CONCLUSION

In conclusion, the approach in treating carcinoid flush should include avoiding precipitating food and alcohol. Somatostatin analogues are the drugs of choice, and if tachyphylaxis develops, increases in dose can be attempted. If this strategy is ineffective, interferon alone, or combined interferon and somatostatin analogies, should be considered. In patients with flush caused by a foregut carcinoid, $H_1$- and $H_2$-receptor blockers can be added.

Last, although most patients will require medical therapy, surgical procedures to remove solitary tumors or debulk large metastases should be considered, along with other means of reducing the tumor burden in the liver, such as embolization and radiofrequency ablation.

## REFERENCES

1. Lubarsch O: Ueber den primaren Krebs des Ileum, nebst Bemerkungen über das gleichzeitige Vorkommen von Krebs und Tuberkuolose. Virchow Arch Pathol Anat Physiol Klin Med 111:280–317, 1867.
2. Ransom W: A case of primary carcinoma of the ileum. Lancet 2:1020–1023, 1890.
3. Oberndorfer S: Karzenoide Tumoren des Dünndarms. Frankf Zschr Pathol 1:426–430, 1907.
4. Gosset A, Masson, P: Tumeurs endocrines de l'appendice. Presse Med 25:237–239, 1914.
5. Lembeck F: 5-Hydroxytryptamine in carcinoid tumor. Nature 172:910–911, 1943.
6. Thorson A, Biorck G, Bjorkman G, Waldenstrom J: Malignant carcinoid of the small intestine with metastases to the liver, valvular disease of the right side of the heart (pulmonary stenosis and tricuspid regurgitation without septal defects), peripheral vasomotor symptoms, bronchoconstriction, and an unusual type of cyanosis: A clinical and pathologic syndrome. Am Heart J 47:795–817, 1954.
7. Williams ED, Sandler M: The classification of carcinoid tumours. Lancet 1:238–239, 1963.
8. Norheim I, Theodorsson-Norheim E, Brodin E, Oberg K: Tachykinins in carcinoid tumors: Their use as a tumor marker and possible role in the carcinoid flush. J Clin Endocrinol Metab 63:605–612, 1986.
9. Modlin IM, Lye KD, Kidd M: A 5-decade analysis of 13,715 carcinoid tumors. Cancer 97:934–959, 2003.
10. Hemminki K, Li X: Incidence trends and risk factors of carcinoid tumors: A nationwide epidemiologic study from Sweden. Cancer 92:2204–2210, 2001.
11. Berge T, Linell F: Carcinoid tumours: Frequency in a defined population during a 12-year period. Acta Pathol Microbiol Scand [A] 84:322–330, 1976.
12. Wilander E, Lundqvist M, Oberg K: Gastrointestinal carcinoid tumours: Histogenetic, histochemical, immunohistochemical, clinical and therapeutic aspects. Prog Histochem Cytochem 19:1–88, 1989.
13. Kloppel G, Heitz PU, Capella C, Solcia E: Pathology and nomenclature of human gastrointestinal neuroendocrine (carcinoid) tumors and related lesions. World J Surg 20:132–141, 1936.
14. Solicia C, Capella C, Buffa R, et al: Endocrine cells of the digestive system. In Johnson L (ed): Physiology of the Gastrointestinal Tract. New York, Raven Press, 1981, pp 39–58.
15. Hocker M, John M, Anagnostopoulos J, et al: Molecular dissection of regulated secretory pathways in human gastric enterochromaffin-like cells: An immunohistochemical analysis. Histochem Cell Biol 112:205–214, 1999.
16. Wiedenmann B: New molecular aspects for the clinical control of hypersecretion and proliferation in neuroendocrine tumor disease. In Mignon M, Colombel JF (eds): Recent Advances in the Pathophysiology and Management of Inflammatory Bowel Diseases and Digestive Endocrine Tumors. Montrouge, John Libbey, 1999, pp 280–282.
17. Wiedenmann B, John M, Ahnert-Hilger G, Riecken E: Molecular and cell biological aspects of neuroendocrine tumors of the gastroenteropancreatic system. J Mol Med 76:637–647, 1998.
18. Solcia E, Fiocca R, Rindi G, et al: The pathology of the gastrointestinal endocrine system. Endocrinol Metab Clin North Am 22:795–821, 1993.
19. Qvigstad G, Qvigstad T, Westre B et al: Neuroendocrine differentiation in gastric adenocarcinomas associated with severe hypergastrinemia and/or pernicious anemia. APMIS 110:132–139, 1992.
20. Larsson C, Skogseid B, Oberg K, et al: Multiple endocrine neoplasia type 1 gene maps to chromosome 11 and is lost in insulinoma. Nature 332:85–87, 1977.
21. Latif F, Tory K, Gnarra J, et al: Identification of the von Hippel-Lindau disease tumor suppressor gene. Science 260:1317–1320, 1993.
22. Jakobsen AM, Andersson P, Saglik G, et al: Differential expression of vesicular monoamine transporter (VMAT) 1 and 2 in gastrointestinal endocrine tumours. J Pathol 195:463–472, 2001.
23. Solcia E, Kloppel G, Sobin L: Histological typing of endocrine tumours. In (eds): New York, Springer, 2000, pp 38–74.
24. Zhao J, de Krijger RR, Meier D, et al: Genomic alterations in well-differentiated gastrointestinal and bronchial neuroendocrine tumors (carcinoids): Marked differences indicating diversity in molecular pathogenesis. Am J Pathol 157:1431–1438, 2000.
25. Granberg D, Wilander E, Oberg K, Skogseid B: Prognostic markers in patients with typical bronchial carcinoid tumors. J Clin Endocrinol Metab 85:3425–3430, 2000.
26. Kytola S, Hoog A, Nord B, et al: Comparative genomic hybridization identifies loss of 18q22-qter as an early and specific event in tumorigenesis of midgut carcinoids. Am J Pathol 158:1803–1808, 2001.
27. Shimizu T, Tanaka S, Haruma K, et al: Growth characteristics of rectal carcinoid tumors. Oncology 59:229–237, 2000.
28. Sturm N, Rossi G, Lantuejoul S, et al: Expression of thyroid transcription factor-1 in the spectrum of neuroendocrine cell lung proliferations with special interest in carcinoids. Hum Pathol 33:175–182, 2002.
29. Oliveira AM, Tazelaar HD, Wentzlaff KA, et al: Familial pulmonary carcinoid tumors. Cancer 91:2104–2109, 2001.
30. Feldman JM, O'Dorisio TM: Role of neuropeptides and serotonin in the diagnosis of carcinoid tumors. Am J Med 81:41–48, 1986.
31. Smith RA: Bronchial carcinoid tumours. Thorax 24:43–50, 1969.
32. Feldman JM: Carcinoid tumors and syndrome. Semin Oncol 14:237–246, 1987.
33. Tiensuu Janson EM, Oberg KE: Carcinoid tumours. Baillieres Clin Gastroenterol 10:589–601, 1996.
34. Creutzfeldt W, Stockmann F: Carcinoids and carcinoid syndrome. Am J Med 82:4–16, 1987.
35. Bean WB, Olch D, Weinberg HB: The syndrome of carcinoid and acquired valve lesions of the right side of the heart. Circulation 12:1–6, 1955.
36. Levin R, Elsas L, Duvall C, et al: Malignant carcinoid tumors with and without flushing. JAMA 186:905–907, 1963
37. Freedman RR, Woodward S, Sabharwal SC: Alpha 2-adrenergic mechanism in menopausal hot flushes. Obstet Gynecol 76:573–578, 1990.
38. Freedman RR, Norton D, Woodward S, et al: Core body temperature and circadian rhythm of hot flashes in menopausal women. J Clin Endocrinol Metab 80:2354–2358, 1995.
39. Wyon Y: Vasomotor symptoms in postmenopausal women. Linköping, Linköping University, 2002.
40. Demis DJ: The mastocytosis syndrome: Clinical and biological studies. Ann Intern Med 59:194–206, 1963.
41. Parker C, Cryer P, Kissane J: Systemic mastocytosis. Am J Med 61:671–680, 1976.
42. Roberts LJ 2nd, Sweetman BJ, Lewis RA, et al: Increased production of prostaglandin $D_2$ in patients with

systemic mastocytosis. N Engl J Med 303:1400–1404, 1980.

43. Matuchansky C, Launay JM: Serotonin, catecholamines, and spontaneous midgut carcinoid flush: Plasma studies from flushing and nonflushing sites. Gastroenterology 108:743–751, 1995.

44. Emson PC, Gilbert RF, Martensson H, Nobin A: Elevated concentrations of substance P and 5-HT in plasma in patients with carcinoid tumors. Cancer 54:715–718, 1984.

45. Schaffalitzky De Muckadell OB, Aggestrup S, Stentoft P: Flushing and plasma substance P concentration during infusion of synthetic substance P in normal man. Scand J Gastroenterol 21:498–502, 1986.

46. Robertson JI, Peart WS, Andrews TM. The mechanism of facial flushes in the carcinoid syndrome. Q J Med 31:103–123, 1962.

47. Frolich JC, Bloomgarden ZT, Oates JA, et al: The carcinoid flush: Provocation by pentagastrin and inhibition by somatostatin. N Engl J Med 299:1055–1057, 1978.

48. Furschgott R, Zawadski JU: The obligatory role of endothelial cells in the relaxation of arterial smooth muscle by acetylcholine. Nature 288:373–376, 1980.

49. Jensen RT: Overview of chronic diarrhea caused by functional neuroendocrine neoplasms. Semin Gastrointest Dis 10:156–172, 1999.

50. Donowitz M, Binder HJ: Jejunal fluid and electrolyte secretion in carcinoid syndrome. Am J Dig Dis 20:1115–1122, 1975.

51. Debonguie J, Philips S: Capacity of the human colon to absorb fluid. Gastroenterology 74:698–703, 1978.

52. von der Ohe MR, Camilleri M, Kvols LK, Thomforde GM: Motor dysfunction of the small bowel and colon in patients with the carcinoid syndrome and diarrhea. N Engl J Med 329:1073–1078, 1973.

53. Lundin L, Norheim I, Landelius J, et al: Carcinoid heart disease: Relationship of circulating vasoactive substances to ultrasound-detectable cardiac abnormalities. Circulation 77:264–269, 1988.

54. Roberts WC, Sjoerdsma A: The cardiac disease associated with the carcinoid syndrome (carcinoid heart disease). Am J Med 36:5–34, 1964.

55. Ferrans VJ, Roberts WC: The carcinoid endocardial plaque: An ultrastructural study. Hum Pathol 7:387–409, 1976.

56. Lundin L, Landelius J, Andren B, Oberg K: Transoesophageal echocardiography improves the diagnostic value of cardiac ultrasound in patients with carcinoid heart disease. Br Heart J 64:190–194, 1990.

57. Robiolio PA, Rigolin VH, Wilson JS, et al: Carcinoid heart disease: Correlation of high serotonin levels with valvular abnormalities detected by cardiac catheterization and echocardiography. Circulation 92:790–795, 1995.

58. Waltenberger J, Lundin L, Oberg K, et al: Involvement of transforming growth factor-beta in the formation of fibrotic lesions in carcinoid heart disease. Am J Pathol 142:71–78, 1993.

59. Hua X, Lundberg JM, Theodorsson-Norheim E, Brodin E: Comparison of cardiovascular and bronchoconstrictor effects of substance P, substance K and other tachykinins. Naunyn Schmiedebergs Arch Pharmacol 328:196–201, 1984.

60. Gardner B, Dollinger M, Silen W, et al: Studies of the carcinoid syndrome: Its relationship to serotonin, bradykinin, and histamine. Surgery 61:846–852, 1967.

61. Vinik AI, McLeod MK, Fig LM, et al: Clinical features, diagnosis, and localization of carcinoid tumors and their management. Gastroenterol Clin North Am 18:865–896, 1989.

62. Andaker L, Lamke LO, Smeds S: Follow-up of 102 patients operated on for gastrointestinal carcinoid. Acta Chir Scand 151:469–473, 1985.

63. Stridsberg M, Oberg K, Li Q, et al: Measurements of chromogranin A, chromogranin B (secretogranin I), chromogranin C (secretogranin II) and pancreastatin in plasma and urine from patients with carcinoid tumours and endocrine pancreatic tumours. J Endocrinol 144:49–59, 1995.

64. Nobels FR, Kwekkeboom DJ, Coopmans W, et al: Chromogranin A as serum marker for neuroendocrine neoplasia: Comparison with neuron-specific enolase and the alpha-subunit of glycoprotein hormones. J Clin Endocrinol Metab 82:2622–2628, 1997.

65. Oberg K, Stridsberg M: Chromogranins as diagnostic and prognostic markers in neuroendocrine tumours. Adv Exp Med Biol 482:329–337, 2000.

66. Grossmann M, Trautmann ME, Poertl S, et al: Alpha-subunit and human chorionic gonadotropin-beta immunoreactivity in patients with malignant endocrine gastroenteropancreatic tumours. Eur J Clin Invest 24:131–136, 1994.

67. Oberg K, Grimelius L, Lundqvist G, Lorelius LE: Update on pancreatic polypeptide as a specific marker for endocrine tumours of the pancreas and gut. Acta Med Scand 210:145–152, 1981.

68. Mani S, Modlin IM, Ballantyne G, et al: Carcinoids of the rectum. J Am Coll Surg 179:231–248, 1994.

69. Baudin E, Gigliotti A, Ducreux M, et al: Neuron-specific enolase and chromogranin A as markers of neuroendocrine tumours. Br J Cancer 78:1102–1107, 1998.

70. Wallace S, Ajani JA, Charnsangavej C, et al: Carcinoid tumors: Imaging procedures and interventional radiology. World J Surg 20:147–156, 1996.

71. Ricke J, Klose KJ, Mignon M, et al: Standardisation of imaging in neuroendocrine tumours: results of a European delphi process. Eur J Radiol 37:8–17, 2001.

72. Kwekkeboom D, Krenning EP, de Jong M: Peptide receptor imaging and therapy. J Nucl Med 41:1704–1713, 2000.

73. Bombardieri E, Maccauro M, De Deckere E, et al. Nuclear medicine imaging of neuroendocrine tumours. Ann Oncol 12(Suppl 2):S51–61, 2001.

74. Krenning EP, de Jong M, Kooij PP, et al: Radiolabelled somatostatin analogue(s) for peptide receptor scintigraphy and radionuclide therapy. Ann Oncol 10(Suppl 2):S23–S29, 1999.

75. Balon HR, Goldsmith SJ, Siegel BA, et al: Procedure guideline for somatostatin receptor scintigraphy with (111)In-pentetreotide. J Nucl Med 42:1134–1138, 2001.

76. Virgolini I, Traub T, Novotny C, et al: New trends in peptide receptor radioligands. Q J Nucl Med 45:153–159, 2001.

77. Orlefors H, Sundin A, Ahlstrom H, et al: Positron emission tomography with 5-hydroxytryprophan in neuroendocrine tumors. J Clin Oncol 16:2534–2541, 1998.

78. Erasmus JJ, McAdams HP, Patz EF Jr, et al: Evaluation of primary pulmonary carcinoid tumors using FDG PET. AJR Am J Roentgenol 170:1369–1373, 1998.

79. Kaltsas G, Korbonits M, Heintz E, et al: Comparison of somatostatin analog and meta-iodobenzylguanidine radionuclides in the diagnosis and localization of advanced neuroendocrine tumors. J Clin Endocrinol Metab 86:895–902, 2001.

80. Hellman P, Lundstrom T, Ohrvall U, et al: Effect of surgery on the outcome of midgut carcinoid disease with lymph node and liver metastases. World J Surg 26:991–997, 2002.

81. Eriksson BK, Larsson EG, Skogseid BM, et al: Liver embolizations of patients with malignant neuroendocrine gastrointestinal tumors. Cancer 83:2293–2301, 1998.

82. Ruszniewski P, Malka D: Hepatic arterial chemoembolization in the management of advanced digestive endocrine tumors. Digestion 62(Suppl 1):79–83, 2000.

83. Berber E, Flesher N, Siperstein AE: Laparoscopic radiofrequency ablation of neuroendocrine liver metastases. World J Surg 26:985–990, 2002.

84. Pless J, Bauer W, Briner U, et al: Chemistry and pharmacology of SMS 201-995: A long-acting octapeptide analogue of somatostatin. Scand J Gastroenterol Suppl 119:54–64, 1986.

85. Kutz K, Nuesch E, Rosenthaler J: Pharmacokinetics of SMS 201-995 in healthy subjects. Scand J Gastroenterol Suppl 19:65–72, 1986.

86. Jensen RT: Recent advances in the use of somatostatin and other peptide receptor agonists and antagonists. In Lewis J, Dubois A (eds): Current Clinical Topics in Gastrointestinal Pharmacology. Malden, Mass, Blackwell Science, 1997, p 144.

87. Harris AG, O'Dorisio TM, Woltering EA, et al: Consensus statement: Octreotide dose titration in secretory diarrhea: Diarrhea Management Consensus Development Panel. Dig Dis Sci 40:1464–1473, 1995.

88. Oberg K. Advances in chemotherapy and biotherapy of endocrine tumors. Curr Opin Oncol 10:58–65, 1998.

89. Ruszniewski P, Ducreux M, Chayvialle JA, et al: Treatment of the carcinoid syndrome with the long-acting somatostatin analogue lanreotide: A prospective study in 39 patients. Gut 39:279–283, 1996.

90. Rubin J, Ajani J, Schirmer W, et al: Octreotide acetate long-acting formulation versus open-label subcutaneous octreotide acetate in malignant carcinoid syndrome. J Clin Oncol 17:600–606, 1999.

91. Tomassetti P, Migliori M, Gullo L: Slow-release lanreotide treatment in endocrine gastrointestinal tumors. Am J Gastroenterol 93:1468–1471, 1998.

92. Frank M, Klose KJ, Wied M, et al: Combination therapy with octreotide and alpha-interferon: Effect on tumor growth in metastatic endocrine gastroenteropancreatic tumors. Am J Gastroenterol 94:1381–1387, 1999.

93. Eriksson B, Renstrup J, Imam H, Oberg K: High-dose treatment with lanreotide of patients with advanced neuroendocrine gastrointestinal tumors: Clinical and biological effects. Ann Oncol 8:1041–1044, 1997.

94. Schonfeld WH, Eikin EP, Woltering EA, et al: The cost-effectiveness of octreotide acetate in the treatment of carcinoid syndrome and VIPoma. Int J Technol Assess Health Care 14:514–525, 1998.

95. Bajetta E, Carnaghi C, Ferrari L, et al: The role of somatostatin analogues in the treatment of gastro-enteropancreatic endocrine tumours. Digestion 57(Suppl 1):72–76, 1996.

96. Stewart PM, Stewart SE, Clark PM, Sheppard MC: Clinical and biochemical response following withdrawal of a long-acting, depot injection form of octreotide (Sandostatin-LAR). Clin Endocrinol (Oxf) 50:295–299, 1999.

97. Oberg K, Norheim I, Theodorsson E: Treatment of malignant midgut carcinoid tumours with a long-acting somatostatin analogue octreotide. Acta Oncol 30:503–507, 1991.

98. Arnold R, Frank M: Gastrointestinal endocrine tumours: Medical management. Baillieres Clin Gastroenterol 10:737–759, 1996.

99. Yamada Y, Post SR, Wang K, et al: Cloning and functional characterization of a family of human and mouse somatostatin receptors expressed in brain, gastrointestinal tract, and kidney. Proc Natl Acad Sci U S A 89:251–255, 1992.

100. Yamada Y, Reisine T, Law SF, et al: Somatostatin receptors, an expanding gene family: Cloning and functional characterization of human SSTR3, a

protein coupled to adenylyl cyclase. Mol Endocrinol 6:2136–2142, 1992.

101. Yamada Y, Kagimoto S, Kubota A, et al: Cloning, functional expression and pharmacological characterization of a fourth (hSSTR4) and a fifth (hSSTR5) human somatostatin receptor subtype. Biochem Biophys Res Commun 195:844–852, 1933.

102. O'Carroll AM, Lolait SJ, Konig M, Mahan LC: Molecular cloning and expression of a pituitary somatostatin receptor with preferential affinity for somatostatin-28. Mol Pharmacol 42:939–946, 1992.

103. Reubi JC, Kvols LK, Waser B, et al: Detection of somatostatin receptors in surgical and percutaneous needle biopsy samples of carcinoids and islet cell carcinomas. Cancer Res 50:5969–5977, 1990.

104. Krenning EP, Kwekkeboom DJ, Bakker WH, et al. Somatostatin receptor scintigraphy with [$^{111}$In-DTPA-D-Phe1]- and [$^{123}$I-Tyr3]-octreotide: The Rotterdam experience with more than 1000 patients. Eur J Nucl Med 20:716–731, 1993.

105. Janson ET, Westlin JE, Eriksson B, et al: [$^{111}$In-DTPA-D-Phe1]octreotide scintigraphy in patients with carcinoid tumours: The predictive value for somatostatin analogue treatment. Eur J Endocrinol 131:577–581, 1994.

106. Harris AG, Redfern JS. Octreotide treatment of carcinoid syndrome: Analysis of published dose-titration data. Aliment Pharmacol Ther 9:387–394, 1995.

107. Kalkner KM, Janson ET, Nilsson S, et al: Somatostatin receptor scintigraphy in patients with carcinoid tumors: Comparison between radioligand uptake and tumor markers. Cancer Res 55:5801s–5804s, 1995.

108. Kvols LK, Martin JK, Marsh HM, Moertel CG: Rapid reversal of carcinoid crisis with a somatostatin analogue. N Engl J Med 313:1229–1230, 1985.

109. Oberg K NI, Lundqvist G, Wide L: Treatment of the carcinoid syndrome with SMS 201-995, a somatostatin analogue. Scand J Gastroenterol 119:191–192, 1986.

110. Gillis JC, Noble S, Goa KL: Octreotide long-acting release (LAR): A review of its pharmacological properties and therapeutic use in the management of acromegaly. Drugs 53:681–699, 1997.

111. Ruszniewski PI-SS, Wymenga M, et al: Rapid and sustained relief from the symptoms of carcinoma syndrome: Results from an open 6-month study of the 28-day prolonged-release formulation of lanreotide. Neuro-endocrinology 80:244–251, 2004.

112. Eriksson B, Oberg K: Summing up 15 years of somatostatin analog therapy in neuroendocrine tumors: Future outlook. Ann Oncol 10(Suppl 2):S31–S38, 1999.

113. Trendle MC, Moertel CG, Kvols LK: Incidence and morbidity of cholelithiasis in patients receiving

chronic octreotide for metastatic carcinoid and malignant islet cell tumors. Cancer 79:830–834, 1997.

114. Oberg K, Funa K, Alm G: Effects of leukocyte interferon on clinical symptoms and hormone levels in patients with mid-gut carcinoid tumors and carcinoid syndrome. N Engl J Med 309:129–133, 1983.

115. Oberg K, Eriksson B: The role of interferons in the management of carcinoid tumors. Acta Oncol 30:519–522, 1991.

116. Zhou Y, Wang S, Gobl A, Oberg K: The interferon-alpha regulation of interferon regulatory factor 1 (IRF-1) and IRF-2 has therapeutic implications in carcinoid tumors. Ann Oncol 11:707–714, 2000.

117. Moertel CG, Rubin J, Kvols LK: Therapy of metastatic carcinoid tumor and the malignant carcinoid syndrome with recombinant leukocyte A interferon. J Clin Oncol 7:865–868, 1989.

118. Hanssen LE, Schrumpf E, Kolbenstvedt AN, et al: Treatment of malignant metastatic midgut carcinoid tumours with recombinant human alpha2b interferon with or without prior hepatic artery embolization. Scand J Gastroenterol 24:787–795, 1989.

119. Bartsch DK SF, Arnold R: Treatment of metastatic carcinoid tumours by recombinant interferon-alfa results from a phase II study. J Cancer Res Clin Oncol 116:305, 1990.

120. Valimaki M, Jarvinen H, Salmela P, et al: Is the treatment of metastatic carcinoid tumor with interferon not as successful as suggested? Cancer 67:547–549, 1991.

121. Jakobsen M, Hansen LE, Kolmannskog F, et al: Interferon-alfa 2b, with or without prior hepatic artery embolization: Clinical response and survival in midgut carcinoid patients. Scand J Gastroenterol 30:789–796, 1995.

122. Bajetta E, Zilembo N, Di Bartolomeo M, et al: Treatment of metastatic carcinoids and other neuroendocrine tumors with recombinant interferon-alpha-2a: A study by the Italian Trials in Medical Oncology Group. Cancer 72:3099–3105, 1993.

123. Tiensuu Janson EM, Ahlstrom H, Anderson T, et al: Octreotide and interferon alfa: A new combination for the treatment of malignant carcinoid tumours. Eur J Cancer 28A:1647–1650, 1992.

124. Janson ET, Oberg K. Long-term management of the carcinoid syndrome: Treatment with octreotide alone and in combination with alpha-interferon. Acta Oncol 32:225–229, 1993.

125. Moertel CG: Treatment of the carcinoid tumor and the malignant carcinoid syndrome. J Clin Oncol 1:727–740, 1983.

126. Melmon KL, Sjoerdsma A, Oates JA, Laster L: Treatment of malabsorption and diarrhea of the carcinoid

syndrome with methysergide. Gastroenterology 48:18–24, 1965.

127. Vroom FQ, Brown RE, Dempsey H, Hill SR Jr: Studies on several possible antiserotonin compounds in a patient with the functioning carcinoid syndrome. Ann Intern Med 56:941–945, 1962.

128. Schworer H, Munke H, Stockmann F, et al: Treatment of diarrhea in carcinoid syndrome with ondansetron, tropisetron, and clonidine. Am J Gastroenterol 90:645–648, 1995.

129. Roberts LJ 2nd, Marney SR Jr, Oates JA: Blockade of the flush associated with metastatic gastric carcinoid by combined histamine $H_1$ and $H_2$ receptor antagonists: Evidence for an important role of $H_2$ receptors in human vasculature. N Engl J Med 300:236–238, 1979.

130. Buscombe JR, Caplin ME, Hilson AJ: Long-term efficacy of high-activity [111]In-pentetreotide therapy in patients with disseminated neuroendocrine tumors. J Nucl Med 44:1–6, 2003.

131. Kwekkeboom DJ, Bakker WH, Kooij PP, et al: [[177]Lu-DOTAOTyr3]octreotate: Comparison with [[111]In-DTPAo]octreotide in patients. Eur J Nucl Med 28:1319–1325, 2001.

# Ectopic Hormone Syndromes

## David W. Ray

## HISTORY

Tightly regulated production of hormones from specialized endocrine glands is usually under the control of higher centers, ultimately the brain, and is normally subject to negative feedback. This affords a mechanism for influencing diverse tissue function throughout the body. Apparently, inappropriate hormone production by nonendocrine tissue causes a spectrum of rare syndromes. These disorders are important because they may be the first manifestation of an underlying tumor, and the hormonal manifestations can induce morbidity and affect quality of life. Ectopic hormone secretion also sheds light on mechanisms of tissue-specific gene expression and regulation. Ectopic hormone production reveals important linkage between cell differentiation and gene expression. Ectopic expression of a peptide may also be useful as a tumor marker (e.g., human chorionic gonadotropin, α-fetoprotein).

Initial reports of endocrine activity associated with tumors appeared in the 1920s. These examples included features of parathyroid-like activity with disseminated carcinoma and adrenocortical activity in patients with lung and thymic tumors.[1-3] At the same time, initial reports of tumor-associated hypoglycemia were documented.[4,5] Later, based on the metabolic similarities to hyperparathyroidism, Albright and Reifenstein[6] proposed the secretion of parathyroid-like hormone activity in a patient with renal cell carcinoma as the cause of hypercalcemia.

Proof of tumor-derived endocrine factors had to await development of accurate and sensitive hormone assays. These assays allowed identification of adrenocorticotropic hormone (ACTH), and antidiuretic hormone secretion from tumors causing ectopic ACTH syndrome and the syndrome of inappropriate antidiuretic hormone secretion (SIADH), respectively.[7-10] Since these breakthroughs, further advances in cell and molecular biology have sought to explain how and why such ectopic hormone production occurs and its consequences.

## THEORETICAL CONSIDERATIONS

Circulating hormones are almost exclusively derived from specialized cells in endocrine glands. However, low-level hormone production or gene expression, at the very least, can be found much more widely. For example, the gene encoding ACTH is expressed at a high level in anterior pituitary corticotroph cells, but its expression has also been detected in a wide array of normal and tumoral extrapituitary tissues. This "ectopic" expression can give rise to the clinical syndrome of ectopic ACTH production, a cause of Cushing's syndrome. However, it is also possible that POMC gene expression may have a role in healthy tissue, especially in the placenta, lymphocytes, testes, and lung.

There must be compelling evidence that the hormone is produced by the tissue or tumor in question for the diagnosis of ectopic hormone production to be secure. Production is the most fundamental level of hormone control. Thus, mRNA or the peptide should be demonstrated in tissue sections or hormone secretion can be shown to persist in vitro in primary cell culture or there may be an arteriovenous gradient of hormone across the tissue in vivo. Other criteria, such as reduction in hormone level postresection, are weaker because the tumor may express a hormone secretogogue (e.g., growth hormone–releasing hormone [GHRH] rather than growth hormone [GH] itself).

Hormones most frequently associated with ectopic production tend to be those with the most widespread distribution. The *POMC* gene is widely expressed in nontumorous, nonendocrine tissues and is frequently overexpressed in tumors, giving rise to the ectopic ACTH syndrome. Insulin is almost never produced ectopically by tumors, consistent with its restricted expression only in specialized β cells within the pancreatic islets.

Peptide hormones are often processed differently in tumors compared with their usual organs of production. They may undergo incomplete proteolytic cleavage or altered glycosylation, but the peptides themselves are the products of the same genes responsible for their production in their normal cells. Tumors that produce one hormone ectopically frequently express other hormones and proteins inappropriately; however, it is rare to have clinically significant secretion of more than one peptide.

## THEORIES OF THE ORIGIN OF ECTOPIC HORMONES

With the development of sophisticated molecular techniques, low levels of hormone gene expression have been documented in a wide range of normal tissues.[11] Therefore, it is not surprising that tumors arising from these tissues can give rise to ectopic hormone-producing syndromes. If hormone production in the tumor remained under physiologic control, ectopic hormone production would not pose a clinical problem. Sometimes aberrant control has an obvious mechanism (e.g., lack of specific neural connection, physical distance from a portal system, absence of receptors for hormonal modulators of gene expression).

Several theories have been proposed to explain ectopic hormone production.

### Derepression Hypothesis[12–20]

A variety of normally quiescent genes are activated as a result of malignant cell transformation. This observation suggests that a tumor is capable of producing any hormone, which is clearly not the case, but it does predict correctly that regulated expression of genes may be lost. In fact, transformed cells frequently modify portions of their genome to exert long-term effects on gene expression (e.g., gene methylation).

### Dedifferentiation Hypothesis[21]

The dedifferentiation hypothesis is a refinement of the derepression hypothesis. It suggests that terminally differentiated cells in a normal organ, because of malignant transformation, reacquire characteristics of the pluripotent progenitor cells from which they are derived. This process is accompanied by a loss of differentiated function, well known to accompany neoplastic change. However, this theory lacks hard data support, and it seems unlikely that dedifferentiation is an orderly process because malignant cells do not share many features of progenitor cells. In addition, it is unclear whether cells can become dedifferentiated; it is more likely that transformation of a progenitor cell, with greater proliferative capacity, is the underlying process in tumorigenicity.

### Oncogene Hypothesis

Neoplastic cells frequently overexpress cell growth- and division-promoting genes, or oncogenes. Morphologically, malignant cells often have multiple copies of chromosomal segments, shown as extrachromosomal structures, also known as double minutes. These amplified sections of the genome result in increased expression of the genes coded on them. These genes are often oncogenes, but they may also encode peptide hormone genes. Some peptide hormone genes are known to map close to known oncogenes. Amplification might explain some features of ectopic hormone syndromes, but there is not enough hard evidence to support this theory as a common cause of ectopic hormone production.

### Amine Precursor Uptake and Decarboxylation Hypothesis[22–26]

A number of endocrinologically active cells are dispersed through normal tissues but they are not usually considered to be endocrinologically active. These cells share amine precursor uptake and decarboxylation (APUD) properties. At one time, these cells were thought to derive from a common source in the embryonic neural crest. Although an appealing concept, evidence of this common origin is lacking. Nonetheless, their common features suggest that they may respond to transformation in a similar way. Many ectopic hormone-producing tumors have features of APUD cells, and these tumors may originate from APUD precursor cells. However, other ectopic hormone-producing tumors have no features of APUD tissue, and these tumors are often the most aggressive, secreting high levels of hormone, evidence that contradicts the importance of APUD characteristics for hormone production.

### Dysdifferentiation Theory[27–33]

Problems with the previous theories have led to the dysdifferentiation hypothesis. It proposes that neoplastic changes occur in progenitor cells rather than in terminally differentiated cells. As a result of one or more mutations, the transformed progenitor cell undergoes variable differentiation. If this theory holds true, it predicts a tumor with a mixed population of cells at different stages of development. Depending on the blocks to normal differentiation, a subset of cells may develop into an endocrine cell type and give rise to an endocrine-type tumor. This model explains why some tissues produce particular hormones because the tumor would tend to transcribe the same genes as its parent tissue, although these may be expressed aberrantly (Fig. 195-1).

Extrapituitary expression of the *ACTH* gene (pro-opiomelanocortin [POMC]) is described in detail in the following. Ectopic ACTH production shares many features of other ectopic hormone syndromes and may provide a paradigm for understanding general mechanisms of ectopic hormone production.

## HORMONES IN SMALL CELL LUNG CARCINOMA

Small cell lung carcinoma (SCLC) is the most common and aggressive neuroendocrine tumor. Patients with SCLC seldom present to the endocrinologist, but, because there is evidence of hormone expression, it is a useful model from which to extrapolate to other, less common, syndromes.

The normal adult lung contains a diffuse population of cells that synthesize very low levels of peptide hormones including ACTH, GHRH, and gastrin-releasing hormone. In fetal life, these cells are more densely represented and produce higher concentrations of hormones, suggesting a possible role in differentiation. These scattered endocrine cells have APUD properties and comprise part of a diffuse neuroendocrine system.

SCLC, a bronchogenic tumor, produces most of the hormones found in normal bronchial epithelium. ACTH, vasopressin, and calcitonin secretion have been studied most extensively because of the clinical syndromes that they cause and because they produce potential disease markers that can be used for diagnosis or response to treatment. In a study of 157 primary lung tumor extracts, 83% expressed at least one peptide hormone. Multiple hormone production is common and includes ectopic ACTH syndrome in 20% of cases, although production of one hormone tends to dominate the clinical picture.[34,35] However, only approximately 1% of patients with SCLC have clinical features of cortisol excess, possibly because of the short duration of disease.[36] Peptide hormones often undergo incomplete processing. In particular, POMC is not efficiently cleaved to ACTH, resulting in high-molecular-weight forms of ACTH in tumor extracts and in the circulation.[34,37] It is now clear that these alternate

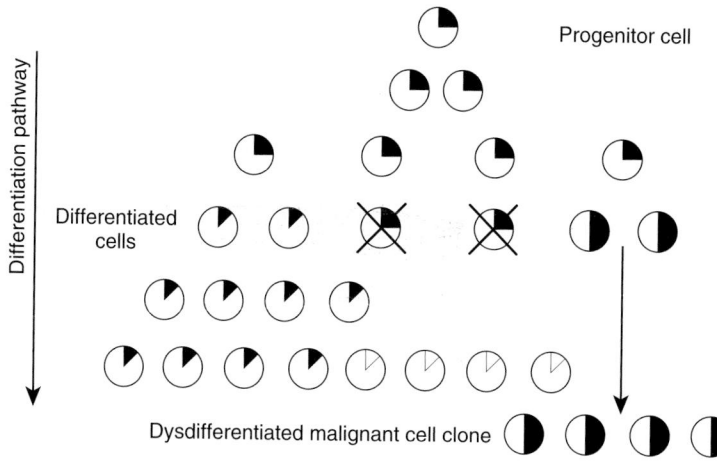

Progenitor cell

Differentiation pathway

Differentiated cells

Dysdifferentiated malignant cell clone

**Figure 195-1**   Dysdifferentiation results in aberrant gene expression. The malignant transformation of a progenitor cell results in a clonal population of cells that have undergone atypical differentiation. These cells share some features with their progenitor cells (*shaded areas*) and may continue to express genes associated with these immature, incompletely differentiated cells. Malignant transformation of a cell can lead to persistent, or enhanced, hormone gene expression in the clone of proliferating cells (*heavily shaded area*).

forms represent the prohormones POMC and pro-ACTH. The abnormal protein processing may result from a lack of specific cleavage enzymes, prohormone convertases 1 and 2, which are expressed only in specialized endocrine tissue or from a switch from the regulated secretory pathway to the constitutive one.[38]

## ECTOPIC ADRENOCORTICOTROPIC HORMONE SYNDROME

### THE POMC GENE

Pituitary corticotroph cells are the only cells that express the *POMC* gene at a high level. The human *POMC* gene is encoded in three exons on chromosome 2. The first exon is noncoding. The second exon contains the signal peptide, which targets the protein product to the regulated secretion pathway. The third exon encodes the majority of the mature protein, including ACTH.[39] The mature mRNA from the *POMC* gene is 1200 nucleotides. In addition, a short form of the mRNA has been found at low levels in most tissues analyzed. This arises from a transcription start site 5′ to exon 3 and thus only includes the coding sequence for exon 3.[40] Therefore, this transcript lacks a signal peptide and does not give rise to the mature POMC molecule. There is no evidence that this transcript produces a peptide product, and its physiologic role is unclear. A third POMC transcript has also been described that is longer than the pituitary form (~1500 nucleotides). It arises from a site, or multiple sites, within the 5′ flanking region of the human POMC promoter.[41–43] This mRNA species includes the entire coding region of the peptide and does give rise to a secreted peptide product. This "long" form of the POMC mRNA is particularly found in extrapituitary tissues and tumors.

### REGULATION OF POMC GENE EXPRESSION

Expression of the *POMC* gene appears to be predominantly controlled at the level of gene transcription.[44–46] The rat *POMC* gene has been most extensively studied, and pituitary expression is conferred by the 5′ flanking region of the gene. It has recently been found that pituitary corticotroph expression of POMC requires the action of a tightly restricted transcription factor, a member of the T-box family, termed Tpit.[47] This factor acts with the homeodomain protein PitX1 and promotes recruitment of SRC family coactivators to the POMC promoter, leading to enhanced gene transcription.[48]

Corticotropin-releasing hormone (CRH) acts on pituitary corticotroph cells to increase cyclic adenosine monophosphate (cAMP) accumulation and activates mitogen-activated protein kinases. There is also evidence of activation of the orphan nuclear receptor nerve growth factor–induced clone B (or Nur 77)[49–51] leading to enhanced POMC transcription through the recruitment of SRC coactivators to nerve growth factor–induced clone B.[48,52] As nerve growth factor–induced clone B and Tpit act synergistically, this suggests the formation of a regulatory complex on the POMC promoter with Tpit, NGFI-B and SRC coactivators.[48] It is important that expression of Tpit promotes corticotroph cell differentiation and that its expression is more limited than that of POMC. Therefore, there is no Tpit expression in hypothalamic POMC-expressing neurons, suggesting that Tpit is specific for corticotroph-specific expression of POMC; other mechanisms are responsible for expression elsewhere. Tpit expression has been found specifically in human pituitary corticotroph adenomas.[47]

Glucocorticoids repress transcription of the *POMC* gene by binding to two DNA elements in the 5′ flanking region of the promoter. The more proximal element, an imperfect palindrome 63 nucleotides upstream from the transcription start site, is thought to bind three glucocorticoid receptor molecules in an unusual trimer formation.[53–55] This conformation of receptors on DNA directs repression of transcription rather than enhancement. Further upstream, between −480 and −320, there is another glucocorticoid-regulated element, suggesting that these two DNA elements interact to achieve the full effect of glucocorticoid repression.[56] It is interesting that Tpit expression, essential to the corticotroph cell type and to POMC expression, is not affected by glucocorticoids, in contrast to POMC, which is repressed.[57] Because Tpit is not part of the mechanism allowing glucocorticoid repression of POMC, the lack of Tpit in ectopic ACTH syndrome causing tumors cannot explain the failure of glucocorticoid repression characteristic of the disorder. However, the mechanism underlying POMC induction by CRH in some well-differentiated carcinoid tumors causing ectopic ACTH syndrome is not yet defined. Although the expression of nerve growth factor–induced gene B and Tpit in such tumors is not definitively addressed, other pathways, such as mitogen-activated protein kinase activation, cAMP activation, and induction of c-fos may be important.[58–62]

A number of other hypothalamic factors act on the pituitary corticotroph to influence POMC expression. However, their modes of action are not well defined. In particular, arginine vasopressin stimulates POMC expression rather weakly but augments CRH action. The intracellular pathways activated by arginine vasopressin appear to be protein kinase C dependent, but arginine vasopressin also potentiates the action of CRH on cAMP generation.[44,63]

Evidence points to intrapituitary factors as important modulators of corticotroph function. One such factor is the proinflammatory cytokine leukemia inhibitory factor, which signals through the Janus kinase/signal transducers and activators of transcription pathway.[64–67] Leukemia inhibitory factor has been shown to act on the *POMC* gene through a specific response element that overlaps with the −166 CRH response element.[68] In addition to stimulating POMC, transcription leukemia inhibitory factor also appears to trigger a "switch" in cell phenotype from proliferative to synthetic.[69]

However, many other peptide growth factors and cytokines are capable of activating cAMP, mitogen-activated protein kinase and Janus kinase/signal transducers and activators of transcription signaling cascades and thus are potentially capable of regulating POMC expression in nonpituitary tissue. Although extrapituitary tissues lack expression of corticotroph-specific transcription factors, activation of common signaling cascades might be expected to result in *POMC* gene expression. In extrapituitary tissues, the *POMC* gene may be modified to render it transcriptionally silent. One such irreversible modification is DNA methylation. The loss of methylation in tumor tissue may allow transcription of the gene to be activated by the common signaling pathways described previously. There is some evidence that such changes in DNA methylation do occur in cell line models of ectopic ACTH syndrome.[70–72] It seems likely that POMC expression per cell is less in most extrapituitary tumors compared with the pituitary corticotroph, but this relative inefficiency of expression is compensated for by the greater number of cells expressing the gene in extrapituitary tumors.

## ECTOPIC ADRENOCORTICOTROPIC HORMONE SYNDROME

ACTH immunoreactivity has been recognized to show size heterogeneity for many years, with the presence of high molecular weight forms detected in human plasma.[19,20,73–75] Ectopic ACTH syndrome was the first of the ectopic hormone syndromes to be recognized. In its most florid form, it is rare, in one study affecting 4.5% of patients with SCLC, although there is evidence of derangement in the hypothalamic-pituitary-adrenal axis in the majority of patients with SCLC[73,76,77] (Table 195-1). Analysis of tumor tissue surprisingly suggests the presence of immunoreactive ACTH, even in the absence of clinical features of hormone excess.[14,19] ACTH is present predominantly in a high molecular weight form of approximately 20 kilodaltons, but this purified material can be cleaved to mature ACTH (4.5 kilodaltons) by the action of trypsin. Further work identified the presence of immunoreactive ACTH-like peptide in a variety of normal tissues, suggesting that extrapituitary ACTH expression is less ectopic than it is inappropriately regulated. The ACTH immunoreactivity was found to have no biologic activity and was assumed to be "big" ACTH. However, identification of predominantly high-molecular-weight forms of ACTH in the circulation of patients with clinically apparent Cushing's syndrome suggests that the precursors of ACTH may have some activity at the ACTH receptor.

## PRO-OPIOMELANOCORTIN PROCESSING

The *POMC* gene leads to the generation of a pre-pro hormone, POMC. This protein undergoes a series of proteolytic cleavages at dibasic amino acid residues to give rise to a series of small molecules, including ACTH, melanocyte-stimulating hormone, and β-endorphin.[78–80] In the anterior pituitary, ACTH is cleaved by the action of a specific protease, termed PC1 (for prohormone convertase type 1).[81] In the rodent intermediate lobe melanotroph, the POMC molecule undergoes more comprehensive digestion to give smaller fragments, melanocyte-stimulating hormone, β-endorphin, and corticotropin-like intermediate lobe peptide as a result of cleavage by prohormone convertase 2. Expression of prohormone convertase 2 and thus detection of circulating ACTH fragments have been described in ectopic ACTH syndrome tumors.[82]

In the majority of extrapituitary tumors that cause ectopic ACTH syndrome, processing of the preprohormone is incomplete. Therefore, ectopic ACTH syndrome is characterized by high-molecular-weight forms of ACTH in the circulation.[35,37] It is likely that the extent of processing correlates with the degree of neuroendocrine differentiation of the tumor, and hormonal manifestations are probably only seen in tumors with significant hormone-processing capacity. A number of small, highly differentiated, slow-growing tumors (typically bronchial carcinoid) have been shown to process POMC in the neurointermediate lobe manner, giving rise to small fragments in the circulation, such as corticotropin-like intermediate lobe peptide and α-melanocyte-stimulating hormone. These have been used to aid diagnosis in some cases of Cushing's syndrome, although the series are small.[9,83]

## DYSREGULATION OF POMC GENE EXPRESSION IN EXTRAPITUITARY TUMORS

In contrast to *POMC* gene expression in pituitary corticotroph cells, expression in extrapituitary tumors is characteristically resistant to glucocorticoid.[8,84] This is the basis of the high-dose glucocorticoid suppression test used to distinguish eutopic from ectopic sources of ACTH in Cushing's syndrome. As the test has approximately 10% false-positive and 10% false-negative rates, it has largely been superseded by sophisticated imaging and inferior petrosal sinus sampling for differential diagnosis.[85] With the availability of recombinant CRH, responses of extrapituitary tumors to this peptide have been measured. In general, only pituitary corticotrophs stimulate POMC expression in response to CRH, but exceptions are increasingly being identified.[86–88]

As pituitary expression of POMC was defined with the aid of a cell line model, so a cell line model was sought for extrapituitary expression. To this end, a panel of human SCLC cell lines was established. These cell lines express the *POMC* gene, and expression is resistant to glucocorticoid suppression.[34,89–93] Further, the cell lines secrete predominantly unprocessed POMC and partially processed forms, again reflecting the pattern of activity characterized in vivo.[89,94]

It is intriguing that the majority of extrapituitary tumors are resistant to glucocorticoid inhibition of POMC expression. Receptors for glucocorticoids are present in most cells, including malignant cells, so exploring the mechanisms of glucocorticoid resistance was important. Using the panel of cell lines, expression of glucocorticoid receptor was identified using both Western blot with a polyclonal anti–glucocorticoid receptor antibody, and ligand-binding assays using tritiated dexamethasone.[92,93,95] To determine whether the receptors were sufficient for glucocorticoid signaling, a synthetic, glucocorticoid-responsive gene was used. This gene was trans-

| Table 195-1 | Types of Tumors Causing Ectopic Adrenocorticotropic Hormone Secretion |
| --- | --- |

Small cell lung carcinoma
Carcinoid tumors (bronchus, thymus, small intestine)
Pancreatic islet cell tumor
Pheochromocytoma
Medullary carcinoma of the thyroid
Carcinomas (breast, gastrointestinal tract [esophageal, gastric, colorectal], ovarian, cervical, prostate)

fected into the cells, and the effects of glucocorticoid incubation on expression of the reporter measured. In contrast to the brisk induction of expression seen in control pituitary cells, none of the human SCLC cells responded to either natural or synthetic glucocorticoids.[92,95] Thus, resistance of the *POMC* gene to glucocorticoid is only part of a global resistance of malignant cells to glucocorticoid action. High concentrations of wild-type receptor in the cells was found to be sufficient to restore glucocorticoid signaling, thereby suggesting that resistance resides at the level of the endogenous receptor.[92] Because one of the actions of glucocorticoids on pituitary corticotrophs is to inhibit proliferation and in the developing lung glucocorticoids act to promote differentiation, it is possible that evasion of glucocorticoid signaling confers a survival advantage on the malignant cells. As yet, a single, unifying molecular mechanism of glucocorticoid resistance in the human SCLC cell lines remains to be defined.

It is interesting that well-differentiated carcinoid tumors causing ectopic ACTH syndrome sometimes show appropriate POMC suppression to supraphysiologic glucocorticoid levels, as in pituitary-dependent Cushing's disease, but these tumors express high levels of the glucocorticoid receptor.[96]

## DIAGNOSIS

The diagnosis of Cushing's syndrome and the differential diagnosis of ACTH-dependent Cushing's syndrome are described elsewhere (see Chapter 24). Dynamic endocrine testing is required to diagnose Cushing's syndrome, and detection of ACTH using a sensitive two-site immunoradiometric assay is useful for making the diagnosis of ACTH-dependent Cushing's syndrome. A variety of dynamic endocrine and imaging protocols is used to identify a pituitary or extrapituitary source of the ACTH excess (Tables 195-2 and 195-3). These all have variable sensitivity and specificity. The most reliable test is bilateral inferior petrosal sinus sampling, which has an accuracy of nearly 100%, if performed when the patient is hypercortisolemic.

Most occult tumors are carcinoid, pheochromocytoma, or medullary thyroid carcinoma and originate in the neck, chest, or abdomen. Computed tomography or magnetic resonance imaging can be used to detect chest tumors in patients with a normal chest radiograph. There has been some success in using indium-labeled octreotide scanning to identify occult neuroendocrine tumors, although experience is still limited.[97–103]

### Table 195-2 Laboratory Investigation of Ectopic Adrenocorticotropic Hormone Syndrome

| Investigation | Test Results |
|---|---|
| ACTH | Higher in ectopic disease; partially processed forms more common in ectopic disease |
| Cortisol | Higher in ectopic disease |
| Hypokalemia (<3.2 mmol/L) and alkalosis | Nearly 100% in ectopic ACTH secretion; ~10% in Cushing's disease |
| High-dose dexamethasone testing (8 mg) | No suppression in 89% of ectopic disease; suppression in 78% of pituitary-dependent disease |
| CRH test | Absent response in ectopic disease; exaggerated response in pituitary-dependent disease |
| Tumor markers | Presence of elevated calcitonin, hCG, α-fetoprotein, 5-HIAA suggests ectopic disease |

ACTH, adrenocorticotropic hormone; CRH, corticotropin-releasing hormone; hCG, human chorionic gonadotropin, 5-HIAA, 5-hydroxyindoleacetic acid.

### Table 195-3 Features of Different Causes of Ectopic Cushing's Syndrome

| | Small Cell Lung Carcinoma | Carcinoid |
|---|---|---|
| ACTH | Very high | Similar to pituitary-dependent disease |
| Cortisol | Very high | Similar to pituitary-dependent disease |
| Features | Not cushingoid | Cushingoid |
| Potassium | Marked hypokalemia | Potassium <3.2 mmol/L |

ACTH, adrenocorticotropic hormone.

## TREATMENT

Treatment is based on two objectives: (1) to control endocrine manifestations and (2) to manage the underlying tumor. Individual patients will present with different priorities. The ideal treatment is curative resection of the primary tumor, achieving both objectives. If this is not possible, patients with small, occult primary tumors may be managed by chemical or surgical adrenalectomy; in most cases, the primary tumor is not life threatening. Patients with extensive carcinoma, for example, small cell carcinoma where ACTH excess coexists, may be best managed by chemotherapy, which indirectly reduces ACTH expression. Chemotherapy should be tailored for the cell type and tumor stage, regardless of hormone excess.

In some patients with florid Cushing's syndrome, control of cortisol production may help in preparation for surgery. In these cases, treatment with metyrapone, mitotane, or ketoconazole, in combination or individually, is helpful.[104–108] Side effects are common with these agents in the doses required, and so combinations (e.g., ketoconazole and metyrapone) may allow more effective control. There are case reports of good responses to long-acting somatostatin analogues[109,110] (Table 195-4).

## ECTOPIC CORTICOTROPIN-RELEASING HORMONE SECRETION

It has been more than 30 years since the original description of ectopic CRH secretion,[111] and it is now clear that true, isolated secretion of CRH is very rare (Table 195-5). In tumors secreting ACTH peptides, there are frequent reports of CRH immunoreactivity, which may play a paracrine role in the development of the hormone syndrome, but such a role has not been defined.[112–115] CRH is expressed outside the central nervous system, particularly in sites of inflammation, and may subserve other roles, including vasodilatation. CRH is seldom measured in the peripheral blood during the workup

### Table 195-4 Medical Therapy of Cushing's Syndrome Caused by Ectopic Adrenocorticotropic Hormone

| Drug | Mechanism of Action |
|---|---|
| Metyrapone | Inhibition of 11β-hydroxylase |
| Ketoconazole | Inhibition of several steps of cortisol synthesis |
| Aminoglutethimide | Inhibition of cholesterol conversion to pregnenolone |
| Octreotide | Inhibition of adrenocorticotropic hormone secretion |
| Etomidate | Adrenolytic agent |
| RU486 | Glucocorticoid receptor antagonist |
| Mitotane | Adrenolytic agent |

**Table 195-5** Tumors Associated with Ectopic Corticotropin-Releasing Hormone Secretion

Pancreatic tumors
Small cell lung carcinoma
Prostate carcinoma
Hypothalamic gangliocytoma
Medullary thyroid carcinoma
Bronchial carcinoid

**Table 195-7** Tumors Associated with Syndrome of Inappropriate Antidiuretic Hormone Secretion

| Tumor |
| --- |
| Small cell lung carcinoma |
| Pancreas |
| Duodenum |
| Urethra |
| Prostate |
| Bladder |
| Lymphoma and other hematologic malignancies |

of Cushing's syndrome or in inflammatory disease, and so evidence is lacking of a true endocrine role of this hormone in the peripheral circulation.

The clinical features are typical of Cushing's syndrome, and the hormonal features may resemble either pituitary secretion of ACTH (if the ectopic source secretes purely CRH) or ectopic ACTH syndrome (if the tumor cosecretes ACTH-related peptides). Measurement of CRH is probably best left to those cases with definitive pituitary ACTH production and confirmed corticotroph hyperplasia by histology.

## SYNDROME OF INAPPROPRIATE ANTIDIURETIC HORMONE SECRETION

SIADH is the most common cause of hyponatremia, and one of the most frequent hormone syndromes associated with malignant disease (Table 195-6). It may be caused by a wide range of underlying disorders that can be categorized into three broad groups, including malignancies, neurologic disorders, and lung disease. These conditions cause hyponatremia as a result of abnormal hypothalamic vasopressin, when secretion comes under aberrant control from either neuronal inputs or circulating humoral factors.

The vasopressin gene is expressed in a number of separate neuronal nuclei and peripheral tissues. Regulation of vasopressin expression is dependent on the site. For example, hyperosmolality increases vasopressin expression in the supraoptic nucleus and the magnocellular division of the paraventricular nucleus, but vasopressin mRNA in other sites is unaltered. For example, vasopressin expression in the suprachiasmatic nucleus is under diurnal regulation. Androgens upregulate expression of vasopressin in the striae terminalis, and glucocorticoids suppress expression in the parvocellular division of the paraventricular nucleus. Differential regulation, even within anatomically related sites, likely results from differential expression of hormone receptors in the cells and different neuronal afferents. Vasopressin gene transcription is under positive regulation by cAMP and protein kinase C pathways. Little is known about regulation of vasopressin outside the central nervous system, but glucocorticoids have been shown to suppress its expression in an SCLC cell line.

Ectopic secretion of vasopressin occurs in squamous cell carcinoma; small cell carcinoma; neuroblastoma; pancreatic, duodenal, prostatic, and urothelial tumors; and undifferentiated carcinoma[116-118] (Table 195-7). In one series, 16% of

patients with SCLC had hyponatremia (<130 mmol/L) at diagnosis compared with 0% of patients with non-SCLC. Hyponatremia was found to be an independent predictor of poor prognosis in extensive stage disease. In vitro studies found that 7 of 11 tumors in culture produced vasopressin, 9 of 11 tumors produced atrial natriuretic factor, and 5 of 11 tumors produced both hormones. All the cells studied from patients with hyponatremia produced one of the two hormones.[115]

The active hormone, vasopressin, is the product of a precursor peptide cleavage, which also gives rise to neurophysin II, and a C-terminal glycopeptide. Similar to the identification of partially processed forms of ACTH in the circulation in ectopic ACTH syndrome, the vasopressin-neurophysin precursor has been found in plasma from patients with SIADH due to SCLC.[119] This is in contrast to patients with SIADH caused by central nervous system disease. Differential hormone processing may provide an additional diagnostic test for the underlying cause of SIADH.

### DIAGNOSIS

Hyponatremia presents with features of neuropsychiatric dysfunction in most cases (Table 195-8). The elderly and the young are more likely than others to be symptomatic. The absolute sodium concentration is less reliable as a predictor of symptoms than the rate of decrease in sodium concentration, although almost all symptomatic patients will have plasma sodium concentration of less than 120 mmol/L. Clinical features include lethargy, fatigue, impaired conscious level, coma, seizures, and psychosis. Hyponatremia may cause death as a result of cerebral edema, uncontrolled seizures and the consequences of coma. Although mild hyponatremia (>125 mmol/L) is usually regarded as a straightforward condition, which may not require specific treatment, hyponatremia should not be regarded as benign.

A set of diagnostic criteria must be fulfilled before a secure diagnosis is reached (see Table 195-8). The underlying cause is then sought. Neurologic, lung-related, drug-related, and

**Table 195-6** Diagnostic Criteria for the Syndrome of Inappropriate Antidiuretic Hormone Secretion

Hyponatremia
Inappropriately increased urine osmolality (> 100 mOsm/kg)
Persistent sodium excretion in urine (> 20 mmol/L)
Normal renal, thyroid, and adrenal function
No hypovolemia, edema, or diuretic use

**Table 195-8** Clinical Features of Hyponatremia

Headache
Lethargy
Weakness
Nausea/vomiting
Mood swings
Confusion
Drowsiness
Hyporeflexia
Positive Babinski's sign
Convulsions
Coma

miscellaneous causes can result in dysregulation of vasopressin regulation in the hypothalamus and should not, therefore, be regarded as ectopic hormone secretion states. In contrast, a variety of tumors (see Table 195-7) has been shown to aberrantly secrete vasopressin and express the vasopressin gene inappropriately. There is evidence from $T_1$-weighted magnetic resonance imaging scans of the pituitary that such ectopic vasopressin secretion results in central suppression of vasopressin synthesis.

## MANAGEMENT

The management of this disorder falls into two parts. The first is to diagnose and treat the underlying cause, and the second is to remove excess, free body water. Discussion of specific therapy on the variety of underlying tumors is beyond the scope of this chapter, but surgical cure or debulking, chemotherapy, and radiotherapy have all been applied. In general, the circulating vasopressin concentration bears a direct relationship to tumor bulk in an individual patient, but there is a low correlation across a patient cohort, presumably reflecting intertumor differences in cellular differentiation and hormone production. Decisions about the acute correction of hyponatremia are complicated by the occurrence of both pontine and extrapontine myelinolysis as consequences of therapy. The risk of myelinolysis is linked to the rate of change in sodium concentration. Therefore, a prudent approach is always justified. In symptomatic patients, treat with furosemide and hypertonic saline until convulsions cease and the level of consciousness improves. This is usually achieved by an increase in sodium concentration of 10% (~10 mmol/L) and subsequent water restriction. In asymptomatic patients, the condition is almost always chronic; these patients should be treated by water deprivation initially.

Specific approaches to antagonize the action of vasopressin usually rely on demeclocycline, in divided doses up to 1200 mg daily, or lithium carbonate, an alternative with more toxicity. These agents induce a state of nephrogenic diabetes insipidus. Alternatively, oral sodium supplementation, up to 3 g daily, with furosemide, 40 to 80 mg, results in net loss of free water. In the future, specific vasopressin $V_2$ receptor antagonists may be a more specific therapeutic approach.[120,121]

## HUMORAL HYPERCALCEMIA OF MALIGNANCY

Hypercalcemia is a common complication of malignancy (Table 195-9). It may result from the direct lytic effect of bony metastases or the action of tumor-derived humoral factors, although it is now clear that a spectrum of disorders lies between these two extremes, and, in most cases, there is a humoral component. Calcitonin has been detected in peripheral blood in a number of patients with malignancy and appears to be incompletely processed, in a manner similar to ACTH, with higher molecular weight variants.[122] However, there is no clinical syndrome ascribed to such ectopic production. Calcitonin secretion appears to be most commonly associated with a multihormonal secretory phenotype, with other peptide hormones including ACTH and gastrin[42,90,122-135] (Table 195-10).

## PARATHYROID HORMONE–RELATED PROTEIN

The humoral syndrome has been explained by the isolation and characterization of a peptide hormone, parathyroid hormone related protein (PTHrP). This hormone is closely related in amino acid sequence to parathyroid hormone (PTH) in its N-terminal region (amino acids 1–34), but after residue 34, the two peptides have unique sequences. The discovery of PTHrP as the circulating mediator of hypercalcemia in malig-

nancy ruled out earlier theories that ectopic production of PTH was the cause. There have been isolated reports of ectopic PTH production by tumors, but these are rare. There is convincing evidence of PTH production in SCLC,[136] an ovarian tumor,[137] thymoma,[138] and neuroectodermal tumor.[139] In most cases, patients with malignancy and hypercalcemia with increased PTH concentrations will have coincident primary hyperparathyroidism rather than ectopic PTH secretion. As many as 70% of cases of hypercalcemia in malignancy are caused by excess PTHrP secretion.[140-145]

PTHrP is seldom detectable in the circulation of normal subjects, but its expression has been shown in a number of normal tissues. PTHrP may be regarded as a product of the diffuse paracrine system and may have evolved to perform quite different physiologic roles compared with the structurally related PTH. Under these circumstances, it is hard to describe production of PTHrP from a tumor arising from any tissue as truly ectopic because no definite eutopic source for the peptide has been defined. However, humoral hypercalcemia of malignancy is most conveniently considered with the group of ectopic hormone secretion syndromes.

### Table 195-9 Mechanisms of Malignancy-Associated Hypercalcemia

| Mechanism | Agent | Tumor Type |
|---|---|---|
| Lytic metastases | TGF-β | Squamous cell carcinoma of the lung |
| | IL-1 | Breast |
| | TNF | Kidney |
| | Lymphotoxin | Myeloma |
| | PTHrP | |
| Humoral effects | PTHrP | Solid tumors, particularly squamous cell carcinoma of the skin, lung, kidney, and head and neck |
| | PGE | Solid tumors |
| | TNF | Multiple myeloma |
| | TGF-β | |
| | IL-1 | |
| | Lymphotoxin | |
| | 1,25-Dihydroxy-vitamin D | T-cell lymphoma |
| | | Non-Hodgkin's lymphoma |
| | | Hodgkin's lymphoma |
| | | Melanoma |
| | | Small cell lung carcinoma |
| | Ectopic PTH (very rare) | Small cell lung carcinoma |
| Coexistent other causes of hypercalcemia | Primary hyper-parathyroidism | Ovarian cancer |
| | Sarcoidosis | |
| | Vitamin D mediated | |

TGF-β, transforming growth factor beta; 1,25-DHCC, 1,25-dihydroxycholecalciferol; IL-1, interleukin-1; TNF, tumor necrosis factor; PGE, prostaglandin E; PTH, parathyroid hormone; PTHrP, parathyroid hormone–related protein.

### Table 195-10 Tumors That Produce Ectopic Calcitonin

Pheochromocytomas
Pancreatic neuroendocrine tumors
Adrenocortical carcinoma
Neuroendocrine tumor of esophagus
Acute leukemia
Lung cancer (27% small cell lung carcinoma or adenocarcinoma)
Cervical carcinoma
Prostatic carcinoma
Breast cancer
Renal carcinoma
Gastrointestinal tract tumors

PTH and PTHrP share a common receptor that they recognize through their homologous N-terminal sequences. The PTH/PTHrP receptor mediates the action of both peptides in bone and kidney and is a member of the G-protein-coupled seven-transmembrane receptor family. The common receptor explains how PTHrP is able to generate cAMP in membrane preparations of PTH-sensitive renal tubule and, further, why the humoral hypercalcemia of malignancy syndrome resulted in hypercalcemia with hypophosphatemia. In addition, there are receptors that specifically recognize PTHrP, and these are presumed to be the natural targets for the peptide within the tissues in which it is produced.[146,147] In the past, there was controversy about 1,25-dihydroxyvitamin D levels in primary hyperparathyroidism versus humoral hypercalcemia of malignancy syndrome. PTHrP and 1,25-dihydroxyvitamin D appear to be loosely correlated in humoral hypercalcemia of malignancy syndrome, suggesting that PTHrP shares with PTH the capacity to induce 1α-hydroxylase. Occasionally, reported discrepancies may stem from the action of other tumor-derived, circulating factors, from the metabolic consequences of malignancy, or from some other mechanism related to hypercalcemia.[148,149]

PTHrP may also play a role in hypercalcemia related to osseous metastases in that the hypercalcemia associated with bony metastases has a significant humoral component. Furthermore, expression of PTHrP by primary tumors is a predictor of bony, metastatic disease development. This suggests that the local production of PTHrP by bone micrometastases may facilitate bony invasion and destruction.[150–153] PTHrP expression is under complex regulation. A number of cytokines and growth factors have been shown to induce its expression, and both glucocorticoids and 1,25-dihydroxycholecalciferol, which have an antiproliferative effect on epithelial cells, inhibit expression.[154–157]

## HYPERCALCEMIA IN HEMATOLOGIC MALIGNANCY

Hypercalcemia occurs in as many as 30% of patients with multiple myeloma. Skeletal involvement causes extensive bone destruction with pain and risk of pathologic fracture. Histologic evidence suggests that the bone disease is caused by increased osteoclastic activity in the absence of significant osteoblastic activity. Loss of osteoblastic activity is also supported by the characteristically negative bone scan and suppressed circulating osteocalcin concentration. A number of cytokines, produced by activated immune cells, have been shown to have direct effects promoting bone resorption. Such cytokines include tumor necrosis factor alpha, tumor growth factor beta, interleukin-1, and leukemia inhibitory factor. A superseded generic term for these factors was osteoclast-activating factor. However, it is noteworthy that in three of nine patients with multiple myeloma complicated by hypercalcemia, there was an elevation in circulating PTHrP, suggesting that a mechanism similar to humoral hypercalcemia of malignancy syndrome may be operating in at least some patients with hematologic malignancy associated hypercalcemia.[24,144,158,159]

Generally, hypercalcemia is rare in lymphoma, with the exception of adult T-cell leukemia/lymphoma. This disease occurs in Japan and the West Indies and is caused by infection with the human T-cell lymphotrophic virus type I. At least one fourth of patients will develop hypercalcemia, which is associated with suppressed 1,25-dihydroxyvitamin D. Hypercalcemia predicts outcome and is implicated in causing patient mortality. There is strong evidence that the hypercalcemia is mediated by PTHrP.[160–163]

## DIAGNOSIS

Hypercalcemia is the most common metabolic complication of malignant disease and the cause of much morbidity (Table 195-11). Most cases are due to humoral mechanisms, principally PTHrP, rather than direct damage of bone by malignant cells. This is clear from the observation that even patients who have bone metastases and hypercalcemia have a poor correlation between extent of skeletal involvement and calcium concentration in the circulation.

The presentation of hypercalcemia may be confusing and may be attributed to the underlying disease process itself. Patients may be nonspecifically unwell and may complain of constipation, nausea, vomiting, confusion, or dehydration. Hypercalcemia induces a diuresis and may cause profound dehydration, particularly in association with vomiting or drowsiness. Further manifestations include lethargy, depression, poor concentration, and drowsiness.

It is sometimes necessary to distinguish malignancy-induced hypercalcemia from other causes of hypercalcemia, such as hyperparathyroidism. PTH levels are low in hypercalcemia of malignancy. An elevated PTHrP level confirms the diagnosis, and it is increased in approximately 80% of patients with hypercalcemia with cancer. 1,25-Dihydroxyvitamin D levels may be increased in patients with lymphoma. Recognition of hypercalcemia and its appropriate treatment allow retrospective allocation of symptoms in an individual patient. Therefore, it is almost always worth treating such patients, irrespective of their underlying disease prognosis.

## TREATMENT

There is little evidence that hypercalcemia is a significant cause of premature mortality in cancer, but it is a significant cause of morbidity.[164] Even if the underlying malignancy is beyond cure, effective relief of hypercalcemia is a most useful palliative intervention. There are few patients in whom treatment should not be seriously considered because intervention is quick, easy, and largely free of serious complications. In the past, calcitonin and/or mithramycin were used, but these have been replaced by the bisphosphonate drugs, in conjunction with rehydration with intravenous saline.[165] The saline promotes a calcium diuresis. Usually, single infusions of pamidronate or clodronate are sufficient, with a suggestion that pamidronate is slightly more effective.[166,167] There are newer bisphosphonates that have become available (e.g., ibandronate), but further head-to-head comparisons are lacking.[168] These drugs are usually administered by slow intravenous infusion. There may be a transient febrile reaction within the first 24 hours, but this is usually self-limiting. The calcium response is typically rapid and may last as long as 1 month. In patients in whom a more rapid acute effect is desired, bisphosphonates can be combined with calcitonin.[169]

The bisphosphonates are rapidly cleared from the circulation and concentrated in bone. They appear to inhibit osteoclast activity and may induce osteoclast apoptosis. Their duration of action is significantly longer than predicted by

| Table 195-11 | Symptoms and Signs of Hypercalcemia |
| --- | --- |
| Polyuria | |
| Thirst | |
| Nausea | |
| Anorexia | |
| Constipation | |
| Confusion | |
| Drowsiness | |
| Headache | |
| Coma | |

their plasma half-life, reflecting their distribution and mode of action.[168]

## ONCOGENIC OSTEOMALACIA

Osteomalacia associated with malignancy was first described in 1947.[170] It is characterized by hypophosphatemia, normal or low calcium, elevated alkaline phosphatase, and suppressed 1,25-dihydroxyvitamin D. It is usually found with benign mesenchymal tumors, of which hemangiopericytomas are the most common. The disorder exhibits biochemical features similar to those seen with inactivating mutations in the *PHEX* gene, the cause of hereditary X-linked hypophosphatemia. The *PHEX* gene encodes a protease that activates phosphatonins, including the protein fibroblast growth factor type 23, which seems to be the phosphaturic factor produced by tumors that cause oncogenic osteomalacia.

## ECTOPIC GROWTH HORMONE–RELEASING HORMONE

Ectopic GHRH-releasing tumors, often the bronchial or upper gastrointestinal carcinoid cell type, are a very rare cause of acromegaly (Table 195-12). In patients who present with acromegaly, the syndrome is usually of several years' duration to allow development of the typical clinical features. Accordingly, it is not surprising that the underlying tumors are usually small and benign. Clinical features are similar to those of typical acromegaly. Pituitary imaging is unhelpful because the radiographic features reveal an enlarged pituitary or an asymmetric mass that can be confused with an adenoma.[171] The histologic identification of true pituitary somatotroph hyperplasia, with a preserved reticulin network, led to the identification of GHRH in extracts from islet cell tumors.[172–175] Since then, many tumors and tumor cell lines have been shown to express or secrete GHRH.[176–180] For example, 25 of 97 carcinoid tumors expressed GHRH in one study,[181] 17% of gastrointestinal and pancreatic tumors stained for GHRH in another,[182] and 63% of endometrial adenocarcinomas expressed GHRH.[183] In addition, subtle abnormalities in GH secretion and regulation may be found in patients harboring carcinoid tumors.[184] GH secretion has been associated with the development of several malignant tumors, notably prostate and colon adenocarcinoma. Therefore, a complex long feedback loop may confer survival advantage on these tumors.

It has been suggested that all patients with acromegaly should be screened for ectopic GHRH because measurements in the plasma of greater than 0.3 ng/mL are virtually diagnostic of GHRH production by a tumor.[185] However, the assays are not widely available and currently remain research tools. In addition, the incidence is rare. In one series of 177 unselected patients with acromegaly, only one had detectable GHRH concentrations in plasma.[174,186]

Most commonly, the diagnosis is made after hypophysectomy, when histology shows somatotroph hyperplasia. In these cases, measurement of GHRH is necessary, as is the search for its source. The best treatment is curative resection of the primary tumor, but in cases in which the tumor is elusive or metastatic, success has been achieved using long-acting somatostatin analogues.[171,187–189]

## NON–ISLET CELL TUMOR HYPOGLYCEMIA

Fasting hypoglycemia may arise as a consequence of non–islet cell tumor formation (see Chapter 193) (Table 195-13). Such tumors do not express insulin, which appears to be very tightly regulated in its tissue distribution, but rather the insulin-related molecules insulin-like growth factor (IGF)-1 or, more commonly, IGF-2 (Table 195-14). These two growth factors are members of the insulin family of peptide hormones along with relaxin, and both are capable of signaling through the IGF-1 receptor or the insulin receptor. IGF-1 is the liver-derived circulating mediator of GH action, whereas IGF-2 has a more important role in development. In normal subjects, IGF-1 and IGF-2 circulate at much higher concentrations than insulin and, if unopposed, cause profound hypoglycemia due to their actions through the insulin receptor. That this does not occur is due to the presence of high-affinity, high-capacity, circulating IGF binding proteins.[190,191] These result in very low concentrations of free IGFs, and they act to chaperone the IGFs and deliver them to their tissue beds of action.

A number of tumors, typically of mesenchymal origin, have been identified as the cause of non–islet cell hypoglycemia. The apparent mechanism is overproduction of IGF-2.[192] In addition to aberrant overproduction of IGF-2, there is also secretion of a partially processed form of IGF-2, "big" IGF-2, which includes a C-terminal extension peptide and frequently an abnormal glycosylation pattern.[193,194] The circulating IGF-2 would be expected to cause few problems if it were effectively sequestered by IGF binding proteins, but this does not occur.[195,196] IGF-2 exerts a negative

---

**Table 195-13  Tumors Associated with Nonislet Cell Tumor Hypoglycemia**

| Carcinoma | Mesenchymal |
|---|---|
| Hepatocellular, hepatoma | Fibroma, fibrosarcoma |
| Adrenocortical | Mesothelioma |
| Pancreatic | Rhabdomyosarcoma |
| Gastric | Neurofibroma, neurofibrosarcoma |
| Colon | Leiomyosarcoma |
| Lung (small cell, squamous) | Others |
| Kidney | Hemangiopericytoma |
| Prostate | Hematologic |
|  | Lymphoma |

---

**Table 195-12  Tumors Associated with Growth Hormone–Releasing Hormone Secretion**

| | |
|---|---|
| Carcinoid tumors (e.g., bronchial) | Pheochromocytomas |
| Pancreatic islet tumors | Adrenal adenomas |
| Small cell lung carcinoma | Hypothalamic gangliocytomas |

---

**Table 195-14  Nonislet Cell Tumor Hypoglycemia Versus Insulinoma**

| | Nonislet Cell | Insulinoma |
|---|---|---|
| IGF-1 | ↔ | ↔ |
| IGF-2 | ↑ | ↔ |
| IGFBP-3 | ↓ | ↔ |
| Insulin | ↓ | ↑ |
| Glucose | ↓ | ↓ |
| Growth hormone | ↓ | ↔ or ↑ |
| β-Hydroxybutyrate | ↓ | ↓ |

IGF, insulin-like growth factor; IGFBP, insulin-like growth factor–binding protein. ↑, increased; ↓, decreased; ↔, equivocal.

feedback at the pituitary somatotroph to suppress GH secretion. GH is the key regulator of hepatic IGF-binding protein 3, a component of the principal, ternary circulating IGF complex (Fig. 195-2). Therefore, in the absence of effective GH drive to IGF-binding protein 3 production, the tumor-derived IGF-2 is left in a free state and is thus capable of acting through the insulin receptor and causing hypoglycemia.[197]

## DIAGNOSIS

The diagnosis is based on the recognition that the patient's symptoms are due to hypoglycemia, which involves a detailed history and confirmation of either hypoglycemia occurring during a symptomatic episode or fasting hypoglycemia. The typical biochemical accompaniment to hypoglycemia is suppressed insulin, suppressed ketone bodies (ß-hydroxybutyrate), and suppressed GH. In addition, IGF-2 is usually elevated or normal, with suppression of IGF-binding protein 3 as a consequence of low GH.[192,198]

Most tumors are large and intra-abdominal, although thoracic tumors have also been reported.[199] The underlying tumor may be benign, in which case curative resection is the aim. Histologic confirmation of the diagnosis is by specific immunostaining of a biopsy for IGF-2.

## MANAGEMENT

Effective management requires either surgical excision or debulking of the tumor. This is best achieved by close consultation between oncologist, surgeon, and interventional radiologist, who may be able to perform tumor embolization. These tumors tend not to be radiosensitive, although there are isolated case reports of therapeutic response. Because these tumors are rare, management is tailored to the individual patient and is usually based on pragmatic approaches. In patients whose tumors are inoperable, relief of hypoglycemia can be achieved by using glucocorticoid, usually dexamethasone, either alone or with recombinant human GH.[197,200]

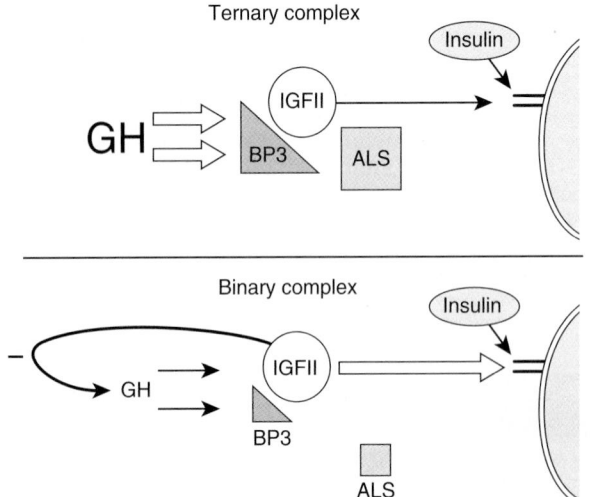

**Figure 195-2** Formation of the ternary complex between insulin-like growth factors (IGFs), IGF-binding protein 3 (BP3), and the acid-labile subunit (ALS). Normal physiology (top) in ectopic production of IGF (usually IGF-2) by tumor (bottom). Increased activity of IGF inhibits pituitary production of growth hormone (GH) and so reduces hepatic production of ALS and IGF-BP3. The resulting binary complex has increased insulin-like activity and, acting through the insulin receptor, causes hypoglycemia.

Glucocorticoids exert a direct anti-insulin and anti-IGF effect, and GH acts both by its anti-insulin action and also by increasing the IGF binding protein concentration, which then acts to "mop up" the excess IGF.

## OTHER PITUITARY ECTOPIC HORMONES

The two pituitary hormones prolactin and GH are of interest because they have wide extrapituitary expression and yet are very seldom the cause of clinically significant ectopic hormone syndromes. Prolactin is expressed in decidualized endometrium, T lymphocytes, mammary epithelial cells, skin, sweat glands, and the brain. It is the same gene that is transcribed in all these cases, rather than the related placental lactogen-type gene, but the regulation of the gene appears completely different.[201] Whereas in the pituitary lactotroph cell, prolactin is under the transcriptional control of the pituitary-specific factor Pit1, in extrapituitary tissues, Pit1 is not expressed, and the pituitary promoter of the prolactin gene is silent. The gene is transcribed from an upstream promoter, which gives rise to a slightly longer mRNA, with a unique 5′ end but, after processing, results in a protein with the same amino acid sequence. Because the gene is transcribed from a different promoter, the control of gene transcription, its basal rate and regulation by external signals, is different. For example, in T-lymphocyte prolactin, gene transcription is responsive to the immunophilins, including cyclosporin A. The function of this extrapituitary prolactin is subject to debate, and it is not clear why such widespread expression is accompanied by such rarity of overexpression in malignant disease, in contrast to ACTH or vasopressin expression. Because prolactin receptors are found in a variety of tissues that cannot be reconciled with an exclusive action on mammary milk production, prolactin may have a more diverse role than so far determined.

Ectopic prolactin secretion is a rare occurrence.[202] There are reports of ectopic prolactin secretion from a bronchial tumor,[203] a gonadoblastoma,[204] a renal cell carcinoma,[205] and undifferentiated lung cancer.[205] However, breast cancers have been shown to express both prolactin and prolactin receptors.[206–208] There is some evidence of a weak tumor-promoting effect of prolactin on breast adenocarcinoma cells[209,210] that has led to the suggestion of a paracrine role for prolactin in the development or progression of breast malignancy. Prolactin may have other activities in addition to its best characterized function on lactation, and, in particular, a 16-kilodalton fragment of prolactin has antiangiogenic potential and may influence tumorigenesis.[211,212] In addition, prolactin can activate nuclear factor-κB, a survival-promoting transcription factor.[213]

GH is also found in extrapituitary tissues, again in cells of hematopoietic lineage. This expression has been suggested to result in paracrine signaling, although hard data are lacking.

Ectopic GH secretion was first described in 1968 in a man with lung cancer. Resection of the tumor caused a decrease in GH concentrations, although GH was not measured in the primary tumor.[214] There are very few cases in which the criteria are met for true ectopic secretion of GH. One such case was described by Melmed and coworkers,[215] who carefully showed GH secretion from a pancreatic islet tumor, with demonstration of a gradient of GH across the tumor in vivo and resolution of abnormal GH and IGF-1 after tumor resection. They also showed GH expression in tumor sections, at both the mRNA and protein level. It is interesting that there is hypertrophic osteoarthropathy in cases of ectopic GH secretion, although this is not a feature of acromegaly; it may result from other humoral factors secreted by the tumors or from neural influences.[215–217]

## GONADOTROPINS

Human chorionic gonadotropin is expressed in trophoblast and from both germ cell and trophoblast tumors. The most frequent nontrophoblast tumor associated with human chorionic gonadotropin overproduction is lung,[218] but other tumors have been described including adrenal, breast, bladder, maxilla, hepatoblastoma, osteosarcoma, and lymphoma.[219-223]

The production of human chorionic gonadotropin in men causes gynecomastia as a result of increased estrogen secretion and may cause precocious puberty in children.[224]

## ECTOPIC GUT HORMONE SYNDROMES

Clinical syndromes associated with ectopic production of gut hormones by tumors are very rare, but vasoactive intestinal polypeptide causing typical watery diarrhea has been described (see Chapter 193). Tumors of the lung, medullary thyroid carcinoma, pheochromocytoma, and neuroendocrine tumors of the kidney have all been reported to produce vasoactive intestinal polypeptide.[225-227]

### ECTOPIC RENIN SECRETION

Renin production is usually tightly restricted to the juxtaglomerular apparatus of the kidney, and true ectopic secretion by nonrenal tumors is very rare (Table 195-15). In cases

| Table 195-15 | Tumors Associated with Ectopic Renin Secretion |
|---|---|

Kidney (Wilms' tumor, renal cell carcinoma)
Lung (small cell lung carcinoma, adenocarcinoma, leiomyosarcoma)
Pancreatic carcinoma
Ovarian tumors
Liver (hepatocellular carcinoma, hamartoma)
Ileal carcinoma
Adrenal paraganglioma
Orbital hemangiopericytoma

described, hypertension is a feature, along with hypokalemia.[228] As is often the case with ectopic production of usually processed hormones, renin precursors are described, with an increased prorenin-renin ratio.[229-231] Resection of the primary tumor affords cure, if identified, but medical therapy with angiotensin-converting enzyme inhibitors or with angiotensin-blocking agents may be beneficial in noncurable disease.[232]

Extrarenal tumors secreting renin include lung,[233-235] pancreas,[231] ovary,[236,237] liver,[238] ileum,[239] adrenal,[240] and orbital hemangiopericytoma.[241]

## Acknowledgments
The author is grateful to Professor Wass and Dr. Turner, who wrote the previous version of this chapter, for inspiration and for the use of tables.

## REFERENCES

1. Klemperer P: Parathyroid hyperplasia and bone destruction in generalised carcinomatosis. Surg Gynaecol Obstet 36:11, 1923.
2. Brown WH: A case of pluriglandular syndrome: Diabetes of bearded women. Lancet 2:1022–1028, 1928.
3. Leyton O, Turnbull AM, Bratton AB. Primary cancer of the thymus with pluriglandular disturbance. J Pathol 34:635, 1931.
4. Nadler WH, Wolfer JA: Hepatogenic hypoglycemia in primary carcinoma of the liver. Arch Intern Med 44:700, 1929.
5. Crawford WH: Hypoglycemia with coma in a case of primary carcinoma of the liver. Am J Med Sci 181:496, 1931.
6. Albright F, Reifenstein EC: The parathyroid glands and metabolic bone disease—selected studies. Baltimore, Williams & Wilkins, 1948.
7. Meador CK, Liddle GW, Island DP, et al: Cause of Cushing's syndrome in patients with tumors arising from "nonendocrine" tissue. J Clin Endocrinol Metab 22:693–703, 1962.
8. Liddle GW, Nicholson WE, Island DP, et al: Clinical and laboratory studies of ectopic humoral syndromes. Recent Prog Horm Res 25:283–314, 1969.
9. Orth DN, Nicholson WE, Mitchell WM, et al: Biologic and immunologic characterization and physical separation of ACTH and ACTH fragments in the ectopic ACTH syndrome. J Clin Invest 52:1756–1769, 1973.
10. Amatruda TT Jr, Mulrow PJ, Gallagher JC, Sawyer WH: Carcinoma of the lung with inappropriate antidiuresis. Demonstration of antidiuretic-hormone-like activity in tumor extract. N Engl J Med 269:544–549, 1963.
11. DeBold CR, Menefee JK, Nicholson WE, Orth DN: Proopiomelanocortin gene is expressed in many normal human tissues and in tumors not associated with ectopic adrenocorticotropin syndrome. Mol Endocrinol 2:862–870, 1988.
12. Gelhorn A: The unifying thread. Cancer Res 23:961–970, 1963.
13. Odell WD: Ectopic ACTH secretion. A misnomer. Endocrinol Metab Clin North Am 20:371–379, 1991.
14. Odell WD, Saito E: Protein hormone-like materials from normal and cancer cells—"ectopic" hormone production. Prog Clin Biol Res 132E:247–258, 1983.
15. Odell WD, Wolfsen AR: Humoral syndromes associated with cancer. Annu Rev Med 29:379–406, 1978.
16. Odell WD, Wolfsen AR: Hormones from tumors: Are they ubiquitous? Am J Med 68:317–318, 1980.
17. Odell WD, Wolfsen AR: Humoral syndromes associated with cancer: Ectopic hormone production. Prog Clin Cancer 8:57–74, 1982.
18. Odell WD: Endocrine/metabolic syndromes of cancer. Semin Oncol 24:299–317, 1997.
19. Saito E, Iwasa S, Odell WD: Widespread presence of large molecular weight adrenocorticotropin-like substances in normal rat extrapituitary tissues. Endocrinology 113:1010–1019, 1983.
20. Saito E, Odell WD: Corticotropin/lipotropin common precursor-like material in normal rat extrapituitary tissues. Proc Natl Acad Sci U S A 80:3792–3796, 1983.
21. Shields R: Ectopic hormone production by tumours. Nature 272:494, 1978.
22. Pearse AG: Common cytochemical and ultrastructural characteristics of cells producing polypeptide hormones (the APUD series) and their relevance to thyroid and ultimobranchial C cells and calcitonin. Proc R Soc Lond B Biol Sci 170:71–80, 1968.
23. Pearse AG, Polak JM: Endocrine tumours of neural crest origin: neurolophomas, apudomas and the APUD concept. Med Biol 52:3–18, 1974.
24. Pearse AG: The APUD cell concept and its implications in pathology. Pathol Annu 9:27–41, 1974.
25. Takor TT, Pearse AG: Cytochemical identification of human and murine pituitary corticotrophs and somatotrophs as APUD cells. Histochemie 37:207–214, 1973.
26. Welbourn RB, Pearse AG, Polak JM, et al: The APUD cells of the alimentary tract in health and disease. Med Clin North Am 58:1359–1374, 1974.
27. Abeloff MD, Eggleston JC, Mendelsohn G, et al: Changes in morphologic and biochemical characteristics of small cell carcinoma of the lung. A clinicopathologic study. Am J Med 66:757–764, 1979.
28. Abeloff MD, Trump DL, Baylin SB: Ectopic adrenocorticotrophic (ACTH) syndrome and small cell carcinoma of the lung-assessment of clinical implications in patients on combination chemotherapy. Cancer 48:1082–1087, 1981.
29. Baylin SB, Mendelsohn G: Ectopic (inappropriate) hormone production by tumors: Mechanisms involved and

the biological and clinical implications. Endocr Rev 1:45–77, 1980.

30. Baylin SB, Mendelsohn G: Time-dependent changes in human tumors: Implications for diagnosis and clinical behavior. Semin Oncol 9:504–512, 1982.

31. Berger CL, Goodwin G, Mendelsohn G, et al: Endocrine-related biochemistry in the spectrum of human lung carcinoma. J Clin Endocrinol Metab 53:422–429, 1981.

32. Berger CL, de Bustros A, Roos BA, et al: Human medullary thyroid carcinoma in culture provides a model relating growth dynamics, endocrine cell differentiation, and tumor progression. J Clin Endocrinol Metab 59:338–343, 1984.

33. Goodwin G, Shaper JH, Abeloff MD, et al: Analysis of cell surface proteins delineates a differentiation pathway linking endocrine and nonendocrine human lung cancers. Proc Natl Acad Sci U S A 80:3807–3811, 1983.

34. White A, Clark AJ: The cellular and molecular basis of the ectopic ACTH syndrome. Clin Endocrinol (Oxf) 39:131–141, 1993.

35. White A, Clark AJ, Stewart MF: The synthesis of ACTH and related peptides by tumours. Baillieres Clin Endocrinol Metab 4:1–27, 1990.

36. Delisle L, Boyer MJ, Warr D, et al: Ectopic corticotropin syndrome and small-cell carcinoma of the lung. Clinical features, outcome, and complications. Arch Intern Med 153:746–752, 1993.

37. Stewart PM, Gibson S, Crosby SR, et al: ACTH precursors characterize the ectopic ACTH syndrome. Clin Endocrinol (Oxf) 40:199–204, 1994.

38. Gumbiner B, Kelly RB: Two distinct intracellular pathways transport secretory and membrane glycoproteins to the surface of pituitary tumor cells. Cell 28:51–59, 1982.

39. Drouin J, Chamberland M, Charron J, et al: Structure of the rat pro-opiomelanocortin (POMC) gene. FEBS Lett 193:54–58, 1985.

40. Clark AJ, Lavender PM, Coates P, et al: In vitro and in vivo analysis of the processing and fate of the peptide products of the short proopiomelanocortin mRNA. Mol Endocrinol 4:1737–1743, 1990.

41. Clark AJ, Lavender PM, Besser GM, Rees LH: Pro-opiomelanocortin mRNA size heterogeneity in ACTH-dependent Cushing's syndrome. J Mol Endocrinol 2:3–9, 1989.

42. Clark AJ: Ectopic hormone production. Baillieres Clin Endocrinol Metab 2:967–986, 1988.

43. De Keyzer Y, Bertagna X, Luton JP, Kahn A: Variable modes of proopiomelanocortin gene transcription in human tumors. Mol Endocrinol 3:215–223, 1989.

44. Lundblad JR, Roberts JL: Regulation of proopiomelanocortin gene expression in pituitary. Endocr Rev 9:135–158, 1988.

45. Drouin J, Nemer M, Charron J, et al: Tissue-specific activity of the pro-opiomelanocortin (POMC) gene and repression by glucocorticoids. Genome 31:510–519, 1989.

46. Gagner JP, Drouin J: Tissue-specific regulation of pituitary proopiomelanocortin gene transcription by corticotropin-releasing hormone, 3',5'-cyclic adenosine monophosphate, and glucocorticoids. Mol Endocrinol 1:677–682, 1987.

47. Lamolet B, Pulichino AM, Lamonerie T, et al: A pituitary cell-restricted T box factor, Tpit, activates POMC transcription in cooperation with Pitx homeoproteins. Cell 104:849–859, 2001.

48. Maira M, Couture C, Le Martelot G, et al: The T-box factor Tpit recruits SRC/p160 co-activators and mediates hormone action. J Biol Chem 278:46523–46532, 2003.

49. Drouin J, Maira M, Philips A: Novel mechanism of action for Nur77 and antagonism by glucocorticoids: A convergent mechanism for CRH activation and glucocorticoid repression of POMC gene transcription. J Steroid Biochem Mol Biol 65:59–63, 1998.

50. Philips A, Maira M, Mullick A, et al: Antagonism between Nur77 and glucocorticoid receptor for control of transcription. Mol Cell Biol 17:5952–5959, 1997.

51. Philips A, Lesage S, Gingras R, et al: Novel dimeric Nur77 signaling mechanism in endocrine and lymphoid cells. Mol Cell Biol 17:5946–5951, 1997.

52. Maira M, Martens C, Batsche E, et al: Dimer-specific potentiation of NGFI-B (Nur77) transcriptional activity by the protein kinase A pathway and AF-1-dependent coactivator recruitment. Mol Cell Biol 23:763–776, 2003.

53. Drouin J, Trifiro MA, Plante RK, et al: Glucocorticoid receptor binding to a specific DNA sequence is required for hormone-dependent repression of pro-opiomelanocortin gene transcription. Mol Cell Biol 9:5305–5314, 1989.

54. Drouin J, Sun YL, Nemer M: Glucocorticoid repression of pro-opiomelanocortin gene transcription. J Steroid Biochem 34:63–69, 1989.

55. Drouin J, Sun YL, Chamberland M, et al: Novel glucocorticoid receptor complex with DNA element of the hormone-repressed POMC gene. EMBO J 12:145–156, 1993.

56. Riegel AT, Lu Y, Remenick J, et al: Proopiomelanocortin gene promoter elements required for constitutive and glucocorticoid-repressed transcription. Mol Endocrinol 5:1973–1982, 1991.

57. Vallette-Kasic S, Figarella-Branger D, Grino M, eta l: Differential regulation of proopiomelanocortin and pituitary-restricted transcription factor (TPIT), a new marker of normal and adenomatous human corticotrophs. J Clin Endocrinol Metab 88:3050–3056, 2003.

58. Boutillier AL, Sassone-Corsi P, Loeffler JP: The protooncogene c-fos is induced by corticotropin-releasing factor and stimulates proopiomelanocortin gene transcription in pituitary cells. Mol Endocrinol 5:1301–1310, 1991.

59. Boutillier AL, Monnier D, Koch B, Loeffler JP: Pituitary adenyl cyclase-activating peptide: A hypophysiotropic factor that stimulates proopiomelanocortin gene transcription, and proopiomelanocortin-derived peptide secretion in corticotropic cells. Neuroendocrinology 60:493–502, 1994.

60. Boutillier AL, Monnier D, Lorang D, et al: Corticotropin-releasing hormone stimulates proopiomelanocortin transcription by cFos-dependent and -independent pathways: Characterization of an AP1 site in exon 1. Mol Endocrinol 9:745–755, 1995.

61. Boutillier AL, Gaiddon C, Lorang D, et al: Transcriptional activation of the proopiomelanocortin gene by cyclic AMP-responsive element binding protein. Pituitary 1:33–43, 1998.

62. Jin WD, Boutillier AL, Glucksman MJ, et al: Characterization of a corticotropin-releasing hormone-responsive element in the rat proopiomelanocortin gene promoter and molecular cloning of its binding protein. Mol Endocrinol 8:1377–1388, 1994.

63. Abou-Samra AB, Harwood JP, Manganiello VC, et al: Phorbol 12-myristate 13-acetate and vasopressin potentiate the effect of corticotropin-releasing factor on cyclic AMP production in rat anterior pituitary cells. Mechanisms of action. J Biol Chem 262:1129–1136, 1987.

64. Auernhammer CJ, Chesnokova V, Bousquet C, Melmed S: Pituitary corticotroph SOCS-3: Novel intracellular regulation of leukemia-inhibitory factor-mediated proopiomelanocortin gene expression and adrenocorticotropin secretion. Mol Endocrinol 12:954–961, 1998.

65. Bousquet C, Susini C, Melmed S: Inhibitory roles for SHP-1 and SOCS-3 following pituitary proopiomelanocortin induction by leukemia inhibitory factor. J Clin Invest 104:1277–1285, 1999.

66. Bousquet C, Melmed S: Critical role for STAT3 in murine pituitary adrenocorticotropin hormone leukemia inhibitory factor signaling. J Biol Chem 274:10723–10730, 1999.

67. Ray DW, Ren SG, Melmed S: Leukemia inhibitory factor (LIF) stimulates proopiomelanocortin (POMC) expression in a corticotroph cell line. Role of STAT pathway. J Clin Invest 97:1852–1859, 1996.

68. Bousquet C, Ray DW, Melmed S: A common pro-opiomelanocortin-binding element mediates leukemia inhibitory factor and corticotropin-releasing hormone transcriptional synergy. J Biol Chem 272:10551–10557, 1997.

69. Stefana B, Ray DW, Melmed S: Leukemia inhibitory factor induces differentiation of pituitary corticotroph function: An

immuno-neuroendocrine phenotypic switch. Proc Natl Acad Sci U S A 93:12502–12506, 1996.

70. Newell-Price J: Proopiomelanocortin gene expression and DNA methylation: Implications for Cushing's syndrome and beyond. J Endocrinol 177:365–372, 2003.

71. Newell-Price J, King P, Clark AJ: The CpG island promoter of the human proopiomelanocortin gene is methylated in nonexpressing normal tissue and tumors and represses expression. Mol Endocrinol 15:338–348, 2001.

72. Newell-Price J: Proopiomelanocortin gene expression and DNA methylation: Implications for Cushing's syndrome and beyond. J Endocrinol 177:365–372, 2003.

73. Wolfsen AR, Odell WD: ProACTH: Use for early detection of lung cancer. Am J Med 66:765–772, 1979.

74. Yalow RS, Berson SA: Size heterogeneity of immunoreactive human ACTH in plasma and in extracts of pituitary glands and ACTH-producing thymoma. Biochem Biophys Res Commun 44:439–445, 1971.

75. Yalow RS, Berson SA: Characteristics of "big ACTH" in human plasma and pituitary extracts. J Clin Endocrinol Metab 36:415–423, 1973.

76. Shepherd FA, Laskey J, Evans WK, et al: Cushing's syndrome associated with ectopic corticotropin production and small-cell lung cancer. J Clin Oncol 10:21–27, 1992.

77. Hansen M, Pedersen AG: Tumor markers in patients with lung cancer. Chest 89:219S–224S, 1986.

78. Mains RE, Eipper BA: Biosynthesis of adrenocorticotropic hormone in mouse pituitary tumor cells. J Biol Chem 251:4115–4120, 1976.

79. Mains RE, Eipper BA, Ling N: Common precursor to corticotropins and endorphins. Proc Natl Acad Sci U S A 74:3014–3018, 1977.

80. Mains RE, Eipper BA: Coordinate synthesis of corticotropins and endorphins by mouse pituitary tumor cells. J Biol Chem 253:651–655, 1978.

81. Marcinkiewicz M, Day R, Seidah NG, Chretien M: Ontogeny of the prohormone convertases PC1 and PC2 in the mouse hypophysis and their colocalization with corticotropin and alpha-melanotropin. Proc Natl Acad Sci U S A 90:4922–4926, 1993.

82. Vieau D, Seidah NG, Mbikay M, et al: Expression of the prohormone convertase PC2 correlates with the presence of corticotropin-like intermediate lobe peptide in human adrenocorticotropin-secreting tumors. J Clin Endocrinol Metab 79:1503–1506, 1994.

83. Vieau D, Massias JF, Girard F, et al: Corticotrophin-like intermediary lobe peptide as a marker of alternate pro-opiomelanocortin processing in ACTH-producing non-pituitary tumours. Clin Endocrinol (Oxf) 31:691–700, 1989.

84. Liddle GW, Givens JR, Nicholson WE, Island DP: The ectopic ACTH syndrome. Cancer Res 25:1057–1061, 1965.

85. Isidori AM, Kaltsas GA, Mohammed S, et al: Discriminatory value of the low-dose dexamethasone suppression test in establishing the diagnosis and differential diagnosis of Cushing's syndrome. J Clin Endocrinol Metab 88:5299–5306, 2003.

86. Newell-Price J, Morris DG, Drake WM, et al: Optimal response criteria for the human CRH test in the differential diagnosis of ACTH-dependent Cushing's syndrome. J Clin Endocrinol Metab 87:1640–1645, 2002.

87. Nieman LK, Cutler GB Jr, Oldfield EH, et al: The ovine corticotropin-releasing hormone (CRH) stimulation test is superior to the human CRH stimulation test for the diagnosis of Cushing's disease. J Clin Endocrinol Metab 69:165–169, 1989.

88. Malchoff CD, Orth DN, Abboud C, et al: Ectopic ACTH syndrome caused by a bronchial carcinoid tumor responsive to dexamethasone, metyrapone, and corticotropin-releasing factor. Am J Med 84:760–764, 1988.

89. White A, Stewart MF, Farrell WE, et al: Pro-opiomelanocortin gene expression and peptide secretion in human small-cell lung cancer cell lines. J Mol Endocrinol 3:65–70, 1989.

90. Bertagna XY, Nicholson WE, Pettengill OS, et al: Ectopic production of high molecular weight calcitonin and corticotropin by human small cell carcinoma cells in tissue culture: Evidence for separate precursors. J Clin Endocrinol Metab 47:1390–1393, 1978.

91. Bertagna XY, Nicholson WE, Sorenson GD, et al: Corticotropin, lipotropin, and beta-endorphin production by a human nonpituitary tumor in culture: Evidence for a common precursor. Proc Natl Acad Sci U S A 75:5160–5164, 1978.

92. Ray DW, Littlewood AC, Clark AJ, et al: Human small cell lung cancer cell lines expressing the proopiomelanocortin gene have aberrant glucocorticoid receptor function. J Clin Invest 93:1625–1630, 1994.

93. Clark AJ, Stewart MF, Lavender PM, et al: Defective glucocorticoid regulation of proopiomelanocortin gene expression and peptide secretion in a small cell lung cancer cell line. J Clin Endocrinol Metab 70:485–490, 1990.

94. Stewart MF, Crosby SR, Gibson S, et al: Small cell lung cancer cell lines secrete predominantly ACTH precursor peptides not ACTH. Br J Cancer 60:20–24, 1989.

95. Ray DW, Davis JR, White A, Clark AJ: Glucocorticoid receptor structure and function in glucocorticoid-resistant small cell lung carcinoma cells. Cancer Res 56:3276–3280, 1996.

96. Florkowski CM, Wittert GA, Lewis JG, et al: Glucocorticoid responsive ACTH secreting bronchial carcinoid tumours contain high concentrations of glucocorticoid receptors. Clin Endocrinol (Oxf) 40:269–274, 1994.

97. Briganti V, Mannelli M, La Cava G, et al: Characterizing an ectopic secreting carcinoid with indium-111-DTPA-D-Phe-pentetreotide. J Nucl Med 38:711–714, 1997.

98. Christin-Maitre S, Chabbert-Buffet N, Mure A, et al: Use of somatostatin analog for localization and treatment of ACTH secreting bronchial carcinoid tumor. Chest 109:845–846, 1996.

99. Cremonini N, Furno A, Sforza A, et al: 111In-octeotide scintigraphy in endocrine tumors. Preliminary data. Q J Nucl Med 39:116–120, 1995.

100. de Herder WW, Krenning EP, Malchoff CD, et al: Somatostatin receptor scintigraphy: Its value in tumor localization in patients with Cushing's syndrome caused by ectopic corticotropin or corticotropin-releasing hormone secretion. Am J Med 96:305–312, 1994.

101. Filosso PL, Rena O, Ruffini E, Oliaro A: Ectopic ACTH-producing tumors of the chest and octreotide scintigraphy. Eur J Cardiothorac Surg 21:1126–1127, 2002.

102. Torpy DJ, Chen CC, Mullen N, et al: Lack of utility (of111n)-pentetreotide scintigraphy in localizing ectopic ACTH producing tumors: Follow-up of 18 patients. J Clin Endocrinol Metab 84:1186–1192, 1999.

103. Tsagarakis S, Giannakenas C, Vassilakos PJ, et al: Successful localization of an occult ACTH-secreting bronchial carcinoid tumour with 111indium-DTPA labelled octreotide. Clin Endocrinol (Oxf) 43:763–767, 1995.

104. Engelhardt D, Jacob K, Doerr HG: Different therapeutic efficacy of ketoconazole in patients with Cushing's syndrome. Klin Wochenschr 67:241–247, 1989.

105. Hoffman DM, Brigham B: The use of ketoconazole in ectopic adrenocorticotropic hormone syndrome. Cancer 67:1447–1449, 1991.

106. Sonino N, Boscaro M, Paoletta A, et al: Ketoconazole treatment in Cushing's syndrome: Experience in 34 patients. Clin Endocrinol (Oxf) 35:347–352, 1991.

107. Tabarin A, Navarranne A, Guerin J, et al: Use of ketoconazole in the treatment of Cushing's disease and ectopic ACTH syndrome. Clin Endocrinol (Oxf) 34:63–69, 1991.

108. Winquist EW, Laskey J, Crump M, et al: Ketoconazole in the management of paraneoplastic Cushing's syndrome secondary to ectopic adrenocorticotropin production. J Clin Oncol 13:157–164, 1995.

109. De Rosa G, Testa A, Liberale I, et al: Successful treatment of ectopic Cushing's syndrome with the long-acting somatostatin analog octreotide. Exp Clin Endocrinol 101:319–325, 1993.

110. Gill GV, Yong A, Power E, Ramage J: Carcinoid-associated ectopic ACTH syndrome with variable response to

octreotide. Postgrad Med J 75:98–100, 1999.

111. Upton GV, Amatruda TT Jr: Evidence for the presence of tumor peptides with corticotropin-releasing-factor-like activity in the ectopic ACTH syndrome. N Engl J Med 285:419–424, 1971.

112. Becker M, Aron DC: Ectopic ACTH syndrome and CRH-mediated Cushing's syndrome. Endocrinol Metab Clin North Am 23:585–606, 1994.

113. Muller OA, von Werder K: Ectopic production of ACTH and corticotropin-releasing hormone (CRH). J Steroid Biochem Mol Biol 43:403–408, 1992.

114. Young J, Deneux C, Grino M, et al: Pitfall of petrosal sinus sampling in a Cushing's syndrome secondary to ectopic adrenocorticotropin-corticotropin releasing hormone (ACTH-CRH) secretion. J Clin Endocrinol Metab 83:305–308, 1998.

115. Gross AJ, Steinberg SM, Reilly JG, et al: Atrial natriuretic factor and arginine vasopressin production in tumor cell lines from patients with lung cancer and their relationship to serum sodium. Cancer Res 53:67–74, 1993.

116. Ghandur-Mnaymneh L, Satterfield S, Block NL: Small cell carcinoma of the prostate gland with inappropriate antidiuretic hormone secretion: Morphological, immunohistochemical and clinical expressions. J Urol 135:1263–1266, 1986.

117. Moses AM, Notman DD: Diabetes insipidus and syndrome of inappropriate antidiuretic hormone secretion (SIADH). Adv Intern Med 27:73–100, 1982.

118. Kaye SB, Ross EJ: Inappropriate anti-diuretic hormone (ADH) secretion in association with carcinoma of the bladder. Postgrad Med J 53:274–277, 1977.

119. Yamaji T, Ishibashi M, Hori T: Propressophysin in human blood: A possible marker of ectopic vasopressin production. J Clin Endocrinol Metab 59:505–512, 1984.

120. Arroyo V, Jimenez W: Clinical need for antidiuretic hormone antagonists in cirrhosis. Hepatology 37:13–15, 2003.

121. Verbalis JG: Vasopressin V2 receptor antagonists. J Mol Endocrinol 29:1–9, 2002.

122. Zajac JD, Martin TJ, Hudson P, et al: Biosynthesis of calcitonin by human lung cancer cells. Endocrinology 116:749–755, 1985.

123. Asa SL, Kovacs K, Killinger DW, et al: Pancreatic islet cell carcinoma producing gastrin, ACTH, alpha-endorphin, somatostatin and calcitonin. Am J Gastroenterol 74:30–35, 1980.

124. Bishop JW, Osamura RY, Tsutsumi Y: Multiple hormone production in an oat cell carcinoma of the larynx. Acta Pathol Jpn 35:915–923, 1985.

125. di Sant'Agnese PA: Neuroendocrine differentiation in carcinoma of the prostate. Diagnostic, prognostic, and therapeutic implications. Cancer 70:254–268, 1992.

126. Ellison ML, Hillyard CJ, Bloomfield GA, et al: Ectopic hormone production by bronchial carcinomas in culture. Clin Endocrinol (Oxf) 5(Suppl):397S–406S, 1976.

127. Himsworth RL, Bloomfield GA, Coombes RC, et al: "Big ACTH" and calcitonin in an ectopic hormone secreting tumour of the liver. Clin Endocrinol (Oxf) 7:45–62, 1977.

128. Inoue T, Yamaguchi K, Suzuki H, et al: Production of immunoreactive-polypeptide hormones in cervical carcinoma. Cancer 53:1509–1514, 1984.

129. Lamberts SW, Hackeng WH, Visser TJ: Dissociation and association between calcitonin and adrenocorticotropin secretion. J Clin Endocrinol Metab 50:565–568, 1980.

130. Monsieur I, Meysman M, Noppen M, et al: Non-small-cell lung cancer with multiple paraneoplastic syndromes. Eur Respir J 8:1231–1234, 1995.

131. Porto DP, Wick MR, Ewing SL, Adams GL: Neuroendocrine carcinoma of the larynx. Am J Otolaryngol 8:97–104, 1987.

132. Rees LH, Ratcliffe JG: Ectopic hormone production by non-endocrine tumours. Clin Endocrinol (Oxf) 3:263–299, 1974.

133. Saw EC, Yu GS, Wagner G, Heng Y: Synchronous primary neuroendocrine carcinoma and adenocarcinoma in Barrett's esophagus. J Clin Gastroenterol 24:116–119, 1997.

134. Schwartz KE, Wolfsen AR, Forster B, Odell WD: Calcitonin in nonthyroidal cancer. J Clin Endocrinol Metab 49:438–444, 1979.

135. Viale G, Dell'Orto P, Moro E, et al: Vasoactive intestinal polypeptide-, somatostatin-, and calcitonin-producing adrenal pheochromocytoma associated with the watery diarrhea (WDHH) syndrome. First case report with immunohistochemical findings. Cancer 55:1099–1106, 1985.

136. Yoshimoto K, Yamasaki R, Sakai H, et al: Ectopic production of parathyroid hormone by small cell lung cancer in a patient with hypercalcemia. J Clin Endocrinol Metab 68:976–981, 1989.

137. Nussbaum SR, Gaz RD, Arnold A: Hypercalcemia and ectopic secretion of parathyroid hormone by an ovarian carcinoma with rearrangement of the gene for parathyroid hormone. N Engl J Med 323:1324–1328, 1990.

138. Rizzoli R, Pache JC, Didierjean L, et al: A thymoma as a cause of true ectopic hyperparathyroidism. J Clin Endocrinol Metab 79:912–915, 1994.

139. Strewler GJ, Budayr AA, Clark OH, Nissenson RA: Production of parathyroid hormone by a malignant nonparathyroid tumor in a hypercalcemic patient. J Clin Endocrinol Metab 76:1373–1375, 1993.

140. Budayr AA, Nissenson RA, Klein RF, et al: Increased serum levels of a parathyroid hormone-like protein in malignancy-associated hypercalcemia. Ann Intern Med 111:807–812, 1989.

141. Broadus AE, Mangin M, Ikeda K, et al: Humoral hypercalcemia of cancer. Identification of a novel parathyroid hormone-like peptide. N Engl J Med 319:556–563, 1988.

142. Burtis WJ, Wu T, Bunch C, et al: Identification of a novel 17,000-dalton parathyroid hormone-like adenylate cyclase-stimulating protein from a tumor associated with humoral hypercalcemia of malignancy. J Biol Chem 262:7151–7156, 1987.

143. Burtis WJ, Brady TG, Orloff JJ, et al: Immunochemical characterization of circulating parathyroid hormone-related protein in patients with humoral hypercalcemia of cancer. N Engl J Med 322:1106–1112, 1990.

144. Firkin F, Schneider H, Grill V: Parathyroid hormone-related protein in hypercalcemia associated with hematological malignancy. Leuk Lymphoma 29:499–506, 1998.

145. Grill V, Ho P, Body JJ, et al: Parathyroid hormone-related protein: Elevated levels in both humoral hypercalcemia of malignancy and hypercalcemia complicating metastatic breast cancer. J Clin Endocrinol Metab 73:1309–1315, 1991.

146. Karaplis AC: PTHrP: Novel roles in skeletal biology. Curr Pharm Des 7:655–670, 2001.

147. Wysolmerski JJ, Philbrick WM, Dunbar ME, et al: Rescue of the parathyroid hormone-related protein knockout mouse demonstrates that parathyroid hormone-related protein is essential for mammary gland development. Development 125:1285–1294, 1998.

148. Ralston SH, Cowan RA, Robertson AG, et al: Circulating vitamin D metabolites and hypercalcaemia of malignancy. Acta Endocrinol (Copenh) 106:556–563, 1984.

149. Fraher LJ, Hodsman AB, Jonas K, et al: A comparison of the in vivo biochemical responses to exogenous parathyroid hormone-(1-34) [PTH-(1-34) and PTH-related peptide-(1-34) in man. J Clin Endocrinol Metab 75:417–423, 1992.

150. Bundred NJ, Walls J, Ratcliffe WA: Parathyroid hormone-related protein, bone metastases and hypercalcaemia of malignancy. Ann R Coll Surg Engl 78:354–358, 1996.

151. Bundred NJ, Walker RA, Ratcliffe WA, et al: Parathyroid hormone related protein and skeletal morbidity in breast cancer. Eur J Cancer 28:690–692, 1992.

152. Chirgwin JM, Guise TA: Molecular mechanisms of tumor-bone interactions in osteolytic metastases. Crit Rev Eukaryot Gene Expr 10:159–178, 2000.

153. Guise TA, Yin JJ, Thomas RJ, et al: Parathyroid hormone-related protein (PTHrP)-(1-139) isoform is efficiently

secreted in vitro and enhances breast cancer metastasis to bone in vivo. Bone 30:670–676, 2002.

154. Ikeda K, Lu C, Weir EC, et al: Transcriptional regulation of the parathyroid hormone-related peptide gene by glucocorticoids and vitamin D in a human C-cell line. J Biol Chem 264:15743–15746, 1989.

155. Lu C, Ikeda K, Deftos LJ, et al: Glucocorticoid regulation of parathyroid hormone-related peptide gene transcription in a human neuroendocrine cell line. Mol Endocrinol 3:2034–2040, 1989.

156. Eto M, Akishita M, Ishikawa M, et al: Cytokine-induced expression of parathyroid hormone-related peptide in cultured human vascular endothelial cells. Biochem Biophys Res Commun 249:339–343, 1998.

157. Urena P, Iida-Klein A, Kong XF, et al: Regulation of parathyroid hormone (PTH)/PTH-related peptide receptor messenger ribonucleic acid by glucocorticoids and PTH in ROS 17/2.8 and OK cells. Endocrinology 134:451–456, 1994.

158. Seymour JF, Grill V, Martin TJ, et al: Hypercalcemia in the blastic phase of chronic myeloid leukemia associated with elevated parathyroid hormone-related protein. Leukemia 7:1672–1675, 1993.

159. Zeimer H, Firkin F, Grill V, et al: Assessment of cellular expression of parathyroid hormone-related protein mRNA and protein in multiple myeloma. J Pathol 192:336–341, 2000.

160. Richard V, Lairmore MD, Green PL, et al: Humoral hypercalcemia of malignancy: Severe combined immunodeficient/beige mouse model of adult T-cell lymphoma independent of human T-cell lymphotropic virus type-1 tax expression. Am J Pathol 158:2219–2228, 2001.

161. Obagi S, Derubertis F, Brown L, Deng JS: Hypercalcemia and parathyroid hormone related protein expression in cutaneous T-cell lymphoma. Int J Dermatol 38:855–862, 1999.

162. Moseley JM, Danks JA, Grill V, et al: Immunocytochemical demonstration of PTHrP protein in neoplastic tissue of HTLV-1 positive human adult T cell leukaemia/lymphoma: Implications for the mechanism of hypercalcaemia. Br J Cancer 64:745–748, 1991.

163. Bunn PA Jr, Schechter GP, Jaffe E, et al: Clinical course of retrovirus-associated adult T-cell lymphoma in the United States. N Engl J Med 309:257–264, 1983.

164. Ralston SH, Gallacher SJ, Patel U, et al: Cancer-associated hypercalcemia: morbidity and mortality. Clinical experience in 126 treated patients. Ann Intern Med 112:499–504, 1990.

165. Ralston SH, Gardner MD, Dryburgh FJ, et al: Comparison of aminohydroxypropylidene diphosphonate, mithramycin, and corticosteroids/calcitonin in treatment of cancer-associated hypercalcaemia. Lancet 2:907–910, 1985.

166. Gallacher SJ, Ralston SH, Fraser WD, et al: A comparison of low versus high dose pamidronate in cancer-associated hypercalcaemia. Bone Miner 15:249–256, 1991.

167. Ralston SH, Gallacher SJ, Patel U, et al: Comparison of three intravenous bisphosphonates in cancer-associated hypercalcaemia. Lancet 2:1180–1182, 1989.

168. Ralston SH, Thiebaud D, Herrmann Z, et al: Dose-response study of ibandronate in the treatment of cancer-associated hypercalcaemia. Br J Cancer 75:295–300, 1997.

169. Ralston SH, Alzaid AA, Gardner MD, Boyle IT: Treatment of cancer associated hypercalcaemia with combined aminohydroxypropylidene diphosphonate and calcitonin. Br Med J 292:1549–1550, 1986.

170. McCance RA: Osteomalacia with Looser's nodes (Milkman's syndrome) due to raised resistance to vitamin D acquired about the age of 15 years. Q J Med 16:33–47, 1947.

171. Drange MR, Melmed S: Long-acting lanreotide induces clinical and biochemical remission of acromegaly caused by disseminated growth hormone-releasing hormone-secreting carcinoid. J Clin Endocrinol Metab 83:3104–3109, 1998.

172. Guillemin R, Brazeau P, Bohlen P, et al: Growth hormone-releasing factor from a human pancreatic tumor that caused acromegaly. Science 218:585–587, 1982.

173. Rivier J, Spiess J, Thorner M, Vale W: Characterization of a growth hormone-releasing factor from a human pancreatic islet tumour. Nature 300:276–278, 1982.

174. Thorner MO, Perryman RL, Cronin MJ, et al: Somatotroph hyperplasia. Successful treatment of acromegaly by removal of a pancreatic islet tumor secreting a growth hormone-releasing factor. J Clin Invest 70:965–977, 1982.

175. Thorner MO, Rivier J, Spiess J, et al: Human pancreatic growth-hormone-releasing factor selectively stimulates growth-hormone secretion in man. Lancet 1:24–28, 1983.

176. Sano T, Saito H, Yamasaki R, et al: Production and secretion of immunoreactive growth hormone-releasing factor by pheochromocytomas. Cancer 57:1788–1793, 1986.

177. Doga M, Bonadonna S, Burattin A, Giustina A: Ectopic secretion of growth hormone-releasing hormone (GHRH) in neuroendocrine tumors: relevant clinical aspects. Ann Oncol 12(suppl 2):S89–S94, 2001.

178. Othman NH, Ezzat S, Kovacs K, et al: Growth hormone-releasing hormone (GHRH) and GHRH receptor (GHRH-R) isoform expression in ectopic acromegaly. Clin Endocrinol (Oxf) 55:135–140, 2001.

179. Sano T, Yamasaki R, Saito H, et al: Growth hormone-releasing hormone (GHRH)-secreting pancreatic tumor in a patient with multiple endocrine neoplasia type I. Am J Surg Pathol 11:810–819, 1987.

180. Schulte HM, Benker G, Windeck R, et al: Failure to respond to growth hormone releasing hormone (GHRH) in acromegaly due to a GHRH secreting pancreatic tumor: Dynamics of multiple endocrine testing. J Clin Endocrinol Metab 61:585–587, 1985.

181. Sano T, Asa SL, Kovacs K: Growth hormone-releasing hormone-producing tumors: Clinical, biochemical, and morphological manifestations. Endocr Rev 9:357–373, 1988.

182. Dayal Y, Lin HD, Tallberg K, et al: Immunocytochemical demonstration of growth hormone-releasing factor in gastrointestinal and pancreatic endocrine tumors. Am J Clin Pathol 85:13–20, 1986.

183. Chatzistamou I, Schally AV, Pafiti A, et al: Expression of growth hormone-releasing hormone in human primary endometrial carcinomas. Eur J Endocrinol 147:381–386, 2002.

184. Oberg K, Norheim I, Wide L: Serum growth hormone in patients with carcinoid tumours; basal levels and response to glucose and thyrotrophin releasing hormone. Acta Endocrinol (Copenh) 109:13–18, 1985.

185. Faglia G, Arosio M, Bazzoni N: Ectopic acromegaly. Endocrinol Metab Clin North Am 21:575–595, 1992.

186. Thorner MO, Frohman LA, Leong DA, et al: Extrahypothalamic growth-hormone-releasing factor (GRF) secretion is a rare cause of acromegaly: Plasma GRF levels in 177 acromegalic patients. J Clin Endocrinol Metab 59:846–849, 1984.

187. Melmed S: Extrapituitary acromegaly. Endocrinol Metab Clin North Am 20:507–518, 1991.

188. Melmed S, Ziel FH, Braunstein GD, et al: Medical management of acromegaly due to ectopic production of growth hormone-releasing hormone by a carcinoid tumor. J Clin Endocrinol Metab 67:395–399, 1988.

189. Lefebvre S, De Paepe L, Abs R, et al: Subcutaneous octreotide treatment of a growth hormone-releasing hormone-secreting bronchial carcinoid: Superiority of continuous versus intermittent administration to control hormonal secretion. Eur J Endocrinol 133:320–324, 1995.

190. Marks V, Teale JD: Tumours producing hypoglycaemia. Diabetes Metab Rev 7:79–91, 1991.

191. Teale JD: Non-islet cell tumour hypoglycaemia. Clin Endocrinol (Oxf) 51:147, 1999.

192. Teale JD, Marks V: Inappropriately elevated plasma insulin-like growth factor II in relation to suppressed insulin-like growth factor I in the diagnosis of non-islet cell tumour

hypoglycaemia. Clin Endocrinol (Oxf) 33:87–98, 1990.

193. Daughaday WH, Wu JC, Lee SD, Kapadia M: Abnormal processing of pro-IGF-II in patients with hepatoma and in some hepatitis B virus antibody-positive asymptomatic individuals. J Lab Clin Med 116:555–562, 1990.

194. Daughaday WH, Trivedi B, Baxter RC: Serum "big insulin-like growth factor II" from patients with tumor hypoglycemia lacks normal E-domain O-linked glycosylation, a possible determinant of normal propeptide processing. Proc Natl Acad Sci U S A 90:5823–5827, 1993.

195. Frystyk J, Skjaerbaek C, Zapf J, Orskov H: Increased levels of circulating free insulin-like growth factors in patients with non-islet cell tumour hypoglycaemia. Diabetologia 41:589–594, 1998.

196. Moller N, Frystyk J, Skjaerbaek C, et al: Systemic and regional tumour metabolism in a patient with non-islet cell tumour hypoglycaemia: Role of increased levels of free insulin-like growth factors. Diabetologia 39:1534–1535, 1996.

197. Teale JD, Blum WF, Marks V: Alleviation of non-islet cell tumour hypoglycaemia by growth hormone therapy is associated with changes in IGF binding protein-3. Ann Clin Biochem 29:314–323, 1992.

198. Daughaday WH, Deuel TF: Tumor secretion of growth factors. Endocrinol Metab Clin North Am 20:539–563, 1991.

199. Masson EA, MacFarlane IA, Graham D, Foy P: Spontaneous hypoglycaemia due to a pleural fibroma: Role of insulin like growth factors. Thorax 46:930–931, 1991.

200. Teale JD, Marks V: Glucocorticoid therapy suppresses abnormal secretion of big IGF-II by non-islet cell tumours inducing hypoglycaemia (NICTH). Clin Endocrinol (Oxf) 49:491–498, 1998.

201. Ben Jonathan N, Mershon JL, Allen DL, Steinmetz RW: Extrapituitary prolactin: Distribution, regulation, functions, and clinical aspects. Endocr Rev 17:639–669, 1996.

202. Molitch ME, Schwartz S, Mukherji B: Is prolactin secreted ectopically? Am J Med 70:803–807, 1981.

203. Rees LH, Bloomfield GA, Rees GM, et al: Multiple hormones in a bronchial tumor. J Clin Endocrinol Metab 38:1090–1097, 1974.

204. Hoffman WH, Gala RR, Kovacs K, Subramanian MG: Ectopic prolactin secretion from a gonadoblastoma. Cancer 60:2690–2695, 1987.

205. Turkington RW: Ectopic production of prolactin. N Engl J Med 285:1455–1458, 1971.

206. Jahnke GD, Trempus CS, Kari FW, DiAugustine RP: Expression of a prolactin-like factor in preneoplastic and neoplastic mouse mammary gland and cells. J Mol Endocrinol 17:247–256, 1996.

207. Clevenger CV, Chang WP, Ngo W, et al: Expression of prolactin and prolactin receptor in human breast carcinoma. Evidence for an autocrine/paracrine loop. Am J Pathol 146:695–705, 1995.

208. Clevenger CV, Furth PA, Hankinson SE, Schuler LA: The role of prolactin in mammary carcinoma. Endocr Rev 24:1–27, 2003.

209. Clevenger CV, Plank TL: Prolactin as an autocrine/paracrine factor in breast tissue. J Mammary Gland Biol Neoplasia 2:59–68, 1997.

210. Kwa HG, Cleton F, Wang DY, et al: A prospective study of plasma prolactin levels and subsequent risk of breast cancer. Int J Cancer 28:673–676, 1981.

211. Clapp C, Martial JA, Guzman RC, et al: The 16-kilodalton N-terminal fragment of human prolactin is a potent inhibitor of angiogenesis. Endocrinology 133:1292–1299, 1993.

212. Ferrara N, Clapp C, Weiner R: The 16K fragment of prolactin specifically inhibits basal or fibroblast growth factor stimulated growth of capillary endothelial cells. Endocrinology 129:896–900, 1991.

213. Macotela Y, Mendoza C, Corbacho AM, et al: 16K prolactin induces NF-kappaB activation in pulmonary fibroblasts. J Endocrinol 175:R13–R18, 2002.

214. Steiner H, Dahlback O, Waldenstrom J: Ectopic growth-hormone production and osteoarthropathy in carcinoma of the bronchus. Lancet 1:783–785, 1968.

215. Melmed S, Ezrin C, Kovacs K, et al: Acromegaly due to secretion of growth hormone by an ectopic pancreatic islet-cell tumor. N Engl J Med 312:9–17, 1985.

216. Melmed S, Rushakoff RJ: Ectopic pituitary and hypothalamic hormone syndromes. Endocrinol Metab Clin North Am 16:805–821, 1987.

217. Greenberg PB, Martin TJ, Beck C, Burger HG: Synthesis and release of human growth hormone from lung carcinoma in cell culture. Lancet 1:350–352, 1972.

218. Yokotani T, Koizumi T, Taniguchi R, et al: Expression of alpha and beta genes of human chorionic gonadotropin in lung cancer. Int J Cancer 71:539–544, 1997.

219. Broder LE, Weintraub BD, Rosen SW, et al: Placental proteins and their subunits as tumor markers in prostatic carcinoma. Cancer 40:211–216, 1977.

220. Scholl PD, Jurco S, Austin JR: Ectopic production of beta-HCG by a maxillary squamous cell carcinoma. Head Neck 19:701–705, 1997.

221. McArthur JW, Toll GD, Russfield AB, et al: Sexual precocity attributable to ectopic gonadotropin secretion by hepatoblastoma. Am J Med 54:390–403, 1973.

222. Ordonez NG, Ayala AG, Raymond AK, et al: Ectopic production of the beta-subunit of human chorionic gonadotropin in osteosarcoma. Arch Pathol Lab Med 113:416–419, 1989.

223. Senba M, Watanabe M: Ectopic production of beta-subunit of human chorionic gonadotropin in malignant lymphoma. Zentralbl Pathol 137:402–404, 1991.

224. Treves N: Gynecomastia; the origins of mammary swelling in the male: An analysis of 406 patients with breast hypertrophy, 525 with testicular tumors, and 13 with adrenal neoplasms. Cancer 11:1083–1102, 1958.

225. Mendelsohn G, Eggleston JC, Olson JL, et al: Vasoactive intestinal peptide and its relationship to ganglion cell differentiation in neuroblastic tumors. Lab Invest 41:144–149, 1979.

226. Said SI, Faloona GR: Elevated plasma and tissue levels of vasoactive intestinal polypeptide in the watery-diarrhea syndrome due to pancreatic, bronchogenic and other tumors. N Engl J Med 293:155–160, 1975.

227. Hamilton I, Reis L, Bilimoria S, Long RG: A renal vipoma. BMJ 281:1323–1324, 1980.

228. Hollifield JW, Page DL, Smith C, et al: Renin-secreting clear cell carcinoma of the kidney. Arch Intern Med 135:859–864, 1975.

229. Soubrier F, Devaux C, Galen FX, et al: Biochemical and immunological characterization of ectopic tumoral renin. J Clin Endocrinol Metab 54:139–144, 1982.

230. Atlas SA, Hesson TE, Sealey JE, et al: Characterization of inactive renin ("prorenin") from renin-secreting tumors of nonrenal origin. Similarity to inactive renin from kidney and normal plasma. J Clin Invest 73:437–447, 1984.

231. Ruddy MC, Atlas SA, Salerno FG: Hypertension associated with a renin-secreting adenocarcinoma of the pancreas. N Engl J Med 307:993–997, 1982.

232. Aurell M, Rudin A, Tisell LE, et al: Captopril effect on hypertension in patient with renin-producing tumour. Lancet 2:149–150, 1979.

233. Hauger-Klevene JH: High plasma renin activity in an oat cell carcinoma: A renin-secreting carcinoma? Cancer 26:1112–1114, 1970.

234. Genest J, Rojo-Ortega JM, Kuchel O, et al: Malignant hypertension with hypokalemia in a patient with renin-producing pulmonary carcinoma. Trans Assoc Am Physicians 88:192–201, 1975.

235. Kawai K, Fukamizu A, Kawakami Y, et al: A case of renin producing leiomyosarcoma originating in the lung. Endocrinol Jpn 38:603–609, 1991.

236. Anderson PW, Macaulay L, Do YS, et al: Extrarenal renin-secreting tumors: Insights into hypertension and ovarian renin production. Medicine (Baltimore) 68:257–268, 1989.

237. Tetu B, Lebel M, Camilleri JP: Renin-producing ovarian tumor. A case report with immunohistochemical and electron-microscopic study. Am J Surg Pathol 12:634–640, 1988.

238. Cox JN, Paunier L, Vallotton MB, et al: Epithelial liver hamartoma, systemic arterial hypertension and renin hypersecretion. Virchows Arch A Pathol Anat Histol 366:15–26, 1975.

239. Saito T, Fukamizu A, Okada K, et al: Ectopic production of renin by ileal carcinoma. Endocrinol Jpn 36:117–124, 1989.

240. Fried G, Wikstrom LM, Hoog A, et al: Multiple neuropeptide immunoreactivities in a renin-producing human paraganglioma. Cancer 74:142–151, 1994.

241. Yokoyama H, Yamane Y, Takahara J, et al: A case of ectopic renin-secreting orbital hemangiopericytoma associated with juvenile hypertension and hypokalemia. Acta Med Okayama 33:315–322, 1979.

# ENDOCRINE TESTING AND ENDOCRINE DRUG

# Endocrine Testing

## Delbert A. Fisher and Esther Carlton

INTRODUCTION

IN VITRO ENDOCRINE TESTS

## INTRODUCTION

The diagnosis and management of endocrine disorders are heavily dependent on the quantification of circulating hormone and growth factor species and subspecies. The 20th century heralded development of hormone bioassay systems that provided our early understanding of hormone systems physiology and contributed importantly to the evolution of the clinical discipline. However, it was the development during the past 30 years of several generations of sensitive and specific immunoassay methods for in vitro hormone measurements that transformed the science of endocrinology and enabled the growth and subspecialization of clinical endocrinology. Molecular technologies have further advanced the basic and clinical endocrine fields and will increasingly contribute to our clinical diagnostic toolbox and therapeutic armamentarium. This chapter is designed to provide an overview of current in vitro endocrine test menus, normative data, and interpretive guidelines to complement the specialized chapter discussions. The generally available endocrine and selected metabolic tests are considered in several endocrine system categories. The test methods and reference values as developed by the Quest Diagnostics–Nichols Institute are provided.[1] Specific methods and reference ranges for other laboratories may vary. Stimulation or suppression tests are sometimes helpful in patient diagnosis and management. These are described in the individual chapters and other texts.[1-4] Endocrine research techniques have been discussed in a text edited by de Pablo and colleagues.[5]

## IN VITRO ENDOCRINE TESTS

Available endocrine tests are listed by name and method and reference ranges are provided for adults and pediatric age groups. Tests are arranged in categories as follows:

Adrenocortical Function Tests
Endocrine-Related Autoantibody Tests
Catecholamines
Gastrointestinal Hormone-Related Tests
Gonad Function Tests
Growth and Growth Hormone Tests
Hypothalamic-Pituitary Tests
Parathyroid/Bone Tests
Renal and Fluid Balance Tests
Thyroid Function Tests
Genetic Tests

Abbreviations are used as follows:

Ac = acid hydrolysis
Ch = column chromatography
E = extraction
ED = equilibrium dialysis
EL = electrophoresis
ELISA = enzyme-linked immunosorbent assay
Enz = enzyme hydrolysis
HPLC = high-pressure liquid chromatography
ICMA = immunochemiluminometric assay
IRMA = immunoradiometric assay
MEIA = microparticle enzyme immunoassay
NA = not available
P = ammonium sulfate precipitation
PEG = polyethylene glycol precipitation
Postmen. = postmenopausal
Premen. = premenopausal
RBA = radiobinding assay
RIA = radioimmunoassay
RRA = radioreceptor assay

## Adrenocortical Function Tests

| Test | Method (units) | Reference Range — Adult |  |  | Reference Range — Pediatric |  |  |
|---|---|---|---|---|---|---|---|
|  |  | Condition | Male | Female | Condition | Male | Female |
| Adrenocorticotropic hormone (*see Hypothalamic-Pituitary Tests*) |  |  |  |  |  |  |  |
| Aldosterone, serum | E, Ch, RIA (ng/dL) | Upright<br>Normal sodium diet<br>8:00–10:00 A.M.<br>4:00–6:00 P.M.<br>Supine<br>Postfludrocortisone suppression or saline infusion | 3–35<br>2–21<br>2–9<br>≤4 | 3–35<br>2–21<br>2–9<br>≤4 | Upright<br>Normal sodium diet<br><1 yr<br>1–5 yr<br>6–12 yr<br>Tanner stage<br>II–III<br>IV–V<br>Ref. 10 | 2–130<br>2–37<br>3–21<br>1–13<br>3–14 | 2–130<br>2–37<br>3–21<br>2–20<br>4–32 |
| Aldosterone, 24-hr urine | Ac, E, RIA (µg/24 hr) | Random sodium diet<br>Postfludrocortisone suppression or saline infusion | 2.3–21<br>≤5 | 2.3–21<br>≤5 | Random sodium diet<br>2–7 yr<br>8–11 yr<br>12–16 yr | 0.5–5.7<br>0.5–10.2<br>0.5–15.6 | 0.5–5.7<br>0.5–10.2<br>0.5–15.6 |
| Androstenedione, serum | E, Ch, RIA (ng/dL) | Postmen. | 50–250 | 50–250<br>16–120 | <1 yr<br>1–5 yr<br>6–12 yr<br>Tanner stage<br>II–III<br>IV–V<br>Ref. 9 | 6–78<br>5–51<br>7–68<br>17–82<br>57–150 | 6–78<br>5–51<br>17–68<br>43–180<br>73–220 |
| Corticosterone, serum | E, Ch, RIA (ng/dL) | 8:00–10:00 A.M.<br>4:00–6:00 P.M. | 100–700<br>40–260 | 100–700<br>40–260 | Prepubertal<br><1 yr<br>1–5 yr<br>6–12 yr<br>Tanner stage<br>II, III<br>IV, V<br>Ref. 10 | 78–1750<br>120–1290<br>235–1370<br>115–1220<br>110–600 | 89–1200<br>160–2040<br>155–1100<br>1475–5065<br>1725–5110 |
| Corticotropin-releasing hormone (*see Hypothalamic-Pituitary Tests*) |  |  |  |  |  |  |  |
| Cortisol, serum | RIA (µg/dL) | 8:00–10:00 A.M.<br>4:00–6:00 P.M. | 8–24<br>2–17 | 8–24<br>2–17 | <1 yr<br>1–5 yr<br>6–12 yr<br>Tanner stage<br>II–III<br>IV–V<br>Ref. 9 | 3–23<br>6–25<br>3–15<br>4–13<br>5–15 | 3–23<br>6–25<br>3–15<br>4–16<br>6–15 |
| Cortisol, free, serum | ED, RIA (µg/dL) | 8:00–10:00 A.M.<br>4:00–6:00 P.M. | 0.6–1.6<br>0.2–0.9 | 0.6–1.6<br>0.2–0.9 | 6–9 yr<br>10–11 yr<br>12–14 yr<br>15–17 yr<br>Ref. 9 | 0.37–1.62<br>0.27–1.12<br>0.23–1.67<br>0.43–1.77 | 0.37–1.62<br>0.27–1.12<br>0.23–1.67<br>0.43–1.77 |
| Cortisol-binding globulin, serum (transcortin) | RIA (mg/L) |  | 19–45 | 19–45 | Preterm infants <8 days | 6–26 | 6–26 |
| Cortisol, free, 24-hr urine | E, HPLC (µg/24 hr) |  | ≤50 | ≤50 | 2–7 yr<br>8–12 yr<br>13–17 yr | 1.4–18<br>1.6–21<br>2.1–38 | 1.4–18<br>1.6–21<br>2.1–38 |

| Test | Specimen/Method (Units) | Condition | Value | Value | Value | Value |
|---|---|---|---|---|---|---|
| Cortisone, serum | E, HPLC (µg/dL) | A.M. | 0.7–2.7 | 0.7–2.7 | NA | NA |
| | | P.M. | 0.6–2.3 | 0.6–2.3 | | |
| Cortisone, 24-hr urine | E, P, HPLC (µg/24 hr) | | ≤96 | ≤96 | NA | NA |
| Deoxycorticosterone, serum | E, Ch, RIA (ng/dL) | | 3.5–11.5 | | | |
| | | Follicular | | 1.5–8.5 | | |
| | | Luteal | | 3.5–13.0 | | |
| | | Pregnancy | | | | |
| | | 1st trimester | | 5–25 | | |
| | | 2nd trimester | | 10–75 | | |
| | | 3rd trimester | | 30–110 | | |
| | | <1 yr | | | 7–57 | 7–57 |
| | | 1–5 yr | | | 4–49 | 4–49 |
| | | 6–12 yr | | | 9–34 | 2–13 |
| | | Tanner stage | | | | |
| | | II–III | | | 4–30 | 2–12 |
| | | IV–V | | | 5–14 | 5–10 |
| 11-Deoxycortisol, serum (compound S) | E, Ch, RIA (ng/dL) | | 20–130 | 20–130 | | |
| | | Postmetyrapone | >5000 (>5 µg/dL) | >5000 (>5 µg/dL) | | |
| | | Ref. 9 | | | | |
| | | 1–3 days | | | 13–150 | 13–150 |
| | | <1 yr | | | 10–200 | 10–200 |
| | | 1–5 yr | | | 7–210 | 7–210 |
| | | 6–12 yr | | | 14–140 | 14–140 |
| | | Tanner stage | | | | |
| | | II–III | | | 15–130 | 15–130 |
| | | IV–V | | | 17–120 | 17–120 |
| | | Ref. 9 | | | | |
| Dexamethasone, serum | E, HPLC, RIA (ng/dL) | After 1 mg dexamethasone (8:00 P.M.) overnight 8:00–10:00 A.M. | <20 | <20 | NA | NA |
| Dehydroepiandrosterone, serum (DHEA) | E, Ch, RIA (ng/dL) | | 180–550 | 180–550 | | |
| | | | 180–1250 | 130–980 | | |
| | | <1 yr | | | 26–585 | 26–585 |
| | | 1–5 yr | | | 9–42 | 9–42 |
| | | 6–12 yr | | | 11–155 | 11–155 |
| | | Tanner stage | | | | |
| | | II–III | | | 25–300 | 69–605 |
| | | IV–V | | | 100–400 | 165–690 |
| | | Ref. 9 | | | | |
| Dehydroepiandrosterone sulfate, serum (DHEA-SO$_4$) | RIA (µg/dL) | 18–30 yr | 125–619 | 45–380 | | |
| | | 31–50 yr | 59–452 | 12–379 | | |
| | | 51–60 yr | 20–413 | <245 | | |
| | | 61–83 yr | 10–285 | <115 | | |
| | | Cord blood | | | <380 | <380 |
| | | 1–5 days | | | 10–250 | 10–250 |
| | | 1–5 mo | | | ≤41 | 5–55 |
| | | 6–11 mo | | | 5–20 | 5–30 |
| | | 1–5 yr | | | ≤40 | ≤20 |
| | | 6–9 yr | | | ≤145 | ≤140 |
| | | 10–11 yr | | | 15–115 | 15–260 |
| | | 12–14 yr | | | 20–500 | 20–535 |
| | | 15–17 yr | | | 30–555 | 35–535 |
| | | Tanner stage | | | | |
| | | I | | | 5–265 | 5–125 |
| | | II | | | 15–380 | 15–150 |
| | | III | | | 60–505 | 20–535 |
| | | IV | | | 65–562 | 35–485 |
| | | V | | | 165–500 | 75–530 |
| Endorphin (see Hypothalamic-Pituitary Tests) | | | | | | |
| 17-Hydroxycorticosteroids, 24-hr urine | Modified Porter-Silber (mg/24 hr) (mg/g Cr) | | 4–11 / 1.9–9.5/ g Cr | 3–10 / 1.9–9.5/ g Cr | | |
| | | 2–17 yr | | | 1.1–7.5 / 0.9–9.5/ g Cr | 1.1–7.5 / 0.9–15.3/ g Cr |

Continued

## Adrenocortical Function Tests—cont'd

| Test | Method (units) | | Adult | | Reference Range | Pediatric | |
|---|---|---|---|---|---|---|---|
| | | | Male | Female | | Male | Female |
| 18-Hydroxycorticosterone, serum | E, Ch, RIA (ng/dL) | 8:00–10:00 A.M. | | | <1 yr | 5–310 | 5–310 |
| | | Supine | 4–37 | 4–37 | 1–5 yr | 7–155 | 7–155 |
| | | Ambulatory | 5–80 | 5–80 | 6–12 yr | 10–74 | 10–74 |
| | | | | | Tanner stage | | |
| | | | | | II, III | 5–73 | 11–82 |
| | | | | | IV, V | 14–62 | 11–68 |
| | | | | | Ref. 10 | | |
| 6β-Hydroxycortisol, 24-hr urine | HPLC (μg/24 hr) (μg/g Cr) | | 40–330 | 40–330 | 0–2 mo | 3–6 μg/g Cr | 3–6 μg/g Cr |
| | | | | | 2 mo–3 yr | 3–49 μg/g Cr | 3–49 μg/g Cr |
| | | | | | 3–8 yr | 15–95 μg/g Cr | 15–95 μg/g Cr |
| | | | | | 9–12 yr | 24–197 μg/g Cr | 24–197 μg/g Cr |
| | | | | | 13–17 yr | 44–350 μg/g Cr | 41–350 μg/g Cr |
| | | | | | (Calculated per 140 g Cr) | | |
| 18-Hydroxydeoxycorticosterone, serum | E, Ch, RIA (ng/dL) | 8:00 A.M. | 3–13 | 3–13 | | NA | NA |
| | | 6:00 P.M. | 3–8 | 3–8 | | | |
| 17-Hydroxypregnenolone, serum | E, Ch, RIA (ng/dL) | | 20–450 | 20–450 | <1 yr | 14–830 | 14–830 |
| | | | | | 1–5 yr | 10–100 | 10–100 |
| | | | | | 6–12 yr | 10–190 | 10–190 |
| | | | | | Tanner stage | | |
| | | | | | II–III | 20–360 | 58–450 |
| | | | | | IV–V | 32–300 | 53–540 |
| | | | | | Ref. 9 | | |
| 17-Hydroxyprogesterone, serum | E, RIA (ng/dL) | Follicular | 50–250 | 20–100 | 1–5 days | 80–420 | 80–420 |
| | | Mid-cycle | | 100–250 | <1 yr | 11–170 | 11–170 |
| | | Luteal | | 100–500 | 1–5 yr | 4–115 | 4–115 |
| | | Postmen. | | ≤70 | 6–12 yr | 7–69 | 7–69 |
| | | | | | Tanner stage | | |
| | | | | | II–III | 12–130 | 18–220 |
| | | | | | IV–V | 51–190 | 36–200 |
| | | | | | Ref. 9 | | |
| 17-Ketosteroids (see Gonadal section) | | | | | | | |
| Pregnenolone, serum | E, Ch, RIA (ng/dL) | | 10–200 | 10–230 | <1 yr | 10–140 | 10–140 |
| | | | | | 1–5 yr | 10–48 | 10–48 |
| | | | | | 6–12 yr | 15–45 | 15–45 |
| | | | | | Tanner stage | | |
| | | | | | II–III | 10–45 | 15–84 |
| | | | | | IV–V | 11–50 | 20–77 |
| | | | | | Ref. 10 | | |
| Progesterone, serum | E, RIA (ng/dL) | Follicular | 10–50 | ≤50 | <1 yr | 5–80 | 5–80 |
| | | Luteal | | 300–2500 | 1–5 yr | 8–64 | 8–64 |
| | | Postmen. | | ≤40 | 6–12 yr | 5–93 | 5–93 |
| | | Pregnancy | | | Tanner stage | | |
| | | 1st trimester | | 725–4400 | II, III | 64–115 | 6–680 |
| | | 2nd trimester | | 1950–8250 | IV, V | 17–145 | 16–1290 |
| | | 3rd trimester | | 6500–22,900 | Ref. 10 | | |

Cr, creatinine.

**Endocrine-Related Autoantibody Tests**

| Test | Method (units) | Reference Range | | | | | |
|------|----------------|--------|--------|-----------|--------|
| | | Adult | | Pediatric | | | |
| | | Male | Female | Male | Female |
| Antiadrenal antibody, serum (monkey adrenal) | IFA (titer) | <10 | <10 | <10 | <10 |
| Antiparietal cell antibody, serum (mouse stomach) | IFA (titer) | <20 | <20 | <20 | <20 |
| Antitriiodothyroxine antibody, serum | RBA (titer) | Negative | Negative | Negative | Negative |
| Antithyroxine antibody, serum | RBA (titer) | Negative | Negative | Negative | Negative |
| Antithyroglobulin antibody (sensitivity 0.6 IU/mL), serum | ICMA (IU/mL) | <2.0 | <2.0 | <2.0 | <2.0 |
| Antithyroid peroxidase antibody, serum (sensitivity 0.2 IU/mL) | ICMA (IU/mL) | <2.0 | <2.0 | <2.0 | <2.0 |
| Anti–thyroid-stimulating hormone antibody, serum | RBA (titer) | Negative | Negative | Negative | Negative |
| Anti–glutamic acid decarboxylase 65 autoantibody, serum | RBA (IU/mL) | <1.0 | <1.0 | <1.0 | <1.0 |
| Growth hormone antibody, serum | RBA (titer) | Negative | Negative | Negative | Negative |
| 21Hydroxylase antibody, serum | RBA (titer) | <1.0 | <1.0 | <1.0 | <1.0 |
| Insulin antibody (for high-titer autoantibodies in diabetic patients), serum | RBA (titer) | Negative | Negative | Negative | Negative |
| Insulin antibody (highly sensitive for assessment of prediabetic patients), serum | RBA (% insulin antibody) | <1.1% | <1.1% | <1.1% | <1.1% |
| Islet cell antibody, serum (monkey pancreas) | IFA (titer) | Negative | Negative | Negative | Negative |
| Islet cell antigen 512, serum (IA2) | RBA (index vs. control) | <0.07 | <0.07 | <0.07 | <0.07 |
| Parathyroid hormone antibody, serum | RBA (titer) | Negative | Negative | Negative | Negative |
| Thyroid growth-stimulating immunoglobulin | Bioassay, RBA (% stimulation of basal thymidine uptake) | <130 | <130 | <130 | <130 |
| Thyrotropin-binding inhibitory immunoglobulin, serum | RRA human recombinant TSH receptor (% inhibition of TSH binding) | <10 | <10 | <10 | <10 |
| Thyrotropin-blocking antibody, serum | Bioassay, RIA (human TSH receptor transfected CHO cells) (% inhibition of TSH-stimulated cyclic AMP) | <10 | <10 | <10 | <10 |
| Thyroid-stimulating immunoglobulin, serum | Bioassay, RIA (human TSH receptor transfected CHO cells) (% stimulation of basal cyclic AMP production) | <130 | <130 | <130 | <130 |

cyclic AMP, cyclic adenosine monophosphate; CHO, chinese hamster ovary; TSH, thyroid-stimulating hormone.

## Catecholamines

| Test | Method (units) | Reference Range Adult | | | Pediatric | |
|---|---|---|---|---|---|---|
| | | | **Male** | **Female** | **Male** | **Female** |
| Catecholamines, plasma | HPLC (pg/mL)<br>E, epinephrine<br>N, norepinephrine<br>D, dopamine | Supine<br>E<br>N<br>D<br>Total (E+N) | <50<br>112–658<br><10<br>123–671 | <50<br>112–658<br><10<br>123–671 | Supine<br>3–15 yr<br>E<br>N<br>D<br>Total (E+N)<br>Ref. 40 | ≤464<br>≤1251<br>≤60<br>≤1715 | ≤464<br>≤1251<br>≤60<br>≤1715 |
| | | Upright<br>E<br>N<br>D<br>Total (E+N) | <95<br>217–1109<br><20<br>242–1125 | <95<br>217–1109<br><20<br>242–1125 | | | |
| Catecholamines, urine | HPLC (µg/24 hr)<br>(µg/g Cr)<br>E, epinephrine<br>N, norepinephrine<br>D, dopamine | E<br><br>N<br><br>D<br><br><br>Total E+N | 2–24<br>2–16/g Cr<br>15–100<br>7–65/g Cr<br>52–480<br>40–390/g Cr<br><br>26–121<br>9–74/g Cr | 2–24<br>2–16/g Cr<br>15–100<br>7–65/g Cr<br>52–480<br>40–390/g Cr<br><br>26–121<br>9–74/g Cr | <6 mo<br>E<br>N<br>D<br>Total (E+N)<br>7–11 mo<br>E<br>N<br>D<br>Total (E+N)<br>1–2 yr<br>E<br>N<br>D<br>Total (E+N)<br>3–8 yr<br>E<br><br>N<br><br>D<br><br>Total (E+N)<br><br>9–12 yr<br>E<br><br>N<br><br>D<br><br>Total (E+N)<br><br>13–17 yr<br>E<br><br>N<br><br>D<br><br>Total (E+N) | 2–45/g Cr<br>12–286/g Cr<br>107–2180/g Cr<br>24–322/g Cr<br><br>5–45/g Cr<br>19–250/g Cr<br>96–2441/g Cr<br>10–295/g Cr<br><br>1–49/g Cr<br>25–210/g Cr<br>86–1861/g Cr<br>30–263/g Cr<br><br>1–7<br>4–32/g Cr<br>5–41<br>20–108/g Cr<br>80–378<br>295–1123/g Cr<br>9–51<br>30–130/g Cr<br><br>≤8<br>1–15/g Cr<br>5–50<br>20–73/g Cr<br>51–474<br>164–744/g Cr<br>9–71<br>25–90/g Cr<br><br>≤11<br>1–10/g Cr<br>12–88<br>15–58/g Cr<br>51–645<br>156–551/g Cr<br>13–90<br>20–70/g Cr | 2–45/g Cr<br>12–286/g Cr<br>107–2180/g Cr<br>24–322/g Cr<br><br>5–45/g Cr<br>19–250/g Cr<br>96–2441/g Cr<br>10–295/g Cr<br><br>1–49/g Cr<br>25–210/g Cr<br>86–1861/g Cr<br>30–263/g Cr<br><br>1–7<br>4–32/g Cr<br>5–41<br>20–108/g Cr<br>80–378<br>295–1123/g Cr<br>9–51<br>30–130/g Cr<br><br>≤8<br>1–15/g Cr<br>5–50<br>20–73/g Cr<br>51–474<br>164–744/g Cr<br>9–71<br>25–90/g Cr<br><br>≤11<br>1–10/g Cr<br>12–88<br>15–58/g Cr<br>51–645<br>156–551/g Cr<br>13–90<br>20–70/g Cr |
| Chromogranin A, serum | ICMA (ng/mL) | | 6.0–39 | 6.0–39 | | NA | NA |
| Homovanillic acid, urine | HPLC (mg/24 hr)<br>(mg/g Cr) | | 1.6–7.5<br>1.4–5.3/g Cr | 1.6–7.5<br>1.4–5.3/g Cr | <6 mo<br>7–11 mo<br>1–2 yr<br>3–8 yr<br><br>9–12 yr<br><br>13–17 yr | 9.1–36/g Cr<br>11.2–33/g Cr<br>8.5–38/g Cr<br>0.5–6.7<br>1.7–17/g Cr<br>1.1–6.8<br>3.2–9.7/g Cr<br>1.4–7.2<br>2.0–6.2/g Cr | 9.1–36/g Cr<br>11.2–33/g Cr<br>8.5–38/g Cr<br>0.5–6.7<br>1.7–17/g Cr<br>1.1–6.8<br>3.2–9.7/g Cr<br>1.4–7.2<br>2.0–6.2/g Cr |

**Catecholamines—*cont'd***

| Test | Method (units) | | Adult | | | Pediatric | |
|---|---|---|---|---|---|---|---|
| | | | **Reference Range** | | | | |
| | | | Male | Female | | Male | Female |
| Metanephrines, urine | HPLC (μg/24 hr) (μg/g Cr) M, metanephrine N, normetanephrine | M | 26–230 *20–150/g Cr* | 19–140 *30–165/g Cr* | <6 mo M N Total | *83–523/g Cr* *574–3856/g Cr* *865–4173/g Cr* | *83–523/g Cr* *574–3856/g Cr* *865–4173/g Cr* |
| | | N | 44–450 *70–335/g Cr* | 52–310 *105–375/g Cr* | 7–11 mo M N Total | *45–419/g Cr* *527–2730/g Cr* *730–2980/g Cr* | *45–419/g Cr* *527–2730/g Cr* *730–2980/g Cr* |
| | | Total | 90–690 *110–480/g Cr* | 95–475 *150–510/g Cr* | 1–2 yr M N Total | *78–509/g Cr* *233–2000/g Cr* *311–2509/g Cr* | *78–509/g Cr* *233–2000/g Cr* *311–2509/g Cr* |
| | | | | | 3–8 yr M N Total | 9–86 *57–237/g Cr* 20–186 *124–516/g Cr* 47–260 *256–1528/g Cr* | 9–86 *57–237/g Cr* 20–186 *124–516/g Cr* 47–260 *256–1528/g Cr* |
| | | | | | 9–12 yr M N Total | 26–156 *38–188/g Cr* 10–319 *46–517/g Cr* 72–410 *219–1364/g Cr* | 26–156 *38–188/g Cr* 10–319 *46–517/g Cr* 72–410 *219–1364/g Cr* |
| | | | | | 13–17 yr M N Total | 31–156 *34–126/g Cr* 71–395 *45–324/g Cr* 130–520 *110–510/g Cr* | 31–156 *34–126/g Cr* 71–395 *45–324/g Cr* 130–520 *110–510/g Cr* |
| Vanillylmandelic acid, urine | HPLC (mg/24 hr) *(mg/g Cr)* | | ≤6.0 *1.1–4.1/g Cr* | ≤6.0 *1.1–4.1/g Cr* | <6 mo 7–11 mo 1–2 yr 3–8 yr 9–12 yr 13–17 yr | *5.5–26/g Cr* *6.1–20/g Cr* *2.5–21/g Cr* ≤2.3 *1.7–6.5/g Cr* ≤3.4 *1.4–5.1/g Cr* ≤3.9 *1.5–3.6/g Cr* | *5.5–26/g Cr* *6.1–20/g Cr* *2.5–21/g Cr* ≤2.3 *1.7–6.5/g Cr* ≤3.4 *1.4–5.1/g Cr* ≤3.9 *1.5–3.6/g Cr* |

Cr, Creatinine.

## Gastrointestinal/Hormone-Related Tests

| Test | Method (units) | Reference Range — Adult Male | Adult Female | Age/Notes | Pediatric Male | Pediatric Female |
|---|---|---|---|---|---|---|
| α Subunit (see Hypothalamic Pituitary Tests) | | | | | | |
| Calcitonin (see Thyroid Function Tests) | | | | | | |
| C peptide, plasma | RIA (ng/mL) | 0.5–2.0 | 0.5–2.0 | 5–17 yr / Ref. 6 | 0.7–2.8 | 0.7–2.8 |
| C peptide, 24-hr urine | ICMA (ng/mL) | 0.8–3.1 | 0.8–3.1 | 2–7 yr | NA | NA |
| | RIA (µg/g Cr) | 11–53 | 11–53 | | 14–129 | 14–129 |
| | ICMA (ng/mL) | 10.8–108 | 10.8–108 | | NA | NA |
| Fructosamine, serum | Colorimetry (µmol/L) | 190–270 | 190–270 | | 190–270 | 190–270 |
| Gastrin, serum | RIA (pg/mL) | <42 | <42 | 1–2 wk | 69–190 | 69–190 |
| | | | | 1–24 mo | 55–186 | 55–186 |
| | | | | Pre/postpubertal | | |
| | | | | Fasting | 2–168 | 2–168 |
| | | | | 3–4 hr | 3–117 | 3–117 |
| | | | | 5–6 hr | 1–125 | 1–125 |
| | | | | >8 hr | | |
| | | | | Ref. 25, 26 | | |
| Glucagon, serum | E, RIA (pg/mL) | 20–100 | 20–100 | Cord blood | 0–215 | 0–215 |
| | | | | 3 days | 0–1750 | 0–1750 |
| | | | | 1–17 yr | 20–100 | 20–100 |
| | | | | Ref. 6 | | |
| Glycated albumin, plasma | Affinity Ch (%) | 0.8–1.4 | 0.8–1.4 | | 0.8–1.4 | 0.8–1.4 |
| Human chorionic gonadotropin-β subunit (see Gonad Function Tests) | | | | | | |
| Hemoglobin A1c (Bio Rad) | Cation Ch/HPLC (%) | 4.3–6.1 | 4.3–6.1 | 2–10 yr | 4.3–5.9 | 4.3–5.9 |
| | | | | >10 yr | ≤8 | ≤8 |
| 5-Hydroxyindoleacetic acid, 24-hr urine | HPLC (mg/24 hr) | ≤6 | ≤6 | | ≤6 | ≤6 |
| Insulin | RIA µU/mL | ≤20 | ≤20 | Ref. 6 | 3.8–21 | 3.8–21 |
| Insulin, total (free + bound), serum | E, PEP, RIA (µU/mL) | ≤20 | ≤20 | 1–18 yr | ≤20 | ≤20 |
| Insulin, free, serum | PEP, RIA (µU/mL) | 4–20 | 4–20 | 1–18 yr | 4–20 | 4–20 |
| Microalbumin, urine 24-hr or random | Turbidometric (mg/24 hr) | ≤30 | ≤30 | | ≤30 | ≤30 |
| | (mg/24 hr) | ≤24/g Cr | ≤24/g Cr | | ≤24/g Cr | ≤24/g Cr |
| Neuron-specific enolase, serum | RIA (µg/L) | ≤12.5 | 12.5 | | NA | NA |
| Pancreatic polypeptide, plasma | E, RIA (pg/mL) | 26–158 | 26–158 | 20–29 yr | NA | NA |
| | | 55–284 | 55–284 | 30–39 yr | | |
| | | 64–243 | 64–243 | 40–49 yr | | |
| | | 51–326 | 51–326 | >50 yr | | |
| Pepsinogen I, serum | RIA (ng/mL) | 25–100 | 25–100 | 1–18 yr | NA | NA |
| Proinsulin, serum | E, RIA (ng/mL) | ≤0.20 | ≤0.20 | | ≤0.20 | ≤0.20 |
| | ELISA (pmol/L) | ≤19.1 | ≤8.8 | | NA | NA |
| Parathyroid hormone-related protein (see Parathyroid/Bone Tests) | | | | | | |
| Somatostatin (see Hypothalamic-Pituitary Tests) | | | | | | |
| Vasoactive intestinal peptide, plasma | E, RIA (pg/mL) | <50 | <50 | 1–18 yr | <50 | <50 |

## Gonad Function Tests

| Test | Method (units) | Reference Range Adult | | Reference Range Pediatric | | |
|---|---|---|---|---|---|---|
| α Subunit (*see Hypothalamic-Pituitary Tests*) | | | | | | |
| | | **Male** | **Female** | | **Male** | **Female** |
| 3α-Androstanediol glucuronide, serum | E, Enz, Ch, RIA (ng/dL) | 260–1500 | 60–300 | Prepubertal | 10–60 | 10–60 |
| Dihydrotestosterone, total, serum | E, Ch, RIA (ng/dL) | 25–75 | 5–30 | Cord blood | < 2–8 | <2–8 |
| | | | | 1–2 mo | 12–85 | <5 |
| | | | | 7 mo–puberty | <5 | <5 |
| | | | | Tanner stage | | |
| | | | | I | <5 | <5 |
| | | | | II–III | 3–33 | 5–19 |
| | | | | IV–V | 22–75 | 4–30 |
| | | | | Ref. 39 | | |
| Dihydrotestosterone, free, serum | ED, E, Ch, RIA (ng/dL) | 1.0–6.2 | 0.3–1.9 | | NA | NA |
| | (% free) | *0.62–1.10%* | *0.47–0.68%* | | | |
| Estradiol, bioavailable, serum | P, E, Ch, RIA (pg/mL) | 10.5–28.5 | | | NA | NA |
| | (% bioavailable) | *37.5– 73.4%* | | | | |
| | | Follicular | 7.1–46 | | | |
| | | | *13.4–44.5%* | | | |
| | | Mid-cycle | 35–120 | | | |
| | | | *14.3–43.5%* | | | |
| | | Luteal | 8.2–52 | | | |
| | | | *14.6–40.6%* | | | |
| | | Postmen. | ≤4.7 | | | |
| | | | *9.3–52.9%* | | | |
| Estradiol, free, serum | ED, E, Ch RIA (pg/mL) | 0.30–0.90 | | | NA | NA |
| | (% free) | *1.7–2.1%* | | | | |
| | | Follicular | 0.6–3.2 | | | |
| | | | *1.5–2.0%* | | | |
| | | Mid-cycle | 0.49–1.1 | | | |
| | | | *1.6–2.1%* | | | |
| | | Luteal | 0.30–4.1 | | | |
| | | | *1.5–2.0%* | | | |
| | | Postmen. | ≤0.23 | | | |
| | | | *1.5–2.9%* | | | |
| Estradiol, automated, serum (sensitivity 25 ng/L) (Abbott IMX) | MEIA (ng/L) | <50 | | | NA | NA |
| | | Follicular | <145 | | | |
| | | Mid-cycle | 112–443 | | | |
| | | Luteal | 48–241 | | | |
| | | Postmen. | <59 | | | |
| Estradiol, total, serum (sensitivity 3 pg/mL) | E, Ch, RIA (pg/mL) | 10–50 | | 1–5 yr | 3–10 | 5–10 |
| | | Follicular | | 6–9 yr | 3–10 | 5–60 |
| | | Early | 20–150 | 10–11 yr | 5–10 | 5–300 |
| | | Late | 40–350 | 12–14 yr | 5–30 | 25–410 |
| | | Mid-cycle | 150–750 | 15–17 yr | 5– 45 | 40–410 |
| | | Luteal | 30–450 | | | |
| | | Postmen. | ≤20 | | | |
| | | | | Tanner stage | | |
| | | | | I | 3–15 | 5–10 |
| | | | | II | 3–10 | 5–115 |
| | | | | III | 5–15 | 5–180 |
| | | | | IV | 3–40 | 25–345 |
| | | | | V | 15–40 | 25–410 |
| Estradiol, 24-hr urine (sensitivity 10 pg/mL) | Enz, Ch, RIA (µg/g Cr) | 1–4 | | 2–10 yr | ≤0.6 | ≤0.6 |
| | | Follicular | 1–13 | 11–17 yr | ≤1.5 | ≤7.2 |
| | | Mid-cycle | 4–20 | | | |
| | | Luteal | 1–17 | | | |
| Estrogen, total, serum | E, RIA (pg/mL) | Assay not recommended for use in males | | | Assay not recommended for use in prepubertal children | |
| | | Follicular | | | | |
| | | Early | 70–400 | | | |
| | | Late | 100–900 | | | |
| | | Luteal | 70–700 | | | |
| | | Postmen. | ≤130 | | | |

*Continued*

**Gonad Function Tests**—*cont'd*

| Test | Method (units) | Adult Male | Adult Female | Pediatric Male | Pediatric Female |
|------|----------------|------------|--------------|----------------|------------------|
| | | **Reference Range** | | | |
| | | Male | Female | Male | Female |
| Estrogen, total, 24-hr urine | Enz, RIA (µg/g Cr) | 4–23 | | NA | NA |
| | | Follicular | 7–65 | | |
| | | Mid-cycle | 32–104 | | |
| | | Luteal | 8–135 | | |
| Estrogens, fractionated, serum | E, Ch, RIA (pg/mL) | Estrone 15–65 | | NA | NA |
| | | Follicular | | | |
| | | Early | 15–150 | | |
| | | Late | 100–250 | | |
| | | Luteal | 15–200 | | |
| | | Postmen. | 15–55 | | |
| | | Estradiol 10–50 | | | |
| | | Follicular | | | |
| | | Early | 20–150 | | |
| | | Late | 40–350 | | |
| | | Mid-cycle | 150–750 | | |
| | | Luteal | 30–450 | | |
| | | Postmen. | <20 | | |
| | | Estriol | | | |
| | | Nonpregnant | <0.1 | | |
| Estrogens, total and fractionated, 24-hr urine Sensitivities Estrone: 0.2 µg/g Estradiol: 0.02 µg/g Estriol: 0.3 µg/g Total: 0.5 µg/g | A, E, Ch, RIA (µg/g cr) | Estrone 2–8 | | NA | NA |
| | | Estradiol 1–4 | | | |
| | | Estriol 2–19 | | | |
| | | Total 4–23 | | | |
| | | Estrone | | | |
| | | Follicular | 2–39 | | |
| | | Mid-cycle | 11–46 | | |
| | | Luteal | 3–52 | | |
| | | Estradiol | | | |
| | | Follicular | 1–13 | | |
| | | Mid-cycle | 4–20 | | |
| | | Luteal | 1–17 | | |
| | | Estriol | | | |
| | | Follicular | 3–48 | | |
| | | Mid-cycle | 20–130 | | |
| | | Luteal | 9–60 | | |
| | | Total | | | |
| | | Follicular | 7–65 | | |
| | | Mid-cycle | 32–104 | | |
| | | Luteal | 8–135 | | |
| Estrone, bioavailable, serum | Pt, Ch, RIA (pg/mL) (% bioavailable) | 18–54 50–81% | | NA | NA |
| | | Follicular | 7–55 25–61% | | |
| | | Luteal | 15–63 21–61% | | |
| Estrone, free, serum | ED, Ch, RIA (pg/mL) (% free) | 0.9–2.3 2.6–4.0% | | NA | NA |
| | | Follicular | 0.8–3.2 2.2–3.2% | | |
| | | Luteal | 1.1–4.3 2.0–3.7% | | |
| | | Postmen. | 0.2–2.2 2.2–3.8% | | |

**Gonad Function Tests—*cont'd***

| Test | Method (units) | Reference Range | | | | |
|------|----------------|------|------|------|------|------|
| | | **Adult** | | **Pediatric** | | |
| | | Male | Female | | Male | Female |
| Estrone, serum | E, Ch, RIA (pg/mL) | 15–65 | | Cord blood | 9000–34,000 | 9000–34,000 |
| | | Follicular | | 1–4 days | 15–300 | 15–300 |
| | | Early | 15–250 | Children | 5–15 | 5–15 |
| | | Late | 100–250 | | | |
| | | Luteal | 15–200 | Tanner stage | | |
| | | Postmen. | 15–55 | II | 10–22 | 10–33 |
| | | | | III | 17–25 | 15–43 |
| | | | | IV | 21–35 | 16–77 |
| | | | | V | 18–45 | 29–77 |
| | | | | Ref. 27 | | |
| Estrone sulfate, serum | A, Ch, RIA (pg/mL) | 230–2200 | | NA | NA | |
| | | Follicular | 300–2600 | | | |
| | | Luteal | 100–3200 | | | |
| | | Postmen. | 100–1300 | | | |
| Estrone, 24-hr urine | En, Ch, RIA (µg/g Cr) | 2–8 | | 2–10 yr | ≤1.2 | ≤1.2 |
| | | Follicular | 2–39 | | | |
| | | Mid-cycle | 11–46 | 11–17 yr | ≤3.1 | ≤16.0 |
| | | Luteal | 3–52 | | | |
| FSH (automated), serum (sensitivity 0.1 IU/L) (Bayer Centaur) | ICMA (IU/L) | 1.6–8.0 | | | NA | NA |
| | | Follicular | 2.5–10.2 | | | |
| | | Mid-cycle | 3.1–17.7 | | | |
| | | Luteal | 1.5–9.1 | | | |
| | | Postmen. | 23–116 | | | |
| FSH 3rd generation, serum (sensitivity 0.02 IU/L) | ICMA (IU/L) | 1.5–14.3 | | 2 wk | 1.2–5.2 | 2.1–30 |
| | | Follicular | 1.4–9.9 | 1–18 mo | 0.2–3.0 | 1.1–14 |
| | | Mid-cycle | 6.2–17.2 | 19 mo–7.9 yr | 0.3–1.9 | 0.7–3.4 |
| | | Luteal | 1.1–9.2 | 8–9.9 yr | 0.3–1.7 | 0.3–5.6 |
| | | Postmen. | 15–124 | 10–11.9 yr | 0.2–5.8 | 0.7–7.3 |
| | | | | 12–14.9 yr | 0.2–10.4 | 1.0–9.2 |
| | | | | 15–18 yr | 0.8–8.2 | 0.3–10.5 |
| | | | | Tanner stage | | |
| | | | | I | 0.2–1.9 | 0.5–2.4 |
| | | | | II | 0.7–4.6 | 1.7–4.7 |
| | | | | III | 1.2–10.4 | 2.5–7.0 |
| | | | | IV | 1.7–10.4 | 1.3–7.4 |
| | | | | V | 1.5–7.0 | 1.0–9.2 |
| hCG-β subunit, quantity pregnancy, serum (Abbott, AXYM) | MEIA (mIU/mL) | Wk of gestation | Female | Wk of gestation | | Female |
| | | 3–4 | 9–130 | 3–4 | | 9–130 |
| | | 4–5 | 75–2600 | 4–5 | | 75–2600 |
| | | 5–6 | 850–20,800 | 5–6 | | 850–20,800 |
| | | 6–7 | 4000–100,200 | 6–7 | | 4,000–100, 200 |
| | | 7–12 | 11,500–289,000 | 7–12 | | 11,500–289, 000 |
| | | 12–16 | 18,300–137,000 | 12–16 | | 18,300–137,000 |
| | | 16–29 | 1400–53,000 | 16–29 | | 1,400–53,000 |
| | | 29–41 | 940–60,000 | 29–41 | | 940–60,000 |
| hCG-β subunit, quantity tumor, automated, serum (Abbott, AXYM) | MEIA (mIU/mL) | <5 | <5 | | <5 | <5 |
| 17-Ketosteroids, 24-hr urine | Modified Zimmerman (mg/24 hr) *(mg/g Cr)* | 7–20 *3.5–12.3 g Cr* | 5–15 *3.5–12.3 g Cr* | 2–17 yr | 0.8–8.1 *1.3–13.1 g Cr* | 0.8–8.1 *1.3–13.1 g Cr* |
| LH, automated, serum (sensitivity 0.3 IU/L) (Bayer Centaur) | ICMA (IU/L) | 1.5–9.3 | | | NA | NA |
| | | Follicular | 1.9–12.5 | | | |
| | | Mid-cycle | 8.7–76 | | | |
| | | Luteal | 0.5–17 | | | |
| | | Postmen. | 5.0–52 | | | |

*Continued*

**Gonad Function Tests—*cont'd***

| Test | Method (units) | Reference Range | | | | |
|---|---|---|---|---|---|---|
| | | **Adult** | | **Pediatric** | | |
| | | Male | Female | | Male | Female |
| LH 3rd generation, serum (sensitivity 0.02 IU/L) | ICMA (IU/L) | 0.95–5.6 | | 2 wk | 4.9–10 | 0.3–7.9 |
| | | | Follicular 1.7–15 | 1–18 mo | 0.04–3.0 | 0.02–1.8 |
| | | | Mid-cycle 22–57 | 19 mo–7.9 yr | 0.02–1.0 | 0.03–0.6 |
| | | | Luteal 0.6–16 | 8–9.9 yr | 0.02–0.8 | 0.02–0.2 |
| | | | Postmen. 9.0–52 | 10–11.9 yr | 0.03–4.4 | 0.02–4.1 |
| | | | | 12–14.9 yr | 0.25–4.8 | 0.3–29 |
| | | | | 15–18 yr | 0.7–7.2 | 0.1–29 |
| | | | | Tanner stage | | |
| | | | | I | 0.02–0.4 | 0.01–0.2 |
| | | | | II | 0.3–4.8 | 0.3–4.1 |
| | | | | III | 0.6–3.7 | 0.2–4.1 |
| | | | | IV | 0.6–7.2 | 0.7–15 |
| | | | | V | 1.5–7.0 | 0.3–29 |
| Pregnenolone (*see Adrenal Section*) | | | | | | |
| Progesterone (see Adrenal Section) | | | | | | |
| Sex hormone–binding globulin, serum | ICMA (nmol/L) | 7–50 | 17–120 | 2–8 yr | 29–141 | 41–137 |
| | | | | 9–14 yr | 32–92 | 15–123 |
| | | | | Refs. 41, 42 | | |
| Testosterone, bioavailable, serum | P, E, Ch, RIA (ng/dL) (% bioavailable) | 66–417 12.3–63% | | | NA | NA |
| | | | Premen. 0.6–5.0 2.4–12.9% | | | |
| | | | Postmen. 0.2–4.3 1.8–20.0% | | | |
| Testosterone, free, serum | ED, E, Ch, RIA (pg/mL) (% free) | 50–210 1.0–2.7% | | Cord blood | 5–22 2.0–4.4% | 4–16 2.0–3.9% |
| | | | Premen. 1.0–8.5 0.5–1.8% | 1–5 d | 1.5–31 0.9–1.7% | 0.5–2.5 0.8–1.5% |
| | | | Postmen. 0.6–6.7 0.8–1.9% | 1–3 mo | 3.3–18 0.4–0.8% | 0.1–1.3 0.4–1.1% |
| | | | | 3–5 mo | 0.7–14 0.4–1.1% | 0.3–1.1 0.5–1.0% |
| | | | | 5–7 mo | 0.4–4.8 0.4–1.0% | 0.2–0.6 0.5–0.8% |
| | | | | 1–5 yr | 0.15–0.6 0.4–0.9% | 0.15–0.6 0.4–0.9% |
| | | | | 6–9 yr | 1.3–3.2 0.9–1.7% | 0.1–0.9 0.9–1.4% |
| | | | | 10–11 yr | 0.6–5.7 1.0–1.9% | 1.0–5.2 1.0–1.9% |
| | | | | 12–14 yr | 1.4–156 1.3–3.0% | 1.0–5.2 1.0–1.9% |
| | | | | 15–17 yr | 80–159 1.8–2.7% | 1.0–5.2 1.0–1.9% |
| | | | | Refs. 28, 29 | | |
| Testosterone, total, serum (sensitivity <1 ng/dL) | E, Ch, RIA (ng/dL) | 260–1000 | | 1–5 mo | 1–177 | 1–5 |
| | | | Premen. 15–70 | 6–11 mo | 2–7 | 2–5 |
| | | | Postmen. 5–51 | 1–5 yr | 2–25 | 2–10 |
| | | | | 6–9 yr | 3–30 | 2–20 |
| | | | | 10–11 yr | 5–50 | 5–25 |
| | | | | 12–14 yr | 10–570 | 10–40 |
| | | | | 15–17 yr | 220–800 | 5–40 |
| | | | | Tanner stage | | |
| | | | | I | 2–23 | 2–10 |
| | | | | II | 5–70 | 5–30 |
| | | | | III | 15–280 | 10–30 |
| | | | | IV | 105–545 | 15–40 |
| | | | | V | 265–800 | 10–40 |

Cr, creatinine; FSH, follicle-stimulating hormone; hCG-β, human chorionic gonadotropin-β; LH, luteinizing hormone.

## Growth and Growth Hormone Tests

| Test | Method (units) | Reference Range — Adult Male | Adult Female | Pediatric (age) | Pediatric Male | Pediatric Female |
|---|---|---|---|---|---|---|
| Acid labile subunit, serum (DSL assay) | ELISA (µg/mL) | 13–44 | 13–44 | <1 yr<br>1–4 yr<br>5–9 yr<br>10–16 yr<br>Ref. 7 | 1–14<br>2–20<br>5–31<br>11–41 | 1–14<br>2–20<br>5–31<br>11–41 |
| GH, serum (measures 22 + 20K GH) | ICMA (ng/mL) | ≤10 | ≤10 | ≤13 | ≤13 | |
|  |  | Fasting<br>Because of diurnal variability, random GH values are not reliable for diagnosis of GH deficiency or acromegaly. See Table 196-16; Ref. 23. | | Because of diurnal variability, random GH values are not reliable for diagnosis of GH deficiency or gigantism. See Table 196-16; Refs. 21–24. | | |
| GH-binding protein, serum | Ligand-mediated immunofunctional assay (pmol/L) | 66–306 | 66–306 | 3–5 yr<br>6–9 yr<br>10–15 yr | 57–282<br>60–619<br>52–783 | 62–519<br>58–572<br>72–965 |
| GH-releasing hormone, plasma | E, RIA (pg/mL) | <50 | <50 | | <50 | <50 |
| IGF-1 serum | ICMA (ng/mL) | 16–24 yr 182–780<br>25–39 yr 114–492<br>40–54 yr 90–360<br>>55 yr 71–290 | 182–780<br>114–492<br>90–360<br>71–290 | 2 mo–5 yr<br>6–8 yr<br>9–11 yr<br>12–15 yr | 17–248<br>88–474<br>110–565<br>202–957 | 17–248<br>88–474<br>117–771<br>261–1096 |
|  |  |  |  | Tanner stage<br>I<br>II<br>III<br>IV<br>V | 109–485<br>174–512<br>230–818<br>396–776<br>402–839 | 128–470<br>186–695<br>292–883<br>394–920<br>308–1138 |
| IGF-2, plasma | E, RIA (ng/mL) | 18–54 yr 405–1085<br>55–65 yr 230–970<br>>65 yr 210–750 | 405–1085<br>230–970<br>210–750 | 2 mo–5 yr<br>6–9 yr<br>10–17 yr | 300–860<br>520–1050<br>530–1140 | 300–860<br>520–1050<br>530–1140 |
| IGF-binding protein 1, serum | RIA (ng/mL) | Fasting 13–73 | 13–73 | 5–10 yr<br>10–15 yr<br>15–18 yr<br>Ref. 30 | 20–105<br>10–70<br>10–40 | 20–105<br>10–70<br>10–40 |
| IGF-binding protein 2, serum | RIA (ng/mL) | 18–49 yr 55–240<br>>49 yr 28–444 | 55–240<br>28–444 | 1–9 yr<br>10–17 yr | 69–480<br>50–326 | 69–480<br>50–326 |
| IGF-binding protein 3, serum | RIA (ng/mL) | 19–55 yr 2000–4000<br>56–82 yr 900–3700 | 2000–4000<br>900–3700 | 2–23 mo<br>2–7 yr<br>8–11 yr<br>12–18 yr | 700–2300<br>900–4100<br>1500–4300<br>2200–4200 | 700–2300<br>900–4100<br>1500–4300<br>2200–4200 |

GH, growth hormone; IGF, insulin-like growth factor.

## Hypothalamic Pituitary Tests

| Test | Method (units) | Reference Range (Adult) | Adult Male | Adult Female | Reference Range (Pediatric) | Pediatric Male | Pediatric Female |
|---|---|---|---|---|---|---|---|
| ACTH (sensitivity 2 pg/mL), plasma | ICMA (pg/mL) | 7:00–10:00 A.M. | 9–52 | 9–52 | Prepubertal<br>Pubertal | 7–28<br>2–49 | 7–27<br>2–49 |
| ACTH (sensitivity 10 pg/mL, recognizes precursors and fragments), plasma | E, RIA (pg/mL) | Metyrapone stimulated<br>Dexamethasone suppressed<br>Females on oral contraceptives<br>8:00–10:00 A.M. | 112–466<br>2–8<br><br>≤130 | 112–466<br>2–8<br>5–29<br>≤130 |  | NA | NA |
| α Subunit, serum | RIA (ng/mL) | Mid-cycle<br>Postmen.<br>Pregnancy | <1.0 | <3.6<br><3.6<br>Varies with human chorionic gonadotropin | Prepubertal | <1.0 | <1.0 |
| Arginine vasopressin, plasma (2.5 pg = 1 µU) (sensitivity 1 pg/mL) | E, RIA (pg/mL) | See Figure 196-1 | 1–13 | 1–13 | See Figure 196-1 | 1–13 | 1–13 |
| Arginine vasopressin, urine (2.5 pg = 1 µU) (sensitivity 4.2 pg/mL) | RIA (pg/mL) | See Figure 196-2 | ≤112 | ≤112 | See Figure 196-2 | ≤112 | ≤112 |
| Corticotropin-releasing hormone, plasma | E, RIA (pg/mL) | 6:00–10:00 A.M. | 24–40 | 24–40 |  | NA | NA |
| Endorphin (β-endorphin/lipotropin), plasma | E, RIA (pg/mL) |  | 16–48 | 16–48 |  | NA | NA |
| Follicle-stimulating hormone (see Gonad Function Tests) |  |  |  |  |  |  |  |
| Growth hormone (see Growth and Growth Hormone Tests) |  |  |  |  |  |  |  |
| Luteinizing hormone (see Gonad Function Tests) |  |  |  |  |  |  |  |
| Prolactin, serum (Bayer Centaur) | ICMA (ng/dL) |  | 3–14.7 | 3.8–23.2 | Cord blood<br>Prepubertal<br>Tanner stage<br>II, III<br>IV, V | 45–539<br><10<br><br><6.1<br>2.8–11 | 45–539<br>3.6–12<br><br>2.6–18<br>3.2–20 |
| Somatostatin, plasma | E, RIA (pg/mL) |  | 10–22 | 10–22 |  | NA | NA |
| Thyrotropin-releasing hormone, plasma | RIA (pg/mL) |  | <5.0 | <5.0 |  | NA | NA |
| Thyroid-stimulating hormone (see Thyroid Functions Tests) |  |  |  |  |  |  |  |

ACTH, adrenocorticotropic hormone.

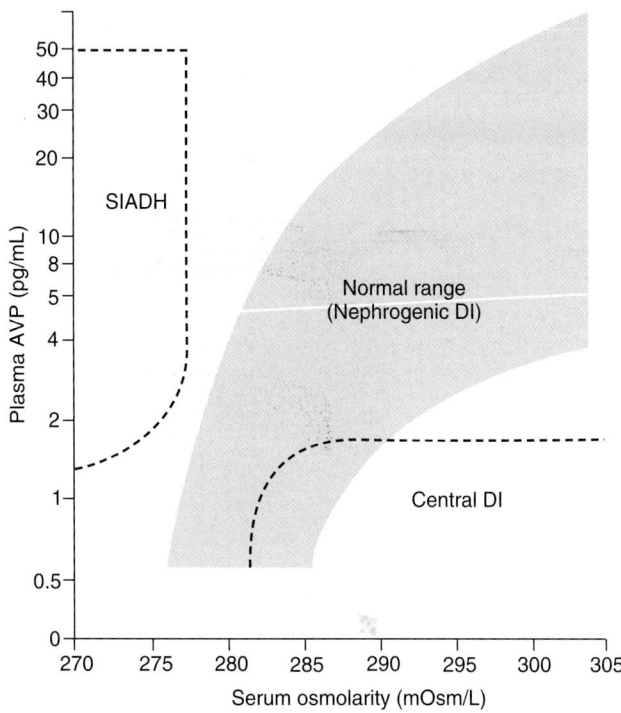

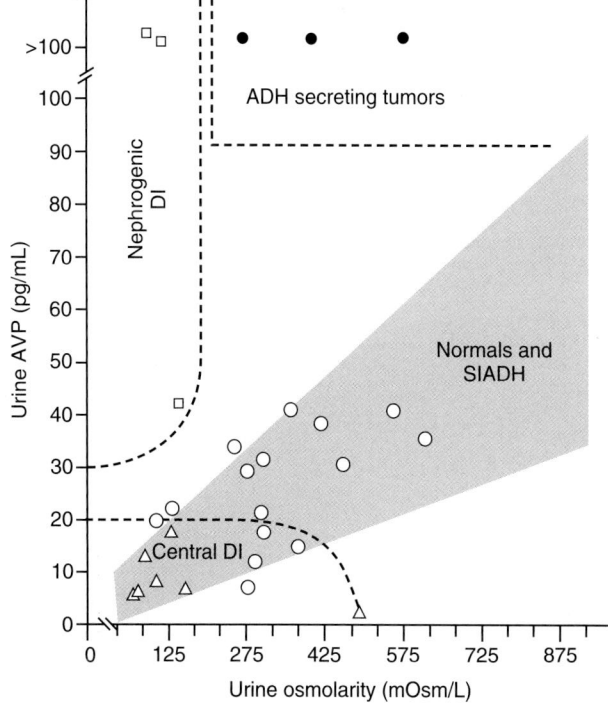

**Figure 196-1** Relationship of serum osmolarity and plasma arginine vasopressin (AVP) levels in normal subjects and patients with central and nephrogenic diabetes insipidus (DI) and the syndrome of inappropriate antidiuretic hormone or (vasopressin) secretion (SIADH). The nephrogenic diabetes insipidus range and the normal range are similar. (From Fisher DA [ed]: Endocrinology: Test Selection and Interpretation. Teterboro, NJ, Quest Diagnostics, 1998.)

**Figure 196-2** Relationship of urine osmolarity and urine arginine vasopressin (AVP) levels in normal subjects and patients with central and nephrogenic diabetes insipidus (DI) (Nichols Institute values of urine AVP and osmolarity). The syndrome of inappropriate antidiuretic hormone (or vasopressin) secretion (SIADH) and antidiuretic hormone (ADH)-secreting tumors. (From Fisher DA [ed]: Endocrinology: Test Selection and Interpretation. Teterboro, NJ, Quest Diagnostics, 1998.)

Nichols Institute values for urine AVP and Osmolarity
- ○ 15 patients with SIADH
- △ 6 patients with central DI
- □ 3 patients with nephrogenic DI
- ● ADH immunoreactivity in 3 patients with ADH secreting tumors

## Parathyroid/Bone Tests

| Test | Method (units) | Adult | | | Pediatric | | |
|------|---------------|-------|--|--|-----------|--|--|
| | | | **Male** 6–23 | **Female** | 8–17 yr | **Male** 13.7–136 | **Female** 13.7–136 |
| Alkaline phosphatase, bone specific, serum | IRMA (µg/L) | Premen. | | 4–15 | Tanner stage | | |
| | | Postmen. | | 6–24 | I, II | 20–88 | 20–88 |
| | | | | | III, IV | 20–160 | 20–160 |
| | | | | | V | 4–46 | 4–46 |
| | Immunoenzymatic (µg/L) | | 8.8–30 | 5.7–22 | 2–24 mo | 25.4–124 | 25.4–124 |
| | | | | | 2–9 yr | 24.2–89.5 | 24.2–89.5 |
| | | | | | Tanner stage | | |
| | | | | | I–II | 19.5–87.5 | 19.5–87.5 |
| | | | | | III–IV | 19.5–156 | 19.5–156 |
| | | | | | Refs. 43, 44 | | |
| Calcitonin serum (*see Thyroid Function Tests*) (thyrocalcitonin) | | | | | | | |
| Collagen cross-linked N telopeptide, 2nd void, urine | EIA nmol BCE/ mmol Cr | Premen. | 11–103 | 10–110 | | NA | NA |
| Collagen cross-linked N telopeptide, 24-hr urine | EIA nmol BCE/ mmol Cr | Premen. | 5–87 | 5–79 | | NA | NA |
| Cyclic AMP, nephrogenous, random urine, plasma | E, RBA, colorimetry | Nephrogenous cyclic AMP (nmol/dL) | 1.4–5.0 | 1.4–5.0 | | NA | NA |
| | | Urine cyclic AMP (µmol/L) | 0.6–12.0 | 0.6–12.0 | | | |
| | | Plasma cyclic AMP (nmol/L) | 6.3–13.7 | 6.3–13.7 | | | |
| Hydroxyproline, 24-hr urine (free and total) | Colorimetry (mg/24 hr) | Total | 9–73 | 7–49 | | NA | NA |
| | | Free | ≤2.7 | ≤2.7 | | | |
| Osteocalcin (bone α-carboxyglutamic acid protein, β-glycerophosphatase), serum | IRMA (ng/mL) | | 11.3–35.4 | | Prepubertal | | |
| | | Premen. | | 7.2–27.9 | 2 mo–1 yr | 27–149 | 27–149 |
| | | | | | 1.1–4 yr | 23–105 | 23–105 |
| | | | | | 5–9 yr | 24–123 | 24–123 |
| | | | | | Tanner stage | | |
| | | | | | I | 20–89 | 20–89 |
| | | | | | II | 26–91 | 44–144 |
| | | | | | III | 48–123 | 31–90 |
| | | | | | Ref. 33 | | |
| PTH C-terminal (midmolecule), serum | RIA (pg/mL) | | 50–330 | 50–330 | 1–16 yr | 54–226 | 54–226 |
| PTH, intact, serum | ICMA (pg/mL) | See Figure 196-3 | 10–65 | 10–65 | Cord blood | <10 | <10 |
| | | | | | 3 d–1 yr | ≤56 | ≤56 |
| | | | | | 2–17 yr | 9–52 | 9–52 |
| PTH, BioIntact (amino acids 1–84) | pg/mL | | 6–40 | 6–40 | | NA | NA |
| PTH-related protein, plasma | IRMA (pmol/L) | | ≤1.3 | ≤1.3 | | NA | NA |
| Pyridinium collagen crosslinks PYD, DPYD, 2-hr morning urine | HPLC (nmol/mmol Cr) | PYD | 23–65 | | 2–10 yr | | |
| | | DPYD | 6–26 | | PYD | 150–400 | 150–400 |
| | | Premen. | | | DPYD | 40–120 | 40–120 |
| | | PYD | | 25–83 | 11–17 yr | | |
| | | DPYD | | 6–23 | PYD | 17–410 | 17–410 |
| | | | | | DPYD | 2–118 | 2–118 |
| Pyridinium collagen crosslinks PYD, DPYD, 24-hr urine | HPLC (nmol/mmol Cr) | PYD | 20–61 | | 2–10 yr | | |
| | | DPYD | 4–19 | | PYD | 160–440 | 160–440 |
| | | Premen. | | | DPYD | 31–110 | 31–110 |
| | | PYD | | 22–89 | 11–14 yr | | |
| | | DPYD | | 4–21 | PYD | 105–400 | 105–400 |
| | | | | | DPYD | 17–100 | 17–100 |
| | | | | | 15–17 yr | | |
| | | | | | PYD | 42–200 | 42–200 |
| | | | | | DPYD | ≤59 | ≤59 |

**Parathyroid/Bone Tests—*cont'd***

| Test | Method (units) | Reference Range | | | | | |
|------|----------------|------|------|------|------|------|------|
| | | **Adult** | | | **Pediatric** | | |
| | | Male | Female | | | Male<br>NA | Female<br>NA |
| Pyrilinks D, DPYD,<br>  free urine | EIA<br>(nmol/mmol Cr) | 1.8–5.8 | | Premen. | | | |
| | | | 2.8–8.2 | | | | |
| Vitamin D, 25-hydroxy,<br>  serum | E, Ch, RBA (ng/mL) | 9–54 | 9–54 | | Cord blood | ≤30 | ≤30 |
| | | | | | 1 mo–17 yr | 13–67 | 13–67 |
| Vitamin D, 1,25-dihydroxy,<br>  serum | E, Ch, RBA (pg/mL) | 15–60 | 15–60 | | Cord blood | ≤40 | ≤40 |
| | | | | | 1 mo–17 yr | 27–71 | 27–71 |

Cr, creatinine; cyclic AMP, cyclic adenosine monophosphate; DPYD, deoxypyridinoline; PTH, parathyroid hormone; PYD, pyridinoline.

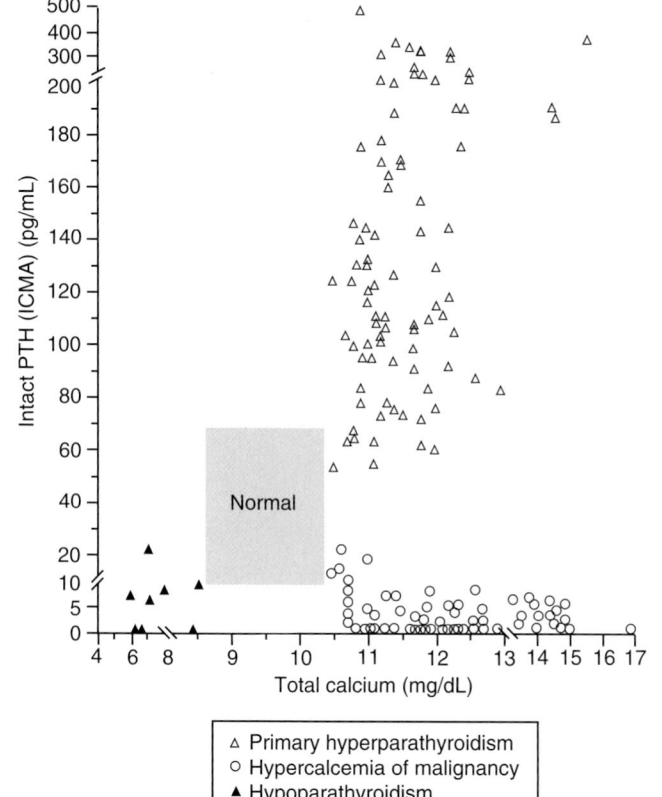

***Figure 196-3*** Relationship of serum (total) calcium and intact parathyroid hormone (PTH) concentrations in patients with primary hyperparathyroidism, hypoparathyroidism, and hypercalcemia of malignancy. Patients with hypercalcemia of malignancy usually also have elevated levels of parathyroid hormone-related protein. ICMA, immunochemiluminometric assay. (From Fisher DA [ed]: Endocrinology: Test Selection and Interpretation. Teterboro, NJ, Quest Diagnostics, 1998.)

△ Primary hyperparathyroidism
○ Hypercalcemia of malignancy
▲ Hypoparathyroidism

## Renal and Fluid Balance Tests

| Test | Method (units) | Adult | | | Pediatric | | |
|---|---|---|---|---|---|---|---|
| | | | | | | | |
| Aldosterone, serum (*see Adrenal Tests*) | | | | | | | |
| Aldosterone, urine (*see Adrenal Tests*) | | Male | Female | | | Male | Female |
| Angiotensin-converting enzyme, serum | Kinetic assay (U/L) | 9–67 | 9–67 | | <3 yr | 25–67 | 25–67 |
| | | | | | 3–5 yr | 20–76 | 20–76 |
| | | | | | 6–8 yr | 23–70 | 23–70 |
| | | | | | 9–11 yr | 24–67 | 24–67 |
| | | | | | 12–14 yr | 22–72 | 22–72 |
| | | | | | 15–18 yr | 17–60 | 17–60 |
| | | | | | Ref. 37 | | |
| Arginine vasopressin (*see Hypothalamic-Pituitary Tests*) | | | | | | | |
| Atrial natriuretic hormone or factor, plasma | E, RIA (pg/mL) | 25–77 | 25–77 | | | NA | NA |
| Corticosterone (*see Adrenal Tests*) | | | | | | | |
| Deoxycorticosterone (*see Adrenal Tests*) | | | | | | | |
| Plasma renin activity | Angiotensin I generation, RIA (ng/mL/hr) | Supine | 0.65–5.0 | 0.65–5.0 | *Supine* Premature | | |
| | | | | | 1–7 days | ≤34 | ≤34 |
| | | | | | Term newborn | ≤26 | ≤26 |
| | | | | | 3 mo–1 yr | ≤15 | ≤15 |
| | | | | | 1–4 yr | ≤10 | ≤10 |
| | | | | | 4–6 yr | ≤7.5 | ≤7.5 |
| | | | | | 7–9 yr | ≤5.9 | ≤5.9 |
| | | | | | 10–12 yr | ≤5.3 | ≤5.3 |
| | | | | | 13–15 yr | ≤4.4 | ≤4.4 |
| | | | | | Refs. 34–36 | | |
| Prorenin, plasma | IRMA (mU/L) | 21–35 yr | 57–285 | 57–285 | | NA | NA |
| | | >35 yr | 48–224 | 48–224 | | | |
| Renin, direct or immunoreactive, plasma | ICMA (mU/L) | Supine | 12–79 | 12–79 | *Supine* | | |
| | | Upright | 13–114 | 13–114 | Cord blood | 39–617 | 39–617 |
| | | | | | Term newborn | | |
| | | | | | 2–4 days | 11–759 | 11–759 |
| | | | | | 5–7 days | 4–246 | 4–246 |
| | | | | | 2 wk–3 mo | 11–148 | 11–148 |
| | | | | | 4 mo–1 yr | 17–174 | 17–174 |
| | | | | | 1–3 yr | 21–102 | 21–102 |
| | | | | | 3–5 yr | 20–123 | 20–123 |
| | | | | | 5–7 yr | 20–129 | 20–129 |
| | | | | | 7–11 yr | 15–102 | 15–102 |
| | | | | | 11–15 yr | 14–105 | 14–105 |
| | | | | | 15–18 yr | 14–72 | 14–72 |
| | | | | | Ref. 38 | | |

## Thyroid Function Tests

| Test | Method (units) | | Reference Range — Adult | | | Reference Range — Pediatric | |
|---|---|---|---|---|---|---|---|
| | | | **Male** | **Female** | | **Male** | **Female** |
| Calcitonin, serum (thyrocalcitonin) | ICMA (pg/mL) | Basal Provocative test (see Table 196-22) | ≤4 | ≤8 | | NA | NA |
| $T_3$, total, serum | RIA (ng/dL) | | 87–180 | 87–180 | Cord blood | 43–99 | 43–99 |
| | | Pregnancy | | | 1–3 days | 100–740 | 100–740 |
| | | 1st trimester | | 81–190 | 1–11 mo | 105–245 | 105–245 |
| | | 2nd, 3rd trimesters | | 100–260 | 1–4 yr | 105–269 | 105–269 |
| | | | | | 5–9 yr | 94–241 | 94–241 |
| | | | | | 10–14 yr | 82–213 | 82–213 |
| | | | | | 15–19 yr | 80–210 | 80–210 |
| | | | | | See Tables 196-18 and 196-19 | | |
| | ICMA (ng/dL) | | 60–181 | 60–181 | 1–9 yr | 127–221 | 127–221 |
| | | | | | 10–13 yr | 123–211 | 123–211 |
| | | | | | 14–18 yr | 97–186 | 97–186 |
| $T_3$, free (nondialysis), serum (Bayer Centaur) | ICMA (pg/dL) | | 290–410 | 245–360 | 1–9 yr | 337–506 | 337–506 |
| | | | | | 10–13 yr | 335–480 | 335–480 |
| | | | | | 14–18 yr | 287–455 | 287–455 |
| $T_3$, free (tracer dialysis), serum | ED, RIA (pg/dL) | | 210–440 | 210–440 | 1–9 yr | 296–325 | 296–325 |
| | | Pregnancy | | 200–380 | 10–13 yr | 290–547 | 290–547 |
| | | | | | 14–18 yr | 240–546 | 240–546 |
| $T_3$, reverse, serum | RIA (ng/dL) | | 10–24 | 10–24 | Cord blood | 102–342 | 102–342 |
| | | | | | 1 mo–20 yr | 10–35 | 10–35 |
| $T_4$, total, serum (ACS-180) | ICMA (µg/dL) | | 5.6–13.7 | 5.6–13.7 | Premature Cord blood | See Table 196-18 | See Table 196-18 |
| | | Pregnancy | | | | | |
| | | 1st trimester | | 8.0–17.1 | (>37 wk) | 5.9–15.0 | 5.9–15.0 |
| | | 2nd trimester | | 8.0–17.8 | 0–4 days | 14–28 | 14–28 |
| | | 3rd trimester | | 8.0–20.1 | 2–20 wk | 8.1–15.7 | 8.1–15.7 |
| | | | | | 21 wk–20 yr | 5.6–14.9 | 5.6–14.9 |
| $T_4$, free (nondialysis), serum (Bayer Centaur) | ICMA (ng/dL) | | 0.8–1.8 | 0.8–1.8 | 1–9 yr | 0.9–1.6 | 0.9–1.6 |
| | | | | | 10–18 yr | 0.9–1.4 | 0.9–1.4 |
| $T_4$ free (direct dialysis), serum | ED, RIA (ng/dL) | | 0.8–2.7 | 0.8–2.7 | Premature (25–30 wk) | | |
| | | Pregnancy | | | 0–7 days | 0.5–3.3 | 0.5–3.3 |
| | | 1st trimester | | 0.7–2.0 | (31–36 wk) | | |
| | | 2nd trimester | | 0.5–1.6 | 0–7 days | 1.3–4.7 | 1.3–4.7 |
| | | 3rd trimester | | 0.5–1.6 | Cord blood | | |
| | | | | | (>37 wk) | 1.2–2.2 | 1.2–2.2 |
| | | | | | 1–4 days | 2.2–5.3 | 2.2–5.3 |
| | | | | | 2 wk–20 yr | 0.8–2.0 | 0.8–2.0 |
| $T_4$-binding proteins, serum | EL, serial immunoassays | *See Figure 196-4* | Male and female | | 10–19 yr | | Male and female similar to adult values |
| | | $T_4$ | 5.6–13.7 µg/dL | | | | |
| | | TBG-bound $T_4$ | 3.6–8.4 µg/dL | | | | |
| | | Prealbumin-bound $T_4$ | 0.6–2.0 µg/dL | | | | |
| | | Albumin-bound $T_4$ | 0.5–1.2 µg/dL | | | | |
| | | TBG | 1.7–3.6 mg/dL | | | | |
| | | Prealbumin | | | | | |
| | | Male | 21–43 mg/dL | | | | |
| | | Female | 17–34 mg/dL | | | | |
| | | Albumin | 3700–5100 mg/dL | | | | |
| | | $\dfrac{\text{TBG-bound } T_4}{\text{TBG}}$ | 1.9–3.5 µg/mg | | | | |
| | | $\dfrac{\text{Prealbumin-bound } T_4}{\text{Prealbumin}}$ | 0.02–0.07 µg/mg | | | | |
| | | $\dfrac{\text{Albumin-bound } T_4}{\text{Albumin}}$ | 0.11–0.28 µg/g | | | | |

*Continued*

**Thyroid Function Tests—cont'd**

| Test | Method (units) | Reference Range | | | | | |
|---|---|---|---|---|---|---|---|
| | | Adult | | | Pediatric | | |
| | | Male | Female | | | Male | Female |
| TBG, serum | RIA (mg/dL) | 1.7–3.6 | 1.7–3.6 | | Cord blood | 2.1–3.7 | 2.1–3.7 |
| | | | | | 1–5 days | 2.2–4.2 | 2.2–4.2 |
| | | | | | 1–11 mo | 1.6–3.6 | 1.7–3.7 |
| | | | | | 1–9 yr | 1.2–2.8 | 1.5–2.7 |
| | | | | | 10–19 yr | 1.4–2.6 | 1.4–3.0 |
| TBG assessment ($T_3$ uptake), serum | Solid-phase talc uptake, radioassay (ratio to standard serum pool) | 20–49 yr  0.92–1.14 | 0.83–1.15 | | 1–9 yr | 0.61–1.13 | 0.68–0.96 |
| | | 50–90 yr  0.87–1.11 | 0.80–1.04 | | 10–19 yr | 0.67–1.09 | 0.64–1.00 |
| Thyroglobulin, serum (sensitivity 0.5 ng/mL) | ICMA (ng/mL) | 3.5–56.0 | 3.5–56.0 | | Cord blood | 15–101 | 15–101 |
| | | | | | Birth–2 yr | 11–92 | 11–92 |
| | | | | | 2–16 yr | 2.3–40 | 2.3–40 |
| Thyroid-stimulating hormone, 3rd generation, serum | ICMA (mU/L) | 0.4–5.5 | 0.4–5.5 | | Premature | See Table 196-17 | See Table 196-17 |
| | | Pregnancy | | | Cord blood | 2.3–13 | 2.3–13 |
| | | 1st trimester | 0.3–4.5 | | 1–2 days | 3.20–34.7 | 3.20–34.7 |
| | | 2nd trimester | 0.5–4.6 | | 3–4 days | 0.70–15.4 | 0.70–15.4 |
| | | 3rd trimester | 0.8–5.2 | | 2–20 wk | 1.7–9.1 | 1.7–9.1 |
| | | | | | 21 wk–20 yr | 0.7–6.4 | 0.7–6.4 |
| | | See Figure 196-4 | | | | | |

$T_3$, triiodothyroxine; $T_4$, thyroxine; TBG, thyroxine-binding globulin.

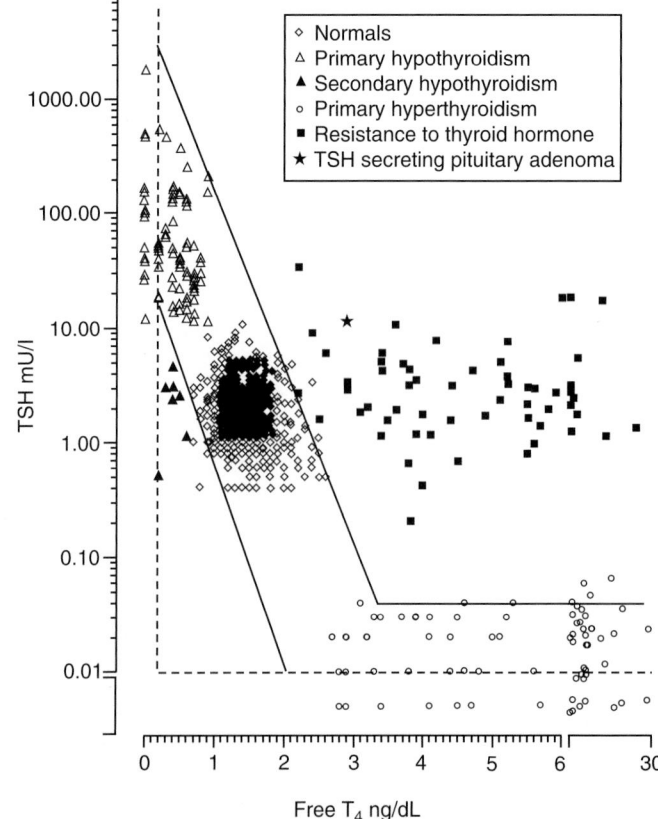

*Figure 196-4* Relationship of serum free thyroxine ($T_4$) (direct dialysis) and thyroid-stimulating hormone (TSH) concentrations in normal subjects and patients with thyroid disorders. The log linear relationship is shown whereby a linear change in serum free $T_4$ produces a logarithmic change in serum TSH concentration. Normal values are shown for 589 normal subjects (289 children 5 months to 20 years of age and 300 adults 21 to 54 years of age), 84 hypothyroid and 116 hyperthyroid patients obtained through the Nichols Institute Clinical Correlations Division. The samples from patients with thyroid hormone resistance were provided by Dr. Samuel Refetoff of The University of Chicago. Samples from patients with central hypothyroidism were provided by Dr. Peter Singer of the University of Southern California, Dr. Mary Samuels of Oregon Health Sciences University, Dr. Susan Clark of Loma Linda University, and Dr. Arlan Rosenbloom of the University of Florida. All patients were sampled before treatment, thus representing the native disease state. (From Fisher DA [ed]: Endocrinology: Test Selection and Interpretation. Teterboro, NJ, Quest Diagnostics, 1998.)

## Genetic Tests

| Test | Method (units) | Reference Range Adult Male | Adult Female | Pediatric Male | Pediatric Female |
|------|---------------|----------|----------|----------|----------|
| Androgen insensitivity | PCR and DNA sequencing | Negative | Negative | Negative | Negative |
| CAH (21-hydroxylase deficiency) common mutations (whole blood, amniotic fluid, CVS) | PCR and mutation detection | Negative | Negative | Negative | Negative |
| CAH (21-hydroxylase deficiency) rare mutations (whole blood, amniotic fluid, CVS) | PCR and DNA sequencing | Negative | Negative | Negative | Negative |
| Carney complex (whole blood) | PCR and mutation analysis or DNA sequencing | Negative | Negative | Negative | Negative |
| Central diabetes insipidus (whole blood) | PCR and DNA sequencing | Negative | Negative | Negative | Negative |
| Chromosome-specific (1-22, X, Y) centromere (whole blood) | FISH | Normal | Normal | Normal | Normal |
| Di George syndrome, (whole blood) | FISH | Normal | Normal | Normal | Normal |
| Kallmann's syndrome, (whole blood) | FISH | Normal | Normal | Normal | Normal |
| McCune-Albright syndrome (whole blood) | PCR and mutation analysis | Negative | Negative | Negative | Negative |
| MEN1 (whole blood) | PCR and DNA sequencing or linkage analysis | Negative | Negative | Negative | Negative |
| MEN2 and familial medullary thyroid cancer mutations, exons 10, 11, 13–16 (whole blood) | PCR and DNA sequencing | Negative | Negative | Negative | Negative |
| Nephrogenic diabetes insipidus (X-linked) mutations (whole blood) | PCR and DNA sequencing | Negative | Negative | Negative | Negative |
| Prader-Willi syndrome (whole blood) | FISH | Normal | Normal | Normal | Normal |
| Pheochromocytoma, VHL gene mutations (whole blood) | PCR and DNA sequencing | Negative | Negative | Negative | Negative |
| Pheochromocytoma, SDHB gene mutations (whole blood) | PCR and DNA sequencing | Negative | Negative | Negative | Negative |
| Pheochromocytoma, sudden death heart disease gene mutations (whole blood) | PCR and DNA sequencing | Negative | Negative | Negative | Negative |
| Resistance to thyroid hormone (whole blood) | PCR and DNA sequencing | Negative | Negative | Negative | Negative |
| SRY sequences detection (whole blood) | PCR, gel electrophoresis | Normal | Normal | Normal | Normal |
| Williams syndrome (whole blood) | FISH | Normal | Normal | Normal | Normal |

CAH, congenital adrenal hyperplasia; CVS, chorionic villi sampling; FISH, fluorescence in situ hybridization; MEN, multiple endocrine neoplasia; PCR, polymerase chain reaction.

**Table 196-1** Rapid Adrenocorticotropic Hormone Stimulation Results in Normal Adults: (250-μg Intravenous Bolus 1–24 ACTH) Glucocorticoid Pathway*†

| Steroid | Blood Level (ng/dL) Except Cortisol 0 | 60 min |
|---------|---|--------|
| 17-Hydroxypregnenolone | 20–450 | 290–910 |
| 17-Hydroxyprogesterone | 17–104 | 42–250 |
| Dehydroepiandrosterone | 230–955 | 545–1845 |
| Androstenedione | 56–135 | 72–290 |
| 11-Deoxycortisol | 21–130 | 82–290 |
| Cortisol (μg/dL) | 6–19 | 14–41 |

*Quest Diagnostics Nichols Institute: 10 females, 10 males, healthy young adults, results are observed ranges.
†Adrenocorticotropic hormone (1–24) 250-μg intravenous bolus.
From Fisher DA (ed): Endocrinology: Test Selection and Interpretation. Teterboro, NJ, Quest Diagnostics, 1998.

**Table 196-2** Mineralocorticoid Pathway*

| Steroid | Blood Level (ng/dL) 0 | 60 min |
|---------|---|--------|
| Progesterone | 5–50 | 21–44 |
| Deoxycorticosterone | 3–10 | 14–33 |
| 18-Hydroxycorticosterone | 11–46 | 54–161 |
| Aldosterone | 2–9 | 5–20 |

*Quest Diagnostics Nichols Institute: 10 females, 10 males, healthy young adults, results are observed ranges.
From Fisher DA (ed): Endocrinology: Test Selection and Interpretation. Teterboro, NJ, Quest Diagnostics, 1998.

**Table 196-3** Rapid Adrenocorticotropic Hormone Stimulation Results in Normal Children and Adolescents: (250-μg Intravenous Bolus 1–24 ACTH) Glucocorticoid Pathway*†

| | Blood Levels (ng/dL) Except Cortisol | | | | | | | |
| | Male and Female (1–5 yr, n = 22) | | Male and Female (6–12 yr, n = 15) | | Pubertal | | | |
| | | | | | Male, n = 23 | | Female, n = 19 | |
| Steroid | 0 | 60 min | 0 | 60 min | 0 | 60 min | 0 | 60 min |
|---|---|---|---|---|---|---|---|---|
| 17-Hydroxypregnenolone | 10–100 | 45–740 | 11–190 | 70–660 | 20–360 | 88–860 | 53–540 | 250–1600 |
| 17-Hydroxyprogesterone | 4–115 | 50–350 | 7–69 | 75–220 | 12–190 | 69–310 | 18–220 | 80–420 |
| Dehydroepiandrosterone | 9–42 | 21–98 | 11–155 | 34–320 | 25–400 | 69–690 | 62–510 | 95–1460 |
| Androstenedione | 5–51 | 12–68 | 7–68 | 12–98 | 17–150 | 29–215 | 43–220 | 58–320 |
| 11-Deoxycortisol | 7–210 | 98–360 | 14–140 | 95–320 | 11–150 | 87–280 | 15–130 | 78–250 |
| Cortisol (μg/dL) | 6–25 | 22–40 | 3–15 | 17–28 | 4–15 | 15–27 | 4–16 | 16–35 |

*Adrenocorticotropic hormone (1–24) 250-μg intravenous bolus.
†Testing from 8:00 to 10:00 A.M. Results are observed ranges.
Data from Adrenal steroid response to ACTH. Pediatrics, Endocrine Sciences. Calabassas Hills, CA, May 1991; and Lashansky G, Saenger P, Fishman K, et al: Normative data for adrenal steroidogenesis in a healthy pediatric population: Age and sex related changes after adrenocorticotropin stimulation. J Clin Endocrinol Metab 73:674–686, 1991.

**Table 196-4** Mineralocorticoid Pathway*

| | Blood Levels (ng/dL) | | | | | | | |
| | Male and Female (1–5 yr, n = 22) | | Male and Female (6–12 yr, n = 15) | | Pubertal | | | |
| | | | | | Male, n = 23 | | Female, n = 20 | |
| Steroid | 0 | 60 min | 0 | 60 min | 0 | 60 min | 0 | 60 min |
|---|---|---|---|---|---|---|---|---|
| Progesterone | 8–64 | 51–230 | 5–93 | 38–200 | 17–145 | 35–225 | 6–1290 | 32–1080 |
| Deoxycorticosterone | 4–49 | 26–140 | 2–34 | 19–140 | 4–30 | 12–74 | 2–12 | 13–63 |
| 18-Hydroxycorticosterone | 7–155 | 49–370 | 10–74 | 79–360 | 5–73 | 73–1475 | 11–82 | 69–320 |
| Aldosterone | 2–37 | 13–85 | 3–21 | 14–50 | 1–14 | 10–33 | 2–32 | 10–34 |

*Testing from 8:00 to 10:00 A.M. Results are observed ranges.
Data from Lashansky G, Saenger P, Dimartino-Nardi J, et al: Normative data for the steroidogenic response of mineralocorticoids and their precursors to adrenocorticotropin in a healthy pediatric population. J Clin Endocrinol Metab 75:1491–1496, 1992.

**Table 196-5** Low-Dose Short Synacthen Testing

Indications
    Suspected HPA axis impairment
    Suspected cortisol deficiency
    Alternative to ITT
Testing
    Baseline blood sample for plasma cortisol measurement
    1.0 μg tetracosactrin (ACTH 1–24) intravenously
    Blood samples for plasma cortisol at 0, 20, 30 min
Expected results
    A peak plasma cortisol level of 2.17 μg/dL (600 nmol/L) indicates
      an intact HPA axis
Comment*
    There is a high correlation between the ITT and LDSST peak cortisol
      responses ($r = 0.89$; $P < 0.0001$)
    Sensitivity of the LDSST approximates 100%

*See Abdir et al.[11]
ACTH, adrenocorticotropic hormone; HPA, hypothalamic-pituitary-adrenal;
ITT, insulin tolerance testing; LDSST, low-dose short synacthen testing.

**Table 196-6** Overnight Dexamethasone Suppression Testing

Indications
    Suspected Cushing's syndrome
    Suspected dexamethasone-suppressible hyperaldosteronism
    Differentiation of pituitary vs. ectopic Cushing's syndrome
    Assess adrenal source of androgen in polycystic ovary syndrome
Overnight testing
    Diagnosis of Cushing's syndrome
        Dexamethasone 20 μg/kg (max, 1 mg) at 11P.M.–12 A.M.
        Serum sampling at 8:00 A.M.
        Normal responses
            Serum cortisol <5 μg/dL
            Serum aldosterone <5 ng/dL
            Serum dexamethasone 125–1277 μg/dL
        A serum cortisol >10 ng/dL suggestive of Cushing's syndrome
    Differentiation of pituitary vs. ectopic Cushing's syndrome
        Dexmathasone 200 μg/kg (max, 8 mg) at 10:00 P.M.
        Serum sampling at 8:00 A.M.
        Expected serum cortisol responses
            Pituitary disease >60% suppression
            Ectopic disease <60% suppression

From Findling JW, Raff H, Aron DC: The low dose dexamethasone
suppression test: A reevaluation in patients with Cushing's syndrome.
J Clin Endocrinol Metab 89:1222–1226, 2003.

**Table 196-7** Standard 6-Day Dexamethasone Suppression Testing

Indications
  Suspected Cushing's syndrome
  Differentiation of pituitary vs. nonpituitary Cushing's syndrome
Low-dose phase: days 0, 1, 2 (diagnosis of Cushing's syndrome)
  Dexamethasone 10 μg/kg (max, 0.5 mg) q 6 hr × 2 days
  8:00 A.M. serum cortisol days 0, 1, and 2
  24-hr urine free cortisol on days 0 and 2 (2nd low-dose day)
  Normal responses
    Serum cortisol <5 μg/dL
    Urine free cortisol <20 μg/dL
High-dose phase: days 3, 4, 5 (pituitary vs. nonpituitary Cushing's syndrome)
  Dexamethasone 50 μg/kg (max, 2 mg) q 6 hr × 2 days
  8:00 A.M. serum cortisol days 3, 4, and 5
  24-hr urine free cortisol on day 4 (2nd high-dose day)
  Normal responses (pituitary Cushing's syndrome)
    Serum cortisol suppressed >50% from day 2 baseline
    Urine free cortisol suppressed > 50% from day 2 baseline
Comments
  ACTH-dependent Cushing's syndrome is inhibited by high-dose dexamethasone
  Cortisol is not suppressed in patients with adrenal tumors or most cases of ectopic ACTH secretion
  Based on >90% suppression of urine free cortisol, the sensitivity and specificity for the diagnosis of Cushing's syndrome are 79% with 100% specificity; diagnostic accuracy is 83% (68%–93%)[31]

ACTH, adrenocorticotropic hormone.

**Table 196-8** Aldosterone Suppression Testing

Indications
  Diagnosis of primary hyperaldosteronism
  Patients with serum aldosterone >15 ng/dL, plasma renin activity <0.5 ng/mL/hr, serum potassium low (usually <3.6 mEq/L)
Testing
  Saline loading
    2 L isotonic saline over 2 hr intravenously
    Blood sampling for serum cortisol, aldosterone, and 18-hydroxy-corticosterone at baseline and 2 hr
    Expected responses
      In patients with primary hyperaldosteronism, serum aldosterone remains >8 ng/dL with aldosterone/cortisol (ng/dL/μg/dL) and 18-hydroxycorticosterone/cortisol (ng/dL/ng/dL) ratios >3.0
  Fludrohydrocortisone testing
    Fludrohydrocortisone (Florinef) 0.4 mg orally per day × 2 days
    Blood sampling for serum cortisol, aldosterone, and 18-hydroxycorticosterone at baseline and after 48 hr
    Expected responses
      Similar to saline loading (see above)
Comments
  Either test is useful to assess aldosterone suppression
  Saline loading is more useful to differentiate adrenal adenoma and IAH
  In patients with IAH, the above ratios are <3.0. Aldosterone and 18-hydroxycorticosterone are more angiotensin II and volume dependent than cortisol and less suppressed in IAH than in patients with an adenoma

IAH, idiopathic adrenal hyperplasia.

**Table 196-9** Angiotensin-Converting Enzyme Inhibition Testing

Indication
  Diagnosis of primary hyperaldosteronism
Testing
  Normal salt diet × 3 days
  1-hr recumbent subject
  50 mg captopril orally
  Blood sampling for PRA and aldosterone measurements at 0 and 90 min
Expected results
  Aldosterone/PRA ratio (ng/dL/ng/mL/hr) <20 in normal subjects after angiotensin-converting enzyme inhibition
  Aldosterone/PRA ratio >20 and aldosterone >15 ng/dL in patients with primary hyperaldosteronism
Comment
  Test 92% specific and 95% predictive for primary hyperaldosteronism[32]

PRA, plasma renin activity.

**Table 196-10** Adrenal Steroid Biosynthetic Enzyme Precursor/Product Ratios in Infants and Children with Documented Deficiencies of Adrenal Enzymes*

| | Type 1 | Type 2 | Reference Value (normal) |
|---|---|---|---|
| Cytochrome P-450 c21 (CYP21A2), adrenal 21-hydroxylase | | | |
| Progesterone | 200 | 4 (10) | <10 |
| Deoxycorticosterone | | | |
| 17-Hydroxyprogesterone | 250 | 20 (10) | <5 |
| 11-Deoxycortisol | | | |
| Cytochrome P-450 c11 (CYP11B1), adrenal 11-hydroxylase | | | |
| 11-Deoxycortisol | 850 | | <12 |
| Cortisol | | | |
| Cytochrome P-450 c11ase (CYP11B2), adrenal aldosterone synthase | | | |
| 18-Hydroxycorticosterone | 150 | | <15 |
| Aldosterone | | | |
| Cytochrome P-450 c17 (CYP17), adrenal and gonadal 17-hydroxylase | | | |
| Pregnenolone | 15 (35) | | <5 |
| 17-Hydroxypregnenolone | | | |
| Progesterone | 22 (16) | | <5 |
| 17-Hydroxyprogesterone | | | |
| 3β-hydroxysteroid dehydrogenase | | | |
| 17-Hydroxypregnenolone | † | | <22 |
| 17-Hydroxyprogesterone | | | |
| Dehydroepiandrosterone | † | | <15 |
| Androstenedione | | | |

*Values listed are averages. Numbers in parentheses are post–adrenocorticotropic hormone stimulation.
†Average values not available; ratios exceeding normal by twofold are suspect.
Data from Fisher DA (ed): Endocrinology: Test selection and Interpretation. Teterboro, NJ, Quest Diagnostics, 1998; and Adrenal steroid response to ACTH. Pediatrics, Endocrine Sciences. Calabassas Hills, CA, May 1991.

**Table 196-11** Criteria for Interpretation of Oral Glucose Tolerance Test*

| Category | Blood Glucose (mg/dL) | | | |
|---|---|---|---|---|
| | Fasting | 1 hr | 2 hr | 3 hr |
| Impaired glucose tolerance | >100, <125 | | 140–199 | |
| Gestational diabetes[†] | ≥105 | ≥190 | ≥165 | ≥145 |
| Diabetes | ≥126 | | ≥200 | |
| Normal | <100 | | <140 | |

*See Genuth et al.[20] Values for a 75-g carbohydrate load: National Diabetes Data Group criteria. For children, the oral dose is 1.75 g/kg body weight to a maximal 75-g dose.
[†]One hundred-gram carbohydrate load: positive if any two or four values meet criteria.

**Table 196-12** Risk of Development of Overt Type 1 Diabetes Mellitus in First-Degree Relatives of Patients with Type 1 Diabetes Relative to the Presence of Insulin, Glutamic Acid Decarboxylase, and/or ICA512 (1A2) Autoantibodies

| No. of Autoantibodies | Risk of Type 1 Diabetes Within | | |
|---|---|---|---|
| | 3 yr (%) | 5 yr (%) | 10 yr (%) |
| 0 | <1 | <1 | <1 |
| 1 | 8 | 15 | 23 |
| 2 | 30 | 43 | 72 |
| 3 | 49 | >95 | |

Data from Verge CF, Gianani R, Kawasaki E, et al: Prediction of type I diabetes in first degree relatives using a combination of insulin, GAD and ICA512 bdc/IA2 autoantibodies. Diabetes 45:926–933, 1996.

**Table 196-13** Laboratory Features of Primary Disorders of Salt and Water Metabolism

| Disorder | Serum Na⁺ | Serum K⁺ | Serum Aldo | Urine Aldo | Urine Na | Plasma OSM | Plasma AVP | Urine OSM | Urine AVP | Plasma ANH | Plasma renin |
|---|---|---|---|---|---|---|---|---|---|---|---|
| Diabetes insipidus (central) | ↑ | N | N | N | N | ↑ | ↓ | ↓ | ↓* | — | N |
| SIADH | ↓ | N | N | N | N | ↓ | ↑[†] | ↑ | ↑[†] | ↑ | N |
| Nephrogenic diabetes insipidus (AVP resistance) | ↑ | N | N | N | N | ↑ | ↑ | ↓ | ↑ | — | N |
| Psychogenic polydipsia | ↓ | N | N | N | N | ↓ | ↓ | ↓ | ↓ | — | N |
| Primary aldosteronism | N | ↓ | ↑ | ↑ | N-↓ | N | N | N | N | ↑ | ↓ |
| Hypoaldosteronism | ↓ | ↑ | ↓ | ↓ | ↑ | N | N | N | N | — | ↑ |
| Hyporeninemic hypoaldosteronism | N | ↑ | ↓ | ↓ | ↑ | N | N | N | N | — | N or ↓ |
| Pseudohypoaldosteronism | ↓ | ↑ | ↑ | ↑ | ↑ | N | N | N | N | — | ↑ |

*Decreased or normal relative to urine osmolarity; see Figure 196-2 and Fisher.[1]
[†]Increased relative to plasma osmolarity but normal relative to urine osmolarity.
Aldo, aldosterone; ANH, atrial natriuretic hormone; AVP, arginine vasopressin; OSM, osmolality; SIADH, syndrome of inappropriate vasopressin (antidiuretic hormone) secretion.

**Table 196-14** Gonadatropin-Releasing Hormone Stimulation Test Responses in Normal Children*

| Tanner Stage | Luteinizing Hormone | | Follicle-Stimulating Hormone | |
|---|---|---|---|---|
| | Male | Female | Male | Female |
| Prepubertal | 1.8 ± 1.3 | 1.8 ± 1.3 | | |
| I | 3.2 ± 3.0 | 2.0 ± 1.5 | 4.7 ± 2.2 | 21 ± 5.5 |
| II, III | 15 ± 6.3 | 21 ± 17 | 3.4 ± 2.2 | 10 ± 5.0 |
| IV, V | 42 ± 23 | 33 ± 20 | 11 ± 5.6 | 11 ± 3.3 |

*Ultrasensitive immunochemiluminometric assay: 0-, 30-, 60-, and 90-minute samplings after 100 µg gonadotropin-releasing hormone (Factrel) intravenously; results as mean peak response ± SD.
Data from Neely EK, Hintz RL, Wilson DM, et al: Normal ranges for immunochemiluminometric gonadotropin assays. J Pediatr 127:40–46, 1995.

**Table 196-15** Gonadotropin-Releasing Hormone Stimulation Test Responses in Children with Central Precocious Puberty*

| | CPP | Non-CPP |
|---|---|---|
| Peak LH after IV GnRH | 26 ± 13 | 2.9 ± 2.6 |
| LH after SC GnRH | 30 ± 18 | 2.8 ± 2.4 |

*Ultrasensitive immunochemiluminometric assay: 0-, 30-, 60-, and 90-minute samplings after 100 µg gonadotropin-releasing hormone (Factrel) intravenously or 40-minute sampling after 100 µg subcutaneously; results as mean peak response ± SD.
CPP, central precocious puberty; GnRH, gonadotropin-releasing hormone; IV, intravenous; LH, luteinizing hormone; SC, subcutaneous.
Data from Eckert KL, Wilson DM, Bachrach LK, et al: A single sample, subcutaneous gonadotropin releasing hormone test for central precocious puberty. Pediatrics 97:517–519, 1996.

| Table 196-16 | Criteria for Diagnosis of Growth Hormone Deficiency and Gigantism/Acromegaly |
|---|---|

**Random GH**
  Characterized by marked variability
  Levels >10 ng/mL with a normal insulin-like growth factor 1
    (IGF-1) concentration exclude a diagnosis of GH deficiency
**GH stimulation testing**
  GH deficiency is likely in children if the peak serum GH
    concentration in response to two or more stimulation tests is
    <5 ng/mL and possible if the peak response is >5 and <10 ng/mL
    (see Refs. 19, 20)
  In adults, the preferred stimulation tests are insulin and GHRH +
    arginine. GH deficiency is likely if the peak serum GH
    concentration in response to stimulation is <3 ng/mL and possible
    if the response is >3 and <5 ng/mL (see Ref. 22)
  The stimulation tests include (fasting)
    Arginine infusion, L-arginine hydrochloride 0.5 g/kg (max 30 g) IV
    Insulin 0.10 U/kg IV; 0.05 U/kg IV if high degree of suspicion
    Levodopa, orally
      125 mg if <15 kg
      250 mg if <30 kg
      500 mg if >30 kg
    Propranolol 0.75 mg/kg (max 40 mg) orally
    Clonidine 5 µg/kg (max 300 µg) orally
    GHRH 1.0 µg/kg IV
      Blood sampling for GH assay is usually conducted at 0, 30, 60,
        90, and 120 minutes
**Accuracy**
  Single agent tests in general have an accuracy of 86% at a cut-off
    level of 3 ng/mL and 75% at a cut-off of 10 ng/mL. Thus, at least
    two tests have been recommended to confirm GH deficiency. The
    combined insulin-arginine test (given sequentially) has an
    accuracy close to 100% at a cut-off of 10 ng/mL. The sequential
    combination of levodopa and propranolol has been used to avoid
    the complications and higher risk of insulin-arginine testing; the
    accuracy at a cut-off of 7–10 ng/mL probably approximates
    90%–95%. The specificity of GHRH testing approximates 95% at
    a cut-off of 7–10 ng/mL but sensitivity is only 30%. In most
    children, the GH secretory dysfunction appears to be at the
    hypothalamic rather than the pituitary level. The GHRH test is
    most useful in distinguishing hypothalamic and pituitary disease
    because GHRH acts at the pituitary level.
**GH suppression testing**
  Elevated blood glucose levels normally suppress GH secretion.
    Autonomous GH hypersecretion is likely if the serum GH is not
      suppressed in response to glucose loading
    Glucose 1.75 g/kg (max 75 g) orally after overnight fasting
      (or nothing by mouth after midnight)
    Blood sampling at 0, 30, 60, 90, and 120 minutes. Serum GH
      normally suppressed to <1.0 ng/mL

See Refs. 21–23.
GH, growth hormone; GHRH, growth hormone-releasing hormone; IV,
intravenously; max, maximum.
From Guistina A, Barkan A, Casanueva FF, et al: Criteria for cure of
acromegaly: A consensus statement. J Clin Endocrinol Metab 85:526–529,
2000.

| Table 196-17 | Normal Ranges for IGF-1, IGFBP-2, IGFBP-3, and IGFBP-2/IGF-I and IGFBP-2/IGFBP-3 Ratios |
|---|---|

| | Age | Normal Range (ng/mL) |
|---|---|---|
| **IGF-1** | 2 mo–5 yr | 17–248 |
| | 6–8 yr | 88–474 |
| | 9–11 yr | 110–771 |
| | 12–18 yr | 202–1096 |
| | 18–39 yr | 114–492 |
| | 40–54 yr | 90–360 |
| | >55 yr | 71–290 |
| **IGFBP-2** | 1–9 yr | 69–480 |
| | 10–18 yr | 50–326 |
| | 18–49 yr | 55–240 |
| | >50 yr | 28–444 |
| **IGFBP-3** | 2–23 mo | 905–2634 |
| | 2–7 yr | 1173–4329 |
| | 8–11 yr | 2517–4729 |
| | 12–18 yr | 2859–5295 |
| | 19–55 yr | 2000–4000 |
| | >55 yr | 900–3700 |
| | | **95% range** |
| **IGFBP-2/IGF-1 ratio** | 2–23 mo | 1.1–42.9 |
| | 2–5 yr | 1.1–9.0 |
| | 6–8 yr | 0.4–1.9 |
| | 9–11 yr | 0.2–1.9 |
| | 12–18 yr | 0.01–1.0 |
| **IGFBP-2/IGFBP-3 ratio** | 2–23 mo | 0.07–0.41 |
| | 2–5 yr | 0.05–0.19 |
| | 6–8 yr | 0.03–0.08 |
| | 9–11 yr | 0.03–0.09 |
| | 12–18 yr | 0.02–0.07 |

IGF-1, insulin-like growth factor 1; IGFBP, insulin-like growth factor–binding
protein.
Data from Nichols Institute Clinical Correlations Division.

**Table 196-18** | Changes in Thyroid Function Parameters with Age

| Age | Serum Concentrations* | | | | T₄ Utilization (µg/kg/day) |
|---|---|---|---|---|---|
| | $T_4$ (µg/dL) | $FT_4$ (ng/dL) | TSH (mU/L) | TBG (ng/dL) | $T_4$ Utilization (µg/kg/day) |
| **Fetus** | | | | | |
| 12–20 wk | 0.4–3.9 | 0–0.4 | 1–8 | 0.2–2.3 | 1.0 |
| 21–30 wk | 2.7–7.8 | 0.4–0.9 | 1.9–8.8 | 0.8–3.3 | 2.0 |
| 31–40 wk | 5.4–14.0 | 0.9–1.7 | 3–12 | 1.5–5.0 | 5.0 |
| **Infant** | | | | | |
| 1–4 days | 14.0–28.4 | 2.2–5.3 | 1–39 | 2.2–4.2 | 10.0 |
| 1–4 wk | 8.1–15.7 | 0.9–2.3 | 1.7–9.1 | — | 7.0 |
| 1–12 mo | 5.6–14.9 | 0.8–2.0 | 0.8–8.2 | 1.6–3.6 | 6.0 |
| **Child** | | | | | |
| 1–5 yr | 5.6–14.9 | 0.8–2.0 | 0.7–5.7 | 1.2–2.8 | 6.0 |
| 6–10 yr | 5.6–14.9 | 0.8–2.0 | 0.7–5.7 | 1.2–2.8 | 4.0 |
| 11–15 yr | 5.6–14.9 | 0.8–2.0 | 0.7–5.7 | 1.4–3.0 | 3.0 |
| 16–20 yr | 5.6–14.9 | 0.8–2.0 | 0.7–5.7 | 1.4–3.0 | 2.0 |
| **Adult** | | | | | |
| 21–50 yr | 5.6–13.7 | 0.8–2.7 | 0.4–4.2 | 1.7–3.6 | 1.5 |
| 51–80 yr | 5.6–13.7 | 0.8–2.7 | 0.4–4.2 | 1.7–3.6 | 1.5 |

*Values as 2-SD range.

$FT_4$, freethyroxine; $T_4$, thyroxine; TBG, thyroxine-binding globulin; TSH, thyroid-stimulating hormone.

Data from Nelson JC, Clark SJ, Borut DL, et al: Age related change in serum free thyroxine during childhood and adolescence. J Pediatr 124:899–905, 1993; Adams LM, Emery JR, Clark SJ, et al: Reference ranges for newer thyroid function tests in premature infants. J Pediatr 126:122–127, 1995; Thorpe-Beeston JG, Nicolaides KH, McGregor AM: Fetal thyroid function. Thyroid 2:207–217, 1992; Delange F, Fisher DA: The thyroid gland. In Brook CGD (ed): Clinical Pediatric Endocrinology, 3d ed. Oxford, Blackwell Scientific, 1995, pp 397–433; and Quest Diagnostics Nichols Institute Clinical Correlations Division.

**Table 196-19** | Changes in Thyroid Function Parameters with Age

| Age | $T_3$ (ng/dL) | $rT_3$ (ng/dL) | Thyroglobulin (ng/mL) | $T_4$ Utilization (µg/kg/day) |
|---|---|---|---|---|
| **Fetus** | | | | |
| 12–20 wk | 3.2–25 | — | — | 1.0 |
| 21–30 wk | 6.5–49 | — | 6–230 | 3.0 |
| 31–40 wk | 13–97 | 97–500 | 2–54 | 5.0 |
| **Infant** | | | | |
| 1–4 days | 100–740 | — | 15–101 | 10.0 |
| 1–4 wk | — | 26–292 | — | 7.0 |
| 1–12 mo | 105–245 | 11–130 | 11–92 | 6.0 |
| **Child** | | | | |
| 1–5 yr | 105–269 | 15–71 | 5.6–42 | 5.0 |
| 6–10 yr | 94–241 | 17–78 | 5.6–42 | 4.0 |
| 11–15 yr | 82–213 | 19–84 | 2.3–40 | 3.0 |
| 16–20 yr | 80–210 | 25–78 | 2.3–40 | 2.0 |
| **Adult** | | | | |
| 21–50 yr | 71–200 | 30–78 | 3.5–56 | 1.5 |
| 51–80 yr | 39–182 | 30–78 | 3.5–56 | 1.5 |

$rT_3$, reverse triiodothyronine.

Data from Nelson JC, Clark SJ, Borut DL, et al: Age related change in serum free thyroxine during childhood and adolescence. J Pediatr 124:899–905, 1993; Adams LM, Emery JR, Clark SJ, et al: Reference ranges for newer thyroid function tests in premature infants. J Pediatr 126:122–127, 1995; Thorpe-Beeston JG, Nicolaides KH, McGregor AM: Fetal thyroid function. Thyroid 2:207–217, 1992; Delange F, Fisher DA: The thyroid gland. In Brook CGD (ed): Clinical Pediatric Endocrinology, 3d ed. Oxford, Blackwell Scientific, 1995, pp 397–433; and Quest Diagnostics Nichols Institute Clinical Correlations Division.

**Table 196-20**  Hormones in Multiple Endocrine Neoplasia Syndromes

| MEN Type | Parathyroid | Pituitary | Pancreas Gastroinestinal | Adrenal Medulla | Thyroid |
|---|---|---|---|---|---|
| MEN1 (Werner's syndrome) | PTH | PRL<br>GH<br>ACTH | Gastrin<br>Insulin<br>Glucagon<br>GHRH<br>VIP<br>SRIF<br>PP | | |
| MEN2 or -2A (Sipple's syndrome) | PTH | | | CAT<br>Met<br>ChrA | CT<br>CEA<br>ChrA<br>† |
| MEN2B or -3* | PTH (rare) | | | CAT<br>Met<br>VMA<br>ChrA | CT<br>CEA<br>ChrA<br>† |

*Multiple endocrine neoplasia type 3 (2B) includes mucosal ganglioneuromas, marfanoid habitus.
†Ectopic hormones sometimes secreted by medullary thyroid carcinomas: serotonin, vasoactive intestinal peptide, somatostatin, adrenocorticotropic hormone.
CAT, catecholamines; CEA, carcinoembryonic antigen; ChrA, chromogranin A; CT, calcitonin; GH, growth hormone; GHRH, growth hormone–releasing hormone; 5-HT, serotonin; MEN, multiple endocrine neoplasia; Met, metanephrines; PP, pancreatic polypeptide; PRL, prolactin; PTH, parathyroid hormone; SRIF, somatostatin; VIP, vasoactive intestinal polypeptide; VMA, vanillylmandelic acid.
From Fisher DA (ed): Endocrinology: Test Selection and Interpretation. Teterboro, NJ, Quest Diagnostics, 1998.

**Table 196-21**  Frequency of Hormonal Secretions in Apparently Sporadic Neuroendocrine Tumors According to Primary Site*

| Hormone | Foregut | Pancreas | Midgut | Hindgut | Unknown | Overall* |
|---|---|---|---|---|---|---|
| Neuron-specific enolase | 42 | 45 | 42 | 2/3 | 65 | 47 |
| 5-HIAA | 44 | 10 | 85 | 1/3 | 55 | 46 |
| α Subunit | 30 | 26 | 0 | 1/3 | 15 | 19 |
| Calcitonin | 28 | 13 | 3 | 0 | 10 | 14 |
| hCG-β | 17 | 21 | 0 | 0 | 10 | 12 (89) |
| Urine free cortisol | 9 | 10 | 0 | 0 | 0 | 6 (64) |
| Somatostatin | 9 | 0 | 0 | 0 | 0 | 3 (64) |
| PTHrP | 3 | 0 | 0 | 0 | 0 | <1 |

*Results in percentage of 130 patients studied except as indicated in parentheses and for hindgut tumors. There were only three patients with hindgut tumors and absolute numbers are shown.
hCG-β, human chorionic gonadotropin-β; 5-HIAA, 5-hydroxyindoleacetic acid; PTHrP, parathyroid hormone-related protein.
From Baudin E, Bidart JM, Rougier P, et al: Screening for multiple endocrine neoplasia type 1 and hormonal production in apparently sporadic neuroendocrine tumors. J Clin Endocrinol Metab 84:69–75, 1999.

**Table 196-22**  Calcitonin Pentagastrin Stimulation Test* (Quest Diagnostics–Nichols Institute Immunochemiluminometric Assay)

| Blood Samples† | Adult Males (n = 10) | Adult Females (n = 10) |
|---|---|---|
| Basal | ≤8.0 | ≤4.0 |
| 1 min | ≤324 | ≤41 |
| 2 min | ≤491 | ≤70 |
| 5 min | ≤343 | ≤39 |
| 10 min | ≤112 | ≤23 |

*Values in pg/mL, 2-SD range.
†Calcium gluconate, 20 mg/kg  body weight
Data from Nichols Institute Clinical Correlations Division. (2 mg elemental calcium intravenously over 1 minute followed by 0.5 µg/kg pentagastrin as a bolus over 5 seconds). Nothing by mouth after midnight, patient supine.

## REFERENCES

1. Fisher DA (ed): Endocrinology: Test Selection and Interpretation. Teterboro, NJ, Quest Diagnostics, 1998.
2. Dons RF: Endocrine and Metabolic Testing Manual, 3d ed. Boca Raton, FL, CRC Press, 1998.
3. Ginsberg LJ: A practical approach to tolerance testing in children. In Lifshitz F (ed): Pediatric Endocrinology, 2d ed. New York, Marcel Dekker, 1990, pp 953–982.
4. Bertrand J, Rappoport R, Sizonenko PC: In Bertrand J, Rappaport R, Sizonenko PC (eds): Pediatric Endocrinology, 2d ed. Baltimore, Williams & Wilkins, 1993, pp 658–681.
5. de Pablo F, Seanes CG, Weintraub BD: Handbook of Endocrine Research Techniques. San Diego, Academic Press, 1993.
6. Meites S: Pediatric Clinical Chemistry, Reference (Normal) Values, 3d ed. Washington, DC, AACC Press, 1989.
7. Baxter RC: Circulating levels and molecular distribution of acid labile subunit of the high molecular weight insulin-like growth factor binding protein complex. J Clin Endocrinol Metab 70:1347–1353, 1990.
8. Adrenal steroid response to ACTH, Pediatrics, Endocrine Sciences, Calabassas Hills, CA, May 1991 catalogue.
9. Lashansky G, Saenger P, Fishman K, et al: Normative data for adrenal steroidogenesis in a healthy pediatric population: Age and sex related changes after adrenocorticotropin stimulation. J Clin Endocrinol Metab 73:674–686, 1991.
10. Lashansky G, Saenger P, Dimartino-Nardi J, et al: Normative data for the steroidogenic response of mineralocorticoids and their precursors to adrenocorticotropin in a healthy pediatric population. J Clin Endocrinol Metab 75:1491–1496, 1992.
11. Abdir TAM, Elhadd TA, Neary R, Clayton RN: Comparison of the low dose short synacthen test (1 μg), the conventional dose short synacthen test (250 μg), and the insulin tolerance test for assessment of the hypothalamic-pituitary-adrenal axis in patients with pituitary disease. J Clin Endocrinol Metab 84:838–843, 1999.
12. Verge CF, Gianani R, Kawasaki E, et al: Prediction of type 1 diabetes in first degree relatives using a combination of insulin, GAD and ICA512 bdc/IA2 autoantibodies. Diabetes 45:926–933, 1996.
13. Neely EK, Hintz RL, Wilson DM, et al: Normal ranges for immunochemiluminometric gonadotropin assays. J Pediatr 127:40–46, 1995.
14. Eckert KL, Wilson DM, Bachrach LK, et al: A single sample, subcutaneous gonadotropin releasing hormone test for central precocious puberty. Pediatrics 97:517–519, 1996.
15. Nelson JC, Clark SJ, Borut DL, et al: Age related change in serum free thyroxine during childhood and adolescence. J Pediatr 124:899–905, 1993.
16. Adams LM, Emery JR, Clark SJ, et al: Reference ranges for newer thyroid function tests in premature infants. J Pediatr 126:122–127, 1995.
17. Thorpe-Beeston JG, Nicolaides KH, McGregor AM: Fetal thyroid function. Thyroid 2:207–217, 1992.
18. Delange F, Fisher DA: The thyroid gland. In Brook CGD (ed): Clinical Pediatric Endocrinology, 3d ed. Oxford, Blackwell Scientific, 1995, pp 397–433.
19. Baudin E, Bidart JM, Rougier P, et al: Screening for multiple endocrine neoplasia type 1 and hormonal production in apparently sporadic neuroendocrine tumors. J Clin Endocrinol Metab 84:69–75, 1999.
20. Genuth S, Alberti KG, Bennett P, et al: Follow-up report on the diagnosis of diabetes mellitus. Diabetes Care 26:3160–3167, 2003.
21. Sizonenko PC, Clayton PE, Cohen P, et al: Diagnosis and management of growth hormone deficiency in childhood and adolescence. Part 1: Diagnosis of growth hormone deficiency. Growth Horm IGF Res 11:137–165, 2001.
22. Growth Hormone Research Society: Consensus guidelines for the diagnosis and treatment of growth hormone (GH) deficiency in childhood and adolescence: summary statement of the GH Research Society. J Clin Endocrinol Metab 85:3990–3993, 2000.
23. Consensus guidelines for the diagnosis and treatment of adults with growth hormone deficiency: Summary statement of the Growth Hormone Research Society workshop on adult growth hormone deficiency. J Clin Endocrinol Metab 83:379–381, 1998.
24. Giustina A, Barkan A, Casanueva FF, et al: Criteria for cure of acromegaly: A consensus statement. J Clin Endocrinol Metab 85:526–529, 2000.
25. Sann L, Chayvialle JAP, Bremond A, Lambert R: Serum gastrin-level in early childhood. Arch Dis Child 50:782–785, 1975.
26. Janik JS, Akbar AM, Burrington JD, Burke G: Serum gastrin-levels in infants and children. Pediatrics 60:60–64, 1977.
27. Bidlingmaier F, Wagner-Barnak M, Butenandt O, Knorr D: Plasma estrogens in childhood and puberty under physiologic and pathologic conditions. Pediatr Res 7:901–907, 1973.
28. Forest MG, Sizonenko PC, Cathiard AM, Bertrand J: Hypophyso-gonadal function in humans during the first year of life. I. Evidence for testicular activity in early infancy. J Clin Invest 53:819–828, 1974.
29. Forest MG, Cathiard AM, Bertrand JA: Total and unbound testosterone levels in the newborn and in normal and hypogonadal children: Use of a sensitive radioimmunoassay for testosterone. J Clin Endocrinol Metab 36:1132–1142, 1973.
30. Juul A, Dalgaard P, Blum WF, et al: Serum Levels of Insulin-like growth factor (IGF)-binding protein 3 (IGFBP-3) in healthy infants, children, and adolescents: The relation to IGF-I, IGF-II, IGFBP-1, IGFBP-2, age sex, body mass index, and pubertal maturation. J Clin Endocrinol Metab 80:2534–2542, 1995.
31. Dicheck HL, Nieman LK, Oldfield EH, et al: A comparison of the standard high dose dexamethasone suppression test and the overnight 8 mg dexamethasone suppression test for the differential diagnosis of adrenocorticotropin-dependent Cushing syndrome. J Clin Endocrinol Metab 78:418–422, 1994.
32. Naomi S, Umeda T, Iwaoka T, Sato T: Effects of sodium intake on the captopril test for primary aldosteronism. Jpn Heart J 28:357–365, 1987.
33. Tommasi M, Bacciottini L, Benucci A, et al: Serum biochemical markers of bone turnover in healthy infants and children. Int J Biol Markers 11:159–164, 1996.
34. Sulyok E, Nemeth M, Tenji I, et al: Postnatal development of renin-angiotensin-aldosterone system, RAAS, in relation to electrolyte balance in premature infants. Pediatr Res 13:817–820, 1979.
35. Stalker HP, Holland NH, Katchen JM, Kotchen TA: Plasma renin activity in healthy children. J Pediatr 89:256–258, 1976.
36. Fukushige J, Shimomura K, Ueda K: Influence of upright activity on plasma renin activity and aldosterone concentration in children. Eur J Pediatr 153:284–286, 1994.
37. Rodriguez GE, Shin BC, Abernathy RS, Kendig EL: Serum angiotensin-converting enzyme activity in normal children and in those with sarcoidosis. J Pediatr 99:68–72, 1981.
38. Kruger C, Rauh M, Dörr HG: Immunoreactive renin concentrations in healthy children from birth to adolescence. Clin Chem Acta 274:15–27, 1998.
39. Pang S, Levine LS, Chow D, et al: Dihydrotestosterone and its relationship to testosterone in infancy and childhood. J Clin Endocrinol Metab 48:821–826, 1979.
40. Candito M, Albertini M, Politano S, et al: Plasma catecholamine levels in children. J Chromatogr 617:304–307, 1993.
41. Bolton NJ, Tapanainen J, Koivisto M, Vihko R: Circulating sex hormone-binding globulin and testosterone in newborns and infants. Clin Endocrinol 31:201–207, 1989
42. Lee IR, Lawder LE, Townsend DC, et al: Plasma sex hormone binding globulin concentration and binding capacity in children before and during puberty. Acta Endocrinol 109:276–280, 1985.

43. Tommasi M, Bacciottini L, Benucci A, et al: Serum biochemical markers of bone turnover in healthy infants and children. Int J Biol Markers 11:159–164, 1996.

44. Mora S, Pitukcheewanont P, Kaufman FR, et al: Biochemical markers of bone turnover and the volume and density of bone in children at different stages of sexual development. J Bone Miner Res 14:1664–1671, 1999.

45. Findling JW, Raff H, Aron DC: The low dose dexamethasone suppression test: A reevaluation in patients with Cushing's syndrome. J Clin Endocrinol Metab 89:1222–1226, 2003.

# Index

Note: Page numbers followed by f indicate figures; those followed by t indicate tables; those followed by b indicate boxed material.